Readers' Guide to
Periodical Literature

MARCH 1971—FEBRUARY 1972

READERS' GUIDE TO PERIODICAL LITERATURE

Cumulated Volumes

READERS' GUIDE TO PERIODICAL LITERATURE

An Author and Subject Index

MARCH 1971—FEBRUARY 1972

Edited by
ZADA LIMERICK

Assistant Editor
LINDA LACK HOY

Indexers
ANN F. DIETZ
ANNE W. FURNESS
MARY HUMPHREY
LOVISA J. JENKINS
MURIEL M. PHILLIPS
BERTA PISCIOTTANO

THE H. W. WILSON COMPANY
NEW YORK   **1972**

ACKNOWLEDGMENTS

In addition to the staff members whose names appear on the title page we wish to acknowledge the contributions of Ilene S. Goldstein who indexed for this volume.

Z. L.

PREFATORY NOTE

The READERS' GUIDE TO PERIODICAL LITERATURE is a cumulative author subject index to periodicals of general interest published in the United States.

The Committee on Wilson Indexes of the American Library Association's Reference Services Division advises the publisher on indexing and editorial policy by means of in-depth contents studies conducted at intervals of several years. The Committee as part of its study prepares a list of periodicals, representative of all subject areas included in the Index, for consideration by the subscribers.

Selection of periodicals for indexing is accomplished by subscriber vote. In voting their preferences subscribers are asked to place primary emphasis on the reference value of the periodicals under consideration. They are also asked to give particular consideration to subject balance in order to insure that no important field be overlooked in proportion to overall index coverage.

Suggestions for additions or deletions of titles should be brought to the attention of the Committee in care of The H. W. Wilson Company.

SUGGESTIONS FOR THE USE OF THE
READERS' GUIDE TO PERIODICAL LITERATURE

Arrangement

Authors and subjects are arranged in one alphabet. Under authors and subjects, titles are arranged also in alphabetical order by the first word, initial articles being disregarded. Under personal names titles *by* author precede those *about* him. Subdivisions of a subject are arranged alphabetically under the subject. Geographical subheads follow the other subdivisions in a separate alphabet.

Cross References

See references are made from various forms of personal names and subject headings to the most generally accepted forms appearing in the first issue, after made, and thereafter in but one quarterly issue, until the annual volume. They are also made from titles of dramas, operas, and stories to names of authors and composers.

See also references are made from a subject to related subjects under which additional material may be found.

Dramas

Dramas are indexed under the dramatist's name with a *see* reference from the title of the drama; titles are also listed under the heading—Dramas—Criticisms, plots, etc.—Single works.

Fiction

Novels and short stories are indexed under the author's name with a *see* reference from the title to the author. Subject entries are made for selected types of fiction, e.g. Historical fiction; Christmas stories; etc.

Moving Pictures

Moving picture plays are indexed only under the headings Moving picture plays—Criticisms, plots, etc.—Single works, or Moving pictures—Documentary films—Criticisms, plots, etc. No title references are made.

Musical comedies, revues, etc.

Musical comedies, revues, etc. are indexed under the heading Musical comedies, revues, etc.—Criticisms, plots, etc. with a *see* reference from the title of the work.

Operas, Operettas

Operas, Operettas are indexed under the composer's name with a *see* reference from the title of the opera or operetta; titles are also listed under the headings Operas—Criticisms, plots, etc., or Operettas—Criticisms, plots, etc.

Sample entry: NEGRO athletes
    Assessment of black is best. M. Kane. il
    Sports Illus 34:72-6+ Ja 18 '71

An illustrated article on the subject **NEGRO athletes** entitled "Assessment of black is best," by M. Kane, will be found in volume 34 of Sports Illustrated, pages 72-6 (continued on later pages of the same issue) the January 18, 1971 number

PERIODICALS INDEXED

March 1971—February 1972

All data as of latest issue received

Aging—$2.50. m (bi-m F-Mr, Jl-Ag, N-D) Aging, Superintendent of Documents, U.S. Government Printing Office, Washington, D.C. 20402

America—$10. w (bi-w Jl, Ag and year-end issue) America Press, 106 W 56th St, New York 10019

American Artist—$11. m American Artist, 2160 Patterson St, Cincinnati, Ohio 45214

The American City—$15. m The American City Magazine, Buttenheim Publishing Corp, Berkshire Common, Pittsfield, Mass. 01201

American Education—$4.50. m (bi-m Ja-F, Ag-S) American Education, Superintendent of Documents, U.S. Government Printing Office, Washington, D.C. 20402

American Forests—$7.50. m American Forestry Association, 1319 18th St, NW, Washington, D.C. 20036

*American Heritage—$20. bi-m American Heritage, 383 W Center St, Marion, Ohio 43302

The American Historical Review—$20. free to members of the American Historical Association. 5 times a yr (O, D, F, Ap, Je) American Historical Association, 400 A St, SE, Washington, D.C. 20003

American Home—$4. m American Home, Flushing, New York 11357

American Imago—$10. q Wayne State Univ. Press, 5980 Cass Av, Detroit, Mich. 48202

American Libraries—available only to members. m (bi-m Jl-Ag) American Library Association, 50 E Huron St, Chicago 60611

The American Record Guide—$6. m American Record Guide, P.O. Box 319, Radio City Station, New York 10019

The American Scholar—$5. q United Chapters of Phi Beta Kappa, 1811 Q St, NW, Washington, D.C. 20009

The American West—$9. bi-m American West Pub. Co, 599 College Av, Palo Alto, Calif. 94306

Américas—$6. m General Secretariat of the Organization of American States, Washington, D.C. 20006

The Annals of the American Academy of Political and Social Science—$12. free to members. bi-m American Academy of Political and Social Science, 3937 Chestnut St, Philadelphia 19104

Antiques—$16. m Straight Enterprises, Inc, 551 5th Av, New York 10017

The Architectural Forum—$12. m (bi-m Ja-F, Jl-Ag) The Architectural Forum, 130 E 59th St, New York 10022

Architectural Record—$7.50. m (semi-m My) Architectural Record, P.O. Box 430, Hightstown, N.J. 08520

Art in America—$15. bi-m Art in America, 115 Tenth St, Des Moines, Ia. 50304

Art News—$13. m (S-My) Art News, 444 Madison Av, New York 10022

*The Atlantic—$10.50. m Atlantic, 125 Garden St, Marion, Ohio 43302

Audubon—$8.50. bi-m National Audubon Society, 1130 5th Av, New York 10028

Aviation Week & Space Technology—$20. w Aviation Week, P.O. Box 430, Hightstown, N.J. 08520

Better Homes and Gardens—$4. m Better Homes and Gardens, 1716 Locust St, Des Moines, Ia. 50336

Bulletin of the Atomic Scientists—$8.50. m (S-Je) Bulletin of the Atomic Scientists, 24 E 58th St, Chicago 60637

Business Week—$12. w Business Week, P.O. Box 430, Hightstown, N.J. 08520

Camping Magazine—$9. free to members of the American Camping Association. m (Ja-Je, bi-m S-D) Camping Magazine, 5 Mountain Av, N Plainfield, N.J. 07060

The Catholic World—$8. m Catholic World, 400 Sette Drive, Paramus, N.J. 07652

Ceramics Monthly—$6. m (S-Je) Ceramics Monthly, P.O. Box 4548, Columbus, Ohio 43212

*Changing Times—$7. m Changing Times, The Kiplinger Magazine, Editors Park, Md. 20782

Chemistry—$6. m (bi-m Jl-Ag) American Chemical Society, 1155 16th St, NW, Washington, D.C. 20036

The Christian Century continuing New Christian—$12. w Christian Century Foundation, 407 S Dearborn St, Chicago 60605

Christianity Today—$7.50. fortn. Christianity Today, 1014 Washington Building, Washington, D.C. 20005

The Clearing House—$5. m (S-My) The Clearing House, 205 Lexington Av, Sweet Springs, Missouri 65351

Commentary—$10. m American Jewish Committee, 165 E 56th St, New York 10022

Commonweal—$14. w (bi-w year-end issue, Je-mid-S) Commonweal Pub. Co, Inc, 232 Madison Av, New York 10016

Congressional Digest—$12.50. m (bi-m Je-Jl, Ag-S) Congressional Digest Corp, 3231 P St, NW, Washington, D.C. 20007

Conservationist (Albany)—$2. bi-m The New York State Conservationist, Circulation Dept, New York State Conservation Department, Albany, N.Y. 12201

*Consumer Bulletin—$8. m Consumers' Research, Inc, Washington, N.J. 07882

*Consumer Reports—$8. m Consumers Union of U.S, Inc, 256 Washington St, Mount Vernon, N.Y. 10550

Craft Horizons—$10. bi-m American Craftsmen's Council, 44 W 53d St, New York 10019

Current—$10. m (except Jl) Current, Plainfield, Vermont 05667

Current History—$9.50. m Current History, Inc, 1822 Ludlow St, Philadelphia 19103

Dance Magazine—$10. m Dance Magazine, 268 W 47th St, New York 10036

The Department of State Bulletin—$16. w Department of State Bulletin, Superintendent of Documents, U.S. Government Printing Office, Washington, D.C. 20402

Design—$7. 6 times a yr Design Magazine, 1100 Waterway Blvd, Indianapolis, Ind. 46202

Dun's—$7. m Dun & Bradstreet Pub. Corp, P.O. Box 3088, Grand Central Station, New York 10017

*Ebony—$8. m Ebony, 820 S Michigan Av, Chicago 60605

The Education Digest—$7. m (S-My) Prakken Publications, Inc, 416 Longshore Drive, Ann Arbor, Michigan 48107

Electronics World—$7. m Electronics World, P.O. Box 1093, Flushing, New York 11352
Incorporated in Popular Electronics Ja '72

English Journal—$12. m (S-My) National Council of Teachers of English, 1111 Kenyon Road, Urbana, Illinois 61801

Environment—$10. m (bi-m Ja-F, Jl-Ag) Environment, 438 N Skinker Blvd, St Louis, Missouri 63130

Esquire—$8.50. m Esquire, Portland Pl, Boulder, Colo. 80302

*Farm Journal (Central edition)—$2. m Farm Journal, Inc, 230 W Washington Sq, Philadelphia 19105

Field & Stream—$5. m Holt, Rinehart and Winston, Inc, 383 Madison Av, New York 10017

Film Quarterly—$5. q University of California Press, Berkeley, Calif. 94720

Flying—$7. m P.O. Box 1094, Flushing, New York 11352

Focus—$3.50 m (S-Je) American Geographical Society, Broadway at 156th St, New York 10032

Forbes—$9.50. semi-m Forbes, 60 Fifth Av, New York 10011

*Foreign Affairs—$10. q Council on Foreign Relations, Inc, 58 E 68th St, New York 10021

Fortune—$16. m Fortune, 541 N Fairbanks Court, Chicago 60611

*Good Housekeeping—$5. m Good Housekeeping, Box 517, New York 10019

Harper's Bazaar—$7. m Harper's Bazaar, P.O. Box 552, New York 10019

*Harper's Magazine—$8.50. m Harper's Magazine, 381 W Center St, Marion, Ohio 43302

Harvard Business Review—$12. bi-m Harvard Business Review, 108 10th St, Des Moines, Ia. 50305

*Harvest Years—$6. m Harvest Years, 150 E 58th St, New York 10022

*High Fidelity and Musical America—$14. m High Fidelity, 2160 Patterson St, Cincinnati, Ohio 45214

Hobbies—$6. m Lightner Pub. Corp, 1006 S Michigan Av, Chicago 60605

*Holiday—$7. m (bi-m D-Ja, My-Je, Jl-Ag) Holiday, 1100 Waterway Blvd, Indianapolis, Ind. 46202

Home Garden & Flower Grower—$5.40. 9 times a yr (Ja, F, Mr, Ap, My, Je, Ag, O, D) Home Garden, Portland Pl, Boulder, Colo. 80302

*Horizon—$20. q Horizon, 379 W Center St, Marion, Ohio 43302

The Horn Book Magazine—$7.50. bi-m Horn Book, Inc, 585 Boylston St, Boston 02116

Horticulture—$7. m Horticulture, 125 Garden St, Marion, Ohio 43302

Hot Rod—$7.50. m Petersen Pub. Co, 8490 Sunset Blvd, Los Angeles 90069

House & Garden incorporating Living for Young Homemakers—$7. m House & Garden, Box 5202, Boulder, Colo. 80302

House Beautiful—$7. m House Beautiful, P.O. Box 560, New York 10019

International Conciliation—$4. 5 times a yr (S, N, Ja, Mr, My) Carnegie Endowment for International Peace, 345 E 46th St, New York 10017

*Ladies' Home Journal—$5.94. m Ladies' Home Journal, Flushing, New York 11357

Library Journal—$15. semi-m (m Jl, Ag) R. R. Bowker Co, 1180 Avenue of the Americas, New York 10036

Life—$10. w (except one issue at the beginning and one issue at the year end) Life, 541 N Fairbanks Court, Chicago 60611

The Living Wilderness—$7.50. q The Wilderness Society, 729 15th St, NW, Washington, D.C. 20005

*Look—$3. bi-w Look, Box 857, Des Moines, Ia. 50304
Discontinued publication O 19 '71

McCall's—$3.95. m McCall's, P.O. Box 771, Muscatine, Iowa 52761

Mademoiselle—$6. m Mademoiselle, P.O. Box 5204, Boulder, Colo. 80302

Mechanix Illustrated—$4. m Fawcett Publications, Inc, Fawcett Pl, Greenwich, Conn. 06830

Mental Hygiene—$10. q Mental Hygiene, 49 Sheridan Av, Albany, New York 12210

Space World—$8. m Space World, Amherst, Wisconsin 54406

Sports Car Graphic. See Motor Trend

*****Sports Illustrated**—$12. w (except one issue at year end) Sports Illustrated, 541 N Fairbanks Court, Chicago 60611

Successful Farming (Midwest edition)—$2. m (semi-m F, Mr, bi-m Je-Jl, N-D) Successful Farming, 1716 Locust St, Des Moines, Ia. 50336

Sunset (Central edition)—$4. m Calif, Ore, Wash, Idaho, Ariz, Nev, Utah, Hawaii, Alaska. $6. in other states m Sunset Magazine, Menlo Park, Calif. 94025

Time—$14. w Time, 541 N Fairbanks Court, Chicago 60611

Today's Education—available only to members. m (S-My) National Education Association of the United States, 1201 16th St, NW, Washington, D.C. 20036

*****Today's Health**—$5. m Today's Health, 535 N Dearborn St, Chicago 60610

Trans-Action—$9.75. m (bi-m Jl-Ag) Trans-action, Box A, Rutgers—The State University, New Brunswick, N.J. 08903

Travel—$6. m Travel, Travel Bldg, Floral Park, N.Y. 11001

UN Monthly Chronicle—$9.50. m (bi-m Ag-S) United Nations Publications, Room LX-2300, New York 10017

The UNESCO Courier—$5. m (bi-m Ag-S) UNESCO Pub. Center, Box 433, New York 10016

*****U.S. News & World Report**—$12. w U.S. News & World Report, 435 Parker Av, Dayton, Ohio 45401

Vital Speeches of the Day—$10. semi-m City News Pub. Co, Inc, Box 606, Southold, N.Y. 11971

Vogue—$10. semi-m (m My-Jl, D) Vogue, Box 5201, Boulder, Colo. 80302

Weatherwise—$7. bi-m American Meteorological Society, 45 Beacon St, Boston, Mass. 02108

Wilson Library Bulletin—$9. m (S-Je) The H. W. Wilson Co, 950 University Av, Bronx, N.Y. 10452

*****The Writer**—$7. m The Writer, Inc, 8 Arlington St, Boston 02116

Writer's Digest—$4. m Writer's Digest, 22 E 12th St, Cincinnati, Ohio 45210

Yachting—$8.50. m Yachting Pub. Corp, 50 W 44th St, New York 10036

The Yale Review—$6. q Yale Review, 28 Hillhouse Av, New Haven, Conn. 06520

---

* Available for blind and other physically handicapped readers on talking books, in braille, or on magnetic tape. For information address Division for the Blind and Physically Handicapped, Library of Congress, Washington, D.C. 20542

ABBREVIATIONS OF PERIODICALS INDEXED

For full information, consult pages IX-XII

Aging—Aging
Am Artist—American Artist
Am City—American City
Am Ed—American Education
Am For—American Forests
*Am Heritage—American Heritage
Am Hist R—American Historical Review
Am Home—American Home
Am Imago—American Imago
Am Lib—American Libraries
Am Rec G—American Record Guide
Am Scholar—American Scholar
Am West—American West
America—America
Américas—Américas
Ann Am Acad—Annals of the American Academy of Political and Social Science
Antiques—Antiques
Arch Forum—Architectural Forum
Arch Rec—Architectural Record
Art in Am—Art in America
Art N—Art News
*Atlan—Atlantic
Audubon—Audubon
Aviation W—Aviation Week & Space Technology

Bet Hom & Gard—Better Homes and Gardens
Bsns W—Business Week
Bul Atom Sci—Bulletin of the Atomic Scientists

Camp Mag—Camping Magazine
Cath World—Catholic World
Ceram Mo—Ceramics Monthly
*Changing T—Changing Times
Chem—Chemistry
Chr Cent—Christian Century continuing New Christian
Chr Today—Christianity Today
Clear House—Clearing House
Commentary—Commentary
Commonweal—Commonweal
Cong Digest—Congressional Digest
Cons—Conservationist (Albany)
*Consumer Bul—Consumer Bulletin
*Consumer Rep—Consumer Reports
Craft Horiz—Craft Horizons
Cur—Current
Cur Hist—Current History

Dance Mag—Dance Magazine
Dept State Bul—Department of State Bulletin
Design—Design
Duns—Dun's

*Ebony—Ebony
Ed Digest—Education Digest
Electr World—Electronics World
    Incorporated in Popular Electronics Ja '72
Engl J—English Journal
Environ—Environment
Esquire—Esquire

*Farm J—Farm Journal (Central edition)
Field & S—Field & Stream
Film Q—Film Quarterly
Flying—Flying
Focus—Focus
*For Affairs—Foreign Affairs
Forbes—Forbes
Fortune—Fortune

*Good H—Good Housekeeping

*Har Yrs—Harvest Years
Harp Baz—Harper's Bazaar
*Harper—Harper's Magazine
Harvard Bsns R—Harvard Business Review
*Hi Fi—High Fidelity and Musical America
Hobbies—Hobbies
*Holiday—Holiday
Home Gard—Home Garden & Flower Grower
*Horizon—Horizon
Horn Bk—Horn Book Magazine
Horticulture—Horticulture
Hot Rod—Hot Rod
House & Gard—House & Garden incorporating Living for Young Homemakers
House B—House Beautiful

Int Concil—International Conciliation

*Ladies Home J—Ladies' Home Journal
Library J—Library Journal
    Includes School Library Journal
Life—Life
Liv Wildn—Living Wilderness
*Look—Look
    Discontinued publication O 19 '71

McCalls—McCall's
Mech Illus—Mechanix Illustrated
Ment Hy—Mental Hygiene
Mlle—Mademoiselle
Mo Labor R—Monthly Labor Review
Mod Phot—Modern Photography

Motor B & S—Motor Boating & Sailing
Motor T—Motor Trend
Mus Q—Musical Quarterly

N Y Times Mag—New York Times Magazine
*__Nat Geog__—National Geographic Magazine
Nat Parks & Con Mag—National Parks & Conservation Magazine
Nat R—National Review (44p issue only, pub. in alternate weeks)
Nat Wildlife—National Wildlife
Nation—Nation
Nations Bsns—Nation's Business
*__Natur Hist__—Natural History
Negro Hist Bul—Negro History Bulletin
New Repub—New Republic
New Yorker—New Yorker
*__Newsweek__—Newsweek

Opera N—Opera News
Org Gard & Farm—Organic Gardening and Farming
Outdoor Life—Outdoor Life

PTA Mag—PTA Magazine
Parents Mag—Parents' Magazine & Better Family Living
Parks & Rec—Parks & Recreation
Phys Today—Physics Today
Plays—Plays
Poetry—Poetry
Pop Electr—Popular Electronics
    Incorporating Electronics World Ja '72
*__Pop Mech__—Popular Mechanics
Pop Phot—Popular Photography
Pop Sci—Popular Science Monthly
Pub W—Publishers' Weekly

Radio-Electr—Radio-Electronics
Ramp Mag—Ramparts Magazine
*__Read Digest__—Reader's Digest
Redbook—Redbook
Rod & Custom. See Hot Rod

*__Sat R__—Saturday Review
Sch & Soc—School and Society
Sch Arts—School Arts
Schol Teach—Scholastic Teacher
    Bound in Senior Scholastic
Schol Teach Jr/Sr High—Scholastic Teacher Junior/Senior High Teacher's Edition
School Library Journal. See Library Journal
*__Sci Am__—Scientific American
Sci Digest—Science Digest
Sci N—Science News
Science—Science
Sea Front—Sea Frontiers
*__Seventeen__—Seventeen
Sky & Tel—Sky and Telescope
Space World—Space World
Sports Car Graphic. See Motor Trend
*__Sports Illus__—Sports Illustrated
Sr Schol—Senior Scholastic (Teacher edition)
Suc Farm—Successful Farming (Midwest edition)
Sunset—Sunset (Central edition)

Time—Time
Todays Ed—Today's Education
*__Todays Health__—Today's Health
Trans-Action—Trans-Action
Travel—Travel

UN Mo Chron—UN Monthly Chronicle
UNESCO Courier—UNESCO Courier
*__U S News__—U.S. News & World Report

Vital Speeches—Vital Speeches of the Day
Vogue—Vogue

Weatherwise—Weatherwise
Wilson Lib Bul—Wilson Library Bulletin
*__Writer__—Writer
Writers Digest—Writer's Digest

Yachting—Yachting
Yale R—Yale Review

* Available for blind and other physically handicapped readers on talking books, in braille, or on magnetic tape. For information address Division for the Blind and Physically Handicapped, Library of Congress, Washington, D.C. 20542

ABBREVIATIONS

*	following name entry, a printer's device		jr	junior
+	continued on later pages of same issue		jt auth	joint author
abp	archbishop		ltd	limited
abr	abridged		m	monthly
Ag	August		Mr	March
Ap	April		My	May
arch	architect		N	November
assn	association		no	number
Aut	Autumn		O	October
av	avenue		por	portrait
bart	baronet		pseud	pseudonym
bibliog	bibliography		pt	part
bibliog f	bibliographical foot-notes		pub	published, publisher, publishing
bi-m	bimonthly		q	quarterly
bi-w	biweekly		rev	revised
bldg	building		S	September
bp	bishop		sec	section
co	company		semi-m	semimonthly
comp	compiled, compiler		soc	society
cond	condensed		Spr	Spring
cont	continued		sq	square
corp	corporation		sr	senior
D	December		st	street
dept	department		Sum	Summer
ed	edited, edition, editor		sup	supplement
F	February		supt	superintendent
Hon	Honorable		tr	translated, transla-tion, translator
il	illustrated, illustra-tion, illustrator		v	volume
inc	incorporated		w	weekly
introd	introduction, intro-ductory		Wint	Winter
Ja	January		yr	year
Je	June			
Jl	July			

READERS' GUIDE TO
PERIODICAL LITERATURE
MARCH 1971—FEBRUARY 1972

A. Philip Randolph institute
Vote mobilization for the 1970s. il por Ebony 26:84-6 Jl '71
AA. See Alcoholics anonymous
AAAS. See American association for the advancement of science
AADC. See Association of American dance companies
AAES. See American association of evangelical students
AAHA. See American association of homes for the aging
AALS. See Association of American library schools
AAP. See Agribusiness accountability project (organization); Association of American publishers
AAPC. See American association of pastoral counselors
AAPT. See American association of physics teachers
AASA. See American association of school administrators
AASCU. See American association of state colleges and universities
AASL. See American association of school librarians
AAU. See Amateur athletic union of the United States
AAUP. See American association of university professors; Association of American university presses
AAVSO. See American association of variable star observers
A and P company. See Great Atlantic and Pacific tea company
ABA. See American bar association; American basketball association; American booksellers association
ABC. See American broadcasting companies
ABCC. See Atomic bomb casualty commission
ABCD (Action for Boston community development) See Boston—Public welfare
ABM (anti-ballistic missile) See Guided missiles—Defenses
ABT. See American ballet theatre
ACA. See American camping association
ACC. See American crafts council
ACCC. See American council of Christian churches
ACDA. See United States—Arms control and disarmament agency
AC/DC; drama. See Williams, H.
ACE. See American council on education
ACLU. See American civil liberties union
ACONDA. See American library association—Activities committee on new directions for ALA
ACP. See Associated church press (organization)
ACPE. See Association for clinical pastoral education
ACS. See American chemical society
ACT. See Action for children's television (organization)
ACTH
Calcium as a mediator of adrenocorticotrophic hormone action on adrenal protein synthesis. R. V. Farese. bibliog il Science 173: 447-50 Jl 30 '71
Mineral element correlation with adenohypophyseal-adrenal cortex function and stress. A. Flynn and others. bibliog il Science 173:1035-6 S 10 '71
Stress and behavior. S. Levine. il Sci Am 224:26-31 bibliog(p 122) Ja '71

ADA. See Americans for Democratic action
ADR system. See Amortization deductions
AEC. See United States—Atomic energy commission
AECT. See National education association—Association for educational communication and technology
AFA. See American forestry association
AFDC (aid to families with dependent children) See Child welfare—United States
AFL-CIO. See American federation of labor and Congress of industrial organizations
AFSC. See American Friends service committee
AFSCME. See American federation of state, county and municipal employees
AFTRA. See American federation of television and radio artists
AGMA. See American guild of musical artists
AHRA national races. See Drag racing
AI. See Artificial insemination
AIA. See Aerospace industries association of America, inc; American institute of architects
AIA-Sunset Western home awards. See Western home awards
AIBS. See American institute of biological sciences
AICPA. See American institute of certified public accountants
AID. See United States—Agency for international development
AIP. See American institute of physics
ALA. See Alliance for labor action; American library association
ALA catalog rules. See Cataloging
ALD (aminolevulinate dehydratase) See Enzymes
ALPA. See Air line pilots association. International
ALPO. See Association of lunar and planetary observers
ALSEP (Apollo lunar service experiments package) See Moon—Exploration—Equipment
AMA. See American management association
AMC. See American motors corporation; American music conference
AMF, inc.
Rejoicing at leisure. il Forbes 108:42 N 1 '71
Rodney C. Gott of AMF: interview. R. C. Gott. il pors Nations Bsns 59:52-4+ N '71
AMP. See Adenosine monophosphate
ANZUS (Australia, New Zealand, United States) council. See Anzus council
APA. See American psychiatric association; American psychological association
APBA. See American power boat association
APG bowmen. See Sports clubs
APS. See American physical society
APTA. See Aerospace professional and technical association
ARPA. See United States—Defense, Department of—Advanced research projects agency
ARTS (advanced radar traffic system) See Radar in aviation
ASA. See American sociological association
ASC. See American security council
ASCE. See American society of Christian ethics
ASCS. See United States—Agricultural stabilization and conservation service
ASIS. See American society for information science
ASNLH. See Association for the study of Negro life and history

ASR (airport surveillance radar) See Radar in aviation

AT & T. See American telephone and telegraph company

ATA. See Air transport association of America

ATC satellites. See Artificial satellites—Air traffic control use

ATET (advanced technology experimental transport) See Airplanes, Experimental

ATP. See Adenosine triphosphate

ATV (all-terrain vehicles) See Motor vehicles, Amphibious

AWACS (airborne warning and control system) See Airplanes, Military—Radar equipment

AACH, Herb
Arts and the human environment. Craft Horiz 31:38 F '71
How color sensitive are you? quiz. House & Gard 140:10-11+ S '71
Structure of color. Craft Horiz 31:54+ Je '71

AAMODT, Kim
Book notes and reviews. See issues of Yachting

AARON, Benjamin
Employee rights under an agreement: a current evaluation. bibliog Mo Labor R 94:52-6 Ag '71

AARON, Chloe
Video underground. il Art in Am 59:74-9+ My '71

AARON, Henry, 1934-
Annual baseball roundup: the last of the big bats. il pors Ebony 26:92-4+ Je '71 *
Babe Ruth derby. il por Time 97:58+ My 10 '71*
Babe, Willie and Hank. il por Newsweek 77:67 My 10 '71 *

AARON, Jonathan
Consequences of a dime; poem. New Yorker 47:46 D 11 '71
Introduction to the sleepers; poem. Esquire 76:45 D '71
Running; poem. Esquire 76:84 O '71

AARONSON, Stuart A. and others
Induction of murine C-type viruses from clonal lines of virus-free BALB/3T3 cells. bibliog il Science 174:157-9 O 8 '71

AARONSON, Terri
Black box. bibliog il Environ 13:10-18 D '71
Gamble. il Environ 13:20-4+ S '71
Mercury in the environment. il Environ 13:16-23 My '71
Tour of Vietnam. bibliog il Environ 13:34-43 Mr '71

ABADY, Robert
Nobody touches me with impunity. R. H. Boyle. il Sports Illus 34:74-7+ Mr 15 '71 *

ABANDONED buildings. See Buildings, Abandoned

ABANDONED farms. See Farms, Worn-out

ABANDONED towns
In Idaho's Bayhorse, old beehives. il Sunset 146:58 Mr '71
Western ghost towns. il Sunset 147:88-91 N '71

ABBEY, Edward
Living on the last whole earth. il Natur Hist 80:84-8 N '71
Park that caught urban blight. il Life 71:40+ S 3 '71

ABBEYS
Aalto's second American building: an abbey library for a hillside in Oregon; Mount Angel abbey library, St Benedict, Ore. il Arch Rec 149:111-16 My '71
Ann of Mount Angel abbey. L. Robinson. il pors Ebony 26:29-30+ F '71

ABBOTSFORD international air show. See Aviation—Exhibitions

ABBOTT, William L.
Public worker transforms labor. Nation 212:648-52 My 24 '71

ABBOTT laboratories
Case of bottled death; contaminated intravenous-feeding bottles. il Newsweek 77:57 Mr 29 '71
Drugmaker tries to recapture a market. il Bsns W p22-3 Jl 31 '71
Food and drug administration: is protecting lives the priority? contaminated IV feeding bottles. R. J. Bazell. Science 172:41-3 Ap 2 '71; Reply with rejoinder. C. C. Edwards. 173:379 Jl 30 '71
Tainted products. Newsweek 78:45 Ag 2 '71

ABDEL-HAMEED, F. and Shoffner, R. N.
Intersexes and sex determination in chickens. bibliog il Science 172:962-4 My 28 '71

ABDUCTION. See Kidnapping

ABDUL-JABBAR, Kareem
We've got to spread a little anarchy; interview. ed. by J. Olsen. il por Sports Illus 34:36-8+ Ap 19 '71

about
Annual basketball roundup: Milwaukee Bucks, an instant dynasty? L. J. Banks. il pors Ebony 26:83-6+ Ja '71 *
Kareem of the crop. H. L. Masin. por Sr Schol 99:16-17 D 6 '71; 20-1 Ja 10 '72 *
Lew is not enough. P. Carry. il por Sports Illus 34:14-17 F 8 '71 *
No member from the wedding. P. Carry. il Sports Illus 34:32-3 Je 7 '71 *
Take a bow, Lew Alcindor. J. Stewart-Gordon. il por Read Digest 98:118-22 Ja '71 *
With Oscar and Lew, Milwaukee is basketball's best, but... P. Wilkes. pors Look 35:68-70 Ap 6 '71 *

ABDUL and the Caliph's treasure; drama. See Heshmati, L. B.

ABEL, Bill
Turntable Junction. il Travel 136:73 S '71

ABEL, Elie. See Kalb, M. jt. auth.

ABEL, Ernest L.
Marihuana and memory: acquisition or retrieval? bibliog il Science 173:1038-40 S 10 '71

ABEL, I. W.
Decent guys a little too long; interview. ed. by T. Joyce and J. Lowell. por Newsweek 77:51 F 1 '71
Steelworkers conservation program. il por Nat Parks & Con Mag 45:25-8 F '71

about
Steelworkers' chief sees a bitter fight. por Bsns W p 16 Ja 23 '71 *
Trying to avoid an unwanted strike. il pors Time 97:77-8 My 24 '71 *

ABEL, Josef
He types portraits. H. Meyer. il pors Design 73:20-3 Wint '71 *

ABELARD and Heloise; drama. See Millar, R.

ABELES, F. B. and others
Fate of air pollutants: removal of ethylene, sulfur dioxide, and nitrogen dioxide by soil. bibliog il Science 173:914-16 S 3 '71

ABELIAS
Three visitors from Mexico: red yucca, Mexican abelia and red cestrum. il Sunset 147:184 S '71

ABELL, George O.
Bye-bye, galaxies: the universe may be twice as large as thought. Sci N 101:22 Ja 8 '72 *

ABELSON, Philip H.
Geophysicists in Moscow: signs of easier relations. Science 173:797-800 Ag 27 '71

ABERCROMBIE, Thomas J.
Morocco: land of the farthest west. il Nat Geog 139:834-65 Je '71

ABERNATHY, Ralph David
Abernathy woos Communist as U.S. backing drops. Chr Today 16:43 O 22 '71 *
Black study. J. Osborne. New Repub 164:11 Mr 13 '71 *

ABERRATION (optics)
Seeing and scintillation. A. T. Young. bibliog il Sky & Tel 42:139-41+ S '71

ABE'S winkin' eye; drama. See Fisher, A.

ABHAU, Elliot
Getting religion; poem. Am Scholar 40:512 Sum '71
Penta-gone; poem. Am Scholar 40:304 Spr '71

ABILENE, Tex.

Parks and playgrounds
Every playground has a theme. il Am City 86:32 Ja '71

ABILITIES, inc.
School that love built. J. Reddy. por Read Digest 99:149-50+ S '71

ABILITY
See also
Athletic ability
Creative ability
Great men
Learning, Psychology of
Success

ABILITY grouping in education
Ability grouping: out or in?... G. Rinehart. Ed Digest 36:49-51 F '71
Grouping for motivation in mathematics. K. F. George. Clear House 46:81 O '71
My sweet Caroline: a failure in second grade. L. G. Anderson. il por Redbook 137:24+ My '71
Programmed for social class: tracking in high school. W. E. Schafer and others. il Trans-Action 7:39-46+ O '70
See also
Ungraded classes

---

* Printer's device

ABILITY tests. See Aptitude tests

ABKHASIANS
Why they live to be 100, or even older. In Abkhasia. S. Benet. il N Y Times Mag p3+ D 26 '71

ABLON, Joan
Cultural conflict in urban Indians. bibliog Ment Hy 55:199-205 Ap '71

ABNAKI Indians
Red power in Maine; TRIBE high school for Indian dropouts. Newsweek 77:55 My 31 '71

ABNER Crane from Hayseed lane; drama. See Dias, E. J.

ABNORMALITIES (animals)
Teratogenic effects of a chelating agent and their prevention by zinc. H. Swenerton and L. S. Hurley. bibliog il Science 173:62-4 Jl 2 '71; Reply with rejoinder. R. D. Hamilton. 174:102-3 O 8 '71

ABNORMALITIES (birds)
Early warning of the terns. H. Hays and R. W. Risebrough. il Natur Hist 80:38-47 N '71

ABORIGINES, Australian. See Australia—Native races

ABORTION
Abortion and public opinion: the 1960-70 decade. J. Blake. bibliog il Science 171:540-9 F 12 '71
Abortion: how it's working. il Newsweek 78:50-2 Jl 19 '71
Abortion: what you should know. P. M. Sarrel and L. J. Sarrel. Vogue 158:93-4 Ag 1 '71
Alternative to abortion. L. N. Bell. Chr Today 15:17-19 Je 18 '71
Birthright: alternative to abortion. J. B. Breslin. America 125:116-19 S 4 '71; Discussion. 125:217, 273 O 2, 16 '71
Guide for women. A. J. Margolis and S. Loebl. Redbook 136:26 Ja '71
Legal abortion: who, why and where. il Time 98:67-70 S 27 '71
Nurses and abortion. Time 97:60 My 31 '71
Politics of death. R. Kirk. Nat R 23:315 Mr 23 '71
Report on the abortion capital of the country; New York city. S. Edmiston. il N Y Times Mag p 10-11+ Ap 11 '71; Discussion. p22+ My 2; 80 My 9; 16 My 23 '71
Stormy aftermath of abortion reform. C. Remsberg and B. Remsberg. Good H 172:86-7+ F '71
They take care of their own; abortion loan fund of University of Maine students. E. Scribner. Nation 212:230 F 22 '71
What every woman should know about abortion. J. E. Brody. Read Digest 98:119-22 F '71
What we do, and don't know about miscarriage. S. Olds. il Todays Health 49:42-5 F '71

Laws and legislation
Abortion and suicidal behaviors: observations on the concept of endangering the mental health of the mother. H. L. P. Resnik and B. J. Wittlin. bibliog Ment Hy 55:10-20 Ja '71
Abortion and the reverence for life. P. W. Rahmeier. Chr Cent 88:556-60 My 5 '71; Reply. R. H. Hamill. 88:957-8 Ag 11 '71
Abortion battle. Newsweek 77:110 My 3 '71
Abortion: law, choice and morality, by D. Callahan. Review
Chr Cent il 88:166+ F 3 '71. D. W. Stump
Abortion-law reform is inevitable, even in Texas. J. C. Evans. Chr Cent 88:548-9 My 5 '71; Discussion. 88:1051-2, 1424-6 S 8, D 1 '71
Abortion rap, by D. Schulder and F. Kennedy. Review
Nation 213:342-3 O 11 '71. C. Dreifus
Abortion reform and the courts; Florida and Michigan Supreme court decisions. America 125:52 Ag 7 '71
Abortion: rhetoric and reality. Chr Cent 88:871 Jl 21 '71; Discussion. 88:1052-3 S 8 '71
Ambivalence on abortion. por Time 97:40 My 3 '71
Catholics and liberalized abortion laws. N. J. Rigali. il Cath World 213:283-5 S '71; Discussion. 214:101-2 D '71
Cause and effect; decline in birthrate with new abortion law. Sci Am 225:42 O '71
Guide to abortion laws in the United States. L. Lader. Redbook 137:51-8 Je '71
Legal abortion: who, why and where. il Time 98:67-70 S 27 '71
President on abortion; executive order to military hospitals. Newsweek 77:129+ Ap 19 '71
Roundup on abortion reform. America 125:134-5 S 11 '71

Secular case against abortion on demand. R. Stith. Commonweal 95:151-4 N 12 '71
Supreme court and abortion. America 124:443 My 1 '71
Teacher opinion poll; liberalizing abortion law. Todays Ed 60:5 My '71
Two books on abortion and the questions they raise. C. B. Luce; discussion. America 124:62 Ja 23 '71; Nat R 23:116, 176, 198-9, 232 F 9-Mr 9 '71

Canada
Abortion statements in Canada: Catholic clarity, Protestant ambivalence. G. Lane. Chr Cent 88:1303-4 N 3 '71

France
Free abortions, now! proposed reforms. il Newsweek 77:54+ Ap 19 '71

Germany (Federal Republic)
Parting shots: well-kept-secret weapon in the sexual revolution. W. A. McWhirter. il por Life 71:69 Jl 9 '71

Moral and religious aspects
Abortion and morality. P. R. Ehrlich and J. P. Holdren. Sat R 54:58 S 4 '71
Abortion and pluralist society. C. F. Magistro. il Nat R 23:476-8+ My 4 '71
Abortion and the reverence for life. P. W. Rahmeier. Chr Cent 88:556-60 My 5 '71; Reply. R. H. Hamill. 88:957-8 Ag 11 '71
Abortion issue. D. Kucharsky. Chr Today 15:36 Ap 23 '71
Abortion: law, choice and morality, by D. Callahan. Review
Chr Cent il 88:166+ F 3 '71. D. W. Stump
Abortion-law reform is inevitable, even in Texas. J. C. Evans. Chr Cent 88:548-9 My 5 '71; Discussion. 88:1051-2, 1424-6 S 8, D 1 '71
Abortion: rhetoric and reality. Chr Cent 88:871 Jl 21 '71; Discussion. 88:1052-3 S 8 '71
Abortion: the crunch; How to protest abortion. W. F. Buckley, jr. Nat R 23:444-5 Ap 20 '71
Anti-abortion campaign. il Time 97:70+ Mr 29 '71
Catholics and liberalized abortion laws. N. J. Rigali. il Cath World 213:283-5 S '71; Discussion. 214:101-2 D '71
Morality of abortion, ed. by J. T. Noonan, jr. Review
Chr Cent 88:165-6 F 3 '71. A. Seaburg
Now-generation churchmen and the unborn. H. B. Kuhn. Chr Today 15:38 Ja 29 '71
Plain meaning of abortion. G. L. Hallett. America 124:632-3 Je 19 '71
Public policy making: why the churches strike out. V. C. Blum. America 124:224-8 Mr 6 '71
Rationales for feticide. D. W. Louisell. Cath World 212:318-19 Mr '71
Religious pacifist looks at abortion. G. C. Zahn. Commonweal 94:279-82 My 28 '71; Discussion. 94:395+ Ag 6 '71
Right to life: who is to decide? J. L. Arehart. il Sci N 100:298-300 O 30 '71
Secular case against abortion on demand. R. Stith. Commonweal 95:151-4 N 12 '71
Two books on abortion and the questions they raise. C. B. Luce; discussion. America 124:62 Ja 23 '71; Nat R 23:116, 176, 198-9, 232 F 9-Mr 9 '71
Why are nurses shook-up over abortion? I. Fischl. Look 35:66 F 9 '71

Psychological aspects
Abortion's psychological price. K. J. Sharp. Chr Today 15:4-6 Je 4 '71
Emotional scars of abortion. H. S. Arnstein. il Ladies Home J 88:121+ My '71

ABORTION information services. See Information services

ABPLANALP, Robert H.
President's other friend. R. G. Hummerstone. il pors Life 70:55-6+ Mr 5 '71 *

ABRAHAMSEN, David
Is there a bit of Calley in us? Look 35:76-7 Je 1 '71

ABRAMOWITZ, Emanuel
Auxiliary; interview. New Yorker 47:28-30 D 18 '71

ABRAMOWITZ, Susan Isaacs
Opinion: on left turning right, the new conservative. por Mlle 74:24+ Ja '72

ABRAMS, Arnold
Quiet heroes of South Vietnam. Read Digest 99:142-6 O '71

ABRAMS, Charles
Guide to the language of cities; excerpts from The language of cities. por Fortune 83:121-2 Mr '71

ABRAMS, Creighton Williams, 1914-
General v. the system. il Time 97:26-7 F 15
'71 *
Withdrawal pains. il Newsweek 77:41 Je 7
'71 *
ABRAMS, Harry Nathan
Book business; interview, ed. by A. Green.
Sat R 54:43+ N 27 '71
ABRAMS, Harry N, inc.
Book business; interview, ed. by A. Green.
H. N. Abrams. Sat R 54:43+ N 27 '71
ABRASIVE blasting. See Sand blast
ABRASIVE wheels. See Grinding wheels
ABRASIVES
See also
Norton company
ABRAVANEL, Maurice
Summer experience. il por Hi Fi 21:MA12-13
F '71
ABS, Hermann Josef
Talk with Europe's top banker; interview,
ed. by B. van Voorst. por Newsweek 77:
72-3 F 22 '71
ABSCISIC acid
Asymmetry, its importance to the action
and metabolism of abscisic acid. E. Sond-
heimer and others. bibliog il Science 174:
829-31 N 19 '71
ABSENTEEISM
Absenteeism: worse than strikes. U S News
71:67 Ag 23 '71
Every day is Sunday; Italy. il Time 97:84
Mr 29 '71
ABSHIRE, David M.
Offshore oil activities in the Viet-Nam area;
text of letters. Dept State Bul 64:491-4 Ap
5 '71
ABSORPTION (physiology)
2-Thiophenecarboxylic acid: inhibitor of bone
resorption in tissue culture. V. S. Fang and
others. bibliog il Science 172:163-5 Ap 9 '71
ABSORPTION (plants)
See also
Plants—Absorption of water
ABSORPTION in soils. See Soil absorption
ABSTRACT art. See Art, Abstract
ABSTRACT photography. See Photography,
Artistic
ABSTRACTION
Free recall and abstractness of stimuli. W.
Bevan and J. A. Steger. bibliog il Science
172:597-9 My 7 '71
ABSURD, The
Mildly absurd. R. Hattersley. il Pop Phot
69:88-91 S '71
ABT, Clark C.
Outside consultant for government. por Bsns
W p69 N 27 '71 *
ABU DHABI
See also
Irrigation—Abu Dhabi
ABU SIMBEL. Temples of
Nubia: victory of international solidarity. A.
M. El Sawi. il UNESCO Courier 24:60-2
Ag '71
ABUTILON. See Flowering maples
ABYSS; ballet. See Ballets—Criticisms
ABYSSINIAN church. See Ethiopic church
ABZUG, Bella
Fighting hard. por Vogue 157:94-5 Je '71
Unfinished business of America. Look 35:61
Jl 13 '71
about
Bellacose Abzug. pors Time 98:14+ Ag 16
'71 *
ACACIAS, Silky. See Silk trees
ACADEMIC achievement. See Student achieve-
ments
ACADEMIC degrees. See Degrees, Academic
ACADEMIC freedom
AASCU statement on academic responsi-
bility. Sch & Soc 99:204 Ap '71
Academic freedom, alive and ... P. Steinfels.
Commonweal 93:440 F 5 '71
Dogma of absolute truth. J. E. Krug and J.
A. Harvey. Am Lib 2:638-40 Je '71
Free speech and Catholic university; Ti-
Grace affair. America 124:306 Mr 27 '71
Freedom and funding; Skinner support
queried. por Sci N 100:420-1 D 25 '71
Intellectual freedom and the university. D. R.
Goddard and L. C. Koons. bibliog Science
173:607-10 Ag 13 '71
Newer concepts of academic freedom. W. W.
Brickman. Sch & Soc 99:72-3 F '71
Promotion of chaos: the three major cata-
lysts; address. July 17. 1971. R. E. L. Eaton.
Vital Speeches 37:687-90 S 1 '71
Race, evolution and Mormonism. C. W.
Quaintance. Chr Cent 88:589-6 My 12 '71
Responsible professors. T. H. Clancy; reply.
B. F. Reilly. America 124:133 F 13 '71

ACADEMIC tenure. See College professors and
instructors—Tenure; Teachers—Tenure
ACADEMIE française. See French academy
ACADEMIES of science. See Scientific socie-
ties
ACADEMY awards (moving pictures)
Importance of being Oscar. C. L. Westerbeck,
jr. il Commonweal 94:139-44 Ap 16 '71
Prize day at Global Village. il Time 97:53-4
Ap 26 '71
Reluctant Oscars; interviews, ed. by C. Irving.
G. C. Scott; G. Jackson. pors McCalls 98:
12+ Jl '71
Story behind: Oscar. il Changing T 25:30
Mr '71
ACADEMY of music, Brooklyn
Theatre grows in Brooklyn; Chelsea theater
center. M. Gottfried. Vogue 157:130 Ap 15
'71
ACADEMY of music, Philadelphia
Current chronicle; Philadelphia musical acad-
emy centennial anniversary celebration. D.
Chittum. il Mus Q 57:129-41 Ja '71
House at Broad and Locust: Academy of
music. F. W. Stokes. il Opera N 35:8-12 Ja
23 '71
ACADEMY of sciences of the USSR
Space meteorology; cooperation between
NASA and the Russian academy of sci-
ences. Space World H-7-91:33-5 Jl '71
ACADIA NATIONAL PARK
Acadia National park: where Maine's moun-
tains meet the sea on Mount Desert Island.
B. Schill and B. Schill. il Yachting 129:54-
5+ Je '71
ACANTHASTER planci. See Starfishes
ACAPULCO, Mexico
24-hour going traveler: Acapulco. S. Cuneo.
Mlle 74:76-7 Ja '72

Hotels, restaurants, etc.
Acapulco: more in the jet setters' playpen.
Bsns W p45 Ja 1 '72
ACCADEMIA musicale Chigiana, Siena, Italy.
See Music schools
ACCELERATION in education. See Education-
al acceleration
ACCELERATION of particles. See Particles
(nuclear physics)—Acceleration
ACCELERATORS (electrons, etc)
Accelerating heavy ions in the Bevatron. D.
E. Thomsen. il Sci N 100:266-8 O 16 '71
Acceleration of heavy ions at the bevatron.
H. A. Grunder and others. il Science 174:
1128-9 D 10 '71
Acceleration of nitrogen ions to 7.4 Gev in
the Princeton particle accelerator. M. G.
White and others. bibliog il Science 174:
1121-3 D 10 '71
Accelerator for Japan. Sci N 99:300 My 1 '71
American physicists worry; heavy-ion ac-
celerators. il Sci N 99:178-9 Mr 13 '71
Boost for Bevatron. Time 98:60-1 S 13 '71
Brookhaven AGS modification has 200-MeV
linac. il Phys Today 24:21 Ja '71
CERN: final planning begins for Europe's
big machine. N. Hawkes. Science 172:653
My 14 '71
Crucial year; superconducting linear accel-
erators. Sci N 99:163 Mr 6 '71
Double and redouble; superconducting tubes
at the National accelerator laboratory. D.
E. Thomsen. il Sci N 99:199 Mr 20 '71
Extra zip for atom smashers; intersecting
storage rings. il Bsns W p78+ Mr 27 '71
Heavy ions for cancer; Princeton-Penn accelerator. Sci N 99:248 Ap 10 '71
High energy physics: in-group talks funds,
possible closeouts. D. Shapley. Science 173:
897-9 S 3 '71
How to build a machine to produce low-
energy protons and deuterons; accelerator
using a Van de Graaff generator. L. Cress.
il Sci Am 225:106-8+ Ag '71
ISR collisions at CERN; experiments start
this summer. G. B. Lubkin. il Phys Today
24-17 Ap '71
LAMPF meson factory calls for beam-time
proposals. J. T. Scott. il Phys Today 24:
19-20 F '71
Livermore's new linear accelerator. G. B.
Lubkin. il Phys Today 24:19 Ag '71
Loops in the linear; proposal for the Stanford linear accelerator center. il Sci N 99:
414 Je 19 '71
Princeton-Pennsylvania accelerator: end of
an era in particle physics. D. P. Teter. il
Science 173:36-9 Jl 2 '71
Relevance of particle accelerators to national
goals; adaptation of address. March 1971.
L. Rosen. bibliog il Science 173:490-7 Ag 6
Ring records; CERN storage-ring complex.
Sci Am 224:47 Ja '71

ACCELERATORS (electrons, etc)—*Continued*
SLAC proposes to boost energy above 50 GeV without superconductors. il Phys Today 24:18-19 O '71
300-GeV machine approved; CERN proton accelerator. Sci N 99:143 F 27 '71
300 GeV or 1,000; CERN accelerator. Sci Am 224:49-50 Ap '71
Toward asymptopia; CERN use of ISR atom smasher. il Time 99:45-6 Ja 10 '72
See also
National accelerator laboratory

Medical use
Another way to treat cancer; medical linacs. il Bsns W p86 D 18 '71

ACCESS to the children; story. See Trevor, W.
ACCESSORIES, Household. See Household furnishings
ACCIDENTS
Home unsafe home. R. Nader. Ladies Home J 89:70+ Ja '72
Moonstruck scientists; claim accident rates influenced by natural phenomena. il Time 99:48 Ja 10 '72
Needed: more help for accident victims. J. R. Miller. Read Digest 98:83-7 Ja '71
Ten deadliest household products. L. David. il Mech Illus 67:64-6+ F '71
See also
Electricity, Injuries from
First aid in illness and injury
Shipwrecks
Traffic accidents
Traumatism
also subhead Accidents or Accidents and injuries under various subjects, e.g. Boats and boating—Accidents

Prevention
Accidents that don't have to happen: what parents should know. B. Schanzer. il Redbook 137:60-1+ Jl '71
Children's safety measures. L. W. Sauer. PTA Mag 65:21-2 My '71
Christmas time with Willie. il Consumer Bul 54:13-14 D '71
Dangerous fallacy of the accident-prone child. D. Klein. il Parents Mag 46:78-9+ N '71
Holiday hazards; quite avoidable. Sunset 147:120 D '71
Home is where accidents happen. il Changing T 25:37-8 D '71
Household hazards. Consumer Bul 54:33-4 Ag '71
How to fall-proof your home. H. Farkas. il Mech Illus 68:90-1+ Ja '72
How to keep your home safe for your children. V. E. Pomeranz and D. Schultz. il Todays Health 49:32-4 O '71
How to prevent most home accidents. il Good H 173:141 Ag '71
Municipal safety program that works; Kansas City, Mo. M. D. Calkins. il Am City 86:67-8 Ag '71
National safety council's accident-prevention checklist. il Parents Mag 46:52 N '71
Safety starts at home. D. Schultz. Ladies Home J 88:170 S '71
Why should a child swallow drain cleaner? il Consumer Rep 36:528-31 S '71
See also subhead Safety devices and measures under various subjects, e.g. Automobiles—Safety devices and measures

ACCIDENTS, Industrial
See also
Insurance, Workmens compensation

Prevention
See Industrial safety
ACCIDENTS, Liability for. See Liability (law)
ACCOUNTABILITY. See Responsibility
ACCOUNTABILITY (education)
Accountability and the classroom teacher. il Todays Ed 60:41-55 Mr '71
Accountability; at what cost? address, November 1970. F. E. Ratliff. Engl J 60:485-90 Ap '71
Accountability is here to stay. W. D. Boutwell. PTA Mag 66:13-14 N '71
Accountability, the next deadly nostrum in education? R. J. Nash. bibliog Sch & Soc 99:501-4 D '71
Accountability: watchword for the 70's. J. E. Morris. bibliog Clear House 45:323-8 F '71
Accountable to whom? For what? J. Cass. Sat R 54:41 Mr 20 '71
After all. H. Bain. Todays Ed 60:80 Mr '71
In education, are publishers accountable? R. H. Smith. Pub W 199:39 Ja 18 '71
It's time for accountability in education. L. Lessinger. il Nations Bsns 59:54-7 Ag '71

Some misgivings about teacher accountability. H. Bain. por Parents Mag 46:40 Mr '71
Why insist on accountability? W. D. Boutwell. PTA Mag 66:9-10 D '71
See also
Performance contracts (education)
ACCOUNTANTS
Why accountants need to tell a fuller story; auditor's liability. il Bsns W p86-7 F 6 '71
ACCOUNTING
See also
American institute of certified public accountants
Institutional accounting
also subhead Accounting under various subjects, e.g. Corporations—Accounting

Mechanical aids
See also
Computers—Business use
ACCOUNTING, Household. See Budget, Household
ACCREDITATION, College. See Colleges and universities—Accreditation
ACCREDITATION of library schools. See Library schools and education
ACCREDITED library schools. See Library schools and education
ACCULTURATION
Persistent cultural systems. E. H. Spicer. bibliog Science 174:795-800 N 19 '71
ACE, Goodman
Top of my head. See issues of Saturday review
ACETALDEHYDE
Induction of liver acetaldehyde dehydrogenase: possible role in ethanol tolerance after exposure to barbiturates. G. Redmond and G. Cohen. bibliog il Science 171:387-9 Ja 29 '71
ACETAMIDE
Chemically induced porphyria: increased microsomal heme turnover after treatment with allylisopropylacetamide. U. A. Meyer and H. S. Marver. bibliog il Science 171:64-6 Ja 8 '71
ACETATES
Phenylthioacetate: a useful substrate for the histochemical and colorimetric detection of cholinesterase. G. M. Booth and R. L. Metcalf; reply. W. D. McEnroe. Science 171:928 Mr 5 '71
Sex pheromone of the almond moth and the Indian meal moth: cis-9, trans-12-tetradecadienyl acetate. Y. Kuwahara and others. bibliog Science 171:801-2 F 26 '71
Sex stimulant and attractant in the Indian meal moth and in the almond moth. U. E. Brady and others. bibliog il Science 171:802-4 F 26 '71
See also
Sodium acetate
ACETOXYCYCLOHEXIMIDE
Acetoxycycloheximide enhances audiogenic seizures in DBA/2J mice. H. D. Jameson and others. bibliog il Science 173:249-51 Jl 16 '71
ACETYLCHOLINE
Acetylcholine binding to torpedo electroplax: relationship to acetylcholine receptors. M. E. Eldefrawi and others. bibliog il Science 173:338-40 Jl 23 '71
Acetylcholine liberation from cerebral cortex during paradoxical (REM) sleep. H. H. Jasper and J. Tessier. bibliog il Science 172:601-2 My 7 '71
Conductance changes produced by acetylcholine in lipidic membranes containing a proteolipid from electrophorus. M. Parisi and others. bibliog il Science 172:56-7 Ap 2 '71
Kinetics of acetylcholine synthesis and hydrolysis in myasthenia gravis. R. N. Rosenberg and others. bibliog il Science 173:644-5 Ag 13 '71
ACETYLCHOLINESTERASE
Diisopropylphosphorofluoridate and Tabun: enzymatic hydrolysis and nerve function. F. C. G. Hoskin. bibliog il Science 172:1243-5 Je 18 '71
ACETYLHISTIDINE. See Histidine
ACETYLTRANSFERASE. See Transferases
ACHEBE, Chinua
Study of Chinua Achebe's Things fall apart in mid-America. J. Leach. Engl J 60:1052-6 N '71 *
ACHESON, Dean Gooderham
Eclipse of the State department. For Affairs 49:593-606 Jl '71
Pungent memories from Mr Acheson; excerpts from interview, ed. by K. Harris. il pors Life 71:51-2+ Jl 23 '71

ACHESON, Dean Gooderham—*Continued*

about

Complexity of Acheson. P. Steinfels. Commonweal 95:102 O 29 '71 *
Diplomat who did not want to be liked. il pors Time 98:19-20 O 25 '71 *
Obituary
  Nat R 23:1219-20 N 5 '71
  Newsweek por 78:52 O 25 '71. R. Boeth
Whatsoever things are true. D. Brudnoy. il Nat R 23:1310-11 N 19 '71 *

ACHIEVEMENTS, Student. See Student achievements

ACID-base equilibrium
  See also
  Buffer solutions

ACID soils. See Soil acidity

ACIDITY
  See also
  Antacids

ACIDS
  See also names of acids and acid groups, e.g. Polyadenylic acid

ACIDS, Fatty
Tall oil, a valuable by-product. J. T. Geoghegan and W. E. Bambrick. bibliog il pors Chem 44:6-10 Ja '71
Unstirred water layers in intestine: rate determinant of fatty acid absorption from micellar solutions. F. A. Wilson and others. bibliog il Science 174:1031-3 D 3 '71
  See also
  Prostaglandins

ACKERMAN, James S.
Religion in the public schools. PTA Mag 65:2-5 bibliog(p33) My '71

ACKLEY, Gardner
Economy. See issues of Dun's, December 1971-

about

Dun's newest faces. Duns 98:3 N '71 *

ACKLEY, S. F. and Itagaki, K.
Distribution of icing in the Northeast's ice storm of 26-27 December 1969. bibliog il Weatherwise 23:274-9 D '70

ACKLEY, Sheldon
To overcome discrimination now. Cur 129:35-8 My '71

ACOSTA, Mary J.
Can rubbings be creative? il Design 72:30-1 mid-Wint '71
Designing a class mural. il Design 72:32-3 Spr '71

ACOUSTIC phenomena in nature
  See also
  Thunderstorms

ACOUSTIC research, inc.
Component maker meets record company: the AR/DGG contemporary music project. D. Henahan. Hi Fi 21:96-7 F '71

ACOUSTIC waves. See Sound waves

ACOUSTICS, Architectural
Auditory backward inhibition in concert halls. G. Von Békésy. bibliog il Science 171:529-36 F 12 '71
Guidelines for good sound. I. W. Wood. il Arch Rec 150:123-5 Jl '71
Predicting ballast noise from H.I.D. lighting systems. A. C. McNamara, jr. il Arch Rec 149:139-42 My '71
  See also
  Orchestra shells

ACOUSTOELECTRONICS. See Electroacoustics

ACQUISITIONS, College library. See College libraries—Acquisitions

ACQUISITIONS, Library. See Libraries—Acquisitions

ACRIDINE orange. See Stains and staining (microscopy)

ACROBATS; drama. See Horovitz, I.

ACROBATS and acrobatism
Ritual acrobats of Persia, Brooklyn academy of music. D. Hering. Dance Mag 46:28 Ja '72

ACRYLIC painting. See Painting

ACTING
Don't call me madam! interview, ed. by G. Loney. U. Hagen. il por Opera N 35:6-7 Ja 23 '71
How handsome the hero, how romantic his fate! interviews, ed. by E. Miller. T. Dalton; R. O'Neal. il pors Seventeen 29:110-11+ D '70
If it's Monday, it must be Tuesday; interview, ed. by M. Ronan. T. Weld. por Sr Schol 99:24 D 13 '71
Is there a new now? interview, ed. by M. Ronan. A. MacGraw. por Sr Schol 98:3+ F 15 '71

Mistaken identity Ann-Margret and R. Harris. M. Ronan. por Sr Schol 98:30+ F 15 '71
Nicholas and Alexandra quartet; interview with four budding actresses, ed. by E. Miller. il Seventeen 30:102-3 N '71
On location; interview, ed. by E. Miller. J. Agutter. por Seventeen 30:62 N '71
On location; interview, ed. by. E. Miller. S. Duncan. por Seventeen 30:72+ S '71
On location; interview, ed. by E. Miller. D. Halprin; B. Davison. por Seventeen 30:52 O '71
Our local correspondents; afternoons with Hopper. J. Stevenson. New Yorker 47:116+ N 13 '71
Stepin Fetchit talks back; interview, ed. by J. McBride. S. Fetchit. pors Film Q 24:20-6 Sum '71
Zero in; interview, ed. by S. Jenkins. Z. Mostel. por Opera N 35:14-15 F 13 '71
  See also
  Moving picture acting
  Pantomime

ACTINOMYCIN
Acridine orange potentiation of actinomycin D uptake and activity. E. F. Roth, jr. and J. Kochen. bibliog il Science 174:696-8 N 12 '71
Actinomycin D: renewed RNA synthesis after removal from mammalian cells. A. Schluederberg and others. bibliog il Science 172:577-9 My 7 '71
Now visible, in 3-D; how actinomycin binds to DNA. il por Sci N 99:436 Je 26 '71
Sea urchin embryos are permeable to actinomycin. G. A. Greenhouse and others. bibliog il Science 171:686-9 F 19 '71

ACTION corps (proposed) See United States—Action corps (proposed)

ACTION for children's television (organization)
She ACTs against television. M. Meade. il McCalls 99:46 D '71

ACTION in art
  See also
  Mobiles

ACTIONS and defenses
Alaska's Tongass suit: the exercise at Juneau; Sierra club vs. Hardin. M. Miller. il Am For 77:28-31+ Mr '71
Barbara Ringer wins round one in Copyright office fight. S. Wagner. Pub W 200:42 S 27 '71
Carey is new copyright head; Ringer sues, charging bias. Pub W 200:29 S 6 '71
Case of the Hayden, Stone letter. C. J. Loomis. Fortune 83:143+ Mr '71
Conservationists go to court. R. D. Butcher. il Am For 77:32-5+ Je; 32-5 Jl '71
Courtroom shootouts; emergence of the environmental trial lawyers. J. B. Craig. Am For 77:11 Jl '71
If you are mad enough to sue. . . il Changing T 25:19-21 Je '71
It's Moody versus Moody in the struggle for American national. A. M. Louis. il por Fortune 83:108-12+ Mr '71
Legal strategies for environmental control. S. Lawrence. Field & S 75:12+ F '71
One for all; class actions. il Time 98:38 D 13 '71
$108-million suit filed against Beech. Aviation W 94:21 Je 28 '71
Phantom charges that haunt hotels; class actions for refunds. Bsns W p40-1 D 25 '71
To the boondocks; environmental litigation to federal district courts. S. J. Ungar. New Repub 165:11-12 O 2 '71
21 authors file suit against Britannica. Pub W 200:30-1 Ag 9 '71
Viking, Esquire, dropped from Calley law suit. Pub W 199:37 Ja 18 '71
  See also
  Libel and slander
  Torts

ACTIVATED carbon. See Carbon, Activated

ACTIVATED sludge method. See Sewage purification—Activated sludge method

ACTIVISTS, Student. See Student militants

ACTIVITIES committee on new directions for ALA. See American library association—Activities committee on new directions for ALA

ACTON, Harold Mario Mitchell
Art of memory. G. Steiner. New Yorker 47:63-4 Ja 1 '72 *
Memoirs of an aesthete 1939-69, by H. Acton. Review
  Sat R 54:27-8 My 8 '71. G. Gersh *

ACTORS, Animal. See Animals as actors

ACTORS and actresses
It's my turn to be lucky; Broadway understudies. P. Bosworth. il pors Todays Health 49:24-7+ D '71
Profiles: D. Lefkowitz: show business autograph collector. W. Whitworth. New Yorker 47:38-42+ D 18 '71
　See also
Acting
Actors' equity association
Children as actors
Moving picture actors and actresses
Television broadcasting—Performers
　also names of actors and actresses, e.g.
J. E. Jones

Political activities
What's behind those beautiful blue eyes? interview, ed. by E. Miller. P. Newman. Seventeen 29:124-5+ N '70
ACTORS' equity association
Do you call that a union? D. Weinstein. Nation 213:242-5 S 20 '71
ACTRESS glass. See Glassware
ACTS of the apostles. See Bible—New Testament—Acts
ACUITY, Visual. See Sight
ACUPUNCTURE
Acupuncture. F. Lang. il Ramp Mag 10:12+ O '71
Acupuncture: myth cure? il Vogue 159:94-5+ Ja 1 '72
Battle over stickpins. il Sci Digest 71:20 Ja '72
Chinese surgeons. il Newsweek 77:78 Je 7 '71
More than herbs and acupuncture. E. G. Dimond. il Sat R 54:17-19+ D 18 '71
Place in American medicine? il Sci N 99:400 Je 12 '71
Prickly panacea called acupuncture; with report by J. Saar. il Life 71:32-5 Ag 13 '71
Yang, yin and needles. il Time 98:37-8 Ag 9 '71
AD hoc committees. See Committees
AD hoc council committee on ACONDA. See American library association—Ad hoc council committee on ACONDA
ADAMO, N. J. and Ratner, A.
Monosodium glutamate: lack of effects on brain and reproductive function in rats. bibliog il Science 169:673-4; 172:294 Ag 14 '70, Ap 16 '71
ADAMO, S. J.
Press. See Issues of America
ADAMS, Alice
Ripped off; story. New Yorker 47:40-3 My 22 '71
Swastika on our door; story. New Yorker 47:36-44 S 11 '71
ADAMS, Andrew
Summer diplomat, U.S.A. por Seventeen 29:270-1+ Ag '70
ADAMS, Ansel
Ansel Adams revisited: something old, something new. M. Mann. il Pop Phot 68:49+ My '71 •
ADAMS, Carolyn H.
Emperor's fish; story. Todays Ed 60:29 Ap '71
ADAMS, Charlotte
Four seasons cookbook; excerpts. il Ladies Home J 88:140-1+ N '71
ADAMS, E. Sherman
Case for an incomes policy, now; address, April 23, 1971. Vital Speeches 37:546-9 Jl 1 '71
ADAMS, George R.
Black militant drama. bibliog f Am Imago 28:107-28 Sum '71
ADAMS, Hazard
Above Carra; poem. Am Scholar 40:599-600 Aut '71
ADAMS, John B. and McCord, T. B.
Alteration of lunar optical properties: age and composition effects. bibliog il Science 171:567-71 F 12 '71
ADAMS, Martha
Class reunions: dare we? il Har Yrs 11:28-9 S '71
ADAMS, Paul W.
Saga of the Antilles. il Yachting 129:62-3+ My '71
ADAMS, Phoebe Lou
Short reviews: books. See Issues of Atlantic
ADAMS, Ruth C.
Gaspé: source of organically-raised foods. Org Gard & Farm 18:74-9 N '71
Recycling nut answers the backlashers. il Org Gard & Farm 18:50-3 Je '71
ADAMS, Thelma F.
Model for teaching valuing. bibliog il Clear House 45:507-9 Ap '71

ADAMS, Tony
Restorations experts speak their minds; interview. House & Gard 140:6+ Ag '71
ADAMSON, George
Freeing the big cats. W. Nussey and H. Reuter. il pors Sci Digest 69:46-8 Je '71 •
ADAMSON, Jack H.
Tools of our tools; address, August 14, 1971. Vital Speeches 37:720-3 S 15 '71
ADAMSON, Joy
Freeing the big cats. W. Nussey and H. Reuter. il pors Sci Digest 69:46-8 Je '71 •
ADAPTABILITY (psychology)
Patient's views on relocation; reactions of psychiatric patients to urban renewal. P. Sifneos. Ment Hy 55:495-8 O '71
ADAPTATION (biology)
Allelochemics: chemical interactions between species. R. H. Whittaker and P. P. Feeny. bibliog il Science 171:757-70 F 26 '71; Discussion. 172:1362; 173:945 Je 25, S 3 '71
What natural mechanisms does man use to adapt to changes in his environment? Sci Digest 69:89 Je '71
ADAPTATION, Social. See Adjustment, Social
ADAPTATION, Visual. See Eye—Accommodation and refraction
ADAPTERS, Radio. See Radio apparatus
ADARKAR, Vivek
Mr Stevenson, sir; story. Seventeen 30:150-1 Mr '71
ADDERLEY, Terence E.
Distress call changed the temporary help industry. il pors Nations Bsns 59:70-1 Ja '71
ADDICTS, Drug. See Narcotic addicts
ADDIE Pray; story. See Brown, J. D.
ADDITIONS, House. See Houses, Remodeled
ADDITIVES. See Food additives; Gasoline—Additives; Lubrication and lubricants—Additives
ADDRESS to the orgiasts; story. See Rogin, G.
ADELAIDE, Australia

Music
Quist and Copland in Adelaide, S.A. I. Kolodin. Sat R 54:33 Jl 3 '71
ADELMAN, Maurice, Jr
Biography (cont) America 124:549-51, 125:432+ My 22, N 20 '71
ADELPHI university, Garden City, N.Y.

School of business
Learning on wheels: Adelphi university's graduate course in Principles of marketing given on a Long Island railroad train. il Time 98:66-7 N 1 '71
ADELSEN, Charles E.
Holocaust on the Golden Horn. il Opera N 35:14-16 Ja 30 '71
Road to Ani; with biographical sketch. il Natur Hist 80:4, 62-73 N '71
ADELSON, Joseph
Inventing the young. Commentary 51:43-8 My '71
ADENO-associated satellite viruses. See Viruses
ADENOMAS. See Tumors
ADENOSINE monophosphate
Adenosine 3',5'-monophosphate in nervous tissue: increase associated with synaptic transmission. D. A. McAfee and others. bibliog il Science 171:1156-8 Mr 19 '71
Adenosine 3',5'-monophosphate increases capacity for RNA synthesis in rat liver nuclei. L. A. Dokas and L. J. Kleinsmith. bibliog il Science 172:1237-8 Je 18 '71
Adenosine 3',5'-monophosphate phosphodiesterase in the growth medium of physarum polycephalum. A. W. Murray and others. bibliog il Science 171:496-8 F 5 '71
Adenosine 3',5'-monophosphate phosphodiesterase multiple molecular forms. E. Monn and R. O. Christiansen. bibliog il Science 173:540-2 Ag 6 '71
Cyclic adenosine and guanosine monophosphates and glucagon: effect on liver membrane potentials. N. Friedmann and others. bibliog il Science 171:400-2 Ja 29 '71
Cyclic adenosine monophosphate and norepinephrine; effects on transmembrane properties of cerebellar Purkinje cells. G. R. Siggins and others. bibliog il Science 171:192-4 Ja 15 '71; Reply with rejoinder. 174:1257-9 D '71
Cyclic adenosine monophosphate: function in photoreceptors. W. H. Miller and others. bibliog il Science 174:295-7 O 15 '71

ADENOSINE monophosphate—*Continued*
Cyclic adenosine monophosphate in brain areas: microwave irradiation as a means of tissue fixation. M. J. Schmidt and others. bibliog il Science 173:1142-3 S 17 '71
Cyclic adenosine 3',5'-monophosphate during glucose repression in the rat liver. O. Sudilovsky and others. bibliog il Science 174: 142-4 O 8 '71
Histamine augments leukocyte adenosine 3',5'-monophosphate and blocks antigenic histamine release. H. R. Bourne and others. bibliog il Science 173:743-5 Ag 20 '71
1971 Nobel prize for physiology or medicine. I. H. Paston. por Science 174:392-3 O 22 '71
1971 Nobel prizes in science. por Chem 45: 22-3 Ja '72
Nobelist in Nashville; research in cyclic AMP. por Newsweek 78:109-10 O 25 '71
Norepinephrine stimulated increase of cyclic AMP levels in developing mouse brain cell cultures. N. W. Seeds and A. G. Gilman. bibliog il Science 174:292 O 15 '71
Potassium ion release and enzyme secretion: adrenergic regulation by α- and β-receptors. S. Batzri and others. bibliog il Science 174:1029-31 D 3 '71
Role of cyclic AMP in cell function, ed. by P. Greengard and E. Costa. Review
  Science 171:1229-30 Mr 26 '71. A. P. Somlyo
Second messenger: prize in medicine and physiology. por Time 98:63 O 25 '71
Sutherland's cyclic AMP work brings him 1971 Nobel prize. por Sci N 100:278 O 23 '71
Urinary adenosine 3',5'-monophosphate in the switch process from depression to mania. M. I. Paul and others. bibliog il Science 171:300-3 Ja 22 '71

ADENOSINE triphosphate
[³H]adenosine triphosphate: release during stimulation of enteric nerves. C. Su and others. bibliog il Science 173:336-8 Jl 23 '71
Glycerinated muscle fibers: relation between isometric tension and adenosine triphosphate hydrolysis. W. J. Bowen and L. Mankelkern. bibliog il Science 173:239-40 Jl 16 '71

ADENYL cyclase. See Enzymes

ADHESIVE-backed tiles. See Tiles

ADHESIVE tape
New tapes for the handyman. R. Day. il Mech Illus 67:112-14+ My '71
Tapes: new workhorses for your home. House B 113:16+ S '71
There's a tape for almost any task. A. Francekevich. il Pop Phot 68:18+ F '71
Two-faced tapes do honest shop jobs. J. Hand. il Pop Sci 198:94-5+ Mr '71

ADHESIVES
All you need to know about adhesives; with tables. R. C. Snogren. Pop Sci 199:92-7 D '71
Glues and adhesives: an up-to-date use guide. Good H 172:179 Mr '71
One drop of glue does the trick; new type plastic adhesives. il UNESCO Courier 24: 18-19 Je '71
3M's new adhesives: strong, versatile, fast. il Consumer Rep 36:65-6 F '71
Which glue for which job? Here are some guidelines. Sunset 147:122-3 O '71
  See also
Glue

ADIPOCYTES. See Cells

ADIRONDACK MOUNTAINS
Noah John Rondeau: Adirondack hermit, by M. C. DeSormo. Review
  Liv Wildn por 35:42-4 Spr '71. W. K. Verner
Reporter at large. B. Bernstein. il New Yorker 47:100+ N 27 '71
To Hanging Spear Falls with Zahnie. P. Schaefer. il Liv Wildn 34:23-7 Wint '70

ADIRONDACK MOUNTAINS in art
Art and the Adirondacks. W. K. Verner. il Antiques 100:84-92 Jl '71

ADIRONDACK park. See New York (state)—Parks and reserves

ADISESHIAH, Malcolm S.
Brain drain from the Arab world; adaptation of address, December 22, 1969. Sch & Soc 99:367-9 O '71

ADJUSTMENT (psychology)
  See also
Adaptability (psychology)

ADJUSTMENT, Social
How to cope with Future shock; ed. by W. Kirk and A. Harris. A. Toffler il Seventeen 30:146-7+ Mr '71
Social variables and their effect on psychiatric emergency situations among children. W. C. Sze. bibliog il Ment Hy 55:437-43 O '71

Therapy in the gym; Academy of physical and social development, Boston. il por Time 97:47 F 15 '71
  See also
Aged—Adjustment problems
College students—Adjustment
Maturity
School children—Adjustment
Widows—Adjustment

ADKINS, Jan
Letter from Cape Cod. Harper 243:48+ O '71

ADLER, Alfred
Man who gave us inferiority complex, compensation, overcompensation, aggressive drive and style of life. M. Scarf. il pors N Y Times Mag p 10-11+ F 28 '71 *

ADLER, Billy
Pap art. il pors Time 98:90 N 1 '71 *

ADLER, Felix
Toward common ground, by H. B. Radest. Review
  Commentary 51:71-6 Mr '71. M. A. Meyer; Discussion. 52:28+ Ag '71 *

ADLER, Frederick
Dispassionate venturer. A. Hershman. por Duns 97:64+ Je '71 *

ADLER, Norman A.
Sounds of executive silence. il Harvard Bsns R 49:100-5 Jl '71

ADLER, Norman T. and Zoloth, S. R.
Copulatory behavior can inhibit pregnancy in female rats. bibliog il Science 168:1480-2; 171:311-12 Je 19 '70, Ja 22 '71

ADLER, Renata
Air. New Yorker 47:46-9 D 25 '71
Downers and séances; story. New Yorker 46: 32-6 F 13 '71
Quiet. New Yorker 47:36-42 Ap 24 '71

ADMINISTRATION
  See also
Efficiency, Administrative

ADMINISTRATION, Public. See Public administration

ADMINISTRATION of Justice. See Justice, Administration of

ADMINISTRATIVE advisory bodies. See Executive advisory bodies

ADMINISTRATIVE assistants to the president. See Public officers

ADMINISTRATIVE efficiency. See Efficiency, Administrative

ADMINISTRATIVE law
  See also
Executive advisory bodies

ADMINISTRATIVE remedies
  See also
Ombudsman

ADMINISTRATOR-teacher relationships. See Teacher-administrator relations

ADMINISTRATORS, College. See College officials

ADMIRAL'S cup race. See Yacht racing

ADMIRALTY ISLAND (Alaska)
Warning: the chain saw cometh. P. Brooks. il Atlan 228:95-9 D '71

ADOLESCENCE
New world of the adolescent. R. Erickson. Clear House 46:227-30 D '71
When I was 17; interviews, ed. by B. Kevles. pors Seventeen 30:130-1+ O '71
  See also
Boys
Girls
High school students
Puberty
Youth

           Psychology
Adolescent suicide; results of study by P. Cantor. Time 99:57 Ja 3 '72
Postponing adolescence. il Time 98:60 N 29 '71
Ten teenage troubles; with study-discussion program, by C. Smallenburg and H. Smallenburg. J. D. Johnson. bibliog il PTA Mag 65:2-4, 35 Ap '71

ADOLESCENT literature. See Young adults literature

ADOLESCENT medicine. See Youth—Health and hygiene

ADOLESCENTS. See Youth

ADOLPH Coors company. See Coors, Adolph, company

ADOPTED children. See Children, Adopted

ADOPTION
Adopting a lover. Time 98:50 S 6 '71
Adoption shortage called acute. M. Smith. McCalls 98:41 S '71
Alternative to abortion. L. N. Bell. Chr Today 15:17-18 Je 18 '71
Another modest proposal: baby brokering. W. F. Rickenbacker. Nat R 23:1355 D 3 '71
Baby Lenore; the Nick DeMartinos-Olga Scarpetta case. il Newsweek 77:118 Je 7 '71
Children no one wanted. J. Devaney. il Redbook 138:68-70+ D '71

ADOPTION—*Continued*
Computer with a heart. N. Morgan. il Mc-Calls 98:46 Je '71
Day Bobby learned about love. C. Alvarado. il por Redbook 136:10+ F '71
Fight for baby Lenore. E. L. Hughes. il pors Ladies Home J 88:58+ S '71
Frontier of faith, geography of joy: a librarian's testament; with editorial comment. P. Willey. il pors Wilson Lib Bul 45:856-63 My '71
How Ngoc-Lan became Melissa, ed. by E. Mulligan. S. Cummings. il Parents Mag 46:44-7+ Ap '71
Interracial adoptions: how are they working? I. Doig. il Parents Mag 46:62-5 F '71
Mother's love; legal questions arising from the DeMartino case. J. Morgenstern. Newsweek 77:11 Je 21 '71
Multiracial family. G. Brooten. il N Y Times Mag p78+ S 26 '71
New face of adoption. J. Morgenstern. il Newsweek 78:66-8+ S 13 '71
One parent, better than none. J. C. Hefley and M. Hefley. il Todays Health 59:33-5+ Mr '71
Paging Solomon; natural mother vs. foster mother. G. Ace. Sat R 54:8 F 27 '71
Population bomb and how to defuse it. J. L. Block. il Good H 172:80-3+ My '71
Revolution in our adoption laws. R. Kramer. il Parents Mag 46:37-9+ D '71
Two cribs for baby Lenore; with introd. J. DeMartino; O. Scarpetta. il Life 70:34-6 Je 11 '71
White parents, black children; transracial adoption. il Time 98:42+ Ag 16 '71
  See also
Children, Adopted

ADRENAL glands
I am Joe's adrenal gland. J. D. Ratcliff. il Read Digest 98:127-30 My '71
  See also
ACTH
Adrenalin

ADRENALIN
Adrenal release mechanisms. il Sci N 100:106 Ag 14 '71

ADRENOCORTICOTROPIC hormone. See ACTH

ADRIAN H. Muller and son. See Muller, Adrian H. and son

ADSORPTION
Adsorption. J. H. S. Haggin. il Chem 44:6-9 Ap '71
Steady-state sieving across membranes. E. H. Bresler and others. bibliog il Science 172:858-9 My 21 '71

ADULT-child relationship. See Child-adult relationship

ADULT education
Adult education and economic planning as weapons against unemployment. T. Kristensen. Sch & Soc 99:232-4 Ap '71
Adult education and the urban crisis. R. F. Olson. il Todays Ed 60:24-6 F '71
Adult learning: motivation key to success. V. A. Gallo. bibliog f Clear House 46:239-44 D '71
College credits for life experiences; program for adults at Brooklyn college. Sch & Soc 99:271-2 Sum '71
Early efforts toward educating the black adult. L. McGee. bibliog Negro Hist Bul 34:88-90 Ap '71
Hollywood community adult school. E. Blangsted. il Sch Arts 70:36-7 F '71
Year 1991; necessity for lifelong education; adaptation of address. T. H. Bell. il Am Ed 7:23-6 Ja '71
  See also
Aged—Education
Illiteracy
Labor and laboring classes—Education
Lectures and lecturing
Radio in education
Television in education
University extension

China (People's Republic)
May 7 schools. P. Stursberg. il Newsweek 77:50+ Je 14 '71

Great Britain
Britain's university of the air. Bsns W p79 Ja 16 '71
Britain's university of the second chance; Open university. R. I. Lester. il Am Ed 7:7-11 Ag '71
College of the second chance. I. Crichton. il Sch & Soc 99:443-5 N '71
Everyman's alma mater; Britain's Open university. il Newsweek 77:52+ Ja 25 '71
Open university. P. Davidson. Nation 212:474-6 Ap 12 '71

Open university: breakthrough for Britain? J. Walsh. il Science 174:675-8 N 12 '71
When college is open to all: the experiment in Britain; Open university. il U S News 70:63-4 Mr 1 '71

ADULT-youth relationship. See Youth-adult relationship

ADULTERY
Are we a nation of adulterers? H. Colton. Harp Baz 104:124-6 O '71

ADVANCE schools, inc.
Technique for teaching technicians. V. Louviere. Nations Bsns 59·14 Ja '71

ADVANCED research projects agency. See United States—Defense, Department of—Advanced research projects agency

ADVENT
Expectation and preparation. V. P. McCorry. America 125:468 N 27 '71
  See also
Second advent

ADVENT services. See Church services

ADVENTISTS, Seventh-day. See Seventh-day Adventists

ADVENTURES, Joint. See Joint adventures

ADVERTISEMENT writing. See Advertising copy

ADVERTISEMENTS. See Advertising

ADVERTISING
Advertising that comes à la carte; advertising cartels. il Bsns W p44+ My 1 '71
Businessmen look hard at advertising. S. A. Greyser and B. B. Reece. bibliog f il Harvard Bsns R 49:18-20+ My '71
Madison avenue (cont) Sat R 54:59+ Je 12 '71
New era: creativity plus plain talk. il Bsns W p72-4 F 20 '71
News behind the ads. See every other issue of Changing times
Remember when? nostalgia craze. il Newsweek 77:77-8 Mr 1 '71
Six memorable ones. il Forbes 108:16 Ag 15 '71
Vulnerable media. Nation 212:195 F 15 '71
  See also
Animals in advertising
Premiums
Radio advertising
Religious advertising
Samples (merchandising)
Television advertising
  also subhead Advertising under various subjects, e.g. Airlines—Advertising

Bibliography
Books in communications. S. W. Little. See issues of Saturday review

Laws and regulations
Blind people do not fear snakes; advertising: is it legal, moral & ethical? address, May 25, 1971. M. Stephenson. Vital Speeches 37:583-6 Jl 15 '71
Right to quote: using reviews in book and theater advertising; letter to the editor. J. Weidman. Pub W 200:23 N 15 '71

Moral aspects
  See Advertising ethics

Prize contests
Biggest sweepstakes; FTC files complaint against the Digest. il Newsweek 77:61 Ja 18 '71

Social aspects
Adman battles society's ills. il por Bsns W p 108+ S 11 '71
Guilty until proven innocent; advertising & the consumer; address, April 15, 1971. L. S. Matthews. Vital Speeches 37:505-9 Je 1 '71

Study and teaching
Is advertising education relevant? J. J. Russell. Sat R 54:95+ Mr 13 '71

Testimonials
Doubling a player's dollar. il por Forbes 108:66-7 O 15 '71

ADVERTISING, Direct mail
Direct-mail ads will get more direct. il Bsns W p84+ N 27 '71
  See also
Mailing lists

ADVERTISING, Fraudulent
Advertising claims to get closer scrutiny. U S News 70:53 Je 21 '71
Before you believe those exercise and diet ads read the following report. R. Sherrill. il Todays Health 49:34-6+ Ag '71
Burden of proof; FTC ruling. Newsweek 77:72+ Je 21 '71

ADVERTISING, Fraudulent—*Continued*
Chevron's pollution solution; Scott Carpenter and his F310 additive. S. Berman. Commonweal 93:546-8 Mr 5 '71
End to puffery? FTC charges against Continental baking company. il Newsweek 77:88-9 Mr 29 '71
FTC gets tougher on misleading ads. Bsns W p35 D 11 '71
FTC zooms in on the better buys. il Bsns W p20-1 F 20 '71
Justice dusts off a sharp weapon; criminal contempt actions. Bsns W p30 O 9 '71
Profile bread: a test for corrective ads. Consumer Rep 36:525 S '71
Promoting self-policing; actions to root out deceptive ads. Time 97:81-2 Je 14 '71
Tanks but no tanks; fairness doctrine and Chevron's claims. T. Asher. New Repub 164:17-19 Je 26 '71
These work-at-home schemes are fakes. il Changing T 25:21-3 O '71
ADVERTISING, Industrial
Industrial ads: a debate heats up. il Bsns W p68-9 Jl 17 '71
ADVERTISING, Magazine
Selling death: cigarette ads in the magazines. T. Whiteside. New Repub 164:15-17 Mr 27 '71
ADVERTISING, Mail. See Advertising, Direct mail
ADVERTISING, Newspaper
Right to turn down advertising. R. L. Tobin. Sat R 54:55-6 Je 12 '71
ADVERTISING, Outdoor
   See also
Billboards
ADVERTISING, Political
   See also
Television in politics
ADVERTISING, Public service
Brouhaha over POWs. L. Sloane. Sat R 54: 97 N 13 '71
ADVERTISING agencies
Leo the lion; founder of Chicago-based Leo Burnett co. por Time 97:78 Je 21 '71
New era: creativity plus plain talk. il Bsns W p72-4 F 20 '71
Promise them anything, but. . ; why computers didn't produce miracles. Bsns W p74 Je 5 '71
   See also
American association of advertising agencies
Government investigations—Advertising agencies
   also names of advertising agencies, e.g. Ogilvy and Mather, inc.

Securities
Institutions discover the ad stocks. il Bsns W p81 Je 19 '71
When an ad agency goes public. L. Sloane. Sat R 54:76 O 9 '71
ADVERTISING and women
Airline's ad encounters some turbulence. il Life 71:75-6 O 29 '71
Is television messing with your mind? N. Johnson. Vogue 158:92 Jl '71
ADVERTISING as a profession
How I learned to stop worrying and like advertising. S. Christie. Mlle 74:211+ N '71
ADVERTISING awards
Cold shoulders for Andy, Effy, Clio. il Bsns W p30 F 13 '71
SR's nineteenth annual advertising awards. R. L. Tobin. Sat R 54:51-5 Ap 10 '71
ADVERTISING cards
Racers have arrived; Fleer/AHRA drag champs bubble gum cards. il Hot Rod 24: 94 S '71
ADVERTISING characters
Anybody give a hoot? Federal government's cartoon characters Johnny Horizon and Woodsy the Owl. il Time 98:8 Ag 16 '71
ADVERTISING copy
Freelance job idea, writing paperback cover copy. P. Sellers. il Writers Digest 52:26 Ja '72
What Volkswagon, Revlon, and Ayd's candies can tell you about writing. L. McDougall. Engl J 60:479-80 Ap '70
ADVERTISING council
Brouhaha over POWs. L. Sloane. Sat R 54:97 N 13 '71
ADVERTISING ethics
Ally for admen against the FTC. Bsns W p39 Je 19 '71
Blind people do not fear snakes; advertising: is it legal, moral & ethical? address, May 25, 1971. M. Stephenson. Vital Speeches 37:583-6 Jl 15 '71
Closer and cleaner? Newsweek 78:58 S 6 '71
San Francisco. Sodom revisited; Examiner editorial. Chr Today 15:23 Ja 29 '71
   See also
Advertising, Fraudulent
National advertising review board

ADVERTISING mediums
Magnetic tape players
Squawk box; Audio commercial message repeating unit. New Repub 164:13-14 Ap 10 '71
Pamphlets
Freelance job aid: promotion packet. C. G. Welton. il Writers Digest 51:27 Ag '71
Paperback books
Ads in paperbacks: are they necessary? E. Lottman. Pub W 200:14-16 N 1 '71; Reply. S. S. Baker. 200:26 N 15 '71
ADVERTISING men
High wind on Madison avenue. L. E. Sissman. Atlan 228:20+ Jl '71
ADVERTISING premiums. See Premiums
ADVERTISING signs. See Billboards; Signs and signboards
ADVISORY commission on civil disorders. See United States—National advisory commission on civil disorders
ADVISORY committees, commissions, etc. See Executive advisory bodies
ADVISORY council on European affairs. See United States—State, Department of—Advisory council on European affairs
ADVISORY council on executive organization. See United States—President's advisory council on executive organization
ADVISORY panel on international law. See United States—State, Department of—Advisory panel on international law
AEGEAN ISLANDS
Yachting in the Greek isles. D. Marley. il Harp Baz 104:64+ Mr '71
AEGYPTOPITHECUS. See Apes, Fossil
AENEID. See Virgil
AERATION of sewage. See Sewage purification—Aeration
AERATION of water. See Water—Aeration
AERIAL bombing. See Bombing, Aerial
AERIAL bombs. See Bombs, Aerial
AERIAL cableways. See Cableways
AERIAL corn planting. See Corn—Seeding
AERIAL lifts. See Cranes, derricks, etc.
AERIAL mapping. See Mapping, Aerial
AERIAL photography. See Photography, Aerial
AERIAL reconnaissance
   See also
Artificial satellites—Military use

Equipment
Beep, blink and thrum of spy gadgetry. il Newsweek 78:38 N 22 '71
AERO propulsion laboratory. See United States—Air force—Aero propulsion laboratory
AEROBATIC airplanes. See Airplanes, Aerobatic
AEROBIC sewage treatment. See Sewage purification—Aeration
AEROBICS. See Exercise
AEROCARS. See Airplanes, Light—Automobile combinations
AERODYNAMICS
Vectored-thrust maneuverability explored. D. A. Brown. il Aviation W 95:36-9 D 13 '71
AERODYNAMICS, Supersonic
   See also
Shock waves
AEROFLOT (airline) See Airlines—Russia
AERONAUTIC instruments
Back to basics: engine instruments. K. E. Gardner and P. Garrison. Flying 88:88-9 Je '71
Horizontal situation indicator in F-15 uses digital technology. il Aviation W 96:56-7 Ja 10 '72
Product news. See issues of Flying
What's it all about, alpha? angle of attack. R. Blodget. Flying 89:38+ N '71
   See also
Airplanes—Instrument boards
Airplanes, Military—Radio equipment
Compass
Detectors, Infrared
Inertial guidance systems
Navigation, Aerial—Aids and devices
Proximity warning indicators
Radio beacons

Display systems
Advanced moving map displays explored. B. M. Elson. il Aviation W 95:38-40 Jl 26 '71
Color display aimed at air, ground roles. K. J. Stein. il Aviation W 95:52-3 N 8 '71
French attitude indicator offers color symbols. K. J. Stein. il Aviation W 94:53-4 Mr 22 '71

AERONAUTIC laboratories
Test facility needs cited in study. M. L. Yaffee. Aviation W 95:44-5 D 6 '71
See also
Cornell aeronautical laboratory, inc.

AERONAUTIC meteorology. See Meteorology, Aeronautic

AERONAUTIC museums
Aerospace museums. W. D. Siuru and W. G. Holder. il Travel 136:58-65 Jl '71
From the film world two barns full of nostalgic cars, planes; Buena Park, Calif. il Sunset 147:38 O '71
Military aviation museum. J. L. Stoughtenburgh. il Hobbies 75:156 F '71
Wings of brave men; Air force museum. K. V. Brown. il Pop Mech 136:62-6 Jl '71

AERONAUTIC research
Air transport goals; excerpts from address. R. P. Jackson. Aviation W 94:9 My 24 '71
Broad civil aviation R&D urged by panel. D. A. Brown. Aviation W 94:20-1 My 10 '71
Research and development; address, February 16, 1971. G. S. Brown. Vital Speeches 37:331-4 Mr 15 '71
See also
Aeronautic laboratories
United States—Air force—Aero propulsion laboratory
United States—Arnold engineering development center

AERONAUTICAL satellites. See Artificial satellites—Air traffic control use

AERONAUTICAL systems division. See United States—Air force—Systems command

AERONAUTICS
See also
Aviation
Kites

Accidents
See Aviation—Accidents

History
All the daring young men: aviation comes to the West. J. F. Hood. il Am West 8:10-15+ Jl '71
Lift-off from San Francisco Bay; homemade flying machine. A. G. Sutro. il Read Digest 99:110-14 D '71
Plane that broke the profit barrier; Douglas DC-3. D. J. Lloyd-Jones. il por Nations Bsns 59:44-5 Ja '71
Those early airplanes. J. Gilbert. il Flying 89:34-40+ D '71

Laws and regulations
See Aviation—Laws and regulations

Study and teaching
Flying lessons: exciting, but the price is high. Bsns W p61-2 Jl 3 '71
Maine's Camp Solo puts young aviators in the pilot's seat; with editorial comment. il Life 71:1, 60-3 Ag 27 '71
See also
Air pilots—Training

AERONAUTICS, Commercial
See also
Air freight service
Airports
International civil aviation organization

International aspects
See Aviation—International aspects

Alaska
See also
Airlines—Alaska

Arab states
See also
Airlines—Arab states

Australia
See also
Airlines—Australia

Canada
Canada plans national STOL drive. C. Brownlow. il Aviation W 94:14-15 Mr 22 '71
See also
Airlines—Canada

Chile
See also
Airlines—Chile

China (People's Republic)
China orders six Trident 2Es. Aviation W 95:21 Ag 30 '71
Chinese jet bid may cloud trade policy. L. Doty. Aviation W 94:30 Mr 15 '71
Wings for China? il Forbes 108:25-6 S 15 '71
Wings of Mao. il Time 97:82 My 24 '71

Denmark
See also
Airlines—Denmark

Egypt
See also
Airlines—Egypt

Ethiopia
See also
Airlines—Ethiopia

Europe, Western
Europe: the new commercial challenge; symposium, with editorial comment. il Aviation W 94:21, 56-61+ My 31 '71

Finland
See also
Airlines—Finland

France
See also
Airlines—France

Germany (Federal Republic)
See also
Airlines—Germany (Federal Republic)

Great Britain
See also
Airlines—Great Britain

Iceland
See also
Airlines—Iceland

Israel
See also
Airlines—Israel

Japan
Japan pushes airways modernization plan. il Aviation W 95:80-2 N 1 '71
See also
Airlines—Japan

Libya
See also
Airlines—Libya

Pakistan
See also
Airlines—Pakistan

Russia
Soviet aviation growth creating markets. H. J. Coleman. Aviation W 94:46-7 My 24 '71
See also
Airlines—Russia

United States
See also
Airlines—United States
Fixed base operators

AERONAUTICS, Military
See also
Aviation—Formation flying
Bombing, Aerial
Bombs, Aerial
Helicopters—Military use

Europe, Western
See also
Airplanes, Military—Europe, Western

France
French plan five-year hardware program. il Aviation W 94:35-6 Mr 8 '71
See also
Airplanes, Military—France

Germany (Federal Republic)
See also
Airplanes, Military—Germany (Federal Republic)

India
See also
India—Air force

Israel
See also
Israeli-Arab war, 1967- —Aerial operations

Italy
Italy thrust into crucial European role. E. H. Kolcum. il Aviation W 94:29-30+ Mr 8 '71

Japan
See also
Airplanes, Military—Japan
Japan—Air force

Netherlands
See also
Airplanes, Military—Netherlands

Russia
See also
Airplanes, Military—Russia

Sweden
See also
Airplanes, Military—Sweden

AERONAUTICS, Military—*Continued*
Switzerland
See also
Airplanes, Military—Switzerland

United States
See also
Airplanes, Military—United States

Vietnam (Republic)
See also
Vietnamese war, 1957- —Aerial operations

AERONAUTICS, State departments of. See
Aviation, State departments of

AEROSAT system. See Artificial satellites—
Air traffic control use

AEROSOL oven cleaners. See Cleaning compositions

AEROSOL packaging. See Pressure packaging

AEROSOLS
Atmospheric aerosol: does a background level exist? W. M. Porch and others; reply.
W. H. Fischer. Science 171:828-9 F 26 '71
Atmospheric carbon dioxide and aerosols:
effects of large increases on global climate. S. I. Rasool and S. H. Schneider.
bibliog il Science 173:138-41 Jl 9 '71; Discussion. 173:982-3 S 10 '71
Don't breathe aerosol. Newsweek 77:42 My 31
'71
Is man changing earth's temperature? Sky
& Tel 42:272 N '71
Particle formation during water-vapor photolysis. I. D. Clark and J. F. Noxon. bibliog Science 174:941-4 N 26 '71
Question for the (ice) ages; effects of aerosols in the atmosphere. Sci N 100:39 Jl 17
'71

AEROSPACE industries
Laurels for 1971; people who made significant contributions. R. Hotz. Aviation W 95:9
D 20 '71
See also
Airplane industry
Guided missile industries
Industrial demobilization

Directories
Marketing directory section. Aviation W 95:
27+ D 27 '71

Employees
Aerospace in crisis; California bubble. M.
Gellen. Nation 212:232-5 F 22 '71
Brains on the shelf. il Nations Bsns 59:66-9
My '71
Employment decline predicted by AIA. Aviation W 95:20 O 4 '71
First aid for the recession's casualties. il
Bsns W p24-5 Mr 27 '71
Jobless scientists bus to Washington; testimonies before the House subcommittee on
science, research, and development. il Bsns
W p22 Je 26 '71
Over 40. . .and fired. E. H. Graham. il por
Mech Illus 67:69-71+ My '71
Pace of aerospace layoffs slows. W. H. Gregory. il Aviation W 95:14-15 Jl 12 '71
Shock waves from a surplus plane. il Newsweek 77:62+ Ap 5 '71
Southern California: a pickup in jobs. Bsns
W p47 N 13 '71
Victims of a good, glamorous cause. il Time
97:78-9 Ap 5 '71
See also
Aerospace professional and technical association
International association of machinists and
aerospace workers

Retraining
See Retraining, Occupational

Federal aid
Future aerospace funding studied. J. P. Woolsey. Aviation W 94:14-15 Je 21 '71
L-1011 pacts signed with lenders, airlines.
Aviation W 95:31 S 20 '71
Lift for Lockheed. il Time 98:70+ Ag 16 '71
Perils of Lockheed. Newsweek 77:76 Mr 1 '71
Shedding the albatross. Newsweek 77:76+ My
3 '71

Finance
Aerospace and defense; with yardsticks of
management performance. il Forbes 109:183-
4 Ja 1 '72
Aerospace: another year of shrinking markets. Bsns W p49 D 25 '71
Aerospace: the troubled blue yonder. il
Time 97:76-80+ Ap 5 '71
Airlines and aerospace; the debt load factor.
il Bsns W p70-1 Je 26 '71
Lockheed's rough ride with Rolls-Royce. il
Time 97:68-9 F 15 '71
On the skids: Rolls goes bankrupt. il Sr Schol
98:14-15 Mr 8 '71

Pollution control activities
For some, pollution is the answer. Bsns W
p25 Mr 27 '71

Public relations
Industry, government seek ways to gain
public support of shuttle. Aviation W 94:
38-9 Ap 5 '71

Real estate operations
Douglas launches a real estate rocket. il Bsns
W p25-6 O 9 '71

Securities
Fasten your seat belts. C. Morgello. il Newsweek 77:78 Ap 5 '71

Wages and hours
Aerospace pact tests the Pay board. Bsns W
p34 D 11 '71
Now the Pay board trips over aerospace.
Bsns W p31 D 18 '71
Pay board irks aerospace unions. Aviation
W 96:21 Ja 10 '72
Pay board postpones action on aerospace
wages. Aviation W 96:16 Ja 3 '72
Pay board puts off the aerospace issue. Bsns
W p 19 D 25 '71

Canada
Canadian aerospace industry ailing. C.
Brownlow. il Aviation W 94:36-8 Ap 19 '71
Dassault may gain Canadian entry. Aviation W 95:16-17 S 27 '71

Europe, Western
Europe focuses on civil, space projects. il
Aviation W 95:13-14 D 27 '71
Europe: the new commercial challenge; symposium, with editorial comment. il Aviation W 94:21, 56-61+ My 31 '71
Europeans urge retaliatory import duties. D.
E. Fink. Aviation W 95:19-20 O 25 '71

France
France keys growth to civil aircraft. Aviation W 94:69-70 My 31 '71
French export orders set record. D. E. Fink.
Aviation W 94:14-15 Ja 25 '71

Germany (Federal Republic)
Germans press trade law change. E. H. Kolcum. il Aviation W 94:61+ My 31 '71
Mergers key to German aerospace drive. il
Aviation W 94:205+ My 31 '71

Great Britain
Concorde, RB.211 spark U.K. R&D crisis. H. J.
Coleman. il Aviation W 94:67-9 My 31 '71
See also
Society of British aerospace companies

Italy
Italy to modernize aerospace industry. il Aviation W 94:73+ My 31 '71

Japan
Japanese aerospace industry nears parity
with the west. il Aviation W 95:34-7 N 1
'71

Russia
Soviets in Paris. R. Hotz. Aviation W 94:9 Je
21 '71

Sweden
Sweden's Saab-Scania seeks civil project.
Aviation W 94:75 My 31 '71

Switzerland
Swiss fighter competition scene shifts from
technical to political. E. H. Kolcum. Aviation W 95:18 Ag 30 '71

United States
Aerospace crowds into mass transit; Pittsburgh's annual International conference. il
Bsns W p20-1 S 18 '71
Aerospace dinosaurs. P. Barnes. New Repub
164:17-19 Mr 27 '71
Aerospace game. Nation 211:642-3 D 21 '70
Aerospace industry: its formula for survival.
il U S News 70:32-3 F 15 '71
Aerospace is diversifying again. il Bsns W
p 124-6 S 11 '71
Aerospace: the troubled blue yonder. il
Time 97:76-80+ Ap 5 '71
Aerospace's urban role debated; report of
Urban technology conference. W. H. Gregory. Aviation W 94:62-4+ Je 7 '71
Breaking with tradition; excerpts from address. E. G. Uhl. Aviation W 95:9 Ag 2
'71
Ecological problem. R. Hotz. Aviation W
94:11 Ap 12 '71

AEROSPACE industries—United States—
Continued
Future programs provide glimmerings of
aerospace industry resurgence. W. H. Greg-
ory. Aviation W 94:12-13 Mr 8 '71
Midyear outlook. R. Hotz. Aviation W 95:9
Jl 26 '71
More government-industry efforts urged.
Aviation W 95:22-3 O 11 '71
New challenge; excerpts from address. D. L.
Williams. Aviation W 94:9 F 22 '71
Nixon's economic Immelmann. R. Hotz. Avia-
tion W 95:11 S 13 '71
Outlook for 1972. R. Hotz. Aviation W 96:7
Ja 3 '72
Scientific starvation today; a second-rate na-
tion tomorrow; address, April 14, 1971. R.
Anderson. Vital Speeches 37:502-5 Je 1 '71;
Excerpts. Aviation W 94:9 My 17 '71
Urban areas called lean aerospace market.
Z. Strickland. Aviation W 95:56-7 N 8 '71
See also
Collective bargaining—Aerospace industries
Fairchild Hiller corporation
Lockheed aircraft corporation
North American Rockwell corporation
Rohr corporation
Thiokol chemical corporation
Tool research and engineering corporation
United aircraft corporation
AEROSPACE industries association of America,
inc.
Contract guidelines change asked. Aviation
W 96:61 Ja 10 '72
Returns fail to match aerospace capital
needs, risks, AIA says. Aviation W 95:19
Jl 19 '71
AEROSPACE museums. See Aeronautic muse-
ums
**AEROSPACE professional and technical asso-
ciation**
Labor board rejects engineers bid for col-
lective bargaining right. Aviation W 95:
24 N 15 '71
AEROSPACE telemetry
Telemetry system may cut F-14 test time. K.
J. Stein. il Aviation W 95:54-7 D 20 '71
AEROSPACE workers. See Aerospace indus-
tries—Employees
AEROTRAINS. See Air cushion vehicles
AESTHETICS
Need for beauty. House & Gard 139:81 My '71
Oh, say, can you see? P. K. Scholl. il Sch
Arts 70:12-13 Ap '71
State of taste (cont) R. Lynes. por Art in Am
59:19 Ja '71
Those *longeurs* in Japanese films. B. Wolf.
Nation 213:152-4 Ag 30 '71
See also
Art—Philosophy
Nature (aesthetics)
AETNA life and casualty company
Crowbar governor was a man of many parts.
O. D. Smith. pors Nations Bsns 59:42-3 Ja
'71
AFAR triangle. See Danakil
AFFECTIVE learning. See Learning, psychol-
ogy of—Emotional aspects
AFGHANISTAN
Church in Kabul. Chr Today 16:46 Ja 7 '72
See also
Hindu Kush
Sports—Afghanistan
United Nations—Afghanistan
Description and travel
Afghanistan is a land that answers to dreams.
F. D. Chu. il Travel 136:40-5 N '71
AFGHANS (coverlets)
Make a cozy afghan. V. P. Guild. il Good H
173:100-1+ S '71
AFLATOXIN. See Toxins and antitoxins
AFRICA
French tie that binds; G. Pompidou's visit
to former colonies. il Time 97:37 F 15 '71
Reports & comment: French Africa; former
colonies in black Africa. S. Meisler. Atlan
228:6+ S '71
See also
Children—Africa
Cities and towns—Africa
English language in Africa
Guerrillas—Africa
Hunting—Africa
Science—Africa
Socialism—Africa
Student demonstrations—Africa
Technical assistance in Africa
United Nations—Africa
Wildlife conservation—Africa
Antiquities
See also
Carthage

Civilization
Independence of Africa and cultural decolonization. J. Ngugi. il UNESCO Courier 24:
25-6+ Ja '71

Description and travel
Hovercraft to the heart of Africa; Transafrican hovercraft expedition. il Sci Digest
70:38-45+ D '71

Economic conditions
See also
United Nations—Economic commission for
Africa
Foreign relations
France
See France—Foreign relations—Africa

History
Problems of writing African history; Unesco's
General History of Africa project. O. Bhely-
Quenum. Sch & Soc 99:101-2 F '71
Yambo Ouologuem on violence, truth and
black history; interview, ed. by L. Kuehl.
Y. Ouologuem. por Commonweal 94:311-14
Je 11 '71
Maps
Africa & Middle East. Sr Schol 99:11 O 4 '71
Portrait of a continent, its people and its
past. il Nat Geog 140:737, sup(folded map)
D '71
Nationalism
Black Africa a decade later. il Time 97:37-8+
F 1 '71
Englishman tries to understand apartheid.
T. Stacey. il Nat R 23:581-4 Je 1 '71
Independence of Africa and cultural decolo-
nization. J. Ngugi. il UNESCO Courier 24:
25-6+ Ja '71
Native races
See also
Drum language
Negroes in Africa
Zulus
also subhead Native races under names
of African countries, e.g. Kenya—Native
races
Politics
Africa, 1971; symposium. bibliog f Cur Hist
60:129-67+ Mr '71
Black Africa a decade later. il Time 97:37-8+
F 1 '71
Detours on Africa's freedom road. R. Gib-
son. Commonweal 95:172-3 N 19 '71
Francophone Africa. W. H. Lewis. Cur Hist
60:142-5+ Mr '71
Predictable Africa. America 124:139-40 F 13
'71
What they're talking about in the Middle
East & Africa. il Sr Schol 99:10 O 4 '71
See also
Pan-Africanism
Population
Population pressure in tropical Africa. T. E.
Dow, jr. bibliog f il Cur Hist 60:136-41+
Mr '71
Race question
See also subhead Race question under
names of African countries, e.g. South Af-
rica—Race question
Religious institutions and affairs
Africa: independent churches thrive but face
hurdles. O. Okite. Chr Today 15:54-5 Mr 12
'71
See also
Catholic church in Africa
Christians in Africa
AFRICA, CENTRAL
See also
Chad, Lake
Malawi
AFRICA, EAST
See also
Automobile racing—Africa, East
East Indians in East Africa
Hunting—Africa, East
Mozambique
National parks and reserves—Africa, East
Railroads—Africa, East
Tourist trade—Africa, East
Description and travel
Bright journey in East Africa. M. E. Murie.
il Liv Wildn 34:38-43 Aut '70
Native races
God's ears; ear customs of the Masai of
Kenya and Tanzania. il Esquire 75:116-
19 Je '71

AFRICA, EAST—*Continued*
Politics
Itching for a fight. Newsweek 77:36+ My 24 '71
Shock waves. il Newsweek 77:40 F 15 '71
Religious institutions and affairs
Target/Lengo: open window on East Africa. K. Strong. Chr Cent 88:1451-2 D 8 '71
AFRICA, NORTH
See also
Economic assistance in North Africa
Libya
Morocco
AFRICA, SOUTHEAST
See also
Swaziland
AFRICA, SOUTHERN
See also
Botswana
United Nations—Africa, Southern
Foreign relations
United States
See United States—Foreign relations—Africa, Southern
Politics
Future of Africa South. C. P. Potholm. bibliog f Cur Hist 60:146-50+ Mr '71
Hazardous courses in southern Africa. G. F. Kennan. For Affairs 49:218-36 Ja '71; Same abr. with title What policies toward southern Africa? Cur 127:50-63 Mr '71
Race question
Africa and America: the seventies; address, March 1971. S. Khama. Vital Speeches 37:679-83 S 1 '71
AFRICA, WEST
See also
Ashanti
Ghana
Portuguese Guinea
Sierra Leone
Visitors, Foreign—Africa, West
Description and travel
Portals to West Africa. N. Lynn. il Travel 136:40-5+ D '71
AFRICA in literature
Africa's past: another version. C. R. Larson. Nation 212:697-9 My 31 '71
AFRICAN art. See Art, African
AFRICAN cookery. See Cookery, African
AFRICAN daisies (dimorphotheca) See Cape marigolds
AFRICAN dancing. See Dancing, African
AFRICAN drum language. See Drum language
AFRICAN fiction
Books. J. Updike. New Yorker 47:187-8+ N 13 '71
AFRICAN hair styles. See Hairdressing
AFRICAN literature
Amos Tutuola: emerging African literature. P. Neumarkt. bibliog Am Imago 28:129-45 Sum '71
AFRICAN Methodist Episcopal church
Funds misuse charge of black church. Negro Hist Bul 34:117-18 My '71
AFRICAN sculpture. See Sculpture, African
AFRICAN students
See also
Student demonstrations—Africa
AFRICAN students in the United States. See Foreign students in the United States
AFRICAN studies
Africa: frontier for summer study. J. Mandelstam. il Schol Teach Jr/Sr High p 17-19 Ja 11 '71
AFRICAN track team. See Track athletics
AFRICAN violets
Favorite African violets. Horticulture 49:52 F '71
How to keep African-violets blooming all winter. C. Fischer. il Home Gard 58:38+ O '71
Your garden indoors. F. S. David. il Home Gard 58:48 Mr '71
AFRICANS in art
Pictures from an African journey; P. Collins west African life. il pors Ebony 26:174-6+ O '71
AFRO-AMERICAN group attack team (organization) See Narcotics. Control of
AFRO-AMERICAN healers. See Folk medicine
AFRO-AMERICAN history week. See Negro history week
AFRO-AMERICAN literature. See Negro literature

AFRO-AMERICAN studies
Afro-American research unit for Harvard. Negro Hist Bul 33:170 N '70
Black Americana studies. C. L. Lee. Negro Hist Bul 34:114-15 My '71
Black culture: a reading program develops better understanding. I. W. Hale. Clear House 45:269-72 Ja '71
Black studies crisis. J. H. Harris. Negro Hist Bul 34:6 Ja '71
Ideas for teaching about black Americans. Todays Ed 60:57-8 Ja '71
Ideas for teaching about black Americans. il Negro Hist Bul 34:35-6 F '71
Teaching black studies with independent study. il Negro Hist Bul 34:4-5 Ja '71
Negro colleges and universities—Curriculum
AFRO-AMERICANS. See Negroes
AFRO-ASIAN festival. See Dance festivals
AFTER images
Stereoscopic depth aftereffect produced without monocular cues. C. Blakemore and B. Julesz. bibliog il Science 171:286-8 Ja 22 '71
AFTER six, inc.
Tuxedo maker promotes the casual look. il Bsns W p66-7 Ap 17 '71
AFTEREFFECTS, Figural. See Figural aftereffects
AFZAL, Manuchehr
Teheran university and the government of Iran. bibliog Sch & Soc 99:369-73 O '71
AGAGIANIAN, Gregory Peter, cardinal
Obituary
Chr Cent 88:684 Je 2 '71
AGAR
This seaweed gelatin is an Oriental cook's secret; kanten. il Sunset 146:146+ F '71
AGATES
Pocketful of treasure; agate supplies of Iowa and the shores of Lake Superior. L. Seamer. por Hobbies 75:144 F '71
AGAVES
See also
Sisal hemp
AGAZZARI, Agostino
Agazzari's Eumelio, a dramma pastorale. M. F. Johnson. bibliog f il Mus Q 57:491-505 Jl '71 *
AGE
See also
Aging
Longevity
Middle age
Old age
AGE (fishes)
Residues of total mercury and methylmercuric salts in lake trout as a function of age. C. A. Bache and others. bibliog il Science 172:951-2 My 28 '71
AGE (psychology)
See also
Age and intelligence
AGE, School. See School age
AGE, Voting. See Suffrage—United States
AGE and employment
AoA Title III project employs older people with Love to share; project in Fort Smith, Ark. il Aging 201:19 Jl '71
Florida firm hires older workers, places them in temporary positions. il Aging 200:14 Je '71
Is there life after forty? S. Margetts. il Duns 98:55 D '71
Late-blooming career women. V. Cadden. il McCalls 99:88-9+ O '71
Man needs to work; Harvey Gamage, Maine boat builder. G. Goodman. Look 35:44 Ja 12 '71
SRS-aided Long Island project finding jobs for 55+ seniors. il Aging 195:8-9 Ja '71
Social-security swingers; policy of Texas refinery corp. il Newsweek 79:37 Ja 3 '72
Volunteers operate senior program in state employment office; Iowa. il Aging 204:14 O '71
See also
Forty plus clubs
Retirement
Working life, Length of
AGE and intelligence
Intelligence and blood pressure in the aged. F. Wilkie and C. Eisdorfer. bibliog il Science 172:959-62 My 28 '71
AGE and mental ability. See Age and intelligence
AGE and sex. See Aged—Sexual behavior; Middle age—Sexual behavior
AGE determination by radioactivity. See Radioactive dating

AGHAJANIAN, George K. and Asher, I. M.
Histochemical fluorescence of raphe neurons: selective enhancement by tryptophan. bibliog il Science 172:1159-61 Je 11 '71
AGING
Age-associated changes in the DNA of mouse tissue. G. B. Price and others. bibliog il Science 171:917-20 Mr 5 '71
Aging: ten years of progress or procrastination? E. Harger. por Har Yrs 11:18-22 Mr '71
Double standard. I. P. Bell. il Trans-Action 8:75-80 N '70
Growing old, and how to cope with it. A. Deeken. America 124:315-18 Mr 27 '71
House names committee to study aging needs. T. Schuchat. Har Yrs 11:4 N '71
Imperatives on aging. W. C. Fitch. Har Yrs 11:54-5 Ag 71
New perspectives on aging. D. H. Gustafson. Cur 132:40-2 S '71
Shot of youth for the ills of age. il por Bsns W p60+ N 20 '71
Youth pill. P. M. McGrady, jr. il Ladies Home J 88:72-4+ Jl '71
See also
Gerontology
AGING (periodical)
Growing concern for older Americans recorded in twenty years of Aging. Aging 200:3-4 Je '71
AGING, Administration on. See United States —Aging, Administration on
AGING, Conferences on
Community White House conferences discuss future of all Americans. il Aging 200:9 Je '71
Conference calendar. See issues of Aging
Leisure and gerontology conferences held in Rhode Island and Florida. Aging 198:12 Ap '71
National organizations agree on plan for action for elderly. il Aging 205:7 N '71
President and Cabinet members meet with representatives of older people. il Aging 200:6 Je '71
State conferences on aging hardworking, also festive. il Aging 201:16-17 Jl '71
State executives from states, territories, meet in Washington. il Aging 195:5 Ja '71
Theme of 24th Ann Arbor conference on aging to be Care of old people. Aging 198:4 Ap '71
24th annual Michigan conference discusses care for the aged. il Aging 201:7-8 Jl '71
See also
National council on the aging
White House conference on aging, 1971 (proposed)
AGNELLI, Giovanni, 1921-
Embattled prince of Fiat. W. McQuade. il pors Fortune 84:124-6+ Ag '71 •
Outsider for Agnelli's IFI. il por Bsns W p70+ O 30 '71 •
AGNELLI, Susanna
Fighting words: American women are lousy lovers. Vogue 158:91+ Jl '71
One woman's adventures with her three decorators. il por House & Gard 140:116-23+ O '71
AGNEW, Elinor Isobel (Judefind)
Don't be ashamed to call yourself housewife! interview, ed. by J. C. G. Conniff. il pors Todays Health 49:20-3+ Jl '71
Private world of Judy Agnew. W. McLendon. il pors McCalls 98:102-7 F '71 •
AGNEW, H. W. jr. See Webb, W. B. jt. auth.
AGNEW, Irene
Russian press reports on Soviet science. See issues of Science digest
AGNEW, Ken
One of the comrades is missing; ed. by K. Schaefer. il Read Digest 98:78-82 Ap '71
AGNEW, Spiro Theodore
Not infected with the conceit of infallibility; ed. by J. Underwood. il pors Sports Illus 34:60-2+ Je 21 '71
United States concern for prisoners of war; address, May 17, 1971. Dept State Bul 64:803-6 Je 21 '71; Excerpts. U S News 70:73 My 31 '71
Vice President Agnew visits 10 nations; statements. June 26-July 28, 1971. Dept State Bul 65:229-34 Ag 30 '71
Vice President Agnew visits Turkey, Iran, and Greece; statements, October 1971. Dept State Bul 65:621-2 N 29 '71
We've not given up on POW's; excerpts from address, May 17, 1971. U S News 70:73 My 31 '71
about
Agnew agonistes. il Newsweek 78:27 N 29 '71 •
Agnew axis. por Newsweek 78:42+ N 1 '71 •
Agnew, by R. Marsh. Review
Nat R 23:710-11+ Je 29 '71. G. F. Will •

Appointment in Gargalianoi. il por Time 98:20 N 1 '71 •
Arrow in the air. Newsweek 77:111 Mr 29 '71 •
Attica and Mr Agnew. N. Cousin. Sat R 54:36 O 16 '71 •
Dump Agnew? il por Newsweek 78:16 Ag 2 '71 •
Is Spiro Agnew necessary? Time 98:11-12 Ag 16 '71 •
Jackie and Ari and Tom and George and Spiro and . . . R. Fitch. il pors Ramp Mag 10:38-47+ Ja '72 •
Low profile. por Newsweek 77:23-4 Mr 22 '71 •
Mr Agnew goes home again; trip to Greece. T. Theodoracopulos. Nat R 23:1412+ D 17 '71 •
New role for Vice President Agnew. il pors U S News 70:62-4+ Ap 19 '71 •
Notes from the cavern. J. Osborne. New Repub 165:13-14 D 4 '71 •
Save our Spiro. Newsweek 79:15 Ja 3 '72 •
Shepherd to the wordsmith; press secretary. V. Gold. il pors Time 98:77 O 18 '71 •
Short rein of Spiro T. Agnew. Time 97:10-11 Ja 25 '71 •
Spiro. F. Trippett. il Look 35:28-9 S 7 '71 •
Spiro and the Buchwald blues. W. O'Toole. Commonweal 93:465 F 12 '71 •
Spiro's homecoming. il por Newsweek 78:53 O 25 '71 •
Thanks for the memory. A. Wright. il pors Sports Illus 34:12-15 F 22 '71 •
Two-China policy? Newsweek 77:28-9 My 3 '71 •
Will Agnew dump himself? K. Phillips. il pors N Y Times Mag p36-7+ N 14 '71 •
Worries on a traveler's mind. H. Sidey. por Life 71:2 O 29 '71 •

Anecdotes, facetiae, satire, etc.
Day they stole the Agnew. P. Steinfels. Commonweal 93:390+ Ja 22 '71

World tour, 1971
In his country's service; visit to Korea. Newsweek 78:44 Jl 12 '71
On the road with Agnew; report. H. Gorey. il por Time 98:20 Jl 26 '71
Parting shots: Spiro Agnew's month-long $1.2 million non-event. H. Sidey. il por Life 71:61 Ag 6 '71
Round-the-world stroking. Time 98:9-10 Jl 12 '71
Safari. Newsweek 78:30 Jl 26 '71
Strange, strange bedfellows. il por Ebony 26:142-3 S '71
Vice President Agnew visits 10 nations; statements. June 26-July 28, 1971. S. T. Agnew. Dept State Bul 65:229-34 Ag 30 '71
AGNEW, Spiro Theodore, family
Don't be ashamed to call yourself housewife! interview, ed. by J. C. G. Conniff. E. I. Agnew. il pors Todays Health 49:20-3+ Jl '71
AGNON, Samuel Joseph
Agnon's last word. R. Alter. Commentary 51:74-81 Je '71 •
AGNON, Shmuel Yosef. See Agnon, S. J.
AGONIS
Word for it is graceful; peppermint tree or Australian willow myrtle. il Sunset 147:143 Ag '71
AGREEMENTS, Trade. See Trade agreements
AGRIBUSINESS accountability project (organization)
Group charges pesticides were tested on people. G. Reynolds. Farm J 95:38 Ap '71
AGRICULTURAL administration

China (People's Republic)
Food and agriculture in mainland China. Y. L. Wu. bibliog f Cur Hist 61:160-4 S '71

Peru
Revolutionary nationalism in Peru. M. Niedergang. For Affairs 49:454-63 Ap '71

Underdeveloped areas
See Underdeveloped areas—Agriculture

United States
Agri-welfare roll. il Ramp Mag 10:10+ O '71
America's quiet crimes against people: tobacco subsidies. C. Rogers. Chr Cent 88:769 Je 23 '71
Beyond the wage-price freeze. Farm J 95:19-21+ O '71
Brighter outlook for farmers; interview. C. M. Hardin. il por U S News 70:58-62 Je 28 '71
Butz appointment. Nation 213:644-5 D 20 '71

AGRICULTURAL administration—United States
   Continued
Growing unrest on the farm; with interview
   with W. J. Scherle. il por Time 98:20-1 N
   22 '71
Land of milk and money; dairy farmers con-
   tribute to presidential campaign funds. F.
   Wright. Nation 213:657-9 D 20 '71
Last minute report straight from Washing-
   ton. See issues of Farm journal
Opinion. See issues of Farm journal
'72 feed grain program. R. D. Wennblom.
   Farm J 95:15 D '71
Washington report. See issues of Successful
   farming
What farmers think of family farms; na-
   tional survey on big farms, programs, bar-
   gaining and credit; with editorial comment.
   C. W. Gifford. Farm J 95:17, 50 Je '71
Who's the farmers' friend? New Repub 165:
   5-6 D 4 '71
Your letters do make a difference. W. E.
   Swegle. Suc Farm 69:no5 L4 Mr '71
      See also
Farm produce—Prices
United States—Agriculture, Department of
AGRICULTURAL assistance
When North and West try to help. R. L. To-
   bin. Sat R 54:26 My 1 '71
AGRICULTURAL chemicals
Chemicals: what would it cost to . . . M.
   Hood. il Suc Farm 69:26-7 N '71
How to tank-mix sprays that save trips,
   cut costs. il Farm J 95:24B-24C Ag '71
New chemistry of food. G. Gregory. il
   UNESCO Courier 24:8-12 Je '71
Ways to save time: when using chemicals.
   G. L. Earle. il Suc Farm 69:no4 36-7 Mr
   '71
      See also
Fungicides
Herbicides
Insecticides
Pesticides
AGRICULTURAL chemistry
      See also
Plants—Chemical analysis
Soil acidity
Soil fertility
AGRICULTURAL conferences
Potential is great, but profits won't come
   easy; report of Midwest beef cattle confer-
   ence. W. Kester. il Farm J 95:32 O '71
AGRICULTURAL contracts. See Contracts,
   Agricultural
AGRICULTURAL cooperation. See Agriculture,
   Cooperative
AGRICULTURAL credit
Crisis in country banks. F. Bailey, jr. il Suc
   Farm 69:10-11 S '71
More competition to lend you money; rural
   banks, PCAs and land banks. G. Reynolds.
   Farm J 95:10 Ja '71
AGRICULTURAL economics. See Agriculture—
   Economic aspects
AGRICULTURAL education
Obsolete dream machine. L. Soth. il Nation
   212:687-90 My 31 '71
      See also
4-H clubs
AGRICULTURAL exhibitions
April 23 and 24 in San Luis Obispo, a college
   carnival and rodeo. il Sunset 146:75 Ap '71
Get more from a fair. Suc Farm 69:G28 S '71
State fair: she crawls on her belly like a
   reptile; two Texases and the fair. M. Good-
   man. il Time 98:28 N 1 '71
      See also
Flevohof, Netherlands
AGRICULTURAL extension work
      See also
4-H clubs
AGRICULTURAL forecasting
Big corn acreage went in fast and early.
   D. Wennblom. il Farm J 95:18-19 Je '71
Farmcast. See issues of Farm journal
How 1971 looks now; with editorial comment.
   C. W. Gifford. Farm J 95:20-1, 58 Ja '71
How to predict livestock prices. Suc Farm
   69:no2 51-5 F '71
1971: biggest guess ever. C. W. Gifford. Farm
   J 95:29-31 Mr '71
What you should know before you plant.
   C. W. Gifford. Farm J 95:22-3 My '71
AGRICULTURAL information services. See
   Agriculture—Information services
AGRICULTURAL insurance. See Insurance,
   Agricultural
AGRICULTURAL machinery
Big power for faster tillage. il Farm J 95:
   36-7 Mr '71
Geniuses down on the farm. W. Kester and
   G. Logsdon. il Farm J 95:20-1+ Je '71
How Europeans get more work from farm
   machines. il Farm J 95:49 F '71
How to be fair when you share machinery.
   Farm J 95:14 My '71

Machinery management. P. B. Jones. See is-
   sues of Successful farming
Machinery parade; photographs. See issues of
   Farm journal
Machinery preview 1971. G. W. Wormley. il
   Farm J 95:22-7 Ja '71
Technical words we have trouble with (title
   varies) Suc Farm 69:B18 My; D16 O '71
Three ways to screen fines. il Suc Farm 69:B16
   Je '71
What's ahead in farm machinery. il Suc
   Farm 69:no2 A4 F '71
      See also
Augers
Farm mechanization
Feed grinders and grinding
Grain handling
Harvesting machinery
Hay stackers
Irrigation machinery
Planters (farm machines)
Silage handling
Spraying apparatus
Tractors
      Cost of operation
Machinery costs can make or break you. M.
   Hood. il Suc Farm 69:no2 32-3 F '71
Machinery: what would it cost to . . . P. B.
   Jones. il Suc Farm 69:32-3 N '71
      Depreciation
   See Depreciation
      Equipment
Good hitch ideas. il Suc Farm 69:no2 50 F
   '71
How to choose machinery options. P. B.
   Jones. il Suc Farm 69:no2 36-7 F '71
      Leasing and renting
Cheaper to rent or hire machinery? Suc
   Farm 69:C16 O '71
How to get good service from your custom
   operator. T. McCartney and M. Hood. il
   Suc Farm 69:L1 Ag '71
Rent or lease: an alternative to owning. R.
   Krumme. il Suc Farm 69:no2 34-5 F '71
When to own, when to custom hire. R.
   Krumme. il Suc Farm 69:no 4 C22 Mr '71
      Maintenance and repair
Get your equipment ready for the field. G.
   L. Earle. il Suc Farm 69:no5 M16 Mr '71
How to keep your engine cool. il Suc Farm
   69:D8 Je '71
Mechanics' ideas to keep machinery running.
   G. L. Earle. il Suc Farm 69:no2 30-1 F '71
New is nice, but is it really necessary? C.
   Atwell. il Har Yrs 11:26-7 Ag '71
Two ways to clean your equipment. il Suc
   Farm 69:M4 Ag '71
      See also
Welding

   Anecdotes, facetiae, satire, etc.
How I trained my wife to buy repairs. H. R.
   Betzelberger. Farm J 95:39 Je '71
      Safety devices and measures
Coming big push for machinery safety. P. B.
   Jones. il Suc Farm 69:no2 29 F '71
Don't duel V-belts, put guards on them.
   Suc Farm 69:no4 C4 Mr '71
      Storage
Dollars and cents of machinery storage. M.
   Hood. il Suc Farm 69:A1 S '71
AGRICULTURAL machinery industry
      See also
Deere and company
International harvester company
Massey-Ferguson, ltd.
AGRICULTURAL meteorology. See Meteorol-
   ogy, Agricultural
AGRICULTURAL pests
      See also
Grain, Stored—Diseases and pests
Poison baits
      also subhead Diseases and pests under
   names of crops, e.g. Corn—Diseases and
   pests; *also* names of agricultural pests, e.g.
   Borers (insects)
AGRICULTURAL production. See Production,
   Agricultural
AGRICULTURAL products. See Farm produce
AGRICULTURAL research
Agricultural research and the small farm. R.
   Steffen. Org Gard & Farm 18:84-5 My '71
      See also
Plant breeding
AGRICULTURAL societies
      See also
American society of agronomy
National farmers organization

AGUALLO, Thomaline—*Continued*
  Place between; story. Seventeen 30:116-17
    N '71
  Underground; story. Seventeen 30:106-7 Jl
    '71
  When strangers meet; story. Good H 172:100-1
    My '71
AGUSTA (firm) See Helicopter industry—Italy
AGUTTER, Jenny
  On location; interview. ed. by E. Miller. por
    Seventeen 30:62 N '71
AH See and the six-colored heaven; drama
  See Boiko, C.
AHERN, James F. and Bernstein, V. H.
  How we handcuff our police. Redbook 136:
    79+ Ap '71
AHMAD, Aijaz
  Bloody surgery of Pakistan. Nation 212:815-
    19 Je 28 '71
AHMAD, Eqbal
  Theory and fallacies of counterinsurgency.
    il Nation 213:70-85 Ag 2 '71

              about
  How the kidnap conspiracy was hatched.
    L. Lockwood. il pors Life 70:26-30 My 21
    '71 *
AHUJA AKS, Ameena
  (tr) See Chekhov, A. P. Three short stories
AICHI, Kiichi
  U.S. and Japan sign agreement on rever-
    sion of Okinawa; letter. June 17, 1971.
    Dept State Bul 65:39-40 Jl 12 '71
AID to families with dependent children (pro-
    gram) See Child welfare—United States
AIDA; opera. See Verdi G.
AIDES, Psychiatric hospital. See Hospitals,
    Psychiatric—Staff
AIDES, Teachers. See Teachers aides
AIDS in teaching. See Teaching—Aids and de-
    vices
AIDS to navigation. See Navigation—Aids
    and devices
AIGNER, Jean S. and others
  Early racial and cultural identifications in
    southwestern Alaska. bibliog Science 171:
    87-8 Ja 8 '71
AIGRAIN, Pierre
  Two views of US technology and world
    trade. S. M. Hein. pors Phys Today 24:69-
    70 D '71 *
AIKEN, Conrad
  Life carved to a pointed end. B. DeMott.
    Sat R 54:23-5 Ja 30 '71
AILEY, Alvin
  All hail Ailey. W. Terry. il Sat R 54:36 N
    6 '71 *
  Of time and Alvin Ailey. N. M. Stoop. il
    por Dance Mag 45:28-33 D '71 *
AILEY, Alvin, American dance theatre. See
    Alvin Ailey American dance theatre
AILSA Mellon Bruce collection. See Art—
    Private collections; Silverware—Collectors
    and collecting
AIMS in education. See Education—Aims and
    objectives
AINT supposed to die a natural death; musical
    comedy. See Musical comedies, revues, etc.
    —Criticisms, plots, etc.
AIR
              Analysis
    See also
  Air pollution—Measurement
AIR, Ionized
  Air ionizer. J. Darr. il Radio-Electr 42:32-
    Je '71
AIR agreements. See Aviation—International
    aspects
AIR bags. See Automobiles—Safety devices and
    measures
AIR bases
  Military exchanges think black; Westover
    air force base. il Ebony 26:54-6+ Jl '71
AIR buildings. See Air-supported structures
AIR buses. See Airplanes, Jet
AIR cargo containers. See Containers for
    shipping
AIR cleaners. See Air filters
AIR conditioning
  Central air conditioning; how to get the most
    cool for your money. D. Quentzel. Good H
    172:198 My '71
  How to get your money's worth from cen-
    tral air conditioning; excerpt from The
    home owner's survival kit. A. M. Watkins.
    House & Gard 139:56+ My '71
    See also
  Air filters
  School buildings—Air conditioning
AIR conditioning equipment
  Air conditioners. il Consumer Bul 54:19-24
    Jl '71
  Cool your whole house with one window
    unit? compact high-BTU air conditioners.
    J. R. Free. il Pop Sci 198:92-4+ My '71

  Cooling salts; thermal energy storage. Sci
    Am 225:46 Ag '71
  Engines do double duty; refrigeration or
    standby power. il Arch Rec 149:151-2 Mr '71
  Getting the most out of your room air con-
    ditioner. Bet Hom & Gard 49:115 My '71
  Know your cooling system. R. L. Bly. il Am
    City 86:80+ Ap '71
  Low-cost air conditioners. J. Hand. il Mech
    Illus 67:94-5+ Jl '71
  Room air-conditioners. il Consumer Rep 36:
    369-75 Je '71
    See also
  Air diffusers
  Dehumidifiers
  Humidifiers
AIR conditioning industry
    See also
  Carrier corporation
AIR coolers. See Air conditioning equipment
AIR currents. See Winds
AIR cushion landing system. See Airplanes—
    Landing gear
AIR cushion vehicles
  Air cushion cargo craft tested in Canada.
    M. L. Yaffee. il Aviation W 95:58-60 D 20
    '71
  Air cushion to Dulles. Sci N 99:144 F 27 '71
  Build the yellow jacket for $400. R. Q. Riley.
    il Pop Mech 135:126-9+ Mr '71
  Drive for modern navy, warships that fly;
    surface-effect ships. il U S News 71:53-4
    D 6 '71
  Hovercraft military market emphasized. il
    Aviation W 94:44-5 Je 7 '71
  Hovercraft to the wilderness; Amazonas ho-
    vercraft expedition. D. Smithers. il por Sci
    Digest 70:8-17+ N '71
  Leading international surface effect machines
    (title varies) tables (cont) Aviation W 94:99
    Mr 8 '71
  Magnetic force studied for intercity travel.
    il Aviation W 94:50-1 Mr 22 '71
  New use for SK-5. J. H. Super. il Sea Front
    17:272-3 S '71
  Riding on air; U.S. train of the future? il U S
    News 70:84 Mr 15 '71
  Surface-effect ships. B. Kocivar. il Pop Sci
    199:46-7 Jl '71
  Trial runs for a 100-knot navy; surface-ef-
    fects ships. il Bsns W p 110 N 6 '71
AIR defenses
    See also
  United States—Defenses
AIR diffusers
  Three new variable air volume systems; com-
    fort, economy. il Arch Rec 149:153-4 Mr '71
AIR filters
  Can charged water clear our air? charged
    aerosol purifier. E. A. Zadig. il Pop Sci
    199:32 O '71
  Electronic way to a clean-air house. il Bet
    Hom & Gard 49:112 O '71
  Electrostatic air cleaner. J. Darr. il Radio-
    Electr 42:32+ Jl '71
  Facts about air cleaners for the home. il
    Good H 173:158 Jl '71
  Good-bye to dust; new air cleaners. M. K.
    Spencer. il Am Home 74:48 Mr '71
  90% clean air at home, electronically. il
    Changing T 25:35-6 O '71
  Roundy-round corner; filtration unit for
    race car engines. S. Kelly. il Hot Rod 24:
    92 Ag '71
  View from Kramer. A. Kramer. Mod Phot
    35:18+ Ap '71
    See also
  Purolator, inc
AIR force academy. See United States air
    force academy. Colorado Springs
AIR force bases. See Air bases
AIR force museum. See Aeronautic museums
AIR force systems command. See United States
    —Air force—Systems command
AIR France. See Airlines—France
AIR freight containerization. See Containeri-
    zation (freight)
AIR freight forwarders. See Forwarding com-
    panies
AIR freight service
  CAB denies added cargo rights. Aviation W
    95:18 N 22 '71
  New rates, containers spur cargo efforts.
    R. S. Kahn. il Aviation W 95:28-30 D 20 '71
  Pacific air tonnage soars as dock strike con-
    tinues. W. S. Hieronymus. Aviation W 95:32
    S 13 '71
  Sagging cargo, economy cut use of QCs.
    H. D. Watkins. Aviation W 95:27+ Ag 2
    '71
  Second business at our airports; theft. D.
    Walsh. il Life 70:16-23 F 12 '71
    See also
  Airlift international, inc.
  Airplanes. Freight
  Emery air freight corporation
  Flying Tiger, inc.

AIR freight service—*Continued*

Rates

BOAC may block Atlantic cargo rate plan. D. E. Fink. Aviation W 95:26-7 D 6 '71

IATA leaves cargo rates open. E. H. Kolcum. Aviation W 94:26-7 Je 21 '71

IATA parley to weigh freight increases. E. H. Kolcum. Aviation W 94:29 My 10 '71

Passenger, cargo surcharges set to offset new navigation fees. E. H. Kolcum. Aviation W 94:27 Ja 25 '71

Statistics

Growth in North Atlantic air cargo and mail; year 1970 over 1969; table. Aviation W 94:37 Mr 22 '71

North Atlantic air cargo and mail data; tables. Aviation W 95:40-1 Jl 19; 34-5 N 8 '71

U.S. airline mail and cargo, 1970; table. Aviation W 94:47 Je 14 '71

Lebanon

From desert airlift to global caravan; Trans Mediterranean airways. il Bsns W p36-7 O 9 '71

AIR glow. See Airglow

AIR hitchhiking. See Air travel

AIR inlets (jet planes) See Jet airplane engines—Air intakes

AIR lanes. See Airways

AIR line pilots association, International
Pilots ask $1.5-billion airport plan. Aviation W 95:27 N 15 '71

Pilots spur anti-hijacking drive. Aviation W 94:19 Ja 18 '71

AIR locks
Manned space laboratory airlock passes preflight tests. il Space World H-3-87:38-9 Mr '71

AIR mail service
Airline schedule reductions spark delivery problem for post office. J. Woolsey. Aviation W 94:28 Ja 18 '71

Promises, promises. il Newsweek 77:77 Ap 26 '71
   See also
Pigeon post

Statistics

Growth in North Atlantic air cargo and mail; year 1970 over 1969; table. Aviation W 94:37 Mr 22 '71

North Atlantic air cargo and mail data; tables. Aviation W 95:40-1 Jl 19; 34-5 N 8 '71

U.S. airline mail and cargo, 1970; table. Aviation W 94:47 Je 14 '71

AIR microbiology
Fort Detrick: a top laboratory is threatened with extinction. P. M. Boffey. Science 171: 262-4 Ja 22 '71

AIR museums. See Aeronautic museums

AIR navigation. See Navigation, Aerial

AIR pilots
Pro's nest. T. H. Block. See issues of Flying
Who's in charge here? T. H. Block. Flying 88:105 Ap '71
   See also
Air line pilots association, International
Airplanes—Piloting
Children as air pilots
Drinking and airplane accidents
Negro air pilots
Physicians as air pilots

Anecdotes, facetiae, satire, etc.

Framed! W. V. Mull. il Flying 89:73-9+ N '71

Political activities

Pilots pro or con; Pilots for Nixon. R. B. Parke. Flying 88:32 Mr '71

Qualifications

New pilot qualifications proposed. Aviation W 94:46 Ap 5 '71

Testing

Those pesky writtens. R. L. Collins. Flying 89:88 N '71

Training

Brand-new way to learn to fly; Cessna integrated flight training system. N. Aubuchon. il por Pop Sci 199:50-2 D '71

Flight unlimited. il pors Ebony 26:123-4+ O '71

Follow me through. See issues of Flying
Harrier program seeks broad VTOL data. D. A. Brown. il Aviation W 95:47-8+ O 25 '71
Student pilot. H. Jason. Flying 88:118 Je; 89: 120 Ag; 24 O '71
   See also
Aeronautics—Study and teaching
Airplanes, Training

AIR piracy. See Airplane hijacking

AIR plants
Plants you can grow on walls. il Sunset 146: 254+ Ap '71

AIR pollution
Cloud comes to Quibbletown. D. Jackson. il Life 71:72-4+ D 10 '71
Environment; symposium on air pollution. Sci N 99:90 F 6 '71
Fate of air pollutants: removal of ethylene, sulfur dioxide, and nitrogen dioxide by soil. F. B. Abeles and others. bibliog il Science 173:914-16 S 3 '71
Global circulation of atmospheric pollutants. R. E. Newell. il Sci Am 224:32-42 Ja '71
Heat barrier; thermal air pollution. P. R. Ehrlich and J. P. Holdren. Sat R 54:61 Ap 3 '71
Invisible particles in air. il Chem 44:27 Jl '71
Lead balloon; NAS report on lead in the air. Newsweek 78:73-4 D 6 '71
Lead in the air; industry weight on Academy panel challenged. R. Gillette. Science 174:800-2 N 19 '71
Leaden atmosphere. il Chem 44:26 Jl '71
Mercury in the air. Sci N 99:280 Ap 24 '71
Mercury in the air. bibliog il Environ 13: 24+ My '71
Polluting the atmosphere with asbestos. Sci N 100:261 O 16 '71
Some air pollution myths. R. B. Carroll. Nat R 23:1233-4 N 5 '71
Threat of the unseen. V. J. Schaefer. il Sat R 54:55-7 F 6 '71
Which way will you be lead? letters. Natur Hist 80:6-7 D '71
Worse, not better. Sci N 99:80-1 Ja 30 '71
   See also
Airplanes—Pollution
Automobiles—Pollution
Electric plants—Pollution
Factories—Pollution
Plants, Effect of air pollution on
Smog
Smoke
Steel works—Pollution
Telephone—Air pollution reports
   also subhead Air pollution under names of cities, e.g. Los Angeles—Air pollution

Conferences

Steelworkers conservation program. I. W. Abel. il por Nat Parks & Con Mag 45: 25-8 F '71

Trying to clear the air on air pollution; report of Airlie house seminar. R. H. Gilluly. Sci N 100:332 N 13 '71

Control

Air pollution control news. See issues of American city

Clean air effort gets youth backing; policy of Neenah foundry co, Neenah, Wis. il Am City 86:78 O '71

Cleaner way to make coke. il Bsns W p42 Jl 31 '71

Radio network nabs air-pollution violators; Allegheny County, Pa. R. Chleboski. il Am City 86:89-90 D '71

To protect yourself against air pollution. E. H. McCleary. Read Digest 99:41-2 S '71
   See also
Air filters
Airplanes—Pollution control devices
Electronics in pollution control
Industry and the environmental movement
Motor vehicles—Pollution control devices
Odors—Control
Smoke prevention

Economic aspects

Pollution tax is boomeranging; tax on sulfur emissions. por Bsns W p40-1 Ap 10 '71

Skeleton in the garage; memorandum. Economics of clean air. J. Lear. Sat R 54:47-8 Je 5 '71

Laws and legislation

Blueprint for breathing; 1970 Clean air act. Time 97:46 My 17 '71

Cities face decisions on autos; national ambient air standards. Sci N 99:314 My 8 '71

Clean air act cuts more teeth. il Bsns W p 18-19 My 8 '71

Copper counts the cost of clean air. il Bsns W p 104 Jl 17 '71

AIR pollution—Laws and legislation—*Continued*
How I fought city hall, and won. M. Boyd. il por Redbook 138:24+ N '71
What have we done? Look 35:30 My 4 '71

Measurement

ASTRA project monitors atmospheric pollution. G. B. Lubkin. il Phys Today 24:20 Ja '71; Discussion. bibliog 24:11+ Ag '71
Decreasing transparency of our atmosphere. il Sky & Tel 41:272 My '71
Detection of air pollutants with tunable diode lasers. E. D. Hinkley and P. L. Kelley. bibliog il Science 171:635-9 F 19 '71
Lasers measure air pollution. S. Lindsay. il Sat R 54:52 Ag 7 '71
Little tester that sniffs air pollution. E. F. Lindsley. il Pop Sci 198:12 F '71
New eye on the air; correlation spectrometer. A. Coble and others. bibliog il por Environ 13:34-41 My '71
Nitric oxide air pollution: detection by optoacoustic spectroscopy. L. B. Kreuzer and C. K. N. Patel. bibliog il Science 173: 45-7 Jl 2 '71

Physiological effects

Cloud comes to Quibbletown. D. Jackson. il Life 71:72-4+ D 10 '71
Episode 104. V. Brodine. bibliog il Environ 13:2-24+ Ja '71
Lead poisoning: combating the threat from the air. R. J. Bazell. Science 174:574-6 N 5 '71
Mene, mene; boys at play afflicted in New Jersey. Nation 213:292 O 4 '71
Metals in the air. H. A. Schroeder. bibliog il por Environ 13:18-24+ O '71
Poisons in the air, what they can do to you. B. Ford. il Sci Digest 70:73-8+ S '71
Special burden. V. Brodine. il Environ 13: 22-4+ Mr '71

Research

Autos, emission reports and the public. Sci N 99:280 Ap 24 '71
Clean air; an R&D gap; il Sci N 99:177-8 Mr 13 '71; Reply. F. W. Bowditch. 99:276 Ap 24 '71
Climate change study by NOAA. il Weatherwise 24:63 Ap '71
Mysterious open air factor. Chem 44:24-5 F '71

Statistics

Air; EQ index. il Nat Wildlife 9:30-1 O '71

Germany (Federal Republic)

Knapsack packs up. Newsweek 78:57 Jl 26 '71

Southwestern states

Cloud on the desert. R. Craig. bibliog il Environ 13:20-4+ Jl '71; Discussion. 13:50 N '71
Hello, energy; goodbye, big sky; smokestacks invade the Southwest. J. Neary. il Life 70:61-4+ Ap 16 '71

AIR pollution and cancer. See Cancer—Causes
AIR pressure. See Atmospheric pressure
AIR purification
    See also
Odors—Control
AIR races. See Airplane racing
AIR raids
    See also
London—Air raids
Vietnamese war, 1957- —Aerial operations
AIR routes. See Airlines—International services; Airlines—United States—Routes; Airways
AIR safety. See Aviation—Safety devices and measures
AIR-sea interaction. See Ocean-atmosphere interaction
AIR shows. See Aviation—Exhibitions
AIR shuttles. See Airlines—Shuttle service
AIR-soil interaction. See Soil-atmosphere interaction
AIR stewardesses. See Airlines—Hostesses
AIR-supported structures
Air support structures. il Parks & Rec 6:34-5 My '71
Inflatable, portable house. il Vogue 158:116-17 Ag 1 '71
Momentary community for a mobile era; whiz bang Quick city. W. McQuade. il Life 71:8 Jl 23 '71
AIR taxi service
CAB unit urges new air taxi standards. H. D. Watkins. Aviation W 94:29-30 Ap 26 '71
Potential market seen in eased taxi rules. H. D. Watkins. Aviation W 95:26 O 4 '71
    See also
Executive jet aviation, inc.

AIR tools. See Pneumatic tools
AIR traffic. See Airlines—Traffic
AIR traffic control
Avionics giant seeks ATC superiority; Thomson-CSF. il Aviation W 94:173-80 My 31 '71
Design-operations study seeks to obviate special procedures; Concorde. il Aviation W 94:107+ F 8 '71
Double lesson; stand by vs. go-around. R. L. Collins. Flying 89:70 S '71
Shift of ATC design from FAA urged. P. J. Klass. Aviation W 94:20-1 Mr 15 '71
System versus area navigation. R. L. Collins. il Flying 88:41-5 Mr '71
VFR minimums. R. L. Collins. Flying 89: 14-15 D '71
    See also
Airports—Traffic control
Artificial satellites—Air traffic control use
Radar in aviation

Europe, Western

Eurocontrol plans shift in SST routing studies. Aviation W 94:111 F 8 '71

France

France's ATC automation near schedule. Aviation W 94:192-4 My 31 '71

Italy

Italy launches ATC automation program. Aviation W 94:190 My 31 '71

AIR traffic controllers (persons)
Controller standards proposed in Senate. Aviation W 94:20-1 My 17 '71
House passes controller bill. Aviation W 95: 30 O 11 '71
AIR transport agreements. See Aviation—International aspects
AIR transport association of America
Airlines oppose U.S./ESRO aerosat. P. J. Klass. Aviation W 95:22-3 O 25 '71
Nonskeds soar with CAB ruling. il Bsns W p 18-19 F 6 '71
AIR travel
Air-esses: our fasten-your-seatbelt survey of flying women. il Ladies Home J 88: 62 My '71
Airlines study wholesaling own tours. Aviation W 95:28 Ag 30 '71
Hitchhiking by air; report. M. Knox. il Time 98:49 Ag 16 '71
Leapfrogging the SST: an alternative. S. A. Kallis, jr. Nat R 23:419-20 Ap 20 '71
Martinis at Mach 2. R. Hotz. Aviation W 94: 9 Je 7 '71
Thumb-tripping by air. L. Gage. Esquire 76:56+ N '71
Tour New York by air. S. Wilkinson. il Flying 89:S12-16 Ag '71
Triple play; Anchorage, Honolulu and Los Angeles. M. Miller. il Travel 136:74-5 Ag '71
    See also
Aviation consumer action project
Private flying

Physiological aspects
    See Aviation—Physiological aspects

Radiation hazards
    See Aviation—Radiation hazards

Statistics

Growth in U.S. air passengers; table. Aviation W 95:30 Ag 30 '71
1970 air passengers between the United States, other countries by flag of carrier; table. Aviation W 95:32-3 Jl 26 '71
AIR travel with children. See Travel with children
AIR weapons training centers. See Bombing and gunnery ranges
AIRASIAN, Peter W.
Behavioral objectives and the teaching of English. Engl J 60:495-9 Ap '71
AIRBOATS, Fishing. See Fishing—Implements and appliances
AIRBORNE display systems. See Aeronautic instruments—Display systems
AIRBUSES. See Airplanes, Jet
AIRCRAFT
    See also
Airplanes
Airships
Balloons
Gliders (aeronautics)
Helicopters
AIRCRAFT carriers
    See also
Airplanes, Military—Landing on carriers

AIRD, Catherine
  Pen to paper. Writer 84:14-16 O '71
AIRFOILS
  See also
  Airplane wings
  Flaps, Airplane
AIRGLOW
  Spectrum of the airglow. M. F. Ingham. il
  Sci Am 226:78-85 Ja '72
AIRLIFT International, Inc.
  Airlift international pushes to cut losses. H.
  D. Watkins. Aviation W 95:36-8 Jl 19 '71
  Wobbly cargo line keeps its wings. il Bsns W
  p36-7 Ap 17 '71
AIRLINE hostesses. See Airlines—Hostesses
AIRLINE mergers. See Airlines—Consolida-
  tions and mergers
AIRLINE schedules. See Airlines—Management
AIRLINES
  See also
  Air travel
  International air transport association

Accounting
Airlines wary of accounting change for leased
  equipment. W. H. Gregory. Aviation W
  95:25-6 O 25 '71

Advertising
Airlines focus on special interest groups.
  W. H. Gregory. il Aviation W 95:32-4 Ag 2
  '71
National on the offensive. il Newsweek 78:
  96+ N 15 '71
Stew at 30,000 feet; feminists protest cam-
  paigns. D. Butwin. il Sat R 54:72-6 D 4 '71

Automation
See also
Airlines—Luggage handling
Airlines—Reservation systems
Computers—Airline use

Communication systems
Uses, area of airline data link expanded. B.
  M. Elson. il Aviation W 95:60-1+ O 25 '71

Consolidations and mergers
American expects early Caribbean profit.
  W. H. Gregory. Aviation W 94:29 Mr 15 '71
American-Western merger opposed. L. Doty.
  Aviation W 96:20 Ja 3 '72
Board affirms merger position; proposed
  Northeast-Northwest merger. Aviation W
  94:187 Mr 8 '71
CAB examiner urges approval of Northeast
  merger with Delta. Aviation W 95:28 N 1 '71
Can a hotelman run an airline? il Fortune
  83:31-2 F '71
Diverging on merging; American-Western.
  Time 98:80 S 13 '71
Examiner approves Hawaiian merger. Avia-
  tion W 94:24 Mr 1 '71
Foggy guidelines for airline mergers. il Bsns
  W p22 S 4 '71
Merger opinion may alter labor clauses. H.
  D. Watkins. Aviation W 95:28 N 8 '71
Mergers threaten trunk structure; tentative
  merger agreement between Northwest and
  National. H. D. Watkins. il Aviation W 95:
  24-6 S 13 '71
New airline merger policy blurred. H. D.
  Watkins. Aviation W 95:22-4 S 6 '71
Northwest, National merger filed. Aviation
  W 95:22 O 4 '71
Requiem for a merger? American and West-
  ern airlines. il Newsweek 78:92 S 13 '71
Rivals hit American/Western merger. Avi-
  ation W 94:31 Je 28 '71
Troubled airlines try a fresh tack. il U S News
  70:44 Ja 18 '71
Winged colossus? Pan American world air-
  ways and Trans World airlines. il News-
  week 78:57 Jl 26 '71

Cooperation
Arab airlines buying transports as regional
  cooperation grows. E. H. Kolcum. Aviation W 95:25 Jl 12 '71

Cost of operation
Flying the American way. R. Fink. New
  Repub 164:19-22 F 13 '71
  See also
Airplanes, Jet—Cost of operation

Employees
Eastern bids employes cooperate to avoid
  large-scale furloughs. Aviation W 94:25 Ap
  5 '71
Merger opinion may alter labor clauses. H.
  D. Watkins. Aviation W 95:28 N 8 '71
  See also
Airlines—Hostesses
Airlines—Wages and hours

Equipment and supplies
  See also
Airports—Equipment

Fares
Air fare war roars on. il Bsns W p40 Je 19 '71
Air-fare warfare. il Time 98:64-5 Jl 5 '71
Air war. W. F. Buckley, jr. Nat R 23:1199
  O 22 '71
Airline that thrives on discounting; Ice-
  landic airlines. il Bsns W p68+ Jl 24 '71
Airlines raise fares to Hawaii. Aviation W
  94:25 My 17 '71
Atlantic passenger fares set; cargo tariffs
  open. Aviation W 95:26-7 D 20 '71
Bargains in air travel as price war spreads.
  il U S News 71:37-8 N 1 '71
CAB allows more flexibility in discounts. H.
  D. Watkins. Aviation W 95:27-8 S 20 '71
CAB issues fare ruling deluge; major new
  bids hang on case. H. D. Watkins. Aviation
  W 94:21-2 Ja 18 '71
CAB orders fare reasonableness action. Avia-
  tion W 94:187 Mr 8 '71
CAB pushes for international fares power. L.
  Doty. Aviation W 95:24 O 25 '71
Charter carriers gird to maintain position as
  rate war threatens. Aviation W 95:29 S 27
  '71
Cuts coming in air fares abroad. il U S News
  71:71 Ag 23 '71
Eastern fare proposals rejected. Aviation W
  94:40 My 31 '71
Eastern seeking family fare approval. R. S.
  Kahn. Aviation W 94:32 My 3 '71
Easy fliers; youth fare program abused.
  il Newsweek 77:86+ F 8 '71
European flags oppose Lufthansa. E. H.
  Kolcum. Aviation W 95:24-5 Ag 23 '71
European youth fare directives intensify
  IATA-government rifts. Aviation W 94:30
  Je 14 '71
Exodus 1971: new bargains in the sky. il
  Time 98:62-4+ Jl 19 '71
Fare cuts ahead. Newsweek 78:66+ Ag 23 '71
Fare hikes will not halt the tailspin. Bsns W
  p26 Ja 16 '71
Fare level spurs sharp divergence. H. D.
  Watkins. Aviation W 94:24 F 1 '71
Fare war in Texas. Newsweek 78:56+ Jl 5
  '71
Fasten your seat belts. R. Robertson, 3d.
  New Repub 164:17-18 Ja 2 '71; Discussion.
  164:34-5 F 13 '71
Flying the cheap way to Europe. il Time 97:
  74 Je 21 '71
For air travelers: rising fares ahead. il U S
  News 70:64 Ap 26 '71
German roulette. Newsweek 78:67-8 O 4 '71
Giving the CAB transatlantic power. il Bsns
  W p26-7 O 16 '71
Government edicts guide agenda for IATA.
  L. Doty. il Aviation W 94:28-9 Je 28 '71
Great air fare war. il Newsweek 77:71 Je
  21 '71
High-level mess. Time 98:98 O 11 '71
IATA members aim at charters. R. S. Kahn.
  Aviation W 95:22-5 Ag 2 '71
Just one more time. il Newsweek 77:78+ Ap
  26 '71
Lufthansa topples the fare structure. il Bsns
  W p25 S 18 '71
More North Atlantic talks to dominate IATA
  parley. E. H. Kolcum. Aviation W 95:27-8
  S 6 '71
New military rates aid revenue; Hawaii fare
  bids founder again; with table. H. D. Wat-
  kins. Aviation W 94:31 My 15 '71
North Atlantic fare increases approved. Avi-
  ation W 94:29 Mr 29 '71
North Atlantic fares war spurs government
  aid bid. L. Doty. Aviation W 95:24-5 O 4
  '71
Northeast airlines' family fare plan rejected
  by CAB. Aviation W 94:30 Je 7 '71
Open rate situation looms in North Atlantic
  market. Aviation W 95:32 Ag 16 '71
Pan Am seeks lower North Atlantic fares.
  Aviation W 94:28 My 24 '71
Passenger, cargo surcharges set to offset new
  navigation fees. E. H. Kolcum. Aviation W
  94:27 Ja 25 '71
Price of victory in the air fare war. il Bsns
  W p84 O 2 '71
Prices down over the Atlantic. Time 98:86
  S 27 '71
Promotional fares aimed at traffic lag. H. D.
  Watkins. Aviation W 95:31 Ag 16 '71
Red Baron strikes again. Time 98:49 Ag 23
  '71
Rulings add incentive for capacity cuts. H.
  D. Watkins. il Aviation W 94:28-9 Ap 19 '71
SAS, Alitalia file new Atlantic fares. Avia-
  tion W 95:25 N 15 '71
Seating surcharge range urged. Aviation W
  95:30 O 11 '71

AIRLINES—Fares—*Continued*
Soon: lower air fares to Europe. U S News
71:45 S 27 '71
Supplementals bracing for IATA action. R.
G. O'Lone. Aviation W 95:20-1 Jl 19 '71
TWA proposing lower North Atlantic fares.
Aviation W 94:28-9 Je 7 '71
Thank you, Red Baron; Lufthansa changing
transatlantic fares. il Newsweek 78:90+ S
27 '71
Transatlantic open rate expected as IATA
fare talks hit impasse. Aviation W 95:
27 N 8 '71
Uncertain sky. il Time 98:58-9 S 6 '71
Unfair air fares. R. Fink. New Repub 165:
13-15 S 11 '71
War no more. Newsweek 78:86 N 29 '71
Youth fare battle hits government level.
Aviation W 94:26 Je 21 '71
Youthfare scramble. il Sr Schol 99:7-9 S 20
'71

Federal aid
Good old government. New Repub 166:11 Ja
1 '72
See also
Local service airlines—Federal aid

Feeder airlines
See Local service airlines

Finance
Airline income, expense; tables (cont) Avia-
tion W 94:59 My 10; 95:35 Jl 12; 31 O 18
71; 96:35 Ja 3 '72
Airlines and aerospace: the debt load fac-
tor. il Bsns W p70-1 Je 26 '71
Airlines, CAB examine effects of Phase 2.
J. P. Woolsey. Aviation W 95:23 N 22 '71
Airlines' fiscal woes buffet airports. H. D.
Watkins. il Aviation W 95:38-43 N 15 '71
Airlines' troubles: search for a cure. il U S
News 70:58-9 Mr 1 '71
American, TWA, Braniff report increased
third quarter profits. Aviation W 95:23 O
25 '71
Capacity, earnings woes stalk carriers. Avia-
tion W 94:26 Mr 22 '71
Carriers differ on remedy for fiscal woes.
L. Doty. Aviation W 94:22 F 8 '71
Carriers' financial outlook clouded. H. D.
Watkins. il Aviation W 95:21-3 Jl 26 '71
Carriers show mixed second-quarter results.
Aviation W 95:27 Ag 2 '71
Crying the blues; Senate hearings. News-
week 77:64-5 F 15 '71
Debt obligations hit $6.8 billion for U.S.
certificated carriers. Aviation W 95:26 Jl
19 '71
Fasten your seat belts. R. Robertson, 3d.
New Repub 164:17-18 Ja 2 '71; Discussion.
164:34-5 F 13 '71
Freedom and enterprise; address. February
24, 1971. F. D. Hall. Vital Speeches 37:430-4
My 1 '71
Increases in airline operating revenues; table.
Aviation W 94:34 My 10 '71
Third quarter results hint downtrend halt;
with tables. Aviation W 95:29 N 1 '71
Transportation: with vardsticks of manage-
ment performance. il Forbes 109:186-9 Ja
1 '72
Troubled airlines try a fresh tack. il U S
News 70:44 Ja 18 '71
Trunkline profit, loss; tables (cont) Aviation
W 94:24 Ap 19; 50 My 31; 95:23 Ag 30; 28
N 22 '71
U.S. airline increases in operating revenues;
tables. Aviation W 95:33 O 18 '71
U.S. airline revenues and expenses; table.
Aviation W 95:30 N 1 '71
U.S. scheduled airline operating revenues
and expenses, 1970; table. Aviation W 94:
34-5 My 17 '71
Wall Street beat. R. Brady. Duns 97:81 F '71
See also
Airlines—Accounting
Airlines—Fares

Freight service
See Air freight service

History
See Aeronautics—History

Hostesses
Beauty on the wing; flight attendants. P.
Van Wagenen. il Parents Mag 46:64-8 My
'71
Longer stewardess careers spark gains,
frustrations for airlines. L. Doty. il Aviation W 94:29+ My 17 '71
Play now, fly later; fun at Sun Valley, Idaho
il Sports Illus 34:16-17 Ja 18 '71

Stew at 30,000 feet; training. D. Butwin.
il Sat R 54:72-6 D 4 '71
Stewardesses: what the pros do when they
fly for fun. M. Kunz. il Ladies Home J
88:58 My '71

Information services
BOAC, BEA offer U.K. business contact
data to passengers. Aviation W 94:30 F 22
'71

Insurance
Higher liability limit set in new protocol.
Aviation W 94:36 Ap 12 '71
Tangled aftermath: destruction of planes by
Arab guerrillas, September 1970. il News-
week 77:39-40 F 8 '71

International services
Whatever happened to Moscow-New York
airline service? il U S News 70:87 F 22 '71

Asia
Obstacles bar red China routes. L. Doty.
Aviation W 94:23-4 Ap 26 '71

European-Asiatic
SAS inaugurates transsiberian service. D. E.
Fink. il Aviation W 94:25-7 Ap 19 '71

Latin America
Pan American cuts Caribbean frequencies to
200/week. Aviation W 94:30 My 10 '71

Transatlantic
Competition spurs Miami-London traffic. H.
D. Watkins. il Aviation W 95:30-2 N 22
'71
Cuts coming in air fares abroad. il U S News
71:71 Ag 23 '71
First KLM DC-10s will serve Toronto be-
ginning in late 1972. Aviation W 95:30 O 4
'71
Miami-London carriers vary cabin service. H.
D. Watkins. Aviation W 95:29-30 N 29 '71

Transpacific
Air Micronesia gets island route. J. P. Woolsey. Aviation W 95:31-2 Ag 16 '71
South Pacific capacity dispute makes Qantas
shift 747 route. R. G. O'Lone. Aviation W
95:25 Ag 23 '71

Western hemisphere
Carriers may seek truce soon in San Juan-
New York battle. J. P. Woolsey. Aviation
W 96:29-30 Ja 10 '72
Competition stiffens in Caribbean. J. P.
Woolsey. Aviation W 95:23-4 O 4 '71

Load factor
See Airlines—Traffic

Luggage handling
Airport roller coaster gives your bags a
fast ride. E. F. Lindsley. il Pop Sci 198:
34+ My '71
New baggage system planned by airport;
Seattle-Tacoma international airport. R. S.
Kahn. il Aviation W 94:34-5 Ja 18 '71

Management
Airline schedule reductions spark delivery
problem for post office. J. P. Woolsey. Avia-
tion W 94:28 Ja 18 '71
CAB control of scheduling feared. L. Doty.
il Aviation W 95:19-20 Ag 30 '71
Carriers press own schedule cuts. L. Doty.
Aviation W 94:25-6 Ja 25 '71
DC-10 bows, bringing lots more seats to fill.
il Bsns W p94-7 Ag 14 '71
Dismal outlook spurs capacity cut drive.
L. Doty. Aviation W 94:29 Ap 12 '71
Opposition may stall agreement on flight
cuts. Aviation W 94:28 Mr 29 '71

Non-scheduled operations
Beware charter-flight cheats. J. H. Win-
chester. Read Digest 98:97-100 Ja '71
CAB non-affinity proposal adds fuel to charter
feud. R. S. Kahn. Aviation W 95:25-6 Ag 30
'71
CAB to scrutinize European charters. L. Doty.
Aviation W 95:26-7 S 6 '71
Cannon upholds supplemental carriers. H. D.
Watkins. Aviation W 94:25-6 Mr 1 '71
Charter carriers gird to maintain position as
rate war threatens. Aviation W 95:29 S 27
'71
Charter flights. il Newsweek 77:86+ My 17
'71
Charters force revised airport standards. H.
J. Coleman. il Aviation W 95:113+ N 15 '71
Charters impact strongly in Europe. E. H.
Kolcum. il Aviation W 94:24-7 Je 28 '71

AIRLINES—Non-Scheduled operations—*Cont.*
Europeans ponder charter limits. L. Doty.
  Aviation W 94:27-8 My 24 '71
Fly charter and save, but be careful! il
  Changing T 25:15-18 Mr '71
IATA members aim at charters. R. S. Kahn.
  Aviation W 95:22-5 Ag 2 '71
International charters agreement sought. L.
  Doty. Aviation W 94:28 F 22 '71
Non-skeds go after charter pacts. il Bsns W
  p36+ Ap 3 '71
Nonskeds soar with CAB ruling. il Bsns W
  p 18-19 F 6 '71
Supplementals bracing for IATA action. R.
  G. O'Lone. Aviation W 95:20-1 Jl 19 '71
U.S. acts to ease charter rights. L. Doty.
  Aviation W 94:24 Mr 22 '71
What you should know about charter flights.
  Good H 172:172-3 Je '71
  See also
Air taxi service
Local service airlines
Overseas national airways
Purdue airlines

Finance

Supplemental airline revenues and expenses;
  tables (cont) Aviation W 94:30 My 3; 95:37
  Jl 19 '71

Passenger service

Air lounge war. il Newsweek 78:64 S 6 '71
Airlines concentrate on passenger service.
  il Aviation W 95:11-12 D 27 '71
DC-10 bows, bringing lots more seats to fill.
  il Bsns W p94-7 Ag 14 '71
DC-10 demonstrates scheduling versatility;
  with tables. H. D. Watkins. il Aviation W
  96:26-30 Ja 3 '72
Does your flight seem different lately? il
  Time 97:78-9 F 8 '71
Miami-London carriers vary cabin service.
  H. D. Watkins. Aviation W 95:29-30 N 29
  '71
Some aspects of DC-10 draw criticism. H.
  D. Watkins. il Aviation W 95:32-6 D 20 '71
Why TWA is the Sears of the air. il Bsns W
  p68 Ap 17 '71
  See also
Aviation consumer action project

Passenger traffic

See Airlines—Traffic

Public relations

Airlines split over public relations effort.
  L. Doty. Aviation W 95:27-8 D 13 '71
Consumer pressure spurs CAB scrutiny. Avi-
  ation W 94:32-4 Mr 29 '71

Rates

See Air freight service—Rates; Airlines—
  Fares

Regulations

See Aviation—Laws and regulations

Reservation systems

Board allows conditional reservation test.
  H. D. Watkins. Aviation W 95:26 Jl 5 '71
If an airline should "bump" you. Good H
  174:142 Ja '72
JAL extends automation of reservation system. il Aviation W 95:83-5 N 1 '71
Perspective on consumerism; excerpts from
  address. S. G. Tipton. Aviation W 95:9 Jl
  12 '71

Safety devices and measures

See Aviation—Safety devices and measures

Schedules

See Airlines—Management

Securities

Airline shares look for gains. il Bsns W
  p82-4 O 30 '71
Stocks boom despite earnings dip. W. H.
  Gregory. Aviation W 94:25-6 My 3 '71

Shuttle service

Air-shuttle revisions under way. Aviation W
  94:32 Ja 25 '71
For quick hops between big cities, look at
  Canada's plan. il U S News 70:76 Je 7 '71
Initial public satisfaction found with shuttle
  pre-ticketing, drinks. Aviation W 94:28 Mr
  15 '71
Rejiggering the air shuttle to make it pay.
  il Bsns W p42 Ja 30 '71

Statistics

Airline traffic; tables. See occasional issues of
  Aviation week & space technology
Four-engine turbojet/fan aircraft 1970 traffic
  and load factors; operating factors; tables.
  Aviation W 94:34-8 My 24 '71

Four-engine turbojet/fan load factors; table.
  Aviation W 95:23 S 6 '71
Growth in North Atlantic air traffic and
  service; year 1970 over 1969; table. Aviation W 94:37 Mr 22 '71
Growth in North Atlantic traffic and service,
  first months of 1971 over 1970; table. Aviation W 95:29 N 29 '71
Mainland-Hawaii market analysis, year 1970;
  table. Aviation W 94:28 Ap 12 '71
Mainland-Hawaii market participation; ta-
  bles (cont) Aviation W 94:43 F 1; 34 Ap 19;
  30 Ap 26; 33 Je 7; 31 Je 28; 95:24 Jl 19; 23
  Ag 30; 26 S 20; 32 O 18; 30 N 29; 36 D 20 '71
North Atlantic air passengers, load factors;
  tables. Aviation W 95:32-3 N 1 '71
North Atlantic air passenger load factors,
  year 1970; table. Aviation W 94:38-9 Mr 22
  '71
North Atlantic charter flights years 1969,
  1970; table. Aviation W 94:40 Mr 22 '71
Passenger boardings by U.S. carriers; tables.
  Aviation W 95:35-7 D 6 '71
Trunkline load factors, tables (cont) Aviation
  W 94:26 F 22; 28 Mr 22; 23 Ap 19; 28 My 24;
  47 Je 28; 95:23 Jl 19; 24 Ag 23; 31 O 4; 30
  O 11; 28 N 15; 27 D 13 '71
Trunkline on-time performance; tables (title
  varies) (cont) Aviation W 94:28 F 22; 33
  Mr 29; 31 Ap 12; 30 My 10; 33 Je 7; 32 Je
  28; 95:33 Ag 2; 24 S 6; 31 O 4; 28 N 1; 28
  N 29 '71; 96:30 Ja 10 '72
Turboprop aircraft 1970 traffic & load fac-
  tors; operating factors; tables. Aviation
  W 94:42-3 Je 28 '71
Two and three engine turbojet/fan aircraft
  1970 traffic and load factors; operating
  factors; tables. Aviation W 94:36+ Je 14
  '71
Two/three engine turbojet/fan load factors;
  tables. Aviation W 95:40 S 13 '71
U.S. airline scheduled service load factors;
  table. Aviation W 95:32 S 6 '71
U.S. airline scheduled service traffic growth;
  table. Aviation W 95:33 S 6 '71
U.S. airline traffic and operations; year 1970;
  table. Aviation W 94:34-5 Mr 15 '71
U.S. airline traffic growth; table. Aviation W
  94:35 Mr 22 '71
U.S.-North Atlantic passenger traffic; tables
  (cont) Aviation W 94:32 Ja 18; 44 F 1; 34
  Mr 29; 29 Ap 26; 25 My 10; 95:29 Jl 5; 36
  Jl 19; 24-5 Ag 2; 36 S 27; 31 N 29 '71; 96:
  34 Ja 10 '72

Traffic

April traffic shows increase, but upward
  trend still uncertain. Aviation W 94:24 My
  17 '71
Carriers wrestle with capacity control. H. D.
  Watkins. il Aviation W 94:118-20+ Mr 8 '71
Florida, Caribbean traffic lags. R. S. Kahn.
  Aviation W 94:26-8 Ap 12 '71
Great weekend for most airlines. il Bsns W
  p22 Jl 10 '71
Grim traffic marks fourth quarter. L. Doty.
  Aviation W 94:20-1 Ja 18 '71
Holiday surge boosts trunk profit hopes. R.
  S. Kahn. Aviation W 36:24-5 Ja 10 '72
Holiday traffic shows sharp gain. L. Doty.
  Aviation W 95:24-5 D 6 '71
International air traffic decline foreseen. L.
  Doty. Aviation W 95:19 Ag 23 '71
July 4 holiday traffic dampens hopes for
  reversal of downtrend. Aviation W 95:26
  Jl 12 '71
May extends trunk traffic slump. L. Doty.
  Aviation W 94:29 Je 14 '71
North Atlantic bookings up slightly. R. S.
  Kahn. Aviation W 94:22-4 My 10 '71
North Atlantic traffic outlook dim. R. S.
  Kahn. Aviation W 95:24-5 O 11 '71
October gains ease traffic gloom. J. P. Wool-
  sey Aviation W 95:26-7 N 8 '71
Strong traffic revival expected in 1972. H.
  D. Watkins. il Aviation W 93:27-9 Ja 10
  '72
Traffic dip raises recovery doubt. W. H.
  Gregory. il Aviation W 95:20-2 Jl 5 '71
Traffic shows no recovery signs. L. Doty. Avi-
  ation W 95:22-3 O 18 '71
Traffic slump clouds regulation. L. Doty. Avi-
  ation W 95:25 S 20 '71
Trunk loads plummet for March. L. Doty.
  Aviation W 94:23-4 Ap 19 '71
  See also
Local service airlines—Traffic

Wages and hours

Wages in the scheduled airlines industry;
  with tables. E. J. Caramela. Mo Labor R
  94:68-72 D '71

Alaska

Alaska route changes proposed. Aviation W
  94:24 Ap 5 '71
  See also
Alaska airlines

AIRLINES—*Continued*

Arab states

Arab airlines buying transports as regional cooperation grows. E. H. Kolcum. Aviation W 95:25 Jl 12 '71

Australia

Australian carriers upgrading equipment. il Aviation W 94:34-5 Ja 25 '71

Australian domestic carriers expect steady growth rate; Ansett airlines of Australia and Trans Australia airlines. R. G. O'Lone. Aviation W 95:30-1 S 20 '71

Qantas cutting costs to stay profitable. Aviation W 94:30 Ap 26 '71

Qantas plans multi-phase market drive. R. G. O'Lone. il Aviation W 95:28-31 S 13 '71

South Pacific capacity dispute makes Qantas shift 747 route. R. G. O'Lone. Aviation W 95:25 Ag 23 '71

Canada

For quick hops between big cities; look at Canada's plan. il U S News 70:76 Je 7 '71

Chile

LAN resists government on purchasing Soviet jets. L. Doty. Aviation W 95:28-9 S 27 '71

Denmark

Sterling studies long-haul aircraft needs. D. E. Fink. il Aviation W 95:28-30 Jl 5 '71

Egypt

U.S, USSR vie for Egyptair order. E. H. Kolcum. Aviation W 96:22-3 Ja 10 '72

Ethiopia

Ethiopian plays major role in economy. J. P. Woolsey. il Aviation W 95:26-8 Jl 26 '71

Ethiopian pushing for African leadership. J. P. Woolsey. il Aviation W 95:30-1 Ag 9 '71

Finland

Charter firm has Moscow rights; Nordair oy. D. A. Brown. il Aviation W 94:52 My 17 '71

France

BOAC, Air France in final Concorde talks. Aviation W 94:34-5 My 31 '71

Germany (Federal Republic)

European flags oppose Lufthansa. E. H. Kolcum. Aviation W 95:24-5 Ag 23 '71

Lufthansa forces IATA into experiment. E. H. Kolcum. Aviation W 95:26 S 20 '71

Lufthansa topples the fare structure. il Bsns W p25 S 18 '71

Red Baron strikes again. Time 98:49 Ag 23 '71

Thank you, Red Baron; Lufthansa changing transatlantic fares. il Newsweek 78:90+ S 27 '71

Great Britain

BOAC, BEA offer U.K. business contact data to passengers. Aviation W 94:30 F 22 '71

U.K. carrier orders 2L-1011s; Court line aviation. Aviation W 95:28 N 1 '71

See also
British overseas airways corporation
Caledonian-BUA airways

Iceland

Airline that thrives on discounting; Icelandic airlines. il Bsns W p68+ Jl 24 '71

Case of the agile flea; Icelandic airlines. il Forbes 108:20-1 Jl 15 '71

Ireland

U.S, Irish clash on Dublin rights. L. Doty. Aviation W 95:25-6 D 20 '71

Israel

El Al stresses terrorist security, advises other airlines in Tel Aviv. Aviation W 95:26 S 13 '71

Japan

JAL extends automation of reservation system. il Aviation W 95:83-5 N 1 '71

Lebanon

See also
Air freight service—Lebanon

Libya

Libyan airline will use all-Boeing fleet. Aviation W 96:23 Ja 10 '72

Netherlands

First KLM DC-10s will serve Toronto beginning in late 1972. Aviation W 95:30 O 4 '71

Pakistan

Pan Am, Pakistan airlines hurt by war. J. P. Woolsey. Aviation W 96:24 Ja 3 '72

Russia

Moscow makes the going tough. il Bsns W p20-1 My 8 '71

Soviets plan to remove Aeroflot operationally from ministry. Aviation W 94:27 Ap 19 '71

Scandinavia

See also
Scandinavian airlines system, inc.

United States

Costs, recession dim airline outlook. L. Doty. il Aviation W 94:107-9+ Mr 8 '71

Different crisis; excerpts from address, February 1971. F. D. Hall. Aviation W 94:9 Mr 1 '71

Freedom and enterprise; address, February 24, 1971. F. D. Hall. Vital Speeches 37:430-4 My 1 '71

It's an ill wind. il Forbes 107:22-3 Mr 15 '71

Plane that arrived too soon: Boeing 747. Bsns W p46 Ja 30 '71

Rail trends spur airline concern. H. D. Watkins. Aviation W 95:26-7 N 1 '71

What is needed to get the airlines out of trouble; interview. G. A. Spater. il por U S News 71:62-7 Ag 9 '71

See also
Air transport association of America
Collective bargaining—Airlines
Local service airlines
also names of airlines, e.g. American airlines

Routes

Alaska route changes proposed. Aviation W 94:24 Ap 5 '71

Northwest-Northeast link hangs on Miami-Los Angeles authority. J. P. Woolsey. Aviation W 94:26-7 Ja 25 '71

AIRLINES, Local service. See Local service airlines

AIRLINES, Supplemental. See Airlines—Nonscheduled operations

AIRLOCKS. See Air locks

AIRPLANE accidents. See Aviation—Accidents

AIRPLANE cabins
American plans new 707 interior. Aviation W 95:24 Ag 16 '71

AIRPLANE cockpits
Eased DC-10 crew chores expected. R. R. Ropelewski. il Aviation W 94:40-3 Mr 29 '71

AIRPLANE decoration
Back to the old drawing board for the 747. E. Allen and M. Benoff. il Esquire 76:74-81 Jl '71

AIRPLANE engines
Is twin-engine safety a myth? R. L. Collins. il Flying 89:68-71+ Ag '71
See also
Franklin engine company
Jet airplane engines

Exhaust

See also
Jet airplane engines—Exhaust

Specifications

U.S. reciprocating engines; tables (cont) Aviation W 94:82-3 Mr 8 '71
See also
Jet airplane engines—Specifications

Starting

See Airplanes—Starting

Superchargers

Is the turbocharger here to stay? R. L. Collins. il Flying 89:48-51 Jl '71

AIRPLANE fares. See Airlines—Fares

AIRPLANE hangars. See Hangars

AIRPLANE hijacking
Bandit who went out into the cold; Northwest airlines flight 305, Washington, D. C. to Seattle. il Time 98:20 D 6 '71

Bringing skyjackers down to earth; views of psychiatrist D. G. Hubbard. Time 98:64-5 O 4 '71

Calculated risk; skyjacker of TWA jetliner killed by FBI marksman. il Newsweek 78:24 Ag 2 '71

Command posts manned by key Braniff officials during hijack. Aviation W 95:20 Jl 12 '71

Deadly dilemma; controversy over the FBI's handling of incident in Jacksonville, Fla. il Newsweek 78:21 N 1 '71

Death at the terminal; R. A. Obergfell shot by FBI agent at La Guardia airport. il Time 98:18 Ag 2 '71

AIRPLANE hijacking—*Continued*
Hijacker parachutes from Northwest **727**.
Aviation W 95:22 D 6 '71
Quantum leap: Northwest airlines flight 305
to Seattle. il Newsweek 78:25-6 D 6 '71
Ransom growth seen in air piracy cases.
Aviation W 96:15 Ja 3 '72
Skyjacker; with excerpt from The skyjacker,
by David G. Hubbard. F. Knebel. il Look
35:22-6 F 9 '71
Take me along; American airlines 747 jumbo
jet. il Newsweek 78:47-8 N 8 '71
Tangled aftermath; destruction of planes by
Arab guerrillas, September 1970. il News-
week 77:39-40 F 8 '71
Terrorizing terrorists; Costa Rica. por Time
98:33-4 D 27 '71
This is a hijacking! condensation. J. A.
Elten. il Read Digest 99:213-17+ Jl '71
U.S. supports U.N. resolution condemning
aerial hijacking; statement, with text of
resolution. R. H. Gimer. Dept State Bul
64:32-3 Ja 4 '71
We were hijacked! teen travelers in Jordan-
ian desert and Amman. S. Finkelstein; P.
Burt. pors Seventeen 29:170 D '70
What makes a skyjacker? Sci Digest 71:21-2
Ja '72

Prevention
Convention on aviation sabotage adopted by
Montreal conference; statements, Septem-
ber 15 and 22, 1971; with text of convention.
C. N. Brower. Dept State Bul 65:464-8 O 25
'71
Department urges Senate advice and consent
to ratification of hijacking convention;
statement, June 7, 1971. J. R. Stevenson.
Dept State Bul 65:84-8 Jl 19 '71
El Al stresses terrorist security, advises other airlines in Tel Aviv. Aviation W 95:26
S 13 '71
Foiled sky marshals. D. Zwerdling. New
Repub 165:10-11 N 27 '71
International conference on air law approves
convention on aircraft hijacking; statements, with text of convention. J. R. Stevenson; J. B. Rhinelander. Dept State Bul
64:50-5 Ja 11 '71
Pilots spur anti-hijacking drive. Aviation W
94:19 Ja 18 '71
President asks Senate approval of aircraft
hijacking convention; message to the Senate, April 15, 1971; with Secretary Rogers'
report of March 24, 1971. Dept State Bul
64:654-5 My 17 '71
Progress in war on skyjackers. il U S News
71:25 Ag 9 '71
U.S. deposits ratification of hijacking convention. Dept State Bul 65:371 O 4 '71
X-rays can ruin your outing! screening of
luggage. J. Samson. il Field & S 75:16 Ap
'71

AIRPLANE industry
Foreign accent. J. Fricker. See occasional
issues of Flying
See also
Helicopter industry

Consolidations and mergers
Merger to spur Dassault fiscal strength. D.
E. Fink. Aviation W 95:16-17 O 18 '71

Directories
Marketing directory section. Aviation W 95:
27+ D 27 '71

Finance
Business aircraft sales slump continues.
C. E. Schneider. il Aviation W 95:18-19 Jl
26 '71
80% financing to be offered for A-300B.
Aviation W 94:32 Ap 26 '71
Industry working to stem profit erosion;
manufacturers of light aircraft. Aviation
W 95:17 D 27 '71

Statistics
U.S. business & utility aircraft shipments;
tables. See occasional issues of Aviation
week & space technology

Canada
Canada's plane makers fly low. il Bsns W
p36 N 6 '71

Czechoslovakia
Turbojet sales in West pushed. Aviation W
94:23 Je 14 '71

France
Merger to spur Dassault fiscal strength. D. E.
Fink. Aviation W 95:16-17 O 18 '71

Germany (Federal Republic)
Short-range planes for the long haul. il
Bsns W p37 F 20 '71
VFW-614 program pace hinges on M45H. il
Aviation W 94:100+ My 31 '71

Great Britain
See also
Britten-Norman. ltd.
JetStream aircraft, ltd.
Rolls-Royce, ltd.

Greece, Modern
U.S, France vie for Greek facility award.
E. H. Kolcum. Aviation W 95:21-2 D 13 '71

Israel
Israel spurs Commodore, Arava marketing. il
Aviation W 94:201 My 31 '71
Where aerospace still flies high; Israel avia-
tion industries. il Bsns W p51 Ap 17 '71

Italy
Italy emphasizes effort on civil transport. il
Aviation W 94:202-3 My 31 '71

Japan
Japan mapping advanced transport plans.
D. E. Fink il Aviation W 94:29-30 My 3 '71
New programs entering production stage. il
Aviation W 95:71-5 N 1 '71

Netherlands
Up from the ashes: Fokker. il Forbes 107:40+
Je 1 '71

Rumania
Yugoslavia, Rumania consider joint effort.
Aviation W 94:26 Je 7 '71

United States
Domestic business aircraft boost seen in investment tax credit. C. E. Schneider. Aviation W 95:20 Ag 23 '71
General aviation industry senses upturn. C.
E. Schneider. Aviation W 94:16-17 Ap 26
'71
See also
Helicopter industry—United States
also names of airplane manufacturing
companies, e.g. Grumman corporation

Yugoslavia
Yugoslavia, Rumania consider joint effort.
Aviation W 94:26 Je 7 '71
AIRPLANE instruments. See Aeronautic in-
struments
AIRPLANE manuals. See Airplanes—Hand-
books, manuals, etc.
AIRPLANE models
Flip, flop, the ornithop. il Esquire 75:120-3
Ap '71
AIRPLANE museums. See Aeronautic muse-
ums
AIRPLANE racing
Fly away on ladies' day; Powder puff derby.
J. Bruce. il Sports Illus 35:44+ Jl 19 '71
Leather ladies. G. Baxter. il Flying 89:130 O
'71
Return to Reno. P. Garrison. il Flying 89:
44-7 S '71
AIRPLANE seats. See Airplanes—Seats
AIRPLANE service stations
Gassing up the VIPs; Exec air, inc. R. Levy.
por Duns 98:60 Jl '71
See also
Fixed base operators
AIRPLANE travel. See Air travel
AIRPLANE turbochargers. See Airplane en-
gines—Superchargers
AIRPLANE wakes. See Atmospheric turbu-
lence
AIRPLANE wings
A-300B airbus wing delivery on target. il
Aviation W 94:86 My 31 '71
Composite slats evaluated on USAF C-5s. il
Aviation W 95:47-9 Jl 12 '71
F-8 flies with NASA supercritical wing. il
Aviation W 94:48 Mr 22 '71
New wing technology study will use F-111.
Aviation W 95:19 Jl 12 '71
SST engine, wing changes weighed. R. G.
O'Lone. il Aviation W 94:36-8 Mr 15 '71
Supercritical wing tested. il Sci N 99:196 Mr
20 '71
USAF, NASA to test new airfoil on F-111A.
E. J. Bulban. il Aviation W 95:20-1 N 29
'71
See also
Flaps, Airplane
AIRPLANES
See also
Autogiros
Aviation
Helicopters
Seaplanes

Accidents
See Aviation—Accidents

AIRPLANES—*Continued*

Airworthiness
See Airplanes—Standards

Cabins
See Airplane cabins

Certification
See Airplanes—Standards

Chartering
Executive jet CAB filing seeks to stop Pan Am Falcon charters. C. E. Schneider. Aviation W 95:17 Ag 30 '71
See also
Airlines—Non-scheduled operations

Cockpits
See Airplane cockpits

Collectors and collecting
Bad baron flies again; Palen collection. il Life 70:62-5 Ja 29 '71

Control
Vectored-thrust maneuverability explored. D. A. Brown. il Aviation W 95:36-9 D 13 '71
See also
Airplanes, Military—Control

Cost
See Airplanes—Prices

Decoration
See Airplane decoration

Design
See also
Airplane cabins

Electronic equipment
French challenge U.S. dominance. P. J. Klass. il Aviation W 94:167-71 My 31 '71
See also
Automatic pilot (airplanes)
Computers—Aeronautic use
Navigation, Aerial—Aids and devices

Equipment
Give yourself a Christmas present. il Flying 89:30-1 D '71
Product news. See issues of Flying

Escape devices
How science helps combat fliers escape over enemy territory. W. R. Kreh. il Sci Digest 69:16-19 Mr '71
Wing fabric separation cited as ejection seat crash cause. Aviation W 94:59 F 22 '71

Flaps
See Flaps, Airplane

Fueling
See Airplanes—Refueling

Handbooks, manuals, etc.
Knots and pounds; need for standard-format manuals. R. B. Parke. Flying 90:36 Ja '72
Owner's manuals are for the birds. R. L. Collins. Flying 90:79-81 Ja '72

History
See Aeronautics—History

Ice protection
Back to basics: induction-system icing. J. Diblin. Flying 89:82-3 Jl '71
Ice. T. H. Block. il Flying 89:26-7 D '71
Safety check; frosted feathers. R. Collins. Flying 88:104 Mr '71

Instrument boards
Distractions. R. Blodget. Flying 89:102+ D '71
Safety check. R. Blodget. Flying 89:104 Jl '71

Instrument flying
See Aviation—Instrument flying

Instruments
See Aeronautic instruments

Interior decoration
See Airplane decoration

Landing
Automatic visual range reporting tested. K. J. Stein. il Aviation W 94:48-50 Ap 12 '71
Contact approach or visual approach: what's the difference? W. Berkley. Flying 88:69-70 Mr '71
Follow me through. R. Blodget. il Flying 88:100-1 Je '71

4 microwave ILS designs evaluated. Aviation W 94:194 My 31 '71
How not to fly a localizer. V. Marra. Flying 88:73 Mr '71
Landing slumps. T. H. Block. il Flying 90:30+ Ja '72
Pro's nest; the ILS approach. T. H. Block. il Flying 89:32-3 N '71
Radiometer ILS monitor studied. il Aviation W 94:42-3+ My 17 '71
Safety check; too low approach. R. L. Collins. Flying 88:87 My '71
Wheels down? R. L. Collins. Flying 89:26 Ag '71
See also
Airplanes, Jet—Landing
Airplanes, Military—Landing

Landing gear
Canadians, USAF evaluating air cushion landing device. Z. Strickland. il Aviation W 95:66-7+ S 27 '71

Laws and regulations
See Aviation—Laws and regulations

Leasing and renting
Airplanes for rent; Lease-a-plane international. P. Garrison. il Flying 89:49-51+ D '71
This plane for hire; Lease-a-plane international. il por Time 97:80+ Mr 29 '71

Lightning hazards
See Aviation—Lightning hazards

Loading and unloading
See Loading and unloading

Manufacture
See also
Airplanes, Jet—Manufacture
Airplanes, Military—Manufacture
Airplanes, Supersonic—Manufacture

Marketing
Banking groups to finance export orders; Concorde. il Aviation W 94:113-15 F 8 '71
Cessna alters marketing of single-engine aircraft. E. J. Bulban. il Aviation W 96:58-9 O 11 '71
Cessna changes basic marketing. C. E. Schneider. il Aviation W 96:58 Ja 3 '72
Cessna Citation marketing emphasizes aircraft utility. C. E. Schneider. Aviation W 94:60-2 F 22 '71
Corporate jet sales upturn seen. Aviation W 95:56 S 20 '71
Fokker, VFW form new marketing group. il Aviation W 94:209+ My 31 '71
Hopes rise for A-300B U.S. penetration. il Aviation W 94:95+ My 31 '71
International pact drive widens. il Aviation W 94:51-5 Je 21 '71
Manufacturers mount aggressive campaign for improved sales in 1972. E. J. Bulban. il Aviation W 95:58-60+ S 20 '71
Mitsubishi expands market share; Mitsubishi aircraft international. C. E. Schneider. Aviation W 94:54-5 Ja 25 '71
Northrop P-530 fighter sales drive aimed at Holland, Italy. il Aviation W 95:19 Jl 12 '71
Sales programs, methods scrutinized for overhauling; business aviation manufactureres. C. E. Schneider. il Aviation W 94:151+ Mr 8 '71
Soviet plane for the West; Yak-40. il Bsns W p84 Mr 20 '71

Materials
Lightning and the plastic airplane. R. Markson; T. Sim. Flying 89:6-7 Jl '71
Titanium castings studied by USAF. W. S. Hieronymus. il Aviation W 95:52-4 Jl 19 '71
See also
Airplanes, Light—Materials
Airplanes, Military—Materials
Airplanes, Supersonic—Materials

Noise
Airport noise rules may be top SST test. Aviation W 94:30-1 Ap 12 '71
Airport operators push engine retrofits. J. P. Woolsey. Aviation W 94:20 Mr 1 '71
Concorde spurs basic research on noise. il Aviation W 94:74-7 F 8 '71
Economics of noise rules studied. M. L. Yaffee. il Aviation W 94:40-2 Ap 12 '71
Engine inlet change designed for reduced 747 noise levels. il Aviation W 94:28 My 10 '71
Lockheed research aims at 50% attenuation in turbofan noise. il Aviation W 95:54-5 Jl 19 '71

AIRPLANES—Noise—*Continued*

New landing method aimed at reduction in approach noise. W. S. Hieronymus. il Aviation W 94:46-7 Mr 1 '71

New noise regulations possible for SSTs. J. P. Woolsey. Aviation W 94:32 Ap 19 '71

Noise factor to pace STOL effort. R. G. O'Lone. il Aviation W 94:48-9 Je 7 '71

Noise study takes legislator to U.K. Aviation W 94:58 Mr 1 '71

Operators, FAA seek jet noise solution. J. P. Woolsey. il Aviation W 95:50-1+ S 20 '71

Psychology: a closer look at jet aircraft noise. il Bsns W p43 Ja 1 '72

Quiet fan test promises cut in noise levels. Aviation W 94:21 Ap 5 '71

Reduced-noise approach profiles tested. il Aviation W 95:38-40 S 13 '71

Stein's sound barrier; threat to Concorde. il por Newsweek 77:78 Mr 1 '71

See also

Helicopters—Noise

Noise control

Photographs

Jaguar prototypes carry varied stores. Aviation W 95:56-7 Jl 19 '71

Piloting

Aviation's most dangerous myth; hands-off flying. R. Blodget. il Flying 90:56-9+ Ja '72

How to handle multi-engine emergencies. S. Wilkinson. Flying 89:55+ N '71

I flew the world's biggest plane; C-5A. B. Kocivar. il Pop Sci 198:50-2+ Je '71

I learned about flying from that. See issues of Flying

It's the perfect days that get you. J. Spencer. Flying 88:93 Je '71

See also

Aviation—Instrument flying

Drinking and airplane accidents

Meteorology, Aeronautic

Pollution

Environment issues stunt airport growth. J. P. Woolsey. il Aviation W 95:46-8+ N 15 '71

See also

Airplanes, Jet—Pollution

Airplanes, Supersonic—Environmental effects

Airplanes, Supersonic—Pollution

Pollution control devices

USAF broadens pollutant control studies; fixed-bed catalytic combustor concept. M. L. Yaffee. Aviation W 95:34-6 N 22 '71

Prices

Why light planes cost so much. P. Garrison. il Flying 89:S6-8+ Ag '71

Purchasing

Perfect airplane store. R. L. Collins. Flying 88:13-14 Mr '71

Racing

See Airplane racing

Radio equipment

See also

Airplanes, Military—Radio equipment

Radio telephone on aircraft

Refueling

SST may need air refueling. Aviation W 95:29-30 O 25 '71

See also

Airplane service stations

Safety devices and measures

Anti-collision cost may be $250 million. P. J. Klass. Aviation W 95:27-8 Ag 16 '71

Anti-collision systems fight anticipated. P. J. Klass. Aviation W 95:29 N 15 '71

Coming: a computerized collision-avoidance system. M. Schultz. il Pop Mech 135:90-3+ F '71

High equipment cost may block collision avoidance system use. D. C. Winston. Aviation W 95:17 D 6 '71

Time/frequency CAS data may be sent via TV. Aviation W 95:63 S 27 '71

See also

Airplanes—Ice protection

Aviation—Safety devices and measures

Seats

CAB reopens tentative seating decisions. Aviation W 95:25 Jl 5 '71

Seat layouts heighten competition. R. S. Kahn. il Aviation W 95:21-4 Jl 12 '71

Seating surcharge range urged. Aviation W 95:30 O 11 '71

Specifications

Leading international aircraft; tables (cont) Aviation W 94:101-4 Mr 8 '71

Leading turbine-powered business aircraft; tables (cont) Aviation W 94:98 Mr 8 '71

U.S. and Canadian STOL aircraft; tables (cont) Aviation W 94:84 Mr 8 '71

U.S. and Canadian VTOL aircraft; tables (cont) Aviation W 94:83 Mr 8 '71

U.S. business, personal and utility aircraft; tables (cont) Aviation W 94:96 Mr 8 '71

U.S. commercial transports; tables. Aviation W 94:69 Mr 8 '71

U.S. military aircraft; tables (cont) Aviation W 94:61-2 Mr 8 '71

USSR military and civil aircraft; tables (cont) Aviation W 94:70 Mr 8 '71

Stalling

What's it all about, alpha? angle of attack. R. Blodget. Flying 89:38+ N '71

Standards

Europeans to revise certification. E. H. Kolcum. Aviation W 94:14 Ja 18 '71

Transport rule coverage expansion urged. Aviation W 94:19 Mr 15 '71

See also

Airplanes, Business—Standards

Airplanes, Jet—Standards

Starting

Contact. W. Wells. il Flying 90:54-5+ Ja '72

Storage

See also

Hangars

Take-off

Back to basics; figuring take-off distance. P. Garrison. il Flying 89:57-9 S '71

Balanced field lengths. A. Trammell. il Flying 89:60-4 O '71

On top; takeoff minimums. R. L. Collins. Flying 88:10-12 Je '71

Pro's nest; abort. T. H. Block. Flying 88:20 My '71

Testing

Aviation week pilot report: Trislander offers big aircraft handling. il Aviation W 94:217-19 My 31 '71

See also

Airplanes, Business—Testing

Airplanes, Jet—Testing

Helicopters—Testing

Wings

See Airplane wings

AIRPLANES, Aerobatic

Czechs unveil new aerobatic trainers. il Aviation W 95:46-7 Jl 5 '71

Great ones. A. Trammell. il Flying 88:76-83 My '71

Pilot report: Cessna 150 Aerobat. A. Trammell. il Flying 88:72-3 Je '71

AIRPLANES, Amphibious

Coming, the incredible Skyshark: first amphibious jet. M. Caidin. il Pop Mech 135:77-80+ Ap '71

Dear Mr Hefner: Catalina Pelican. N. Aubuchon. il Flying 89:78-84 Ag '71

Pilot report: Lake Buccaneer. R. L. Collins. il Flying 89:74-9 O '71

Those flying amphibians are back. K. Brown. il Mech Illus 67:55-7 Ag '71

Turboprop Goose in flight tests. il Aviation W 96:58-9 Ja 10 '72

AIRPLANES, Business

BH-125-600 on U.S. market late in 1971. Aviation W 94:215 My 31 '71

Citation: the jet that Cessna built. A. Trammell. il Flying 88:49-54+ Je '71

Commodore set for U.S. debut; photographs. Aviation W 94:50 Je 7 '71

Foreign accent; Dassault Falcon 10 and Aérospatiale Corvette. J. Fricker. il Flying 89:24-6+ Jl '71

French start SN-600 production. Aviation W 95:17 O 18 '71

Maker strives to regain SN-600 pace. il Aviation W 94:220-3 My 31 '71

Plane that could teach an industry to fly; Cessna Citation. P. Siekman. il Fortune 83:96-9+ Ap '71

Rallye aimed at growing European market. il Aviation W 95:76-7 S 27 '71

Ted Smith company plans new aircraft. Aviation W 95:59 Ag 16 '71

See also

Airplanes in business

AIRPLANES, Business—*Continued*

Design

Certification of TFE-731-2 nears. W. S. Hieronymus. il Aviation W 95:44-6 N 22 '71
Falcon 20T aimed at new market. D. E. Fink. il Aviation W 94:49-52 Ap 19 '71
Mirage wing technology aids Falcon 10. il Aviation W 94:228-9 My 31 '71

Marketing
See Airplanes—Marketing

Specifications
See Airplanes—Specifications

Standards
FAA chary on new rules' impact; operating and maintenance standards of large aircraft. C. E. Schneider. Aviation W 94:54 Mr 29 '71

Testing
Aviation week pilot report:
  A100 reflects shift in marketing. C. E. Schneider. il Aviation W 95:50-1+ D 13 '71
  Cessna aims Citation at turboprop market. C. E. Schneider. il Aviation W 94:44-8 Mr 15 '71
  Merlin 3 stresses range, speed. C. E. Schneider. il Aviation W 94:60-3 F 1 '71
  SN-600 design stresses simplicity. D. E. Fink. il Aviation W 94:53-7 Ap 12 '71
  Sabre 75 retains handling qualities. C. E. Schneider. il Aviation W 95:58-61+ N 8 '71
Pilot report:
  BH 125. R. L. Collins. il Flying 88:32-7+ Ap '71
  Beech Duke. R. L. Collins. il Flying 88:34-7 Mr '71
  Britten-Norman Islander. A. Trammell. il Flying 89:40-5+ N '71
  Cessna Turbo Centurion II. R. L. Collins. il Flying 89:48-51 Jl '71
  MU-2G. R. L. Collins. il Flying 89:42-7 Jl '71

AIRPLANES, Convertible
KLM, Sabena using main deck of 747s for cargo/baggage. il Aviation W 95:25 D 6 '71

AIRPLANES, Drone
Remotely flown vehicles stir wide interest. il Aviation W 94:26 Je 14 '71
U.S. & Canadian drones and target missiles (title varies) tables (cont) Aviation W 94:89 Mr 8 '71

AIRPLANES, Experimental
Advanced technology transport delayed. D. A. Brown. Aviation W 94:22 Mr 22 '71
XMC: Cessna's two-place mystery pusher plane. B. Kocivar. il Pop Sci 199:50-1+ Ag '71

AIRPLANES, Freight
New IL-76 built to Aeroflot specifications. il Aviation W 94:29-31 My 31 '71
747F will test air cargo market potential. Aviation W 95:25-6 N 29 '71
  See also
Airplanes, Convertible

AIRPLANES, Hijacking of. See Airplane hijacking

AIRPLANES, Hypersonic. See Airplanes, Supersonic

AIRPLANES, Jet
American, National drop 13 DC-10 transport options. Aviation W 94:21 My 10 '71
DC-10 demonstrates scheduling versatility; with tables. H. D. Watkins. il Aviation W 96:26-30 Ja 3 '72
DC-10 meeting operational goals. H. D. Watkins. il Aviation W 95:23-6 D 13 '71
DC-10 orders reported at 238. Aviation W 94:19 F 8 '71
Decision nears for Japan airbus partner. il Aviation W 95:76-7 N 1 '71
Delivery schedules revised for L-1011. Aviation W 94:27 My 3 '71
Falcon 20T program redirected toward high-bypass fan engines. Aviation W 96:17 Ja 10 '72
High hopes for latest jetliner: the DC-10. il U S News 71:61 Ag 9 '71
Introducing the new superjet set. il Time 98:66-9 S 20 '71
Lockheed L-1011 makes first European visit. H. J. Coleman. Aviation W 94:24-5 Je 7 '71
McDonnell Douglas studies DC-11 to challenge A-300B airbus. Aviation W 95:27 O 4 '71
Mercure pushed for worldwide market. il Aviation W 94:106+ My 31 '71
Now: big, quiet buses for the airlanes. J. Goodrum. il Pop Mech 135:90-3 Ap '71
Plane that arrived too soon: Boeing 747. Bsns W p46 Ja 30 '71

Seven Yak-40s reported sold following West German tour. Aviation W 94:18 Mr 15 '71
Short-range planes for the long haul; A 300-B airbus. il Bsns W p37 F 20 '71
Some aspects of DC-10 draw criticism. H. D Watkins. Aviation W 95:32-6 D 20 '71
Soviet plane for the West; Yak-40. il Bsns W p84 Mr 20 '71
VFW 614, Mercure aid challenge to U.S. il Aviation W 94:19 Ap 12 '71
VFW-614 program pace hinges on M45H. il Aviation W 94:100+ My 31 '71
Whatever happened to the airbus? trijet. L. Buckwalter. il Mech Illus 67:83-5+ Ap '71
What's wrong with the 747? M. Schultz. il Mech Illus 67:60-1+ Je '71
  See also
Airplanes, Business

Certification
See Airplanes, Jet—Standards

Control
  See also
Inertial guidance systems

Cost of operation
Boeing 747 aircraft operations and cost data; table. Aviation W 95:30 Jl 5 '71
Four engine turbojet/fan operating costs; table. Aviation W 95:30 O 25 '71
Four engine turbojet/turbofan transports; 1970 hourly costs: cents per mile costs; tables. Aviation W 94:36-8 My 24 '71
Turboprop transports 1970 hourly costs; cents per mile costs; tables. Aviation W 94:38-9+ Je 28 '71
Two and three engine turbojet/fan aircraft 1970 cents per mile costs; hourly costs; tables. Aviation W 94:43-5 Je 14 '71
Two/three engine turbojet/fan operating costs; table. Aviation W 95:29 O 25 '71
Yak-40 flight and fixed costs are estimated. Aviation W 95:59 Ag 16 '71

Design
Commuter version extends Falcon line. il Aviation W 94:224-5 My 31 '71
Convair evolves design concepts for NASA transport research. E. J. Bulban. il Aviation W 94:28-9 Je 21 '71
Il-62M200 held key to Aeroflot goals. D. C. Winston. il Aviation W 94:24-5 Je 14 '71
747 growth keyed to revitalized market. R. G. O'Lone. il Aviation W 95:28-30 Jl 12 '71

Engines
See Jet airplane engines

Landing
Early touchdown cited in 747 incident. il Aviation W 94:60-5 Mr 1 '71
New landing method aimed at reduction in approach noise. W. S. Hieronymus. il Aviation W 94:46-7 Mr 1 '71
Reduced-noise approach profiles tested. il Aviation W 95:38-40 S 13 '71

Manufacture
Cessna Citation jet production started; photographs. Aviation W 94:52-3 Je 7 '71
Details shown of final assembly steps for VFW-614. il Aviation W 94:98-9 My 31 '71
Long-range series 20 DC-10 assembled. il Aviation W 95:32-3 S 20 '71
Production is on original schedule for A-300B airbus. il Aviation W 94:78-9+ My 31 '71
Work progresses on mockup, pre-series versions of the Franco-German A-300B. il Aviation W 94:76-7 My 31 '71

Marketing
See Airplanes—Marketing

Noise
See Airplanes—Noise

Photographs
New transports flown at Paris. Aviation W 94:30-1 Je 21 '71

Pollution
Air force laboratory studies jet engine pollution control. M. L. Yaffee. Aviation W 94:58-9 F 1 '71
Airlines evaluate modification to eliminate jet fuel dumping. Aviation W 94:26 F 1 '71
Improved-performance engines raise nitric oxide emissions. Aviation W 94:57-8 Mr 1 '71
Mike Frome. M Frome. Am For 77:7+ F '71
Technique detects nitric oxide emissions. R. S. Kahn. il Aviation W 96:44-5 Ja 3 '72

AIRPLANES, Jet—*Continued*

Standards

Soviets grant Yak-40 plant visits; airworthiness certification barriers. E. H. Kolcum. Aviation W 95:58 Ag 16 '71

Testing

Aviation week pilot report:
DC-10 minimizes crew workload. R. R. Ropelewski. il Aviation W 95:36-9+ Ag 30 '71
L-1011 shows docile handling qualities. R. R. Ropelewski. il Aviation W 96:36-9 Ja 3 '72
ST-27 stresses ruggedness, simplicity. H. J. Coleman. il Aviation W 95:46-9 Ag 2 '71
Turbolet single-engine capability explored. H. J. Coleman. il Aviation W 95:44-5 Jl 5 '71
Data handling system cuts DC-10 testing. W. S. Hieronymus. il Aviation W 94:43+ Ap 12 '71
Flight test program for L-1011 realigned. R. R. Ropelewski. il Aviation W 95:16-17 Jl 5 '71
Reduced-noise approach profiles tested. il Aviation W 95:38-40 S 13 '71
747 fatigue tests help solve problems. R. G. O'Lone. il Aviation W 94:24-5 Ja 18 '71

Wings

See Airplane wings

AIRPLANES, Light

Another look at the BD-4. P. H. Poberezny. il Flying 89:71-3 Jl '71
Cessna Cardinal RG. il Flying 88:46-8 Mr '71
Champ; Aeronca 7AC. S. Wilkinson. il Flying 88:40-3 F '71
Flying rail: a twin-engine pusher you can build. B. Kocivar. il Pop Sci 199:55-7+ O '71
Is this the world's best airplane? Cessna Skyhawk/172. S. Wilkinson. il Flying 88:38-40 Ap '71
Man-powered flight. P. Wahl. il Pop Sci 198:43-5+ Ja '71
Monsieur Druine's marvelous Turbulent. J. Gilbert. il Flying 89:62-9 Jl '71
Newest Aero Commander; Commander 112. il Flying 88:38-40 Mr '71
Now: teenie two! VW-powered plane. K. Brown. il Pop Mech 135:94-101 My '71
Piper Cherokee Flite Liner. C. Knight. il Flying 88:42-4+ My '71
Report from Europe: new look in small planes. B. Kocivar. il Pop Sci 199:66-8 O '71
See also
Airplanes, Aerobatic

Automobile combinations

This car really flies; Aerocar III. B. Grant; F. A. Tinker. il Pop Mech 136:87-91+ Ag '71

Design

Roll your own (cont) P. Garrison. il Flying 89:58-63 Ag '71

Marketing

See Airplanes—Marketing

Materials

Bellanca: the Bugatti of airplanes. S. Wilkinson. il Flying 89:28-34 S '71
Windecker's fantastic plastic plane. N. Aubuchon. il Pop Sci 198:73-5+ Ja '71

Prices

See Airplanes—Prices

Specifications

See Airplanes—Specifications

Testing

Crash destroys first Corvette. Aviation W 94:18 Mr 29 '71
Pilot report:
Aero Commander. R. L. Collins. il Flying 89:40-3+ S '71
Bellanca Champion. S. Wilkinson. il Flying 89:28-34 S '71
Cessna Stationair. S. Wilkinson. il Flying 89:58-61+ N '71
Cessna 340. R. L. Collins. il Flying 90:38-44 Ja '72
Piper Seneca. S. Wilkinson. il Flying 89:48-55 O '71
Robertson Twin Comanche. R. L. Collins. il Flying 89:80-4 N '71
Traveler. S. Wilkinson. il Flying 89:70-5 D '71
Piper Aztec E. T. H. Block. il Flying 88:40-5 Je '71
Retractable musketeer; Beech Super R. S. Wilkinson. il Flying 88:34-9 F '71

Used airplanes

See Airplanes, Used

AIRPLANES, Military

See also
Airplanes, Drone
Airplanes, Short take-off and landing
Airplanes, Training

Armaments

Lasers aid delivery of weapons. B. Miller. il Aviation W 94:48-53 My 3 '71
New weapons delivery aid tested; close air support system. B. Miller. il Aviation W 95:39+ N 22 '71
See also
Bombs, Aerial
Guided missiles—Launching from airplanes
Helicopters—Armaments

Control

NASA F-8 to test fly-by-wire. il Aviation W 94:44 Ap 5 '71
New microwave guidance unit has combat, VTOL capabilities; Madge system. il Aviation W 95:40-1+ D 6 '71

Cost

B-1 bomber. B. Rice. il Sat R 54:20-2+ D 11 '71
Efforts made to control B-1 costs. Aviation W 95:44 Jl 26 '71
How many millions should an F-14 cost? il Life 71:36-7 Ag 6 '71
Rising cost of capability. il Fortune 83:164-5 My '71
Up, up, up; F-14 overrun. il Newsweek 77:80+ Je 14 '71

Design

B-1 design keyed to future growth. R. R. Ropelewski. il Aviation W 95:34-7 N 29 '71
B-1 designed to new standards. W. S. Hieronymus. il Aviation W 95:42-5 Jl 26 '71
B-1 performance unaffected by cost cuts. W. S. Hieronymus. Aviation W 95:43-5 S 6 '71
Beech proposes Bonanza strike version. il Aviation W 96:42-3 Ja 3 '72
Beech to enter modified Debonair in USAF Pave Coin competition. Aviation W 94:71 Je 14 '71
Control vanes aid B-1 low-level role. il Aviation W 94:48-9 Je 21 '71
Design review of B-1 favorable. Aviation W 95:17 N 8 '71
F-5E keyed to agility for combat. R. R. Ropelewski. il Aviation W 95:41-3 Jl 12 '71
F-14A subcomponent accessibility shown; photographs. Aviation W 94:40-1 Ja 25 '71
Maximum design leeway marks AX effort. Aviation W 94:18 Ap 19 '71
Northrop seeks aid abroad for fighter. B. Miller. il Aviation W 94:20-1 F 1 '71
S-3A facing program milestones; anti-submarine aircraft. R. R. Ropelewski. il Aviation W 95:38-40 S 27 '71

Electronic equipment

A-7E bombing accuracy displayed. R. R. Ropelewski. il Aviation W 94:60-1+ My 10 '71
Airborne military avionics gear emerging from Europe. il Aviation W 94:196-8 My 31 '71
ECM capabilities for EA-6B broadened. il Aviation W 94:18-19 F 8 '71
MRCA spurs U.S., European bidding. P. J. Klass. Aviation W 94:52-5 Ap 26 '71
Modified P-2 tests electro-optics. il Aviation W 94:42-3 Ap 5 '71
Weapon delivery aid flexibility sought. B. Miller. il Aviation W 94:75-6+ My 10 '71
See also
Airplanes, Military—Radio equipment

Equipment

See also
Aeronautic instruments

Instrument flying

See Aviation—Instrument flying

Landing

C-5A autoland tests successful. K. J. Stein. il Aviation W 95:52-5+ Ag 16 '71
Category 2 solid-state ILS in USAF use. Aviation W 95:43 D 6 '71
Landing aid for army progresses; A-Scan landing guidance units. K. J. Stein. il Aviation W 95:42-4 O 4 '71

Landing on carriers

Jaguar finishes second carrier evaluation. D. E. Fink. Aviation W 95:21-2 N 8 '71
Marines fit Harrier to own tactics. D. A Brown. il Aviation W 95:38-44 O 18 '71

AIRPLANES, Military—*Continued*

Manufacture

Production of S-3A wing, aft body shown. il Aviation W 96:66-7 Ja 10 '72

Marketing

See Airplanes—Marketing

Materials

Avco bets on boron tape. Bsns W p 124+ Ap 10 '71

Avco readies new boron plant as demand for composites lags. Aviation W 94:48 Ap 19 '71

Composite slats evaluated on USAF C-5s. il Aviation W 95:47-9 Jl 12 '71

New materials will be used on F-15 windshield, canopy. il Aviation W 94:49 My 17 '71

USAF outlines composite plans. Aviation W 94:44 My 3 '71

Photographs

Initial Mirage G8 displayed in flight. Aviation W 94:20-1 Je 21 '71

Mirage F1 prototypes flown with stores. Aviation W 95:44-5 Jl 12 '71

Radar equipment

It protects the surface from six miles up! AWACS. M. E. Dowd. il Pop Mech 135:73-5+ Mr '71

Radio equipment

Navy to unveil integrated avionics plan. P. J. Klass. il Aviation W 94:51-3 Je 28 '71

Specifications

See Airplanes—Specifications

Stunt flying

See Aviation—Stunt flying

Testing

Accelerated testing set for F-14A. D. A Brown. il Aviation W 95:49-53 D 20 '71

Harrier flexibility displayed at Paris. il Aviation W 95:52-5 Jl 5 '71

Harrier program seeks broad VTOL data. D. A. Brown. il Aviation W 95:47-8+ O 25 '71

Mirage G8 prototype testing to begin. D. E. Fink. il Aviation W 94:45-6 My 3 '71

Saab-Scania Viggen in final stage of flight test program. Aviation W 96:45 Ja 3 '72

Telemetry system may cut F-14 test time. K J. Stein. il Aviation W 95:54-7 D 20 '71

USAF stiffens test requirements. Aviation W 94:49-50 My 17 '71

Wings

See Airplane wings

Europe, Western

Competition intensifies in fighter market. E. H. Kolcum. Aviation W 94:23 Je 7 '71

Italy thrust into crucial European role. E. H. Kolcum. il Aviation W 94:29-30+ Mr 8 '71

MRCA avionics awards planned as cost curtailment is sought. Aviation W 95:23 Ag 16 '71

France

Agreement may open parts line to Israel. D. E. Fink Aviation W 95:15-16 N 22 '71

Mirage G8 demonstrates variable wing. il Aviation W 95:52-3 Jl 26 '71

Mirage G8 prototype testing to begin. D. E. Fink. il Aviation W 94:45-6 My 3 '71

Germany (Federal Republic)

Bundestag fund limit spurs talk on quantity in F-4E (F) purchase. Aviation W 95:18 Jl 5 '71

Germans choose F-4 for interim role. E. H. Kolcum. Aviation W 94:17-18 Mr 29 '71

Great Britain

Jump jet: the shape of wings to come; Harrier. P. Browne. il Read Digest 99:174-6+ O '71

Japan

Japan plans to buy 895 aircraft. Aviation W 94:47 My 24 '71

New hardware planned for Japan defense. il Aviation W 95:47-8+ N 1 '71

New programs entering production stage. il Aviation W 95:71-5 N 1 '71

Netherlands

Dutch to evaluate four new fighters. Aviation W 94:25 Ap 5 '71

Russia

Fighter capabilities; effectiveness of U.S. fighter F-14 versus the Russian MiG-23 Foxbat; letter to the editor. T. O'Connor and N. Criss. Aviation W 95:64 S 13 '71; Discussion. 95:62 O 11; 54 O 18 '71

MiG-21s display agility on French visit. il Aviation W 95:20-1 S 13 '71

Russia's MiG-23: unbeatable? with excerpt from Thud ridge by Jack Broughton. D. J. Holford. il Pop Mech 136:90-4 N '71

Soviet MiG-21 team performs for French. il Aviation W 95:22-3 S 20 '71

Soviet swinger; Backfire bomber. il Time 98:34 S 20 '71

Soviets continue stress on tactical air. il Aviation W 94:27-8 Mr 8 '71

Soviets flying Mach 2 strategic bomber. il Aviation W 95:16 S 13 '71

Soviets push advances in fighters. C. Brownlow and B. Miller. il Aviation W 95:34-7 O 18 '71

USSR military and civil aircraft; tables (cont) Aviation W 94:70 Mr 8 '71

World's hottest plane? advanced jet fighters to Egypt. il Newsweek 77:39 Ap 26 '71

Sweden

Viggen shows takeoff, landing capability; photographs. Aviation W 95:56-8 Jl 5 '71

Switzerland

A-4 in second place after A-7 in Swiss attack aircraft program. Aviation W 94:18-19 My 10 '71

Swiss fighter competition scene shifts from technical to political. E. H. Kolcum. Aviation W 95:18 Ag 30 '71

United States

Another opening; B-1 program. il Newsweek 78:90+ N 15 '71

B-1 bomber. B. Rice. il Sat R 54:20-2+ D 11 '71

B-1 mockup is unveiled. il Aviation W 95:14-16 N 8 '71

Costs to spur F-14 contract change. C. Brownlow. Aviation W 94:14-15 Ap 26 '71

Defense cut bid threatens B-1 bomber. D. C. Winston. Aviation W 94:16-17 My 10 '71

Eight subcontracts awarded for B-1. Aviation W 95:55 Jl 19 '71

F-14 costs, missions. Aviation W 96:70 Ja 10 '72

Fighter capabilities; effectiveness of U.S. fighter F-14 versus the Russian MiG-23 Foxbat; letter to the editor. T. O'Connor and N. Criss. Aviation W 95:64 S 13 '71; Discussion 95:62 O 11; 54 O 18 '71

Fighter programs hit by Proxmire group. D. C. Winston. Aviation W 94:17-18 My 17 '71

Grumman's whipsaw? F-14. il Forbes 108:32-3 D 15 '71

How many millions should an F-14 cost? il Life 71:36-7 Ag 6 '71

Latest worry: plight of nation's H-bombers. il U S News 71:50-1 D 27 '71

Lockheed expects S-3A development below cost ceiling; anti-submarine warfare aircraft. il Aviation W 95:18-19 N 15 '71

Lockheed rolls out an antisub jet; S-3A. Bsns W p36-7 N 6 '71

NASA to use U-2s. Aviation W 94:25 Ap 12 '71

NASA using U-2s as ERTS simulators. il Aviation W 95:16 O 25 '71

Northrop puts on a show to sell Cobras. il Bsns W p71 S 4 '71

Prop-jet fighter at a bargain price; Piper Enforcer. il Bsns W p51 Jl 3 '71

Reliability, effectiveness shown by A-7E. C. Brownlow. Aviation W 94:20 Ap 5 '71

Survival as a free country depends on modern weapons; interview. B. K. Holloway. il por U S News 71:52-5 D 27 '71

Three-engine RA-5 proposed to air force in interceptor role. il Aviation W 95:42 S 6 '71

AIRPLANES, Military, Theft of

Plot to steal a fighter plane; excerpts from KGB. J. Barron. il Read Digest 96:69-74 F '71

AIRPLANES, Military transport

Another flight of fancy; the C-5A. P. D. H. Stockton and B. Newman. Nation 212:653-6 My 24 '71

C-5A demonstration at Paris stresses STOL capabilities. il Aviation W 94:60-5 Je 28 '71

C-5A, go away. New Repub 165:8-9 D 25 '71

C-5A, postmortem on a mess. B. Rice. Look 35:80-1 My 18 '71

Edsel of the airways? C-5A. il Newsweek 78:91 O 25 '71

AIRPLANES, Supersonic—*Continued*
SST's point of no return. il Bsns W p88+ F 27 '71
Secret OST report released. Sci N 100:141 Ag 28 '71
Shock waves from a surplus plane. il Newsweek 77:62+ Ap 5 '71
Showdown on the SST. il Time 97:13-14 Mr 29 '71
Slowdown in the technology of haste. il Time 97:11 Ap 5 '71
Soviet SST, delegation expected at U.S. transportation exhibit. Aviation W 96:19 Ja 3 '72
Soviets press Tu-144 marketing with east Europe comecon bloc. Aviation W 95:28 S 20 '71
Special report on Concorde; symposium, with editorial comment. il Aviation W 94:11, 28-33+ F 8 '71
Supersonic counterattack. il Time 97:15 Mr 22 '71
Supersonic shock wave. R. Hotz; discussion. Aviation W 94:70 Ja 11; 58 Ja 18; 58 Ja 25; 128 F 8 '71
U.K. government backs Concorde as commercially viable project. H. J. Coleman. Aviation W 95:16-17 D 20 '71
U.S. superjet for Japan? Time 98:59 Jl 26 '71
See also
Sonic boom

Cost
Concorde price set at $31.2 million. Aviation W 95:14 D 13 '71
Let's ground the SST. il Life 70:40 Mr 19 '71
SST program faces major slips despite request for $235 million. Aviation W 94:19 F 1 '71
Ziegler confirms Concorde price. Aviation W 95:16 D 20 '71

Design
Designers study evolution of Concorde. il Aviation W 94:41-3+ F 8 '71
Major Tu-144, Concorde differences cited. D. E. Fink. il Aviation W 94:36-7+ Je 21 '71

Electronic equipment
Packaging gains spur advanced concepts; Concorde. il Aviation W 94:86-7+ F 8 '71

Engines
See Jet airplane engines

Environmental effects
Concorde environmental effects studied. il Aviation W 94:78-9+ F 8 '71
DOT using mathematical models to study SST climate effects. Aviation W 94:42 Ja 25 '71
Politics of environmental disruption. Fortune 83:69-70 Ja '71

Manufacture
Concorde 01 rolled out during labor strife. il Aviation W 95:25-6 S 27 '71
Planning eases complex production task. il Aviation W 94:116-23 F 8 '71
SST prototype hardware, tooling programs progress despite continuing controversy. R. G. O'Lone. il Aviation W 94:20-2 Ja 25 '71

Marketing
See Airplanes—Marketing

Materials
Weight, cost balanced in materials study; Concorde. il Aviation W 94:124-5 F 8 '71

Noise
See Airplanes—Noise

Photographs
Tu-144 makes first appearance in west. il Aviation W 94:32-3 My 31 '71

Pollution
Eighteen-hundred-and-froze-to-death: pollution of the stratosphere by the SST? G. S. Fichter. il Sci Digest 69:62-6 F '71

Refueling
See Airplanes—Refueling

Testing
Concorde autoland tests start; flights follow operational profile. Aviation W 94:20 My 24 '71
Concorde meets airline-like tour schedule. D. E. Fink. il Aviation W 95:26-8 S 27 '71
Concorde tested in subsonic traffic. Aviation W 94:34 My 31 '71
Concorde tour tests systems performance. D. E. Fink. Aviation W 95:48+ O 11 '71

Flight testing started by Soviets on Tu-144 production prototypes. Aviation W 95:28 O 4 '71
Testing probes critical Mach 2 areas. il Aviation W 94:48-51+ F 8 '71
Up there at 1,300 m.p.h.; Anglo-French Concorde test-flight report. W. Rademaekers. il Time 97:80 Je 14 '71

AIRPLANES, Theft of
See also
Airplanes, Military, Theft of

AIRPLANES, Training
Alpha jet enters prototype development. D. E. Fink. il Aviation W 94:20-2 Je 7 '71
American aviation builds a slick new trainer. A. Trammell. il Flying 89:35-9 S '71
Aviation week pilot report:
  Italian trainer fills varied roles. H. J. Coleman. il Aviation W 95:52-4 S 6 '71
In-flight simulator capabilities tested; total in-flight simulator. D. A. Brown. il Aviation W 95:35-8 Ag 9 '71

AIRPLANES, Used
Foreign accent; the Dragon and I. J. Fricker. il Flying 90:70-1+ Ja '72
Mighty Mooney Mite. B. M. Rogers. il Flying 88:60-4 Je '71
Twin Beech: ancient but honorable. T. H. Block. il Flying 89:65-72 O '71

Marketing
Aircraft swaps spice recession. Aviation W 95:63+ S 20 '71
Eastern successful in used aircraft sales. H. D. Watkins. il Aviation W 94:28-9 Ja 25 '71

Testing
Pilot report:
  Cessna 195. N. Aubuchon. il Flying 89:41-8+ D '71
Remember Sky King? Cessna 310. P. Garrison. il Flying 88:70-5 Ap '71
Used-airplane pilot report:
  Bellanca 260A. P. Garrison. il Flying 90:45-9 Ja '72
  Mooney Mark 21. P. Garrison. il Flying 88:60-5 F '71

AIRPLANES, Vertical take-off and landing
Aircraft in the balance; STOL/VTOL concept. K. H. Hohenemser. bibliog il Environ 13:42-9 D '71
German firms agree on V/STOL. E. H. Kolcum. il Aviation W 95:32-3 O 4 '71
Germany studies five V/STOL concepts. il Aviation W 94:136+ My 31 '71
V/STOL technology exploitation principle gets German backing. Aviation W 94:32 Ap 26 '71
See also
Airplanes, Military

Specifications
See Airplanes—Specifications

AIRPLANES in agriculture
Duster. S. Wilkinson. Flying 88:48-56 F '71
U.S. agricultural aircraft; tables. Aviation W 94:84 Mr 8 '71
See also
International flying farmers (association)

AIRPLANES in business
Better climate seen ahead in business flying operations. Aviation W 95:18-19 S 27 '71
Business flying seeks recession antidote. E. J. Bulban. il Aviation W 94:145-7+ Mr 8 '71
Business flying's new requirements; symposium; with editorial comment. il Aviation W 95:11, 38-9+ S 20 '71
Recession boosting aircraft utilization. Aviation W 95:67+ S 20 '71
See also
Airplanes, Business
National business aircraft association

AIRPLANES in education
Ag class in the sky. R. Miller. Ed Digest 36:32-3 Ap '71
Airplane as a teaching tool. T. Taylor. Flying 89:54-6 D '71

AIRPLANES in forest fire protection
Flying fire engine. J. Joseph. il Mech Illus 67:68+ F '71

AIRPLANES in hunting and fishing
Canada clamps down on aircraft. B. East. Outdoor Life 147:6 Mr '71

AIRPLANES in hydrologic research
Airplanes and hydrologists: a beneficial alliance. J. M. Whipple. il Cons 26:17-21 O '71

AIRPLANES in lumbering
See also
Helicopters in lumbering

AIRPLANES in medical service
See also
Helicopters, Ambulance

AIRPLANES in moving
We turn Piper's aerial station wagon into
a moving van. P. Garrison. il Flying 89:62
N '71

AIRPLANES in police work
Flying vigilantes help stop rustlers. E. E.
Wirt. il Farm J 95:19 F '71

AIRPORT and airway development act. See
Aviation—Laws and regulations

AIRPORT buildings
Kansas City will test gate arrival plan. D. C.
Winston. il Aviation W 95:104-5+ N 15 '71
Nation's newest airport complex; Tampa, Fla,
international airport. il Am City 86:76+ S
'71
Pavilion at Kennedy; the National airlines
terminal at New York's JFK airport. il
Arch Forum 135:18-25 O '71

AIRPORT fees. See Airports—Finance

AIRPORT surveillance radar. See Radar in
aviation

AIRPORT thefts
Second business at our airports: theft. D.
Walsh. il Life 70:16-23 F 12 '71
Tigers reduce cargo losses due to thefts.
Aviation W 95:56-7 Ag 30 '71

AIRPORTS
Special report: facing the airport challenge;
symposium, with editorial comment. il
Aviation W 95:11, 34-6+ N 15 '71
See also
Airways
Heliports
Seaplane bases

Automation
Reactions to automated support gear vary.
R. S. Kahn. il Aviation W 95:121-2+ N 15
'71

Buildings
See Airport buildings

Design
Transfer at Tampa; Florida airport terminal.
il Arch Forum 135:34-7 O '71

Equipment
Curing terminal fatigue. il Time 97:70+ Je
21 '71
Driverless automated trains improve air pas-
senger mobility; Houston, Tex. il Am City
86:109-10 Ap '71
How's your airport standby power? Hopkins
international airport, Cleveland; diesel elec-
tric sets. G. E. Katzmar. il Am City 86:96
D '71
Reactions to automated support gear vary.
R. S. Kahn. il Aviation W 95:121-2+ N
15 '71
Tampa design keyed to shuttle system. Z.
Strickland. il Aviation W 95:91+ N 15 '71

Federal aid
Airport, airways funding status remains
clouded. J. P. Woolsey. Aviation W 94:
135-7+ Mr 8 '71
Congressional conferees restrict aviation
trust fund expenditures. D. C. Winston.
Aviation W 95:16-17 Ag 2 '71
House unit asks airport aid boost. Aviation W
96:22 Ja 3 '72
Senate unit reports amendment limiting user
fund expenditures; 1970 Airport and airway
development act. D. C. Winston. Aviation
W 95:28 O 4 '71
Senate would halt trust fund loss. D. C.
Winston. Aviation W 95:14-15 Jl 26 '71
Volpe pledges aviation tax fund integrity.
C. E. Schneider. Aviation W 94:23-4 My 3
'71

Finance
Airlines face burgeoning user, airport fees.
Aviation W 95:51 N 15 '71
See also
Airports—Federal aid
Motor fuels—Taxation

Fires and fire protection
Scale fire services to airport use. Am City
86:36 N '71

Laws and regulations
Industry pressure builds on Nixon to sign
user tax restraints bill. Aviation W 95:28
N 15 '71
Senate sponsor sees Nixon veto of trust fund
use restriction. Aviation W 95:26 O 18 '71

Location
Superjet airports run into trouble. il U S
News 70:30-2 Mr 22 '71

Luggage handling
See Airlines—Luggage handling

Maintenance departments
Los Angeles builds separate helicopter facility. J. Purko. il Am City 86:97 Je '71

Planning
Airlines' fiscal woes buffet airports. H. D.
Watkins. il Aviation W 95:38-43 N 15 '71
Environmental constraints delay airport/air-
way developments. Aviation W 94:20-1 Mr
1 '71
Fiscal, social obstacles slow airport ad-
vances. il Aviation W 95:34-6 N 15 '71
How to plan regionally for a regional air-
port; Kansas City, Mo. W. G. Roeseler. il
Am City 86:70+ Mr '71

Safety devices and measures
See also
Radar in aviation

Security measures
How the airlines hope to stop bombs and
bomb scares. M. Schultz. il Pop Mech 135:
94-7+ Mr '71
See also
Airplane hijacking—Prevention

Standards
Charters force revised airport standards.
H. J. Coleman. il Aviation W 95:113+
N 15 '71
FAA readies inspection program, standards
of safety for airports. Aviation W 94:24 Ja
25 '71
Softened airport standards impact sought.
K. Johnsen. Aviation W 95:102 N 15 '71

Traffic control
DOT seen impeding landing aid program.
C. E. Schneider. il Aviation W 95:53-4
N 15 '71
FAR sight; regulated traffic patterns. A.
Trammell. il Flying 89:104 S '71
On top. R. L. Collins. Flying 88:12 Mr '71
Two new TCAs; New York and Los Ange-
les. il Flying 89:34-5 Jl '71

Transportation problems
Vought to build airport transit system;
Dallas/Ft Worth airport. E. J. Bulban. il
Aviation W 95:16-17 Jl 19 '71

California
Land squeeze, traffic spur airport plans. W.
S. Hieronymus. il Aviation W 94:57-8 Mr
22 '71
See also
Los Angeles—Airports
San Francisco—Airports
Santa Barbara, Calif.—Airports

Europe, Western
Airlines face burgeoning user, airport fees.
Aviation W 95:51 N 15 '71

Florida
Where wildlife and jets coexist; Everglades
airstrip. il Bsns W p88 O 16 '71
See also
Tampa, Fla.—Airports

France
See also
Paris—Airports

Georgia
See also
Atlanta—Airports

Germany (Democratic Republic)
See also
Berlin (East Berlin)—Airports

Germany (Federal Republic)
See also
Frankfort on the Main—Airports

Great Britain
See also
Great Britain—British airports authority
London—Airports

Hong Kong
Traffic sparks Hong Kong airport growth.
R. R. Ropelewsi. il Aviation W 96:32-3 Ja
10 '72

Illinois
See also
Chicago—Airports

Japan
See also
Tokyo—Airports

Maine
Esthetics yielding to function in design
of new Maine airport; Bangor international airport. Aviation W 95:54 N 15 '71

AIRPORTS—*Continued*

Missouri
See also
Kansas City, Mo.—Airports
St Louis—Airports

New Jersey
See also
Newark, N.J.—Airports

New York (state)
See also
New York (city)—Airports

Ohio
See also
Cleveland—Airports

Russia
Krasnodar draws Soviet consumer ire. Aviation W 95:60 N 15 '71

Texas
See also
Dallas—Airports
Houston, Tex.—Airports

United States
Environment issues stunt airport growth. J. P. Woolsey. il Aviation W 95:46-8+ N 15 '71
See also
Fixed base operators
also subhead Airports under names of cities, e.g. St Louis—Airports

AIRPORTS, Stealing from. See Airport thefts

AIRSHIPS
All the daring young men; aviation comes to the West. J. F. Hood. il Am West 8: 10-15+ Jl '71
Etymology of blimp. R. P. Smyers. Aviation W 96:62 Ja 3 '72
Other end of the spectrum; ride in the Goodyear blimp Mayflower. R. Hotz. Aviation W 95:11 N 1 '71

AIRWAY communications stations. See United States—Federal aviation administration—Flight service stations

AIRWAYS
Cleared as filed; how to choose the proper IFR route. W. Berkley. il Flying 89:54-5 Jl '71
Japan pushes airways modernization plan. il Aviation W 95:80-2 N 1 '71
New aviation growth blocked at New York; Northeast corridor. Aviation W 95:31 O 4 '71

Traffic control
See Air traffic control

AIRWORTHINESS regulations for helicopters. See Helicopters—Standards

AITKEN, William I.
Cancer; address, April 5, 1971. Vital Speeches 37:552-6 Jl 1 '71

AJO, Ariz.
Life with Big Daddy. Newsweek 78:71+ Ag 23 '71

AKADEMGORODOK, Siberia
Science in Siberia. W. R. Shelton. il Bul Atom Sci 27:23-8 F '71

AKEROYD, Richard
Alternative information. bibliog Wilson Lib Bul 46:103 S '71

AKO castle. See Castles

AKRON, Ohio
Edifice rex; grubstaking the Gospel. por Chr Today 16:42-3 O 8 '71

Parks and playgrounds
Rating a neighborhood park. W. S. Hendon. il Am City 86:70-1 Ap '71

AKSEL, Sophie C.
Will Shakespeare knew that all along. il por Wilson Lib Bul 45:754-7 Ap '71

AL-AMRI, Hassan. See Amri, H.

AL-GHAZZALI, Muhammad. See Ghazzali, M.

AL-QADDAFI, Muammar. See Qaddafi, M.

ALABAMA
See also
Education—Alabama
Greene County
Hunting—Alabama
Justice, Administration of—Alabama

Description and travel
Alabama's Tennessee playground. B. Thomas. il Travel 135:46-7 Je '71

Parks and reserves
Sequoyah country. G. G. Ripple. il Travel 136:26-7 D '71

Race question
See also
Birmingham, Ala.—Negroes

ALABAMA. University, Tuscaloosa
New beat in the heart of Dixie. P. Schrag. il por Sat R 54:42-5+ Mr 20 '71
Pick the fraternity housemother. il Life 70: 81-4 Ap 16 '71
Pride in the red jersey, Alabama's Crimson Tide. P. Putnam. il Sports Illus 35:18-21 O 11 '71

ALAMEDA COUNTY, Calif, library, Hayward

Branches
Books in the suburbs; branch library, San Lorenzo, Calif. il Arch Forum 135:46-7 N '71

ALANINE aminotransferase. See Transferases

ALARM clock in the cupboard; story. See Baranskaya, N.

ALARMS
School control, statistical aids devised from space technology; mobile ultrasonic alarm system. Aviation W 94:19 My 24 '71
See also
Burglar alarms
Electric alarms
Fire alarms

ALASKA
Japan's foothold in Alaska. il U S News 71:36 S 27 '71
Last frontier (cont) S. Wright. il pors Am West 8:24-7 Mr; 36-9 Jl; 16-19 N '71
Will oil and tundra mix? W. S. Ellis. il Nat Geog 140:484-517 O '71
See also
Admiralty Island
Airlines—Alaska
Aleutian Islands
Barrow
Brooks Range
Conservation of resources—Alaska
Ecology—Alaska
Forests and forestry—Alaska
Gustavus
Hunting—Alaska
Indians of North America—Alaska
Juneau
Justice, Administration of—Alaska
Ketchikan
Land tenure—Alaska
Libraries—Alaska
Mount McKinley National Park
Petroleum—Alaska
Point Barrow
Public lands—Alaska
Wilderness areas—Alaska
Wildlife sanctuaries—Alaska

Antiquities
Archeology along the pipeline. R. J. Trotter. il Sci N 100:396-7 D 11 '71
See also
Eskimos—Antiquities

Description and travel
Alaska, where the fabulous is routine. R. Atcheson. il Holiday 49:52-5+ Ap '71

Economic conditions
Second purchase; federal government compensates Eskimos, Aleuts and Indians. Time 98:11 D 27 '71
Showdown nears for Alaska pipeline. il U S News 71:80-2 S 13 '71
State teetering between hope and despair. N. J. Margolin. il U S News 70:53-4 Mr 15 '71
Why Alaskans are upset about conservation. il U S News 71:43-5 O 4 '71

Native races
See Indians of North America—Alaska

ALASKA airlines
Revised operating factors; table. Aviation W 95:34 Ag 2 '71

ALASKA pipeline. See Petroleum—Pipe lines

ALASKAN brown bear hunting. See Bear hunting

ALATEEN (organization)
My parents drink too much; questions and answers. A. Wood. Seventeen 30:168+ Ap '71

ALAWI, Adnan A. and Pak, W. L.
On-transient of insect electroretinogram; its cellular origin. bibliog il Science 172:1055-7 Je 4 '71

ALBANIA
Fear that guards the vineyard. il Time 98: 30-1 S 6 '71

ALBANY, N.Y.
Computerized traffic control. F J. Fuller and others. il Am City 86:109-11 O '71

ALBANY, N.Y.—*Continued*

City planning

Edifice complex? South Mall project. il Newsweek 77:24-5 Mr 1 '71

What price glory on the Albany Mall? E. Carruth. il por Fortune 83:92-5+ Je '71

Crime

Cops can't find the pusher. K. S. Christianson. Nation 213:562-4 N 29 '71

ALBARET, Céleste

Woman in Proust's life. S. de Gramont. il Harp Baz 104:54-5 Je '71 *

ALBEDO, Planetary. See Earth—Radiation

ALBEE, Edward

All over. Criticism
America 124:593-5 Je 5 '71 *
Commonweal 94:166-7 Ap 23 '71 *
Nat R 23:602-4 Je 1 '71 *
Nation 212-476-7 Ap 12 '71 *
Nation 212:571-2 My 3 '71 *
New Repub 164:24+ Ap 17 '71 *
New Yorker 47:95 Ap 3 '71 *
Newsweek il 77:52 Ap 5 '71 *
Sat R 54:54 Ap 17 '71 *
Time il 97:69 Ap 5 '71 *

ALBERDI, Juan Bautista

Precursors of the inter-American system. por Américas 23:S8-9 Ja '71 *

ALBERS, Josef

Homage to Albers. D. Shapiro. il por Art N 70:30-3+ N '71 *

Man of a thousand squares. D. Davis. il por Newsweek 77:77-8 Ja 18 '71 *

ALBERS, Marjorie K.

Benjamin Randolph, cabinetmaker. il Design 72:8-9 Spr '71 *

Historical view of the window. il Design 72:12-15 Sum '71 *

ALBERT, Carl

Excerpt from debate, September 16, 1971. Cong Digest 50:271+ N '71

about

Albert has dashed the reformers' hopes. por Bsns W p32-3 D 11 '71 *

Coming battle between President and Congress. il pors Time 97:12-14+ F 1 '71 *

ALBERT and Mary Lasker foundation

Lasker awards for medical research. il Sci N 100:342 N 20 '71

ALBERT Herring; opera. See Britten, B.

ALBERTA

See also
Banff
Booksellers and bookselling—Alberta

ALBERTS, Donald

Spread oil on the Sound's troubled waters and you'll be in hot water with the chief. S. Singer. il pors Todays Health 49:35-9+ O '71 *

ALBERTS, Robert C.

Business of the highest magnitude; or, Don't put off until tomorrow what you can ram through today. il Am Heritage 22:48-53+ F '71

ALBERTSON, Chris

Lil Hardin Armstrong, a fond remembrance. il pors Sat R 54:66-7 S 25 '71

Unmasking of Miles Davis. il pors Sat R 54:67-9+ N 27 '71

ALBERTY, John

Three reconnoitering artists. J. Livingston. il Art in Am 59:114-17 My '71 *

ALBIZZIA julibrissin. See Silk trees

ALBORNOZ, Miguel

Dialogue for understanding. pors Américas 23:12-15 Mr '71

ALBRECHT, R. See Noell, W. K. jt. auth.

ALBRIGHT and Wilson, ltd.

Carry on! Forbes 108:36 Jl 1 '71

ALBUQUERQUE, Edson X. and Warnick, J. E.

Electrophysiological observations in normal and dystrophic chicken muscles. bibliog il Science 172:1260-3 Je 18 '71

—and others

Batrachotoxin: chemistry and pharmacology. bibliog il Science 172:995-1002 Je 4 '71

ALBUQUERQUE, N.Mex.

Libraries

Albuquerque's free-wheeling library. L. Waugh and J. Waugh. il Am Ed 7:33-5 Ag '71

Riots

Let's give 'em a riot. il Newsweek 77:38 Je 28 '71

ALCAN aluminium, ltd.

Why Alcan spends so much. il Bsns W p78+ Jl 10 '71

ALCATRAZ (island)

Anomie at Alcatraz; report. W. Marmon. il Time 97:21 Ap 12 '71

ALCHEMY

Alchemical symbols; table. Chem 44:27 O '71

ALCHEMY symbols. See Symbolism in medicine

ALCINDOR, Lewis. See Abdul-Jabbar, K.

ALCOA. See Aluminum company of America

ALCOA Seaprobe (ship) See Ships, Research

ALCOHOL

Drugs of habit & the drugs of belief; with editorial comment. S. McCracken. bibliog f Commentary 51:4, 43-52 Je '71

Physiological effects

Alcohol dependence and opiate dependence: lack of relationship in mice. A. Goldstein and B. A. Judson. bibliog il Science 172:290-2 Ap 16 '71

Alcohol dependence produced in mice by inhalation of ethanol: grading the withdrawal reaction. D. B. Goldstein and N. Pal. bibliog il Science 172:288-90 Ap 16 '71

Ethanol stimulates triglyceride synthesis by the intestine. E. A. Carter and others. bibliog il Science 174:1245-7 D 17 '71

Heavenly cure; Hangover heaven, Atlanta. il Time 97:62 F 15 '71

See also
Alcoholism
Drinking and airplane accidents

ALCOHOL, Denatured

Industrial alcohol from waste paper. Chem 44:23 N '71

ALCOHOL, Industrial. See Alcohol, Denatured

ALCOHOL breath tests. See Alcohol in the body

ALCOHOL dehydrogenase. See Dehydrogenases

ALCOHOL in the body

Alcohol breath tests: gross errors in current methods of measuring alveolar gas concentrations. N. H. Spector. bibliog il Science 172:57-9; 174:772+ Ap 2, N 19 '71

Alcoholism, alcohol, and drugs. E. Rubin and C. S. Lieber. bibliog il Science 172:1097-102 Je 11 '71

Induction of liver acetaldehyde dehydrogenase: possible role in ethanol tolerance after exposure to barbiturates. G. Redmond and G. Cohen. bibliog il Science 171:387-9 Ja 29 '71

On-the-scene sobriety tests; Baton Rouge, La. E. O. Bauer, jr. Am City 86:20 Ja '71

Synergy of ethanol and a natural soporific—gamma hydroxybutyrate. E. R. McCabe and others. bibliog il Science 171:404-6 Ja 29 '71

ALCOHOLIC beverages

Blend in the flavor of summer. E. Greenberg. il House B 113:128+ My '71

Fresh new flavors for cooling summer drinks. J. Ellis. House & Gard 139:100-1 Je '71

Help for the home bartender. L. V. Power. il Am Home 74:62 N '71

Warm your spirits with festive cheer. il Ebony 27:110+ Ja '72

Wine and spirit gifts and drinks for holiday parties; with recipes. J. Ellis. House & Gard 140:34+ D '71

Your liquid assets: drinks for parties; excerpt from Complete guide to creative entertaining. House & Gard 140:130+ O '71

See also
Cocktails

ALCOHOLICS

Diary of an alcoholic wife. J. Gage. il por Ladies Home J 88:128-9+ My '71

When alcoholism is a family problem. C. Levine. Parents Mag 46:74-6+ F '71

ALCOHOLICS anonymous

Anonymous ally. il por Time 97:52 F 8 '71

ALCOHOLISM

Alcoholism, alcohol, and drugs. E. Rubin and C. S. Lieber. bibliog il Science 172:1097-102 Je 11 '71

Alcoholism analyzed. G. D. Everett. Chr Today 15:38-9 F 26 '71

Drugs and drinking in the business world; interview. H. Johnson. por U S News 70:70-3 Mr 22 '71

Robert Young's toughest role. B. Ellison. il pors Todays Health 49:25-7+ My '71

U.S. journal: Gallup, N.Mex; drunken Navahos. C. Trillin. New Yorker 47:108+ S 25 '71

See also
Alateen (organization)

ALCOHOLISM—*Continued*

Research

Alcoholism research and resistance to understanding the compulsive drinker. P. Verden and D. Shatterly. bibliog Ment Hy 55:331-6 Jl '71

Beliefs about disease and alcoholism. P. J. Blizard. bibliog Ment Hy 55:184-9 Ap '71

Ethanol preference in the rat as a function of photoperiod. I. Geller. bibliog il Science 173:456-9 Jl 30 '71

Therapy

Alcohol addicts. Sci N 100:8 Jl 3 '71

Cocktail lounge that keeps you sober. il Sci Digest 69:78 My '71

Farewell to alcohol. W. McIlwain. il Atlan 229:29-35 Ja '72

Training to be sober; therapeutic imbibing at Patton state hospital, San Bernardino, Calif. il Time 97:54 Mr 15 '71

See also

Alcoholics anonymous

ALCORN, James Lusk

Hundred years of history. G. A. Sewell. bibliog il pors Negro Hist Bul 34:78-9 Ap '71 *

ALCORN agricultural and mechanical college, Lorman, Miss.

Hundred years of history. G. A. Sewell. bibliog il pors Negro Hist Bul 34:78-9 Ap '71

ALCYONE, pseud. See Krishnamurti, J.

ALDABRA ISLAND

Island for science. Sci N 100:141 Ag 28 '71

ALDAN, Daisy

Words of the tribe. Poetry 118:35-40 Ap '71

ALDANA E., Guillermo

Mesa del Nayar's strange Holy week. il por Nat Geog 139:780-95 Je '71

ALDEBURGH festival. See Music festivals—England

ALDEHYDE dehydrogenases. See Dehydrogenases

ALDEHYDES

See also

Acetaldehyde

ALDEN, Vernon R.

Boston co: a string of matched pearls. il por Bsns W p36+ F 6 '71 *

ALDERSON, Wendell

Down among the sheltering palms. il Opera N 35:6-10 Mr 13 '71

ALDERSON, William T.

Tennessee, a historical introduction. il Antiques 100:378-81 S '71

ALDOLASE

Subunit structure of aldolase. E. G. Heidner and others. bibliog il Science 171:677-80 F 19 '71

ALDRICH, Samuel

Who'll call the tune on pollution control? interview, ed. by B. Coffman. por Farm J 95:G1 Ap '71

ALDRIDGE, John W.

Egalitarian snobs. Sat R 54:21-4 My 8 '71

Writer's demotion to solid-citizen status. il Sat R 54:36-6+ S 18 '71

ALDRIN

Aldrin and dieldrin. C. F. Wurster. bibliog il Environ 13:33-41 O '71

ALEGRIA, Fernando

Most significant decade in Latin American fiction. bibliog Pub W 200:pt2 166-8 S 27 '71

ALENIKOFF, Frances

Performance. Craft Horiz 31:13+ D '71

ALESHIRE, Robert A.

Case for free transit. Cur 135:19-22 D '71

ALEUTIAN ISLANDS

North Pacific circumnavigation; are the Aleutians cold? H. Roth. il Yachting 130: 54-5+ S '71 (to be cont)

See also

Amchitka Island

Earthquakes—Aleutian Islands

ALEXANDER, Clifford L. 1933-

Clifford Alexander, chief, black political fund. Negro Hist Bul 33:171 N '70 *

ALEXANDER, E. C. Jr. and others

Plutonium-244: confirmation as an extinct radioactivity. bibliog il Science 172:837-40 My 21 '71

ALEXANDER, Garrett E. See Fuster. J. M. jt. auth.

ALEXANDER, George

Little engine that could be an answer to pollution. il N Y Times Mag p 18-19+ O 3 '71

ALEXANDER, Guy

Chemist in industry. por Chem 45:19-21 Ja '72

ALEXANDER, Judd H.

Silent servant; address, October 4, 1971. Vital Speeches 38:112-15 D 1 '71

ALEXANDER, Lloyd

High fantasy and heroic romance; address, October 1969. bibliog f Horn Bk 47:577-84 D '71

SLJ meets Lloyd Alexander; interview. il por Library J 96:1421-3 Ap 15 '71

about

Classic hero in a new mythology. M. Carr. il Horn Bk 47:508-13 O '71 *

Lloyd Alexander in Lexington, Massachusetts. il Horn Bk 47:102-3 F '71 *

NBA winner stresses seriousness of fantasy. Library J 96:1412-13 Ap 15 '71 *

ALEXANDER, Raymond Pace

Blacks and the law. por Negro Hist Bul 34: 109-13 My '71

ALEXANDER, Rickey

In my opinion. por Seventeen 30:212 O '71

ALEXANDER, Shana

Where the women are. il McCalls 98:85-7 F '71

ALEXANDER, Stewart F.

Disaster at Bari; excerpts. G. Infield. il por Am Heritage 22:64+ O '71 *

ALEXANDER, Tom

Defusing the world population bomb. il Fortune 84:112-16+ O '71

Hard road to soft automation. il Fortune 84:95-7+ Jl '71

There are sex differences in the mind, too. il Fortune 83:76-9+ F '71

ALEXANDER, William M.

What's the score on: middle schools? Todays Ed 60:67 N '71

ALEXANDRE, Marc

Man on the ground floor. pors Forbes 107:37-9 Ja 15 '71 *

ALEXANDROV, A.

Earth to spacecraft; integrated command and measuring complexes. Space World H-6-90:6-7 Je '71

ALEXANDROVICH, Rivka

Cries for liberty grow louder. D. Kucharsky. por Chr Today 15:34 Je 18 '71 *

ALFA-Romeo company. See Automobile industry—Italy

ALFALFA

Establishing and managing alfalfa seedlings. R. Steffen. Org Gard & Farm 18:114-17 N '71

$250 net an acre from alfalfa pasture. G. Lorang. il Farm J 95:28+ My '71

Will alfalfa survive? C. E. Sommers. Suc Farm 69:G30 Ap '71

ALFALFA leaf-cutting bees. See Bees

ALFALFA leafhoppers. See Leafhoppers

ALFALFA weevils

Alfalfa weevil keeps spreading. il Suc Farm 69:no3 W29 F '71

ALFONSO, Jordi Gussinyer. See Gussinyer Alfonso, J.

ALFRED, William

Ourselves alone: Irish exiles in Brooklyn. il por Atlan 227:53-8 Mr '71

ALFREY, Elsie V.

There's a time and a way to prune. il Org Gard & Farm 18:94-9 Ja '71

ALFVÉN, Hannes

Apples in a spacecraft. bibliog il Science 173: 522-5 Ag 6 '71

Fission and fusion reactors: the Alfven memorandum. Bul Atom Sci 27:36 S '71

Plasma physics applied to cosmology. bibliog il Phys Today 24:28-31+ F '71

Plasma physics, space research, and the origin of the solar system; Nobel lecture, December 11, 1970. il Science 172:991-4 Je 4 '71

about

Toro makes a threesome with earth and moon. G. B. Lubkin. il Phys Today 24: 17-18 D '71 *

ALGAE

Artificial microfossils: experimental studies of permineralization of blue-green algae in silica. J. H. Oehler and J. W. Schopf. bibliog il Science 174:1229-31 D 17 '71

Plasmalemma: the seat of dual mechanisms of ion absorption in chlorella pyrenoidosa. S. Kannan. bibliog il Science 173:927-9 S 3 '71

To control algae, consider carbon. Am City 86:36 Mr '71

See also

Diatoms

Euglena

Kelp

Lichens

Red tide

Sargassum

Seaweed

Water bloom

ALLEN, Francis A.
Freedom, order and justice. Cur Hist 60:321-6+ Je '71

ALLEN, George
Allen's red-hot Redskins. il por Newsweek 78:54-6+ N 1 '71 *
Ice-cream man cometh. J. Underwood. il Sports Illus 35:71-2+ O 25 '71 *
King of the Ramskins. il por Life 71:40-1 O 15 '71 *

ALLEN, Ivan, 1911-
Civic boosterism. J. Yardley. New Repub 165:26 Ag 21 '71 *

ALLEN, J. W.
Best seller bamboozle. Sat R 54:14-15+ Jl 31 '71

ALLEN, James E. and Rasmussen, Howard
Human red blood cells: prostaglandin E₂, epinephrine, and isoproterenol alter deformability. bibliog il Science 174:512-14 O 29 '71

ALLEN, James Edward, 1911-1972
Crisis in confidence; the public and its schools. PTA Mag 66:18-20+ bibliog(p36) O '71
Reading, the fundamental R: what parents can do to upgrade school programs. por Parents Mag 46:32 My '71
Recasting of public education; address. July 5, 1971. Vital Speeches 37:654-8 Ag 15 '71

ALLEN, L. H. Jr, and others
Plant response to carbon dioxide enrichment under field conditions: a simulation. bibliog il Science 173:256-8 Jl 16 '71

ALLEN, Larry
Color TV goes modular for '72. il Radio-Electr 43:33-7+ Ja '72
Stereo cassettes, the electronic side. il Radio-Electr 42:39-42 Mr '71
Stereo cassettes, the mechanical side. il Radio-Electr 42:37-40 Ap '71
What's a frequency synthesizer? il Radio-Electr 42:50-2 F '71

ALLEN, Linda
(ed) The look you like; questions and answers. See issues of Todays health

ALLEN, Margaret
In the name of creation. il PTA Mag 66:18-20 D '71

ALLEN, Milton B.
Milton B. Allen, the first black states attorney. E. P. Burrell. por Negro Hist Bul 34:63-7 Mr '71 *

ALLEN, Muriel
Washington, spare that pesticide! New Repub 164:14-15 Je 12 '71
—and Schnittker, John
Milking the consumer. New Repub 165:17-18 Jl 17 '71

ALLEN, Paul E.
Night of the cottonmouth. il por Outdoor Life 148:58-61+ Jl '71

ALLEN, Penny
5 who fight pollution. C. Remsberg and B. Remsberg. pors Seventeen 30:128+ Ap '71 *

ALLEN, Robert Day, and others
Direct test of the positive pressure gradient theory of pseudopod extension and retraction in amoebae. bibliog il Science 174:1237-40 D 17 '71

ALLEN, Robert H.
Something out of nothing. il Forbes 107:40 Je 15 '71 *

ALLEN, Sarah Van Alstyne
Old music box; poem. Cath World 213:120 Je '71
Plea from a reader; poem. Commonweal 93:496 F 19 '71

ALLEN, Walter
Swan of Avon bites chickens. Nation 213:22-4 Jl 5 '71

ALLEN, William J.
Day camp runs night program. il Camp Mag 43:18 Ja '71

ALLEN, Woody
Schmeed memoirs. New Yorker 47:36-7 Ap 17 '71
about
Current cinema. P. Gilliatt. New Yorker 47:127-9 My 15 '71 *
Getting even, by W. Allen. Review
Commonweal 95:164 N 12 '71. J. A. Pratt-leback *
Woody Allen: the power of an imperfectionist. M. Rosin. il por Harp Baz 105:62-3 D '71 *

ALLENDE GOSSENS, Salvador
Allende: a special kind of Marxist. P. Young. il pors Life 71:38-40 Jl 16 '71 *
Allende's hundred days. il por Time 97:33+ F 22 '71
Allende's unorthodox road to socialism. il Bsns W p88 Ap 10 '71 *
Chile going Marxist? il por Sr Schol 98:8-15 F 1 '71 *

Chile: it's half and half. il por Newsweek 77:60+ Ap 19 '71 *
Chile under Marxism: does it work? J. Barnes. il por Newsweek 78:43-4+ N 15 '71 *
Chile's reasonable revolution: Allende after a year. J. Radford. Nation 213:422-4 N 1 '71; Reply with rejoinder. J. A. Menz. 213:642 D 20 '71
Growing pains. Newsweek 78:34+ Ag 23 '71 *
Letter from Santiago. J. Kraft. New Yorker 46:80-9 Ja 30 '71 *
Making an impression. il Newsweek 78:35 S 13 '71 *
Mandate for Allende. il pors Time 97:24+ Ap 19 '71 *
Road to socialism: a rough one for Chile. il por U S News 71:73-5 O 25 '71 *
Setback for a native son. Time 98:31 Ag 2 '71 *
Trend that failed. J. Barnes. il por Newsweek 78:4+ D 20 '71 *
You're going great, Chicho. il por Time 98:37 N 15 '71 *

ALLENDE meteorite. See Meteorites

ALLENTOWN, Pa.
Superclinic, science-fiction structure takes the pain out of medical treatment. N. Schaffer. il Arch Forum 135:30-5 N '71

ALLENTOWN college of St Francis De Sales
Libraries
Allentown college library suffers $100,000 flood loss. Library J 96:3553-4 N 1 '71

ALLER, Margo F.
Promethium in the star HR 465. il Sky & Tel 41:220-2 Ap '71

ALLERGIC encephalomyelitis. See Encephalomyelitis

ALLERGY
Allergenic mechanism. il Chem 44:23-4 My '71
Allergies: not to be sneezed at! W. J. Papp. il Har Yrs 11:30-3+ Ap '71
Histamine augments leukocyte adenosine 3',5'-monophosphate and blocks antigenic histamine release. H. R. Bourne and others. bibliog il Science 173:743-5 Ag 20 '71
Reporter at large; enigmatic enzyme. P. Brodeur. New Yorker 46:42-8+ Je 16 '71
Warning on enzymes. Newsweek 77:42 F 1 '71
See also
Drug allergy
Food allergy
Hay fever
Hives (urticaria)

ALLEVA, John J. and others
Calcium carbonate concretions: cyclic occurrence in the hamster vagina. bibliog il Science 174:600-3 N 5 '71

ALLEY, Jeanette
Roommate; poem. Seventeen 30:132 Jl '71

ALLEY, Robert D. See Chaffee, L. M. jt. auth.

ALLIANCE for labor action
Firm support for a shaky alliance. il Bsns W p97 Mr 6 '71
Some events to watch in the unions. B. L. Masse. America 125:81 Ag 21 '71

ALLIANCE for progress
Beyond the Alliance; excerpt from address, April 14, 1971. G. Plaza. il Américas 23:2-4 My '71
CIAP protests protectionism. Américas 23:44 Ja '71
New decade of inter-American cooperation; statement, August 17, 1971; with editorial comment. G. Plaza. il Américas 23:1, 44 S '71
President marks 10th anniversary of the Alliance for progress; statement, August 17, 1971. R. M. Nixon. Dept State Bul 65:334 S 27 '71

ALLIANCE of figurative artists
Of, by, and for artists. K. Kuh. Sat R 54:88-9 Ja 23 '71

ALLIANCES
See also
International organizations, Regional
Nato

ALLIED stores corporation
Looks like up. por Forbes 108:54 O 15 '71

ALLIGATORS
Alligator, ugly old king of survival. H. V. L. Bloomfield. il Am For 77:40-3 Ag '71
They're still not safe. L. Line. il Audubon 73:12-13 Jl '71

ALLIONE, Sylvie
Horrifying fall from a balloon; death of S. Allione. il Life 71:28-9 Ag 6 '71 *

ALLIS-Chalmers manufacturing company
  Allis: the turnaround got stuck. il por Bsns W
    p96-7 Mr 13 '71
  Out of the shadow of big Allis. il Bsns W
    p22 Jl 24 '71
  White frees Allis in record stock sale. Bsns W
    p25-6 F 13 '71
ALLISON, Roy
  Get the most from your speakers; questions
    and answers. Hi Fi 21:48-50 Je '71
ALLISON and Busby (firm) See Publishers
    and publishing—Great Britain
ALLON, Yigal
  Talk with Yigal Allon. H. Krosney. il Nation
    212:550-2 My 3 '71 *
ALLOPHANES. See Aluminum silicates
ALLOWANCES, Childrens. See Childrens al-
    lowances
ALLOWAY, Lawrence
  Art. See issues of Nation
  Frankenthaler as pastoral. il Art N 70:
    66-8+ N '71
ALLOYS
  Memorious metal; Nitinol. Sci Am 224:47 Mr
    '71
  New superconductors. T. H. Geballe. il Sci
    Am 225:22-33 N '71
  Shhh: new noiseless alloys will make it easy
    on your ears. D. Hellyer. il Pop Sci 199:38+
    Jl '71
    See also
  Lead alloys
ALLSTATE insurance company
  You're in good hands with safety; public-
    service advertising. S. W. Little. il Sat R
    54:76 D 11 '71
ALLYLISOPROPYLACETAMIDE. See Aceta-
    mide
ALMA desk company
  Alma desk. il Nations Bsns 59:74-6 S '71
ALMANACS
  Weather-wise; Old farmer's almanac. il News-
    week 78:69 D 6 '71
  Your Harvest years almanac for 1971. K. Hill-
    yard. Har Yrs 11:23-9 Ja '71
ALMIRANTE, Giorgio
  Almirante is no M-s---l-- yet. M. S. Davis.
    il por N Y Times Mag p27+ Je 6 '71 *
ALMOND, Richard
  Therapeutic community; with biographical
    sketch. il Sci Am 224:14, 34-5 bibliog(p 124)
    Mr '71
ALMOND moths. See Moths
ALMQUIST, Ray
  Signs of our time. il Design 72:38-9 Sum '71
ALOES
  Euphorbia and aloe as living sculpture. il
    Sunset 147:252+ N '71
ALONSO, Alicia
  Alicia Alonso, the flower of Cuba. M.
    Horosko. il pors Dance Mag 45:43-58 Ag
    '71 *
  Brava, Alicia. W. Terry. il pors Sat R 54:31
    Jl 10 '71 *
  Dance, N. Goldner. Nation 213:91-3 Ag 2 '71 *
  Pilgrimage to Montreal: Alicia Alonso and
    Ballet nacional de Cuba. G. Fitzgerald. il
    por Dance Mag 45:8 Ag '71 *
ALPERT, Barbara A.
  Ethiopian perplex. Cur Hist 60:151-6+ Mr '71
ALPERT, Helen
  Make-it-yourself holiday gifts. il Har Yrs
    11:24-33 D '71
  Why get married? Har Yrs 11:6-10+ Ap '71
  Women doctors preferred? il Har Yrs 11:36-40
    Ag '71
  You can cut medical costs. bibliog il Har
    Yrs 11:6-10 Jl '71
ALPERT, Hollis
  Cassette man cometh. il Sat R 54:42-4+ Ja
    30 '71
  Diversification of Shirley MacLaine. il pors
    Sat R 54:43-5+ F 27 '71
  Film. il Sat R 54:43-5+ F 27; 48-9+ Ap 24;
    61-3+ S 25 '71
  SR goes to the movies. See issues of Saturday
    review
ALPERT, Jonathan L.
  Legal guide to buying. Har Yrs 11:35-7 F '71
ALPHA waves. See Brain waves
ALPHABET
  I.T.A. vs. traditional orthography. Sch &
    Soc 99:270-1 Sum '71
ALPHAND, Nicole Mérenda
  At home in Paris—with Madame Herve Al-
    phand. G. Perint. por Harp Baz 104:179 F
    '71 *
ALPINE climbing. See Mountaineering
ALPINE flora
  Growing alpines under glass. J. P. Osborne. il
    Horticulture 49:34-5 F '71
  Springtime in the Rockies. M. Sprague. il
    Nat Wildlife 9:26-8, 29-31 Ap '71
ALPS
  Shaping the Alps. il Sci N 100:7 Jl 3 '71

ALSOP, Joseph
  Joe Alsop story. B. L. Collier. il pors N Y
    Times Mag p22-3+ My 23 '71 *
ALSOP, Stewart
  [Column on public affairs] See issues of
    Newsweek
  God tempers the wind; report on illness. por
    Newsweek 78:84 Ag 30; 76 S 6 '71
  Radical chic is dead. Read Digest 98:103-4 F
    '71
  Worse than My Lai. Newsweek 77:108 My
    24 '71; Same abr. with title Drugs and
    the GI in Vietnam. Read Digest 99:159-61
    Ag '71
    about
  Anticantian imperative. Chr Cent 88:415 Mr
    31 '71 *
ALSTON, E. Deedom
  Systems approach to street sweeping. il Am
    City 86:91-2+ N '71
ALSTON, Elizabeth
  Florida: the natives swing to Cuban cooking.
    il Look 35:46-9 Ap 6 '71
  Where the buys are in your food market. il
    Look 35:64-5 Ap 20 '71
ALTAR pieces
  Hidden treasure; religious art collection of
    St Leonard's church, Zoutleeuw. il Time
    98:46-8 D 27 '71
ALTBACH, Philip G. and Laufer, R. S.
  (eds) Students protest. bibliog f il Ann Am
    Acad 395:1-194 My '71
—and Peterson, Patti
  Before Berkeley: historical perspectives on
    American student activism. bibliog f Ann
    Am Acad 395:1-14 My '71
ALTER, Robert
  Agnon's last word. Commentary 51:74-81 Je
    '71
  Appropriating the religious tradition. Com-
    mentary 51:47-54 F; 24+ Je '71
ALTERNATIVE life style. See Counter culture
ALTERNATIVE service. See Service, Com-
    pulsory non-military
ALTERNATORS. See Electric generators, Al-
    ternating current
ALTES, Richard A.
  Computer derivation of some dolphin echo-
    location signals. bibliog il Science 173:
    912-14 S 3 '71
ALTIERY, Mason
  At peace with pidgin. il Am Ed 7:32-6 O '71
ALTMAN, Joseph. See Das, G. D. jt. auth.
ALTMAN, Robert
  Current cinema. P. Kael. New Yorker 47:
    40-4 Jl 3 '71 *
  15th man who was asked to direct M*A*S*H
    (and did) makes a peculiar western. A.
    Hermetz. il por N Y Times Mag p 10-11+
    Je 20 '71
ALTRUISM
  Altruism is rewarding. R. F. Weiss and oth-
    ers. bibliog il Science 171:1262-3 Mr 26 '71
    See also
  Helping behavior
ALTSCHULER, Martin D.
  Geometry of the coronal magnetic field. il
    Sky & Tel 41:146-50 Mr '71
ALUMINUM
  Conductor design with thin-film insulated
    aluminum. H. D. Walker. il Electr World
    86:39+ D '71
ALUMINUM company of America
  Second thoughts. il Forbes 108:68 O 15 '71
ALUMINUM company of Canada. See Alcan
    aluminium, ltd.
ALUMINUM industry
  Aluminum attacks its overcapacity. il Bsns
    W p24 S 18 '71
    Wages and hours
  Raises in aluminum: latest pattern? U S
    News 70:66 Je 14 '71
    Canada
    See also
  Alcan aluminium, ltd.
    United States
    See also
  Aluminum company of America
  Reynolds metals company
ALUMINUM silicates
  Amorphous clay materials; allophanes. H.
    Van Olphen. Science 171:91-2 Ja 8 '71
ALUMINUM storm doors. See Doors
ALUMINUM storm windows. See Windows
ALUMNI. See College graduates
ALUMNI funds. See Colleges and universities—
    Gifts, legacies, etc.
ALVARADO, Catherine
  Day Bobby learned about love. il por Red-
    book 136:10+ F '71

ALVARADO, Juan Velasco. See Velasco Alvarado, J.
ALVAREZ, A.
  Attempt; excerpt from The savage God. il Atlan 227:84-6+ Ap '71
  Night out; story. New Yorker 47:26-31 S 4 '71
ALVAREZ, Luis Echeverria. See Echeverría Alvarez, L.
ALVAREZ, Walter Clement
  Looking at medicine (cont) Look 35:18 F 23; 12-13 Je 29; 54 Ag 24 '71
ALVES, Márcio Moreira
  Brazil; what terror is like. Nation 212:337-41 Mr 15 '71
ALVIN Ailey American dance theater
  Alvin Ailey American dance theater, ANTA theater, NYC. T. Borek. Dance Mag 45: 84-5 Ap '71
  Alvin Ailey American dance theater, City center of music and drama, NYC. N. Mason. Dance Mag 45:23-4 Jl '71
  Dance; Choral dances and Cry. J. Maskey. il Hi Fi 21:MA8 S '71
  Dance; performances at the Apollo in New York. il Time 97:72-3 F 8 '71
  Musical events; season at the ANTA theatre. W. Sargeant. New Yorker 46:93 F 6 '71
  Spirit of Mary Lou; performance of Mary Lou's Mass. H. Saal. il por Newsweek 78: 67 D 20 '71
  World of dance; American dance season program. W. Terry. Sat R 54:45+ F 13 '71
ALWAN, Ameen
  Humus; poem. Nation 212:798 Je 21 '71
ALWIN Nikolais dance company
  American dance season. W. Terry. il Sat R 54:79 Mr 13 '71
  Nikolais dance theatre in Scenario, ANTA theatre, NYC. D. Hering. Dance Mag 45:20 Je '71
AMA (Japanese women divers) See Skin diving
AMABILE, George
  Networks; poem. New Yorker 47:97 Mr 27 '71
AMADON, Dean
  Clutch of the falconer; with biographical sketch. il Natur Hist 80:6, 28-30 Mr '71
AMAKER, Norman C.
  Public school desegregation; legal perspectives. Negro Hist Bul 33:174-7 N '70
AMANA furniture. See Furniture, American
AMANA society
  Old Amana furniture, by M. K. Albers. Review
    Antiques il 99:908+ Je '71. K. D. Barron
AMANTADINE hydrochloride
  Dopamine: release from the brain in vivo by amantadine. P. F. Von Voigtlander and K. E. Moore. bibliog il Science 174:408-10 O 22 '71
L'AMANTE Anglaise; drama. See Duras, M.
AMAR, Wesley F.
  Self-confrontation: rehearsal for renaissance. Clear House 45:294-6 Ja '71
AMARAL, Anthony
  Threat to the free spirit. il Am West 8:13-17+ S '71
  Wild horse, worth saving? il Nat Parks & Con Mag 45:21-4 Mr '71
AMARILLO, Tex.
  Power plant to run on reclaimed water. il Am City 86:24 F '71
AMARYLLIS
  See also
  Blood lilies
AMATEUR art. See Art, Amateur
AMATEUR astronomers. See Astronomers, Amateur
AMATEUR athletic union of the United States
  Firstest, fastest and mostest; AAU track and field championships in Eugene, Ore. P. Putnam and S. Myslenski. il Sports Illus 35:18-21 Jl 5 '71
  Mr America; Amateur athletic union-sponsored contest. il pors Ebony 26:80-2+ My '71
  No bird, no plane, just Superjack. J. Underwood. il pors Sports Illus 34:32-5+ My 10 '71
AMATEUR moving pictures. See Moving pictures, Amateur
AMATEUR opera. See Opera, Amateur
AMATEUR photographers. See Photographers
AMATEUR radio operators. See Radio operators, Amateur
AMATEUR theatricals. See College and school drama
AMATEUR trapshooting association
  Grand American; trapshooting tournament. B. A. Foxworthy. il Holiday 49:52-6 Jl '71
AMATEUR yacht research society
  Amateur yacht research society. W. D. Teague. il Motor B & S 127:90-1+ Mr '71

AMATEURISM (sports)
  Ineligible married man; Toomey the best decathlete, now a professional. W. F. Reed. il por Sports Illus 34:42-4+ Ap 12 '71
  Jack Kelly speaks out on shamateurism. Sports Illus 34:34-5 My 10 '71
  See also
  Amateur athletic union of the United States
  Sports—Economic aspects
AMATUZIO, Anna
  Creative writing; poem. Seventeen 29:62 S '70
AMAUROTIC family idiocy
  Genetics for the community; Tay-Sachs disease and Jews in the Baltimore-Washington area. il Time 98:54 S 13 '71
  Jewish disease; Tay-Sachs disease. il por Newsweek 77:39 My 31 '71
  Tay-Sachs disease: prenatal diagnosis. J. S. O'Brien and others. bibliog il Science 172: 61-4 Ap 2 '71
AMAYA, Mario
  International art critics' conference. il Art in Am 59:130-1 Ja '71
  Toronto. il Art in Am 59:122-3 My; 102-5 S '71
  Trays by ten artists. il Art in Am 59:48-57 Ja '71
AMAZONAS hovercraft expedition. See Scientific expeditions
AMBASSADORS
  Chinese ambassador; Huang arrives in Canada. il por Newsweek 78:15 Ag 2 '71
  Mao's new America watcher; Communist China's ambassador to Canada. por Time 97:27 Je 21 '71
  Our man in Athens. il por Newsweek 77:48+ My 3 '71
  Sudden celebrities; Peking's ambassador to Canada. il por Time 98:43 O 18 '71
  Undiplomatic behavior; J. G. Hurd in South Africa. il por Newsweek 78:35 Jl 26 '71
  See also
  Negro ambassadors
  United States—Diplomatic and consular service
AMBASSADORS wives
  See also
  Cromer, E. H. B.
AMBER, Betty K.
  Father to daughter; story. Good H 172:94-5 Je '71
AMBERG, William
  Alone to Hawaii. il pors Yachting 130:50-1+ S '71
AMBROSE, Myles J.
  Gains in the war against drug smugglers; interview. il por U S News 70:60-2+ Je 21 '71
AMBROSINO, Lillian
  Runaways. il Todays Ed 60:26-8 D '71
AMBULANCE helicopters. See Helicopters, Ambulance
AMBULANCES
  Rescue squad; Sun City Center, Fla. R. G. King. il Har Yrs 11:28-9 N '71
AMCHITKA ISLAND
  From Milrow to Cannikin; Amchitka tests. il Sci N 99:350 My 22 '71
AMCO industries, inc.
  Swartzberg's misfortune. G. R. Rosen. por Duns 98:74 S '71
AMEBAS
  Direct test of the positive pressure gradient theory of pseudopod extension and retraction in amoebae. R. D. Allen and others. bibliog il Science 174:1237-40 D 17 '71
  Infectious agent from a free-living soil amoeba, naegleria gruberi. T. H. Dunnebacke and F. L. Schuster. bibliog il Science 174:516-18 O 29 '71
AMELANCHIER arborea. See Serviceberries (tree)
AMEND, Mary W. and others
  Literature program for students. Engl J 60: 65-9 Ja '71
AMENDMENTS to the Constitution. See United States—Constitution—Amendments
AMERICA
  Our America. G. de Zendegui. il Américas 22: S1-48 N '70
  See also
  Latin America
  United States

Antiquities
  See also
  Paleo-Indians

Discovery and exploration
  Before Columbus, by C. H. Gordon. Review Sat R 54:52+ S 25 '71. G. F. Ekholm
  Did blacks beat whites to America? African civilization brought to America before Columbus. Negro Hist Bul 34:117 My '71
  Epic of the New World; symposium, ed. by G. de Zéndegui. il Américas 23:S1-16 O '71

AMERICA—Discovery and exploration—*Cont.*
European discovery of America, by S. E.
Morison. Review
Sat R 54:61-2 S 4 '71. J. Lear
Time 97:77 Ap 19 '71. M. Maddocks
Land hol H. Martinez-Montero. il Américas
23:S11-13 O '71
Old man of the western sea; Juan de Fuca.
K. C. Tessendorf. il Américas 23:25-32 S
'71
Semites first in America? B. Ford. il Sci
Digest 71:43-8+ Ja '72
Trial of Coronado. W. J. Buchanan. il Amér-
icas 23:28-38 Ja '71
See also
Kensington rune stone

AMERICA (periodical)
Of many things; retirement of B. L. Masse.
D. R. Campion. America 125:inside cover
Jl 24 '71; Discussion 125:133 S 11 '71
Thoughts on leaving the America staff. B. L.
Masse. America 125:25 Jl 24 '71

AMERICAN academy of arts and letters
Holding the fort on Audubon Terrace. M.
Cowley. il Sat R 54:17+ Ap 3 '71

AMERICAN airlines
American advances STOL studies. Aviation
W 94:24 Mr 29 '71
American expects early Caribbean profit. W.
H. Gregory. Aviation W 94:29 Mr 15 '71
American, National drop 13 DC-10 transport
options. Aviation W 94:21 My 10 '71
American plans new 707 interior. Aviation W
95:24 Ag 16 '71
American reorganization: same faces, new
jobs. Aviation W 74:25 Je 21 '71
American, TWA ponder stock offerings as
market declines. W. H. Gregory. Aviation
W 94:29 Je 28 '71
American-Western merger opposed. L. Doty.
Aviation W 96:20 Ja 3 '72
Competition stiffens in Caribbean. J. P.
Woolsey. Aviation W 95:23-4 O 4 '71
DC-10 bows, bringing lots more seats to fill.
il Bsns W p94-7 Ag 14 '71
DC-10 demonstrates scheduling versatility;
with tables. H. D. Watkins. il Aviation W
96:26-30 Ja 3 '72
DC-10 meeting operational goals. H. D. Wat-
kins. il Aviation W 95:23-6 D 13 '71
DC-10s delivered to United, American. il Avi-
ation W 95:26 Ag 2 '71
Plane that broke the profit barrier; Douglas
DC-3. D. J. Lloyd-Jones. il por Nations
Bsns 59:44-5 Ja '71
Western holders favor merger. Aviation W 94:
27 Mr 29 '71

AMERICAN airlines-Western air lines merger.
See Airlines—Consolidations and mergers

AMERICAN anthropological association
Behavioral sciences; summary of papers. Sci
N 100:392 D 11 '71
Camelot revisited; study of ethical aspects of
assistance to counterinsurgency efforts. Sci
Am 224:45-6+ My '71
Ethics and anthropology. Sci Am 226:47 Ja
'72

AMERICAN architecture. See Architecture,
American

AMERICAN art. See Art, American

AMERICAN artists. See Artists, American

AMERICAN association for the advancement
of science
AAAS:
Facing the questions of what it should be
and do. P. M. Boffey. Science 172:453-
6+ Ap 30 '71
Is order of magnitude expansion a reasonable goal? P. M. Boffey. Science 172:
656-8 My 14 '71
What it is and what it tries to do. P. M.
Boffey. Science 172:542-7 My 7 '71
AAAS council resolutions. F. B. Wood. Science 173:769 Ag 27 '71
AAAS names five to freedom panel. R. Gillette. Science 173:129 Jl 9 '71
AAAS officers, committees, and representa-
tives for 1971. Science 171:712-16 F 19 '71
Defoliation in Chicago: AAAS report on military use of defoliants in Vietnam. Sci Am
224:44 F '71
General scientific association; a bridge to so-
ciety at large; adaptation of address, March
22, 1971. W. Bevan. Science 172:349-52 Ap 23
'71
Governance of the association. L. M. Rieser.
Science 171:755 F 26 '71
Herbicides in Vietnam: AAAS study finds
widespread devastation. P. M. Boffey. il
Science 171:43-7 Ja 8 '71
Herbicides in Vietnam: violating the laws,
starving our allies. C.-G. McDaniel. Chr
Cent 88:195-7 F 10 '71

On the use and misuse of science. A. W.
Galston. Yale R 60:458-63 Spr '71; Same
with title Education of a scientific in-
nocent. Natur Hist 80:16-18+ Je '71
Protecting the scientist. Sci N 100:61 Jl 24 '71
Starvation as a policy; report of the Science-
herbicide assessment commission. P. R.
Ehrlich and J. P. Holdren. Sat R 54:91 D
4 '71
Tour of Vietnam. T. Aaronson. bibliog il
Environ 13:34-43 Mr '71

Meetings
AAAS; highlights of some papers. Sci N
101:26 Ja 8 '72
AAAS meeting in Mexico City. A. Spilhaus.
Science 174:549 N 5 '71
Brief prospectus of the 1971 AAAS annual
meeting; with editorial comment. W. G.
Berl. Science 174:777, 847-56 N 19 '71
Confusion and confrontation. il Sci N 101:
5-6 Ja 1 '72
New path for the scientists. il Bsns W p42-3
Ja 1 '72
Philadelphia story; 138th annual meeting.
Time 99:45 Ja 10 '72
Searching for goals, examining ethics. Sci N
101:21-3 Ja 8 '72

Meetings, 1970
AAAS convention: radicals harass the establishment. P. M. Boffey. Science 171:47-9 Ja 8
'71
AAAS council meeting, 1970. W. Bevan. il Science 171:709-11 F 19 '71
Chicago meeting. P. H. Abelson. Science 171:
239 Ja 22 '71
Debacle disruptions, demagogues; letters. Science 171:230 Ja 22 '71
Looking backward: Chicago AAAS annual
meeting. W. G. Berl. Science 171:716-17 F 19
'71

AMERICAN association of advertising agencies
Making of a profession? L. L. L. Golden. Sat
R 54:74 O 9 '71

AMERICAN association of evangelical students
What evangelical students think. R. Chandler. Chr Today 15:38+ Ap 23 '71

AMERICAN association of homes for the aging
AAHA holds ninth annual conference plus
training program for administrators. il Aging
195:7 Ja '71

AMERICAN association of library schools. See
Association of American library schools

AMERICAN association of nurserymen
Asia in Alabama and a garden in the sky;
awards. il Nations Bsns 59:63 D '71

AMERICAN association of pastoral counselors
Counseling confab explores counterculture,
women's liberation and homosexuality. C. J.
Edson. Chr Cent 88:1473-4 D 15 '71

AMERICAN association of physics teachers
APS-AAPT meet in New York. M. S. Rothenberg. il Phys Today 24:25+ Ja '71
Employment debated at meeting. il Phys Today 24:65-6 Ap '71

AMERICAN association of school adminis-
trators
AASA's nonacademic academy. L. L. Gray.
Am Ed 7:21-4 O '71
Schoolman of the hour; P. D. Salmon selected
by AASA. por Newsweek 77:80 My 31 '71

AMERICAN association of school librarians
AASL: search for a stand. E. Geller. il Li-
brary J 96:2832-7 S 15 '71
More on AASL; letter to the editor. D. Burns.
Library J 96:671 F 15 '71
On minority materials: school librarians move.
R. H. Smith. Pub W 199:61 F 8 '71
Previews: AASL, CSD, YASD. E. Geller and
P. Schuman. Library J 96:2460 Ag '71
Shadow and substance; ALA midwinter, Jan-
uary 16-22. P. Schuman. il Library J 96:
1091-5 Mr 15 '71

AMERICAN association of state colleges and
universities
AASCU statement on academic responsibil-
ity. Sch & Soc 99:204 Ap '71
Responsible professors. T. H. Clancy; reply.
B. F. Reilly. America 124:133 F 13 '71

AMERICAN association of university presses.
See Association of American university
presses

AMERICAN association of university professors
Faculty collective bargaining at the City
university of New York. S. Jacobson. Sch
& Soc 99:346-9 O '71
Newer concepts of academic freedom. W. W.
Brickman. Sch & Soc 99:72-3 F '71
Responsible professors. T. H. Clancy; reply.
B. F. Reilly. America 124:133 F 13 '71

AMERICAN civil liberties union
For liberty and equality. N. Hill. Cur 129:32-5 My '71
To overcome discrimination now. S. Ackley. Cur 129:35-8 My '71
AMERICAN coins. See Coins
AMERICAN college theater festival. See Drama festivals
AMERICAN Communist party. See Communist party (United States)
AMERICAN conservatism. See Conservatism
AMERICAN cookery. See Cookery, American
AMERICAN correspondents. See Foreign correspondents
AMERICAN council of Christian churches
ACCC: new leaders, new goals. R. Chandler. Chr Today 16:39-40+ N 19 '71
McIntire's mélange. E. E. Plowman. Chr Today 15:36 My 7 '71
AMERICAN council on education
ACE: rating of graduate programs shows little change in status quo. J. Walsh. Science 171:49-50 Ja 8 '71
Evaluation of graduate school programs; report. Sch & Soc 99:264-5 Sum '71
AMERICAN crafts council
America house: an appreciation; with editorial comment. H. Cohen. Craft Horiz 31:11+ Ap '71
AMERICAN cyanamid company
Cyanamid crashes the glamour markets. il Bsns W p74-5 S 4 '71
Synergetic Cyanamid. il Forbes 107:46 Ap 1 '71
See also
Lederle laboratories
AMERICAN dance camp. See Dance camps
AMERICAN dance season. See Dance festivals
AMERICAN dancing. See Dancing
AMERICAN design. See Design
AMERICAN distilling company
Light touch. R. Levy. Duns 97:70 Mr '71
AMERICAN documentation institute. See American society for information science
AMERICAN eagles. See Eagles
AMERICAN economic assistance. See Economic assistance, American
AMERICAN economic association
Convention that went Galbraithian. il por Bsns W p 16-17 Ja 1 '72
AMERICAN educational publishers institute. See Association of American publishers
AMERICAN express company
In quest of Utopia. H. L. Clark. il pors Nations Bsns 59:48-9 Ja '71
AMERICAN farm bureau federation
Farm bureau steps up environmental crusade. D. Seim. Farm J 95:37 My '71
AMERICAN federation of labor and Congress of industrial organizations
Angry unions aim for a deal with Nixon. il por Bsns W p52-5+ Ag 28 '71
Battle lines drawn for '72 election; union, White House showdown. il por U S News 71:11-13 D 6 '71
Battle of Bal Harbour. Time 98:16 D 6 '71
Being Meany to Nixon. J. Hill. Commonweal 95:268-9 D 17 '71
Controls that labor would buy. Bsns W p48+ S 11 '71
George Meany; fight over the freeze; with interview with G. Meany. il pors Newsweek 78:46+ S 6 '71
Hints at wage controls: unions prepare to fight back. il U S News 70:60-2 Mr 1 '71
If you freeze wages, freeze everything. Bsns W p29 Ag 14 '71
Jockeying for Meany's job begins. il por Bsns W p64+ D 18 '71
Labor can make or break the stabilization program. A. M. Louis. il Fortune 84:140-3+ N '71
Labor goes along, for now. Time 98:24 O 25 '71
Labor's disturbing challenge: President Nixon and G. Meany as speakers at AFL-CIO convention. pors Time 98:29 N 29 '71
Living with the Pay board. strategy of big unions. il U S News 71:59-60 N 29 '71
Mr Inside at the AFL-CIO; J. L. Kirkland. por Newsweek 78:50 S 6 '71
Mr Nixon knows what he can do. il pors Newsweek 78:16-18 N 29 '71
Nix on Nixon. il Newsweek 78:60 Ag 23 '71
Nixon and labor widen the breach. por Bsns W p 18-19 N 27 '71
Rediscovering American labor; intellectuals and labor. P. Kemble. Commentary 51:45-52 Ap '71; Reply with rejoinder. H. A. Gray. 52:22 Ag '71
Show biz in Miami; AFL-CIO convention. Nation 213:578-9 D 6 '71

Unions approach showdown: what to do about Pay board; looking ahead to the AFL-CIO convention. il U S News 71:85-6 N 22 '71
Unions demand more jobs. il Bsns W p63-4 Jl 17 '71
What labor wants. Nations Bsns 59:24-6 Mr '71
United farm workers organizing committee
Chavez strikes again; suit against the Defense department. il por Newsweek 77:64+ Ja 25 '71
Farm workers and city unions. R. P. Gibbons. New Repub 165:12-13 Jl 24 '71; Reply with rejoinder. G. Grant. 165:32-3 S 11 '71
Lettuce boycott reaches New York; first of lawsuits against the Pentagon. T. J. O'Connell. America 124:148-9 F 13 '71
Salad days at the Pentagon. J. Drake and G. Gersmehl. Commonweal 93:485-6 F 19 '71
To die standing: Cesar Chavez and the Chicanos. J. G. Dunne. por Atlan 227:33-45 Je '71; Reply with rejoinder. J. Angell. 228:36 S '71
Why Chavez spurns the Labor act. R. B. Taylor. il Nation 212:454-6 Ap 12 '71
AMERICAN federation of state, county and municipal employees
Taking the politics out of the paycheck. Bsns W p22 My 22 '71
AMERICAN federation of television and radio artists
Progress report: Buckley vs. AFTRA. W. F. Buckley, jr. Nat R 23:330 Mr 23 '71
William F. Buckley, jr. talks about compulsory unionism; interview. W. F. Buckley, jr. pors Nations Bsns 59:32-4+ Je '71
AMERICAN festival orchestra. See Orchestras
AMERICAN fiction
See also
Best sellers
AMERICAN film institute
Treasure of L'enfant plaza. A. Knight. il Sat R 54:40-1 Jl 31 '71
Unloved one. E. Callenbach. Film Q 24:42-54 Sum '71
AMERICAN flag. See Flags—United States
AMERICAN folk music. See Folk music, American
AMERICAN folk songs. See Folk songs, American
AMERICAN football league
Goodby to the alka-seltzer and aspirin bowl; NFL the prouder. T. Maule. Sports Illus 34:50-1 F 1 '71
AMERICAN forestry association
AFA annual meeting awards. il pors Am For 77:6-7 D '71
AFA Distinguished service award to Henry Clepper. il por Am For 77:39 Ja '71
AFA to move. il Am For 77:12-13 My '71
Amendments to the bylaws. Am For 77:3 Je '71
Man called Pink: citizen of the year; adaptation of address, February 25, 1971. H. Clepper. por Am For 77:3+ My '71
Report from Atlanta. il Am For 77:36-8+ Ja '71
See also
Trail riders of the wilderness
AMERICAN forests (periodical)
Timber mining: accusation or prospect? R. W. Behan. il Am For 77:4-6+ N '71
AMERICAN freedom from hunger foundation
Helping foot; walks for development. il Sr Schol 98:17 Mr 1 '71
Youth, dollars, and development; walks for development of the Young world development. R. R. Nathan. Sat R 54:24-5+ My 1 '71
AMERICAN Friends service committee
On doing good. by G. Jonas. Review New Repub 164:25-6 My 15 '71. **P. Caws**
Reporter at large. G. Jonas. New Yorker 47:92+ Mr 13; 99-104+ Mr 20 '71
AMERICAN furniture. See Furniture, American
AMERICAN geophysical union
Earth sciences; report of meeting. Sci N 99:274 Ap 24 '71
AMERICAN glass. See Glassware
AMERICAN guild of musical artists
Report: Opera house. F. Merkling. Opera N 35:35 Ap 17 '71
AMERICAN heritage (periodical)
Letter from the editor. O. Jensen. il Am Heritage 22:2 Ag '71
AMERICAN heritage dictionary of the English language. See English language—Dictionaries
AMERICAN historians. See Historians, American

AMERICAN historical association
American historical association in 1970; adaptation of address, December 28, 1970. R. R. Palmer. Am Hist R 76:1-15 F '71
Roche paper. Newsweek 77:20 Ja 18 '71
AMERICAN homeowners association
How to get a repairman. Newsweek 77:89-90 Je 7 '71
R for homeowners. McCalls 98:44 Mr '71
AMERICAN hospital supply corporation
Doing it the hard way. il Forbes 107:22-3 Je 1 '71
AMERICAN house decoration. See House decoration, American
AMERICAN humor. See Humor, American
AMERICAN institute of architects
A.I.A. convention report; with editorial comment. il Arch Rec 150:9-10, 35-8+ Ag '71
A.I.A. starts debating goals for architecture, and the America. W. F. Wagner, jr. Arch Rec 150:9-10 Jl '71
Architects and social responsibility: good beginning, and a big boost. W. F. Wagner, jr. Arch Rec 149:9 F '71
More on architects and social responsibility. J. Morgan. Arch Rec 149:10 Ap '71
Some random thoughts on the eve of the convention. W. F. Wagner, jr. Arch Rec 149:9-10 Je '71
Student and the practitioner: communication, accomplishment; Association of student chapters. W. F. Wagner, jr. Arch Rec 149:9 My '71
AMERICAN institute of biological sciences
Biological sciences; summaries of papers. Sci N 100:176 S 11 '71
AMERICAN institute of certified public accountants
It's not material! il Forbes 107:37-8 Ap 15 '71
Methodical man. por Forbes 107:54 Mr 15 '71
Why accountants need to tell a fuller story. il Bsns W p86-7 F 6 '71
AMERICAN institute of graphic arts childrens book show. See Book exhibits
AMERICAN institute of graphic arts fifty books exhibit. See Book exhibits
AMERICAN institute of physics
AIP annual report: 1970. il Phys Today 24:38-42+ Je '71
Current physics information. H. W. Koch. bibliog il Science 174:918-22 N 26 '71
Keeping up with what's going on in physics; AIP's Current physics information program; with editorial comment. A. Herschman. bibliog il Phys Today 24:23-9, 80 N '71

History
AIP 40 years. il Phys Today 24:29-37 Je '71
AMERICAN institute of steel construction
Municipal buildings award winners. il Am City 86:35 Ap '71
AMERICAN Irish. See Irish Americans
AMERICAN iron and steel institute
Steel's past ills linger tenaciously. il Bsns W p20 My 29 '71
AMERICAN legion
U.S. journal: Manhattan and Atchison, Kan; the Maes family. C. Trillin. New Yorker 47:90-5 Je 12 '71
AMERICAN liberalism. See Liberalism
AMERICAN libraries (periodical)
Administrative? Council vote to distribute the organizational manual to all members? letter to the editor. Am Lib 2:683-4 Jl '71
Executive board passes new policy statements for American libraries. Am Lib 2:555 Je '71
AMERICAN library association
ALA award winners; the 90th annual conference at Dallas. il Am Lib 2:851-8 S '71
ALA awards. il Wilson Lib Bul 46:15 S '71
ALA awards and scholarships. Library J 96:3802 N 15 '71
ALA awards, citations, scholarships, and grants for 1971. R. F. Delzell and J. F. Krug. Am Lib 2:1075-80 N '71
ALA ExBoard nixes minority recruiter. W. R. Eshelman. Wilson Lib Bul 46:305+ D '71
ALA Executive Board nominees state positions. Wilson Lib Bul 46:394 Ja '72
ALA executive board: thy name is action. W. R. Eshelman. Wilson Lib Bul 45:909+ Je '71
ALA nominating committee report for 1972. il Am Lib 2:1199-203 D '71
ALA officers and awards. Library J 96:2820 S 15 '71
ALA reorganization: questions. M. Boaz. Am Lib 2:454-5 My '71

ALA seeks broad support on copyright: Williams & Wilkins case; excerpts from address, June 22, 1971, ed. by G. Krettek and E. D. Cooke. W. D. North. Am Lib 2:1182-5 D '71
AV task force survey report. C. W. Stone; discussion. Am Lib 1:44-5; 2:149-50 Ja '70, F '71
Administrative? Council vote to distribute the organizational manual to all members? letter to the editor. Am Lib 2:683-4 Jl '71
Arizona LA annual convention, March 1971. D. Snyder. Am Lib 2:564 Je '71
Awards and citations ALA, 1971. il Library J 96:2458-9 Ag '71
Barred from LC, ALA team interviews underground; investigating racism charges. Wilson Lib Bul 46:389 Ja '72
Editor's choice: Program of action. J. G. Burke. Am Lib 2:457 My '71
Future is up to you; address, June 25, 1971. K. Doms. por Am Lib 2:987-90 O '71
Hearing for Doiron. J. Berry. Library J 96:3931 D 1 '71
Media fragments and ALA. A. B. Martin. il Library J 96:1339 Ap 15 '71
New ALA officers. il Library J 96:2453 Ag '71
New program proposed for council adoption. Am Lib 2:435 My '71
Overdue: a student to Dallas speaks out on ALA, with editorial comment. D. R. Dowell. il Wilson Lib Bul 46:27, 79-80 S '71
Returns of the 1971 ALA election. Am Lib 2:752-4 Jl '71
Spring meeting hops: ALA executive board. il Am Lib 2:555-7 Je '71
Statement of policy regarding gifts and bequests to libraries; reprint. Am Lib 2:721 Jl '71
Students to Dallas; symposium. Library J 96:2454-7 Ag '71
See also
American association of school librarians

Meetings
First responsibility; letter to the editor. M. Boaz. Am Lib 2:1035 N '71

Anecdotes, facetiae, satire, etc.
Hooper heads for Dallas. K. Nyren. il Library J 96:1337 Ap 15 '71
Hooper in Dallas. K. Nyren. Library J 96:1686 My 15; 2059 Je 15 '71
Meeting. R. B. Moses. Am Lib 2:244-5 Mr '71
Midwinter night's bummer dream. Am Lib 2:23 Ja '71

Meetings, 1971
ALA Dallas conference addenda. il Am Lib 2:991-8 O '71
ALA midwinter: post-analytic depression. A. Plotnik and W. R. Eshelman. il Wilson Lib Bul 45:622-4+ Mr '71
ALA 1971: membership and budgetary problems/response to social responsibilities. Pub W 200:26-8 S 6 '71
ALA 1971: notes & comments. il Wilson Lib Bul 46:8-28 S '71
ALA: the core of power; annual conference. E. Geller. il Library J 96:2825-31 S 15 '71
Annual conference highlights. il Am Lib 2:861-75 S '71
Come together: alternative in Dallas. il Library J 96:1932-3 Je 1 '71
Conference roundup; symposium. Library J 96:2431-61+ Ag '71
Conference wrap-up. Am Lib 2:557-8 Je '71
Conservative caucus planned for ALA-Dallas. Library J 96:1311 Ap 15 '71
Council cop-out: moods of ALA mid-winter. J. Berry; S. Havens. il Library J 96:905, 918-31 Mr 15 '71
Going to Texas early? Wilson Lib Bul 45:831 My '71
Headin' for the last roundup; Los Angeles midwinter, January 18-22, 1971. G. R. Shields and others. il Am Lib 2:243-73 Mr '71
Highlights of ALA conference, response to a restive world. Library J 96:1751 My 15 '71
Intellectual freedom show: on prime time in Dallas. Library J 96:1901+ Je 1 '71
1971 ALA conference, Dallas, June 20-26; announcement. Am Lib 2:112-16 Ja '71
1000 microphones in Dallas; council meetings. R. Parsons; H. Renthal. Am Lib 2:341-2 Ap '71; Reply. E. Yates. 2:570-1 Je '71
Periscope on Dallas. K. Nyren. il Library J 96:1927-32 Je 1 '71
Response to a restive world; conference program. il Am Lib 2:505-21 My '71

AMERICAN library association—Meetings, 1971
—*Continued*
Shadow and substance; ALA midwinter, January 16–22. P. Schuman. il Library J 96:1091–5 Mr 15 '71
Toward a two-party system for ALA council? W. R. Eshelman. Wilson Lib Bul 45:814 My '71
Up the down concourse; Dallas 1971. il Am Lib 2:797–835 S '71

Meetings, 1972
1972 ALA midwinter meeting. il Am Lib 2:1204–5 D '71
1972 midwinter meeting Chicago, Palmer House, January 23–29. Am Lib 2:888–9 S '71

Activities committee on new directions for ALA
ACONDA-ANACONDA joint report. Am Lib 2:523–5 My '71
ACONDA revised recommendations on democratization and reorganization; report for midwinter meeting, January 1971. il Am Lib 2:81–91 Ja '71
ACONDA: worth its weight? ALA midwinter. G. R. Shields and others. il Am Lib 2:253–6+ Mr '71
ALA executive board accepts ACONDA report. Library J 96:1914 Je 1 '71
ALA midwinter: stupor bowl. W. R. Eshelman. il Wilson Lib Bul 45:628+ Mr '71
Council cop-out; moods of ALA mid-winter. J. Berry. il Library J 96:918–24 Mr 15 '71
Saving the summer frolic. J. Berry, 3d. Library J 96:1899 Je 1 '71
Viewpoint. A. B. Martin. il Library J 96:609 F 15 '71

Anecdotes, facetiae, satire, etc.
CANACONDA? R. Moses. por Library J 96:915–17 Mr 15 '71

Ad hoc council committee on ACONDA
ACONDA-ANACONDA joint report. Am Lib 2:523–5 My '71
ALA executive board accepts ACONDA report. Library J 96:1914 Je 1 '71
ANACONDA gets there; ALA midwinter. G. R. Shields and others. il Am Lib 2:256–9+ Mr '71
Recommendations from ANACONDA; report for midwinter meeting, January 1971. il Am Lib 2:92–6 Ja '71
Saving the summer frolic. J. Berry, 3d. Library J 96:1899 Je 1 '71

Adult services division
1970 notable books list released by ALA. Library J 96:774 Mr 1 '71; Same. Am Lib 2:401–2 Ap '71
Notable books, 1944–1969. E. Eatenson. Am Lib 2:105–9 Ja '71; Reply. M. L. Reynolds. 2:347–8 Ap '71
Notable nominations (cont) Am Lib 2:124, 645, 762, 897, 1010, 1109, 1225 Ja, Je-D '71
Public library service to the aging; ASD special report. G. M. Casey. il Am Lib 2:999–1004 O '71
RSD and ASD: getting it all together. M. J. Lynch. bibliog Am Lib 2:501–3 My '71

Anecdotes, facetiae, satire, etc.
Editor's choice. G. R. Shields. Am Lib 2:581 Je '71

Children's services division
ALA lists 1970's notable children's books. il Pub W 199:58 Ag 12 '71; Same. Am Lib 2:404–6 Ap '71; Library J 96:1764 My 15 '71
Getting with it; 1971 ALA conference. P. Schuman. il Library J 96:2838–41 S 15 '71
Previews: AASL, CSD, YASD. E. Geller and P. Schuman. Library J 96:2460 Ag '71

Constitution
ALA constitution and bylaws. Am Lib 2:1093–101 N '71

Constitution and bylaws committee
Constitution and bylaws committee report. Am Lib 2:529–30 My '71

Council
ALA midwinter: council capers. W. R. Eshelman. il Wilson Lib Bul 45:630+ Mr '71
ALA 1971: the rise and demise of the Council. W. R. Eshelman. il Wilson Lib Bul 46:18–20 S '71
Council; ALA midwinter. G. R. Shields and others. il Am Lib 2:260–71 Mr '71
Council cop-out; moods of ALA mid-winter. J. Berry. il Library J 96:918–24 Mr 15 '71
Improving council effectiveness. I. B. Moon. Am Lib 2:455 My '71

1000 microphones in Dallas. R. Parsons; H. Renthal. Am Lib 2:341–2 Ap '71; Reply. E. Yates. 2:570–1 Je '71
Resolutions adopted by ALA council. Am Lib 2:270–1 Mr '71
Resolutions adopted by ALA membership and council. Am Lib 2:257 Mr '71
Time to say no; statement, June 1971. P. Sullivan. Am Lib 2:802–3 S '71
Toward a two-party system for ALA council? W. R. Eshelman. Wilson Lib Bul 45:814 My '71
Up the down concourse; Dallas 1971. il Am Lib 2:809–22 S '71

Finance
ALA 1971: mandates unmanned. W. R. Eshelman. il Wilson Lib Bul 46:21–4 S '71
ALA treasurer's report. Am Lib 2:1206–12 D '71
Budget requests and recommendations. D. H. Clift. Am Lib 2:605–7 Je '71
Executive session board: fall meeting; with report by L. Gaertner. il Am Lib 2:1127–9 D '71
John Carter's budget appeal to ALA membership; statement, June 1971. J. Carter. por Library J 96:2436 Ag '71
1971–72 budget. L. J. Gaertner. Am Lib 2:837–9 S '71

Intellectual freedom committee
Curious counsels. E. Geller. Library J 96:2811 S 15 '71; Discussion. 96:4129–32 D 15 '71
Intellectual freedom; ALA midwinter. G. R. Shields and others. il Am Lib 2:247–50 Mr '71
Intellectual freedom and the jurisdictional jungle; ALA midwinter and intellectual freedom committee. S. Havens. Library J 96:925–9 Mr 15 '71
Intellectual freedom at Dallas. S. Havens. il Library J 96:2447–9 Ag '71
Intellectual freedom committee. J. F. Krug and J. A. Harvey. Am Lib 2:352 Ap '71
Intellectual freedom show: on prime time in Dallas. Library J 96:1901+ Je 1 '71
Report of the Intellectual freedom committee to council, Dallas, June 25, 1971; ed. by J. F. Krug and J. A. Harvey. D. K. Berninghausen. Am Lib 2:891–2 S '71
Statement on the IFC report. E. J. Josey. por Library J 96:2828–31 S 15 '71

Library administration division
Tenure investigation: library adminstration division's report concerning nonrenewal of contracts of five librarians, University of Missouri library; discussion. Am Lib 2:150–2 F '71

Library technology program
LTP news. F. Carhart. Am Lib 2:178 F '71

Mediation, arbitration and inquiry, Staff committee on
Staff committee on mediation, arbitration and inquiry. Am Lib 2:1069 N '71

Membership
ALA membership slides 6,471. W. R. Eshelman. Wilson Lib Bul 45:525 F '71
ALA midwinter: business and the brotherhood. W. R. Eshelman. il Wilson Lib Bul 45:627–8 Mr '71
ALA 1971: the membership style. A. Plotnik. il Wilson Lib Bul 46:10–14+ S '71
ALA salary survey: personal members. il Am Lib 2:409–17 Ap '71
Editor's choice: our very own design for a dues scale. Am Lib 2:935 O '71
Librarian or citizen? G. Dunbar. por Library J 97:42–3 Ja 1 '72
Membership; ALA midwinter. G. R. Shields and others. Am Lib 2:250–2+ Mr '71
Membership in ALA; letter to the editor. D. Heron. Am Lib 2:925 O '71
1970 ALA membership statistics. Am Lib 2:418–19 Ap '71
Professionalism in ALA; letter to the editor. J. T. Thomas. Am Lib 2:1139 D '71
Resolutions adopted by ALA membership and council. Am Lib 2:257 Mr '71
Shadows of the future; Dallas meeting. J. Berry and K. Nyren. il Library J 96:2431–46 Ag '71
Time to say no; statement, June 1971. P. Sullivan. Am Lib 2:802–3 S '71
Up the down concourse; Dallas 1971. il Am Lib 2:804–9 S '71

Notable books council
See American library association—Adult services division

AMERICAN library association—*Continued*

Office for intellectual freedom
Curious counsels. E. Geller. Library J 96:2811 S 15 '71; Discussion. 96:4129-32 D 15 '71
Defending the defenders of intellectual freedom; ed. by J. F. Krug and J. A. Harvey. D. Berninghausen. bibliog Am Lib 2:18-21 Ja '71
James A. Harvey, librarian for intellectual freedom. il pors Wilson Lib Bul 45:740-1 Ap '71
Office for intellectual freedom. J. F. Krug and J. A. Harvey. Am Lib 2:352-3 Ap '71
Opening those closed shelves: advisory statement concerning restricted circulation of library materials. J. F. Krug and J. A. Harvey. Am Lib 2:755 Jl '71; Reply with rejoinder. E. J. Gaines. 2:923-4 O '71

Program evaluation and support, Committee on
Coping with COPES on LSD; services to disadvantaged at ALA meeting. E. Geller. il Library J 96:2825-9 S 15 '71
NJLA cuts ALA support: COPES' tight budget cited. Library J 96:3934-5 D 1 '71
1971-72 budget. L. J. Gaertner. Am Lib 2:837-9 S '71
Shadows of the future; Dallas meeting. J. Berry and K. Nyren. il Library J 96:2431-5 Ag '71

Publishing department
Publishing board meets. Am Lib 2:1129-30 D '71
See also
Choice (periodical)

Reference services division
Hypothetic dialogues; RSD preconference. B. Geller. Library J 96:2450-1 Ag '71
RSD and ASD: getting it all together. M. J. Lynch. bibliog Am Lib 2:501-3 My '71

Social responsibilities round table
ALA/SRRT goes to Washington; meeting of the Acton council. Wilson Lib Bul 46:304-5 D '71
Bay area SRRT's sensitive survey. W. R. Eshelman. Wilson Lib Bul 46:395-6 Ja '72
Come together: alternative in Dallas. il Library J 96:1932-3 Je 1 '71
East coast SRRT conclave sets new action targets. Library J 96:2029 Je 15 '71
For the socially responsible only: the names and addresses of 1971-72 task force coordinators. Wilson Lib Bul 46:107 S '71
Gay is: SRRT Task force on gay liberation at ALA conference. il Wilson Lib Bul 46:17 S '71
Putting the cart before the blecch: meeting on Social effectiveness. A. Plotnik. Wilson Lib Bul 45:909 Je '71
SRRT $200 for Angela Davis approved by ALA exec board. Library J 96:1913 Je 1 '71
Social responsibilities: what it's all about. B. DeJohn. bibliog il Am Lib 2:300-2 Mr '71
Social responsibility: the neighborhood alternative. J. Berry. Library J 96:929-30 Mr 15 '71

Young adult services division
Getting with it; 1971 ALA conference. P. Schuman. il Library J 96:2838-41 S 15 '71
Previews: AASL, CSD, YASD. E. Geller and P. Schuman. Library J 96:2460 Ag '71
34 choice teen books announced by ALA. Library J 96:1764 My 15 '71

AMERICAN light whiskey. See Whiskey
AMERICAN lions. See Pumas
AMERICAN literature
See also
American poetry
Mexican American literature
Negro literature
Periodicals—United States

Study and teaching
From puritans to panthers. J. E. Smith, jr. Clear House 46:125-6 O '71
Ray Bradbury's Dandelion wine: themes, sources, and style. M. E. Mengeling. bibliog f Engl J 60:877-87 O '71
Yankee imperialist in King Arthur's court. J. Smith. Commonweal 95:334-5 Ja 7 '72
See also
Short story—Study and teaching
AMERICAN Lutheran church. See Lutheran church in the United States

AMERICAN machine and foundry company. See AMF, inc.
AMERICAN management association
First on the spot; AMA Meeting on doing business with red China. New Yorker 47:47-8 N 13 '71
AMERICAN medical association
Decline of an American institution? AMA convention. Sci N 100:6 Jl 3 '71
TRB from Washington. New Repub 164:4 Mr 27 '71
Thunder in the AMA. il por Newsweek 78:52-3 Jl 5 '71
AMERICAN merchant marine. See Merchant marine—United States
AMERICAN meteorological society
Educational film program of the American meteorological society; with list of films. M. Toyli and J. Gerhardt. Weatherwise 24:228-9+ O '71
AMERICAN military assistance. See Military assistance, American
AMERICAN mime theatre
American mime theatre, Library & museum of the performing arts, NYC. D. Hering. Dance Mag 45:90 N '71
American mime theatre, New York Shakespeare public theatre. L. Pastore. Dance Mag 45:82 D '71
AMERICAN minorities. See Minorities
AMERICAN motors corporation
American flits ahead. Time 98:78+ N 29 '71
American motors' road looks bumpier. Bsns W p23 Ap 24 '71
New AMC warranty. Newsweek 78:65 Ag 23 '71
UAW agrees to settle for less. Bsns W p34 Ap 17 '71
AMERICAN museum of natural history, New York
Museum auction. New Yorker 47:46-7 D 4 '71
New Hall. New Yorker 47:32-3 Ap 10 '71
Our new Hall of the Pacific: 45 years in the making. M. Mead. il Redbook 137:54+ My '71
Peoples of the Pacific; ed. by M. Mead and P. McClanahan. bibliog il pors Natur Hist 80:33-70 My '71
AMERICAN music. See Music, American
AMERICAN music conference
Making music; Chicago's summer youth music competition. T. M. McCarty. il Parks & Rec 6:25-6+ Ap '71
AMERICAN national insurance company
It's Moody versus Moody in the struggle for American national. A. M. Louis. il por Fortune 83:108-12+ Mr '71
Shock waves rock a Texas insurer. il Bsns W p84-7 Ja 16 '71
AMERICAN Negro academy
Editorial. il Negro Hist Bul 33:156-7 N '70
AMERICAN Negro visitors in Africa. See Visitors, Foreign—Africa
AMERICAN Negroes. See Negroes
AMERICAN newspapers. See Newspapers—United States
AMERICAN oil company
Always leave 'em smiling. il Newsweek 79:36-7 Ja 3 '72
Saving a small town. L. L. L. Golden. Sat R 54:94 N 13 '71
AMERICAN opera center. See Lincoln Center for the performing arts, New York—Juilliard school
AMERICAN opera company
Advance guard. Q. Eaton. il Opera N 35:28-31 F 27 '71
AMERICAN ospreys. See Ospreys
AMERICAN painting. See Painting, American
AMERICAN people. See Americans; United States—Population
AMERICAN pharmaceutical association
Buying drugs; question of posting prices. New Repub 166:13 Ja 1 '72
Prescription prices lose their mystery. il Bsns W p21-2 D 18 '71
AMERICAN philosophical association
Philosophers and politics. America 124:626 Je 19 '71
AMERICAN physical society
APS-AAPT meet in New York. M. S. Rothenberg. il Phys Today 24:25+ Ja '71
Employment debated at meeting. il Phys Today 24:65-6 Ap '71
Greening of the American physical society. D. E. Thomsen. il Sci N 99:167-8 Mr 6 '71
Hippocrates' physic. D. Shapley. Science 172:544 My 7 '71; Reply. P. Noyes. 173:475 Ag 6 '71
Physical sciences. Sci N 99:322 My 8 '71
Physical sciences; annual meeting. Sci N 99:115, 129 F 13-20 '71
Physical sciences; summary of papers. Sci N 100:150 Ag 28 '71

AMERICAN place theatre. See New York
   (city)—Theater
AMERICAN poetry
   Alone with America, by R. Howard. Review
      Poetry 117:258-61 Ja '71. D. Sheehan
   Law of order, the promise of poetry. L. Un-
      termeyer. Sat R 54:18-20+ Mr 20 '71
   Leaping ghazals and inside jokes concealed
      in tropes. J. Whitehead. Sat R 54:37-41+ D
      18 '71
   Poetry today: low profile, flatted voice. A.
      T. Baker. il Time 98:61+ Jl 12 '71
   Shared language in the poet's tongue. D.
      Jaffe. il Sat R 54:31-3+ Ap 3 '71
   Voice that is great within us, ed. by H. Car-
      ruth. Review
         Commentary 51:88+ F '71. D. Bromwich
   See also
   Negro poetry
   Poets, American
AMERICAN poets. See Poets, American
AMERICAN Poles. See Polish Americans
AMERICAN pork congress
   Who said the industry couldn't do it again?
      R. Wilmore. Farm J 95:H24 Ap '71
AMERICAN portraits. See Portraits, American
AMERICAN pottery. See Pottery, American
AMERICAN power boat association
   Escape from the humdrum; APBA regattas.
      E. Crimmin. il Motor B & S 127:35+ Ap '71
   More power to you. M. Crook. See issues of
      Yachting
AMERICAN press institute
   Twenty-five years of the API. J. Hohenberg.
      il Sat R 54:72-3+ D 11 '71
AMERICAN prints. See Prints
AMERICAN propaganda. See Propaganda
AMERICAN property in Vietnam (Republic)
   What the U.S. is leaving behind in Viet-
      nam. C. G. Burck. il Fortune 84:82-7 O '71
AMERICAN psychiatric association
   Behavioral sciences. Sci N 99:333 My 15 '71
   May day at the APA. Sci N 99:315-16 My 8 '71
AMERICAN psychological association
   Behavioral sciences; summaries of papers.
      Sci N 100:190-1 S 18 '71
   Psychologist as social engineer; annual meet-
      ing. Sci N 100:166 S 11 '71
   Psychologists beset by feelings of futility,
      self-doubt. C. Holden. Science 173:1111 S 17
      '71; Discussion. 174:890-2 N 26 '71
AMERICAN public opinion. See Public opinion
   —United States
AMERICAN Red cross. See Red cross—United
   States
AMERICAN revolution. See United States—
   History—Revolution
AMERICAN scene in literature. See United
   States in literature
AMERICAN scholar (periodical)
   Raskolnikov, the Scholar, and fresh air;
      introd. to fortieth anniversary issue. P. P.
      Hallie. Am Scholar 40:579-82 Aut '71
   See also
   Military post schools, American
AMERICAN sculpture. See Sculpture, Ameri-
   can
AMERICAN security council
   Cold-war college. B. Rice. Nation 213:304-8
      O 4 '71
   See also
   Freedom studies center
AMERICAN Shakespeare festival theatre and
   academy, Stratford, Conn.
   Improvisational techniques: Center for thea-
      tre techniques in education, or CTTE. T.
      Mofford and J. Mofford. biblp il Schol
      Teach Jr/Sr High p 14-16 Ja '72
   Picnicking with the Bard; summer produc-
      tions. J. Kroll. il Newsweek 77:85 Je 28 '71
   Theater; production of Mourning becomes
      Electra. H. Hewes. Sat R 54:33 Ag 7 '71
AMERICAN silverware. See Silverware
AMERICAN slang. See Slang
AMERICAN society for information science
   ASIS: information science in motion; 34th
      annual meeting. S. M. Newman. il Wilson
      Lib Bul 46:475-7 Ja '72
   Bellies and ASIS; annual meeting. T. Sara-
      cevic. il Library J 96:167-8 Ja 15 '71
   SLA-ASIS merger friction aired by New
      Jersey SLA. Library J 96:1184 Ap 1 '71
AMERICAN society of agronomy
   Protein "fertilizer" boosts soybean yields;
      report of annual meeting. Farm J 95:36
      O '71
AMERICAN society of Christian ethics
   Ethicists examine conspiracy laws. Chr Cent
      88:213-14 F 17 '71
AMERICAN society of newspaper editors
   Right to protect a news source; ASNE's drive
      to protect reporters from court procedures.
      R. L. Tobin. Sat R 54:45-6 My 8 '71

AMERICAN sociological association
   Sociologyorama; annual convention. F. Lang.
      Ramp Mag 10:9-10+ N '71
AMERICAN soybean association
   Soybeans' newest ambassador; interview. ed.
      by B. Coffman. H. Kuehn. il Farm J 95:35 O
      '71
AMERICAN standard, inc.
   Eberle of American standard. por Forbes
      107:65 My 15 '71
   Lure of the land fades for companies. Bsns
      W p38 Jl 17 '71
AMERICAN sterilizer company
   Robot orderlies. il Newsweek 78:44 S 6 '71
AMERICAN stock exchange
   Time for a switch. por Time 97:78 Mr 29 '71
AMERICAN strategy. See Strategy
AMERICAN students in foreign countries
   See also
   Foreign study
AMERICAN students in Germany. See For-
   eign students in Germany
AMERICAN symphony orchestra
   Musical events:
      Concert in Carnegie Hall. W. Sargeant.
         New Yorker 47:64-5 D 25 '71
AMERICAN teachers in Canada
   Americanization of Canadian universities. C.
      Cocking. il Sat R 54:44-5+ Ag 21 '71
   Maple leaves among the ivy. V. M. Johnson.
      Commonweal 95:35-7 O 8 '71
AMERICAN teachers in Germany (Federal Re-
   public)
   Teacher exodus; Germany takes U.S. sur-
      plus. il Newsweek 78:76 Ag 9 '71
   Transplanting teachers; Germany imports
      U.S. surplus. il Time 98:45 Ag 9 '71
AMERICAN telephone and telegraph company
   AT&T opens up its wideband lines. Bsns W
      p23-4 Jl 31 '71
   AT&T pushes advanced satcom research.
      Aviation W 95:51 Jl 12 '71
   Corporate baby-sitting. il Forbes 107:19-20
      Je 1 '71
   H. I. Romnes of AT&T; interview. H. I.
      Romnes. por Nations Bsns 59:56-60+ Ap '71
   Is preferred the right word? il Forbes 108:46
      Jl 1 '71
   Justice dept. slows AT&T system case. il
      Aviation W 95:38-40 Ag 23 '71
   Ma Bell, male chauvinist. Newsweek 78:80
      D 13 '71
   Phone company papers; a peek at the books.
      J. C. Goulden. il Nation 214:37-41 Ja 10 '72
   Romnes of AT&T. il por Forbes 107:54 My
      15 '71
   Target, yes. Sitting duck, no. Forbes 107:43
      Ja 15 '71
   What's the outlook for AT&T stocks and
      bonds? S. Meisenberg. il Har Yrs 11:52-3
      D '71
   Why Bell system wants higher rates. il
      Bsns W p36-7 F 27 '71
   Why your phone bill is going to go up. il
      U S News 71:78-9 N 22 '71
AMERICAN tobacco company. See American
   brands, inc.
AMERICAN tourists. See Travelers
AMERICAN tradition. See Tradition
AMERICAN visitors in China (People's Repub-
   lic); American visitors in France; etc.
   See Visitors, Foreign—China (People's
   Republic); Visitors, Foreign—France; etc.
AMERICAN walnut manufacturers association
   Mike Frome; question of the vanishing Amer-
      ican black walnut. M. Frome. Am For 77:
      7+ My '71
AMERICAN wind symphony orchestra
   Barge man. il Time 98:54 Jl 26 '71
AMERICAN wines. See Wine
AMERICAN women. See Women—United
   States
AMERICAN writers congress. See Congress
   of American writers
AMERICANISM
   Why we fly the flag; It's my country, too!
      D. Seim; G. Logsdon. il Farm J 95:19-20 Jl
      '71
AMERICANS
   America may be in its last phase of ado-
      lescence. J. Lukacs. il N Y Times Mag
      p48+ D 5 '71
   Average man might fool you. R. Coles. por
      Life 70:4 My 7 '71
   Case for optimism. N. Cousins. Sat R 54:
      28-9 N 20 '71
   Cooling of America; symposium. il Time 97:
      10-19 F 22 '71
   Family portraits U.S.A. A. Gagnebin. il
      Look 35:22-9 Ja 26 '71
   How America lives:
      Making ends meet in paradise; Hawaii.
         L. Tornabene. il Ladies Home J 88:
         82-3+ Ja '71

AMERICANS—*Continued*
Hunting for America. R. W. Murphy. Harper 242:16-18+ Je '71
Listening to America. B. Moyers; discussion. Harper 242:6+ F '71
Listening to America, by B. Moyers. Review New Repub 164:30+ Ap 17 '71. J. Walt
Middle Americans, by R. Coles. Review Nat R 23:879-80 Ag 10 '71
On rising to the occasion. R. L. Tobin. Sat R 54:20 F 27 '71
Rebirth: Americans moving on; symposium. Look 35:33-8+ Ja 12 '71
Strong economy and a strong national defense; address, August 19, 1971. R. M. Nixon. Dept State Bul 65:273-6 S 13 '71
We are all ethnics now. Chr Cent 88:1039 S 8 '71
What is the American talent for living? Seven candid opinions. B. Russell. House & Gard 139:46-7+ F '71
White ethnic. M. Novak. il Harper 243:44-6+ S '71; Discussion. 243:6 N; 14-15 D '71
Working-class majority; end of the myth of the middle class majority. A. Levison. il Nation 213:626-8 D 13 '71
See also
Armenian Americans
Polish Americans
Westerners
AMERICANS for Democratic action
ADA and Nixon. W. F. Buckley, jr. Nat R 23:608-9 Je 1 '71
AMERICANS in Armenia
I want to go home. il Newsweek 77:42+ My 17 '71
AMERICANS in Belgium
Waterloo: old name for a new Scarsdale. Bsns W p31 Jl 3 '71
AMERICANS in Canada
America's sad young exiles; draft evaders and deserters in Canada. K. Fleming. il Newsweek 77:28-30 F 15 '71
Amnesty when? Vietnam war resisters and deserters. R. Gardner. New Repub 165:12-13 D 25 '71
Canadian Christians primed for ministry to U.S. draft refugees. C. de Mestral. Chr Cent 88:73 Ja 20 '71
New exiles, by R. N. Williams. Review New Repub 164:26-8 Je 19 '71. R. Cassidy
See also
American teachers in Canada
AMERICANS in Chile
Land grab; peasants seize farm of the Lewis family. J. Barnes. Newsweek 77:40 F 1 '71
AMERICANS in China
Recollections of a cultural imperialist (j.g.) J. C. Thomson, jr. Atlan 228:35-9 Ag '71
AMERICANS in Czechoslovakia
How to get kicked out of Prague. A. Levy. il pors N Y Times Mag p28-9+ My 16 '71
AMERICANS in England
Americans: making it in London. J. Crosby. Vogue 157:118-19 Mr 15 '71
Oxford visit. B. Vroom. New Yorker 47:112-15 My 8 '71
AMERICANS in Europe
See also
United States—Armed forces—Forces in Europe
AMERICANS in foreign countries
Devaluation needn't sour that overseas plum. Bsns W p51 D 25 '71
Notes for the corporate nomad:
Getting in from the airport. il Fortune 83:42 Ap '71
Guide to company hierarchies. Fortune 84:38-9 Jl '71
How much to tip. il Fortune 83:94 My '71
Learning languages. Fortune 83:42 Mr '71
Moving electrically. il Fortune 84:82-3 Ag '71
Scarcer household help. Fortune 83:44 F '71
Taking pets overseas. Fortune 84:50 O '71
Those unwritten social rules. Fortune 83:52 Ja '71
What to do between appointments. Fortune 84:98 N '71
What Americans are doing abroad: case histories in their own words. il U S News 70:22-5 F 1 '71
AMERICANS in France
American family arrives in Paris. W. A. McWhirter. il Life 70:59-60+ Je 25 '71
AMERICANS in Germany (Federal Republic)
Yankees in Valhalla; American singers in Germany. W. Hutton. il Opera N 35:8-11 Mr 20 '71
See also
United States—Army Forces in Europe

AMERICANS in Hong Kong
Executives like their new outpost. il Bsns W p42+ D 4 '71
AMERICANS in Iran
Peace corps: a firsthand view. J. Starke. por Sr Schol 98:15 F 15 '71
AMERICANS in Italy
Authors & editors: A. Cornelisen as social worker in Lucania. B. A. Bannon. por Pub W 200:9-11 N 1 '71
AMERICANS in Japan
Myths that mislead U.S. managers in Japan. Y. Tsurumi. Harvard Bsns R 49:118-27 Jl '71
Tokyo: the problem city after the shock. il Bsns W p66-9 O 9 '71
AMERICANS in London. See Americans in England
AMERICANS in Paris. See Americans in France
AMERICANS in Russia
Bully tactics. il Newsweek 77:34 Ja 18 '71
AMERICANS in Tunisia
Peace corps: a firsthand view. J. Scovill. por Sr Schol 98:14 F 15 '71
AMERICANS in Vietnam
See also
United States—Armed forces—Forces in Vietnam
United States—Army—Forces in Vietnam
AMERICA'S #1 husband; story. See Stein, G.
AMERICUS, Ga.
Small victories in Americus. M. Frady. il Life 70:46B-46D+ F 12 '71
AMERSON, Lucius D.
Rough justice. por Newsweek 77:25 Mr 1 '71 *
AMES, B. Charles
Dilemma of product/market management. il Harvard Bsns R 49:66-74 Mr '71
AMES, Kenneth
Gardner & company of New York. il Antiques 100:252-5 Ag '71
AMES, Morgan
In brief. Hi Fi 21:108 Ja '71
—and others
Lighter side. See issues of High fidelity and Musical America
AMES, Ia.
Full-depth asphalt to the rescue; stabilized bases. A. O. Chantland. il Am City 86:68+ D '71
AMES International orchestra festival. See Music festivals—Iowa
AMEX. See American stock exchange
AMFT, M. J.
Merry Christmas, Mary Kay; story. Seventeen 29:114-15 D '70
More like a friend; story. Seventeen 29:132-3 O '70
AMIDEI, Rosemary
Ingredients for life in outer space. bibliog il Sci Digest 70:24-9 S '71
AMIDES
See also
Acetamide
AMIN DADA, Idi
Big daddy takes charge. il pors Time 97:38 F 8 '71 *
Gold-dust twins. il por Newsweek 77:35 F 8 '71 *
Itching for a fight. Newsweek 77:36+ My 24 '71 *
Naked repression. il por Time 98:31 Ag 2 '71 *
Shock waves. il Newsweek 77:40 F 15 '71 *
AMINES
Social behavior of monkeys selectively depleted of monoamines. D. E. Redmond, jr. and others. bibliog il Science 174:428-31 O 22 '71
See also
Catecholamines
Choline
Nitrosamines
AMINO acids
Amino acid analyses of the Murchison, Murray, and Allende carbonaceous chondrites. J. R. Cronin and C. B. Moore. bibliog il Science 172:1327-9 Je 25 '71
Amino acid composition of proteins as a product of molecular evolution. T. Ohta and M. Kimura. bibliog il Science 174:150-3 O 8 '71
Amino acids from outer space. il Chem 44:24 F '71
Amino acids in both moon and meteorite. G. B. Lubkin. bibliog il Phys Today 24:17-19 F '71
Amino acids in meteorites. Sky & Tel 42:84 Ag '71
Amino acids indigenous to the Murray meteorite. J. G. Lawless and others. bibliog il Science 173:626-7 Ag 13 '71

AMINO acids—*Continued*
Evidence for compounds hydrolyzable to amino acids in aqueous extracts of Apollo 11 and Apollo 12 lunar fines. K. Harada and others. bibliog il Science 173:433-5 Jl 30 '71
Extraterrestrial amino acids. Sci N 99:435 Je 26 '71
How protein-like compounds could evolve in space. Sci N 100:323 N 13 '71
Life beyond the earth? Sci Digest 69:31 Mr '71
Long-wavelength ultraviolet photoproduction of amino acids on the primitive earth. C. Sagan and B. N. Khare. bibliog il Science 173:417-20 Jl 30 '71
More evidence for life in space. il Sci Digest 70:30-1 S '71
Origin in space; Murchison amino acids. Sci N 99:195 Mr 20 '71
Possible pattern for origin of life. Space World H-9-93:47-8 S '71
Racemization of amino acids in marine sediments. J. Wehmiller and P. E. Hare. bibliog il Science 173:907-11 S 3 '71
Rule of amino acids in ribosomal RNA synthesis. Sci N 100:374 D 4 '71
Specialization of rabbit reticulocyte transfer RNA content for hemoglobin synthesis. D. W. E. Smith and A. L. McNamara. bibliog il Science 171:577-9 F 12 '71; Correction. 171:1040 Mr 12 '71
Synthesis of amino acids by the heating of formaldehyde and ammonia. S. W. Fox and C. R. Windsor; discussion. bibliog il Science 174:1038-41 D 3 '71
Synthesis of amino acids from gases known in space. Sci N 100:357 N 27 '71
See also
Arginine
Dopa
Histidine
Peptides
Tryptophan
AMINOLEVULINATE dehydratase. See Enzymes
AMISH Mennonites. See Mennonites
AMMER, Dean S.
What businessmen expect from the 1970's. il Harvard Bsns R 49:41-52 Ja '71
AMMETERS
EW lab report: volt-ohm milliammeters. J. D. Hirsch. il Electr World 85:34-8 Mr '71
Forgotten gauges. il Hot Rod 24:46-8 N '71
Solid-state V.O.M.'s. J. D. Hirsch. il Electr World 85:39-42+ Ap '71
AMMONIA in the body
Ammonia production in muscle: the purine nucleotide cycle. J. Lowenstein and K. Tornheim. bibliog il Science 171:397-400 Ja 29 '71
Ammonium and chloride extrusion: hyperpolarizing synaptic inhibition in spinal motoneurons. H. D. Lux. bibliog il Science 173:555-7 Ag 6 '71
AMMONIOBORITE. See Borates
AMMONS, A. R.
Eternal city; poem. Harper 242:60 Ap '71
Terminus; poem. Harper 242:97 Ja '71
AMMUNITION
See also
Cartridges
AMNESIA
Amnesia produced by spreading depression and ECS: evidence for time-dependent memory trace localization. R. M. Paolino and H. M. Levy. bibliog il Science 172:746-9 My 14 '71
Electroshock effects on brain protein synthesis: relation to brain seizures and retrograde amnesia. C. W. Cotman and others. bibliog il Science 173:454-6 Jl 30 '71
Retrograde amnesia: electroconvulsive shock effects after termination of rapid eye movement sleep deprivation. W. Fishbein and others. bibliog il Science 172:80-2 Ap 2 '71
Selective recovery from retrograde amnesia produced by hippocampal spreading depression. B. S. Kapp and A. M. Schneider. bibliog il Science 173:1149-51 S 17 '71
AMNESTY for draft resisters. See Military service, Compulsory—Draft resisters
AMNIOCENTESIS. See Fetus—Diseases—Diagnosis
AMNIOTIC liquid
Histidase activity in cultivated human amniotic fluid cells. S. B. Melancon and others. bibliog il Science 173:627-8 Ag 13 '71
AMOEBAS. See Amebas
AMON, Christopher Arthur
Chris Amon on Can-Am; interview, ed. by K. Ludvigsen. il por Motor T 23:80+ Mr '71
AMONKAR, S. V. and Banerji, A.
Isolation and characterization of larvicidal principle of garlic. bibliog il Science 174:1343-4 D 24 '71

AMORPHOUS ice. See Ice
AMORPHOUS semiconductors. See Semiconductors
AMORTIZATION deductions
Behind the fight against tax break for business. il U S News 70:85-6 My 3 '71
Book for business; revised depreciation regulations. Duns 97:96 F '71
Boost for growth, a slap at prices. il Bsns W p22-3 Ja 16 '71
Faster write-offs finally emerge. Bsns W p22-3 Je 26 '71
Feud over faster write-offs. Bsns W p27-8 My 1 '71
Mr Nixon's tricky bonanza; ADR system. R. Nader. Nation 212:774-6 Je 21 '71
New depreciation rules O.K.'d, but still face challenges. U S News 71:44 Jl 5 '71
TRB from Washington; R. Nader and others file suit to block fast depreciation allowances. New Repub 165:6 Jl 17 '71
Tax break. New Repub 164:11 My 1 '71
Tax break for businessmen, and others. il U S News 70:78-9 Ja 25 '71
Utilities get in on the write-off bill. Bsns W p41 F 27 '71
Trade winds. See issues of Saturday review
AMORY, Cleveland
AMOS 'n' Andy (radio program) See Radio broadcasting—Humor
AMPEX corporation
Ampex and instant publishing. I. Berger. Sat R 54:47-8 Ag 28 '71
Ampex buys its own in semiconductors. Bsns W p24 Ap 24 '71
AMPHETAMINES
Adrenal release mechanisms. il Sci N 100:106 Ag 14 '71
Amphetamine abuse; report of meeting. E. H. Ellinwood and S. Cohen. Science 171:420-1 Ja 29 '71
Beware the amphetamines: speed kills. W. Cole. il Parents Mag 46:74-5+ N '71
Crackdown on pep pills. Newsweek 77:77 Je 7 '71
Drugs for children; the Omaha program and resulting political involvement. H. Vinnedge. New Repub 164:13-15 Mr 13 '71; Discussion. 164:28-9 Ap 10; 37-8 Ap 17 '71
How speed kills athletic careers. W. B. Furlong. Todays Health 49:30-3+ F '71
Methamphetamine-induced insulin release. E. M. McMahon and others. bibliog il Science 174:66-8 O 1 '71
Panel sanctions amphetamines for hyperkinetic children. R. J. Bazell. Science 171:1223 Mr 26 '71
Putting some limits on speed. R. Loving, jr. Fortune 83:99+ Mr '71
Speed: downhill all the way. M. English. il Look 35:88-9 Je 1 '71
Uses, and misuses, of common mood drugs. G. G. Greer. Bet Hom & Gard 49:4+ Ja '71
AMPHIBIA
See also
Nervous system—Amphibia
AMPHIBIANS (airplanes) See Airplanes, Amphibious
AMPHIBIOUS airplanes. See Airplanes, Amphibious
AMPHIBIOUS motor vehicles. See Motor vehicles, Amphibious
AMPLIFIERS
All American sports amplifier; TV antenna preamp. R. B. Cooper. il Pop Electr 35:29-35+ S '71
Amplifier quiz. W. R. Shippee. Electr World 86:51 D '71
Audio amplifiers quiz. A. G. Nelson. Electr World 85:41 F '71
Break through radio pollution: use of etched coils in FM preamp. R. B. Cooper, jr. il Radio-Electr 42:33-7 Je '71
Build R-E's 4-channel IC power amplifier. G. D. Hanchett. il Radio-Electr 42:37-40 O '71
Build R-E's 4-channel IC preamp. L. Kaplan. il Radio-Electr 42:41-5 O '71
Build the five forty power amplifier. D. Meyer. il Pop Electr 34:49-53+ My '71
Hi-fi amplifier module; use of Sinclair model Z-30 audio amplifier. A. Trauffer. il Pop Electr 35:59-60 D '71
Inside linear ICs. W. G. Jung. il Radio-Electr 42:50-1 D '71
New quickie kits for hi-fi. S. M. Gallager and S. M. Gallager. il Pop Mech 135:116-17 F '71
New solid-state device could improve amplifier performance; gallium arsenide field effect transistors. il Aviation W 95:42 N 29 '71
Operational amplifier: what it is & how it works. R. Tenny. il Pop Electr 35:30-5+ Ag; 61-6 S '71

AMPLIFIERS—*Continued*
Plastic tiger audio power amplifier. D. Meyer. il Pop Electr 35:27-34+ O '71
Portable sound systems for performers. D. L. Patten. il Electr World 86:38-40 S '71
Power amplification. R. Berkovitz. il Hi Fi 21:58-62+ S '71
10 keys specs for effective PA. M. S. Sumberg. il Radio-Electr 42:45-7 My '71
    See also
Lasers
Man amplifiers
Traveling wave tubes

Design
Amateur scientist; on the differential operational amplifier, a device that simulates almost anything. S. Froud. il Sci Am 224:110-16 Ja '71
Designing solid-state stereo amplifiers (title varies) M. Horowitz. See issues of Radio-electronics

Noise
Design for stereo. M. Horowitz. il Radio-Electr 42:50-4+ O '71
Noise filters in hi-fi amplifiers. J. D. Hirsch. il Electr World 85:44+ Je '71

Testing
Hi-fi product report:
Harman-Kardon Citation 12 stereo amplifier. il Electr World 85:12+ Mr '71
Sony TA-1144 integrated stereo amplifier. il Electr World 85:8+ My '71

AMPUTEES
Technical dilemma; operation of robots by legless men in film by D. Trumbull. il Esquire 76:130-5 S '71

al-AMRI, Hassan
Crossed wires. por Newsweek 78:53 S 20 '71 •
Crossed wires. il por Time 98:35 S 20 '71 •

AMSCARS (carts) See Hospitals—Equipment and supplies

AMSTERDAM, Netherlands

Music
Behind the scenes. E. Greenfield. Hi Fi 21:21-2 D '71

AMSTERDAM, Fort. See Ghana—Historic houses, etc.

AMSTERDAM concertgebouw orchestra
Mirrors of our time; interview, ed. by R. Hemming. Sr Schol 98:19 My 17 '71
Musical events appearance in Carnegie Hall. W. Sargeant. New Yorker 47:112 My 1 '71

AMSTERDAM news, New York. See Negro press

AMTRAK. See National railroad passenger corporation

AMTRAK trains. See Railroads—Trains

AMULETS
Riddle of the abraxas amulets. il UNESCO Courier 24:8-9 My '71

AMUSEMENT parks
Come on over; Palisades amusement park. Fort Lee, N.J. New Yorker 47:19-20 Ag 21 '71
Family playground; Playland amusement park, Rye, N.Y. F. A. Seitz. il Parks & Rec 6:42-3+ Ap '71
Fight to claim Missouri's Six flags. il Bsns W p26 Ap 24 '71
Fun house fun; San Francisco's Playland-at-the-beach. il Sunset 147:32-3 Jl '71
Ride back into San Francisco's past; Enchanted world on Fisherman's Wharf. il Sunset 147:42 Ag '71
    See also
Disney world, Fla.

Employees
Magic mountain for the jobless. il Bsns W p24 My 8 '71

AMUSEMENTS
    See also
Camping—Activities
Childrens amusements
Games
Mathematical recreations
Moving pictures
Night clubs
Puzzles

AMYLOIDOSIS
Amyloid fibril proteins: proof of homology with immunoglobulin light chains by sequence analyses. G. G. Glenner and others. bibliog il Science 172:1150-1 Je 11 '71
Creation of "amyloid" fibrils from Bence Jones proteins in vitro. G. G. Glenner and others. bibliog il Science 174:712-14 N 12 '71

ANABIOSIS. See Cryptobiosis
ANACHARIS
Environmental control of photosynthetic enhancement. T. Punnett. bibliog il Science 171:284-6 Ja 22 '71
ANACONDA. See American library association—Ad hoc council committee on ACONDA
ANACONDA company
Anaconda turns to a money man. por Bsns W p24-5 My 22 '71
Bad scene at Mike horse mine. J. N. Miller. Read Digest 98:75-9 F '71
Banking on an outsider. E. J. Tracy and others. por Fortune 83:33 Je '71
Montana versus the mining companies: new awakening or impractical idealism. R. H. Gilluly. il Sci N 100:235-7 O 2 '71
Reading the small print; OPIC insurance of Chilean property. il Forbes 107:22-3 Mr 15 '71
Two ways to do it. il Forbes 109:24-5 Ja 1 '72
ANACOSTIA neighborhood museum. See Smithsonian institution
ANAHEIM, Calif.

Street traffic
Mickey mouse traffic-signal interconnect. E. F. Granzow. il Am City 86:55-7 Ag '71
ANALGESIA
Analgesia from electrical stimulation in the brainstem of the rat. D. J. Mayer and others. bibliog il Science 174:1351-4 D 24 '71
Radio signal relieves pain. A. J. Snider. Sci Digest 71:69 Ja '72
ANALGESICS
Excedrin: what that clinical study really shows; with editorial comment. Consumer Rep 36:464-5, 492 Ag '71
    See also
Aspirin
Morphine
ANALOGY
Analogies in chemistry (cont) Chem 44:31 N '71
ANALOGY (rhetoric) See Figures of speech
ANALYSIS (philosophy)
Analytic philosophy in the 20th century. T. M. Reed. bibliog Am Lib 2:1161-8 D '71
ANALYTICAL economics. See Economics
ANALYTICAL philosophy. See Analysis (philosophy)
ANANIA, Michael
Comment. J. Atlas. Poetry 119:46-7 O '71 •
ANARCHISM and anarchists
Anarchism, past and future. D. Rosenthal. Nation 213:439-40 N 1 '71
    See also
Terrorism
ANATOL, A. pseud. See Kuznefsov, A. V.
ANATOMICAL models
Finger bone connected to . . ; plastic skeleton models. il Sci Digest 69:inside cover, 88-9 Mr '71
ANATOMY
Three-dimensional structure identified from single sections; adaptation of address, August 1971 H. Elias. bibliog il Science 174:993-1000 D 3 '71
    See also names of organs and regions of the body, e.g. Brain
ANCESTRY. See Genealogy
ANCHORAGE, Alaska
Anchorage: on the oil frontier. il Bsns W p 156 My 15 '71
ANCHORAGE
Bit about anchoring. D. Lazarus. il Yachting 129:69+ Ap '71
Important tips on rafting. L. Fay. il Motor B & S 128:88+ Jl '71
    See also
Marinas
ANCHORING. See Anchorage
ANCHORS
Bit about anchoring. D. Lazarus. il Yachting 129:69+ Ap '71
ANCHOVIES
    See also
Cookery—Fish
ANCIENT civilization. See Civilization, Ancient
ANCIENT coins. See Coins, Ancient
AND Miss Reardon drinks a little; drama. See Zindel, P.
AND they put handcuffs on the flowers; drama. See Arrabal, F.
AND whose little boy are you? drama. See Parker. R.
ANDEAN condors. See Condors
ANDERMATT, Paul
How does a plant synthesize a molecule? il Chem 45:23-4 Ja '72

ANEMIA—*Continued*
Counterattack on a killer; sickle cell anemia. il Ebony 26:84-6+ O '71
Detecting an old killer; sickle-cell anemia. il Time 98:57 O 4 '71
Disease that always killed; ed. by J. D. Ratcliff. G. H. Whipple. Read Digest 99:169-70+ N '71
Now Eddie Smith has a better chance of getting his Rhodes scholarship; sickle cell anemia. S. Murata. il Todays Health 49:54-6 D '71
Progress in treating sickle cell anemia. il Chem 44:21-2 Ap '71
Sickle cell anemia: an interesting pathology. M. G. Michaelson. il Ramp Mag 10:52-8 O '71
Silent hemoglobin alpha genes in apes: potential source of thalassemia. S. H. Boyer and others. bibliog il Science 171:182-5 Ja 15 '71
See also
Favism
Leukemia

ANEMOMETERS
Amateur scientist; experiments with wind: a pendulum anemometer and miniature tornadoes. P. L. Clemens. il Sci Am 225:108-10 O '71

ANEMONES
It makes sense, takes courage; Japanese anemone. il Sunset 146:133 Ja '71
New faces for a spring garden; ed. by E. Haraszty. R. E. Atkinson. il McCalls 98:30 F '71

ANEMONES, Sea. See Sea anemones

ANESTHESIA
Anesthesia and analgesia during childbirth; ed. by S. Olds. F. Ostapowicz. Redbook 136:12+ Ap '71
Anesthesia by dissociation. Sci Am 224:56 Je '71

ANESTHETICS
Beware the vapors; causing miscarriages among surgical nurses and female anesthetists. Newsweek 78:109 O 25 '71
Warning on anaesthetics; effect on pregnant women. Time 98:63 O 25 '71
See also
Lidocaine hydrochloride

ANGEL ISLAND state park. See California— Parks and reserves

ANGELL, Alan
Chile: from Christian democracy to Marxism? bibliog f Cur Hist 60:84-9+ F '71

ANGELL, Madeline
Play it straight with your children. il Parents Mag 46:49-51+ O '71

ANGELL, Roger
Achievement. New Yorker 47:24-8 Ag 21 '71
Sporting scene (cont) il New Yorker 47:92-9 F 20: 73-82 Je 19: 138+ N 6 '71

ANGELS (baseball) See Baseball clubs

ANGER
Express anger, lower anxiety. A. J. Snider. il Sci Digest 71:70 Ja '72
Look back on anger; Time essay. M. Maddocks. il Time 98:40 Ag 16 '71
On using anger. R. A. Gardner. Harp Baz 104:64+ Jl '71
What parent doesn't wonder about the right and wrong way to discipline children? B. Bettelheim. Ladies Home J 88:18+ F '71

ANGIOKERATOMA
Fabry's disease: antenatal detection. R. O. Brady and others. bibliog il Science 172:174-5 Ap 9 '71

ANGIONEUROTIC edema. See Edema

ANGIOTENSIN
Angiotensin-forming enzyme in brain tissue. D. Ganten and others. bibliog il Science 173:64-5 Jl 2 '71
Angiotensin II: rapid localization in nuclei of smooth and cardiac muscle. A. L. Robertson, jr. and P. A. Khairallah. bibliog il Science 172:1138-9 Je 11 '71
Intrarenal formation of angiotensin I. H. D. Itskovitz and C. Odya. bibliog il Science 174:58 O 1 '71

ANGKOR, Cambodia
Angkor, by J. Myrdal and G. Kessle. Review Nation 212:187-8 F '71. J. Gutmann

ANGLE of repose; story. See Stegner, W.

ANGLICAN church. See Church of England

ANGLICAN church in South Africa. See Church of England in South Africa

ANGLICAN church of Canada. See Church of England in Canada

ANGLICAN consultative council
Anglican council approves WCC grants, ordination of women. M. M. Kelleran. Chr Cent 88:534 Ap 28 '71

ANGLING. See Fishing

ANGLO-AMERICAN catalog rules. See Cataloging

ANGLUND, Joan (Walsh)
Authors & editors. B. A. Bannon. por Pub W 199:35-6 Ja 11 '71 •

ANGUILLA (island)
Bay of Piglets revisited. il Time 98:31 Jl 26 '71
In Anguilla it's the spirit of '71. D. E. Westlake. il N Y Times Mag p24-5+ My 23 '71
Rejoining the fold. Newsweek 78:35 Jl 19 '71

ANGUS, Robert
Newest: 4-channel stereo. il Mech Illus 67:118-20+ N '71
Tapester's timer. il Pop Phot 68:47+ Ja '71

ANHEUSER-Busch, inc.
Busch of Anheuser-Busch. il por Forbes 107:49 My 15 '71

ANI, Turkey (ancient city)
Road to Ani. C. E. Adelsen. il Natur Hist 80:62-73 N '71

ANICO. See American national insurance company

ANIMAL actors. See Animals as actors

ANIMAL behavior. See Animals—Habits and behavior

ANIMAL calling
About face! M. Burnham. il Outdoor Life 147:90-3 Ap '71

ANIMAL communication
Language in chimpanzee? D. Premack. bibliog il Science 172:808-22 My 21 '71
No thanks, said the ape. il Newsweek 78:101 D 20 '71
Reporter at large; chimpanzees and language. E. Hahn. New Yorker 47:54-6+ D 11 '71
Sarah language? Learn. Sci Am 225:44-5 Jl '71
Wolf music. J. B. Theberge. il Natur Hist 80:36-43 bibliog(p 84) Ap '71
Your dog talks back. L. Mueller. il Field & S 75:196-8+ Mr '71
See also
Animal sounds

ANIMAL defenses. See Defense mechanisms (biology)

ANIMAL experimentation
Debate: animal experimentation and evolution; antivivisection: the reluctant hydra. C. Roberts; R. J. White. Am Scholar 40:497-512 Sum '71
In my opinion animal torture must be stopped! L. Dawkins. por Seventeen 30:166 Mr '71
Probing the brain il Newsweek 77:60-2+ Je 21 '71; Same abr. with title Awesome prospects of the brain probers. Read Digest 99:98-102 S '71
Social setting: influence on the physiological response to electric shock in the rat. R. B. Williams and B. Eichelman. bibliog il Science 174:613-14 N 5 '71
What man owes the baboon. C. N. Barnard. il por Sci Digest 70:36-41 S '71
See also
Animals—Treatment
Emory university, Atlanta, Ga.—Yerkes primate research center
Laboratory animals
Stimulation (physiology)
Stimulus and response
Vivisection

ANIMAL extinction. See Animals, Extinct

ANIMAL introduction
Game bird search. Cons 25:39 F '71

ANIMAL language. See Animal communication

ANIMAL learning
Present shock: experiments in learning. D. M. Rorvik. il Esquire 76:48+ D '71
See also
Memory

ANIMAL locomotion
See also
Insects—Flight

ANIMAL lore
Another cliché, ah, bites the dust; fox in the chicken coop. il Life 71:80 S 17 '71

ANIMAL luminescence. See Bioluminescence

ANIMAL migration. See Animals—Migration

ANIMAL odors. See Odors of animals

ANIMAL parks. See Menageries

ANIMAL poisoning. See Poisons

ANIMAL populations
Where the wolves are and how they stand. L. D. Mech. Natur Hist 80:26-9 Ap '71

Control
Elephant trouble: too many in Uganda, disappearing in Ceylon. Sr Schol 98:14 Mr 8 '71
See also
Animals, Predatory—Control

ANIMAL sculpture
Anne Arnold. C. Ratcliff. il por Craft Horiz 31:18-21+ Je '71
David Gilhooly; ceramist for the frog world. J. Arneson. il Craft Horiz 31:20-1+ Ag '71
Manhattan safari. K. Simmon. il Natur Hist 80:72-7 My '71

ANIMAL sounds
Songs of humpback whales. R. S. Payne and S. McVay. bibliog il Science 173:585-97 Ag 13 '71
    See also
Phonograph records—Animal sounds

ANIMAL tagging
Dial-a-bison; Wind Cave project. A. F. Joy. il Parks & Rec 6:118-19+ Ja '71
Never say never; campground bears. E. Harger. il por Outdoor Life 147:60-3+ Mr '71
Polar bear: lonely nomad of the North. T. Larsen. il Nat Geog 139:574-90 Ap '71

ANIMAL tissue. See Tissues

ANIMAL tracks and trails
Stories in the snow. H. Borland. il Audubon 73:inside cover Ja '71

ANIMAL training. See Animals—Training

ANIMALS
    See also
Circus animals
Hybridization
Mammals
Odors of animals
Photography of animals
Rare animals
Wildlife
    also names of animals, e.g. Rhinoceros

Coloration
    See Color of animals

Diseases and pests
    See also
Communicable diseases in animals
Leptospirosis
Veterinary medicine
    also Swine—Diseases and pests, and similar headings

Food and feeding
Bare zone between California shrub and grassland communities: the role of animals. B. Bartholomew; reply with rejoinder. C. H. Muller and R. Del Moral. bibliog il Science 173:462-3 Jl 30 '71
Bears, dumps and people. G. T. Chase. il Cons 26:5 Ag '71
Carnivorous tendencies among primates. S. J. Fleming. il Sci Digest 70:89-92 Ag '71
Diners of unlimited diversity; excerpts from Beastly inventions. J. C. George. il Natur Hist 80:42-53, bibliog(p84) Ja '71
Illness-induced aversions in rat and quail: relative salience of visual and gustatory cues. H. C. Wilcoxon and others. bibliog il Science 171:826-8 F 26 '71
Suppression of food intake with intragastric loading: relation to natural feeding cycle. D. Quartermain and others. bibliog il Science 173:941-3 S 3 '71

Habits and behavior
Lot of bull for a buck. H. C. Corley. il Outdoor Life 148:60-2+ D '71
Mammalian scent marking. K. Ralls. bibliog il Science 171:443-9 F 5 '71
Olfactory bulb removal eliminates maternal behavior in the mouse. R. Gandelman and others. bibliog il Science 171:210-11 Ja 15 '71
Our far-flung correspondents; visit to pig farm called Real farms, inc. in Tipton, Pa. W. Whitworth. il New Yorker 46:64+ Ja 30 '71
Reporter at large; primate behavior, especially the chimpanzee. E. Hahn. New Yorker 47:46-8+ Ap 17; 46-50+ Ap 24 '71
Social behavior of monkeys selectively depleted of monoamines. D. E. Redmond, jr. and others. bibliog il Science 174:428-31 O 22 '71
    See also
Animals as artists
Biotelemetry
Birds—Habits and behavior
Displacement activity (animal behavior)
Hibernation
Love, Maternal

Language
    See Animal communication

Markings
    See Color of animals

Migration
Grazing ecosystem in the Serengeti. R. H. V. Bell. il Sci Am 225:86-93 Jl '71
Winter the antelope moved to town. B. Eckerson. il Outdoor Life 147:62-3+ F '71
    See also
Crustaceans—Migration

Photographs
Icy escape; photographer saving deer out of river. R. A. Benson. il Nat Wildlife 9:30-1 F '71
Impala's struggle for life brings a hippo to the rescue. Life 70:70-4 Je 4 '71
Jungle adventure in Ceylon. E. A. Bauer. il Outdoor Life 148:46-9+ D '71
One dinner coming up; leopard with a gazelle. J. Allan. il Outdoor Life 147:60-3 My '71
Terriers. Life 70:38-45 F 12 '71
    See also
Photography of animals

Protection
Good guys, bad guys and the bighorn. E. Zern. il por Sports Illus 34:20-2+ Je 28 '71
    See also
Animals—Treatment
Game laws
Wildlife conservation

Sight
    See Sight (animals)

Tracks
    See Animal tracks and trails

Training
Animal guidance systems; use of Skinner box. L. G. Lawrence. il Electr World 86:27-9+ D '71
Animal trainer who's big on love; Africa, U.S.A. il pors Ebony 26:120-2+ S '71
Big cat with big cats; animal trainer G. Gebel-Williams of the Ringling bros. and Barnum & Bailey circus. il por Time 97:67 My 24 '71
Cat tricks: dog tricks. il Ladies Home J 88:40 Ap '71
Gebel-Williams burning bright; circus trainer. R. Schickel. Harper 243:18+ Ag '71
Peerless potentate of pachydermia. N. F. Busch. il Read Digest 99:133-7 N '71
Soul of the tiger; G. Gebel-Williams. E. Hoagland. il pors Esquire 76:88-93+ Jl '71
    See also
Animals as actors

Transportation
Parting shots; an outrage at sea; shipping of wild animals. il Life 70:66A-66B+ Mr 19 '71

Treatment
Animal welfare act of 1970. M. B. Visscher. Science 172:916-17 My 28 '71
Ride 'em cowboy, gently. il Newsweek 77:83 Je 28 '71
    See also
Hunting—Ethical aspects
Vivisection

ANIMALS, Color of. See Color of animals
ANIMALS, Cruelty to. See Animals—Treatment
ANIMALS, Domestication of. See Domestication
ANIMALS, Extinct
Magnetic reversals and biological extinctions. L. Purrett. il Sci N 10:300-1 O 30 '71
    See also
Birds, Extinct
Dinosaurs
Mastodons
Paleontology
ANIMALS, Food habits of. See Animals—Food and feeding
ANIMALS, Geographical distribution of. See Geographical distribution of animals and plants
ANIMALS, Germfree. See Germfree life
ANIMALS, Infancy of
Effects of brief separation from mother on rhesus monkeys. R. A. Hinde and Y. Spencer-Booth. bibliog il Science 173:111-18 Jl 9 '71
ANIMALS, Mythical
    See also
Loch Ness monster
ANIMALS, Predatory
Poisoning of the West; excerpt from Slaughter the animals, poison the earth. J. Olsen. il Read Digest 99:69-74 Ag '71
    See also
Foxes

ANIMALS, Predatory—*Continued*
Control
Eagle killings and their end result. M. Frome. il Field & S 76:44-5+ D '71
It's time to give the predators a break. W. E. Towell. Am For 77:8-9 N '71
Poisoning of the West; predator control programs. J. Olsen. il Sports Illus 34:80-4+ Mr 8; 36-40+ Mr 15; 34-6+ Mr 22 '71
Predator control: a study in overkill. M. Frome. Field & S 75:18+ Ja '71
War on wildlife. F. McNulty. il Nat Parks & Con Mag 45:11-17 Mr '71

ANIMALS, Rare. See Rare animals
ANIMALS, Tattooing of. See Tattooing
ANIMALS, Training of. See Animals—Training
ANIMALS, Treatment of. See Animals—Treatment
ANIMALS, War use of
Animal guidance systems; piloting air-to-air missiles. L. G. Lawrence. il Electr World 86:27-9+ D '71

ANIMALS and children. See Children and animals
ANIMALS as actors
Ham actors in furs and feathers. H. Kaye. il Sci Digest 71:30-4 Ja '72
ANIMALS as artists
Ape artists: what they tell us about origins of human tool use. S. S. McKern and T. W. McKern. il Science Digest 70:28-33 O '71
ANIMALS as carriers of infection
Mother, put the cat out; toxoplasmosis. il Newsweek 78:67-8 N 29 '71
Toxoplasmosis. D. A. Schanche. McCalls 99: 56+ N '71
Urban pollution: many long years ago. J. A. Tarr. il Am Heritage 22:65-9+ O '71

ANIMALS in advertising
Animal crackers. il Time 98:59 Jl 26 '71
ANIMALS in art
Armadillo man; interview. J. Franklin. New Yorker 47:41-2 D 11 '71
See also
Animal sculpture
Horses in art
ANIMALS in captivity. See Menageries; Zoological gardens
ANIMALS in fiction. See Animals in literature
ANIMALS in literature
Authors & editors: Mary Poppins and Friend Monkey; interview, ed. by P. Bragg. P. L. Travers. por Pub W 200:7-9 D 13 '71
Beast of Gévaudan. C. H. D. Clarke. bibliog Natur Hist 80:44-51+ Ap '71
Pigs are beautiful. E. Geller. il Library J 96:1065 Mr 15 '71
T.R. and the nature fakers; imaginative nature writers. G. Carson. il por Am Heritage 22:60-5+ F '71

Anecdotes, facetiae, satire, etc.
Destroy! Destroy! depiction of animals as people as in Sylvester and the magic pebble; letter to the editor. N. Toy. Am Lib 2:688 Jl '71

ANIMALS in the Bible. See Bible—Natural history
ANIMALS in war. See Animals, War use of
ANIMATED cartoons. See Moving pictures—Animated cartoons; Television broadcasting—Animated cartoons
ANIMATED dial clocks. See Clocks
ANISFIELD-Wolf awards
SR's 1971 Anisfield-Wolf awards. D. Dempsey. Sat R 54:30 Je 12 '71
ANITA Louise Beslin, Sister. See Beslin, A. L.
ANKERMANN, Horst A.
Using an impedance tester. il Radio-Electr 42:82-3+ Je '71
ANN-ELIZABETH
Fair woman; poem. New Yorker 47:93 F 27 '71
ANN-MARGRET
Most wanted, 1971: sexy Ann-Margret. pors Vogue 157:100-1 Je '71
about
Ann-Margret suddenly blooming. P. F. Kluge. il pors Life 71:30-5 Ag 6 '71 •
Ann-Margret the prude & the passion. H. Ehrlich. il pors Look 35:48-53+ Je 15 '71 •
Mistaken identity. M. Ronan. por Sr Schol 98:30 F 15 '71 •
Mouse that roared. por Newsweek 78:78 Jl 19 '71 •
Ordeal of Ann-Margret. il pors Time 98:57-8 Jl 19 '71 •

ANN ARBOR, Mich.
Parking garage over a city street. il Am City 86:120 My '71
ANNE, princess of Great Britain
Forthright young princess comes of age; with editorial comment. pors Life 71:3, 30-3 Ag 20 '71 •
H.R.H. the Princess Anne; photographs. N. Parkinson. Vogue 158:54-7 Ag 15 '71 •
Into the African bush with Anne and Charles. il por Time 97:27 F 22 '71 •
ANNE Schnoebelen, Sister. See Schnoebelen, A.
ANNELIDS
Reef-building worms; honeycomb worms or sabellariid worms. D. W. Kirtley. il Sea Front 17:102-7 Mr '71
See also
Leeches
ANNES, Tom
Build a pocket pipper. il Radio-Electr 42:46-8 F '71
14 ways to use R-E's tone-burst generator. il Radio-Electr 42:32-5+ Ag '71
Tune up your stereo: build a tone-burst generator. il Radio-Electr 42:22-7 Jl '71
ANNESE, Louis E.
Principal as a change agent. bibliog Clear House 45:273-7 Ja '71
ANNEXATION (municipal government)
Cure for city blight, the Jacksonville story: merger of city and county governments; And a look at three other areawide governments. il U S News 72:34-6 Ja 3 '72
Fight to claim Missouri's Six flags. il Bsns W p26 Ap 24 '71
ANNIVERSARIES
See also
Centennials
Fourth of July
Wedding anniversaries
ANNONACEAE
Unique type of angiosperm pollen from the family annonaceae. J. W. Walker. bibliog il Science 172:565-7 My 7 '71
ANNUAL meetings, Stockholders. See Stockholders meetings
ANNUAL reports. See Corporation reports; Reports
ANNUALS (plants)
Color summer with annuals. R. M. Peters. il Home Gard 58:26-34 Ap '71
Now's the time to start your own winter-spring annuals. il Sunset 147:122 Ag '71
Sowing now in open ground. Sunset 147:263 O '71
ANNUALS, College. See College annuals
ANNUALS, Photographic. See Photographic literature
ANNUNCIATORS, Electric. See Electric annunciators
ANOMALOUS water. See Water
ANOMY
Design of discord: studies of anomie, by E. H. Powell. Review
America 124:658-9 Je 26 '71. R. McCormick
ANOREXIA. See Appetite
ANORTHOSITE
Earth twin for a rock from the moon. Sci N 100:325 N 13 '71
Lunar anorthosites: rare-earth and other elemental abundances. H. Wakita and R. A. Schmitt. bibliog il Science 170:969-74 N 27 '70; Correction. 172:184 Ap 9 '71; reply. W. D. Romey. 172:292 Ap 16 '71
ANOTHER mother for peace (organization)
Sunflower that grew and grew. D. Silverton. por McCalls 98:44 My '71
ANOUILH, Jean
Ne reveillez pas madame. Criticism
Nation 213:90 Ag 2 '71 •
ANSCOCHROME films. See Photography—Films
ANSELMI, Giuseppe
Giuseppe Anselmi. A. Favia-Artsay. il pors Hobbies 76:35-6+ N '71 •
ANSETT airlines of Australia. See Airlines—Australia
ANSHEN, Ruth Nanda
Woman behind great thinkers. H. Rosenberg. por Vogue 158:72 Ag 1 '71 •
ANSON, Thomas Patrick John, 5th earl of Lichfield. See Lichfield, T. P. J. A.
ANT venom. See Venom
ANTACIDS
Antacid analysis. J. M. Miller and D. V. Zahniser. bibliog il pors Chem 44:28 Jl '71
ANTARCTIC REGIONS
Antarctica. P. Lernoux. il Travel 136:40-5+ S '71
Antarctica's nearer side. S. W. Matthews. il Nat Geog 140:622-55 N '71
See also
Ice—Polar Regions
Paleontology—Antarctic Regions
South Pole

ANTARCTIC research
Antarctica: the world's greatest laboratory. L. M. Gould. Am Scholar 40:402-15 Sum '71
Big bubble atop the South Pole; polar home for Operation Deep Freeze. M. Walker. il Pop Sci 199:56-9 Ag '71
U.S. inspection team to visit Antarctic research stations. Dept State Bul 64:205 F 15 '71

ANTARCTIC treaty
U.S. marks 10th anniversary of the Antarctic treaty. Department announcement; with statement by President Nixon. R. M. Nixon. Dept State Bul 65:82-3 Jl 19 '71

ANTELOPES
African round-up; Operation Oryx. W. Nussey and H. Reuter. il Sci Digest 69:42-5 Je '71
Way to extinction: the giant sable antelope. il Audubon 73:44-5 My '71
Winter the antelope moved to town. B. Eckerson. il Outdoor Life 147:62-3+ F '71

ANTENNAS (electronics)
See also
Radar—Antenna and scanning mechanisms
Radio antennas
Television antennas

ANTHES, Richard A. and others
Three dimensional particle trajectories in a model hurricane. il Weatherwise 24:174-8 Ag '71

ANTHOLOGY film archives, N.Y. See Moving picture film collections

ANTHONY, Albert S.
Some unprinciples for successful innovation. Ed Digest 37:32-3 N '71
Twenty unprinciples for successful innovation. Clear House 46:32-4 S '71

ANTHONY, Evelyn
Tamarind seed; story. Redbook 137:131-53 Jl '71

ANTHONY, Felix C. pseud.
"Pound", a new unity sign. America 124:147-8 F 13 '71

ANTHONY, Lynn
Coffee-can magic. il Org Gard & Farm 18:118-19 Ap '71

ANTHONY, Mary
Mary Anthony dance theater. Fashion institute of technology, NYC. T. Borek. Dance Mag 45:78 F '71 *

ANTHONY, Robert N.
Can nonprofit organizations be well managed? address, February 18, 1971. Vital Speeches 37:442-5 My 1 '71

ANTHRAMYCIN. See Antibiotics

ANTHRAX
Ecology of anthrax. G. B. Van Ness. bibliog Science 172:1303-7 Je 25 '71

ANTHROPOLOGICAL museums
See also
Ethnological museums and collections

ANTHROPOLOGISTS
See also
Róheim, G.

ANTHROPOLOGY
See also
Acculturation
American anthropological association
Archeology
Evolution
Fingerprints
Man
Man, Prehistoric
Society, Primitive

ANTHURIUMS
Exotic anthuriums. P. Granberry. Horticulture 49:18-19 D '71

ANTI-AMERICAN opinion. See United States —Foreign opinion

ANTI-AMERICAN propaganda. See Propaganda

ANTI-BALLISTIC missile system. See Guided missiles—Defenses

ANTIBIOTIC feed supplements
Are you within the law on drug withdrawal? R. J. Fee. il Suc Farm 69:23 S '71
Feed additives on the firing line. J. Russell. Farm J 95:H16 My '71

ANTIBIOTICS
Chemosterilant action of anthramycin: a proposed mechanism. S. B. Horwitz and others. bibliog il Science 174:159-61 O 8 '71
Freezing and melting of lipid bilayers and the mode of action of nonactin, valinomycin, and gramicidin. S. Krasne and others. bibliog il Science 174:412-15 O 22 '71

Layman's guide to antibiotics. il Changing T 25:13-15 F '71
Some medicines you may want to avoid; FDA list of ineffective drugs. Consumer Rep 36:114-17 F '71
See also
Actinomycin
Chloramphenicol
Cycloheximide
Erythromycin
Filipin
Fungi—Resistance and sensitivity
Tetracyclines

ANTIBODIES. See Antigens and antibodies

ANTIBODIES, Fluorescent
Nonencapsidated infectious DNA of adenosatellite virus in cells coinfected with herpesvirus. D. W. Boucher and others. bibliog il Science 173:1243-5 S 24 '71

ANTICOAGULANTS
Anemia in sleep-deprived rats receiving anticoagulants. R. R. Drucker-Colin and others. bibliog il Science 174:505-7 O 29 '71

ANTI-COLLISION systems. See Airplanes—Safety devices and measures

ANTI-COMMUNIST measures. See Communism —Anti-Communist measures

ANTI-COMMUNIST movements

Thailand
Counterinsurgency's proving ground M. T. Klare. Nation 212:527-31 Ap 26 '71

ANTI-CRIME legislation. See Crime prevention

ANTIDEPRESSANTS
Rubidium and lithium: opposite effects on amine-mediated excitement. B. J. Carroll and P. T. Sharp. bibliog il Science 172:1355-7 Je 25 '71

ANTI-DEPRESSION measures. See United States—Economic policy

ANTIFERROMAGNETISM. See Magnetism

ANTIFOULING paint. See Paint, Protective

ANTI-FOULING research. See Marine fouling

ANTIFREEZE solutions
Consumer's guide to antifreeze. il Mech Illus 67:69 N '71

ANTIGENS and antibodies
Activation of spontaneous murine leukemia virus-related antigen by lymphocytic choriomeningitis virus. M. B. A. Oldstone and others. bibliog il Science 174:843-5 N 19 '71
Cancer breakthrough; CEA test for cancer of the colon. J. Kirschy. il por Life 70:28-31 Ap 23 '71
Cell dissociation: univalent antibodies as a possible alternative to proteolytic enzymes. H. Beug and others. bibliog il Science 173:742-3 Ag 20 '71
Cell surface antigens: serial sectioning of single cells as an approach to topographical analysis. C. W. Stackpole and others. bibliog il Science 172:472-4 Ap 30 '71
Compositional relatedness between histocompatibility antigens and human serum lipoproteins. K. Berg. bibliog il Science 172:1136-8 Je 11 '71
Density gradient separation of marrow cells restricted for antibody class. H. C. Miller and G. Cudkowicz. bibliog il Science 171:913-15 Mr 5 '71
Density gradient separation of marrow precursor cells restricted for antibody specificity. H. C. Miller and G. Cudkowicz. bibliog il Science 173:156-8 Jl 9 '71
Detection of an antigen associated with acute leukemia. D. L. Mann and others. bibliog il Science 174:1136-7 D 10 '71
Fat antibody. R. H. Berg. McCalls 99:37 N '71
Herpesvirus antigens on cell membranes detected by centrifugation of membrane-antibody complexes. B. Roizman and P. G. Spear. bibliog il Science 171:298-300 Ja 22 '71
Immunogenicity of glucagon: determinants responsible for antibody binding and lymphocyte stimulation. G. Senyk and others. bibliog il Science 171:407-8 Ja 29 '71
Production of hemadsorption-negative areas by serums containing Australia antigen. D. H. Carver and D. S. Y. Seto. bibliog il Science 172:1265-7 Je 18 '71
Salt extraction of soluble HL-A antigens. R. A. Reisfield and others. bibliog il Science 172:1134-6 Je 11 '71
Selective stimulation of allelic expression: effect of antibodies to allotypic markers on lymphoid cells. A. Frensdorff and others. bibliog il Science 171:391-4 Ja 29 '71

ANTIGENS and antibodies—*Continued*
Stimulation in vitro with protein carrier of antibodies against a hapten. A. Sulica and others. bibliog il Science 171:1165-7 Mr 19 '71
Tracing the breakdown of immunity in cancer. il Sci N 100:260-1 O 16 '71
  See also
Complements (immunity)
Gamma globulin
Immunoglobulins
ANTIGONE; drama. See Sophocles
ANTIGUA (island)
Bye-bye. Bird Time 97:41 F 22 '71
ANTIHISTAMINES
Cold that can kill; cold urticaria treatment by cyproheptadine. il Newsweek 78:52 D 27 '71
ANTI-INFLATION measures. See Inflation (finance)
ANTI-LEWIS B factor. See Blood groups
ANTILLES fire. See Ships—Fires and fire protection
ANTILYMPHOCYTIC serum
Homograft rejection delayed by treatment of donor tissue in vitro with antilymphocyte serum. R. M. Burde and others. bibliog il Science 173:921-3 S 3 '71
ANTIMATTER. See Matter, Interstellar
ANTIMETABOLITES
  See also
Acetoxycycloheximide
ANTIMISSILE defense system. See Guided missiles—Defenses
ANTIN, David
Alex Katz and the tactics of representation. il Art N 70:44-7+ Ap '71
Art and the corporations. il Art N 70:22-6+ S '71
Déjà-vu. il Art N 70:50-1+ Sum '71
It reaches a desert in which nothing can be perceived but feeling. bibliog il Art N 70:38-41+ Mr '71
ANTI-NAZI movement
Anti-Nazi resisters: a few remain. E. E. Turner. Chr Cent 88:1266-7 O 27 '71
ANTIOXIDANTS
Dietary trace elements and antioxidants. il Chem 44:23-4 Ja '71
ANTIPERSONNEL weapons. See Weapons
ANTIPERSPIRANTS. See Deodorants
ANTI-POLLUTION patents. See Pollution—Control—Patents
ANTI-POVERTY program, 1964-1969
Phony war on poverty in the Great society. R. M. Pious. bibliog f il Cur Hist 61:266-72 N '71
ANTI-PRIVACY. See Privacy, Right of
ANTIPUT, Samuel N.
AIGA fifty books show; a sharp critique. il Pub W 199:34-7 My 10 '71
ANTIQUE automobiles
  Collectors and collecting
  See Automobiles—Collectors and collecting
ANTIQUE dealers
  See also
Parke-Bernet galleries, inc.
ANTIQUE dolls. See Dolls
ANTIQUE jewelry. See Jewelry
ANTIQUES
Antiquing: the incurable disease. H. H. Carr. Hobbies 75:68-9+ Ja '71
Clues and footnotes. W. D. Garrett. See issues of Antiques
In a memorable house, antiques aren't just to look at. L. Grundy. il House B 113:44-7 Ag '71
Living with antiques:
  Castlefinn farm, the Pennsylvania home of Mrs James Rawle II. L. H. Solis-Cohen. il Antiques 99:386-90 Mr '71
  Château near Liége, Belgium. E. D. Flory. il Antiques 99:398-403 Mr '71
  Chicago apartment of Marshall Field. D. A. Hanks. il Antiques 100:116-19 Jl '71
  Everard Benjamin house, New Haven, Conn. W. D. Garrett. il Antiques 101:185-92 Ja '72
  Fairvue, Tennessee. T. K. Connor. il Antiques 100:606-10 O '71
  Harpeth house, Nashville, Tenn. il Antiques 100:602-5 O '71
  Nashville home of Dr and Mrs Benjamin H. Caldwell, jr. O. W. June. il Antiques 100:433-41 S '71
  Stewart Gregory's Connecticut barn. J. Lipman. il Antiques 99:112-21 Ja '71
Living with antiques in New York state. E. Gaines. il Antiques 99:892-5 Je '71

Questions & answers: antiques. L. A. Boger. See issues of House & garden incorporating Living for young homemakers
Rummaging. R. Berenson. Nat R 23:1004-5 S 10 '71
  See also
Collectors and collecting
Music boxes
Samplers

  Bibliography
Books about antiques. See issues of Antiques
Books reviewed. See issues of Hobbies

  Collectors and collecting
Age is all the rage. Nations Bsns 59:82 My '71
Antiques: what's new? M. Gough. House B 113:89+ S '71
Should you invest in antiques now? M. Roche. bibliog il House & Gard 140:102-3+ N '71

  Exhibitions
Best of show; seventeenth annual winter antiques show. N. Skurka. il N Y Times Mag p54-5+ Ja 17 '71
Calendar of shows. See issues of Antiques
Current and coming. S. B. Sherrill. See issues of Antiques
ANTIQUES (periodical)
Perspective; a history of the magazine commemorating the magazine's 50th anniversary. A. Winchester. il Antiques 101:144-52 Ja '72
ANTIQUITIES, Byzantine. See Byzantine antiquities
ANTIQUITIES, Forgery of. See Forgery of works of art
ANTI-RIOT devices. See Police—Equipment and supplies
ANTI-SEMITISM
Anti-Semitism without Jews, by P. Lendvai. Review
  Commentary 52:88-90 Jl '71. M. Friedberg
  Sat R 54:30+ F 13 '71. S. M. Lipset
Certain anxiety; address. N. Podnoretz. Commentary 52:4+ Ag '71
God's first love, by F. Heer. Review
  Commentary 51:91-2+ Mr '71. A. R. Eckardt; Discussion. 52:18+ Ag '71
Jesus and Israel, by J. Isaac. Review
  Commentary 52:92-5 S '71
Jews and the early church. J. J. Magee. Cath World 214:113-16 D '71
Middle East: from polemic to accommodation. W. G. Oxtoby. bibliog il por Chr Cent 88:1192-7 O 13 '71
Necessary cruelty; the emergence of official anti-Semitism in Poland, 1936-39. E. D. Wynot, jr. bibliog f Am Hist R 76:1035-58 O '71
Never again! M. Himmelfarb. Commentary 52:73-6 Ag '71
Socialism of fools: the new left calls it anti-Zionism. S. M. Lipset; discussion. N Y Times Mag p39 Ja 31; 16+ Mr 14 '71
Superstar attacked by Jewish groups. Chr Cent 88:1255 O 27 '71

  Protests, demonstrations, etc. against
Bully tactics. il Newsweek 77:34 Ja 18 '71
Close call; sniper attack on the building housing the Soviet mission. Newsweek 78:40+ N 1 '71
Jewish outcry; protests against Leningrad trial. il Newsweek 77:51-2 Ja 18 '71
New tension between Russia and U.S; anti-Russian violence. il U S News 70:20-1 Ja 25 '71
President and Jewish leaders decry violence against Soviet facilities; exchange of messages. R. M. Nixon. Dept State Bul 64:166 F 8 '71
ANTISERUM
  See also
Antilymphocytic serum
ANTI-SLAVERY movement. See Slavery—United States
ANTI-SMOKING devices. See Smoking
ANTI-STRIKE legislation. See Labor laws and legislation—United States
ANTI-SUBMARINE airplanes. See Airplanes, Military
ANTITRUST division. See United States—Justice, Department of—Antitrust division
ANTITRUST legislation. See Trusts, Industrial—Law
ANTI-VIETNAM demonstrations. See Vietnamese war, 1957- —Protests, demonstrations, etc. against

ANTIVIRAL agents. See Viruses—Inactivation

ANTIVIRAL proteins. See Interferon

ANTIVIVISECTION. See Vivisection

ANTLERS
Trophies without guns; collecting shed antlers. Cons 26:38 D '71

ANTONACCI, Greg
Dance wi' me; or, The fatal twitch. Criticism
New Yorker 47:51 Je 19 '71 *

ANTONICH, George
How to turn fact into fiction. il Writers Digest 51:37-9+ Ap '71

ANTONIONI, Michelangelo
Antonioni: two decades of film. C. T. Samuels. il Art in Am 59:72-7 Ja '71 *

ANTONY and Cleopatra; opera. See Barber, S.

ANTREI, Albert
Western phenomenon. il Am West 8:42-7+ Mr '71

ANTS
Attack by pheromone. Sci Am 225:45 Jl '71
Big schemes for little ants; fire ants. A. Wolff. il Audubon 73:120-4 Mr '71
Chemical communication and propaganda in slave-maker ants. F. E. Regnier and E. O. Wilson. bibliog il Science 172:267-9 Ap 16 '71
Communication between ants and their guests. B. Hölldobler. il Sci Am 224:86-3 Mr '71
Eradicate them one more time: fire ant eradication program. G. Laycock. Field & S 76:46-7+ D '71
Fire ant control under fire; EDF vs. USDA. D. Shapley. Science 171:1131 Mr 19 '71
Homing in the harvester ant pogonomyrmex badius. B. Hölldobler. bibliog il Science 171: 1149-51 Mr 19 '71
Mirex and the fire ant: decline in fortunes of perfect pesticide. D. Shapley. il Science 172:358-60 Ap 23 '71

ANTUN, Doris
Indian diary. il por Mlle 73:182 Je '71

ANXIETY
Express anger, lower anxiety. A. J. Snider. il Sci Digest 71:70 Ja '72
Final-exam jitters. il Newsweek 77:49 My 24 '71
See also
Fear
Peace of mind
Worry

ANZUS council
ANZUS council holds 21st meeting at New York; text of communique, October 4, 1971. Dept State Bul 65:462-3 O 25 '71

AOKI, Hiroaki
What makes Rocky run. por Newsweek 77: 104+ Ap 19 '71 *

AOUDAD hunting. See Mountain sheep hunting

APARICIO, Luis
Even the President worried. R. Fimrite. Sports Illus 34:54+ Je 14 '71 *

APARTHEID. See South Africa—Race problems

APARTMENT houses
Apartments: adapting to a changing market. R. M. Young. il Arch Rec 149:60 F '71
Apartments of the year. il Arch Rec 149:82-98 mid-My '71
See also
Housing management
Row houses

Condominium plan ownership

In Florida: an ancient concept, a new lifestyle. J. De Long. il House B 113:64-9 F '71
What's the difference between co-op and condominium housing? Good H 173:221 N '71
Worry-free comfort in an apres-ski apartment: condominium approach in Vermont. R. Fitzgerald. il House B 113:96-7 Ap '71

Cooperative ownership

What's the difference between co-op and condominium housing? Good H 173:221 N '71

Garden apartments

Best homes of '71; The Californian. Tustin, Calif. N. Gray. il Am Home 74:81-5+ S '71
Corning, N.Y; Spring Pond apartments. il Arch Forum 134:34-7 My '71
Suburbia was never like this; Sixty-01. Redmond, Wash. B. Plumb. il Am Home 74: 70-5 F '71

APARTMENT houses, Prefabricated
Building types study. il Arch Rec 149:115-38 Ap '71
Structure for change and growth. H. C. Schulitz. il Arch Forum 134:60-3 Mr '71

APARTMENTS
All together now; environmental design. N. Skurka. il N Y Times Mag p48-9 Ap 11 '71
Apartment boom: still going, but running into trouble. il U S News 71:38-40 Ag 2 '71
Bachelor's way: with modest means. il House B 113:156-7 O '71
Breaking out of a box; designs of Rubén de Saavedra. N. Skurka. il N Y Times Mag p74-5 F 21 '71
Breaking out; one-room studio. N. Skurka. il N Y Times Mag p30-1 Jl 11 '71
Bridging the decoration gap. N. Skurka. il N Y Times Mag p 100-1 N 21 '71
City living for the 1970's. B. Plumb. il Am Home 74:50-1 Jl '71
Classic modern setting for a fascinating woman; designed for F. Dunaway. il pors House & Gard 140:60-3 Jl '71
Country garden in the city, bright and informal. N. Schram. il House B 113:42-3 Ag '71
Designing eye at work. N. Schram. il House B 113:94-6 S '71
Discoveries: living machines. il House & Gard 139:94-7 Ap '71
Double-duty units expand a country condominium. H. Brown. il Am Home 74:59-62 F '71
Easy-care decorating; two apartments designed for minimum maintenance. M. Kraft. il Good H 172:120-7 Je '71
End of the box. il House B 113:24-7 Jl '71
Family living in a gala mood. il House & Gard 140:104-9 N '71
First furnishings, first apartment; Brooklyn, N.Y. brownstone apartment. A. Walker. il Am Home 74:40-3 Ag '71
Flexible planning creates a world of uses for city living. R. S. Wurman. il Am Home 74:56-8+ F '71
Flourishing transplant. N. Skurka. il N Y Times Mag p36-7 My 30 '71
For Van Day Truex a scrapbook of souvenirs. N. Schram. il House B 113:48-50 Ag '71
Here today, gone tomorrow; Subhash Paranjpe's Washington, D.C. apartment. N. Skurka. il N Y Times Mag p52-3 F 14 '71
Hideout in the city. A. Wiglama. il House B 113:56-9 F '71
How to pick an apartment. il Changing T 25:15-17 Ap '71
Icy chic of status modern. N. Skurka. il N Y Times Mag p36-7 Ag 29 '71
Islands for today. N. Skurka. il N Y Times Mag p66-7 My 23 '71
Joan Harwood: fresh breeze from the Midwest. S. Nirenberg. il House B 113:58-9+ Ag '71
Lighting an underground mix; ethnic art and art deco. N. Skurka. il N Y Times Mag p78-9 Ap 25 '71
Line-and-form: the New York apartment of Mr and Mrs Alexander Vagliano. il Vogue 157:178-9 F 1 '71
Lofty design on a low budget; Greenwich Village loft. H. Brown. il Am Home 74: 38-9 Ag '71
Mr and Mrs Gardner Cowles's New York apartment. V. Lawford. il Vogue 158:180-7+ O 1 '71
Oasis in Paris: country peace of Yves Saint Laurent's thirties duplex. il Vogue 158: 158-63 N 1 '71
On and off the avenue; A. Kasuba's apartment. J. Malcolm. New Yorker 47:115-17 S 25 '71
One woman's adventures with her three decorators. S. Rattazzi. il por House & Gard 140:116-23+ O '71
Pattern on pattern; Manhattan apartment, designed by Seymour Avigdor. N. Skurka. il N Y Times Mag p54-5 Ja 31 '71
Personal statement; Harrison Cultra's duplex. N. Skurka. il N Y Times Mag p46-7 F 7 '71
Self in chambered space; A. Kasuba. M. Shorr. il Craft Horiz 31:26-9+ Ag '71
Sleek dream by the sea; A. Belfers' Palm Beach apartment. L. Grundy. il House B 113:130-5 O '71
Space-and-light: the New York apartment of Fred Mueller. il Vogue 157:174-7 F 1 '71
Splash of graphics. il House B 113:40-3 Jl '71
That brownstone feeling; New York duplex. N. Skurka. il N Y Times Mag p42-3 Ag 15 '71
Touch of worldliness; Park avenue duplex. N. Skurka. il N Y Times Mag p80-1 Mr 7 '71
Urbane triumph by the Golden Gate: Tony Hail's apartment in San Francisco. L. Grundy. il House B 113:60-3 Mr '71
Wanted: room with view. Sci Digest 69:82 Ap '71

APARTMENTS—*Continued*
World of rich color. il House & Gard 140:
110-13 S '71
Young apartment with decorating ideas by
the dozen. M. Kraft. il Good H 173:118-22+
Jl '71
Your first apartment. P. Bartlett. il Mlle 72:42
Ja '71
APARTMENTS, Remodeled
Making sense out of a jigsaw apartment. A.
Wiglama. il House B 113:92-3 My '71
Raising the roof in the midst of Manhattan.
il House B 113:119-21 My '71
6 interiors; A. Kasuba's New York apart-
ment. il Arch Rec 150:93-5 Ag '71
Where did all the laundry go? N. Schram. il
House B 113:108-9 My '71
APE men. See Man, Prehistoric
APÉRITIF wines. See Wine
APES
Carnivorous tendencies among primates. S. J.
Fleming. il Sci Digest 70:89-92 Ag '71
See also
Chimpanzees
Gorillas
Monkeys

Anecdotes, facetiae, satire, etc.
He's big! He's bashful! He smells bad! great
skunk ape of south Florida. P. Putnam.
il Sports Illus 35:44-6 Ag 30 '71
APES, Barbary. See Monkeys
APES, Fossil
Earliest ape; Aegyptopithecus. il Sci N 100:
24 Jl 10 '71
Extinct ape puzzle pieces finally fit; dryopi-
thecus. il Sci Digest 69:88-9 F '71
Gorilla-sized ape from the miocene of India;
Dryopithecus indicus. E. L. Simons and
D. Pilbeam. bibliog il Science 173:23-7 Jl 2
'71
APES as artists. See Animals as artists
APGAR, Mahlon, 4th
New business from new towns? il Harvard
Bsns R 49:90-109 Ja '71
APHORISMS and apothegms
Sayings of poor Russell. R. Baker. il Harper
244:64-5 Ja '72
APHRODISIACS
Can love medicines make you sexier? A.
West. il Vogue 158:160-1+ O 1 '71
APOCHROMATIC lenses. See Lenses, Photo-
graphic
APOLLO 11 flight. See Space flight to the
moon—Manned flights—Apollo 11 flight
APOLLO 14 flight. See Space flight to the moon
—Manned flights—Apollo 14 flight
APOLLO 15 flight. See Space flight to the
moon—Manned flights—Apollo 15 flight
APOLLO 17 (flight proposed) See Space flight
to the moon—Manned flights—Apollo 17
flight (proposed)
APOLLO flight training. See Astronauts—
Training
APOLLO lunar surface experiments package.
See Moon—Exploration—Equipment
APOLLO project. See Space flight to the moon
APOLLO theatre, Harlem. See Theater, Negro
APOLOGETICS
History of apologetics, by A. Dulles. Review
America 125:45-6 Jl 24 '71. G. Baum
APOPLEXY. See Cerebrovascular disease
APOSTAL, Robert A.
Personality descriptions of mental health
center patients for use as pre-therapy in-
formation. Ment Hy 55:119-20 Ja '71
APOSTLES. Acts of. See Bible—New Testa-
ment—Acts
APOTHEGMS. See Aphorisms and apothegms
APPALACHIAN furniture. See Furniture,
American
APPALACHIAN REGION
Alternative service locates in Appalachia. J.
DeMuth. il America 125:374-5 N 6 '71
Appalachia; cultural values. L. Jones. il To-
days Ed 60:54-5 Ap '71
Helping out in Appalachia; work vacation
of 35 New Jersey students. il Good H 172:
60-1 Je '71
Price of strip mining. il Time 97:47 Mr 22 '71
Strip mining. J. Trawick. il Nat Parks &
Con Mag 45:10-14 Jl '71; Same abr. with
title Ravaging land by strip mining. Cur
132:31-5 S '71
Stripping for pleasure and profit. J. Brans-
come. Commonweal 95:229-31 D 3 '71
Threats to southern Appalachia. M. Frome.
il Nat Parks & Con Mag 45:6-9 Jl '71
See also
Arts and crafts—Appalachian Region
Coal mines and mining—Appalachian Region
Education—Appalachian Region
Mountaineers (southern states)
Public health—Appalachian Region

Photographs
Gallery: Doris Ulman's The Appalachian
photographs. Life 71:8-9 O 1 '71

Social conditions
Change in rural Appalachia, ed. by J. D. Pho-
tiadis and H. K. Schwarzweller and Appa-
lachia's children, by D. H. Looff. Reviews
Nation 213:216+ S 13 '71. H. S. Arnow
APPALACHIAN TRAIL
Long, long trail awinding. P. Whitley. il por
Am For 77:16-18+ F '71
Trails: so who needs them? D. B. Huyck. il
Am For 77:22-4+ O '71
APPARENT movement illusion. See Optical
illusions
APPARITIONS
See also
Mediums
APPEAL. See Appellate procedure
APPEL, Alfred, Jr
Nabokov: a portrait. il pors Atlan 228:77-
9+ S '71
APPEL, Benjamin
Two views from two sides of the generation
fence. il Pub W 199:23+ Je 7 '71
APPEL, Gary L. and Schlenker, R. E.
Analysis of Michigan's experience with work
incentives. bibliog il Mo Labor R 94:15-22
S '71
APPEL, George J.
Plastic trash carts to the rescue. il Am City
86:77-8 Jl '71
APPELLATE procedure
Decisions. Time 98:60 S 20 '71
APPETITE
Lateral hypothalamus: reevaluation of func-
tion in motivated feeding behavior. L. D.
Devenport and S. Balagura. bibliog il Sci-
ence 172:744-6 My 14 '71
Norepinephrine: reversal of anorexia in rats
with lateral hypothalamic damage. B. D.
Berger and others. bibliog il Science 172:
281-4 Ap 16 '71
APPETIZERS
Cheese pastries with tomato on top. il Sun-
set 147:172 D '71
Conversation food; with recipes. F. Guth. il
House & Gard 139:85-91 F '71
Cooking game, fast paced. M. McKendry. il
Vogue 158:206 S 1 '71
Finger food. E. Marlowe. il Am Home 74:72
N '71
Food. J. Hewitt. il N Y Times Mag p 105+
D 5 '71
For vegetables: a vegetable dip. il Sunset 147:
158 D '71
Hibachi appetizers. il Bet Hom & Gard 49:11
Je '71
Hot shrimp puffs, easily made. il Sunset
146:186 Je '71
Make an unexpected feast; eight freshly east-
ern appetizers. E. Alston and others. il
Look 35:36 S 21 '71
Making your own Liptauer; cheese dip. il
Sunset 147:187 O '71
Pickled onions as appetizer. il Sunset 146:106
Ja '71
Sauerkraut and ham balls. il Sunset 147:
176 N '71
This appetizer idea is Chinese; water chest-
nut tumble. il Sunset 146:188 Je '71
APPIA, Adolphe
Let there be light. M. J. Matz. il pors Opera
N 35:8-11 Ap 3 '71 •
APPLAUSE
Applause. G. R. Marek. il Opera N 36:6-7 D 18
'71
APPLAUSE; musical comedy. See Musical com-
edies, revues, etc.—Criticisms, plots, etc.
APPLE, Raymond Walter, 1934-
Is McCloskey the McCarthy of '72? il pors
N Y Times Mag p28-9+ Ap 18 '71
APPLE cider. See Cider
APPLE trees
Apples are ready! L. Hill. il Org Gard & Farm
18:62-5 S '71
Doctoring old apple trees. J. Vivian. il por
Org Gard & Farm 18:65-7 D '71
APPLE worms. See Codling moths
APPLEMAN, Philip
Love poem. Nation 212:152 F 1 '71
Persistence of memory; poem. Nation 213:
124 Ag 16 '71
APPLES
Apples are ready! Duchess apples. L. Hill.
il Org Gard & Farm 18:62-5 S '71
See also
Cookery—Fruit

APPLESAUCE. See Cookery—Fruit

APPLEWHITE, James
Roadside notes in ragged hand driving from South Carolina: poem. Harper 243:81 S '71
Scorned; Highwater; poems. Poetry 118: 195-7 Jl '71

APPLIANCE rollers. See Casters, glides, etc (hardware)

APPLIANCE warranties. See Warranty

APPLICATIONS for positions
How poverty area residents look for work. H. J. Hilaski. il Mo Labor R 94:41-5 Mr '71
If you wind up in the ranks of the unemployed. Bsns W p73 Jl 10 '71
9 big do's and don'ts for the 1971 job hunter. C. Mangel. Look 35:21-3 My 18 '71; Same abr. with title How to land the job you want. Read Digest 99:197-8+ O '71
Top executive hunts for a job. M. Durham. il pors Life 70:44-50C Mr 19 '71
See also
Video recorders and recording—Business use

APPORTIONMENT (election law)
Coming shake-up in Congress: redistricting signals big changes: il U S News 71:78-81 N 29 '71
Illinois gerrymander. Nation 213:323-4 O 11 '71
It's a different political ball game; redistricting. Nations Bsns 59:38-9+ Ap '71
See also
Gerrymander

APPRAISAL of books. See Book reviews

APPRAISAL of employees. See Employees—Rating

APPRECIATION of art. See Art—Appreciation

APPRECIATION of music. See Music—Appreciation

APPRENTICES
Apprenticeships for graphic designers. D. Holden. Am Artist 35:56-8 My '71

APPROPRIATIONS. See subhead Appropriations and expenditures under names of countries and departments of government, e.g. United States—Armed forces—Appropriations and expenditures

APTHEKER, Herbert
Souls of black folk: a comparison of the 1903 and 1952 editions; address. October, 1970. por Negro Hist Bul 34:15-17 Ja '71

APTITUDE tests
How to cure a major cause of unrest. D. Lawrence. U S News 70:96 Je 21 '71
How to tell whether you're in the right job. S. Bacon. il Mech Illus 67:39-41+ Ag '71
Learning languages; modern language aptitude test. Fortune 83:42 Mr '71
Predicting college success of the educationally disadvantaged; adaptation of address, June 1970. J. C. Stanley. bibliog Science 171:640-7 F 19 '71; Discussion. 173: 1079; 174:1278-9 S 17. D 24 '71

AQUACULTURE. See Fish culture

AQUARIUMS
How to make and keep a smart fish bowl under the table. J. Hand. il Pop Sci 199: 78-9+ Jl '71
Miniature ecosystem. M. Andolina. il Cons 25:48-9+ Je '71
Starting a home aquarium. Good H 173:140 Ag '71

AQUATIC plants
For variety in your water garden. il Sunset 146:217 Je '71
See also
Algae
Anacharis
Aquariums
Marine flora
Water gardens
Water milfoil

AQUATIC sports
Cypress Gardens rides again. M. E. Slate. il Motor B & S 127:10-11 Mr '71
Octopush. il Life 70:89-90 My 14 '71
Red cross national aquatic and small-craft schools (cont) Camp Mag 43:30-1 Ap '71
Watersports; ed. by G. F. Hammond. See issues of Motor boating & sailing to July 1971
See also
Boats and boating
Diving
Sailing
Skin diving
Swimming
Water skis and skiing

AQUATIC weed control
Control those water weeds. il Suc Farm 69: no4 C30 Mr '71
Hay bales: an answer to pond weeds. R. Martin. Org Gard & Farm 18:70-1 N '71

Out with the algae, safely: Delavan Lake. il Am City 86:84+ Je '71
Striking the balance; TVA use of 2,4-D to control Eurasian watermilfoil. E. Hirst and H. Bank. bibliog il Environ 13:34-41 N '71

AQUINAS, Thomas, Saint. See Thomas Aquinas, Saint

ARAB countries. See Arab states

ARAB-Israeli war, 1967-. See Israeli-Arab war, 1967

ARAB-Jewish relations. See Jewish-Arab relations

ARAB REPUBLICS, Federation of
Federated Arabs. Time 98:33 S 13 '71
Mideast troika. Nat R 23:462 My 4 '71
No. 4: the Union of Arab republics. il Newsweek 77:39-40 My 3 '71

ARAB states
What is an Arab? J. Morris. il Horizon 13:4-17 Sum '71
Where sheiks are sheiks, and money flows: sheikdom states of the Persian Gulf. A. de Borchgrave. il Newsweek 77:30 Ja 18 '71
See also
Airlines—Arab states
Banks and banking—Arab states
Guerrillas—Arab states
Immigration and emigration—Arab states
Jewish-Arab relations
Panarabism
Union of Arab republics (proposed)
Women—Arab states

Foreign relations
Arabs' attitude to the west. M. Berger. Yale R 61:207-25 D '71
United States
See United States—Foreign relations—Arab states

Israeli occupation, 1967-
Bulldozers carve out Israel's new frontiers. M. Orshefsky. il Life 70:32-4 Mr 12 '71
See also
United Nations—Special committee to investigate Israeli practices affecting the human rights of the population of the occupied territories

Nationalism
See also
Panarabism

Politics
Arab world in turmoil. E. von Kuehnelt-Leddihn. Nat R 23:993 S 10 '71
Arabs v. Communists: thanks but no thanks. il Time 98:26-7 Ag 9 '71
New danger signals in Mideast. il U S News 71:11-12 Ag 9 '71
Persian Gulf: after the British raj. D. Holden. il For Affairs 49:721-35 Jl '71

ARABIA
See also
Oman

ARABIAN beauty; story. See Hoyer, L. G.

ARABIAN nights entertainments
Thousand and one nights or the secret of Scheherazade. M. Léturmy. il UNESCO Courier 24:40-3 O '71

ARABS
Arabs' attitude to the west. M. Berger. Yale R 61:207-25 D '71
What is an Arab? J. Morris. il Horizon 13:4-17 Sum '71
See also
Jewish-Arab relations

ARABS in Israel. See Palestinian Arabs

ARABS in Morocco
Mohammed: the prophet armed. S. De Gramont. il Horizon 13:18-23 Sum '71

ARABS of Palestine. See Palestinian Arabs

ARACHNIDS
See also
Harvestmen
Spiders

ARAKAWA, Shusaku
Can epistemology be entertaining? J. G. Bowles. il por Art N 70:34-5+ My '71 •

ARAN ISLANDS
Arans, Ireland's invincible isles. V. Thomas. il Nat Geog 139:544-73 Ap '71

ARANA OSORIO, Carlos Manuel
Guatemala: terror in silence. J. C. Goulden. Nation 212:365-8 Mr 22 '71 •
When the blood began to run. il por Time 97: 33 Mr 22 '71 •

ARANSON, Jack
Moby Dick; dramatization of novel by H. Melville. Criticism
Time il por 97:74 Ap 26 '71 •

ARANT, Willard D.
Yardstick has to measure up. por Nations Bsns 59:75 My '71

ARARAT, MOUNT
Ark fever. J. W. Montgomery. Chr Today 15: 38-9 Jl 2 '71
ARBANAS, Fred
These major-leaguers succeeded in spite of . . . E. Kiester. il pors Todays Health 49: 49-50 O '71 *
ARBITRAGE
Arbitrage, headiest game in the street. A. Hershman. il Duns 93:52-4+ Je '69
ARBITRATION, Industrial
Who cares about the public interest? compulsory arbitration; reprint. D. Lawrence. U S News 70:84 My 31 '71
See also
Collective bargaining

United States
High-level search for a better way. Bsns W p80 F 20 '71
Unfair practices and arbitration. bibliog Mo Labor R 94:64-6 N '71
See also
United States—Federal mediation and conciliation service
ARBITRATION, International
World and U.S. problems; address. July 6, 1971. R. M. Nixon. Vital Speeches 37:611-15 Ag 1 '71; Excerpts. U S News 71:46-7 Ag 2 '71
ARBITRATION, Judicial. See Procedure (law)
ARBITRATION and award
Court of his peers; Hoffman-Forcade case. Time 98:59 O 4 '71
ARBORVITAE
Diethylamide of thujic acid: a potent repellent of aedes aegypti; substance from bark of Western red cedar. V. Hach and E. C. McDonald. bibliog il Science 174:144-5 O 8 '71
ARCHAEOPTERYX. See Birds, Fossil
ARCHEOLOGICAL expeditions
Once more into the past; planned expedition by L. S. B. Leakey to East Africa. il por Sci N 100:259 O 16 '71
ARCHEOLOGICAL pillage. See Pillage
ARCHEOLOGICAL research. See Archeology—Methodology
ARCHEOLOGY
New archeology: toward a social science. A. L. Hammond. Science 172:1119-20 Je 11 '71
Pyramids from France? theories of C. Renfrew. il Newsweek 77:50 Ap 5 '71
See also
Bible—Antiquities
Cave drawings and paintings
Cities and towns, Ruined, extinct, etc.
Excavations (archeology)
Man—Origin and antiquity
Man, Prehistoric
Mummies
Petroglyphs
Pyramids
Stone implements and weapons
X rays—Archeological use
also subhead Antiquities under names of continents, countries, states, etc. e.g. Turkey—Antiquities

Methodology
Ancient impressions; fingerprints used in dating. il Time 97:55 Je 7 '71
Application of the physical sciences to archeology. F. H. Stross. Science 171:831-2+ F 26 '71
Archeological methodology and remote sensing. G. J. Gumerman and T. R. Lyons. bibliog il Science 172:126-32 Ap 9 '71
Finding records of ancient man in the soil. J. Zimmerman. il Chem 44:12-14 My '71
In the footsteps of ancient man: Archaeology research center in Lejre, Denmark. J. Zimmerman. il Chem 44:16-17 F '71
Prehistoric domestication of animals: effects on bone structure. I. M. Drew and others. bibliog il Science 171:280-2 Ja 22 '71
Tools for archeology: aids to studying the past. A. L. Hammond. Science 173:511-12 Ag 6 '71
What new methods are being developed for dating the past? Sci Digest 70:88-9 S '71
See also
Radioactive dating
Radiocarbon dating
ARCHEOLOGY, Submarine
Byzantine trading venture. G. F. Bass. il Sci Am 225:22-33 bibliog(p 120) Ag '71
Deep-water archeology. W. Bascom. bibliog il Science 174:261-9 O 15 '71
Salvaging ancient ships; Alcoa Seaprobe. il Newsweek 78:84 N 22 '71

ARCHEOLOGY and the World war. See World war, 1939-1945—Science
ARCHER, Jeff
From: songs for wayfarers and invalids. Sr Schol 98:8 My 17 '71
ARCHER, Michael C. and others
Environmental nitroso compounds: reaction of nitrite with creatine and creatinine. bibliog il Science 174:1341-3 D 24 '71
ARCHERY
How are you on archery? questions and answers. D. Du Bois. Outdoor Life 148:82-4 S '71
Sport of all seasons. G. H. Gillelan. il Outdoor Life 147:118+ My '71
Women in archery. G. H. Gillelan. il Outdoor Life 147:16+ Ap '71
See also
Fishing with bow and arrow
Hunting with bow and arrow

Competitions
Unusual archery club. G. H. Gillelan. il Outdoor Life 147:36+ Mr '71

Equipment
Big little gizmo imbroglio: mechanical releases. H. Weiskopf. il Sports Illus 34:52+ F 15 '71
ARCHES NATIONAL MONUMENT
Arches. il Sunset 146:92-5 My '71
Arches National Monument. E. H. Colner. il Parks & Rec 6:36-7 N '71
ARCHIBALD, Paul B.
Some delightful engines driven by the heating of rubber bands. il Sci Am 224:118-22 Ap '71
ARCHITECTS
Architect's role in preservation. R. Jensen. il Arch Rec 150:82-3+ D '71
Architects want a voice in redesigning America. G. Breckenfeld. il Fortune 84:144-7+ N '71
Building team, and other ill-defined ideas. W. F. Wagner, jr. Arch Rec 149:9 Ap '71
Professional construction management and project administration; with editorial comment. W. B. Foxhill. il Arch Rec 149:9-10, 69-70 Je '71
See also
American institute of architects
Architecture as a profession
Naval architects
Negro architects
also names of architects, e.g. S. White
Licenses and registration
State registration laws can trip you. J. W. Giles. Arch Rec 149:55 My '71
See also
National council of architectural registration boards
Training
See also
Architectural education
ARCHITECTS offices. See Offices
ARCHITECTURAL acoustics. See Acoustics, Architectural
ARCHITECTURAL decoration. See Decoration and ornament, Architectural
ARCHITECTURAL designs. See Architecture—Designs and plans
ARCHITECTURAL drawing
Architectural firm uses half-size drawing system. il Arch Rec 149:58 My '71
ARCHITECTURAL education
Beyond habitat, by M. Safdie. Review Arch Forum 135:10 Jl '71. R. Banham
See also
Frank Lloyd Wright school of architecture
ARCHITECTURAL firms
Are architectural employees headed for unionism? E. K. Thompson. Arch Rec 149: 10 My '71
Pros and cons of corporate professional practice. Arch Rec 149:66+ Mr '71
See also names of architectural firms, e.g. Yearwood and Johnson, inc.
ARCHITECTURAL follies. See Follies (architecture)
ARCHITECTURAL lighting. See Lighting, Architectural and decorative
ARCHITECTURAL plans. See Architecture—Designs and plans
ARCHITECTURAL space. See Space (architecture)
ARCHITECTURAL symbols. See Symbols
ARCHITECTURE
Architecture. M. Josephson. il Art in Am 59: 108-9 Mr '71
Architecture. G. McCue. il Art in Am 59:96-7 My; 98-9 S '71
Focus; monthly review of notable buildings. See issues of Architectural forum

ARCHITECTURE, Domestic—See also—*Cont.*
Hillside architecture
House construction
Houses, Prefabricated
Houses, Remodeled
Housing
Porches
Row houses
Studios
Vacation houses

Conservation and restoration

See Architecture—Conservation and restoration

Designs and plans

Computer house: a house to match our age; with editorial comment. J. Ingersoll. il House B 113:20. 45-55+ F '71
Custom design for modern living. il McCalls 98:88-91+ Ag '71
Four good no-nonsense houses. S. Mead. il Bet Hom & Gard 49:48-55+ S '71
House that grows; Diaz-Infante's modular house of plastic polyester. J. Sanger. il por Américas 23:16-24 Mr '71
House with growing room; 14th Mothers' conference home. J. R. Cary. il Parents Mag 46:54-5 Jl '71
Record houses of 1971. il Arch Rec 149:21-81 mid-My '71
Six-level house for $11,200 for materials and land. il House & Gard 139:112-15 Ap '71
Well-built house. J. H. Ingersoll. See issues of House beautiful

Arizona

Desert house within a wild mesquite grove. il Sunset 146:56-7 Ja '71

Arkansas

Looking-glass house; James Lambeth's design for his family home. B. Plumb. il Am Home 74:62-5 Mr '71

Australia

Australia's terrace houses. K. Woolley. il Arch Forum 134:46-51 My '71

Bahama Islands

House of Grace, countess of Dudley, in Nassau. V. Lawford. il por Vogue 157:142-7+ Mr 1 '71

Block Island

Block Island sanctuary. B. Plumb. il Am Home 74:86-9 S '71

California

As much to view inside as out; beachfront house of the David Martins. il House B 113: 64-7 Mr '71
Double serenity in two art-filled homes of H. Wallis. M. Miller. il House B 113:27-33 Ag '71
Fresh look for the Mexican heritage; house of the Thomas Inches. M. Miller. il House B 113:48-55 Mr '71
House with disappearing walls. il Sunset 147: 92-3 N '71
New house with the warmth of the land; Kipp Stewart's house on Monterey Peninsula. il House & Gard 140:42-51 Ag '71
Paseo houses: Valencia, Calif. S. Mead. il Bet Hom & Gard 49:40-1 Ag '71
Pueblo freshly defined: California bicentennial house, design of Raul Garduno. il House B 113:78-81 Mr '71
Riley house, Inverness. il Arch Rec 149:26-7 mid-My '71
Stevens house, Malibu colony, Malibu Beach. il Arch Rec 149:44-7 mid-My '71
Unusual city house, screened from the street yet open to its grand view of San Francisco Bay. il Sunset 146:80-1 Je '71
What a wonderful space to be in. il Sunset 147:80-1 O '71
What's unusual about this house? Its many unusual windows. il Sunset 147:62-3 S '71

Canada

House which enhances its site. il Arch Rec 149:119-22 F '71
Well-built house: T-shaped for Toronto lakeside. J. H. Ingersoll. il House B 113:190 O '71

Caribbean Region

Season it Caribbean. J. Peter. il Look 35: 70-1 O 19 '71

Colorado

Bridge house for skiers by Eliot Noyes. il Arch Rec 149:125-8 Mr '71
Grossman house, Denver. il Arch Rec 149:32-3 mid-My '71

Living in a scalloped foam shell. J. Levy. il Am Home 74:86-7 Ap '71
Well-built house; E. Folsom's house on Pike's Peak. J. H. Ingersoll. il House B 113:6 Ag '71

Connecticut

Andrew Wyeth kind of house. N. Skurka. il N Y Times Mag p42-3 Jl 25 '71
Barn becomes a home. il Am Home 74:90-1 My '71
Burnham house, Stamford. il Arch Rec 149: 76-7 mid-My '71
Graham house, Fairfield County. il Arch Rec 149:64-5 mid-My '71
Special house for a handicapped owner. il Arch Rec 149:122-4 My '71

Denmark

Danish modern is classic; home of Hans Wegner. N. Skurka. il N Y Times Mag p96-7 O 17 '71
New kind of urban sprawl for relaxed city living. S. G. Lewin. il House B 113:34-7 Ag '71

England

Uppark, Sussex: a property of the English national trust. C. Musgrave. il Antiques 99: 848-53 Je '71

Fire Island

Combs house. il Arch Rec 149:70-1 mid-My '71
It's great when entertaining. A. Wiglama. il House B 113:158-61 O '71

Florida

Custom design for modern living. il McCalls 98:88-91+ Ag '71
Dual drama; spatial excitement within a sculptured form. S. G. Lewin. il House B 113:105-12 N '71
Exposed pilings support eight-level wood frame house. il Arch Rec 150:135-8 S '71
In Florida: an ancient concept, a new lifestyle. J. De Long. il House B 113:64-9 F '71
Pretty colors: a woman's best friend; the Thomas Shevlins' house. il House & Gard 140:100-5 S '71
Schmidt house, Coconut Grove. il Arch Rec 149:56-7 mid-My '71

Georgia

Charles Tallman 1848 house in Savannah. il House & Gard 140:64-5 Ag '71
Debutante look for a depressed dowager; Ansley park, Atlanta. J. H. Ingersoll. il House B 113:78-85 My '71
Our dollar-saving idea house. V. D. Hahn. il Am Home 74:76-81 Ap '71

Great Britain

Americans in London: mews houses belonging to Hugh Chisholm and John Galliher. il Vogue 158:118-21 S 15 '71

Guadeloupe (islands)

Jungle jewel box; live-and-work studios of J. Schlumberger. V. Lawford. il por Vogue 157:112-19+ F 15 '71

Illinois

Haid house, Evanston. il Arch Rec 149:48-9 mid-My '71
Well-built house; separate sleeping and living areas. J. H. Ingersoll. il House B 113: 12 N '71

Indiana

Well-built house. il House B 113:10 Je '71

Italy

There's a small palazzo by a Grand Canal. il N Y Times Mag p 104-5 S 12 '71

Long Island

Barn with a spirit all its own. S. G. Lewin. il House B 113:86-9 My '71
Closed and open. N. Skurka. il N Y Times Mag p62-3 O 10 '71
Honest heirs to an urbane past. il House B 113:136-8 O '71
House, ahoy! il N Y Times Mag p32 Jl 18 '71
Perlbinder house, Sagaponac. il Arch Rec 149:34-7 mid-My '71
Remodeled garage beside Long Island's waters. L. Grundy. il House B 113:70-4 F '71
Residence in East Hampton. il Arch Rec 149: 72-5 mid-My '71
Sabel house, Bridgehampton. il Arch Rec 149: 22-5 mid-My '71
Secluded weekend house for city dwellers. il Arch Rec 149:120-1 My '71
Treehouse deep in the woods. il House B 113: 45-9 Ja '71

ARCHITECTURE, Domestic—*Continued*

Louisiana

1830 landmark lights up. il Am Home 74:92-5 My '71

Maryland

Patio houses. S. Mead. il Bet Hom & Gard 49:76-7 Ap '71

Residence in eastern shore. il Arch Rec 149: 50-3 mid-My '71

Mississippi

History in towns; ante bellum houses in Columbus. P. T. Murfee. il Antiques 100: 914-18 D '71

Missouri

Architect's answer to an impossible dream. J. DeLong. il House B 113:84-8 S '71

New England

At journey's end: the house she couldn't find. N. Craig and M. Sutphen. il House B 113:114-21 Ap '71

New Hampshire

Six-level house for $11,200 for materials and land. il House & Gard 139:112-15 Ap '71

New Jersey

Cabin adds a wing. V. D. Hahn. il Am Home 74:96-7 My '71

Frankel house, Margate. il Arch Rec 149:54-5 mid-My '71

Parker house, Mendham. il Arch Rec 149:40-3 mid-My '71

Rescuing a homestead from the wrath of time. E. McDonald. il House B 113:98-9 My '71

Timeless modern house; Lakewood. N.J; with introd. by J. D. Morgan. il Arch Rec 150: 113-18 O '71

Wide-open spaces. N. Skurka. il N Y Times Mag p68-9 O 31 '71

New York (state)

Far cry from hay and horses; 19th-century barn/carriage house. il House B 113:90-1 My '71

Four levels for living in the treetops; M. Goldfinger house. il House & Gard 139:76-81 Je '71

Goldfinger house, Waccabuc. il Arch Rec 149: 78-81 mid-My '71

House designed for play; home of Eliot and Sheila Gerber. il House B 113:34-9 Jl '71

House next to nature. il House & Gard 140: 126-9 O '71

Residence in central New York state. il Arch Rec 149:58-9 mid-My '71

Residence in Harrison. il Arch Rec 149:66-9 mid-My '71

Residence in Waccabuc. il Arch Rec 149:28-31 mid-My '71

Shafer house, Annandale-on-Hudson. il Arch Rec 149:60-3 mid-My '71

See also

Architecture, Domestic—Long Island

New York (city)—Architecture

Ohio

Hallmark house 1971. il House & Gard 140: 90-101 N '71

Quebec (province)

Foam domes expand a $12,500 house. B. Plumb. il Am Home 74:82-5 Ap '71

Rhode Island

Adventures for the eye in a young family's hilltop house. il House & Gard 140:122-5 S '71

Alfred Van Liew 1860 house in Providence. il House & Gard 140:56-7 Ag '71

See also

Architecture, Domestic—Block Island

South Carolina

New shape for the Old South. F. Heard. il House B 113:80-9 F '71

Rufus Barkley 1772 house in Charleston. il House & Gard 140:58-9 Ag '71

Tennessee

Domestic architecture in Middle Tennessee. A. W. Hutchinson, jr. il Antiques 100:402-7 S '71

Jones house, Memphis. il Arch Rec 149:38-9 mid-My '71

Texas

Computer house: a house to match our age; with editorial comment. J. Ingersoll. il House B 113:20, 45-55+ F '71

Farmhouse opens to the Texas sky. B. Plumb. il Am Home 74:84-9 My '71

Old Texas farmhouse restored for a family of five. il House & Gard 140:68-71 Ag '71

Well-built house; J. Zemanek residence, Houston. J. H. Ingersoll. il House B 113:6 Jl '71

Tobago (Island)

Place to raise rainbows; Mr and Mrs Norman Parkinson's house. W. Parkinson. il Vogue 157:106-11 Ja 15 '71

United States

Art of architecture. C. Gwathmey. il Art in Am 59:92-7 Ja '71

Barefoot, see-through house; house of Mr and Mrs Thomas Britt. il House & Gard 139:100-7 My '71

California look: a thriving transplant. il Bsns W p44-5 Ag 14 '71

When an architect builds for himself. W. McQuade. il Fortune 84:148-55 N '71

See also subhead Architecture under names of cities, e.g. Columbus, Ind.—Architecture

Vermont

Snug house for snow lovers. B. Plumb. il Am Home 74:56-7+ D '71

Virgin Islands

Vacation house to catch the breeze. il House & Gard 140:72-7 D '71

Virginia

House at ease in any season. J. H. Ingersoll. il House B 113:76-9 D '71

Well-built house; Richmond row house. J. H. Ingersoll. il House B 113:46 My '71

Washington (state)

Beside the lake, beneath the trees. J. DeLong. il House B 113:78-83 Je '71

Design tailored to the trees; home of Donna and Jack Melill. B. Plumb. il Am Home 74:66-9 Mr '71

Western states

See also

Western home awards

Wisconsin

Cliffhanging retreat for a three-career man; Ben Heineman's summer home on Green Bay. W. McQuade. il Fortune 83:105-7 Mr '71

Real cliffhanger. il Arch Forum 134:62-5 Ja '71

ARCHITECTURE, English

See also

Architecture, Domestic—England

ARCHITECTURE, Fantastic

Futurescapes of the 21st century. il UNESCO Courier 24:16-21 Ap '71

Old French postman's dream; F. Cheval's palace of fantasy, France. il por Life 70: 70-3 Mr 12 '71

U.S. journal: Watts, the towers. C. Trillin. New Yorker 47:136+ D 4 '71

ARCHITECTURE, Georgian

Notable American houses: going by the book in designs and practices; excerpt from The American heritage history of notable American houses. M. B. Davidson. il Antiques 100:580-5 O '71

ARCHITECTURE, Gothic

American Gothic; with portfolio of the works of A. J. Davis. W. Andrews. Am Heritage 22:26-47+ O '71

ARCHITECTURE, Hillside. See Hillside architecture

ARCHITECTURE, Hotel. See Hotels, taverns, etc.

ARCHITECTURE, Italian

Notable American houses: going by the book in designs and practices; Palladian style; excerpt from The American heritage history of notable American houses. M. B. Davidson. il Antiques 100:580-5 O '71

ARCHITECTURE, Latin American

Colonial art in Latin America; architecture; symposium. il Américas 23:S1-24 Ap '71

ARCHITECTURE, Modern

Kenzo Tange, 1946-1969, architecture and urban design. ed. by U. Kultermann. Review

Arch Forum 135:8 O '71. R. Boyd

Less is more: Mies van der Rohe; less is a bore: Robert Venturi. P. Goldberger. il N Y Times Mag p34-7+ O 17 '71

New architecture: building for man. il Newsweek 77:78-88+ Ap 19 '71

You can't see the foyer for the trees. W. Von Eckardt. il pors Horizon 13:40-7 Sum '71

Young families like modern: Looking-glass house; Design tailored to the trees. B. Plumb. il Am Home 74:61-9 Mr '71

ARCHITECTURE, School. See School buildings

ARCHITECTURE, Spanish colonial. See Architecture, Latin American

ARCHITECTURE as a profession
Your career in architecture. C. Peet. il Sci Digest 69:60-4 Je '71

ARCHIVES
  See also
Documents

Great Britain
Day in the life; childrens' accounts of census day, April 25, 1971, to be preserved. H. R. Mayes. Sat R 54:10+ N 6 '71

United States
  See also
Presidential libraries
United States—National archives

Vietnam (Republic)
Diem documents. il por Time 98:29 Ag 2 '71

ARCOLOGIES. See City planning

ARCTANDER, Erik H.
Minicycle: a whole new breed of bike! il Pop Mech 136:140-3 O '71

ARCTIC enterprises, inc.
Dynamic growth companies. il Nations Bsns 59:70-2 F '71

ARCTIC OCEAN
Submarine pingos in the Beaufort Sea. J. M. Shearer and others. bibliog il Science 174: 816-18 N 19 '71
Unveiling an ocean of ice. Nat Geog 140:518-19. sup(folded map) O '71

ARCTIC owls. See Owls

ARCTIC REGIONS
  See also
Alaska
Aleutian Islands
Aviation—Arctic Regions
Baffin Island
Eskimos
Fishing—Arctic Regions
Ice—Polar Regions
Paleontology—Arctic Regions
Shipping—Arctic Regions

Maps
Unveiling an ocean of ice. Nat Geog 140:518-19. sup(folded map) O '71

ARCTIC wildlife range. See Wildlife sanctuaries—Alaska

ARCTIIDAE. See Moths

ARDOIN, John
Symphonic debacle; a new butterfly. Hi Fi 21:MA28-9 Ap '71

AREA navigation. See Navigation, Aerial

AREA studies
  See also
African studies

ARECIBO telescope. See Radio telescopes

ARENA stage. See Washington, D.C.—Theater

ARENS, Richard
Attica: part of an overall pattern. Commonweal 95:52-3 O 15 '71

ARFONS, Art
Art was my copilot. R. Guldahl, jr. il por Hot Rod 24:84-5 D '71 *

ARGENTINA
  See also
Astronomical observatories—Argentina
Automobile racing—Argentina
Hospitals—Argentina
Investments, Foreign (in Argentina)
Paraná River
Periodicals—Argentina
Tierra del Fuego

Economic conditions
Investors shy from a shaky economy. il Bsns W p31 S 4 '71

Industries
  See also
Meat industry—Argentina

Politics and government
Magic in the Pink House. por Time 97:34+ Ap 5 '71
Peron: the homesick dictator. R. O'Mara. Nation 213:14-15 Jl 5 '71
Whatever happened to dictator Peron: gone but not forgotten. il pors U S News 70:86 My 24 '71

History
Guillermo Rawson's idealistic vision of the United States. J. Villaverde. il pors Américas 23:25-35 Ag '71

ARGENTINA and the United States
Guillermo Rawson's idealistic vision of the United States. J. Villaverde. il pors Américas 23:25-35 Ag '71

ARGININE
Specific enzymic methylation of an arginine in the experimental allergic encephalomyelitis protein from human myelin. G. S. Baldin and P. R. Carnegie. bibliog il Science 171:579-81 F 12 '71

ARGO petroleum corporation
Two-drill dentist; Argo petroleum. por Newsweek 78:72 Ag 30 '71

ARGONNE national laboratory
Change in Argonne national laboratory: a case study. A. Mozley. bibliog Science 174: 30-8 O 1 '71

ARGOW, Keith A. See Griessman, B. E. jt. auth.

ARI; musical comedy. See Musical comedies, revues, etc.—Criticisms, plots, etc.

ARIAS, Juan
What a fiesta we will have! W. F. Reed. il pors Sports Illus 34:26-8+ My 31 '71 *

ARIAS
  See also
Phonograph records—Arias

ARID regions
Jungle, desert, icebergs, and hunger; forecast by the FAO. R. L. Tobin. il Sat R 54:20 O 23 '71; Reply. N. J. Rosenberg. 54:30 N 20 '71

ARIMURA, Akira, and others
Ovulation induced by synthetic luteinizing hormone-releasing hormone in the hamster. bibliog il Science 174:511-12 O 29 '71

ARIODANTE; opera. See Händel, G. F.

ARITHMETIC
Unsolved problems in arithmetic. H. DeLong. il Sci Am 224:50-60 bibliog(p 124) Mr '71
  See also
Numbers, Real

Study and teaching
What happened to elementary school arithmetic? G. W. Brown. Ed Digest 37:38-40 S '71
  See also
Number concept

ARIZONA
  See also
Black Mesa
Grand Canyon
Hunting—Arizona
Recreation areas—Arizona
Saguaro National Monument
Wildlife conservation—Arizona
Wupatki National Monument

Description and travel
Copper horseshoe route. Travel 135:9 Je '71

Parks and reserves
Arizona public parks law. H. E. Gillmore. il Parks & Rec 6:23+ F '71
Lyman Lake an Arizona stopover. il Sunset 146:32 My '71

Politics and government
Taking over the OEO; Governor Williams's attempt to take control of OEO programs. J. R. Hood. Nation 213:646-9 D 20 '71

ARIZONA. University, Tucson

Environmental research laboratory
Arid land agriculture: Shaikh up in Arizona research. R. J. Bazell. il Science 171:989-90 Mr 12 '71

ARK, Noah's. See Noah's ark

ARKANSAS
  See also
Architecture, Domestic—Arkansas
Arts and crafts—Arkansas
Cossatot River
Fishing—Arkansas
Hunting—Arkansas
Ouachita River
Prisons—Arkansas

Description and travel
Treasures of the Ozarks. A. J. Runsick. il por Travel 136:50-4 Ag '71

Economic conditions
Reports & comment: Arkansas. B. Herget. Atlan 227:14+ F '71

Politics and government
Reports & comment: Arkansas. B. Herget. Atlan 227:14+ F '71

ARKANSAS library association
Of note; forty-ninth annual conference. G. Nelson and C. Wyatt. Am Lib 2:1135-6 D '71

ARKANSAS RIVER WATERWAY
Honeymoon on a houseboat. G. Reiger. il
Pop Mech 135:102-5+ F '71
What? Oklahoma a coastal state? McClellan-
Kerr Arkansas River navigation system.
il U S News 70:60 F 22 '71

ARKIN, Alan
Current cinema. P. Kael. New Yorker 47:
92+ Mr 6 '71 *

ARKING, Albert. See Hansen, J. E. jt. auth.

ARKING, Linda
(ed) See Lipchitz, J. Visit with Jacques
Lipchitz

ARLECCHINO; opera. See Busoni, F.

ARLEN, Michael J.
Sight & sound: a few sensible words about
children's TV. McCalls 98:34+ F '71
Standing in the wind. il McCalls 99:54+ O '71

ARLEN realty and development corporation
Will the store be minded? merger of
Korvette with the Arlen group. il Forbes
108:44 Ag 15 '71

ARLINGTON, Mass.
You can't see your best snow fighting tool;
public cooperation. J. E. Bowler. il Am
City 86:81-2 D '71

ARLINGTON, Tex.
Carnival in Texas. Newsweek 78:98 D 13 '71
33 cubic yards per trailer load; city ordinance requiring plastic bags. il Am City
86:29 O '71

ARLINGTON, Va.

Libraries

Va. school & library join to form community
library; Aurora Hills library. Library J
96:3061 O 1 '71

National cemetery

See also
Unknown soldiers

ARLINGTON HEIGHTS, Ill.
Still another Mount Trashmore. il Am City
86:32 S '71

ARMADILLOS
Armadillo helps leprosy research. Sci N 100:
138 Ag 28 '71
Meet the armored spoof. M. S. Haverstock. il
Nat Wildlife 10:52-5 D '71

ARMADILLOS in art. See Animals in art

ARMAMENT industries. See Munitions industries

ARMAMENTS
See also
Airplanes, Military—Armaments
Munitions
Tanks, Military

ARMBRISTER, Trevor
How Chile chose Marxism. Read Digest 98:
69-74 Je '71
I think I'll try the White House. il Read
Digest 98:71-5 My '71
Lonely struggle of the black cop. Read Digest
98:123-7 Mr '71

ARMBRUSTER, Carl J. and Begley, J. J.
Hidden thorns. Commonweal 94:60-4 Mr 26 '71

ARMCO steel corporation
Water polluters tangle with the law, and lose.
il Bsns W p64-5 O 9 '71

ARMED forces
See also subhead Armed forces under
names of countries, e.g. United States—
Armed forces

Appropriations and expenditures

Unreordered priority; world military expenditures. Sci Am 225:42 Jl '71

ARMED forces staff college. See United States
—Armed forces staff college

ARMENIA
Letter from Armenia. F. J. Dyson. New Yorker
47:126-30+ N 6 '71
See also
Americans in Armenia
Ani, Turkey (ancient city)
Astronomical observatories—Armenia

ARMENIAN Americans
I want to go home. il Newsweek 77:42+ My
17 '71

ARMENIAN Soviet Republic. See Armenia

ARMERDING, Carl Edwin
Ancient Israel and her neighbors. Chr Today 15:21-2 F 12 '71
Books on the Old Testament, 1970. Chr Today 15:11-12+ F 26 '71
Religion and theology of Israel. Chr Today
15:27-9 My 21 '71

ARMIES

Officers

See also
Generals

ARMILLAS, Pedro
Gardens on swamps. bibliog il Science 174:
653-61 N 12 '71

ARMISTICE, Korean. See Korean war, 1950-
1953—Peace and mediation

ARMITAGE, Frank
Brain; drawings. Life 71:42-59 O 1; 42-56+
O 22; 57-65+ N 12 '71 (to be cont)

about

Delicate art of illustrating the brain. R.
Graves. il por Life 71:3 O 22 '71 *

ARMOUR, Lawrence A.
Pro basketball. Sports Illus 34:70+ Mr 15 '71

ARMOUR, Leslie
Aliens in their own land. Nation 212:750-3 Je
14 '71

ARMOUR, Richard
Be good to your authors. Pub W 200:23
Ag 9 '71
Confessions of a cold-cure collector. il Read
Digest 99:55-6 O '71
Is Dr Doctor in? Read Digest 99:114-15 Jl '71
My backward youth. Sat R 54:4-5 Ag 28 '71
Short note on long hair. Sat R 54:4 Je 19 '71
Why I'm not a bird watcher. Sat R 54:58
O 30 '71

ARMOUR, Toby
Dances by Toby Armour, Riverside church
theatre, NYC. L. Pastore. Dance Mag 45:
78 Jl '71 *

ARMOUR and company
His Greyhound goes to Phoenix. Bsns W p59
Jl 3 '71

ARMS control. See Disarmament

ARMS control and disarmament agency. See
United States—Arms control and disarmament agency

ARMS control legislation. See Firearms—Laws
and regulations

ARMS trade. See Munitions

ARMSTRONG, Anne
Berlin revisited. Nat R 23:1057 S 24 '71

ARMSTRONG, Hamilton Fish
Authors that bloom in the spring; excerpts
from press conference. il por Pub W 199:
22-3 Mr 22 '71

about

Foreign substance. A. Cooper. por Newsweek 77:86+ Je 28 '71 *

ARMSTRONG, Henry
Whatever happened to hammerin' Henry
Armstrong. il pors Ebony 26:122 Jl '71 *

ARMSTRONG, Herbert W.
Examining his Worldwide church of God. J.
M. Hopkins. Chr Today 16:6-9 D 17 '71 *

ARMSTRONG, John A.
Lasers; applications in physics research. bibliog il Phys Today 24:34-9 Mr '71

ARMSTRONG, Lillian Hardin
Lil Hardin Armstrong, a fond remembrance.
C. Albertson. il pors Sat R 54:66-7 S 25 '71 *

ARMSTRONG, Louis
Funeral of Louis Armstrong. W. Conover.
il Sat R 54:43 Jl 31 '71 *
Good-by, Louis. H. Saal. il por Newsweek
78:76 Jl 19 '71 *
Last trumpet for the first trumpeter. il por
Time 98:34-5 Jl 19 '71 *
Musical events. W. Balliett. New Yorker
47:75-7 Ag 28 '71 *
Obituary
America 125:24-5 Jl 24 '71
Ebony il pors 26:31-4+ S '71. P. Garland
Negro Hist Bul 34:139 O '71
New Yorker 47:21 Jl 17 '71
Parting shots: Satchmo, the greatest of all,
is gone. R. Meryman. il pors Life 71:70-1
Jl 16 '71 *
Scanning the history of jazz. por Esquire 76:
184-7+ D '71
Unforgettable Satchmo. T. Glenn. il por Read
Digest 99:81-5 D '71 *

ARMSTRONG, Marion
Movies (title varies) See occasional issues of
Christian century continuing New Christian

ARMSTRONG, O. K.
Beware the commercialized faith healers.
Read Digest 98:179-80+ Je '71

ARMSTRONG, Richard
Passion that rules Ralph Nader. il por Fortune 83:144-7+ My '71

ARMSTRONG, W. McD. and Lee, C. O.
Sodium and potassium activities in normal
and sodium-rich frog skeletal muscle. bibliog il Science 171:413-15 Ja 29 '71

ARMSTRONG, Willis Coburn
Our foreign economic crisis; address, February 22, 1971. Vital Speeches 37:327-31 Mr
15 '71

ARMSTRONG-JONES, Antony Charles Robert,
1st earl of Snowdon. See Snowdon, A. C. R.
A.-J.

ARMSTRONG cork company
Armstrong cork bets on residential housing.
il por Bsns W p 122-4 O 23 '71

ARMY

Materiel command
See United States—Army—Materiel command

ARMY and air force exchange services. See United States—Armed forces—Post exchanges

ARMY engineers. See United States—Army—Corps of engineers

ARMY investigations. See Government investigations

ARMY libraries. See United States—Army—Libraries

ARMY life. See Military life

ARMY mathematics research center. See Wisconsin. University—Madison campus

ARMY medical corps. See United States—Army—Medical corps

ARMY posts. See Military posts

ARMY service clubs. See Clubs

ARMY special services. See United States—Army—Special services

ARNAUD, Claude, and others
Serum parathyroid hormone in X-linked hypophosphatemia. bibliog il Science 173:845-7 Ag 27 '71

ARNAZ, Desi, 1917-
My mother, Lucille Ball; interview, ed. by J. N. Bell. D. Arnaz, jr. il pors Good H 172:14+ Mr '71 *

ARNAZ, Desi, 1953-
My mother, Lucille Ball; interview, ed. by J. N. Bell. il pors Good H 172:14+ Mr '71
Desi Arnaz, jr. talks turkey. il pors Seventeen 30:98+ Ja '71 *

ARNDT, Rudolf G.
Copperhead in New York. il Cons 25:18-19 Ap '71

ARNDT, Walter W.
—And bring your autoharp. il pors Har Yrs 11:44-6 N '71

ARNESON, Jeannette
David Gilhooly. il Craft Horiz 31:20-1+ Ag '71

ARNESS, James
Gunsmoke's mysterious. V. Scott. il pors Ladies Home J 88:90+ My '71 *

ARNETT, David W
Receptive field organization of units in the first optic ganglion of diptera. bibliog il Science 173:929-31 S 3 '71

ARNHEM, Battle of, 1944
Hell's highway to Arnhem. S. W. Sears. il Am Heritage 22:60-3+ Je '71

ARNOLD, Anne
Anne Arnold. C. Ratcliff. il por Craft Horiz 31:18-21+ Je '71 *

ARNOLD, Arnold
Gail E. Haley. por Horn Bk 47:369-72 Ag '71

ARNOLD, Rus
Sunday travel page markets. il Writers Digest 51:31+ My '71
Writer with a camera (cont) por Writers Digest 51:14-16 F; 18-20 Ap; 16-18 Jl; 14+ S; 34-5+ N '71; 52:34-5 Ja '72

ARNOLD engineering development center. See United States—Arnold engineering development center

ARNOLDO Mondadori editore. See Publishers and publishing—Italy

ARNOW, Harriette (Simpson)
No rats in the mines. il Nation 213:401-4 O 25 '71

ARNSTEIN, Helene S.
Emotional scars of abortion. il Ladies Home J 88:121+ My '71

AROFFO, Armand
I never dreamed medicine would be like this! il pors Todays Health 49:40-5 O '71 *

AROMATIC hydrocarbons. See Hydrocarbons

ARON, William I, and Smith, S. H.
Ship canals and aquatic ecosystems. bibliog il Science 174:13-20 O 1 '71

ARONE, Frank T.
Toward greater success in team teaching. Clear House 45:501-2 Ap '71

ARONOW, Don
In the old days she ran full of rum. H. D. Whall. il Sports Illus 35:34-5 S 6 '71 *

ARONS, Stephen
Joker in private school aid. il Sat R 54:45-7+ Ja 16 '71

ARONSON, Eric, and Rosenbloom, Shelley
Space perception in early infancy; perception within a common auditory-visual space. bibliog il Science 172:1161-3 Je 11 '71

ARONSON, Harvey
(ed) See Bailey, F. L. F. Lee Bailey's strangest murder case
(ed) See Bailey, F. L. F. Lee Bailey's The defense never rests

ARONSON, Henry M.
At war with the army. il por Time 97:48 F 8 '71 *

ARONSON, Leonard J.
Psychologist and minimal brain dysfunction: ten steps to maximum incompetence. Ment Hy 55:523-5 O '71

ARP, Halton
Observational paradoxes in extragalactic astronomy. bibliog il Science 174:1189-200 D 17 '71

ARPINO, Gerald
Dance. N. Goldner. Nation 213:635 D 13 '71 *

ARRABAL, Fernando
And they put handcuffs on the flowers. Criticism
Nation 213:573-4 N 29 '71 *
New Yorker 47:102-3 O 30 '71 *

ARRANGEMENT of flowers. See Flowers, Arrangement of

ARRANGEMENT of furniture. See Furniture, Arrangement of

ARRAU, Claudio
Fox meets the rabbit. H. Goldsmith. il pors Hi Fi 21:61-2 My '71 *

ARREST
Annals of the law; false arrest of black T. Goins by Bronx police on narcotics charge. E. J. Kahn, jr. New Yorker 46:76-84 F 6 '71
If your child is arrested. M. Brenton. McCalls 98:41 Mr '71
Victimless crimes. il Newsweek 78:83 N 29 '71
What to do if your child gets arrested. J. S. Lobenthal, jr. Harp Baz 104:174-5 S '71
See also
Bail
Habeas corpus

ARREST records. See Police records

ARRICK, Larry
Unlikely heroes; dramatization of three stories by P. Roth. Criticism
America 125:427 N 20 '71 *
Nation 213:507 N 15 '71 *
New Yorker 47:115 N 6 '71 *
Newsweek il 78:104 N 8 '71 *
Sat R 54:12-13 N 13 '71 *
Time il 98:85 N 8 '71 *

ARRIGONI, Edward A.
Experiments in cryogenics. bibliog il por Chem 44:23-6 O '71

ARROW points. See Arrowheads

ARROW worms. See Arrowworms

ARROWHEADS
Indian arrow heads. C. Miles. il Hobbies 75: 154-5+ F '71
Test for broadheads. G. H. Gillelan. il Outdoor Life 147:22+ Ja '71

ARROWSMITH, William
Great academic refusal; address, May 21, 1971. Vital Speeches 37:592-7 Jl 15 '71

ARROWWORMS
Deadly arrow worm. M. Reeve. il Sea Front 17:175-83 My '71

ARROYO, Martina
Real Martina; interview, ed. by S. Jenkins. por Opera N 36:16-17 N '71

about
Met's Martina. H. Saal. por Newsweek 77:73 Je 14 '71 *
Recordings. M. Mayer. Esquire 75:30 F '71 *

ARROYO SECO, N.Mex.
U.S. journal. C. Trillin. New Yorker 47:103-4+ S 18 '71

ARRUPE, Pedro
Questions for a globe-trotting general; interview, with editorial comment. il America 125:inside cover, 55-8 Ag 7 '71

ARSENIC
Arsenic in detergents: possible danger and pollution hazard. E. E. Angino and others; discussion. Science 168:1525-6; 170:870-2; 171:234 Je 26, N 20 '70, Ja 22 '71
See also
Water supply—Arsenic content

ARSON
Insurers get burned on ghetto policies. il Bsns W p38 N 6 '71

ART
See also
The Arts
Children in art
Childrens art
Christian art and symbolism
Computers—Art use
Creation (literary, artistic, etc)
Cubism
Design
Graffiti
Illustration of books and periodicals
Impressionism (art)
Modernism (art)

ART—See also—*Continued*
Multiple art
Mural painting and decoration
Nature in art
Negroes in art
Nude in art
Painting
Paintings
Photography, Artistic
Prints
Realism in art
Sculpture
Space flight in art
Surrealism
Symbolism in art
Vietnamese war, 1957- —Art
West Indies in art

Appreciation

Art and the mass audience. E. Van Den Haag. il Art in Am 59:52-7 Jl '71
Art appreciation in the elementary school. B. Wasserman. il Sch Arts 70:12-13 Mr '71
Art education and the public taste. M. E. Shaw. Am Artist 35:5 Ag '71; Discussion. 35:11 N '71
If you look very closely. T. B. Hess. Art N 70:21 Sum '71
Museum and the democratic fallacy. B. Robertson. il Art in Am 59:58-65 Jl '71
Public and modern art; Unesco-backed inquiry; with report by D. F. Cameron. il UNESCO Courier 24:4-34 Mr '71
Why we can't understand art. R. Henkes. il Design 72:16-19 Spr '71
    See also
Art criticism

Bibliography

Art books. L. Alloway. Nation 213:664-8 D 20 '71
Art books of 1970 (cont) L. Kirstein. Nation 211:663-4+ D 21 '70
Book reviews. See issues of American artist to April 1971
Books. J. Jacobs. See issues of Art in America
Recommended reading. il Am Artist 35:21+ Je; 54-6+ Ag; 16+ S; 10+ O; 64+ N; 20-1+ D '71; 36:64-6+ Ja '72
Reviewer's choice. See issues of Design
Season's art books: a Browser's guide. P. S. Prescott. il Newsweek 78:103-4+ D 13 '71
25 years of Unesco publications on art. UNESCO Courier 24:35-6 Mr '71
    See also
Art literature

Collections

See Art—Galleries and museums; Art—Private collections

Collectors and collecting

Dilemmas of the curator. E. F. Fry. il Art in Am 59:72-7 Jl '71
Gold rush in Western art. il U S News 70:81-2 My 17 '71
Interview with J. Paul Getty; ed. by M. Gendel. J. P. Getty. il por Art N 70:44-5+ S '71
    See also
Art—Private collections
Art as an investment

Competitions

Competitions and awards. See issues of American artist
1971 art awards. Sr Schol 98:2, 6-7 My 17 '71

Conservation and restoration

Mind preserved; Unesco missions. W. McEwing. il UNESCO Courier 24:48-53 Ag '71
Restoring a rare work of art; bronze bust of Lucius Aurelius Verus. il Life 71:83-4 D 3 '71

Criticism

See Art criticism

Education

See Art education

Exhibitions

Art. L. Alloway. See issues of Nation
Art and the corporations; Los Angeles County museum of art show. D. Antin. il Art N 70:22-6+ S '71
Art world (cont) H. Rosenberg. New Yorker 46:71-5 Ja 30; 47:73-7 Mr 6; 117-20 Mr 27; 102-5 My 8; 101-5 Je 12; 201-4+ N 20 '71; 43-6 Ja 1 '72
Artists vs. museums; Haacke-Guggenheim affair. E. C. Baker. Art N 70:25+ My '71; Discussion. 70:21+ S '71
Between two worlds; exhibition of Florentine art at the Cleveland and Metropolitan museums. D. Davis. il Newsweek 78:58-9 Ag 2 '71

Black artists: two generations; exhibition at the Newark museum. il Sch Arts 71:21-8 D '71
Brief utopia; Art in revolution at the New York cultural center. D. Davis. Newsweek 78:79 O 4 '71
Bulletin board. See issues of American artist
Butterfly and the old ox; Whistler and his circle, exhibition at Wildenstein. T. Reff. il pors Art N 70:26-31+ Mr '71
Coming soon. See issues of Design
Current and coming. S. B. Sherrill. See issues of Antiques
Esthetic valence of cubism; at the Metropolitan museum. M. Kozloff. il Art N 70:34-7+ Ap '71
European art finds R. Bernier. Vogue 158:90+ S 15 '71
False faces; exhibition at New York's Whitney museum, 200 years of North American Indian art. D. Davis. il Newsweek 78:79 N 29 '71
Gallery-hopping in New York. D. Davis. il Newsweek 78:36-7 D 27 '71
Goings on about town. See issues of New Yorker
How to organize an outdoor art show. C. S. Nutt. il Am Artist 35:24-9 Je '71
In a black bind; exhibit at New York's Whitney museum called Black artists in America. il Time 97:64 Ap 12 '71
It reaches a desert in which nothing can be perceived but feeling; The four elements, exhibition at Boston museum. D. Antin. bibliog il Art N 70:38-41+ Mr '71
Lasers in L.A; exhibition at Los Angeles County museum of art. il Newsweek 77:56 My 31 '71
Machined mosaics; Paolozzi retrospective at the Tate gallery. R. Hughes. il Time 98:86-7 O 11 '71
Making the gallery scene; ancient art of the New World. B. Wasserman. il Sch Arts 71:30-3 O '71
Man and machine; Los Angeles County museum's exhibition called Art and technology. il por Time 97:60-3 Je 28 '71
Man of a thousand squares; Princeton university art museum displays works by J. Albers. D. Davis. il por Newsweek 77:77-8 Ja 18 '71
Master's legacy; E. Hopper's exhibition at New York city's Whitney museum. D. Davis. il por Newsweek 78:98-9 S 27 '71
Museums U.S.A. il Harp Baz 104:90-1 O '71
Nature tame, nature wild; exhibition of English landscapes at the Metropolitan museum of art. D. Davis. il Newsweek 78:78 Jl 26 '71
New York. G. Glueck. See issues of Art in America
Paint it black; exhibition at Rice university, Houston. D. McConathy. il Vogue 157:127 Ap 15 '71
Potpourri: new art season in New York. R. Berenson. Nat R 23:1367 D 3 '71
Professional page:
    Approaching galleries for display. B. Chamberlain. Am Artist 35:11-12 S '71
    Business matters. B. Chamberlain. Am Artist 35:46+ O '71
    Concerning copy cats. B. Chamberlain. Am Artist 35:54 N '71
    Finding outlets for your work. B. Chamberlain. Am Artist 35:16+ Ag '71
    One man, one show. B. Chamberlain. Am Artist 35:15 D '71
    Placement: do it yourself. B. Chamberlain. Am Artist 36:16 Ja '72
Retrospectives and prospectives. C. J. McNaspy. America 124:263 Mr 13 '71
Reviews and previews. See issues of Art news
Roughneck's gang; Caravaggio and his followers at the Cleveland museum. D. Davis. il Newsweek 78:120 N 8 '71
Sanguinary saga; Some American history exhibition. T. W. Moore. il Chr Cent 88:864-5 Jl 14 '71
Screen stars; exhibition of Rimpa art at Japan house. D. Davis. il Newsweek 78:79 O 4 '71
Second incarnation of Ben Heller; Beyond Europe exhibition. H. A. La Farge. il Art N 70:38-9+ Ap '71
Tempest in a samovar; Art in revolution; exhibition at the Hayward gallery, London. il Newsweek 77:53 Ap 5 '71

ART—Exhibitions—*Continued*
Where and when to exhibit. See issues of
Art news
  See also
Art—Galleries and museums
Childrens art—Exhibitions
Drawings—Exhibitions
Etchings—Exhibitions
Photography—Exhibitions
Pottery—Exhibitions
Prints—Exhibitions
  also names of museums, e.g. Brooklyn museum

Expertising
Anyone here want to buy a Rubens? D. Saxon. Esquire 75:58+ Ja '71

Federal aid
See Art and state

Galleries and museums
Art; the Tanager, a cooperative gallery. L. Alloway. Nation 214:29-30 Ja **3** '72
Ivory tower versus the discotheque; differing conceptions of T. Hoving and S. Lee. G. Glueck. il pors Art in Am 59:80-5 My '71
Museum accessions. R. Davidson. See issues of Antiques
Special museum issue; symposium, with introd. by B. O'Doherty. bibliog il Art in Am 59:25-99+ Jl '71
  See also
College art galleries and museums
Museums and schools
  also names of museums, e.g. San Francisco museum of art; *also* subhead Galleries and museums under names of cities, e.g. New York (city)—Galleries and museums

Acquisitions
Art; problem of unseen permanent collections. L. Alloway. Nation 212:125-6 Ja 25 '71
Message to museums; modern art monopoly. E. K. Belmont. Am Artist 35:11 D '71

Trustees, boards, committees, etc.
Power and esthetics: the trustee. G. Glueck. il Art in Am 59:78-83 Jl '71

History
Museums and radicals: a history of emergencies. L. Nochlin. bibliog il Art in Am 59:26-39 Jl '71

Study and teaching
Creative art history. J. Comins. il Sch Arts 70:44 Je '71
NAA revision of the CAA. E. F. Fry. Art in Am 59:31-2 Mr '71

Philosophy
Education of the un-artist. A. Kaprow. il Art N 69:28-31+ F '71 (to be cont)
On the de-definition of art. H. Rosenberg. Art N 70:23 D '71
  See also
Aesthetics

Prices
Displaced values. R. Hughes. il Time 97:53 Je 21 '71
Expensive nineteenth century. G. Keen. Art in Am 59:29 S '71
Who needs masterpieces at those prices? Time essay. R. Hughes. il Time 98:52-3 Jl 19 '71

Private collections
Ailsa Mellon Bruce collection in Pittsburgh; Museum of art of Carnegie institute. R. Davidson. il Antiques 100:330 S '71
Art for everybody; interview. ed. by M. Roche. C. Cowles. House & Gard 140:31+ O '71
Art world; Stein family collection at Museum of modern art. H. Rosenberg. New Yorker 46:71-5 Ja 30 '71
At home with art; Lee Anderson's Renwick Point house. il Art in Am 59:86-9 Ja '71
Carl Kempe collection; exhibition at New York's Asia house gallery. J. Brzostoski. il Craft Horiz 31:22-6 Je '71
Cézanne without tears; Phillips collection exhibition. B. F. Forgey. il pors Art N 70:56-9+ Ap '71
Collector collects; Gaston de Havenon collection. L. Hess. il Harp Baz 104:186 S '71
Dance of the Chi Wara; Gaston de Havenon collection. B. Forgey. il Art N 70:46-9+ Sum '71
Four patron saints in one great act; the Steins. T. Prideaux. il por Life 70:56-60+ Ap 23 '71
G.M.P. J. Ashbery. il Art N 69:44-7+ F '71
Lehman legacy. il Life 70:40-7 Ja 29 '71
London; Dutch pictures from the Royal collection. J. Russell. il Art N 70:38+ Sum '71

Migrant masterpieces; art in Great Britain. J. Russell. il Art in Am 59:106-9 S '71
Second incarnation of Ben Heller; classic and Asiatic sculpture. H. A. La Farge. il Art N 70:38-9+ Ap '71
  See also
Art in the home
Prints—Collectors and collecting

Psychology
Art in everyday life uncoils springs of tension. G. Von Kantor. il Sch Arts 70:22-3 Ap '71
Why parents can't understand Johnny's picture. R. Henkes. il Sch Arts 71:18-21 S '71

Scholarships and fellowships
Competitions. See issues of Art news
Competitions and awards. See issues of American artist

Social aspects
See Art and society

Study and teaching
Art and the small community. B. H. Belton. il Sch Arts 70:26-8 Mr '71
Art classrooms without walls in the Toledo, Ohio public schools. M. Ryan. il Sch Arts 70:40 Je '71
Art in everyday life uncoils springs of tensions. G. Von Kanto. il Sch Arts 70:22-3 Ap '71
Art open lab. R. Imhoff. il Sch Arts 70:38-40 F '71
Clipboard. V. G. Timmons. See issues of School arts
Doing your own thing. B. A. Gurr. il Sch Arts 70:34-6 Mr '71
Enriching the elementary art program; tape and slide programs. S. Liby. il por Sch Arts 71:14-15 S '71
For the elementary teacher: time for art. T. P. Foote. il Sch Arts 71:8-9 O '71
For the elementary teacher: your art program. L. C. Leatherbury. il Sch Arts 71:6-7 N '71
How and why of classroom art. R. Henkes. il Design 72:21-3 mid-Sum '71
Program at Centennial elementary school, Wapakoneta, Ohio. J. R. Carter. il Sch Arts 70:42 Je '71
Relating art to the secondary student's environment. J. A. Varmecky. il Sch Arts 71:38-9 S '71
S.I.T.E: a suggested answer to the pollution in art teacher development. A. W. Beck. il Sch Arts 71:36-7 S '71
Structure needn't stifle. P. K. Scholl. il Sch Arts 71:12-13 S '71
To feel y'self gettin' better. P. K. Scholl. il Sch Arts 71:30-1 D '71
  See also
Art—Appreciation
Art education
Artists as teachers
Design—Study and teaching
Drawing—Study and teaching
Moving pictures—Art films
Painting—Study and teaching
Posters
Sculpture—Study and teaching

Materials
Don't buy it, beg it. G. Graves. il Sch Arts 70:42-3 Ap '71
Organizing for art. V. G. Timmons. il Sch Arts 70:12-13 F '71
Pitfalls and promises. H. Haessner. il Sch Arts 71:22-5 Ja '72
  See also
Papier-mâché
Sculpture—Study and teaching—Materials

Projects
Art at auction; primary grades at St Andrew's Episcopal day school, Jacksonville, Fla. contribute to community art auction. C. Dorman. il por Sch Arts 71:48 Ja '72
Art for the self-contained classroom; packet or unit plan. A. J. Levin. il Sch Arts 71:10-11 S '71
Bottoms of things. S. Geisert. il Sch Arts 71:22-3 N '71
Create creativity; balsawood Victorian houses. R. Guthrie. il Sch Arts 71:28-30 S '71
For the elementary teacher: holiday stereotypes. V. J. Popolizio. il Sch Arts 71:8-9 S '71
Luminal art. R. M. Farrell. il Sch Arts 71:18-19 O '71
Not-so-still life. M. Heinrich. il Sch Arts 71:20-1 N '71

ART—Study and teaching—Projects—*Continued*
Patterned objects. M. Panchal. il Sch Arts
71:30 Ja '72
Projects from plaster. L. J. Miller. il Design
72:34-5 mid-Sum '71
See also
Calendars
Christmas projects
Collage
Glass painting and staining
Kites
Masks (for the face)
Mosaics
Mural painting and decoration
Mural painting and decoration, Exterior
Prints—Technique
Puppets and puppet plays
Rubbings

Technique

How and why of classroom art. R. Henkes. il
Design 72:21-3 mid-Sum '71
See also
Chiaroscuro
Modeling
Painting—Technique

Themes

Response to an urban environment; with
paintings and drawings by Edward Gray.
R. N. Day. il Sch Arts 70:4-7 My '71
See also
Animals in art
Birds in art
Chemistry in art
Dancing in art
Flowers in art
Hunting in art
Indians in art
Negroes in art
Slave trade in art
South in art
Venice in art
West in art
Women in art
Words in art

Therapeutic use

See Art therapy

California

Art surprises at Half Moon Bay. il Sunset
146:25-6 Ja '71
See also
Los Angeles—Art

England

See Art—Great Britain

Europe, Western

European potpourri. K. Kuh. Sat R 54:60-2
O 9 '71

France

Museums and radicals: a history of emergencies. L. Nochlin. bibliog il Art in Am
59:26-39 Jl '71

Great Britain

Migrant masterpieces. J. Russell. il Art in
Am 59:106-9 S '71
See also
Art, British

India

Green is for coolness, yellow for good auspices. F. A. Zimmer. il Natur Hist 80:54-9
Ja '71

Italy

Italy. M. Gendel. Art N 70:56 My '71
Rome. M. Gendel. Art N 70:43 Ap '71
See also
Art—Sicily

Russia

Failed utopia: Russian art 1917-32. J. E.
Bowlt. bibliog il Art in Am 59:40-51 Jl '71
See also
Painting, Russian

Sicily

To Sicily with love. C. J. McNaspy. America
125:95-6 Ag 21 '71

United States

See also
Art, American
also subhead Art under names of cities,
e.g. Chicago—Art

Vermont

Art out of the attic. C. Davidson. il Am
Heritage 23:66-71 D '71
ART, Abstract
Art; Lyrical abstraction exhibition at the
Whitney. L. Alloway. Nation 212:733-4 Je 7
'71
Art; Structure of color exhibition at Whitney
museum. L. Alloway. Nation 212:477-8 Ap
12 '71

Déjà-vu; abstract-expressionism of the 1970s.
D. Antin. il Art N 70:50-1+ Sum '71
Kelly, collage and color. D. Waldman. bibliog
il Art N 70:44-7+ D '71
Structure of color; show at the Whitney
museum. H. Aach. Craft Horiz 31:54+ Je
'71
Structure of colour show at the Whitney mu-
seum. B. Rose. Vogue 157:128 Ap 15 '71
See also
Art, Abstract
Constructivism
ART, African
Totem and taboo; Museum of African art,
Washington, D.C. il Newsweek 77:85-6 Je
21 '71
See also
Art, Guinean
ART, Amateur
Joys of being a Sunday painter. il Changing T
25:45-7 N '71
People's art. R. Sommer. il Natur Hist 80:
40-5 F '71
Sanford Darling paints his house; harbor
scenes, mountains, etc. on outside walls. T.
Tyler. il por Time 97:17 Ap 5 '71
Walls belong to the people; photographs by
Elihu Blotnick. Ramp Mag 9:30-2 Mr '71
ART, American
American artists at Midtown galleries; thir-
ty-ninth anniversary exhibition. il Design
72:16-17 Sum '71
At home with art: Lee Anderson's Renwick
Point house. il Art in Am 59:86-9 Ja '71
Gold rush in Western art. il U S News 70:
81-2 My 17 '71
News & views. Design 73:9+ Wint '71
Profiles: H. Geldzahler, curator of Metro-
politan's Department of contempory art.
C. Tomkins. por New Yorker 47:58-60+ N
6 '71
See also
Art, Negro (American)
Painting, American
Pottery, American
Whitney museum of American art, New
York
ART, Ancient
See also
Sculpture, Ancient
ART, Asian
Second incarnation of Ben Heller; Beyond
Europe exhibition. H. A. La Farge. il Art
N 70:38-9+ Ap '71
ART, Baroque
See also
Painting, Baroque
ART, British
Art; New York cultural center's exhibition
of the British avant-garde. L. Alloway.
Nation 212:797-8 Je 21 '71
London; youth will be served; Art spectrum
shows. J. Russell. Art N 70:23+ O '71
See also
Painting, British
Pottery, English
ART, Chinese
Carl Kempe collection; exhibition at New
York's Asia house gallery. J. Brzostoski.
il Craft Horiz 31:22-6 Je '71
See also
Pottery, Chinese
ART, Christian. See Christian art and sym-
bolism
ART, Commercial
See also
Illustration of books and periodicals
ART, Egyptian
See also
Sculpture, Egyptian
ART, English. See Art, British
ART, Eskimo. See Eskimos—Art
ART, Florentine. See Art, Italian
ART, Gothic
See also
Painting, Gothic
ART, Graphic. See Graphic arts
ART, Guinean
Baga and the inscrutable Nimba. L. Ban-
goura. bibliog il Negro Hist Bul 34:30-2 F
'71
ART, Indonesian
Local genius of classical Java. J. Fontein. il
Art N 70:50-5 O '71
ART, Iranian. See Art, Persian
ART, Italian
Between two worlds; exhibition of Florentine
art at the Cleveland and Metropolitan mu-
seums. D. Davis. il Newsweek 78:58-9
Ag 2 '71
See also
Milan, Italy—Art

ART, Japanese
Screen stars; exhibition of Rimpa art at
Japan house. D. Davis. il Newsweek 78:
79 O 4 '71
See also
Painting, Japanese

ART, Jewish
Jewish ceremonial art and religious obser-
vance, by A. Kanof. Review
Cath World 213:51-2 Ap '71. S. Kellner

ART, Latin American
Colonial art; symposium, ed. by G. de Zénde-
gui. il Américas 23:S1-24 Ap '71
Hemisphere art. See issues of Américas

ART, Medieval
See also
Metropolitan museum of art, New York—
Cloisters

ART, Modern
Art; artists' use of new media. L. Alloway.
Nation 212:413-14 Mr 29 '71
Art; Conceptual art works at Everson mu-
seum, Syracuse. L. Alloway. Nation 213:
477-8 N 8 '71
Art; decline of easel painting. L. Alloway.
Nation 213:60-1 Jl 19 '71
Art world; dead art movements and vital
works produced by them. H. Rosenberg.
New Yorker 47:73-7 Mr 6 '71
Arte povera, amore mio; conceptual and eco-
logical art. M. Gendel. il Art N 69:38-9+
F '71
Different drummer; the work of Rafael Fer-
rer. il Art N 70:48-51 D '71
Dublin muslin; opening of Rosc. New Yorker
47:45 N 6 '71
If someone says his work is art, it's art.
T. Meehan. il Horizon 13:4-15 Aut '71
It reaches a desert in which nothing can be
perceived but feeling; The four elements.
D. Antin. bibliog il Art N 70:38-41+ Mr '71
Message to museums; modern art monopoly.
E. K. Belmont. Am Artist 35:11 D '71
Profiles; H. Geldzahler, curator of Metro-
politan's Department of contemporary art.
C. Tomkins. por New Yorker 47:58-60+
N 6 '71
Public and modern art; Unesco-backed in-
quiry; with report by D. F. Cameron. il
UNESCO Courier 24:4-34 Mr '71
Self in city space and in clothed space; City-
senses exhibition at Museum of contempo-
rary crafts. B. Schwartz. il por Craft Horiz
31:30-5 Ag '71
Visual illusions. M. Shaw. il Sch Arts 71:
40 N '71
What is post-modernism? B. O'Doherty. Art
in Am 59:19 My '71
See also
Constructivism
Cubism
Environment (art)
Multiple art

ART, Municipal
Our environment: awareness and commitment. il Sch Arts 70:27-34 Ap '71

ART, Negro (American)
Art; Whitney museum's Contemporary black
artists in America. L. Alloway. Nation 212:
604-5 My 10 '71
Artists portray a black Christ. il Ebony 26.
176-8+ Ap '71
Black artists: two generations; exhibition at
the Newark museum. il Sch Arts 71:21-8 D
'71
In a black bind; exhibit at New York's
Whitney museum called Black artists in
America. il Time 97:64 Ap 12 '71
It's not enough to say black is beautiful. F.
Bowling. il Art N 70:53-5+ Ap '71
See also
Negroes in art

ART, Norwegian
See also
Arts and crafts—Norway

ART, Oriental
See also
Art, Asian

ART, Persian
Romance of Varghe and Golshah. A. S. Me-
likian-Chirvani. il UNESCO Courier 24:26-
9 O '71
Sacred art in Persian culture. S. H. Nasr.
il UNESCO Courier 24:16-25 O '71
See also
Sculpture, Persian

ART, Peruvian
See also
Painting, Peruvian

ART, Pre-Columbian
Pre-Columbian America: Mesoamerica; sym-
posium. il Américas 23:S1-40 Je '71
See also
Sculpture, Pre-Columbian

ART, Primitive
See also
Art, Pre-Columbian
Cave drawings and paintings
ART, Religious. See Art, Jewish; Christian
art and symbolism

ART, Renaissance
See also
Painting, Renaissance
ART, Romantic. See Romanticism

ART, Russian
Brief utopia; Art in revolution at the New
York cultural center. D. Davis. Newsweek
78:79 O 4 '71
Tempest in a samovar; Art in revolution; ex-
hibition at the Hayward gallery, London.
il Newsweek 77:53 Ap 5 '71
See also
Painting, Russian
ART, Spanish American. See Art, Latin Ameri-
can

ART, Turkish
Roots of Turkish art. K. Kuh. il Sat R 54:
20-6+ N 20 '71
ART and communism. See Communism and art

ART and industry
See also
Art in factories
Business in the arts award
ART and libraries. See Libraries and art

ART and photography
Casual comparisons; comp. by J. Lipman.
il Art in Am 59:68-71 Ja '71
Collecting source material with a camera.
J. DeSoto. il Design 72:22-3 Sum '71
Kodachrome II, f/11-1/250 sec? Riverside mu-
seum show. Paintings from the photo. J.
Dreyfuss. il Mod Phot 35:62-3 F '71
Photo draw. R. K. Hillis. il Design 72:24-6
Spr '71
See also
Photography, Artistic
ART and religion
Can art be used? dedication of Rothko chapel.
T. B. Hess. Art N 70:33 Ap '71
ART and science
See also
Art and technology
ART and society
Art critic as social reformer, with a ques-
tion mark: G. Swenson. G. Battcock. il por
Art in Am 59:26-7 S '71
Culture and the people; Museo del bario,
Puerto Rican experiment. R. Ortiz. Art in
Am 59:27 My '71
New conservatism in the seventies? B.
O'Doherty. Art in Am 59:23 Mr '71
Public and modern art; Unesco-backed in-
quiry; with report by D. F. Cameron. il
UNESCO Courier 24:4-34 Mr '71
Special museum issue; symposium, with in-
trod. by B. O'Doherty. bibliog il Art in
Am 59:25-99+ Jl '71
ART and state
First in war, first in space, and last in sup-
port for the arts? D. Preiss. il Am Artist
35:5 Ap '71
How best to support artists? C. Cutler. Art
in Am 59:47 Ja '71
Museums and radicals: a history of emer-
gencies. L. Nochlin. bibliog il Art in Am
59:26-39 Jl '71
Toward a community of artists; National art
workers community. A. Gross. Am Artist
35:5 Je '71
WPA art: rescue of a U.S. treasure. il U S
News 70:75-8 Je 21 '71
See also
Art and society
ART and technology
Art and the corporations. D. Antin. il Art N
70:22-6+ S '71
Man and machine; Los Angeles County mu-
seum's exhibition. il por Time 97:60-3 Je
28 '71
ART appreciation. See Art—Appreciation

ART as a profession
Sexual politics, art style. L. R. Lippard.
Art in Am 59:19-20 S '71
ART as an investment
Graphics: fair game for the treasure-
seekers. A. Ogden. House B 113:22+ D '71
ART auctions. See Art sales
ART books. See Art literature
ART centers
See also
Walker art center, Minneapolis
ART clubs and societies
See also
Alliance of figurative artists
National art workers community
Print council of America
Salmagundi club, New York
ART collecting. See Art—Collectors and col-
lecting

ART collectors. See Art—Collectors and collecting
ART colonies. See Artists colonies
ART competitions. See Art—Competitions
ART criticism
Art world. H. Rosenberg. New Yorker 47: 62-5 Jl 24 '71
See also
Photography—Criticism, interpretation, etc.
ART critics
See also
International association of art critics
Swenson, G.
ART dealers
See also
Fischer, K.
Parke-Bernet galleries, inc.
Sotheby and company
ART déco
Art deco. S. B. Sherrill. il Antiques 100:154+ Ag '71
Art deco; of the '20s and '30s. il Life 70:70-4 F 19 '71
Art; exhibition at the Minneapolis institute of arts. L. Alloway. Nation 213:124+ Ag 16 '71
New antiques: art deco and modernism. J. S. Johnson. il Antiques 101:230-6 Ja '72
On and off the avenue; show at the Minneapolis institute of arts. J. Malcolm. New Yorker 47:111-15 S 18 '71
Return of the '30's, sweet and sharp; Art deco exhibition. A. Kazin. il Vogue 157:55 Ja 15 '71
ART education
Art education and the public taste. M. E. Shaw. Am Artist 35:5 Ag '71; Discussion. 35:11 N '71
Education of an artist; excerpt from The shape of content. B. Shahn. Am Artist 35:5 My '71
How and why of classroom art. R. Henkes. il Design 72:21-3 mid-Sum '71
Right philosophy. R. Henkes. Design 72:38-9 mid Wint '71
See also
Art—Appreciation
Art—Study and teaching
Art schools
Japan
Elementary art education in Osaka, Japan. E. Penn. il Sch Arts 70:46-9 Ap '71
ART exhibitions. See Art—Exhibitions
ART forgeries. See Forgery of works of art
ART galleries and museums. See Art—Galleries and museums
ART in factories
Art against the wall. il Newsweek 78:69 Ag 2 '71
Art for the worker's sake. V. Louvière. il Nations Bsns 59:17 O '71
Art on the line; paintings in Holland's Turmac tobacco plant. il Newsweek 77:80-3 Ap 12 '71
ART in the home
Double serenity in two art-filled homes of H. Wallis. M. Miller. il Home B 113:27-33 Ag '71
How much is that painting in the window? L. S. Bernstein. House B 113:38+ N '71
Space-and-light. the New York apartment of Fred Mueller. il Vogue 157:174-7 F 1 '71
See also
Garden ornaments
ART in the schoolroom. See Art—Study and teaching
ART jargon. See Jargon
ART juries. See Juries, Art
ART literature
Library books for leftover class time; reading tables at Monona public schools, Madison, Wis. J. W. Stewig. bibliog il por Wilson Lib Bul 45:681-4 Mr '71; Correction. 45:836 My '71
New gift and art books; with portfolio. A. H. Johnston. Pub W 200:43-62 Ag 23 '71
See also
Publishers and publishing—Art literature
ART materials. See Artists materials
ART medal. See Medals
ART metal work
Artist with nails. R. Fox. il pors Design 72: 16-17 mid-Wint '71
Designs in steel; 1970-1 Design in steel award program. il Design 72:4-7 Sum '71
Kalpa tarou; found art sculpture, Kokomo, Ind. il Design 72:29-30 mid-Sum '71

Mechanic turns artist; metal parts sculpture of L. Lefton. F. Worth. il por Design 72: 11 mid-Sum '71
Workshop: photofabrication. E. Moty. bibliog f il Craft Horiz 31:12-17 Je '71
See also
Damascening
Enamel and enameling
Jewelry
Pewter
Wire sculpture
ART metal workers
See also
Jewelers
ART museums. See Art—Galleries and museums
ART nouveau (movement)
Let's enjoy Emile Galle's glass. L. F. Reals il Hobbies 76:91 My '71
Living in styles: turn-of-the-century. il Redbook 136:122-6 Mr '71
See also
Art déco
ART objects
See also
Art in the home
Display of antiques, art objects, etc.

Collectors and collecting
Limited editions for love and money. A. Ogden. il House B 113:56+ N '71
Tabletop art; Warner and Kay LeRoy collection of art nouveau and art deco. R. Reif. il N Y Times Mag p82-3 Mr 28 '71
Wrightsman collection. R. Davidson. il Antiques 99:702-11 My '71

Conservation and restoration
See Art—Conservation and restoration
ART objects, Chinese
Chinese gold, silver, and porcelain; exhibit at Asia house, New York. S. B. Sherrill. il Antiques 99:630+ My '71
ART objects, Photography of. See Photography of works of art
ART objects, Victorian
Victoria's return. il Newsweek 78:90+ N 8 '71
ART of living. See Conduct of life
ART patronage
Four patron saints in one great act: the Steins. T. Prideaux. il por Life 70:56-60+ Ap 23 '71
Under the corporate wing. M. Kozloff. il Art in Am 59:92-9 Jl '71
ART prices. See Art—Prices
ART publishing
See also
Transworld art, inc.
ART sales
Antiques at auction; highlights of the 1970-1971 season across the country. D. Ellesin. il Antiques 100:532-4+ O '71
Coming auctions. See issues of Art news
See also
Art—Prices
Parke-Bernet galleries, inc.
ART schools
Art school directory. il Am Artist 35:29-52 Mr '71
See also
California institute of the arts, Valencia
Haystack Mountain school of crafts, Deer Isle, Me.
San Francisco art institute
ART shows. See Art—Exhibitions
ART thefts
Lost, and sadly found; a Vermeer on loan from Amsterdam's Rijksmuseum taken from Brussels' Palais des beaux-arts. il Time 98:66 O 18 '71
Vanishing treasure. il Time 98:54 S 20 '71
ART therapy
Relieving anxiety through art activity in an inner city school. E. Scott. bibliog il Sch Arts 70:44-6 Mr '71
ART trade
Anyone here want to buy a Rubens? D. Saxon. Esquire 75:58+ Ja '71
See also
Art sales
ART typing
He types portraits; work of J. Abel. H. Meyer. il pors Design 73:20-3 Wint '71
ARTEMIA. See Shrimps
ARTERIOSCLEROSIS
Now the villain is protein. il Sci N 100:123-4 Ag 21 '71
What killed Chuck Hughes. Newsweek 78:74 N 8 '71

ARTHRITIS
Answers to the most commonly asked questions about arthritis. G. M. Knox. Bet Hom & Gard 49:30+ O '71
Noel Charron's courage alone makes him the toughest kid on the block; living with rheumatoid arthritis. B. Lindeman. il Todays Health 49:46-51 S '71
What parents need to know about juvenile arthritis care; excerpt from The truth about arthritis care. J. J. Calabro and J. Wykert. Parents Mag 46:50-1+ Ap '71
You and your arthritis. H. Alpert. il Har Yrs 11:42-6 O '71

Therapy
Two more possibilities; histidine and prostaglandins. Sci N 99:44+ Ja 16 '71
ARTHRITIS in swine. See Swine—Diseases and pests
ARTHUR, King (romances, etc)
In quest of King Arthur. R. Wickerd and F. Wickerd. il Travel 136:54-61 S '71
ARTHUR, Paul
Color: the silent language of vision; interview, ed. by M. Roche. House & Gard 140: 22+ S '71
ARTHUR, Robert Alan
Wit and sass of Harry S. Truman. il pors Esquire 76:62-7+ Ag '71
ARTHUR, William, Jr, and Paddock, Polly
Nursing Nixon. Nation 213:453-4 N 8 '71
ARTHUR D. Little, Inc. See Little, Arthur D. inc.
ARTICHOKES
Three vegetables that come back. il Sunset 146:158+ F '71
See also
Cookery—Vegetables
ARTICLES, Thirty-nine. See Church of England—Articles of religion
ARTICLES for periodicals. See Periodical articles
ARTIFACTS, Indian. See Indians of North America—Implements
ARTIFICIAL diamonds. See Diamonds, Artificial
ARTIFICIAL fog. See Fog, Artificial
ARTIFICIAL fur. See Fur, Artificial
ARTIFICIAL hearts. See Hearts, Artificial
ARTIFICIAL insemination
How I make artificial insemination work. S. Hunewill. il por Suc Farm 69:no3 D5-7 F '71
Newest way to spot cows in heat; use of Gomer bull and chin-ball marker. G. Reynolds. il Farm J 95:22 D '71
Saving birds from DDT. il Newsweek 77:47 My 31 '71
Tips on A.I. from a real pro. P. Swan. pors Suc Farm 69:no3 D10 F '71
What AI can do for you. T. McCartney. Suc Farm 69:no5 B18 Mr '71
ARTIFICIAL insemination, Human
See also
Semen
ARTIFICIAL intelligence
Age of thinking machines. il Bsns W p90-2+ O 30 '71
ARTIFICIAL islands
Another SST? artificial deep-water port. il Forbes 107:21-2 Ap 15 '71
Holocaust on platform B; Shell oil company's drilling platform in Gulf of Mexico. J. P. Blank. il Read Digest 99:80-4 N '71
Oil islands, one way to disguise off-shore oil rigs. E. Cargile. il Sci Digest 69:34-5 Je '71
Oilmen at sea: life on South Marsh Island 73; American scene. L. Janos. il Time 97:16 Mr 1 '71
See also
Cities and towns, Floating
ARTIFICIAL kidneys. See Kidneys, Artificial
ARTIFICIAL lakes. See Lakes, Artificial
ARTIFICIAL leather. See Leather substitutes
ARTIFICIAL light gardening
Gain an extra growing season with artificial lighting L. W. Patterson. il Org Gard & Farm 18:41-3 D '71
Start your vegetable seeds under lights. D. Flegenheimer Home Gard 58:48 F '71
Winter gardening under lights. D. Flegenheimer. il Home Gard 58:30-1+ D '71
ARTIFICIAL marble. See Marble, Artificial
ARTIFICIAL satellite models
Lockheed leads team of 16 firms on satcom demonstration model. K. Johnsen. Aviation W 95:21 N 1 '71

ARTIFICIAL satellites
Perpetual motor of the universe. S. Khabarov. Space World H-8-92:38-9 Ag '71
Satellite report; tables. See issues of Space world
What next in space? J. P. Wiley, jr. il Natur Hist 80:74-5 Ag '71
See also
Space stations

Agricultural use
How satellite works for you. Suc Farm 69: no4 40 Mr '71

Air traffic control use
Aeronautical satellite negotiations planned. Aviation W 94:30 Je 14 '71
Aerosat controversy. P. J. Klass. Aviation W 95:9 N 8 '71
Aerosat progresses, but obstacles remain. il Aviation W 95:35-6 Ag 23 '71
Aerosat specifications delineated. P. J. Klass. il Aviation W 95:53-4+ O 11 '71
Airlines oppose U.S./ESRO aerosat. P. J. Klass. Aviation W 95:22-3 O 25 '71
Balloons used in aerosat tests. P. J. Klass. il Aviation W 94:56-9 Je 21 '71
Compromise on aerosat appears emerging. P. J. Klass. Aviation W 96:16-17 Ja 3 '72
Comsat offers aerosat patterned on Intelsat global network. K. Johnsen. Aviation W 96:17 Ja 3 '72
Congress boosts aerosat problems. K. Johnsen. Aviation W 95:16 D 6 '71
Domestic ATC satellite plans accelerate. P. J. Klass. il Aviation W 94:167+ Mr 8 '71
IATA threatens action in court to stop mandatory UHF aerosat. E. H. Kolcum. Aviation W 95:24 Jl 5 '71
Joint aerosat to be sought to avoid ICAO argument. P. J. Klass. Aviation W 94:17-18 Ap 12 '71
Ministerial-level parley initiates joint aerosat development plan. Aviation W 94:21 Je 28 '71
U.S. indecision on aerosat plans spurs impatience of Europeans. Aviation W 96:20 Ja 10 '72

Astronomical use
Explorer 43; IMP-I. il Space World H-6-90:36-42 Je '71
Lockheed experiment will map sun's X-rays; X-ray heliometer experiment. Space World H-11-95:43 N '71
New interplanetary monitoring platform. R. N. Watts, jr. il Sky & Tel 41:281-2 My '71
OAO-B: world's largest space astronomy telescope. il Space World H-4-88:10-15 Ap '71
OSO-H to continue study of the sun. il Space World H-12-96:4-11 D '71
OSO 7 begins observations. R. N. Watts, jr. il Sky & Tel 42:346 D '71
OSO to study sun in quiet period. R. R. Ropelewski. il Aviation W 95:34-6 Jl 26 '71
OSO will provide own eclipse. Aviation W 95:17 S 20 '71
Seventh OSO in orbit. R. N. Watts, jr. Sky & Tel 42:271+ N '71
Strange discoveries from our X-ray observatories in space. W. Von Braun. il Pop Sci 199:61-3 S '71
What two sun-observing satellites tell us. R. J. Thomas and S. P. Maran. il pors Sky & Tel 41:268-72 My '71
X-ray results from Uhuru. il Sky & Tel 41: 341-3 Je '71

Communication use
See Communications satellites

International aspects
Italy to launch U.S. satellites. Space World H-2-86:46 F '71
U.S. indecision on aerosat plans spurs impatience of Europeans. Aviation W 96:20 Ja 10 '72
U.S. offers launch assistance to Europeans; Department announcement, November 1, 1971; with text of letter to T. Lefevre, September 1, 1971, and summary of amplifying comments. Dept State Bul 65:624-7 N 29 '71

Launching
Italy to launch U.S. satellites. Space World H-2-86:46 F '71

Mapping use
See also
International satellite geodesy experiment

Meteorological use
French weather satellite. R. N. Watts, jr. il Sky & Tel 42:212 O '71
Italian San Marco-C. il Space World H-8-92: 28-30 Ag '71

ARTIFICIAL satellites—Meteorological use
—*Continued*
Lightning: observations by satellite. il Sci N 100:142 Ag 28 '71
Nimbus weather satellites: remote sounding of the atmosphere. G. L. Wick. Science 172:1222-3 Je 18 '71

Military use
Recon satellite assumes dual role. P. J. Klass. Aviation W 95:12-13 Ag 30 '71
Role of reconnaissance satellites in the arms race. P. Morrison. Sci Am 225:229-30+ S '71
Secret war in space, where U.S. trails Russia. il U S News 72:69 Ja 10 '72
Soviets trying mid-air satellite recovery. P. J. Klass. Aviation W 95:16 O 4 '71
Spies above. il Time 98:20+ Ag 30 '71
See also
Ballistic missile early warning system

Navigational use
USAF plans to orbit 621B navsats. Aviation W 94:52 F 22 '71

Orbits
USAF satellite uses new orbit. Aviation W 94:19 Ap 26 '71

Propulsion systems
See Space vehicles—Propulsion systems

Radio equipment
See Space vehicles—Radio equipment

Use in rescue work
Low-cost locator system pushed; global rescue alarm net for locating downed aircraft. C. E. Schneider. il Aviation W 95:46-7 Ag 9 '71

Use in research
Big eye in the sky. P. Briggs. il Nat Wildlife 9:35-9 F '71
CARETS: remote sensing for environmental studies. il Sci N 99:413-14 Je 19 '71
ERTS: satellites to serve man. il Electr World 85:27-9+ My '71
Exploring the earth by satellite. il Chem 44:25-6 Je '71
Eye in the sky; Earth resources technology satellite useful to foresters. E. Hay. il Am For 77:20-3 Ja '71
Gulf Stream and middle Atlantic bight: complex thermal structure as seen from an environmental satellite. P. K. Rao and others. il Science 173:529-30 Ag 6 '71
Infrared exploration, new light on the environment. J. Lear. il Sat R 54:53-7 Ap 3 '71
Pick up the phone and learn the earth's secrets. C. V. Glines. il Nations Bsns 59:48-51 D '71
Satellites: environmental sentries. il Space World H-3-87:16-19 Mr '71
Satellites to monitor earth resources. I. J. Sattinger. il Parks & Rec 6:10-13+ D '71
Saving earth's resources with photos from space. W. Von Braun. il Pop Sci 198:77-9+ Je '71
Techniques tomorrow; earth resources satellite photography. B. Sherman. Mod Phot 34:30+ N '70

ARTIFICIAL satellites, Canadian
Ionosphere satellite ISIS-B. il Space World H-7-91:38-41 Jl '71
ARTIFICIAL satellites, Chinese
Chinese in space again. Sci N 99:179 Mr 13 '71
ARTIFICIAL satellites, European
Intercosmos: space program of socialist countries. B. Petrov. Space World H-4-88:36-7 Ap '71
ARTIFICIAL satellites, French
L'affaire Eole. R. Gillette. Science 174:477 O 29 '71
French weather satellite; Eole. R. N. Watts, jr. il Sky & Tel 42:212 O 71
ARTIFICIAL satellites, Italian
Italian San Marco-C. il Space World H-8-72:28-30 Ag '71
ARTIFICIAL satellites, Russian
400 Cosmos satellites. A. Bessonov. il Space World H-8-92:24-5 Ag '71
Recent Cosmos believed advanced hardware test. Aviation W 94:18 Mr 15 '71
Soviet cosmonauts and satellites; photographs. Space World H-6-90:21-32 Je '71
Soviets trying mid-air satellite recovery. P. J. Klass. Aviation W 95:16 O 4 '71
ARTIFICIAL turf. See Turf, Artificial
ARTIFICIAL uterus. See Uterus, Artificial
ARTIS, William, jr
Solitary hunter stands in the way. il por Look 35:70-1 Ap 6 '71

ARTISTIC photography. See Photography, Artistic
ARTISTS
See also
Cartoonists
Illustrators
Women as artists
ARTISTS, American
Double vision of David Levine. P. A. Dreyfus. il por Am Artist 35:34-9+ N '71
See also
Alberty, J.
Bearden, R.
Crutchfield, W.
Grieger, S.
Heizer, M.
Hesse, E.
Hogan, P.
Jones, H.
Kent, R.
Madsen, R. P.
National art workers community
Neiman, L.
Painting, American
Schwartz, D.
Volunteer lawyers for the arts
Warhol, A.
ARTISTS, Animal. See Animals as artists
ARTISTS, British
See also
Painting, British
Paolozzi, E.
ARTISTS as teachers
Richard Lack's atelier system of training painters. D. Jardine. il por Am Artist 35:48-53+ Je '71
ARTISTS colonies
Community of crafts:
Peters Valley, N.J. M. Rhodes. il Craft Horiz 31:38+ Ap '71
Redwood Mountain; Calif. C. McCann. il Craft Horiz 31:37+ Ap '71
ARTISTS materials
Art mart. See issues of American artist
Clipboard V. G. Timmons. See issues of School arts
Experiment in sculpture; use of epoxy material. G. E. Toles. il Design 73:32-3 Wint '71
New sources, new materials (cont) Art N 70:74 Sum; 66 S; 98 N '71
Oil crayon. H. S. Paston. il Design 72:11 mid-Wint '71
Ralph Mayer's technical question & answer page. R. Mayer. See issues of American artist
What's new, where to buy it. See issues of Design
See also
Drawing materials
Paper
ARTISTS rights
New deal for art? il Newsweek 77:65+ Mr 29 '71
ARTISTS studios
Home for the working artist; residence and studio of K. Noland. N. Skurka. il N Y Times Mag p68-9 O 3 '71
Last studios; Manhattan's SoHo. il Time 98:52-6 Jl 5 '71
The ARTS
Arts and the human environment. H. Aach. Craft Horiz 31:38 F '71
Arts flash from Europe. R. Orrick. Vogue 158:72-4 N 1 '71
Greedy underground. J. Gruen. Vogue 157:136 F 1 '71
See also
Performing arts

Social aspects
See The Arts and society

Study and teaching
Adventures in the multi-disciplinary world of the arts and humanities. N. C. Polos. il Sch Arts 71:34-5 S '71
Care and feeding of an arts administrator. F. Taylor. Hi Fi 21:MA10-11 S '71
Columbus arts IMPACT; interdisciplinary model programs in the arts for children and teachers. il Todays Ed 60:20-4 N '71
Willingly to school. N. Hanks. il PTA Mag 65:18-21 Ap '71
See also
California institute of the arts, Valencia
Creative education

ARTS and crafts
Kid crafts. il Bet Hom & Gard 49:20+ Ag '71
New light from old bottles; easy to make hanging lamps. il Design 73:29 Wint '71
 See also
Batik
Block printing
Folk art
Handicraft
Ironwork
Jewelry
Mosaics
Needlework
Papier-mâché
Plaster work (craft)
Plastics work
Pyrography
Silverware
Stencil work
Tapestries
Woodworking
World crafts council

Bibliography
Books. See issues of Craft horizons
New books. See issues of School arts
Resource materials. V. G. Timmons. See issues of School arts
Reviewer's choice. See issues of Design

Exhibitions
Arts and crafts show for fun and money. il Sunset 147:79-80 Ag '71
Calendar. See issues of Craft horizons
Come to the crafts fairs. il McCalls 98:42 S '71
Craftsmen of the Piedmont. il Design 73:30-1 Wint '71
Exhibitions. See issues of Craft horizons
Furs and feathers; New York's Museum of contemporary crafts. R. Elman. il Craft Horiz 31:43-7 Ap '71
Objects & crafts; Indiana crafts; with comments by artists. il Design 73:24-6 Fall '71
October display of Hawaii crafts; Hawaii craftsmen annual. il Sunset 147:66 O '71
Sterling in the '70s; Sterling silver design competition at New York's Lever house. D. Smith. Craft Horiz 31:12-17 O '71
Young America arts fair; Milwaukee, Wis. il Design 73:40-1 Wint '71

Study and teaching
Community of crafts: Peters Valley; N.J. M. Rhodes. il Craft Horiz 31:38+ Ap '71
Expressions in three-dimensional design. S. R. Rainey. il Sch Arts 71:6-7 Ja '72
Handcrafts and the teacher. E. Mattil. il Design 72:36-9 mid-Sum '71
Travel and study directory. Craft Horiz 31: 26-30+ Ap; 44-9 Je '71
 See also
Haystack Mountain school of crafts, Deer Isle, Me.
Moving pictures—Art films

Appalachian Region
Appalachian folk school. J. M. Ramsay. il Nat Parks & Con Mag 45:22-4 Jl '71

Arizona
Learning at the zoo; Phoenix zoo's children's natural history and art program. F. J. Turkowski. il Parks & Rec 6:25-6 N '71

Arkansas
Molding history; good old days with paper. R. J. Lynch. il por Har Yrs 11:41-3 Ag '71

Indonesia
Ancient art of batik making. G. E. Toles. il Design 72:8-10 mid-Sum '71

Iran
Craftsmanship of early Iran. il UNESCO Courier 24:45 O '71

Italy
Rome: milieu for ceramics; Centro internazionale di ceramica. il Craft Horiz 31:35 Ap '71

Latin America
Artists and artisans. E. Hollstein. il Américas 22:25-9 N '70

Norway
Norwegian craft revitalized; rosemaling. J. H. Hood. il por Design 72:40-1 mid-Sum '71

Poland
Polish paper cutting. E. Mitsch. il Am Artist 35:58-9 Ap '71

Switzerland
Bookbinding at Ascona. il Craft Horiz 31:36+ Ap '71

Tunisia
Mats of Nabeul. E. Rossbach. il Craft Horiz 31:33-4+ Ap '71

United States
North Carolina's mountain craftsmen. J. Goodrum. il Travel 135:48-51 Je '71
 See also
American crafts council
ARTS and crafts, Indian. See Indians of North America—Industries
The ARTS and industry
Companies lend their expertise to the arts. il Bsns W p 102 My 15 '71
The ARTS and libraries. See Libraries and the arts
The ARTS and society
Arts & society; culture for the majority; address, November 15, 1970. M. Straight. Vital Speeches 37:394-8 Ap 15 '71
Sensibility in the 70's; excerpt from The disjunction of culture and social structure. D. Bell. Commentary 51:63-73 Je '71
The ARTS and state
Man who's made the most solid contribution to the arts of any president since F.D.R. F. Getlein. il por N Y Times Mag p 14-16+ F 14 '71; Reply. M. R. Rogers. p36 Mr 28 '71
Working with foundations: how to start a local arts council. D. J. Sager. bibliog il Wilson Lib Bul 45:744-9 Ap '71
ARTS education. See The Arts—Study and teaching
ARTSAY, Aida Favia-. See Favia-Artsay, A.
ARTSIMOVICH, Lev Andreevich
Comments of Lev Artsimovich, chief, Soviet thermonuclear project; interview. por Bul Atom Sci 27:50-1 O '71
ARTZ, Robert M.
Citizen leadership. Parks & Rec 6:109-10+ Ja '71
ARUBA (island)
Discovery of Aruba and Curacao. S. Cuneo. Mlle 73:216+ My '71
ARVEY, Jacob M.
Where are they now? il pors Newsweek 77: 12 Ap 5 '71 *
ARYAN languages
Aryan myth. M. D. Biddiss. il por Horizon 13:96-101 Sum '71
 See also
Indo-Aryan languages
ARYANS
Aryan myth. M. D. Biddiss. il por Horizon 13:96-101 Sum '71
Echoes of the Aryans. F. V. Grunfeld. il Horizon 13:102-4 Sum '71
ARYLAMINONAPHTHALENESULFONATES. See Sulfonates
AS the hippiest doctor almost grooved; story. See Erhart, S.
AS we have learnt from Freud, there are no jokes; story. See Gilliatt, P.
ASA, Thomas N.
Greenhouses unlimited. il Org Gard & Farm 18:63 F '71
ASBELL, Bernard
Day America could have used a psychiatrist. il por Todays Health 49:24-9+ Ag '71
ASBESTOS
Polluting the atmosphere with asbestos. Sci N 100:261 O 16 '71
Talc-treated rice and Japanese stomach cancer. R. R. Merliss. bibliog il Science 173:1141-2 S 17 '71
Technology; danger of asbestos. M. Villecco. il Arch Forum 133:50-2 D '70
ASBESTOSIS. See Lungs—Dust diseases
ASBURY, Barbara. See Galvin, H. R. jt. auth.
ASBURY college, Wilmore, Ky.
Asbury revisited J. F. Nelson. Chr Today 15:51+ F 12 '71
ASBURY PARK, N.J.
Cop named Joe; community relations project. F. Knebel. il Look 35:15-19 Jl 27 '71
ASCENSION ISLAND stamps. See Postage stamps
ASCHER, Amalie Adler
Gladioli in modern arrangements. il Horticulture 49:39-40 S '71
ASCHOFF, J. and others
Human circadian rhythms in continuous darkness; entrainment by social cues. bibliog il Science 171:213-15 Ja 15 '71
ASCORBIC acid. See Vitamins—Vitamin C
ASH, Lee
Ash's brief lives. W. R. Eshelman. Wilson Lib Bul 45:722+ Ap '71*

ASH, Michael E. and others
System of planetary masses. bibliog il Science 174:551-6 N 5 '71

ASH, Roy L.
Why the federal government needs restructuring. Fortune 83:64+ Mr '71

ASH, Sam
Sam Ash. J. Walsh. il pors Hobbies 76:37+ Mr '71 *

ASH, Volcanic. See Volcanic ash, tuff. etc.

ASHANIN, Charles B.
American Orthodox Christians in search of mission. Chr Cent 88:465-6 Ap 14 '71

ASHANTI
  History
Ashanti. J. Morris. il Horizon 13:74-91 Spr '71

ASHBERY, John
All the birds and the beasts were there. il por Art N 70:36-7+ Mr '71
G.M.P. il Art N 69:44-7+ F '71

ASHBROOK, John Milan
By all means; Ashbrook urged to enter the primary. Nation 214:4 Ja 3 '72 *
Off and running for '72. il pors Time 99:11-12 Ja 10 '72 *
Small Paul Revere. por Time 98:10-11 D 20 '71 *

ASHBROOK, Joseph
Astronomical scrapbook. See issues of Sky and telescope

ASHE, Arthur, 1943-
Once and future diplomat. F. Deford. il por Sports Illus 34:62-6+ Mr 1 '71 *

ASHE, Warren K. and others
Interaction of rheumatoid factor with infectious herpes simplex virus-antibody complexes. bibliog il Science 172:176-7 Ap 9 '71

ASHEIM, Lester
I'm glad you asked that; questions and answers. Am Lib 2:597-9 Je '71

ASHER, Irving M. See Aghajanian, G. K. jt. auth.

ASHER, Thomas R.
Tanks but no tanks. New Repub 164:17-19 Je 26 '71

ASHES
Fly ash: friend or foe? Mech Illus 67:38 Ap '71

ASHLAND, Ore, Shakespeare festival. See Shakespeare festivals

ASHLAND, Wis.
Focus on the future: the small town: address, January 28, 1971. J. W. Joanis. Vital Speeches 37:275-9 F 15 '71

ASHLEY, Nova Trimble
Time study; poem. Good H 173:36 D '71

ASHLEY, Robert P.
What makes a good novel? Engl J 60:596-8+ My '71

ASHLEY, Terry, and Gennaro, J. F. jr
Fly in the sundew; with biographical sketches. il Natur Hist 80:3-4, 80-5+ D '71

ASHMEAD, Hal
Illustrator in the courtroom: Hal Ashmead. M. Schaefer. il por Am Artist 36:30-5+ Ja '72 *

ASHTON, Beverly
Practical reading course for the slow learner in high school. il Engl J 60:97-101 Ja '71

ASHTON, Harris John
He's in the market for a meatpacker. por Bsns W p70 Jl 10 '71 *

ASIA
Asia's moves toward red China. U S News 71:41 Ag 2 '71
  See also
Agriculture—Asia
Communism—Asia
English language in Asia
Gambling—Asia
Hindu Kush
Military assistance, American—Asia
Pollution—Asia
United Nations—Economic commission for Asia and the Far East
United States—Armed forces—Forces in Asia
World war, 1939-1945—Asia
  Foreign relations
New balance of power in Asia and the Pacific. H. Bull. For Affairs 49:669-81 Jl '71
  Maps
Asia (cont) Sr Schol 99:9 O 4 '71
  Politics
As power lineup shifts in a key part of the world. il U S News 71:64-6 O 11 '71
Korea and the emerging Asian power balance. P. C. Hahm. For Affairs 50:339-50 Ja '72
What they're talking about in Asia. il Sr Schol 99:8+ O 4 '71
Who can make peace now in Asia? D. Lawrence. U S News 71:92 D 20 '71
  See also
Balance of power

  Religious institutions and affairs
  See also
Catholic church in Asia

ASIA, CENTRAL
  See also
Afghanistan
Iran

ASIA, SOUTHEASTERN
Lands and peoples of Southeast Asia; symposium. il Nat Geog 139:295-365, sup(folded map) Mr '71
Southeast Asia, 1971; symposium. il Cur Hist 61:321-56+ D '71
  See also
Chinese in southeastern Asia
Indochina
Opium trade—Asia, Southeastern
Petroleum—Asia, Southeastern
Russians in southeastern Asia
United States—Foreign relations—Asia, Southeastern
Visitors, Foreign—Asia, Southeastern
  Antiquities
New light on a forgotten past. W. G. Solheim, 2d. il Nat Geog 139:330-9 Mr '71
  Defenses
  See also
Southeast Asia treaty organization
  Foreign relations
New tides in Southeast Asia. W. P. Bundy. For Affairs 49:187-200 Ja '71
    United States
  See United States—Foreign relations—Asia, Southeastern
  Industries
Wealth and power of the overseas Chinese. L. Kraar. il Fortune 83:78-81+ Mr '71
  Maps
Lands and peoples of southeast Asia. il Nat Geog 139:295-365. sup(folded map) Mr '71
  Politics
Asia: how stand the dominoes? M. Parker. il Newsweek 78:47+ S 27 '71
Collective security in Asia; address, August 31, 1971. J. S. McCain, jr. Vital Speeches 37:749-57 O 1 '71
What price Asian elections? W. P. Bundy. Newsweek 77:56 My 10 '71

ASIA, SOUTHERN
  Foreign relations
Super powers and southern Asia. Cur 130:11-14 Je '71
  Politics
Nehru's plan for peace. S. S. Harrison. New Repub 164:17-22 Je 19 '71
New worries for U.S. in Asia, aftermath of Indian-Pakistani war. il U S News 72:14-17 Ja 3 '72

ASIADOLLARS. See Money—International aspects

ASIAN American students. See Oriental American students

ASIAN art. See Art, Asian

ASIAN music. See Music, Asian

ASIAN students in the United States. See Foreign students in the United States

ASIANS
  See also
Abkhasians

ASIATIC-European airline services. See Airlines—International services—European-Asiatic

ASIMOV, Isaac
Bookworm. Sat R 54:70 Ja 23 '71
Hidden rhythms that make nature's clock tick. il Nat Wildlife 10:36-40 D '71
Isaac Asimov explains: questions and answers. See issues of Science digest
No space for women? il Ladies Home J 88:115+ Mr '71
World's most deadly poison. il Sci Digest 71:8-11 Ja '72

ASINOF, Eliot
Craig & Joan: two lives for peace; story, excerpt from novel. McCalls 98:155-66 F '71

ASKEW, Reubin
Mod populist. il por Newsweek 79:15-16 Ja 3 '72 *
Reubin Askew of Florida. por Time 97:18-19 My 31 '71 *

ASKOV, Eunice, and others
Decade of research in handwriting. Ed Digest 36:43-6 Mr '71

ASSUMPTION of the Virgin Mary. See Mary,
   Virgin
ASSYRO-BABYLONIAN maps. See Maps, As-
   syro-Babylonian
ASTARTE (goddess) See Mythology, Assyro-
   Babylonian
ASTARTE; ballet. See Ballets—Criticisms
ASTEROIDS
   Asteroid conference in Tucson. M. S. Mat-
      thews. il Sky & Tel 42:22-4 Jl '71
   Bountiful November for asteroid watchers.
      il Sky & Tel 42:318-19 N '71
   Minor planet 1971 FA. Sky & Tel 41:351
      Je '71
   Newly named asteroids. Sky & Tel 41:279
      My '71
   Toro makes a threesome with earth and
      moon. G. B. Lubkin. il Phys Today 24:
      17-18 D '71
   Vesta: the brightest asteroid. il Sky & Tel
      41:395 Je '71
ASTHMA
   Pharmacological differentiation of allergic
      and classically conditioned asthma in the
      guinea pig. D. R. Justesen and others;
      discussion. bibliog Science 173:82 Jl 2 '71
ASTIN, Alexander W.
   Open admissions: the real issue. Science
      173:1197 S 24 '71
ASTOR, Gerald
   Agonized American Jews. il Look 35:17-19
      Ap 20 '71
   New York ten. il N Y Times Mag p32-5
      D 12 '71
   No recession in the skin trade. il Look 35:27-
      36 Je 29 '71
   TV's Dr Marcus Welby. il pors Look 35:56-9
      Mr 23 '71
   What's different about public TV? il Look
      35:14-15 S 7 '71
—and Mothner, Ira
   How 10 cities fight drugs. Look 35:73-4+ F 23
      '71
ASTOR family
   Who owns New York? il Forbes 107:24-6+
      Je 1 '71
ASTROLOGY
   Astrology: horoscopes (title varies) M. Wood-
      ruff. See issues of McCall's
   Birth control by astrology; excerpt from
      Psychic discoveries behind the iron cur-
      tain. S. Ostrander and L. Schroeder. Harp
      Baz 104:104-5 F '71
   Eye on the sky. X. Pové. See issues of
      Harper's bazaar
   Horoscope. M. E. Crummere. See issues of
      Vogue
   If you're an Aries; an astrological guide for
      librarians. E. Hoffman. bibliog il Library J
      96:241-4 Ja 15 '71
   Jupiter's brain: notes on sexual compatibility
      and astrology. R. Phelps. il Mlle 73:130-1+
      S '71
   Starcast. M. L. Fiel. Mlle 74:132-3 Ja '72
   Why astrology stays sky-high! L. Sherr. il
      Seventeen 29:126-7+ N '70

   Anecdotes, facetiae, satire, etc.
   Censor's horoscope. R. Knudson. Am Lib 2:
      180-5 F '71
   Night my stars got crossed. T. Bolton. il
      Read Digest 99:123-5 D '71
ASTRONAUTS
   Astronaut careers turn to be closed-ended.
      E. Driscoll. il Sci N 99:234-6 Ap 3 '71
   Biographical data on the Soyuz 10 crew. il
      Space World H-8-92:8-9 Ag '71
   Communes on the moon? C. H. Simonds.
      Nat R 23:1118 O 8 '71
   Cosmonaut family album; excerpts from Rus-
      sians in space. il Life 71:48-52 N 5 '71
   Foreign astronauts may help man U.S.
      spacecraft in mid-1970s. Z. Strickland.
      Aviation W 95:19 O 4 '71
   Latest patch of unemployment: astronauts
      for space missions. il U S News 71:40-1 Ag
      16 '71
   Requiem for the scientist-astronauts. R. S.
      Lewis. Bul Atom Sci 27:17-18 My '71
   Russians in space. by E. Riabchikov. Re-
      view
      Harper 243:138+ N '71
   Soviet cosmonauts visit United States. il
      Space World H-3-87:46 Mr '71
   Three Soviet heroes; cosmonauts of Soyuz
      11 lying in state. il Life 71:30-1 Jl 16 '71
   Who will fly to Mars? B. Ford. il Sci Digest
      70:47-52 N '71
      See also
   Space flight to the moon—Manned flights
   Women as astronauts
      also names of astronauts, e.g. A. B. Shep-
      ard

Clothing
   Apollo 16 spacesuit mobility, fit tested. il
      Aviation W 95:51 N 8 '71
   Astronauts and cosmic rays; study of Apollo
      helmets. il Chem 44:22 Jl '71
   Cosmic-ray tracks in plastics: the Apollo hel-
      met dosimetry experiment. G. M. Com-
      stock and others. bibliog il Science 172:154-7
      Ap 9 '71
      Food
   See Space flight—Food problems
      Photographs
   Soviet cosmonauts and satellites. Space World
      H-6-90:21-32 Je '71
      Training
   Alan Shepard gets set for the moon. L.
      Wainwright. por Read Digest 98:88-92 Ja '71
   News from the world of space exploration;
      Skylab 56-day test. Space World H-8-92:44
      Ag '71
   With the Apollo astronauts: training for the
      moon. R. Gannon. il Pop Sci 199:52-4+ Jl '71
ASTRONOMERS
   See also names of astronomers, e.g. H.
      Shapley
ASTRONOMERS, Amateur
   Amateur activities in South Vietnam. R. W.
      Sinnott. il Sky & Tel 41:159-60 Mr '71
   Amateur astronomers. See issues of Sky and
      telescope
   Amateur scientist; groups are organized to
      observe the eclipse of stars by the moon.
      T. E. Bell. il Sci Am 226:108-11 Ja '72
   Gleanings for ATM's; ed. by R. E. Cox. See
      issues of Sky and telescope
   Join the star-struck generation. J. Galub. il
      Am Home 74:32+ My '71
   New England amateurs visit the Southland.
      il Sky & Tel 41:224-8 Ag '71
      See also
   Association of lunar and planetary observers
   Western amateur astronomers (organization)
ASTRONOMICAL conferences
   Apollo rendezvous and telescope fair in Ohio.
      il Sky & Tel 42:107-11 Ag '71
   Asteroid conference in Tucson. M. S. Mat-
      thews. il Sky & Tel 42:22-4 Jl '71
   1971 AL-ALPO convention plans. W. J. Bus-
      ler. il Sky & Tel 41:229 Ap '71
   Stellafane holds Porter centennial. D. Milon.
      il por Sky & Tel 42:208-11 O '71
   Telescope makers meet at Riverside, Cali-
      fornia. il Sky & Tel 41:359-60 Je '71
ASTRONOMICAL distances
   Bye-bye, galaxies: the universe may be twice
      as large as thought. Sci N 101:22 Ja 8 '72
ASTRONOMICAL education. See Astronomy—
   Study and teaching
ASTRONOMICAL instruments
   Sun machine previews shadows; Heliolux. P.
      Wahl. il Pop Sci 199:121 Ag '71
      See also
   Sextants
   Spectrohelioscope
   Telescopes
ASTRONOMICAL league
   Memphis memorandum; report of annual con-
      vention. il Sky & Tel 42:266-9 N '71
ASTRONOMICAL observations. See Astron-
   omy—Observations
ASTRONOMICAL observatories
   Club observatory in Indiana. J. C. Thomas
      and R. Miller. il Sky & Tel 42:217-18 O '71
   Darkness. A. W. Smith. Nat Parks & Con
      Mag 45:2+ Jl '71
   Four amateur observatories. il Sky & Tel
      42:280-2 N '71
   Observatory-planetarium at Kutztown, Penn-
      sylvania: Gruber-Knedler planetarium and
      observatory. A. Kiasat and C. R. Cham-
      bliss. il Sky & Tel 42:76-7 Ag '71
   Two amateurs set up an observatory-tele-
      scope cooperative. A. E. Morton. il Sky
      & Tel 42:374-7 D '71
      Location
   Blinding the big eyes; glare of city lights,
      an astronomical disaster. il Time 97:48 Ap
      12 '71
   Star bright, street light, which will they see
      tonight? R. J. Bazell. il Science 171:461 F 5
      '71
      Argentina
   First century of Cordoba observatory. J. L.
      Sersic. il Sky & Tel 42:347-50 D '71
      Armenia
   Byurakan observatory in Societ Armenia. E.
      E. Khachikian and D. W. Weedman. il Sky
      & Tel 41:217-19 Ap '71
   Letter from Armenia; Byurakan astrophysi-
      cal observatory. F. J. Dyson. New Yorker
      47:130+ N 6 '71

ASTROPHYSICS—*Continued*
Social uses of astrophysics. Sky & Tel 41: 79 F '71
Spotting an invisible black hole; collapsars. J. P. Wiley, jr. il Natur Hist 80:62-3 Ap '71
Stellar old age: black holes and gravitational collapse. A. L. Hammond. Science 171:1228 Mr 26 '71
Through a black hole darkly. Sci Am 224:46 Mr '71
When is a hole not a hole? black hole theory. Mech Illus 67:38 My '71
See also
Neutron stars
Stars—Evolution
Universe

ASTROS (baseball) See Baseball clubs

ASWAN HIGH DAM
Aswan dam looses a flood of problems. C. Sterling. il Life 70:46-46A F 12 '71
Aswan disaster. C. Sterling. il Nat Parks & Con Mag 45:10-13 Ag '71
Damned if you dam. Nation 212:230 F 22 '71
Fifteen years later. Commonweal 93:436 F 5 '71
New life from the Nile. il Time 97:31 Ja 25 '71
Price of progress. il Newsweek 77:37+ Ja 25 '71

ASYLUM, Right of
Futile leap; would-be defector. Simas Kudirka. Sr Schol 97:5 Ja 11 '71
Right of sanctuary: then and now. J. Hennesey. America 125:482-3 D 4 '71

ASYLUMS. See Hospitals, Psychiatric

ASYMMETRY. See Symmetry (biology)

ATCHESON, Richard
Alaska, where the fabulous is routine. il Holiday 49:52-5+ Ap '71
Down and out in Dinkelsbühl. il Sat R 54: 42+ Mr 13 '71
Galapagos: the way the world was. il Holiday 48:52-5+ S '70
Rubbing the right way. Holiday 49:22+ D '70

ATCHISON, Topeka and Santa Fe railway
Man who met the longhorns with a railroad. J. S. Reed. il por Nations Bsns 59:50-1 Ja '71
Miracle of rare device; Santa Fe's Super chief. K. R. Zimmermann. Nat R 23: 655+ Je 15 '71

ATHEISM
Gods of atheism, by V. P. Miceli. Review Cath World 214:43-4 O '71. H. Gow Nat R 23:813-14 Jl 27 '71. W. Herberg

ATHENS, Greece
Letter from Athens. A. Bailey. New Yorker 47:130+ N 20 '71
Music
Orpheus in Athens, and Fausto Cleva's death. S. Fleming. il Hi Fi 21:MA15 N '71

ATHENS, Ohio
Education
Our high school reading center; Athens high school. E. Elmore. Todays Ed 60:40 Ja '71

ATHEROSCLEROSIS. See Arteriosclerosis

ATHLETES
Debunking a myth; Ogilvie-Tutko study. Time 98:77 O 11 '71
Jack Scott draws blood from sportsmanship. P. Axthelm. Vogue 157:163 Ap 1 '71
New stars leap toward the Olympics. il Life 71:34-5 Jl 16 '71
Not the triumph but the struggle; condensation from Deep water. D. Schollander and D. Savage. il pors Read Digest 98:221-4+ Je '71
Sports; making athletics a masculinity rite. J. Scott. Ramp Mag 10:64 Ja '72
They still swing a mean paddle; red China's athletes at the World table tennis championship. D. Miles. il Sports Illus 34:32-3 Ap 12 '71
Trading game. A. S. Young. il Ebony 26: 139-42+ Ap '71
Woolf at the door. il por Time 98:69 N 29 '71
See also
Amateurism (sports)
Baseball players
Basketball players
Fellowship of Christian athletes
Football players
Negro athletes
Sports halls of fame
Women as athletes
Ability testing
See Athletic ability

Health and hygiene
Champs don't win on diets. J. Chamberlin. il Sci Digest 70:64-8 S '71
These major-leaguers succeeded in spite of . . . E. Kiester. il pors Todays Health 49: 46-51 O '71
We have a neurotic in the backfield, doctor; consulting psychologists at San Jose state college. J. Jares. il pors Sports Illus 34:30-4 Ja 18 '71
Mental hygiene
See Athletes—Health and hygiene
Recruiting
Legal license to steal the stars; NBA's four-year rule declared illegal. W. Johnson. il Sports Illus 34:34-6+ Ap 12 '71
Salaries, pensions, etc.
See also
Basketball players—Salaries, pensions, etc.

ATHLETES agents
Men behind the men who make money in sports. P. Axthelm. il Vogue 157:186-7+ My '71

ATHLETES as authors
When sports figures turn author: jocks and their ghosts. H. Higdon. il Sat R 54:48-9+ Ag 14 '71

ATHLETIC ability
Testing for athletic talent. D. Newlands. il Look 35:67 Je 1 '71
We have a neurotic in the backfield, doctor; consulting psychologists at San Jose state college. J. Jares. il pors Sports Illus 34:30-4 Ja 18 '71

ATHLETIC buildings. See Gymnasiums

ATHLETIC fields
Lighting
Low-budget sports lighting; Riverdale, San Joaquin Valley, Calif. il Am City 86:72 Ja '71

ATHLETICS
See also
Amateur athletic union of the United States
Athletes
Boxing
Pan American games
Running
School athletics
Sports
Sportsmanship
Track athletics
Medical aspects
See Sports medicine

ATHLETICS (baseball) See Baseball clubs

ATKINS, Janina
I love America. Read Digest 98:187-8 Mr '71

ATKINSON, Bob
Setting sail for yesterday. il Audubon 73:73-9 Mr '71

ATKINSON, Brooks
Another world, another time. il Audubon 73: 66-71 Ja '71

ATKINSON, Claudene D.
New approach: drama in the classroom. Engl J 60:947-51+ O '71

ATKINSON, Keith W.
Communication: closing the widening gap. Clear House 46:27-31 S '71

ATKINSON, Richard C. and Shiffrin, R. M.
Control of short-term memory; with biographical sketches. il Sci Am 225:13. 82-90 bibliog(p 120) Ag '71

ATKINSON, Robert E.
Gardener's almanac; ed. by E. Haraszty (cont) il McCalls 98:30 F '71

ATLANTA
Airports
Atlanta TCA revisited. Flying 89:19-20+ N '71
Banks
Making depositors into shareholders; Citizens & Southern national bank. Bsns W p75 Jl 31 '71
Bookstores
See Booksellers and bookselling—Georgia
Description
Atlanta: black mecca of the South. P. Garland. il Ebony 26:152-7 Ag '71
Step by step through Atlanta. R. Deardorff. il Travel 136:28-31+ O '71
Economic conditions
Nixon's price freeze heats up Atlanta's lots. T. Thompson. il Life 71:34-7 O 8 '71
Music
S.R.O. in Atlanta; traveling Carmen. B. Thebom. il Opera N 36:27-9 D 25 '71

ATLANTA—*Continued*

Negroes

Atlanta: black mecca of the South. P. Garland. il Ebony 26:152-7 Ag '71

Parks and playgrounds

Spring swing to playgrounds; imaginative playground equipment. J. C. Delius. il Parks & Rec 6:48-9+ O '71

Politics and government

Mayor, by I. Allen jr, ed. by P. Hemphill. Review
　New Repub 165:26 Ag 21 '71. J. Yardley
Win for Mayor Sam. por Newsweek 78:76+ D 6 '71

Sanitary affairs

Sticker condemns that old garbage can. il Am City 86:32 S '71
Wheeled refuse containers please everyone. R. Hulsey. il Am City 86:113 S '71
Will test home trash smashing. il Am City 86:34 Mr '71

Social conditions

Life and death of Atlanta's hip strip. J. T. Wooten. il N Y Times Mag p34-5+ Mr 14 '71
New day a'coming in the South. il por Time 97:14-20 My 31 '71

Transit systems

Road, rail and racism. Nation 213:515 N 22 '71

ATLANTA 500. See Automobile racing
ATLANTA Hawks (basketball team) See Basketball teams
ATLANTIC and Pacific tea company. See Great Atlantic and Pacific tea company
ATLANTIC cement company. See Cement industry
ATLANTIC coast
　See also
Sea Islands
ATLANTIC flights. See Aviation—Transatlantic flights
ATLANTIC OCEAN
　See also
Gulf Stream
Jamaica Bay
Labrador Sea
ATLANTIC recording corporation
Soul kaleidoscope: Aretha at the Fillmore. M. Lydon. il pors Ramp Mag 10:30-9 O '71
ATLANTIC states
　See also
Gardens—Atlantic states

Description and travel

Mountains east. il Bet Hom & Gard 49:145-50 O '71

ATLANTIS
New thought on lost Atlantis. il Chem 44:5 Ja '71
ATLAS, Charles
Indoor exercises to keep you fit this winter. il Mech Illus 67:53-5 D '71
ATLAS, James
Diary of Gustav Janouch; Isaac Rosenfeld thinks about his life; poems. Poetry 118:211-15 Jl '71
Modern poets: an American-British anthology, ed. by J. M. Brinnin and B. Read. Review
　Poetry 119:169-71 D '71
What is to be done? Poetry 119:45-51 O '71
ATLAS chemical industries, inc.
What Atlas has that ICI wants. Bsns W p33 Ap 24 '71
ATLASES
National atlas of the United States. Review
　Weatherwise il 24:204-7 O '71. A. Court

Bibliography

Great gift is the question-answerer: a good atlas. il Sunset 147:46 D '71
ATMOSPHERE
Normal atmosphere: large radical and formaldehyde concentrations predicted. H. Levy, 2d. bibliog il Science 173:141-3 Jl 9 '71
Primordial oil slick. A. C. Lasaga and others. bibliog il Science 174:53-5 O 1 '71
Recent volcanism and the stratosphere. J. F. Cronin. bibliog il Science 172:847-9 My 21 '71
Sulfur isotopes in Swaziland system barites and the evolution of the earth's atmosphere. E. C. Perry, jr. and others. bibliog il Science 171:1015-16 Mr 12 '71
　See also
Atmospheric pressure
Counterglow
Winds

ATMOSPHERE, Color of. See Sky, Color of
ATMOSPHERE, Upper
Halo for the earth; magnetoglow. Sci N 99:114 F 13 '71
Magnetoglow: a new geophysical resource. C. Y. Johnson and others. bibliog il Science 171:379-81 Ja 29 '71
Thunderstorms: effects on ionosphere. il Sci N 100:142 Ag 28 '71
　See also
Airglow
ATMOSPHERE-ocean interaction. See Ocean-atmosphere interaction
ATMOSPHERE-soil interaction. See Soil-atmosphere interaction
ATMOSPHERIC aerosols. See Aerosols
ATMOSPHERIC carbon dioxide. See Carbon dioxide
ATMOSPHERIC dust. See Dust
ATMOSPHERIC electricity
　See also
Auroras
Lightning
St Elmo's fire
Thunderstorms
ATMOSPHERIC ions. See Ions
ATMOSPHERIC models. See Meteorological models
ATMOSPHERIC nucleation
Clustering of sulfur dioxide and water vapor about oxonium and nitric oxide ions. A. W. Castleman, jr. and others. bibliog il Science 173:1025-6 S 10 '71
ATMOSPHERIC oxygen. See Oxygen
ATMOSPHERIC pollution. See Air pollution
ATMOSPHERIC pressure
Extremes of atmospheric pressure. il Weatherwise 24:130-1 Je '71
More or less under pressure. A. K. Blackadar. il Weatherwise 23:283-5+ D '70
ATMOSPHERIC research
Climate cycles. C. Emiliani. il Sea Front 17:108-20 Mr '71
Climatic changes: some evidence and implications. J. E. Newman. il Weatherwise 24:56-62 Ap '71
Modifying the ionosphere with intense radio waves. W. F. Utlaut and R. Cohen. bibliog il Science 174:245-54 O 15 '71
New theory on excitations between spheres of the globe. A. Osipov. Space World H-12-96:46 D '71
Priorities for the 1970's. Sci N 99:384 Je 5 '71
　See also
Rockets—Meteorological use
United States—National oceanic and atmospheric administration
ATMOSPHERIC temperature
Heat barrier. P. R. Ehrlich and J. P. Holdren. Sat R 54:61 Ap 3 '71
　See also
Global temperature changes
Temperature inversions
ATMOSPHERIC transparency
Decreasing transparency of our atmosphere. il Sky & Tel 41:272 My '71
ATMOSPHERIC turbidity
Solar radiation: absence of air pollution trends at Mauna Loa. H. T. Ellis and R. F. Pueschel. bibliog il Science 172:845-6 My 21 '71
ATMOSPHERIC turbulence
Follow me through; wake turbulence. R. Blodget. il Flying 89:28-9 N '71
On the track of CAT: clear air turbulence. K. V. Brown. il Sci Digest 70:62-6 N '71
On top; wake turbulence. R. L. Collins. Flying 89:12-14 Jl '71
Riding a giant's coattails. T. J. Storli. Flying 89:82+ O '71
Warning to flyers: watch the wake! B. Kocivar. il Pop Sci 198:76-7+ Ap '71
ATOLLS. See Coral reefs and islands
ATOM smashing apparatus. See Accelerators (electrons, etc)
ATOMIC absorption spectrometer. See Spectrometers
ATOMIC attack, Survival after. See Survival after airplane accidents, shipwrecks, etc.
ATOMIC blasting
Sharing the atom; Soviet nuclear projects. il Time 98:60 S 13 '71
ATOMIC bomb casualty commission
After the bomb. il Chem 44:22-3 N '71
ATOMIC bomb shelters
Effects of fallout shelter confinement on mental health. M. P. Beussee and others. Ment Hy 55:121-3 Ja '71
ATOMIC bombs
Black-market A-bombs? il Newsweek 77:59 Ap 26 '71

ATOMIC bombs—*Continued*

Physiological effects
See Radioactivity—Physiological effects

Testing, Detection of
Detection of underground tests. Sci Am 225: 46-8 N '71
Seismology meets politics. il Sci N 100:22-3 Jl 10 '71
Testing boom begins to fade. il Bsns W p45 N 13 '71

Testing, Underground
Alaskan atom test, why all the furor. il U S News 71:38 S 27 '71
Amchitka and tribalism. N. Cousins. Sat R 54:30 S 25 '71
Amchitka bomb goes off. il Time 98:15 N 15 '71
Amchitka H-test: was it worth it? il U S News 71:72 N 22 '71
Amchitka nuclear blast. il Newsweek 78: 30-1 N 15 '71
Amchitka; Operation Cannikin. A. W. Smith. Nat Parks & Con Mag 45:2+ Ag '71
Autopsy on Cannikin. Time 98:84 N 22 '71
Cannikin's 7.0 explosion causes local damage only. Sci N 100:323 N 13 '71
Conflict over underground nuclear tests. il Sci N 100:307 N 6 '71
Confusion on Amchitka. Nation 213:229 S 20 '71
Crunch on Cannikin decision near. C. Holden. Science 173:1004 S 10 '71
Explosion effects and earthquakes in the Amchitka Island Region. E. R. Engdahl. bibliog il Science 173:1232-5 S 24 '71
From Milrow to Cannikin; Amchitka tests. il Sci N 99:350 My 22 '71
Good news on the arms front. N. Cousins. Sat R 54:16 Ag 28 '71
Green light on Cannikin. il Time 98:74 N 8 '71
Hell in a very small place; Amchitka blast. W. K. Wyant, jr. Nation 213:132 Ag 30 '71
Is this blast necessary? Amchitka. il Newsweek 78:99 N 1 '71
Notes and comment: test at Amchitka. New Yorker 47:45-6 N 20 '71
Nuclear test that may fizzle; Cannikin test. il Bsns W p 117-18+ S 25 '71
Nuclear tests: big Amchitka shot target of mounting opposition. R. J. Bazell. il Science 172:1219-21 Je 18 '71
Round 2 at Amchitka; environmentalists suit against the AEC. Time 98:41 Jl 19 '71
Why are they smiling? two daughters of James Schlesinger, near Amchitka blast to prove test is safe. il Sr Schol 99:15 D 6 '71

ATOMIC energy. See Atomic power
ATOMIC energy agency. See International atomic energy agency
ATOMIC energy commission. See United States—Atomic energy commission
ATOMIC energy industries. See Atomic power industry
ATOMIC fuels. See Nuclear fuels
ATOMIC industries. See Atomic power industry
ATOMIC medicine
Nuclear physics in medicine. G. L. Brownell and R. J. Shalek; reply. P. R. Almond. Phys Today 24:9 Ja '71
ATOMIC nuclei
Concepts of nuclear structure; adaptation of address, October 29, 1970. A. Bohr. il Science 172:17-21 Ap 2 '71
Superheavy nuclei from Orsay's Alice. Sci N 100:373 D 4 '71

Energy levels
See Energy levels (quantum mechanics)
ATOMIC power
Atomic power: is it really necessary? E. Flattau. Sci Digest 70:15-20 O '71
Energy crisis: symposium. Bul Atom Sci 27:2-53 S '71
See also
Nuclear fusion
Nuclear reactors
United States—Congress—Joint committee on atomic energy

Economic aspects
Atoms and dollars. il Forbes 108:24-6+ O 1 '71
New goals for atomic energy. V. L. Parsegian. por Bul Atom Sci 27:2-7 O '71
Nonproliferation and control: peaceful uses of atomic energy. G. C. Delcoigne and G. Rubinstein. il Bul Atom Sci 27:5-7 F '71

Nuclear energy and the Malthusian dilemma. D. R. Inglis. Bul Atom Sci 27:14-18 F '71; Reply with rejoinder. A. M. Weinberg. 27:3+ Je '71
Seeking a convergent view; the unfinished detective story. W. B. Lewis and A. M. Marko. pors Bul Atom Sci 27:50-2 N '71
See also
Atomic blasting
Atomic power industry
Atomic power plants

Industrial aspects
See Atomic power—Economic aspects

International aspects
Nuclear energy: a prelude to H. G. Wells' dream. A. M. Weinberg. For Affairs 49:407-18 Ap '71
Sharing the atom; U.S. and the Soviet Union. il Time 98:60 S 13 '71
See also
International atomic energy agency

Medical use
See Atomic medicine

Social aspects
Nuclear energy and the Malthusian dilemma. D. R. Inglis. Bul Atom Sci 27:14-18 F '71; Reply with rejoinder. A. M. Weinberg. 27:3+ Je '71
Nuclear tyranny and the divine right of kings. G. E. Christianson. il Bul Atom Sci 27:44-6 Ja '71

India
Will India go nuclear? K. Nanda. il Bul Atom Sci 27:39-41 D '71

Russia
Nuclear energy in the Soviet Union. V. S. Emelíanov. il por Bul Atom Sci 27:38-41 N '71
Nuclear power in the U.S.S.R: American visitors find surprises. R. Gillette. il Science 173:1003-6 S 10 '71

ATOMIC power industry
AEC to nuclear industry: we're no longer your protector. Sci N 100:290 O 30 '71
AEC to referee, not promote, industry; excerpts from address, October 1971. J. R. Schlesinger. Science 174:478 O 29 '71
Employment in the atomic energy field. J. M. Lukasiewicz. bibliog il Mo Labor R 94:51-4 O '71
Plutonium: reactor proliferation threatens a nuclear black market. D. Shapley. bibliog f Science 172:143-6 Ap 9 '71; Reply. R. L. Stetson. 173:7 Jl 2 '71

Public relations
Nuclear power: the information communication predicament; address, February 17, 1971. F. Costagliola. Vital Speeches 37:436-41 My 1 '71
Radiation controversy; address, July 15, 1971. P. Turner. Vital Speeches 37:696-9 S 1 '71

Europe, Western
Westinghouse cracks the nuclear power market; Wenese S.A. il Bsns W p58 N 13 '71

Great Britain
Britain: nuclear power industry faces critical choice on reactor. N. Hawkes. Science 174:681-2 N 12 '71

ATOMIC power plant simulators. See Simulators
ATOMIC power plants
Atomic power: what are our alternatives? R. Gannon. il Sci Digest 70:18-23 D '71
Electric power crisis in America; interview. C. Starr. Look 35:37-40+ Ag 10 '71
Electric power from nuclear fission; adaptation of address, April 1971. M. Benedict. bibliog il por Bul Atom Sci 27:8-16 S '71
Four big fears about nuclear power. R. E. Lapp. il N Y Times Mag p 16-17+ F 7 '71; Discussion. p79-80 Mr 21 '71
Impacts of nuclear power plants on the environment. A. W. Eipper and others. bibliog f il Liv Wildn 34:5-12 Aut '70
Living with atomic power, and liking it; Yankee atomic nuclear power station, Rowe, Mass. il U S News 70:67-9 Mr 29 '71
Nuclear power: a brighter power source tomorrow. il Nations Bsns 59:35-6 Jl '71
Nuclear power plants, boon or blight? G. T. Seaborg; B. Commoner. il por Nat Wildlife 9:21-3 Ap '71
On misunderstanding the atom; adaptation of address, March 22, 1971. G. T. Seaborg. Bul Atom Sci 27:46-53 S '71

ATOMIC power plants—*Continued*
Underground nuclear power plants. F. C. Rogers. il por Bul Atom Sci 27:38-41+ O '71
Utilities burn over cooling towers. il Bsns W p52+ Ap 3 '71
See also
Nuclear reactors

Accidents

Radioactive accidents: Pile no. 1 at Windscale, England. G. Williams. 3d. il Sci Digest 70:10-14 Ag '71
What are the dangers? R. Gannon. il Sci Digest 71:36-42 Ja '72

Laws and legislation

Palisades protest: a pattern of citizen intervention. F. Gendlin. il Bul Atom Sci 27:53-6 N '71

Location

Nuclear plant controversy. R. E. Lapp. New Repub 164:18-21 Ja 23; 20-3 F 6; 17-21 F 27 '71; Same abr. with title Nuclear power for electricity. Cur 127:42-9 Mr '71
Nuclear power loses a battle in court. Bsns W p24 Jl 31 '71
Palisades protest: a pattern of citizen intervention. F. Gendlin. il Bul Atom Sci 27: 53-6 N '71
Vermont: a power deficit raises pressure for new plants. J. Walsh. il Science 173: 1110+ S 17 '71
Vermont: forced to figure in big power picture. J. Walsh. Science 174:44-7 O 1 '71

Pollution

Delaying nuclear power. Time 98:56+ S 13 '71
Great nuclear debate: are our newborn babies' lives in danger? M. Hope and J. Young. Redbook 138:16+ Ja '72
What are the dangers? R. Gannon. il Sci Digest 71:36-42 Ja '72

Regulation

AEC's new environmental rules for nuclear plants may open new debate, extend delays, raise plant costs. R. Gillette. Science 173:1112-13 S 17 '71

Safety devices and measures

Another summer of power worries. il Bsns W p29 Je 26 '71
Safety and nuclear power plants: a British view. F. R. Farmer. por Bul Atom Sci 27:47-9 N '71
ATOMIC power plants (space vehicles) See Space vehicles—Atomic power plants
ATOMIC powered rockets. See Rockets, Atomic powered
ATOMIC powered ships. See Ships, Atomic powered
ATOMIC radiation. See Radioactivity
ATOMIC research
Pentagon salesman: J. S. Foster. Nation 212:676 My 31 '71
See also
Accelerators (electrons, etc)
Hanford works, Richland, Wash.

Europe, Western

See also
European organization for nuclear research

Great Britain

See also
Great Britain—Atomic energy authority

Russia

Science in Siberia. W. R. Shelton. il Bul Atom Sci 27:23-8 F '71
ATOMIC research laboratories
See also
Argonne national laboratory
California. University—Lawrence radiation laboratories
ATOMIC theory
Atomic theory in the ancient world. il Chem 44:17-18 Ap '71
ATOMIC warfare
See also
Atomic weapons

Defenses

Balance of terror, by E. Bottome. Review
New Repub 164:28-9 Je 12 '71. P. Passell
Holes in U.S. defense against nuclear assault. il U S News 70:26-8 Mr 8 '71
Nuclear diplomacy: Britain, France and America. A. J. Pierre. For Affairs 49:283-301 Ja '71

Strategic balance; the future of freedom; address, April 15, 1971. H. M. Jackson. Vital Speeches 37:482-5 Je 1 '71
Time dimension of military forces; address, May 14, 1971. J. C. Meyer. Vital Speeches 37:518-21 Je 15 '71

Ethical aspects

Hiroshima after 25 years; we are all survivors. B. Nelson. Science 171:556-7 F 12 '71
Is the ABM moral? An argument for the affirmative. E. S. Boylan. Commonweal 94:303-6 Je 11 '71; Discussion 94:418-19+ Ag 20 '71
Reporter at large; atom bomb on Indochina. D. Lang. New Yorker 46:52-61 Ja 9 '71
ATOMIC waste. See Radioactive waste disposal
ATOMIC weapons
On the march to oblivion? F. Barnaby. il Cur 128:59-63 Ap '71
State of the bomb. bibliog il Environ 13:38-43 Jl '71
When red China becomes a nuclear superpower. il U S News 71:46-8 S 27 '71
See also
Atomic bombs
Guided missiles

International control

Bridging the gap. Newsweek 78:55 N 22 '71
Disarmament and arms limitation: Pugwash assessment. Bul Atom Sci 27:20-3 Mr '71
Japan and the world of SALT. R. Imai. por Bul Atom Sci 27:13-16 D '71
No deep secrets; banning seabed weapons. Sr Schol 98:13-14 Mr 8 '71
Nonproliferation and control: peaceful uses of atomic energy. G. C. Delcoigne and G. Rubinstein. il Bul Atom Sci 27:5-7 F '71
Scorpion and the tarantula: the struggle to control atomic energy 1945-1949, by J. I. Leiberman. Review
Bul Atom Sci 27:47 My '71. H. L. Anderson

Testing, Detection of

Extending the nuclear-test ban. H. R. Myers. il Sci Am 226:13-23 bibliog(p 122) Ja '72

Testing, Suspension of

Extending the nuclear-test ban. H. R. Myers. il Sci Am 226:13-23 bibliog(p 122) Ja '72
How the Pentagon blocks arms pacts. J. J. Wadsworth and J. Pomerance. Cur 133:45-7 O '71

Testing, Underground

Underground nuclear explosions: tectonic utility and dangers. M. N. Toksöz and H. H. Kehrer. bibliog il Science 173:230-3 Jl 16 '71
ATOMIC weapons and disarmament
Advantages of a comprehensive nuclear test ban and the question of verification; statement, July 22, 1971. P. J. Farley. Dept State Bul 65:182-5 Ag 16 '71
Arms control and supra-nationalism: a comment on foreign policy thinking. D. M. Schwartz. Bul Atom Sci 27:38-41 Ap '71
Can nuclear weapons be abolished? D. Lawrence. U S News 71:96 S 27 '71
Can the U.S. take unilateral steps? excerpt from Balance of terror: a guide to the arms race. E. M. Bottome. Cur 130:60-3 Je '71
Defense: the savings of accommodation. T. C. Schelling. Sat R 54:38 Ja 23 '71
Disarmament and arms limitation: Pugwash assessment. Bul Atom Sci 27:20-3 Mr '71
Good news on the arms front. N. Cousins. Sat R 54:16 Ag 28 '71
Make the test ban total! Chr Cent 88:611 My 19 '71
New Soviet jab at Peking; call for UN world disarmament conference. U S News 71:48 S 27 '71
Shocks and shivers; Russia-U.S. spiral. New Repub 165:7-8 O 30 '71
See also
Strategic arm limitations talks
ATOMIC weights
Notes from IUPAC. il Chem 44:22 O '71
See also
Periodic law
ATOMS
Free atoms; a whole new basic chemistry. il por Sci N 100:390 D 11 '71
See also
Atomic nuclei
Atomic theory
Atomic weights

ATOMS—See also—*Continued*
  Magnetic resonance
  Mesons
  Neutrinos
  Neutrons
  Protons
      Space arrangement
      See Stereochemistry
ATOMS for peace. See Atomic power—International aspects
ATONEMENT
  Atonement, God's way. L. N. Bell. Chr Today 15:28 Ag 6 '71
ATROCITIES
  Beyond atrocity; excerpt from introd. to Crimes of war. R. J. Lifton. Sat R 54:23-5+ Mr 27 '71; Same abr. with title Reflections on Hiroshima and beyond. Cur 130:48-54 Je '71
      See also
  Pakistan—Army—Atrocities
  Vietnamese war, 1957- —Atrocities
ATROCITIES, Military. See War crimes
ATROPHIC rhinitis in swine. See Swine—Diseases and pests
ATTACHED houses. See Row houses
ATTACK on Pearl Harbor. See Pearl Harbor, Attack on, 1941
ATTAIGNANT, Pierre. See Attaingnant, P.
ATTAINGNANT, Pierre
  Pierre Attaingnant, royal printer of music, by D. Hertz. Review
    Mus Q 57:155-62 Ja '71. P. H. Lang *
ATTENTION
  Attention-related increases in cortical responsivity dissociated from the contingent negative variation. M. W. Donald, jr, and W. R. Goff. bibliog il Science 172:1163-6 Je 11 '71
  Human auditory attention: a central or peripheral process? T. W. Picon and others. bibliog il Science 173:351-3 Jl 23 '71
  Visual attention in the tree shrew: an ablation study of the striate and extrastriate visual cortex. H. Killackey and I. T. Diamond. bibliog il Science 171:696-9 F 19 '71
ATTIC insulation. See Insulation (heat)
ATTIC sales. See Sales
ATTICA, N.Y.
  Attica in the aftermath. il Time 98:22-3 S 27 '71
ATTICA prison. See Prisons—New York (state)
ATTICS
  Carefree attic. V. Troiano. il Mech Illus 68:64-8+ Ja '72
  How to turn your attic into a movie theater. T. Hook. il Mech Illus 67:90-2 Mr '71
ATTITUDE (psychology)
      See also
  Attitude change
ATTITUDE change
  Attitudes of teachers and the public toward mental illness. W. K. Bentz and others. bibliog il Ment Hy 55:324-30 Jl '71
ATTITUDE director indicator. See Aeronautic instruments—Display systems
ATTITUDES
  Public reaction to crime in the streets. F. F. Furstenberg, jr. il Am Scholar 40:601-10 Aut '71
  Quality of life: malaise or divine discontent? Sci N 101:23 Ja 8 '72
      See also
  Aged—Attitudes
  Children—Attitudes
  Frustration
  Moral attitudes
  Political attitudes
  Public opinion
  Race attitudes
  Students—Attitudes
  Youth—Attitudes
ATTITUDES (psychology)
      See also
  Value (psychology)
ATTNEAVE, Fred
  Multistability in perception: with biographical sketch. il Sci Am 225:10, 62-71 D '71
ATTORNEY General (United States) See United States—Justice, Department of
ATTORNEYS. See Lawyers
ATTRIBUTES of God. See God—Attributes
ATTUCKS, Crispus
  Boston massacre and Crispus Attucks. il Negro Hist Bul 34:52-4 Mr '71 *
  Crispus Attucks, one of America's first and noblest heroes. J. W. Dobbs. il por Negro Hist Bul 34:55-6 Mr '71 *
  St Louis public school named for Crispus Attucks. J. Davis. Negro Hist Bul 34:57 Mr '71 *

ATTWOOD, Simone
  Women inside China. il pors McCalls 99:78+ N '71
ATWATER, James
  Free world must avoid a trade war. Read Digest 99:75-9 S '71
ATWELL, Charles
  New is nice, but is it really necessary? il Har Yrs 11:26-7 Ag '71
ATWOOD, H. L. See Sherman, R. G. jt. auth
ATWOOD, Margaret
  Poetry of Margaret Atwood. R. Brown. Nation 212:824-6 Je 28 '71 *
AUBREY, James Thomas, 1918-
  Uprising at MGM. Time 98:49 D 27 '71 *
AUBUCHON, Norbert
  Across the Atlantic in a light twin. il pors Pop Sci 199:78-81+ N '71
  Brand-new way to learn to fly. il por Pop Sci 199:50-2 D '71
  Prop-jet gives new lift to STOL plane. il Pop Sci 198:66-7+ F '71
  Windecker's fantastic plastic plane. il Pop Sci 198:73-5+ Ja '71
AUBUSSON tapestries. See Tapestry
AUCHINCLOSS, Louis
  Ghost of Hamlet's ghost; story. Harp Baz 104:66-9 Je '71
AUCTIONEERS
      See also names of auctioneers, e.g. H. Brooks
AUCTIONS
  Bidding for Adolf. il pors Time 97:29 Ap 19 '71
  High cost of sipping; third annual wine auction in San Francisco. il Time 97:76 Je 7 '71
  Is it crooked or straight? Keeneland fall yearling sale. J. Kirshenbaum. il Sports Illus 35:79+ S 27 '71
  Lion at bay; auction at Metro-Goldwyn-Mayer's Culver City studio. T. H. Watkins. il Am West 8:30-5+ Ja '71
  Parting shots; $5,000 bet on a bottle of wine. il Life 70:74-5 Je 18 '71
  Real choosy about the Doozy; auction of antique and classic cars, Radnor, Pa. R. F. Jones. il Sports Illus 34:22-5 My 10 '71
  Saratoga auction: the very elegant crap game; report. C. Winfrey. il Time 98:12 Ag 23 '71
  Sell land at auction? interview. L. Erickson. por Suc Farm 69:10 Ag '71
  $72 a sip; wine auction, San Francisco. Newsweek 77:118 Je 7 '71
  To sell real estate fast try an auction. Bsns W p66 Jl 31 '71
      See also
  Parke-Bernet galleries, inc.
AUCTIONS, Art. See Art sales
AUDEN, Wystan Hugh
  Academic graffiti; poem. New Yorker 47:40 My 8 '71
  Books (cont) New Yorker 47:117-23 F 20 '71
  Encounter; poem. Horizon 13:112 Aut '71
  Ode to the medieval poets; poem. Poetry 119:63 N '71
  Talking to dogs; poem. Harper 242:110 Mr '71

      about
  As he is. R. B. Shaw. Poetry 118:349-51 S '71 *
  Comment. R. Howard. Poetry 119:36-9 O '71 *
  On Audenstrasse, in the autumn of the age of anxiety. A. Levy. pors N Y Times Mag p 10-11+ Ag 8 '71 *
AUDIENCES
  Applause, applause; Hospital audiences, inc. McCalls 98:46 Ag '71
  Audiences, what's happened to them? F. Taylor. Hi Fi 20:MA10-12+ D '70
  Yes, yes, yes, yes, yes: revival of On the town and theatre party ladies. New Yorker 47:33-4 Ap 17 '71
      See also
  Applause
  Moving picture audiences
  Television audiences
AUDIO amplifiers. See Amplifiers
AUDIO commercial message repeating unit. See Advertising mediums—Magnetic tape players
AUDIO compressors. See Sound—Apparatus
AUDIO fairs
  Journey to judgment, an audiomusical tour of Europe. L. Marcus. Hi Fi 21:4+ D '71
AUDIO generators. See Signal generators
AUDIO mixers. See Sound—Apparatus
AUDIO oscillators. See Oscillators

AUDIO-visual aids
  Audiovisual guide; comp. by P. Levy. Library J 96:1443-4+, 3824-6+ Ap 15, N 15 '71
  A-V clinic; questions and answers (cont) D. Molner. Schol Teach Jr/Sr High p25 F 1; 38 Mr 8; 23 Ap 5; 46 S; 58 O; 21 N '71
  A-V roundup (cont) D. Molner. il Schol Teach Jr/Sr High p22 F 1 '71
  Resource materials. V. G. Timmons. See issues of School arts
  Resources for women's studies. Schol Teach Jr/Sr High p 13 N '71
  Screenings; media mix (cont) Library J 96: 1791, 3454, 4173 My 15, O 15, D 15 '71
    See also
  Camps and audio-visual materials
  Education market
  English language—Study and teaching—Aids and devices
  Film strips
  Humanities—Study and teaching—Aids and devices
  Instructional materials centers
  Libraries and audio-visual materials
  Literature—Study and teaching—Aids and devices
  Magnetic recorders and recording—Educational use
  Pictures in education
  Transparencies
AUDIO visual aids in selling. See Salesmen and salesmanship—Audio visual aids
AUDIO-visual equipment
  Planning disciplines for audio-visual facilities; symposium. il Arch Rec 149:137-44 Je; 150:123-8 Jl '71
    Exhibitions
  Color TV from a video disc; Berlin. P. Moor. Sat R 54:73 S 25 '71
AUDIO-visual instruction
  Electrified term papers. D. McCoy. Engl J 60:107-10 Ja '71
    See also
  Camps and audio-visual materials
  Computers—Educational use
  Libraries and audio-visual materials
  Moving pictures in education
  Television in education
  Video recorders and recording—Educational use
AUDIO-visual script authorship
  Expanding new market; audio visuals. T. Crone. il Writers Digest 51:22-4+ S '71
AUDIO-visual systems. See Audio-visual equipment
AUDIOGENIC seizures. See Epilepsy
AUDITING
    See also
  Tax auditing
AUDITORIUMS
  Guidelines for good seeing. R. H. Wadsworth. il Arch Rec 149:137-44 Je '71
    See also
  Concert halls
AUDITORS. See Accountants
AUDITORY perception. See Sound perception
AUDITORY signal detection. See Signal detection (psychology)
AUDUBON, John James
  Audubon. J. Shepherd. il Look 35:26-8 O 19 '71 *
AUDUBON (periodical)
  Letter from the editor. L. Line. Audubon. 73:2 Mr '71
AUDUBON nature camps
  Camp; the ideal place for teaching environmental urgencies. E. J. Stahr. il Camp Mag 43:20+ Mr '71
AUERBACH, Arnold M.
  Brief (mercifully so) encounter. Sat R 54: 84 N 13 '71
  42nd street, 1971 style. Sat R 54:18 My 29 '71
AUERBACH, Pamela, and Carlton, P. L.
  Retention deficit correlated with a deficit in the corticoid response to stress. bibliog il Science 173:1148-9 S 17 '71
AUFFENBERG, Walter
  We lived with dragons; ed. by W. Hartley and E. Hartley. il Sci Digest 70:32-8 Ag '71
AUGER, Pierre
  Jean Perrin. UNESCO Courier 23:45 D '70
AUGERS
  Auger ideas you can use. G. L. Earle. il Suc Farm 69:H14 S '71
  Earth augers; fast way to dig a hole. E. F. Lindsley. il Pop Sci 198:144+ My '71
  Unloading augers that save backwork; photographs. Farm J 95:22H S '71
AUGUST, Bill
  Aiming the gun of Bill August. C. Goren. il Sports Illus 35:88-9 S 20 '71 *

AUGUSTA, Ga.
    Music
    See also
  Augusta opera company
AUGUSTA national golf club course. See Golf courses
AUGUSTA opera company
  Report:
    Madame Butterfly. H. E. Phillips. Opera N 36:26 N '71
AUKS
  Funk Island. F. Bruemmer. il Natur Hist 80:52-7 Je '71
AUL, Henry B.
  Iris in the landscape. il Horticulture 49:28-9+ My '71
AURELIAN, Laure, and others
  Herpesvirus type 2 isolated from cervical tumor cells grown in tissue culture. bibliog il Science 174:704-7 N 12 '71
AURELIO, Richard R.
  Stalking of the president. R. Wool. il Esquire 76:85-7+ Jl '71 *
AURORAS
  Bright aurora of April 14th. il Sky & Tel 41:386-9 Je '71
    See also
  Airglow
AURTHUR, Robert Alan
  Harry Truman chuckles dryly. il Esquire 76:136-9+ S '71
AURUM, pseud.
  Letter from London. Bul Atom Sci 27:42-3 F; 24+ Mr; 29-30 Ap; 41-2 My; 25-6 Je; 31-2 N; 21-2 D '71
AUSTIN, Charles M.
  Drama. Chr Cent 88:412-13, 938 Mr 31, Ag 4 '71
  Movies (title varies) Chr Cent 88:261-2, 508, 1299-300, 1529-30 F 24, Ap 21, N 3, D 29 '71
AUSTIN, John Paul
  Austin of Coca-Cola. il por Forbes 107:70 My 15 '71 *
AUSTIN, Nancy
  Big business. il por Time 98:72 N 29 '71 *
AUSTIN, Phil
  Watercolor page; with biographical sketch. il por Am Artist 35:48-51 O '71
AUSTIN, Tex.
    Education
  Austin story. J. Osborne. New Repub 165: 13-15 Ag 21 '71
AUSTRALIA
    See also
  Airlines—Australia
  Alice Springs
  Botany—Australia
  Christmas—Australia
  Drag racing—Australia
  Fishing—Australia
  Golf courses—Australia
  Great Barrier Reef
  Mines and mineral resources—Australia
  Music—Australia
  Opera—Australia
  Public opinion—Australia
  Religious conferences—Australia
  Securities—Australia
  Torres Strait
  Tourist trade—Australia
  Victoria
  Visitors, Foreign—Australia
  Yacht racing—Australia
    Description and travel
  Australia: big, bold, bursting. S. Cuneo. il Mlle 73:149-50+ O '71
  Australia: the city life. I. Kolodin. il Sat R 54:48-50 O 23 '71
  Where living still counts: Australia. M. Cantwell. il Mlle 73:138-47+ O '71
    Economic conditions
  Australia: she'll be right, mate, maybe. il Time 97:34-8 My 24 '71
    Foreign population
  Mix that goes into Australia's melting pot. I. Kolodin. Sat R 54:32 Ag 7 '71
    Foreign relations
  Australians divided on South Africans' rugby, cricket tours. R. Mathias. Chr Cent 88:668-9 My 26 '71
    China (People's Republic)
  Australia responds to ping-pong policy. R. Mathias. Chr Cent 88:842 Jl 7 '71
    Industries
    See also
  Mining industry and finance—Australia
  Petroleum industry—Australia
  Photographic apparatus and supplies industry—Australia

AUSTRALIA—*Continued*

Native races

Peoples of the Pacific; ed. by M. Mead and P. McClanahan. bibliog il pors Natur Hist 80:48-9 My '71

Politics and government

Fall of the larrikin. il pors Time 97:26 Mr 22 '71

Good-by John, hello Billy. il por Newsweek 77:38 Mr 22 '71

What's wrong with Australia? M. Parker. il por Newsweek 79:24-6 Ja 3 '72

Race question

Cricket controversy: sport and social protest. W. Clarnette. Chr Cent 88:1267-8 O 27 '71

Religious institutions and affairs

Pope's visit Down Under: stress on unity. R. Mathias. Chr Cent 88:198 F 10 '71

Worldaround. Chr Cent 88:933-4 Ag 4 '71

AUSTRALIA, New Zealand, United States treaty council. See Anzus council

AUSTRALIA antigen. See Antigens and antibodies

AUSTRALIAN ballet company

Australian ballet, New York city center. M. Marks. il Dance Mag 45:76-7 Ap '71

World of dance; productions in New York. W. Terry. il Sat R 54:39 F 20 '71

AUSTRALIAN broadcasting commission

How Australians learn their ABCs. I. Kolodin. Sat R 54:48 Jl 24 '71

AUSTRALIAN cookery. See Cookery, Australian

AUSTRALIAN cranes. See Cranes (birds)

AUSTRALIAN fairy penguin. See Penguins

AUSTRALIAN opera company. See Opera—Australia

AUSTRALIAN willow myrtle. See Agonis

AUSTRALIANS

Where living still counts: Australia. M. Cantwell. il Mlle 73:138-47+ O '71

AUSTRALITES. See Tektites

AUSTRALOPITHECUS. See Man, Prehistoric

AUSTRIA

See also
Automobile racing—Austria
Ballet—Austria
Elections—Austria
Forests and forestry—Austria
Hunting—Austria
Music festivals—Austria
Publishers and publishing—Austria
Salzkammergut

AUSTRIAN cookery. See Cookery, Austrian

AUSTRIAN music. See Music, Austrian

AUTHORITY

After the revolution, by R. A. Dahl. Review Nation 213:117-21 Ag 16 '71. T. Gitlin
See also
Divine right of kings

AUTHORITY (religion)

See also
Catholic church—Infallibility
Popes—Infallibility
Tradition (theology)

AUTHORS

Artist and his country. E. O'Brien. por Vogue 158:232-3+ S 1 '71

Authors & editors. See Issues of Publishers' weekly

Conscience of the writer; report of panel discussion. il Pub W 199:26-8 Mr 22 '71

How to promote your book on radio and TV interviews. R. Hull. il Writers Digest 51: 28-30+ Ag '71

T.R. and the nature fakers; imaginative nature writers. G. Carson. il por Am Heritage 22:60-5+ F '71

Tax checklist. Writers Digest 51:21 Ap '71
See also
Authorship
Children as authors
Copyright
Dramatists
Editors and editing
Executives as authors
Humorists
Literary agents
PEN club
Poets
Prisoners as authors
Royalties
Strikes—United States—Authors

Caricatures and cartoons

Authors at work. W. Hamilton. Horizon 13: 112-13 Wint '71

Childrens literature

Rewards of writing. Z. Sutherland. Sat R 54: 56 O 16 '71

Homes and haunts

See Literary landmarks

Psychology

Living with a writer. L. Conger. Writer 84: 9-10 S '71

Portrait of the artist as an oyster. L. Conger. Writer 84:9-10 Ap '71

Seventh thing; writer's need for a thick skin. L. Conger. Writer 85:6-8 Ja '72

AUTHORS, African
See also
African literature

AUTHORS, American

If an artist wants to be serious and respected and rich, famous and popular, he is suffering from cultural schizophrenia. R. Brustein. il N Y Times Mag p 12-13+ S 26 '71; Discussion. p 16 O 24 '71

Yale faculty makes the scene. T. Meehan. il N Y Times Mag p 12-13+ F 7 '71; Discussion. p4 F 28; 12+ Mr 7 '71
See also
Bolton, I.
Bradbury, R.
Clemens, S. L.
Dahlberg, E.
De Vries, P.
Didion, J.
Fitzgerald, F. S. K.
Ford, J. H.
Hemingway, E.
Hoffer, E.
Howells, W. D.
Jackson, S.
James, H.
Jones, J.
Kerouac, J.
Macdonald, R. pseud.
Mailer, N.
Mencken, H. L.
Metalious, G.
O'Connor, F.
Odets, C.
Poets, American
Roth, P.
Stein, G.
Stratemeyer, E.
Thurber, J
Vonnegut, K. jr
Welty, E.
Wilson, E.
Wolfe, T. K.
Wouk. H.

AUTHORS, Argentine
See also
Borges, J. L.

AUTHORS, English
See also
Belloc, H.
Dickens, C.
English literature
Ford, F. M.
Forster, E. M.
Galsworthy, J.
Greene, G.
Lawrence, D. H.
Lewis, C. S.
Monsarrat, N
Pater, W.
Read, H. E.
Russell, B. R.
Thackeray, W. M.

AUTHORS, French
See also
Beauvoir, S. de
Camus, A.
Cocteau, J
Colette, S. G.
Flaubert, G.
Malraux, A.
Mérimée, P.
Proust, M.
Sartre, J. P.

AUTHORS, German

West German writers move toward an industrial trade union for culture. D. Lattmann. Pub W 200:pt2 177 S 27 '71
See also
Mann, T.

AUTHORS, Greek
See also
Fakinos, A.
Kazantzakis, N.

AUTHORS, Israeli
See also
Ben-Amotz, D.

AUTHORS, Nigerian
See also
Achebe, C.

AUTHORS, Norwegian
　See also
　Ibsen, H.
AUTHORS, Persian
　Ageless voices of poets & writers. il UNESCO
　　Courier 24:44 O '71
AUTHORS, Polish
　See also
　Kosinski, J. N.
AUTHORS, Russian
　Sign of a thaw? il por Newsweek 78:29-30
　　Jl 19 '71
　Would you buy a used manuscript from
　　this man? H. Gold. il por N Y Times Mag
　　p 12-13+ Ja 31 '71
　　See also
　Pushkin, A. S.
　Solzhenitsyn, A. I.
AUTHORS, Scottish
　See also
　Scott, W.
AUTHORS, Uruguayan
　See also
　Rodó, J. E.
AUTHORS agents. See Literary agents
AUTHORS and libraries. See Libraries and
　authors
AUTHORS and publishers
　Albert Camus and the men of the stone, by
　　R. Proix. Review
　　Pub W il por 200:42-4 N 1 '71. P. Standard
　Book business; contracts. A. Green. Sat R 54:
　　49+ O 30 '71
　Case of the wrejected writer. P. Cooper. Pub
　　W 199:19 My 10 '71
　Market newsletter. See issues of Writer
　New York market letter. H. B. Jacobs. See
　　issues of Writer's digest
　Reference notebook: how books get pub-
　　lished. Writers Digest 51:31 Ap '71
　Trade winds: interview. ed. by C. Amory.
　　S. Stein; O. Lange. Sat R 54:12 My 1 '71
　Where to sell manuscripts. See issues of Writ-
　　er
　Where's the money: hard cover or paper-
　　back? S. Marlowe. il Writers Digest 51:28-
　　30+ S '71
　Writer's market; late news! See issues of
　　Writer's digest
　Writing & selling the nonfiction book. H. E.
　　Neal. Writers Digest 51:28-31 Ap '71
　　See also
　Literary agents
　Negro authors and publishers
　Royalties

　　　　Anecdotes, facetiae, satire, etc.
　Rent-a-script caper. M. Bennett. Pub W 200:
　　40 Ag 2 '71
AUTHORS colonies
　MacDowell colony. M. Mannes. il por Pub W
　　199:32-4 My 17 '71
AUTHORS conferences
　Black writers sponsor conference in N.Y.C.
　　Pub W 200:31 Ag 9 '71
　Gathering at Bunnymede; Playboy interna-
　　tional writers' convocation. R. Todd. Atlan
　　229:86-8 Ja '72
　Hows and whys of writers' conferences. K.
　　McCormick. Writer 84:27-8 My '71
　1971 writers' conferences. Writers Digest 51:
　　38-42 My '71
　The O'Neill; National playwright's confer-
　　ence. S. K. Obereck. il Newsweek 78:75-6
　　Ag 16 '71
　Playboy bust; 1971 Playboy writers' convo-
　　cation. il Newsweek 78:128 O 18 '71
　Playboy's literary ego-trip; International wri-
　　ters' convocation. L. L. King. Pub W 200:
　　17-18 N 1 '71
　Writers' conferences and literary pilgrim-
　　ages. W. B. Faherty. il Writers Digest 51:
　　34-8 My '71
　Writers' conferences 1971. Writer 84:29-35 My
　　'71
　　See also
　Congress of American writers
AUTHORS league of America, inc.
　What boundaries for federal censorship?
　　memo to FCC. R. H. Smith. Pub W 199:39
　　My 3 '71
AUTHORS lectures. See Lectures and lecturing
AUTHORS markets. See Authors and pub-
　lishers
AUTHORS notebooks. See Notebooks
AUTHORS rights
　Legal rights for writers. J. Pollett. Writer
　　84:22-4 Ap '71
AUTHORSHIP
　Apology for literature. P. Goodman. Com-
　　mentary 52:39-46 Jl '71
　Best selling novelist tells why she keeps a
　　notebook; excerpt from Slouching towards
　　Bethlehem. J. Didion. il por Writers Digest
　　51:26-7+ D '71

Dig for buried treasure. A. W. Lyons. Writer
　84:15-17 Je '71
Faith of a writer; remarks, December 2, 1971.
　E. B. White. Pub W 200:29 D 6 '71
Fiction techniques in nonfiction writing. N.
　B. Gerson. Writer 84:13-14+ D '71
Freelance job aid: promotion packet. C. G.
　Welton. il Writers Digest 51:27 Ag '71
Freelance job idea: family histories. K. Car-
　vell. il Writers Digest 51:30-1+ Jl '71
Freelance market report: Harcourt Brace and
　Jovanovich trade journals. M. W. Fedo. il
　Writers Digest 51:28-30 N '71
Help! The editor of Writers digest answers
　your questions. See issues of Writer's Di-
　gest
How I do it; helpful tips from writer-
　readers. See issues of Writer's digest
How much your freelance time is worth. T.
　Crone. il Writers Digest 51:28-9+ Mr '71
How to establish a retainer. B. Palmer.
　Writers Digest 51:30 D '71
Million words of practice writing. M. L. Fal-
　kowski. Writer 84:23-5 Mr '71
Presenting the past. A. Vivante. Writer 84:
　9-11 My '71
Reference notebook: what is your writing ob-
　jective? L. Camomile. Writers Digest 51:27
　Mr '71
SLJ meets Lloyd Alexander; interview. L.
　Alexander. il por Library J 96:1421-3 Ap 15
　'71
Secret of full-time freelancing: get a retain-
　er. T. Rakstis. il Writers Digest 51:28-30+
　D '71
Way of seeing. J. H. Kay. Writer 84:24-6 My
　'71
When to follow the rules. S. Bauer. Writer
　84:23 Je '71
Where to find ideas. C. Stephens. il Writers
　Digest 51:33-5 Mr '71
Writers and money. L. Conger. Writer 84:7-8
　My '71
Writer's demotion to solid-citizen status. J.
　W. Aldridge. il Sat R 54:35-6+ S 18 '71
　See also
Advertising copy
Audio-visual script authorship
Authors conferences
Childrens literature—Technique
Creative writing
Detective and mystery stories—Authorship
Drama—Technique
Fiction—Authorship
Fiction—Technique
Journalism—Authorship
Literary research
Literature—Technique
Moving picture authorship
Periodical articles
Plots (drama, novel, etc)
Short story
Technical writing
Television authorship

　　　　　　Bibliography
Books for writers (cont) Writers Digest 51:
　11+ F; 8 My; 52 Je; 37-8 Jl; 52-3 S; 18-19+
　N '71; 52:54 Ja '72
Writer's library. See occasional issues of
　Writer

　　　　　　Collaboration
Keys to the as-told-to article, or book;
　adaptation of address. B. Day. Writers Di-
　gest 51:30-2+ Mr '71
When sports figures turn author: jocks and
　their ghosts. H. Higdon. il Sat R 54:48-9+
　Ag 14 '71

　　　　　　Competitions
　See Literature—Competitions
AUTO expo Mexico. See Automobiles—Exhibi-
　tions
AUTO-train. See Railroads—Trains
AUTO-train corporation
　Auto-train miracle. il Newsweek 79:38 Ja 3
　　'72
　Train that takes your auto along; combina-
　　tion passenger and auto-ferry service to
　　Florida. il Bsns W p26-7 O 30 '71
AUTOGIROS
　Charles King and his magnificent flying
　　machine; gyrocopter Midnight Mover. il
　　Ebony 27:94-6+ N '71
　Everybody loves an autogyro; McCulloch
　　J-2. P. Garrison. il Flying 88:66-8 F '71
　Tri-motor gyro? P. M. Eckstein. il Mech
　　Illus 67:40+ N '71
AUTOGRAPHS
　Profiles: D. Lefkowitz: show business col-
　　lector. W. Whitworth. New Yorker 47:38-
　　42+ D 18 '71
AUTOHARP
　—And bring your autoharp. W. W. Arndt. il
　　pors Har Yrs 11:44-6 N '71

AUTOIMMUNE diseases
See also
Encephalomyelitis
AUTOMATA theory. See Machine theory
AUTOMATED cars. See Computers—Automotive use
AUTOMATIC coffee makers. See Coffee pots, percolators, etc.
AUTOMATIC control
See also
Sewage disposal plants—Automatic control
AUTOMATIC data processing, inc.
Electronic accountant Wall Street likes. il Bsns W p52+ Mr 20 '71
AUTOMATIC flight control system. See Automatic pilot (airplanes)
AUTOMATIC ice makers. See Ice—Manufacture
AUTOMATIC indexing. See Computers—Indexing use
AUTOMATIC pilot (airplanes)
Flight controls incorporate self-testing; automatic flight controls for the Concorde. il Aviation W 94:98-100+ F 8 '71
AUTOMATIC sprinklers. See Sprinklers
AUTOMATIC tint control. See Television receivers, Color—Tuning
AUTOMATIC transmission. See Motor trucks—Transmission
AUTOMATIC transmission fluid. See Automobiles—Transmission
AUTOMATIC turntables. See Phonograph—Record changers
AUTOMATIC washing machines. See Washing machines
AUTOMATION
Hard road to soft automation. T. Alexander. il Fortune 84:95-7+ Jl '71
See also
Automobile factories—Automation
Computers—Industrial use
Garment factories—Automation
Libraries—Automation
AUTOMATON theory. See Machine theory
AUTOMATONS
Hard road to soft automation. T. Alexander. il Fortune 84:95-7+ Jl '71
AUTOMOBILE accidents. See Traffic accidents
AUTOMOBILE air filters. See Air filters
AUTOMOBILE alarms. See Automobiles—Protection against theft
AUTOMOBILE assembly plants. See Automobile factories
AUTOMOBILE auctions. See Auctions
AUTOMOBILE batteries. See Storage batteries
AUTOMOBILE boat trailers
Boat trailer light bar. P. McLain. il Field & S 75:44+ Ap '71
Trailing your mini-yacht. G. S. Hensley. il Yachting 130:60-1+ Ag '71

Maintenance and repair
Trailer maintenance. J. Duffett. il Motor B & S 127:102 Ap '71
AUTOMOBILE brakes. See Brakes, Automobile
AUTOMOBILE burglar alarms. See Automobiles—Protection against theft
AUTOMOBILE buying. See Automobiles—Purchasing
AUTOMOBILE camping. See Camping
AUTOMOBILE clubs
MI at large: grandpa was a better man; Long Island Old car club's run for the sea for pre-1914 cars. il Mech Illus 67:44+ Mr '71
National street rod association. B. Miller. Hot Rod 24:116 Ag '71
World's largest car club; Ford motorsports association. Hot Rod 24:102 Mr '71
AUTOMOBILE cylinder heads. See Automobile engines—Cylinders
AUTOMOBILE dealers
Black car dealers struggle to exist; with editorial comment. il Bsns W p54+, 128 Ap 10 '71
From showroom to service shop. il Consumer Rep 36:203-6 Ap '71
L.A. shows off its mini mania. il Bsns W p27 Je 12 '71
See also
National automobile dealers association
United auto brokers, inc.
AUTOMOBILE decoration
How to make a turn for the better. B. Bryan. il Hot Rod 24:88-9 D '71
Tape tricks. S. Green. il Hot Rod 24:78 S '71
Yipes, stripes! il Hot Rod 24:83 N '71
AUTOMOBILE drivers
See also
Chauffeurs

Licenses
Face to face with a boy who took his own case to court. G. W. Pratt, 3d. por Seventeen 30:139 Jl '71
Let's fight the bad-driver menace. C. T. Rowan and D. M. Mazie. Read Digest 99:123-6 O '71

Psychology
Psychology of auto accidents. E. Timm. il Sci Digest 70:38-42 O '71
AUTOMOBILE driving
Drivin' with Dan; questions and answers. D. Gurney. See issues of Popular mechanics
Facing winter like an expert. B. Behme. il Field & S 76:138-40 N '71
How to cope with the worst driving crises. il Good H 172:188-9 My '71
How to steer clear! E. D. Fales, jr. il Pop Mech 136:53-6+ Jl '71
How you can drive a small car safely. J. P. Norbye. il Pop Sci 199:90-1+ Jl '71
Learn about winter driving from the ice racers! D. Bauer. il Pop Mech 136:76-9+ D '71
Making it through the summer without a dent; turnpike and freeway driving. B. Behme. il Field & S 76:92-4 Jl '71
Manners of the road: excerpt from The new Seventeen book of etiquette and young living. E. A. Haupt. Seventeen 30:146 N '71
Muzzling winter's bite. C. Packard. il Motor T 23:92-6+ N '71
National driver survey: asleep at the wheel. B. Ford. il Sci Digest 70:36-43 Jl '71
New ways to stay safe on the road. Bsns W p85-6 F 20 '71
Safe driving is no sin. America 125:136 S 11 '71
Safety tips for cold weather driving. Good H 173:222 N '71
Six keys to safer driving. D. McCluggage. il Am Home 74:48+ O '71
Skillful driver:
If a car jumps the guardrail. il Pop Sci 198:20 Ap '71
If a head-on crash seems imminent. il Pop Sci 199:46 S '71
If a truck pulls out suddenly. il Pop Sci 198:12 Mr '71
If you lose a wheel. il Pop Sci 198:42 My '71
If you meet a wrong way car. il Pop Sci 198:24 Ja '71
If your car gets into a tailskid. il Pop Sci 198:38 F '71
If your car is on fire. il Pop Sci 199:12 Ag '71
If you're caught by crosswind. il Pop Sci 198:36 Je '71
If you're hydroplaning. il Pop Sci 199:33 Jl '71
10 driving tips that could save your life. E. D. Fales, jr. il Pop Mech 135:69-73+ Ap '71
Your car's in a skid! What do you do? il Changing T 25:19-20 N '71

Competitions
Explorer scout road rallye. Hot Rod 24:100 Mr '71
Fun's in the run! gymkhanas, rodeos and rallies. J. Calvin. il Hot Rod 24:102-7 Ag '71

Study and teaching
Ready to drive? M. L. Miles. il Parents Mag 46:44+ Jl '71
That driver education boondoggle. R. Kirk. Nat R 23:932 Ag 24 '71

Stunt driving
Caution: beware of angels at work. F. Deford. il Sports Illus 34:84-8+ My 17 '71
AUTOMOBILE engineering
Engineering: the car that must not fail. A. B. Shuman. il Motor T 23:41-2+ F '71
AUTOMOBILE engines
Ah so, more go for Datsun! J. Thawley. il Hot Rod 24:102-4 Ap '71
Black's magic; mini MoPar. S. Green. il Hot Rod 24:42-5 Ap '71
Bossing the 351. S. Kelly. il Hot Rod 24:62-5 F '71
Bulletproof pushrod. R. Guldahl, jr. il Hot Rod 24:61 Jl '71
Chevy 372. S. Green. il Hot Rod 24:24-5 D '71
D.O.H.C. small-block Chevy. J. Dianna il Hot Rod 24:34-7 Ag '71
Displacement guide; table. J. Dianna. Hot Rod 24:141-2 O '71
Drag engines: Chevy 366, Ford 366. J. Dianna. il Hot Rod 24:28-31 My '71
Engine basics. E. K. von Delden. il Hot Rod 24:62-5 S '71

AUTOMOBILE engines—*Continued*
GM joins the rotary club. J. Christy. il Motor
  T 23:32-4 D '71
Grab a V8 Grabber. S. Kelly. il Hot Rod 24:
  114-15 Ap '71
Hot air engine runs quietly and cleanly. G.
  Wilkins. il Mech Illus 67:68+ O '71
It's just another 340: Colt. il Hot Rod 24:48-
  50 D '71
Lift for the auto; engine-flywheel hybrids.
  J. McCaull. il Environ 13:35-41 D '71
Little engine that could be an answer to
  pollution; Wankel engines. G. Alexander.
  il N Y Times Mag p 18-19+ O 3 '71
Look under the hoods of tomorrow's cars.
  B. Hartford. il Pop Mech 135:98-101+ Je '71
Low-pollution engines. Sci Am 225:80+ S
  '71
Performance engineering for the '72s. S.
  Kelly. il Hot Rod 24:88-9 Ag '71
Pick a size for Chevy. J. Thawley. il Hot Rod
  24:38-40 Mr '71
Project Maverick. S. Green. il Hot Rod 24:
  84-6 S; 48-9 O; 50 N '71
Project street bug. J. Dianna. il Hot Rod
  24:42-4 S '71
Report on safety in cars of the future;
  excerpt from address, November 3, 1971.
  E. N. Cole. il por U S News 71:76-7 N 22
  '71
Stage-five Pinto: quick & clean. S. Kelly. il
  Hot Rod 24:57-9 Ap '71
Street rod tips; plumbing. J. Thawley. il
  Hot Rod 24:100-1 S '71
Super six on a shoestring. S. Kelly. il Hot
  Rod 24:92-5 Mr '71
Those little 4-cylinder engines: can you have
  durability and performance? R. Hunting-
  ton. il Pop Mech 135:94-7+ Ap '71
Tom McCahill tests (title varies)
  Hot Wankel-engine Mazda RX-12. T. Mc-
  Cahill. il Mech Illus 67:60-2+ Ag '71
Vega trickery. S. Green. il Hot Rod 24:59
  Jl '71
Volvo 142-RS: 140 inches=140 horses. il Motor
  T 23:52-4 S '71
Vrod project report (title varies) J. Thaw-
  ley. il Hot Rod 24:112-14 Jl; 110-11 S '71
Your pollution-free car of 1975. M. J. Schultz.
  il Sci Digest 69:48-54 My '71
  See also
Antifreeze solutions
Automobiles—Cams
Carburetors
Cranks and crankshafts
Gas turbines, Automotive
Manifolds
Tachometers
Air filters
See Air filters

Air supply
Fresh air for U; placing intake for carburetor
  air ducts or hood scoop. S. Green. il Hot
  Rod 24:58 Ag '71
High-pressure approach. S. Kelly. il Hot Rod
  24:110-11 F '71
  See also
Automobile engines—Superchargers

Cleaning
How to clean up dirty mechanical problems.
  M. Schultz. il Pop Mech 135:116-19 Ap '71

Cooling
Cooling and oiling; VW engine modifications.
  J. Thawley. il Hot Rod 24:120-1 Mr '71
Heat increases on auto coolants. il Bsns W
  p21 Jl 24 '71
Help your car keep its cool. Changing T 25:
  19-20 Ag '71
Hot facts on those cool radiator additives.
  R. Day. il Pop Sci 198:38+ Je '71
Summer cool additives and treatments: are
  they necessary? radiator coolant additives.
  il Consumer Bul 54:27-8 My '71

Cylinders
50 easy horses. J. Dianna. il Hot Rod 24:120-1
  Ap '71
Racing head science. B. Lang. il Hot Rod
  24:116-19 F '71
Right slant; slanted-plug Chevy heads. J.
  Thawley. il Hot Rod 24:122 F '71

Design
Engineering preview '72. A. B. Shuman. il
  Motor T 23:82-4+ Ag '71
How clean a car and how soon. il Life 70:32
  Mr 26 '71
Is this the little steam engine that can?
  Hinckley rotary engine. J. Enking. il Pop
  Sci 199:50+ N '71

Olds super rocket. S. Green. il Hot Rod 24:
  92+ My '71
Twelve to go; new Jaguar engine. K. Ludvig-
  sen. il Motor T 23:80+ My '71
Why Detroit is doing a double take on the
  Wankel. J. P. Norbye. il Pop Sci 198:54-5+
  Ja '71

Exhaust
A 4-2-1 punch; Hedman's header/collector
  combination. J. Dianna. il Hot Rod 24:63-4
  O '71
Auto pollution: what can we really do about
  it? Bet Hom & Gard 49:39-40+ Ap '71
Ecology headers. S. Green. il Hot Rod 24:78
  Je '71
Exhaust-system service center for your car.
  R. Day. il Pop Sci 199:107+ N '71
Headers and mufflers. il Hot Rod 24:36-41
  Jl '71
Outside job; external exhaust system. S. Kelly.
  il Hot Rod 24:98 F '71
Tougher tests to make autos come clean. il
  Bsns W p 100+ N 6 '71
  See also
Automobiles—Pollution
Carbon monoxide
Motor vehicles—Pollution control devices
Plants, Effect of smog on

Fuel
Great gas conversion. il Newsweek 78:54
  Ag 30 '71
Motor fleets ride on vapor fuels. il Bsns W
  p 124 Je 19 '71
New pollution solution: dual-fuel Cal-gas
  car. J. P. Zmuda. il Pop Sci 198:12 Ap '71
Washington's clean air cars. Time 98:33 Ag
  30 '71
  See also
Gasoline

Fuel consumption
How to save 1½ gallons of gas every tankful.
  M. Schultz. il Pop Mech 135:146-9 Je '71
What does the G.T. energy chamber do? il
  Consumer Rep 36:220 Ap '71

Fuel feeding
Strictly for stocks; race car fuel system. J.
  Dianna. il Hot Rod 24:94 O '71

Ignition
Dwell extender for your car. R. M. Ben-
  rey. il Pop Sci 199:104-5 O '71
Improved capacitive-discharge ignition sys-
  tem. R. L. Carroll. il Electr World 85:78 F
  '71
Pointers on points. T. Tappett. il Mech Il-
  lus 67:82-4+ Jl '71
Why you should hop up your ignition. R.
  Huntington. il Pop Mech 136:128-31+ O '71
  See also
Spark plugs

Lubrication
See Automobiles—Lubrication

Maintenance and repair
How to save 1½ gallons of gas every tankful.
  M. Schultz. il Pop Mech 135:146-9 Je '71
Shop talk. J. Dianna. See issues of Hot rod
Supertune super-Q-ship Corolla. J. Christy.
  il Motor T 23:96-9 D '71
Troubleshoot the tough ones. M. Schultz.
  il Pop Mech 136:126-9 D '71

Mounting
Biggest recall; GM mounts. Newsweek 78:94
  O 25; 88 D 13 '71

Mufflers
For car owners: basics on mufflers, tail-
  pipes. il Changing T 25:21-2 F '71
Headers and mufflers. il Hot Rod 24:36-41
  Jl '71

Parts
See Automobile parts

Superchargers
Budget turbo: 5 easy pieces. B. Hellmuth. il
  Hot Rod 24:40-1 D '71
Doubly fast. il Hot Rod 24:72+ O '71
Mickey's bottle baby: thermocharger com-
  pressed-air boost system. S. Green. il Hot
  Rod 24:76-8 D '71
New equalizers; turbocharged cars. S. Kel-
  ly. il Hot Rod 24:130-3 O '71
Ohio George blows it! S. Green. il Hot Rod
  24:38-40 S '71
Pressuring the Pinto; turbo kit. S. Kelly.
  il Hot Rod 24:59 S '71
Turbocharged Vega. S. Kelly. il Hot Rod
  24:98-9 My '71

AUTOMOBILE engines—*Continued*

Testing

Tougher tests to make autos come clean. il Bsns W p 100+ N 6 '71
See also
Dynamometers

Valves

Cams, valves and valve gear. K. Ludvigsen. il Hot Rod 24:42-5 D '71
RPM+ for 351 Fords; Manley adjustable rockers. J. Dianna. il Hot Rod 24:44-5 Ag '71
Repairing the ravages of no-lead gas. T. Tappett. il Mech Illus 67:97-9+ Ag '71
Straight shaft for Chevy; rocker shaft. J. Thawley. il Hot Rod 24:60-1 Ap '71
Strictly for stocks; modifications to rocker arm shaft bosses. J. Dianna. il Hot Rod 24:104-5 D '71

AUTOMOBILE engines, Remodeled. See Automobile engines

AUTOMOBILE equipment. See Automobiles—Equipment

AUTOMOBILE equipment industry
See also
Dana corporation

AUTOMOBILE exhaust catalysts. See Catalysts

AUTOMOBILE factories

Automation

Lot more computers in Detroit's future. il Bsns W p84+ Je 5 '71

Employees

See Automobile industry workers

AUTOMOBILE financing. See Instalment plan

AUTOMOBILE gages. See Gages

AUTOMOBILE graveyards
See also
Western antique auto supply (firm)

AUTOMOBILE headlights. See Automobiles—Lighting

AUTOMOBILE ice racing. See Automobile racing

AUTOMOBILE industry
See also
Automobile factories
Motor truck industry

Advertising

Detroit tries to close its credibility gap. il Bsns W p46+ O 2 '71
Motor trend interview: the Vega and other adventures. D. E. Davis, jr. il pors Motor T 23:78+ F '71
Tell it like it is; automakers ordered to produce documentation for advertising claims. Newsweek 78:63 Jl 26 '71

Finance

Automotive; with yardsticks of management performance. il Forbes 109:151-2 Ja 1 '72
Belt-tightening paid off for Detroit. il Bsns W p21 Jl 31 '71
Car sickness. Fortune 83:51 Ja '71
Detroit gets its chance to shine. il Bsns W p66-7 Ag 21 '71
Detroit's model year grinds to a close. il Bsns W p23 Ag 7 '71
Topsy-turvy time for the new models. il Bsns W p 18-19 S 4 '71

History

Back to Methuselah. S. Novick. il Environ 13:50-2 O '71
What grandfather built; Fiat. il Fortune 84:127-8 Ag '71

Imports problem

Despite Detroit's minicars, the imports keep booming. il U S News 70:18+ Je 7 '71
First round to the foreigners. il Time 97:74 Mr 1 '71
Imports race for the middle market. il Bsns W p 15 Ap 3 '71

International aspects

Detroit's Asia strategy. J. Ridgeway. il Ramp Mag 10:20-1 S '71

Statistics

For October, a big boom in automobile sales. il U S News 71:25 N 8 '71

Study and teaching

See also
General motors institute, Flint, Mich.

Used cars

Lot of transportation for a little money. B. Davis. il Mech Illus 67:48-50+ Ag '71

Brazil

Automóvel do Brasil. K. Ludvigsen. il Motor T 23:74-6+ Ap '71
Following GM's profit formula. il Bsns W p36+ N 27 '71

Europe, Western

Toughest auto market is now in Europe. il Bsns W p48-9+ Je 12 '71

France

Satisfied stockholder; Renault automobile company. il por Forbes 107:34+ Ap 1 '71

Germany (Federal Republic)

Cars of Germany. K. Ludvigsen. il Motor T 23:39-45+ D '71
Detroit way doesn't work at VW. Bsns W p38+ My 1 '71
Marking time; visit to BMW. E. Dahlquist. il Motor T 23:8 N '71
Sturm und drang at VW. Newsweek 78:89 S 13 '71
Troubled giant; Volkswagen. por Time 98:86-7 S 27 '71
VW drops the driver. il Bsns W p34 S 18 '71

Great Britain

Auto makers look for help in Japan; new sources of components. Bsns W p53 Ap 10 '71
See also
British Leyland motor corporation
Brown, David, corporation
Ford motor company, ltd.
Rolls-Royce motors, ltd.

Italy

Changing Fiat with a fine Italian hand. il Bsns W p58+ F 20 '71
Embattled prince of Fiat. W. McQuade. il pors Fortune 84:124-6+ Ag '71
Ford gains on Fiat and Alfa. Bsns W p41 N 20 '71
Hot wheels Italian style; Ferrari, de Tomaso, Lamborghini and Maserati. D. J. Hamblin. il Sports Illus 35:24-9 Ag 30 '71

Japan

Auto industry goes into shock. il Bsns W p34 Ag 7 '71
Detroit gets a toe in Japanese waters. il Bsns W p36 Je 19 '71
How the Japanese blitzed the California auto market. il Forbes 108:28-9 S 15 '71
Japan's big drive in autos. il Newsweek 77:72-4+ My 3 '71

Latin America

Weeding out auto plants. il Bsns W p36 My 22 '71

Russia

Fiats are coming. il Newsweek 77:76 Je 21 '71

Sweden

Accelerating Volvo's pace. G. J. Berkwitt. por Duns 97:58-9 F '71
Cars of Sweden. E. Dahlquist. il Motor T 23:50-6 S '71
Tough Swede; Volvo's sales in the U.S. il Forbes 107:35 Je 15 '71

United States

Autos: a hazardous stretch ahead. D. Cordtz. il Fortune 83:68-71+ Ap '71
Autos, emission reports and the public. Sci N 99:280 Ap 24 '71
Detroit is nearly sure of a great new year. il Bsns W p 17-18 D 25 '71
Detroit listening post. R. Lund. See issues of Popular mechanics
Detroit report. J. Dunne. See issues of Popular science monthly
Detroit's Asia strategy. J. Ridgeway. il Ramp Mag 10:20-1 S '71
Detroit's hope for 1971: the mini-cars. il Ebony 26:64-9 Ja '71
Detroit's sales race ahead of profits. il Bsns W p32 N 6 '71
Favored Detroit in a mixed mood; impact of the President's economic program. il Newsweek 78:20-1 Ag 30 '71
If you're buying a new car. il U S News 71:20-1 S 13 '71
If your auto is called back—. il U S News 71:28 D 20 '71
Imports continue to make inroads. il Bsns W p20 Jl 10 '71
Inside Detroit. See issues of Motor trend
Minicar invasion. il Newsweek 78:64-5 Ag 23 '71
Off to good start; 1971 auto sales. il U S News 70:79 Mr 1 '71

AUTOMOBILE industry—United States—*Cont.*
Record year that tastes bitter. il Bsns W
p26-7 Je 12 '71
Richard Nixon, car salesman; today's boom.
Time 98:86 O 25 '71
Story behind the book: Wheels; interview,
ed. by P. A. Farrell. A. Hailey. Pub W 200:
32 O 18 '71
See also
Automobile dealers
Automobiles—Prices
United automobile, aerospace and agricul-
tural implement workers of America
also names of automobile manufacturing
companies, e.g. General motors corporation
AUTOMOBILE industry workers
Assembly line. W. Serrin. il Atlan 228:62-8+
O '71
Disassembling the line. Time 99:58-9 Ja 17
'72
See also
United automobile, aerospace and agricul-
tural implement workers of America
AUTOMOBILE inspection. See Automobiles—
Inspection
AUTOMOBILE insurance. See Insurance, Auto-
mobile
AUTOMOBILE jacks. See Jacks
AUTOMOBILE laws and regulations
See also
Insurance, Automobile
Traffic violations
AUTOMOBILE license plates. See Automobiles
—License plates
AUTOMOBILE lighting. See Automobiles—
Lighting
AUTOMOBILE loans. See Loans, Personal
AUTOMOBILE mechanics (persons)
Close doesn't count; Plymouth trouble shoot-
ing contest. S. Kelly. il Hot Rod 24:88-9
S '71
Pit crew; Wood brothers best in stock car
racing. il Life 70:65-8 Mr 26 '71
See also
Bignotti, G.
AUTOMOBILE models
5/8 of a '32 Chevy. il Mech Illus 67:8 O '71
Small-scale car, big-scale thrills; Heath's
radio-controlled model racer. S. M. Gal-
lager. il Pop Mech 136:84-6 Jl '71
Zingers! il Hot Rod 24:80-2 Jl '71

Racing
Now you can be a race driver, at any age;
radio-controlled racing. B. Grant. il Pop
Mech 136:69-71+ D '71
AUTOMOBILE museums
From the film world two barns full of nos-
talgic cars, planes, Buena Park, Calif. il
Sunset 147:38 O '71
AUTOMOBILE ownership
See also
Automobiles—Purchasing
Automobiles—Selling
AUTOMOBILE painting. See Automobiles—
Painting
AUTOMOBILE parking
How to be a defensive parker. Bet Hom &
Gard 49:14+ Mr '71
On parking. D. McCluggage. Am Home 74:
42+ Mr '71
Park-and-ride rail station; Woodbridge, N.J.
S. Lindsay. il Sat R 55:72 Ja 1 '72
Parking problems in residential areas;
Skokie, Ill. J. Matzer, jr. il Am City 86:
68 Jl '71
Room for your car and a garden too; with
editorial comment. il Horticulture 49:20,
24-6 Ap '71
See also
Garages
Garages, Municipal
Parking meters
AUTOMOBILE parts
Auto makers look for help in Japan; new
sources of components. Bsns W p53 Ap 10
'71
Cams & valve trains. il Hot Rod 24:34-8 Je '71
Packaged power; compatibility tested en-
gine parts. B. Neumann. il Hot Rod 24:
46-50 F '71
Product trends. See issues of Motor trend
to July 1971
Spherical rod ends. S. Green. il Hot Rod 24:
94-5 D '71
U.S. ingredients in foreign recipes. Bsns W
p20 Jl 24 '71
See also
Genuine parts company
Western antique auto supply (firm)
AUTOMOBILE race starting devices. See Speed-
ways—Equipment

AUTOMOBILE racing
¡ Ay chihuahua! What a race; Daytona
race. R. F. Jones. il por Sports Illus 34:
20-1 F 8 '71
Bad day for underdogs; Questor Grand prix.
J. Lamm. il Motor T 23:76-9+ Je '71
California 500: a fine day for underdogs.
J. Lamm. il Motor T 23:82-5 N '71
Can Am '71. D. Grey. il Motor T 23:58-60
S '71
Can-do Scot in the Can-Am; Canadian-
American challenge cup series. R. F. Jones.
il por Sports Illus 35:22-3 Jl 5 '71
Captain Marvel presents Captain Nice; Po-
cono raceway. B. Yates. il por Sports Illus
35:18-19 Jl 12 '71
Chris Amon on Can-Am; interview, ed. by
K. Ludvigsen. C. A. Amon. il por Motor T
23:80+ Mr '71
Cyclone levels Ontario. J. Brokaw. il Motor
T 23:26-9+ My '71
Darlington's 22nd Southern 500. S. Kelly.
il Hot Rod 24:72-4 N '71
Daytona 50; World series of mini-stock rac-
ing. J. Lamm. il Motor T 23:85 My '71
Daytona 500. S. Kelly. il Hot Rod 24:32-5 My
'71
Daytona 500: round two. J. Lamm. il Motor
T 23:32-4+ Ap '71
Earthly delights of stock-car racing. W. Mc-
Ilwain. Harper 243:22+ S '71
Fast last fling for an old girl: Sebring's
sports car competition. R. F. Jones. il
Sports Illus 34:16-21 Mr 29 '71
Ford black flags racing. J. Brokaw. il Motor T
23:65-7+ F '71
Great white dyno; Bonneville national speed
trials; with table. J. Thawley. il Hot Rod
24:42-4 N '71
Harvey on the lam; S. McQueen, racing en-
thusiast. R. F. Jones. por Sports Illus 35:
55-6+ Ag 23 '71
Hoist a bottle to leadfoot U; California 500.
R. F. Jones. il por Sports Illus 35:26-7 S
20 '71
How to last eleven laps and be happy; Mid-
Ohio Canadian-American challenge cup
race, Lexington, Ohio. H. Whall. il
por(cover) Sports Illus 35:43-5 S 6 '71
I'm retiring from driving, but I'll never quit
racing! interview. D. Gurney. il pors Pop
Mech 135:86-9+ Mr '71
Independent's day; Motor trend 500. J. Bro-
kaw. il Motor T 23:56-9+ Mr '71
It's not how long you wear your hair but.. ;
Questor Grand prix between U.S. and Eu-
ropean cars. G. S. Brown. il por Sports
Illus 34:70-1 Ap 5 '71
Johnny Lightning drives through the wreck-
age; Indy 500. R. F. Jones. il por Sports
Illus 34:26-9 Je 7 '71
Lime Rock Trans-Am. C. Koch. il Motor T
23:48-50+ Jl '71
MI at large; days at the races, Daytona
Beach, Fla. il Mech Illus 67:132-4 Ag '71
Million-dollar Sunday driver; R. Petty in
Atlanta's Dixie 500. R. Blount. il por Sports
Illus 35:16-17 Ag 9 '71
Motor trend 500: farmers subsidy. S. Kelly.
il Hot Rod 24:34-7 Mr '71
Motor trend interview. A. Unser.
il pors Motor T 23:72+ Mr '71
Motor trend interview; evolution of stock
car racing. F. Lorenzen. il pors Motor T
23:26+ Je '71
No conflict; no way; Questor Grand prix. il
Hot Rod 24:128-9 Je '71
No recession for Mr Petty; Daytona 500.
R. F. Jones. Sports Illus 34:56 F 22 '71
Old man of the brickyard tries again and
again and again; A. J. Foyt wanting fourth
win at Indy. M. Spiegel. il por Mech Illus
67:57-9+ My '71
One+A= mismatch: race at California's On-
tario motor speedway. il Time 97:60 Ap 12
'71
Ontario 500. S. Kelly. il Hot Rod 24:36-8 M
'71
Peter, Peter, Donohue beater; practice for
the 500. R. F. Jones. il por Sports Illus
34:34-6+ My 24 '71
Racetrack is still Detroit's best test track!
interview, ed. by D. O'Reilly. J. Passino.
il pors Pop Mech 136:76-9+ Ag '71
Rap 'n 'pinion; need for associations. B.
France. por Motor T 23:12 Mr '71
Re: Daytona an open letter to the boss. M.
Spiegel. il Sr Schol 98:30-2 Ap 26 '71
Roddin' at random. See issues of Hot rod
Roundy-round corner. S. Kelly. See issues of
Hot rod
Schaefer 500 at Pocono. il Motor T 23:84-7+
S '71
'71 championship racing preview: year of the
triple crown. B. Hartford. il Pop Mech 135:
82-5+ My '71

AUTOMOBILE racing—*Continued*
'71 racing preview; symposium. il Motor T 23:20-2+ Mr '71
Show & go. See issues of Hot rod to June 1971
Slide-rule boys at Indy: R. Penske and M. Donohue. R. F. Jones. il pors Sports Illus 34:32-4+ My 31 '71
Speed costs money; Indianapolis 500. S. Kelly. il Hot Rod 24:64-7 Ag '71
Swift happening at the Glen, U.S. Grand prix, Watkins Glen. R. F. Jones. il Sports Illus 35:73+ O 11 '71
Technical victory; the McLaren cars at Indianapolis. A. B. Shuman. il Motor T 23:68-71+ Ag '71
They slip & slide for the fun of it; New England ice racing. D. Bauer. il Mech Illus 67:84-6+ F '71
To be king of the mountain; Chimney Rock hillclimb. S. Wilkinson. il Sports Illus 34:84-6+ Ap 19 '71
Trackside '71. See issues of Motor trend
U.S. Grand prix. K. Ludvigsen. il Motor T 23:46-9 D '71
Who caught the brass ring? National 500. J. Brokaw. il Motor T 23:88-90 D '71
  See also
Automobile speed records
Automobiles, Racing
Computers—Sports use
Drag racing
Grand prix drivers association
Motor vehicle racing
Speedways

Accidents and injuries
  See also
Drag racing—Accidents and injuries

History
Marking time. E. Dahlquist. il Motor T 23:6 Mr '71
Roundy-round corner; Gulf-Miller rear-engine Indy car. S. Kelly. il Hot Rod 24:70 S '71

Rules
Daytona 500: big year for the little guys? B. Hartford. il Pop Mech 135:66-9 F '71

Africa, East
White magic in a noble black land; East African safari auto rally. R. F. Jones. il Sports Illus 35:48-57 Ag 2 '71

Argentina
Rafaelapolis. S. Smith. il Motor T 23:48-50+ Je '71

Austria
Austrian and Italian Grands prix. B. Cahier. il Motor T 23:98-100 N '71

Germany (Federal Republic)
'Ring; der grosser preis von Deutschland. B. Cahier. il Motor T 23:56-8+ O '71

Great Britain
Lift a pint to the king, luv; Jackie Stewart, master of Grand prix racing. R. F. Jones. il por Sports Illus 35:14-17 Jl 26 '71

Italy
Austrian and Italian Grands prix. B. Cahier. il Motor T 23:100 N '71

Monaco
Monaco! J. Lamm. il Motor T 23:56-8+ Ag '71

Spain
XVII gran premio de España. A. B. Shuman. il Motor T 23:34-6+ Jl '71

AUTOMOBILE racing drivers
Daytona 500: big year for the little guys? B. Hartford. il Pop Mech 135:66-9 F '71
Mod squad; modified production classes. J. Dianna. il Hot Rod 24:66-75 D '71
Now, when I am world champion . . . K. Chaplin. il Sports Illus 35:32-4+ N 1 '71
'71 pro stocks in action. il Hot Rod 24:96-8+ Je '71
'71 racing preview; symposium. il Motor T 23:20-2+ Mr '71
To be king of the mountain; Chimney Rock hillclimb. S. Wilkinson. il Sports Illus 34:84-6+ Ap 19 '71
  See also names of racing drivers, e.g. A. Vanke

AUTOMOBILE racing movies. See Moving pictures—Sports films

AUTOMOBILE racing timers. See Timing devices

AUTOMOBILE rallies. See Automobile driving —Competitions

AUTOMOBILE ramps. See Ramps
AUTOMOBILE renting. See Automobiles—Leasing and renting
AUTOMOBILE research
  See also
Automobiles, Experimental
AUTOMOBILE safety belts. See Automobiles—Safety belts
AUTOMOBILE salesmen
Nixon's price freeze heats up Atlanta's lots. T. Thompson. il Life 71:34-7 O 8 '71
  See also
Automobile dealers
AUTOMOBILE sealing compounds. See Sealing compounds
AUTOMOBILE service stations
Diagnosing the used car. il Motor T 23:36-7 Je '71
New garage where you pocket the labor costs; do-it-yourself emporium. J. H. Pickerell. il Pop Mech 135:88-9 Je '71
AUTOMOBILE speed records
Bobby Isaac sweeps Bonneville. il Hot Rod 24:62 D '71
Bonneville records; tables. Hot Rod 24:147 N '71
How we captured the world land speed record for electric cars; MI's Silver Eagle. B. Wennerstrom. il Mech Illus 67:72-5+ D '71
Records, wet and dry. E. Crimmin. il Hot Rod 24:120-1 Je '71
We break the world land and speed record! MI's Silver Eagle. il Mech Illus 67:84-5 N '71
AUTOMOBILE speedways. See Speedways
AUTOMOBILE stealing. See Automobiles, Theft of
AUTOMOBILE stickers. See Labels
AUTOMOBILE styling. See Automobiles—Design
AUTOMOBILE thefts. See Automobiles, Theft of
AUTOMOBILE tires. See Tires, Automobile
AUTOMOBILE touring

Anecdotes, facetiae, satire, etc.
You can't miss it! D. Williamson. Sat R 54:18 Ag 7 '71

California, Lower
Back from Baja. W. R. C. Shedenhelm. il Motor T 23:50-1 F '71
If you plan to drive Baja. il Sunset 146:46+ Mr '71
One rough road; Baja peninsula in Condor, 4-wheel-drive home. B. Behme. il Field & S 75:156+ Mr '71

Mexico
  See also
Automobile touring—California, Lower

Morocco
Morocco: more than a place, a world. L. Lee. Mlle 73:148-54+ Je '71

Texas
Shunpiking through Texas. N. D. Ford. il Har Yrs 11:6-13+ F '71

United States
Drive-in-islands. N. D. Ford. bibliog il Har Yrs 11:6-13+ My '71
I drove our first coast-to-coast interstate, the campers' expressway. D. Francis. il Pop Sci 198:78-9+ Mr '71
That cross-country trip by mobile home was so much fun, he's doing it again. L. Barry. Pop Phot 69:65+ O '71
AUTOMOBILE touring with children. See Travel with children
AUTOMOBILE traffic. See Road traffic
AUTOMOBILE trailers
Consumer's guide to camping trailers. il Mech Illus 67:84 My '71
Fold-up trailer you can build. W. J. Hawkins. il Pop Sci 199:60-1 Ag '71
For your mini-compact; build the PS mini-camper. F. Wojcik. il Pop Sci 198:100-2 My '71
Great new ideas for motor camping. J. M. Liston. il Pop Mech 135:147-8+ My '71
How to leave home without leaving it. D. McCluggage. Am Home 74:40+ Je '71
How to select a recreational travel vehicle. C. M. Edwards. il Consumer Bul 54:4+ Mr '71
Live-aboard trailering. M. Rizer. il Motor B & S 127:89+ My '71
New way to hitch your trailer; fifth-wheel trailers. J. Copeland. il Pop Sci 199:102+ Ag '71
Tent-camper revolution. H. Shuldiner. il Pop Sci 198:84-5 Mr '71

AUTOMOBILE trailers—*Continued*
Tiny trailers for tiny cars. F. K. Coffee. il Mech Illus 67:74-5+ My '71
Winter use for your camper. G. L. Earle. il Suc Farm 69:C18 N '71
See also
Automobile boat trailers
Houseboats—Automobile trailer combination

Maintenance and repair
Smart ways to improve your recreational vehicle. V. L. Oertle. il Pop Mech 135:156+ My '71

Towing
See Towing
AUTOMOBILE trips. See Automobile touring
AUTOMOBILE trucks. See Motor trucks
AUTOMOBILE warranty. See Warranty
AUTOMOBILE winches. See Winches
AUTOMOBILES
AMC gets it all together. R. Lund. il Pop Mech 136:116-18+ O '71
Aiming straight; AMC. il Motor T 23:46-9+ S '71
Annual model change is alive and well in Detroit. J. Dunne. il Pop Sci 199:58-9+ Jl '71
Broken field 'Runner. J. Brokaw. il Motor T 23:60+ Jl '71
Buick 1972. J. Lamm. il Motor T 23:40-2 O '71
Cadillac: qualified excellence. J. Lamm. il Motor T 23:47-9 O '71
California dreamin'; Chevrolet. C. Koch. il Motor T 23:36-9 O '71
Cars. D. Gregg. See issues of Better homes and gardens
Cars of the year. il Motor T 23:92-5 D '71
Centurion-Monterey face off. J. Brokaw. il Motor T 23:60-2+ Mr '71
Chrysler sets some standards. R. Lund. il Pop Mech 136:124-6+ O '71
Circle game; Pontiac's '71½ Ventura II. E. Dahlquist. il Motor T 23:50-2 Mr '71
Commonsense Roadrunner. J. Brokaw. il Motor T 23:26-9+ F '71
Continental Mark IV. A. B. Shuman. il Motor T 23:36-40 Ag '71
Convertible folds up. B. Sanders. il Motor T 23:42-5+ N '71
Detroit preview: what's new for '72. R. Lund. il Pop Mech 135:63-5+ Je '71
Ford gets with it. J. Brokaw. il Motor T 23:36-41+ S '71
4 intermediate cars; Plymouth Satellite, Chevrolet Chevelle, Ford Torino, AMC Matador. il Consumer Rep 36:86-92 F '71
From Pinto to Pantera; Ford, Lincoln-Mercury lineup for '72. B. Hartford. il Pop Mech 136:98-101+ S '71
Full-sized sedans; Chevrolet Impala, Pontiac Catalina Brougham, Ford Galaxie 500, and Plymouth Fury III. il Consumer Rep 36: 149-55 Mr '71
GM holds the line. M. Lamm. il Pop Mech 136:119-23+ O '71
Gone with the wind; convertibles. il Newsweek 78:65 S 6 '71
Great Pontiac conspiracy. C. Koch. il Motor T 23:30-2 O '71
High price spread; Chevrolet Caprice and Cadillac de Ville. il Motor T 23:63-6 My '71
How to drive like a millionaire. il T. Hogg. Esquire 76:142-5+ D '71
Intermediate cars for 1971. il Consumer Bul 54:16-21+ Je '71
Intermediate cars; Full-sized, low-priced cars; High-priced cars; Specialty cars. il Consumer Rep 36:212-17 Ap '71
Invisible cars; 350 Chevelle, 351 Torino and 318 Satellite. J. Brokaw. il Motor T 23:80-5 Je '71
Last ride for a status symbol; convertibles. il Time 97:88 Ap 12 '71
Luxury line; Oldsmobile. C. Koch. il Motor T 23:44-6 O '71
MI's color portfolio of the 1972 cars. il Mech Illus 67:65-8 N '71
Machinery management (cont of) Truck and car news. P. B. Jones. See issues of Successful farming
Montego, Monte Carlo, Charger, Cutlass; are they coming or going? J. Brokaw. il Motor T 23:36-41 N '71
Name of the game is change: Look's sixteenth annual new car preview. A. Rothenberg. il Look 35:44-53+ S 21 '71
New cars have that old magic; with report by T. Thompson. il Life 71:32-7 O 8 '71
1972 cars. il Changing T 25:25-32 D '71
1972 cars. il Mech Illus 67:20 Je; 55-7+ O '71
1972 Detroit model review. R. Huntington. il Consumer Bul 54:7-12 O '71

Olds F-80: shooting for the three-pointed star? il Motor T 23:58-9 N '71
PM owners report:
Plymouth Satellite. M. Lamm. il Pop Mech 135:88-91 My '71
Pontiac Grand Ville. M. Lamm. il Pop Mech 136:102-5 Ag '71
Pontiac Firebird, Ford Mustang, Mercury Capri, Opel 1900 and Peugeot 304. il Consumer Rep 36:447-55 Jl '71
Seven year car; Chevrolet Nova. J. Brokaw. il Motor T 23:76-81 S '71
'72 cars. il Ebony 27:64-9 Ja '72
'72 cars: why you should buy now. B. Hartford. il Pop Mech 136:114-15 O '71
'72 new car preview. il Motor T 23:24-9 Jl '71
'72 performers. il Hot Rod 24:40-7 O '71
'72 performers; AMC, Dodge, Ford, Lincoln-Mercury. il Hot Rod 24:30-7 S '71
Sneak preview: '72 high-performance movers! S. Kelly. il Hot Rod 24:34-5 Jl '71
Three for the money; Riviera, Thunderbird and Jaguar XJ6. J. Brokaw. il Motor T 23: 68-73+ D '71
Three full size 1971 cars: Chevrolet Impala, Ford LTD, Plymouth Fury. Consumer Bul 54:7-13 My '71
Topsy-turvy time for the new models. il Bsns W p18-19 S 4 '71
View down the road. J. P. Norbye. il Pop Sci 199:14 O; 54 N; 36 D '71
What you see is what you get; Chrysler. W. Wyss. il Motor T 23:42-5+ S '71
What's new in the '72 cars. J. P. Norbye and J. Dunne. il Pop Sci 199:52-5 S '71
Where there's smoke, there's hope; muscle cars. il Motor T 23:108-11 O '71
See also
Automobile engineering
Jeep automobiles
Motor trucks
Sports cars
Station wagons
Taxicabs

Accessories
See Automobiles—Equipment

Accidents
See Traffic accidents

Advertising
See Automobile industry—Advertising

Air conditioning
Readers report on auto air-conditioning. il Consumer Rep 36:430-1 Jl '71

Airplane combinations
See Airplanes, Light—Automobile combinations

Axles
Strictly for stocks; use of Summers brothers Hy-Tuff axles in narrowed housings. J. Dianna. il Hot Rod 24:86 Ap '71
Time for a quick change; funny car axle assembly. S. Green. il Hot Rod 24:58-9 Mr '71

Batteries
See Storage batteries

Brakes
See Brakes, Automobile

Bumpers
Bumper crop for safety's sake. il Bsns W p32-3 N 6 '71
5 mph barrier. il Motor T 23:20 S '71
New bumpers will take the ouch out of your auto repair bills. J. Dunne. il Pop Sci 199: 43-5 Jl '71
Search for the perfect bumper. il Life 71: 36-9 Ag 13 '71

Camping equipment
Build a cartop camper. N. Schawn. il Mech Illus 67:69-71 Je '71
See also
Automobile trailers

Cams
Cams & valve trains. il Hot Rod 24:34-8 Je '71

Carburetors
See Carburetors

Care
See Automobiles—Maintenance and repair

Clutches
Clutch can cooler. R. Guldahl, jr. il Hot Rod 24:128 F '71

AUTOMOBILES—*Continued*

Collectors and collecting

Body beautiful; Reuter coach works. K. Prentiss. il Holiday 48:84-7 S '70
Chase for classic cars. E. Herzberg. il Duns 98:65-6 Jl '71
MI at large: grandpa was a better man; Long Island Old car club's run for the sea for pre-1914 cars. il Mech Illus 67:44+ Mr '71
Real choosy about the Doozy; auction of antique and classic cars, Radnor, Pa. R. F. Jones. il Sports Illus 34:22-5 My 10 '71

Control

See also
Computers—Automotive use

Decoration

See Automobile decoration

Design

Backstage Detroit. J. P. Norbye and J. Dunne. il Pop Sci 199:90-6 O '71
Changes to expect in the '72 autos. il U S News 70:56-8 My 17 '71
Collusion of style; Big three's annual restyling practices. B. C. Bradford. Nation 213:5 Jl 5 '71
Detroit de-emphasizes the styling game. Bsns W p 16 Ap 3 '71
First of the '72 cars. il Mech Illus 67:55-8 S '71
Meade in Italy. G. Borgeson. il por Motor T 23:66+ Ap '71
Motor trend interview; styling operations. W. L. Mitchell; C. Jordan. il pors Motor T 23:88+ Jl '71
1972 cars: what to expect in new autos. il U S News 71:38-9 Ag 23 '71
Past, present and future; 1972 Olds 98, Electra 225, Mercury Marquis. J. Brokaw. il Motor T 23:76-9+ Ag '71
Safety upstages styling. il Time 98:50-1 Ag 23 '71
'72's: tamed but still tough. M. Spiegel. il Sr Schol 99:26-7+ O 25 '71
Something special: intermediate Oldsmobile Cutlass, 1971. M. Spiegel. il Sr Schol 98: 40+ Mv 17 '71
We unveil the 1972 cars. R. W. Irvin. il Mech Illus 67:52-4+ Jl '71
See also
Automobiles—Safety devices and measures

Driving

See Automobile driving

Electric equipment

Paser magnum. il Consumer Rep 37:18-19 Ja '72
VR12 voltage regulator. C. R. Ball, jr. il Pop Electr 34:65-70+ Ap '71

Electronic equipment

More solid-state electronics for the new cars. J. D. Drummond. il Pop Electr 1: 63-7 Ja '72
Tail light monitor for your car. R. F. Graf and G. J. Whalen. il Radio-Electr 42:60-1 Ag '71
Travel computer, electronic navigation for your car. R. M. Benrey. il Pop Sci 198:79-81 Mv '71
2 safety aid projects for your car; low-fuel-level alarm; and automatic parking light operator. R. M. Marston. il Radio-Electr 42:44-7 Ap '71
What's new in car electronics. F. W. Holder. il Radio-Electr 42:33-6 Ap '71
See also
Automobiles—Protection against theft
Computers—Automotive use

Equipment

Choosing the options. il Consumer Rep 36: 200-2 Ap '71
Clear your drive the easy way; homemade snowplow attached to car bumper. F. M. Butrick. il Pop Mech 136:166+ D '71
Does optional equipment increase a new car's value? A. Lee. Bet Hom & Gard 49:55+ N '71
Eyes in the back of your rig. B. Behme. il Field & S 76:86-7+ D '71
Gift guide. il Motor T 23:62-4+ D '71
New skin-deep beauty for your car. T. Tappett. il Mech Illus 67:86-8+ Ap '71
Prettified Pinto. S. Green. il Hot Rod 24:111 Mv '71
Product trends. See issues of Motor trend to July 1971
What's new. See issues of Hot rod
See also
Automobiles—Electric equipment
Automobiles—Tape equipment
Specialty equipment manufacturers association
Speedometers

Exhibitions

Auto expo Mexico '71. T. C. Browne. il Motor T 23:74-6 N '71
Geneva. E. Seidler. il Motor T 23:96-8+ Jl '71
Oakland roadster show '71. il Hot Rod 24: 104-5 Jl '71
'71 auto show. il Motor T 23:22-7 Ap '71
Show & go. See issues of Hot rod to June 1971
See also
Recreational vehicles—Exhibitions

Fires and fire protection

Is your car a fire hazard? D. L. Gregg. Bet Hom & Gard 49:95+ Jl '71

Four wheel drive

See also
Station wagons—Four wheel drive

Front wheel drive

Is front-wheel drive best for small cars? J. P. Norbye. il Pop Sci 198:58-60 Mr '71

Fuel

See Automobile engines—Fuel

Fuel systems

See Automobile engines—Fuel feeding

Gages

See Gages

Gearing

Low where it counts: high where it cruises; Ultra-Low gears. S. Kelly. il Hot Rod 24: 60-1 S '71
See also
Automobiles—Transmission

Handbooks, manuals, etc.

Your first car tool: factory shop manual. P. McCafferty. il Pop Sci 199:103+ O '71

History

America adopts the automobile, 1895-1910, by J. Flink. Review
Fortune 83:160-1 Ja '71. C. G. Burck
End of an affair; 1904 Oldsmobile. J. Lamm. il Motor T 23:46-8+ Ap '71
In retrospect:
1941 Lincoln Continental Cabriolet. J. Christy. il Motor T 23:64-6+ S '71
150-grand comparison; Stutz vs. Mercer. E. Dahlquist. il Motor T 23:86-8+ Mr '71
Tom McCahill tests (title varies)
45-year-old Chrysler. T. McCahill. il Mech Illus 67:85-7+ Mr '71
1948 Tucker. T. McCahill. il Mech Illus 67:88-91+ F '71
Tucker: a modern American tragedy. A. B. Shuman. il pors Motor T 23:68-70+ My' 71

Ignition

See Automobile engines—Ignition

Inspection

Computer spots defective autos; vehicle inspection station in the District of Columbia. Am City 86:32-3 O '71
How to make your own safety inspection. M. Schultz. il Pop Mech 135:122-5 My '71
How to swat the bugs in a new car. E. F. Lindsley. il Pop Sci 198:90-2 Je '71

Insurance

See Insurance, Automobile

Leasing and renting

Co-op cars; Montpellier, France. il Newsweek 78:54+ S 13 '71
Know-how you need in renting a car. il Changing T 25:15-17 My '71
Select-a-car; automated car loan system. il Motor T 23:81 Jl '71
They don't try harder; Soviet domestic rent-a-car garages phased out. Time 97:24 Mr 1 '71
Who's on first? Hertz-Avis-National advertising rivalry. S. W. Little. Sat R 54:59+ Je 12 '71
See also
Avis rent a car system, inc.
Hertz corporation

License plates

License plates of Burning Tree; Washington. D. C. New Yorker 46:20-2 Ja 30 '71

Lighting

Are extra driving lights necessary? T. Tappett. il Mech Illus 67:92-4+ F '71
T lights. T. Medley. il Hot Rod 24:46-7 D '71

AUTOMOBILES—*Continued*

Loading

What happens when you overload your car?
D. L. Gregg. il Bet Hom & Gard 49:70+
Jl '71

Lubrication

How to change your oil. il Motor T 23:74 My
'71
How to set up and run a home auto-lube
center. R. Day. il Pop Sci 198:98-100+ F
'71
Spec reading made easy. T. Tappett. il Mech
Illus 68:94-6+ Ja '72

Maintenance and repair

Automobile clinic; questions and answers.
M. Schultz. See issues of Popular mechan-
ics
Beginner's guide to car care. T. Tappett.
il Mech Illus 67:109-11+ S '71
Car care. T. Tappett. See issues of Mechanix
illustrated
Checklist complete, will travel. J. Davis. il
Pop Sci 198:74-5 My '71
Dam the water; cure for leaks. T. Tappett.
il Mech Illus 67:98-100+ Mr '71
Do all of your own routine service and main-
tenance! M. Schultz. il Pop Mech 136:122-
5+ S '71
Doing it:
How to change points. il Motor T 23:82
O '71
How to change spark plugs. il Motor T
23:71 Jl '71
How to change your oil. il Motor T 23:74
My '71
Don't ignore these indicators of auto trouble.
D. L. Gregg. Bet Hom & Gard 49:12+ Mr '71
Facing winter like an expert. B. Behme.
il Field & S 76:138-40 N '71
How to avoid auto repair headaches. D. L.
Gregg. Bet Hom & Gard 49:96-7 Ag '71
Muzzling winter's bite. C. Packard. il
Motor T 23:92-6+ N '71
Old cars can be dangerous. Consumer Bul
54:27 N '71
Preparing your car for a trip. Good H 173:
159 Jl '71
Saturday mechanic. M. Schultz. See issues
of Popular mechanics
Say, Smokey; questions and answers. S.
Yunick. See issues of Popular science
monthly
Servicing the self-service cars. T. Tappett. il
Mech Illus 67:106-8+ My '71
Shop talk. J. Dianna. See issues of Hot rod
Taking care of your car. See issues of Popular
science monthly
Ten time-saving tips for weekend mechanics.
T. Tappett. il Mech Illus 67:124-6+ N '71
See also
Antifreeze solutions
Automobile mechanics (persons)
Automobile service stations

Manufacture

See also
Automobile factories
Automobile parts

Noise

Is your car a hypochondriac? D. McCluggage.
Am Home 74:42+ N '71

Painting

Save money: do your own auto touch-up. W.
C. Leckey. il Pop Mech 136:192+ O '71

Parking

See Automobile parking

Parts

See Automobile parts

Periodicals

See also
Hot rod (periodical)
Motor trend (periodical)

Pollution

Big hassle: your car vs. clean air. A. Rothenberg. Look 35:51-2+ Mr 23 '71
Can automotive air pollution be curbed? J. K.
Hawley. il Cons 25:9-12 Ap; 10-12 Je '71
Environment, autos and the public. il Sci N
100:371-2 D 4 '71
Exhaustive test for Detroit. por Time 98:
51 Jl 12 '71
How clean a car and how soon. il Life 70:
32 Mr 26 '71
How GM reacts to the pressure. il por Newsweek 77:76-7 My 24 '71
How to make your car a good clean-air
citizen. D. Gregg. il Bet Hom & Gard 49:
32+ F '71

I love my car, which pollutes the air. il
Sr Schol 99:6, 12-15 S 20 '71
Lead from automobile exhaust. R. W.
Medeiros. bibliog il por Chem 44:7-9 N '71
Marking time. E. Dahlquist. Motor T 23:8
S '71
Modest proposal: Electricart. C. Ogburn. il
Harper 243:106-7 O '71
NRC auto emissions study: scope too limited?
Sci N 100:224 O 2 '71
Pollution, the no-lead myth. D. Hill. Hot
Rod 24:120-1 F '71
Practical problems remain; 1976 nitrogen
oxides standards. Sci N 100:8 Jl 3 '71
Rap 'n 'pinion. T. B. Tom. por Motor T 23:
12 F '71
Skeleton in the garage; memorandum. Econ-
omics of clean air. J. Lear. Sat R 54:47-8
Je 5 '71
Threat of the unseen. V. J. Schaefer. il
Sat R 54:55-7 F 6 '71
What future for the auto? EPA hearings. il
Sci N 99:329-30 My 15 '71
Who's really in tune? AC tune-in for cleaner
air program of General motors. M. Spiegel.
il Sr Schol 99:40 S 27 '71
Will the new gasolines lick auto pollution?
il Consumer Rep 36:156-9 Mr '71
See also
Plants. Effect of smog on

Prices

Auto price boosts respond to control. Bsns W
p37 D 4 '71
High gear. Newsweek 78:87 D 6 '71
Higher prices for '72 cars, why. il U S
News 71:41 Jl 26 '71
If you're buying a new car. il U S News
71:20-1 S 13 '71
Price break for U.S. cars: a look at the boom
to come. il U S News 71:55-6 Ag 30 '71
What you will pay for safer cars of future;
interview. L. A. Iacocca. il por U S News
70:32-6 Mr 8 '71

Protection against theft

Car alarm has siren voice. E. F. Lindsley. il
Pop Sci 199:41 N '71
Don't make it easy for thieves to steal your
car. Good H 173:191 O '71
Improved vehicular intrusion alarm. S.
Mentler. il Electr World 86:38-9 Ag '71

Purchasing

Annual roundup for new-car buyers. il Con-
sumer Rep 36:196-226 Ap '71
Art of buying a car. il Changing T 25:25-8
Mr '71
Before you buy a '72 car..; with tables.
J. P. Norbye and J. Dunne. il Pop Sci 199:
86-9 O '71
Buying a good car in retirement. N. D. Ford.
il Har Yrs 11:6-13 O '71
Europeans play the game of car-buying. il
Bsns W p52-4 Je 12 '71
How to get the best deal on your next new
car. D. L. Gregg. Bet Hom & Gard 49:30+
S '71
How to save a pile of money when you buy
a new car. D. MacDonald. il Mech Illus
68:39-41+ Ja '72
Know the auto sales agreement before you
sign. A. Lee. Bet Hom & Gard 49:46+ N '71
Motor trend guide:
How to buy your new Javelin. il Motor T
23:54-5 Mr '71
New car buyer's guide. il Motor T 23:68-74
O '71
Should you buy a leftover new car? D.
Gregg. il Bet Hom & Gard 49:32+ O '71
Tips for the bargain-hunting car buyer.
Bsns W p69 S 4 '71
See also
Automobiles, Used—Purchasing

Radio equipment

VHF frequency converter. L. E. Greenlee.
il Pop Electr 35:52-3+ D '71

Rattles

See Automobiles—Noise

Repairing

See Automobiles—Maintenance and repair

Safety belts

How to belt your kid, and save his life. B.
Hartford. il Pop Mech 136:100-3 Jl '71
New safety belt you can't ignore. H. Shul-
diner. il Pop Sci 198:61 Mr '71

Safety devices and measures

Air bag faces a showdown fight. il Bsns W
p74-5 Ag 14 '71
Crash program that is changing Detroit. il
Bsns W p78-82+ F 27 '71

AUTOMOBILES—Safety devices and measures
  —*Continued*
Full of air. P. J. Slovan. New Repub 164:9
  Mr 20 '71; Reply. D. D. Campbell. 164:33 My
  1 '71
Great air-bag debate. il Time 98:87 S 27 '71
Great airbag hassle. R. S. Strother. Nat R
  23:812+ Jl 27 '71; Same abr. Read Digest
  99:53+ N '71
How to belt your kid, and save his life. B.
  Hartford. il Pop Mech 136:100-3 Jl '71
Kick for air bags, a boost for belts. il Bsns W
  p72 O 9 '71
Making your car safer, latest moves. il U S
  News 71:58 O 11 '71
New life for air bags with seat belts. Con-
  sumer Rep 36:268-9 My '71
Price of safety. il Time 98:86 O 25 '71
Report on safety in cars of the future;
  excerpt from address. November 3, 1971.
  E. N. Cole. il por U S News 71:76-7 N 22
  '71
Safety cars are coming, the safety cars are
  coming; with editorial comment. A. B.
  Shuman. il Motor T 23:6, 32-6 My '71
Safety cars make their bow. il U S News 71:
  26-7 D 20 '71
Safety cars: the origin of the species. K. Lud-
  vigsen. il Motor T 23:37-8+ My '71
Safety: the argument over air bags. Consumer Rep 36:221-2 Ap '71
Safety upstages styling. il Time 98:50-1 Ag
  23 '71
Small size, big risk; test crashes by Insur-
  ance institute for highway safety. il Time
  98:75-6 N 29 '71
Styling for safety. il Newsweek 78:92 N 8
  '71
What ever happened to air bags? R. Lund.
  il Pop Mech 135:63-5+ F '71
What the revised safety rules will mean to
  you. J. P. Norbye. Pop Sci 198:44 My '71
What you will pay for safer cars of future;
  interview. L. A. Iacocca. il por U S News
  70:32-6 Mr 8 '71
  See also
Automobiles—Bumpers
Automobiles, Foreign—Safety devices and
  measures
Brakes, Automobile

Anecdotes, facetiae, satire, etc.
Driving you to drink; devices to keep the
  drunken driver off the road. D. Williamson.
  Sat R 54:4 D 25 '71

Selling
Sell your car yourself and get more. il Changing T 25:32 Je '71

Shock absorbers
New shocks and you save $22! M. Schultz.
  il Pop Mech 136:120-3 Jl '71

Skidding
Learn to skid, and you'll drive more safely
  on ice. J. P. Norbye. il Pop Sci 199:65-7 N
  '71
Your car's in a skid! What do you do? il
  Changing T 25:19-20 N '71

Social aspects
America adopts the automobile, 1895-1910, by
  J. Flink. Review
  Fortune 83:160-1 Ja '71. C. G. Burck
Americans put the car in its place. il Bsns
  W p66+ S 18 '71
Fade out for private cars? A. Peccei. Cur 134:
  52-5 N '71

Specifications
Important characteristics, specifications, and
  test data, 1971 intermediate and semi-sport
  automobiles. Consumer Bul 54:22-3 Je '71
Spec reading made easy. T. Tappett. il Mech
  Illus 68:94-6+ Ja '72

Speed
  See also
Automobile speed records
Speedometers

Springs and suspension
Drag racing suspensions. S. Green. il Hot
  Rod 24:61-3 Ag '71
Street rod tips; Corvair suspension modifica-
  tions. J. Thawley. il Hot Rod 24:104-5 O
  '71

Stability and stabilizers
Road-holding: design or accident? J. P. Norbye. il Pop Sci 199:43-5 Ag '71

Standards
Lemon-aid. Nader style. Time 97:79-80 F 8
  '71

Steering gear
Roundy-round corner; power steering for
  race cars. S. Kelly. il Hot Rod 24:82 O '71
Street rod tips; Jaguar steering units. B.
  Bryan. il Hot Rod 24:118-19 Ag '71

Styling
  See Automobiles—Design

Tape equipment
Packaged music in the car; automobile tapes.
  A. Carter. il Hi Fi 21:55-61 D '71
Stereo on wheels. E. Walters. il Radio-Electr
  42:41-3 Ap '71

Testing
Crash-testing for safety with world's larg-
  est linear motor. D. Scott. il Pop Sci 198:
  64-5 F '71
For executives only; Chrysler 300 and Pontiac
  Grand Ville. J. Brokaw. il Motor T 23:88-
  92+ Ap '71
Hot rod road test:
  Chevrolet Nova. il Hot Rod 24:70-1 N
    '71
  Cutlass is class. R. Guldahl, jr. il Hot
    Rod 24:42-3 Ag '71
  Dodge Charger Super Bee. S. Kelly. il
    Hot Rod 24:42-4 F '71
  Pontiac GT-37. S. Kelly. il Hot Rod 24:
    40-2 Je '71
  SS Camaro. S. Kelly. il Hot Rod 24:32-3
    Jl '71
How CU tests cars. Consumer Rep 36:207 Ap
  '71
King of the hill: Eldo-Mark III revisited.
  J. Lamm. il Motor T 23:52-4+ Jl '71
Last roundup; ponycars? W. Wyss. il Mo-
  tor T 23:76-81 O '71
Road tests on four 1972 cars; Dodge Coro-
  net, Chevrolet Chevelle Malibu, Ford Gran
  Torino, AMC Matador. il Changing T 26:25-9
  Ja '72
Something special: intermediate Oldsmobile
  Cutlass, 1971. M. Spiegel. il Sr Schol 98:40+
  My 17 '71
Tom McCahill tests (title varies)
  All-new Toronado. T. McCahill. il Mech
    Illus 67:64-6+ Je '71
  Chevrolet Malibu. T. McCahill. il Mech
    Illus 68:73-5+ Ja '72
  Continental Mark IV. T. McCahill. il
    Mech Illus 67:88-90+ D '71
  Dodge Coronet. T. McCahill. il Mech Illus
    67:66-8 My '71
  Dodge Polara Custom. T. McCahill. il
    Mech Illus 67:97-9 N '71
  45-year-old Chrysler. T. McCahill. il
    Mech Illus 67:85-7+ Mr '71
  1972 Buick GS. T. McCahill. il Mech Illus
    67:80-2 N '71
  1972 Ford Torino. T. McCahill. il Mech
    Illus 67:73-4+ S '71
  1972 Plymouth. T. McCahill. il Mech
    Illus 67:92-4 S '71
  1972 Pontiac Catalina. T. McCahill. il
    Mech Illus 67:43-5+ O '71
  We test the Matador. T. McCahill. il
    Mech Illus 67:76+ Ap '71
Two morsels from the lap of luxury; Cougar
  and Monte Carlo. A. B. Shuman. il Motor
  T 23:68-71+ Mr '71
  See also
Automobiles, Foreign—Testing

Tires
  See Tires, Automobile

Trailers
  See Automobile trailers

Transmission
All about your car's automatic shift. il
  Changing T 25:15-18 S '71
Ford C-4 trans in a Vega. J. Thawley. il
  Hot Rod 24:102-3 S '71
Lenco's latest: underdrive; dragster trans-
  mission. il Hot Rod 24:50+ Ag '71
Mr Gasket's supershifter. J. Dianna. il Hot
  Rod 24:74+ Ap '71
Ramrod: racer's hardware; straight-pattern,
  four-speed shifter. S. Kelly. il Hot Rod
  24:124-5 S '71
Trans progression; bolt-ins for street auto-
  matics. J. Dianna. il Hot Rod 24:126-9 O
  '71
Trick shift; high-performance racing
  transmission fluid. J. Dianna. il Hot Rod
  24:68+ My '71
Two-speeds are better than one. J. Thawley.
  il Hot Rod 24:116-17 Mr '71
  See also
Automobiles—Gearing

AUTOMOBILES—*Continued*

Transportation

See also
Automobiles, Racing—Transportation
Auto-train corporation

Upholstery
'29 Highboy project report. B. Bryan. il Hot
Rod 24:108-10 Ag '71

Warranty
See Warranty

Windshield washers
How to install a windshield-washer gauge.
C. J. Baker. il Pop Sci 199:108 Ag '71

Windshield wipers
Windshield wiper pause control. P. Schultz. il
Radio-Electr 42:52-3 D '71

Wrecking
Car-crushing, for your community? J. J.
Brown. il Cons 25:5 Ap '71
Good riddance to auto hulks; projects of
Padnos iron and metal company, Mich.
and General motors. S. Lindsay. il Sat R
54:58-9 F 6 '71
Safe way to wreck a car; researchers simu-
lating head-on collisions. il Mech Illus 67:
70 Ja '71
AUTOMOBILES, Automated. See Computers—
Automotive use
AUTOMOBILES, Compact
Compact and sub-compact cars. il Con-
sumer Bul 54:13-20 Ap '71
Compact cars: Dodge Dart, Chevrolet Nova,
AMC Hornet, Mercury Comet. il Consumer
Rep 36:303-9 My '71
Despite Detroit's minicars, the imports keep
booming. il U S News 70:18+ Je 7 '71
Detroit's hope for 1971: the mini-cars. il
Ebony 26:64-9 Ja '71
Is your small car really more dangerous? H.
Shuldiner. il Pop Sci 198:47-9+ My '71
L.A. shows off its mini mania. il Bsns W p27
Je 12 '71
Little Pontiac and a little. .; Ventura II. S.
Kelly. il Hot Rod 24:118-19 Mr '71
Mini car buyer's guide. C. Koch. il Motor T
23:38-41 Jl '71
Mini (hemi) magnum; Dodge Colt. J.
Christy. il Motor T 23:48-9+ Ag '71
New sub-compact cars; Pinto, Vega 2300,
Volkswagen Super Beetle 1131. il Consumer
Bul 54:16-22 F '71
1971 car of the year; Chevrolet Vega 2300.
il Motor T 23:38-47 F '71
Now that America has decided to buy the
small car. . . T. Hogg. Esquire 75:68+ Je
'71
PM owners report:
    AMC Gremlin. M. Lamm. il Pop Mech
    135:112-15 Je '71
    Dodge Dart. M. Lamm. il Pop Mech 135:
    76-9 Je '71
    Lincoln-Mercury Capri. M. Lamm. il Pop
    Mech 135:82-5 Ap '71
Putting the Mustang out to pasture. il Time
98:77 D 13 '71
'72 performers. il Hot Rod 24:40-7 O '71
Small size, big risk; test crashes by Insurance
institute for highway safety. il Time 98:75-6
N 29 '71
Subcompact cars. il Consumer Rep 36:208-11
Ap '71
Two small cars; Cricket; Hornet SST. il Con-
sumer Bul 54:14-16 Jl '71
U.S. minicars trail on the first lap. il Bsns W
p20 F 6 '71
Vega 2300: Chevy's sporty mini. M. Spiegel.
il Sr Schol 97:26+ Ja 18 '71
Vega Z-29. J. Christy. il Motor T 23:50-1
O '71
Wankel-engine sport coupe for under $2,500
and 16 other cars you can buy for under
$2,000. R. Connor. il Mech Illus 67:39-43
Ja '71
Who's winning the small-car race now. il
U S News 70:56-7 F 1 '71
See also
Automobiles, Foreign

Design
Little big car; 1971 Mercury Comet. M.
Spiegel. il Sr Schol 98:38+ My 17 '71

Testing
Five subcompacts: Toyota Corona, Dodge
Colt, VW Fastback, Chevrolet Vega, Ford
Pinto. il Consumer Rep 37:42-9 Ja '72
Hot rod road test:
    Project Comet: stage one. S. Green. il
    Hot Rod 24:46-8 Ap '71

Little big car; 1971 Mercury Comet. M.
Spiegel. il Sr Schol 98:38+ My 17 '71
Mazda Wankel vs. Comet 302. W. Wyss. il
Motor T 23:76-8+ My '71
PM's coast-to-coast test: Pinto vs. Vega. I.
Dolin. il Pop Mech 135:76-80+ Mr '71
Popular science car test:
    Pinto and Vega: 10,000 miles later. J. P.
    Norbye and others. il Pop Sci 198:12+
    Ja '71
    '71 compacts. J. P. Norbye and J. Dunne.
    il Pop Sci 198:40+ F '71
    Top-line compacts: Mercury Comet, Pon-
    tiac Ventura II, and the Dodge Demon.
    J. P. Norby and J. Dunne. il Pop Sci
    198:24+ Je '71
Real small ones, basic economic transporta-
tion? il Consumer Bul 55:7-12 Ja '72
Tom McCahill tests (title varies)
    Mercury's Comet. T. McCahill. il Mech
    Illus 67:56-8+ Mr '71
    Pontiac's new economy car. T. McCahill.
    il Mech Illus 67:77-9+ My '71
AUTOMOBILES, Electric
Electric cars: the battery problem; adapta-
tion of address, December, 1970. V. Wouk.
il Bul Atom Sci 27:19-22 Ap '71
Great voltage war; International electric
vehicle symposium and exposition. il News-
week 78:101+ N 22 '71
How we captured the world land speed record
for electric cars; MI's Silver Eagle. B.
Wennerstrom. il Mech Illus 67:72-5+ D '71
Let's mass produce an electric car now. C.
R. Whiting. il Sci Digest 70:67-71 Ag '71
Modest proposal: Electricart. C. Ogburn. il
Harper 243:106-7 O '71
New electrics make performance break-
throughs. J. P. Zmuda. il Pop Sci 198:55-6
F '71
Next sound you hear will be your electric
car. C. Packard. il Motor T 23:94-7 Ag '71
AUTOMOBILES, Experimental
Amazing car that comes apart: the Barrcar.
il Mech Illus 67:84 D '71
Inside the Minicar think tank. W. Wyss. il
Motor T 23:78-81 Jl '71
Lamborghini Countach! il Motor T 23:98-100
S '71
Safety cars make their bow. il U S News 71:
26-7 D 20 '71
We drive the new Williams turbine-engine
clean-air car. J. P. Norbye and J. Dunne.
il Pop Sci 199:59-61+ N '71
AUTOMOBILES, Flying. See Airplanes, Light—
Automobile combinations
AUTOMOBILES, Foreign
Bavaria; BMW. W. Wyss. il Motor T 23:56+
Je '71
Cars for splendid winter driving. E. Dahl-
quist. il Motor T 23:96-7 N '71
Cars of Germany. K. Ludvigsen. il Motor T
23:39-45+ D '71
Cars of the world:
    Brazil. K. Ludvigsen. il Motor T 23:74-6+
    Ap '71
    England. J. Brokaw. il Motor T 23:42-
    6+ Jl '71
    France. J. Lamm. il Motor T 23:52-3+
    F '71
    Sweden. E. Dahlquist. il Motor T 23:
    50-6 S '71
Datsun also rises. il Hot Rod 24:101 N '71
Electric blue ego machine; Alpine Renaults.
J. Lamm. il Motor T 23:52-3 Je '71
Fiat 128: the new Beetle. W. Wyss. il Motor
T 23:72-5 Jl '71
411 series: Volkswagen's luxury line. G. Hart-
ford. il Pop Mech 135:92-3 Mr '71
450 SL: *sicherheit* and *lauterkeit*. A. B. Shu-
man. il Motor T 23:44-7+ Je '71
Front-engine VW. E. Seidler. il Motor T
23:68-71 F '71
Front-wheel drive to the fore! Renault 12.
B. Hartford. il Pop Mech 136:126-9 N '71
How the Japanese blitzed the California auto
market. il Forbes 108:28-9 S 15 '71
Import report. See issues of Motor trend
Imports race for the middle market. il Bsns
W p 15 Ap 3 '71
Is front-wheel drive best for small cars?
Citroën GS and Peugeot 304: J. P. Norbye.
il Pop Sci 198:58-60 Mr '71
It really is possible to design a car without
compromise! Mercedes-Benz 350SL. B.
Hartford. il Pop Mech 136:58+ O '71
Mini car buyer's guide. C. Koch. il Motor T
23:38-41 Jl '71
Minicar invasion. il Newsweek 78:64-5 Ag 23
'71
Morris Marina. E. Seidler. il Motor T 23:
102-3 Ag '71
Neretti: both ears and a tail. T. C. Browne.
il Motor T 23:86-7 O '71

AUTOMOBILES, Foreign—*Continued*
125 calibre Colt. il Motor T 23:62 F '71
Opel supertune. J. Christy. il Motor T 23:
90-1+ N '71
PM owners report:
Buick Opel. M. Lamm. il Pop Mech 136:
74-7 Jl '71
Honda 600. M. Lamm. il Pop Mech 136:
96-9 N '71
Mazda rotary-engined coupe. M. Lamm.
il Pop Mech 136:100-3 O '71
Plymouth Cricket; Dodge Colt. il Pop
Mech 136:76-9+ S '71
Toyota Corona. M. Lamm. il Pop Mech
136:96-9 Ag '71
Reflections on a three-pointed star; Mercedes
280 SEL 4.5. A. B. Shuman. il Motor T 23:
100-2+ O '71
Renault 15/17. E. Seidler. il Motor T 23:
92-4+ S '71
Rotary-engine car is catching on; Mazda.
il Bsns W p20 Jl 10 '71
Shrewd engineering keeps Fiat 128 light and
simple. J. P. Norbye. il Pop Sci 199:
64-5 S '71
Subaru: is it here to stay? B. Hartford. il
Pop Mech 135:24+ My '71
Surprise package; Toyota Corolla 1600. S.
Green. il Hot Rod 24:42 Jl '71
Tough Swede; Volvo's sales in the U.S. il
Forbes 107:35 Je 15 '71
Triumph's transcendent three: TR6, GT6,
Spitfire. J. Christy. il Motor T 23:46-8+ N
'71
Two Volvos; 1962 PV544 and the 142E. J.
Lamm. il Motor T 23:48-50+ My '71
Ultimate Capri; the 2300 GT. B. Cahier. il
Motor T 23:30-1 Ap '71
Wankel challenge; Japan selling compact
models. il Time 97:84 Ap 5 '71
Wankel-engine sport coupe for under $2,500
and 16 other cars you can buy for under
$2,000. R. Connor. il Mech Illus 67:39-43 Ja
'71
What's a Marcos? K. Ludvigsen. il Motor T
23:88-9 Je '71
World's fastest production cars; Fer-
rari, Maserati, and Lamborghini. J. P.
Norbye. il Pop Sci 198:64-5+ My '71
See also
Sports cars

Anecdotes, facetiae, satire, etc.
How to keep your Volkswagen alive, by J.
Muir. Review
Life il 71:10 Jl 23 '71. J. Kastner

Design
Fiat does it again; new Fiat 127. il Motor T
23:22-3 Je '71
Front-drive cars in VW's future. J. P.
Norbye. il Pop Sci 199:10+ O '71
Hot wheels Italian style; Ferrari, de Tomaso,
Lamborghini and Maserati. D. J. Hamblin.
il Sports Illus 35:24-9 Ag 30 '71

History
In retrospect:
MG-TC. J. Lamm. il Motor T 23:60-2+
N '71
Mercedes-Benz 300SL Gullwing coupe. il
Motor T 23:60-2+ Ag '71
Phil Hill's Blower Bentley. E. Dahlquist.
il Motor T 23:62-4+ Jl '71

Safety devices and measures
Beetles; R. Nader's report on Volkswagens.
G. Lardner. New Repub 165:17-19 O 9 '71
Hatching of a safer Beetle. il Bsns W p35
Je 19 '71
Volkswagen's armored cars. E. Seidler. il
Motor T 23:78-81 N '71

Testing
Alfa Romeo. il Motor T 23:30-4+ S '71
Citroën's super machine. J. Lamm. il Mo-
tor T 23:52-5 O '71
Ferrari Dino 246 GT vs. Porsche 911S. E.
Dahlquist. il Motor T 23:30-3 Jl '71
5 imported subcompact sedans: Fiat 124B;
Toyota Corolla 1200; Datsun 1200; Volks-
wagen 111; Plymouth Cricket. il Consumer
Rep 36:543-9 S '71
French entry; Renault 12. J. Lamm. il Motor
T 23:72-5 Ag '71
Great expectations; Subaru Star. W. Wyss.
il Motor T 23:104-6 O '71
Hot rod road test:
Cricket, stock and southern-style. S.
Green. il Hot Rod 24:64-6 Je '71
MG: Morris garages. J. Christy. il Motor T
23:91-2+ O '71

Popular science car test:
Citröen DS-21. Jaguar XJ-6 and Mer-
cedes-Benz 250. J. P. Norbye and J.
Dunne. il Pop Sci 199:18+ D '71
Colt, Cricket, Opel 1900 and Capri. J. P.
Norbye and J. Dunne. il Pop Sci 198:16+
My '71
Opel 1900, Renault R-12 and Peugeot 304.
J. P. Norbye and J. Dunne. il Pop Sci
199:16+ N '71
Super-Beetle, Subaru FF-1 and Fiat 128.
J. P. Norbye and J. Dunne. il Pop Sci
199:26+ S '71
Real small ones, basic economic transporta-
tion? il Consumer Bul 55:7-12 Ja '72
Return of the native; Toyota Celica. W.
Wyss. il Motor T 23:50-2 Ag '71
Stalemate, not checkmate; Capri 2000 and
Opel 1900. C. Koch. il Motor T 23:28-31+
Ap '71
Tom McCahill tests (title varies)
Hot Wankel-engine Mazda RX-2. T.
McCahill. il Mech Illus 67:60-2+ Ag '71
Subaru FF-1G. T. McCahill. il Mech
Illus 67:72+ O '71
VW's Super Beetle. T. McCahill. il Mech
Illus 67:81-3+ Ja '71
Very, very expensive Lamborghini Es-
pada. T. McCahill. il Mech Illus 67:62-
4+ Ap '71
Volkswagen 411. T. McCahill. il Mech
Illus 68:52+ Ja '72
Ultimate Christmas gift: a Ferrari 365 GTS/4
Daytona. C. Queener. il Motor T 23:52-4+
D '71
Volkswagen 411. il Consumer Rep 36:737-9
N '71
You can get more than you pay for; Peugeot
304, Datsun 1200, Subaru Star and Toyota
Corolla. C. Koch. il Motor T 23:72-6+ F '71
AUTOMOBILES, Miniature. See Automobile
models
AUTOMOBILES, Old

Collectors and collecting
See Automobiles—Collectors and collect-
ing
AUTOMOBILES, Police
Patrol car console cuts driver risks. il Am
City 86:26 Ja '71
What's black and white and can save you
money? il Motor T 23:37-8 Je '71
AUTOMOBILES, Racing
All-star funny cars. il Hot Rod 24:90-4+ Ap
'71
Art was my copilot; a ride in Cyclops two
jet car. R. Guldahl, jr. il por Hot Rod 24:
84-5 D '71
Ask Herb's wife if we can take her car
racing. A. B. Shuman. il Motor T 23:
88-90+ S '71
C/MP 'Vette threat. J. Dianna. il Hot Rod
24:46-8Ag '71
Complete guide to unracing; bracket racing.
S. Green. il Hot Rod 24:86-7 D '71
Construction report: E-body Plymouth pro
stocker. J. Dianna. il Hot Rod 24:138-9 N '71
Driving impressions: Chaparral-engined
March STP 707. K. Ludvigsen. il Motor T
23:78-80 Mr '71
First of the light-heavyweights; small-block
Vega pro stock. J. Dianna. il Hot Rod 24:
102-4 N '71
Fittipaldi 3200! K. Ludvigsen. il Motor T
23:52+ Ag '71
Flicker of the Blue Flame. B. Wennerstrom.
il Mech Illus 67:57-8+ Ap '71
4-speed record changer. J. Dianna. il Hot Rod
24:84+ N '71
Funny winder; fourth-generation Chrisman
Sidewinder. R. Guldahl. il Hot Rod 24:36-9
N '71
Gas digger; twice-motored, rear-type! il Hot
Rod 24:66-7 O '71
How they did with what they had; California
500. il Hot Rod 24:76 N '71
How to throw the Javelin. J. McFarland.
Motor T 23:47 Mr '71
Little engine that could, almost; 305 Charger.
il Motor T 23:34-5 Ap '71
Look at what AMC's up to, again. S. Kelly. il
Hot Rod 24:90-1 D '71
Mod squad; modified production classes. J.
Dianna. il Hot Rod 24:66-75 D '71
Redwood racer. il Hot Rod 24:90 S '71
Roddin' at random. See issues of Hot rod
Roundy-round corner; LSR Can-Am car. S.
Kelly. il Hot Rod 24:110 N '71
'71 pro stocks in action. il Hot Rod 24:96-8+
Je '71
'71 racing preview; symposium. il Motor T
23:20-2+ Mr '71
622.407 MPH. R. Guldahl, jr. il por Hot Rod
24:90-2 F '71

AUTOMOBILES, Racing—*Continued*
Strange flight of the Silver Eagle. B. Wennerstrom. il Mech Illus 67:53-6+ Ap '71
Technical victory; the McLaren cars at Indianapolis. A. B. Shuman. il Motor T 23:68-71+ Ag '71

Brakes
See Brakes, Automobile

Design
Big daddy's E.T. element. il por Hot Rod 24:8 N '71
Breedlove's rocket racers. E. K. von Delden. il pors Hot Rod 24:112-17 My '71
Garlits up front. R. Guldahl, jr. il por Hot Rod 24:52-3+ My '71
Roundy-round corner; Aero-structures formula racers. S. Kelly. il Hot Rod 24:123 Je '71

Equipment
Strictly for stocks. J. Dianna. See issues of Hot rod

Fuel systems
See Automobile engines—Fuel feeding

Maintenance and repair
Big man with Indy wrench. K. Chapin. il pors Sports Illus 34:40-5 My 24 '71
See also
Automobile mechanics (persons)

Models
See Automobile models

Photographs
Hair they are! Hot Rod 24:76-7 Jl '71

Safety devices and measures
Total containment; safety bellhousing. J. Dianna. il Hot Rod 24:82 Ap '71

Springs and suspension
See Automobiles—Springs and suspension

Steering gear
See Automobiles—Steering gear

Tires
See Tires, Automobile

Transmission
See Automobiles—Transmission

Transportation
Strictly for stocks. J. Dianna. il Hot Rod 24:72 Ag '71
AUTOMOBILES, Remodeled
Personalized Pontiac; SSJ Hurst. J. Dianna. il Hot Rod 24:59 Je '71
Project Comet: stage two. S. Kelly. il Hot Rod 24:40-3 My '71
Project Demon. S. Green. il Hot Rod 24: 118-20 My; 44-6 Je; 46-8 Jl '71
Project street Bug: stage two. J. Dianna. il Hot Rod 24:68-70 O '71
Right out of the roaring twenties. D. S. Powell. il Pop Mech 136:76H N '71
Shadetree musclecars. J. Fuchs. il Hot Rod 24:32-4 D '71
Steel Stingray; Datsun-Chevy hybrid. A. B. Shuman. il Hot Rod 24:40-1 N '71
Street rod nationals scrapbook. il Hot Rod 24:117-24+ N '71
Tale of two Pintos. S. Green. il Hot Rod 24:30-3 Mr '71
'29 Highboy project report. B. Bryan. il Hot Rod 24:108-10 Ag '71
See also
Automobiles, Racing
AUTOMOBILES, Restored
In retrospect:
1931 Duesenberg Model J Tourster. J. Lamm. il Motor T 23:62-4+ O '71
Old cars in Fossil, Oregon. il Sunset 146:91 My '71
Special delivery; 1940 Ford sedan il Hot Rod 24:106-8 Jl '71
See also
Western antique auto supply (firm)
AUTOMOBILES, Steam
Damn the smog, full steam ahead! Forbes 107:36 F 1 '71
Lear: the steam king? K. Ludvigsen. il pors Motor T 23:30-2+ F '71
New try to revive the steam car. Bsns W p45 Mr 13 '71
Steam engine that might. il Time 97:76+ Mr 29 '71

AUTOMOBILES, Theft of
Electronic help for lost cars; National automobile theft bureau. P. M. Eckstein. Mech Illus 67:16 Jl '71
Hot Porsche caper. il Time 98:12 D 20 '71
Stealing cars is a growth industry. P. Hellman. il pors N Y Times Mag p7+ Je 20 '71
Stealing your car. A. Rothenberg. il pors Look 35:74-6 Je 29 '71
See also
Automobiles—Protection against theft
AUTOMOBILES, Three wheel
We test a $1,000 car; Bond Bug. G. Wilkins. il por Mech Illus 67:58-9 Je '71
AUTOMOBILES, Used
Chase for classic cars. E. Herzberg. il Duns 98:65-6 Jl '71
Lot of transportation for a little money. B. Davis. il Mech Illus 67:48-50+ Ag '71
Used car as a hedge against inflation; special interest cars. il Motor T 23:38-41 Je '71

Purchasing
How to buy a used car. D. McCluggage. Am Home 74:52+ Ap '71
1971 used car buyer's guide. il Motor T 23:35-42 Je '71
AUTOMOBILES, Winter conditioning of. See Automobiles—Maintenance and repair
AUTOMOBILES in art
Car art; Art around the automobile exhibition at Hofstra university's gallery in Long Island. D. Davis. Newsweek 78:77 Jl 5 '71
AUTOMOTIVE diesel engines. See Diesel engines. Automotive
AUTOMOTIVE engineering. See Automobile engineering
AUTOMOTIVE gas turbines. See Gas turbines, Automotive
AUTOMOTIVE industries

Finance
Automotive; with yardsticks of management performance. il Forbes 109:151-2 Ja 1 '72
AUTOPSY
Art of autopsy. B. J. Friedman. Esquire 76: 96+ D '71
AUTRET, Jean
(ed) See Proust, M. Proust's prefaces to Ruskin
AUTUMN
Most beautiful time of the year. H. Norris. il Nat Wildlife 9:4-9 O '71
See also
November
AUTUMN photography. See Nature photography
AUXILIARY heaters. See Heaters
AUXILIARY marine engines. See Marine engines
AUXINS
Auxins in citrus: a reappraisal. E. E. Goldschmidt and others. bibliog Science 174: 1256-7 D 17 '71
AVAILABLE-light photography. See Photography—Light
AVALANCHES
Man who busts avalanches. il Mech Illus 68: 97+ Ja '72
See also
Landslides
AVANCE, Lyonel D.
Vee vee the one, two . . . il Parks & Rec 6:28-9+ N '71
AVANT, John Alfred
Slouching toward criticism. il por Library J 96:4055-9 D 15 '71
AVANT-garde dancing. See Dancing
AVANT-garde films. See Moving pictures, Experimental
AVANT-garde music. See Music
AVANT-garde theater. See Theater, Experimental
AVARICE
Pride goes before avarice: social change and the vices in Latin Christendom. L. K. Little. bibliog f il Am Hist R 76:16-49 F '71
AVCO corporation
Avco bets on boron tape. Bsns W p 124+ Ap 10 '71
Avco readies new boron plant as demand for composites lags. Aviation W 94:48 Ap 19 '71
Avco soups up its recovery drive. il Bsns W p40+ O 9 '71
AVEDON, Luciana
Secrets of a million-dollar face; excerpt from Beautiful people's beauty book. por Ladies Home J 88:74-5+ Ja '71
—and Molli, Jeanne
Your looks are as good as your discipline; excerpt from The beauty book. il Vogue 157:86-7+ Ja 15 '71

AVEDON, Luciana—*Continued*

about

Mirror, mirror. por Time 97:49-50 Mr 15 '71 •

AVEDON, Richard
Three classic beauties; photographs. Vogue 158:64-9 Ag 1 '71

AVERAGES, Stock. See Stocks—Price indexes and averages

AVERY, Peter
Iran: cultural crossroads for 2,500 years. il UNESCO Courier 24:4-9 O '71

AVERY products corporation
Avery's profit establishment. T. J. Murray. Duns 98:54-5 Ag '71

AVIARIES
Doctor Swan's finches get to fly from one aviary to another. il Sunset 146:102-4 Je '71
No caged birds; Richmond, Va. il Am City 86:28 Ap '71

AVIATION
See also
Air travel
Airports
Airships
Airways
Balloon ascensions
Gliding and soaring
Private flying
Radio in aviation
Television in aviation
also headings beginning Aeronautic, Aeronautics, Airplane, Airplanes

Accident prevention
See Aviation—Safety devices and measures

Accidents
Board probing 747 takeoff accident. il Aviation W 95:26-7 Ag 9 '71
Early touchdown cited in 747 incident; Renton airport, Renton, Wash, December 13, 1969. il Aviation W 94:60-5 Mr 1 '71
Information lack revealed in 747 probe. Aviation W 95:21-4 Ag 30 '71
Is twin-engine safety a myth? R. L. Collins. il Flying 89:68-71+ Ag '71
NTSB broadens 747 investigation. il Aviation W 95:29-30 Ag 16 '71
Over-trimming cited in Corvette crash. Aviation W 94:221 My 31 '71
Preliminary report planned on mid-air; collision between American airlines Boeing 707 and Cessna 150. Aviation W 94:43 Ja 25 '71
Safety check. R. L. Collins. See issues of Flying
Was the Wichita state crash avoidable? C. S. Wren. il Look 35:73-6 Mr 9 '71
Worst ever; All Nippon airways Boeing 727. Time 98:30 Ag 9 '71
See also
Drinking and airplane accidents
Helicopters—Accidents

Bibliography
Books. See issues of Flying

Clubs
See Aviation clubs

Cold weather conditions
See Aviation—Winter flying

Economic aspects
Rules, economics hold keys to future growth. C. E. Schneider. il Aviation W 95:39+ S 20 '71

Exhibitions
Air show that Europe stole; Paris air show. il Bsns W p40-1 Je 5 '71
Antique fly-in is coming to Watsonville May 14, 15, 16. il Sunset 146:81-2 My '71
British Columbia's grand air show the August 14 weekend; Abbotsford international air show. il Sunset 147:32+ Ag '71
Export drive highlights Paris show. il Aviation W 94:26-8 My 31 '71
Ilyushin Il-76 exhibit planned at Paris show. D. E. Fink. il Aviation W 94:17 My 24 '71
Japan show draws east, west. Aviation W 95:92 N 1 '71
LeBourget Paris show facilities expanded. D. E. Fink. Aviation W 96:18-19 Ja 10 '72
Paris 1971: a vintage year. J. Fricker. Flying 89:104-7 O '71
Reading. G. Baxter. il Flying 88:75-8 Je '71
Red stars at Le Bourget. il Time 97:68-9 Je 7 '71
SST's on show; Paris's Le Bourget airfield. il Newsweek 77:65-6 My 31 '71
Show and tell; Paris air show. R. B. Parke. Flying 89:22 S '71
Some perspective on Paris. R. Hotz. Aviation W 94:11 Je 28 '71

Special report: Paris air show; with editorial comment. il Aviation W 94:14-26+ Je 7; 9, 14-23 Je 14 '71
Tu-144 expected to be displayed at Paris. D. E. Fink. Aviation W 94:18-19 Ap 5 '71

Flight planning
See Aviation—Safety devices and measures

Fog problem
They'll never know. F. W. Gibson. Flying 88:69-70 F '71

Formation flying
MiG-21 pilots show precision flying ability. il Aviation W 95:56-7 D 6 '71

History
See Aeronautics—History

Ice problem
See Airplanes—Ice protection

Instrument flying
Cleared as filed: how to choose the proper IFR route. W. Berkley. il Flying 89:54-5 Jl '71
IFR DCA to JFK; flight log. R. Peterson. il Flying 89:88-92 O '71
Military to fly IFR wherever practicable. Aviation W 94:23 Je 28 '71
Poor-man's IFR; single-radio IFR. A. Trammell. il Flying 88:41-3+ Ap '71
Pro's nest; selection of alternate airports. T. H. Block. Flying 89:29+ O '71

International aspects
Air agreement with Ireland to be modified, Department announcement. Dept State Bul 65:270-1 S 6 '71
Charter firm has Moscow rights; Nordair oy. D. A. Brown. il Aviation W 94:52 My 17 '71
Costs, recession dim airline outlook. L. Doty. il Aviation W 94:107-9+ Mr 8 '71
Current policy problems in international aviation; address, November 17, 1970. B. W. Rein. Dept State Bul 64:15-18 Ja 4 '71
European group challenges U.S. supplemental influx. L. Doty. Aviation W 95:21-2 Jl 19 '71
Inter-governmental charter talks may be base for future accord. L. Doty. Aviation W 94:23 Ap 5 '71
International charters agreement sought. L. Doty. Aviation W 94:28 F 22 '71
Non-skeds go after charter pacts. il Bsns W p36 Ap 3 '71
Restriction drive sparks friction. Aviation W 94:32 Ap 19 '71
U.S. acts to ease charter rights. L. Doty. Aviation W 94:24 Mr 22 '71
U.S. and Dominican Republic amend air transport agreement. Dept State Bul 65:539 N 8 '71
U.S. Australia discuss capacity, but positions appear hardening. R. G. O'Lone. Aviation W 95:20 Ag 30 '71
U.S. Australia reach air service agreement. Aviation W 95:31 S 27 '71
U.S. British governments reach accord on Atlantic capacity cut. Aviation W 95:25 Jl 5 '71
U.S. Irish clash on Dublin rights. L. Doty. Aviation W 95:25-6 D 20 '71
U.S. signs protocol revising Warsaw convention rules in regard to air carried liability to passengers; Department announcement; with text of protocol. Dept State Bul 64:555-9 Ap 26 '71
United States and Korea amend air transport agreement. Dept State Bul 64:515 Ap 12 '71
United States and Switzerland amend air transport agreement. Dept State Bul 64:35 Ja 4 '71
See also
Airlines—International services
International air transport association
International civil aviation organization
Warsaw convention

Laws and regulations
Are you legal? P. Garrison. Flying 88:57-9+ Je '71
Civil aviation bills facing uncertain fate in Congress. D. C. Winston. Aviation W 95:54-5 S 20 '71
On top; takeoff minimums. R. L. Collins. Flying 88:10-12 Je '71
Pilot's rights. W. Berkley. Flying 89:94-6 O '71
Rules, economics hold keys to future growth. C. E. Schneider. il Aviation W 95:39+ S 20 '71

AVIATION—Laws and regulations—*Continued*
Senate unit reports amendment limiting user fund expenditures; 1970 Airport and airway development act. D. C. Winston. Aviation W 95:28 O 4 '71
Slick clique. R. B. Parke. Flying 88:34 Je '71
Teaching teachers; FAA overhauling licensing system. R. B. Parke. Flying 88:33 F '71
Traffic slump clouds regulation. L. Doty. Aviation W 95:25 S 20 '71
Transport rule coverage expansion urged. Aviation W 94:19 Mr 15 '71
See also
Air traffic control
Airports—Laws and regulations
Airports—Traffic control
United States —Civil aeronautics board
United States—Federal aviation administration

Lightning hazards
Lightning and the plastic airplane. R. Markson; T. Sim. Flying 89:6-7 Jl '71
When lightning strikes, are you safe in a plane? excerpt from Understanding lightning. M. A. Uman. il Sci Digest 70:69-72 D '71
See also
Medical aspects
Motion sickness

Meteorological aspects
See Meteorology, Aeronautic

Night flying
Fun & fear of night flight. L. Buckwalter. il pors Mech Illus 67:89-91+ N '71
One good scare. J. Lemmart. Flying 89:60-1 S '71
Safety check; fly by night. R. L. Collins. il Flying 89:112 N '71
When the sun goes down. D. Lowery. il Flying 90:50-1+ Ja '72

Physiological aspects
Hunt for traveler's pill; Project Pegasus research on jet-lag fatigue. B. Kocivar. McCalls 98:41 My '71
Jet lag: how time-zone changes can shake up travellers' health. D. Moreau. Vogue 157: 102+ Ap 15 '71
See also
Aviation—Radiation hazards

Public relations
See also
Airlines—Public relations

Radiation hazards
Radiation exposure in air travel. H. J. Schaefer. bibliog il Science 173:780-3 Ag 27 '71

Records
See Aviation records

Safety devices and measures
Back to basics; declaring an emergency. P. Garrison. il Flying 89:56-8 O '71
Five safety proposals result from NTSB's 747 accident probe. Aviation W 96:21-2 Ja 3 '72
Pro's nest; selection of alternate airports. T. H. Block. Flying 89:29+ O '71
Tougher safety rules urged for general aviation. Aviation W 95:20-1 O 11 '71
See also
Airplanes—Ice protection
Airplanes—Safety devices and measures
Proximity warning indicators
Radar in aviation
Radio beacons
United States—Federal aviation administration—Flight service stations

Storm hazards
VFR to IFR. M. Catalan. Flying 89:77+ N '71
See also
Aviation—Lightning hazards

Study and teaching
See Aeronautics—Study and teaching

Stunt flying
A-7D flight demonstrations at Le Bourget tailored to low ceiling, show restrictions. il Aviation W 94:48-50 Je 28 '71
Last barnstormer. G. Baxter. Flying 88:102 F '71
Tallman speaking; interview, ed. by P. Garrison. F. Tallman. il pors Flying 88:44-51 Ap '71

Transatlantic flights
Across the Atlantic in a light twin. N. Aubuchon. il pors Pop Sci 199:78-81+ N '71
How not to fly the Atlantic; excerpts from Oceans, Poles and airmen. R. Montague. il pors Am Heritage 22:42-7+ Ap '71

Winter flying
Busy Beaver. L. V. DeBlicquy. il Flying 89:62-3 D '71
Winter winds. R. L. Collins. il Flying 89: 52-3+ D '71
See also
Airplanes—Ice protection

Arctic Regions
World of Weldy Phipps. S. Wilkinson. il Flying 88:54-63 Mr '71

Canada
See also
Aeronautics, Commercial—Canada

Kenya
Modern Masai. H. Reuter. il pors Ebony 26: 87-91 Ap '71

Russia
See also
Aeronautics, Commercial—Russia

United States
Customer. R. B. Parke. Flying 89:32 D '71
In debt; general aviation. R. B. Parke. Flying 88:40 My '71
See also
Airlines—United States
Aviation, State departments of
United States—President's aviation advisory committee

AVIATION, State departments of
Your state aviation director: what has he done for you lately? R. Hoffman. Flying 88: S1-4+ My '71

AVIATION associations
Aerospace calendar. See issues of Aviation week & space technology
Calendar. See issues of Flying
See also names of aviation associations, e.g. International flying farmers (association)

AVIATION clubs
How to run a flying club. R. Blodget. il Flying 89:54-5 S; 80-1 D '71
How to start a flying club for fun and profit. R. Blodget. il Flying 88:46-8 Je '71

AVIATION conferences
See also
European civil aviation conference

AVIATION consumer action project
Nader group formed for airline users. Aviation W 94:25 My 17 '71

AVIATION education
See also
Aeronautics—Study and teaching
Air pilots—Training

AVIATION fuel taxes. See Motor fuels—Taxation

AVIATION instruments. See Aeronautic instruments

AVIATION museums. See Aeronautic museums

AVIATION records
Army claims eight records for CH-54B. Aviation W 95:55 D 6 '71
How not to fly the Atlantic; excerpts from Oceans, Poles and airmen. R. Montague. il pors Am Heritage 22:42-7+ Ap '71
Lift-off from San Francisco Bay; homemade flying machine. A. G. Sutro. il Read Digest 99:110-14 D '71

AVIATION research. See Aeronautic research

AVIATION schools
See also
Flight unlimited, inc.

AVILA, Gustavo
What a fiesta we will have! W. F. Reed. il pors Sports Illus 34:26-8+ My 31 '71 *

AVIONICS
Exhibitions
U.S. avionics show exceeds expectations. Aviation W 95:91-2 N 1 '71

Testing
Military expertise applied to civil uses; automatic test equipment for airline avionics. P. J. Klass. il Aviation W 96:54-6 Ja 10 '72

AVIONICS industry
Semiconductor market recovery anticipated. B. M. Elson. il Aviation W 94:174-9 Mr 8 '71
See also
Collins radio company
Narco avionics (firm)

AVIONICS industry—*Continued*

Europe, Western

Diverse trends shape European avionics. Aviation W 94:183-5 My 31 '71
European avionics firms focus on space applications projects. il Aviation W 94:186-9 My 31 '71

France

Avionics giant seeks ATC superiority; Thomson-CSF. il Aviation W 94:173-80 My 31 '71
French challenge U.S. dominance. P. J. Klass. il Aviation W 94:167-71 My 31 '71

Japan

Japanese press avionics growth. il Aviation W 95:38-9+ N 1 '71

AVIONS Marcel Dassault. See Airplane industry—France

AVIS rent a car system, inc.
McCahill vs Hertz (Chevrolet) vs Avis (Plymouth) il Mech Illus 67:56-8+ Jl '71
Now Avis thinks it can become no. 1. il Bsns W p46+ F 6 '71
That clerk could be a president in disguise. V. Louviere. il Nations Bsns 59:23 S '71

AVOCADOS
Almost certain way to grow a practically perfect avocado plant; excerpt from The after-dinner gardening book. R. W. Langer. Redbook 136:86+ Mr '71
Avocado incognito, the secret weapon beauty fruit. il Harp Baz 104:108-9 O '71
Avocados sell at any price. il Bsns W p46 O 16 '71

AVOIDANCE (psychology)
Infant responses to impending collision: optical and real. W. Ball and E. Tronick. bibliog il Science 171:818-20 F 26 '71
Preavoidance blood pressure elevations accompanied by heart rate decreases in the dog. D. E. Anderson and J. V. Brady. bibliog il Science 172:595-7 My 7 '71
Regional blood-flow changes during 72-hour avoidance schedules in the monkey. R. P. Forsyth. bibliog il Science 173:546-8 Ag 6 '71

AVORN, Jerry
1971 B.C: what the new living is like in a Boston commune. il Look 35:54+ Ag 10 '71

AWAD, Mohamed
Other person's skin. UNESCO Courier 24:20-2 N '71

AWARDS. See Rewards, prizes, etc.

AWNINGS
Awnings make their stable a party house. il Sunset 147:96-7 Jl '71

AWOONOR, Kofi
Books. J. Updike. New Yorker 47:187-8+ N 13 '71 *

AWRAMIK, Stanley M.
Precambrian columnar stromatolite diversity: reflection of metazoan appearance. bibliog il Science 174:825-7 N 19 '71

AX, Paul
Newport librarian resigns: cites lack of funds. Library J 96:2680 O 1 '71 *

AXELBANK, Albert
How we bombed Tokyo's press. Nation 213:205-6 S 13 '71
Japan's way with protest. Nation 212:684 My 31 '71

AXELROD, George
Trade winds; interview, ed. by C. Amory. Sat R 54:14+ S 11 '71

AXELROD, Julius
Noradrenaline: fate and control of its biosynthesis; Nobel lecture, December 12, 1970. bibliog il Science 173:598-606 Ag 13 '71
—See Weinshilboum, R. jt. auth.

AXLES
See also
Automobiles—Axles
Motor trucks—Axles

AXTHELM, Pete
Men behind the men who make money in sports. il Vogue 157:186-7+ My '71
Sports (cont) Vogue 157:115 Mr 1; 163 Ap 1 '71

AYALA, Francisco J.
Competition between species: frequency dependence. bibliog il Science 171:820-4 F 26 '71

AYALA, G. F. and others
Penicillin as an epileptogenic agent: effect on an isolated synapse. bibliog il Science 171:915-17 Mr 5 '71

AYALA, Ramón Pérez de. See Pérez de Ayala, R.

AYALA, Ruben S.
Look at our judicial system; address. Vital Speeches 37:374-6 Ap 1 '71

AYCKBOURN, Alan
How the other half loves. Criticism
New Yorker 47:95 Ap 3 '71 *
Time 97:78 Ap 12 '71 *

AYER, LaNeil
We did it. il House B 113:24+ Ap '71

AYLOR, Donald E.
Plants filter noises. Horticulture 49:28+ F '71

AYLOR, Kay E.
Peephole into the world of work. il Am Ed 7:29-30 Mr '71

AYLWARD, Jim
All-purpose Lindsay comment. Sat R 54:4 D 25 '71

AYMOND, A. H.
Science and technology; address, April 30, 1971. Vital Speeches 37:492-4 Je 1 '71

AYO, Nicholas
At night in prayer. il Chr Cent 88:1494-7 D 22 '71

AYRES, James E.
British folk art at Freshford manor. il Antiques 99:866-71 Je '71

AZALEAS
Azalea, outside beauty plus indoor bloom. J. G. Bowman. il Org Gard & Farm 18:90+ Ap '71
Novel approaches to azalea culture. F. W. Wright, jr. il Horticulture 49:30-3 Ap '71

AZHDANOV tailors; story. See Stead, C.

AZO compounds
Soil transforms; metabolism of aniline-based pesticides to TCAB and other azo compounds. D. Pramer. il Environ 13:42-6 My '71

AZTECS
Gardens on swamps. P. Armillas. bibliog il Science 174:653-61 N 12 '71

B

B and F enterprises (firm)
B&F, where surplus goods reign supreme. N. Goldberg. il Pop Phot 69:54+ S '71

B-1 (airplane) See Airplanes, Military—United States

BART (Bay area rapid transit) See San Francisco—Transit systems

BATS (ballistic aerial target system) See Guided missiles

B. F. Goodrich company. See Goodrich, B. F. company

BIA. See United States—Indian affairs, Bureau of

BIS. See Bank for international settlements

BLET. See United States—Education, Office of —Libraries and educational technology, Bureau of

BLS. See United States—Labor statistics, Bureau of

BMEWS. See Ballistic missile early warning system

BMI. See Book manufacturers' institute

BMW (Bayerische motoren werke) See Automobile industry—Germany (Federal Republic)

BOAC. See British overseas airways corporation

BOMEX (Barbados oceanographic and meteorological experiment) See Weather research

BP oil corporation. See British petroleum company

BSA (Birmingham small arms) company. See Motorcycle industry

BAARSLAG, Karl
Peking's other face. Nat R 23:991+ S 10 '71

BAATH Socialist party. See Iraq—Politics and government

BABBITT, Natalie
Good king; story. il Redbook 138:74-6 D '71
Happy endings. Writer 84:12-14+ Je '71
How can we write children's books if we don't know anything about children? il Pub W 200:64-6 Jl 19 '71

BABCOCK and Wilcox company
Live training in nuclear power. V. Louviere. il Nations Bsns 59:18 D '71

BABIGIAN, Haroutun. See Harper, D. jt. auth.

BABOONS
What man owes the baboon. C. N. Barnard. il por Sci Digest 70:36-41 S '71

BABY care. See Infants—Care and hygiene

BABY carriages
Stroller for the baby. il Consumer Bul 54:10-13 Jl '71

BABY cribs. See Cribs (beds)
BABY foods. See Infants food
BABY sitter; story. See Fremlin, C.
BABY sitter who didn't love children; story.
    See Madocs, R.
BABY sitters
    Try a babysitting co-op. L. Liblen. il Par-
      ents Mag 46:32-3+ Jl '71
    What really counts in choosing a baby sit-
      ter. Il Good H 173:222-3 N '71
BABY talk. See Children—Language
BABYLON, N.Y.
    Treat septic-tank wastes separately. R. Mac-
      Callum. il Am City 86:48-9 Ja '71
BABYLONIAN maps. See Maps, Assyro-Baby-
    lonian
BABYLONIAN mythology. See Mythology, As-
    syro-Babylonian
BACCALAUREATE addresses
    Commencement talk. W. F. Buckley, jr. Nat
      R 23:889 Ag 10 '71
    Get lost, class of '71: commencement address-
      es; quotations. Nat R 23:690 Je 29 '71
BACH, Fritz H. See Zoschke, D. C. jt. auth.
BACH, G. L.
    Price stability and full employment too?
      il Harvard Bsns R 49:68-78 S '71
BACH, Johann Sebastian
    From the best Weihnachtsoratorium, the best.
      P. L. Miller. il Am Rec G 37:210 D '70 *
    How slow is fast? W. F. Rickenbacker. Nat
      R 23:772 Jl 13 '71 *
    Johann Sebastian Bach. F. V. Grunfeld.
      il por Horizon 13:58-65 Wint '71 *
    Meanwhile, in nearby Brattleboro. P. L. Mil-
      ler. Am Rec G 37:290 Ja '71 *
    Music to my ears; Bach by Rostropovich.
      I. Kolodin. Sat R 54:60 D 25 '71*
    New research on Bach's Musical offering.
      C. Wolff. bibliog f il Mus Q 57:379-408 Jl
      '71 *
    Saint Matthew sweepstakes, by Philadelphia,
      Stuttgart, Pro Arte. J. Hiemenz. Hi Fi 21:
      MA25 Jl '71 *
    Three North American keyboard virtuosos
      give Bach a young look. C. F. Gilmore.
      Il Hi Fi 21:86-7 S '71 *
    Total victory in the Bach revolution. C. F.
      Gilmore. il Hi Fi 21:67-8 Jl '71 *
BACH, Richard
    Voices: writing Jonathan Livingston Seagull.
      P. S. Nathan. Pub W 200:34 O 18 '71 *
BACH family
    Reviews of records; Bach family: organ
      works. L. Noss. Mus Q 57:163-6 Ja '71
BACH festivals
    Music to my ears; Stuttgart's Bach collegium
      and Gaechinger kantorei at Carnegie Hall.
      I. Kolodin. Sat R 54:18 My 1 '71
BACHARACH, Burt
    Burt Bacharach special. M. Harriton. Dance
      Mag 45:95 My '71 *
BACHE, C. A. and others
    Residues of total mercury and methylmer-
      curic salts in lake trout as a function of
      age. bibliog il Science 172:951-2 My 28 '71
BACHELORS. See Single men
BACHNER, Saul
    Literature in the ghetto school. Clear House
      46:147-50 N '71
BACILLUS subtilis
    Regulation of chromosome replication in ba-
      cillus subtilis: marker frequency analysis
      after amino acid starvation. J. C. Copeland.
      bibliog il Science 172:159-61 Ap 9 '71
    Toxic factors in enzymes used in laundry
      products. R. Dubos. il Science 173:259-60
      Jl 16 '71
BACK
    See also
    Spine
BACK BAY national wildlife refuge. See Wild-
    life sanctuaries—Virginia
BACK RIVER
    Never in anger, by J. L. Briggs. Review
      Natur Hist il 80:74-5 Ja '71. S. A. Freed
BACK yards
    Well-built house; remodeled enclosed yard. J.
      H. Ingersoll. il House B 113:54 S '71
    See also
    City gardens
    Outdoor rooms
BACKACHE
    All about backaches: latest advice from
      a specialist; interview. H. L. Feffer. il
      por U S News 71:74-8 S 20 '71; Same abr.
      Read Digest 99:203-4+ D '71
BACKBONE. See Spine
BACKEN, James J.
    Flexible scheduling: facts, fantasies, and
      fads; address, November 1970. Engl J 60:
      363-8+ Mr '71

BACKES, Ruth. See Lewis, D. O. jt. auth.
BACKGROUND in fiction. See Fiction—Tech-
    nique
BACKGROUND in literature. See Local color
    in literature
BACKHAUS, Wilhelm
    Super great recordings of the century: Back-
      haus. R. Kammerer. por Am Rec G 37:
      430-1 Mr '71 *
BACKPACKING. See Walking
BACKSTER, Cleve
    Do you chat with your plants? M. Pines. il
      McCalls 98:44-5 F '71 *
    Plants have feelings, too. . . L. G. Lawrence.
      il Org Gard & Farm 18:64-7 Ap '71 *
    Startling new research from the man who
      talks to plants. J. Robbins and C. Robbins.
      il pors Nat Wildlife 9:21-4 O '71 *
BACKWARD children. See Slow learning chil-
    dren
BACKYARDS. See Back yards
BACON, E. M.
    Make your woodlands work for you. il
      Camp Mag 43:13-14 Ja '71 *
BACON, Francis
    Francis Bacon: a retrospective and a pre-
      view; with portfolio. J. Russell. por Hori-
      zon 13:78-95 Aut '71 *
    Out of the black hole. R. Hughes. il por
      Time 98:66-7 D 13 '71 *
BACON, James
    (ed) See Davis, S. jr. How Frank Sinatra
      taught me friendship
BACON, Leslie
    Material witness. por Newsweek 77:26-27B
      My 10 '71 *
BACON, Martha
    Death of the white bear; poem. Atlan 227:92
      Mr '71
    Prosody of beasts; poem. Atlan 228:59 O '71
BACON, Roger
    Doctor Mirabilis, by J. Blish. Review
      America 125:269 O 9 '71. J. S. Brusher *
BACON, Steve
    Disaster at Hurricane creek. il Pop Mech
      136:85-9+ O '71
    How to tell whether you're in the right job.
      il Mech Illus 67:39-41+ Ag '71
    I became a bum to understand their prob-
      lems. il pors Sci Digest 69:40-7 My '71
    Now they're probing the hidden depths of
      your mind. il Pop Mech 136:62-5+ Ag '71
    They throw money away on purpose. il
      Sci Digest 69:39-44 F '71
BACON, W. Stevenson
    How they'll pump energy from the sea. il
      Pop Sci 198:38 Mr '71
BACOT, H. Parrott, and Lambdin, B. B.
    Nineteenth-century silver in Natchez. il An-
      tiques 99:412-17 Mr '71
BACTERIA
    Bacterial differentiation; cell cycle of
      caulobacter. L. Shapiro and others. bib-
      liog il Science 173:884-92 S 3 '71
    See also
    Bacillus subtilis
    Clostridium botulinum
    Escherichia coli
    Mycobacterium
    Pseudomonas
                        Culture
    Coevolution of escherichia coli and bacte-
      riophages in chemostat culture. M. T.
      Horne; reply with rejoinder. M. J. B. Payn-
      ter and H. R. Bungay, 3d. bibliog Science
      172:405 Ap 23 '71
    Cultivation of borrelia hermsi. R. Kelly. bib-
      liog il Science 173:443-4 Jl 30 '71
    Pseudomonas aeruginosa: growth in distilled
      water from hospitals. M. S. Favero and
      others. bibliog il Science 173:836-8 Ag 27
      '71
BACTERIA, Fossil. See Micropaleontology
BACTERIA, Pathogenic
    Cultivation of borrelia hermsi. R. Kelly. bib-
      liog il Science 173:443-4 Jl 30 '71
    Lead suppression of mouse resistance to
      salmonella typhimurium. F. E. Hemphill
      and others. bibliog il Science 172:1031-2 Je
      4 '71
BACTERIA, Photosynthetic
    Interchangeability of phosphorylation coup-
      ling factors in photosynthetic and respira-
      tory energy conversion. B. A. Melandri and
      others. bibliog il Science 174:514-16 O 29 '71
BACTERIAL cells
    See also
    Cell division (bacteriology)
BACTERIAL degradation. See Degradation
    (biology)
BACTERIAL differentiation. See Differentia-
    tion (biology)
BACTERIAL endotoxins. See Toxins and anti-
    toxins

BACTERIAL proteins
Periplasmic galactose binding protein of escherichia coli. H. M. Kalckar. bibliog il Science 174:557-65 N 5 '71
BACTERIAL viruses. See Bacteriophage
BACTERIOLOGY
See also
Filters and filtration (bacteriology)
Toxins and antitoxins
BACTERIOPHAGE
Bacteriophage and the toxigenicity of clostridium botulinum type C. M. W. Eklund and others. bibliog il Science 172:480-2 Ap 30 '71
Coevolution of escherichia coli and bacteriophages in chemostat culture. M. T. Horne; reply with rejoinder. M. J. B. Paynter and H. R. Bungay, 3d. bibliog Science 172:405 Ap 23 '71
Genetics: a friendly virus. il Newsweek 78:109 O 25 '71
Transfer of bacterial genes to human cells. Sci N 100:276 O 23 '71
BACTERIURIA. See Kidneys—Diseases
BADA, Jeffrey L. and others
Marine sediments: dating by the racemization of amino acids. bibliog il Science 170:730-2; 172:503 N 13 '70, Ap 30 '71
BADASH, Lawrence
Importance of being Ernest Rutherford. Science 173:873 S 3 '71
BADEN-BADEN
Baden-Baden: a cure for what ails you. M. Gough. House B 113:21+ Mr '71
Getting soothed on the Oos. H. Sutton. il Sat R 54:37-9 Ja 30 '71
Soaking therapy in Germany's great, happy elegant spa. D. Messinesi. Vogue 158:111+ Ag 15 '71
BADER, Barbara
Barbara Bader's column. Wilson Lib Bul 46:227, 322-3, 446-7+ N '71-Ja '72
BADGERS
No one badgers the badger. J. D. Scott. il Nat Wildlife 9:18-20 F '71
BADHAM, Michael
Soothing lethargy. il Yachting 129:64+ F '71
BADMINTON (game)
What kind of racket is this? Houston badminton tournament. D. Levin. Sports Illus 35:82-4 N 22 '71
BAER, Betty
Safe and lovable toys. il por Am Home 74:94-5+ S '71
BAEZ, Joan
Baez on film. C. E. Fager. Chr Cent 88:206 F 10 '71
Peace of mind. por Look 35:23 Jl 27 '71
When I was 17; interview. ed. by B. Kevles. pors Seventeen 30:130+ O '71
about
Changing life of Joan Baez. K. D. Fury. il Redbook 137:77-9+ My '71 *
BAFFIN ISLAND
High adventure in high latitudes. J. McEachern. il por Motor B & S 128:70-3+ S '71
BAGA (native race) See Guinea—Native races
BAGELS. See Bread
BAGG, Robert
Playing the wheel in Juan; poem. Atlan 228:71 N '71
BAGG, Terry R.
Pavlov; poem. Poetry 117:231 Ja '71
BAGGAGE. See Luggage
BAGLEY, Richard
Perfect anchorage. Yachting 130:55+ Ag '71
BAHAISM
Baha'is report increased assemblies doubling of membership in the U.S. Chr Cent 88:616 My 19 '71
BAHAMA ISLANDS
See also
Architecture, Domestic—Bahama Islands
Bimini Islands
Fishing—Bahama Islands
Paleontology—Bahama Islands
Seaside resorts—Bahama Islands
Description and travel
Bahamas bound; with editorial comment. A. Trammell. il Flying 89:4, 40-5+ N '71
BAHAMAS 500 race. See Motor boat racing
BAHIA (city) See Salvador, Brazil
BAHR, Edith-Jane
Just call me honey; story. Ladies Home J 88:127 My '71
Miss Witherspoon regrets; story. Ladies Home J 88:108-9 O '71

BAHR, Gunter F. See Golomb, H. M. jt. auth.
BAHREIN
See also
United Nations—Bahrein
BAIKAL, LAKE
Even in Siberia it's the age of ecology. R. Richardson. il por Am For 77:24-7+ Mr '71
Our far-flung correspondents; pollution. M. I. Goldman. New Yorker 47:58-66 Je 19 '71
Saving Lake Baikal. Newsweek 78:52+ N 22 '71
BAIL
Fair trial for Angela Davis? J. H. Skolnick and S. A. Brick. por Nation 213:48-9 Jl 19 '71
Pretrial and nontrial in the lower criminal courts. R. M. Pious. bibliog f Cur Hist 61:20-6+ Jl '71
BAILEY, Anthony
Everything you always wanted to know about the dodo. il Horizon 13:92-3 Spr '71
Letter from Athens. New Yorker 47:130+ N 20 '71
Profiles: Stonington. Conn. New Yorker 47:36-44+ Jl 24; 38-52+ Jl 31 '71
BAILEY, Arila S.
Christmas in the Berkshires. il Horticulture 49:40-1 D '71
BAILEY, Bob
Lost men of Muldoon Canyon. J. Neary. il pors Life 70:50D-50F+ Mr 19 '71 *
BAILEY, Francis Lee
F. Lee Bailey's The defense never rests; excerpt from The defense never rests; ed. by H. Aronson. il pors Ladies Home J 88:93-5+ O '71; 122-3+ N '71
about
Bailey's breakthrough. Newsweek 78:43 S 27 '71 *
Days in court. A. Cooper. il por Newsweek 78:96+ D 20 '71 *
Hef Lee Bailey. Newsweek 79:50 Ja 3 '72 *
BAILEY, J. Martyn
Jupiter: its captured satellites. bibliog il Science 173:812-13 Ag 27 '71
BAILEY, John T.
Case for a custom job too well done. il Radio-Electr 42:54 N '71
How to locate buried-conductor faults. il Electr World 85:42+ Mr '71
Using silicon diode rectifiers as power resistors. il Electr World 85:38+ My '71
BAILEY, Peter
Getting it together at the Point. il Ebony 27:136+ D '71
Lady takes charge. il pors Ebony 27:156-8+ N '71
Miracle worker on campus. il pors Ebony 26:80-1+ S '71
BAIN, Helen Pate
After all. Todays Ed 60:80 Mr '71
Some misgivings about teacher accountability. por Parents Mag 46:40 Mr '71
What do you want from NEA? il por Todays Ed 60:26-9+ Ja '71
BAIN, Romany
(ed) See Burton, R. Our marriage after 7 years
(ed) See Taylor, E. Our marriage after 7 years
BAINBRIDGE, John
Profiles: P. R. Sawyer, police constable. por New Yorker 47:40-50+ Ag 14 '71
BAINTON family
Bainton coat-of-arms. H. K. Eilers. il Hobbies 75:152-3 F '71
BAIRD, Pat
Grand Funk Railroad; con. il Sr Schol 99:23-4 S 27 '71
Poco's comin' up fast. il Sr Schol 98:26 My 17 '71
BAIRD, Ron
Victoria's hanging baskets. il Horticulture 49:24 Jl '71
BAIT
Supply your own natural bait. B. J. Minsky. il Field & S 76:20+ D '71
What to feed an ice hole. H. G. Tapply. il Field & S 75:60 Ja '71
You never know when you might need a mullet. C. Phinizy. il pors Sports Illus 34:54-6+ Ap 5 '71
See also
Earthworms
Grasshoppers
Minnows
BAITS, Poison. See Poison baits
BAJA CALIFORNIA. See California, Lower
BAKAL, Carl
Failure of federal gun control. il Sat R 54:12-15+ Jl 3 '71
BAKALIS, Michael J.
Rocking the boat. il por Newsweek 78:81 D 6 '71 *

BAKER, Augusta
C. L. Skinner award goes to Augusta Baker. por Library J 96:3802 N 15 '71 *
BAKER, Carl G.
Cancer conquest program; letter. Science 174:980-1 D 3 '71
BAKER, D. James, Jr
Density gradients in a rotating stratified fluid: experimental evidence for a new stability. bibliog il Science 172:1029-31 Je 4 '71
BAKER, Dwight L.
Bible prophecy in the prophets' city. Chr Today 15:29-30 Jl 16 '71
BAKER, E. M. 3d, and others
Ascorbate sulfate: a urinary metabolite of ascorbic acid in man. bibliog il Science 173:826-7 Ag 27 '71
BAKER, Elizabeth C.
Critics choice: Daniel Buren. Art N 70:25+ Mr '71
Frank Stella, revival and relief. il Art N 70:34-5+ N '71
Glass of fashion and the mold of form. il Art N 70:40-1+ Ap '71
Los Angeles, 1971. il Art N 70:27-39 S '71
BAKER, George L.
Game never stops. il Nation 213:114-16 Ag 16 '71
BAKER, Ginger
Rock family affair. il por Life 71:52 S 24 '71 *
BAKER, Henry G.
Baker's dozen of heroic vitalists; address, June 4, 1971. Vital Speeches 37:586-92 Jl 15 '71
BAKER, Henry J. Jr, and others
Neuronal GM₁ gangliosidosis in a Siamese cat with β-galactosidase deficiency. bibliog il Science 174:838-9 N 19 '71
BAKER, Howard Henry, 1925-
Excerpt from address, February 9, 1971. Cong Digest 50:108+ Ap '71
TV tapes as research materials; with text of bill. Am Lib 2:951-2 O '71

about

Senator Baker to head committee on U.N. environment conference. Dept State Bul 64:333 Mr 15 '71 *
BAKER, James
Making of a civic space. il Arch Forum 135:40-5 N '71
BAKER, Luther G. Jr
Male role in home economics. Ed Digest 37:48-9 D '71
BAKER, Richard H. and others
Linkage group-chromosome correlation in culex tritaeniorhynchus. bibliog il Science 171:585-7 F 12 '71
BAKER, Robert Gene
Reflections on the way to jail. H. Sidey. il pors Time 97:22-3 Ja 25 '71 *
BAKER, Russell
Observing the observer: the serene Russell Baker; interview, ed. by S. Nirenberg. House B 113:46-8 S '71
Sayings of poor Russell. il Harper 244:64-5 Ja '72
What boys don't know about girls, and why. il McCalls 98:49+ Je '71

about

Daily sanity. R. Z. Sheppard. por Time 99:63 Ja 17 '72 *
BAKER, Samm Sinclair. See Stillman, I. M. jt. auth.
BAKER, Tom
Tom Baker. il pors Look 35:60-2 O 19 '71 *
BAKER, Willis M.
Adventures in retirement. il pors Am For 77:28-31+ Je: 38-9+ Ag: 36-9+ S '71
BAKERS and bakeries
How to make money in your spare time; Christmas cakes. J. Kuh. il Ladies Home J 88:115 D '71
See also
American bakeries company
ITT Continental baking company
BAKERSFIELD fuel and gas championship race. See Drag racing
BAKING
Oven dinners: easy, economical cooking at its best, with recipes. Z. Coulson. il Good H 174:80-96 Ja '72
See also
Bread
Cake
Cookies
Crackers
Gingerbread
Ovens
Pastry
Pie

BAKING soda. See Sodium bicarbonate
BAKKER, Robert T.
Swamp-dweller or landlubber? brontosaurus. il Sci N 99:79 Ja 30 '71 *
BAKSHIAN, Aram, Jr
Film chronicle (title varies) Nat R 23:489-90 My 4 '71
Lovely battle: Nat R 23:1128-9 O 8 '71
BALAGURA, Saul. See Devenport, L. D. jt. auth.
BALAKIAN, Anna
Andre Breton, by A. Balakian. Review
Sat R 54:23 My 29 '71. L. S. Roudiez *
BALANCE meters, Stereophonic. See Stereophonic sound systems—Equipment
BALANCE of nature. See Ecology
BALANCE of payments
Bankers try to head off a crisis. il Bsns W p38 Ap 10 '71
Building walls abroad; the unsettled trading world. il Time 98:35-6 N 1 '71
Capital is something that doesn't love a wall. S. Rose. il Fortune 83:100-3+ F '71
Connally's blunt talk on trade and the dollar; excerpts from address, November 16, 1971. J. B. Connally, jr. por U S News 71:88-9 N 29 '71
Deadlock over the dollar; with editorial comment. il Bsns W p82-6+, 144 S 25 '71
Dollar arrogance. Nation 212:356-7 Mr 22 '71
Dollar at bay. Duns 97:104 Je '71
Dollar crisis: floating toward reform? il Time 97:85-6+ My 17 '71
Dollar goes begging. il Newsweek 77:75-7 My 17 '71
Dollar's dilemma. Time 97:74 Ap 19 '71
Exchanges in turmoil. H. C. Wallich. Newsweek 77:88 My 17 '71
Military spending & dollars abroad. R. W. Stevens. il Nation 213:554-7 N 29 '71
Money: the dangers of the U.S. hard line. il por Time 98:34-5 S 27 '71
Mutual responsibility for maintaining a stable monetary system; address, May 28, 1971. J. B. Connally. Dept State Bul 65:42-6 Jl 12 '71; Excerpts with title Tough talk to U.S. Allies on trade, defense. U S News 70:51-3 Je 14 '71
New troubles for the dollar? J. Ross-Skinner. il Duns 97:49-51 Mr '71
Nixon's power play. R. B. Du Boff. Commonweal 95:86-7 O 22 '71
Plight of the dollar: now another setback. U S News 70:21 My 31 '71
Revolt against the dollar. Life 70:32 My 21 '71
Saga of the dollar. New Repub 164:7 My 22 '71; Reply with rejoinder. B. McCrea. 165:32-3 Jl 3 '71
Still a stalemate; International banking conference. il Newsweek 77:82 Je 7 '71
Sunny side of the deficit. il Forbes 109:24-9 Ja 1 '72
Things are so bad, they're good. por Forbes 107:50-1 Je 1 '71
Tough talk to U.S. allies on trade, defense; excerpts from address, May 28, 1971. J. B. Connally. il pors U S News 70:51-3 Je 14 '71
Wall Street:
Rising above the dollar. C. Morgello. il Newsweek 77:80 My 10 '71
Why dollars piled up in Europe. il Bsns W p 116-17 My 15 '71
World inflation and the international payments system; address, January 14, 1971. P. A. Volcker. Dept State Bul 64:212-18 F 15 '71
See also
Balance of trade
BALANCE of power
Mysterious mushiness; Winston Churchill's view on American power vs. Soviet power. S. Alsop. Newsweek 77:88 My 31 '71
New balance of power in Asia and the Pacific. H. Bull. For Affairs 49:669-81 Jl '71
Our new five-cornered world. il Life 71:4 Ag 6 '71
Our strategic-arms advantage is fading fast. C. J. V. Murphy. Read Digest 98:94-8 F '71
Path to Peking; with editorial comment. W. C. McWilliams. Commonweal 94:395-397-8 Ag 6 '71
Strategic balance; the future of freedom: address, April 15, 1971. H. M. Jackson. Vital Speeches 37:482-5 Je 1 '71
U.S. superiority has ended; summary of statement by Citizens' panel on defense. il U S News 70:49-50+ Ap 5 '71
Whose serve? J. Burnham. Nat R 23:469 My 4 '71
Will success sober Moscow? il Newsweek 78:30-1 N 1 '71
See also
World politics

BALANCE of trade
Campaign to right the trade balance. il **Bsns**
W p28-9 **Ag** 21 '71
General electric chairman Fred Borch lays it
on the line; address. F. Borch. por Forbes
108:27-8+ N 15 '71
Our strange new hard line on trade. S. Rose.
il Fortune 84:136-9+ N '71
Sounding the alarm; testimony of M. Stans.
il Newsweek 78:57-8 Ag 9 '71
Tough, risky U.S. trade offensive. il News-
week 77:81 Je 7 '71
Trade surplus that vanished. il Fortune 84:
22 Ag '71
Two views of US technology and world
trade. S. M. Hein. pors Phys Today 24:69-
70 D '71
U.S. gains an edge. il Bsns W p 14-16 D
25 '71
BALANCHINE, George
Choreographic partners; interview. New
Yorker 47:28-30 My 22 '71
about
Effervescent foolery. J. T. Elson. Time 97:66
Je 28 '71 *
BALAND, Timothy
(tr) See Hernandez, M. To smile with the
joyful sadness of the olive tree
BALASURIYA, Tissa
Insurrection in Ceylon. Commonweal 94:300-1
Je 11 '71
BALBOA, Calif.
Balboa and the fun zone. T. H. Garver. il
Art in Am 59:58-67 S '71
BALCANOFF, Eugene J.
Psychiatrist in a superior court setting.
bibliog Ment Hy 55:45-50 Ja '71
BALD eagles. See Eagles
BALDANI, Ruza
Ruza; interview, ed. by H. E. Phillips. por
Opera N 35:16 F 6 '71
BALDNESS
How to use your head when your hair starts
falling out; hair loss in women. J. Snyder.
il Todays Health 49:32-4+ Jl '71
Shiny pate need not mean an indoor sum-
mer; wigless ways to cover up. Bsns W
p85 Je 26 '71
BALDWIN, C. Stephen
Bangla Desh: on the brink of survival. il
Sat R 54:32-3+ N 6 '71
BALDWIN, Carl R.
Courbet and the column. il Art N 70:36-8 My
'71
It floats. il Art N 70:36-7+ N '71
P.M. at 100. il Art N 70:26-8+ D '71
BALDWIN, Carson, Jr
Green gold from the forest. il Am For 77:
40-3 Ap '71
BALDWIN, E. Colin
Turning an art into science. il por Nations
Bsns 59:88-9 Ja '71
BALDWIN, Frank Stephen
Abacus, American style. J. Sheridan. il pors
Nations Bsns 59:76-7 Ja '71 *
BALDWIN, G. S. and Carnegie, P. R.
Specific enzymic methylation of an arginine
in the experimental allergic encephalo-
myelitis protein from human myelin. bib-
liog il Science 171:579-81 F 12 '71
BALDWIN, Hanson Weightman
Keys to the Pacific. Read Digest 99:164-5
D '71
Vietnam: the facts and the falsehoods. Read
Digest 99:211-12+ N '71
BALDWIN, James
Rap on race; excerpts. pors McCalls 98:84-
5+ Je '71
about
Black literature revisited: Sonny's blues. E.
R. Ognibene. Engl J 60:36-7 Ja '71 *
How Margaret Mead and James Baldwin got
together for A rap on race. B. A. Bannon.
pors Pub W 199:104-5 My 31 '71 *
Muffled voices. G. Wolff. pors Newsweek 77:
100+ My 24 '71 *
Parting shots: after years of futility Baldwin
explodes again. W. A. McWhirter. por Life
71:63 Jl 30 '71 *
Rap on race: how James Baldwin and I
talked a book. M. Mead. il por Redbook
137:70-2+ S '71 *
BALDWIN, Nancy
Bird feeders. il Ceram Mo 19:16-20 O '71
BALDWIN, Ralph
Mr Goshen's glory week. L. Simross. Sports
Illus 35:48-9 Jl 19 '71 *
BALDWIN, William
Decorator speaks his mind. See issues of
House & garden incorporating Living for
young homemakers

about
One-room living with Billy Baldwin. C.
Kriebel. il por Harp Baz 105:146 N '71 *
BALDWIN HILLS DAM failure. See Dams—
Failures
BALDWIN-Montrose chemical company
DDT stopped, suit dropped. E. P. Jones.
Science 173:38 Jl 2 '71
BALEARIC ISLANDS
See also
Ibiza (island)
BALED hay. See Hay
BALFOUR, Robert Arthur, 2d baron Riverdale.
See Riverdale, R. A. B.
BALI
Bali: the last Eden. D. Butwin. il Sat R 54:
40-1 O 23 '71
Java, Bali: the exotic isles. M. Litton. il
Holiday 49:42-7+ Jl '71
BALI company
Fight vandals with light. il Am City 86:118 My
'71
BALIN, Robert P.
[Electronics quiz] (cont) il Pop Electr 34:50+
Mr '71
BALINT, Nicholas G.
(comp) As others see us. See issues of Satur-
day review
(comp) Letters to the world's editors. See is-
sues of Saturday review
BALKAN PENINSULA
Changing the old script. il Time 98:42+ N 29
'71
BALKAN STATES
See also
Bosnia and Herzegovina
BALL, C. R. Jr
VR12 voltage regulator. il Pop Electr 34:65-
70+ Ap '71
BALL, C. W.
Add this sander table to your faceplate
lathe. il Pop Mech 136:143 Jl '71
BALL, Charles E. and Porter, Phil
Milk pays the bills, beef makes the profit.
il Farm J 95:18-19+ D '71
BALL, Colleen
Train; poem Seventeen 31:90 Ja '72
BALL, Donald W.
Cats & dogs & people. il Trans-Action 8:44-7
F '71
BALL, Edward
Break in Florida's nine-year strike. por
Bsns W p 18 D 25 '71 *
Why strikers fear Ed Ball. por Bsns W p 102
O 16 '71 *
BALL, Fred
Herbert Sanders. il por Ceram Mo 19:14-17 N
'71
Primitive pottery at Red Dog. il Ceram Mo
19:29-32 My '71
BALL, George W.
[Column] See issues of Newsweek
Exit the cold warrior? por Newsweek 77:45
F 8 '71
In defense of the military. Newsweek 78:48
Jl 5 '71; Same abr. with title Let's get off
our soldiers' backs! Read Digest 99:155-6 O
'71
Packing the trunks for China. il Newsweek
78:53+ S 27 '71
Voices of spring. por Newsweek 77:43 Mr 1
'71
about
20-20 hindsight; Vietnamese war stance. New
Repub 164:9 Ap 17 '71 *
BALL, Lucille
Lucille Ball, the star that never sets; inter-
view, ed. by L. Bergquist. pors Look 35:
54-7+ S 7 '71
about
My mother, Lucille Ball; interview, ed. by
J. N. Bell. D. Arnaz, jr. il pors Good H
172:14+ Mr '71 *
BALL, Michael
Veteran comes home, to limbo. C. Leinster.
il pors Life 70:28-38 Ap 16 '71 *
BALL, Robert
Conservatism's new British accent. il For-
tune 83:80-3+ Ap '71
Secret life of Hoffmann-LaRoche. il Fortune
84:130-5+ Ag '71
BALL, Robert M.
Social security. Todays Ed 60:24-6 Ap '71
BALL, Samuel. See Bogatz, G. A. jt. auth.
BALL, William, and Tronick, Edward
Infant responses to impending collision: op-
tical and real. bibliog il Science 171:818-20
F 26 '71
BALL
See also
Handball

BALL lightning. See Lightning
BALLAD, Richard
(ed) See Downs, H. Hugh Downs to Frank McGee: the big switch on the Today show
(ed) See McGee, F. Hugh Downs to Frank McGee: the big switch on the Today show
BALLADS, American
See also
Folk songs, American
BALLARD, Holley
Second thoughts on the subject of mother; story. Redbook 137:62-3 Jl '71
BALLENGER, Martha D.
Physician's assistants and the licensing issue. Mo Labor R 94:62-3 Ap '71
BALLENTINE, Leslie E.
Formalism is not the interpretation. por Phys Today 24:36-8 Ap '71
BALLER, William, and Lower, Earl
Informative feedback: an educational controversy. bibliog Sch & Soc 99:417-19 N '71
BALLET
Ballet for the man who enjoys Wallace Stevens. I. Howe. Harper 242:102-6+ My '71
Ballet unlimited. H. Saal. il por Newsweek 77:48+ F 8 '71
Béjart: the lingering impact. R. Philp. il Dance Mag 45:26-8 Ap '71
Dance. J. Maskey. See issues of High fidelity and Musical America
Dance: interview, ed. by E. Miller. G. Kirkland. por Seventeen 30:138 Ag '71
Encounter with an athlete. M. Kram. il pors Sports Illus 35:92-4+ S 27 '71
From the wonderful folk who gave you the Swan queen: rock-ballet as synthesis of forms. S. W. McDermott. il Dance Mag 45:38-45+ O '71
International book of ballet, by P. Brinson and C. Crisp. Review
　Dance Mag 45:96 O '71. M. Marks
Is an opera house a home? Afterthoughts on the Stuttgart ballet's New York season. D. Hering. il Dance Mag 45:57-63 Jl '71
Presstime news. See issues of Dance magazine
Reviews. See issues of Dance magazine
Shocks and ceremonies; New York programs. il Time 97:72 F 8 '71
World of dance. W. Terry. See issues of Saturday review
See also
Choreography
Moving pictures—Dance films
Television programs—Dance programs

History
Kchessinska at ninety-nine. O. Maynard. il pors Dance Mag 45:22-4 N '71
Stravinsky and the natures of ballet and opera. G. Martin. Yale R 61:193-206 D '71
Les sylphides. O. Maynard. il por Dance Mag 45:43-66 D '71

Study and teaching
Classes in classical ballet; excerpt, tr. by O. Briansky. A. Messerer. il pors Dance Mag 46:40-5 Ja '72 (to be cont)
In Paris and many other places it's Grantzeva; interview, ed. by N. M. Stoop. T. Grantzeva. il pors Dance Mag 45:26-31 Jl '71
Markova on mime. W. Terry. il por Sat R 54:40-1 Ag 28 '71

Austria
Vienna state opera ballet, Blossom music center, Cleveland. B. Anthony. Dance Mag 45:94-5 O '71

Cambodia
Classical Khmer ballet of Cambodia, Brooklyn academy of music, NYC. L. Pastore. Dance Mag 45:88 D '71
Dance: at the Brooklyn academy of music. N. Goldner. Nation 213:507-9 N 15 '71
Hands of time; Classical Khmer ballet at the Brooklyn academy of music. H. Saal. il Newsweek 78:97 N 1 '71

Canada
Les grands ballets canadiens in Hip and straight and Tommy, New York city center. D. Hering. il Dance Mag 45:79-81 Je '71
Les grands ballets canadiens: Tommy & Hip and straight, New York city center. J. Anderson. Dance Mag 45:90-1 N '71
Idea, image and purpose: ballet in Canada today; with editorial comment. O. Maynard. il Dance Mag 45:31, 32-65+ Ap '71

Musical events; Tommy, presented by Les grands ballets canadiens at the City center. W. Sargeant. New Yorker 47:102 Ap 24 '71
Purpose: Ludmilla Chiriaeff and Les grands ballets canadiens. O. Maynard. il por Dance Mag 45:56-65 Ap '71
See also
National ballet of Canada
Royal Winnipeg ballet

Cuba
Alicia Alonso, the flower of Cuba. M. Horosko. il pors Dance Mag 45:43-58 Ag '71
See also
Ballet nacional de Cuba

France
World of dance; Ballet théâtre contemporain. W. Terry. il Sat R 54:59 S 18 '71

Great Britain
Bosman's follies. S. W. McDermott. il pors Dance Mag 45:32-7 My '71

Mexico
World of dance. W. Terry. il Sat R 54:59+ S 18 '71
See also
Ballet clásico 70 (ballet company)

Netherlands
See also
Netherlands dance theater

Russia
In the shadow of Russian tradition: interview, ed. by M. Horosko. F. Doubrovska. il pors Dance Mag 45:40-2 F '71
In the shadow of Russian tradition: interview, ed. by M. Horosko. A. Federova. il pors Dance Mag 45:24-8 My '71
Presence of Russian dance. il Dance Mag 45:42-75 N '71

Sweden
Dance in Sweden; Royal Swedish ballet, Cramér ballet company. L. Svedin. il Dance Mag 45:50-61 My '71

United States
Lucia Chase: first lady of American ballet. O. Maynard. il pors Dance Mag 45:28-33 Ag '71
BALLET, Photography of. See Photography of dancing
BALLET, Underwater. See Swimming, Synchronized
BALLET, Water. See Swimming, Synchronized
BALLET clásico 70 (ballet company)
Doña Amalia's at it again. D. Hering. il por Dance Mag 45:47-9 Je '71
BALLET companies
Ballet of the 20th century, NY city center. J. Anderson. Dance Mag 46:76+ Ja '72
Ballet West, Aspen, Colorado. A. Barzel. Dance Mag 45:84 S '71
Ballet West off to Europe. il Dance Mag 45:26 Je '71
Béjart; repertoire of Ballet of the twentieth century. New Yorker 46:23-5 F 6 '71
Dance; Béjart's Ballet of the 20th century. N. Goldner. Nation 212:348-9 Mr 15 '71
Dance largess; M. Béjart's Ballet of the 20th century W. Terry. il Sat R 54:39 F 20 '71
Dance; Rose for Emily. J. Maskey. il Hi Fi 21:MA11+ My '71
Downtown ballet company, New York university, Hall of fame playhouse. L. Pastore. Dance Mag 46:26 Ja '72
Garden state ballet, Symphony hall, Newark, N.J. J. Gale. Dance Mag 45:25+ Je '71
Musical events; Maurice Béjart's ballet of the twentieth century all-Stravinsky program at the City center of music and drama. W. Sargeant. New Yorker 47:133-4 D 4 '71
Musical events; Maurice Béjart's Ballet of the twentieth century at the Brooklyn academy of music. W. Sargeant. New Yorker 46:93 F 6 '71
Niagara ballet, Auditorium, Rochester, NY. A. Barzel. Dance Mag 45:80 Jl '71
St Louis civic ballet, John Burroughs school, St Louis. D. Hering. Dance Mag 45:80 Jl '71
Salt Lake City is on its toes; Ballet West. V. Louviere. il Nations Bsns 59:15 Ag '71
See also
American ballet company
American ballet theatre
Australian ballet company
Ballet nacional de Cuba
Boston ballet company
City center Joffrey ballet
Dance theater of Harlem
Eglevsky ballet company
New York city ballet
Pennsylvania ballet

BALLET dancers. See Dancers
BALLET exercises. See Exercise
BALLET festivals. See Dance festivals
BALLET music
　Dancer's composer; with comments by bal
　lerinas. W. Terry. il Sat R 54:42-3+ My 29
　'71
　　See also
　Phonograph records—Ballet music
BALLET nacional de Cuba
　Pilgrimage to Montreal; Alicia Alonso and
　Ballet nacional de Cuba. G. Fitzgerald. il
　por Dance Mag 45:8 Ag '71
BALLET of the twentieth century (organiza
　tion) See Ballet companies
BALLET théâtre contemporain. See Ballet
　—France
BALLET West (dance company) See Ballet
　companies
BALLETS
　Ballet for the man who enjoys Wallace
　Stevens. I. Howe. Harper 242:102-6+ My
　'71
Choreographies
　See Choreography

Criticisms
Abyss
　Dance Mag 45:93 My '71
　Hi Fi 21:MA9 Jl '71
Astarte
　Dance Mag il 45:38-45+ O '71
Carmen
　Hi Fi 21:MA9 S '71
　New Yorker 47:91 My 8 '71
　Newsweek il 77:121 My 10 '71
　Opera N 35:28 Je 12 '71
　Time il 97:70 My 10 '71
Concert
　Nation 214:58+ Ja 10 '72
　Sat R il 55:8 Ja 1 '72
　Time 98:55 D 20 '71
Concerto for jazz band and orchestra
　New Yorker 47:140 My 15 '71
Consort
　Hi Fi 21:MA18 Mr '71
Deaths and entrances
　Hi Fi 21:MA6 Ja '71
Don Quixote
　Nation 212:252 F 22 '71
Eugene Onegin
　Life il 70:10 My 21 '71
　New Yorker 47:110 My 1 '71
　Sat R il 54:41 My 8 '71
Every soul is a circus
　Hi Fi 21:MA6-7 Ja '71
Four last songs
　Nation 212:251-2 F 22 '71
Goldberg variations
　Hi Fi il 21:MA10 O '71
　Nation 213:28-9 Jl 5 '71
　New Yorker 47:121 Je 5 '71
　Newsweek 77:72 Je 7 '71
　Sat R il 54:32 Jl 3 '71
　Time il 97:69 Je 21 '71
Kettentanz
　Nation 213:635 D 13 '71
Letter to the world
　Hi Fi 21:MA6-7 Ja '71
Mary Lou's Mass
　Newsweek 78:67 D 20 '71
Mendelssohn symphony
　Hi Fi 21:MA13 N '71
Mingus dancers
　Time 98:95 N 8 '71
Miraculous mandarin
　Hi Fi 21:MA7+ N '71
Mutations
　Dance Mag il 45:55-9 F '71
Nijinsky: Clown of God
　Dance Mag il 45:34-41 D '71
Nutcracker
　Sat R il 54:35 Ja 16 '71
Objects
　Hi Fi 21:MA19 Mr '71
Octandre
　Hi Fi 21:MA10 O '71
On the move
　Newsweek il 77:81 Ja 25 '71
PAMTGG
　Newsweek il 77:95 Je 28 '71
　Time 97:66 Je 28 '71
Poem forgotten
　Hi Fi 21:MA18 Mr '71
Poème de l'extase
　Dance Mag 45:86 S '71
　Hi Fi il 21:MA11 O '71
　Newsweek il 78:81 Ag 2 '71
　Sat R il 54:43 S 4 '71
　Time 98:51 Ag 2 '71
Poppy
　Dance Mag 45:102 N '71
Reflections
　Dance Mag 45:92 My '71
　Hi Fi 21:MA9 Jl '71

River
　Newsweek 78:89 Jl 12 '71
　Sat R il 54:65 S 25 '71
Romance
　Nation 212:636-7 My 17 '71
Romeo and Juliet
　Hi Fi il 21:MA7 N '71
　New Yorker 47:110 My 1 '71
　Sat R il 54:65 S 25 '71
Rose for Miss Emily
　Hi Fi 21:MA11+ My '71
　New Yorker 46:79 Ja 9 '71
Signals
　Hi Fi 21:MA19 Mr '71
Square dance
　Dance Mag 45:93 My '71
　Hi Fi 21:MA9 Jl '71
　Sat R 54:30 Ap 10 '71
Still point
　Hi Fi 21:MA7 Ja '71
Suite no. 3
　Hi Fi 21:MA18 Mr '71
　Sat R 54:35 Ja 16 '71
Les sylphides
　Dance Mag il por 45:43-66 D '71
Tommy
　Dance Mag 45:38-45+ O '71
　Dance Mag 45:90-1 N '71
　New Yorker 47:102 Ap 24 '71
Trinity
　Dance Mag il 45:38-45+ O '71
　Hi Fi 21:MA7 Ja '71
Les vainqueurs
　Opera N 35:31 Ap 3 '71
Valentine
　Dance Mag 45:93 My '71
Weewis
　Dance Mag il 46:38-9+ Ja '72
　Time il 98:95 N 8 '71

Photographs
Astarte. H. Migdoll. Horizon 13:19-26 Spr '71

Production and direction
　See Dance production
BALLEW, Kenyon F.
　Ballew raid. J. Mann. New Repub 165:12-13
　S 11 '71 *
BALLIETT, Whitney
　Jazz records. New Yorker 47:160-6+ N 6 '71
　Musical events (cont) New Yorker 47:76+
　Jl 17 '71
　Profiles; M. Gordon and B. Josephson; night
　club owners. pors New Yorker 47:50-6+ O 9
　'71
　Profiles; Modern jazz quartet. New Yorker
　47:62-4+ N 20 '71
　Reporter at large. New Yorker 47:42-4+
　My 29; 40-5 D 25 '71
BALLISTIC missile early warning system
　Early warning satellites seen operational. P.
　J. Klass. il Aviation W 95:18-20 S 20 '71
　Now, instant warning if U.S. is attacked. il
　U S News 71:108-9 N 15 '71
　Satellites provide early warning of ICBMs.
　Aviation W 95:14 O 25 '71
　Warning satellite achieves successful orbit.
　Aviation W 94:23 Je 28 '71
Un BALLO in maschera; opera. See Verdi, G.
BALLOON ascensions
　Across Grand Canyon in a basket. il Life 71:
　88-9 N 26 '71
Accidents
　Horrifying fall from a balloon; death of S.
　Allione. il Life 71:28-9 Ag 6 '71
BALLOON astronomy. See Balloons—Research
　use
BALLOONS
　Hot air balloons go to work; use in aerial
　photography. il Mech Illus 68:56 Ja '72
　　See also
　Balloon ascensions

Research use
　Balloons used in aerosat tests. P. J. Klass.
　il Aviation W 94:56-9 Je 21 '71
　Instrumentation balloons carry electronic pay
　loads. L. G. Lawrence. il Electr World
　86:13-15 D '71
　News from the world of space exploration;
　Stratoscope II. Space World H-9-93:45 S
　'71
　Telescope in a balloon; how it works; Strato
　scope II. il Space World H-11-95:4-10 N '71
BALLOT
　　See also
　Suffrage

BALLPARKS. See Stadiums

BALLROOM dancing. See Dancing

BALLS
Balls of fire: inflammable plastic-foam balls.
il Consumer Rep 37:4-5 Ja '72
This ball is a ball of fire; Nerf ball. il
Consumer Rep 36:132 Mr '71
See also
Billiard balls
Tennis balls
BALLS (parties)
Everything is everything: costume ball. New
Yorker 47:23 Je 19 '71
Sterling ball funds ghetto scholarships. il
Ebony 26:72-4+ Jl '71
BALLY, C. F, ltd. See Shoe industry
BALSA
Balsa. E. A. Menninger. il **Am For** 77:38-9+
Ap '71
BALTIMORE
Abandoned vehicles couldn't wait. il **Am City**
86:16 Ap '71

Economic conditions
Winning is a many splendored thing. il
Nations Bsns 59:70-2 D '71

Fire department
Safety shelters for fire apparatus.   C. R.
Warfield. il Am City 86:10 D '71

Libraries
See also
Enoch Pratt free library, Baltimore

Politics and government
Black and white in Baltimore; liberal electoral success. Nation 211:652-3 D 21 '70

Theater
Baltimore homecoming; performance of Trial
of the Catonsville nine at the Center
stage. G. Owens. Nation 213:600-1+ D
6 '71
BALTIMORE Bullets (basketball team) See
Basketball teams
BALTIMORE Colts (football club) See Football
clubs
BALTIMORE Orioles (baseball) See Baseball
clubs
BALTIMORE symphony orchestra
Music to my ears; concert in Carnegie Hall.
I. Kolodin. Sat R 54:52 My 22 '71
Musical events; Baltimore symphony at
Carnegie Hall. W. Sargeant. New Yorker
47:136+ My 15 '71
BALUCHITHERIUM; story. See Updike. J.
BALYOGESHWAR (Indian guru)
Boy guru. por Newsweek 78:72 Ag 2 '71•
BAMBARA, Toni Cade
I ain't playin, I'm hurtin; story. Redbook
138:90-1 N '71
Raymond's run; story. Redbook 137:82-3 Je
'71
BAMBERGER, David
(ed) Opera for grownups: Hansel and Gretel.
il Opera N 36:15-18 D 25 '71
BAMBOO
How to put the brakes on golden bamboo.
il Sunset 146:244 Je '71
Will the giant bamboos all bloom at once,
and maybe die? il Sunset 147:174 S '71
BAMBOO grass. See Grasses
BAMBRICK, W. E. See Geoghegan, J. T. jt.
auth.
BAMFORD, Larry
Lion of a lifetime. il **Field & S** 76:64-5+
Ag '71
BANANAS, Joe. See Bonanno, J.
BANANAS
See also
Cookery—Fruit
BANCROFT, Ruth M.
Pool in the parlor. il Har Yrs 11:41 S '71
BAND music
Pied Piper. A. M. Lingg. il pors Opera N
36:10-14 D 25 '71
See also
Military music
BAND-tail pigeon shooting. See Pigeon shoot-
ing
BAND theory of solids. See Energy band theory
of solids
BANDA, Hastings Kamuzu
Red carpet for a black man. por **Time** 98:28
Ag 30 '71 •
BANDARANAIKE, Sirimavo
Che Guevarist uprising. Time 97:21 Ap 19 '71
Insurrection in Ceylon. T. Balasuriya. Com-
monweal 94:300-1 Je 11 '71
Making new friends. il Newsweek 77:36+ Ap
26 '71 •
Three women leaders beset by problems. por
U S News 70:42 My 10 '71 •

BANDEL, Hannskarl
Innovative engineering leads to new stadium
designs. il Arch Rec 150:139-42 N '71
BANDLER, Michael J.
Paperback revolution. jr. Commonweal 95:
132-5 N 19 '71
BANDLER, Richard, Jr, and Flynn, J. P.
Visual patterned reflex present during hy-
pothalamically elicited attack. bibliog il Sci-
ence 171:871-18 F 26 '71
BANDS (music)
Big bands cash in on nostalgia. il Bsns W
p20 Ja 1 '72
Follow the fifers! Deep River, Conn. R. A.
Dow. il Travel 136:44-7+ Jl '71
Music to talk by; TV studio bands. il News-
week 77:60-1 Ap 26 '71
Rosenkavaliers; Michigan and Stanford uni-
versity bands. il Newsweek 79:46 Ja 3 '72
Whoops of joy; Thad Jones-Mel Lewis big
band. il por Time 97:73 Mr 15 '71
See also
Band music
Rock groups
BANERJI, A. See Amonkar, S. V. jt. auth.
BANFF, Alberta
When you're in Banff, man, you're in Nelson
Eddy country! G. Malko. il Holiday 48:70-1
S '70
BANGLADESH
Anguished birth of Bangladesh. il Life 71:
2-5 D 31 '71
Bangla Desh: on the brink of survival. C.
S. Baldwin. il Sat R 54:32-3+ N 6 '71
Bangladesh: out of war, a nation is born. il
Time 98:20-2+ D 20 '71
Birth pangs of Bangladesh. il Newsweek 79:
20-1 Ja 3 '72
Bloody birth of a nation. America 125:546
D 25 '71
In wake of India's victory, storm signals
still flying; political and economic condi-
tions in Bangla Desh and West Pakistan.
J. N. Wallace. il U S News 71:20-3 D 27 '71
Mujib's road from prison to power. il por
Time 99:22-5 Ja 17 '72
Talk with Indira Gandhi; excerpts from
interview, ed. by E. Behr. I. Gandhi. por
Newsweek 79:23 Ja 3 '72
War nobody stopped.   V. G. Kiernan; R.
Sobhan; V. P. Nanda. il Nation 213:682-91
D 27 '71
Will you welcome now no. 139. Bangla-
desh. Newsweek 78:24 D 27 '71
See also
Terrorism—Bangladesh
BANGLADESH refugees benefit concert. See
Benefit performances
BANGOR, Me.
To pigeon-proof downtown, try pigeon
birth control. il Am City 86:81 Jl '71
BANGOR international airport. See Airports—
Maine
BANGOR Punta corporation
Bangor Punta shrinks to manageable size.
Bsns W p 100+ D 11 '71
BANGOURA, Lorraine
Baga and the inscrutable Nimba. bibliog il
Negro Hist Bul 34:30-2 F '71
BANHAM, Reyner
Defending Los Angeles. il Time 98:41 Ag 9
'71 •
BANK, Harvey. See Hirst, E. jt. auth.
BANK architecture. See Bank buildings
BANK buildings
Branch of the Fidelity bank, Philadelphia in-
ternational airport. il Arch Rec 149:88-9 Ja
'71
First city national bank of Binghamton,
New York. il Arch Rec 150:112-13 Jl '71
BANK checks. See Checks
BANK credit cards. See Credit cards
BANK deposits, Foreign
Business, privacy and hot money; Foreign
bank secrecy act. Duns 98:80 D '71
BANK employees
Salaries in the banking industry; with tables.
H. W. Jack. Mo Labor R 94:57-9 Ap '71
Squeeze is on, and payrolls feel it. Bsns W
p 19-20 Ap 24 '71
BANK examination
Banks and consumers. New Repub 165:12
Jl 17 '71
BANK failures
Founder; Sharpstown state bank failure. il
por Time 97:18+ F 15 '71
BANK for international settlements
Bankers try to head off a crisis. il Bsns W
p38 Ap 10 '71
First step to curb the Eurodollar mart. Bsns
W p35 Je 19 '71

BANK holding companies
Profit motive and the public interest: Wright Patman vs. the bankers. W. Shapiro. il Ramp Mag 9:16-20 My '71
Texas banks make a bid for the big time. il Bsns W p60+ D 4 '71
See also
Depositors corporation

Laws and legislation
Fed acts cautiously on one-bank issue. Bsns W p20 Ja 30 '71
Law opens a multifrontier; Banking holding company act. Bsns W p38 F 27 '71
BANK inspection. See Bank examination
BANK loans. See Loans, Bank
BANK of America national trust and savings association
Antiwar bank. New Repub 164:12-13 Ap 10 '71
Bank of America is not for burning. J. Davenport. il Fortune 83:91-3+ Ja '71
Biggest bank bets more on high risk. il Bsns W p80+ My 22 '71
Clausen of Bank of America. por Forbes 107:73 My 15 '71
Largest bank was once a plank on the waterfront. A. W. Clausen. il pors Nations Bsns 59:54-5 Ja '71
BANK of British Columbia. See Banks and banking—Canada
BANK of Sark. See Banks and banking—Great Britain
BANK premiums. See Premiums
BANK rates. See Interest
BANK robberies. See Robberies and assaults
BANK stocks. See Banks and banking—Securities
BANKERS
See also
Women as bankers
BANKING. See Banks and banking
BANKING and currency committee. See United States—Congress—House—Banking and currency, Committee on; United States—Congress—Senate—Banking and currency, Committee on
BANKING law
Another round; Banking reform act of 1971. Forbes 107:58 Je 1 '71
Business, privacy and hot money; Foreign bank secrecy act. Duns 98:80 D '71
Multiple warhead aimed at the banks; bank reform bill. por Bsns W p 19 Ap 24 '71
See also
Bank holding companies—Laws and legislation
BANKRUPTCY
Penury without tears; lavish life-style of J. M. King. il por Time 99:59-60 Ja 17 '72
Rising worry: what happens when companies go broke. il U S News 70:60-1 Mr 22 '71
Who's going bankrupt and why; personal bankruptcies. il U S News 71:83-4 Jl 19 '71
See also
Business failures
BANKS, Charles Wells
Wells, Fargo's Jekyll and Hyde. R. H. Dillon. il por Am West 8:28-33+ Mr '71 •
BANKS, Edna Hill
Edna Hill Banks, exemplary elementary school librarian. il pors Wilson Lib Bul 45:946-7 Je '71 •
BANKS, George. See Severtson, S. jt. auth.
BANKS, John
It's money in the bank. T. Maule. il por Sports Illus 35:36-8+ N 29 '71 •
BANKS, Lacy J.
Annual basketball roundup: Milwaukee Bucks, an instant dynasty? il pors Ebony 26:83-6+ Ja '71
Austin Carr rides again. il pors Ebony 26:60-2+ Mr '71
Big man, big bat, big heart. il pors Ebony 26:132-4+ O '71
Biggest fight in history. il pors Ebony 26:134-6+ Mr '71
Black admiral signals new look for U.S. Navy. il pors Ebony 26:72-4+ S '71
Buddy Miles: going thru changes. il pors Ebony 27:74-6+ D '71
Case for the defense. il Ebony 27:170-2 N '71
Cinderellas of the superstars. il pors Ebony 27:70-3 Ja '72
Miracle of the Miracles. il pors Ebony 26:164-6+ O '71
Rev Richardson's football farm. il pors Ebony 27: 104-9 D '71
Winner, the loser, the crowd. il pors Ebony 26:132-4+ My '71
World's leading heart transplant sets super pace. il pors Ebony 26:106-8+ Ap '71

BANKS, Coin
Old mechanical banks. F. H. Griffith. See issues of Hobbies
Who invented the piggy bank? Good H 172:164 F '71
BANKS and banking
Fifty largest commercial banks outside the U.S. T. Alexander. il Fortune 84:156-8 Ag '71
See also
Agricultural credit
Bank examination
Checks
Clearing houses
Computers—Banking use
Credit
Foreign exchange
Interest
Investment banking
Loans, Bank
Safe deposit boxes
Savings and loan associations

Automation
Auto teller brings you 24-hour banking. F. Lowe. il Pop Sci 199:42 D '71

Bill payment service
Banks move into multipurpose checks. il Bsns W p88 F 13 '71

Branch banking
Big-city banks follow people to the suburbs. il U S News 70:78-9 Mr 29 '71
See also
Banks and banking—Foreign business

Checking accounts
Parting shots; living high on a $528,471 booboo. il pors Life 70:78-9 Je 4 '71
See also
Checks

Customer relations
Begging for borrowers. il Time 97:71 F 1 '71
Waiting game. Newsweek 77:67 Ja 18 '71

Employees
See Bank employees

Finance
Earnings picture is a bit blurred; with tables. Bsns W p50 O 23 '71
Finance; with yardsticks of management performance. Forbes 109:93-6 Ja 1 '72
Profits start to convalesce; with table. Bsns W p32 Ap 17 '71
Quality of credit is strained. il Bsns W p70-2+ Je 26 '71
Squeeze is on, and payrolls feel it. Bsns W p 19-20 Ap 24 '71

Float
Europe learns to cut its float. Bsns W p41-2 Ap 3 '71

Foreign branches
See Banks and banking—Foreign business

Foreign business
Big push on the Swiss banks; First national city bank of New York. J. Ross-Skinner. il Duns 98:46-8 Jl '71
Foreign banks thrive in California. il Bsns W p 104+ Ap 10 '71
New U.S. bankers abroad; merchant banks in London. J. Ross-Skinner. Duns 97:51-2+ F '71
U.S. banks abroad; one-stop shopping? S. I. Davis. Harvard Bsns R 49:75-84 Jl '71
Yank banks have landed; branches in Britain and the Continent. S. G. Slappey. il Nations Bsns 59:66-71 Mr '71

Holding companies
See Bank holding companies

Law
See Banking law

Location
See Location in business and industry

Public relations
See also
Banks and banking—Customer relations

Securities
Investors line up to go into banking. Bsns W p80+ Ja 16 '71
Making depositors into shareholders; Citizens & Southern national bank. Bsns W p75 Jl 31 '71
Misjudged industry. il Fortune 84:137-9 S '71
Overlooked. il Forbes 108:17 Ag 1 '71

BANKS and banking—*Continued*

Services

Look at new ways banks are luring customers. il U S News 71:66-7 D 6 '71

Statistics

50 largest commercial banking companies; with directory. Fortune 83:192-3 My '71

Travel departments

Sinologist at St Paul; travel unit of First national bank of St Paul. R. Levy. Duns 98:61 O '71

Trust departments

Battle over $300-billion in bank trusts. il por Bsns W p64-7 Jl 24 '71

Patman's new threat to the bankers. por Bsns W p20 Ap 3 '71

Wages and hours

Salaries in the banking industry; with tables. H. W. Jack. Mo Labor R 94:57-9 Ap '71

Arab states

Paris helps the Arabs build; unique Franco-Arab bank. il Bsns W p38 My 1 '71

California

Foreign banks thrive in California. il Bsns W p 104+ Ap 10 '71
See also
Bank of America national trust and savings association
San Francisco—Banks

Canada

New bank challenges Canada's giants; Bank of British Columbia. il Bsns W p37-8 S 18 '71

Europe, Western

Europe learns to cut its float. Bsns W p41-2 Ap 3 '71

Florida

Florida banks combine to prosper. il Bsns W p40-1 Ap 3 '71

France

Paris helps the Arabs build; unique Franco-Arab bank. il Bsns W p38 My 1 '71

Georgia

See also
Atlanta—Banks

Germany (Federal Republic)

Virtuoso German banker moves center stage. pors Bsns W p56-7 Mr 27 '71

Great Britain

Multinational swindle born of tight money; worthless flood of paper from Guernsey's Bank of Sark. il Bsns W p46-7+ Jl 10 '71
See also
Barclays bank. ltd.
London—Banks

Hawaii

Hawaiian bank gets behind the badge. V. Louviere. il Nations Bsns 59:15 Jl '71

Idaho

See also
Boise, Idaho—Banks

Illinois

See also
Chicago—Banks

Massachusetts

See also
Boston—Banks

Michigan

More tremors jolt a shaky empire. por Bsns W p24-5 F 20 '71

Minnesota

See also
St Paul—Banks

New York (state)

See also
New York (city)—Banks

Pennsylvania

See also
Philadelphia—Banks

Rhode Island

Pair of S&Ls bedevils the Fed. Bsns W p38 S 18 '71

Sweden

Wallenberg grip. il Time 98:79 O 4 '71

Switzerland

Big push on the Swiss banks. J. Ross-Skinner. il Duns 98:46-8 Jl '71

Brazilian prelate hits banking procedures, stirs controversy in Switzerland. Chr Cent 88:970 Ag 18 '71

Dead letter; Rheinkapital GmbH solicits foreign accounts. por Newsweek 78:84+ S 20 '71

How the big Swiss banks manage $60-billion. il Bsns W p80-4 Ap 17 '71

Texas

Texas banks make a bid for the big time. il Bsns W p60+ D 4 '71
See also
Houston, Tex.—Banks

United States

Choose your bank carefully, then use it right. il Changing T 25:7-10 D '71

Factors borrow a touch of class; acquisition by commercial banks. il Bsns W p88-9 Mr 6 '71

Financing federal projects, plan for another U.S. bank; Federal financing bank. il U S News 71:96-7 N 22 '71
See also
Bank of America national trust and savings association
Export-import bank of the United States of America
Federal deposit insurance corporation
Morgan guaranty trust company
United States—Federal reserve board
also subhead Banks under names of cities, e.g. Boston—Banks

BANKS and banking, Cooperative
See also
Credit unions

BANKS and banking, International
Better than marriage; French-German-Italian bank. il Time 97:74 F 1 '71

Boom in London's bank consortiums. il Bsns W p42-3 D 18 '71

Rise of consortium banking. M. Von Clemm. il Harvard Bsns R 49:125-36+ My '71

Soviet gold; State bank subsidiaries. Nation 212:677-8 My 31 '71
See also
Bank for international settlements
Banks and banking—Foreign business
Barclays bank ltd.
Eurobond market
Eurodollar market
Export-import bank of the United States of America
Money—International aspects

BANNERS. See Flags

BANNON, Barbara A.
(ed) See Fisher, M. F. K. Art of eating, the art of living

BANOVITCH, Milenko
Travels with Banovitch. S. Robin. pors Dance Mag 45:36-7 Je '71 *

BANTA, Martha
Benjamin, Edgar, Humbert, and Jay. Yale R 60:532-49 Je '71

BANTAM books, inc.
Bantam books launches its lecture bureau. Pub W 200:19 N 1 '71

Bantam introduces new series of all-color paperbacks. Pub W 200:35 S 20 '71

BANUELOS, Romana A.
Hot tamale. il por Newsweek 78:36 O 18 '71 *

Old-fashioned U.S. success story. il pors U S News 71:80 O 4 '71 *

Romana's *mojados.* il por Time 98:37 O 18 '71 *

BANZER SUAREZ, Hugo
Another Guatemala? Nation 213:196 S 13 '71 *

Coup for the colonel. il por Time 98:31 S 6 '71 *

New regime. il Newsweek 78:31-2 S 6 '71 *

BANZHAF, John F. 3d
How you can make big business care about the little man; ed. by J. C. G. Conniff. por Today's Health 49:66 D '71

about

Man behind the ban on cigarette commercials. J. E. Roper. por Read Digest 98:213-14+ Mr '71 *

BAPTISM
Baptism by theater. il Time 99:49 Ja 3 '72

BAPTISTS in Great Britain
British Baptists divided. J. D. Douglas. Chr Today 16:46 Ja 7 '72

British Baptists in disarray. T. Beeson. Chr Cent 88:1487 D 22 '71

BAPTISTS in the United States
Baptist convention opens quietly. R. Chandler. Chr Today 15:30 Je 18 '71
Baptist parking lot case; Diffenderfer **v.**
Central Baptist church of Miami. **T. M.**
Gannon. il America 125:480-1 D 4 '71
Black and white gather at the river; Baptist church of the Covenant, Birmingham, Ala.
il por Life 71:44-6 N 5 '71
Negro Baptist leader calls black theology racist. Chr Cent 88:1128 S 29 '71
Peace breaks out at ABC convention. C. Rogers. Chr Cent 88:682 Je 2 '71; Discussion.
88:955-6 Ag 11 '71
Southern Baptists act on issues, review Bible commentary controversy. Chr Cent 88:770
Je 23 '71
Sticky thicket snares Broadman commentator. R. Chandler. il Chr Today 15:32-3 Jl
2 '71
Texas togetherness. E. E. Plowman. Chr Today 16:46 N 19 '71
Threatening picture; Sunday school board of the Southern Baptist convention suppresses picture. il Newsweek 78:105 N 15 '71
Year of the woman for Baptists. Presbyterians. E. E. Plowman. por Chr Today 15:27 Je 4 '71
BAR-ILLAN, David
Haunting of Philharmonic Hall. R. Freedman. il por Life 71:14 O 29 '71 *
BAR associations
See also
American bar association
National bar association (Negro)
BARAJAS, Luciano
Renin secretion: an anatomical basis for tubular control. bibliog il Science 172:485-7 Ap 30 '71
BARAM, Michael S.
Social control of science and technology. bibliog il Science 172:535-9 My 7 '71
BARAN, Paul Alexander
Confronting reality with reason. P. Clecak. Nation 212:245-8+ F 22 '71 *
BARANCO, Vic
Big Vic. C. H. Simonds. Nat R 23:1471 D 31 '71 *
BARANSKAIA, Natalíia
Alarm clock in the cupboard; story, tr. by B. Stillman. Redbook 136:179-201 Mr '71
BARANY, George
Hoping against hope: the enlightened age in Hungary. bibliog f il Am Hist R 76:319-57 Ap '71
BARASH, Julia
She's just one of the guys. B. Sales. il pors Todays Health 49:19-22+ Ap '71 *
BARBADOS
Description and travel
Washington's retreat: Barbados. J. Koenig, jr. il Travel 136:70-4 Jl '71
BARBADOS oceanographic and meteorological experiment. See Weather research
BARBARY apes. See Monkeys
BARBARY sheep hunting. See Mountain sheep hunting
BARBECUE carts. See Serving carts
BARBECUE cookery
Barbecue ideas hot off the grill. D. Eby. il Bet Hom & Gard 49:54-61+ Je '71
Barbecue lesson: southern barbecued chicken. il N Y Times Mag p84 Je 6 '71
Desserts hot off the grill. il Bet Hom & Gard 49:83 Ag '71
Easy grillwork. F. M. Crawford. il Am Home 74:56+ Ag '71
Hibachi cooking. il Ebony 26:156+ My '71
How to barbecue lobster tails. il Bet Hom & Gard 49:10 Ag '71
How'd you like to chew on some dinosaur bones? il Sunset 147:155 S '71
Keys that release barbecue secrets: sauces, marinades and butters. H. McCully. il House B 113:72+ Jl '71
Open-fire cooking. R. Olney. il House & Gard 139:92-9 Je '71
Things mother never taught you. il Ladies Home J 88:106 Jl '71
BARBECUE grills
Indoor grills; indoor electric. Bet Hom & Gard 49:120-1 O '71
Light it, and your barbecue's ready; gas-fired outdoor barbecue. W. C. Leckey. il Pop Mech 135:136-8+ My '71
Outdoor grills: which one for you? J. Heckroth. il Bet Hom & Gard 49:90 Je '71
See also
Smoke ovens

BARBECUE sauces. See Sauces
BARBER, Anthony
International monetary system; address, September 28, 1971. Vital Speeches 38:61-3 N 1 '71
BARBER, Benjamin R.
Switzerland: progress against the communes. il Trans-Action 8:27-31+ F '71
BARBER, D. J. and others
Extralunar dust in Apollo cores? bibliog il Science 171:372-4 Ja 29 '71
BARBER, Lawrence
Hijacked! il Yachting 129:59+ Mr '71
Mighty Columbia. il Yachting 129:60-1+ My '71
BARBER, Raymond. See Meyers, J. jt. auth.
BARBER, Samuel
Antony and Cleopatra. Criticism
New Yorker 47:116 D 18 '71 *
Lovers. Criticism
Sat R 54:14 O 23 '71 *
BARBER of Seville; opera. See Rossini, G.
BARBERS and barbershops
See also
Haircutting
BARBEZAT, Gilbert O. and Grossman, M. I.
Intestinal secretion: stimulation by peptides. bibliog il Science 174:422-4 O 22 '71
Il BARBIERE di Siviglia; opera. See Rossini, G.
BARBIROLI, Bruno, and Potter, V. R.
DNA synthesis and interaction between controlled feeding schedules and partial hepatectomy in rats. bibliog il Science 172:738-41 My 14 '71
BARBITURATES
Barbiturates: radioimmunoassay. S. Spector and E. J. Flynn. bibliog il Science 174:1036-8 D 3 '71
Drug abuse: now it's downers. il U S News 71:44 D 27 '71
See also
Phenobarbital
BARBOSA, Luiz Horta-. See Horta-Barbosa, L.
BARCELONA
Music
Report:
Aufstieg und fall der stadt Mahagonny and La Cenerentola. G. Price. Opera N 35:32-3 Mr 27 '71
Bellini's Il Pirata. G. Price. Opera N 35:32 F 27 '71
Una cosa rara, by V. Martín y Soler. G. Price. Opera N 35:30 Ja 23 '71
Donizetti's Lucrezia Borgia, Parsifal and Eugene Onegin. G. Price. Opera N 35:30 F 13 '71
La Gioconda and La Bohème. G. Price. il Opera N 35:30 Mr 13 '71
BARCLAYS bank, ltd.
John Thomson of Barclays bank ltd; interview. J. Thomson. il pors Nations Bsns 59:44-8 Ag '71
Sun still sets on Barclays. Forbes 108:42 D 1 '71
BARD, Bernard
College bound: a study in success. il Parents Mag 46:66-7+ S '71
BARD, C. R. inc.
Growing up. il Forbes 108:41 N 1 '71
BARDA, William R.
Parent conferences: guidelines for the counselor. Clear House 45:520-3 My '71
BARDIN, Shlomo
Brandeis effect. il por Time 98:58-9 Jl 5 '71 *
BARDOT, Brigitte
Fetching new symbol of France. il por Time 97:32 Mr 22 '71 *
BARE, Colleen Stanley
Slip up; poem. Good H 172:44 F '71
BARENBOIM, Daniel
Music to my ears; duple Barenboim. I. Kolodin. Sat R 54:14 Ja 30 '71 *
Music to my ears; program devoted to works of Mendelssohn, Goehr and Beethoven. I. Kolodin. Sat R 54:14 Ja 16 '71 *
Musician of the month. S. Fleming. il por Hi Fi 20:MA8-9 D '70 *
BARGE carriers. See Freighters
BARGE concerts. See Concerts
BARGE lines
Teacher's pet. il Forbes 107:50-1 Mr 1 '71
BARGE-tug systems. See Freighters
BARGES
Now: traffic jams on U.S. rivers. il U S News 71:66-8 S 20 '71
BARGHOORN, Elso S.
Oldest fossils; with biographical sketch. il Sci Am 224:12, 30-42 bibliog(p 132) My '71

BARI, Italy
Disaster at Bari; excerpts. G. Infield. il por
Am Heritage 22:60-4+ O '71
Music
Report:
Ballo in maschera at Teatro Petruzzelli.
S. Gould. Opera N 35:31 Mr 20 '71
BARILLET, Pierre, and Grédy, J. P.
Four on a garden; adapted by A. Burrows.
Criticism
New Yorker 46:72 F 6 '71 •
Time il 97:60 F 15 '71 •
BARING, Maurice
Maurice Baring restored, by P. Horgan.
Review
New Yorker 47:128+ S 18 '71. E. Wilson •
BARISCH, Sylvia
Parting look at the National register. il Phys
Today 24:40-3+ O '71
BARITE
Sulfur isotopes in Swaziland system barites
and the evolution of the earth's atmo-
sphere. E. C. Perry, jr. and others. bibliog
il Science 171:1015-16 Mr 12 '71
BARIUM silicates
Eight-membered cyclosilicate rings in murite.
A. A. Khan and W. H. Baur. bibliog il
Science 173:916-18 S 3 '71
BARIUM sulfate
See also
Barite
BARK, Dennis L.
Changing East-West relations in Europe; ad-
dress, December 18, 1970. Vital Speeches
37:216-18 Ja 15 '71
BARKAN, Robert
Big brother. il Ramp Mag 10:10+ S '71
War toys for adults. New Repub 165:7-8
D 11 '71
BARKER, B. Devereux, 3d
Deep water racing. See issues of Yachting
(ed) See issues of Yachting
BARKER, Clyde F. and others
Lymph node cells: their differential ca-
pacity to induce tolerance of heart and
skin homografts in rats. bibliog il Sci-
ence 172:1050-2 Je 4 '71
BARKER, Jeffery L. and Carpenter, D. O.
Thermosensitivity of neurons in the sensori-
motor cortex of the cat. bibliog il Science
169:597-8; 172:1361-2 Ag 7 '70, Je 25 '71
—and Levitan, Herbert
Salicylate: effect on membrane permeability
of molluscan neurons. bibliog il Science
172:1245-7 Je 18 '71
—and others
Supraoptic neurosecretory cells: adrenergic
and cholinergic sensitivity. bibliog il Sci-
ence 171:208-10 Ja 15 '71
Supraoptic neurosecretory cells: autonomic
modulation. bibliog il Science 171:206-7 Ja
15 '71
BARKER, John Jesse
John Jesse Barker of New Brunswick. E.
Gaines. il Antiques 100:129 Jl '71 •
BARKER, John W.
Cantiones sacrae 1575. pors Am Rec G 37:344-
5+ F '71
BARKER, Robinson Franklin
Ability to compete, address, November 4,
1971. Vital Speeches 38:157-60 D 15 '71
BARKER, Terry
Filming poetry. il Schol Teach Jr/Sr High p
10-11 Ap 5 '71
BARKEY, Anton M.
This die holder makes thread cutting easy.
il Pop Mech 135:155 F '71
BARLEV, Haim
On to the political wars. il por Time 98:44+
N 22 '71 •
BARLOW, Elizabeth
Once and future island. il Audubon 73:59-60+
Mr '71
BARLOW, Klara
Music to my ears; Metropolitan debut in
Fidelio. I. Kolodin. Sat R 54:44 F 20 '71 •
BARLOW, Robert B. jr, and Kaplan, Ehud
Limulus lateral eye: properties of receptor
units in the unexcised eye. bibliog il
Science 174:1027-9 D 3 '71
BARMASH, Isadore
Are you in your husband's will? Harp Baz
104:96 Je '71
Credit cards: spend now, pay later. Harp
Baz 104:187 S '71
Is there a shoplifter in your family? Harp
Baz 104:127 O '71
Trade winds; interview. ed. by C. Amory. Sat
R 54:10+ S 25 '71
Wafting through Europe on the floating dol-
lar. Harp Baz 105:101 N '71
BARN sales. See Sales
BARNABY, Frank
On the march to oblivion? il Cur 128:59-63
Ap '71

BARNACLES
Barnacles and hormones. D. Tighe-Ford. il
Sea Front 17:243-50 Jl '71
Barnacles have shells, but they are not
mollusks. A. G. Melvin. il Hobbies 76:124-5
S '71
BARNARD, Christiaan Neethling
What man owes the baboon. il por Sci Digest
70:36-41 S '71
What women should know about heart
attacks; excerpt from Heart attack:
you don't have to die. il por Ladies Home J
89:92-3+ Ja '72
about
Barnard touch. por Newsweek 78:62-3 Ag 9
'71 •
Barnard's bullet. por Time 98:37 Ag 9 '71 •
Heartbreak, by L. Barnard. Review
Newsweek il por 78:48+ S 20 '71 •
Transplant slump. il por Newsweek 77:69 My
17 '71 •
BARNARD, John, 1917-
What you should know about mutual funds;
interview. il por U S News 70:44-8 Ap 26 '71
BARNARD college, New York
Libraries
Barnard's alternative library. il Library J
96:1572 My 1 '71
BARNDS, William J.
Pakistan's agony. il America 124:508-9+ My
15 '71
BARNEA, Joseph
Geothermal power; with biographical sketch.
il Sci Am 26:10, 70-7 bibliog(p 122) Ja '72
BARNES, Aaron, and others
Permanent lunar surface magnetism and its
deflection of the solar wind. bibliog il Sci-
ence 172:716-18 My 14 '71
BARNES, Ben F.
Big Ben. il por Newsweek 77:36+ Je 28 '71 •
BARNES, Charles M. jr
Doubling a player's dollars. il por Forbes
108:66-7 O 15 '71 •
Men behind the men who make money in
sports. P. Axthelm. il Vogue 157:186-7+ My
'71 •
BARNES, Clive
Germany's elegant troupe of storytellers. il
por Life 70:10 My 21 '71
BARNES, Djuna
Walking-mort; poem. New Yorker 47:34
My 15 '71
BARNES, Joanna
Trade winds; interview. ed. by C. Amory.
Sat R 54:8+ F 20 '71
BARNES, John
Colonel Herbert tried to go by the book in
Vietnam: how a supersoldier was fired from
his command. J. T. Wooten. il pors N Y
Times Mag p 10-11+ S 5 '71 •
BARNES, Louis B. See White, B. F. jt. auth.
BARNES, Peter
Aerospace dinosaurs. New Repub 164:17-19
Mr 27 '71
California is wide open. New Repub 164:16-17
F 6 '71
Cooperatives that work. New Repub 165:12-13
D 18 '71; 166:17-19 Ja 1 '72
Land reform. New Repub 164:19-23 Je 5;
21-4 Je 12; 13-17 Je 19 '71
Oil everywhere. New Repub 165:21-3 N 6 '71
Oregon for the Oregonians. New Repub 164:
10-11 Mr 20 '71
Reagan versus the poverty lawyers. New Re-
pub 164:15-17 Ja 23 '71
Rescuing California. New Repub 165:12-13 S
18 '71
Starting a fourth party. New Repub 165:19-21
Jl 24 '71
Unfreezing Alaska. New Repub 165:15-17 S
11 '71
Water, water for the wealthy. New Repub
164:9-10+ My 8 '71
Withholding war taxes. New Repub 164:15-17
Ap 10 '71
BARNES, Peter (playwright)
Ruling class. Criticism
Sat R il 54:64 Mr 27 '71 •
Time il 97:60-1 F 15 '71 •
BARNET, Richard Joseph
Game of nations. il Harper 243:53-9 N '71
BARNETT, A. Doak
How to live with both Peking and Taiwan.
por Life 71:17 Ag 13 '71
BARNETT, Correlli
How not to win a war. il Horizon 13:48-53
Sum '71
Mao's long march. il pors Horizon 13:72-9
Wint '71
BARNETT, Jonathan
Beginning the debate on a national planning
policy. Arch Rec 149:117-18 My '71

BARNETT, Lincoln
Case of John Peter Zenger. il pors Am
Heritage 23:33-41+ D '71
BARNETT, Michael P.
IFLA in Liverpool: return of the native.
Wilson Lib Bul 46:469-70 Ja '72
BARNETT, Robert Warren
What about Taiwan? Cur 130:7-11 Je '71
BARNETT, T. P. and others
Bispectrum analysis of electroencephalogram
signals during waking and sleeping. bib-
liog il Science 172:401-2 Ap 23 '71
BARNETTE, Henlee
Agony and amnesty. il Chr Cent 88:1133-4 S
29 '71
BARNETTE, Rachel
Operation facelift. Har Yrs 11:22-3 F '71
BARNEY, Dick
Men against the sea. il Pop Mech 136:92-7+
D '71
BARNEY the Bookie, pseud.
Bookie rates off-track betting; ed. by J. Le-
bow. il Look 35:46+ Ag 10 '71
BARNEY'S girl; story. See Aguallo, T.
BARNS and stables
Barn for car, storage, or pony! il Mech
Illus 67:78-80 D '71
Hen house to calf barn for $400. il Suc Farm
69:D12 My '71
Modern tips for stanchion barns. R. G. Gar-
rett. il Farm J 95:6 Ja '71
New stall barn, full of ideas. J. R. Borcher-
ding. il Suc Farm 69:no4 D6-7 Mr '71
Plan your move to free stalls. Suc Farm
69:no2 D6 F '71

Floors
This converted barn has a slatted holding
pen. B. Eftink. il Suc Farm 69:H6 N '71

Heating and ventilation
Are warm dairy barns worth the cost? N.
Reeder. il Farm J 95:12-13 Je '71

Sanitation
These calves have water in their basements.
il Farm J 95:18 N '71
BARNSTORMING. See Aviation—Stunt flying
BAROMETERS
Amateur scientist; how to ensure a good
hologram and how to build an unusual
kind of barometer. E. E. Muehlner. il Sci
Am 225:111-14 Jl '71
BAROMETRIC pressure. See Atmospheric pres-
sure
BAROODY, Jamil Murad
Jamil the irrepressible. il por Time 98:32+
D 13 '71
BAROQUE marble; story. See Proulx, E. A.
BAROQUE painting. See Painting, Baroque
BARR, Audrey
Daytime island: Caladesi. il Travel 137:46-9
Ja '72
BARR, Browne
Lineaments of seminary renewal. Chr Cent
88:97-101 Ja 27 '71
BARR, Donald
Barr plan. J. K. Footlick. il por Newsweek
78:121 S 27 '71
Dalton brawl. il por Time 97:44-5 Ap 5 '71
Notes from a controversialist. por Time 98:
39 Ag 30 '71
BARR, John C.
New boy's baseball policy for Los Angeles.
il Parks & Rec 6:35+ Je '71
BARRACKS
Something new in barracks; coast guard, in
Alameda, Calif. il Arch Forum 164:68-70
Mr '71
BARRACUDA fishing
Splash fishing for cuda. G. Heinold. il Out-
door Life 147:18+ Ja '71
BARRETT, Marvin
Television. il Vogue 158:91 S 15 '71
BARRETT, Peter
Hat and the sprig. il Outdoor Life 148:50-3+
Jl '71
Return to the Roaring Kill. il Field & S 76:
62-3+ My '71
BARRETT, Tom
Dining out in the park. il Parks & Rec 6:19-
22+ Ap '71
BARRIER REEF, GREAT. See Great Barrier
Reef
BARRIERS, Median. See Roads—Safety guards
BARRON, John
Plot to steal a fighter plane; excerpts from
KGB. il Read Digest 98:69-74 F '71
Soviet plot to destroy Mexico; excerpt from
KGB. il Read Digest 99:227-32+ N '71
BARRON, Karen D.
Books about antiques (cont) Antiques 99:
230+, 650+; 100:354+, 920+ F, My, S, D '71

BARROW, Thomas Davies
Striking it big, the unorthodox way. il pors
Nations Bsns 59:68-9 Ja '71
BARROW, Alaska
Barrow, Alaska: cold frontier. K. Pra-
ger. il Time 99:31 Ja 3 '72
BARRY, Jay
Rose bowl star, 56 years ago. il por Ebony
27:100-2+ Ja '72
BARRY, Julian
Lenny. Criticism
Life 70:16 Je 25 '71 •
Nation 212:798 Je 21 '71 •
New Repub 165:26+ Jl 17 '71 •
New Yorker 47:100 Je 5 '71 •
Newsweek 77:75+ Je 7 '71 •
Sat R 54:36 Jl 10 '71
Time 97:62 Je 7 '71 •
Vogue il 158:75 Ag 1 '71
BARRY, Les
Traveler's camera. See issues of Popular pho-
tography
BARS and barrooms
And a merrie olde pint for thee; photographs
by Gerry Cranham; with account by P.
Knight. Sports Illus 34:50-5 Ap 19 '71
Demon drink rides again; plan to denation-
alize state pubs in Carlisle, England. C.
Brogan. Nat R 23:1237-8 N 5 '71
Oscar's. E. Waldron. il Holiday 48:91-2 S '70

Automation
Electronic bartender. F. W. Holder. il
Electr World 85:31 Je '71
BARS for the home
Handsome buffet that leads a double
life. W. C. Leckey. il Pop Mech 136:140-3+
D '71
BARSS, Currie
Joshua's tomorrows. il Redbook 137:84-5+ O
'71
BARSTOW, C. A. See Eidelberg, E. jt. auth.
BART, Pauline
Mother Portnoy's complaints. il Trans-Action
8:69-74 N '70
BARTA, Russell
Are the rules changing? America 125:341-5 O
30 '71
BARTEL, Constance
Good-looking homemaker. See issues of
American home up to December 1971
BARTEL, Virginia
When teachers strike. il Parents Mag 46:68-
70+ Mr '71
BARTELS, Eva, and Rosenberry, T. L.
Snake neurotoxins: effect of disulfide re-
duction on interaction with electroplax.
bibliog il Science 174:1236-7 D 17 '71
BARTER
Anyone for succotash? services swapping
ideas. L. M. Cottin. Har Yrs 11:21-3 Jl '71
They swap & talk & sell. il Mech Illus 67:6
D '71
BARTH, Charles A. and Hord, C. W.
Mariner ultraviolet spectrometer: topography
and polar cap. bibliog il Science 173:197-201
Jl 16 '71
BARTH, Karl
Pale ghost of Barth; Union theological semi-
nary colloquium. C. F. H. Henry. Chr
Today 15:40+ F 12 '71 •
Theology of Karl Barth, by H. U. von Bal-
thasar. Review
America 125:18 Jl 10 '71. M. A. Fahey •
Chr Today 15:14-16 Jl 16 '71. D. W. Day-
ton •
BARTHA, Dénes
On Beethoven's thematic structure. bibliog f
il Mus Q 56:759-78 O '70
BARTHEL, Joan
Bob Hope: the road gets rougher. il pors
Life 70:48-50+ Ja 29 '71
Notes in a viewer's album. il Life 71:60-7
S 10 '71
On being a Catholic. il pors Life 70:55-60+
Ap 30 '71
Quartet of queens. il pors Life 70:60-2+
F 19 '71

about
No preconceived notions and lots of note-
books. R. Graves. por Life 70:1 Ja 29 '71 •
BARTHELME, Donald
Catechist; story. New Yorker 47:49-51 N 13
'71
Critique de la vie quotidienne; story. New
Yorker 47:26-9 Jl 17 '71
Departures; story. New Yorker 47:42-4 O 9
'71
Engineer-Private Paul Klee misplaces an air-
craft between Milbertshofen and Cambrai.
March 1916; story. New Yorker 47:33-4 Ap
3 '71
Flying to America; story. New Yorker 47:
50-8 D 4 '71

BARTHELME, Donald—*Continued*
  Genius. New Yorker 47:38-40 F 20 '71
  Mothball fleet; story. New Yorker 47:34-5 S
    11 '71
  Natural history. il Harper 243:44-5 Ag '71
  Perpetua; story. New Yorker 47:40-2 Je 12
    '71
  Story thus far; New Yorker 47:42-5 My 1 '71
  Subpoena; story. New Yorker 47:33 My 29
    '71
BARTHELMES, Wes
  Cry, our beloved country. Commonweal 94:
    186-7 Ap 30 '71
BARTHOLOMEW, Bruce
  Bare zone between California shrub and
    grassland communities: the role of ani-
    mals. bibliog il Science 170:1210-12; 173:463
    D 11 '70. Jl 30 '71
BARTHOLOMEW, Robert
  Rapid concept communication. il Design 73:
    37-9 Fall '71
BARTL, Charles P. and Peltier, G. L.
  Academic underachiever in an industrialized
    world. bibliog Sch & Soc 99:24-7 Ja '71
BARTLETT pears. See Pears
BARTNETT, Robert A.
  Summer dog days walleye. il Field & S 76:
    82-3+ Je '71
BARTÓK, Béla
  Bartok and the second revolution. R. Evett.
    New Repub 164:38-40 Ja 2 '71
BARTON, Henry A.
  Four decades of AIP. por Phys Today 24:
    29 Je '71
BARTON, Joseph
  Theatre. America 125:516-17 D 11 '71
BARTON, Sam B.
  Compromise agreements as a means of work
    injury settlement. bibliog il Mo Labor R
    94:51-3 S '71
BARTON, Thomas H.
  New windows on the world. Harvard Bsns R
    49:136-8+ S '71
BARTON brands, inc.
  Why Barton toasts its liquidation. il Bsns W
    p45 S 11 '71
BARTOSHUK, L. M. and others
  Taste of water in the cat: effects on sucrose
    preference. bibliog il Science 171:699-701
    F 19 '71
BARTZ, Wayne R. and others
  Mental hospitals and the winds of change.
    Ment Hy 55:266-9 Ap '71
BARZEL, Rainer
  Challenger with two hats. por Time 98:45-6
    O 18 '71 •
  Choice not an echo. il por Newsweek 78:
    41 D 20 '71 •
BASALT
  Deep sea drilling: age and composition of an
    Atlantic basaltic intrusion. D. Macdougall.
    bibliog il Science 171:1244-5 Mr 26 '71
  Lunar and terrestrial ilmenite basalt. S. S.
    Goldich. bibliog il Science 171:1245-6 Mr 26
    '71
BASCOM, Willard
  Deep-water archeology. bibliog il Science
    174:261-9 O 15 '71
BASEBALL
  Brat is a winner for old USA: baseball coach
    E. Stanky. R. Fimrite. il por Sports Illus
    34:62-3 My 3 '71
  Dropout with a big future; B. Hooton of
    University of Texas. R. Fimrite. por
    Sports Illus 34:68+ My 31 '71
  I'm glad you didn't take it personally;
    excerpt. ed. by L. Shecter. J. Bouton.
    il por Look 35:34-8+ Je 15 '71
  New baseball. G. Keillor. New Yorker 47:
    35 My 15 '71
  New boy's baseball policy for Los Angeles.
    J. C. Barr. il Parks & Rec 6:35+ Je '71
  Week; baseball. J. Jares. Sports Illus 34:62+
    Ap 26 '71
    See also
  Little leagues
  National baseball hall of fame and museum
  Pitching (baseball)
  Radio broadcasting—Sports
  Softball
  World series (baseball)

  Accidents and injuries
  Show me the way to go home; T. Conigliaro.
    R. Fimrite. il por Sports Illus 35:16-17 Jl
    19 '71

  **Anecdotes, facetiae, satire,
  etc.**
  Boog! The big baseball musical; with edi-
    torial comment. B. Ottum. il Sports Illus
    35:4,50-4+ Jl 19 '71

  Bibliography
  Books for young people. Z. Sutherland. Sat R
    54:36 Jl 17 '71

  Photographs
  Dance in the dust. il Sports Illus 35:32-7
    Jl 19 '71
  Songs and music
    See also
  Phonograph records—Baseball—Songs and
    music
  Study and teaching
  Baseball where the players are; Cincinnati
    junior baseball program. J. Twyman. il
    Parks & Rec 6:27+ S '71
  School's in: watch out for baseball players;
    Kansas City Royals baseball academy, Sara-
    sota, Fla. W. Leggett. il Sports Illus 35:38-9
    Ag 23 '71
  Japan
  Learning by doing. il Time 97:54+ Mr 29 '71
BASEBALL; story. See Nagle, C.
BASEBALL, Commissioner of. See Baseball
  clubs—Organization and administration
BASEBALL accidents. See Baseball—Accidents
  and injuries
BASEBALL clubs
  Alex and the angry Angels. il por Time 97:64
    Je 28 '71
  And they're off and swinging. R. Blount, jr.
    Sports Illus 34:62 Ap 26 '71
  Annual baseball roundup: the last of the
    big bats. il pors Ebony 26:92-4+ Je '71
  Babe Ruth derby. il por Time 97:58+ My 10
    '71
  Baseball's amazing Vida Blue; Oakland
    Athletics to top of American league's pen-
    nant race. il pors Ebony 26:94-9 S '71
  Baseball's odd couple meets the wild bunch;
    Washington Senators. J. Mann. il
    pors Look 35:71-2+ My 4 '71
  Baseball's week. H. Weiskopf. Sports Illus
    35:107 S 27; 84 O 4 '71
  Beep! Beep! R. Garr, Atlanta Braves. por
    Time 98:43 Jl 5 '71
  Best damn team in baseball: the Orioles. F.
    Deford. il Sports Illus 34:78-82 Ap 12 '71
  Beware of the cliff dwellers; Mets. W.
    Leggett. il Sports Illus 34:22-4+ Je 21 '71
  Big man, big bat, big heart; Pittsburgh's W.
    Stargell. L. J. Banks. il pors Ebony 26:132-
    4+ O '71
  Billy the kid as peacemaker; manager of
    Detroit Tigers. R. Fimrite. il por Sports
    Illus 34:18-19 Je 28 '71
  Blue blazer; Oakland Athletics. por Time
    97:88 My 24 '71
  Blue speed; V. Blue, the best young
    pitcher. il pors Life 70:30-3 Je 18 '71
  Bolt of Blue lightning. il pors Time 98:40-4
    Ag 23 '71
  Bronx cheer-up for Yankees. D. Levin. Sports
    Illus 35:40 Jl 19 '71
  Bucs and Birds in a breeze; divisional play-
    offs: Pittsburgh Pirates vs. San Francisco
    Giants and Baltimore Orioles vs. Oakland
    A's. il Time 98:92 O 18 '71
  Cincinnati's big Red clunk: Cincinnati
    Reds. W. F. Reed. il Sports Illus 34:69+
    Je 7 '71
  Curtain up on a mod new act: thoroughly
    modern Phillies. R. Blount, jr. il Sports
    Illus 34:30-3 Ap 19 '71
  Eerie September, camaraderie and the Fox
    who says no; Dodgers vs Giants in the
    Western division race. R. Fimrite. il Sports
    Illus 35:15-17 Ag 30 '71
  Enter an all-round Wise gut; Phillies pitcher.
    W. Leggett. il por Sports Illus 35:40 Jl 5
    '71
  Fate and the Giants. il Newsweek 77:53
    Je 7 '71
  Few hundred words from the front office; in-
    terview. ed. by A. S. Young. W. O'Malley.
    il pors Ebony 26:44-6+ Ja '71
  For failure to give his best, A. Johnson of
    California Angels suspended for indiffer-
    ence. R. Fimrite. il pors Sports Illus 35:12-
    17 Jl 5 '71
  $40 million body shuffle; player trading
    by big league managers. W. Leggett. il
    Sports Illus 35:22-3 D 13 '71
  Four honest Birds; Baltimore Orioles pitching
    stars. il Newsweek 78:73 O 11 '71
  Gomer is tops in the tepee; Indians. H.
    Hodge. G. Curry. por Sports Illus 35:51
    Jl 26 '71
  Good one for the books: Houston pitcher
    L. Dierker. R. Fimrite. il por Sports
    Illus 34:62 My 24 '71
  Humming a rhapsody in Blue; Oakland A's
    21-year-old lefthander. R. Blount. il pors
    Sports Illus 35:22-3 Jl 12 '71
  In Greek it's Los Angeles; Dodgers the team
    to watch. W. Leggett. il Sports Illus 34:22-
    4+ Mr 22 '71

BASEBALL players—*Continued*
On the lam with the Three rivers gang;
  Pittsburgh Pirates. R. Blount. il Sports
  Illus 35:12-17 Ag 2 '71
Pitcher: baseball's tormented magician. B.
  Surface. il Read Digest 99:115-18 Ag '71
Red, white and who? NBA-ABA inter-league
  exhibition games. P. Carry. il Sports Illus
  35:20-3 O 4 '71
Return of the natives: Perry boys of Wil-
  liamston, N.C. R. Blount, jr. il pors Sports
  Illus 34:56-60+ Mr 29 '71
School's in: watch out for baseball players;
  Kansas City Royals baseball academy, Sara-
  sota, Fla. W. Leggett. il Sports Illus 35:
  38-9 Ag 23 '71
Some kind of a comeback: Pirates the World
  champions. W. Leggett. il Sports Illus 35:
  18-23 O 25 '71
Sporting scene. R. Angell. il New Yorker
  47:92-9 F 20; 73-82 Je 19 '71
Sporting scene; Pirates' victory over the
  Orioles. R. Angell. il New Yorker 47:138+
  N 6 '71
Three kids warm up chilly city; San Fran-
  cisco Giants again. R. Fimrite. il Sports
  Illus 34:18-21 My 17 '71
Tightening-up at the Fens: Boston Red
  Sox. W. Leggett. il Sports Illus 34:26-
  8+ My 24 '71
Tightening up in Baltimore. M. Mulvoy.
  Sports Illus 35:42 Jl 12 '71
Watch the Dodgers. il Newsweek 77:76 Ap
  19 '71
Who's in charge here? Boston's Red Sox.
  il por Newsweek 78:61 Jl 12 '71
Year of the player; Baseball 1971. W. Leggett.
  il Sports Illus 34:52-4+ Ap 12 '71
  See also
National baseball hall of fame and museum
  also names of baseball players, e.g. V.
  Blue
Names
Call him Willie, or Carlos or Lee. Every-
  body does. D. Delliquanti. Sports Illus 35:
  68 S 20 '71
Photographs
Those seventh-inning blues; American league
  playoff games, Baltimore vs Oakland. R.
  Fimrite. il Sports Illus 35:22-5 O 11 '71
Rating
It's hot-stove warmup time. W. Leggett.
  Sports Illus 35:85-6 O 11 '71
Recruiting
  See Baseball scouting
BASEBALL players association. See Major
  league baseball players association
BASEBALL scouting
Scouting reports: AL West and East. Sports
  Illus 34:74-7 Ap 12 '71
Scouting reports; NL East and West. Sports
  Illus 34:62+ Ap 12 '71
BASEBALL stadiums. See Stadiums
BASEBALL teams. See Baseball clubs
BASEBALL uniforms. See Uniforms, Sports
BASEBOARD heating. See Heating
BASEMENT recreation rooms. See Recreation
  rooms
BASEMENTS and cellars
This home-made cold cellar is a money
  saver. T. Fenstermacher il Org Gard &
  Farm 18:48-50 D '71
BASES (chemistry)
Immunochemical detection of minor bases in
  nucleic acids. D. L. Sawicki and others.
  bibliog il Science 174:70-2 O 1 '71
BASES, Military. See Military bases
BASHFULNESS
Helping the shy child. il por Newsweek 78:
  40 Ag 23 '71
BASHLINE, L. James
Boat-in bucks. il Field & S 76:48-9+ O '71
Little salmon. il Field & S 76:38 Je '71
Minnesota for muskies. il Field & S 75:78-9+
  Ap '71
Play it again, Sam. il Field & S 76:32-3+
  D '71
.22 rimfire: still the fun gun. il Field & S
  76:100-1+ O '71
Winter is the time for steelhead. il Field & S
  75:40-1+ Ja '71
BASIC training of Pavlo Hummel; drama.
  See Rabe, D.
BASIDIOMYCETES
Genetic restriction of energy conservation in
  schizophyllum. R. M. Hoffman and J. R.
  Raper. bibliog il Science 171:418-19 Ja 29 '71
BASKET making
  See also
Indians of North America—Basket making

BASKETBALL
Austin Carr rides again; Notre Dame basket-
  ball captain. L. J. Banks. il pors Ebony 26:
  60-2+ Mr '71
Camille goes under again; USC vs UCLA.
  J. Jares. il Sports Illus 34:14-17 F 15 '71
Case of the capering Croat; Brigham Young's
  K. Cosic. C. Kirkpatrick. il por Sports Illus
  35:65-6 D 13 '71
Close one at last; UCLA's fifth NCAA title.
  J. Jares. il Sports Illus 34:24-7 Ap 5 '71
Coach's garden of curses; Tennessee state
  and Kentucky state rivalry. J. Jares. il
  Sports Illus 34:46-7 F 22 '71
College basketball (cont) Sports Illus 35:46-
  62+ N 29; 110 D 20 '71
Crazy cat and his curious Warriors; Mar-
  quette Warriors. C. Kirkpatrick. il Sports
  Illus 34:32-6 Ja 25 '71
Far out in middle America; Kansas Jayhawks.
  C. Kirkpatrick. il Sports Illus 34:20-1 Mr 1
  '71
Geriatric memoirs of a basketballer. J.
  Flaherty. il Life 70:10 Ap 9 '71
Give Lefty a V, a V and . .; Lefty Driesell
  of University of Maryland. S. Treadwell.
  Sports Illus 34:42 Ja 25 '71
Good times come to Cajun country; Univer-
  sity of Southwestern Louisiana vs Long
  Beach state college. W. F. Reed. il por
  Sports Illus 35:20-1 D 20 '71
Lady in the shower? Dr Robbins of St Peter's
  of N.J. P. Jordon. por Sports Illus 34:50
  Mr 1 '71
Long jump to the baskets; B . Beamon of
  Adelphi university squad. D. Delliquanti. il
  por Sports Illus 34:38 Ja 11 '71
Love story on Rose hill; coach D. Phelps of
  Fordham. L. Keith. il Sports Illus 34:48 F
  15 '71
McGuire's Marquette. il por Newsweek 77:
  96-7 Mr 1 '71
Red-hot new pistol in Rebel land; Johnny
  Neumann of Ole Miss. C. Kirkpatrick. il
  pors Sports Illus 34:42-5 F 8 '71
Score one for friendship; Riverview and Sara-
  sota high schools' eight day basketball
  game. Sr Schol 97:8 Ja 18 '71
Seven Yanks at Oxford. il Newsweek 79:46
  Ja 10 '72
There's no place like home; Jacksonville uni-
  versity's Dolphins vs Houston Cougars. J.
  Jares. il Sports Illus 34:65-6 Mr 8 '71
They're no hair-raisers, but they win; Uni-
  versity of Pennsylvania basketball play-
  ers. J. Jares. il Sports Illus 34:56-7 Ja 18 '71
Week; college basketball (cont) J. Jares.
  Sports Illus 34:59-60 Mr 15 '71
Week; college basketball. L. Keith. Sports
  Illus 35:84+ N 29 '71
Week; college basketball. C. Kirkpartick.
  Sports Illus 34:38-9 Ja 11 '71
Week; college basketball. H. Peterson. Sports
  Illus 34:57-8 Ja 18; 42-3 Ja 25; 44 F 1; 45-6
  F 8; 48-9 F 15; 35-66+ D 13 '71
Week; college basketball. S. Treadwell.
  Sports Illus 34:47-8 F 22; 50-1 Mr 1; 66+
  Mr 8 '71
  See also
American basketball association

Equipment
7 ways to put up a basketball backboard. il
  Pop Sci 198:83 Ja '71
BASKETBALL coaches. See Coaches (ath-
  letics)
BASKETBALL courts
Building a backyard basketball court. E.
  McGough. il Mech Illus 67:102+ O '71
BASKETBALL players
Basketball's black entrepreneur: M. Haynes
  of Fabulous Magicians. A. S. Young. il pors
  Ebony 26:96-8+ Mr '71
Cinderellas of the superstars; B. Love and
  R. Brown. L. J. Banks. il pors Ebony
  27:70-3 Ja '72
College basketball (cont) il Sports Illus 35:
  46-62+ N 29 '71
1971 All-American H.S. basketball squad.
  H. L. Masin. Sr Schol 98:28 My 17 '71
Pro basketball: mighty match-ups make it
  go: photographs by W. Iooss, jr; with ac-
  count by P. Carry. Sports Illus 35:32-40+ O
  25 '71
Russians, thanks be, are leaving; Soviet
  national basketball team in Paintsville,
  Ky. J. Kirshenbaum. il Sports Illus 34:
  76+ Je 7 '71
Sports brighten a silent world; deaf-mute.
  B. Fuller. il pors Ebony 27:44-6+ D '71
Winner gets to play Alcindor; Baltimore Bul-
  lets vs New York Knicks. P. Carry. il
  Sports Illus 34:22-4+ Ap 26 '71
  See also names of basketball players, e.g
  C. Murphy

BASKETBALL players—*Continued*

Recruiting
See Basketball scouting

Salaries, pensions, etc.
Instant millionaires from the basketball war; with account by D. Fisher. il Life 70:32-4 Ap 23 '71
Tall men, tall prices; ed. by M. Kane. Sports Illus 34:5+ F 1 '71

BASKETBALL scouting
Anybody else care to bid for Spencer Haywood? an Olympic hero. P. Carry. il por Sports Illus 34:52-3 Ja 25 '71
Body snatchers. Time 97:60+ Ap 12 '71
Elmore the Great. il por Newsweek 77:67 Mr 29 '71
Thinking small pays big. il Time 97:35-6 Mr 22 '71
Top 20; college basketball scouting reports. il Sports Illus 35:50-62+ N 29 '71

BASKETBALL teams
Annual basketball roundup: Milwaukee Bucks, an instant dynasty? L. J. Banks. il pors Ebony 26:83-6+ Ja '71
Back door into the big time: pro basketball without help of an alma mater. P. Carry. il por Sports Illus 35:26-7 N 1 '71
Best team, ever: Milwaukee Bucks. P. Carry. il Sports Illus 35:24-7 N 15 '71
Beware, little big man is here: Chicago Bulls. D. Motta, NBA coach of the year. F. Deford. por Sports Illus 35:46-7+ O 25 '71
Big time for the Bucks. il Time 97:54 Mr 29 '71
Bucks in a breeze. il Time 97:58 My 10 '71
Bully for the Bullets. il por Newsweek 77:91 My 3 '71
Celtic Lakers; Los Angeles Lakers. il Time 98:51 D 27 '71
Fortunes of a new tough cookie: rookie E. Smith of Buffalo Braves. P. Carry. il por Sports Illus 35:76+ N 22 '71
Getting up and going after a title: Lakers coach B. Sharman proves that practice makes perfect. P. Carry. il Sports Illus 35:24-6+ D 13 '71
Hawks: fouled up but flourishing. F. Deford. il Sports Illus 34:26-8+ Mr 8 '71
It was a brief time-out; Boston Celtics fighting for place in playoffs. P. Carry. il pors Sports Illus 34:22-3 Ja 11 '71
Lakers roll on. il Time 99:56+ Ja 10 '72
Lew is not enough; Bucks third to beat the Knicks. P. Carry. il por Sports Illus 34:14-17 F 8 '71
Little big man. il por Time 97:66 F 1 '71
Playing the comedy circuit: NBA central division. P. Carry. il Sports Illus 35:62+ N 8 '71
Pro basketball: mighty match-ups make it go; photographs by W. Iooss, jr; with account by P. Carry. Sports Illus 35:32-40+ O 25 '71
Pro basketball roundup. L. J. Banks. il Ebony 27:74+ Ja '72
Red, white and who? NBA-ABA inter-league exhibition games. P. Carry. il Sports Illus 35:20-3 O 4 '71
San Diego's Calvin Murphy: pro basketball's tiny giant. il pors Ebony 26:38-40+ F '71
Toughing it out around the purgatory league; Allentown Jets vs Camden Bullets in EBA. L. A. Armour. il Sports Illus 34:70+ Mr 15 '71
We can punch, we can dance; Bullets vs Knicks in the NBA playoffs. P. Carry. il Sports Illus 34:30-1 Ap 12 '71
We've got to spread a little anarchy: Bucks vs Knicks; interview. ed. by J. Olsen. L. Alcindor. il por Sports Illus 34:36-8+ Ap 19 '71
Why L.A. loves the Lakers. il por Newsweek 78:73 D 13 '71
Winner gets to play Alcindor; Baltimore Bullets vs New York Knicks. P. Carry. il Sports Illus 34:22-4+ Ap 26 '71
With Oscar and Lew, Milwaukee is basketball's best, but . . . P. Wilkes. pors Look 35:68-70 Ap 6 '71
See also
All-Star basketball game
American basketball association
National basketball association

BASKETBALL tournaments
Just forget UCLA, the man said. C. Kirkpatrick. il Sports Illus 34:22-5 Mr 29 '71
Most conventional win for the Thorobreds; Kentucky state in NAIA finals. S. Treadwell. il Sports Illus 34:58+ Mr 22 '71
Perennial problem: stop UCLA. J. Jares. il Sports Illus 34:12-17 Mr 22 '71
Toughing it out around the purgatory league; Allentown Jets vs Camden Bullets in EBA. L. A. Armour. il Sports Illus 34:70+ Mr 15 '71

BASKETS
Food in baskets to delight the senses. il House & Gard 140:30-1 Jl '71
Making baskets into play tables, patio tables, end tables. il Sunset 146:105-6 Mr '71
See also
Hanging baskets

BASKIN, Darryl
Old home town. New Repub 165:11 N 6 '71

BASKING sharks. See Sharks

BASQUE separatists trial. See Trials—Spain

BASQUES
No firing squads in Spain; Burgos trial. E. von Kuehntlt-Leddihn. Nat R 23:134 F 9 '71

BAS-relief printing. See Photography—Printing processes

BASS, George F.
Byzantine trading venture; with biographical sketch. il Sci Am 225:13, 22-33 bibliog(p 120) Ag '71

BASS
See also
Cookery—Fish

BASS fishing
All you need to know about catching bass, with a fly rod. T. Nixon. il Field & S 75:72-3+ Ap '71
Barse man from Texas. B. Geagan. il Field & S 76:66-7+ N '71
Best bass bait in the world. B. Underwood. il Outdoor Life 147:74-5+ Mr '71
Bugging is more fun. S. Fagerstrom. il Outdoor Life 147:102-3+ Ap '71
Bugs and bogs and immortal bass: St Vincent Island. D. Levin. il Sports Illus 34:36-8+ F 22 '71
Casting on a sea of memories: Sakonnet Point revisited. T. McGuane. il Sports Illus 35:42-4+ S 27 '71
Conowingo, Maryland's neglected bass lake. C. B. Pfeiffer. il Field & S 76:162-4+ My '71
Doc psychs big bass. T. Weber, jr. il por Outdoor Life 147:86-8+ Je '71
Don't doodlesock 'em. C. Elliott. il Outdoor Life 148:42-3+ Jl '71
Field & stream interviews: the Nation's best topwater bass fisherman? interview. E. Todtenbier. il por Field & S 76:36-7+ D '71
Fishing's newest twist . . . spoonfeeding bass. B. Brister. il Field & S 76:56-7+ Je '71
Florida's lunker bass lake. B. Underwood. il Field & S 75:56-7+ F '71
Go camping to catch more fish. E. A. Bauer. il por Outdoor Life 147:82-3+ Mr '71
Hidden lakes of Long Island. T. Kerasote. il pors Outdoor Life 147:74-7+ My '71
Late season largemouth. S. Fagerstrom. il por Field & S 76:50-1+ S '71
Magic on the Withlacoochee; largemouth bass. R. Kennedy. il Time 97:67 My 3 '71
Not a place that appeals to everyone; centuries-old millpond in tidewater Virginia. E. White. il Sports Illus 34:40-2+ My 31 '71
Pole fishing the bass bushes. B. Holiday. il Field & S 75:66-7+ Mr '71
Popping for stripers. G. Heinold. il Outdoor Life 147:180+ Ap '71
Potomac: smallmouth paradise. C. B. Pfeiffer. il Field & S 76:52-3+ Mr '71
Reservoir right at home. M. Caraher. il pors Outdoor Life 148:72-3+ Ag '71
Riddle of Miccosukee. C. Elliott. il por Outdoor Life 148:88-9+ O '71
Rock riot at Nags Head. K. Osborne. il pors Outdoor Life 148:56-7+ N '71
Saltwater combos. G. Heinold. il Outdoor Life 147:30+ Je '71
Shortcut to smallmouth. S. Marking. il Field & S 76:74-5+ My '71
Smallmouth, the fighter. J. Brooks. il Outdoor Life 147:68-9+ Je '71
Strangest bass fishing on earth. E. A. Bauer. il Field & S 75:48-9+ Ja '71
Striped bass with a fly. R. Chatham. il Field & S 75:62-3+ Ap '71
Stripers come big. V. Evanoff. il Motor B & S 127:37+ Ap '71
Taking smallmouths from the deep. W. Davis. il Mech Illus 67:48+ My '71
This year hang a trophy bass. J. A. Moorhouse. il Field & S 76:42-3+ Jl '71
What our own bass tell us. B. W. Dalrymple. il pors Outdoor Life 147:52-5+ Ja '71
World's best bass fisherman; interview. B. Dance. il pors Field & S 76:58-9+ My '71

BASSHAM, James A.
Control of photosynthetic carbon metabolism. bibliog il Science 172:526-34 My 7 '71

BASSMAN, Lillian
Gallery; photographs. Life 71:8-9 Ag 20 '71

BASSO, Renaldo
Two poets; photographs. il pors Am Lib 2:1045-9 N '71

BASSOGIGAS. See Fishes

BASTIAN, Linda
Filmmaking and social criticism. il Sch Arts 71:38-9 D '71
Filmmaking in the classroom. il Sch Arts 70: 10-11 Je 5 '71

BASTIAT, Claude Frédéric. See Bastiat, F.

BASTIAT, Frédéric
Frederic Bastiat, by G. C. Roche, 3d. Review Nat R 23:938-40 Ag 24 '71 B. Peterson *

BASTOGI (firm) See Holding companies—Italy

BATAVIA accelerator. See National accelerator laboratory

BATES, William L.
Love/hate relationship between press and school. Ed Digest 36:22-4 Ap '71

BATH, N.Y.
Try units to finance sewerage construction. L. E. Bower. Am City 86:10 My '71

BATH houses. See Bathhouses

BATH preparations
Beauty & the bath. S. Lindsay. il House B 113:40+ My '71

BATH rooms. See Bathrooms

BATH tubs. See Bathtubs

BATHHOUSES
Build this cabana now, use it all year. D. Shiner. il Pop Mech 135:154-7 Ap '71
It's the next thing to a family resort; cabana facilities. il Sunset 147:66 Ag '71
Living around a pool. il House & Gard 139: 66-7 Je '71
Well-built house; poolhouse. J. H. Ingersoll. il House B 113:30-1 Ja '71

BATHING. See Baths

BATHING suits
Julia models a look for the beach. il pors Ebony 26:106-9 Ja '71

History
Once more on to the beach; with paintings. G. Carson. il Am Heritage 22:58-80+ Ag '71

BATHROOM fixtures
Care of fiberglass in the bathroom. Sunset 147:90 Jl '71
See also
Plumbing
Toilets

BATHROOM furnishings. See Household furnishings

BATHROOM scales. See Scales (weighing instruments)

BATHROOMS
Bathrooms go plastic. A. Lees. il Pop Sci 199: 86-7 S '71
Four very personal baths. il House B 113: 68-9 Mr '71
How the other half bathes. il Time 97:62-6 Mr 29 '71
How to defrost a bathroom. il Bet Hom & Gard 49:136 D '71
Idea from Hawaii, the bath that seems half out-of-doors. il Sunset 146:148 Ap '71
Move the bath into the hall and gain space. A. Lees. il Pop Sci 198:96-7 Ap '71
New ideas for beautiful bathrooms. M. Kraft. il Good H 173:108-12+ Ag '71
New private life. R. Warfield. il House & Gard 139:84-5+ My '71
New super bath. il House & Gard 139:50-3 Ja '71
Planning a better bathroom. N. Seney. il Bet Hom & Gard 49:42-9 Ag '71
To share or not to share? B. Russell. il House & Gard 139:98-9+ My '71
2 baths that turn yesterday's space to today's use. S. Lindsay and H. Ingersoll. il House B 113:94-7 My '71

BATHS
••••ing is no longer a dirty word. M. McEachern. il Todays Health 49:24-7 My '71
Superconditioned body: the big soak. il Mlle 72:240-1 Ap '71
See also
Bath preparations
Hydrotherapy

BATHS, Finnish. See Sauna

BATHS, Vapor
See also
Sauna

BATHTUBS
Party-time tubs. il Life 72:40-2 Ja 14 '72

BATIK
Ancient art of batik making. G. E. Toles. il Design 72:8-10 mid-Sum '71
Batik: a short cut. M. C. McMurray. il por Sch Arts 70:20-1 Ap '71

BATKI, John
Strange-dreaming Charlie, cow-eyed Charlie; story. New Yorker 47:36-41 Mr 20 '71

BATON ROUGE, La.
Police
On-the-scene sobriety tests. E. O. Bauer, jr. Am City 86:26 Ja '71
Turn police files into information centers. E. B. Bauer, jr. and E. B. Morel. il Am City 86:105 My '71

BATRACHOTOXIN. See Toxins and antitoxins

BATS
Artibeus jamaicensis: delayed embryonic development in a neotropical bat. T. H. Fleming. bibliog il Science 171:402-4 Ja 29 '71

BATSHEVA dance company. See Dancing, Israeli

BATTCOCK, Gregory
Art critic as social reformer, with a question mark. il por Art in Am 59:26-7 S '71

BATTELLE, Kenneth
How to get the haircut you want. il pors Redbook 136:82-5+ F '71 *

BATTELLE memorial institute, Columbus, Ohio
See also
Holotron corporation

BATTEN, Alan H. and Plavec, Miroslav
Two new chapters in the story of U Cephei. il Sky & Tel 42:147-50, 213-15 S-O '71

BATTEN, James K.
Sam Ervin and the privacy invaders. il New Repub 164:19-23 My 8 '71

BATTEN, William Milfred
Batten of J. C. Penney. il por Forbes 107:66 My 15 '71 *

BATTERBERRY, Ariane, and Batterberry, Michael
Art: give multiples. il Harp Baz 105:72-3 D '71
—See Batterberry, M. jt. auth.

BATTERBERRY, Michael, and Batterberry, Ariane
Escaping escaping gas. il Harp Baz 104:71 Ag '71
Women artists? Harp Baz 104:73 Jl '71
—See Batterberry, A. jt. auth.

BATTERED child syndrome. See Cruelty to children

BATTERIES, Electric. See Electric batteries

BATTERIES, Solar. See Solar batteries

BATTERS, Baseball. See Baseball players

BATTERSBY, Mark
How to smooth the path to college. il Mech Illus 67:87-8+ N '71

BATTERY chargers. See Storage battery chargers

BATTERY charging. See Electric batteries—Charging; Storage batteries—Charging

BATTERY-operated clocks. See Clocks

BATTERY Park city. See New York (city)—City planning

BATTLE of the sexes. See Women and men

BATTLES
See also
War

BATZRI, Samuel, and others
Potassium ion release and enzyme secretion: adrenergic regulation by α- and β-receptors. bibliog il Science 174:1029-31 D 3 '71

BAUDO, Serge
Moving quickly; interview, ed. by B. Fischer-Williams. por Opera N 35:16 Ap 10 '71

BAUER, Arnold J.
Chilean rural labor in the nineteenth century. bibliog f il Am Hist R 76:1059-83 O '71

BAUER, Dick
Learn about winter driving from the ice racers! il Pop Mech 136:76-9+ D '71
They slip & slide for the fun of it. il Mech Illus 67:84-6+ F '71

BAUER, E. O. jr. and Morel, E. B.
Turn police files into information centers. il Am City 86:105 My '71

BAUER, Erwin A.
Big secret. il Outdoor Life 148:78-81+ O '71
Bulls of the midnight pond. il Outdoor Life 147:78-9+ Je '71
Camp by boat. il Outdoor Life 147:64-5+ Ja '71
Changing pheasant. il Outdoor Life 148:60-3+ N '71
Free-for-all ducks. il Outdoor Life 148:34-7+ D '71
Go camping to catch more fish. il por Outdoor Life 147:82-3+ Mr '71
Jumping jacks. il Outdoor Life 147:82-5+ Ap '71
Jungle adventure in Ceylon. il Outdoor Life 148:46-9+ D '71
Strangest bass fishing on earth. il Field & S 75:48-9+ Ja '71
Strategy for whitetails. il Outdoor Life 148: 52-5+ S '71

BAUER, Erwin A.—*Continued*
Tragedy of India's wildlife. il Outdoor Life
147:49-53+ F '71
Work while the fish are biting; ed. by J. B.
Smith. il por Writers Digest 51:36-7+ Je
'71
BAUER, Parker
Too easy to catch. il Nat Wildlife 9:10-11 Je
'71
BAUER, Shirley
When to follow the rules. Writer 84:23 Je
'71
BAUGH, Laura Zonetta
And, in a prettier part of the forest ... J.
Jares. il por Sports Illus 35:16-17 S 6 '71 •
BAUGHMAN, James P.
Plain talk about interest. por Nations Bsns
59:96 Ja '71
BAUM, Gregory
Earl Neiman: a great artist. il Cath World
213:69-74 My '71
Infallibility beyond polemics. Commonweal
94:103-5, 294 Ap 9, My 28 '71
about
Hans Küng replies to Gregory Baum. H.
Küng. Commonweal 94:326-30 Je 25 '71 •
BAUMAN, John F.
Scope of the poverty problem. bibliog f Cur
Hist 61:284-9+ N '71
BAUMAN, Zygmunt
Uses of information: when social information
becomes desired. bibliog f Ann Am Acad
393:20-31 Ja '71
BAUMEL, Rachael Ball
West Coast symphony, in purple. il Hi Fi
20:MA24-5 D '70
BAUMGARTEN, Murray
(tr) See Pérez De Ayala, R. Ruera street
BAUMGARTNER, Leona
Crisis in American medicine. il Parents Mag
45:59-61+ N '71
BAUR, Werner H. See Khan, A. A. jt. auth.
BAUSCH and Lomb, inc.
Bausch & Lomb focuses on a new lens; soft
plastic contacts. il Bsns W p68+ My 15 '71
Market as contact (lens) sport. S. H. Brown.
il Life 71:8 Ag 13 '71
BAUSI, Luciano
Happy mayor; interview. New Yorker 47:33-4
My 8 '71
BAVAGNOLI, Carlo
Gallery; photographs. Life 70:6-7 Ap 2 '71
BAVIER, Robert Newton, 1918-
From the cockpit. See issues of Yachting
Record fastnet. il Yachting 130:53+ O '71
BAXANDALL, Lee
Brecht returns as a classic. Nation 212:501-3
Ap 19 '71
BAXTER, Gordon
Bax seat. See issues of Flying
BAXTER, John D. and others
Glucocorticoid receptors in lymphoma cells
in culture: relationship to glucocorticoid
killing activity. bibliog il Science 171:189-91
Ja 15 '71
BAY, Christian
Violence as a negation of freedom. Am
Scholar 40:634-41 Aut '71
BAY area rapid transit. See San Francisco—
Transit systems
BAY COUNTY, Mich.
County land-records support local develop-
ment. E. M. Nearing. il Am City 86:103
My '71
BAY LAUREL, Alicia, pseud.
Bookmaking. D. N. Mount. il Pub W 199:72-3
Ap 19 '71
BAYANIHAN Philippine dance company. See
Dancing, Philippine
BAYER, Frederick M.
Coral; with biographical sketch. Natur Hist
80:6+, 42-7 Mr '71
BAYH, Birch Evans, 1928-
Excerpt from address, October 7, 1970. Cong
Digest 50:10+ Ja '71
Toward juvenile justice; address, July 12,
1971. Am Scholar 40:662-6 Aut '71
about
Bayh bows out. il por Newsweek 78:27 O 25
'71 •
Birch Bayh's bid. por Newsweek 77:43 Ap 19
'71 •
Exit Bayh. il por Time 98:16 O 25 '71 •
Lifestyle. il pors Am Home 74:10+ S '71 •
Recipe for a Washington dinner party. W.
McLendon and S. Smith. il pors Ladies
Home J 88:110+ My '71 •
Young man from Indiana. P. R. Wieck. New
Repub 164:23-7 Je 26 '71; Reply. B. Bayh.
165:32-3 Jl 24 '71 •

BAYH, Marvella
Recipe for a Washington dinner party. W.
McLendon and S. Smith. il pors Ladies
Home J 88:110+ My '71 •
BAYHORSE, Idaho. See Abandoned towns
BAYLISS, Frank T. and Vinopal, R. T.
Selection of ribosomal mutants by antibiotic
suppression in yeast. bibliog il Science 174:
1339-41 D 24 '71
BAYNTON-COX, Elisabeth
Mrs Cox's double life. M. Kasindorf. il por
Newsweek 77:101 My 10 '71
BAYÓN, Damián
Many faces of colonial art. Américas 23:S14-
17 Ap '71
BAYONET practice
Army goes mod. Chr Cent 88:1215 O 13 '71
BAYREUTH
Description
Wagner lives. B. Evans. Nat R 23:1427-8 D 17
'71
BAYREUTH festival
Operatic impass: Bayreuth and Munich
festivals. P. G. Davis. il Hi Fi 21:MA26-7
N '71
Report:
Wagnerian wonders. J. H. Sutcliffe. Opera
N 36:28-9 O '71
BAZAARS, Charitable
Bazaar: dozens of ingenious things to make
and bake. M. B. Smith. il Bet Hom &
Gard 49:70-3 S '71
Talk of the town: bazaar to prevent cutting
back rehabilitation programs of Livingston
school. New Yorker 47:41-3 O 30 '71
BAZELI, Frank P.
Creating group cohesion in inner city class-
rooms. bibliog Clear House 45:547-50 My '71
BAZELL, Robert
Behind the cancer campaign. il Ramp Mag
10:28-34 D '71
BAZELON, David T.
Toward a culture of unreason? Cur 131:51-6
Jl '71
BAZIN, André
Two types of film theory. B. Hender-
son. Film Q 24:33-42 Spr '71 •
BAZIOTES, William A.
Art world: exhibition at the Marlborough
gallery. H. Rosenberg. New Yorker 47:
76-7 Mr 6 '71 •
BEA, Augustin, cardinal
Augustin Cardinal Bea, ed. by S. Schmidt.
Review
Cath World 214:44-5 O '71. E. M. Jung •
BEACH architecture
Color built-in. il House & Gard 140:94-5 S
'71
Combs house, Fire Island Pines, N.Y. il Arch
Rec 149:70-1 mid-My '71
Designed into nature. R. J. O'Gara. il Design
73:10-11 Wint '71
House, ahoy! il N Y Times Mag p32 Jl 18 '71
Perlbinder house, Sagaponac, L.I. il Arch Rec
149:34-7 mid-My '71
Sand castles for keeps. J. Peter. il Look 35:
84-6 Je 1 '71
Stevens house, Malibu colony, Malibu Beach,
Calif. il Arch Rec 149:44-7 mid-My '71
BEACH erosion
Our moving beaches. W. F. Tanner. il
Américas 23:2-8 O '71
BEACH mats. See Cushions
BEACHES
Beach-combing. M. E. Slate. il Motor B & S
128:50-1 bibliog(p58) Jl '71
Birth of a beach. B. Einsohn. il Motor B & S
128:56-7 bibliog(p58) Jl '71
In Hilo good beaches for children. il Sunset
147:52 O '71
Long Island's ocean beaches. C. J. Schuberth.
il Sea Front 17:350-62 N '72
Low tide walking on Hawaii beaches. il Sun-
set 146:40 Je '71
Place to stretch your soul; Washington's
Olympic beach. R. Kirk. il Nat Wildlife 9:
42-7 Je '71
Southern California beaches. L. Burton. il
Travel 135:28-35+ Ap '71
BEACONS. Radar. See Radar in aviation
BEAD pictures. See Pictures
BEADLE, Gina
Kitchens. M. Davidson. il pors Ladies Home
J 88:25 Je '71 •
BEADS
Raku beads. S. Hyman. il Ceram Mo 19:28-30
O '71
See also
Beadwork
BEADWORK
Uses of beads; excerpt from The universal
bead. J. M. Erikson. il Craft Horiz 31:18-
21+ O '71

BEAUTIFYING of cities. See Municipal improvement
BEAUTY. See Aesthetics
BEAUTY, Personal
American good looks; eight women's beauty routines. Vogue il 157:164-9 F 1 '71
Art of looking beautiful; excerpts from Joan Crawford: my way of life. J. Crawford. il pors McCalls 98:55-7+ Jl '71
Beautiful people's beauty book, by Princess L. Pignatelli, ed. by J. Molli. Review
  Commentary 51:90+ My '71. A. Hollander
Beauty bulletin. See issues of Vogue
Beauty checkout. See issues of Vogue
Beauty: fresh lemon twists. S. Obre. il Ladies Home J 88:48+ Je '71
Beauty: how to have more than you started with. il Vogue 158:128-37 O 1 '71
Beauty ifs. il Seventeen 30:68-73+ Ja '71
Beauty in our time; reprint of May 1961 article. A. Liberman. Vogue 158:115-16 O 1 '71
Beauty, 1 year later. il Seventeen 31:68-73 Ja '72
Beauty secrets from the ballet girls. il Vogue 158:108-11+ Ag 1 '71
Beauty while you wait; mid-pregnancy pick up. il Ladies Home J 88:128-9 Mr '71
Beauty with a gilt edge; tips by top beauty experts, ed. by S. Obre. il Ladies Home J 88:76-7+ Ja '71
Best-dressed face list. il Harp Baz 104:54-61 Jl '71
Face maintenance. G. Klinger. il Harp Baz 104:36 Mr '71
Good-looking homemaker. C. Bartel. See issues of American home up to December 1971
Good looks & good health. R. Warfield. See issues of House & garden incorporating Living for young homemakers
Guest editor journal: beauty marathon. il Mlle 73:322-7 Ag '71
Happy returns; working mothers. S. Obre and T. Owett. il Ladies Home J 88:116-23 S '71
Herb chart for health and beauty and fun. il Mlle 72:166-9 Mr '71
How to be divine all over. il Mlle 74:118-20 Ja '72
How to have a beautiful summer. il Redbook 137:90-1+ Je '71
I need help! N. Craig. il McCalls 99:98-101 O '71
In my opinion; the natural look is a charade. A. Spinale. por Seventeen 30:346 Ag '71
It's time to give nature a chance. il Harp Baz 104:116 Mr '71
The look you like; questions and answers, ed. by L. Allen. See issues of Today's health
Mirror, mirror; L. Pignatelli's pursuit of beauty. por Time 97:49-50 Mr 15 '71
Mutual admiration society. il Harp Baz 105:78-81 D '71
New look at yourself. il Vogue 159:86-9 Ja 1 '72
Of skin and hair and water power. il Vogue 157:116-21 Mr 1 '71
Out of the swim and into the fall. S. Lindsay. House B 113:12 Ag '71
Personal appearance. Harp Baz 104:162-3 Mr '71
Pretty woman uses all the help she can get; 25 good ideas. Vogue 157:118-19+ Ap 1 '71
Project: you. il Ladies Home J 88:47 Ja; 28 Mr; 26 My; 133 Jl; 68 S; 74 D '71
Redbook beauty report: Ginnie Hibbard. il Redbook 138:84-7+ Ja '72
Redbook helps three women with one goal; how to look better. il Redbook 137:89-91 My '71
Redbook's illustrated guide to being better-looking. Redbook 137:93-6 My '71
Secrets of a million-dollar face; excerpt from Beautiful people's beauty book. L. Pignatelli. por Ladies Home J 88:74-5+ Ja '71
Sex appeal is a state of mind. Vogue 157:102 Ap 1 '71
Sex appeal 1971. G. Guinness. Harp Baz 104:196-7 S '71
Stay young and beautiful (title varies) P. Van Wagenen. See issues of Parents' magazine & better family living
10 minutes to be beautiful. Mlle 73:150-1 S '71
Think beauty all the way. N. Craig. il McCalls 99:91-5 N '71
Travel and beauty care. J. Clark. Holiday 49:104+ F; 18 Mr; 16 Ap; 17 My '71
What I learned from my sister Johnna. G. Kirkland. il por Seventeen 29:79 Jl '70
What is a beautiful woman? G. Guinness. il Harp Baz 104:124-5 Ap '71
Which way does the wind blow? il Vogue 158:272-9 S 1 '71

You can be what you want to be. il Seventenn 30:86-91 Jl '71
Your looks are as good as your discipline; excerpt from The beauty book. L. Avedon and J. Molli. il Vogue 157:86-7+ Ja 15 '71
  See also
Baths
Beauty shops
Cosmetics
Exercise
Hair
Hairdressing
Hand
Make-up
Mouth

Bibliography

Beauty by the book. Mlle 73:32 Jl '71

Equipment and supplies

Project: you, electric beauty. il Ladies Home J 88:47 Ja '71
BEAUTY contests
Beauty pageants are pathetic auctions! E. Crabtree. por Seventeen 29:230 S '70
Dollar signs in Miss America's eyes. il Bsns W p46-7 S 11 '71
Night Miss America vanished; excerpt from There she is: the life and times of Miss America. F. Deford. il por Ladies Home J 88:104-5+ S '71
Pageant! Miss Teenage America. il Seventeen 29:102-3+ Jl '70
There she is: Miss America 1940; with interview, ed. by A. Hollister. il Life 70:45-8 F 5 '71
There she is: the life and times of Miss America, by F. Deford. Review
  Newsweek il 78:99+ S 13 '71. A. Cooper
  Time il 98:62 S 6 '71. R. Z. Sheppard
Trade winds; Miss America; interviews, ed. by C. Amory. F. Deford; M. Weisinger. Sat R 54:8+ O 2 '71
BEAUTY operators
Beauty sense and nonsense; hairstylists. il Harp Baz 105:44 N '71
L.A: A to Z. Vogue 158:22 Ag 1 '71
  See also
Klinger, G.
Manzoni, P.
BEAUTY preparations. See Cosmetics
BEAUTY queens. See Beauty contests
BEAUTY resorts. See Health resorts, watering places, etc.
BEAUTY shops
In-most places. P. D. Dibble. Ladies Home J 88:66 My '71
6 interiors; Vidal Sassoon salon in Toronto. il Arch Rec 150:96-7 Ag '71
  See also
Beauty operators
BEAUVOIR, Simone de
Joie de vivre; excerpts from The coming of age. il Harper 244:33-40 Ja '72
  about
Europe's first feminist has changed the second sex. C. Cate. il pors N Y Times Mag p4-5+ Jl 11 '71 *
BEAVERS
Beaver in New York. G. C. Champagne. il Cons 26:18-21 Ag '71

Anecdotes, facetiae, satire, etc.

Dissertation on the beaver; excerpts from The great fur opera. K. Dobbs. il Natur Hist 80:8+ Je '71
BEAZLEY, George G. Jr
In defense of Louvain's pluralism. Chr Cent 88:1305 N 3 '71
BECK, Alan M.
Life and times of Shag, a feral dog in Baltimore; with biographical sketch. il Natur Hist 80:3, 58-65 O '71
BECK, Albert W.
S.I.T.E: a suggested answer to the pollution in art teacher development. il Sch Arts 71:36-7 S '71
BECK, Alfred D.
Teleguide. il Sr Schol Teach ed 99:5 N 15 '71
BECK, Charles F.
How to store your food crops. il Org Gard & Farm 18:84-92 S '71
BECK, Julian
This is theater. por Newsweek 78:40 Ag 16 '71 *
BECK, William R. and Rosenberger, D. S.
Chairman: where does he fit in? Clear House 46:48-51 S '71
BECK Industries, Inc.
Who says bankers aren't friendly? loan to purchase Beck's shoe and handbag operation. por Forbes 107:15-16 F 1 '71

BECKER, Benjamin M.
Myth of arms control and disarmament. Bul
Atom Sci 27:5-8+ Ap '71
BECKER, Herman F.
Digging in Montana's evolutionary past. il
Am For 77:44-7+ Ap '71
BECKER, Kenneth
There's oil in Alaska; poem. Liv Wildn
34:62 Wint '70
BECKER, Robert Otto
Limb regeneration in mammals. il por Sci N
100:322-3 N 13 '71 •
BECKER-CARSTEN, Wolfgang
Current chronicle; tr. by L. Wallach. Mus
Q 57:314-17 Ap '71
BECKETT, Elizabeth G.
Where the white whales play. il Yachting
129:65+ F '71
BECKETT, Samuel
Waiting for Godot. Criticism
Chr Cent 88:603-4 My 12 '71 •
Commentary 51:78 Ap '71 •
Nation 212:253-4 F 22 '71 •
New Yorker 46:78+ F 13 '71
Time il 97:61 F 15 '71 •
BECKHARD, Herbert
Two houses by Herbert Beckhard. il Arch
Rec 149:119-24 My '71 •
BECKMAN, Don
Song of the lark. por Opera N 35:6-7 F 27 '71
BECKMAN, Norman
Congressional information processes for na-
tional policy. bibliog f Ann Am Acad 394:
84-99 Mr '71
BECKMAN, Wanda
Fat. Mlle 73:186+ Ag '71
BÉCQUER, Gustavo Adolfo
Gustavo Adolfo Bécquer. A. B. Carisomo. por
Américas 23:9-10 Ja '71 •
BED linens. See Linen, Household
BED-sitting rooms. See Bedrooms
BEDAU, Hugo Adam
Broils and civil commotions. Nation 212:757-9
Je 14 '71
BEDDING
Mattresses, pads, and pillows. Parents Mag
46:57 Jl '71
Sleeping around. E. Sheppard. Harp Baz
105:138-9 N '71
See also
Quilts
Sheets
BEDE the Venerable
Father of English history. P. W. Schmidt-
chen. il por Hobbies 75:134-6+ Ja '71
BEDFORD park. See California—Parks and
reserves
BEDFORD-Stuyvesant restoration corporation,
Brooklyn
Superblock: new life on the street. il Arch
Forum 134:66-8 Ja '71
See also
Design works of Bedford-Stuyvesant
BEDQUILTS. See Quilts
BEDROOM furnishings. See Household furnish-
ings
BEDROOM furniture
See also
Beds
BEDROOMS
Beautiful bedrooms: romantic, individual,
nostalgic. il House B 113:51-7 Ag '71
Bedrooms: how to make the most of small
space. P. Rumely and R. E. Dittmer. il
Bet Hom & Gard 49:30-9 Ag '71
Doubling up; do and don't decorating ideas
when sharing a room. il Seventeen 30:134-
7+ Ap '71
How you can create a romantic bedroom,
sheet mix-up. il House & Gard 139:42-9 Ja
'71
Make mine romantic. il Seventeen 29:118-21
O '70
Master bedroom. il Redbook 138:88-91 Ja '72
One room living for one, two and three. il
Seventeen 30:132-7 O '71
Plugged-in circuit. il Seventeen 30:260-5 Ag
'71
Room for new ideas. il Seventeen 31:82-3 Ja
'72
So the depression has hit your room. il Sev-
enteen 30:112-13 Jl '71
To share or not to share? B. Russell. il
House & Gard 139:98-9+ My '71
See also
Childrens rooms
Guest rooms
BEDS
Beware the waterbed. McCalls 98:46 Ag '71
Bunk beds. Spanish style. il Mech Illus 67:
94-6 O '71
Facts about those new waterbeds. Good H
173:201 S '71
Headboard for night owls. W. Sill. il Pop
Sci 198:102-3 Mr '71

Lots of Queen Anne beds. E. Gaines. il An-
tiques 100:233-5 Ag '71
Make your bed and float on it; Waterbed.
C. P. Gilmore. il Pop Sci 199:75+ Jl '71
One place the water bed takes to is the out-
of-doors: on a deck, on a terrace, even
afloat in the pool. il Sunset 146:86-7 Ap '71
Stitch a flowered headboard. M. Gough. il
House B 113:76-7 Ja '71
Water beds. Consumer Bul 54:14 O '71
Waterbed squishes in; with report by W.
Zinsser. il Life 70:52-4 Mr 12 '71
Waterbeds: a rising tide. il Time 97:71 F 8
'71
See also
Bedding
Cribs (beds)
Hospital beds
BEDSPREADS. See Coverlets
BEDSTEADS. See Beds
BEDTIME story telling. See Story telling
BEE culture
Honey makes money. W. Wagner. il Har Yrs
11:11-13 Ap '71
BEECH aircraft corporation
Beech spurs single-engine effort. C. E. Sch-
neider. Aviation W 95:61-2 D 20 '71
Hatchet job; product-liability suit. R. L. Col-
lins. Flying 89:18-19 N '71
$108-million suit filed against Beech. Avia-
tion W 94:21 Je 28 '71
Retrial ruled in Beech fuel case. Aviation W
95:17 Ag 30 '71
BEECHAM group, ltd.
Beecham tries to buy a top spot in drugs;
bid for Glaxo group. Bsns W p52 D 11 '71
BEECHEY, Gwilym
Memoirs of Dr William Boyce. bibliog f il por
Mus Q 57:87-106 Ja '71
BEEF
Close look at hamburger. il Consumer Rep
36:478-82 Ag '71
Price of beef; diethylstilbestrol residues. D.
Cottrell. bibliog il Environ 13:44-7+ Jl '71
See also
Cookery—Meat

Prices
See Meat—Prices
BEEF cattle. See Cattle, Beef
BEEF grading.   See Meat—Grading and
standardization
BEEF industry. See Meat industry
BEEF measles. See Measles in cattle
BEEFSTEAK. See Cookery—Meat
BEEKEEPING. See Bee culture
BEELER, Kent D. and Eberle, A. W.
Paradoxes in higher education. Sch & Soc
99:217-18 Ap '71
BEELEY, Sir Harold
Changing role of British international propa-
ganda. Ann Am Acad 398:124-9 N '71
BEER, Michael. See Huse, E. F. jt. auth.
BEER
Will beer really get slugs, snails? Sunset 146:
253 Ap '71
See also
Brewing industries
Cookery—Beer
BEERBOHM, Sir Max
Benevolent dandy. por Newsweek 77:96A F 22
'71 •
Gold for all its glitter. C. L. Markmann. Na-
tion 212:311-12 Mr 8 '71 •
BEES
Bees. L. Schroeder. il Horticulture 49:24-5+ F
'71
Euglossine bees as long-distance pollinators
of tropical plants. D. H. Janzen. bibliog il
Science 171:203-5 Ja 15 '71
Fierce bee menaces humans and animals; Af-
rican honeybee. il Sci Digest 70:24-5 D '71
He raises alfalfa leaf-cutting bees. V. H.
Maas. il Suc Farm 69:no3 B6 F '71

Anecdotes, facetiae, satire, etc.
Insectual politics. B. Everett. Sat R 54:68 N
20 '71
BEES (cooperative gatherings)
Old-style threshing bees this month and
next. il Sunset 147:62-3 Ag '71
BEESLEY, Jesse C.
Beesley and his bronze children. D. Cochrane.
il por Am Artist 35:54-9+ S '71 •
BEESON, Trevor Randall
Sum and substance. See issues of Christian
century continuing New Christian
Theology en masse. Chr Cent 88:1016-17 S 1
'71

BEETHOVEN, Ludwig van
Beethoven by the bushel from DGG. P. G. Davis. Hi Fi 20:116 D '70 •
Beethoven on records:
  Piano music. H. Goldsmith. Hi Fi 21:61-2 Ja '71 •
  Symphonies. P. H. Lang. Hi Fi 20 49-50+ D '70 •
Beethoven violin concerto for piano. H. Goldsmith. Hi Fi 21:92 N '71 •
Fidelio. Criticism
  Hi Fi il 21:MA15-16+ Ap '71 •
  Nation 212:157-8 F 1 '71 •
  Sat R 54:44 F 20 '71 •
  Sat R 54:24 Mr 13 '71 •
In a class by itself: Bishop's Emperor. M. N. Kanny. il Am Rec G 37:240 D '70 •
Jakob Gimpel: there is no mistaking the mastery. M. N. Kanny. Am Rec G 38:712 Je '71 •
Ludwig van Beethoven, ed. by J. Kerman. Review
  Mus Q 57:323-9 Ap '71. P. H. Lang
Recording the Beethoven sketchbooks; recording projects in London. T. Heinitz. Sat R 54:52 Jl 31 '71 •
Recordings. M. Mayer. Esquire 75:174-5 Ap '71 •
Report:
  Fidelio, by East Berlin's Staatsoper. J. H. Sutcliffe. Opera N 35:32 F 27 '71
Serkin and Beethoven's Hammerklavier. H. Goldsmith. Hi Fi 21:86 D '71 •
Special issue celebrating the bicentennial of the birth of Beethoven; with introd. by P. H. Lang. bibliog il por Mus Q 56:505-793 O '70 •
Truly great Beethoven by Schmidt-Isserstedt. M. N. Kanny. Am Rec G 37:762-3 Jl '71 •
200 years of B. Schott's söhne. E. Helm. il por Hi Fi 21:55-60 Ja '71 •
Why Beethoven became deaf. Sci Digest 70:26-7 D '71 •

Manuscripts
Little-known Beethoven sketch in Moscow. B. Schwarz. bibliog f il Mus Q 56:539-50 O '70

BEETLES
Cereal leaf beetle keeps moving. il Suc Farm 69:no3 W25 F '71
Communication between ants and their guests. B. Hölldobler. il Sci Am 224:86-93 Mr '71
  See also
  Flour beetles

BEETS
Beets are good from top to bottom. R. Tirrell. Org Gard & Farm 18:68-9 D '71
Kohlrabi and beets can grow in the same row. Org Gard & Farm 18:62-3 Ag '71

BEFORE your very eyes; drama. See Boiko, C.

BEGINNER'S luck: story. See Quinn, G.

BEGINNINGS; story. See Coover, R.

BEGLEY, John J. See Armbruster, C. J. jt. auth.

BEHAN, Brendan
Two poems: Jim Larkin; The versemaker's wish; tr. by U. O'Connor. Atlan 227:67 Je '71

    about
Brendan, by U. O'Connor. Review
  Cath World 213:296-7 S '71. J. O'Connell •
  Look 35:76 My 4 '71. W. Kennedy •
  Sat R il por 54:37 My 1 '71. T. MacIntyre •

BEHAN, R. W.
Timber mining: accusation or prospect? il Am For 77:4-6+ N '71

BEHANNA, Gertrude Florence (Ingram) See Burns, E. pseud.

BEHAVIOR (psychology)
Behavioral theory vs. reality. J. A. Lee. bibliog f Harvard Bsns R 49:20-2+ Mr '71; Discussion. 49:31-2 S '71
Beyond freedom and dignity, by B. F. Skinner. Review
  Atlan 228:122-5 O '71. G. Kateb
  Cur 135:9-18 D '71. C. Lehmann-Haupt; D. C. Anderson; R. Claiborne
  Nat R 23:1160+ O 22 '71
  Nat R 23:1247-8 N 5 '71. M. S. Gazzaniga
  New Repub 165:32-4 O 16 '71. P. Caws
Biology of behavior. R. J. Williams. Sat R 54:17-19 Ja 30 '71
Cardiac activity preparatory to overt and covert behavior. G. E. Schwartz and J. D. Higgins. bibliog il Science 173:1144-6 S 17 '71
Despairing optimist. R. Dubos. Am Scholar 41:16-18+ Wint '71
End of sadness and history. J. V. Schall. il Cath World 213:222-6 Ag '71

Freedom of the mind and other essays, by S. Hampshire. Review
  New Repub 165:24-5+ O 23 '71. P. Caws
He envisions a happier age. C. McCarry. il McCalls 99:35 N '71
Imperial animal, by L. Tiger and R. Fox. Review
  Natur Hist il 80:90-2+ O '71. J. Shapiro
  Sat R 54:40+ N 20 '71. B. J. Siegel
Nice new world of B. F. Skinner; interview, ed. by A. Gross. B. F. Skinner. pors Mlle 74:90-3+ Ja '72
Problems of strong people. America 125:446 N 27 '71
Researching the parables. P. Steinfels. Commonweal 94:230 My 14 '71
Stress and behavior. S. Levine. il Sci Am 224:26-31 bibliog(p 122) Ja '71
What is normal behavior? Sci Digest 70:27-8 D '71
  See also
  Displacement (psychology)
  Social norm

BEHAVIOR, Animal. See Animals—Habits and behavior

BEHAVIOR, Group. See Groups (sociology)

BEHAVIOR modification
Ethical issues in biomedicine; choices on everyone's conscience; ed. by R. J. Trotter. il Sci N 100:275-6 O 23 '71

BEHAVIOR of animals. See Animals—Habits and behavior

BEHAVIOR problems (children) See Problem children

BEHAVIOR therapy
Behavior modified? E. Canning. il Sci Digest 70:26-31 Jl '71
How to help troubled children cope with fears and problems. B. P. McCarthy. il Parents Mag 46:44-5+ Ag '71
How to teach your child good habits; behavior therapy. A. Lake. il Redbook 137:74+ Je '71
Neurosis: just a bad habit? il Time 98:41 Ag 2 '71

BEHAVIORAL research. See Psychological research

BEHAVIORAL research laboratories
Will this boy's curriculum manager deserve an apple this year? Gary, Ind. Banneker school. B. Kaufman. il Todays Health 49:20-3 S '71

BEHAVIORAL sciences
Behavioral sciences. See issues of Science news
  See also
  Behavior (psychology)

BEHAVIORISM
Skinner's utopia: panacea, or path to hell? il pors Time 98:47-52+ S 20 '71
Ultimate conclusions of a mod behaviorist. R. J. Trotter. por Sci N 100:96-7 Ag 7 '71; Discussion. 100:134+ Ag 28 '71

BEHIND-the-lens meters. See Exposure meters

BEHME, Bob
Expanding world of snowmobiles. il Field & S 76:S1-4+ O '71
Vehicles. See issues of Field & stream

BEHOLD! Cometh the Vanderkellans; drama. See Mackey, W. W.

BEHREND, Ernst Richard
Marketing change that meant everyone won. R. D. DeVitt. il pors Nations Bsns 59:64-5 Ja '71 •

BEHRENS, Richard
Barium glazes. Ceram Mo 19:27 O '71
Basic matt glazes for cone 4. Ceram Mo 19:33 D '71
Cone 6 reduction glazes. il Ceram Mo 20:12 Ja '72
Fluoride glazes for cones 06, 4 and 6. il Ceram Mo 19:33 S '71
Formulary of leadless glazes. Ceram Mo 19:24+ F '71
Low temperature frit porcelain. il Ceram Mo 19:33 N '71
Nepheleine syenite glazes. il Ceram Mo 19:33 Je '71
Rosy gold glazes. Ceram Mo 19:26+ Mr '71
Some glaze faults, and their correction. il Ceram Mo 20:28-9 Ja '72 (to be cont)
Terra sigillata. Ceram Mo 19:31 Ja '71
Two-component glazes. Ceram Mo 19:33 My '71

BEHRMAN, Daniel
Trieste: world rendezvous for physicists. il UNESCO Courier 24:12-16+ My '71

BEICHMAN, Arnold
Six 'big lies' about America. il N Y Times Mag p32-3+ Je 6 '71

BEINBRACH family
Sleuthing for ancestors. M. R. Bonebrake. il Hobbies 76:152-3+ Jl '71

BEISNER, Robert L.
Commune in East Aurora. il pors Am Heritage 22:72-7+ F '71

BÉJART, Maurice
Béjart; interview. New Yorker 46:23-5 F 6 '71
about
Ballet bitcheries. W. Terry. Sat R 54:79 Mr 13 '71 *
Ballet of the 20th century. NY city center. J. Anderson. Dance Mag 46:76+ Ja '72 *
Ballet unlimited. H. Saal. il por Newsweek 77:48+ F 8 '71 *
Béjart: the lingering impact. R. Philp. il Dance Mag 45:26-8 Ap '71 *
Béjart's Nijinsky: Clown of God; tr. by N. M. Stoop. M. F. Christout. il Dance Mag 45:34-41 D '71 *
Dance. N. Goldner. Nation 212:348-9 Mr 15 '71 *
Dance largess. W. Terry. il Sat R 54:39 F 20 '71 *
Dance laughter. W. Terry. il Sat R 55:8 Ja 1 '72 *
Dance: Les vainquerurs. R. Zachary. il Opera N 35:31 Ap 3 '71 *
Mudra: Maurice Béjart's gesture. N. M. Stoop. il pors Dance Mag 45:30-7 N '71 *
Pick your side of the ocean. D. Hering. Dance Mag 45:24-5+ Ap '71 *

BEKIERKUNST, A. and others
Suppression of urethan-induced lung adenomas in mice treated with trehalose-6,6-dimycolate (cord factor) and living bacillus Calmette Guérin. bibliog il Science 174:1240-2 D 17 '71

BELAFONTE, Harry
Durango: Poitier meets Belafonte. G. Goodman. il pors Look 35:56-60+ Ag 24 '71 *

BEL AIR, Md.
Music
See also
Harford theater association

BELANGER, Jerome D.
Raising rabbits right. il Org Gard & Farm 18:120-1 Ap '71 *

BEL canto. See Singing

BELDEN, Louise C.
Sallie Morris' silver. il Antiques 100:214-16 Ag '71

BELDEN, Stanley D.
Labor of love. il Org Gard & Farm 18:66-7 Mr '71

BELDING, Robert E.
Norway's district colleges. Sch & Soc 99:54-5 Ja '71

BELEN, N.Mex
Expendable Americans; Vietnamese war casualties. J. Rowen. Ramp Mag 10:8-9 N '71

BELFAST
Knights in the shebeen; report. J. Wilde. il Time 97:31 Ap 5 '71
Ulster: in the green hell. M. Kupfer. il Newsweek 77:42+ Ap 5 '71

Riots
Night in Ardoyne. Newsweek 77:40 F 15 '71
Northern Ireland: the children's war. il Time 97:27-8 F 22 '71
Northern Ireland: the powder keg. il por Time 97:26-32 Ap 5 '71
Nothing but violence. A. Deming. il Newsweek 77:42 F 22 '71

BELGIAN castles. See Castles

BELGIAN cattle herders (dogs) See Bouviers des Flandres

BELGIUM
See also
Americans in Belgium
Churches—Belgium
Holding companies—Belgium
Investments, Foreign (in Belgium)

Description and travel
Castles in Belgium. N. Hazelton. il Nat R 23:1251 N 5 '71

Economic conditions
Belgian boom goes on. G. R. Rosen. il Duns 98:81-2+ S '71

Economic policy
See also
Wage-price policy—Belgium

Languages
Belgium moves toward unity. T. Beeson. Chr Cent 88:1126 S 29 '71

Politics and government
Belgium moves toward unity. T. Beeson. Chr Cent 88:1126 S 29 '71

BELIEF and doubt
See also
Truth

BELIEF in God. See Faith

BELITT, Ben
Soundings. Block Island; poem. New Yorker 47:29 Ag 21 '71
(tr) See Neruda, P. Four poems

BELIVEAU, Jean
Get mad and win. il Newsweek 77:86-7 My 31 '71 *

BELIZE
Belize, the awakening land. L. De La Haba. il Nat Geog 141:124-46 Ja '72

BELL, Alphonzo
Can we afford the loss of momentum in the Nation's aerospace program? Space World H-9-93:36-7 S '71

BELL, Barbara
Tortola. il Travel 136:60-3 D '71

BELL, Charles A.
1700-foot outfall laid in one day. il Am City 86:66-7 S '71

BELL, Charles G.
Fly bait; poem. Sat R 54:70 F 20 '71

BELL, Clara, and Dray, Sheldon
Expression of allelic immunoglobulin in homozygous rabbits injected with RNA extract. bibliog il Science 171:199-201 Ja 15 '71

BELL, Daniel
Sensibility in the 60's; excerpt from The disjunction of culture and social structure. Commentary 51:63-73 Je '71

BELL, David V. J. and Goodman, A. E.
Vietnam and the American revolution. Yale R 61:26-34 O '71

BELL, Eugene
Informational DNA synthesis distinguished from that of nuclear DNA by inhibitors of DNA synthesis. bibliog il Science 174:603-6 N 5 '71

BELL, Inge Powell
Double standard. il Trans-Action 8:75-80 N '70

BELL, Jess
Outdoor makeup, you say? Well, tan my hide! A. Verschoth. il por Sports Illus 35:86-7 N 22 '71 *

BELL, Joseph N.
Danger: smut. Good H 172:85+ Ap '71
New crisis in medical care. Good H 174:62-3+ Ja '72
Secret family of Father Duryea. il pors Good H 173:80-1+ Ag '71
Take your troubles to the Hotline. il Seventeen 29:242-3+ Ag '70
Those mushrooming food fads. il Seventeen 30:110-11+ Jl '71
(ed) See Andrews, J. My friend, Carol Burnett
(ed) See Arnaz, D. jr. My mother, Lucille Ball

BELL, L. Nelson
Layman and his faith. See issues of Christianity today
about
Founder of Presbyterian journal resigns over withdrawal plan. Chr Cent 88:1043 S 8 '71 *

BELL, Marvin
Song: the organic years. New Yorker 47:42 Je 5 '71
Travels we took in our time; Temper; Getting lost in nazi Germany; Constant feelings; poems. Poetry 117:304-7 F '71
What the doctor ordered; poem. Nation 212:442 Ap 5 '71

BELL, Richard H. V.
Grazing ecosystem in the Serengeti; with biographical sketch. il Sci Am 225:14, 86-93 Jl '71

BELL, Robert M. and Koshland, D. E. jr
Covalent enzyme-substrate intermediates. bibliog il Science 172:1253-6 Je 18 '71

BELL, Terrel Howard
Year 1991; adaptation of address. il Am Ed 7:23-6 Ja '71

BELL, Trudy E.
Groups are organized to observe the eclipse of stars by the moon. il Sci Am 226:108-11 Ja '72

BELL and Howell company
Bell & Howell to microfilm Women's lib materials. Library J 96:3933 D 1 '71
Digestion and indigestion. il por Forbes 108:35 S 1 '71
He'll put snap into Bell & Howell. il por Bsns W p28+ F 20 '71

BELL boys. See Hotels, taverns, etc.—Employees

BELL holders
Bell ringing project. D. Shiner. il Design 72:30-1 Spr '71

BELL telephone laboratories
Behind "number, please" the story of W. Lincoln Hawkins. S. P. Massie. il por Chem 44:16 O '71
Bell labs swings to minis. il Bsns W p 118-19 Je 5 '71
How Bell labs answers calls for help. il Bsns W p38-41+ Ja 23 '71

BELL telephone system. See American telephone and telegraph company
BELLA VILLA, Mo.
Plastic trash carts to the rescue. G. J. Appel.
il Am City 86:77-8 Jl '71
BELLAK, Leopold
Our unsure society; address, October 16, 1970.
Vital Speeches 37:279-82 F 15 '71
La BELLE telephone; drama. See Boiko, C.
BELLESEN, Paul
Idea from below nowhere. E. Crimmin. il
por Motor B & S 127:12+ My '71 *
BELLEVUE, Wash.

Education
Bellevue education association. L. E. Saylor.
Todays Ed 60:66 Mr '71
BELLINI, Vincenzo
Norma. Criticism
Newsweek 77:95 Je 28 '71 *
BELLO, Francis. See Schmidt, M. jt. auth.
BELLOC, Hilaire
Belloc, ed. by H. van Thal. Review
Commonweal 94:67-9 Mr 26 '71. M.
Ward *
BELLOCQ, E. J.
Gallery; photographs. Life 70:6-9 Mr 26 '71

about
E. J. Bellocq: storeyville portraits, by L.
Friedlander and J. Szarkowski. Review
Commonweal 94:409-10 Ag 6 '71. S.
Cohen *
BELLOW, Saul
Midtown and the Village. A. Kazin. il
Harper 242:82-9 Ja '71 *
Mr Sammler and the God of Our fathers. J.
W. Sire. Chr Today 15:6-9 Je 4 '71 *
BELLOWS
Camera collector; Turner bellows inc. J.
Schneider. il Mod Phot 35:104+ S '71
Schwalberg on bellowsmanship. B. Schwalberg. il Pop Phot 69:62-5+ Jl '71
BELLS
Ring out, ring out, ye merry bells. D.
Powills. il Hobbies 76:140-1+ D '71

Collecting and collectors
Welcome to Bell haven. L. Springer. il Hobbies 76:152-3 O '71
BELLWORTS
Wild oats can be controlled. Suc Farm 69:
no4 C36 Mr '71
BELMONT, Eleanor (Robson)
Lady without whom we would not be here
today; excerpt from intermission talk on
the Texaco-Metropolitan opera broadcast,
March 13, 1971. F. Robinson. Opera N 35:6-
7 My 15 '71 *
BELMONT, Elsie K.
Message to museums. Am Artist 35:11 D '71
BELMONT stakes. See Horse racing
BELT, Byron
JFK center for the performing arts. il Hi Fi
21:52-7 S '71
Wolf Trap, a gala opening. por Hi Fi 21:
MA20+ O '71
BELT, Forest H.
Antenna lead-ins for TV. il Electr World
86:32-4 Ag '71
Automatic tint correction in color TV. il
Electr World 86:45-8 Ag '71
Cable TV: where it is & where it's going. il
Pop Electr 1:26-30 Ja '72
Color-bar generators for servicing. il Electr
World 86:34-7+ S '71
Color TV for 1971. il Electr World 85:23-6+
F; 43-4+ Mr '71
How to select a TV antenna. il Electr World
85:32-5+ My '71
Television scene. Pop Electr 1:112-15 Ja '72
Testing IC's in TV receivers. il Electr World
86:49-52+ N '71
They've changed the rules for marine radio;
with tables. il Pop Sci 199:65-7+ D '71
Transistor testers for servicing. il Electr
World 86:40-3 Jl '71
Trinitron versus shadowmask. il Radio-Electr
43:38-41 Ja '72
What's happened to educational TV? il Pop
Electr 35:31-5 D '71
BELTING
How to service your V-belt power drives.
Suc Farm 69:no5 D2 Mr '71
BELTON, Betty H.
Art and the small community. il Sch Arts
70:26-8 Mr '71
BELTON, John
Crucified lovers of Mizoguchi. il Film Q 25:
15-19 Fall '71
BELTRAN house. See Lima, Peru—Historic
houses, etc.
BELTS
Leather belt you make in less than an hour.
il Sunset 147:82+ D '71
One square knot after another; macramé belt.
il Sunset 146:83-4+ F '71

BEN, Philip
Making ends meet. New Repub 164:14 Ja 30
'71
BEN-AMOTZ, Dan
Israel postscript: two writers. D. N. Mount.
Pub W 199:31 Je 7 '71 *
BEN-GURION, David
Peace is more important than real estate;
interview, ed. by J. M. Roots. il por
Sat R 54:14-16 Ap 3 '71

about
Desert sage. por Time 98:46 O 18 '71 *
BEN-ZVI, Seymour
Danger in the hospital. A. S. Freese. il Pop
Mech 135:80-3 F '71 *
BEN-ZVI, Zvi, and others
6β-Hydroxy-Δ¹-tetrahydrocannabinol synthesis
and biological activity. bibliog il Science
174:951-2 N 26 '71
BEN Heller collection. See Art—Private collections
BENCE Jones proteins. See Proteins
BENCH grinders. See Grinding machines
BENCHES
For work, for lunch, even for a nap; it's a
superbench. il Sunset 147:124 O '71
Fun-to-build block bench. D. Houser. il Pop
Sci 199:134 O '71
It's three levels for lunch, but just one level
for lounging. il Sunset 146:140 My '71
Shelling bench. M. Stilwell. il por Org Gard
& Farm 18:66 Ag '71
You can build this early American gossip
bench. W. C. Leckey. il Pop Mech 135:152-
4+ Mr '71
See also
Work benches
BENCHLEY, Nathaniel
House; story. Ladies Home J 88:126-7 N '71
BENCHLEY, Peter
Bermuda: balmy, British and beautiful. il
Nat Geog 140:93-121 Jl '71
Central America. il Holiday 48:62-6 N '70
New Zealand's bountiful South Island. il Nat
Geog 141:92-123 Ja '72
Palm Springs. il Holiday 49:56-9+ D '70
BENDING of tubes. See Tube bending
BENDING of wood. See Wood bending
BENDIX corporation
Bendix plots a new course. il por Bsns W
p93-4+ Jl 17 '71
BENDOW, Burton
Are you in the ketchup trade also? Nation
213:533-5 N 22 '71
Poet's duty. Nation 212:469-71 Ap 12 '71
BENEDICT, J.
Battle royal over inkblot tests: are they
useless? il Sci Digest 70:43-8+ O '71
BENEDICT, Manson
Electric power from nuclear fission; adaptation of address, April 1971. bibliog il por Bul
Atom Sci 27:8-16 S '71
BENEDICT, William F. and Karon, Myron
Chromatid breakage: cytosine arabinoside-
induced lesions inhibited by ultraviolet irradiation. bibliog il Science 171:680-2 F 19
'71
BENEDIKT, Michael
Tragic landscape; Elegy for the insects;
poems. Poetry 117:363-4 Mr '71
BENEFIT performances
Colossal event. G. Harrison and R. Shankar
benefit performance at Madison Square
Garden for people of Bangla Desh. J.-C.
Costa. il pors Sr Schol 99:32-4 S 27 '71
Concert: benefit for the George Harrison and
Ravi Shankar special emergency relief fund
for displaced persons of Bangla Desh. New
Yorker 47:28-30 Ag 14 '71
Rarest rock show of all; George Harrison
and his friends. il pors Life 71:20-3 Ag 13
'71
See also
Phonograph records—Benefit performances
BENÉT, Stephen Vincent
Devil and Daniel Webster; dramatization. See
MacLeish, A. Scratch
BENET, Sula
Why they live to be 100, or even older, in
Abkhasia. il N Y Times Mag p3+ D 26 '71
BENEVOLENT and protective order of elks.
See Elks, Benevolent and protective order
of
BENFEY, Theodor
Western alchemy symbols in a Japanese
medical work. bibliog il Chem 44:14-18 S '71
BENFORD, Gregory, and Book, David
Sky color; with biographical sketches. bibliog
il Natur Hist 80:6, 32-9+ F '71
BENFORD, John Q.
Philadelphia project. il por Library J 96:
2041-7 Je 15 '71
BENGALI refugees. See Refugees. Pakistan
BENGALI restaurant. See New York (city)—
Hotels, restaurants, etc.

BENGALIS
People apart: the complex Bengalis. il Newsweek 77:32 Ap 5 '71
BENGALIS in the United States
Talk of the town; party at new Bengali restaurant. New Yorker 47:24-5 D 25 '71
BENGELSDORF, Irving S.
Are we running out of fuel? il Nat Wildlife 9:4-9 F '71
BENI Immobili Italia. See Italy—Industries
BENIHANA of Tokyo, Inc.
What makes Rocky run. por Newsweek 77:104+ Ap 19 '71
BENISKOS, J. M.
Person teacher. Ed Digest 36:34-6 Ap '71
BENJAMIN, Ben
Beauty sense and nonsense. Harp Baz 104:20 My '71
BENJAMIN, Edward B.
Houseboat that sails. il Yachting 130:55+ Jl '71
BENJAMIN, Joel
New repertory dance theater. the Cubiculo, NYC.   T. Borek. Dance Mag 45:82+ S '71 •
BENJAMIN, Richard
Hollywood scene; interview, ed. by E. Miller. pors Seventeen 29:46 Jl '70
BENN, Anthony Wedgwood
Technical power and people. Bul Atom Sci 27:23-6 D '71
BENNETT, Benjamin K.
Riverside park; Jardin du Luxembourg; Ajax; poems. Poetry 118:25-6 Ap '71
BENNETT, John B.
Case of the president's predicament. il Harvard Bsns R 49:16-18+ Ja '71
BENNETT, John Coleman
C and C in crisis. Newsweek 77:97-8 Mr 22 '71 •
BENNETT, Sir John Wheeler Wheeler-. See Wheeler-Bennett, J. W.
BENNETT, Joseph
Monsoon: Return to sea-level; poems. Poetry 117:357-60 Mr '71
BENNETT, Lerone, Jr
Making of black America (cont) il Ebony 26:56-8+ N '70; 44-6+ F '71
Old illusions and new Souths. il Ebony 26:35-8+ Ag '71
Sweetback in wonderland. il por Ebony 26:106-8+ S '71
White hopes and other coalitions; adaptation of address. il Ebony 26:33-4+ O '71
BENNETT, Margaret, pseud.
Rent-a-script caper. Pub W 200:40 Ag 2 '71
BENNETT, Ralph Kinney
Angela Davis: the making of a martyr. pors Read Digest 98:108-12 Mr '71
Terrorists among us. il Read Digest 99:115-20 O '71
Why we have a fuel and power shortage. Read Digest 98:74-8 Ja '71
BENNETT, Robert A.
NCTE counciletter. Engl J 60:1131-2 N '71
NCTE: 1971; address, November 1970. Engl J 60:455-7 Ap '71
BENNETT, Timothy
Pumpkin fever. il Travel 136:46-7 S '71
BENNETT, William Tapley, 1917-
U.N. defers consideration of Korea until 27th General assembly; statement, September 25, 1971. Dept State Bul 65:430 O 18 '71
U.S. supports Security council resolution on Namibia; statement. October 20, 1971. Dept State Bul 65:609-12 N 22 '71
U.S. urges international community to continue relief to south Asia; statement, November 19, 1971. Dept State Bul 65:717-19 D 20 '71
BENNION, Adam
Oil in Vietnam. il Ramp Mag 9:8+ My '71
BENNIS, Warren G.
Searching for the perfect university president. il Atlan 227:39-44+ Ap '71
BENOFF, Mitchell. See Allen, E. jt. auth.
BENOMYL. See Fungicides
BENREY, Ronald M.
Add-on converter turns your B&W TV into a color set. il Pop Sci 199:45-7 D '71
Appliance tester you can build. il Pop Sci 199:124+ S '71
Dwell extender for your car. il Pop Sci 199:104-5 O '71
Enlarge your rooms with light. il Pop Sci 199:98-9+ S '71
How electronics can lock power tools. il Pop Sci 199:98-9+ D '71
How to beat those football blackouts. il Pop Sci 199:57-9+ S '71
Instant darkroom. il Pop Sci 199:114 O '71
Make holograms at home, at a budget price. il Pop Sci 198:84-6 Ja '71
Microelectronics in the '70s. il Pop Sci 199:83-5+ O '71

Three-range electronic thermometer. il Pop Sci 198:102-3 F '71
Travel computer. il Pop Sci 198:79-81 My '71
Writing for the science and mechanics magazines. Writer 84:26-7 N '71
BENSEN, Donald R.
(ed) See Wodehouse, P. G. Exclusive interview
BENSON, Bruce
Hobie cat national championship. Motor B & S 127:37 F '71
Piracy in the Pacific! il Motor B & S 128:46-7+ O '71
BENSON, Charles
Deterrence through defense. il Nat R 23:251-9 Mr 9 '71
BENSON, D. John
Please, before I hit the ground. Chr Today 15:11-12+ S 10 '71
BENSON, Edward Frederic
Story behind the books: Lucia is alive and well. E. Erdosi. Pub W 200:49 Ag 9 '71 •
BENSON, Elizabeth P.
Before Cortés. il Américas 23:S2-11 Je '71
BENSON, George A.
Church needs Christian lovers, not oedipal boys; ordination sermon. Chr Cent 88:101-4 Ja 27 '71
BENSON, Herbert
—and others
Decreased systolic blood pressure through operant conditioning techniques in patients with essential hypertension. bibliog il Science 173:740-2 Ag 20 '71

about

Mind over drugs. il Time 98:51 O 25 '71 •
BENSON, Robert A.
Icy escape. il Nat Wildlife 9:30-1 F '71
BENT, Henry A.
Haste makes waste: pollution and entropy. bibliog il por Chem 44:6-15 O '71
BENTHAM, Jeremy
Mummy's curse. J. W. Burrow. il por Horizon 13:42-7 Aut '71
BENTHOS
Deep, deep sea floor; excerpt from The face of the deep. B. C. Heezen and C. D. Hollister. il Natur Hist 80:30-3 bibliog (p 104) My '71
Tektite unlocks secrets from the ocean's floor. C. B. Jackson. il Nat Wildlife 9:50-5 Ap '71
BENTLEY, David R.
Genetic control of an insect neuronal network. bibliog il Science 174:1139-41 D 10 '71
BENTLEY, Wilson Alwyn
Lifetime of snowflakes; photographs. Audubon 73:61-4 Ja '71

about

Wilson Bentley, the snowflake man. D. C. Blanchard. bibliog il pors Weatherwise 23:260-9 D '70 •
BENTON, Robert. See Newman, D. jt. auth.
BENTZ, W. Kenneth, and others
Attitudes of teachers and the public toward mental illness. bibliog il Ment Hy 55:324-30 Jl '71
BEQUEST to the nation; drama. See Rattigan, T.
BEQUIA (island)
Report from Bequia. P. Cronin. il Travel 135:56-9 Mr '71
BEREAVEMENT
Therapeutic friendship. il Time 97:45 My 3 '71
BERELSON, Bernard
Trends in world population; address, February 24, 1971. Vital Speeches 37:349-52 Mr 15 '71
BERENBERG, William
What's happening to today's children; interview. il por U S News 70:82-5 F 15 '71
BERENDT, John
From those wonderful people who gave you Kent state. Esquire 75:38+ Ap '71
BERENSON, Ruth
In the Midwest. Nat R 23:94-5 Ja 26 '71
Pillow talk. Nat R 23:1190-1 O 22 '71
Rummaging. Nat R 23:1004-5 S 10 '71
BERENSTAIN, Janice. See Berenstain, S. jt. auth.
BERENSTAIN, Stanley, and Berenstain, Janice
It's all in the family (cont) il Good H 172:64-5 Ap; 86-7 My; 173:76-7 Ag; 72-3 D '71
BERG, Alban
From Alban to Helene. G. Perle. il por Sat R 54:38-9+ Ag 28 '71 •
BERG, Kare
Compositional relatedness between histocompatibility antigens and human serum lipoproteins. bibliog il Science 172:1136-8 Je 11 '71

BERG, Louis
Founders & fur traders. Commentary 51:77-81 My '71
BERG, Marianne
In my opinion. Seventeen 30:62 S '71
BERG, Raymond
Drunk deterrent. Newsweek 77:84+ Mr 1 '71 •
BERG, Roland H.
Over-medicated woman. il McCalls 98:67+ S '71
There's more than cholesterol behind heart attacks. Look 35:51-2 F 9 '71
Will my baby be normal? McCalls 98:52+ Ag '71
BERGAMINI, David
Japan's imperial conspiracy; interview, ed. by A. H. Johnston. il por Pub W 200:26-7 O 4 '71

about

Is Hirohito the war's real villain? il por Time 98:43-4 O 4 '71 •
BERGDORF Goodman company. See New York (city)—Stores
BERGE, Carol
Comment. J. Martin. Poetry 118:345-6 S '71 •
BERGEN, Candice
Candice Bergen and her California house. il pors Vogue 157:74-9+ Je '71
Candy Bergen: what can you say about a sleeping beauty? interview, ed. by J. Greenfeld. por Redbook 137:58+ Jl '71
Lee Marvin and Paul Newman. pors Vogue 158:146-7+ O 1 '71
She's a great girl! interview, ed. by E. Miller. il pors Seventeen 29:240-1+ Ag '70
BERGEN COUNTY, N.J.
How to make digesters work faster. Am City 86:26 D '71
BERGER, Allen. See Nathan, N. jt. auth.
BERGER, Barry D. and others
Norepinephrine: reversal of anorexia in rats with lateral hypothalamic damage. il bibliog il Science 172:281-4 Ap 16 '71
BERGER, Bob
Apartment ping-pong table. il Mech Illus 67:102-3 D '71
Cap-eating shark. il Mech Illus 67:118 F '71
Everything you always wanted to know about the micrometer. il Mech Illus 67:95-7+ S '71
House hunting with a Polaroid. il Mech Illus 68:86 Ja '72
Welding equipment for the home shop. il Mech Illus 67:106-7+ D '71
BERGER, Brigitte. See Berger, P. L. jt. auth.
BERGER, Bruce
Point of music; poem. Commonweal 95:347 Ja 14 '72
BERGER, Harold
Neutron radiography for nondestructive testing. il Electr World 86:40-1+ Ag '71
Now N rays show what X rays can't. il por Pop Sci 198:57-9+ Je '71
BERGER, Ivan
Audio. il Sat R 54:76 Mr 27; 49+ Jl 31; 47-8 Ag 28, 84 O 30; 91 N 27 '71
Cassette-TV. il Sat R 54:45-7 Ja 30; 51 F 27 '71
Someday morning for the culture cans. il Sat R 54:45-7 Ja 30 '71
BERGER, Morroe
Arab's attitude to the west. Yale R 61:207-25 D '71
BERGER, Peter L.
Call for authority in the Christian community; address. Chr Cent 88:1257-63 O 27 '71
—and Berger, Brigitte
Blueing of America. New Repub 164:20-3 Ap 3 '71; Same. Cur 131:56-62 Jl '71

about

Death of relevance. Time 98:64 O 11 '71 •
Religious renascence? J. Deedy. Commonweal 95:170 N 19 '71 •
BERGER, Phil
What makes Ryun run again? il pors Look 35:56-8+ Jl 27 '71
BERGER, Roland
Beckoning a new generation. Nation 213:361-7 O 18 '71
BERGER, William
Insufficient evidence. Time 97:44 Ap 12 '71 •
Justice, Italian style. il por Time 97:52 Ap 5 '71 •
BERGERAC, Michel C.
ITT's bigger push in Europe. il por Time 98:70+ D 20 '71 •
BERGES, Ruth
Dear Saxon. por Opera N 35:6-7 Mr 20 '71

BERGMAN, Ingmar
Bergman about love. P. Gilliatt. New Yorker 47:57-8 Jl 24 '71 •
Bergman's odyssey. R. E. Lauder. America 125:119-20 S 4 '71 •
Disappointing Bergman. J. Cocks. il Time 98:50-1 Jl 26 '71 •
I live at the edge of a very strange country. R. Meryman. il pors Life 71:60-60B+ O 15 '71 •
BERGQUIST, Laura
Keeping up with Rose Kennedy at 81. il por McCalls 98:92-3+ S '71
(ed) See Ball, L. Lucille Ball, the star that never sets
BERGSTEN, C. Fred
Crisis in U.S. trade policy. bibliog f For Affairs 49:619-35 Jl '71
New economics and U.S. foreign policy. For Affairs 50:199-222 Ja '72
BERGUS, Donald
Middle East: dead but not buried. pors Time 98:23 Jl 12 '71 •
BERINGER, Doris
Student art used on calendar. il Sch Arts 70:11 Ap '71
BERIO, Luciano
Musical events; concert with the American symphony orchestra in Philharmonic Hall. W. Sargeant. New Yorker 47:122 My 22 '71 •
BERK, Donald M.
Four-channel stereo sound. il Consumer Bul 54:29-30 My '71
BERK, Harvey D.
Audio-visual aids can help you pep up staff meetings. il Camp Mag 43:12-13 Ap '71
BERKA, L. H. See Christian, P. A. jt. auth.
BERKE, Joel S.
Crisis in school finance. Ed Digest 37:5-8 N '71
BERKELEY, Busby
Busby Berkeley's girls glitter again. H. Wingo. il por Life 70:42-3 F 19 '71 •
BERKELEY, David S.
Science at the second coming; poem. Chr Today 15:8 My 21 '71
BERKELEY, Gail
Darkness; poem. Seventeen 30:194 S '71
BERKELEY, Calif.

Education

Living lab for high school students; Nursery teacher aide training program at Berkeley, Calif. high school. M. P. Larson. il Todays Ed 60:22-4 Mr '71

Elections

Berkeley votes. New Repub 164:11 Ap 17 '71
Comes the revolution; victory for the April coalition. il Newsweek 77:44 Ap 19 '71
Radicals use the system, and find that it works. il U S News 70:37 Ap 19 '71
Welcome to the system; Mayor Widener and radical council members. il por Time 97:16 Ap 19 '71

Parks and playgrounds

Sod creates instant park. J. E. Howland. il Parks & Rec 6:27+ N '71

Police

Neighborhood police. J. H. Skolnick. Nation 212:372-3 Mr 22 '71

Politics and government

Berkeley: a tale of one city. P. Seabury. Commentary 52:66-72 Ag '71
Berkeley city council will never be the same. S. Stern. il N Y Times Mag p 14-16+ Ag 28 '71
Guard changes in Berkeley; April coalition. J. Slater. il pors Ebony 26:74-6+ O '71
New blood and brains. J. Morgenstern. Newsweek 77:17 My 10 '71
People's Republic of Berkeley. J. R. Coyne, jr. Nat R 23:260+ Mr 9 '71
See also
Berkeley, Calif.—Elections

Social conditions

Halfway between dropping out and dropping in. S. V. Roberts. il N Y Times Mag p44-6+ S 12 '71
BERKELEY bookstores. See Booksellers and bookselling—California
BERKELEY campus. See California. University—Berkeley campus
BERKLEY, William
Cleared as filed: how to choose the proper IFR route. il Flying 89:54-5 Jl '71
Contact approach or visual approach: what's the difference? Flying 88:69-70 Mr '71

BERKLEY, William—*Continued*
Everything you always wanted to know about radar. il Flying 88:44-6 F '71
Pilots rights. Flying 89:94-6 O '71
Radar and the VFR pilot. Flying 88:57-8 My '71

BERKMAN, Alexander
Lesson out of the past. P. Caws. New Repub 164:23-4 Ja 16 '71 •

BERKMAN, Harry A.
National ski patrol. il Cons 26:20-1 D '71

BERKOVITZ, Robert
Power amplification. il Hi Fi 21:58-62+ S '71

BERKOWITZ, Norton
Search for design. il Sch Arts 71:16-18 D '71

BERKSHIRE boy choir. See Choirs

BERKWITT, George J.
Modern industry. il Duns 97:83-4+ Mr; 98:61-2+ Ag; 83-4+ N '71

BERL, Kathe
Fun jewelry. il Ceram Mo 19:29 Ja; 27 Ap '71
Liquid enamels for background and texture. il Ceram Mo 19:30 N '71

BERL, Walter G.
Brief prospectus of the 1971 AAAS annual meeting. Science 174:847-56 N 19 '71
Looking backward: Chicago AAAS annual meeting. Science 171:716-17 F 19 '71

BERLAND, Theodore
Giving more of our infants the lives they deserve. il Todays Health 49:16-19+ Ag '71

BERLE, Adolf Augustus, 1895-1971
Corporate giants. P. A. Samuelson. Newsweek 77:88 Mr 29 '71 •

BERLE, Anton
Teleguide. il Schol Teach Jr/Sr High p31 Ja '72

BERLIN, Edward. See Craig, P. P. jt. auth.

BERLIN, Newton N.
Watching the corn grow. il Org Gard & Farm 18:62-3 Jl '71

BERLIN

History
Russian blockade
Berlin blockade and the use of the United Nations. P. C. Jessup. bibliog f For Affairs 50:163-73 O '71

BERLIN (East Berlin)

Airports
Airports across the wall; East Berlin's Schönefeld airport. Time 98:50 Ag 23 '71

Music
Fiddler in Berlin. Newsweek 77:39 F 8 '71
Fiddler on an East Berlin roof. G. R. Marek. il Sat R 54:46-7+ F 27 '71
Report:
Fiddler on the roof. J. H. Sutcliffe. Opera N 35:31 Mr 20 '71
Fidelio, by East Berlin's Staatsoper. J. H. Sutcliffe. Opera N 35:32 F 27 '71
Massenet's Don Quichotte in East Berlin's Komische oper. J. H. Sutcliffe Opera N 36:29-30 D 11 '71
Verdi's Forza del destino and Strauss' Frau ohne schatten at East Berlin's Komische oper and Staatsoper. J. H. Sutcliffe. il Opera N 35:25 Je 12 '71

BERLIN (West Berlin)
Berlin revisited. A. Armstrong. Nat R 23:1057 S 24 '71
Deal with Russia? not for Berliners. R. A. Haeger. il U S News 70:88-9 Mr 29 '71

Music
Report:
Beverly Sills in Traviata. J. H. Sutcliffe. Opera N 35:31 Mr 6 '71
Boris Godunov at West Berlin's Deutsche oper. J. H. Sutcliffe. Opera N 35:31 Mr 13 '71
Reimann's Melusine, Henze's The wearisome way into Natasha Ungeheuer's apartment, and Stravinsky's Historie du soldat. J. H. Sutcliffe. Opera N 36:29 D 11 '71

BERLIN festival. See Music festivals—Germany (Federal Republic)

BERLIN question, 1945-
Agreement on Berlin. H. J. Morgenthau. New Repub 165:16-18 D 25 '71
At last, Berlin agreement. il U S News 71:24-5 S 6 '71
Beginning of the end? il Newsweek 78:30 Ag 23 '71
Berlin agreement: an assessment; address, September 22, 1971. K. Rush. Dept State Bul 65:489-97 N 1 '71
Berlin breakthrough. Time 98:42 D 20 '71
Berlin breakthrough. T. Beeson. Chr Cent 88:1073-4 S 15 '71

Berlin getting off dead center. New Repub 165:7-9 Jl 24 '71
Berlin on their mind. Newsweek 77:46+ Je 28 '71
Berlin: shaping agreements. il Time 98:25-6 Ag 30 '71
Breakthrough in Berlin. il Newsweek 78:34+ Ag 30 '71
Breakthrough on Berlin? Time 98:26-7 Ag 16 '71
Divided Berlin: America's lingering problem in long division. il Sr Schol 98:3-8 Mr 8 '71
Don't go, comrade Ulbricht. Time 98:38 D 6 '71
End of the short fuse; signing of a preliminary agreement. il Time 98:26+ S 13 '71
End to Berlin crisis? draft accord. il Newsweek 78:27+ S 6 '71
Entering a new realm. Newsweek 77:43 Mr 1 '71
Fissures in the other wall. Nat R 23:1046 S 24 '71
Interested bystanders. Time 98:26 S 6 '71
Peace as a process. Nation 213:195 S 13 '71
Quadripartite agreement on Berlin signed at Berlin concluding first phase of negotiations; statements, with text of quadripartite agreement and related documents and Exchange of notes, September 3, 1971. W. P. Rogers; K. Rush. Dept State Bul 65:317-25 S 27 '71
Round two. New Repub 165:9 S 4 '71
Scattered chips. il Time 98:47 N 29 '71
See also
Berlin wall, 1961-

BERLIN wall, 1961-
After 10 years, Communist wall in Berlin has a permanent look. il U S News 71:62 Ag 16 '71
Berlin wall: ten years later. J. R. Moskin. il Look 35:58-9+ Ag 10 '71
Fighting over a few words. il Time 98:21 Ag 23 '71

BERLINRUT, Peter
Notes of a substitute teacher. Commentary 51:53-62 Ap '71

BERLIOZ, Hector
Music to my ears; sections of Béatrice et Bénédict performed by New York philharmonic. I. Kolodin. Sat R 54:33+ My 8 '71 •

BERMAN, Bertha
Character parts in the drama of English grammar. Clear House 45:380-2 F '71

BERMAN, Eleanor
Mothers help out at school. il Parents Mag 46:58+ Ap '71

BERMAN, Ruth
Computative oak; poem. Sat R 54:6 Mr 20 '71
Soundstage; poem. Sat R 54:21 Ja 30 '71

BERMAN, Sanford
Children, idiots, the underground, and others; excerpts from Prejudices and antipathies. bibliog f il por Library J 96:4162-7 D 15 '71
Let it all hang out. il Library J 96:2054-8 Je 15 '71

BERMAN, Susan
Chevron's pollution solution. Commonweal 93:546-8 Mr 5 '71

BERMUDA
Bermuda: balmy, British and beautiful. P. Benchley. il Nat Geog 140:93-121 Jl '71

Description and travel
Bermuda on two wheels a day. D. Butwin. il Sat R 54:64+ O 16 '71

BERMUDIAN furniture. See Furniture, Bermudian

BERMUDIAN silver. See Silverware

BERN (city)
I remember the bears. M. D. Ross. il Har Yrs 11:46-7 F '71

BERNAL, John Desmond
Obituary
Phys Today por 24:65-7 D '71. A. Mackay

BERNARD, Burton
Radio operated fire alarm system. il Radio-Electr 42:47 D '71

BERNARD, Jack
(tr) See Revel, J. F. Without Marx or Jesus

BERNARD, Thomas L.
Brain drain: mountain or molehill? bibliog Sch & Soc 99:43-5 Ja '71

BERNE, Dale L.
High school remembers the senior citizen. Clear House 45:545-6 My '71

BERNE, Eric
Sex education in America. Harp Baz 104:140-1 Mr '71

BERNE (city) See Bern

BERNE copyright convention. See Copyright

BERNETTA Quinn, Sister. See Quinn, B.

BERNHARD, Berl
Manager for Muskie. pors Time 97:13 Mr 1 '71 *

BERNHEIMER, Martin
Contempo '71, calm and becalmed. il Hi Fi 21:MA24-5 Ag '71
Villa-Lobos' Yerma bogs down. Hi Fi 21: MA16-17 N '71

BERNIER, Rosamond
European art finds. Vogue 158:90+ S 15 '71

BERNINGHAUSEN, David Knipe
Defending the defenders of intellectual freedom; ed. by J. F. Krug and J. A. Harvey. bibliog Am Lib 2:18-21 Ja '71
Report of the Intellectual freedom committee to council, Dallas, June 25, 1971; ed. by J. F. Krug and J. A. Harvey. Am Lib 2:891-2 S '71

BERNS, Gabriel
(tr) See Pérez De Ayala, R. Ruera street

BERNS, Michael W. and others
Chromosome lesions produced with an argon laser microbeam without dye sensitization. bibliog il Science 171:903-5 Mr 5 '71

BERNSTEIN, Abraham
Cultural clash, crash, and cash; address, November 1970. Engl J 60:773-7 S '71

BERNSTEIN, Burton
Reporter at large. il New Yorker 47:100+ N 27 '71

BERNSTEIN, Edward Morris
Things are so bad, they're good. por Forbes 107:50-1 Je 1 '71 *

BERNSTEIN, Irwin D. and others
Tumor immunity: tumor suppression in vivo initiated by soluble products of specifically stimulated lymphocytes. bibliog il Science 172:729-31 My 14 '71

BERNSTEIN, Jeremy
Reporter at large (cont) New Yoker 47:118-32+ O 30 '71

BERNSTEIN, Leonard
Bernstein talks about his work; interview, ed. by R. T. Zadikov. il Time 98:42 S 20 '71
Leonard Bernstein; interview, ed. by J. Gruen. il por Vogue 158:252-3+ S 1 '71

about

At JFK center. S. Fleming. il Hi Fi 21: MA10-11 D '71 *
Bernstein-Ginastera premieres at Kennedy center. I. Kolodin. il Sat R 54:74-5 S 25 '71 *
Bernstein's Mass: no word from the Lord. C. A. Forbes. il Chr Today 16:40-1 O 8 '71 *
Bernstein's Mass opens Kennedy center. C. J. McNaspy; J. Gallen. il America 125:228-9 O 2 '71 *
Candide. Criticism
  Nat R 23:1427 D 17 '71 *
  Sat R 54:75 N 20 '71 *
Catching Lenny. R. Kotlowitz. il pors N Y Times Mag p6-7+ D 19 '71 *
Celebration of the spirit; first performance of Mass. H. Saal. il por Newsweek 78:29-30+ S 20 '71 *
Mass for everyone, maybe. W. Bender. il Time 98:41-3 S 20 '71 *
Media is the mass. R. Thibodeau. Commonweal 95:17-18 O 1 '71 *
Music; Mass. D. Hamilton. Nation 213:317-18 O 4 '71 *
Musical events; thousandth concert with New York philharmonic, and TV documentary: Beethoven's birthday. W. Sargeant. New Yorker 47:64 D 25 '71 *
Radical chic and Mau-Mauing the flak catchers, by T. Wolfe. Review
  Commentary 51:98+ Mr '71. J. Epstein *

BERNSTEIN, Leonard S.
How much is that painting in the window? House B 113:38+ N '71
How to make a million dollars on your vacation. Holiday 49:26-7 Jl '71

BERNSTEIN, Peter. See Bernstein, T. jt. auth.

BERNSTEIN, Theodore M.
Word with you, Miss Thistlebottom; excerpt from Miss Thistlebottom's hobgoblins. Read Digest 98:39-40+ My '71

BERNSTEIN, Tom, and Bernstein, Peter
Pleasures and pitfalls of getting out the vote. il Seventeen 31:122+ Ja '72

BERNSTEIN, Victor H.
Coming soon: the three-day weekend, every week. il Redbook 138:77+ Ja '72
How to succeed though innocent. Nation 212:376-8 Mr 22 '71
Our transportation system that gets us nowhere. Redbook 136:89+ Mr '71
—See Ahern, J. F. jt. auth.

BERRIAULT, Gina
Last of life... il Esquire 75:118-19+ My '71

BERRIES
See also
Cookery—Fruit
Miracle fruit
  also names of berries, e.g. Strawberries

BERRIGAN, Daniel
Dialogue with radical priest Daniel Berrigan; excerpts from The geography of faith. pors Time 97:16-17 Mr 22 '71

about

Bearing the burden of the Berrigan brothers. E. Duff. New Repub 164:18-23 Mr 6 '71 *
Berrigan still in good standing in Jesuit order, superior says. Chr Cent 88:615 My 19 '71 *
Harboring of Daniel Berrigan. R. Wool. il Esquire 76:156-61+ N '71 *
How the kidnap conspiracy was hatched. L. Lockwood. il pors Life 70:24-30 My 21 '71 *
Inversion of tradition. S. M. Smith. Nat R 23:817+ Jl 27 '71 *
Minotaur or man? M. Maddocks. por Time 97:89+ Je 14 '71 *
Notes and comment; concerning message addressed to the weathermen. New Yorker 47:29 Mr 27 '71 *
Stringfellow-Towne indictment; with statement. J. R. Nelson. Chr Cent 88:60-1 Ja 20 '71 *
Trial of the Catonsville nine. Criticism
  America 124:208-9 F 27 '71 *
  Chr Cent 88:412-13 Mr 31 '71 *
  Commonweal 93:525 F 26 '71 *
  Life il 70:16-17 Ap 16 '71 *
  Nat R 23:490-1 My 4 '71 *
  Nation 212:254 F 22 '71 *
  New Repub 164:28-30 Mr 6 '71 *
  New Yorker 47:90 F 20 '71 *
  Newsweek 77:14-15 Mr 1 '71 *
  Newsweek il 77:67 F 22 '71 *
  Sat R 54:21 Mr 6 '71 *
  Time il 97:52 F 22 '71 *
  Vogue il 157:126 Ap 15 '71 *

BERRIGAN, Philip
Berrigan letters. il por Newsweek 77:27B My 10 '71 *
Drama inside the Berrigan circle; with report by L. Lockwood. il pors Life 70:22-31 My 21 '71 *
How to grab the brain child. il pors Time 97:15-16 My 10 '71 *
Kissinger kidnap plot revisited. America 124:503 My 15 '71 *
Philip Berrigan, ten others moved to Springfield prison. Chr Cent 88:1018 S 1 '71 *

BERRIGAN brothers
Anti-government kidnap, bomb plot? il U S News 70:28 Ja 25 '71 *
Belling the Berrigans. H. M. Engel and others. pors Cath World 213:227-31 Ag '71 *
Berrigan informer. il pors Time 97:20 F 1 '71
Berrigan plot. il pors Newsweek 77:28-9 Ja 25 '71 *
Berrigans: conspiracy and conscience. il pors Time 97:12-17 Ja 25 '71 *
Berrigans in focus. Nat R 23:184-6 F 23 '71 *
Berrigans: radical activism personified (cont) G. C. Zahn. Cath World 212:285 Mr '71
Berrigans vs the United States. M. Geltman. il Nat R 23:470-4 My 4 '71 *
Harrisburg indictments. Commonweal 93:435-6 F 5 '71
How about it, Sister? Nat R 23:516-17 My 18 '71
Kissinger kidnap plot; reactions to the indictment. America 124:80 Ja 30 '71; Reply. P. Steinfels. 124:134 F 13 '71
Knowing the Berrigans; Gallup survey. J. Deedy. Commonweal 95:74 O 22 '71 *
Lord's commands to a congressman. W. R. Anderson. Chr Cent 88:182-3 F 10 '71 *
Metamorphosis of a hawk: why an ex-navy hero from Tennessee attacked J. Edgar Hoover. R. Wool. il pors N Y Times Mag p22-3+ Ap 25 '71 *
New dove: W. R. Anderson. New Yorker 47:28-30 Ap 3 '71 *
No parole for Berrigans. America 125:78 Ag 21 '71 *
Old cause, new need. Commonweal 95:338 Ja 14 '72
Skipper sticks to his guns; W. R. Anderson support. M. McGrory. America 124:138 F 13 '71
Tales of two brothers. J. Sullivan. Cath World 213:150-1 Je '71

BERRY, Donald L.
Inner and outer freedom. Chr Cent 88:775-6 Je 23 '71

BERRY, H. M.
Breadfruit tree. il Horticulture 49:19+ Mr '71

BERRY, James R.
How we're reading nature's secrets from the sky. il Pop Mech 136:68-72 S '71

BERRY, Marcellus
In quest of Utopia. H. L. Clark. il pors
Nations Bsns 59:48-9 Ja '71 •
BERRY, R. Stephen
Option for survival. Bul Atom Sci 27:22-7 My
'71
BERRY, Wendell
For two friends fallen in love; poem. Mlle
72:102 Ja '71
One-inch journey; excerpt from The un-
foreseen wilderness. il Audubon 73:4-11 My
'71
Prayer after eating; Anger against beasts;
Homecoming; poems. Poetry 119:67-8 N '71
Wild geese; poem. Esquire 75:146 Mr '71
        about
Comment. W. H. Pritchard. Poetry 119:162-
3 D '71 •
BERRY bearing plants
Plan now to grow a feast for the birds. il
Home Gard 58:50 Mr '71
BERRYMAN, John
Ecce homo; poem. New Yorker 47:38 Ap 10
'71
Form; poem. Esquire 75:18 My '71
Tampa stomp; poem. Esquire 75:181 Ap '71
Washington in love; poem. Esquire 75:172 Ap
'71
        about
Love, art and money. H. Carruth; discussion.
Nation 211:546; 212:98 N 30 '70, Ja 25 '71 •
BERSHADSKAYA, Lyubov Leontyevna
24 years in the life of Lyuba Bershadskaya.
T. Vocse. il por N Y Times Mag p27-9+
Mr 14 '71 •
BERSON, Lenora E.
Toughest cop in America campaigns for may-
or of Philadelphia. il pors N Y Times Mag
p30-1+ My 16 '71
BERSON, Minnie P.
Inside the open classroom. il Am Ed 7:11-15
My '71
Mending lives at a PCC. il Am Ed 7:22-7 D
'71
BERTELSMANN company. See Publishers and
publishing—Germany (Federal Republic)
BERTHOFF, Warner
Fictions and events, by W. Berthoff. Review
Sat R il 55:36 Ja 8 '72. L. Graver •
BERTINE, K. K. and Goldberg, E. D.
Fossil fuel combustion and the major sedi-
mentary cycle. bibliog il Science 173:233-5
Jl 16 '71
BERTINO, J. R. and others
Inhibition of growth of leukemia cells by
enzymic folate depletion. bibliog il Science
172:161-2 Ap 9 '71
BERTRAM, Richard
Organizing for offshore. il Motor B & S 128:
26+ O '71
BERUBE, Maurice R.
Defeat of the Great black hope. Common-
weal 94:54-5 Mr 26 '71
Trouble with vouchers. Commonweal 93:
414-17; 94:46-7 Ja 29, Mr 19 '71
BERVEN, Leroy
5 who fight pollution. C. Remsberg and B.
Remsberg. pors Seventeen 30:128+ Ap '71 •
BERYLLIUM
Beryllium. J. E. House, jr. il por Chem 44:10-
13 D '71
BESHARA, Dennis
East vs. west. il por Newsweek 78:52-3 Ag
30 '71 •
BESLIN, Sister Anita Louise
Alleluia! English has risen! Engl J 60:607-9
My '71
BESOZZO, Michelino Molinari da
Luminous messenger. R. Hughes. il Time
97:64-5 My 3 '71 •
BESSERMAN, Laura
Whole earth view of bookselling; excerpts
from The whole earth catalog. por Pub W
200:21-2 S 6 '71
BESSONOV, Alexander
400 Cosmos satellites. il Space World H-8-92:
24-5 Ag '71
BEST, Gordon, and Weeks, John
Search for flexibility in hospital design. Arch
Rec 150:66+ S '71
BEST books. See Books and reading—Best
books
BEST dressed women. See Clothing and dress
BEST friend; story. See Kean, G.
BEST sellers
Best seller bamboozle; how best seller lists
are compiled. J. W. Allen. Sat R 54:14-
15+ Jl 31 '71
Best sellers. See issues of Publishers' weekly
Checking the literary scene from 35,000 books
up. M. Maddocks. il Life 71:25 D 31 '71

Hardcover best sellers of 1970: the year of the
love story. A. P. Hackett. il Pub W 199:34-7
F 8 '71
1970: some surprises in paperback best sellers.
il Pub W 199:38-41 F 8 '71
Pickwick buyer urges best seller list for West
coast; interview, ed. by B. A. Bannon. A.
Kahn. Pub W 199:51-2 Je 28 '71
        **Anecdotes, facetiae, satire,
        etc.**
Hugo Flesch worst seller list. Wilson Lib
Bul 45:779 Ap '71
BESTER, Alfred
Europe in Canada's front yard. il Holiday 49:
40-1 My '71
BESTUZHEV-LADA, Igor V.
Soviet scientist looks at futurology. il
UNESCO Courier 24:22-7 Ap '71
BETHEL report. See Coal mines and mining—
Accidents and explosions
BETHELL, John T.
President's chair. il Am Heritage 23:110 D '71
BETHELL, Tom
Hoffa and the witness. Nation 212:678-9 My
31 '71
BETHLEHEM steel corporation
Bethlehem caper. Newsweek 78:66 Ag 23 '71
Bethlehem's strategist. por Bsns W p67
Ja 23 '71
Cort of Bethlehem steel. il por Forbes 107:72
My 15 '71
Jawbone hits steel. Newsweek 77:63-4 Ja 25
'71
Why Bethlehem acts that way. il Bsns W
p86-7 Ap 24 '71
BETHUNE, Mary McLeod
Lady who left us hope. M. M. McGlynn. il
por Look 35:57 F 9 '71 •
Memorable woman. Chr Today 15:39 Mr 12
'71 •
BETJEMAN, John
Crematorium; poem. Poetry 119:98 N '71
Loneliness; poem. New Yorker 47:45 Ap 17
'71
Winter seascape; poem. Ladies Home J 88:
126 F '71
BETSCH, Carolyn
(comp) Catalogue raisonné of Warhol's ges-
tures. Art in Am 59:47 My '71
BETTELHEIM, Bruno
Bruno Bettelheim (cont of) Dialogue with
mothers. See issues of Ladies' home journal
BETTER business bureaus
Better business bureaus prepare for action;
Council of better business bureaus. il
Changing T 25:21-3 N '71
What business has to do about consumerism;
Council of Better business bureaus. E.
Gray. 2d. Look 35:68+ Mr 9 '71
BETTER to know you; story. See Shiek. H.
BETTING. See Book making (betting); Gam-
bling; Horse race betting
BETTY, Maurice Moore-. See Moore-Betty, M.
BETWEEN love and longing; story. See Ros-
siter, E.
BEUG, H. and others
Cell dissociation: univalent antibodies as a
possible alternative to proteolytic enzymes.
bibliog il Science 173:742-3 Ag 20 '71
BEUM, Robert
Les Americains; poem. Chr Cent 88:1344 N 17
'71
Sources; poem. Commonweal 94:112 Ap 9 '71
To a father, at his retirement; poem. Chr
Cent 88:583 My 12 '71
BEUSSEE, Mary P. and others
Effects of fallout shelter confinement on
mental health. Ment Hy 55:121-3 Ja '71
BEVAN, William
AAAS council meeting. 1970. il Science 171:
709-11 F 19 '71
General scientific association: a bridge to
society at large; adaptation of address,
March 22, 1971. Science 172:349-52 Ap 23 '71
—and Steger, J. A.
Free recall and abstractness of stimuli. bib
liog il Science 172:597-9 My 7 '71
BEVATRON. See Accelerators (electrons, etc)
BEVERAGES
DEP, cancer and beverages. Sci N 100:422 D
25 '71
Diethyl pyrocarbonate: formation of urethan
in treated beverages. G. Löfroth and T.
Gejvall. bibliog il Science 174:1248-50 D 17
'71
Drinks that bloom with fruit and flowers.
H. P. McNulty. House & Gard 140:76 Ag
'71
How fresh are our milk and eggs, and what
goes into cola drinks? il Consumer Bul 54:
31-2 Ag '71

BEVERAGES—*Continued*
How to make switched-on drinks. House & Gard 139:132-3+ Ap '71
Thirst-quenchers. M. Happel. il Ladies Home J 88:84+ Ag '71
See also
Alcoholic beverages
Cider
Coffee
Punch (beverage)
Soft drink industry
Tea
Wine
BEVERIDGE, James J.
Selecting and using a backpack and frame. il Field & S 76:60-1+ Jl '71
BEVINEAU, William A.
Am but black who wears a black mask; poem. Negro Hist Bul 34:116 My '71
Life line; poem. Negro Hist Bul 33:169 N '70
BEWICK, Thomas
Conservationists find contemporary interest in Bewick prints. P. Standard. il Pub W 199: 60-2 Mr 8 '71
BEYER, N. Lee
Which computer: time-sharing. il Electr World 86:46-8+ N '71
BEYTAGH, Gonville Auble Ffrench-. See Ffrench-Beytagh, G. A.
BEZAK, Ladislaw
Do-it-yourself escape; Czechoslovakian defector. por Time 99:41 Ja 3 '72 •
BHATHAL, R. S.
Science and government in Singapore. Bul Atom Sci 27:20-1+ Ja '71
BHELY-QUENUM, Olympe
Problems of writing African history. Sch & Soc 99:101-2 F '71
BHUTAN
See also
United Nations—Bhutan
BHUTTO, Zulfikar Ali
Bhutto: the voice of Pakistan; interview. ed. by D. Coggin. Time 99:29 Ja 10 '72

about

Ali Bhutto begins to pick up the pieces. il por Time 99:32+ Ja 3 '72 •
Pakistan's new order. il Newsweek 79:21-2 Ja 3 '72 •
Pakistan's top man: now, kind words for U.S. por U S News 72:17 Ja 3 '72 •
President on a tightrope. il por Newsweek 79:25-7 Ja 10 '72 •
Toward a revolution. il por Time 99:25 Ja 17 '72 •
Whiz kid. por Newsweek 79:22 Ja 3 '72 •
BIAGGINI, Benjamin Franklin
Five keys to railroad productivity and service; address, November 8, 1971. Vital Speeches 38:130-4 D 15 '71
Future of passenger trains; interview. il por U S News 72:44-8 Ja 3 '72
Railroad industry; address, December 14, 1970. Vital Speeches 37:212-16 Ja 15 '71
BIANCHI, Eugene C.
Of celibacy and stipends. Cath World 213:35-8 Ap '71
BIANCO, Celso, and Nussenzweig, Victor
Theta-bearing and complement-receptor lymphocytes are distinct populations of cells. bibliog il Science 173:154-6 Jl 9 '71
BIBB, Philip C.
Water movement in plants. il Horticulture 49:2-3+ Mr '71
BIBB lettuce. See Lettuce
BIBLE
Let's update Bible and sermon. P. R. Gastonguay. il Cath World 213:232-5 Ag '71
See also
Jews
Prophets

Antiquities
Story behind the book: a great photographer narrates the story of Jesus; with photographs. A. H. Johnston. Pub W 201:28-9 Ja 3 '72
See also
Noah's ark

Bibliography
Ancient Israel and her neighbors. C. E. Armerding. Chr Today 15:21-2 F 12 '71
1971 books on the Bible. R. J. Clifford. America 125:460-6 N 27 '71

Chronology
Europe's "discovery" of China and the writing of world history. E. J. Van Kley. bibliog f Am Hist R 76:358-85 Ap '71

Criticism, interpretation, etc.
My conscience is bound by the word of God; thoughts on Luther, address, April 17, 1971. C. L. Manschreck. bibliog Vital Speeches 37:540-4 Je 15 '71

Distribution
See Bible—Publication and distribution

Examinations, questions, etc.
Story behind the book: Revell's Bible quiz book. B. A. Bannon. il Pub W 200:36 S 20 '71

Food
See also
Wine in religion, folklore, etc.

Illustrations
See Bible—Pictorial illustrations

Interpretation
See Bible—Criticism, interpretation, etc.

Literary character
Bringing Job into the twentieth century. M. Meador. Engl J 60:921-3 O '71

Natural history
. . .And God saw that it was good. P. Spier. il Nat Wildlife 10:26-7 D '71

Pictorial illustrations
Story behind the book: a great photographer narrates the story of Jesus; with photographs. A. H. Johnston. Pub W 201:28-9 Ja 3 '72

Prophecies
Lamp of prophecy; the Jerusalem conference on Biblical prophecy. C. F. H. Henry. Chr Today 15:34-5 Ap 9 '71
Prophetic hope; Jerusalem conference on biblical prophecy. C. F. H. Henry. Chr Today 15:40-1 S 10 '71

Publication and distribution
Iron curtain bibles: smugglers too smug? P. Geiger. Chr Today 15:35 Jl 16 '71; Discussion. 15:15 Ag 27 '71

Teachings
See Bible—Theology

Themes
See also
Cities and towns—Biblical teaching

Theology
Christians and the Old Testament. G. O'Collins. America 124:291-2 Mr 20 '71

Translations
See Bible—Versions

Versions
Bear's Bible. G. Cabrera Leiva. il Américas 23:19-24 Je '71
Forty-seven writers: most read, least known; King James Bible. L. Conger. Writer 84:7-8 Jl '71
Latest word in Bibles. D. Wharton. il Read Digest 98:119-22 Je '71
Living Bible: a record. E. E. Plowman. Chr Today 15:42 S 10 '71
New Bible versions break language barriers. J. J. Van Capelleveen. Chr Today 15:32 Je 4 '71
Old wine in new bottles. R. G. Bratcher. il Chr Today 16:16-19 O 8 '71
Protestant debut; new Ukrainian New Testament and psalms. D. Kucharsky. Chr Today 15:40 Ag 6 '71
Updating the Bible; K. N. Taylor's Living Bible. il por Newsweek 78:102 S 27 '71

Women
See Women in the Bible

Old Testament
Christians and the Old Testament. G. O'Collins. America 124:291-2 Mr 20 '71

Bibliography
Books on the Old Testament, 1970. C. E. Armerding. Chr Today 15:11-12+ F 26 '71
Religion and theology of Israel. C. E. Armerding. Chr Today 15:27-9 My 21 '71

Manuscripts
See also
Dead Sea scrolls

Genesis
Evolution as a scientific theory. G. Vanderkool. Chr Today 15:13-14 My 7 '71
See also
Noah's ark

Job
Bringing Job into the twentieth century. M. Meador. Engl J 60:921-3 O '71
Dimensions of Job. ed. by N. Glatzer. Review Commonweal 94:19-21 Mr 12 '71. J. Riemer

BIBLE—Old Testament—*Continued*
Psalms
Psalms of struggle, by E. Cardenal. Review Commonweal 94:484-6 S 17 '71. J. Riemer

New Testament
Bibliography
Books on the New Testament, 1970. R. P. Martin. Chr Today 15:6-11 F 26 '71
Gospels
Burying the Gospel. D. G. Bloesch. Chr Today 15:8-11 S 24; 16:12-14 O 8 '71
Gospels without myth, by L. Evely. Review Cath World 213:149 Je '71. G. Baum Commonweal 94:307-10 Je 11 '71. J. L. McKenzie
Who has the good news straight? il Time 98: 44-5 D 27 '71
See also
Jesus Christ—Teachings
Matthew
Epiphany counterpoint. V. P. McCorry. America 125:inside back cover D 25 '71
Mark
Mark's special Easter emphasis. R. P. Meye. Chr Today 15:4-6 Mr 26 '71
Luke
Luke the theologian. L. Morris. Chr Today 15:39 Ag 27 '71
John
Gospel of John, by R. Bultmann, and The Gospel according to John, by R. E. Brown. Reviews
Chr Today 15:13 Jl 16 '71. J. M. Boice
Witness of the Baptist. V. P. McCorry. America 126:inside back cover Ja 8 '72
Acts
Luke the theologian. L. Morris. Chr Today 15:39 Ag 27 '71
BIBLE as literature. See Bible—Literary character
BIBLE quizzes. See Bible—Examinations, questions. etc.
BIBLE smuggling. See Smuggling
BIBLICAL archeology. See Bible—Antiquities
BIBLIOGRAPHY
See also subhead Bibliography under various subjects, e.g. Science—Bibliography
Fine editions
See Books—Fine editions
BIBLIOGRAPHY, National
United States
See also
Cumulative book index
BICARBONATE of soda. See Sodium bicarbonate
BICENTENNIAL of the Republic. See United States—Centennial celebrations, etc.
BICENTENNIAL photography contest. See Photography—Competitions
BICKEL, Alexander M.
Judging the Chicago trial. bibliog f Commentary 51:31-40 Ja; 14+ My '71
Sharing responsibility for war. New Repub 165:15-17 S 25 '71
BICKNELL, Mary
Build your own first mortgage. Har Yrs 11: 34-5 Je '71
BICYCLE industry
Bike boom: a way out for commuters? il U S News 71:84-5 D 6 '71
They like bikes. il Time 97:81 Je 14 '71
BICYCLE polo
Polo on wheels. il Time 98:25 Ag 23 '71
Rajahs' game falls on hard times. G. Plimpton. il Sports Illus 35:20-2+ Jl 19 '71
BICYCLE routes. See Cycling
BICYCLE trips. See Cycling
BICYCLES
Big boom in the hot new bikes. A. J. Hand. il Pop Sci 199:72-4+ Jl '71
Buying guide for bicycles. il Good H 173:220 N '71
Children's bicycles. il Consumer Rep 36:649-55 N '71
Choosing a bike for easy riding il Mech Illus 67:74-5 Ap '71
Havoc in your household; dangerous highrise bicycles. S. Klein. il Sci Digest 69:14-19 My '71
How to buy a used mini bike. M. Schultz. il Mech Illus 67:76-7 Jl '71
How to pick a machine from a store's cluttered racks. il Life 71:32-3 Jl 30 '71

Look, ma, no engine il Esquire 76:169-73 D '71
Saddle up! ride your bike for fun and health. J. Galub. House B 113:42+ Ap '71
Tom McCahill tests:
World's greatest bike. T. McCahill. il Mech Illus 67:47-9+ D '71
See also
Cycling
Equipment
Bike bags bring home the groceries. il Sunset 147:94-5 Jl '71
Mudbacks. D. Williamson. Sat R 54:6 Ja 30 '71
BICYCLING. See Cycling
BIDDING, Competitive. See Municipal contracts
BIDDISS, Michael D.
Aryan myth. il por Horizon 13:96-101 Sum '71
BIEL, Heinz H.
Stock analysis. See issues of Forbes
BIELA'S comet. See Comets
BIEMILLER, Andrew J.
Excerpt from testimony, March 17, 1970. Cong Digest 50:94-5 Mr '71
BIENNALE, Venice. See Music festivals—Italy
BIENVENU, Millard J.
Adolescent grievances: at home. il PTA Mag 66:18-20 bibliog(p35) S '71
BIFOLD doors. See Doors
BIG BEND NATIONAL PARK
Chisos Mountains: an ecological island. J. Gillette. il Nat Parks & Con Mag 45:4-8 F '71
Mysterious Chisos. J. Gillette. il Nat Parks & Con Mag 45:4-10 Ja '71
BIG business
America, inc. by M. Mintz and J. S. Cohen. Review
Bsns W p 13+ Je 12 '71. E. W. Kintner
Vogue 158:59 Ag 15 '71. A. Schlesinger, jr
Antitrust: new life in an old issue. il Time 97:70-2 Je 28 '71
Corporate snare. M. J. Ulmer. New Repub 165:23-5 S 18 '71
Story behind the book; America, inc. S. Wagner. il Pub W 200:60-1 N 15 '71
Views on bigness are contradictory. il Bsns W p58-63 Ag 7 '71
See also
Competition
BIG CYPRESS SWAMP
Coalition defends Big Cypress Swamp; letter. Nat Parks & Con Mag 45:37-8 My '71
Newest trouble on Everglades waters. il Bsns W p44+ Je 5 '71
Saving the Big Cypress Swamp. il Time 98: 50 D 6 '71
BIG game. See Game
BIG Paul Bunyan; drama. See Thane, A.
BIG sister; story. See Edson, L.
BIG sister program. See Volunteer service
BIG THICKET
Big Thicket: crossroads of nature. E. W. Teale. il Audubon 73:12-32 My '71
BIG trees. See Sequoia. Giant
BIGGS, Ken
Come out from behind your viewfinder and see. M. Edelson. il Pop Phot 68:97-9 Ja '71 *
BIGHAM, Helen
Dyeing yarn for weaving. il Sch Arts 70:16-17 F '71
BIGHORN hunting. See Mountain sheep hunting
BIGHORNS. See Mountain sheep
BIGNAMI, A. and Parry, H. B.
Aggregations of 35-nanometer particles associated with neuronal cytopathic changes in natural scrapie. bibliog il Science 171: 389-90 Ja 29 '71
BIGNOTTI, George
Big man with an Indy wrench. K. Chapin. il pors Sports Illus 34:40-5 My 24 '71 *
BIGOTRY. See Toleration
BIGWOOD, Catherine
(ed) See Chesler, P. Tyranny of the male therapist
BIKE routes. See Cycling
BIKEWAYS. See Cycling
BIKING. See Cycling
BILAK, Vasil
How to overrun Czechoslovakia. A. Martin. il Nat R 23:1408-11+ D 17 '71 *
BILE
Cholestasis: lamellar structure of the abnormal human serum liporotein. R. L. Hamilton and others. bibliog il Science 172:475-8 Ap 30 '71

BILEK, Frank
Some downwind thoughts: the surfing boat. il Yachting 129:52-3+ Je '71
Surfing or seakindliness? il Yachting 130:64-5+ Jl '71
BILINGUAL education. See Education, Bilingual

BILL, James A.
Challenge of change: petroleum and planning in the Middle East. bibliog il Focus 22:1-5 S '71
BILL of rights day
Bill of rights day. Human rights day; proclamation. R. M. Nixon. Dept State Bul 63:774 D 28 '70
BILLBOARDS
Billboard caper: Michigan's interstate highways. Time 97:48 Mr 22 '71
Billboards are falling! K. O. Gilmore. Read Digest 99:53-4+ D '71
Editorial: abolishing billboards. J. Samson. il Field & S 75:6 Mr '71
Great billboard battle. C. G. Rogers. il McCalls 99:36 N '71
See America; compensating owners for signs removed. il New Repub 166:15 Ja 1 '72
Sign busters; Denver. il Newsweek 77:116+ Je 7 '71
BILLIARD balls
Snooker for Froyennes fats? Belgian billiard-ball hustlers vs. Albany billiard ball co. of Albany, N.Y. il Time 97:79-80 Mr 15 '71
BILLIARDS
Clutch of odd birds. P. Jordan. il Sports Illus 35:56-60+ Ag 30 '71
Pool in the parlor. R. M. Bancroft. il Har Yrs 11:41 S '71
Wimpy tackles an ex-tiger; Kelly vs Lassiter. J. Morgan. il pors Sports Illus 34:52-3 F 8 '71
BILLING
Daily control replaces cycle billing; Hollywood, Fla. D. J. Giordano. il Am City 86:109-10 My '71
Write it once and retain it; computer and optical character recognition. D. W. Brown. il por Am City 86:81-2 N '71

Anecdotes, facetiae, satire, etc.

Fold! Spindle! Mutilate! A. Drubdovi. Nat R 23:1252 N 5 '71
BILLINGTON, Raymond John
Expulsion of an outsider. T. Beeson. Chr Cent 88:849 Jl 14 '71 *
BILLS (birds)
Aluminum beak saves stork's life. il Sci Digest 69:66-7 My '71
BILLS (legislation) See Legislation
BILSKI, Catherine
Exciting new products. See issues of Popular mechanics
Publications worth writing for. See issues of Popular mechanics
BIMINI ISLANDS
Bimini: island in the stream. J. Groene and G. Groene. il Motor B & S 127:54+ Je '71
BIMS, Hamilton
Black veteran: battle on the home front. il Ebony 27:35-8+ N '71
Neighborhood center: newest public health remedy. il Ebony 26:124-6+ N '70
BINAPHTHYL. See Dinaphthyl
BINARY stars. See Stars, Double
BINDING (books) See Bookbinding
BINDING energy, Molecular. See Chemical bonds
BING, Arthur
Controlling weeds in groundcovers. il Horticulture 49:20-3 Je '71
BING, Sir Rudolf
Musical events: tomorrow is another day. W. Sargeant. New Yorker 47:83 Je 19 '71 *
Sir Rudolf. New Yorker 47:33-4 O 2 '71 *
BINGHAM, Hiram, 1789-1869
Mad Jack and the missionaries. L. McKee. il pors Am Heritage 22:30-7+ Ap '71*
BINGHAM, Jonathan B.
Replacing the draft. New Repub 164:17-21 Ja 16: 34 F 13 '71
BINGHAM, Sallie
Fear: story. Mlle 74:126 Ja '72
BINGHAM, Stephen
Jackson's legacy. il Newsweek 78:17-18 S 13 '71 *
BINGHAM, Thomas R.
Ten neglected rock classics. il Hi Fi 21:28+ O '71
BINGHAM, Walter
Golf (cont) Sports Illus 34:59-60 Mr 1 '71
My drive to be a champion. il Sports Illus 35:74-7+ O 4 '71
Pro who runs the tour. il pors Sports Illus 34:52-5 Mr 15 '71

Tennis (cont) Sports Illus 34:59 F 22 '71
Waltz at Wimbledon. il pors Sports Illus 35:14-17 Jl 12 '71
World's greatest gamesman. il pors Sports Illus 34:28-30+ Ja 11 '71
BINGHAMTON, N.Y.
Parking facility award winner. il Am City 86:88 Jl '71

Banks

First city national bank of Binghamton, New York. il Arch Rec 150:112-13 Jl '71

Bridges

Who would know that it was 82 years old? Court street bridge. il Am City 86:87 N '71

Music

See also
Tri-Cities opera (Binghamton, Endicott and Johnson City, N.Y.)
BINKLEY, Sue, and others
Pineal function in sparrows: circadian rhythms and body temperature. bibliog il Science 174:311-14 O 15 '71
BINNS, James Hazlett
Armstrong cork bets on residential housing. il por Bsns W p 122-4 O 23 '71 *
BINOCULAR cameras. See Cameras
BINOCULARS. See Field glasses
BINZEN, Bill
Gallery; photographs. Life 70:8-9 F 19 '71
BINZEN, Peter. See Friedman, M. jt. auth.
BIOCHEMISTRY
Allelochemics: chemical interactions between species. R. H. Whittaker and P. P. Feeny. bibliog il Science 171:757-70 F 26 '71; Discussion. 172:1362; 173:945 Je 25, S 3 '71
See also
Alcohol in the body
Bioenergetics
Biosynthesis
Chemoreceptivity
Immunochemistry
Metabolism
Neurochemistry
Synergism
BIODEGRADABLE plastics. See Plastics—Deterioration
BIOELECTRONICS
Signal averaging techniques. S. L. Silver. il Electr World 85:45-8+ My '71
BIOENERGETICS
Flow of energy in a hunting society. W. B. Kemp. il Sci Am 225:104-15 S '71
Flow of energy in an agricultural society. R. A. Rappaport. il Sci Am 225:116-22+ bibliog(p244) S '71
Time, energy, and territoriality of the anna hummingbird (calypte anna) F. G. Stiles. bibliog il Science 173:818-21 Ag 21 '71
BIOEROSION. See Erosion
BIOFEEDBACK. See Biological control systems
BIOGENESIS. See Life (biology)—Origin
BIOGRAPHICAL dictionaries
Index to young readers' collective biographies, by J. Silverman. Review
Library J 96:1095 Mr 15 '71. M. M. Murray; Reply. J. Silverman. 96:1742 My 15 '71
See also
Biographical directory of librarians in the United States and Canada
BIOGRAPHICAL directory of librarians in the United States and Canada
Ash's brief lives. W. R. Eshelman. Wilson Lib Bul 45:722+ Ap '71
BIOGRAPHICAL films. See Moving pictures—Biographical films
BIOGRAPHIES
See also
Publishers and publishing—Biographies
BIOGRAPHY
How & where to find biographical information. C. MacLeod. il Writers Digest 52:28-30 Ja '72
See also
Genealogy
Obituaries
Television programs—Biographical programs

Bibliography

Biographies they can read; junior high level. J. Higgins. il Library J 96:1431-2 Ap 15 '71
Biography (cont) M. Adelman, jr. America 124:549-51, 125:432+ My 22, N 20 '71
BIOLOGICAL and chemical weapons. See Chemical and biological weapons

BIOLOGICAL assay

Barbiturates: radioimmunoassay. S. Spector and E. J. Flynn. bibliog il Science 174: 1036-8 D 3 '71

Disposition of morphine in man: radioimmunoassay study. S. Spector and E. S. Vesell. bibliog il Science 174:421-2 O 22 '71

Radioimmunoassay for prostaglandins. B. M. Jaffe and others. bibliog il Science 171:494-6 F 5 '71

BIOLOGICAL clocks. See Biology—Periodicity

BIOLOGICAL conferences

Man and environment: a national biological congress. K. V. Thimann. Science 172: 1366-7 Je 25 '71

BIOLOGICAL control of insects. See Insect control—Biological control

BIOLOGICAL control systems

Brain power: the case for bio-feedback training. B. L. Collier. il Sat R 54:10-13+ Ap 10 '71

Listen to your head. R. J. Trotter. il Sci N 100:314-16 N 6 '71

Mind over body, mind over mind. G. Luce and E. Peper. il N Y Times Mag p34-5+ S 12 '71

Perception of changes in certain exteroceptive stimuli. J. M. Notterman and others. bibliog il Science 173:1206-11 S 24 '71

Stress and behavior. S. Levine. il Sci Am 224:26-31 bibliog(p 122) Ja '71

They've found a wish switch in your brain. D. Lampe. por Pop Sci 198:30+ Ja '71

BIOLOGICAL cycles. See Biology—Periodicity

BIOLOGICAL erosion. See Erosion

BIOLOGICAL laboratories

See also

United States—National institutes of health —Rocky Mountain laboratory

BIOLOGICAL luminescence. See Bioluminescence

BIOLOGICAL physics

Mössbauer spectroscopy and biophysics. C. E. Johnson. bibliog il Phys Today 24:35-40 F '71

BIOLOGICAL research

Dr Hsu's frozen zoo; preserving cells of animals doomed to extinction. Time 98:57 D 6 '71

Magnetism as a tool in biology. D. E. Thomsen. il Sci N 99:117-18 F 13 '71

See also

Brain research

Computers—Biological use

Ecological research

Embryology, Experimental

Germfree life

Roche institute of molecular biology

BIOLOGICAL rhythms. See Biology—Periodicity

BIOLOGICAL societies

See also

American institute of biological sciences

BIOLOGICAL telemetry. See Biotelemetry

BIOLOGICAL transport

DDT: disrupted osmoregulatory events in the intestine of the eels anguilla rostrata adapted to seawater. R. H. Janicki and W. B. Kinter. bibliog il Science 173:1146-8 S 17 '71

Erythrocyte metabolism: interaction with oxygen transport. G. J. Brewer and J. W. Eaton. bibliog il Science 171:1205-11 Mr 26 '71

Periplasmic galactose binding protein of escherichia coli. H. M. Kalckar. bibliog il Science 174:557-65 N 5 '71

Sugar transport: effect of temperature on concentrative uptake of α-methylglucoside by kidney cortex slices. P. McNamara and others. bibliog il Science 172:1033-4 Je 4 '71

Theoretical and experimental basis for a specific countertransport system in membranes. E. L. Cussler and others. bibliog il Science 172:377-9 Ap 23 '71

Transport of nitrogen mustard on the transport-carrier for choline in L5178Y lymphoblasts. G. J. Goldenberg and others. bibliog il Science 172:1148-9 Je 11 '71

Unstirred water layers in intestine: rate determinant of fatty acid absorption from micellar solutions. F. A. Wilson and others. bibliog il Science 174:1031-3 D 3 '71

Vitamin D: a cholecalciferol metabolite highly active in promoting intestinal calcium transport. J. F. Myrtle and A. W. Norman. bibliog il Science 171:79-82 Ja 8 '71

See also

Blood-brain barrier

Osmosis

BIOLOGICAL transport (plants) See Plants, Motion of fluids in

BIOLOGICAL warfare

See also

Chemical and biological weapons

BIOLOGY

See also

Adaptation (biology)

American institute of biological sciences

Clones (biology)

Ecology

Environment

Eugenics

Evolution

Genetics

Hybridization

Life (biology)

Molecular biology—Conferences

Morphogenesis

Mutation (biology)

Neurobiology

Polymorphism (biology)

Regeneration (biology)

Reproduction

Species

Struggle for existence

Symbiosis

Classification

Origins of taxonomy. P. H. Raven and others. bibliog Science 174:1210-13 D 17 '71

History

La logique du vivant, by F. Jacob. Review Science 172:364-6 Ap 23 '71. A. W. Ravin

Methodology

Three-dimensional structure identified from single sections; adaptation of address, August 1971. H. Elias. bibliog il Science 174: 993-1000 D 3 '71

Periodicity

Annual biological clocks. E. T. Pengelley and S. J. Asmundson. il Sci Am 224:72-9 Ap '71

Biological clocks; adapted from Biological rhythms in psychiatry and medicine. G. Luce. il Todays Ed 60:40-2+ O '71

Biological sciences; highlights of some papers from a symposium of the International society for the study of biological rhythms. Sci N 100:343 N 20 '71

Body time; excerpt (title varies) G. G. Luce. Vogue 158:156-7+ N 1; 132-3+ N 15 '71

Circadian rhythm: population of interacting neurons. J. W. Jacklet and J. Geronimo. bibliog il Science 174:299-302 O 15 '71

Day people vs. night people. W. A. Nolen. il McCalls 98:6 S '71

Destiny and geomagnetism. W. Garrison. il Pop Electr 35:41-6 Jl '71

Fish otoliths: daily growth layers and periodical patterns. G. Pannella. bibliog il Science 173:1124-7 S 17 '71

Hidden rhythms that make nature's clock tick. I. Asimov. il Nat Wildlife 10:36-40 D '71

Human circadian rhythms in continuous darkness: entrainment by social cues. J. Aschoff and others. bibliog il Science 171: 213-15 Ja 15 '71

Monitoring of body rhythms: ticking loudly will not do; report of meeting. Sci N 100: 342 N 20 '71

Moonstruck scientists; claim accident rates influenced by natural phenomena. il Time 99:48 Ja 10 '72

Photosensitivity of the circadian rhythm and of visual receptors in carotenoid-depleted drosophila. W. F. Zimmerman and T. H. Goldsmith. bibliog il Science 171:1167-9 Mr 19 '71

Pineal function in sparrows: circadian rhythms and body temperature. S. Binkley and others. bibliog il Science 174:311-14 O 15 '71

Search for clues to the rhythms of life. J. L. Arehart. il Sci N 100:178-9 S 11 '71

Throwing the biological clock off by altering a single gene. Sci N 100:226 O 2 '71

What makes us tick, so mysteriously. W. B. Furlong. il Todays Health 49:28-31+ My '71

See also

Photoperiodism

Study and teaching

Junior high school people launch an unusual attack on pests and weeds. il Sunset 147: 230-1 N '71

Race, evolution and Mormonism. C. W. Quintance. Chr Cent 88:586-9 My 12 '71

See also

Nature study

BIOLUMINESCENCE

Finding fish by fire. il Sea Front 17:94 Mr '71

Light production in the luminous fishes photoblepharon and anomalops from the Banda Islands. Y. Haneda and F. I. Tsuji. bibliog il Science 173:143-5 Jl 9 '71

BIOLUMINESCENCE—*Continued*
Light to hide by: ventral luminescence to camouflage the silhoutte. J. W. Hastings. bibliog il Science 173:1016-17 S 10 '71
Nature's night lights: probing the secrets of bioluminescence. P. A. Zahl. il Nat Geog 140:45-69 Jl '71
See also
Fireflies
BIOMAGNETICS. See Magnetic fields—Physiological effects
BIOME projects. See International biological program
BIOMEDICAL engineering
Biomedical engineer: the roles he can play. J. D. Bronzino. bibliog il Science 174:1001-3 D 3 '71
Engineers & doctors, a new partnership. P. Reichert. Radio-Electr 42:39 F '71
New biology: what price relieving man's estate? L. R. Kass. bibliog Science 174:779-88 N 19 '71
BIOMEDICAL research. See Medical research
BIONICS
See also
Artificial intelligence
BIOPHYSICS. See Biological physics
BIORHYTHM. See Biology—Periodicity; Botany—Periodicity
BIOSYNTHESIS
Attempts to map a process evolution of peptide biosynthesis. F. Lipmann. bibliog il Science 173:875-84 S 3 '71
Calcium as a mediator of adrenocorticotrophic hormone action on adrenal protein synthesis. R. V. Farese. bibliog il Science 173:447-50 Jl 30 '71
Cell-free protein synthesizing system from yeast mitochondria. A. H. Scragg and others. bibliog il Science 171:908-10 Mr 5 '71
How does a plant synthesize a molecule? P. Andermatt. il Chem 45:23-4 Ja '72
Organic production on Mars. Sci N 99:210 Mr 27 '71
Ribosome-catalyzed polyester formation. S. Fahnestock and A. Rich. bibliog il Science 173:340-3 Jl 23 '71
Synthesis of amino acids by the heating of formaldehyde and ammonia. S. W. Fox and C. R. Windsor; discussion. bibliog il Science 174:1038-41 D 3 '71
Synthesis of amino acids from gases known in space. Sci N 100:357 N 27 '71
Thymine: a possible prebiotic synthesis. E. Stephen-Sherwood and others. bibliog il Science 173:446-7 Jl 30 '71
BIOTELEMETRY
Wiring the king for sound. il Sci Digest 71:25-7 Ja '72
BIPHENYL compounds. See Diphenyl compounds
BIRCH, Adolpho A. Jr
Black judges in the South. il por Ebony 26 31-4+ Mr '71 •
BIRCHLEAF mountain mahogany. See Mountain mahogany
BIRD, Caroline
Recession special: ten grand is yours to spend... Esquire 75:142-3 Je '71
Myths that keep women down. Ladies Home J 88:68+ N '71
BIRD, Vere Cornwall
Bye, bye, Bird. Time 97:41 F 22 '71 •
BIRD breeding. See Birds—Breeding
BIRD calling
How to call spring gobblers. J. M. Vance. il Field & S 75:64-5+ F '71
BIRD dogs
Dogs. D. M. Duffey. See issues of Outdoor life
Dove dog. R. Starnes. Field & S 75:8+ Ap '71
Grouse and woodcock dog. G. B. Evans. il Field & S 76:126+ Jl '71
Love me, love my dog. H. G. Tapply. il Field & S 76:70 O '71
See also
Pointers (dogs)
Retrievers
Setters
Training
See Dogs—Training
BIRD feeders
Bird feeders. N. Baldwin. il Ceram Mo 19:16-20 O '71
BIRD flight. See Birds—Flight
BIRD gardens
Gardening with birds. E. Mullins. il Horticulture 49:38-40 Je '71

BIRD houses
Gourds make attractive bird houses. C. Hanley. il Org Gard & Farm 18:54-5 Ag '71
Great purple martin controversy! J. Star. il por Look 35:24-6 Ag 10 '71
Landlord of the birds; building apartment houses for purple martins. T. Fenstermacher. il Org Gard & Farm 18:52-3 Ap '71
BIRD hunting. See Shooting
BIRD migration. See Birds—Migration
BIRD names. See Birds—Nomenclature
BIRD photography. See Photography of birds
BIRD populations
Control
To pigeon-proof downtown, try pigeon birth control; Bangor, Me. il Am City 86:81 Jl '71
BIRD prints. See Birds in art
BIRD protection. See Birds—Protection
BIRD sanctuaries
New York (state)
See also
Great Gull Island
BIRD songs. See Birds—Song
BIRD study
... And a partridge in a palm tree; annual Audubon bird count, Cocoa, Fla. P. Ryan. Sports Illus 34:44 Ja 11 '71
Birding by boat. B. Shemella. il Motor B & S 128:52-3 bibliog(p58) Jl '71
Land birds at sea. A. C. Jensen. il Sea Front 17:48-56 Ja '71
Tips for would-be bird watchers. Changing T 25:38 S '71
See also
Photography of birds
BIRD tracks. See Animal tracks and trails
BIRD urine. See Urine
BIRD watching. See Bird study
BIRDHOUSES. See Bird houses
BIRDOFF, Harry
Elusive Jenny Lind record. il por Hobbies 75:35-6+ F '71
Voice of Harriet Beecher Stowe. il por Hobbies 76:35-6+ Jl '71
BIRDS
Who laid the egg? quiz. il Nat Wildlife 9:12-15+ Ap '71
See also
Abnormalities (birds)
Aviaries
Bird houses
Embryology—Birds
Game birds
Hearing (birds)
Photography of birds
Respiratory organs—Birds
Water birds
also names of birds, e.g. Martins

Accidents and hazards
Barehanded battle to cleanse the Bay. P. T. White. il Nat Geog 139:866-81 Je '71

Anatomy
See also
Bills (birds)

Breeding
Business for the birds. O. Henry. il pors Har Yrs 11:19-22 Ag '71
See also
Artificial insemination

Eggs
See Birds eggs

Flight
Why are birds the fastest creatures? Sci Digest 70:76 N '71

Food and feeding
Illness-induced aversions in rat and quail: relative salience of visual and gustatory cues. H. C. Wilcoxon and others. bibliog il Science 171:826-8 F 26 '71
Plan now to grow a feast for the birds. il Home Gard 58:50 Mr '71
Small-seeded sunflowers, for sunshine on the wing. M. Miller. il Org Gard & Farm 18:72-6 Ap '71
See also
Bird feeders
Bird gardens

Habits and behavior
Social order of turkeys. C. R. Watts and A. W. Stokes. il Sci Am 224:112-18 Je '71
See also
Courtship of birds

BIRDS—*Continued*

Migration

Land birds at sea. A. C. Jensen. il Sea Front 17:48-56 Ja '71

Mysterious journey. T. Trueblood. il Field & S 75:6+ Ja '71

Woodcock! Flights and fancies. F. Woolner. il Field & S 76:62-3+ N '71

See also
Orientation

Nests

See Nests

Nomenclature

How's your wildlife terminology? G. A. Sylvester. il Field & S 75:32 Mr '71

Orientation

See Orientation

Photographs

Cutwater. F. K. Truslow. il Audubon 73:8-11 Jl '71

Down the hatch; great blue heron. J. H. Carmichael, jr. il Nat Wildlife 9:50-1 O '71

Gallery; royal terns in Texas sanctuary. G. Silk. Life 70:6-7 Mr 19 '71

On the beach; a stroll through a seaside nursery. W. D. Griffin. il Audubon 73:33-5 My '71

Protection

Her home is a sanctuary for injured wildlife; R. Collett of Florida. W. Hartley and E. Hartley. il pors Good H 173:78+ O '71

New hope at Patuxent. D. Farney. il Nat Wildlife 9:44-7 O '71

See also
Birds of prey—Protection

Reproduction

See Reproduction

Song

Elusive seringo. D. Zochert. il Natur Hist 80:8-10 D '71

Florida

... And a partridge in a palm tree; annual Audubon bird count, Cocoa. P. Ryan. Sports Illus 34:44 Ja 11 '71

Swallowtails of Royal Palm; with photographs by M. Wright. R. Green and N. Reed. Audubon 73:40-9 Ja '71

India

See also
Jungle fowls

Latin America
Bibliography

Birds of the Americas; comp. by S. S. Benson. il Américas 23:38-40 O '71

Long Island

Ookpikjuak comes to Long Island; snowy owl. R. Caras. il Nat Wildlife 9:10-11 F '71

BIRDS, Effect of solar radiation on

Roadrunners: energy conservation by hypothermia and absorption of sunlight. R. D. Ohmart and R. C. Lasiewski. bibliog il Science 172:67-9 Ap 2 '71

BIRDS, Extinct

Extinct (and hence very rare) birds of Sergio Gonzales Tornero. il Audubon 73:72-5 Ja '71

See also
Dodo
Passenger pigeons

BIRDS, Fossil

Record in the rocks; find of archaeopteryx; with photographs by B. Ratcliffe. R. Moore. Audubon 73:13-29 Ja '71

See also
Penguins, Fossil

BIRDS, Predatory. See Birds of prey

BIRDS, Rescue of. See Birds—Protection

BIRDS and pesticides. See Pesticides and wildlife

BIRDS eggs

You can get killed shooting birds' eggs. H. H. Harrison. il Nat Wildlife 9:10-15 Ap '71

See also
Egg shells

BIRDS in a summer garden; story. See Oppenheimer, J.

BIRDS in art

Embossed pictures of Samuel Dixon and his imitators. A. L. Leask. il Antiques 100:120-3 Jl '71

Fuertes sampler. F. G. Marcham. il Natur Hist 80:38-43 Je '71

BIRD'S nest lichens. See Lichens

BIRDS nests. See Nests

BIRDS of prey

DDE residues and eggshell changes in Alaskan falcons and hawks. T. J. Cade and others. bibliog il Science 172:955-7 My 28 '71

See also
Condors

Protection

Mass killing of eagles alarms Senate unit. il Sr Schol 99:14 O 11 '71

Slaughter of the eagles; testimonies before Senate environmental subcommittee. il Newsweek 78:23 Ag 16 '71

Sluicing the eagles; slaughtering of eagles from helicopters in Wyoming. il Time 98:36 Ag 16 '71

BIRDWATCHING. See Bird study

BIRDYSHAW, W. L.

Unmanned satellite water plants. il Am City 86:97-9 Ag '71

BIRGITTA, princess of Sweden

Princess Birgitta's royal Swedish shape-up; excerpts from Spänsta med Birgitta. il pors Ladies Home J 88:36 Ja '71

BIRIUKOV, IUrii

Rocket ships; from Kibalchich to Korolev. Space World H-6-90:4-6 Je '71

BIRKEN, June

Keep your eye on color. il por Vogue 158:120-3 N 15 '71

BIRKERTS, Gunnar

Subterranean systems as a framework for a new urban planning policy. Arch Forum 135:58-9 N '71

about

New directions for Gunnar Birkerts; with introd. by M. F. Schmertz. il Arch Rec 150:97-110 O '71 *

BIRMAN, Paul

Digitally controlled power supplies. il Electr World 86:28-9 O '71

BIRMINGHAM, Stephen

But the new generation doesn't want to mind the store. il pors N Y Times Mag p 16-17+ S 26 '71

Fort Lauderdale. il Holiday 49:60-3+ D '70

BIRMINGHAM, Ala.

Theaters framing a square; Civic center. il Arch Forum 134:44-7 Mr '71

Air pollution

Bad air over Birmingham. Time 98:49 N 29 '71

Birmingham's grim lesson. il Bsns W p20-1 N 27 '71

Clearing the air. S. Lindsay. Sat R 55:72 Ja 1 '72

Showdown on smog. Newsweek 78:82 N 29 '71

Churches

Black and white gather at the river; Baptist church of the Covenant. il por Life 71:44-6 N 5 '71

Negroes

Birmingham revisited. F. L. Shuttlesworth. il pors Ebony 26:114-18 Ag '71

BIRMINGHAM small arms company. See Motorcycle industry

BIRNBAUM, Norman

Modern master. Commentary 52:72-7 Jl '71

BIRNIE, William A. H.

Eternal garden of Monsieur Redon. il Read Digest 99:122-8 S '71

Norman Rockwell album. il pors Read Digest 98:145-54 Ap '71

Where a bird nests. il Read Digest 98:150-5 Je '71

BIRREN, Faber

Palettes of the old masters. il Am Artist 35:38-43+ F '71

BIRSTEIN, Ann

Books. Vogue 158:176 O 1 '71

Movies (title varies) Vogue 157:75 Mr 15; 160 Ap 1; 159 My; 158:89 Jl; 60 Ag 15; 170 N 1 '71

Television. Vogue 158:74 Ag 1 '71

BIRTH. See Childbirth

BIRTH, Multiple

See also
Quintuplets

BIRTH control

Another approach to population control? N. De Nevers. Bul Atom Sci 27:34 Mr '71

Biological tyranny; OEO's family planning projects in West Virginia. W. Hern. New Repub 164:15-17 F 27 '71

Defusing the world population bomb; new birth-control techniques. T. Alexander. il Fortune 84:112-16+ O '71

Giving reason to rhythm; inducing ovulation. Sci N 100:310 N 6 '71

How many children are we entitled to have? A. L. Goodstadt. il por Redbook 136:12+ Mr '71

BIRTH control—*Continued*
Licensing: for cars and babies. B. M. Russett; discussion. Bul Atom Sci 27:2-3 My '71
Lost genius debate. P. R. Ehrlich and J. P. Holdren. Sat R 54:61 My 1 '71
Making rhythm work. il Newsweek 78:74 S 27 '71
Planning ahead. S. Ramos. il N Y Times Mag p83-4+ N 14 '71; Reply. C. Keller. p 14 D 26 '71
Population bomb and how to defuse it. J. L. Block. il Good H 172:80-3+ My '71
Population control: your child's future depends on it. E. Foote. por Parents Mag 46:26 Je '71
Toward the reduction of unwanted pregnancy; adaptation of address. January 21, 1971. F. S. Jaffe. bibliog il Science 174:119-27 O 8 '71
Trends in world population; factors accounting for progress to date; address, February 24, 1971. B. Berelson. Vital Speeches 37:349-52 Mr 15 '71
Who makes the babies? P. R. Ehrlich and J. P. Holdren. il Sat R 54:60 F 6 71
See also
Abortion
Contraceptives
Malthusianism
Planned parenthood-world population (organization)

Anecdotes, facetiae, satire, etc.
Sad, sad tale. R. W. O'Donnell. Nat R 23:369 Ap 6 '71

Laws and legislation
Fight over what every little girl shouldn't know; New York couple arrested for subjecting child to the corrupting influence of birth control information. il Life 71:65 Ag 20 '71
Population act: proponents dismayed at funding levels. R. Gillette. Science 171:1221-2+ Mr 26 '71

Religious aspects
Plague of children. M. Himmelfarb. Commentary 51:37-43 Ap '71; Discussion. 51:6, 37-43 Ap; 52:14+ S '71
Rhythm lobby. Time 97:54 F 1 '71
Right to choose: Vatican's concern. T. Beeson. Chr Cent 88:277 Mr 3 '71

China (People's Republic)
China: Politics in command slogan. H. Yu. Chr Cent 88:142 Ja 27 '71
Neither Marx nor Malthus. P. R. Ehrlich and J. P. Holdren. Sat R 54:88 N 6 '71
Population care and control. E. Snow. New Repub 164:20-2 My 1 '71

Czechoslovakia
Birth control by astrology; excerpt from Psychic discoveries behind the iron curtain. S. Ostrander and L. Schroeder. Harp Baz 104:104-5 F '71

Ecuador
Ecuador: birth-controlling the people. R. Cowan. il Ramp Mag 10:20-3 O '71

Ireland
Irish rebellion. il Newsweek 77:65 Je 7 '71

Japan
How many people? Sci Am 225:43-4 Jl '71

Latin America
Family planning in Latin America: image and reality. T. G. Sanders. il America 124:203-7 F 27 '71

United States
See Birth control
BIRTH defects. See Deformities
BIRTH rate
Avoiding the problem. P. R. Ehrlich and J. P. Holdren. Sat R 54:56 Mr 6 '71
Predicting and preventing population problems. R. J. Trotter. il Sci N 100:114-15 Ag 14 '71
See also
Birth control
Population, Increase of

United States
Birth dearth? Chr Cent 88:1374 N 24 '71
Bye-bye, baby boom. T. Kelly. il Nations Bsns 59:52-5 D '71
Looking ahead to U.S. in year 2000. il U S News 71:56 N 22 '71

Man and his environment; adaptation of address, March 19, 1970. A. J. Coale; discussion. Science 171:15 Ja 8 '71
Survival of nations and civilization. G. Hardin. Science 172:1297 Je 25 '71; Discussion. bibliog 173:381; 174:1077-8 Jl 30, D 10 '71
Z.P.G. Sci Am 224:50 Ap '71
BIRTHDAY party; drama. See Pinter, H.
BIRTHRIGHT centers
Birthright: alternative to abortion. J. B. Breslin. America 125:116-19 S 4 '71; Discussion 125:217, 273 O 2, 16 '71
Birthright centers; finding alternatives to abortion. J. Deedy. Commonweal 93:410 Ja 29 '71
BIRYUKOV, Yuri. See Biriūkov, IŪ.
BISHOP, Barry C. See Bishop, L. M. jt. auth.
BISHOP, Budd H.
Three Tennessee painters. il Antiques 100:432-7 S '71
BISHOP, Elizabeth
Crusoe in England; poem. New Yorker 47:48-9 N 6 '71
In the waiting room; poem. New Yorker 47:34 Jl 17 '71
(tr) See Cardozo, J. Cemetery of childhood
(tr) See De Moraes, V. Sonnet of intimacy
BISHOP. Jordan
Agriculture, like politics, is not an exact science. even in Cuba. Commonweal 93:472-4 F 12 '71
BISHOP, Joseph W. jr
Will Mr William Kunstler please step down? il pors Esquire 75:115-17+ Ap '71
BISHOP, Lila M. and Bishop, B. C.
Karnali, roadless world of western Nepal. il Nat Geog 140:656-89 N '71
BISHOP, Morris
Carême, ou la crème de la crème. il por Horizon 13:70-1 Wint '71
Four Indian kings in London. il Am Heritage 23:62-5 D '71
Liberation of Mme de Tencin. por Horizon 13:54-6 Sum '71
Perfide Mansion and abbé Prévost. il por Horizon 13:76-7 Aut '71
Scoundrel who invented credit. por Horizon 13:110-11 Spr '71
BISHOP, Thomas Edward
You are the target; address, December 3, 1970. Vital Speeches 37:238-41 F 1 '71
BISHOP HILL, Ill.
Bishop Hill; a colony of Swedish pietists in Illinois. R. E. Nelson. il Antiques 99:140-7 Ja '71
BISHOPS
Baffled bishops. R. G. Hoyt. il Harper 243:76-81 O '71
Bishops in the dock. por Newsweek 77:62+ Je 28 '71
Bishops under attack. il por Time 97:58 Je 28 '71
Can the bishops lead the church? America 125:473-4 D 4 '71
Hoyt on bishops. J. Deedy. Commonweal 95:26 O 8 '71
Silent hierarchy; bishops distrustful of Catholic press. S. J. Adamo. America 124:411-12 Ap '71
See also
National conference of Catholic bishops
Synod of bishops, 1971

Selection
CLSA asks wider participation in selecting bishops. Chr Cent 88:1288 N 3 '71
BISON, American. See Buffaloes
BISON, Fossil
Here we go again; Paleo-Indian bison kill. Sci Am 224:59 Je '71
BISQUES. See Soups
BISSONETTE, David
Christmas light; poem. America 125:558 D 25 '71
Foot; poem. America 125:403 N 13 '71
BIT of capital; story. See Bonham, M.
BITMAN, Joel, and others
Nonconversion of o,p'-DDT to p,p'-DDT in rats, sheep, chickens, and quail. bibliog il Science 174:64-6 O 1 '71
BITO, Laszlo Z. and others
Cholinergic sensitivity: normal variability as a function of stimulus background. bibliog il Science 172:583-5 My 7 '71
BITS, Boring. See Drilling and boring machinery
BITTERROOT national forest, Mont. See National forests
BITTLE, Camilla R.
Man who came home; story. Good H 173:88-9 Jl '71

BLACK skimmers. See Skimmers (birds)
BLACK students union. See Negro students
BLACK studies. See Afro-American studies
BLACK swans. See Swans
BLACK tailed deer hunting. See Deer hunting
BLACK terror; drama. See Wesley, R.
BLACK theology. See Theology
BLACK walnut trees. See Walnut trees
BLACK widow spider venom. See Venom
BLACK world (periodical)
  The scene. L. Ruth. Engl J 60:656-8 My '71
BLACK writers conference. See Authors conferences
BLACKADAR, Alfred K.
  More or less under pressure. il Weatherwise 23:283-5+ D '70
BLACKBERRIES
  Our own blackberry patch. M. Burns. il Org Gard & Farm 18:78 Jl '71
BLACKBURN, Paul
  Agape; poem. Nation 212:124 Ja 25 '71
  Surrogate; poem. Nation 212:220 F 15 '71
BLACKBURN, Robin
  (ed) See Ono, Y. and Lennon, J. Lennon: the working-class hero turns red
BLACKBURN, Thomas R.
  Sensuous-intellectual complementarity in science. bibliog Science 172:1003-7; 173:1194-5 Je 4, S 24 '71
BLACKISTONE, Zachariah D.
  Bloom is still on at age 100. V. Louviere. il por Nations Bsns 59:21 Ap '71 *
BLACKLISTING
  Open letter to the Honorable Richard Ichord. J. Ciardi. Sat R 54:14-15+ My 15 '71
  Through the years with the blacklist. O. Bean. il Nat R 23:193-5+ F 23 '71
  See also
  Boycott
BLACKLOCK, Don
  Troubleshooting reed-relay logic. il Radio-Electr 42:39-42 D '71
BLACKMAN, Bob
  Musical poets of the '70s. il Seventeen 30:36 Ja '71
BLACKMAN, Robert L.
  Ivy league Lombardi gets a Big ten jolt. R. Blount, jr. il por Sports Illus 35:66+ O 18 '71 *
BLACKMAN, Samuel G.
  Strange case of libel. Sat R 54:48-9+ Ap 10 '71
BLACKMUN, Harry Andrew
  Justice Blackmun's dissent. W. F. Buckley, jr. Nat R 23:828-9 Jl 27 '71 *
BLACKOUT; story. See Ernst, P.
BLACKOUTS (electric power) See Electric power failures
BLACKPOOL, England
  Snobberies of the left: abusive articles. P. Worsthorne. Nat R 23:76 Ja 26 '71
BLACKWATER RIVER
  Channelization: a case study: Blackwater River in Johnson County, Mo. J. W. Emerson. bibliog il Science 173:325-6 Jl 23 '71
BLACKWELDER, JoAnne
  (comp) Coming events. il Motor B & S 127:156-8 My '71
BLADDER cancer. See Cancer
BLADES, Saw. See Saws
BLAGONRAVOV, Anatolii Arkad'evich
  Progress of space exploration and research. il Space World H-9-93:12-21 S '71
  Space platforms: why they should be built. Space World H-8-92:34-5 Ag '71
BLAIKIE, Robert J.
  Where the action is. C. F. H. Henry. Chr Today 15:41-2 Mr 12 '71 *
BLAINE, Betty Gray
  Rosy-cheeked ghost; drama. Plays 31:52-6, 72 O '71
BLAIR, Allen M.
  Readability, what it is and isn't. Ed Digest 37:50-1 O '71
BLAIR, Dike
  Booksellers bemoan shrinking margins and profits. Pub W 200:32-3 N 22 '71
BLAIR, Eric. See Orwell, G. pseud.
BLAIR, William L.
  Crystal calibrator for the ham and SWL. il Pop Electr 35:59-62 Ag '71
BLAIR, William Sutherland
  Hang-up at Harper's. pors Time 97:41 Mr 15 '71 *
  What happened at Harper's. S. Little. il por Sat R 54:43-7+ Ap 10 '71 *
BLAKE, Betty
  Steamin' up the River: how the Queen was saved. D. Butwin. il Sat R 54:44-6+ Je 5 '71 *

BLAKE, Eubie
  Mr Ragtime. H. Saal. por Newsweek 77:99 F 22 '71 *
BLAKE, Fay
  Useful academic librarian; remarks, April 1971. il por Library J 96:3731-3 N 15 '71
BLAKE, Harriet Train
  Leisurely cities. Harp Baz 104:52-3 My '71
BLAKE, James
  Riot in the penitentiary. Am Scholar 40:672-3 Aut '71
BLAKE, Judith
  Abortion and public opinion: the 1960-70 decade. bibliog il Science 171:540-9 F 12 '71
BLAKE, Robert. See Thorp, R. jt. auth.
BLAKE, Robert W.
  New English: hot stuff or cool, man, cool? address, November 1970. Engl J 60:728-34 S '71
BLAKE, Wendon
  Acrylics: the opaque technique; excerpt from Complete guide to acrylic painting. il Am Artist 36:52-9+ Ja '72
BLAKE, William
  New (?) romanticism. J. Jerome. Writers Digest 51:14-17 N '71 *
BLAKEMORE, Colin, and Julesz, Bela
  Stereoscopic depth aftereffect produced without monocular cues. bibliog il Science 171:286-8 Ja 22 '71
BLAKESLEE, Alton L.
  Today's health news. See issues of Today's health to July 1971
BLAKESLEE, Sandra
  It's a virus. House & Gard 139:74-5 Ja '71
BLANCHARD, Duncan C.
  Borderland of burning bubbles. il Sat R 55:60-3 Ja 1 '72
  Wilson Bentley, the snowflake man. bibliog il pors Weatherwise 23:260-9 D '70
BLANCHARD, Margot
  Karen Park's ceramic wall reliefs. il por Ceram Mo 19:24-6 O '71
BLANCHARD, Maurice
  Right answers, wrong questions. Chr Today 15:8-10 Ag 6 '71
  Touchstone of truth and value in religions. Chr Today 15:10-13 Ja 29 '71
BLANCHARD, Tinkie
  (comp) Coming events. Motor B & S 128:22+ Jl; 10+ Ag; 24+ S '71
BLANCHETTE, V. G.
  Experiments with wind: a pendulum anemometer and miniature tornadoes. ;l Sci Am 225:110-12 O '71
Les BLANCS; drama. See Hansberry, L.
BLANDA, George
  Decade of revenge; ed. by J. Olsen. Sports Illus 35:36-8+ Jl 26 '71
  I keep getting my kicks; ed. by J. Olsen. il Sports Illus 35:26-31 Jl 19 '71
  That impossible season; ed. by J. Olsen. il Sports Illus 35:30-6 Ag 2 '71
BLANGSTED, Eleanor
  Hollywood community adult school. il Sch Arts 70:36-7 F '71
BLANK, Joseph P.
  Almost-perfect kidnaping. Read Digest 98:140-4 Je '71
  Holocaust on platform B. il Read Digest 99:80-4 N '71
  Terrible wave. il Read Digest 98:90-4 My '71
  Town that disappeared. il Read Digest 99:86-90 D '71
  Who mourns for Herbie Wirth? il Read Digest 99:67-71 Jl '71
BLANKENBURG, Richard M.
  Civil rights of public school students. Cur 131:35-42 Jl '71
BLANKETS
  Rayon-blend blankets: not acceptable. il Consumer Rep 36:238-9 Ap '71
BLANTON, William. See Fay, L. jt. auth.
BLANZACO, André
  VD. Todays Ed 60:41 D '71
BLASBERG, Robert W.
  Grueby art pottery. il Antiques 100:246-9 Ag '71
  (ed) See Irvine, S. Sadie Irvine letters: a further note on the production of Newcomb pottery
BLASE, Melvin G. See Staub, W. J. jt. auth.
BLASI, Vince
  Privilege in a time of violence. Nation 211:653-6 D 21 '70
        about
  Reporters, subpoenas, immunity, and the Court. R. L. Tobin. Sat R 54:63-4 D 11 '71 *
BLASS, Bill
  Bill Blass. J. Brady. por Harp Baz 105:68-9 N '71 *

BLAST cleaning. See Sand blast
BLASTING
  See also
  Atomic blasting
BLATAS, Arbit
  Meeting of minds. S. Jenkins. il pors Opera
    N 35:6-9 Ap 17 '71 *
BLATCHFORD, Joseph H.
  U.S. presents initial contribution to U.N.
    volunteers fund; statement, June 17, 1971.
    Dept State Bul 65:139 Ag 2 '71
                    about
  Agents of the new empire. M. Windmiller.
    Nation 212:592-6 My 10 '71 *
  Getting it all together in the name of Action;
    merger of the Peace corps, VISTA and
    smaller government volunteer groups. il
    por Time 97:11-12 Je 7 '71 *
BLATTY, William Peter
  Trade winds; interview, ed. by C. Amory.
    Sat R 54:10+ O 23 '71 *
BLAUNER, Robert
  Chicano sensibility. Trans-Action 8:51-6+ F
    '71
BLAUSTEIN, Esther
  She fought to teach. il pors Good H 173:56+
    S '71
BLAUSTEIN, M. P.
  Preganglionic stimulation increases calcium
    uptake by sympathetic ganglia. bibliog il
    Science 172:391-3 Ap 23 '71
BLAZE, Phil
  Any season: hop aboard the Hope. il Travel
    135:63-5 My '71
BLAZERS. See Clothing and dress—Sports
    clothes
BLEACHING materials
  See also
  Clorox company
BLECHMAN, Fred
  Speaker monitor for your tape recorder. il
    Radio-Electr 42:45+ N '71
BLEDSOE, Jerry C.
  Brother's keeper. Esquire 76:81-2+ N '71
BLEEDERS disease. See Hemophilia
BLEEDING pig disease. See Swine—Diseases
    and pests
BLEGEN, Judith
  Musician of the month. G. Movshon. por
    Hi Fi 21:MA6-7 Jl '71 *
BLEI, Norbert
  Phantom of the library; reprint. il Am Lib
    2:367-9 Ap '71
BLEICH, David
  More's Utopia: confessional modes. bibliog
    f Am Imago 28:24-52 Spr '71
BLENDER cookery. See Cookery
BLENDERS, Electric. See Household appli-
    ances, Electric
BLENKINSOPP, Joseph
  My entire soul is a cry. Commonweal 93:514-
    18 F 26 '71
  Why keep on celebrating Christmas? Com-
    monweal 95:302-3 D 24 '71
BLESSING, Richard R.
  Contractor refuse collection wouldn't do. il
    Am City 86:46+ Jl '71
BLESSITT, Arthur O.
  World witness walk. Chr Today 15:41 S 24
    '71 *
BLEY, Karl
  One of the comrades is missing; ed. by K.
    Schaefer. K. Agnew. il Read Digest 98:78-
    82 Ap '71 *
BLIMPS. See Airships
BLIND
  White cane. G. Yunge. il por Good H 172:
    71+ Je '71
  See also
  American blind bowling association
  College libraries—Services to blind
  Libraries—Services to blind
              Education
  Don't let this go to waste. M. K. Murphy
    and C. E. Kozoll. il Am Ed 7:6-9 Mr '71
  From unteachable to Ph.D; W. Butts. por
    Sch & Soc 99:272-3 Sum '71
  Making learning real fun for blind children.
    E. Freund. il UNESCO Courier 24:28-31
    My '71
              Employment
  See also
  Blind, Occupations for the
              Recreation
  See Recreation for the blind
BLIND, Apparatus for the
  Now a machine that lets you see with your
    back; Tactile vision substitution system. R.
    Teresi. il Mech Illus 67:42+ F '71
  Sam Genensky's marvelous seeing machine;
    Randsight. G. A. Boehm. il Read Digest
    98:27-8+ Ja '71

BLIND, Books for the
  See also
  Talking books
BLIND, Nature trails for the. See Trails
BLIND, Occupations for the
  Visually handicapped now work as SERVE
    volunteers. il Aging 203:10-11 S '71
BLIND junkie; musical comedy. See Musical
    comedies, revues, etc.—Criticisms, plots,
    etc.
BLINDERMAN, Abraham
  On sidestepping proselytism. Chr Cent 88:
    655-6+ My 26 '71
BLINDNESS
  See also
  Blind
  Eye banks
BLINDS, Duck. See Duck blinds
BLINKING lights. See Electric lamps, Flash-
    ing
BLINTZES. See Griddle cakes
BLISS, Shepherd
  Christian educationists parley in Peru. Chr
    Cent 88:968 Ag 18 '71
BLISTERS
  Cure for cold sores? il Time 98:41 Jl 12 '71
  New light on cold sores. il Newsweek 78:81
    Jl 12 '71
BLITZ, Thelma
  They laughed when I quit my job. por Red-
    book 136:10+ Ja '71
BLIVEN, Bruce
  Not lost in the stars; poem. Atlan 227:82 Ap
    '71
                    about
  Editor reminisces. New Repub 164:32+ Ja 2
    '71 *
BLIZARD, Peter J.
  Beliefs about disease and alcoholism. bib-
    liog Ment Hy 55:184-9 Ap '71
BLIZZARDS. See Snowstorms
BLOCH, R.
  Good stereo at a glance. il Pop Mech 135:
    126-8 Ap '71
BLOCHMAN, Lawrence G.
  Unforgettable Stanley Stein. il por Read
    Digest 98:88-92 My '71
BLOCK, Ellery B.
  Accomplishment/cost: better project control.
    il Harvard Bsns R 49:110-24 My '71
BLOCK, Gerald B.
  New president to repair Republic. pors
    Bsns W p40+ F 13 '71 *
BLOCK, Jean Libman
  How to enjoy spending more for less. il
    Todays Health 49:55-6 Mr '71
  Makonde sculpture. il Craft Horiz 31:31-2+
    Ap '71
  Population bomb and how to defuse it. il
    Good H 172:80-3+ My '71
  What schoolgirls want to know about sex.
    il Good H 173:64-5+ Ag '71
  —and Stein, Jane
  Miracle baby of Carolyn Sinclair. il por
    Good H 172:86-7+ Je '71
BLOCK, Lawrence
  We call our place Rabbit run. il Org Gard
    & Farm 18:104-10 F '71
BLOCK, Thomas H.
  Pro's nest. See issues of Flying
BLOCK, Victor
  Missing chapter in American history. il
    Parents Mag 46:64-5+ S '71
BLOCK front furniture. See Furniture, Amer-
    ican
BLOCK ISLAND
  Block Island: sanctuary out of time. P. R.
    Marunas. il Motor B & S 127:50-3+ Je
    '71
  See also
  Architecture, Domestic—Block Island
BLOCK ISLAND race week. See Regattas
BLOCK printing
  Printing with tiles; use of clay tiles for
    blocks. I. Kettner. il Ceram Mo 19:30-1 D
    '71
  See also
  Linoleum block printing
BLODGET, Robert
  Follow me through. See issues of Flying
  How to run a flying club. il Flying 89:80-1
    D '71
  Safety check. Flying 89:104 Jl '71
BLOEME, Allyn Rice
  Robert Davis: painter of the sea. il por Am
    Artist 35:50-5 F '71
  Virtuoso technique of Richard Schmid. il
    por Am Artists 35:20-7+ Ag '71
BLOESCH, Donald G.
  Burying the Gospel. Chr Today 15:8-11 S
    24: 16:12-14 O 8 '71
  Misunderstanding of prayer. Chr Cent 88:
    1492-4 D 22 '71

BLOK, Aleksandr Aleksandrovich
Comment. J. Atlas. Poetry 119:50-1 O '71 •
BLOND hair. See Hair
BLONDELL, Joan
Quartet of queens. J. Barthel. il pors Life 70: 60-2 F 19 '71 •
BLOOD

Analysis and chemistry
Portal blood factor as the humoral agent in liver regeneration. B. Fisher and others. bibliog il Science 171:575-7 F 12 '71

Circulation
See also
Blood-brain barrier
Blood flow

Circulation, Artificial
Terry and the parents; alternative to blood transfusion. il Newsweek 77:43 Ja 18 '71

Circulation, Disorders of
Duchenne muscular dystrophy: functional ischemia reproduces its characteristic lesions. J. R. Mendell and others. bibliog il Science 172:1143-5 Je 11 '71
See also
Hypertension

Coagulation
See also
Anticoagulants
Embolism

Corpuscles and platelets
Ultraviolet light: a new stimulus for the induction of platelet aggregation. R. C. Dickson and others. bibliog il Science 172: 1140-2 Je 11 '71
See also
Erythrocytes
Leukocytes
Lymphocytes

Dialysis
See Kidneys, Artificial

Diseases
See also
Anemia
Galactosemia
Hemophilia
Leukemia
Von Willebrand's disease

Flow
See Blood flow

Formation
See also
Marrow

Pigments
See also
Hemoglobin

Plasma
See also
Blood substitutes

Pressure
See Blood pressure

Proteins
Circulating immunoglobulin M: increased concentrations in endemic and sporadic goiter. S. C. Werner and others; reply. W. T. London and R. L. Vought. Science 171: 928 Mr 5 '71
Expression of allelic immunoglobulin in homozygous rabbits injected with RNA extract. C. Bell and S. Dray. bibliog il Science 171:199-201 Ja 15 '71
See also
Cytochromes
Gamma globulin
Immunoglobulins
Transferrin

Storage
See also
Blood, Frozen

Sugar
See Blood sugar

Testing
Factor VIII detection by hemagglutination inhibition: hemophilia A and von Willebrand's disease. D. P. Stites and others. bibliog il Science 171:196-7 Ja 15 '71
More insurance against hepatitis; hemagglutination inhibition test for serum hepatitis. il Bsns W p 116+ Ap 10 '71

Transfusion
Each to his own blood; self-transfusion. Sci Am 226:47+ Ja '72
Letter to the editor: a veteran in Viet-Nam on racial labels of blood. Negro Hist Bul 33:164 N '70

New fight to make blood transfusions safer. Good H 172:169-71 Je '71
See also
Blood—Circulation, Artificial
Blood banks
Blood donors
BLOOD, Artificial. See Blood substitutes
BLOOD, Frozen
Frozen blood. il por Newsweek 78:47 S 13 '71
BLOOD banks
Blood banks, a matter of life and death. il Changing T 25:31-4 N '71
Gift of blood; excerpt from The gift relationship. R. Titmuss. il Trans-Action 8:18-26+ Ja '71
See also
Blood donors
BLOOD-brain barrier
Reversible osmotic opening of the blood-brain barrier. S. I. Rapoport and others. bibliog il Science 173:1026-8 S 10 '71
BLOOD donors
Blood and malaria; donation of blood by drug addicts. Time 97:62+ Mr 15 '71
Blood; British and American policies. P. A. Samuelson. Newsweek 78:94 S 13 '71
Excessive anonymity; letter. H. Gershowitz. Science 172:427 Ap 30 '71
Gift of blood; excerpt from The gift relationship. R. Titmuss. il Trans-Action 8:18-26+ Ja '71
On stimulating the gift of blood. W. Bevan. Science 173:583 Ag 13 '71
See also
Blood—Transfusion
BLOOD filters. See Filters and filtration (biological products)
BLOOD flow
Human red blood cells: prostaglandin E₂ epinephrine, and isoproterenol alter deformability. J. E. Allen and H. Rasmussen. bibliog il Science 174:512-14 O 29 '71
Regional blood-flow changes during 72-hour avoidance schedules in the monkey. R. P. Forsyth. bibliog il Science 173:546-8 Ag 6 '71
BLOOD groups
Precious blood of Joe Thomas; anti-Lewis B factor. il pors Ebony 26:72-4+ My '71
BLOOD lilies
Above and beyond the call of duty. il Sunset 146:120-1 Ja '71
BLOOD meal as feed
Mammalian blood, new food for oysters. S. V. Jones. il Sci Digest 70:69 O '71
BLOOD poisoning
Food and drug administration: is protecting lives the priority? contaminated IV feeding bottles. R. J. Bazell. Science 172:41-3 Ap 2 '71; Reply with rejoinder. C. C. Edwards. 173:379 Jl 30 '71
BLOOD pressure
Clue to senility. Newsweek 78:40 Ag 23 '71
Preavoidance blood pressure elevations accompanied by heart rate decreases in the dog. D. E. Anderson and J. V. Brady. bibliog il Science 172:695-7 My 7 '71
See also
Hypertension
BLOOD substitutes
Artificial blood, new lifeline for man. R. Davids. il Sci Digest 70:11-14 S '71
BLOOD sugar
Beauty sense and nonsense; excerpt from Low blood sugar and you. C. Fredericks and H. Goodman. Harp Baz 104:82 O '71
Hypoglycemia. M. S. Welch. Ladies Home J 88:98+ N '71
Low blood sugar: fact and fiction. Consumer Rep 36:444-6 Jl '71
Methamphetamine-induced insulin release. E. M. McMahon and others. bibliog il Science 174:66-8 O 1 '71
BLOOD tests. See Blood—Testing
BLOOD vessels

Transplantation
Saving the heart; vein grafts from leg to bypass atherosclerotic deposits. il Newsweek 78:50 Jl 26 '71
BLOODHOUNDS
Man is fair game. C. Gammon. il Sports Illus 34:74-6+ Mr 22 '71
BLOODSTAINS; story. See Oates, J. C.
BLOOM, Arthur D. and others
Immunoglobulin production by human lymphocytoid lines and clones: absence of genic exclusion. bibliog il Science 172:382-3 Ap 23 '71
BLOOM, Claire
Claire Bloom as Nora and Hedda. T. Prideaux. pors Life 70:10 Mr 12 '71 •

BLOOM, Gordon F.
Productivity: weak link in our economy.
bibliog f Harvard Bsns R 49:4-6+ Ja '71
BLOOM, Joel
Values of a good camping experience. por
Camp Mag 43:4 Ap '71
BLOOM, Murray Teigh
Highest interest; lowest risks. il Har Yrs
11:30-2 My '71; Same abr. with title How
to get the most out of your savings. Read
Digest 98:211-12+ My '71
Pittsburgh's program for efficient courts.
Read Digest 98:215-16+ Je '71
Want more income from your savings? Read
Digest 99:109-11 S '71
BLOOM, Ruth
Home is for sharing; story. Good H 172:108-9
Ap '71
BLOOMFIELD, Howard V. L.
Alligator, ugly old king of survival. il Am
For 77:40-3 Ag '71
Paper's pollution problems. il Am For 77:10-
13+ N '71
BLOOMFIELD, Lincoln P.
After neo-isolationism, what? Bul Atom Sci
27:9-13 Ap '71
BLOOMINGTON, Minn.
Municipal improvement
Add 1% for esthetics. S. H. Hobbs. il Am
City 86:107-8+ S '71
BLOOMSTEIN, Morris J.
American jury system. Cur Hist 60:357-61+
Je '71
BLOT test. See Personality tests
BLOUNT, Nathan S.
Summary of investigations relating to the
English language arts in secondary educa-
tion: 1970. bibliog Engl J 60:633-40+ My
'71
—See Searles, J. R. jt. ed.
BLOUNT, Roy, Jr
And now for the resurrection. il por Sports
Illus 34:96-100+ Ap 12 '71
Baseball (cont) il Sports Illus 34:46-7 Mr 29;
62 Ap 26; 64+ My 17 '71
College football. Sports Illus 35:66+ O 18;
60+ O 25 '71
Curtain up on a mod new act. il Sports Illus
34:30-3 Ap 19 '71
Garden of versatile stars. Sports Illus 34:23
My 31 '71
Humming a rhapsody in Blue. il pors Sports
Illus 35:22-7 Jl 12 '71
Magic number is Sixkiller. il pors Sports
Illus 35:34-7 O 4 '71
Million-dollar Sunday driver. il por Sports
Illus 35:16-17 Ag 9 '71
More Joan of Arc than Shirley Temple. il
pors Sports Illus 35:30-1 S 20 '71
On the lam with the Three rivers gang.
il Sports Illus 35:12-17 Ag 2 '71
Out of this I am getting not a nyickl. il por
Sports Illus 34:62-4+ My 31 '71
Return of the natives. il pors Sports Illus 34:
58-60+ Mr 29 '71
Week; baseball. Sports Illus 35:58-9 Ag 16 '71
BLOUNT, Winton Malcolm
Let's put the smut merchants out of busi-
ness. il Nations Bsns 59:34-6+ S '71
What new mail service means to you; inter-
view. il por U S News 71:46-51 Jl 5 '71
BLOUSTEIN, Edward J.
Why we ought to join our kids. Look 35:46-
7 Ja 26 '71
BLOWFLIES
Blowflies: alteration of adult taste re-
sponses by chemicals present during de-
velopment. V. G. Dethier and N. Goldrich.
bibliog il Science 173:242-4 Jl 16 '71
BLOY, Myron B. Jr
Counter-culture: it just won't go away. Com-
monweal 95:29-34 O 8 '71
BLUE, Janice
Without end; poem. Seventeen 30:81 Ja '71
BLUE, Vida
Baseball's amazing Vida Blue. il pors Ebony
26:94-9 S '71 •
Blue blazer. por Time 97:88 My 24 '71 •
Blue speed. il pors Life 70:30-3 Je 18 '71 •
Bolt of Blue lightning. il pors Times 98:
40-4 Ag 23 '71 •
How to throw the ultimate fast ball. W.
Twombly. il pors N Y Times Mag p22-4+
Jl 25 '71 •
Humming a rhapsody in Blue. R. Blount.
il pors Sports Illus 35:22-7 Jl 12 '71 •
Is Vida Blue really true? por Newsweek 77:
65 My 24 '71 •
What if they had a world series and no-
body came? L. Shecter. Look 35:22+ O 5
'71 •
Where Vida Blue grew. J. Lebow. il pors
Look 35:73-6+ S 21 '71 •

BLUE and white bus company
How to throw the ultimate fast ball. W.
p40 S 25 '71
BLUE collar workers. See Labor and laboring
classes
BLUE cross hospital services. See Insurance,
Hospitalization
BLUE LAKE. See Lakes—New Mexico
BLUE laws. See Sunday legislation
BLUE Petes (birds) See Gallinules
BLUE RIDGE hydroelectric project. See Hydro-
electric plants
BLUE whales. See Whales
BLUEBERRIES
Who says you can't grow blueberries in
Kansas? J. Stockinger and N. F. Stock-
inger. il por Org Gard & Farm 18:50-3 F
'71
See also
Cookery—Fruit
Huckleberries
BLUEFISH fishing
Bedlam in blue. G. Heinold. il Outdoor Life
148:76-7+ O '71
Fly-rodding the blues. G. Grant. il Field & S
76:120+ Je '71
Get ready to follow the blues, great battlers
on light tackle. V. Evanoff. Motor B & S
127:137+ Mr '71
Homecoming blues. H. H. Edel. il Outdoor
Life 148:54-5+ Jl '71
Saltwater combos. G. Heinold. il Outdoor Life
147:30+ Je '71
Slammer blues of Oyster Bay. T. Kerasote.
il pors Outdoor Life 148:58-9+ Ag '71
BLUEGILL fishing. See Sunfish fishing
BLUES (songs, etc)
B.B. bringing the blues back home. V. Gibbs.
pors Sr Schol 97:23-5 Ja 18 '71
Who took the blues from its owners? T.
Glover. il Sr Schol 98:46-7 My 17 '71
See also
Phonograph records—Blues (songs, etc)
BLUHDORN, Charles G.
Conglomerateur comes back. por Bsns W
p67 D 18 '71 •
BLUM, Etta
Beit Guvrin; Only because; poems. Poetry
118:209-10 Jl '71
BLUM, Sam
How we met and why we married. il Red-
book 136:62-3+ Ja '71
Oh! Fashion! One man's look at the preen-
ing of America. il Redbook 136:79+ Ap '71
One man no woman ever escapes. Redbook
136:73+ Ap '71
Ralph Nader: the man who makes waves. il
pors Redbook 138:70+ N '71
BLUM, Virgil C.
Public policy making: why the churches
strike out. America 124:224-8 Mr 6 '71
BLUM, Zevi
Canterbury album; drawings. Horizon 13:
48-56 Spr '71
about
Personal imagery of Zevi Blum. J. Wechsler.
il por Am Artist 36:46-51+ Ja '72 •
BLUMBERG, Philip S.
Latin: requiescat in pace. Clear House 45:
314-16 Ja '71
BLUMBERG, Stanley A. See Owens, G. jt.
auth.
BLUME, Delorys E. See Blume, R. jt. auth.
BLUME, Robert, and Blume, D. E.
Camping with inner-city kids. il Todays Ed
60:32-3 Mr '71
BLUMEN, Jean Lipman-. See Lipman-Blum-
en, J.
BLUMER, Max, and others
Small oil spill. bibliog il Environ 13:2-12 Mr
'71
BLY, Nellie, pseud. See Cochrane, E.
BLY, Robert
Dream on the night of first snow; After long
busyness; Caterpillar on the desk; poems.
Poetry 118:33-4 Ap '71
Return of political poetry. T. Gitlin. Com-
monweal 94:375-80 Jl 23 '71 •
BLY, Robert L.
Know your cooling system. il Am City 86:
80+ Ap '71
BLYDEN, Edward Wilmot
Black is beautiful: an old idea. T. H. Hen-
riksen. bibliog il Negro Hist Bul 34:150-2
N '71 •
BLYDEN, Herbert X.
Two men from cell block D. pors Time 98:
21 S 27 '71 •
BOABAB trees. See Bottle trees
BOALS, Kay
Opinion. por Mlle 72:56+ Ap '71

BOARD games. See Games
BOARD to investigate the Vietnamese war (proposed) See Commission to investigate the Vietnamese war (proposed)
BOARD-up services. See Service industries
BOARDMAN, John
Back-to-nature movement a threat? letter. il Phys Today 24:9 F; 67-8 My '71
BOARDS of directors. See Corporations—Directors
BOARDS of education. See School boards
BOARS. See Swine
BOAS, Maxwell
Inside Los Angeles: the coroner's report. il por Ramp Mag 10:30-5 Jl '71
BOAS, Orlando Villas. See Villas Boas, O.
BOAT accessories. See Boats—Equipment
BOAT building. See Boatbuilding
BOAT buying. See Boats—Purchasing
BOAT clubs
Snug Harbor, where the only tide is yule; seagoing midsummer yuletide celebration. N. Levy. il Motor B & S 127:16+ Je '71
BOAT engines. See Marine engines
BOAT hijacking. See Ship hijacking
BOAT hulls. See Hulls (naval architecture)
BOAT loaders. See Loading and unloading
BOAT models. See Ship and boat models
BOAT racing
Parting shots: aboard the good ship Pasteurized. il Life 71:62-3 Ag 13 '71
  See also
Catamaran racing
Hydroplane racing
Motor boat racing
Sailboat racing
Yacht racing
BOAT repairing. See Boats—Maintenance and repair
BOAT shelters. See Shelters
BOAT shows. See Boats—Exhibitions
BOAT signals. See Signals and signaling
BOAT surfing. See Surf riding
BOAT toilets. See Boats—Toilet facilities
BOAT tools. See Tools
BOAT trade. See Boating industry
BOAT trailer lights. See Automobile boat trailers—Lighting
BOAT trailers. See Automobile boat trailers
BOATBUILDING
Aquarod. H. Kelly. il Mech Illus 67:66-70+ Mr '71
Boating business. W. Robberson. See issues of Yachting
Build the Scottish schooner. H. Kelly. il Mech Illus 67:42-7+ Ag '71
Build Tom's Quacker; a nimble lightweight skimmer for duck hunters. H. Kelly. il Mech Illus 67:70-2 N '71
Building a cartop trimaran. M. F. Danials. il Mech Illus 67:72-4+ Mr '71
Can you and should you build your own boat? Z. Taylor. Motor B & S 127:52-5 F '71
  See also
Hulls (naval architecture)
  Anecdotes, facetiae, satire, etc.
So you're going to build an ocean liner; reprint. J. H. Slate. il Motor B & S 127:55+ F '71
BOATING clothes. See Clothing and dress—Sports clothes
BOATING for women. See Women in boating
BOATING industry
Boat builders eye consumers' course. Bsns W p 18 Ja 23 '71
How not to sell your boat. D. Fenwick. il Motor B & S 128:85-6+ O '71
What can you do in a canoe? law against sales to citizens of Communist countries. D. Sanford. New Repub 164:17-18 My 29 '71
BOATS
  Chartering
  See Boats—Leasing and renting
  Cleaning
Clues to shipshape clean-up. J. Duffett. Motor B & S 127:90-1 Ap '71
  Design
Beauty boats. il Mech Illus 67:72 My '71
Boats by Purdy. W. C. Hadley. il Yachting 130:68-9+ N '71
Designs & new boats (title varies) ed. by T. Gibbs. See issues of Motor boating & sailing

Experts advise you: how to pick a safe boat. D. D. Vigren. il Pop Sci 198:58-9+ Ja '71
New boats. T. Gibbs. il Motor B & S 127:77 F '71
New designs. T. Gibbs. il Motor B & S 127:72-6 F '71
  Displacement (ships)
  See Displacement (ships)
  Electric equipment
Basic wiring for accessories. E. L. Slepian. il Motor B & S 128:74 O '71
Don't get hung up in your boat's wiring. C. Miller. Motor B & S 127:120+ Mr '71
More electrical power; auxiliary generator. C. F. Kelley. il Yachting 130:62+ Jl '71
  See also
Electric motors
Motor boats—Electric equipment
  Maintenance and repair
Electrical system. C. Miller. il Motor B & S 127:98-9 Ap '71
  Electronic equipment
Marine electronics (title varies) See issues of Motor boating & sailing to August 1971
  Equipment
Cabin talk. M. Wiley. See issues of Yachting
Gadgets and gilhickies. J. Smith. See issues of Yachting
It's new. See issues of Yachting
New boat accessories. Outdoor Life 147:108 Ja '71
New boating products. R. Kinson. il Pop Mech 135:124-5 Mr '71
New gear and gadgets for fun afloat. F. M. Paulson. il Field & S 75:134-7+ F '71
Outfitting for offshore. W. Tompkins, jr. il Motor B & S 128:46-7+ Ag '71
Sail for your dinghy. V. Crane. il Motor B & S 128:76+ O '71
Tips on stowing gear. J. A. Emmett. il Outdoor Life 148:32+ Ag '71
Waterfront news. See issues of Yachting
What's new. P. R. Marunas. See issues of Motor boating & sailing
Yachting's boat show (cont) il Yachting 129:206-11 F '71
  See also
Boats—Roofs
Depth indicators
Radio telephone on ships, boats, etc.
Sailboats—Equipment
  Exhibitions
Boat-show calendar. Outdoor Life 147:109 Ja '71
Sailing away: National boat show '71, at the Coliseum. New Yorker 46:27-8 F 13 '71
They do go near the water: United States sailboat show, Annapolis. H. D. Whall. il Sports Illus 35:89-90 O 25 '71
Yachting's preview of 1972 sailboats and sailboat shows. il Yachting 130:63-71+ S '71
  Fires and fire protection
Fires and explosions. C. F. Kelley. Yachting 130:66+ Ag '71
  Hulls
  See Hulls (naval architecture)
  Leasing and renting
Charming charter on the Thames. C. Howland. il Motor B & S 128:60-1+ Jl '71
Ten tips for the rental boatman. B. McKeown. il Mech Illus 67:84+ Mr '71
  Maintenance and repair
Boatowner's guide to repair compounds. H. B. Notrom. il Pop Mech 135:106-9 Je '71
Care of teak. J. Emmett. Motor B & S 128:66+ S '71
How to repair a fiberglass boat. M. J. Schultz. il Pop Mech 135:116-19+ Mr '71
Instant rubber for boat repairs. J. Duffett. Motor B & S 128:74+ O '71
Maintenance; symposium. il Motor B & S 127:89-104 Ap '71
Repairing your fiberglass boat. E. H. Moore. il Cons 25:48-9 Ap '71
Something new in winter boat cover. D. Fenwick. il Motor B & S 128:75+ O '71
When storm warnings go up! M. Johnson. il Motor B & S 128:8+ S '71
  Materials
Boat-building woods. il Motor B & S 127:100-1 Ap '71
Concrete hull is not a boat. R. Koci. Motor B & S 127:54+ F '71
Fiberglass hulls: to paint or not to paint. B. Cobb, jr. il Yachting 129:56-7+ Ap '71

BOATS—Materials—*Continued*
How to repair a fiberglass boat. M. J. Schultz. il Pop Mech 135:116-19+ Mr '71
Improving fibreglass boats. J. A. Emmett. il Outdoor Life 147:26+ F '71
World's first structured plastic boat; Spoacraft Chub. D. D. Vigren. il Pop Sci 198:60 Je '71

Mooring
See Anchorage

Painting
Fiberglass hulls: to paint or not to paint. B. Cobb, jr. il Yachting 129:56-7+ Ap '71
How much paint do you need? excerpts from How to paint your boat. il Motor B & S 127:94-5 Ap '71
Painting and refinishing. J. A. Emmett. il Outdoor Life 147:28+ Mr '71
Your guide to the perfect paint job. F. C. Clark, jr. il Motor B & S 127:83-90 F '71

Protection against theft
Build a $5 vehicle alarm system. H. Phillips. il Radio-Electr 42:35-6 N '71

Purchasing
Money side of boats. B. McKeown. il Mech Illus 67:80+ Ja '71
See also
Yachts—Purchasing

Radio equipment
See Radio apparatus on ships, boats, etc.

Refrigerators
See Refrigeration on boats

Renting
See Boats—Leasing and renting

Roofs
Ragtop to hardtop. V. J. DeArmond, jr. il Motor B & S 127:116+ Mr '71

Sanitation
EPA drops the other shoe; federal water quality standards. P. Smyth. Motor B & S 127:2+ Je '71
EPA speaks: what's ahead. P. Smyth. Motor B & S 128:2 Ag '71
Pre-season plumbing; engine systems, potable water systems, and marine toilets. J. Duffett. Motor B & S 127:102-3 Ap '71
See also
Boats—Toilet facilities

Speed
Speed curves. J. West. il Yachting 130:58-9+ Ag '71
See also
Motor boats—Speed

Stability and stabilizers
See also
Tabs (boats)

Steering gear
Hladky fiberglass rudder; best type rudder for a small racing sailboat. D. Rose. il Yachting 130:32-3+ O '71
John Oakeley discusses rudders; excerpts from Winning. il Yachting 129:64+ My '71

Storage
Ways to store small boats. F. M. Paulson. il Field & S 76:146-50 N '71

Toilet facilities
How to install a holding tank on your boat. K. Weldy. il Mech Illus 67:100+ Ap '71

Towing
To tow a boat. A. Anderson. il Yachting 129:68+ Ap '71
Towing techniques. C. R. Myer. il Motor B & S 128:14+ Ag '71

Transportation
See also
Automobile boat trailers

Water supply
Make your water tank from wood. G. Groene and J. Groene. il Motor B & S 128:74-8 Ag '71

Windshields
Easy-to-make automatic windshield washer. G. P. Manning. il Motor B & S 127:89 Je '71

BOATS, Jet
New jet-powered boats. il Pop Mech 135:115 Mr '71

BOATS, Police. *See* Police boats
BOATS, Submarine. *See* Submarine boats
BOATS, Theft of
See also
Boats—Protection against theft
BOATS, Used
How not to sell your boat. D. Fenwick. il Motor B & S 128:85-6+ O '71
Three ways to buy a used boat. Motor B & S 128:120 S '71
BOATS and boating
Barnegat Bay sneak box; one man duck boat. F. M. Paulson. il Field & S 76:148-9+ O '71
Boating. J. A. Emmett. See issues of Outdoor life
Boating; ed. by F. M. Paulson. See issues of Field & stream
Boatman's world; symposium. bibliog il Motor B & S 128:43-58 Jl '71
Boats & boating. B. McKeown. See issues of Mechanix illustrated
Boats I remember. J. A. Emmett. il Outdoor Life 148:32-4+ N '71
Boats with a purpose, under $100; Water wagon G. W. Reiger. il Pop Mech 136:102-4+ S '71
Calendar of coming events. See issues of Motor boating & sailing
Calendar of major power and sail events. See issues of Yachting
Captain Spry's boat; picket boats used in tunnel construction. New Yorker 47:29-30 My 15 '71
Carry your boat to the water in a bag; lightweight inflatables. R. Hill. il por Pop Sci 198:118-20+ Ap '71
Delightful dinghy. F. M. Paulson. il Field & S 76:120-3 S '71
Dollar-a-pound dinghy; lightweight Chub dinghy. il Field & S 75:162 Mr '71
Fresh look at fresh water; future planning for the Great Lakes basin. A. Limburg. il Motor B & S 127:10-12+ Ap '71
From the cockpit. R. N. Bavier, jr. See issues of Yachting
I'll bet you don't know this one or do you? Test yourself. E. A. Zadig. il Motor B & S 127:62-5 F '71
Inshore seamanship; surf fishing. J. A. Emmett. il Outdoor Life 148:20+ Jl '71
In-use boat report. See issues of Motor boating & sailing
Lure of dark water. T. F. Norton. il Motor B & S 128:54-5+ S '71
More fun for your money. il Pop Sci 198:87-9 F '71
Motor boating & sailing USA. See issues of Motor boating & sailing to June 1971
New boats for sportsmen. F. M. Paulson. il Field & S 75:148-50+ Ap '71
New guide to inflatable boats. F. M. Paulson. il Field & S 76:100-4 Jl '71
New 1971 boats. il Pop Mech 135:108-11 Mr '71
News from yachting centers. See issues of Yachting
1972 boats. B. McKeown. il Mech Illus 68:48-9+ Ja '72
Photo safari by boat. F. M. Paulson. il Field & S 75:42-5+ Ja '71
Rogue River float. F. M. Paulson. il Field & S 76:54-7+ N '71
Scuttlebutt. G. F. Hammond. See issues of Motor boating & sailing
Season stretchers for boatmen. B. McKeown. il Mech Illus 67:40+ D '71
Three new fun boats. il Mech Illus 67:113 N '71
Troubled water over bridges; encroachments on the waters used for pleasure boating. B. Robinson. Yachting 130:31 D '71
What readers ask; question-and-answer. J. A. Emmett. il Outdoor Life 148:78-80+ D '71
What's new. P. R. Marunas. See issues of Motor boating & sailing
See also
Boatbuilding
Boating industry
Canoe trips
Canoes and canoeing
Cruising
Fishing boats
Houseboats
Kayaks
Marinas
Motor boats
Navigation
Regattas
River trips
Sailboats
Sailing
Sails
Seamanship
Trimarans
United States power squadron, inc.
Women in boating
Yachts and yachting

BOATS and boating—*Continued*

Accidents

Pleasures of sailing. A. Stanford. Motor B & S 127:76-7+ Mr '71
Sunk by a whale! G. Webb. il por Motor B & S 128:38-40+ Ag '71
Unusual catch; Bahamas cruise turned into a rescue operation. A. Redding. il Yachting 130:54-5 N '71
When in trouble: lessons from three rescue operations and a severe squall. S. Chasalow; R. Williams; G. J. Hess. il Yachting 129:60-4+ Je '71

Anecdotes, facetiae, satire, etc.

Mystery of the musical motor. R. Humphrey. Motor B & S 128:69+ S '71

Bibliography

Book notes and reviews. K. Aamodt. See issues of Yachting
Book shelf. T. Gibbs. See issues of Motor boating & sailing
Bookshelf for boatmen. il Mech Illus 67:76 Mr '71

Economic aspects

28 ways to stretch your boating buck. W. Juettner. Motor B & S 127:114-15+ Mr '71

Laws and regulations

At last: the 1968-69-70 Federal boat safety act of 1971 passes. T. Gibbs. Motor B & S 128:48-9+ S '71
Beware the bureaucrats. B. Robinson. Yachting 130:33 N '71
Don't make waves; action against U.S. boat speeders in Wallaceburg, Ont. il Newsweek 78:42 Ag 9 '71
I.O.R. rule is being changed. B. Bavier. Yachting 130:48 N '71
Those dangerous encounters. D. M. Saunders. Yachting 130:44+ N '71
Washington report. W. T. Stone. See issues of Yachting
See also
National association of state boating law administrator

Lightning hazards

How to protect your boat against lightning. C. Miller. il Motor B & S 127:114-15+ Ap '71
Lightning protection; ground system for a boat. J. Smith. Yachting 130:71 D '71

Photographs

Gallery. Motor B & S 127:79-85 Mr '71

Safety devices and measures

Distress signals; safety equipment for boats. E. Robberson. il Yachting 129:70-2+ My '71
Experts advise you: how to pick a safe boat. D. D. Vigren. il Pop Sci 198:58-9+ Ja '71
How to handle offshore water. B. McKeown. il Mech Illus 67:46+ F '71
Keeping your head above water. A. Limburg. il Motor B & S 128:83-5 Jl '71
Man overboard, you! B. McKeown. il Mech Illus 67:54+ N '71
Safer boats on the way? J. Roe. il Pop Sci 199:60+ S '71
Using survival equipment? B. D. Barker. 3d. il Yachting 130:68-9 Jl '71
When in trouble: lessons from three rescue operations and a severe squall. S. Chasalow; R. Williams; G. J. Hess. il Yachting 129:60-4+ Je '71
See also
Boats and boating—Lightning hazards
Life preservers
Life saving equipment

Study and teaching

Idea from below nowhere; P. Bellesen and his youth organization. E. Crimmin. il por Motor B & S 127:12+ My '71
See also
Sailing—Study and teaching

Terminology

Nautical talk. F. M. Paulson. il Field & S 75:142-4+ Mr '71

BOAZ, Martha
First responsibility; letter to the editor. Am Lib 2:1035 N '71

BOB Hope desert classic. See Golf—Tournaments

BOB Jones university, Greenville, S.C.
Most unusual: no time for a change. Chr Today 16:34 D 17 '71

BOB Marshall wilderness area. See Wilderness areas—Montana

BOBBITT, Mayme
Arkansas shallots stay versatile. il Org Gard & Farm 18:82-3 My '71

BOBCAT hunting
Bobcat paradise. D. J. Anderson. il Field & S 76:68-9+ N '71
Cat comes calling. J. Wootters. il Outdoor Life 148:70-1+ O '71

BOBCATS
Bobcat facts; excerpt from The bobcat of North America. S. P. Young. il Field & S 76:28 Je '71

BOBECK, Andrew H. and Scovil, H. E. D.
Magnetic bubbles; with biographical sketches. il Sci Am 224:16, 78-90 Je '71

BOBICK, Duane
Good things come in large packages. P. Putnam. il pors Sports Illus 35:16-18+ Ag 23 '71

BOBROW, Michael L.
Evolution of nursing space planning for efficient operation. il Arch Rec 150:151-4 S '71

BOBROWSKI, Barbara
How I escaped a time clock. por Redbook 136:38+ Ap '71

BOBROWSKY, Kenneth
Teleguide. il Schol Teach Jr/Sr High p28 Ja '72

BOBST, Elmer H.
Elmer Bobst tells his Nixon story. por Bsns W p54-5 Jl 31 '71

BOBWHITE shooting. See Quail shooting

BOCA RATON, Fla.

Architecture

IBM in Boca Raton: Breuer builds on Florida's flood plain. il Arch Rec 149:113-18 F '71

BOCCIE. See Bowling

BOCHENSKI, Judy
Ping pong diplomat. il por Seventeen 30:142+ O '71

BOCHER, Main Rousseau. See Mainbocher

BOCK, Joleen
Two-year academic library buildings. il Library J 96:3986-9 D 1 '71

BODE, Carl
Friday fence; poem. Commonweal 94:330 Je 25 '71
Transposition; poem. Nation 213:92 Ag 2 '71

BODE, Ken
Blacks, Democrats and the '72 convention. New Repub 165:11-15 O 16 '71
Democratic party reform. New Repub 165:19-23 Jl 10 '71
Dilemma of the lesser Democrats. New Repub 165:14-16 D 25 '71
Favorite sons in '72. New Repub 165:17-20 N 6 '71
Party loyalty in '72. New Repub 165:13-15 N 20 '71

BODENHEIMER, Susanne
Inside a state of siege: legalized murder in Guatemala. il Ramp Mag 9:50-2 Je '71

BODENSTEIN, Bennett, and Keppler, Herbert
Camera flare: the real enemy? il Mod Phot 36:86-9 Ja '72
—See Schneider, J. jt. auth.

BODINE, Aldine Aubrey
Pictorialism. E. Scully. il Mod Phot 35:94-9 Ja '71 *

BODY, Human
Body-typing to help you improve your body-image. il Vogue 159:90-1 Ja 1 '72
Fashionable body; excerpt from The unfashionable human body. B. Rudofsky. il Horizon 13:56-65 Aut '71

BODY fat. See Fat

BODY fluids
See also
Edema
Lymph
Perspiration

BODY image
Chimp with a self concept? il Sci Digest 70:46-50 Jl '71

BODY lice. See Lice

BODY odors. See Odors

BODY paint. See Indians of North America—Costume and adornment

BODY size
Mini-people, inc? H. Manchester. Sat R 54:6+ O 16 '71

BODY surfing. See Surf riding

BODY temperature. See Temperature, Animal and human

BODY weight. See Weight (physiology)

BOEHM, George A. W.
Firefighting: better equipment for the big ones. il Pop Mech 136:114-17+ N '71
Sam Genensky's marvelous seeing machine. il Read Digest 98:27-8+ Ja '71

BOEING company
Aerospace dinosaurs. P. Barnes. New Repub 164:17-19 Mr 27 '71
Aerospace giant tries earthwork. il Time 98:79 N 15 '71

BOEING company—*Continued*
Boeing, Boeing, bong. SST battle. Sr Schol 97:3 Ja 11 '71
Boeing earnings up slightly in quarter. Aviation W 94:21 My 3 '71
Boeing expects to diversify. Aviation W 94: 53 Mr 29 '71
Boeing pulls back subcontract work. Aviation W 94:20 My 24 '71
Boeing sows diversification seed in desert. R. G. O'Lone. il Aviation W 95:44-6 N 29 '71
Boeing's earnings up, McDonnell Douglas' dip. Aviation W 95:14 Ag 2 '71
Boeing's surplus is on the block. il Bsns W p35-6 Ap 17 '71
Conversion pains. Newsweek 77:76-7 Mr 1 '71
Faint hopes of U.S. supersonic transport restart haunt Boeing termination efforts. R. G. O'Lone. il Aviation W 94:18-21 My 3 '71
How to win by losing. Forbes 107:20 Je 15 '71
Lunar rover program spurred. R. G. O'Lone. il Aviation W 94:49-51 F 15 '71
Packing up the SST; with report on the Concorde by W. A. McWhirter. il Life 70: 85-6+ My 28 '71
SST stops short. Sr Schol 98:16-17 Ap 19 '71
SST termination process begins; with editorial comment. Aviation W 94:9, 14-16 Mr 29 '71
Wilson of Boeing. il por Forbes 107:53 My 15 '71
BOEKI Daigaku. See Business schools and colleges—Japan
BOER war. See South African war, 1899-1902
BOFFEY, Philip M.
Nader to sponsor study of Academy. Sci N 99:247 Ap 10 '71 •
BOG ecology. See Marsh ecology
BOG vegetation. See Marsh plants
BOGATZ, Gerry Ann, and Ball, Samuel
Some things you've wanted to know about Sesame street. il Am Ed 7:11-15 Ap '71; Same. Ed Digest 37:23-6 S '71
BOGDANOVIC, Bogomir
Watercolor page; with biographical sketch. il por Am Artist 35:57 D '71
BOGDANOVICH, Peter
Current cinema. P. Kael. New Yorker 47: 145-7+ O 9 '71 •
Festival prize. il por Time 98:80+ O 11 '71 •
It won't be his last picture show, with report by J. Watters. il pors Life 71:43-4+ N 26 '71 •
Movies in the round. P. D. Zimmerman. il por Newsweek 78:108+ O 18 '71 •
BOGEN, Robert W. See Smith, S. jt. auth.
BOGEN, S. A.
18 months of nuisance-free operation. il Am City 86:71-3 Je '71
BOGER, Louise Ade
Questions & answers: antiques. See issues of House & garden incorporating Living for young homemakers
BOGGAN, Tim
How to play winning ping-pong. il por Mech Illus 67:82-3+ S '71
BOGGS, Hale
Inefficient Congress? rebuttal from Capitol hill; interview. por U S News 70:80-1 Mr 22 '71

about

Boggs file. Newsweek 77:29 My 3 '71 •
Byrd and Boggs. New Repub 164:10 Ja 30 '71 •
Mayors revolt. il Newsweek 77:94 My 24 '71 •
Road to power in Congress. L. L. King. Harper 242:39-42+ Je '71 •
What's bugging Boggs. por Newsweek 77: 35+ Ap 19 '71 •
BOGGS, Peggy Ann
Sweet surprise. il Org Gard & Farm 18:53 Ag '71
BOGOMIL funerary art. See Sepulchral monuments
BOGORAD, Lawrence. See Mets, L. J. jt. auth.
BOGOTÁ, Colombia

Buildings

Bogotá builds. J. Sanger. il Américas 23: 25-30 Je '71
BOHANNAN, Paul
Beyond civilization; with biographical sketch. il Natur Hist 80:10, 50-67 F '71
La BOHEME; opera. See Puccini, G.
BOHEMIANISM
See also
Beatniks
BOHLING, Al
Tallgrass prairie park. il Nat Parks & Con Mag 45:6-10 Mr '71

BÖHM, Georg
Reviews of records. L. Noss. Mus Q 57:166-9 Ja '71 •
BÖHM, Karl
Interview of the week, ed. by R. Hemming. Sr Schol 98:22 F 8 '71

about

Music to my ears; conducting the New York philharmonic in performance of Bruckner's Symphony no. 8. I. Kolodin. Sat R 54:18 Mr 27 '71 •
BOHN, Hinrich L.
Clean new gas. bibliog il Environ 13:4-9 D '71
BOHNEN, Michael
Mail and reviews. A. Favia-Artsay. por Hobbies 76:36+ Mr '71 •
BOHR, Aage
Concepts of nuclear structure; adaptation of address, October 29, 1970. il Science 172: 17-21 Ap 2 '71
BOIARSKY, Carolyn, and Pedersen, Nelda
Youth speaks out about teachers. il Todays Ed 60:44-6 N '71
BOICE, James Montgomery
Presbyterians weigh pacts. Chr Today 15:29 Je 18 '71
BOIGNY, Félix Houphouet-. See Houphouet-Boigny, F.
BOIKO, Claire
Ah See and the six-colored heaven; dramatization of Chinese fairy tale. Plays 30:65-70, 78 Mr '71
Before your very eyes; drama. Plays 30:1-8 Ap '71
La Belle telephone; drama. Plays 30:13-20 F '71
Ghost wanted; drama. Plays 31:17-26, 36 O '71
How mothers came to be; dramatization of an Indian legend. Plays 30:73-6 My '71
Monkey business; dramatization of an Indian folktale. Plays 31:73-6 O '71
My cousin from Tycho; drama. Plays 31: 37-46 N '71
On camera, Noah Webster! drama. Plays 31: 57-62 N '71
Star fever; drama. Plays 30:15-24 Mr '71
Tall tale tournament; drama. Plays 31:67-72 D '71
Trick or treat for UNICEF; drama. Plays 31: 57-62 O '71
BOISE, Idaho

Banks

Going to pieces in Boise; sorting cut-up checks. il Time 98:59 Ag 2 '71

Education

Citizens endorse change. il Sat R 54:53 Je 19 '71
BOISE Cascade corporation
Boise Cascade shifts toward tighter control. il Bsns W p86+ My 15 '71
Lessons from the land; ventures in leisure-time communities. il Time 97:86 Ap 12 '71
Report to the readers; history of ownership of Saturday review. N. Cousins. Sat R 54: 16-17 Jl 31 '71
BOITO, Arrigo
He and Lenor. M. J. Matz. il pors Opera N 35:11-13 F 13 '71 •
Mefistofele. Criticism
Hi Fi 20:MA16 D '70 •
BOK, Bart J.
Gum nebula. il por Sky & Tel 42:64-9 Ag '71
Harlow Shapley, cosmographer. Am Scholar 40:470-4 Sum '71
BOK, Derek Curtis
Harvard picks a president; with interview, ed. by E. Kern. il pors Life 70:34-6 Ja 22 '71

about

Harvard: new president's task to unify, preside over change. T. P. Southwick. Science 171:264-6 Ja 22 '71 •
Harvard picks a president. il por Newsweek 77:70-2 Ja 18 '71 •
Harvardization of Derek Bok. Newsweek 77: 71 Ja 18 '71 •
Harvard's quiet man. il por Time 97:60-1 Ja 25 '71 •
BOKASSA, Jean Bedel
Tale of two daughters. il por Time 97:34 Ja 25 '71 •
BOLAM, Irene
Amelia Earhart lives, by J. Klaas. Review Flying 88:25+ Mr '71. F. W. Gibson •
BOLCH, Jennifer Ann
Therapy of sharing. il Har Yrs 11:10+ Mr '71

BOND, Edward
Narrow road to the Deep North. Criticism
Time 99:47 Ja 17 '72 •
Saved. Criticism
Commonweal 93:397 Ja 22 '71 •
BOND, Harold
Impasse; poem. Horn Bk 47:358 Ag '71
BOND, Horace Julian. See Bond, J.
BOND, Julian
Rising stock of Julian Bond. E. Clift. por
McCalls 98:40 My '71 •
Sowing the seeds of power. il pors Ebony
26:104-8+ O '71 •
Up, uppity and away. J. Neary. por Esquire
75:109-11+ My '71 •
BONDARCHUK, Sergei
Current cinema. P. Gilliatt. New Yorker 47:
130+ Ap 10 '71 •
BONDI, Joseph
Middle school requires some direction. Clear
House 45:568 My '71
Verbal patterns of teachers in the class-
room. Ed Digest 37:44-5 S '71
BONDS
Bond bulls roared, then lost. A. Hershman.
il Duns 98:35 Ag '71
Bonds in '72: higher yields; interview. J. H.
Sedlmayr. por U S News 72:60-1 Ja 10 '72
Bonds: you can get taken here, too. por
Forbes 108:42-3 Jl 15 '71
Fund operators rush into bonds. il Bsns
W p57 Jl 24 '71
Hope for bonds. C. Morgello. il Newsweek
78:96 N 29 '71
Making money work; are bonds still good
for safety and income? S. Meisenberg. il
Har Yrs 11:36-8 Jl '71
Nonstop prosperity? il Forbes 107:33 Mr 1 '71
Want more income from your savings? M.
T. Bloom. Read Digest 99:109-11 S '71
See also
Chemical bonds
Municipal bonds

Rating
Economy: 1065 and all that. il Newsweek
77:77 Mr 15 '71
Rising rates mark a bond rally's end. il
Bsns W p42 F 27 '71

Redemption
How to call your convertibles. A. B. Miller.
Harvard Bsns R 49:66-70 My '71

Yields
Why bond yields are important. J. W. Schulz.
il Forbes 108:84-5 O 1 '71
BONDS, Convertible
Convertibles. C. Morgello. il Newsweek 77:91
Ap 12 '71
How to call your convertibles. A. B. Miller.
Harvard Bsns R 49:66-70 My '71
Making money work; should you buy con-
vertible stocks and bonds? S. Meisenberg.
Har Yrs 11:44-5 Ag '71
BONDS, Government
Are U.S. savings bonds a better deal now?
il Changing T 25:17-18 Je '71
Purchasing-power bonds. M. Friedman. News-
week 77:86 Ap 12 '71
Savings (?) bonds. J. Phillips. Ramp Mag
9:8+ Mr '71
Treasury offers market-traded bonds. U S
News 71:70 Ag 2 '71
Uncle Sam brings small investors treasury
bonds at high interest. T. Schuchat. Har
Yrs 11:4 S '71
See also
Foreign bondholders protective council
Municipal bonds

China
Chinese bonds take a great leap forward.
Bsns W p26+ Jl 31 '71

Germany (Federal Republic)
U.S. brings Young loan dispute before arbi-
tral tribunal. Dept State Bul 65:55 Jl 12
'71

Hungary
Hungary readies a Eurobond issue. Bsns W
p27-8 Mr 6 '71
Man who put Hungary into Eurobonds. por
Bsns W p52 Jl 17 '71

Russia
Questionable bargain in bonds; Russian
Tsarist bonds. G. J. Henry. por Forbes 107:
67 Mr 1 '71
BONDS, Municipal. See Municipal bonds
BONDS, School. See School finance
BONE
Prehistoric domestication of animals; effects
on bone structure. I. M. Drew and others.
bibliog il Science 171:280-2 Ja 22 '71; Reply
with rejoinder. D. McConnell and D. W.
Foreman, jr. 172:971-3 My 28 '71

BONE marrow. See Marrow
BONE meal
From bone manure to superphosphate. V.
Schatz and A. Schatz. il Org Gard & Farm
18:140-7+ Mr '71
BONE resorption. See Absorption (physiology)
BONEBRAKE, Marie R.
Sleuthing for ancestors. il Hobbies 76:152-
3+ Jl '71
BONEFISH fishing
Bonefish behavior. A. J. McClane. il Field &
S 76:102-3+ Je '71
Bonefish break the rules. M. Gadsden. il Field
& S 76:80-1+ Je '71
Catch bonefish on your own! L. Kreh. il
por Field & S 76:60-1+ My '71
BONES, Jim
Big Thicket; photographs. Audubon 73:13-
24 My '71
BONES
See also
Fractures
Joints

Diseases
See also
Osteogenesis imperfecta
Paget's disease
Rickets
BONES, Fossil. See Paleontology
BONES of contention; story. See Trott, S.
BONFANTE, Jordan
Germaine Greer. il por Life 70:30-3 My 7 '71
I would be willing to do anything at all. Life
71:29-30 D 3 '71
BONGARTZ, Roy
Deformità perfetta of Richard Nixon, Lyn-
don Johnson and other heroes. pors Esquire
75:70-5 F '71
Fleet of landlocked schooners on the Amer-
can sea. il Holiday 49:32-3+ My '71
Go North to Gaspé. il Holiday 49:42-5 My '71
I don't want to waste time, says Louise
Nevelson at 70. il pors N Y Times Mag
p 12-13+ Ja 24 '71
Mountain versus Korczak Ziolkowski. il Es-
quire 75:112-13+ Mr '71
Pitchman for free (and freewheeling) thea-
ter. il pors N Y Times Mag p 12-13+ Ag
15 '71
BONHAM, Margaret
Bit of capital; story. Redbook 137:64-5 Jl
'71
BONHAM, Roger D.
Ceramic sculpture of Joe Ann Cousino. il
Ceram Mo 19:16-17 My '71
Joe Ann Cousino demonstrates sculpture
from coils. il Ceram Mo 19:18-20 My '71
BONHAM, Ruth C.
Air pollution and chrysanthemums. il Horti-
culture 49:30-1 O '71
BONHOEFFER, Dietrich
ABC: Assy, Bonhoeffer, Carswell. R. M.
Brown. il Chr Cent 88:369-71 Mr 24 '71 •
BONILLA, Antulio Parrilla-. See Parrilla-Bon-
illa, A.
BONING of poultry. See Poultry, Dressing of
BONNE Bell cosmetics. See Cosmetics
BONNER, Harry
Fish from the rocks! il Field & S 76:64-5+
My '71
BONNER, Thomas Neville
Meet the press. il por Newsweek 78:84 Ag 23
'71 •
BONNETS. See Hats
BONNEVILLE national speed trials. See Auto-
mobile racing; Motorcycle racing
BONNEY, Weston
Maine idea in banking. A. Hershman. por
Duns 97:68 Ap '71 •
BONNIE; story. See Ephron, N.
BONNIWELL, Bernard L.
Social control of pornography and sexual
behavior. bibliog f Ann Am Acad 397:97-104
S '71
BONO, Agostino
No muscle is the message. Commonweal 95:
316-17 Ja 7 '72
BONOMI-BOLCHINI, Anna
Lady magnate of Milan. il por Time 97:73
Je 7 '71 •
BONOMO, Victor A.
Pepsi's whiz kid. por Bsns W p80 F 6 '71 •
BONSAI. See Trees, Dwarf
BONUS system
Bonuses as usual, but not for all. Bsns W p 19
Ja 1 '72
Crunch that stole Christmas. Time 98:69 D 20
'71
What's wrong with bonuses. J. Perham. il
Duns 97:42-4+ Ap '71

BOOGAARD, Mary Augusta, and Chaney, E. R.
From not so different worlds. Engl J 60:226-8+ F '71
BOOK, David. See Benford, G. jt. auth.
BOOK advertising. See Books—Advertising
BOOK awards, National. See National book awards
BOOK bazaars. See Book fairs
BOOK binding. See Bookbinding
BOOK bulletins. See Library publications
BOOK buying
Publisher's practical plan; book budgets. Chr Cent 88:1399 N 24 '71
BOOK buying for libraries. See Libraries—Acquisitions
BOOK censorship. See Censorship
BOOK clerks. See Booksellers and bookselling—Employees
BOOK clubs
European scene; Club Français du livre. H. R. Lottman. Pub W 200:21 Jl 5 '71
Playboy forms book club; firm will go public soon. Pub W 199:45-6 Je 21 '71
Why won't it work? F. H. Brown. Pub W 199:28-30 Mr 29 '71
See also
Book-of-the-month-club
BOOK collecting
See also
Book rarities
BOOK covers
Illustration is alive and well on paperback covers. M. R. Kraner. bibliog il Pub W 199:54-6 Je 28 '71
BOOK decoration. See Book ornamentation
BOOK dedications
Trade winds. C. Amory. Sat R 54:20 N 27 '71
BOOK design
American heritage dictionary: pictures at a definition; a marginal critique; with reply by W. Morris. J. B. White. il Wilson Lib Bul 45:674-80 Mr '71
Book designers are a pain in the neck. G. Stevens. Sat R 54:20 F 6 '71
Companionable design for definitive Thoreau; Princeton university press edition. C. B. Grannis. il por Pub W 200:44+ O 4 '71
Graphic design in Israel. E. Reichl. il Pub W 199:48-9 Je 7 '71
Wide open approach to the wide open spaces; publication of The art of the Old West, by David C. Hunt and Paul A. Rossi. A. De Mirjian, jr. il Pub W 200:30-3 N 1 '71
BOOK discarding. See Libraries—Book discarding
BOOK donations. See Libraries—Gifts, legacies, etc.
BOOK editors. See Editors and editing
BOOK ends and bookracks
Adjustable book rack for desk. S. Koren. il Pop Sci 199:132 O '71
Quickie designs that keep the sawdust flying; colonial bookrack. il Pop Mech 135:156-7 Mr '71
BOOK exhibits
AAUP design: clear traditional mold. il Pub W 199:47-9 My 3 '71
AIGA fifty books show: a sharp critique. S. N. Antiput. il Pub W 199:34-7 My 10 '71
Chicago book clinic show. il Pub W 199:61-3 My 24 '71
New England book show, the mixture as before. il Pub W 199:135-6 F 22 '71
Panorama of children's book design; AIGA children's book show. D. Klemin. il Pub W 199:56-8+ F 1 '71
See also
Book fairs
Library exhibits
BOOK fairs
Bookbang in Bedford square brings together buyers and authors. B. Kolins. il Pub W 199:50-1 Je 28 '71; Reply. M. Goff. 200:59-61 Jl 19 '71
Building up for the Frankfurt buchmesse. H. R. Lottman. Pub W 200:27 Ag 9 '71
European scene: Brussels book fair. H. R. Lottman. Pub W 199:31-2 Ap 5 '71
Frankfurt '71. H. R. Lottman. il Pub W 200:19 N 8 '71
International book fairs 1972; table. Pub W 200:pt2 141 S 27 '71
Jerusalem international book fair. D. N. Mount. il Pub W 199:20-4 My 17 '71
Jerusalem: Int'l book fair and publishing conference. Pub W 199:57 Ap 12 '71
New England book festival draws record crowds. Pub W 200:28-30 O 25 '71
New England book festival to be held October 1-3. Pub W 200:28 S 20 '71
Nice: over before it gets off the ground? H. R. Lottman. il Pub W 199:40-1 Je 28 '71

1971 Frankfurt book fair bigger than last year's. Pub W 200:28 S 20 '71
Prison escape; Connecticut department of correction paperback book fair, conducted and sponsored by the Connecticut state library. E. W. Strain. il por Library J 96:169-70 Ja 15 '71
BOOK forums. See Forums (discussion and debate)
BOOK illustration. See Illustration of books and periodicals
BOOK imports. See Books—Importation
BOOK industries
Book business. A. Green. Sat R 54:25 My 29; 21-2 Je 26; 23-4 Jl 31; 25 Ag 28; 40+ S 25; 48-9+ O 30 '71
Bookmaking. See issues of Publishers' weekly
See also
Book fairs
Books—Marketing
Books—Prices
Booksellers and bookselling
Copyright
Printing
Printing industry

Advertising

See Books—Advertising

Employees

Occupational employment survey in printing and publishing; with tables. G. T. Silvestri. Mo Labor R 94:56-8 N '71

Finance

Wage-price freeze and the book industry. R. H. Smith. Pub W 200:241 Ag 30 '71

International aspects

See also
Association for the promotion of the international circulation of the press

Law

But can you do that? H. F. Pilpel and K. P. Norwick. See issues of Publisher's weekly to March 29, 1971
You can do that. H. F. Pilpel and A. U. Schwartz. Pub W 200:37 Ag 2 '71; 201:30-2 Ja 3 '72

Statistics

Book trade in 1972: wary but hopeful. C. B. Grannis. Pub W 200:28 D 20 '71

Austria

See also
Publishers and publishing—Austria

Canada

See also
Publishers and publishing—Canada

Denmark

See also
Booksellers and bookselling—Denmark

France

See also
Publishers and publishing—France

Great Britain

See also
Publishers and publishing—Great Britain

Iran

Persian book trade prepares for nation's 2500th anniversary. W. F. Courtney. il Pub W 200:pt2 181-3 S 27 '71

Israel

See also
Publishers and publishing—Israel

Russia

See also
Publishers and publishing—Russia

Spain

See also
Publishers and publishing—Spain

United States

See also
Book manufacturers' institute
Publishers and publishing—United States
BOOK jobbers. See Book wholesalers
BOOK lending, Library. See Libraries—Circulation, loans, etc.
BOOK lists. See Books and reading—Best books; Children's literature——Bibliography
BOOK making (betting)
Little bet shop around the corner? il Forbes 107:48+ Ap 15 '71
See also
Coral index, ltd.
Horse race betting
Off-track betting corporation, New York

BOOK manufacturers' institute
BMI: 39th annual meeting. il Pub W 200:20-5 D 13 '71

BOOK of hours of Catherine of Cleves. See Hours, Books of

BOOK of Job. See Bible—Old Testament—Job

BOOK-of-the-month club
Fitzgerald moves to BOM; club will expand shortly. Pub W 200:35 Ag 16 '71

BOOK orders, Library. See Libraries—Acquisitions

BOOK ornamentation
Fore-edge: the collectors new passion? P. Ingraham. il Pub W 200:260+ Ag 30 '71

BOOK packagers. See Publishers and publishing

BOOK postage. See Postal rates—United States

BOOK prices. See Books—Prices

BOOK processing in libraries. See Libraries—Technical processes

BOOK promotion. See Books—Advertising

BOOK purchasing, Government. See Purchasing, Government

BOOK rarities
See also
Booksellers and bookselling—Book rarities
Hours, Books of

Collections
See College libraries—Special collections

Facsimiles
Standards proposed: Rare book libraries' conference on facsimiles. Am Lib 2:1131 D '71

BOOK reports
Ubiquitous book report. L. Millsap. Ed Digest 36:52-4 F '71

BOOK restoration. See Books—Conservation and restoration

BOOK reviewers and reviewing
Rhode Island project: book reviews by older citizens. J. Drickhamer. bibliog il por Library J 96:2737-43 S 15 '71

BOOK reviews
Right to quote: using reviews in book and theater advertising; letter to the editor. J. Weidman. Pub W 200:23 N 15 '71
School children and book selection; use of elementary student reviewers for Learning resource centers in Canton, Ohio. W. Measel and L. L. Crawford. il pors Am Lib 2:955-7 O '71
Slouching toward criticism. J. A. Avant. il por Library J 96:4055-9 D 15 '71
See also
Books in Canada (periodical)
Choice (periodical)
Kirkus bulletin (periodical)
Literary criticism
New York review of books (periodical)
New York times book review

BOOK sections of newspapers. See Newspapers—Sections, columns, etc.

BOOK selection
Against the dogmatists: a sceptical view of libraries. D. Gore; discussion. Am Lib 2:16, 147-8, 343-4 Ja-F, Ap '71
Ideological balance in the Free library of Philadelphia book collections; ed. by J. F. Krug and J. A. Harvey. G. Wilson. Am Lib 2:156-7 F '71
Let's add diversity. K. F. Kister. Library J 96:2745 S 15 '71; Discussion. 96:3927 D 1 '71
Pornography collection; excerpts from Magazine selection. B. Katz. bibliog il Library J 96:4060-6 D 15 '71
Selection of library materials; letter to the editor. Am Lib 2:451-2 My '71
Slouching toward criticism. J. A. Avant. il por Library J 96:4055-9 D 15 '71
See also
Booksellers and bookselling—Stock
Kirkus bulletin (periodical)
School libraries—Book selection

Anecdotes, facetiae, satire, etc.
Manly art: book rejection. B. E. Richardson. il Library J 96:446-9 F 1 '71

BOOK series. See Series, Book

BOOK stacks. See Library furniture and equipment

BOOK storage. See Books—Storage

BOOK thefts
See also
Library protection systems

BOOK titles. See Titles of books, stories, etc.

BOOK week
Children's book week promotions announced. Pub W 200:38-40 Ag 23 '71
Turning on parent power. S. C. Silberberg. Sat R 54:58-9 N 13 '71

BOOK wholesalers
Unfair competition from wholesaler-owned stores; letter to the editor. L. M. Marrone. Pub W 200:24-6 N 15 '71
See also
Feffer and Simons, inc.

BOOKBINDING
Bookbinding at Ascona; Centro del bel libro, Switzerland. il Craft Horiz 31:36+ Ap '71
Bookbinding kit. il Consumer Bul 54:26 Mr '71
Getting your book into a fine bind; Lauriat's bookstore in Boston. P. Ingraham. Pub W 200:49 Ag 2 '71
Hot books of a new kind: Sendor bindery, New York. il Pub W 200:48-9 O 4 '71
How to rebind a book. R. Capotosto. il Mech Illus 67:100-1+ D '71

BOOKCASES
Bookcases that can grow. J. Capotosto. il Mech Illus 67:94-5 Ja '71

BOOKER, Christopher
Candet in medio litterarum mundo prelum universitatis oxoniensis. il Esquire 76:100-3+ Jl '71

BOOKER, Simeon
America mourns Whitney M. Young jr. il pors Ebony 26:31-4+ My '71
Black business is tops in South. il Ebony 26:56-8+ Ag '71
Black caucus. il Ebony 26:100-2+ S '71
Two blacks discover lost African world. il Ebony 27:47-8+ N '71

BOOKLETS. See Pamphlets

BOOKMOBILES
Bookmobiles: a somewhat closer look. E. Healy. il Am Lib 2:72-8 Ja '71

BOOKRACKS. See Book ends and bookracks

BOOKS
See also
Best sellers
Book manufacturers' institute
Copyright
Manuscripts
Royalties
Textbooks
Title pages

Advertising
AAP seminar focuses on direct mail. P. A. Farrell. Pub W 200:16-17 N 29 '71
Captivity on the promo circuit. R. Dudman. New Repub 165:27-8 Jl 24 '71
Close your eyes and buy a book; device with taped message of the critics, produced by Booksounds. P. A. Farrell. il Pub W 200:39-40 O 4 '71
FTC says book ads have free speech guarantees. S. Wagner. Pub W 200:29-30 Jl 26 '71
Fall announcements. il Pub W 200:203-32 Ag 30 '71
Higbee's rounds up 14 publishers for book promotion first; meet the experts event. Pub W 199:36 Ap 19 '71
How to promote your book on radio and TV interviews. R. Hull. il Writers Digest 51:28-30+ Ag '71
New service offers CATV author interviews. il Pub W 200:25 D 6 '71
Spring highspots; February through May. il Pub W 199:187-216 Ja 25 '71
See also
Book reviews
Book week
Booksounds, inc.

Classification
See Classification

Conservation and restoration
Allentown college library suffers $100,000 flood loss. Library J 96:3553-4 N 1 '71
Preserving the past. A. M. Cunningham. Mlle 74:169+ N '71
See also
Books—Fine editions

Editions

Exhibitions
See Book exhibits

Fine editions
Book business; book packagers. A. Green. Sat R 54:48-9 O 30 '71

BOOKS—*Continued*

Importation

Hauling cartons and swatting mosquitoes: a night with the U.S. customs. R. H. Smith. Pub W 200:96-7 Jl 19 '71

Walkout maroons a sea of books. il Bsns W p47 N 13 '71

Marketing

Book distribution and marketing; highlights of panel discussion, June 2, 1971. Pub W 199:38+ Je 21 '71

Mutilation, defacement, etc.

Anecdotes, facetiae, satire, etc.

Dewey damsel system. J. Breen. Wilson Lib Bul 45:770-1 Ap '71

Paper covered books

See Paperback books

Prices

AAP argues against book price ceiling as First amendment infringement. S. Wagner. Pub W 200:27 O 25 '71

Wage-price freeze: Phase two. R. H. Smith. Pub W 200:21 O 25 '71

What price a book? R. E. Bye. Library J 96:2279 Jl '71

See also
Books—Reprints
Libraries—Finance

Reprints

Reprint wish-fulfillment; letter to the editor. S. Crane; discussion. Library J 96:150-1 Ja 15 '71

See also
Paperback books

Anecdotes, facetiae, satire, etc.

Gold fever. J. Ciardi. Sat R 54:10+ F 13 '71

Bibliography

Books to come (cont) il Library J 96:2216+, 2689-90+; 97:99+ Je 15, S 1 '71, Ja 1 '72

Statistics

See Book industries—Statistics

Storage

Little boxes: book storage by Randtriever, that locates and delivers books in seconds, automatically. D. Dickinson. Am Lib 2:422 Ap '71; Reply. M. Cart. 2:575-6 Je '71

See also
Warehouses

Anecdotes, facetiae, satire, etc.

Encyclopedia behind the eggs. H. Briggs. House B 113:76 O '71

Translations

See Translations and translating

Transportation

Dock strike: effects on overseas shipping. Pub W 200:19 N 1 '71

BOOKS, Art. See Art literature

BOOKS, Censorship of. See Censorship

BOOKS, Filmed. See Moving picture adaptations

BOOKS, Illustrated. See Illustrated books

BOOKS, Illustration of. See Illustration of books and periodicals

BOOKS, Paper covered. See Paperback books

BOOKS, Rare. See Book rarities

BOOKS, Secondhand

See also
Booksellers and bookselling—Secondhand books

BOOKS and reading

Books. M. Muggeridge. See issues of Esquire

Books in the field (cont) bibliog il por Wilson Lib Bul 45:653-73 Mr '71

Constant rereader's five-foot shelf. L. E. Sissman. Atlan 228:32-4 O '71

Exploring books; Provo, Utah. Senior center class. R. McDougall. il Har Yrs 11:48-9 O '71

Looking at books. P. S. Prescott. See issues of Look

Peripatetic reviewer. E. Weeks. See issues of Atlantic

This matter of media; address. E. Geller. bibliog il por Library J 96:2048-53 Je 15 '71

Trade winds; interview, ed. by C. Amory. A. McMahon. Sat R 54:12-13 Jl 31 '71

What's happening. G. Shalit. See issues of Ladies' home journal

Will the book survive? letter to the editor. B. H. Stewart. Am Lib 2:1145 D '71

See also
Art literature
Biography
Book buying
Book reviews
Book selection
Books as gifts
Childrens literature
Childrens reading
College students—Reading
Detective and mystery stories
Fiction
High school students—Reading
Illustrated books
International book year, 1972 (proposed)
Libraries
Libraries and readers
Literary criticism
National book committee
Picture books
Readability (literary style)
Reading
Religious literature
Travel literature

Best books

Book review; ed. by J. Serebnick and others. See issues of Library journal

Dean Downs on influential books; comp. by R. B. Downs. Wilson Lib Bul 45:921 Je '71

1970 notable books list released by ALA. Library J 96:774 Mr 1 '71; Same. Am Lib 2:401-2 Ap '71; Todays Ed 60:53 My '71

Notable books, 1944-1969. E. Eatenson. Am Lib 2:105-9 Ja '71; Reply. M. L. Reynolds. 2:347-8 Ap '71

Notable nominations (cont) Am Lib 2:124, 645, 762, 897, 1010, 1109, 1225 Ja, Je-D '71

Reviewer's choice (cont) M. Maddocks. il Life 70:6-7 F 12 '71

Selection of the year's best books. Time 99: 70 Ja 3 '72

See also
Best sellers
Book selection
Childrens literature

Bibliography

All kinds of gift books. il Changing T 25:13-14 D '71

Betsy's book bazaar. Harp Baz 104:64 Jl '71

Betsy's book bazaar. B. Freund. Harp Baz 104:74-5 Je; 66 Ag; 186 S; 150 O; 105:123 N; 76 D '71

Book marks. C. McWilliams. Nation 213: 345-6+, 700-1 O 11, D 27 '71

Books. See issues of Business week

Books and records to give for Christmas. J. Herbert. House & Gard 140:38+ D '71

Books by Nation contributors. Nation 211: 667-9 D 21 '70; 212:538+; 213:121-2, 636-8 Ap 26, Ag 16, D 13 '71

Books to come. il Library J 96:513-14+, 2153+, 3171-2+ F 1, Je 15, O 1 '71

Booktrucking about town. Wilson Lib Bul 46:117+, 213-14+ O-N '71

Critics' choices for Christmas. Commonweal 95:232-9 D 3 '71

Deck the halls with books worth reading. S. Powell. il Bsns W p 11-12 D 18 '71

Deck the shelves; for $275 and under. il Time 98:90-2+ D 20 '71

Fall announcements. il Pub W 200:203-32 Ag 30 '71

Fall book roundup. America 125:428-30+ N 20 '71

For the future LJ takes notice of. Library J 96:3645, 4034; 97:89 N 1, D 1 '71, Ja 1 '72

Headiest, happiest holiday gifts: books. Sat R 54:44+ N 27 '71

New fall books. J. B. Breslin. America 125: 236-8+ O 2 '71

New Yorker lists at this season some books by its contributors published during the year (cont) New Yorker 47:164-5 D 11 '71

Not what they used to be; Christmas gift books. C. H. Simonds. Nat R 23:1420+ D 17 '71

Notable. See issues of New republic

PW forecasts. See issues of Publishers' weekly

Reviewer's choice. H. Kenner. il Life 71:8 D 10 '71

Reviewer's choice. M. Maddocks. Life 70:8-9 Ap 2 '71

Selected titles from the world's leading publishers October 1971-April 1972. il Pub W 200:pt2 82-120+ S 27 '71

Selected titles to be published during June, July and August. il Pub W 199:26-40 Ap 26 '71

BOOKS and reading—Bibliography—*Continued*
Short reviews: books. P. Adams. See issues of Atlantic
Spring book roundup. America 124:543-51 My 22 '71
Spring highspots; February through May. il Pub W 199:187-216 Ja 25 '71
Spring previews! January-June 1972. il Pub W 200:22-41 S 27 '71
Summer previews; June through September. il Pub W 199:217-26 Ja 25 '71
This week. See issues of Christian century continuing New Christian
Weekly record. See issues of Publishers' weekly
What's coming in September-December. il Pub W 199:75-102 My 31 '71
Year in books: a personal report. P. S. Prescott. il Newsweek 78:57+ D 27 '71

Reading aloud
Of books and love; reading to children. H. Ross. il PTA Mag 65:24-5 Ap '71

Study and teaching
See Literature—Study and teaching

United States
See Books and reading

BOOKS and reading, Influence of. See Literature, Influence of

BOOKS as gifts
Deck the shelves: for $275 and under. il Time 98:90-2+ D 20 '71
Seed collection: how to increase the sale and use of books. Pub W 200:47 N 1 '71
See also
Books and reading
Childrens literature—Bibliography

BOOKS for children. See Childrens literature

BOOKS for girls. See Childrens literature

BOOKS in Canada (periodical)
New magazine deals with books in Canada. Pub W 199:104-6 My 31 '71

BOOKS on microfilm
See also
Booksellers and bookselling—Books on microfilm

BOOKSELLERS and bookselling
Blasting off at curr-like booksellers, in 1709 yet; excerpt. A. Hill. Pub W 199:43 Mr 29 '71
Censorship: what a bookseller can do about it. R. D. Hale. Pub W 200:26-7 Jl 26 '71
How to become a bookseller. G. R. Smith. Pub W 200:25-7 N 29 '71
Whole earth view of bookselling; excerpt from The whole earth catalog. D. Shugart; L. Besserman. por Pub W 200:20-2 S 6 '71
See also
Book clubs
Books—Advertising
Books—Marketing
Books—Prices
College bookstores

Book rarities
Kraus offers new list of unusual books and MSS. C. B. Grannis. Pub W 200:42 O 25 '71
Kraus sets $2 1/2-million price on Gutenberg Bible. Pub W 200:33 N 22 '71
Stalking the back roads in search of rare books: Coventry bookstore. C. Connelly. il Pub W 199:133 F 22 '71

Books on microfilm
Book business. A. Green. Sat R 54:23-4 Jl 31 '71

Childrens literature
Pre-ABA conference on children's books. il Pub W 199:40-1 Je 21 '71
Tiny bookshop quenching affluent young's thirst for knowledge; Paperbacks plus in Riverdale. Pub W 200:107-8 Jl 19 '71

Cookbooks
Macrobiotic cookbooks turn ecology outside in. P. A. Farrell. il Pub W 199:40-2 Mr 29 '71

Counter culture literature
This is earth calling Berkeley. P. Welsh and P. Liepman. il pors Pub W 200:38-40 Jl 5 '71

Employees
300 apply in Boston for $115 bookstore job. P. Ingraham. Pub W 199:62 Mr 15 '71

Finance
Affluent communities feeling pinch but not in book sales. Pub W 199:69 Ap 12 '71

Garden literature
Macrobiotic cookbooks turn ecology outside in. P. A. Farrell. il Pub W 199:40-2 Mr 29 '71

Greeting cards
Anderson's roundup on 1970 P.G. season. Pub W 199:70 Ap 12 '71

Immoral literature and pictures
Porno comes to Beacon Hill: Mod books. P. Ingraham. Pub W 200:39 O 18 '71

Mexican American literature
Chicano movement and its books; Hornet bookstore, Sacramento state college. R. Duval. il Pub W 199:53-4 Ja 11 '71

Paperback books
Changing paperback book market; highlights of panel discussion, May 31, 1971. il Pub W 199:30-1 Je 21 '71
How to make money in your spare time; secondhand paperback bookstores. L. Greenhalgh. il Ladies Home J 88:169 S '71
Returns. E. Lottman. Pub W 200:16-17 D 20 '71

Photographic literature
View from Kramer; searching for old photobooks. A. Kramer. il Mod Phot 35:56+ D '71

Reference books
Blitzing the supermarket customer with books. P. A. Farrell. Pub W 200:71-2 Ag 23 '71

Religious literature
Hackman's Bible store outgrows old quarters. il Pub W 199:41 Je 14 '71
See also
Christian booksellers association

Secondhand books
Used books are recycled books. R. Duval. Pub W 200:38-40 S 6 '71

Statistics
Census data on bookselling: they aren't all they might be. C. B. Grannis. Pub W 200:72-3 Ag 23 '71
What sort of year was 1970? with tables. Pub W 200:21-3 D 20 '71

Stock
How many books make a bookstore? G. R. Smith. il Pub W 200:18-20 D 20 '71
Unraveling the inventory control mystery; highlights of panel discussion, June 1, 1971. il Pub W 199:31-4 Je 21 '71

Terminology
Bookseller's glossary. G. R. Smith. il Pub W 200:20 D 20 '71

Textbooks
Big textbook caper. N. Gover. Nation 213:468-9 N 8 '71
College textbook crisis of the 1970's. R. W. Vanderhoef. Pub W 200:24-5 O 4 '71; Discussion. 200:24, 63-4 N 15; 10 D 13 '71
Used books are recycled books. R. Duval. Pub W 200:38-40 S 6 '71

Africa
Hachette sees firm future in Africa. H. R. Lottman. Pub W 200:21 S 20 '71
Longman and Colin team up in Africa. H. R. Lottman. Pub W 200:29 S 20 '71

Alberta
Bookshop staff stages surprise anniversary party; honors to E. De Mille, owner of three bookstores in Calgary and Vancouver. P. A. Farrell. Pub W 200:40 O 18 '71

British Columbia
Bookshop staff stages surprise anniversary party; honors to E. De Mille, owner of three bookstores in Calgary and Vancouver. P. A. Farrell. Pub W 200:40 O 18 '71

California
This is earth calling Berkeley. P. Welsh and P. Liepman. il pors Pub W 200:38-40 Jl 5; 62-3 Jl 12 '71
West coast publishing: San Francisco. D. N. Mount. Pub W 200:14-17 D 13 '71
West coast publishing scene: Los Angeles. D. N. Mount. Pub W 200:19-22 D 6 '71
Yab Yum, a sensory experience in 4000 sq. ft; Yab Yum artifacts, crafts and bookshop, San Diego. M. Clark. il Pub W 199:43-5 My 3 '71

BOOKSELLERS and bookselling—*Continued*

Canada

Lumberjacks, miners, tourists keep a unique bookstore busy and solvent; Highway book shop. J. R. Hunt. il por Pub W 199:57-8 Mr 8 '71

U.S. book sales up, but nationalist spirit rising. Pub W 199:63-4 F 15 '71

See also
Canadian booksellers association

Connecticut

Bazaar bookshop in an empty nest community; Village Green shopping center in Heritage Village, Southbury. il Pub W 199:246-8 Ja 25 '71

Stalking the back roads in search of rare books; Coventry bookstore. C. Connelly. il Pub W 199:133 F 22 '71

Denmark

Danish that's 75 years old; Arnold Busck. H. R. Lottman. il Pub W 200:51-2 O 11 '71

Georgia

Success story in Atlanta; Elson book stores. P. Bragg. il Pub W 200:26-7 S 20 '71

Great Britain

American designer looks at European bookstores. K. White. il Pub W 199:117-19 My 31 '71

Idaho

How to make money in your spare time; secondhand paperback bookstores. L. Greenhalgh. il Ladies Home J 88:169 S '71

Illinois

Bookselling at the center of the world; Leekley bookstore, Winthrop Harbor. M. J. O'Hanlon. il Pub W 199:45 Mr 1 '71

K&B kicks off fall book presentation; meeting of sales staff and publishers' representatives in Chicago. il Pub W 200:41 O 25 '71

Italy

Bookshop where Italian rebels meet: new link in the Feltrinelli chain in Parma. H. R. Lottman. il Pub W 200:35 D 6 '71

Long Island

See Booksellers and bookselling—New York (state)

Massachusetts

Brattle book shop goes exotic; Ecuadorian and Galapagos Islands curio center in Boston antiquarian bookstore. P. Ingraham. Pub W 199:52 Je 28 '71

Getting your book into a fine bind; Lauriat's bookstore in Boston. P. Ingraham. Pub W 200:49 Ag 2 '71

Introducing a new formula: free time+interest=profit; Mr Wizard science center, Wellesley. Pub W 199:62-3 Mr 15 '71

Porno comes to Beacon Hill; Mod books. P. Ingraham. Pub W 200:39 O 18 '71

Missouri

Alternate bookstore in St Louis, Missouri; Left bank book store. M. J. O'Hanlon. Pub W 199:40 Je 14 '71

Name's the same but not the face; Bennett Schneider, inc, Kansas City. il Pub W 199:44-5 Ja 18 '71

Special fixturing creates interest areas; Herald book and gift shop, Independence. il Pub W 199:59-60 Je 21 '71

Netherlands

American designer looks at European bookstores. K. White. il Pub W 199:117-19 My 31 '71

Dutch bookman invades the seabed; d'Ailly boekhandel, Emmeloord. S. Greene. il Pub W 199:43-5 Mr 22 '71

Feffer and Simons builds up European operations. H. R. Lottman. il Pub W 200:43-4 S 13 '71

New York (state)

High rent forces bookshop out after 45 years; William Floyd's Lenox hill book shop. Pub W 199:60-1 Je 21 '71

Kraus offers new list of unusual books and MSS. C. B. Grannis. Pub W 200:42 O 25 '71

Kraus sets $2 1/2-million price on Gutenberg Bible. Pub W 200:33 N 22 '71

McGraw-Hill moves to Sixth avenue includes plans for mammoth bookstore. P. A. Farrell. il Pub W 200:52-4 S 13 '71

Macrobiotic cookbooks turn ecology outside in; Greenwich Village shops. P. A. Farrell. il Pub W 199:40-2 Mr 29 '71

Macy's opens bargains bookshop in the underground. P. A. Farrell. Pub W 200:40 Jl 26 '71

Publishing execs open bookstore in East Hampton. R. H. Smith. Pub W 200:262-3 Ag 30 '71

Tiny bookshop quenching affluent young's thirst for knowledge; Paperbacks plus in Riverdale. Pub W 200:107-8 Jl 19 '71

Ohio

Higbee's rounds up 14 publishers for book promotion first. Pub W 199:36 Ap 19 '71

Pennsylvania

Hackman's Bible store outgrows old quarters. il Pub W 199:41 Je 14 '71

Scandinavia

Scandinavia's lively literary agents. P. Nathan. Pub W 200:pt2 175-6 S 27 '71

United States

Bookselling prospered in 1970's gloomy economy; dramatic increase in bookshop closings in 1970. il Pub W 199:68-70 F 8 '71

Bookstores forming up for better management. H. D. Greene, 3d. Pub W 199:40-2 Ap 5 '71

Publisher-bookseller issues: bookselling problems; highlights of panel discussion, June 1, 1971. il Pub W 199:34-5+ Je 21 '71

Retailing. See issues of Publishers' weekly

Seed collection: how to increase the sale and use of books. Pub W 200:47 N 1 '71

Unfair competition from wholesaler-owned stores; letter to the editor. L. M. Marrone. Pub W 200:24-6 N 15 '71

See also
American booksellers association
Christian booksellers association

Vermont

Booksellers bemoan shrinking margins and profits. D. Blair. Pub W 200:32-3 N 22 '71

BOOKSELLING in college libraries
Toward the library-bookstore. S. Severtson and G. Banks. bibliog il pors Library J 96:163-6 Ja 15 '71

BOOKSELLING in libraries
Five ways to sell books in libraries. P. A. Farrell. Pub W 200:38 N 8 '71

See also
Bookselling in college libraries

BOOKSOUNDS, inc.
Close your eyes and buy a book. P. A. Farrell. il Pub W 200:39-40 O 4 '71

BOOKSTACKS. See Library furniture and equipment

BOOKSTORES. See Booksellers and bookselling; College bookstores

BOOMS, Real estate. See Real estate investment

BOONE, Pat
Pat Boone and the charismatics; interview, ed. by D. M. Lynch. Chr Cent 88:1167+ O 6 '71

BOONTON, N.J.

Water supply

Don't color the water black. F. J. Costabile and C. H. Perron. il Am City 86:46-7 Ja '71

BOORSTIN, Daniel J.
TV's impact on society. il Life 71:36-9 S 10 '71

about
Consciousness and ideology in American history: the burden of Daniel J. Boorstin. J. P. Diggins. bibliog f Am Hist R 76:99-118 F '71; Reply with rejoinder. O. Berland. 76:1245-54 O '71 *

BOOSTERS for space vehicles. See Space vehicles—Propulsion systems

BOOTH, A. D. See Webb, S. J. jt. auth.

BOOTH, Arch Newell
Honor America day. Nations Bsns 59:72 Jl '71

BOOTH, Yvette Spencer-. See Spencer-Booth, Y.

BOOTLEG records. See Phonograph records—Recording—Unauthorized recording

BOOTS and shoes. See Shoes

BOQUEN monastery. See Monasteries

BORATES
Ammonioborite: near borate polyion and its structure. S. Merlino and F. Sartori. bibliog il Science 171:377-9 Ja 29 '71

BORCH, Fred J.
Fred J. Borch of General electric; interview. il pors Nations Bsns 59:30-3+ F '71
General electric chairman Fred Borch lays it on the line; address. por Forbes 108:27-8+ N 15 '71

about

Borch of General electric. por Forbes 107:59-60 My 15 '71 •
SR's businessman of the year. R. L. Tobin. por Sat R 54:55-7 Ja 23 '71 •

BORCHERDING, James R.
Dairy management. See issues of Successful farming
(ed) Successful dairy management. il por Suc Farm 69:D1 My; D1 S '71

BORCHERT, Donald Marvin
Future of religion in a Marxist society; adaptation of address. Chr Cent 88:1129-33 S 29 '71

BORDEAUX wines. See Wine

BORDELON, Marvin
Bishops and just war. America 126:17-19 Ja 8 '72

BORDEN, Inc.
Crackerjacks in Japan. il Forbes 108:24-5 Jl 1 '71
See also
Sacramento foods (firm)

BOREDOM
Longing for Armageddon. L. H. Lapham. il Harper 243:10+ Ag '71
Toward a culture of unreason? D. Bazelon. Cur 131:51-6 Jl '71
When you're all tired out. W. A. Nolen. McCalls 98:20 Je '71

BORERS (Insects)
Corn borer comeback. D. Seim. Farm J 95:23 D '71

BORES (persons)
Are you a bore? reprint. I. A. R. Wylie. Read Digest 98:128-30 Mr '71

BORG, Ganni
Malta: radical priests outwit foes of reform. America 125:35-6 Jl 24 '71

BORG-Warner corporation
Borg-Warner sheds a list of losers. Bsns W p22 My 1 '71

BORGER, John
Co-ed housing. il Todays Ed 60:34-6 O '71

BORGER, Tex.

Municipal Improvement

Downtown dresses up. il Am City 86:128 Ap '71

BORGES, Jorge Luis
Anxieties; tr. by N. T. Di Giovanni and the author. New Yorker 47:41-2 F 20 '71
Congress; story, tr. by N. T. Di Giovanni and the author. New Yorker 47:50-7 N 6 '71
Dialogue for understanding. pors Américas 23:12-15 Mr '71
Elder lady; story, tr. by N. T. Di Giovanni and the author. New Yorker 47:46-8 S 25 '71
End of the duel; story, tr. by N. T. Di Giovanni and the author. New Yorker 47:34-5 Mr 13 '71
Gospel according to Mark; story, tr. by N. T. Di Giovanni and the author. New Yorker 47:40-2 O 23 '71
Israel 1969; poem, tr. by N. T. Di Giovanni. Nation 213:346 O 11 '71
Juan Muraña; story, tr. by N. T. Di Giovanni and the author. New Yorker 47:40-1 Mr 27 '71
Southside; Rose; tr. by N. T. Di Giovanni. New Yorker 47:40 My 15 '71
Tom Castro, the implausible impostor; story, tr. by N. T. Di Giovanni and the author. Harper 243:82-4 O '71
Twice-told tales; tr. by N. T. Di Giovanni and the author. il New Yorker 47:25-9 Ja 1 '72
Unworthy friend; story, tr. by N. T. Di Giovanni and the author. Harper 242:62-4 Ja '71

about

Borges, a blind writer with insight; reprint. I. Shenker. il por Pub W 199:20-1 My 10 '71 •
Old tricks, and new. P. S. Prescott. por Newsweek 79:55-6+ Ja 3 '72 •

BORGESON, Griffith
Meade in Italy. il por Motor T 23:66+ Ap '71

BORGHESE, Iunio Valerio
Pasta putsch. por Time 97:32+ Ap 5 '71 •

BORIS Godunov; opera. See Musorgskii, M. P.

BORISOV, Mikhail
En route to Mars. Space World H-12-96:41 D '71

BORISSOFF, Vladimir A.
Soviet system of protected natural areas. il Nat Parks & Con Mag 45:8-14 Je '71

BORKH, Inge
Ladies' week in the world of music. I. Kolodin. Sat R 54:44 F 13 '71 •

BORLAND, Hal
Echoes in a conch shell. il Audubon 73:12-13 Mr '71
Lifetime of snowflakes. Audubon 73:59-65 Ja '71
Live better electrically? il Audubon 73:68-9 Jl '71

BORLAUG, Norman Ernest
Green revolution: for bread and peace; address, December 1971. por Bul Atom Sci 27:6-9+ Je '71
Without pesticides, the world population will starve; excerpts from address, October 7, 1971. il por U S News 71:93 N 1 '71

about

Father of the green revolution. S. Seegers and K. Seegers. por Read Digest 98:134-8 Mr '71 •
Who's for DDT? por Time 98:84 N 22 '71 •

BORMANN, Martin
Bormann enigma. pors Time 98:36+ S 20 '71 •
Mixed motives; Gehlen memoirs. il por Newsweek 78:26+ S 13 '71 •

BORNEMEIER, Walter Carl
Shapers of the future; address, November 29, 1970. Vital Speeches 37:315-18 Mr 1 '71

BORNEO
See also
Brunei (sultanate)

BORNSTEIN, Paul. See Ross, R. jt. auth.

BORON
Avco bets on boron tape. Bsns W p 124+ Ap 10 '71
Avco readies new boron plant as demand for composites lags. Aviation W 94:48 Ap 19 '71
See also
Plants. Effect of boron on

BOROSON, Warren
Parent and child (cont) il N Y Times Mag p91+ D 5 '71

BOROV, Abbe
Organic; interview. New Yorker 47:30-2 My 22 '71

BOROWSKI, Ron
Homage to Norman Rockwell; photographs. Esquire 75:84-5 Ap '71

BORRELIA hermsi. See Bacteria, Pathogenic

BORROFF, Marie
Creativity, poetic language, and the computer. Yale R 60:481-513 Je '71

BORROWING of money. See Credit

BORSCH, Frederick H.
Fragging the beast. Chr Cent 88:720-2 Je 9 '71

BORSCHT. See Soups

BORSKY, Paul
Psychology and noise pollution. Sci N 101:6-7 Ja 1 '72 •

BORTEN, Per
Indiscreet traveler. Newsweek 77:50+ Mr 15 '71 •
Price of a lie. Time 97:38-9 Mr 15 '71 •

BOSC, Robert
Development: a Soviet countermodel. il America 124:504-8 My 15 '71
Third world development, can east and west agree? il America 124:532-4 My 22 '71

BOSCH, C. A.
Redwoods: a population model. bibliog il Science 172:345-9 Ap 23 '71

BOSE corporation
Is testing fair at Consumers union? il Bsns W p41-2 F 27 '71

BOSMAN, Petrus
Bosman's follies. S. W. McDermott. il pors Dance Mag 45:32-7 My '71 •

BOSNIA AND HERZEGOVINA
Stones with the raised hands; funerary art of the Bogomils. M. Krleza. il UNESCO Courier 24:17-22 My '71

BOSONS. See Particles (nuclear physics)

BOSSCHA observatory. See Astronomical observatories—Indonesia

BOSTON
Boston's graffiti board. C. Bratley. il Am City 86:138+ Ap '71

Air pollution

Boston's sufferance of sulfur dioxide. J. J. MacKenzie. Science 172:792 My 21 '71

Architecture

North Harvard in Boston: a concrete panel system improves with age. il Arch Rec 149:120-1 Ap '71

Art

Boston (cont) J. Koethe. Art N 70:18+ Sum '71

BOSTON—*Continued*

Banks

Cool cash from Coolidge. il Time 98:70+ S 20 '71

Oldest bank's newest innovator; First national bank of Boston. por Bsns W p 112 S 11 '71

Bookstores

See Booksellers and bookselling—Massachusetts

City planning

Boston sets the pace for livability. il Bsns W p 150-1+ N 13 '71

Clubs

6 interiors; Madison Square Garden club. il Arch Rec 150:98-9 Ag '71

Education

Blot for Boston; charge of maintaining segregated schools. il Newsweek 78:62 D 13 '71

Finance

A city gears for austerity. J. E. Curtis. il Parks & Rec 6:37-8+ Mr '71

Fire department

Telescoping boom moves indoors. J. M. Murphy. il Am City 86:46 Je '71

Galleries and museums

See also
Boston children's museum
Boston museum of fine arts

Gardens

Garden in the clouds; with editorial comment. S. N. Shurcliff. il Horticulture 49: 20, 22-5 My '71

Hospitals

Annals of medicine; outbreak of salmonella cubana at Massachusetts general hospital caused by contaminated carmine dye. B. Roueché. New Yorker 47:66-72+ S 4 '71

Boston hospital dispute: Harvard rectifies expansionist policies. R. J. Bazell. il Science 171:358-61 Ja 29 '71

Last-ditch fight for life; Respiratory intensive care unit at Massachusetts general. E. M. Wylie. il Good H 172:98-9+ My '71

Hotels, restaurants, etc.

Eating in Boston: fine views and delicious fare. Bsns W p8 2Ap 3 '71

Housing

Boston hospital dispute: Harvard rectifies expansionist policies. R. J. Bazell. il Science 171:358-61 Ja 29 '71

Model services system developed in Boston housing for the elderly; Castle Square housing development. il Aging 200:10-11 Je '71

Intellectual life

Literary lights were always bright at 148 Charles street. B. Rotundo. il pors Am Heritage 22:10-15 F '71

Libraries

See also
Boston public library

Music

DGG's new studio. P. G. Davis. il Hi Fi 21:21 My '71

Report:
Monteverdi's Orfeo. H. Neville. il Opera N 35:30 Ap 10 '71

See also
Boston symphony orchestra
New England conservatory of music
Opera company of Boston

Newspapers

See also
Globe (Boston)
Phoenix (newspaper)

Police

Soul patrol; black Tactical patrol force unit. il Newsweek 79:41 Ja 3 '72

Politics and government

It has always been enough to say You know where I stand; L. Hicks running for mayor. R. Brigham. il Life 71:36 O 29 '71

Poor

See also
Boston—Public welfare

Protests, demonstrations, etc.

Judge George Sullivan: lawbreaker for peace; interview, ed. by C. E. Fager. G. A. Sullivan, jr. il Chr Cent 88:852-5 Jl 14 '71

Public welfare

Vote in the action; Action for Boston community development. Time 97:24+ Je 14 '71

Publishers and publishing

See Publishers and publishing—Massachusetts

Recreation

Adopt an island; Lovell's island in Boston harbor. L. D. Harris. il Am For 77:4-5 My '71

A city gears for austerity. J. E. Curtis. il Parks & Rec 6:37-8+ Mr '71

Converge; agency to pool the city's recreation resources. R. L. Pilla. Parks & Rec 6:29+ O '71

Park programs on a bare-bones budget. J. E. Curtis. il por Am City 86:51-3 D '71

Schools

See Boston—Education

Social work

Model cities program as a field placement for graduate students in mental health nursing. J. A. Collins. Ment Hy 55:308-11 Jl '71

Stores

See also
Pierce, S. S, company

Transit systems

See also
Massachusetts Bay transportation authority

BOSTON after dark (newspaper)
War of the weeklies. il Time 98:74+ N 15 '71

BOSTON ballet company
Boston ballet, Savoy theatre, Boston. S. Smoliar. Dance Mag 45:100 Ap; 23-4 Je; 80 Jl '71

BOSTON Bruins (hockey team) See Hockey teams

BOSTON children's museum
Children's museum. il Arch Forum 135:32-3 S '71
Please touch! il Parents Mag 46:38-9+ Jl '71

BOSTON company
Boston co: a string of matched pearls. il por Bsns W p36+ F 6 '71

BOSTON marathon. See Running

BOSTON massacre, 1770
Boston massacre and Crispus Attucks. il Negro Hist Bul 34:52-4 Mr '71

BOSTON museum of fine arts
Breakthrough in Boston; Elements of art exhibition. D. Davis. il Newsweek 77:90 F 15 '71
Fine arts of the kitchen; excerpts from Fine arts cookbook. il McCalls 98:88-94+ Ap '71
Golden links to the bronze age; display at the Museum of fine arts, Boston. E. Vermeule. il Horizon 13:50-3 Wint '71
Textiles at Boston's museum of fine arts. S. B. Sherrill. il Antiques 100:654+ N '71

BOSTON public library
Boston's public library: a keeper with many keys; print collection. J. H. Kay. il Art in Am 59:78-81 Ja '71

Branches

Library designed for intensive community use; Brighton branch library, Brighton, Mass. il Arch Rec 149:109-14 Ap '71

BOSTON Red Sox (baseball) See Baseball clubs

BOSTON symphony chamber players. See Chamber orchestras

BOSTON symphony orchestra
DGG in Boston. D. Hamilton. il Hi Fi 20:85-6 D '70
If it's Thursday and La valse, this must be Wuppertal; European tour. R. Hemming. il Sr Schol 98:18 My 10 '71
Musical events:
Mahler's Sixth symphony in Philharmonic Hall. W. Sargeant. New Yorker 47: 159-60 N 6 '71
Performance at New York Philharmonic Hall, conducted by Michael Tilson Thomas. W. Sargeant. New Yorker 47: 94 Mr 27 '71
On the upbeat. il por Newsweek 77:67 Mr 1 '71

BOSTON tea party, 1773
Dorothea's story, transcribed from her account, ed. by M. A. Downie. D. Gamsby. Horn Bk 47:192-8 Ap '71

BOSTON university
Quest for a silver unicorn; search for a new president; with editorial comment. E. Kern. il pors Life 70:3, 54-5+ Je 4 '71

BOSWELL, James
Boswell in extremes, 1776-1778, ed. by C. M.
Weis and F. A. Pottle. Review
Sat R 54:26+ F 6 '71. R. Halsband
BOSWORTH, Patricia
It's my turn to be lucky. il pors Todays
Health 49:24-7+ D '71
BOTANICAL chemistry
See also
Photosynthesis
BOTANICAL gardens
See also
Brooklyn botanic garden
Milwaukee—Mitchell park horticultural con-
servatory
New York botanical garden
BOTANICAL research
Do you chat with your plants? M. Pines. il
McCalls 98:44-5 F '71
Plants have feelings, too. . . L. G. Lawrence.
il Org Gard & Farm 18:64-7 Ap '71
Rhythm of the flowers. J. D. Palmer. il
Natur Hist 80:64-73 Ag '71
Startling new research from the man who
talks to plants. J. Robbins and C. Rob-
bins. il pors Nat Wildlife 9:21-4 O '71
BOTANY
See also
Alpine flora
Buds
Cave fauna and flora
Chromosomes (botany)
Evolution
Grasses
Lichens
Pollen
  also headings beginning Botanical, Plant,
Plants
Anatomy
See also
Trichomes
Veins (botany)
Ecology
See also
Plant introduction
Plant succession
Periodicity
Potassium flux: a common feature of albizzia
leaflet movement controlled by phytochrome
or endogenous rhythm. R. L. Satter and A.
W. Galston. bibliog il Science 174:518-20
O 29 '71
Rhythm of the flowers. J. D. Palmer. il
Natur Hist 80:64-73 Ag '71
See also
Tree rings
Physiology
See also
Chloroplasts
Dormancy (plants)
Photosynthesis
Plants—Absorption of water
Plants—Metabolism
Plants, Motion of fluids in
Roots
Australia
Photoperiod evidence in the introduction of
xanthium (cocklebur) to Australia. C. Mc-
Millan. bibliog il Science 171:1029-31 Mr
12 '71
See also
Bottle trees
Spear lilies
California
Bare zone between California shrub and
grassland communities: the role of animals.
B. Bartholomew; reply with rejoinder. C.
H. Muller and R. Del Moral. bibliog il
Science 173:462-3 Jl 30 '71
Hawaii
Disjunct foliar veins in Hawaiian euphor-
bias. D. Herbst. bibliog il Science 171:
1247-8 Mr 26 '71
South Africa
Desiccation-tolerant flowering plants in south-
ern Africa. D. F. Gaff. bibliog il Science
174:1033-4 D 3 '71
BOTANY, Economic
See also
Plant introduction
BOTANY, Medical
See also
Ginseng
Hallucination and illusion producing plants
Herbs
BOTANY as a profession
Opportunities in plant science. P. H. Abel-
son. Science 172:1195 Je 18 '71
BOTANY industries, inc.
Bold cutter trims Botany's losers. por Bsns W
p67 F 20 '71
BOTSFORD, Keith
New European man runs France. por N Y
Times Mag p9+ Ag 29 '71

BOTSFORD, Ward
About baseball giants, and the great Leon-
tyne Price. por(p273) Am Rec G 37:296-7+
Ja '71
BOTSWANA
Passage through Botswana. E. McCarthy.
Commonweal 95:131-2 N 5 '71
BOTTEL, Helen
Do drag racers need to know how to read?
il Am Ed 7:3-7 O '71
13 questions on becoming a syndicated col-
umnist. Writers Digest 51:32-4 Ap '71
BOTTICELLI, Sandro
Pines of Ravenna. N. T. Mirov. il Natur Hist
80:24-6 Ja '71 *
BOTTINI, Egidio, and others
Favism: association with erythrocyte acid
phosphatase phenotype. bibliog il Science
171:409-11 Ja 29 '71
BOTTLE cap removers. See Cap removers
BOTTLE caps and seals
10-minute danger test. il Life 71:40C-40D O
22 '71
BOTTLE gardens. See Gardens, Miniature
BOTTLE trees
Boabab trees: strange remnants of prehis-
tory. il Sci Digest 70:37 D '71
BOTTLED water. See Water, Bottled
BOTTLES
Battle over bottles & cans. il Changing T
25:45-6 D '71
Bottle bonanza. D. F. Robinson. il Field &
S 76:128-9 S '71
Bottles, flasks and Dr Dyott, by H. Mc-
Kearin. Review
Antiques il 100:196+ Ag '71. E. Gaines
Nostalgia comes to the kitchen: jars and bot-
tles with an old-time flavor. il House B
113:54 N '71
Collectors and collecting
Empties are better. il por Time 97:62 Mr 22
'71
BOTTLES, Intravenous-feeding. See Hospi-
tals—Equipment and supplies
BOTTLING industry
See also
Coca-Cola bottling company of Los Angeles
BOTTO, Louis
Confessions of the world's lousiest spy. il
Look 35:76+ O 19 '71
Executive mother. il pors Look 35:73+ Ja 26
'71
Prince & his follies. il pors Look 35:34-8 My
18 '71
Ruby Keeler is alive and tapping. il pors Look
35:70-4 F 9 '71
Selling of the president, 1976. il Look 35:
52-3 S 7 '71
That family sure has its share of problems.
il por Look 35:64-5 S 7 '71
BOTTOME, Edgar M.
Can the U.S. take unilateral steps? excerpt
from Balance of terror: a guide to the arms
race. Cur 130:60-3 Je '71
BOTTOMLEY, Thomas R.
Taking the iceberg to Ensenada. il Motor B
& S 127:78-81+ Ap '71
BOTTS, Roderic
What means this end? Some unexamined
classroom practices. Engl J 60:88-92 Ja '71
BOTULISM
Botulism: an unnecessary menace. Consumer
Rep 36:540-2 S '71
Botulism pushes the panic button. R. War-
field. House & Gard 140:46+ O '71
Canned menace called botulism; with report
by J. Howard. il Life 71:26-9 S 10 '71
Deadly soup. il Newsweek 78:67-8 Jl 19
'71
Death in cans; spoiled vichyssoise prepared
by Bon Vivant soups, inc. il Time 98:36+
Jl 19 '71
Double trouble at Campbell soup. il Bsns W
p26 Ag 28 '71
When Americans are a swallow away from
death. B. Rensberger; B. Rouché. il To-
days Health 49:40-3+ S '71
See also
Clostridium botulinum
BOUCHER, D. Wark, and others
Nonencapsidated infectious DNA of adeno-
satellite virus in cells coinfected with her-
pesvirus. bibliog il Science 173:1243-5 S 24
'71
BOUCOT, A. J. See Gray, J. jt. auth.
BOUDIN, Kathy
Leonard Boudin: the left's lawyer's lawyer.
P. Wilkes. il pors N Y Times Mag p38-40+
N 14 '71 *
BOUDIN, Leonard B.
Leonard Boudin: the left's lawyer's lawyer.
P. Wilkes. il por N Y Times Mag p38-40+
N 14 '71; Reply. C. Lamont. p 125 D 5
'71 *

BOUDON, Raymond
Sources of student protest in France. il **Ann**
Am Acad 395:139-49 My '71
BOUDREAU, Robert
Barge man. il Time 98:54 Jl 26 '71 *
BOULANGER, Georges Ernest Jean Marie
Boulanger, by J. Harding. Review
Time por 98:55+ Ag 23 '71. T. Foote *
BOULANGER, Nadia
France's great teacher is honored. D. Noakes.
il por Hi Fi 21:MA22-3 D '71 *
BOULAT, Pierre, and others
Shah's princely party; photographs. **Life** 71:
22-30 O 29 '71
BOULDER, Colo.

Water supply
Reservoir designed not to be seen. R. G.
Westdyke. il Am City 86:19 S '71
BOULDER, Colo, public library
McLaren film festival. J. Heckel. il Am Lib
2:1195-7 D '71
BOULDING, Kenneth E.
Dodo didn't make it: survival and better-
ment. Bul Atom Sci 27:19-22 My '71
BOULER, André
Fine arts. C. J. McNaspy. America 124:263
Mr 13 '71 *
BOULEZ, Pierre
Style or idea? tr. by D. Noakes. il Sat R
54:39-41+ My 29 '71
Who wants Parsifal in the morning? inter-
view, ed. by W. Bender. por Time 98:
62 S 27 '71

about
Boulez and new breezes. A. Satz. por Hi Fi
21:MA12+ Ag '71 *
Boulez at the Philharmonic. I. Kolodin. Sat
R 54:18 My 1 '71 *
Boulez to the attack. H. Saal. il pors News-
week 78:86-8+ O 11 '71 *
Fold and rap. R. Jones. por Time 97:78-9
F 22 '71 *
Haunting of Philharmonic Hall. R. Freed-
man. il por Life 71:14 O 29 '71 *
Masterwork by Boulez. R. P. Morgan. por
Hi Fi 21:70-1 Ag '71 *
Music. D. Hamilton. Nation 213:413-14 O 25
'71 *
Music. H. C. Schonberg. Harper 243:96-7
Jl '71 *
Music: concerts with the New York phil-
harmonic. D. Hamilton. Nation 212:637-8
My 17 '71 *
Music to my ears. I. Kolodin. Sat R 54:20
O 9 '71 *
Music to my ears; performances of Liszt's
The legend of St Elizabeth and The poli-
tics of harmony. I. Kolodin. Sat R 54:38+
O 16 '71 *
Musical events; opening concerts of Phil-
harmonic. W. Sargeant. New Yorker 47:
120-1 O 2 '71 *
New music man. J. Downs. il pors Life 71:
41-2+ N 12 '71 *
BOULOS, Mervet S. and Manuel, O. K.
Xenon record of extinct radioactives in the
earth. bibliog il Science 174:1334-6 D 24 '71
BOULTBEE, Winifred
Some personal recollections of Beatrix Pot-
ter. il Horn Bk 47:586-8 D '71
BOULWARE, Lemuel R.
Harvest years hall of fame: Lemuel R.
Boulware. por Har Yrs 11:45+ Ja '71 *
BOUMA, Mary
Liberated mothers. Chr Today 15:4-6 My 7 '71
BOUNDARY waters canoe area. See Wilder-
ness areas—Minnesota
BOUQUETS
How to make your own corsage. il Sunset
147:121 Ag '71
BOURBON whiskey. See Whiskey
BOURDEAUX, Michael
Alexander Solzhenitsyn: religious writer. Chr
Cent 88:202-3 F 10 '71
Russian orthodoxy in crucial council. Chr
Cent 88:646-7 My 26 '71
Yuri Titov: profile of a Soviet artist. Chr
Cent 88:1264-6 O 27 '71
BOURDET, Claude
Alignments after the revolution. Nation 212:
461-4 Ap 12 '71
Experiments with liberty. Nation 213:234-8
S 20 '71
BOURDON, David
Warhol as filmmaker. il Art in Am 59:48-53
My '71
BOURDON, Joseph A.
Lone scout. Sat R 54:19 Mr 13 '71
BOURJAILY, Monte, jr
Pretty good teacher, for a cat. il Read Digest
98:82-6 Mr '71

BOURKE, George
From tip to top in Florida. See issues of
Travel
BOURKE-WHITE, Margaret
Gallery; photographs. Life 70:6-9 Ja 29 '71
Obituary
Sat R 54:28-9 S 11 '71. N. Cousins
Time il pors 98:46 S 6 '71
Obituary; with editorial comment. il pors
Life 71:3, 34+ S 10 '71
BOURNE, Henry R. and others
Histamine augments leukocyte adenosine
3',5'-monophosphate and blocks antigenic
histamine release. bibliog il Science 173:
743-5 Ag 20 '71
BOURRIDE. See Chowder
BOUSSAC, Marcel
Boussac tries to save his empire. por Bsns W
p31 Jl 3 '71 *
Wrong century. il por Forbes 107:54 Mr 1
'71 *
BOUTIQUES. See Specialty stores
BOUTON, James Alan. See Bouton, Jim
BOUTON, Jim
Authors that bloom in the spring; excerpts
from press conference. il por Pub W 199:
24 Mr 22 '71
I'm glad you didn't take it personally; ex-
cerpt, ed. by L. Shecter. il por Look 35:
34-8+ Je 15 '71
BOUTWELL, Jane P.
New man at the Met. il pors N Y Times
Mag p40-1+ S 12; 30 O 17 '71
(ed) See Brilioth, H. Rare bird
BOUTWELL, William D.
English in a sea of science; address, No-
vember 1970. Engl J 60:326-32 Mr '71
Happenings in education. See issues of PTA
magazine
Putting parents into the reading picture.
il PTA Mag 66:6-8+ bibliog(p35) O '71
Three-way communication; administrators,
teachers, and parents need to talk; ad-
dress, 1971. il PTA Mag 65:10-13 My '71;
Same abr. with title Achieving effective
communication. Ed Digest 37:20-2 S '71
BOUVIERS des Flandres
Nobody touches me with impunity. R. H.
Boyle. il Sports Illus 34:74-7+ Mr 15 '71
BOW and arrow
See also
Archery
Crossbow
BOW hunting. See Hunting with bow and ar-
row
BOWATER, Sir Eric Vansittart
Spellbinder. por Forbes 107:53 F 15 '71 *
BOWATER paper corporation, ltd.
Let the customer help. il Forbes 107:53-4
F 15 '71
BOWDEN, George T.
Underwater battle. il Parks & Rec 6:23-4
Jl '71
BOWDEN, James H.
Garden of worldly delights; poem. Chr Cent
88:826 Jl 7 '71
Item; poem. Chr Cent 88:371 Mr 24 '71
Massacre of the innocents; poem. Chr Cent
88:1490 D 22 '71
BOWDEN, Mary
Different track. See issues of House beauti-
ful
BOWDITCH, Nathaniel
Episode in early American astronomy: the
Weston meteorite. J. Ashbrook. bibliog
por Sky & Tel 41:223+ Ap '71 *
BOWEN, John
Downstate Delaware. il Travel 136:48-51+ N
'71
Other side of the James. il Travel 135:42-7
Ap '71
BOWEN, W. J. and Mandelkern, L.
Glycerinated muscle fibers: relation between
isometric tension and adenosine triphos-
phate hydrolysis. bibliog il Science 173:239-
40 Jl 16 '71
BOWEN, William
Books & ideas (cont) il Fortune 84:131-2 S
'71
BOWEN, William Gordon
Fiscal Houdini for Princeton. il por Bsns W
p78+ D 4 '71 *
From Goheen to "Boheen". por Time 98:42
D 13 '71 *
BOWEN family
Bowen coat-of-arms. H. K. Eilers. Hobbies
76:158-9 Ja '72
BOWER, George
First cold Saturday in October; poem. Atlan
228:121 O '71
BOWER, T. G. R.
Object in the world of the infant; with
biographical sketch. il Sci Am 225:12, 30-8
bibliog(p 120) O '71

BOWERMAN, Bill
Secrets of speed; ed. by G. S. Brown. Il Sports Illus 35:22-9 Ag 2 '71
BOWERS, Lucille. See Bowers, W. F. jt. auth.
BOWERS, Warner F.
Leaves: nature's autumn dividend. il Org Gard & Farm 18:44-5 O '71
——and Bowers, Lucille
Our composting program. il por Org Gard & Farm 18:54-7 Ja '71
BOWERS mansion (county park) See Nevada— Parks and reserves
BOWFISHING. See Fishing with bow and arrow
BOWIE knives
Beautiful blades; sports knives. W. Page. il Field & S 75:58-61+ Ap '71
Never lay it down; hunting knives. T. Trueblood. il Field & S 76:12+ Je '71
BOWKER, Albert Hosmer
Bowker for Berkeley. il por Time 97:81 Ap 26 '71 •
BOWKER, R. R, company
See also
Carey-Thomas award
BOWL football games. See Football
BOWLER, John E.
You can't see your best snow fighting tool. il Am City 86:81-2 D '71
BOWLES, Chester
America and Russia in India. For Affairs 49:636-51 Jl '71
Five major blunders by the U.S. in Asia. il por Sat R 54:28-31 N 6 '71
Promises to keep, by C. Bowles. Review Sat R 54:23+ Je 26 '71. J. M. Allison •
BOWLES, Jerry G.
Can epistemology be entertaining. il por Art N 70:34-5+ My '71
BOWLES, Paul
Happenings in Morocco. D. J. Soria. por Hi Fi 21:MA4-5+ Ag '71 •
BOWLING, Frank
It's not enough to say black is beautiful. il Art N 70:53-5+ Ap '71
BOWLING
Bowling, the ideal exercise. il Harp Baz 104: 22 My '71
New life for an old ball game; boccie. G. McCormick. il Sports Illus 35:36-41 Jl 12 '71
Obviously it's a leftist plot; southpaw bowlers vs righthanders. K. Chapin. il Sports Illus 34:24-6+ My 3 '71
Superfingers vs. the chauvinists: Dotty Fothergill in competitive bowling. H. Weiskopf. il Sports Illus 35:44-5 Ag 2 '71
To the victor go the spares: PBA tournament. J. Jares. il Sports Illus 35:92+ O 25 '71
See also
American blind bowling association
BOWLING GREEN, Ky.
Water reservoir shows its colors. il Am City 86:16 Jl '71
BOWLY, John E.
Failed utopia: Russian art 1917-32. bibliog il Art in Am 59:40-51 Jl '71
BOWMAN, Eldon G.
Cop image. il Parks & Rec 6:34-6 Ja '71
BOWMAN, Jean G.
Azalea, outside beauty plus indoor bloom. il Org Gard & Farm 18:90+ Ap '71
Kohlrabi and chard: two early and easy vegetables. il por Org Gard & Farm 18:56-7 F '71
Tiny table trees from Christmas trimmings. il Horticulture 49:38-9 D '71
BOWMAN, M. Bruce
Drawing with mixed media. il Sch Arts 71: 14-15 N '71
BOWMAN, Robert L. See Ito, Y. jt. auth.
BOWSER, Hallowell
Against provocation. Sat R 54:22 Mr 20 '71
Dispossessed. Sat R 54:14 Ap 10 '71
BOX gardening. See Container gardening
BOXER, Lady Arabella (Stuart)
Someone's in the kitchen with Maxime. M. McKendry. il por Vogue 158:80+ D '71 •
BOXERS
In defense of the sweet science. J. P. Heinz. il Sports Illus 35:70-4+ Ag 16 '71
Where are they now? ex-heavyweight champs. il Newsweek 77:16 Mr 22 '71
See also names of boxers, e.g. C. Clay
BOXES, cases, etc.
See also
Jewelry boxes, cases, etc.
Key cases, holders, etc.
Mailboxes

BOXES, Music. See Music boxes
BOXING
Album of great heavyweight fights. il Time 97:64-5 Mr 8 '71
Ali-Frazier crunch. P. Axthelm. Vogue 157: 115 Mr 1 '71
Ali-Frazier fight; with editorial comment. N. Mailer. il pors Life 70:3, 18F-19+ Mr 19 '71
Ali on Peachtree; fight vs. Quarry. J. Richardson. il Harper 242:46-9+ Ja '71
Ali vs. Frazier: a show-biz approach. por Bsns W p27 F 13 '71
All the Scotsman managed to lose was $2; K. Buchanan vs M. Ramos. P. Putnam. il pors Sports Illus 34:54-5 F 22 '71
And then there was one; C. Clay vs. J. Frazier. il pors Time 97:35 Mr 22 '71
At the bell. . . Frazier-Ali fight. M. Kram. il pors Sports Illus 34:18-21 Mr 8 '71
Battered face of a winner; Ali-Frazier fight; photographs, with report by M. Kram. Sports Illus 34:16-21 Mr 15 '71
Battle of the undefeated giants; Ali-Frazier preview; with editorial comment. T. Thompson. il pors Life 70:3, 40-9 Mr 5 '71
Big fight; Muhammad Ali-Joe Frazier. il Life 71:32-3 D 31 '71
Biggest fight in history; C. Clay vs. J. Frazier. L. J. Banks. il pors Ebony 26:134-6+ Mr '71
Boxer and the slugger; with sketches of famous fights by R. Handville. M. Kane. Sports Illus 34:38-47 Mr 1 '71
Bull v. butterfly: a clash of champions; C. Clay vs. J. Frazier. il pors Time 97:63+ Mr 8 '71
Bundini: Svengali in Ali's corner; D. Brown. E. Shrake. pors Sports Illus 34:32-6 F 15 '71
Defeat of the Great black hope; Joe Frazier's victory. M. R. Berube. Commonweal 94: 54-5 Mr 26 '71
End of a beautiful friendship; Muhammad Ali-J. Ellis fight. T. Maule. il por Sports Illus 35:10-11 Ag 2 '71
Everything's rosy with Jose; Backus vs Napoles welterweight championship fight. R. H. Boyle. il pors Sports Illus 34:22-3 Je 14 '71
Fight: Ali-Frazier battle. New Yorker 47:32-5 Mr 20 '71
Fight of century has few losers; Ali-Frazier match. il Bsns W p44 Mr 13 '71
Fighting carpenter from Scotland: lightweight champion K. Buchanan. H. McIlvanney. il pors Sports Illus 34:30-2+ F 8 '71
Got to look good to Allah: Muhammad Ali vs. Buster Mathis. T. Maule. il pors Sports Illus 35:28-9 N 29 '71
He has heavy things on his mind; J. Ellis vs Muhammad Ali. T. Maule. il por Sports Illus 35:24-6 Jl 26 '71
I got a surprise for Clay; interview, ed. by M. Sharnik. J. Frazier. por Sports Illus 34:28-30+ F 22 '71
In this corner Jerry Perenchio; interview, ed. by L. Gross. A. G. Perenchio. il pors Look 35:92-3+ Je 1 '71
It's gonna be the champ and the tramp; Muhammad Ali-J. Frazier fight. T. Maule and M. Sharnik. il pors Sports Illus 34:14-17 F 1 '71
Looking for kicks and a few bucks, too; kickboxing. D. Levin. il pors Sports Illus 34:38-40+ Ap 26 '71
Mentor of the mighty mites; Nápoles-Lewis welterweight title bout. il Time 98:52 D 27 '71
Mountain to molehill; Ali-Mathis fight in Houston. il por Time 98:69 N 29 '71
Nice story about boxing. J. Lebow. il pors Look 35:64-7 Ag 24 '71
No requiem for a heavyweight; Ali-Frazier fight. G. Plimpton. il por Sports Illus 34: 84-6+ Ap 5 '71
Now there is one champion; Ali-Frazier fight. il pors Newsweek 77:72-6 Mr 22 '71
Our 'enery gets the 'ook: Cooper vs Bugner. J. Kirshenbaum. pors Sports Illus 34:26-7 Mr 29 '71
Out of this I am getting not a nyickl; G. Parnassus, fight promoter. R. Blount. il por Sports Illus 34:62-4+ My 31 '71
Purse snatchers; J. Frazier to meet C. Clay. il pors Time 97:65-6 Ja 25 '71
Requiem for a grandfather; H. Johnson vs. Herschel Jacobs. il por Newsweek 77:74-5 Ap 12 '71
Scot was a cut or two above the challenger; K. Buchanan vs Ismael Laguna. M. Kram. por Sports Illus 35:74+ S 27 '71
Scots wha hae; Buchanan-Laguna fight. il por Newsweek 78:101 S 27 '71

BOXING—*Continued*
Sport's $5 million payday; Ali-Frazier fight. J. Kirshenbaum. il por Sports Illus 34:20-3 Ja 25 '71
Take the money and run; Muhammad Ali-Joe Frazier fight promotors. il por Newsweek 77:94-5 Mr 8 '71
Winner, the loser, the crowd; Muhammad Ali-Joe Frazier contest. L. Banks. il por Ebony 26:132-4+ My '71

History
In defense of the sweet science. J. P. Heinz. il Sports Illus 35:70-4+ Ag 16 '71

Laws and regulations
Should professional boxing be banned? Senior youthview. il Sr Schol 98:12-13 My 3 '71

Moral aspects
Should professional boxing be banned? Senior youthview. il Sr Schol 98:12-13 My 3 '71

Photographs
Ali-Frazier fight. il pors Life 70:20-7 Mr 19 '71

BOY choirs. See Choirs
BOY scouts
Establishment's secret weapon. McCalls 99:38 N '71
Lone scout. J. A. Bourdon. Sat R 54:19 Mr 13 '71
Scouting blazes a trail into the ghetto. il Life 70:38-42 Je 4 '71
Scouts can help; Project SOAR. T. Trueblood. il Field & S 75:16+ F '71
Scouts soar with anti-litter project. Sr Schol 99:14 N 8 '71
See also
Keep America beautiful day

Anecdotes, facetiae, satire, etc.
On my honor, I am middle-aged. R. Woodley. Esquire 76:118+ D '71

BOYARSKY, Bill
Mayor Sam Yorty's one-man bandwagon. New Repub 165:14+ D 18 '71
BOYCE, Ernest F.
Pragmatic supermarketer. por Duns 97:62 Je '71 *
BOYCE, William
Memoirs of Dr William Boyce. G. Beechey. bibliog f il por Mus Q 57:87-106 Ja '71 *
BOYCOTT
Lettuce boycott reaches New York. T. J. O'Connell. America 124:148-9 F 13 '71
Salad days at the Pentagon. J. Drake and G. Gersmehl. Commonweal 93:485-6 F 19 '71
Superfluous boycott; effect of boycott by Arab countries. il Time 98:17-18 Jl 19 '71
Unions move against the multinationals. Bsns W p48-9+ Jl 24 '71
BOYD, Andrew
Orange bullies & British Tories. il Nation 212:521-4 Ap 26 '71
Stormont on Britain's back. Nation 213:560-2 N 29 '71
Ulster: a kind of plague. Nation 213:176-8 S 6 '71
BOYD, George N.
Movie (title varies) Chr Cent 88:985, 1066, 1093, 1213-14, 1274 Ag 18, S 8-15, O 13, 27 '71
BOYD, Josephine
How one woman tackles her grocery bill. Bet Hom & Gard 49:146-8 N '71
BOYD, Malcolm
Peace of mind. por Look 35:30 Jl 27 '71
BOYD, Mary
How I fought city hall, and won. il por Redbook 138:24+ N '71
BOYD, Waldo T.
Q W E R T U I O P ? * ! ? Dvorak simplified keyboard. il Writers Digest 51:37+ F '71
BOYER, Ernest L. and Keller, G. C.
Big move to non-campus colleges. il Sat R 54:46-9+ Jl 17 '71
BOYER, Samuel H. and others
Silent hemoglobin alpha genes in apes: potential source of thalassemia. bibliog il Science 171:182-5 Ja 15 '71
BOYER, Susan
Blazing a new trail. Sat R 54:53 Ja 16 '71
Day-care jungle. il Sat R 54:50-1 F 20 '71
Eye on Fourth street. il Sat R 54:46-7 Ag 21 '71
Performance contracting; Texarkana and Gary. il Sat R 54:64-5 S 18 '71
BOYER, William H.
Education for survival. Ed Digest 36:1-4 Mr '71

BOYLAN, Edward S.
Is the ABM moral? Commonweal 94:303-6, 438-9 Je 11, Ag 20 '71
BOYLE, Kay
Comment. M. L. Rosenthal. Poetry 119:101 N '71 *
BOYLE, Magdalene
Woman behind the man. il Har Yrs 11:22-3 Ap '71
BOYLE, Robert
Great moments in chemistry; tr. by R. E. Oesper. F. Szabadvary. il pors Chem 44:14-17 D '71 *
BOYLE, Robert H.
Absolutely stuck on stamps. il por Sports Illus 35:32-7 Ag 23 '71
Champion of the armchair athletes. il pors Sports Illus 34:20-2+ F 22 '71
Everything's rosy with Jose. il pors Sports Illus 34:22-3 Je 14 '71
Fishing (cont) il Sports Illus 35:46-7 Jl 12 '71
Grab the goat and ride, Omar! il Sports Illus 34:58-61 My 17 '71
Hudson River lives. il Audubon 73:14-17+ Mr '71
Late summer madness. il Sports Illus 35:18-21 S 13 '71
Mud flies all over the track. il por Sports Illus 35:30-1 N 1 '71
Nobody touches me with impunity. il Sports Illus 34:74-7+ Mr 15 '71
Pro football. Sports Illus 35:84+ N 15 '71
There's no need to pity the Pats. il Sports Illus 35:30-2+ O 18 '71
(ed) These are times of technical adjustment. Sports Illus 35:95-6+ O 18 '71
Trick or *truite*: here comes Joe Hyde. il Sports Illus 35:44-6+ N 8 '71
With a quack, quack here. il por Sports Illus 35:50-3+ S 27 '71
BOYLE, Tony. See Boyle, W. A.
BOYLE, William Anthony
Anarchy threatens the kingdom of coal. T. O'Hanlon. il por Fortune 83:78-82+ Ja '71 *
Bombshell from the Yablonski trial. Bsns W p30 Je 26 '71 *
Boyle's law. New Repub 164:7-8 Mr 27 '71 *
Coal walks out before it bargains. por Bsns W p37 Je 19 '71 *
Ghost of John L. por Newsweek 77:86+ My 10 '71 *
Indictment for Boyle. il por Newsweek 77:78+ Mr 15 '71 *
More trouble for Tony. il por Time 97:26 Mr 15 '71 *
BOYNTON, Lindsay
Some documented pieces of English furniture. il Antiques 99:562-7 Ap '71
BOYS
Boys in your world; excerpts from The new Seventeen book of etiquette and young living. E. A. Haupt. por Seventeen 29:128-31+ N '70
Little boy taught me. . . T. Guyant. il Nat Wildlife 10:13-15 D '71
Secret wish of unwed fathers; interview. ed. by L. David. N. Littner. Seventeen 29:128-9+ O '70
What boys don't know about girls, and why. R. Baker. il McCalls 98:49+ Je '71
Young living; questions and answers. A. Wood. See issues of Seventeen
See also
Newsboys
Runaway boys and girls
BOYS, Tall. See Stature
BOYS as actors. See Children as actors
BOYS choirs. See Choirs
BOYS clothing. See Clothing and dress—Children
BOYS clubs
See also
Boy scouts
BOYS haircuts. See Haircutting
BOYS homes. See Homes, Institutional
BOYS nation. See Citizenship, Education for
BOYS rooms. See Childrens rooms
BOYS states. See Citizenship, Education for
BOYSE, E. A. See Leckband, E. jt. auth.
BRA. See Brassieres
BRAASCH, Willette
Two times remembered; poem. Seventeen 31: 91 Ja '72
BRABYN, Howard
Coptic voices from the past. il UNESCO Courier 24:11 My '71
Environmental control and economic systems. il UNESCO Courier 24:24-7 Jl '71
Unesco in the second development decade. il UNESCO Courier 24:12-16 F '71
BRACE, Russell W.
Along the Maine line. il Travel 136:64+ N '71

BRACELAND, Mrs F. J.
God helps those . . . . ; poem. Cath World 213:147 Je '71
Mother; poem. Cath World 213:12 Ap '71; Same. 213:231 Ag '71

BRACELETS
Copper bracelets and the gullibility gap. Consumer Rep 36:133 Mr '71

BRACEWELL, R. N. and others
Stanford's high-resolution radio interferometer. il pors Sky & Tel 42:4-9 Jl '71

BRACHIOPODS
Recent brachiopod-coralline sponge communities and their paleoecological significance. J. B. C. Jackson and others. bibliog il Science 173:623-5 Ag 13 '71

BRACHT, Nell F. See Evans, P. P. jt. auth.

BRACKEEN, Margaret
Integration and acceptance; excerpt from The forum for residential therapy. por Camp Mag 43:12-14 F '71

BRACKEN, Peg
Resolutions, anyone? il Read Digest 98:129-31 Ja '71

BRACKMAN, Jacob
Films. See issues of Esquire

BRADBURY, Ray
How, instead of being educated in college, I was graduated from libraries; or Thoughts from a chap who landed on the moon in 1932; address, with questions and answers. il por Wilson Lib Bul 45:842-51 My '71
These unsparked flints, these uncut gravestone brides; poem. il por Wilson Lib Bul 45:842-3 My '71

about

Ray Bradbury's Dandelion wine: themes, sources, and style. M. E. Mengeling. bibliog f Engl J 60:877-87 O '71 •

BRADBURY, Will
Mystery of memory. il Life 71:66+ N 12 '71

BRADEN, Waldo W.
Beyond the campus gate; address, April 29, 1971. Vital Speeches 37:572-4 Jl 1 '71

BRADERMAN, Eugene M.
New directions in international production and intellectual property; address, May 6, 1971. Dept State Bul 64:772-7 Je 14 '71

BRADFORD, J. C, and company
Regionals put it into narrow focus. il Bsns W p53-4 Ag 7 '71

BRADFORD, Jean
Getting the most out of odd moments. Read Digest 98:82-4 Je '71

BRADLEY, Cornelius B.
Some problems relating to the giant trees; reprint from 1886 article. il por Am For 77:29-31+ My '71

BRADLEY, Sam
Catch; poem. Chr Cent 88:587 My 12 '71
Let nothing divide; poem. Chr Cent 88:1490 D 22 '71
Poor man's plaint; poem. Nation 212:350 Mr 15 '71

BRADNER, Enos
Sagebrush rainbows. il Field & S 75:62-3+ F '71

BRADOW, Judith
Flower shop in the backyard. il Horticulture 49:36-8 My '71

BRADSHAW, George
Puerto Rico: where the past grows young. il Vogue 157:88-9+ Ja 15 '71
Quiche subverted; excerpt from Soufflés, quiches, mousses and the random egg. Vogue 157:44+ Ap 1 '71
Sea gift, a cruise into irresponsibility. Vogue 157:38 F 15 '71

BRADSHAW, Hank
Little Sioux is big on cats. il pors Outdoor Life 148:64-6+ Jl '71
South Dakota's golden geese. il Outdoor Life 148:52-5+ N '71
Tullibee, the surprise fish. il Field & S 75:80-1+ Ap '71
Where raccoons come tough. il Field & S 75:56-7+ Ja '71
—and Bradshaw, Vera
All about game and how to hunt it. il Field & S 76:68-71+ Ag '71
Free booklets, films, maps, etc, for snowmobilers. il Field & S 75:38-9+ Ja '71
Hawkeye outdoorsmen of Wilson junior high. il Field & S 76:78-9+ My '71

BRADSHAW, Thornton Frederick
Power crisis: electricity, oil, coal; interview. il por U S News 70:84-6+ My 10 '71

BRADSHAW, Vera. See Bradshaw, H. jt. auth.

BRADY, Anna
Who will be the next pope? il(p 112) Cath World 213:75-8 My '71

BRADY, Bruce H.
Mr Bob is full of beans. il Outdoor Life 147:72-3+ F '71

BRADY, Elizabeth
One times two; poem. Ladies Home J 88:72 Ap '71

BRADY, James
Fashion influentials. por Harp Baz 104:102-3 O; 105:68-9 N; 53 D '71

about

Editor's guest book. por Harp Baz 105:81 N '71 •

BRADY, Joseph V. See Anderson, D. E. jt. auth.

BRADY, Raymond
Late tape. See issues of Dun's

BRADY, Roscoe O. and others
Fabry's disease: antenatal detection. bibliog il Science 172:174-5 Ap 9 '71

BRADY, U. Eugene, and others
Sex stimulant and attractant in the Indian meal moth and in the almond moth. bibliog il Science 171:802-4 F 26 '71

BRAGG, Sir Lawrence
Obituary
Phys Today por 24:64-5+ O '71. P. P. Ewald

BRAHM, Walter
Knights and windmills. il Library J 96:3096-8 O 1 '71

BRAHMS, Johannes
Brahms by Arrau: two of his finest recorded performances. M. N. Kanny. Am Rec G 37:714 Je '71 •
Dvořák's relations with Brahms and Hanslick. J. Clapham. pors Mus Q 57:241-54 Ap '71 •
Fox meets the rabbit. H. Goldsmith. il pors Hi Fi 21:61-2 My '71 •
Music to my ears; Ludwig-Bernstein recital in Carnegie Hall. I. Kolodin. Sat R 54:27 N 13 '71
One of the great ones, Haitnik's Brahms Third. M. N. Kanny. Am Rec G 37:503-4 Ap '71 •
Truly extraordinary Brahms. M. N. Kanny. Am Rec G 37:364 F '71 •
Very rich, thoroughly convincing Brahms. M. N. Kanny. Am Rec G 37:288+ Ja '71 •

BRAILLE trails. See Trails

BRAIN, George B.
National assessment moves ahead. Todays Ed 60:45 F '71

BRAIN
Brain. il Life 71:42-59 O 1; 42-56+ O 22; 55-66+ N 12; 46-8+ N 26 '71 (to be cont)
Brain as a parallel coherent detector. A. Trehub. bibliog il Science 174:722-3 N 12 '71
Cerebrospinal fluid production by the choroid plexus and brain. T. H. Milhorat and others. bibliog il Science 173:330-2 Jl 23 '71
Lame-brains. J. Morgenstern. por Newsweek 77:18-19 Mr 29 '71
Recurrent excitation of secondary olfactory neurons: a possible mechanism for signal amplification. R. A. Nicoll. bibliog il Science 171:824-6 F 26 '71
Synaptic adjustment after deafferentation of the superior colliculus of the rat. R. D. Lund and J. S. Lund. bibliog il Science 171:804-7 F 26 '71
See also
Brain waves
Cerebellum
Cerebral cortex
Consciousness
Electroencephalography
Hypothalamus
Limbic system
Memory
Optic thalamus
Sleep

Analysis and chemistry

Angiotensin-forming enzyme in brain tissue. D. Ganten and others. bibliog il Science 173:64-5 Jl 2 '71
Brain histamine: rapid apparent turnover altered by restraint and cold stress. K. M. Taylor and S. H. Snyder. bibliog il Science 172:1037-9 Je 4 '71
Cyclic 3',5'-nucleotide phosphodiesterase: cytochemical localization in cerebral cortex. N. T. Florendo and others. bibliog il Science 173:745-7 Ag 20 '71
Differences in the distribution of catecholamine varicosities in cat and rat reticular formation. J. R. Sladek, jr. bibliog il Science 174:410-12 O 22 '71
Dopamine: release from the brain in vivo by amantadine. P. F. Von Voigtlander and K. E. Moore. bibliog il Science 174:408-10 O 22 '71
Electroshock effects on brain protein synthesis: relation to brain seizures and retrograde amnesia. C. W. Cotman and others. bibliog il Science 173:454-6 Jl 30 '71

BRAIN—Analysis and chemistry—*Continued*
Hydrocortisone-mediated increase of norepinephrine uptake by brain slices. J. W. Maas and M. Mednieks. bibliog il Science 171:178-9 Ja 15 '71
Inhibition of biogenic amine uptake by hydrogen peroxide: a mechanism for toxic effects of 6-hydroxydopamine. R. Heikkila and G. Cohen. bibliog il Science 172:1257-8 Je 18 '71
Isolation of filaments from brain. M. L. Shelanski and others. bibliog il Science 174:1242-5 D 17 '71
[^{3}H]Lysergic acid diethylamide: cellular autoradiographic localization in rat brain. I. M. Diab and others. bibliog il Science 173:1022-4 S 10 '71
Memory chemical isolated; scotophobin. Sci Digest 69:81-2 Ap '71
Narcotic tolerance and dependence: lack of relationship with serotonin turnover in the brain. D. L. Cheney and others. bibliog il Science 171:1169-70 Mr 19 '71
Norepinephrine pools in rat brain: differences in turnover rates and pathways of metabolism. J. J. Schildkraut and others. bibliog il Science 172:587-9 My 7 '71
Nuclear localization of histamine in neonatal rat brain. A. B. Young and others. bibliog il Science 173:247-9 Jl 16 '71
Perinatal undernutrition: accumulation of catecholamines in rat brain. W. J. Shoemaker and R. J. Wurtman. bibliog il Science 171:1017-19 Mr 12 '71
Transcription of nonrepeated DNA in mouse brain. W. E. Hahn and C. D. Laird. bibliog il Science 173:158-61 Jl 9 '71

Diseases

Susceptibility of mink to sheep scrapie; similarity to mink encephalopathy. R. P. Hanson and others. bibliog il Science 172:859-61 My 21 '71
See also
Amaurotic family idiocy
Cerebrovascular disease
Leukodystrophy
Parkinson's disease

Inflammation
See Encephalitis

Localization of functions

Amnesia produced by spreading depression and ECS: evidence for time-dependent memory trace localization. R. M. Paolino and H. M. Levy. bibliog il Science 172:746-9 My 14 '71
Brain; miracle and mysteries. A. Hope. il Life 71:42-59 O 1 '71
Differential cerebral processing of noise and verbal stimuli. R. Cohn. bibliog il Science 172:599-601 My 7 '71
Dissociation of impairment after lateral and medial prefrontal lesions in dogs. J. Dabrowska. bibliog il Science 171:1037-8 Mr 12 '71
Hemispheric asymmetry of electrocortical responses to speech stimuli. L. K. Morrell and J. G. Salamy. bibliog il Science 174:164-6 O 8 '71
How does the striate cortex begin the reconstruction of the visual world? D. A. Pollen and others. bibliog il Science 173:74-7 Jl 2 '71
Language production: electroencephalographic localization in the normal human brain. D. W. McAdam and H. A. Whitaker. bibliog il Science 172:499-502 Ap 30 '71; Reply with rejoinder. L. K. Morrell and D. A. Huntington. 174:1359-61 D 24 '71
Loci of memory. Sci Am 225:48-9 N '71
Mind in action; with reports by R. Gore and W. Bradbury. il Life 71:55-66+ N 12 '71
Olfactory bulb removal eliminates maternal behavior in the mouse. R. Gandelman and others. bibliog il Science 171:210-11 Ja 15 '71
Pathways in the brain. L. Heimer. il Sci Am 225:48-57+ Jl '71
Rhesus monkey vestibular cortex: a biomodal primary projection field. D. W. F. Schwarz and J. M. Fredrickson. bibliog il Science 172:280-1 Ap 16 '71
Superior colliculus cell responses related to eye movements in awake monkeys. R. H. Wurtz and M. E. Goldberg. bibliog il Science 171:82-4 Ja 8 '71
Superior colliculus: some receptive field properties of bimodally responsive cells. B. G. Wickelgren. bibliog il Science 173:69-72 Jl 2 '71
Taste pathways in rat brainstem. R. Norgren and C. M. Leonard. bibliog il Science 173:1136-9 S 17 '71

Thermosensitivity of neurons in the sensorimotor cortex of the cat. J. L. Barker and D. O. Carpenter; reply with rejoinder. J. S. Eisenman and H. M. Edinger bibliog Science 172:1360-2 Je 25 '71
Unilateral ablation of the auditory cortex in the cat impairs complex sound localization. J. Cranford and others. bibliog il Science 172:286-8 Ap 16 '71
Visual and auditory inputs into the cuneate nucleus. S. J. Jabbur and others. bibliog il Science 174:1146-7 D 10 '71

Metabolism

Urinary adenosine 3',5'-monophosphate in the switch process from depression to mania. M. I. Paul and others. bibliog il Science 171:300-3 Ja 22 '71

Photographs

Brain, L. Nilsson. Life 71:44-59 O 1; 42-56+ O 22 '71 (to be cont)
Photographing the brain as no one ever has. R. Graves. il por Life 71:3 O 1 '71

Surgery

Brain surgery for addicts; cingulumotomy. Ramp Mag 10:15 S '71
Freezing aids brain surgery. A. J. Snider. Sci Digest 70:58-9 S '71
Recovery of function after serial ablation of prefrontal cortex in the rhesus monkey. J. Rosen and others. bibliog il Science 173:353-6 Jl 23 '71

Weight

Never too late; increase in brain weight in mature rats by environmental stimulation. Sci Am 225:84 S '71
BRAIN-blood barrier. See Blood-brain barrier
BRAIN catecholamines. See Catecholamines
BRAIN damage
Cerebral atrophy in marijuana smokers. Sci N 100:406 D 18 '71
See also
Minimal brain dysfunction
BRAIN damaged children
Words for a deaf daughter, by P. West. Review
Commentary 51:106-7 Ja '71. J. Kaplan; Discussion. 51:10+ Ap '71
BRAIN drain
Brain drain and development. A. A. Michie. Sch & Soc 99:102-3 F '71
Brain drain from the Arab world; adaptation of address, December 22, 1969. M. S. Adiseshiah. Sch & Soc 99:367-9 O '71
Brain drain in the Philippines; a case study. A. Muriel; reply. M. J. Moravcsik. Bul Atom Sci 27:36 F '71

History

Brain drain: mountain or molehill? T. L. Bernard. bibliog Sch & Soc 99:43-5 Ja '71
BRAIN research
Mind; from memory pills to electronic pleasures beyond sex. il Time 97:45-7 Ap 19 '71
Now they're probing the hidden depths of your mind. S. Bacon. il Pop Mech 136:62-5+ Ag '71
Probing the brain. il Newsweek 77:60-2+ Je 21 '71; Same abr. with title Awesome prospects of the brain probers. Read Digest 99:98-102 S '71
Violence and the brain, by V. H. Mark and F. R. Ervin. Review
Nation 212:664-6 My 24 '71. J. Gliedman
BRAIN stimulation. See Electronic behavior control; Stimulation (physiology)
BRAIN surgery. See Brain—Surgery
BRAIN waves
Alpha waves of the future. il por Time 98:33 Jl 19 '71
Brain power: the case for bio-feedback training. B. L. Collier. il Sat R 54:10-13+ Ap 10 '71
Listen to your head. R. J. Trotter. il Sci N 100:314-16 N 6 '71
New test for the brain. Newsweek 78:67-8 D 13 '71
Now they're probing the hidden depths of your mind. S. Bacon. il Pop Mech 136:62-5+ Ag '71
They've found a wish switch in your brain. D. Lampe. por Pop Sci 198:30+ Ja '71
See also
Electroencephalography
BRAINARD, Franklin
. . .Rather than scream. il pors Todays Health 49:32-7 Je '71
BRAKES
Little brake stops power tools, fast. C. P. Gilmore. il Pop Sci 199:69 N '71

BRAKES, Automobile
New story on disc brakes. T. Tappett. il
Mech Illus 67:109-11+ Ja '71
Now: the world's safest brake system; Tel-
dix anti-bloc. J. P. Norbye. il Pop Sci 198:
74-5 Ap '71
Roundy-round corner; disc brakes on race
cars. S. Kelly. il Hot Rod 24:110 Ap '71
Stove stoppers; disc brakes for the early
Chevy. J. Thawley. il Hot Rod 24:98-9
D '71
We have ways of making you stop; Mercedes'
anti-skid brake system. A. B. Shuman. il
Motor T 23:40-2+ Ap '71

Maintenance and repair
Doing it: brake reline. il Motor T 23:86 Je '71
Roundy-round corner; brake job for racing
cars. S. Kelly. il Hot Rod 24:94-5 Jl '71
Save up to $47 on the cost of power-brake
repair. M. Schultz. il Pop Mech 136:152+
Ag '71

BRAMLEY, Arthur
Obituary
Phys Today 24:73 S '71. H. A. Barton
BRANAN, Karen
Getting high on high school. il Schol Teach
Jr/Sr High p12-14+ F 1 '71
High school alternatives: stepping out into
the sunshine. il Schol Teach Jr/Sr High
p8-11 D '71
I get a very different feeling in that class.
il Schol Teach Jr/Sr High p8-10 My 3
'71; Same abr. Ed Digest 37:9-11 S '71
Vouchers: schools in the marketplace. Schol
Teach Jr/Sr High p6-8 Ja 11 '71
What can I do about. .? Schol Teach Jr/Sr
High p26+ S; 26 O; 20 N '71; 30 Ja '72
BRANCH, C. H. Hardin
Pollution of the psychological environment.
bibliog Ment Hy 55:519-22 O '71
BRANCH, William McKinley
Judge Branch of Greene County. il pors
Ebony 26:82-5 Ag '71 *
BRANCH banking. See Banks and banking—
Branch banking
BRANCH stores. See Department stores—
Branch stores
BRAND, Ludwig. See Seliskar, C. J. jt. auth.
BRAND, Millen
Selfish gathering; poem. Nation 212:827 Je
28 '71
BRAND name goods. See Branded merchandise
BRAND names. See Trade marks and trade
names
BRANDED merchandise
Consumer goods; with yardsticks of manage-
ment performance. il Forbes 109:154+ Ja 1
'72
See also
Private brands
BRANDEIS university, Waltham, Mass.
Brandeis sets up unit on gerontology policy
with private, AoA funds. Aging 195:10 Ja
'71
Roy. J. A. Lukas. il pors Esquire 75:122-6+
Mr '71
BRANDING
See also
Swine—Branding
BRANDO, Marlon
Shooting The Godfather. il Newsweek 77:89
Je 28 '71 *
BRANDON, Henry
(ed) See Moynihan, D. P. Moynihan report:
after six months of benign neglect
(ed) See Nicholson, M. Renaissance
BRANDON, Liane
Using media creatively in the English class-
room. Engl J 60:1231-3 D '71
BRANDS, Private. See Private brands
BRANDT, N. B. and Ginzburg, N. I.
Superconductivity at high pressure; with bio-
graphical sketches. il Sci Am 224:14, 83-8+
Ap '71
BRANDT, Nat
New York is worth twenty Richmonds. il
Am Heritage 22:74-80+ O '71
To the flag. il Am Heritage 22:72-5+ Je '71
BRANDT, Willy
Why U.S. must stay in Europe; interview,
ed. by R. Haeger. il pors U S News 70:
39-42+ Je 14 '71
about
As Willy Brandt looks east: worries for U.S.
and Germany. il por U S News 70:55-6 F 8
'71 *
Brandt and the peace prize. Nation 213:452-
3 N 8 '71 *
Fourth corner. B. van Voorst. por Newsweek
77:34-5 Je 21 '71 *
Hectoring Herr Brandt. New Repub 164:7-8
Ja 23 '71 *
Honors beyond bitterness. Chr Cent 88:1283
N 3 '71 *

President entertains the chancellor. il por
Time 99:12-13 Ja 10 '72 *
Prize for a German peacemaker. il por Time
98:48 N 1 '71 *
Prize for a good neighbor. Newsweek 78:35+
N 1 '71 *
Willy Brandt walks a tightrope. por Read
Digest 98:96-100 Ap '71 *
Willy Brandt wins Nobel peace prize. por
Sr Schol 99:16-17 N 15 '71 *
BRANDY
Brandy goes native. E. Greenberg. il House
B 113:189+ O '71
Classic fruit brandies. C. Ray. il Holiday
49:76-8 Mr '71
Cognac: to put the cook in good spirits. H.
McNulty. House & Gard 140:126+ S '71
BRANDYWINE RIVER museum
Brandywine school. D. Davis. il Newsweek
77:93 Je 28 '71
BRANHAM, J. M. and others
Coral-eating sea stars acanthaster planci in
Hawaii. bibliog il Science 172:1155-7 Je 11
'71
BRANIFF international airways
Braniff expects small traffic growth. Avia-
tion W 95:22 O 18 '71
Braniff to refurbish, expand 727 fleet. R. G.
O'Lone. il Aviation W 95:30 S 27 '71
Command posts manned by key Braniff offi-
cials during hijack. Aviation W 95:20 Jl
12 '71
LTV begins sale of Braniff holdings. Avia-
tion W 94:27 Mr 22 '71
BRANN, Henry Walter
(tr) See Mann, T. Letters of Thomas Mann
to Henry Walter Brann
BRANNIGAN, William A.
Communist parties of Israel. Nation 213:
398-401 O 25 '71
BRANSCOMB, Lewis M.
Taming technology address, December 27,
1970. bibliog Science 171:972-7 Mr 12 '71
BRANSCOME, James
Appalachia, like the flayed back of a man.
il N Y Times Mag p30-1+ D 12 '71
Stripping for pleasure and profit. Common-
weal 95:229-31 D 3 '71
BRANSON, Roy
(ed) See Sullivan, C. If not Charles Evers,
who?
(ed) See Swann, J. If not Charles Evers,
who?
BRANT. See Geese, Wild
BRAQUE, Georges
Picasso and Braque, their cubist years. R.
Phelps. Vogue 157:125+ Ap 1 '71 *
BRASESCO, Emilio
University cheesecake; interview. New York-
er 47:32-4 Mr 27 '71
BRASH, Edward
My götterdämmerung; poem. Mlle 73:146 My
'71
BRASÍLIA, Brazil
Gateway to a rich heartland. il Bsns W p92-
3 Mr 13 '71
BRASS rubbings. See Rubbings
BRASS work
Bits of brass; photographs of some objects
in the collection of M. Davidson. M. B.
Davidson. il Antiques 101:193-200 Ja '72
BRASSAI
Master at 90, Picasso's great age seems only
to stir up the demons within. il pors N Y
Times Mag p30-1+ O 24 '71
BRASSARD, Roger
Restorations experts speak their minds; in-
terview. House & Gard 140:6+ Ag '71
BRASSIERES
Answers to your questions about the new
bras and girdles. V. Griffin. il Good H 172:
152 Mr '71
BRASSWORK. See Brass work
BRATHWAITE, George
My China visit as a ping pong diplomat. il
pors Ebony 27:84-6+ N '71
BRATLEY, Carol
Boston's graffiti board. il Am City 86:138+
Ap '71
BRATT, Elmer C.
Economic growth and fluctuations. bibliog f
Ann Am Acad 393:122-31 Ja '71
BRAUDY, Leo
Difficulties of Little big man. il Film Q 25:
30-3 Fall '71
BRAUDY, Susan
James Taylor, a new troubadour. il pors
N Y Times Mag p28-9+ F 21 '71
BRAUN, Ernest
Gallery; photograph. Life 70:8-9 Ap 9 '71
Water, man, and nature; photographs. il Am
West 8:18-29 Ja '71
BRAUN, Henry
Scholars on vacation; Old groups; On read-
ing late; poems. Poetry 118:23-4 Ap '71

BRAUN, Moodie E. Jr
Make your own gemstone faceting machine.
il Pop Mech 135:156-61+ F '71

BRAUN, Saul
Shazam! Here comes Captain Relevant. il
por N Y Times Mag p32-3+ My 2 '71

BRAUTIGAN, Richard
Homage to the San Francisco YMCA; story.
il Vogue 158:96-7 Jl '71
Old bus; story; excerpt from Revenge of the
lawn. Vogue 157:192 F 1 '71
Poem: Crow maiden. Harper 243:58 O '71

about

Still loving. J. Yardley. New Repub 164:24
Mr 20 '71 •

BRAVES (basketball team) See Basketball
teams

BRAWER, Catherine C.
Don Reitz. il pors Ceram Mo 19:19-26 D '71
(ed) See Breckenridge, B. Conversation with
Don Reitz and Bruce Breckenridge
(ed) See Reitz, D. Conversation with Don
Reitz and Bruce Breckenridge

BRAXTON, Dorothy
Macquarie Island; with biographical sketch.
il Sea Front 17:224-9, 255 Jl '71

BRAY, John Roger
Solar-climate relationships in the post-pleistocene. bibliog Science 171:1242-3 Mr 26 '71

BRAYBROOKE, Neville
Poets at Bethlehem. Chr Cent 88:1497-8 D
22 '71
Vocation in the desert. Commonweal 94:88-9
Ap 2 '71

BRAYER, Yves
Yves Brayer. J. Opalak. il Design 72:27-9
mid-Wint '71 •

BRAYERS
Painting with a brayer. J. Macey. il Sch
Arts 71:8 D '71

BRAZELTON, T. Berry
What childbirth drugs can do to your child.
il por Redbook 136:65+ F '71
—and Main, Mary
Are there too many sights and sounds in
your baby's world? il Redbook 137:91+
S '71

BRAZIL
See also
Brasília
Coffee industry—Brazil
Economic assistance in Brazil
Education—Brazil
Forests and forestry—Brazil
Investments, Foreign (in Brazil)
Iron mines and mining—Brazil
Land tenure—Brazil
Mato Grosso
Opera—Brazil
Paraná River
Police—Brazil
Political prisoners—Brazil
Poor—Brazil
Recife
Roads—Brazil
Salvador
Terrorism—Brazil

Antiquities
Women's lib, Amazon style; artifacts of war-
like women. il Time 98:54 D 27 '71

Commerce
Export list grows and grows. il Bsns W p46
Je 12 '71

Economic conditions
After the miracle. Nation 213:645-6 D 20 '71
Booming Brazil finds a key to growth; with
editorial comment. il Bsns W p90-3, 136
Mr 13 '71
Don't underestimate Brazil. S. Rodman. il
Nat R 23:860-3 Ag 10 '71
See also
Brazil—Industries

Bibliography
Economics and development of modern Brazil. F. J. Munch. il Américas 23:37-40 Mr
'71

Economic policy
Ailing giant starts a comeback: will it last?
il U S News 71:59-61 Ag 30 '71

Industries
Great sisal scheme. D. R. Gross. il Natur
Hist 80:48-55 Mr '71
See also
Automobile industry—Brazil

Native races
See Indians of South America—Brazil

Politics and government
Brazil: all power to the generals. H. J.
Steiner and D. M. Trubek. For Affairs
49:464-79 Ap '71
Brazil: what terror is like. M. M. Alves. Na-
tion 212:337-41 Mr 15 '71
Brazil's third government of the revolution.
R. E. Poppino. Cur Hist 60:102-7+ F '71
Don't underestimate Brazil. S. Rodman. il
Nat R 23:860-3 Ag 10 '71
Economic torture? il por Forbes 107:50 F 1 '71

Religious institutions and affairs
World around us (title varies) (cont) Chr
Cent 88:291, 604+, 1056+ Mr 3, My 12, S 8
'71
See also
Catholics in Brazil
Evangelical congregational church in Brazil

Social conditions
Ailing giant starts a comeback: will it last?
il U S News 71:59-61 Ag 30 '71
See also
Poor—Brazil

BRAZILIAN architecture. See Architecture,
Brazilian
BRAZILIAN fishermen. See Fishermen
BRAZILIAN literature
See also
Brazilian poetry
BRAZILIAN opera. See Opera—Brazil
BRAZILIAN philosophy. See Philosophy, Braz-
ilian
BRAZILIAN poetry

Translations Into English
Two Brazilian poems: Cemetery of childhood
by J. Cardozo; Sonnet of intimacy by
V. De Moraes; tr. by E. Bishop. New
Yorker 47:52 N 27 '71

BRAZILIANS
Homage to Iemanjá; pagan practices. il Time
99:44-5 Ja 10 '72

BRAZILLER, George
Authors & editors; interview. ed. by A. H.
Johnston. Pub W 200:17-19 O 11 '71

BRAZILLER, George, Inc.
Authors & editors; interview. ed. by A. H.
Johnston. G. Braziller. Pub W 200:17-19
O 11 '71

BREAD
ABC's of cinnamon rolls. il Am Home 74:86
F '71
Bake it, don't fake it! with recipes. il Seven-
teen 31:94-5+ Ja '72
Baking your own health breads. Sunset 146:
193-4 Mr '71
Bazaar foods. il Bet Hom & Gard 49:74-5+
S '71
Better with bread. J. Hewitt. il N Y Times
Mag p56 Ap 11 '71
Bread; course in bread baking. New Yorker
47:30-2 Ap 3 '71
Bread for a cookout. il Bet Hom & Gard
49:71 Ag '71
Bread sticks. J. Hewitt. il N Y Times Mag
p36 Jl 18 '71
Breads & cereals; questions and answers;
with recipes. R. H. Smithies. il Good H
173:144+ D '71
Breads, beautiful breads. H. McCully. il
House B 113:82-3+ Ja '71
Building and baking in your own pueblo
oven. il Sunset 147:50-3 Ag '71
Come for coffee, afternoon cards, a commit-
tee meeting. il Bet Hom & Gard 49:64-5+
Ja '71
Cooking lesson: the versatile brioche. J. Jaff-
ry. il Am Home 74:90-1+ Mr '71
Fruit breads to bake ahead for the holidays.
il Sunset 147:204 N '71
German dark rye bread. il Bet Hom & Gard
49:96 D '71
Hot breads in less than 10 minutes. il Farm
J 95:54 Ap '71
How to make your own crusty *bolillos*. il
Sunset 147:216 O '71
Made, with love, by hand. M. F. K. Fisher.
il McCalls 98:94-5+ S '71
More fun than play dough. B. B. Smith. il
Todays Health 49:58-61 F '71
Pop, top and bake; with recipes. il Seventeen
29:146-7+ N '70
They're still the way to start the day;
bacon 'n' corn bread, lemon bread. il N Y
Times Mag p72 S 26 '71
This article tells you how to make bagels
in interesting shapes and sizes. il Sunset
146:76-7 Mr '71
Tower from Russia, an egg-crown from
Greece, here are bread surprises for Eas-
ter. il Sunset 146:88-9 Ap '71
See also
Gingerbread
Toast

BREAD—*Continued*

Advertising
Admen burn over baker's bow to FTC. Bsns
W p25-6 Jl 10 '71
Mea culpa, sort of; Profile bread's TV ad.
Newsweek 78:98 S 27 '71

BREAD, Frozen
See also
Dough, Frozen

BREAD sticks. See Bread

BREADFRUIT
Breadfruit tree. H. M. Berry. il Horticulture
49:19+ Mr '71

BREAKFAST foods. See Cereal foods

BREAKFASTS
Back-to-school breakfasts. Bet Hom & Gard
49:101 O '71
Beautiful breakfasts; menus and recipes. il
House & Gard 139:123-4+ Mr '71
Better breakfast ideas (cont) il Bet Hom
& Gard 49:124-5 Ap '71
Country breakfasts. F. M. Crawford. il Am
Home 74:104-5+ O '71
Quiet revolution at breakfast time. il Sunset
146:58-62 Ja '71
Thoughts for the hostess. M. M. Hemingway.
House & Gard 139:22 Je '71
Wake up to color and breakfast. il House &
Gard 139:106-11 Mr '71
See also
Brunches

BREAST
Surgery
Controversy over breast cancer; radical
mastectomy. A. Q. Maisel. Read Digest
99:151-6 D '71
How Silastic transformed breast surgery. J.
Star. Look 35:12 Jl 27 '71
I was a cancer coward; facing radical mas-
tectomy. E. B. Thompson. il por Ebony
26:64-8+ S '71
Operation women fear most; mastectomy.
W. A. Nolen. McCalls 98:52+ Ap '71
Silicone used in breast surgery. Sci Digest
69:56 Je '71

BREAST cancer. See Cancer

BREAST feeding
Breast feeding. D. Reuben. McCalls 98:64+
My '71
Mothers' milk or other milk? W. E. Homan.
il N Y Times Mag p75+ Je 6 '71; Discus-
sion. p 15+ Jl 4 '71
Scientists and the press: cancer scare story
that wasn't. N. Wade. Science 174:679-80
N 12 '71
Why mothers should breast-feed their ba-
bies. Princess Grace of Monaco. por La-
dies Home J 88:56+ Ag '71

BREAST milk. See Milk, Human

BREATHING. See Respiration

BRECHT, Bertolt
Brecht returns as a classic. L. Baxandall.
Nation 212:501-3 Ap 19 '71 •
St Joan of the stockyards. Criticism
Newsweek il 77:123 My 10 '71 •

BRECK, George D. and Trager, W. F.
Oxidative N-dealkylation: a mannich intermediate in the formation of a new metabolite of lidocaine in man. bibliog il Science
173:544-6 Ag 6 '71

BRECKENFELD, Gurney
Architects want a voice in redesigning Amer-
ica. il Fortune 84:144-7+ N '71
How the Arabs changed the oil business. il
Fortune 84:112-16+ Ag '71

BRECKENRIDGE, Bruce
Conversation with Don Reitz and Bruce
Breckenridge; ed. by C. Brawer. il pors
Ceram Mo 19:17-19 Mr '71

BREDEMUS, James C.
Swimtime; when a camp director needs a
friend. il Camp Mag 43:23+ Ap '71

BREDTHAUER, Oscar
Big man for a big job. W. Kester. pors Farm
J 95:B-5 My '71 •

BREED (motorcycle gang) See Gangs

BREEDER reactors. See Nuclear reactors

BREEDING
See also
Birds—Breeding
Cattle breeding
Dog breeding
Plant breeding
Reproduction
Swine breeding
Tree breeding

BREEDLOVE, C. H. Jr
Chemical basis for a common type of drain
cleaner. il por Chem 44:25 S '71

BREEDLOVE, Craig
Breedlove's rocket racers. E. K. von Delden.
il pors Hot Rod 24:112-17 My '71 •

BREEDS of cattle. See Cattle—Breeds

BREEN, John
What a priceless possession is heritage.
Read Digest 98:172-4 Ja '71

BREEN, Jon L.
Dewey damsel system. Wilson Lib Bul 45:
770-1 Ap '71
World of mysteries. Wilson Lib Bul 46:404+
Ja '72

BREIVIK, Patricia Senn
Beyond full-time faculties. bibliog il por Library J 96:1197-9 Ap 1 '71

BREMER, Otto A.
Is business the source of new social values?
Harvard Bsns R 49:121-6 N '71

BRENBERGER, Richard W.
Valley's their business. il Am For 77:44-6+
My '71

BRENDEL, Alfred
Elegant thunderer. por Time 98:36 Ag 23 '71 •

BRENGEL, Fred L.
Consistent capitalist. M. F. Brdlik. il por
Duns 93:65+ Je '69 •

BRENNAN, Donna
Quietude; poem. Ladies Home J 88:143 F '71

BRENNAN, Harold J.
Jurying: science, art, or gamble? por Ceram
Mo 19:31-2 O '71

BRENNAN, Matthew J.
Making tomorrow now. Ed Digest 36:13-15
F '71

BRENNER, Ed
General purpose power supplies. il Electr
World 86:30-3 O '71

BRENT, Madeleine
Escape! story. il Good H 173:61-3 Ag '71

BRENTON, Myron
Mothers & daughters. il Seventeen 30:92-
3+ D '71
Troubled teachers whose behavior disturbs
our kids. il Todays Health 49:16-19+ N '71
You can be more creative! il Seventeen 29:
244-5+ Ag '70
(ed) See Rabinowitz, O. How to talk to your
parents about sex

BRESLER, E. H. and others
Steady-state sieving across membranes. bibliog il Science 172:858-9 My 21 '71

BRESLIN, Edward H.
Microelectronic soldering. il por Electr World
86:53 N '71

BRESLIN, John B.
Birthright; alternative to abortion. America
125:116-19 S 4 '71
New fall books. America 125:236-8+ O 2 '71
Three faces of war. America 125:314-16 O 23
'71

BRESNICK, David. See Lachman, S. P. jt.
auth.

BRESSLER, Marvin
American college; some problems and choices;
address, April 1971. bibliog f Ann Am Acad
396:57-69 Jl '71

BRESSON, Henri Cartier-. See Cartier-Bresson, H.

BRESSON, Robert
Current cinema. P. Gilliatt. New Yorker 47:
79-81 My 29 '71 •

BRETHREN, Church of the. See Church of
the Brethren

BRETON, André
André Breton, by A. Balakian. Review
Sat R 54:23 My 29 '71. L. S. Roudiez •
André Breton: magus of surrealism, by A.
Balakian. Review
America 125:327-8 O 23 '71. J. D.
Gauthier •
Comment. P. Schjeldahl. Poetry 117:262-4 Ja
'71 •

BRETT, Grace Neff
Kate Greenaway. il Hobbies 76:76+ D '71

BRETT, James J.
Pathways for the blind. il Cons 25:13-16 Je
'71

BRETTON WOODS conference, 1944. See
United Nations monetary and financial conference

BREUER, Stephen E.
Program goals or administrative needs?
Camp Mag 43:23-4 My '71

BREUGHEL, Peeter. See Brueghel, P.

BREWER, Gene C.
He won Riegel for Southwest. por Bsns W
p42 Je 19 '71 •

BREWER, George J. and Eaton, J. W.
Erythrocyte metabolism: interaction with oxygen transport. bibliog il Science 171:1205-
11 Mr 26 '71

BREWER, William Miles
Obituary
Negro Hist Bul por 33:173 N '70
BREWERIES
Not fit for horses; Löwenbräu beer wagons returning during Munich Oktoberfest. il Time 97:33 F 22 '71
BREWING industries
Those vanishing brews. Forbes 107:26 My 1 '71
See also
Anheuser-Busch, inc.
Coors, Adolph, company
Lucky breweries, inc.
Watney Mann, ltd.

Denmark
Skol! Carlsberg foundation. il Forbes 108: 44+ S 1 '71
BREZHNEV, Leonid Il'ich
Soviet statement on disarmament; excerpts from address, June 11, 1971. Cur Hist 61:240 O '71
about
Brezhnev no. 1. il por Sr Schol 98:16 My 3 '71 *
Brezhnev's big show. Newsweek 77:56 Ap 19 '71 *
Charmer in Paris. il por Time 98:38+ N 8 '71 *
Collective or personal rule in the U.S.S.R? D. T. Cattell. Cur Hist 61:235-9 O '71 *
Feathers and foie gras; visit to France. il pors Newsweek 78:54 N 8 '71 *
Man from Moscow. il por Newsweek 78:44+ O 4 '71 *
More power for Brezhnev: what it means to U.S. por U S News 70:18 Ap 26 '71 *
Six hours with Leonid Brezhnev. il por Newsweek 77:47-8 Ap 12 '71 *
Soviet Union: something for everyone. il por Time 97:22-3 Ap 12 '71 *
Super B and the new Soviet surge. il pors Newsweek 78:29-30+ N 1 '71 *
That's show biz. Newsweek 78:74 D 13 '71 *
Whoa, comrade Brezhnev. il por Time 98: 38 D 6 '71 *
BRIAND, Georgette
Hair arts. il por Harp Baz 104:41 F '71
BRIANSKY, Oleg
(tr) See Messerer, A. Classes in classical ballet
BRIBERY
See also
Politics, Corruption in
BRIBERY in child training. See Children— Management and training
BRICK, Steven A. See Skolnick, J. H. jt. auth.
BRICKER amendment. See United States— Treaties
BRICKMAN, William W.
Books for educators; U.S. and foreign. Sch & Soc 99:472-86+ D '71
Drug addiction and the schools. Sch & Soc 99:146-7 Mr '71
Educational literature review: U.S. and foreign. Sch & Soc 99:294-6+ Sum '71
Input-output language in education. Sch & Soc 99:394 N '71
Instant and relevant curricula. Sch & Soc 99:207 Ap '71
Newer concepts of academic freedom. Sch & Soc 99:72-3 F '71
Professionalism in higher education. Sch & Soc 99:466-7 D '71
Study of higher education. Sch & Soc 99: 266-7 Sum '71
BRICKS
End product; bricks from manure. il Newsweek 78:62 Jl 26 '71
BRIDEGROOM and daddy; story. See Chekhov, A.
BRIDES
New brides ring out the old traditions. il Bsns W p 114-15 Je 19 '71
BRIDGE (game)
Bridge. A. Truscott. See issues of New York times magazine
Bridging the generation gap with a new deal; International junior pairs championship. C. Goren. il Sports Illus 34:52 Mr 1 '71
Checkmate at a little no-trump slam. C. Goren. il Sports Illus 35:46 Ag 2 '71
Goren's Christmas quiz (cont) C. Goren. il Sports Illus 35:74-6+ D 20 '71
Now you see them, now you don't. C. Goren. il Sports Illus 34:60+ Je 14 '71
Show of hands proved aces were high. C. Goren. il Sports Illus 34:54 Je 21 '71
Staking a claim on one club; Precision system. C. Goren. il Sports Illus 34:64+ Mr 15 '71

BRIDGE design. See Bridges—Design
BRIDGE players
Cutting some uppity kids down to size. C. Goren. il Sports Illus 35:76+ O 18 '71
Now you see them, now you don't. C. Goren. il Sports Illus 34:60+ Je 14 '71
Six aces are hard to beat; Contract bridge league's spring national tournament. C. Goren. il Sports Illus 34:94-5 Ap 12 '71
See also
August, B.
BRIDGE tournaments
Bridging the generation gap with a new deal; International junior pairs championship. C. Gore. il Sports Illus 34:52 Mr 1 '71
Forecast: cloudy, but clearing in October; Summer National championships in Chicago. C. Goren. il Sports Illus 35:48 Ag 9 '71
New empire is on the rise, but first an older one has to fall: Ira Corn's Aces in Bermuda bowl competition. C. Goren. il Sports Illus 35:70+ N 8 '71
One ace to trump in Taiwan; world team championship. C. Goren. il Sports Illus 34:62 My 10 '71
Six aces are hard to beat; Contract bridge league's spring national tournament. C. Goren. il Sports Illus 34:94-5 Ap 12 '71
Staking a claim on one club; Precision system. C. Goren. il Sports Illus 34:64+ Mr 15 '71
Two for the Aces in Taipei; world bridge championship team of U.S. R. Frey. il Sports Illus 34:76+ My 31 '71
BRIDGER, C. See Helfand, L. A. jt. auth.
BRIDGES, Annetta Hereford
Hello, my children, good-by. Read Digest 99:157-60 O '71
Where did the years all fly? il PTA Mag 66:14-16 O '71
BRIDGES, Harry
Harry Bridges veers right. por Bsns W p50 My 1 '71 *
BRIDGES, Linda
High price of fanaticism. Nat R 23:1297-8 N 19 '71
BRIDGES
Troubled water over bridges; encroachments on the waters used for pleasure boating. B. Robinson. Yachting 130:31 D '71
See also
Chesapeake Bay bridge-tunnel
also subhead Bridges under names of rivers, cities, etc, e.g. San Francisco Bay —Bridges
Design
Morandi's bridges. il Arch Forum 135:48-53 O '71
Shaken faith in bridges; investigating the safety of box-girder design. il Bsns W p38 Ag 7 '71
Foundation and piers
Who would know that it was 82 years old? Court street bridge. il Am City 86:87 N '71
Lighting
High lighting for an upper level; San Francisco-Oakland Bay bridge. il Am City 86: 70 Ja '71
Great Britain
Shaken faith in bridges; investigating the safety of box-girder design. il Bsns W p38 Ag 7 '71
BRIDGES, Concrete
Morandi's bridges. il Arch Forum 135:48-53 O '71
BRIDGES, Wooden
See also
Covered bridges
BRIEFER, Charles
How New York's pioneer classical station has fallen upon sorry Times. il pors Hi Fi 21:74-9 S '71
BRIEN, Sidney
Music to my eyes. il Sch Arts 70:30-1 Mr '71
BRIGANDS and robbers
Presenting the next great western movie; alleged perpetrators of robberies against the Southern Pacific railroad during the early 1890s. L. E. Sissman. Atlan 228:40+ D '71
BRIGGS, Peter
Big eye in the sky. il Nat Wildlife 9:35-9 F '71
BRIGHAM, Robert
Crisis at sea: the threat of no more fish. il Life 71:60-8 D 3 '71
It has always been enough to say You know where I stand. il Life 71:36 O 29 '71
BRIGHT, John, pseud.
Southern-side up. Commonweal 94:76-7 Ap 2 '71

BRIGHT, Willard Mead
  Boston grudge fight may lead to a merger.
  il por Bsns W p58+ N 6 '71 *
BRIGHTBILL, Dorothy
  This month in American home. F. R. Smith.
  por Am Home 74:8 N '71 *
BRIGHTMAN, Robert
  How to choose and use binoculars. il Pop
  Mech 136:88-91+ S '71
BRIGHTMAN, Samuel C.
  Democrats open the door. Nation 212:552-5
  My 3 '71
  Something bad for everyone. Nation 213:11-
  13 Jl 5 '71
BRIGHTON, Carl T.
  Low charge for fractures. il Newsweek 78:
  74+ N 8 '71 *
BRIGHTON branch library. See Boston public
  library—Branches
BRILHART, Barbara L.
  Oral communication for the Indian student;
  address, April 1970. Engl J 60:629-32 My
  '71
BRILIOTH, Helge
  Rare bird; interview. ed. by J. Boutwell. por
  Opera N 35:12-13 F 20 '71
          about
  Music to my ears; performance in Tristan.
  I. Kolodin. Sat R 54:25 D 18 '71 *
BRILL, Debbie
  She gets her back up. A. Verschoth. por
  Sports Illus 34:52-3 F 22 '71 *
BRILL, Norman Q. See Weinstein, R. M. jt.
  auth.
BRILLEMAN, Edna Lane
  Why the yacht broker? il Motor B & S
  128:112 Ag '71
BRILOFF, Abraham J.
  Cool look at hot-pants accounting; interview,
  ed. by R. Brady. il por Duns 98:8-9+ O
  '71
BRIMHALL, Dean R.
  Brimhall saga. F. Brodie. il por Am West
  8:4-9+. 18-23+ Jl, S '71 *
BRIMMER, Andrew-Felton
  Persistent professional. por Bsns W p99 Jl
  17 '71 *
BRINER, Bob
  But it looked like a great new racket; ed.
  by F. Deford. il Sports Illus 34:56-8+ Ap
  19 '71
BRINHART, Betty
  Big bargain in bulbs, the beautiful Dutch
  iris. il Home Gard 58:38-9 D '71
  Bushels of late potatoes. il Org Gard & Farm
  18:39-41 My '71
  Cow manure? il Org Gard & Farm 18:89-91
  Mr '71
BRINKMAN, Grover
  Road. il Liv Wildn 34:18-22 Wint '70
BRINKMANN, R. T.
  Mars: has nitrogen escaped? bibliog il Sci-
  ence 174:944-5 N 26 '71
BRINNIN, John Malcolm
  Sway of the grand saloon; excerpts. il Am
  Heritage 22:12-19+ O '71
BRIOCHE. See Bread
BRISCOE, Robert
  Utopians in the marketplace. bibliog f
  Harvard Bsns R 49:4-6+ S '71
BRISCOE, Rudel
  How to get the haircut you want. il pors
  Redbook 136:82-5+ F '71 *
BRISTER, Bob
  Best fishing spots in Mexico. il Field & S 76:
  85+ My '71
  Bobwhite is no gentleman anymore! il Field
  & S 75:34-5+ Ja '71
  Brown bear the hard way. il Field & S 76:30-
  1+ D '71
  Fishing's newest twist . . . spoonfeeding bass.
  il Field & S 76:56-7+ Je '71
  Ptarmigan. il Field & S 76:36-7+ S '71
          about
  Two new shooting editors for a growing
  sport. M. J. O'Neill and C. Conley. pors
  Field & S 76:8-9 O '71 *
BRISTOL, Esther
  I got a letter! il PTA Mag 65:26-7 Ap '71
BRITISH
  See also
  English
BRITISH airports authority. See Great Britain
  —British airports authority
BRITISH art. See Art, British
**BRITISH association for the advancement of
  science**
  Funereal occasion: annual meeting of BSSRS.
  Aurum. Bul Atom Sci 27:29 Ap '71

BRITISH automobiles. See Automobiles, For-
  eign
BRITISH broadcasting corporation
  Is Sesame authoritarian? Newsweek 78:68+
  S 20 '71
BRITISH Caledonian airways. See Caledonian-
  BUA airways
BRITISH COLUMBIA
  See also
  Booksellers and bookselling—British Colum-
  bia
  Gulf Islands
            Antiquities
  Men out of Asia. Sci Am 226:51 Ja '72
            Commerce
  Boom in Canada's far west, and no end in
  sight. N. J. Margolin. il U S News 70:88-90
  My 17 '71
            Description and travel
  Beauty of British Columbia. R. S. Kane. il
  Harp Baz 104:26+ Je '71
  Desolation Sound. B. Crabtree. il Yachting
  129:52-3+ My '71
  Vacation getaways. F. Shemanski. il Schol
  Teach Jr/Sr High p22 My 3 '71
            Economic conditions
  Boom in Canada's far west, and no end in
  sight. N. J. Margolin. il U S News 70:88-90
  My 17 '71
            Parks and reserves
  It's a turn-of-the-century Kootenay ghost;
  Fort Steele historic park. il Sunset 146:86
  My '71
            Religious institutions and
            affairs
  Worldaround. Chr Cent 88:982 Ag 18 '71
BRITISH COLUMBIA university press
  Univ. of British Columbia launches scholarly
  press. Pub W 199:41+ Ap 26 '71
BRITISH communications satellites. See Com-
  munications satellites, British
BRITISH cookery. See Cookery, English
BRITISH council of churches
  Rhodesian proposals under fire by British
  churchmen. Chr Cent 88:1488 D 22 '71
BRITISH folk art. See Folk art
BRITISH Ford. See Ford motor company, ltd.
BRITISH Grand prix. See Automobile racing—
  Great Britain
BRITISH HONDURAS
  See also
  Belize
BRITISH ISLES (ship) See Sailing vessels
BRITISH Labor party. See Labor party (Great
  Britain)
BRITISH Leyland motor corporation
  Motor trend interview. D. G. S. Stokes of Ley-
  land. il pors Motor T 23:86+ Ag '71
BRITISH library association. See Library as-
  sociation
BRITISH money. See Money—Great Britain
BRITISH Open golf tournament. See Golf—
  Tournaments
BRITISH overseas airways corporation
  BOAC, Air France in final Concorde talks.
  Aviation W 94:34-5 My 31 '71
  BOAC may block Atlantic cargo rate plan.
  D. E. Fink. Aviation W 95:26-7 D 6 '71
  BOAC profit outlook diminishes after tum-
  bling last fiscal year. Aviation W 95:26 Ag
  30 '71
  Miami-London carriers vary cabin service.
  H. D. Watkins. Aviation W 95:29-30 N 29
  '71
BRITISH painting. See Painting, British
BRITISH petroleum company
  BP's embattled chairman. por Bsns W p79 D
  11 '71
  Ties that may keep two oil giants apart;
  proposed merger of Continental oil co. with
  Britain's Burmah oil co. Bsns W p30 Mr
  6 '71
BRITISH poetry
  Recent developments in British poetry. M.
  Mott. Poetry 118:102-14 My '71
  Verse: a muchness of modernity. L. Coxe.
  New Repub 165:26-30 O 16 '71
BRITISH press council. See Newspapers—Great
  Britain
BRITISH propaganda. See Propaganda, British
BRITISH royal collection. See Art—Private col-
  lections
BRITISH society for social responsibility
  Funereal occasion: annual meeting of BSSR.
  Aurum. Bul Atom Sci 27:29 Ap '71
BRITISH student Christian movement. See
  Student Christian movements
BRITISH united airways. See Caledonian-BUA
  airways

BRITISH VIRGIN ISLANDS
Diving cruise to Horse Shoe reef. C.
Mitchell. il Yachting 130:58-60+ N '71
See also
Tortola (island)

BRITTANNY spaniels. See Spaniels

BRITTEN, Benjamin
Albert Herring. Criticism
Hi Fi il 21:MA16 D '71 •
Nation 213:350 O 11 '71 •
New Yorker 47:118-19 S 25 '71 •
Britten's Britons. J. W. Stedman and G.
McElroy. il por Opera N 36:18-20 N '71 •
Britten's Prodigal. R. Jacobson. Sat R 54:57
My 29 '71 •
Britten's The rape of Lucretia. D. Harris. il
Hi Fi 21:80-1 O '71 •
King of the May. G. Martin. il Opera N
36:16-17 S '71 •
Opera *mundi*. W. Bender. il Time 97:74 My
24 '71 •
Tippett's Knot garden, Britten's Owen Win-
grave. E. Greenfield. il Hi Fi 21:MA30-1 Ag
'71 •

BRITTEN-Norman, ltd.
Bank forces Britten-Norman receivership.
H. J. Coleman. Aviation W 95:18-19 N 1
'71
High flyer lands in receivership. il Bsns W
p29 O 30 '71

BRITTINGHAM, Marion
Natural resources in the English curriculum.
Engl J 60:927-30 O '71

BROAD bean poisoning. See Favism

BROADHEADS. See Arrowheads

BROADWAY, New York (theater district) See
New York (city)—Theater

BROADWAY actors and actresses. See Actors
and actresses

BROADWAY-Hale stores, inc.
Broadway-Hall makes it to Fifth avenue; to
acquire Bergdorf Goodman. il Bsns W p68+
Ap 3 '71

BROBERG, Pete
They're out of their classes. J. Jares. pors
Sports Illus 34:51 Je 28 '71 •

BROBSTON, Stanley Heard
Good music: an enriching addition to your
camp program. Camp Mag 43:18 Mr '71

BROCCOLI
Broccoli comes before lettuce. J. R. Coggins.
il Org Gard & Farm 18:63-4 Ja '71

BROCHURES. See Pamphlets

BROCK, Guy Clutton-. See Clutton-Brock, G.

BROCK, Stanley E.
Jungle cowboy; condensation. il pors Read
Digest 98:233-9+ F '71

BROCK, William Emerson, 1930-
Annals of politics. R. E. Harris. New Yorker
47:34-54 Jl 10 '71 •

BRODE, Wallace R.
Manpower in science and engineering, based
on a saturation model; adaptation of address, November 23, 1970. bibliog il Science
173:206-13 Jl 16 '71

BRODER, Gloria Kurian
Elena, unfaithful; story. il Harper 243:86-90
D '71

BRODERICK, Dorothy M.
Censorship: reevaluated. bibliog Library J 96:
3816-18 N 15 '71
In focus. por Library J 96:2852-3, 3448-9,
4168 S 15, O 15. D 15 '71
Lessons in leadership. il Library J 96:699-
701 F 15 '71

BRODEUR, Paul
Department of amplification. New Yorker 47:
147-51+ O 23 '71
Reporter at large. New Yorker 46:42-8+ Ja 16
'71

BRODIE, Fawn
Brimhall saga. il por Am West 8:4-9+, 18-
23+ Jl, S '71

BRODIE, John
Prime of Mr John Brodie. R. F. Jones. por
Sports Illus 35:62-6 S 20 '71 •

BRODINE, Virginia
Episode 104. bibliog il Environ 13:2-24+
Ja '71
Special burden. il Environ 13:22-4+ Mr '71

BRODNEY, Kay
Invocation. Wilson Lib Bul 45:777 Ap '71

BRODO, Irwin M.
Lichens and air pollution. il Cons 26:22-6 Ag
'71

BRODOVITCH, Alexey
Obituary
Pop Phot por 69:60 S '71. C. Reynolds

BRODY, Jane E.
What every woman should know about abortion. Read Digest 98:119-22 F '71

BRODY, Sidney
Light touch. Todays Ed 60:23 F '71
Pringle's pride; story. Todays Ed 60:28-9 N
'71

BROGAN, Colm
Can Heath hold the line? Nat R 23:634+ Je
15 '71
Demon drink rides again. Nat R 23:1237-
8 N 5 '71
Wilson agonistes. Nat R 23:930+ Ag 24 '71

BROGGI, Giuliana
Rise of Signora Broggi. H. Lottman. Pub W
199:30 Je 14 '71 •

BROKEN bones. See Fractures

BROKEN broomstick; drama. See Miller, H. L.

BROKEN homes
See also
Children of divorced parents

BROKERS
Aftershocks; big board's suit against Orvis
brothers & co. Newsweek 78:68+ Jl 12 '71
Big buyers start to bargain; block trading. il
Bsns W p74 Ap 3 '71
Confessions of a stockbroker. Brutus. il Atlan
226:46-51 Je '71
Hard look at why brokers fail. Bsns W p54-5
Ag 7 '71
Less room to play with customer cash. Bsns
W p41 N 13 '71
Mad rush to go public. Bsns W p58 Mr 13
'71
Meeting the volume test. C. Morgello. il
Newsweek 77:80 F 22 '71
Other people's money. New Repub 164:9-10
Ja 23 '71
Ready to peddle life insurance. Bsns W p80+
Mr 20 '71
Street's pipeline to Japanese stocks. il
Bsns W p66+ My 29 '71
Why the little guy feels neglected. Bsns
W p86 Ap 17 '71
See also
Bradford, J. C. and company
Daniels and Bell (firm)
Donaldson, Lufkin and Jenrette, inc.
DuPont, F. I, Glore Forgan and company
First Harlem securities corporation
Hayden. Stone. inc.
Loeb, Rhoades and company
Merrill Lynch Pierce, Fenner and Smith, inc.
Reynolds and company
Saunders-Stiver and company
Stock exchange
Walston and company
Witter, William D, inc.

Commissions
Brokerage-fee changes proposed. il U S News
71:85 Jl 19 '71
Confusing debut for negotiated rates. il Bsns
W p39 Ap 10 '71
Double blow for the big board. il Time 97:
75-6 Ap 19 '71
Down to the wire on brokerage fees. il Bsns
W p75 Jl 17 '71
Free trade comes to Wall Street. il News-
week 77:97-8 Ap 19 '71
New schedule of stockbrokerage fees. il U S
News 71:92 O 11 '71
Rating the new rates. C. Morgello. il News-
week 78:100 O 25 '71
Rolling with the punches. por Forbes 107:
59-60 Ap 15 '71
Smooth transition. C. Morgello. il Newsweek
77:82 Je 21 '71
Surcharge helps brokerage profits. Bsns W
p22+ My 8 '71
Wails of Wall Street. Duns 98:84 Ag '71
Wall Street revisited. Nat R 23:466 My 4 '71
Will new fees aid small investors? U S News
71:75-6 Jl 26 '71

Consolidations and mergers
Unbelievable last months of Hayden. Stone.
C. J. Loomis. il Fortune 83:114-16+ Ja '71

Finance
Bandwagon: rush to take the public in as
partners. Forbes 108:16-17 S 1 '71

Insurance
Big board starts defogging; special trust fund
payments to houses in liquidation. il Bsns
W p80 Ja 16 '71

Security measures
Hallway for stock thieves; Sensitrace pass-
ageway. il Bsns W p66 O 16 '71

BROLGA. See Cranes (birds)

BROMELIADS
Bromeliads. J. Kramer. il Horticulture 49:
24-7 Mr '71
See also
Spanish moss

BROMFIELD, E. A.
Technicians in Britain. Electr World 86:36 Jl
'71

BROMIDES
Inhibitors of DNA polymerases of murine leukemia viruses: activity of ethidium bromide. S. Z. Hirschman. bibliog il Science 173:441-3 Jl 30 '71
BROMIGE, David
Comment. S. Dobyns. Poetry 117:392-4 Mr '71 *
BROMILEY, Geoffrey W.
Books on church history and theology. 1970. Chr Today 15:4-6 F 26 '71
Curious anniversary. Chr Today 16:5-6 O 22 '71
Six certainties about the Lord's Supper. Chr Today 15:5-8 Jl 16 '71
BROMKE, Adam
Beyond the Gomulka era. For Affairs 49:480-92 Ap '71
BROMODEOXYURIDINE
Murine leukemia virus: high-frequency activation in vitro by 5-iododeoxyuridine and 5-bromodeoxyuridine. D. R. Lowy and others. bibliog il Science 174:155-6 O 8 '71
BROMWICH, David L.
Reading Robert Lowell. Commentary 52:78-83 Ag '71
BRONFENBRENNER, Urie
Parents bring up your children! excerpts from Two worlds of childhood U.S. and U.S.S.R. Look 35:45-6 Ja 26 '71
BRONFMAN, Samuel
Mister Sam's succession. por Time 98:59+ Jl 26 '71 *
BRONSON, David B.
Story of an English elective program. Engl J 60:1086-90 N '71
BRONSON, William
It's about too late for Tahoe. il Audubon 73:46-62+ My '71
BRONTOSAURUS. See Dinosaurs
BRONX zoo. See New York zoological park
BRONZE age gold jewelry. See Jewelry, Ancient
BRONZES
Renaissance reunion; Saint Christopher carrying the Christ Child with the globe of the world. il Newsweek 77:70 Mr 1 '71
BRONZINO, Joseph D.
Biomedical engineer: the roles he can play. bibliog il Science 174:1001-3 D 3 '71
BROOK, Peter
Circus in the Forest of Arden. T. Prideaux. por Life 70:12 F 26 '71 *
Current cinema. P. Kael. New Yorker 47:135-9 D 11 '71 *
Theatre; production of Midsummer night's dream. H. Clurman. Nation 212:188-9 F 8 '71 *
BROOK, Randy
Hitching a ride across America. il pors Life 71:36-43 Ag 27 '71
BROOK, Simon Bryden-. See Bryden-Brook, S.
BROOK trout fishing. See Trout fishing
BROOKE, Edward William
My mother, right or wrong. il por McCalls 98:70 My '71
about
Brooke scenario. il por Time 98:13 D 13 '71 *
BROOKE Bond Liebig, ltd.
People's drink. il Forbes 107:40 Ap 15 '71
BROOKGREEN gardens. See Gardens—South Carolina
BROOKHAVEN, N.Y.
From a dump of sorts to a spot for sports. J. Kaplan. il Sports Illus 35:52-3 Ag 23 '71
Phoenix plan at Brookhaven. K. P. Goldbach. Cons 25:30 F '71
BROOKHISER, Richard
Young Conservative looks at Nixon and China. por Nat R 23:1056+ S 24 '71
BROOKHOUSE, Christopher
Scattered craft. J. Galassi. Poetry 118:290 Ag '71 *
BROOKLYN

Architecture
Community resources center; East New York M. Villecco. il Arch Forum 134:54-4 Ap '71

Education
Love project: Thomas Jefferson high school. A. Lorrance. il Todays Ed 60:60-2 S '71

Housing
East New York: this place makes Bedford-Stuyvesant look beautiful. R. Rogin. il N Y Times Mag p30-1+ Mr 28 '71

Riots
90-cent riot; Brooklyn's Brownsville section. il Newsweek 77:94 My 17 '71
BROOKLYN academy of music. See Academy of music, Brooklyn

BROOKLYN botanic garden
Lawns. H. W. Indyk. New Yorker 47:27-9 S 18 '71
BROOKLYN college. See New York (city). City university—Brooklyn college
BROOKLYN museum
Making the gallery scene; Japanese prints at the Brooklyn museum. B. Wasserman. il Sch Arts 71:28-31 N '71
Myth, muse and mom; Pride and prejudice: A woman's exhibition. S. K. Oberbeck. il Newsweek 77:85 Je 21 '71
BROOKLYN public library
Voices of Brooklyn: report on a project funded by the National endowment for the humanities. D. Nyren. il por Wilson Lib Bul 46:443-5 Ja '72

Branches
Working in public libraries; Prospect district library. A. M. Cunningham. Mile 74:168+ N '71
BROOKLYNITES. See New Yorkers
BROOKS, Alan
Sculpture on a grand scale. il por Sch Arts 71:38-40 O '71
BROOKS, Albert
Albert Brooks' Famous school for comedians. il por Esquire 75:89-94 F '71
BROOKS, Charles M.
Need for legislation; address, April 26, 1971. Vital Speeches 37:563-6 Jl 1 '71
BROOKS, Edward M.
Weather prospects for the 1972 total solar eclipse. il Sky & Tel 41:290-1 My '71
BROOKS, Glenn
Glenn Brooks, Interboro civil ballet, Clark center, N.Y. T. Borek. Dance Mag 45:85-6 My '71 *
BROOKS, Gwendolyn
Dreams of a black Christmas; excerpt from The autobiography. McCalls 99:136+ D '71
In Montgomery; with photographs by M. Sleet, jr. il Ebony 26:42-8 Ag '71
BROOKS, H. K. See Purdy, B. A. jt. auth.
BROOKS, Harvey
Can science survive in the modern age? bibliog Science 174:21-30 O 1 '71
BROOKS, Henry
Charon's toll. por Forbes 107:25-6 My 1 '71 *
BROOKS, James
Art world; exhibition at Martha Jackson. H. Rosenberg. New Yorker 47:75-6 Mr 6 '71 *
Beyond control. H. Rosenstein. il Art N 69:48-9+ F '71 *
BROOKS, Joe
Fishing. See issues of Outdoor life
BROOKS, John
Return from the drug scene. il pors Ebony 26:50+ S '71 *
BROOKS, John, 1920-
Marts of trade. New Yorker 47:138+ O 9 '71
Reporter at large. New Yorker 47:117-18+ O 23 '71
BROOKS, Lois
Workshop: adire eleko. il Craft Horiz 31:12-15 Ag '71
BROOKS, Maurice
West Virginia: the paradox of a forgotten state. il Nat Wildlife 10:56-63 D '71
BROOKS, Oscar
(ed) See Ochoa, M. Day the rebels attacked
BROOKS, Patricia
Fairy-tale atmosphere of Danish inns. il Holiday 49:60-1+ F '71
How to eat in Chinese. il Sat R 54:38-9+ O 23 '71
Inns for all seasons. il Holiday 48:82-3+ S '70
Pilgrims' trail. Nat R 23:1003-4 S 10 '71
BROOKS, Paul, 1909-
Warning: the chain saw cometh. il Atlan 228:95-9 D '71
BROOKS, Richard
On closed sets. il Harp Baz 104:66-7 Jl '71
BROOKS RANGE
Eskimo village. S. Wright. il Liv Wildn 34:3-9 Wint '70
Nameless valleys, shining mountains; excerpts. J. P. Milton. il Liv Wildn 34:10-17 Wint '70
BROOKS RANGE wilderness area. See Wilderness areas—Alaska
BROOME COUNTY, N.Y.
Saving Broome County's environment. D. F. Newton. Cons 25:20-1 Ap '71
BROOME-Murie awards. See Wilderness society
BROOTEN, Gary
Parent and child. il N Y Times Mag p78+ S 26 '71

BROPHY, Jere E. See Good, T. L. jt. auth.

BROSIO, Manlio
President presents Medal of freedom to NATO Secretary General Brosio; remarks, September 29, 1971. Dept State Bul 65:488 N 1 '71

about

Western explorer heads for Moscow. il por Time 98:38+ O 18 '71 •

BROSNAN, Jim
What we're losing by our craze for winning. il Todays Health 49:16-19 My '71

BROTEN, G. A. and Twardokens, G. R.
Dream came true. il Parks & Rec 6:111+ Ja '71

BROTHERHOOD of man
Courage to see; religious implications of the new sisterhood. M. Daly. Chr Cent 88:1108-11 S 22 '71
Man for all souls. B. Burwell. il Am Heritage 23:13-16 D '71
Violence or brotherhood? A religious dilemma. S. A. Fineberg. il Cath World 213:17-20 Ap '71

Bibliography

Books for brotherhood. Commonweal 93:520-3 F 26 '71

BROTHERS, Joyce
On being a woman. See issues of Good housekeeping
Teaching children the habit of success. il por Good H 173:72+ O '71
True confessions: should you disclose & expose? il Harp Baz 105:100+ N '71

BROTHERS, Lisa
Streamlines: how to fight collegiate fat. por Seventeen 30:290 Ag '71

BROTHERS and sisters. See Siblings

BROTMAN, Herman B.
Aging population up 63.1% in 20-year Aging lifetime. il Aging 200:5 Je '71

BROUN, Heywood Hale
Life sports review. il Life 71:12 Ag 20 '71
Should anyone really play to win? Yes, or else. . . Vogue 157:130-1 My '71

BROUWER, Jack H.
How to tame a wild river. il Am City 86:84+ D '71

BROUWER, L. G. See Edwards, H. W. jt. auth.

BROWDER, Earl Russell
Marx's disenchanted salesman; interview, ed. by H. Stein. por Am Heritage 23:58-61+ D '71

BROWER, Brock
Dylan's boathouse. il Esquire 75:96-7+ Ja '71
Ed Muskie asks you to trust him. il pors Life 71:58-60+ N 5 '71
Play it again, Sam Bogie, Harry, Wendell, Claude. il Esquire 76:120-1+ N '71
Taking the kids and surviving it: a case for togetherness. il Life 71:26-1 S 3 '71
Where have all the leaders gone? il Life 71:68-9+ O 8 '71

BROWER, Charles N.
Convention on aviation sabotage adopted by Montreal conference; statements, September 15 and 22, 1971. Dept State Bul 65:464-5 O 25 '71

BROWER, David Ross
Conservationist speaks his mind; interview. por U S News 71:64-5 Jl 5 '71

about

Encounters with the archdruid, by J. McPhee. Review
Am For 77:35-6 N '71. M. Bush •
Profiles. J. McPhee. por New Yorker 47:42-8+ Mr 20; 42-8+ Mr 27; 41-4+ Ap 3 '71

BROWN, Alfred E. and Reinhart, K. A.
Polyester fiber: from its invention to its present position. bibliog il Science 173:287-93 Jl 23 '71

BROWN, Barbara
Alpha wave of the future. il por Time 98:33 Jl 19 '71 •

BROWN, Bertram S.
Mental health of our children: we must conserve our most precious natural resource. por Parents Mag 46:24 Jl '71

BROWN, Beverly S.
Snake chief; text. Negro Hist Bul 34:70-1 Mr '71

BROWN, Bruce
On any Sunday. C. S. Ashworth. il pors Hot Rod 24:126-7 Je '71 •

BROWN, Carolyn
In celebration of Carolyn Brown. O. Maynard. il pors Dance Mag 45:35-42 Jl '71 •

BROWN, Colin
Unfulfilled prophecies of Karl Marx. Chr Today 15:4-6 Jl 2 '71

BROWN, Courtney C.
Inflation: the dangerous sedative. Sat R 54:22-3 Mr 6 '71

BROWN, D. W.
Write it once and retain it. il por Am City 86:81-2 N '71

BROWN, David, corporation
New driver for David Brown corp. il Bsns W p50 Jl 17 '71

BROWN, David G. and Coffey, D. S.
Release of nuclear DNA template restrictions by specific polyribonucleotides. bibliog il Science 171:176-8 Ja 15 '71

BROWN, Dean
Presenting Dean Brown; photographs. Art in Am 59:82-5 Ja '71

BROWN, Dee Alexander
Bury my heart at Wounded Knee; story behind the book. L. P. Freilicher. il Pub W 199:34-5 Ap 19 '71 •

BROWN, Denise Scott
Crosstown is dead, long live the crosstown? il Arch Forum 135:42-4 O '71
—See Venturi, R. jt. auth.

BROWN, Dennis A.
New plants from old. il Home Gard 58:26-31 Je '71

BROWN, Dorothy Foster
Button collecting. See issues of Hobbies

BROWN, Douglas
New defenders of the old mass; reprint. Nat R 23:1235 N 5 '71

BROWN, Douglass Vincent
Legalism in U.S. industrial relations. Mo Labor R 94:51-3 Mr '71

BROWN, Drew
Bundini: Svengali in Ali's corner. E. Shrake. pors Sports Illus 34:32-6 F 15 '71 •

BROWN, Duane
California design XI. il Craft Horiz 31:24-5 Ap '71 •

BROWN, Edmund G. Jr
Full disclosure. Nation 214:36 Ja 10 '72 •

BROWN, F. Harry
Why won't it work? Pub W 199:28-30 Mr 29 '71

BROWN, George Edward, 1920-
Physics and social change; adaptation of address, June 1971. il pors Phys Today 24:23-7 O '71

BROWN, George Hay
Patterns of change in the United States; address, January 25, 1971. Vital Speeches 37:261-3 F 15 '71; Excerpts. por U S News 70:25 F 8 '71

BROWN, George S.
Realistic deterrence; address, April 12, 1971. Vital Speeches 37:514-16 Je 15 '71
Research and development; address, February 16, 1971. Vital Speeches 37:331-4 Mr 15 '71
USAF development policies; excerpts from address. Aviation W 95:9 S 6 '71
Viability of the United States; address, September 17, 1971. Vital Speeches 38:53-6 N 1 '71

BROWN, George W.
George Brown toy sketchbook, ed. and introd. by E. F. Barenholtz. Review
Antiques 100:354+ S '71. K. D. Barron •

BROWN, Gerald W.
What happened to elementary school arithmetic? Ed Digest 37:38-40 S '71

BROWN, Gwilym S.
Cross-country. il por Sports Illus 35:94-5 D 6 '71
Golf. Sports Illus 35:88-90 S 27; 85-6 O 25 '71
He was more like a regiment. il por Sports Illus 35:28-9 O 18 '71
I'm going to punish them for last year. il pors Sports Illus 35:30-2+ Ag 30 '71
Is a mustache just peanuts? il por Sports Illus 34:38-40+ Je 14 '71
Motor sports. il por Sports Illus 34:70-1 Ap 5 '71
Owners can be tackled, too. il Sports Illus 34:18-21 Mr 22 '71
Platform tennis. il Sports Illus 34:81-2 Ap 19 '71
Pro skiing. Sports Illus 35:92+ D 20 '71
Still something of a summit meeting. il Sports Illus 35:20-1 Jl 12 '71
Tennis (cont) Sports Illus 34:60+ Ja 18 '71
Two for money, one for show. il pors Sports Illus 35:28-9 N 8 '71
Week; college football (cont) Sports Illus 35:57-9 N 1; 72+ N 15 '71
(ed) See Bowerman, B. Secrets of speed

BROWN, H. Douglas
Gems and minerals. See issues of Hobbies

BROWN, H. Rap
Cherry pie. Time 98:19 O 25 '71 •
Out of invisibility. il por Newsweek 78:50 O 25 '71 •
Violent harvest for black militants. il pors Life 71:41-2 O 29 '71 •

BROWN, Harold O. J.
Dreams of a third age. Chr Today 15:3-5 Jl 16 '71
BROWN, Harrison
After the population explosion. il Sat R 54:11-13+ Je 26 '71
Scenario for an American renaissance; excerpt from address. Sat R 54:18-19 D 25 '71
Science, technology and the developing countries; statement to House committee on science and astronautics at meeting with Panel on science and technology. Jan. 26-28, 1971. por Bul Atom Sci 27:10-14 Je '71
BROWN, Harvey
You don't just execute the enemy. por Life 70:27 Ap 23 '71 *
BROWN, Helen Gurley
What it will be like when we elect a woman president; interview, ed. by D. Sendler. il por Todays Health 49:26-31 Jl '71
BROWN, Henry James
Virginia planter-painter Henry James Brown. L. M. Watson. il Antiques 100:591-5 O '71 *
BROWN, James H.
Desert pupfish; with biographical sketch. il Sci Am 225:12, 104-10 N '71
BROWN, Jesse LeRoy
Navy secretary names first ship for black naval officer. por Negro Hist Bul 34:62 Mr '71 *
BROWN, Jimmy
Waves for family fun. il Am City 86:101-2 O '71
BROWN, Joan G.
Law and punishment status of state statutes. Clear House 46:106-9 O '71
Tenure and the teacher. Clear House 45:355-60 F '71
BROWN, Joe David
Addie Pray; story. McCalls 98:105-14 Jl '71
BROWN, John, 1800-1859
To purge this land with blood, by S. B. Oates. Review
Nation 212:405-7+ Mr 29 '71. T. Nelson; Reply. S. B. Oates. 212:546 My 3 '71 *
BROWN, John Anthony
Human reach; address, February 7, 1971. Vital Speeches 37:398-401 Ap 15 '71
BROWN, John J.
Car-crushing, for your community? il Cons 25:5 Ap '71
BROWN, Joseph Stanley-. See Stanley-Brown, J.
BROWN, Kevin V.
Company for dinner? il pors Todays Health 49:46-9+ My '71
Now: teenie two! il Pop Mech 135:94-101 My '71
On the track of CAT: clear air turbulence. il Sci Digest 70:62-6 N '71
Those flying amphibians are back. il Mech Illus 67:55-7 Ag '71
Wings of brave men. il Pop Mech 136:62-6 Jl '71
BROWN, Les
Trade winds; interview, ed. by C. Amory. Sat R 54:14+ N 13 '71
about
[Dollar signs] S. Kanfer. il por Time 98:90+ N 1 '71 *
BROWN, Lester R.
Social impact of the green revolution. bibliog f il pors Int Concil 581:5-61 Ja '71
BROWN, Lillian
Before our very eyes. il PTA Mag 65:18-20 My '71
BROWN, Louis M.
Family legal matters (cont) Bet Hom & Gard 49:100 My '71
Using a lawyer for a personal-injury claim. Bet Hom & Gard 49:12+ Ap '71
BROWN, Louise C.
Sons of the sea goddess. il Américas 23:36-7 O '71
BROWN, Maurice J. E.
Schubert: discoveries of the last decade. bibliog f il por Mus Q 57:351-78 Jl '71
BROWN, Michael
Drug scene, has it changed? il PTA Mag 66:4-5 bibliog(p35) D '71
BROWN, N. H.
Miniature wide-range V. L. F. tuner. il Electr World 86:61 Jl '71
BROWN, Norman B. See Huff, W. H. jt. auth.
BROWN, Peter C.
Snake pottery. R. Goettsch. il Ceram Mo 19:16-17 F '71 *
BROWN, Randy
AEC has something for Kansas. Nation 212:712-16 Je 7 '71

BROWN, Rap. See Brown, H. R.
BROWN, Robert McAfee
ABC: Assy, Bonhoeffer, Carswell. il Chr Cent 88:369-71 Mr 24 '71
Bob Brown: reluctant radical; interview, ed. by R. M. Herhold. il por Chr Cent 88:745-7 Je 16 '71
BROWN, Roger
Cinderellas of the superstars. L. J. Banks. il pors Ebony 27:70-3 Ja '72 *
BROWN, Roger K.
Sound planning stretches capital funds; questions and answers. Parks & Rec 6:37-8+ Jl '71
BROWN, Roland G.
Moral dilemma, a teaching unit for slow learners. Engl J 60:924-6+ O '71
BROWN, Rosellen
Poetry of Margaret Atwood. Nation 212:824-6 Je 28 '71
BROWN, Rosemary
Supernatural symphonies; excerpt from Unfinished symphonies. il por Ladies Home J 88:92+ S '71
about
Liszt's lament? Beethoven's bagatelle? Or Rosemary's babies? G. Gould. il pors Hi Fi 20:87-8+ D '70 *
BROWN, Royal S.
Prokofiev blockbuster. Hi Fi 21:88+ Ja '71
Shostakovich's fourteenth, a new protest? por Hi Fi 21:64-5 F '71
BROWN, Russell A.
Loci of conflict and compromise; address, December 5, 1970. Vital Speeches 37:247-9 F 1 '71
BROWN, Russell Richards
Light touch. R. Levy. Duns 97:70 Mr '71 *
BROWN, Sam W. jr
Same old gang turns up in Washington. por Life 70:2 Ja 29 '71
BROWN, Samuel C. jr
I am a househusband but call me mister. il por Redbook 137:80+ My '71
BROWN, Sonny
Song of freedom. por Newsweek 77:115 My 17 '71 *
BROWN, Stanley H.
Buy now, play later boom. il Life 71:8 D 3 '71
Market as contact (lens) sport. il Life 71:8 Ag 13 '71
BROWN, Stephen W. and Dyer, R. F.
Ombudsman in the educational hierarchy. bibliog il Clear House 46:234-8 D '71
BROWN, Thomas
Use defense installations as models for recycling. Org Gard & Farm 18:53 Je '71
BROWN, Thomas M.
Natives may win one: the great Alaskan real-estate deal. il N Y Times Mag p42-3+ O 17 '71
BROWN, Virginia L. See Farr, R. jt. auth.
BROWN, Willard W.
Parks & recreation essay. Parks & Rec 6:38-9 Je '71
BROWN, William E. and Wold, Finn
Alkyl isocyanates as active site-specific inhibitors of chymotrypsin and elastase. bibliog il Science 174:608-10 N 5 '71
BROWN, William P.
Golden arm of the law. il Nation 213:392-7 O 25 '71
BROWN, Worth A.
Callas, past, present and future. il Horticulture 49:38+ Mr '71
BROWN lung. See Lungs—Dust diseases
BROWN pelicans. See Pelicans
BROWN trout fishing. See Trout fishing
BROWN university, Providence, R.I.
Bio-medical center
Providence, R.I. il Arch Forum 134:36-9 Je '71
BROWNE, Alan K.
Way to finance environmental protection. Am City 86:6 Ja '71
about
Bonds: you can get taken here, too. por Forbes 108:42-3 Jl 15 '71 *
BROWNE, Geoffrey S.
If Britain goes into the Common market . . . il Nations Bsns 59:44-7 F '71
BROWNE, Peter
Jump jet: the shape of wings to come; Harrier. il Read Digest 99:174-6+ O '71
There's no one quite like David Frost. por Read Digest 98:91-5 Mr '71
BROWNE, Robert
Yale's summer school. il Hi Fi 21:MA12-14 My '71

BROWNE, Secor D.
Stormy weather for CAB's Secor Browne. il pors Nations Bsns 59:73-5 Mr '71

about

Aero-elephantiasis? pors Forbes 108:82 N 15 '71 •

BROWNE, T. C.
Neretti: both ears and a tail. il Motor T 23: 86-7 O '71

BROWNELL, S. M.
Desirable characteristics of decentralized school systems. Ed Digest 36:8-11 Ap '71

BROWNING, Frank
Cable, TV: turn on, tune in, rip off. il Ramp Mag 9:32-8 Ap '71
Senator Scoop Jackson: Pentagon populist. por Ramp Mag 10:54-7 Ja '72
—and Garrett, Banning
New opium war. il Ramp Mag 9:32-9 My '71

BROWNING, Howard B.
City maps that work. il Am City 86:74-5 Je '71

BROWNING arms company
Country gunshop. W. Page. il Field & S 75: 116-18+ F '71

BROWNING guns. See Rifles

BROWNSTEIN, Michael
Comment. J. Atlas. Poetry 119:48-9 O '71 •

BROWNSVILLE. See Brooklyn

BROWNSVILLE, Tex.

Riot, 1906

Congressman cites Norton book as basis for bill to clear black battalion. L. P. Freilicher. Pub W 199:65 Ap 12 '71

BROWSING in libraries. See Libraries and readers

BROY, Anthony
New sparkle in crystals. il Duns 97:89-90+ My '71

BRUCE, David K. E.
Ambassador Bruce discusses problem of U.S. prisoners of war in southeast Asia; text of news conference, December 1, 1970. il Dept State Bul 63:737-45 D 21 '70
Ambassador Bruce resigns as head of U.S. delegation to Paris talks; with exchange of letters, July 28, 1971. Dept State Bul 65:179 Ag 16 '71
Plenary session on Vietnam held at Paris. See issues of Department of state bulletin

BRUCE, Evangeline (Bell)
Two literary travellers: a dialogue. pors Vogue 157:122-3 Ap 15 '71

BRUCE, George
Conservative's dilemma. Nat R 23:1224 N 5 '71
Philadelphia story: the Tasker homes. il America 124:652-4 Je 26 '71

BRUCE, Jeannette
Air racing. il Sports Illus 35:44+ Jl 19 '71
Himalayan trek or treat. il Sports Illus 34:86-8+ Je 7 '71

BRUCE, Lenny
Broken taboo breaker. D. Auchincloss. il Time 97:62 Je 7 '71 •
Bruce boomlet. il por Time 97:73 My 31 '71 •
Lenny lives. J. Kroll. il por Newsweek 77:75+ Je 7 '71 •
What Lenny Bruce was all about. A. Goldman. il pors N Y Times Mag p 12-13+ Je 27 '71 •

BRUCE, Mellon, collection. See Art—Private collections

BRUCHAC, Joseph
Mountain dreams; poem. Nation 212:190 F 8 '71

BRUCKNER, Anton
Flashes of greatness from the 25-year-old Bruckner: a moving, masterly Requiem. J. Diether. por Am Rec G 37:428-9+ Mr '71 •
Music to my ears; performance of Symphony No. 8. I. Kolodin. Sat R 54:43 Mr 6 '71 •

BRUCKNER, D. J. R.
Precarious state of America's big city parks. il Parks & Rec 6:36+ S '71

BRUDNOY, David
Broadway. Nat R 23:1129-30 O 8 '71
Film chronicle (title varies) Nat R 23:381-2, 662, 822-3, 941, 1191-2, 1250, 1368 Ap 6, Je 15, Jl 27, Ag 24, O 22-N 5, D 3 '71
Good Dreele easier; poem. Nat R 23:1097 O 8 '71
Peking buddies; poem. Nat R 23:970 S 10 '71
Television (cont) Nat R 23:269-70 Mr 9 '71
Ungluing of San Francisco. il Nat R 23:593 Je 1 '71

BRUEGHEL, Peeter, the elder
Games children play. A. Eliot. il Sports Illus 34:46-51+ Ja 11 '71 •

BRUEMMER, Fred
Funk Island; with biographical sketch. il Natur Hist 80:5, 52-7 Je '71

BRUI, William
Refreezing the thaw. J. Rubenstein. il por Art N 70:40-1+ D '71 •

BRUMBAUGH, Thomas B.
Horatio Greenough in the classic mold. il por Antiques 99:252-6 F '71

BRUNAIS, Augustin. See Brunias, A.

BRUNCHES
Football brunch. P. Tamor. il Todays Health 49:40-3 N '71
New Year's day brunch. il Bet Hom & Gard 49:60-1+ Ja '71
Sunday breakfast is Sunday lunch; menus and recipes. H. McCully. il House B 113: 112-13+ S '71

BRUNDAGE, Avery
Brundage backs down. Newsweek 78:84 Ag 2 '71 •

BRUNEAU, Thomas C.
Brazil's people of God, prophets or martyrs? America 124:91-4 Ja 30 '71

BRUNEAU dunes state park. See Idaho—Parks and reserves

BRUNEI (sultanate)
Brunei. E. Sandberg-Diment. il Travel 136: 32-9+ O '71

BRUNETTE hair. See Hair

BRUNIAS, Agostino
Colonial life in the West Indies as depicted in prints. N. Connell. il Antiques 99:732-7 My '71 •

BRUNING, Heinrich
End of the Weimar republic. J. Wheeler-Bennett. For Affairs 50:351-71 Ja '72 •

BRUNK, Jeffrey A.
Phantom of record. il por Outdoor Life 148: 49-51+ N '71

BRUNK, Max E.
Meddlesome seventies; address. November 17, 1970. Vital Speeches 37:200-4 Ja 15 '71

BRUNNER, Hans R. and Kirshman, J. D.
Hypertension of renal origin: evidence for two different mechanisms. bibliog il Science 174:1344-6 D 24 '71

BRUNNER, John
Building four-dimensional people in science fiction. Writer 84:21-4 D '71

BRUNO, Jerry
Advance man; interview. New Yorker 47:30-1 Je 12 '71
Advance man; interview, ed. by D. N. Mount. il Pub W 199:46-7 Je 21 '71

about

Advance man, by J. Bruno and J. Greenfield. Review
Life il por 70:11 My 28 '71. V. S. Navasky •

BRUNS, Bill
Fans boo him everywhere, and he loves it. Life 70:48-51 Ap 9 '71
Mad golfer. il pors Life 71:34-5 Jl 2 '71

BRUNS, Renee
At the Smithsonian, photography is treated with sophistication. il Pop Phot 68:52+ Ja '71
How the McLuhan generation speaks. il Pop Phot 68:106-9 Ja '71

BRUSH fires
How to outmaneuver a firestorm. J. Joseph. il Todays Health 49:34-9+ S '71

BRUSHES
Hardworking household brushes. il Bet Hom & Gard 49:120-1 D '71

BRUSHING of teeth. See Teeth—Care and hygiene

BRUSILOW, Anshel
Symphonic debacle; a new butterfly. J. Ardoin. Hi Fi 21:MA28-9 Ap '71 •

BRUSILOW, William
Your big chance. por Yachting 129:41+ Mr '71

BRUSSELS

Music

Report:
L'incoronazione di Poppea. L. Mueller. Opera N 35:32 F 13 '71
Purcell's Dido and Aeneas and John Blow's Venus and Adonis. L. Mueller. Opera N 35:32 Ap 10 '71

BRUSSELS international book fair. See Book fairs

BRUSSELS sprouts
Wanted: brussels sprouts in Oklahoma. L. Riotte. il Org Gard & Farm 18:56-7 Ag '71
See also
Cookery—Vegetables

BRUSTEIN, Robert
If an artist wants to be serious and respected and rich, famous and popular, he is suffering from cultural schizophrenia. il N Y Times Mag p 12-13+ S 26 '71
Theater. New Repub 165:26+ Jl 17 '71

BRUTUS, pseud.
Confessions of a stockbroker. il Atlan 227:46-51 Je '71
BRUYN, Louise
One woman's walk for peace. A. Lake. il pors Good H 173:70-1+ Jl '71 •
BRYAN, Bud
'29 Highboy project report. il Hot Rod 24:108-10 Ag '71
BRYAN, Frank M.
Catholic education aid: Yankee style. il America 125:174-5 S 18 '71
BRYAN, J. 3d
Algarve. il Holiday 49:48-9+ F '71
Hot dice, spinning wheels, and spurious beginnings have made Deauville. il Holiday 49:26-31+ My '71
Necropolis. il Nat R 23:821-2 Jl 27 '71
Pillow for el Caudillo? Nat R 23:1314-15 N 19 '71
BRYAN, Marcus R.
Secret of the sequence report. Flying 89:70-1+ N '71
BRYANS, Charles I. Jr
High blood pressure during pregnancy; ed. by E. Jacobs. Redbook 136:20+ F '71
BRYANT, Beth
San Francisco scene. il Mlle 72:180+ F '71
BRYANT, Jerry H.
Politics and the black novel. Nation 213:660-2 D 20 '71
BRYANT, Nelson
Lure of the surf. Atlan 227:108+ My '71
BRYANT, Peter
Piaget undermined? pors Newsweek 78:61-2 S 13 '71 •
BRYANT, William Cullen
Poems: Africa; Jomo Kenyatta; African chief. Negro Hist Bul 34:36-7 F '71
BRYANT park. See New York (city)—Parks and playgrounds
BRYDEN-BROOK, Simon
Catholic renewal in England. Chr Cent 88:372-5 Mr 24 '71
BRYN, Katherine
Sins of Salem. Sci Digest 69:29-31 My '71
BRZEZINSKI, Zbigniew
[Column] See issues of Newsweek
Japan's global engagement. For Affairs 50:270-82 Ja '72
BRZOSTOSKI, John
Carl Kempe collection. il Craft Horiz 31:22-6 Je '71
BUBBLE birth. See Childbirth
BUBBLE gum trading cards. See Advertising cards
BUBBLES
Borderland of burning bubbles. D. C. Blanchard. il Sat R 55:60-3 Ja 1 '72
BUBECK, Robert C. and others
Runoff of deicing salt: effect on Irondequoit Bay, Rochester, New York. bibliog il Science 172:1128-32 Je 11 '71
BUBEL, Michael. See Bubel, N. W. jt. auth.
BUBEL, Nancy W.
Chickens before eggs. il Org Gard & Farm 18:44-7 D '71
Columbines in the rhubarb. il Org Gard & Farm 18:56-7 My '71
Complete acre, or, Keep your dream and make it real! il Org Gard & Farm 18:40-4 Ap '71
Gardening with rock minerals. Org Gard & Farm 18:69-71 O '71
Notes by a new goat-keeper. il por Org Gard & Farm 18:104-11 Mr '71
Succeeding with succession crops. il Org Gard & Farm 18:44-9 Ja '71
What we learned about soybeans. il por Org Gard & Farm 18:60-3 Je '71
Wood chips hold our garden together. il por Org Gard & Farm 18:38-41 N '71
—and Bubel, Michael
Small-time hay-making. il Org Gard & Farm 18:98-101 Ag '71
BUBER, Martin
Martin Buber, by A. Hodes. Review
Sat R por 54:22 Jl 31 '71. M. Levin •
Martin Buber: friend of the court. D. J. Moore. il America 124:231-4 Mr 6 '71; Reply. J. M. Oesterreicher. 124:301 Mr 27 '71 •
BUBONIC plague. See Plague
BUCHAN, Perdita
Lotus; story. New Yorker 47:36-42 Mr 13 '71
BUCHANAN, Kenny
All the Scotsman managed to lose was $2. P. Putnam. il pors Sports Illus 34:54-5 F 22 '71 •
Fighting carpenter from Scotland; lightweight champion K. Buchanan. H. McIlvanney. il pors Sports Illus 34:30-2+ F 8 '71 •
Scot was a cut or two above the challenger. M. Kram. por Sports Illus 35:74+ S 27 '71 •
Scots wha hae. il por Newsweek 78:101 S 27 '71 •

BUCHANAN, William J.
Trial of Coronado. il Américas 23:28-38 Ja '71
BUCHER, Carl
Carl and Heidi Bucher need your body. B. Schwartz. il Craft Horiz 31:27-9+ Je '71 •
BUCHER, Giovanni Enrico
Price goes up. Newsweek 77:44 Ja 24 '71 •
BUCHER, Heidi
Carl and Heidi Bucher need your body. B. Schwartz. il Craft Horiz 31:27-9+ Je '71 •
BUCHER, Lloyd Mark
For Lloyd Bucher, a new job and haunting memories. R. Woodbury. por Life 71:97 D 10 '71 •
BUCHSBAUM, Arnold
By freighter to the Inca. il Américas 23:18-24 O '71
BUCHSBAUM, Walter H.
Attachments to your telephone. il Electr World 86:27-9+ Jl '71
CATV: its future starts now. il Electr World 85:39-41 Mr '71
Understand the system. il Pop Electr 35:52-3+ S '71
BUCHWALD, Art
Pro-football murder mystery; excerpt from Getting high in government circles. il Read Digest 99:78-9 N '71
Scholastis adolescum: a disease every kid has the cure for; excerpts from Sons of the great society. il Todays Health 49:44-5 S '71
about
Cruise director on the Titanic. T. Meehan. il pors N Y Times Mag p10-11+ Ja 2 '72 •
Spiro and the Buchwald blues. W. O'Toole. Commonweal 93:465 F 12 '71 •
BUCK, Clayton A. and others
Glycopeptides from the surface of control and virus-transformed cells. bibliog il Science 172:169-71 Ap 9 '71
BUCK, Joan
Friends as mirrors. Mlle 72:142-3+ F '71
BUCK, Pearl (Sydenstricker)
Coming of Jesus; excerpt from The story Bible. Ladies Home J 88:83+ D '71
Gifts of joy; story. Good H 173:66-7 D '71
Historic basis of friendship. Cur 130:3-5 Je '71
Visit with Pearl Buck; interview, ed. by C. Renshaw, jr. il pors Nat Wildlife 10:28-32 D '71
BUCK ISLAND REEF NATIONAL MONUMENT
Buck Island: underwater jewel. J. Greenberg and I. Greenberg. il Nat Geog 139:674-83 My '71
BUCKETS (pails)
Beyond the pail; inexpensive and colorful containers. N. Mandelbaum. il Ladies Home J 88:74-5 Je '71
BUCKINGHAM, Nash
Feeling like a goose. il por Outdoor Life 148:76-9+ S '71
BUCKLAND, Raymond
Witches are rising. B. Vachon. il pors Look 35:42-3 Ag 24 '71 •
BUCKLEY, Emerson
Place in the sun. F. Stevenson. il por Opera N 35:12-13 Mr 13 '71 •
BUCKLEY, Fergus Reid
Give power to the students. Nat R 23:424-5+ Ap 20 '71
Return to Lanzarote. Nat R 23:883 Ag 10 '71
Sham in the bullring. il Nat R 23:920-2 Ag 24 '71
BUCKLEY, James L.
Erosion of U.S. military strength; address, July 14, 1971. Vital Speeches 37:642-4 Ag 15 '71
about
Columbia conservatives for Buckley. J. Collins. Mlle 72:138 Ja '71 •
Education of freshman Senator Buckley. L. C. Dubois. il pors N Y Times Mag p8-9+ Ag 15 '71 •
Mr Buckley goes to Washington. C. Rabb. Commonweal 94:181-2 Ap 30 '71 •
BUCKLEY, Jim
No place to go but up. il pors Time 97:65 Ap 19 '71 •
BUCKLEY, John William
Other Buckley minds the business. il por Bsns W p54 Ja 30 '71 •
BUCKLEY, Kevin P.
Puppet pulls the strings. il Newsweek 78:25 O 4 '71
BUCKLEY, Marylou
Boris, dog of Formentera; poem. America 124:344 Ap 3 '71
Gifts; poem. America 125:559 D 25 '71
La iglesia de San Fernando; poem. America 125:234 O 2 '71

BUCKLEY, Patricia (Taylor)
Mrs William F. Buckley, jr. il pors Vogue 159:44-9 Ja 1 '72 *
BUCKLEY, Priscilla L.
Theater. Nat R 23:440 Ap 20 '71
BUCKLEY, Tom
Captain who commanded Lieutenant Calley. il por N Y Times Mag p8-9+ Je 20 '71
Is this written in the stars? See it through with Nguyen van Thieu. il pors N Y Times Mag p 14-15+ S 26 '71
Mafia tries a new tune. il Harper 243:46-7+ Ag '71
Murphy among the meat-eaters. il pors N Y Times Mag p 10-11+ D 19 '71
Palm Beach is the big stadium... il N Y Times Mag p26-9+ Mr 21 '71
BUCKLEY, Walter B.
Fire-alarm system guards a police station. il Am City 86:86+ Mr '71
BUCKLEY, William Frank, 1881-1958, family
Battling Buckley women. S. Sheehan. il Mc-Calls 99:82-3+ O '71
BUCKLEY, William Frank, 1925-
End of the United Nations? address, October 29, 1971. il Nat R 23:1300-1+ N 19 '71
Notes & asides. See issues of National review
On the right. See issues of National review
Say it isn't so, Mr President. il pors N Y Times Mag p8-9+ Ag 1 '71
Week's journal. New Yorker 47:36-43+ Ag 21; 36-42+ Ag 28 '71
William F. Buckley jr talks about compulsory unionism; interview. pors Nations Bsns 59:32-4+ Je '71

about

Bill Buckley: blithe spirit of the right. J. Reddy. por Read Digest 99:112-6 S '71 *
Buckley papers. Newsweek 78:21-2 Ag 2 '71 *
Buckley's brief; AFTRA membership. Newsweek 77:61 Ja 25 '71 *
Buckley's prank. por Time 98:43 Ag 2 '71 *
Cruising speed, by W. F. Buckley, jr. Review
Harper 243:134-6 N '71. L. DuBois *
Department of amplification. E. McCormack. New Yorker 47:121-3 D 18 '71 *
Firing line goes public. Cyclops. por Life 71:11 Jl 16 '71 *
Man in motion. D. K. Mano. Nat R 23:1121+ O 8 '71 *
BUCKNER, Sally
Christmas lullaby. Chr Cent 88:1491-2 D 22 '71
BUCKS (basketball team) See Basketball teams
BUCKWALTER, Len
Appliance repairs anyone can make. il Mech Illus 67:98-101+ O '71
Basics of washer repair. il Mech Illus 67:91-3+ D '71
Fun & fear of night flight. il pors Mech Illus 67:89-91+ N '71
Portable TVs you can play at a picnic, on a patio, by a pool. il Pop Mech 136:104-7 Jl '71
Truly instant heating element. il Mech Illus 67:90-1+ Ja '71
What cable TV may mean to you. il Mech Illus 68:76-8+ Ja '72
Whatever happened to the airbus? il Mech Illus 67:83-5+ Ap '71
Worldwide adventures on the airwaves. il Pop Sci 198:60+ Ap '71
BUCKWHEAT
Buckwheat does it all. R. M. Robinson. il Org Gard & Farm 18:33-5 Je '71
BUDAPEST string quartet
Four decades of the Budapest quartet: a discography, 1926-1966. S. Smolian. il Am Rec G 37:220-4+ D '70
BUDD, David
David Budd: continental drift. L. Anderson. il por Art N 70:32-3+ Sum '71 *
BUDDHA and Buddhism
Appeal of Buddhism: a Christian perspective. D. K. Swearer. il Chr Cent 88:1289-93 N 3 '71
Church and state in Cambodia. J. C. Haughey. il America 125:279-81 O 16 '71
See also
Zen Buddhism
BUDDHISTS
Buddhist role in South Vietnam. J. C. Haughey. il America 125:259-62 O 9 '71
BUDGE, Donald
Commercial. il New Yorker 47:21-3 Ag 7 '71 *
BUDGET
See also
Program budgeting

Great Britain
Britain faces up to recession. G. J. Henry. Forbes 107:51 My 1 '71
Two-nations budget? il Time 97:37 Ap 12 '71

United States
Big jump foreseen in deficit: why. U S News 71:106 S 20 '71
Budget game. Nation 212:227-8 F 22 '71
Budget of the United States government, fiscal year 1972; excerpts. Dept State Bul 64:242-5 F 22 '71
Budget that looks like a campaign burden. il Bsns W p32 Jl 17 '71
Budgeting toward a new prosperity. il por Newsweek 77:68-70 F 8 '71
Cut, cut, cut, for a bigger budget. il Newsweek 79:49 Ja 10 '72
Deficit or a surplus? U S News 71:46 Ag 9 '71
Double-talk bookkeeping; military budget. R. F. Kaufman. Nation 213:429-32 N 1 '71
Doubts about an iffy budget. R. J. Saulnier. por Nations Bsns 59:37 Jl '71
Federal R&D: domestic problems get new efforts but little money. A. L. Hammond. Science 171:657-8+ F 19 '71
5 presidents and red ink: Nixon's deficits setting a new record. il U S News 71:24-5 Ag 16 '71
Hiding billions from Congress. L. Fisher. Nation 213:486-90 N 15 '71
Lift from the budget is mostly behind us. il Fortune 83:22 Je '71
Mr Nixon's course? F. S. Meyer. Nat R 23:86 Ja 26 '71
Nixon spends to spur faster growth; with editorial comment. il Bsns W p66-9, 88 Ja 30 '71
Nixon's secret plan: the budget. R. Du Boff. Commonweal 93:543-5 Mr 5 '71
Nixon's spending plan for 1972. il Time 97:12 F 8 '71
Policy of self-fulfilling prophecy. il Time 97:76-7 F 8 '71
Rosy projection for fiscal 1972. America 124:140 F 13 '71
'72 budget: Nixon proposes modest increases for science. J. Walsh. il Science 171:459-60+ F 5 '71
Special report; fiscal 1972 budget; symposium, with editorial comment. il Aviation W 94:9, 14-19 F 1 '71
To be first in everything. il Sci N 99:93-6 F 6 '71
To soup up the economy: 229 billions. il U S News 70:15-16 F 8 '71
U.S. budget and the trillion-dollar economy. il Sr Schol 98:18-19 Ap 5 '71
U.S. is running out of money. il Time 99:26 Ja 10 '72
See also
United States—Appropriations and expenditures
BUDGET, Household
Family money management. See issues of Better homes and gardens
How a practical family managed its money. il Changing T 25:6-11 My '71
How one woman tackles her grocery bill. J. Boyd. Bet Hom & Gard 49:146-8 N '71
How to enjoy spending more for less. J. L. Block. il Todays Health 49:55-6 Mr '71
New way to manage family finances. Y. Postelle. il Mech Illus 67:65-7+ S '71
1971 ways to save money. H. Alpert. il Har Yrs 11:6-13+ Ja '71
Spring 1970 cost estimates for urban family budgets; with table. E. Ruiz. Mo Labor R 94:59-61 Ja '71
BUDGET, Municipal. See Municipal finance
BUDGET, Personal
See also
Childrens allowances
BUDGET, School. See School finance
BUDGETS, Library. See Libraries—Finance
BUDGETS, School library. See School libraries —Finance
BUDINGER, Thomas F. and others
Visual phenomena noted by human subjects on exposure to neutrons of energies less than 25 million electron volts. bibliog il Science 172:868-70 My 21 '71
BUDORCAS. See Takins
BUDS
Greening of a woodland. il Nat Wildlife 9:19 Ap '71
BUDWORM moths. See Moths
BUECHNER, Frederick
Authors & editors. B. A. Bannon. por Pub W 199:11-12 Mr 29 '71 *
BUECHNER, Robert D.
Warring of the green. il Parks & Rec 6:57+ My '71

BUEDING, Ernest. See Rogers, S. H. jt. auth.

BUELER, Lois E.
Limbo; or, Who the devil is Ruth Gordon? Sat R 54:58 O 30 '71

BUELNA, Joseph L.
Creative writing. the inner eye, il Wilson Lib Bul 45:750-3 Ap '71

BUENOS AIRES
Description
Silent tour of Buenos Aires. G. Nogués. il Américas 23:24-31 O '71

History
May revolution. O. González Roura. il Américas 23:36-9 My '71

BUENOS AIRES opera house. See Opera houses

BUETER, Robert J.
Television. Chr Cent 88:1530-1 D 29 '71

about
Third Haselden fellow. Chr Cent 88:826 Jl 7 '71 *

BUETTNER, Carl F.
Money down the drain. il Am City 86:60-3 Ag '71

BUFANO, Beniamino Benvenuto
Bufano; work of San Francisco's own sculptor. il Sunset 147:32+ D '71 *

BUFFALO, N.Y.
Graders take on the big drifts. il Am City 86:22 Ja '71
Spreading out Buffalo's burden of snow. il Sci N 100:341 N 20 '71

Police
Lineups in blue; antagonism between blacks and police. Time 98:35 Jl 26 '71

BUFFALO Bills (football club) See Football clubs

BUFFALO Braves (basketball team) See Basketball teams

BUFFALO hunting
Killing buffalo to save buffalo. W. Davis. il Mech Illus 67:86+ O '71

BUFFALO tagging. See Animal tagging

BUFFALOES
Mountain bison. G. M. Christman. il Am West 8:44-7 My '71
See also
National bison range

BUFFER solutions
Buffer combinations for mammalian cell culture. H. Eagle. bibliog il Science 174: 500-3 O 29 '71
Stress collisions and constants. D. L. Morris. il Chem 44:15-19 My '71

BUFFET meals
Bachelor buffet. il Bet Hom & Gard 49:26 F '71
Rice table idea. il Sunset 147:58-9 Ag '71
Well-planned buffet. with recipes. J. Jaffry. il Am Home 74:60+ N '71
See also
Christmas meals

BUFFETS (furniture)
Build a buffet for plug-in parties, formal & informal. J. Heckroth and D. Ashe. il Bet Hom & Gard 49:60-3 Mr '71
Handsome buffet that leads a double life. W. C. Leckey. il Pop Mech 136:140-3+ D '71

BUFFUM, Marjorie
Watercolor effect with enamels. il Ceram Mo 19:27-9 D '71

BUG traps. See Insect traps

BUGGING. See Electronics in criminal investigation, espionage, etc.

BUGNER, Joe
Our 'enery gets the 'ook. J. Kirshenbaum. pors Sports Illus 34:26-7 Mr 29 '71 *

BUGS, Artificial. See Fishing lures, flies, etc.

BUHRMASTER, Kenneth E.
Association and the school board. pors Todays Ed 60:48-50 My '71

BUILDING
See also
Building sites
Foundations
Helicopters in building
House construction
Insulation (heat)
Shoring and underpinning
Systems building
Wind-pressure

Contracts and specifications
New method to cut building costs; construction-manager approach. il U S News 71: 74-5 Ag 9 '71
Recommendations on payment practices issued by construction industry council. Arch Rec 150:57-8 Ag '71

Cost
Budget control of the phased construction project; excerpt from Professional construction management and project administration. W. B. Foxhall. il Arch Rec 150: 67-8 O '71
Building costs; indexes and indicators. W. H. Edgerton. See issues of Architectural record
Construction markets; cross-section and perspective. J. E. Carlson. Arch Rec 150:76 O '71
Let me make one thing clear; New Orleans $130 million pleasure dome. J. Kirshenbaum. il Sports Illus 34:34-6+ Je 7 '71
New method to cut building costs; construction-manager approach. il U S News 71:74-5 Ag 9 '71
See also
School buildings—Cost

Estimates
Budget control of the phased construction project; excerpt from Professional construction management and project administration. W. B. Foxhall. il Arch Rec 150: 67-8 O '71

Finance
See also
Housing finance
Mortgages

Standards
Big battles over rules for builders; federal standards for local building codes. il Bsns W p48-9 Ja 1 '72
Performance criteria in building. J. R. Wright. il Sci Am 224:16-25 Mr '71

BUILDING, Iron and steel
Last cast iron; New York city. C. Robinson. il Arch Forum 135:46-9 S '71

BUILDING and earthquakes. See Earthquakes and building

BUILDING codes. See Building laws and regulations

BUILDING costs. See Building—Cost

BUILDING estimates. See Building—Estimates

BUILDING failures
Parting shots; the 14 victims of Sallen. R. Chelminski. il Life 70:78-9 Je 11 '71

BUILDING fittings
Building components. il Arch Rec 149:153-4 Mr; 150:127-8 Ag '71
Product reports. See issues of Architectural record

BUILDING industry. See Construction industry

BUILDING laws and regulations
Big battles over rules for builders; federal standards for local building codes. il Bsns W p48-9 Ja 1 '72
Performance criteria in building. J. R. Wright. il Sci Am 224:16-25 Mr '71
Why builders donate schools. Bsns W p58 O 9 '71
See also
Zoning law

BUILDING machinery. See Construction machinery

BUILDING materials
Big decorative build-up. il House & Gard 139:72-3 Ja '71
Building components. il Arch Rec 149:153-4 Mr; 150:127-8 Ag '71
Ideas to build on. J. H. Ingersoll. See issues of House beautiful
Mud below, brass above. il Newsweek 77:108+ Ap 12 '71
New money-saving materials. B. Gladstone. il Am Home 74:62+ My '71
Product reports. See issues of Architectural record
Products to make your job look professional. R. F. Dempewolff. il Pop Mech 135:110-11+ My '71
Standard-sizes chart. Am Home 74:76 My '71
See also
Fireproof construction
Lumber
Plastics in building
Plywood
Wood

BUILDING materials industry
See also
United States plywood-Champion papers, inc.

BUILDING materials industry—*Continued*

Finance

Building materials: mostly bright, with a few clouds. il Bsns W p44-6 D 25 '71

Building materials; with yardsticks of management performance. il Forbes 109:113-14 Ja 1 '72

BUILDING sites

Ever watch your farm disappear? G. Logsdon. Farm J 95:53 Mr '71

Goldfinger house, Waccabuc, N.Y. il Arch Rec 149:78-81 mid-My '71

Residence in Waccabuc, N.Y. il Arch Rec 149:28-31 mid-My '71

   See also

Hillside architecture

Housing projects—Site planning

BUILDING trades unions. See Construction trades unions

BUILDING workers. See Construction workers

BUILDINGS

Focus; monthly review of notable buildings. See issues of Architectural forum

Forum; monthly review of events and ideas. See issues of Architectural forum

   See also

Airport buildings

Architecture

Building failures

Public buildings

Skyscrapers

   also subhead Buildings under names of cities, e.g. Dallas—Buildings

Equipment

   See Building fittings

BUILDINGS, Abandoned

Housing abandonment. Arch Forum 134:42-5 Ap '71

They board up the windows. il Bsns W p90 My 1 '71

BUILDINGS, Fireproof. See Fireproof construction

BUILDINGS, Moving of. See Moving of structures, etc.

BUILDINGS, Prefabricated

Architect speaks his mind; interview. ed. by A. Stagg. M. Goldfinger. por House & Gard 139:16+ Je '71

Efficient multi-story space frame built from a few basic components; Mah-LeMessurier system. il Arch Rec 149:139-44 Ap '71

Steel prefabs that can be stacked; motel built of Anvan modules. il Bsns W p27 O 30 '71

Technology; Depondt component building system. il Arch Forum 135:66-9 Jl '71

Technology, first U.S. systems-built highrise; Futura in Yonkers, N.Y. M. Villecco. il Arch Forum 135:68-70 N '71

Technology; Hardy Holzman Pfeiffer projects. M. Villecco. il Arch Forum 134:52-5 Ap '71

Technology; Operation Breakthrough. M. Villecco. il Arch Forum 134:58-62 My '71

   See also

Houses, Prefabricated

School buildings, Prefabricated

BUILDINGS, Remodeled

How do railroad stations retire? V. A. Schlich. il Har Yrs 11:14-16 D '71

New schools at a bargain rate. il Life 71: 72-4 O 22 '71

   See also

Houses, Remodeled

BUILDINGS, Restoration of. See Architecture —Conservation and restoration

BUILDINGS, Round

   See also

Geodesic domes

BUILT in furniture. See Furniture, Built in

BUKALSKI, Peter J.

Collecting classic films; with filmography. il Am Lib 2:475-9 My '71

BULAT, M. and Živković, B.

Origin of 5-hydroxyindoleacetic acid in the spinal fluid. bibliog il Science 173:738-40 Ag 20 '71

BULBS

Autumn color from bulbs. J. Hudak. il Horticulture 49:38+ Ag '71

Bulbs go in and out of the bins. Sunset 147: 242 O '71

Bulbs: plant now for a spectacular spring. H. Mason. il Bet Hom & Gard 49:72-7+ O '71

Expert gives advice on bulb planting. D. Feldon. il Home Gard 58:16+ O '71

Five bulbs for gardeners who seek unusual color or form. il Sunset 147:189+ S '71

Keeping bulbs turned on. T. Cruso. il McCalls 98:48+ My '71

Little bulbs. il Sunset 147:94-7 N '71

Little-known bulbs. W. B. Harris. House & Gard 140:12+ Jl; 26+ Ag '71

Seven little bulb gardens you can plant on a budget! il Home Gard 58:28-31 O '71

Uncommon bulbs for indoors. L. Cutak. il Horticulture 49:32-6 O '71

   See also

Forcing (plants)

Geest industries, ltd.

Narcissus

Nerines

Ornithogalums

Tulips

BULBS, Light. See Electric lamps, Incandescent

BULGARIA

   See also

Opera—Bulgaria

BULGER, Paul G.

Youth education in conservation, a vital force. Cons 26:33 Ag '71

BULKELEY, Morgan Gardner

Crowbar governor was a man of many parts. O. D. Smith. pors Nations Bsns 59:42-3 Ja '71 *

BULKHEADS

Otter-proof bulkheading. E. W. Jones. il Parks & Rec 6:43-4+ My '71

BULL, Hedley

New balance of power in Asia and the Pacific. For Affairs 49:669-81 Jl '71

BULL Bailey, I love you; story. See Tauke, M. S.

BULL fights. See Bullfights

BULL sharks. See Sharks

BULLARD, E. John

John Sloan as an illustrator. il Am Artist 35:52+ O '71

BULLETIN boards

For the elementary teacher: bulletin boards and a learning environment. il Sch Arts 71:6-7 D '71

For the elementary teacher: holiday stereotypes. V. J. Popolizio. il Sch Arts 71:8-9 S '71

BULLETINS, Library. See Library publications

BULLETS

Strange ways of bullets. W. Davis. il Mech Illus 67:82+ F '71

   See also

Cartridges

BULLFIGHTERS

Hats off at the comeback of an old renegade: Antonio Bienvenida. J. McCormick. por Sports Illus 35:56-7 Jl 26 '71

Old master back in the ring; L. M. Dominguin; with photographs by G. Parks. Life 71:74-9 N 5 '71

Real Escamillo. R. D. Daniels. il Opera N 35: 14-15 F 6 '71

Sham in the bullring. F. R. Buckley. Nat R 23:920-2 Ag 24 '71

   See also

Fulton, J.

Ordóñez, A.

BULLFIGHTS

Graceful ritual of bloody death; black matador R. Chibanga. il pors Ebony 26:78-80+ Mr '71

Hats off at the comeback of an old renegade: Antonio Bienvenida. J. McCormick. il Sports Illus 35:56-7 Jl 26 '71

Old master back in the ring; L. M. Dominguin; with photographs by G. Parks. Life 71:74-9 N 5 '71

On offering the bull his body; matador Ordóñez in Madrid plaza, Las Ventas. J. McCormick. il pors Sports Illus 34:26-8+ Je 14 '71

Sham in the bullring. F. R. Buckley. Nat R 23:920-2 Ag 24 '71

BULLHEADS

Chemical languages of fishes. J. H. Todd. il Sci Am 224:98-106+ My '71

BULLINS, Ed

Fabulous Miss Marie. Criticism

   New Yorker 47:94-5 Mr 20 '71 *

In New England winter. Criticism

   New Yorker 46:72 F 6 '71 *

BULLOCK, Michael

(tr) See Krolow, K. Love poem

BULLS

Using growth records to buy a bull. B. Eftink. il Suc Farm 69:no3 D14 F '71

BULL'S eye and the scorpion; story. See Diamond, S.

BULWER-LYTTON, Edward

Are we the coming race? R. L. Wolff. Atlan 228:104-6 S '71 *

BUMPER stickers. See Labels
BUMPERS, Dale
Dale Bumpers of Arkansas. por Time 97:19
My 31 '71 *
Reports & comment: Arkansas. B. Herget.
Atlan 227:14+ F '71 *
BUMPERS, Automobiles. See Automobiles—
Bumpers
BUMPUS, Jerry
In Utica; story. il Esquire 76:58-9+ Ag '71
BUMS. See Tramps
BUNCHE, Ralph Johnson
Man without color. por Time 98:34+ D 20
'71 *
Never did he despair. por Newsweek 78:44+
O 11 '71 *
Notes and comment. New Yorker 47:15-21
Ja 1 '72 *
Obituary
Nation 213:677 D 27 '71
Newsweek por 78:33 D 20 '71
Soon-to-be-forgotten peacemaker? Chr Cent
88:1517 D 29 '71 *
BUNDESWEHR (West German armed forces)
See Germany (Federal Republic)—Armed
forces
BUNDY, Mary Lee
Crisis in library education. il por Library J
96:797-80 Mr 1 '71
BUNDY, William P.
[Column] See issues of Newsweek
Death of doctrine. por Newsweek 77:44 F 15
'71
New tides in Southeast Asia. For Affairs 49:
187-200 Ja '71
about
Brouhaha at Foreign affairs. Time 98:15-16
S 6 '71 *
Test for an editor. il por Newsweek 78:74
S 6 '71 *
BUNK beds. See Beds
BUNKER, Ellsworth
Can South Vietnam survive without U.S? in-
terview, ed. by W. S. Merick. il por U S
News 71:24-6 Jl 5 '71
Review of progress and problems in Viet-
Nam; address, January 21, 1971. Dept State
Bul 64:206-11 F 15 '71
Vietnamese election campaign; instruction to
U.S. personnel in Vietnam. Dept State Bul
65:9 Jl 5 '71
about
Anguish of a Yankee gentleman. S. Cloud.
il por Time 98:12 S 13 '71 *
Democracy in reverse? Newsweek 78:45 Ag
30 '71 *
New blow to U.S. goals in Vietnam. il por
U S News 71:26 S 6 '71 *
Politics vs. democracy. Newsweek 78:25 S
6 '71 *
Still a Thieu-way race in South Viet Nam.
il por Time 98:23-4 Ag 30 '71 *
BUNKS. See Beds
BUNN, H. Franklin
Differences in the interaction of 2,3-di-
phosphoglycerate with certain mam-
malian hemoglobins. bibliog il Science
172:1049-50 Je 4 '71
BUNSEN, Robert Wilhelm Eberhard
Bunsen, the man behind the burner. por
Chem 44:4 Ap '71 *
BUNSTER, Enrique
Cape Horn. il Américas 23:2-11 Mr '71
BUNT, John S.
New lab beneath the Bahamian Sea; with
biographical sketch. il por Sea Front 17:
171-4, 190 My '71
BUNTING, Basil
Struggler in the wilderness. R. Guedalla.
Nation 212:216-18 F 15 '71 *
BUNTING, John Richard, 1925-
Economic rationale for social involvement;
address, September 24, 1971. Vital Speeches
38:51-3 N 1 '71
about
Bunting's bet. por Time 97:72 Je 28 '71 *
BUNTON twins. See Siamese twins
BUNYAN, Paul (legendary hero)
Drama
Big Paul Bunyan. A. Thane. Plays 30:29-36
Ap '71
BURAWA, Alexander W.
4-channel stereo is here. il Pop Electr 35:
47-51 Jl '71
Look at the PC market. il Pop Electr 1:
46-50 Ja '72
Surplus scene. il Pop Electr 1:116 Ja '72
BURBANK, R. D. and Jones, G. R.
Xenon hexafluoride: structural crystallogra-
phy of tetrameric phases. bibliog il Science
171:485-7 F 5 '71

BURCH, Lucius E. Jr
Little wisdom gathered from much folly. Liv
Wildn 35:32-3 Spr '71
BURCH, Monte
How to customize your hunting-knife han-
dle. il Pop Mech 136:110-12 D '71
BURCH, Robert
New realism. bibliog f il Horn Bk 47:257-
64 Je '71
BURCHENAL, Joseph H.
Can leukemia be cured? il Parents Mag 46:
68-9+ N '71
BURCHETT, Wilfred
Poor Wilfred Burchett. W. F. Buckley.
jr. Nat R 23:668 Je 15 '71 *
BURCHFIEL, J. L. See Duffy, F. H. jt. auth.
BURCK, Charles G.
Books and ideas. Fortune 83:160-1 Ja '71
Happy days for California wines. il Fortune
84:78-82+ S '71
How the Tisches run their little store. il
por Fortune 83:158-61+ My '71
Little railroad that could. il Fortune 84:74-7
Jl '71
—and others
Businessmen in the news. See issues of For-
tune
BURCK, Gilbert
Famine years for the arms makers. il For-
tune 83:162-7+ My '71
That ever expanding pension balloon. il For-
tune 84:100-3+ O '71
Transportation's troubled abundance. il For-
tune 84:59-62+ Jl '71
Union power and the new inflation. il For-
tune 83:65-9+ F '71; Same abr. with title
High cost of wage inflation. Read Digest 98:
139-43 Ap '71
BURDE, Ronald M. and others
Homograft rejection delayed by treatment of
donor tissue in vitro with antilymphocyte
serum. bibliog il Science 173:921-3 S 3 '71
BURDEN, Carter
Carter Burden question. T. Meehan. il por
N Y Times Mag p33+ N 7 '71; Discussion.
p6+ N 28 '71 *
Responsibilities of Carter Burden. W. F.
Buckley, jr. Nat R 23:557 My 18 '71 *
BURDEN, Charles A.
Who employs the mentally restored and
why? Ment Hy 55:487-91 O '71
BURDEN, Ernest
Slide presentations; excerpt from Architec-
tural delineations, a photographic approach
to presentation. il Arch Rec 150:55-8 Jl '71
BUREAU of Indian affairs. See United States
—Indian affairs, Bureau of
BUREAU of international commerce. See
United States—International commerce, Bu-
reau of
BUREAU of labor statistics. See United States
—Labor statistics, Bureau of
BUREAU of land management. See United
States—Land management, Bureau of
BUREAU of sport fisheries and wildlife. See
United States—Fish and wildlife service
BUREAU of veterinary medicine. See United
States—Food and drug administration—
Veterinary medicine, Bureau of
BUREAUCRACY
Bureaucratic odyssey of a space mapping
camera; with editorial comment. E. Driscoll.
Sci N 100:354, 362-3 N 27 '71
Down the bureaucracy! M. P. Dumont.
Trans-Action 7:10-12+ O '70
Environment and the bureaucracy; Hart-
McGovern bill. J. L. Sax. New Repub
164:9-10 Je 19 '71
Is bureaucracy out of control? il U S News
70:61-4 My 17 '71
Mess in Washington: how it got that way;
excerpts from message to Congress, March
25,1971. R. M. Nixon. il por U S News 70:
78-80 Ap 12 '71
Red-tape jungle: spreading, costing billions.
il U S News 71:29-31 Jl 19 '71; Same abr.
with title Red tape on the Potomac. Read
Digest 99:110-12 O '71
BUREAUCRATS. See Public officers
BUREN, Daniel
Critics choice: Daniel Buren. E. C. Baker.
Art N 70:25+ Mr '71 *
BURFORD, Lolah
Story behind the book: Vice avenged. B. A.
Bannon. por Pub W 200:52-3 Jl 12 '71 *
BURFORD, William S.
Gymnos; poem. Nation 213:604 D 6 '71
(ed) See Proust, M. Lunch
(ed) See Proust, M. Proust's prefaces to Rus-
kin
BURG, Mike. See Burg, S.
BURG, Sumner
Therapy in the gym. il por Time 97:47 F
15 '71 *

BURGER, Warren Earl
Burger: don't look for courts to reshape society; excerpts from address, September 17, 1971. por U S News 71:19 O 4 '71
Chief justice looks at crime and the courts; interview. por Read Digest 98:113-16 Ap '71; Same with title Our creaking courts. 98:217-19+ My '71
Court reform; address, March 12, 1971. Vital Speeches 37:386-90 Ap 15 '71
Racial balance in every school is not required; excerpts from remarks, August 31, 1971. por U S News 71:23 S 13 '71
Slow justice is inadequate justice; interview. il por Forbes 108.21-3 Jl 1 '71
State of the federal judiciary; address, August 10, 1970. Forbes 108:15-18 Jl 1 '71
Three points of view from the Court. Time 98:10-11 Jl 12 '71
Unruly lawyers are menace; excerpts from address, May 18, 1971. por U S News 70:83 My 31 '71; Same. Cur Hist 61:111+ Ag '71
Words for a contentious profession; excerpts from address. Time 97:52 My 31 '71

about

From Burger: a call for action to stop freeing the guilty. por U S News 71:33 Jl 5 '71 •
Plea for civility. por Time 97:52 My 31 '71 •
BURGESS, Anthony, pseud.
Canterbury tales; with drawings by Z. Blum. Horizon 13:44-59 Spr '71
Is America falling apart? il N Y Times Mag p99-104 N 7 '71
Letter from Europe (cont) Am Scholar 40: 514+; 41:139-42 Sum, Wint '71

about

Algonquin legend. M. Duffy. por Time 97:80+ Mr 22 '71 •
MF. R. McInery. Commonweal 94:290-1 My 28 '71 •
BURGESS, Jackson
How I gave up fly fishing and became a credit to the community. il Field & S 75: 70-1+ Mr '71
BURGESS, Lorraine Marshall
Fuchsias. il Horticulture 49:38-9 Jl '71
BURGESS, Robert F.
Shark vs porpoise. bibliog il Sci Digest 69: 36-40 Je '71
BURGHARDT, Gordon M.
Chemical-cue preferences of newborn snakes: influence of prenatal maternal experience. bibliog il Science 171:921-3 Mr 5 '71
BURGIN, Bryan E.
Hunting accident report for 1970. il Cons 26:9 Ag '71
BURGLAR alarms
Build a multi-sensor alarm. C. R. Lewart. il Radio-Electr 42:58-9 N '71
Burglar alarms for the home: choose with care. Bsns W p87 Mr 27 '71
Campguard, intruder alarm for campers. J. G. Busse. il Pop Sci 198:114-15 Ap '71
Electronic security systems. J. Frye. por Electr World 85:47-8 F '71
How electronics can guard your home. R. M. Benrey. il Pop Sci 198:92-5 Ja '71
Inexpensive alarms scare off burglars. H. Wicks. il Pop Mech 136:144-5 Jl '71
Pick the right system for you. J. Squires. il Radio-Electr 42:23-7+ N '71
Professional intruder; fire alarm. G. Meyerle. il Pop Electr 35:61-5 D '71
Reliable electronic intrusion alarm. G. M. Presson. il Electr World 86:31 S '71
Rising wages of fear. il Time 97:80+ My 24 '71
24 easy-to-build burglar alarms. R. M. Marston. il Radio-Electr 42:23-6 Je; 38-41 Jl; 46-9 Ag: 54-7 S '71
Ultrasonic alarm shoos off intruders. R. Day. il Pop Sci 199:115 D '71
BURGLAR alarms, Automobile. See Automobiles—Protection against theft
BURGLAR alarms, Boat. See Boats—Protection against theft
BURGLAR alarms, Motorcycle. See Motorcycles—Protection against theft
BURGLARY and burglars
Burglars in the suburbs. Newsweek 78:102 O 4 '71
BURGLARY insurance. See Insurance, Burglary
BURGLARY protection
Check these security measures before renting an apartment. Good H 173:192 O '71
Fortress on 78th street; with account by K. Thorsen. editorial comment and questionnaire. il Life 71:3; 26-36 N 19; 3 D 10 '71
Giving robbers the cold shoulder. Todays Health 49:41 F '71

Here's a plan thieves don't like: Operation Identification. Bet Hom & Gard 49:126 Mr '71
How to protect your home with lights. R. Day. il Mech Illus 67:120+ Mr '71
How you help the burglar. L. Torok. il por Pop Mech 136:86-7 S '71
Security for your home; more urgent than ever. J. H. Ingersoll. House B 113:62+ N '71
Some minimum security precautions. Consumer Rep 36:103 F '71
See also
Burglar alarms
Cameras—Protection against theft
BURGNER, Jack W.
Children's sculpture. il Sch Arts 71:42-4 O '71
BURGOS trial. See Trials—Spain
BURGUNDY (wines) See Wine
BURIAL at sea
Deep six; trend to burials at sea. il Newsweek 79:43 Ja 10 '72
BURIAL grounds. See Cemeteries
BURIAN, Jarka M.
Scenic world of Joseph Svoboda. il por Sat R 54:35-7+ Ag 28 '71
BURIED treasure. See Treasure trove
BURK, C. John
Outer Banks revisited. il Nat Parks & Con Mag 45:4-7 Je '71
BURK, Dale A.
Mining the national forests. il Nation 212:110-13 Ja 25 '71
Timber vs. trout. Field & S 75:12+ Ja '71
BURKARD, Michael
Elkin poems; Roots; poems. Poetry 118: 156-61 Je '71
Three lost poems. Poetry 119:144-7 D '71
BURKE, Frances Marie. See Kenney, F. M. B.
BURKE, James A.
Excerpt from letter, March 1, 1971. Cong Digest 50:115+ Ap '71
BURKE, Michael
Sports. R. Kahn. il Esquire 76:20 Ag '71 •
BURKE, R. E. and others
Mammalian motor units: physiological-histochemical correlation in three types in cat gastrocnemius. bibliog il Science 174: 709-12 N 12 '71
BURKE, Roseanne
Odyssey in an antique land. il Travel 136:48-53 Jl '71
BURKE CANYON strike, 1892. See Coeur d' Alene strike, 1892
BURKERT, George
Cops as pushers. il Time 98:17-18 N 8 '71 •
BURKETT, Jessie
Molding history. R. J. Lynch. il por Har Yrs 11:41-3 Ag '71 •
BURKHART, Kitsi
Women in prison. il Ramp Mag 9:20-9 Je '71
BURKS, David D.
Cuba today. Cur Hist 60:108-11+ F '71
BURLING tract. See Fairfax County, Va.—Parks and reserves
BURLINGTON, N.C.
Man who was cut out for the job; excerpt from Black coach. P. Jordan. il Sports Illus 35:90-4+ O 11 '71
BURLINGTON COUNTY, N.J. library, Mount Holly
Mount Holly, N.J: a new county center. il Library J 96:3985 D 1 '71
BURLINGTON Industries, Inc.
Burlington's reach for identity. J. Poindexter. il Duns 97:69-70+ F '71
Clarence Finley's magic carpet ride; black man president of Charm-Tred-Monticello division. il pors Ebony 26:58-60+ F '71
BURLINGTON Northern, Inc.
Merger that started on the right track. il Bsns W p70-1 Je 12 '71
BURLS, Redwood. See Redwood burls
BURMA
See also
Guerrillas—Burma
Pagan
Rangoon
World war, 1939-1945—Campaigns and battles —Burma
BURNAND, Audrey B.
What bird's nests are these? il Nat Wildlife 9 :24 Ag '71
BURNE-JONES, Sir Edward Coley, bart
Book that never was, by J. R. Dunlap. Review
Pub W il 200:45-6 D 6 '71. C. B. Grannis •
BURNELL, Brian, jr
Follow-up: command performance. M. Davidson. il por Good H 172:50+ Je '71 •

BURNERS, Gas. See Gas burners—Control
BURNETT, Carol
Carol Burnett has never looked better. il
pors Ladies Home J 88:100-1+ D '71 *
Carol Burnett show. Cyclops. il por Life 70:
10 Ap 2 '71 *
Here's to you, Mrs Hamilton; with report
by J. Downs. il pors Life 70:92-5+ My 14
'71 *
My friend, Carol Burnett; ed. by J. N. Bell.
J. Andrews. il pors Good H 174:57-9+ Ja
'72 *
BURNETT, Guy J.
Behind the UL label. il Electr World 85:25-7+
Ap '71
BURNETT, Dame Ivy Compton-. See Compton-
Burnett, I.
BURNETT, Leo
Leo the lion. por Time 97:78 Je 21 '71 *
BURNETT, Leo, company. See Advertising
agencies
BURNETT, Robin
DDT residues: distribution of concentra-
tions in emerita analoga (stimpson) along
coastal California. bibliog il Science 174:
606-8 N 5 '71
BURNETT, Virgil
Mummy; poem. Poetry 118:342 S '71
BURNEY, Victoria K.
Home visitation and parent involvement. To-
days Ed 60:10-11 O '71
BURNHAM, Donald Clemens
Corporate do-gooder at the top. por Bsns W
p66 O 2 '71 *
BURNHAM, J. Bernard
What liberals don't understand about Viet-
nam. Nat R 23:77-80 Ja 26 '71
BURNHAM, James
Letter from Greece. Nat R 23:1169-70 O 22
'71
Notes from the road. Nat R 23:191 F 23 '71
Protracted conflict. See issues of National
review
SST: dead duck or phoenix? Nat R 23:361 Ap
6 '71
about
Cheerful James. Nation 213:643-4 D 20 '71 *
BURNHAM, Murry
About face! il Outdoor Life 147:90-3 Ap '71
BURNHAM, Sophy
Heroin babies: going cold turkey at birth.
il N Y Times Mag p 18-19+ Ja 9 '72
BURNING of land
See also
Shifting cultivation
BURNING Tree golf club. See Washington,
D.C.—Clubs
BURNS, Arthur Frank
Arthur Burns explains policy on dividends,
interest rates; excerpts from testimony
before the Senate committee on banking,
housing and urban affairs, November 2,
1971. por U S News 71:91-2 N 15 '71
Burns on business: recovery, but new dan-
gers of inflation; excerpts from testimony,
February 19, 1971. por U S News 70:55-7
Mr 1 '71
Economy at midyear: a size-up by Arthur
Burns; statement before the Joint econom-
ic committee, July 23, 1971. por U S News
71:49-52 Ag 9 '71
Restoration of confidence; excerpt from ad-
dress. Sat R 54:45 Ja 23 '71
about
Administration takes on the Fed; with edi-
torial comment. pors Bsns W p 18-19,
80 Jl 31 '71 *
Arthur the independent. il por Time 97:70
Mr 1 '71 *
Changes at Federal reserve under Arthur
Burns. il por U S News 71:60-3 Ag 23 '71 *
High marks for the Fed's freshman boss. il
por Bsns W p38-9 Ja 30 '71 *
Practical politician at the Fed. L. Malkin.
il por Fortune 83:148-51+ My '71 *
Shooting at the bluebirds of happiness. il pors
Time 98:17-18 Ag 9 '71 *
TRB from Washington. New Repub 164:6 Ap
17 '71 *
What Mr Burns really said; testimony be-
fore Joint congressional economic commit-
tee. America 124:223 Mr 6 '71 *
BURNS, Eileen
Prompter. il pors Opera N 35:27-9 Mr 27 '71
BURNS, Elizabeth, pseud.
Late Liz: metamorphosis of a rich alcoholic.
M. Moss. Chr Today 16:34-5 O 22 '71 *
BURNS, James MacGregor
Nixon tightrope. il pors Life 70:48B-48D+
Ap 2 '71

BURNS, Jim
Self in city space and in clothed space. B.
Schwartz. il por Craft Horiz 31:30-5 Ag
'71 *
BURNS, John M. 3d
Burns case. il por Time 97:43 Ja 25 '71 *
BURNS, Martin
Our own blackberry patch. il Org Gard &
Farm 18:78 Jl '71
BURNS, Pamela
Pam designs her way to the Daisy award. il
pors Seventeen 29:168 O '70 *
BURNS, R. Hugh, and McCullen, Audrey
Teachers look at classroom behavior prob-
lems, a survey. Ment Hy 55:504-6 O '71
BURNS, Richard
Classroom exercise; poem. Commonweal 94:
135 Ap 16 '71
—and Harrell, R. L.
Game of one downsmanship or one upsman-
ship down. Clear House 46:96-7 O '71
BURNS, Robert F.
Ecumenical rebellion in Chicago. Chr Cent
88:1461 D 15 '71 *
BURNS, Robert Grant
Holding; poem. New Yorker 47:40 D 18 '71
Saviors; poem. Poetry 119:151-4 D '71
BURNS, Robert I.
Christian-Islamic confrontation in the west:
the thirteenth-century dream of conver-
sion. bibliog f il Am Hist R 76:1386-434 D
'71
BURNS, Robert R.
Scanning for sales. A. Hershman. por Duns
98:48 D '71 *
BURNS, Scott
How to make money while relaxing in the
country. Vogue 159:12 Ja 1 '72
BURNS and scalds
Better care for burn victims. il Time 97:38
Mr 1 '71
Skin substitute holds promise for burn vic-
tims. Todays Health 49:65 My '71
BURNSIDE, Irene Mortenson
Adolescent; poem. Ment Hy 55:412 Jl '71
Loneliness in old age. bibliog Ment Hy 55:
391-7 Jl '71
BURNSIDE, William
Gallery; photographs. Life 71:6-7 Jl 23 '71
BURNT wood works. See Pyrography
BURNUP and Sims, Inc.
Busy signal at Burnup & Sims. R. Levy.
Duns 97:78 My '71
BURRELL, Evelyn P.
Milton B. Allen, the first black states attor-
ney. por Negro Hist Bul 34:63-7 Mr '71
BURRELL, Walter Price
Hollywood stunt girl. il pors Ebony 27:147-
8+ D '71
BURRITOS. See Cookery, Mexican
BURROUGHS, John
Maximat V10: one-tool machine shop. il
Pop Mech 136:146-8+ Ag '71
BURROUGHS, R. H. See Heirtzler, J. R. jt.
auth.
BURROUGHS, William Seward, 1914-
Life with father. W. Burroughs, jr. por
Esquire 76:113-15+ S '71 *
BURROUGHS, William Seward, jr
Life with father. por Esquire 76:113-15+ S '71
BURROW, J. W.
Mummy's curse. il por Horizon 13:42-7 Aut
'71
BURROWS, Abe
Four on a garden; adaptation. See Barillet,
P. and Grédy, J. P.
BURROWS, David
Music and the nausea delle cose cotidiane.
bibliog f il Mus Q 57:230-40 Ap '71
BURROWS, Larry
Frantic night on the edge of Laos; photo-
graphs. Life 70:26-31 F 19 '71
Lau goes home to Vietnam; photographs. il
Life 70:18B-27 Ja 29 '71
Vietnam: a compassionate vision; photo-
graphs. por Life 70:34-45 F 26 '71
about
Edge of the sword. il por Newsweek 77:55
F 22 '71 *
Larry Burrows: a photographer's own story.
E. H. Needham. il pors Pop Phot 69:98-9+
Jl '71
Larry Burrows, photographer. R. Graves. por
Life 70:3 F 19 '71 *
This strange war fascinates me. il por Time
97:70 F 22 '71 *
BURSTON and Texas commerce bank, ltd.
See London—Banks
BURT, Alvin Victor, 1927-
Miami: the Cuban flavor. il Nation 212:299-
302, 450 My 8, Ap 12 '71
BURT, Peggy
We were hijacked! pors Seventeen 29:170 D
'70

BURTON, Bozzie Bryant, 3d
Miranda extended. Time 99:58 Ja 10 '72 •
BURTON, Dwight L.
English in no man's land: some suggestions for the middle years. Engl J 60:23-30 Ja '71
—and Fillion, Bryant
Literature program for the middle school. Clear House 45:524-7 My '71
BURTON, Lou
Southern California beaches. il Travel 135:28-35+ Ap '71
BURTON, Richard
Dauntless travelers. il por Vogue 158:130-3 O 15 '71
Our marriage after 7 years; interview, ed. by R. Bain. por Ladies Home J 88:89+ Ap '71
Travelling with Elizabeth. il pors Vogue 157:68-71 Ap 15 '71
BURTON, Robert E.
Weatherman looks at the redwood tree: California fog drinker. il Weatherwise 24:120-4 Je '71
BURTON, Robin
Helgoland underwater laboratory. il Sea Front 17:335-41 N '71
BURTON, Virginia Lee
Virginia Lee Burton's trip to Japan. M. Ishii. il Horn Bk 47:147-56 Ap '71 •
BURTON, Walter E.
Add an indexing attachment to your lathe. il Pop Mech 135:170-6 Mr '71
Carriage chuck mount for your lathe. il Pop Mech 136:60 N '71
Lathe ball-turning attachment. il Pop Mech 136:138-42 Jl '71
Little tool with a big bite. il Pop Mech 135:168-70 Ap '71
Make a center indicator for lathe work. il Pop Mech 135:126-9+ My '71
New jaws for an old vise. il Pop Sci 198:136 Mr '71
Tired of turning metals? Try rigid plastic. il Pop Mech 135:160-4 Je '71
BURWELL, Basil
Man for all souls. il Am Heritage 23:13-16 D '71
BURWELL, Robert L. Jr. See Haensel, V. jt. auth.
BURY ST EDMUNDS cross. See Cross and crosses
BURZIO, Eugenia
Mail and reviews. A. Favia-Artsay. por Hobbies 76:35-6 Mr '71 •
BUS accidents. See Traffic accidents
BUS lines. See Motor bus lines
BUS wagons. See Station wagons
BUSBY, Margaret
London's most remarkable publishing firm. il pors Ebony 26:43-6+ Mr '71 •
BUSCH, August A. 1899-
Busch of Anheuser-Busch. il por Forbes 107:49 My 15 '71 •
BUSCH, Daryle H.
Metal ion control of chemical reactions. bibliog il Science 171:241-8 Ja 22 '71
BUSCH, Noel F.
Peerless potentate of pachydermia. il Read Digest 99:133-7 N '71
Savvy skipper of protocol. por Read Digest 99:161-5 O '71
BUSCH gardens. See Tampa, Fla.—Parks and playgrounds
BUSER, Robert L.
Student activities in the schools of the seventies. Ed Digest 37:48-50 N '71
BUSH, Geoffrey
Higher forms of the new thriller. Sat R 54:18 My 29 '71
BUSH, George Herbert Walker
Ambassador; interview. New Yorker 47:33-4 O 16 '71
Challenges facing the economic and social council; statement. July 7, 1971. Dept State Bul 65:122-6 Ag 2 '71
Chinese representation items inscribed on U.N. General assembly agenda; statements, September 22 and 24, 1971. Dept State Bul 65:425-7 O 18 '71
Environment and development; the interlocking problems; remarks, May 24, 1971. Dept State Bul 65:21-2 Jl 5 '71
Expanding international cooperation in space activities; address, May 3, 1971. Dept State Bul 64:709-10 My 31 '71
Humanitarian and social concerns of the United Nations; address, June 28, 1971. Dept State Bul 65:99-102 Jl 26 '71
Policy on two Chinas; interview. il por U S News 71:47-8 S 20 '71
Proposal to discuss Puerto Rico rejected by U.N General assembly; statements, September 23 and 24, 1971. Dept State Bul 65:427-9 O 18 '71

Two Chinas in the U.N. the U.S. states its case; excerpts from statement, October 18, 1971. il por U S News 71:74-5 N 1 '71
U.N. defers consideration of Korea until 27th General assembly; statement, September 23, 1971. Dept State Bul 65:429 O 18 '71
U.N. force in Cyprus extended through December 1971; statement, May 26, 1971. Dept tate Bul 64:842-3 Je 28 '71
United Nations admits Oman to membership, statement, October 7, 1971. Dept State Bul 65:607 N 22 '71
United Nations votes to seat People's Republic of China and expel representatives of Republic of China; statements, October 18 and 25, 1971. Dept State Bul 65:548-56 N 15 '71
U.S. calls for agreed guidelines for U.N. peacekeeping; statement, April 1, 1971. Dept State Bul 64:626 My 10 '71
U.S. condemns shooting incident at Soviet mission to the U.N; statement, October 21, 1971. Dept State Bul 65:598 N 22 '71
U.S. presents initial contribution to U.N. volunteers fund; statement, and text of letter, June 17, 1971. Dept State Bul 65:138 Ag 2 '71
U.S. reiterates position on Jerusalem; statement, September 25, 1971. Dept State Bul 65:469 O 25 '71
U.S. reviews financial plight of the United Nations; statement, October 15, 1971. Dept State Bul 65:556-8 N 15 '71
U.S. supports admission of Bahrain to the United Nations; statement, August 18, 1971. Dept State Bul 65:294 S 13 '71
U.S. supports admission of Qatar to the United Nations; statement, September 15, 1971. Dept State Bul 65:468 O 25 '71
U.S. urges stronger U.N. efforts in narcotics control; statement, May 3, 1971. Dept State Bul 64:769-71 Je 14 '71
U.S. welcomes People's Republic of China to the United Nations; statement, November 15, 1971. Dept State Bul 65:715 D 20 '71
United States presents $1 million to U.N. drug abuse control fund; statement, April 1, 1971. Dept State Bul 64:574-5 My 3 '71

about

Burden of George Bush. W. F. Buckley, jr. Nat R 23:1198-9 O 22 '71 •
China & the U.S: the twain shall meet. A. H. Grossman. il Harper 243:86-8+ O '71 •
New stripe at the U.N. por Time 98:14-15 S 20 '71 •
Our man at the U.N. A. Tuckerman. Nation 212:389 Mr 29 '71 •
There goes Taipei; with report by P. Young and editorial comment. il pors Life 71:28-36 N 5 '71 •
BUSH, Jack Hamilton
Jack Bush: illusions of transparency. K. Moffett. il por Art N 70:42-5 Mr '71 •
BUSH, Karen, and others
Deuterium effects on binding of reduced coenzyme alcohol dehydrogenase isoenzyme EE. bibliog il Science 172:478-80 Ap 30 '71
BUSH, Monroe
Denver's conservation library. il Am For 77:12-15 Ap '71
Reading about resources. See issues of American forests
BUSH, Vannevar
Dictation to science by laymen; excerpt from 1946 Carnegie institution of Washington yearbook. Science 174:11 O 1 '71
BUSH Negroes. See Negroes in Surinam
BUSHNELL, Louise
Pride in America; address, October 30, 1971. Vital Speeches 38:142-5 D 15 '71
BUSINESS
See also
Advertising
Airplanes in business
Big business
Capitalism
Christmas business
Competition
Corporations
Efficiency, Industrial
Free enterprise
Location in business and industry
Retail trade
Stock exchange
Television in business

BUSINESS—*Continued*

Bibliography

Books to come (cont) Library J 96:890-4, 2399-400+, 3686-8+ Mr 1, Jl, N 1 '71

Business & related subjects; a selection of books planned for publication November, 1971 through May, 1972. il Pub W 200:43-8 N 15 '71

Business books of 1970; comp. by J. B. Woy. il por Library J 96:793-6 Mr 1 '71

1971's economy is mirrored here; high spot titles April through September. il Pub W 199:48-56 Ap 12 '71

Federal aid

Lockheed stirs up the ghost of RFC. Bsns W p23 Je 26 '71

Should the government rescue companies? comments by members of presidents' panel, ed. by N. A. Martin. il Duns 98:43-4 S '71

Why the drive to bail out businesses in trouble. il U S News 70:41-4 My 24 '71

See also
Reconstruction finance corporation

Forms, blanks, etc.

See also
Moore corporation

International aspects

Fortune multinational report. See issues of Fortune

International business. See issues of Dun's

Peace needs world business; address, July 29, 1971. E. M. De Windt. Vital Speeches 37:726-9 S 15 '71

See also
Japan—California association

Periodicals

See also
Business week (periodical)
Dun's (periodical)

Political aspects

G.O.P.'s strange appeal to business. R. D. Corwin and L. Gray. il Fortune 84:127-8 Jl '71

Sounds of executive silence. N. A. Adler. il Harvard Bsns R 49:100-5 Jl '71; Discussion. 49:21+ N '71

Why local reform is a businessman's concern. W. G. Colman. il Nations Bsns 59: 70-1 Jl '71

See also
Lobbying

Public relations

American corporation under fire. il Newsweek 77:74-6+ My 24 '71

Business takes on its critics. il U S News 70:52-4 Ap 26 '71

How should business respond to its critics? address, May 7, 1971. C. B. McCoy. por U S New 70:65-7 My 31 '71

See also
Corporate image

Social aspects

Accelerated generation moves into management. J. Gooding. il Fortune 83:100-4+ Mr '71

American corporation under fire. il Newsweek 77:74-6+ My 24 '71

Anatomy of activism for executives. S. A. Culbert and J. M. Elden; discussion. Harvard Bsns R 49:34+ Mr '71

At Xerox; giving but not forcing. V. Louviere. Nations Bsns 59:18 D '71

Business and society; address, January 27, 1971. R. W. Sarnoff. Vital Speeches 37: 273-5 F 15 '71

Business and the revolution; CED report on the social responsibilities of business corporations. R. Gelatt. Sat R 54:32 Jl 24 '71

Business fights the social ills: in a recession. il Bsns W p51-4+ Mr 6 '71

Competitive system; to work, to preserve, to protect; address, March 25, 1971. J. M. Roche. il por Vital Speeches 37:445-8 My 1 '71; Same abr. with title Let's stop blaming business! Read Digest 99:123-5 Jl '71; Excerpts. U S News 70:91-3 Ap 12 '71

Corporate responsibility: group rates company social performance. C. Holden. Science 171:463-6 F 5 '71

Corporate responsibility movement is alive and well. C. Holden. Science 172:920 My 28 '71

Corporate underground. T. H. Ingram. Nation 213:206-12 S 13 '71

Economic rationale for social involvement: a corporate must; address, September 24, 1971. J. R. Bunting. Vital Speeches 38:51-3 N 1 '71

Executives as community volunteers. D. H. Fenn, jr. il Harvard Bsns R 49:4-6+ Mr '71

How a library project got off the shelf; Stran-steel employees involved in community improvement. V. Louviere. Nations Bsns 59:21 N '71

How should business respond to its critics? address, May 7, 1971. C. B. McCoy. por U S New 70:65-7 My 31 '71

How to cope with critics. C. B. McCoy. por Nations Bsns 59:24 S '71

IBM's quiet aid for college blacks. il Bsns W p28 D 18 '71

Is business the source of new social values? O. A. Bremer. Harvard Bsns R 49:121-6 N '71

Killing the goose; responsibility vs. irresponsibility in business. D. Fife. il Environ 13:20-2+ Ap '71

Marts of trade; proposed anti-corporation for the public interest. J. Brooks. New Yorker 47:13K+ O 9 '71

Moral issues in investment policy. B.G. Malkiel and R. E. Quandt. bibliog f Harvard Bsns R 49:37-47 Mr '71

New business from new towns? M. Apgar, 4th. il Harvard Bsns R 49:90-109 Ja '71

Next step for business: social audit. B. L. Masse. America 124:335 Ap 3 '71

Not strictly business. Nations Bsns 59:24 N '71

Public concerns of private enterprise; address, February 3, 1971. J. W. Hull. Vital Speeches 37:367-70 Ap 1 '71

Relativism in organizations. G. F. F Lombard. bibliog f Harvard Bsns R 49:55-65 Mr '71

Responsibility beyond profit. Time 98:55-6 Jl 12 '71

Turn public problems to private account. R. C. Rockefeller. Harvard Bsns R 49:131-8 Ja '71

Utopians in the marketplace. R. Briscoe. bibliog f Harvard Bsns R 49:4-6+ S '71

Why of Xerox. L. L. L. Golden. Sat R 54: 53-4 Ag 14 '71

Xerox's social concern; new Social service leave program. America 125:219 O 2 '71

See also
Business and race problems
Council on economic priorities

BUSINESS, Retirement from. See Retirement

BUSINESS airplanes. See Airplanes, Business

BUSINESS and education
Leisure & education; with yardsticks of management performance. il Forbes 109: 174+ Ja 1 '72

Reexamination of trustee responsibility; address, March 17, 1971. H. T. Mudd. Vital Speeches 37:472-4 My 15 '71

See also
Colleges and universities—Gifts, legacies, etc.
Education market
Performance contracts (education)

BUSINESS and government. See Industry and state

BUSINESS and professional women
Let's put women in their place like, for instance, city hall. J. Mayer. McCalls 98: 74+ F '71

You still have a long way to go, baby. il Bsns W p74-6+ S 25 '71

See also
Married woman—Employment
Secretaries
Women as executives
Women as scientists

BUSINESS and race problems
Dilemma for the American corporation; American investment in South Africa. America 124:586 Je 5 '71

Race relations is their business (cont) S. Friedman. N Y Times Mag p4+ F 14 '71; Reply. J. A. Morsell. N Y Times Mag p93 Mr 7 '71

Wide-awake time down South; Memphis, Tenn. il Nations Bsns 59:54-9 F '71

See also
National alliance of businessmen

BUSINESS and state. See Industry and state

BUSINESS and the arts. See The Arts and industry

BUSINESS and the community. See Business—Social aspects

BUSINESS and the environmental movement. See Industry and the environmental movement

BUSINESS committee for the arts (BCA) See Business in the arts award

BUSINESS communication. See Communication in management

BUSINESS forecasting—*Continued*
1972: a mixed bag for key industries. il Bsns W p44-9 D 25 '71
Quarterly outlook survey; views of top executives. il Nations Bsns 59:26-8+ Ja; 72-5 Ap; 20-3 Jl; 24-6+ O '71
Solid signs of revival. il Time 98:56 D 27 '71
See also
Economic forecasting
Sales forecasting
Stocks—Price forecasting

BUSINESS hours
Retailers move toward the 168-hour week. il Bsns W p96+ O 16 '71
To whom do Sundays go? Pub W 199:59-60 My 24 '71
See also
Hours of labor
Business—Hours of opening

BUSINESS in the arts award
Esquire-BCA fifth annual Business in the arts awards; with editorial comment. Esquire 76:6, 132-3 Jl '71
Fifth annual business in the arts awards competition; with editorial comment. il Esquire 75:6, 150-1 Ja '71

BUSINESS insurance. See Insurance, Business
BUSINESS journals. See Trade journals
BUSINESS liquidation. See Liquidation

BUSINESS literature
See also
Business—Bibliography

BUSINESS location. See Location in business and industry

BUSINESS machines. See Office equipment and supplies

BUSINESS management and organization
Accelerated generation moves into management. J. Gooding. il Fortune 83:100-4+ Mr '71
Accomplishment/cost: better project control. E. B. Block. il Harvard Bsns R 49:110-24 My '71
Caught in a closely held company. H. Smith, pseud. Duns 98:57-8 D '71
Companies create Phase II staffs. Bsns W p32-3 N 20 '71
Don't solve problems, prevent them. J. J. Cribbin. il Nations Bsns 59:57-8 O '71
Executive trends. J. Costello. See issues of Nation's business
Forum; problems of the manager. J. D. Robertson Duns 98:73 Ag '71
How to redeploy assets. R. H. Hillman. il Harvard Bsns R 49:95-103 N '71
Is the policy manual obsolete? G. J. Berkwitt. il Duns 93:55-6+ Je '69
Make way for the new organization man. M. Hanan. il Harvard Bsns R 49:128-38 Jl '71; Reply. J. D. Hobbs. 49:19+ N '71
Make your MBO pragmatic; Wells Fargo bank program. J. B Lasagna. Harvard Bsns R 49:64-9 N '71
Measuring management: 1971. il Forbes 109: 92 Ja 1 '72
Relativism in organizations. G. F. F. Lombard. bibliog f Harvard Bsns R 49:55-65 Mr '71
Situational theory of management. R. J. Mockler. bibliog Harvard Bsns R 49:146-8+ My '71
Symptoms of a sick management; views of top executives; symposium. il Nations Bsns 59:70-5 Ap '71
Teamwork through conflict; management by Matrix. il Bsns W p44-5+ Mr 20 '71
Top management is getting tough. G. Berkwitt. il Duns 97:44-6 My '71
Understand your overseas work force; with folded charts. D. Sirota and J. M. Greenwood. il Harvard Bsns R 49:53-60 Ja '71
What do young people think about managers? invitation to participate in study. Harvard Bsns R 49:96+ Jl '71
Who wants corporate democracy? analysis of subscribers' views. D. W. Ewing. bibliog f il Harvard Bsns R 49:12-14+ S '71
See also
Airlines—Management
American management association
Bonus system
Business consultants
Business planning
Business records
Communication in management
Computers—Business use
Conflict of interests (business)
Corporations
Credit management
Diversification in industry
Executives
Inventories
Location in business and industry
Marketing
Organizational change
Personnel management

Case studies
Problems in review (cont) il Harvard Bsns R 49:16-18+ Ja; 148-50+ Jl; 128-30+ N '71
Programmed case: the misfired missive; Dashman case (cont) A. M. Hodgson and W. R. Dill. Harvard Bsns R 49:140-2+ Ja '71

Employee participation
See Employees representation in management

History
Genesis. il por Forbes 107:198-201 My 15 '71

Germany (Federal Republic)
Two-tier board in West Germany. Bsns W p57 My 22 '71

Japan
How to negotiate in Japan. H. F. Van Zandt; reply. W. M. Wallace. Harvard Bsns R 49: 167-8 Mr '71
Myths that mislead U.S. managers in Japan. Y. Tsurumi. Harvard Bsns R 49:118-27 Jl '71
What we can learn from Japan. E. Goldston. il por Fortune 84:137+ O '71
What we can learn from Japanese management P. F. Drucker. Harvard Bsns R 49: 110-22 Mr '71

Russia
Picking the capitalist brains. il Bsns W p40-1 Mr 27 '71

Sweden
Project management, Swedish style. P. Jonason. Harvard Bsns R 49:104-9 N '71

BUSINESS meetings
How to meet with success; management conferences. N. B. Sigband. il Nations Bsns 59:76-8 Mr '71

BUSINESS ombudsman. See Ombudsman
BUSINESS organization. See Business management and organization

BUSINESS planning
Catalytic agent for effective planning; coordinator's role. J. C. Chambers and others. il Harvard Bsns R 49:110-19 Ja '71
Formulating strategy in smaller companies. F. F. Gilmore. bibliog f il Harvard Bsns R 49:71-81 My '71
How to make the least of planning. M. W. Pennington. il Nations Bsns 59:78-9 Je '71
Make TF serve corporate planning. P. H. Thurston. Harvard Bsns R 49:98-102 S '71
Problems in planning the information system. F. W. McFarlan. il Harvard Bsns R 49:75-89 Mr '71

BUSINESS recession. See Business depression
BUSINESS records
Mountainous defense by IBM; collection of proprietary records of data processing companies. Bsns W p26+ D 18 '71
See also
Microfilm records

BUSINESS research
See also
Operations research

BUSINESS schools and colleges
Institutions of corporate learning. V. Louviere. il Nations Bsns 59:13 Ja '71
Managing with the monster; computer courses. il Bsns W p94-8 Je 5 '71
Student tastes shift to the executive suite. il Nations Bsns 59:32-3 My '71
See also
Adelphi university, Garden City, N.Y.—School of business
California. University—Los Angeles campus—Graduate school of business administration
Pepperdine university, Los Angeles—School of business
Southern Methodist university, Dallas, Tex.—School of business administration

Finance
B-schools scramble for Perot's cash. por Bsns W p47-8 S 11 '71

Graduates
B-school grads face a tighter market. il Bsns W p122-3+ F 27 '71
Job-hopping and the MBA. J. A. De Pasquale and R. A. Lange. il Harvard Bsns R 49: 4-8+ N '71

Europe, Western
Big boom in European B-schools. il Bsns W p64+ N 20 '71

Japan
Steak, yes, martinis, no; Boeki Daigaku. B. Szuprowicz. il Duns 98:71-2+ O '71
Trade U; Boeki Daigaku. il Newsweek 79: 55-6 Ja 10 '72

BUSINESS schools and colleges—*Continued*

Russia

Picking the capitalist brains; first business school, the Institute for management of the national economy. il Bsns W p40-1 Mr 27 '71

BUSINESS seminars. See Seminars

BUSINESS stabilization. See Economic stabilization

BUSINESS statistics
Figures of the week. See issues of Business week
See also
Business forecasting

BUSINESS travel
New ruling on travel expenses. U S News 71:72 S 27 '71
Notes for the corporate nomad:
Shipping things home. Fortune 84:48 S '71
Two cultures note: criticism of NINDS director for travel on government time and money. J. Walsh. Science 174:128-9 O 8 '71
When is a wife deductible? Duns 98:63 Jl '71
See also
Airplanes in business

BUSINESS trips. See Business travel

BUSINESS uniforms. See Uniforms

BUSINESS week (periodical)
Publisher's memo; Business week awards for business citizenship. C. C. Randolph. il Bsns W p5 Ja 1 '72

BUSINESS writing. See Authorship

BUSINESSMEN
Businessmen in the news. C. Burck and others. See issues of Fortune
Businessmen who weather the winter in Nanyang. C. Mydans. il Fortune 83:82-7 Mr '71
Faces behind the figures. See issues of Forbes
Money men. See issues of Forbes
SR's businessman of the year. R. L. Tobin. por Sat R 54:55-7 Ja 23 '71
Spare us those cocktail parties! interviews with Japanese businessmen. Forbes 108: 20-1 D 15 '71
10 greatest men of American business, as you picked them. il Nations Bsns 59:44-6+ Mr '71
See also
Executives
Japan-California association
Negro businessmen

Health and hygiene

Drugs and drinking in the business world; interview. H. Johnson. por U S News 70: 70-3 Mr 22 '71
Staying healthy: a regimen for executives. Bsns W p85 My 1 '71
See also
Executives—Health programs

BUSINESSMEN as presidential advisers. See Presidential advisers

BUSING and integration. See School children —Transportation for integration

BUSING of school children. See School children—Transportation for integration

BUSKIN, Judith. See Singer, L. J. jt. auth.

BUSONI, Ferruccio
Arlecchino. Criticism
New Yorker 47:93 Mr 27 '71 *

BUSSARD, Ray
Fastest man afloat; D. Edgar and his coach. W. F. Reed. il por Sports Illus 34:16-19 Mr 1 '71 *

BUSSE, James G.
Campguard, intruder alarm for campers. il Pop Sci 198:114-15 Ap '71
Experiments you can make with amazing activated charcoal. il Pop Sci 199:96-8 Ag '71

BUT she must be perfect; story. See Coxhead, N.

BUTANE
See also
Liquefied petroleum gas

BUTCHER, Russell D.
Conservationists go to court. il Am For 77: 32-5+ Je; 32-5 Jl '71 (to be cont)

BUTINOV, Nikolai A.
(ed) See Miklukha-Maklaï, N. N. 19th century champion of anti-racism in New Guinea

BUTLER, Charles F.
U.S. to participate in conference on revision of Warsaw convention; text of letter, November 17, 1970. Dept State Bul 63:751 D 21 '70

BUTLER, John
All the strange things: John Butler on opera choreography among other kinds of dance; ed. By G. Loney. il por Dance Mag 45:22-7 Ag '71

BUTLER, Josephine Elizabeth (Grey)
Singular iniquity, by G. Petrie. Review
Sat R 55:28 Ja 1 '72. M. Haynes *

BUTLER, Kirk
Zener diodes & voltage-regulator design. il Electr World 86:32-4+ D 71

BUTLER, Michael
Weekend with Chief Michael Butler and his inner tribe. H. Lawrenson. il Esquire 76: 165-8+ N '71 *

BUTLER, Neil A.
Black mayor in Florida town. il pors Ebony 26:98-100+ Ag '71 *

BUTLER, Patrick
Catching up with the wig lady. il Wilson Lib Bul 45:775 Ap '71

BUTLER, Robert F. and Cox, A. V.
Mechanism for producing magnetic remanence in meteorites and lunar samples by cosmic-ray exposure. bibliog il Science 172: 939-41 My 28 '71

BUTLER-McCook homestead. See Hartford, Conn.—Historic houses, etc.

BUTRICK, Frank M.
Clear your drive the easy way. il Pop Mech 136:166+ D '71
Do patents pay? il Pop Mech 135:68-9+ Je '71

BUTSCHER, Edward
Unknown soldier; poem. Nation 212:186 F 8 '71

BUTTER
House beautiful chef. J. Pépin. il House B 113:85 Ja '71

BUTTERFLIES
Butterfly feeding on lycopsid. M. C. Singer and others. bibliog il Science 172:1341-2 Je 25 '71
Butterfly show; American museum of natural history's exhibit. New Yorker 47:30-1 My 15 '71
Juvenile hormone induces vitellogenin synthesis in the monarch butterfly. M. L. Pan and G. R. Wyatt. bibliog il Science 174: 503-5 O 29 '71
See also
Caterpillars

BUTTERNUT squash. See Squashes

BUTTONS
Button collecting. D. F. Brown. See issues of Hobbies
Buttons; history of buttonmaking; summary of address. H. C. Marshall. il Hobbies 76: 128-30 Ag; 129-30 S; 129-30 O '71
Everglade state; historical events on buttons. D. F. Brown. il Hobbies 75:129-30 Ja '71
Pilgrims. D. F. Brown. il Hobbies 76:130 D '71
Put on a happy face; Smilie button. il Time 98:36 Ag 30 '71

BUTTS, William
From unteachable to Ph.D. por Sch & Soc 99: 272-3 Sum '71 *

BUTWELL, Richard
Nixon doctrine in southeast Asia. bibliog f Cur Hist 61:321-6+ D '71

BUTWIN, David W.
Booked for travel. See issues of Saturday review

BUTYROLACTONE
Synergy of ethanol and a natural soporific— gamma hydroxybutyrate. E. R. McCabe and others. bibliog il Science 171:404-6 Ja 29 '71

BUTZ, Earl Lauer
Butz appointment. Nation 213:644-5 D 20 '71 *
Down on the farm. il por Newsweek 78:22 D 6 '71 *
Growing unrest on the farm. il por Time 98: 20-1 N 22 '71 *
Nixon's top man at agriculture now, a close-up. por U S News 71:86-7 D 13 '71 *
Who's the farmers' friend? New Repub 165: 5-6 D 4 '71 *

BUTZ, J. S. Jr
Exciting product of the excited atom. il Nations Bsns 59:78-82 S '71

BUYERS guides. See Consumer education

BUYING. See Shopping and shoppers

BUYING clubs. See Purchasing, Cooperative

BUYING motives. See Market research

BUZKASHI. See Sports—Afghanistan

BYARS, Betsy (Cromer)
Newbery award acceptance; address, June 21, 1971. il Horn Bk 47:354-8 Ag '71
Newbery/Caldecott awards; excerpts from addresses, ed. by P. Bragg. Pub W 200:28 S 6 '71
about
Betsy Byars. E. F. Byars. il por Horn Bk 47:359-62 Ag '71 *
Viking and Atheneum authors are 1970 Newbery and Caldecott winners. L. Russ. il pors Pub W 199:116-18 F 22 '71 *

BYARS, Edward F.
Betsy Byars. il por Horn Bk 47:359-62 Ag '71

BYE, Richard E.
Bye lines (cont) Library J 96:805, 1585, 2279, 2605, 3577 Mr 1, My 1, Jl, S 1, N 1 '71

BYERLY, Rich
Walking a coyote track. il Outdoor Life 147:50-1+ Ja '71

BYLINSKY, Gene
Cancer cells begin to yield their secrets. il Fortune 84:156-9+ N '71
Little chips invade the memory market. il Fortune 83:100-4+ Ap '71
Metallic menaces in the environment. il Fortune 83:110-13+ Ja '71
Mounting bill for pollution control. il Fortune 84:87-9+ Jl '71

BYOBU. See Painting, Japanese

BYRAM, E. T. and others
X-ray survey of Centaurus A. bibliog il Science 169:366-8; 171:501 Jl 24 '70, F 5 '71

BYRD, Helen B.
New era in preservation. il Nat Parks & Con Mag 45:21-2+ My '71

BYRD, Robert
Portfolio of Robert Byrd. D. Klemin. il por Am Artist 35:54-9 Je '71 *

BYRD, Robert Carlyle
School busing and forced integration; address. September 8, 1971. Vital Speeches 38: 7-11 O 15 '71

about

Byrd and Boggs. New Repub 164:10 Ja 30 '71 *
Cloud on the Kennedy horizon. pors U S News 70:18 F 1 '71 *
Embodiment of poor white power. R. Sherrill. il pors N Y Times Mag p9+ F 28 '71 *
Man who toppled Teddy. por Newsweek 77: 19 F 1 '71 *
President and the Court. Nation 213:388 O 25 '71
Tortoise and the hare. il por Newsweek 77: 18-20 F 1 '71 *

BYRD, William
Cantiones sacrae 1575. J. W. Barker. pors Am Rec G 37:344-5+ F '71 *

BYRNE, Mary
Color it red and call it Christmas. il Nat Wildlife 10:24-5 D '71
Hop skip, jump and a pounce. il Nat Wildlife 9:40-1 Je '71

BYRNE, Robert
Bless me, father; excerpt from Memories of a non-Jewish boyhood. Commonweal 93:519+ F 26 '71

BYRNES, George
Keep in trim. il Motor B & S 127:64-5+ Je '71

BYRNES, Robert Francis
Russia in eastern Europe: hegemony without security. For Affairs 49:682-97 Jl '71

BYRON, George Gordon Noël Byron, 6th baron
Lovers; excerpt from The nympho and other maniacs. I. Wallace. pors Ladies Home J 88:127-33 F '71 *

BYRON, William J.
Three ingredients of graft. il America 125: 532-3 D 18 '71

BYSSINOSIS. See Lungs—Dust diseases

BYURAKAN astrophysical observatory. See Astronomical observatories—Armenia

BYZANTINE antiquities
Byzantine trading venture. G. F. Bass. il Sci Am 225:22-33 bibliog(p 120) Ag '71

BYZANTINE shipwrecks. See Shipwrecks

BYZANTINE studies
International Byzantine congress: East-West communication. C. S. Calian. Chr Cent 88: 1472-3 D 15 '71

C

C-5A (airplane) See Airplanes, Military transport

C and O Canal national historical park. See Chesapeake and Ohio Canal National Historical Park

CAB. See United States—Civil aeronautics board

CAI (computer-assisted instruction) See Computers—Educational use

CAINS (carrier aircraft inertial navigation system) See Inertial guidance systems

CAL. See Cornell aeronautical laboratory, inc.

CALA. See Canadian association for Latin America

CAS (collision avoidance systems) See Airplanes —Safety devices and measures

CAT (clear air turbulence) See Atmospheric turbulence

CATV system
CATV and the wired city. W. G. Salm. il Radio-Electr 42:36-8 My '71
CATV: its future starts now. W. H. Buchsbaum. il Electr World 85:39-41+ Mr '71
CATV: new dimensions in communications. J. K. Flagg. il Parks & Rec 6:30-3+ O '71
CATV: visual library service. B. L. Kenney and F. W. Norwood. bibliog il Am Lib 2: 723-6 Jl '71
Cable capers; Cox cable after contract in Fort Wayne, Ind. Newsweek 78:84 D 20 '71
Cable revisions. R. L. Shayon. Sat R 54: 14 D 11 '71
Cable: shape of things to come? J. Kronenberger. il Look 35:66 S 7 '71
Cable television. W. T. Knox. il Sci Am 225: 22-9 O '71
Cable TV: a common carrier or not? J. Castelli. il America 125:397-400 N 13 '71
Cable TV: omission by commission: recommendations of the Sloan commission on cable communications. S. W. Dean, jr. Nation 213:691-3 D 27 '71
Cable television proposals. G. Krettek and E. D. Cooke. Wilson Lib Bul 46:200-1 O '71
Cable TV: turn on, tune in, rip off. F. Browning. il Ramp Mag 9:32-8 Ap '71
Cable TV: where it is & where it's going. F. H. Belt. il Pop Electr 1:26-30 Ja '72
Do-it-yourself TV; Open channel in New York city. il Newsweek 79:49-50 Ja 3 '72
Future for cable TV. Newsweek 78:79 N 22 '71
Get into CATV picture, ALA urges libraries. Library J 96:3709-10 N 15 '71
Lid comes off the box. B. Dunn. il Life 70: 42-6+ Ap 2 '71
Lot of new services in store for TV viewers. il U S News 72:40-2 Ja 3 '72
New service offers CATV author interviews. il Pub W 200:25 D 6 '71
Pact that cuts little ice for CATV. Bsns W p78-9 N 27 '71
Ruling the rule-makers. R. L. Shayon. Sat R 54:16 Je 19 '71
Scandal clouds the CATV picture. il Bsns W p88 N 6 '71
Special feature on cable television. il Todays Ed 60:52-6 N '71
What cable TV may mean to you. L. Buckwalter. il Mech Illus 68:76-8+ Ja '72

CATV system and copyright. See Copyright —Broadcasting rights

CB radio. See Citizens radio service

CBE. See Council for basic education

CBI. See Cumulative book index

CBS. See Columbia broadcasting system, inc.

CBW research. See Chemical and biological weapons

CCAR. See Central conference of American rabbis

CCD (Conference of the committee on disarmament) See United Nations—Committee on disarmament

CCI. See Christian camping international

CCLD. See New York (state)—Education, Department of—Commissioner's committee on library development

CDU (Christian democratic union) See Political parties—Germany (Federal Republic)

CEA. See United States—Council of economic advisers

CEI. See Committee for environmental information

CEP. See Council on economic priorities

CEQ. See United States—Council on environmental quality

CERN (conseil européen pour la recherche nucléaire) See European organization for nuclear research

CETI (communication with extraterrestrial intelligence) See Interstellar communication

C. F. Bally ltd. See Shoe industry

C. F. Murphy associates. See Murphy, C. F, associates

CHA. See Christian holiness association

CIA. See United States—Central intelligence agency

CIAP (Inter-American committee on the Alliance for progress) See Alliance for progress

CIC. See National council of churches—Corporate information center

CICOP (Catholic Inter-American cooperation program) See Religious conferences

CIDOC. See Center of intercultural documentation

CIECC. See Inter-American council for education, science, and culture

CIO. See Congress of industrial organizations
CLASS (close air support system) See Airplanes, Military—Armaments
CLC. See United States—Cost of living council
CLR.   See Council on library resources, inc.
CLSA. See Canon law society of America
CMSM. See Conference of major superiors of men
CNA financial corporation
   CNA chooses a chief and loses a top V-P. il por Bsns W p35 Jl 17 '71
   Insurers ride herd on medical care fees. V. Louviere. Nations Bsns 59:16 Ag '71
CNES (Centre national d'études spatiales) See France—National center for space studies
COCU. See Consultation on church union
COPE program. See Cope program
COPES. See American library association—Program evaluation and support. Committee on
COR. See Committee of responsibility to save war-burned and war-injured Vietnamese children
CORE. See Congress of racial equality
COS. See Central opera service
COSPAR. See International council of scientific unions—Committee on space research
CPC (Christian peace conference) See Peace conferences
CPC International, inc.
   Company that fled New York. il por Newsweek 78:97-8 O 18 '71
CPM (critical path method) See Critical path analysis
CRLA (California rural legal assistance program) See Legal aid
CRS. See Catholic relief services
CSD. See American library association—Childrens services division
CU. See Consumers union of United States
CUNY. See New York (city). City university
CWA. See Communications workers of America
CAAMAÑO, Roberto
   Temple of the opera. il Américas 23:17-24 Ja '71
CABALLÉ, Montserrat
   Caballé and early Bellini. H. Weinstock. Sat R 54:55 Ap 24 '71 *
CABALQUINTO, Luis, and Pancho, Juan
   Magnificent medinilla. il Horticulture 49:46-7 F '71
CABANAC, Michel
   Physiological role of pleasure. bibliog il Science 173:1103-7 S 17 '71
CABANAS. See Bathhouses
CABANNE, Pierre
   (ed) See Duchamp. M. Marcel Duchamp
CABBAGE, Flowering. See Flowering cabbage
CABBAGES
   See also
   Brussels sprouts
   Kohlrabi
CABET, Étienne
   Communism and the working class before Marx: the Icarian experience. C. H. Johnson. bibliog f il Am Hist R 76:642-89 Je '71 *
CABIN cruisers. See Cruisers (pleasure boats)
CABINET (United States) See United States—Cabinet
CABINET committee on aging. See United States—Cabinet committee on aging
CABINET officers
   Midterm minuet: firing of Walter J. Hickel; replacement of David Kennedy. Sr Schol 97:4 Ja 11 '71

   Appointment, qualifications, tenure, etc.
   Oil slick on the Potomac: selection of Connally. S. Houston. Commonweal 93:436-8 F 5 '71
CABINET work
   See also
   Cabinetmakers
   Joinery
   Veneers and veneering
CABINETMAKERS
   Cincinnati cabinet- and chairmakers, 1819-1830; with list of cabinet- and chairmakers. D. Streifthau. il Antiques 99:896-905 Je '71
   Tennessee cabinetmakers and chairmakers through 1840. E. Beasley. il Antiques 100:612-21 O '71
   Tennessee furniture and its makers. E. Beasley. il Antiques 100:425-31 S '71
   Work of an anonymous Carolina cabinetmaker; colonial North Carolina. F. L. Horton. il Antiques 101:169-76 Ja '72
   See also
   Phyfe. D.
   Randolph, B.

CABINETS (furniture)
   Dutch hutch. R. C. Sickler. il Mech Illus 67:64-6 Ag '71
   Early American server with a secret. H. Wicks. il Pop Mech 136:156-61+ N '71
   File works; home-furniture finds. M. Emmerling. il Mile 72:54-5 Mr '71
   Fine-furniture filing cabinets. R. Sickler. il Mech Illus 67:110+ Ap '71
   Four-file cabinet costing less than $25. il Sunset 147:112 S '71
   Mix and match storage units, easily built. il Sunset 147:156+ O '71
   See also
   High fidelity sound systems—Cabinets
   Kitchen cabinets
CABINS
   Astonishing wooden tent. il Sunset 146:96-9 My '71
CABLE, Harold
   That time of year; drama. Plays 31:23-30, 44 D '71
CABLE television. See CATV system
CABLES, Submarine
   Cable vs. satellite in an FCC showdown. Bsns W p29-30 Je 12 '71
CABLEWAYS
   By air-car to the top of Germany: Zugspitze. il Sunset 146:74+ My '71
CABOT corporation
   Why not call a spade a spade? F. C. Foy. Forbes 107:84-5 Mr 15 '71
CABRAL, Elizabeth
   Tell-tale portals. Har Yrs 11:27 Je '71
CABRERA LEIVA, Guillermo
   Bear's Bible. il Américas 23:19-24 Je '71
CACOYANNIS, Michael
   Current cinema. P. Kael. New Yorker 47:155-6+ O 16 '71 *
CACTUS
   Almost-perfect house plant; Christmas cactus. V. McDonald. il Org Gard & Farm 18:54-6 D '71
   Cactus in pots are easy, interesting. il Sunset 146:255 My '71
   Growing cactus seed in sphagnum moss or brick dust. il Sunset 146:293 Ap '71
   Saguaro. L. Payne. il Nat Parks & Con Mag 45:29-31 Ap '71
   See also
   Prickly pears
CADAQUÉS, Spain
   What is the best bargain in Europe? Maybe Cadaqués in Spain. W. A. Krauss. il Holiday 49:74-6+ F '71
CADDEN, Vivian
   Late-blooming career women. il McCalls 99:88-9+ O '71
   Politics of marriage: a delicate balance. il Redbook 137:55+ Jl '71
   Yes to love and joyful faces. il Life 71:68+ D 17 '71
CADDY spoons. See Spoons
CADE, Tom J. and others
   DDE residues and eggshell changes in Alaskan falcons and hawks. bibliog il Science 172:955-7 My 28 '71
CADIEUX, Charles L.
   Great Lakes of the Missouri. il Yachting 129:58-9+ Je '71
   Highland lakes of Texas. il Yachting 130:54-5+ O '71
   Small boat passage. il Yachting 129:68-9+ F '71
CADMIUM
   And now, cadmium; tragic results of Japan's unchecked pollution. Time 97:35 Mr 8 '71
   Building a shorter life. J. McCaull. bibliog f il Environ 13:2-15+ S '71
CADMIUM poisoning
   Building a shorter life. J. McCaull. bibliog f il Environ 13:2-15+ S '71
   Cadmium crisis. Newsweek 78:68 Jl 5 '71
   Cadmium watch. Sci Am 225:47 Ag '71
CAESAR, Orville Swan
   With several ways to go, he chose up. R. F. Shaffer.   il pors Nations Bsns 59:60-1 Ja '71 *
CAESAR salad. See Salads
CAETANO, Marcello
   Bread-and-butter politics. por Newsweek 77:46 Je 28 '71 *
CAFARAKIS, Christian
   Onassis servant tells all he knows, and then some. W. A. McWhirter. il por Life 71:85 N 12 '71 *
CAFFEINE
   How fresh are our milk and eggs, and what goes into cola drinks? il Consumer Bul 54:31-2 Ag '71
   Striated muscle fibers: facilitation of contraction at short lengths by caffeine. R. Rüdel and S. R. Taylor. bibliog il Science 172:387-8 Ap 23 '71

CAFFREY, Thomas A.
Do Humanae vitae and infallibility stand or
fall together? T. A. Caffrey. America 125:
66-7 Ag 7 '71
CAHALAN, John I. and others
Polymers can relieve surcharged sewers.
Am City 86:87-8+ S '71
CAHIER, Bernard
'Ring: der grosser preis von Deutschland. il
Motor T 23:56-8+ O '71
Ultimate Capri. il Motor T 23:30-1 Ap '71
CAHILL, Joe
We will stop at nothing. por Newsweek
78:46 S 20 '71 •
CAHILL, Marianne
Virginity was my problem. por Redbook 137:
38+ Ag '71
CAHILL, William Thomas
How two influential fathers turned family
drug tragedies into a triumph for the pub-
lic. R. Sullivan. il Todays Health 49:42-5
My '71 •
CAHIR, John J. See Myers, J. N. jt. auth.
CAHN, Anne H.
Student's view of Pugwash. Bul Atom Sci
27:36-7 Ap '71
CAIDIN, Martin
Coming, the incredible Skyshark: first am-
phibious jet. il Pop Mech 135:77-80+ Ap
'71
CAILLIET, Emile
Ultimate spring of solitude; excerpt from
Alone at high noon. Chr Today 15:12 Jl 16
'71
CAIN, Edward R.
Protest and foreign policy. il Chr Cent 88:
742-4 Je 16 '71
CAIN, Emily
Episode on a July morning; story. Redbook
137:66-7 Jl '71
Our things fell off the mountain; story. Red-
book 137:80-1 Je '71
CAIN, Roy E. and others
Habituation of electrically induced readi-
ness to gnaw. bibliog il Science 173:262-4
Jl 16 '71
CAIN, Thomas H.
Wild flowers on a balcony. il Horticulture 49:
24-5+ S '71
CAIRNGORM MOUNTAINS, Scotland
Cairngorm wildlands of Scotland. H. A. Raup.
il Liv Wildn 35:24-9 Spr '71
CAIRO, Ill.

Education
Ghost town. Nation 212:644-5 My 24 '71

Race question
Bad day at Cairo, Ill. J. A. Lukas. il N Y Times
Mag p22-3+ F 21 '71
Civil war in Cairo, Ill: a dispatch from the
front. H. Kohn. il Ramp Mag 9:46-51 Ap
'71
Doesn't anyone care about Cairo? T. A. Knopf.
Commonweal 93:510-12 F 26 '71
CAIRO opera house. See Opera houses
CAKE
As busy as a bee; choice of three cakes. il
Ladies Home J 88:106-7+ O '71
Bakeshop banana cakes; with recipes. il
Seventeen 29:128-9+ D '70
Botany of a fruitcake. M. A. Gamble. il Hor-
ticulture 49:50-4 Mr '71
Bûche de Nöel; Christmas yule log; with
recipe. J. Pépin. il House B 1J3:74-5+ D
'71
Coffee-flavored pound cake. il Sunset 146:166
Mr '71
Cooking with cool; chocolate cake roll. il
Seventeen 29:186 S '70
Fine texture and buttery flavor; Swiss al-
mond cake. il Sunset 146:170 Je '71
Fruitcake to fit your family. il McCalls 99:
38-9+ D '71
Grand glorious tortes. J. Uetz. il Am Home
74:102-3+ S '71
Holiday cakes: nuts and fruit; with recipes.
il Sunset 147:156 D '71
Introducing two thirsty cakes. Sunset 147:
147 S '71
Just baked and ready to travel. Sunset
147:105 Ag '71
Make mine butter-scotch. il Bet Hom &
Gard 49:88 Ap '71
Mashed-potato spice cake. il McCalls 98:82-3
Jl '71
Maxicalorie masterpiece; Coach house choco-
late cake. il N Y Times Mag p32 My 30 '71
Most elegant; Savarin: rum cake. R. A.
Sokolov. il N Y Times Mag p29 Ja 2 '72
Most seductive dessert; kirsch torte. C. Clai-
borne. il N Y Times Mag p72-3 My 2 '71
Party angels. il Farm J 95:40 Ag '71
Poundcake: penny-wise and pound-wise, too;
recipe. il McCalls 98:96+ Ap '71

Sauce seeps into the cake; apricot sauce
cake. il Sunset 146:192 Ap '71
Spectacular way to end a meal; flour tortilla
torte. il Sunset 146:212 My '71
Starting point is a remarkable and easy recipe;
whole egg sponge cake. il Sunset 146:114+ F
'71
Strawberry salute; nut torte. J. Hewitt. il
N Y Times Mag p63 My 9 '71
This cake ends up under the broiler; caramel-
pecan oatmeal cake. il Sunset 146:128 F '71
Twelve baking days to Christmas; fruitcake.
il N Y Times Mag p88 D 12 '71
See also
Cheesecake
Gingerbread
Pastry
CAL ARTS. See California institute of the
arts, Valencia
CAL STANDARD. See Standard oil company of
California
CALABRO, John J. and Wykert, John
What parents need to know about juvenile
arthritis; excerpt from The truth about
arthritis care. Parents Mag 46:50-1+ Ap
'71
CALADESI ISLAND. See Florida
CALAM, John
New books. See issues of Saturday review
CALAMITIES. See Disasters
CALARESU, Franco R. and Henry, J. L.
Sex difference in the number of sympathe-
tic neurons in the spinal cord of the cat.
bibliog il Science 173:343-4 Jl 23 '71
CALATRELLO, Robert L.
Reflections on a sociologist in a school of
education. Sch & Soc 99:419-20 N '71
CALCIFICATION
Phospholipid-calcium phosphate complex: en-
hanced calcium migration in the presence
of phosphate. J. M. Cotmore and others.
bibliog il Science 172:1339-41 Je 25 '71
CALCITONIN
Thyrocalcitonin: stimulation of secretion by
pentagastrin. C. W. Cooper and others. bibliog il Science 172:1238-40 Je 18 '71
CALCIUM in the body
Calcium as a mediator of adrenocorticotrophic hormone action on adrenal protein
synthesis. R. V. Farese. bibliog il Science
173:447-50 Jl 30 '71
Calcium: is it required for transmitter secretion? D. M. J. Quastel and others. bibliog il Science 172:1034-6 Je 4 '71
Calcium requirement for melanophore-
stimulating hormone action on melano-
phores. D. L. Vesely and M. E. Hadley.
bibliog il Science 173:923-5 S 3 '71
Vitamin D₃: induction of calcium-binding
protein in embryonic chick intestine in vi-
tro. R. A. Corradino and R. H. Wasserman.
bibliog il Science 172:731-3 My 14 '71
See also
Calcification
CALCULATING devices
See also
Monroe calculating machine company
Slide rule
CALCULATING machines, Electronic
Calculators slim down in size and price. il
Bsns W p50 O 9 '71
Electronic slide rules; pocket-sized electronic
calculators. J. Frye. Electr World 86:48+
O '71
Microelectronics shrinks the calculator. J. R.
Free. il Pop Sci 198:74-6+ Je '71
Which computer, the programmable cal-
culator? P. Asmus. il Electr World 86:27-30
S '71
See also
Wang laboratories, inc.
CALCULI, Biliary
Farewell to gallstones? il Newsweek 79:66
Ja 10 '72
CALCUTTA
Can urban guerrilla warfare succeed? H.
Tinker. Cur 129:52-7 My '71
Every day St Valentine's day; bitter feuding
between Marxist Communist party and Nax-
alites. Time 97:31-2 Mr 15 '71
Millions of refugees, calamity for India. J.
Wallace. il U S News 70:41 Je 28 '71
CALDECOTT medal
Caldecott award acceptance; address, June
21, 1971. G. E. Haley. Horn Bk 47:363-8
Ag '71
Newberry? L. N. Gerhardt. Library J 96:
4135 D 15 '71
Newbery-Caldecott awards. il Library J 96:
1094 Mr 15 '71
Newbery/Caldecott awards; excerpts from
addresses, ed. by P. Bragg. G. Haley; B.
Byars. Pub W 200:28 S 6 '71
Viking and Atheneum authors are 1970 New-
bery and Caldecott winners. L. Russ. il pors
Pub W 199:116-18 F 22 '71

CALDECOTT medal—*Continued*

Anecdotes, facetiae, satire, etc.

Up for discussion; a modest proposal for the very first worst children's book award ever. L. N. Gerhardt. Library J 96:1136-7 Mr 15 '71

Up for discussion; Finn Pin picked & Budd Button popped. L. N. Gerhardt. Library J 96:1525 Ap 15 '71

CALDER, Alexander
Artful camera of Ugo Mulas. M. R. Weiss. il pors Sat R 54:44-5 Je 12 '71 *
Calder tapestries. M. Welish. il Craft Horiz 31:40-1 D '71 *

CALDERONE, Mary (Steichen)
Sex education for the whole society. Ed Digest 37:43-5 O '71

CALDWELL, Benjamin Hubbard, 1935-
Tennessee silversmiths. il Antiques 100:382-5 S '71
Tennessee silversmiths prior to 1860; a check list. il Antiques 100:906-13 D '71

about

Living with antiques. O. W. June. il Antiques 100:438-41 S '71 *

CALDWELL, Bettye M.
Timid giant grows bolder. il Sat R 54:47-9+ F 20 '71

CALDWELL, Dean
Inch by inch up El Capitan. il Read Digest 98:64-9 Mr '71

about

Because it's nowhere. H. Peterson. il pors Sports Illus 34:76-8+ My 3 '71
Lady of the mountain. F. G. Loyd. il por Todays Health 49:37 F '71 *

CALDWELL, Earl
Freedoms to write and read and be informed. R. H. Smith. Pub W 200:29 D 13 '71 *

CALDWELL, Gwendolyn D.
I? poem. Negro Hist Bul 34:87 Ap '71

CALDWELL, Philip
From Philco to Ford. por Bsns W p75 O 2 '71 *

CALDWELL, Sarah
Druids in Boston. H. Saal. il por Newsweek 77:95 Je 28 '71 *

CALEDONIAN-BUA airways
Caledonian to declare $2.5-million profit. Aviation W 95:29 N 8 '71

CALENDAR
See also
Time

CALENDARS
Student art used on calendar. D. Beringer. il Sch Arts 70:11 Ap '71

CALF barns. See Barns and stables

CALF feeding contracts. See Contracts, Agricultural

CALIAN, Carnegie Samuel
Can eastern Christians survive under Marx or Islam? il Cath World 212:249-52+ F '71

CALIBRATION
How to calibrate your sprayer. il Suc Farm 69:no4 C32 Mr '71
Swing your compass. D. B. Richards. il Flying 88:57-8 F '71

CALIBRATORS
Building and using the 2XY calibrator; double-axis oscilloscope calibrator. G. Windolph. il Pop Electr 34:34-5+ Mr '71
Crystal calibrator for the ham and SWL. W. L. Blair. il Pop Electr 35:59-62 Ag '71

CALIFANO, Joseph Anthony, 1931-
Excerpt from testimony, September 17, 1969. Cong Digest 50:59+ F '71
Excerpt from The case against an all-volunteer army, February 21, 1971. Cong Digest 50:145+ My '71

CALIFORNIA
California on my mind; facts and fancies gleaned from varied sources, and quotations. House B 113:76-7 Mr '71
Life in a land of legends; symposium. il House B 113:47-98+ Mr '71
See also
Agriculture—California
Airports—California
Architecture, Domestic—California
Art—California
Banks and banking—California
Bolinas Lagoon
Booksellers and bookselling—California
Cascade Range
Colleges and universities—California
Contra Costa County
Death Valley
Divorce—California
Education—California
Environmental policy—California
Fishing—California

Gardening—California
Gardens—California
Geology—California
Hetch Hetchy Valley
Housing—California
Hunting—California
Insurance, Unemployment—California
Irrigation—California
Justice, Administration of—California
Land—California
Medical service, State—California
Mojave Desert
Music festivals—California
Napa Valley
Owens Valley
Pinnacles National Monument
Prisons—California
Public health—California
Public welfare—California
Publishers and publishing—California
Recreation areas—California
Redwood National Park
Roads—California
Sacramento County
San Diego County
San Francisco Bay
Santa Catalina Island
Santa Monica Mountains
School laws and legislation—California
School libraries—California
Shasta Lake
Sierra Nevada Mountains
Squaw Valley
Tahoe, Lake
Taxation—California
Tomales Bay
Transportation—California
Unemployment—California
Water pollution—California
Water supply—California
Wildlife conservation—California
Yosemite National Park
Yosemite Valley

Description and travel

California talk for on-lookers and doers. Vogue 157:88 My '71
Tour California by air. P. Garrison. il Flying 90:62-5 Ja '72
West coast sights and delights. H. Brown. Am Home 74:44 Je '71

Economic conditions

Aerospace in crisis. M. Gellen. Nation 212:232-5 F 22 '71
Southern California: the end of sunny growth. il Bsns W p88-92 Jl 17 '71

Education, Department of

California's new education boss. L. Robinson. il pors Ebony 26:54-6+ My '71

History

Gardener in Eden; notes from a native son on beginning a history of the Golden state. T. H. Watkins. Am West 8:42-7 N '71
See also
California—Missions
San Francisco—History

Industries

See also
Wine industry

Land tenure

See Land tenure—United States

Legislature

Rescuing California; survey by R. Nader. P. Barnes. New Repub 165:12-13 S 18 '71

Joint fact-finding committee on un-American activities

Locking up the Tenney files. J. R. Mills. Nation 213:10-11 Jl 5 '71

Missions

Building a new world; the white man's mighty effort to civilize the first Californians. D. Lavender. il Am West 8:36-41+ N '71

Parks and reserves

Coe is usually uncrowded. il Sunset 146:34+ Mr '71
For Cal from Uncle Sam, with well; leasing of marines Camp Pendleton and San Onofre beachfront to the state of California. R. W. Johnston. Sports Illus 35:86+ S 13 '71
In the lee of Angel Island. E. St Davids. il Motor B & S 127:56-7+ Je '71
Newest California state park; Castle Rock park. il Sunset 146:55 Mr '71
Park with a gold mine in it; Bedford park. il Sunset 147:23 Ag '71

CALIFORNIA—Parks and reserves—*Cont.*
San Simeon's treats go beyond art and architecture. il Sunset 146:272-3 My '71
To the Marin headlands for a winter picnic. il Sunset 146:54-5 Ja '71

Photographs
Balboa and the fun zone. T. H. Garver. il Art in Am 59:58-67 S '71

Politics and government
California's mad mix. M. E. Leary. Nation 212:685-7 My 31 '71
Chavez machine. W. F. Buckley, jr. Nat R 23:888-9 Ag 10 '71
Crisis facing key states: what Reagan, Rockefeller are doing. pors U S News 70:41-2 My 17 '71
Democratic new guard. M. E. Leary. Nation 212:302-5 Mr 8 '71
Jess Unruh and his moment of truth. J. Larner. pors Harper 242:62-8 Ap '71
Reagan and reality, by E. G. Brown. Review
    Nat R 23:91+ Ja 26 '71. G. F. Will
Ronald Reagan's slow fade. K. Fleming. il por Newsweek 78:28-9 D 20 '71

Population
Is California's boom over? il U S News 70:37-8 Je 21 '71
Paradise lost? il Newsweek 78:52 Ag 2 '71

Religious institutions and affairs
Church alive and changing: southern California suburbs. J. C. Hough, jr. il Chr Cent 89:8-12 Ja 5 '72

Social life and customs
American thing: a view of southern California. C. Holland. Mlle 72:207+ Ap '71

Theater
See Theater—United States

CALIFORNIA, GULF OF
Love affair south of the border. E. Gibbons. Org Gard & Farm 18:122-7 Ap '71
Lure of Baja. C. West. il Yachting 129:48-9+ Ap '71
Small boat passage. C. L. Cadieux. il Yachting 129:68-9+ F '71

CALIFORNIA, LOWER
Baja California. N. Morgan. il Holiday 48:48-51+ N '70
Lure of Baja. C. West. il Yachting 129:48-9+ Ap '71
    See also
Automobile touring—California, Lower
Fishing—California, Lower

Description and travel
Holiday below the Baja border and up in the Baja foothills. il Sunset 146:36+ Ap '71

CALIFORNIA Angels (baseball) See Baseball clubs
CALIFORNIA beaches. See Beaches
CALIFORNIA children's lobby. See Pressure groups

CALIFORNIA CITY, Calif.
Images for a new California City. R. Jensen. il Arch Rec 149:117-20 Je '71

CALIFORNIA college of podiatric medicine, San Francisco, Calif.
San Francisco, Calif. il Arch Forum 134:46-7 Je '71
CALIFORNIA design show. See Design—Exhibitions
CALIFORNIA 500. See Automobile racing

CALIFORNIA. Fresno state college, Fresno
Strangulation of Fresno state. B. Hillenbrand. Commonweal 94:136-8 Ap 16 '71

CALIFORNIA gray whales. See Whales
CALIFORNIA Indians. See Indians of North America

CALIFORNIA institute of the arts, Valencia, Calif.
Cal Arts: freedom is the password; no grades, no exams. K. Monson. il Hi Fi 21:MA10-12 Je '71
Disney's dream school. il Newsweek 78:67-8 N 8 '71

CALIFORNIA medical association
Medical association sues California over cuts in care. R. J. Bazell. Science 171:360 Ja 29 '71

CALIFORNIA rural legal assistance program. See Legal aid
CALIFORNIA sea lions. See Seals (animals)

CALIFORNIA. State college, Long Beach

Department of dance
New climate for dance, Cal State Long Beach. V. H. Swisher. il Dance Mag 45:29-30 My '71

CALIFORNIA. State polytechnic college. San Luis Obispo
April 23 and 24 in San Luis Obispo, a college carnival and rodeo. il Sunset 146:75 Ap '71

CALIFORNIA trail
Incident at Tragedy Springs; an unsolved mystery of the California trail. F. Egan. il Am West 8:36-9 Ja '71

CALIFORNIA. University

Berkeley campus
Beginning: Berkeley, 1964, by M. Heirich. Review
    Nation 212:599-600 My 10 '71. B. Aptheker
Berkeley scene, 1971: patching up the ivory tower. R. J. Bazell. Science 173:1006-8 S 10 '71
Window boxes do a lot for an old building as this Berkeley student action shows. il Sunset 146:78-9 Mr '71

School of librarianship
Reconstitution for peace and relevancy; 1970 crisis in southeast Asia. C. MacLeod. il pors Library J 96:1192-6 Ap 1 '71

Irvine campus
Department of dance
Cunningham on campus. O. Maynard. il por Dance Mag 45:32-4 Jl '71

Lawrence radiation laboratories
Berkeley debate; nuclear weapons research. Nation 212:134 F 1 '71
Man-made cosmic rays. il Newsweek 78:61 S 6 '71

Libraries
See also
California. University—Los Angeles campus —Libraries
California. University—San Diego campus—Libraries

Los Angeles campus
Perennial problem: NCAA basketball playoffs. J. Jares. il Sports Illus 34:12-17 Mr 22 '71
UCLA graduate dance center. V. H. Swisher. il Dance Mag 45:76-9 D '71

Graduate school of business administration
Entrepreneurs teach others how to do it; Project enterprise course. il Bsns W p 124+ N 13 '71

Libraries
Moratorium history committee; UCLA. R. Trager. il Am Lib 2:1157-60 D '71
Undergraduate library, for undergraduates! UCLA experience; address, 1970. N. E. Jones. il por Wilson Lib Bul 45:584-90 F '71

San Diego campus
Libraries
UCSD: the new central library. W. B. Kuhn. il Am Lib 2:168-73 F '71

Santa Barbara campus
California's Isla Vista: From anathema to dialogue; Student service center. N. Cousins. Sat R 54:22-4 Je 5 '71

Santa Cruz campus
Santa Cruz mystique. A. Gross. il Mlle 74:102-3+ Ja '72
U. of California at Santa Cruz: new deal for undergraduates? L. J. Carter. il Science 171:153-7 Ja 15 '71

CALIFORNIA wines. See Wine

CALIPERS
Handiest tool in my shop: vernier caliper. J. Miller. il Pop Sci 199:134 O '71

CALISHER, Hortense
House; story. Mlle 73:144-5 Je '71
1971 Gigi looks at sex; story; excerpt from Queenie. Vogue 157:121 Ap 1 '71
    about
Trade winds. C. Amory. Sat R 54:6+ My 8 '71 •

CALISTHENICS. See Gymnastics

CALKINS, Frank
Many seasons of South Pass. il Field & S 76:62-3+ Ag '71

CALKINS, Hugh
Financing education in the 70's. Todays Ed 60:30-2 F '71

CALKINS, Myron D.
Municipal safety program that works. il Am City 86:67-8 Ag '71

CALL; story. See O'Connor, F.

CALLA lilies
Callas, past, present and future. W. A. Brown. il Horticulture 49:38+ Mr '71

CALLAGHAN, Morley Edward
Authors & editors. T. Chastain. por Pub W 199:15-17 Je 7 '71 *

CALLAHAN, Daniel
Making the ethical case against abortion. pors Time 97:70 Mr 29 '71 *

CALLAHAN, David
His biggest commodity: publicity. por Bsns W p25 Jl 31 '71 *

CALLAHAN, Leslie G. Jr
Science of war? Nat R 23:313 Mr 23 '71

CALLAHAN, Michael A.
Can Quaker Oats rescue Hollywood? America 125:121-2 S 4 '71

CALLAHAN, William E.
America first; interview. il Forbes 108:43 Ag 1 '71

CALLAND, Chad
Incredible ordeal of Chad Calland, M.D. A. Hano. il Redbook 137:94+ S '71 *

CALLARD, Eric John
Arrival of enemy no. 1. por Fortune 83:65 My '71 *

CALLARD, Jack. See Callard, E. J.

CALLAS, Constantine
Build a Wheatstone bridge substitution box. il Pop Electr 34:62-5+ F '71

CALLAS, Maria
Callas on the record; interview, ed. by H. Saal. por Newsweek 77:90-1 F 15 '71
Processo alla Callas; interview. New Yorker 47:31-2 Ap 24 '71
   about
Artist life. D. J. Soria. il por Hi Fi 21:MA4-5+ Jl '71 *
Fiery Maria Callas is a pianissimo professor. J. Downs. por Life 71:91 N 26 '71 *
Reality of Maria. por Harp Baz 104:94-5 Ag '71 *

CALLAWAY, Ely R.
Friend at Burlington. por Bsns W p92 Mr 20 '71 *

CALLAWAY gardens. See Gardens—Georgia

CALLEJÓN DE HUAYLAS. See Huaylas, Callejón de

CALLENBACH, Ernest
Recent film writing: a survey. bibliog Film Q 24:11-32 Spr '71
Unloved one. Film Q 24:42-54 Sum '71

CALLEY, William Laws, Jr
Confessions of Lieutenant Calley; interview, ed. by J. Sack (cont) Esquire 75:59-9+ F '71; 76:85-9+ S '71
I fired into the ditch also, sir; excerpts from testimony. Life 70:28 Mr 5 '71
   about
Calley affair. il Time 97:13-14 Ap 19 '71 *
Calley and the public conscience. P. Steinfels. Commonweal 94:128 Ap 16 '71 *
Calley case re-examined. S. Lesher. il pors N Y Times Mag p6-7+ Jl 11 '71 *
Calley on the couch. Newsweek 77:25 F 1 '71 *
Calley story. A. Cooper. il por Newsweek 78:90+ S 20 '71 *
Calley takes the stand. il pors Life 70:22-7 Mr 5 '71 *
Calley's confession. por Newsweek 77:21-2 Mr 1 '71 *
Calley's defense: anger, hate, fear, orders. por Newsweek 77:51-2 Mr 8 '71 *
Coddled criminal. New Repub 164:10-11 Ap 17 '71 *
Court-martial of Lt Calley, by R. Hammer. Review
   Time por 98:55 Ag 23 '71. E. Magnuson *
Day America could have used a psychiatrist. B. Asbell. il por Todays Health 49:24-9+ Ag '71 *
Hero Calley. por Time 97:14 F 15 '71 *
Is there a bit of Calley in us? D. Abrahamsen. Look 35:76-7 Je 1 '71 *
Judgment at Fort Benning. il pors Newsweek 77:27-9 Ap 12 '71 *
Lieutenant Calley and the President. Life 70:40 Ap 16 '71 *
My Lai and Lieut Calley: the wounds of war. il por Sr Schol 98:11-12+ My 10 '71 *
Mysterious Lieutenant Calley. T. Mayer. il Life 71:14 O 1 '71 *
Reduction for Calley. Time 98:20 Ag 30 '71 *
Rusty Calley: unlikely villain; report. P. Range. il por Time 97:17 Ap 12 '71 *
Second thoughts about Calley. Newsweek 77:29-30 Ap 19 '71 *
Two soldiers. J. Morgenstern. Newsweek 77:18-19 Mr 15 '71 *

Viking, Esquire, dropped from Calley law suit. Pub W 199:37 Ja 18 '71 *
Viking press explains position on publication of Lieutenant Calley. A. J. Johnston. il por Pub W 199:42 Ap 26 '71; Reply. W. Greenhaw. 199:14 My 17 '71 *
Who is responsible for My Lai? por Time 97:18-19 Mr 8 '71 *
With Calley at My Lai. il Newsweek 77:32-3 Ja 25 '71 *

CALLEY trial. See Courts martial and courts of inquiry

CALLEY verdict. See Courts martial and courts of inquiry—Verdicts

CALLING cards. See Visiting cards

CALLISON, Charles H.
National outlook. See issues of Audubon

CALLOWAY, Doris
Food for thought. McCalls 98:54+ My; 68 Je; 18 Ag; 30 S; 99:30 O; 40 D '71

CALLUNA. See Heathers

CALMANN-LÉVY (firm) See Publishers and publishing—France

CALOGERAS, Roy C.
Gèza Róheim: psychoanalytic anthropologist or radical Freudian? bibliog Am Imago 28:146-57 Sum '71
—See Schupper, F. X. jt. auth.

CALORIES, Food. See Diet

CALORIMETERS and calorimetry
Determining specific heats by ice calorimetry. H. W. Edwards and L. G. Brouwer. bibliog il pors Chem 44:23-4 Ap '71

CALVAYRAC, Regis, and others
Euglena gracilis: formation of giant mitochondria. bibliog il Science 173:252-4 Jl 16 '71

CALVÉ, Emma
I remember Emma. P. Wood. por Opera N 35:26-9 F 6 '71 *

CALVES
Testing pays 50 extra tons of calf per crop. C. Peterson, jr. il Suc Farm 69:no5 B13 Mr '71

   Care
Fall calves pay on Idaho ranch. B. M. Wilkinson. Suc Farm 69:L6-7 N '71
He starts dairy-beef calves. W. Waltner and E. Waltner. il Suc Farm 69:L10 N '71
Master plan for healthier calves. W. Kester. il Farm J 95:B6-7+ O '71

   Feeding
Colostrum timing important in calf disease control. Suc Farm 69:no2 D8 F '71
They raise 'em, he feeds 'em. il Suc Farm 69:D6 Ap '71

CALVIN, John
Social welfare in Calvin's Geneva; adaptation of address, December 30, 1968. R. M. Kingdon. bibliog f Am Hist R 76:50-69 F '71 *

CALVING
Keep heifers calving on schedule. C. E. Ball. il Farm J 95:B11+ O '71 *

CAMARA, Helder Pessôa, abp
Brazilian prelate hits banking procedures, stirs controversy in Switzerland. Chr Cent 88:970 Ag 18 '71 *
Dom Helder Camara as a symbolic man. B. Tyson. Cath World 213:178-82, 235-9 Jl-Ag '71 *
Dom Helder Câmara, by J. de Broucker. Review
   Chr Cent por 88:700-1 Je 2 '71. C. F. Stoerker *
Little priest who stands up to Brazil's generals. J. A. Page. il por N Y Times Mag p26-7+ My 23 '71 *

CAMBODIA
Cambodia. W. A. Withington. bibliog il Focus 21:1-9 F '71
   See also
Ballet—Cambodia
Church and state in Cambodia
Hospitals—Cambodia
Military assistance, American—Cambodia
Natural resources—Cambodia
United States—Foreign relations—Cambodia

   Army
Pinching the arteries. il Time 97:35 Ja 25 '71
Why they call Lon Nol the mayor of Pnompenh. D. Kirk. il N Y Times Mag p26-7+ Je 27 '71

   Foreign relations
   United States
   See United States—Foreign relations—Cambodia

CAMBODIA—*Continued*
Politics and government
Change of guard. il Newsweek 77:36 F 22 '71
Man behind the symbol. por Time 97:39 My 17 '71
Meaning of coup in Thailand. il U S News 71:91 N 29 '71
Return of Lon Nol. M. Proffitt. Newsweek 77:46-7 Ap 26 '71
With Sihanuok in Peking; interview, ed. by A. Casella. Norodom Sihanouk. Nation 212: 305-8 Mr 8 '71
Year one. Time 98:44 O 18 '71

Religious institutions and affairs
See also
Buddha and Buddhism
CAMBODIAN minorities. See Minorities
CAMBODIAN refugees. See Refugees, Cambodian
CAMBODIAN-Vietnamese conflict
Cambodia: triumph and terror. il Time 97: 22+ F 1 '71
Guerrilla war; attack on Phnom Penh airport. Newsweek 77:27 F 1 '71
In for the duration. il Time 98:39 D 20 '71
Keeping them guessing; ARVN moves into Cambodia. Time 98:35 D 6 '71
Letter from Indo-China (cont) R. Shaplen. New Yorker 47:85-7 Mr 6; 121-3+ Ap 24 '71
Reason for confidence in Cambodia. W. C. Moore. por U S News 70:20-1 F 8 '71
Why they call Lon Nol the mayor of Pnompenh. D. Kirk. il N Y Times Mag p26-7+ Je 27 '71

Aerial operations
Cambodia: growing debacle. Nation 212:130-1 F 1 '71

American participation
Cambodia: key to U.S. plan for Vietnam pullout. il U S News 71:36-7 N 29 '71
Cambodia: why U.S. is getting in deeper; with report by W. S. Merick. il U S News 70:19-20 F 1 '71
Debate over Cambodia. il Newsweek 77:26 F 1 '71
Just looking on; military equipment delivery teams. Nation 212:194 F 15 '71
Proxy war. il Newsweek 77:49 Ja 25 '71
Remember Cambodia? Nation 213:418-19 N 1 '71
Secretary Rogers' news conference of January 29, 1971. W. P. Rogers. Dept State Bul 64:189-97 F 15 '71

Campaigns and battles
Bloody reminder. il Newsweek 78:54 D 13 '71
CAMBRIDGE, Godfrey MacArthur
What the F.B.I. has on me. por Esquire 76:140-1+ D '71 •
CAMBRIDGE, University
Quest at Cambridge. N. Pittenger. Chr Cent 88:150 F 3 '71

Cavendish laboratory
Recollections of Rutherford and the Cavendish; adaptation of address, August 1971. S. Devons. il pors Phys Today 24:38-45 D '71
CAMDEN, N.J.
Campbell stays with Camden; with editorial comment il por Bsns W p66-8, 94 F 6 '71
Rehabilitator of its hometown. il Bsns W p60 Mr 6 '71
CAMELLIA exhibits. See Flower exhibits
CAMELLIAS
Camellia with flower garlands; camellia lutchuensis. il Sunset 147:213 D '71
Camellias in the landscape. H. E. Dryden. il Horticulture 49:28-9+ D '71
New developments in camellias. D. L. Feathers. il Horticulture 49:22-3+ S '71
Petaled perfection. L. V. Power. il Am Home 74:36 Mr '71
Retics, the show stoppers. il Sunset 146:82-5 Mr '71
Shishi-gashira; do-it-all camellia. il Sunset 147:192 D '71
CAMELS
How can camels go without water for such long periods of time? Sci Digest 70:84 O '71
CAMEOS
From slave to siren. D. J. Janson. il Art N 70:49-53 My '71
Great men in American history honored in sulphides or cameo encrustations. T. H. Marsh. il Hobbies 75:116-17 Ja '71
CAMERA backs. See Cameras—Loading
CAMERA bags. See Photography—Apparatus and supplies

CAMERA bellows. See Bellows
CAMERA cases
Camera bags I have known. N. Rothschild. il Pop Phot 69:68-70+ Ag '71
CAMERA industry. See Photographic apparatus and supplies industry
CAMERA lenses. See Lenses, Photographic
CAMERA shutters
View from Kramer; behind-the-lens shutters. A. Kramer. il Mod Phot 35:38+ N '71
Control
Keppler on the SLR; electronically controlled shutters. H. Keppler. il Mod Phot 35:10+ Jl '71
CAMERA tools. See Tools
CAMERA tripods
Feininger. A. Feininger. Mod Phot 35:52+ F '71
How shaky is your camera? J. Schneider and B. Bodenstein. il Mod Phot 35:90-3 My '71
3 legs are better than 2. J. Schneider. il Mod Phot 35:84-7 Ap '71
Tripods are up to new tricks. J. Hand. il Pop Mech 135:140-3+ Mr '71
View from Kramer; portable tripod for view cameras. A. Kramer. il Mod Phot 35:26+ O '71
CAMERAS
And now the M5! B. Schwalberg. il Pop Phot 69:106-9+ O '71
Annual guide to 47 top cameras (cont) il Mod Phot 35:75-122 D '71
Behind the scenes. See occasional issues of Modern photography
Binocular camera takes spotlight. il Travel 136:74-5 O '71
Electric-eye 35mm cameras. il Consumer Bul 54:31-8 D '71
First look. See issues of Popular photography
4 Seagulls. 1 Pearl River from China. M. Tsuji. il Mod Phot 35:16+ N '71
In the good old days when the 4x5 press camera was king. S. Nathan. il Pop Phot 69:58+ Jl '71
Large-format cameras: does bigger mean better? N. Rothschild. il Pop Phot 68:61-7+ Ap '71
Last look at Photokina '70. N. Goldberg. il Pop Phot 68:74-5 F '71
Modern photography's annual guide to 46 top cameras. il Mod Phot 34:85-130 D '70
NASA develops new underwater camera. Aviation W 94:20 Ap 19 '71
Our stone-age cameras. N. Goldberg. il Pop Phot 68:69-73 F '71
Photokina 70. il Pop Phot 68:81-96 Ja '71
Readers' report:
Leicas. il Mod Phot 35:102-3+ Je '71
Rolleis that didn't make it! H. Keppler. il Mod Phot 35:66 Je '71
Swinging lens camera; Panon-Panox-Panophic. S. Nathan. il Pop Phot 68:44+ Ja '71
Taking circular underwater photos; panoramic camera. M. W. Martin. il Sea Front 17:202-3 Jl '71
35mm rangefinder camera with behind-lens meter? Yup, the Leica M5. J. Schneider. il Mod Phot 35:32+ O '71
Two dozen compact 35s: how they compare. L. Drukker. il Pop Phot 69:92-7+ S '71
View from Kramer; Kardan 45S, Arca Swiss Basic B view cameras. A. Kramer. il Mod Phot 35:46+ Ag '71
View from Kramer; Toyo field view camera. A. Kramer. il Mod Phot 35:59+ My '71
What's new? Look! il Mod Phot 35:63-78 Ja '71
See also
Moving picture cameras
Polaroid Land cameras
Single-lens reflex cameras
Twin-lens cameras

Collectors and collecting
Camera collector:
American turn-of-the-century classics. J. Schneider. il Mod Phot 35:52+ My '71
Brunning's of High Holborn, London. J. Schneider. il Mod Phot 35:58+ N '71
Japanese classics and Konica-made folders from the middle 1930's. J. Schneider. il Mod Phot 35:36+ Mr '71
Konicas. J. Schneider. il Mod Phot 35: 36+ Mr: 62+ Ap '71
Pigeon 35, JEM jr. 120 and Deceptive angle graphic. J. Schneider. il Mod Phot 35:60+ O '71
Pre-Minox minis. J. Schneider. il Mod Phot 35:48+ Ag '71
Quartet of classic stereos from the Olden collection. J. Schneider. il Mod Phot 35:58+ D '71
Unidentifiable camera quiz. J. Schneider. il Mod Phot 35:46+ Je '71

CAMERAS—*Continued*

Control
See Camera shutters—Control

Design
Human engineering. N. Goldberg. il Pop Phot 69:61-3+ Ag '71

Loading
Cutting time and cost with 70-mm; camera back. P. Gowland. il Pop Phot 68:24 Ja '71

Maintenance and repair
Techniques tomorrow; camera repair. B. Sherman. il Mod Phot 35:40+ Ap '71

Manufacture
What's so special about the 'Goldberg stand-off?' Plenty! N. Goldberg. il Pop Phot 69:80+ O '71

Mounting
How shaky is your camera? J. Schneider and B. Bodenstein. il Mod Phot 35:90-3 My '71

Protection against theft
Write your own camera theft policy. E. Meyers. il Pop Phot 68:60+ My '71

Testing
Camera flare: the real enemy? B. Bodenstein and H. Keppler. il Mod Phot 36:86-9 Ja '72
How to field test your camera. E. Scully. il Mod Phot 35:36+ D '71
Keppler on the SLR. H. Keppler. il Mod Phot 35:12+ Mr '71
Lab report:
Canonet QL17. N. Rothschild; N. Goldberg. il Pop Phot 68:100-1+ Mr '71
Fujica G690. N. Goldberg and L. Kean. il Pop Phot 68:100-1+ Ap '71
Modern tests. See issues of Modern photography

CAMERAS, Used
Buying a used camera. J. Reynolds. il Consumer Bul 54:28-32 N '71
Camera collector; how to sell an old camera. J. Schneider. il Mod Phot 35:130-1 Jl '71
CAMERAS on space vehicles. See Space vehicles—Equipment

CAMERON, A. G. W.
Spotting an invisible black hole. J. P. Wiley, jr. il Natur Hist 80:62-3 Ap '71 •

CAMERON, Bruce
Peaceful progress. il Yachting 130:57+ Ag '71

CAMERON, Duncan F.
Public puts its cards on the table. UNESCO Courier 24:15+ Mr '71

CAMERON, Eleanor
High fantasy: A wizard of Earthsea; address, October 1969. bibliog f Horn Bk 47:129-38 Ap '71

CAMERON, Gail
Rose; excerpts. il pors Ladies Home J 88:87-9+ Jl; 67-9+ Ag '71

CAMERON, James, 1817-1882
Three Tennessee painters. B. H. Bishop. il Antiques 100:432-7 S '71 •

CAMERON, Juan
Boston Brahmin in Heartbreak house. il pors Fortune 84:88-91+ O '71
How the interstate changed the face of the Nation. il Fortune 84:78-81+ Jl '71
Our gravest military problem is manpower. il Fortune 83:60-3+ Ap '71

CAMERON, Melvin
Stealing your car. A. Rothenberg. il pors Look 35:74-6 Je 29 '71 •

CAMEROON REPUBLIC
See also
Trials—Cameroon Republic

CAMHI, Jeffrey M.
Flight orientation in locusts; with biographical sketch. il Sci Am 225:13, 74-81 bibliog(p 120) Ag '71

CAMOMILE, Leo
Reference notebook: what is your writing objective? Writers Digest 51:27 Mr '71

CAMP activities. See Camping—Activities
CAMP administration. See Camps—Administration

CAMP children
I got a letter! help for campers' homesickness. E. Bristol. il PTA Mag 65:26-7 Ap '71
Post-season camp for alumni proves success. S. M. Dickhaus and S. O. Cohen. Camp Mag 43:22 F '71

Transportation
New camp transportation policy. W. R. Hawkins. il Camp Mag 43:15-16 My '71

CAMP chores
Put fun into camp dining room clean-up. J. D. Orr. il Camp Mag 43:50 Mr '71

CAMP cookery
Camp chef. C. B. Colby. See issues of Outdoor life
Camp cooking. il Sunset 146:78-83 Ap '71
Camp cooks say keep it simple. il Sunset 146:184+ Ap '71
Campfire cooking with foil. A. Old. Redbook 137:32 My '71
Food outlook for 1971. Camp Mag 43:18 My '71
Good housekeeping practices in camp food storage. il Camp Mag 43:18+ Ap '71
How your camp kitchen can cope with electrical emergencies; excerpts from Highlights: food marketing and management. Camp Mag 43:16-17 Ja '71
New egg products save you time and space. il Camp Mag 43:18-19 Je '71
One-pot or no-pot camp meal. Sunset 147:121-2 Jl '71
Positives outweigh negatives for camps using convenience foods. J. A. Schwartz. il Camp Mag 43:20-2 My '71
See also
Cookery, Outdoor
CAMP-cooking utensils. See Kitchen utensils

CAMP counselors
Audio-visual aids can help you pep up staff meetings. H. D. Berk. il Camp Mag 43:12-13 Ap '71
Camp staff members, just as campers, need individual guidance; excerpts from address. F. Hamilton. il Camp Mag 43:8-9 Ap '71
Foreign counselors come to camp; Camp Mohawk, Wis. W. J. Cullen. Camp Mag 43:26-7 Ja '71
How to give real meaning to CIT programs. S. Sterk. il Camp Mag 43:15-16 Mr '71
Human relations training for camp staff members. C. B. Rotman and C .S. Clayman. il Camp Mag 43:10+ Ap '71
Professionalizing your staff development. M. Silverman. il Camp Mag 43:13-14 Mr '71
What are today's college-age counselors really like? excerpts from address. O. E. Jones. il por Camp Mag 43:11-12+ Ja '71

CAMP discipline
What will your counselors communicate to campers? D. Webb. Camp Mag 43:14+ Ap '71

CAMP equipment. See Camping—Outfits, supplies, etc.

CAMP fires
Campfires. R. Cochran. il Field & S 76:20 Jl '71

CAMP food storage. See Food—Storage
CAMP intruder alarms. See Burglar alarms
CAMP management. See Camps—Administration

CAMP revival meetings. See Revivals

CAMP sanitation
Campers vs. litter: practical ecology in camp. A. H. Seed, jr. il Camp Mag 43:13+ Je '71
Most camps need better garbage disposal facilities. M. Melamed. il Camp Mag 43:25-6 My '71

CAMP sites, facilities, etc.
Asphalt forest; Campland, off San Diego freeway. il Time 98:46 Ag 2 '71
Brave new world of private campgrounds. B. Behme. il Field & S 76:124-6 S '71
Condominium camping. P. R. Martin. il Har Yrs 11:18-21 My '71
Crisis in our campgrounds. B. Behme. Field & S 75:130-1 F '71
LP-gas aids longer camp seasons. J. P. Linehan. Camp Mag 43:16 N '71
Make your woodlands work for you. E. M. Bacon. il Camp Mag 43:13-14 Ja '71
New camping stop on Interstate 5; northern California. il Sunset 147:27 S '71
Playing with blocks; day camp, Mt Olive, N.J. E. P. Berkeley. il Arch Forum 135:38-41 Jl '71
Private forest camping sites the public can use. Good H 172:172-3 Je '71
Unique design solves rainy day problems; Camp Greylock, Mass. il Camp Mag 43:12 S '71

CAMP Solo, Maine. See Camps—Maine

CAMP stoves
Camp cooking fires you carry with you. il Sunset 147:54-7 Jl '71

CAMPA, Justiniano F. and Engel, W. K.
Histochemical and functional correlations in anterior horn neurons of the cat spinal cord. bibliog il Science 171:198-9 Ja 15 '71

CAMPAIGN desks. See Desks

CAMPAIGN funds
Annals of politics. R. E. Harris. New York-
er 47:37-40+ Ag 7 '71
Campaign costs: floor, not ceiling; Time es-
say. Time 97:18-19 My 17 '71
Campaign expense problem. W. F. Buckley,
jr. Nat R 23:1434-5 D 17 '71
Campaign funding. W. Pincus. New Repub
165:17-19 D 11 '71
Can Congress really control election spend-
ing? il U S News 70:33-6 Ap 26 '71
Candidate with the built-in edge; scheme to
finance campaigns with tax dollars. il por
Newsweek 78:21-2 D 13 '71
Coming: taxpayer subsidy of presidential
candidates? il U S News 71:14+ D 6 '71
Dirty little secret. Nation 213:645 D 20 '71
$400 million election machine; political con-
tributors. il Newsweek 78:23-4+ D 13 '71
Full disclosure; expenses of California's can-
didates. Nation 214:36 Ja 10 '72
Green revolution; plan for financing presi-
dential campaigns from tax revenues. News-
week 78:19-20 N 29 '71
High price of campaigning. America 125:472
D 4 '71
Honesty in politics. W. Pincus. New Repub
165:9-10+ D 4 '71
Land of milk and money; dairy farmers con-
tribute to presidential campaign funds. F.
Wright. Nation 213: 657-9 D 20 '71
Money and politics. Nation 213:3-4 Jl 5 '71
Nixon's feudal friends in Carolina. E. Torn-
quist. Ramp Mag 10:16+ O '71
Paying to get elected. New Repub 165:7-8 O
16 '71
Political inflation. New Repub 165:9-10 Ag
7 '71
Politics for rich & poor. N. D. Reece. New
Repub 164:8-9 Ja 16 '71; Reply. M. Gravel.
164:32-3 F 20 '71
Politics: who should pay? Of fat cats and
other angels. il Time 98:14-15 N 29 '71
Put the lid on: financing the '72 Democratic
primaries. J. R. Schmidt and W. W. Whalen.
New Repub 164:16-17 Je 5 '71; Reply. A. J.
Rosenthal. 164:7-9 Je 19 '71
Reports & comment: Washington. E. B.
Drew. Atlan 227:18+ Mr '71
Something bad for everyone. S. C. Bright-
man. Nation 213:11-13 Jl 5 '71
Spending in the '72 campaign; a whole
new set of rules. il U S News 71:42-3
D 27 '71
Tax subsidy for political candidates? U S
News 70:58 Ap 12 '71

Anecdotes, facetiae, satire, etc.
Cut-rate president. G. Ace. Sat R 55:4 Ja 1
'72

CAMPAIGN issues
Conservation: new political power or plati-
tude? M. Frome. Field & S 75:34+ Mr '71
Crime & the liberal audience. J. Q. Wilson;
discussion. Commentary 51:26+ My '71
Organizing the new politics: a proposal. S.
Lynd. Ramp Mag 10:14-15+ D '71
Top issue for '72; quality of Richard Nixon's
leadership. Nation 213:675-6 D 27 '71

CAMPAIGN management
Advance man. by J. Bruno and J. Green-
field. Review
Life il por 70:11 My 28 '71. V. S. Navasky
Advance man; interview. J. Bruno. New
Yorker 47:30-1 Je 12 '71
Advance man; interview, ed. by D. N. Mount.
J. Bruno. il Pub W 199:46-7 Je 21 '71

CAMPAIGN organizers. See Campaign management

CAMPAIGN slogans. See Slogans

CAMPAIGN songs
Songs America voted by. ed. by L. Silber.
Review
New Repub 165:32-4 D 4 '71

CAMPAIGNS, Money raising. See Fund raising

CAMPBELL, Colin
Prayer. Chr Today 15:10 Ag 6 '71

CAMPBELL, E. Simms
Obituary
Negro Hist Bul 34:92 Ap '71
Passing of a pillar of the original Esquire.
A. Gingrich. Esquire 75:6 My '71 *

CAMPBELL, J. Phil, 1917-
Trees for a better environment; address,
October 4, 1970. por Am For 77:10+ Ja '71

CAMPBELL, John Coert
Soviet-American relations. bibliog f Cur Hist
61:193-7+ O '71

CAMPBELL, Joseph
Need for new myths. G. Clarke. il por Time
99:50-1 Ja 17 '72 *

CAMPBELL, Jule
Sporting look (cont) il Sports Illus 34:62-3
Mr 22; 58-61 Ap 26; 35:42-3 Ag 23 '71

CAMPBELL, Kenneth
Happy hunting ground. il pors Outdoor Life
148:72-5+ O '71

CAMPBELL, Lawrence
Edward Hopper, and the melancholy of Robinson Crusoe. il Art N 70:36-9+ O '71 *
Things are thoughts in America. il Art N
69:34-7+ F '71

CAMPBELL, Robert
Chemistry of madness. il Life 71:66-8+ N 26
'71
about
Trying to make a wild river stand still. R.
Graves. por Life 71:3 N 26 '71 *

CAMPBELL, Robert D.
Records (title varies) (cont) Chr Cent 88:1009
Ag 25 '71

CAMPBELL, William Wallace
W. W. Campbell and a puzzling object. J.
Ashbrook. il por Sky & Tel 41:352-3 Je
'71 *

CAMPBELL folk school. See John C. Campbell folk school, Brasstown, N.C.

CAMPBELL soup company
Campbell stays with Camden; with editorial
comment. il por Bsns W p66-8, 94 F 6
'71
Double trouble at Campbell soup. il Bsns W
p26 Ag 28 '71
Making haste slowly. il Forbes 107:16-17 Ja
15 '71
Rehabilitator of its hometown. il Bsns W
p60 Mr 6 '71

CAMPERS. See Camp children

CAMPERS (trailers) See Automobile trailers

CAMPERS and coaches, Truck
Back-country camper. V. L. Oertle. il Pop
Mech 136:58 S '71
Buying a used camping vehicle. D. Gregg.
il Bet Hom & Gard 49:6+ Ap '71
Camper Americans love; Volkswagen camp-
mobile il Bsns W p33 My 29 '71
Camping in style. M. K. Spencer. il Am Home
74:60-1+ Je '71
Fine art of mating a camper and pickup.
J. Copeland. il Pop Sci 198:74-5+ Mr '71
Fleet of landlocked schooners on the Ameri-
can sea. R. Bongartz. il Holiday 49:32-3+
My '71
From van to camper, $340. J. W. Daum. il
Pop Mech 135:148-52+ F '71
Great new ideas for motor camping. J. M.
Liston. il Pop Mech 135:147-8+ My '71
Home on the road. il Field & S 75:107 Ja '71
How to leave home without leaving it. D.
McCluggage. Am Home 74:40+ Je '71
How to match your truck and camper. J.
Parry. il Pop Mech 135:166D+ My '71
How to see America and never leave home.
G. Helgeland. il Nat Wildlife 9:46-9 Ap '71
How to select a recreational travel vehicle.
C. M. Edwards. il Consumer Bul 54:4+
Mr '71
Maine to Mexico in a camper, without get-
ting out. B. McKeown. il pors Mech Illus
67:89-91+ Ap '71
Making the van go. il Time 98:36+ S 6 '71
Mini-est of mobile camps; new pickup
trucks. B. W. Dalrymple. il Field & S
75:62-3+ Mr '71
One rough road; Baja peninsula in Condor,
4-wheel-drive home. B. Behme. il Field
& S 75:156+ Mr '71
Recreation vehicles for 1971; what's new in
campers, trailers and motor homes. B.
Behme. il Field & S 75:66-9+ Ap '71
Slick new RVs offer you all the comforts
of home-on wheels. H. Shuldiner. il Pop
Sci 198:82-3 Mr '71
Splendor in the grass; with travel notes.
R. Joseph. il Esquire 76:102, 169-75 N '71
Start a rebellion: build a calico camper. W.
B. Reyer. il Pop Sci 199:76-7+ Jl '71
Those second-generation motor homes. F.
Coffee. il Mech Illus 67:53-5+ Je '71
$1200 camper from a kit for $800. il Pop
Mech 136:128-31 Jl '71
We did it; conversion of a dry-cleaning
van to a mobile home for four. B. Tunder.
il House B 113:38 Mr '71
West coast vans. S. Green. il Hot Rod 24:
82-6 Ag '71
Winter use for your camper. G. L. Earle.
il Suc Farm 69:C18 N '71

Maintenance and repair
Getting a camper or motor home ready for
winter storage. Sunset 147:64 N '71
Smart ways to improve your recreational vehicle. V. L. Oertle. il Pop Mech 135:156+ My
'71

CAMPHOR tree
Lament for the camphor tree. K. Lucas. il
Am For 77:34-6 Ap '71

CAMPING
Camping. C. B. Colby. See issues of Outdoor life
Camping in style; camping with a camper van. M. K. Spencer. il Am Home 74:60-1+ Je '71
Camping out in comfort; recreational vehicle camping. A. F. Rush. il McCalls 98:104-5+ Je '71
1971 camping; symposium. il Pop Sci 198:74-85 Mr '71
On-the-go camping. V. L. Oertle. See issues of Popular mechanics to July 1971
Today's campers should learn how to be lazy on trips. E. F. Schmidt. il Camp Mag 43:16 Je '71
Try woodland camping, family style. K. Jeans. il Parents Mag 46:44-5+ Je '71
Wilderness program for one-week campers. J. H. Reyburn. il Camp Mag 43:14 Je '71
See also
Camp cookery
Camp fires
Camp sites, facilities, etc.
Camps
Outdoor life
Wilderness survival

Activities
Day camp runs night program; teen night camp at Camp Massasoit. W. J. Allen. il Camp Mag 43:18 Ja '71
Diversification can solve many camp problems; year-round programs. E. R. Guerard. il Camp Mag 43:10-11 N '71
Good music an enriching addition to your camp program. S. H. Brobston. Camp Mag 43:18 Mr '71
Informal dramatics can provide the means; expression of individuality. R. Telleen. il Camp Mag 43:12-13 My '71
More tested ideas to spark your camp program. Camp Mag 43:25-7 Je '71
When will they ever learn; relevant topics used in show. L. Mozzi. Camp Mag 43:28 F '71

Anecdotes, facetiae, satire, etc.
Backyard safari. P. F. McManus. il Field & S 76:60-1+ Je '71

Bibliography
Books. Camp Mag 43:19 S; 19 N '71
Current reading (cont) Camp Mag 43:30-1 Ja; 30-1 F; 45 Mr; 32-3 Ap; 28-9 My; 21 Je '71

Educational aspects
Feeling one's way across the chasm; city kids in day camp. W. Service. il Sports Illus 35:62-4+ Jl 26 '71
How to think about the extended school year; with comment by E. F. Schmidt. il Camp Mag 43:4. 8-12 S '71
See also
Conservation of resources—Study and teaching
Nature study

Health aspects
Camp environment checklist. W. H. Wadsworth. Camp Mag 43:11-12 Je '71
Camping with a coronary. W. L. Trotter. il Har Yrs 11:37-8 Mr '71
How your camp kitchen can cope with electrical emergencies; excerpts from Highlights; food marketing and management. Camp Mag 43:16-17 Ja '71
Sedentary camper syndrome. W. P. Marley. por Camp Mag 43:14 My '71

Outfits, supplies, etc.
Beat the trip spoilers. C. B. Colby. il Outdoor Life 147:54+ Ap '71
Camping with all the comforts. Bet Hom & Gard 49:42 Ap '71
Colorful camping scene. il Mech Illus 67:74-5 Je '71
Don't forget these camping accessories. il Bet Hom & Gard 49:60 Ag '71
How to outfit for a wilderness canoe trip. N. Karas. il Pop Mech 135:100-3 Ap '71
New camping gear. C. B. Colby. il Outdoor Life 147:28+ My; 10+ Je 11 '71
New for the outdoorsman. il Mech Illus 67:48 N '71
New gear that makes roughing it soft. il Life 71:44-7+ S 3 '71
Selecting and using a backpack and frame. J. J. Beveridge. il Field & S 76:60-1+ Jl '71
Splendor in the grass; with travel notes. R. Joseph. il Esquire 76:102, 169-75 N '71
Trail camping: new gear makes the simple life simpler. A. Lees. il Pop Sci 198:80-1+ Mr '71

Travel takes. il Seventeen 30:20+ Jl '71
Try station wagon camping. R. Tinsley. il Nat Wildlife 9:20-3 Ag '71
What's new (title varies) See issues of Camping Magazine
See also
Automobiles—Camping equipment
Camp cookery
Camp stoves
Coleman company
Knapsacks
Sleeping bags
Tents

Leasing and renting
Rent a camping trip. C. B. Colby. il Outdoor Life 147:12+ F '71

Protection against theft
Thieves are after your gear. J. Weiss. il Field & S 76:48+ My '71

Religious life and activities
Ministry to campers: the gospel on the go. R. Chandler. Chr Today 15:31-2 Je 18 '71
See also
Christian camping international

Safety devices and measures
How to keep in touch; maintaining contact with home while camping. C. B. Colby. il Outdoor Life 148:12+ Jl '71
How to protect your camp from electrical fires. L. Short and A. Short. Camp Mag 43:18-19+ F '71
Let's put an end to lost camper hazards on trips. A. J. Stolz. Camp Mag 43:14 Mr '71
Swimtime; when a camp director needs a friend; Camp Birchwood, Minn. J. C. Bredemus. il Camp Mag 43:23+ Ap '71
Youth camp safety act. A. Ribicoff. por Parks & Rec 6:23+ S '71

Study and teaching
Camp staff members, just as campers, need individual guidance; excerpts from address. F. Hamilton. il Camp Mag 43:8-9 Ap '71
Human relations training for camp staff members. C. B. Rotman and C. S. Clayman. il Camp Mag 43:10+ Ap '71
Snow camping school will open at Badger Pass. il Sunset 146:16+ Ja '71

Denmark
On the backpack trail: the siege of Copenhagen; Green camp. D. Butwin. il Sat R 54:40-2 S 4 '71

Europe
Le camping: the cheapest way to go. M. Pugh. il Holiday 49:70-1+ F '71

Europe, Western
European camping, a big travel bargain. D. Huff. il Pop Sci 198:76-8+ My '71

Middle Western states
Best vacation camping in mid-America. G. Greer. il Bet Hom & Gard 49:101-6 My '71

New York (state)
Canoe-camping the Adirondacks. S. Netherby. il Field & S 76:56-7+ Jl '71

United States
Big change in camping. C. B. Colby. il Outdoor Life 147.12-13+ Ja '71
Camp by boat. E. A. Bauer. il Outdoor Life 147:64-5+ Ja '71
Camping spree in America: it's a billion-dollar market. il U S News 70:39-41 My 10 '71
Family camping. Bet Hom & Gard 49:42 Ap '71
Giving camping a second chance. C. B. Colby. il Outdoor Life 148:12+ S '71
Misery kit. P. McManus. il Field & S 76:68-9+ My '71
Organized camping looks to 1971. A. F. Luehrs. por Camp Mag 43:4 Mr '71
Plea for keeping camping both relevant and sane. D. Shellenberger. il Camp Mag 43:11-12 Mr '71
Private forest camping sites the public can use. Good H 172:172-3 Je '71
The seventies, years of challenge. F. M. Levine. il Camp Mag 43:8-10 F '71
Simple joys of roughing it. S. Udall. il McCalls 98:106 Je '71
See also
American camping association

Virginia
Wilderness beach camping. P. McLain. il Field & S 76:70-1+ My '71

CAMPING—*Continued*

Western states

In the California, Arizona, Sonora low desert, spring signals the time to camp. il Sunset 146:70-5 Mr '71

CAMPING, Value of

Eight values camps can give. B. Charpentier and H. Charpentier. Camp Mag 43:14 S '71

How summer camp changes a child. M. Mead. il Redbook 137:45+ Ag '71

Program goals or administrative needs? S. E. Breuer. Camp Mag 43:23-4 My '71

Values of a good camping experience. J. Bloom. por Camp Mag 43:4 Ap '71

What camping means to kids. S. H. Webb. il Parents Mag 46:42-3+ Ap '71

Written goals, clearly stated, help staff understand objectives. R. R. Schmatz. Camp Mag 43:14 N '71

CAMPING equipment. See Camping—Outfits, supplies, etc.

CAMPING shelters. See Shelters

CAMPION, Nardi Reeder

Unforgettable Harry Emerson Fosdick. por Read Digest 98:69-73 Ja '71

CAMPO, Johnny

Staking a claim for big John. T. Maule. por Sports Illus 34:34-6+ My 3 '71 •

CAMPS

Feeling one's way across the chasm; city kids in day camp. W. Service il Sports Illus 35:62-4+ Jl 26 '71

Which summer camp is right for your child. T. J. Rakstis. il Todays Health 49:35-7+ My '71

See also

American camping association

Audubon nature camps

Camp sites, facilities, etc.

Dance camps

Activities

See Camping—Activities

Administration

Camp staff members, just as campers, need individual guidance; excerpts from address. F. Hamilton. il Camp Mag 43:8-9 Ap '71

New friends, new ideas, a new direction and a new horizon; New England camp director's institute. D. Fillpot. Camp Mag 43:12 Mr '71

Program goals or administrative needs? S. E. Breuer. Camp Mag 43:23-4 My '71

Swimtime: when a camp director needs a friend; Camp Birchwood, Minn. J. C. Bredemus. il Camp Mag 43:23+ Ap '71

Audio-visual materials

See Camps and audio-visual materials

Counselors

See Camp counselors

Desegregation

Integration and acceptance; excerpt from The forum for residential therapy. M. Brackeen. por Camp Mag 43:12-14 F '71

Dining halls

Indoor-outdoor mess hall. il Arch Forum 135:54-5 O '71

Winterized dining hall provides for 11 different functions; Camp Bethel, Va. R. R. Jones. il Camp Mag 43:13 S '71

Finance

Board trims ACA finance sails to weather credit crunch. Camp Mag 43:6-7+ My '71

Costs of camping. H. P. Galloway. il Camp Mag 43:8-11 My '71

Diversification can solve many camp problems; year-round programs. E. R. Guerard. il Camp Mag 43:10-11 N '71

Great cost cutback. B. Henderson and others. Camp Mag 43:8-10 N '71

State of the economy and the future of camping. W. L. Casey, jr. and C. F. Medford. Camp Mag 43:8-10 Ja '71

Public relations

Can good P.R. sell your camp? It sure can help! Camp Naticook, N.H. R. Wasserman. il Camp Mag 43:12-13 N '71

Standards

ACA accreditation through a revised standards visitation program. T. Morash. Camp Mag 43:19-20 Ja '71

It's already time to think about summer camp. il Changing T 25:46 F '71

Rough draft of the proposed new ACA standards. Camp Mag 43:21-5 Ja '71

Volunteer workers

Training volunteer camp staff. V. Gillespie. il Camp Mag 43:16+ Ap '71

Illinois

Real camp program in a city park day camp. R. Papich. il Camp Mag 43:20-1 F '71; Reply. D. M. Lonheim. 43:30 Je '71

Maine

Maine's Camp Solo puts young aviators in the pilot's seat; with editorial comment. il Life 71:1, 60-3 Ag 27 '71

Massachusetts

When will they ever learn; relevant topics used in show. L. Mozzi. Camp Mag 43:28 F '71

Minnesota

Swimtime: when a camp director needs a friend. J. C. Bredemus. il Camp Mag 43: 23+ Ap '71

New Hampshire

Can good P.R. sell your camp? It sure can help! Camp Naticook. R. Wasserman. il Camp Mag 43:12-13 N '71

Pennsylvania

Counselors' post-camp Canadian canoe trip brings staff back again next year; Camp Fairfield. B. T. Vance. il Camp Mag 43:16-17 Je '71

Wilderness program for one-week campers. J. H. Reyburn. il Camp Mag 43:14 Je '71

Rhode Island

Day camp runs night program; Teen night camp at Camp Massasoit. W. J. Allen. il Camp Mag 43:18 Ja '71

United States

You can't win 'em all. C. B. Colby. il Outdoor Life 148:10+ N '71

Virgin Islands

Tent for rent on an island in the sun; Cinnamon Bay camp, Cruz Bay, St John. J. H. Mofford. il Schol Teach Jr/Sr High p26-7+ F 1 '71

Virginia

Winterized dining hall provides for 11 different functions; Camp Bethel. R. R. Jones. il Camp Mag 43:13 S '71

Washington (state)

City camping calls for coordination; day camps in Seattle. D. M. Lonheim. Camp Mag 43:20-1 Ap '71

Wisconsin

Foreign counselors come to camp; Camp Mohawk. W. J. Cullen. Camp Mag 43:26-7 Ja '71

CAMPS and audio-visual materials

Audio-visual aids can help you pep up staff meetings. H. D. Berk. il Camp Mag 43: 12-13 Ap '71

CAMPS for the socially handicapped

Stretch camps' responsibility to include disadvantaged. L. Maisel, 2d. Camp Mag 43:8-10 Mr '71

CAMPUS planning

Building types study; New York state university construction fund; with editorial comment. M. F. Schmertz. il Arch Rec 149: 105-28 Ja '71

CAMPUS police. See Colleges and universities —Security measures

CAMPUS press. See College and school journalism

CAMPUS recruiting programs. See Recruiting of employees

CAMS

See also

Automobiles—Cams

CAMUS, Albert

Albert Camus and the men of the stone, by R. Proix. Review

Pub W il por 200:42-4 N 1 '71. P. Standard •

CAN crushers. See Refuse and refuse disposal —Apparatus

CAN I count you in? story. See Faessler, S.

CANADA

Canada: an immensely boring country, until now. M. Richler. il Life 70:54-54B+ Ap 9 '71

Darkness in the North. T. Pembroke. il Nat R 23:868-70+ Ag 10 '71

See also

Abortion—Laws and legislation—Canada

Aeronautics, Commerical—Canada

Airlines—Canada

Airplane industry—Canada

American teachers in Canada

CANADA—See also—*Continued*
  Americans in Canada
  Architecture, Domestic—Canada
  Back River
  Ballet—Canada
  Banks and banking—Canada
  Booksellers and bookselling—Canada
  British Columbia
  Church union—Canada
  Civil rights—Canada
  Coal mines and mining—Canada
  Collective bargaining—Canada
  Colleges and universities—Canada
  Drag racing—Canada
  Fishing—Canada
  Flood prevention and control—Canada
  Gold mines and mining—Canada
  Hunting—Canada
  Immigrants in Canada
  Investments, Foreign (in Canada)
  Libraries—Canada
  National parks and reserves—Canada
  Natural resources—Canada
  Nova Scotia
  Petroleum—Canada
  Prince Edward Island
  Public opinion—Canada
  Public works—Canada
  Publishers and publishing—Canada
  Railroads—Canada
  Rocky Mountains—Canadian Rockies
  Saguenay River
  Sailboat racing—Canada
  Skis and skiing—Canada
  Taxation—Canada
  Television broadcasting—Canada
  Trade unions—Canada
  Unemployment—Canada
  War and emergency powers—Canada
  Waterways—Canada
  Wilderness areas—Canada

Antiquities
See also
British Columbia—Antiquities

Armed forces
How two allies fare with volunteers. il U S News 70:35 Mr 1 '71

Bibliography
Canadian club. N. Magid. Commonweal 95: 327-30 Ja 7 '72

Commerce
Canada gets a cold shoulder. Bsns W p64-5 Ag 28 '71
Chinese like to buy Canadian. Bsns W p33 Jl 24 '71
Lament for lost U.S. markets. il Bsns W p40 O 30 '71
Looking to open new trade doors. Bsns W p34-5 S 18 '71
Second birthday for an export boom. il Bsns W p34+ Ag 7 '71

Defenses
Canada switches targets. D. Coxe. Nat R 23: 1177 O 22 '71

Description and travel
Guest editor journal, Canada: the fresh free life; with G.E. comments. Mlle 73:328+ Ag '71

Economic conditions
Canada: a troubled nation. J. R. Mutchmor. Chr Cent 88:189-92 F 10 '71
Cold wind from Canada, the Gray report. E. Cowan. Nation 213:613-16 D 13 '71
Exporting political trouble. W. P. Bundy. Newsweek 78:39 S 13 '71
New strains between Canada and U.S. il U S News 71:58-60 O 25 '71
Upbeat economy north of the border. il Bsns W p38 F 13 '71

Economic policy
See also
Wage-price policy—Canada

Economic relations
Latin America
See also
Canadian association for Latin America

United States
See United States—Economic relations—Canada

Foreign population
See also
Immigrants in Canada

Foreign relations
Canada. G. S. Tomkins. bibliog il Focus 21:1-8 Je '71
Foreign policy of the new Canada. I. L. Head. For Affairs 50:237-52 Ja '72
My friend Trudeau. il por Time 98:51 N 1 '71

China (People's Republc)
Chinese ambassador; Huang arrives in Canada. il por Newsweek 78:15 Ag 2 '71

Russia
See Russia—Foreign relations—Canada

United States
See United States—Foreign relations—Canada

History
Canada. G. S. Tomkins. bibliog il Focus 21:1-8 Je '71

Industries
See also
Aerospace industries—Canada
Airplane industry—Canada
Construction industry—Canada
Forest products industry
International nickel company of Canada
Massey-Ferguson, ltd.
Nickel industry—Canada
Petroleum industry—Canada
Steel company of Canada
Tobacco industry—Canada

Intellectual life
Idea, image and purpose: ballet in Canada today; with editorial comment. O. Maynard. il Dance Mag 45:31, 32-7+ Ap '71

National parks service
See also
National park personnel

Nationalism
Americanization of Canadian universities. C. Cocking. il Sat R 54:44-5+ Ag 21 '71
Is Canada turning away from U.S? il U S News 71:66-7 Jl 19 '71
Maple leaves among the ivy. V. M. Johnson. Commonweal 95:35-7 O 8 '71
Oh! Canada! The eruption of a revolution. R. Salutin. Harper 243:26-31 Jl '71; Discussion. 243:9-10 S '71
Sounds of nationalism grow louder. il Bsns W p58 O 30 '71
Thawing of Canada. P. C. Newman. il Sat R 54:15-18+ Mr 13 '71
See also
Front for the liberation of Quebec

Politics and government
Canada: a troubled nation. J. R. Mutchmor. Chr Cent 88:189-92 F 10 '71
TRB from Washington. New Repub 165:4 D 18 '71
Trudeau in power, by W. Stewart. Review Sat R por 55:30-1 Ja 8 '72. C. Cocking
See also
French Canadians

Religious institutions and affairs
Revival in Canada. R. Greenslade and E. E. Plowman. il Chr Today 16:31-2 D 17 '71
Worldaround. Chr Cent 88:860 Jl 14 '71
See also
Catholic church in Canada
Pentecostal churches in Canada
Presbyterian church in Canada
Reformed church in Canada
United church of Canada

Social conditions
Meditations of a landed immigrant. E. Z. Friedenberg. Nation 212:656-60 My 24 '71

Treaties
Russia
See Russia—Treaties—Canada

CANADA and the United States
Oh! Canada! The eruption of a revolution. R. Salutin. Harper 243:26-31 Jl '71; Discussion. 243:9-10 S '71

CANADA geese. See Geese. Wild

CANADIAN-American challenge cup series. See Automobile racing

CANADIAN artificial satellites. See Artificial satellites, Canadian

CANADIAN association for Latin America
Canada looks southward; setting up of CALA. M. R. Lubbock. il Américas 23: 2-8 Ja '71

CANADIAN booksellers association
Canadian booksellers grapple with nationalism. Pub W 199:41-2+ Je 7 '71

CANADIAN communications satellites. See Communications satellites, Canadian

CANADIAN council of churches
Canadian Christians primed for ministry to U.S. draft refugees. C. de Mestral. Chr Cent 88:73 Ja 20 '71

CANCER cells
Human leukemic cells: in vitro growth of colonies containing the Philadelphia (Ph[1]) chromosome. P. A. Chervenick and others. bibliog il Science 174:1134-6 D 10 '71
Inhibition of growth of leukemia cells by enzymic folate depletion. J. R. Bertino and others. bibliog il Science 172:161-2 Ap 9 '71
Junctions between cancer cells in culture: ultrastructure and permeability. R. G. Johnson and J. D. Sheridan. bibliog il Science 174:717-19 N 12 '71

CANCER inhibiting substances
Camptothecin. Chem 44:4 My '71
Free radical inhibitory effect of some anticancer compounds. K. K. Georgieff. bibliog il Science 173:537-9 Ag 6 '71
Suppression of urethan-induced lung adenomas in mice treated with trehalose-6,6-dimycolate (cord factor) and living bacillus Calmette Guérin. A. Bekierkunst and others. bibliog il Science 174:1240-2 D 17 '71
See also
Asparaginase
Methotrexate

CANCER producing substances
Carcinogen and microsomal membrane interactions: changes in membrane density and ability to bind nucleic acids. H. Kubinski and C. B. Kasper. bibliog il Science 171:20λ-3 Ja 15 '71
See also
Maleic hydrazide
Nitrosamines
Urethanes

CANCER research
Behind the cancer campaign. R. Bazell. il Ramp Mag 10:29-34 D '71
Best way to attack cancer. il Bsns W p62 Ap 3 '71
Breast cancer and virus. il Time 97:40 My 24 '71
Campaign against cancer. Sci N 99:80 Ja 30 '71
Campaign conquers Senate: Conquest of cancer act. R. J. Bazell. Science 173:218 Jl 16 '71
Cancer and transplants; study of tumor-destroying lymphocytes. il pors Newsweek 77:98 My 10 '71
Cancer breakthrough; CEA test for cancer of the colon. J. Kirschy. il Life 70:28-31 Ap 23 '71
Cancer cells begin to yield their secrets. G. Bylinsky. il Fortune 84:156-9+ N '71
Cancer conquest program; letter. C. G. Baker. Science 174:980-1 D 3 '71
Cancer cure; bill to create new cancer-fighting agency. New Repub 165:11-12 Jl 17 '71
Cancer hearings: legislative medusa. il Sci N 100:243-4 O 9 '71
Cancer legislation: pro-NIH bill advances in House. N. Wade. Science 174:388-9 O 22 '71
Cancer: quest for a virus. il Newsweek 78:64 D 13 '71
Cancer research and the scientfic community. S. S. Cohen. Science 172:1212-14 Je 18 '71
Cancer research goes political. Sci N 99:347-8 My 22 '71
Cancer research proposals: new money, old conflicts. R. J. Bazell. Science 171:877-9 Mr 5 '71
Cancer researchers finally get Ft Detrick. Sci N 100:278 O 23 '71
Cancer; the problems and progress; address, April 5, 1971. W. I. Aitken. Vital Speeches 37:552-6 Jl 1 '71
Conquer cancer: now a top priority in Washington. U S News 70:91 My 24 '71
Exciting clues for cancer cure. il Bsns W p76+ Ag 28 '71
Federal support of cancer research. P. H. Abelson. Science 172:15 Ap 2 '71
Four Nobelists zap senator. N. Wade. Science 173:1114 S 17 '71
Good Dr Nixon. Nation 212:645 My 24 '71
Hiroshima time bomb; research by the Atomic bomb casualty commission. il Time 97:73 Je 14 '71
Isolation and culture of a virus from human cancer tissue. il Sci N 100:21 Jl 10 '71
Money won't solve everything. G. A Silver. il Nation 213:110-14 Ag 16 '71
More candidates for a human cancer virus. il Sci N 100:388-9 D 11 '71
Nixon embraces principle of separate cancer authority, but original proponents say they are not yet convinced. R. J. Bazell. Science 172:922-3 My 28 '71

Politics of cancer. Nation 213:549 N 29 '71
Politics of cancer. Time 98:40-1 Jl 5 '71
Politics of cancer; which strategy for the war against cancer? L. Eisenberg. il Harper 243:100-2+ N '71
Progress on breast cancer. il por Newsweek 77:129 Ap 19 '71
Progress on cancer. il Time 98:40 D 13 '71
Pus bona et laudabile. S. Alsop. Newsweek 78:116 D 13 '71
Race for human cancer virus: odds against Houston team lengthen. N. Wade. Science 173:1220-2 S 24 '71
Report on cancer. il Chem 44:20-1 My '71
Scientists and the press: cancer scare story that wasn't. N. Wade. Science 174:679-80 N 12 '71
Search for a cancer cure. il Time 97:44 Ap 19 '71
Tracing the breakdown of immunity in cancer. il Sci N 100:260-1 O 16 '71
War on cancer: progress report. il Newsweek 77:84-6+ F 22 '71
What's happening in cancer research? H. E. Skipper. il Sat R 54:16-19 Ja 16 '71
See also
United States—National cancer institute

CANCER tests. See Cancer—Diagnosis

CANCRO, Robert
Preserving the species. Sat R 54:50-1 Mr 6 '71

CANDIDATES, Political
Candidates answer Senior's queries: black American as a presidential or vice-presidential candidate in 1972? il Sr Schol 99:6-7 N 1 '71
If not Charles Evers, who? interviews. ed. by R. Branson. J. Swan; C. Sullivan. Chr Cent 88:906-8 Jl 28 '71
Running back into the past; mayoral candidates, Boston and Philadelphia; with reports by J. Pekkanen and R. Brigham. il pors Life 71:32-4+ O 29 '71
Senator Muskie's gaffe; Negro candidates. W. F. Buckley, jr. Nat R 23:1198 O 22 '71
Those who vote may also run; youthful candidates. il Newsweek 78:35 O 25 '71
Urban quartet: mayoralty races. il Time 98:21-2 N 1 '71
See also
Presidential candidates
Vice-Presidential candidates
also subhead Politics and government under names of countries, states, cities, etc. e.g. Philadelphia—Politics and government

CANDIDE; operetta. See Bernstein, L.

CANDIED fruit. See Confectionery

CANDLE holders. See Candlesticks

CANDLES
Details that make the difference. W. Baldwin. House & Gard 139:10+ My '71
Don't forget the candles; uses in camping. J. Dexter. il Field & S 76:12+ N '71
Make your own decorative candles. il Consumer Bul 54:24+ N '71
More power to the candle. il Time 97:72 Je 21 '71

CANDLESTICKS
Can't hold a candle to candle holders. il Consumer Rep 36:404 Jl '71
Elegance right out of the scrap bin; Christmas candle lights. il Sunset 147:58-9 D '71

CANDY, Graham
Quest for the little America's cup. il por Yachting 129:56-8+ Mr '71

CANDY
Easy homemade candies. il Bet Hom & Gard 49:90 Mr '71
She's reaching for peanut crunch but also there's toffee; with recipes. il Sunset 147:152 D '71
Taffy is kids' stuff. il Ladies Home J 88:102-3+ O '71
See also
Confectionery

Prices
Sweet inflation. il Time 97:79 F 8 '71

CANDY containers, Glass. See Glass containers

CANDY industry
See also
Mars, inc.

CANE, Melville
Ladies of the Dial; excerpt from Eloquent April. Am Scholar 40:316-21 Spr '71
Law and justice. Am Scholar 40:583 Aut '71

CANFIELD, Cass
Trade winds; interview. ed. by C. Amory. Sat R 54:12 D 25 '71

about
Mister Tomorrow in publishing. J. Leggett. New Repub 165:26-8+ D 4 '71 *
Peripatetic reviewer. E. Weeks. Atlan 228:150-2 N '71 *

CANFIELD, Gabriella
Someone's in the kitchen with Maxime. M. McKendry. il por Vogue 158:90+ N 1 '71 •
CANNABIS. See Marijuana
CANNABIS sativa. See Hemp
CANNED food
Little puddings in dangerous cans. il Consumer Rep 36:406-7 Jl '71
Upsetting facts about our diet; sugar added to processed foods. B. T. Hunter. il Consumer Bul 54:4+ Jl '71
See also
Cookery—Canned food
CANNED food industry
See also
Heinz, H. J, company
CANNERY ROW, Monterey, Calif. See Monterey, Calif.
CANNIKIN project. See Atomic bombs—Testing, Underground
CANNING, Elizabeth
Behavior modified? il Sci Digest 70:26-31 Jl '71
CANNING and preserving
Introduction to home canning. il Redbook 137:82-6 Jl '71
It's the month to rediscover the joys of fruit canning. il Sunset 147:60-5 bibliog(p 108) Jl '71
Preserved perfection. il McCalls 98:96-7+ S '71
See also
Jelly, jam, etc.
Pickles and relishes
CANNON, Dyan
Skin touch. il pors Time 99:46 Ja 17 '72 •
CANNON, Howard Walter
Liftoff to economy: the space shuttle. il Space World H-11-95:11-15 N '71
about
Cannon upholds supplemental carriers. H. D. Watkins. Aviation W 94:25-6 Mr 1 '71 •
CANNON, Maureen
First day of school; poem. Ladies Home J 88:84 S '71
Sycophant; poem. Cath World 214:104 D '71
Young wife at midnight; Birthday party; poems. Ladies Home J 88:147, 159 O '71
CANNON, Poppy
Poppy Cannon's meal-a-day menus. See issues of Ladies' home journal
CANOE camping. See Camping
CANOE trips
Canoe trails of North America. F. M. Paulson. il Field & S 76:138-41 My '71
Counselors' post-camp Canadian canoe trip brings staff back again next year; Camp Fairfield, Pa. B. T. Vance. il Camp Mag 43:16-17 Je '71
High adventure in high latitudes. J. McEachern. il por Motor B & S 128:70-3+ S '71
How to outfit for a wilderness canoe trip. N. Karas. il Pop Mech 135:100-3 Ap '71
Hunt silently by canoe. N. Nelson, jr. il pors Outdoor Life 148:72-5+ N '71
Instant wilderness; New Jersey's Oswego River. R. A. Lodge. il por Parks & Rec 6:19-22+ F '71
Paddle your own canoe. S. K. Summers and A. P. Teton. il por Parks & Rec 6:35-6 Jl '71
Yellowstone canoe trip. R. Thomas. il Travel 136:37-9+ Jl '71
See also
Canoes and canoeing
CANOES and canoeing
Comeback of the canoe. J. George. Read Digest 99:193-4+ Jl '71
Ducks from a red canoe. J. B. Robinson. il Outdoor Life 148:64-5+ O '71
Float note; canoeing on Ouachita River. Travel 137:27 Ja '72
How to choose a canoe. J. A. Emmett. il Outdoor Life 147:34+ Ap '71
Rediscovery of New York city; 80-mile canoe trip over New York waterfront. C. Phinizy. il Sports Illus 35:98-101+ N 22 '71
See also
Canoe trips
CANON, Bradley C.
British, French and American systems of justice compared. bibliog f Cur Hist 61:97-104+ Ag '71
CANON law
Basic law found wanting. T. Beeson. Chr Cent 1101-2 S 22 '71
Canon law: justice by variety. M. J. McManus. America 125:257-9 O 9 '71
For Catholics, another 95-point crisis. R. L. Peck. Chr Today 15:34 Ag 27 '71
Fundamental law: old skin for new wine. America 125:26-7 Jl 24 '71

Lex ecclesiae fundamentalis controversy and a pertinent postscript. W. Triggs. Chr Cent 88:896-7 Jl 28 '71
Sign of fear in Rome? Lex fundamentalis. il Time 98:38-9 Ag 30 '71
Strait jacket for the mystical body. F. X. Murphy. America 124:611-13 Je 12 '71
Trying to undo the Council; the Fundamental law issue on bishops' agenda. H. T. Kortenaar. Commonweal 94:348-9 Jl 9 '71
See also
Marriage—Annulment (canon law)
CANON law society of America
CLSA asks wider participation in selecting bishops. Chr Cent 88:1288 N 3 '71
CANS
Don't throw away that can. R. Wrenn. il Design 72:28-9 Spr '71

Manufacture
See also
Continental can company
National can corporation
CANT
Oliver. A. Pospisil. Sat R 54:84 N 13 '71
CANTATAS
Cantata of peace premiered at church music meeting. Chr Cent 88:1018 S 1 '71
CANTERBURY, Arthur Michael Ramsey, abp of. See Ramsey, A. M.
CANTERBURY tales. See Chaucer, G.
CANTON trade fair. See Exhibitions
CANTOR, Lon
Chemicals for electronics. il Pop Electr 34:25-8+ Ap; 63-6 My '71
CANTOR, Michael B.
Signaled reinforcing brain stimulation facilitates operant behavior under schedules of intermittent reinforcement. bibliog il Science 174:610-13 N 5 '71
CANTOR, Richard
Patient is feeling better but he isnt' really cured; interview. por Forbes 108:42-3 Jl 1 '71
CANTU, Xavier Gutierrez. See Gutierrez Cantu, X.
CANTWELL, Mary
Eat. See issues of Mademoiselle
Living off the land. il Mlle 73:126-9 Je '71
Open the shutters and let the godforce through. il Mlle 74:142-3+ D '71
Opinion: thoughts after an evening with Norman Mailer, Germaine Greer, Diana Trilling, Jill Johnston, Jacqueline Ceballos and a cast of thousands. Mlle 73:36+ Jl '71
CANTWELL, Robert
Bobby clears the board for the title. il por Sports Illus 35:30-2+ N 8 '71
In the mood for baseball. il Sports Illus 34:54-6+ Je 7 '71
Maybe you can win them all. il Sports Illus 35:18-19 Ag 2 '71
CANVAS
See also
Awnings
CANVASBACKS. See Ducks, Wild
CANVASSING
Cooling-off proposed for door-to-door sales. R. H. Smith. Pub W 199:33 Mr 22 '71
Door-to-door sales: industry proposal better. R. W. Frase. Pub W 199:18-19 My 3 '71
Encyclopedia sales frauds. il Consumer Rep 36:172-4 Mr '71
FTC postpones hearings on door-to-door sales. Pub W 199:46 F 1 '71
FTC takes new tack on door-to-door book sales. S. Wagner. Pub W 200:29 Jl 26 '71
Knock, knock; direct selling. il Forbes 108:26 Ag 1 '71
CANYONLANDS NATIONAL PARK
Canyonlands. J. W. Krutch. il Audubon 73:32-51 Jl '71
Canyonlands: realm of rock and the far horizon. R. Findley. il Nat Geog 140:71-91 Jl '71
Gallery; lonely beauty of the Canyonlands. J. Leongard. Life 71:6-9 Ag 6 '71
CANYONS
See also
Grand Canyon
CANYONS, Submarine. See Submarine valleys
CANZONERI, Robert
Reflections; story. McCalls 98:100-1 Mr '71
CAP removers
Cap-eating shark. B. Berger. il Mech Illus 67:118 F '71
CAPACITANCE, Electric. See Electric capacitance
CAPACITIVE-discharge Ignition. See Automobile engines—Ignition

CAPACITOR testers. See Testing instruments
CAPACITY and disability
   See also
  Guardian and ward
CAPE ANN, Mass.
  Cape Ann, by H. Kenny. Review
    Nat R 23:878 Ag 10 '71. F. Russell
CAPE CANAVERAL, Fla.
  McIntire: on the gateway to the stars; new
    freedom center. W. Willoughby. Chr To-
    day 15:30-1 Ja 29 '71
CAPE COD
  Thoreau and the endless beach. E. Kinkead.
    il Sat R 54:40+ Mr 13 '71
  Trees of Cape Cod. G. S. Smith. il Am For 77:
    6-7 Je '71
    See also
  Gardens—Cape Cod

        History
  Wellfleet tavern. E. Ekholm and J. Deetz. il
    Natur Hist 80:48-57 Ag '71
CAPE COD NATIONAL SEASHORE
  Making of a seashore: Cape Cod. M. H.
    Koehler. il Travel 136:60-7 Ag '71
CAPE colored people. See Colored people
  (South Africa)
CAPE HORN. See Horn, Cape
CAPE marigolds
  For a grand color show next April to June.
    il Sunset 147:250 N '71
CAPEHART, Homer Earl
  Where are they now? pors Newsweek 77:8
    Ja 25 '71 •
CAPEN, Charles F.
  Martian yellow clouds, past and future. il
    Sky & Tel 41:117-20 F '71
        about
  Stormy weather on Mars. il Sci N 100:245 O
    9 '71 •
CAPES
  All cloaked up. il Time 97:49 Mr 15 '71
CAPITAL
    See also
  Liquidity (economics)
CAPITAL, Venture
  Biggest bank bets more on high risk. il Bsns
    W p80+ My 22 '71
  Dispassionate venturer. A. Hershman. por
    Duns 97:64+ Je '71
  Venture capital for minority publishers? R.
    H. Smith. Pub W 199:35 Ap 5 '71; Same abr.
    with title Another chance for publishing.
    Cur 129:22-3 My '71
CAPITAL investments
  Bit more confidence in spending plans. il
    Bsns W p30-1 N 6 '71
  Capital goods may get a growing share;
    relationships between capital and output.
    L. A. Mayer. il Fortune 83:96-9+ Je '71
  Capital spending; hope and caution. il Bsns W
    p28-9 My 1 '71
  Great cost cutback; comments by members
    of Dun's presidents' panel. N. A. Martin.
    il Duns 97:63-5 Mr '71
  Plans hold steady despite the storm. il
    Bsns W p30 S 4 '71
  Recovery in capital spending will wait a
    while. il Fortune 83:18+ Je '71
  What's behind the capital spending boom?
    J. C. Perham. il Duns 93:31-3 Je '69
CAPITAL punishment
  Above and beyond capital punishment. G.
    Stevens. il Sat R 54:28-9 S 25 '71
  Act of mercy; Senator Hart's proposal. Nation
    212:772-3 Je 21 '71
  Bring back "old sparky"; opinions of
    thousands of Texans. Time 97:25 Mr 15
    '71
  Church groups file brief against death pen-
    alty. Chr Cent 88:1044 S 8 '71
  Churches and the noose. Nation 213:228 S
    20 '71
  Criminal violence; how about the victim?
    address, May 12, 1971. T. L. Sendak. Vital
    Speeches 37:574-6 Jl 1 '71
  Death by degrees. R. L. Massie. Esquire 75:
    179-80 Ap '71
  Death penalty: a world survey. il U S News
    70:38-40 My 31 '71
  Death sentence for Manson clan, but—. il
    U S News 70:26 Ap 12 '71
  Death takes a holiday. W. J. Lassers. Trans-
    Action 8:10+ Ja '71
  Death to capital punishment. New Repub
    164:12 F 20 '71
  Due process and the death penalty. America
    124:501 My 15 '71
  Fatal decision; Supreme court on death pen-
    alty. il Time 97:64 My 17 '71
  McGautha v. California, May, 1971. Cur Hist
    61:40-2+ Jl '71

Question of life or death. il Newsweek 77:30-
  2 My 17 '71
Signs of an end to death row: U.S. joining
  trend? il U S News 70:37-8 My 31 '71
Ultimate question. Nation 212:610 My 17 '71
Wistful goodbye to capital punishment. D.
  A. Zoll. Nat R 23:1351-4 D 3 '71; Discus-
  sion. 23:1445 D 31 '71
CAPITAL spending. See Capital investments
CAPITALISM
  Economics of sex bias. B. M. Gray. Nation
    212:742-4 Je 14 '71
  Phase II of the capitalist system. R. L.
    Heilbroner. il N Y Times Mag p30-1+ N
    28 '71
    See also
  Big business
  Black capitalism
  Free enterprise
CAPITALISM and communism. See Commu-
  nism and democracy
El CAPITAN climb. See Mountaineering
CAPITOL (United States) See United States
  —Capitol
CAPITOL bombing case. See Terrorism
CAPITOL records, inc.
  Another president on Capitol's turntable. il
    Bsns W p23 My 1 '71
  Capitol punishment. il Forbes 108:44+ Jl 15
    '71
CAPITOLS
    See also
  United States—Capitol
CAPLIN, Mortimer M.
  14 ways you can legally cut your taxes;
    interview, ed. by J. R. Moskin. Look 35:
    15-17 Mr 23 '71
CAPON, Robert Farrar
  Equality seesaw: how men fail their wives
    and daughters. il Redbook 137:73+ Je '71
CAPONE, Alphonse
  Browsing in gangland; with editorial com-
    ment. J. Epstein. Commentary 53:4+, 46-
    55 Ja '72 •
CAPOTE, Truman
  Truman Capote on Christmas, places, mem-
    ories; interview. il por Mlle 74:122-3+
    D '71
  White rose. il por Ladies Home J 88:96-7+
    Jl '71
CAPOTOSTO, John
  And now, a gazebo with storage! il Mech Illus
    67:91-5+ Ag '71
  Basic 2x4 workbench. il Mech Illus 67:99-102
    My '71
  Bookcases that can grow. il Mech Illus 67:
    94-5 Ja '71
  Bottle garden, the easy way. il Mech Illus
    67:73 My '71
  Campaign desk. il Mech Illus 67:102-3 F '71
  Den for men. il Mech Illus 67:83-6 Je '71
  Martini table. il Mech Illus 67:90+ My '71
  Space-saving dinette. il Mech Illus 67:65-7
    Jl '71
  Tiny turned tables. il Mech Illus 67:106-8 N
    '71
CAPOTOSTO, Rosario
  Basics of wood bending. il Mech Illus 67:
    78-80 Jl '71
  Colonial chair you can build for $53. il
    Pop Mech 136:144-9 D '71
  Cutting party knockdowns from single ply-
    wood sheets. il Pop Sci 198:108-10 Ap '71
  $45 worth of beauty and convenience you can
    build for $21. il Pop Mech 135:134-7 Je '71
  Happiness is a warm shop. il Mech Illus
    67:97-9+ D '71
  How to rebind a book. il Mech Illus 67:
    100-1+ D '71
  Make a grand entry. il Pop Mech 135:144-7+
    Mr '71
  Mod clock of manmade marble. il Pop Sci
    199:86-9 D '71
  Telescoping wood rings turn into lamp. il
    Pop Sci 199:109-10+ O '71
  Wall that changes with the seasons. il
    Mech Illus 67:104-5 D '71
CAPP, Al
  TV; address, March 30, 1971. Vital Speeches
    37:477-8 My 15 '71
CAPPS, Gene T.
  Humanities-science: a natural for team
    teaching. Clear House 45:361-4 F '71
CAPRA, Frank
  Trade winds; interview, ed. by C. Amory.
    Sat R 54:4 Jl 10 '71
        about
  Authors & editors. D. N. Mount. por Pub W
    200:31-3 Ag 2 '71 •
  Frank Capra, by F. Capra. Review
    Sat R 54:27+ Jl 3 '71. B. Bendow •
CAPRIO, Joseph M.
  How lilacs and other plants time their
    blooming. Horticulture 49:26-7+ S '71

CAPRON, Marion, and Mazer, Gwen
Bazaar's bazar. il Harp Baz 104:164-5 Mr '71
CAPS, Bottle. See Bottle caps and seals
CAPTIVE animals. See Zoological gardens
CAR parks, Underwater. See Garages, Underwater
CAR stereo tapes. See Automobiles—Tape equipment
CARAHER, Michele
Reservoir right at home. il pors Outdoor Life 148:72-3+ Ag '71
CARAMEL apples. See Confectionery
CARAMOOR festivals. See Music festivals—New York (state)
CARANDELL, Jose Maria
Barrio Gaudi. il Arch Forum 134:22-7 My '71
CARAS, Roger
Ookpikjuak comes to Long Island. il Nat Wildlife 9:10-11 F '71
Trade winds; interview. ed. by C. Amory. Sat R 54:14 F 13 '71
CARAVAGGIO, Michelangelo Merisi da
First bohemian. R. Hughes. il por Time 98: 54-5 N 15 '71 •
Pseudo-Caravaggisti. R. E. Spear. il Art N 70:38-41+ N '71 •
Roughneck's gang; Caravaggio and his followers at the Cleveland museum. D. Davis. il Newsweek 78:120 N 8 '71 •
CARAVAGGIO; drama. See Straight, M.
CARAVANS
Erin a la cart; tour in Irish tinker's cart. E. H. Urban. il Travel 135:52-4 F '71
CARBARYL. See Insecticides
CARBINES. See Rifles
CARBOHYDRATE metabolism
Brain serotonin content: increase following ingestion of carbohydrate diet. J. D. Fernstrom and R. J. Wurtman. bibliog il Science 174:1023-5 D 3 '71
CARBON
New materials science of carbon and graphite; report of meeting. G. L. Montet. Science 172:87 Ap 2 '71
See also
Graphite
CARBON, Activated
Experiments you can make with amazing activated charcoal. J. G. Busse. il Pop Sci 199:96-8 Ag '71
CARBON, Structural
High-temperature resistant carbon. il Space World H-10-94:50 O '71
CARBON black
From rice hulls to carbon black. il Bsns W p 18 Jl 3 '71
CARBON compounds
See also
Hydrocarbons
CARBON dioxide
Atmospheric carbon dioxide and aerosols; effects of large increases on global climate. S. I. Rasool and S. H. Schneider. bibliog il Science 173:138-41 Jl 9 '71; Discussion. 173: 982-3 S 10 '71
Is man changing earth's temperature? Sky & Tel 42:272 N '71
Mystery of the one-way heat trap; greenhouse effect. I. Asimov. Sci Digest 69:82-3 My '71
See also
Photosynthesis
Plants, Effect of carbon dioxide on
CARBON dioxide laser. See Lasers
CARBON fibers. See Fibers
CARBON monoxide
Carbon monoxide: association of community air pollution with mortality. A. C. Hexter and J. R. Goldsmith. bibliog il Science 172: 265-7 Ap 16 '71; Discussion. 173:576+ Ag 13 '71
Carbon monoxide in rainwater. J. W. Swinnerton and others. bibliog il Science 172: 943-5 My 28 '71
Carbon monoxide in the Corvair. Consumer Rep 36:572-4 S '71
Carbon monoxide: its role in photochemical smog formation. K. Westberg and others. bibliog il Science 171:1013-15 Mr 12 '71
Kindly killer. il Mech Illus 67:144-6 N '71
See also
Soils—Carbon monoxide content
CARBON tetrachloride
Warning about carbon tetrachloride. Chem 44:3 Je '71
CARBONATED beverages. See Beverages
CARBONATES
See also
Sodium carbonates
CARBONIC anhydrase
Carbonic anhydrase interaction with DDT, DDE, and dieldrin. Y. Pocker and others. bibliog il Science 174:1336-9 D 24 '71

Does DDT inhibit carbonic anhydrase? B. H. Dvorchik and others. bibliog il Science 172: 728-9 My 14 '71
CARBOXYLIC acids
2-Thiophenecarboxylic acid: inhibitor of bone resorption in tissue culture. V. S. Fang and others. bibliog il Science 172: 163-5 Ap 9 '71
CARBOXYPEPTIDASES
Inhibition of growth of leukemia cells by enzymic folate depletion. J. R. Bertino and others. bibliog il Science 172:161-2 Ap 9 '71
CARBURETORS
Answer to a prayer; Rochester quadrajet carburetor. il Hot Rod 24:53-6 Mr '71
Auto shop series carburetors. D. Hill. il Hot Rod 24:90-3 O '71
Boss induction; Autolite's in-line four-holers. J. Dianna. il Hot Rod 24:86+ Je '71
Path to performance; Carter thermo-quad. J. Dianna. il Hot Rod 24:74+ Je '71
Tunable carbs. J. Dianna. il Hot Rod 24:64-5 Jl '71
Vrod progress report. J. Thawley. il Hot Rod 24:110-11 S '71
CARCINOGENS. See Cancer producing substances
CARCINOMA. See Cancer
CARD, Charles, Jr
Honest Charley hisself. R. Guldahl, jr. il pors Hot Rod 24:42-4 Mr '71 •
CARD sharping. See Cardsharping
CARD tables. See Tables
CARD weaving. See Weaving
CARDBOARD. See Paperboard
CARDÉ, Ring T. See Roelofs, W. L. jt. auth.
CARDENAS, Lázaro
Obituary
Américas 22:1 N' 70
CARDIAC glycosides
See also
Ouabain
CARDIAC pacers. See Pacemaker, Artificial (heart)
CARDIAC patients. See Cardiacs
CARDIAC rhythm. See Heart beat
CARDIACS
Heart care at home. Newsweek 78:74 S 27 '71
Sudden death victim types. A. J. Snider. Sci Digest 70:58 N '71
Weak heart? Don't drink. il Newsweek 79:50 Ja 3 '72
CARDIOGRAPHY
Magnetocardiography of direct currents: S-T segment and baseline shifts during experimental myocardial infarction. D. Cohen and others. bibliog il Science 172:1329-33 Je 25 '71
CARDONA, Carlo
Elections in Malta. America 124:609-10 Je 12 '71
CARDONA-HINE, Alvaro
Center; poem. Nation 213:218 S 13 '71
CARDOZO, Joaquim
Cemetery of childhood; poem. New Yorker 47:52 N 27 '71
CARDPLAYERS; story. See Lurie, M.
CARDS
American bicentennial, 1776-1976. D. Powills. il Hobbies 76:156-7 Jl '71
Fads and foibles of the past: the game of Old maid. D. Martin. il Hobbies 76:156-7+ Ag '71
Mr President, United States of America. D. Powills. il Hobbies 75:146-7+ F; 76:146-7+ Mr '71
Origin of playing cards. A. J. Ryan. il Hobbies 76:142-4 My; 142-3+ Je '71
Origin of the suits. A. J. Ryan. il Hobbies 76:156-7+ S '71
Playing cards. D. Powills. See issues of Hobbies
Playing cards and medicine. D. Powills. il Hobbies 76:156-7 O '71
See also
Cardsharping
Gambling
Tarot
Collectors and collecting
Card sharks; baseball cards. il Time 98:105+ O 11 '71
CARDS, Advertising. See Advertising cards
CARDS, Catalog. See Catalog cards
CARDS, Greeting. See Greeting cards
CARDSHARPING
How card hustlers make the game. E. L. Mahigel and G. P. Stone. bibliog(p8) il Trans-Action 8:40-5 Ja '71
CARE, Norman S.
University as an investor. New Repub 165: 12-13 O 2 '71

CAREER counseling. See Vocational guidance
CAREER education. See Vocational education
CAREER stories. See Childrens literature
CAREERS. See Occupations; Professions
CAREERS for Negro women. See Negro women
—Occupations
CAREERS for women. See Woman—Occupations
CARÊME, Marie Antonin
Carême, ou la crème de la crème. M. Bishop.
il por Horizon 13:70-1 Wint '71 *
CARESS, Charles W.
Teacher recruitment. Clear House 45:392-6
Mr '71
CAREY, Eileen. See O'Casey, E. R.
CAREY, George D.
Barbara Ringer wins round one in Copyright
office fight. S. Wagner. Pub W 200:42 S 27
'71 *
Carey is new copyright head; Ringer sues,
charging bias. Pub W 200:29 S 6 '71 *
CAREY, John T.
Go-for-broke in Groton. il por Library J 96:
1684-5 My 15 '71
Overdue. bibliog por Wilson Lib Bul 45:593-4
F '71
about
Groton, Conn. library board rejects Carey
ouster. Library J 96:2251-2 Jl '71 *
Nevergreen in Groton: special news analysis.
S. C. Scott. il pors Wilson Lib Bul 45:818-
20+ My '71 *
CAREY, Steve
Comment. P. Schjeldahl. Poetry 117:269 Ja
'71 *
CAREY, William Daniel
Science policy: an insider's view of LBJ,
Dubridge, and the budget. P. M. Boffey.
Science 171:874-6 Mr 5 '71 *
CAREY-Thomas award
Random, Wesleyan, Harper win Carey-
Thomas awards. Pub W 199:103 My 31 '71
CARGAS, Harry J.
Holocaust literature: today's burning bush.
il America 125:458-9 N 27 '71
(ed) See McAlister, E.   Sister Elizabeth Mc-
Alister
CARGO airlines. See Air freight service
CARGO cults. See Cults
CARGO planes. See Airplanes, Freight
CARGO planes, Military. See Airplanes, Military
transport
CARGO ships. See Freighters
CARIBBEAN cookery. See Cookery, West Indian
CARIBBEAN REGION
See also
Architecture, Domestic—Caribbean Region
Cruising—Caribbean Region
Geology—Caribbean Region
Hotels, taverns, etc.—Caribbean Region
Leeward Islands
Negroes in the Caribbean Region
West Indies
Yachts and yachting—Caribbean Region
Description and travel
Going things; Caribbean islands. il Mlle 73:
128-32 My '71
CARIBBEAN SEA
Birth of the Caribbean. L. Purrett. il Sci
N 99:169-70 Mr 6 '71
Passaging south: experiences in the infamous
Bermuda Triangle. B. Cameron. il Yachting
130:56-7+ Ag '71
CARIBOU
See also
Reindeer
CARIBOU hunting
Drive-in caribou: province of Saskatchewan.
S. Netherby. il Field & S 76:164-6+ N '71
Top of the world. L. L. Eddy. il Outdoor
Life 148:42-5+ D '71
CARICATURES and cartoons
Cartoonist Q's. J. Markow. See issues of
Writer's digest
Jules Feiffer (cont) J. Feiffer. New Repub
164:30 Ja 2; 27 Ja 23; 23 F 13; 19 Mr 20; 23
Je 5; 23 Je 19; 165:25 Jl 17; 21 O 30; 21 N
27; 25 D 25 '71
Parting shots: Walt Kelly canines with a
little extra bite; Pogo's political carica-
tures. Life 71:61 Ag 13 '71
Some cartoons of 1971. il Nation 214:16-17
Ja 3 '72
Uncle Tom: that enduring old image. il Am
Heritage 23:50-7 D '71
See also
Comics (books, strips, etc)
also subhead Caricatures and cartoons
under various subjects, e.g. Travel—Carica-
tures and cartoons

Competitions
Winners in WD's first annual cartoon & gag
writing contest. R. Rosenthal. Writers Di-
gest 51:32-3 My '71
Exhibitions
Cartoonist's bite; J. Held display at New
York's Graham gallery. D. Davis. il News-
week 77:106-7 My 24 '71
Rube Goldberg; exhibition at the New uni-
versity art museum, Berkeley, Calif. il De-
sign 72:10-13 Spr '71
CARIES, Dental. See Dental caries
CARIGNAN, R. Don
Poem for Christmas. Horn Bk 47:585 D '71
CARINGELLA, Charles
Distortionless audio compressor. il Pop Electr
35:25-30 D '71
CARISOMO, Arturo Berenguer
Gustavo Adolfo Bécquer. por Américas 23:
9-10 Ja '71
CARL Kempe collection. See Art—Private col-
lections
CARLE, Wayne M.
Cut back or close down? il Newsweek 78:65
N 1 '71 *
CARLETON, R. Milton
Soil know-how: your key to beautiful plants.
il Home Gard 58:41-7+ Mr '71
CARLINSKY, Dan
Heard any new (old) jokes lately? il Seven-
teen 30:114-15 O '71
Nostalgia: who says it's only for over-30's?
il Seventeen 30:114-15+ Jl '71
Surprise! Holiday greetings. il Seventeen
30:98-9 D '71
CARLISLE, Norman
They like impossible jobs. il Pop Mech 135:
76-9+ F '71
CARLISLE, Olga
Poems over power. il Vogue 157:58-9+ Ja 15
'71
CARLISLE, Thomas John
Subpoena; poem. Chr Cent 88:191 F 10 '71
CARLISLE, England
Demon drink rides again: plan to denation-
alize state pubs. C. Brogan. Nat R 23:1237-
8 N 5 '71
CARLO Erba (firm) See Drug industry—Italy
CARLOTA, consort of Maximilian, emperor of
Mexico. See Charlotte
CARLQUIST, Bill
Digital music maker. il Electr World 85:60
Ap '71
CARLSBAD CAVERNS NATIONAL PARK
Carlsbad Caverns National Park. E. H. Coin-
er. il Parks & Rec 6:120-1 Ja '71
CARLSON, Carl
Plastic water main for hot soil. il Am City
86:70 Je '71
CARLSON, D. A. and others
Sex attractant pheromone of the house fly:
isolation, identification and synthesis. bib-
liog il Science 174:76-8 O 1 '71
CARLSON, Edward Elmer
Carlson moves to decentralize United. H. D.
Watkins. Aviation W 94:28-9 My 17 '71 *
Is this any way to run an airline? por Time
98:101 N 8 '71 *
CARLSON, James E.
Current trends in construction. Arch Rec
149:60 Ja; 70 Mr; 63 My; 76 Je; 62 Ag;
150:75 S; 76 O; 60 D '71
CARLTON, Peter L. See Auerback, P. jt. auth.
CARMANY, George W.
Barrier Reef marlin. il Field & S 75:86+
Mr '71
CARMEAN, Harry
Harry Carmean: teacher of classical figure
drawing. R. Parola. il por Am Artist 35:
58-65+ Mr '71 *
CARMEL, Calif.
Field of artichokes. il Newsweek 78:77 S 27
'71
CARMELITES
What would Teresa say? decree for the Car-
melites. America 125:304 O 23 '71; Reply.
G. Wilkinson. 125:332 O 30 '71
CARMEN; ballet. See Ballets—Criticisms
CARMEN; opera. See Bizet, G.
CARMER, Carl
Irving and the misty valley. il Sat R 54:
41+ Mr 13 '71
CARMICHAEL, James H. Jr
Down the hatch. il Nat Wildlife 9:50-1 O '71
Nature's jewels; photographs. Am For 77:44-5
Ja '71
CARNEGIE, Andrew
Andrew Carnegie, by J. F. Wall. Review
Nat R 23:154-5 F 9 '71. J. B. Burnham *
CARNEGIE, P. R. See Baldwin, G. S. jt. auth.

CARNEGIE commission on higher education
Faculty-student views on colleges. Sch & Soc 99:262+ Sum '71
Higher education: reinforcement from the Carnegie commission. J. Walsh. Science 174:1215-17 D 22 '71
Less time and more options in higher education: conclusions of report. Sch & Soc 99:285-6 Sum '71
Medical education: Carnegie panel urges expansion, acceleration. J. Walsh; discussion. Science 171:846 Mr 5 '71
Separate but better; report on black colleges. il Time 97:56 Mr 1 '71
Stop and go. Newsweek 78:72 O 18 '71
Up from isolation; report on black colleges. Newsweek 77:68-9 Mr 1 '71
CARNEGIE corporation of New York
Private institutions in jeopardy. R. G. Smith. Pub W 199:54 Mr 15 '71
CARNEGIE Hall. See New York (city)—Carnegie Hall
CARNEGIE institute, Pittsburgh
Ailsa Mellon Bruce collection in Pittsburgh; Museum of art of Carnegie institute. R. Davidson. il Antiques 100:330 S '71
Greening of Pittsburgh. H. A. La Farge. il Art N 70:39-43+ My '71
CARNEGIE library of Pittsburgh
Construction halt to end at Pittsburgh library; racial balance requirement on Squirrel hill library project. Library J 96:2720 S 15 '71
CARNEGIE museum, Pittsburgh. See Carnegie institute, Pittsburgh
CARNER, Mosco
Witches' cauldron. il Opera N 35:24-6 F 27 '71
CARNIVAL
Carnival in Trinidad. H. La Fay. il Nat Geog 140:690-701 N '71
Fat Tuesday; New Orleans Mardi gras. il Newsweek 77:57 Mr 8 '71
Mas'; Trinidad's carnival. S. Rodman. Nat R 23:371 Ap 6 '71
CARNIVORA
See also
Badgers
CARNOW, Bertram Warren
Special burden. V. Brodine. il Environ 13:22-4+ Mr '71 *
CAROLS
See also
Christmas carols
CAROTENOIDS
Photosensitivity of the circadian rhythm and of visual receptors in carotenoid-depleted drosophila. W. F. Zimmerman and T. H. Goldsmith. bibliog il Science 171:1167-9 Mr 19 '71
CAROUSEL inertial navigation system. See Inertial guidance systems
CARP
Breeding carp with fewer bones. il Sci Digest 69:91-3 F '71
CARPATHIAN walnut trees. See Walnut trees
CARPENTER, David O. See Barker, J. L. jt. auth.
CARPENTER, Don
Pistol; story. Mlle 73:246-9 My '71
CARPENTER, E. Brodie
Agriculture and teeth; reprint. Org Gard & Farm 18:88-91 Ag '71
CARPENTER, Elizabeth
Education. Vogue 158:62 Ag 15 '71
CARPENTER, Regan
Vector theory of curriculum development. Sch & Soc 99:30-2 Ja '71
CARPENTERS
See also
Cabinetmakers
CARPENTERS; drama. See Tesich, S.
CARPENTIERI, C.
Tan now, pay in 1986. il Mech Illus 67:62-3+ Jl '71
CARPENTRY
See also
Joinery
Joints (carpentry)
Tenoning machines
Woodworking
CARPER, Jean
Beware the pitfalls in the fine print. Read Digest 98:123-6 F '71
Beware those quick-reducing gadgets. Read Digest 99:60-3 S '71
CARPET cleaning. See Rugs and carpets—Care
CARPETS. See Rugs and carpets
CARR, Archie
In praise of snakes. il Audubon 73:18-27 Jl '71
CARR, Austin
Austin Carr rides again. L. J. Banks. il pors Ebony 26:60-2+ Mr '71 *

Carr with all the optionals! H. L. Masin. por Sr Schol 98:19 F 8 '71 *
Irish Carr moves into high gear. C. Kirkpatrick. il por Sports Illus 34:42-4 F 1 '71 *
CARR, Fred
Woes of Wall Street; interview. ed. by R. Brady. il por Duns 98:8-9+ S '71
CARR, Gladys
Trade winds; interview. ed. by C. Amory. Sat R 54:16-17 D 11 '71
CARR, Harriet H.
Antiquing. Hobbies 75:68-9+ Ja '71
CARR, Marion
Classic hero in a new mythology. il Horn Bk 47:508-13 O '71
CARR, Robert
New way of life. il por Newsweek 77:44 Ja 25 '71
CARR, William E. See Gurin, S. jt. auth.
CARR, William Henry
Living with lions. il Am For 77:4-5+ F '71
CARRIAGES
See also
Coaches and coaching
CARRIAGES, Doll. See Doll carriages
CARRIER, James A.
Spring in the Scottish highlands. il Travel 135:40-5 F '71
CARRIER, Willis Haviland
Keeping cool at ringside. C. V. Fenn. il pors Nations Bsns 59:56-7 Ja '71 *
CARRIER aircraft inertial navigation system. See Inertial guidance systems
CARRIER corporation
Keeping cool at ringside. C. V. Fenn. il pors Nations Bsns 59:56-7 Ja '71
CARRIERS
Transportation; with yardsticks of management performance. il Forbes 109:186-9 Ja 1 '72
See also
Forwarding companies
Transportation
United States—Interstate commerce commission
CARRIERS of infection
See also
Animals as carriers of infection
CARRINGTON, Frank G. See Inbau, F. E. jt. auth.
CARRINGTON, John F.
Talking drums of Africa; with biographical sketch. il Sci Am 225:10, 90-4 bibliog(p 120) D '71
CARRO, Geraldine
Ali; life story. il pors Ladies Home J 88:86-9+ F '71
Crisscross crown; story. Ladies Home J 88:90 D '71
CARROLL, Bernard J. and Sharp, P. T.
Rubidium and lithium: opposite effects on amine-mediated excitement. bibliog il Science 172:1355-7 Je 25 '71
CARROLL, Charles
Charles Carroll of Carrollton, by T. O. Hanley. Review
America 124:266 Mr 13 '71. A. M. Greeley *
Cath World 213:297-8 S '71. R. F. Jones *
CARROLL, Diahann
Julia models a look for the beach. il pors Ebony 26:106-9 Ja '71 *
CARROLL, Douglas, 3d. See Reich, C. A. jt. auth.
CARROLL, Frances Laverne, and Friday, Margaret
Stirrings in a new school library movement. Wilson Lib Bul 45:983-6 Je '71
CARROLL, Hanson. See Robinson, J. B. jt. auth.
CARROLL, Irwin R. See Stern, L. jt. auth.
CARROLL, James D.
Participatory technology. bibliog Science 171:647-53 F 19 '71
CARROLL, Lewis, pseud.
Alice. D. F. Brown. il Hobbies 76:129-30 Mr '71 *
Alice in Wonderland; dramatization. See Gregory, A.
CARROLL, Paul
Laureate of the day after. Poetry 117:338-40 F '71
Rhapsode from cinci. Poetry 119:104-6 N '71
about
Comment. A. Williamson. Poetry 118:169-70 Je '71 *
CARROLL, Richard
Ice cream man; story. Américas 23:33-6 S '71
CARROLL, Richard B. pseud.
Some air pollution myths. Nat R 23:1233-4 N 5 '71
CARROLL, Ronald L.
Improved capacitive-discharge ignition system. il Electr World 85:78 F '71

CARROLL, Ted
New breed principal brings peace to Pelton. il pors Ebony 27:144-6+ N '71 *
CARROLL COUNTY, Md.
Cellular glass floats support twin intake lines. il Am City 86:32 Ag '71
CARROTS
Crazy about carrots! R. L. Hawks. il Home Gard 58:34-5 My '71
Our colossal carrots. T. J. Marcou. il Org Gard & Farm 18:50-1 Ap '71
Triple-row carrots. D. Foraker. Org Gard & Farm 18:105 Ag '71
See also
Cookery—Vegetables
CARRUTH, Eleanore
Big move to new towns. il Fortune 84:94-7+ S '71
New York hangs out the for-rent sign. il Fortune 83:86-90+ F '71
What price glory on the Albany Mall? il por Fortune 83:92-5+ Je '71
CARRUTH, Hayden
New England tradition. bibliog il Am Lib 2:690-700, 938-48 Jl, O '71
Storm at White Sands, N.M; poem. Esquire 75:75 F '71
CARRY, Peter
Africa was right on in Dixie. il Sports Illus 35:20-3 Jl 26 '71
Back door into the big time. il por Sports Illus 35:26-7 N 1 '71
Baseball (cont) Sports Illus 35:42 Ag 2 '71
Best team, ever. il Sports Illus 35:24-7 N 15 '71
Getting up and going after a title. il Sports Illus 35:24-6+ D 13 '71
Gooood kids on the way. il Sports Illus 35:12-15 Ag 9 '71
Hey, look, ma! Only one hand. il Sports Illus 34:26-8+ My 10 '71
It was a brief time-out. il pors Sports Illus 34:22-3 Ja 11 '71
Lacrosse. il Sports Illus 34:58-9 Je 14 '71
Lew is not enough. il por Sports Illus 34:14-17 F 8 '71
No member from the wedding. il Sports Illus 34:32-3 Je 7 '71
Pro basketball (cont) Sports Illus 34:52-3 Ja 25; 69+ Mr 22; 68+ My 24; 35:74+ S 20; 62+ N 8; 76+ N 22 '71
Red, white and who? il Sports Illus 35:20-3 O 4 '71
We can punch, we can dance. il Sports Illus 34:30-1 Ap 12 '71
Week: baseball. Sports Illus 35:39-40 Ag 23 '71
Winner gets to play Alcindor. il Sports Illus 34:22-4+ Ap 26 '71
CARRY me back to Chicago; story. See Klein, J.
CARS. See Railroads—Cars
CARS (automobiles) See Automobiles
CARSON, Gerald
Once more on the beach. il Am Heritage 22:58-64+ Ag '71
Sweet extract of hokum. il pors Am Heritage 22:18-27+ Je '71
T.R. and the nature fakers. il por Am Heritage 22:60-5+ F '71
CARSON, Rachel Louise
Deadly dust: the unhappy history of DDT. K. S. Davis. il pors Am Heritage 22:44-7+ F '71 *
CARSON, Robert T.
Honesty in politics. W. Pincus. New Repub 165:9-10+ D 4 '71 *
CARSTEN, Wolfgang Becker-. See Becker-Carsten, W.
CARSWELL, George Harrold
Decision, by R. Harris. Review
Sat R 54:37-8 My 1 '71. H. Mitgang *
CARTELS, International. See Trusts, Industrial—International trusts
CARTER, Alan
Packaged music in the car. il Hi Fi 21:55-61 D '71
CARTER, Albert Howard, 3d
Christmas question; poem. Chr Cent 88:1491 D 22 '71
CARTER, Albert Howard, 1913-1970
And now; poem. Chr Cent 88:458 Ap 14 '71
CARTER, Angela
Tokyo, directed by Fellini. il Nation 212:114-16 Ja 25 '71
CARTER, Clarence Holbrook
Egg and eye. S. K. Oberbeck. il por Newsweek 77:56+ My 31 '71 *
Tomb with a view. L. Campbell. il por Art N 70:54-5+ My '71 *
CARTER, Dorothy
Dorothy Carter, prison librarian, emeritus. il pors Wilson Lib Bul 46:408-10 Ja '72 *

CARTER, Edward A. and others
Ethanol stimulates triglyceride synthesis by the intestine. bibliog il Science 174:1245-7 D 17 '71
CARTER, Elliott, 1908-
Carter's Concerto for orchestra, a gripping musical experience. D. Hamilton. Hi Fi 21:82 Mr '71 *
His own man, the music of Elliott Carter. A. Cohn. il por Am Rec G 37:756-9 Jl '71 *
Music to my ears; concert at McMillin theatre of Columbia university. I. Kolodin. Sat R 54:33 My 8 '71 *
CARTER, Jimmy
I say to you the time for discrimination is over. il pors Life 70:30-1 Ja 29 '71 *
New day. pors Newsweek 77:33 F 15 '71 *
New day a'coming in the South. il por Time 97:14-20 My 31 '71 *
CARTER, John Mitchell
John Carter's budget appeal to ALA membership; statement. June 1971. por Library J 96:2436 Ag '71
CARTER, Joseph R.
Program at Centennial elementary school, Wapakoneta, Ohio. il Sch Arts 70:42 Je '71
CARTER, Leon J. 3d
Shades of gray; poem. Negro Hist Bul 34:141 O '71
CARTER, Lillie Mae
America, America; poem. Negro Hist Bul 34:157 N '71
Half-still; poem. Negro Hist Bul 34:87 Ap '71
CARTER, Manfred A.
Night time; poem. Chr Cent 88:224 F 17 '71
Quiet months; Blitz; Foes on the rimrock; Tension; Light after light; Wet Wings; Eternal snow; poems. Chr Cent 88:741 Je 16 '71
CARTER, Richard
(ed) See Flood, C. My rebellion
CARTER, Robert S.
Red star over Cynthia R. il Motor B & S 127:60-1+ My '71
CARTER, Verlon E.
Forest management on National wildlife refuges. il Am For 7:22-5+ Ag '71
CARTER, Willie Mae
Recipe for a Washington dinner party. W. McLendon and S. Smith. il pors Ladies Home J 88:110+ My '71 *
CARTHAGE, Africa
Carthage must not be destroyed; symposium. il UNESCO Courier 23:4-44 D '70

History
See also
Punic wars
CARTHAGINIAN civilization. See Civilization, Phoenician
CARTHAGINIANS
Adventures of Hanno the navigator. il UNESCO Courier 23:14-16 D '70
CARTHEW, Anthony
Red and the green: the divided I.R.A. il N Y Times Mag p22-3+ Mr 28 '71
CARTIER, John O.
Crows like wildfire. il Outdoor Life 147:42-3+ Ja '71
Deer for my pains. il pors Outdoor Life 148:76-7+ N '71
New ice-fishing action. il por Outdoor Life 147:58-9+ Mr '71
Nothing like doves. il Outdoor Life 148:70-1+ S '71
CARTIER-BRESSON, Henri
Cartier-Bresson's France; photographs. Pop Phot 68:92-9 F '71

about
Cartier-Bresson's France. M. R. Weiss. il Sat R 54:46-8 F 13 '71 *
Henri Cartier Bresson: a lyrical view of life. E. Haas. il Mod Phot 35:88-97+ N '71 *
Master of the moment. il Time 97:52+ F 15 '71 *
Metaphors of motion. L. Kirstein. Nation 212:345-6 Mr 15 '71 *
CARTO, Willis A.
Willis Carto. C. H. Simonds. il por Nat R 23:978-89 S 10 '71 *
CARTOGRAPHY
He maps the way to success. W. Lowenberg, jr. il pors Har Yrs 11:36-9 D '71
Map-making at Hammond. A. DeMirjian, jr. il Pub W 200:69-76 S 13 '71
CARTOONISTS
Jobs for cartoonists. J. Markow. Writers Digest 51:43-6 Ap '71
See also
Caricatures and cartoons
Dunn, B.
Goldberg, R. L.
Held, J. jr
Levine, D.
Mauldin, B.
Mullin, W. H.
Nast, T.

CARTOONS. See Caricatures and cartoons;
  Moving pictures—Animated cartoons
CARTOP campers. See Automobiles—Camping
  equipment
CARTOSCELLI, Richard M.
  RC time constants in UJT circuits. il Electr
    World 86:23 D '71
CARTRIDGE tape recorders. See Magnetic re-
  corders and recording
CARTRIDGE television. See Video playback
  systems
CARTRIDGES
  New handgun shot shell. D. O. Moreton. il
    Field & S 76:16+ N '71
  New .17 caliber. J. O'Connor. il Outdoor Life
    148:96+ Jl '71
  7mm. Remington magnum. J. O'Connor. il
    Outdoor Life 147:166+ Mr '71
  Shooter's guide to 22 ammo; with tables. P.
    Wahl. il Pop Sci 199:62-3+ O '71
  Small holes. W. Page. il Field & S 76:96-8
    Jl '71
  Twenty-eight little Indians. W. Page. il Field
    & S 76:142-6 My '71
CARTRIDGES, Stereo. See Phonograph—Ster-
  eophonic pickup
CARTS
  See also
  Serving carts
CARTS, Motor. See Motor vehicles
CARTTER, Allan Murray
  Aftereffects of blind eye to telescope. Ed
    Digest 36:15-18 Mr '71
  Scientific manpower for 1970-1985; adapta-
    tion of address, December 27, 1970. bibliog
    il Science 172:132-40; 173:7 Ap 9, Jl 2 '71
CARTWRIGHT, Gary
  Tin star state. il Esquire 75:95-9+ F '71
CARTWRIGHT, Rufus
  Ask Rufus; questions and answers. See is-
    sues of Mechanix illustrated
CARUBA, Alan
  Ecology books: a doomsday bibliography. il
    Pub W 200:28-30 Ag 16 '71
  Splurge of photo books. il Pub W 199:24-34
    My 3 '71
  Two views from two sides of the generation
    fence. il Pub W 199:22+ Je 7 '71
CARVELL, Kevin
  Freelance job idea: family histories. il Writ-
    ers Digest 51:30-1+ Jl '71
CARVELL, Lyn
  5 who fight pollution. C. Remsberg and B.
    Remsberg. pors Seventeen 30:129+ Ap '71 *
CARVER, David H. and Seto, D. S. Y.
  Production of hemadsorption-negative areas
    by serums containing Australia antigen.
    bibliog il Science 172:1265-7 Je 18 '71
CARVER, Raymond
  Deschutes River; poem. Esquire 76:76 Ag '71
  Fat; story. Harp Baz 104:198-9 S '71
  Hunter; poem. Esquire 76:18 Jl '71
  Neighbors; story. Esquire 75:137-9 Je '71
CARVING (art industries)
  Coal sculpture. J. McCaughey. il Design 72:
    14-15 Spr '71
  Root work is fun to him. G. Pacheco. il por
    Mech Illus 67:72 Ap '71
  See also
  Cameos
CARVING (meat, etc)
  ABC's of carving. il Am Home 74:129 N '71
  Beginner's guide to carving. il Redbook 137:
    62+ My '71
  How to carve a leg of lamb and a baked
    ham. J. Pépin. il House B 113:73 Jl '71
CARVONE
  Odor differences between enantiomeric isom-
    ers. G. F. Russell and J. I. Hills; bibliog il
    Science 172:1043-4 Je 4 '71
  Odor incongruity and chirality. L. Friedman
    and J. G. Miller. bibliog il Science 172:1044-6
    Je 4 '71
CARY, Bob
  Lakers on the breakup. il Outdoor Life 147:
    108-9+ Ap '71
CARY, George D.
  Barbara Ringer endorsed by former copy-
    right chief. S. Wagner. Pub W 200:30 O 18
    '71 *
  Cary appointed register: action contested by
    Ringer. Library J 97:12+ Ja 1 '72 *
  Cary renamed register of copyrights. S. Wag-
    ner. Pub W 200:29 N 8 '71 *
  Race & sex bias are issues as Ringer takes
    LC to court. pors Library J 96:3262-3 O 15
    '71 *
CARY, William Lucius
—and Werner, Walter
  Outlook for securities markets. Harvard Bsns
    R 49:16-18+ Jl '71
    about
  Another voice. por Forbes 108:47 S 1 '71 *

CASALS, Pablo
  Americas pay tribute to Casals. il por Améri-
    cas 23:45 Je '71 *
  Casals. A. Matilla. il pors Américas 23:5-9
    My '71 *
  Music from Marlboro. M. Kanny. il por Am
    Rec G 37:282-7 Ja '71 *
  Pablo Casals: a tribute. D. W. Moore. por
    Am Rec G 37:280-1 Ja '71 *
CASALS festival. See Music festivals—Puerto
  Rico
CASAROLI, Agostino, abp
  Papal diplomat in the Kremlin. America
    124:249 Mr 13 '71 *
CASCADE RANGE
  Volcano watchers. il Newsweek 78:123 S 27 '71
CASE, Elizabeth
  Burton Silverman captures the moment. il
    por Am Artist 35:36-43+ Je '71
CASE, Margaret
  Obituary
    Vogue por 158:114 O 1 '71
CASE, Robert N.
  Experimental models for school library
    media education. bibliog il por Library J 96:
    4151-6 D 15 '71
  Who should do what in the media center. por
    Wilson Lib Bul 45:852-5 My '71
—and Lowrey, A. M.
  School library manpower project: a report on
    phase 1. il Am Lib 2:98-101 Ja '71
CASE for two spies; drama. See Murray, J.
CASE hardening
  Tuff stuff; Tufftriding and nitriding. S. Green.
    il Hot Rod 24:122-3 Ap '71
CASE studies. See subhead Case studies under
  specific subjects, e.g. Business management
  and organization—Case studies
CASELLA, Alessandro
  (ed) See Norodom Sihanouk. With Sih-
    anouk in Peking
CASELLI, Ron
  Defining racism. Clear House 46:98-101 O '71
  Keys to standard English. Ed Digest 36:30-1
    Ja '71
CASERIO, Martin Joseph
  Right on. Establishment, address, October 11,
    1971. Vital Speeches 38:86-90 N 15 '71
CASEWIT, Curtis W.
  Black Africa: the white man's future. il
    America 125:15-17 Jl 10 '71
CASEY, Brian
  There was a time: poem. America 125:100
    Ag 21 '71
CASEY, Frank
  How to improve your credit rating. Mech Il-
    lus 67:64-5+ My '71
  12 convenience items worth buying. il Mech
    Illus 67:74-5 Jl '71
  Which records should your family keep? il
    Mech Illus 68:46-7+ Ja '72
CASEY, Genevieve M.
  Public library service to the aging. il Am
    Lib 2:999-1004 O '71
CASEY, John
  Testimony and demeanor; story. New Yorker
    47:24-40 Je 19 '71
CASEY, John P.
  Independent study, a plan for all pupils. Clear
    House 46:173-7 N '71
CASEY, Kenneth L.
  Somatosensory responses of bulboreticular
    units in awake cat: relation to escape-
    producing stimuli. bibliog il Science 173:
    77-80 Jl 2 '71
CASEY, Michael
  Knowledge; Road hazard; poems. America
    125:403 N 13 '71
  LZ gator body collector; Hoa Binh; Free
    love; Bagley; poems. Nation 213:695 D 27
    '71
CASEY, Richard G. and Nagy, George
  Advances in pattern recognition; with bio-
    graphical sketches. il Sci Am 224:14, 56-
    64 Ap '71
CASEY, Samuel Brown
  Big switch at Pullman. A. A. Butkus. il
    por Duns 98:30-3 D '71 *
CASEY, William J.
  What's wrong with stock markets; inter-
    view. il por U S News 71:50-4 Ag 16 '71
    about
  Casey: an SEC chairman Wall Street loves;
    with editorial comment. il por Bsns W p70-
    3, 104 O 16 '71 *
  Casey at the bat. por Newsweek 77:64 F 15
    '71 *
  Casey at the bat. por Time 97:74 Mr 22 '71 *
  Casey safe on first. por Newsweek 77:90
    Mr 22 '71 *
  Casey the reformer? Newsweek 77:64-5 My 31
    '71 *

CASEY, William J. —about—*Continued*
Dying breed? por Forbes 108:17 Jl 15 '71 *
Full count for Casey? Newsweek 77:79 Mr 8 '71 *
New man to guide the troubled SEC. por Bsns W p 18 F 6 '71 *
Past haunts an SEC nominee. Bsns W p35 F 27 '71 *
Strike two for Casey? Wall Street journal discloses 1962 violations. Newsweek 77:70+ F 22 '71 *
Tough task for new SEC chief. por U S News 70:77 F 15 '71 *
Wall Street's favorite bureaucrat, now. por Time 98:99 N 22 '71 *

CASEY, William L. Jr. and Medford, C. F.
State of the economy and the future of camping. Camp Mag 43:8-10 Ja '71

CASH, Johnny
Johnny Cash: I'm growing, I'm changing, I'm becoming. D. Gallagher. il por Redbook 137:61+ Ag '71
Small talk with Johnny Cash; interview, ed. by E. Miller. il pors Seventeen 29:122-3+ O '70
about
Winners got scars too; condensation. C. S. Wren. por McCalls 98:99-106 Ag '71 *

CASH, W. B. See Wheatley, B. C. jt. auth.

CASH discounts. See Discount

CASH registers, Electronic
Battle of the cash registers. il Bsns W p67-8 Ap 10 '71
Three-way free-for-all. A. A. Butkus. il Duns 98:68-9 S '71

CASINOS
Life without Hughes. K. Fleming. Newsweek 78:88+ N 8 '71
School for gamblers; novel Nevada jobs program. L. Deni. il Ebony 27:55-6+ D '71
See also
Recrion corporation

CASPARY, Vera
My Laura and Otto's. il Sat R 54:36-7 Je 26 '71

CASPER, Frank
Sailor's sailor. S. Chasalow and H. Chasalow. il por Yachting 129:82+ Mr '71 *

CASPIAN SEA
Pollution kills fish in Caspian Sea. I. Agnew. Sci Digest 71:54 Ja '72

CASS, James
Board room and the campus. il Sat R 54:46-7 Mr 20 '71
—and others
Education in America. See issues of Saturday review

CASS scenic railroad. See Railroads, Short line

CASSAVETES, John
On actors & directors. Harp Baz 104:72 Jl '71
about
Merry nepotism, 1971. John Cassavetes. N. Gittelson. il pors Harp Baz 105:74-5 D '71 *
Oh, those husbands! Cassavetes, Gazzara and Falk. N. Gittelson. Harp Baz 104:34+ F '71 *

CASSEGRAIN telescope. See Telescopes

CASSELL, Eric J.
Public health authority talks about food scares. House & Gard 140:58+ Jl '71

CASSELL, Kay Ann
Legal status of women. bibliog il Library J 96:2600-3 S 1 '71

CASSENA
Yaupon. J. V. Watkins. il Horticulture 49:20 F '71

CASSEROLE cookery
Beef tongue in a sweet-strong sauce. Sunset 147:218 O '71
California casserole. il McCalls 98:80-1 Jl '71
For a hot picnic the Dutch oven is a happy traveler. il Sunset 146:154-5 Mr '71
Guess what's coming for dinner; covered-dish suppers. il McCalls 98:92-8+ My '71
Luscious budget trimmers. E. W. Manning. il Farm J 95:44-5 Ja '71

CASSETTE recordings. See Tape recordings

CASSETTE tape. See Magnetic tape

CASSETTE tape players. See Magnetic tape players

CASSETTE tape recorders. See Magnetic recorders and recording

CASSETTE television. See Video playback systems

CASSETTES, Video. See Video tape recordings

CASSIDY, David
David. por Newsweek 78:82-3 Ag 30 '71 *
David; with editorial comment. J. Fayard. il pors Life 71:1, 70-3 O 29 '71 *

CASSIDY, Jerry
Positive use for negatives. il Design 73:12-14 Wint '71

CASSIDY, Michael
South African Christian confronts apartheid. Chr Today 16:3-6 N 19 '71

CASSIDY, Robert
Ever been arrested? New Repub 165:14-16 D 4 '71
Housing black workers. New Repub 165:16-17 Jl 17 '71
Hunting scapegoats in Kentucky. New Repub 164:15-16 F 13 '71
Solidarity. New Repub 164:14-16 Mr 6 '71
Trouble with property taxes. New Repub 164:15-16 My 15 '71

CASSITY, Turner
Scenes from Alexander Raymond; or, The return of Ming the merciless; poem. Poetry 118:276-86 Ag '71

CASSREINO, John, and others
High-performance incinerator. il Am City 86: 54-7 Ja '71

CAST iron building. See Building, Iron and steel

CAST off! story. See Jordan, P.

CASTANEDA, Carlos
Further conversations with Don Juan; excerpt from A separate reality. il Esquire 75:75-89+ Mr '71
about
Sorcerer's apprentice. W. Madsen and C. Madsen. il Natur Hist 80:74-6+ Je '71 *

CASTELFRANCO, Giorgione da. See Giorgione da Castelfranco

CASTELLI, Jim
Abuse of myth. il Cath World 213:88-92 My '71
Cable TV: a common carrier or not? il America 125:397-400 N 13 '71
Inside the prison-industrial complex. Commonweal 95:124-5 N 5 '71
National service: worse than the draft. Chr Cent 88:315-16 Mr 10 '71
Will health beat Nixon in '72? Commonweal 94:108-12 Ap 9 '71
Wounded wait in line. Nation 213:178-80, 322+ S 6, O 11 '71
Year of the prisons. Commonweal 94:494-7 S 24 '71

CASTELLO, Hugo
But what else do you do? D. Dellinquanti. il por Sports Illus 34:76+ Mr 8 '71 *

CASTERS, glides, etc (hardware)
Modernize your refrigerator-freezer; appliance rollers. il Consumer Bul 54:4 My '71; Correction. 54:40 Jl '71
Retractable casters for your shop machine stands. W. G. Waggoner. il Pop Mech 136: 155 D '71

CASTING (fishing)
See also
Fly casting

CASTING, Continuous. See Continuous casting

CASTINGS. See Metal castings

CASTLE, Jerome
Jerry Castle's ordeal. por Forbes 108:20-1 Jl 15 '71 *

CASTLE ROCK park. See California—Parks and reserves

CASTLEMAN, A. W. Jr. and others
Clustering of sulfur dioxide and water vapor about oxonium and nitric oxide ions. bibliog il Science 173:1025-6 S 10 '71

CASTLES
Castles in Belgium. N. Hazelton. il Nat R 23:1251 N 5 '71
Chateaux of France. G. Trotta. il Harp Baz 104:34-5 Ag '71
From Martinique to Malmaison. M. Simons. il por Sat R 54:49-50+ Mr 13 '71
Have you never lived in a castle? M. Gough. House B 113:14-15+ Ja '71
Japanese Gothic: Ako castle. L. Namioka. il Travel 136:52-7 N '71
Living with antiques; château near Liège, Belgium. E. D. Flory. il Antiques 99:398-403 Mr '71
Shelter for a dark age. B. Rudofsky. il Horizon 13:62-73 Spr '71

CASTRO, Emilio
Same cells, the same barracks. Chr Cent 88:1022-4 S 1 '71

CASTRO, Fidel
Castro's big drive to win friends. il por U S News 71:39 N 22 '71 *
End to isolation; visit to Chile. il por Newsweek 78:61 N 22 '71 *
Fidel the silent. il pors Time 98:40-2 N 29 '71 *
Journey for a homebody; visit to Chile. il por Time 98:42 N 22 '71 *

CASTRO, Fidel—*Continued*
Look, mama, only 38 days. W. F. Buckley, jr. Nat R 23:668-9 Je 15 '71 *
On the road. il pors Newsweek 78:40 N 29 '71 *
Soother in Havana. il pors Time 98:40+ N 8 '71 *
Trend that failed. J. Barnes. il por Newsweek 78:44+ D 20 '71 *

CASTRO, Rosalia de
Nasin cand' as prantas nasen. . ; tr. by J. F. Nims; excerpt from Sappho to Valéry: poems in translation. Am Scholar 40:284 Spr '71

CASUALTIES, Vietnamese war. See Vietnamese war, 1957- —Casualties

CAT family. See Felidae

CATALAN, Morrie
VFR to IFR. Flying 89:77+ N '71

CATALINA ISLAND. See Santa Catalina Island

CATALOG cards
Cataloging-in-publication awaiting funds; role of LC. A. Plotnik. Wilson Lib Bul 45:526 F '71
Problem of LC cataloging; excerpts from Melcher on acquisition. D. Melcher. Am Lib 2:701-4 Jl '71

CATALOG codes. See Cataloging

CATALOGING
Cataloging-in-publication awaiting funds; role of LC. A. Plotnik. Wilson Lib Bul 45:526 F '71
Cataloging, processing, and automation; excerpts from Melcher on acquisition. D. Melcher. Am Lib 2:701-13 Jl '71; Discussion. 2:927-8 O '71
Greatest invention since the title-page? autobibliography from incipit to cataloging-in-publication. V. W. Clapp. bibliog il Wilson Lib Bul 46:348-59 D '71
Library of Congress launches cataloging in publication program. S. Wagner. Pub W 200:41-2 Ag 2 '71
1976 minus 6 . . . 5 . . . need for perfected edition of rules in time for bicentennial of American librarianship. S. Lubetzky. il por Library J 96:450-1 F 1 '71
Overdue: elementary school librarian questions the Anglo-American cataloging rules for nonbook materials. C. L. Palovic. Wilson Lib Bul 46:268-9 O '71; Discussion. 46:399-400 Ja '72
See also
Indexing
Subject headings

Anecdotes, facetiae, satire, etc.
Cataloging on the wall. D. Peele. Wilson Lib Bul 45:772-4 Ap '71
Editor's choice: a story told in the temple ruins. G. R. Shields. Am Lib 2:581 Je '71
Invocation. K. Brodney. Wilson Lib Bul 45:777 Ap '71

CATALOGING, Computerized. See Libraries—Automation

CATALOGS
See also
Children's catalog (publication)

CATALOGS, Mail order
Good parts of the Whole earth. D. Schiller. il Pop Phot 68:86-7+ Mr '71

CATALOGS, Publishers
Librarians scrutinize publishers' catalogs. Pub W 200:51-3 N 15 '71

CATALOGS, Seed and plant
Garden mart. House & Gard 139:146-7 F '71

CATALOGS, Trade
Making Christmas one for the books; Christmas retail catalogs. il Bsns W p24-5 N 20 '71

CATALYSIS
Catalysis. V. Haensel and R. L. Burwell, jr. il Sci Am 225:46-58 D '71
See also
Enzymes

CATALYSTS
Promising catalyst for auto exhaust. W. F. Libby. il Science 171:499-500 F 5 '71; Reply. R. C. Vickery. 172:86 Ap 2 '71

CATAMARAN racing
Hobie cat national championship. B. Benson. Motor B & S 127:37 F '71
Quest for the little America's cup; International catamaran trophy. G. Candy. il por Yachting 129:56-8+ Mr '71

CATAMARANS
Catamarans catch on! il Pop Mech 136:92-3 Ag '71

CATARACT surgery. See Eye—Surgery

CATASTROPHE Clarence; drama. See Shore, M.

CATBOAT racing. See Sailboat racing

CATCHBASINS. See Gutters

CATE, Curtis
Europe's first feminist has changed the second sex. il pors N Y Times Mag p4-5+ Jl 11 '71

CATE, William B.
Ecumenism on Main Street. U.S.A. Chr Cent 88:1339-40 N 17 '71

CATECHETICS
Catechetical congress cites problems. Chr Cent 88:1223 O 20 '71
Catechetics R.I.P. G. Moran; discussion. Commonweal 93:459+ F 12 '71
Catechetics, theology and religious education. M. A. Lang. America 125:39-41 Jl 24 '71
Getting it together: the International catechetical congress. C. J. Pfeifer. America 125:287-9 O 16 '71

CATECHIST; story. See Barthelme, D.

CATECHOLAMINES
Differences in the distribution of catecholamine varicosities in cat and rat reticular formaton. J. R. Sladek, jr. bibliog il Science 174:410-12 O 22 '71
Effects of long-term reserpine treatment on brain tyrosine hydroxylase and behavioral activity. D. S. Segal and others. bibliog il Science 173:847-9 Ag 27 '71
Electrical activity of the hypothalamus: effects of intraventricular catecholamines. R. J. Weiner and others. bibliog il Science 171:411-12 Ja 29 '71
Perinatal undernutrition: accumulation of catecholamines in rat brain. W. J. Shoemaker and R. J. Wurtman. bibliog il Science 171:1017-19 Mr 12 '71
See also
Adrenalin
Dopamine
Norepinephrine

CATERERS and catering
Food strategy: garden party an l a Midsummer night fête at the Cloisters. N. Hazelton. Nat R 23:881-2 Ag 10 '71
See also
Carter, W. M.

CATERO, Fred
Classical recording techniques. il por Electr World 85:43+ My '71

CATERPILLAR tractor company
Caterpillar: virtue unrewarded? il Forbes 109:27 Ja 1 '72
Wages of virtue. il Forbes 108:34-5 D 15 '71

CATERPILLARS
Butterfly-plant coevolution: has passiflora adenopoda won the selectional race with heliconiine butterflies? L. E. Gilbert. bibliog il Science 172:585-6 My 7 '71
Detoxication enzymes in the guts of caterpillars: an evolutionary answer to plant defenses? R. I. Krieger and others. bibliog il Science 172:579-81 My 7 '71
Great caterpillar war and the ecopolitics of pesticides. P. Montague and K. Montague. il Audubon 73:50-8 Ja '71
See also
Gypsy moths
Loopers
Silkworms

CATFISH fishing
How the champ catches cats. G. Laycock. il Field & S 76:72-3+ My '71
Little Sioux is big on cats. H. Bradshaw. il pors Outdoor Life 148:64-6+ Jl '71
Tidewater cats G. E. Wolfe. il Outdoor Life 148:62-3+ S '71

CATFISHES
Gross $28,000 on catfish in a barn! B. Coffman. Farm J 95:22D Jl '71
Jumping catfish! il Newsweek 78:90 S 27 '71
Now they're herding catfish. H. Manchester. il Read Digest 98:19-22+ Je '71
Taste, smell and ecology. R. H. Gilluly. il Sci N 100:98 Ag 7 '71
See also
Bullheads

CATHEDRAL Gorge state park. See Nevada—Parks and reserves

CATHEDRAL of St John the Divine. See New York (city)—St John the Divine, Cathedral of

CATHEDRALS
On building cathedrals and tearing them down. J. V. Schall. il Cath World 212:301-6 Mr '71

England
See also
London—St Paul's cathedral

Italy
See also
Rome (city)—St Peter's cathedral

CATHEDRALS—*Continued*

United States

See also subhead Churches under names of cities, e.g. San Francisco—Churches

CATHER, Willa Sibert
Song of the lark. D. Beckman. por Opera N 35:6-7 F 27 '71 *

CATHERINE of Cleves, Book of hours of. See Hours, Books of

CATHODE ray tubes
See also
Television receivers. Color—Picture tubes

CATHOLIC church
Can the bishops lead the church? America 125:473-4 D 4 '71
Catch-up leadership; Vatican's pastoral instruction on public communications. Commonweal 94:323 Je 25 '71
Catholic crisis. E. H. Smith. Commonweal 95:320-3 Ja 7 '72
Catholics and the communications revolution. T. Beeson. Chr Cent 88:714 Je 9 '71
Christianity with a human face; interview, ed. by C. F. Jullien. H. Küng. Commonweal 94:106-7 Ap 9 '71
Church and communications; pastoral instruction on the means of social communication. America 124:622 Je 19 '71
Church as inkblot; result of questionnaire on changes within Catholicism. J. N. Kotre. America 124:196-200 F 27 '71
Decline and fall of radical Catholicism, by J. Hitchcock, and Authority and rebellion, by C. E. Rice. Reviews
    Cath World 214:37-8 O '71. G. C. Hay, jr
End to serenity. P. Steinfels. Commonweal 95:78 O 22 '71
Lex ecclesiae fundamentalis controversy and a pertinent postscript. W. Triggs. Chr Cent 88:896-7 Jl 28 '71
Needed: a new posture. Commonweal 94:419-20 Ag 20 '71
New Roman church: a modest proposal. J. R. Kelly. Commonweal 95:222-6 D 3 '71
Of many things; need for improved communication within the church. D. R. Campion. America 124:inside cover Je 5 '71
Power and the glory are passing. J. Roddy. il Look 35:21-5 O 19 '71
Secrecy; Vatican's instruction on communications. S. J. Adamo. America 124:638 Je 19 '71
Toward a more fallible church; Time essay. M. Mohs. il Time 98:84-5 N 15 '71
Watch your umbrella. Theophilus Protestantus. Cath World 213:87 My '71
Why I am staying in the church. H. Küng. il America 124:281-3 Mr 20 '71; Discussion. 124:358 Ap 10 '71
See also
Canon law
Church renewal—Catholic church
Ecumenical movement
Laity—Catholic church
Mass
Pastoral letters
Religious orders
Synod of bishops, 1971
Vatican council, 2d

Apologetics
See Apologetics

Authority
See Church—Authority

Byzantine rite (Ukrainian)
Bolting bishops; Ukrainian Catholics. Chr Today 16:46 N 19 '71
No revelation in Rome; Ukrainian defiance. il Time 98:84 N 15 '71
Of many things; case of the Ukrainians. D. R. Campion. America 125:384 N 13 '71
Ukrainians on the march. G. A. Maloney. por Cath World 214:109-12 D '71

Clergy
See also
Bishops
Priests

Discipline
See also
Congregation for the doctrine of the faith
Dispensation (canon law)

Education
Catholic educators face new options. C. A. Koob. America 124:366 Ap 10 '71
Hidden agenda. G. Elford. America 124:560-2 My 29 '71
New frontiersmen in religious education; religious educators. J. C. Neiman. America 124:378-80 Ap 10 '71

Undiscussed alternatives. C. A. Koob. America 125:168-70 S 18 '71
See also
Catholic colleges and universities
Catholic schools
Theological seminaries, Catholic

Eucharist
Corpus Christi; aspect of the eucharist. V. P. McCorry. America 124:620 Je 12 '71
Mass accord; agreement on doctrine of eucharist between Roman Catholic church and Church of England. Time 99:44 Ja 10 '72

Finance
Catholic church is one of the least efficient investment institutions in the world; interview. J. Gollin. por Forbes 108:53-4+ N 1 '71
Catholics and credibility. Chr Today 16:24 D 17 '71
God's mammon; findings of J. Gollin. Time 98:92-3 N 8 '71
Worldly goods, by J. Gollin. Review
    America 125:492-3 D 4 '71. D. E. Meier

Government
After the synod. A. M. Greeley. America 125:424-6 N 20 '71
Does the church need a constitution? views of Cardinal Suenens. J. B. Sheerin. Cath World 214:3-4 O '71
Suenens proposal; regional synods. J. Deedy. Commonweal 95:170 N 19 '71

History
Future: does it need a prologue? J. T. Ellis. Cath World 214:21-6 O '71
See also
Trent, Council of, 1545-1563

Infallibility
Celebrating infallibility; letter to the editor. C. M. Murphy. Commonweal 94:51+ Mr 26 '71; Reply. P. Misner. 94:179+ Ap 30 '71
Do Humanae vitae and infallibility stand or fall together? T. A. Caffrey. America 125:66-7 Ag 7 '71
Exploring infallibility. America 124:137 F 13 '71
Follow-up on the Küng-Rahner feud. Chr Cent 88:997-1000 Ag 25 '71
Hans Küng replies to Gregory Baum. H. Küng. Commonweal 94:326-30 Je 25 '71
Has Küng opened the dikes? J. B. Sheerin. Cath Wold 213:3-4 Ap '71
Infallibility beyond polemics. G. Baum. Commonweal 94:103-4 Ap 9 '71; Reply with rejoinder. M. Gallagher. 94:293-4 My 28 '71
Infallible? by H. Küng. Review
    Cath World 213:244-5 Ag '71. M. Ward
    Chr Cent 88:631-3 My 19 '71. D. Tracy
    Sat R il 54:17-19 Ap 10 '71. M. Barth; Discussion. 54:32 My 1 '71
Küng and Rahner: dueling over infallibility. B. Van Voorst. por Chr Cent 88:617-22 My 19 '71
Küng on infallibility. C. Davis. Commonweal 93:445-7 F 5 '71; Correction. 93:555 Mr 5 '71; Reply. F. Simons. 94:295 My 28 '71
Küng-Rahner debate. G. C. Berkouwer. Chr Today 15:45-6 My 7 '71
Question of infallibility. por Time 97:54+ Ap 5 '71
Symposium on Hans Küng's Infallible? an inquiry. A. Dulles; M. A. Fahey; G. A. Lindbeck. America 124:427-33 Ap 24 '71
See also
Popes—Infallibility

Liturgy and ritual
Failure of imagination. il Newsweek 78:87-8 O 4 '71
Instant church. W. H. Cleary. Commonweal 94:426-7 Ag 20 '71; Discussion. 95:51+ O 15 '71
Liturgical reform again? J. Gallen; reply. J. Morris. America 124:133-4 F 13 '71
See also
Chants (Gregorian, plain, etc)
Liturgical language
Mass

Missions
Rome and colonialism; the protesting missionaries in Mozambique. W. Triggs. Chr Cent 88:824-5 Jl 7 '71

Modernism
See Modernism

Negroes
Detroit's black Catholics. America 124:603 Je 12 '71

CATHOLIC church—*Continued*

Oriental rites
East vs. west; married priests. il por Newsweek 78:52-3 Ag 30 '71

Parishes
See Parishes

Relations

Church of England
Mass accord; agreement on doctrine of eucharist. Time 99:44 Ja 10 '72
Underlines; and more cardinals. I. Eldad. Chr Cent 88:777 Je 23 '71

Jews
Catholics, Jews and Israel. J. B. Sheerin. Cath World 213:115-16 Je '71; Discussion. 214:5, 101 O, D '71
Jews and the early church. J. J. Magee. Cath World 214:113-16 D '71

Protestant churches
Protestants and the Pope. L. Morris. Chr Today 15:53-4 F 26 '71
Rome-Geneva: a long and difficult way. W. Triggs. Chr Cent 88:582-3 My 12 '71

Relations (diplomatic)

China (People's Republic)
China and the Holy See. America 124:601 Je 12 '71
Of many things. D. R. Campion America 124:inside cover Ap 24 '71

Europe, Eastern
Pope faces east. T. Beeson. Chr Cent 88:549 My 5 '71
Vatican's ostpolitik. Newsweek 78:58 D 6 '71

Russia
Improbable triumvirate: Khrushchev, Kennedy, and Pope John. N. Cousins, pors Sat R 54:24-35 O 30 '71
Papal diplomat in the Kremlin. America 124:249 Mr 13 '71

United Nations
United Nations and the Holy See. J. A. Lucal; reply with rejoinder. E. C. Tatnall. America 124:178-80 F 20 '71

United States
United States-Vatican relations in the 1970's. W. O. Peterfi. il America 125:89-93 Ag 21 '71

Renewal
See Church renewal—Catholic church

Societies
See also
Knights of Columbus
National council of Catholic laity

Theology
See Theology

Ukrainian rite
See Catholic church—Byzantine rite (Ukrainian)

CATHOLIC church and communism
Cassocks and communism; Latin America. R. Peter. Nat R 23:1468-9 D 31 '71
Working group 7; Catholics and Communists in Hong Kong. N. Hunter; reply with rejoinder. F. Hsu. Commonweal 94:23 Mr 12 '71

CATHOLIC church and race problems. See Church and race problems

CATHOLIC church and social problems. See Church and social problems

CATHOLIC church and the press. See Church and the press

CATHOLIC church and war. See War and religion

CATHOLIC church in Africa
New world language? a chance to mediate the Christian message. A. Deeken. il America 126:11-14 Ja 8 '72

CATHOLIC church in Asia
New world language? a chance to mediate the Christian message. A. Deeken. il America 126:11-14 Ja 8 '72

CATHOLIC church in Bolivia
Bolivia: prayers before a coup. F. Jerez. Commonweal 94:469-70 S 17 '71
See also
Church and state in Bolivia

CATHOLIC church in Brazil
Brazil's people of God, prophets or martyrs? T. C. Bruneau. America 124:91-4 Ja 30 '71
See also
Church and state in Brazil

CATHOLIC church in Canada
Quebec. C. de Mestral. Chr Cent 88:1526-8 D 29 '71

CATHOLIC church in Chile
Chilean Catholics debate Allende's socialism. P. Zottele. Chr Cent 88:778 Je 23 '71

CATHOLIC church in Colombia
See also
Church and state in Colombia

CATHOLIC church in France
See also
Church and state in France

CATHOLIC church in Germany (Federal Republic)
Noted German Catholic weekly dropped by hierarchy; Publik. Chr Cent 88:1408 D 1 '71
Publik: death of a nice try. B. Daley. il America 125:507-10 D 11 '71

CATHOLIC church in Great Britain
Britain's Catholic schools take stock. T. Beeson. Chr Cent 88:583-4 My 12 '71
Catholic renewal in England. S. Bryden-Brook. Chr Cent 88:372-5 Mr 24 '71
When silence is not golden; arms sales to South Africa. T. Beeson. Chr Cent 88:645 My 26 '71

CATHOLIC church in Hong Kong
Working group 7; Catholics and Communists in Hong Kong. N. Hunter; reply with rejoinder. F. Hsu. Commonweal 94:23 Mr 12 '71

CATHOLIC church in Ireland
Ireland's changing Church. Newsweek 78:72 Ag 2 '71
See also
Church and state in Ireland

CATHOLIC church in Italy
Red and the black: two Italian priests. L. Cunningham. Commonweal 94:502-4 S 24 '71
See also
Church and state in Italy

CATHOLIC church in Latin America
Cassocks and communism. R. Peter. Nat R 23:1468-9 D 31 '71
Family planning in Latin America: image and reality. T. G. Sanders. il America 124:203-7 F 27 '71
Liberation of men and nations. America 125:53-4 Ag 7 '71
See also
Church and state in Latin America

CATHOLIC church in Malta
Making Malta modern. J. D. Douglas. Chr Today 15:33 Je 18 '71
Malta: radical priests outwit foes of reform. G. Borg. America 125:35-6 Jl 24 '71
See also
Church and state in Malta

CATHOLIC church in Paraguay
See also
Church and state in Paraguay

CATHOLIC church in Portugal
Portuguese church changes patriarchs, ordains married Protestant minister. Chr Cent 88:740 Je 16 '71
See also
Church and state in Portugal

CATHOLIC church in Quebec. See Catholic church in Canada

CATHOLIC church in Rhodesia
Divided church of Rhodesia. America 124:556 My 29 '71
See also
Church and state in Rhodesia

CATHOLIC church in South America. See Catholic church in Latin America

CATHOLIC church in Spain
See also
Church and state in Spain
Opus Dei (secular institute)

CATHOLIC church in Switzerland
Europe's Tibet: Switzerland, a military democracy. E. M. von Kuehnelt-Laddihn. il Cath World 214:120-3 D '71

CATHOLIC church in the Netherlands
Is it true what they say about Holland? J. E. Kerns. il Cath World 213:30-4 Ap '71
Papal politics; new Bishop of Rotterdam. Newsweek 77:52 Ja 18 '71

CATHOLIC church in the United States
Baffled bishops. R. G. Hoyt. il Harper 243:76:81 O '71
Catholic nostalgia. America 125:336-7 O 30 '71
Catholic priest in the United States, ed. by J. T. Ellis. Review
America 125:406 N 13 '71. J. Hennesey
Catholics and credibility. Chr Today 16:24 D 17 '71
Detroit's Cardinal Dearden: a cautious progressive. A. O. Sigur. Chr Cent 88:671-3 My 26 '71
God's mammon; findings of J. Gollin. Time 98:92-3 N 8 '71
Great Catholic upheaval; significance of Catholic opposition to war. G. Zahn. il Sat R 54:24-7+ S 11 '71

CATHOLIC church in the United States
—Continued
Hidden agenda. G. Elford. America 124:560-2
My 29 '71
Memories of a Catholic boyhood. G. Wills. il
Esquire 75:102-5+ F '71
More U.S. Catholics, but fewer schools and
priests. il U S News 70:72 My 24 '71
Priest-bishop relations: American perspective.
J. C. Haughey. America 124:518-20 My 15 '71
Two Christian styles. T. E. Clarke. America
124:177-8 F 20 '71
What really happened in the 1960's? J. Hitch-
cock. America 124:449-53 My 1 '71
Where to find the leaders? il Newsweek 78:
82-3 O 4 '71
See also
Catholics in the United States
Knights of Columbus
United States Catholic conference
CATHOLIC church in Uganda
See also
Church and state in Uganda
CATHOLIC church in Vietnam (Democratic
Republic)
Clearly anti-Catholic; K. Woodward's article
on the Catholic church in North Vietnam.
S. J. Adamo. America 125:127 S 4 '71
Our Catholic enemies. R. B. Griffin. Com-
monweal 94:402-4 Ag 6 '71
CATHOLIC church in Vietnam (Republic)
Church's changing face. R. J. Willis. Com-
monweal 95:204-5 N 26 '71
Vietnam after the election. T. Fox. Com-
monweal 95:203-7 N 26 '71
CATHOLIC colleges and universities
America's directory of colleges, 1971. America
125:370-2 N 6 '71
Catholic universities flunk the Ph.D. exam;
ACE study. America 124:84 Ja 30 '71; Re-
ply. 124:442 My 1 '71
Changing student in the Catholic college;
excerpt from Catholic higher education in
America: a history. E. J. Power. bibliog f
Sch & Soc 99:493-6 D '71
Future for Catholic colleges? R. E. Christin.
America 125:179-80 S 18 '71
Theology, university and a brave new world.
L. M. Orsy. America 124:606-8 Je 12 '71
See also
Allentown college of St Francis De Sales
Catholic university of America
Dallas. University, Dallas
St Louis university, St Louis, Mo.

Federal aid
Win one, lose one: the Supreme court. W. C.
McInnes. America 125:170-3 S 18 '71

State aid
Department of amplification: W. F. Buckley
on Blaine amendment. E. McCormack.
New Yorker 47:121-3 D 18 '71
CATHOLIC dissenters. See Dissenters, Reli-
gious
CATHOLIC education. See Catholic church—
Education
CATHOLIC hospitals. See Hospitals
CATHOLIC Indian missions. See Indians of
North America—Missions
CATHOLIC inter-American co-operation pro-
gram (CICOP) See Religious conferences
CATHOLIC junior colleges
Directory of junior colleges. America 124:out
side back cover My 8 '71
CATHOLIC laymen. See Laity—Catholic church
CATHOLIC library association
CLA golden anniversary April, 1971. J. Vigle.
Am Lib 2:564 Je '71
Catholic LA: restructure, retrenchment; re-
port. E. Corry. Wilson Lib Bul 45:914+
Je '71
CATHOLIC literature

Bibliography
Critics' choices; selections for religious book
week. Commonweal 93:526-9 F 26 '71
Lenten reading suggestions (cont) America
124:181-8 F 20 '71
Religion (cont) E. S. Stanton. America 124:
547-8. 125:437-8 My 22. N 20 '71
CATHOLIC newspapers. See Catholic press
CATHOLIC parishes. See Parishes
CATHOLIC peace fellowship. See Vietnamese
war. 1957- —Protests, demonstrations, etc,
against
CATHOLIC periodicals. See Catholic press
CATHOLIC press
Exceptions: National Catholic register take-
over by Twin circle publishing company.
S. J. Adamo; discussion. America 124:70-1,
217 Ja 23, Mr 6 '71

Lost ideal; Catholic newspapers dying. S. J.
Adamo. America 125:564 D 25 '71
Noted German Catholic weekly dropped by
hierarchy; Publik. Chr Cent 88:1408 D 1 '71
Our troubled press; diocesan newspapers. S. J.
Adamo. America 125:467 N 27 '71
Press. S. J. Adamo. See issues of America
Publik: death of a nice try. B. Daley. il
America 125:507-10 D 11 '71
Vanishing Catholic press. J. Deedy. Common-
weal 95:127-30 N 5 '71; Discussion. 95:242-
3+ D 10 '71
See also
National Catholic reporter
CATHOLIC press association
Of many things. D. R. Campion. America
124:inside cover My 29 '71
CATHOLIC public officers. See Public officers
CATHOLIC radical movement. See Radicalism
CATHOLIC relief services
Work of CRS. America 124:112 F 6 '71
CATHOLIC schools
Britain's Catholic schools take stock. T.
Beeson. Chr Cent 88:583-4 My 12 '71
Brooklyn's little giant of Catholic education;
Msgr. Molloy. G. A. Kelly. America 125:
312-14 O 23 '71
Can Catholic schools survive? by W. E. Brown
and A. M. Greeley. Review
Cath World 212:277 F '71. B. Downey
Catholic school crisis. il Newsweek 78:83-4 O
4 '71
Catholic schools: alive, kicking. America 125:
164-5 S 18 '71
Decline in Catholic schools enrollment re-
ported. Chr Cent 88:1255 O 27 '71
Devil and Catholic education. D. A. Erick-
son. America 124:367-71 Ap 10 '71
Division X: Catholic response to dull, drab
classrooms. G. Elford. America 124:376-8
Ap 10 '71
For want of pupils. Commonweal 95:290 D
24 '71
Growing up Catholic in mid-century Ameri-
ca. C. Rivers. il pors N Y Times Mag p
16-17+ O 10 '71; Discussion. p 10+ O 31
'71
Historical perspectives and contemporary
realities of Catholic education; adaptation
of address, April 1, 1970. F. Cordasco. bib-
liog Sch & Soc 99:149-52 Mr '71
Is this school necessary? Gary report. M. R.
Berube. Commonweal 95:341-2 Ja 14 '72
Rechartering Catholic schools; symposium.
America 124:560-70 My 29 '71; Discussion.
124:641+ Je 26 '71
Should Catholic schools survive? J. Deedy.
New Repub 164:15-18 Mr 13 '71
Trying to save the schools; symposium. Com-
monweal 93:411-12+ Ja 29 '71
What is a Catholic school? E. Doerr. Ed
Digest 36:37-9 F '71; Discussion. 36:53-4
Ap '71
See also
Jesuits—Education
National Catholic educational association

Desegregation
Catholic segregation; it's almost 1954; Opel-
ousas, La. J. A. Cozzi; reply with rejoinder. R. V. Mouton. Commonweal 93:435+
F 5 '71

Federal aid
Bad way to pay for schools. Life 71:42 D 10
'71
Catholic strategy; views of R. M. Nixon. il
Newsweek 78:52 Ag 30 '71
Church and state united. il Sat R 54:52 Ja
16 '71
High price of fanaticism. L. Bridges. Nat R
23:1297-8 N 19 '71
Politics and parochiaid. M. Friedman and
P. Binzen. New Repub 164:12-15 Ja 23 '71;
Discussion. 164:33-4 F 20 '71
Rechartering Catholic schools; symposium.
America 124:560-70 May 29 '71; Discussion.
124:641+ Je 26 '71
Untangling parochial schools. il Time 98:32+
Jl 12 '71
Win one, lose one: the Supreme court. W. C.
McInnes. America 125:170-3 S 18 '71

Finance
Bishops call for educational tax credits, end
to war. Chr Cent 88:1407 D 1 '71
Can parochial schools survive? il U S News
71:26-8 Jl 12 '71
Parochiaid and taxes. J. M. Swomley, jr.
Chr Cent 88:1024-5 S 1 '71; Reply. E.
Bartell. 88:1238 O 20 '71
Tax credits for education; proposals of Cath
olic bishops. America 125:474-5 D 4 '71
Untangling parochial schools. il Time 98:32+
Jl 12 '71

CATHOLIC schools—*Continued*

State aid

Catholic education aid: Yankee style; Vermont plan. F. M. Bryan. il America 125:174-5 S 18 '71; Reply. R. A. Adams. 125:217 O 2 '71

Parochiaid and taxes. J. M. Swomley, jr. Chr Cent 88:1024-5 S 1 '71; Reply. E. Bartell. 88:1238 O 20 '71

Schools' crisis. J. Deedy. Commonweal 94:394 Ag 6 '71

CATHOLIC theologians. See Theologians

CATHOLIC university of America

Free speech and Catholic university; Ti-Grace affair. America 124:306 Mr 27 '71

CATHOLIC world (periodical)

Father Sheerin retires as editor. K. A. Lynch. Cath World 214:100 D '71

CATHOLICISM. See Catholic church

CATHOLICS

Ambivalent Catholicism. R. Houghton. Cath World 214:7-8 O '71

On being a Catholic; experience of a priest and a woman looking back. J. Barthel. il pors Life 70:55-60+ Ap 30 '71

CATHOLICS, Ukrainian, in the United States

Patriarch for Ukrainians? America 124:601 Je 12 '71

Ukrainians on the march. G. A. Maloney. por Cath World 214:109-12 D '71

CATHOLICS in Brazil

Miracle at Josaseiro, by R. della Cava, and Catholic radicals in Brazil, by E. de Kadt. Reviews

　Commonweal 94:389-90 Jl 23 '71. V. Freehafer

CATHOLICS in the United States

American and Catholic, by R. Leckie. Review

　Cath World 212:325-6 Mr '71. G. MacEoin

Church as inkblot; result of questionnaire on changes within Catholicism. J. N. Kotre. America 124:196-200 F 27 '71

Has the church lost its soul? survey. il Newsweek 78:80-4+ O 4 '71

Holy secularity in a rural parish. L. R. Ward. il Cath World 212:259-63 F '71

Memories of a Catholic boyhood. G. Wills. il Esquire 75:102-5+ F '71

Middle Catholic's anguish. P. C. Rule. il America 125:96-9 Ag 21 '71

Theological weather report from the mediating left. W. H Dodd. America 124:403-6 Ap 17 '71

History

Charles Carroll of Carrollton, by T. O. Hanley. Review

　Cath World 213:297-8 S '71. R. F. Jones

CATHOLICS in Vietnam

Catholics in Vietnam. il Newsweek 77:56+ Je 21 '71

North Viet Catholics urged to follow both Christ and Ho Chi Minh. Chr Cent 88:715 Je 9 '71

Viet Catholics for peace. J. Deedy. Commonweal 94:124 Ap 16 '71

CATIONS

Cation disorder in shocked orthopyroxene. R. W. Dundon and S. S. Hafner. bibliog il Science 174:581-3 N 5 '71

CATKINS

What are those yellow clusters on my pines? il Sunset 146:168 F '71

CATLEDGE, Turner

Averted gaze. J. Chamberlain. Nat R 23:263+ Mr 9 '71 *

CATLING, Patrick Skene

Life and loves of the American beach bum. Vogue 158:52-3+ Ag 15 '71

Sex on the go. il Vogue 157:100+ Ap 15 '71

CATO, pseud.

Letter from Washington (cont) Nat R 23:74 132, 190, 243, 302, 354, 410, 468, 522, 625, 688, 740, 794, 910, 1045, 1096, 1160, 1213, 1278, 1342, 1394, 1451 Ja 26-My 18, Je 15-Jl 27, Ag 24, S 24-D 31 '71

CATOIR, John T.

When the courts don't work. America 125:254-7 O 9 '71

CATON, Hiram

Mau-mauing at Penn state. Nat R 23:428 Ap 20 '71

CATS

Anomalous retinal pathways in the Siamese cat: an inadequate substrate for normal binocular vision. R. E. Kalil and others. bibliog il Science 174:302-5 O 15 '71

Cats & dogs & people. D. W. Ball. il Trans-Action 8:44-7 F '71

Centrality of the cat; views of radicals, ed. by H, Herzberg. il Esquire 75:66-9 F '71

Development of polysensory responses in association cortex of kitten. K. S. Mayers and others. bibliog il Science 171:1038-40 Mr 12 '71

Electroencephalographic and behavioral alterations produced by Δ¹-tetrahydrocannabinol. C. H. Hockman and others. bibliog il Science 172:968-70 My 28 '71

Neural pathways associated with hypothalamically elicited attack behavior in cats. C. C. Chi and J. P. Flynn. bibliog il Science 171:703-6 F 19 '71

Neuronal GM_1 gangliosidosis in a Siamese cat with β-galactosidase deficiency. H. J. Baker, jr. and others. bibliog il Science 174:838-9 N 19 '71

Of cats and men; study of Waardenburg's syndrome. Sci Am 225:50 N '71

Sex difference in the number of sympathetic neurons in the spinal cord of the cat. F. R. Calaresu and J. L. Henry. bibliog il Science 173:343-4 Jl 23 '71

Somatosensory responses of bulboreticular units in awake cat: relation to escape-producing stimuli. K. L. Casey. bibliog il Science 173:77-80 Jl 2 '71

Taste of water in the cat: effects on sucrose preference. L. M. Bartoshuk and others. bibliog il Science 171:699-701 F 19 '71

Unilateral ablation of the auditory cortex in the cat impairs complex sound localization. J. Cranford and others. bibliog il Science 172:286-8 Ap 16 '71

Visual patterned reflex present during hypothalamically elicited attack. R. Bandler, jr. and J. P. Flynn. bibliog il Science 171:817-18 F 26 '71; Reply. A. Trehub. 173:1041 S 10 '71

Food and feeding

Guide to: consumer's cat & dog foods. Mech Illus 67:64 S '71

What should you feed your cat? D. M. Lidster. Bet Hom & Gard 49:38+ Mr '71

What you should know about feeding your dog or cat. L. Coe. Read Digest 98:119-22 Mr '71

CATS as carriers of infection. See Animals as carriers of infection

CATS vision. See Sight (animals)

CATTARAUGUS CREEK

Shadows on the wall. K. M. Wigren. il Cons 26:30-1 Ag '71

CATTELL, David T.

Collective or personal rule in the U.S.S.R.? Cur Hist 61:235-9 O '71

CATTLE

Cattle feeding, and lassoed investors. il Duns 98:33-7 S '71

　See also

Bulls

Calves

Cows

Pastures

Breeding

　See Cattle breeding

Breeds

Brood cows: the better half of the new exotic breeds. il Farm J 95:24-6 N '71

How good are the exotics? interview, ed. by R. Sanders. D. L. Good. por Suc Farm 69:B2-3 Ag '71

How the new breeds may work. il Suc Farm 69:no3 D16 F '71

New lines for crossing. direct from Europe. L. Palmer. il Farm J 95:B24-5 S '71

Care

Animal health; handling newly arrived feeder cattle. R. Lutz. il Suc Farm 69:B24 O '71

Confinement methods

How much confinement can you afford? W. Kester. il Farm J 95:B8-9+ O '71

Diseases and pests

　See also

Cattle, Beef—Preconditioning

Leptospirosis

Measles in cattle

Feeding

Are testing programs on the right track? J. A. Rohlf. il Farm J 95:B9 S '71

Be a weight watcher! Those extra pounds may cut feeding profits. R. Reiman. Suc Farm 69:B8 Ag '71

Custom feeding hedges feeder margins. W. Waltner and E. Waltner. il Suc Farm 69:B22 O '71

Easiest way yet to winter a cow herd. D. K. O'Brien. il Farm J 95:B16-17 S '71

Feed whole-plant soybean pellets? J. D. Boyd. il Farm J 95:B10 O '71

CAVAFY, Constantine Peter
Cavafy: the art of the dramatic. W. Burford. Nation 212:438-40 Ap 5 '71 *
CAVAGNARO, David
Gallery; photographs. Life 71:8-9 Jl 16 '71
Water, man, and nature. il Am West 8:18-29 Ja '71
CAVALIERE, A. and others
Rapidly changing radio images. bibliog il Science 173:525-8 Ag 6 '71
CAVALLERIA rusticana; opera. See Mascagni, P.
CAVANAH, Frances
More souvenirs of Jenny Lind. il Hobbies 75:138-40+ Ja '71
CAVANAUGH, Gordon
People are part of the input. America 124: 589-90 Je 5 '71
CAVANDER, Kenneth
Astarte phenomenon. il Horizon 13:14-18+ Spr '71
CAVE, Hugh
One touch of magic; story. Good H 173:100-1 N '71
Secret treasure; story. Good H 172:64-5 F '71
Three's a family; story. Good H 173:94-5 S '71
CAVE drawings and paintings
Exploring Spanish caves for cave-man art; tr. by K. Young. J. V. Pico. il Sci Digest 70:6-11 Jl '71
Mayan mystery of the Onima caves. E. Hartley. il Sci Digest 69:9-13 Ag '71
Those mysterious cave paintings; cave of Altamira. R. Schiller. il Read Digest 98:154-9 Mr '71; Same abr. with title Europe's cave paintings. Travel 135:60-2+ Mr '71
CAVE fauna and flora
Entrance, twilight, and dark life of the cave. G. Nicholas. il Natur Hist 80:30-5 bibliog(p84) Ap '71
CAVENDISH laboratory. See Cambridge. University—Cavendish laboratory
CAVERLY, Joseph
Plan for action. il Parks & Rec 6:18-19+ N '71
CAVES
Cave development during a catastrophic storm in the Great Valley of Virginia. D. O. Doehring and R. C. Vierbuchen. bibliog il Science 174:1327-9 D 24 '71
See also
Ice caves
Wind Cave National Park
CAVETT, Dick
Back here; interview. New Yorker 47:34-5 Je 5 '71
Dick Cavett talks about . . . interview, ed. by C. Trillin. il Vogue 158:94-5 Jl '71
It isn't as easy as it looks; interview, ed. by J. Birnbaum. il pors Time 97:83-5 Je 7 '71
about
Cavett's complaint; White House pressure. Newsweek 77:59 Ap 5 '71 *
Dick Cavett: the art of show and tell. il pors Time 97:80-3 Je 7 '71 *
Late-night hope for the republic. Cyclops. por Life 71:12 D 10 '71 *
CAVIAR
Champagne & caviar. S. Spitzer. il Holiday 49:72-3+ D '70
CAWELTI, Gordon, and McCloud, Paul
Tests your child takes. il PTA Mag 65:6-9 bibliog(p35) Mr '71
CAYMAN ISLANDS
Deep dive for black coral. J. R. Parks. il Field & S 76:114-16+ D '71
CAYÖNÜ excavations. See Turkey—Antiquities
CAYUGA LAKE
Residues of total mercury and methylmercuric salts in lake trout as a function of age. C. A. Bache and others. bibliog il Science 172:951-2 My 28 '71
CAZZATI, Maurizio
Cazzati vs. Bologna: 1657-1671. A. Schnoebelen. bibliog f il Mus Q 57:26-39 Ja '71 *
CEAUSESCU, Nicolae
Crimean summit. por Time 98:25-6 Ag 16 '71 *
Nixon confuses. Chou. Nation 212:771 Je 21 '71 *
Turn of the screw. il por Newsweek 78:36+ Ag 9 '71 *
CECIL, Andrew R.
Campus unrest; address, February 19, 1971. bibliog Vital Speeches 37:340-5 Mr 15 '71
CECROPIA
Glycogen plastids in Müllerian body cells of cecropia peltata, a higher green plant. F. R. Rickson. bibliog il Science 173:344-7 Jl 23 '71
CEDAR
They live within and behind a six-year-old forest of deodars. il Sunset 146:170-1 F '71

CEDAR, Red. See Juniper
CEDERBLAD 201. See Nebulae
CELAN, Paul
Eleven poems, tr. by M. Hamburger. Poetry 119:134-41 D '71
Poems: In the shape of a boar; Thread-suns; By all means; Today and tomorrow; tr. by J. Neugroschel. Harper 242:93 Mr '71
CELEBRATION; story. See Ullian, R.
CELEBRATIONS
Pirates win; then jubilant celebration or mass brawl? il Sr Schol 99:15-16 N 15 '71
What riot? contrasting news reports of Pittsburgh's post-World series victory celebration. il Newsweek 78:82 N 1 '71
See also
United States—Centennial celebrations, etc.
CELEBRITIES
American greats: L. Bernstein, A. Ailey, D. Ellington. il Vogue 158:252-5 S 1 '71
Before the colors fade (cont) Am Heritage 22:38-43+ Ag; 23:58-61+ D '71
Best-dressed face list. il Harp Baz 104:54-61 Jl '71
Celebrity spotlight. E. N. Mintz. See issues of Travel
Eleven o'clock: Tuesday, January 12, 1971; an ordinary morning for celebrities of New York. New Yorker 46:26-7 Ja 23 '71
Four love stories; photographs. Esquire 75: 93-6 Je '71
Guest editor journal; talking to . . ; quotations. il Mlle 73:318-21 Ag '71
Purposeful people. E. Sheppard. Harp Baz 104:134-5 F '71
Scene/seen. L. Lerman. See issues of Mademoiselle
Senior achievement awards. il Har Yrs 11:26-9 My '71
What I learned from my first child; seven celebrated parents describe their first-time around boners, ed. by R. Wacker, jr. il Good H 173:114-17 N '71
What teenagers think about the 16 people and the dog on our cover; Senior youth-view. il Sr Schol 99:16-18 S 20 '71
See also
Great men
Negro celebrities
Women, Famous

Anecdotes, facetiae, satire, etc.
Winners! results of contest in matching the titles of familiar books to familiar persons. N. Hazelton. Nat R 23:314+ Mr 23 '71
CELESTIAL mechanics. See Mechanics, Celestial
CELESTIAL navigation. See Navigation
CELIBACY
Celibacy: the foundations have shifted. J. C. Schwarz. Cath World 212:254-8 F '71; Reply. Father Patrick. 213:61 My '71
Crisis in the Catholic church. J. A. O'Brien. Chr Cent 88:1233-4 O 20 '71
Forbidden topic. Newsweek 78:127 O 25 '71
NFPC's celibacy stand. J. C. Haughey. America 124:341-3 Ap 3 '71; Discussion. 124:441-2 My 1 '71
Of celibacy and stipends. E. C. Bianchi. Cath World 213:35-8 Ap '71
Of salary and celibacy. D. Kucharsky. Chr Today 15:52 S 10 '71
On eating our cake and having it too. J. J. Hughes. Cath World 213:83-6 My '71
Optional celibacy; Canon law society of America report. America 125:221 O 2 '71
Optional celibacy; letter to editor. W. F. Meersman. Commonweal 94:487 S 17 '71
Priestly celibacy supported by Rome synod. Chr Cent 88:1287 N 3 '71
Question of freedom. Time 97:73 Ap 26 '71
To be or not to be celibate. Chr Today 16:33 O 8 '71
CELL aggregation
Cell dissociation: univalent antibodies as a possible alternative to proteolytic enzymes. H. Beug and others. bibliog il Science 173: 742-3 Ag 20 '71
CELL banks. See Tissue banks
CELL dissociation. See Cell aggregation
CELL division (bacteriology)
Regulation of chromosome replication in bacillus subtilis: marker frequency analysis after amino acid starvation. J. C. Copeland. bibliog il Science 172:159-61 Ap 9 '71
CELL junctions. See Junctions (physiology)
CELL membranes. See Membranes (biology)
CELL movement. See Cells—Motility

CELL nuclei
Ribosomal RNA synthesis and the multiple, atypical nucleoli in cleaving embryos. C. P. Emerson, jr. and T. Humphreys. bibliog il Science 171:898-901 Mr 5 '71

CELLARS. See Basements and cellars

CELLER, Emanuel
Celler's slingshot misses the giants. por Bsns W p44 S 11 '71 *

CELLISTS
See also
Casals, P.
Rostropovich, M.

CELLO music
See also
Phonograph records—Cello music

CELLS
Adenosine 3',5'-monophosphate dependent protein kinase of cultured mammalian cells. M. I. Klein and M. H. Makman. bibliog Science 172:863-4 My 21 '71
Biochemical and cytological evidence for triple hybrid cell line formed from fusion of three different cells. F. Ricciuti and F. H. Ruddle. bibliog il Science 172:470-2 Ap 30 '71
Biology: new answers to some fundamental questions. Bsns W p42 Ja 1 '72
DNA repair. il Sci N 99:415 Je 19 '71
Embryonic and neoplastic cell surfaces: availability of receptors for concanavalin A and wheat germ agglutinin. A. A. Moscona. bibliog il Science 171:905-7 Mr 5 '71; Reply with rejoinder. A. Sivak. 173:264-5 Jl 16 '71
Glycopeptides from the surface of control and virus-transformed cells. C. A. Buck and others. bibliog il Science 172:169-71 Ap 9 '71
Human thymidine kinase gene locus: assignment to chromosome 17 in a hybrid of man and mouse cells. O. J. Miller and others. bibliog il Science 173:244-5 Jl 16 '71
Insulin and microtubules in rat adipocytes. D. Soifer and others. bibliog il Science 172:269-71 Ap 16 '71
Kinetic differences in unresponsiveness of thymus and bone marrow cells. J. M. Chiller and others. bibliog il Science 171:813-15 F 26 '71
Symbiosis and evolution: origin of organelles. L. Margulis. il Sci Am 225:48-57 bibliog(p 120) Ag '71
Synthesis of 5S and 4S RNA in metaphase-arrested HeLa cells. E. A. Zylber and S. Penman. bibliog il Science 172:947-9 My 28 '71
See also
Cancer cells
Chromatin
Differentiation (biology)
Epithelium
Germ cells
Golgi apparatus
Macrophages
Melanophores
Membranes (biology)
Osmosis
Peroxisomes
Phagocytes and phagocytosis
Rod and cone cells
Thymocytes
Tumor cells

Culture
See Tissues—Culture

Inclusions
See also
Mitochondria

Motility
How living cells change shape. N. K. Wessells. il Sci Am 225:76-82 O '71

Preservation
See Tissues—Preservation

CELLULAR automata theory. See Machine theory

CELLULAR differentiation. See Differentiation (biology)

CELLULAR therapy
Shot of youth for the ills of age. il por Bsns W p60+ N 20 '71

CELTIC sculpture. See Sculpture, Ancient

CELTS
Sacred source of the Seine. S. A. Deyts. il Sci Am 225:65-73 Jl '71

CEMBURA, Albert
Empties are better. il por Time 97:62 Mr 22 '71 *

CEMENT
See also
Concrete

CEMENT boats. See Boats—Materials

CEMENT gun
See also
Gunite

CEMENT industry
Cement plant, anyone? Atlantic cement. Forbes 107:48 Je 15 '71
Climbing out of the gully; with table. il Forbes 107:59-60 Mr 15 '71
See also
Martin-Marietta corporation
Penn Dixie cement corporation

CEMENT work. See Concrete work

CEMENTS, Adhesive
Household cements (cont) il Consumer Bul 54:36-7 F '71

CEMETERIES
Let sleeping bones lie; Indians' graves. Chr Cent 88:1157 O 6 '71

CEMETERY workers strike. See Strikes—United States—Cemetery workers

CENOZOIC period. See Geology, Stratigraphic—Cenozoic; Paleontology—Cenozoic

CENSORSHIP
Banning of Billy Pilgrim; Michigan court on Vonnegut's Slaughterhouse five. Chr Cent 88:681 Je 2 '71
Censorship and public understanding. R. R. Gard. bibliog Engl J 60:255-9 F '71
Censorship and teacher responsibility. J. F. Symula. Engl J 60:128-31 Ja '71
Everything you always wanted to know about censorship (but were afraid to ask) explained. E. M. Oboler. bibliog il Am Lib 2:194-8 F '71
New waves of censorship. R. H. Smith. Pub W 200:34 Jl 26 '71
Phantasy and facts: censorship & schools. F. C. Ellenburg. bibliog f Clear House 45:515-19 My '71
Social control of pornography and sexual behavior. B. L. Bonniwell. bibliog f Ann Am Acad 397:97-104 S '71
Story behind the book: The little red schoolbook. L. P. Freilicher. pors Pub W 200:32-3 D 13 '71
Threats to intellectual freedom; address. June 1971. E. T. Moore. il por Library J 96:3563-7 N 1 '71; Same abr. with title Rise of a new censorship? Cur 135:3-8 D '71
What a bookseller can do about it. R. D. Hale. Pub W 200:26-7 Jl 26 '71
What boundaries for federal censorship? R. H. Smith. Pub W 199:39 My 3 '71
See also
Freedom of the press
Government and the press
Immoral literature and pictures
Information, Freedom of
Intellectual liberty
Moving picture censorship
Obscenity (law)
Postal censorship
also subhead Censorship under various subjects. e.g. Radio broadcasting—Censorship

Great Britain
England restricts freedom to publish; Little red school book. M. Reynolds. Pub W 200:27-8 Jl 26 '71

Russia
Reality and socialist realism: two versions of Babi Yar. by A. Kuznetsov. T. Solotaroff. Sat R 54:59-62 Ja 23 '71
Russian book publishing: inexorably wedded to censorship. S. Jacoby. il Pub W 200:pt2 169-71 S 27 '71
Science censored. D. Shapley. Science 174:273 O 15 '71

South Africa
Ghettoizing culture in South Africa. I. Robertson and J. Fishkin. Commonweal 94:156-7 Ap 23 '71
M*A*S*H*E*D; entertainments amendment bill. Newsweek 77:45-6 F 22 '71

United States
See Censorship

CENSUS
See also
Great Britain—Census
United States—Census

CENTENARIANS
Bloom is still on at age 100; Z. D. Blackistone of Washington, D.C. V. Louviere. il por Nations Bsns 59:21 Ap '71
5,253 centenarians on social security; up 2,053 in 2 years. il Aging 200:12-13 Je '71
When you're 100 and have three wishes. B. B. Beard. il por Har Yrs 11:40-3 F '71

CENTENNIALS
See also
United States—Centennial celebrations, etc.

CENTER for concern (proposed)
Center for concern; study of world peace, justice and development. America 124:531 My 22 '71
CENTER for intercultural documentation. See Center of intercultural documentation
CENTER for modern dance education, Bergen County, N.J. See Dance schools
CENTER for policy research
MINERVA: a participatory technology system. E. Leonard and others. il Bul Atom Sci 27:4-12 N '71
CENTER for short-lived phenomena. See Smithsonian institution—Center for short-lived phenomena
CENTER for the study of power and peace
New presence in Washington. Chr Cent 88: 991 Ag 25 '71
CENTER of intercultural documentation
CIDOC: alternatives in design and education. R. M. Golder. il Arch Rec 150:117-18 Jl '71
CENTER of population. See United States— Population
CENTER of the eye, Aspen, Colo. See Photography—Study and teaching
CENTER opera company, Minneapolis
Faust and loose; production of Faust counter Faust. il Newsweek 77:91 F 15 '71
Faust counter Faust. J. Gerstel. il Hi Fi 21:MA26-7 My '71
Report:
Faust counter Faust. P. Gainsley. il Opera N 35:29 Mr 13 '71
Postcard from Morocco, by Dominick Argento. L. Hollister. Opera N 36:28 D 11 '71
Virgil Thomson's Mother of us all. C. J. Luten. Opera N 36:23 S '71
Revolution comes to opera. C. L. Osborne. il Hi Fi 21:62-70 N '71
CENTER stage theater. See Baltimore—Theater
CENTERING
Make a center indicator for lathe work. W. E. Burton. il Pop Mech 135:126-9+ My '71
CENTERPIECES. See Table decoration
CENTERS for the performing arts
Anti-city beautiful movement. W. Von Eckardt. New Repub 164:32-3 Ap 3 '71
See also
Bombay—National centre for the performing arts
Heinz Hall for the performing arts, Pittsburgh
John F. Kennedy center for the performing arts, Washington, D.C.
Wolf Trap Farm Park for the performing arts
CENTO. See Central treaty organization
CENTRAL AMERICA
See also
Canals—Central America
Indians of Central America

Description and travel
Central America. P. Benchley. il Holiday 48: 62:6 N '70
CENTRAL Baptist theological seminary, Kansas City, Kan.
Ferment at Central Baptist. J. S. Tinney. Chr Today 15:46 My 21 '71
CENTRAL conference of American rabbis
Mixed marriage feelings. Newsweek 78:52 Jl 5 '71
CENTRAL EUROPE
See also
Transylvania
CENTRAL Florida regional library, Ocala
Ocala, Florida: a skylit hexagon. il Library J 96:3981 D 1 '71
CENTRAL intelligence agency. See United States—Central intelligence agency
CENTRAL KANSAS library system, Great Bend, Kan.
Library almanac. D. Johnson. il Am Lib 2: 1194-5 D '71
CENTRAL nervous system. See Nervous system
CENTRAL opera service
NOA, COS conferences. R. Mercer. Opera N 36:41 D 25 '71
CENTRAL park. See New York (city)—Parks and playgrounds
CENTRAL Park precinct. See New York (city)—Police department—Central Park precinct
CENTRAL park zoo. See New York (city)—Parks and playgrounds
CENTRAL treaty organization
Secretary Rogers attends SEATO and CENTO meetings and visits four Arab states, Israel and Rome; statements, transcripts of interviews, and texts of communiques, April 26-May 9, 1971. W. P. Rogers. Dept State Bul 64:681-702 My 31 '71
CENTRALIZATION in government. See Decentralization in government

CENTRIFUGAL chromatography. See Chromatographic analysis
CENTRIFUGATION
Carcinogen and microsomal membrane interactions: changes in membrane density and ability to bind nucleic acids. H. Kubinski and C. B. Kasper. bibliog il Science 171:201-3 Ja 15 '71
Density gradient separation of marrow cells restricted for antibody class. H. C. Miller and G. Cudkowicz. bibliog il Science 171: 913-15 Mr 5 '71
Density gradient separation of marrow precursor cells restricted for antibody specificity. H. C. Miller and G. Cudkowicz. bibliog il Science 173:156-8 Jl 9 '71
Herpesvirus antigens on cell membranes detected by centrifugation of membrane-antibody complexes. B. Roizman and P. G. Spear. bibliog il Science 171:298-300 Ja 22 '71
CENTRO intercultural de documentacion. See Center of intercultural documentation
CEPHEIDS. See Stars, Variable
CERAM, C. W. pseud.
Last stone age American; excerpt from The first American. il pors Am Heritage 22:14-19+ Ag '71
CERAMIC beads. See Beads
CERAMIC coating. See Enamel and enameling
CERAMIC costume jewelry. See Jewelry
CERAMIC materials
See also
Electronic ceramics
CERAMIC sculpture
Ceramic sculpture from wheel-thrown parts. L. Helmuth. il Ceram Mo 19:22-5 My '71
Ceramic sculpture of Joe Ann Cousino. R. D. Bonham. il Ceram Mo 19:16-17 My '71
David Gilhooly; J. Arneson. il Craft Horiz 31:20-1+ Ag '71
Karen Park's ceramic wall reliefs. M. Blanchard. il por Ceram Mo 19:24-6 O '71
Laugh-in in clay; Clayworks: 20 Americans, exhibition at the Museum of contemporary crafts. R. Slivka. il Craft Horiz 31:39-47 O '71
Monumental ceramic sculpture for Southern Illinois campus. il Ceram Mo 19:28-9 Ap '71
CERAMIC tiles. See Tiles
CERAMICS. See Pottery
CERAMICS, English. See Pottery, English
CERCOCARPUS. See Mountain mahogany
CEREAL foods
Breads & cereals; questions and answers; with recipes. R. H. Smithies. il Good H 173:144+ D '71
See also
Cookery—Cereals
CEREAL leaf beetles. See Beetles
CEREBELLUM
Cerebellar hypoplasia in neonatal rats caused by lymphocytic choriomeningitis virus. A. A. Monjan and others. bibliog il Science 171:194-6 Ja 15 '71
Human fetal cerebellar cortex: organization and maturation of cells in vitro. L. W. Lapham and W. R. Markesbery. bibliog il Science 173:829-32 Ag 27 '71
CEREBRAL cortex
Acetylcholine liberation from cerebral cortex during paradoxical (REM) sleep. H. H. Jasper and J. Tessier. bibliog il Science 172:601-2 My 7 '71
Cyclic 3,5'-nucleotide phosphodiesterase: cytochemical localization in cerebral cortex. N. T. Florendo and others. bibliog il Science 173:745-7 Ag 20 '71
Development of polysensory responses in association cortex of kitten. K. S. Mayers and others. bibliog il Science 171:1038-40 Mr 12 '71
Fortification illusions of migraines. W. Richards. il Sci Am 224:88-94+ bibliog(p 132) My '71
Retention deficit correlated with a deficit in the corticoid response to stress. P. Auerbach and P. L. Carlton. bibliog il Science 173:1148-9 S 17 '71
Rhesus monkey vestibular cortex: a bimodal primary projection field. D. W. F. Schwarz and J. M. Fredrickson. bibliog il Science 172:280-1 Ap 16 '71
Selective recovery from retrograde amnesia produced by hippocampal spreading depression. B. S. Kapp and A. M. Schneider. bibliog il Science 173:1149-51 S 17 '71
Shift in binocular disparity causes compensatory change in the cortical structure of kittens. R. Shlaer. bibliog il Science 173: 638-41 Ag 13 '71

CEREBRAL cortex—*Continued*
Visual attention in the tree shrew: an abla-
tion study of the striate and extrastriate
visual cortex. H. Killackey and I. T. Dia-
mond. bibliog il Science 171:696-9 F 19 '71
CEREBROSPINAL fluid
Cerebrospinal fluid production by the choroid
plexus and brain. T. H. Milhorat and oth-
ers. bibliog il Science 173:330-2 Jl 23 '71
Origin of 5-hydroxyindoleacetic acid in the
spinal fluid. M. Bulat and B. Živković.
bibliog il Science 173:738-40 Ag 20 '71
See also
Blood-brain barrier
CEREBROVASCULAR disease
Candidates for stroke. Sci Digest 71:23 Ja '72
CEREGHINO, Edward J.
Administrator: target for today. Clear House
45:528-31 My '71
CEREMONIES. See Rites and ceremonies
CERF, Bennett
Obituary
Pub W por 200:30-1 S 6 '71
Sat R 54:28 S 11 '71. N. Cousins
CERN (conseil européen pour la recherche
nucléaire) See European organization for
nuclear research
CERRA, Frances
Guided tour of the balance sheet. il Nation
212:562-4 My 3 '71
CERRO corporation
Breaking ranks. il Forbes 108:27 S 15 '71
CERRUTI, Eugene. See Donner, F. J. jt. auth.
CERRUTI, James
Britain's "French" Channel Islands. il Nat
Geog 139:710-40 My '71
Chelsea, London's haven of individualists. il
Nat Geog 141:28-55 Ja '72
Sea Islands. il Nat Geog 139:366-93 Mr '71
CERTAIN-Teed products corporation
Concept at Certain-Teed. il Duns 98:49 D '71
CERTIFICATES, Teachers. See Teachers—Cer-
tification
CERTIFICATION of airplanes. See Airplanes
—Standards
CERTIFICATION of airports. See Airports—
Standards
CERTIFICATION of commercial products. See
Commercial products, Certification of
CERTIFICATION of helicopters. See Helicop-
ters—Standards
CERUMEN. See Earwax
CERVICAL cancer. See Cancer
CESSNA aircraft company
Cessna changes basic marketing. C. E.
Schneider. il Aviation W 96:58 Ja 3 '72
Cessna Citation marketing emphasizes air-
craft utility. C. E. Schneider. Aviation W
94:60-2 F 22 '71
Protests spark Cessna facility location shift.
E. J. Bulban. Aviation W 95:20-1 O 4 '71
CESTRUMS
Three visitors from Mexico; red yucca, Mex-
ican abelia and red cestrum. il Sunset 147:
184 S '71
CETACEA
See also
Whales
CEYLON
See also
Zoology—Ceylon

Description and travel
Firewalkers of Udappawa. V. Perera. Harper
242:18+ My '71

Economic conditions
Ceylon: the bitter harvest. E. Gilliland. Nation 212:582-4 My 10 '71

Politics and government
Ceylon: the bitter harvest. E. Gilliland. Na-
tion 212:582-4 My 10 '71
Che Guevarist uprising. Time 97:21 Ap 19
'71
Civil war in Ceylon. T. Deutscher. il Ramp
Mag 10:26-9 Jl '71
Insurrection in Ceylon. T. Balasuriya. Com-
monweal 94:300-1 Je 11 '71
Making new friends. il Newsweek 77:36+
Ap 26 '71
Out of touch. E. Behr. il Newsweek 77:59 Ap
19 '71
CÉZANNE, Paul
Cézanne without tears; Phillips collection
exhibition. B. F. Forgey. il pors Art N 70:
56-9+ Ap '71
CHAD
See also
Guerrillas—Chad
Hunting—Chad

CHAD, LAKE
Hovercraft to the heart of Africa; Trans-
african hovercraft expedition. il Sci Digest
70:38-45+ D '71
CHADWICK, H. Joseph
Earn greeting card money selling promotion
ideas. il Writers Digest 51:22-3+ Ag '71
Short story checklist. Writers Digest 51:33
N '71; 52:27 Ja '72
CHADWICK, Hal
Last resort. il Todays Health 49:50-2 My '71
CHADWICK, Thomas A.
Vermont bear hunt. il por Outdoor Life 148:
64-5+ N '71
CHAETOGNATHA. See Arrowworms
CHAFFEE, Leonard M. and Alley, R. D.
Strike one! Yer' out! A short count for
the student teacher in a school strike?
Clear House 45:503-6 Ap '71
CHAFFIN, LaJean, and others
Cross-lined transfer RNA functions in all
steps of the translation process. bibliog il
Science 172:854-5 My 21 '71
CHAFING dish cookery
Cooking at the table. il Sunset 146:148-9 Je
'71
CHAIN saws. See Saws
CHAIN stores
Big stores begin another great migration. il
Bsns W p66-7 My 22 '71
Gibson's l'il ole billion-dollar business; dis-
count stores. il pors Bsns W p60-1+ Mr 20
'71
See also
Broadway-Hale stores, inc.
Eckerd, Jack, corporation
Federated department stores, inc.
Grocery trade
Penney, J. C, company
Pier 1 imports, inc.
Safeway stores, inc.
Silo, inc.
Sixty nine cents shops
Supermarkets
Supermarkets general corporation
Toronto—Stores

Securities
Making money work; retail trade industry in-
vestments. S. Meisenberg. il Har Yrs 11:44-
5 My '71
CHAIRS
Cincinnati cabinet- and chairmakers, 1819-
1830. D. Streifthau. il Antiques 99:896-905
Je '71
Colonial chair you can build for $53. R.
Capotosto. il Pop Mech 136:144-9 D '71
Form and frame: new thoughts on the
American easy chair; today called a wing
chair; with editorial comment. M. H.
Heckscher. il Antiques 100:885, 886-93 D '71
Good looking and comfortable, it is lami-
nated wood, canvas, glue, and big dowels.
il Sunset 147:76 Jl '71
Hardwood, cotton duck, and a comfortable
roll of foam. il Sunset 147:112+ N '71
Rocking chair in America. E. Gaines. il
Antiques 99:238-40 F '71
Rocking chair in Victorian England. J.
Gloag. il Antiques 99:241-4 F '71
Tennessee cabinetmakers and chairmakers
through 1840. E. Beasley. il Antiques 100:
612-21 O '71
What's new in casual furniture. il Bet Hom
& Gard 49:72+ Je '71
Windsor chair in Nova Scotia; with list of
chairmakers. G. MacLaren. il Antiques 100:
124-7 Jl '71
You can make this chair for $15; wrought
iron furniture. W. C. Leckey. il Pop Mech
136:152-4+ Jl '71
See also
Wheelchairs

Repairing
Uplift for a sagging chair. B. Duggan. il
Mech Illus 68:92-3 Ja '72
CHAISSON, John R.
Parting shots: a marine who could handle
the tank. por Life 71·69 Jl 16 '71 *
CHALFANT, Arnold R.
Ecology primer. bibliog il Nat Wildlife 9:
38-9 Ag; 10-11 O '71
Water rules the world. bibliog il Nat Wild-
life 9:38-41 Ag '71
CHALIDZE, Valerii N.
To the president of the U.S.S.R. Supreme
Soviet: on the persecution of repatriate
Jews. Sat R 54:31 S 18 '71
CHALLENER, R. D.
Which way America? Dulles always knew;
ed. by J. Fenton. il pors Am Heritage
22:12-13+ Je '71

CHALLENGER expedition, 1872-1876
Her Majesty's fauna on the bounding main;
with excerpts from Notes by a naturalist
on the Challenger, by H. N. Moseley. S.
Schlee. il Natur Hist 80:76-80 O '71
CHALLINOR, R. A.
Variations in the rate of rotation of the
earth. bibliog il Science 172:1022-5 Je 4 '71
CHAMBER music
It's the group that counts today; R. Hem-
ming interviews the Guarneri quartet. il
Sr Schol 98:20 Mr 15 '71
Musical events; Music from Marlboro series,
in Alice Tully Hall. W. Sargeant. New
Yorker 47:114 F 20 '71
See also
Phonograph records—Chamber music
CHAMBER music festival. See Washington,
D.C.—Music
CHAMBER music society of Lincoln Center
Music to my ears; latest exercises in Alice
Tully Hall. I. Kolodin. Sat R 54:44 F 20 '71
Music to my ears; season's first concert. I.
Kolodin. Sat R 54:68 N 6 '71
CHAMBER of commerce of the United States
of America
Archie K. Davis of Wachovia bank & trust;
interview. A. K. Davis. il pors Nations
Bsns 59:34-41 My '71
CHAMBER orchestras
Boston symphony chamber players: Schubert-
Milhaud-Hindemith miscellany. A. Cohn.
il Am Rec G 37:424-6 Mr '71
CHAMBERED nautilus. See Nautilus
CHAMBERLAIN, Anne
Coming to terms with a character. Writer
84:25-6+ Ag '71
CHAMBERLAIN, Betty
Professional page. Am Artist 35:16+ Ag; 11-
12 S; 46+ O; 54 N; 15 D '71; 36:16 Ja '72
CHAMBERLAIN, Gary M.
City owned and operated TV stations. il
Am City 86:103-4+ Ap '71
Traffic signals come of age. il Am City 86:
93-4+ Ag '71
(ed) See Howard, J. P. How to solve the
police crisis
(ed) See Kelley, C. M. How to solve the
police crisis
(ed) See Wilson, J. V. How to solve the
police crisis
CHAMBERLAIN, John
Edith Efron's murderous adding machine.
Nat R 23:1225-6+ N 5 '71
Harry Luce and the Russian century. Nat R
23:524-5+ My 18 '71
CHAMBERLAIN, Neil Wolverton
Stabilization of labor relations? address,
April 1971, with questions and answers.
Ann Am Acad 396:79-89 Jl '71
CHAMBERLAIN, Richard
Alas, poor Ilyich. por Vogue 157:70 Mr 15 '71 •
New Barrymore. T. E. Kalem. por Time
97:74 Ap 26 '71 •
CHAMBERLAIN, Samuel
Hastings house is 35: high standards and a
touch of nostalgia. M. R. Kraner. il Pub W
200:12-14 N 29 '71 •
CHAMBERLIN, Anne
Panty hose; see how they run. McCalls 98:
24+ Mr '71
CHAMBERLIN, Clarence Duncan
How not to fly the Atlantic; excerpts from
Oceans, Poles and airmen. R. Montague. il
pors Am Heritage 22:42-7+ Ap '71 •
CHAMBERLIN, Jo
Champs don't win on diets. Sci Digest 70:
64-8 S '71
CHAMBERS, Bradford
Book publishing: a racist club? il Pub W 199:
40-4 F 1 '71; Same abr. Cur 129:16-22 My
'71
Interracial books: background of a challenge.
il Pub W 200:23-9 O 11 '71
Minority publishing: bringing the record up
to date. Pub W 201:27 Ja 3 '72
(ed) Why minority publishing? il pors Pub W
199:35-50 Mr 15 '71
CHAMBERS, Carl D. and Schultz, Dodi
Women and drugs (title varies) il Ladies
Home J 88:130-1+ N; 66+ D '71
CHAMBERS, Ernest W.
Drugs for children; the Omaha program and
resulting political involvement. H. Vinn-
edge. New Repub 164:13-15 Mr 13 '71; Dis-
cussion. 164:28-9 Ap 10: 37-8 Ap 17 '71 •
CHAMBERS, John C. and others
Catalytic agent for effective planning. il
Harvard Bsns R 49:110-19 Ja '71
How to choose the right forecasting technique.
bibliog f il Harvard Bsns R 49:45-74 Jl '71
CHAMBERS, M. M.
Trend toward separate governing boards.
Sch & Soc 99:349-50 O '71

CHAMBERS, Whittaker
Alger Hiss case revisited. A. Weinstein. Am
Scholar 41:121-32 Wint '71 •
Ten years dead. R. De Toledano. Nat R 23:
793 Jl 27 '71 •
CHAMBERS, isolation. See Isolation chambers
CHAMBLISS, Carison R. See Kiasat, A. jt.
auth.
CHAMELEON who ended up not knowing what
to turn; story. See Monterroso, A.
CHAMOIS hunting
Hat and the sprig. P. Barrett. il Outdoor
Life 148:50-3+ Jl '71
CHAMOT, Mary
Palace of Pavlovsk, near Leningrad. il An-
tiques 99:725-31 My '71
CHAMPAGNE, Glenn C.
Beaver in New York. il Cons 26:18-21 Ag '71
CHAMPAGNE
Champagne: a mood, a myth, a miracle. G.
Gaskill. Read Digest 99:162-5 Ag '71
Champagne & caviar. S. Spitzer. il Holiday
49:72-3+ D '70
Champagne: psychological magic. H. P. Mc-
Nulty. House & Gard 139:79+ My '71
Contest, and champagne. N. Hazelton. il Nat
R 23:1426 D 17 '71
Do you speak basic champagne? R. J. Misch.
House B 113:84 Ja '71
Just one more for the road. s'il vous plait:
second annual Rallye des champions,
France. R. F. Jones. il Sports Illus 35:26-
8+ O 25 '71
CHAMPAIGN, III.
Education
Inside the open classroom; Booker T. Wash-
ington elementary school. M. P. Berson. il
Am Ed 7:11-15 My '71
CHAMPIONS golf club course, Houston. See
Golf courses
CHAMPLAIN, LAKE
Gunkholing on Lake Champlain. G. P. Man-
ning. il Motor B & S 128:50-1 Ag '71
CHAMPLIN, Charles
Sunset over the fable factory. il Sat R 54:52+
Mr 13 '71
CHANCELLOR, John William
Chancellor on his own. il por Newsweek 78:
71 Ag 2 '71 •
Iron Chancellor. por Time 89:55 Ag 2 '71 •
CHANDLER, Albert Benjamin
Gunned down by the heavies; ed. by J. Under-
wood. il pors Sports Illus 34:52-4+ My 3
'71
How I jumped from clean politics into dirty
baseball; ed. by J. Underwood. il pors
Sports Illus 34:72-4+ Ap 26 '71
CHANDLER, Mary Kay
Introspection; poem. Seventeen 30:108 Ag '71
CHANDLER, Russell
Campers stake future. il Chr Today 16:42-3
N 19 '71
CHANDLER, Ariz.
Make it show leadership. G. D. Christy. il
Am City 86:83 Mr '71
CHANDRA, G. S. Sharat
Second journey; Of my 33rd birthday; poems.
Poetry 119:65-6 N '71
CHANEL, Coco. See Chanel, G.
CHANEL, Gabrielle
Chanel, 1883-1971; photographs by C. Beaton.
Vogue 157:76-9 F 15 '71 •
Chanel no. 1. il pors Time 97:54 Ja 25 '71 •
Chanel's régime d'exubérance. Vogue 157:12
Mr 15 '71 •
Christmas at the Ritz. P. O'Higgins. il por
Harp Baz 105:100-1 D '71 •
Grande mademoiselle Chanel. H. Lazareff. il
por Harp Baz 104:160-1 Mr '71 •
CHANEY, Ed
Catastrophe brewing in quiet waters. il Nat
Wildlife 9:4-7 Ag '71
CHANEY, Emily R. See Boogaard, M. A. jt.
auth.
CHANG, Diana
Secular piety; poem. Am Scholar 40:266 Spr
'71
CHANG, Sherwood, and others
Carbon, carbides, and methane in an Apollo
12 sample. bibliog il Science 171:474-7 F 5
'71
CHANGE
Forum. R. W. Anderson. Duns 97:91 Je '71
Rebirth; symposium. il Look 35:15-38+ Ja
12 '71
See also
Educational innovations
Social change
Technological change
CHANGE (psychology)
Hazards of change. Time 97:54 Mr 1 '71
CHANGE of heart; story. See Cochrane. S. G.
CHANGE of life in men. See Climacteric

CHANGE of life in women. See Menopause

CHANGE of sex
Transsexualism and sex reassignment, ed. by R. Green and J. Money. Review
Trans-Action 7:54-5 O '70. J. H. Gagnon

CHANGNON, Stanley A. Jr. and Wilson J. W.
Record severe storms in a dense meteorological network. bibliog il Weatherwise 24:152-63 Ag '71

CHANNEL electron multipliers. See Photoelectric multipliers

CHANNEL ISLANDS (English Channel)
Britain's "French" Channel Islands. J. Cerruti. il Nat Geog 139:710-40 My '71

CHANNELS (hydraulic engineering)
Channelization: a case study; Blackwater River in Johnson County, Mo. J. W. Emerson. bibliog il Science 173:325-6 Jl 23 '71

CHANOVER, E. Pierre
(comp) Psychological bibliography of Jean Racine. Am Imago 28:84-90 Spr '71

CHANTCYS. See Sailors songs

CHANTLAND, Arnold O.
Full-depth asphalt to the rescue. il Am City 86:68+ D '71

CHANTS (Gregorian, plain, etc)
Early trope repertory of Saint Martial de Limoges, by P. Evans. Review
Mus Q bibliog f 57:519-23 Jl '71. A. E. Planchart
Lux de luce: the origin of an Italian sequence. K. Levy. bibliog f il Mus Q 57:40-61 Ja '71

CHAPEL services. See Church services

CHAPELS
Chapel in the dell; Mount Vernon college, Washington, D.C. il Arch Forum 134:56-9 Mr '71
See also subhead Chapels under names of cities, e.g. Houston, Tex.—Chapels

CHAPIN, Dwight
It's tough to beat this Queen of diamonds. il pors Todays Health 49:35-9+ Jl '71

CHAPIN, Katherine Garrison
Twentieth century renaissance woman. New Repub 164:25-8 My 8 '71
Years end; poem. New Repub 165:22 D 18 '71

CHAPIN, Kim
Big man with an Indy wrench. il pors Sports Illus 34:40-5 My 24 '71
Now, when I am world champion . . . il Sports Illus 35:32-4+ N 1 '71
Obviously it's a leftist plot. il Sports Illus 34: 24-6+ My 3 '71

CHAPLAINS, Industrial
Industrial mission comes of age; British industrial chaplains. Chr Cent 88:547 My 5 '71

CHAPLAINS, Military
Chaplains as oilers. Chr Cent 88:1374 N 24 '71
Chaplains' parley: what price freedom? Military chaplains association. W. Willoughby. Chr Today 15:30 Je 4 '71
Onward Christian soldiers: dehumanization and the military chaplain. R. E. Klitgaard; discussion. Chr Cent 87:1569; 88:20, 467-8, 956-7 D 30 '70-Ja 6, Ap 14, Ag 11 '71
Plowshares into swords; Bishop Hobgood's consecration. T. W. Moore. il Chr Cent 88: 294+ Mr 3 '71

CHAPLIN, Charles, 1889-
Grand rerun for Charlie Chaplin. W. A. McWhirter. il pors Life 71:93-6 D 3 '71 *

CHAPMAN, Anne M.
Lola; with biographical sketch. il Natur Hist 80:6, 32-41 Mr '71

CHAPMAN, Hank, and Chapman, Toni
Midas of New Mexico. bibliog il pors Am West 8:4-9+ Ja '71

CHAPMAN, Robert M. and others
Alpha and kappa electroencephalogram activity in eyeless subjects. bibliog il Science 171:1159-61 Mr 19 '71

CHAPMAN, Toni. See Chapman, H. jt. auth.

CHAPMAN award. See Motor boating and sailing (periodical)

CHAPPELL, Warren
Art vs. adventitious circumstances. il Horn Bk 47:456-61 O '71

CHAPRALIS, Jim C.
New hotspot for big black marlin. il Field & S 76:84+ Je '71

CHARACTER
See also
Personality
Responsibility
Temperament
Typology (psychology)

CHARACTER analysis
See also
Palmistry

Anecdotes, facetiae, satire, etc.
Old horizons in education. L. D'Angelo. Sat R 54:67 D 4 '71

CHARACTER education. See Moral education

CHARACTER reading. See Graphology; Physiognomy

CHARACTERIZATION
Building four-dimensional people in science fiction. J. Brunner. Writer 84:21-4 D '71
Coming to terms with a character. A. Chamberlain. Writer 84:25-6+ Ag '71
Getting it together. H. Crews. Writer 84:9-11 Je '71
I live my novel. A. Walden. Writer 84:26-8 O '71
Mannequins, or characters? J. Z. Owen. Writer 84:17-19 S '71
People and characters. B. Deal. Writer 84: 16-18 Ap '71

CHARACTERS in literature
Authors & editors: Mary Poppins and Friend Monkey; interview, ed. by P. Bragg. P. L. Travers. por Pub W 200:7-9 D 13 '71
Back to the gore of yore; reprinting of Doc Savage stories. B. Darrach. il por Time 98:70-1 Jl 5 '71
Coin Harvey, O. Stephens. il por Am West 8:4-9 S '71
Ibsen's Nora and ours. J. Richardson. Commentary 52:77-80 Jl '71
Life and times of Horatio Hornblower, by C. N. Parkinson. Review
New Repub 165:27 Jl 10 '71. J. Yardley
No kisses for Achmed Bond. Time 97:26-7 F 22 '71
Shooting star; Goethe's autobiographical Sorrows of young Werther. F. Stevenson. il Opera N 35:24-6 Mr 27 '71
Uncle Tom: that enduring old image. il Am Heritage 23:50-7 D '71
Verne hero lives; Phileas Fogg rides again. il por Sr Schol 98:6 F 1 '71
See also
Animals in literature
Characterization
Women in literature

CHARACTERS in opera
How to say it: a pronunciation guide for the Metropolitan opera's 1971-72 broadcasts. Opera N 36:28-9 D 18 '71
Many faces of Orpheus. M. Springer. Opera N 35:16 Ja 23 '71
Meet Keikobad; father of the Empress in Strauss' Frau ohne schatten. A. M. Lingg. Opera N 35:16 Ja 16 '71
Opera by the book. M. Ponzo. il Wilson Lib Bul 46:335-7 D '71
Real Escamillo. R. D. Daniels. il Opera N 35:14-15 F 6 '71
Rousseau, Beaumarchais, and Figaro. A. Livermore. bibliog f il Mus Q 57:466-90 Jl '71

CHARAN, Ram, and Wormald, Nicola
Case of the offending effluent. il Harvard Bsns R 49:148-50+ Jl '71

CHARCOAL, Activated. See Carbon, Activated

CHARCOAL drawing
Douglas Graves: painter with charcoal. D. C. Hines. il por Am Artist 35:58-63+ N '71

CHARD
Kohlrabi and chard: two early and easy vegetables. J. G. Bowman. il por Org Gard & Farm 18:56-7 F '71

CHARDIN, Pierre Teilhard de. See Teilhard de Chardin, P.

CHARGAFF, Erwin
Preface to a grammar of biology. bibliog Science 172:637-42 My 14 '71

CHARGE accounts (retail trade)
Battle brewing over interest on charge accounts. Pub W 199:42 Mr 29 '71

CHARGE-coupled devices. See Semiconductors

CHARGERS, Battery. See Storage battery chargers

CHARISMATIC leadership. See Leadership

CHARITIES
Time for giving. il Ebony 26:126-7 Je '71
See also
Corporations—Charitable contributions
Foundations. Charitable and educational
Fund raising
Giving
National conference of Catholic charities

CHARITY balls. See Balls (parties)

CHARLEROI, Pa.
Rubber RR crossing an unqualified success. D. S. Bosson. il Am City 86:20 Jl '71

CHARLES, prince of Wales
How to choose a royal bride. F. V. Grunfeld. il por Horizon 13:118-19 Spr '71 *
Into the African bush with Anne and Charles. il por Time 97:27 F 22 '71 *

CHARLES, Alan F.
Case of Ritalin. New Repub 165:17-19 O 23 '71

CHARLES, David
Blue rotating beacon? Flying 88:93-4 Ap '71
CHARLES-PICARD, Gilbert
Eight centuries of Carthaginian civilization.
il UNESCO Courier 23:17-21+ D '70
CHARLES' law. See Gases
CHARLESTON, S.C.

Hotels, restaurants, etc.
Bed and board: Mills Hyatt house. P. Fiori.
il Holiday 49:81-2 Mr '71
CHARLESTON, W.Va.
Women's clubs win street lighting awards. il
Am City 86:80 F '71
CHARLOTTE, consort of Maximilian, emperor
of Mexico
Cactus throne, by R. O'Connor. Review
Nat R 23:322-4 Mr 23 '71. A. Bakshian, jr
CHARLOTTE Elisabeth, princess Palatine and
duchess of Orleans
Letters from Liselotte, ed. by M. Kroll.
Review
Sat R 54:36+ Ap 3 '71. B. Levy
CHARLTON, Robert W.
Elk paid me off. il pors Outdoor Life 148:60-
3+ Ag '71
CHARLTON, W. R.
Cesium properties of puns. il Chem 44:25 Ap
'71
CHARM-Tred-Monticello division. See Burling-
ton industries, inc.
CHARMS
See also
Amulets
CHARNEY, Nicolas H.
Report to the readers. por Sat R 54:26-7 D
11; 26-7 D 18; 20-1 D 25 '71

about
New owners for SR, McCall book division.
Pub W 200:95 Jl 19 '71 •
New tycoons. pors Newsweek 78:64 Jl 26 '71 •
Report to the readers. N. Cousins. Sat R 54:
16-17 Jl 31 '71 •
Report to the readers. J. J. Veronis. Sat R
54:32-3 D 4 '71 •
Revamping the Review. il pors Time 98:62 N
22 '71 •
CHARPENTIER, Bruce, and Charpentier, Helen
Eight values camps can give. Camp Mag 43:
14 S '71
CHARPENTIER, Gustave
Friend of the working girl. H. E. Phillips.
por Opera N 35:28-30 Mr 6 '71 •
Louise. Criticism
New Yorker 47:127-8 Mr 13 '71 •
CHARPENTIER, Helen. See Charpentier, B. jt.
auth.
CHARTENER, William H.
Excerpt from testimony before the Subcom-
mittee on constitutional rights, May 2, 1969.
Cong Digest 50:248+ O '71
CHARTER airlines. See Airlines—Non-sched-
uled operations
CHARTER of the United Nations. See United
Nations—Charter
CHARTERING of airplanes. See Airplanes—
Chartering
CHARTERING of boats. See Boats—Leasing
and renting
CHARTERING of yachts. See Yachts—Char-
tering
CHARTS, Calculating
See also
Nomography (mathematics)
CHARTS, Nautical. See Nautical charts
CHASALOW, Harold. See Chasalow, S. jt.
auth.
CHASALOW, Shirley
Anatomy of a rescue. il Yachting 129:60-1+
Je '71
—and Chasalow, Harold
Sailor's sailor. il por Yachting 129:82+ Mr '71
CHASE, Greenleaf T.
Bears, dumps and people. il Cons 26:5 Ag '71
—See Spofford. W. R. jt. auth.
CHASE, Lucia
Lucia Chase: first lady of American ballet.
O. Maynard. il pors Dance Mag 45:28-33 Ag
'71 •
CHASE, Salmon P.
Puget Sound's war within a war. I. Doig. il
Am West 8:22-7 My '71 •
CHASE, Stuart
Two cheers for technology. Sat R 54:20-1+
F 20 '71
CHASE, W. Calvin
William H. Ferris criticizes Booker T. Wash-
ington (1898); reprint from a Negro news-
paper of 1898. G. P. Marks, 3d. il por
Negro Hist Bul 33:162-3 N '70 •

CHASE, William W.
Off-the-shelf schoolhouses. il Am Ed 7:8-10
Ja '71; Same abr. Ed Digest 36:19-21 Ap
'71
CHATAIN, Robert
Curare; poem. Poetry 118:91 My '71
Map; Crawl; Sane; poems. Poetry 118:313-15
S '71
CHATEAUX. See Castles
CHATHAM press, inc.
Chatham press extends its sights beyond Cape
Cod. il Pub W 199:36-7 Je 28 '71
CHATTOOGA RIVER
Turnabout on the Chattooga; with editorial
comment. D. G. Cullimore. il Am For 77:
12-15+ F '71
CHAU, Tran-ngoc-. See Tran-ngoc-Chau
CHAUCER, Geoffrey
Canterbury tales; with drawings by Z. Blum.
A. Burgess. Horizon 13:44-59 Spr '71 •
CHAUFFEURS
I drive for money. R. French. Har Yrs 11:54
S '71
CHÁVEZ, César
Chavez machine. W. F. Buckley, jr. Nat R
23:888-9 Ag 10 '71 •
Chavez strikes again. il por Newsweek 77:
64+ Ja 25 '71 •
Lettuce boycott reaches New York. T. J.
O'Connell. America 124:148-9 F 13 '71 •
To die standing: Cesar Chavez and the
Chicanos. J. G. Dunne. por Atlan 227:39-
45 Je '71; Reply with rejoinder. J. Angell.
228:36 S '71 •
Why Chavez spurns the Labor act. R. B.
Taylor. il Nation 212:454-6 Ap 12 '71 •
CHAYES, Antonia
Disarmed at middle age. Atlan 228:72-3 N '71
CHEATING
See also
Fraud
CHEATING at cards. See Cardsharping
CHEATING in school work
Cheating in high school. K. Montor. Sch &
Soc 99:96-8 F '71
Plagiarism and originality: some remedies.
R. G. Martin. bibliog f Engl J 60:621-5+ My
'71
Term-paper hustlers. il Time 97:67 Ap 19 '71
Writer: men who sell term papers. G. Ace.
Sat R 54:3 Ag 28 '71
CHEATING in sports. See Sportsmanship
CHECK forgery. See Forgery
CHECK-off plan in farm produce advertising.
See Farm produce—Advertising
CHECKERED lilies. See Fritillaries
CHECKING accounts. See Banks and banking
—Checking accounts
CHECKS
Going to pieces in Boise; sorting cut-up
checks. il Time 98:59 Ag 2 '71
What you need to know about checks. El.
L. Harms. Suc Farm 69:36 O '71
see also
Banks and banking—Float
Clearing houses

Anecdotes, facetiae, satire, etc.
Check and supercheck. W. Zinsser. il Life 71:
14 O 22 '71
CHECKS and balances (government) See Se-
paration of powers
CHECKUP, Medical. See Physical examinations
CHEEK, Frances E. and others
Carpeting the ward: an exploratory study in
environmental psychiatry. bibliog Ment Hy
55:109-18 Ja '71
CHEEK, James Edward
College presidents and students; interview.
Mlle 73:245+ Ag '71
CHEERLEADERS. See Cheerleading
CHEERLEADING
G-R-A-double N-Y; D. Heitz. S. Elder. pors
Har Yrs 11:14-15 S '71
CHEESE
Molded cheeses with fruit from Russia,
France, Italy. il Sunset 146:96-7 Je '71
See also
Cookery—Cheese
CHEESE dishes. See Glassware
CHEESECAKE
Cheesecake for almost any meal. il Sunset
147:150 S '71
Cheesecake: three easy steps; with recipes.
M. Happel. il Ladies Home J 88:96-7+ Ap
'71
Chocolate on top and chocolate inside; choco-
late chip cheesecake. il Sunset 146:188 Mr '71
Cold power cooking: no-baking strawberry
cheesecake; recipe. il McCalls 98:50-1 Jl '71
Strawberry cheesecake pie. il Bet Hom &
Gard 49:8 Ag '71

CHEESECAKE—*Continued*
University cheesecake; interview with cafeteria manager of City university's Graduate school. E. Brasesco. New Yorker 47:32-4 Mr 27 '71
CHEETAH charter bus service company
Where blacks own the bus. il Bsns W p78 My 15 '71
CHEETAHS
Cheetah. R. L. Eaton. il Nat Parks & Con Mag 45:18-22 Je '71
Cheetah, nature's speed king. E. D'Aulaire and O. D'Aulaire. il Read Digest 98:208-12 Mr '71
Freeing the big cats. W. Nussey and H. Reuter. il pors Sci Digest 69:46-8 Je '71
CHEFS. See Cooks
CHEFS hats. See Hats
CHEKHOV, Anton Pavlovich
Bridegroom and daddy; story. Mlle 74:120 D '71
Night in the cemetery; story. Mlle 74:118-19 D '71
Three short stories; tr. by A. Ahuja Aks. Mlle 74:118-21+ D '71
Woman's luck; story. Mlle 74:121 D '71
about
Uncle Vanya. Criticism
Time 97:52 F 22 '71 *
CHELATING agents. See Sequestering agents
CHELLIS, Ken
There's money in the air. il Pop Phot 68:80-1+ F '71
CHELMINSKI, Rudolph
Savior of old movies. il pors Life 71:45-6+ D 10 '71
CHELSEA, London. See London
CHELSEA theater center. See Academy of music, Brooklyn
CHEMABRASION. See Chemosurgery
CHEMICAL additives in food. See Food additives
CHEMICAL and biological weapons
Budget gives the game away; with editorial comment. A. Kanegis and L. Richards. Nation 213:325, 337-40 O 11 '71
Department urges Senate approval of Geneva protocol on poisonous gases and biological warfare; statement, March 5, 1971. W. P. Rogers. Dept State Bul 64:455-9 Mr 29 '71
Destroying the germs of war; with editorial comment. il Life 71:3, 38-41 Jl 30 '71
Ethnic weapons. F. Lang. Ramp Mag 10:4 N '71
Getting the bugs out. New Repub 166:11-12 Ja 1 '72
Legal limits on the use of chemical and biological weapons, by A. V. Thomas and A. J. Thomas, jr. Review
Bul Atom Sci 27:42-3 Ap '71. A. R. Seith
Never in any circumstances. Sci Am 225:46 N '71
See also
Gases, Asphyxiating and poisonous
Tear gas
International control
Ban on biologicals. Time 98:26 Ag 16 '71
Bottling the Satan bug; Soviet proposal. il Newsweek 77:48 Ap 12 '71
CBW ban: Nixon would exclude tear gas and herbicides. R. J. Bazell. Science 172:246-8 Ap 16 '71
Ecocide and the Geneva protocol. L. C. Johnstone. For Affairs 49:711-20 Jl '71
Geneva protocol. Time 97:12 Mr 8 '71
Good news on the arms front. N. Cousins. Sat R 54:16 Ag 28 '71
Soviet support for ban on germ warfare. Sci N 99:245 Ap 10 '71
United States welcomes Soviet move toward biological weapons ban; statement read to news correspondents by C. W. Bray. Dept State Bul 64:549 Ap 26 '71
CHEMICAL bonds
Chemical bond and solid-state physics; adaptation of address, March 1969. J. C. Phillips; reply with rejoinder. L. Pauling. bibliog il Phys Today 24:9+ F '71
Core binding energy difference between bridging and nonbridging oxygen atoms in a silicate chain. L. I. Yin and others. bibliog il Science 173:633-5 Ag 13 '71
Hydrogen-bond stereochemistry and anomalous water. B. Kamb. bibliog il Science 172:231-42 Ap 16 '71; Discussion. 173:1252 S 24 '71
Ion binding by synthetic macrocyclic compounds. J. J. Christensen and others. bibliog il Science 174:459-67 O 29 '71
CHEMICAL compounds
See also
Cyclic compounds

CHEMICAL elements
How should periodic groups be numbered? R. T. Sanderson. il por Chem 44:17-18 N '71
See also
Atomic weights
Periodic law
Transuranium elements
also names of chemical elements, e.g. Oxygen
Atomic no. 112
Element 112 evidence starts a rush on proton beam stops. G. B. Lubkin. Phys Today 24:17-19 My '71
Evidence for element 112. Sci N 99:127-8 F 20 '71
On the trail of a new element. Bsns W p90 Mr 6 '71
CHEMICAL equilibrium
Making tubes for NO_2—N_2O_4 equilibrium reaction. E. C. Sutton. il por Chem 45:28 Ja '72
CHEMICAL fertilizers. See Fertilizers and manures
CHEMICAL genetics
Central dogma of molecular biology reexamined. il Chem 44:21-2 F '71
CHEMICAL industries
Sneaking up on Europe's giants. il Bsns W p52+ F 27 '71
See also
American cyanamid company
Atlas chemical industries, inc.
Dow chemical company
Du Pont de Nemours, E. I, and company
GAF corporation
Grace, W. R, and company
Lubrizol corporation
Monsanto company
National starch and chemical corporation
Olin corporation
Rohm and Haas company
Stauffer chemical company
Union carbide corporation
Finance
Chemicals: a turnabout in profits and productivity. il Bsns W p44 D 25 '71
Chemicals; with yardsticks of management performance. il Forbes 109:106-8 Ja 1 '72
France
Back in the race; Rhône-Poulenc. Forbes 108:71+ D 1 '71
Great Britain
See also
Albright and Wilson, inc.
Imperial chemical industries, ltd.
Iceland
Hot springs fuel Iceland's hopes; proposed chemical complex. il Bsns W p 124 Ap 10 '71
Italy
Big showdown at Montedison. Bsns W p52 Ap 10 '71
$7.2-billion spur for petrochemicals; state-inspired investment plan. il Bsns W p26 D 25 '71
Japan
Japan's free-trader; head of Sumitomo chemical co. N. Martin. por Duns 98:55-6 Ag '71
CHEMICAL literature
See also
Pharmocopoeias
CHEMICAL plants
Importing expertise from Warsaw; building sulfuric acid plant in Germany. Bsns W p41 Ag 14 '71
CHEMICAL reactions
Metal ion control of chemical reactions. D. H. Busch. bibliog il Science 171:241-8 Ja 22 '71
Xenon as a nucleophile in gas-phase displacement reactions: formation of the methyl xenonium ion. D. Holtz and J. L. Beauchamp. bibliog il Science 173:1237-8 S 24 '71
See also
Catalysis
CHEMICAL reagents
See also
Isocyanates
CHEMICAL research
See also
Gordon research conferences
CHEMICAL societies
See also
American chemical society
CHEMICAL tools. See Tools
CHEMICAL warfare
See also
European war, 1914-1918—Chemical warfare
Vietnamese war, 1957- —Chemical warfare

CHEMICAL wastes. See Trade waste

CHEMICALS
See also
Agricultural chemicals
Plasticizers

Transportation
Fighting fire with a computer. il Sci N 100: 91 Ag 7 '71

CHEMISTRY
Chemistry. Sci N 100:93, 215, Ag 7, S 25 '71
Chemistry, an interdisciplinary science. M. Gardner. Chem 44:2 Ja '71
Magic of modern chemistry. G. Gregory. il UNESCO Courier 24:4-23 bibliog(p27) Je '71
See also
Alchemy
Bases (chemistry)
Computers—Chemical use
Decomposition (chemistry)
Immunochemistry
Phlogiston theory
Photochemistry
Radicals (chemistry)
Stereochemistry

Experiments
Lab bench. See issues of Chemistry

History
Caricature and the chemist. W. B. Jensen. bibliog il Chem 44:6-9 D '71
Doebereiner and the University of Jena; tr. by R. E. Oesper. W. Schütz. il pors Chem 45:10-11 Ja '72
Great moments in chemistry; tr. by R. E. Oesper (cont) F. Szabadvary. il por Chem 44:18-20 Je; 14-17 D '71
That chart on the laboratory wall. G. Teterin and C. Terlon. il pors UNESCO Courier 24:24-7+ Je '71
Unintentional discoveries. J. A. Sears. bibliog il por Chem 44:16-18 Ja '71

CHEMISTRY (periodical)
Editor's page. T. Benfey. Chem 44:2 S '71
Keeping up with Chemistry; using the magazine as required reading for chemistry students. Chem 44:4 S '71

CHEMISTRY, Analytic
Analyzing metallic mixtures. P. H. Mogul and S. B. Portnoy. il pors Chem 44:27-9 Mr '71
Lab bench. See issues of Chemistry
See also
Fluorimetry
Spectrophotometry
Water—Analysis

CHEMISTRY, Forensic. See Chemistry, Legal

CHEMISTRY, Legal
Sherlock Holmes lives again. J. Stewart-Gordon. Read Digest 98:203-6+ F '71

CHEMISTRY, Organic
See also
Cyclic compounds
Polymers
Synthesis

CHEMISTRY, Physical and theoretical
See also
Adsorption
Atomic weights
Atoms
Catalysis
Coordination compounds
Diffusion
Emulsions
Periodic law
Solution (chemistry)

CHEMISTRY, Technical
Catalysis. V. Haensel and R. L. Burwell, jr. il Sci Am 225:46-58 D '71
See also
Adhesives
Alcohol, Denatured
Cleaning compositions
Gums and resins

CHEMISTRY as a profession
Career opportunities in chemistry. H. L. Youmans. bibliog il por Chem 44:18-20 Mr '71

CHEMISTRY in art
Caricature and the chemist. W. B. Jensen. bibliog il Chem 44:6-9 D '71

CHEMISTS
Chemist in industry. G. Alexander. por Chem 45:19-21 Ja '72
Chemists' involvement in society (cont) R. Ferreira. bibliog pors Chem 44:18-20 F '71
See also
Chemistry as a profession
Ferguson, L. N.
Hall, L. A.
Hill, H. A.
Women as chemists

Supply and demand
Doesn't anybody need a Ph.D. chemist? il por Life 71:34 N 5 '71
Future? W. C. Fernelius. Chem 44:2 Ap '71

CHEMORECEPTIVITY
Chemoreception in nassarius obsoletus: the role of specific stimulatory proteins. S. Gurin and W. E. Carr. bibliog il Science 174:293-5 O 15 '71
Sea life's chemical senses. Sci N 100:186 S 18 '71
Taste, smell and ecology. R. H. Gilluly. il Sci N 100:98 Ag 7 '71

CHEMOSURGERY
Skin peel before & after. S. Lord. il Harp Baz 104:112-13 O '71
Treat yourself to a brand-new skin; chemabrasion. N. Craig. McCalls 98:78-9+ Ag '71
You're not Mrs Hatfield. B. Lindeman. pors Todays Health 49:25-7+ F '71

CHEN, Chi
Chen Chi: the way of the heart. D. Marron. il por Am Artist 36:40-5 Ja '72 *

CHEN, Lung-chu
Let Taiwan decide. New Repub 164:16 My 29 '71
U.N. plebiscite for Taiwan. Chr Cent 88:952-3 Ag 11 '71

CHEN, Percy
Marco Polo's mixer. por Time 99:41 Ja 10 '72 *

CHEN, Shi-han, and Giblett, E. R.
Polymorphism of soluble glutamic-pyruvic transaminase; a new genetic marker in man. bibliog il Science 173:148-9 Jl 9 '71

CHENERY, Janet D.
Selecting a manuscript for publication. Writer 84:24-5 O '71

CHENEY, D. L. and others
Narcotic tolerance and dependence: lack of relationship with serotonin turnover in the brain. bibliog il Science 171:1169-70 Mr 19 '71

CHENEY, Frances Neel
Current reference books. See issues of Wilson library bulletin

CHENFELD, Mimi Brodsky
My son a nursery school dropout. Todays Ed 60:75 S '71

CHENG, Chu-yuan
China's industry: advances and dilemma. bibliog f Cur Hist 61:154-9+ S '71

CHENG, Roger J.
Water drop freezing: ejection of microdroplets. bibliog il Science 170:1395-6; 173: 849-50 D 25 '70, Ag 27 '71

CHERKIN, Arthur. See Riege, W. H. jt. auth.

CHERMAK, Sylvia
Peter and the wolf; dramatization of a Russian folk tale. Plays 30:67-70 Ap '71

CHEROKEE, Ia.
Education
Hawkeye outdoorsmen of Wilson junior high. H. Bradshaw and V. Bradshaw. il Field & S 76:78-9+ My '71

CHEROKEE Indians
Cherokee tragedy, by T. Wilkins. Review Natur Hist il 80:76-8 Ap '71. N. O. Lurie Sat R 54:50 F 13 '71. R. D. Fogelson

CHERRY, Kelly
Covenant; story. Commentary 51:49-60 My '71

CHERRY trees
Plan now for the cherry that blooms in the autumn. F. Frederick. il House B 113:112 Jl '71

CHERT
Artificial microfossils: experimental studies of permineralization of blue-green algae in silica. J. H. Oehler and J. W. Schopf. bibliog il Science 174:1229-31 D 17 '71
Thermal alteration of silica minerals: an archeological approach. B. A. Purdy and H. K. Brooks. bibliog il Science 173:322-5 Jl 23 '71

CHERVENICK, Paul A. and others
Human leukemic cells: in vitro growth of colonies containing the Philadelphia (Ph[1]) chromosome. bibliog il Science 174:1134-6 D 10 '71

CHESAPEAKE AND OHIO CANAL NATIONAL HISTORICAL PARK
Biking through history; Chesapeake and Ohio Canal. B. Thomas. il Parents Mag 46:46-9+ Mv '71
C&O Canal becomes a park. W. O. Douglas. il Nat Parks & Con Mag 45:4-8 My '71
C&O Canal: our newest national park. K. Jeans. il Am For 77:24-7 Ap '71

CHESAPEAKE BAY
Chesapeake Bay. C. Holden; A. L. Hammond. il Science 172:825-30 My 21 '71; Reply. J. R. Schubel and D. W. Pritchard. 173:943-5 S 3 '71

CHESAPEAKE BAY—*Continued*
Conference of remote sensing of the Chesapeake bay. Space World H-6-90:49-50 Je '71
Time to pick up the decoys. R. Cave. Sports Illus 35:41 D 13 '71
CHESAPEAKE BAY bridge-tunnel
Season-off peak: Chesapeake. il Travel 136: 68-9 S '71

CHESAPEAKE BAY REGION
Season off-peak: Chesapeake. il Travel 136: 68-9 S '71
CHESHIRE, Maxine
Ethel & Andy. il pors Ladies Home J 88:86+ O '71
(ed) See Dallas, R. My 8 years as Kennedys' private nurse
CHESLER, Phyllis
Tyranny of the male therapist; interview, ed. by C. Bigwood. Harp Baz 104:52-3 Jl '71
CHESS, Stella
Why some bright children have trouble in school. il Parents Mag 46:42-3+ My '71
CHESS
Bobby clears the board for the title: world championship. R. Cantwell. il por Sports Illus 35:30-2+ N 8 '71
Bobby makes his move; Bobby Fischer vs. T. Petrosian in Buenos Aires. il pors Time 98:68+ N 8 '71
Chess corner. A. Horowitz. See issues of Saturday review
Maybe you can win them all; Fischer vs Bent Larsen in Denver. R. Cantwell. il Sports Illus 35:18-19 Ag 2 '71
On to Moscow· B. Fischer vs. T. Petrosian. Newsweek 78:80 N 8 '71
Peacock vs. the wren; Petrosian-Fischer game, Buenos Aires match. il por Newsweek 78:87-8+ O 18 '71
Six moves toward a world championship; world chess tournament, Vancouver, British Columbia. L. Evans. il por Sports Illus 34:58-9 Je 21 '71
Strange malady called Fischer fear. H. C. Schonberg. il pors N Y Times Mag p32-3+ N 14 '71
CHESS players
Computerized steamroller. il pors Time 98:54 Ag 2 '71
Parting shots: Mr Fischer, demon of the chess world. B. Darrach. il por Life 71:61 Jl 23 '71
Six moves toward a world championship; world chess tournament, Vancouver, British Columbia. L. Evans. il por Sports Illus 34:58-9 Je 21 '71
See also
Fischer, B.
CHESSIN, Henry. See Vonnegut, B. jt. auth.
CHESTNUT blight
King is dead, long live the king. W. B. Sayers. il Am For 77:20-3+ N; 22-3+ D '71
New hope for the American chestnut. P. M. Tilden. il Nat Parks & Con Mag 45:25-8 Jl '71
CHESTNUT trees
Chestnut tree is good looking, and the nuts are delicious. il Sunset 147:177 S '71
New hope for the American chestnut. P. M. Tilden. il Nat Parks & Con Mag 45:25-8 Jl '71
Diseases and pests
See also
Chestnut blight
CHESTNUTS
See also
Cookery—Nuts
CHESTS
Spanish-style chest with a marproof top. R. Wortham. il Pop Mech 136:148-50 S '71
CHESTS, Jewel. See Jewel boxes, cases, etc.
CHEVAL, Ferdinand
Old French postman's dream. il por Life 70: 70-3 Mr 12 '71 *
CHEVALIER, Maurice
Obituary
Newsweek por 79:68 Ja 10 '72. A. Cooper
Reserved for the stage. por Time 99:74 Ja 10 '72 *
CHEVROLET motor company. See General motors corporation—Chevrolet division
CHEVRON oil company
Chevron's pollution solution; Scott Carpenter and his F310 additive. S. Berman. Commonweal 93:546-8 Mr 5 '71
CHEW, Effie
His and hers super spa. il pors Vogue 157:174-7 My '71 *
CHEW, Peter
Mostest hoss. il Am Heritage 22:24-9+ Ap '71

CHEW, Samuel, Jr
His and hers super spa. il pors Vogue 157:174-7 My '71 *
CHEYFITZ, Eric
For commander Bucher, & A company, 196th light brigade; poem. Esquire 76:20 Ag '71
CHI, Carl Chungming, and Flynn, J. P.
Neural pathways associated with hypothalamically eilcited attack behavior in cats. bibliog il Science 171:703-6 F 19 '71
CHIANG, Kai-shek
Chiang's last redoubt; future uncertain. il pors Time 98:32-3 N 8 '71 *
Meanwhile, in Taiwan. il por Time 98:14 Ag 2 '71 *
Parrying a policy. por Time 97:23-4 Mr 29 '71 *
Taiwan: reality intrudes on a dogged dream. il Newsweek 78:24 N 8 '71 *
CHIAO, Kuan-hua
People's Republic of China; address, November 15, 1971. Vital Speeches 38:98-101 D 1 '71
about
Madison avenue Maoists. il por Time 98:36+ N 22 '71 *
CHIAROSCURO
David A. Leffel: 20th century old master. D. Cochrane. il por Am Artist 35:20-5 O '71
CHIBANGA, Ricardo
Graceful ritual of bloody death. il pors Ebony 26:78-80+ Mr '71 *
CHICAGO
Code inspectors and computers work well together. J. E. Fitzgerald. il Am City 86:42 Ap '71
Airports
Sluggish traffic slows revival of Mid-way. H. D. Watkins. il Aviation W 94:37-9+ Je 28 '71
Art
Art news in Chicago. F. Schulze. il Art N 70:45-55 N '71
Banks
Cadillacs for free? First state bank of Chicago. il Time 97:89 F 22 '71
Bookstores
See Booksellers and bookselling—Illinois
Buildings
Down comes a masterpiece; Louis Sullivan's old Stock exchange building. il Life 71:40-1 N 5 '71
One long fight that preservationists lost; Chicago stock exchange building. J. Shaw. il Arch Rec 150:10 D '71
See also
Chicago—McCormick Place
City planning
Chicago's South Commons: an urban reawakening. J. H. Ingersoll. il House B 113:109-11 O '71
Proposal to change the urban landscape by redistributing a city's office space into 152-story superframe towers. A. T. Swenson. il Arch Forum 135:58-60 S '71
Courts
Mayor Daley's way with justice. J. R. Waltz. il Nation 213:460-8 N 8 '71
Description
Visiting Chicago? Bsns W p97-8 O 23 '71
Education
Aqui estoy . . . here I am; storefront English language center for Spanish speakers. A. Gaber. il por Am Ed 7:18-22 Ja '71
Second-chance academy; Christian action ministry academy. il Ebony 26:39-42 Ja '71
Sensitivity training; Raymond school project. R. L. Jerrems. Ed Digest 37:26-9 O '71
Wingspread: where people are people; black-white student exchanges. M. Cleary. il Am Ed 7:21-4 Ap '71
See also
Chicago city college
Education, Board of
Education of a school board member. J. Witkowsky. il por Sat R 54:90-2 N 20 '71
Elections
Daley: shaken but secure. Nation 212:356 Mr 22 '71
Daley way. Newsweek 77:43-4 Ap 19 '71
Mayor Daley's flip-flop. New Repub 164:15-16 My 29 '71; Discussion. 165:32-3 Jl 10 '71

CHICAGO—*Continued*

Fire, October 1871

Fire; anniversary. il Newsweek 78:36-7 O 18 '71

Story behind the book. L. P. Freilicher. il Pub W 200:36-7 O 25 '71

Galleries and museums

Art news in Chicago. F. Schulze. il Art N 70:45-55 N '71

Historic houses, etc.

Where are they now? Robie house. il Newsweek 77:20 Ap 19 '71

History

See also
Chicago—Fire, October 1871

Hospitals

Caring for the community; merger of two small private hospitals in Chicago's west side ghetto. il por Time 97:45 F 15 '71

Chicago hires a black top doc; Cook County hospital. il pors Ebony 26:76-8+ Ap '71

Cook County hospital: the terrible place. J. Star. il Look 35:24-30+ My 18 '71

Provident hospital. il por Ebony 26:64-6+ Je '71

Housing

Chicago, Ill; Woodlawn gardens. E. P. Berkeley. il Arch Forum 134:38-41 My '71

Daley news; public housing sites. T. M. Gray. New Repub 164:16-18 Ap 3 '71; Reply with rejoinder. L. W. Hill. 165:32-3 Jl 10 '71

Foot-dragging in Daley's Chicago. Bsns W p24 O 9 '71

Reporter at large; American Friends service committee in ghetto housing. G. Jonas. New Yorker 47:92+ Mr 13 '71

Shlaes north side townhouses. il Arch Rec 149:88-9 mid-My '71

Libraries

See also
Chicago public library

McCormick Place

Graceful solution to controversy; Chicago's new McCormick place exhibition. il Arch Forum 135:36-57 N '71

McCormick Place on-the-lake, Chicago. il Arch Rec 149:102-5 My '71

Music

See also
Chicago symphony orchestra

Negroes

Cook County hospital: the terrible place. J. Star. il Look 35:24-30+ My 18 '71

Family under siege. W. B. Furlong. il pors Good H 172:106-7+ Ap '71

Reporter at large; American Friends service committee in ghetto housing. G. Jonas. New Yorker 47:92+ Mr 13 '71

Newspapers

Chicago's war of the losers. il Time 98:52-3 Ag 9 '71

See also
Chicago tribune

Noise

SSSHHICAGO. il Time 98:91 O 11 '71

Parks and playgrounds

Precarious state of America's big city parks; Lincoln park. D. J. R. Bruckner. il Parks & Rec 6:36+ S '71

Police

I, pig. by J. Muller. Review
Time il 98:106+ O 11 '71. R. Z. Sheppard

Lonely fear of a policeman's wife; life of Mary Ellen Streske. G. Sheehy. il McCalls 98:96-9+ Mr '71

See also
Helicopters in police work

Police department

Fire-alarm system guards a police station. W. B. Buckley. il Am City 86:86+ Mr '71

Politics and government

Boss. by M. Royko. Review
Nation 212:507-8 Ap 19 '71. S. D. Alinsky

New Repub 164:28-9 Ap 17 '71. R. M. Fisher

New Yorker 47:137-42 My 8 '71. R. Harris

Sat R 54:28 Ap 24 '71. D. Walker

Sat R 54:29 Ap 24 '71. P. L. Weed

Challenge to Daley. por Time 97:14-15 Ap 5 '71

Chicago's Daley; how to run a city. il pors Newsweek 77:80-4 Ap 5 '71

Clearing the slate. il Newsweek 79:14 Ja 3 '72

Cracks in Daley. P. Yessne. Nation 212:360-5 Mr 22 '71

Dick Daley: the business candidate. il por Bsns W p81-2 Ap 10 '71

Mayor Daley's way with justice. J. R. Waltz. il Nation 213:460-8 N 8 '71

Take heart from the heartland. A. M. Greeley; discussion. New Repub 163:9-11 D 26 '70; 164:43 Ja 2 '71

See also
Chicago—Elections

Race question

Lawlor on the line. il por Newsweek 78:54 S 13 '71

Rapid transit

See Chicago—Transit systems

Recreation

See also
Chicago—Parks and playgrounds

Religious institutions and affairs

Chicago ecumenism: changes in style and agenda. R. L. Rogers. il Chr Cent 88:626-31 My 19 '71

Ecumenical rebellion in Chicago. Chr Cent 88:1461 D 15 '71

Sanitary affairs

Chicago moves from truck cranes to back-hoe-loaders. J. T. Mattucci. il Am City 86:38 Mr '71

Social conditions

Charity; case worker in Chicago. S. Dybeck. Commonweal 95:248-52 D 10 '71

See also
North side cooperative ministry

Stations

Chicago's new rapid transit extensions. il Arch Rec 150:129-32 N '71

Stockyards

Chicago stockyards; photograph. H. Kluetmeier. Life 70:4-5 F 26 '71

Streets

Chicago's magnificent mile: North Michigan avenue. il Time 98:96-7 D 6 '71

Festive lights for a famous street; North Michigan ave. il Am City 86:92+ D '71

Strikes

See also
Strikes—United States—Teachers

Theater

Sin is in; the Goodman's second professional season. H. Hewes. Sat R 54:33 Ag 7 '71

Theater; productions at the Goodman and Ivanhoe theaters. Sat R 54:14 D 11 '71

Transit systems

Chicago's new rapid transit extensions. il Arch Rec 150:129-32 N '71

Low maintenance transit stations. il Am City 86:122 S '71

Vigilance committees

See Vigilance committees—Illinois

Water supply

Computer assures pinpoint water control. J. W. Jardine. il Am City 86:82+ S '71

CHICAGO (rock group) See Rock groups

CHICAGO Bears (football club) See Football clubs

CHICAGO book clinic annual exhibit. See Book exhibits

CHICAGO Bulls (basketball team) See Basketball teams

CHICAGO city college

Malcolm X campus

Intellectual black power. il por Time 98:50+ Ag 16 '71

Monument to blackness. il por Newsweek 78:46-7 Ag 2 '71

CHICAGO civic opera house. See Opera houses

CHICAGO journalism review

New voices of newsmen: local journalism reviews. D. Rose. il Nation 214:43-6 Ja 10 '72

CHICAGO lyric opera. See Lyric opera of Chicago

CHICAGO-Mackinac race. See Yacht racing

CHICAGO public library
Price of a landmark: $28 million. W. R. Eshelman. Wilson Lib Bul 45:526+ F '71

Anecdotes, facetiae, satire, etc.
Phantom of the library; reprint. N. Blei. il Am Lib 2:367-9 Ap '71

CHICAGO RIVER
Paddle your own canoe. S. K. Summers and A. P. Teton. il por Parks & Rec 6:35-6 Jl '71

CHICAGO stock exchange. See Stock exchange —Chicago

CHICAGO stock exchange building. See Chicago—Buildings

CHICAGO symphony orchestra
Music. D. Hamilton. Nation 213:670 D 20 '71
Music to my ears; concert version of Wagner's Das Rheingold performed under direction of G. Solti. I. Kolodin. Sat R 54:19 My 15 '71
Music to my ears; performance in Carnegie Hall. I. Kolodin. Sat R 54:38 D 4 '71
Musical events; concert in Carnegie Hall, conducted by G. Solti. W. Sargeant. New Yorker 47:97 N 27 '71
Musical events; Wagner's Das Rheingold, in concert form. W. Sargeant. New Yorker 47:91-2 My 8 '71
Report:
Concert performance of Rheingold, Georg Solti conducting. S. Jenkins. Opera N 35:22 Je 12 '71
Solti is special. R. C. Marsh. por Hi Fi 21 MA26-7 Ap '71

CHICAGO thoroughbred enterprises, inc.
Race-track scandal; case of O. Kerner. il por Time 98:15 D 13 '71

CHICAGO tribune
No more frater trafic; end of simplified spelling. Time 97:47 Ja 25 '71

CHICAGO. University
For the class of '71, the party's over. W. B. Furlong. il N Y Times Mag p34-5+ Je 6 '71

Libraries
Graduate research library in the humanities and social sciences; Joseph Regenstein library. il Sch & Soc 99:12+ Ja '71

CHICAGO White Sox (baseball) See Baseball clubs

CHICANO students. See Mexican American students

CHICANOS. See Mexican Americans

CHICHESTER-CLARK, James Dawson
P.M. resigns. por Time 97:39 Mr 29 '71 •

CHICK embryos. See Embryology—Birds

CHICKEN
Prices
See Poultry—Prices

CHICKEN, Cutting of. See Poultry. Dressing of

CHICKEN as food. See Cookery—Poultry

CHICKENS. See Poultry

CHICKERING, Arthur W.
Best colleges have the least effect. il Sat R 54:48-50+ Ja 16 '71

CHICKERING, Sherman B.
Staying hip. il Harper 243:62-5 S '71

CHIEF executive officer (corporations) See Executives

CHIHULY, Dale
Dale Chihuly: the fluid breath of glass. D. Manzella. il por Craft Horiz 31:22-6 D '71 •

CHILAQUILES. See Cookery. Mexican

CHILD abuse. See Cruelty to children

CHILD-adult relationship
Before you say no. A. B. Heath. Nat R 23: 1459-60 D 31 '71
Experiment for the White House; experiment conducted at the Detroit free press for the White House conference on children; address, February 23, 1971. T. R. Peters. Vital Speeches 37:379-82 Ap 1 '71
See also
Parent-child relationship

CHILD art. See Childrens art

CHILD beating. See Cruelty to children

CHILD care centers. See Day nurseries

CHILD delinquency. See Juvenile delinquency

CHILD health. See Children—Care and hygiene

CHILD labor
United States
Child labor, 1971. il Newsweek 77:83+ Ap 12 '71

CHILD labor laws and legislation
United States
Child labor: a barbarism we must not tolerate. E. E. Cohen. por Parents Mag 46:34 Ag '71

CHILD molesters
My daughter was molested. il Good H 173: 14+ S '71
Safe on the streets; with study-discussion program, by E. Harris and D. Harris. G. Randall. bibliog il PTA Mag 65:5-7, 34-5 Ap '71

CHILD obesity. See Corpulence

CHILD photography. See Photography of children

CHILD portraiture. See Portrait painting

CHILD psychiatry
Serum magnesium differences: further evidence for discontinuity between adult and childhood schizophrenia. M. Gittelman and J. Cleeman. bibliog il Ment Hy 55:492-4 O '71
Social variables and their effect on psychiatric emergency situations among children. W. C. Sze. bibliog il Ment Hy 55:437-43 O '71
Therapy in the gym; Academy of physical and social development, Boston. il por Time 97:47 F 15 '71
See also
Child psychotherapy
Mentally ill children
Schizophrenia
School phobia

CHILD psychology. See Child study

CHILD psychotherapy
Helping the shy child. il por Newsweek 78:40 Ag 23 '71

CHILD study
Belfast and the psyche. il Time 97:47 Mr 29 '71
Bruno Bettelheim. B. Bettelheim. See issues of Ladies' home journal
Fear of failure and other handicaps; with study-discussion program, by E. Harris and D. Harris. E. D. Wagner. il PTA Mag 66: 24-6+ N '71
How to exercise dogs and minds; research project of British psychologist Edward de Bono. il Time 98:60 D 6 '71
Is this crib necessary? views of R. Feinbloom. il Time 98:87 N 8 '71
Launching healthy children; symposium. il Life 71:61+ D 17 '71
Measuring young minds. D. Elkind. por Horizon 13:32-7 Wint '71
New understanding of childhood. M. Mead. il Redbook 138:49+ Ja '72
Positive carriers of violence among children: detection by speech deviations; with replies by B. Fraser and E. Roberts. R. Filippi and C. L. Rousey. bibliog Ment Hy 55: 157-64 Ap '71
Psychologist and minimal brain dysfunction: ten steps to maximum incompetence. L. J. Aronson. Ment Hy 55:523-5 O '71
Quiet ones, the noisy ones. J. D. Noshpitz. il Todays Ed 60:24-7 S '71; Same abr. Ed Digest 37:45-7 N '71
Reinforcement approach to the elimination of a child's school phobia. C. V. Edlund. bibliog Ment Hy 55:433-6 O '71
Search for the truth about day care. S. Cole. il N Y Times Mag p84+ D 12 '71
Teachers look at classroom behavior problems, a survey. R. H. Burns and A. McCullen. Ment Hy 55:504-6 O '71
What makes children the way they are. il Time 97:49 Je 14 '71
When mother goes away; how young children learn to cope with separations. E. Limmer. il Parents Mag 46:42-3+ D '71
Youngsters' need to love; with study-discussion program, by M. M. Conant. S. F. Ward. bibliog il PTA Mag 66:12-14, 33 D '71
See also
Child psychotherapy
Children—Language
Emotional problems of children
Parent-child relationship
Play
Playmates
Underachievers

CHILD welfare
See also
Adoption
Children—Institutional care
Childrens villages
Cruelty to children
Day nurseries
Orphans and orphan asylums
United Nations children's fund

Italy
Nobody's children; orphans in Rome. il Time 97:27 Mr 8 '71

CHILDREN—*Continued*

Imprisonment

How to make a criminal out of a child. C. Mangel. il Look 35:49+ Je 29 '71

Institutional care

Mental hygiene influences in children's institutions; organization and technology for treatment. J. K. Whittaker. bibliog Ment Hy 55:444-50 O '71

Jealousy
See Jealousy

Language

Research in the teaching of English. D. V. Gunderson. bibliog Engl J 60:547-53 Ap '71

Say it right and they will too; David Pushaw's developmental language and speech center, Grand Rapids, Mich. M. Lloyd. il Am Ed 7:5-7 Ja '71

That magical moment when baby starts to talk. M. K. Omar. il Parents Mag 46:54-5+ S '71

Law

Another modest proposal: baby brokering. W. F. Rickenbacker. Nat R 23:1355 D 3 '71

Miranda extended; case of B. B. Burton. Time 99:58 Ja 10 '72

Wayward winners; Wayward minor statute declared unconstitutional. Time 99:59 Ja 10 '72

See also
Adoption
Curfew law
Guardian and ward
Juvenile delinquency
Youth—Law

Management and training

Are your children independent? B. Bettelheim. Ladies Home J 88:26+ Ja '71

Bringing up mother; interview, tr. by A. Foukle. F. Mallet-Joris. Vogue 158:68+ O 1 '71

Does your child want to grow up to be just like mommy or daddy? B. Bettelheim. Ladies Home J 88:30+ Jl '71

Don't blame me! answers to accusations of permissiveness. B. Spock. Look 35:37-8 Ja 26 '71; Same abr. with title Doctor Spock speaks out. Cur 127:19-23 Mr '71

Family clinic, ed. by P. B. Katz. See issues of Parents' magazine & better family living

Family forum; a creative method of settling differences. C. D. Giles. il Parents Mag 46:54-5+ Ap '71

Father takes care of the baby. L. Weeks. il Parents Mag 46:60-1+ F '71

Growing pains; questions and answers. See issues of Today's health

Helping the procrastinating child. B. Spock. il Redbook 136:20+ Ja '71

How can you teach your kids about money? M. Daly. Bet Hom & Gard 49:6 N '71

How to grow a genius. Sci Digest 69:19-20 Je '71

Male chauvinist Spock recants, well, almost. B. Spock. N Y Times Mag p98+ S 12 '71

Parents bring up your children! excerpts from Two worlds of childhood U.S. and U.S.S.R. U. Bronfenbrenner. Look 35:45-6 Ja 26 '71

Raising your child to have a good marriage. B. Spock. Redbook 137:29+ Je '71

Sensitivity training starts early; with study-discussion program, by M. M. Conant. P. B. Wood. bibliog il PTA Mag 65:20-2+, 32 Je '71

Spirit of Christmas and Chanukah. B. Spock. Redbook 138:24+ D '71

Teaching children the habit of success. J. Brothers. il por Good H 173:72+ O '71

Teaching lovingness to children. B. Spock. il Redbook 137:26+ Jl '71

Touch sparks love. il Good H 173:14+ Ag '71

What do a small child's sexual "advances" toward a parent mean? B. Bettelheim. Ladies Home J 88:24+ Ag '71

What I learned from my first child; seven celebrated parents describe their first-time around boners ed. by R. Wacker, jr. il Good H 173:114-17 N '71

What parents should know about punishing their children. N. M. Lobsenz. il Redbook 138:64-5+ Ja '72

What preschoolers need most; parent-child agreements. D. Elkind. il Parents Mag 46:37-9+ My '71

When should parents push? B. Bettelheim. Ladies Home J 88:56-7 Mr '71

See also
Camp discipline
Child study
Childrens allowances
Discipline
Moral education
Parent-child relationship
Parent education

Bibliography

Books for parents; comp. by P. Pinson. See issues of Parents' magazine & better family living

Nutrition

Feeding children in the family, with recipes. R. H. Smithies. il Good H 172:144+ Mr '71

Ignorance and apathy vs. food abundance. Sch & Soc 99:9 Ja '71

Someone's in the kitchen with Maxime; Rusty Holzer, age two. M. McKendry. il pors Vogue 159:34 Ja 1 '72

See also
Infants—Nutrition

Photographs

Child; the camera reaches into a secret world. il Life 71:21-40 D 17 '71

Out of the crib; opera stars as children. Opera N 36:14-16 D 18 '71

See also
Photography of children

Preparation for medical and dental care

Preparing a child for the hospital or dentist. Good H 174:141 Ja '72

Psychology
See Child study

Religion

Helping children of different ages to understand religion. B. Spock. Redbook 136:58+ F '71

Sayings

Faith, hope and hilarity; excerpts. D. Van Dyke. Read Digest 98:231-2 F '71

Science gives me joy-feels all over. H. Dunn. il Sci Digest 69:30-3 Je '71

Sleepwalking
See Somnambulism

Social and economic status

Experiment for the White House; experiment conducted at the Detroit free press for the White House conference on children; address, February 23, 1971. T. R. Peters. Vital Speeches 37:379-82 Ap 1 '71

Planning a children's advocacy system. Cur 125:3-4 Ja '71

See also
Socially handicapped children

Speech
See Children—Language

Surgery

See also
Orthopedia

Africa

At play in African villages. E. Leacock. il Natur Hist 80:60-5 D '71

China

Playing grownup; Sung dynasty. E. H. Schafer. il Horizon 13:20-3 Wint '71

Europe, Western

Creativity among west European pupils. E. J. Ogletree and J. A. Rackauskas. bibliog Sch & Soc 99:377-8 O '71

Great Britain

Day in the life; childrens' accounts of census day, April 25, 1971, to be preserved. H. R. Mayes. Sat R 54:10+ N 6 '71

Nigeria

Biafra one year later. il Life 70:40-1 My 14 '71

Northern Ireland

Ulster: the children of violence; with excerpts from essays by children. il Newsweek 77:46-50+ Ap 19 '71

Russia

See also
Preschool children—Russia

CHILDREN—*Continued*

United States

Children of women in the labor force; with tables. E. Waldman and K. R. Gover. bibliog f Mo Labor R 94:19-25 Jl '71
See also
Child labor—United States
Negro children

Vietnam (Republic)

Amer-Asian children in Vietnam. D. Luce. Chr Cent 88:996-7 Ag 25 '71; Discussion. 88:1181-2 O 6 '71
Lau goes home to Vietnam; and the case of Ngu Van Xia; with editorial comment. il Life 70:18B-28 Ja 29 '71
Suffer the little ones..: Vietnam children's care agency. J. Deedy. Commonweal 95: 122 N 5 '71
See also
Vietnamese war, 1957- —Children

CHILDREN, Adopted
Family of his own; Donny, age 9, is adopted at last. B. Dunn. il Life 71:130-8 D 17 '71
Search for myself. il Seventeen 30:118-19+ N '71

CHILDREN, Adoption of. See Adoption
CHILDREN, Arrest of. See Arrest
CHILDREN, Backward. See Slow learning children
CHILDREN, Blind. See Blind
CHILDREN, Cruelty to. See Cruelty to children
CHILDREN, Delinquent. See Juvenile delinquency
CHILDREN, Epileptic. See Epileptics

CHILDREN, Exceptional
Learning disabilities. F. R. Vellutino and E. R. Sipay. Ed Digest 36:35-8 Mr '71
See also
Children, Gifted
Children, Handicapped
Minimal brain dysfunction

CHILDREN, Gifted
Confessions of an ex-quiz kid: a vote for children's lib. L. E. Sissman. Atlan 227:34+ Mr '71
Growing up gifted. K. Feinberg. Ed Digest 36:44-5 Ap '71
See also
Children as musicians
High school students, Mentally superior

Education

What's good for the gifted is good for everyone. S. Levitin. il Parents Mag 46: 62-3+ S '71

CHILDREN, Handicapped
Hidden threats to your child's learning ability. M. Pines. Read Digest 98:29-30+ F '71
Toys for the handicapped. il Time 97:48 Ap 26 '71
See also
Recreation for the handicapped

Education

Children who had to be found; Indiana, Pa, preschool project; interview, ed. by W. E. Densham A. Davis. il Am Ed 7:11-14 Mr '71
Deprivation and disadvantage in developing countries. Sch & Soc 99:359+ O '71
Ending the isolation of the handicapped; teacher training programs under the Education professions development act. W. L. Smith. il Am Ed 7:29-33 N '71
Grants to states for handicapped children. il Am Ed 7:32 Ap '71
See also
Special classes and special schools

Recreation

See Recreation for the handicapped
CHILDREN, Hemophilic. See Hemophilia
CHILDREN, Hyperactive. See Hyperkinesis
CHILDREN, Illegitimate. See Illegitimacy
CHILDREN, Mentally handicapped. See Mentally handicapped children
CHILDREN, Missing. See Missing persons
CHILDREN, Painting of. See Portrait painting
CHILDREN, Photography of. See Photography of children
CHILDREN, Retarded. See Mentally handicapped children
CHILDREN, Runaway. See Runaway boys and girls
CHILDREN, Shy. See Bashfulness
CHILDREN, Sick. See Sick children

CHILDREN and adults. See Child-adult relationship

CHILDREN and animals
Can your child cope with an unruly dog? Bet Hom & Gard 49:138 O '71
Children and pets. B. Spock. il Redbook 138: 26+ Ja '72
What is a pet? excerpts. L. P. McGrath and J. Scobey. Good H 173:90-1 Jl '71

CHILDREN and death
Pretty good teacher, for a cat. M. Bourjaily, jr. il Read Digest 98:82-6 Mr '71

CHILDREN and music
Good music: an enriching addition to your camp program. S. H. Brobston. Camp Mag 43:18 Mr '71
Music and the environment. J. C. Hoem. il Cons 25:2-4 Ap '71

CHILDREN and parents. See Parent-child relationship
CHILDREN and pets. See Children and animals
CHILDREN and race cooperation. See Interracial cooperation
CHILDREN and religion. See Children—Religion

CHILDREN and science
Investigating children's science learning. M. Dunfee. Ed Digest 36:34-7 Ja '71
Science gives me joy-feels all over. H. Dunn. il Sci Digest 69:30-3 Je '71

CHILDREN and television. See Television broadcasting and children

CHILDREN and war
Ulster: the children of violence; with excerpts from essays by children. il Newsweek 77:46-50+ Ap 19 '71
War and children; study on loyalties of American children. J. Deedy. il Commonweal 95:74 O 22 '71
See also
Committee of responsibility to save war-burned and war-injured Vietnamese children
Vietnamese war, 1957- —Children

CHILDREN as actors
See the young artists at work; Touchstone center for children, inc, New York. il Parents Mag 46:52-3+ Ag '71
Steven Paul: twelve-year-old actor-playwright; interview. S. Paul. New Yorker 46: 28-31 F 13 '71
Two boys get into the movies; sons of actor Dan O'Herlihy. C. Terry. il Good H 172:38 Ap '71
See also
Childrens plays

CHILDREN as air pilots
Maine's Camp Solo puts young aviators in the pilot's seat; with editorial comment. il Life 71:1, 60-3 Ag 27 '71

CHILDREN as artists
See the young artists at work; Touchstone center for children, inc, New York. il Parents Mag 46:52-3+ Ag '71

CHILDREN as authors
Steven Paul: twelve-year-old actor-playwright; interview. S. Paul. New Yorker 46: 28-31 F 13 '71
See also
Children as poets

CHILDREN as magicians
Is there a magician in the house? T. Prideaux. il Life 71:114-16+ D 17 '71

CHILDREN as musicians
Little Boy Blue: Lucky Peterson. por Newsweek 77:73 Je 14 '71
On stage with Little Lucky. il pors Ebony 26:94-6+ O '71
Whatever happened to "Sugar Chile" Robinson? il pors Ebony 26:178 Je '71
Young man with a horn. por Time 98:64 S 13 '71

CHILDREN as photographers
Showing and telling in photographs by kids. il Life 71:54-6 D 17 '71

CHILDREN as poets
Are children poets? B. Wallenstein. Commonweal 93:448-50 F 5 '71

CHILDREN as prisoners. See Children—Imprisonment

CHILDREN in art
Beesley and his bronze children. D. Cochrane. il por Am Artist 35:54-9+ S '71
Children as seen by their fathers: portfolio. Horizon 13:24-31 Wint '71

CHILDREN in boating
Junior yachting. See issues of Yachting
Welcome aboard. Cherie. S. Parenteau. il pors Motor B & S 127:54-5 My '71

CHILDREN in literature
See also
Negro children in literature

CHILDREN in the morning; story. See Shertzer, K.

CHILDREN of divorced parents
Boys and girls book about divorce; excerpts. R. A. Gardner. il Harp Baz 104:118-21 F '71
How divorced parents can help their children adjust. B. Spock. il Redbook 136:33-4+ Mr '71

CHILDREN of God (movement)
Generation gap. il Newsweek 78:89-90 N 22 '71
Home for Christmas? Chr Today 16:35 D 17 '71
Where have all the children gone? with editorial comment. J. F. Jordan and E. Plowman. il Chr Today 16:31, 38-40 N 5 '71

CHILDREN of migrant laborers
Child labor: a barbarism we must not tolerate. E. E. Cohen. por Parents Mag 46:34 Ag '71
Sending a boy to do a job you wouldn't even wish on a man; with photographs by R. Simmons. A. E. Woolley. Todays Health 49:44-9 Jl '71

Education
Cultivating student teachers in the Yakima Valley; Center for the study of migrant and Indian education, Central Washington state college. C. H. Potter. il Am Ed 7:27-31 My '71
Grants to states for migrant children. il Am Ed 7:32 Je '71
Teaching for the real world; Micro-social learning center; Vineland, N.J. L. Rich. il Am Ed 7:3-6 Ag '71
Teaching migrant children. A. Lund. Todays Ed 60:49-51 O '71

CHILDREN of missionaries
Recollections of a cultural imperialist (j.g.) J. C. Thomson, jr. Atlan 228:35-9 Ag '71

CHILDREN of service men
Education
See also
Military post schools. American

CHILDREN'S aid society, New York
House in place of home; residence for underprivileged children. il Arch Forum 134:56-7 My '71

CHILDRENS allowances
How children learn to handle money. G. L. Wohlner. il Parents Mag 46:46-7+ Je '71

CHILDRENS amusements
See also
Camping—Activities
Christmas projects
Games
Piñatas
Play
Playgrounds, Home—Equipment
Playhouses
Toys
History
Playing grownup. E. H. Schafer. il Horizon 13:20-3 Wint '71

CHILDRENS art
Hands: inky fun with your fingers; with illustrations by B. Shein and R. Tallon. il Life 71:156-60 D 17 '71
International language of peace: children's art: exchange of paintings by Russian and American youngsters. il Parents Mag 46:46-7 D '71
School artists. See issues of School arts
Showcase '71. il Sch Arts 70:14-18+ My '71
What children tell us through their art. A. Hurwitz. il PTA Mag 65:24-5 My '71
Who painted what? schoolchildren from Russia and United States. il Life 71:76-9 O 15 '71
Why parents can't understand Johnny's picture. R. Henkes. il Sch Arts 71:18-21 S '71
Worlds only children can create. il Life 71:46-51 D 17 '71

Exhibitions
Car art; Art around the automobile exhibition at Hofstra university's gallery in Long Island. D. Davis. Newsweek 78:77 Jl 5 '71
Closing the gap: psychedelic art. G. S. Smith. il Sch Arts 70:29 Mr '71
Youth art month really works. T. Gallagher. il Sch Arts 71:24-5 N '71
Youth art show; La Crosse, Wis. R. Sherin. il Sch Arts 70:32-3 F '71

CHILDRENS beds. See Cribs (beds)
CHILDRENS book departments. See Booksellers and bookselling—Childrens literature
CHILDRENS book exhibits. See Book exhibits
CHILDRENS book series. See Series, Book
CHILDRENS book week. See Book week
CHILDRENS books. See Childrens literature

CHILDRENS bookshops. See Booksellers and bookselling—Childrens literature
CHILDRENS camps. See Camps
CHILDRENS card games. See Cards
CHILDREN'S catalog (publication)
Lessons in leadership. D. Broderick. il Library J 96:699-701 F 15 '71
CHILDRENS crafts. See Arts and crafts
CHILDRENS emotional problems. See Emotional problems of children
CHILDRENS exhibitions
See also
Childrens art—Exhibitions
CHILDRENS fantasies
Should parents encourage their children to believe in Santa Claus? B. Bettelheim. Ladies Home J 88:14+ D '71
CHILDRENS fears. See Fear
CHILDRENS fishing. See Fishing
CHILDRENS friends. See Playmates
CHILDRENS furniture. See Furniture, Childrens
CHILDRENS gardens
Hub box: growing things. C. B. Lees. il Horticulture 49:30-1+ Mr '71
Indoor planting adventures for children. il Sunset 146:164-5 F '71
Lighting the fires. M. Perry-Miller. Horticulture 49:34+ D '71
Mother-of-the-gardener: what it takes to succeed. E. Harnett. House B 113:30+ Mr '71
Plants for little people. il Bet Hom & Gard 49:76+ Ag '71
Young garden prizewinners of 1970. il Sunset 146:262-3 Ap '71
CHILDRENS homes. See Homes, Institutional; Orphans and orphan asylums
CHILDRENS homesickness. See Nostalgia
CHILDRENS librarians
Children's librarians in 1970; address. A. R. Izard. bibliog il Am Lib 2:973-6 O '71
CHILDRENS libraries. See Libraries, Childrens
CHILDRENS literature
Barbara Bader's column: show and tell. B. Bader. Wilson Lib Bul 46:227 N '71
Bringing Chicken Licken up to date. J. Karl. por Pub W 199:81-3 F 22 '71
Changing role of science fiction in children's literature. S. L. Engdahl. il Horn Bk 47:449-55 O '71
Children's literature award announced by NBA jury. il Library J 96:1067 Mr 15 '71
Count-down on the 1-2-3's: counting and mathematical-concept books for the primary level. D. Thomas. bibliog il Library J 96:1083-90 Mr 15 '71
Critique of the Critical history. B. Bader. Wilson Lib Bul 46:446-7+ Ja '72
Down the rabbit hole, by S. G. Lanes. Review
    Nation 213:183-4 S 6 '71. R. Sklar
Feminist look at children's books. il Library J 96:235-40 Ja 15 '71; Discussion. 96:1401+ Ap 15 '71
Happy endings. N. Babbitt. Writer 84:12-14+ Je '71
Harmful lessons little girls learn in school. B. Miles. il Redbook 136:86-7+ Mr '71
High fantasy: A wizard of Earthsea; address, October 1969. E. Cameron. bibliog f Horn Bk 47:129-38 Ap '71
How can we write children's books if we don't know anything about children? N. Babbitt. il Pub W 200:64-6 Jl 19 '71
I still would plant my little apple-tree; excerpts from address. June 1970. M. C. Livingston. bibliog f Horn Bk 47:75-84 F '71
In literary terms; excerpt from A sense of story. J. R. Townsend. bibliog Horn Bk 47:347-53 Ag '71
Innocence is a cop-out. J. B. Mercer. il Wilson Lib Bul 46:144-6 O '71
LAPL racism workshop reaction to SLJ feature; excerpts from report on the institute sent to SLJ by B. Tate. Library J 96:1752+ My 15 '71
Library books for leftover class time; art reading tables at Monona public schools. Madison, Wis. J. W. Stewig. bibliog il por Wilson Lib Bul 45:681-4 Mr '71; Correction. 45:836 My '71
No bargain for Frances: children's trade books and consumer education. K. M. Heylman. bibliog il por Library J 96:3433-8 O 15 '71
Peter Rabbit, say good-bye to Snow White. J. Yolen. il por Pub W 199:79-80 F 22 '71
Psychiatrists helping young mommas understand baby; new read-together books for parents and children, interview, ed. by P. A. Farrell. R Switzer; J. C. Hirschberg. il pors Pub W 199:38-9 Je 28 '71

CHILDRENS literature—*Continued*
Realism, truth, and honesty; address, July 1970. M. Q. Steele. Horn Bk 47:17-27 F '71
Run, Dick, run! research by the Feminist collective. L. Haber. Sat R 54:6 Je 12 '71
SLJ meets Lloyd Alexander; interview. L. Alexander. il por Library J 96:1421-3 Ap 15 '71
Second golden age? in a time of flood? adaptation of address, October 1970. V. Haviland. Horn Bk 47:409-19 Ag '71
Sexism (Sic) in children's books; report of panel discussion. il Pub W 199:20-2 Mr 22 '71
Sugar and spice: childrens books. P. Schuman. Library J 96:221 Ja 15 '71
What, if anything, is a children's book? B. Bader. Wilson Lib Bul 46:322-3 D '71
Who should write for young readers? M. Wojciechowska. Writer 84:19-20 Ap '71
Write for children. J. Frank. il Writers Digest 51:24-5+ F '71
Writing the career novel. M. M. Freer. Writer 84:14-16+ Mr '71
See also
Authors—Childrens literature
Book week
Booksellers and bookselling—Childrens literature
Childrens poems (by children)
Childrens poems (for children)
Childrens reading
Childrens stories
Council on interracial books for children
Fairy tales
Negroes in childrens literature
Newbery medal
Paperback books
Picture books for children
Publishers and publishing—Childrens literature
Scientific literature for children
Series, Book
Story telling

Awards and prizes
See also
Caldecott medal

Bibliography
ALA lists 1970's notable children's books. il Pub W 199:58 Ap 12 '71; Same. Am Lib 2:404-6 Ap '71; Library J 96:1764 My 15 '71
American children's books for teachers in England; comp. by E. L. Heins. Horn Bk 47:630-5 D '71
Best books for spring 1971; ed. by L. N. Gerhardt and others. il Library J 96:1780-2 My 15 '71
Best books of 1971; selected by SLJ book review's editors. L. N. Gerhardt and others. il Library J 96:4157-61 D 15 '71
Book review; ed. by L. N. Gerhardt and others. See second issue of each month of Library journal
Booklist (title varies) comp. by P. Heins and others. See issues of Horn book magazine
Books for boys and girls. H. Wilson. See occasional issues of Parents' magazine & better family living
Books for young people. Z. Sutherland. See issues of Saturday review
Books to come; ed. by A. Yazejian. Library J 96:1145-71. 3497-527 Mr 15. O 15 '71
Caboose thoughts and celebrities. T. Foote. il Time 98:60+ D 27 '71
Child-sized primers for survival. S. G. Lanes. il Life 71:44+ D 17 '71
Children's books. See issues of Publishers weekly
Children's books at Christmastime. E. Sheehan. il America 125:486-91 D 4 '71
Children's books for Christmas. J. Stafford. New Yorker 47:177-84+ D 4 '71
Children's books for spring. Z. Sutherland. il Sat R 54:45-8 My 15 '71
Children's books: highlights of the spring. E. M. Graves. Commonweal 94:263-6 My 21 '71
Children's books to remember (cont) Pub W 199:46 Ja 11; 33 Mr 29 '71
Children's books to stimulate a sense of religion. M. E. Marty. il Chr Cent 88:1383+ N 24 '71
Children's paperbacks (cont) Library J 96: 297-9, 1837-9. 2863-5 Ja 15, My 15, S 15 '71
Christmas books for '71. D. G. Stavn. il Library J 96:3482-7 O 15 '71
Family reading: books rated AA (acceptable to adults) P. S. Prescott. Look 35:16 Ja 26 '71
Fanfare 1971: the Horn book's honor list; books of 1970. Horn Bk 47:500-1 O '71
Few ornaments on the tree; Christmas books. Z. Sutherland. Sat R 54:45 D 11 '71

Index to young readers' collective biographies, by J. Silverman. Review
Library J 96:1095 Mr 15 '71. M. M. Murray; Reply. J. Silverman. 96:1742 My 15 '71
1970 children's books of international interest. Todays Ed 60:74-6 N '71
Once upon a time. L. J. Robb. il Ladies Home J 88:62+ N '71
Parade of children's books. il Pub W 200:70-93 Jl 19 '71
Prize-winning children's books. il PTA Mag 65:30-1 Mr '71
Reality clashes head on with fantasy in the children's hour; spring titles, January through June. il Pub W 199:84-114 F 22 '71
Selected list of children's books (cont) E. M. Graves. il Commonweal 94:266-71; 95:185-91 My 21, N 19 '71
Year of the witch. E. M. Graves. Commonweal 95:179-82 N 19 '71

Book reviews
See Book reviews

Censorship
See Censorship

Exhibitions
See Book exhibits

History and criticism
Down the rabbit hole, S. G. Lanes. Review Horn Bk 47:343-5 Ag '71
Early record; address, October 30, 1970. E. Nesbitt. bibliog f Horn Bk 47:268-74 Je '71
Juvenile incunabula. E. Quayle. il por Wilson Lib Bul 46:326-34 D '71

Readability
See Readability (literary style)

Technique
Authors & editors; interview. ed. by P. Bragg. S. O'Dell. por Pub W 200:21-3 N 15 '71
Maybe you can write a children's book! J. Beatty, jr. Redbook 136:78+ Ap '71
Newbery award acceptance; address, June 21, 1971. B. Byars. il Horn Bk 47:354-8 Ag '71
Selecting a manuscript for publication. J. D. Chenery. Writer 84:24-5 O '71

Themes
Children's books; year of the witch. E. M. Graves. Commonweal 95:179-82 N 19 '71
See also
Frontier and pioneer life—United States—Childrens literature

Translations and translating
Adventure in translation. E. Shub. Horn Bk 47:265-7 Je '71
Onward and upward with the arts; a study of Alice's adventures in wonderland and Jabberwocky as translated in German and French, with selections. V. Proetz. New Yorker 47:95-107+ My 22 '71
Story behind the book: Mother Goose gets the French treatment; interview. ed. by P. Bragg. O. De Kay, jr. il Pub W 200:18-19 D 13 '71

Germany
Freedom books. il Newsweek 78:124+ N 22 '71

Great Britain
Children's books in Britain: aiming hard for a new golden age. J. R. Townsend. il Pub W 200:67-9 Jl 19 '71

Iceland
Search for children's books in Iceland. L. Kingman. il Horn Bk 47:462-9 O '71

Russia
Confessions of an old story-teller; tr. by L. G. Leighton (cont) K. I. Chukovskii. il por Horn Bk 47:28-39 F '71
CHILDRENS literature, Immoral. See Immoral literature and pictures
CHILDRENS literature, Influence of
Moral values and children's literature; excerpts from address, October 16, 1971. D. Broderick. Library J 96:4168 D 15 '71
CHILDRENS museums
See also
Boston children's museum
CHILDRENS opinions
Class of 1984. N. Gittelson. Harp Baz 104:47+ Mr '71
War and children; study on loyalties of American children. J. Deedy. il Commonweal 95:74 O 22 '71
See also
Children—Attitudes

CHILDRENS periodicals (by children)
Eye on Fourth street; Lower East side high
school students edit The Fourth street
i. S. Boyer. il Sat R 54:46-7 Ag 21 '71
    See also
Hot owl (periodical)
Kids (periodical)
CHILDRENS pets. See Pets
CHILDRENS phonograph records. See Phono-
graph records—Childrens records
CHILDRENS plays
Close to somebody; Children's theatre: work-
shop at the City center of music and
drama. New Yorker 47:36-8 O 23 '71
Informal dramatics can provide the means;
expression of individuality. R. Telleen. il
Camp Mag 43:12-13 My '71

Texts
Middle grades; lower grades. See issues of
Plays
CHILDRENS poems (by children)
Horn book league. See issues of Horn book
magazine to August 1971
Worlds only children can create. il Life 71:
46-51 D 17 '71
CHILDRENS poems (for children)
Children's corner. J. Ciardi. Sat R 54:34 D 4
'71
    See also
Mother Goose
Nursery rhymes
CHILDRENS poetry
Confessions of an old story-teller; tr. by
L. G. Leighton (cont) K. I. Chukovskii.
il por Horn Bk 47:28-39 F '71
    See also
Childrens poems (by children)
Childrens poems (for children)

Bibliography
Children as poets. Z. Sutherland. Sat R 54:
26 Ag 21 '71
CHILDRENS reading
Bookworm. I. Asimov. Sat R 54:70 Ja 23 '71
English children's choices: Black beauty,
Little women. Library J 96:4137 D 15 '71
Letter to the editor; thin books vs. thick
books. B. K. Walker. Horn Bk 47:558-9 O
'71
Literature program for the middle school.
D. L. Burton and B. Fillion. Clear House
45:524-7 My '71
Tales young readers cherish. S. G. Lanes.
il Parents Mag 46:50-1+ My '71
What's so funny about it? Z. Sutherland.
Sat R 54:48 S 18 '71
    See also
Childrens literature
Right to read program
CHILDRENS rooms
Bunk beds, drawer stack, desk for two
boys. il Sunset 146:161 Ap '71
Children's corner, for reading, dreaming,
growing. il McCalls 98:114-15 F '71
Children's rooms have a built-in future. il
Sunset 146:169 Ap '71
Easy-care ideas for bright and lively chil-
dren's rooms. J. R. Cary. il Parents Mag
46:76-9 Je '71
Living with children. il Redbook 137:114-
17 O '71
26 dollar-saving ideas for children's rooms.
C. L. Crane. Am Home 74:26-8 S '71
Wishbook of dream rooms. M. Sutphen.
House B 113:118+ My '71
    See also
Playrooms
CHILDRENS safety seats. See Automobiles—
Safety devices and measures
CHILDRENS sayings. See Children—Sayings
CHILDRENS services division, American li-
brary association. See American library
association—Children's services division
CHILDRENS shoes. See Shoes
CHILDRENS songs
    See also
Mother Goose
CHILDRENS sports. See Sports for children
CHILDRENS stories
Christmas message. E. J. Keats. Redbook
138:73 D '71
Crisscross crown. G. Carro. il Ladies Home
J 88:90 D '71
Eliot Miles does not wish you a Merry
Christmas because. E. L. Konigsburg. Red-
book 138:78 D '71
Magic mask. A. Moray. il Redbook 138:71-3 D
'71
Seeds. R. Levin. Ladies Home J 88:80 My '71
Soul of Christmas. H. H. King. Ebony 27:
172-6 D '71

Unfinished story. See issues of Today's edu-
cation
What I told Ophelia and Lucy about God.
R. Dahl. il Redbook 138:76-8 D '71
    See also
Story telling
CHILDRENS success. See Success
CHILDRENS thefts. See Shoplifting
CHILDREN'S underground press. See Private
presses
CHILDRENS villages
Father to the orphans of three continents;
SOS children's villages. M. Moyal. il por
Chr Cent 88:752-4 Je 16 '71
CHILDS, John F.
Games companies play. por Forbes 108:68+
S 15 '71
CHILDS, Sister Maryanna
Three gifts for a godchild; poem. Cath
World 213:221 Ag '71
CHILDS, Richard Spencer
Businessman who brought the pro to city
hall. W. M. Wringle. il por Nations Bsns
59:30-2 D '71 *
CHILDS, Theodore F.
Miracle worker on campus. P. Bailey. il pors
Ebony 26:80-1+ S '71 *
CHILE
Image of Chile. G. de Zéndegui. il Américas
23:S1-S24 Mr '71
    See also
Airlines—Chile
Elections—Chile
Government ownership—Chile
Guerrillas—Chile
Indians of South America—Chile
Investments, Foreign (in Chile)
Labor and laboring classes—Chile
Land tenure—Chile
Moving pictures—Chile
Protests, demonstrations, etc.—Chile
Science and state—Chile
Skis and skiing—Chile
Technology—Chile

Cabinet
Growing pains. Newsweek 78:34+ Ag 23 '71
Economic conditions
Chile con Allende; with editorial comment.
D. D. Ranstead. Commonweal 95:244-5, 253-
6 D 10 '71
Chile: from Christian democracy to Marx-
ism? A. Angell. bibliog f Cur Hist 60:84-9+
F '71
Chile is not Cuba, or is it? R. Kuttner. Com-
monweal 94:405-7 Ag 6 '71
Chile: it's half and half. il por Newsweek
77:60+ Ap 19 '71
Growing pains. Newsweek 78:34+ Ag 23 '71
Growing woes of socialist-led Chile. il U S
News 71:76 D 20 '71
Operation Tranquilizer. il Newsweek 77:39-40
Je 21 '71
Economic policy
Andes: a nationalist surge. il Time 98:32 Jl
26 '71
Can Marxists now go all the way in Chile?
il U S News 70:39-40 Ap 19 '71
Chile: a good neighbor. R. O'Mara. Nation
212:180-1 F 8 '71
Chilean revolution: the bullet or the ballot.
M. Zeitlin. il Ramp Mag 9:20-8 Ap '71
Closing the curtain. W. F. Buckley, jr. Nat
R 23:276-8 Mr 9 '71
Fast take-over in Chile. U S News 70:70 Ja
18 '71
Expropriation policy
Chile: the big grab. il Time 98:97 O 11 '71
Chilean notes. Nat R 23:1219, 1283 N 5-19 '71
Copper crisis. Newsweek 78:77 O 11 '71
Expropriation: why do they do it? interview.
O. Letelier. pors Forbes 108:33-5 Jl 15 '71
U.S. responds to Chilean decision on com-
pensation for expropriation; statement,
October 13, 1971. W. P. Rogers. Dept State
Bul 65:478 N 1 '71

Foreign relations
Making an impression; President's tour of
neighboring countries. Newsweek 78:35 S
13 '71
    Cuba
Castro's big drive to win friends. il por U S
News 71:39 N 22 '71
End to isolation; visit of F. Castro. il por
Newsweek 78:61 N 22 '71
Fidel the silent; visit to Chile. il pors Time
98:40-2 N 29 '71
    United States
    See United States—Foreign relations—
Chile

CHILE—*Continued*

History

Chilean rural labor in the nineteenth century. A. J. Bauer. bibliog f il Am Hist R 76: 1059-83 O '71

Industries

See also
Copper industry—Chile

Politics and government

Allende: a special kind of Marxist. P. Young. il pors Life 71:38-40 Jl 16 '71

Allende's hundred days. il por Time 97:33+ F 22 '71

Allende's unorthodox road to socialism. il Bsns W p88 Ap 10 '71

Chile *con* Allende; with editorial comment. D. D. Ranstead. Commonweal 95:244-5, 253-6 D 10 '71

Chile: from Christian democracy to Marxism? A. Angell. bibliog f Cur Hist 60:84-9+ F '71

Chile going Marxist? What it means to the U.S. il por Sr Schol 98:8-15 F 1 '71

Chile under Marxism: does it work? J. Barnes. il por Newsweek 78:43-4+ N 15 '71

Chilean experiment. C. Véliz. For Affairs 49:442-53 Ap '71

Chilean family chronicle: living through the Allende revolution. S. Davidson. il N Y Times Mag p33+ O 17 '71

Chilean notes. Nat R 23:1398 D 17 '71

Chilean revolution: the bullet or the ballot. M. Zeitlin. il Ramp Mag 9:20-8 Ap '71

Chile's reasonable revolution: Allende after a year. J. Radford. Nation 213:422-4 N 1 '71; Reply with rejoinder. J. A. Menz. 213: 642 D 20 '71

China and Chile. Nation 212:516 Ap 26 '71

Closing the curtain. W. F. Buckley, jr. Nat R 23:276-8 Mr 9 '71

Empty pots and Yankee plots. il Time 98:26 D 13 '71

How Chile chose Marxism. T. Armbrister. Read Digest 98:69-74 Je '71

In with the outs; haven for exiled revolutionaries in Santiago. il por Time 97:36 Ja 25 '71

Journey for a homebody; F. Castro's visit. il por Time 98:42 N 22 '71

Letter from Santiago. J. Kraft. New Yorker 46:80-9 Ja 30 '71

Mandate for Allende. il pors Time 97:24+ Ap 19 '71

March of the empty pots; demonstration against the Allende government. il Newsweek 78:53-4 D 13 '71

Operation Tranquilizer. il Newsweek 77:39-40 Je 21 '71

Road to socialism: a rough one for Chile. il por U S News 71:73-5 O 25 '71

Setback for a native son. Time 98:31 Ag 2 '71

You're going great, Chicho. il por Time 98:37 N 15 '71

See also
Elections—Chile
Political parties—Chile

Religious institutions and affairs

World council head. others confer with Chilean President Allende. Chr Cent 88:946 Ag 11 '71

See also
Catholic church in Chile
Pentecostal churches in Chile

CHILE trench. See Submarine valleys

CHILEAN poetry

Translations into English

Disburdened; excerpt from Selected poems. tr. by D. Dana. G. Mistral. Mlle 72:20 Ja '71

Four poems: Falling; Enemy; On the road; Song with landscape and a river; tr. by B. Belitt. P. Neruda. New Yorker 47:54 N 20 '71

CHILEAN propaganda. See Propaganda, Chilean

CHILES, Lawton
He won in a walk. F. Trippett. Look 35:46-7 Ja 12 '71 *

CHILES amendment.   See Vietnamese war, 1957- —American troop withdrawals

CHILLER, Jacques M. and others
Kinetic differences in unresponsiveness of thymus and bone marrow cells. bibliog il Science 171:813-15 F 26 '71

CHILTON, W. E. 3d
Break for West Virginia. Nation 213:390-2 O 25 '71

CHIME Rinpoche, 1939-
Lama in exile: prospects for an expatriate tradition. M. Jeschke. por Chr Cent 88:443-6 Ap 7 '71 *

CHIMNEY ROCK hillclimb. See Automobile racing

CHIMPANZEES
Authors & editors; interview. ed. by L. P. Freilicher. J. G. van Lawick. il por Pub W 200:7-9 N 22 '71

Chimp with a self concept? il Sci Digest 70:46-50 Jl '71

Clues about carriers; gonorrhea experiments. il Newsweek 78:53 Jl 5 '71

In the shadow of man, by I. van Lawick-Goodall. Review
Time il por 98:104+ N 8 '71. B. Darrach

Jane of the apes; excerpt from In the shadow of man. J. G. van Lawick. il por Ladies Home J 88:78+ O '71

Language in chimpanzee? D. Premack. bibliog il Science 172:808-22 My 21 '71

No thanks, said the ape. il Newsweek 78:101 D 20 '71

Reporter at large. E. Hahn. New Yorker 47: 46-8+ Ap 17; 46-50+ Ap 24; 54-6+ D 11 '71

Sarah language? Learn. Sci Am 225:44-5 Jl '71

CHIMSKY, Jean
5 writing problems in the short story. il Writers Digest 51:24-7+ My '71

1971 poetry contest. Writers Digest 51:32-3+ O '71

CH'IN Shih-huang-ti, emperor of China, 259-210 B.C.
World's most evil man. P. W. Schmidtchen. il Hobbies 76:134-6+ Mr '71 *

CHINA
See also
Bonds, Government—China
Children—China
Chinese studies (Sinology)
Libraries—China
Missions—China
World war, 1939-1945—China

Antiquities

China's amazing art discoveries, jade and gold body suits; with photographs by M. Riboud. Vogue 158:94-7 O 15 '71

Civilization

See also
China—Intellectual life

History

After ping-pong what next with Peking? O. E. Clubb. Sat R 54:19-22 My 29 '71

Mao's long march. C. Barnett. il pors Horizon 13:72-9 Wint '71

Historiography

Europe's "discovery" of China and the writing of world history. E. J. Van Kley. bibliog f Am Hist R 76:358-85 Ap '71

Historical analogism, public policy, and social science in eleventh- and twelfth-century China. R. M. Hartwell. bibliog f il Am Hist R 76:690-727 Je '71

Intellectual life

Historical analogism, public policy, and social science in eleventh- and twelfth-century China. R. M. Hartwell. bibliog f il Am Hist R 76:690-727 Je '71

Military policy

Probing the Chinese mind: reports from two U.S. experts. J. K. Fairbank; J. Cohen. pors U S News 71:80-1 S 6 '71

Religious institutions and affairs
See also
Confucius and Confucianism

CHINA (People's Republic)
Beckoning a new generation. R. Berger. Nation 213:361-7 O 18 '71

Communist China 1949-1969. ed. by F. N. Trager and W. Henderson. Review
Nat R 23:816 Jl 27 '71. D. Brudnoy

800,000,000: the real China; excerpts. R. Terrill. il Atlan 228:90-6+ N '71; 229:39-54+ Ja '72

Inside China; eyewitness report by J. Saar. photographs by F. Fischbeck; with editorial comments and E. Snow's talk with Mao. Life 70:3-4, 22-34+ Ap 30 '71

That Chinese threat; adaptation of address. A. S. Whiting. New Repub 164: 18-20 Ap 3 '71

See also
Adult education—China (People's Republic)
Aeronautics, Commercial—China (People's Republic)
Agricultural administration—China (People's Republic)
Birth control—China (People's Republic)
Catholic church—Relations (diplomatic)—China (People's Republic)

CHINA (People's Republic)—See also—*Cont.*
Christians in China
Collective settlements—China (People's Republic)
Colleges and universities—China (People's Republic)
Communism—China (People's Republic)
Communist party (China [People's Republic])
Education—China (People's Republic)
Libraries—China (People's Republic)
Medicine—China (People's Republic)
Missions—China (People's Republic)
Physics—China (People's Republic)
Political prisoners—China (People's Republic)
Public health—China (People's Republic)
Research—China (People's Republic)
Science—China (People's Republic)
Tourist trade—China (People's Republic)
United Nations—China (People's Republic)
United States—Commerce—China (People's Republic)
United States—Foreign relations—China (People's Republic)
Villages—China (People's Republic)
Visitors, Foreign—China (People's Republic)
Women—China (People's Republic)
Youth—China (People's Republic)

Armed forces

Army and the party. E. Snow. New Repub 164:9-12 My 22 '71
Close-up of red China: now a real leap forward. il U S News 70:68-71 F 15 '71
Visit to Peking university, what the cultural revolution was all about. B. M. Frolic. il N Y Times Mag p29+ O 24 '71

Boundaries

See also
Sino-Indian border dispute, 1957-

Commerce

Can we do business with China? interview, ed. by J. Ross-Skinner. L. Norris and C. Luff. il Duns 97:14-16+ Je '71
China trade: how big how fast? Newsweek 77:71 My 3 '71
Chinese like to buy Canadian. Bsns W p33 Jl 24 '71
Concorde sales to China explored. H. J. Coleman. Aviation W 95:24 S 27 '71
Doing business with red China: myth or reality? il U S News 70:14-16 My 10 '71
Push to Peking. Newsweek 78:62+ O 4 '71
Pushing on the trade door. il Bsns W p38 O 2 '71
Red China: the economy behind the open door. il Bsns W p46-7 Jl 24 '71
U.S. faces a reluctant dragon; with editorial comment. il Bsns W p 16-17, 94 Ap 24 '71

United States

See United States—Commerce—China (People's Republic)

Defenses

When red China becomes a nuclear superpower. il U S News 71:46-8 S 27 '71

Description and travel

All you need to know for a trip to China. L. W. Snow. il Sat R 54:36-9 O 23 '71
China: a traveler's diary. P. Stursberg. il Newsweek 77:48+ My 17 '71
Closeup on China. por Time 98:72+ N 15 '71
Return to changing China. A. Topping. il por Nat Geog 140:800-33 D '71
Women inside China; with introduction. S. Attwood; J. Garavente. il pors McCalls 99:77-9+ N '71

Diplomatic and consular service

Now red China has a watchtower over U.S; embassy in Canada. il pors U S News 71:67-9 S 13 '71
See also
Ambassadors

Economic conditions

Aftermath of the cultural revolution. E. Snow. New Repub 164:18-21 Ap 10 '71
Behind the turmoil in red China; with comments by T. Durdin. il U S News 71:32-5 O 18 '71
Communist China, 1971; symposium. bibliog f Cur Hist 61:129-76+ S '71
L'economie Chinoise, by J. Deleyne. Review Nation 214:22-3 Ja 3 '72. A. Segal
Fundamentals of the economy; address, November 1, 1971. L. J. Mulkern. Vital Speeches 38:148-51 D 15 '71
Life inside a Chinese commune; interview, ed. by K. M. Chrysler. M. Wakabayashi. il por U S News 70:70-1 F 15 '71

Life under Mao: Spartan but better. G. Ringwald. il Bsns W p 10-11 N 20 '71
Red China: the economy behind the open door. il Bsns W p46-7 Jl 24 '71

Economic policy

China; youth and the economic development goals. H. Yu. Chr Cent 88:810 Je 30 '71

Economic relations

China; Sino-Japanese relations. H. Yu. Chr Cent 88:414 Mr 31 '71
See also
China (People's Republic)—Commerce

Foreign opinion
American

Drumfire on China. New Repub 165:11 S 25 '71

Foreign relations

Asia's moves toward red China. U S News 71:41 Ag 2 '71
Barriers to a deal between U.S. and red China; interview. R. MacFarquhar. il por U S News 70:30-2 My 3 '71
China; Mao's tactics in war and peace, in international relations. H. Yu. Chr Cent 88:542 Ap 28 '71
China: normalizing of relations with the nations and peoples of the world. H. Yu. Chr Cent 88:1278 O 27 '71
China: open door to what? R. Larson. Chr Today 15:3-5 Ag 27 '71
China will talk from a position of strength; with editorial comment. E. Snow. il pors Life 71:20-1, 22-7 Jl 30 '71
China's strategic shift. O. E. Clubb. Cur 132:58-64 S '71
Close-up of red China: now a real leap forward. il U S News 70:68-71 F 15 '71
Communist China, 1971; symposium. bibliog f Cur Hist 61:129-76+ S '71
Conversaton with Mao Tse-tung. E. Snow. il por Life 70:46-8 Ap 30 '71
800,000,000: the real China; excerpts. R. Terrill. il por Atlan 229:39-54+ Ja '72
Games nations play. Newsweek 77:56 Ap 19 '71
Image and reality in Indochina. H. E. Salisbury. For Affairs 49:381-94 Ap '71
New China. W. F. Buckley, jr. Nat R 23:497 My 4 '71
Pleasures of victory. il Newsweek 78:27-8 N 8 '71
Recognizing China. J. A. Cohen. For Affairs 50:30-43 O '71
Red China's chance to win worldwide friendship. D. Lawrence. U S News 70:92 Mr 1 '71; Same. 70:88 My 3; 71:80 Ag 2 '71
Strategies of Peking. M. Oksenberg. For Affairs 50:15-29 O '71
What is behind red China's smile? C. J. V. Murphy. Read Digest 99:69-73 O '71
What new role for the People's Republic of China? R. C. Hottelet. il Sat R 54:27-30 S 18 '71
Will China intervene? Newsweek 77:19-20 Mr 1 '71
Will red China now risk war? intervention in Indo-China. il U S News 70:17 Mr 8 '71
Worldgram; excerpts from interview. E. L. Chou. U S News 71:37-8 Jl 5 '71
See also
China (People's Republic)—Diplomatic and consular service
Communist strategy

Asia

Red giants battle over Asia. J. N. Wallace. il U S News 71:42-5 S 20 '71

Asia, Southeastern

Asia: how stand the dominoes? M. Parker. il Newsweek 78:47+ S 27 '71

Asia, Southern

Super powers and southern Asia. Cur 130:11-14 Je '71

Cambodia

With Sihanouk in Peking; interview, ed. by A. Casella. Norodom Sihanouk. Nation 212:305-8 Mr 8 '71

Canada

See Canada—Foreign relations—China (People's Republic)

Hong Kong

Marco Polo's mixer; Hong Kong westerners meet with officials of the People's Republic of China. por Time 99:41 Ja 10 '72
View from red China's border. E. Sparn. il Sr Schol 99:9 S 20 '71

CHINA (People's Republic)—Foreign relations
—*Continued*

India

China's relations with India and Pakistan. N. D. Palmer. bibliog f Cur Hist 61:148-53 S '71
See also
Sino-Indian border dispute, 1957-

Japan

Bad dream come true. il Time 98:29-30 Ag 9 '71
Don't miss the bus; Japan. il Newsweek 77:42+ My 3 '71
Fateful triangle: the United States, Japan and China. E. O. Reischauer. il N Y Times Mag p 12-13+ S 19 '71
Playing ping pong with Peking. W. P. Bundy. Newsweek 77:62 Ap 19 '71

Laos

Future of Laos; interview, ed. by G. M. Kahin. Souvanna Phouma. New Repub 165:15-16 Jl 24 '71

Pakistan

China's relations with India and Pakistan. N. D. Palmer. bibliog f Cur Hist 61:148-53 S '71
Peking's double game. J. M. Van Der Kroef. Nat R 23:928-9 Ag 24 '71

Rumania

Nixon confuses Chou. Nation 212:771 Je 21 '71
Visit to China that may help East-West ties. U S News 70:59 Je 14 '71

Russia

See Russia—Foreign relations—China (People's Republic)

United States

See United States—Foreign relations—China (People's Republic)

Vietnam (Democratic Republic)

Three ifs and two buts; significance of Chou's consultations in Hanoi. W. P. Bundy. Newsweek 77:49 Mr 29 '71

Industries

China's industry: advances and dilemma. C. Y. Cheng. bibliog f Cur Hist 61:154-9+ S '71

Military policy

Probing the Chinese mind: reports from two U.S. experts. J. K. Fairbank; J. Cohen. pors U S News 71:80-1 S 6 '71

Photographs

China: a sense of initiative. M. Riboud. il Newsweek 78:28-35 S 13 '71
China: three photographic insights. M. Riboud. Vogue 158:156-61 D '71
Curtain going up? Travel 136:66-9 Jl '71
Gallery; timeless glimpse of China; photograph. Life 70:6-7 My 28 '71
Great wall comes down. Life 70:22-31 Ap 30 '71

Politics and government

Aftermath of China's cultural revolution. M. Goldman. Cur Hist 61:165-70+ S '71
Alive and well in Peking; Mao back in sight. il por Time 98:40 O 18 '71
China. H. Yu. See issues of the Christian century continuing New Christian
China: signs of internal strife. il Time 98:28-9 O 4 '71
China: something must be happening. ' il Newsweek 78:31-2 O 4 '71
Clues to fight for power in red China. il pors U S News 71:29 N 22 '71
Conversation with Mao Tse-tung. E. Snow. il por Life 70:46-8 Ap 30 '71
Dialogues with Chou. pors Newsweek 77:59 Ap 12 '71
If ever the twain shall meet. B. P. Clark. il Sat R 54:14-16+ D 18 '71
Inside China: in the wake of the cultural revolution. J. Gittings. il Ramp Mag 10:10-19 Ag '71
Mao wipes the slate clean. America 125:359 N 6 '71
Mao's great revolution. by R. S. Elegant. Review
Nat R 23:535-6 My 18 '71. J. M. Van Der Kroef
More pieces in the Chinese puzzle. il Time 98:37 O 11 '71
Mystery deepens. il Newsweek 78:35 O 11 '71
Open door; summary of interview with Chou En-lai. E. Snow. New Repub 164:20-3 Mr 27 '71

Republic of China; address, October 25, 1971. S. K. Chow. Vital Speeches 38:101-2 D 1 '71
Round-trip ticket to Peking. il por Newsweek 78:51-2 O 18 '71
See also
Communism—China (People's Republic)
Communist party (China [People's Republic])

Religious institutions and affairs

China. H. Yu. Chr Cent 88:1534 D 29 '71
Nixon visit and religion in China. J. B. Sheerin. Cath World 213:259-60 S '71
See also
Christians in China

Social conditions

Achieving a new stability; life after the Mao's great proletarian cultural revolution. T. Durdin. Cur 133:48-64 O '71
Biologist's view of China. A. W. Galston. Yale R 61:139-46 O '71
China: a sense of initiative. M. Riboud. il Newsweek 78:28-35 S 13 '71
China; decentralization program. Hwa Yu. Chr Cent 88:914 Jl 28 '71
China's new mood: relaxation, self-confidence. E. van Heuvel. il N Y Times Mag p 10-11+ Jl 25 '71
Inside China: in the wake of the cultural revolution. J. Gittings. il Ramp Mag 10:10-19 Ag '71
Mao's attempt to remake man. il por Time 98:24-5 Jl 12 '71
Protestant ethic, Chinese style. Nation 213:67-8 Ag 2 '71
What they saw and didn't see. il Time 97:27 My 3 '71
See also
Communism—China (People's Republic)
Women—China (People's Republic)

CHINA (People's Republic) and Japan

Table tennis, anyone? Peking's ping pong team in Japan. S. Liu. il Newsweek 77:57+ Ap 12 '71

CHINA (People's Republic) and the United States

Backspin on the Chinese serve. Chr Cent 88:483 Ap 21 '71
China: more signals. il Time 97:26 My 3 '71
Meeting the Chinese. S. C. Rose. Chr Cent 88:1516 D 29 '71
Notes and comment; opening of China to the United States table-tennis team. New Yorker 47:31 Ap 24 '71
Peek into Peking; ping-pong gambit. Sr Schol 98:15 Ap 26 '71
Ping heard round the world; American ping pong players in China. il Time 97:25-8+ Ap 26 '71
Ping pong anyone? Nation 212:514 Ap 26 '71
Ping pong diplomat. J. Bochenski. il por Seventeen 30:142+ O '71
You have opened a new page. il Newsweek 77:16-18+ Ap 26 '71

CHINA news analysis (periodical) See Periodicals—Hong Kong

CHINA records project. See Yale university—Libraries

CHINA scholars. See Scholars

CHINA trade porcelain. See Pottery, Chinese

CHINA vote. See United Nations—Voting

CHINAMPAS

Gardens on swamps. P. Armillas. bibliog il Science 174:653-61 N 12 '71

CHINESE

Photographs

Great wall comes down. Life 70:22-31 Ap 30 '71

CHINESE art objects. See Art objects, Chinese

CHINESE artificial satellites. See Artificial satellites, Chinese

CHINESE athletes. See Athletes

CHINESE bonds. See Bonds, Government—China

CHINESE businessmen. See Businessmen

CHINESE civilization. See Civilization, Chinese

CHINESE cookery. See Cookery, Chinese

CHINESE cucumbers. See Cucumbers

CHINESE delegates to the United Nations. See United Nations—Delegates

CHINESE economic assistance. See Economic assistance, Chinese

CHINESE egg rolls. See Cookery, Chinese

CHINESE fortune cookies. See Cookies

CHINESE gooseberries. See Yantaos

CHINESE imports. See Imports

CHINESE in southeastern Asia

Wealth and power of the overseas Chinese. L. Kraar. il Fortune 83:78-81+ Mr '71

CHINESE-Indian border dispute, 1957-. See
Sino-Indian border dispute, 1957-
CHINESE-Japanese war, 1931-1932
Shanghai crisis of 1932: the basis of British
policy. C. Thorne; reply. G. B. Ostrower.
Am Hist R 76:1265-7 O '71
CHINESE Joinery. See Joinery
CHINESE junks. See Junks
CHINESE language

Writing
American children with reading problems can
easily learn to read English represented
by Chinese characters. P. Rozin and others.
bibliog il Science 171:1264-7 Mr 26 '71; Dis-
cussion. 173:190-1 Jl 16 '71
Language corner. A. Gottfurcht. il Chem 44:18
D '71
CHINESE Lowestoft. See Pottery, Chinese
CHINESE medicine. See Medicine—China
(People's Republic)
CHINESE military assistance. See Military as-
sistance, Chinese
CHINESE missile program. See Guided missiles
CHINESE poetry

Translations into English
Prison diary of Ho Chi Minh, tr. by A. Palm-
er. Review
New Repub 165:27-8 Ag 7 '71. R. Whitte-
more; Reply. Huynh Sanh Thong. 165:
32 S 18 '71
CHINESE pottery. See Pottery, Chinese
CHINESE students in the United States. See
Foreign students in the United States
CHINESE studies (sinology)
China scholars. il Time 98:44+ Ag 9 '71
Learning about China. Newsweek 78:56-7 D
20 '71
CHINESE styled clothes. See Costume design
CHINESE tapestry. See Tapestry
CHINESE trade fair. See Exhibitions
CHINESE village life. See Village life
CHINESE visitors in Japan. See Visitors,
Foreign—Japan
CHINESE writing. See Chinese language—Writ-
ing
CHINNOCK, Frank W.
Sensible new plan to fight drugs in our
schools; excerpt from The nightmare route:
the truth about drugs in suburbia. Ladies
Home J 88:68-70+ Ap '71
CHINOOK salmon fishing. See Salmon fishing
CHIP circuits. See Electronic circuits, Inte-
grated
CHIP logs. See Logs (nautical instruments)
CHIP memories. See Memory devices (com-
puters)
CHIPMAN, Abram
Self-analysis of a music addict. por Hi Fi
21:20 F '71
CHIPPOKES plantation state park. See Vir-
ginia—Parks and reserves
CHIRIAEFF, Ludmilla
Purpose: Ludmilla Chiriaeff and Les grands
ballets canadiens. O. Maynard. il por Dance
Mag 45:56-65 Ap '71 •
CHIROPRACTORS
Should chiropractors be paid with your tax
dollars? A. Q. Maisel. Read Digest 99:76-81
Jl '71
What can a chiropractor do for you? L. Da-
vid. il Mech Illus 67:67-9+ Ap '71
CHIRVANI, Assadullah Souren Melikian-. See
Melikian-Chirvani, A. S.
CHISEL plowing. See Tillage
CHISHOLM, Margaret
MARC: what is it? Ed Digest 36:42-4 My '71
CHISHOLM, Shirley A.
Excerpt from statement to House armed ser-
vices committee, March 11, 1971. Cong Di-
gest 50:154+ My '71
Excerpt from testimony before the Consti-
tutional amendments subcommittee, May
5, 1970. Cong Digest 50:20+ Ja '71
Love is not enough. il por Parents Mag 46:
52+ D '71

about
Clear it with Shirley. il por Newsweek 78:35-
6 O 18 '71 •
In search of a black strategy. por Time 98:
9-10 D 20 '71 •
On the Chisholm campaign trail. P. R. Wieck.
New Repub 165:16-18 D 4 '71 •
Shaker-upper wants to be Madame Presi-
dent Chisholm. J. Howard. por Life 71:81
N 5 '71 •
CHISOLM, J. Julian, Jr
Lead poisoning; with biographical sketch. il
Sci Am 224:12, 15-23 bibliog(p 130) F '71

CHISOS MOUNTAINS
Chisos Mountains: an ecological island. J.
Gillette. il Nat Parks & Con Mag 45:4-8
F '71
Mysterious Chisos. J. Gillette. il Nat Parks
& Con Mag 45:4-10 Ja '71
CHITTUM, Donald
Current chronicle. il Mus Q 57:129-41 Ja '71
CHITWOOD family
Caution: beware of angels at work. F. De-
ford. il Sports Illus 34:84-8+ My 17 '71
CHLEBOSKI, Ronald
Radio network nabs air-pollution violators.
il Am City 86:89-90 D '71
CHLORAMPHENICOL
Special dispensation; overseas sales of chlo-
romycetin. S. Sesser. New Repub 164:16-17
Mr 6 '71
CHLORELLA. See Algae
CHLORIDES in the body
Ammonium and chloride extrusion: hyper-
polarizing synaptic inhibition in spinal
motoneuron. H. D. Lux. bibliog il Science
173:555-7 Ag 6 '71
CHLOROMYCETIN. See Chloramphenicol
CHLOROPLASTS
Environmental control of photosynthetic en-
hancement. T. Punnett. bibliog il Science
171-284-6 Ja 22 '71
Hybrid ribosome formation from escherichia
coli and chloroplast ribosome subunits. S.
G. Lee and W. R. Evans. bibliog il Sci-
ence 173:241-2 Jl 16 '71
CHMELIK, Lee
John Stobart, marine artist. il por Am Artist
35:46-51+ N '71
CHOATE, Robert B. Jr
My phony neighbors and yours. Sedulus.
New Repub 164:36-7 Ap 17 '71 •
CHOCO Indians. See Indians of Central Amer-
ica
CHOCOLATE
See also
Cookery—Chocolate
CHOCOLATE desserts. See Desserts
CHOCOLATE roll. See Cake
CHOCOLATE soufflés. See Soufflés
CHOICE (periodical)
Choice editor fired by ALA; P. M. Doiron.
Library J 96:2715 S 15 '71
Dismissal appealed. Am Lib 2:915 O '71
Editor of Choice fired; P. M. Doiron. W. R.
Eshelman. Wilson Lib Bul 46:5 S '71
Firing of Choice editor raises protest storm.
Library J 96:3061 O 1 '71
Hearing for Doiron. J. Berry. Library J 96:
3931 D 1 '71
CHOICE (psychology)
See also
Decision making
CHOICE by lot
Randomization and social affairs: the 1970
draft lottery. S. E. Fienberg. bibliog il
Science 171-255-61 Ja 22 '71
CHOICE of college. See College, Choice of
CHOICE of occupation. See Occupations
CHOIRS
Boys in the choir; Berkshire boy choir. il
Newsweek 78:83 Ag 30 '71
CHOKES, Shotgun. See Shotguns
CHOLECALCIFEROL. See Vitamins—Vitamin
D
CHOLERA
Cholera. N. Hirschhorn and W. B. Gre-
enough, 3d. il Sci Am 225:15-21 Ag '71
Faces emptied of all hope; Pakistan refugees
endure chaos and cholera. J. Saar. il Life
70:22-9 Je 18 '71
New cure for cholera; massive intravenous
infusions of water and salts. il Time 97:75
Ap 5 '71
Why cholera is the disease nations try to
hide. L. M. Rhodes. il Todays Health 49:
51-3 Je '71
CHOLERA, Hog. See Hog cholera
CHOLESTASIS. See Bile
CHOLESTEROL
Antibiotics as pesticides. il Chem 44:23 F '71
Growing worry over cholesterol. il Changing
T 25:37-9 Jl '71
On vitamin C, cholesterol, and heart attack.
il Chem 44:24-5 Je '71
Questions and answers on fats and choles-
terol. R. H. Smithies. il Good H 172:139-40
F '71
There's more than cholesterol behind heart
attacks; triglyceride problem. R. H. Berg.
il Look 35:51-2 F 9 '71

CHOLINE
Transport of nitrogen mustard on the transport-carrier for choline in L5178Y lymphoblasts. G. J. Goldenberg and others. bibliog il Science 172:1148-9 Je 11 '71
See also
Acetylcholine

CHOLINESTERASE
Nerve trophic function: in vitro assay of effects of nerve tissue on muscle cholinesterase activity. T. L. Lentz. bibliog il Science 171:187-9 Ja 15 '71
Phenylthioacetate: a useful substrate for the histochemical and colorimetric detection of cholinesterase. G. M. Booth and R. L. Metcalf; reply. W. D. McEnroe. Science 171:928 Mr 5 '71
Sex and population differences in the incidence of a plasma cholinesterase variant. A. H. Lubin and others. bibliog il Science 173:161-4 Jl 9 '71

CHOMSKY, Noam
Chomsky is difficult to please. . ; I. Shenker. il por Horizon 13:104-9 Spr '71 *
Onward and upward with the arts; linguistics. V. Mehta. il New Yorker 47:44-8+ My 8 '71

CHONDRITES. See Meteorites

CHONDRULES. See Meteorites

CHONES, Jim
Big one who stayed. C. Kirkpatrick. il por Sports Illus 35:46-50 N 29 '71 *

CHOPIN, Frédéric François
From the Musical heritage society, the complete works of Chopin. L. Richmond. il pors Am Rec G 37:488-93+ Ap '71 '
Sergei Rachmaninoff. L. Gerber. il Am Rec G 37:438-9 Mr '71 *

CHOPSTICKS
How to use chopsticks. il Bet Hom & Gard 49:118 N '71

CHORAL groups and societies
New resonances from Stockhausen's Stimmung; performed by the Collegium vocale of Cologne. I. Kolodin. Sat R 54:19 D 11 '71

CHORAL music
See also
Phonograph records—Choral music

CHORAL singing
See also
Choirs

CHORDATA
See also
Tunicates

CHOREA, Huntington's. See Huntington's chorea

CHOREOGRAPHY
All the strange things: John Butler on opera choreography among other kinds of dance; ed. by G. Loney. J. Butler. il por Dance Mag 45:22-7 Ag '71
Choreographic partners: Concerto for jazz band and orchestra; interview. G. Balanchine; A. Mitchell. New Yorker 47:28-30 My 22 '71
Dance: Broadway rhythm; dance in musical comedy. H. Saal. il Newsweek 78:76-7 D 13 '71
Not a Swan lake swan; M. Sappington's Weewis. N. M. Stoop. il por Dance Mag 46:36-9+ Ja '72
Robbins: Goldberg variations; interview. J. Robbins. New Yorker 47:21-3 Je 19 '71
See also
Dance notation

CHORES, Camp. See Camp chores

CHOROID plexus. See Brain

CHORUS in opera. See Opera—Chorus

CHORUSES, Sacred
Memoirs of Dr William Boyce. G. Beechey. bibliog f il por Mus Q 57:87-106 Ja '71

CHOU, En-lai
Worldgram: excerpts from interview. U S News 71:37-8 Jl 5 '71

about

After-dinner speech. il Newsweek 78:47-8 Jl 5 '71 *
China will talk from a position of strength; with editorial comment. E. Snow. il pors Life 71:20-1, 22-7 Jl 30 '71 *
Chou gives a nod to science swap. D. Shapley. Science 173:616 Ag 13 '71 *
Chou's shopping list. il por Newsweek 78:31 Ag 23 '71 *
Clues to fight for power in red China. il pors U S News 71:29 N 22 '71 *
Dialogues with Chou. pors Newsweek 77:59 Ap 12 '71 *
800,000,000: the real China; excerpts. R. Terrill. il por Atlan 229:39-54+ Ja '72 *
No. 1 dancer: Chou En-lai. il por Newsweek 77:21-2 Ap 26 '71 *

Open door; summary of interview. E. Snow. New Repub 164:20-3 Mr 27 '71 *
Peking's indispensable man. il por Newsweek 78:19 Jl 26 '71 *
Please don't eat the lotus leaves; J. Reston interview. il por Time 98:32 Ag 23 '71 *
Reston and Chou. Nat R 23:912 Ag 24 '71 *
Scrutability in Life. Nat R 23:974 S 10 '71 *
Uses of charm and chill. il por Time 98:29 Ag 9 '71 *

CHOU, Wen-chung
Asian concepts and twentieth-century western composers. bibliog f il Mus Q 57:211-29 Ap '71

CHOW, Shu-kai
Republic of China; address. October 25, 1971. Vital Speeches 38:101-2 D 1 '71

CHOWDER
Chowders: thick and creamy. il Bet Hom & Gard 49:78-9+ S '71
Crab chowder supreme. il Bet Hom & Gard 49:12 O '71
Delicious choice in chowders: crab, oyster, shrimp. Sunset 147:212 O '71
Holiday soup; bourride. il Sunset 147:138-9 D '71
Soup and fish. il Sunset 146:90-1 Mr '71

CHRAMBACH, A. and Rodbard, D.
Polyacrylamide gel electrophoresis. bibliog il Science 172:440-51 Ap 30 '71

CHRISS, Nicholas C.
Bad day in Memphis. Nation 213:653-4 D 20 '71
Bombs to the right of them. Nation 212:243-4 F 22 '71
Catching up with Natchez. Nation 213:592-3 D 6 '71
Lyndon gets his library. Nation 212:710-12 Je 7 '71
New chapter in horror. il Nation 214:49-50 Ja 10 '72

CHRIST. See Jesus Christ

CHRISTAKIS, George
Common-sense diet that works. il Read Digest 98:159-63 Ap '71
Perfect diet. il Redbook 136:54-5+ Ja '71

CHRISTENSEN, Bonniejean
Adventures in manipulation. Engl J 60:359-60 Mr '71

CHRISTENSEN, H. D. and others
Activity of Δ^8-andΔ^9-tetrahydrocannabinol and related compounds in the mouse. bibliog il Science 172:165-7 Ap 9 '71

CHRISTENSEN, Harold T.
Comparative sex norms in U.S. and Danish students. Sch & Soc 99:333-4 O '71 *

CHRISTENSEN, J. J. and others
Ion binding by synthetic macrocyclic compounds. bibliog il Science 174:459-67 O 29 '71

CHRISTENSEN, Sherman T.
Technique for teaching technicians. V. Louviere. Nations Bsns 59:14 Ja '71 *

CHRISTENSON, Reo M.
On breaking the black impasse; resettling low-income families. il Chr Cent 88:902-6 Jl 28 '71

CHRISTIAENS, Louis
Combating la drug scene, in France. America 125:286-7 O 16 '71

CHRISTIAN, Marcus
Dark heritage; poem. Negro Hist Bul 34:140 O '71
Southern share-cropper; Birth of a Communist; poems. Negro Hist Bul 34:157 N '71

CHRISTIAN, P. A. and Berka, L. H.
Preparing polywater and other anomalous liquids. bibliog il pors Chem 44:25-8 Ja '71

CHRISTIAN action ministry academy. See Chicago—Education

CHRISTIAN and missionary alliance
Tooling up for world revival. D. Kucharsky. Chr Today 15:28-9 Je 4 '71

CHRISTIAN antiquities
See also
Byzantine antiquities

CHRISTIAN art and symbolism
Earl Neiman: a great artist. G. Baum. il Cath World 213:69-74 My '71
See also
Altar pieces
Cross and crosses
Illumination of books and manuscripts
Religious articles

Exhibitions
Tinfoil tribute to God; The throne of the third heaven. il Chr Today 15:21 Ag 27 '71

CHRISTIAN booksellers association
Religion is big business as Christian booksellers meet in Denver. S. Peckham. il Pub W 200:46-7 Ag 16 '71

CHRISTIAN camping international
Campers stake future. R. Chandler. il Chr
Today 16:42-3 N 19 '71
CHRISTIAN camps. See Church camps
CHRISTIAN century (periodical)
Century goes up. J. Deedy. Commonweal 95:
314 Ja 7 '72
Fa la la la la. Chr Cent 88:1439 D 8 '71
Letter from the editor. A. Geyer. Chr Cent
88:515 Ap 28 '71
New editors at large. Chr Cent 88:277-8 Mr 3
'71
CHRISTIAN century foundation
Third Haselden fellow. Chr Cent 88:826 Jl
7 '71
CHRISTIAN church, Disciples of Christ
Disciples in Louisville: democracy at work.
H. E. Fey. Chr Cent 88:1426-8 D 1 '71
CHRISTIAN colleges. See Church colleges
CHRISTIAN democratic union (Germany) See
Political parties—Germany (Federal Re-
public)
CHRISTIAN democrats (Chile) See Political
parties—Chile
CHRISTIAN education. See Religious educa-
tion
CHRISTIAN endeavor union. See World's
Christian endeavor union
CHRISTIAN ethics
Christian apathy. F. J. Quinlivan. il Cath
World 213:187-8 Jl '71
E. M. Forster, homosexuality and Christian
morality. N. Pittenger. Chr Cent 88:1468-71
D 15 '71
Ecology of the spirit. L. N. Bell. Chr Today
15:19 Ja 29 '71
Ethical ambivalence. Chr Today 15:32-3 My
21 '71
Flexibility on the social, fixity on the per-
sonal; statement concerning moral ques-
tions issued by English bishops. T. Beeson.
Chr Cent 88:62 Ja 20 '71
Grace to say no! L. N. Bell. Chr Today 15:
36-7 Mr 12 '71
Moral theology: hope for revival? F. Colborn.
America 124:312-15 Mr 27 '71
New commandment: thou shalt not, maybe.
il Time 98:73-4 D 13 '71
Responsible freedom: guidelines for Chris-
tian action, by L. H. DeWolf. Review
Commonweal 95:306-8 D 24 '71. R. L.
Shinn
Word. V. P. McCorry. See issues of America
See also
American society of Christian ethics
Church and social problems
Conscience
Humility
Sin
War and religion
CHRISTIAN fellowship. See Fellowship of the
Spirit
CHRISTIAN herald
Changing the masthead at the Christian
herald. R. Chandler. Chr Today 15:34-5 Mr
26 '71
CHRISTIAN holiness association
Distinguishing holiness; National holiness
association name change. J. S. Tinney.
Chr Today 15:42 My 7 '71
CHRISTIAN humanism. See Humanism
CHRISTIAN leadership
Leaders we need. W. L. Doty. il Cath World
214:124-7 D '71
CHRISTIAN life
After commencement what? Christian's sta-
tion in life. Chr Today 15:20-1 Je 18 '71
Christian endurance. L. N. Bell. Chr Today
16:20-1 O 22 '71
Christian growth. E. Glynn. America 124:
153-4 F 13 '71
Christian nonviolent workshop. J. Pisani.
Cath World 214:31-4 O '71
Last word. Chr Today 16:27 Ja 7 '72
Merely servants. V. P. McCorry. America
125:inside back cover S 25 '71
New monasticism. R. Haughton. Cath World
214:103-4 D '71
Renewal: testing the assumptions. T. Dubay.
America 125:124-6 S 4 '71
Thank God, this is the day. Chr Today 16:28
N 19 '71
Trouble is chronic. Chr Today 15:25 Ag 6 '71
Vanishing religious order and the new hu-
man community. R. Ruether. Chr Cent 88:
425-9 Ap 7 '71
See also
Christian ethics
Prayer
Spiritual life
CHRISTIAN life communities. See National
federation of Christian life communities
CHRISTIAN love. See Love (theology)
CHRISTIAN missions. See Missions

CHRISTIAN movements, Student. See Student
Christian movements
CHRISTIAN peace conference. See Peace con-
ferences
CHRISTIAN reformed church. See Reformed
churches
CHRISTIAN Science
Christian Scientists seek extension of Eddy
copyright. Pub W 200:28 O 4 '71
CHRISTIAN science monitor (newspaper)
Out of the cloister. il por Newsweek 78:51
Ag 23 '71
CHRISTIAN service corps
Walking inn; new headquarters. Chr Today
15:45 F 12 '71
CHRISTIAN union. See Church union
CHRISTIAN witness. See Witness bearing
(Christianity)
CHRISTIANITY
Finding a new stride. C. F. H. Henry. Chr
Today 15:29-30 Jl 2 '71
Greening of Christianity. G. O'Collins.
America 124:410 Ap 17 '71
Love and life ever upwelling; excerpt from
God at large. C. Walsh. Chr Cent 88:332
Mr 17 '71
On moving with the times; excerpt from God
in the dock. C. S. Lewis. Chr Today 15:4-6
Mr 12; 13-15 Mr 26 '71
Touchstone of truth and value in religions.
M. Blanchard. Chr Today 15:10-13 Ja 29
'71
See also
Christian ethics
Church
Church history
Grace (theology)
Jesus Christ
Kingdom of God
Sociology, Christian
Theology
CHRISTIANITY and communism. See Catholic
church and communism; Communism and
religion
CHRISTIANITY and crisis (periodical)
C and C in crisis. Newsweek 77:97-8 Mr 22
'71
Thirty and beyond. B. Thompson. Chr Cent
88:422 Ap 7 '71
CHRISTIANITY and international affairs. See
Church and international relations
CHRISTIANITY and law. See Religion and
law
CHRISTIANITY and magic
Religion and the decline of magic, by K.
Thomas. Review
America 125:73 Ag 7 '71. D. A. Drennen
CHRISTIANITY and other religions
Can eastern Christians survive under Marx
or Islam? C. S. Calian. il Cath World
212:249-52+ F '71
Christian-Islamic confrontation in the west:
the thirteenth-century dream of conver-
sion. R. I. Burns. bibliog f il Am Hist
R 76:1386-434 D '71
Ecumenism: threat to Judaism? America
124:253 Mr 13 '71
Evangelical-Jewish dialogue. Chr Today 15:
36 Ja 29 '71
From proclamation to dialogue: a new pro-
file for Christians. J. C. Haughey. America
124:483-5 My 8 '71
German church seeks to bring Jews, Chris-
tians and Moslems together. Chr Cent 88:
899 Jl 28 '71
God's first love, by F. Heer. Review
Commonweal 94:218-20 My 7 '71. A. A.
Cohen
Going east: neomysticism and Christian
faith. G. Fackre. il Chr Cent 88:457-61 Ap
14 '71
Jesus and Israel, by J. Isaac. Review
Cath World 213:246-7 Ag '71. J. T. Paw-
likowski
Commonweal 94:314-16 Je 11 '71. G. Baum
New syncretistic dialogue. O. F. Stahlke. Chr
Today 16:8-9 D 3 '71
Paganism-Christianity-Judaism, by M. Brod.
Review
Commentary 51:85-6 My '71. A. A. Cohen
Right answers, wrong questions. M. Blan-
chard. Chr Today 15:8-10 Ag 6 '71
Touchstone of truth and value in religions.
M. Blanchard. Chr Today 15:10-13 Ja 29
'71
Winds from the East; youth and countercults.
J. Needleman. il Commonweal 94:188-90
Ap 30 '71
CHRISTIANITY and politics. See Church and
politics
CHRISTIANITY and science. See Religion and
science
CHRISTIANITY and social problems. See
Church and social problems

CHRISTIANITY and the world. See Church and the world

CHRISTIANITY and war. See War and religion

CHRISTIANS
Christians and tomorrow's world. H. B. Kuhn. Chr Today 15:38-9 Jl 16 '71
Liberty in Christ. V. P. McCorry. America 124:661 Je 26 '71
Merely, militantly Christian. E. M. Blaiklock. Chr Today 15:6 My 7 '71

CHRISTIANS and Jews. See Christianity and other religions

CHRISTIANS in Africa
Black Africa: blacks move to the city. J. Derrick. il America 125:13-14 Jl 10 '71
Christianity's future. America 124:220-1 Mr 6 '71

CHRISTIANS in China
Churches and China. America 125:50-1 Ag 7 '71
Lift for the bamboo cross. D. Kucharsky. Chr Today 15:47 My 21 '71
Will thaw in China mean comeback for Christianity? il U S News 71:66-8 Jl 5 '71

CHRISTIANS in Israel
Anxiety in Israel. D. L. Baker. Chr Today 15:35 Je 18 '71

CHRISTIANS in Japan
See also
United church of Christ in Japan

CHRISTIANS in Russia
Open letter to the Kremlin; reprint. V. I. Kozlov. America 124:346-8 Ap 3 '71

CHRISTIANS in South Africa
South African Christian confronts apartheid. M. Cassidy. Chr Today 16:3-6 N 19 '71

CHRISTIANSEN, Robert O. See Monn, E. jt. auth.

CHRISTIANSON, Gale Edward
Nuclear tyranny and the divine right of kings. il Bul Atom Sci 27:44-6 Ja '71

CHRISTIANSON, K. Scott
Cops can't find the pusher. Nation 213:562-4 N 29 '71

CHRISTIE, George A.
Current trends in construction. Arch Rec 149:76 Ap; 62 Jl '71

CHRISTIE, Julie
Warren and Julie: together at last. H. Ehrlich. pors Look 35:70-4 Je 1 '71 •

CHRISTIE, Sherry
How I learned to stop worrying and like advertising. Mlle 74:211+ N '71

CHRISTIN, Robert E.
Future for Catholic colleges? America 125:179-80 S 18 '71

CHRISTMAN, Gene M.
Mountain bison. il Am West 8:44-7 My '71

CHRISTMAS, Joyce S.
Three little kittens' Christmas; drama. Plays 31:73-6, 88 D '71

CHRISTMAS
Animals of Christmas. G. Kopecky. Ladies Home J 88:76 D '71
C is for . . . il Ladies Home J 88:84-95+ D '71
Christmas counterpoint. V. P. McCorry. America 125:545 D 18 '71
Christmas is a time for loving; symposium. McCalls 99:75-7+ D '71
Christmas sun: a memory. M. A. Rodgers. il Good H 173:58+ D '71
Death of Christmas, ed. by K. Heise and A. Allan. Review
Chr Cent 88:1479 D 15 '71
Festival of flame and fire. H. W. Dengler. il Am For 77:4-5+ D '71
Hope and joy of Christmas; message. C. Wedel. Chr Cent 88:1460 D 15 '71
Hospital holiday; army's Valley Forge general hospital; excerpt from How to say yes to life. C. L. Miller. il Good H 173:68-9+ D '71
How the best-known holiday traditions began il Good H 173:172 D '71
Mystery of Christmas. Chr Cent 88:1483 D 22 '71
Someday, a real Christmas; excerpt from issue of December 23, 1955. D. Lawrence. U S News 72:72 Ja 3 '72
Special gift of Mary Perkins; Florida girl who cared about homeless black kids. W. Hartley and E. Hartley. il por Seventeen 30:110+ D '71
Two Christmas stories. S. A. Mateer. il Chr Today 16:5-7 D 3 '71
Vital signs of Christmas. R. Warfield. House & Gard 140:52+ N '71
Wonder of Christmas. M. Gough. il House B 113:31-42 D '71

Wyeths' kind of Christmas magic; excerpts from letters, ed. by R. Meryman. il por Life 71:122-9 D 17 '71
See also
Christmas eve
Jesus Christ—Nativity
Santa Claus

Anecdotes, facetiae, satire, etc.
Notes and comment. New Yorker 47:27 D 18 '71
Truman Capote on Christmas, places, memories; interview. T. Capote. il por Mlle 74:122-3+ D '71

Australia
Christmas with corals. G. Durrell. House & Gard 140:70-1+ D '71

Mexico
See also
Piñatas

United States
American family Christmas. il Bet Hom & Gard 49:54-71+ D '71
Be gentle, be happy and give your child the stars for Christmas. J. West. il Redbook 138:66-7+ D '71
Boyhood joys of Christmas; holiday joys of H. Reasoner and his family. J. Egan. il pors Good H 173:44+ D '71
Christmas at the White House. P. R. Nixon. il House & Gard 140:62-9 D '71
Christmas; tour of the Christmas season. il Redbook 138:88-109+ D '71
Peaceful people. M. Evans. il Am Home 74:44-9+ D '71
Snug Harbor, where the only tide is yule; seagoing midsummer yuletide celebration. N. Levy. il Motor B & S 127:16+ Je '71
Special gifts of Christmas. D. Hardie. il House & Gard 140:86+ D '71
White House Christmas, 1971; photo report. U S News 71:40-1 D 27 '71

CHRISTMAS banners. See Flags

CHRISTMAS bonuses. See Bonus system

CHRISTMAS books, Childrens. See Childrens literature

CHRISTMAS business
Christmas shopping: biggest ever; outlook by merchants. il U S News 71:26-8 N 29 '71
Christmas trade: a blockbuster. il U S News 71:13-15 D 27 '71
Signs of cheer for Christmas. il Time 98:22 D 6 '71
Stores add up a merry selling season. il Bsns W p 18-19 Ja 1 '72
This year Santa is really packing them in. il Bsns W p24-5 D 4 '71

CHRISTMAS cactus. See Cactus

CHRISTMAS cake. See Cake

CHRISTMAS cards
Anthony Saris: variations on an angel's theme. N. Meglin. il Am Artist 35:22-5 D '71
Christmas & note cards produced by libraries. R. Bartnofsky. il Wilson Lib Bul 46:248-55 N '71
Christmas card syndrome. S. K. Johnson. il N Y Times Mag p38-9+ D 5 '71; Discussion. p 15 D 26 '71
Christmascardmanship. Sci Am 224:48 Mr '71
No trees destroyed: Recycled paper products co. of Chicago. McCalls 99:46-7 D '71
Sociology of Christmas cards. S. K. Johnson. Trans-Action 8:27-9 Ja '71
Surprise! Holiday greetings; samples of cards you'd expect to get from famous folks. D. Carlinsky. il Seventeen 30:98-9 D '71
Ways to reuse Christmas cards and decorations. Good H 173:169 D '71

CHRISTMAS carols
Poets at Bethlehem. N. Braybrooke. Chr Cent 88:1497-8 D 22 '71

CHRISTMAS cookery
Christmas as you like it. il Redbook 138:110-18 D '71
Christmas cookbook. Redbook 138:119-26 D '71
Christmas cookbook. il Am Home 74:67-74 D '71
Christmas foods from many lands. Z. Coulson. il Good H 173:76-91 D '71
Cook it now for holiday giving; for holiday eating. il Redbook 138:118-22+ N '71
Fast and fancy holiday desserts il Bet Hom & Gard 49:81-2 D '71
Here come the holidays! with recipes. Z. Coulson. il Good H 179:126-41 N '71
Holiday heirloom recipes. E. W. Manning. il Farm J 95:36-7+ D '71
Merry eating & drinking; with menus and recipes. H. McCully. il House B 113:67-9+ D '71

CHRISTMAS cookery—*Continued*
Treasury of Christmas recipes. D. Eby and J. McCloskey. il Bet Hom & Gard 49:42-51+ D '71
See also
Christmas dinners
Christmas meals
Cookery, Ornamental

CHRISTMAS cookies. See Cookies

CHRISTMAS decorations
American family Christmas. E. D. Craster. il Bet Hom & Gard 49:54-71+ D '71
Beautiful Christmas you make yourself. il House & Gard 140:42-9 D '71
Christmas as you like it. il Redbook 138:110-18 D '71
Easy instant decorating. H. Brown. il Am Home 74:80 N '71
Easy-to-make posies to trim your tree. V. P. Guild. il Good H 1773:132+ D '71
Five for Christmas. il Farm J 95:34-5 D '71
Gonfalons. il Sunset 147:70-3 D '71
Holiday decorations that cost practically nothing to make. il Pop Mech 136:136-8 D '71
Just dowels and popcorn wool; wooden lambs. il Sunset 147:110 D '71
Lighting up in safety. il McCalls 99:52 D '71
Ornaments made from cornstarch. il Sunset 147:109 D '71
Rooms ready for celebrating. il House & Gard 140:50-61 D '71
Still with us: popcorn strings. il Sunset 147:96 D '71
Welcome to Williamsburg for Christmas. il Horticulture 49:30-3 D '71
Wrap up your holiday home with warmth & festivity. L. Grundy. il House B 113:49-58 D '71
See also
Christmas projects
Christmas trees
Christmas wreaths

CHRISTMAS decorations, Outdoor
Christmas in the Berkshires. A. S. Bailey. il Horticulture 49:40-1 D '71
Festive lights for a famous street; North Michigan ave. in Chicago. il Am City 86:92+ D '71
Keep outdoor holiday lighting safe Good H 173:167 D '71
Outdoor decorations from mirror plastic. il Pop Mech 136:159 D '71
Santa's helper spotlights your door. il Pop Mech 136:139 D '71
This Christmas wish the world peace. W. C. Leckey. il Pop Mech 136:152-5+ N '71

CHRISTMAS desserts. See Desserts

CHRISTMAS dinners
Bountiful holiday feast; with recipes. F. M. Crawford. il Am Home 74:58-9+ D '71
Christmas dinner not complete without a sweet potato dish. il Ebony 27:158+ D '71

CHRISTMAS eve
Christmas eve picnic around the tree. il House & Gard 140:88 D '71
TRB from South Lee: memories of Christmas. New Repub 165:4 D 25 '71

CHRISTMAS gift catalogs. See Catalogs, Trade

CHRISTMAS gifts
Art: give multiples. A. Batterberry and M. Batterberry. il Harp Baz 105:72-3 D '71
Artful gift. A. Ogden. il House B 113:62-3 D '71
Arts-and-crafts-kit presents for the entire family. il Good H 173:168 D '71
Best buy gifts 1971. il Consumer Rep 36:668-72 N '71
Choose a handsome robe for him or her. A. Holmes. il Good H 173:142 D '71
Christmas as you like it. il Redbook 138:110-18 D '71
Christmas gift computer. Field & S 76:52+ D '71
Christmas shopping guide. il Am Artist 35:12-14 D '71
Editorial: gifts for gardeners. C. B. Lees. Horticulture 49:20 D '71
Fashion gifts, up to $5 and under $10. il Good H 173:100-1 D '71
For Christmas gifts that are different. il Changing T 25:6 N '71
41 marvelous make it yourself gifts. il Good H 173:154-8+ N '71
Fragrant decorations and presents of herbs and spices. il House & Gard 140:87+ D '71
GH's bright-idea gift list. il Good H 173:20+ D '71
GH's famous gift list. il Good H 173:14+ N '71
Gala presents. il House & Gard 140:110-21 N '71
Get ready in November to give in December. F. Henle. Harp Baz 105:130-1 N '71

Gift baskets. il Good H 173:116-17 D '71
Gift guide. il Motor T 23:62-4+ D '71
Gift of music. il Sunset 147:62-3 D '71
Gifts to make. il House B 113:92-101+ N '71
Gifts to please the traveler. il Holiday 49:84-5 D '70
Gifts to sew. il Parents Mag 46:80 N '71
Gifts you can make. il Mlle 74:154-7 N '71
Givings; $7 to $25. il Mlle 74:158-9+ N '71
Hints for Santa's helpers. S. McBee. McCalls 99:49 D '71
Holiday for givers. E. Frances. il Ladies Home J 88:29+ D '71
It mails as a Christmas card, becomes a doll after arrival. il Sunset 147:106 N '71
Late arrivals: relax and rejoice. il Esquire 75:124-7 Ja '71
Make-it-yourself holiday gifts. H. Alpert. il Har Yrs 11:24-33 D '71
129 great gifts. il Am Home 74:50-5 D '71
Pin-money presents; pincushions to make. il Good H 173:134+ D '71
Puzzlery; toys and games for adults. S. G. Lewin. il House B 113:66 D '71
Quandary gifts. il Harp Baz 105:120-1 D '71
Redbook's guide to Christmas gifts. il Redbook 138:100-8 N '71
Ring out, sweet sound; electronic equipment. E. McDonald. il House B 113:59-61 D '71
Scents for all. il Seventeen 30:154 D '71
Sea shell pillows: needlepoint kits to give as presents. il House & Gard 140:78-9 D '71
Shopping around for gourmet gifts. il House & Gard 140:208-11 N: 150-2 D '71
Shopping around's Christmas in New York. il House & Gard 140:180-1 N '71
Silver thoughts. il House B 113:80 N '71
Stereo stocking stuffers, for under $23. R. Long. il Hi Fi 21:66-70 D '71
This Christmas; 89 ideas from the editors. il Vogue 158:124-31 N 15 '71
To coddle the ego; suggestions by a group of department store executives and designers. N. Skurka. il N Y Times Mag p40-1 D 19 '71
What's in a gift? Chr Today 16:30-1 D 3 '71
See also
Christmas projects
Food as gifts
Plants as gifts
Wine as gifts
Wrapping of packages

CHRISTMAS gifts for children
For the young beauty. T. Pavlik. il Good H 173:158 D '71
From the wood workshop a garageful of toys. il Sunset 147:114+ D '71
Give him the makings for projects il Sunset 147:64-5 D '71
Instant gifts, making Christmas child's play. il Harp Baz 105:98-9 D '71
New surge in toys that teach. il Ebony 26:114-16+ N '70
On and off the avenue (cont) New Yorker 47:109-10+ D 11 '71
100 inexpensive gifts that have pleased children for years. il Good H 173:165-7 D '71
Spirit of Christmas and Chanukah. B. Spock. Redbook 138:24+ D '71
Toys and games to give this Christmas. J. R. Cary. il Parents Mag 46:28-31 D '71
What's new in toys? il Ebony 27:135-6+ N '71
See also
Dolls
Toys

CHRISTMAS gifts for men
Christmas gift ideas for the good-looking husband. Am Home 74:26 D '71
Christmas toys for really big boys. il Mech Illus 67:68-9 D '71
For today's man. T. Pavlik. il Good H 173:141 D '71
On and off the avenue. New Yorker 47:56+ D 18 '71
What not to buy dad for his car this Christmas. A. Lee. Bet Hom & Gard 49:20+ D '71

CHRISTMAS gifts for the home
Corporate gift giving. N. Hazelton. Nat R 23:992+ S 10 '71
Gifts for up-to-date living. L. Chapman. il Good H 173:144-5+ N '71
Gifts you couldn't give before. N. Craig. il House B 113:80-2 D '71
Great house gifts. il House & Gard 140:133-5 N '71
Holiday-timed gifts for the home. J. Randolph. il Parents Mag 46:49-51 N '71
More small wonders. N. Schram. il House B 113:47-8 D '71
On and off the avenue (cont) New Yorker 47:145-8+ D 4 '71

CHRISTMAS gifts for women
Beauty & the bath. S. Lindsay. il House B 113:74+ N '71

CHRISTMAS gifts for women—*Continued*
Beauty wrap-up. P. Van Wagenen. il Parents Mag 46:34 D '71
Gentleman's guide to giving the swell smells. R. Warfield. House & Gard 140:24+ D '71
Glamour gifts for her T. Pavlik. il Good H 173:150 D '71
Instant gifts. il Harp Baz 105:84-7 D '71
On and off the avenue (cont) New Yorker 47: 157-68+ N 27 '71

CHRISTMAS greens
Greens from the forest. N. Smith. il Nat Wildlife 10:16 D '71
See also
Christmas decorations
Christmas trees
Holly

CHRISTMAS lighting. See Christmas decorations

CHRISTMAS lights
Control
See Electric lighting—Control

CHRISTMAS literature, Childrens. See Childrens literature

CHRISTMAS meals
Christmas eve supper with friends; with recipes. House B 113:70-1 D '71
Great entertaining, buffet style; with recipes. Z. Coulson. il Good H 173:102-15 D '71
See also
Christmas dinners

CHRISTMAS message; story. See Keats, E. J.

CHRISTMAS pageants. See Pageants

CHRISTMAS parties. See Entertaining

CHRISTMAS plays
Texts
Nurnberg stove; dramatization of story by L. De La Ramée. H. L. Howard. Plays 31: 35-43 D '71
Reindeer on the roof; reprint from December 1952 issue. M. Hark and N. McQueen. Plays 31:45-57, 95 D '71
Room for a King. G. DuBois. Plays 31:13-22, 44 D '71
That time of year. H. Cable. Plays 31:23-30, 44 D '71
Three little kittens' Christmas. J. S. Christmas. Plays 31:73-6, 88 D '71
Twelve days of Christmas; drama. D. G. Wright. Plays 31:77-80, 95 D '71

CHRISTMAS poetry
C. S. Lewis on the meaning of Christmas; excerpts from Mere Christianity, ed. by K. Futch. C. S. Lewis. Chr Today 16:10+ D 17 '71
Christmas medley. L. Lewisohn. Good H 173: 38 D '71
Day after Christmas. B. Jacobson. Chr Today 16:9 D 17 '71
Poem for Christmas. R. D. Carignan. Horn Bk 47:585 D '71
Poems for Christmas. America 125:558-9 D 25 '71
Xmas: and it came to pass. Chr Cent 88: 1490 D 22 '71

CHRISTMAS poinsettia. See Poinsettias

CHRISTMAS presents. See Christmas gifts

CHRISTMAS projects
Christmas crafts. il Parents Mag 46:22-3 N '71
Santa and the summer rotisserie. M. B. Green, jr. il Design 73:24-7 Wint '71
Special joy: family traditions. il House B 113:6+ D '71

CHRISTMAS puddings. See Puddings

CHRISTMAS shopping
See also
Christmas business

CHRISTMAS stamps. See Postage stamps

CHRISTMAS stockings. See Christmas decorations

CHRISTMAS stories
Come let us adore him. S. Lardner. il Seventeen 30:102-3 D '71
Gifts of joy. P. S. Buck. il Good H 173: 66-7 D '71
Good king. N. Babbitt. il Redbook 138:74-6 D '71
Holy Child is everywhere. J. Wahtera. il Redbook 138:161-83 D '71
Joyful noises. E. Ibbotson. il Redbook 138: 80-1 D '71
Lost angel. E. Goudge. il Ladies Home J 88: 98-9 D '71
Merry Christmas, Mary Kay. M. J. Amft. il Seventeen 29:114-15 D '70
Mr Lawrence. G. Munson. il Seventeen 29: 126-7 D '70
Surprising stranger. F. J. Soman. il Good H 173:70-1 D '71

Troubadours. P. D. Boles. il Seventeen 30:96-7 D '71
Young girl's heart. L. Dowty. il Good H 173:92-3 D '71

CHRISTMAS stories, Childrens. See Childrens stories

CHRISTMAS story writing. See Short story

CHRISTMAS suppers. See Christmas meals

CHRISTMAS table decoration. See Table decoration

CHRISTMAS table setting. See Table setting

CHRISTMAS tree ornaments. See Christmas decorations

CHRISTMAS tree stands
If you have a spare spare. il Sunset 147:100 D '71

CHRISTMAS trees
Choosing and caring for Christmas trees. il Bet Hom & Gard 49:38-9 D '71
Christmas time with Willie; holiday safety. il Consumer Bul 54:13-14 D '71
Christmas tree as a symbol. C. A. Connaughton. Am For 77:9 D '71
Christmas tree for the White House. J. D. Boyd. il Farm J 95:27 D '71
Christmas trees in America. M. K. Koelling and J. J. Kielbaso. il Horticulture 49:24-7+ D '71
Environments. M. Emmerling. Mlle 74:167 D '71
Good old Monterey pine, why not? il Sunset 147:76-8 D '71
Grow-and-cut your own Christmas trees. H. Kline. il pors Har Yrs 11:46-9 Ja '71
How to keep life in your Christmas tree. E. McDonald. House B 113:150 D '71
Live tree for Christmas. M. Franz. il Org Gard & Farm 18:116-18 D '71
Living Christmas trees. il Sunset 147:190-1 D '71
Living tree. il House B 113:43 D '71
Living tree comes indoors. il Sunset 147:200 D '71
Plastic trees are sprouting fast. il Bsns W p35 D 11 '71
Recycling of the greens. B. Gilford. il Org Gard & Farm 18:74-5 D '71
Tiny table trees from Christmas trimmings. J. G. Bowman. il Horticulture 49:38-9 D '71
Trimmed to perfection, a tiny tree under glass. il House & Gard 140:86 D '71
What you should know when buying a Christmas tree. il Good H 173:171 D '71

CHRISTMAS window displays. See Show windows

CHRISTMAS wrappings. See Wrapping of packages

CHRISTMAS wreaths
Bright wreath of peppers and chiles. il Sunset 147:131 D '71
It's time to think Christmas. H. A. Kline. il Home Gard 58:41 D '71

CHRISTO
Curtain time. il por Newsweek 78:37-8 O 18 '71 *

CHRISTOLOGY. See Jesus Christ

CHRISTOUT, Marie Françoise
Béjart's Nijinsky: Clown of God; tr. by N. M. Stoop. il Dance Mag 45:34-41 D '71

CHRISTY, Gale D.
Make it show leadership. il Am City 86:83 Mr '71

CHROMATIDS. See Chromosomes

CHROMATIN
Heterochromatin, satellite DNA, and cell function. J. J. Yunis and W. G. Yasmineh. bibliog il Science 174:1200-9 D 17 '71
Polymorphism of human constitutive heterochromatin. A. P. Craig-Holmes and M. W. Shaw. bibliog il Science 174:702-4 N 12 '71

CHROMATOGRAPHIC analysis
Countercurrent chromatography with flow-through coil planet centrifuge. Y. Ito and R. L. Bowman. bibliog il Science 173:420-2 Jl 30 '71
Enzymes bound to artificial matrixes. K. Mosbach. il Sci Am 224:32-3 bibliog(p 124) Mr '71
Frontal analysis in chromatography. W. Husain. il por Chem 44:25 D '71
Lab bench; markers for chromatography. V. Heines. il por Chem 44:25 N '71
Marihuana: identification of cannabinoids by centrifugal chromatography. D. G. Petcoff and others. bibliog il Science 173:824-6 Ag 27 '71

CHROMATOPHORES
See also
Melanophores

CHROMIUM ores
Chrome plated blunder. New Repub 165:7 N 27 '71
Why the U.S. ban on chrome was lifted. il Bsns W p23 N 27 '71

CHROMIUM plating
Chromium plating on plastics. N. R. Roobol. il por Chem 44:10-13 N '71

CHROMO lithographs. See Lithographs

CHROMOSOMES
Acetylsalicylic acid: no chromosome damage in human leukocytes. I. Mauer and others; discussion. bibliog Science 171:829-30 F 26 '71

Add six years to your life; sulfur compounds to combat free radicals. il Sci Digest 70:76-7 D '71

Chromatid breakage: cytosine arabinoside-induced lesions inhibited by ultraviolet irradiation. W. F. Benedict and M. Karon. bibliog il Science 171:680-2 F 19 '71

Chromosome lesions produced with an argon laser microbeam without dye sensitization. M. W. Berns and others. bibliog il Science 171:903-5 Mr 5 '71

DNA constancy in heteroploidy and the stem line theory of tumors. P. M. Kraemer and others. bibliog il Science 174:714-17 N 12 '71

Epithelial origin of polyoma salivary tumors in mice: evidence based on chromosome-marked cells. C. J. Dawe and others. bibliog il Science 171:394-7 Ja 29 '71

Height and antisocial behavior in XY and XYY boys. E. B. Hook and D. S. Kim. bibliog il Science 172:284-6 Ap 16 '71

Human thymidine kinase gene locus: assignment to chromosome 17 in a hybrid of man and mouse cells. O. J. Miller and others. bibliog il Science 173:244-5 Jl 16 '71

Identification of each human chromosome with a modified Giemsa stain. S. R. Patil and others. bibliog il Science 173:821-2 Ag 27 '71

LSD and genetic damage. N. I. Dishotsky and others. bibliog il Science 172:431-40 Ap 30 '71

Linkage group-chromosome correlation in culex tritaeniorhynchus. R. H. Baker and others. bibliog il Science 171:585-7 F 12 '71

Linkage groups II and XII of the mouse: cytological localization by fluorochrome staining. M. Nesbitt and U. Francke. bibliog il Science 174:60-2 O 1 '71

Mapping of human chromosomes. V. A. McKusick. il Sci Am 224:104-13 Ap '71

Scanning electron microscopic observations of surface structure of isolated human chromosomes. H. M. Golomb and G. F. Bahr. bibliog il Science 171:1024-6 Mr 12 '71

Sorting out chromosomes; use of Giemsa stain. il Sci N 100:200 S 25 '71

Speculative model for cell biology. il Sci N 100:324 N 13 '71
See also
Chromatin
Linkage (genetics)

CHROMOSOMES (botany)
Multiple genotypes in individuals of Claytonia virginica. W. H. Lewis and others. bibliog il Science 172:564-5 My 7 '71

CHRONIN, Jack
Lifeline for a man with a dying heart. E. Gore. il pors Life 70:51-4+ F 5 '71 *

CHRONOLOGY, Biblical. See Bible—Chronology

CHRYSANTHEMUMS
Air pollution and chrysanthemums. R. C. Bonham. il Horticulture 49:30-1 O '71

Chrysanthemums in Japan. L. Greene. il Horticulture 49:26+ N '71

Miraculous mums. il Home Gard 58:21 Ag '71

CHRYSLER corporation
Chrysler reshuffles to whittle costs. il Bsns W p25-6 Ja 16 '71

Detroit gets a toe in Japanese waters. il Bsns W p36 Je 19 '71

How Chrysler fights a skid. il Bsns W p72-3+ Ap 17 '71

Unexpected cut in Chrysler's prime rate. Bsns W p34 Mr 27 '71

CHU, Franklin D.
Afghanistan is a land that answers to dreams. il Travel 136:40-5 N '71

CHUBB, Dell
Maia Wojciechowska: controversial and committed. Writer 84:21 Ap '71

CHUBB and son, inc.
Chubb's conservatism. A. Hershman. Duns 98:58 N '71

CHUCK hunting. See Woodchuck hunting

CHUCKS
Carriage chuck mount for your lathe. W. E. Burton. il Pop Mech 136:60 N '71

CHUI, Lim-ming
How to play ping-pong like a Chinese champ. il pors Esquire 76:122-7 N '71

CHUKOVSKII, Kornei Ivanovich
Confessions of an old story-teller; tr. by L. G. Leighton (cont) il por Horn Bk 47:28-39 F '71

CHUMLEY, John Wesley
Lyric brush of John Chumley. O. Findsen. il por Am Artist 35:30-5+ Je '71 *

CHURCH, Frank
Farewell to foreign aid; address, October 29. 1971. Vital Speeches 38:66-73 N 15 '71; Same abr. New Repub 165:14-17 N 13 '71

Impounding congressional policy. Nation 213:519-20 N 22 '71

Senator Church views the conference; interview. pors Har Yrs 11:9-12 N '71

CHURCH, Ron
Deepstar explores the ocean floor. il por Nat Geog 139:110-29 Ja '71

CHURCH
Christians and tomorrow's world. H. B. Kuhn. Chr Today 15:38-9 Jl 16 '71
See also
Christianity
Mission of the church
Women and the church

Authority

Authority and conscience. A. T. Padovano. il Cath World 213:79-82 My '71

Authority and rebellion, by C. E. Rice. Review
Nat R 23:1182-3 O 22 '71. W. Herberg

Authority. Protestantus. Cath World 213:146-7 Je '71

Conserving the faith; Pope Paul on the function of theologians. Chr Today 15:35 F 12 '71

Does God speak through men? G. C. Berkouwer. Chr Today 15:57-8 F 12 '71

Infallibility fight. pors Newsweek 77:57 Ja 25 '71

My conscience is bound by the word of God; thoughts on Luther, address, April 17, 1971. C. L. Manschreck. bibliog Vital Speeches 37:540-4 Je 15 '71

On the rise of demotheology. R. S. Tapp. Chr Cent 88:153-6 F 3 '71

Survival of dogma, by A. Dulles. Review
Commonweal 95:45-7 O 8 '71. G. MacRae
See also
Popes—Primacy

History
See also
Catholic church—History

Mission
See Mission of the church

Purpose
See Mission of the church

CHURCH, Negro. See Negroes—Religion

CHURCH and education
See also
Church schools
Public schools and religion

CHURCH and international relations
Burying an epoch of ecumenical politics. J. Hilke. Chr Cent 88:493-5 Ap 21 '71 Reply. A. R. Booth. 88:729-30 Je 9 '71

Mission eastern Europe: toward a new agenda. C. C. West. Chr Cent 89:13-15 Ja 5 '72
See also
Catholic church—Relations (diplomatic)—United Nations
United Nations—Non-governmental organizations

CHURCH and labor
As churches strive for relevancy; study program on collective bargaining at St John college, Cleveland. B. L. Masse. America 124:604 Je 12 '71
See also
Chaplains, Industrial

CHURCH and politics
ABC: Assy, Bonhoeffer, Carswell. R. M. Brown. il Chr Cent 88:369-71 Mr 24 '71

Bearing the burden of the Berrigan brothers. E. Duff. New Repub 164:18-23 Mr 6 '71

Christianity recrudescent? D. K. Mano. Nat R 23:1452 D 31 '71

Churches' role in Washington. E. F. Snyder. Chr Cent 88:69-71 Ja 20 '71

Confronting church lobbyists. Chr Today 16:32 N 5 '71

John Lindsay looks at the church; interview, ed. by T. Early. J. Lindsay. Chr Cent 88:400-3 Mr 31 '71

Politics and conscience; views of M. O. Hatfield and J. B. Anderson. por Time 98:80 S 27 '71
See also
Center for the study of power and peace
Church and international relations

CHURCH and race problems
Angela and the Presbyterians. Chr Cent 88:823 Jl 7 '71; Discussion. 88:979-80 Ag 18 '71
Black government aide denounces church retreat on civil rights. Chr Cent 88:851 Jl 14 '71
Black theology of James Cone. R. Ruether. por Cath World 214:18-20 O '71
Blacks and COCU: a new honesty. C. Rogers; reply. F. Mulkey. Chr Cent 88: 136 Ja 27 '71
Must our churches finance revolution? C. W. Hall. Read Digest 99:95-100 O '71; Reply. Chr Cent 88:1219 O 20 '71
Pursuit of souls: betrayal of soul. J. T. Ryan. Cath World 212:245-8 F '71
Skirmish among Catholics; Cairo, Ill. racial tensions. J. Deedy. Commonweal 93:511 F 26 '71
Tale of two cities. H. H. Mitchell and E. S. O'Neal. Chr Cent 88:156-8 F 3 '71; Reply. C. D. Tripp. 88:379+ Mr 24 '71
Through different spectacles; WWC grants. J. D. Douglas. Chr Today 15:45-6 Mr 26 '71
Your God is too white, by C. Salley and R. Behm. Review
    Chr Today 15:26-8 Je 18 '71. J. S. Tinney
    See also
Interreligious foundation for community organization

CHURCH and race problems in Rhodesia
Rubbish problem in Rhodesia; Catholic stance on multiracial schools. America 124:220 Mr 6 '71

CHURCH and race problems in South Africa
Apartheid: condemned by resolutions, aided by inaction. C. Rogers. Chr Cent 88:921-2 Ag 4 '71
Cut it out; trial of G. A. Ffrench-Beytagh. por Newsweek 78:40+ Ag 16 '71
South Africa: sanctioning U.S. business? Chr Today 15:47-8 S 24 '71
South African Christian confronts apartheid. M. Cassidy. Chr Today 16:3-6 N 19 '71

CHURCH and social problems
Bearing the burden of the Berrigan brothers. E. Duff. New Repub 164:18-23 Mr 6 '71
Can Christians aid violence? P. J. Riga. il Cath World 212:232-6 F '71
Church alive and changing: southern California suburbs. J. C. Hough, jr. il Chr Cent 89:8-12 Ja 5 '72
Discerning power realities; interview. ed. by S. C. Rose. S. Alinsky. por Chr Cent 88: 622-6 My 19 '71
Get ready for economics! Chr Cent 88:451 Ap 14 '71
Lord's commands to a congressman. W. R. Anderson. Chr Cent 88:182-3 F 10 '71
Might the synod surprise? H. ten Kortenaar. Commonweal 95:4-5 O 1 '71
New "encyclical" on social justice. P. P. McDermott. por Chr Cent 88:748-51 Je 16 '71
New politics for Christians; address. R. Tucci. America 125:112-16 S 4 '71
New turn on campus, the Christian commune. J. F. Conway. America 124:479-81 My 8 '71; Reply. G. A. Buckley. 124:621 Je 19 '71
On being a Catholic; experience of a priest and a woman looking back. J. Barthel. il pors Life 70:55-60+ Ap 30 '71
On the rise of demotheology. R. B. Tapp. Chr Cent 88:153-6 F 3 '71
Politics of the kingdom of God. R. Stone. Chr Cent 88:337-40 Mr 17 '71
Pope Paul's letter. Commonweal 94:299-300 Je 11 '71
Pope Pius XI on rebuilding the social order; Rerum novarum and Quadragesimo anno. B. L. Masse. America 124:559 My 29 '71
Primeau on pulpits; socio-political questions. E. Primeau. Commonweal 95:74 O 22 '71
Public policy making: why the churches strike out. V. C. Blum. America 124:224-8 Mr 6 '71; Discussion. 124:348-9 Ap 3 '71
Quadragesimo anno: forty years after. J. R. Jennings. il America 125:208-10 S 25 '71
Religious education-community. G. Moran. America 124:86-9 Ja 30 '71; Discussion. 124: 189 F 27 '71
Revolution through peace, by D. H. Camara. Review
    America 125:158-9 S 11 '71. J. C. Hawley
Scripture sanctioned revolution. V. Fiddes. Chr Today 15:16 My 21 '71
Should churches use their funds to force social change? il U S News 71:71-2 S 20 '71
Social reform: an evangelical imperative. C. Thompson. Chr Today 15:8-12 Mr 26 '71
Un-service station. D. M. Kelley. Chr Cent 88:799-801 Je 30 '71

Urgency of doing justice. C. T. McIntire. Chr Today 15:22-4+ S 24 '71
Worldaround. See issues of Christian century continuing New Christian
    See also
Church and labor
Church and politics
Church and race problems
Church work with homosexuals
Interreligious foundation for community organization
Social action
Sociology, Christian

Great Britain
Man of vision; the case of Nicolas Stacey. T. Beeson. Chr Cent 88:825-6 Jl 7 '71
Public ministry in a London suburb; Roundshaw experiment. D. Jones. Chr Cent 88: 1309-10 N 3 '71

Latin America
Modest proposal; church's wealth and Cardinal Maurer. Commonweal 95:2 O 1 '71
Theology of revolution for the third world. A. Pérez-Esclarin. il Cath World 213:277-82 S '71

Philippines
Filipino voice for justice echoes in Manila. America 124:190 F 27 '71
Social action in the P.I. America 125:359 N 6 '71

Puerto Rico
Issue of the Puerto Rican copper mines. R. W. Gillett. Chr Cent 88:857-9 Jl 14 '71

CHURCH and state
Churches' role in Washington. E. F. Snyder. Chr Cent 88:69-71 Ja 20 '71
Growing church lobby in Washington, by J. L. Adams. Review
    Chr Cent 88:76-7 Ja 20 '71. J. M. Swomley, jr
New confusion on church-state school issue. R. H. Smith. Pub W 200:33 Jl 5 '71
Religion and education: cooperation or conflict? G. A. Kizer. bibliog Sch & Soc 99: 152-6 Mr '71
    See also
Catholic schools
Church property
Public schools and religion

CHURCH and state in Bolivia
Theology of the coup d'etat? J. Algeria. Commonweal 95:340-1 Ja 14 '72

CHURCH and state in Brazil
Dom Helder Camara as a symbolic man. B. Tyson. Cath World 213:178-82, 235-9 Jl-Ag '71

CHURCH and state in Cambodia
Church and state in Cambodia; important role of Buddhism. J. C. Haughey. il America 125:279-81 O 16 '71

CHURCH and state in Colombia
Angelic rhetoric; reactions to Pastrana's statement. J. Deedy. Commonweal 95:122 N 5 '71
Colombia's church-state rite denounced by Catholic churchmen. S. Bliss and E. Holsteyn. Chr Cent 88:1178 O 6 '71

CHURCH and state in Finland
Church-state separation proposed in Finland. Chr Cent 88:1224 O 20 '71

CHURCH and state in France
French hierarchy resists government interference. A. Woodrow. Chr Cent 88:227 F 17 '71

CHURCH and state in Germany (Federal Republic)
    See also
Church tax—Germany (Federal Republic)

CHURCH and state in Guatemala
Matter of conscience. il por Newsweek 78:127 O 25 '71

CHURCH and state in Ireland
Ireland: church-state tensions over education. J. Horgan. Chr Cent 88:469 Ap 14 '71
Ireland's rocky road to pluralism. T. P. O'Mahony. il America 124:513-16 My 15 '71

CHURCH and state in Italy
Roman question and Italian politics. P. M. Spoletini. il America 124:336-40 Ap 3 '71

CHURCH and state in Jamaica
Free to be itself; disestablishment of the Church of England in the West Indies. G. D. Everett. Chr Today 15:33 Je 18 '71

CHURCH and state in Latin America
Latin America's own work corps: 180,000 religious. J. F. Talbot. il America 124:343-4 Ap 3 '71

CHURCH and state in Malta
Elections in Malta. C. Cardona. America 124: 609-10 Je 12 '71

CHURCH and state in Norway
Attack Norwegian state church. Chr Cent 88: 1224 O 20 '71

CHURCH and state in Paraguay
Distaff thugs in Paraguay. America 124:396 Ap 17 '71
Paranoid Paraguay. J. Deedy. Commonweal 94:204 My 7 '71
Peril in Paraguay. J. Deedy. Commonweal 94:98 Ap 9 '71

CHURCH and state in Portugal
Rome and colonialism; the protesting missionaries in Mozambique. W. Triggs. Chr Cent 88:824-5 Jl 7 '71

CHURCH and state in Rhodesia
Church-state countdown in Rhodesia. A. J. Jolson. America 124:481-3 My 8 '71
Hard dilemma in Rhodesia. America 124:395 Ap 17 '71
Rhodesia: the church hesitant. E. McCarthy. Commonweal 93:460-1 F 12 '71

CHURCH and state in Russia
See also
Orthodox Eastern church, Russian

CHURCH and state in South Africa
Crackdown in South Africa. il Time 97:42 Mr 22 '71
South Africa wracked by conflict between state, liberal clergy. J. Squire. Chr Cent 88: 406-7 Mr 31 '71

CHURCH and state in Spain
Reins in Spain: Le Monde interview; excerpts. C. Just. Commonweal 93:386 Ja 22 '71
Slap in the face for Franco. A. Woodrow. Commonweal 95:100-1 O 29 '71
Turnabout in Spain. Newsweek 78:102 S 27 '71

CHURCH and state in Sweden
Sweden faces church-state, ecumenical problems. J. E. Wikström. Chr Cent 88:258-9 F 24 '71

CHURCH and state in the Netherlands
Dutch pillar system still stands. H. Biersteker. Chr Cent 88:759 Je 16 '71

CHURCH and state in Uganda
Coup in Uganda; church divided. J. H. Okullu. Chr Cent 88:278 Mr 3 '71

CHURCH and the press
Forever fascinating; condition of the American episcopacy. S. J. Adamo. America 125: 292-3 O 16 '71
See also
Vatican and the press

CHURCH and the world
Call for authority in the Christian community; address. P. L. Berger. Chr Cent 88: 1257-63 O 27 '71; Reply. J. Deedy. Commonweal 95:170 N 19 '71
Death of relevance. Time 98:64 O 11 '71
Dreams of a third age. H. O. J. Brown. Chr Today 15:3-5 Jl 16 '71
Expansive man and the church of the '70s. G. B. Noyce. Chr Cent 88:1377-9 N 24 '71
Geolatry, topolatry and chronolatry. E. M. von Kuehnelt-Leddihn. Cath World 212: 237-9 F '71
Wisdom, cry out! T. E. Clarke. il America 125:151-2 S 11 '71

CHURCH architecture
First Unitarian church of Richmond, Virginia. il Arch Rec 150:108-9 Jl '71
Saint Mary's cathedral, San Francisco. E. K. Thompson. Arch Rec 150:113-20 S '71
Suburban church: St Thomas Aquinas church, St Paul Park, Minn. il Arch Forum 134:60-2 Je '71
Three religious buildings. il Arch Rec 149: 111-16 Je '71
See also
Chapels
Mosques

Philosophy
Environmental workbook on church space. B. Rogers. il Chr Cent 88:948-51 Ag 11 '71

CHURCH attendance
Electric chimes or rams' horns; reprint. A. N. Wilder. Chr Cent 88:103 Ja 27 '71
Mass every Sunday? support from H. Küng. J. Deedy. Commonweal 95:266 D 17 '71

CHURCH camps
See also
Christian camping international

CHURCH colleges
Are Christian colleges worth the trouble? C. G. Fry. Chr Today 15:6-10 F 12 '71
Campus unrest; address, February 19, 1971. A. R. Cecil. bibliog Vital Speeches 37:340-5 Mr 15 '71
Evangelical colleges plan consortium. D. Kucharsky. il Chr Today 15:44-5 Ap 9 '71
Faith-affirming colleges; future of evangelical colleges. C. F. H. Henry. Chr Today 15:32-3 My 7 '71
Shall the Christian colleges die? Chr Today 15:33 My 21 '71

What's new: Christian higher education. Chr Today 15:44-5 S 24 '71
See also
Bob Jones university, Greenville, S.C.
Lubbock Christian college, Lubbock, Tex.
Shelton college, Cape May, N.J.

Federal aid
School aid decisions. C. M. Whelan. America 125:8-11 Jl 10 '71
Will churches give up their colleges? C. S. Lowell. Ed Digest 37:24-5 O '71

Finance
Crisis in Christian education. F. E. Gaebelein. Chr Today 15:4-7 My 21 '71

CHURCH decoration and ornament
See also
Altar pieces

CHURCH facilities
Planning
Environmental workbook on church space. B. Rogers. il Chr Cent 88:948-51 Ag 11 '71

CHURCH finance
Churches and their portfolios. America 124: 219 Mr 6 '71
Conscience and the portfolios. Time 97:57 F 15 '71
Corporate critics gain new allies; church investments. Bsns W p29 F 13 '71
Issue of the Puerto Rican copper mines; implications for American churches in aiding Third world development. R. W. Gillett. Chr Cent 88:857-9 Jl 14 '71
Money squeeze tightens on U.S. churches. il U S News 70:42-4 F 8 '71
Pacifist portfolios? investments in companies with defense contracts. il Time 99: 52 Ja 17 '72
Portfolio power. Chr Today 15:22 Je 18 '71
Should churches use their funds to force social change? il U S News 71:71-2 S 20 '71
See also
Catholic church—Finance
Church property

CHURCH going. See Church attendance

CHURCH government
See also
Catholic church—Government

CHURCH history
Ecumenical "if"; Council of Trent and letter of Diego Lainez. C. J. McNaspy. il America 124:655-6 Je 26 '71
Emergence of the Catholic tradition (100-600) by J. Pelikan. Review Newsweek 78:62 S 6 '71

Bibliography
Books on church history and theology, 1970. G. W. Bromiley. Chr Today 15:4-6 F 26 '71

Middle ages
Christian-Islamic confrontation in the west: the thirteenth-century drama of conversion. R. I. Burns. bibliog f il Am Hist R 76: 1386-434 D '71

CHURCH history, Hypothetical
Sending parable; if St Paul had traveled east to the Orient instead of west. J. Gillies. Chr Cent 88:253-6 F 24 '71

CHURCH libraries. See Libraries, Church

CHURCH lobby. See Lobbyists

CHURCH lobbying. See Lobbying

CHURCH membership
Membership plateaus. Chr Today 15:36 Mr 26 '71
ZPG in the churches. Newsweek 77:96 Mr 15 '71
See also
Confirmation

CHURCH models
Sharing his hobbies has made thousands happy; O. M. Tand, of Tavares, Fla. S. A. Parvin. il Hobbies 76:140-1 My '71

CHURCH music
At the corner of Glory avenue and Hallelujah street; concert of white gospel music. W. C. Martin. Harper 244:95-9 Ja '72
Memoirs of Dr William Boyce. G. Beechey. bibliog f il por Mus Q 57:87-106 Ja '71
Real thing; All nite soul at St Peter's Lutheran church, N.Y. M. E. Marty. Chr Cent 88:1311 N 3 '71
Shape of church music in the '70s. C. F. Schalk; reply. B. Gluskin. Chr Cent 88: 194 F 10 '71
Stravinsky's sacred music. R. Thibodeau. il Commonweal 94:384-5 Jl 23 '71
See also
Choirs
Hymns
Mass (music)
Phonograph records—Church music
Religion and music

CHURCH of England
Can the Church of England be renewed? E. James. Chr Cent 88:313-15 Mr 10 '71
Dismal synod at York. T. Beeson. Chr Cent 88:920-1 Ag 4 '71
Pummeling the prelates. J. D. Douglas. Chr Today 15:51-2 S 24 '71
Showing who's boss; Ramsey at general synod. J. D. Douglas. Chr Today 15:40-1 Mr 26 '71
See also
Anglican consultative council
Catholic church—Relations—Church of England
Church union—Great Britain
Marriage—Church of England

Articles of religion
Curious anniversary; Thirty-nine articles. G. W. Bromiley. Chr Today 16:5-6 O 22 '71

Clergy
Clergy misdemeanors. T. Beeson. Chr Cent 88:213 F 17 '71
Urban training, English style; Urban ministry project. R. H. Luecke. Chr Cent 88:1348-51 N 17 '71

CHURCH of England in Canada
New Canadian hymnal brings Anglican-UCC union a step closer. G. Lane. Chr Cent 89:18-19 Ja 5 '72

CHURCH of England in South Africa
Church leaders hail Anglican stand in South Africa. Chr Cent 88:1440 D 8 '71
Outside critics polarize opinion. J. Squire. Chr Cent 88:883-5 Jl 21 '71

CHURCH of God
Assemblies' line; Assemblies of God. J. S. Tinney. Chr Today 15:45-6 S 10 '71

CHURCH of Jesus Christ of Latter-day saints. See Mormons and Mormonism

CHURCH of Scotland
War and the kirk. J. D. Douglas. Chr Today 15:30 Je 18 '71

CHURCH of the Brethren
Brethren conference takes some steps, defers others. O. D. Mitchell. Chr Cent 88:1005-6 Ag 25 '71

CHURCH property
Property and propriety; Good Shepherd Baptist church legal scrape with Wisconsin Evangelical Lutheran synod. Chr Cent 88:731 Je 9 '71; Reply. R. G. Doll. 88:865 Jl 14 '71

Taxation
Baptist parking lot case; Diffenderfer v. Central Baptist church of Miami. T. M. Gannon. il America 125:480-1 D 4 '71
Pivotal parking lot. D. Kucharsky. il Chr Today 16:42 Ja 7 '72

CHURCH-related colleges. See Church colleges
CHURCH related schools. See Church schools
CHURCH renewal
Christianity and change. G. O'Collins. America 124:264 Mr 13 '71
Modesty is the best policy. Chr Cent 88:1015 S 1 '71
New face for the church, by O. Richards. Review
Chr Today 15:28 Mr 26 '71. N. H. West
Reform of church, by D. G. Bloesch. Review
Commonweal 93:404 Ja 22 71. R. P. McBrien
Second chance for the neo-orthodox. J. P. Crossley. jr. Chr Cent 88:1048-51 S 8 '71
See also
Mission of the church

Catholic church
Aggiornamento has failed; excerpt from The decline and fall of radical Catholicism. J. Hitchcock. Commonweal 94:231-5 My 14 '71; Discussion. 94:228, 299+, 323+ My 11, Je 11, 25 '71
Catechetics R.I.P. G. Moran; discussion. Commonweal 93:411+ Ja 29; 459+ F 12 '71
Catholic renewal in England. S. Bryden-Brook. Chr Cent 88:372-5 Mr 24 '71
Catholics get the spirit. E. E. Plowman. il Chr Today 15:31-2 Jl 16 '71
Church eyes future shock. T. R. Haney. America 124:174-7 F 20 '71
Day after aggiornamento. B. J. Nauer; discussion. America 124:105 F 6 '71
Ill-tempered Christians. F. Sontag. Chr Cent 88:316-17 Mr 10 '71
New vs. old, the struggle among Catholics. il U S News 71:31-3 N 1 '71
No problem for Sister Editha. America 125:108 S 4 '71
Resist your funeral. Theophilus Protestantus. Cath World 212:312 Mr '71

Tensions in a church alive. J. B. Sheerin; reply. O. R. Link. Cath World 212:285-6 Mr '71
See also
Mission of the church

CHURCH schools
Vision realized; Stony Brook school, N.Y. Chr Today 15:31 S 10 '71
See also
Catholic schools
Education and state

Federal aid
Lessons from the school aid decisions. C. M. Whelan. America 125:32-3 Jl 24 '71
Parochaid disallowed; with editorial comment. D. Kucharsky. il Chr Today 15:23, 34 Jl 16 '71
Parochaid; drawing the lines. Chr Today 15:43 S 10 '71
School aid decisions. C. M. Whelan. America 125:8-11 Jl 10 '71
School aid; shift to politics. America 124:364-5 Ap 10 '71
School aid; will Illinois find a way? four experts explore the constitutionality of such aid. P. J. Weber. America 124:534-8 My 22 '71
Supreme court cases; questions and answers. C. M. Whelan. America 124:372-5 Ap 10 '71
See also
Catholic schools—Federal aid

State aid
Aid to parochial schools. Sch & Soc 99:198+ Ap '71
Can parochial schools survive? il U S News 71:26-8 Jl 12 '71
High price of free exercise. America 125:360-1 N 6 '71
Joker in private school aid; with editorial comment. S. Arons. il Sat R 54:41, 45-7+ Ja 16 '71
Parochaid decision. L. Pfeffer. Todays Ed 60:63-4+ S '71
Parochaid, more legal turmoil ahead. Ed Digest 37:23-5 N '71
Parochial opinion; Supreme court ruling on state aid. il Newsweek 78:55 Jl 12 '71
Parochial school aid; Supreme court decision. New Repub 165:7 Jl 10 '71
Parochial school tangle; Supreme court decisions. il Sat R 54:48 Ag 21 '71
Parochial schools. Nat R 23:744 Jl 13 '71
Return to the marketplace; Michigan vote against public funds for nonpublic schools. O. J. Murdick. il America 124:565-7 My 29 '71
U.S. Supreme court as prophet; Pennsylvania and Rhode Island laws furnishing aid to church-related schools declared unconstitutional. W. W. Brickman. Sch & Soc 99:330-1 O '71

CHURCH services
Celebration, not sensation; Advent service at Southern Methodist university chapel. J. C. Evans. Chr Cent 89:4-6 Ja 5 '72
Glide to glory; Glide memorial united Methodist church. L. Robinson. il por Ebony 26:44-6+ Jl '71
Hey, pastor! L. M. Green. Chr Cent 88:126-8 Ja 27 '71
Let's put life in church services. E. E. Plowman. Chr Today 15:22-3 Mr 26; 31-2 Ap 23 '71
Life in church services. R. C. Stedman. Chr Today 15:38-9 My 21 '71
Troubadours for God; Hair mass; Manhattans's Episcopal Cathedral of St John the Divine. il Time 97:46+ My 24 '71
See also
Liturgies

Anecdotes, facetiae, satire, etc.
Beautiful lethargy. Chr Cent 88:915 Jl 28 '71
CHURCH statistics
See also
Church membership
CHURCH tax

Germany (Federal Republic)
Cutting the church's cut. Time 97:69 My 10 '71
Germany's leading publisher loses church tax suit. E. E. Turner. Chr Cent 88:980-1 Ag 18 '71
CHURCH union
Place to stand. T. Protestantus. Cath World 213:286 S '71
We're still shooting our own troops. T. Protestantus. Cath World 213:39 Ap '71
See also
Church renewal
Consultation on church union
Ecumenical movement
World council of churches

CHURCH union—*Continued*

Canada
Canadian Anglicans and United churchmen consider union. J. R. Mutchmor. Chr Cent 88:436-8 Ap 7 '71
Canadian union drive: down shifting? L. K. Tarr. Chr Today 16:43 Ja 7 '72
Cupid's dart falls short; United church and the Anglican church. L. K. Tarr. Chr Today 15:34+ F 26 '71
See also
United church of Canada

Germany (Federal Republic)
Grass-roots ecumenism sprouts at Augsburg congress. F. Lüpsen. Chr Cent 88:931-2 Ag 4 '71

Great Britain
Before the dry bones decay; Anglican-Methodist unity scheme. T. Beeson. Chr Cent 88:308-9 Mr 10 '71
England awaits the word. Chr Today 16:22 O 22 '71
English Free churches in the melting pot. B. Duckworth. Chr Cent 88:340-2 Mr 17 '71
Open letter to Archbishop Lord Fisher of Lambeth, Anglican-Methodist reunion. T. Beeson. Chr Cent 88:244-5 F 24 '71

New Zealand
Church union plans finalized. R. O'Grady. Chr Cent 88:1359 N 17 '71

United States
Liturgy for a divided household; sacrament of unity. A. P. Ware. Chr Cent 88:496-7 Ap 21 '71; Discussion. 88:730 Je 9 '71

CHURCH work
See also
Christian service corps
Church and social problems
Mass media in religion
Missions
Pastoral theology

CHURCH work with homosexuals
Church and Gay liberation. E. Wright. il Chr Cent 88:281-5 Mr 3 '71
Churches and the homosexual; San Francisco's gay community. J. A. Coleman. America 124:113-17 F 6 '71; Discussion. 124:inside cover, 273 F 6, Mr 20 '70

CHURCH work with the aged
Miami church program seeks to change image of retirement. Aging 204:15 O '71

CHURCH work with the handicapped
When clergymen help the mentally ill. Good H 172:174 Je '71

CHURCH work with tourists, travelers, etc.
Ministering to holidaymakers. T. Beeson. Chr Cent 88:768 Je 23 '71

CHURCH work with youth
Church and youth; Bishop Worlock at Isle of Wight rock festival. Commonweal 94:442 S 3 '71
See also
Coffee house ministry

CHURCHES
See also
Cathedrals
Church architecture
Country churches

Membership
See Church membership

Belgium
Hidden treasure; religious art collection of St Leonard's church, Zoutleeuw. il Time 98:46-8 D 27 '71

Cuba
Church-hopping in Havana. D. Peerman. Chr Cent 88:1435-8 D 8 '71

Italy
See also
Venice—Churches

New England
Churches receive national landmark status. G. Everett. Chr Today 15:46-7 Ap 9 '71

Rumania
Roumania: angels among the roses; painted churches of Moldavia. M. Sulzberger. Vogue 157:194 My '71

United States
Big churches? Yes and no! E. L. Towns; J. A. Davey. Chr Today 16:6-8+ N 5 '71
See also subhead Churches under names of cities, e.g. San Francisco—Churches

CHURCHES, Friend
Raising the meetinghouse in Webster, New Hampshire, 1791; excerpt from The history of Boscawen and Webster, New Hampshire. C. C. Coffin. il Antiques 100:714 N '71

CHURCHES, Suburban. See Suburban churches

CHURCHES and the United Nations. See United Nations—Non-governmental organizations

CHURCHILL, Jennie (Jerome) lady
Jennie, by R. G. Martin. Review
Atlan 228:148 N '71. E. Weeks •
Nat R il por 23:1472-3 D 31 '71. A. Bakshian, jr •
Sat R por 54:44 N 6 '71. A. Whitman •

CHURCHILL, Randolph Frederick Edward Spencer
Grand original, ed. by K. Halle. Review
Nat R 23:1360-1 D 3 '71. A. Lejeune •

CHURCHILL, Sir Winston Leonard Spencer
Winston Churchill on revolution; excerpt from Great contemporaries. Read Digest 98:195-6 F '71
about
Day the iron curtain fell. il por Sr Schol 98:18 Mr 8 '71 •
History in books. P. W. Schmidtchen. il pors Hobbies 76:134-6+ Ja '72 •
Jennie, by R. G. Martin. Review
Nat R il por 23:1472-3 D 31 '71. A. Bakshian, jr •

CHUSSIL, Yale
Teacher-administrator relations: a continuing hiatus. bibliog f Clear House 45:387-91 Mr '71

CHUTES, Cattle. See Cattle handling equipment

CHWAST, Seymour
Seymour Chwast: a Coney Island of the head. D. Preiss. il por Am Artist 35:40-5+ O '71 •

CIARDI, John
Children's corner: Man who lived in a house too big; About making speeches; Thing about a hero; poems. Sat R 54:37 F 6 '71
Children's corner; poems. Sat R 54:34 D 4 '71
Graph; poem. Sat R 54:18-19 Ap 3 '71
Manner of speaking. See occasional issues of Saturday review
Of fish and fishermen; poem. Sat R 54:23 Mr 13 '71
Open letter to the Honorable Richard Ichord. Sat R 54:14-15+ My 15 '71
about
Humanism and the Orphic voice. J. W. Hughes. il por Sat R 54:31-3 My 22 '71 •

CICADAS
Periodical cicada: mechanism of sound production. K. H. Reid. bibliog il Science 172:949-51 My 28 '71
Periodical cicada: sound production and hearing. J. A. Simmons and others. il Science 171:212-13 Ja 15 '71

CICHLIDS
Pavón paradise. A. J. McClane. il Field & S 75:49-51+ F '71

CIDER
Pressing your own cider. il Sunset 147:96-7 O '71

CIDOC. See Center of intercultural documentation

CIENFUEGOS naval base. See Navy yards and naval stations

CIGAR industry
See also
General cigar company

CIGAR store Indians. See Indians, Wooden

CIGARETTE smoking. See Smoking

CIGARETTE smoking and youth. See Smoking and youth

CIGARETTE vending machines. See Vending machines

CIGARETTES
Hazardous substances. New Repub 164:11 Ap 3 '71

Advertising
After the blackout. il Time 97:73-4 Mr 22 '71
Case to watch; ban of cigarette advertising in the electronic media. Nation 213:485 N 15 '71
Cigarette ads go to the races. Bsns W p 19 F 6 '71
Cigarette advertising & federal law. R. L. Tobin. il Sat R 54:89-90 Mr 13 '71
Cigarette makers do great without TV. il Bsns W p56-7 My 29 '71
Man behind the ban on cigarette commercials: J. F. Banzhaf, 3d. J. E. Roper. por Read Digest 98:213-14+ Mr '71

CIGARETTES—Advertising—*Continued*
Selling death: cigarette ads in the magazines. T. Whiteside. New Repub 164:15-17 Mr 27 '71
Squawk box; Audio commercial message repeating unit. New Repub 164:13-14 Ap 10 '71
Where cigarette makers spend ad dollars now. il Bsns W p56-7 D 25 '71
Will the ad ban spread north? il Bsns W p24-5 My 1 '71

Taxation
Filtering out theft and tax increases. il Bsns W p22 Ap 3 '71

CIGARS
Inorganic particles in cigars and cigar smoke. A. M. Langer and others. bibliog il Science 174:585-7 N 5 '71

CINCINNATI
Lighting adds color to new stadium. il Am City 86:82 F '71

Art
See also
Cincinnati art museum

City planning
See also
Cincinnati—Municipal improvement

Galleries and museums
See also
Cincinnati art museum

History
Historymobile. H. M. Stock. Parks & Rec 6:25+ Jl '71

Municipal improvement
Details make the difference. il Am City 86:59 Ja '71

Theater
Portrait of artist; production of Caravaggio at the Playhouse in the park. H. Hewes. Sat R 54:34 Jl 24 '71

CINCINNATI art museum
Cincinnati's new look. K. Kuh. il Sat R 54:34-5 F 27 '71

CINCINNATI Bengals (football club) See Football clubs

CINCINNATI cabinetmakers. See Cabinetmakers

CINCINNATI milacron, Inc.
Machine maker with optimism. Bsns W p46+ N 20 '71

CINCINNATI Reds (baseball) See Baseball clubs

CINEMA. See Moving pictures

CINEMA rooms. See Recreation rooms

CINEMATHEQUE Française, Paris. See Moving picture film collections

CINEMATOGRAPHY. See Moving picture photography

CINGULUMOTOMY. See Brain—Surgery

CINNAMON rolls. See Bread

CINQUEFOIL
It makes an interesting lawn substitute; potentilla verna. il Sunset 146:258 My '71

CINTA Larga Indians. See Indians of South America—Brazil

CIRCADIAN rhythms. See Biology—Periodicity

CIRCUIT breakers, Electric. See Electric circuit breakers

CIRCULARLY polarized light. See Polarization (light)

CIRCULATION departments in libraries. See Libraries—Circulation, loans, etc.

CIRCUMCISION
Moses encounters the daemonic aspect of God. D. F. Zeligs. bibliog Am Imago 27:379-91 Wint '70

Anecdotes, facetiae, satire, etc.
Foreskin saga; spoof by J. Harnes. Time 98:59 S 20 '71

CIRCUS
Big cat with big cats; animal trainer G. Gebel-Williams of the Ringling bros. and Barnum & Bailey circus. il por Time 97:67 My 24 '71
Dauntless travelers; outrageous day in Mexico. R. Burton. il por Vogue 158:130-3 O 15 '71
For visitors to Russia a treat not to miss is the circus. il Sunset 146:37 Ja '71
Here comes the circus; with report by E. Hoagland. il Life 70:66-70A Ap 23 '71
Orphan-boys circus. M. Del Castillo. il por Vogue 158:104-7+ D '71

CIRCUS animals
Training
See Animals—Training

CIRCUS performers
Soul of the tiger. E. Hoagland. il pors Esquire 76:88-93+ Jl '71
See also
Clowns

CIRCUS world museum, Baraboo, Wis.
Circus museum at the water works. R. G. Wolkowski. il Am City 86:40 Ap '71

CISCO fishing
Tullibee, the surprise fish. H. Bradshaw. il Field & S 75:80-1+ Ap '71

CISSIE
Woman's way. See issues of Today's health to June 1971

CITELLUS. See Ground squirrels

CITIBANK. See New York (city)—Banks

CITIES and towns
City and suburb; instead of shouting, how about talking? W. F. Wagner, jr. Arch Rec 150:9-10 O '71
See also
Annexation (municipal government)
Business districts
City and town life
Cleaning of cities, towns, etc.
Education, Urban
New cities and towns
Parks
Playgrounds
Slums

Biblical teaching
Meaning of the city, by J. Ellul. Review Commonweal 94:351-7 Jl 9 '71. H. Cox

Federal aid
See Federal and municipal relations

Finance
See Municipal finance

Growth
Is bigger also better? R. D. Lamm. New Repub 164:17-19 Je 5 '71
Poor lands spawn big squalid cities. B. L. Masse. America 124:166 F 20 '71
Rural & urban growth. New Repub 165:12-13 S 25 '71
Rural exodus: new census report. il U S News 70:37 F 22 '71
See also
Metropolitan areas
Suburbs

Lighting
See Street lighting

Names
See Names, Geographical

Planning
See City planning

Protection
U.S. gets its first walled city; Sugar Creek, Tex, electronically fortified. il Bsns W p28 Mr 6 '71

Transportation
See Urban transportation

Water supply
See Water supply

Zone system
See Zoning

Africa
Black Africa: blacks move to the city. J. Derrick. il America 125:13-14 Jl 10 '71

Australia
Australia: the city life. I. Kolodin. il Sat R 54:48-50 O 23 '71

France
See also
New cities and towns

Great Britain
See also
New cities and towns

Mexico
Citizen-city interaction south of the border. P. D. Eimon. il Am City 86:78+ Ja '71

Middle East
Cities of the Middle East and their problems. R. S. Harrison. bibliog il Focus 22:1-8 N '71

Singapore
See also
Housing—Singapore

Spain
See also
New cities and towns

CITIES and towns—*Continued*

Switzerland

Switzerland: progress against the communes. B. R. Barber. il Trans-Action 8:27-31+ F '71

United States

Are big cities worth saving? interview. G. S. Sternlieb. il por U S News 71:42-6+ Ji 26 '71

Are our cities dying? E. Raskin; S. Tenenbaum; R. Reeves. Read Digest 99:167-8+ Ag '71

Black takeover of U.S. cities? A. Poinsett. il Ebony 26:76-9+ N '70

Cities are finished. S. Alsop. Newsweek 77:100 Ap 5 '71

Cities: forecast for summer. il Time 97:12 My 31 '71

Cities where business is best; with tables. il U S News 71:76-9 S 27 '71

City woes: easing a bit, mayors say. il U S News 70:32 Je 28 '71

Liberal mayor's advice to blacks: think white; excerpts from address, October 6, 1971. S. Massell. por U S News 71:94-5 N 1 '71

Urban environment: cities made for people. Sr Schol 98:9-10 F 8 '71

See also
All-America cities
Metropolitan areas
National league of cities
Urban renewal

CITIES and towns, Floating
Cities on the sea? J. Lear. il Sat R 54:80-6+ D 4 '71

CITIES and towns, Medieval
Landlord and the economic revival of the middle ages in northern Europe, 1000-1250. R. G. Witt. bibliog f Am Hist R 76:965-88 O '71

CITIES and towns, Ruined, extinct, etc.
Vanishing Guarani treasures. A. Ibáñez Padilla. il Américas 23:32-5 O '71
See also
Ani, Turkey (ancient city)
Portobelo, Panama

CITIES and towns in literature. See Literature —Themes

CITIES service oil company
Gallop-in-place. il Forbes 107:65 Ap 15 '71

CITIZEN crime commission. See Crime prevention—Citizen participation

CITIZEN of the year award. See American forestry association

CITIZENS and Southern national bank of Atlanta. See Atlanta—Banks

CITIZENS associations
Citizens' corporations as true community mental retardation and mental health centers; Intercommunity action, inc. R. C. Stephanos. Ment Hy 55:410-12 Jl '71

Situation ethnics; new ethnic community organizations. P. Freiberg. Commonweal 94:81-3 Ap 2 '71
See also
Crime prevention—Citizen participation

CITIZENS' committee on public transportation
Constituency for mass transit. C. Holden. Science 172:1118 Je 11 '71

CITIZENS corporations. See Citizens associations

CITIZENS' panel on defense
U.S. superiority has ended; summary of statement. il U S News 70:49-50+ Ap 5 '71

CITIZENS radio service
CB and the coast guard. R. Humphrey. il Pop Electr 35:42-4 S '71
See also
React (organization)

Equipment

CB troubleshooter's casebook; comp. by A. J. Mueller. See issues of Radio-electronics to April 1971
See also
Radio antennas
Radio telephone

CITIZENSHIP
Downgrading citizens. il Time 97:42 My 10 '71
New dimensions in citizenship; address, May 1971. R. Nader. il PTA Mag 66:12-15 S: 10-13 O '71
See also
Patriotism

CITIZENSHIP, Education for
Learning to cope in Prince Georges County; new course on Teen-agers' rights and responsibilities for all eighth-graders. B. L. Collier. il Sat R 54:64-5+ My 22 '71

Orphan-boys circus; Bemposta republic. M. Del Castillo. il por Vogue 158:104-7+ D '71

This way to the voting booth; preparing teenagers. W. D. Boutwell. PTA Mag 65:16 Ap '71
See also
Education and democracy
Political science—Study and teaching

CITROEN (automobile) See Automobiles, Foreign

CITRUS fruit industry
OJ play: tough and tangy; frozen orange juice futures. A. Hershman. il Duns 97:55-7 Ap '71

CITRUS fruits
Auxins in citrus: a reappraisal. E. E. Goldschmidt and others. bibliog Science 174:1256-7 D 17 '71
See also
Oranges

CITY and country
Suburbs have to open their gates. L. Davidoff and others. il N Y Times Mag p40-4+ N 7 '71
See also
Village life

CITY and town life
Big city, small city: how the living compares. il Changing T 25:13-15 Jl '71

Fear in the streets. J. Wideman. Am Scholar 40:611-22 Aut '71

Focus on the future: the small town; address, January 28, 1971. J. W. Joanis. Vital Speeches 37:275-9 F 15 '71

Main street: 1971; small towns can be an alternate way of life-if... R. Hoffmann. il Mlle 73:124-5+ Je '71

Walking my dog on the West side. J. Yglesias. il Esquire 75:120-3 Je '71
See also
Church and social problems
Village life

History

Families against the city and The uses of disorder, by R. Sennett. Reviews
Commentary 51:86-90 My '71. M. Dubofsky

CITY center Joffrey ballet
All hail Alley: fall season. W. Terry. il Sat R 54:36 N 6 '71

City center Joffrey ballet in Reflections; The abyss; Valentine and Square dance. Dance Mag 45:92-3+ My '71

Dance; Reflections, Square dance and Abyss. J. Maskey. Hi Fi 21:MA9 Jl '71

Dance; Trinity and Still point. J. Maskey. il Hi Fi 21:MA7 Ja '71

Her feet go wickety-wack; production of Square dance. W. Terry. il Sat R 54:30 Ap 10 '71

Joffrey journey; highlights of the fall season. D. Hering. il Dance Mag 46:30-5 Ja '72

Love on the rock. J. T. Elson. il Time 98:95 N 8 '71

Musical events; new ballets: Reflections and Valentine. W. Sargeant. New Yorker 47:135 Mr 20 '71

World of dance; performance of Weewis, and Kettentanz. W. Terry. Sat R 54:74 N 20 '71

CITY center of music and drama, inc.
Drama at Lincoln Center; future of the Forum and the Beaumont. S. Kauffmann. New Repub 165:20+ O 23 '71; Reply with rejoinder. D. Schary. 165:29-30 N 27 '71

Tale of two centers; take over of the Vivian Beaumont theater. il Newsweek 77:45 F 1 '71

CITY churches
See also
Suburban churches

CITY cleaning. See Cleaning of cities, towns, etc.

CITY-county cooperation. See Intercommunity cooperation

CITY emblems. See Emblems, City

CITY employees. See Municipal employees

CITY gardens
City oases; New York gardens. N. Skurka. il N Y Times Mag p40-1 Je 27 '71

Flowers on Avenue D. C. A. Lewis. il Horticulture 49:30-1+ Ag '71

Room for your car and a garden too; with editorial comment. il Horticulture 49:20, 24-6 Ap '71
See also
Roof gardens

CITY government. See Municipal government

CITY growth. See Cities and towns—Growth

CITY halls
Government center instead of city hall; Kettering, Ohio. il Am City 86:65 Je '71

Office rentals pay for half of new city hall; Hayward, Calif. il Am City 86:40 Mr '71

CITY houses
Brownstoning: an alternative for foes of sub-
urbia. Bsns W p 101 Je 5 '71
John R. Little residences, San Anselmo, Calif.
il Arch Rec 149:94-5 mid-My '71
Manhattan country house. N. Skurka. il N Y
Times Mag p82-3 My 16 '71
Rainy-weather cheer; London townhouse of
Mary Gilliat. il N Y Times Mag p92-3
D 12 '71
Shlaes north side townhouses, Chicago. il
Arch Rec 149:88-9 mid-My '71
Town houses. S. Mead. il Bet Hom & Gard
49:56-7 Mr '71
Truly sensuous house; Victorian townhouse.
S. G. Lewin. il House B 113:118-21 N '71
Unusual city house, screened from the street
yet open to its grand view of San Francisco
Bay. il Sunset 146:80-1 Je '71
Up and down house; New York Lawrence
Horowitz's remodeled West side townhouse.
R. Reif. il N Y Times Mag p90-1 N 14 '71
See also
Row houses
CITY improvement. See Municipal improve-
ment
CITY investing company
Chameleon. il Forbes 107:20-1 Je 1 '71
CITY life. See City and town life
CITY manager plan
Businessman who brought the pro to city
hall. W. M. Wringle. il por Nations Bsns
59:30-2 D '71
CITY managers
How councilmen select city managers. Am
City 86:98-9 Jl '71
CITY maps. See Municipal maps
CITY models. See Models of cities, towns, etc.
CITY ordinances. See Municipal ordinances
CITY parks. See Parks
CITY planning
Architects want a voice in redesigning Amer-
ica. G. Breckenfeld. il Fortune 84:144-7+
N '71
Architecture of urban space. K. R. Schnei-
der. Arch Forum 134:48-51+ Je '71
Architecture with inner meaning, notes
toward a definition of urban design. A.
Mayer. il Arch Forum 135:60-3 N '71
Beyond civilization; P. Soleri's arcologies.
P. Bohannan. il Natur Hist 80:50-67 F '71
Books. H. H. Waechter. Arch Forum 135:76
S '71
Culture of cities, by L. Mumford. Review
New Repub 165:29-30 O 23 '71. H. J.
Muller
More greenspace for urban America. J. J.
Shomon. il Cons 26:14-17 D '71
On urbanization: a worldwide process; ex-
cerpts from address, November 1970. B.
Ward. por Sr Schol Teach ed 97:3 Ja 11
'71
Soleri's arcology: a new design for the city?
S. Kostof. il Art in Am 59:90-5 Mr '71
Subterranean systems as a framework for
a new urban planning policy. G. Birkerts.
Arch Forum 135:58-9 N '71
See also
Business districts
Housing
Municipal improvement
Regional planning
Rural planning
Suburbs
Traffic engineering
Urban renewal
also subhead City planning under names
of cities, e.g. New Haven, Conn.—City
planning
History
Town and revolution: Soviet architecture and
city planning, 1917-1935, by A. Kopp. Re-
view
Arch Forum 134:76+ Mr '71. K. Framp-
ton
Terminology
Guide to the language of cities; excerpts from
The language of cities. C. Abrams. por
Fortune 83:121-2 Mr '71

Europe, Western
Humans and cities: the European answer. il
Sci N 100:308-9 N 6 '71

Russia
Town and revolution: Soviet architecture and
city planning, 1917-1935, by A. Kopp. Re-
view
Arch Forum 134:76+ Mr '71. K. Frampton
CITY services. See Municipal services
CITY symbols. See Emblems, City

CITY traffic
See also
Traffic engineering
Traffic signals
also subhead Street traffic under names
of cities, e.g. Indianapolis—Street traffic
Automatic control
See also
Computers—Traffic control use
CITY transit. See Local transit
CITY transportation. See Urban transportation
CITY trees. See Trees in cities
CITY university of New York. See New York
(city). City university
CIVIC centers. See Municipal centers
CIVIC opera house, Chicago. See Opera houses
CIVICS. See Political science—Study and
teaching
CIVIL aeronautics board. See United States—
Civil aeronautics board
CIVIL disobedience. See Government, Re-
sistance to
CIVIL liberties union, American. See American
civil liberties union
CIVIL liberty. See Liberty
CIVIL marriage ceremonies. See Marriage cus-
toms and rites
CIVIL procedure
See also
Arbitration and award
Jury
CIVIL rights
Assembly decisions on human rights ques-
tions. UN Mo Chron 8:74-8 Ja '71
Economic and social council adopts resolu-
tions on human rights. UN Mo Chron 8:
59-68 Je '71
See also
Free speech
Human rights day and week
Information, Freedom of
Intellectual liberty
Liberty
Privacy, Right of
Searches and seizures
Trials (civil rights)
United Nations—Commission on human
rights
Universal declaration of human rights
Woman—Equal rights
also subhead Civil rights under vari-
ous subjects, e.g. Employees—Civil rights
Canada
Strong-arm rule in Canada; effect of the
War measures act. R. N. Williams. New
Repub 164:15-18 Ja 30 '71; Discussion. 164:
33-4 F 27 '71
Northern Ireland
Battle of the Boyne II. J. Wyatt. Common-
weal 94:162-5 Ap 23 '71
Russia
Dissent in Russia: the thin wedge. il por
Newsweek 77:29-34 F 1 '71
Medvedev papers, by Z. A. Medvedev. Re-
view
Science 174:937 N 26 '71. R. Pipes
United States
Civil liberties, by W. Spinrad. Review
Nation 212:505-6 Ap 19 '71. C. L. Mark-
mann; Reply. W Spinrad. 212:802 Je 28
'71
Civil rights: little progress. America. 125:471
D 4 '71
Grand jury network; how the Nixon admin-
istration has secretly perverted a tradi-
tional safeguard of individual rights. F. J.
Donner and E. Cerruti. il Nation 214:5-
15+ Ja 3 '72
Lawyer's brief. Time 97:18 Je 21 '71
Notes and comment; anti-democratic trends
in the government. New Yorker 47:21-2 Jl
24 '71
Question of neglect; Commission on civil
rights report. Commonweal 95:268 D 17 '71
Telltale bullets; case of J. L. Crowder. Time
97:53 Ap 5 '71
See also
Indians of North America—Civil rights
Negroes—Civil rights
United States—Commission on civil rights
United States—Constitution—Bill of rights
CIVIL rights commission. See United States—
Commission on civil rights
CIVIL rights demonstrations
Catching up with Natchez. N. C. Chriss.
Nation 213:592-3 D 6 '71
See also
Negroes—Segregation, Resistance to

CIVIL rights division. See United States—Justice, Department of—Civil rights division

CIVIL rights organizations
    See also
    American civil liberties union
    Italian-American civil rights league
    Medical committee for human rights
    National welfare rights organization
    Scholarship, education and defense fund for racial equality
    Southern Christian leadership conference

Russia

Sakharov on human rights; principles and aims of the Committee on human rights. A. D. Sakharov and others. Sat R 54:24 Ja 16 '71

CIVIL service
    See also
    Bureaucracy
    Government employees
    Municipal employees
    Patronage, Political
    Public officers

United States

Civil service reform: science agency heads balk at Nixon plan. R. Gillette. Science 172:652-5 My 14 '71
Double standard; sex discrimination in civil service employment. New Repub 164:12+ My 29 '71
New labor policies in the Civil service; interview. R. E. Hampton. il por Nations Bsns 59:70-2+ Je '71
Role of civil service. F. A. Cosgrove and R. Kraus. il Parks & Rec 6:27-9+ Je '71

CIVIL service pensions
    See also
    Municipal employees—Pensions
    State employees—Pensions

CIVIL war
    See also
    Insurgency

CIVIL war (United States) See United States—History—Civil war

CIVILIAN military relations. See United States—Armed forces—Relations with civilians

CIVILIAN morale. See Morale, National

CIVILIZATION
Beyond civilization. P. Bohannan. il Natur Hist 80:50-67 F '71
Easing our burden. R. Haughton. Cath World 213:119-20 Je '71
For a better world. P. Medawar. Vogue 159: 64-5 Ja 1 '72
In Bluebeard's castle, by G. Steiner. Review Nat 213:1477-8 D 31 '71. E. Vivas
NCTE presidential address: imagination and the health of everyman; November 1970. J. E. Miller, jr. Engl J 60:189-98 F '71
Passing of the modern age, by J. Lukacs. Review
    Nation 213:86-8 Ag 2 '71. R. Lilienfeld
    See also
    Acculturation
    Archaeology
    Culture
    History
    Humanism
    Intellectual life
    Popular culture
    Progress
    Social change
    Social progress
    Social sciences
    Technology and civilization
    also subhead Civilization under names of countries, e.g. United States—Civilization

History

Planetary planning; address, November 13, 1969. R. B. Fuller. Am Scholar 40:285-304 Spr '71
Planetary vistas. W. I. Thompson. bibliog il Harper 243:71-8 D '71
    See also
    Europe, Western—Civilization—History

Philosophy

Planetary planning; address, November 13, 1969. R. B. Fuller. Am Scholar 40:285-304 Spr '71
Toward a culture of unreason? D. Bazelon. Cur 131:51-6 Jl '71

CIVILIZATION, Ancient
Carbon 14 and the prehistory of Europe. C. Renfrew. il Sci Am 225:63-70+ bibliog (p 120) O '71
    See also
    Civilization, Iranian
    Mayas

CIVILIZATION, Carthaginian. See Civilization, Phoenician

CIVILIZATION, Chinese
Science and civilisation in China, by J. Needham. Review
    Sci Am il 226:113-18 Ja '72. N. Sivin

CIVILIZATION, Iranian
Iran: cultural crossroads for 2,500 years. P. Avery. il UNESCO Courier 24:4-9 O '71

CIVILIZATION, Modern. See Civilization

CIVILIZATION, Persian. See Civilization, Iranian

CIVILIZATION, Phoenician
Eight centuries of Carthaginian civilization. G. C. Picard. il UNESCO Courier 23:17-21+ D '70
Grandeur and decline of the Punic city-state; rise of Carthage. H. Slim. il UNESCO Courier 23:9-16 D '70

CIVILIZATION and science. See Science and civilization

CIVILIZATION and technology. See Technology and civilization

CLACKERS (toys) See Toys

CLAD metals. See Metals, Clad

CLAIBORNE, Craig
Authors & editors; interview, ed. by L. P. Freilicher. por Pub W 200:13-15 N 8 '71
Cooking with herbs & spices; excerpts. il por Ladies Home J 88:84+ Je '71
Craig Claiborne cooks for a crowd. il por Harp Baz 104:78-9+ Ag '71
Eastertide tradition. il N Y Times Mag p90 Ap 4 '71
New York times international cookbook; excerpts. il Ladies Home J 88:102-3+ D '71
—See Lee, V. jt. auth.

about

In search of Craig Claiborne. G. Carro. por Ladies Home J 88:112 D '71 •
Kitchens. M. Davidson. il pors Ladies Home J 88:21 Je '71 •

CLAIMS
    See also
    Insurance—Adjustment of claims

CLAIR, René
René Clair in Hollywood: an interview, ed. by R. C. Dale. il Film Q 24:34-40 Wint '70

CLAIRE, William F.
Thinking of Anais Nin; poem. Nation 212:414 Mr 29 '71

CLAIRMONT, Claire. See Clairmont, C. M. J.

CLAIRMONT, Clara Mary Jane
Lovers; excerpt from The nympho and other maniacs. I. Wallace. pors Ladies Home J 88:127-33 F '71 •

CLAIRVOYANCE. See Extrasensory perception

CLAMPS
New universal clamp is three clamps in one. il Pop Mech 136:190 N '71

CLAMS
    See also
    Cookery—Shellfish

CLAMS, Fresh water. See Mussels, Fresh water

CLANCY, Roger
Landlocked sailors. il Sea Front 17:241-2 Jl '71

CLANCY, Thomas H.
College of your choice. America 124:89-91 Ja 30 '71
Communications. America 124:262-3 Mr 13 '71
Ignatius Loyola: a soldier-saint? America 125:317-18 O 23 '71
Lincoln's almost chosen people. il por America 124:145-7 F 13 '71
Showdown on the volunteer army. America 124:647-8 Je 26 '71

CLAPHAM, John
Dvořak's relations with Brahms and Hanslick. pors Mus Q 57:241-54 Ap '71

CLAPP, Verner W.
Greatest invention since the title-page? autobibliography from incipit to cataloging-in-publication. bibliog il Wilson Lib Bul 46:348-59 D '71

about

Verner W. Clapp, library ombudsman. il pors Wilson Lib Bul 45:554-5 F '71 •

CLAPTON, Eric
Rock family affair. il por Life 71:49 S 24 '71 •

CLAQUE. See Applause

CLARION music society, Inc.
Music to my ears; concert performance of Olimpiade, by A. Hasse. I. Kolodin. Sat R 54:42 Ap 3 '71

CLARION music society, inc.—*Continued*
Musical events; concert in Alice Tully Hall.
W. Sargeant. New Yorker 47:97-8 N 27 '71
Report:
Olimpiade. F. Merkling. Opera N 35:22
My 15 '71
Two by Hasse: Clarion's L'Olimpiade. Barnard's Gentleman. P. J. Smith. Hi Fi 21:
MA27 Je '71

CLARK, Blake
Hawaii, the aloha state. il Read Digest 98:
146-52 Ja '71

CLARK, Bronson Pettibone
If ever the twain shall meet. Sat R 54:14+
D 18 '71

CLARK, Dane
Dane Clark: adobe landscapes in acrylic and
watercolor. J. Jellico. il por Am Artist 35:
52-7+ Ap '71 *

CLARK, David D.
Shape isomers and the double-humped
barrier. biblíog il Phys Today 24:23-31 D
'71

CLARK, Earl
John F. Stevens: pathfinder for western railroads. biblíog il pors Am West 8:28-33+ My
'71
Shootout in Burke Canyon. il Am Heritage
22:44-8+ Ag '71

CLARK, Fred C. Jr
Cathedral in the canyon. il Motor B & S 127:
94-7+ Mr '71
Single-screw handling: it's easier than you
think. il Motor B & S 128:62-3+ Jl '71
Your guide to the perfect paint job. il
Motor B & S 127:83-90 F '71

CLARK, Howard Longstreth
In quest of Utopia. il pors Nations Bsns
59:48-9 Ja '71

CLARK, Ian D. and Noxon, J. F.
Particle formation during water-vapor photolysis. biblíog Science 174:941-4 N 26 '71

CLARK, James Dawson Chichester-. See Chichester-Clark, J. D.

CLARK, John
Space program: pro and con: address. Space
World H-12-96:32-5 D '71

CLARK, Joseph G.
Feedlot health. See issues of Farm Journal

CLARK, June
Travel and beauty care. Holiday 49:124+ D
'70; 104+ F; 18 Mr; 16 Ap; 17 My '71

CLARK, Keith
Linder collection of the works and drawings
of Beatrix Potter. il Horn Bk 47:554-5 O
'71

CLARK, Kenneth Mackenzie Clark, baron
TV is civilisation. pors Look 35:50 S 7 '71
about
Kenneth Clark: a man for all media. P.
Quennell. il por Sat R 54:10-12+ Ag 28
'71 *

CLARK, Madilyn
American dance camp: a summer road to
dance. N. M. Stoop. il Dance Mag 45:64-5
Je '71 *

CLARK, Milo
Yab Yum, a sensory experience in 4000 sq. ft.
il Pub W 199:43-5 My 3 '71

CLARK, Phil
Mexican gardens. il Horticulture 49:26-7+ F
'71

CLARK, Ramsey
Demeaning human dignity. Sat R 54:29-30+
Ap 17 '71
about
Causes and prevention of Ramsey Clark.
E. Van Den Haag. Nat R 23:316-18 Mr 23
'71 *
Of Hoover and Clark. por Time 97:16-17 My 3
'71 *

CLARK, Richard
Two men from cell block D. pors Time 98:21
S 27 '71 *

CLARK, Robert B.
American holly. il Horticulture 49:22-3 D '71

CLARK, Robert M. and others
Manage solid wastes as a utility. il Am City
86:45-7 F '71

CLARK, William
See also
Lewis and Clark expedition

CLARK COUNTY, Nev. library. Las Vegas
Las Vegas, Nevada: a winner in the desert.
il Library J 96:8983 D 1 '71

CLARK oil and refining corporation
Over a barrel. Forbes 107:18-19 F 1 '71

CLARK university, Worcester, Mass.
Training teachers of teachers; an agent of
change; Office of education program. J. A.
Plaisted. il Am Ed 7:33-5 Ja '71

CLARKE, C. H. D.
Beast of Gévaudan; with biographical sketch.
biblíog Natur Hist 80:10, 44-51+ Ap '71

CLARKE, Gerald
JFK, bitter memories of a cold day. New
Repub 164:13-15 Ja 16 '71
Sob story; or, A bestseller bested: Time essay. Time 97:78 Mr 1 '71

CLARKE, John
Electronics with superconducting junctions.
biblíog il Phys Today 24:30-7 Ag '71

CLARKE, Sanford
Middle school, specially trained teachers are
vital to its success. biblíog f Clear House
46:218-22 D '71

CLARKE, Thomas E.
Faith in focus. America 124:177-8; 125:151-2,
232-3 F 20, S 11, O 2 '71
Meet the new deacon. America 124:260-2 Mr
13 '71
Renewal in the church: two mentalities in
conflict. America 124:234-7 Mr 6 '71

CLARKSON, John
M.I.T. professor challenges garden clubs.
Horticulture 49:32-5 Je '71

CLASS actions. See Actions and defenses

CLASS discussions. See Discussion method
(education)

CLASS reunions. See High school graduates

CLASSICAL ballet. See Ballet

CLASSICAL education
See also
Humanities
Latin language—Study and teaching

CLASSICAL Khmer ballet. See Ballet—Cambodia

CLASSICAL music. See Music

CLASSICAL Rome. See Rome

CLASSICISM in music
Classical nature of Schubert's lieder. W. Gray.
biblíog f Mus Q 57:62-72 Ja '71

CLASSIFICATION
Instant classification: improving reference service in research libraries. D. A. Diefenbach.
por Library J 96:801-2 Mr 1 '71; Discussion.
96:1547 My 1 '71
See also
Biology—Classification

Anecdotes, facetiae, satire, etc.
Cataloging on the wall. D. Peele. Wilson Lib
Bul 45:772-4 Ap '71
Invocation. K. Brodney. Wilson Lib Bul 45:
777 Ap '71

CLASSIFICATION, Decimal
Dewey 18: a preview and a report to the
profession. W. E. Matthews. il por Wilson
Lib Bul 45:572-7 F '71

CLASSIFICATION of movies. See Moving pictures—Classification

CLASSIFIED defense information. See Defense
information, Classified

CLASSIFIED documents. See Security classification (government documents)

CLASSROOM films. See Moving pictures in
education

CLASSROOM management
Beginning teacher's soliloquy. M. Tener.
Clear House 45:379 F '71
Classroom control should be a vital part of
teacher education. D. A. Wesley. biblíog
Clear House 45:346-9 F '71
Creating group cohesion in inner city classrooms. F. P. Bazeli. biblíog Clear House 45:
547-50 My '71
My first year of teaching; excerpt from
Don't smile until Christmas, ed. by K.
Ryan. W. Crawford. Todays Ed 60:46-7 F
'71
School behavior: whose problem? with studydiscussion program, by E. Harris and D.
Harris. C. Smallenburg and H. Smallenburg. biblíog il PTA Mag 65:18-21, 35 F '71
Using drugs in classrooms. N. Hentoff. Cur
126:40-5 F '71

CLASSROOMS
Happy classroom home; kindergarten environment. C. Winterton and J. Winterton.
Todays Ed 60:69 S '71
Learning on wheels: Adelphi university's
graduate course in Principles of marketing
given on a Long Island railroad train. il
Time 98:66-7 N 1 '71
Paint a what? Paint a bus! E. J. Erdahl.
il Sch Arts 71:12-13 N '71
See also
Open plan schools

CLAUSEN, Alden Winship
Largest bank was once a plank on the
waterfront. il pors Nations Bsns 59:54-5
Ja '71

CLAUSEN, Alden Winship—*Continued*
Quest for values in a world of facts; address, December 6, 1971. Vital Speeches 38:182-6 Ja 1 '72

about

Clausen of Bank of America. por Forbes 107: 73 My 15 '71 *

CLAUSEWITZ, Karl von
How not to win a war. C. Barnett. il Horizon 13:48-53 Sum '71 *

CLAXTON, Philander P. Jr
Development of institutions to meet the world population crisis; address, March 12, 1971. Dept State Bul 65:165-72 Ag 16 '71

CLAY, Cassius
My mother, right or wrong. McCalls 98:111 My '71

about

Ali-Frazier crunch. P. Axthelm. Vogue 157: 115 Mr 1 '71 *
Ali-Frazier fight; with editorial comment. N. Mailer. il pors Life 70:3, 18F-19+ Mr 19 '71 *
Ali on Peachtree. J. Richardson. il Harper 242:46-9+ Ja '71 *
And then there was one. il pors Time 97: 35 Mr 22 '71 *
At the bell... M. Kram. il pors Sports Illus 34:18-21 Mr 8 '71 *
Battered face of a winner; Ali-Frazier fight; photographs, with report by M. Kram. Sports Illus 34:16-21 Mr 15 '71 *
Battle of the undefeated giants; with editorial comment. T. Thompson. il pors Life 70:3, 40-9 Mr 5 '71 *
Biggest fight in history. L. J. Banks. il pors Ebony 26:134-6+ Mr '71 *
Bull v. butterfly: a clash of champions. il pors Time 97:63+ Mr 8 '71 *
Bundini: Svengali in Ali's corner. E. Shrake. pors Sports Illus 34:32-6 F 15 '71 *
Decision for Allah; Supreme court ruling on draft exemption. por Newsweek 78:61+ Jl 12 '71 *
Defeat of the Great black hope. M. R. Berube. Commonweal 94:54-5 Mr 26 '71 *
Disintegration of a folk hero. P. Hamill. por Harp Baz 104:104-5 My '71 *
Don't call me champ; Supreme court decision. Nation 213:37 Jl 19 '71 *
End of a beautiful friendship; Muhammad Ali-J. Ellis fight. T. Maule. il por Sports Illus 35:10-11 Ag 2 '71 *
Fall and rise of Muhammad Ali. L. Schecter. il pors Look 35:62-6 Mr 9 '71 *
Fight. New Yorker 47:32-5 Mr 20 '71 *
$500,000 workout. por Newsweek 78:75 Ag 9 '71 *
Got to look good to Allah. T. Maule. il pors Sports Illus 35:28-9 N 29 '71 *
He has heavy things on his mind. T. Maule. il por Sports Illus 35:24-6 Jl 26 '71 *
I don't have to be what you want me to be, says Muhammad Ali. R. Lipsyte. il pors N Y Times Mag p24-5+ Mr 7 '71 *
It's gonna be the champ and the tramp. T. Maule and M. Sharnik. il pors Sports Illus 34:14-17 F 1 '71 *
Mountain to molehill. il por Time 98:69 N 29 '71

No requiem for a heavyweight. G. Plimpton. il por Sports Illus 34:84-6+ Ap 5 '71 *
Now there is one champion. il pors Newsweek 77:72-6 Mr 22 '71 *
Parting shots: fastest gun in the gym grows old. por Life 71:69 Jl 9 '71 *
Purse snatchers. il pors Time 97:65-6 Ja 25 '71 *
Quiet family life of Muhammad Ali; photographs by I. Sutton. Ebony 26:118-22 Ja 71 *
. . . Sting like a bee, by J. Torres. Review Sat R 54:46-7 N 6 '71. W. Kennedy *
Winner if not champ. por Time 98:53 Jl 12 '71 *
Winner, the loser, the crowd. L. Banks. il pors Ebony 26:132-4+ My '71 *

CLAY, Frédéric
Gilbert without Sullivan; recording of Ages ago. R. Jacobson. Sat R 54:58 F 27 '71 *

CLAY, Grady
New environment of the South. Arch Forum 133:42-5 D '70

CLAY, Henry
Precursors of the inter-American system. por Américas 23:S9-10 Ja '71 *

CLAY, Landon T.
Golden links to the bronze age. E. Vermeule. il Horizon 13:50-3 Wint '71 *

CLAY, Nanine
Miniparks: diminishing returns. il Parks & Rec 6:22-6 Ja '71

CLAY, William Lacy
Live wire in the caucus. il por Newsweek 77: 32 Je 7 '71 *

CLAY
Amorphous clay materials. H. Van Olphen. Science 171:91-2 Ja 8 '71
Balloon forms from buttered clay. F. Staryos. il Ceram Mo 19:31 Mr '71
Primitive pottery at Red Dog. F. Ball. il Ceram Mo 19:29-32 My '71
Where and how to find clay; excerpts from Keramos, the teaching of pottery. F. Kriwanek. il Ceram Mo 19:16-19 Ja '71

CLAY beads. See Beads
CLAY medallions. See Jewelry
CLAY modeling. See Modeling
CLAY sculpture. See Ceramic sculpture

CLAYMAN, Charles S. See Rotman, C. B. jt. auth.

CLAYTON, Donald. See Robinson, D. jt. auth.

CLAYTON, J. F.
Overlooked space program benefits; excerpts from address. Aviation W 94:11 Mr 15 '71

CLAYTON, Xernona
Atlanta's charmer on channel 5. il pors Ebony 26:134-6+ N '70 *

CLAYTONIA. See Spring beauties

CLEAN air act. See Air pollution—Laws and legislation

CLEAN-up campaigns. See Cleaning of cities, towns, etc.

CLEANERS. See Cleaning compositions

CLEANERS, Drain. See Drain cleaners

CLEANING
Good spot remover for prelaundering use. Consumer Rep 36:133-4 Mr '71
Leather cleaner that delivers the goods. il Consumer Rep 36:270-1 My '71
Spot remover that works; K2r spot-lifter. Consumer Bul 54:39 Je '71
Stamp out laundry stains! il Bet Hom & Gard 49:139 D '71
See also
Boats—Cleaning
Brushes
Furniture—Care
Kitchen utensils—Care
Metal cleaning
Rugs and carpets—Care
Sewer cleaning

CLEANING compositions
Chemicals for electronics. L. Cantor. il Pop Electr 34:25-8+ Ap '71 (to be cont)
Clean that oven! aerosol oven cleaners. il Consumer Bul 54:11-13 F '71
Consumer's guide to chemical cleaners for home & shop. il Mech Illus 67:85 Jl '71
Scouring pads and powders. il Consumer Rep 36:489-91 Ag '71
See also
Polishing materials

CLEANING of books. See Books—Conservation and restoration

CLEANING of cities, towns, etc.
Clean-up mood sweeps the Nation. il Life 70:30-5 Mr 5 '71
How street sweepers perform today; 152 cities responding to sweeper survey. C. W. Laird and J. Scott. il Am City 86:58-62 Mr '71
Ways to save this fair and sweet land. R. Dubos. Vogue 158:52-3+ Ag 15 '71
See also
Street cleaning

CLEANLINESS
See also
Baths

CLEANSING creams. See Cosmetics

CLEAR air turbulence. See Atmospheric turbulence

CLEARCUTTING. See Forest thinning

CLEARING houses
Checks that come back fast; Fed's check-clearing system. il Bsns W p72+ N 27 '71

CLEARING of lakes, rivers, etc.
Mud-weed gobbler. il Mech Illus 67:46 N '71

CLEARING of land
Land clearance in the Irish neolithic: new evidence and interpretation. J. R. Pilcher and others. bibliog il Science 172:560-2 My 7 '71
Leveling the jungle; landclearing operations in Vietnam. A. H. Westing. il Environ 13: 8-12 N '71
Wasteland: South Vietnam. W. Haseltine and A. H. Westing. New Repub 165:13-15 O 30 '71

CLEARWATER, Fla.
Sanitary affairs
Odor-prevention insurance. L. A. McDowell. il Am City 86:54+ F '71
Penguin litter receptacle. il Am City 86:32 Ja '71

CLEARWATER (sloop) See Sloops

CLEARY, Maryell
Wingspread: where people are people. il Am
Ed 7:21-4 Ap '71

CLEARY, Robert E.
Are civic education courses worth keeping?
bibliog Sch & Soc 99:35-9 Ja '71
Elections and image building. il Todays Ed
60:30-2+ D '71

CLEARY, William H.
Instant church. Commonweal 94:426-7; 95:71
Ag 20, O 15 '71

CLEAVER, Kathleen
Panthers in Frankfurt. il por Newsweek 78:
37 Jl 19 '71 *

CLECAK, Peter
Confronting reality with reason. Nation 212:
245-8+ F 22 '71

CLEEMAN, James. See Gittelman, M. jt. auth.

CLEM, Charles Douglass
Poet with a purpose. J. R. Sherman. bibliog
Negro Hist Bul 34:163-4 N '71 *

CLEMATIS
Clematis, aristocrat of vines. R. E. Farrell.
il Home Gard 58:46-7+ F '71

CLEMENS, Cyril
Did Mark Twain originate famous weather
remark? Hobbies 76:138-9 Jl '71
Mark Twain & John F. Kennedy. il Hobbies
76:138-9 Mr '71
Mark Twain & Rudyard Kipling. Hobbies 76:
151 S '71

CLEMENS, P. L.
Experiments with wind; a pendulum anemometer and miniature tornadoes. il Sci Am
225:108-10 O '71

CLEMENS, Samuel Langhorne
Huckleberry Finn; dramatization. See Du-
Bois, G.

about
Did Mark Twain originate famous weather
remark? C. Clemens. Hobbies 76:139+ Jl
'71 *
Mark Twain & John F. Kennedy. C. Clem-
ens. il Hobbies 76:138-9 Mr '71 *
Mark Twain and journalistic humor today;
address, November 1970. J. B. McCullough.
Engl J 60:591-5 My '71 *
Mark Twain & Rudyard Kipling. C. Clemens.
Hobbies 76:151 S '71 *
Mark Twain, by M. Geismar. Review
Commentary 51:87-90 Mr '71. P. Shaw;
Discussion. 52:23-4 Ag '71 *
Sat R 54:27-8 F 27 '71. B. Weber. *

CLEMENS, Walter C. Jr
Sakharov: a man for our times. il Bul Atom
Sci 27:4-6+ D '71

CLEMENT, Paul W.
Helping the shy child. il por Newsweek 78:
40 Ag 23 '71 *

CLEMENT, R. D. and Starliper, R. L.
Relaxation oscillators, old and new. il Electr
World 85:36-7 My '71

CLEMENT, Robert M.
Gay church. il Time 98:39 Ag 23 '71 *

CLEMENTE, Roberto Walker
Champagne and aspirin. pors Newsweek 78:
75 O 25 '71 *
Some kind of a comeback. W. Leggett. il
Sports Illus 35:18-23 O 25 '71 *

CLEMENTI, Muzio
Great master of sonata form. S. Lincoln. il
pors Am Rec G 37:228-34 D 70

CLEMENTS, Geoffrey
How Geoffrey Clements photographs fine
art; interview, ed. by S. E. Meyer. il Am
Artist 35:24-6 My '71

CLEMENTS, Robert J.
European literary scene. See issues of Satur-
day review
Neruda laureate. por Sat R 54:50-1 N 13 '71

**La CLEMENZA di Tito; opera. See Mozart,
J. C. W. A.**

CLEPPER, Henry
Man called Pink: citizen of the year; adap-
tation of address, February 25, 1971. por
Am For 77:3+ My '71
Probing the secrets of the woods. il Am For
77:26-9+ Ag '71

about
AFA Distinguished service award to Henry
Clepper. il por Am For 77:39 Ja '71 *

CLERCQ, E. de, and Somer, P. de
Antiviral activity of polyribocytidylic acid
in cells primed with polyriboinosinic acid.
bibliog il Science 173:260-2 Jl 16 '71

CLERGUE, Lucien
Lucien Clergue: master of the sensuous
image. E. Scully. il Mod Phot 36:92-7 Ja
'72 *

CLERGY
Clergy under stress; report by J. Koval.
Newsweek 77:58 Ja 25 '71
Cultural strain and Protestant liberalism;
liberal movement in American theology
from 1875 to World war I. W. R. Hutchi-
son. bibliog f il Am Hist R 76:386-411 Ap
'71; Reply with rejoinder. D. E. Bigham.
76:1631-3 D '71
Now a clergy gap; the Koval-Mills-Bell
study. J. Deedy. Commonweal 93:410 Ja 29
'71
Pastor as cultural apologist. C. Miller. Chr
Today 15:27-8 Ja 29 '71
See also
Armstrong, H.
Chaplains, Military
Church of England—Clergy
Confidential communications—Clergy
Missionaries
Pastoral theology
Preaching
Priests
Protestant Episcopal church—Clergy
Seminarians
Theological education
Women as ministers

Appointment, call and election
In the service: a Christmas story. A. W.
Greeley. il por Am For 77:10-11+ D '71

Dismissal
Theology for swingers. Chr Cent 88:447 Ap 7
'71

Salaries, allowances, etc.
How well do you support your pastor? Chr
Today 15:30 S 10 '71
On not paying priests; the non-stipendiary
clergy. America 125:500 D 11 '71
Social security proposals may alter clergy
status. Chr Cent 88:1043 S 8 '71

Vocation
*See Clergy—Appointment, call and elec-
tion*

CLERGY in literature
Portraits of the preacher in American fiction. W. Martens. Chr Today 16:12-13 D
3 '71

CLERGYMEN as tour guides. See Guides

CLERICAL workers. See Office workers

CLEVA, Fausto
Meanwhile, back at the Met . . ; Cleva's 50th.
Council's 20th. il por Opera N 35:18-19 Je 12
'71 *
Orpheus in Athens, and Fausto Cleva's death.
S. Fleming. il Hi Fi 21:MA15 N '71 *

CLEVELAND
Gale-tested marina. R. H. Anderson and F.
W. Reusswig. il Am City 86:130+ Ap '71

Airports
How's your airport standby power? G. E.
Katzmar. il Am City 86:96 D '71

Education
Lowering the dropout rate; transition
classes. M. Schuster. Clear House 45:329-
32 F '71
Peephole into the world of work; Kennard
junior high school, Vocational information
program. K. E. Aylor. il Am Ed 7:29-30
Mr '71

Galleries and museums
See also
Cleveland museum of art

Housing
HUD's other shoe drops on Cleveland. Bsns
W p22+ Ja 30 '71

Libraries
See also
Cleveland public library

Music
Lutoslawski comes to town. B. Murray. il
por Hi Fi 21:MA24 S '71
See also
Cleveland orchestra
Lake Erie opera theater

Negroes
As the blacks move in, the ethnics move out.
P. Wilkes. il por N Y Times Mag p9-11+
Ja 24 '71

Social conditions
See also
Cleveland—Negroes

**CLEVELAND Indians (baseball) See Baseball
clubs**

CLEVELAND museum of art
Education in the arts; education wing. il Arch Forum 135:20-5 S '71
Ivory tower versus the discotheque. G. Glueck. il pors Art in Am 59:80-5 My '71
New addition to the Cleveland museum of art. il Design 72:4-7 Spr '71
CLEVELAND orchestra
Ethnic nights are a box office hit. il Bsns W p94 O 23 '71
CLEVELAND public library
Branches
Jumping the eighteenth century barrier: Carnegie West library; letter to the editor. F. Stein. Am Lib 2:1146 D '71
CLEVITE corporation
Westinghouse get torpedoed. Bsns W p 19 Jl 10 '71
CLIBBON, Sheila, and Sachs, M. L.
Creating consolidated clinical techniques spaces for an expanding role in health care. bibliog il Arch Rec 149:105-12 F '71
CLIFF, Edward P.
Forest service in the seventies. por Am For 77:11 Ja '71
More trees for people. il Am For 77:16-19+ Ap '71
Our research natural areas. il Am For 77:36-8+ O '71
CLIFF ISLAND
Saving an island school; report. P. Taubman. il Time 98:52-3 Ag 16 '71
CLIFFORD, Clark McAdams
Clark Clifford sounds the alarm. P. Anderson. il pors N Y Times Mag p8-9+ Ag 8 '71 •
Clifford interview. Nation 213:133 Ag 30 '71 •
CLIFFORD, John
Dancing gypsy. H. Saal. il Newsweek 77:81 Ja 25 '71 •
CLIFFORD, Richard J.
1971 books on the Bible. America 125:460-6 N 27 '71
CLIFFORD, William
How to read a wine label. il House B 113: 88-9+ Je; 74-6 Jl; 68+ Ag '71
CLIFT, David Horace
Clift balks at Davis gift voted by SRRT council. Library J 96:1553 My 1 '71 •
CLIFTON, Lucille
End of love is death & the end of death is love; story. Atlan 227:65-7 Mr '71
CLIMACTERIC
Male menopause is a very real thing. T. I. Rubin. Ladies Home J 88:52 N '71
CLIMATE
Climate cycles. C. Emiliani. il Sea Front 17: 108-20 Mr '71
Climatic changes: some evidence and implications. J. E. Newman. il Weatherwise 24: 56-62 Ap '71
Global circulation of atmospheric pollutants. R. E. Newell. il Sci Am 224:32-42 Ja '71
Man-made climatic changes. H. E. Landsberg; reply with rejoinder. A. N. Dingle. bibliog il Science 173:461-2 Jl 30 '71
Man's impact on climate: what is ahead? SMIC international study. il Sci N 100:73 Jl 31 '71
See also
Paleoclimatology
Weather
also subhead Climate under names of continents, countries, cities, etc. e.g. Montreal—Climate
CLIMATE, Geological. See Paleoclimatology
CLIMATE and health. See Weather—Mental and physiological effects
CLIMATE-solar relationships. See Sun and meteorology
CLIMATOLOGY. See Climate
CLIMBING plants
Ivy for everyone; municipal improvement project. P. Ertresvaag. Good H 173:163 Jl '71
Upholding vines and trees. il Sunset 146:96-9 Ap '71
Woody vines. D. Wyman. il Horticulture 49: 32-3+ Ag '71
See also
Clematis
Passion flowers
CLINE, Howard Francis
Obituary
Am Hist R 76:1639-40 D '71. C. C. Griffin
CLINICAL laboratories. See Medical laboratories
CLINICAL research. See Medical research
CLINICS. See Health facilities
CLINICS, Reading. See Reading clinics
CLINTON youth and family center. See New York (city)—Community centers
CLIPPERS, Hair. See Hair clippers

CLIPPERS, Hedge. See Hedge clippers
CLIVIAS
Clivia is happy indoors or outdoors, almost anywhere except in the sun. il Sunset 146: 72-3 F '71
CLOCK and watch museum, Germany. See Museums
CLOCK paradox. See Relativity (physics)
CLOCK radios
Different track; three-in-one clock, lamp and radio. M. Bowden. il House B 113:23 Ap '71
FM/AM clock radios. il Consumer Rep 36: 532-5 S '71
CLOCK timers. See Timing devices
CLOCK towers. See Towers
CLOCKS
Animated dial clocks. F. H. Griffith. il Hobbies 76:48-50+ Ja '72
Battery-operated clocks. il Consumer Bul 54: 25-6 N '71
Bily brothers' clocks. O. R. Hagans. il Hobbies 76:125-8 D '71
Make this charming colonial wall clock. il Pop Mech 136:132-4 Jl '71
Mod clock of manmade marble; grandfather clock. R. Capotosto. il Pop Sci 199:86-9 D '71
On time. O. R. Hagans. See issues of Hobbies
Popular science introduces the picture clock. R. P. Stevenson. il Pop Sci 198:90-3 Mr '71
Sportsman's wall clock with plywood face. il Pop Mech 136:166-7 N '71
Collectors and collecting
Clocks have personality. il Hobbies 76:123 O '71
Some Japanese clocks. O. R. Hagans. il Hobbies 76:126-7 Ap; 127-8 My; 126-7 Je; 125-7 Jl '71
CLOISONNÉ
Footed cloisonne bowl. P. Rothenberg. il Ceram Mo 19:25-7 F '71
CLOISTERS (museum) See Metropolitan museum of art, New York—Cloisters
CLONES (biology)
Cloning: the ethical question. il Sci Digest 70:58-9 Ag '71
Moving toward the clonal man. J. D. Watson. il Atlan 227:50-3 My '71
Prospect of carbon-copy humans. H. B. Kuhn. Chr Today 15:11-12+ Ap 9 '71
CLOPTON family
Clopton coat-of-arms. H. K. Eilers. il Hobbies 76:152-3 Mr '71
CLOROX company
Clorox makes it on its own. il Bsns W p 119-20 F 27 '71
CLOSE air support system. See Airplanes, Military—Armaments
CLOSE-up photography. See Photography, Close-up
CLOSED circuit television. See Television, Closed circuit
CLOSED-end investment companies. See Investment trusts
CLOSED shelves in libraries. See Open and closed shelves
CLOSET lighting. See Electric lighting
CLOSETS
Order out of chaos: closets. il Pop Sci 199: 95-7 S '71
You get more storage if you divide up the space. il Sunset 146:170+ Ap '71
See also
Storage in the home
Equipment
See also
Clothes racks
CLOSSON, Fred I.
Delinquency: its prevention rests upon the academic community. bibliog Clear House 45:290-3 Ja '71
CLOSTRIDIUM botulinum
Bacteriophage and the toxigenicity of clostridium botulinum types C. M. W. Eklund and others. bibliog il Science 172:480-2 Ap 30 '71
This is C. botulinum and a list of simple precautions to follow. il Life 71:30-1 S 10 '71
World's most deadly poison: the botulin spore. I. Asimov. il Sci Digest 71:8-11 Ja '72
CLOTFELTER, James
Millions for defense but . . . il Nation 212: 108-10 Ja 25 '71
Notes on the new isolationists. Bul Atom Sci 27:37 F '71
CLOTH cutting. See Garment cutting

CLOTHES dryers
Compact washing machines; and a dryer. il Consumer Bul 54:7-10 F '71
For laundry that needs tender loving care. il House B 113:60 O '71

CLOTHES racks
Spin-around storage; clothes closet with an electric rack. il House & Gard 139:98-9 Mr '71

CLOTHES washing machines. See Washing machines

CLOTHING, Cold weather
See also
Underwear

CLOTHING, Protective
See also
Clothing, Waterproof
Helmets

CLOTHING, Waterproof
Foul-weather gear. J. A. Emmett. il Outdoor Life 148:42+ S '71

CLOTHING and dress
Best dressed women of 1971. il Ebony 26: 162-4+ My '71
Bright lips of yesterday; look of the '30s and '40s resurfaces. il Life 70:52-6 F 19 '71
Fashion '71: anything goes. il Newsweek 77: 68-78 Mr 29 '71
Fashions in GH: practical as well as pretty. il Good H 172:6 Je '71
Feminine fashions. K. Fraser. New Yorker 47: 101-2+ Ap 3 '71
Hot pants: a short but happy career. il Life 71:14-15 D 31 '71
Hot pants: legs are back. il Time 97:48-50 F 1 '71
Hot pants? Right next to the hockey sticks. J. Campbell. il Sports Illus 34:58-61 Ap 26 '71
Hot pants; shorts. il Life 70:36-9 Ja 29 '71
Hotpants: the heat's off! S. Edmiston. Seventeen 30:157 Jl '71
In my opinion; the midi must go! G. Stone. por Seventeen 29:216 N '70
Industry still wins; chaos in women's clothing. il Bsns W p 112-13 F 27 '71
It's Minnie mouse and Donald duck and love and peace and stars and stripes forever! A.-M. Schiro. il N Y Times Mag p20-1 Jl 4 '71
Looking backward. il Newsweek 78:77-8 O 18 '71
Minneapolis look. il Time 98:48+ Ag 16 '71
Mrs William F. Buckley, jr. il pors Vogue 159:44-9 Ja 1 '72
Museum fashions. il Time 97:62 My 24 '71
New fashion is sans fashion. il Bsns W p25 F 6 '71
On and off the avenue. K. Fraser. New Yorker 47:66-8 Jl 24 '71
Pants outfits in public? A. Vanderbilt. il Ladies Home J 88:24 Ja '71
Parents provide the fall sales action. il Bsns W p40-1 S 11 '71
Short and shorter; Paris shows 1971 spring collections. il Newsweek 77:86 F 8 '71
Summer clothes that make good travelers. M. Dahlerus. il Good H 173:142 Jl '71
Vietnam vogue; military look dominating French scene. il Newsweek 78:58 Jl 12 '71
Working-order wardrobe. il Seventeen 29:229 S '70
See also
Bathing suits
Capes
Clothing industry
Costume
Costume design
Costume designers
Fashion
Garment cutting
Hats
Hosiery
Indians of North America—Costume and adornment
Models (persons)
Nightgowns, pajamas, etc.
Sewing
Shoes
Sweaters
Uniforms
Uniforms, Military
Veils
Vests
Wedding clothes

Children
Buying boy's slacks. M. Foy. il Good H 173: 126 Ag '71

History
Great change in children. J. H. Plumb. il Horizon 13:4-13 Wint '71

Cleaning
See Cleaning

History
See also
Clothing and dress—Children—History

Maternity clothes
Bellies are beautiful. il Time 97:58 My 31 '71
Big mama goes couture. M. Smith. il McCalls 99:33 N '71

Men
Advice for men. il McCalls 98:45 Ap '71
Brown suit; popularity among Italians. J. Ferris. Sat R 54:4 Ag 14 '71
Dashing young men. E. Sheppard. il Harp Baz 104:132 Mr '71
Earl of Lichfield presents: instant elegance. I. Bauer. il pors Look 35:78-80 Mr 23 '71
High style disrupts the men's wear industry. W. McQuade. il Fortune 83:70-2+ F '71
His bazaar. C. Kriebel. See issues of Harper's bazaar
Knits: something new in menswear. Changing T 25:19-20 S '71
On and off the avenue. New Yorker 47:56+ D 18 '71
What well-knit men will wear. il Bsns W p89 Ja 23 '71
See also
Neckties
Shirts
Underwear

Psychological aspects
Why some women prefer daring fashions. J. Brothers. Good H 173:58+ Jl '71

Renting
Rented uniforms cheaper than buying work clothes. il Suc Farm 69:34 N '71

Size
Big business; N. Austin's custom-designed fat-lady clothes. il por Time 98:72 N 29 '71

Sports clothes
Blaze orange/camouflage reversible package down jacket. C. Conley. il Field & S 76:167 Je '71
Blue jeans are the hot pants. il Bsns W p32-3 Ap 24 '71
Catch it, net it, put it in your pocket. J. Campbell. il Sports Illus 34:62-3 Mr 22 '71
Flotation jacket. il Yachting 129:60-1+ Ap '71
Patchwork fashions; custom patching of jeans. il Time 98:46-7 Jl 12 '71
What in blue blazers? Also red, gray. J. Campbell. il Sports Illus 35:42-3 Ag 23 '71

Students
In my opinion; the natural look is a charade. A Spinale. por Seventeen 30:346 Ag '71
Student dress codes. E. G. Scriven and A. Harrison, jr. Ed Digest 36:40-1 F '71
We left them laughing. S. Marsh. il Har Yrs 11:24-5 S '71

Work clothes
Rented uniforms cheaper than buying work clothes. il Suc Farm 69:34 N '71

CLOTHING industry
See also
Garment factories
Tailors

Wages and hours
Wages in men's and boys' suit and coat manufacturing. M. J. Tighe. il Mo Labor R 94:76-7 Je '71

Rumania
Wheeling and dealing in Rumania. il por Newsweek 77:39 Ap 5 '71

United States
High style disrupts the men's wear industry. W. McQuade. il Fortune 83:70-2+ F '71
If you wear it, it's selling well. il Bsns W p21 Jl 10 '71
Industry still wins; chaos in women's clothing. il Bsns W p 112-13 F 27 '71
Women's lib, ready-to-wear division. il Forbes 108:18-19 Jl 15 '71
See also
After six, inc.
Botany industries, inc.
Genesco, inc
Hart Schaffner and Marx (firm)
Interco, inc.
International ladies' garment workers' union
Strauss, Levi, and company

CLOTURE rule. See United States—Senate—Rules and practice

CLOUD seeding. See Rain making; Weather control

CLOUDS
These clouds bring storms. R. Lutz. il Suc Farm 69:B8 My '71

CLOVE apples, oranges, etc.   See Pomanders

CLOWNS
Subject was laughter; first woman clown. P. Williams. L. Foster. McCalls 98:40 Ag '71
Two clowns. E. Hoagland. il Life 70:70A Ap 23 '71

CLUB Français du livre. See Book clubs

CLUB Méditerranée. See Vacation villages

CLUB of Rome
What are man's prospects? D. L. Meadows. Cur 133:3-9 O '71

CLUBB, Oliver Edmund
China and the United States: beyond ping-pong. bibliog f Cur Hist 61:129-34+ S '71
China's plans: an informed guess. Nation 212:613-15 My 17 '71
China's strategic shift. Cur 132:58-64 S '71

about
Where are they now? il pors Newsweek 78: 10 Ag 9 '71 *

CLUBS
Club talk; service clubs. il Newsweek 77:81 F 15 '71
Colonel and the lady; Mme Phuong's on-post steam bath and massage parlor in Vietnam. il Time 97:29 Mr 15 '71
Roasted goose in the Tower of London; American beefeater club. C. Ray. il Holiday 48:12-13 N '70
See also
Automobile clubs
Aviation clubs
Boat clubs
Book clubs
Country clubs
Forty plus clubs
Garden clubs
Health clubs
Investment clubs
London—Clubs
Marco Polo club
Negroes—Clubs, societies, etc.
Yacht clubs

CLURMAN, Harold
Performing arts. Harper 242:28-34 F; 16, 30+ My '71
Theatre. See issues of Nation

CLUSTER housing. See Housing projects—Site planning

CLUTCHES, Automobile. See Automobiles—Clutches

CLUTTON-BROCK, Guy
Cold comfort. il por Newsweek 77:41 F 15 '71

CLYDE shipyards. See Shipyards

CNIDUS excavations. See Turkey—Antiquities

COACHES (athletics)
But what else do you do? NYU fencing coach. D. Delliquanti. il por Sports Illus 34:76+ Mr 8 '71
Getting up and going after a title; Lakers coach B. Sharman proves that practice makes perfect. P. Carry. il Sports Illus 35:24-6+ D 13 '71
Greening of U NO who—or do you? Priva-teers' coach R. Greene. L. Keith. por Sports Illus 34:58-9 Mr 15 '71
In the footsteps of Knute. D. Jenkins. il Sports Illus 35:44-51 S 13 '71
I've never taught a boy how to lose; ski coach W. Schaffler. il pors Life 70:46-9 Mr 12 '71
Only the game has changed; baseball coaches; photographs by James Drake; with account by R. Blount, jr. il Sports Illus 34:44-9 My 10 '71
See also
Allen, G.
Blackman, B.
Devaney, B.
Devine, G.
Evans, J.
McGuire, A.
Prothro, J. T. jr
Rauch, J.
Royal, D.
Weiskopf, H.

COACHES and coaching
American stagecoaches, where are they now? J. Frizzell and M. Frizzell. il Hobbies 76:98K-98M Ja '72
Legendary Concords. S. B. Duncan. il por Am West 8:16-17+ Ja '71

COAGULATION, Water. See Water purification

COAL
See also
Coke industry
Gasification
See Coal gasification

COAL carving. See Carving (art industries)

COAL gasification
Gas from coal: progress in technology and funding. Sci N 100:356-7 N 27 '71
Making synthetic fuel gas. Sci N 100:90-1 Ag 7 '71
Scramble to turn coal into gas. il Bsns W p20-1 S 4 '71

COAL industry
United States
Comeback king. il Time 97:73-4 Je 28 '71
Competitive comeback of coal. R. H. Gilluly. il Sci N 99:84-6 Ja 30 '71; Discussion. 99: 160 Mr 6 '71
Energy's Cinderella? il Forbes 109:140+ Ja 1 '72
Japan corners Alabama's coal. il Bsns W p45 My 15 '71
New boom for an old industry. il U S News 70:60-2 Mr 29 '71
See also
Coal mines and mining—United States
Collective bargaining—Coal industry
Peabody coal company
Pittston company
Westmoreland coal company

COAL miners
Bleak life of skilled diggers; portfolio. Fortune 83:83-5 Ja '71
Coal the killer. P. J. Nyden. Nation 213: 238-42 S 20 '71
Dusty death in Kentucky; black-lung run-around. D. Holwerk. il Nation 211:657-9 D 21 '70
Eccles no. 6; working the seam in a West Virginia coal mine. L. Leamer. il Harper 243:100-2+ D '71
Solidarity; reformers in West Virginia. R. Cassidy. New Repub 164:14-16 Mr 6 '71
See also
Coal mines and mining—Wages and hours
Collective bargaining—Coal industry
Strikes—United States—Coal mines and min-ing
United mine workers of America

COAL mines and mining
See also
Coal miners
Strip mining

Accidents and explosions
American tragedy. Nation 211:645 D 21 '70
Blood on the coal. D. Lockard. Nation 212: 207 F 15 '71
Disaster at Hurricane creek. S. Bacon. il Pop Mech 136:85-9+ O '71
Hunting scapegoats in Kentucky; Bethel re-port. R. Cassidy. New Repub 164:15-16 F 13 '71
See also
Coal mines and mining—Safety devices and measures

Safety devices and measures
Experts; Advisory committee on coal mine safety research. Ramp Mag 9:15 My '71
Mine safety slips through a loophole. Bsns W p 19 Ja 30 '71
No rats in the mines. H. S. Arnow. il Nation 213:401-4 O 25 '71

Stripping operations
See Strip mining

Wages and hours
What the soft-coal decision means. Bsns W p37 D 4 '71

Appalachian Region
Appalachia, like the flayed back of a man. J. Branscome. il N Y Times Mag p30-1+ D 12 '71

Canada
How Kaiser dug a hole for itself; Kaiser re-sources, Elkview operation. il Bsns W p98+ Je 19 '71
Kaiser calls for help; Japanese deal with Kaiser resources. Fortune 83:43-4 F '71

France
Letter from Paris; strike. Genêt. New York-er 47:91 F 27 '71

United States
Coal companies rediscover the West. il Bsns W p92+ D 13 '71
King coal. Ramp Mag 9:4 Mr '71
See also
Coal industry—United States

COAL strikes (United States) See Strikes—United States—Coal mines and mining

COAL supply
Coal: you can paint a rock black and sell it. il Nations Bsns 59:33-5 Jl '71

COALE, Ansley J.
Man and his environment; adaptation of address, March 19, 1970. Science 170:132-6; 171: 15 O 9 '70, Ja 8 '71

COAST changes
Net kinetic energy in littoral transport. W. F. Tanner. bibliog Science 172:1231 Je 18 '71
See also
Beach erosion

COAST guard. See United States—Coast guard

COASTAL marshes. See Marshes, Tide

COASTAL states gas producing company
Gas price rule hits a maverick. Bsns W p20 Ap 3 '71

COASTERS. See Table mats, tiles, etc.

COASTS
Mexico
Down the Mexican coast. C. Mitchell. il Motor B & S 128:52-5+ O '71
United States
Threatened coastlines. il Time 98:32-3 Ag 30 '71

COATED lenses. See Lenses, Photographic

COATS
Jacket fit for a tiger; Sherpa jacket. J. Milligan. Holiday 49:30 Jl '71
See also
Capes

COAXIAL cables
See also
Television cables

COBALAMIN. See Vitamins—Vitamin B₁₂

COBALT
Isotopes
Recycled water: pure enough to drink because of cobalt-60. E. Hartley. il Sci Digest 70:82-6 N '71

COBB, Boughton, Jr
Fiberglass hulls: to paint or not to paint. il Yachting 129:56-7+ Ap '71

COBB, Mary
Nursery school on wheels. il Parents Mag 46: 60-1+ S '71

COBB, Tom
Earthquakes and eucalypts in Peru. il Am For 77:20-1+ S '71

COBEAN, Robert H. and others
Obsidian trade at San Lorenzo Tenochtitlan, Mexico. bibliog il Science 174:666-71 N 12 '71

COBEN, Stanley
Scientific establishment and the transmission of quantum mechanics to the United States, 1919-32. bibliog f Am Hist R 76: 442-66 Ap '71

COBLE, Anna, and others
New eye on the air. bibliog il por Environ 13:34-41 My '71

COBRA venom. See Venom

COCA-COLA bottling company of Los Angeles
Late tape. R. Brady. Duns 97:10-11 Je '71

COCA-COLA company
Austin of Coca-Cola. il por Forbes 107:70 My 15 '71
Company that helps migrants. il Bsns W p61 Mr 6 '71
Have a Coke, world; commercial jingle becomes popular hit. Newsweek 79:47 Ja 3 '72
Let them drink Pepsi; closing of the bottling plant in Italy. Newsweek 78:98 O 18 '71
Place in the sun for the migrant; Coca-Cola's housing project. il Nations Bsns 59:70-3 S '71

COCAINE
Doctor Jekyll and Mr Cocaine. Sci N 99:264 Ap 17 '71
It's the real thing. il Newsweek 78:124 S 27 '71

COCHITI LAKE, N.Mex. (proposed) See New cities and towns

COCHLEA. See Labyrinth (ear)

COCHRAN, Clay L.
Scandal of rural housing. Arch Forum 134: 52-5 Mr '71

COCHRAN, Leonard
Theological verse, done after the manner of Miss Dickinson; poem. Cath World 213:242 Ag '71

COCHRANE, Diane
Beesley and his bronze children. il por Am Artist 35:54-9+ S '71
David A. Leffel: 20th century old master. il por Am Artist 35:20-5 O '71

COCHRANE, Elizabeth
Oh, my, that Nellie Bly! V. Kelly. por Read Digest 99:33-4+ D '71

COCHRANE, Shirley Graves
Change of heart; story. Good H 172:86-7 Ap '71

COCK fighting
Blood and bets. Newsweek 78:49 Ag 23 '71

COCKBURN, Alexander
Down and out in London: the Common market dilemma. il Ramp Mag 10:48-51 O '71

COCKER, Joe
Rock family affair. il por Life 71:52-3 S 24 '71 *

COCKETTES (rock group) See Rock groups

COCKFIGHTING. See Cock fighting

COCKING, Clive
Americanization of Canadian universities. il Sat R 54:44-5+ Ag 21 '71

COCKLEBURS
Photoperiod evidence in the introduction of xanthium (cocklebur) to Australia. C. McMillan. bibliog il Science 171:1029-31 Mr 12 '71

COCKROACH control
Non-hazardous cockroach control; utilizing Drione. E. H. Paisley. il Am City 86:60-1 Ja '71
Notes and comment: geckos as protection. New Yorker 46:19-20 Ja 30 '71

COCKROACHES
Extermination
See Cockroach control

COCKTAIL tables. See Tables

COCKTAILS
Top of the morning party drinks. J. Wilson. House & Gard 139:54+ Mr '71
When the recipe sells what's in the drink; Harvey Wallbanger. il Bsns W p35 Jl 3 '71

COCOA, Fla.
Water supply
Water was too hard. G. C. Folkes and J. Sellers. il Am City 86:49+ Jl '71

COCONUT
Coconut, it's a house plant surprise. il Sunset 146:220 Mr '71
See also
Cookery—Coconut

COCTEAU, Jean
Cocteau, by F. Steegmuller. Review
New Yorker 47:130+ Mr 13 '71. N. Bliven *
La vie du poète. R. Winegarten. Commentary 51:89-92 Ap '71 *

COD, CAPE. See Cape Cod

CODLING moths
Codling moths beget apple worms. il Sunset 146:283 Ap '71
Sex attractant of the codling moth: characterization with electroantennogram technique. W. Roelofs and others. bibliog Science 174:297-9 O 15 '71

CODRESCU, Andrei
Best side of me; Accident; Truth & ruffles; Thieves, seasons; poems. Poetry 119:74-6 N '71

CODY, John, cardinal
Bishops in the dock. por Newsweek 77:63 Je 28 '71

COE, Henry W, state park. See California—Parks and reserves

COE, Kenton
Artist life. D. J. Soria. il por Hi Fi 21: MA4-6+ N '71 *

COE, Lee
What you should know about feeding your dog or cat. Read Digest 98:119-22 Mr '71

COE, Michael D.
Shadow of the Olmecs. il Horizon 13:66-75 Aut '71

COE, Ralph T.
Breaking through the sound barrier. il Art N 70:44-5+ Sum '71

CO-ED dormitories. See Dormitories

COEDUCATION
Best of both worlds. il Newsweek 77:86 Ap 5 '71
Colleges going co-ed: a trend that keeps rising. il U S News 70:70-1 F 8 '71
From coeducation to equality. il Time 98: 60+ D 6 '71
Lady is a tiger. D. Leff. il Seventeen 29:124-5+ O '70

COELENTERATES
See also
Jellyfish
Sea anemones
Siphonophora
Sponges
Zoanthus

COENZYMES
Vitamin B₁₂. T. C. Stadtman. bibliog il Science 171:859-67 Mr 5 '71

COEUR D'ALENE LAKE
Offshore in Idaho. R. S. Larringan. il Yachting 129:58+ My '71

COEUR D'ALENE strike, 1892
Shootout in Burke Canyon. E. Clark. il Am Heritage 22:44-8+ Ag '71
COEXISTENCE policy. See United States— Foreign relations—Russia
COFFEE, Frank K.
Bike comes back. il Mech Illus 67:73-4+ Ap '71
Buried treasure, hot new hobby for RVers. il Mech Illus 67:100-2+ S '71
Can you afford to invest in the stock market? il Mech Illus 67:57-9+ F '71
Can you cut your fuel bill in half? il Mech Illus 67:132-3+ N '71
Coffee mill comes back. il Mech Illus 67:50-1 D '71
Drinking man's guide to water filters. il Mech Illus 67:86-7+ S '71
Facts on prefinished paneling. il Mech Illus 67:87-9+ Ja '71
Happiness is a humidified home. il Mech Illus 67:118-19+ Ja '71
How to brave Disney's new world. il Mech Illus 67:46+ O '71
Super lift from supercopters. il Mech Illus 68:50-1+ Ja '72
Those second-generation motor homes. il Mech Illus 67:53-5+ Je '71
Tiny trailers for tiny cars. il Mech illus 67:74-5+ My '71
COFFEE
Coffee and your health. Consumer Bul 54:22 Ap '71
Coffee talk: 8 ways to brew a good cup. M. Cubisino. il Good H 173:198-9+ D '71
For gentle coffee, the cold water idea. il Sunset 146:118 F '71
How to make a good cup of coffee. Redbook 136:66+ Ap '71
Story of coffee. W. J. Thompson. il Horticulture 49:20-1+ N '71
Suppliers of coffee beans. Consumer Bul 54:2 F '71
What, coffee, too? linked to cancer of the bladder. Newsweek 78:82 Jl 12 '71
COFFEE cake
Come for coffee, afternoon cards, a committee meeting. il Bet Hom & Gard 49:64-5+ Ja '71
Fast and fancy coffee cakes. il Bet Hom & Gard 49:103-4 Ap '71
COFFEE grinders, Electric. See Coffee mills
COFFEE house ministry
Opinion: the Potter's house: a coffeehouse church. N. Legge. por Mlle 73:66+ S '71
COFFEE industry
See also
International coffee agreement

Brazil
United States and Brazil conclude agreement on soluble coffee; Department announcement, text of U.S. note. Dept State Bul 64:627-8 My 10 '71

Japan
Instant profits for coffee. il Bsns W p40 My 1 '71
COFFEE mills
Coffee mill comes back. F. Coffee. il Mech Illus 67:50-1 D '71
Electric coffee grinders. il Consumer Bul 54:15-17 Ag '71
COFFEE pots, percolators, etc.
Coffee makers for the seventies. il Consumer Bul 54:17-23 O '71
COFFEE table books. See Picture books
COFFEE tables. See Tables
COFFER, Helene Lewis
With all my heart; story. Good H 173:72-3 Jl '71
COFFEY, Donald S. See Brown, D. G. jt. auth.
COFFIN, Anne
(ed) See Nixon, R. M. Father and the bride
(ed) See Nixon, T. Father and the bride
COFFIN, Patricia
(ed) American family. il Look 35:21-40+ Ja 26 '71
Happy family. il Look 35:30-4 Ja 26 '71
Young unmarrieds. il Look 35:63-4+ Ja 26 '71
COFFIN, Tristram
Big rock-candy mountain. Nation 213:262-4 S 27 '71
On power as a disease. Nation 213:649-53 D 20 '71
COGAN, Berlind, Weill and Levitt, inc.
Unbelievable last months of Hayden, Stone. C. J. Loomis. il Fortune 83:114-16+ Ja '71
COGER, Leslie Irene
Readers theatre. il Schol Teach Jr/Sr High p24-5 O '71
COGGIN, Joseph
New test detects cancer quickly. McCalls 98:42 Jl '71 *

COGGINS, Dessie-Ellen. See Coggins, J. R. jt. auth.
COGGINS, Jack Roland
A-frame for plants. Org Gard & Farm 18:47 Jl '71
Broccoli comes before lettuce. il Org Gard & Farm 18:63-4 Ja '71
Huckleberries, anyone? il Org Gard & Farm 18:64-5 F '71
Terrace gardens are easy with a tiller. il Org Gard & Farm 18:58-9 Je '71
Try earlier planting. il Org Gard & Farm 18:46-7 Mr '71
Yes, you can have fine roasting ears by the 4th! il Org Gard & Farm 18:48-9 Ap '71
—and Coggins, D.-E.
Our family fights pollution. il Parents Mag 46:54-5+ Mr '71
COGNITION
Learned ape; experiments to study dyslexia. il Newsweek 78:78 O 25 '71
COHABITATION
Young unmarrieds: Theresa Pommett and Charles Walsh, college graduates living together. P. Coffin. il Look 35:63-4+ F 5 '71
COHEA, Barbara
Plea; story. Sr Schol 98:10 My 17 '71
COHEN, Abraham
Screenings: 8mm (cont) Library J 96:2860-1, 3454 S 15, O 15 '71
COHEN, Alexander H.
Winner is, the losers are... il pors Time 97:50-1+ Mr 29 '71 *
COHEN, Alvin
Bolivia: internal instability and international dependence. bibliog f Cur Hist 60:78-83 F '71
COHEN, Carl
Poisonous tree. Nation 212:231-2 F 22 '71; Same with title How far electronics surveillance? Cur 129:3-6 My '71
COHEN, Daniel
Sea serpents: what they really are. il Sci Digest 69:27-8 Mr '71
Sir Alister Hardy: science and religious experiences. il por Sci Digest 70:18-23 S '71
Sweepstakes route. il Sci Digest 69:8-13 Mr '71
Witches in our midst. il Sci Digest 69:22-6 Je '71
COHEN, David, and others
Magnetocardiography of direct currents: S-T segment and baseline shifts during experimental myocardial infarction. bibliog il Science 172:1329-33 Je 25 '71
COHEN, Eli, 1924-1965
Shattered silence, by Aldouby and Ballinger. Review
Bsns W il por p 11 Jl 10 '71. M. A. Reichek *
COHEN, Eli E.
Child labor: a barbarism we must not tolerate. por Parents Mag 46:34 Ag '71
COHEN, Gerald. See Heikkila, R; Redmond, G. jt. auths.
COHEN, Harold
Learning to cope in Prince Georges County. B. L. Collier. il Sat R 54:64-5+ My 22 '71 *
COHEN, Harriet
America house: an appreciation. Craft Horiz 31:11+ Ap '71
COHEN, Jerome Alan
Probing the Chinese mind. por U S News 71:81 S 6 '71
Recognizing China. For Affairs 50:30-43 O '71
COHEN, Jerry
Story behind the book: America, inc. S. Wagner. il Pub W 200:60-1 N 15 '71 *
COHEN, Larry
Rosebloom's here. il Sat R 54:50-1 Ja 30 '71
COHEN, Lita H. Solis-. See Solis-Cohen, L. H.
COHEN, Marcia
Dear driver; poem. Ladies Home J 88:198 S '71
May days; poem. Ladies Home J 88:187 My '71
COHEN, Martin
How our strangers in paradise like us now. il Todays Health 49:40-3+ Jl '71
How the heavens influence our lives. il Todays Health 49:16-19 O '71
Postscript to tragedy: a father's crusade. il Redbook 137:76-7+ Je '71
COHEN, Morrel H.
Theory of amorphous semiconductors: adaptation of address, February 1971. bibliog il Phys Today 24:26-32 My '71
COHEN, Nathan
Congressman convicted; case of J. Dowdy. por Time 99:13-14 Ja 10 '72 *
COHEN, Nathan Marshall
OE library agency aide heads resurgent union. Library J 96:578 F 15 '71 *

COHEN, Paul
Erosion of surface naval power. For Affairs 49:330-41 Ja '71
COHEN, Robert. See Utlaut, W. F. jt. auth.
COHEN, Seymour S.
Cancer research and the scientific community. Science 172:1212-14 Je 18 '71
COHEN, Sidney
Drug scene. il PTA Mag 65:20-3 Ja '71
COHEN, Steve O. See Dickhaus, S. M. jt. auth.
COHEN, Stewart
Creativity: an implicit goal in education. bibliog Sch & Soc 99:174-6 Mr '71
COHEN, Wilbur J.
Welfare reform: a persistent quest. Cur Hist 61:257-60+ N '71
COHEN, Ze'eva
Ze'eva Cohen, the Cubiculo, NYC. L. Pastore. Dance Mag 45:77 Je '71 •
COHN, Arthur
Boston symphony chamber players. il Am Rec G 37:424-6 Mr '71
His own man, the music of Elliott Carter. il por Am Rec G 37:756-9 Jl '71

about

Strong, assertive voice: the music of Arthur Cohn. D. W. Moore. por Am Rec G 37:554 My '71 •
COHN, Edward S. and others
Ethacrynic acid effect on the composition of cochlear fluids. bibliog il Science 171:910-11 Mr 5 '71
COHN, Haim Hermann
Plea of innocence. il por Newsweek 77:101 Mr 15 '71 •
COHN, Marcus
Should the FCC reward stations that do a good job? il Sat R 54:45-7 Ag 14 '71
COHN, Nudie
Nudie the tailor. il por Newsweek 78:90 S 13 '71 •
COHN, Robert
Differential cerebral processing of noise and verbal stimuli. bibliog il Science 172:599-601 My 7 '71
COHN, Roy Marcus
Conservative's civil liberties. M. S. Evans. Nat R 23:936-7 Ag 24 '71 •
COHN, Victor
Vital hour: your physical exam. Ladies Home J 88:74 Ap '71
Where are we at now? Cur 125:15-19 Ja '71
COIFFURE. See Hairdressing
COILS, Induction. See Induction coils
COIN (literary character) See Characters in literature
COIN banks. See Banks, Coin
COIN collecting. See Numismatics
COIN-operated washers and dryers. See Laundries, Commercial
COINAGE. See Coins; Silver as money
COINER, Elizabeth H.
Arches National Monument. il Parks & Rec 6:36-7 N '71
Carlsbad Caverns National Park. il Parks & Rec 6:120-1 Ja '71
COINS
Attempts to unite the world's coinages; convention in Paris, 1867 to decide upon an international gold piece. C. French. Hobbies 76:132+ S '71
Coin quiz. C. F. French. See issues of Hobbies
Gold coins glitter in investors' eyes. Bsns W p85-6 O 16 '71
Ike dollar: it's coming on the market, but may be hard to find. il U S News 71:68 Ag 9 '71
Let's talk about our coinage. C. F. French. Hobbies 76:132 Je '71
New monetary system after the revolution. C. French. Hobbies 76:132+ Ag '71
200th anniversary of our independence. C. French. Hobbies 76:132 Ja '72
Whatever happened to those millions of Eisenhower dollars? il U S News 76:62 Ja 10 '72
See also
Franklin mint

Collectors and collecting
See Numismatics
COINS, Ancient
Life during ancient times; silver tetradrachm. C. F. French. il Hobbies. 76:132 My '71
Tetradrachms of Phoenicia. C. F. French. il Hobbies 76:132 Ap '71

COIRO, Cynthia
Ecology: what we must do now. il Har Yrs 11:6-12+ Je '71
Mobile homes today. il Har Yrs 11:19-23+ S '71
On the road to sensitivity. Har Yrs 11:7 Mr '71
Why a National caucus on the black aged? il Har Yrs 11:12-18 N '71
COKE, Van Deren
Talk with Van Deren Coke, new man at the George Eastman house. J. Deschin. por Pop Phot 69:24+ Ag '71
COKE industry
Cleaner way to make coke. il Bsns W p42 Jl 31 '71
Kaiser calls for help; Japanese deal with Kaiser resources. Fortune 83:43-4 F '71
COKE plants
See also
Steel works
COLA beverages. See Beverages
COLBERT, Francis T.
Lasater ranch: applied range ecology. il Nat Parks & Con Mag 45:18-20 Mr '71
COLBORN, Francis
Moral theology: hope for revival? America 124:312-15 Mr 27 '71
COLBY, Carroll B.
Camp chef. See issues of Outdoor life
Camping. See issues of Outdoor life
COLD
See also
Low temperatures

Physiological effects
How your body adapts to cold; excerpt from Freezing point: cold as a matter of life and death. L. Kavaler. Read Digest 98:125-8 Ja '71
Survival at 70 below: it's easier these days. B. Hildenbrand. il Todays Health 49:46-9+ F '71
See also
Fishes, Effect of temperature on
Shivering
COLD (disease)
C is for controversy. Newsweek 78:102+ D 6 '71
Can vitamin C really prevent and cure colds? il Good H 172:173-5 Mr '71
Cure for the cold? T. J. Murray. Duns 97:64 Je '71
Vitamin C and the common cold, by L. Pauling. Review
Nation 212:440-2 Ap 5 '71. D. Planz
Vitamin C on the cold front: cure or craze? Sr Schol 98:8 F 8 '71

Anecdotes, facetiae, satire, etc.
Confessions of a cold-cure collector. R. Armour. il Read Digest 99:55-6 O '71
Give in to a cold? Not me! E. Bombeck. il Good H 172:48+ Mr '71
COLD cellars. See Basements and cellars
COLD creams. See Cosmetics
COLD drinks. See Beverages
COLD frames
A-frame for plants. J. R. Coggins. Org Gard & Farm 18:47 Jl '71
I call my cold frame indispensable. K. MacReynolds. il por Org Gard & Farm 18:53-5 O '71
Make a baled-hay cold frame. A. Alexander. il Org Gard & Farm 18:90 My '71
See also
Hotbeds
COLD remedies. See Medicines, Patent, proprietary, etc.
COLD resistance in plants. See Plants—Frost resistance
COLD sores. See Herpes simplex
COLD soups. See Soups
COLD urticaria. See Hives (urticaria)
COLD war (United States and Russia) See United States—Foreign relations—Russia
COLD war college (proposed) See Freedom studies center (organization)
COLDS. See Cold (disease)
COLDWATER, Mich., public library
Censorship in Coldwater; letter to the editor. R. H. Rosichan. Library J 96:3256 O 15 '71
COLE, Alison
Graffiti; poem. Seventeen 29:146 Jl '70
COLE, Edward N.
Report on safety in cars of the future; excerpt from address, November 3, 1971. il por U S News 71:76-7 N 22 '71
COLE, Flora
Soft sell. Engl J 60:931-2 O '71

COLE, Glen F.
Stalking the grizzly, stalking the elk. J.
L. Arehart. il Sci N 100:251 O 9 '71 *
COLE, John N.
Letter from Maine. il Harper 243:42+ N '71
COLE, Sheila
Parent and child. N Y Times Mag p84+ D 12
'71
COLE, William
Beware the amphetamines: speed kills. il
Parents Mag 46:74-5+ N '71
Joined at birth, separated they thrive. il
Good H 173:60+ O '71
Mary Litty's 25-year struggle to help epilep-
tics. pors il Good H 173:48+ Jl '71
New understanding, new hope, for children
with epilepsy. Parents Mag 46:52-3+ My
'71
COLEMAN, D. L.
Linkage of genes controlling the rate of syn-
thesis and structure of aminolevulinate de-
hydratase. bibliog il Science 173:1245-6 S 24
'71
COLEMAN, John A.
Churches and the homosexual. America 124:
113-17 F 6 '71
COLEMAN, Kate
Carnal knowledge: a portrait of four hook-
ers. il Ramp Mag 10:16-28 D '71
COLEMAN, Robert E.
Coming world revival? Chr Today 15:10-12 Jl
16 '71
COLEMAN, Rodney
White House fellow. il pors Ebony 26:98-
100+ My '71 *
COLEMAN, Sheldon
Merchandising the outdoors. il por Bsns W
p68+ My 22 '71 *
COLEMAN company
Merchandising the outdoors. il por Bsns W
p68+ My 22 '71
COLES, Christie Lund
Willow in winter; poem. Ladies Home J 88:
138 F '71
COLES, Robert
Average man might fool you. por Life 70:4
My 7 '71
Dialogue with radical priest Daniel Berrigan;
excerpts from The geography of faith. pors
Time 97:16-17 Mr 22 '71
Domain of sorts; excerpt from Children of
crisis: migrants, sharecroppers and moun-
taineers. il Harper 243:116-18+ N '71
"I am a maid, and what do I know?" Atlan
228:64-8 Ag '71
Mondale of Minnesota. New Repub 165:21-3
D 25 '71
On the meaning of work. Atlan 228:103-4
O '71
(ed) Policeman complains; interview; excerpt
from Middle Americans. il N Y Times Mag
p 11+ Je 13 '71
COLETTE, Sidonie Gabrielle
White rose. T. Capote. il por Ladies Home J
88:96-7+ Jl '71 *
COLEUS
Good pot plant: colorful coleus. il Sunset 147:
154 Jl '71
COLGATE, Stephen
How to win the Admiral's cup. il Yachting
130:52+ O '71
COLIC
Handling colicky babies. A. J. Snider. il Sci
Digest 70:72 O '71
COLIJN, Helen
To the beautiful isle. il Yachting 130:58-9+
D '71
COLIN, Patrick L.
Other reef; with biographical sketch. il por
Sea Front 17:160-70, 191 My '71
COLIN, R. R. Drucker-. See Drucker-Colin, R.
R.
COLISEUM, Richmond, Va. See Richmond, Va.
—Coliseum
COLISH, A, inc.
Fine press talents combined at A. Colish. C.
B. Grannis. il Pub W 200:42-3 D 6 '71
COLL, Dick
Sellers of Sellersville. il Am City 86:64 Jl '71
COLL, Edward
One man's peace corps. por Time 98:12 Jl 19
'71 *
COLLABORATION, Literary. See Authorship
—Collaboration
COLLAGE
Contemporary scene in creative expression.
L. J. Miller. il Sch Arts 70:16-17 Ap '71
Experiments in collage. il Design 72:34-5
mid-Wint '71
Gingham checks in; excerpt from Gloria Van-
derbilt book of collage. G. Vanderbilt. il
por Ladies Home J 88:80-1 Ap '71
How to make a rainbow; Cornell's collages.
A. C. Anderson. il Art N 69:50-2+ F '71

Kelly, collage and color. D. Waldman. bib-
liog il Art N 70:44-7+ D '71
Masterpiece in the mail? New York corres-
pondance school. C. Troy. il McCalls 98:44
Ag '71
Mixed media collage. J. Comins. il Sch Arts
71:10-11 N '71
Recreating the mediocre and the discard. B.
Stubbins. il Sch Arts 70:11 Mr '71
COLLAGEN
Collagen polypeptides: normal release from
polysomes in the absence of proline hy-
droxylation. E. Lazarides and L. N. Lukens.
bibliog il Science 173:723-5 Ag 20 '71
Sight saver; replacing vitreous humor. il
Time 97:40 My 24 '71
COLLECTIVE agreements. See Trade agree-
ments
COLLECTIVE bargaining
Bargaining chill deepens. il Bsns W p 108+
S 25 '71
Collective bargaining; address, February 24,
1971. J. D. Hodgson. Vital Speeches 37:382-4
Ap 1 '71
Icy disregard for the wage freeze. il Bsns W
p70+ Ag 21 '71
Is there hope for collective bargaining? the
inflation threat; address, May 7, 1971. R. H.
Larry. Vital Speeches 37:537-40 Je 15 '71
Lighter bargaining calendar ahead; with
table. Bsns W p54-5 D 25 '71
More labor troubles for two vital industries:
dockworkers and coal miners. il U S News
71:99-101 O 11 '71
Now it's my turn. il Newsweek 77:50-2 F 1 '71
Productivity is the sticking point. il Bsns W p
17-19 Jl 10 '71
Rival approaches to strikes, talks; forum
sponsored by the Institute of collective bar-
gaining and group relations. U S News 70:
85 Je 7 '71
Should collective bargaining be revamped?
symposium. bibliog Mo Labor R 94:42-59 Ag
'71
Unions aim still higher. il Bsns W p 106 Mr
13 '71
Unions spurn the inflation alert. il Bsns W
p72-3 Ap 24 '71
Wage spiral: too late to slow it down in '71?
U S News 70:86-7 Je 21 '71
See also
Arbitration, Industrial
Trade agreements

Aerospace industries

Aerospace unions demanding increases in
wages, benefits. Aviation W 95:17 Jl 19 '71
Aerospace unions pick a target. Bsns W
p84 O 9 '71
Aircraft unions hold their fire. il Bsns W
p 118 My 15 '71
Negotiating with a hard-hit industry. Bsns
W p98 Mr 6 '71
Policy blocks labor talks in aerospace. Avia-
tion W 95:18 Ag 23 '71

Airlines

Airlines, Administration face first test on
wage portion of Phase 2. Aviation W 95:
26 N 29 '71
Airlines move into closer formation. por
Bsns W p98 Ag 14 '71
Carriers push new labor law. L. Doty. Aviation W 94:40-1 My 31 '71

Automobile industry

Chrysler reshuffles to whittle costs. il Bsns
W p25-6 Ja 16 '71

Coal industry

Signs of peace. Newsweek 78:97-8 N 22 '71

College professors and instructors

Collective bargaining on the college campus.
Todays Ed 60:44-5 D '71
Faculty collective bargaining at the City
university of New York. S. Jacobson. Sch &
Soc 99:346-9 O '71

Construction industry

Wage madness in the construction industry.
C. Stevenson. Read Digest 98:47-51 Ja '71

Farm labor

Why Chavez spurns the Labor act. R. B.
Taylor. il Nation 212:454-6 Ap 12 '71

Government employees

Public employee relations; address, March
19, 1971. J. R. Van De Water. Vital Speeches 37:556-63 Jl 1 '71
Public worker transforms labor. W. L. Abbott. Nation 212:648-52 My 24 '71

COLLECTIVE bargaining—*Continued*

Maritime workers

Dock disputes heat up again. Bsns W p21 Ja 1 '72

ILWU won't freeze. M. E. Leary. Nation 213: 174-6 S 6 '71

Nixon will use no hooks on dockers. il Bsns W p66 Mr 20 '71

Signs of peace. Newsweek 78:97-8 N 22 '71

Railroads

Fight shaping up on rail labor law. il Bsns W p45 Ja 23 '71

Is anyone listening? address, May 20, 1971. 1971. J. S. Reed. Vital Speeches 37:569-72 Jl 1 '71

New plea to curb transport strikes. U S News 70:79-80 F 15 '71

On the way: another railroad crisis. il U S News 70:80-1 F 8 '71

Steel industry

Down to the wire in steel bargaining. Bsns W p 19-20 Jl 31 '71

How the steel strike was averted. il Bsns W p 17-19 Ag 7 '71

Key steel question: administration role. il U S News 70:55 My 17 '71

Midnight cliffhanger in steel. il Time 98: 56-7 Ag 9 '71

Peace in the mills? Newsweek 78:55-6 Jl 26 '71

Price of peace. Time 98:57 Ag 2 '71

Rumblings of a steel strike get louder. il Bsns W p69 F 27 '71

Steel settlement: brighter chances. U S News 71:50-1 Jl 19 '71

Steel settles in for some long talks. il Bsns W p50 Je 26 '71

Steel: the thaw before the freeze. R. W. Gibbons. Commonweal 94:444-5 S 3 '71

Steelworkers' chief sees a bitter fight. por Bsns W p 16 Ja 23 '71

Steelworkers set guidelines for 1971 pay talks. U S News 70:81 Ap 12 '71

USW whets its c-o-l clause; unlimited cost-of-living. Bsns W p82 F 20 '71

Warm-up fight for steelworkers. Bsns W p28 Ja 16 '71

Teachers

Governance is integral to accountability. L. Williams. Todays Ed 60:59-60 Ap '71

Telephone companies

TV carries a call for a phone strike. Bsns W p20 My 29 '71

Tougher tone in phone talks. Bsns W p78 My 8 '71

Canada

Canadians try to catch up again. il Bsns W p90 Ja 16 '71

COLLECTIVE farms
See also
Collective settlements

Rhodesia

Cold comfort: multiracial farm society. il Newsweek 77:41 F 15 '71

COLLECTIVE labor agreements. See Trade agreements

COLLECTIVE security. See International security

COLLECTIVE settlements

After the fall: what this country needs is a good counter counterculture culture. D. French. il N Y Times Mag p20-1+ O 3 '71; Discussion. p26 O 24; 98 N 7; 22+ N 21 '71

Apocalypse is a nice place to visit, but. .; communal living in New Mexico. C. Rotmil. Sat R 54:4+ N 27 '71

Authors & editors: writing of Getting back together; interview. ed. by D. N. Mount. R. Houriet. por Pub W 200:33-5 S 13 '71

Big Vic; operator of Institute of human abilities More Houses. C. H. Simonds. Nat R 23:1471 D 31 '71

Commune: child of the 1970's. J. C. Haughey. America 124:254-6 Mr 13 '71

Commune information: the People's information center, Brooklyn, New Yorker 47:32 O 16 '71

Commune way keeps spreading because: maybe it'll be different here; New Buffalo commune, Taos County, N.Mex. W. Hedgepeth. il Look 35:63-6+ Mr 23 '71

Communes: a firsthand report on a controversial new life style. S. G. Lanes. il Parents Mag 46:61-3+ O '71

Communes and the work crisis. L. M. Andrews. Cur 126:34-9 F '71

Communes go to court. il Time 97:53-4 F 1 '71

Communes: the alternative life-style; with list of types of communes and report on the Good Earth commune. Ore. H. A. Otto. il Sat R 54:16-21 Ap 24 '71; Same abr. Cur 130:15-22 Je '71

Could you make it in a commune? McCalls 98:45 S '71

Family: the story of Charles Manson's dune-buggy attack battalion, by E. Sanders. Review Nat R 23:1311-12 N 19 '71. C. H. Simonds

Halfway between dropping out and dropping in. S. V. Roberts. il N Y Times Mag p44-6+ S 12 '71

In transit (literally) religious bands form semi-communal state. Chr Today 15:35 Ap 23 '71

Life inside a hippie commune. L. Robinson. il Ebony 26:88-91+ N '70

New trail to Santa Fe. D. Butwin. il Sat R 54:35-6 Jl 3 '71

1971 B.C: what the new living is like in a Boston commune. J. Avorn. il Look 35: 54+ Ag 10 '71

Notes from Rainbow farm. Ramp Mag 10: 49-51 Ag; 58-60 S '71

Open the shutters and let the godforce through; Brotherhood of the spirit commune in Massachusets. M. Cantwell. il Mlle 74:142-3+ D '71

Our commune in suburbia. N. Jackson. il por Redbook 138:44+ Ja '72

Poetry of new community. J. Jerome. Writers Digest 51:18-19 Ag '71

Rainbow farm (cont of) Notes from rainbow farm. Ramp Mag 10:60-3 D '71

Rapping with the Jesus people; Senior youthview, ed. by A. Rubin. il Sr Schol 99:12-14 D 13 '71

Trade winds; interview, ed. by C. Amory. R. Houriet. Sat R 54:18+ S 18 '71

Twin Oaks: on to Walden two. il Time 98: 48-9 S 20 '71

U.S. journal: Manhattan and Atchison, Kan; the Maes family. C. Trillin. New Yorker 47:90-5 Je 12 '71

Vibes: Brotherhood of the spirit commune, Warwick, Mass. and the New York branch of the Fort Hill community, Roxbury, Mass. New Yorker 47:24-5 Ag 7 '71

Wear and tear in the communes. A. Solnit. il Nation 212:524-7 Ap 26 '71; Same abr. Cur 130:22-6 Je '71

Young people. are they America's new peasantry? R. Rodale. il Org Gard & Farm 18:30-3 My '71

See also
Amana society
Bishop Hill, Ill.

China (People's Republic)

China's 70,000 communes. E. Snow. New Republic 164:19-23 Je 26 '71

Israel

Israeli kibbutz: model for religious orders? J. C. Fleck. America 125:143-6 S 11 '71

What has to be said: a personal statement; librarian drops 6,000 miles out. A. Sable. il Wilson Lib Bul 46:338-47 D '71

COLLECTIVISM

Is socialism the wave of the future. B. L. Masse. America 124:280 Mr 20 '71

COLLECTORS and collecting

Antiques' travel guide. See occasional issues of Antiques

Collectibles: hunting treasures. J. Dhai. House B 113:131-3 Ap '71

Collectors' notes; ed. by E. Gaines. See issues of Antiques

How to sell your valuables. R. J. Fornwalt. il Har Yrs 11:19-23 N '71

Personal signatures; designer-collectors. N. Schram. il House B 113:75-9 F '71

See also
Autographs
Bottles
Display of antiques, art objects, etc.
Miniature objects
Paperweights

also subhead Collectors and collecting under various subjects, e.g. Postage stamps —Collectors and collecting

COLLEEN Moore doll house. See Doll houses

COLLEGE, Choice of

College & careers. G. C. Keller. il Seventeen 30:23+ S '71

College of your choice. T. H. Clancy. America 124 :89-91 Ja 30 '71

COLLEGE administration. See Colleges and universities—Administration

COLLEGE administrators. See College officials

COLLEGE admission. See Colleges and universities—Entrance requirements

COLLEGE All-Star game. See All-Star football game

COLLEGE alumni. See College graduates

COLLEGE and business. See Business and education

COLLEGE and school drama
Curtain going up! S. D. Stutz. il Parents Mag 46:60-1+ Mr '71
Play's the thing: theater and dramatic arts in secondary schools. C. M. Kirkton. bibliog Engl J 60:533-9 Ap '71
Segregated drama in integrated schools. D. Evans. Engl J 60:260-3 F '71
Theater; Florida state university's production of Is anybody listening? H. Hewes. Sat R 54:16+ F 20 '71

Texts
Junior and senior high. See issues of Plays

COLLEGE and school journalism
Alternative: publication of the party of the Right at Yale. W. F. Buckley, jr. Nat R 23:331 Mr 23 '71
Analysis of a high school underground paper. F. K. Heussenstamm. Ed Digest 36:53-4 Ja '71
Campus newspapers: journalistic atrocities with captive readership and a guaranteed income. Nat R 23:71 Ja 26 '71
Evangelical college students: an opinion sampler; excerpts from college newspapers. D. J. Riggall. Chr Today 15:11-14 My 21 '71
High school confidential; FPS, a national news service. M. Smith. McCalls 98:44 Ag '71
High school newsreels; Redmond, Wash. J. A. Newman. il Schol Teach Jr/Sr High p22-3 Mr 8 '71
Old new journalism; campus press. J. Tebbel. Sat R 54:96-7 Mr 13 '71; Discussion. 54:42+ Ap 10 '71
Reluctant rebels; high school underground newspapers. R. J. Sullivan. il Parents Mag 46:56-7+ Ap '71
Responsible freedom for the secondary school press: a cooperative effort. E. M. Deal. Engl J 60:960-2 O '71
Underground newspaper, what's it all about? C. Hughes. bibliog Clear House 46:155-7 N '71
See also
College annuals

COLLEGE and the community. See Colleges and universities—Public relations

COLLEGE annuals
Gumbo in the soup; Louisiana state university's yearbook. il Newsweek 77:77 Je 14 '71

COLLEGE aptitude tests. See Aptitude tests

COLLEGE architecture
Building types study; New York state university construction fund; with editorial comment. M. F. Schmertz. il Arch Rec 149:105-28 Ja '71
Cafe, Yale freshman commons. il Arch Rec 149:100-1 Ja '71
College arts complex shaped by a strong master plan; Rochester institute of technology, Rochester, N.Y. il Arch Rec 149:93-100 Ap '71
College construction: the emphases is on classrooms. J. E. Carlson. il Arch Rec 150:75 S '71
Made for walking; student union at Stony Brook. il Arch Forum 135:58-61 Jl '71
Malcolm X community college, Chicago. il Arch Rec 149:98-9 My '71
Multicategorical and animal research laboratory, Ithaca, New York. il Arch Rec 150:114-16 Jl '71
University of Rochester psychology building, Rochester, New York. il Arch Rec 149:100-1 My '71

COLLEGE art association of America
See also
New art association

COLLEGE art galleries and museums
Coming soon: art exhibits. Design 73:3 Fall '71
University museum: accidental past, purposeful future? J. R. Spencer. il Art in Am 59:84-90 Jl '70

COLLEGE athlete recruiting. See Athletes—Recruiting

COLLEGE athletics
College sports feel budget ax. Bsns W p38-9 Ag 28 '71
Legal license to steal the stars; NBA's four-year rule declared illegal. W. Johnson. il Sports Illus 34:34-6+ Ap 12 '71

Tough talk from prexy; W. Tate, president of Southern Methodist university. M. Kane. Sports Illus 35:11 Jl 12 '71
See also
Baseball
Football
Lacrosse
National collegiate athletic association
Rowing

COLLEGE attendance. See Colleges and universities—Attendance

COLLEGE bands. See Bands (music)

COLLEGE bookstores
Books are on the second floor; University of Miami bookstore. M. J. O'Hanlon. Pub W 199:37-8 Ap 19 '71
Campus bookselling: a complete service. C. B. McCaleb. Pub W 199:30-1 Ja 18 '71
Chicano movement and its books; Hornet bookstore, Sacramento state college. R. Duval. il Pub W 199:53-4 Ja 11 '71
College bookstore rush and how to cope with it. R. Duval. Pub W 199:50-2 Ap 26 '71
Paperback is king at Eisenhower college. D. MacGlashan. il Pub W 199:31-2 My 10 '71
See also
Booksellers and bookselling—Textbooks
Bookselling in college libraries
National association of college stores

COLLEGE broadcasts. See Television in education

COLLEGE buildings. See College architecture

COLLEGE chapels. See Chapels

COLLEGE cheers. See Cheerleading

COLLEGE clubs and societies
See also
College fraternities

COLLEGE consortiums. See Colleges and universities—Cooperation

COLLEGE counselors. See Student counselors

COLLEGE credits. See Grading and marking (students)

COLLEGE degrees. See Degrees, Academic

COLLEGE discipline
Dissent vs. disruption; Miami university. Sch & Soc 99:7-8 Ja '71
Is a mustache just peanuts? University of Tennessee vs Bill Skinner. G. S. Brown. il por Sports Illus 34:38-40+ Je 14 '71
Rough spring ahead? recommendations of the Carnegie commission on higher education. Newsweek 77:64 Mr 22 '71

COLLEGE dormitories. See Dormitories

COLLEGE dropouts. See Dropouts

COLLEGE education
Call for higher education reform; excerpts from address, June 1971. A. Pifer. por Sch & Soc 99:327-8 O '71
Class-conscious. Nations Bsns 59:22 Mr '71
Faculty-student views on colleges; Carnegie commission on higher education survey. Sch & Soc 99:262+ Sum '71
Has the bubble really burst? J. Cass. Sat R 54:61 Ap 17 '71
Hello, my children, good-by. A. H. Bridges. Read Digest 99:157-60 O '71
Higher education faces real disaster; address, January 28, 1971. E. A. Walker. Vital Speeches 37:270-3 F 15 '71
Higher education: new report takes an unconventional approach. C. Holden. Science 171:1129-30 Mr 19 '71
Human reach; address, February 7, 1971. J. A. Brown. Vital Speeches 37:398-401 Ap 15 '71
Less time and more options in higher education; conclusions of report by the Carnegie commission on higher education. Sch & Soc 99:285-6 Sum '71
Let's break the go-to-college lockstep. E. K. Faltermayer. Read Digest 98:154-7 F '71
New depression in higher education, by E. F. Cheit. Review
America 124:573+ My 29 '71. T. H. Clancy
New directions in higher education; recommendations of the Assembly on university goals and governance and the Carnegie commission on higher education. J. Cass. Sat R 54:45 F 20 '71
On the death of college. G. F. Kreyche. Sch & Soc 99:223-4 Ap '71
Paradoxes in higher education. K. D. Beeler and A. W. Eberle. Sch & Soc 99:217-18 Ap '71
Pressures for change. J. Cass. Sat R 54:77 N 20 '71
Professionalism in higher education; Newman report. W. W. Brickman. Sch & Soc 99:466-7 D '71
Prophets whisper fearful change. W. B. Martin. Ed Digest 36:49-52 Ap '71

COLLEGE education—*Continued*
Reexamination of trustee responsibility; address, March 17, 1971. H. T. Mudd. Vital Speeches 37:472-4 My 15 '71
What higher education is all about. J. Cass. Sat R 54:59+ My 22 '71
What's going on in schools & colleges. See every other issue of Changing times
See also
Carnegie commission on higher education
Colleges and universities—Attendance
Colleges and universities—Curriculum
Humanities
Independent study
Junior colleges

Aims and objectives

Any future for private colleges? interview. J. A. Howard. il por U S News 71:43-6 S 6 '71
Changes and new demands in higher education. C. B. Grannis. Pub W 199:57 F 15 '71
College presidents and students: are their heads ever in the same place? symposium. Mlle 73:244-7+ Ag '71
Degradation of the academic dogma, by R. Nisbet. Review
  Nat R 23:541+ My 18 '71. S. J. Tonsor
Deluge of humanitarianism in the American university; excerpt from Degradation of the academic dogma. R. Nisbet. Sch & Soc 99:241-4+ Ap '71
Educational technocrat. J. G. Lawler. Commonweal 95:343-7 Ja 14 '72
Escapes from freedom; universities' effort to help people; address, May 22, 1971. R. W. Lyman. Vital Speeches 37:757-9 O 1 '71
Give power to the students. F. R. Buckley. Nat R 23:424-5+ Ap 20 '71
Great academic refusal; address, May 21, 1971. W. Arrowsmith. Vital Speeches 37:592-7 Jl 15 '71
Higher education in a turbulent society; adaptation of address, December 14, 1969. A. W. Cordier. Sch & Soc 99:88 F '71
How to change colleges, by H. Taylor. Review
  New Repub 164:23-4 Ap 24 '71. L. Coxe;
  Same abr. Cur 130:35-9 Je '71
Involved in the relevant. M. S. Marshall. Sch & Soc 99:89-90 F '71
My father's shoebox; a hidden curriculum for today's education; address, October 1971. P. Crow. Vital Speeches 38:134-6 D 15 '71
Ortega y Gasset: the partly faithful professor; excerpt from Man and his circumstances; Ortega as educator. R. McClintock. bibliog Sch & Soc 99:304-15 Sum '71
Rationale for the Christian college. C. F. H. Henry. Chr Today 15:7-8+ My 21 '71
Survival and after: the outlook for higher education; excerpts from From riot to reason. E. L. Johnson. Todays Ed 60:65-7 S '71
Toward radical reform; excerpts from How to change colleges. H. Taylor. Cur 130:27-35 Je '71

Cost

Can you afford college? Costs up and headed higher. il U S News 70:25-8 F 22 '71
How to smooth the path to college; short-term pay-out trust plan for your child's college education. M. Battersby. il Mech Illus 67:87-8+ N '71
Study now, pay later: Yale's Pay as you earn plan. Time 98:66 N 1 '71

COLLEGE education, Experimental
Big move to non-campus colleges. E. L. Boyer and G. C. Keller. il Sat R 54:46-9+ Jl 17 '71
Get ready for off-campus colleges. G. C. Keller. il Seventeen 30:23+ S '71
Higher learning moves off the campus. il Bsns W p78-9 Ja 16 '71
Two new college options: California's Thomas Aquinas college and New college. America 125:165 S 18 '71

COLLEGE education, Value of
Sheepskin psychosis and campus unrest. Sch & Soc 99:6-7 Ja '71
Should everyone go to college? S. Jantzen. il Sr Schol 99:4-9 N 15 '71

COLLEGE enrollment. See Colleges and universities—Attendance

COLLEGE entrance examination board

Scholastic aptitude test

Buried under a sea of troubles; USC and UCLA football teams. R. Fimrite. il Sports Illus 35:28-31 N 15 '71

COLLEGE entrance requirements. See Colleges and universities—Entrance requirements

COLLEGE faculties. See College professors and instructors

COLLEGE fees. See Colleges and universities—Finance

COLLEGE football. See Football

COLLEGE football players. See Football players

COLLEGE fraternities
Memoirs of a fraternity man; a year as a member of Phi epsilon pi at University of Illinois. J. Epstein. Commentary 52:59-64 Jl '71
Pick the fraternity housemother. il Life 70:81-4 Ap 16 '71

COLLEGE freshmen. See College students

COLLEGE graduates
Class of '68 revisited: a cooler anger. il Time 97:55-6 My 17 '71
Graduates and jobs: a grave new world. il Time 97:49-52+ My 24 '71
I hunt for lost alumni. L. Beauchamp. por Har Yrs 11:21 Je '71
On the up and up. New Repub 164:5-6 Je 19 '71
See also
Business schools and colleges—Graduates
College education. Value of
Colleges and universities—Graduate work

Employment

Aftereffects of blind eye to telescope; lack of academic openings for Ph.D. A. M. Cartter. Ed Digest 36:15-18 Mr '71
For the class of '71, the party's over. W. B. Furlong. il N Y Times Mag p34-5+ Je 6 '71
Jobs for college graduates. il U S News 71:30-3 D 27 '71
Main street: 1971; small towns can be an alternate way of life-if. . . R. Hoffmann. il Mlle 73:124-5+ Je '71
Mortarboard in hand. Newsweek 78:66 Jl 5 '71
On graduation and dislocation. Chr Cent 88:679 Je 2 '71
On the job: after graduation anything? Mlle 73:80 Je '71
Our intellectual proletariat. R. Kirk. Nat R 23:1119 O 8 '71
Plumber from Yale. il Sr Schol 99:9+ N 15 '71
Recession hits the campus: fewer jobs for graduates. il U S News 70:22-3 Mr 15 '71
'71 grads find a hard world waiting. il U S News 70:19-20 Je 28 '71
Tough year to launch a career. il Time 99:57 Ja 17 '72
Working without the system: common laborers. il Esquire 76:166-7 S '71

COLLEGE grounds
See also
Campus planning

COLLEGE investments. See Colleges and universities—Investments

COLLEGE journalism. See College and school journalism

COLLEGE librarians
Divine right of kings: academic status. R. Horn. il Am Lib 2:625-9 Je '71
Faculty status for librarians; address, November 7, 1970. E. J. Josey. bibliog por Library J 96:1333-6 Ap 15 '71; Discussion. 96:2022 Je 15 '71
Floating academic librarian. R. P. Haro. bibliog il Am Lib 2:1169-73 D '71
Sixth year study and the academic librarian. M. L. Dimmock. bibliog por Library J 96:2731-3 S 15 '71
Status in New Jersey; letter to the editor. M. Villavecchia. Am Lib 2:16 Ja '71
Useful academic librarian; remarks. April 1971. F. Blake. il por Library J 96:3731-3 N 15 '71
View from the front. K. F. Kister. bibliog il por Library J 96:3283-6 O 15 '71; Discussion. 97:3 Ja 1 '72
Who is the culprit? letters to the editor. C. S. Webber; J. R. Beard. Library J 96:3055-6 O 1 '71
Women in academic libraries. H. W. Tuttle. Library J 96:2594-6 S 1 '71; Discussion. 96:3255 O 15 '71

Anecdotes, facetiae, satire, etc.

Faculty status for the librarians at Arbuthnot. D. Gore. Am Lib 2:283-95 Mr '71; Discussion. 2:567-9, 683, 783, 785 Je-S '71

Salaries

Anecdotes, facetiae, satire, etc.
Catching up with the wig lady. P. Butler. il Wilson Lib Bul 45:775 Ap '71

Tenure

Tenure investigation: library administration division's report concerning nonrenewal of contracts of five librarians, University of Missouri library; discussion. Am Lib 2:150-2 F '71

COLLEGE libraries
Along the academic way. E. Mason. il por Library J 96:1671-6 My 15 '71; Discussion. bibliog 96:1657, 2408-9, 3277-82, 3699 My 15, Ag, O 15, N 15 '71
Floating academic librarian. R. P. Haro. bibliog il Am Lib 2:1169-73 D '71
Library-university. L. Shores. Sch & Soc 99: 163-6 Mr '71
Renaissance of academic library building 1967-1971. J. Orne. il por Library J 96:3947-67 D 1 '71
Two-year academic library buildings. J. Bock. il Library J 96:3986-9 D 1 '71
Undergraduate library; symposium, with editorial comment. bibliog il Library J 96: 1551, 1567-83 My 1 '71
Unserved: academic library style. R. M. Dougherty. il Am Lib 2:1055-8 N '71
See also
Conference of eastern college librarians
Research libraries
also subhead Libraries or Library under names of colleges, e.g. Howard university, Washington, D.C.—Library

Acquisitions
Librarian vs. publisher. J. Kesselman; discussion. Library J 96:759 Mr 1 '71

Anecdotes, facetiae, satire, etc.
Memo to the building committee. H. D. Jones. Library J 96:1579 My 1 '71

Architecture
See Library architecture

Federal aid
Congress debates Higher education act. Pub W 199:35-6 My 3 '71
Higher education bill clears Senate. G. Krettek and E. D. Cooke. Am Lib 2:965-6 O '71
Higher eduction legislation delayed. S. Wagner. Pub W 200:23-4 D 6 '71
Libraries look to the state agency. A. L. McNeal. bibliog il Am Lib 2:739-41 Jl '71
Senate passes four-year HEA extension bill. G. Krettek and E. D. Cooke. Wilson Lib Bul 46:99 S '71

Instruction in use
See Libraries—Instruction in use

Reference work
Building Northwestern's Core: noncirculating duplicate collection aimed particularly at the undergraduate. K. Horny. il por Library J 96:1580-3 My 1 '71

Reports
See Library reports

Services to blind
Hartwick serves blind. C. Wolf and J. Miller. il Am Lib 2:1193-4 D '71

Special collections
Approach to special collections; project of Washington university library Rare book department. W. Matheson. il Am Lib 2: 1151-6 D '71
Building Northwestern's Core: noncirculating duplicate collection aimed particularly at the undergraduate. K. Horny. il por Library J 96:1580-3 My 1 '71

Standards
Divine right of kings: academic status. R. Horn. il Am Lib 2:625-9 Je '71
Faculty status for librarians; address, November 7, 1970. E. J. Josey. bibliog por Library J 96:1333-6 Ap 15 '71; Discussion. 96: 2022 Je 15 '71
Who is the culprit? letters to the editor. C. S. Webber; J. R. Beard. Library J 96:3055-6 O 1 '71

Anecdotes, facetiae, satire, etc.
Faculty status for the librarians at Arbuthnot. D. Gore. Am Lib 2:283-95 Mr '71; Discussion. 2:567-9, 683, 783, 785 Je-S '71
COLLEGE libraries and booksellers
See also
Bookselling in college libraries
COLLEGE libraries and publishers
Librarian vs. publisher. J. Kellelman; discussion. Library J 96:759 Mr 1 '71
Scholarly publishing and the university library; address, May 1971. R. E. Ellsworth. il por Library J 96:3568-72 N 1 '71
COLLEGE libraries and research. See Libraries and research
COLLEGE libraries and state
See also
College libraries—Federal aid

COLLEGE library administration
See also
College librarians—Tenure
COLLEGE library architecture. See Library architecture
COLLEGE library reports. See Library reports
COLLEGE marketing and research corporation
Campus conquistador. por Time 97:71 Mr 8 '71
COLLEGE museums. See College art galleries and museums
COLLEGE newspapers. See College and school journalism
COLLEGE officials
Educational technocrat. J. G. Lawler. Commonweal 95:343-7 Ja 14 '72
See also
College presidents
Ombudsman (education)
COLLEGE operas, revues, etc.
Report:
La Bohème at Hunter college. R. D. Daniels. Opera N 35:33 F 20 '71
COLLEGE periodicals. See College and school journalism
COLLEGE presidents
Changed role of the modern university president. R. M. Spector. bibliog Sch & Soc 99:276-9 Sum '71; Same abr. Ed Digest 37: 46-9 O '71
College presidents and students: are their heads ever in the same place? symposium. Mlle 73:244-7+ Ag '71
Making of college presidents. C. N. Parkinson. Cur 125:25-9 Ja '71
President's chair; troubles of Harvard's early presidents. J. T. Bethell. il Am Heritage 23:110 D '71
See also
Bok, D. C
Walker, H.

Selection and appointment
Quest for a silver unicorn; Boston university's search for a new president; with editorial comment. E. Kern. il pors Life 70: 3, 54-5+ Je 4 '71
Searching for the perfect university president; with editorial comment. W. G. Bennis. il Atlan 227:4, 39-44+ Ap '71; Discussion. 227:32-5 Je '71
COLLEGE professors and instructors
Arrogance on the campus, by L. B. Mayhew.
Review
Sat R 54:72 Ap 17 '71. P. Woodring
Here's what junior-college faculties think. Todays Ed 60:67-8 Mr '71
Man in the middle: the college professor. R. W. Tobin. il America 125:176-8 S 18 '71
Moonlight dims for professors. il Bsns W p52-5 Jl 3 '71
Parting shots; a professor dresses up zoology; R. Eakin of Berkeley campus. il pors Life 71:62-3 Jl 23 '71
Professor, I am unhappy with you; professor of education. W. M. Davis. Clear House 45:340 F '71
Research, teaching, and faculty fate. J. R. Hayes. bibliog il Science 172:227-30 Ap 16 '71; Discussion. 172:1082-5 Je 11 '71
Short course in the three types of radical professors. J. Hitchcock. il N Y Times Mag p30-1+ F '21 '71; Discussion. p80 Mr 21 '71
Student response to faculty power. L. G. Geiger. Sch & Soc 99:424-6 N '71
See also
American association of university professors
Collective bargaining—College professors and instructors
Colleges and universities—Administration—Faculty participation
Negro college professors and instructors
Teachers and students
Women as college professors and instructors

Political activities
Inciting to violence; H. B. Franklin fired by Stanford university. il por Time 99:41 Ja 17 '72
Limits of academic freedom; case of radical professor H. B. Franklin at Stanford university. il por Time 97:51 Mr 15 '71
Living through the revolution; demonstrations at MLA. D. Grumbach. Commonweal 93:412-13 Ja 29 '71
See also
New university conference

Publications
Professors are too sophisticated. A. Kazin. Sat R 54:23-4+ My 22 '71
Yale faculty makes the scene. T. Meehan. il N Y Times Mag p 12-13+ F 7 '71; Discussion. p4 F 28; 12+ Mr 7 '71

COLLEGE professors and instructors—*Cont.*

Rating

Evaluating college professors by scientific methods. E. Kossoff. Am Scholar 41:79-93 Wint '71

Rating by students

College teaching effectiveness; survey of college students. E. McDaniel and J. F. Feldhusen. Todays Ed 60:27 Mr '71

Differences in course grades and student ratings of teacher performance. R. G. Weigel and others. bibliog Sch & Soc 99:60-2 Ja '71

Student evaluation of university professors. F. N. Kerlinger. Sch & Soc 99:353-6 O '71

Recruiting

Women in academia; study of the hiring decision in departments of physical science. A. Y. Lewin and L. Duchan. bibliog Science 173:892-5 S 3 '71

Salaries, allowances, etc.

Faculty salary pinch worsens. C. Holden. Science 172:658 My 14 '71

Selection and appointment

Aliens in their own land; Canadians who teach in Canadian universities. L. Armour. il Nation 212:750-3 Je 14 '71

On academic blood tests. A. Etzioni. Science 172:1087 Je 11 '71; Discussion. 174:101-2 O 8 '71

Profesor and his wife; anti-nepotism rules. L. Kanowitz. McCalls 98:42 Ag '71

Social status

Proposal for professional control of educator performance. J. C. Walden. bibliog Sch & Soc 99:39-41 Ja '71

Tenure

Faculty featherbedding. Time 97:62+ My 10 '71

Women, students, and tenure. F. Moog. Science 174:983 D 3 '71

Unions

See Teachers unions

COLLEGE reports and records

Library reports

See Library reports

COLLEGE scholarships. See Scholarships and fellowships

COLLEGE sports. See College athletics

COLLEGE STATION, Tex.

Ground tires reduce pavement cracking. L. L. James. il Am City 86:64-5+ F '71

COLLEGE student opinion. See Student opinion

COLLEGE students

Best colleges have the least effect; Project on student development in small colleges. A. W. Chickering. il Sat R 54:48-50+ Ja 16 '71

Changing student in the Catholic college; excerpt from Catholic higher education in America: a history. E. J. Power. bibliog f Sch & Soc 99:493-6 D '71

College presidents and students: are their heads ever in the same place? symposium. Mlle 73:244-7+ Ag '71

Cooling it: The Americanization of the college campus, '71-'72. il Esquire 76:159-71 S '71

Dropouts, drifters, the lock step: a critical report on colleges; excerpts from Stanford university Report on higher education. il U S News 70:62-3 Mr 22 '71

Four Mlle editors go to ten campuses to find out what they're like in 1971. il Mlle 73:248-53+ Ag '71

Getting used to the system; letter from a freshman. E. Vasquez. Nat R 23:587-8+ Je 1 '71

Joys and terrors of sending the kids to college. H. Swados. il N Y Times Mag p 12-13+ F 14 '71

Opinion: on the subtle chauvinism of Princeton males. K. Boals. por Mlle 72:56+ Ap '71

Students with lawyers; student-financed public interest groups. New Repub 164:10 Je 26 '71

U.S. journal: Florida; student spring vacations in Fort Lauderdale and Daytona Beach. C. Trillin. New Yorker 47:104+ My 1 '71

What my students taught me; ed. by J. C. G. Conniff. H. H. Humphrey. il por Todays Health 49:20-3+ Ag '71

See also
Coeducation
College fraternities
College students and war
Foreign students in the United States
German students
Law students
Self government in education
Student Christian movements
Student demonstrations
Student militants
Student movement
Young Americans for freedom (organization)

Adjustment

Freedom: the booby trap for students; excerpt from The college student's handbook. A. H. Lass and E. S. Wilson. Today's Ed 60:27-8 Ap '71; Same abr. Ed Digest 37:30-1 S '71

Getting through the college daze; questions and answers. A. Wood. Seventeen 29:148+ N '70

Long way from Vietnam; veterans on the GI bill. il Newsweek 78:50+ O 4 '71

Aid

See Student aid; Student loans

Attitudes

See Students—Attitudes

Conduct of life

Campus exodus. A. H. Leitch. Chr Today 15:38-9 Je 4 '71

Students all quiet on the campus front. G. Wierzynski. il Time 97:14-15 F 22 '71

Demonstrations

See Student demonstrations

Discipline

See College discipline

Employment

See Student employment

Federal aid

See Student aid

Food

College campus, new home for organic foods. M. C. Goldman. il Org Gard & Farm 18:86-7 Ag '71

Grading

See Grading and marking (students)

Health and hygiene

Innovations in college mental health. R. B. Falk. Ment Hy 55:451-5 O '71

Streamlines: how to fight collegiate fat. L. Brothers. por Seventeen 30:290 Ag '71

They take care of their own; abortion loan fund of University of Maine students. E. Scribner. Nation 212:230 F 22 '71

Housing

Commune for conservatives; Schuyler Hall, New York. il Time 97:59 Mr 1 '71

Where the young and old live together, happily; Syracuse campus. L. Kassman. McCalls 98:42-3 Ag '71

See also
Dormitories

Political activities

Anatomy of activism for executives. S. A. Culbert and J. M. Elden; discussion. Harvard Bsns R 49:34+ Mr '71

Beginning: Berkeley, 1964, by M. Heirich. Review
Nation 212:599-600 My 10 '71. B. Aptheker

Campus vote; residency requirements. Nation 212:354-6 Mr 22 '71

College-town worry: will 18-to-21 voters take over? il U S News 71:38-41 S 6 '71

Columbia conservatives for Buckley. J. Collins. Mlle 72:138 Ja '71

Home is where the vote is. R. G. Singer. Nation 213:202-5 S 13 '71

Student faith in democracy. Sch & Soc 99:6 Ja '71

Student power in East Lansing. il Time 98:18 N 15 '71

Students a marginal elite in politics. F. A. Pinner. bibliog f Ann Am Acad 395:127-38 My '71

Students against campus violence; excerpt from The riot makers. E. H. Methvin. Read Digest 98:62-6 Ja '71

COLLEGE students—Political activities—*Cont.*
Turn from campus violence, the reasons. il
U S News 71:40-3 O 25 '71
See also
Student movement
Students for a democratic society (organiza-
tion)
Vietnamese war, 1957- —Protests, demon-
strations, etc, against

Reading
Why not-ers and what they are reading. D.
J. Leary. il Cath World 212:240-4 F '71

Religion
Challenge of student idealists. P. A. Ward.
Chr Today 15:8-9 Ja 29 '71
From freaks to followers. Chr Today 16:33-
4 O 22 '71
Mother church and her wandering children.
B. Gibbs. il Cath World 213:274-6 S '71
Quest at Cambridge. N. Pittenger. Chr Cent
88:150 F 3 '71
See also
Colleges and universities—Religious life

Selection
See Student selection

Sexual behavior
Comparative sex norms in U.S. and Danish
students; findings of H. T. Christensen.
Sch & Soc 99:333-4 O '71
How new ideas about sex are changing our
lives. J. Cuber. Redbook 136:85+ Mr '71
Psychosocial analysis of sex-policing on cam-
pus; address, December 7, 1965. J. P. Fell.
Ed Digest 36:38-41 Ja '71
Sex in the college dorm. Chr Today 15:33 My
21 '71

Suicide
See Suicide

Transportation
Moving people on campus today, and tomorrow. Ed Digest 37:50-1 D '71

Travel
See Student travel

Volunteer service
See Volunteer service
COLLEGE students, Jewish. See Jewish stu-
dents
COLLEGE students, Women
Newest campus crusade: equal rights for
women; with address by A. Pifer. il U S
News 71:79-82 D 13 '71
See also
Education of women
Negro students, Women
COLLEGE students and business
Youth and establishment collaboration? Yan-
kelovich survey. Cur 127:15-19 Mr '71
COLLEGE students and environmental prob-
lems. See Environmental movement
COLLEGE students and war
General and the Christian college: where was
the dissent? army conduct in Vietnam. D.
M. Lynch. Chr Cent 88:724-6 Je 9 '71
COLLEGE students as guides. See Guides
COLLEGE students life insurance policies. See
Insurance, Life—Policies
COLLEGE students opinion. See Student opin-
ion
COLLEGE teachers. See College professors and
instructors
COLLEGE teaching. See Colleges and uni-
versities—Teaching
COLLEGE textbooks. See Textbooks
COLLEGE trustees
Hysteria on the campus: who is responsible?
address, March 2, 1971. L. Fertig. Vital
Speeches 37:454-9 My 15 '71
COLLEGE verse
Undergraduate poems; comp. by J. Moffitt.
America 124:510-11 My 15 '71
COLLEGE work-study program. See Education,
Cooperative
COLLEGE yearbooks. See College annuals
COLLEGES, Small. See Small colleges
COLLEGES and universities
See also
Academic freedom
Catholic colleges and universities
Church colleges
College education
College students
Liberal education
Negro colleges and universities
Schools of education
Student movement
    also types of colleges, e.g. Medical col-
leges

Accreditation
University extension and accreditation. E.
J. Durnall. Sch & Soc 99:87-8 F '71

Administration
Conflict between politics and evaluation in
higher education. R. G. Cope. bibliog Sch
& Soc 99:218-20 Ap '71
Great academic refusal; address, May 21,
1971. W. Arrowsmith. Vital Speeches 37:
592-7 Jl 15 '71
New tensions on campus. W. J. McGill. por
Life 71:55 O 8 '71
On the art of university pruning. A. Etzioni.
Science 172:429 Ap 30 '71; Discussion. 173:
103 Jl 9 '71
Strangulation of Fresno state. B. Hillen-
brand. Commonweal 94:136-8 Ap 16 '71
Student protest and university response. J.
R. Gusfield. bibliog f Ann Am Acad 395:
26-38 My '71
Survival and after: the outlook for higher
education; excerpts from From riot to
reason. E. L. Johnson. Todays Ed 60:65-7
S '71
To reform the academy. R. M. Ohmann. Sat
R 54:54-5 Jl 17 '71
Whither United States universities? G. E.
Pake. Science 172:908-16 My 28 '71; Dis-
cussion. 174:7-9 O 1 '71
See also
College discipline
College officials
College presidents
Ombudsman (education)
Self government in education

Faculty participation
Faculty as enemy. A. W. Godfrey. America
124:630-2 Je 19 '71; Reply. R. W. Tobin.
125:49 Ag 7 '71
Team approach to academic administration.
T. J. Diener. bibliog Sch & Soc 99:504-7
D '71

Student participation
Eva Jefferson: young voice of change; Associated student government of Northwestern university, Evanston, Ill. H. H.
King. il pors Ebony 26:71-4+ Ja '71

Admission standards
See Colleges and universities—Entrance
requirements

Attendance
Choosing careers: the big shift. il U S News
70:22-4 My 31 '71
Easier to get into college? Results of a sur-
vey. il U S News 70:37-9 F 15 '71
Enrollment survey to appear in February is-
sue. G. G. Parker. Sch & Soc 99:19 Ja '71
Interstate student migration. Sch & Soc 99:
268+ Sum '71
Now it's colleges seeking students. il U S
News 71:42 S 6 '71
Record year on American campuses. il U S
News 71:38 S 20 '71
Statistics of attendance in American univer-
sities and colleges, 1970-71. G. G. Parker.
bibliog f il Sch & Soc 99:105-26 F '71
Stop and go; Carnegie report on enrollment.
Newsweek 78:72 O 18 '71
See also
Student selection

Business schools
See Business schools and colleges

Choice
See College, Choice of

Cooperation
Colleges unite in troubled times. il Bsns W
p90 Ap 3 '71
See also
Hampshire college

Curriculum
Instant and relevant curricula. W. W. Brick-
man. Sch & Soc 99:207 Ap '71
My father's shoebox; a hidden curriculum
for today's education; address, October
1971. P. Crow. Vital Speeches 38:134-6
D 15 '71
Proper study of womankind is . . . women.
L. Friedrich. McCalls 98:42 S '71
Toward relevancy, curriculum, and the social
order. R. N. Reynolds. Sch & Soc 99:29-30
Ja '71
Woman's place is in the curriculum. J. L.
Trecker. il Sat R 54:83-6+ O 16 '71
Women's studies. R. M. Somerville. Todays
Ed 60:35-7 N '71

COLLEGES and universities—Curriculum
—*Continued*
Women's studies; San Diego state college.
R. Salper. il Ramp Mag 10:56-60 D '71
See also
Independent study
Liberal education

Departments of dance
Dance with a liberal education; dance program at York university. Toronto. G. Thomson. il por Dance Mag 45:66-7 Ap '71
See also
California. State college, Long Beach—Department of dance
California. University—Irvine campus—Department of dance

Departments of physics
Physics department ratings: another evaluation. C. F. Elton and S. A. Rodgers. bibliog il Science 174:565-8 N 5 '71

Enrollment
See Colleges and universities—Attendance

Entrance requirements
Bipolarity on the campus. A. B. Grobman. Science 174:457 O 29 '71
Black professor says: colleges are skipping over competent blacks to admit authentic ghetto types. T. Sowell; discussion. N Y Times Mag p6+ Ja 24 '71
College admissions policies. R. W. Young. Ed Digest 36:19-21 Ja '71
Freshman sabbatical; deferred admission. il Newsweek 78:48 Jl 19 '71
Let's break the go-to-college lockstep. E. K. Faltermayer. Read Digest 98:154-7 F '71
Open admissions: a mixed report; experience of City university of New York. il Time 98:50+ N 29 '71
Open admissions: the real issue. A. W. Astin. Science 173:1197 S 24 '71
Predicting college success of the educationally disadvantaged; adaptation of address, June 1970. J. C. Stanley. bibliog Science 171:640-7 F 19 '71; Discussion. 173:1079; 174:1278-9 S 17, D 24 '71
Report card on open admissions: remedial work recommended; City university of New York. S. Resnik and B. Kaplan. il N Y Times Mag p26-8+ My 9 '71; Discussion. p21+ Je 6 '71
Reverse discrimination; Seattle court decision. Time 98:78 O 11 '71
These colleges still have room. il Changing T 25:21-4 My '71
What's wrong with college admissions? E. R. Weidlein. Ed Digest 37:35-8 D '71
See also
College entrance examination board—Scholastic aptitude test
Student selection

Extension
See University extension

Faculties
See College professors and instructors

Federal aid
Basic grants and fellowships backed in House debate. G. Krettek and E. D. Cooke. Wilson Lib Bul 46:375-6 D '71
Congressional fight looms over higher education. Pub W 199:35 Mr 1 '71
Higher education act; September 30, 1971 extension and amendments. G. Krettek and E. D. Cooke. Wilson Lib Bul 46:284 N '71
Higher education bill. America 125:417 N 20 '71
Higher education: funds rise while basic changes are debated. D. P. Teter. il Science 173:309-11 Jl 23 '71
Higher education legislation delayed. S. Wagner. Pub W 200:23-4 D 6 '71
Higher education: reinforcement from the Carnegie commission. J. Walsh. Science 174:1215-17 D 17 '71
Higher education: will federal aid favor students or institutions? J. Walsh. Science 171:1219-21 Mr 26 '71
Out of pocket in academe. Sat R 54:70-1 Ap 17 '71
Recommendations for national action affecting higher education; statement of policy adopted by the National association of state universities and land-grant colleges and the American association of state colleges and universities. November 1970. Sch & Soc 99:379-81 O '71
Soon, new type of federal aid for colleges. U S News 71:86 N 15 '71

Steps toward a national policy for academic science. C. M. York. bibliog il Science 172:643-8 My 14 '71
See also
Church colleges—Federal aid
College libraries—Federal aid
United States—National foundation for higher education (proposed)

Finance
Austerity on the campus. G. H. Wierzynski. il Time 97:52-4 Je 14 '71
Boost for out-of-state students in South. Sch & Soc 99:464-5 D '71
College costs: more green for the halls of ivy. il Bsns W p107 Je 19 '71
A communication; state colleges and fee financing; letter. F. R. McKenna. New Repub 164:31-2 Ja 23 '71
Cost squeeze in higher learning. C. Holden. Science 171:1225 Mr 26 '71
Fund shortages restrict programs at state colleges and universities. Sch & Soc 99:70 F '71
Grim run to fiscal daylight; college football in financial squeeze. P. Ryan. il Sports Illus 34:18-20+ F 1 '71
Hard times. Sci Am 224:44 My '71
Money pinch for colleges: impact on students, campuses. il U S News 70:28-9 My 10 '71
Ohio plan succumbs to lack of popular and institutional support. Sch & Soc 99:399 N '71
Private higher education; St Louis university self-security. America 125:500 D 11 '71
Private institutions in jeopardy. Sat R 54:49 Mr 20 '71
Purely academic depression. Fortune 83:108 F '71
Recession hits the colleges. il Newsweek 77:63-4 Mr 22 '71
Who should pay for higher education? R. Kirk. Nat R 23:534 My 18 '71
See also
Church colleges—Finance
College education—Cost
Colleges and universities—Gifts, legacies, etc.
Colleges and universities—Investments

Gifts, legacies, etc.
Better year for fund raising. Bsns W p92 Ap 10 '71
Board room and the campus; Corporate 1% program for higher education. J. Cass. il Sat R 54:46-7 Mr 20 '71

Graduate work
ACE: rating of graduate programs shows little change in status quo. J. Walsh. Science 171:49-50 Ja 8 '71
Boom in religion studies. por Time 98:83-4 O 18 '71
Evaluation of graduate school programs: report by the American council on education. Sch & Soc 99:264-5 Sum '71
Supernatural department. D. Wolfle. Science 173:109 Jl 9 '71; Discussion. 174:1279-80 D 24 '71

Investments
Battle of the yield tables; Minnesota university's endowment fund. il Forbes 107:62 Mr 15 '71
Enhancing endowments; The common fund for non-profit organizations. Sat R 54:69 My 22 '71
University as an investor. N. S. Care. New Repub 165:12-13 O 2 '71

Physics departments
See Colleges and universities—Departments of physics

Political control
Distinguishing fact from fiction in social crises. W. P. Moellenberg. bibliog Sch & Soc 99:420-4 N '71

Public relations
Beyond the campus gate; the communication problems of the elite; address, April 29, 1971. W. W. Braden. Vital Speeches 37:572-4 Jl 1 '71
Community relations for special programs in higher education. R. D. Wilkinson. Sch & Soc 99:170-2 Mr '71
Eggheads under the hard hats? R. W. Gibbons. Commonweal 94:4-5 Mr 12 '71; Reply. L. Perlis. 94:199 Ap 30 '71

Publications
See also
University presses

Religious life
Evangelical college students: an opinion sampler; excerpts from college newspapers. D. J. Riggall. Chr Today 15:11-14 My 21 '71

COLLEGES and universities—Religious life
—*Continued*
New turn on campus, the Christian commune.
J. F. Conway. America 124:479-81 My 8 '71;
Reply. G. A. Buckley. 124:621 Je 19 '71
Religion in higher education. M. Novak.
Commonweal 93:395-6 Ja 22 '71
Religion on the campus. R. T. Osborn. il Chr
Cent 88:1161-3 O 6 '71; Reply. R. L Johnson.
88:1474-6 D 15 '71
See also
College students—Religion
Inter-varsity Christian fellowship

Research
Berkeley debate; nuclear weapons research.
Nation 212:134 F 1 '71
Campus research: a giant in trouble; with
views of J. Wiesner. il U S News 71:33-7
D 20 '71
Colleges in action. See issues of Science di-
gest
Interdisciplinary problem-oriented research in
the university. F. A. Long. Science 171:961
Mr 12 '71
Michigan war research charged. R. J. Bazell.
Science 171:656 F 19 '71

Security measures
Crime wave hits colleges. il U S News 71:24-6
N 22 '71

Social rooms
See Student lounges

Statistics
See also
Colleges and universities—Attendance

Student recruiting
Recruitment: forum or bazaar? F. E. Wagner. Sch & Soc 99:86-7 F '71

Teaching
Student participation in college teaching. Sch
& Soc 99:463 D '71
See also
College professors and instructors

Trustees
See College trustees

Alabama
See also
Alabama. University, Tuscaloosa

Arizona
See also
Arizona. University, Tucson

California
Two new college options: California's Thomas
Aquinas college and New college. America
125:165 S 18 '71
See also
California. Fresno state college, Fresno
California. State college, Long Beach
California. State polytechnic college, San
Luis Obispo
California. University
La Verne college
Pepperdine university, Los Angeles
Riverside university
Southern California university, Los Angeles
Stanford university, Palo Alto

Canada
Aliens in their own land; Canadians who
teach in Canadian universities. L. Armour.
il Nation 212:750-3 Je 14 '71
Americanization of Canadian universities. C.
Cocking il Sat R 54:44-5+ Ag 21 '71
Dance with a liberal education; dance pro-
gram at York university, Toronto. G.
Thomson. il por Dance Mag 45:66-7 Ap '71
See also
McMaster university, Hamilton, Ontario

China (People's Republic)
China: future of the university. C. M. Martin. Bul Atom Sci 27:11-15 Ja '71

Connecticut
See also
Yale university

England
See also
Cambridge. University

Florida
See also
Miami. University, Coral Gables

Georgia
See also
Morehouse college, Atlanta

Great Britain
British university library buildings. E. B.
Stanford. bibliog il por Library J 96:4067-71
D 15 '71
See also
Adult education—Great Britain
Theological seminaries—Great Britain

Illinois
A communication; state colleges and fee
financing; letter. F. R. McKenna. New
Repub 164:31-2 Ja 23 '71
See also
Chicago city college
Chicago. University
Illinois. University
Northwestern university, Evanston
Rockford college, Rockford

India
Umbrellas for Chandigarh; Punjab university Fine arts museum. il Arch Forum 135:
26-7 S '71

Indiana
See also
Manchester college, North Manchester
Vincennes university

Iran
Shah vs. bureaucrats; Pahlavi university. G.
H. Muller. Nation 212:240-3 F 22 '71
Teheran university and the government of
Iran. M. Afzal. bibliog Sch & Soc 99:369-73
O '71

Japan
Sports showcase; Japan dental college gym,
Tokyo. il Arch Forum 135:42-5 Jl '71

Kansas
See also
Kansas state university, Manhattan

Kentucky
See also
Asbury college, Wilmore

Latin America
History
Role of the colonial university. L. A.
Sánchez. il Américas 23:S6-8 Ag '71

Louisiana
See also
Louisiana state university, Baton Rouge
Tulane university, New Orleans

Maryland
See also
Goucher college, Baltimore

Massachusetts
Public higher education in Massachusetts.
J. W. Lederle. il Sch & Soc 99:51-4 Ja '71
See also
Boston university
Brandeis university, Waltham
Clark university, Worcester
Hampshire college
Harvard university
Massachusetts institute of technology, Cam-
bridge
Massachusetts. University, Amherst

Michigan
See also
Detroit. University
General motors institute, Flint
Michigan. University, Ann Arbor
Western Michigan university, Kalamazoo

Minnesota
See also
Minnesota. University, Minneapolis

Mississippi
See also
Alcorn agricultural and mechanical college,
Lorman
Jackson state college, Jackson

Missouri
See also
Missouri. University, Colombia
St Louis university
Washington university, St Louis

New Hampshire
See also
New Hampshire. University, Durham

New Jersey
See also
Princeton university
Shelton college, Cape May

COLLEGES and universities—*Continued*

New York (state)

See also
Barnard college
Columbia university
Eisenhower college, Seneca Falls
Hamilton college, Clinton
Hartwick college, Oneonta
Hofstra university, Hempstead
Rochester, N.Y. University
Syracuse university
Yeshiva university, New York

North Carolina

See also
Johnson C. Smith university, Charlotte
North Carolina Wesleyan college, Rocky
Mount

Norway

Norway's district colleges. R. E. Belding.
Sch & Soc 99:54-5 Ja '71

Ohio

See also
Miami university, Oxford
Oberlin college
Ohio. Kent state university
Wilberforce university

Oregon

See also
Eastern Oregon college, La Grande

Pennsylvania

See also
Allentown college of St Francis De Sales
Lincoln university, Oxford
Pennsylvania state university
Swarthmore college
Temple university, Philadelphia

South Carolina

See also
Bob Jones university, Greenville
South Carolina. University, Columbia

South Dakota

See also
Sioux Falls college, Sioux Falls

Southern states

Boost for out-of-state students in South.
Sch & Soc 99:464-5 D '71
Views on state aid to private colleges; study
done for the Southern regional education
board. Sch & Soc 99:325-7 O '71
See also
Negro colleges and universities

Switzerland

See also
University of the New World

Tennessee

See also
Vanderbilt university, Nashville

Texas

See also
Dallas. University
Lubbock Christian college
Southern Methodist university, Dallas
Texas. University

Turkey

Storm over the Bosporus; Robert college. T.
Cosmades. Chr Today 15:33 Ja 29 '71

United States

Academe and its models. G. F. Kreyche. Sch
& Soc 99:410 N '71
American college: some problems and choices;
address, April 1971. M. Bressler. bibliog f
Ann Am Acad 396:57-69 Jl '71
Austerity on the campus. G. H. Wierzynski.
il Time 97:52-4 Je 14 '71
Changes in the traditional concepts of higher
education. A. S. Knowles. Sch & Soc 99:
405-9 N '71
College ferment '71; symposium. il Todays
Health 49:25-40 Ap '71
Four Mlle editors go to ten campuses to
find out what they're like in 1971. il Mlle
73:248-53+ Ag '71
From coeducation to equality. il Time 98:60+
D 6 '71
Future of the university; excerpt from ad-
dress, February 1970. R. Nisbet. Commen-
tary 51:62-71 F '71
How to change colleges, by H. Taylor. Re-
view
Nat R 23:602 Je 1 '71. M. S. Gazzaniga
President's view of campus unrest. A. S.
Knowles. Sch & Soc 99:81-4 F '71
Reform rears its lovely head; Newman re-
port. R. Kirk. Nat R 23:429 Ap 20 '71

Signs of the times. R. Kirk. Nat R 23:653
Je 15 '71
Union and campus: talking together. J. Hig-
gins. Nation 213:171-4 S 6 '71
University as paradox. E. B. Schick. Sch &
Soc 99:84-6 F '71
What lies ahead for our universities; ad-
dress, February 16, 1971. W. J. McGill. Vital
Speeches 37:337-40 Mr 15 '71; Same. Sch &
Soc 99:337-41 O '71
What's going on in schools & colleges. See
every other issue of Changing times
Whither United States universities? G. E.
Pake. Science 172:908-16 My 28 '71; Dis-
cussion. 174:7-9 O 1 '71
See also
Church colleges
Coeducation
Colleges and universities. State
Colleges for women
Engineering colleges
Foreign students in the United States
Negro colleges and universities
Small colleges
Theological seminaries

Washington, D.C.

See also
Howard university, Washington, D.C.
Washington, D.C. Federal city college

Washington (state)

See also
Washington (state). University, Seattle

Wisconsin

See also
Wisconsin. University

COLLEGES and universities, Experimental
Experimental colleges and communes. R.
Kirk. Nat R 23:147 F 9 '71
Internationalized university without walls;
grants to Union for experimenting colleges
and universities. Sch & Soc 99:397-8 N '71
See also
Hampshire college
La Verne college, La Verne, Calif.
New York (state). State university—College
at Old Westbury
Riverside university, Riverside, Calif.

COLLEGES and universities, Municipal
See also
New York (city). City university

COLLEGES and universities, State
Developing state colleges and universities:
current status and future roles. F. H.
Harcleroad and others. Sch & Soc 99:157-
60 Mr '71
Fund shortages restrict programs at state
colleges and universities. Sch & Soc 99:70 F
'71
Trend toward separate governing boards. M.
M. Chambers. Sch & Soc 99:349-50 O '71
See also
American association of state colleges and
universities
Kansas state university, Manhattan

Massachusetts

Public higher education in Massachusetts.
J. W. Lederle. il Sch & Soc 99:51-4 Ja '71

New Jersey

Status in New Jersey; letter to the editor.
M. Villavecchia. Am Lib 2:16 Ja '71
Who is the culprit? letters to the editor. C. S.
Webber; J. R. Beard. Library J 96:3055-6
O 1 '71

Ohio

Financing higher education in Ohio. P. N.
Reid. New Repub 164:13-14 Je 12 '71
Gilligan plan. Newsweek 77:73 Ap 12 '71

COLLEGES for women
Best of both worlds. il Newsweek 77:86 Ap
5 '71
Future of the women's college; Catholic
women's college. America 125:304 O 23 '71
What would Teresa say? decree for the Car-
melites. America 125:304 O 23 '71
See also
Goucher college, Baltimore

COLLEGIUM vocale of Cologne. See Choral
groups and societies

COLLETT, Rosemary
Her home is a sanctuary for injured wildlife.
W. Hartley and E. Hartley. il pors Good H
173:78+ O '71 *

COLLIER, Barnard Law
Brain power: the case for bio-feedback
training. il Sat R 54:10-13+ Ap 10 '71
Joe Alsop story. il pors N Y Times Mag p22-
3+ My 23 '71
Learning to cope in Prince Georges County.
il Sat R 54:64-5+ My 22 '71

COLLIER, Barnard Law—*Continued*
　Road to Peking; or, How does this Kissinger do it? il pors N Y Times Mag p34-5+ N 14 '71
　Story of a teen-age Nader raider. il pors N Y Times Mag p30-1+ Mr 14 '71
COLLIER, James Lincoln
　Me and my presidents. il Read Digest 98:102-5 Je '71
COLLIER, Jo-Etha
　Senseless killing. por Time 97:13-14 Je 7 '71 *
COLLIER, Peter
　Salmon fishing in America: the Indians vs. the state of Washington. il Ramp Mag 9: 29-31+ Ap '71
　(ed) See Deloria, V. jr. American thing: white society is breaking down around us
COLLIER, Richard
　Wish upon a star: the magical kingdoms of Walt Disney; condensation. il Read Digest 99:221-4+ O '71
COLLIES
　Cyclic urinary leukopoietic activity in gray collie dogs. D. C. Dale and others. bibliog il Science 173:152-3 Jl 9 '71
COLLIN, Michel
　Pope Clement XV. il por Time 97:66 Mr 15 '71 *
COLLINS, Arthur Andrews
　Collins radio loses its Collins. Bsns W p31 D 4 '71 *
COLLINS, Bessie F.
　And the sun shines down; poem. Horn Bk 47:302 Je '71
COLLINS, Bill
　Mining the musical underground. il Hi Fi 21:74-6 N '71
COLLINS, Bud
　Tennis. il Sports Illus 35:65-7 Ag 16 '71
COLLINS, Chapin
　25 years later: the circle that works. il Am For 77:15-20+ O '71
COLLINS, Chuck
　Chicago's Underground news. Cyclops. Life 71:14 Jl 2 '71 *
COLLINS, Dabney Otis
　Battle for Blue Lake. il Am West 8:32-7 S '71
COLLINS, Floyd, and Shieh, C. Y.
　More water from the same plant. il pors Am City 86:96-7 O '71
COLLINS, Jean
　Columbia conservatives for Buckley. Mlle 72: 138 Ja '71
COLLINS, Jerome A.
　Model cities program as a field placement for graduate students in mental health nursing. Ment Hy 55:308-11 Jl '71
COLLINS, John
　How to use operator "j". il Radio-Electr 42:49 F '71
COLLINS, Michael, 1930-
　Earth from far away, and close up; interview, ed. by P. Goldberger. por Sr Schol 98:16 Mr 15 '71
COLLINS, Paul
　Pictures from an African journey. il pors Ebony 26:174-6+ O '71 *
COLLINS, Peter M.
　Sex education in the secondary curriculum: problems and pseudo-problems. Sch & Soc 99:357-9 O '71
COLLINS, Richard L.
　Back to basics. il Flying 89:52-3+ D '71
　Flying visit. il Flying 88:108-9 Je '71
　On top. See issues of Flying
　Safety check. See issues of Flying
COLLINS, Sid
　Sid Collins. R. Guldahl, jr. il pors Hot Rod 24:44-6 My '71 *
COLLINS, Thomas
　Inquiring about retiring; questions and answers. See issues of Harvest years
COLLINS radio company
　Collins radio finds a friend with money. il Bsns W p 111-12 Je 19 '71
　Collins radio loses its Collins. Bsns W p31 D 4 '71
　Collins reports $41-million loss. Aviation W 95:18 Jl 5 '71
　Collins, Rockwell explore affiliation. Aviation W 94:20 My 24 '71
　North American Rockwell, Collins reach accord. Aviation W 94:27 Je 7 '71
　Reorganization set at Collins radio. Aviation W 95:24 D 20 '71
COLLISION avoidance systems. See Airplanes—Safety devices and measures
COLLISIONS, Automobile. See Traffic accidents
COLLOGRAPHS. See Prints
COLLOIDS
　See also
　Aerosols
　Electrophoresis
　Emulsions
　Gelatin

COLMAN, William Gerald
　Why local reform is a businessman's concern. il Nations Bsns 59:70-1 Jl '71
COLO, Rosa Lee
　Beginning teacher; interview. il por Todays Ed 60:54-9 S '71
COLOGNE for men. See Perfumes for men
COLOMBEY-LES-DEUX-EGLISES, France
　De Gaulle in a crystal ball. Time 98:48 N 22 '71
　Selling of de Gaulle. A. Tillier. il Newsweek 78:26 S 13 '71
COLOMBIA
　See also
　Church and state in Colombia
　Fishing—Colombia
　Popayán

　　　Politics and government
　La capitana. il pors Time 98:43-4+ D 6 '71
　Coalition in Colombia. M. Deas. Cur Hist 60:90-4+ F '71
　Colombia: Latin America's best bet. W. F. Buckley, jr. Nat R 23:216-17 F 23 '71

　　　Religious institutions and affairs
　See also
　Church and state in Colombia
COLOMBIAN cookery. See Cookery, Colombian
COLOMBIAN poets. See Poets, Colombian
COLOMBO, Emilio
　Prime Minister Colombo of Italy visits the United States; exchange of greetings, toasts, February 18, 1971. Dept State Bul 64:329-33 Mr 15 '71

　　　about
　Can Italian democracy survive? J. Navone. Commonweal 95:323-5 Ja 7 '72
　Trying to take wing. por Time 97:28+ F 22 '71 *
COLOMBO, Joe
　Discoveries: living machines. il House & Gard 139:94-7 Ap '71 *
COLOMBO, Joseph
　Capo who went public. Time 98:16-17 Jl 12 '71 *
　Colombo. por Time 98:13 Jl 19 '71 *
　Family man. Nation 212:454 Ap 12 '71 *
　How one family stamped out the M——. il pors Newsweek 77:22-3 Ap 5 '71 *
　It's Joe! They got Joe! il por Newsweek 78:30-1 Jl 12 '71 *
　Mafia: back to the bad old days? il pors Time 98:14-18+ Jl 12 '71 *
　Mafia tries a new tune; with report by E. Harvey. T. Buckley. il Harper 243:46-7+ Ag '71 *
　Night for Colombo. il por Time 97:16 Ap 5 '71 *
　Parting shots: Unity day that split the mob. il pors Life 71:70-1 Jl 9 '71 *
　What d'ya hear from the mob? P. Axthelm. il por Newsweek 78:31-2 Jl 12 '71 *
COLÓN theater, Buenos Aires. See Opera houses
COLONIAL furniture. See Furniture, American
COLONIAL gardens. See Gardens, Colonial
COLONIAL life and customs
　See also
　Williamsburg, Va.
COLONIAL stores, inc.
　Pragmatic supermarketer. por Duns 97:62 Je '71
COLONIAL Williamsburg garden symposium
　Virginia, where garden lovers come to look and learn. M. Perry. il Home Gard 58:26-9 Mr '71
COLONIES
　See also
　United Nations—Special committee on the situation with regard to the implementation of the declaration on the granting of independence to colonial countries and peoples
　United Nations—Trusteeship council
　also subhead Colonies under names of countries, e.g. France—Colonies
COLONIES, Artists. See Artists colonies
COLONNESE, Louis M.
　Unwarranted dismissal. Chr Cent 88:1102 S 22 '71 *
　Writing on the wall: Colonnese go home; with editorial comment. G. Maceoin. Commonweal 94:492-3 S 24 '71 *
COLOR
　Canvases brimming with color. il Life 71: 74-9 S 24 '71
　Color it springtime. il Ladies Home J 88: 30+ Mr '71
　Color: the silent language of vision; interview, ed. by M. Roche. P. Arthur. House & Gard 140:22+ S '71
　See also
　Palettes (colors)

COLOR—*Continued*

Psychology

How color sensitive are you? quiz. H. Aach. House & Gard 140:10-11+ S '71

COLOR-bar generators. See Testing instruments

COLOR blindness

Prolonged color blindness induced by intense spectral lights in rhesus monkeys. R. S. Harwerth and H. G. Sperling. bibliog il Science 174:520-3 O 29 '71

COLOR codes

Black is white and white is black; color-coding of wires. J. Darr. il Radio-Electr 43:22+ Ja '72

COLOR films. See Photography—Films

COLOR filters. See Light filters

COLOR in architecture

Color: the silent language of vision; interview, ed. by M. Roche. P. Arthur. House & Gard 140:22+ S '71

New directions in color, indoors and out. il House & Gard 140:88-93 S '71

COLOR-in-color process. See Copying processes

COLOR in gardens. See Gardens—Color

COLOR in house decoration

Color & how people live with it. P. Rumely. il Bet Hom & Gard 49:59-71 Ap '71

Color: we present the pace setters. il House B 113:90-3 Ap '71

Decorate-it-yourself inspiration; G. Vanderbilt's summer house. il House & Gard 139:86-93 Ap '71

Deep livable powerful color. L. Grundy. il House B 113:76-83 S '71

Flower colors make a house vibrate with summer. il House & Gard 139:82-5 Je '71

Garden fantasy to bring inside. il House & Gard 139:92-7 Mr '71

How to color it yourself with House & garden colors 1972. il House & Gard 140:79-97+ S '71

How to use color now; Joy of summer garden color. il House & Gard 139:75-85 Mr '71

Ideas with go from Americans at home and abroad. il House & Gard 139:56-61 F '71

Living in a garden indoors and out; Maine houses, and garden of Mr and Mrs Henry Parish II. il House & Gard 139:86-91 Mr '71

Monticello colors for today. V. D. Hahn. il Am Home 74:32+ Jl '71

Peaches; pick of the crop. N. Mandelbaum. il Ladies Home J 88:76-7 Ag '71

Putting together the pace setter colors. L. Grundy. il House B 113:94-5 Ap '71

Yellow; sunstreaking. N. Mandelbaum. il Ladies Home J 88:82-3 F '71

COLOR music. See Music and color

COLOR negative films. See Photography—Films

COLOR now with Europe; story. See King, J.

COLOR of animals

Eye marks in vertebrates; aids to vision. R. W. Ficken and others. bibliog il Science 173:936-9 S 3 '71

Splendor of iridescence; the makng of H. Simon's new book. il Pub W 199:35-8 Mr 22 '71

COLOR of fishes

Reflectors in fishes. E. Denton. il Sci Am 224:64-72 Ja '71

COLOR of food

Cook by eye: the eat-appeal of colour. M. McKendry. Vogue 157:66+ Mr 1 '71

COLOR of man

Other person's skin. M. Awad. UNESCO Courier 24:20-2 N '71

See also
Hair

COLOR of music. See Music and color

COLOR photography

Case of the near-sighted seers. J. Deschin. Pop Phot 69:61+ Jl '71

Ed Scully on color. E. Scully. See issues of Modern photography

Feininger. A. Feininger. Mod Phot 35:30+ Jl '71

Power of one-color color. C. Steinberg. il Pop Phot 69:72-7 Jl '71

Competitions

See Photography—Competitions

COLOR photography printing. See Photography—Printing processes

COLOR prejudice. See Race prejudice

COLOR print processor. See Photography—Processing—Apparatus and supplies

COLOR prints

See also
Linoleum block printing

COLOR sense

Color- and edge-sensitive channels in the human visual system; tuning for orientation. R. Held and S. R. Shattuck. bibliog il Science 174:314-16 O 15 '71

COLOR television. See Television, Color

COLOR television receivers. See Television receivers, Color

COLOR vision. See Color sense

COLORADO

See also
Architecture, Domestic—Colorado
Florissant Fossil Beds National Monument
Hunting—Colorado
Land—Colorado
Music festivals—Colorado
Petroleum—Colorado
Rocky Mountain National Park
Skis and skiing—Colorado

Description and travel

Colorado, the American family vacation state. J. O'Reilly. il Holiday 49:42-9+ Mr '71

Colorado: the state nearest heaven. P. Friggens. il Read Digest 98:158-64 F '71

COLORADO library association

Colorado LA conference draws well, talks change. D. W. Brunton. Wilson Lib Bul 46:309-12 D '71

Of note; conference. Am Lib 2:1138 D '71

COLORADO opera festival. See Music festivals—Colorado

COLORADO RIVER

Profiles; F. Dominy and D. Brower. J. McPhee. por New Yorker 47:41-4+ Ap 3 '71

Rip-roaring river. M. Litton. il Holiday 49:50-3 My '71

U.S. and Mexico extend agreement on Colorado River salinity; Department announcement. Dept State Bul 63:732 D 14 70

Why the sands aren't red; canyonlands. H. Lansford. il Sci Digest 69:61-5 My '71

See also
Grand Canyon
Powell, Lake

COLORADO SPRINGS

Education

Colorado Springs teachers association. B. R. Dickinson. Todays Ed 60:50 D '71

Sanitary affairs

Portable plant meets tertiary requirements. il Am City 86:63 Mr '71

COLORADO strike, 1913-14. See Strikes—United States—Coal mines and mining

COLORADO tick fever. See Rocky Mountain spotted fever

COLORED illustrations. See Illustration of books and periodicals

COLORED people (South Africa)

Not quite black or white; Cape coloreds. E. Peter, jr. New Repub 165:13 D 25 '71

COLORS. See Color

COLOSTRUM

Colostrum timing important in calf disease control. Suc Farm 69:no2 D8 F '71

COLSON, Charles Wendell

Man who is in. por Newsweek 78:16 S 6 '71 *

COLSON, Frank A.

Workshop; kiln building with space age materials. il Craft Horiz 30:46-8 Ag '70; 31:8 Ag '71

COLSON, J. G.

Baron Barnaby's box; drama; reprint from March 1955 issue. Plays 30:57-62 Ap '71

COLT, Jon

Don't throw good power diodes away. il Radio-Electr 42:37 Jl '71

Dynamic dwell/tachometer. il Electr World 85:78-80 My '71

COLTER, Gordon

Schwabing; Germany's Greenwich Village. il Holiday 49:62-3+ F '71

COLTON, Helen

Are we a nation of adulterers? Harp Baz 104:124-6 O '71

Sex & the law. Harp Baz 104:108-9+ Ag '71

COLTS (football club) See Football clubs

COLUMBIA, Md.

Columbia and the new cities, by G. Breckenfeld. Review
New Repub 165:31-2 S 4 '71. G. Gappert

Fresh scene in the clean dream. W. Von Eckardt. il Sat R 54:21-3 My 15 '71

COLUMBIA, Md.—*Continued*

Tale of one city. J. Rosenthal. il N Y Times Mag p4-5+ D 26 '71

Tidesfall townhouses. il Arch Rec 149:92-3 mid-My '71

Education

Case for permissipline; informal teaching at Wilde Lake middle school. il Time 97:54 Je 21 '71

Lighting

Bright life for a new city. il Am City 86:114 O '71

COLUMBIA, S.C.

Historic houses, etc.

History in houses: the Hampton-Preston house. W. Seale. il Antiques 100:241-5 Ag '71

COLUMBIA broadcasting system, inc.

Arrow in the air. Newsweek 77:111 Mr 29 '71

CBS gets an expert in diversification. por Bsns W p22 S 18 '71

CBS versus Congress. W. F. Buckley, jr. Nat R 23:829 Jl 27 '71

Day in the life of Walter Cronkite. P. Hudson. il pors Sr Schol 99:10-11+ O 18 '71

Getting CBS; House commerce investigations subcommittee demands materials used in making The selling of the Pentagon. Newsweek 77:95 Ap 19 '71

Harassing of CBS. Commonweal 94:206 My 7 '71

How a network boss picks shows. T. Thompson. il pors Life 71:46-50+ S 10 '71

Melvin Laird and CBS; question of editing. Sedulus. New Repub 165:29-30 Jl 10 '71; Reply. K. D. Tiven. 165:33 Jl 24 '71

Selling of Congress. il por Newsweek 78:24-5 Jl 26 '71

Selling of the Selling of the Pentagon. R. J. Irvine. Nat R 23:855-7+ Ag 10 '71

Stanton's no. por Time 98:68 Jl 5 '71

Station break at CBS. Newsweek 78:82 S 20 '71

Unblinking eye of CBS; case of controversial documentary The selling of the Pentagon. Time 98:19 Jl 26 '71

Where is Prof. Greet? J. C. Ottinger. Nat R 23:943 Ag 24 '71

Who is big brother? The selling of the Pentagon materials; hearing before House commerce investigations subcommittee. por Newsweek 78:25-6 Jl 5 '71

COLUMBIA records, inc.

Meeting: new single records. New Yorker 47:41-3 N 27 '71

COLUMBIA RIVER

Mighty Columbia. L. Barber. il Yachting 129:60-1+ My '71

New Astoria bridge opens up winter beach adventure. il Sunset 146:65 Mr '71

Will we let the pink and silver warrior die? J. Hemingway. il pors Nat Wildlife 9:34-7 Ag '71

COLUMBIA university

Columbia reactor gets thumbs down. G. B. Lubkin. il Phys Today 24:61-2 Je '71

Columbia's lion gets a bearding. Bsns W p48 N 13 '71

New tensions on campus. W. J. McGill. por Life 71:55 O 8 '71

Reaction on Morningside Heights; denial of reactor permit. R. J. Bazell. Science 174:575 N 5 '71

Segregation comes to Columbia; granting of Malcolm X liberation center and other student groups' demand for lounges. F. K Lowell. Nat R 23:1236 N 5 '71

See also
Barnard college, New York

Libraries

Nevins papers and library at Columbia. Sch & Soc 99:462-3 D '71

Urban center

New directions for Columbia's urban center. il Sch & Soc 99:202-4 Ap '71

COLUMBINES

Columbines in the rhubarb. N. W. Bubel. il Org Gard & Farm 18:56-7 My '71

COLUMBUS, Christopher

Columbus' melting pot of 1492. il por Sr Schol 99:4-5 S 27 '71 •

First letter from the New World. M. A. Lubin. il Américas 23:2-12 Ap '71 •

Land ho! H. Martínez-Montero. il Américas 23:S11-13 O '71 •

What did Columbus mean to Europe? S. de Madariaga. il Américas 23:S14-15 O '71 •

Drama

Sail on! Sail on! L. Olfson. Plays 31:77-81 O '71

COLUMBUS, Ind.

Architecture

Discovering Columbus. K. Kuh. il Sat R 54:36-7 Ag 21 '71

Making of a civic space. J. Baker. il Arch Forum 135:40-5 N '71

Post office as a pacesetter. il Arch Forum 133:46-9 D '70

What's all this top architecture doing out on the prairie? J. L. O'Neill. il Am Home 74:48-51+ Ag '71

COLUMBUS, Miss.

History in towns; ante bellum houses. P. T. Murfee. il Antiques 100:914-18 D '71

COLUMBUS, Ohio

Education

Columbus arts IMPACT; Interdisciplinary model programs in the arts for children and teachers. il Todays Ed 60:20-4 N '71

Galleries and museums

This museum is mainly for kids; Historical center. il Arch Rec 150:85-90 Jl '70

COLUMNISTS. See Journalists

COLUMNS (newspapers) See Newspapers—Sections, columns, etc.

COLUMNS (periodicals) See Periodicals—Sections, columns, etc.

COLWIN, Laurie

Elite viewer; story. Mlle 73:149 S '71

Girl with the harlequin glasses; story. Redbook 138:88-9 N '71

(tr) See Singer, I. B. Day in Coney Island
(tr) See Singer, I. B. Magazine
(tr) See Singer, I. B. Third one

COMBINATION locks. See Locks and keys

COMBINATION rooms. See Rooms

COMBINATIONS

Combinatorial richness of folding a piece of paper. M. Gardner. il Sci Am 224:110-12+ My; 122-3 Je '71

COMBINED immune deficiency. See Deficiency diseases

COMBINES. See Harvesting machinery

COMBUSTION

• Fossil fuel combustion and the major sedimentary cycle. K. K. Bertine and E. D. Goldberg. bibliog il Science 173:233-5 Jl 16 '71

See also
Fuel
Phlogiston theory
Smoke

COMBUSTION engineering, inc.

Stewart Jackson: instant pro? with photographs. B. Nemser. por Pop Phot 69:102-5 O '71

COME home with me; story. See Coulter, J.

COME let us adore him; story. See Lardner, S.

COME out and play day. See Special days, weeks, and months

COME to the fair! drama. See Murray, J.

COMEDIANS

See also
Allen, W
Bruce, L.
Cavett, D.
Frye, D.
Smothers brothers
Steinberg, D.

COMEDY

End of sadness and history. J. V. Schall. il Cath World 213:222-6 Ag '71

See also
Humor

Study and teaching

Anecdotes, facetiae, satire, etc.

Albert Brooks' Famous school for comedians. A. Brooks. il por Esquire 75:89-94 F '71

COMER, James P.

—See Poussaint, A. F. jt. auth.

about

Wanted: a Dr Spock for black mothers. J. Dann. il por N Y Times Mag p78-80+ Ap 18 '71 •

COMER, Nancy Axelrad

Career is all in your head. Mlle 72:119+ Ja '71

Jobs that can change your world. il Mlle 73:132-4+ S '71

On campus. il por Mlle 73:202+ My '71

Surviving outward bound. il por Mlle 73:180-1+ O '71

Whole sell catalogue. Mlle 72:188-90 Mr '71

COMETS
Comets did it. Time 98:40+ S 6 '71
Comets of 1970; with table. Sky & Tel 41: 222 Ap '71
Comets: production mechanisms of hydroxyl and hydrogen halos. A. H. Delsemme. bibliog Science 172:1126-7 Je 11 '71
New light on Biela's comet. il Sky & Tel 41: 84 F '71
Why do comets have tails? I. Asimov. Sci Digest 70:82-3 Ag '71

Observations
Visual observation of comets. J. Rahe and B. Donn. il Sky & Tel 41:214-16 Ap '71

COMIC books. See Comics (books, strips, etc)
COMIC opera. See Opera
COMIC strips. See Comics (books, strips, etc)

COMICS (books, strips, etc)
Art; exhibition of 75 years of the comics. L. Alloway Nation 213:157-8 Ag 30 '71
Comics; exhibition to celebrate diamond jubilee of comic strips. New Yorker 47: 32-3 My 1 '71
Comics on the couch. G. Clarke. il Time 98: 70-1 D 13 '71
Dirigible (cont) G. Viertel. il Harp Baz 104: 124-5 F; 156-7 Mr ; 140:1 Ap; 144-5 My '71
Fascinating funnies. F. Dickenson. il Read Digest 99:201-4+ N '71
Good grief, $150 million! the Peanuts empire. il pors Newsweek 78:40-44 D 27 '71
King features syndicate. J. Markow. Writers Digest 51:18-19 My '71
@&%#!! or, Takin' the lid off the id. H. Kurtzman. il Esquire 75:128-36 Je '71
Shazam! Here comes Captain Relevant. S. Braun. il por N Y Times Mag p32-3+ My 2 '71; Discussion. p6 My 30 '71
Wow! There's a kaboom in old comic books! il Changing T 26:36 Ja '72

COMINS, Jeremy
Creative art history. il Sch Arts 70:44 Je '71
Found object sculpture. il Sch Arts 70:14-15 F '71
Mixed media collage. il Sch Arts 71:10-11 N '71

COMISSIONA, Sergiu
My life was like a game of Russian roulette; interview, ed. by R. Hemming. por Sr Schol 99:22-3 O 25 '71

about
Music to my ears; concert in Carnegie Hall. I. Kolodin. Sat R 54:52 My 22 '71 *

COMMAGER, Henry Steele
Misuse of power. New Repub 164:17-21 Ap 17 '71
Roots of lawlessness. por Sat R 54:17-19+ F 13 '71

COMMANDAY, Robert
Vienna is a state of mind. il Hi Fi 21: MA26-7 O '71

COMMEMORATIVE buttons. See Buttons
COMMEMORATIVE glassware. See Glassware
COMMEMORATIVE medals. See Medals
COMMEMORATIVE stamps. See Postage stamps
COMMENCEMENT addresses. See Baccalaureate addresses

COMMENCEMENTS
Fond farewell; speakers. Newsweek 77:98 Je 7 '71

COMMENTARY (periodical)
Come on in, the water's fine; disassociation of Jews from left radicalism. Nat R 23:249-50 Mr 9 '71
Cooling of the intellectuals. P. Steinfels. Commonweal 94:255-61 My 21 '71; Discussion. 94:365-7, 418 Jl 9, Ag 20 '71
My Jewish problem, and ours; Israel, the left, and the Jewish establishment. S. Stern. il Ramp Mag 10:38-40 Ag '71

COMMERCE
Building walls abroad; the unsettled trading world. il Time 98:35-6 N 1 '71
International trade issues for the seventies; statement, May 20, 1971. N. Samuels. Dept State Bul 64:807-12 Je 21 '71
Now, a trade hassle. Time 98:27 D 27 '71
Protectionism or free trade: a decision for our time; address, May 3, 1971. K. Rush. Dept State Bul 64:749-53 Je 7 '71
Retaliation against surcharge? il U S News 71:26 D 13 '71
Technology and world trade: is there cause for alarm? P. M. Boffey. il Science 172:37-41 Ap 2 '71
Trade collides with ecology. il Bsns W p72-3+ Ja 23 '71

World trade: looking ahead. R. A. Peterson. Duns 93:25 Je '69
See also
Balance of trade
Communist countries—Commerce
Competition, International
Dumping (commercial policy)
Foreign trade regulation
Free trade and protection
Ports
Raw materials
Smuggling
Waterways
World trade institute
World trade week
also subhead Commerce under names of countries, e.g. United States—Commerce
COMMERCIAL banks. See Banks and banking

COMMERCIAL law
See also
Foreign trade regulation
Landlord and tenant
Trusts, Industrial—Law
COMMERCIAL paper. See Negotiable instruments

COMMERCIAL products
Consumer goods; with yardsticks of management performance. il Forbes 109:154+ Ja 1 '72
Identity crisis in the consumer markets. C. E. Silberman. il Fortune 83:92-5+ Mr '71
Price of progress; conclusions of B. Commoner. Time 98:79 N 1 '71
See also
Commodity exchanges
Private brands
Products, New
Quality of products
Surplus products

Endorsements
See Advertising—Testimonials

Safety devices and measures
Havoc in your household; how to prevent it. S. Klein. il Sci Digest 69:14-19 My '71
Lawn mowers & other killers. S. Klein. il Nation 212:402-4 Mr 29 '71
More killers. Nation 212:422 Ap 5 '71

Standards
See also
United States—Standards, National bureau of

Testing
See also
Consumers union of United States
COMMERCIAL products, Certification of
Labeling the label; seals of approval. Consumer Bul 54:2+ N '71
Labels and seals: Good housekeeping. Parents' magazine. il Consumer Bul 54:14 Ag '71
Labels and seals: what do they mean to the consumer? household appliances. il Consumer Bul 54:37-8 Je '71

COMMERCIAL treaties and agreements
See also
General agreement on tariffs and trade
United States—Commercial treaties and agreements
COMMERCIALS. See Radio advertising; Television advertising

COMMISSION merchants
See also
Factors
COMMISSION of the churches on international affairs. See World council of churches
COMMISSION on campus unrest. See United States—President's commission on campus unrest
COMMISSION on personnel interchange. See United States—President's commission on personnel interchange
COMMISSION to investigate the Vietnamese war (proposed)
Wanted: an inquiry into the war. New Repub 164:5-6 My 22 '71
COMMISSIONER of baseball. See Baseball clubs—Organization and administration
COMMISSIONER of education. See United States—Education, Office of
COMMISSIONER'S committee on library development. See New York (state)—Education, Department of—Commissioner's committee on library development
COMMISSIONS, Independent regulatory. See Independent regulatory commissions

COMMISSIONS of inquiry
Bloodied Lindsay; Knapp commission testimony by J. Kriegel. Time 99:29 Ja 3 '72
Cops as pushers; findings of Knapp commission. Time 98:17-18 N 8 '71
Knapp commission didn't know it couldn't be done. B. Davidson. il N Y Times Mag p 16-17+ Ja 9 '72

COMMISSIONS of inquiry—*Continued*
Red-handed men in blue; Knapp commission hearings. il Newsweek 78:77-8 N 8 '71
What's a rat bite got to do with Thomas Jefferson? presidential fact-finding commissions decisions, but no action; with three viewpoints. il Sr Schol 99:4-10 O 11 '71
    See also
Commission to investigate the Vietnamese war (proposed)

COMMISSIONS of inquiry, International
    See also
International commission of enquiry into United States crimes in Indochina

COMMISSIONS of the United Nations. See name of the commission as subhead under United Nations, e.g. United Nations—Commission on human rights

COMMISSIONS of the United States government. See name of the commission as subhead under United States, e.g. United States—Commission on government procurement

COMMITTEE for economic developments
Business and the revolution; report on the social responsibilities of business corporations. R. Gelatt. Sat R 54:32 Jl 24 '71
Can we afford tomorrow? symposium, with introd. by W. C. Stolk. il Sat R 54:35-8+ Ja 23 '71

COMMITTEE for environmental information
Critics weigh EPA herbicide report, find it wanting; 2,4,5-T controversy. C. Holden. Science 173:312 Jl 23 '71
Gamble; making public the advisory committee report on 2,4,5-T. T. Aaronson. il Environ 13:20-4+ S '71

COMMITTEE of responsibility to save war-burned and war-injured Vietnamese children
Bach Anh walks back home again. il Sr Schol 99:17 O 18 '71
Lau goes home to Vietnam; and the case of Ngu Van Xia; with editorial comment. il Life 70:18B-28 Ja 29 '71

COMMITTEE of twenty-four. See United Nations—Special committee on the situation with regard to the implementation of the declaration on the granting of independence to colonial countries and peoples

COMMITTEE on environment and development. See United States—Agency for international development

COMMITTEE on new directions for ALA. See American library association—Activities . committee on new directions for ALA

COMMITTEE on scientific freedom and responsibility. See American association for the advancement of science

COMMITTEE on space research. See International council of scientific unions—Committee on space research

COMMITTEE on the challenges of modern society. See NATO—Committee on the challenges of modern society

COMMITTEE to investigate assassinations
Irregulars take the field. F. J. Cook. Nation 213:40-6 Jl 19 '71

COMMITTEES

Anecdotes, facetiae, satire, etc.
Ad hoc. J. Ferris. Sat R 54:89 S 25 '71

COMMITTEES, Congressional. See United States—Congress—Committees

COMMITTEES of the United Nations. See name of the committee as subhead under United Nations, e.g. United Nations—Committee on the elimination of racial discrimination

COMMITTEES of the United States government. See name of committee, inverted, as subhead under United States, e.g. United States—Health service industry, Committee on the

COMMODITY control

Germany (Democratic Republic)
Fifth of the GNP is black market. il Bsns W p35 My 8 '71

COMMODITY exchanges
Bright futures in cotton trading; New York cotton exchange. il Bsns W p44 Je 5 '71
Commodities: plenty of action for high rollers. Bsns W p83 Ap 24 '71
Commodity traders work in the dark. il Bsns W p76 Ag 21 '71
Gold bug; futures trade in British sovereigns on the West Coast commodity exchange. il Newsweek 78:62 Ag 2 '71
Harvest from a new commodity contract; Chicago mercantile exchange's milo campaign. il Bsns W p70+ S 18 '71
His biggest commodity: publicity; West Coast commodity exchange. pors Bsns W p25 Jl 31 '71

OJ play: tough and tangy; frozen orange juice futures. A. Hershman. il Duns 97: 55-7 Ap '71
Should you try corn futures? F. Bailey, jr. il Suc Farm 69:B20 Je '71
Watching futures for profit; corn futures. F. Bailey, jr. il Suc Farm 69:31 Je '71
What you should know about delivering on a future contract; cattle futures. W. Kester. il Farm J 95:B10-11 Ag '71
Wildest game is also the safest; futures trading. il Bsns W p74 F 6 '71

COMMON cause (political organization)
Birthday for common cause. por Time 98:14 Ag 16 '71
Common cause. New Repub 164:5-7 Mr 20 '71
Common cause flexes its muscles. Bsns W p29 F 13 '71
Common cause: the yeas and nays have it. il Bsns W p92+ O 23 '71
John W. Gardner. New Yorker 47:30-2 F 27 '71

COMMON market in western Europe. See European economic community

COMMONER, Barry
Economic growth and ecology: a biologist's view; with tables. bibliog Mo Labor R 94:3-13 N '71
Nuclear power plants, boon or blight? il por Nat Wildlife 9:21-3 Ap '71
Reporter at large. New Yorker 47:49-54+ S 25; 44-8+ O 2 '71
—and others
Causes of pollution. bibliog il Environ 13: 2-19 Ap '71

    about
Pentagon has the money. Nation 213:100 Ag 16 '71 •
Price of progress. Time 98:79 N 1 '71 •

COMMONWEAL (periodical)
Best editorial, 1970. Commonweal 94:342 Je 25 '71
Case of Commonweal. Commonweal 95:129 N 5 '71

COMMONWEALTH prime ministers conference. See Prime ministers conferences

COMMONWEALTH united corporation
Spinoff to break a fall. il Bsns W p38-9 S 25 '71

COMMUNAL living. See Collective settlements

COMMUNAL penance. See Confession

COMMUNE; drama. See Schechner, R.

COMMUNES. See Collective settlements

COMMUNICABLE diseases
    See also
Animals as carriers of infection
Streptococcal infections
    also names of communicable diseases, e.g. Cholera

COMMUNICABLE diseases in animals
Susceptibility of mink to sheep scrapie. R. P. Hanson and others. bibliog il Science 172:859-61 My 21 '71

COMMUNICATION
Communications; ed. by R. L. Tobin. See Communications issues of Saturday review
Neglected science of mass communication; address, November 11, 1971. P. Lesly. Vital Speeches 38:117-20 D 1 '71
To describe it all, growl softly. W. J. Reynolds. Engl J 60:267-9 F '71
    See also
Interlibrary communication
Knowledge, Sociology of
Language and languages
Mass media
Popular culture
Self disclosure
Sign language
Speech

International aspects
Information systems and inter-organizational space; social problems. A. J. N. Judge. bibliog f Ann Am Acad 393:47-64 Ja '71
Sharing the mind; Unesco role. W. McEwing. il UNESCO Courier 24:54-6 Ag '71

Social aspects
Transcultural aspects of community psychiatry. J. Hartog. bibliog Ment Hy 55: 35-44 Ja '71
What did you say? address, July 17, 1971. W. A. Nail. Vital Speeches 37:723-6 S 15 '71
    See also
MINERVA system

COMMUNICATION (theology)
Catholics and the communications revolution. T. Beeson. Chr Cent 88:714 Je 9 '71
Of many things; communication problem within the church. D. R. Campion. America 125:inside cover O 30 '71

COMMUNICATIONS satellites, Russian
Soviets expanding satcom capabilities. il
Aviation W 95:51-2 Ag 23 '71
COMMUNICATIONS workers

Wages and hours
Wages of telephone and telegraph workers.
M. J. Tighe. il Mo Labor R 94:61-2 Ja '71
COMMUNICATIONS workers of America
TV carries a call for a phone strike. Bsns W
p20 My 29 '71
Tougher tone in phone talks. Bsns W p78
My 8 '71
COMMUNION. See Lords Supper
COMMUNISM
Confession was within the logic of Stalinism.
D. Howard. Commonweal 93:550+ Mr 5 '71
Harry Luce and the Russian century. J.
Chamberlain. Nat R 23:524-5+ My 18 '71
New Democratic theory, by K. A. Megill. Re-
view
Nat R 23:268 Mr 9 '71. H. Caton
State of communism. Z. Brzezinski. News-
week 77:56 Mr 15 '71
Unfulfilled prophecies of Karl Marx. C. Brown.
Chr Today 15:4-6 Jl 2 '71
What's a Marxist? Sr Schol 98:10 F 1 '71
See also
Collective settlements
Communist parties
Socialism

Anti-Communist measures
After Vietnam, another witchhunt? L. J.
Halle. il N Y Times Mag p36-8+ Je 6 '71
Through the years with the blacklist. O.
Bean. il Nat R 23:193-5+ F 23 '71
See also
United States—Foreign relations—Anti-Com-
munist measures

Asia
Asia beyond Vietnam: half the world's people
in turmoil. il U S News 70:32-3 My 31 '71

China (People's Republic)
Ant hill: Maoland. J. Burnham. Nat R 23:580
Je 1 '71
China as it is today. L. La Dany. America
125:87-8 Ag 21 '71
China's strategic shift. O. E. Clubb. Cur 132:
58-64 S '71
Maoism in east Europe? E. V. Kohak. Com-
monweal 95:275-7 D 17 '71
Massacre of history. Time 98:22 Ag 23 '71

Cuba
Worker's paradise Cuban style. E. McDowell. il Nat R 23:1063-4 S 24 '71

Czechoslovakia
People dissolved. il por Time 97:18 Je 7 '71
Prague, spring '71. H. Sutton. il Sat R 54:19-
21+ Je 5 '71
Reports and comment: Prague. F. Lewis.
Atlan 228:14-16+ Ag '71
See also
Communist party (Czechoslovakia)

Europe, Eastern
Eastern Europe: the red reformation continues.
E. Klein. il Newsweek 78:39 Jl 5 '71
Maoism in east Europe? E. V. Kohak. Com-
monweal 95:275-7 D 17 '71

Europe, Western
Europe: the revolution that failed. il Time
97:36-7 F 8 '71

France
See also
Communist party (France)

History
Communism and the working class before
Marx: the Icarian experience. C. H. John-
son. bibliog f il Am Hist R 76:642-89 Je '71

Greece, Modern
To understand Greece, go to Lia. N. Gage. il
pors N Y Times Mag p 16-17+ Ja 31 '71

Italy
See also
Communist party (Italy)

Latin America
Cassocks and communism. R. Peter. Nat R
23:1468-9 D 31 '71
Crumbling hemisphere. D. Lawrence. U S
News 70:88 F 22 '71
What drives Latin Americans left? S. Rod-
man. il Nat R 23:1348-50+ D 3 '71

Philippines
Marcos and the Communists. J. de Herrerra.
il America 126:6-10 Ja 8 '72

Poland
See also
Communist party (Poland)

Russia
Let history judge, by R. A. Medvedev. Re-
view
Newsweek il 79:55 Ja 3 '72. S. K. Ober-
beck
Sat R il pors 55:25-8 Ja 8 '72. R. C.
Tucker
Time il por 99:66+ Ja 17 '72. S. Talbott
Rise and fall and rise of Leon Trotsky. E.
Taylor. il pors Horizon 13:34-43 Spr '71
See also
Communist party (Russia)

Thailand
Who says Thailand's next? W. A. O'Neil.
New Repub 164:23-7 Ja 2 '71

United States
TRB from Washington: the spook; J.
McCarthy. New Repub 165:6 Ag 21 '71
See also
Communist party (United States)

Anti-Communist measures
See also
Conservatism
Internal security
United States—Subversive activities control
board

Vietnam (Republic)
Anti-Communist measures
See also
Vietnamese war, 1957-
COMMUNISM and art
Failed utopia: Russian art 1917-32. J. E. Bowlt.
bibliog il Art in Am 59:40-51 Jl '71
Refreezing the thaw; the artist W. Brui and
the Soviet authorities. J. Rubenstein. il
por Art N 70:40-1+ D '71
Social radicalism and the arts, by D. D.
Egbert. Review
Nation 211:660-1 D 21 '70. G. Woodcock
COMMUNISM and democracy
Capitalism vs. communism. Chr Today 15:
34-5 F 12 '71
New left: why violence? J. Ciardi. Sat R
54:12+ Ja 23 '71
Pulling away, W. F. Buckley, jr. Nat R
23:163 F 9 '71
Right to leave: difference between Com-
munist regimes and ours. J. Burnham.
Nat R 23:306 Mr 23 '71
COMMUNISM and religion
Can eastern Christians survive under Marx
or Islam? C. S. Calian. il Cath World
212:249-52+ F '71
Dead-end dialogue; Marxists and Christians.
S. M. Smith. Nat R 23:367-8 Ap 6 '71
Future of religion in a Marxist society; adaptation of address. D. M. Borchert. Chr Cent
88:1129-33 S 29 '71
God and man in the dialogue with Marxism.
A. J. Conyers. Chr Today 15:6-8 Jl 2 '71
Marxism and radical religion, by J. C. Raines
and T. Dean. Review
Chr Cent 88:783-4 Je 23 '71. J. M. Swom-
ley, jr
Marxists on the spot; International sympo-
sium on religion and atheism in Commu-
nist societies. B. Hruby. Chr Today 15:
40 My 7 '71
Patriarch and prophets, by M. Bourdeaux
and The urgency of Marxist Christian dia-
logue, by H. Aptheker. Review
Chr Today 15:30 My 21 '71. B. Hruby
Same cells, the same barracks. E. Castro.
Chr Cent 88:1022-4 S 1 '71
Which way the World council of churches.
C. W. Hall. Read Digest 99:177-8+ N '71
See also
Catholic church and communism
COMMUNISM and the Catholic church. See
Catholic church and communism
COMMUNIST countries
See also
China (People's Republic)
Europe, Eastern
Investments, Foreign (in Communist coun-
tries)

Commerce
Nobody here but us Marxists? il Forbes 108:
48+ Jl 15 '71
Satisfying a desire for western gifts. Bsns W
p25-6 D 25 '71
See also
Europe, Eastern—Commerce

COMMUNIST countries—*Continued*

Religious institutions and affairs

Future of religion in a Marxist society; adaptation of address. D. M. Borchert. Chr Cent 88:1129-33 S 29 '71
See also
Europe, Eastern—Religious institutions and affairs

COMMUNIST parties
Crimean summit. por Time 98:25-6 Ag 16 '71

Purges
See also
Communist party (China [People's Republic])—Purges

COMMUNIST party (Bolivia)
Cuba's second Vietnam: Bolivia. M. D. Gensler. Yale R 60:342-65 Mr '71

COMMUNIST party (China [People's Republic])
After ping-pong what next with Peking? O. E. Clubb. Sat R 54:19-22 My 29 '71
Aftermath of the cultural revolution. E. Snow. New Repub 164:18-21 Ap 10 '71
China: the struggle for power. A. S. Whiting. New Repub 165:19-21 D 4 '71
Power struggle in Peking. il Newsweek 78: 26-7 N 8 '71
Struggle in China. America 125:277 O 16 '71
Therefore it will crash; how the anti-Mao plotters met their death. S. Alsop. Newsweek 78:104 D 20 '71

Purges
China: the fall of Mao's heir. il por Time 98: 35-6 N 22 '71

COMMUNIST party (Czechoslovakia)
Czechoslovakia three springs later. V. E. Mares. bibliog f Cur Hist 60:282-9+ My '71
How to overrun Czechoslovakia. A. Martin. il Nat R 23:1408-11+ D 17 '71

COMMUNIST party (France)
Communist funfest. il Time 98:48 S 27 '71

COMMUNIST party (India)
What future for India's Naxalities? E. Haubold. Cur 129:57-61 My '71

COMMUNIST party (Israel)
Communist parties of Israel. W. A. Brannigan. Nation 213:398-401 O 25 '71

COMMUNIST party (Italy)
Opportunity a *sinistra*. P. Freiberg. Commonweal 95:76-7 O 22 '71

COMMUNIST party (Poland)
Beyond the Gomulka era. A. Bromke. For Affairs 49:485-8 Ap '71
Needed: all hands, all brains; sixth party congress. il Time 98:41-2 D 20 '71
New course in Communist-ruled Poland? R. F. Staar. bibliog f il Cur Hist 60:269-75 My '71

COMMUNIST party (Russia)
Brezhnev no. 1; 24th congress. il por Sr Schol 98:16 My 3 '71
Brezhnev's big show; 24th congress. Newsweek 77:56 Ap 19 '71
Report to the Presidium; excerpt from year-end report by the Secretariat of the Politburo; ed. by J. Burnham. Nat R 23:75 Ja 26 '71
Six hours with Leonid Brezhnev; 24th congress. il por Newsweek 77:47-8 Ap 12 '71
Soviet Union: something for everyone; 24th party congress. il por Time 97:22-3 Ap 12 '71
Twenty-fourth Soviet party congress. A. Ulam. Cur Hist 61:222-6+ O '71
Uncle Leonid; Communist party congress. Nat R 23:412-13 Ap 20 '71
Week on the town; 24th congress. il Newsweek 77:34 Ap 5 '71
Whoa, comrade Brezhnev. il por Time 98:33 D 6 '71
See also
Russia—Politics and government

Political bureau
And then there was one; 24th Soviet party congress announcing new order of precedence in the Politburo. il Time 97:26+ Ap 19 '71
Return of Stalin's mustache on a higher level. R. Lowenthal. il N Y Times Mag p26-7+ Mr 28 '71
Soviet Union: the risks of reform; meeting of 24th congress of the Soviet Communist party. il Time 97:27-30+ Mr 29 '71

COMMUNIST party (Sudan)
Revenge in the Sudan; Communists, army officers executed. il por Time 98:26-7 Ag 9 '71

COMMUNIST party (United States)
Marx's disenchanted salesman; interview, ed. by H. Stein. E. R. Bowder. por Am Heritage 23:58-61+ D '71

Red decade, by E. Lyons. Review
Nat R 23:435-6 Ap 20 '71. R. De Toledano

Caricatures and cartoons
Whatever became of the Communist party, U.S.A? cartoons. Cath World 213:148 Je '71

COMMUNIST party (Vietnam)
See also
Viet Cong

COMMUNIST party congress. See Communist party (Russia)

COMMUNIST strategy
Deceitful peace, by G. Niemeyer. Review
Nat R 23:374-5 Ap 6 '71. G. F. Will
Tactics of terror: where reds will strike next; interview, ed. by J. Fromm. B. Crozier. il por U S News 70:75-8 Mr 1 '71
That Chinese threat; adaptation of address. A. S. Whiting. New Repub 164:18-20 Ap 3 '71
Who says Thailand's next? W. A. O'Neil. New Repub 164:23-7 Ja 2 '71
Winston Churchill on revolution; excerpt from Great contemporaries. W. L. S. Churchill. Read Digest 98:195-6 F '71

COMMUNISTIC settlements. See Collective settlements

COMMUNITARIAN movement. See Collective settlements

COMMUNITY action agencies. See United States—Economic opportunity, Office of

COMMUNITY and business. See Business—Social aspects

COMMUNITY and the school. See School and the community

COMMUNITY antenna television system. See CATV system

COMMUNITY centers
See also
Senior centers
also subhead Community centers under names of cities, e.g. New York (city)—Community centers

COMMUNITY colleges. See Junior colleges

COMMUNITY control of schools. See School management and organization

COMMUNITY cooperation. See Intercommunity cooperation

COMMUNITY development

United States
Urban field service; Harvard graduate school of design. C. W. Hartman. Arch Forum 135:50-3 S '71

COMMUNITY development corporation
Spring swing to playgrounds; imaginative playground equipment in Atlanta. J. C. Delius. il Parks & Rec 6:48-9+ O '71

COMMUNITY fallout shelters. See Atomic bomb shelters

COMMUNITY health centers. See Health facilities

COMMUNITY hospital, Rural. See Hospitals, Rural

COMMUNITY life
See also
Bees (cooperative gatherings)
Church and social problems
Social education

COMMUNITY mental health centers. See Mental health centers

COMMUNITY mental health service. See Mental health service

COMMUNITY news service
Reporting from the ghettos. M. L. Stein. Sat R 54:95-6 N 13 '71

COMMUNITY of true inspiration. See Amana society

COMMUNITY of work. See Collective settlements

COMMUNITY outreach. See Volunteer service

COMMUNITY planning. See City planning

COMMUNITY-police relations. See Police—Public relations

COMMUNITY psychiatry. See Social psychiatry

COMMUNITY service
Community action. See occasional issues of Sunset
Executives as community volunteers. D. H. Fenn, jr. il Harvard Bsns R 49:4-6+ Mr '71
Final report from SERVE project includes broad recommendations. il Aging 205:14-15 N '71
Most precious gift a father can give to his son; ed. by S. O'Quin. S. I. Hayakawa. il por Todays Health 49:21-3 Je '71
Oregon Title III self-help program is community activity. il Aging 205:18 N '71
Seniors. Girl scouts cooperate for community service in N.Y. town: Friendship club of senior citizens. Clarence, Erie County. il Aging 203:6 S '71

COMMUNITY service—*Continued*
Visually handicapped now work as SERVE
volunteers. il Aging 203:10-11 S '71
See also
Volunteer service

Northern Ireland
Northern Ireland's Corrymeela community.
R. Davey. Chr Cent 88:1240-1 O 20 '71

COMMUTER airlines. See Local service airlines

COMMUTER income tax. See Income tax, Municipal

COMMUTERS
Agony of the commuter. il Newsweek 77:
44-7+ Ja 18 '71
Learning on wheels; Adelphi university's
graduate course in Principles of marketing
given on a Long Island railroad train. il
Time 98:66-7 N 1 '71
Pedal power; urban bike commuting. R.
Hanneman. il Parks & Rec 6:28-33 Ja '71
See also
Railroads—Commuter service

COMPACT cars. See Automobiles, Compact

COMPACTORS. See Refuse and refuse disposal
—Apparatus

COMPAGNIE Lambert. See Holding companies—Belgium

COMPANION crops
Kohlrabi and beets can grow in the same
row. Org Gard & Farm 18:62-3 Ag '71

COMPANIONATE marriage. See Marriage,
Companionate

The COMPANY. See Los Angeles—Theater

COMPANY; musical comedy. See Musical
comedies, revues, etc.—Criticisms, plots,
etc.

COMPANY presidents (in business) See Executives

COMPANY publications. See Employees magazines, handbooks. etc.

COMPANY secretaries. See Corporation secretaries

COMPANY towns
Corporation towns. J. Ridgeway. il Ramp
Mag 10:23+ Ja '72
End of a company town; Saltville, Va; with
editorial comment. J. Newcombe. il Life
70:3, 36-45 Mr 26 '71
See also
Ajo, Ariz.

COMPARATIVE education. See Education,
Comparative

COMPARATIVE religion. See Religions

COMPARATO, Frank
Modern technology and modern publishing;
excerpts from Books for the millions. Pub
W 200:34+ N 1 '71

COMPARISON shopping. See Shopping and
shoppers

COMPARTMENTS, Isolation. See Isolation
chambers

COMPASS
Adjust your compass. J. B. Kane. il Motor B
& S 127:80+ Je '71
Lost at sea, and what to do about it. B. Mc-
Keown. il Mech Illus 67:72+ Jl '71
Swing your compass. D. B. Richards. il
Flying 88:57-8 F '71
See also
Orienteering (sport)

COMPATIBILITY (marriage) See Marriage

COMPENSATION (law)
See also
Insurance, Workmens compensation

COMPENSATION, Unemployment. See Insurance, Unemployment

COMPENSATION for victims of crime. See
Reparation

COMPETITION
Farmers and the competitive spirit. il Farm
J 95:54 O '71
He wants to lengthen antitrust's reach; sup-
ply space concept. por Bsns W p38+ My
22 '71

COMPETITION (biology) See Struggle for existence

COMPETITION (psychology)
Advice from a pediatrician. J. Lebow. il
Look 35:64 Je 1 '71

COMPETITION, International
Ability to compete, costs & benefits; address,
November 4, 1971. R. F. Barker. Vital
Speeches 38:157-60 D 15 '71
Fresh strategy to win world markets. il Bsns
W p 19-20 My 22 '71
High stakes of international poker. il Time
98:22-3 S 20 '71
Lifelines for import victims. il Nations Bsns
59:28+ Je '71
Road to economic survival; address, Novem-
ber 15, 1971. R. C. Firestone. Vital Speeches
38:155-7 D 15 '71

World trade: a clash of wills. il Time 98:21-2
S 20 '71
See also
Free trade and protection

COMPETITION, Unfair
See also
Dumping (commercial policy)

COMPETITIONS
It's fun for all at pee-wee tractor pulls. N.
Reeder. il Farm J 95:18 S '71
Just one more for the road, s'il vous plait;
second annual Rallye des champions.
France. R. F. Jones. il Sports Illus 35:
26-8+ O 25 '71
Should we enter that contest? G. R. Weldy.
Ed Digest 37:39-41 D '71
They wanted wings; birdmen in flying con-
test. il Time 98:25 Ag 23 '71
Yeeow! third annual National (actually in-
ternational) hollerin' contest, Spivey's Corn-
er, N.C.   H. Peterson. il Sports Illus 35:44-5
Jl 12 '71
See also
Beauty contests
Tournaments
also subhead Competitions under vari-
ous subjects, e.g. Photography—Competi-
tions

COMPLAINTS
Buyer vs. seller in small claims court. il Consumer Rep 36:624-31 O '71
They promise action on consumer complaints.
il Changing T 26:16-18 Ja '72
When you and your doctor disagree; medical
grievance committees. Bet Hom & Gard
49:128 Ap '71

COMPLEMENTS (immunity)
C1 inhibitor; evidence for decreased hepatic
synthesis in hereditary angioneurotic edema. A. M. Johnson and others. bibliog il
Science 173:553-4 Ag 6 '71

COMPLEX numbers. See Numbers, Complex

COMPLEXES (psychology)
Ulysses complex. L. P. R. Santiago. bibliog il Am Imago 28:158-86 Sum '71

COMPLEXION. See Beauty, Personal

COMPOSERS
Beyond the avant garde. E. Siegmeister. il
Hi Fi 21:MA13-14+ D '71
Lives of the great composers, by H. C.
Schonberg. Review
Sat R 54:29-30 F 6 '71. M. Goldin
Musical poets of the '70s. B. Blackman. il
Seventeen 30:36 Ja '71
Songwriter & the record business today. A.
Shaw. il Writers Digest 51:24-7+ N '71
See also
Women as musicians

COMPOSERS, American
See also
Bacharach, B.
Bowles, P.
Coe, K.
Crumb, G.
Davidovsky, M.
Gershwin, G.
Guiraud, E.
Hoiby, L.
Ives, C. E.
Kirchner, L.
Menotti, G. C.
Perle, G.
Rorem, N.
Sousa, J. P.
Thomson, V.

COMPOSERS, Austrian
See also
Berg, A.
Haydn, F. J.
Mahler, G.
Mozart, J. C. W. A.
Schönberg, A.
Schubert, F. P.
Webern, A. von

COMPOSERS, Brazilian
See also
Villa-Lobos, H.

COMPOSERS, British
See also
Walton, W. T.

COMPOSERS, Czech
See also
Dvořák, A.
Janáček, L.
Smetana, B.

COMPOSERS, English
See also
Britten, B.
Holst, G.
Tallis, T

COMPOSERS, Finnish
See also
Sibelius, J. J. C.

COMPOSERS, Flemish
See also
Deprès, J.

COMPOSERS, French
See also
Alkan, C. H. V.
Boulez, P.
Charpentier, G.
Gounod, C. F.
L'Héritier, J.
Lully, J. B.
Massenet, J.
Messiaen, O.
Philidor, F. A. D.
Poulenc, F.
Satie, E.

COMPOSERS, German
See also
Bach, J. S.
Beethoven, L. van
Brahms, J.
Händel, G. F.
Hasse, J. A.
Henze, H. W.
Mayr, S.
Mendelssohn, F.
Meyerbeer, G.
Offenbach, J.
Orff, C.
Praetorius, M.
Wagner, R.

COMPOSERS, Hungarian
See also
Kodály, Z.
Liszt, F.

COMPOSERS, Italian
See also
Agazzari, A.
Berio, L.
Cazzati, M.
Clementi, M.
Corelli, A.
Frescobaldi, G.
Maderna, B.
Mercadante, S.
Rossini, G.
Vivaldi, A.

COMPOSERS, Polish
See also
Chopin, F. F.
Lutolawski, W.
Penderecki, K.

COMPOSERS, Russian
Soviet composers and the development of Soviet music, by S. D. Krebs. Review Am Rec G il 37:632-4 My '71. D. W. Moore
See also
Shostakovich, D. D.
Stravinsky, I. F.
Tchaikovsky, P. I.

COMPOSERS theater festival. See Music festivals—New York (state)

COMPOSITE materials
Broadcloth production process could reduce composite costs. Aviation W 94:47 Ap 26 '71
USAF outlines composite plans. Aviation W 94:44 My 3 '71

COMPOSITE photography. See Photomontage

COMPOSITION (music)
Alec Wilder; interview. A. Wilder. New Yorker 47:22-4 S 4 '71
Beethoven's new way and the Eroica. P. G. Downs. bibliog il Mus Q 56:585-604 O '70
Diary of two deadlines; G. C. Menotti's Most important man and Maria Golovin. F. Rizzo. Opera N 35:26-8 Mr 13 '71
Electronic creativity in the elementary classroom. A. D. Modugno. il Todays Ed 60:62-4 Mr '71
Interview of the week, ed. by R. Hemming. K. Bohm. Sr Schol 98:22 F 8 '71
Prodigies and music. H. C. Schonberg. Harper 242:113-14 My '71
See also
Musical forgeries and mystifications
Musical form

COMPOSITION (photography)
Composition, the mind's eye in the camera's shutter. F. Rohr. il Travel 136:74-6 S '71
Feininger. A. Feininger. Mod Phot 35:64+ D '71
Feininger; static and dynamic composition. A. Feininger. il Mod Phot 36:60+ Ja '72

COMPOSITION, English. See English language—Composition

COMPOST
Art and science of composting. A. S. Taormina. il Cons 26:48-9+ O '71
Compost is what makes the Cooper garden go. il Sunset 146:236+ My '71
Composting for the new generation. G. Furlow. il Org Gard & Farm 18:58-60 Ap '71
Confessions of a reluctant composter. L. M. Cottin. Org Gard & Farm 18:96-7 O '71
From leaves to compost in 14 days. il Home Gard 58:36-7+ O '71

Heaped bonuses. C. Sauerland. Org Gard & Farm 18:101 O '71
How to compost leaves; Maplewood, N.J. R. Walter. il por Am City 86:115-17 Je '71
Making your own compost. il Sunset 146:224-5 Mr '71
Nationwide composting campaign: symposium. il Org Gard & Farm 18:48-53 Mr '71
No garbage problem when you compost. D. Goldman. Org Gard & Farm 18:34 O '71
Our composting program. W. Bowers and L. Bowers. il por Org Gard & Farm 18:54-7 Ja '71
Our rotating compost. M. Wills. Org Gard & Farm 18:81 My '71
This town accepts the composting challenge; Brookhaven, Long Island. M. Franz. il Org Gard & Farm 18:36-40 Jl '71
Turn your garbage can into a composter. H. Elmore. Org Gard & Farm 18:126 D '71
See also
Humus
Refuse as fertilizer

Preservation and storage
Compost piles: large, middle-sized and small. O. R. Griffin. il Org Gard & Farm 18:47-9 Je '71
Three kinds of compost bin. Org Gard & Farm 18:98-100 O '71

COMPOST bins. See Compost—Preservation and storage

COMPOST grinders and grinding
Chomping machine chews up yard waste. E. F. Lindsley. il Pop Sci 198:22 F '71
If you have prunings that need chomping up. il Sunset 146:50-3 Ja '71
Shredder-grinder: a little machine that makes quick compost of garden waste. J. M. Liston. il Pop Mech 136:73-5 S '71

COMPOST piles. See Compost—Preservation and storage

COMPOST shredders. See Compost grinders and grinding

COMPREHENSION
To describe it all, growl softly. W. J. Reynolds. Engl J 60:267-9 F '71

COMPREHENSIVE designers, inc.
Comprehensive designers, inc. il Nations Bsns 59:50-2 Jl '71

COMPRESSED air
See also
Pneumatic tools

COMPRESSED speech
How we can listen faster with compressed speech. C. M. Rossiter, jr. il Sci Digest 70:66-8 D '71

COMPRESSORS, Audio. See Sound—Apparatus

COMPTON, Gail W.
Mad hatter disease: mercury poisoning. il Sci Digest 69:61-6 Mr '71
—See Zeiller, W. jt. auth.

COMPTON-BURNETT, Dame Ivy
Household tyrants. M. Duffy. il por Time 98:73 Ag 16 '71 *

COMPULSORY arbitration. See Arbitration, Industrial

COMPULSORY education
Amish win important Court decision; question of compulsory school attendance. Chr Cent 88:95 Ja 27 '71
Who teaches? Catholic and Amish parents vs. schools over compulsory attendance. Sr Schol 98:10-11 Mr 29 '71

COMPULSORY labor. See Labor, Compulsory

COMPULSORY military service. See Military service, Compulsory

COMPULSORY non-military service. See Service, Compulsory non-military

COMPUTER-assisted instruction. See Computers—Educational use

COMPUTER-based service companies
See also
University computing company

COMPUTER billing. See Billing

COMPUTER equipment industry
IBM's price war hurts the independents. Bsns W p53-4+ D 18 '71

COMPUTER graphics
Computer graphics as an aid to learning. K. R. Hammond. bibliog il Science 172:903-8 My 28 '71
Creative electronics. A. DeMirjian, jr. il Pub W 201:46-7 Ja 3 '72
Management by computer graphics. K. Shostack and C. Eddy. il Harvard Bsns R 49:52-63 N '71

COMPUTER industry
Big-time beckons minicomputers. il Bsns W p32+ Ja 30 '71
Challenging the jolly gray giant: Honeywell competes with IBM. il Time 99:62-3 Ja 3 '72

COMPUTER industry—*Continued*
Growth industry grows up. il Time 97:72+
Mr 1 '71
Prospects are good. il Bsns W p 129+ Je 5
'71
  See also
Control data corporation
Data general corporation
Data trends, inc.
Digital equipment corporation
General automation, inc.
Honeywell, inc.
International business machines corporation
RCA corporation
Scan-Data corporation
Sperry Rand corporation—Univac division

Consolidations and mergers
Dirty dozen outfit cleans up in Itel deal.
por Bsns W p21 Ja 23 '71

Finance
Information processing; with yardsticks of
management performance. il Forbes 109:
144+ Ja 1 '72

Europe, Western
Late tape. R. Brady. il Duns 98:9 Ag '71

Germany (Federal Republic)
German effort to challenge IBM; Telefunken
computer GMBH. Bsns W p37 D 11 '71

Great Britain
  See also
International computers, ltd.

Japan
Data general's coup in minicomputers. il
Bsns W p54 Je 19 '71

COMPUTER languages
Hemisphere-wide standardization of computer
language sought. il Américas 23:46 S '71

COMPUTER printers. See Computers—Print-
out equipment

COMPUTER process control. See Computers—
Industrial use

COMPUTER program languages. See Computer
languages

COMPUTER programming
Programming new frontiers. il Bsns W p 118-
19+ Je 5 '71
  See also
Computing and software, inc.

COMPUTER schools. See Trade schools

COMPUTER systems management
Managing the system. il Bsns W p62-3+ Je
5 '71

COMPUTER tapes. See Data tapes

COMPUTER television, inc.
Films check in to motel rooms. il Bsns W
p79 O 9 '71
Motel Bijou. il Newsweek 78:43 Ag 9 '71

COMPUTER translating. See Machine translating

COMPUTERS
Computer in perspective. W. McQuade. il
Life 70:12 Ap 30 '71
Eames and the mythic monster; exhibition
at IBM display center. K. Kuh. il Sat R
54:34+ My 29 '71
It's here, the computer revolution. P. T.
White. Read Digest 98:133-7 My '71
  See also
Calculating machines, Electronic
Computer languages
Control data corporation
Data processing service centers
Electronic data processing
Memory devices (computers)

Aeronautic use
ATC computer to test collision avoidance.
K. J. Stein. il Aviation W 95:34-5 D 13 '71
Horizontal situation indicator in F-15 uses
digital technology. il Aviation W 96:56-7
Ja 10 '72
New airborne computer system. il Pop Electr
35:67-8 Ag '71
News from the world of space exploration;
electronic control system for future aircraft.
il Space World H-7-91:47 Jl '71
Raytheon ATC computer contract terms
changed. Aviation W 94:28 Mr 22 '71
  See also
Airlines—Communication systems

Agricultural use
Computer gives farmers advice on herbicides. il Suc Farm 69:B6 S '71
Fast way to sharpen management; swine
farms. J. Russell. il Farm J 95:H6-7+ Ap
'71

SPAM: a computer views a cornfield. il Sci N
100:292-3 O 30 '71
Sun's work in a cornfield; SPAM model. E.
Lemon and others. bibliog il Science 174:
371-8 O 22 '71
You can hire these accounting systems. R.
Krumme. Suc Farm 69:32-3 Ag '71

Air traffic control use
  See Computers—Aeronautic use

Airline use
Airlines stress cost-effective computers. K. J.
Stein. il Aviation W 94:140+ Mr 8 '71
New test equipment saves time. B. M. El-
son. il Aviation W 94:41-3 Ap 19 '71
  See also
Airlines—Communication systems

Architectural use
Artificial intelligent architecture: computers
in design. T. P. Moran. bibliog f il Arch
Rec 149:129-34 Mr '71
Computerized architecture. il Sci Digest 69:
22-3 F '71
Computers: tools for construction management; excerpt from Professional construction management and project administration. W. B. Foxhall. il Arch Rec 150:53-4
D '71

Art use
Artist and the computer. D. Davis. il por
Newsweek 78:78-81 S 13 '71
Contemporary art by computer. il Design 73:
18-19 Wint '71

Astronomical use
Computer-run radio telescope spectrograph;
Onsala space observatory. A. Winnberg. il
Sky & Tel 42:274-6 N '71

Automotive use
I rode a driverless car! S. Bacon. il Mech
Illus 67:166-70 N '71

Banking use
Cashless society isn't here. il Bsns W p 104-6
Je 5 '71

Biological use
Computer derivation of some dolphin echolocation signals. R. A. Altes. bibliog il Science 173:912-14 S 3 '71
Extremely rapid visual search: the maximum
rate of scanning letters for the presence
of a numeral. G. Sperling and others. bibliog il Science 174:307-11 O 15 '71
Mimicking the placenta with computer models. il Sci N 100:205 S 25 '71
They've found a wish switch in your brain.
D. Lampe. por Pop Sci 198:30+ Ja '71

Business use
Business takes a second look at computers.
il Bsns W p59-63+ Je 5 '71
Electronic accountant Wall Street likes. il
Bsns W p52+ Mr 20 '71
Low-cost way to keep books by computer. il
Bsns W p 106+ O 23 '71
Management by computer graphics. K. Sho-
stack and C. Eddy. il Harvard Bsns R 49:
52-63 N '71
Southern's system for using the computer. V.
Louviere. Nations Bsns 59:15 Jl '71
  See also
Billing
Information systems, Management

Cataloging use
  See Libraries—Automation

Chemical use
Computers and chemistry. D. D. Edman and
others. bibliog il pors Chem 45:6-9 Ja '72

Circuits
Fastest computer. D. L. Slotnick. il Sci Am
224:76-87 F '71
R-E's logic laboratory; parts and suppliers.
Radio-Electr 42:87 F '71

Cooperative use
  See Computers—Time sharing systems

Digital computers
Battle of the giant brains; or, Electronics
conquers all. F. Y. Dill. bibliog il Pop
Electr 34:39-43+ Ap '71
Computers and chemistry. D. D. Edman and
others. bibliog il pors Chem 45:6-9 '72
Little known creators of the computer;
ENIAC system. J. Costello. il pors Nations
Bsns 59:56-62 D '71

COMPUTERS—*Continued*

Economic use

Economists play the numbers game; computerized models. il Bsns W p 125+ Je 5 '71

Educational use

Beware of false gods; utilizing technology in guidance. E. P. Dworkin. Ed Digest 36: 27–9 Ja '71

Computer graphics as an aid to learning. K. R. Hammond. bibliog il Science 172: 903–8 My 28 '71

Computers in the classroom. S. Umans. il Parents Mag 46:62–3+ Mr '71

DOVACK's machines help children read. M. Wills. il por Am Ed 7:3–8 Je '71

Educational usages of the computer. T. R. Nee. Clear House 46:63–4 S '71

Essay grading by computer: a laboratory phenomenon? H. B. Slotnick and J. V. Knapp. bibliog f Engl J 60:75–80+ Ja '71

IBM computer for Navajo language textbooks. il Sch & Soc 99:468–9 D '71

Spreading the basic knowledge. il Bsns W p94–8 Je 5 '71

Use of computers for instruction. Ed Digest 36:49 My '71

Employment use

Computers jobhunt for undergrads. il Bsns W p 123 F 27 '71

Employment application tests; excerpt from The assault on privacy, by A. R. Miller. Sat R 54:30 Ap 17 '71

Engineering use

Portable computer tests engines in the field. il Am City 86:73 S '71

Errors

If a computer fouls up your charge account. Read Digest 98:139–42 Ja '71

Unidentifed stationary objects. C. G. Tierney. Sat R 54:30 D 18 '71

Gambling use

Can a computer beat the horses. J. Morgan. il Look 35:33 Je 1 '71

Government use

For social security, it works like a dream. il Bsns W p 110+ Je 5 '71

Has big brother got your number? il Sr Schol 98:12–16 Mr 29 '71

Washington cracks down on computer costs. il Bsns W p73–4 O 23 '71

History

Battle of the giant brains; or, Electronics conquers all. F. Y. Dill. bibliog il Pop Electr 34:39–43+ Ap '71

Little known creators of the computer; ENIAC system. J. Costello. il pors Nations Bsns 59:56–62 D '71

Home economics use

Prugh's computer: machine owned by Thomas Prugh, Defense department engineer. New Yorker 46:30–1 Ja 16 '71

Hospital use

Models for financially healthy hospitals. G. C. Forsyth and D. G. Thomas. il Harvard Bsns R 49:106–17 Jl '71

Indexing use

ICC announces automatic indexing system. Pub W 199:61 F 1 '71

Industrial use

Automating the factory. il Bsns W p82–4+ Je 5 '71

Easier way to pick parts in a warehouse. il Bsns W p43 Jl 31 '71

Rise of the blue-collar computer. A. R. Dooley and T. M. Stout. Harvard Bsns R 49:85–95 Jl '71

Input-output equipment

Computers that talk back to you. il Bsns W p60+ S 25 '71

See also
Cash registers, Electronic

Investment use

Higher meaning of NASDAQ; market for over-the-counter stocks. il Fortune 83:141–2+ Ap '71

Midwest solution for back-office paper; Signet 80. Bsns W p36–7 Je 19 '71

NASDAQ we love you. R. Stovall. il por Forbes 107:84–5 Ap 15 '71

New way to trade. C. Morgello. il Newsweek 77:93 Je 7 '71

Present and future shock. Time 97:87 F 22 '71

Quotes that irk exchanges; NASDAQ systems. Bsns W p95 Ap 10 '71

Radical changes for Wall Street. Bsns W p 108 Je 5 '71

Tussle over automatic OTC trading. il Bsns W p72+ Ja 30 '71

Library use

See Libraries—Automation

Literary use

Creativity, poetic language, and the computer. M. Borroff. Yale R 60:481–513 Je '71

Lesson of IBM 7094-7040 DCS. L. Conger. Writer 84:9–10 O '71

Programmed poetry. Time 97:77 F 22 '71

Marketing use

Picking customers out of the mob. il Bsns W p71-2 Je 5 '71

Mathematical use

Longest root; square root of 2 to more than one million places. il por Time 98:59+ O 25 '71

Mechanical engineering use

See Computers—Engineering use

Medical use

Automated radiological diagnosis system. il Pop Electr 1:97 Ja '72

Computer as doctor. Newsweek 78:52 D 27 '71

Computer-based interviewing system dealing with nonverbal behavior as well as keyboard responses. W. Slack. bibliog il Science 171: 84–7 Ja 8 '71

Doctor-machines; automated multiphasic health testing. E. McCleary. il McCalls 98:39 My '71

Image analysis: application to automated medical diagnosis. A. L. Hammond. il Science 174:1011–12 D 3 '71

NASA computer development may aid care of heart patients. Aviation W 94:57 My 3 '71

News from the world of space exploration; cardiac computer. Space World H-8-92:47-8 Ag '71

News from the world of space exploration; viewing the heart in action. Space World H-7-91:48 Jl '71

System measures your drug reaction. il Sci Digest 70:14-15 Jl '71

Tiny bedside monitor watches all patients. A. J. Snider. Sci Digest 70:58 D '71

Your next doctor may be a computer. M. W. Martin. il Sci Digest 69:39-43 Ap '71

Military use

Soviets closing gap in avionics, computer science military development. C. Brownlow and B. Miller. il Aviation W 95:40-3+ O 25 '71

Toward computerized warfare. C. Foley. Cur 132:20-3 S '71

You can't run wars with a computer. il Bsns W p 122 Je 5 '71

Miniaturization

Bell labs swings to minis. il Bsns W p 118-19 Je 5 '71

Data general's coup in minicomputers. Bsns W p54 Je 19 '71

Thinking small. il Newsweek 78:71+ Jl 12 '71

Which computer, the minicomputer? R. Katz. il Electr World 86:23-5+ O '71

Municipal use

Code inspectors and computers work well together; Chicago. J. E. Fitzgerald. il Am City 86:42 Ap '71

Computer assures pinpoint water control at Chicago's central filtration plant. J. W. Jardine. il Am City 86:82+ S '71

Computer improves recycling process. Am City 86:36 S '71

Computerized total-cost bidding; Palo Alto, Calif. J. W. Wear. il Am City 86:60-1 F '71

Electronic data processing in urban government; symposium. il Am City 86:69-75+ My '71

Local governments share a computer; Owensboro, Ky. M. N. Rhoads. il Am City 86:52 F '71

See also
Computers—Traffic control use

COMPUTERS—*Continued*

Musical use

Computer organ has virtually unlimited voicing. il Pop Electr 35:66-7 Ag '71

Optical equipment

See also
Optical scanners

Police use

Computerized police communications; Indianapolis, Ind. il Am City 86:32 My '71
Computerized police systems in the U.S.? L. Webb. Cur 132:14-20 S '71
Electronic help for lost cars; National automobile theft bureau. P. M. Eckstein. Mech Illus 67:16 Jl '71

Political use

Computerizing Soviet society. V. Zorza. Cur 132:23-30 S '71
New technology. Time 99:12-13 Ja 10 '72

Prices

Washington cracks down on computer costs. il Bsns W p73-4 O 23 '71

Print-out equipment

Cheaper printer for minicomputers. Bsns W p64+ O 16 '71

Publishing use

Book making trends for the 21st century; excerpts from address, 1971. W. C. Lamparter. il Pub W 200:38+ N 1 '71
How publishers can benefit from the new minicomputers. J. D. Seick. il Pub W 200: 24-6 Ag 9 '71
Modern technology and modern publishing; excerpts from Books for the millions. F. Comparato. Pub W 200:34+ N 1 '71

Reliability

Self-heal capability could aid airborne computer reliability. Aviation W 94:64 Je 14 '71

Social science use

Club of Rome; computerizing the world. il Bsns W p42 Ap 10 '71

Social use

Choose the right roommate; by computer. W. Kempthorne. Seventeen 29:14+ S '70
Computer with a heart; adoption. N. Morgan. il McCalls 98:46 Je '71

Space flight use

Man in space or chip in space? R. Jastrow. il N Y Times Mag p 14-15+ Ja 31 '71

Speed

Fastest computer. D. L. Slotnick. il Sci Am 224:76-87 F '71

Sports use

Computerized scoring and timing system for auto racing; Ontario motor speedway system. P. Harms. il Electr World 86:22-3 N '71
See also
Computers—Gambling use

Statistical use

AR 24; what the real job is. il Forbes 108:9 N 1 '71

Stock exchange use

See Computers—Investment use

Time sales

Welcome buck from surplus time. Bsns W p90+ Je 5 '71

Time sharing systems

Local governments share a computer; Owensboro, Ky. M. N. Rhoads. il Am City 86:52 F '71
Shopping for a time-sharing service. H. Elkholy; reply. R. E May. Phys Today 24-13+ Ja '71
Which computer: time-sharing. N. L. Beyer. il Electr World 86:46-8+ N '71

Trade union use

Bargaining by electronics. il Bsns W p78+ Je 5 '71

Traffic control use

Computerized signal settings speed traffic flow; Kansas City, Mo. Am City 86:126 Ap '71
Computerized traffic control; Albany, N.Y. F. J. Fuller and others. il Am City 86:109-11 O '71
Electronic traffic cops take on bigger jobs. il Bsns W p51-2 Jl 10 '71

Low-cost computer halves driving time; Indianapolis. C. A. Venable. il Am City 86: 105-6 Mr '71
Now computers guide you through traffic snarls. S. Solomon. il Pop Sci 198:51-3+ Ja '71
VASCAR, the computer that catches speeders. Changing T 25:33 O '71

COMPUTING and software, inc.
Wizard of software. T. J. Murray. Duns 98: 60-1 O '71

COMSAT. See Communications satellite corporation

COMSTOCK, Anthony
Comstock's nemesis. D. Brudnoy. Nat R 23: 1064+ S 24 '71 *

COMSTOCK, G. M. and others
Cosmic-ray tracks in plastics: the Apollo helmet dosimetry experiment. bibliog il Science 172:154-7 Ap 9 '71

CON, Nguyen-truong-. See Nguyen-truong-Con

CONANT, Margaret M.
How to's for leaders and members (cont) PTA Mag 65:36 F; 36 Mr 34 My; 33 Je '71
Play-in, teach-in for parents. il PTA Mag 65:14-17 bibliog(p34) Mr '71

CONAWAY, James
André Watts on André Watts: I'm doing all right, I'm never good enough, but I'm not standing still. il pors N Y Times Mag p 14-15+ S 19 '71
Memphis. Atlan 228:24+ N '71
Milos Forman's America is like Kafka's, basically comic. il pors N Y Times Mag p8-12 Jl 11 '71

CONCANAVALINS
Embryonic and neoplastic cell surfaces: availability of receptors for concanavalin A and wheat germ agglutinin. A. A. Moscona. bibliog il Science 171:905-7 Mr 5 '71; Reply with rejoinder. A. Sivak. 173:264-5 Jl 16 '71

CONCENTRATION. See Attention

CONCENTRATION camps
Story behind the book: The book of Alfred Kantor; interview. ed. by D. G. Maryles. A. Kantor. il Pub W 200:28-9 O 25 '71

Northern Ireland

Prisoner's view of a British internment camp. il Life 71:36-7 N 12 '71

Russia

See also
Prison camps—Russia

United States

Co-opting the oppressors: the case of the Japanese-Americans. R. O. Haak. il Trans-Action 7:23-31 O '70
Detention camps; Title II of the McCarran act. Nation 212:421-2 Ap 5 '71

CONCEPTUAL art. See Art, Modern

CONCERT; ballet. See Ballets—Criticisms

CONCERT audiences. See Audiences

CONCERT halls
New hall for St Paul: I. O. O'Shaughnessy auditorium. il Hi Fi 21:MA18-19 S '71
See also
Opera houses
Sarasota, Fla—Van Wezel performing arts hall

Acoustics

See Acoustics, Architectural

CONCERTGEBOUW orchestra, Amsterdam. See Amsterdam concertgebouw orchestra

CONCERTO for jazz band and orchestra; ballet. See Ballets—Criticisms

CONCERTOS
Beethoven's unfinished piano concerto of 1815: sources and problems. L. Lockwood. bibliog f il Mus Q 56:624-46 O '70
See also
Phonograph records—Concertos

CONCERTS
Barge man; American wind symphony orchestra barge concerts. il Time 98:54 Jl 26 '71
Goodbye to rock; B. Graham gets out of rock concert business. M. Durham. il pors Life 70:62-4+ My 14 '71
Rock concerts: a perilous profit. il Bsns W p54 Ja 16 '71
Rock, etc. concert at Monticello raceway. E. Willis. New Yorker 47:130+ S 25 '71
Videomagnifier: Stephen Stills rock concert at Madison Square Garden; interview. J. White New Yorker 47:19-20 Ag 28 '71
Young people's concert: how not to win friends. Hi Fi 21:MA24 My '71
See also
Benefit performances
Dance concerts
also subhead Music under names of cities, e.g. New York (city)—Music

CONCESSIONS (food, etc)
Dining out in the park; Busch gardens, Tampa, Fla. T. Barrett. il Parks & Rec 6: 19-22+ Ap '71
CONCILIATION courts. See Small claims courts
CONCORD, Mass.
Reunion in Concord. O. Friedrich. il Harper 242:87-94+ My '71
CONCORD, N.H.
Industries
History
Legendary Concords. S. B. Duncan. il por Am West 8:16-17+ Ja '71
CONCORD, Battle of, 1775
Voices of Lexington and Concord; eyewitness accounts; excerpts from Voices of 1776, comp. by R. Wheeler. il Am Heritage 22:8-13+ Ap '71
CONCORD coaches. See Coaches and coaching
CONCORDE airliner. See Airplanes, Supersonic
CONCORDIA theological seminary, St Louis
Preus on Concordia: no progress reports. R. Chandler. Chr Today 15:48 F 26 '71
CONCRETE
Removing stains from concrete. Sunset 146: 126 Je '71
Chemistry
Slowest polymerization reaction; clinker mineral and water in portland cement. K. E. Daugherty and J. Skalny. il pors Chem 45: 12-15 Ja '72
Testing
Driveway patching compounds. il Consumer Rep 36:606-11 O '71
CONCRETE, Precast
Concrete panels may make it after all; Go-Con process. Bsns W p89 O 2 '71
CONCRETE boats. See Boats—Materials
CONCRETE construction
See also
Bridges—Foundations and piers
Bridges, Concrete
CONCRETE houses
Architecture shaped by nature; P. Soleri's Cat cast house. il por House & Gard 139: 50-5 Je '71
Residence in central New York state. il Arch Rec 149:58-9 mid-My '71
Residence in Harrison, N.Y. il Arch Rec 149: 66-9 mid-My '71
Schmidt house, Coconut Grove, Fla. il Arch Rec 149:56-7 mid-My '71
Stevens house, Malibu colony, Malibu Beach, Calif. il Arch Rec 149:44-7 mid-My '71
CONCRETE pavements. See Pavements, Concrete
CONCRETE roofs. See Roofs
CONCRETE testing. See Concrete—Testing
CONCRETE tiles. See Tiles
CONCRETE work
How to work with today's materials. il Bet Hom & Gard 49:50 Jl '71
Anecdotes, facetiae, satire, etc.
Cement mixing made easy. D. Williamson. Sat R 54:12 Ap 17 '71
CONDEMNATION of land. See Eminent domain
CONDEMNATION of property. See Eminent domain
CONDENSATION
Possible prebiotic condensation of mononucleotides by cyanamide. J. D. Ibanez and others. bibliog il Science 173:444-6 Jl 30 '71
Preparing polywater and other anomalous liquids. P. A. Christian and L. H. Berka. bibliog il pors Chem 44:25-8 Ja '71
See also
Atmospheric nucleation
CONDITIONED reflexes. See Conditioned responses
CONDITIONED responses
Behavioral sensitivity to microwave irradiation. N. W. King and others. bibliog il Science 172:398-401 Ap 23 '71
Classical conditioning of a complex skeletal response. E. Gamzu and D. R. Williams. bibliog il Science 171:923-5 Mr 5 '71; Reply with rejoinder. B. F. Skinner. 173:752-3 Ag 20 '71
Decreased systolic blood pressure through operant conditioning techniques in patients with essential hypertension. H. Benson and others. bibliog il Science 173:740-2 Ag 20 '71
Habituation of electrically induced readiness to gnaw. R. E. Cain and others. bibliog il Science 173:262-4 Jl 16 '71

How to break habits that make you unhappy; excerpt from The will to happiness. A. A. Hutschnecker. il Ladies Home J 88:134+ F '71
Melatonin: effect on punished and nonpunished operant behavior of the pigeon. R. I. Schoenfeld. bibliog il Science 171:1258-60 Mr 26 '71
Operant conditioning of specific patterns of neural and muscular activity. E. E. Fetz and D. V. Finocchio. bibliog il Science 174: 431-5 O 22 '71
Retention deficit correlated with a deficit in the corticoid response to stress. P. Auerbach and P. L. Carlton. bibliog il Science 173:1148-9 S 17 '71
See also
Reinforcement (psychology)
CONDOMINIUM campsites. See Camp sites, facilities, etc.
CONDOMINIUM plan ownership. See Apartment houses—Condominium plan ownership
CONDON, Richard
Authors & editors; imaginary interview about The vertical smile. por Pub W 200:193-6 Ag 30 '71 *
CONDON report. See Flying saucers
CONDORS
Condor, soaring spirit of the Andes. J. McGahan. il por Nat Geog 139:684-709 My '71
CONDUCT of court proceedings
Move to curb disorder in court trials. U S News 71:59 Jl 19 '71
Plea for civility; courtroom decorum. por Time 97:52 My 31 '71
Unruly lawyers are menace; excerpts from address, May 18, 1971. W. E. Burger. por U S News 70:83 My 31 '71; Same. Cur Hist 61:111+ Ag '71
See also
Video recorders and recording—Court use
CONDUCT of life
Christian father. E. Elliot. Chr Today 15:3-4 Je 18 '71
Civilization. R. Haughton. Cath World 213: 119-20 Je '71
Eight steps to a new life. N. V. Peale. Read Digest 99:121-4 N '71
Gifts of the spirit. E. Mallory. por PTA Mag 66:11 D '71
How to survive life: the cynic's guide. M. Tumin. Mlle 73:290-1+ Ag '71
Lesson of the fire flowers. J. Hill. il Read Digest 99:119-22 Ag '71
Man from another time; excerpt from Plant dreaming deep. M. Sarton. il Read Digest 98:61-4 Je '71
On rising to the occasion. R. L. Tobin. Sat R 54:20 F 27 '71
Remembrance of things present. D. Newman and R. Benton. Mlle 73:16 O '71
Rule is the situation. P. W. Schmidtchen. il Hobbies 76:134-6+ O '71
Test pattern for living. N. Johnson. il por Sat R 54:12-15+ My 29 '71
Try talking to yourself. W. D. Ellis. Read Digest 99:134-7 Jl '71
Warning: danger ahead. L. N. Bell. Chr Today 15:23-4 Je 4 '71
Who are the addicted? excerpt from The high holy day message of the Jewish theological seminary of America. B. Mandelbaum and V. M. Ratner. Read Digest 98:137-8 Ja '71
Who mourns for Herbie Wirth? J. P. Blank. Read Digest 99:67-71 Jl '71
Your soggy day survival kit. S. Costa. Har Yrs 11:51-3 Je '71
See also
Anger
Avarice
Christian life
College students—Conduct of life
Conscience
Culture
Duty
Early rising
Ethics
Faith
Habits
Human relations
Humility
Life
Love
New Years resolutions
Patriotism
Responsibility
Spiritual life
Sportsmanship
Success
Temptation
Time, Use of
Virtue
Work
Worth
Youth—Conduct of life

CONDUCT unbecoming; drama. See England,
B.
CONDUCTORS (music)
Becoming a conductor. J. Krips. Opera N 35:
14-15 Mr 20 '71
How to say it: a pronunciation guide for the
Metropolitan opera's 1971-72 broadcasts.
Opera N 36:28-9 D 18 '71
Mirrors of our time; black conductors in
Europe and the US; interview, ed. by R.
Hemming. D. Dixon. por Sr Schol 98:17 Mr
22 '71
Musical events; symphony conductors (cont)
W. Sargeant. New Yorker 46:68-9 Ja 23 '71
See also
Bernstein, L.
Boulez, P.
Cleva, F.
Davis, C.
Dorati, A.
Felsenstein, W.
Furtwängler, W.
Karajan, H. von
Levine, J.
Maazel, L.
Mester, J
Priestman, B.
Rudel, J.
Solti, G.
Thomas, M. T.
Waart, E. de
Women as musicians
CONDUCTORS, Electric. See Electric conductors
CONDUITS. See Electric conduits
CONE, A. Lynn. See Dierks-Ventling, C. jt.
auth.
CONE, Edward T.
Schubert's Beethoven. bibliog f il Mus Q 56:
779-93 O '70
CONE, James H.
—and Hordern, William
Dialogue on black theology. Chr Cent 88:
1079-80+ S 15 '71
about
Black theology of James Cone. R. Ruether.
por Cath World 214:18-20 O '71 *
James Cone and the Methodists. C. Rogers.
Chr Cent 88:1340 N 17 '71 *
CONE cells. See Rod and cone cells
CONE snails. See Snails
CONES, Volcanic. See Volcanoes
CONFECTIONERY
Caramel apples for fund raising. il Sunset
147:228+ O '71
See also
Candy
CONFEDERACY of the six nations. See Iroquois Indians
CONFEDERATE States of America
See also
United States—History—Civil war
Army
Yankee Quaker Confederate general, by C. M.
Cummings. Review
Sat R 54:39 My 22 '71
CONFEDERATION of Latin American religious. See Religious conferences—Latin
America
CONFERENCE centers
Getting with it, away from it all. W. Martin.
il Nations Bsns 59:38-41 N '71
CONFERENCE committees, Congressional. See
United States—Congress—Committees
CONFERENCE halls. See Auditoriums
CONFERENCE of American rabbis. See Central conference of American rabbis
CONFERENCE of eastern college librarians
Death at 56; epithets and an epitaph. Wilson
Lib Bul 45:719-20 Ap '71
CONFERENCE of European churches. See
Religious conferences—Europe
CONFERENCE of major superiors of men
CMSM's 14th annual assembly. J. L. Connor. America 125:12 Jl 10 '71
CONFERENCE of state executives on aging.
See Aging, Conferences on
CONFERENCE on Asian environments. See Environment—Conferences
CONFERENCE on biblical prophecy. See Religious conferences—Israel
CONFERENCE on labor statistics. See North
American conference on labor statistics
CONFERENCE on the law of the sea. See
United Nations conference on the law of
the sea, 1973
CONFERENCE on the law of treaties. See
United Nations conference on the law of
treaties

CONFERENCE on the peaceful uses of atomic
energy. See International conference on the
peaceful uses of atomic energy, 4th Geneva, 1971
CONFERENCES
Coming events. See issues of Parks & recreation
Conventions: when & where. See issues of
American city
See also
Agricultural conferences
Authors conferences
Conventions
International conferences
Library conferences
Music conferences
Peace conferences
Photographic conferences
Technical conferences
CONFERENCES on science and world affairs.
See Pugwash conferences on science and
world affairs
CONFESSION
Communal penance: an update. P. E. Fink.
America 124:202 F 27 '71
Communal penance: what are the options?
P. F. Palmer. America 124:64-6 Ja 23 '71;
Discussion. 124:133, 411 F 13, Ap 17 '71
Confusion over confession. America 124:81 Ja
30 '71
Seal of confession. America 124:218-19 Mr 6
'71
Sin and forgiveness. V. P. McCorry. America
124:419-20 Ap 17 '71
To re-mythologize forgiveness. G. R. Fitzgerald. li Cath World 213:269-73 S '71
See also
Confidential communications—Clergy
Anecdotes, facetiae, satire, etc.
Bless me, father; excerpt from Memories of
a non-Jewish boyhood. R. Byrne. Commonweal 93:519+ F 26 '71
CONFESSION story. See Short story
CONFIDENCE men. See Fraud
CONFIDENCES, Personal. See Confidential
communications
CONFIDENTIAL communications
Strictly academic; S. Popkin challenges government's methods in investigation of D.
Ellsberg. il por Newsweek 78:47 N 8 '71
True confessions: should you disclose & expose? J. Brothers. il Harp Baz 105:100+
N '71
See also
Official secrets
Privacy, Right of
Clergy
Religious and the right to secrecy; case of
Sister Margaret Murtha. America 125:82-3
Ag 21 '71
Press
Ex-reporter's privilege; case of W. Farr.
Newsweek 78:42 Ag 9 '71
Privilege in a time of violence; Caldwell
ruling and press subpoenas. V. Blasi. Nation 211:653-6 D 21 '70
Reporters, subpoenas, immunity, and the
Court; views of V. Blasi. R. L. Tobin. Sat
R 54:63-4 D 11 '71
Right to protect a news source; ASNE's
drive to protect reporters from court procedures. R. L. Tobin. Sat R 54:45-6 My 8
'71
Third installment; J. Sack and the William
L. Calley tapes. il por Newsweek 77:44 F
1 '71
Television
Who is big brother? The selling of the Pentagon materials; hearing before House
commerce investigations subcommittee.
por Newsweek 78:25-6 Jl 5 '71
CONFINEMENT feeding of cattle. See Cattle
—Confinement methods
CONFINEMENT feeding of swine. See Swine—
Confinement methods
CONFIRMATION
Confirmation demilitarized; new Roman Catholic rite. il Time 98:80 S 27 '71
CONFLICT, Social. See Social conflict
CONFLICT of generations. See Generation gap
CONFLICT of interests (business)
CAB financial advisors disbanded. L. Doty.
Aviation W 94:28 Je 7 '71
Consultants clash over ownership. il Bsns W
p66-72 N 27 '71
House report puts Penphil under fire. Bsns W
p22 F 20 '71
CONFLICT of interests (public office)
Non-exposé; case of J. Connally. por Time
97:52 F 15 '71
Rescuing California; survey by R. Nader. P.
Barnes. New Repub 165:12-13 S 18 '71

CONFLICT of interests (public office)—*Cont.*
Spoils of politics? M. K. Udall to investigate why the President's former law firm might have received preferential treatment. Newsweek 78:53-4 Ag 9 '71
Such good friends; investigation over choice of underwriters for postal bonds. Newsweek 78:82+ O 11 '71

CONFORMITY
See also
Social values

CONFRONTATION and communication associates
Doctor to the cities; I. Goldaber. il por Newsweek 78:36 S 6 '71

CONFUCIUS and Confucianism
Confucius say... P. W. Schmidtchen. il Hobbies 76:135-8+ Jl '71

CONGDON, Charles C.
Bone marrow transplantation. bibliog il Science 171:1116-24 Mr 19 '71

CONGENITAL deafness. See Deafness

CONGENITAL heart defects. See Heart—Abnormities and deformities

CONGER, Clement Ellis
Grand acquisitor. il por Newsweek 77:26+ Mr 1 '71 *

CONGER, Cornelia
Loveliest rooms I've ever seen. House & Gard 140:38+ O '71

CONGER, Fred M.
Sewage reservoir solves overflow problem. il Am City 86:103 N '71

CONGER, Lesley
Off the cuff. See issues of Writer

CONGLOMERATE corporations
Rise of the conglomerchant. R. Tillman. il Harvard Bsns R 49:44-51 N '71
See also
Avco corporation
Bangor Punta corporation
Commonwealth united corporation
Government investigations—Conglomerate corporations
Gulf and Western industries, inc.
International telephone and telegraph corporation
Kidde, Walter, and company
Ling-Temco-Vought, inc.
Litton industries, inc.
Loews corporation
Rock Island corporation
Signal companies
Simon, Norton, inc.
Slater, Walker securities, ltd.
Textron, inc.
White consolidated industries, inc.
Whittaker corporation

Finance
Multicompanies; with yardsticks of management performance. il Forbes 109:125-9 Ja 1 '72

CONGO (Democratic Republic)
Note:
For material after October 1971, see Zaïre (Democratic Republic)
See also
Ruwenzori Mountains

Politics and government
Comeback in the Congo. D. Reed. por Read Digest 98:134-8 Ap '71
Reports & comment: Congo. S. Meisler. Atlan 227:26+ Mr '71

CONGREGATION for the doctrine of the faith
Rome unbends a bit; dealing with theologians. Chr Cent 88:309 Mr 10 '71

CONGRESS; story. See Borges. J. L.

CONGRESS (United States) See United States—Congress

CONGRESS for recreation and parks
Congress notes; with editorial comment. il Parks & Rec 6:14, 28-9 S '71
Delegate involvement; ladies events; with calendar of events and list of exhibitors. il Parks & Rec 6:36-42 O '71
Highlights; 1971 Congress for recreation & parks. il Parks & Rec 6:25-40 D '71
Will NRPA survive? remarks before the 1971 Congress for recreation and parks. D. F. Rettie. Parks & Rec 6:23-4+ D '71

CONGRESS of American writers
Two views from two sides of the generation fence. A. Caruba; B. Appel. il Pub W 199:22-8 Je 7 '71

CONGRESS of industrial organizations
Labor radical. by L. De Caux. Review
Nation 212:631-2 My 17 '71. L. Fenster

CONGRESS of racial equality
Separatism unacceptable. Negro Hist Bul 33:171 N '70

CONGRESS of the Soviet Communist party. See Communist party (Russia)

CONGRESSIONAL committees. See United States—Congress—Committees

CONGRESSIONAL cup race. See Yacht racing

CONGRESSIONAL hearings. See United States—Congress—Committees

CONGRESSIONAL investigations. See Government investigations

CONGRESSIONAL library. See United States—Library of Congress

CONGRESSIONAL reorganization. See United States—Congress—Reorganization

CONGRESSMEN
Congress: a family business. J. Volz. Nation 212:819-20 Je 28 '71
Congressional chairmen. il Todays Ed 60:40-2 My '71
Legislators on tour: record this year? il U S News 71:41 Ag 30 '71
One day in the life of Guy Vander Jagt (R.-Mich.) J. Corry. por Harper 242:70-9 Ap '71
People to watch in the 92nd Congress. il Sr Schol 98:4-6 Mr 1 '71
President vs. the 92nd Congress. il Newsweek 77:16-18+ Ja 25 '71
Who's new in the Congress. il Time 97:15 F 1 '71
Who's who in the Congress. il Sr Schol 99:13 O 4 '71
Your congressman: myth and reality. il Sr Schol 98:9-11 Mr 1 '71
See also
Conflict of interest (public office)
Members of Congress for peace through law
Negro congressmen
Senators
also names of congressmen, e.g. M. McCormack

Ethics
See Political ethics

Salaries, allowances, etc.
Watch on the Potomac. K. T. Tomlinson and G. Denison. Read Digest 99:25-7+ Jl '71

CONGRESSMEN, Letters to. See Lobbying

CONGRESSWOMEN
Bellacose Abzug. pors Time 98:14+ Ag 16 '71

CONIFERS
See also
Pine

CONIGLIARO, Tony
Show me the way to go home. M. Mulvoy and R. Fimrite. il por Sports Illus 35:16-17 Jl 19 '71 *

CONIL-LACOSTE, Michel
Paris. See issues of Art news

CONJUGAL visits for convicts. See Prisons—Visits with inmates

CONJURING
Is there a magician in the house? T. Prideaux. il Life 71:114-16+ D 17 '71

CONN, Stewart
Marriage a mountain ridge; poem. Poetry 118:198-200 Jl '71

CONNALLY, John Bowden, 1917-
As Connally explains policy on wage-price controls; excerpts from testimony before House banking and currency committee, February 23, 1971. por U S News 70:76-7 Mr 8 '71
As Connally sees his Cabinet job; excerpts from testimony before the Senate finance committee. por U S News 70:36 F 15 '71
Boards of governors of the IMF and IBRD meet at Washington; statement. September 30, 1971. Dept State Bul 65:453-7 O 25 '71
Connally explains how new tax plan will help people; excerpts from testimony before House ways and means committee. il por U S News 71:83-5 S 20 '71
Connally's blunt talk on trade and the dollar; excerpts from address, November 16, 1971. por U S News 71:88-9 N 29 '71
Mutual responsibility for maintaining a stable monetary system; address, May 28, 1971. Dept State Bul 65:42-6 Jl 12 '71; Excerpts with title Tough talk to U.S. allies on trade, defense. U S News 70:51-3 Je 14 '71
Nixon's new chief spokesman sizes up the economy; excerpts from news conference, June 29, 1971. por U S News 71:76-8 Jl 12 '71
Recovery controls, taxes, trade war; interview. il pors U S News 70:52-7 Ap 12 '71
Tough talk to U.S. allies on trade, defense; excerpts from address. May 28, 1971. il pors U S News 70:51-3 Je 14 '71

about
Administration takes on the Fed; with editorial comment. pors Bsns W p 18-19, 80 Jl 31 '71 *
Connally of the treasury: accent on the I. por Forbes 107:52 Ap 1 '71 *

CONNALLY, John Bowden, 1917- —about
—Continued
Connally's hard sell against inflation. il pors Bsns W p62-6 Jl 10 '71 *
Connally's high-stakes poker game. il por Newsweek 78:20-1 O 11 '71 *
Connally's waltz; Senate finance committee hearing. por Newsweek 77:70+ F 8 '71 *
Deal with Japan. il por Newsweek 78:101 N 22 '71 *
Drive to beat inflation, and Democrats; Blurry banner for Phase II; program presented by President Nixon, October 7, 1971. il por Time 98:10-12+ O 18 '71 *
Governor Connally named member, Foreign intelligence advisory board. Dept State Bul 64:84 Ja 18 '71 *
John Connally. H. Sidey. il pors Life 70:38-41 My 7 '71 *
John Connally comes on strong. il pors Newsweek 77:56-7 F 15 '71 *
John Connally: Mr Nixon's no. 2 man? il pors Newsweek 78:16-20 Ag 9 '71 *
John Connally: Nixon's new quarterback. R. Dugger. Atlan 228:82-6+ Jl '71; Reply with rejoinder. D. L. Shapiro. 228:40+ O '71 *
Money: a move toward disarmament. il por Time 98:26 O 11 '71 *
Money: the dangers of the U.S. hard line. il por Time 98:34-5 S 27 '71 *
New U.S. campaign. por Newsweek 77:63 My 31 '71 *
Nixon-Connally arrangement. R. J. Whalen. por Harper 243:29-33+ Ag '71 *
Nixon's four-point do-nothing plan. il pors Newsweek 78:67 Jl 12 '71 *
Non-exposé. por Time 97:52 F 15 '71 *
Oil slick on the Potomac. S. Houston. Commonweal 93:436-8 F 5 '71 *
Phase two: living with controls. il pors Newsweek 78:26-32 O 18 '71 *
Relentless breeze; stopover in Japan. il por Time 98:33 N 22 '71 *
Return of a Texas twister. il por Time 97:17-18 My 10 '71 *
Rising star from Texas. il pors Time 98:18+ O 18 '71 *
Rough road to the Treasury. por Bsns W p 17 F 6 '71 *
Solving a crisis: John Connally superstar. il por Newsweek 78:85-6+ D 13 '71 *
Tough talk and an ominous deadline. il por Newsweek 78:82-4 S 27 '71 *
Washington question: what's ahead for John Connally? il pors U S News 71:22-3 Jl 19 '71 *
Well-oiled. New Repub 164:10-11 F 13 '71 *
Who's in charge here. H. Sidey. il Life 71:4 D 10 '71 *

CONNAUGHTON, Charles A.
AFA's new president. por Am For 77:6 My '71 *

CONNECTICUT
See also
Architecture, Domestic—Connecticut
Booksellers and bookselling—Connecticut
Express highways—Connecticut
Fishing—Connecticut
Gardens—Connecticut
Prisons—Connecticut
Unemployment—Connecticut

Politics and government
Reaganism in Connecticut. J. Quinn. New Repub 164:17 My 29 '71

CONNECTICUT college American dance festival. See Dance festivals

CONNECTICUT state library, Hartford
Prison escape; Connecticut department of correction paperback book fair. E. W. Strain. il por Library J 96:169-70 Ja 15 '71

CONNECTIVE tissues
See also
Collagen
Elastic tissues

Diseases
See also
Scleroderma

CONNELL, Elizabeth B.
Expectant mother. por Redbook 137:10+ Ag; 50+ O '71
Modern obstetric care. por Redbook 137:16+ Je '71
Your health. por Redbook 137:14+ Jl; 57+ S; 138:36+ N; 11-12+ Ja '72

CONNELL, Neville
Colonial life in the West Indies as depicted in prints. il Antiques 99:732-7 My '71
Some early printed views of the West Indies. il Antiques 99:127-31 Ja '71

CONNELLY, Claire
Stalking the back roads in search of rare books. il Pub W 199:133 F 22 '71

CONNELLY, Dolly
Everybody is up in arms. il Sports Illus 34:32-4+ Ap 5 '71

CONNELLY, Joel
Candidacy of Senator Jackson. por Nation 213:490-3 N 15 '71

CONNELLY, Patrick M.
Con con. Todays Ed 60:57 My '71

CONNER, David C.
Light-operated bistable switch. il Pop Electr 34:70 Mr '71

CONNER, John W.
Book marks. See issues of English journal

CONNIFF, James C. G.
(ed) See Agnew, E. I. Don't be ashamed to call yourself housewife
(ed) See Humphrey, H. H. What my students taught me

CONNOLLY, Stephen, and Shapiro, Peter
Staging area imperialism. Nation 213:330-4 O 11 '71

CONNOR, James L.
CMSM's 14th annual assembly. America 125:12 Jl 10 '71

CONNOR, John T.
Financing social revolutions; address. October 28, 1971. Vital Speeches 38:105-9 D 1 '71

CONNOR, Robert
Wankel-engine sport coupe for under $2,500 and 16 other cars you can buy for under $2,000. il Mech Illus 67:39-43 Ja '71

CONNOR, Thomas K.
Living with antiques. il Antiques 100:606-10 O '71

CONOVER, Willis
Funeral of Louis Armstrong. il Sat R 54:43 Jl 31 '71

CONQUEST, Joe
Lost men of Muldoon Canyon. J. Neary. il pors Life 70:50D-50F+ Mr 19 '71 *

CONRAD, Anne
Home on the range. il Seventeen 30:108+ Ja '71

CONRAD, C. Carson
Tone up the swimming-pool way. C. Mitchell. il Read Digest 99:143-5 Ag '71 *

CONRAD, John P.
Need for prison reform. Cur Hist 61:87-91 Ag '71

CONRAD, Randall
Diaries of two chambermaids. il Film Q 24:48-51 Wint '70

*CONRAD, Thomas M.
Politics of gullibility. Commonweal 95:13-15 O 1 '71
about
Seekers after justice. P. Steinfels. Commonweal 95:150 N 12 '71 *

CONROY, Sarah Booth
What kind of a man has Tricia married? pors Good H 173:14-16+ Jl '71

CONSCIENCE
Authority and conscience. A. T. Padovano. il Cath World 213:79-82 My '71
Conscience: good or bad guide? Chr Today 16:25 Ja 7 '72
My conscience is bound by the word of God; thoughts on Luther, address, April 17, 1971. C. L. Manschreck. bibliog Vital Speeches 37:540-4 Je 15 '71

CONSCIENTIOUS objectors
All or nothing for C.O.s. il Time 97:52 Mr 22 '71
Alternative service locates in Appalachia. J. DeMuth. il America 125:374-5 N 6 '71
American Catholic bishops support selective conscientious objection. Chr Cent 88:1320 N 10 '71
Amnesty as reconciliation. Chr Cent 88:1371 N 24 '71
Benefits for COs. New Repub 165:10-11 N 20 '71
Bishops, the CO's and amnesty. America 125:362-3 N 6 '71
CO's attract wider support. America 125:108 S 4 '71
Conscientious objection. New Repub 164:7 Mr 27 '71
Conscientious objection: no longer un-Catholic. J. Pisani. Chr Cent 88:876-8 Jl 21 '71; Reply. R. Horton. 88:1026 S 1 '71
Great disappointment: the Negré-Gillette decision. Chr Cent 88:363 Mr 24 '71
Man the world forgot; G. Elder. S. Grady. il pors Ebony 26:154-6+ O '71
Pentagon broadens C.O. guidelines. Chr Cent 88:1075 S 15 '71
Revised draft rules for COs, seminarians issued. Chr Cent 88:1375 N 24 '71
Selective conscientious objectors decision. America 124:278 Mr 20 '71
Spain incarcerates Catholic C.O. Chr Cent 88:585 My 12 '71
Viet objectors overruled; Court decision on draft. Sr Schol 98:12 Mr 22 '71

CONSCIOUSNESS
Consciousness-makers and the autonomy of consciousness. E. Pols. Yale R 60:514-31 Je '71
Expansive man and the church of the '70s. G. B. Noyce. Chr Cent 88:1377-9 N 24 '71
New consciousness. C. F. H. Henry. Chr Today 16:28-9 O 8 '71
      See also
Self

CONSCIOUSNESS-expanding drugs. See Hallucinogenic drugs

CONSCRIPTION. See Military service, Compulsory

CONSCRIPTION, Civilian. See Service, Compulsory non-military

CONSERVATION associations
Conservation: how can you help? E. Welke. Bet Hom & Gard 49:46 F '71
Hudson's many friends. Audubon 73:102 Mr '71
Hunters and conservationists share goals; official policy toward hunting. il Nat Wildlife 9:18-19 O '71
Tax issue; refusal of tax exempt status for organizations engaged in efforts to protect or restore the environment. Liv Wildn 34:3 Aut '70
      See also
American forestry association
Environmental associations, committees, etc.
National wildlife federation
Sierra club

CONSERVATION commissions, Municipal
Aid for local conservationists. S. Lindsay. Sat R 55:72-3 Ja 1 '72

CONSERVATION education. See Conservation of resources—Study and teaching; Environmental education

CONSERVATION exhibits, Traveling. See Exhibitions, Traveling

CONSERVATION law. See Conservation of resources—Laws and legislation

CONSERVATION library center. See Denver public library—Conservation library center

CONSERVATION movement. See Environmental movement

CONSERVATION of resources
Conservation. M. Frome. See issues of Field & stream
Conservation and the minerals industry. P. H. Abelson. Science 173:9 Jl 2 '71
Conservation, for whom? L. C. Watkins. Liv Wildn 34:51-2 Aut '70
Conservation news (cont of) News and commentary. See issues of National parks & Conservation magazine
Conservationist speaks his mind; interview. D. Brower. por U S News 71:64-5 Jl 5 '71
Ecocatastrophe, by the editors of Ramparts. Review
      Trans-Action 8:58-60 F''71. J. McEvoy, 3d
Getting it together. M. Frome. Field & S 76:28+ S '71
Is anybody in Washington really listening? M. Frome. Field & S 76:38+ Ag '71
Making of a conservationist; excerpt from Who owns America? W. J. Hickel. il Sat R 54:65-7 O 2 '71
Making peace with the earth; excerpt from Earthkeeping. G. Harrison. il Sat R 54:77+ N 6 '71
National outlook. C. H. Callison. See issues of Audubon
National parks and conservation association; report of the president and general counsel, May 20, 1971. A. W. Smith. Nat Parks & Con Mag 45:23-6 My '71
News items of interest. See issues of Living wilderness
1971 EQ index. il Nat Wildlife 9:25-40 O '71
Personal testimony on the standard of living. D. Lambert. il Nat Parks & Con Mag 45:23-6 Je '71
Potomac prospect. A. W. Smith. Nat Parks & Con Mag 45:2 F '71
Recycling: an old idea with new significance. R. Andrus and S. P. Mathur. il Cons 25:28-31 Je: 26:10-11 Ag '71
Technology and society: a challenge to private enterprise; address, April 1971. I. K. MacGregor. Vital Speeches 37:525-9 Je 15 '71
This land is our land. il Sr Schol 98:16-17 F 1 '71
Toward a policy of energy conservation. S. D. Freeman. por Bul Atom Sci 27:8-12 O '71
Visit with Pearl Buck; interview, ed. by C. Renshaw, jr. P. Buck. il pors Nat Wildlife 10:28-32 D '71
      See also
Conservation associations
Environmental movement
Environmental policy

Forest conservation
Landscape protection
Natural resources
Nature conservation
Reclamation of land
Soil conservation
United States—Interior, Department of
Water conservation
Wilderness areas
Wildlife conservation

Bibliography
Among the books (title varies) See issues of Living wilderness
Books. Nat Parks & Con Mag 45:45 My '71

History
Home for the spirit. R. Nash. bibliog il Am West 8:40-7 Ja '71

Laws and legislation
Home for the spirit. R. Nash. bibliog il Am West 8:40-7 Ja '71
How conservation has fared in the 91st Congress (as of October 14, 1970) Liv Wildn 34:63 Aut '70
Message from the President of the United States; transmitting the sixth annual report on the National wilderness preservation system, August 5, 1970. R. M. Nixon. Liv Wildn 34:2 Aut '70
National outlook; record for the 91st Congress. C. H. Callison. Audubon 73:96-7 Ja '71
Wilderness system gains twenty-three new units. Liv Wildn 34:60 Aut '70
      See also
Wildlife conservation—Laws and legislation

Periodicals
Ecology, conservation, etc; ed. by B. Katz, E. Schwartz. Library J 96:3304-6 O 15 '71
      See also
Conservationist (periodical)

Study and teaching
Camp: the ideal place for teaching environmental urgencies. E. J. Stahr. il Camp Mag 43:20+ Mr '71
Scouts can help; Project SOAR. T. Trueblood. il Field & S 75:16+ F '71
Your camp ecology program. S. Van Matre. il Camp Mag 43:8-10 Je '71
Youth education in conservation, a vital force. P. G. Bulger. Cons 26:33 Ag '71
      See also
United States—Youth conservation corps

Alaska
Alaska's Tongass suit: the exercise at Juneau. M. Miller. il Am For 77:28-31+ Mr '71
America must have the Alaskan oil. S. G. Slappey. il Nations Bsns 59:40-3 S '71
Conservationists urge Alaska land freeze; letter to R. M. Nixon. Nat Parks & Con Mag 45:29-30 F '71
Fight for the trees in the Tongass. M. Miller. il Am For 77:16-19 Jl '71
Letter from Alaska: plan or plunder for the American Arctic? R. B. Weeden. il Liv Wildn 35:35-40 Sum '71
Little wisdom gathered from much folly. L. E. Burch, jr. Liv Wildn 35:32-3 Spr '71
Pipeline. New Repub 164:9 Ja 30 '71

Florida
Blocking Florida's ditch. il Newsweek 77:55-6 F 1 '71
Florida: Nixon halts canal project, cites environment. J. Walsh. il Science 171:357 Ja 29 '71
Nixon stops up a barge canal. Bsns W p 19 Ja 23 '71

Kentucky
Second rape of Appalachia. P. Primack. Nation 213:530-2 N 22 '71

Montana
Montana versus the mining companies: new awakening or impractical idealism? R. H. Gilluly. il Sci N 100:245-7 O 2 '71

New Jersey
Progress toward points of no return; excerpts from letter, August 17, 1970. T. M. Edison. Liv Wildn 34:52-3 Wint '70

New York (state)
      See also
New York (state)—Environmental conservation, Department of

Oregon
Oregon for the Oregonians. P. Barnes. New Repub 164:10-11 Mr 20 '71

CONSERVATION of resources—*Continued*

Rhode Island

Tempting of a small town; Tiverton and the oil refinery. R. Vaughan. il Life 71:50-1+ Jl 30 '71; Same abr. Read Digest 99:207-8+ O '71

Russia

Attitudes toward conservation in the Soviet Union. C. W. Luscher. il Liv Wildn 34:13-19 Aut '70

Southwestern states

Murder of the Southwest. A. M. Josephy, jr. il Audubon 73:52-67 Jl '71

Ukraine

Ukraine's nation-wide movement to protect its natural resources; interview. B. Voltovski. il UNESCO Courier 24:26-9 Jl '71

CONSERVATION of wildlife. See Wildlife conservation

CONSERVATION of works of art. See Art—Conservation and restoration

CONSERVATIONIST (periodical)
Facing the future. Cons 25:1 Ap '71
Quarter-century of concern; with editorial comment. il Cons 26:1, 12-13 Ag '71

CONSERVATISM
Confessions of a street-corner conservative. W. F. Gavin. il Nat R 23:1345-7 D 3 '71
Declaration: suspension of support of R. Nixon by twelve conservative spokesmen. Nat R 23:842 Ag 10 '71; Discussion. 23:908-9 Ag 24 '71
Disenchanted; Republicans denounce R. Nixon. il Newsweek 78:35+ N 8 '71
Opinion: on left turning right, the new conservative. S. I. Abramowitz. por Mlle 74:24+ Ja '72
Right of center. J. M. Hillard. Wilson Lib Bul 46:229 N '71
Say it isn't so, Mr President. W. F. Buckley, jr. il pors N Y Times Mag p8-9+ Ag 1 '71
Week's journal. W. F. Buckley, jr. New Yorker 47:36-43+ Ag 21; 36-42+ Ag 28 '71
Wisdom of conservatism, ed. by P. Witonski. Review
Nat R 23:995+ S 10 '71. M. S. Evans
See also
Young Americans for freedom (organization)

CONSERVATIVE; story. See Yglesias, J.

CONSERVATORSHIP care. See Guardian and ward

CONSOLIDATED Edison company of New York
Wintertime mini-crisis. il Newsweek 77:73 F 15 '71

CONSOLIDATIONS, Business. See Business consolidations and mergers

CON SON prison. See Prisons—Vietnam (Republic)

CONSORT: ballet. See Ballets—Criticisms

CONSORTIUM for graduate study in business for blacks. See Negro executives—Training

CONSORTIUM of publishers for employment. See Cope program

CONSPIRACY
Anti-government kidnap, bomb plot? Catholic antiwar militants. il U S News 70:28 Ja 25 '71
Arraignment in Harrisburg. R. Stone. Chr Cent 88:589-92 My 12 '71
Berrigan defense. il Newsweek 77:28 Mr 22 '71
Berrigan letters. il por Newsweek 77:27B Mv 10 '71
Berrigan plot; indictments against Roman Catholic radicals. il pors Newsweek 77:28-9 Ja 25 '71
Berrigans: conspiracy and conscience. il pors Time 97:12-17 Ja 25 '71
Drama inside the Berrigan circle; with report by L. Lockwood. il pors Life 70:22-31 My 21 '71
Ethicists examine conspiracy laws. Chr Cent 88:213-14 F 17 '71
Guide to a curious case: Harrisburg six; interviews. ed. by C. Roberts. il Newsweek 77:30-2 My 3 '71
Harrisburg conspiracy. Nation 212:133 F 1 '71
Harrisburgh indictments. Commonweal 93:435-6 F 5 '71
Hazards of journalism; charges against foreign journalists in Northern Ireland. Nation 212:773 Je 21 '71
Hoover-Berrigan-Wills. Nat R 23:578 Je 1 '71
How to grab the brain child; charges of conspiring to kidnap H. Kissinger. il pors Time 97:15-16 My 10 '71
Kissinger kidnap plot: reactions to the indictment. America 124:80 Ja 30 '71; Reply. P. Steinfels. 124:134 F 13 '71

Kissinger kidnap plot revisited. America 124:503 My 15 '71
Laws of men and the law of God. G. W. Glick. Chr Cent 88:1225-9 O 20 '71
Notes and comments; the eight charged with plan to kidnap Dr Kissinger. New Yorker 47:27-8 My 15 '71
Plausible and the wacky. L. P. Ribuffo. Nation 213:251-4 S 20 '71
Problem of conspiracy. il Time 97:48 F 15 '71
Study in contrasts; various reactions to Harrisburg indictments. J. Deedy. Commonweal 93:434 F 5 '71; Reply. A. Wolsky. 94:3+ Mr 12 '71
Trial by headline; Harrisburg conspiracy case. Nation 212:707 Je 7 '71; Reply with rejoinder. L. Lockwood. 213:66 Ag 2 '71
What goes on in Harrisburg; Harrisburg six pretrial hearings. J. Freed. Nation 212:464-6 Ap 12 '71
See also
Trials (conspiracy)

Anecdotes, facetiae, satire, etc.

Day they stole the Agnew. P. Steinfels. Commonweal 93:390+ Ja 22 '71

CONSPIRACY; drama. See Thane, A.

CONSTANT of gravitation. See Gravitation

CONSTANTINOPLE. See Istanbul

CONSTANTS. See Units

CONSTIPATION
Five steps to regularity. K. Anderson. Har Yrs 11:49-52 Mr '71

CONSTITUTION (United States) See United States—Constitution

CONSTITUTIONAL amendments. See United States—Constitution—Amendments

CONSTITUTIONAL conventions
Thomas Jefferson, won't you please come home? proposed urban constitutional convention; address, April 1971, with questions and answers. L. N. Cutler. bibliog f Ann Am Acad 396:25-39 Jl '71
See also
United States—Constitutional convention, 1787

CONSTITUTIONAL law
See also
Police power
Rule of law

CONSTRUCTION. See Building

CONSTRUCTION (art) See Assemblage (art)

CONSTRUCTION contracts. See Building—Contracts and specifications

CONSTRUCTION industry
Another boom year for builders. il Bsns W p52-3 Ja 1 '72
Big buildup in housing. il Time 98:105 N 1 '71
Building snaps back with a bang. il Bsns W p34-5 Ap 10 '71
Building team, and other ill-defined ideas. W. F. Wagner, jr. Arch Rec 149:9 Ap '71
Building with the Buffalo boys. il Time 98:21-2 Ag 30 '71
Construction industry; address, January 20, 1971. J. D. Hodgson. Vital Speeches 37:258-60 F 15 '71
Current trends in construction. See issues of Architectural record
Home building: is the boom hollow? il Forbes 108:28-30+ N 1 '71
Labor requirements for construction of single-family houses. R. Ball and L. Ludwig. il Mo Labor R 94:12-14 S '71
New method to cut building costs; construction-manager approach. il U S News 71:74-5 Ag 9 '71
Prehire agreements in construction. bibliog Mo Labor R 94:66-8 O '71
Professional construction management and project administration; with editorial comment. W. B. Foxhill. il Arch Rec 149:9-10 69-70 Je '71
Where, oh where, are the management skills? W. F. Wagner, jr. Arch Rec 150:9 D '71
Why builders donate schools. Bsns W p58 O 9 '71
See also
Fuller, George A, company
Houses, Prefabricated
Levitt and sons, inc.
Shapell industries, inc.
Strikes—United States—Construction industry
Swindell-Dressler company
Walter, Jim, corporation

Employees

Boost, blast for Philadelphia plan. U S News 70:63 My 10 '71
Construction industry; manpower; address, January 20, 1971. J. D. Hodgson. Vital Speeches 37:258-60 F 15 '71

CONSTRUCTION industry—Employees—*Cont.*

Construction labor in the sixties: the phenomenon of scarcity. J. E. Carlson. Arch Rec 149:76 Je '71

Construction manpower needs by 1980. W. F. Hahn. bibliog f il Mo Labor R 94:12-18 Jl '71

Now a U.S. hiring plan for San Francisco. U S News 70:88-9 Je 21 '71

See also
Construction industry—Wages and hours
Construction workers

Finance

F. W. Dodge construction outlook: 1972. il Arch Rec 150:67-70 N '71

Labor conditions

See also
Strikes—United States—Construction industry

Securities

Building group. C. Morgello. il Newsweek 78:71 Jl 19 '71

Making money work. S. Meisenberg. Har Yrs 11:34-5 Ja '71

Statistics

Surveying the gaps in construction statistics: report of Cabinet committee on construction. S. Swerdloff. Mo Labor R 94:33-7 F '71

Wages and hours

As builders brace for strikes, higher wages—. il U S News 70:87-8 Mr 22 '71

As construction industry sets own pay pattern. il U S News 71:78 D 6 '71

Bat in Mr Nixon's hand. il por Newsweek 77:75 Mr 1 '71

Braking to be slow on construction pay. U S News 70:47-8 My 31 '71

Builders' pay pact to test controls. U S News 71:30 Je 28 '71

Builders put a lid on overtime pay. Bsns W p38 Je 19 '71

Building-wage plan to get court test. U S News 70:54 My 3 '71

Building wages begin to stabilize. Bsns W p 16 Jl 3 '71

Can a wage board work? Construction industry stabilization committee. Nations Bsns 59:38-9 O '71

Construction wages burden arms talks; slowdown in building third Safeguard site. Bsns W p28 Ag 14 '71

Damper on building wages. U S News 71:75 Jl 5 '71

Fight over a freeze on building costs. il Newsweek 77:69-70 F 22 '71

Guideposts for hardhats. Time 97:85-6 Ap 12 '71

Hard hats are talking tougher. il Bsns W p 105 Mr 13 '71

Hints at wage controls: unions prepare to fight back. il U S News 70:60-2 Mr 1 '71

Holding down raises: the latest proposal. U S News 70:86 Ap 5 '71

Inflationary woes of the construction industry after the wage price freeze; address, August 1971. J. E. Healy, 2d. Vital Speeches 37:762-5 O 1 '71

Is a pattern already set for Pay board's wage controls? il U S News 71:76-8 N 1 '71

Is Nixon moving toward more controls? il U S News 70:17-18 Ap 12 '71

Living with the phases. J. E. Carlson. Arch Rec 150:60 D '71

Loose lid on construction pay. Bsns W p60+ My 22 '71

Mr Nixon's puzzling wage ploy. il Newsweek 77:79 Mr 8 '71

More unions cut their raises. U S News 71:106 D 13 '71

Next moves in the battle to hold down pay and prices; suspension of the Davis-Bacon act. il U S News 70:23-4 Mr 8 '71

Nixon opts for intervention. il Bsns W p34-5 F 27 '71

Nixon puts more teeth in the jawbone. il Bsns W p 14 Ap 3 '71

Nixon's drive to curb pay in building: can it succeed? il U S News 70:52-4 F 1 '71

Nixon's half swing at construction costs. il Time 97:74+ Mr 8 '71

Pass the barrel of worms, please; reinstated Davis-Bacon act. Nat R 23:413 Ap 20 '71

Proposal to outlaw hiring halls; Construction users anti-inflation round-table proposals. il U S News 70:79 F 15 '71

Showdown nearing over pay curbs in construction. il U S News 70:82-4 My 24 '71

Testing ground for inflation control; Construction industry stabilization committee. il Bsns W p30-1 Ag 14 '71

Turning off hardhats: suspension of the Davis-Bacon act. New Repub 164:9 Mr 6 '71

Uncertainty leads to higher wages. Bsns W p 17-18 My 8 '71

Unions' worry: White House crackdown on wage demands. il U S News 70:63-4 F 22 '71

Wage controls in building get their first test. il U S News 70:108-9 Ap 19 '71

Wage freeze in construction. por Bsns W p94 N 20 '71

Wage madness in the construction industry. C. Stevenson. Read Digest 98:47-51 Ja '71

Wage-price plan. il Newsweek 77:65+ Ap 5 '71

Wage-price restraints in construction. M. H. Moskow. Mo Labor R 94:46-7 S '71

Will Nixon freeze construction wages? il Bsns W p25-6 F 20 '71

Canada

Programs for providing winter jobs in construction. E. J. Howenstine. bibliog Mo Labor R 94:24-32 F '71

Europe, Western

Programs for providing winter jobs in construction. E. J. Howenstine. bibliog Mo Labor R 94:24-32 F '71

Germany (Federal Republic)

From union-made to union-owned; Neue Heimat companies. Bsns W p34 Ap 3 '71

Poland

Importing expertise from Warsaw; building sulfuric acid plant in Germany. Bsns W p41 Ag 14 '71

United States

See Construction industry

CONSTRUCTION industry affairs council of Kansas City

Recommendations on payment practices issued by construction industry council. Arch Rec 150:57-8 Ag '71

CONSTRUCTION machinery

Marketing

Liebherr digs the U.S. market. por Bsns W p40 Je 26 '71

CONSTRUCTION trades unions

Nixon's half swing at construction costs. il Time 97:74+ Mr 8 '71

U.S. v. construction workers. il Time 97:72+ F 15 '71

CONSTRUCTION workers

Keep this under your hat; the long-haired hard hat. K. Fleming. il Newsweek 78:30-1 Jl 26 '71

Longhair hard hat. W. J. McKean. Look 35:38+ Ja 12 '71

Topping out the world's tallest building. R. Gannon. il Pop Sci 198:82-3+ My '71

U.S. v. construction workers. il Time 97:72+ F 15 '71

See also
Construction industry—Wages and hours

CONSTRUCTIVISM

Art; exhibition of Russian art of the revolution, at the Brooklyn museum. L. Alloway. Nation 213:29-30 Jl 5 '71

Russian revolutionary art; New York cultural center. B. Rose. il Vogue 158:177-8 O 1 '71

When the renaissance came to Russia. A. Hilton. bibliog il Art N 70:34-9+ D '71

CONSULAR service. See United States—Diplomatic and consular service

CONSULTANTS

See also
Business consultants
Educational consultants
Psychiatric consultants

CONSULTATION on church union

Blacks and COCU: a new honesty. C. Rogers; discussion. Chr Cent 88:136, 195 Ja 27, F 10 '71

COCU: a loss of nerve? Chr Today 16:35 O 22 '71

COCU continues to draw support. Chr Cent 88:1518 D 29 '71

COCU: hope in Denver. S. C. Rose. Chr Cent 88:1189-90 O 13 '71

COCU plan of union and Catholicity. J. T. Ford. Chr Cent 88:1229-32 O 20 '71

Call for authority in the Christian community; address. P. L. Berger. Chr Cent 88:1257-63 O 27 '71

How will COCU resolve the church's real problems? W. R. McGeary, jr. Chr Today 15:16 Mr 26 '71

CONSUMERS—*Continued*
Why consumers will spend. L. H. Olsen. por Nations Bsns 59:66 S '71
Why the recovery lags. il Newsweek 78:63-4 Jl 19 '71
See also
Consumer education
Consumer protection
Negro market
Old age market
Youth market
CONSUMERS, Department of (proposed) See United States—Consumer affairs, Department of (proposed)
CONSUMERS cooperative of Berkeley, inc.
Democratic, up to a point. P. Barnes. New Repub 166:17-19 Ja 1 '72
CONSUMERS union of United States
CU's grant to develop consumer education. Consumer Rep 36:132 Mr '71
Consumer library. K. Nyren. il Library J 96:3295-7 O 15 '71
How CU works; 35th anniversary issue; with introd. by C. E. Warne. il Consumer Rep 36:679-710 N '71
Is testing fair at Consumers union? il Bsns W p41-2 F 27 '71
Members elect eight to CU's board. Consumer Rep 36:587 O '71
Other Ralph Nader. R. Levy. por Duns 98:42-3 D '71
Quiet watchdog. il Newsweek 77:85 Mr 15 '71
CONSUMPTION (economics)
Boom of gloom ahead? Consumer spending could be the key. il Sr Schol 98:13-15 Ap 5 '71
Buy, brother, buy. il Forbes 107:36 Mr 1 '71
Cautious consumers, wary executives. il Time 97:76-7 Mr 15 '71
Customer holds the key to 1971, but will he use it? il U S News 70:22-3 Ja 18 '71
Giving the customers what they want. il Fortune 83:18 Mr '71
Man and his environment; adaptation of address, March 19, 1970. A. J. Coale; discussion. Science 171:15 Ja 8 '71
Solid base of national support. il Bsns W p 17-18 Ag 28 '71
See also
Consumer surveys
Consumers
Purchasing power
CONTACT lenses
Contact lenses for people who can't wear contact lenses. il Vogue 158:105-6+ Ag 1 '71
Contact lenses that are easy on the eyes. F. C. Kilburn. il Mech Illus 48:84-5+ Ja '72
Eye, the jury; soft contact lenses. il Time 97:80 My 31 '71
Facts about those new soft contact lenses. Good H 173:219 N '71
New soft contact lens. C. Conley. il Field & S 76:158 N '71
Truth about contact lenses, by J. Baker. Review
Consumer Bul 55:33+ Ja '72
Wall Street latches on to soft lenses. il Bsns W p70 My 15 '71
CONTAINER gardening
Containers for easy patio gardening. L. V. Power. il Am Home 74:88-91+ Ap '71
Growing grapes in containers? il Sunset 146:114-15 Ja '71
Wild flowers on a balcony. T. H. Cain. il Horticulture 49:24-5+ S '71
See also
Flower boxes, planters, etc.
Hanging baskets
House plants
Indoor gardening
Plants, Potted
Vegetable gardening. Home
CONTAINER industry
Odd shape that sold Japan; Tetra pak international. il Bsns W p30-1 Ja 30 '71
CONTAINERIZATION (freight)
Forwarders ask container incentives. R. S. Kahn. Aviation W 94:40-1 F 22 '71
CONTAINERS
Battle over bottles & cans. il Changing T 25:45-6 D '71
Deposit on litter; bill banning throwaway bottles and cans in Oregon. Nation 213:6 Jl 5 '71
Food carriers. il Bet Hom & Gard 49:71 Je '71
See also
Bottles
Glass containers
Thermos containers
CONTAINERS, Pressurized. See Pressure packaging

CONTAINERS for shipping
Emery introduces new garment container. R. S. Kahn. il Aviation W 95:32-3 D 13 '71
New rates, containers spur cargo efforts. R. S. Kahn. il Aviation W 95:28-30 D 20 '71
CONTAMINATED food. See Food contamination
CONTEMPLATION. See Meditation
CONTEMPLATION, Religious. See Meditation
CONTEMPLATIVE orders
Contemplation in a world of action, by T. Merton. Review
America 124:490-1 My 8 '71. P. J. Fleming
Contemplative life and the sociologist. M. Rowe; discussion. Chr Cent 88:20,319 Ja 6, Mr 10 '71
Contemplative life in the modern world. G. Fourez. il Cath World 213:27-9 Ap '71
CONTEMPORARY furniture. See Furniture
CONTEMPORARY music. See Music
CONTEMPT of court
Justice dusts off a sharp weapon; criminal contempt actions. Bsns W p30 O 9 '71
Les CONTES d'Hoffmann; opera. See Offenbach J.
CONTI, P. S. See Heuvel, E. P. J. van den, jt. auth.
CONTINENTAL airlines
Air Micronesia gets island route. J. P. Woolsey. Aviation W 95:31-2 Ag 16 '71
Best buy in the sky. Newsweek 77:88 My 17 '71
Bob Six show rolls on. T. J. Murray. il por Duns 97:34-7+ Je '71
Eastern, Continental report 1970 profits. Aviation W 94:26 F 1 '71
CONTINENTAL baking company. See ITT Continental baking company
CONTINENTAL can company
Concan challenge. J. Ross-Skinner. il Duns 98:61-2+ D '71
Concan is caught in an antitrust test. Bsns W p37+ D 18 '71
Trustbusters fire at a U.S. target. Bsns W p41 Mr 27 '71
CONTINENTAL Congress. See United States—Continental Congress
CONTINENTAL drift
Continental drift and the diversity of species. L. Purrett. il Sci N 100:394-5 D 11 '71
Continents are adrift! Glomar Challenger. R. Schiller. il Read Digest 98:101-6 Ap '71
Geophysical garbage dump. il Time 97:70 Ap 5 '71
Hot spots and crust motion; mantle convection. Sci N 99:180 Mr 13 '71
Madagascar's paleoposition: new data from the Mozambique Channel. J. R. Heirtzler and R. H. Burroughs. bibliog il Science 174:488-90 O 29 '71
Other extreme; Gondwana reconstructions. il Sci N 99:49 Ja 16 '71
Those shifty continents. R. S. Dietz. bibliog il Sea Front 17:204-12 Jl '71
Will the continents quit drifting in a billion years? Sci N 100:325 N 13 '71
CONTINENTAL oil corporation
Betting the odds. il Forbes 107:30 Ja 15 '71
CONTINENTALS (soldiers) See United States—History—Revolution—American forces
CONTINENTS
See also
Continental drift
CONTINUOUS casting
One-trip sheetmaking goes on stream; tandem casting-rolling mill. il Bsns W p55 O 9 '71
CONTINUOUS sessions. See School year
CONTOS, Catherine
Brava, maestra! il Hi Fi 21:MA7-10 My '71
CONTRA COSTA COUNTY, Calif.
Renovated wastewater for industry? il Am City 86:118+ Je '71
CONTRABAND trade. See Smuggling
CONTRACEPTION. See Birth control
CONTRACEPTIVES
Beyond the pill. D. M. Rorvik. Look 35:17-19 Je 15 '71
Defusing the world population bomb; new birth-control techniques. T. Alexander. il Fortune 84:112-16+ O '71
Hallelujah the pill? R. B. Dixon. il Trans-Action 8:44-9+ N '70
Morning-after pill; diethylstilbestrol. Sci N 100:293 O 30 '71
Morning-after pill; diethylstilbestrol. Time 98:67 N 8 '71
Morning-after pill; diethylstilbestrol. il Newsweek 78:74 N 8 '71
New contraceptives. il Newsweek 78:47-8 S 13 '71

CONTRACEPTIVES—*Continued*
Pot. pills and the pill: how they affect your skin, hair and health. Mlle 73:254-5 Ag '71
Questions you ask most about birth control. A. Lake. Seventeen 30:84-5+ Ja '71
Toward birth control by peptides. por Sci N 100:37 Jl 17 '71
  See also
Prostaglandins
CONTRACT bridge. See Bridge (game)
CONTRACT bridge league's spring national tournament. See Bridge tournaments
CONTRACT plan (education)
Middle school tries contractual reading. L. L. Smith and J. Riebock. Clear House 45: 404-6 Mr '71
CONTRACTILITY (biology)
Contraction of granulation tissue in vitro: similarity to smooth muscle. G. Majno and others. bibliog il Science 173:548-50 Ag 6 '71
  See also
Cells—Motility
CONTRACTOR; drama. See Storey, D.
CONTRACTORS
  See also
Fischbach and Moore, inc.
CONTRACTS
Beware the pitfalls in the fine print. J. Carper. Read Digest 98:123-6 F '71
Legal guide to buying. J. L. Alpert. Har Yrs 11:34-7 F '71
  See also
Instalment contracts
Labor contracts
Land contracts
Municipal contracts
Put and call transactions
Trade agreements
CONTRACTS, Agricultural
Backgrounding on contract; calf feeding contracts. N. Reeder. il Farm J 95:B8 Mr '71
Livestock integration: a tough way to get ahead; broiler contracting and sow-leasing. R. Wilmore; J. D. Ritchie. il Farm J 95:16-17+ Ag '71
CONTRACTS, Government
Aftermath of Lockheed's defeat. Bsns W p22-3 F 6 '71
Big rock-candy mountain. T. Coffin. Nation 213:262-4 S 27 '71
Biggest racket; GAO report on defense contract profits. Nation 212:452-3 Ap 12 '71
Business of war; defense contracts report by the Council on economic priorities. Nation 212:517 Ap 26 '71
Business of war; study by the Council on economic priorities. il Ramp Mag 9:7-8 Je '71
Congress probes Rover fund cuts. K. Johnsen. Aviation W 94:14-15 Mr 1 '71
Congress urged to base profits on investments. K. Johnsen. Aviation W 94:15 My 10 '71
Costs to spur F-14 contract change. C. Brownlow. Aviation W 94:14-15 Ap 26 '71
DOD urged to find cost overrun causes. K. Johnsen. il Aviation W 94:21-2 Mr 29 '71
Defense department lists leading 100 contractors for fiscal 1971; table. Aviation W 95: 50-1+ D 6 '71
Eight subcontracts awarded for B-1. Aviation W 95:55 Jl 19 '71
Fight delays NASA shuttle. Bsns W p78 Ag 28 '71
Gravy train; defense contracts report by Council on economic priorities. New Repub 164:9 Ap 24 '71; Discussion. 164:37, 39 My 15 '71
Grumman's F-14 draws more flak. il Bsns W p25 O 9 '71
Lockheed accepts $200-million C-5 loss. il Aviation W 94:20-1 F 8 '71
Maximum design leeway marks AX effort. Aviation W 94:18 Ap 19 '71
New battle over defense profits. il Time 97: 70-1 Mr 8 '71
New design for the bottom line; change in Pentagon's system for negotiating profits. Bsns W p66+ Mr 27 '71
Running down overruns. il Time 97:74-5 Je 21 '71
SEC wants more disclosure. Bsns W p21-2 My 8 '71
Settlement cuts Sanders' equity. Aviation W 95:17 Jl 26 '71
Shuttle engine awarded to Rocketdyne. Aviation W 95:12 Jl 19 '71
Status of major U.S, European defense, aerospace programs (cont) Aviation W 94:14-18 Mr 8 '71
Tighter bridle on defense R&D. Bsns W p58+ O 16 '71

Tighter rein on financing. il Bsns W p78-9 Ja 23 '71
  See also
Purchasing, Government
United States—Commission on government procurement
United States—National aeronautics and space administration—Procurement
  Accounting
LeBourget Paris show facilities expanded. D. E. Fink. Aviation W 96:18-19 Ja 10 '72
  Anecdotes, facetiae, satire, etc.
Parting shots: my 19,000 per cent overrun. W. Zinsser. il Life 70:59-60 F 12 '71
  Labor problems
Black workers & unemployment: court orders must be policed; address, July 8, 1971. H. Hill. Vital Speeches 37:658-62 Ag 15 '71
  Renegotiation
What Grumman has learned from Lockheed. il Bsns W p74-5 Je 12 '71
  Subcontracting
Major B-1 subcontractors. Aviation W 95:17 N 8 '71
CONTRACTS, Land. See Land contracts
CONTRACTS, Municipal. See Municipal contracts
CONTRIBUTORS, Political. See Campaign funds
CONTROL data corporation
Control data's bold design. A. A. Butkus. il Duns 98:32-5+ Jl '71
Winded? Or resting? il Forbes 107:22-3 Mr 1 '71
CONTROL of insects. See Insect control
CONTROL panels (airplanes) See Airplanes—Instrument boards
CONTROL systems, Biological. See Biological control systems
CONTROLLED fusion. See Nuclear fusion
CONUS. See Snails
CONVALESCENCE
Recuperation from illness: flavor enhancement for rats. K. F. Green and J. Garcia. bibliog il Science 173:749-51 Ag 20 '71
CONVALESCENT homes. See Nursing homes
CONVENIENCE foods. See Food—Ready-to-cook food
CONVENIENCE stores. See Food stores
CONVENTION delegates. See National conventions (political)
CONVENTIONS
Conventions: when & where. See issues of American city
Traveling on the IRS; trend to overseas conventions. il Newsweek 78:52-3 Jl 26 '71
CONVENTIONS, Constitutional. See Constitutional conventions
CONVENTIONS, Political. See National conventions (political)
CONVENTS and nunneries
Social life space of nuns in the seventies; address, April 1970. T. Hickey. il Cath World 212:292-6 Mr '71
  See also
Nuns
CONVERSATION
  See also
Gossip

  Anecdotes, facetiae, satire, etc.
There's no mayonnaise in Ireland. W. Stanton. il Read Digest 98:153-4+ My '71
CONVERSATION television programs. See Television programs—Conversation programs
CONVERSION
On becoming a Catholic; excerpt from A sort of life. G. Greene. Commonweal 94:451-3 S 3 '71
On sidestepping proselytism. A. Blinderman. Chr Cent 88:655-6+ My 26 '71
Right to convert. D. H. C. Read. Chr Today 15:9-12 Ag 27 '71
  See also
Evangelistic work
Revivals
CONVERSION (defense industries) See Industrial demobilization
CONVERSION of energy. See Force and energy
CONVERTERS, Radio. See Radio converters
CONVERTERS, Television. See Television apparatus
CONVERTERS, Thermionic. See Thermionic converters
CONVERTIBLE bonds. See Bonds, Convertible

CONVERTIBLE debentures. See Bonds, Convertible
CONVERTIBLE sofas. See Furniture, Convertible
CONVERTIBLES (automobiles) See Automobiles
CONVICT labor
Danbury strikes. Commonweal 94:442 S 3 '71
Reflections from the pig farm; Lewisburg federal penitentiary. T. Lewis. Commonweal 94:499-500 S 24 '71
CONVICTS. See Prisoners
CONVOCATION of United Methodists for evangelical Christianity. See Religious conferences
CONVULSIONS
See also
Epilepsy
CONWAY, James F.
New turn on campus, the Christian commune. America 124:479-81 My 8 '71
CONWAY, John Horton
On cellular automata, self-reproduction, the Garden of Eden and the game, life. M. Gardner. il Sci Am 224:112-17 F '71 *
CONYERS, A. J.
God and man in the dialogue with Marxism. Chr Today 15:6-8 Jl 2 '71
CONYERS, John, 1929-
Eulogies and evasions. R. Sherrill. Nation 212:197-200 F 15 '71 *
COODY, Charles
Poor boy makes good. il por Newsweek 77:67 Ap 26 '71 *
There went the slam. D. Jenkins. il por Sports Illus 34:16-19 Ap 19 '71 *
COOK, Ann, and Mack, Herbert
Discovery center hustle. Ed Digest 36:50-3 Mr '71
COOK, Bruce
Ross Macdonald: the prince in the poorhouse. por Cath World 214:27-30 O '71
COOK, Chauncey William Wallace
He dishes out advice. por Bsns W p84 Mr 6 '71 *
COOK, Don
Scandinavia. Atlan 229:6+ Ja '72
COOK, Earl Ferguson
Flow of energy in an industrial society; with biographical sketch. il Sci Am 225: 28, 134-42+ bibliog(p244) S '71
COOK, Fred J.
Black Mafia moves into the numbers racket. il N Y Times Mag p26-7+ Ap 4 '71
Irregulars take the field. Nation 213:40-6 Jl 19 '71
Mayor Kenneth Gibson says: wherever the central cities are going, Newark is going to get there first. il N Y Times Mag p7-9+ Jl 25 '71
COOK, Geoffrey
New Delhi intercontinental hotel; poem. Nation 212:246 F 22 '71
COOK, James
Man who mapped the Pacific. A. Villiers. il por Nat Geog 140:297-349 S '71 *
COOK, Joan
Marriage. il Ladies Home J 88:192+ S '71
COOK, Margery L. See Stevens, J. G. jt. auth.
COOK, Marlow Webster
Excerpts from address, February 10, 1971. Cong Digest 50:112+ Ap '71
COOK, Robert E.
Mist that rolled into the trenches: chemical escalation in World war I. Bul Atom Sci 27:34-8 Ja '71
COOK, Theirrie
Giving peace a chance. Ramp Mag 9:16-17, Ap '71
COOK, Thomas
Fruits of temperance. por Forbes 107:23 Mr 1 '71 *
COOK, Thomas, and son
Plum for the picking. Forbes 107:22-3 Mr 1 '71
COOK books. See Cookbooks
COOK COUNTY, Ill.
Sulfur dioxide emissions from power plants: their effect on air quality. J. Golden and T. R. Mongan. il Science 171:381-3 Ja 29 '71
COOK COUNTY hospital. See Chicago—Hospitals
COOK ISLANDS
Wells, Fargo's Jekyll and Hyde. R. H. Dillon. il por Am West 8:28-33+ Mr '71
COOKBOOKS
Books in the field. A. Muffoletto. bibliog il por Wilson Lib Bul 45:653-63 Mr '71
Elizabeth David, England's first lady of the kitchen. H. McCully. por House B 113:190 S '71
Food and drink; with portfolio. A. H. Johnston. Pub W 200:24-9 O 18 '71

Mrs Beeton's book of household management, by I. Beeton. Review
Nat R 23:942-3 Ag 24 '71. F. Russell
See also
Booksellers and bookselling—Cookbooks

Bibliography
Cookbook for every palate. il Pub W 199:20-7 Mr 29 '71
Cookbooks 1971. H. McCully. House B 113: 147-9 N '71
Feast of cookbooks. il Changing T 25:41-4 Je '71
COOKE, Betty Lou
Bleeder; poem. Chr Cent 88:581 My 12 '71
Delivery; poem. Chr Cent 88:94 Ja 27 '71
COOKE, Eileen D. See Krettek, G. jt. auth.
COOKE, Hereward Lester, jr
France's palace of the arts. il Nat Geog 139: 796-831 Je '71
COOKE, Jack Kent
Purse snatchers. il pors Time 97:65-6 Ja 25 '71 *
Take the money and run. il por Newsweek 77:94-5 Mr 8 '71 *
COOKE, Lloyd M.
Story of Lloyd M. Cooke. S. P. Massie. il Chem 44:11 My '71 *
COOKE, Strathmore Ridley Barnott
35-mm camera for astrophotography. il Sky & Tel 41:109-13 F '71
COOKE, Terence James, cardinal
Peace of mind. por Look 35:23 Jl 27 '71

about
Variations on a theme; abortion pastoral. Commonweal 94:229 My 14 '71 *
COOKERS, Solar. See Solar cookers
COOKERY
Anticipating a busy summer? excerpts from Busy woman's cookbook. E. W. Manning and P. A. Ward. il Farm J 95:64-5+ Mr '71
Aquarian recipes. Sr School 98:26 F 15 '71
Barefoot in the kitchen; excerpts. M. Wallace. il Am Home 74:64-72+ Je '71
Blue ribbon beauties; recipes. E. W. Manning. il Farm J 95:44-5 N '71
Cooking lesson. J. Jaffry. See issues of American home
Cooking tips and kitchen secrets. il House & Gard 140:42+ Jl '71
Cooking: why the experts succeed; excerpts from Cooking with Helen McCully beside you. H. McCully. il Ladies Home J 88:100+ Ap '71
Cooking with a wok. il Sunset 146:74-8 F '71
Countdown for summer slimness; with recipes. il Todays Health 49:58-61 Ap '71
Date with a dish. See issues of Ebony
Easy meals for two; recipes for bake-in-the-oven meals. il Redbook 136:38+ Ja '71
Eat. M. Cantwell. See issues of Mademoiselle
Eating-out favorites you can fix at home. R. Molter. il Parents Mag 46:74-7+ Mr '71
Entertaining American style; an American summer cookbook; comp. by N. Haslam. S. Duwyenie. il House & Gard 140:76-7+ Ag '71
Festive feasting for the holidays. L. Driggs. il Har Yrs 11:36-9+ N '71
Flaming desserts, an introduction. Sunset 146:140+ F '71
Food. See issues of New York times magazine
Food gazette. M. McKendry. See issues of Vogue
Food questions you ask. See occasional issues of American home
Four seasons cookbook; excerpts. C. Adams. il Ladies Home J 88:140-1+ N '71
Freeze-ahead recipes. Z. Coulson. il Good H 172:98-113 Mr '71
From our kitchen; with recipes (title varies) L. Driggs. See issues of Harvest years
Happy New Year! with recipes. N. Hazelton. Nat R 23:1480-1 D 31 '71
House beautiful chef. J. Pépin. See issues of House beautiful
How to run a kitchen. Redbook 138:36+ Ja '72
Journal cookbook of the month. See issues of Ladies' home journal
Lessons from 2 great cooking schools; J. Dannenbaum and M. Moore-Betty. il pors House & Gard 140:72-6+ Jl '71
Living off the fat of the land; food jobs you've heard of and some you haven't. A. M. Cunningham. il Mlle 72:178-9+ F '71
[Month] menus; with recipes. See issues of Sunset
My family's favorite dish; with recipes. E. W. Manning. il Farm J 95:52-3 Ap '71

COOKERY—*Continued*

New York times international cookbook; excerpts. C. Claiborne. il Ladies Home J 88:102-3+ D '71

Nobody ever tells you these things. H. McCully. See issues of House beautiful

Oven meals that won't bruise the budget; with menus and recipes. D. Eby. il Bet Hom & Gard 49:72-8 F '71

Penny pincher's gourmet cookbook. il McCalls 98:104-10+ Mr '71

Quick and easy raw food cookbook; excerpts. M. Hodgson. il Ladies Home J 88:80-1+ Ag '71

Readers' choice, most popular recipes of 1971. il N Y Times Mag p54-5 Ja 9 '72

Redbook cookbook; excerpts. il Redbook 137: 98-103+ S '71

Redbook reader Mrs James A. Grace, an amateur who cooks like a pro; with menus and recipes. il por Redbook 136:106-12+ Ap '71

Redbook's timesaver cookbook. il Redbook 136:104-14 Mr '71

Saving graces. F. M. Crawford. See issues of American home

Seven who love to cook; with recipes. H. McCully. il House B 113:134-9+ N '71

Short-cut cooking. Z. Coulson. il Good H 172:104-21 My '71

Skillet-ry; with recipes. il Ladies Home J 88:94-5+ Ap '71

Special-occasion cookbook. Z. Coulson. il Good H 172:90-105 F '71

Sunset's kitchen cabinet. See issues of Sunset

Whole family cooks! Z. Coulson. il Good H 173:86-101 Ag '71

Why do we cook the food we eat? Sci Digest 69:83-4 My '71

Work wonders with blenders; with recipes. il Ladies Home J 88:148+ My '71

See also
Appetizers
Baking
Barbecue cookery
Bread
Breakfasts
Cake
Candy
Casserole cookery
Caterers and catering
Chafing dish cookery
Chowder
Christmas cookery
Coffee
Confectionery
Cookbooks
Cookies
Desserts
Diet
Dinners and dining
Dumplings
Electric cookery
Fondues
Frying
Griddle cakes
Ice cream, ices, etc.
Jelly, jam, etc.
Kitchen utensils
Liver as food
Macaroni
Meals
Meringue
Noodles
Pastry
Pickles and relishes
Pie
Puddings
Salads
Sandwiches
Sauces
Soufflés
Soups
Spreads (food)
Steaming (cookery)
Suppers
Tarts
Television programs—Cookery programs
Thanksgiving dinners
Toast
Waffles
Wedding meals

Bibliography
See Cookbooks—Bibliography

Competitions
Winners! McCall's cooking contest; with recipes. il McCalls 98:78-84+ Jl '71

Measurements
How many cups in a can? chart. Consumer Bul 54:13 My '71

Study and teaching
For Paris visitors, an afternoon at Le Cordon Bleu. il Sunset 147:235 O '71

Street cooking; California street cooking school, San Francisco. il Newsweek 77:67 My 17 '71

Anecdotes, facetiae, satire, etc.

Mastering cooking classes; attending Simone Beck classes. J. Davis. il Life 70:10-11 F 19 '71

Beer
Beer on a bun. il Bet Hom & Gard 49:24 Ap '71

Now you're cooking with beer. Field & S 76: 40 Je '71

Canned food
Creative cooking with canned foods. il Ebony 26:110+ Ja '71

Just living out of cans, and managing to live very well. il Sunset 146:184+ My '71

Work wonders with canned soups. il Ladies Home J 88:90+ Ja '71

Cereals
Cereals start and end the day right. Parents Mag 46:40+ N '71

It's crunchy and it's versatile. Sunset 146: 184 Je '71

Cheese
Cheese it, Italian style; mozzarella. C. Claiborne. il N Y Times Mag p72 Mr 7 '71

Cheese: the good life; with recipes. il Ladies Home J 89:94-5 Ja '72

Feasting with feta. C. Claiborne. il N Y Times Mag p72 Mr 21 '71

Fireside supper tonight is flowing gold, *raclette*. il Sunset 146:70-1 F '71

Golden cheese entrees. il Bet Hom & Gard 49:74 My '71

See also
Cheesecake

Chocolate
Chocolate cake, clouds, charlotte. Sunset 146: 191 Je '71

How to use chocolate. S. Whittier. il Good H 172:128 Mr '71

Coconut
Coconut: in a flan, in a sherbet. il Sunset 146:183 Mr '71

Corn meal
What's cooking?
    Cornmeal on the menu. M. C. Goldman. Org Gard & Farm 18:126-8 F '71

Cream, Sour
Sour cream specials. il Bet Hom & Gard 49: 121 Ap '71

Eggs
Cooking with eggs. il Good H 172:120-35 Ap '71

Egg as decoration; with recipes. House & Gard 139:24+ Ap '71

New egg products save you time and space. il Camp Mag 43:18-19 Je '71

See also
Omelets
Soufflés

Fish
Beyond fish 'n' chips; Dover sole veronique. M. Woodward. il Travel 136:18 N '71

Boneless trout. C. B. Colby. il Outdoor Life 147:58 Ap '71

Classic but quite simple; paupiettes de sole Dugléré. H. McCully. il House B 113:164-5 O '71

Classic fish dish: braised bass in red wine. R. A. Sokolov. il N Y Times Mag p89 O 24 '71

Crappie specials. C. B. Colby. il Outdoor Life 148:16 Jl '71

Eastertide tradition; red snapper creole. C. Claiborne. il N Y Times Mag p90 Ap 4 '71

Fine kettle of fish. C. B. Colby. il Outdoor Life 147:16 F '71

Fish your family can't resist. D. Eby. il Bet Hom & Gard 49:68-75+ Mr '71

Fishman talks about fish; ed. by H. McCully. J. Enea. il por House B 113:166+ O '71

France in the Caribbean; *blaff* Martiniquais. M. Woodward. il Travel 136:14 Ag '71

Northern Italian food; bagna cauda. M. Woodward. il Travel 137:76 Ja '72

Poached salmon in aspic. J. Jaffry. il Am Home 74:52-3+ Ag '71

Shrimp mousse with sole. il McCalls 99:59-60 O '71

Shrimp-stuffed flounder. il Bet Hom & Gard 49:34 D '71

COOKERY—Fish—*Continued*

Sole! The salmon! The cream! Sublime! dilled fish pate. J. Hewitt. il N Y Times Mag p79 N 14 '71

Sophisticated eel; eel matelote with raisins. R. A. Sokolov. il N Y Times Mag p57 S 19 '71

Soup and fish. il Sunset 146:90-1 Mr '71

Whitefish and grunion. C. B. Colby. il Outdoor Life 148:158 Ag '71

See also
Chowder
Cookery—Shellfish
Fish as food

Flowers

Flowers in a salad, leaves into fish packets; nasturtiums. il Sunset 146:208 My '71

Rose geranium in the kitchen. il Sunset 146:194 My '71

Fruit

Add a slice of sunshine; use of oranges. J. Uetz. il Am Home 74:84+ F '71

April's strawberries in refreshing cup desserts. il Sunset 146:188 Ap '71

Bakeshop banana cakes; with recipes. il Seventeen 29:128-9+ D '70

Blueberries baked in a torte. il Sunset 147:132 Jl '71

Blueberry time. il Ebony 26:162+ Je '71

Canned magic. il Redbook 136:66+ Mr '71

Cranberries; three courses. il Bet Hom & Gard 49:106-7 D '71

Fast and fancy banana desserts. il Bet Hom & Gard 49:75-6 Ja '71

Fast and fancy date desserts. il Bet Hom & Gard 49:97-8 O '71

Fresh pineapple: a tropical pinecone. il Bet Hom & Gard 49:93 Je '71

Fresh taste of spring; rhubarb and strawberries. E. W. Manning. Farm J 95:48-9 My '71

Fruits & vegetables; answers to your questions, plus recipes. R. H. Smithies. Good H 172:137-8+ Je '71

Hot papaya, icy papaya. il Sunset 146:201 My '71

Irresistible raisins! il Bet Hom & Gard 49:89 O '71

It's the time to taste fresh figs. il Sunset 147:140 S '71

Luscious fruit. A. D. Hawkes. il House & Gard 139:127-8+ My '71

Merry month of melons. il Ladies Home J 88:100-1+ Jl '71

Nature's table; the apple harvest. Seventeen 30:162 O '71

New cranberry turkey trimming. il Sunset 147:169 N '71

To celebrate with strawberries,three glorious ways to go. il Sunset 146:162-3 Je '71

Touch of fresh raspberry. il Sunset 147:102 Ag '71

What could be peachier? with recipes. il Seventeen 30:116-17+ Jl '71

What's cooking?

So who needs perfect apples? R. Tirrell. Org Gard & Farm 18:130+ O '71

Winning ways with dried fruits. J. Uetz. il Am Home 74:110+ O '71

Work wonders with applesauce. il Ladies Home J 88:138+ S '71

Work wonders with cranberries. il Ladies Home J 88:142+ N '71

See also
Canning and preserving

Game

Chuck bonus. C. B. Colby. il Outdoor Life 147:26 Je '71

Cook with a can opener; add can of soup. B. K. Fraser. il Field & S 75:46 Mr '71

Cooking venison? Keep it simple. F. Luks. il Outdoor Life 147:214 Mr '71

Deer liver on a stick. W. H. Hohensee. il Outdoor Life 148:84 N '71

First get yourself two rabbits. Sunset 146:227 My '71

Game dinner comin' up. H. G. Tapply. il Field & S 76:74 N '71

Good any time; roast venison with poivrade sauce and sweet and sour cabbage. C. Claiborne. N Y Times Mag p49 F 14 '71

Grin and bear it. C. B. Colby. Outdoor Life 147:16 Ja '71

Hunter cooks. H. J. Samuels. il Outdoor Life 157:84+ F '71

Pheasant family-style; Escoffier's pheasant with sour cream; and Ed Giobbi's fagiano al modo mio. R. A. Sokolov. il N Y Times Mag p34 D 19 '71

Reindeer recipes. C. B. Colby. il Outdoor Life 147:46 Mr '71

We love venison. C. J. Anderson. il Field & S 75:76-7+ F '71

Garnishes

Things mother never taught you about garnishes. il Ladies Home J 88:150 My '71

Leftovers

After yesterday's feast, what can you do for an encore? il Redbook 137:116-18+ My '71

Day after; a brand new dish. Sunset 147:164 D '71

Magic with leftovers. F. M. Crawford. il Am Home 74:108+ My '71

Second-time ham. N. Hopkins. il Bet Hom & Gard 49:124 N '71

Turkey makes a tempting comeback. il Parents Mag 46:92-4+ N '71

Marshmallows

Work wonders with marshmallows; with recipes. il Ladies Home J 88:98+ Ap '71

Meat

ABC's of steak. il Am Home 74:110 Mr '71

April fool! fancy foods. il Ebony 26:170+ Ap '71

Bachelor buffet; rice-apricot stuffed pork. il Bet Hom & Gard 49:26 F '71

Beef 'n' brew. il McCalls 98:78-9 Jl '71

Big chuck roast comes home and then comes apart. il Sunset 146:170 Mr '71

Budget steaks. il Ladies Home J 88:144-5+ My '71

Burgers but different. il Bet Hom & Gard 49:112-13 Ap '71

Buy it big, cut it small. M. Happel. il Ladies Home J 88:136-7+ S '71

Cookout franks. P. Pollock. il Bet Hom & Gard 49:62 Je '71

Dining at a German spa; sauerbraten Kaiserhof. M. Woodward. il Travel 135:75 F '71

Discovery of beef heart. Sunset 146:87 Ja '71

Easy oven ways with ribs. Sunset 146:98 Ja '71

Elegant braised beef. il McCalls 98:106+ My '71

Fast and fancy ground beef dishes. il Bet Hom & Gard 49:89-90 S '71

Fast and fancy steaks. il Bet Hom & Gard 49:77-8 Jl '71

First you pound your veal then you sauté it quickly. il Sunset 146:208 Ap '71

Flank steak, for the cook in a hurry. il Sunset 146:158 Mr '71

From Florence, savory liver pâté. Sunset 147:170 O '71

Go Greek with lamburgers. il Seventeen 30:164-5+ S '71

Good rich potpies; meat pies. il Redbook 138:94-6+ Ja '72

Ground lamb into meatballs; spiced, lively. il Sunset 146:106 F '71

Hamburger: America's sweetheart; excerpt from Hamburger. N. Hazelton. il Ladies Home J 88:88-9+ Ja '71

Hearty main dishes that make the most of your money. R. Molter. il Parents Mag 46:103-6+ S '71

Home at 6; dinner at 7; meatballs. il Redbook 137:120-2+ O '71

If you think you are ready for tripe. Sunset 147:191 N '71

It's called zampino; zampino or ham with beans bretonne. il N Y Times Mag p93 O 17 '71

It's the sauce that makes the meatballs. il Sunset 147:114 Jl '71

Korean way with hamburger. il Sunset 147:206 O '71

Lamb ideas for dinner tonight. il Sunset 146:182 My '71

Lamb shanks baked with rice or limas. Sunset 147:202 O '71

Make mine falafel; flat bread; lamb kebabs; spiced ground lamb. J. Hewitt. il N Y Times Mag p34 Ag 29 '71

Many guises of the hamburger. J. Hewitt. il N Y Times Mag p49 Ag 22 '71

Meatballs international; with recipes. M. Happel. il Ladies Home J 88:138-9+ N '71

On a bed of spinach; sweetbreads Florentine. il N Y Times Mag p96 N 21 '71

Out of the oven, your own jerky. Sunset 147:157 S '71

Picnic meat loaves. il Sunset 147:84-5 Ag '71

Plump cherries with the veal. Sunset 146:160 Je '71

Pork balls with cheese overtones. Sunset 146:173 Je '71

Pork loin becomes a meat roll. il Sunset 146:207 Ap '71

Pot roast. S. Whittier. il Good H 173:86 O '71

Puerto Rican pot roast. E. Alston. il Look 35:42-3 Mr 9 '71

COOKERY—Meat—*Continued*

Put it to soak the night before; **Portuguese roast beef.** Sunset 146:202 My '71

Roasts; with roasting time and temperature chart. D. Eby. il Bet Hom & Gard 49:78-86+ O '71

Sellouts for summer meals. R. Molter. il Parents Mag 46:45-8+ Jl '71

Serving boiled beef the Austrian way. il Mc-Calls 98:34 Mr '71

Special on meat: the new pork and how to cook it. L. Wing. il Good H 174:129 Ja '72

Splurge or save with steak. il Bet Hom & Gard 49:87 Mr '71

Steak au Poivre. J. Jaffry. il Am Home 74:110-11 Ap '71

Steak; the American way. **M. McKendry.** Vogue 157:88+ F 1 '71

Summer baked ham. il McCalls 98:34-5 Ag '71

Summer rib round-up. M. Happel. il Ladies Home J 88:102-3+ Jl '71

Things mother never taught you about roasting. il Ladies Home J 88:92 Ja '71

Things mother never taught you about stuffing; with recipes. il Ladies Home J 88:60+ F '71

To a Texan's taste; roasted kid. C. Claiborne. il N Y Times Mag p85 My 16 '71

Tongue, not all that mysterious. Sunset 146:197 Mr '71

Versatile sausage. F. M. Crawford. il Am Home 74:80-1+ F '71

Wiener schnitzel. J. Jaffry. il Am Home 74:100-1 S '71

See also
Barbecue cookery
Cookery—Game
Stew

Milk

Dairy delights. L. Driggs. il Har Yrs 11:46-50 Je '71

Nuts

Froth of chestnuts. C. Claiborne. il N Y Times Mag p59-60 Ja 24 '71

Instead of peanut butter. il Sunset 147:221 N '71

Nuts before dessert; with vegetables. J. Hewitt. il N Y Times Mag p89+ Mr 28 '71

Organic food

Nature's table: seeds not just for the birds. il Seventeen 30:142 N '71

Reality food; menu, recipes, tips for an organic dinner. il Vogue 158:72-3 N 15 '71

Someone's in the kitchen with Maxime: Rusty Holzer, age two. M. McKendry. il pors Vogue 159:34 Ja 1 '72

Poultry

Chicken, always a bargain. il Bet Hom & Gard 49:66-7+ My '71

Chicken in every pot au feu. C. Claiborne. il N Y Times Mag p42 F 7 '71

Chicken, ready for company. D. Eby and P. Pollock. il Bet Hom & Gard 49:64-5+ My '71

Chicken trick: roast it with butter under the skin; with recipe. il McCalls 98:54+ Mr '71

Chicken with apricot, avocado. il Sunset 147:116 Jl '71

Eat; chicken in champagne. M. Cantwell. Mlle 73:80+ My '71

Game hens, five good ways to go. Sunset 146:210+ Ap '71

Good and cheap; chicken giblet stew; chicken noodle soup. J. Hewitt. il N Y Times Mag p57 F 28 '71

How to truss a bird two ways. J. Pepin. il House B 113:90-1 Je '71

Imperial Peking duck. J. Jaffry. il Am Home 74:106-8 O '71

It's roast duckling for dinner, with mushrooms or with red cabbage. il Sunset 146:190 Ap '71

Like drumsticks, tiny appetizers. il Sunset 147:124 S '71

Money-saving chicken dishes; recipes. il Good H 172:174 F '71

No-cook chicken dinners. M. Happel. il Ladies Home J 88:82-3+ Ag '71

Other birds for the big day. J. McCloskey. il Bet Hom & Gard 49:96 N '71

Pei-Mei's cold (and hot) salads. R. A. Sokolov. il N Y Times Mag p39 Jl 25 '71

Revisionist Peking duck. C. Claiborne. il N Y Times Mag p72+ Ap 25 '71

Smart cooks choose chicken. F. M. Crawford. il Am Home 74:98-9+ S '71

Step by step to perfect pan-fried chicken. il Bet Hom & Gard 49:82 My '71

Tasty canard: duck Nivernaise. il N Y Times Mag p76 O 31 '71

Things mother never taught you about roasting. il Ladies Home J 88:92 Ja '71

Things mother never taught you about stuffing; with recipes. il Ladies Home J 88:60+ F '71

Turkey comes to the table in its own hot roasting pot. il Sunset 147:162-3 N '71

Turkey roasting chart. Bet Hom & Gard 49:122 N '71

Turkey stuffings using rice. Sunset 147:202 N '71

Turkey: the varieties you can buy; How to roast a whole turkey. il Good H 173:218 N '71

Would you believe croquettes? chicken croquettes. C. Claiborne. il N Y Times Mag p82 Ap 18 '71

See also
Barbecue cookery
Cookery—Game
Thanksgiving dinners

Rhubarb

Fresh taste of spring. E. W. Manning. il Farm J 95:48-9 My '71

Rhubarb, delectable for dessert. il Bet Hom & Gard 49:70-1+ My '71

Rice

Fast and fancy rice main dishes. il Bet Hom & Gard 49:91-2 F '71

Rice: a lot for a little. il Parents Mag 46:92+ O '71

Winning ways with rice. J. Uetz. il Am Home 74:112+ Ap '71

Sea food

It's a seafood stroganoff. il Sunset 146:168 Je '71

See also
Cookery—Fish
Cookery—Shellfish

Shellfish

Bounty from the sea; with recipes. il Ladies Home J 88:136-7 Mr '71

Fish your family can't resist. D. Eby. il Bet Hom & Gard 49:68-75+ Mr '71

Good word for squid. il N Y Times Mag p61-2 My 23 '71

Hot saucy crab. il Sunset 146:122-3 My '71

How to barbecue lobster tails. il Bet Hom & Gard 49:10 Ag '71

Joy of eating in Belgium; baked eggs and shrimp. M. Woodward. il Travel 135:16 Ap '71

Light touch with oysters. il Sunset 146:238 Ap '71

Seafood pies with crab or shrimp. Sunset 146:164 Mr '71

Small shrimp: in aspic, in salad. il Sunset 146:215 Ap '71

Snails

Flourishes with food; equip yourself for snails. il McCalls 98:70 F '71

Vegetables

Art of precooking vegetables. il Sunset 146:224 My '71

Art of the artichoke. C. Claiborne. il N Y Times Mag p68-9 Mr 14 '71

Artichokes: how to eat a thistle and love it. il Bet Hom & Gard 49:96 Mr '71

Asparagus, a spring-tender treat. il Bet Hom & Gard 49:68+ My '71

At the root of the matter; with recipes. il Ladies Home J 89:104+ Ja '72

Benevolent bean. H. McCully. il House B 113:94-6+ F '71

Brussels sprouts bonanza. il Bet Hom & Gard 49:101 Ap '71

Camp chef; potato variety. C. B. Colby. il Outdoor Life 148:20 O '71

Christmas dinner not complete without a sweet potato dish. il Ebony 27:158+ D '71

Cool Italian idea, cook-ahead vegetables in halves, quarters, slices. il Sunset 147:174-5 O '71

Corn: America's most amazing plant. R. Rodale. il por Org Gard & Farm 18:30-5 Jl '71

Dried and delicious; nutritious peas and beans. il Ebony 26:188+ O '71

Dried split peas and lentils. il Redbook 136:106-7+ F '71

Fast and fancy corn dishes. il Bet Hom & Gard 49:73-4 Ag '71

Fine crop of prized potato dishes. E. W. Manning. il Farm J 95:74-5 F '71

Four delicious ways to make potatoes from scratch. il Sunset 146:146-7 Mr '71

Fresh vegetables! Z. Coulson. il Good H 173:94-106 Jl '71

Fresh vegetables highlight spring meals. R. Molter. il Parents Mag 46:60-3+ My '71

Fruits & vegetables; answers to your questions, plus recipes. R. H. Smithies. Good H 172:137-8+ Je '71

COOKERY—Vegetables—*Continued*
George Bernard Shaw's vegetarian recipes. R.
J. Minney. il por Harp Baz 104:151-3 O '71
Have a vegetable festival. il Ebony 26:96+
Jl '71
How to make vegetables unforgettable. F.
M. Crawford. il Am Home 74:102-4+ Ap
'71
Introduction to soybeans. Sunset 146:226+ Ap
'71
It's time for green tomato pie. il Sunset
147:134 S '71
Last of all you eat the container. il Sunset
147:198 O '71
Learn about leeks. il Bet Hom & Gard 49:
114 O '71
New seasoners add new life to fall vegetables.
Parents Mag 46:100 O '71
Nuts before dessert. J. Hewitt. il N Y Times
Mag p89+ Mr 28 '71
On a bed of spinach; sweetbreads Florentine.
il N Y Times Mag p96 N 21 '71
On the trail of the three sisters; food plants
of the original Americans; with recipes by
F. Gibbons. E. Gibbons. Natur Hist 80:
14-16+ F '71
Onion, gentle giant. H. McCully. il House
B 113:122-3+ Ap '71
Onions for holiday meals. il Bet Hom &
Gard 49:78 D '71
Pommes soufflées; puffed potatoes. J. Jaffry.
il Am Home 74:82-3 F '71
Preparing cucumbers, for salad and as a
vegetable. J. Pepin. il House B 113:79 Ag
'71
Prime time for summer vegetables. il Red-
book 137:96-7+ Ag '71
Pumpkin means more than pie. il Parents
Mag 46:96+ N '71
Some like them cooked; lettuce, radishes.
R. A. Sokolov. il N Y Times Mag p34 Ag
1 '71
Squash is to put things into. il Sunset 147:
154 D '71
Summer starter, a chilly slush. Sunset 147:
161 S '71
Tasty canard: duck Nivernaise. il N Y Times
Mag p76 O 31 '71
Tomatoes. il Ebony 26:144+ S '71
Vegetable casseroles for November. Sunset
147:179 N '71
Vegetables from the oven. il Bet Hom &
Gard 49:132 D '71
What's cooking?
Carrots, genuine garden gold. L. Riotte.
Org Gard & Farm 18:140+ Ap '71
Chinese wok for crisper vegetables. K.
McReynolds. il Org Gard & Farm 18:
127-9 D '71
Radishes are a must. K. Geneson. Org
Gard & Farm 18:126-7 N '71
Seven ways to stuff a pepper. E. Parsons.
Org Gard & Farm 18:94-5 Je '71
Spring treats, Chinese style. J. W. Holm.
il Org Gard & Farm 18:98-101 My '71
Surprises in the green patch. Org Gard
& Farm 18:132-3 Mr '71
Vacation sprouts. A. J. Cooley. Org Gard
& Farm 18:90-1 Jl '71
With fresh, green, tender asparagus. il Sun-
set 146:172-3 My '71
With leeks it's just a matter of knowing how.
il Sunset 147:208 N '71
See also
Canning and preserving

Anecdotes, facetiae, satire, etc.
Gourmet of the golden browns; french fried
potatoes. C. Trillin. il Life 71:14 Ag 27 '71
COOKERY, African
Gathering of West African dishes. il Good
H 173:164 Ag '71
Kitchen safari; excerpts. H. Hachten. il La-
dies Home J 88:140-1+ Mr '71
Thebouidienne: fish and rice dish at the
African chef in Harlem; interview. W.
Werner. New Yorker 47:44-5 N 6 '71
COOKERY, American
California cuisine in a capsule. H. McCully.
il House B 113:94-5+ Mr '71
Classic meals of the South. il Ebony 26:
174+ Ag '71
Cross-country tour of great American cook-
ing. il Good H 173:120-35 O '71
Great American cookout; western cookery.
C. Pepper. il Travel 136:56-61 O '71
Historic recipes from Mammy Pleasant. il
por Ebony 26:108+ F '71
Incomparable Creole cooking. F. M. Craw-
ford. il Am Home 74:84-5 Mr '71
Southern heirlooms. R. A. Sokolov. il N Y
Times Mag p 16 Jl 4 '71
Vibes from Verta Mae; soul gourmet cookery.
P. Garland. il pors Ebony 26:86-8+ Mr '71

What's new besides hamburgers? Great
American snacks; with recipes. il Seventeen
30:144-7+ Ap '71
COOKERY, Australian
Eat. M. Cantwell. Mlle 73:56+ O '71
COOKERY, Austrian
Wiener schnitzel. J. Jaffry. il Am Home 74:
100-1 S '71
COOKERY, Belgian
Joy of eating in Belgium; baked eggs and
shrimp. M. Woodward. il Travel 135:16 Ap
'71
COOKERY, Chinese
Chinese sweetness in pork, chicken. il Sun-
set 147:137 D '71
Chinese wok cookery. il Bet Hom & Gard
49:116 O '71
Cook-as-you-go Chinese lunch. V. Lee and
C. Claiborne. il pors House & Gard 140:
52-3+ Jl '71
Craig Claiborne cooks for a crowd; Mongol-
ian hot pot and chrysanthemum pot. C.
Claiborne. il por Harp Baz 104:78-9+ Ag
'71
Food from afar; Chinese egg rolls. il Bet Hom
& Gard 49:80 My '71
How to eat in Chinese. P. Brooks. il Sat R
54:38-9+ O 23 '71
Nobody ever tells you these things. H.
McCully. House B 113:38-9 S '71
Pei-Mei's cold (and hot) salads. R. A. Soko-
lov. il N Y Times Mag p39 Jl 25 '71
Revisionist Peking duck. C. Claiborne. il
N Y Times Mag p72+ Ap 25 '71
This appetizer idea is Chinese; water chest-
nut tumble. il Sunset 146:188 Je '71
COOKERY, Colombian
Discover Colombian cooking! il Good H
172:154 Mr '71
COOKERY, Creole. See Cookery, American
COOKERY, Cuban
Florida: the natives swing to Cuban cook-
ing. E. Alston. il Look 35:46-9 Ap 6 '71
COOKERY, Dutch
Variety dining in Holland; with recipes. M.
Woodward. il Travel 135:14 Je '71
COOKERY, Electric. See Electric cookery
COOKERY, English
English finesse; Mrs D. Mlinaric in her hus-
band's London studio. M. McKendry. il
por Vogue 158:34 S 15 '71
Nobody ever tells you these things. H. Mc-
Cully. House B 113:130-1 My '71
Someone's in the kitchen with Maxime; Lady
Arabella Boxer. M. McKendry. il por
Vogue 158:80+ D '71
Someone's in the kitchen with Maxime:
Penelope Gilliatt. M. McKendry. il por
Vogue 158:66 O 15 '71
Stately-home cooking. M. McKendry. Vogue
157:22 Mr 15 '71
COOKERY, Finnish
Dining in Finland. M. Woodward. il Travel
136:26 S '71
COOKERY, Foreign. See Cookery, Interna-
tional
COOKERY, French
Accent is garlic; daube. il N Y Times Mag
p47 Je 27 '71
Bûche de Nöel; Christmas yule log; with
recipe. J. Pépin. il House B 113:74-5+ D
'71
Carême, ou la crème de la crème. M. Bishop.
il por Horizon 13:70-1 Wint '71
Chicken in every pot au feu. C. Claiborne.
il N Y Times Mag p42 F 7 '71
Cook laughing; recipes of Michel Warren
and Yves Larsen. M. McKendry. Vogue
157:84 Ap 1 '71
Cooking lesson. J. Jaffry. See issues of Amer-
ican home
Food from afar: France; chocolate soufflé
with grand marnier sauce. il Bet Hom &
Gard 49:126 Ap '71
France in the Caribbean; blaff Martiniquais.
M. Woodward. il Travel 136:14 Ag '71
Gallic wedding treat; croquembouche, cream
puffs. R. A. Sokolov. il N Y Times Mag
p45 Ag 8 '71
Madeleine recaptured. R. A. Sokolov. il N Y
Times Mag p66 Je 13 '71
Mexican enchiladas wrapped in French
crêpes. il Sunset 147:176+ O '71
Most elegant; Savarin: rum cake. R. A.
Sokolov. il N Y Times Mag p29 Ja 2 '72
Quiche subverted; excerpt from Soufflés,
quiches, mousses and the random egg. G.
Bradshaw. Vogue 157:44+ Ap 1 '71
Rich, robust and rewarding; the food of
Normandy. B. H. Fussell. il Holiday 49:
54-5+ Mr '71
Secret of great women chefs. W. Root and
M. Eckley. il McCalls 98:70-7+ Ag '71

COOKERY, French—*Continued*
Sole! The salmon! The cream! Sublime! dilled fish pate. J. Hewitt. il N Y Times Mag p79 N 14 '71
Sophisticated eel; eel matelote with raisins. R. A. Sokolov. il N Y Times Mag p57 S 19 '71

Terminology
How to get and keep the upper hand with a French menu. C. Stinnett. Holiday 49:8+ F '71

COOKERY, German
Dining at a German spa; sauerbraten Kaiserhof. M. Woodward. il Travel 135:75 F '71
German dark rye bread. il Bet Hom & Gard 49:96 D '71

COOKERY, Greek
Feasting with feta. C. Claiborne il N Y Times Mag p72 Mr 21 '71
Go Greek with lamburgers. il Seventeen 30: 164-5+ S '71
How the Greeks make honey puffs. il Sunset 147:214 O '71

COOKERY, Indian (East Indian)
Gastronomy of India. M. Woodward. il Travel 136:12 Jl '71

COOKERY, Indonesian
Here are Indonesian party recipes. Sunset 147:86-7 Ag '71
Rice table idea. il Sunset 147:58-9 Ag '71

COOKERY, International
All manner of food; excerpts. M. Field. il Ladies Home J 88:92-3+ F '71
Food gazette (cont) M. McKendry. Vogue 157:29+ F 15 '71
International chef. M. Woodward. See issues of Travel
Introduction to fresh green coriander. Sunset 146:168+ My '71
Joys of ethnic cooking. il McCalls 98:116-21+ F '71
Take home recipes make great travel souvenirs. il Ladies Home J 88:68 My '71
See also
Christmas cookery

COOKERY, Iranian
Persian treat. J. Hewitt. il N Y Times Mag p79 O 10 '71

COOKERY, Israeli
Israeli cooking: multi-national mix. L. Wing. il Good H 173:240 N '71

COOKERY, Italian
Arabella Lacloche cooks Italian. M. McKendry. il por Vogue 158:108+ O 1 '71
Cool Italian idea, cook-ahead vegetables in halves, quarters, slices. il Sunset 147:174-5 O '71
Doing your own pizza. il Bet Hom & Gard 49:20 Ja '71
Food of Italy, by W. Root. Review Newsweek il 78:116+ D 6 '71. S. K. Oberbeck
From Florence, savory liver pâté. Sunset 147:170 O '71
It's called zampino: zampino or ham with beans bretonne. il N Y Times Mag p93 O 17 '71
It's torta rustica. il Sunset 147:110-11 Jl '71
Man, oh, manicotti, what a pasta! il McCalls 98:26+ Je '71
Northern Italian food; bagna cauda. M. Woodward. il Travel 137:76 Ja '72
Palate revolution. il Forbes 107:35+ F 15 '71
Pasta al pesto. J. Jaffry. il Am Home 74: 56-7 Jl '71
Pizza of your own. R. A. Sokolov. il N Y Times Mag p86 N 7 '71
Pizzas: two easy ways to go. Sunset 147: 99 Ag '71
Rise of the pizza. il Newsweek 78:78 O 18 '71
Rosemary stew. il N Y Times Mag p47 Ag 15 '71
Sauces for spaghetti lovers. il Redbook 136:104-5+ F '71
Someone's in the kitchen with Maxime: Gabriella Canfield. M. McKendry. il por Vogue 158:90+ N 1 '71
Tuscan dumpling: malfatti. J. Hewitt. il N Y Times Mag p36 Jl 18 '71
See also
Macaroni

COOKERY, Jewish
Dumplings in the soup are Jewish matzo balls. il Sunset 147:232 O '71

COOKERY, Korean
Korean way with hamburger. il Sunset 147: 206 O '71

COOKERY, Mexican
Chicken enchiladas. il Bet Hom & Gard 49: 10 N '71
Company begs for this main dish; enchiladas. il Farm J 95:46 Ja '71

Eggs, tortillas, cheese go together. il Sunset 147:198+ N '71
Fiesta dining in Guadalajara; guacamole. M. Woodward. il Travel 135:63 Mr '71
Food from afar: Mexico; gazpacho. il Bet Hom & Gard 49:80 Je '71
How to make your own crusty *bolillos*. il Sunset 147:216 O '71
In Mexico much is up to the cook; quesadillas. il Sunset 147:204 O '71
Mexican patio party; with recipes. il Sunset 147:60-1 S '71
Out of the fire-pan and into you; burritos. il Sunset 146:84-5 Ja '71
Out of the pumpkin, Aztec soup from Mexico. il Sunset 147:100-1 O '71
South of the border soup; corn soup and guacamole. il N Y Times Mag p29 S 5 '71

COOKERY, Middle Eastern
Make mine falafel; flat bread; lamb kebabs; spiced ground lamb. J. Hewitt. il N Y Times Mag p34 Ag 29 '71
Taking liberties with moussaka. Sunset 147:166 D '71
Wild and cool life of the Mideast brought West. il Look 35:34 S 21 '71

COOKERY, North African
Arabs' delight; couscous. C. Claiborne. il N Y Times Mag p59 Ja 17 '71
Coucous, a North African delight. il House B 113:19 Jl '71

COOKERY, Norwegian
Young and hungry; excerpts. S. Taylor. il Ladies Home J 88:146-7+ My '71

COOKERY, Oriental
Chopstick soups. il Sunset 146:106-7 My '71
Skillet-ry: with recipes. il Ladies Home J 88:94-5+ Ap '71
See also
Cookery, Chinese

COOKERY, Ornamental
Easy prefab approach to cooky house architecture. il Sunset 147:60-1 D '71
Fine arts of the kitchen; excerpts from Fine arts cookbook. il McCalls 98:88-94+ Ap '71
House Hansel and Gretel found. il Ladies Home J 88:104 D '71
See also
Cookery—Garnishes
Cookies

COOKERY, Outdoor
Camp chef. C. Colby. See issues of Outdoor life
Camp cooking home style. D. Eby. il Bet Hom & Gard 49:54-9+ Ag '71
Cookout franks. P. Pollock. il Bet Hom & Gard 49:62 Je '71
Eat freely. M. McKendry. Vogue 158:46 Jl '71
Picnic menus without chicken. Bet Hom & Gard 49:70 Je '71
Pot that does it all; the Dutch oven. T. Trueblood. il Field & S 75:20+ Ap '71
Right fire; open-fire cooking. C. B. Colby. il Outdoor Life 148:15 N '71
Trail cookery simplified. R. J. Whitcomb. il Outdoor Life 147:74-7+ Je '71
What's cooking?
Underground recipes for cool summer cookery. Org Gard & Farm 18:110-11 Ag '71
See also
Barbecue cookery
Camp cookery
Outdoor meals
Smoke ovens

Equipment and supplies
Build this patio appliance center. W. C. Leckey. il Pop Mech 136:124-7 Ag '71

COOKERY, Philippine
Carne asada the Philippine way. Sunset 147:173 O '71
Filipina cuisine. M. Woodward. il Travel 135: 26 My '71
Lumpia is a wrapper with a pork-shrimp filling. il Sunset 147:192 N '71
Quick introduction to the Philippines. Sunset 146:109 F '71

COOKERY, Puerto Rican
Puerto Rican pot roast. E. Alston. il Look 35:42-3 Mr 9 '71

COOKERY, Quantity
Cooking for the dozens; with menus and recipes. L. Driggs. il Har Yrs 11:25-32 Mr '71

COOKERY, Scandinavian
See also
Cookery, Norwegian

COOKERY, Southern. See Cookery, American

COOKERY, Spanish
Conversation food. F. Guth. il House & Gard 139:85-91 F '71
Variation on coffee and. . ; Spanish hot chocolate and churros. R. A. Sokolov. il N Y Times Mag p 82 O 3 '71

COOKERY, Swiss
Fireside supper tonight is flowing gold, *raclette*. il Sunset 146:70-1 F '71
Reward: lunch at the Fondue pot. New Yorker 47:33 Ap 17 '71
Something to yodel about; veal-in-cream with rösti potatoes. C. Claiborne. il N Y Times Mag p59 Ja 31 '71

COOKERY, Viennese. See Cookery, Austrian

COOKERY, West Indian
Season it Caribbean. E. Alston. il Look 35: 68-9 O 19 '71
Stew surprises from the Caribbean. Sunset 146:139 F '71

COOKERY books. See Cookbooks

COOKERY by children
Frozen dough to stretch, knead, cut, twist, bake, show off, and serve for Easter breakfast. il Sunset 146:182-3 Ap '71
Susan, our beginning cook. S. Whittier. See issues of Good housekeeping
12-year-old chef makes Caesar salad at the table while everybody watches. il Sunset 146:110-11 F '71

COOKERY by men
Authors & editors; interview. ed. by L. P. Freilicher. C. Claiborne. por Pub W 200: 13-15 N 8 '71
Chefs of the West. See issues of Sunset
Company for dinner? Engine 310, Ladder 174, Brooklyn, that is. K. V. Brown. il pors Todays Health 49:46-9+ My '71
Eat; bachelor on a budget. W. Beckman. Mlle 73:186+ Ag '71
He cooks! See issues of Better homes and gardens
My brother's cooking; with recipes. S. Peirce. por Seventeen 30:162 Mr '71
Trick or *truste*: here comes Joe Hyde; New York's dashing sportsman-chef. R. H. Boyle. il por Sports Illus 35:44-6+ N 8 '71

COOKERY contests. See Cookery—Competitions

COOKERY for animals. See Feeding and feeding stuffs—Cookery

COOKFAIR, Arthur S.
Patent talk. Radio-Electr 42:53+ F '71

COOKIES
At long last Chinatown's secret is out; fortune cookies. il Sunset 146:48-9 Ja '71
Bazaar foods. il Bet Home & Gard 49:74-5+ S '71
Collection of the best cookies ever baked; excerpt from Homemade cookies. E. W. Manning. il Farm J 95:44-5+ O '71
Crèche of Christmas cookies. il McCalls 99: 108+ D '71
Eat; Christmas cookies. M. Cantwell. Mlle 74:167-8 D '71
Elephant cutout cookies from single cooky sheets with no waste at all. il Sunset 147:178 D '71
Extra nutrients, but they still taste as oatmeal cookies should. il Sunset 146:162 Mr '71
Fancy but easy cookies as gifts. il Sunset 147:161-2 D '71
Hand-painted Christmas cookies. il Farm J 95:38 D '71
Holiday cookies. R. Molter. il Parents Mag 46:74-8+ D '71
How to make our Raggedy Ann & Andy cookies. il Good H 173:10 D '71
Madeleine recaptured. R. A. Sokolov. il N Y Times Mag p66 Je 13 '71
Pie-bar cookies. Farm J 95:42 N '71
Pine nuts add the crunch. il Sunset 146:210 My '71
Shortbread for your coffee break. il Sunset 146:190 Mr '71
Spicy cookies in slices or squares. Sunset 146:184 Mr '71
These cookies are bone hard on purpose. il Sunset 146:202 Ap '71
These sturdy cookies can survive the adventurous trip to school. Sunset 147:209-10 O '71

COOKING. See Cookery

COOKING kettles. See Kettles

COOKING schools. See Cookery—Study and teaching

COOKING thermometers. See Thermometers, Cooking

COOKING utensils. See Kitchen utensils

COOKING utensils, Electric. See Household appliances, Electric

COOKS
Secret of great women chefs. W. Root and M. Eckley. il McCalls 98:70-7+ Ag '71
See also
Carême, M. A.
Dannenbaum, J.
Hyde, J.
Kerr, G.
Moore-Betty, M.

COOKWARE. See Kitchen utensils

COOLANTS for automobile radiators. See Automobile engines—Cooling

COOLEY, Alfaretta Johnson
What's cooking? Org Gard & Farm 18:90-1 Jl '71

COOLEY, Candace. See Dankman, L. jt. auth.

COOLEY, Denton Arthur
Hearts, by T. Thompson. Review
Bsns W por p 12 O 9 '71. S. Brown •
Time pors 98:94-6 O 25 '71. K. R. Johnson •

COOLIDGE bank and trust company. See Boston—Banks

COOLING
See also
Air conditioning
Automobiles engines—Cooling
Gas and oil engines—Cooling
Heat transmission

COOLING equipment
See also
Air conditioning equipment

COOLING of livestock. See Livestock, Cooling of

COOLING towers
Cooling towers. R. D. Woodson. il Sci Am 224:70-8 My '71
Utilities burn over cooling towers. il Bsns W p52+ Ap 3 '71

COOMBE, B. G.
GA₃₃: a polar gibberellin with high biological potency. bibliog il Science 172:856-7 My 21 '71

COOMBES, J. P.
New ways to attack old snow-ice problems. il por Am City 86:63-5 N '71

COOMBS, Arthur E.
Australian 12½-inch Buchroeder relay telescope. il Sky & Tel 42:302-8 N '71

COOMBS, Donald J.
Information exchange. il Wilson Lib Bul 45: 1010-11 Je '71

COOMBS, Orde
Soul in suburbia. il Harper 244:24-6+ Ja '72
(ed) See Samuelson, P. Where has all the money gone?

COON hounds. See Hounds

COONS, William N.
Attica graduate tells his story. il por N Y Times Mag p20-1+ O 10 '71

COONS. See Raccoons

COOPER, Alan F. jr. See Crowe, J. H. jt. auth.

COOPER, Alice
Rock in the androgynous zone. A. Goldman. por Life 71:16 Jl 30 '71 •

COOPER, Bette
Night Miss America vanished; excerpt from There she is: the life and times of Miss America. F. Deford. il por Ladies Home J 88:104-5+ S '71 •

COOPER, Cary W. and others
Thyrocalcitonin: stimulation of secretion by pentagastrin. bibliog il Science 172:1238-40 Je 18 '71

COOPER, Charles R.
New climate for personal responses to literature in the classroom. Engl J 60:1063-71 N '71

COOPER, Chester L.
CIA and decision-making. For Affairs 50: 223-36 Ja '72

COOPER, David
Topography of love; excerpt from The death of the family. Vogue 157:104-5+ Ja 15 '71

COOPER, Douglas
Daddy's travels with a diaper bag. il Good H 172:69-70+ Ap '71
To Alaska in 3½ days. il Yachting 129:56-7+ My '71

COOPER, Ed
Nature's jewels; photographs. Am For 77: 44-5 Mr '71

COOPER, Gloria (Vanderbilt) See Vanderbilt, G.

COOPER, Henry
Our 'enery gets the 'ook. J. Kirshenbaum. pors Sports Illus 34:26-7 Mr 29 '71 •

COOPER, Henry S. F. jr
Letter from the space center (cont) New Yorker 46:66-74 Ja 9; 47:120+ Ap 17; 40-2+ Jl 17 '71

COOPER, James Fenimore
James Fenimore Cooper and the environment. D. R. Noble. il por Cons 26:3-7 O '71 •

COOPER, Jane
Life on De Witt. il por Time 99:73 Ja 10
'72 *
COOPER, Kenneth Hardy
Art of aerobics. il por Time 97:60 Mr 8 '71 *
COOPER, Martin
Average sensual man. il por Opera N 35:6-
11 Mr 27 '71
COOPER, Paulette
Case of the wrejected writer. Pub W 199:19
My 10 '71
COOPER, R. Conrad
Airlines move into closer formation. por
Bsns W p98 Ag 14 '71 *
COOPER, Richard A. and Uzmann, J. R.
Migrations and growth of deep-sea lobsters,
homarus americanus. bibliog il Science 171:
288-90 Ja 22 '71
COOPER, Robert B. Jr
All American sports amplifier. il Pop Electr
35:29-35+ S '71
Break through radio pollution: use etched
coils in FM preamp. il Radio-Electr 42:33-7
Je '71
COOPER, Sidney A.
Appliance dealer with a real clout. il por
Bsns W p76+ N 6 '71 *
COOPER, Washington Bogart
Three Tennessee painters. B. H. Bishop. il
Antiques 100:432-7 S '71 *
COOPER, Wyatt
Does everybody want to be somebody. il
Harp Baz 104:134-5 My '71
COOPER-Hewitt museum of decorative arts
and design. See Cooper union for the ad-
vancement of science and art
COOPER union for the advancement of science
and art
Cooper-Hewitt museum: progress report. S.
B. Sherrill. il Antiques 101:114 Ja '72
COOPERATION
See also
Agriculture, Cooperative
Bees (cooperative gatherings)
Collective settlements
Colleges and universities—Cooperation
Intercommunity cooperation
Interracial cooperation
Library cooperation
Religious cooperation
COOPERATIVE agriculture. See Agriculture,
Cooperative
COOPERATIVE apartment houses. See Apart-
ment houses—Cooperative ownership
COOPERATIVE art galleries. See Art—Galleries
and museums
COOPERATIVE associations
Closing ranks on poverty. il Ebony 26:86-7+
Ag '71
Cooperatives that work:
Democratic, up to a point. P. Barnes.
New Repub 166:17-19 Ja 1 '72
Health care in Seattle. P. Barnes. New
Repub 165:12-13 D 18 '71
Scrimping together; food cooperatives. il
Newsweek 77:68 Ap 5 '71
Unorthodox ministry of Leon H. Sullivan.
P. Garland. il pors Ebony 26:112-14+ My
'71
See also
Credit unions
Dairymens associations
Mantua industrial development corporation
Marketing, Cooperative
COOPERATIVE buying. See Purchasing, Co-
operative
COOPERATIVE credit associations. See Credit
unions
COOPERATIVE education. See Education, Co-
operative
COOPERATIVE living establishments. See Col-
lective settlements
COOPERATIVE marketing. See Marketing, Co-
operative
COOPERATIVE purchasing. See Purchasing,
Cooperative
COOPERATIVE societies. See Cooperative as-
sociations
COOPERSTOWN, N.Y.
See also
National baseball hall of fame and museum
Hospitals
Mini-medical center; Mary Imogene Bassett
hospital. il Time 97:56 Ja 25 '71
COORDINATES
Celestial coordinates. J. Stokley. il Sci N
100:217 S 25 '71
Sky full of lines; how to read celestial co-
ordinates. K. L. Franklin. il Sci Digest 70:
22-9 Ag '71

COORDINATION compounds
Antiprismatic coordination about xenon:
the structure of nitrosonium octafluorox-
enate(VI) S. W. Peterson and others. bib-
liog il Science 173:1238-9 S 24 '71
Quadratic elongation: a quantitative measure
of distortion in coordination polyhedra.
K. Robinson and others. bibliog il Science
172:567-70 My 7 '71
COORS, Adolph, company
How one company trains in the great out-
doors. il Bsns W p40-1+ Jl 24 '71
COORS, William
Coors cleans up despite his anger. il Bsns W
p70+ N 20 '71 *
COOVER, Robert
Beginnings; story. Harper 244:82-7 Ja '72
COPAN, Honduras
Lost world of Copan. W. B. Alig. il Américas
23:S32-5 Je '71
COPE, Edward Drinker
Professor Cope vs. Professor Marsh. J. Pe-
nick. il pors Am Heritage 22:4-13+ Ag
'71 *
COPE, Myron
Golf. Sports Illus 35:44+ Ag 9 '71
Often bloody, but uncowed. por Sports Illus
34:50-2+ My 10 '71
COPE, Robert G.
Conflict between politics and evaluation in
higher education. bibliog Sch & Soc 99:
218-20 Ap '71
COPE program
COPE expands its program: from trainee to
professional. A. DeMirjian, jr. il Pub W
201:50 Ja 3 '72
COPELAND, James C.
Regulation of chromosome replication in
bacillus subtilis: marker frequency analy-
sis after amino acid starvation. bibliog il
Science 172:159-61 Ap 9 '71
COPELAND, Jerry
Fine art of mating a camper and pickup. il
Pop Sci 198:74-5+ Mr '71
New way to hitch your trailer. il Pop Sci
199:102+ Ag '71
Tag axle: one more for the road. il Pop Sci
199:52 O '71
COPELAND, Lammot du Pont, 1905-
Moving down at Du Pont. pors Time 97:84-
5 My 3 '71 *
COPELAND, Lammot du Pont, 1933?-
Moving down at Du Pont. pors Time 97:84-
5 My 3 '71 *
COPELAND, LaVon
Nonstop Timmy, our two-year-old terror.
il Redbook 137:38+ O '71
COPELAND, Peter
Dress parade; excerpts from America's fight-
ing men; paintings. Am Heritage 22:4-11
O '71
COPELAND, Ronald M. and others
Use LIFO to offset inflation. bibliog f il Har-
vard Bsns R 49:91-100 My '71
COPENHAGEN
Description
Copenhagen. J. D. Weaver. il Holiday 49:56-
9+ F '71
Music
Report:
Monteverdi's Ritorno d'Ulisse in patria.
R. Croan. Opera N 35:26-7 My 15 '71
Wozzeck; Simon Boccanegra and Han-
del's Samson. R. Croan. Opera N 35:32
Mr 27 '71
Theater
Byways of Europe: Copenhagen. G. Loney. il
Opera N 35:29 F 13 '71
COPILOTS. See Air pilots
COPLAND, Jeri
(ed) See Crews, E. Help wanted: foster moth-
ers
COPPER bracelets. See Bracelets
COPPER enameled mosaics. See Mosaics
COPPER in the body
Biological function of copper. G. W. Evans.
Chem 44:10-11 Je '71
COPPER industry
See also
Anaconda company
Cerro corporation
Kennecott copper corporation
Chile
Chile: the big grab. il Time 98:97 O 11 '71
Copper crisis. Newsweek 78:77 O 11 '71
Copper pays the price of nationalism. il Bsns
W p38+ Ag 21 '71
Sticking point; implications of nationaliza-
tion on American companies. il Newsweek
78:38+ Jl 26 '71
COPPER jewelry. See Jewelry

COPPER mines and mining
Profiles: C. Park and D. Brower. J. McPhee.
  por New Yorker 47:42-8+ Mr 20 '71
    See also
Anaconda company
Kennecott copper corporation

Chile
Breaking ranks. il Forbes 108:27 S 15 '71

Mexico
Instant millionaire: Colonel W. C. Greene in
  fact and folklore. C. L. Sonnichsen. bibliog
  il pors Am West 8:4-9+ N '71
COPPERHEADS
Copperhead in New York. R. G. Arndt. il
  Cons 25:18-19 Ap '71
COPPOLINO, Carl Anthony
  F. Lee Bailey's strangest murder case; ex-
  cerpt from The defense never rests; ed. by
  H. Aronson. F. L. Bailey. il por Ladies
  Home J 88:122-3+ N '71 •
COPTIC church
    See also
Copts
COPTIC manuscripts. See Manuscripts, Coptic
  (papyri)
COPTS
True Jews. il por Newsweek 78:48 N 29 '71
COPY writing. See Advertising copy
COPYING processes
Architectural firm uses half-size drawing sys-
  tem. il Arch Rec 149:58 My '71
Copier for the home office. il Consumer Bul
  55:26-7 Ja '72
Scholarship, piracy and the copying machine.
  C. B. Grannis. Pub W 199:34 Je 14 '71
Turn on with 3M's color-in-color machine.
  A. Francekevich. il Pop Phot 69:32+ S '71
Universal Xerox life compiler machine. W.
  Jovanovich. Am Scholar 40:249-55 Spr '71
    See also
Microfilms
Mimeograph
Xerox corporation
COPYRIGHT
Downgrading the protection of international
  copyright; Universal copyright and Berne
  conventions. I. Karp. Pub W 200:pt2 143-7
  S 27 '71
Historic revision of world copyright. Pub W
  200:29-30 Ag 9 '71
International copyright turns another corner;
  Berne copyright convention and Stockholm
  protocol. B. Ringer. Pub W 200:22-5 N
  8 '71
Legal rights for writers. J. Pollett. Writer 84:
  24 Ap '71
New deal in int'l copyright? Stockholm pro-
  tocol, Berne copyright union and Univer-
  sal copyright convention. R. H. Smith. Pub
  W 200:33 N 8 '71
Sci-tech publishers wary about proposed
  UNESCO information network: World sci-
  ence information system, UNISIST. Pub W
  200:28 N 8 '71
Universal Xerox life compiler machine. W.
  Jovanovich. Am Scholar 40:249-55 Spr '71
    See also
Royalties
UNESCO—International copyright information
  center
World intellectual property organization

Broadcasting rights
Copyright extended one more year; com-
  promise on the CATV issue. S. Wagner.
  Pub W 200:15 N 29 '71
FCC proposals on CATV and copyright. G.
  Krettek and E. D. Cooke. Am Lib 2:966-7
  O '71
Hope for copyright in CATV settlement. R.
  H. Smith. Pub W 200:20 N 29 '71
New copyright challenge to cable television.
  R. H. Smith. Pub W 200:40 O 11 '71

Conferences
Conference poses liberalized world copyright.
  Pub W 200:41 Ag 2 '71
Paris conference considers Berne and UCC
  revisions. H. R. Lottman. Pub W 200:30-1
  Jl 26 '71

Duration
Christian Scientists seek extension of Eddy
  copyright. Pub W 200:28 O 4 '71

Phonograph records
Copyright protection of recordings favored by
  Department. B. C. Ladd, jr. Dept State Bul
  65:67 Jl 12 '71

Renewal
See Copyright—Duration

Television rights
See Copyright—Broadcasting rights

Unauthorized reprints
Thou shalt not copy, right? with editorial
  comment. C. A. Forbes. il Chr Today 15:32,
  44 S 10 '71

Video records and tapes
Get yourself a lawyer; report of meeting; Salt
  Lake City. D. N. Mount. il Pub W 199:29-32
  Mr 1 '71; Reply. H. M. Jones. 199:13-14 My
  17 '71

United States
ALA seeks broad support on copyright: Wil-
  liams & Wilkins case; excerpts from ad-
  dress, June 22, 1971, ed. by G. Krettek and
  E. D. Cooke. W. D. North. Am Lib 2:1182-5
  D '71
Bill introduced to extend subsisting copy-
  rights. S. Wagner. Pub W 200:31 Ag 9 '71
Breakthrough for copyright revision? S.
  Wagner. Pub W 200:94 Jl 19 '71
Copyright commission in the public interest?
  R. H. Smith. Pub W 199:35 My 17 '71
Copyright extended one more year. S. Wag-
  ner. Pub W 200:15 N 29 '71
Copyright, fair use, permissions; current and
  pending laws. M. Nicholson. Writers Di-
  gest 51:22-3 N '71
Copyright problems: revision, photocopying;
  AAP general meeting. il Pub W 200:33 O
  11 '71
[Copyright] quagmire. D. Lacy. Sat R 54:24-8
  N 27 '71
Copyright revision bill introduced. Pub W
  199:35-6 Mr 1 '71
Copyright schizophrenia. R. E. Bye. Library
  J 96:805 Mr 1 '71
Copyright: the situation now. D. N. Mount.
  Pub W 200:24-7 Jl 5; 46-8 Jl 12 '71
Librarians and copyright legislation; the
  historical background. C. Kim. bibliog il
  Am Lib 2:615-22 Je '71
Privacy, publishing and you. H. F. Pilpel
  and A. U. Schwartz. Pub W 201:30-2 Ja 3
  '72
Rights and permissions. P. S. Nathan. See
  issues of Publishers' weekly
Royalties, copyrights freed from price con-
  trols. S. Wagner. Pub W 200:19 N 22 '71
Scholarship, piracy and the copying machine.
  C. B. Grannis. Pub W 199:34 Je 14 '71
    See also
United States—Copyright office
COPYRIGHT and television. See Copyright—
  Broadcasting rights
COPYRIGHT office. See United States—Copy-
  right office
CORA Indians. See Indians of Mexico
CORA Indians Holy week celebrations. See Pas-
  sion plays
CORAL index, ltd.
  Making book on the Dow. E. Herzberg. por
  Duns 97:75-6 Je '71
CORAL reefs and islands
Curious controversy over coral reefs. S.
  Schlee. il por Sea Front 17:214-23 Jl '71
    See also
Buck Island Reef National Monument
Great Barrier Reef
CORAL SEA
Rugged run to New Guinea. P. Fitzgerald. il
  por Motor B & S 127:58-9+ F '71
CORALLINE sponges. See Sponges
CORALS
Coral; photographs by D. Faulkner. F. M.
  Bayer Natur Hist 80:42-7 Mr '71
Recent brachiopod-coralline sponge commu-
  nities and their paleoecological significance.
  J. B. C. Jackson and others. bibliog il
  Science 173:623-5 Ag 13 '71
CORBALLIS, Michael C. and Beale, I. L.
  On telling left from right; with biographical
  sketches. il Sci Am 224:14, 96-104 bibliog(p
  124) Mr '71
CORBIN, Kendall W. See Uzzell, T. jt. auth.
CORBIN, Patricia
  Notes to help you decorate-it-yourself; ques-
  tions and answers. House & Gard 139:40+
  Ap; 24+ My; 140:52+ S; 70 O '71
CORBY, Colleen
  When I was 17; interview, ed. by B. Kevles.
  pors Seventeen 30:131+ O '71
CORBY, Molly
  What I learned from my sister Colleen. il
  por Seventeen 29:78 Jl '70
CORCORAN gallery of art, Washington, D.C.
  Artists as critics; biennial exhibition. D.
  Davis. il Newsweek 77:65 Mr 29 '71

CORN—*Continued*

Seeding

Aerial corn planting takes off. R. Sanders. il Suc Farm 69:no5 M20 Mr '71

Big corn acreage went in fast and early. D. Wennblom. il Farm J 95:18-19 Je '71

Crops look good in the corn belt. R. D. Wennblom. Farm J 95:31 Jl '71

Cut soil losses on soybean land. Suc Farm 69:no2 B9 F '71

He likes no-till corn. B. J. Czartoski. il Suc Farm 69:no 4 B4 Mr '71

High-speed planters "pit-stop" refills to... beat the blight. il Farm J 95:30-3 Ap '71

Plant corn in standing wheat. B. Coffman. il Farm J 95:24-5 O '71

Should you replant corn? Suc Farm 69:G8 Ap '71

Timeliness. il Suc Farm 69:no4 27-33 Mr '71

What you should know before you plant. C. W. Gifford. Farm J 95:22-3 My '71

Storage

Blight-damaged grain takes extra management. Suc Farm 69:no2 B13 F '71

Important: check that stored corn now. il Suc Farm 69:D4 Ap '71

Yield

See Crop yields

CORN, Sweet

Watching the corn grow. N. H. Berlin. il Org Gard & Farm 18:62-3 Jl '71

Yes, you can have fine roasting ears by the 4th! J. R. Coggins. il Org Gard & Farm 18:48-9 Ap '71

See also
Cookery—Vegetables

CORN blight. See Corn—Diseases and pests

CORN borers. See Borers (insects)

CORN bread. See Bread

CORN cobs. See Corncobs

CORN earworms. See Bollworms

CORN exchanges. See Commodity exchanges

CORN futures. See Commodity exchanges

CORN grits
Grits. G. Moore. Sat R 54:56 O 9 '71

CORN husking
Cornhusking bees in America, 1836. Antiques 99:88+ Ja '71

CORN meal
See also
Cookery—Corn meal

CORN planting. See Corn—Seeding

CORN products
See also
Corn grits

CORN rootworms
Do you have to live with rootworms? Suc Farm 69:no3 W12 F '71

CORN silage. See Silage

CORN surplus. See Surplus products, Agricultural

CORNCOBS
Worthless corncob. Org Gard & Farm 18:88 My '71

CORNELIA, Sister
Sister Fuzz. il pors Life 70:50-1 Mr 12 '71 *

CORNELISEN, Ann
Authors & editors. B. A. Bannon. por Pub W 200:9-11 N 1 '71 *

CORNELL, Joseph
How to make a rainbow. A. C. Anderson. il Art N 69:50-2+ F '71*

CORNELL aeronautical laboratory, inc,
Techniques tomorrow; Cornell aeronautical laboratories. B. Sherman. il Mod Phot 35:60+ Je '71

CORNELL university, Ithaca, N.Y.

School of veterinary medicine

Multicategorical and animal research laboratory, Ithaca. New York. il Arch Rec 150:114-16 Jl '71

On the track of doped horses. il Bsns W p85 S 18 '71

CORNELY, Paul B.
Prevention: the healthiest way to control rising costs of medical care. por Parents Mag 46:16 Ap '71

CORNET, Antonio Gaudi y. See Gaudi y Cornet, A.

CORNFELD, Bernard
Cornfeld's farewell. Newsweek 77:52+ F 1 '71

Do you sincerely want to be rich? by C. Raw and others. Review
Bsns W il p 15 Ag 14 '71. G. Williams *
Life por 71:6 Ag 27 '71. J. Brooks *
Sat R 54:32+ S 4 '71. S. W Clements *
Sticks and stones... il Forbes 108:9 O 1 '71 *

CORNHUSKING. See Corn husking

CORNING, N.Y.
Corning, N.Y.; Spring Pond apartments. il Arch Forum 134:34-7 My '71

CORNING glass center, Corning, N.Y.
20th anniversary at Corning museum. Hobbies 76:151 O '71

CORNING glass works
Penalty of success. il Forbes 108:22-3 Ag 15 '71

CORNING museum of glass. See Corning glass center, Corning, N.Y.

CORNSTALK rot. See Corn—Diseases and pests

CORNWALL, England
Cornwall: sea and moors. A. Bester. il Holiday 49:64-9 F '71

CORNWALLIS, Charles Cornwallis, 1st marquis
Surrender at Yorktown: the world turn'd upside down. T. Fleming. il Read Digest 98:162-4+ Ja '71 *

CORNWELL, John
Is the Mediterranean dying? il N Y Times Mag p24-5+ F 21 '71

CORONA, Juan V.
Anatomy of a murder suspect. il por Time 97:24 Je 14 '71 *

Corona in court. por Newsweek 77:37 Je 14 '71 *

Death in the orchards. il por Time 97:14 Je 7 '71 *

Grisly harvest of the orchard. il por Life 70:38-9 Je 11 '71 *

Massacre at Yuba City. il por Newsweek 77:28-9 Je 7 '71 *

CORONA, Solar. See Sun—Corona

CORONADO, Francisco Vázquez de. See Vázquez de Coronado, F.

CORONERS
See also
Noguchi, T. T.

CORPORAL punishment
Bottoms up in big D; Dallas public-school system. il Newsweek 77:99 My 17 '71

Law and punishment status of state statutes. J. G. Brown. Clear House 46:106-9 O '71

CORPORATE airplanes. See Airplanes, Business

CORPORATE day care centers. See Day nurseries

CORPORATE debt
Companies in bondage to debt. R. Jallow. por Nations Bsns 59:77 Je '71

CORPORATE development executives. See Executives

CORPORATE giving. See Corporations—Charitable contributions

CORPORATE image
Companies face an identity crisis. il Bsns W p52-5 F 20 '71

Uniformity pays off for career clothes. il Bsns W p38-9 Jl 24 '71

What's your corporate image? R. Leys. Nations Bsns 59:61 S '71

CORPORATE information center. See National council of churches—Corporate information center

CORPORATE liquidation. See Liquidation

CORPORATE ombudsman. See Ombudsman

CORPORATE 1% program for higher education. See Colleges and universities—Gifts, legacies, etc.

CORPORATE planning. See Business planning

CORPORATE recruiting. See Recruiting of employees

CORPORATE secretaries. See Corporation secretaries

CORPORATION for public broadcasting
See also
Public broadcasting service

CORPORATION lawyers. See Lawyers

CORPORATION records. See Business records

CORPORATION reports
Annual reports bare long-hidden facts. il Bsns W p65-6 Ap 3 '71

Let's call a cost a cost; social costs. F. C. Foy. Forbes 108:66-7 Jl 1 '71

Selective reporting? Forbes 107:51+ Mr 15 '71

Stewart Jackson: instant pro? with photographs. B. Nemser. por Pop Phot 69:102-5 () '71

Why not call a spade a spade? F. C. Foy. Forbes 107:84-5 Mr 15 '71

CORPORATION secretaries
Embattled corporate secretaries. J. Perham. il Duns 98:36-8 Jl '71

CORPORATIONS

Alphabetical index of the 1000 largest industrial corporations. il Fortune 83:122-7 Je '71

Corporate giants. P. A. Samuelson. Newsweek 77:88 Mr 29 '71

Dynamic growth companies. See issues of Nation's business

Is your company lonesome? il Nations Bsns 59:74-5 F '71

Peter Drucker attacks: out top-heavy corporations; interview, ed. by T. J. Murray. P. F. Drucker. por Duns 97:38-41 Ap '71

Toward a reappraisal of corporate purpose. W. S. Rukeyser. Fortune 83:235-6 My '71

See also
Business consolidations and mergers
Conglomerate corporations
Corporation secretaries
Executives
Family corporations
Farm corporations
Limited partnership
Negro companies
Proxies
Stockholders
Trusts, Industrial

Accounting

Accounting for premature profits; land development companies. Bsns W p87 Ja 23 '71

Cool look at hot-pants accounting; interview, ed. by R. Brady. A. J. Briloff il por Duns 98:8-9+ O '71

It's not material! il Forbes 107:37-8 Ap 15 '71

Threat to the booming leasing business. il Bsns W p42+ S 4 '71

Use LIFO to offset inflation. R. M. Copeland and others. bibliog f il Harvard Bsns R 49:91-100 My '71; Discussion. 49:35+ S '71

Agricultural operations

Vanishing small farmer. P. Barnes. New Repub 164:21-4 Je 12 '71

Charitable contributions

Gifts and questions; Gulf-Western industries gift. America 125:499 D 11 '71

Pound foolish tax policy; manufacturing companies to deduct goods donated to charity. America 125:499 D 11 '71

See also
Foundations, Charitable and educational

Directories

Dimensions of American business. Forbes 107:128-61 My 15 '71

500 biggest corporations by assets. Forbes 107:103-4+ My 15 '71

500 biggest corporations by market value. Forbes 107:91-2+ My 15 '71

500 biggest corporations by profits. Forbes 107:115-16+ My 15 '71

500 biggest corporations by revenues. Forbes 107:79-80+ My 15 '71

Fortune directory of the 500 largest industrial corporations; with introd. by C. G. Burck. Fortune 83:170-204 My '71

Fortune directory of the second 500 largest industrial corporations; with introd. by L. Adam. il Fortune 83:100-27 Je '71

Fortune directory; 200 largest industrials outside the U.S. Fortune 84:150-5 Ag '71

Who's where in American industry; tables. Forbes 109:31-6 Ja 1 '72

Directors

Black woman joins three boards. por Bsns W p22 My 29 '71

Board: it's obsolete unless overhauled; with editorial comment. il Bsns W p50-1+, 90 My 22 '71

Directors: myth & reality. by M. L. Mace. Review
Bsns W il p 14+ S 25 '71. D A Fausch

Power to which people? lack of black and Mexican-American executives in California-based corporations. New Repub 164:9-10 F 20 '71

Employees

See Employees

Finance

As Nixon looks beyond the freeze; remarks. September 23, 1971. R. M. Nixon. il por U S News 71:77-9 O 4'71

Big fall in profits: what it means to the economy. D. Lawrence. U S News 70:80 Ja 18 '71

Big squeeze. Newsweek 77:72 F 8 '71

Earnings picture is a bit blurred; with tables. Bsns W p50 O 23 '71

Ferment in fringes. J. Perham. il Duns 98:34-6 D '71

Framework for financial decisions. W. W. Sihler. bibliog f il Harvard Bsns R 49:123-35 Mr '71

Games companies play. J. F. Childs. por Forbes 108:68+ S 15 '71

Great profits deflation. Time 98:58-9 Ag 2 '71

Healthier profits begin to show up. Bsns W p36 Jl 17 '71

How to redeploy assets. R. H. Hillman. il Harvard Bsns R 49:95-103 N '71

Inflated view of company profits. il Bsns W p26 D 18 '71

Last quarter was bittersweet. Bsns W p26-7 F 13 '71

Lesson of the credit crisis. C. J. Loomis. il Fortune 83:141-3+ My '71

Lots of ways to lose money; 12 losers. Fortune 83:171 Je '71

Mixed bag. il Newsweek 78:88 N 8 '71

Modest comeback for profits; with table. Bsns W p24 Mr 6 '71

New profit figures shock the experts. il Bsns W p57 Jl 31 '71

1970 was rough for biggest firms. il U S News 70:74 Mr 22 '71

Postwar law of margins. Time 97:77 Mr 15 '71

Profitable, but not very; European companies; with table. Bsns W p60 O 23 '71

Profits now: starting a slow climb. il U S News 70:95-6 My 10 '71

Profits picture: looking better. il U S News 70:52-3 F 15 '71

Profits: some big gains, but—. il U S News 71:28-9 Ag 2 '71

Profits start to convalesce; with table. Bsns W p32 Ap 17 '71

Report on American industry. il Forbes 109:31-6+ Ja 1 '72

Right to know; questions of disclosure. Newsweek 77:85-6 Ap 12 '71

Tight-money financing. R. F. Vandell and R. M. Pennell. il Harvard Bsns R 49:82-97 S '71

Top companies that can't raise prices. Bsns W p30+ N 20 '71

Wall Street:
Name of the game. C. Morgello. il Newsweek 77:90 My 17 '71

What's good for profits can be bad for prices. il Fortune 84:18 Ag '71

Where profits took an abrupt fall; with table. Bsns W p 17-18 Ja 30 '71

Year of the big bath; with table. Forbes 107:42-3 Mr 1 '71

See also
Bankruptcy
Capital investments
Corporate debt
Corporations—Accounting
Corporations—Valuation
Corporations, International—Finance
Dividends
Employees as stockholders
Profit
Securities—Marketing
Small business—Finance

Statistics

500 biggest corporations by assets; with directory. Forbes 107:103-4+ My 15 '71

500 biggest corporations by profits; with directory. Forbes 107:115-16+ My 15 '71

500 biggest corporations by revenues; with directory. Forbes 107:79-80+ My 15 '71

Fortune directory of the 500 largest industrial corporations; with introd. by C. G. Burck. Fortune 83:170-204 My '71

Fortune directory of the second 500 largest industrial corporations; with introd. by L. Adams. il Fortune 83:100-27 Je '71

Quarterly survey of corporate performance; with tables. Bsns W p41-52+ My 8; 47-54+ Ag 14; 71-8+ N 13 '71

Who's where in profitability; tables. Forbes 109:40-2+ Ja 1 '72

Foreign business

Myths that mislead U.S. managers in Japan. Y. Tsurumi. Harvard Bsns R 49:118-27 Jl '71

One way to connect on the Continent; Business associations S.A. (BASSA) Bsns W p35 Jl 31 '71

Sunny side of the deficit. il Forbes 109:24-9 Ja 1 '72

See also
Export trade

Foreign subsidiaries

Understand your overseas work force; with folded charts. D. Sirota and J. M. Greenwood. il Harvard Bsns R 49:53-60 Ja '71

CORPORATIONS—*Continued*

History
Great moments & great men of American business; symposium, ed. by S. G. Slappey. Nations Bsns 59:41-5+ Ja '71

Location
See Location in business and industry

Presidents
See Executives

Public relations
See Business—Public relations

Real estate operations
Corporate move to leisure towns. E. Carruth. il Fortune 83:72-9 Ap '71
Land sales: a lower key. il Bsns W p84+ Ja 23 '71
Lure of the land fades for companies. Bsns W p38 Jl 17 '71
New business from new towns? M. Apgar, 4th. il Harvard Bsns R 49:90-109 Ja '71

Size
Dimensions of American business; a roster of the country's biggest corporations. Forbes 107:128-61 My 15 '71
See also
Big business

Social aspects
See Business—Social aspects

Taxation
Can business pay taxes? M. Friedman. Newsweek 78:91 N 29 '71
Let's take a harder look at business taxes. Fortune 83:134 My '71
Pound foolish tax policy; manufacturing companies to deduct goods donated to charity. America 125:499 D 11 '71
See also
Excess profits tax
Public utilities—Taxation

Valuation
500 biggest corporations by market value; with directory. Forbes 107:91-2+ My 15 '71
Who's where in the stock market; tables. Forbes 109:64-6+ Ja 1 '72

CORPORATIONS, Foreign
Fortune directory; 200 largest industrials outside the U.S. Fortune 84:150-5 Ag '71
See also
Corporations, International

CORPORATIONS, Government
See also
Overseas private investment corporation

CORPORATIONS, International
Business survival in the seventies: is the world company the answer? address, February 25, 1971. E. M. De Windt. Vital Speeches 37:363-7 Ap 1 '71
Coming of the cosmocorp. J. E. Kenney. il America 125:450-2 N 27 '71
Global view; concern over growth of multinational corporations. il Newsweek 77:77-8 My 17 '71
How multinationals play it. il Bsns W p 101-2+ S 25 '71
Invisible empires, by L. Turner. Review Bsns W p 12 F 27 '71. C. P. Kindleberger
Living with the Nixon measures. Fortune 84:49-50 O '71
Multinational corporation; address, May 3, 1971. P. H. Trezise. Vital Speeches 37:494-6 Je 1 '71; Same with title Some policy implications of the multinational corporation. Dept State Bul 64:669-72 My 24 '71
Multinational enterprise: power versus sovereignty; excerpts from Sovereignty at bay. R. Vernon. For Affairs 49:736-51 Jl '71
Multinationals take it in stride; tariff surcharge. il Bsns W p59 Ag 28 '71
New rules for investing in the LDC's. il Newsweek 78:80-2 S 20 '71
New view: build here and export. il Bsns W p29-30 Ja 1 '72
On the way: companies more powerful than nations. il U S News 71:38-41 Jl 19 '71
Science and policy for a new decade. C. P. Haskins. bibliog f For Affairs 49:237-70 Ja '71
Unions move against the multinationals. Bsns W p48-9+ Jl 24 '71
See also
Eaton Yale & Towne, inc.
International basic economy corporation
Mitsubishi
Nestlé company

Finance
Multinational profits; with table. Forbes 108:77+ N 15 '71

CORPORATIONS, Nonprofit
See also
Rand corporation

CORPORATIONS, Stealing from. See Stealing

CORPS of engineers. See United States—Army—Corps of engineers

CORPULENCE
Are weight-loss belts effective? Good H 173:145 Ag '71
Before you believe those exercise and diet ads read the following report. R. Sherrill. il Todays Health 49:34-6+ Ag '71
Dept of weights and measures; sweat pants and slenderizing shakes. il Vogue 157:70 My '71
Fat antibody. R. H. Berg. McCalls 99:37 N '71
Fat child. C. M. Young. Todays Ed 60:58-9 Mr '71
Fitness program for overweight teen-agers; excerpts from The handbook of adolescence; a complete medical guide. M J. Gersh and I. F. Litt. il Parents Mag 46:50-1+ Ag '71
Self-hypnosis diet. E. Frances. il Ladies Home J 88:52+ Je '71
Spontaneous reduction; wrapping method. il Time 97:46 My 10 '71
U.S. journal: Manhattan; the ordeal of Fats Goldberg. C. Trillin. New Yorker 47:57-8+ Jl 3 '71
What a wonderful beauty idea; definition, causes and control of cellulite. Harp Baz 104:22 Ja; 50 F; 42 Mr '71

CORPUS CHRISTI, Tex.
Libraries
Hurricane Celia damage. il Am Lib 2:138 F '71

CORPUS luteum. See Ovaries

CORRADINO, R. A. and Wasserman, R. H.
Vitamin D₃: induction of calcium-binding protein in embryonic chick intestine in vitro. bibliog il Science 172:731-3 My 14 '71

CORRECTIONAL institutions. See Reformatories

CORRELATION (education)
More than a space science center; space science lab for elementary school complex in Middletown, R.I. N. D. Field. il Todays Ed 60:32-3 O '71

CORRELATION spectrometer. See Spectrometers

CORRELL, Charles James
Where are they now? Newsweek 78:23 N 15 '71 *

CORRESPONDENCE. See Letter writing

CORRESPONDENCE schools and courses
Learning by mail: writing and allied subjects. Writers Digest 51:32-3+ S '71
Some correspondence schools are plain gyps. il Changing T 25:31-4 Jl '71
See also
Advance schools, inc.
FAS international, inc.
Famous photographers school
Famous writers school
University extension

CORRESPONDENTS, Foreign. See Foreign correspondents

CORRESPONDENTS, War. See War correspondents

CORROSION and anticorrosives
Mystery of the rustless pillar; monument of wrought iron erected in ancient Delhi. il Chem 44:5 S '71

CORRUPTION, Police. See Police corruption

CORRUPTION in politics. See Politics, Corruption in

CORRY, Emmett
Catholic LA: restructure, retrenchment; report. Wilson Lib Bul 45:914+ Je '71

CORRY, John
Mrs Lieberman of Baltimore. por Harper 242:92-5 F '71
One day in the life of Guy Vander Jagt (R.-Mich.) por Harper 242:70-9 Ap '71
about
That homey touch. Time 98:77 O 18 '71 *

CORRY, Will. See Wurlitzer. R. jt. auth.

CORRYMEELA community. See Community service—Northern Ireland

CORSAGES (flowers) See Bouquets

CORSICA
Description and travel
To the beautiful isle. H. Colijn. il Yachting 130:58-9+ D '71

CORT, Stewart Shaw
Free trade? Yes, but! por Nations Bsns 59: 54-7 Jl '71
about
Bethlehem's strategist. por Bsns W p67 Ja 23 '71 •
Cort of Bethleham steel. il pors Forbes 107: 72 My 15 '71 •
CORTE, Arturo E. See Higashi. A. jt. auth.
CORTESE, James
Mississippi's ante-bellum itinerary. il Travel 135:28-33 Mr '71
CORTEX, Cerebral. See Cerebral cortex
CORTÉZ, SEA OF. See California, Gulf of
CORTICOSTEROIDS
Glucocorticoid receptors in lymphoma cells in culture: relationship to glucocorticoid killing activity. J. D. Baxter and others. bibliog il Science 171:189-91 Ja 15 '71
Retention deficit correlated with a deficit in the corticoid response to stress. P. Auerbach and P. L. Carlton. bibliog il Science 173:1148-9 S 17 '71
CORVALLIS, Ore.
More water from the same plant. F. Collins and C. Y. Shieh. il pors Am City 86:96-7 O '71
CORVETTE (sports car) See Sports cars
CORWIN, R. D. and Gray, Lois
Books & ideas. il Fortune 84:127-8 Jl '71
COSA nostra. See Mafia
COSBY, Bill
Follow-up: command performance. M. Davidson. il por Good H 172:50+ Je '71 •
Man and boy. L. Robinson. il pors Ebony 26:42-4+ Ap '71 •
COSBY, William
Case of John Peter Zenger. L. Barnett. il pors Am Heritage 23:33-41+ D '71 •
COSELL, Howard
Howard Cosell is just another pretty face. J. Marshall. il por Esquire 76:93-7+ O '71 •
Shall we rule these TV egos guilty of unnecessary roughness? S. Singer. il Todays Health 49:40-3 D '71 •
TV talk. F. Deford. Sports Illus 34:10 Je 28 '71 •
What are they doing with the sacred game of pro football? E. Shrake. pors Sports Illus 35:96-9+ O 25 '71 •
COSGRAVE, Mary Silva
Outlook tower. See issues of Horn book magazine
COSGROVE, Francis A. and Kraus, Richard
Role of civil service. Parks & Rec 6:27-9+ Je '71
COSI fan tutte: opera. See Mozart, J. C. W. A.
COSIC, Kresimir
Case of the capering Croat. C. Kirkpatrick. il por Sports Illus 35:65-6 D 13 '71 •
COSMETIC surgery. See Surgery, Plastic
COSMETICS
Beauty & the bath. S. Lindsay. See issues of House beautiful
Beauty checkout. See issues of Vogue
Beauty: how to have more than you started with. il Vogue 158:128-37 O 1 '71
Cosmetics good enough to eat; natural-cosmetics. C. Chase. McCalls 98:42 My '71
Cosmetics: how to get the most for your money. il Good H 172:164 Mr '71
Do burn lotions help? A. T. Snider. Sci Digest 71:70-1 Ja '72
Elements of beauty; sun tan preparations. P. Van Wagenen. Parents Mag 46:66-7 Jl '71
Facial creams: 150 A.D. to 1971. L. Allen. Todays Health 49:10 F '71
GH poll: how satisfied are women with food and cosmetic products? Good H 172:166 F '71
Instant beauty, the masks which matter. il Harp Baz 104:110-11 O '71
Let your beauty shine through: sheer-tint gels. T. Pavlik. il Good H 173:110-11 Jl '71
Let's make sun worship unfashionable; suntan lotions. Consumer Bul 54:29-30 Je '71
Moisturizers to make you glow. il Redbook 137:90-1+ Ag '71
Natural beauty. C. Bartel. il Am Home 74:14+ Ag '71
Natural cosmetics: are they really better? Good H 173:189 O '71
New sparkle for skin; brighter eyes fresh beauty. Harp Baz 104:82-3 My '71
Organic shops move into the big stores. il Bsns W p76-7 Jl 10 '71

Outdoor makeup, you say? Well, tan my hide! Bonne Bell cosmetics for skiing. A. Verschoth. il por Sports Illus 35:86-7 N 22 '71
Sane sun worship; prevent sunburn. Harp Baz 104:19 Je '71
Sun-worshiper's strategy. Ladies Home J 88: 133 Jl '71
Suntan preparations. il Consumer Rep 36: 408-11 Jl '71
Travel and beauty care; suntanning preparations. J. Clark. Holiday 49:124+ D '70
See also
Beauty, Personal
Lipstick
Make-up
Toilet preparations

Testing
Testing suntan preparations. J. A. Vinson. il por Chem 44:27 Je '71
COSMETICS for men
See also
Perfumes for men
COSMETICS industry
Ugly truths about today's beauty aids. E. Kiester, jr. il Todays Health 49:16-20+ Je '71; Reply. J. B. Jerome. 49:70-1 S '71
See also
Koscot interplanetary, inc.

Japan
Cosmetics maker counterattacks; Shiseido co. il Bsns W p48+ O 16 '71
COSMIC antimatter. See Matter, Interstellar
COSMIC physics
See also
Astrophysics
Magnetic fields (cosmic physics)
Solar wind
COSMIC rays
Cosmic- muon flux and the W particle. G. B. Lubkin. Phys Today 24:17-18 N '71
Man-made cosmic rays. il Newsweek 78:61 S 6 '71
Mechanism for producing magnetic remanence in meteorites and lunar samples by cosmic-ray exposure. R. F. Butler and A. V. Cox. bibliog il Science 172:939-41 My 28 '71
Olivines: revelation of tracks of charged particles. S. Krishnaswami and others. bibliog il Science 174:287-91 O 15 '71
Origins of cosmic rays. R. Cowsik and P. B. Price. bibliog il Phys Today 24:30-8 O '71
Very heavy solar cosmic rays: energy spectrum and implications for lunar erosion. R. L. Fleischer and others. bibliog il Science 171:1240-2 Mr 26 '71

Measurement
Astronauts and cosmic rays; study of Apollo helmets. il Chem 44:22 Jl '71
Cosmic-ray tracks in plastics: the Apollo helmet dosimetry experiment. G. M. Comstock and others. bibliog il Science 172: 154-7 Ap 9 '71
COSMOGONY
See also
Creation
Universe
COSMOLOGY
Arguments concerning relativity and cosmology. O. Klein. bibliog il Science 171:339-45 Ja 29 '71
Experimental cosmology. Sci Am 224:54-6 Je '71
Introducing the black hole; excerpt from The significance of space research for fundamental physics. R. Ruffini and J. A. Wheeler. bibliog il Phys Today 24:30-6+ Ja '71
Red herring of the three-story universe. J. W. Duddington. Chr Today 16:13-14+ N 5 '71
See also
Creation
Life on other planets
Universe
COSMONAUTS. See Astronauts
COSMOS satellites. See Artificial satellites, Russian
COSSATOT RIVER
Cossatot River, another legal milestone; Gillham Dam and reservoir project. D. G. Cullimore. il Am For 77:8-10+ My '71
COST
Get more for your money; opportunity cost. Suc Farm 69:C20 N '71
See also
Labor cost
Value (economic theory)
also subhead Cost under various subjects, e.g. College education—Cost

COST benefit analysis. See Cost effectiveness
COST effectiveness
Accomplishment/cost: better project control. E. B. Block. il Harvard Bsns R 49:110-24 My '71
Morals and measurements: Christian ethics and cost benefit analysis. D. Munby. il Commonweal 95:271-5 D 17 '71
COST of food. See Food—Prices
COST of living
    See also
Budget, Household
Domestic finance
Income
Purchasing power
Standard of living

Hawaii
How America lives: making ends meet in paradise. L. Tornabene. il Ladies Home J 88:82-3+ Ja '71

Russia
    See also
Purchasing power—Russia

United States
Anatomy of price change in 1970. W. J. Layng and T. Nakayama. il Mo Labor R 94:38-41 F '71
Coping with inflation: what readers report. il Changing T 25:35-9 Ag '71
Here's what's been happening to your living costs. Changing T 25:7-14 Ap '71
Prices; tables. See issues of Monthly labor review
Spring 1970 cost estimates for urban family budgets; with table. E. Ruiz. Mo Labor R 94:59-61 Ja '71
What inflation is costing Americans. il U S News 70:23-5 My 17 '71
    See also
Food—Prices
Price indexes
Prices—United States

COST of living council. See United States—Cost of living council
COST of medical service. See Medical service, Cost of
COSTA, Jean-Charles
Buffalo Springfield: this time around. il Sr Schol 98:24-5 My 17 '71
Colossal event. il pors Sr Schol 99:34 S 27 '71
COSTA, Simeon
Your soggy day survival kit. Har Yrs 11:51-3 Je '71
COSTABILE, Frank J. and Perron, C. H.
Don't color the water black. il Am City 86:46-7 Ja '71
COSTA-GAVRAS
Agent provocateur of films. M. S. Davis il pors N Y Times Mag p32-4+ Mr 21 '71 •
COSTAGLIOLA, Francesco
Nuclear power; address, February 17, 1971. Vital Speeches 37:436-41 My 1 '71
COSTA RICA
    See also
Fishing—Costa Rica

Politics and government
Freelance diplomacy. il por Time 97:29 Mr 8 '71
COSTELLO, John
Executive trends. See issues of Nation's business
COSTELLO, Timothy William
Library urban info network scheme explained to NYLA; summary of statement, 1971. por Library J 96:3707 N 15 '71
COSTO, Rupert
Why minority publishing? ed. by B. Chambers. il pors Pub W 199:40-1 Mr 15 '71 •
COSTS (law)
    See also
Insurance, Litigation
COSTUME
    See also
Fashion
Millinery

Exhibitions
Carl and Heidi Bucher need your body; exhibition at the Museum of contemporary crafts. B. Schwartz. il Craft Horiz 31:27-9+ Je '71
Self in city space and in clothed space; exhibition at Museum of contemporary crafts. B. Schwartz. il por Craft Horiz 31:30-5 Ag '71
    See also
Metropolitan museum of art, New York—Costume institute

Far East
Costumes of the East; excerpt.W. A. Fairservis, jr. il Natur Hist 80:28-37 N '71
United States
Politics of the costume. B. Sabol and L. K. Truscott, 4th. il Esquire 75:123-34 My '71
COSTUME, Theatrical
Reenter Werther; photographs of Rudolf Heinrich's costumes for Massenet's Werther. Opera N 35:28-9 Ja 16 '71
COSTUME balls. See Balls (parties)
COSTUME design
Chicom chic. il Time 98:90 D 6 '71
Chinese look. il Newsweek 78:56 S 20 '71
How to look like a cool coolie. il Life 71:59-65 D 10 '71
Mainbocher; great gentleman of fashion. il Harp Baz 104:70-3 Je '71
On and off the avenue; American designers showing their fall collections. K. Fraser. New Yorker 47:60+ Jl 10 '71
On and off the avenue; Narcissa, designer boutique. K. Fraser. New Yorker 47:122+ N 20 '71
Ungaro's triumph. il por Newsweek 78:45 Ag 9 '71
COSTUME designers
Fashion influentials. J. Brady. por Harp Baz 104:102-3 O; 105:68-9 N; 53 D '71
Shotgun approach. il Forbes 108:19 Jl 15 '71
Under $50; where high fashion is happening. T. Owett. il Ladies Home J 88:84-5 Ja '71
    See also
Chanel, G.
Eula, J.
Johnson, B.
Mainbocher
Olly
St Laurent, Y. M.
Schiaparelli, E.
Sweeney, J. J.
Whyte, J. B.
COSTUME institute. See Metropolitan museum of art, New York—Costume institute
COSWAY, Maria (Hadfield)
Thomas Jefferson and Maria Cosway. C. B. Van Pelt. il pors Am Heritage 22:22-5+ Ag '71 •
COSWAY, Richard
Romance: Richard Cosway saw it; engravings. il pors Am Heritage 22:26-7 Ag '71
Thomas Jefferson and Maria Cosway. C. B. Van Pelt. il pors Am Heritage 22:22-5+ Ag '71 •
COTE, Carol K.
Walt Whitman: poet of democracy; drama. Plays 30:77-84+ F '71
COTE d'Azur. See Riviera
COTLER, Gordon
One and only Radio City music hall. il Holiday 49:78-9+ D '70
Real life Grenada. il Holiday 48:45+ N '70
COTMAN, Carl W. and others
Electroshock effects on brain protein synthesis: relation to brain seizures and retrograde amnesia. bibliog il Science 173:454-6 Jl 30 '71
COTMORE, John M. and others
Phospholipid-calcium phosphate complex: enhanced calcium migration in the presence of phosphate. bibliog il Science 172:1339-41 Je 25 '71
COTT, Ed
Fruits for harsh climates. il Horticulture 49:36-7+ S '71
COTTAGE industries
When can a home be used for business? L. M. Brown. Bet Hom & Gard 49:100 My '71
    See also
Pier 1 imports, inc.
COTTAGES, Summer. See Summer homes
COTTEN, Donald, and Donn, W. L.
Sound from Apollo rockets in space. bibliog il Science 171:565-7 F 12 '71
COTTER, Donald J.
Building a hobby greenhouse. il Horticulture 49:42-5 My '71
COTTER, James F.
Poets are remembering it well. America 125:514-16 D 11 '71
COTTER HIRSCHBERG, J. See Hirschberg, J. C.
COTTIN, Louis M.
Anyone for succotash? Har Yrs 11:21-3 Jl '71
Confessions of a reluctant composter. Org Gard & Farm 18:96-7 O '71
My complaint; poem. Har Yrs 11:38 My '71
COTTLE, Thomas J.
In the car shop. il Sat R 54:49-51+ Je 19 '71
True creativity can emerge anytime, at age 6, or at 40. il Life 71:52-3 D 17 '71
White House conference on children. il Sat R 54:56-7+ F 20 '71

COTTON

Diseases and pests

Melancholy addiction of Ol'King Cotton. R. Van Den Bosch. il Natur Hist 80:86-91 bibliog(p 120) D '71

Prices

Bright futures in cotton trading. il Bsns W p44 Je 5 '71

COTTON exchanges. See Commodity exchanges

COTTON fabrics

See also

Denim

COTTON growing

Game never stops; subsidies to California cotton growers. G. L. Baker. il Nation 213:114-16 Ag 16 '71

COTTON industry

U.S. and the Philippines sign cotton textile agreement. Dept State Bul 63:766 D 21 '70

U.S. cotton heads overseas. il Bsns W p 142 My 15 '71

United States and Portugal sign cotton textile agreement. Dept State Bul 63:764 D 21 '70

COTTON mills

Employees

Cotton-mill killer. R. Nader. Nation 212:335-7 Mr 15 '71

COTTON textile workers. See Cotton mills— Employees

COTTONMOUTH moccasin. See Snakes

COTTONSEED meal

Good deal, cottonseed meal. L. W. Patterson. Org Gard & Farm 18:102-3 S '71

COTTONTAIL hunting. See Rabbit hunting

COTTRELL, Dorothy

Price of beef. bibliog il Environ 13:44-7+ Jl '71

COTTRELL, John

My search for the Holy Grail. il Ladies Home J 88:58+ Ap '71

COTZIAS, George Constantin, and others

Melatonin and abnormal movements induced by L-dopa in mice. bibliog il Science 173: 450-2 Jl 30 '71

COUCHES. See Sofas

COUGAR hunting. See Puma hunting

COUGARS. See Pumas

COUGH medicines. See Medicine, Patent, proprietary, etc.

COUGHLIN, Charles Edward

Where are they now? pors Newsweek 78:15 O 4 '71 *

COULETTE, Henri

BRRR; Today I begin my first novel; Prince of frogs; Situation comedy; At the hotel Des saints pères; poems. Poetry 117:366-70 Mr '71

COULOMB, Charles Augustin de

Measurement of the man-day. E. S. Ferguston. il Sci Am 225:99-101 O '71 *

COULOMB, Jean

Good use of scientists; adaptation of address. Bul Atom Sci 27:39-41 Ja '71

COULTER, Jeanne

Come home with me; story. Good H 174:74-5 Ja '72

COULTER, Olivia W. and Lewis, D. J.

Invitation to design a world; second reader. il Aging 199:13-28 My '71

COUNCIL for basic education

Council for basic education. R. Kirk. Nat R 23:762 Jl 13 '71

Down to basics. Newsweek 78:48-9 Jl 19 '71

COUNCIL-manager government. See City manager plan

COUNCIL of better business bureaus. See Better business bureaus

COUNCIL of churches of the city of New York

Family of man award recipients named. Chr Cent 88:1127 S 29 '71

Representing New York. Newsweek 77:56 My 17 '71

COUNCIL of economic advisers. See United States—Council of economic advisers

COUNCIL of Europe

Europe on the move. P. Hebblethwaite. il America 124:169-71 F 20 '71

COUNCIL of Trent. See Trent, Council of, 1545-1563

COUNCIL on economic priorities

Business of war. il Ramp Mag 9:7-8 Je '71

Business of war; defense contracts report. Nation 212:517 Ap 26 '71

Corporate responsibility; group rates company social performance. C. Holden. Science 171:463-6 F 5 '71

Environmental advertising; a question of integrity; CEP report. Sci N 100:356 N 27 '71

Gravy train; defense contracts report. New Repub 164:9 Ap 24 '71; Discussion. 164:37, 39 My 15 '71

Stocks without sin. W. Goodman. il Harper 243:61-7 Ag '71

COUNCIL on environmental quality. See United States—Council on environmental quality

COUNCIL on foreign relations

Council on foreign relations, is it a club? Seminar? Presidium? Invisible government? J. A. Lukas. il N Y Times Mag p34-5+ N 21 '71

Inside the CFR. Nat R 23:1074-5 S 24 '71

COUNCIL on international economic policy. See United States—Council on international economic policy

COUNCIL on interracial books for children

Development and insurance funds proposed for minority-owned book firms. Pub W 199: 29 Ap 19 '71

Interracial books: background of a challenge. B. Chambers. il Pub W 200:23-9 O 11 '71

Minority publishing: bringing the record up to date. B. Chambers. Pub W 201:27 Ja 3 '72

Minority publishing fund proposed at conference. Library J 96:2030 Je 15 '71

Why minority publishing? ed. B. Chambers. il pors Pub W 199:35-50 Mr 15 '71

COUNCIL on library resources, inc.

Verner W. Clapp, library ombudsman. il pors Wilson Lib Bul 45:554-5 F '71

COUNCILS and synods

See also

Synod of bishops, 1971

Vatican council, 2d

COUNSELING

Legacy of David Scull; Emergency homes, inc. J. E. Roper. por Read Digest 99:33-6 Ag '71

Psychiatry comes of age. G. W. Weinstein. il Parents Mag 46:66-7+ N '71

Who gets counseled and for what? J. W. M. Rothney. Ed Digest 37:41-4 N '71

Young living; questions and answers. A. Wood. See issues of Seventeen

See also

Genetic counseling

Marriage counseling

Pastoral counseling

Personnel service in education

Telephone in counseling

Vocational guidance

COUNSELING, Financial. See Financial services

COUNSELORS

See also

Camp counselors

Mental health counselors

Personnel service in education

Student counselors

COUNTER culture

After the fall: what this country needs is a good counter counterculture culture. D. French. il N Y Times Mag p20-1+ O 3 '71; Discussion. p26 O 24; 98 N 7; 22+ N 21 '71

Communes on the moon? C. H. Simonds. Nat R 23:1118 O 8 '71

Communes: the alternative life-style. H. A. Otto. il Sat R 54:16-21 Ap 24 '71; Same abr. Cur 130:15-22 Je '71

Counterculture at Kickapoo Creek. G. L. Heath. bibliog Sch & Soc 99:247-50 Ap '71

Counter culture: groupthink or liberation? J. Marks. Mlle 72:166-7+ F '71

Counter-culture: it just won't go away. M. B. Bloy, jr. Commonweal 95:29-34 O 8 '71

End of the youth revolt? il U S News 71: 26-31 Ag 9 '71

Family: the story of Charles Manson's dune-buggy attack battalion, by E. Sanders. Review

Nat R 23:1311-12 N 19 '71. C. H. Simonds

Great white son turns left. E. G. Dalbey, jr. il Chr Cent 88:716-20 Je 9 '71

Halfway between dropping out and dropping in. S. V. Roberts. il N Y Times Mag p44-6+ S 12 '71

Impossibility of dropping out. A. Hartley. il Horizon 13:104-5 Aut '71

Liberal antecedents of the revolt; excerpt from Youth and dissent. K. Keniston. Cur 134:3-20 N '71

Making the van go. il Time 98:36+ S 6 '71

Movement toward a new America, ed. by M. Goodman. Review

Fortune 84:173-4 Ag '71. I. Kristol

Out of tune and lost in the counterculture. T. Tyler. Time 97:15-16 F 22 '71

COUNTER culture—*Continued*

Revolution as a trip: symbol and paradox; address, 1970. B. G. Myerhoff. bibliog f Ann Am Acad 395:105-16 My '71

Ripping off, the new life style. M. Drosnin. il N Y Times Mag p 12-13+ Ag 8 '71

Stances and substances. J. R. Seeley. Ann Am Acad 395:95-104 My '71

Streets, actions, alternatives, raps, by J. Stickney. Review Newsweek 78:112+ N 8 '71. R. Boeth

Trade winds; interview, ed. by C. Amory. R. Houriet. Sat R 54:18 S 18 '71

Why we ought to join our kids. E. J. Bloustein. Look 35:46-7 Ja 26 '71

Winds from the East; youth and counter-cults. J. Needleman. il Commonweal 94: 188-90 Ap 30 '71

Bibliography

Alternative information R. Akeroyd. bibliog Wilson Lib Bul 46:103 S '71

New perspectives on the counter-culture. S. M. Lipset. Sat R 54:25-8 Mr 20 '71

Caricatures and cartoons

Countering the counterculture. Time 97:62 My 10 '71

COUNTER culture literature

Living on the last whole earth. E. Abbey. il Natur Hist 80:84-8 N '71

Up from the underground; EST: The steersman handbook. P. S. Nathan. Pub W 200: 40 O 25 '71

See also
Booksellers and bookselling—Counter culture literature

COUNTER culture slang. See Slang

COUNTERCULTURE. See Counter culture

COUNTERCURRENT chromatography. See Chromatographic analysis

COUNTERFEITS and counterfeiting

See also
Forgery of works of art
Fraud

COUNTERGLOW

No local dust cloud? study of gegenschein particles. Sky & Tel 41:213 Ap '71

Woher der gegenschein? Sci Am 225:47 Ag '71

COUNTERINSURGENCY. See Insurgency

COUNTERTENORS. See Singers

COUNTING machines and devices

Heath IB-101 frequency counter. il Electr World 85:76-7 My '71

Heathkit frequency counter, Model IB-101. il Radio-Electr 42:82 Ag '71

More about electronic counters. D. L. Steinbach. il Electr World 85:32-3+ Mr '71

Novel counter, decoder, readout. F. H. Tooker. il Electr World 86:40-2 D '71

Ultimate decimal counter. D. Meyer. il Pop Electr 34:45-8+ F '71

COUNTRIES. See Nations

COUNTRY and city. See City and country

COUNTRY churches

Saving an American tradition: little country churches on post cards. V. L. George. il Hobbies 76:158-9 N '71

See also
Suburban churches

COUNTRY clubs

Country clubs fall short of the green. il Bsns W p77-8 Mr 6 '71

Golf and country, Champions golf club, Houston, Texas. C. Price. Holiday 49:84-5 Mr '71

Our ailing country clubs. il Forbes 107:42-4 Mr 15 '71

COUNTRY doctors. See Medical service, Rural; Physicians

COUNTRY estates

Cornè, McIntire, and the Hersey Derby farm; Michel Cornè's painting of a Salem, Mass. country estate. N. F. Little. il Antiques 101:226-9 Ja '72

England

Country house in flower; Radziwill's Turville Grange. P. Devlin. il pors Vogue 158:100-7+ Jl '71

COUNTRY hospitals. See Hospitals, Rural

COUNTRY inns. See Hotels, taverns, etc.

COUNTRY life

Adventures in retirement; North Carolina. W. M. Baker. il pors Am For 77:28-31+ Je; 38-9+ Ag; 36-9+ S '71

City shepherd's calendar. L. E. Sissman. Atlan 227:40-1 F '71

Couple who live in the clouds; Kate and Peter Worsley. B. Wein. il Redbook 138: 51+ D '71

Opinion: on living in the country. L. Ullman. por Mlle 72:20+ F '71

Uncle Wes and the boll weevils. R. Starnes. Field & S 75:8+ F '71

See also
Bees (cooperative gatherings)
Farm life
Village life

COUNTRY music. See Folk music, American

COUNTRY music; story. See Maynard, J.

COUNTRY singers. See Singers

COUNTRY town life. See Village life

COUNTRYMAN, Vern

Computers and dossiers; reprint. il Nation 213:134-49 Ag 30 '71

COUNTY buildings

County government center by Paul Rudolph; Orange County, N.Y. il Arch Rec 150:83-92 Ag '71

See also
Courthouses

COUNTY centers. See County buildings

COUNTY jail libraries. See Prison libraries

COUNTY parks and reserves

See also
Fairfax County, Va.—Parks and reserves

COUNTY records on microfilm

County land-records support local development; Bay County, Mich. E. M. Nearing. il Am City 86:103 My '71

Microfilm improves the revenue column; Luzerne County, Pa. T. P. Garrity. il Am City 86:92+ My '71

COUPLINGS, Electric

TV-set couplers. il Consumer Rep 36:144-5 Mr '71

COURAGE

Courage. New Repub 164:14 Ja 2 '71

See also
Heroes

COURBET, Gustave

Courbet and the column. C. R. Baldwin. il Art N 70:36-8 My '71 *

COURSES of study

Curriculum for people. Todays Ed 60:42-4 F '71

Curse of courses. M. S. Marshall. Sch & Soc 99:32-5 Ja '71; Same abr. Ed Digest 36: 37-9 Ap '71

See also
Afro-American studies
Colleges and universities—Curriculum
Curriculum planning
Elective system in education
High schools—Curriculum
Junior high schools—Curriculum
Schedules, School

COURT buildings. See Courthouses

COURT houses. See Courthouses

COURT line aviation. See Airlines—Great Britain

COURT martial. See Courts martial and courts of inquiry

COURT procedure. See Procedure (law)

COURT reporting (by newspapers) See Newspaper court reporting

COURT theater. See Copenhagen—Theater

COURT use of video tape recordings. See Video recorders and recording—Court use

COURTHOUSES

Frank Lloyd Wright's Hall of justice; Marin County, Calif. R. Montgomery. il Arch Forum 133:54-9 D '70

COURTING disaster (or. Serious in the fifties) story. See Roth. P.

COURTNEY, Winifred F.

Persian book trade prepares for nation's 2500th anniversary. il Pub W 200:pt2 181-3 S 27 '71

COURTROOM decorum. See Conduct of court proceedings

COURTROOM illustrators. See Illustrators

COURTS

British. French and American systems of justice compared. B. C. Canon. bibliog f Cur Hist 61:97-104+ Ag '71

See also
Appellate procedure
Contempt of court
Criminal procedure
Grand jury
Jury
Small claims courts

California

See also
Justice, Administration of—California

COURTS—*Continued*

Illinois

Indicted prosecutor. New Repub 165:9-10 S 11 '71

Jam-up: crisis in our criminal courts. J. Star. il Look 35:32-4+ Mr 23 '71

Panther raid coverup. J. W. Singer and T. J. Dolan. New Repub 165:21-3 Jl 24 '71

New York (state)

Trial courts in urban politics, by K. M. Dolbeare. Review
Trans-Action 8:96+ N '70. W. K. Muir, jr

United States

Chief justice looks at crime and the courts; interview. W. E. Burger. por Read Digest 98:113-16 Ap '71

Court reform; address, March 12, 1971. W. E. Burger. Vital Speeches 37:386-90 Ap 15 '71

Criminal court logjam; excerpts from Justice denied. L. Downie, jr. Cur Hist 61:82-6+ Ag '71

Defending the environment, by J. L. Sax. Review
New Repub 165:27-8 Jl 3 '71. R. A. Jones

Federal courts. bibliog f Cur Hist 60:347-52+ Je '71

Judge for a day; antidote to court congestion. il Time 98:71-2 O 18 '71

Nixon's other judges. il Time 98:57 N 29 '71

Our creaking courts; interview. W. E. Burger. por Read Digest 98:217-19+ My '71

System of state and local courts. H. R. Glick. Cur Hist 60:341-6 Je '71

See also
Courts martial and courts of inquiry
Justice, Administration of—United States
United States—Supreme court
also subhead Courts under names of cities, e.g. Pittsburgh—Courts

COURTS (for games)

Back-yard games: how to lay them out. il Pop Mech 136:136 Ag '71

Penny's pavilion, concepts in concrete. C. M. Pendleton, jr. il Parks & Rec 6:42+ My '71

See also
Basketball courts
Tennis courts

COURTS, Ecclesiastical. See Ecclesiastical courts

COURTS, International

See also
International court of justice, The Hague

COURTS martial and courts of inquiry

As others see us; the Calley case; comp. by N. G. Balint. Sat R 54:36-7 My 8 '71

Bailey's breakthrough; Medina trial. Newsweek 78:43 S 27 '71

Black cadet at West Point; J. C. Whittaker case. J. F. Marszalek, jr. il pors Am Heritage 22:30-7+ Ag '71; Reply. T. J. Fleming. 22:111 O '71

Calley affair. il Time 97:13-14 Ap 19 '71

Calley and company. New Repub 164:10-11 Ap 10 '71

Calley on the couch. Newsweek 77:25 F 1 '71

Calley takes the stand; with excerpts from testimony. il pors Life 70:22-8 Mr 5 '71

Calley: the existential problem. Nat R 23:245 Mr 9 '71

Calley verdict. Nation 212:450-2 Ap 12 '71

Calley's confession. por Newsweek 77:21-2 Mr 1 '71

Calley's defense: anger, hate, fear, orders. por Newsweek 77:51-2 Mr 8 '71

Captain and the President; A. Daniel's letter to the President in contrast to the President's TV address of April 7. Nation 212:482-3 Ap 19 '71

Case against Medina. il Newsweek 78:24 Ag 30 '71

Clamor over Calley: who shares the guilt? il Time 97:14-16+ Ap 12 '71

Confessions of Lieutenant Calley; interview, ed. by J. Sack. W. L. Calley, jr. Esquire 76:85-9+ S '71

End of the affair; Medina trial. il por Newsweek 78:22 O 4 '71

Guilty, sort of; case of T. Culver and the anti-war demonstration. por Newsweek 78:26 Jl 26 '71

Henderson in the dock. il por Newsweek 78:17-18 S 6 '71

I couldn't kill. . . ; Calley trial. por Newsweek 77:26 Mr 29 '71

Inside the jury room; Calley's day of judgment. S. Lesher. il Newsweek 77:33-4 Ap 12 '71

Judging Calley is not enough. T. Taylor. il Life 70:20-3 Ap 9 '71

Judgment at Fort Benning: the Calley verdict. il pors Newsweek 77:27-9 Ap 12 '71

Lies about My Lai. Time 98:25 N 29 '71

Medina's story; with excerpts from testimony. il Newsweek 77:24-6 Mr 22 '71

Military justice is to justice as military music is to music, by R Sherrill. Review
Commentary 51:91-2+ Je '71. J. W. Bishop, jr; Discussion. 52:4+ S '71

More about My Lai; Medina trial. Time 98:32 S 27 '71

My Lai: a question of orders. il pors Time 97:24 Ja 25 '71

My Lai: now only five. Time 97:24 F 8 '71

One is lying; trial of W. L. Calley. por Time 97:16 Mr 22 '71

Postscript to the Medina trial. K. Reich. Nation 213:433-5 N 1 '71

Power of the press; second trial of R. V. Johnson. Nation 211:645 D 21 '70

Verdict that troubled a nation; Calley trial. U S News 70:25 Ap 12 '71

War is hell; Calley trial. D. Lawrence. U S News 70:96 Ap 26 '71

Who is responsible for My Lai? por Time 97 18-19 Mr 8 '71

Why the Calley case opens up worldwide debate. D. Lawrence. U S News 70:96 Ap 12 '71

With Calley at My Lai. il Newsweek 77:32-3 Ja 25 '71

Young peers of Long Binh; most unusual jury in military memory. il Time 98:81+ N 8 '71

Your witness: prosecution witnesses and the Medina trial. Newsweek 78:18 S 6 '71

See also
Military law

Verdicts

After Vietnam, another witchhunt? L. J. Halle. il N Y Times Mag p36-8+ Je 6 '71

Battle hymn of Lt Calley and the Republic. M. Novak. Commonweal 94:183-6 Ap 30 '71

Calley. N Cousins Sat R 54:22 Ap 24 '71

Calley case re-examined. S. Lesher. il pors N Y Times Mag p6-7+ Jl 11 '71

Calley for president? reactions to the Calley verdict. Nat R 23:408+ Ap 20 '71

Case that will not go quietly away; the Calley verdict. il Life 70:22-6 Ap 23 '71

Cases of conscience; reactions to Calley verdict. J. Ciardi. Sat R 54:4+ My 1 '71

Court adjourns on My Lai; Col O. K. Henderson not guilty of covering up tragedy. il Time 98:8 D 27 '71

Day America could have used a psychiatrist. B. Asbell. il por Todays Health 49:24-9+ Ag '71

End of the affair; acquittal for O. K. Henderson. por Newsweek 78:18-19 D 27 '71

In the uproar over Calley's conviction. il U S News 70:20 Ap 19 '71

Lieutenant Calley and the tragedy of violence; reactions to verdict. T. M. Gannon. America 124:399 Ap 17 '71

Meaning of Calley. J. Goldstein. New Repub 164:13-14 My 8 '71

Medina goes free. il Time 98:18 O 4 '71

My Lai and Lieut Calley: the wounds of war. il por Sr Schol 98:11-12+ My 10 '71

Mylai case: Rusty Calley, convicted of murder. por Life 71:34-5 D 31 '71

My Lai killings: 12 out of 13 accused are free. il U S News 71:101 O 4 '71

Notes and comment; Nixon's actions in the Calley case. New Yorker 47:31-3 Ap 17 '71

COURTS of appeal. See Appellate procedure

COURTS of inquiry. See Courts martial and courts of inquiry

COURTS of small claims. See Small claims courts

COURTSHIP

Anecdotes, facetiae, satire, etc.

Eating and making love. . . Q. Crewe. il Vogue 158:93-4 Jl '71

COURTSHIP of birds

Courtship of storks. M. P. Kahl. il Natur Hist 80:36-45 O '71

COUSCOUS. See Cookery, North African

COUSINO, Joe Ann

Ceramic sculpture of Joe Ann Cousino. R. D. Bonham. il Ceram Mo 19:16-17 My '71 *

COUSINS, Margaret

Love story; runaway hit: why? il Vogue 157:130-2+ Mr 1 '71

Remembrance of things future; story. Ladies Home J 88:110-11 O '71

COUSINS, Norman

Death of Look. U S News 71:104+ O 11 '71

Final report to the readers. Sat R 54:32-3 N 27 '71

COUSINS, Norman—*Continued*
Improbable triumvirate: Khrushchev, Kennedy, and Pope John. pors Sat R 54:24-35 O 30 '71
Linus Pauling and the vitamin controversy. Sat R 54:37-40+ My 15 '71
Report to the readers. Sat R 54:16-17 Jl 31 '71

about
Bargaining for a baby. por Time 98:30 Jl 19 '71 *
Cousins quits. Time 98:58 N 29 '71 *
End of an era. il Newsweek 78:51 N 29 '71 *
New tycoons. pors Newsweek 78:64 Jl 26 '71 *
Report to the readers. J. J. Veronis. Sat R 54:32-3 D 4 '71 *
Revamping the Review. il pors Time 98:62 N 22 '71 *

COUSTEAU, Jacques Yves
Dying oceans, poisoned seas; views presented at United Nations symposium on the environment. Time 98:74+ N 8 '71
—and Cousteau, Phillipe
Shark; excerpt from The shark: splendid savage of the sea. il Read Digest 99:103-8 S '71

COUSTEAU, Philippe. See Cousteau, J. Y. jt. auth.

COUTURE, Alfred E.
Death ran with the river. il pors Outdoor Life 147:53-7+ My '71

COUTURE, Thomas
Thomas Couture, painter and teacher of painters; with editorial comment. M. E. Landgren. il Antiques 99:772, 877-81 Je '71 *

COVARRUBIAS, Miguel
Divided world of Miguel Covarrubias. T. Grieder. il Américas 23:19-24 My '71 *

COVENANT; story. See Cherry, K.

COVENT Garden. See London—Covent Garden

COVENT Garden opera company. See Royal opera, Great Britain

COVER crops
Cover crop as green manure. Sunset 147:232 N '71
See also
Vetch

COVER design. See Book covers

COVER plants
Controlling weeds in groundcovers. A. Bing. il Horticulture 49:20-3 Je '71
It flowers yellow in spring, it isn't very demanding, and it covers the ground; hypericum coris. il Sunset 147:229 N '71
See also
Cinquefoil
Knotweeds
Wood sorrel

COVERED bridges
Covered bridges: historic reminders. W. N. Savage. il Am For 77:40-3+ Je '71

COVERLETS
Bounce-proof bedspreads for boys and girls. C. Houck. il Parents Mag 46:18-19 O '71
See also
Afghans (coverlets)

COVERS, Book. See Book covers

COVERT behavior. See Behavior (psychology)

COW. See Cows

COWAN, Edward
Cold wind from Canada, the Gray report. Nation 213:613-16 D 13 '71

COWAN, Gary
Look what Gary found in the cup! J. Jares. il por Sports Illus 35:24-5 S 13 '71 *

COWAN, George M.
Overcoming Babel. Chr Today 15:8-10 Jl 16 '71

COWAN, Glenn
Ping-pong star's get-rich plans. il por Bsns W p26 My 8 '71 *
Youth view from Chou. il por Sr Schol 98:15-16 My 10 '71 *

COWAN, Joel
Job for patient money. por Forbes 107:45+ F 15 '71 *

COWAN, Richard. See Poppy, J. jt. auth.

COWAN, Zélide. See Teague, M. jt. auth.

COWART, Clarence R. Jr
Dumps are signs of poor administration. il Am City 86:54+ D '71

COWBOYS
Jungle cowboy; condensation. S. E. Brock. il pors Read Digest 98:233-9+ F '71
See also
Rodeos

COWBOYS (football club) See Football clubs

COWEN, Robert C.
Does it recycle through black holes? Cur 133:30-3 O '71

COWENS, Dave
It was a brief time-out. P. Carry. il pors Sports Illus 34:22-3 Ja 11 '71 *

COWES, Roberto A.
Gold of Coclé. il Américas 23:S36-40 Je '71

COWICHAN VALLEY forest museum. See Open-air museums

COWLES, Charles
Art for everybody; interview, ed. by M. Roche. House & Gard 140:31+ O '71

COWLES, Gardner
Last Look. por Time 98:55 S 27 '71 *
Look suspends publication after 34 years. Pub W 200:42-3 S 27 '71 *

COWLES, Jan
Mr and Mrs Gardner Cowles's New York apartment. V. Lawford il Vogue 158:180-7+ O 1 '71 *

COWLES, John, 1929-
After the fall. il por Newsweek 77:69 Mr 22 '71 *
Hang-up at Harper's. pors Time 97:41 Mr 15 '71 *
What happened at Harper's. S. Little. il por Sat R 54:43-7+ Ap 10 '71 *

COWLES book company
Regnery, Chicago firm, buys Cowles book company. Pub W 199:49 Mr 8 '71

COWLES communications, inc.
Last Look. il Newsweek 78:78 S 27 '71
What finally crippled the Cowles empire. il Bsns W p 122-3+ S 25 '71

COWLEY, Malcolm
Holding the fort on Audubon Terrace. il Sat R 54:17+ Ap 3 '71
Storytelling's tarnished image. Sat R 54:25-7+ S 25 '71
We had such good times. New Repub 165:27-8 D 25 '71

COWLEY, Robert
Their work is child's play. il pors Horizon 13:14-15 Wint '71

COWS
Amazing things they find in cows. il Sci Digest 69:13-15 Je '71
Finky cows I have known. M. Miner. il por Farm J 95:D7-8 D '71
See also
Dairying
Heifers

Anecdotes, facetiae, satire, etc.
How now? C. Tomkins. New Yorker 46:28 Ja 23 '71

Care
Animal health: hints for high producers. J. R. Borcherding. il Suc Farm 69:D6 My '71

Diseases and pests
See also
Mastitis

Feeding
Best way to fuel up cows: complete feed. il Farm J 95:D6+ Je '71
No-hay rations can spell trouble. B. Guss. il Suc Farm 69:D2-4 My '71
Young dairyman hits the top. il Suc Farm 69:D8 My '71

Milk production
See Milk—Production

COWS, Cooling of. See Livestock, Cooling of

COWSIK, Ramanath, and Price, P. B.
Origins of cosmic rays. bibliog il Phys Today 24:30-8 O '71

COX, Allan V. See Butler, R. F; Doell, R. R. jt. auths.

COX, David F.
Some comments on linguistics. Chr Cent 88:1498-9 D 22 '71

COX, Edward Finch
June wedding in the White House. il pors Time 97:11-12 Mr 29 '71 *
Love story. il pors Newsweek 77:24-5 Mr 29 '71 *
Mr Cox takes a June bride. il pors Time 97:16 Je 21 '71 *
Simple spectacular at the White House. il pors Time 97:13-17 Je 14 '71 *
Tricia Nixon's romance with Ed Cox. il pors Life 70:18-23 Ja 22 '71 *
Wedding in the garden. il pors Newsweek 77:20-1 Je 21 '71 *
What kind of a man has Tricia married? S. B. Conroy. pors Good H 173:14-16+ Jl '71 *
When Tricia Nixon marries—. il por U S News 70:54 Je 14 '71 *
White House wedding. il pors Newsweek 77:30-4 Je 14 '71 *

COX, Elisabeth Baynton-. See Baynton-Cox, E.

COX, Georgia Lee
Confessions of a wicked stepmother. il Ladies Home J 88:104+ Mr '71
COX, Harvey
Ungodly city. il Commonweal 94:351-7 Jl 9 '71
COX, Hubert K.
Beginner on elk. il Field & S 76:46-7+ Ag '71
COX, James J.
Why cry? il Todays Health 49:28-32 Mr '71
COX, Jeff
How much technology in the kitchen? il Org Gard & Farm 18:100-4 Ja '71
Make sure your soil has trace minerals. Org Gard & Farm 18:58-61 Jl '71
They don't try too hard. il Org Gard & Farm 18:46-7 My '71
COX, Robert E.
(ed) Gleanings for ATM's. See issues of Sky and telescope
COX, Roy L. and Ramer, E. M.
Trends in state-level curriculum requirements. Clear House 45:309-11 Ja '71
COX, Tricia (Nixon)
Where's Tricia? L. Winter. por Ladies Home J 88:76+ N '71 *
White House wedding. il pors Life 71:10-11 D 31 '71 *
COXE, Donald
Canada switches targets. Nat R 23:1177 O 22 '71
Great pipeline flap. Nat R 23:703+ Je 29 '71
COXHEAD, Nona
But she must be perfect; story. Ladies Home J 88:98-9 Jl '71
COYNE, John R. jr
People's republic of Berkeley. Nat R 23:260+ Mr 9 '71
Slates and hamsters. il Nat R 23:309-11 Mr 23 '71
COYNE, Patricia S.
Teaching the teacher. Nat R 23:1302+ N 19 '71
COYOTE hunting
Walking a coyote track. R. Byerly. il Outdoor Life 147:50-1+ Ja '71
COYOTES. Photography of. See Photography of animals
COZZI, Juliet A.
Catholic segregation: it's almost 1954. Commonweal 93:317, 435+ D 25 '70, F 5 '71
CRAB cactus. See Cactus
CRAB fisheries. See Shellfish fisheries
CRAB lice. See Lice
CRABB, Henry Alexander
Henry A. Crabb, filibuster or colonizer? J. A. Stout. il pors Am West 8:4-9 My '71 *
CRABB, Lawrence J. jr
New scientific thought: data and dogma as compatible. Chr Today 15:7-8 Mr 12 '71
CRABS
DDT residues: distribution of concentrations in emerita analoga (stimpson) along coastal California. R. Burnett. bibliog il Science 174:606-8 N 5 '71
See also
Cookery—Shellfish
King crabs
CRABS eye. See Eye (crustaceans)
CRABTREE, Bruce
By the mark. See issues of Yachting
Control points. See issues of Yachting to June 1971
Desolation Sound. il Yachting 129:52-3+ My '71
Destination Diamond Head. il Yachting 129:50-1+ Je '71
CRABTREE, Eloise
Beauty pageants are pathetic auctions! por Seventeen 29:230 S '70
CRACKERS
You can make your own crackers. il Sunset 146:220+ My '71
CRAFT fairs. See Arts and crafts—Exhibitions
CRAFTS, Edward C.
Men and events behind the Redwood National Park. il Am For 77:20-8+ My '71
CRAFTS. See Arts and crafts; Handicraft
CRAFTSMANSHIP
Craftsmen of the Piedmont; 8th annual fair. il Design 73:30-1 Wint '71
CRAFTSMENS colonies. See Artists colonies
CRAGUN, Richard
Team. W. Terry. il pors Sat R 54:42 Je 5 '71 *
CRAIG, Hardin
Hardin Craig: professor. N. L. Henry. Am Scholar 40:305-8 Spr '71 *
CRAIG, Jack
TV talk. Sports Illus 35:11 N 8 '71
CRAIG, James B.
Washington lookout. Am For 77:8+ D '71

CRAIG, Norma
I need help! il McCalls 99:98-101 O '71
Treat yourself to a brand-new skin. McCalls 98:78-9+ Ag '71
CRAIG, Paul P.
Lead, the inexcusable pollutant. il Sat R 54:68-70+ O 2 '71
—and Berlin, Edward
Air of poverty. bibliog il Environ 13:2-9 Je '71
CRAIG, Roy
Cloud on the desert. bibliog il Environ 13:20-4+ Jl; 50 N '71
CRAIG-HOLMES, Ann P. and Shaw, M. W.
Polymorphism of human constitutive heterochromatin. bibliog il Science 174:702-4 N 12 '71
CRAIG & Joan; story. See Asinof, E.
CRAIN, David Jason
Umbrella; poem. America 125:100 Ag 21 '71
CRAMER ballet company. See Ballet—Sweden
CRAMER electronics, inc.
When the other guy pauses, we charge! il por Bsns W p42+ F 6 '71
CRAMPS. See Menstruation—Disorders
CRANBERRIES
See also
Cookery—Fruit
CRANE, Carol L.
How to choose an interior designer. Am Home 74:72+ My '71
26 dollar-saving ideas for children's rooms. Am Home 74:26-8 S '71
CRANE, Clinton Hadley
Great yacht designers. B. Robinson. il por Yachting 129:72+ F '71 *
CRANE, H. Richard
Opportunities in geophysics. il Phys Today 24:23-6 F '71
CRANE, Hart
Hart Crane and the contemporary search. P. J. Sheehan. Engl J 60:1209-13 D '71 *
CRANE, Verne
Sail for your dinghy. il Motor B & S 128:76+ O '71
CRANE community college. See Chicago city college—Malcolm X campus
CRANES (birds)
Brolga dancing bird. il Sci Digest 70:35 S '71
CRANES, derricks, etc.
Revolutionary aerial lift. il Parks & Rec 6:39 My '71
CRANFORD, J. and others
Unilateral ablation of the auditory cortex in the cat impairs sound localization. bibliog il Science 172:286-8 Ap 16 '71
CRANKO, John
Dance. N. Goldner. Nation 212:731-2 Je 7 '71 *
Germany's elegant troupe of storytellers. C. Barnes. il por Life 70:10 My 21 '71 *
Goyas and dolls. il Time 97:70 My 10 '71 *
Selected short Crankos. H. Saal. il Newsweek 77:72 Je 7 '71 *
Stuttgart ballet. R. Zachary. Opera N 35:28 Je 12 '71 *
Who ever heard of a German ballet company? H. Saal. il por N Y Times Mag p 10-12+ Jl 18 '71 *
CRANKS and crankshafts
Tuff stuff; Tufftriding and nitriding. S. Green. il Hot Rod 24:122-3 Ap '71
VW crank thing. J. Thawley. il Hot Rod 24:108-9 F '71
CRANSTON, Alan
Excerpt from debate, September 17, 1970. Cong Digest 50:84+ Mr '71
Great trip-wire delusion. Sat R 54:14 Je 19 '71
Ordeal of the wounded veteran. Redbook 136:78+ Ap '71
CRAPPIE fishing
New trick for crappie. C. Nansen. il Field & S 75:58-9+ Mr '71
CRAPPIES
See also
Cookery—Fish
CRASSUS, Marcus Licinius
M. Licinius Crassus, loser; excerpt from the jaws of victory. C. Fair. il Horiz 13:112-17 Spr '71 *
CRASSWELLER, Robert D.
Darkness in Haiti. For Affairs 49:315-29 Ja '71
CRATERS
See also
Sunset Crater National Monument
CRATERS, Moon. See Moon—Surface
CRAVEN, John Piña
Cities on the sea? J. Lear. il Sat R 54:80-6+ D 4 '71 *

CRAVENS, Jay H.
Feeling our way to a good environment. il Am Ed 7:25-8 O '71
New Hampshire's Great Gulf, a wilderness area in trouble. il Am For 77:30-2+ S '71

CRAVIOTO, J. and others
Sex differences in I.Q. pattern of children with congenital heart defects. bibliog il Science 174:1042-3 D 3 '71

CRAW, Julia
U.S. wildlife refuges. il Travel 136:46-51 D '71

CRAWFORD, Frances M.
Saving graces. See issues of American home

CRAWFORD, Jim
Heads 'n' tails. il Pop Electr 1:35-7 Ja '72

CRAWFORD, Joan
Art of looking beautiful; excerpts from Joan Crawford: my way of life. il pors Mc-Calls 98:55-7+ Jl '71

about

Joan Crawford refuses to play Miss Mushy Mouth. T. Moore. por Life 71:81 O 15 '71 *

CRAWFORD, John S.
North country red. il Outdoor Life 148:38-41+ Jl; 68-71+ Ag '71

CRAWFORD, L. Lucille. See Measel. W. jt. auth.

CRAWFORD, M. H.
Hemoglobin polymorphism. Science 171:706 F 19 '71

CRAWFORD, Michael
Invective against the anti-metaphorites; poem. Commonweal 95:331 Ja 7 '72

CRAWFORD, R. D.
One IC audio generator. il Radio-Electr 42: 37-8 F '71

CRAWFORD, Robert W.
Walk-to swimming pools. il Am City 86:51-2 Ja '71

CRAWFORD, Wylie
My first year of teaching; excerpt from Don't smile until Christmas, ed. by K. Ryan. Todays Ed 60:46-7 F '71

CRAWFORD COUNTY, Ind.
Staying serene in Indiana. B. Watt. Travel 135:9 My '71

CRAYFISH
Neuronal circuit mediating escape responses in crayfish. R. S. Zucker and others. bibliog il Science 173:645-50 Ag 13 '71

CRAYFISH culture. See Shellfish culture

CRAYON drawing
Children in pastel. I. E. Weidenaar. il Design 72:32-3 mid-Wint '71

CRAYON marks on the wall; story. See Farrington, C. G.

CRAYON painting. See Encaustic painting

CRAYONS
Oil crayon. H. S. Paston. il Design 72:11 mid-Wint '71

CRAZY Horse (Sioux chief)
Custer myth. A. M. Josephy, jr. il por Life 71:48-52+ Jl 2 '71 *

Statues, portraits, etc.
Mountain versus Korczak Ziolkowski. R. Bongartz: il Esquire 75:113+ Mr '71

CREAM masks. See Cosmetics

CREAM puffs. See Pastry

CREAMS, Masking. See Cosmetics

CREAMS for the face. See Cosmetics

CREATINE
Environmental nitroso compounds: reaction of nitrite with creatine and creatinine. M. C. Archer and others. bibliog il Science 174:1341-3 D 24 '71

CREATININE
Environmental nitroso compounds: reaction of nitrite with creatine and creatinine. M. C. Archer and others. bibliog il Science 174:1341-3 D 24 '71

CREATION
Creation. W. Hedgepeth. il Look 35:16-29 Ja 12 '71

CREATION (literary, artistic, etc)
Creativity, poetic language, and the computer. M. Borroff. Yale R 60:481-513 Je '71
In the name of creation. M. Allen. il PTA Mag 66:18-20 D '71
Let's be creative:
Making a cardboard print. il Todays Ed 60:66 N '71
Making an accordion book. il Todays Ed 60:56 O '71
True creativity can emerge anytime, at 6, or at 40. T. J. Cottle. il Life 71:52-3 D 17 '71

Working with your hands. A. A. Hutschnecker. Vogue 158:114+ Jl '71
See also
Creative ability
Creative writing

Anecdotes, facetiae, satire, etc.
Flash! Famous novelist OD's on coffee! L. Hutchinson. Sr Schol 98:36 My 17 '71

CREATIVE ability
Creative kids: how to help them. il Changing T 25:41-4 Mr '71
You can be more creative! M. Brenton. il Seventeen 29:244-5+ Ag '70

CREATIVE dramatics. See Childrens plays; Dramatization in education

CREATIVE education
Creativity in the humanities class; program at Booker T. Washington high school, Atlanta. J. H. Whatley. il Todays Ed 60:10-12+ D '71
Let's be creative. il Todays Ed 60:56 O '71
Place where learning happens; Escarosa humanities center in Pensacola, Fla. S. K. DeMarko. il Am Ed 7:21-3 My '71
See also
Education, Experimental

CREATIVE imagination. See Imagination

CREATIVE photography
Creativity: the wrong exposure at the right time; with photographs. M. Edelson. Pop Phot 68:91-8 My '71
Stay young with photography. R. Hattersley. il Pop Phot 69:90-3+ O '71

CREATIVE playthings, inc.
Toy in your future. P. Steinfels. Commonweal 95:270 D 17 '71

CREATIVE thinking. See Thought and thinking

CREATIVE writing
See also
English language—Composition

Study and teaching
About creative writing. R. M. Stern. Writer 84:9-10 Jl '71
Art of word forms. H. Friedlander. Clear House 46:62 S '71
Autobiography: the gold of writing power. D. M. Wolfe. Engl J 60:937-46 O '71
Creative writing: the inner eye; publication of Lincoln Heights branch of the Los Angeles public library. J. L. Buelna. il Wilson Lib Bul 45:750-3 Ap '71
Film stimuli, an approach to creative writing. P. Dauterman and R. Stahl. Engl J 60:1120-2 N '71
Learning by mail. Writers Digest 51:32-3+ S '71
Reading, writing, and creativity. R. J. Smith. bibliog f il Clear House 45:350-4 F '71
What writers advise on the teaching of creative writing. J. Harris. bibliog Engl J 60: 345-62 Mr '71

CREDENTIALS committee of the United Nations. See United Nations—Credentials committee

CREDIT
Before you borrow or say charge it. il Changing T 26:33-5 Ja '72
Credit outlook: enough money, probably, and perhaps not too much. il Fortune 84:18 N '71
Growing fight over easy money. il U S News 70:35-6 Mr 15 '71
Lesson of the credit crisis. C. J. Loomis. il Fortune 83:141-3+ My '71
Scoundrel who invented credit. M. Bishop. por Horizon 13:110-11 Spr '71
Using credit: key words you need to know. il Changing T 25:37-8 N '71
See also
Agricultural credit
Charge accounts (retail trade)
Debtor and creditor
Discount
Export credit
Government lending
Loans, Bank
Negotiable instruments

Information services
See Credit bureaus

Rating
How to improve your credit rating. F. Casey. Mech Illus 67:64-5+ My '71
Your credit rating: how to check its accuracy. Good H 173:206 S '71

Regulation
Credit act cools mortgage men. Bsns W p84 My 22 '71

CRIME and criminals—Great Britain—*Cont.*

Hermit of Les Ecréhous; Edward Paisnel convicted of sex crimes on the island of Jersey. il por Time 98:32 D 13 '71

See also
London—Crime

History

Rufflers and ripping coves. J. Skow. por Time 97:92+ My 24 '71

Illinois

Black man leads Illinois' crime fight. il pors Ebony 26:64-6+ My '71

Iowa

U.S. journal: Center Junction; Jim, Tex, and the one-armed man. C. Trillin. New Yorker 47:100-2+ F 20 '71

Israel

Crime issue. il pors Newsweek 78:32-3 N 29 '71

Italy

Failure of a brave and foolish act. il Life 71:78-9 S 17 '71

See also
Mafia

Japan

Badge of courage. il Newsweek 77:42 Mr 22 '71

Inheritors; thieves of Fujigase. il Newsweek 77:42+ F 15 '71

See also
Tokyo—Crime

New England

See also
Mafia

New Jersey

See also
Mafia

Sicily

See also
Mafia

United States

America the violent? America 124:448 My 1 '71

Are you personally afraid of crime? Readers speak out. il Life 72:28-31 Ja 14 '72

Backfire on crime. il Time 98:33-4 O 18 '71

Browsing in gangland; with editorial comment. J. Epstein. Commentary 53:4+, 46-55 Ja '72

Crime and business. Nation 213:677-8 D 27 '71

Crime in America, by R. Clark. Review Commonweal 94:41-3 Mr 19 '71. I. Silver Fortune il 83:140-1 F '71. S. Hook Nat R 23:316-18 Mr 23 '71. E. Van Den Haag

Crime in the office building. J. Perham. il Duns 98:29-33 O '71

Crime: 1 in 36 is a victim. il U S News 71:54-5 S 13 '71

Crime wave hits colleges; High schools, too, have a crime problem. il U S News 71:24-6 N 22 '71

Crimes without victims. A. B. Smith and H. Pollack. Sat R 54:27-9 D 4 '71

Flood of responses to our crime questionnaire. R. Graves. il Life 71:3 D 10 '71

Has crime passed its peak? City-by-city report. il U S News 70:13-17 Ja 18 '71

Law that is still within us. Life 70:46 My 7 '71

New crimes for old. G. M. Sykes. Am Scholar 40:592-8 Aut '71

Park that caught urban blight. E. Abbey. il Life 71:40+ S 3 '71

Public reaction to crime in the streets. F. F. Furstenberg, jr. il Am Scholar 40:601-10 Aut '71

Study rules out crime relationship to color. Negro Hist Bul 33:171 N '70

Victimless crimes. il Newsweek 78:83 N 29 '71

Watched in the wild: crime in national parks. P. Barnes. New Repub 165:12-13 Ag 21 '71

What is the business of organized crime? T. C. Schelling. bibliog f Am Scholar 40:643-53 Aut '71

See also
Automobiles, Theft of
Criminal statistics
Gangs
Government investigations—Crime and criminals
Mafia
Police—United States
Prisons—United States
United States—Federal bureau of investigation
also subhead Crime under names of cities, e.g. New York (city)—Crime

History

Medicare mob; four grand old felons from the golden age of crime. il pors Esquire 76:98-101 Ag '71

CRIME and criminals, Sexual. See Sex crimes

CRIME and narcotics. See Narcotics and crime

CRIME and punishment; opera. See Petrovics, E.

CRIME and the press

Police, the press & the legend; call it Mafia. E Ruffini. il Nation 213:520-4 N 22 '71

Pretrial crime news: to curb or not to curb? J. Lofton. Cur Hist 61:71-4+ Ag '71

Sheppard v. Maxwell, 1966. Cur Hist 61:106-10+ Ag '71

See also
Newspaper court reporting

CRIME control laws and legislation. See Crime prevention

CRIME in literature

See also
Detective and mystery stories

CRIME insurance, Government. See Insurance, Government

CRIME novels. See Detective and mystery stories

CRIME prevention

Crime and law-and-order. H. Zeisel. Am Scholar 40:624-33 Aut '71

Crime and punishment. Sci Am 224:50-1 My '71

Has crime passed its peak? City-by-city report. il U S News 70:13-17 Ja 18 '71

Legislation proposed to protect U.S. officials and foreign diplomats; Department of justice announcement, with text of letter by Attorney General Mitchell and Secretary Rogers. Dept State Bul 65:268-70 S 6 '71

New war against crime. C. Rogers. Chr Cent 88:276-7 Mr 3 '71

TRB from Washington: congressional hearings. New Repub 164:6 Je 12 '71

There's more to crime control than the get tough approach. D. L. Skoler. bibliog f Ann Am Acad 397:28-39 S '71

Washington's capital crime-stopper; police chief J. Wilson. R. MacLeish. Read Digest 98:53-4+ My '71

Where war against crime is being won; interview. J. N. Mitchell. il pors U S News 70:38-42 Mr 22 '71

Year of the prisons. J. Castelli. Commonweal 94:494-7 S 24 '71

See also
Juvenile delinquency—Prevention
United States—Justice, Department of—Law enforcement assistance administration

Citizen participation

Citizens' war on crime. il U S News 71:23-5 D 20 '71

Failure of a brave and foolish act; Genoa, Italy. il Life 71:78-9 S 17 '71

CRIME wave. See Crime and criminals—United States

CRIMES, War. See War crimes

CRIMES aboard aircraft
See also
Airplane hijacking

CRIMINAL investigation

Secret witness: new weapon against crime; Detroit News program. J. Stewart-Gordon. il Read Digest 99:190-1+ N '71

See also
Chemistry, Legal
Detectives
Electronics in criminal investigation, espionage, etc
New York (state)—Legislature—Joint committee on crime, its causes, control and effect on society
Television in criminal investigation
United States—Federal bureau of investigation
Voiceprints

CRIMINAL justice, Administration of. See Justice, Administration of

CRIMINAL law

American justice at work; symposium. bibliog f Cur Hist 61:1-39+ Jl '71

Burger court & the penal system. S. Rubin. Nation 212:785-8 Je 21 '71

Freedom, order and justice. F. A. Allen. Cur Hist 60:321-6+ Je '71

See also
Capital punishment
Conspiracy
Contempt of court
Criminal procedure
Indeterminate sentence
Libel and slander
Obscenity (law)
United States—National commission on reform of federal criminal laws

CRIMINAL lawyers. See Lawyers
CRIMINAL procedure
British, French and American systems of justice compared. B. C. Canon. bibliog f Cur Hist 61:97-104+ Ag '71
Case for the so-called hard line approach to crime. F. E. Inbau and F. G. Carrington. bibliog f Ann Am Acad 397:19-27 S '71
Death takes a holiday. W. J. Lassers. Trans-Action 8:10+ Ja '71
Delaying the game; C. Jones avoids trial. il por Time 99:58-9 Ja 10 '72
Justice British style: lessons U.S. lawyers see. il U S News 71:36-7 Ag 2 '71
Law & order; address, August 4, 1971. H. O. Reed. Vital Speeches 37:730-6 S 15 '71
Look at our judicial system; address. R. S. Ayala. Vital Speeches 37:374-6 Ap 1 '71
Pre-posthumous conversation with myself. E. Smith. pors Esquire 75:112-15+ Je '71
    See also
Arrest
Bail
Courts martial and courts of inquiry
Defense (criminal procedure)
Grand jury
Indeterminate sentence
Jury
Pleas (criminal procedure)
Pre-trial procedure
Preventive detention
Probation
Searches and seizures
Speedy trial
CRIMINAL psychology
    See also
Forensic psychiatry
Psychology, Pathological
CRIMINAL statistics
Progress in the battle against crime. il U S News 71:38 Jl 12 '71
CRIMINALS. See Crime and criminals
CRIMINOLOGY. See Crime and criminals
CRIMMIN, Eileen
Escape from the humdrum. il Motor B & S 127:35+ Ap '71
Idea from below nowhere. il por Motor B & S 127:12+ My '71
San Juan: pride of the Northwest. il Motor B & S 127:55+ Je '71
CRIMP, Douglas
Quartered and drawn. il Art N 70:48-9+ Mr '71
CRINKLEY, Richmond
Theater (cont) Nat R 23:155-6, 324, 602-4, 1427 F 9, Mr 23, Je 1, D 17 '71
CRIPPLES
    See also
Amputees
CRISPENS, Chris
Lifestyle. il por Am Home 74:20 D '71 •
CRISSCROSS crown; story. See Carro, G.
CRIST, Raymond E.
Popayán revisited. il Américas 23:25-32 Ap '71
CRITCHFIELD, Richard
Impact in Hanoi. Nation 213:102-5 Ag 16 '71
CRITES, Stephen
Jack be nimble; poem. Chr Cent 88:768 Je 23 '71
CRITICAL path analysis
Management rediscovers CPM. G. J. Berk-witt. il Duns 97:57-9 My '71
CRITICAL path method. See Critical path analysis
CRITICAL point
Critical phenomena; report of conferences. R. E. Mills and others. Science 174:1260-1 D 17 '71
Solution of eight-vertex model excites critical-point theorists. G. B. Lubkin. bibliog il Phys Today 24:17+ S '71
CRITICAL thinking. See Thought and thinking
CRITICISM
Speaking and hearing the truth in love. K. S. Roundhill. Chr Today 16:7-9 Ja 7 '72
    See also
Art criticism
Dramatic criticism
Educational criticism
Literary criticism
Moving picture criticism
Musical criticism
Television criticism
CRITICISM, Personal. See Self evaluation
CRITICS
Current cinema. P. Kael. New Yorker 46:76-80 Ja 23 '71
Movie audiences don't change; interview. ed. by M. Ronan. D. Lean. por Sr Schol 98:18 F 15 '71
    See also
Book reviewers and reviewing
Kael, P.
Literary criticism

CRITIQUE de la vie quotidienne; story. See Barthelme, D.
CRITTENDEN, Jordan
Day Mr Claycomb's wife left home; story. Harp Baz 104:122-3 My '71
CROCE, Arlene
Performing arts. Harper 242:30+ Ap '71
Sexism in the head. bibliog f Commentary 51:63-8 Mr '71
CROCE, Joseph Santa-. See Santa-Croce, J.
CROCHETING
How to get hooked on crochet. il House & Gard 139:104-7 Ap '71
Introduction to the simple art of crochet il House & Gard 139:140-2 Ap '71
Nostalgic crochet for your home. V. P. Guild. il Good H 173:106-7 Ag '71
Redbook guide. il Redbook 137:104-12 O '71
    See also
Knitting
CROCKETT, George William, 1909-
Reflections of a jurist on civil disobedience. Am Scholar 40:584-91 Aut '71
CROCKETT, James Underwood
In your greenhouse. See issues of Horticulture
CROCODILES
    See also
Alligators
CROESUS and the witch; musical comedy. See Musical comedies, revues, etc.—Criticisms, plots, etc.
CROFT, A. Russell
Romance of perched soil. il Am For 77:38-9+ Mr '71
CROKE, E. J. and Roberts, J. J.
Air resource management and regional planning. il Bul Atom Sci 27:8-12 F '71
CROLL, Tina
Tina Croll and dance company, the Cubiculo, NYC. N. Mason. Dance Mag 45:72+ F '71 •
Tina Croll and dance company, Washington Square church, NYC. T. Borek. Dance Mag 45:77 Jl '71 •
CROMER, Esmé (Harmsworth) Baring, countess of
Countess of Cromer. G. Perint. Harp Baz 104:58 Mr '71 •
CROMIE, Robert Allen
Story behind the book. L. P. Freilicher. il Pub W 200:36-7 O 25 '71 •
CROMWELL, Oliver
Bess and old Noll. A. Fraser. pors Horizon 13:106-11 Aut '71 •
CRONE, Tom
Expanding new market: audio visuals. il Writers Digest 51:22-4+ S '71
How much your freelance time is worth. il Writers Digest 51:28-9+ Mr '71
CRONIN, John F.
Recent volcanism and the stratosphere. bibliog il Science 172:847-9 My 21 '71
CRONIN, John R. and Moore, C. B.
Amino acid analyses of the Murchison, Murray, and Allende carbonaceous chondrites. bibliog il Science 172:1327-9 Je 25 '71
CRONIN, Paula
Report from Bequia. il Travel 135:56-9 Mr '71
CRONIN, Sean
Everyone but the terrorists. Commonweal 94:470-1 S 17 '71
CRONIN, Thomas E. and Thomas, N. C.
Federal advisory processes: advice and discontent. bibliog il Science 171:771-9 F 26 '71
CRONIN, Timothy X.
When the other guy pauses, we charge! il por Bsns W p42+ F 6 '71 •
CRONIN, Vincent
Humanists. il Horizon 13:80-103 Wint '71
CRONKITE, Walter, 1916-
Authors & editors; interview. ed. by A. Johnston. por Pub W 199:15-17 My 3 '71
Cronkite retort; excerpt from address. por Time 97:71 My 31 '71
    about
Day in the life of Walter Cronkite. P. Hudson. il pors Sr Schol 99:10-11+ O 18 '71 •
Prime time of Walter Cronkite. P. O'Neil. il pors Life 70:50-50B+ Mr 26 '71 •
You are there. Cyclops. por Life 71:20 O 3 '71 •
CROOK, Mel
More power to you. See issues of Yachting 1972 outboards. il Yachting 130:64-5+ O '71
CROP; story. See O'Connor, F.
CROP forecasts. See Agricultural forecasting
CROP insurance. See Insurance, Agricultural
CROP waste as feed. See Feeding and feeding stuffs—Waste products

CROP yields
Big corn crop: no boon for hogmen. R. Wilmore. il Farm J 95:H24 O '71
Don't cut yields when you cut costs. Suc Farm J 95:36 O '71
Easy way to estimate yields. C. E. Sommers. il Suc Farm 69:B8 S '71
5-billion-bushel corn crop. B. Coffman. Farm J 95:19 S '71
Higher yields lower costs. Suc Farm 69:no5 34 Mr '71
How floods cut corn yields. J. C. Herman. Suc Farm 69:no2 46-7 F '71
Protein "fertilizer" boosts soybean yields. Farm J 95:36 O '71
Should you raise oats? R. Lutz. il Suc Farm 69:no4A4 Mr '71
10-ton forage yields are his challenge. J. Davis. il Suc Farm 69:no5 H8 Mr '71
These factors cut corn yields. Suc Farm 69: D18 O '71
You can get 10 more bushels from every acre; ed. by R. Lutz. il Suc Farm 69:SB3-5 N '71

CROPS
Crop management. C. E. Sommers. See issues of Successful farming
Which to plant: corn, beans, or grain sorghum? il Suc Farm 69:no4 12 Mr '71
    See also
Companion crops
Cover crops
Double cropping
Forage plants
Harvesting
    also names of crops, e.g. Milo

Marketing
See Farm produce—Marketing

Prices
See Farm produce—Prices

CROPS, Surplus. See Surplus products, Agricultural

CROQUET
Right out of their league. J. Mathewson. Sports Illus 34:62-4 Ap 5 '71

CROSBY, D. G. and others
Photodecomposition of chlorinated dibenzo-p-dioxins. bibliog il Science 173:748-9 Ag 20 '71

CROSBY, David
Rock family affair. il por Life 71:54 S 24 '71 •

CROSBY, John
Americans: making it in London. Vogue 157: 118-19 Mr 15 '71

CROSBY, John O'Hea
Pilgrim's progress; interview, ed. by F. Merkling. por Opera N 35:12-13 Je 12 '71

CROSBY, Robert M. N.
Dyslexic child. Todays Ed 60:46-8 O '71

CROSS, Alan
Capital gets some culture. il Am For 77:14-19 N '71

CROSS, Charles A.
Mariners' 1969 closeup map of Mars. il Sky & Tel 42:16-17 Jl '71

CROSS, James Richard
Diplomat freed. Sr Schol 97:6-7 Ja 11 '71 •

CROSS and crosses
Cross-bearers. A. Eggebroten. il Chr Today 15:33-4 Ag 27 '71
Getting it together; New York's Metropolitan museum and Norway's Oslo museum of applied art to join basic components of the Bury St Edmunds cross. il Newsweek 78:58 Ag 2 '71
    See also
Crucifixion

CROSS country running. See Running

CROSS country skiing. See Skis and skiing

CROSS eyes. See Strabismus

CROSS FLORIDA BARGE CANAL
Blocking Florida's ditch. il Newsweek 77:55-6 F 1 '71
Canal abandoned. il Sr Schol 98:8 F 15 '71
End of the barge canal. Time 97:61 F 1 '71
Florida: Nixon halts canal project, cites environment. J. Walsh. il Science 171:357 Ja 29 '71
Nixon stops up a barge canal. Bsns W p 19 Ja 23 '71
President's action halts Florida's favorite folly. Audubon 73:115 Mr '71

CROSSBOW
Cross-bow, an example of longevity. C. Worman. il Hobbies 76:154-5 O '71
Look what they've done to the crossbow! P. Wahl. il Pop Sci 198:36 Ap '71

CROSSBREEDING. See Hybridization

CROSSBREEDING of cattle. See Cattle breeding

CROSSES. See Cross and crosses

CROSSING the Alps; story. See Drabble, M.

CROSSLEY, John P. Jr
Second chance for the neo-orthodox. Chr Cent 88 :1048-51 S 8 '71

CROSSMAN, Richard
Regal cheek? il pors Newsweek 77:50 Je 14 '71 •

CROTALE (missile) See Guided missiles

CROUTONS. See Toast

CROW, Porter
My father's shoebox; address, October 1971. Vital Speeches 38:134-6 D 15 '71

CROW, Trammell
Trammell Crow: Big, Bigger Biggest? por Forbes 107:53-4+ Ap 15 '71 •

CROW Indians
How 114 washing machines came to the Crow reservation; excerpt from The death of the Great Spirit. E. Shorris. Atlan 227:73-7 F '71
    See also
Plenty Coups (Indian chief)

CROW shooting
Crows like wildfire. J O. Cartier. Outdoor Life 147:42-3+ Ja '71
Float trip for crows. J. B. Robinson. il pors Outdoor Life 147:66-7+ My '71

CROWDER, James Lee
Telltale bullets. Time 97:53 Ap 5 '71 •

CROWDS
U.S. journal: Pasadena; waiting for the roses. C. Trillin. New Yorker 46:85-9 Ja 16 '71

CROWE, John H. and Cooper, A. F. Jr
Cryptobiosis; with biographical sketches. il Sci Am 225:10, 30-6 D '71

CROWN agents for oversea governments and administrations
Serving a new empire. J. Ross-Skinner. il Duns 97:79-80+ Je '71

CROWN and Eagle mills, North Uxbridge. See Massachusetts—Historic houses. etc.

CROWN-of-thorns starfish. See Starfishes

CROWTHER, Betty, and Pantleo, P. M.
Marathon therapy and changes in attitude toward treatment and behavior ratings. bibliog Ment Hy 55:165-70 Ap '71

CROZAZ, G. and Walker, R. M.
Solar particle tracks in glass from the Surveyor 3 spacecraft. bibliog il Science 171: 1237-9 Mr 26 '71

CROZIER, Andrew
Comment. P. Schjeldahl. Poetry 117:274 Ja '71 •

CROZIER, Brian
Tactics of terror: where reds will strike next; interview. ed. by J. Fromm. il por U S News 70:75-8 Mr 1 '71

CRUCIFERAE
We grow the biggest mustard. O. Raney. Org Gard & Farm 18:74 S '71

CRUCIFIXES. See Cross and crosses

CRUCIFIXION
Rite of crucifixion. il Newsweek 77:52-3 Ja 18 '71

CRUCIFIXION of Christ. See Jesus Christ—Crucifixion

CRUELTY
    See also
Atrocities

CRUELTY to children
Battered child; reprint. S. R. Zalba. il Sci Digest 70:8-13+ D '71

CRUICKSHANK, Alexander M.
Gordon research conferences. Science 171: 1041-58+ Mr 12 '71
Gordon research conferences: winter program, 1972. Science 174:730+ N 12 '71

CRUIKSHANK, Nelson H.
NCSC re-elects Cruikshank, urges WHCOA every 3 years. il por Aging 201:9-10 Jl '71 •

CRUISE missiles. See Guided missiles—Launching from ships

CRUISERS (pleasure boats)
Houseboat that sails. E. B. Benjamin. il Yachting 130:55+ Jl '71
Is this any way to plan a retirement? H. M. Winters. Motor B & S 128:90 S '71
One man's boat. A. W. Moffat. il Yachting 129:63+ Mr '71
Streak of adventure. M. J. Hayes. il por Yachting 129:54-5+ Mr '71
"Yachting" eyes a boat:
    Chris-Craft 35' Commander. J. Smith. il Yachting 130:72-3+ N '71
    Stamas V26 americana sedan cruiser. R. Marston. il Yachting 130:66-7+ D '71
    Uniflite 42' double cabin sedan. A. Hemenway. il Yachting 130:70-1+ Jl '71
    Winner 280. il Yachting 129:72-3+ Ap '71

CRUISERS (pleasure boats)—*Continued*

Design

Breeding tells: latest 42' Constellations. il Motor B & S 128:60-1 Ag '71
Deliveries: special and otherwise; from Niagara to Florida's Gold Coast. P. Smyth. il Motor B & S 127:68-71+ F '71
Designs; ed. by B. D. Barker, 3d. See issues of Yachting
For all seasons. A. Hemenway. il Yachting 129:54-5+ My '71
It's the little things that count; offshore diesel powered cruiser Sans Terre. C. Mitchell. il Motor B & S 127:66-71+ Ap '71
Retire afloat. P. Smyth. il Motor B & S 128:42-5+ S '71
Surfing or seakindliness? F. Bilek. il Yachting 130:64-5+ Jl '71

Materials
See Boats—Materials

Noise
Noise aboard. E. H. Nabb. il Yachting 129:54-5+ Ap '71

Painting
See Boats—Painting

Pollution
Hysteria over heads. il Time 97:57-8 My 3 '71
Time for action. B. Robinson. Yachting 129:33 My '71

Stability and stabilizers
Anti-roll devices. E. Monk. il Yachting 129:64-5+ Mr '71

CRUISES. See Cruising

CRUISING
Any season; hop aboard the Hope. P. Blaze. il Travel 135:63-5 My '71
Armchair cruising; symposium. il Yachting 129:56-69+ F '71
Autumn and winter cruises from the West coast. Sunset 147:72-3 O '71
Betterments of cruising, including the Scandinavian. A. Gingrich. Esquire 75:6 Ap '71
Block Island; sanctuary out of time. P. R. Marunas. il Motor B & S 127:50-3+ Je '71
Can you squeeze in a weekend cruise between two work weeks? You can. il Sunset 146:42-4 Mr '71
Cathedral in the canyon. F. C. Clark. jr. il Motor B & S 127:94-7+ Mr '71
Cruise to Alaska, so many choices. il Sunset 146:16+ Ap '71
Cruising Lake Michigan. J. Roe. il por Yachting 130:58-9+ Jl '71
Desolation Sound. B. Crabtree. il Yachting 129:52-3+ My '71
Down the Mexican coast. C. Mitchell. il Motor B & S 128:52-5+ O '71
Gulf coast guide. G. Marston. il Yachting 130:62-3+ N '71
Gunkholing on Lake Champlain. G. P. Manning. il Motor B & S 128:50-1 Ag '71
Highland lakes of Texas; a series of impoundments of the Colorado River. C. L. Cadieux. il Yachting 130:54-5+ O '71
History hopping down the I.C.W. G. Merrill. bibliog il Motor B & S 128:50-1+ S '71
Letter from Long Island Sound. M. Hunt. New Yorker 47:62+ Ag 28 '71
Logistics of glut; world cruise aboard the S.S. France. J. Wechsberg. il Esquire 76:188-93+ D '71
Mariner's guide to cruising the waters of the world. J. Harman and H. E. Harman. 3d. il Holiday 49:50-1 Jl '71
No chicken counting; Nova Scotia cruise. T. Sturges. il Yachting 129:68-9+ My '71
Offbeat cruises. Newsweek 79:42 Ja 3 '72
Pareu parade; Society Islands. C. Pepper. il Travel 135:48-52+ Ap '71
Red star over Cynthia R. R. S. Carter. il Motor B & S 127:60-1+ My '71
Rugged run to New Guinea. P. Fitzgerald. il por Motor B & S 127:58-9+ F '71
Run away to sea, with the whole family. J. Higgins and S. R. Higgins. il Todays Health 49:36-9 Mr '71
San Juan; pride of the Northwest. E. Crimmin. il Motor B & S 127:55+ Je '71
Superior cruising. G. E. Miller. il Motor B & S 127:62-5+ My '71
Travel notes. R. Joseph. Esquire 75:20+ My '71
Voyage to the Hebrides. R. Feeley. il Yachting 129:56-7+ Je '71
When a lady cruises solo. J. M. Lang. il por Yachting 130:56-7+ S '71

Wilderness waterway; through Florida's 10,000 islands. J. Martenhoff. il Yachting 130:64+ N '71
See also
River trips
Voyages

Caribbean Region
Bareboating in the Grenadines. E. Horan. il Yachting 130:56-7+ N '71
Bimini: island in the stream. J. Groene and G. Groene. il Motor B & S 127:54+ Je '71
Cruising from the port of Miami. il Holiday 49:54-5 My '71
Diving cruise to Horse Shoe reef. C. Mitchell. il Yachting 130:58-60+ N '71
Reefing through the Leewards. W. D. Teague. il Yachting 130:52-3+ N '71
Sea gift, a cruise into irresponsibility. G. Bradshaw. Vogue 157:38 F 15 '71
Yacht chartering. C. Mitchell. il Holiday 48:44+ N '70

Islands of the Pacific
I'd love to get you on a slow boat to Vava'u. il Sat R 54:79 O 23 '71

Latin America
By freighter to the Incas. A. Buchsbaum. il Américas 23:18-24 O '71

Mediterranean Region
To the beautiful isle: Corsica. H. Colijn. il Yachting 130:58-9+ D '71

Mexico
Strange doings! D. Huffman; R. Bagley. il Yachting 130:55+ Ag '71

Scandinavia
Danish way; new charter service. B. Robinson. il Yachting 130:51-3+ D '71
New approach to an ancient route; Denmark's Zealand via the Gota Canal to Stockholm. J. Wynne. il Yachting 130:54-5+ D '71

Turkey
Odyssey in an antique land. R. Burke. il Travel 136:49-53 Jl '71

CRUISING houseboats. See Houseboats
CRUM, William J.
* Money king of Viet Nam. il por Time 97:19 Mr 8 '71 *
CRUMB, George
Toy pianos, musical saws and a great vocal tour de force. D. Hamilton. Hi Fi 21:78 Ag '71 *
CRUMB, Jan B.
Portrait of a protester. H. Mitgang. New Repub 164:14-15 My 8 '71 *
CRUMMERE, Maria Elise
Horoscope. See issues of Vogue
CRUSADE; story. See Oz, A.
CRUSH, Marion A.
Noble savage, 1971: suggestions for survival reading. bibliog il por Wilson Lib Bul 45:864-9 My '71
We threw away our tennis shoes. il Am Lib 2:207 F '71
CRUSO, Thalassa
5 easy garden ideas you can do yourself. il por House & Gard 139:80-5 Ag '71
How my garden grows. McCalls 98:48+ My; 73+ Je; 28+ Jl; 48+ Ag; 34+ S; 99:66+ N '71
Lady who talks to plants; interview, ed. by M. Mercer. il pors McCalls 98:80-1+ Ap '71
CRUSTACEANS
See also
Barnacles
Crabs
Eye (crustaceans)
Nervous system—Crustaceans
Sexual behavior—Crustaceans

Migration
Migrations and growth of deep-sea lobsters, homarus americanus. R. A. Cooper and J. R. Uzmann. bibliog il Science 171:288-90 Ja 22 '71
CRUSTACEANS, Fossil
See also
Trilobites
CRUTCHFIELD, William
Crutchfield phenomenon. J. Livingston. il por Art in Am 59:124-7 Ja '71 *
CRY from the heart: story. See Duncan, L.
CRYING
Treating excessive weepers. A. J. Snider. Sci Digest 69:70-1 My '71
Why cry? J. J. Cox. il Todays Health 49:28-32 Mr '71

CRYOBIOLOGY
  See also
  Cryonics
CRYOGENICS. See Low temperatures
CRYONICS
  Immortality and the freezing of human bodies. J. P. Wiley, jr; J. K. Sherman. il Natur Hist 80:12-18+ D '71
CRYPTOBIOSIS
  Cryptobiosis. J. H. Crowe and A. F. Cooper, jr. il Sci Am 225:30-6 D '71
CRYPTOGAMS
  See also
  Lichens
CRYSTAL, Richard
  Newport, the third of July. il Hi Fi 21:62-5 D '71
CRYSTAL cameos. See Cameos
CRYSTAL CITY, Tex.
  Education
  U.S. journal: Mexican American students. C. Trillin. New Yorker 47:102+ Ap 17 '71
CRYSTAL optics
  Reflectors in fishes. E. Denton. il Sci Am 224:64-72 Ja '71
CRYSTAL oscillators. See Oscillators, Crystal
CRYSTALLINE lens
  Eye lens color. formation and function. S. Zigman. bibliog il Science 171:807-9 F 26 '71; Reply with rejoinder. D. Kennedy and R. Milkman. 173:654-5 Ag 13 '71
CRYSTALLOGRAPHY
  Chemical bond and solid-state physics; adaptation of address, March 1969. J. C. Phillips; reply with rejoinder. L. Pauling. bibliog il Phys Today 24:9+ F '71
  Crystallography of the hexagonal ferrites. J. A. Kohn and others. bibliog il Science 172:519-25 My 7 '71
  Space groups not always derivable by parallelohedra and subdivision into stereohedra. W. Nowacki. bibliog il Science 174:52-5 O 1 '71
  Xenon hexafluoride: structural crystallography of tetrameric phases. R. D. Burbank and G. R. Jones. bibliog il Science 171:485-7 F 5 '71
  See also
  Crystal optics
  Crystals
  X ray studies
  Crystal structure of a naturally occurring dinucleoside monophosphate: uridylyl (3',5') adenosine hemihydrate. J. Rubin and others. bibliog il Science 174:1020-2 D 3 '71
CRYSTALS
  Crystal stores holograms. il Radio-Electr 42:2+ O '71
  Crystals and data storage. il Chem 44:22 S '71
  New sparkle in crystals. A. Broy. il Duns 97:89-90+ My '71
  X-ray parametric conversion: two photons for one; use of beryllium crystal. M. S. Rothenberg. Phys Today 24:17+ Ap '71
  Optical properties
  See Crystal optics
  Surfaces
  Surface microtopography; adaptation of address, March 1971. R. D. Young. bibliog il Phys Today 24:42-9 N '71
CSOKONAI VITÉZ, Mihály
  Hoping against hope: the enlightened age in Hungary. G. Barany. bibliog f il Am Hist R 76:319-57 Ap '71 *
CSURI, Charles
  Artist and the computer. D. Davis. il por Newsweek 78:78-81 S 13 '71 *
CUBA
  Cuba is there; Torriente's plans to invade Cuba. Nation 213:517-18 N 22 '71
  Cuba: the pursuit of freedom. by H. Thomas. Review
    America 125:378-9 N 6 '71. J. F. Thorning
  See also
  Agriculture—Cuba
  Ballet—Cuba
  Communism—Cuba
  Economic assistance in Cuba
  Education—Cuba
  Jews in Cuba
  Russians in Cuba
  Technical assistance, Russian—Cuba
  Visitors, Foreign—Cuba
  Defenses
  Soviet moves highlight Guantanamo role. C. Brownlow. il Aviation W 94:16-17 Ja 25 '71

Economic conditions
  Kosygin in Cuba: a visit with a high-priced ally. il U S News 71:60 N 8 '71
  Russia tightens grip on Castro. il U S News 71:34-5 Ag 23 '71
  Stronger voice now for Russia in Cuba. il U S News 70:26 Ja 18 '71
  Why Castro is halting the airlift. U S News 71:91 S 13 '71
  Economic policy
  Mortgaged island. il Time 97:38+ F 8 '71
  Foreign relations
  Cuba today. D. D. Burks. Cur Hist 60:108-111+ F '71
  Cuba's second Vietnam: Bolivia. M. D. Gensler. Yale R 60:342-65 Mr '71
  Chile
  See Chile—Foreign relations—Cuba
  Russia
  See Russia—Foreign relations—Cuba
  United States
  See United States—Foreign relations—Cuba
  Politics and government
  Agriculture, like politics is not an exact science, even in Cuba. J. Bishop. Commonweal 93:472-4 F 12 '71
  Cuba today. D. D. Burks. Cur Hist 60:108-111+ F '71
  Guerrillas in power, by K. S. Karol. Review
    Nation 212:693-5 My 31 '71. E. Hakim
  Religious institutions and affairs
  Religion in Cuba today, ed. by A. L. Hageman and P. E. Wheaton. Review
    Chr Cent 88:953 Ag 11 '71. L. M. Colonnese
  See also
  Churches—Cuba
CUBA and the United States
  After China, can Cuba be far behind? work of Cuba resource center. B. Thompson. Chr Cent 88:944-5 Ag 11 '71
  Attack in the Caribbean; piratical act of Cuban patrol boat. Time 98:33 D 27 '71
CUBAN cookery. See Cookery, Cuban
CUBAN crisis, 1962
  Global intelligence: the Democratic society; address, April 14, 1971. R. Helms. Vital Speeches 37:450-4 My 15 '71; Excerpts. il por U S News 70:34-6 Ap 26 '71
  Nuclear tyranny and the divine right of kings. G. E. Christianson. il Bul Atom Sci 27:44-6 Ja '71
  Son's defense; Kremlin issues official version. il Newsweek 78:41-2 Ag 9 '71
  Straight from the bear's mouth. M. Lazo; N. S. Khrushchev. Nat R 23:70-1 Ja 26 '71
CUBAN dancing. See Dancing, Cuban
CUBAN refugees. See Refugees, Cuban
CUBANS in the United States
  How the immigrants made it in Miami. il Bsns W p88-9 My 1 '71
  Making it in Miami, Cuban-style. il Life 71:36-41 D 10 '71
  Romeo & Julieta; growing up among Cuban relatives in Tampa, Fla. J. Yglesias. New Yorker 47:107-8+ O 16 '71
  See also
  Refugees, Cuban
CUBER, John Frank
  How new ideas about sex are changing our lives. Redbook 136:85+ Mr '71
CUBIC corporation
  Elevator to profits. T. J. Murray. Duns 97:78+ My '71
CUBISM
  Art; exhibition at the Metropolitan museum. L. Alloway. Nation 212:540-2 Ap 26 '71
  Art world; exhibition: the Cubist epoch at the Metropolitan museum. H. Robenberg. New Yorker 47:102-5 My 8 '71
  Cubism: making a new reality. il Vogue 157:122-5 Ap 1 '71
  Cubist epoch. H. Kramer. il Art in Am 59:51-7 Mr '71
  Esthetic valence of cubism. M. Kozloff. il Art N 70:34-7+ Ap '71
  Onward and upward with the arts; exhibition: the Cubist epoch at the Los Angeles County museum of art. F. Steegmuller. New Yorker 46:70-5 Ja 23 '71
  Painters' painting: cubism. R. McMullen. il Am Scholar 40:432-46 Sum '71
CUCCIA, James W.
  Princeps puzzle. il Pop Electr 34:26-32 My '71

CUCKOOS
  See also
  Road runners (birds)
CUCUMBERS
  Chinese cucumbers as big as zucchini. A. S. Dixon. il Org Gard & Farm 18:84-5 Jl '71
  Cucumber beetle resistance and mite susceptibility controlled by the bitter gene in cucumis sativus L. C. P. Da Costa and C. M. Jones. bibliog il Science 172:1145-6 Je 11 '71
  Grow more cucumbers, use less space. P. E. Mahan. il Org Gard & Farm 18:51 My '71
  Morphactin-induced parthenocarpy in the cucumber. R. W. Robinson and others. bibliog il Science 171:1251 Mr 26 '71
  See also
  Cookery—Vegetables
CUDKOWICZ, Gustavo. See Miller, H. C. jt. auth.
CULBERTSON, D. H.
  Baseball, the conglomerate way. Duns 98: 81 N '71
CULBERTSON, Tom, and Culbertson, Tom, 3d
  Lahaina charter. il Yachting 129:52-3+ Mr '71
CULBERTSON, Tom, 3d. See Culbertson, Tom, jt. auth.
CULBERTSON, William
  Obituary
  Chr Today 16:32 D 3 '71
CULEBRA ISLAND
  Culebra: island besieged; chapel-building demonstration against U.S. navy bombing. R. Swann. Nation 212:262-5 Mr 1 '71
  Culebran protest: what of the navy's peace treaty with the islanders? S. Bliss. Chr Cent 88:262-4 F 24 '71
  Operation Rescue Culebra: islanders halt U.S. navy. B. Bliss. Chr Cent 88:235-7 F 17 '71
CULEX. See Mosquitoes
CULHANE, Eugene K.
  Colonialism lives in South America. il America 125:67-9 Ag 7 '71
CULHANE, John
  En garde, pessimists! Enter Réné Dubos. il pors N Y Times Mag p44-6+ O 17 '71
CULLEN, William J.
  Foreign counselors come to camp. Camp Mag 43:26-7 Ja '71
CULLER, Floyd L.
  Radioactive salt mine; comment. il Bul Atom Sci 27:31 Je '71
CULLEY, Betty
  Tapestries: a versatile approach. il Sch Arts 71:10-11 Ja '72
CULLIMORE, Don G.
  Cossatot River, another legal milestone. il Am For 77:8-10+ My '71
  Turnabout on the Chattooga. il Am For 77: 12-15+ F '71
CULLINAN, Elizabeth
  Only human; story. New Yorker 46:28-37 F 6 '71
CULLMAN, Edgar Meyer
  Winning a losing battle. il Forbes 108:50 S 15 '71
CULLY, Iris V.
  Curriculum scandal. Chr Cent 88:879-82 Jl 21 '71
CULTIVATION. See Tillage
CULTIVATION of corn. See Corn—Cultivation
CULTIVATION of soybeans. See Soybeans—Cultivation
CULTIVATORS
  Terrace gardens are easy with a tiller. J. R. Coggins. il Org Gard & Farm 18:58-9 Je '71
CULTS
  Persistence of smalltown saints; cults of King San Pascual and San Simón. J. Luján Muñoz. il Américas 23:10-15 My '71
  Waiting for that Cargo. il Time 98:23-4 Jl 19 '71
  See also
  Satanism
CULTURAL centers
  See also
  Centers for the performing arts
CULTURAL differences. See Ethnopsychology
CULTURAL education. See Intercultural education
CULTURAL evolution. See Social change
CULTURAL relations
  Cultural policy: a modern dilemma; Unesco's intergovernmental conference on administrative, institutional and financial aspects of cultural policies; symposium. il UNESCO Courier 24:4-32 Ja '71
  Mind creating: Unesco's projects in world culture. W. McEwing. il UNESCO Courier 24:44-7 Ag '71
CULTURAL revolution. See Social revolution
CULTURALLY deprived children. See Socially handicapped children

CULTURE
  Authenticity and the modern unconscious. L. Trilling. Commentary 52:39-50 S '71
  In Bluebeard's castle: some notes towards the redefinition of culture, by G. Steiner. Review
    Nation 214:53-4 Ja 10 '72. R. S. Picciotto
  Thousand and one facets of culture. il UNESCO Courier 24:21-4 Ja '71
  See also
  Civilization
  Indians of North America—Culture
    also subheads Civilization; Intellectual life; Popular culture under names of countries, e.g. United States—Civilization
CULTURE, American. See United States—Civilization
CULTURE, British. See Great Britain—Popular culture
CULTURE, European. See Europe—Civilization
CULTURE, Russian. See Russia—Intellectual life
CULTURE contacts. See Acculturation
CULTURE media
  Buffer combinations for mammalian cell culture. H. Eagle. bibliog il Science 174:500-3 O 29 '71
CULTURE media (bacteria) See Bacteria—Culture
CULTURE pearls. See Pearls
CULVER, Eloise Crosby
  Crispus Attucks; poem. Negro Hist Bul 34: 58 Mr '71
CULVER, Thomas
  Guilty, sort of. por Newsweek 78:26 Jl 26 '71 •
CULVER CITY, Calif.
  Lion at bay; auction at Metro-Goldwyn-Mayer's Culver City studio. T. H. Watkins. il Am West 8:30-5+ Ja '71

Parks and playgrounds
  Can you make it into a park? S. Kronenthal. il Am City 86:115-16 S '71
CULVERHOUSE, Gary
  Wire tapestry. il Sch Arts 71:14-15 Ja '72
CUMBERLAND GAP
  People of Cumberland Gap. J. Fetterman. il Nat Geog 140:591-621 N '71
CUMBERLAND ISLAND
  Profiles; C. Fraser and D. Brower. J. McPhee. pors New Yorker 47:42-8+ Mr 27 '71
CUMMING, Joseph B. Jr
  Been down home so long it looks like up to me. il Esquire 76:84-90+ Ag '71
CUMMINGS, Susan
  How Ngoc-Lan became Melissa; ed. by E. Mulligan. il Parents Mag 46:44-7+ Ap '71
CUMMINS prison farm. See Prisons—Arkansas
CUMULATIVE book index
  National bibliography??? D. Dickinson. Am Lib 2:537-8 My '71
CUNA Indians. See Indians of Central America
CUNARD steamship company
  Broadside at Cunard; takeover bid. il Newsweek 78:68 Jl 19 '71
CUNEATE nucleus. See Brain
CUNEIFORM inscriptions
  Stone tablets of Cyrus and Darius. il UNESCO Courier 24:30-1 O '71
CUNEO, Sara
  Corfu and Crete. Mlle 73:92+ Jl '71
  Discovery of Aruba and Curacao. Mlle 73: 216+ My '71
  Going things; getting to Greece. il por Mlle 73:58-60 Jl '71
  Look at the U.S. Virgin Islands. Mlle 73:215+ My '71
  New England. il Mlle 72:244-6 Ap '71
  Ski touring. Mlle 74:170-1+ N '71
  Travel: the going things. il Mlle 74:100-2+ N; 78-80+ D '71; 40-2 Ja '72
  24-hour going traveler: Acapulco. Mlle 74: 76-7 Ja '72
CUNNINGHAM, Ann Marie
  Library jobs: out of the stacks into the streets. il Mlle 74:168-9+ N '71
  Living off the fat of the land. il Mlle 72: 178-9+ F '71
  Southwest. Mlle 72:272-3 Ap '71
  Superconditioned body: women in sports. il Mlle 72:238-9+ Ap '71
  31 enterprising ways to work/live. il Mlle 74:69-71+ Ja '72
CUNNINGHAM, Eugene
  Lightning and color TV sets. il Radio-Electr 42:48 Jl '71
CUNNINGHAM, Imogen
  Imogen Cunningham; portrait of a candid cook. E. Alston. il pors Look 35:36-7 F 9 '71 •
  Imogen Cunningham; with photographs. M. Mann. por Pop Phot 68:102-5 My '71 •

CUNNINGHAM, John T.
How are you going to keep them down on the farm? address, January 27, 1971. Vital Speeches 37:345-9 Mr 15 '71
CUNNINGHAM, Katharine S.
From page to stage, recording dance for the future. il Dance Mag 45:32-5 Je '71
Why am I driven? il por Dance Mag 46:56-61 Ja '72
CUNNINGHAM, Lawrence S.
Red and the black: two Italian priests. Commonweal 94:502-4 S 24 '71
CUNNINGHAM, Merce
Cunningham on campus. O. Maynard. il por Dance Mag 45:32-4 Jl '71 •
CUNNINGHAM, Walter
Astronaut Cunningham resigns. Space World H-9-93:47 S '71 •
CUNNINGHAM, William Dean
William Dean Cunningham, university librarian. il pors Wilson Lib Bul 46:236-7 N '71 •
CUPBOARDS
See also
Cabinets (furniture)
Kitchen cabinets
CUPID on the loose; drama. See Miller, H. L.
CUPS
Ron Nagle: the potter. J. Pugliese. il Craft Horiz 31:35-7 Je '71
CURAÇAO (island)
Discovery of Aruba and Curacao. S. Cuneo. Mlle 73:216+ My '71
CURATORS. See Museum directors
CURB painting. See Traffic markings
CURB peddlers. See Street trades
CURBS
We tried gunite to repair spalled curbs; Manchester, Conn. W. D. O'Neill. il Am City 86:69 Ja '71
CURFEW law
Is curfew the cure? Washington, D.C. il Newsweek 78:36+ S 6 '71
CURING of meat. See Meat—Preservation
CURLEY, August, and others
Organic mercury identified as the cause of poisoning in humans and hogs. bibliog il Science 172:65-7 Ap 2 '71
CURRENCY. See Money
CURRENCY question
Another monetary crisis. America 124:530-1 My 22 '71
Devaluation economics. P. A. Samuelson. Newsweek 78:69 Ag 23 '71
Dollar at bay. Duns 97:104 Je '71
Dollar devaluation. il Newsweek 78:16-18 Ag 30 '71
Exaggerated fuss over U.S. dollar devaluation. Time 98:22-3 O 4 '71
Gloomy prelude to the IMF meeting; with editorial comment. il Bsns W p20, 96 S 18 '71
Hardening lines. il Newsweek 78:61 O 4 '71
High price of national pride. R. Lekachman. Duns 98:13 Jl '71
Money: the dangers of the U.S. hard line. il por Time 98:34-5 S 27 '71
Revolt against the dollar. Life 70:32 My 21 '71
Rising worry about the dollar. il U S News 71:26-8 Ag 16 '71
Signs of worldwide business crisis. il U S News 71:15-17 O 4 '71
Tough talk and an ominous deadline. il por Newsweek 78:82-4 S 27 '71
What to expect next in world's money crisis. il U S News 71:89-91 O 11 '71
See also
Inflation (finance)
CURRENT, Charles E.
Acquisition of maps for school and other small libraries. bibliog il por Wilson Lib Bul 45:578-83 F '71
CURRENT events
Month in review. See issues of Current history
The Nation/the world (cont of) People and events. See issues of Senior scholastic
News & views. J. Deedy. See issues of Commonweal
Parting shots. See issues of Life
People and events. See issues of Senior scholastic
Press section; notes and comment on the news. See issues of Reader's digest
Photographs
Beat of life. Life 72:2-9 Ja 14 '72
CURRICULUM. See Colleges and universities
—Curriculum; Courses of study; High schools—Curriculum
CURRICULUM planning
Are curriculum guides passé? R. L. Hamm. Clear House 46:249 D '71

Educational change and pedagogical validity. H. K. Heger. bibliog Clear House 45:563-7 My '71
Educational philosophy and behavioral objectives. R. B. Kimball. bibliog il Clear House 45:496-500 Ap '71
Helping spend school dollars wisely; teachers councils on curriculum development. D. J. Stangel. Todays Ed 60:38-9 Ja '71
Open curriculum; student-planned programs. M. L. Patton. il Schol Teach Jr/Sr High p20-3 S '71
Students lay it on the line. C. H. Harrison. il Schol Teach Jr/Sr High p8+ Ap 5 '71
Vector theory of curriculum development. R. Carpenter. Sch & Soc 99:30-2 Ja '71
CURRIE, Elliott
Repressive violence. Trans-Action 8:12-14+ F '71; Same abr. with title Violent America: a new myth? Cur 128:29-33 Ap '71
CURRY, George
Baseball il Sports Illus 35:51 Jl 26 '71
Track & field (title varies) il Sports Illus 34:66+ My 3 '71
CURRY, Holly
Rock painting for fun and profit. J. Windle. il pors Design 72:20-1 mid-Wint '71 •
CURRY, Peggy (Simson)
Detail makes the difference. Writer 84:13-15+ N '71
Viewpoint: a persuasive light; excerpt from Creating fiction from experience. Writer 84:17-18+ Mr '71
CURTAINS and draperies
New beauty treatments for your windows. il House & Gard 139:76-81 Ja '71
Tips on shower curtains. A. M. Dahlerus. il Good H 172:144 F '71
Work wonders with your windows. il House B. 113:99-108 Ap '71
CURTIN, Phyllis
Music's handmaiden. H. Saal. por Newsweek 77:50 Ja 18 '71 •
CURTIN, Tom
Questions ACA, and you, need to ask. por Camp Mag 43:4 N '71
CURTIS, Carl Thomas
New domestic spending bills: address, April 5, 1971. Vital Speeches 37:486-8 Je 1 '71
CURTIS, Gerald L.
Conservative dominance in Japanese politics. Cur Hist 60:207-12+ Ap '71
CURTIS, Harold T.
One form for all tax receipts. il Am City 86:62 Ja '71
CURTIS, Joseph E.
A city gears for austerity. il Parks & Rec 6:37-8+ Mr '71
Park programs on a bare-bones budget. il por Am City 86:51-3 D '71
CURTIS, Mike
Super bowl. M Sharnik. il por Sports Illus 34:19-20+ Ja 18 '71 •
CURTIS, Neville
South Africa: the politics of fragmentation. il For Affairs 50:283-96 Ja '72
CURTIS, Paul
My greatest trout float. il Field & S 75:50-1+ Ap '71
New ways to hunt rabbits. il Field & S 75:36-7+ Ja '71
CURTIS, Walt
Girl with the green eyes; poem. Atlan 227:67 Mr '71
CURTIS, Will C.
Our most beautiful natives. J. A. Lynch. il por Nat Wildlife 9:21-4 Je '71 •
CURTIS, William
How to bag bandtails. il Field & S 76:54-5+ S '71
Kings of the spring. il Outdoor Life 147:64-5+ Mr '71
CURTIS publishing company
Return of the Post. il por Time 97:70 Je 14 '71
CURTISS, Ursula
Over your dead body; story, excerpt from Letter of intent. Redbook 136:143-65 Ap '71
CUSACK, Thomasine
Monetary gold: to have or have not. America 125:555-7 D 25 '71
CUSHING, L. Clark
Fences are out in Murray City park. il Parks & Rec 6:30-1+ Jl '71
CUSHING family
Cushings of Newport. il pors Vogue 157:120-5 My '71
CUSHIONS
Off to the beach with a handy and useful mat you make yourself. il Sunset 147:86-7 Jl '71

CUSHMAN, Robert Everton, 1914-
D 13 '71 *
Commandant Cushman. por Newsweek 78:37
Marines' new chief: a man Nixon never forgot. por U S News 71:39 D 13 71 *
New top leatherneck. por Time 98:13-14 D 13 '71 *

CUSSLER, E. L. and others
Theoretical and experimental basis for a specific countertransport system in membranes. bibliog il Science 172:377-9 Ap 23 '71

CUSTARDS
Caramel on top, coffee flavor inside; coffee flan. il Sunset 146:150 F '71
Custard can gain sophistication. il Sunset 146:109 Ja '71
Puffs on top of custard. il Sunset 146:166 My '71

CUSTER, George Armstrong
Custer myth. A. M. Josephy, jr. il por Life 71:48-52+ Jl 2 '71 *
Echoes of the Little Bighorn. D. H. Miller. il pors Am Heritage 22:28-39 Je '71 *

CUSTINE, Astolphe Louis Léonard, marquis de
Marquis de Custine and his Russia in 1839, by G. F. Kennan. Review
Atlan 228:94 Ag '71. E. Weeks *
Sat R 54:20 Je 19 '71. R. K. Massie *
Reflections. G. F. Kennan. New Yorker 47:46-50+ My 1 '71 *

CUSTODY of children. See Guardian and ward

CUSTOM farming. See Agricultural machinery—Leasing and renting

CUSTOMER relations
Ombudsmen; corporate ombudsman. il Newsweek 78:57+ Jl 26 '71
See also
Customer service
also subhead Customer relations under various subjects, e.g. Banks and banking—Customer relations

CUSTOMER service
Company clout for the consumer. il Nations Bsns 59:52-5+ Je '71

CUSTOMHOUSE brokers
From limousines to casaba melons. M. V. Rosenbloom. Nations Bsns 59:41 Ag '71

CUSTOMS. See Manners and customs

CUSTOMS brokers. See Customhouse brokers

CUSTOMS caper; drama. See Murray, J.

CUSTOMS service

United States
Hauling cartons and swatting mosquitoes: a night with the U.S. customs. R. H. Smith. Pub W 200:96-7 Jl 19 '71

CUSTOMS service and tourists
Gains in the war against drug smugglers; interview. M. J. Ambrose. il por U S News 70:60-2+ Je 21 '71
Vacationing in jail; crackdowns on drug smuggling. il Sr Schol 98:12-13 My 17 '71

CUT flowers. See Flowers—Cut flowers

CUTAK, Ladislaus
Uncommon bulbs for indoors. il Horticulture 49:32-6 O '71

CUTLER, Carol
How best to support artists? Art in Am 59:47 Ja '71

CUTLER, Lloyd Norton
Thomas Jefferson, won't you please come home? address, April 1971, with questions and answers. bibliog f Ann Am Acad 396:25-39 Jl '71

CUTLERY
Redbook guide to cutlery. il Redbook 137:97-100 My '71
See also
Knives

CUTSHALL, Alden
Philippines. bibliog il Focus 21:1-12 Mr '71

CUTTING machines
Abrasive cutoff machine you can make for $15. B. Eckert. il Pop Mech 136:166+ S '71

CUTTING of chicken. See Poultry, Dressing of

CUTTING tools
See also
Knives
Saws

CUTTINGS, Plant. See Plant propagation

CUTWATERS (birds) See Skimmers (birds)

CUYAHOGA FALLS, Ohio
No-drip pipe galleries. il Am City 86:16 Je '71

Recreation
Indoor-outdoor. C. F. Fuerst. il Parks & Rec 6:30-1+ Mr '71

CUZCO school of painting. See Painting, Peruvian

CVANCARA, Alan M. and others
Paleolimnology of late quaternary deposits: Seibold site, North Dakota. bibliog il Science 171:172-4 Ja 15 '71

CYANAMIDE
Possible prebiotic condensation of mononucleotides by cyanamide. J. D. Ibanez and others. bibliog il Science 173:444-6 Jl 30 '71

CYBULSKI, Walter
Bear; poem. America 125:234 O 2 '71

CYCLES, Biological. See Biology—Periodicity

CYCLES, Business. See Business cycles

CYCLIC compounds
Ion binding by synthetic macrocyclic compounds. J. J. Christensen and others. bibliog il Science 174:459-67 O 29 '71

CYCLING
Bicycle madness. il Life 71:28-33 Jl 30 '71
Bike boom: a way out for commuters? il U S News 71:84-5 D 6 '71
Bike comes back. F. Coffee. il Mech Illus 67:73-4+ Ap '71
Bike is back and booming! J. Stewart-Gordon. il Read Digest 99:185-8+ D '71
Biking through history; Chesapeake and Ohio Canal. B. Thomas. il Parents Mag 46:46-9+ My '71
Confession of a biker. R. Finkelstein. il Sr Schol 98:34-5 Ap 26 '71
My new best friend is a bile-green wheel; theories of Luther H. Porter and Eugene A. Sloane. L. Wainwright. il Life 71:36-7 Jl 30 '71
Pedal power; urban bike commuting. R. Hanneman. il Parks & Rec 6:28-33 Ja '71
Pedaling to Shangri-la. R. Hall. il Cons 26:5-7 D '71
Queasy rider. M. Michaelson. il Todays Health 49:44-7+ Je '71
Riding a bike for health, economy, and ecology. Consumer Bul 54:17 Jl '71
Saddle up! ride your bike for fun and health. J. Galub. House B 113:42+ Ap '71
Song of the cyclist. il Newsweek 77:67 Je 28 '71
U.S. journal: Manhattan. C. Trillin. New Yorker 47:120+ O 9 '71

CYCLOHEXIMIDE
Cycloheximide: its effects on activity are dissociable from its effects on memory. D. S. Segal and others. bibliog il Science 172:82-4 Ap 2 '71

CYCLONES
Deadly surge; East Pakistan flood. Sci Am 224:46 Mr '71
Misery's spawning ground; devastation in Orissa State, India. il Time 98:32 N 15 '71

CYCLOPS, pseud.
Life TV review. See issues of Life

CYGNUS loop. See Nebulae

CYLINDER heads, Automobile. See Automobile engines—Cylinders

CYLINDER records. See Phonograph records

CYLINDERS (engines, etc)
See also
Automobile engines—Cylinders

CYMBELINE; drama. See Shakespeare. W.—Plays

CYMBIDIUMS. See Orchids

CYNICISM
How to survive life: the cynic's guide. M. Tumin. Mlle 73:290-1+ Ag '71

CYPRESS, Calif.
Renew that deteriorated pavement. A. W. Schatzeder. il Am City 86:109-10 Je '71

CYPRESS gardens. See Gardens—Florida

CYPRINODON. See Killifishes

CYPRIPEDIUM. See Ladys slippers

CYPROHEPTADINE. See Antihistamines

CYPRUS
No progress. B. Van Voorst. il Newsweek 78:32+ Ag 23 '71
Peace watch on Cyprus. J. C. Fleck. America 124:587-9 Je 5 '71
Reports & comment. E. Drew. Atlan 228:6+ N '71
See also
United Nations—Armed forces—Forces in Cyprus

CYRANO de Bergerac; drama. See Rostand. E.

CYSTICERCUS bovis. See Measles in cattle

CYTOCHALASIN
Microfilaments in cellular and developmental processes. N. K. Wessells and others. bibliog il Science 171:135-43 Ja 15 '71; Reply with rejoinder. R. D. Estensen and others. 173:356-9 Jl 23 '71

CYTOCHROMES
Isolation of liver enzyme; Cytochrome P-450. Sci N 100:55 Jl 24 '71

DNA—*Continued*

Heterochromatin, satellite DNA, and cell
function. J. J. Yunis and W. G. Yasmineh.
bibliog il Science 174:1200-9 D 17 '71
Heterogeneity of murine leukemia virus in
vitro DNA; detection of viral DNA in mammalian cells. L. D. Gelb and others. bibliog
il Science 172:1353-5 Je 25 '71
Informational DNA synthesis distinguished
from that of nuclear DNA by inhibitors of
DNA synthesis. E. Bell. bibliog il Science
174:603-6 N 5 '71
LSD and DNA. il Sci N 100:74 Jl 31 '71
Lymphocyte DNA synthesis inhibition. J. C.
Houck and others. bibliog il Science 173:
1139-41 S 17 '71
Now visible, in 3-D; how actinomycin binds
to DNA. il por Sci N 99:436 Je 26 '71
RNA-directed DNA synthesis. H. M. Temin.
il Sci Am 226:24-33 bibliog(p 122) Ja '72
Release of nuclear DNA template restrictions
by specific polyribonucleotides. D. G.
Brown and D. S. Coffey. bibliog il Science
171:176-8 Ja 15 '71
Reverse transcriptions: one year later. B. J.
Culliton. Science 172:926-8 My 28 '71
Transcription of nonrepeated DNA in mouse
brain. W. E. Hahn and C. D. Laird. bibliog
il Science 173:158-61 Jl 9 '71

DNA polymerase. See Polymerase

DNA viruses. See Viruses

DOT. See United States—Transportation, Department of

DABROWSKA, Jadwiga
Dissociation of impairment after lateral and
medial prefrontal lesions in dogs. bibliog il
Science 171:1037-8 Mr 12 '71

DACCA, Pakistan
Dacca, city of the dead. D. Coggin. il Time
97:28 My 3 '71

DACHAU, Germany
What's in a name. il Newsweek 78:64 Ag 30
'71

DA COSTA, Cyro P. and Jones, C. M.
Cucumber beetle resistance and mite susceptibility controlled by the bitter gene in
cucumis sativus L. bibliog il Science 172:
1145-6 Je 11 '71

DADA, Idi Amin. See Amin Dada, I.

DADAISM
Out of the midden heap; K. Schwitters' retrospective in Düsseldorf, Germany. R. Hughes.
il por Time 97:64-6 Mr 1 '71

DADDARIO, Emilio Quincy
Can democracy cope with man's predicament?
Cur '133:9-16 O '71
National science policy, prelude to global
cooperation. por Bul Atom Sci 27:21-4 Je
'71
U.S. technology: looking for a better mouse-
trap; interview, ed. by R. Nash. il pors
Forbes 108:36-8+ N 15 '71

about

Daddario; scientific community's friend on
the Hill is leaving. D. S. Greenberg; discussion. Science 170:1254; 171:232 D 18 '70,
Ja 22 '71 *

DADDY longlegs. See Harvestmen

DADE COUNTY, Fla.
How to detect vehicle detector problems. M.
Wilcox. il Am City 86:128+ Je '71

DAFFODILS. See Narcissus

DAHL, Gordon J.
Time, work and leisure today. Chr Cent 88:
185-9 F 10 '71

DAHL, Roald
What I told Ophelia and Lucy about God;
story. il Redbook 138:76-8 D '71

DAHLBERG, Edward
Anyone's miserable chagrin. C. Bedient. New
Repub 164:27-8+ F 6 '71 *
Are you in the ketchup trade also? B. Ben-
dow. Nation 213:533-5 N 22 '71 *
Edward Dahlberg: pariah. S. Maloff. por Com-
monweal 93:497-9 F 19 '71 *

DAHLIAS
Dahlias. H. Mason. il Bet Hom & Gard 49:
72-5 Ap '71
Plant matched mates . . . glads and dahlias.
B. Miles. il Horticulture 49:40-1+ Mr '71

DAHLQUIST, Eric
Marking time. See issues of Motor trend

DAICHES, David
What is a Jew? il Horizon 13:24-35 Sum '71

DAIDO steel company. See Steel industry—
Japan

DAIGER, Richard H.
Will pass/fail pass the test? Todays Ed 60:
24 N '71

DAILY mirror, New York. See New York mirror

DAIRMAN, Wallace, and Udenfriend, Sidney
Decrease in adrenal tyrosine hydroxylase and
increase in norepinephrine synthesis in rats
given L-Dopa. bibliog il Science 171:1022-4
Mr 12 '71

D'AIRO, Leonard
Build FM stereo adapter. il Radio-Electr 42:
68-70 Mr '71

DAIRY barns. See Barns and stables

DAIRY cooperative associations. See Dairymens associations

DAIRY farm management
Dairyman gets top returns from poor soil.
B. Eftink. Suc Farm 69:J20 N '71
His goal: ton of milk a day per man. il Suc
Farm 69:J24 N '71
How they built a class-topping herd. C. Peter-
son, jr. il Suc Farm 69:A1 N '71
Look what he does on forty acres. J. R.
Borcherding. il Suc Farm 69:30-1 O '71
Plan now to avoid summer slumps. J. R.
Borcherding. il Suc Farm 69:no5 32-3 Mr
'71
Successful dairy management (cont) il por
Suc Farm 69:no2 D1-3+ F: no4 D1-4+ Mr:
D1 My; D1-6+ S '71
They match crops and cows. J. R. Borcherd-
ing. il Suc Farm 69:30-1 Ag '71

DAIRY farming. See Dairying

DAIRY industry
Guess what the milkman's selling now! G.
Logsdon. Farm J 95:46 F '71

DAIRY lobby. See Lobbying

DAIRY machinery
See also
Milking machines

DAIRY products
See also
Ice cream, ices, etc.
Milk

DAIRYING
Dairy extra. See issues of Farm Journal
Dairy management. J. R. Borcherding. See
issues of Successful farming
Ideas from Ohio's top 20 herds. il Suc Farm
69:D6+ S '71
Ideas ready to use. il Farm J 95:D11 Je '71
See also
Cows—Feeding
Dairy farm management
Milk plants

Economic aspects

What's ahead in financing dairy farming.
Suc Farm 69:D4 S '71

DAIRYING, Cooperative
See also
Dairymen's associations

DAIRYMENS associations
Can dairymen control production? N. Reeder
and C. Machan. Farm J 95:D6+ D '71
Can the super co-ops crash these road-
blocks? N. Reeder. Farm J 95:21+ My '71
Land of milk and money; dairy farmers con-
tribute to presidential campaign funds. F.
Wright. Nation 213:657-9 D 20 '71

D'ALBE, E. M. Fournier. See Fournier d'Albe,
E. M.

DALBEY, E. Gordon, Jr
Great white son turns left. il Chr Cent 88:
716-20 Je 9 '71

DALE, David C. and others
Cyclic urinary leukopoietic activity in gray
collie dogs. bibliog il Science 173:152-3 Jl
9 '71

DALE, Edwin L. Jr
Bitchy society will be an inflationary society, and other responses to a questionnaire. il N Y Times Mag p 18-19+ S 26 '71
How to stop inflation: stop raising wages.
il Look 35:64+ F 23 '71

DALEY, Brian
Publik: death of a nice try. il America
125:507-10 D 11 '71

DALEY, Richard J.
Boss, by M. Royko. Review
  America 124:599 Je 5 '71. W. J. Parente
  Bsns W por p8 Ap 17 '71. A. G. Carlson *
  Commentary 52:86-90 S '71. J. Epstein *
  Nat R por 23:597 Je 1 '71. J. G. Cam-
    paigne, jr *
  Nation 212:507-8 Ap 19 '71. S. D. Alinsky *
  New Repub 164:28-9 Ap 17 '71. R. M.
    Fisher *
  New Yorker 47:137-42 My 8 '71. R.
    Harris *
  Sat R 54:28 Ap 24 '71. D. Walker *
  Sat R 54:29 Ap 24 '71. P. L. Weed *
Challenge to Daley. por Time 97:14-15 Ap 5
  '71 *
Chicago's Daley: how to run a city. il pors
  Newsweek 77:80-4 Ap 5 '71 *
Cracks in Daley. P. Yessne. Nation 212:360-5
  Mr 22 '71 *

DANA, Roger W.
  Forum. Duns 97:113 My '71
DANA corporation
  TV replaces stacks of paperwork. il Bsns **W**
    p48+ Ja 30 '71
DANAKIL
  Final desiccation of the Afar rift, Ethiopia.
    E. Bonatti and others. bibliog il Science 172:
    468-9 Ap 30 '71
DANCE, Bill
  World's best bass fisherman; interview. il
    pors Field & S 76:58-9+ My '71
DANCE, Stanley
  Recordings reports: jazz LPs. See issues of
    Saturday review
DANCE camps
  American dance camp: a summer road to
    dance. N. M. Stoop. il Dance Mag 45:64-
    5 Je '71
DANCE companies
  Dance, the liveliest art. I. Stanger. Harp Baz
    104:150 O '71
  Darkening pond; Paul Sanasardo company.
    D. Hering. il Dance Mag 45:73-4 Ag '71
  Eleo Pomare dance company, ANTA theatre,
    NYC. L. Pastore. Dance Mag 45:96 Ap '71
  Minnesota dance theatre and Claude Kipnis
    mime theatre, Jacob's Pillow dance festi-
    val, Mass. D. Hering. Dance Mag 45:92
    O '71
  New England dance theatre, Boston. S.
    Smoliar. Dance Mag 45:75-6 F '71
  Toronto dance theatre. B. G. Rowes. il Dance
    Mag 45:70-3 Ap '71
  Why Ohio? D. Hering. il Dance Mag 45:47-
    62 S '71
    See also
  Alvin Ailey American dance theatre
  Alwin Nikolais dance company
  Association of American dance companies
  Paul Taylor dance company
  Pearl Lang dance company

Finance
  Tax reform act (cont) I. Fisher. Dance Mag
    45:83 F; 108 Ap '71
DANCE concerts
  Alonso Castro dance theatre, Theatre of
    Riverside church, NYC. L. Pastore.
    Dance Mag 46:28 Ja '72
  American dance in repertory, Mershon audi-
    torium, Ohio state University, Columbus,
    Ohio. B. Anthony. Dance Mag 46:26-7 Ja
    '72
  Ann Halprin & San Francisco dancers'
    workshop, NY city center ballroom. J.
    Anderson. Dance Mag 46:29+ Ja '72
  Ballet players of WPA. WPA workshop of
    the players art, NYC. T. Borek. Dance
    Mag 45:91 N '71
  Barbara Gardner construction co, Cunning-
    ham studio, Westbeth, NYC. L. Pastore.
    Dance Mag 45:86 D '71
  Barbara Roan: the October parade, the Cubi-
    culo, NYC. J. Anderson. Dance Mag 45:
    83 D '71
  Carolyn Biderback, Shawn Avrea and
    Charlotte Honda, the Cubiculo, NYC. L.
    Pastore. Dance Mag 45:84 S '71
  ChoreoConcerts and critiques, the New school,
    NYC. N. Mason anl M. Marks. Dance Mag
    45:83-5 D '71
  ChoreoConcerts repertory company, The new
    school, NYC. N. Mason. Dance Mag 45:
    80 Ag '71
  Choreography of Richard Gain, Sophie Mas-
    low & Richard Kuch, Theatre of the River-
    side church, NYC. L. Pastore. Dance Mag
    45:82-3 Ag '71
  Contemporary choreographers ensemble, the
    Cubiculo, NYC. L. Pastore. Dance Mag
    46:27 Ja '72
  Dance uptown: Elizabeth Keen & Phyllis
    Lamhut, Barnard college gymnasium, NYC.
    J. Anderson. Dance Mag 46:75 Ja '72
  Dance uptown, Minor Latham playhouse,
    NYC. N. Mason. Dance Mag 45:86+ Ap
    '71
  Dances of three continents, the Cubiculo,
    NYC. M. Marks. Dance Mag 45:85 S '71
  Experimental intermediate foundation. NYU
    education auditorium, NYC. T. Borek.
    Dance Mag 45:86+ S '71
  Four evenings of dance, American theatre
    laboratory, NYC. M. Marks. Dance Mag
    45:86 My '71
  Gale Ormiston, Hideko Tano and Lonny Gor-
    don, the Cubiculo, NYC. L. Pastore. Dance
    Mag 45:79 F '71
  Gerda Zimmermann in kammertanz III. L.
    Pastore. Dance Mag 45:71 F '71
  Gudde dancers, Julia Richman high school,
    NYC. L. Pastore. Dance Mag 45:82 Ag '71

  Impulses: a concert of improvisations, the
    Cubiculo, NYC. L. Pastore. Dance Mag
    45:25 Je '71
  Interboro ballet company and guests, Clark
    center for the performing arts, NYC. N.
    Mason. Dance Mag 45:82 Ag '71
  James Cunningham and the Acme dance
    company, Judson memorial church. J. An-
    derson. Dance Mag 46:81 Ja '72
  Jan Van Dyke, Lillo Way & Suzette Mar-
    tinez, the Cubiculo, NYC. N. Mason.
    Dance Mag 45:76-7 Je '71
  Joan Miller and the Chamber arts/dance
    players, Theatre of the Riverside church,
    NYC. D. Hering. Dance Mag 46:26 Ja '72
  Kei Takei and Ben Dolphin, the Cubiculo,
    NYC. M. Marks. Dance Mag 45:86 D '71
  Kenneth Rinker, Jan Van Dyke, Mel Wong,
    the Cubiculo, NYC. D. Hering. Dance Mag
    45:88-9 D '71
  Lar Lubovitch dance company, Stage city,
    NYC. N. Mason. Dance Mag 46:75 Ja '72
  Larry Richardson & dance company, Thea-
    tre of the Riverside church, NYC. J. An-
    derson. Dance Mag 46:81 Ja '72
  Laura Dean dance concert, American theatre
    laboratory, NYC. D. Hering. Dance Mag
    45:89 D '71
  Laura Pawel and Christine Loizeaux, the
    Cubiculo, NYC. L. Pastore. Dance Mag 45:
    88 My '71
  Left of spring, Kaufman concert hall, NYC.
    L. Pastore. Dance Mag 45:79 Jl '71
  Nancy Topf and Jon Gibson, Dance theater
    workshop, NYC. D. Hering. Dance Mag 45:
    93 O '71
  On tap! 92nd street Y, NYC. M. Marks.
    Dance Mag 45:78 Jl '71
  Pat Catterson & Douglas Dunn, Cunningham
    studio, Westbeth, NYC. T. Borek. Dance
    Mag 45:82 D '71
  Sally Bowden & Carolyn Lord, solos Merce
    Cunningham studio, at Westbeth, NYC.
    T. Borek. Dance Mag 45:93 O '71
  Tamburitzans, Hunter college, NYC. N. Ma-
    son. Dance Mag 45:100 Ap '71
  Vessel, an opera epic by Meredith Monk
    and The house, NYC. D. Hering. Dance
    Mag 46:24-5 Ja '72
DANCE festivals
  All hail Ailey; fall season. W. Terry. il Sat
    R 54:36 N 6 '71
  Calendar of international summer dance
    events. il Dance Mag 45:63+ My '71
  Dance; American dance season at the ANTA
    theatre. N. Goldner. Nation 212:443-5 Ap
    5 '71
  Dance, New York dance festival. J. Maskey.
    il Hi Fi 21:MA9+ D '71
  Double festival; Northeast regional ballet
    festival, Jacob's Pillow. W. Terry. il Sat
    R 54:49 Jl 24 '71
  Exotic festival; Afro-Asian festival. W.
    Terry. il Sat R 54:70 D 4 '71
  Festival of black dance, Manhattan theater
    club, NYC. T. Borek. Dance Mag 45:89-90+
    O '71
  Kids can take it; sixth annual Pacific re-
    gional ballet festival; Pasadena, California.
    D. Hering. il Dance Mag 45:68-72 Ag '71
  Land together; twelfth Northeast regional
    ballet festival; Jacob's Pillow and Beaupre.
    D. Hering. il Dance Mag 45:76-81 N '71
  Myth any Thursday: review of Connecticut
    college American dance festival. D. Hering
    and others. il Dance Mag 45:38-41+ N '71
  Neither floods nor. . . Canadian regional bal-
    let festival. D. Hering. il Dance Mag 45:
    74-5 Ap '71
  New York dance festival, Delacorte theater,
    Central park. M. Marks. N. Mason. Dance
    Mag 45:88-90 N '71
  Pillow talk. R. Berenson. Nat R 23:1190-1 O
    22 '71
  Rich, rich palette; Afro-Asian festival at
    the Brooklyn academy of music. W. Terry.
    il Sat R 54:74 N 20 '71
  Special kind of courage; sixteenth annual
    Southeastern regional ballet festival. D.
    Hering. il Dance Mag 45:70-4 Jl '71
  Summer specials; Williamsburg Va; Jacob's
    Pillow; New York; Washington, D.C. W.
    Terry. il Sat R 54:57+ O 9 '71
  Where are the bluebonnets? Southwestern
    regional ballet festival. D. Hering. il Dance
    Mag 45:66-70+ Je '71
DANCE films. See Moving pictures—Dance
  films

DANCE institutes and workshops
Dance theater workshop, American theater laboratory, NYC. T. Borek. Dance Mag 45:87-9 O '71
Nikolais and Louis: a new space; Louis-Nikolais dance theater lab, T. Tobias. il pors Dance Mag 45:46-54 F '71
  See also
School of American ballet, inc.

DANCE music
  See also
Ballet music
Phonograph records—Dance music

DANCE notation
Stillness of Rudy Perez. D. Jowitt. il Art in Am 59:102-3 My '71

DANCE notation bureau, inc.
From page to stage; recording dance for the future. K. S. Cunningham. il Dance Mag 45:32-5 Je '71

DANCE production
And if you're a good girl, I'll take you to a Makarova rehearsal. T. Tobias. il pors Dance Mag 45:38-43 My '71
Rose for Miss Agnes. J. Gale. il pors Dance Mag 45:46-50 O '71

DANCE records. See Phonograph records—Dance music

DANCE schools
Reveille for taps. il Time 98:44-5 Jl 5 '71
Why am I driven? Shirley Ubell's Center for modern dance education. K. S. Cunningham. il por Dance Mag 46:56-61 Ja '72

DANCE teachers
Convention time! N. M. Stoop. il Dance Mag 45:91-3+ S; 18+ O '71

DANCE theatre of Harlem
Black ballet can be beautiful. W. Terry. il por Sat R 54:48-9 F 27 '71
Ceremony of joy. H. Saal. il Newsweek 77:115 My 17 '71
Dance theatre of Harlem, ANTA theatre, NYC. D. Hering. Dance Mag 45:20-2 Je '71
Doing the thing you do best; Harlem dance theater. J. T. Elson. il Time 97:59-60 Mr 22 '71

DANCE theater workshop. See Dance institutes and workshops

DANCE wi' me; or, The fatal twitch; drama. See Antonacci, G.

DANCERS
Beauty secrets from the ballet girls. il Vogue 158:108-11+ Ag 1 '71
Brief biography. S. Goodman. See issues of Dance magazine
Dance: de-sexing women. J. Marks. Vogue 157:157 My '71
In the news. il Dance Mag 45:20 N '71
Obedient dancers; letter. C. Maracci. Nation 212:450+ Ap 12 '71; Discussion. 212:578+ My 10 '71
Presstime news. See issues of Dance magazine
  See also
Alonso, A.
Nijinsky. W.
Villella, E.
     Photographs
Lovely new swan alights; Natalya Makarova. M. Waldman. Life 70:38-43 Ja 22 '71

DANCERS workshop of San Francisco
Raw dance; appearance at the City center. D. Davis. il por Newsweek 78:137 N 22 '71

DANCING
All the strange things: John Butler on opera choreography among other kinds of dance; ed. by G. Loney. J. Butler. il por Dance Mag 45:22-7 Ag '71
Carousel: photo essay on dance around the world (title varies) (cont) il Dance Mag 45:34-9 F; 50-73 My; 38-43 Je; 64-7 Jl; 34-7 Ag; 63-5 S; 67-75 D '71; 46:62-9 Ja '72
Dance. D. Jowitt. il Art in Am 59:102-3 My '71
Dance: Broadway rhythm; dance in musical comedy. H. Saal. il Newsweek 78:76-7 D 13 '71
Dance report. il Vogue 157:192 My '71
Flowers in the garland of Sappho: I. Duncan's The art of the dance. D. Hering. il pors Dance Mag 45:28-33 F '71
In homage to Francois Delsarte: 1811-1871. O. Maynard. il por Dance Mag 45:64-5 Ag '71
Losers: maybe not a winner, but dance-wise not dull. G. Loney. il Dance Mag 45:22 Jl '71
New ecstatics. J. Gruen. il Vogue 157:73 Mr 15 '71
Observations: first U.S. National ballroom championships 1971. il Vogue 158:166 N 1 '71
Performance. F. Alenikoff. Craft Horiz 31:13+ D '71

Post-Judson dance. D. Jowitt. il Art in Am 59:81-7 S '71
Presstime news. See issues of Dance magazine
Reviews. See issues of Dance magazine
Rise and fall and rise of modern dance, by D. McDonagh. Review
  Dance Mag il 45:47-9+ My '71. T. Borek
Shocks and ceremonies; New York programs. il Time 97:72 F 8 '71
World of dance. W. Terry. See issues of Saturday review
  See also
Ballet
Choreography
Dance notation
Moving pictures—Dance films
Tap dancing
Television programs—Dancing
     Photographs
  See also
Photography of dancing
     Study and teaching
Certification: an educational necessity. B. King. il Dance Mag 45:71-3 Je '71
UCLA graduate dance center. V. H. Swisher. il Dance Mag 45:76-9 D '71
  See also
Colleges and universities—Departments of dance
Dance schools

DANCING, African
Festival of black dance, Manhattan theater club, NYC. T. Borek. Dance Mag 45:89-90+ O '71
Senegalese national dance company Brooklyn academy of music. L. Pastore. Dance Mag 46:24 Ja '72
Sierra Leone national dance company, Brooklyn academy of music, NYC. G. Forman. Dance Mag 46:73+ Ja '72
  See also
Olatunji, B.

DANCING, Cuban
Modern dance in Cuba: foothold with a future. M. Manings. il Dance Mag 45:59-63 Ag '71

DANCING, Dutch
  See also
Netherlands dance theater

DANCING, Indian (East Indian)
Kerala Kalamandalum, Kathakali company, Hunter college assembly hall, NYC. M. Marks. Dance Mag 45:23+ F '71
Shakuntala, 92nd street Y, NYC. M. Marks. Dance Mag 45:78 Jl '71
Shapmochan 92nd street Y, NYC. M. Marks. Dance Mag 45:81 Ag '71

DANCING, Israeli
Gift from Israel: Batsheva dance company. W. Terry. Sat R 54:35 Ja 16 '71
Inbal dance theatre of Israel, New York city center. NYC. N. Mason. Dance Mag 45:100 Ap '71
Sabra Graham: Batsheva dance company of Israel. D. Hering. il Dance Mag 45:60-1+ F '71

DANCING, Korean
Little angels, National folk ballet of Korea, Hunter college assembly hall, NYC. N. Mason. Dance Mag 46:76 Ja '72

DANCING, Mexican
  See also
Ballet clásico 70 (ballet company)

DANCING, Moroccan
National dance company of Morocco, Brooklyn academy of music. J. Anderson. Dance Mag 46:25 Ja '72

DANCING, Philippine
Bayanihan Philippine dance company. Alice Tully Hall, NYC. M. Marks. il Dance Mag 45:79 F '71

DANCING, Russian
Siberian dancers & singers of Omsk, Carnegie Hall, NYC. L. Pastore. Dance Mag 45:85-6 Ap '71

DANCING, Spanish
Carlos Ibanez company, Kaufman concert hall, NYC. L. Pastore. Dance Mag 45:79 Jl '71
Dance in Spain. by A. Ivanova. Review Américas il 23:38-9 Ap '71. F. Jackson

DANCING in art
Miriam Winslow: dancer-sculptress. W. Terry. il pors Dance Mag 45:25-7 D '71

DANCING in sculpture. See Dancing in art

DANCING in television. See Television programs—Dancing

DANCING schools. See Dance schools

DANE COUNTY, Wis.
EDP keeps tabs on wife supporters. A. Larson. il Am City 86:82 My '71

DANFORTH, Richard S.
Developing the whole city. Cur 127:39-41 Mr '71
DANG, Howard
Glory returns to Fragrant Harbor. R. Joseph. il pors Esquire 75:87-93 Ap '71 *
D'ANGELO, Lou
Old horizons in education. Sat R 54:67 D 4 '71
DANGEROUS toys. See Toys, Hazardous
DANIALS, M. F.
Building a cartop trimaran. il Mech Illus 67.72-4+ Mr '71
DANIEL, Aubrey, 3d
Greatest tragedy of all; excerpts from letter to President Nixon. il Time 97:13 Ap 19 '71
Captain and the President. Nation 212:482-3 Ap 19 '71 *
Captain who told the President off. por Newsweek 77:30 Ap 19 '71 *
Portrait of a prosecutor. por Time 97:14 Ap 19 '71 *
DANIEL, James
Day care: how good for your child? Read Digest 99:136-40 Ag '71
DANIEL, Oliver
Books. Sat R 54:82-3 S 25 '71
DANIEL, Pete. See Harlan, L. R. jt. auth.
DANIEL Boone regional library, Columbia, Mo.
Overdue; great undoer. H. Kreigh. por Wilson Lib Bul 46:360-1+ D '71
We're counting them in! young adults program. H. Kreigh. il Am Lib 2:208-9 F '71
DANIELS, Bill
Cable TV: turn on, tune in, rip off. F. Browning. il Ramp Mag 9:32-8 Ap '71 *
DANIELS, George E.
Electrical repairs anyone can do. il Mech Illus 67:96-100 Jl '71
New epoxy sealer-patcher with water washup. il Pop Sci 198:100 Ja '71
Running wiring on and through concrete. il Pop Sci 199:102-4+ S '71
See-through saw guard is always in place. il Pop Sci 198:106 Je '71
DANIELS, Malcolm, and Hauswirth, William
Fluorescence of the purine and pyrimidine bases of the nucleic acids in neutral aqueous solutions at 300°K. bibliog il Science 171:675-7 F 19 '71
DANIELS, Robert D.
Hapless queen of Scots. il pors Opera N 35: 10-15 N '71
Real Escamillo. il Opera N 35:14-15 F 6 '71
Tietjens the beloved. por Opera N 35:24-6 Ja 30 '71
DANIELS and Bell (firm)
Making it. il Forbes 108:56 Jl 15 '71
DANISH pastry. See Pastry
DANISH pottery. See Pottery, Danish
DANISH students
Comparative sex norms in U.S. and Danish students; findings of H. T. Christensen. Sch & Soc 99:333-4 O '71
DANKE, O. G.
Spring is for flounders. il Motor B & S 127:35+ Mr '71
DANKMAN, Linda, and Cooley, Candace
Ask him out? il Seventeen 30:94-5 D '71
DANN, George
Water resource leaders. W. S. Foster. il pors Am City 86:67-8 Mr '71 *
DANN, Joanne
Parent and child. N Y Times Mag p78-80+ Ap 18 '71
DANNENBAUM, Julie
Cooking lesson with Julie Dannenbaum. il por House & Gard 140:72-3+ Jl '71 *
DANNER, Ray
Danner feasts on food franchising. il por Bsns W p 120 O 23 '71 *
DANTE Alighieri
Dante and Virgil. R. Montano. Yale R 60: 550-61 Je '71
D'ANTONIO, Lawrence E. and others
Malaria resistance: artificial induction with a partially purified plasmodial fraction. bibliog il Science 168:1117-18; 171:1175-6 My 29 '70, Mr 19 '71
DANVERS, Mass.
They're digging up witch lore in Salem. S. S. McKern. il Sci Digest 69:27-8+ My '71
DANZIG, Aaron L.
International action for the aged? Cur 132: 42-5 S '71
DAPHNIS, Nassos
Canvas 33 stories high. D. Davis. Newsweek 78:65-6 Ag 9 '71 *
D'APRILE, Vincent A.
Noise an emerging hazard. il Cons 25:29-32 Ap '71
DARBEN, Althea (Gibson) See Gibson, A.
DARK glasses. See Sun glasses

DARKROOM equipment. See Photography— Processing—Apparatus and supplies
DARKROOM technique in photography. See Photography—Processing
DARKROOM timers. See Photography—Processing—Apparatus and supplies
DARKROOMS. See Photography—Studios and darkrooms
DARLING, Richard L.
Accountability: notes toward a definition; address, 1971. il por Library J 96:3805-8 N 15 '71
DARLING, Robert Edward
Darling of San Francisco. S. Von Buchau. por Opera N 35:12-13 Mr 20 '71 *
DARLING, Sanford
Mr Darling paints his dream house. il pors Life 70:66-9 Je 25 '71 *
Sanford Darling paints his house. T. Tyler. il por Time 97:17 Ap 5 '71 *
DARMSTADTER, Joel
GNP does matter. il Bul Atom Sci 27:46-8 D '71
DARNELL, J. E. and others
Polyadenylic acid sequences: role in conversion of nuclear RNA into messenger RNA. bibliog il Science 174:507-10 O 29 '71
DAROFF, Michael
Bold cutter trims Botany's losers. por Bsns W p67 F 20 '71 *
DARR, Jack
Build a scope camera for $45. il Radio-Electr 42:43-5 N '71
Home appliance electronics. See issues of Radio-electronics to April 1971
In the shop, with Jack. See issues of Radio-electronics
Replacement transistors. il Radio-Electr 42: 33-6 F; 57-60+ Mr '71
Service clinic; questions and answers. See issues of Radio-electronics
Technician's special (title varies) il Radio-Electr 42:36-40+ Ag; 84-5+ S '71
DARRACH, Brad
Bobby Fischer is a ferocious winner. il pors Life 71:50A-53 N 12 '71
Outrageous Lyle. il pors Life 70:61-4+ Je 11 '71
DARRELL, Robert Donaldson
Great recordings of the decade:
Tapes. il Hi Fi 21:71-3 Ap '71
Nine cassettes to show off and test your tape playback system. Hi Fi 21:48-9 Ag '71
Ormandy declares war (on himself) Hi Fi 21:77 Je '71
Potpourri for Beatrix Potter. il Hi Fi 21:98 O '71
Producer stars in DGG's first Boston Pops recording. il por Hi Fi 20:86-7 D '70
Tape deck. See issues of High fidelity and Musical America
Thrilling live recording. il Hi Fi 21:79 O '71
DARRO, Peter
Saga of the foiled fox. il Nat Wildlife 9: 62-3 O '71
DART games
Darts away. il Time 98:62 Jl 26 '71
DARTS. See Dart games
DARWIN, Charles Robert
Curious controversy over coral reefs. S. Schlee. il por Sea Front 17:214-23 Jl '71 *
Evolution islands. D. C. Fales. il Sci Digest 69:16-21 F '71 *
DAS, Gopal D. and Altman, Joseph
Transplanted precursors of nerve cells: their fate in the cerebellums of young rats. bibliog il Science 173:637-8 Ag 13 '71
D'ASARO, L. A. and Ripper, J. E.
Junction lasers. bibliog il Phys Today 24:42-8 Mr '71
DASSAULT, Marcel, company. See Airplane industry—France
DASSIN, Jules
Current cinema. P. Kael. New Yorker 46:90-2 F 6 '71 *
DATA banks. See Information storage and retrieval systems
DATA general corporation
Data general's coup in minicomputers. il Bsns W p54 Je 19 '71
DATA processing. See Electronic data processing; Information storage and retrieval systems
DATA processing service centers
California cities form data center partnership; San Gabriel Valley municipal data system. L. G. Soper. il Am City 86:113-14 My '71
See also
Automatic data processing, inc.
Electronic data systems corporation
DATA storage retrieval systems. See Information storage and retrieval systems

DATA tapes
Particle that jams more data on tape; Cobaloy. Bsns W p42+ Ap 10 '71
DATA transmission company. See University computing company
DATA transmission systems
Heady dreams at University computing; nationwide microwave network. il por Bsns W p54-5+ My 1 '71
NASA ponders relay satellites. il Aviation W 95:66+ Ag 23 '71
See also
American telephone and telegraph company
Facsimile transmission
Microwave communications, inc.
DATA trends, inc.
Low-cost way to keep books by computer. il Bsns W p 106+ O 23 '71
DATES (fruit)
See also
Cookery—Fruit
DATING
Ask him out? L. Dankman and C. Cooley. il Seventeen 30:94-5 D '71
Boys in your world; excerpts from The new seventeen book of etiquette and young living. E. A. Haupt. por Seventeen 29:128-31+ N '70
Dating around the world. il Seventeen 30:66-7+ Ja '71
Talking it over; questions and answers. Sr Schol 98:20 Ap 19; 19 My 3 '71
See also
Courtship
DATING of foods. See Food—Labeling
DATRAN project. See University computing company
DATSUN (automobile) See Automobiles, Foreign
DAUGHERTY, Charles M.
Charles Reid: the direct approach. il por Am Artist 35:44-9+ D '71
DAUGHERTY, John, and Daugherty, Molly
Quiz. See issues of Science digest
DAUGHERTY, K. E. and Skalny, Jan
Slowest polymerization reaction. il pors Chem 45:12-15 Ja '72
DAUGHERTY, Molly. See Daugherty, J. jt. auth.
DAUGHTERS
See also
Fathers
Girls
DAUGHTERS and mothers. See Parent-child relationship
D'AULAIRE, Emily, and D'Aulaire, Ola
Cheetah, nature's speed king. il Read Digest 98:208-12 Mr '71
D'AULAIRE, Ola. See D'Aulaire, E. jt. auth.
DAUM, Jeffrey W.
From van to camper, $340. il Pop Mech 135:148-52+ F '71
DAUPHIN, Lost. See Louis XVII, king of France
DAUTERMAN, Philip, and Stahl, Robert
Film stimuli, an approach to creative writing. Engl J 60:1120-2 N '71
DAVENPORT, Horace W.
Why the stomach does not digest itself; with biographical sketch. il Sci Am 226:10-11, 86-93 bibliog(p 122) Ja '72
DAVENPORT, John, 1904-
Bank of America is not for burning. il Fortune 83:91-3+ Ja '71
Case against controls: an addendum. Nat R 23:1116 O 8 '71
How to curb union power. il Fortune 84:52+ Jl '71
DAVENPORT, Winthrop
First stop for the U.S. on the road to Havana. J. Jares. il Sports Illus 34:72+ My 17 '71 *
DAVEY, James A.
Big churches? No! Chr Today 16:7+ N 5 '71
DAVID, Anne C.
Effective low cost aftercare. bibliog Ment Hy 55:351-7 Jl '71
DAVID, Edward Emil, 1925-
Coming: fuel crisis; interview. il por U S News 71:53-6 O 18 '71
David on neutrality of NAS, PSAC; excerpts from interview. Science 174:1109 D 10 '71
One objective for science teaching; excerpts from address, March 27, 1971. Science 172:901 My 28 '71
Research and development; address, January 27, 1971. Vital Speeches 37:311-13 Mr 1 '71
U.S. technology: looking for a better mousetrap; interview, ed. by R. Nash. il pors Forbes 108:36-8+ N 15 '71

about
Losing our nerve to experiment? P. M. Boffey. Science 171:875 Mr 5 '71 *
Scientist and public: chapter and verse from David. D. Shapley. Science 172:1010 Je 4 '71 *
DAVID, Elizabeth
Elizabeth David, England's first lady of the kitchen. H. McCully. por House B 113:190 S '71 *
DAVID, F. S.
Your garden indoors. See issues of Home garden & flower grower
DAVID, Lester
Can hypnosis help you? il Seventeen 30:94-5+ Jl '71
50 crafty ways to save money. il Mech Illus 67:62-3+ Je '71
How to cope with being out of work. il Mech Illus 67:53-5+ Mr '71
How to outfox the lawn gyps. il Mech Illus 67:109-11+ My '71
How to save money when you travel. Read Digest 98:53-4+ Je '71
More crafty moneysavers from our readers. il Mech Illus 67:110-11+ N '71
Quick guide to life insurance. il Mech Illus 67:75-7+ Ja '71
Quiet heroism of Dorothy Nichols. il pors Good H 172:114-15+ Ap '71
Ted Kennedy: his triumphs and tragedies; excerpts. por Ladies Home J 89:77+ Ja '72
Ten deadliest household products. il Mech Illus 67:64-6+ F '71
What can a chiropractor do for you? il Mech Illus 67:67-9+ Ap '71
(ed) See Littner, N. Secret wish of unwed fathers
DAVID Brown corporation. See Brown, David, corporation
DAVID McKay company. See McKay, David, company
DAVID R. Godine, publisher. See Godine, David R. publisher
DAVIDOFF, Linda, and others
Suburbs have to open their gates. il N Y Times Mag p40-4+ N 7 '71
DAVIDOVSKY, Mario
Musician of the month. S. Fleming. por Hi Fi 21:MA6-7 Ag '71 *
DAVIS, Ron
Artificial blood, new lifeline for man. il Sci Digest 70:11-14 S '71
Man-made diamonds, who really made them first? il Sci Digest 69:88-90 Ap '71
DAVIDSON, Barbara
Knapp commission didn't know it couldn't be done. il N Y Times Mag p 16-17+ Ja 9 '72
DAVIDSON, Ben
One of the good guys. H. L. Masin. por Sr Schol 99:18 N 8 '71 *
DAVIDSON, Bill
Many faces of Flip Wilson. il pors Good H 172:15+ Ap '71
Shirley Jones: her struggle for family success. il pors Good H 173:30-2+ Ag '71
Trade winds; interview, ed. by C. Amory. Sat R 54:8+ O 30 '71
DAVIDSON, Bruce
Bruce Davidson: East 100th street. M. Edelson. il Pop Phot 69:110-17+ O '71 *
He's face to face with urban blight. J. Deschin. por Pop Phot 68:32+ F '71 *
DAVIDSON, Carla
Art out of the attic. il Am Heritage 23:66-71 D '71
Good Lord, grandpa, it all came true. il Am Heritage 22:70-1 F '71
DAVIDSON, Erika
Great opera houses: Frankfurt. il Opera N 35:12-15 Mr 27 '71
Montserrat; photographs. Opera N 35:14-16 Ap 3 '71
(ed) See Stignani, E. All about Ebe
DAVIDSON, Gerald E.
Treating addicts: you can't fight dope with sermons; interview. por U S News 71:43-4 S 27 '71
DAVIDSON, Jo
American in Paris. J. W. Freeman. il por Opera N 35:24-7 Mr 6 '71
DAVIDSON, L. A.
Time of never was; poem. Cath World 213:82 My '71
DAVIDSON, Marshall B.
Bits of brass. il Antiques 101:193-200 Ja '72
Notable American houses: going by the book in designs and practices; excerpt from The American heritage history of notable American houses. il Antiques 100:580-5 O '71

DAVIDSON, Muriel
Exciting new TV star goes into orbit. il pors Good H 173:102-3+ N '71
Follow-up: command performance. il por Good H 172:50+ Je '71
Mr & Mrs Paul Newman. il pors Good H 173:84-7+ Jl '71
(ed) See Graham, V. Virginia Graham's advice to wives

DAVIDSON, N. R. Jr
El Hajj Malik. Criticism
America 125:534 D 18 '71 *
Nation 213:669 D 20 '71 *
New Yorker 47:102 D 11 '71

DAVIDSON, Pamela
Open university. Nation 212:474-6 Ap 12 '71

DAVIDSON, Ruth
Japanese screens. il Antiques 99:132-9 Ja '71
Museum accessions. See issues of Antiques

DAVIDSON, Sara
Chilean family chronicle: living through the Allende revolution. il N Y Times Mag p33+ O 17 '71
Funny man for this season. il pors N Y Times Mag p26-7+ Ap 25 '71
Happy, happy, happy Nelsons. il pors Esquire 75:97-101+ Je '71
Mick Jagger shoots birds. Atlan 227:96-8+ My '71
Robert Redford: husband, father and sex symbol. por Redbook 137:81+ My '71
Rush for instant salvation. il Harper 243:40-2+ Jl '71

DAVIES, Don
Teacher numbers game. Ed Digest 36:1-4 Ja '71

DAVIES, Jack, family
Lifestyle. il Am Home 74:10+ N '71

DAVIES, John Paton, Jr
Old China hands. pors Time 98:14-15 Ag 2 '71 *

DAVIES, Nigel
Tea with Twiggy; interview. New Yorker 47:30-1 D 18 '71

DAVIES, Peter
Citizens battle for justice. Nation 213:557-9 N 29 '71
Parting shots: man who says he lost two daughters at Kent state. il por Life 71:65 Ag 27 '71 *

DAVIES, Richard Townsend
Department supports congressional resolution on Soviet Jewry; statement, November 9, 1971. Dept State Bul 65:661-7 D 6 '71

about
Degrees of terror. il Time 98:45 N 22 '71 *

DAVIES, Robertson
Authors & editors. B. A. Bannon. por Pub W 199:21-3 Ap 5 '71 *

DAVIES, Rodger Paul
Development aid and security assistance in the Near East and South Asia; statement, July 14, 1971. Dept State Bul 65:204-8 Ag 23 '71
United States policy toward Greece; statement, July 12, 1971. Dept State Bul 65:161-3 Ag 9 '71

DAVIS, Adelle
Adelle Davis celebrates 25 years with Harcourt; interview, ed. by L. P. Freilicher. il por Pub W 199:56 Je 21 '71
Health eaters; interview. il por Vogue 157:166-8 My '71

about
Earth mother to the foodists. J. Howard. il pors Life 71:67-8+ O 22 '71 *
Her believers eat right. B. Falconer. McCalls 98:45 Ag '71 *

DAVIS, Alexander Jackson
American Gothic; with portfolio. W. Andrews. Am Heritage 22:29-47+ O '71 *

DAVIS, Alice
Children who had to be found; interview, ed. by W. E. Densham. il Am Ed 7:11-14 Mr '71

DAVIS, Angela
Angela Davis in prison; interview, ed. by M. Myerson. il por Ramp Mag 9:20-1+ F; 53 Mr '71
Rhetoric vs. reality. il pors Ebony 26:115-18+ Jl '71

about
Angela and the Presbyterians Chr Cent 88:823 Jl 7 '71; Discussion. 88:979-80 Ag 18 '71 *
Angela Davis: the making of a martyr. R. K. Bennett pors Read Digest 98:108-12 Mr '71 *
Campaign to free Angela Davis, and Ruchell Magee. S. Stern. il por N Y Times Mag p8-9+ Je 27 '71 *
Clift balks at Davis gift voted by SRRT council. Library J 96:1553 My 1 '71 *

Day in court; arraignment. il por Newsweek 77:20+ Ja 18 '71 *
Dear Angela; letter. H. Marcuse. Ramp Mag 9:22 F '71 *
Fair trial for Angela Davis? J. H. Skolnick and S. A. Brick. por Nation 213:46-50 Jl 19 '71 *
Miss Davis and Steinem. W. F. Buckley, jr. Nat R 23:1486 D 31 '71 *
Radicalization of Angela Davis. C. L. Sanders. pors Ebony 26:114+ Jl '71 *
SRRT $200 for Angela Davis approved by ALA exec board. Library J 96:1913 Je 1 '71 *
Soviets invited. il Sr Schol 98:5-6 F 1 '71 *
Story behind the book: if they come in the morning. R. H. Smith. por Pub W 200:52-3 N 15 '71 *
Support for Angela Davis. J. English. Library J 96:903 Mr 15 '71 *
Up the down roller coaster: Presbyterians protest Angela. R. Chandler. Chr Today 15:35-6 Jl 2 '71 *
Uproar over the Angela Davis case: the facts, the issues. il por U S News 71:39 O 11 '71 *
Verdict on Poindexter. por Newsweek 77:31 Ap 26 '71 *

DAVIS, Archie K.
Archie K. Davis of Wachovia bank & trust; interview. il pors Nations Bsns 59:34-41 My '71
We must pull together; address, June 30, 1971. Vital Speeches 37:631-4 Ag 1 '71
Welfare reform; address, September 3, 1971. Vital Speeches 37:765-8 O 1 '71

DAVIS, Arnold R.
Videotapes in public schools. Ed Digest 37:52-3 S '71

DAVIS, Benjamin Oliver, 1877-1970
Obituary
Negro Hist Bul por 33:202 D '70

DAVIS, Bert
Lot of transportation for a little money. il Mech Illus 67:48-50+ Ag '71

DAVIS, Charles
Kung on infallibility. Commonweal 93:445-7 F 5 '71; Correction. 93:555 Mr 5 '71

DAVIS, Charles H. and Hiatt, Peter
SDI is for people. bibliog il pors Library J 96:3573-5 N 1 '71

DAVIS, Chester C.
Letters from the invisible billionaire. with sincere regards, Howard Hughes. il por Life 70:24-8 Ja 22 '71 *

DAVIS, Chuck
Chuck Davis dance company, Hunter college assembly hall, NYU. L. Pastore. Dance Mag 45:85 S '71 *

DAVIS, Clinton Leon
Obituary
Am For il por 77:40-1 My '71. J. B. Craig

DAVIS, Colin
Colin Davis' second marriage. R. Wimbush. il por Hi Fi 21:17-18 Ag '71 *
Ordinary bloke. por Time 99:54-5 Ja 3 '72 *

DAVIS, David E. Jr
Motor trend interview. il pors Motor T 23:78+ F '71

DAVIS, Don
Hi-Fi speakers for reverberant sound. il Electr World 85:30-1+ Ap '71

DAVIS, Edward M.
Chief. por Newsweek 77:31-2 Ap 26 '71 *

DAVIS, Elizabeth
S-t-r-e-t-c-h what you know. Writer 85:16-17+ Ja '72

DAVIS, F. S. and others
Ultrahigh-frequency electromagnetic fields for weed control phytotoxicity and selectivity. bibliog il Science 173:535-7 Ag 6 '71

DAVIS, Forest K.
American education as metaphysics: the religious consequence. F. K. Davis. Yale R 61:57-68 O '71

DAVIS, Gwen
Fat vs. thin. por Harp Baz 104:26 My '71

DAVIS, Jack
Parting shots. fantasy for football fans; drawings. Life 70:62A-64 Ja 22 '71

DAVIS, Johanna
Mastering cooking classes. il Life 70:10-11 F 19 '71

DAVIS, Julia
St Louis public school named for Crispus Attucks. Negro Hist Bul 34:57 Mr '71

DAVIS, Keith
Facts about the grouse cycle. il Field & S 76:38+ S '71

DAVIS, Kenneth P.
ABC's of even-aged management. il Am For 77:18-21+ Ag '71

DAVIS, Kenneth S.
Deadly dust: the unhappy history of DDT. il pors Am Heritage 22:44-7+ F '71
Miss Eleanor Roosevelt; excerpts. il pors Am Heritage 22:48-59 O '71

DAY nurseries—*Continued*
  Should a mother feel guilty about wanting
    to send her toddler to a day care center?
    B. Bettelheim. Ladies Home J 88:34+ S
    '71
  Town that closed its doors; battle in Gar-
    den City against day care center. J. Evans.
    il Redbook 136:88-9+ Mr '71
  What's a mother to do? companies and day
    care. il Newsweek 78:61 Jl 5 '71
DAY of judgment. See Judgment day
DAY of the Lhasa Apso; story. See Green-
    burg, D.
DAY the Marsmen landed; drama. See Rybak,
    R. K.
DAY they gave hamsters away; story. See
    Hinchman. J.
DAYAN, Moshe
  Person behind the patch. por Time 98:40 N
    29 '71 •
  Third way. il por Time 98:33 S 13 '71 •
DAYLILIES. See Day lilies
DAYTON. Ohio
  By invitation only; tactics used during visit
    of R. M. Nixon. New Repub 165:9 S 18 '71
        Economic conditions
  Dayton weathers a siege. Bsns W p81+ D 4
    '71
        Education
  Cut back or close down? il Newsweek 78:65
    N 1 '71
  Dayton's school situation. America 125:446
    N 27 '71
        Sanitary affairs
  Winter ice control, art or science? il Am
    City 86:24 Ag '71
DAYTONA BEACH, Fla.
  U.S. journal; student spring vacations. C.
    Trillin. New Yorker 47:104+ My 1 '71
DAYTONA 500. See Automobile racing
DEACONS
  Lay deacons. America 125:249 O 9 '71
  Meet the new deacon. T. E. Clarke. Amer-
    ica 124:260-2 Mr 13 '71
  Permanent diaconate. G. S. Sloyan; C. J.
    Armbruster; J. J. Begley. Commonweal 94:
    56-64 Mr 26 '71; Discussion. 94:227+ My
    14 '71
DEAD, Resuscitation of. See Resuscitation
DEAD SEA scrolls
  New Covenanters of Qumran. S. Talmon. il
    Sci Am 225:72-81 bibliog(p 136) N '71
DEAF
  Words for a deaf daughter, by P. West. Re-
    view
    Commentary 51:106-7 Ja '71. J. Kaplan;
      Discussion. 51:10+ Ap '71
    See also
  Television broadcasting and the deaf
DEAF, Apparatus for the
    See also
  Hearing aids
DEAF-mutes
  Sports brighten a silent world; basketball
    player, B. Fuller. il pors Ebony 27:44-6+
    D '71
DEAFNESS
  Children's ears in health and in disease. L.
    W. Sauer. PTA Mag 65:31-2 Ap '71
  Electronic device treats deafness; transdermal
    electrical treatments. S. V. Jones. il Sci
    Digest 69:79 Je '71
  Ethacrynic acid effect on the composition
    of cochlear fluids. E. S. Cohn and others.
    bibliog il Science 171:910-11 Mr 5 '71
  Hard of hearing; socially acceptable. E. De-
    vine. il Har Yrs 11:30-1 F '71
  Of cats and men; study of Waardenburg's
    syndrome. Sci Am 225:50 N '71
  Why early detection of hearing problems is
    important to children. Good H 173:221 N
    '71
    See also
  Hearing
  Noise—Physiological effects
DEAKYNE, William
  Serving the Pearl of the Orient. il por Wilson
    Lib Bul 45:966-9 Je '71
DEAL, Babs H.
  More to love; story. Good H 173:92-3 O '71
DEAL, Borden
  People and characters; with biographical
    sketch. Writer 84:16-18 Ap '71
DEAL, Elizabeth M.
  Responsible freedom for the secondary
    school press; a cooperative effort. Engl
    J 60:960-2 O '71
DEAL, Walter J. and others
  Conformational equilibria in spin-labeled
    hemoglobin. bibliog il Science 171:1147-9
    Mr 19 '71

DEALERS, Automobile. See Automobile dealers
DEAN, Beth
  Dynamic new impresario in Australia. il por
    Dance Mag 45:44-6 Je '71
DEAN, James
  Painting the spirit of the past; with bio-
    graphical sketch. il por Am Artist 35:90-
    5+ Mr '71
DEAN, Phillip Hayes
  Sty of the blind pig. Criticism
    Nation 213:668 D 20 '71 •
    New Yorker 47:131 D 4 '71 •
    Newsweek il 78:122 D 6 '71 •
    Time 98:81 D 6 '71 •
DEAN, Sidney W. Jr
  Cable TV; omission by commission. Nation
    213:691-3 D 27 '71
DEANE, Ben Cady
  Portrait of an entrepreneur. por Forbes 108:
    36 N 1 '71 •
DEANS, Edwina
  Laboratory approach to elementary mathe-
    matics. il Todays Ed 60:20-2 F '71
DE ANTONIO, Emile
  Radical scavenging; interview, ed. by B.
    Weiner. il por Film Q 25:3-15 Fall '71
        about
  Minor surgery. Time 98:87 O 18 '71 •
DEARDEN, John Francis, cardinal
  Detroit's Cardinal Dearden; a cautious pro-
    gressive. A. O. Sigur. Chr Cent 88:671-3
    My 26 '71 •
DEARDORFF, Robert
  New Orleans. il Travel 135:36-41 F '71
  New winter trails; Switzerland. il Travel 136:
    34-9 D '71
  Step by step through Atlanta. il Travel
    136:28-31+ O '71
  Step by step through Memphis. il Travel 136:
    48-53+ S '71
  Step by step through Phoenix. il Travel 136:
    58-63 N '71
  Step by step through St Louis. il Travel 135:
    56-61 Je '71
DE ARMOND, V. J. Jr
  Ragtop to hardtop. il Motor B & S 127:116+
    Mr '71
DEAS, Malcolm
  Coalition in Colombia. Cur Hist 60:90-4+ F
    '71
DEASY, Mary
  Like fireflies in August; story. Redbook
    137:66-8 Ag '71
DEATH
  Boundaries, by R. J. Lifton. Review
    Sat R 54:28-9+ F 20 '71. E. Capouya
  Death as an event; a commentary on Robert
    Morison; adaptation of address, December
    29, 1970. L. R. Kass. bibliog Science 173:
    698-702 Ag 20 '71
  Death; process or event? adaptation of ad-
    dress, December 29, 1970. R. S. Morison.
    bibliog Science 173:694-8 Ag 20 '71
  Reflections on one's own death as a peak
    experience. M. Hammer. Ment Hy 55:264-5
    Ap '71
  Through the valley of the shadow. B. Gra-
    ham. Read Digest 98:107-10 Ap '71
    See also
  Bereavement
  Children and death
  Euthanasia
  Immortality
  Suicide
        Causes
    See also
  Suicide
  Temperature—Physiological effects
        Psychology
  Learning how to die. D. Dempsey. il N Y
    Times Mag p58+ N 14 '71; Discussion. p 125
    D 5 '71
  Learning to die. T. Powers. il Harper 242:
    72-4+ Je '71
  Ministering in a death-oriented culture. C.
    Miller. Chr Today 16:10-12 N 19 '71
  Some lessons on dying. B. Hale. il por Chr
    Cent 88:1076-9 S 15 '71
DEATH (biology)
  Definitions of death. Sci Am 225:40+ D '71
DEATH, Apparent
    See also
  Resuscitation
DEATH and children. See Children and death
DEATH of dreams; story. See Oates, J. C.
DEATH on the East side; story. See Gold, H.
DEATH penalty. See Capital punishment
DEATH rate. See Mortality
DEATH rate of infants. See Infant mortality
DEATH row prisoners. See Prisoners

DECORATION and ornament
See also
Art déco
Beadwork
Candles
Christmas decorations
Color in architecture
Cookery, Ornamental
Design
Easter eggs
Enamel and enameling
Flowers, Arrangement of
House decoration
Needlework
Stencil work
Table decoration
Textile design
DECORATION and ornament, Architectural
Adair plaques adorn new Rockford library. il Ceram Mo 20:26-7 Ja '72
Manhattan safari; sculptured animals on city's buildings. K. Simmon. il Natur Hist 80:72-7 My '71
See also
Mural painting and decoration
DECORATION and ornament, Middle Eastern
Taste for the East. il Look 35:30-4+ S 21 '71
DECORATION day. See Memorial day
DECORATION of book edges. See Book ornamentation
DECORATION of food. See Cookery—Garnishes
DECORATIONS, Christmas. See Christmas decorations
DECORATIVE plants. See Plants, Ornamental
DÉCOUPAGE
Découpage: cut-out, paste-up art. il House B 113:70-1+ Ja '71
DECOYS (hunting)
Deadliest decoy; diving decoy. C. F. Rees. il Field & S 76:38 My '71
With a quack, quack here; wildfowl decoys. R. H. Boyle. il por Sports Illus 35:50-3+ S 27 '71
DE CRISTOFORO, R. J.
All-purpose planer. il Mech Illus 67:92-3+ Ap '71
How to know a nice vise when you see one. il Mech Illus 67:112-13+ F '71
Ingenious jig for a table saw. il Mech Illus 67:102-4+ Mr '71
Low cost power tools in kits. il Mech Illus 67:100-2+ N '71
Meet the molder. il Mech Illus 67:117-19 My '71
13 tools every man should own. il Mech Illus 67:112-14+ Ja '71
DECTER, Midge
Liberated woman. Commentary 50:33-44 O '70; 51:32-3+ F '71
Look at Israel. Commentary 51:38-42 My '71
about
Standing her ground. S. Braudy. il por Newsweek 78:115+ S 27 '71 •
DEDICATIONS, Book. See Book dedications
DEDIJER, Vladimir
Revolt in the North. Nation 212:726-7 Je 7 '71
DEEDY, John
News & views. See issues of Commonweal
Should Catholic schools survive? New Repub 164:15-18 Mr 13 '71
Vanishing Catholic press. Commonweal 95:127-30, 242 N 5, D 10 '71
DEEKEN, Alfons
Growing old and how to cope with it. America 124:315-18 Mr 27 '71
Man as an image of the Trinity. il Cath World 214:9-13 O '71
New world language. il America 126:11-14 Ja 8 '72
DE ELORZA, Jeff
On the right track; photographs. Pop Phot 69:66-9 Jl '71
DEEP diving simulators. See Simulators
DEEP in the interior and everything and all; story. See Drake, R.
DEEP injection wells. See Trade waste disposal
DEEP research vehicles. See Submarine research vehicles
DEEP sea deposits. See Marine sediments
DEEP sea diving. See Diving, Submarine
DEEP sea drilling. See Underwater drilling
DEEP-sea exploration. See Underwater exploration
DEEP sea fauna. See Marine fauna
DEEP sea fishing. See Salt water fishing
DEEP sea photography. See Photography, Submarine

DEEP-water archeology. See Archeology, Submarine
DEEPSTAR (submersible) See Submarine research vehicles
DEER
Strange white deer of New York; at Seneca army depot. J. Fisk. il Outdoor Life 148:76-7+ Ag '71
What's happening to our deer? K. Heuser. il Field & S 76:56-7+ O '71
See also
Antlers
Elk
Game, Dressing of
Reindeer
Food and feeding
Acorns at seven. R. V. McCormick. il Field & S 76:48-9+ Ag '71
Photographs
See Animals—Photographs
DEER, Dressing of. See Game, Dressing of
DEER hunting
Best method for you. G. H. Gillelan. il Outdoor Life 148:32+ S '71
Big secret. E. A. Bauer. il Outdoor Life 148:78-81+ O '71
Blacktails for beginners. E. Paradzinski. il Field & S 76:52-3+ O '71
Boat-in bucks: Warren County, Pa. J. Bashline. il Field & S 76:48-9+ O '71
Can you really see deer? J. Palmer. il Field & S 76:31+ S '71
Deer for my pains. J. O. Cartier. il por Outdoor Life 148:76-7+ N '71
Double take: deer and antelope. J. R. Olt. il por Outdoor Life 148:72-5+ S '71
East (hunters) meets West (mule deer) B. Grant. il Field & S 76:40-1+ Jl '71
Eye for deer. B. W. Dalrymple. il Outdoor Life 148:30-3+ D '71
Four-year wait, white tall buck. R. Grecar. il por Outdoor Life 147:84-5+ Je '71
Foxholes for bucks. B. Pettingill. il Field & S 76:45+ O '71
Fundamentals of deer stalking. D. Harbour. il Field & S 76:42-3+ Ag '71
Ghost of Shelby forest. D. Johnson. il Outdoor Life 147:72+ My '71
Happy hunting ground; Jicarilla Apache reservation, New Mexico. K. Campbell. il pors Outdoor Life 148:72-5+ O '71
Hunt the off hours. G. H. Gillelan. il Outdoor Life 148:24+ Ag '71
Looping for whitetail. A. Mitchell. il Field & S 76:50-1+ O '71
My most memorable deer hunt. A. Rutledge. il Outdoor Life 148:44-5+ Jl '71
Of space, time and deer. D. J. Anderson. il Field & S 76:48-9+ N '71
Phantom of record; white-antlered buck. J. A. Brunk. il por Outdoor Life 148:49-51+ N '71
Secret of the Rock. J. Wootters. il Outdoor Life 147:60-1+ F '71
See more shootable deer. H. Wixom. il Field & S 76:46-7+ O '71
Stalk your buck to his hideaway. L. A. Anderson. il Field & S 76:34-5+ D '71
Strategy for whitetails. E. A. Bauer. il Outdoor Life 148:52-5+ S '71
Timetable for bowhunters. J. Palmer. il Field & S 76:46-7+ Jl '71
To venison with love. C. J. Anderson. il Field & S 76:62-3+ O '71
Too many deer: South Fox Island, Mich. J. O. Cartier. Outdoor Life 147:161 Je '71
Whitetails have their faults. L. A. Anderson. il Field & S 76:62-3+ Je '71
Whitetails in the black; Black Hills of Wyoming. C. J. Farmer. il Field & S 76:66-7+ Ag '71
DEER meat. See Venison
DEERE and company
Long wait; joint venture with Italy's Fiat, S.p.A. il Forbes 108:55-6 D 1 '71
DEERFIELD, Mass.
Colonial Deerfield village. M. Evans il Am Home 74:98-103 O '71
DEETZ, James. See Ekholm, E. jt. auth.
DEFECTORS, Political
Do-it-yourself escape; Czechoslovakian defector L. Bezak. por Time 99:41 Ja 3 '72
Dubious defector; A. Fedoseyev. Newsweek 78:38+ Jl 5 '71
How our strangers in paradise like us now. M. Cohen. il Todays Health 49:40-3+ Jl '71
Incident at Orly; defection of Chinese diplomat Chang Shi-jung. il Time 97:36 My 10 '71
Right to leave; difference between Communist regimes and ours. Nat R 23:306 Mr 23 '71
Shanghaied in Paris; Chang Shi-jung. il Newsweek 77:44 My 10 '71

DEFELICE, Vincent N.
Snowshoe country. il Am For 77:20-3+ F '71
DEFENSE (criminal procedure)
Will Mr William Kunstler please step down?
a dissenting opinion on the practice of
new left law. J. W. Bishop, jr. il pors
Esquire 75:115-17+ Ap '71
DEFENSE, Department of. See United States
—Defense, Department of
DEFENSE, Self. See Self defense
DEFENSE appropriations. See United States—
Armed forces—Appropriations and expendi-
tures; United States—Defense, Department
of—Appropriations and expenditures
DEFENSE contracts. See Contracts, Govern-
ment
DEFENSE industries
See also
Industrial demobilization
Military-industrial complex
Munitions industries

Conversion
See Industrial demobilization

Employees
Defense engineers; do they have special re-
employment problems? B. C. Eaton. il Mo
Labor R 94:52-4 Jl '71
Roll-call of colonels that industry hires. il
Bsns W p20 N 27 '71

Finance
Aerospace and defense; with yardsticks of
management performance. il Forbes 109:
183-4 Ja 1 '72
DEFENSE information, Classified
After the Pentagon papers; talk with Kistia-
kowsky, Wiesner; interviews. ed. by E.
Langer. J. Wiesner; G. Kistiakowsky. pors
Science 174:923-8 N 26 '71
Again the Pentagon papers. Time 98:30 Jl 19
'71
Case of the Pentagon papers. America 125:6-7
Jl 10 '71
Counter-government and the Pentagon pa-
pers. Nat R 23:739-41 Jl 13 '71
Ellsberg; the battle over the right to know.
il pors Time 98:6-12 Jl 5 '71
Funds asked for declassification of World
war II documents; text of letter, August
3, 1971. R. M. Nixon. Dept State Bul 65:
249 Ag 30 '71
Government vs. the press; Pentagon study
of the war in Vietnam. il por Newsweek
78:17-19 Jl 5 '71
I have in my hand a photostatic copy of. . ;
role of the New York times. Nat R 23:685-
6 Je 29 '71
Key man in the case of leaked papers; D.
Ellsberg. por U S News 71:25 Jl 12 '71
1984: closer than we'd thought? publication
of Vietnam papers. Pub W 199:45 Je 28 '71
Notes and comment; keeping secret the Pentagon study of the war's origins and development. New Yorker 47:17-19 Jl 3 '71
Notes and comment; Pentagon's secret study
on the conduct of the war. New Yorker
47:29-30 Je 26 '71; Same with title Leader-
ship or suspended government? Cur 131:3-5
Jl '71
Pentagon papers. Commonweal 94:347-8 Jl
9 '71
Pentagon papers. Life 71:6 Jl 2 '71
Pentagon papers: a crucial legal battle erupts.
il U S News 71:19 Jl 5 '71
Pentagon papers: and freedom of the press.
M. S. Hayden. Read Digest 99:133-4 S '71
Pentagon papers, as published by the New
York times, and Senator Gravel edition.
The Pentagon papers. Reviews
Nat R 23:141?+ D 17 '71. D. Brudnoy
Pentagon papers: did the public win or lose?
questions and answers. Sr Schol 99:4-5 S 20
'71
Pentagon papers: repercussions for Rand
and other think tanks? J. Walsh. Science
173:311+ Jl 23 '71
Pentagon papers; the secret war. il Time 97:
11-17 Je 28 '71
Q: do the claims of conscience outweigh the
duties of citizenship? five testimonies on
the publishing of the Pentagon papers. il
por Esquire 76:154-9+ D '71
Round 3: more Pentagon disclosures; excerpts from documents. il Time 98:12-13 Jl
12 '71
Secret decisions that altered the Vietnam war;
storm over leaked documents. il U S News
70:21-3 Je 28 '71
Secret history of Vietnam; Pentagon study,
commissioned by R. McNamara. il pors
Newsweek 77:12-22+ Je 28 '71
Secret Pentagon papers. J. B. Sheerin. Cath
World 213:211-12 Ag '71

Secretary Rogers' news conference of July 1:
the duty of the executive branch to protect
the national security. W. P. Rogers. Dept
State Bul 65:78-82 Jl 19 '71
Security information and democracy. J. C.
Hagerty. Cur 131:7-8 Jl '71
TRB from Washington; Pentagon papers.
New Repub 164:6 Je 26 '71
Today's lessons from the Pentagon papers.
L. H. Gelb. por Life 71:34-6 S 17 '71
Trouble with secrets; displayed reaction of
the President and administration to disclos-
ure of the Pentagon papers. J. Osborne.
New Repub 165:11-12 Jl 3 '71
What the rap might be; publication of the
Pentagon papers. por Time 98:35 Jl 26 '71
Which are the true papers? J. Burnham.
Nat R 23:864 Ag 10 '71
Which edition of the Pentagon papers do you
buy? M. Sacharoff. Wilson Lib Bul 46:313-
14+ D '71

Anecdotes, facetiae, satire, etc.
National review papers. W. F. Buckley, jr.
Nat R 23:850 Ag 10 '71
Secret papers they didn't publish; documents
leaked to National review. Nat R 23:798-
811 Jl 27 '71; Discussion. 23:904, 915-18,
975-6 Ag 24-S 10 '71
DEFENSE intelligence agency. See United
States—Defense intelligence agency
DEFENSE mechanisms (biology)
Defense of phalangid; liquid repellent administered by leg dabbing. T. Eisner and
others. bibliog il Science 173:650-2 Ag 13 '71
2,5-Dichlorophenol (from ingested herbicide?)
in defensive secretion of grasshopper. T.
Eisner and others. bibliog il Science 172:
277-8 Ap 16 '71
Giving ants the brush-off; chemical repel-
lent of vonones. il Chem 44:19 N '71
Grasshopper chemical factories, 2,5-dich-
lorophenol from 2,4-D in defensive secre-
tions. R. H. Gilluly. il Sci N 99:406 Je 12 '71
Leech-repellent property of eastern red-
spotted newts, notophthalmus viridescens.
F. H. Pough. bibliog il Science 174:1144-6
D 10 '71
Sensuous symbionts of the sea. L. Thomas.
il Natur Hist 80:28-37+ bibliog(p96) Ag '71
DEFENSE mechanisms (psychology)
See also
Displacement (psychology)
**DEFERRED admissions by colleges and uni-
versities.** See Colleges and universities—
Entrance requirements
DEFICIENCY diseases
Antiseptic baby; case of combined immune
deficiency. il Newsweek 78:61-2 D 20 '71
See also
Goiter
DEFICIT spending. See Government spending
policy
DEFLIESE, Philip Leroy
Methodical man. por Forbes 107:54 Mr 15
'71 *

DEFOLIATION
Defoliation in Chicago; AAAS report on
military use of defoliants in Vietnam. Sci
Am 224:44 F '71
Destruction of Indochina: report of Stanford
biology study group. il Bul Atom Sci 27:
36-40 My '71
Ecocide and the Geneva protocol. L. C. John-
stone. For Affairs 49:711-20 Jl '71
Ecocide in Indochina. A. H. Westing. il Natur
Hist 80:56-61 Mr '71
Herbicides in Vietnam: AAAS study finds
widespread devastation. P. M. Boffey. il
Science 171:43-7 Ja 8 '71
Reporter at large; aerial spraying of trees
in Vietnam (cont) T. Whiteside. New
Yorker 47:54+ Ag 14 '71
Silent Vietnam; how we invented ecocide and
killed a country. O. Schell, jr. il Look 35:
55+ Ap 6 '71
Tour of Vietnam. T. Aaronson. bibliog il
Environ 13:34-43 Mr '71
DEFORD, Frank
Best damn team in baseball. il Sports Illus
34:78-82 Ap 12 '71
Beware, little big man is here. por Sports
Illus 35:46-7+ O 25 '71
Caution: beware of angels at work. il Sports
Illus 34:84-8+ My 17 '71
Hawks: fouled up but flourishing. il Sports
Illus 34:26-8+ Mr 8 '71
Jump ahead of extinction. il Sports Illus
35:36-8+ N 8 '71
(ed) Never sell the horses short. il Sports
Illus 35:87-9+ O 18 '71
Night Miss America vanished; excerpt from
There she is; the life and times of Miss
America. il por Ladies Home J 88:104-5+
S '71

DEFORD, Frank—*Continued*

Once and future diplomat. il por Sports Illus 34:62-6+ Mr 1 '71

Pro basketball (cont) Sports Illus 35:42 Ag 9 '71

TV talk (cont) Sports Illus 34:12 F 8; 14+ Mr 8; 14 Mr 29; 7 Ap 26; 16 My 24; 10 Je 28; 35:10 S 13 '71

Tennis. il Sports Illus 35:47-8 Ag 30 '71

Time for all good men. . . Sports Illus 35: 54+ N 22 '71

Trade winds; Miss America; interview, ed. by C. Amory. Sat R 54:8+ O 2 '71

Will Franklin Mieull spoil success? il pors Sports Illus 34:62-4+ F 15 '71

(ed) See Briner, B. But it looked like a great new racket

DEFORMITIES

Agonizing decision of Joanne and Roger Pell. R. Pell. Good H 174:76-7+ Ja '72

Aspirin and birth defects: fetal cell inhibition. Sci N 100:225 O 2 '71

Monitoring human birth defects and mutations to detect environmental effects. E. B. Hook. Science 172:1363-6 Je 25 '71

New strides in the battle against birth defects; science of genetic counseling. S. M. Spencer. Read Digest 98:159-60+ My '71

DEFORMITIES (birds) See Abnormalities (birds)

DEFORMITIES, Cure of. See Orthopedia

DEFRANCE, Edward, pseud.

Now ain't it just a wonder? story. Liv Wildn 34:53-4 Aut '70

DEGAS, Edgar

Butterfly and the old ox. T. Reff. il pors Art N 70:26-31+ Mr '71 *

DE GAULLE, Charles. See Gaulle, C. de

DEGGINGER, E. R.

In praise of snakes; photographs. Audubon 73:18-24 Jl '71

DEGRADABLE plastics. See Plastics—Deterioration

DEGRADATION (biology)

Deep sea as a food refrigerator. il Chem 44: 25 My '71

Microbial degradation of organic matter in the deep sea. H. W. Jannasch and others. bibliog il Science 171:672-5 F 19 '71

Sandwiches in the deep sea. Sea Front 17: 267 S '71

DE GRAMONT, Nancy (Ryan)

Couple-speak: rape, true and false. pors Vogue 157:109+ Je '71

DE GRAMONT, Sanche

Can a man lose to a woman in a love game? Yes, but. . . Vogue 157:130+ My '71

Couple-speak: rape, true and false. pors Vogue 157:108+ Je '71

Mohammed: the prophet armed. il Horizon 13:18-23 Sum '71

Woman in Proust's life. por Harp Baz 104: 54-5 Je '71

about

Authors & editors. B. A. Bannon. por Pub W 199:7-9 Mr 22 '71 *

DE GRAZIA, Alfred

Brand new: a university to save the world? Mlle 72:282 Ap '71 *

DEGREE mills. See Diplomas, Fraudulent

DEGREES, Academic

Associate degrees conferred by institutions of higher education. W. V. Grant. Am Ed 7:41 N '71

Catholic universities flunk the Ph.D. exam; ACE study. America 124:84 Ja 30 '71; Reply. 124:442 My 1 '71

Changing expectations in the doctorate. L. W. Kline. Sch & Soc 99:93-4 F '71

College degrees have got to go! D. Matthews. Mlle 72:120-1+ Ja '71

D.min: First or second theological degree? L. H. DeWolf; discussion. Chr Cent 87:1388; 88:138+ N 18 '70, Ja 27 '71

Data on degrees. Sch & Soc 99:397 N '71

Doctor of arts degree. H. G. Stever; discussion. Science 171:234-5 Ja 22 '71

Future market for Ph.D.'s. D. Wolfle and C. V. Kidd. bibliog il Science 173:784-93 Ag 27 '71

Less time and more options in higher education; conclusions of report by the Carnegie commission on higher education. Sch & Soc 99:285-6 Sum '71

New professional studies degrees; authorization by New York state board of regents. Sch & Soc 99:330-2 O '71

Pruning the Ph.D.   Sch & Soc 99:8-9 Ja '71

Sheepskin psychosis and campus unrest. Sch & Soc 99:6-7 Ja '71

Trends in the number of doctor's degrees conferred. W. V. Grant. il Am Ed 7:36-inside back cover Jl '71

See also

Diplomas, Fraudulent

Anecdotes, facetiae, satire, etc.

Sam Snodgrass rides again; oversupply of Ph.D.'s. G. Flavin. America 124:406-7 Ap 17 '71

DEGREES, Honorary

Kudos. il Time 97:35-6 Je 7; 54-5 Je 14; 55 Je 21 '71

See also

Diplomas, Fraudulent

DE GROOT, Roy Andries

Do people snigger when you order the wine? Esquire 75:142-3+ My '71

Holiday feast at the Forsytes. il Esquire 75: 130-3+ Ja '71

Mrs Wilkes's boarding house. il Esquire 76: 150-1+ N '71

What goes with what? House B 113:140-1+ N '71

DEHART, P. H. and DeHart, R. M.

Health and vigor depend on the soil. bibliog il Org Gard & Farm 18:102-7 Je '71

DEHART, R. M. See DeHart, P. H. jt. auth.

DEHOFF, Betty Joy

Newport News education association. Today Ed 60:58 O '71

DEHUMIDIFIERS

No-drip pipe galleries; Cuyahoga Falls, Ohio. il Am City 86:16 Je '71

DEHYDRATED potatoes. See Potatoes, Dried

DEHYDRATION (physiology)

Galactose toxicity in the chick; hyperosmolality. J. I. Malone and others. bibliog il Science 174:952-4 N 26 '71

DEHYDROGENASES

Deuterium effects on binding of reduced coenzyme alcohol dehydrogenase isoenzyme EE. K. Bush and others. bibliog il Science 172:478-80 Ap 30 '71

Developmental variation in the isoenzymes of human liver and gastric alcohol dehydrogenase. R. F. Murray, jr. and A. G. Motulsky. bibliog il Science 171:71-3 Ja 8 '71

Genetic aspects of increase in rat liver aldehyde dehydrogenase induced by phenobarbital. R. A. Deitrich. bibliog il Science 173: 334-6 Jl 23 '71

Induction of liver acetaldehyde dehydrogenase: possible role in ethanol tolerance after exposure to barbiturates. G. Redmond and G. Cohen. bibliog il Science 171:387-9 Ja 29 '71

DEI DOLORI, Mario P. See Morton, T. H. jt. auth.

DEIBE, Carlos Feal-. See Feal-Deibe, C.

DEIBER, Paul Emile

Alsatian; interview, ed. by A. M. Lingg. il por Opera N 35:16 Mr 27 '71

DEICHMANN, William B. and others

DDT tissue retention: sudden rise induced by the addition of aldrin to a fixed DDT intake. bibliog il Science 172:275-6 Ap 16 '71

DE-ICING. See Airplanes—Ice protection; Snow and ice removal

DEIMOS (satellite) See Satellites

DEISS, Joseph Jay

Embolism, the puzzling killer. Read Digest 98:201-2+ Mr '71

DEITCH, David

Phase two: will it work? For whom? Nation 213:678-82 D 27 '71

Watershed of the American economy. Nation 213:198-202, 386+ S 13, O 25 '71

DEITRICH, Richard A.

Genetic aspects of increase in rat liver aldehyde dehydrogenase induced by phenobarbital. bibliog il Science 173:334-6 Jl 23 '71

DEJOHN, Bill

Social responsibilities: what it's all about. bibliog il Am Lib 2:300-2 Mr '71

DE KAY, Ormonde, Jr

Rimes de la Mère Oie; French text; excerpts. il Horizon 13:120 Wint '71

Story behind the book: Mother Goose gets the French treatment; interview, ed. by P. Bragg. il Pub W 200:18-19 D 13 '71

DE LA GRANGE, Henry Louis

Music of the East at Royan. Sat R 54:38 Je 26 '71

DE LA HABA, Louis

Belize, the awakening land. il Nat Geog 141:124-46 Ja '72

DELANEY, Robert F.
  Mismanagement of Latin American affairs;
  address, November 6, 1970. Vital Speeches
  37:235-8 F 1 '71
DE-LA-NOY, Michael
  Plummeling the prelates. J. D. Douglas.
  Chr Today 15:51-2 S 24 '71 •
DE LA RAMÉE, Louise
  Nurnberg stove; dramatization. See Howard,
  H. L.
DE LA ROSA, Daniel, and Ebert, D. D.
  Sunbursts and papier-mâché. il Sch Arts 70:
  6-7 Je '71
DELATTRE, Pierre
  Gasp of amazement; story; Excerpt from
  Tales of a Dalai lama. Harp Baz 104:148
  Mr '71
DELAURENTIS, Louise Budde
  Masque for the 20th century; poem. Chr
  Cent 88:462 Ap 14 '71
DELAVAN LAKE
  Out with the algae, safely. il Am City 86:
  84+ Je '71
DELAWARE
    See also
  Chesapeake Bay
  Environmental policy—Delaware
  Gardens—Delaware

    Description and travel
  Downstate Delaware. J. Bowen. il Travel
  136:48-51+ N '71

    Education
    See also
  Wilmington, Del.—Education

    Industries
  He slammed the door in industry's face; in-
  terview. R. Peterson. il por Nat Wildlife 10:
  50-1 D '71
DELAWARE, Ohio
  Doing his jig with the Jug. W. F. Reed. il
  Sports Illus 35:66-7 O 4 '71
DELAWARE BAY
  He slammed the door in industry's face; in-
  terview. R. Peterson. il por Nat Wildlife 10:
  50-1 D '71
DEL CASTILLO, Michel
  Orphan-boys circus. il por Vogue 158:104-7+
  D '71
DELCOIGNE, Georges C. and Rubinstein, G.
  Nonproliferation and control: peaceful uses of
  atomic energy. il Bul Atom Sci 27:5-7 F '71
DELDERFIELD, Ronald Frederick
  Confessions of the long-distance writer; with
  biographical sketch. Writer 84:11-18 S '71
  Theirs was the kingdom; excerpts. McCalls
  98:117-28 S '71
DELEE, Victoria
  Victoria Delee, in her own words: interview.
  ed. by C. Trillin. New Yorker 47:86+ Mr
  27 '71
DELEGATES, Convention. See National con-
  ventions (political)
DELEGATES to the United Nations. See
  United Nations—Delegates
DE LEON, Virginia Lichauco
  Untitled; poem. Ladies Home J 88:109 F '71
DELFIM NETO, Antônio
  Chief architect of a boom. por Bsns W p90-1
  Mr 13 '71 •
DELGADO, Abelardo
  Why minority publishing? ed. by B. Cham-
  bers. il pors Pub W 199:38 Mr 15 '71
DELILLO, Don
  Game plan; story. New Yorker 47:44-7 N 27
  '71
  In the men's room of the sixteenth century;
  story. il Esquire 76:174-7 D '71
DELINQUENT children. See Juvenile delin-
  quency
DELINQUENTS. See Juvenile delinquency
DELISLE, William
  Imaginary geography. W. M. Wiecek. il Am
  West 8:10-12 S '71 •
DELIUS, Frederick
  Delian delight. D. Henahan. por Hi Fi 21:77
  Ap '71 •
  Koanga. Criticism
  Hi Fi 21:MA31 Ap '71 •
DELIUS, Jack C.
  Spring swing to playgrounds. il Parks &
  Rec 6:48-9+ O '71
DELLER, Alfred
  Men of the high C's. il por Newsweek 79:60-1
  Ja 10 '72 •
DELLIQUANTI, Don
  Baseball (cont) il Sports Illus 34:58 My 10;
  68 S 20 '71
  College basketball. il Sports Illus 34:38 Ja 11
  '71
  Fencing. Sports Illus 34:76+ Mr 8 '71

Week; baseball. Sports Illus 35:38-9 S 6;
  84-5 S 13 '71
Week; college football. Sports Illus 35:70+
  D 6 '71
DEL MARCELLE, David J.
  Lebanon Valley. il Travel 136:64-7 D '71
DELONG, Edward K.
  (ed) See Marchetti, V. Former staff officer
  criticizes CIA activities
DELONG, Howard
  Unsolved problems in arithmetic; with bio-
  graphical sketch. il Sci Am 224:14, 50-60
  bibliog (p 124) Mr '71
DELOREAN, John Zachary
  Battle but not war; interview. il por Forbes
  108:49 Ag 1 '71
  Swinger tries to cure Chevrolet's ills. il pors
  Bsns W p60-4 S 18 '71 •
DELORIA, Vine, Jr
  American thing: white society is breaking
  down around us; interview, ed. by P. Col-
  lier. Mlle 72:202-4+ Ap '71
DELOUETTE, Roger
  French connection. il por Time 98:26 N 29
  '71 •
  French connection. il pors Newsweek 78:38
  N 29 '71 •
DELPREORE, Lawrence
  (ed) See Gibson, K. A. Urban leader
DELSARTE, François
  In homage to Francois Delsarte: 1811-1871.
  O. Maynard. il por Dance Mag 45:64-5 Ag
  '71 •
DELSEMME, A. H.
  Comets: production mechanisms of hydroxyl
  and hydrogen halos. bibliog Science 172:
  1126-7 Je 11 '71
DELSTON, Ethel
  I want to see my mother; story. Redbook
  136:102-3 Mr '71
DELTA air lines
  Airline that makes money. il Fortune 83:240
  My '71
  Amazin'-Dixon line. il Time 97:70+ Je 7 '71
  Charles H. Dolson of Delta air lines; inter-
  view. C. H. Dalson. il pors Nations Bsns
  59:50-3+ S '71
  Delta planning to standardize wide-bodied
  transport fleet. Aviation W 95:24 Jl 26 '71
  Delta signs letter for 5 DC-10s as RB.211 en-
  gine talks reopen. J. P. Woolsey. Aviation
  W 94:25-6 Mr 22 '71
  RB.211 talks still inconclusive as L-1011 re-
  sumes flight test. Aviation W 94:22 Ap 12
  '71
  Will Delta ditch Lockheed? Bsns W p27-8
  Mr 27 '71
DELTA booster. See Space vehicles—Propul-
  sion systems
DELTA Queen (steamship) See Steamships
  and steamboats
DELTA-wing kites. See Kites
DELUCA, H. F. See Omdahl, J. L. jt auth.
DE LUIGI, Ludovico
  Venice revisited. G. Highet. il Horizon 13:54-
  7 Wint '71 •
DEL VENTO, Connie
  Dragon slayer of Hemford; poem. Seventeen
  30:194 S '71
  For you; poem. Seventeen 29:62 S '70
  Have pen, will travel; poem. Seventeen 30:
  132 Jl '71
DELZELL, David E.
  Dismal Swamp: its natural history. il Liv
  Wildn 34:29-33 Wint '70
DELZELL, Robert F. and Krug, J. F.
  ALA awards, citations, scholarships, and
  grants for 1971. Am Lib 2:1075-80 N '71
DEMAREE, Allan T.
  Old China hands who know how to live with
  the new Asia. il Fortune 84:132-5+ N '71
  Steel: recasting an industry under stress. il
  Fortune 83:74-7+ Mr '71
DEMARIA, Anthony J. and others
  Ultrafast laser pulses. bibliog il Phys Today
  24:19-26 Jl '71
DEMARKO, Sharon K.
  Place where learning happens. il Am Ed 7:
  21-3 My '71
DEMARTINO, Jean
  Mothers talk about the anguish of their
  fight. pors Life 70:36 Je 11 '71

    about
  Fight for baby Lenore. E. L. Hughes. il
  pors Ladies Home J 88:58+ S '71 •
DEMARTINO, Nicholas
  Fight for baby Lenore. E. L. Hughes. il pors
  Ladies Home J 88:58+ S '71 •
DEMAS, James N.
  Testing power supplies. il Pop Electr 35:67-8
  S '71

DE MENIL, Dominique
Art and faith in Houston. il por Newsweek
77:63 Mr 15 '71 *
DE MENIL, John
Art and faith in Houston. il por Newsweek
77:63 Mr 15 '71 *
DEMETER, Ernie
Kings on the rocks. il Field & S 75:80-1+ F
'71
DE MILLE, Agnes
Rose for Miss Agnes. J. Gale. il pors Dance
Mag 45:46-50 O '71 *
DE MILLE, Evelyn
Bookshop staff stages surprise anniversary
party. P. A. Farrell. Pub W 200:40 O 18
'71 *
DEMIREL, Suleyman
Pride of authorship. il por Time 97:26+ Mr
22 '71 *
Tagmac memorandum. Newsweek 77:42+ Mr
22 '71 *
We won't give up. il por Newsweek 77:36 Ja
18 '71 *
DEMIRJIAN, Arto, Jr
I and the camera. il Pub W 200:42-3 O 4 '71
Map-making at Hammond. il Pub W 200:69-
76 S 13 '71
Who wins the Nobel prize in literature?
il Pub W 200:pt2 152-5 S 27 '71
Wide open approach to the wide open
spaces. il Pub W 200:30-3 N 1 '71
DEMMY, Melody Bundt
Density of population per square mile; poem.
Seventeen 31:90 Ja '72
DEMOBILIZATION, Industrial. See Industrial
demobilization
DEMOCRACY
Case for participatory democracy, ed. by C.
G. Benello and D. Roussopoulos. Review
Nation 213:537-8 N 22 '71. A. Lapan
Democracy, by C. Cohen. Review
Nation 213:213-15 S 13 '71. R. Sampson
Knowledge, power, and Democratic theory.
S. A. Lakoff. bibliog f Ann Am Acad 394:
4-12 Mr '71
Looking back on a golden age, the relevancy
of history; address, November 10, 1971. P.
MacKendrick. Vital Speeches 38:188-92 Ja
1 '72
Meaning of left and right. T. Szamuely. il
Nat R 23:923-7+ Ag 24 '71
Pentagon papers; implications of deceit by
government. N. Cousins. Sat R 54:16 Jl 3
'71
Student faith in democracy. Sch & Soc 99:6
Ja '71
Students & workers speaking the same lan-
guage. L. Perlis. il Parks & Rec 6:23-4+
Ap '71
See also
Communism and democracy
Education and democracy
Liberalism
Liberty
Suffrage
Study and teaching
Menace of ignorance. D. Lawrence. U S News
70:96 Je 7 '71
DEMOCRACY and communism. See Commu-
nism and democracy
DEMOCRACY and education. See Education
and democracy
DEMOCRATIC convention. See National con-
ventions, Democratic
DEMOCRATIC party
All in the family; credentials chairman. por
Newsweek 78:49 O 25 '71
Alternative to Nixon's game plan. U S News
70:66 Ap 12 '71
Around city hall. A. Logan. New Yorker 47:
64-70 Ag 21 '71
As Democrats look to '72. il U S News 71:
24-6 Ag 2 '71
Before the colors fade: the true-blue Demo-
crat; interview. ed. by V. V. Hamilton.
J. A. Farley. il pors Am Heritage 22:38-43+
Ag '71
California is wide open; state convention. P.
Barnes. New Repub 164:16-17 F 6 '71
Conversion of John Lindsay. il pors Time
98:7-9 Ag 23 '71
Defying the bosses in Illinois & Texas. P. R.
Wieck. New Repub 164:11-13 F 27 '71
Democratic party reform. K. Bode. New Re-
pub 165:19-23 Jl 10 '71; Reply D. M. Fraser.
165:31 Ag 21 '71
Democrats are still drifting. il Bsns W
p 18-19 S 18 '71
Democrats' comeback in South: a political
key to '72. il U S News 70:22-4 Mr 29 '71
Democrats in '72: Muskie and the Teddy
boys. J. Ridgeway. Ramp Mag 10:3-4+ Ag
'71
Democrats: on the threshold of adventure.
H. Sidey. il Time 97:16-18 My 17 '71

Democrats open the door. S. C. Brightman.
Nation 212:552-5 My 3 '71
Disorderly Democrats reprise. Chr Cent 88:
919 Ag 4 '71
End of the affair; meeting of the national
committee. New Repub 164:10-11 Mr 6 '71
Exit Lindsay. W. F. Buckley, jr. Nat R 23:
1010-11 S 10 '71
Gentlemen's agreement. il Newsweek 77:24
F 22 '71
Happiness at Ripon. Nat R 23:1011 S 10 '71
How Democrats are getting set for '72. il
U S News 70:19-22 Ap 12 '71
In search of a black strategy. por Time 98:9-
10 D 20 '71
Jackson and the big lie. P. Steinfels. Com-
monweal 94:446 S 3 '71
Labor and the liberals. S. Alsop. Newsweek
78:140 N 22 '71
Latest scoop. il Time 98:13 Ag 16 '71
Left-wing Joe Pewism. S. Alsop. il News-
week 78:128 O 25 '71
Letter from Washington; next year's elec-
tion. R. H. Rovere. New Yorker 47:80-1
Ag 7 '71
Lindsay: a switch in time? il pors Newsweek
78:15-16+ Ag 23 '71
Lindsay balloons. por Time 97:15-16 Mr 8 '71
Looking for presidents. N. Von Hoffman. il
Harper 243:33-5+ S '71
Not really room for one more. M. McGrory.
America 125:221 O 2 '71
One for O'Brien; temporary chairman of the
credentials committee. New Repub 165:9-10
O 23 '71
Party loyalty in '72. K. Bode. New Repub
165:13-15 N 20 '71
Put the lid on: financing the '72 Demo-
cratic primaries. J. R. Schmidt and W.
W. Whalen. New Repub 164:16-17 Je 5 '71;
Reply. A. J. Rosenthal. 164:7-9 Je 19 '71
Setback for the Democrats. Newsweek 78:20-1
Jl 26 '71
Symbol-think. S. Alsop. Newsweek 77:100 Ap
26 '71
Tug of war in Democratic party: meaning for
1972. il U S News 71:91-2 O 25 '71
Two parties and two prospects. M. McGrory.
America 125:549 D 25 '71
Unconventional reform. Time 97:12 Mr 1 '71
See also
National conventions, Democratic
DEMOLITION downtown; drama. See Williams,
T.
DEMONOLOGY
See also
Satanism
Witchcraft
DEMONSTRATIONS against Vietnamese war.
See Vietnamese war, 1957-—Protests, de-
monstrations, etc, against
DE MORAES, Vinicius
Sonnet of intimacy; poem. New Yorker 47:52
N 27 '71
DEMOTT, Benjamin
Looking back on the seventies. Atlan 227:
59-64 Mr '71
One right way to write and think? Am
Scholar 41:53-62 Wint '71
Vonnegut's otherworldly laughter. Sat R 54:
29-32+ My 1 '71
about
Speechless page after page. R. Ostermann.
New Repub 164:28-31 My 1 '71
DEMPEWOLFF, Richard F.
Building a house? 20 tips that save time and
your back. il Pop Mech 135:112-15 My '71
Products to make your job look profession-
al. il Pop Mech 135:110-11+ My '71
Use this easy method to tie-in the roof. il
Pop Mech 135:128-30 Je '71
We added on and saved, so can you! il
Pop Mech 135:104-9+ My '71
—See Young, G. jt. auth.
DEMPSEY, David
Learning how to die. il N Y Times Mag
p58+ N 14 '71
Love and will and Rollo May. il pors N Y
Times Mag p28-9+ Mr 28 '71
Right to read. Sat R 54:22-3 Ap 17 '71
SR's 1971 Anisfield-Wolf awards. Sat R 54:
30 Je 12 '71
DEMPSEY, William H. Jr
Rails flag a new contract negotiator. Bsns
W p30 O 30 '71 *
DEMSCH, Berthold, and Muller, Dan
Games principals shouldn't play with
teachers. Clear House 45:473-5 Ap '71; Same
abr. with title Games that principals
shouldn't play. Ed Digest 37:18-19 S '71
DEMSKE, Dick
7 plumbing repairs anyone can do. il Mech
Illus 67:84-6+ Ja '71
Thrifty man's guide to lawnmowers. il Mech
Illus 67:94+ Je '71

DEMUTH, Charles
Charles Demuth, by E. Farnham. Review
Sat R 54:41 My 22 '71 *
DEMUTH, Christopher
Case for revenue sharing. Cur 128:42-5 Ap
'71
DEMUTH, Jerry
Alternative service locates in Appalachia.
il America 125:374-5 N 6 '71
Some hate, some hope. Commonweal 94:84-6
Ap 2 '71
Subverting the black lung law. America 125:
530-2 D 18 '71
DENARD, Michaël
Étole. N. M. Stoop. pors Dance Mag 45:36-7
S '71 *
DENBY, David
Movies. See issues of Atlantic
DENDROCHRONOLOGY. See Tree rings
DENENBERG, Herbert Sidney
Putting insurers' feet to the fire il Bsns W
p32 Mr 27 '71 *
DE NEVERS, Noel
Another approach to population control? Bul
Atom Sci 27:34 Mr '71
DENGLER, Harry Wm.
Festival of flame and fire. il Am For 77:4-
5+ D '71
DENI, Laura
School for gamblers; novel Nevada jobs
program. il Ebony 27:55-6+ D '71
DENIM
Star-studded denim; ideas for pillows, cur-
tains, spreads. H. Brown. il Am Home 74:
90-1+ S '71
DENISON, George
Smut: the Mafia's newest racket. Read Di-
gest 99:157-60 D '71
Where labor gets its political muscle. Read
Digest 98:98-101 Je '71
—See Tomlinson, K. Y. jt. auth.
DENMARK
See also
Aged—Denmark
Airlines—Denmark
Architecture, Domestic—Denmark
Booksellers and bookselling—Denmark
Education—Denmark
Fyn
Hotels, taverns, etc.—Denmark
Visitors, Foreign—Denmark
Colonies
See also
Faroe Islands
Industries
See also
Brewing industries—Denmark
DENNER, Charles
French taste. S. Kauffmann. New Repub
165:26 Ag 7 '71 *
DENNEY, Reuel
For a late Asian friend; poem. New Repub
165:23 Jl 3 '71
DENNIS, Jeff
Peddling God's country. R. Rapoport. il por
Sports Illus 35:68-9 N 1 '71 *
DENNIS, Landt
Ethel Merman: queen of Broadway. por Read
Digest 98:112-16 Je '71
DENNIS, Lee
Across the board in old American games.
il Hobbies 76:48-9+ Ag '71
DENNISON, Edwin W.
Electronic optical astronomy: philosophy and
practice. Science 174:240-4 O 15 '71
DENOMINATIONAL colleges. See Church col-
leges
DENOMINATIONS, Religious. See Sects
DENOON, David B. H.
Indonesia: transition to stability? bibliog f
il Cur Hist 61:332-8+ D '71
DENS (rooms)
Den for men. J. Capotosto. il Mech Illus
67:83-6 Je '71
6 designers turn their dreams into winning
hideaways. L. Grundy and N. Schram. il
House B 113:84-7 Ap '71
DENSHAM, William E.
(ed) See Davis, A. Children who had to be
found
DENSITOMETERS
Build R-E's photo densitometer. J. A. Gup-
ton, jr. il Radio-Electr 42:48-51 My '71
DENSITY gradient centrifugation. See Cen-
trifugation
DENSITY of stars. See Stars—Density
DENT, Lester
Back to the gore of yore. B. Darrach. il por
Time 98:70-1 Jl 5 '71 *

DENTAL care, Preparation for. See Children—
Preparation for medical and dental care
DENTAL caries
Prevention
Dental caries: prospects for prevention. H.
W. Scherp. bibliog il Science 173:1199-205
S 24 '71
Paint job for teeth. il Newsweek 78:57 O 4
'71
Tooth coating stops decay. Sci Digest 69:
59 Je '71
DENTAL decay. See Dental caries
DENTAL education
Medical and dental education for the health
care crisis. il Sch & Soc 99:71-4 F '71
DENTAL hygiene. See Teeth—Care and hy-
giene
DENTAL instruments and apparatus
See also
Toothpicks, Electric
DENTAL irrigators. See Toothpicks, Electric
DENTIFRICES
19 dentifrices rated on abrasiveness. il Chang-
ing T 25:13-14 My '71
Toothpaste. S. Rapoport. il Consumer Bul
54:7-9 Ag '71
DENTISTRY
Hurrah! Dentists don't hurt anymore. G. M.
Knox. Bet Hom & Gard 49:12 N '71
Teeth teeth teeth, by S. Garfield. Review
Life il 71:11 S 10 '71. M. Seligson
See also
Periodontia
DENTISTS
Supply and demand
How auxiliaries increase productivity of
dentists. J. H. Weiss. Mo Labor R 94:63-4
Ap '71
DENTON, Eric
Reflectors in fishes; with biographical sketch.
il Sci Am 224:12, 64-72 Ja '71
DENTURES, Artificial. See Teeth, Artificial
DENUNZIO, Ralph Dwight
New scenario for the big board. il por Bsns
W p64 My 22 '71 *
DENVER
City-owned and operated TV stations. G.
M. Chamberlain. il Am City 86:103-4+
Ap '71
Helicopter-ambulance inaugurated. il Am City
86:138 Je '71
Olympian snafu at Sniktau. R. Rapoport.
Sports Illus 34:60-1 F 15 '71
Churches
Divine property? Baptist-Lutheran dispute
over Good Shepherd Baptist church. News-
week 78:51 Jl 5 '71
Property and propriety; Good Shepherd
Baptist church legal scrape with Wisconsin
Evangelical Lutheran synod. Chr Cent 88:
731 Je 9 '71; Reply. R. G. Doll. 88:865 Jl
14 '71
Description
Denver's old Larimer square is making a
comeback. il Sunset 146:32 Ja '71
Education
High school fights for its life . . . and a prin-
cipal, for his; George Washington high
school. L. Gross. il pors Look 35:20-5+ Mr 9
'71
Galleries and museums
See also
Denver art museum
Libraries
See also
Denver public library
Municipal improvement
Sign busters. il Newsweek 77:116+ Je 7 '71
Music
See also
Denver symphony orchestra
Sanitary affairs
$4.31 vs. $34 per basin. il Am City 86:38
Ap '71
Streets
Computerized street maintenance. B. Gilbert.
il Am City 86:70-2 O '71
Water supply
Exchange water keeps Denver's taps flowing.
R. E. Wiedemann. il por Am City 86:79-80+
Je '71
Plastic water main for hot soil. C. Carlson.
il Am City 86:70 Je '71

DENVER art museum
Castle in Denver. B. Plumb. il Am Home 74:
74 O '71
Denver art museum's new building. S. B.
Sherrill. il Antiques 100:476+ O '71
Denver's new art museum; two inaugural
exhibitions. il Design 73:12-15 Fall '71
DENVER public library

Conservation library center
Denver's conservation library. M. Bush. il
Am For 77:12-15 Ap '71
DENVER symphony orchestra
Englishman comes to Denver; Priestman's
first year in Rocky Mountain. A. Young
por Hi Fi 21:MA30 Je '71
DEODAR. See Cedar
DEODORANTS
Beauty sense and nonsense; antiperspirants.
Harp Baz 104:4 Je '71
Room deodorizers. il Consumer Bul 54:38-40
Ag '71
Should genital deodorants be used? Con-
sumer Rep 37:39-41 Ja '72
DEONANAN, Carlton R.
Education for peace. Clear House 46:223-6
D '71
DEOXYRIBONUCLEIC acid. See DNA
DEPALMA, Samuel
Future of the United Nations; address,
April 3, 1971. Dept State Bul 64:517-21 Ap
19 '71
Improving the effectiveness of the United
Nations; statement, October 13, 1971. Dept
State Bul 65:569-75 N 15 '71
**DEPARTMENT of environmental conserva-
tion.** See New York (state)—Environmental
conservation, Department of
DEPARTMENT stores
See also
Allied stores corporation
Federated department stores, inc.
Macy, R. H. and company
Retail trade
Shopping centers

Branch stores
Big stores begin another great migration. il
Bsns W p66-7 My 22 '71

Finance
See also
Retail trade—Finance

Management
New breed that runs the big stores; account-
ants and lawyers in top-management spots.
il Bsns W p54-8 Je 26 '71
DEPARTURES; story. See Barthelme, D.
DE PASQUALE, John A. and Lange, R. A.
Job-hopping and the MBA. il Harvard Bsns
R 49:4-8+ N '71
DEPENDENTS schools, Army. See Military
post schools, American
DE PORRES club. See Negroes—Clubs, so-
cieties, etc.
DEPORTATION
Britain deports Rudi Dutschke. P. Oestreich-
er. Chr Cent 88:223-4 F 17 '71
Nation killers: the Soviet deportation of na-
tionalities, by R. Conquest. Review
Nat R 23:483-4 My 4 '71. F. Russell
DEPOSITORS corporation
Maine idea in banking. A. Hershman. por
Duns 97:68 Ap '71
DEPRECIATION
How tax depreciation can work for you. M.
Hood. il Suc Farm 69:30-1 S '71
See also
Amortization deductions
Investment tax credit

Taxation
See Amortization deductions
DEPRÈS, Josquin
Master of the notes. R. Evans. Nat R 23:1316
N 19 '71 *
New York: a week of Josquin. S. T. Som-
mer. il Hi Fi 21:MA14-15 O '71 *
Prince of music. H. Saal. il Newsweek 78:77
N 15 '71 *
Recordings. M. Mayer. Esquire 76:10-11 Jl '71 *
DEPRESSION, Business. See Business depres-
sion
DEPRESSION, Mental
Mother Portnoy's complaints. P. Bart. il
Trans-Action 8:69-74 N '70
R for depression? a sleepless night. News-
week 78:61 Ag 30 '71
25 most distressing events in your life. A.
J. Snider. Sci Digest 69:68 My '71
Where to turn for help. J. Brothers. Good H
172:48+ My '71
See also
Antidepressants

DEPRIVATION, Maternal. See Maternal de-
privation
DEPTH indicators
Fishfinders; electronic gear and especially-
designed boats. D. Fales. il Motor B & S
127:68-71+ My '71
How deep is your ocean? electronic depth
finders. C. Miller. il Motor B & S 127:76-7+
Je '71
Sonar that talks; depth and fish finders.
C. Conley. il Field & S 76:138 S '71
DEPTH of field. See Photography—Focusing
DEPTH perception. See Space perception
DEPUY, William Eugene
Generals of the new army. il por Ramp Mag
10:16-17 S '71 *
DE RAGEOT, Roger H.
Dismal Swamp fish. bibliog il Liv Wildn 34:
37-9 Wint '70
DERDERIAN, Constance E.
Bonsai from seed. il Horticulture 49:42-3+
Ap '71
DERHAM, James
Translation of Act of emancipation manu-
script. il Negro Hist Bul 33:165 N '70
DERINGERS. See Pistols
DERIVATION of words. See English language
—Etymology
DERNESCH, Helga
Recipe for Brünnhilde; interview, ed. by J.
H. Sutcliffe. por Opera N 35:19 My 15 '71
DERRICK, Jonathan
Black Africa: blacks move to the city.
il America 125:13-14 Jl 10 '71
DERRINGERS. See Pistols
DERSHOWITZ, Alan M.
Stretch points of liberty. Nation 212:329-34
Mr 15 '71
Terrorism & preventive detention: the case
of Israel. bibliog f Commentary 50:67-78 D
'70; 51:38+ Je '71
Wiretaps & national security. Commentary
53:56-61 Ja '72
DESAI, I. D. See Raychaudhuri, C. jt. auth.
DE SAINT PHALLE, Anne
Beating the cigarette habit. il Seventeen 30:
108-9+ N '71
DESALINIZATION of sea water. See Sea water
—Desalting
DESALTING of sea water. See Sea water—
Desalting
DESCHIN, Jacob
Viewpoint. See issues of Popular photography
DESDEMONA (literary character) See Shake-
speare, W.—Characters
DESEGREGATION. See Public schools— De-
segregation
DESEGREGATION of camps. See Camps—De-
segregation
DESELL, Paulette Marie
Girl turns page in Senate history. por Sr
Schol 98:16 Mr 1 '71 *
DE SEMPRÚN DONAHUE, Moraima
Poets of rock and sky. il Américas 22:19-24
N '70
DESERT bighorn sheep hunting. See Moun-
tain sheep hunting
DESERT bighorns. See Mountain sheep
DESERT camping. See Camping—Western
states
DESERT classic. See Golf—Tournaments
DESERT pupfish. See Killifishes
DESERT sheep. See Mountain sheep
DESERT survival. See Wilderness survival
DESERT vegetation
See also
Cactus
Prickly pears
DESERTED towns. See Abandoned towns
DESERTION, Military. See United States—
Armed forces—Desertions
DESERTION and non-support
Wives who run away. M. Gunther. il Ladies
Home J 88:66+ F '71
DESERTS
Polar deserts; AAAS symposium, December
29-30, 1971. T. L. Smiley and J. H. Zum-
berge. il Science 174:79-80 O 1 '71
See also
Death Valley
Mojave Desert
Sonoran Desert
DE SICA, Vittorio
Current cinema. P. Kael. New Yorker 47:48+
D 18 '71 *
Viva De Sica. A. Cooper. il por Newsweek
79:58 Ja 10 '72 *

DETECTIVE story writers, American. See
  Novelists, American
DETECTIVES
Detective Egan's new assignment. P. F.
  Kluge. il pors Life 71:85-6+ D 10 '71
Lessons of the street. B. J. Friedman. il
  Harper 243:86-8+ S '71
Madame Sleuth confesses; D. Uhnak, creator
  of Christie Opara. M. Meade. McCalls 98:
  43 Jl '71

  Anecdotes, facetiae, satire, etc.
Confessions of the world's lousiest spy. L.
  Botto. il Look 35:76+ O 19 '71
DETECTORS
Build a moisture sensor. H. St Laurent. il
  Pop Electr 34:67-9 Mr '71
Explosive detection by dogs restudied. Avia-
  tion W 94:16 My 10 '71
Hallway for stock thieves; Sensitrace pas-
  sageway. il Bsns W p66 O 16 '71
How the airlines hope to stop bombs and
  bomb scares. M. Schultz. il Pop Mech 135:
  94-7+ Mr '71
How to detect vehicle detector problems;
  Dade County, Fla. M. Wilcox. il Am City
  86:128+ Je '71
Underwater fish finder. W. L. Green. il Pop
  Electr 35:48-9+ Ag '71
  See also
Metal detectors
DETECTORS, Infrared
Device sees man-made targets; airborne in-
  frared scanner system. il Aviation W 94:40-
  1 Ap 5 '71
DETECTORS, Radiation. See Radiation—
  Measurement
DETENTION centers. See Concentration camps
DETERGENT pollution of rivers, lakes, etc.
Arsenic in detergents; posible danger and
  pollution hazard. E. E. Angino and oth-
  ers; discussion. Science 168:1525-6; 170:870-
  2; 171:234 Je 26, N 20 '70, Ja 22 '71
Eutrophication of lake water microcosms;
  phosphate versus nonphosphate detergents.
  D. Mitchell. bibliog il Science 174:827-9 N
  19 '71
Nitrogen, phosphorus, and eutrophication in
  the coastal marine environment. J. H.
  Ryther and W. M. Dunstan. bibliog il Sci-
  ence 171:1008-13 Mr 12 '71
DETERGENTS
As the soapers' world turns. il Time 97:72
  Mr 8 '71
Back to enzymes. Newsweek 78:62 N 29 '71
Back to phosphates. Newsweek 78:123 S 27 '71
Detergents: the facts from expert. M. E.
  Purchase. House & Gard 140:44+ Jl '71
Hand dishwashing detergents. il Consumer
  Rep 36:469-71 Ag '71
Hand-dishwashing liquids. il Consumer Bul
  54:7-9 S '71
How well do the no-phosphate detergents
  clean? Consumer Bul 54:24-5 F '71
Is cleanliness next to impossible? D. Zwerd-
  ling. il New Repub 165:13-14 O 9 '71
NTA in detergents. il Chem 44:21-3 Ja '71
No-phosphate and low-phosphate detergents.
  il Consumer Bul 54:27-9 Jl '71
No-phosphate detergents. il Good H 173:6 O
  '71
No-phosphate detergents: do they work? il
  Consumer Rep 36:592-4 O '71
Non-enzyme laundry detergents and soaps. il
  Consumer Bul 54:13-16 Mr '71
Phosphate replacements: problems with the
  washday miracle. A. L. Hammond. Science
  172:361-3 Ap 23 '71
Phosphates down but far from out. il Bsns
  W p21 Jl 3 '71
Phosphates make a sudsy comeback. Bsns W
  p25 S 18 '71
Phosphates turnabout. Sr Schol 99:13-14 O 25
  '71
Reporter at large; enigmatic enzyme. P. Bro-
  deur. New Yorker 46:42-8+ Ja 16 '71
Return of the phosphates. Time 98:90 S 27
  '71
Return to phosphates? Consumer Bul 54:12-13
  N '71
Soap opera; ban on Ecolo-G. il Newsweek
  77:88 Mr 22 '71
Toxic factors in enzymes used in laundry
  products. R. Dubos. il Science 173:259-60
  Jl 16 '71
Warning on enzymes; allergic effects.
  Newsweek 77:42 F 1 '71
Washday question; special report on deter-
  gents and phosphates. M. Steinmann. il
  Life 70:35-7 My 21 '71
Why detergent makers are turning gray. il
  Bsns W p64+ F 20 '71
  See also
North American chemicals corporation

DETERIORATION of plastics. See Plastics—
  Deterioration
DETERRENCE (strategy) See Strategy
DETHIER, V. G. and Goldrich, Nancy
Blowflies: alteration of adult taste responses
  by chemicals present during development.
  bibliog il Science 173:242-4 Jl 16 '71
DETLEFSEN, Ellen Gay. See Schuman, P. jt.
  auth.
DETLEFSEN, Gay. See Detlefsen. E. G.
DE TREY, Marianne
Marianne de Trey; Shinners Bridge pottery.
  E. Lewenstein. il pors Chem Mo 19:14-17
  S '71 •
DETROIT
  City planning
Better idea for Detroit; Ford project to
  revive riverfront. il Time 98:52+ D 6 '71
Pairing the old and new. il Time 97:15-16
  Mr 1 '71
  Description
In the heart of downtown 1935. L. E. Sissman.
  Atlan 227:30+ My '71
  Education
Attack on de facto; federal court ruling.
  Time 98:23-4 O 11 '71
Detroit combines students' worlds. E. Rasof.
  Am Ed 7:25-7 Je '71
Sisters desert racist institution; St Ray-
  mond's school. America 124:194 F 27 '71
Spreading the blame; court ruling against
  segregation. Newsweek 78:28 O 11 '71
  Hotels, restaurants, etc.
Dining in/out with Esquire; the Muer's
  restaurants. Esquire 75:56 Je '71
  Libraries
  See also
Detroit public library
  Lighting
Bright spot downtown for Christmas; new
  lighting installed along Washington blvd. il
  Am City 86:94 D '71
  Newspapers
  See also
Detroit free press
Detroit news
  Police
Detroit under STRESS; indiscriminate gun-
  ning down of Negro criminals. il News-
  week 78:75 O 18 '71
Heroin shooting war. il Time 97:18 Je 21 '71
  Religious institutions and affairs
Detroit's black Catholics. America 124:603 Je
  12 '71
  Social conditions
Where rumor raged; Detroit in the winter
  of 1967-68. M. Rosenthal. il Trans-Action
  8:34-43 F '71
DETROIT Edison company
Detroit Edison's profit-minded boss. por Bsns
  W p74 O 2 '71
DETROIT free press
Experiment for the White House; address,
  February 23, 1971. T. R. Peters. Vital
  Speeches 37:379-82 Ap 1 '71
DETROIT Lions (football club) See Football
  clubs
DETROIT news
Money pays off; Secret witness program.
  il Time 97:65 My 17 '71
Our colleagues err on war secrets issue;
  reprint from The Detroit news, June 27,
  1971. U S News 71:88+ Jl 12 '71
Secret witness; new weapon against crime. J.
  Stewart-Gordon. il Read Digest 99:190-1+
  N '71
DETROIT public library
Detroit's top librarian. il pors Ebony 27:
  115-16+ N '71
Emancipated librarian. L. DeView. por Mc-
  Calls 98:46 Ap '71
  Branches
Three branch closings announced by Detroit
  P.L. Library J 96:3547-8 N 1 '71
DETROIT Red Wings (hockey team) See Hoc-
  key teams
DETROIT Tigers (baseball) See Baseball clubs
DETROIT. University
Streetcar strategists. il Time 98:28+ Ag 23
  '71
DETTMER, Roger
Behind the scenes. il Hi Fi 21:20-1 D '71
DEUTCHMAN, Sandra
No bones about it. il Sch Arts 71:42-3 D '71

DEUTCSH, Arthur
Stealing cars is a growth industry. P. Hellman. il pors N Y Times Mag p7+ Je 20 '71 •

DEUTERIUM

Physiological effects
Deuterium effects on binding of reduced coenzyme alcohol dehydrogenase isoenzyme EE. K. Bush and others. bibliog il Science 172:478-80 Ap 30 '71

DEUTSCH, David
View from the Coast. il pors Time 97:58-9 F 1 '71 •

DEUTSCH, J. Anthony
Cholinergic synapse and the site of memory. bibliog il Science 174:788-94 N 19 '71

DEUTSCH, Karl W.
—and others
Conditions favoring major advances in social science. bibliog il Science 171:450-9; 172:1191-2 F 5, Je 18 '71

about
Social science impact. Time 97:47 Mr 29 '71 •

DEUTSCH, Ronald M.
Plain talk about your diet and heart attacks; excerpt from The family guide to better food and health. Bet Hom & Gard 49:4+ Ag '71
Which diet tricks pay off? excerpt from The family guide to better food and better health. Read Digest 99:87-9 N '71

DEUTSCHE Bundesbahn. See Railroads and state—Germany (Federal Republic)

DEUTSCHER, Tamara
Civil war in Ceylon. il Ramp Mag 10:26-9 Jl '71
Exit Gomulka. il por Ramp Mag 9:12+ Mr '71

DEUTSCHMAN, Paul
Pakistan: what never gets said. Nation 213:457-60 N 8 '71

DE VALERA, Eamon
Eamon de Valera, by the Earl of Longford and T. P. O'Neill. Review
America 125:131 S 4 '71. R. J. Thompson •

DE VALOIS, Russell L. and Pease, P. L.
Contours and contrast: responses of monkey lateral geniculate nucleus cells to luminance and color figures. bibliog il Science 171:694-6 F 19 '71

DEVALUATION of currency. See Currency question

DEVALUATION of the dollar. See Money—United States

DEVANEY, Bob
And this man is at the top. J. Underwood. il por Sports Illus 35:52-7 S 13 '71 •

DEVANEY, John
Children no one wanted. il Redbook 138: 68-70+ D '71
—See Earle, S. A. jt. auth.

DE VAUCOULEURS, Gerard
Mars chart for the Mariner flights. il Sky & Tel 41:283-7 My '71
Telescopic observations of Mars in 1971. il Sky & Tel 42:134-5, 263-4; 43:20-1 S, N '71, Ja '72

DEVELOPING (photography) See Photography—Developing and developers

DEVELOPING nations. See Underdeveloped areas

DEVELOPMENT, Biological. See Morphogenesis

DEVELOPMENT, Organizational. See Organizational change

DEVELOPMENT executives. See Executives

DEVELOPMENT of children. See Children—Growth and development; Infants—Growth and development

DEVELOPMENT program of the United Nations. See United Nations—Development programme

DEVELOPMENTAL dyslexia. See Reading disability

DEVELOPMENTAL neurology
Human fetal cerebellar cortex: organization and maturation of cells in vitro. L. W. Lapham and W. R. Markesbery. bibliog il Science 173:829-32 Ag 27 '71
Prenatal cerebral development: effect of restricted diet, reversal by growth hormone. S. Zamenhof and others. bibliog il Science 174:954-5 N 26 '71

DEVENPORT, Lynn D. and Balagura, Saul
Lateral hypothalamus: reevaluation of function in motivated feeding behavior. bibliog il Science 172:744-6 My 14 '71

DEVEREUX, Robert, 2d earl of Essex. See Essex. R. D.

DEVIATION of the compass. See Compass

DEVIL
Cosmic conflict. L. N. Bell. Chr Today 15: 26-7 F 26 '71
Great diverter. L. N. Bell. Chr Today 15:36-7 My 21 '71
Is Satan expendable? H. B. Kuhn. Chr Today 16:48-9 O 22 '71
See also
Satanism

DE VILLENEUVE, Justin. See Davies, N.

DEVINE, Dan
Big names in the biggest game. il por Time 98:60+ O 4 '71 •

DEVINE, Eleanore
Hard of hearing; socially acceptable. il Har Yrs 11:30-1 F '71

DEVINEY, Calvin A.
Fishing tips. il Pop Mech 135:120-1 Ap '71
Inner-tube float fishing. il Pop Mech 136: 74-5 Ag '71

DE VITO, E. B.
Waterfront at night; poem. Cath World 214:13 O '71

DEVITT, Edward James
Excerpt from address before eighth circuit judicial conference. June 28, 1971. Cong Digest 50:216+ Ag '71

DEVITT, Robert D.
Marketing change that meant everyone won. il pors Nations Bsns 59:64-5 Ja '71

DEVLIN, Bernadette
Bernadette Devlin: mother and maverick. Chr Today 15:38 S 24 '71 •

DEVLIN, Polly
Country house in flower; Radziwill's Turville Grange. il pors Vogue 158:100-7+ Jl '71
Movies. Vogue 158:102 O 15 '71

DEVONIAN period. See Geology, Stratigraphic—Devonian

DEVONS, Samuel
Recollections of Rutherford and the Cavendish; adaptation of address, August 1971. il pors Phys Today 24:38-45 D '71

DEVOTION to the Sacred Heart. See Sacred Heart, Devotion to

DEVRIES, Arthur L.
Glycoproteins as biological antifreeze agents in Antarctic fishes. bibliog il Science 172: 1152-5 Je 11 '71

DE VRIES, Peter
High ground; or, Look, ma, I'm explicating; story New Yorker 47:43-5 S 25 '71
Into your tent I'll creep; story; excerpt. McCalls 99:96-7 N '71
Only place there's censorship left is in my dream life. il Holiday 49:94+ D '70

about
Books. P. Gilliatt. New Yorker 46:95-8 Ja 16 '71

DEVRIES, Ted. See Tovatt, A. jt. auth.

DEWEY, Edward Russell
Does the market respond to unknown forces? interview. por Forbes 108:39-40 S 1 '71

DEWEY, Melvil
History of the New York state library, by C. R. Roseberry. Review
Wilson Lib Bul 45:536 F '71 •

DEWEY, Priscilla B.
Rumpelstiltskin revisited; dramatization of a fairy tale. Plays 31:81-8 D '71

DEWEY, Robert Merrill
Old vets. il Am Heritage 22:54-7+ Ap '71

DEWEY, Thomas Edmund
Man who had it won. por Time 97:18 Mr 29 '71 •
Obituary
Nat R 23:358 Ap 6 '71. W. A. Rusher
Newsweek il pors 77:30+ Mr 29 '71

DEWEY classification. See Classification, Decimal

DE WINDT, Edward Mandell
Business survival in the seventies; address, February 25, 1971. Vital Speeches 37:363 7 Ap 1 '71
Peace needs world business; address, July 29, 1971. Vital Speeches 37:726-9 S 15 '71

DEWITT, Bryce S.
Quantum mechanics and reality. bibliog il Phys Today 23:30-5 S '70; 24:41-3 Ap '71

DE WITT'S ISLAND
Life on De Witt; J. Cooper. il por Time 99: 73 Ja 10 '72

DEWLEN, Al
What should a novel be? adaptation of address, 1970. Writer 84:16-17 Jl '71

DEWOLF, Rose
Getting something for the money; Pennsylvania's Blue cross. Nation 213:435-6 N 1 '71

DE WYNGAERT, Laura
Will the real Jimmy please stand up? il Sch Arts 70:24-5 F '71

DEXTER, Peter F.
Bug trap you can make. il Pop Sci 199:106
Ag '71
DEY, Leslie
Things my sister taught me. il por Seventeen 29:76 Jl '70
DEY, Susan
Becoming Susan Dey. B. Vachon. il pors
Look 35:64-6+ Jl 27 '71 *
DEYOUNG, Russell
DeYoung of Goodyear. por Forbes 107:50-1 My 15 '71 *
DEYTS, Simone Antoinette
Sacred source of the Seine; with biographical sketch. il Sci Am 225:14, 65-73 Jl '71
DHAI, Jii
Collectibles: hunting treasures. House B 113:131-3 Ap '71
D'HARNONCOURT, René
Exercises in taste. J. B. Myers; discussion.
Craft Horiz 30:9 Ag '70; 31:6-7 F '71 *
DIAB, I. M. and others
[3H]Lysergic acid diethylamide: cellular autoradiographic localization in rat brain. bibliog il Science 173:1022-4 S 10 '71
DIABETICS diet. See Diet in disease
DIACONATE. See Deacons
DIAGNOSIS
Do-it-yourself medicine. il Newsweek 78:101 D 6 '71
See also
Computers—Medical use
Ultrasonic waves—Medical use
also subhead Diagnosis under names of diseases, e.g. Tuberculosis—Diagnosis
DIAGNOSIS, Radioscopic
Mobile TB X-ray units: an obsolete technology lingers. B. Nelson. Science 174: 1114-15 D 10 '71
DIAGNOSTIC records. See Medical records
DIAL (periodical)
Dial log. Newsweek 78:79 Jl 26 '71
Ladies of the Dial; excerpt from Eloquent April. M. Cane. Am Scholar 40:316-21 Spr '71
DIAL gages. See Gages
DIALECT, Negro. See Negro-English dialects
DIALECTS
See also
English language—Dialects
DIALOGUE
Six functions of dialogue in fiction. C. N. Heckelmann. Writers Digest 51:24-7 Je '71
Sounds of fiction. M. Franco. Writer 84:11-13 O '71
Uses and abuses of dialogue. B. Pronzini.
Writer 84:12-14+ My '71
DIALYSIS
See also
Kidneys, Artificial
DIAMOND, Henry L.
Adirondack park agency. il Parks & Rec 6:14-17+ D '71
DIAMOND, I. T. See Killackey, H. jt. auth.
DIAMOND, Stephen
Bull's eye and the scorpion; story. Atlan 228: 68-71 N '71
DIAMOND, Sylvia
Everyone is dyeing. il Sch Arts 71:20-1 Ja '72
DIAMOND knives. See Knives
DIAMOND mines and mining
Guaniamo diamond miner is nobody's best friend; situation in Venezuela. J. Morgan. il Atlan 227:56-61 Ap '71.
DIAMONDS
Mysterious jinx of the Hope diamond. J. Stewart-Gordon. il Read Digest 99:25-30 Ag '71
DIAMONDS, Artificial
Man-made diamonds, who really made them first? R. Davis. il Sci Digest 69:88-90 Ap '71
DIAMONDS, Industrial
Sintered diamond compacts with a cobalt binder. H. Katzman and W. F. Libby. bibliog il Science 172:1132-4 Je 11 '71
DIAMONSTEIN, Barbaralee
Emphasis (cont) Harp Baz 104:70 F; 171 Mr '71
Here come the brides! il Good H 172:90-3+ Je '71
DIANNA, John
Shop talk. See issues of Hot rod
Strictly for stocks. See issues of Hot rod
DIAPAUSE. See Insects—Development
DIAPER pins. See Pins
DIAPERS, Infants
Disposable diapers. il Consumer Rep 36:81-3 F '71
DIARIES
Treasured diaries. S. B. Saunders. Hobbies 76:141 O '71

DIARY of a scoundrel; drama. See Ostrovskil, A. N.
DIAS, Earl J.
Abner Crane from Hayseed lane; drama; reprint from October 1956 issue. Plays 30:25-38 Mr '71
DIATOMS
Fecal pellets: role in sedimentation of pelagic diatoms. H. J. Schrader. bibliog il Science 174:55-7 O 1 '71
DIAZ, José-Luis, and Huttunen, M. O.
Persistent increase in brain serotonin turnover after chronic administration of LSD in the rat. bibliog il Science 174:62-4 O 1 '71
DIAZ, Maria Eugenia (Rojas) Moreno. See Moreno Diaz, M. E. R.
DIAZ INFANTE, Juan José
House that grows. J. Sanger. il por Américas 23:16-24 Mr '71 *
DIAZ PUMARA, Hazel L.
Plant your tomatoes in mounds. Org Gard & Farm 18:74-5 Mr '71
DIBBLE, Peter Davis
In-most places. Ladies Home J 88:66 My '71
DIBLE, Isabel W.
Teacher in a multi-mediated setting. Ed Digest 36:26-8 F '71
DIBLIN, Joe
Back to basics. Flying 89:82-3 Jl '71
DIBNER, David R.
Washington, D.C. il Arch Forum 134:46-9 Ja '71
DICHLOROMETHANE. See Methylene chloride
DICHLOROPHENOL
Riboflavin photosensitized oxidation of 2,4-dichlorophenol: assessment of possible chlorinated dioxin formation. J. R. Plimmer and U. I. Klingebiel. bibliog il Science 174:407-8 O 22 '71
DICK, Bernard F.
Love story: it's required. Nat R 23:771 Jl 13 '71
DICK, Lois Hoadley
Silver and gold had I; poem. Chr Today 15:9 S 24 '71
DICK, Robert C.
Rhetoric of ante-bellum black separatism.
bibliog il Negro Hist Bul 34:133-7 O '71
DICK Ross and associates. See Ross, Dick, and associates (firm)
DICKENS, Charles
Old curiosity shop; dramatization of excerpt.
See Thane, A. Conspiracy
about
Dickens the novelist, by F. R. Leavis and Q. D. Leavis. Review
Commonweal 94:337-9 Je 25 '71. B. Wicker *
Nat R 23:763-4 Jl 13 '71. J. Braine *
DICKENSON, Fred
Fascinating funnies. il Read Digest 99:201-4+ N '71
Run around the houses. il Américas 23:36-40 Ag '71
DICKERSON, George
Fragments from a broken window; poem.
Mlle 72:114 F '71
DICKERSON, Henri Christophe
Mr America. il pors Ebony 26:80-2+ My '71 *
DICKES, Robert
Desdemona: an innocent victim? bibliog Am Imago 27:279-97 Fall '70
DICKEY, Charles Denston. 1918-
His job: to turn Scott around. por Bsns W p46 Ag 21 '71 *
DICKEY, James
False youth: autumn: clothes of the age;
poem. Atlan 228:67 N '71
For the death of Vince Lombardi; poem. il por Esquire 76:142-3 S '71
about
Comment. R. B. Shaw. Poetry 118:230 Jl '71 *
DICKEY, John Miller
Lincoln university in the nineteenth century.
D. A. Peters. bibliog Negro Hist Bul 34: 80-2 Ap '71 *
DICKEY, R. P.
Comment. F. D. Reeve. Poetry 118:235-6 Jl '71 *
DICKEY, William
House: for Shirley; poem. Sat R 54:29 N 20 '71
More under Saturn; poem. New Yorker 46: Ja 16 '71
Parliamentary procedure; At the middle of it; Bullhorn; poems. Poetry 117:296-8 F '71
DICKHAUS, Steven M. and Cohen, S. O.
Post-season camp for alumni proves success.
Camp Mag 43:22 F '71

DICKINSON, Bruce R.
Colorado Springs teachers association. Todays
Ed 60:50 D '71
DICKINSON, Donald
Aware. il Am Lib 2:120-1, 214, 318-19, 422,
537-8, 641-2, 756-7 Ja-Jl '71
DICKINSON, Emily
Emily Dickinson: A poet for the now genera-
tion. T. D. McFadden. Engl J 60:462-4 Ap
'71 *
Flesh-and-blood face on the commemorative
stamp. A. Rothenberg. il Sat R 54:33-4+ S
11 '71 *
Trade winds. C. Amory. Sat R 54:6 Ag 28
'71 *
DICKINSON, Fairleigh Stanton, 1919-
How two influential fathers turned family
drug tragedies into a triumph for the pub-
lic. R. Sullivan. il Todays Health 49:42-5
My '71
DICKINSON, Joan Younger
Southern comfort for the seventies; Hilton
Head, S.C. il Holiday 49:70-4 Mr '71
DICKINSON, Patric
J. M. farmer and sailor, drowned September,
1970; poem. Esquire 75:34 My '71
DICKINSON, Peter A.
Time for rewards (cont) il pors Har Yrs
11:36-40 Ja: 41-8 Mr; 45-53 Jl; 48-51 D '71
DICKINSON, William R.
Plate tectonics in geologic history. bibliog il
Science 174:107-13 O 8 '71
—and Luth, W. C.
Model for plate tectonic evolution of mantle
layers. bibliog il Science 174:400-4 O 22 '71
DICKSON, Charles
Liquid breathing in humans fact or fiction?
with biographical sketch. il Sea Front 17:
268-71, 319 S '71
DICKSON, Frank A.
Idea a day (cont) por Writers Digest 51:12-13
F: 12 Mr: 18-20 Je: 16-17+ Ag '71
DICKSON, LeRoy D.
Amateur scientist. il Sci Am 225:110-11 Jl '71
DICKSON, R. C. and others
Ultraviolet light: a new stimulus for the
induction of platelet aggregation. bibliog
il Science 172:1140-2 Je 11 '71
DICTATORSHIP
Dictatorship and gerontocracy. G. W. Ball.
Newsweek 78:60 N 8 '71
    See also
Fascism
Totalitarianism
DICTION
    See also
Singing—Diction
DICTIONARIES
Gov't book purchasing: procedural changes
sought. S. Wagner. Pub W 200:30+ Jl 5 '71
Government book purchasing: the dictionary
controversy. S. Wagner. Pub W 199:36-8
My 17 '71
    See also
Encyclopedias
English language—Dictionaries
Publishers and publishing—Dictionaries
    Illustrations
    See Illustration of books and periodicals
DICTIONARY illustration. See Illustration of
books and periodicals
DIDATO, Salvatore V.
Therapy failure: pride and/or predjudice of
the therapist? bibliog Ment Hy 55:219-20
Ap '71
DIDDLEY, Bo
Second coming of Bo Diddley. M. Lydon.
il pors Ramp Mag 9:21-31 My '71 *
DIDION, Joan
Best selling novelist tells why she keeps a
notebook; excerpt from Slouching towards
Bethlehem. il por Writers Digest 51:26-7+
D '71
—and Dunne, J. G.
Panic in Needle park. Harp Baz 104:68 Jl '71
    about
Joan Didion: portrait of a professional. A.
Kazin. Harper 243:112-14+ D '71 *
DIDUR, Adamo
Adamo Didur. A. Favia-Artsay. il pors Hob-
bies 76:35-6 O '71 *
DIE holders. See Holding devices (machine
work)
DIEBOLD, John
Behold Diebold. R. Levy. por Duns 97:59-60
F '71 *
DIEFENBACH, Dale Alan
Instant classification. por Library J 96:801-2
Mr 1 '71

DIEGO GARCIA naval base. See Navy yards
and naval stations
DIELDRIN
Aldrin and dieldrin. C. F. Wurster. bibliog
il Environ 13:33-41 O '71
Induction of microsomal oxidase in F_1 hy-
brids of a high and a low oxidase housefly
strain. L. C. Terriere and others. bibliog
il Science 171:581-3 F 12 '71
DIELECTRICS
Dielectric siphons. T. B. Jones and others.
bibliog il Science 174:1232-3 D 17 '71
DIEM, Ngo-dinh-. See Ngo-dinh-Diem
DIEMER, Eugene
Gardening at 4,000 feet. il Org Gard & Farm
18:72-3 D '71
DIENBIENPHU, Battle of. See Indochina.
French—History—Civil war. 1946-1954
DIENER, Thomas J.
Team approach to academic administration.
bibliog Sch & Soc 99:504-7 D '71
DIERKER, Larry
Good one for the books. R. Fimrite. il por
Sports Illus 34:62 My 24 '71 *
DIERKS-VENTLING, Christa, and Cone, A. L.
Acetoacetyl-coenzyme A thiolase in brain,
liver, and kidney during maturation of
the rat. bibliog il Science 172:380-2 Ap 23
'71
DIES (metal work)
    See also
Tool and die industry
DIESEL electric sets. See Electric generators
DIESEL engines
    Exhaust
Diesel exhaust test improves engine per-
formance. Am City 86:47 N '71
DIESEL engines, Automotive
Now! A diesel wankel from Rolls-Royce. D.
Scott. il Pop Sci 198:80 F '71
DIET
Amazing new you diet. J. Gage. il Ladies
Home J 88:130-1+ Mr '71
Art of looking beautiful; excerpts from Joan
Crawford: my way of life. J. Crawford.
il pors McCalls 98:55-7+ Jl '71
Body battle: five models. il Seventeen 30:126-
9 S '71
Calorie counting on your vacation. il Bet
Hom & Gard 49:92 Je '71
Chewing your way to health, sexual vitality,
peace. A. Gross. Mlle 72:184-5+ Ap '71
Diet that's killing our kids; Zen macrobiotic
diet. F. J. Stare. il Ladies Home J 88:70+
O '71
Dieter's news; with recipes. il Seventeen 29:
166-7+ S '70
Doctor's quick teen-age diet; excerpt. I. M.
Stillman and S. S. Baker. il McCalls 98:
78-9+ Ap '71
50 most asked diet questions, M. B. Glenn.
Ladies Home J 88:72+ My '71; Same abr.
with title What everyone wants to know
about weight control. Read Digest 99:54-7
Ag '71
Fitness program for overweight teen-agers;
excerpts from The handbook of adolescence:
a complete medical guide. M. J. Gersh and
I. F. Litt. il Parents Mag 46:50-1+ Ag '71
Health eaters; interviews. A. Davis and oth-
ers. pors Vogue 157:167-8+ My '71
High-flavor low-calorie snacks for dieters. il
Parents Mag 46:68 Ag '71
How to stop dieting and start living. moving,
and eating. il pors Mlle 72:126-30 Ja '71
How to survive the holidays. D. Calloway.
McCalls 99:40 D '71
It's super diet. Vogue 158:104-5 O 15 '71
Keep-your-husband diet; excerpt from book.
E. Ford. il por Ladies Home J 88:60+ Ja
'71
New wise woman's diet with all-new recipes
for 14 days of well-balanced, weight-
reducing meals and with increased por-
tions that make it also the new wise man's
diet. il Redbook 138:92-3+ Ja '72
Now-and-forever diet; Super diet; with
recipes. J. Pierson. Vogue 157:98-9 F 15
'71
One week of inexpensive, low-calorie menus;
with recipes. Good H 173:115+ Jl '71
Perfect diet. G. Christakis. il Redbook 136:
54-5+ Ja '71
Play the calorie game. M. Weisinger. il Todays Health 49:58-60 Jl '71
Pregnancy: no time to diet. D. Calloway.
il McCalls 98:54+ My '71
Questions and answers on fats and choles-
terol; low-fat, low-cholesterol recipes. R.
H. Smithies. il Good H 172:139-40+ F '71
Quick, low-calorie cooking; with recipes.
R. H. Smithies. Good H 174:148+ Ja '72
Streamlines (cont) Seventeen 29:288 Ag: 155
N '70; 30:172 Ap; 126 Jl; 290 Ag '71

DIET—*Continued*
Those eight-pound blues; a dieter's lament. J. Viorst. il Redbook 136:90-1+ Mr '71
Travel and beauty care. J. Clark. Holiday 49:17 My '71
Vogue's super diet; reprint from June 1970 issue. Vogue 158:148 O 15 '71
Which diet tricks pay off? excerpt from The family guide to better food and better health. R. M. Deutsch. Read Digest 99:87-9 N '71
Which diets work, which don't; interview, ed. by R. Petty. P. L. White. il Todays Health 49:58-62 S '71
Yin, yang, macrobiotics, and me. H. S. Resnik. il Redbook 137:58-9+ Jl '71
You & your diet. R. H. Smithies. See issues of Good housekeeping
See also
College students—Food
Corpulence
Food fads
Food habits
Iron in diet
Nutrition
Oils and fats, Edible
Proteins
Vegetarianism
Vitamins

Anecdotes, facetiae, satire, etc.
My farewell to girth control. S. Levenson. il por Ladies Home J 88:116+ My '71

DIET, Deficient
By-eggs alone. Sci Am 226:50 Ja '72

DIET and heart disease. See Heart—Diseases—Nutritional aspects

DIET in disease
Answers to your questions, plus cake and cookie recipes for allergy diets. R. H. Smithies. il Good H 172:178+ My '71
11 new desserts for diabetics. il Good H 173:122+ Ag '71

DIET pills. See Weight reducing preparations

DIETARY studies. See Diet, Deficient

DIETERICH, Daniel J.
Mod mod world of flexible modular scheduling. bibliog Engl J 60:1264-71 D '71

DIETHER, Jack
Flashes of greatness from the 25-year-old Bruckner: a moving, masterly Requiem. por Am Rec G 37:428-9+ Mr '71
Georg Solti's first Chicago recordings. il Am Rec G 37:346-9 F '71
Music for the season. il Am Rec G 37:204-8 D '70
Souvenir of Sibelius centennial, the first American recording of Luonnotar. por Am Rec G 37:494-5+ Ap '71

DIETHRICH, Edward
Doctor tries a transplant. T. Thompson. il por Sports Illus 34:34-6 My 17 '71 *

DIETHYL pyrocarbonate
DEP, cancer and beverages. Sci N 100:422 D 25 '71
Diethyl pyrocarbonate: formation of urethan in treated beverages. G. Löfroth and T. Gejvall. bibliog il Science 174:1248-50 D 17 '71

DIETHYLSTILBESTOL. See Stilbestrols

DIETS. See Diet

DIETSCH, Robert W.
Invisible bureaucracy. New Repub 164:19-21 F 20 '71
New thoughts on social security. New Repub 165:13-15 N 27 '71
1971 gerrymander. New Repub 164:20-2 My 29 '71
Raising the flag. New Repub 164:18-19 Je 12 '71
Some progress, more myth. Nation 212:615-18 My 17 '71
Trouble in Fantasyland. New Repub 165:13-14 Jl 17 '71
Wide reach of oil. New Repub 164:16-17 Je 26 '71

DIETTERICH, Paul
Phased withdrawal; report on church efforts at the United Nations. Chr Cent 88:1326-9 N 10 '71

DIETZ, John
Capsule fire flares up again. il pors Life 71:24-9 S 17 '71 *

DIETZ, Lew
Spring bear down east. il Field & S 75:56-7+ Mr '71

DIETZ, Robert S.
Those shifty continents. bibliog il Sea Front 17:204-12 Jl '71

DIFFERENCES, Racial. See Racial differences

DIFFERENTIALS, Wage. See Wage differentials

DIFFERENTIATION (biology)
Bacterial differentiation. L. Shapiro and others. bibliog il Science 173:884-92 S 3 '71
DNA synthesis in differentiating skeletal muscle cells: initiation by ultraviolet light. F. E. Stockdale. bibliog il Science 171:1145-7 Mr 19 '71
Developmental variation in the isoenzymes of human liver and gastric alcohol dehydrogenase. R. F. Murray, jr. and A. G. Motulsky. bibliog il Science 171:71-3 Ja 8 '71
See also
Morphogenesis

DIFFERENTIATION (botany)
Nuclear acidic protein changes during differentiation in physarum polycephalum. W. M. LeStourgeon and H. P. Rusch. bibliog il Science 174:1233-6 D 17 '71

DIFFRACTION
See also
X rays—Diffraction

DIFFUSERS, Air. See Air diffusers

DIFFUSION
Motions of molecules in liquids: viscosity and diffusivity. J. H. Hildebrand. bibliog il Science 174:490-3 O 29 '71

DIFFUSION technique (photography)
How to control diffusion. B. Pierce. il Pop Phot 68:120-1+ Ja '71

DI FILIPPI, Arturo
Dr Di's day. G. Fitzgerald. il pors Opera N 35:14-15 Mr 13 '71 *
Place in the sun. F. Stevenson. il por Opera N 35:12-13 Mr 13 '71 *

DIGESTION
See also
Stomach

DIGESTIVE system
See also
Intestines

DIGGERS (racing cars) See Automobiles, Racing

DIGGING tools, Indian. See Indians of North America—Implements

DIGGINS, John P.
Consciousness and ideology in American history: the burden of Daniel J. Boorstin. bibliog f Am Hist R 76:99-118, 1249-54 F, O '71

DIGGS, Alfred
My work; poem. Negro Hist Bul 34:87 Ap '71

DIGGS, Irene
Attitudes toward color in South America. Negro Hist Bul 34:107-8 My '71

DI GIOVANNI, Norman Thomas
(tr) See Borges, J. L. Anxieties
(tr) See Borges, J. L. Congress
(tr) See Borges, J. L. Elder lady
(tr) See Borges, J. L. End of the duel
(tr) See Borges, J. L. Gospel according to Mark
(tr) See Borges, J. L. Israel 1969
(tr) See Borges, J. L. Juan Murafia
(tr) See Borges, J. L. Southside: Rosa
(tr) See Borges, J. L. Tom Castro, the implausible impostor
(tr) See Borges, J. L. Twice told tales
(tr) See Borges, J. L. Unworthy friend

DIGITAL circuits. See Logic circuits

DIGITAL computers. See Computers—Digital computers

DIGITAL control. See Digital electronics

DIGITAL electronics
Digitally controlled power supplies. P. Birman. il Electr World 86:28-9 O '71
Electronics plays the numbers game. J. R. Free. il Pop Sci 199:72-3 O '71

DIGITAL equipment corporation
Which way? Forbes 107:31 My 1 '71

DIGITAL readout displays. See Information display systems

DIGITAL readout tubes. See Electron tubes

DIGITAL voltmeters. See Voltmeters

DIHYDROURIDINE. See Nucleosides

DIHYDROXYCHOLECALCIFEROL. See Vitamins—Vitamin D

DIHYDROXYPHENYLALANINE. See Dopa

DILEMMA
Quantum mechanics and reality; dilemma of indeterminism. R. S. DeWitt; discussion. bibliog il Phys Today 24:36-44 Ap '71

DILL, Frank Y.
Battle of the giant brains; or, Electronics conquers all. bibliog il Pop Electr 34:39-43+ Ap '71

DILL, Laddie John
View from the Coast. il pors Time 97:58-9 F 1 '71 *

DILL, William R. See Hodgson, A. M. jt. auth.

DILLARD, Nancy Hollis
Counter; poem. Chr Cent 88:1373 N 24 '71

DILLON, Betty Crites
President appoints Mrs Dillon to ICAO council. Dept State Bul 65:639 N 29 '71 *
DILLON, Richard H.
Wells, Fargo's Jekyll and Hyde. il por Am West 8:28-33+ Mr '71
DILORENZO, Louis T.
Which way for pre-K: wishes or reality? il Am Ed 7:28-32 Ja '71
DIMBLEBY, Jonathan
Wide open British drug scene. New Repub 164:15-16 Ap 3 '71
DIMENT, Erik Sandberg-. See Langer, R. W. pseud.
DIMMOCK, Mary Laverne
Sixth year study and the academic librarian. bibliog por Library J 96:2731-3 S 15 '71
DIMOND, E. Grey
More than herbs and acupuncture. il Sat R 54:17-19+ D 18 '71
DIMORPHISM (biology)
Sexual dimorphism in the preoptic area of the rat. G. Raisman and P. M. Field. bibliog il Science 173:731-3 Ag 20 '71
DIMORPHOTHECA. See Cape marigolds
DINAPHTHYL
Probability distribution of enantiomorphous forms in spontaneous generation of optically active substances. R. E. Pincock and others. bibliog il Science 174:1018-20 D 3 '71
DINETTE furniture. See Furniture
DINGHIES. See Boats and boating
DINING. See Dinners and dining
DINING clubs. See Clubs
DINING halls
See also
Camps—Dining halls
DINING rooms
Whatever happened to the dining room? W. Baldwin. House & Gard 139:10+ F '71
DINKELOO, John Gerard
You can't see the foyer for the trees. W. Von Eckardt. il pors Horizon 13:40-7 Sum '71 *
DINNERS and dining
Cook-at-the-table dinner for 4; with menu and recipes. D. Eby. il Bet Hom & Gard 49:70-83+ N '71
Cooking game well played by Mrs Stéphane Groueff; with recipes. M. McKendry. il Vogue 158:24 Ag 15 '71
Easy-dinner dishes. Z. Coulson. il Good H 173:112-27 S '71
Eat; Sunday dinner menu. M. Cantwell. Mlle 72:80-1 Mr '71
Eat; Sunday dinner; with recipes. M. Cantwell. Mlle 74:156-7 Ja '72
Great company dinner; with recipes. J. Jaffry. il Am Home 74:110-18+ N '71
Great dinners for 6; with menus and recipes. J. Uetz. il Am Home 74:60+ Jl '71
Holiday feast at the Forsytes; with list of restaurants serving it. R. A. de Groot. il Esquire 75:130-3+ Ja '71
Home at 6: dinner at 7. il Redbook 137:120-2+ O '71
Last-minute entrees; with menus and recipes. H. McCully. il House B 113:126-7+ My '71
Moveable feasts; vacation cooking; with menus and recipes. il McCalls 98:98-103+ Je '71
No-cook chicken dinners. M. Happel. il Ladies Home J 88:82-3+ Ag '71
Oven dinners; easy, economical cooking at its best, with recipes. Z. Coulson. il Good H 174:80-96 Ja '72
Recipe for a Washington dinner party. W. McLendon and S. Smith. il pors Ladies Home J 88:110+ My '71
Swing into spring with an elegant Easter dinner; with recipes. il Parents Mag 46:62-3+ Ap '71
30-minute menu. il Ladies Home J 89:96 Ja '72
See also
Caterers and catering
Christmas dinners
Food, Frozen
Gastronomy
Outdoor meals
Thanksgiving dinners
DINNERWARE. See Pottery; Tableware
DINOSAURS
Bringing the brontosaurs ashore. il Sci Digest 69:34-5 Ap '71
Swamp-dweller or landlubber? brontosaurus. il Sci N 99:79 Ja 30 '71
Up from the ooze; supposedly aquatic sauropods. Sci Am 224:48 Mr '71
DINUCLEOSIDES. See Nucleosides
DIOCESAN newspapers. See Catholic press

DIODE lasers. See Lasers
DIODES
Diode quiz. W. A. Vincent. il Electr World 86:8 S '71
Getting to know varactor diodes. J. Darr. il Radio-Electr 42:62-3 D '71
Inside the LED. il Electr World 86:47 Jl '71
Solid-state probe thermometer, use of silicon diodes. G. Gregg. il Electr World 85:70-1 Mr '71
Speed control resistor? J. Darr. il Radio-Electr 42:26+ Ap '71
Zener diode voltage-regulator nomograms. C. W. Young. il Electr World 86:32-3+ Jl '71
Zener diodes & voltage-regulator design. K. Butler. il Electr World 86:32-4+ D '71
DIOGENES, 412?-323 B.C.
Good and, or virtuous life. P. W. Schmidtchen. il Hobbies 76:134-6 My '71 *
DIPHENYL compounds
Early warning of the terns. H. Hays and R. W. Risebrough. il Natur Hist 80:38-47 N '71
Menace of PCB. Time 98:91-2 O 11 '71
Oceans as alphabet soup; focus on DDT and PCB's. R. H. Gilluly. Sci N 101:30-1 Ja 8 '72
PCB crisis. il Newsweek 78:60 O 11 '71
PCB's: leaks of toxic substances raises issue of effects, regulation. J. Pichirallo. Science 173:899-902 S 3 '71
DIPHOSPHOGLYCERATE
Differences in the interaction of 2,3-diphosphoglycerate with certain mammalian hemoglobins. H. F. Bunn. bibliog il Science 172:1049-50 Je 4 '71
DIPLOMACY
See also
International relations
United States—Diplomatic and consular service
DIPLOMAS, Fraudulent
Honorary spoof; honorary titles from San Francisco's Millard Fillmore institute. por Time 98:46+ Jl 5 '71
Mail-order Ph.D.'s. J. R. Howard and A. W. Howard. Ed Digest 37:32-3 S '71
DIPLOMATIC and consular service
See also
United States—Diplomatic and consular service
DIPLOMATS
See also
United States—Diplomatic and consular service
Protection
Legislation proposed to protect U.S. officials and foreign diplomats; Department of justice announcement, with text of letter by Attorney General Mitchell and Secretary Rogers. Dept State Bul 65:268-70 S 6 '71
DIPLOMATS, Kidnapping of. See Kidnapping
DIPPEL, John V. H.
Getting nowhere through channels. New Repub 164:13-17 My 22 '71
DIPS. See Appetizers
DIPTERA
See also
Flies
Midges
DIRECT current electric generators. See Electric generators, Direct current
DIRECT delivery of books. See Libraries—Circulation, loans, etc.
DIRECT energy conversion
See also
Fuel cells
Solar batteries
DIRECT mail advertising. See Advertising, Direct mail
DIRECT relief foundation
Visit to DRF. N. Cousins. Sat R 54:14 Je 26 '71
DIRECT selling. See Canvassing
DIRECTION, Operatic. See Operatic production and direction
DIRECTION, Theatrical. See Theatrical production and direction
DIRECTORS, Corporation. See Corporations—Directors
DIRECTORS, Moving picture. See Moving picture directors
DIRIGIBLE; comic strip. See Viertel, G.
DIRIGIBLES. See Airships
DISABILITY, Reading. See Reading disability
DISABLED. See Handicapped
DISADVANTAGED children. See Socially handicapped children

DISALLE, Michael Vincent
Full scale wage-price controls? interview.
pors Nations Bsns 59:32-9 O '71

about

Where are they now? pors Newsweek 78:8
S 6 '71 *

DISALVO, F. J.
Along two dimensions. Sci N 100:140 Ag 28
'71 *

DISARMAMENT
Danger of partial disarmament steps. H. F.
York. Cur 133:41-5 O '71
Disarmament: discussion in First committee.
UN Mo Chron 7:47-52 D '70
Soviet statement on disarmament; excerpts
from address, June 11, 1971. L. I. Brezhnev.
Cur Hist 61:240 O '71
U.S. states views on conventional arms re-
straints; statement, August 26, 1971. J. F.
Leonard. Dept State Bul 65:309-15 S 20 '71
See also
Atomic weapons and disarmament
International security
International summer school on disarmament
and arms control
Strategic arms limitations talks
United Nations—Committee on disarmament
United States—Defenses

Conferences
Disarmament conferences: ballets at the
brink. R. H. Ferrell. il Am Heritage 22:4-
5+ F '71

Russia
Moscow and the missile race. B. S. Lambeth. bibliog f Cur Hist 61:215-21+ O '71

DISARMAMENT agency. See United States—
Arms control and disarmament agency

DISASTER insurance. See Insurance, Disaster

DISASTERS
On cyclones and other natural disasters: re-
flections of a geophysicist. E. M. Fournier
d'Albe. il UNESCO Courier 24:24-7 F '71
See also
Building failures
Floods
Hurricanes

DISC brakes. See Brakes, Automobile

DISC jockeys
Hey, radio, help me make it through the
night; personal relationship between young
people and the radio. P. Fornatale. il por
Sr Schol 99:32-4 O 25 '71

DISCARDING of books. See Libraries—Book
discarding

DISCH, Tom
Phaedra; Questionnaire; D. W. Richmond
gives directions to the architect of his
tomb; poems. Poetry 118:216-17 Jl '71

DISCHARGE of employees. See Employees—
Dismissal

DISCHARGED criminals. See Prisoners, Discharged

DISCIPLES of Christ. See Christian church.
Disciples of Christ

DISCIPLINE
Coping with "I won't"; with study-discus-
sion program, by M. M. Conant. D. Graves.
bibliog il PTA Mag 65:12-14, 34 Ap '71
What parent doesn't wonder about the
right and wrong way to discipline chil-
dren? B. Bettelheim. Ladies Home J 88:
18+ F '71
Young defacers; parental neglect. Life 70:34
Ap 9 '71
See also
Camp discipline
Children—Management and training

DISCIPLINE, Library. See Library administration

DISCIPLINE, Military
As fighting slows in Vietnam: breakdown in
GI discipline. il U S News 70:16-17 Je 7 '71
Conscience and command, ed. by J. Finn.
Review
Commonweal 94:289-90 My 28 '71. W. C.
McWilliams
See also
Military training

DISCOUNT
Cash discounts are a paying consumer's
dream. Pub W 200:41 Jl 26 '71
Greening of America; United international
club, inc. Newsweek 78:109+ N 22 '71
Operation stretch your dollar; 10 percent
discounts for the elderly. A. Z. Rose. il por
Har Yrs 11:28-9 F '71

DISCOUNT chain stores. See Chain stores

DISCOUNT houses (retail trade)
French go wild over discount stores. il Bsns
W p40 N 20 '71
See also
Arlen realty and development corporation
Rite aid corporation
Sixty nine cents shops

DISCRIMINATION
See also
Anti-Semitism

DISCRIMINATION, Racial. See Race discrimination

DISCRIMINATION in education
How Jewish quotas began. S. Steinberg. Com-
mentary 52:67-76 S '71; Discussion. 53:16+
Ja '72
Race and education; summary of reports.
M. Perry. bibliog il Am Lib 2:1051-4 N '71
To overcome discrimination now. S. Ackley.
Cur 129:35-8 My '71
U.S. education: glory and shame. America
125:164 S 18 '71
See also
Equalization. Educational

DISCRIMINATION in employment
Bias suits ask for back pay. U S News 71:96
O 4 '71
Case of the borderline black. T. V. Purcell.
il Harvard Bsns R 49:128-30+ N '71
Discrimination in British industry. T. Bee-
son. il Chr Cent 88:1156 O 6 '71
Galbraith plan to promote the minorities.
J. K. Galbraith and others. il N Y Times
Mag p9+ Ag 22 '71; Same with title To-
ward greater minority employment. Cur
133:22-9 O '71; Discussion. N Y Times Mag
p92+ S 12; 10+ O 10 '71
Gloved rap at corporate bigotry; guidelines
to help end religious discrimination. Bsns
W p39 Je 19 '71
Power to which people? lack of black and
Mexican-American executives in California-
based corporations. New Repub 164:9-10 F
20 '71
See also
Blacklisting
Equal pay for equal work
Jews—Employment
Negroes—Employment
United States—Equal employment opportunity
commission
Woman—Employment
Woman—Equal rights

DISCRIMINATION in housing
Battle of the suburbs. il Newsweek 78:61-4+
N 15 '71
Equal housing: Nixon defines his policy; ex-
cerpts from statement, June 11, 1971. R. M.
Nixon. il U S News 70:72 Je 21 '71
Higher wall around suburbia; Supreme court
decision on discriminatory local zoning
ordinances. Bsns W p24 My 1 '71
Iron curtain; suburban opposition to low-
income housing in Potomac, Md. New
Repub 164:7-8 Ap 24 '71
New pressure on housing bias. il Bsns W
p38 Je 19 '71
Residential segregation: its effects on educa-
tion. A. Downs. Ed Digest. 36:12-15 Ap '71
Stroke of the pen; proposal for open low-cost
housing. A. Simon. Commonweal 93:391-5
Ja 22 '71
Suburban snobbery; statement by R. M.
Nixon. New Repub 164:7-9 Je 26 '71
Suburban strategy; question of forcing inte-
grated low-income housing on a communi-
ty. il Newsweek 77:19 Je 21 '71
To end bias in housing. America 124:643-4
Je 26 '71
See also
Housing—Desegregation
Negroes—Housing

DISCRIMINATION in sports. See Segregation
in sports

DISCUS, pseud.
Music in the round. See issues of Harper's
magazine

DISCUSSION
Panel discussions: is there any hope? R. B.
Leighton. il Phys Today 24:30-4 Ap '71
See also
Negotiation

DISCUSSION groups. See Forums (discussion
and debate)

DISCUSSION method (education)
Class discussion and the craft of questioning.
C. M. Kirkton. bibliog Engl J 60:408-13+
Mr '71
Contemporary learning needs participation
training. R. C. Dobbs and V. Wall. Clear
House 45:480-2 Ap '71
Getting passive students to speak up. H.
Weintraub. il Todays Ed 60:21 Mr '71
Getting used to the system; letter from a
freshman. E. Vasquez. Nat R 23:587-8+ Je
1 '71

DISCUSSION method (education)—*Continued*
Shut up, teacher! excerpt from Getting the
teacher to shut up. K. D. Norris. Todays
Ed 60:46 N '71
Student participation in college teaching.
Sch & Soc 99:463 D '71
Team-it: an instructional strategy. L. W.
Howe. Clear House 45:444-6 Mr '71
DISEASE, Diet in. See Diet in disease
DISEASE resistance. See Immunity
DISEASES
They cut her open and then just sewed her
back up. R. Drake. Chr Cent 88:288-9 Mr 3
'71
    See also
Animals as carriers of infection
Deficiency diseases
Epidemics
Venereal diseases
    also names of diseases, e.g. Hepatitis;
    also subhead Diseases under organs and
    parts of the body, e.g. Lungs—Diseases
DISEASES, Hereditary. See Heredity of dis-
ease
DISEASES, Industrial
And now, cadmium; tragic results of Japan's
unchecked pollution. Time 97:35 Mr 8 '71
Dynamite heart; overexposure to nitrogly-
cerin by ammunition plant workers. il
Time 98:41 Jl 12 '71
    See also
Lungs—Dust diseases
DISEASES, Mental. See Mental illness
DISEASES of famous persons
    See also
Porphyria
DISHOTSKY, Norman I. and others
LSD and genetic damage. bibliog il Science
172:431-40 Ap 30 '71
DISHWASHER that brought out the worst in
everybody; story. See Stanton, W.
DISHWASHING and drying machines
Carocelle dishwasher. il Consumer Bul 54:
27-9 Ag '71
Dishwashers. il Consumer Bul 55:16-24 Ja '72
Dishwashers. il Consumer Rep 36:660-7 N
'71
DISHWASHING detergents. See Detergents
DISINFECTION and disinfectants
    See also
Hexachlorophene
DISK Jockey. See Disc jockeys
DISMAL SWAMP
Fabled swamp. D. E. Delzell; B. Meanley;
R. G. De Rageot. il Liv Wildn 34:28-34+
Wint '70
Great Dismal Swamp. M. Payne. il Nat Parks
& Con Mag 45:9-13 F '71
DISMISSAL of employees. See Employees—Dis-
missal
DISMISSAL of librarians. See Librarians—Dis-
missal
DISMISSAL of teachers. See Teachers—Dismis-
sal
DISNEY, Dorothy Cameron
(ed) Can this marriage be saved? See issues
of Ladies' home journal
DISNEY, Walt
Wish upon a star: the magical kingdoms of
Walt Disney; condensation. R. Collier. il
Read Digest 99:221-4+ O '71 *
DISNEY, Walt, productions
Disney's movable feast; Disney on parade.
il Newsweek 78:64-5 S 6 '71
Disney's war against the wilderness;
Mineral King controversy. R. Rapoport. il
Ramp Mag 10:27-33 N '71
Wish upon a star: the magical kingdoms of
Walt Disney; condensation. R. Collier. il
Read Digest 99:221-4+ O '71
DISNEY world, Fla.
Airlines, space center weighing impact of
Disney on Florida tourism. W. H. Gregory.
il Aviation W 95:34-5+ Ag 16 '71
Disney builds the clean, green world of to-
morrow. E. H. McCleary. il Pop Mech 136:
94-9+ O '71
Disney dollars. il Forbes 107:20-3 My 1 '71
Disney moves East. il Life 71:44-50 O 15 '71
Disney world: pixie dust over Florida. il
Time 98:52-3 O 18 '71
How to brave Disney's new world. F. K.
Coffee. il Mech Illus 67:46+ O '71
Land speculators play Disney's money ma-
chine. il Bsns W p80+ S 11 '71
New boom: Disneyland East. il Newsweek
77:103-4 Ap 19 '71
Preview of the new biggest show on earth.
H. Ehrlich. il Look 35:18-25 Ap 6 '71
Riding the coattails of Mickey Mouse; with
editorial comment. il Bsns W p72-3+, 103
S 11 '71
Send-off for a pair of fantasies. il Life 71:
84-5 D 31 '71

Supertoys; with travel notes. R. Joseph. il
Esquire 76:80, 178-83 D '71
U.S. journal. C. Trillin. New Yorker 47:173-
4+ N 6 '71
What hath Disney wrought! J. Morgenstern.
il Newsweek 78:38-43+ O 18 '71
Whistle while you work. D. Butwin. il
Sat R 54:40-3 F 6 '71
Will 10,000,000 people ruin all this? E. Mc-
Cleary. il Nat Wildlife 9:5-9 Je '71
DISPENSATIONS (canon law)
Nonclerical priests; Vatican's new instruc-
tions on dispensation from priestly vows.
T. Beeson. Chr Cent 88:484-5 Ap 21 '71
DISPLACEMENT (psychology)
When things go wrong are you a victim of
displacement behavior? K. Ellison. il Sci
Digest 69:24-6 Mr '71
DISPLACEMENT (ships)
Surfing or seakindliness? F. Bilek. il Yacht-
ing 130:64-5+ Jl '71
DISPLACEMENT activity (animal behavior)
When things go wrong are you a victim of
displacement behavior? K. Ellison. il Sci
Digest 69:24-6 Mr '71
DISPLACEMENT reactions. See Chemical re-
actions
DISPLAY of antiques, art objects, etc.
At home; memories of a happy summer. N.
Mandelbaum. il Ladies Home J 88:76+ Jl
'71
Showcasing; home furnishings. il Mlle 73:
190-3 My '71
DISPLAY systems, Airborne. See Aeronautic
instruments—Display systems
DISPLAYS, Library. See Library exhibits
DISPOSABLE containers. See Containers
DISPOSABLE diapers. See Diapers, Infants
DISPOSAL of radioactive waste. See Radio-
active waste disposal
DISPOSAL of refuse. See Refuse and refuse
disposal
DISSENT, Freedom of. See Free speech
DISSENT, Right of. See Free speech
DISSENTERS
Berrigans; radical activism personified (cont)
G. C. Zahn. Cath World 212:285 Mr '71
Christianity and criminality. J. B. Shepherd.
il Chr Cent 88:796-8 Je 30 '71
Courage. New Repub 165:14 Ja 2 '71
Dissent in three American wars, by S. E.
Morison and others. Review
Trans-Action 8:100-2 N '70. S. Tax
Dissent within a lawful society; address,
December 4, 1970. E. Sevareid. Vital Speech-
es 37:251-3 F 1 '71
Medvedev papers, by Z. A. Medvedev, and A
question of madness, by Z. A. Medvedev
and R. A. Medvedev. Reviews
Sat R pors 54:35-7 N 20 '71. S. Jacoby
Parting shots; some real heroes. il Life 70:
71-2 Ap 9 '71
Psychoadaptation; or, How to handle dissen-
ters; Russia. por Time 98:44-5 S 27 '71
Seekers after justice; T. M. Conrad, J.
Graham, and A. Kaufman. P. Steinfels.
Commonweal 95:150 N 12 '71
    See also
Protests, demonstrations, etc.
DISSENTERS, Religious
Aggiornamento has failed; excerpt from The
decline and fall of radical Catholicism. J.
Hitchcock. Commonweal 94:231-5 My 14 '71;
Discussion. 94:228, 299+, 323+ Je 11, 25 '71
Catholic revolutionaries; part of the solution
or part of the problem? J. Finn. Com-
monweal 94:456-8 S 3 '71
Decline and fall of radical Catholicism, by
J. Hitchcock. Review
Chr Cent 88:887 Jl 21 '71. D. M. Kelley
Divine disobedience, by F. du Plessix Gray.
Review
Nation 212:153-4 F 1 '71. M. Karpatkin
Question of identity. C. F. H. Henry. Chr
Today 15:30 Ag 6 '71
Silent hierarchy; bishops distrustful of Cath-
olic press. S. J. Adamo. America 124:411-12
Ap 17 '71
Theological weather report from the medi-
ating left. W. H. Dodd. America 124:403-6
Ap 17 '71
Whose heaven, whose earth? by T. Melville
and M. Melville. Review
America 124:268 Mr 13 '71. R. Griffin *
DISSOCIATION
    See also
Decomposition (chemistry)
DISSOCIATION of cells. See Cell aggregation
DISSOCIATIVE anesthesia. See Anesthesia
DISTANCES
    Measurements
    See also
Logs (nautical instruments)

DISTANCES, Astronomical. See Astronomical distances

DISTILLED water. See Water, Distilled

DISTILLERIES
Delectations; a visit to the Beam bourbon plant in Kentucky. N. Hazelton. Nat R 23: 533+, 770 My 18, Jl 13 '71
Flying visit; Jack Daniel's still in Lynchburg, Tenn. R. L. Collins. il Flying 88:108-9 Je '71

DISTILLERS corporation-Seagrams, ltd.
Mister Sam's succession. por Time 98:59+ Jl 26 '71

DISTILLING industries. See Liquor industry

DISTINGUISHED service award. See American forestry association

DISTRESS signals. See Signals and signaling

DISTRIBUTION (probability theory)
Fitting discrete probability distributions to evolutionary events. T. Uzzell and K. W. Corbin. bibliog il Science 172:1089-96 Je 11 '71

DISTRIBUTION of goods
See also
National distribution services, inc.

DISTRIBUTION of moving pictures. See Moving pictures—Distribution

DISTRIBUTION of wealth. See Wealth, Distribution of

DISTRIBUTIVE workers of America, National council of
Right defendant; suit against President Nixon and other government officials by District 65. Nation 213:100-1 Ag 16 '71

DISTRIBUTOR points. See Automobile engines —Ignition

DISTRICT 50. See United mine workers of America—District 50

DISTRICT OF COLUMBIA public library. See Washington, D.C, public library

DISTRIGAS corporation
New gas pipe with a long reach. il Bsns W p28 O 30 '71

DI SUVERO, Mark
Truth amid steel elephants. R. Hughes. il Time 98:48 Ag 2 '71 *

DITTES, Ruth
Establishing a standards board. Todays Ed 60:23 D '71

DITTON, Robert B.
Wreckreation in our national forests. il Parks & Rec 6:22-6+ Je '71

DITZEL, Paul
When drinking and driving mix. Read Digest 98:108-12 Ja '71

DIVANS. See Sofas

DIVERS. See Diving, Submarine

DIVERSIFICATION in industry
Aerospace giant tries earthwork: Boeing's new directions. il Time 98:79 N 15 '71
Aerospace is diversifying again. il Bsns W p 124-6 S 11 '71
Look who's playing with toys! il Forbes 108:22-4+ D 15 '71
See also
Conglomerate corporations

DIVERTICULOSIS. See Intestines—Diseases

DIVIDENDS
Cap on dividends won't pinch too much. il Bsns W p75-6 N 27 '71
Different kinds of dividends that stocks pay. il Changing T 25:19-20 O '71
Dividend raisers feel the chill. Bsns W p42-3 S 11 '71
Looking for income. C. Morgello. il Newsweek 78:79 S 20 '71
Miniwar over dividends; Nixon's call for dividend restraint. Time 98:24 S 20 '71
Revised rules on dividends. U S News 72: 30 Ja 3 '72
Rules on dividends; the official guidelines. U S News 71:20-1 N 29 '71
What lid on dividends means to stockholders in '72. il U S News 72:73-4 Ja 10 '72
See also
United States—Interest and dividends, Committee on

DIVIDERS, Room. See Partitions

DIVINE comedy. See Dante Alighieri

DIVINE healing. See Faith cure

DIVINE right of kings
Nuclear tyranny and the divine right of kings. G. E. Christianson. il Bul Atom Sci 27:44-6 Ja '71

DIVING
Ballet off the boards: U.S. girl divers, photographs by Neil Leifer; with account by W. F. Reed. Sports Illus 35:26-33 Ag 16 '71

DIVING, Submarine
Rugged world of the offshore diver. J. F. Pearson. il Pop Mech 135:68-71+ My '71
See also
Skin diving

Physiological aspects
One mile down. Sci Am 225:44 O '71
Study in depth; Pennsylvania experiment in deep diving chamber. Newsweek 78:60-1 S 6 '71

Safety devices and measures
See also
Life support systems (submarine environment)

DIVING apparatus
See also
Submarine vehicles

DIVING platforms, boards, etc.
Slip-proof diving deck plus storage. H. Wicks. il Pop Mech 136:132-5 Ag '71

DIVING test chambers. See Simulators

DIVINITY schools. See Theological seminaries

DI VIRGILIO, James
Our middle schools give the kids a break. il Todays Ed 60:30-2 Ja '71

DIVISION of powers. See Separation of powers

DIVOKY, Diane
New York's mini-schools. Sat R 54:60-1+ D 18 '71

DIVORCE
Amicable divorce; solemnizing the disolution of a marriage with a religious ceremony. M. M. Shideler. il Chr Cent 88:553-5 My 5 '71
High cost of executive divorce. T. J. Murray. il Duns 98:52-4+ O '71
See also
Children of divorced parents
Marriage
Marriage, Companionate
Separation (law)

California
California: is divorce without guilt working? B. Falconer. McCalls 98:41 Ap '71
Do-it-yourself divorce. Newsweek 78:71 N 8 '71

Dominican Republic
Divorce, Caribbean style; quickie divorces. il Time 98:43 Ag 30 '71

Italy
In no hurry. Newsweek 77:34+ F 1 '71
Undoing the Gordian knot. il Time 98:26 Jl 12 '71

United States
Liberty and disunion. B. A. Weisberger. il Am Heritage 22:22-5+ O '71

DIVORCE (canon law)
See also
Marriage—Annulment (canon law)

DIVORCEES
How divorced young mothers learn to stand alone. N. M. Lobsenz. il Redbook 138:83+ N '71

DIXIE 500. See Automobile racing

DIXON, Anthony S.
Chinese cucumbers as big as zucchini. il Org Gard & Farm 18:84-5 Jl '71

DIXON, Dave
But it looked like a great new racket; ed. by F. Deford. B. Briner. il Sports Illus 34:56-8+ Ap 19 '71 *

DIXON, Dean
Mirrors of our time; interview, ed. by R. Hemming. por Sr Schol 98:17 Mr 22 '71
about
Young people's concert; how not to win friends. Hi Fi 21:MA24 My 71 *

DIXON, Joseph K.
Gallery: photographs. Life 71:10-11 Jl 2 '71

DIXON, Ruth B.
Hallelujah the pill? il Trans-Action 8:44-9+ N '70

DIXON, Samuel
Embossed pictures of Samuel Dixon and his imitators. A. L. Leask. il Antiques 100:120-3 Jl '71 *

DJERASSI, Isaac
Pus bona et laudabile. S. Alsop. Newsweek 78:116 D 13 '71 *

DJILAS, Milovan
Girl with the gold tooth; story, tr. by L. Edwards. il Harper 242:87-90 Je '71
Q: do the claims of conscience outweigh the duties of citizenship? por Esquire 76: 156+ D '71

DMITRIEV, A.
Soviet space flights in 1970. Space World H-6-90:34-5 Je '71

DO-cao-Tri
Death of a fighting general. il por Time 97:21 Mr 8 '71 *
DO-it-yourself diagnosis. See Diagnosis
DO-it-yourself work
How to work with today's materials: plywood, acrylic plastic, concrete. il Bet Hom & Gard 49:48-51 Jl '71
100 ideas under $100. il Bet Hom & Gard 49:8+ Jl '71
DOAN, Herbert Dow
Industrialist looks at pollution. il por Chem 44:13-15 Ap '71
DOBBS, John Wesley
Crispus Attucks, one of America's first and noblest heroes. il por Negro Hist Bul 34: 55-6 Mr '71
DOBBS, Kildare
Dissertation on the beaver; excerpts from The great fur opera; with biographical sketch. il Natur Hist 80:4, 8+ Je '71
DOBBS, Ralph C. and Wall, Virginia
Contemporary learning needs participation training. Clear House 45:480-2 Ap '71
DöBEREINER, Johann Wolfgang
Doebereiner and the University of Jena; tr. by R. E. Oesper. W. Schütz. il pors Chem 45:10-11 Ja '72 *
DOBSON, Pamela
Little girl who shared my pregnancy. il por Redbook 137:23-4 Jl '71
DOBYNS, Stephen
Contingencies; When you're dancing, make the whole world dance with you; Taking a crack at it; poems. Poetry 117:385-7 Mr '71
Five poets. Poetry 392-8 Mr '71
DOC Savage (literary character) See Characters in literature
DOCK strikes (United States) See Strikes—United States—Maritime workers
DOCKING in space. See Orbital rendezvous
DOCKING of houseboats. See Houseboats—Handling
DOCKS
See also
Marinas
Ports
DOCTORATES. See Degrees, Academic
DOCTORS assistants. See Medical workers
DOCTRINAL theology. See Theology
DOCTRINE, Religious. See Theology
DOCUMENTARY films. See Moving pictures—Documentary films
DOCUMENTARY phonograph records. See Phonograph records—Documentary records
DOCUMENTARY photography. See Photography, Documentary
DOCUMENTARY television programs. See Television programs, Documentary
DOCUMENTATION
See also
American society for information science
DOCUMENTS
Overdue; laundry slips and primary documentation, sorting and discarding. K. M. Glazier. por Wilson Lib Bul 45:686-7 Mr '71
See also
Archives
Government publications
United States—National archives
DOCUMENTS expediting project. See United States—Library of Congress—Documents expediting project
DODD, J. L. See McCracken, D. A. jt. auth.
DODD, Thomas Joseph
Obituary
Nat R 23:629 Je 15 '71
DODD, William H.
Theological weather report from the mediating left. America 124:403-6 Ap 17 '71
DODGE, Anna (Thompson)
Selling the dredges; Dodge estate. il Newsweek 78:76-7 O 11 '71 *
DODGE, Grenville Mellen
Lincoln's other dream. T. Fleming. il Read Digest 98:134-9 Je '71 *
DODGERS (baseball) See Baseball clubs
DODGSON, Charles Lutwidge. See Carroll, L. pseud.
DODO
Everything you always wanted to know about the dodo. A. Bailey. il Horizon 13:92-3 Spr '71
DODSON, Roy E.
Pure water from sewage. il por Am City 86:43-4 F '71
DOEBEREINER, Johann Wolfgang. See Döbereiner, J. W.
DOEHRING, D. O. and Vierbuchen, R. C.
Cave development during a castastrophic storm in the Great Valley of Virginia. bibliog il Science 174:1327-9 D 24 '71

DOELL, Richard R. and Cox, A. V.
Pacific geomagnetic secular variation. bibliog il Science 171:248-54 Ja 22 '71
DOERGE, John Otto
Swinger who struck out. il por Bsns W p78+ Mr 13 '71 *
DOERR, Edd
What is a Catholic school? Ed Digest 36: 37-9 F '71
DOG breeding
Best of breed; army's German shepherd breeding program. il Newsweek 78:68 Jl 5 '71
Grouse and woodcock dog; breed your own. G. B. Evans. il Field & S 76:126+ Jl '71
DOG feeders. See Dogs—Food and feeding
DOG houses. See Kennels
DOG racing
Another fine madness; Michael Brennan, greyhound breeder and trainer. C. Gammon. il Sports Illus 35:50-6+ S 6 '71
DOG shows
At a dog show you watch dogs and you also can watch their owner-handlers. il Sunset 146:30-2 F '71
DOG stories. See Dogs—Stories
DOG training. See Dogs—Training
DOG trials. See Field trials (dogs)
DOGS
Another sort of love story; reminiscing about a pet's life after his death. L. Wainwright. Life 70:2B Ja 22 '71; Same abr. Read Digest 98:86-8 My '71
Cats & dogs & people. D. W. Ball. il Trans-Action 8:44-7 F '71
Day in the life of a top dog; Ch. De-Go Hubert. il Ladies Home J 88:60+ Je '71
Dissociation of impairment after lateral and medial prefrontal lesions in dogs. J. Dabrowska. bibliog il Science 171:1037-8 Mr 12 '71
Dogs. D. M. Duffey. See issues of Outdoor life
LBJ's best friend: the love story of a man & his dog. L. B. J. Nugent. il pors Ladies Home J 88:77-9+ Ap '71
Last will and testament of Silverdene Emblem O'Neill. E. G. O'Neill. il pors Look 35:39-40 Ap 20 '71; Same abr. Read Digest 99:193-4+ D '71
Life and times of Shag, a feral dog in Baltimore. A. M. Beck. il Natur Hist 80: 58-65 O '71
Niki, a real watch dog; automatic watch to govern activities. O. R. Hagans. il Hobbies 76:127 Mr '71
Nixon treats them like dogs; White House dogs. il Newsweek 79:13 Ja 3 '72
Of dogs; Jim, the wonder dog. R. Rhodes. il Harper 242:94-7 Ap '71; Reply. G. Green. 242:10+ Je '71
On cooling hot dogs. Chem 44:5 My '71
What even your best friend, the dog, won't tell you. R. Schoenstein. il Todays Health 49:50-3 Jl '71
Your dog: Dr Jekyll and Mr Hyde. L. W. Jackson. il Cons 26:30-1 D '71
See also
Bouviers des Flandres
Collies
Field trials (dogs)
Foxhounds
German shepherd dogs
Hounds
Hunting dogs
Pointers (dogs)
Watchdogs

Anecdotes, facetiae, satire, etc.
Arf, arf, and a hearty woof. J. Ferris. Sat R 54:6 Je 12 '71
It's a dog's life. E. Bombeck. Good H 174: 44+ Ja '72

Breeding
See Dog breeding

Food and feeding
Five minute dog feeder. T. Gauba. il Design 72:33 mid-Sum '71
Guide to: consumer's cat & dog foods. Mech Illus 67:64 S '71
What you should know about feeding your dog or cat. L. Coe. Read Digest 98:119-22 Mr '71

Kennels
See Kennels

Laws and legislation
Dog fight; anti-dog-pollution crusader. il Newsweek 77:95 Ap 12 '71

Photographs
See Animals—Photographs

DOGS—*Continued*

Poetry

Talking to dogs. W. H. Auden. Harper 242: 110 Mr '71

Purchasing

Pet news. H. B. Holt. Ladies Home J 88:62+ Jl '71

Stories

Why Lassie can't come home. Cyclops. il Life 71:11 O 29 '71

Training

Another fine madness; Michael Brennan, greyhound breeder and trainer. C. Gammon. il Sports Illus 35:50-6+ S 6 '71

Make your dog mind. D. M. Lidster. Bet Hom & Gard 49:22 D '71

Master's plan for springers. L. Mueller. il Field & S 76:178-80+ N '71

Old dogs as pup trainers? D. M. Duffey. il Outdoor Life 148:134+ Ag '71

Play versus discipline. J. J. Knap. il Field & S 76:184+ My '71

Training or heredity. D. M. Duffey. il Outdoor Life 147:144+ F '71

When your retriever refuses. G. B. Evans. il Field & S 75:220+ Ap '71

DOGS and children. See Children and animals

DOHERTY, Donald E.

Pitfalls in purchasing. il Todays Ed 60:60-1 Mr '71

DOHNANYI, J. S.

Flux of micrometeoroids: lunar sample analyses compared with flux model. bibliog il Science 173:558 Ag 6 '71

DOHRN, Bernardine

Bernardine Dohrn is weighed in the balance and found heavy. L. Van Gelder. il pors Esquire 75:164+ Ap '71 •

DOIG, Herbert E.

The hunting ethic. il Cons 26:15-16 O '71

DOIG, Ivan

Interracial adoptions: how are they working? il Parents Mag 46:62-5 F '71

Puget Sound's war within a war. il Am West 8:22-7 My '71

DOING well; story. See Aguallo, T.

DOIRON, Peter M.

Choice editor fired by ALA. Library J 96:2715 S 15 '71 •

Dismissal appealed. Am Lib 2:915 O '71 •

Editor of Choice fired. W. R. Eshelman. Wilson Lib Bul 46:5 S '71 •

Firing of Choice editor raises protest storm. Library J 96:3061 O 1 '71 •

Hearing for Doiron. J. Berry. Library J 96: 3931 D 1 '71 •

DOISNEAU, Robert

Gallery; photographs. Life 71:8-9 N 5 '71

DOKAS, Linda A. and Kleinsmith, L. J.

Adenosine 3′, 5′-monophosphate increases capacity for RNA synthesis in rat liver nuclei. bibliog il Science 172:1237-8 Je 18 '71

DOLAN, Anthony R.

Anger anyone? Nat R 23:1117 O 8 '71

DOLAN, Edwin

Why not sell the national parks? Nat R 23:362-5 Ap 6 '71

DOLAN, Thomas J. See Singer, J. W. jt. auth.

DOLBY noise reduction system. See Electronic noise; High fidelity sound systems—Noise

DOLE, Hollis Mathews

America's energy needs; address, January 12, 1971. Vital Speeches 37:322-7 Mr 15 '71

DOLE, Robert J.

Dole-ing it out; statements. por Time 97: 20+ My 31 '71

about

New faces. il por Newsweek 77:17-18 Ja 18 '71 •

DOLHINOW, Phyllis

At play in the fields. il Natur Hist 80:66-71 D '71

DOLIN, Irv

PM's coast-to-coast test: Pinto vs. Vega. il Pop Mech 135:76-80P Mr '71

DOLL carriages

Display of dolls and doll carriages. C. H. Fawcett. il Hobbies 75:41 F '71

DOLL clothes

Antique dolls' dressmaker. C. H. Fawcett. il Hobbies 75:44 Ja '71

DOLL hospital. See Dolls—Repairing

DOLL houses

Dream doll houses; Colleen Moore's and other doll houses. M. B. Karter. il Good H 173: 94-9+ D '71

Ganyard doll house. J. Miracle. il Hobbies 76:141+ S '71

Hobbies bridge the generation gap; Clyde Fulton family of Springfield, Mo. S. A. Parvin. il Hobbies 76:144-7 Je '71

New guardian of Mother Lark's miniatures. S. A. Parvin. il Hobbies 75:148-9 F '71

Renaissance of a Victorian doll house. S. Parvin. il Hobbies 76:144-5+ Jl '71

DOLLAR devaluation. See Money—United States

DOLLAR gap. See Balance of payments

DOLLHOUSES. See Doll houses

DOLLIVER, Barbara

Another language; poem. Good H 172:192 Mr '71

DOLLS

Dollology. C. H. Fawcett. See issues of Hobbies

Four fanciful dolls; made by hand. S. Purdy. il Ladies Home J 88:182 S '71

Hang on to your Schoenhuts. C. H. Fawcett. il Hobbies 76:40+ Je '71

Let oriental dolls enliven your collection. C. H. Fawcett. il Hobbies 76:41+ S '71

Lost dauphin of France. C. H. Fawcett. Hobbies 76:45+ Ag '71

Make one, two, or a dozen all different. il Sunset 147:54-7 D '71

Mechanical dolls. C. H. Fawcett. il Hobbies 76:90 Ja '72

Medicine dolls and primitive peoples. K. Severin. il Sci Digest 69:65-9 Je '71

Parian dolls. C. H. Fawcett. il Hobbies 76: 41 O; 41 N; 41 D '71

Sensuous doll. il Time 98:46 D 20 '71

She went through fire. J. F. Stack. il Hobbies 75:45 Ja '71

Some wooden dolls. C. H. Fawcett. il Hobbies 76:44 Ap; 42 My '71

Twenty years ago in the dollology department of Hobbies; reprint. A. Jacobsen. Hobbies 75:44 F '71

Exhibitions

Dawn: plastic doll at sixty-eighth annual American toy fair; creation of the Topper corporation. New Yorker 47:31-2 Mr 20 '71

Repairing

How to make money in your spare time: doll hospital. J. Kuh. il Ladies Home J 88:165 O '71

DOLL'S house; drama. See Ibsen, H.

DOLORES Hart, Mother. See Hart, D.

DOLPH, Carole

Macmillan executive victim of discrimination. Pub W 199:35-6 Je 7 '71 •

DOLPHIN fishing

Dolphin decoy. G. Heinold. il Outdoor Life 147:10+ Mr '71

DOLPHINS (football club) See Football clubs

DOLPHINS (mammals)

Computer derivation of some dolphin echolocation signals. R. A. Altes. bibliog il Science 173:912-14 S 3 '71

Dolphin spectacular. G. L. Beardsley, jr. il Sea Front 17:194-201 Jl '71

Domesticating porpoises. il Chem 44:4 My '71

Pity the poor porpoise. il Newsweek 75:60 S 6 '71

Shark vs porpoise. R. F. Burgess. bibliog il Sci Digest 69:36-40 Je '71

DOLSON, Charles H.

Charles H. Dolson of Delta air lines; interview. il pors Nations Bsns 59:50-3+ S '71

DOMAIN, Eminent. See Eminent domain

DOMAIN structure

Magnetic bubbles. A. H. Bobeck and H. E. D. Scovil. il Sci Am 224:78-90 Je '71

Magnetic world of bubble domains. D. E. Thomsen. il Sci N 99:318-19 My 8 '71

DOME stadium, New Orleans. See Stadiums

DOMES

Bubbles: newest thing in building! W. Langewiesche. il Read Digest 99:39-40+ Ag '71

Dome on the range, on the beach and in the bay. il Esquire 75:76-7 F '71

See also

Air-supported structures

Geodesic domes

DOMESTIC animals

See also

Dogs

DOMESTIC appliances. See Household appliances

DOMESTIC employees. See Household employees

DOMESTIC finance

Can you cut your fuel bill in half? F. Coffee. il Mech Illus 67:132-3+ N '71

Family money management. See issues of Better homes and gardens

DOOR to door selling. See Canvassing

DOORS
Modernize with bifolds and beautify your home. W. C. Leckey. il Pop Mech 136:134-7 S '71
Tell-tale portals. E. Cabral. Har Yrs 11:27 Je '71
See also
Garage doors

Maintenance and repair
Care & repair of aluminum doors & windows. il Mech Illus 67:115-16+ My '71

DOORS, Screen. See Screens (doors, windows, etc)

DOORYARD gardens. See Gardens

DOPA
Decrease in adrenal tyrosine hydroxylase and increase in norepinephrine synthesis in rats given L-dopa. W. Dairman and S. Udenfriend. bibliog il Science 171:1022-4 Mr 12 '71
L-Dopa. a brain pill? A. J. Snider. Sci Digest 69:56 F '71
L-Dopa disaggregation of brain polysomes and elevation of brain tryptophan. B. F. Weiss and others. bibliog il Science 173:833-5 Ag 27 '71
Melatonin and abnormal movements induced by L-dopa in mice. G. C. Cotzias and others. bibliog il Science 173:450-2 Jl 30 '71

DOPAMINE
Dopamine: release from the brain in vivo by amantadine. P. F. Von Voigtlander and K. E. Moore. bibliog il Science 174:408-10 O 22 '71
Dopamine-sensitive adenyl cyclase: possible role in synaptic transmission. J. W. Kebabian and P. Greengard. bibliog il Science 174:1346-9 D 24 '71
Dopamine: stimulation-induced release from central neurons. K. Y. Ng and others. bibliog il Science 172:487-9 Ap 30 '71
Inhibition of biogenic amine uptake by hydrogen peroxide: a mechanism for toxic effects of 6-hydroxydopamine. R. Heikkila and G. Cohen. bibliog il Science 172:1257-8 Je 18 '71
Possible etiology of schizophrenia: progressive damage to the noradrenergic reward system by 6-hydroxydopamine. L. Stein and C. D. Wise. bibliog il Science 171:1032-6 Mr 12 '71

DOPAMINE-β-hydroxylase. See Hydroxylases

DOPE smuggling. See Smuggling

DOPING in sports
Experiment in drugs at Santa Anita; legalizing Butazolidin for thoroughbreds. W. Leggett. il Sports Illus 34:18-19 Ja 25 '71
How speed kills athletic careers. W. B. Furlong. Todays Health 49:30-3+ F '71
It's not how you play the game, but what pill you take. J. Scott. il N Y Times Mag p40-1+ O 17 '71; Discussion. p6 N 14; 26 D 12 '71
On the track of doped horses. il Bsns W p85 S 18 '71
Sports: Get high on sports, not drugs. J. Scott. Ramp Mag 10:67-8 O '71

DORATI, Antal
Musician of the month. R. Lee. por Hi Fi 21: MA4-5 S '71 *

DORAZIO, Priscilla
Washoe County teachers association. Todays Ed 60:53 Ja '71

DORCHESTER COUNTY, S.C.
Victoria Delee, in her own words; interview, ed. by C. Trillin. V. Delee. New Yorker 47: 86+ Mr 27 '71

DORMAN, Chris
Art at auction. il por Sch Arts 71:48 Ja '72

DORMAN, Sonya
Construction site; poem. Sat R 54:38 F 20 '71

DORMANCY (plants)
Dormancy of trees in winter. T. O. Perry. bibliog il Science 171:29-36 Ja 8 '71
Motion-induced inhibition of elongation and induction of dormancy in liquidambar. P. L. Neel and R. W. Harris. bibliog il Science 173:58-9 Jl 2 '71; Reply. R. Turgeon and J A. Webb. 174:961-2 N 26 '71
When plants mark time. N. Smith. il Nat Wildlife 9:29 F '71

DORMITORIES
Away from home: three college girls talk about life in coed dorms. Seventeen 30: 102 Ag '71
Co-ed housing. J. Borger. il Todays Ed 60: 34-6 O '71
Contour dorms; State university college at Oneonta, N.Y. il Arch Forum 133:8 D '70
New dormitory for St Paul's school; Concord, N.H. il Arch Rec 149:115-18 Mr '71

DORRIEN, Tom
Love poem. Commonweal 95:326 Ja 7 '72

DORSEY, George
World's wasteful woodsmen. il Am For 77: 20-3+ Jl '71

DORST, Mary Crowe
Paper world of Mino. il Craft Horiz 31:50-1 Je '71

DORTECH, inc.
Parent firm seeks sale of Dortech. Aviation W 94:22 Ap 12 '71

DORYANTHES. See Spear lilies

DOS PASSOS, John
On the way to the moon shot. Nat R 23: 135-6 F 9 '71
Wizards meet; excerpts from The 42nd parallel. il por Am Heritage 22:96-7 Ap '71

about
John Dos Passos: a stranded American. M. Schorer. Atlan 227:93-6 Mr '71 *

DOSTOEVSKII, Fedor Mikhailovich
Double and Romans 7. B. Ramm. Chr Today 15:14+ Ap 9 '71 *

DOTY, Paul
Community of science and the search for peace; adaptation of address. April 26, 1971. Science 173:998-1002 S 10 '71

DOTY, Roy
Wordless workshop. See issues of Popular science monthly

DOTY, William L.
Leaders we need. il Cath World 214:124-7 D '71

DOUBLE coated adhesive tapes. See Adhesive tapes

DOUBLE cropping
Moisture supply is key to double-cropping. Suc Farm 69:no2 B14 F '71
Plant corn in standing wheat. B. Coffman. il Farm J 95:24-5 O '71
75 bu. sorghum; 40 bu. wheat same year. Suc Farm 69:38 N '71

DOUBLE standard in sexual ethics. See Sexual ethics

DOUBLE stars. See Stars, Double

DOUBLE taxation. See Taxation, Double

DOUBLEDAY and company
Doubleday acquires English rights to Nasser memoir. Pub W 200:233-4 Ag 30 '71
Doubleday entering commercial film production. Pub W 200:35 Ag 16 '71

DOUBROVSKA, Felia
In the shadow of Russian tradition; interview, ed. by M. Horosko. il pors Dance Mag 45:40-2 F '71
Pierre Vladimiroff; a memoir, ed. by M. Horosko. il pors Dance Mag 45:43-5 F '71

DOUCHING. See Woman—Health and hygiene

DOUGH, Frozen
Dough waits in your freezer. il Sunset 147:206 N '71

DOUGHERTY, Richard M.
Unserved: academic library style. il Am Lib 2:1055-8 N '71

DOUGHNUTS
Donuts 1,2,3! M. Happel. il Ladies Home J 88:94-5+ F '71
Morning call doughnuts. il Am Home 74: 88+ Mr '71

DOUGHTY, Paul L.
From disaster to development. il Américas 23:35-35 My '71

DOUGLAS, Boyd F. jr
Anachronisms of another day. W. R. Eshelman. Wilson Lib Bul 45:719 Ap '71 *
Berrigan informer. il pors Time 97:20 F 1 '71 *
How the kidnap conspiracy was hatched. L. Lockwood. il pors Life 70:30 My 21 '71 *
How to grab the brain child. il pors Time 97: 15-16 My 10 '71 *

DOUGLAS, Carlyle C.
Black politics in the new South. il Ebony 26: 27-30+ Ja '71

DOUGLAS, George H.
Dreiser's enduring genius. Nation 212:826-8 Je 28 '71

DOUGLAS, Gilean
Note to the free; poem. Cath World 212:253 F '71

DOUGLAS, J. D.
Ulster: normally abnormal. Chr Today 15:38-9 Je 18 '71

DOUGLAS, John R.
Classic recordings for a song. il por Library J 96:597-607 F 15 '71

DOUGLAS, Paul H.
Three saints in politics. Am Scholar 40:223-32 Spr '71

DOUGLAS, Philip A.
Washington report. Yachting 129:90 Mr '71

DOUGLAS, Russ
Complete guide to work gloves. il Mech Illus 67:86-8+ Jl '71
DOUGLAS, William Orville
C&O Canal becomes a park. il Nat Parks & Con Mag 45:4-8 My '71
Justice Douglas; no evidence to support impeachment. New Repub 164:13-14 Ja 2 '71 *
DOUGLAS-HAMILTON, Iain
Close in among the elephants. il Life 71:40-8 Ag 6 '71
DOUGLAS-HOME, Sir Alexander Frederick
Douglas-Home's oceanic policy. N. A. Sims. por(p481) Chr Cent 88:490-3 Ap 21 '71 *
Far from ideal. Newsweek 78:44+ D 6 '71 *
Having another go. il por Newsweek 78:37 N 29 '71 *
In civilized hands. il por Time 98:37 D 6 '71 *
DOUGLAS aircraft company. See McDonnell Douglas corporation
DOUGLASS, Suzanne
Gift lament; poem. Good H 172:44 F '71
DOULTON stoneware. See Pottery, English
DOVE shooting. See Mourning dove shooting
DOVER, N. H.
300 years on the same piece of land. il pors Life 71:44-53 S 17 '71
DOVES awards. See Phonograph records—Church music
DOW, Leona
Love remembered; poem. Good H 173:172 N '71
DOW, Richard Alan
Follow the fifers! il Travel 136:44-7+ Jl '71
DOW, Thomas E. jr
Population pressure in tropical Africa. bibliog f il Cur Hist 60:136-41+ Mr '71
DOW chemical company
Carl Gerstacker of Dow chemical co; interview. C. A. Gerstacker. por Nations Bsns 59:40-5 Jl '71
Dow cleans up pollution at no net cost. il Bsns W p32-5 Ja 1 '72
Dow spurs a factual approach to pollution. V. Louviere. il Nations Bsns 59:16 Ag '71
Learning from mistakes; Chilean venture. Newsweek 77:45+ My 3 '71

Rocky Flats division
Renovating Rocky Flats. D. Shapley. Science 174:1312 D 24 '71
Rocky Flats: credibility gap widens on plutonium plant safety. D. Shapley. Science 174:569-71 N 5 '71
DOW-Jones averages. See Stocks—Price indexes and averages
DOW Jones news service
Reuters hits Dow with Lightfoot Leo. il Bsns W p40 F 27 '71
DOWD, Douglas F.
Nixonomics. il Ramp Mag 10:13-16 N '71
Political economy of war. Nation 212:811-15 Je 28 '71
Watch out: prosperity is just around the corner (again) il Ramp Mag 9:34-9 Mr '71
DOWD, Merle E.
It protects the surface from six miles up! il Pop Mech 135:73-5+ Mr '71
DOWDEN, Hutchinson and Ross, Inc.
DH&R: new publisher of professional books. il Pub W 200:54 N 15 '71
DOWDY, John
Congressman convicted. por Time 99:13-14 Ja 10 '72 *
DOWEL joints. See Joints (carpentry)
DOWELL, Anthony
Carousel; photo essay. Dance Mag 45:38-9 Je '71 *
DOWELL, David R.
Overdue. il Wilson Lib Bul 46:79-80 S '71
DOWER, William J. See Lasek, R. J. jt. auth.
DOWLING, Harry Filmore
Prescribed environment; excerpt from Medicines for man. Sat R 54:58-60 Ap 3 '71
DOWLING, Tom
Orr effect. il Atlan 227:62-8 Ap '71
DOWNERS and séances; story. See Adler, R.
DOWNES, Mollie Panter-. See Panter-Downes, M.
DOWNIE, Leonard, Jr
Criminal court logjam; excerpts from Justice denied. Cur Hist 61:82-6+ Ag '71
DOWNIE, Mary Alice
(ed) See Gamsby, D. Dorothea's story, transcribed from her account
DOWNING, David
C. S. Lewis: apostle to the imagination. por Chr Today 16:10-12 O 8 '71
DOWNING, Sir George, bart
Placing a name. H. R. Mayes. Sat R 54:5 Ag 7 '71 *

DOWNING, Lewis
Legendary Concords. S. B. Duncan. il por Am West 8:16-17+ Ja '71 *
DOWNS, Anthony
Private investment and the public weal. il Sat R 54:24-6+ My 15 '71
Residential segregation: its effects on education. Ed Digest 36:12-15 Ap '71
DOWNS, G. S. and others
Mars radar observations, a preliminary report. bibliog il Science 174:1324-7 D 24 '71
DOWNS, Hugh
Hugh Downs to Frank McGee: the big switch on the Today show; interview, ed. by R. Ballad. pors Look 35:13-15 O 5 '71
Peace of mind. por Look 35:24 Jl 27 '71

about
Get up with Hugh Downs. J. Reddy. por Read Digest 98:45-6+ F '71 *
DOWNS, Joan
Black/white dating. il Life 70:56-67 My 28 '71
Her idea of grandeur is a home with a backyard. il Life 70:97 My 14 '71
New music man. il pors Life 71:41-2+ N 12 '71
DOWNS, Philip G.
Beethoven's new way and the Eroica. bibliog il Mus Q 56:585-604 O '70
DOWNS, Robert Bingham
(comp) Dean Downs on influential books. Wilson Lib Bul 45:921 Je '71

about
Robert B. Downs retires; with tribute by H. Goldhor. por Wilson Lib Bul 45:920-1 Je '71 *
DOWNSTATE medical center, Brooklyn. See New York (state). Downstate medical center
DOWNTON, David L.
Community discovers its past. il PTA Mag 65:18-20 Mr '71
DOWNTOWN areas. See Business districts
DOWTY, Leonhard
Wise father; poem. Good H 172:190 Je '71
Young girl's heart; story. Good H 173:92-3 D '71
DOYAL, Clyde
Paper sacks prove profitable. il por Am City 86:68-9 N '71
DOYLE, Adrian Conan
Case of the pig in the poke; estate of Sir Arthur Conan Doyle. il Forbes 107:36 Je 1 '71 *
DOYLE, Sir Arthur Conan
Sherlock Holmes and the second stain; dramatization. See Morley, O. J.

about
Case of the pig in the poke; estate of Sir Arthur Conan Doyle. il Forbes 107:36 Je 1 '71 *
DOYLE, Stephen E.
Permanent charter for Intelsat. Dept State Bul 65:415-18 O 18 '71
DOZIER, Carroll T. bp
Peace: gift & task; pastoral letter. Commonweal 95:289+ D 24 '71
DRABBLE, Margaret
Crossing the Alps; story. Mlle 72:154-5 F '71
DRACHKOVITCH, Milorad M.
Selling of the Soviet Pentagon. bibliog f il Nat R 23:694-6 Je 29 '71
DRACULA: Sabbat; drama. See Katz, L.
DRAFT, Military. See Military service, Compulsory
DRAFT lottery. See Military service, Compulsory
DRAFT resisters. See Military service, Compulsory—Draft resisters
DRAFTING instruments. See Drawing instruments
DRAG boat racing. See Motor boat racing
DRAG racing
AHRA grand American. R. Guldahl, jr. il Hot Rod 24:96-8 Mr '71
AHRA'$ point$ final$. J. Thawley. il Hot Rod 24:112-14 F '71
Bakersfield '71. R. Guldahl, jr. il Hot Rod 24:60-2 My '71
Complete guide to unracing; bracket racing. S. Green. il Hot Rod 24:86-7 D '71
Here come the street rods; second annual Street rod nationals. il Hot Rod 24:96-7 Jl '71
Making it; NHRA Summernationals. J. Dianna. il Hot Rod 24:50-4 O '71
NHRA nationals! il Hot Rod 24:90-1+ N '71
OCIR/Hang ten funny car 500. D. Wallace, jr. il Hot Rod 24:90-1 Ag '71

DRAG racing—*Continued*
Roddin' at random. See issues of Hot rod
'71 Gatornationals is here! R. Guldahl, jr. il
Hot Rod 24:30-3 Je '71
'71 pro stocks in action. il Hot Rod 24:96-8+
Je '71
'71 Winternationals. J. Dianna and others. il
Hot Rod 24:34-41 Ap '71
Street rod nationals scrapbook. il Hot Rod
24:117-24+ N '71
Supernationals. R. Guldahl, jr. il Hot Rod 24:
36-41 F '71
Three-alarm race; NHRA's '71 Springnation-
als. R. Guldahl, jr. il Hot Rod 24:46-50
S '71
    See also
National hot rod association

Accidents and injuries
Hot rod racing gallery; Jim Davis' wheelie-
flip at Bakersfield. il Hot Rod 24:52 Je '71

History
Original Ramchargers. J. Dianna. il Hot Rod
24:94-6 F '71

Australia
Meanwhile, in Australia. B. Thomas. il Hot
Rod 24:106 My '71

Canada
Grandnationals. il Hot Rod 24:66-7 N '71

South Africa
South Africa's Summernationals. J. Hadiaris.
il Hot Rod 24:116 Je '71
DRAG racing cars. See Automobiles, Racing
DRAG racing tires. See Tires, Automobile
DRAGON lizards. See Lizards
DRAIN cleaners
Chemical basis for a common type of drain
cleaner. C. H. Breedlove, jr. il por Chem
44:25 S '71
Differences in drain cleaners. Good H 173:6
Jl '71
Right drain cleaner. il Consumer Bul 54:
29-31 Ap '71
DRAINAGE
City-county drainage plans come first; Hous-
ton, Tex. L. Welch. il Am City 86:70+
Ag '71
Ways to get rid of water your crops don't
need. P. B. Jones. il Suc Farm 69:40-1 My
'71
    See also
Runoff
Storm sewers
Streets—Drainage
DRAKE, Betsy. See Grant, B. D.
DRAKE, Carol Christopher
Age in the mountains of November; poem.
Am Scholar 40:653 Aut '71
DRAKE, Eric
BP's embattled chairman. por Bsns W p79
D 11 '71 *
DRAKE, Gilbert
Quest for permit. il Field & S 75:64-5+ Ap
'71
    about
You never know when you might need a
mullet. C. Phinizy. il pors Sports Illus 34:
54-6+ Ap 5 '71 *
DRAKE, Jim, and Gersmehl, Glen
Salad days at the Pentagon. Commonweal 93:
485-6 F 19 '71
DRAKE, Robert
Deep in the interior and everything and all;
story. Chr Cent 88:159-61 F 3 '71
They cut her open and then just sewed her
back up. Chr Cent 88:288-9 Mr 3 '71
DRAMA
    See also
College and school drama
Dramatic criticism
Dramatists
Negro drama
Pantomime

Study and teaching
Don't put it down! A teacher's session with
Hair. J. Swift. Engl J 60:626-8 My '71
Electives in the English high school program:
drama and flexibility. L. Josephs. bibliog
Engl J 60:246-50 F '71
    See also
College and school drama
Shakespeare, W.—Study and teaching

Technique
5 ways to sell your play. S. Smiley. il Writers
Digest 51:22-5 D '71
Man of the theatre; writing Monkey mountain; interview. D. Walcott. New Yorker 47:
30-1 Je 26 '71

Themes
King heroin; Harlem play on destructive
effects of dope addiction in the black com-
munity. il Ebony 26:56-8+ Je '71
Man of the theatre; writing Monkey moun-
tain; interview. D. Walcott. New Yorker 47:
30-1 Je 26 '71
DRAMA and libraries. See Libraries and drama
DRAMA critics circle. See New York drama
critics circle
DRAMA festivals
Singing in the sun; Lincoln Center street
theater festival. J. Kroll. il Newsweek
78:73 S 6 '71
Summer repertory schedule, 1971; comp. by
H. Hewes. il Sat R 54:43 Je 26 '71
Theater; American college theater festival in
the Nation's capital. H. Hewes. Sat R 54:
65 My 1 '71
    See also
International festival of music and drama,
Edinburgh
New York Shakespeare festival
Shakespeare festivals
DRAMA in education. See Dramatization in
education
DRAMAS
Demolition downtown. T. Williams. il Esquire
75:124-7+ Je '71
Snake chief. B. S. Brown. Negro Hist Bul
34:70-1 Mr '71
    See also
Halloween—Drama
Polo, M.—Drama
Science fiction—Drama
Whitman, W.—Drama

Criticisms, plots, etc.
Broadway. Nat R 23:1129-30 O 8 '71
Goings on about town. See issues of New
Yorker
1971's ten best plays. Time 99:57 Ja 3 '72
Off Broadway. E. Oliver. See issues of New
Yorker
Right to quote; using reviews in book and
theater advertising; letter to the editor.
J. Weidman. Pub W 200:23 N 15 '71
Theater. See occasional issues of National
review
Theatre. H. Clurman. See issues of Nation
Theatre. B. Gill. See issues of New Yorker
Theater. H. Hewes. See issues of Saturday
review
Theatre. C. Hughes. See issues of America
Theater. S. Kauffmann. See occasional issues
of New republic
    See also
London—Theater

Single works
    See name of author for full entry
AC/DC. H. Williams
Abelard and Heloise. R. Millar
Acrobats. I. Horovitz
Alice in Wonderland. A. Gregory
All over. E. Albee
L'Amante Anglaise. M. Duras
And Miss Reardon drinks a little. P. Zindel
And they put handcuffs on the flowers. F.
Arrabal
And whose little boy are you? R. Parker
Antigone. Sophocles
Basic training of Pavlo Hummel. D. Rabe
Behold! Cometh the Vanderkellans. W. W.
Mackey
Bequest to the nation. T. Rattigan
Birthday party. H. Pinter
Black girl. J. E. Franklin
Black terror. R. Wesley
Les blancs. L. Hansberry
Caravaggio. M. Straight
Carpenters. S. Tesich
Commune. R. Schechner
Conduct unbecoming. B. England
Contractor. D. Storey
Cyrano de Bergerac. E. Rostand
Dance wi' me; or, The fatal twitch. G. An-
tonacci
Diary of a scoundrel. A. N. Ostrovskii
Doll's house. H. Ibsen
Dracula: Sabbat. L. Katz
Dream on Monkey Mountain. D. Walcott
L'école des femmes. See School for wives,
below
Effect of gamma rays on man-in-the-moon-
marigolds. P. Zindel
Enemy of the people. A. Miller
Fabulous Miss Marie. E. Bullins
Father's day. O. Hailey
Fingernails blue as flowers. R. Ribman
Four on a garden. P. Barillet and J. P.
Grédy
Gingerbread lady. N. Simon
Gun play. Y. Udoff
El Hajj Malik. N. R. Davidson, jr.

DREDGING
Out goes the silt! de-silting lakes of the Erie-Ohio Canal system. il Am City 86: 37 Ag '71
See also
Clearing of lakes, rivers, etc.

DREIFUS, Claudia
BOSS is watching. il Nation 212:102-8 Ja 25 '71
Selling of a feminist. Nation 212:728-9 Je 7 '71

DREISER, Theodore
Dreiser's enduring genius. G. H. Douglas. Nation 212:826-8 Je 28 '71 *
Homage to Theodore Dreiser, by R. P. Warren. Review
Sat R 54:30 S 4 '71. C. Fadiman *

DREISTADT, Roy
Dream your way to success. il Sci Digest 71: 12-17 Ja '72
Optical illusions, how one kind can cancel out another. il Sci Digest 69:10-14 F '71

DRELL, Sidney
Perl, Drell, York differ on SALT future. H. L. Davis. il pors Phys Today 24:57-9 Jl '71 *

DRENNEN, D. A.
More on Teilhard's spirituality. America 124:413-14 Ap 17 '71

DRESDEN
Music
Behind the scenes. P. Moor. il pors Hi Fi 21: 20+ Ap '71

DRESS. See Clothing and dress

DRESS accessories
See also
Belts

DRESS design. See Costume design

DRESS designers. See Costume designers

DRESSERS (tools)
Grinding-wheel dresser assures square edge. K. N. Thornton. il Pop Mech 135:165 Ap '71

DRESSING of game. See Game, Dressing of

DRESSING of game birds. See Game birds, Dressing of

DRESSING of poultry. See Poultry, Dressing of

DRESSING rooms, Theater
Dressing rooms. G. Shalit. il Ladies Home J 88:12+ My '71

DRESSMAKING
From tablecloth to skirt. N. O'Leary. il Ladies Home J 88:72-3+ Je '71
I made it myself! il Forbes 107:43-4 Ap 15 '71
Redbook sewing lesson:
How to gather skirts. il Redbook 136:64 Ap '71
How to set in sleeves. il Redbook 136: 118 F '71
How to sew fur fabrics. il Redbook 138: 137 N '71
How to sew knits. il Redbook 137:117 Je '71
Tips on fitting. il Redbook 137:185-7 S '71
Underlining. il Redbook 136:214 Mr '71
See also
Costume design
Sewing

DREVER, James I.
Magnesium-iron replacement in clay minerals in anoxic marine sediments. bibliog il Science 172:1334-6 Je 25 '71

DREW, Elizabeth Brenner
Added extra. il por Newsweek 78:74-5 D 13 '71 *
Reports & comment: Washington. See occasional issues of Atlantic

DREW, Isabella Milling, and others
Prehistoric domestication of animals: effects on bone structure. bibliog il Science 171:280-2, 172:972-3 Ja 22, My 28 '71

DREWINKO, B. and others
Functional sequences modulated by morphological transitions in human lymphoid cells grown in vitro. bibliog il Science 171:185-6 Ja 15 '71

DREWNOWSKI, Jan
Practical significance of social information. bibliog f Ann Am Acad 393:82-91 Ja '71

DREXLER, Rosalyn
Artists in the peanut gallery. il Sports Illus 34:78-80+ My 10 '71
Damn you, Gloria. por Harp Baz 105:111 D '71
200 years of North American Indian art. bibliog il Craft Horiz 31:30-9+ D '71

DREYFUS, Patricia Allen
Daniel Schwartz the realist's view. il por Am Artist 35:40-8+ My '71
Double vision of David Levine. il por Am Artist 35:34-9+ N '71
Robert McCall, illustrator. il por Am Artist 35:80-5+ Mr '71

DREYFUS, Pierre
Satisfied stockholder. il por Forbes 107:34+ Ap 1 '71 *

DREYFUS corporation
Dreyfus affair. Time 97:70 Ja 25 '71
Lion's roar. Newsweek 77:76 Ja 25 '71
Stein's salon. Newsweek 77:90+ Mr 22 '71

DRICKHAMER, Jewel
Rhode Island project: book reviews by older citizens. bibliog il por Library J 96:2737-43 S 15 '71

DRIED flowers. See Flowers, Dried

DRIED potatoes. See Potatoes, Dried

DRIFTING of continents. See Continental drift

DRIFTWOOD
Driftwood zoo. D. Meier. il Design 72:20-1 Spr '71

DRIGGS, Louise
From our kitchen; with recipes (title varies) See issues of Harvest years
Soups and stews the world over; excerpts. il por Har Yrs 11:35-8 Ap '71

DRILL chucks. See Chucks

DRILL press. See Drilling and boring machinery

DRILL sharpeners. See Sharpeners

DRILLING and boring (earth and rocks)
See also
Rock drills
Underwater drilling

DRILLING and boring machinery
Accessories that turn your electric drill into a workshop. R. J. De Cristoforo. il Pop Sci 199:112-14 N '71
How to get more from your drill. il Bet Hom & Gard 49:22 F '71
Mini drill press for hobbyists. J. R. Eyton. il Pop Mech 135:162-3 Mr '71
Portable electric drills. il Consumer Rep 36: 415-21 Jl '71
Turn your electric drill into a sharpener; grinder attachment. E. F. Lindsley. il Pop Sci 198:113 Mr '71
Two bits for problem jobs; multi-spur and Forstner bits. D. Warren. il Pop Sci 199: 106-7 O '71
Word for the electric drill: versatile. Sunset 146:128+ My '71
See also
Augers
Jigs

Testing
PM shop-tests AMT's radial drill press. W. C. Leckey. il Pop Mech 136:160-1+ S '71

DRILLING platforms. See Artificial islands

DRILLS (machinery) See Drilling and boring machinery

DRINAN, Robert Frederick
Drinan's Bay state volunteers. J. Higgins. Nation 211:648-52 D 21 '70 *
Roman collar in the House. C. Rabb. Commonweal 94:276 My 28 '71 *
TRB from Washington. New Repub 165:4 N 13 '71 *

DRINK question. See Alcoholism

DRINKING and airplane accidents
Follow me through; flying high. R. Blodget. Flying 89:27 O '71

DRINKING and traffic accidents
Drunk deterrent; experiment in Chicago. Newsweek 77:84+ Mr 1 '71
When drinking and driving mix. P. Ditzel. Read Digest 98:108-12 Ja '71

DRINKING customs
Drink; social drinking. A. Fraser. Mlle 73: 102 O '71

DRINKING vessels
Steins and other drinking vessels pictured on stamps. J. G. Lowenstein. il Hobbies 76:89-92 Jl '71

DRINKING water
See also
Water, Bottled
Water reuse

Standards
Is your drinking water safe? il Good H 172: 161 F '71

DRINKS. See Alcoholic beverages; Beverages

DRINNON, Richard
War on violence. bibliog il Wilson Lib Bul 45:68-77, 545 S '70, F '71

DRIONE. See Insecticides

DRISCOLL, Paul W.
Manager who works with Navajos. il por Bsns W p62 Mr 6 '71 *

DRISCOLL, Thomas F.
School around the calendar. il Am Ed 7:21-3 Mr '71

DRISCOLL, William J.
Rationale for independent study degree programs. bibliog Sch & Soc 99:411-13 N '71

DRIVE-in and curb service
See also
McDonald's corporation

DRIVER training courses. See Automobile driving—Study and teaching

DRIVERLESS car. See Computers—Automotive use

DRIVES (machinery) See Power transmission

DRIVEWAYS
Easy edging for blacktop drives; lay asphalt. il Bet Hom & Gard 49:28 Ap '71
Plan a low-upkeep entrance or driveway. H Mason. il Bet Hom & Gard 49:48-53 Mr '71

DRIVING, Automobile. See Automobile driving

DRIVING classes. See Automobile driving—Study and teaching

DRONE airplanes. See Airplanes, Drone

DROPOUTS
As college starts, there go the stop-outs. il Time 98:79 S 27 '71
Dropouts: prevention and cure. R. Theus. Clear House 46:95 O '71
Dropping out of school: problem or symptom? Sci N 100:310 N 6 '71
Employment of high school graduates and dropouts. A. M. Young. il Mo Labor R 94:33-8 My '71
Prescription for junior college dropouts. H. F. Landrith. bibliog Sch & Soc 99:49-51 Ja '71
School dropout problem in Cuba. L. Nelson. Sch & Soc 99:234-5 Ap '71
School dropouts question in Cuba. Sch & Soc 99:382-5 O '71
Second-chance academy; Christian action ministry academy. il Ebony 26:39-42 Ja '71
Ski bums' plight; unemployed college dropouts at Aspen and Vail, Colo. M. Kasindorf. il Newsweek 78:88+ D 20 '71
Time to fail; a time to succeed. C. Easton. il Parents Mag 46:44-5+ D '71
To "stay" with tax-supported love; project in St Louis. K. Marshall. il Am Ed 7:6-10 Ap '71

DROPS
Borderland of burning bubbles. D. C. Blanchard. il Sat R 55:60-3 Ja 1 '72
Water drop freezing: ejection of microdroplets. R. J. Cheng; reply with rejoinder. P. V. Hobbs. bibliog il Science 173:849-50 Ag 27 '71

DROSERA. See Sundews

DROSNIN, Michael
Ripping off, the new life style. il N Y Times Mag D 12-13+ Ag 8 '71

DROSOPHILA
Competition between species: frequency dependence. F. J. Ayala. bibliog il Science 171:820-4 F 26 '71
Genetic polymorphisms in varied environments. J. R. Powell. bibliog il Science 174:1035-6 D 3 '71
Increasing the multiplicity of ribosomal RNA genes in drosophila melanogaster. K. D. Tartof. bibliog il Science 171:294-7 Ja 22 '71
On-transient of insect electroretinogram: its cellular origin. A. A. Alawi and W. L. Pak. bibliog il Science 172:1055-7 Je 4 '71
Photosensitivity of the circadian rhythm and of visual receptors in carotenoid-depleted drosophila. W. F. Zimmerman and T. H. Goldsmith. bibliog il Science 171:1167-9 Mr 19 '71

DROST, Walter H.
ES '70s: the educational innovation of the 1970's? bibliog Sch & Soc 99:224-7 Ap '71

DROUGHT resistance of plants. See Plants—Drought resistance

DROUGHTS
Bitter harvest in the Southwest. il Bsns W p22 Ap 24 '71
Drought, land and ecology; Great Plains states. Sci N 99:316 My 8 '71
Drought returns to the land. C. Holden. Science 172:657 My 14 '71
In Florida, where Everglades are turning dry. il U S News 70:24 My 3 '71
Return of the dust bowl? il U S News 70:22-4 My 3 '71
Southwest bakes in a ruinous drought. il Life 70:26-31 Je 4 '71
See also
Dust storms

DROWNPROOFING. See Swimming—Safety devices and measures

DRUBOVI, Andy
Fold! Spindle! Mutilate! Nat R 23:1252 N 5 '71

DRUCKER, Daniel C.
Engineer in the establishment. Bul Atom Sci 27:31-4 D '71

DRUCKER, Peter F.
Peter Drucker attacks: our top-heavy corporations; interview, ed. by T. J. Murray. por Duns 97:38-41 Ap '71
Saving the crusade. il Harper 244:66-71 Ja '72
Surprising seventies. il Harper 243:35-9 Jl; 7-8 S '71; Same abr. Read Digest 99:49-52 S '71; Same with title What surprises, if any, for the seventies? Cur 134:56-64 N '71
What we can learn from Japanese management. Harvard Bsns R 49:110-22 Mr '71
about
Principles of the unprincipled. P. Caws. New Repub 165:28-31 S 11 '71 •

DRUCKER-COLIN, R. R. and others
Anemia in sleep-deprived rats receiving anticoagulants. bibliog il Science 174:505-7 O 29 '71

DRUG abuse
Drug abuse: a challenge to U.S.-Turkish cooperation in the seventies; address, December 14, 1970. H. R. Wellman. Dept State Bul 64:140-6 F 1 '71
Drug abuse; address, September 14, 1971. A. Linkletter. Vital Speeches 38:22-5 O 15 '71
Drug abuse: now it's downers. il U S News 71:44 D 27 '71
Drug bust in Kansas. T. Miller. Chr Cent 88:332-3 Mr 17 '71
Drug scene. S. Cohen. il PTA Mag 65:20-3 Ja '71
Drug scene, has it changed? with study-discussion program, by C. Smallenburg and H. Smallenburg. D. L. Farnsworth; D. H. Powelson; M. Brown. bibliog il PTA Mag 66:2-5, 34-5 D '71
Drugged Americans: aspirin-poppers not spared. Sci N 101:7-8 Ja 1 '72
Drugs and drinking in the business world; interview. H. Johnson. por U S News 70:70-3 Mr 22 '71
Drugs & us. M. Mead. Harp Baz 104:130-1+ Mr '71
How 10 cities fight drugs. G. Astor and I. Mothner. Look 35:73-4+ F 23 '71
My view of drug use, and drug abuse. B. Spock. Redbook 136:29+ Ap '71
Preventing drug abuse in children. B. Spock. bibliog Redbook 137:36+ My '71
Women and drugs (title varies) C. D. Chambers and D. Schultz. il Ladies Home J 88:130-1+ N; 66+ D '71
See also
Marijuana
Bibliography
Drug abuse: where to find the facts. S. Sierra. il Todays Health 49:57-8 Mr '71
Road to nowhere: drug abuse. C. Leibenguth. il Library J 96:587-92 F 15 '71

DRUG abuse fund. See United Nations fund for drug abuse control

DRUG abuse prevention, Special action office for. See United States—Drug abuse prevention, Special action office for (proposed)

DRUG addicts. See Narcotic addicts

DRUG allergy
Diseases you can get from medicines. J. D. Wassersug. il Sci Digest 69:80-4 Je '71
Penicillin allergy test developed. A. J. Snider. Sci Digest 69:55-6 Je '71
Penicillin news. E. Stukane. McCalls 98:40 Mr '71
R for penicillin. il Newsweek 77:70 F 15 '71

DRUG and hospital employees union (local 1199)
New York, N.Y.; the East River project. il Arch Forum 134:42-5 My '71
Revolt of the hospital workers. il Ebony 26:53-6+ Mr '71

DRUG education. See Narcotics education

DRUG help line. See Telephone in counseling

DRUG-induced diseases. See Drugs—Physiological effects

DRUG industry
Mental health industry: this way lies madness. A. Kopkind and J. Ridgeway. il Ramp Mag 9:38-44 F '71
Pharmaceuticals: valley of the lies. H. Gewirtz and S. Graham; reply. S. N. Whitney. Trans-Action 8:15 F '71
See also
Abbott laboratories
International chemical and nuclear corporation
Lilly, Eli, and company
Searle, G. D. and company
Sterling drug, inc.

DRUG industry—*Continued*

Advertising
Drug advertising and perception of mental illness; with reply by G. Usdin. R. Seidenberg. bibliog Ment Hy 55:21-34 Ja '71
Over-medicated woman. R. H. Berg. il McCalls 98:67+ S '71

Consolidations and mergers
Health market gets a new giant; Parke-Davis/Warner-Lambert merger. il por Bsns W p38-9+ F 20 '71

Italy
Drug company stays at home; Carlo Erba sale to Montecatini-Edison. Bsns W p40 N 27 '71
Italian drugs lose their kick. Bsns W p62+ My 15 '71

Switzerland
See also
Hoffman-La Roche, F, and company

DRUG interactions in the body. See Drugs—Physiological effects

DRUG laws and legislation
How safe is your food? interview. C. C. Edwards. il por U S News 70:50-4 Ap 19 '71
Some medicines you may want to avoid; FDA list of ineffective drugs. Consumer Rep 36:114-17 F '71
Spotlight on pot. Sr Schol 98:16-17 Mr 1 '71
Vindication of John Bricker; Vienna protocol treaty giving U.N. authority over control of psychotropic drugs in U.S. J. Kaplan. Nat R 23:1413-14 D 17 '71
See also
Narcotic laws
United States—Food and drug administration

DRUG metabolism. See Drugs—Metabolism

DRUG research. See Pharmaceutical research

DRUG testing. See Drugs—Testing

DRUG trade. See Drug industry

DRUGS
More drugs to think twice about; FDA list of possibly effective drugs. Consumer Rep 36:180-1 Mr '71
Prescribed environment; excerpt from Medicines for man. H. F. Dowling. Sat R 54: 58-60 Ap 3 '71
Some medicines you may want to avoid; FDA list of ineffective drugs. Consumer Rep 36:114-17 F '71
See also
Antacids
Barbiturates
Cocaine
Doping in sports
Fertility drugs
Medicines, Patent, proprietary, etc.
Narcotic antagonists
Narcotics
Pharmacogenetics
Prescriptions
Psychopharmacology
Tranquilizing drugs
United States—Food and drug administration
also names of drugs, e.g. Methadone

Advertising
See Drug industry—Advertising

Laws and legislation
See Drug laws and legislation

Metabolism
How genes control drugs. J. L. Arehart. il Sci N 99:438-9 Je 26 '71
System measures your drug reaction. il Sci Digest 70:14-15 Jl '71

Physiological effects
Alcoholism, alcohol, and drugs. E. Rubin and C. S. Lieber. bibliog il Science 172: 1097-102 Je 11 '71
Diseases you can get from medicines. J. D. Wassersug. il Sci Digest 69:80-4 Je '71
Drug interactions in a pill-popping age. il Sci N 99:365-6 My 29 '71
Growing health menace of drug interactions il Good H 172:191 My '71
Pot, pills and the pill: how they affect your skin, hair and health. Mlle 73:254-5 Ag '71
What childbirth drugs can do to your child. T. B. Brazelton. il por Redbook 136:65+ F '71

Prices
Buying drugs; question of posting prices. New Repub 166:13 Ja 1 '72
Prescription prices lose their mystery. Bsns W p21-2 D 18 '71

Psychological effects
Over-medicated woman. R. H. Berg. il McCalls 98:67+ S '71
Pills for classroom peace? E. T. Ladd. Ed Digest 36:1-4 F '71
Using drugs in classrooms. N. Hentoff. Cur 126:40-5 F '71
See also
Antidepressants
Hallucinogenic drugs
Psychopharmacology

Research
See Pharmaceutical research

Side effects
See Drugs—Physiological effects

Testing
Technology gap in health: it has to be closed; address, June, 1971. J. L. Pettis. Vital Speeches 37:693-6 S 1 '71

DRUGS, Experimental
Technology gap in health: it has to be closed; address, June, 1971. J. L. Pettis. Vital Speeches 37:693-6 S 1 '71

DRUGS and athletes. See Doping in sports

DRUGS and youth. See Narcotics and youth

DRUGS in feeds. See Feeding and feeding stuffs—Medicated feed

DRUGSTORES
See also
Eckerd, Jack, corporation
Osco drug, inc.

DRUKKER, Leendert
How to choose a projector like an expert. il Pop Phot 68:104-5+ Ja '71
Texture screens: back again. il Pop Phot 68:86-7+ Ap '71

DRUM language
Talking drums of Africa. J. E. Carrington. il Sci Am 225:90-4 bibliog(p 120) D '71

DRUMELLER, Carl C.
Electronics bookshelf. il Pop Electr 35:48-51 D '71

DRUMM, Thomas E. Jr
Fastest scissors in the East? V. Louviere. por Nations Bsns 59:17 D '71 •

DRUMMOND, Gerard
Day in the life of Riverside park. America 125:265 O 9 '71

DRUMMOND, John D.
More solid-state electronics for the new cars. il Pop Electr 1:63-7 Ja '72

DRUNKENNESS. See Alcoholism

DRUNKENNESS testing. See Alcohol in the body

DRURY, Allen
Inside the White House 1971; excerpts from Courage and hesitation. il pors Look 35: 32-42+ O 19 '71
No more tears; story. Good H 172:82-3 F '71

about
Story behind the book: Courage and hesitation. A. H. Johnson. il por Pub W 200:22-3 O 25 '71 •

DRURY, Michael
Mirror, mirror; poem. Good H 173:186 Jl '71
Silence, please; poem. Good H 173:36 D '71
This glorious feeling! Could it be middle age? il Ladies Home J 88:84+ My '71

DRUSKA, John
St Nicholas day; poem. America 125:558 D 25 '71

DRY cell batteries. See Electric batteries

DRY cleaning. See Cleaning

DRY farming
Texas farmers on the organic trail. F. Allen. il Org Gard & Farm 18:106-12 N '71

DRYDEN, Harold E.
Camellias in the landscape. il Horticulture 49:28-9+ D '71

DRYDEN, Ken
Banned in Boston, knighted in Montreal; interview. ed. by J. Olsen. il Sports Illus 35:45-6+ O 18 '71

about
Four-story goalie. il por Newsweek 77:62 My 17 '71 •

DRYER, Stan
Serving up a new game of life. il Sports Illus 34:46-8+ Ap 26 '71

DRYERS. See Clothes dryers

DRYING
See also
Photography—Drying (films and prints)

DRYING (crops)
See also
Corn—Drying
Grain—Drying
DRYOPITHECUS. See Apes, Fossil
D'SOUZA, Jerome
Indira's triumph. il America 124:400-3 Ap 17
'71
DUBAY, Thomas
Renewal: testing the assumptions. America
125:124-6 S 4 '71
DUBČEK, Alexander
Dubcek, by W. Shawcross. Review •
Sat R 54:22-3 Je 26 '71. E. Loebl •
Parting shots; streetcar named disgrace. il
pors Life 70:99-100 My 14 '71 •
DUBLIN
Art
Dublin muslin; opening of Rosc. New Yorker
47:45 N 6 '71
Description
Delights of Dublin. M. Gough. House B 113:
9-10 Ag '71
Irish eyes are still smiling in Dublin. Bsns W
p81 N 27 '71
DU BOFF, Richard B.
Nixon's power play.   Commonweal   95:86-7
O 22 '71
Nixon's secret plan: the budget. Common-
weal 93:543-5 Mr 5 '71
DU BOIS, Donald
Are you up on hounds? questions and an-
swers. Outdoor Life 147:188-9 Mr '71
How are you on archery? questions and an-
swers. Outdoor Life 148:82-4 S '71
DUBOIS, Eugene E. See Frankie, R. J. jt.
auth.
DUBOIS, Graham. See Dubois, H. G.
DUBOIS, H. Graham
Huckleberry Finn; dramatization of a story
by Mark Twain. Plays 30:71-80 Ap '71
Room for a King; drama. Plays 31:13-22, 44
D '71
DUBOIS, L. Clayton
Education of freshman Senator Buckley. il
pors N Y Times Mag p8-9+ Ag 15 '71
Is he really serious about becoming presi-
dent? Yes. il pors N Y Times Mag p26-7+
My 2 '71
DU BOIS, William Edward Burghardt
Quadroon; poem. Negro Hist Bul 34:116 My
'71
Song of the smoke; poem. Negro Hist Bul
33:193 D '70
about
Cheer the lonesome traveler. by L. A. Lacy.
Review
Chr Cent 88:888 Jl 21 '71. F. Herzog •
Prophet unheard. P. S. Prescott. por News-
week 78:75+ Ag 23 '71 •
Souls of black folk: a comparison of the
1903 and 1952 editions; address, October,
1970. H. Aptheker. por Negro Hist Bul 34:
15-17 Ja '71 •
DUBOS, Rene Jules
Despairing optimist. See issues of American
scholar
Is man over adapting to his environment?
Cur 128:34-9 Ap '71
Prophet of optimism; summary of statements,
ed. by A. Anderson. por Time 97:51 My 31
'71
Toxic factors in enzymes used in laundry
products. il Science 173:259-60 Jl 16 '71
Ways to save this fair and sweet land.
Vogue 158:52-3+ Ag 15 '71
about
En garde, pessimists! Enter Réné Dubos.
J. Culhane. il pors N Y Times Mag p44-6+
O 17 '71 •
DUBROVSKA, Fella. See Doubrovska, F.
DUBUFFET, Jean
Jean Dubuffet's landscape for trolls and
ogres. S. Hunter. il pors Vogue 157:62-5+
Ja 15 '71 •
DUC, Ngo-cong-. See Ngo-cong-Duc
DUCHAMP, Marcel
Marcel Duchamp; interview, ed. by P. Ca-
banne; excerpt from Dialogues with Mar-
cel Duchamp. Am Scholar 40:273-83 Spr '71
about
Art world. H. Rosenberg. New Yorker 47:
147-53 O 16 '71 •
DUCHAN, Linda. See Lewin, A. Y. jt. auth.

DUCHÊNE, Françoise
New European defense community. For Af-
fairs 50:69-82 O '71
DUCHENNE dystrophy.   See   Dystrophy,
Muscular
DUCHESS apples. See Apples
DUCK, Harvey
Great muskie hunt. il Field & S 75:58-9+
F '71
DUCK as food. See Cookery—Poultry
DUCK blinds
There's a picture window in my muskrat
house. F. A. Heidelbauer. il por Nat Wild-
life 9:44-6 Ag '71
DUCK decoys. See Decoys (hunting)
DUCK shooting
Duck hunting tips. L. Kreh. il por Pop Mech
136:113 D '71
Ducks from a red canoe. J. B. Robinson. il
Outdoor Life 148:64-5+ O '71
Free-for-all ducks. E. A. Bauer. il Outdoor
Life 148:34-7+ D '71
Northerns are in. N. Strung. il Field & S 76:
52-3+ N '71
Time to pick up the decoys. R. Cave. Sports
Illus 35:41 D 13 '71
DUCKBOAT building. See Boatbuilding
DUCKBOATS. See Boats and boating
DUCKS, Wild
Flitting ghosts of pleasures past: paintings
by F. Golden with account by R. Cave.
Sports Illus 35:36-41 D 13 '71
Mallards by the numbers. U. B. Henderson.
il Outdoor Life 147:48-9+ Ja '71
See also
Duck shooting
DUCKWORTH, Brian
English Free churches in the melting pot.
Chr Cent 88:340-2 Mr 17 '71
DUDDINGTON, John W.
Red herring of the three-story universe. Chr
Today 16:13-14+ N 5 '71
DUDDLESON, William
Miracle of Point Reyes. il Liv Wildn 35:
15-24 Sum '71
DUDE ranches. See Ranch life
DUDIS, Ellen Kirvin
Isadora Duncan at the Parthenon; poem.
Nation 213:597 D 6 '71
DUDLEY, Grace (Kolin) Ward, countess of
House of Grace, countess of Dudley, in Nas-
sau. V. Lawford. il por Vogue 157:142-7+
Mr 1 '71 •
DUDMAN, Richard
Captivity on the promo circuit. New Repub
165:27-8 Jl 24 '71
Waiting for that visa to China. New Repub
165:17-19 Jl 3 '71
DUE process of law
Due process behind prison walls. M. O.
Tobriner. Nation 213:367-9 O 18 '71
DUELING
Pistols for two. C. Worman. il Hobbies 76:
154-5 Ja '72
DUELING pistols. See Pistols
DUFAULT, Peter Kane
At Vera Frost's pony farm; poem.   New
Yorker 47:28 Ja 1 '72
DUFF, Edward
Bearing the burden of the Berrigan brothers.
New Repub 164:18-23 Mr 6 '71
DUFFETT, John
Instant rubber for boat repairs. Motor B & S
128:74+ O '71
DUFFEY, David Michael
Dogs. See issues of Outdoor life
DUFFEY, Richard
All; poem. Cath World 213:216 Ag '71
DUFFY, F. H. and Burchfiel, J. L.
Somatosensory system: organizational hier-
archy from single units in monkey area 5.
bibliog il Science 172:273-5 Ap 16 '71
DUFFY, Martha
Triumph of a tormented poet. il pors Life
71:38A-38B N 12 '71
DUGGAN, Bill
Basics of expanding any room. il Mech Illus
67:115-17+ Ja '71
Uplift for a sagging chair. il Mech Illus 68:
92-3 Ja '72
DUGGAN, Esther Zemborain de Torres
Dialogue for understanding. pors Américas
23:12-15 Mr '71
DUGGER, Ronnie
John Connally; Nixon's new quarterback.
Atlan 228:82-6+ Jl; 45 O '71
DUGUID, Sandra
Resolution; poem. Chr Today 15:16 Mr 26 '71
DUING, Walter, and Johnson, Donald
Southward flow under the Florida current.
bibliog il Science 173:428-30 Jl 30 '71

DUKE, Charles R.
Questions teachers ask: by-passes or thru-ways? Clear House 45:468-72 Ap '71

DULLES, Avery
Hans Küng's Infallible? The theological issues. America 124:427-8 Ap 24 '71

DULLES, John Foster
Which way America? Dulles always knew; ed. by J. Fenton. R. D. Challener. il pors Am Heritage 22:12-13+ Je '71 •

DULLES international airport. See Washington, D.C.—Airports

DULUTH, Minn.

Anecdotes, facetiae, satire, etc.

Untold delights of Duluth; address, January 27, 1871, ed. by D. G. McCullough. J. P Knott. il por Am Heritage 22:76-80 Je '71

DUMAS, Henry
Inner world where poets wander. J. Kessler. Sat R 54:50 O 2 '71 •

DU MAURIER, Daphne
My love affair with Crete. il Holiday 49:68-9+ Mr '71
Shock of recognition; story; excerpt from Don't look now. Ladies Home J 88:70-1 Ag; 114-15+ S '71

about

Daphne du Maurier, romantic. por Ladies Home J 88:102 Ag '71 •

DUMB. See Deaf-mutes

DUMBBELLS. See Exercising equipment

DUMOND, D. E.
Early racial and cultural identifications in southwestern Alaska; reply. bibliog Science 171:88-90 Ja 8 '71

DUMONT, Matthew P.
Down the bureaucracy! Trans-Action 7:10-12+ O '70

DUMP trucks. See Motor trucks

DUMPING (commercial policy)
Glass makers get a break; anti-dumping duties on Japanese glass imports. Bsns W p 109+ Ap 17 '71
Japanese face suit for dumping TV sets. Bsns W p68 Mr 20 '71
One-way street; trade between U.S. and Japan. il Forbes 107:15-16 My 1 '71

DUMPLINGS
Dumplings for dessert. il Farm J 95:62 Mr '71
Dumplings in the soup are Jewish matzo balls. il Sunset 147:232 O '71

DUN, Angus, bp
Obituary
Chr Cent 88:995 Ag 25 '71

DUNAWAY, Faye
Classic modern setting for a fascinating woman. il pors House & Gard 140:60-3 Jl '71 •

DUNAWAY, Vic
Better way to master marlin. il Field & S 76:66-7+ My '71

DUNBAR, Ernest
Black-on-white TV. il Look 35:31 S 7 '71
For men only: foolproof birth control. Look 35:45-6+ Mr 9 '71
Lost black leader. Look 35:76 Ap 20 '71
Rev Jesse Jackson a new kind of black cat. il pors Look 35:16-20 O 5 '71
Sweet appeal of James Taylor. il Redbook 137:75+ Je '71

DUNBAR, Geoffrey
Librarian and/or citizen? por Library J 97:42-3 Ja 1 '72

DUNBAR, Wilbur
Home is down the road. il Américas 23:32-6 Mr '71

DUNCAN, Barbara
Joaquin Torres-Garcia. il pors Américas 22:11-18 N '70

DUNCAN, David Douglas
Gallery; photographs. Life 71:8-11 S 17 '71

about

Letter from the publisher. il por Time 98:11 N 1 '71 •
Seized movement; retrospective show. il por Time 98:54-7 S 20 '71 •

DUNCAN, Isadora
Flowers in the garland of Sappho. D. Hering. il pors Dance Mag 45:28-33 F '71 •
Real Isadora, by V. Seroff. Review
Dance Mag 45:110 N '71. M. Marks •

DUNCAN, Lois
Cry from the heart: story. il Good H 173:78-9 Ag '71
Song for my mother. Good H 173:150 Jl '71
Using an original formula. Writer 84:11-12+ N '71
Woman alone; poem. Good H 172:210 Ap '71

DUNCAN, S. Blackwell
Legendary Concords. il por Am West 8:16-17+ Ja '71

DUNCAN, Sandy
Exciting new TV star goes into orbit. M. Davidson. il por Good H 173:102-3+ N '71 •
On location; interview, ed. by E. Miller. por Seventeen 30:72+ S '71
Show-stealer against the odds. Cyclops. por Life 71:8 N 26 '71 •

DUNCAN, Vera
Easter eggs: their history and variety. il Hobbies 76:49-50+ Ap '71
Valentines. il Hobbies 75:48-9+ F '71

DUNCAN, William
Alaska's apostle. G. D. Everett. Chr Today 15:36 Ag 6 '71 •

DUNCAN Phyfe furniture. See Furniture, American

DUNCANSON, Dennis J.
Whither Indochina? Cur Hist 61:345-9+ D '71

DUNDON, R. W. and Hafner, S. S.
Cation disorder in shocked orthopyroxene. bibliog il Science 174:581-3 N 5 '71

DUNE buggies
Come Josephine in my buggy machine; dune buggies. il Holiday 48:46-7 N '70
Return of the Kubelwagen. W. Wyss. il Motor T 23:76 Jl '71

DUNFEE, Maxine
Investigating children's science learning. Ed Digest 36:34-7 Ja '71

DUNGAN family
Dungan coat-of-arms. H. K. Eilers. il Hobbies 76:158 D '71

DUNHAM, David W.
Occultation highlights (cont) il Sky & Tel 41:327; 42:184; 43:54-6 My, S '71, Ja '72

DUNLOP, Dick
Many faces of Mexico. il Nat Wildlife 10:44-7 D '71

DUNLOP, John T.
Phase II gets the Dunlop touch. por Bsns W p23 O 2 '71
Wage freeze in construction. por Bsns W p94 N 20 '71 •

DUNLOP, Richard
Instant replay: TV's electronic magic. il Pop Mech 136:108-12+ N '71

DUNN, Betty
Family of his own. il Life 71:130-8 D 17 '71
Lid comes off the box. il Life 70:43-6 Ap 2 '71
Socrates of the ironing board. il pors Life 71:66+ O 1 '71

DUNN, Bob
King features syndicate. J. Markow. Writers Digest 51:18-19 My '71 •

DUNN, David J.
Education of Dave Dunn. por Forbes 108:58-60 N 1 '71 •

DUNN, Diana R.
1970: urban recreation and park...data bench mark year. il por Parks & Rec 6:32-7+ F '71
White House conference on children. il Parks & Rec 6:25-8+ Mr '71

DUNN, Harold
Science gives me joy-feels all over. il Sci Digest 69:30-3 Je '71

DUNN, J. R. and others
Paleomagnetic study of a reversal of the earth's magnetic field. bibliog il Science 172:840-5 My 21 '71

DUNN, John
Tennis. il Sports Illus 34:58-9 F 15 '71

DUNN, Stephen
To the upright; poem. New Repub 164:27 F 27 '71

DUNNE, D. Michael
It's a breed, it's a strain, it's superchicken! il Farm J 95:19 N '71

DUNNE, Finley Peter
Mr Dooley on The Hague conference, 1907. Am Heritage 22:6 F '71

DUNNE, George H.
To hell and gone. il America 125:224-7 O 2 '71

DUNNE, Jim
Detroit report. See issues of Popular science monthly

DUNNE, John Gregory
To die standing: Cesar Chavez and the Chicanos. por Atlan 227:39-45 Je; 228:36 S '71
—See Didion, J. jt. auth.

DUNNEBACKE, T. H. and Schuster, F. L.
Infectious agent from a free-living soil amoeba, naegleria gruberi. bibliog il Science 174:516-18 O 29 '71

DUNNING, Harrison F.
Dunning of Scott paper. por Forbes 107:192 My 15 '71 •

DUNNING, John S.
Camera for the birds; excerpt from Portraits of tropical birds. il Américas 23:14-17 O '71

DUNOVAN, Cass
Growing up; story. Good H 173:124-5 N '71

DUN'S (periodical)
Dun's all over; re-publication of Dun's articles. Duns 97:3 My '71
Dun's newest faces. Duns 98:3 N '71

DUNSON, William A.
Sea snakes are coming; with biographical sketch. il Natur Hist 80:4, 52-61 N '71
—and others
Sea snakes: an unusual salt gland under the tongue. bibliog il Science 173:437-41 Jl 30 '71

DUNSTAN, William M. See Ryther, J. H. jt. auth.

DUNTON, Theodore Watts-. See Watts-Dunton, T.

DUODENAL ulcers. See Peptic ulcers

DUONG-van-Minh
Diem document. il por Time 98:29 Ag 2 '71 •
Letter from Saigon. R. Shaplen. New Yorker 47:96+ S 11 '71 •
Mudslingers. il por Newsweek 78:38 Ag 2 '71 •
South Viet Nam: two against Thieu. il pors Time 98:22+ Jl 26 '71 •

DUPIK, Vasily
Soviet space man's menu. Space World H-12-96:42+ D '71

DU PIN GOUVERNET, Henriette Lucie (Dillon) marquise de la Tour. See La Tour du Pin Gouvernet, H. L. D. de

DUPLAN corporation
Bloom is off. il Forbes 108:52-3 O 1 '71

DU PLESSIX, Francine
Theatre. il Vogue 157:126 Ap 15 '71

DUPLEX apartments. See Apartments

DUPONT, F. I, Glore Forgan and company
Big board bows to Perot. Bsns W p22 My 8 '71
How Perot operates duPont, Glore Forgan. il Bsns W p72-3 O 2 '71
Poker game that Ross Perot won. por Bsns W p72-4+ Mr 27 '71
Ross Perot moves in on Wall Street. A. M. Louis. il por Fortune 84:90-3+ Jl '71
Waiting for Perot. Newsweek 78:94+ D 6 '71

DU PONT, Henry Francis, Winterthur museum. See Henry Francis du Pont Winterthur museum

DU PONT, Pierre Samuel, 1870-1954
Pierre S. du Pont and the making of the modern corporation, by A. Chandler and S. Salsbury. Review
Bsns W il por p 11 My 29 '71. W. Kroger •

DU PONT DE NEMOURS, E. I, and company
Changing chemistry of du Pont. A. A. Butkus. por Duns 97:35-7+ Ap '71
Du Pont's Edsel; Corfam. Newsweek 77:84 Mr 29 '71
Elephant and the chickens; report by Nader's raiders. il Time 98:80+ D 13 '71
Moving down at Du Pont. pors Time 97:84-5 My 3 '71
Nader's raiders nip at du Pont. il por Bsns W p31-2 D 4 '71
Old lines fray at Du Pont. Bsns W p21 Ap 24 '71
$100-million object lesson; Corfam problems. il Fortune 83:109 Ja '71
State of du Pont; report by Nader's Raiders. Newsweek 78:88+ D 13 '71
See also
Holotron corporation

DUPREZ, Colette
Pick a spot. pors Forbes 108:57-8+ O 15 '71 •

DU QUOIN, Ill.
Garbage, grit and the Hambletonian miracle; New York's Antonacci family, reinvade Du Quoin. W. F. Reed, jr. il Sports Illus 35: 92-5 S 13 '71

DURABLE press fabrics. See Textile fabrics, Wrinkle resistant

DURAS, Marguerite
L'Amante Anglaise. Criticism
New Yorker 47:93 Ap 24 '71 •

DURATION, intuition of. See Time perception

DURATION of copyright. See Copyright—Duration

DURDIN, Peggy
Political tidal wave that struck East Pakistan. il por N Y Times Mag p24-5+ My 2 '71

DURDIN, Tillman
Achieving a new stability. Cur 133:48-64 O '71
China after Mao. il U S News 71:35 O 18 '71

DUREL, René
Ut an don an al aron. New Yorker 46:30-8+ Ja 9 '71

DÜRER, Albrecht
Albrecht Dürer, 1471-1971. C. H. Krinsky. il Art N 70:22-6+ Sum '71 •
Albrecht Dürer: master draftsman. A. Werner. il por Am Artist 35:24-9+ S '71 •
Dürer 1471-1971. D. McConathy. il Vogue 158:89+ S 15 '71 •
Dürer: humanist, mystic and tourist. R. Hughes. il Time 98:42-3 Jl 12 '71 •
Dürer quincentennial. il Chr Cent 88:643-4 My 26 '71 •
Dürer's five hundredth birthday. S. B. Sherrill. il Antiques 99:638 My '71 •
Man between. D. Davis. il por Newsweek 77: 92-5 My 10 '71 •

DURFEE, Louise
Opinion: saving a town for the future. Mlle 74:66+ D '71

DURHAM, Michael
Goodbye to rock. il pors Life 70:62-4+ My 14 '71
Top executive hunts for a job. il pors Life 70: 44-50C Mr 19 '71

DURHAM, N.H.
Small town incinerator. H. Le Clair. il Am City 86:63-4 My '71

DURIE, Mason, and others
Relationship therapy in vocational rehabilitation. Ment Hy 55:242-5 Ap '71

DURIN, Stan
Better crops with the chisel plow. il Org Gard & Farm 18:86-7+ O '71

DURKIN, Thomas J.
To bring the people of God together. Chr Cent 88:927-30 Ag 4 '71

DURNALL, Edward J.
University extension and accreditation. Sch & Soc 99:87-8 F '71

DUROCHER, Leo
From the top; ed. by R. W. Creamer. Sports Illus 35:13 S 13 '71 •
Gunned down by the heavies; ed. by J. Underwood. A. B. Chandler. il pors Sports Illus 34:52-4+ My 3 '71 •

DUROUSSEAU, Louis J.
LJ proves thoroughbreds are color-blind. G. Jones. il pors Ebony 26:100-2+ N '70 •

DURRELL, Gerald Malcolm
Christmas with corals. House & Gard 140:70-1+ D '71

DÜRRENMATT, Friedrich
Play Strindberg. Criticism
Nation 213:380 O 18 '71 •
New Yorker 47:84 Je 12 '71 •

DURSO, Joseph
Sportswriting, and the all-American dollar. il Sat R 54:65-7+ O 9 '71

DURY, G. H. and Knox, J. C.
Duricrusts and deep-weathering profiles in southwestern Wisconsin. bibliog Science 174:291 O 15 '71

DURYEA, Dorothy S.
Honeymoon in Hetch Hetchy. L. Foster. il pors Am West 8:10-15 My '71 •

DURYEA, Robert
Honeymoon in Hetch Hetchy. L. Foster. il pors Am West 8:10-15 My '71 •

DURYEA, Robert F.
Double life. il por Newsweek 77:97+ Ap 26 '71 •
Just plain Bob. il por Time 97:73 Ap 26 '71 •
Of many things. D. R. Campion. America 124: 469 My 8 '71 •
Secret family of Father Duryea. J. N. Bell. il pors Good H 173:80-1+ Ag '71 •

DUSCHA, Julius
Political pro who runs Defense. il pors N Y Times Mag p 18-19+ Je 13 '71
Stop! In the public interest! il por N Y Times Mag p4+ Mr 21 '71

DUSE, Eleonora
He and Lenor. M. J. Matz. il pors Opera N 35:11-13 F 13 '71 •

DUSSAULT, E.
Guide to hacksaw blades. il Mech Illus 67: 88-9 Ag '71

DUSSELDORF, Germany
Theaters in the round; Dusseldorf playhouse. il Arch Forum 134:38-43 Mr '71

Galleries and museums
Art. D. McConathy. Vogue 158:68 N 1 '71

DUST
Atmospheric dust increase could lower earth's temperature. G. B. Lubkin. il Phys Today 24:17+ O '71
See also
Volcanic ash, tuff, etc.

DUST bowl. See Great Plains

DUST diseases. See Lungs—Dust diseases

DUST storms
Dust bowl 1971. il Newsweek 77:32-3 Ap 26 '71

DUSZYNSKI, Edwin J.
  Grinding refuse is no experiment. il Am City 86:61-3 S '71
DUTCH, Pennsylvania. See Pennsylvania Germans
DUTCH cookery. See Cookery, Dutch
DUTCH elm disease. See Elm—Diseases and pests
DUTCH glass. See Glassware
DUTCH irises. See Irises
DUTCH painting. See Painting, Dutch
DUTCH pottery. See Pottery, Dutch
DUTIES (tariff) See Tariff
DUTKA, Jacques
  Longest root. il por Time 98:59+ O 25 '71 *
DUTSCHKE, Rudi
  Britain deports Rudi Dutschke. P. Oestreicher. Chr Cent 88:223-4 F 17 '71 *
  Preventive expulsion. Newsweek 77:36 F 1 '71 *
  This miserable little case. il por Time 97: 32 F 1 '71 *
DUTTON, Richard W. See Hoffmann, M. jt. auth.
DUTY
  Reflections: the limits of duty; with case histories. C. A. Reich. New Yorker 47: 52-7 Je 19 '71
  See also
  Conscience
DUVAL, Merlin Kearfott, 1922-
  DuVal for Egeberg. por Sci N 99:348 My 22 '71 *
DUVAL, Ron
  Chicano movement and its books. il Pub W 199:53-4 Ja 11 '71
  College bookstore rush and how to cope with it. Pub W 199:50-2 Ap 26 '71
  Used books are recycled books. Pub W 200: 38-40 S 6 '71
DUVALIER, François
  Breaking the spell. il por Time 97:33-4 My 3 '71 *
  Haiti without Papa Doc; new faces, but more of the same. il por U S News 70:39 My 3 '71
  Known evil. E. Peer. il por Newsweek 77: 39+ Ap 26 '71 *
  President for life dies. il por Newsweek 77: 40+ My 3 '71 *
  Relevance of black power in Haiti. C. W. Thomas. New Repub 164:11-13 Je 19 '71 *
  Funeral rites and ceremonies
  Jean-Claude Duvalier; with editorial comment. Life 70:3, 34-6 My 7 '71
DUVALIER, Jean Claude
  Enter Mama Doc. il por Time 97:41 F 22 '71 *
  Intimations of mortality. por Time 97:36 Ja 25 '71 *
  Jean-Claude Duvalier; with editorial comment. il pors Life 70:3, 34-6 My 7 '71 *
DUWYENIE, Star
  Entertaining American style: an American summer cookbook; comp. by N. Haslam. il House & Gard 140:76-7+ Ag '71
DVOŘÁK, Antonín
  Dvořák's relations with Brahms and Hanslick. J. Clapham. pors Mus Q 57:241-54 Ap '71 *
  Temperament and accuracy. D. W. Moore. Am Rec G 37:367 F '71 *
DVORAK typewriter keyboard. See Typewriters
DVORCHIK, Barry H. and others
  Does DDT inhibit carbonic anhydrase? bibliog il Science 172:728-29 My 14 '71
DWARF fruit trees. See Fruit trees, Dwarf
DWARF stars. See Stars, Dwarf
DWARF trees. See Trees, Dwarf
DWELL meters
  Compu-Dwell. Hot Rod 24:109 Ap '71
  Dynamic dwell/tachometer. J. Colt. il Electr World 85:78-80 My '71
  How to use the tach-dwell for perfect tuneups. M. Schultz. il Pop Mech 135:126-9 F '71
DWIGHT, Donald R.
  State's responsibility in the federal system; address, November 15, 1971. Vital Speeches 38:168-71 Ja 1 '72
DWORKIN, Edward Paul
  Beware of false gods. Ed Digest 36:27-9 Ja '71
DWORKIN, Martin S.
  Confrontation; poem. Cath World 213:168 Jl '71
DYAL, Palmer, and Parkin, C. W.
  Magnetism of the moon; with biographical sketch. il Sci Am 225:13, 62-73 bibliog(p120) Ag '71

DYBECK, Stuart
  Charity. Commonweal 95:248-52 D 10 '71
DYER, Daniel
  Alternative for the middle years: English for little big men. Engl J 60:1091-4 N '71
DYER, Frederick C. See Ford, C. W. jt. auth.
DYER, Henry S.
  Command of knowledge should be only one of the objectives of education. Todays Ed 60:50-1 Ap '71
DYER, Russel F. See Brown, S. W. jt. auth.
DYES and dyeing
  Decorate-it-yourself: tie dye. il House & Gard 140:66-7 Ag '71
  Dye from shells. A. G. Melvin. il Hobbies 75:159+ F '71
  Dyeing yarn for weaving. H. Bigham. il Sch Arts 70:16-17 F '71
  Everyone is dyeing. S. Diamond. il Sch Arts 71:20-1 Ja '72
  Make your own dyes from plants. E. C. Flynn. il Horticulture 49:43-5 S '71
  Tie-dye your own designs. E. Taylor. il Good H 172:210 Je '71
  Tying up the best tie-dyes. J. A. Segal. il Look 35:54-60+ My 18 '71
  Tyrian purple. J. P. Robinson, jr. il Sea Front 17:76-82 Mr '71
  Workshop: adire eleko. L. Brooks. il Craft Horiz 31:12-15 Ag '71
  See also
  Hair—Dyeing and bleaching
  Textile painting
DYES as indicators
  Solvent dependence of the luminescence of N-arylaminonaphthalenesulfonates. C. J. Seliskar and L. Brand. bibliog il Science 171:799-800 F 26 '71
DYHRENFURTH, Norman
  Defeat on Everest. M. Sayle. il por Life 71:22-9 Jl 2 '71 *
DYLAN, Bob
  Bob Dylan: a pre-obituary. P. J. McCann. Nat R 23:156-7 F 9 '71 *
  Dylanologist. il por Newsweek 77:123 Ap 12 '71 *
  Dylan's New morning. R. D. Campbell. por Chr Cent 88:1009 Ag 25 '71 *
  Freaky fresco of hell. J. Cocks. Time 97:74 My 24 '71 *
  Won't you listen to the lambs, Bob Dylan? A. Scaduto. il pors N Y Times Mag p34-6+ N 28 '71 *
DYMALE, Herbert R.
  What kind of hope is adequate? Chr Today 15:9-10 Je 18 '71
DYMALLY, Mervyn M.
  Struggle for the inclusion of Negro history in our text-books: a California experience; address, October 24, 1970. Negro Hist Bul 33:188-91 D '70
DYMENT, Robert
  Tankers in the Alps: a school for skippers. il Sea Front 17:72-5 Mr '71
DYNAMICS
  See also
  Force and energy
DYNAMOMETERS
  Go power dyno. J. Thawley. il Hot Rod 24: 78+ Ag '71
DYNODES. See Photoelectric multipliers
DYOTT, Thomas W.
  Bottles, flasks and Dr Dyott. by H. McKearin Review
  Antiques il 100:196+ Ag '71. E. Gaines *
DYRLI, Odvard Egil. See Roberts, A. D. jt. auth.
DYSLEXIA, Developmental. See Reading disability
DYSON, Allan J.
  Textbooks, propaganda, and librarians. bibliog il por Wilson Lib Bul 46:260-7 N '71
DYSON, Freeman John
  Energy in the universe; with biographical sketch. il Sci Am 225:25, 50-9 S '71
  Letter from Armenia. New Yorker 47:126-30+ N 6 '71
  about
  Chemists, please note; on the future of physics. Chem 44:4-5 Ja '71 *
DYSTROPHY, Muscular
  Duchenne muscular dystrophy: functional ischemia reproduces its characteristic lesions. J. R. Mendell and others. bibliog il Science 172:1143-5 Je 11 '71
  Electrophysiological observations in normal and dystrophic chicken muscles. E. X. Albuquerque and J. E. Warnick. bibliog il Science 172:1260-3 Je 18 '71
DZIEWONSKI, Adam M.
  Overtones of free oscillations and the structure of the earth's interior. bibliog il Science 172:1336-8 Je 25 '71
DZU, Ngo. See Ngo Dzu

E

EG&G, inc.
They like impossible jobs. N. Carlisle. il Pop Mech 135:76-9+ F '71
EAGLE, Harry
Buffer combinations for mammalian cell culture. bibliog il Science 174:500-3 O 29 '71
EAGLE, Raymond
National parks in England and Wales. il Liv Wildn 34:33-7 Aut '70
EAGLES
Eagle killings and their end result. M. Frome. il Field & S 76:44-5+ D '71
Eagles are not for killing; illegal use of poison bait in Wyoming. R. Stebbins. il Am For 77:12-14+ O '71
Golden eagle rediscovered. W. R. Spofford and G. Chase. il Cons 26:6-8 Ag '71
Mass killing of eagles alarms Senate unit. il Sr Schol 99:14 O 11 '71
Sheepmen vs. eagles: slaughter in the sky. C. Leinster. il Life 71:36-8 Ag 20 '71
Slaughter of the eagles; testimonies before Senate environmental subcommittee. il Newsweek 78:23 Ag 16 '71
Sluicing the eagles; slaughtering of eagles from helicopters in Wyoming. il Time 98:36 Ag 16 '71
Vanishing eagle. il Chem 44:3 S '71
EAKIN, Richard Marshall
Parting shots; a professor dresses up zoology. il pors Life 71:62-3 Jl 23 '71 *
EAKINS, Thomas
Camera eye of Thomas Eakins. il Life 71:54-9 Jl 23 '71 *
EALEY, Charles, jr
Holy Toledo! Chuck Ealey nearly lost one. J. Jares. il por Sports Illus 35:64+ O 11 '71 *
Toledos' Mr Cool. il por Newsweek 78:80 N 15 '71 *
EAMES, Charles
General motors revisited. il Arch Forum 134:21-8 Je '71

about

Eames and the mythic monster. K. Kuh. il Sat R 54:34+ My 29 '71 *

EAR
Ear popping and how to control it. Good H 173:146 Ag '71
I am Joe's ear. J. D. Ratcliff. il Read Digest 99:131-4 O '71
See also
Deafness
Hearing
Labyrinth (ear)

Care and hygiene
Children's ears in health and in disease. L. W. Sauer. PTA Mag 65:31-2 Ap '71
EAR wax. See Earwax
EARHART, Amelia
Amelia Earhart lives, by J. Klaas. Review
Flying 88:25+ Mr '71. F. W. Gibson *
EARL, Ralph Eleaser Whitesides, 1785?-1837
Portraits by Ralph E. W. Earl. J. R. MacBeth. il Antiques 100:390-3 S '71 *
EARL of Ruston; musical comedy. See Musical comedies revues, etc.—Criticisms, plots, etc.
EARLE, Sylvia A.
Tektite II. il Nat Geog 140:290-96 Ag '71
—and Devaney, John
My two weeks under the sea. il por Redbook 136:75-7+ Ap '71
EARLIMART, Calif.

Education
Education in the grapes of wrath; problems of an elementary school principal. D. H. Mangers. Ed Digest 36:16-18 F '71
EARLS, Betty
Teaching telephone techniques. Todays Ed 60:41 F '71
EARLY, Tom
Comment. W. H. Pritchard. Poetry 119:160-1 D '71 *
EARLY, Tracy
New York crime and the religious sector. Chr Cent 88:977-8 Ag 18 '71
School aid question: Jews take a new look. il Cath World 213:134-8 Je '71
(ed) See Lindsay, J. John Lindsay looks at the church
EARLY marriage. See Teen-age marriage
EARLY rising
Easter sunrise services are for the birds. J. L. Gilmore. Chr Cent 88:433-4 Ap 7 '71
EARLY warning satellites. See Ballistic missile early warning system
EARRING; story. See Graham, W.
EARTH
See also
Atmosphere
Creation
Geodesy
Ocean

Age
Xenon record of extinct radioactivities in the earth. M. S. Boulos and O. K. Manuel. bibliog il Science 174:1334-6 D 24 '71

Internal structure
Composition and evolution of the mantle and core. D. L. Anderson and others. bibliog il Science 171:1103-12 Mr 19 '71
Hot spots and crust motion; mantle convection. Sci N 99:180 Mr 13 '71
Overtones of free oscillations and the structure of the earth's interior. A. M. Dziewonski. bibliog il Science 172:1336-8 Je 25 '71
Pacific geomagnetic secular variation. R. R. Doell and A. Cox. bibliog il Science 171:248-54 Ja 22 '71

Mantle
See Earth—Internal structure

Orbital motion
An experiment to measure the earth's orbital velocity. D. Hoff. il Sky & Tel 43:9-10 Ja '72

Photographs from space
Eye in the sky. E. Hay. il Am For 77:20-3 Ja '71
For a good picture of the U.S. ask the Russians. Life 70:24-5 F 12 '71
Techniques tomorrow; earth resources satellite photography. B. Sherman. Mod Phot 34:30+ N '70

Radiation
Atmospheric dust increase could lower earth's temperature. G. B. Lubkin. il Phys Today 24:17+ O '71
Halo for the earth; magnetoglow. Sci N 99:114 F 13 '71
Magnetoglow: a new geophysical resource. C. Y. Johnson and others. bibliog il Science 171:379-81 Ja 29 '71

EARTH—*Continued*

Rotation

Rotation of the earth. D. E. Smylie and L. Mansinha. il Sci Am 225:80-8 bibliog(p 120) D '71

Variations in the rate of rotation of the earth. R. A. Challinor. bibliog il Science 172:1022-5 Je 4 '71; Reply. J. Gribbin. 173: 558 Ag 6 '71

Wobbling earth. il Sci N 100:108 Ag 14 '71

Surface

See also
Faults (geology)
Ocean bottom

EARTH, Destruction of. See End of the world

EARTH art. See Environment (art)

EARTH augers. See Augers

EARTH movements
Big creep. Chem 44:23 D '71
What do you know about earthflows & landslides? quiz. J. Daugherty and M. Daugherty. il Sci Digest 69:58-9+ My '71
See also
Earthquakes
Seismology

EARTH resources observation satellites. See Artificial satellites—Use in research

EARTH resources satellites. See Artificial satellites—Use in research

EARTH sciences
Earth sciences. See issues of Science news
See also
Climate
Geography
Oceanography

Study and teaching

Students profit from classroom drilling; course at Norris L. Brookens junior high school. Urbana, Ill. V. Louvière. il Nations Bsns 59:17 O '71

EARTH week. See Environmental movement—Earth week

EARTHENWARE. See Pottery

EARTHENWARE, American; Earthenware, English; etc. See Pottery, American; Pottery, English; etc.

EARTHQUAKE insurance. See Insurance, Earthquake

EARTHQUAKE prediction
Earthquake prediction and control. A. L. Hammond. Science 173:316 Jl 23 '71
Old and faithful quake warnings. il Time 98:63-4 O 18 '71
Possibilities of earthquake prediction. L. Purrett. il Sci N 99:131-3 F 20 '71
Quaking earth: what's the fault? San Andreas fault. il Sr Schol 98:14-16 Mr 1 '71
Ready for an earthquake? California. il Newsweek 78:73 D 6 '71
Same thing will happen again, only worse. il Newsweek 77:22 F 22 '71
Seismologist as seer. il Newsweek 77:91 My 24 '71

EARTHQUAKE research. See Earthquakes—Research

EARTHQUAKES
Earthquake at sea. J. E. Hoffmeister. il Sea Front 17:288-91 S '71
Quakes. science and NATO. Sci N 99:383-4 Je 5 '71
Rotation of the earth. D. E. Smylie and L. Mansinha. il Sci Am 225:80-8 bibliog(p 120) D '71
Wobbling earth. il Sci N 100:108 Ag 14 '71
See also
Tidal waves

Prediction

See Earthquake prediction

Research

Reservoir loading and earthquakes. il Sci N 99:368 My 29 '71

Search for safety valves. Sci N 99:263 Ap 17 '71

Seven-year itch; correlation between the earth's wobble and earthquakes. il Newsweek 78:54-5 Ag 30 '71

Shock to seismologists; San Fernando quake. il Time 97:49 F 22 '71
See also
Earthquake prediction
Seismological stations

Aleutian Islands

Explosion effects and earthquakes in the Amchitka Island Region. F. R. Engdahl. bibliog il Science 173:1232-5 S 24 '71

Peru

Doctorcito, don't let them abandon us. D. Rennie. il por Todays Health 49:23-4+ My '71

Earthquakes and eucalypts in Peru. T. Cobb. il Am For 77:20-1+ S '71

Salvador

Microearthquakes in the Ahuachapan geothermal field, El Salvador, Central America. P. L. Ward and K. H. Jacob. bibliog il Science 173:328-30 Jl 23 '71

United States

Ready for an earthquake? California. il Newsweek 78:73 D 6 '71
See also
Los Angeles—Earthquake. 1971
San Francisco—Earthquake and fire, 1906

EARTHQUAKES and building
Lessons from the quake. Sci N 99:211-12 Mr 27 '71

EARTHS, Rare
See also
Promethium

EARTHWORK
See also
Dams
Filling (earthwork)
Foundations
Tunnels and tunneling

EARTHWORMS
Build an earthworm bed. D. Smith. il Field & S 76:18 D '71
Earthworm mystery. il Sunset 147:194 D '71
Easy way to catch worms. il Field & S 75:44 Mr '71
Effect of earthworms on agricultural soil. M. Franz. il Org Gard & Farm 18:82-4 Je '71
Lumbricus terrestris. Chem 44:4 Je '71
Making money with leaves. O. R. Griffin. il Org Gard & Farm 18:42-3 My '71
Money with a wriggle; worm farmers. C. Meyer. McCalls 98:40 Ag '71

EARWAX
Cerumen genetics and human breast cancer. N. L. Petrakis. bibliog il Science 173: 347-9 Jl 23 '71
Earmarked. Sci Am 224:56+ Je '71

EAST, Ben
Alaska's agony. il Outdoor Life 147:33-5+ Ja '71
Set guns kill polar bears, and it's legal! il Outdoor Life 147:58-9 Ja '71

about
Ben East wins award. il por Outdoor Life 148:10 S '71 •
—See Fairhurst, W. A. jt. auth.

EAST (United States) See Atlantic states

EAST AFRICA. See Africa, East

EAST AFRICAN safari auto rally. See Automobile racing—Africa, East

EAST EUROPEAN refugees. See Refugees, European

EAST GERMAN refugees. See Refugees, German

EAST HAMPTON, N.Y. free library
Board silences "No silence" librarian. Wilson Lib Bul 46:389-90 Ja '72

EAST INDIANS in East Africa
Indians of East Africa. S. Lone. New Repub 165:10-11 S 4 '71

EAST LANSING, Mich.
Student power in East Lansing. il Time 98: 18 N 15 '71

EAST NEW YORK. See Brooklyn

EAST ORANGE, N.J.
Low-income, stagnant. K. Prager. il Time 97:19 Mr 15 '71

EAST PAKISTAN. See Pakistan

EAST PAKISTAN relief operation. See United Nations East Pakistan relief operation

EAST PALO ALTO. See Palo Alto, Calif.

EAST Side house settlement, inc.
East Side house settlement; a story of progress. A. Tilt, jr. il Antiques 99:66 Ja '71

EAST-West trade. See Communist countries—Commerce

EASTBURN, David P.
Puzzle for U.S: growth vs. social progress; address. il por U S News 71:64-6 Jl 12 '71

EASTER
Easter is not for everybody! L. Woodrum. Chr Today 15:5-6 Ap 9 '71
Easter sunrise services are for the birds. J. L. Gilmore. Chr Cent 88:433-4 Ap 7 '71

EASTER—*Continued*
Mark's special Easter emphasis. R. P. Meye.
Chr Today 15:4-6 Mr 26 '71
When Easter comes in April. P. B. Price.
PTA Mag 65:17 Ap '71
See also
Jesus Christ—Resurrection and ascension

Drama
Rabbit's foot. H. L. Miller. Plays 30:9-18 Ap
'71

Poetry
Alleluia lamb. R. Slotten. Chr Cent 88:427
Ap 7 '71
See also
Jesus Christ—Poetry

EASTER breads. See Bread
EASTER business. See Retail trade
EASTER dinners. See Dinners and dining
EASTER eggs
Easter: the hand-painted egg. il Ladies
Home J 88:36+ Ap '71
EASTER ISLAND
Easter Island, by J. Dos Passos. Review
Nat R 23:657 Je 15 '71. J. Greenway
Yanqui, come back. J. Barnes. il Newsweek
77:44+ Mr 29 '71
EASTERN airlines
Board allows conditional reservation test.
H. D. Watkins. Aviation W 95:26 Jl 5 '71
Charter boosts Eastern Labor day traffic. L.
Doty. Aviation W 95:27 S 13 '71
Eastern bids employes cooperate to avoid
large-scale furloughs. Aviation W 94:25 Ap
5 '71
Eastern, Continental report 1970 profits. Avia-
tion W 94:26 F 1 '71
Eastern fare proposals rejected. Aviation W
94:40 My 31 '71
Eastern pilots agree to fly extra hours.
Aviation W 94:24 Ap 19 '71
Eastern receives certification for R-Nav. il
Aviation W 94:29-30 My 24 '71
Eastern rehires fuel-dumping objector. Avi-
ation W 94:22 Ja 18 '71
Eastern seeking family fare approval. R. S.
Kahn. Aviation W 94:32 My 3 '71
Eastern successful in used aircraft sales. H.
D. Watkins. il Aviation W 94:28-9 Ja 25 '71
Eastern's leased 747s used to fill gap prior
to L-1011. Aviation W 94:32 Ja 25 '71
Great way to go; fly-and-rent. B. Behme. il
Field & S 76:154-6 Je '71
Initial public satisfaction found with shuttle
pre-ticketing, drinks. Aviation W 94:28 Mr
15 '71
Mike Frome. M. Frome. Am For 77:7+ F '71
New airborne computer system. il Pop
Electr 35:67-8 Ag '71
Pan American sees merger with Eastern as
main domestic hope. Aviation W 94:36 F
15 '71
Rejiggering the air shuttle to make it pay.
il Bsns W p42 Ja 30 '71
See also
National distribution services. inc.
EASTERN basketball association. See Basket-
ball teams
EASTERN churches
Can eastern Christians survive under Marx
or Islam? C. S. Calian. il Cath World 212:
249-52+ F '71
EASTERN college librarians. See Conference of
eastern college librarians
EASTERN Europe. See Europe, Eastern
EASTERN music festival, Greensboro, N.C.
See Music festivals—North Carolina
EASTERN Oregon college, La Grande, Ore.
Race, evolution and Mormonism. C. W.
Quaintance. Chr Cent 88:586-9 My 12 '71
EASTERN Orthodox church. See Orthodox
Eastern church
**EASTERN Orthodox church in the United
States.** See Orthodox Eastern church in the
United States
EASTLUND, Bernard J. See Gough, W. C. jt.
auth.
EASTMAN house of photography. See Photog-
raphy—Galleries and museums
EASTMAN Kodak company
Photo education; Kodak's Riverwood market-
ing education center. E. Scully. Mod Phot
35:32+ N '71
EASTMAN school of music. See Rochester,
N.Y. University—Eastman school of music
EASTON, Caroline
Time to fail; a time to succeed. il Parents
Mag 46:44-5+ D '71
EASTON, Dexter M.
Garfish olfactory nerve: easily accessible
source of numerous long, homogeneous, non-
myelinated axons. bibliog il Science 172:
952-5 My 28 '71

EASTWOOD, Clint
That self-sufficient thing. il pors Time 98:
66 D 6 '71 *
Who can stand 32,580 seconds of Clint East-
wood? J. Fayard. il pors Life 71:44-8 Jl 23
'71 *
EASY chairs. See Chairs
EATENSON, Ervin
Notable books, 1944-1969. Am Lib 2:105-9 Ja
'71
EATING
See also
Appetite
Diet
Gastronomy
Nutrition

Anecdotes, facetiae, satire, etc.
Apple pie and crazy people. W. Saroyan.
Nation 213:629-30 D 13 '71
EATING, Psychology of
Fat vs. thin. G. Davis. por Harp Baz 104:26
My '71
Why do we overeat? M. Mead. Redbook 136:
28+ Ja '71
EATING habits. See Food habits
EATON, B. Curtis
Defense engineers: do they have special re-
employment problems? il Mo Labor R 94:
52-4 Jl '71
EATON, Cyrus Stephen, 1883-
Eaton on Nixon. Nation 213:229 S 20 '71 *
EATON, Jerome A.
Home greenhouse. See issues of Home gar-
den & flower grower
EATON, John L.
Insect photoreceptor: an internal ocellus is
present in sphinx moths. bibliog il Science
173:822-3 Ag 27 '71
EATON, John W. See Brewer, G. J. jt. auth.
EATON, Quaintance
Advance guard. il Opera N 35:28-31 F 27 '71
Oldest school. il Opera N 35:12-16 Ap 17 '71
Stars eat out. il Opera N 35:12-16 Mr 6 '71
(ed) See Schneider-Siemssen, G. Günther
and Eva
EATON, Randall L.
Cheetah. il Nat Parks & Con Mag 45:18-22
Je '71
EATON, Robert Edward Lee
Promotion of chaos: the three major catal-
ysts; address, July 17, 1971. Vital Speeches
37:687-90 S 1 '71
EATON, T, company, ltd. See Toronto—Stores
EATON Yale & Towne, inc.
How to develop multinational executives. il
pors Bsns W p88+ Je 12 '71
Peace needs world business; address, July
29, 1971. E. M. De Windt. Vital Speeches
37:726-9 S 15 '71
EATON'S (firm) See Toronto—Stores
EBBESSON, Sven O. E. and Schroeder, D. M.
Connections of the nurse shark's telen-
cephalon. bibliog il Science 173:254-6 Jl 16
'71
EBEL, Robert L.
Command of knowledge should be the pri-
mary objective of education. il Todays
Ed 60:36-9 Mr '71
EBERHART, Richard
Fischer cat; poem. New Yorker 47:146 O 23
'71
Man and nature; poem. Sat R 54:40 N 13 '71
about
Richard Eberhart, by J. H. Roache. Review
Commonweal 94:242-3 My 14 '71. B. El-
son *
Sat R por 54:25-7 Mr 6 '71. M. L. Rosen-
thal *
EBERLE, August W. See Beeler, K. D. jt. auth.
EBERLE, William Denman
Eberle negotiates at a pell-mell pace. por
Bsns W p 19 D 18 '71 *
Eberle of American standard. por Forbes
107:65 My 15 '71 *
Senate confirms William Eberle as special
trade representative. Dept State Bul 65:627
N 29 '71 *
EBERLING, May Dean
History in towns. il Antiques 100:420-4 S '71
EBERLY, Donald J.
Voluntary service. Chr Cent 88:757 Je 16 '71
EBERT, Darrell D. See De La Rosa, D. jt.
auth.
EBERT, Roger
Last of the schlockmeisters. il pors Esquire
76:152-5+ N '71
EBON, Martin
Party games to test your ESP; excerpts from
Test your ESP. il Ladies Home J 88:78+ My
'71

ECCENTRICS and eccentricities
DDT eaters and other eco-centrics. il Time 98:40 Ag 9 '71
ECCLES, Sir John Carew
What makes me a unique being? M. Gosnell. il por Newsweek 77:66 Je 21 '71 *
ECCLES, Joseph, family
What the neighbors think. A. R. Martin. Newsweek 78:54 N 29 '71
ECCLESIASTICAL courts
When the courts don't work. J. T. Catoir. America 125:254-7 O 9 '71
ECCLESIASTICAL law
See also
Canon law
ECDYSONE
Ovarian maturation in stable flies: inhibition by 20-hydroxyecdysone. J. E. Wright and others. bibliog il Science 172:1247-8 Je 18 '71; Reply. F. Engelmann. 174:1041 D 3 '71
ECHEVERRÍA ALVAREZ, Luis
Showing them who's boss. il por Time 97:38 Je 28 '71 *
ECHINODERMS
See also
Embryology—Echinoderms
Sea urchins
Starfishes
ECHLIN, Edward P.
Crisis in preaching. il Commonweal 94:423-6; 95:71 Ag 20, O 15 '71
ECHOLOCATION (physiology)
Computer derivation of some dolphin echolocation signals. R. A. Altes. bibliog il Science 173:912-14 S 3 '71
Echolocation in bats; signal processing of echoes for target range. J. A. Simmons. bibliog il Science 171:925-8 Mr 5 '71
ECKARDT, A. Roy
Fantasy of reconciliation in the Middle East. bibliog il por Chr Cent 88:1198-202 O 13 '71
ECKERD, Jack, corporation
House that Jack built. il pors Forbes 108:36-7 O 1 '71
ECKERD, Jack M.
House that Jack built. il pors Forbes 108:36-7 O 1 '71 *
ECKERSON, Bill
Winter the antelope moved to town. il Outdoor Life 147:62-3+ F '71
ECKERT, Bob
Abrasive cutoff machine you can make for $15. il Pop Mech 136:166+ S '71
ECKERT, John Presper, 1919-
Little known creators of the computer. J. Costello. il pors Nations Bsns 59:56-62 D '71 *
ECKERT, Wallace J.
Obituary
Sky & Tel por 42:207 O '71. J. A. Ashbrook
ECKHARDT, Robert B.
Population genetics and human origins; with biographical sketch. il Sci Am 8226:11, 94-103 Ja '72
ECKLES, Kathy
Black mother and child; poem. Negro Hist Bul 33:193 D '70
ECKLEY, Mary, and Plant, Gloria
Entertaining: the second thirty years it gets easier. il McCalls 99:104-9 O '71
—See Root, W. jt. auth.
ECKMAN, Fern Marja
How to find and keep a maid. Ladies Home J 88:70+ My '71
Why can't more women be doctors? Redbook 137:77+ My '71
ECKRICH, Catherine
Eden; poem. Cath World 213:262 S '71
ECKSTEIN, Alexander
There's a certain sense of mystery; interview. il por U S News 70:19-20 My 10 '71
ECKSTEIN, Otto
Expert views the freeze and the future; interview. ed. by W. A. McWhirter. por Life 71:22-5 Ag 27 '71
How is the economy doing? interview, ed. by G. Farmer. por Life 71:38-9 O 8 '71
ECLIPSES
Eclipses of 1972. J. Stokley. il Sci N 100:412 D 18 '71
See also
Occultations
ECLIPSES, Lunar
February eclipse of the moon. J. A. Ashbrook. il Sky & Tel 41:209-12, 273-7 Ap-My '71
Lunar eclipse in January. il Sky & Tel 43:60-1 Ja '72
Total eclipse of the moon. J. Stokley. il Sci N 99:68 Ja 23 '71
Total eclipse of the moon on August 6th. il Sky & Tel 42:243-5 O '71

ECLIPSES, Solar
1970 solar eclipse summary. Sky & Tel 41:80 F '71
Solar eclipse of July 10, 1972. il Sky & Tel 43:25-8 Ja '72
Weather prospects for the 1972 total solar eclipse. E. M. Brooks. il Sky & Tel 41:290-1 My '71
ECLIPSING binaries. See Stars, Eclipsing binary
ECLOGITE
Oxygen isotope ratios in eclogites from kimberlites. G. D. Garlick and others. bibliog il Science 172:1025-7 Je 4 '71
L'ÉCOLE des femmes; drama. See Molière, J. B. P.
ECOLOGICAL models
Systems studies of DDT transport. H. L. Harrison and others; discussion. Science 172:84, 213-14 Ap 2, 16 '71
ECOLOGICAL movement. See Environmental movement
ECOLOGICAL research
Environment: preparing for the crunch; findings and recommendations of the Study of critical environmental problems. C. L. Wilson. il Sat R 54:42-3+ Ja 23 '71
Soviets tackle ecology problems. Sci Digest 69:53 Je '71
What are man's prospects? D. L. Meadows. Cur 133:3-9 O '71
See also
Institute of ecology
International biological program
ECOLOGY
Can land be developed without wrecking nature? W. Hartley and E. Hartley. il Sci Digest 71:73-8 Ja '72
Ecology; letter. P. B. Sears. Science 174:360+ O 22 '71
Ecology primer. A. Chalfant. bibliog il Nat Wildlife 9:38-9 Ag: 10-11 O '71
Ecosystems of national parks. D. B. Houston. bibliog Science 172:648-51 My 14 '71
Haste makes waste: pollution and entropy. H. A. Bent. bibliog il por Chem 44:6-15 O '71
Long arm of biological law; or, How Charles Darwin and his lot will inherit the earth. K. E. F. Watt. Natur Hist 80:14-16+ bibliog(p 84) Ap '71
Man; planetary disease; address, March 10, 1971. L. McHarg. Vital Speeches 37:634-40 Ag 1 '71
Paradox of enrichment: destabilization of exploitation ecosystems in ecological time. M. L. Rosenzweig. bibliog il Science 171:385-7 Ja 29 '71
Politics of ecology, by J. Ridgeway. Review Natur Hist 80:102+ F '71. E. F. Roberts
Renaissance; interview, ed. by H. Brandon. M. Nicholson. Sat R 54:53-4+ My 1 '71
Reporter at large. B. Commoner. New Yorker 47:49-54+ S 25 '71
Stability and diversity at three trophic levels in terrestrial successional ecosystems. L. E. Hurd and others. bibliog il Science 173:1164-6 S 17 '71
To trouble a star; the cost of intervention in nature. C. Hardin; reply with rejoinder. R. B. Coffman. Bul Atom Sci 27:2-4 Ap '71
Way of wildness. C. A. Lindbergh. Read Digest 99:90-3 N '71
What ecology is about. E. Gibbons. il Org Gard & Farm 18:106-9 Ag '71
See also
Environment
Food chains (ecology)
Fresh water ecology
Marine ecology
Marsh ecology
Mountain ecology
Paleoecology
Prairie ecology
Religion and ecology
Struggle for existence

Bibliography
Ecology books: a doomsday bibliography. A. Caruba. il Pub W 200:28-30 Ag 16 '71

Study and teaching
Pressing vs. pressed interests: ecology and education. J. Wheeler and N. Shimahara. Sch & Soc 99:426-8 N '71
Survival U is alive and burgeoning in Green Bay, Wisconsin. J. Fischer. Harper 242:20+ F '71; Same abr. with title New university for survival. Cur 128:12-18 Ap '71
Training your staff to handle ecological programs. M. Tener. Camp Mag 43:11 F '71

Africa
See also
Ecology—Tanzania

ECOLOGY—*Continued*

Alaska

Are we about to plunder Alaska. R. Pollak. Cur 129:39-46 My '71

Egypt

Aswan disaster. C. Sterling. il Nat Parks & Con Mag 45:10-13 Ag '71

Florida

Imperiled Everglades. F. Ward. il Nat Geog 141:1-27 Ja '72

Indochina

Starvation as a policy; report of the Science-herbicide assessment commission. P. R. Ehrlich and J. P. Holdren. Sat R 54:91 D 4 '71

Middle East

Desert and the sown: an ecological appraisal of the Middle East. I. R. Manners. bibliog il Focus 22:1-8 O '71

Siberia

Even in Siberia it's the age of ecology. R. Richardson. il por Am For 77:24-7+ Mr '71

Tanzania

Grazing ecosystem in the Serengeti. R. H. V. Bell. il Sci Am 225:86-93 Jl '71

Vietnam

Defoliation in Chicago; AAAS report on military use of defoliants in Vietnam. Sci Am 224:44 F '71

Destruction of Indochina; report of Stanford biology study group. il Bul Atom Sci 27:36-40 My '71

Ecocide and the Geneva protocol. L. C. Johnstone. For Affairs 49:711-20 Jl '71

Ecocide in Indochina. A. H. Westing. il Natur Hist 80:56-61 Mr '71

Herbicides in Vietnam: AAAS study finds widespread devastation. P. M. Boffey. il Science 171:43-7 Ja 8 '71

Herbicides in Vietnam: violating the laws, starving our allies. C.-G. McDaniel. Chr Cent 88:195-7 F 10 '71

Land war. E. W. Pfeiffer; A. H. Westing. il pors Environ 13:2-15 N '71

Reporter at large; defoliation. (cont) T. Whiteside. New Yorker 47:54+ Ag 14 '71

Silent Vietnam: how we invented ecocide and killed a country. O. Schell, jr. il Look 35:55+ Ap 6 '71

Tour of Vietnam. T. Aaronson. bibliog il Environ 13:34-43 Mr '71

Use of herbicides in Viet-Nam to be phased out; White House announcement, December 26, 1970. Dept State Bul 64:77 Ja 18 '71

Virginia

Up with trash. M. MacPherson. McCalls 99:33 N '71

ECOLOGY action (organization) See Environmental associations, committees, etc.

ECOLOGY action of Florida, Inc. See Environmental associations, committees, etc.

ECOLOGY fair. See Environmental movement—Exhibitions

ECONOMETRIC models. See Economic models

ECONOMIC and social council of the United Nations. See United Nations—Economic and social council

ECONOMIC assistance, American

All the king's horses. W. P. Bundy. Newsweek 78:56 N 15 '71

America's posture could be weakened in world affairs. D. Lawrence. U S News 71:100 N 22 '71

Annual report on foreign assistance program transmitted to Congress; letter of transmittal, February 17, 1971. R. M. Nixon. Dept State Bul 64:301-2 Mr 8 '71

Budget of the United States government, fiscal year 1972; excerpts. Dept State Bul 64:242-5 F 22 '71

Development aid and security assistance in the Near East and South Asia; statement, July 14, 1971. R. P. Davies. Dept State Bul 65:204-8 Ag 23 '71

Eclipse of an idea; foreign aid. Commonweal 94:227-8 My 14 '71

Farewell to foreign aid; address, October 29, 1971. F. Church. Vital Speeches 38:66-73 N 15 '71; Same abr. New Repub 165:14-17 N 13 '71; Reply. R. E. Hunter. 165:18-20 N 20 '71

Fiscal 1972 budget request for development assistance and security assistance; statement, September 8, 1971. W. P. Rogers. Dept State Bul 65:336-9 S 27 '71

Foreign aid: end of an era? il U S News 71:20-2 N 15 '71

Foreign aid: scrambling to the rescue; how the Senate foreign aid bill died; with account by N. MacNeil. il Time 98:13-15 N 15 '71

Foreign aid shakes up Congress, and vice versa. il Sr Schol 99:13-15 D 6 '71

Foreign aid: the dawn of a new era; list the Senate tore up. il Newsweek 78:40-1 N 15 '71

Foreign assistance and the U.S. national interest; statements, with transcripts of news conferences, October 30 and November 1 and 2, 1971. W. P. Rogers; J. A. Hannah; M. R. Laird. Dept State Bul 65:577-86 N 22 '71

Foreign assistance program to meet the conditions of the seventies; statement, June 11, 1971. J. N. Irwin, 2d. il Dept State Bul 65:23-7 Jl 5 '71

Global poverty and underdevelopment; address, March 15, 1971. J. E. Rielly. Vital Speeches 37:496-502 Je 1 '71

High stakes of international poker. il Time 98:22-3 S 20 '71

Institutional problems in the developing countries; address, February 15, 1971. J. A. Hannah. Dept State Bul 64:297-301 Mr 8 '71

Leadership and aid. J. Osborne. New Repub 165:11-13 N 13 '71

Letter from Washington. R. H. Rovere. New Yorker 47:157-61 N 13 '71

Misconceptions and outmoded conceptions about foreign aid; address, July 21, 1971. J. A. Hannah. Dept State Bul 65:152-5 Ag 9 '71

Myth of aid, by D. Goulet and M. Hudson. Review
  Cath World 213:292-3 S '71. G. MacEoin

Nixon's NEP and the developing world. P. J. Henriot. il America 125:448-50 N 27 '71

Piece work; foreign aid bill. Newsweek 78:40+ N 22 '71

Plan to streamline. Time 97:16 My 3 '71

Politics of leverage. il Time 98:29 Jl 12 '71

Prescription for foreign aid. America 124:477-8 My 8 '71

Protracted conflict J. Burnham. Nat R 23:1344 D 3 '71

Reform of the U.S. foreign assistance program: message to Congress, April 21, 1971. R. M. Nixon. Dept State Bul 64:614-25 My 10 '71

Revived aid. New Repub 165:11-12 N 20 '71

Revolt on aid: Senate defeats bill. Commonweal 95:171-2 N 19 '71

Scrub it up, don't wipe it out: Senate debate. New Repub 165:5-7 N 13 '71

Senate rebels against foreign aid. il Time 98:14-16 N 8 '71

Senate unveils its hatchet. America 125:390 N 13 '71

Strengthened and revitalized foreign aid program; statement, April 27, 1971. J. N. Irwin, 2d. Dept State Bul 64:657-64 My 24 '71

Sudden death of foreign aid. Newsweek 78:33+ N 8 '71

Surprise politics in reverse: defeat of foreign aid bill. Nation 213:483-4 N 15 '71

Sustaining a meaningful commitment to Latin American development; statement, August 4, 1971. C. A. Meyer. Dept State Bul 65:236-8 Ag 30 '71
  See also
Food relief
United States—Agency for international development

ECONOMIC assistance, Chinese

Foreign aid: the Chinese are coming. J. S. Prybyla. bibliog f il Cur Hist 61:142-7+ S '71

ECONOMIC assistance, Communist
  See also
Economic assistance, Chinese
Economic assistance, Russian

ECONOMIC assistance, Domestic

Governors and mayors view the poverty program. D. H. Haider. bibliog f Cur Hist 61:273-8+ N '71

Shooting Santa Claus. J. Osborne. New Repub 165:10-12 D 25 '71
  See also
Federal aid
Grants-in-aid
Negative income tax
United States—Economic development administration

ECONOMIC assistance, Japanese

Japan and southeast Asia in the 1970's. K. Wakaizumi. il Cur Hist 60:200-6+ Ap '71

Pacific trade challenge; address, March 15, 1971. N. Ushiba. Vital Speeches 37:390-2 Ap 15 '71

ECONOMIC assistance, Russian
Have the Russians bought Cuba? D. Lawrence. U S News 70:100 Mr 15 '71
In Russia, too, doubts about foreign aid. U S News 71:22 N 15 '71
Russia tightens its grip on Egypt. il U S News 70:28-9 Ap 12 '71

ECONOMIC assistance in Asia
Security assistance programs in east Asia; statement, May 4, 1971. M. Green. Dept State Bul 64:714-19 My 31 '71

ECONOMIC assistance in Brazil
World bank craves a slice of Ex-Im's pie. il Bsns W p28 F 13 '71

ECONOMIC assistance in Cuba
Have the Russians bought Cuba? D. Lawrence. U S News 70:100 Mr 15 '71

ECONOMIC assistance in Egypt
Russia tightens its grip on Egypt. il U S News 70:28-9 Ap 12 '71

ECONOMIC assistance in India
Avoiding disaster in South Asia. W. P. Bundy. Newsweek 78:62 O 25 '71

ECONOMIC assistance in Latin America
Latin America: who is to blame? G. MacEoin. Commonweal 94:331-6 Je 25 '71; Reply. A. J. Durelli. 94:463 S 3 '71

ECONOMIC assistance in North Africa
U.S. and North Africa; lessons from the past and future directions; address, November 18, 1971. D. D. Newsom. Vital Speeches 38: 162-6 Ja 1 '72

ECONOMIC assistance in Pakistan
Avoiding disaster in South Asia. W. P. Bundy. il Newsweek 78:62 O 25 '71
Pakistan: the busy bee route to development. T. Nulty and L. Nulty. il Trans-Action 8: 18-26+ F '71
Sins of commission. New Repub 165:10-11 Jl 24 '71

ECONOMIC assistance in underdeveloped areas
Helping the poor nations, or, Helping ourselves? T. Nulty and L. Nulty; G. MacEoin. Commonweal 95:138-42 N 5 '71

ECONOMIC commissions of the United Nations.
See name of commission under United Nations, e.g. United Nations—Economic commission for Asia and the Far East

ECONOMIC conditions
Building walls abroad; the unsettled trading world. il Time 98:35-6 N 1 '71
Canary has fallen silent; reprint. H. E. Daly. Nat Parks & Con Mag 45:27 Je '71
Into a time of stagflation. L. A. Mayer. il Fortune 84:144-9 Ag '71
Slowdown goes global. il Time 97:72-3 Mr 22 '71
See also
Business conditions
Business cycles
Business depression
Poverty
Standard of living
also subhead Economic conditions under names of countries, states, cities, etc. e.g. New York (city)—Economic conditions

ECONOMIC conferences
No muscle in the message; meeting of underdeveloped nations of Africa, Asia and Latin America. A. Bono. Commonweal 95: 316-17 Ja 2 '72

ECONOMIC development
Analysis of socio-economic development through a system of indicators. D. V. McGranahan. bibliog f Ann Am Acad 393: 65-81 Ja '71
Development of nationalism and the nationalism of development; address, February 18, 1971. R. McClintock. Dept State Bul 64: 522-8 Ap 19 '71
Economic growth and fluctuations. E. C. Bratt. bibliog f Ann Am Acad 393:122-31 Ja '71
Luddites were not all wrong. W. Greene and S. Golden. il por N Y Times Mag p40-2+ N 21 '71
Population growth and national development; address, June 14, 1971. D. L. Gamon. Dept State Bul 65:172-8 Ag 16 '71
Practical significance of social information. J. Drewnowski. bibliog f Ann Am Acad 393:82-91 Ja '71
Small is beautiful: toward a theology of enough; address. E. F. Schumacher. Chr Cent 88:900-2 Jl 28 '71
See also
Underdeveloped areas
United States—Economic conditions

ECONOMIC forecasting
At last, the year of real recovery. il Time 99:18-20+ Ja 10 '72
Brighter outlook for business. il Bsns W p 16-17 Ag 28 '71
Broad-based business upturn for 1972; with table. il Bsns W p 12-13 D 25 '71

Burns on business: recovery, but new dangers of inflation; excerpts from testimony, February 19, 1971. A. Burns. por U S News 70:55-7 Mr 1 '71
Can you top this? por Forbes 108:62 D 1 '71
Economic outlook: boomy. il Newsweek 78: 29-31 O 18 '71
Economic snake oil; the President's forecast. P. A. Samuelson. Newsweek 77:81 Mr 8 '71
Economy: plain or fancy comeback? assessment by Time's economists. il Time 97:82-3 F 22 '71
Embarked on the long voyage home. il Fortune 83:21-2+ Ja '71
Foggy forecast from the CEA. il Bsns W p 16-17 F 6 '71
Great year coming? P. A. Samuelson. Newsweek 78:45 D 27 '71
Hidden promise of the 1970s. Time 97:70-1 F 15 '71
How to buck up the U.S. economy. il Newsweek 79:35-6 Ja 3 '72
Inflation, threat of another round. il U S News 70:13-15 Je 28 '71
Is a tax cut coming? interview, ed. by G. R. Rosen, with editorial comment. P. A. Rinfret. por Duns 97:14-16+, 104 Ap '71
Is recovery sputtering out? il U S News 71: 15-16 Ag 23 '71
Jobs, inflation: what Nixon's top economist expects; excerpts from statement before the Joint economic committee, July 8, 1971. P. W. McCracken. il por U S News 71:57-9 Jl 26 '71
Look at the great economy of 1985. il Bsns W p84-5 D 18 '71
Lower productivity threatens growth. il Bsns W p36-7 Ja 1 '72
Monetary outlook: a little tightening. il Bsns W p 15-16 Ja 1 '72
Mood of cautious optimism; international outlook for 1972. il Bsns W p28-9 Ja 1 '72
1971 outlook; address, March 21, 1971. G. G. Hagedorn. Vital Speeches 37:376-9 Ap 1 '71
Nixon's new economic policy: impact on wages, savings, prices, profits. il U S News 71:16-18 Ag 30 '71
Nixon's recovery plan: will it work? il U S News 70:20-1 F 15 '71
No sale on the President's bullish forecast. il Bsns W p68+ Mr 6 '71
$100 billion in growth: a startling forecast. il Time 98:20 O 4 '71
1065 and all that. por Time 97:83 F 22 '71
Outlook, '72: quicker recovery but no boom. il U S News 72:12-14 Ja 10 '72
Outlook, '72: the way it will be where you live. il U S News 72:28-31 Ja 10 '72
Pick a spot. pors Forbes 108:57-8+ O 15 '71
Prospect for profits: still skinny, but healthier. il Fortune 83:20 F '71
Prospects for wages and prices in Phase II. il Fortune 84:18+ O '71
Recovery is showing some momentum; Wharton econometric model. il Bsns W p 15-16 My 29 '71
Second guesses on '71 forecasts; with table. Bsns W p74-5+ D 11 '71
Stimulating the economy. Newsweek 78:19-20 Ag 30 '71
Surprising seventies. P. F. Drucker. il Harper 243:35-9 Jl '71; Same abr. Read Digest 99: 49-52 S '71; Same with title What surprises, if any, for the seventies? Cur 134:56-64 N '71; Discussion. Harper 243:6-8 S '71
Touch of the poet in Washington. Fortune 83:17-18 Mr '71
Trend will be right, if the psychology is. il Fortune 84:5-6+ Jl '71
Wharton is bullish about 1972. il Bsns W p27-8 D 4 '71
What businessmen expect from the 1970's. D. S. Ammer. il Harvard Bsns R 49:41-52 Ja '71
Where will we be 20 years from now? M. H. Stans. por Nations Bsns 59:26-8 F '71
Which crystal ball? M. Friedman. Newsweek 78:62 Jl 5 '71
Why consumers will spend. L. H. Olsen. por Nations Bsns 59:66 S '71
Will the predictions pan out? CEA report. R. Lekachman. Duns 97:9 Mr '71
See also
Business forecasting
Computers—Economic use

ECONOMIC growth. See Economic development

ECONOMIC history

Medieval

Landlord and the economic revival of the middle ages in northern Europe, 1000-1250. R. G. Witt. bibliog f Am Hist R 76:965-88 O '71

ECONOMIC imperialism. See Imperialism

ECONOMIC models
Econometric stab at stock forecasting; Shilling and Keran models. il Bsns W p36+ My 29 '71
Economists play the numbers game; computerized models. il Bsns W p 125+ Je 5 '71
Recovery is showing some momentum; Wharton econometric model. il Bsns W p 15-16 My 29 '71
Shultz presents the money machine. il Bsns W p74 Mr 20 '71
Wharton is bullish about 1972. il Bsns W p27-8 D 4 '71
ECONOMIC opportunity, Office of. See United States—Economic opportunity, Office of
ECONOMIC opportunity act, 1964. See Economic assistance, Domestic
ECONOMIC planning, International
See also
European economic community
Pacific basin economic council
United Nations—Economic and social council
ECONOMIC policy
See also
Economic development
General agreement on tariffs and trade
Inflation (finance)
Social policy
also subhead Economic policy under names of countries, e.g. Great Britain—Economic policy
ECONOMIC publications, State. See State publications
ECONOMIC relations
Behind Nixon's 5 meetings with allies. il U S News 71:19-21 D 13 '71
Exchanges in turmoil. H. C. Wallich. Newsweek 77:88 My 17 '71
International economic policy scene; address, November 15, 1971. N. Samuels. Dept State Bul 65:669-74 D 13 '71
See also
Balance of payments
also subhead Economic relations under names of countries, e.g. Japan—Economic relations
ECONOMIC research
See also
National bureau of economic research
National institute of economic and social research, London
ECONOMIC sanctions. See Sanctions (international law)
ECONOMIC security
See also
Guaranteed annual income
ECONOMIC stabilization
Price stability and full employment too? G. L. Bach. il Harvard Bsns R 49:68-78 S '71
ECONOMIC statistics
Nobel prize for economics: Kuznets and economic growth. M. Abramovitz. bibliog por Science 174:481-3 O 29 '71
Statistical needs for setting policy. A. Rees. Mo Labor R 94:43-5 S '71
See also
North American conference on labor statistics
Unemployment—Statistics
ECONOMIC surveys
See also
Consumer surveys
ECONOMIC theory. See Economics
ECONOMICS
Academic scribblers, by W. Breit and R. L. Ransom. Review
Nat R 23:321 Mr 23 '71. J. B. Burnham
Does economics deserve a Nobel prize? M. Hudson; reply. M. P. Murray. Commonweal 93:387 Ja 22 '71
Economics in the news (cont) Sr Schol 97: 9-14+ Ja 11; 18-19 Ja 18; 98:18 F 1; 16 Mr 22; 99:7-9 S 20; 11-13 O 11 '71
Economics, peace and laughter, by J. K. Galbraith. Review
Bsns W il p8+ My 8 '71. L. Beman
New Repub 164:28+ My 8 '71. M. J. Ulmer
Sat R 54:25-6 My 8 '71. R. Lekachman
Long arm of biological law; or, How Charles Darwin and his lot will inherit the earth. K. E. F. Watt. Natur Hist 80:14-16+ bibliog (p 84) Ap '71
Maximum principles in analytical economics; Nobel lecture, December 11, 1970. P. A. Samuelson. bibliog il Science 173:991-7 S 10 '71
Money and markets, by B. W. Sprinkel. Review
Bsns W il p6 Jl 3 '71. L. Beman

Progress and poverty, by H. George. Review
New Repub 165:29-31 D 11 '71. P. Barnes
See also
American economic association
Business cycles
Competition
Consumption (economics)
Cost
Efficiency, Industrial
Income
Index numbers (economics)
Liquidity (economics)
Malthusianism
Stock exchange
Value (economic theory)
Wealth, Distribution of

Mathematical models
See Economic models

Social and ethical aspects
U.S. economy in an age of uncertainty. C. E. Silberman. il Fortune 83:72-7+ Ja '71; Same abr. with title Era of new uncertainties. Cur 127:3-14 Mr '71

Terminology
Getting on good terms with economics. Sr Schol 98:20-1 Ap 5 '71
ECONOMICS, Agricultural. See Agriculture—Economic aspects
ECONOMICS and politics
Mixing politics and economics. C. H. Madden. por Nations Bsns 59:40+ Mr '71
Politics and the stages of growth, by W. W. Rostow. Review
New Repub 165:27-9 S 4 '71. P. Streeten
ECONOMISTS
Economics newsmakers. il Sr Schol 98:20-1 Ap 5 '71
Economy: plain or fancy comeback? assessment by Time's economists. il Time 97: 82-3 F 22 '71
Tips from experts at the top. Time 98:69 Ag 16 '71
See also
American economic association
Negro economists
also names of economists, e.g. A. H. Hansen
ECOSYSTEMS. See Ecology
ECUADOR
Fishy business; who owns the oceans? D. F. Ross. New Repub 166:19-21 Ja 1 '72
See also
Birth control—Ecuador
Fishing—Ecuador
Galápagos Islands

Antiquities
Venus of Valdivia. F. Samaniego Salazar. il Américas 23:25-31 Mr '71

Foreign relations
United States
See United States—Foreign relations—Ecuador
ECUMENICAL council, 2d. See Vatican council, 2d
ECUMENICAL movement
Catholics and evangelicals: one in the spirit; Montreal's mass rally for Christ. L. K. Tarr Chr Today 15:38-9 Ap 9 '71
Ecumenism on Main Street, U.S.A. W. B. Cate. Chr Cent 88:1339-40 N 17 '71
Ecumenism: who cares? K. McDonnell. Commonweal 95:55-9 O 15 '71; Reply. L. D. Jordahl. 95:147+ N 12 '71
Ecumenists meet in Dublin; Fourth international congress of Jesuit ecumenists. M. A. Fahey. America 125:141-3 S 11 '71
In Dublin's fair city, the Jesuits; Fourth international congress of Jesuit ecumenists. J. R. Nelson. Chr Cent 88:1072-3 S 15 '71
Price of reconciliation. J. R. Nelson. por Chr Cent 88:972-4 Ag 18 '71
See also
Church union
National association of ecumenical staff
Religious cooperation
World council of churches
EDDAS
Elder Edda, a selection; tr. by P. B. Taylor and W. H. Auden. Review
Poetry 117:341-4 F '71. G. Johnston
EDDY, Charles. See Shostack, K. jt. auth.
EDDY, Lowell L.
Top of the world. il Outdoor Life 148:42-5+ D '71
EDDY, Mary (Baker)
Christian Scientists seek extension of Eddy copyright. Pub W 200:28 O 4 '71 •

EDEL, Harry H.
Homecoming blues. il Outdoor Life 148:54-5+ Jl '71

EDEL, Leon
Profiles. G. T. Hellman. por New Yorker 47: 43-6+ Mr 13 '71 *

EDELBROCK, Vic
SEMA scene; excerpts from address. Hot Rod 24:68 Ag '71

EDELMAN, Susanne Popper
Music by Beaumarchais. il por Opera N 35:8-11 F 20 '71

EDELSON, Edward
How science will speed your mail. il Pop Sci 198:53-5+ Mr '71
(ed) See Wolfe, W. M. Question of sterilization

EDELSON, Michael
Hotline. il Pop Phot 69:10+ O '71

EDEMA
C1 inhibitor: evidence for decreased hepatic synthesis in hereditary angioneurotic edema. A. M. Johnson and others. bibliog il Science 173:553-4 Ag 6 '71

EDEN, Dorothy
Wilder garden; story; excerpt from An afternoon walk. Redbook 138:157-79 N '71

EDEY, Helen
Questions parents ask about sterilization. Parents Mag 46:66-7+ Mr '71

EDGAR, Dave
Fastest man afloat. W. F. Reed. il por Sports Illus 34:16-19 Mr 1 '71 *

EDGAR M. Leventritt award. See Leventritt award

EDGARD, La.

Education

High school class faces the future. il Ebony 26:74-6+ Ag '71

EDGE of panic; story. See Kavan, A.

EDGERTON, Jerry
(ed) See Ruckelshaus, W. D. Man in the eye of the storm
—See Edgerton, L. jt. auth.

EDGERTON, Lynn, and Edgerton, Jerry
Lip service vs. action. il Nat Wildlife 9:28-31 Je '71

EDGERTON, Wallace B.
Development of federal assistance to the humanities; address, April 1971, with questions and answers. Ann Am Acad 396:1-12 Jl '71
What NEH has done for libraries, and how it can help yours. il por Wilson Lib Bul 46:427-30 Ja '72

EDGERTON, William H.
Building costs; indexes and indicators. See issues of Architectural record

EDGLEY, Michael
Dynamic new impresario in Australia. B. Dean. il por Dance Mag 45:44-6 Je '71 *

EDIBLE greens. See Greens, Edible

EDIBLE plants. See Plants, Edible

EDIBLE-podded peas. See Peas

EDINBURGH

Music

Report:
King Arthur, by John Dryden. A. Swanson. il Opera N 35:31 F 13 '71
See also
International festival of music and drama, Edinburgh

EDINBURGH festival of music and drama. See International festival of music and drama, Edinburgh

EDISON, Theodore M.
Progress toward points of no return; excerpts from letter, August 17, 1970. Liv Wildn 34: 52-3 Wint '70

EDISON, Thomas Alva
Tom Edison's sales techniques. R. Peters. il pors Nations Bsns 59:52-6 Mr '71 *

EDITING moving pictures. See Moving pictures—Editing

EDITIONS of works of art. See Multiple art

EDITORIALS
Lion, lion, burning bright; new rulings on Fairness doctrine and paid controversial announcements on TV. R. L. Shayon. Sat R 54:18+ S 11 '71

EDITORS and editing
Dilemma; editors involved in political action. S. J. Adamo. America 124:572 My 29 '71
Editors' editor; J. D. Nicola. S. J. Adamo. America 124:154 F 13 '71
First winner picked for Roger Klein young editors' award. B. A. Bannon. il por Pub W 199:22-3 Ap 26 '71
How religious are religion editors? R. L. Peck. il Chr Today 15:36-7 Ap 9 '71

Job idea: poetry editor. N. Jay. Writers Digest 51:27 F '71
Why the need for young editors? R. H. Smith. Pub W 199:24 Ap 26 '71
See also names of editors, e.g. J. W. Michaels

EDLUND, Calvin V.
Reinforcement approach to the elimination of a child's school phobia. bibliog Ment Hy 55:433-6 O '71

EDMAN, Dwight D. and others
Computers and chemistry. bibliog il pors Chem 45:6-9 Ja '72

EDMISTON, Susan
Fumio Yoshimura. il por Craft Horiz 31: 22-5+ Ag '71
Hotpants: the heat's off! Seventeen 30:157 Jl '71
How is women's liberation doing in the high schools? Seventeen 30:48+ Ag '71
Report on the abortion capital of the country. il N Y Times Mag p 10-11+ Ap 11 '71
(ed) See Millett, K. Day in the life of Kate Millett

EDSON, Lee
C particle: a unified theory of cancer. il por N Y Times Mag p28-9+ Mr 7 '71

EDSON, Lisa
Big sister; story. Seventeen 31:84-5 Ja '72

EDUCATION
Free school. A. C. Jurenas. Clear House 45:418 Mr '71
This book is about schools, ed. by S. Repo. Review
New Repub 164:30-2 Ja 16 '71. W. O'Neil
See also
Ability grouping in education
Accountability (education)
Blind—Education
Catholic church—Education
College education
Communication in education
Communication satellites—Educational use
Culture
Education of women
Elective system in education
Foreign study
Illiteracy
Knowledge
Labor and laboring classes—Education
Laboratory method
Learning, Psychology of
Libraries
Mass media in education
Middle schools
Motivation (education)
Moving pictures in education
Nature study
Right to read program
Role playing
Systems analysis in education
Teaching
Textbooks
Trade schools
Underdeveloped areas—Education
Volunteer workers in education
War and education
also Scientific education and similar headings; also headings beginning Educational, School

Aims and objectives

Aims and requirements of modern education. B. Suchodolski. Sch & Soc 99:409-10 N '71
Command of knowledge should be only one of the objectives of education. H. S. Dyer. Todays Ed 60:50-1 Ap '71
Command of knowledge should be the primary objective of education. R. L. Ebel. il Todays Ed 60:36-9 Mr '71
Curriculum for people. Todays Ed 60:42-4 F '71
Does the school exist for the child? G. S. C. Cheong. Clear House 46:135 N '71
Education for survival. W. H. Boyer. Ed Digest 36:1-4 Mr '71
Radical school reform. B. Gross and R. Gross. Sch & Soc 99:28-9 Ja '71
Target; NEA's report, Schools for the 70's and beyond. H. J. Langer. Sat R 54:75 F 20 '71
Teaching without specific objectives. J. D. Raths. Ed Digest 37:9-12 O '71
We can save our schools. R. Peck. il Parents Mag 46:51-3+ S '71
What is humanization? T. Swihart. Engl J 60:1225-7 D '71
See also
College education—Aims and objectives
Educational sociology

Bibliography

Books for educators; U.S. and foreign. W. W. Brickman. Sch & Soc 99:472-86+ D '71
Educational literature review; U.S. and foreign. W. W. Brickman. Sch & Soc 99:294-6+ Sum '71

EDUCATION—Bibliography—*Continued*
New books. J. Calam. See issues of Saturday review
New educational materials. See issues of Educational digest
Outstanding education books of 1969-70; list prepared by Pi lambda theta. Todays Ed 60:77-9 Mr '71

Curricula
See Courses of study

Economic aspects
Record-smashing year for American education. W. V. Grant. il Am Ed 7:29-31 O '71
See also
College education—Cost
Colleges and universities—Finance
School finance

Evaluation
Can students evaluate their education? with study-discussion program, by C. Smallenburg and H. Smallenburg. R. Peck. bibliog il PTA Mag 65:4-7, 35-6 F '71; Same abr. Ed Digest 36:29-31 My '71
Conflict between politics and evaluation in higher education. R. G. Cope. bibliog Sch & Soc 99:218-20 Ap '71
Five clues to a good school. D. Thomas. Ed Digest 36:29-31 F '71
How do you rate your child's school? G. M. Knox. Bet Hom & Gard 49:26+ S '71
How to rate your child's school. A. Silberman. Ladies Home J 88:39-40+ F '71; Same abr. with title How good is your child's school? Read Digest 98:70-4 Mr '71
We can save our schools. R. Peck. il Parents Mag 46:51-3+ S '71
What people know. R. J. Trotter. Sci N 99:306 My 1 '71
See also
Accountability (education)
National assessment of educational progress
Performance contracts (education)

Experimental methods
See Education, Experimental

Federal aid
Center for law and education aids in title 1, student rights. il Library J 96:681+ F 15 '71
Church and state united. il Sat R 54:52 Ja 16 '71
Education special revenue sharing proposal; Commissioner's conferences held by USOE. G. Krettek and E. D. Cooke. Am Lib 2:380-1 Ap '71
Federal funds. See issues of American education
Giving public education a run for its money. R. Goetz. Chr Cent 88:516-17 Ap 28 '71; Discussion. 88:722-4, 889-90 Je 9, Jl 21 '71
How Louisville put it all together. S. Moorefield. il Am Ed 7:30-4 D '71
New tack on school aid. America 124:111-12 F 6 '71
Nixon administration aims at federal education programs. Pub W 199:36 Ja 18 '71
Pyrrhic victory? House vote. il Newsweek 78:83 N 15 '71
Repackaging federal aid. Time 97:66-7 Ap 19 '71
Revenue sharing and your schools. W. D. Boutwell. PTA Mag 65:15-16 Ap '71
School aid question: Jews take a new look. T. Early. il Cath World 213:134-8 Je '71
Schools cry for more federal aid. il Bsns W p56-8 O 9 '71
Trouble with vouchers. M. R. Berube. Commonweal 93:414-17 Ja 29 '71
See also
Catholic schools—State aid
Church colleges—Federal aid
Church schools—Federal aid
College libraries—Federal aid
Colleges and universities—Federal aid
Libraries—Federal aid
Medical education—Federal aid
Private schools—Federal aid
Right to read program
School libraries—Federal aid
Voucher plan in education

Finance
See School finance

History
1971 as a centennial year in the history of education. F. Parker. Sch & Soc 99:94-6 F '71
See also
Education—United States—History

International aspects
Growing mind: Unesco's work. W. McEwing. il UNESCO Courier 24:21-5 Ag '71
Internationalized university without walls; grants to Union for experimenting colleges and universities. Sch & Soc 99:397-8 N '71

International cooperation
U.S.-U.S.S.R. cooperation. Sch & Soc 99:198 Ap '71
When Soviet and American educators meet; symposium; with joint statement. il Todays Ed 60:16-19 My '71

Laws
See Education—Aims and objectives

Objectives
See Education—Aims and objectives

Organization by years
6-4-4+: the ultimate structure. A. Goldberg. il Clear House 46:10-14 S '71
See also
Middle schools

Periodicals
New Hebrew-English educational journal. Sch & Soc 99:402 N '71

Philosophy
American education as metaphysics: the religious consequence. F. K. Davis. Yale R 61:57-68 O '71
Bertrand Russell: Socrates of our age. H. Ozmon. Ed Digest 36:34-6 F '71
Education without schools. M. A. Petrie. Nation 213:505-6 N 15 '71
Educational philosophy and behavioral objectives. R. B. Kimball. bibliog il Clear House 45:496-500 Ap '71
Educational process; address, September 23, 1971. M. J. Shapp. Vital Speeches 38:49-51 N 1 '71
Essentialist challenge to American education. F. A. Shaw. bibliog Sch & Soc 99:210-14 Ap '71
Herbartians, history, and moral education. N. R. Hiner. Ed Digest 37:51-3 N '71
Meaning and pertinence of educational theory. J. B. Harris. Sch & Soc 99:214-17 Ap '71
Pedagogy of the oppressed, by P. Freire. Review
Sat R 54:54-5 Je 19 '71. D. Harman

Research
See Educational research

Societies
See Educational associations

State aid
See State aid to education

Statistics
Comparative expenditures on education. Sch & Soc 99:396 N '71
Magnitude of the American educational establishment, 1971-1972. il Sat R 54:68 D 18 '71
More education for more people: latest report; years of schooling, how 30 areas compare. il U S News 70:49 Je 7 '71
Record-smashing year for American education. W. V. Grant. il Am Ed 7:29-31 O '71
Statistic of the month. See issues of American education
See also
Colleges and universities—Attendance
School attendance

Study and teaching
See also
Teachers—Education

Terminology
Input-output language in education. W. W. Brickman. Sch & Soc 99:394 N '71

Africa, East
See also
Education—Kenya

Alabama
Following through in Macon County. J. Reed. il Am Ed 7:7-12 N '71

Appalachian Region
Nursery school on wheels; Educational laboratory. M. Cobb. il Parents Mag 46:60-1+ S '71

Arkansas
See also
Little Rock, Ark.—Education

EDUCATION—*Continued*

Brazil

Brazilian government priority projects in education. S. E. Fraser. Sch & Soc 99:364-7 O '71

Pedagogy of the oppressed, by P. Freire. Review
Sat R 54:54-5 Je 19 '71. D. Harman

California

California scraps its school tax system. Bsns W p59-60 S 4 '71

Do drag racers need to know how to read? Yuba County reading-learning center. H. Bottel. il Am Ed 7:3-7 O '71

Man who beat Max Rafferty; with interview. ed. by J. Fried. W. Riles. il pors Life 70:30-1 F 26 '71

See also

Berkeley, Calif.—Education
California—Education, Department of
Colleges and universities—California
Earlimart, Calif.—Education
Fresno, Calif.—Education
Hollywood, Calif.—Education
Martinez, Calif.—Education
Monterey Bay, Calif.—Education
Palo Alto, Calif.—Education
Paramount, Calif.—Education
Pasadena, Calif.—Education
Sacramento, Calif.—Education
San Francisco—Education
Santa Monica, Calif.—Education
School laws and legislation—California

Canada

See also

Colleges and universities—Canada
Education—New Brunswick

China (People's Republic)

Aftermath of China's cultural revolution. M. Goldman. Cur Hist 61:168-9 S '71

Draft program for primary and middle schools in the Chinese countryside; text of document. Sch & Soc 99:238-41 Ap '71

Reforms for rural primary middle schools; introd. to text of document. S. E. Fraser. Sch & Soc 99:237-8 Ap '71

Visit to Peking university, what the cultural revolution was all about. B. M. Frolic. il N Y Times Mag p29+ O 24 '71

See also

Adult education—China (People's Republic)
Colleges and universities—China (People's Republic)

Colorado

See also

Colorado Springs—Education

Connecticut

See also

Enfield, Conn.—Education

Cuba

Revolutionizing educational policy in Cuba. R. G. Paulston. bibliog Sch & Soc 99:452-3 N '71

School dropout problem in Cuba. L. Nelson. Sch & Soc 99:234-5 Ap '71

School dropout question in Cuba. Sch & Soc 99:382-5 O '71

Denmark

Towards a freer school. V. Rasmussen. Ed Digest 36:22-5 My '71

District of Columbia

See Washington, D.C.—Education

Florida

See also

Pensacola, Fla.—Education
St Petersburg, Fla.—Education

France

Ralbol! Paris lycée disorders. il Time 98:46 Jl 5 '71

See also

Schools—France

Germany (Federal Republic)

Changing school patterns in West Germany. W. Hahn. bibliog Clear House 45:300-4 Ja '71

Reform of preschool education in West Germany. Sch & Soc 99:288-9 Sum '71

Great Britain

Comprehensive school under fire in Britain. J. B. Montague, jr. bibliog Clear House 46:44-7 S '71; Same abr. with title British comprehensive school under fire. Ed Digest 37:52-4 D '71

English infant school and informal education, by L. Weber. Review
Sat R 54:69 D 18 '71. M. Hapgood

Open classroom: protect it from its friends. M. Hapgood. il Sat R 54:66-9+ S 18 '71

Open schools: the British and us. J. Featherstone. New Repub 165:20-5 S 11; 17-21 S 25 '71; Excerpt. Ed Digest 37:9-12 D '71

Schools are for children, by A. Hertzberg and E. F. Stone. Review
Sat R 54:73-4 S 18 '71. E. Yeomans

Schools where children learn, by J. Featherstone. Review
Commonweal 95:40-2 O 8 '71. M. Hoffman

See also

Adult education—Great Britain
Colleges and universities—Great Britain
Open plan schools

Hawaii

At peace with pidgin; special language of Hawaiian children. M. Altiery. il Am Ed 7:32-6 O '71

Hilo reads with aloha spirit; Hilo reading clinic. Hawaii. T. Kaser. il Am Ed 7:16-20 Ap '71

Illinois

Rocking the boat; school superintendent M. J. Bakalis. il por Newsweek 78:81 D 6 '71

Valley View's 45-15 year-round school. S. C. Thomas. Todays Ed 60:42-3 N '71

See also

Cairo, Ill.—Education
Champaign, Ill.—Education
Chicago—Education

India

See also

Colleges and universities—India

Indiana

Amish schools today. J. Wittmer. Sch & Soc 99:227-30 Ap '71

See also

Gary, Ind.—Education
Indianapolis—Education

Iowa

See also

Waterloo, Iowa—Education

Iran

See also

Illiteracy—Iran

Ireland

Ireland: church-state tensions over education. J. Horgan. Chr Cent 88:469 Ap 14 '71

Israel

Second-class citizens; Eisenstadt-Peres report. il Newsweek 77:40 F 8 '71

Textbooks for Gaza schoolchildren. Sch & Soc 99:268 Sum '71

Italy

Middle school reform in Italy. G. L. Williams. bibliog f Clear House 46:245-9 D '71

Japan

Educational and cultural trends in Japan today. W. S. Morton. Cur Hist 60:213-17 Ap

See also

Colleges and universities—Japan

Kansas

See also

Shawnee, Kan.—Education

Kentucky

See also

Louisville—Education

Kenya

Language and the schools in Kenya. G. E. Urch. bibliog Sch & Soc 99:373-7 O '71

Latin America

Education, population, and the quality of life in Latin America. K. Holland. Sch & Soc 99:439-42 N '71

See also

Inter-American children's institute

Louisiana

See also

New Orleans—Education

Maine

Saving an island school; case of Cliff Island; report. P. Taubman. il Time 98:52-3 Ag 16 '71

See also

Yarmouth, Me.—Education

Malaysia

Possibilities for violence in Malaysia. P. Pedersen. bibliog f Cur Hist 61:339-44+ D '71

EDUCATION—*Continued*

Maryland

Cargo of career education. W. Wood. il **Am Ed** 7:16-20 O '71

Learning to cope in Prince Georges County; new course on Teen-agers' rights and responsibilities for all eight-graders. B. L. Collier. il **Sat R** 54:64-5+ My 22 '71

Maryland's scholarship plan. A. L. Scanlan. **America** 124:563-4 My 29 '71

See also
Howard County. Md.—Education

Massachusetts

See also
Norton. Mass.—Education
Winchester, Mass.—Education

Michigan

See also
Detroit—Education
Grand Rapids Mich.—Education
Oakland County. Mich.—Education
Pontiac Mich.—Education
School laws and legislation—Michigan

Micronesia

Micronesian culture vs. American education. D. F. Smith. bibliog il **Sch & Soc** 99:279-82 Sum '71

Minnesota

Freedom to learn at Wilson campus school. G. Palmer and O. Jensen. **Todays Ed** 60: 47-8 N '71

See also
Minnesota education association
St Cloud. Minn.—Education
St Paul—Education

Mississippi

See also
Jackson. Miss.—Education
Leflore County, Miss.—Education

Missouri

See also
St Louis—Education

Montana

See also
Monarch, Mont.—Education

Nevada

See also
Washoe County, Nev.—Education

New Brunswick

New Brunswick experience. S. Canning. **Sat R** 54:88 N 20 '71

New Hampshire

Wide open for learning; Project SOLVE; schools without walls. R. C. Wing and P. H. Mack. **Ed Digest** 36:19-21 F '71

New Jersey

See also
Newark. N.J.—Education
Vineland. N.J.—Education

New York (state)

All the isms are wasms; Project Redesign; address, July 15, 1971. E. Nyquist. Vital **Speeches** 37:645-50 Ag 15 '71

See also
New York (city)—Education
Port Washington. N.Y.—Education

North Carolina

See also
John C. Campbell folk school, Brasstown

North Dakota

Dakota story; a new vitality. il **Newsweek** 77:65 My 3 '71

New school; teacher preparation program. V. Perrone and W. Strandberg. **Ed Digest** 37:13-16 O '71

Promise of change in North Dakota; programs of the New school for behavioral studies in education. H. S. Resnik. il **Sat R** 54:67-9+ Ap 17 '71

Norway

See also
Colleges and universities—Norway

Ohio

Ohio plan succumbs to lack of popular and institutional support. **Sch & Soc** 99:399 N '71

See also
Athens. Ohio—Education
Columbus. Ohio—Education
Dayton, Ohio—Education

Pennsylvania

Educational process; address, September 23, 1971. M. J. Shapp. Vital **Speeches** 38:49-51 N 1 '71

See also
Philadelphia—Education

Rhode Island

See also
North Kingstown. R.I.—Education

Russia

From Moscow to Irkutsk to Leningrad; interview. D. Morrison; S. Lambert. il **Todays Ed** 60:36-40 D '71

Soviet schooling: a quiet revolution. S. Jacoby. il **Sat R** 54:43-5+ Jl 17 '71; Same abr. **Ed Digest** 37:17-20 D '71

When Soviet and American educators meet; symposium; with joint statement. il **Todays Ed** 60:16-19 My '71

Who raises Russia's children? preschooling. S. Jacoby. il **Sat R** 54:40-3+ Ag 21 '71

History

Nadezhda K. Krupskaya, founder of Soviet public education. L. Goncharov and L. Kunetskaia. por **Sch & Soc** 99:235-7 Ap '71

Southern states

Busing; Supreme court decision on southern schools. **New Repub** 164:11-12 My 1 '71

Dixie schools charade. A. Poinsett. il **Ebony** 26:144-8 Ag '71

Education in the changing South. S. M. Holton. **Ed Digest** 36:5-8 Ja '71

Now Supreme court sets rules for busing students. il **U S News** 70:12-14 My 3 '71

Rebel yell academies. E. Tornquist. il **Ramp Mag** 10:12+ S '71

See also
Colleges and universities—Southern states
Negroes—Education
Public schools—Desegregation

Tennessee

See also
Nashville, Tenn.—Education

Texas

See also
Austin. Tex.—Education
Crystal City. Tex—Education
Dallas—Education

Turkey

See also
Colleges and universities—Turkey

Underdeveloped areas

See Underdeveloped areas—Education

United States

American education as metaphysics: the religious consequences. F. K. Davis. **Yale R** 61:57-68 O '71

Condition of education in the Nation. S. P. Marland, jr. **Am Ed** 7:3-5 Ap '71

Crisis in the classroom, by C. E. Silberman. Review

  Commentary 51:84-7 Mr '71. S. McCracken
  Schol Teach Jr/Sr High p24 Mr 8 '71

Culture of the school and the problem of change, by S. B. Sarason. Review

  Sat R 54:70 My 22 '71. M. M. Tumin

Education in America. J. Cass and others. See issues of Saturday review

Education 1970: a short review. M. Smith. **Ed Digest** 36:29-31 Ap '71

Educational developments in 1970. W. W. Brickman. **Sch & Soc** 99:10-11 Ja '71

Happenings in education. W. D. Boutwell. See issues of PTA magazine

Love/hate relationship between press and school; a small-town publisher looks at today's schools. W. L. Bates. **Ed Digest** 36:22-4 Ap '71

Margaret Mead views education today. M. Mead. **Ed Digest** 37:5-8 D '71

New ideas for better schools; interview. S. P. Marland, jr. il por **U S News** 71:80-5 N 1 '71

News and trends. See issues of Today's education

Public education: is its demise near? R. W. Seltzer. **Clear House** 46:6-9 S '71

Quoting Marland; excerpts from speeches and writings. S. P. Marland. por **Am Ed** 7:3-4 Ja '71

Radical school reform. B. Gross and R. Gross. **Sch & Soc** 99:28-9 Ja '71

Recasting of public education; address. July 5. 1971. J. E. Allen, jr. Vital **Speeches** 37:654-8 Ag 15 '71

EDUCATION—United States—*Continued*
Revolution or anarchy in our schools? D. H. Parker. Ed Digest 36:5-8 F '71
Schools in trouble. S. McCracken. il Parents Mag 46:57-9+ F '71
Schools make news. See issues of Saturday review
Should schools be abolished? por Time 97:33-4+ Je 7 '71
Teacher numbers game. D. Davies. Ed Digest 36:1-4 Ja '71
U.S. education: glory and shame. America 125:164 S 18 '71
Who pushed Humpty Dumpty? by D. Barr. Review
Sat R 54:94 N 20 '71. W. Newton
With education in Washington. T. Schuchat. See issues of Education digest
See also
Adult education
Colleges and universities—United States
Education—Statistics
Education and democracy
Educational innovations
Equalization, Educational
Future teachers of America
Indians of North America—Education
Junior colleges
Labor and laboring classes—Education
National education association
Negroes—Education
Private schools
Public schools—United States
Rural schools
School laws and legislation—United States
Summer schools
United States—Education, Office of
Vocational education

History
American education. by L. A. Cremin. Review
Sat R 54:50-1 Mr 20 '71. T. R. Sizer
Education: the good old days that never were. G. C. Tiffin. Chr Today 15:4-6 F 12 '71
School days, school days, 140 years ago. il Sr Schol 99:10-11 N 15 '71
Traditions in urban school reform. J. H. Spring. bibliog Sch & Soc 99:428-33 N '71

Vermont
Catholic education aid: Yankee style. F. M. Bryan. il America 125:174-5 S 18 '71; Reply. R. A. Adams. 125:217 O 2 '71

Vietnam (Democratic Republic)
Education and science in North Vietnam. A. W. Galston and E. Signer. bibliog Science 174:379-85 O 22 '71

Virginia
See also
Richmond, Va.—Education

Washington (state)
See also
Bellevue, Wash.—Education
Redmond, Wash.—Education
Seattle—Education

Wisconsin
See also
Milwaukee—Education
EDUCATION, Adult. See Adult education
EDUCATION, Agricultural. See Agricultural education
EDUCATION, Art. See Art education
EDUCATION, Bilingual
Degrees in bilingual education; B.S. and master's degrees available at University of Texas college of education. Sch & Soc 99:332 O '71
Lessons from the schools of other nations; two pilot programs of the Office of education's Institute of international studies. D. Sweeney. il Am Ed 7:9-11 O '71
EDUCATION, Boards of. See School boards
EDUCATION, College. See College education
EDUCATION, Commissioner of. See United States—Education, Office of
EDUCATION, Comparative
Lessons from the schools of other nations; two pilot programs of the Office of education's Institute of international studies. D. Sweeney. il Am Ed 7:8-13 O '71
William Torrey Harris: pioneer in comparative education. J. Sakas. bibliog por Sch & Soc 99:230-2 Ap '71
EDUCATION, Compulsory. See Compulsory education
EDUCATION, Consumer. See Consumer education

EDUCATION, Cooperative
Cooperative education program; United States Office of education. il Am Ed 7:36 Ja '71
Detroit combines students' worlds. E. Rasof. Am Ed 7:25-7 Je '71
Earn-and-learn program scores with employers; University of south Florida's cooperative education program. V. Louviere. il Nations Bsns 59:16 F '71
Is hard work going out of style? interview. E. Ginzberg. il por U S News 71:52-6 Ag 23 '71
R for an age-old dilemma: should I take this job for life? Alhambra high school's occupational center, Martinez, Calif. D. Morrison. il Schol Teach Jr/Sr High p24-5+ S '71
To "stay" with tax-supported love; dropout project in St Louis. K. Marshall. il Am Ed 7:10 Ap '71
EDUCATION, Cost of. See Education—Economic aspects
EDUCATION, Elementary
Feeling our way to a good environment. J. H. Cravens. il Am Ed 7:25-8 O '71
For the elementary teacher: bulletin boards and a learning environment. il Sch Arts 71:6-7 D '71
Rocket age, rickety curriculum? Public schools of choice; with study-discussion program, by C. Smallenburg and H. Smallenburg. M. D. Fantini. bibliog il PTA Mag 65:2-5, 33 Ja '71
Schools where children learn, by J. Featherstone. Review
Commonweal 95:40-2 O 8 '71. M. Hoffman
State superintendent teaches first grade. D. Parnell. il por Todays Ed 60:29-30 O '71
See also
Education, Experimental
Nursery schools
Open plan schools
Schools, Experimental
Voucher plan in education
EDUCATION, Experimental
Freedom to learn at Wilson campus school. G. Palmer and O. Jensen. Todays Ed 60:47-8 N '71
Getting high on high school; new alternatives. K. Branan. il Schol Teach Jr/Sr High p 12-14+ F 1 '71
High school alternatives: stepping out into the sunshine; Program for inquiry, involvement and independent study at New Rochelle and Chicago's Metro. K. Branan. il Schol Teach Jr/Sr High p8-11 D '71
Latent talent: the anagram a parent can solve. B. Nikitin. il UNESCO Courier 24:28-32 F '71
Multimedia classroom; Project SPOKE, Norton, Mass. D. C. Steffen. il Am Ed 7:28-30 Ag '71
Student power; want to start a school? il Seventeen 29:132-3+ N '70
Three new faces of English. R. G. Lambert. Engl J 60:909-12+ O '71
See also
College education, Experimental
Educational innovations
Open plan schools
Philadelphia—Education
Schools, Experimental
Ungraded classes
Voucher plan in education
EDUCATION, Higher. See College education
EDUCATION, Individual. See Individual instruction
EDUCATION, Liberal. See Liberal education
EDUCATION, Medical. See Medical education
EDUCATION, Moral. See Moral education
EDUCATION, Office of. See United States—Education, Office of
EDUCATION, Preschool. See Preschool children—Education
EDUCATION, Primary. See Education, Elementary
EDUCATION, Secondary
ES '70s: the educational innovation of the 1970's? W. H. Drost. bibliog Sch & Soc 99:224-7 Ap '71
See also
High schools
EDUCATION, Social. See Social education
EDUCATION, Speech. See Speech education
EDUCATION, State departments of
Social studies: specialists in state education departments. L. F. Psencik. Clear House 45:341-5 F '71
Trends in state-level curriculum requirements. R. L. Cox and E. M. Ramer. Clear House 45:309-11 Ja '71
See also names of education departments, inverted, under states, e.g. California—Education, Department of

EDUCATION, Urban
Ahead for big-city schools: penny-pinching and turmoil. il U S News 71:24-6+ S 13 '71

Imperatives in urban education; address, July 16, 1971. H. B. Scribner. Vital Speeches 37:669-72 Ag 15 '71

Reorganization of education in metropolitan areas. R. J. Havighurst. Ed Digest 36:5-8 My '71

Traditions in urban school reform. J. H. Spring. bibliog Sch & Soc 99:428-33 N '71

Unique approach to inner-city teacher education; Cooperative Urban Teacher Education project. M. Pedram. Clear House 45: 297-9 Ja '71

Urban teachers for urban youth. E. Kruszynski. bibliog Sch & Soc 99:511-13 D '71

EDUCATION, Value of
See also
College education. Value of

EDUCATION, Vocational. See Vocational education

EDUCATION and democracy
Diffusion of innovations: the school and democratic values. M. T. Hinkemeyer. Clear House 45:429-34 Mr '71

Education and democracy. Negro Hist Bul 34:76-7 Ap '71

EDUCATION and manpower
Human resources: retooling our manpower. J. M. Rosow il Sat R 54:40-1+ Ja 23 '71

Preparing youth for reality; address, October 29, 1971. J. D. Hodgson. Vital Speeches 38:166-8 Ja 1 '72

Where the jobs will be in the '70s; excerpts from survey by U.S. Department of labor. il U S News 71:68-71 S 6 '71

EDUCATION and politics. See Politics and education

EDUCATION and public opinion. See School and the community

EDUCATION and social problems. See School and social and economic problems

EDUCATION and sociology. See Educational sociology

EDUCATION and state
See also
Education—Federal aid
School and the community
Voucher plan in education

EDUCATION and technology
Alternative to schooling. I. D. Illich. il Sat R 54:44-8+ Je 19 '71; Same abr. with title For disestablishment of the school. Cur 131:24-34 Jl '71

Dangers in de-schooling. T. Beeson. Chr Cent 88:1341 N 17 '71

Education: a consumer commodity and a pseudo-religion; adaptation of address, 1971. I. Illich. Chr Cent 88:1464-8 D 15 '71

EDUCATION and travel. See Student travel

EDUCATION associations. See Educational associations

EDUCATION for citizenship. See Citizenship, Education for

EDUCATION market
Has the education industry lost its nerve? R. W. Locke. il Sat R 54:42-4+ Ja 16 '71

EDUCATION of adults. See Adult education

EDUCATION of children
Deschooling society, by I. Illich. Review America 125:42 Jl 24 '71. J. P. Fitzpatrick

From Denmark, with love, English publication of The little red schoolbook. H. R. Mayes. Sat R 54:8-9 Jl 3 '71

Keys to success in learning; everyday things parents can do at home. M. Ratz. il Parents Mag 46:56-7+ O '71

Open schools vs. traditional: which is right for your child? H. S. Resnik. Redbook 137: 60+ O '71

See also
Camping—Educational aspects
Childrens literature
Childrens reading
Education, Elementary
Educational acceleration
Moral education
Nature study
Nursery schools
Play
Psychology, Educational
Schools, Experimental
Sex instruction

EDUCATION of Indian children. See Indians of North America—Education

EDUCATION of librarians. See Library schools and education

EDUCATION of Negroes. See Negroes—Education

EDUCATION of the aged. See Aged—Education

EDUCATION of women
Educating women: no more sugar and spice. F. Howe; J. L. Trecker. il Sat R 54:76-7+ O 16 '71

New priorities and old prejudices. E. D. Koontz. Todays Ed 60:25-6 Mr '71; Same abr. Ed Digest 36:32-3 My '71

Newest campus crusade: equal rights for women; with address by A. Pifer. il U S News 71:79-82 D 13 '71

Sex discrimination in schools; outmoded stereotypes still exist. G. T. McLure and others. Todays Ed 60:33-5 N '71

Women's liberation: or, Exploding the fairy princess myth. A. G. West. bibliog f Schol Teach Jr/Sr High p6-11 N '71

Women's studies. R. M. Somerville. Todays Ed 60:35-7 N '71

EDUCATIONAL acceleration
Getting smarter sooner; proposal of W. Riles for California's children. il por Time 98: 38 Jl 26 '71

EDUCATIONAL achievements. See Student achievements

EDUCATIONAL administration. See School management and organization

EDUCATIONAL associations
Association and the school board. K. E. Buhrmaster; E. Erickson. pors Todays Ed 60:48-50 My '71

Local association of the month:
Alfred I. DuPont education association. B. Sarra. Todays Ed 60:56 Ap '71
Bellevue education association. L. E. Saylor. Todays Ed 60:66 Mr '71
Colorado Springs teachers association. B. R. Dickinson. Todays Ed 60:50 D '71
Monterey Bay teachers association. F. Jacobson and others. Todays Ed 60:63 F '71
NEA of Shawnee Mission. N. K. Nichols. Todays Ed 60:54 My '71
Newport News education association. B. J. DeHoff. Todays Ed 60:58 O '71
Orleans educators association. L. Felix. Todays Ed 60:70 N '71
Washoe County teachers association. P. Dorazio. Todays Ed 60:53 Ja '71
Waterloo education association. L. L. Kelley. Todays Ed 60:76 S '71
See also names of educational associations, e.g. American association of school administrators

EDUCATIONAL change. See Educational innovations

EDUCATIONAL conferences
Dates of the month. See issues of Education digest
European seminar on research in education. Sch & Soc 99:290+ Sum '71
Guidelines on pupil records; report of Russell Sage foundation conference. Sch & Soc 99:283-5 Sum '71
Professional calendar (cont) Todays Ed 60:66-7 Ja; 60 My '71
Reform of preschool education in West Germany; Unesco institute for education conference. Sch & Soc 99:288-9 Sum '71
School records can be an invasion of privacy; Russell Sage foundation conference guidelines. V. S. Teitelbaum. Todays Ed 60:43-5 My '71

EDUCATIONAL consultants
Educational technocrat. J. G. Lawler. Commonweal 95:343-7 Ja 14 '72

EDUCATIONAL cooperation
See also
Colleges and universities—Cooperation

EDUCATIONAL correlation. See Correlation (education)

EDUCATIONAL criticism
What school reformers want; with study-discussion program, by C. Smallenburg and H. Smallenburg. N. Naisbitt. il PTA Mag 66:6-8+ N '71

EDUCATIONAL discrimination. See Discrimination in education

EDUCATIONAL equalization. See Equalization, Educational

EDUCATIONAL exchanges
Report on educational and cultural exchange program sent to Congress; message, August 5, 1971. R. M. Nixon. Dept State Bul 65: 250 Ag 30 '71

Return of the Fulbright. Newsweek 77:80 My 31 '71

Twenty-fifth anniversary of the educational exchange program; Department announcement and statement by the Board of foreign scholarships. Dept State Bul 65:386-90 O 11 '71

See also
Foreign students in the United States

EDUCATIONAL experiments. See Education, Experimental; Educational innovations

EDUCATIONAL films. See Moving pictures in education

EDUCATIONAL foundations. See Foundations, Charitable and educational

EDUCATIONAL guidance
See also
Vocational guidance

EDUCATIONAL innovations
Change in education: the new and the not so new. M. S. Vaughan. bibliog Sch & Soc 99:341-5 O '71
Changes in the traditional concepts of higher education. A. S. Knowles. Sch & Soc 99: 405-9 N '71
Columbus arts IMPACT; interdisciplinary model programs in the arts for children and teachers. il Todays Ed 60:20-4 N '71
Cultural evaluation of contemporary educational innovations. S. L. Miller. bibliog Sch & Soc 99:507-8+ D '71
Death of a modern God. C. F. H. Henry. Chr Today 16:36-7 N 5 '71
Give us this day our ABCs. L. Velie. Read Digest 99:126-30 D '71
Innovation: what's it all about? C. Helwig. bibliog Clear House 46:82-5 O '71
Innovations; suggestions sent in by teachers. Schol Teach Jr/Sr High p 18 S; 20 O '71; 12 Ja '72
Is educational reform conceivable? conference of Open court publishing company. R. Kirk. Nat R 23:872 Ag 10 '71
New orthodoxies for old. J. Cass. il Sat R 54:39 Je 19 '71
Science fiction as education for change. L. Ruth. Engl J 60:1243-51+ D '71
Theory and practice: why nothing seems to work. D. A. Erlandson and E. R. House. Ed Digest 37:34-7 S '71
Twenty unprinciples for successful innovation. A. S. Anthony. Clear House 46:32-4 S '71
Two prof's speak out; teacher inability to change. G. Martinez and W. Shreeve. Clear House 46:150 N '71
Undiscussed alternatives; Catholic education overhaul needed. C. A. Koob. America 125: 168-70 S 18 '71
What are the hallmarks of innovation? A hard look at the educational process; address, October 26, 1971. S. M. McMurrin. Vital Speeches 38:115-17 D 1 '71
What can I do about pressures to conform? K. Branan. Schol Teach Jr/Sr High p30 Ja '72
What will the schools become? results of poll educators. H. G. Shane and O. N. Nelson. Ed Digest 37:1-3 O '71
See also
Education, Experimental

Anecdotes, facetiae, satire, etc.
Some unprinciples for successful innovation. A. S. Anthony. Ed Digest 37:32-3 N '71

EDUCATIONAL literature
See also
Publishers and publishing—Educational literature

EDUCATIONAL materials. See Teaching—Aids and devices

EDUCATIONAL organization. See School management and organization

EDUCATIONAL periodicals. See Education— Periodicals

EDUCATIONAL philosophy. See Education— Philosophy

EDUCATIONAL planning
All the isms are wasms; New York state's Project Redesign; address, July 15, 1971. E. Nyquist. Vital Speeches 37:645-50 Ag 15 '71
See also
Curriculum planning
Educational innovations

EDUCATIONAL policy advisers. See Executive advisory bodies

EDUCATIONAL products information exchange institute
Untested textbooks. il Time 97:33 Je 7 '71

EDUCATIONAL psychology. See Psychology, Educational

EDUCATIONAL radio. See Radio in education

EDUCATIONAL records. See School reports and records

EDUCATIONAL research
European seminar on research in education. Sch & Soc 99:290+ Sum '71
Research clues; questions and answers. See issues of Today's education

Study of higher education; report by the Assembly on university goals and governance. W. W. Brickman. Sch & Soc 99:266-7 Sum '71
See also
United States—National institute of education (proposed)

EDUCATIONAL resource centers. See Instructional materials centers

EDUCATIONAL satellite center. See Wisconsin. University—EDSAT center

EDUCATIONAL segregation. See Segregation in education

EDUCATIONAL sociology
Alternative to schooling. I. D. Illich. il Sat R 54:44-8+ Je 19 '71; Same abr. with title For disestablishment of the school. Cur 131: 24-34 Jl '71
Comprehensive school under fire in Britain. J. B. Montague, jr. bibliog Clear House 46: 44-7; S '71; Same abr. with title British comprehensive school under fire. Ed Digest 37:52-4 D '71
Dangers in de-schooling. T. Beeson. Chr Cent 88:1341 N 17 '71
Delinquency: its prevention rests upon the academic community. F. I. Closson. Clear House 45:290-3 Ja '71
Deschooling society, by I. Illich. Review
America 125:42 Jl 24 '71. J. P. Fitzpatrick
Sat R 54:88-9 O 16 '71. C. Greer
Education: a consumer commodity and a pseudo-religion; adaptation of address, 1971. I. Illich Chr Cent 88:1464-8 D 15 '71
Educational change and pedagogical validity. H. K. Heger. bibliog Clear House 45:563-7 My '71
Quest for values in a world of facts; address, December 6, 1971. A. W. Clausen. Vital Speeches 38:182-6 Ja 1 '72
Reflections of a sociologist in a school of education. N. L. Friedman. bibliog Sch & Soc 99:41-3 Ja '71; Reply. R. L. Calatrello. 99:419-20 N '71
Self-confrontation: rehearsal for renaissance. W. F. Amar. Clear House 45:294-6 Ja '71
Toward radical reform; excerpt from How to change colleges. H. Taylor. Cur 130: 27-35 Je '71
See also
College education—Aims and objectives
Education—Aims and objectives

EDUCATIONAL statistics. See Education— Statistics

EDUCATIONAL study tours. See Travel study courses

EDUCATIONAL surveys
See also
National assessment of educational progress

EDUCATIONAL television. See Television in education

EDUCATIONAL testing service
New ways to measure intelligence in infants. S. S. Fremon. il Parents Mag 46:39-41+ Ap '71

EDUCATIONAL tests and measurements
Do thirteen year olds write as well as seventeen year olds? H. B. Slotnick. il Engl J 60:1109-15 N '71
Implications of national assessment writing results. E. J. Farrell. Engl J 60:1116-19 N '71
Testing for accountability. R. W. Tyler. Ed Digest 36:12-14 Mr '71
Tests your child takes; with study-discussion program, by E. Harris and D. Harris. G. Cawelti and P. McCloud. bibliog il PTA Mag 65:6-9, 34-5 Mr '71
See also
Aptitude tests
Educational testing service
Intelligence tests

EDUCATIONAL theory. See Education—Philosophy

EDUCATIONAL toys. See Toys

EDUCATIONAL workshops
Integrated day workshop; University of Rochester summer workshop on open plan schools. A. Muskopf and J. Moss. Ed Digest 36:26-8 My '71

EDUCATORS
See also
College presidents
College professors and instructors
Negro educators
Teachers
also names of educators, e.g. H. Mann

EDWARDIANS. See Great Britain—History— Edwardian period, 1901-1910

EDWARDS, Carl M.
How to select a recreational travel vehicle. il Consumer Bul 54:4+ Mr '71

EDWARDS, Charles Cornell
How safe is your food? interview. il por U S News 70:50-4 Ap 19 '71

about

Hazardous substances. New Repub 164:11 Ap 3 '71 *

EDWARDS, Clifford
Jesus Christ superstar: electric age messiah. Cath World 213:217-21 Ag '71
Zen in the art of archery: a bridge to the East. America 125:31 Jl 24 '71

EDWARDS, Elizabeth
Dedicated teacher is the teaching profession's greatest enemy. Ed Digest 36:22-3 Ja '71

EDWARDS, Ellen
1001 ways to be unsuccessful. Har Yrs 11: 40-1 My '71

EDWARDS, H. W. and Brouwer, L. G.
Determining specific heats by ice calorimetry. bibliog il pors Chem 44:23-4 Ap '71

EDWARDS, Jeff
Fog; poem. Sr Schol 98:8 My 17 '71

EDWARDS, John S. and Palka, John
Neural regeneration: delayed formation of central contacts by insect sensory cells. bibliog il Science 172:591-4 My 7 '71

EDWARDS, Lee
Friends in need. Newsweek 78:20 S 13 '71 *

EDWARDS, Lovett
(tr) See Djilas, M. Girl with the gold tooth

EDWARDS, Margaret Bunel
Turnabout; drama. Plays 31:31-4 D '71

EDWARDS, Mike W.
Mexico to Canada on the Pacific Crest trail. il pors Nat Geog 139:741-79 Je '71

EDWARDS, William J. Jr
Amenities of opening closed doors. Ed Digest 36:9-11 Ja '71

EELS
DDT: disrupted osmoregulatory events in the intestine of the eel anguilla rostrata adapted to seawater. R. H. Janicki and W. B. Kinter. bibliog il Science 173:1146-8 S 17 '71
See also
Cookery—Fish

EELS, Electric. See Electric eels

EFF, Johannes
Butler did it; poem. Nat R 23:420 Ap 20 '71
Cinderella at the ping-pong ball. Nat R 23: 531 My 18 '71
Firing line guest: Santa Claus; De mortuus Nik; poems. Nat R 23:1467, 1469 D 31 '71
Let's carbuncle Sam; poem. Nat R 23:696 Je 29 '71
Lindsay for president? poem. Nat R 23:1170 O 22 '71
President Bok is on the phone to Mr Nixon; poem. Nat R 23:70-1 Ja 26 '71
See Ogden, you can get there from here; poem. Nat R 23:630 Je 15 '71

EFFECT of gamma rays on man-in-the-moon-marigolds; drama. See Zindel, P.

EFFELSBERG telescope. See Radio telescopes

EFFENBACH, Leah
Close look at the Tchaikovsky competition. Hi Fi 20:MA22-3+ D '70

EFFICIENCY, Administrative
Government agencies are failing our people; address, June 29, 1971. D. F. Linowes. Vital Speeches 37:759-62 O 1 '71

EFFICIENCY, Household. See Home economics

EFFICIENCY, Industrial
Big doesn't mean efficient. R. E. Lapp. New Repub 165:25-7 N 20 '71
See also
Factory management
Labor productivity
Work measurement

EFFLER, Donald Brian
Old hearts. new plumbing. il por Time 97:51-2 My 10 '71

EFIRD, Callie Huger. See Farnham, K. G. jt. auth.

EFRON, Edith
Edith Efron's murderous adding machine. J. Chamberlain. Nat R 23:1225-6+ N 5 '71 *
News twisters. Nat R 23:1159 O 22 '71 *

EFRON, Marshall
TV's tiny terror. M. Barrett. il por Vogue 158:91 S 15 '71
Who took the lemons out of mom's pie? il por Bsns W p23 F 6 '71*

EGAN, Anna Maria Gavin
Ourselves alone: Irish exiles in Brooklyn. W. Alfred. il por Atlan 227:53-8 Mr '71 *

EGAN, Eddie
Bad connection. il por Newsweek 78:28 N 29 '71 *
Detective Egan's new assignment. P. F. Kluge. il pors Life 71:85-6+ D 10 '71 *

EGAN, Ferol
Incident at Tragedy Springs. il Am West 8:36-9 Ja '71

EGAN, James
Boyhood joys of Christmas. il pors Good H 173:44+ D '71
Great homes away from home: Mohonk mountain house. il Am Home 74:42+ O '71
Survival in the suburbs. il Good H 172:74-5+ Je '71

EGAN, John J.
Priest power in Baltimore. Commonweal 94: 101-2 Ap 9 '71

EGAN, William Allen
Alaska's governor covets the pipeline. por Bsns W p44 N 13 '71 *

EGAÑA, Juan
Precursors of the inter-American system. por Américas 23:S4-5 Ja '71 *

EGEBERG, Roger Olaf
Egeberg's successor. Time 97:42 Mr 29 '71 *

EGERIA. See Anacharis

EGG cookers, Electric. See Household appliances, Electric

EGG shells
DDE residues and eggshell changes in Alaskan falcons and hawks. T. J. Cade and others. bibliog il Science 172:955-7 My 28 '71
Eggshell thinning in Japanese quail fed mercuric chloride. G. S. Stoewsand and others. bibliog il Science 173:1030-1 S 10 '71
Will the brown pelican survive? H. H. Harrison. il Nat Wildlife 9:25-7 Je '71

EGGS
See also
Birds eggs
Cookery—Eggs
Easter eggs

EGGSHELLS. See Egg shells

EGLER, Frank E.
Romance of roadside ragweed. Cons 26:27 Ag '71

EGLEVSKY ballet company
Eglevsky ballet company of Long Island, Brooklyn academy of music. T. Borek. Dance Mag 45:87-8 My '71

EGO. See Self

EGOTIST; story. See Singer, I. B.

EGYPT
See also
Airlines—Egypt
Arab Republics, Federation of
Ecology—Egypt
Economic assistance in Egypt
Intelligence service—Egypt
Military assistance, Russian—Egypt
Morale, National—Egypt
Newspapers—Egypt
Red Sea
Sharm el Sheikh
Sinai (peninsula)
Suez Canal
United States—Economic relations—Egypt

Antiquities

Golden links to the bronze age; display at the Museum of fine arts, Boston. E. Vermeule. il Horizon 13:50-3 Wint '71
Probing the New Kingdom pharaohs with X-rays. il Sci N 100:245 O 9 '71
See also
Abu Simbel, Temples of
Pyramids
Temples—Egypt

Defenses

Moscow's arms aid to Egypt: 4.5 billions since 1967. il U S News 70:29 Ap 12 '71
Soviets spur arms flow to Egypt; with editorial comment. E. H. Kolcum. il Aviation W 94:9, 14-16 Ap 19 '71
Strategic balance. il Newsweek 77:37-8 Mr 22 '71

Economic conditions

Egypt since Nasser. A. Z. Rubinstein. Cur Hist 62:6-13 Ja '72
Letter from Cairo. J. Kraft. il New Yorker 47:76+ S 18 '71

Foreign relations

Arab Socialist union; address, June 10, 1971. A. Sadat. Vital Speeches 37:580-3 Jl 15 '71

Nationalism

Sadat's Egypt: a new world may be open. M. J. Kubic. il Newsweek 77:40-1 Ap 5 '71
Yassin, my son. Time 97:39 Ap 5 '71

Politics and government

Arab Socialist union; address, June 10, 1971. A. Sadat. Vital Speeches 37:580-3 Jl 15 '71
Egypt: alone at the top. Newsweek 77:30+ My 31 '71

EGYPT—Politics and government—*Cont.*
Egypt moves west. F. Halliday. por **Ramp**
Mag 10:41-4 Ag '71
Egypt: Sadat in the saddle. il por Time 97:
34+ My 31 '71
Egypt's Sadat: cooling the hawks. il por U S
News 70:36 My 31 '71
Letter from Cairo. J. Kraft. il New Yorker
47:76+ S 18 '71
Middle East: the underrated heir. il pors
Time 97:23-6+ My 17 '71
Preemptive purge in Cairo. il Time 97:28+
My 24 '71
Real Sadat and the demythologized Nasser.
E. R. F. Sheehan. il pors N Y Times Mag
p6-7+ Jl 18 '71
Religion and politics in Anwar el Sadat. J.
C. Haughey. America 124:605 Je 12 '71
Reports & comment. G. G. Stevens. Atlan
229:12-16 Ja '72
Sadat's shake-up. il por Newsweek 77:35-6
My 24 '71
See also
Egypt—Nationalism

Social conditions
Egypt since Nasser. A. Z. Rubenstein. Cur
Hist 62:6-13 Ja '72

Treaties
Russia
See Russia—Treaties—Egypt

EGYPTIAN refugees. See Refugees, Egyptian
EGYPTIAN sculpture. See Sculpture, Egyptian
EHRENFEST, Paul
Paul Ehrenfest, by M. Klein. Review
New Yorker 46:95-8 F 6 '71. J. Bern-
stein •
EHRENREICH, Barbara, and Ehrenreich, John
Conscience of a steel worker. il Nation 213:
268-71 S 27 '71
EHRENREICH, John, and Fein, Oliver
National health insurance. Cur 129:24-31 My
'71
—See Ehrenreich, B. jt. auth.
EHRENWALD, Jan
Occult. il Todays Ed 60:28-30 S '71
Prophecy: fluke, fraud or psychological syn-
drome? bibliog Am Imago 28:79-83 Spr '71
EHRICKE, Krafft Arnold
Extraterrestrial imperative; excerpts from
address, February 1971. il Bul Atom Sci 27:
18-26 N '71
EHRLICH, Ava, and Mehr, Sandy
Northwestern university. Mlle 72:60 Mr '71
EHRLICH, Henry
Ann-Margret the prude & the passion. il pors
Look 35:48-53+ Je 15 '71
Dominique Sanda, the mad and the beautiful.
il pors Look 35:66-72+ O 5 '71
Every night at the movies. il Look 35:62-3
S 7 '71
Now blooming Twiggy. il pors Look 35:58-63
My 4 '71
Preview of the new biggest show on earth.
il Look 35:18-25 Ap 6 '71
Susan Hampshire. il pors Look 35:28-31 F 23
'71
Warren and Julie: together at last. pors
Look 35:70-4 Je 1 '71
What hath Disney wrought? il Look 35:26-
8+ Ap 6 '71
EHRLICH, Paul R.
—and Holdren, J. P.
Abortion and morality. Sat R 54:58 S 4 '71
Avoiding the problem. Sat R 54:56 Mr 6 '71
Energy crisis. Sat R 54:50-1 Ag 7 '71
Gypsy moth backlash. il Sat R 54:71 O 2 '71
Heat barrier. Sat R 54:61 Ap 3 '71
Impact of population growth. bibliog il Sci-
ence 171:1212-17 Mr 26 '71
Lost genius debate. Sat R 54:61 My 1 '71
Negative animal. Sat R 54:58-9 Je 5 '71
Neither Marx nor Malthur. Sat R 54:88 N 6
'71
People in the machinery. Sat R 55:71 Ja 1 '72
Starvation as a policy. Sat R 54:91 D 4 '71
Technology for the poor. Sat R 54:46-7 Jl 3
'71
Who makes the babies il Sat R 54:60 F 6 '71
about
Census sense. Newsweek 77:78 Ja 25 '71 •
Following their footsteps. B. A. DeBauche. il
pors Seventeen 30:94-5+ Ja '71 •
EIBY, George A.
Astronomy in New Zealand. il Sky & Tel
42:18-20 Jl '71
EICHELMAN, B. See Williams, R. B. jt. auth.
EICHHOLD, Louis B. and Redmond, J. D.
Labor relations. il Parks & Rec 6:20-2+ N
'71

EIDELBERG, E. and Barstow, C. A.
Morphine tolerance and dependence induced
by intraventricular injection. bibliog il Sci-
ence 174:74-6 O 1 '71
EIDENIER, Elizabeth
Bottom's song: Shakespeare in junior high.
Engl J 60:208-11 F '71
8 items or less; story. See Tuttle, A.
EIGHTEEN-year-old vote. See Suffrage—
United States
EIGHTEENTH century
See also
Enlightenment
EILENBERGER, Robert F.
Ceramic forms from layered slabs. il Ceram
Mo 19:16-18 Je '71
Clay cooking pot. il Ceram Mo 19:20-3 F '71
Decorating with a slip cup. il Ceram Mo
19:26-8 Ja '71
Handbuilt puzzle jugs. il Ceram Mo 19:26-9
S '71
Impromptu plates molded on a carved base.
il Ceram Mo 19:27-9 Mr '71
Relocating a plate rim. il Ceram Mo 19:23-5
N '71
EILERS, Hazel Kraft
At the sign of the crest. See issues of Hob-
bies
EIMAS, Peter D. and others
Speech perception in infants. bibliog il Sci-
ence 171:303-6 Ja 22 '71
EIMON, Pan Dodd
Municipal public relations (cont of) City tells
its story. See issues of American city
Plazas for people. il Am City 86:88+ F '71
EINSOHN, Bruce
Birth of a beach. il Motor B & S 128:56-7
bibliog(p58) Jl '71
EINSTEIN, Albert
Einstein, by R. W. Clark. Review
Life pors 71:14 Ag 20 '71. C. P. Snow •
Nat R 23:1125-6 O 8 '71. W. J. Holman,
3d •
Newsweek por 78:67-8 Ag 9 '71. P. S.
Prescott •
Einstein, by R. W. Clark, and The Born-
Einstein letters; ed. by M. Born. Reviews
Sat R il 54:38+ S 11 '71. D. M. Locke •
Einstein's rejection of quantum theory: a
personal motive. H. M. Schey. bibliog f
il Am Imago 28:186-90 Sum '71 •
Wizards meet; excerpts from The 42nd paral-
lel. J. Dos Passos. il por Am Heritage 22:
96-7 Ap '71 •
EINSTEIN, Charles
Baseball. Sports Illus 35:38 S 6 '71
EINSTEIN theory. See Relativity (physics)
EIPPER, Alfred W. and others
Impacts of nuclear power plants on the en-
vironment. bibliog f il Liv Wildn 34:5-12
Aut '70
EISDORFER, Carl. See Wilkie, F. jt. auth.
EISELEY, Loren
Creature from the marsh; excerpt from The
night country. Natur Hist 80:24+ O '71
Gold wheel; excerpts from The Night coun-
try. il Harper 243:68-71 Ag '71
Scientist as prophet. il Harper 243:96-8 N
'71
Sunflower forest; excerpts from The invisible
pyramid. il Nat Wildlife 9:42-5 Ap '71
about
After us the dragons. O. Friedrich. Time 98:
107-8 D 6 '71 •
EISEN, Carol G.
Clean book; excerpt from Nobody said you
had to eat off the floor. Ladies Home J
88:135-7 Jl '71
EISENBERG, Arlene, and Eisenberg, Howard
How Wanaque got a library. il Good H 172:
47-8+ F '71
Thanksgiving with a Lebanese flavor. il por
Good H 173:84+ N '71
EISENBERG, Howard. See Eisenberg, A. jt.
auth.
EISENBERG, Lucy
Politics of cancer. il Harper 243:100-2+ N
'71
EISENBERG, Norman
What is a professional turntable? Hi Fi 21:
50-1 My '71
EISENHOWER, Dwight David
Dear General; ed. by J. P. Hobbs. R. Whitte-
more. New Repub 164:25-6 Ap 10 '71 •
Eisenhower revisited: a political genius? A
brilliant man? R. H. Rovere. il pors N Y
Times Mag p 14-15+ F 7 '71; Discussion.
p4+ F 28; 12 Mr 7 '71 •
Why Ike didn't capture Berlin: an untold
story. il por U S News 70:70-3 Ap 26 '71 •

ELECTIONS—*Continued*

Korea (Republic)

Choosing the familiar. Newsweek 77:50 My 10 '71

Landslide for Stone Face. il por Time 97:27 My 10 '71

Malta

Elections in Malta. C. Cardona. America 124:609-10 Je 12 '71

Pakistan

Travesty in Bangla Desh; by-elections in East Pakistan. America 125:442 N 27 '71

Philippines

Marcos and the Communists. J. de Herrerra. il America 126:6-10 Ja 8 '72

Prescription for revolution. il por Time 97:38 Ap 12 '71

Trinidad and Tobago

Challenging the boss-men. il Time 97:27 Je 7 '71

Hollow victory? Newsweek 77:52+ Je 7 '71

United States

Clues in off-year elections. il U S News 71:23-5 N 15 '71

Election notes. Nat R 23:1276+ N 19 '71

Elections: assessing the contests. il Time 98:16-17 N 15 '71

Four men for the new season: new governors of the South. pors Time 97:18-19 My 31 '71

Urban voter speaks. il Newsweek 78:129 N 15 '71

Votes go against change. il Bsns W p40 N 6 '71

What the voters wrought. il Newsweek 78:26-30 N 15 '71

See also
Campaign issues
Candidates, Political
National conventions (political)
Presidential candidates
Presidents—United States—Election
Primaries
Suffrage—United States

Uruguay

Leftists lose in Uruguay. America 125:498 D 11 '71

Winning by losing. Time 98:26+ D 13 '71

Vietnam (Democratic Republic)

Time for change in Hanoi? G. Gregory. Nat R 23:427+ Ap 20 '71

Vietnam (Republic)

And then there was one. il Newsweek 78:41 S 13 '71

Controversy over Thieu's one-man victory. por Sr Schol 99:14-15 N 8 '71

Democracy and government. Nat R 23:1280 N 19 '71

Democracy in reverse? Newsweek 78:45 Ag 30 '71

Doing it by the numbers. Newsweek 78:49 O 18 '71

Election preview. il Time 97:30 My 3 '71

Election time comes to Saigon. R. J. Willis. il America 125:400-2 N 13 '71

Election time in Saigon. il Life 71:22-5 S 10 '71

Hollow triumph? Newsweek 78:49 O 11 '71

Is this written in the stars? See it through with Nguyen van Thieu. T. Buckley. il pors N Y Times Mag p 14-15+ S 26 '71

Letter from Saigon. R. Shaplen. New Yorker 47:96+ S 11 '71

Letter from Washington. R. H. Rovere. New Yorker 47:117-18 S 18 '71

Making of a loser. il Time 98:24+ S 13 '71

Making of the president. il Time 98:38 O 11 '71

New blow to U.S. goals in Vietnam. il por U S News 71:26 S 6 '71

No decent exit from Viet Nam for the U.S. il Time 98:11 S 13 '71

Non-contest; with report by J. Larsen. il por Time 98:30 O 4 '71

Notes and comment; two elections: 1967 and 1971. New Yorker 47:31-2 O 16 '71

One for Thieu. New Repub 164:12 My 1 '71; Reply. T. Jacqueney. 164:38 My 15 '71

Politics vs. democracy. Newsweek 78:25 S 6 '71

Puppet pulls the strings. K. Buckley. il Newsweek 78:25 O 4 '71

Saigon shambles. Nation 213:165 S 6 '71

South Viet Nam: no longer a choice. il por Time 98:23-4 S 13 '71

South Viet Nam's fifth no. il Time 98:23-4 S 6 '71

Spectral presence. il por Time 98:22 Ag 23 '71

That other presidential election. il por Time 97:31-2 Je 14 '71

Thieu and democracy. W. F. Buckley, jr. Nat R 23:1136 O 8 '71

Thieu's election. Commonweal 95:52-3 O 15 '71

Thieu's election in context. Nat R 23:1162+ O 22 '71

Too good to be true. Time 98:43 O 18 '71

Two voices in a one-man race; with excerpts from interviews. Nguyen-van-Thieu; Nguyen-cao-Ky. pors Time 98:33-4 S 20 '71

Vietnam after the election; is Thieu losing his Catholic support? T. Fox. Commonweal 95:203-7 N 26 '71

Vietnamese election campaign; instruction to U.S. personnel in Vietnam. E. Bunker. Dept State Bul 65:9 Jl 5 '71

Vietnamization and October 3rd. Nation 213:34-5 Jl 19 '71

You can't win. Nat R 23:972 S 10 '71

See also
Political campaigns—Vietnam (Republic)

ELECTIONS and business conditions. See Business—Political aspects

ELECTIVE system in education

Electives program in a small high school? It works! T. H. Morton and M. P. Dei Dolori. Engl J 60:952-6 O '71

180 days: observations of an elective year. J. E. Smith, jr. Engl J 60:229-30+ F '71

School for the 70's: an immodest proposal. M. C. Olson. Clear House 45:488-92 Ap '71

Story of an English elective program. D. R. Bronson. Engl J 60:1086-90 N '71

ELECTRIC accidents. See Electricity, Injuries from

ELECTRIC alarms

Homemade brownout alarm to protect your appliances. R. M. Benrey. il Pop Sci 199:90-1 Ag '71

Medicine chest alarm. R. Graf and G. J. Whalen. il Mech Illus 67:106-7 Ja '71

See also
Burglar alarms
Fire alarms

ELECTRIC analgesia. See Analgesia

ELECTRIC and musical industries, ltd.

Capitol punishment. il Forbes 108:44+ Jl 15 '71

ELECTRIC annunciators

In-out annunciator. J. S. Simonton, jr. il Pop Electr 34:48-52+ Ap '71

ELECTRIC apparatus and appliances

See also
Electric torches
Induction coils

also subhead Electric equipment under various headings, e.g. Boats—Electric equipment

Maintenance and repair

How to protect your camp from electrical fires. L. Short and A. Short. Camp Mag 43:18-19+ F '71

Spot and fix these electrical problems. Suc Farm 69:G24 Ap '71

ELECTRIC apparatus and appliances, Domestic. See Household appliances, Electric

ELECTRIC apparatus industry. See Electric industries

ELECTRIC automobiles. See Automobiles, Electric

ELECTRIC barbecue grills. See Barbecue grills

ELECTRIC batteries

Batteries for radios and other uses; D-cell batteries. il Consumer Bul 54:27-8+ Je '71

D-cell batteries. il Consumer Rep 36:718-22 N '71

Everything you always wanted to know about all those little batteries. E. F. Lindsley. il Pop Sci 198:46-8+ Ja '71

See also
Fuel cells
Storage batteries

Charging

Anatomy of a powerboat; electrical wiring and battery charging. J. West. il Yachting 129:70-1+ F '71

Build the charge now. A. A. Mangieri. il Pop Electr 34:53+ Ap '71

ELECTRIC blenders. See Household appliances, Electric

ELECTRIC cables

See also
Electric conduits
Electric lines
Television cables

ELECTRIC capacitance
Nomograms aid capacitance calculations. J.
E. McAlister. il Electr World 85:27+ F '71

ELECTRIC charges
Chain of pellets transfers charge in elec-
trostatic accelerator. G. B. Lubkin. Phys
Today 24:18-19 S '71

ELECTRIC circuit breakers
Circuit breakers. W. Rieder. il Sci Am 224:
76-84 Ja '71

ELECTRIC coffee grinders. See Coffee mills

ELECTRIC coffee pots. See Coffee pots, percolators, etc.

ELECTRIC coils
See also
Induction coils

ELECTRIC conductivity
See also
Superconductivity

ELECTRIC conductors
Conductor design with thin-film insulated
aluminum. H. D. Walker. il Electr World
86:39+ D '71

ELECTRIC conduits
Utility conduit doubles as sidewalk; Pittsfield, Mass. C. J. McMahon. il Am City
86:132-3 S '71

ELECTRIC control
See also
Electric switches

ELECTRIC control, Remote. See Remote control

ELECTRIC cookery
Plugged-in circuit; with recipes. il Seventeen 30:260-5+ Ag '71
Switched-on cooking: new recipes, new techniques. House & Gard 139:123-4+ Ap '71

ELECTRIC cords
Extension cords: some advice that will help
to assure safety in use. il Consumer Bul
54:38 Je '71
New appliance cord; short cord. il Consumer Bul 54:27 Mr '71

ELECTRIC couplings. See Couplings, Electric

ELECTRIC current converters
See also
Electric current inverters
Frequency changers

ELECTRIC current inverters
Put a wall outlet in your car or boat. R. F.
Graf and G. J. Whalen. il Pop Mech 135:
168-70 My '71

ELECTRIC current rectifiers
SCR power supplies. G. F. Walker. il Electr
World 86:36-8+ O '71
SCR's and power transformers. J. Darr.
Radio-Electr 42:16 Ag '71
Speed control resistor? J. Darr. il Radio-
Electr 42:26+ Ap '71
Using silicon diode rectifiers as power resis-
tors. J. T. Bailey. il Electr World 85:38+
My '71

ELECTRIC currents
Isaac Asimov explains; electrons and the
speed of light. I. Asimov. Sci Digest 69:88-
9 Je '71

Grounding
Medical electronic equipment and hospital
safety. H. French. il Pop Electr 1:32-4 Ja
'72

ELECTRIC cutting machinery. See Cutting machines

ELECTRIC dishwashers. See Dishwashing and
drying machines

ELECTRIC drills. See Drilling and boring machinery

ELECTRIC eels
Conductance changes produced by acetylcholine in lipidic membranes containing a proteolipid from electrophorus. M. Parisi and
others. bibliog il Science 172:56-7 Ap 2 '71

ELECTRIC egg cookers. See Household appliances, Electric

ELECTRIC equipment. See Electric apparatus
and appliances

ELECTRIC equipment industry. See Electric
industries

ELECTRIC eye systems. See Electric annunciators

ELECTRIC fans
Safe, efficient and expensive fan: Panasonic
F3OEUB. il Consumer Rep 36:526 S '71

ELECTRIC flashlights. See Flashlights, Electric

ELECTRIC floor washers. See Floor machines

ELECTRIC fuses
What every woman should know about
house fuses. il Good H 172:181 Mr '71

ELECTRIC generators
Engines do double duty: refrigeration or
standby power. il Arch Rec 149:151-2 Mr
'71
How to have power when there is none. R.
Nunn. il Pop Mech 136:156-8 D '71
How's your airport standby power? Hopkins
international airport, Cleveland; diesel elec-
tric sets. G. E. Katzmar. il Am City 86:96
D '71
Rockwell Parsons fails to connect; steam
turbine-generator venture. Bsns W p31-2
Ag 14 '71
Standby power units. J. R. Borcherding. il
Suc Farm 69:no2 D12 F '71
See also
Isotopic power generators
Thermionic converters

ELECTRIC generators, Alternating current
Strictly for stocks; new Accel high-performance alternator. J. Dianna. il Hot Rod
24:90 My '71

ELECTRIC generators, Direct current
More electrical power; auxiliary generator.
C. F. Kelley. il Yachting 130:62+ Jl '71

ELECTRIC griddles. See Household appliances,
Electric

ELECTRIC grinders. See Grinding machines

ELECTRIC hair dryers. See Hair dryers

ELECTRIC household appliances. See Household appliances, Electric

ELECTRIC industries
See also
Electric utilities
Emerson electric company
McGraw-Edison company
Reliance electric company
Square D company
Thomas and Betts corporation
Westinghouse electric corporation

Germany (Federal Republic)
Foreign minister; resignation of G. Tacke
from Siemens. por Forbes 108:80 D 1 '71

Italy
Made in Italy; Indùstria A. Zanussi S.p.A. il
Forbes 107:24 My 1 '71

Japan
Konosuke Matsushita of Matsushita elec-
tric; interview. K. Matsushita. pors Na-
tions Bsns 59:32-7 Ja '71
Sanyo's Samurai fight sagging profits. il
Bsns W p41-2 Mr 6 '71

Netherlands
Family switch at Philips lamp. il Bsns W
p80+ My 1 '71

ELECTRIC insulation. See Insulation (electric)

ELECTRIC interference
Change of pace; pacemaker malfunction from
electrical interference. Sci Am 224:59 Je '71

ELECTRIC irons
Spray-steam irons. il Consumer Bul 54:18-22
S '71
Steam/spray irons. il Consumer Rep 36:74-80
F '71

ELECTRIC lamps
Build a Spanish-style lamp the easy way.
J. A. Lackner il Pop Mech 136:166-7 O '71
Heat lamp for the shop; movie light with
quartz-bromide bulb. P. McCafferty. il Pop
Sci 198:120+ Mr '71
Lighting up the big change. il House B 113:
56-7 Jl '71
Mod glow lamp. P. McCafferty. il Pop Sci
199:85 D '71
New light from old bottles; easy to make
hanging lamps. il Design 73:29 Wint '71
See also
Lighting fixtures

Shades
See Lamp shades

ELECTRIC lamps, Arc
Predicting ballast noise from H.I.D. lighting
systems. A. C. McNamara, jr. il Arch Rec
149:139-42 My '71

ELECTRIC lamps, Flashing
Big blinker; emergency highway flasher. G.
Whalen and R. Graf. il Mech Illus 67:130+
My '71
Rugged auto emergency flasher. R. L. Ives.
il Pop Electr 34:67-9+ My '71

ELECTRIC lamps, Fluorescent
Fluorescent droplight. E. C. Wade. il Mech
Illus 67:100+ Ja '71

ELECTRIC lamps, Incandescent
Better way to choose light bulbs. il Changing T 25:21-2 Jl '71
Labeling information that helps you buy
the right light bulb. Good H 173:160 Jl '71
New labels on light bulbs. il Consumer Bul
54:34-6 Ap '71

ELECTRIC lamps, Photoflash
Phototronics; flashcubes. E. Farber. Mod Phot 35:133+ Jl '71
Phototronics; new GE flashcube. E. Farber. Mod Phot 35:64+ My '71

ELECTRIC lamps (incandescent) in art
Luminal art. R. M. Farrell. il Sch Arts 71: 18-19 O '71

ELECTRIC lanterns
Do-everything flashlights. E. F. Lindsley. il Pop Sci 199:60-2+ Jl '71

ELECTRIC lawn mowers. See Lawn mowers

ELECTRIC light bulbs. See Electric lamps, Incandescent

ELECTRIC light fixtures. See Lighting fixtures

ELECTRIC lighting
Wireless closet lights. il Consumer Bul 54: 23-4 D '71
See also
Christmas decorations, Outdoor
Electric lamps
Electric wire and wiring
Electroluminescence
Lighting, Architectural and decorative
Street lighting

Control
Build PM's $30 house watcher. W. C. Leckey. il Pop Mech 135:120-5+ Je '71
Handy light control for your darkroom. M. S. Schroeder. il Pop Mech 136:116-18 S '71
People-at-home light pattern turns burglars away. R. M. Benrey. il Pop Sci 198: 98-100+ Je '71
Sound-operated light controllers. J. F. Kennedy. il Electr World 86:39 N '71
3 dancing light displays you can build yourself; colored flashing lights for Christmas. S. M. Gallager. il Pop Mech 136:119-23+ D '71

ELECTRIC lines
Danger! High voltage! il Changing T 25:24 O '71
Neat packaging for power lines; gas insulation. il Bsns W p58 Mr 20 '71
See also
Electric conduits

Grounds and faults
See Electric power distribution—Grounds and faults

Poles
Parting shots: oh beautiful, for spacious power lines. il Life 71:70-1 Jl 2 '71

Underground lines
How to locate buried-conductor faults. J. T. Bailey. il Electr World 85:42+ Mr '71
Plastic tape warns contractors; Longmont, Colo. il Am City 86:122 Je '71
Why not put all utility lines in tunnels? Am City 86:33 O '71

ELECTRIC measurements
See also
Oscillographs
Wheatstone bridges

ELECTRIC meters
Grid-dip meter extension. W. P. Turner. il Radio-Electr 42:61 S '71
Is that wood dry enough? wood-moisture-content meter. R. M. Benrey. il Pop Sci 199:88-9+ Jl '71
Sencore FE 20 hi-lo field-effect meter. il Radio-Electr 42:16 Je '71
Underground survey meter and metal locator. H. Pallatz. il Pop Electr 35:63-5 Ag '71
See also
Ammeters
Voltmeters
Voltohmmeters
Wattmeters

ELECTRIC motorcycles. See Motorcycles, Electric

ELECTRIC motors
Amazing motor that draws power from the air; electrostatic motor. C. P. Gilmore and W. J. Hawkins. il Pop Sci 198:80-1+ Ap '71
Electrostatic motors you can build. C. P. Gilmore and W. J. Hawkins. il Pop Sci 198: 95-7+ My '71
Your boat's electric motors. C. Miller. il Motor B & S 127:80-2+ F '71
See also
Automobiles, Electric
Frequency changers
Outboard motors

Control
SCR tool-speed control. B. Lange. il Radio-Electr 42:86 F '71

ELECTRIC noise
See also
Electric interference
Electronic noise

ELECTRIC organs in fishes
Acetylcholine binding to torpedo electroplax: relationship to acetylcholine receptors. M. E. Eldefrawi and others. bibliog il Science 173:338-40 Jl 23 '71

ELECTRIC outlets. See Electric wire and wiring

ELECTRIC ovens
See also
Electric stoves

ELECTRIC plants
Masked ball at the power station. G. McCue. il Art in Am 59:98-9 S '71
See also
Atomic power plants
Electric power
Electric utilities
Hydroelectric plants

Interconnection
Vermont: forced to figure in big power picture; proposed New England power pool. J. Walsh. Science 174:44-7 O 1 '71

Location
Environment; report of Forum of the committee on power plant siting of the National academy of engineering. Sci N 99: 218 Mr 27 '71
Murder of the Southwest. A. M. Josephy, jr. il Audubon 73:52-67 Jl '71
Vermont: a power deficit raises pressure for new plants. J. Walsh. il Science 173:1110+ S 17 '71

Pollution
Bad day at Black Mesa, furor over Four Corners plant. il Newsweek 77:39 Je 7 '71
Cloud on the desert. R. Craig. bibliog il Environ 13:20-4+ Jl '71; Discussion. 13:50 N '71
Dilemmas of power; new plants in the desert shared by Arizona, Utah, Nevada and New Mexico. il Time 97:61 Je 7 '71
Hello, energy; goodbye, big sky; smokestacks invade the Southwest. J. Neary. il Life 70:61-4+ Ap 16 '71
High price of supplying power; Four Corners region. il Bsns W p63-4 Je 12 '71
Live better electrically? H. Borland. il Audubon 73:68-9 Jl '71
Power plants on the prairie; Four Corners plant. il Sci N 99:381 Je 5 '71
Smog over the Great Plains; WEST companies in the Four Corners region. J. Waugh. Nation 212:753-5 Je 14 '71
Sulfur dioxide emissions from power plants; their effect on air quality. J. Golden and T. R. Mongan. il Science 171:381-3 Ja 29 '71; Discussion. 172:792; 173:981 My 21, S 10 '71
Wild, wild WEST. J. Waugh. New Repub 164:10 Mr 27 '71

ELECTRIC plants, Emergency
Give all urban services standby power. il Am City 86:23 F '71

ELECTRIC plugs. See Electric wire and wiring

ELECTRIC power
Another summer of power worries. il Bsns W p29 Je 26 '71
Getting more power to the people. il Time 97:72-4 Ap 19 '71
Let there be darkness. Nat R 23:520 My 18 '71
New winter worry; shortage of power. il U S News 70:25 F 15 '71
Official warning; another summer of power shortages. il U S News 70:26-7 Ap 26 '71
Taking a dim view. il Newsweek 77:81-2 My 3 '71
What dimouts do to your electrical equipment. J. R. Free. il Pop Sci 198:58-9+ F '71
Wintertime mini-crisis. il Newsweek 77:73 F 15 '71
See also
Electric plants
Electric utilities

Interruptions
See Electric power failures

United States
See Electric power

Yugoslavia
Power development in Yugoslavia. J. S. Suica. il por Bul Atom Sci 27:42-6 N '71

ELECTRIC power distribution
See also
Electric conduits
Electric lines
Electric plants—Interconnection

Grounds and faults
How to locate buried-conductor faults. J.
T. Bailey. il Electr World 85:42+ Mr '71
ELECTRIC power failures
Blackout! Can science solve our power crisis? C. P. Gilmore. il Pop Sci 199:55-7+
Jl '71
Lemon named Big Allis. Time 98:41 Jl 19 '71
What to do if the lights go out. Redbook
137:66+ Je '71
ELECTRIC power plants. See Electric plants
ELECTRIC power pooling. See Electric plants
—Interconnection
ELECTRIC power production
Blackout! Can science solve our power crisis?
C. P. Gilmore. il Pop Sci 199:55-7+ Jl '71
Decision-making in the production of power.
M. Katz. Sci Am 225:191-2+ bibliog(p246)
S '71
ELECTRIC power production from chemical
action
See also
Fuel cells
ELECTRIC ranges. See Electric stoves
ELECTRIC rectifiers. See Electric current rectifiers
ELECTRIC refrigerators. See Refrigerators,
Electric
ELECTRIC resistance
See also
Wheatstone bridges
ELECTRIC resistors
All about resistors. F. J. Waters. il Radio-Electr 42:58-61 S '71
Different resistance decade. J. A. Fred. il
Pop Electr 34:64-6 Mr '71
ELECTRIC scissors. See Scissors and shears
ELECTRIC sharpeners. See Sharpeners
ELECTRIC shock
Danger: electric shock. H. French. il Sci
Digest 70:66-70 Jl '71
Electroshock effects on brain protein synthesis: relation to brain seizures and retrograde amnesia C. W. Cotman and others.
bibliog il Science 173:454-6 Jl 30 '71
One-trial learning and biphasic time course
of performance in the goldfish. W. H. Riege
and A. Cherkin. bibliig il Science 172:966-8
My 28 '71
Ralph Nader's most shocking exposé. R.
Nader. il Ladies Home J 88:98+ Mr '71
Rat race; cause of ulcers. il por Newsweek
78:74-5 S 27 '71
Retrograde amnesia: electroconvulsive shock
effects after termination of rapid eye movement sleep deprivation. W. Fishbein and
others. bibliog il Science 172:80-2 Ap 2 '71
Social setting: influence on the physiological
response to electric shock in the rat. R. B.
Williams and B. Eichelman. bibliog il Science 174:613-14 N 5 '71
See also
Electricity, Injuries from
ELECTRIC signals
Signal averaging techniques. S. L. Silver. il
Electr World 85:45-8 My '71
ELECTRIC skillets. See Household appliances, Electric
ELECTRIC soldering irons. See Soldering apparatus
ELECTRIC steam irons. See Electric irons'
ELECTRIC stoves
Exciting new ways to cook; smooth-surfaced cooktops. Redbook 137:100+ Ag '71
New ranges with special cooking talents.
J. Mees. il Good H 173:134-5+ S '71
ELECTRIC switches
Action at your fingertips; touch switch. W.
J. Hawkins. il Pop Sci 198:96-7+ Mr '71
Light-operated bistable switch. D. C. Conner. il Pop Electr 34:70 Mr '71
Low-voltage remote power control; two-way
switching system. N. Johnson. il Pop
Electr 35:69-70+ Jl '71
See also
Electric wire and wiring
ELECTRIC timers. See Timing devices
ELECTRIC toasters
Are present day toasters as automatic as we
would like them to be? il Consumer Bul 54:
23-6 My '71
ELECTRIC tools
Low cost power tools in kits. R. J.
DeCristoforo. il Mech Illus 67:100-2+ N '71
One-motor tool families. il Mech Illus 67:
116-17 N '71

Brakes
See Brakes
Control
See Electric motors—Control
Safety devices and measures
How electronics can lock power tools. R. M.
Benrey. il Pop Sci 199:98-9+ D '71
ELECTRIC tools, Portable
See also
Engraving tools
ELECTRIC toothbrushes. See Toothbrushes
ELECTRIC toothpicks. See Toothpicks, Electric
ELECTRIC torches
Heat lamp for the shop; torchlamps. P.
McCafferty. il Pop Sci 198:120+ Mr '71
ELECTRIC tractors. See Tractors
ELECTRIC transformers
SCR's and power transformers. J. Darr.
Radio-Electr 42:16 Ag '71
See also
Tesla coils
ELECTRIC transmission
See also
Electric power
ELECTRIC typewriters. See Typewriters. Electric
ELECTRIC utilities
Electric utilities: the heat's on. G. Berkwitt.
il Duns 97:83-4+ Mr '71
How wrong forecasts hurt the utilities. il
Bsns W p44+ F 13 '71
Utilities: worried about a power shortage.
Bsns W p47-8 D 25 '71
See also
Detroit Edison company
Advertising
Why do utilities advertise? Nation 212:132
F 1 '71
Regulation
Invisible senator; L. Metcalf. R. Sherrill. por
Nation 212:584-9 My 10 '71
ELECTRIC vehicle exhibitions. See Motor
vehicles—Exhibitions
ELECTRIC vehicles
See also
Automobiles, Electric
ELECTRIC voltage. See Voltage
ELECTRIC voltage regulators. See Voltage
regulators
ELECTRIC washing machines. See Washing
machines
ELECTRIC waves
See also
Microwaves
Radio waves
ELECTRIC welders. See Welders
ELECTRIC wire and wiring
Black is white and white is black; color-coding of wires. J. Darr. il Radio-Electr
43:22+ Ja '72
Easy way to check a 3-wire outlet. A. Lees.
il Pop Sci 198:16 Ap '71
Install a three-way switch yourself? Sure
you can. E. L. Frasier. il Pop Mech 136:
182-4+ O '71
Know your housepower. McCalls 98:148 My
'71
Running wiring on and through concrete. G.
Daniels. il Pop Sci 199:102-4+ S '71
See also
Boats—Electric equipment
Electric conduits
Electric cords
Electric switches
Electricity in the home
Motor boats—Electric equipment
Maintenance and repair
Electrical first aid; repairs. il McCalls 98:
114 Je '71
Electrical repairs anyone can do. G. Daniels. il Mech Illus 67:96-100 Jl '71
ELECTRICAL stimulation of the brain. See
Electronic behavior control
ELECTRICITY
See also
Fuel cells
Magnetism
History
Induction coil. G. Shiers. il Sci Am 224:80-7
My '71
Nikola Tesla's bold adventure. H. L. Goldman. il por Am West 8:4-9 Mr '71
ELECTRICITY, Injuries from
Appliance clinic. J. Darr. il Radio-Electr 42:
16+ D '71
How much current is fatal? with table. Pop
Electr 1:31 Ja '72
See also
Electric shock

ELECTRICITY, Static
De-shocking solutions to electric kisses. J. Joseph. il Todays Health 49:14 F '71
Stamping out static electricity in fabrics and carpets. Good H 173:6 Ag '71
Static marks on film: a mystery that still jolts the experts. N. Goldberg. il Pop Phot 68:94-5+ Ap '71

ELECTRICITY in horticulture. See Electrohorticulture

ELECTRICITY in medicine. See Electrotherapy

ELECTRICITY in the home
Juicing up the under-electrified house. il Changing T 26:43-5 Ja '72
See also
Electric wire and wiring

ELECTRICITY on boats. See Boats—Electric equipment; Motor boats—Electric equipment

ELECTROACOUSTICS
Acoustic surface-wave devices. J. R. Fisk. il Pop Electr 34:27-33 Mr '71

ELECTROCONVULSIVE shock. See Electric shock

ELECTROCULTURE of plants. See Electrohorticulture

ELECTROCUTION
See also
Electric shock

ELECTRODES
Potassium-adenosine triphosphate complex: formation constant measured with ion-selective electrodes. G. A. Rechnitz and M. S. Mohan; reply with rejoinder. N. C. Melchior. bibliog il Science 171:1267-8 Mr 26 '71

ELECTROENCEPHALOGRAPHY
Alpha and kappa electroencephalogram activity in eyeless subjects. R. M. Chapman and others. bibliog il Science 171:1159-61 Mr 19 '71
Attention-related increases in cortical responsivity dissociated from the contingent negative variation. M. W. Donald, jr. and W. R. Goff. bibliog il Science 172:1163-6 Je 11 '71
Bispectrum analysis of electroencephalogram signals during waking and sleeping. T. P. Barnett and others. bibliog il Science 172:401-2 Ap 23 '71
EEG responses in regularly menstruating women and in amenorrheic women treated with ovarian hormones. W. Vogel and others. bibliog il Science 172:388-91 Ap 23 '71
Electrical activity of the hypothalamus: effects of intraventricular catecholamines. R. J. Weiner and others. bibliog il Science 171:411-12 Ja 29 '71
Electroencephalographic and behavioral alterations produced by Δ^1-tetrahydrocannabinol. C. H. Hockman and others. bibliog il Science 172:968-70 My 28 '71
See also
Brain waves

ELECTROFORMING
Electroformed enamels. P. Rothenberg. il Ceram Mo 19:22-5 Mr '71

ELECTROHORTICULTURE
Experimental electro-culture. L. G. Lawrence. il Pop Electr 34:66-70+ F '71
More experiments in electroculture. L. G. Lawrence. bibliog il Pop Electr 34:63-8+ Je '71

ELECTROLUMINESCENCE
El Panel driver. N. P. Huffnagle. il Pop Electr 34:43-8 My '71

ELECTROMAGNETIC scattering. See Scattering (physics)

ELECTROMAGNETIC theory
See also
Field theory (physics)
Magneto-optics

ELECTROMAGNETIC waves
See also
Radio waves

ELECTROMAGNETISM
Weak interaction: puzzle of the fourth force. D. E. Thomsen. il ror Sci N 100:252-3 O 9 '71

ELECTRON beams. See Electrons—Beams

ELECTRON microprobe. See Electron probe microanalyzer

ELECTRON microscope and microscopy
Allende meteorite: a high-voltage electron petrographic study. H. W. Green, 2d. and others. bibliog il Science 172:936-9 My 28 '71
Cell surface antigens: serial sectioning of single cells as an approach to topographical analysis. C. W. Stackpole and others. bibliog il Science 172:472-4 Ap 30 '71

Electron microscopy and diffraction of layered, superconducting intercalation complexes. H. Fernández-Morán and others. bibliog il Science 174:498-500 O 29 '71
Endothelial projections as revealed by scanning electron microscopy. U. Smith and others. bibliog il Science 173:925-7 S 3 '71
Erythrocytes: pits and vacuoles as seen with transmission and scanning electron microscopy. B. Schnitzer and others. bibliog il Science 173:251-2 Jl 16 '71
High-resolution scanning electron microscope. A. V. Crewe. il Sci Am 224:26-35 bibliog (p 130) Ap '71
Internal cellular details of euglena gracilis visualized by scanning electron microscopy. H. N. Guttman. bibliog il Science 171:290-2 Ja 22 '71
Kinetics of single-layer graphite oxidation: evaluation by electron microscopy. E. L. Evans and others. bibliog il Science 171:174-5 Ja 15 '71
Scanning electron microscope. T. E. Everhart and T. L. Hayes. il Sci Am 226:54-61+ Ja '72
Scanning electron microscopes. D. L. Heiserman. il Electr World 85:42-4+ F '71
Scanning electron microscopic observations of surface structure of isolated human chromosomes. H. M. Golomb and G. F. Bahr. bibliog il Science 171:1024-6 Mr 12 '71
Surface microtopography: adaptation of address, March 1971. R. D. Young. bibliog il Phys Today 24:42-9 N '71
Viral RNA polymerases: electron microscopy of reovirus reaction cores. S. Gillies and others. bibliog il Science 174:694-6 N 12 '71
See also
Stains and staining (microscopy)

ELECTRON multipliers. See Photoelectric multipliers

ELECTRON optics
Optoelectronic revolution. L. Stern and I. Carroll. il Electr World 86:46-8+ Jl '71
See also
Image intensifiers

ELECTRON paramagnetic resonance. See Magnetic resonance

ELECTRON probe microanalyzer
Microanalysis of individual mitochondrial granules with diameters less than 1000 angstroms. L. V. Sutfin and others. bibliog il Science 174:947-9 N 26 '71

ELECTRON tubes
How digital readouts work: Nixie tubes. G. Flynn. il Radio-Electr 42:50-3 S '71

ELECTRONIC air cleaner. See Air filters

ELECTRONIC apparatus and appliances
Build with IC's: electronic umpire. E. L. Miller; reply. H. E. Schaffer. Radio-Electr 42:16+ Mr '71
Equipment report. See issues of Radio-electronics
New products. See issues of Radio-electronics
New products & literature. See issues of Electronics world
Product gallery. See issues of Popular electronics
See also
Calculating machines. Electronic
Handicapped. Apparatus for the
Metal detectors
Traveling wave tubes
also subhead Electronic equipment under various subjects, e.g. Airplanes—Electronic equipment

Cooling
Chemicals for electronics. L. Cantor. il Pop Electr 34:63-6 My '71

Exhibitions
See also
Avionics—Exhibitions

Maintenance and repair
Chemicals for electronics. L. Cantor. il Pop Electr 34:25-8+ Ap; 63-6 My '71
Service clinic; questions and answers. J. Darr. See issues of Radio-electronics
Spray chemicals for servicing. J. Frye. il Electr World 85:39-42+ My '71
Technotes. See issues of Radio-electronics

Materials
Don't bypass the hobby shop: hard-to-find tools and materials. F. H. Tooker. il Pop Electr 35:50-2+ O '71

Power supply
Diodes isolate two power supply outputs. W. R. Laitinen. il Radio-Electr 43:97+ Ja '72
IC power supplies. W. G. Jung. il Radio-Electr 42:58-9 Ag '71
IC power supplies dual outputs with uA723's. W. G. Jung. il Radio-Electr 42:69-70+ S '71
Laboratory IC power supply. R. J. Valentine. il Pop Electr 34:31-5 Je '71

ELECTRONIC apparatus and appliances—
Power supply—*Continued*
Millie volts power supply; very-low-voltage power source. R. Magriney. il Radio-Electr 42:53 Mr '71
New in power supplies: hybrid IC regulator. W. Roy. il Radio-Electr 42:57 My '71
Power supplies; symposium. il Electr World 86:28-33+ O '71
Power supplies using the uA723. W. G. Jung. il Radio-Electr 42:49-50 Jl '71
Power-supply improvement. F. H. Tooker. il Electr World 86:73 S '71
Testing power supplies. J. N. Demas. il Pop Electr 35:67-8 S '71
V.T.V.M. battery eliminator. W. G. Heller. il Electr World 85:72 Ap '71

Storage
Parts storage made easy. D. J. Holford. il Radio-Electr 42:80 Jl '71

Testing
EW lab tested. See issues of Electronics world

ELECTRONIC apparatus industry. See Electronic industries
ELECTRONIC bartender. See Bars and barrooms—Automation
ELECTRONIC behavior control
Biology of violence: focus on the brain. il Sci N 100:403-4 D 18 '71
Probing the brain. il Newsweek 77:60-2+ Je 21 '71; Same abr. with title Awesome prospects of the brain probers. Read Digest 99: 98-102 S '71
ELECTRONIC brains. See Artificial intelligence
ELECTRONIC calculating machines. See Calculating machines, Electronic
ELECTRONIC cash registers. See Cash registers, Electronic
ELECTRONIC ceramics
Ferroelectric ceramics, new twist with light. J. R. Free. il Pop Sci 198:61-3 My '71
ELECTRONIC circuits
Noteworthy circuits. See issues of Radio-electronics
Understand the system. W. H. Buchsbaum. il Pop Electr 35:52-3+ S '71
See also
Logic circuits
Printed circuits
Switching systems
Television circuits
Transistor circuits

Manufacture
Microcircuit assembly processes spurred. B. M. Elson. il Aviation W 94:44-5+ Ja 18 '71

Plastic embedment
Make your own integrated-circuit modules; potted-in-epoxy assembly. F. H. Tooker. il Electr World 85:62-3 Mr '71
ELECTRONIC circuits, Integrated
Cashing in on a new generation of chips; custom designed LSI chips. il Bsns W p50+ Mr 27 '71
IC potpourri. W. Jung. Radio-Electr 43:68-9 Ja '72
Inside linear IC's. W. G. Jung. il Radio-Electr 42:60-1 N; 50-1 D '71
Make your own integrated-circuit modules. F. H. Tooker. il Electr World 85:62-3 Mr '71
Microelectronics in the '70s: 10,000 parts on the head of a pin. R. M. Benrey. il Pop Sci 199:83-5+ O '71
Minimod, a new type of ic package. il Radio-Electr 42:79 Jl '71
Mounting IC flat-packs. C. D. Gellker. il Radio-Electr 42:64 Je '71
Potpourri of IC applications. W. G. Jung. il Radio-Electr 42:58-60 Je '71
Power supplies using the uA723. W. G. Jung. il Radio-Electr 42:49-50 Jl '71
Testing IC's in TV receivers. F. N. Belt. il Electr World 86:49-52+ N '71
ELECTRONIC components. See Electronic apparatus and appliances
ELECTRONIC control
See also
Camera shutters—Control
Electric motors—Control
Photoelectric cells—Control use
Wheelchairs—Control
ELECTRONIC counters. See Counting machines and devices
ELECTRONIC data processing
Electronic data processing in urban government; symposium. il Am City 86:69-75+ My '71

Information specialist: from data to dollars. J. Poindexter. il Duns 93:34-7 Je '69
See also
Artificial intelligence
Computers
Data processing service centers
Data tapes
Data transmission systems
Information systems, Management

Libraries
See Libraries—Automation

Security measures
Guard that computer. Nations Bsns 59:84-6 Ap '71
ELECTRONIC data systems corporation
Company that put Perot on Wall Street. il Bsns W p74 Mr 27 '71
H. Ross Perot: America's first welfare billionaire. R. Fitch. il pors Ramp Mag 10: 42-51 N '71
ELECTRONIC digital computers. See Computers—Digital computers
ELECTRONIC equipment. See Electronic apparatus and appliances
ELECTRONIC fortification of cities and towns. See Cities and towns—Protection
ELECTRONIC games
Can you beat tic-tac-tronix? D. Lancaster. il Radio-Electr 42:32-5+ D '71
Heads 'n' tails; electronic coin flipper. J. Crawford. il Pop Electr 1:35-7 Ja '72
ELECTRONIC industries
See also
Avionics industry
Computer industry

Finance
Consumer electronics: filled with cautious optimism. il Bsns W p46 D 25 '71
Electronics; with yardsticks of management performance. il Forbes 109:116+ Ja 1 '72

Europe, Western
See also
Avionics industry—Europe, Western

France
See also
Avionics industry—France

Italy
See also
Olivetti

Japan
See also
Avionics industry—Japan

United States
Cashing in on a new generation of chips. il Bsns W p50+ Mr 27 '71
Semiconductor industry: madness? Or method? il Forbes 107:20-2+ F 15 '71
See also
Bendix corporation
Collins radio company
Cramer electronics, inc.
EG&G, inc.
Fairchild camera and instrument corporation
Hughes aircraft company
Motorola, inc.
RCA corporation
Texas instruments. inc.
Transitron electronics corporation
ELECTRONIC light. See Electroluminescence
ELECTRONIC locks. See Locks and keys
ELECTRONIC music. See Music, Electronic
ELECTRONIC musical instruments. See Musical instruments, Electronic
ELECTRONIC noise
All about Dolby. S. Leckerts. il Radio-Electr 42:38-40 Je '71
ELECTRONIC numerical integrator and calculator. See Computers—Digital computers
ELECTRONIC organ. See Organ, Electronic
ELECTRONIC ovens
Be cool: cook with a microwave oven. W. Stocklin. il Electr World 86:44-5 Jl '71
Exciting new ways to cook. Redbook 137:100+ Ag '71
Heathkit GD-29 electronic oven. il Radio-Electr 42:22 S '71
Heathkit microwave oven. il Pop Electr 34: 82-3+ My '71
Microwave cooker you can build from a kit. W. G. Salm. il Pop Mech 136:105 S '71
Microwave ovens. R. M. Benrey. il Mech Illus 68:60+ Ja '72
Microwave ovens. L. Steckler. il Radio-Electr 42:68-70 F '71

ELECTRONIC ovens—*Continued*
Microwave ovens heat up again. il Bsns W
p21 D 25 '71
Report on those speedy electronic ovens. I.
Horowitz. il McCalls 98:28+ Ap '71
ELECTRONIC parts. See Electronic apparatus
and appliances
ELECTRONIC photoflash units. See Photog-
raphy—Electronic equipment
ELECTRONIC photography. See Photography,
Electronic
ELECTRONIC puzzles. See Puzzles
ELECTRONIC research. See Electronics re-
search
ELECTRONIC service associations
See also
National electronic associations
ELECTRONIC switches. See Electric switches
ELECTRONIC technicians
Technician as a mechanic. J. Frye. Electr
World 86:50-1 Ag '71
See also
National electronic associations
Television workers
ELECTRONIC test instruments. See Testing
instruments
ELECTRONIC thermometers. See Thermome-
ters and thermometry
ELECTRONIC tick-tack-toe. See Electronic
games
ELECTRONIC video recording. See Video play-
back systems
ELECTRONIC warfare. See Electronics—Mili-
tary use
ELECTRONIC weighing equipment. See
Weighing machines
ELECTRONICS
Recent developments in electronics. See is-
sues of Electronics world
See also
Avionics
Bioelectronics
Digital electronics
Medical electronics
Oscillators, Crystal
Pulse techniques (electronics)
Semiconductors
Transistors

Bibliography
Books. See issues of Electronics world
Electronics bookshelf. C. C. Drumeller. il Pop
Electr 35:48-51 D '71
Electronics library. See issues of Popular
electronics
New books. See issues of Radio-electronics

Materials
Electronics with superconducting junctions;
Josephson devices. J. Clarke. bibliog il Phys
Today 24:30-7 Ag '71

Military use
Deadly game of electronic warfare. B. Koci-
var. il Pop Sci 198:60-2 F '71
New radars, fire control aids displayed. P. J.
Klass. il Aviation W 94:39-41+ Je 7 '71

Periodicals
See also
Popular electronics (periodical)

Research
See Electronics research

Terminology
Do you know these electronic abbreviations?
S. D. Prensky. il Electr World 86:57 O '71

Tools
See Tools
ELECTRONICS as a profession
Opportunity awareness; questions and an-
swers. D. L. Heiserman. See issues of
Popular electronics
ELECTRONICS in astronomy
Electronic image tubes in astronomy. D.
L. Heiserman. il Electr World 86:34-5
N '71
Electronic optical astronomy: philosophy and
practice. E. W. Dennison. Science 174:
240-4 O 15 '71
ELECTRONICS in aviation. See Avionics
ELECTRONICS in criminal investigation,
espionage, etc.
Big brother; crime deterrent transponder
system. R. Barkan. il Ramp Mag 10:10+
S '71
Bugs for rent. Nation 213:260-1 S 27 '71
Code of fair practises; right of privacy; ad-
dress, June 16, 1971. G. Meany. Vital
Speeches 37:618-21 Ag 1 '71
Has big brother got your number? il Sr
Schol 98:12-16 Mr 29 '71

Overruling Mitchell; legalities of electronic
eavesdropping. Time 97:58-9 Ap 19 '71
Poisonous tree; electronic surveillance of
private citizens, by government agencies.
C. Cohen. Nation 212:231-2 F 22 '71; Same
with title How far electronics surveillance?
Cur 129:3-6 My '71
Privacy and the third-party bug; case of
James White. N. Lewin. New Repub 164:12-
17 Ap 17 '71
Third-party snooping. Time 97:58 Ap 19 '71
Truck hijacking and electronics. M. S. Snit-
zer. Pop Electr 35:7 Ag '71
See also
Wire tapping
ELECTRONICS in medicine. See Medical elec-
tronics
ELECTRONICS in noise control
Electronics fights noise pollution. S. L. Sil-
ver. il Pop Electr 35:61-6 O '71
ELECTRONICS in photography
Day the lion ate franks and beans. J. Des-
chin. il por Pop Phot 68:10+ Je '71
See also
Photography—Electronic equipment
ELECTRONICS in pollution control
Electronics helps fight air pollution. S. L.
Silver. il Electr World 86.41-4+ S '71
ELECTRONICS in postal service
How science will speed your mail. E. Edel-
son. il Pop Sci 198:53-5+ Mr '71
ELECTRONICS in traffic control
Travel quicker on two-lane highways, new
research shows how; passing aid system.
E. H. Arctander. il Pop Sci 198:114+ F '71
ELECTRONICS industry. See Electronic in-
dustries
ELECTRONICS research
Solid-state research pushed for commercial
application; Central research laboratory of
Hitachi, ltd. Aviation W 95:86 N 1 '71
ELECTRONICS work benches. See Work
benches
ELECTRONICS world (periodical)
Merger! W. A. Stocklin. por Electr World
86:6 D '71
Popular electronics, including Electronics
world. M. S. Snitzer. Pop Electr 1:16 Ja '72
ELECTRONS
How does the muon differ from the electron?
M. L. Perl. bibliog il Phys Today 24:34-5+
Jl '71
Isaac Asimov explains; electrons and the
speed of light. I. Asimov. Sci Digest 69:88-9
Je '71
Studying electron behavior; photoelectron
spectroscopy. Sci N 100:187 S 18 '71
See also
Energy band theory of solids
Mesons
Neutrons

Beams
Optical modulation of electron beam. G. B.
Lubkin. il Phys Today 24:17-19 Je '71
ELECTROOPTICS
Modified P-2 tests electro-optics. il Aviation
W 94:42-3 Ap 5 '71
ELECTROPHORESIS
Electrophoresis demonstration planned for
Apollo 14. il Space World H-4-88:28-30 Ap
'71
Polyacrylamide gel electrophoresis. A. Chram-
bach and D. Rodbard. bibliog il Science 172:
440-51 Ap 30 '71
ELECTROPHORUS. See Electric eels
ELECTROPHOTOGRAPHY. See Photography,
Electronic
ELECTROPHYSIOLOGY
Ammonium and chloride extrusion; hyper-
polarizing synaptic inhibition in spinal mo-
toneurons. H. D. Lux. bibliog il Science
173:555-7 Ag 6 '71
Auditory evoked potentials during speech
perception. C. C. Wood and others. bibliog
il Science 173:1248-51 S 24 '71
Calcium: is it required for transmitter
secretion? D. M. J. Quastel and others.
bibliog il Science 172:1034-6 Je 4 '71
Circadian rhythm: population of interacting
neurons. J. W. Jacklet and J. Geronimo.
bibliog il Science 174:299-302 O 15 '71
Conductance changes produced by acetylcholine in lipidic membranes containing a proteolipid from electrophorus. M. Parisi and
others. bibliog il Science 172:56-7 Ap 2 '71
Cyclic adenosine monophosphate and norepinephrine: effects on transmembrane
properties of cerebellar Purkinje cells. G.
R. Siggins and others. bibliog il Science
171:192-4 Ja 15 '71
Development of excitability in embryonic
muscle cell membranes in certain tunicates.
K. Takahashi and others. bibliog il Science
171:415-18 Ja 29 '71

ELECTROPHYSIOLOGY—*Continued*
Electrophysiological observations in normal and dystrophic chicken muscles. E. X. Albuquerque and J. E. Warnick. bibliog il Science 172:1260-3 Je 18 '71
Evoked potential correlates of auditory signal detection. S. A. Hillyard and others. bibliog il Science 172:1357-60 Je 25 '71
Hemispheric asymmetry of electrocortical responses to speech stimuli. L. K. Morrell and J. G. Salamy. bibliog il Science 174:164-6 O 8 '71
Human auditory attention: a central or peripheral process? T. W. Picton and others. bibliog il Science 173:351-3 Jl 23 '71
Maintenance of resting potential in anoxic guinea pig ventricular muscle: electrogenic sodium pumping. T. F. McDonald and D. P. MacLeod. bibliog il Science 172:570-2 My 7 '71
Neural events and the psychophysical law. S. S. Stevens; reply with rejoinder. M. Buchsbaum. Science 172:502 Ap 30 '71
Neuron activity related to short-term memory. J. M. Fuster and G. E. Alexander. bibliog il Science 173:652-4 Ag 13 '71
Quantal mechanism of neural transmitter release; Nobel lecture, December 12, 1970. B. Katz. bibliog il Science 173:123-6 Jl 9 '71
Recurrent excitation of secondary olfactory neurons: a possible mechanism for signal amplification. R. A. Nicoll. bibliog il Science 171:824-6 F 26 '71
Reversal potential for an electrophysiological event generated by conductance changes: mathematical analysis. J. E. Brown and others. bibliog Science 174:318 O 15 '71
Single neuron activity in cat gigantocellular tegmental field: selectivity of discharge in desynchronized sleep. R. W. McCarley and J. A. Hobson. bibliog il Science 174:1250-2 D 17 '71
Slow synaptic excitation in sympathetic ganglion cells: evidence for synaptic inactivation of potassium conductance. F. F. Weight and J. Votava; reply with rejoinder. B. Libet. Science 172:503-4 Ap 30 '71
Somatosensory responses of bulboreticular units in awake cat: relation to escape-producing stimuli. K. L. Casey. bibliog il Science 173:77-80 Jl 2 '71
Summating potential with electrical stimulation of crossed olivocochlear bundles. T. Konishi and J. Slepian. bibliog il Science 172:483-4 Ap 30 '71
Superior colliculus cell responses related to eye movements in awake monkeys. R. H. Wurtz and M. E. Goldberg. bibliog il Science 171:82-4 Ja 8 '71
Synaptic facilitation: long-term neuromuscular facilitation in crustaceans. R. G. Sherman and H. L. Atwood. bibliog il Science 171:1248-50 Mr 26 '71
Telemetered recording of hormone effects on hippocampal neurons. D. W. Pfaff and others. bibliog il Science 172:394-5 Ap 23 '71
    See also
Bioelectronics
Electric organs in fishes
Electroencephalography

ELECTROPHYSIOLOGY of plants
Startling new research from the man who talks to plants. J. Robbins and C. Robbins. il pors Nat Wildlife 9:21-4 O '71

ELECTROPLATING
    See also
Electroforming

ELECTROPLAX. See Electric organs in fishes

ELECTRORETINOGRAPHY
Extracellular recordings from human retinal ganglion cells. G. W. Weinstein and others. bibliog il Science 171:1021-2 Mr 12 '71
On-transient of insect electroretinogram: its cellular origin. A. A. Alawi and W. L. Pak. bibliog il Science 172:1055-7 Je 4 '71
Receptive field mechanism in the vertebrate retina. K. I. Naka. bibliog il Science 171:691-3 F 19 '71

ELECTROSHOCK. See Electric shock

ELECTROSLEEP therapy. See Sleep therapy

ELECTROSTATIC air filters. See Air filters

ELECTROSTATIC gyroscopes. See Gyroscopes

ELECTROSTATIC loudspeakers. See Loud speaking apparatus

ELECTROSTATIC motors. See Electric motors

ELECTROSTATICS
    See also
Electric charges

ELECTROTHERAPY
Electronic device treats deafness; transdermal electrical treatments. S. V. Jones. il Sci Digest 69:79 Je '71
Limb regeneration in mammals. il por Sci N 100:322-3 N 13 '71
Low charge for fractures. il Newsweek 78:74+ N 8 '71

ELEKTRA; opera. See Strauss, R.

ELEMENTARY education. See Education, Elementary

ELEMENTARY particles. See Particles (nuclear physics)

ELEMENTARY school teachers. See Teachers

ELENA, unfaithful; story. See Border, G. K.

ELEO Pomare dance company. See Dance companies

ELEPHANT seals. See Seals (animals)

ELEPHANTS
Close in among the elephants; Lake Manyara National Park; with editorial comment. I. Douglas-Hamilton. il Life 71:1, 40-8 Ag 6 '71
Death of an elephant. il Life 70:60-5 F 26 '71
Elephant spends 30 years in solitary. B. Dunn. il Life 71:79-80 O 22 '71
Elephant trouble: too many in Uganda, disappearing in Ceylon. Sr Schol 98:14 Mr 8 '71
Elephants are hard on trees. F. Heyward. il Am For 77:24-7+ Je '71
Riddle of America's elephants slabs. N. J. Harris. il Sci Digest 69:74-7 Mr '71

ELEPHANTS, Fossil
    See also
Mastodons

ELEVATORS
    See also
Cubic corporation
Otis elevator company

ELFORD, George
Division X: Catholic response to dull, drab classrooms. America 124:376-8 Ap 10 '71
Hidden agenda. America 124:560-2 My 29 '71
School crisis, or parish crisis? Commonweal 93:418-20 Ja 29 '71

ELGIN, Ill.
Elgin clock tower (title varies) O. R. Hagans. il Hobbies 76:125-7 Ag; 126-8 S; 126-7 O '71

ELGIN national watch company
Elgin clock tower (title varies) O. R. Hagans. il Hobbies 76:125-7 Ag; 126-8 S; 126-7 O '71

ELI Lilly and company. See Lilly, Eli, and company

ELIAS, Hans
Three-dimensional structure identified from single sections; adaptation of address, August 1971. bibliog il Science 174:993-1000 D 3 '71

ELIASSEN, Rolf
Power generation and the environment. il por Bul Atom Sci 27:37-42 S '71

ELIOT, Alexander
Games children play. il Sports Illus 34:46-51+ Ja 11 '71

ELIOT, Thomas Stearns
Great edit. W. Clemons. il por Newsweek 78:122+ N 15 '71 *
Invisible poet. R. W. French. Nation 213:470-2 N 8 '71 *
Rhythmical grumblings. F. Kermode. Atlan 229:89-92 Ja '72 *
T. S. Eliot, by R. Sencourt. Review Nat R 23:1186-7 O 22 '71. R. Berman *
Sat R por 54:35-7+ N 27 '71. B. DeMott *

    Manuscripts
Modeling a new mind from a brain-breaking vision; Waste land manuscript. B. DeMott. por Sat R 54:35-7+ N 27 '71
Old Possum revisited; Waste land manuscript. T. Foote. il por Time 98:105-6 D 6 '71
Waste land: a facsimile and transcript of the original drafts, including the annotations of Ezra Pound, by T. S. Eliot. Review America 126:28 Ja 8 '72. P. C. Rule
Where the penty went; Waste land manuscript with the Pound revisions. H. Kenner. New Repub 165:25-6 N 13 '71

ELIOT Miles does not wish you a Merry Christmas because; story. See Konigsburg, E. L.

ELISABETH Charlotte, princess Palatine. See Charlotte Elisabeth

ELITE (social sciences)
Beyond the campus gate; the communication problems of the elite; address, April 29, 1971. W. W. Braden. Vital Speeches 37:572-4 Jl 1 '71

ELITE viewer; story. See Colwin. L.

ELIZABETH II, queen of Great Britain
I went to London to visit the queen! ed. by W. McLendon. M. Mitchell. por Ladies Home J 88:32+ N '71 *
Regal cheek? request for an increase in annual allowance. il pors Newsweek 77:50 Je 14 '71 *
Salary fit for a queen. Time 97:42 Je 14 '71 *

ELIZABETH, princess of Toro
Elizabeth of Toro; with report by M. C. Wrenn. il pors Life 71:70-2+ D 3 '71 *

ELIZABETH McAlister, Sister. See McAlister, E.

ELIZABETH-Newark transportation complex.
See Transportation—New Jersey

ELK
Elk: sultans of the Rockies. G. Heinold. il Sci Digest 69:22-6 My '71
Stalking the grizzly, stalking the elk. J. L. Arehart. il Sci N 100:251 O 9 '71

ELK hunting
Beginner on elk. H. K. Cox. il Field & S 76: 46-7+ Ag '71
Big elk come high and hard. D. Knight. il pors Outdoor Life 148:68-71+ N '71
Elk paid me off. R. W. Charlton. il pors Outdoor Life 148:60-3+ Ag '71

ELKHORN CREEK
Rescue of Elkhorn Creek. R. Herron. il Good H 172:80-1+ Mr '71

ELKIND, David
Early childhood education; a Piagetian perspective. Ed Digest 37:28-31 D '71
Measuring young minds. por Horizon 13:32-7 Wint '71
Sense and nonsense about preschools. il Parents Mag 46:51-3+ Mr '71
What preschoolers need most. il Parents Mag 46:37-9+ My '71
Wilhelm Reich: the psychoanalyst as revolutionary. il pors N Y Times Mag p25-7+ Ap 18; 36+ My 16 '71

ELKOFF, Marvin
Some of my kid's best friends are black. Esquire 76:10+ D '71

ELKS, Benevolent and protective order of
Rogue Elk; Negro membership controversy. il por Newsweek 78:70 D 13 '71
Whites only Elks. America 125:528 D 18 '71

ELLEN, Sister Mary. See Mary Ellen, Sister

ELLEN Murphy, Sister. See Murphy, E.

ELLENA, Nick
This is a vacation? il por Todays Health 49: 34-6+ F '71

ELLENBOGEN, Henry
Pittsburgh's program for efficient courts. M. T. Bloom. Read Digest 98:215-16+ Je '71 *

ELLENBURG, F. C.
Phantasy and facts: censorship & schools. bibliog f Clear House 45:515-19 My '71

ELLERMAN, Carl Paul
Nietzsche's madness: tragic wisdom. bibliog Am Imago 27:338-57 Wint '70

ELLIFF, John T.
Federal law enforcement in America. Cur Hist 60:335-40+ Je '71

ELLINGSON, Marnie
Women's lib, the tooth fairy and other myths; story. Ladies Home J 88:116-17 Mr '71

ELLINGTON, Duke
Three decades of Ellington: a fascinating Decca release. D. W. Moore. por Am Rec G 37:370 F '71 *

ELLIOT, Douglas
New fruit from China via New Zealand. il Horticulture 49:42-3+ F '71

ELLIOT, Elisabeth
Christian father. Chr Today 15:3-4 Je 18 '71

ELLIOT, Charles
Bobwhite leftovers. il Outdoor Life 148:40-1+ D '71
Don't doodlesock 'em. il Outdoor Life 148:42-3+ Jl '71
Magnum boner. il Outdoor Life 147:88 My '71
Mighty river. il Outdoor Life 147:70-3+ Je '71
One for the books? il Outdoor Life 147:94-5+ Ap '71
Riddle of Miccosukee. il por Outdoor Life 148:88-9+ O '71
Team turkey. il por Outdoor Life 147:66-7+ Mr '71

ELLIOTT, Charles (priest)
Dollar crisis and the developing countries. Chr Cent 88:1520-2 D 29 '71

ELLIOTT, Donald H.
Traffic; interview. New Yorker 47:29-30 S 18 '71

ELLIOTT, George Paul
Harbingers. Writer 84:9-10+ N '71
Science and the profession of literature. Atlan 228:105-7+ O '71
about
Comment. J. T. Irwin. Poetry 118:351 S '71 *

ELLIOTT, Lawrence
Ordeal on Mt Kenya. il Read Digest 99:93-7 S '71
Still dying for a smoke? Read Digest 99:49-52 Jl '71

ELLIS, Charles D.
Danger ahead for pension funds. il Harvard Bsns R 49:50-6 My '71
So how would you invest $500 million? interview. pors Forbes 108:68+ N 15 '71

ELLIS, Don D.
Cougar does attack. il Outdoor Life 148:64-7+ S '71

ELLIS, Ernest
Beginning teacher; interview. il por Todays Ed 60:54-9 S '71

ELLIS, H. F.
Was Blücher late at marathon? New Yorker 47:51-2 O 30 '71

ELLIS, Harry
Snakes I met that day. il Nat Wildlife 9:12-15 O '71

ELLIS, Howard T. and Pueschel, R. F.
Solar radiation: absence of air pollution trends at Mauna Loa. bibliog il Science 172:845-6 My 21 '71

ELLIS, John Tracy
Future: does it need a prologue? Cath World 214:21-6 O '71

ELLIS, M. J.
Play and its theories re-examined. Parks & Rec 6:51-5+ Ag '71

ELLIS, Richard A.
Feasibility of public school desegregation. bibliog Sch & Soc 99:433-6 N '71

ELLIS, Susan
Peace corps forestry. il Am For 77:36-8 My '71

ELLIS, William D.
Try talking to yourself. Read Digest 99:134-7 Jl '71

ELLIS, William N.
Crisis in science and UNESCO. Bul Atom Sci 27:33-5 F '71

ELLIS, William S.
Will oil and tundra mix? il Nat Geog 140: 484-517 O '71

ELLIS memorial & Eldredge house, inc, Boston. See Recreation centers

ELLISON, Bob
Robert Young's toughest role. il pors Todays Health 49:25-7+ My '71

ELLISON, Bruce
Back-country Switzerland. il Travel 135:50-3 My '71

ELLISON, David L. and others
Problems in developing a community-based research component for a mental health center. bibliog Ment Hy 55:312-17 Jl '71

ELLISON, Keith
When things go wrong are you a victim of displacement behavior? il Sci Digest 69: 24-6 Mr '71

ELLISTON, Valerie
Girl who ate green jelly for breakfast; story. Redbook 137:69+ Ag '71

ELLO, J. G.
Measuring color-TV generated X-rays. il Electr World 86:37-9+ Jl '71

ELLSBERG, Daniel
Ellsberg talks; interview. ed. by J. R. Moskin. il pors Look 35:31-4+ O 5 '71
Mylai mentality; excerpt from War crimes and the American conscience, ed. by E. Knoll and J. N. McFadden. New Repub 165:19-20 Jl 17 '71
Suspect: a hawk who turned dove; summary of interview. ed. by J. Blocker. por Newsweek 77:16 Je 28 '71
about
After the Pentagon papers, a month in the new life of Daniel Ellsberg. J. A. Lukas. il por N Y Times Mag p29+ D 12 '71 *
Ellsberg affair. P. Schrag. por Sat R 54:34-9 N 13 '71 *
Ellsberg and the new heroism. T. Gitlin. Commonweal 94:447-51 S 3 '71 *
Ellsberg: the battle over the right to know. il pors Time 98:6-12 Jl 5 '71 *
Ellsberg today. il por Newsweek 78:29 D 6 '71 *
Government vs. the press. il por Newsweek 78:17-19 Jl 5 '71 *
Hawk into violent dove. il pors Life 71:30-3 Jl 2 '71 *
I am not guilty. il por Newsweek 78:24+ Ag 30 '71 *

ELLSBERG, Daniel—about—*Continued*
Key man in the case of leaked papers. por
U S News 71:25 Jl 12 '71 *
Leaker, leakee. il por Newsweek 78:26 Jl 26
'71 *
Man who started it all. il por Newsweek 78:
20 Jl 12 '71 *
Man with the monkey wrench. il por Time
97:18-19 Je 28 '71 *
Pentagon papers; repercussions for Rand and
other think tanks? J. Walsh. Science 173:
311+ Jl 23 '71 *
Q: do the claims of conscience outweigh the
duties of citizenship? five testimonies on
the publishing of the Pentagon papers. il
por Esquire 76:154-9+ D '71 *
Strictly academic. il por Newsweek 78:47 N
8 '71 *
La vita nuova. Nat R 23:1456-7 D 31 '71 *
What the rap might be. por Time 98:35 Jl
26 '71 *

ELLSWORTH, Ralph E.
Scholarly publishing and the university li-
brary; address. May 1971. il por Library
J 96:3568-72 N 1 '71

ELLUL, Jacques
Cult of Jacques Ellul. D. D. McFerran. America 124:122-4 F 6 '71 *
Ungodly city. H. Cox. il Commonweal 94:351-
7 Jl 9 '71 *

ELM
Diseases and pests
Elm disease moves west. Sci Digest 70:26 D
'71

ELMAN, Richard
Furs and feathers. il Craft Horiz 31:43-7 Ap
'71

ELMAN, Robert
Mixed bag for bear hunters. il Field & S 75:
46-7+ Ja '71

EL MONTE, Calif.
Low-income, growing. D. Neff. il Time 97:
18 Mr 15 '71

ELMORE, Elizabeth
Our high school reading center. Todays Ed
60:40 Ja '71

ELODEA. See Anacharis

ELON, Amos
Black Panthers of Israel. il N Y Times Mag
p33+ S 12 '71

ELOQUENCE. See Oratory

EL PASO, Tex.
Sanitary affairs
How do you sweep sand? il Am City 86:38 D
'71

EL PASO natural gas company
El Paso merger heads for the hill; 1957 acquisition of Pacific Northwest pipeline
corp. Bsns W p23 My 29 '71
Naked power of monopoly. R. Sherrill. Nation
213:589-92 D 6 '71

ELROM, Ephraim
Tempting target. Time 97:37 My 31 '71 *

ELSON, Alex, and Elson, Miriam
Teaching about law. Todays Ed 60:61-2 Ap
'71

ELSON, Edward
Success story in Atlanta. P. Bragg. il Pub W
200:26-7 S 20 '71 *

ELSON, Miriam. See Elson, A. jt. auth.

ELTEN, Jörg Andrees
This is a hijacking! condensation. il Read
Digest 99:213-17+ Jl '71

ELTON, Charles F. and Rodgers, S. A.
Physics department ratings: another evaluation. bibliog il Science 174:565-8 N 5 '71

ELTON, John
Twinkle twinkle superstar do we know who
you are? M. English. il pors Look 35:50-3+
Jl 27 '71 *

ELVINS, Peter
(ed) See Donath, H. Pure lyric

ELWOOD, Douglas J.
Primitivism or technology: must we choose?
il Chr Cent 88:1413-18 D 1 '71

EL-ZOGHBY, Gamal. See Zoghby, G.

EMANCIPATION of slaves. See Slavery—
United States—Emancipation

EMANS, Elaine V.
With you; poem. Good H 172:170 F '71

EMBARGO
Embargo's end; Britain's economic embargo
of Rhodesia. Fortune 83:41 Ap '71

EMBDEN geese. See Geese

EMBERS glow; story. See Rosenberg, L.

EMBEZZLEMENT
Wells, Fargo's Jekyll and Hyde. R. H. Dillon.
il por Am West 8:28-33+ Mr '71
Why employes steal; interview. N. Jaspan. il
por U S News 70:78-82 My 3 '71; Same abr.
Read Digest 99:83-6 S '71

EMBLEMS, City
Brighten that image; new city symbol. Bar-
tow, Fla. P. D. Eimon. il Am City 86:120-1
N '71

EMBOLISM
Embolism, the puzzling killer. J. J. Deiss.
Read Digest 98:201-2+ Mr '71

EMBOSSING (typography)
Embossed pictures of Samuel Dixon and his
imitators. A. L. Leask. il Antiques 100:
120-3 Jl '71

EMBROIDERY
Art of needle painting. R. K. Stroh. il Design
73:17 Wint '71
Memorial embroideries by American school-
girls; with editorial comment. B. Ring. il
Antiques 100:569, 570-5 O '71
Stitching; basic embroidery to liven up all
your favorite clothes. il Seventeen 30:144 D
'71
See also
Needlework
Samplers

EMBRYOLOGY
Development of excitability in embryonic
muscle cell membranes in certain tunicates.
K. Takahashi and others. bibliog il Sci-
ence 171:415-18 Ja 29 '71
See also
Differentiation (biology)
Embryology, Experimental
Fetu
Morphogenesis
Ovaries
Placenta
Reproduction
Birds
Bilateral symmetry in chick embryo deter-
mination by gravity. S. Kochav and H.
Eyal-Giladi. bibliog il Science 171:1027-9
Mr 12 '71
Echinoderms
Ribosomal RNA synthesis and the multiple,
atypical nucleoli in cleaving embryos. C. P.
Emerson, jr. and T. Humphreys. bibliog
il Science 171:898-901 Mr 5 '71
Sea urchin embryos are permeable to actino-
mycin. G. A. Greenhouse and others. bib-
liog il Science 171:686-9 F 19 '71
Mammals
Artibeus jamaicensis: delayed embryonic de-
velopment in a neotropical bat. T. H. Flem-
ing. bibliog il Science 171:402-4 Ja 29 '71

EMBRYOLOGY, Experimental
Body: from baby hatcheries to Xeroxing hu-
man beings. il Time 97:37-8+ Ap 19 '71
Bridging a gap: implantation stage. por Sci N
99:278 Ap 24 '71
Second genesis, by A. Rosenfeld. Review
Bul Atom Sci 27:47-8 Ja '71. R Henoch
Test-tube baby is coming. D. M. Rorvik. il
pors Look 35:83-6+ My 18 '71
Moral and religious aspects
Homo faber with a vengeance. Commonweal
94:179-80 Ap 30 '71

EMEL'IANOV, Vasilii Semenovich
Nuclear energy in the Soviet Union. il por
Bul Atom Sci 27:38-41 N '71

EMERALD mines and mining
Emeralds and bullets. il Time 98:56 Jl 12 '71

EMERGENCIES, Assistance in. See Assistance
in emergencies

EMERGENCY communication systems
See also
Police communication systems
Radio communication—Emergency use

EMERGENCY electric plants. See Electric
plants, Emergency

EMERGENCY highway flasher. See Electric
lamps, Flashing

EMERGENCY powers. See Presidents—United
States—Powers and duties; War and emergency powers

EMERGENCY preparedness, Office of. See
United States—Emergency preparedness,
Office of

EMERGENCY services, Hospital. See Hospitals
—Emergency services

EMERGENCY squads, Volunteer. See Volunteer service

EMERITA analoga. See Crabs

EMERSON, Charles P. jr, and Humphreys, Tom
Ribosomal RNA synthesis and the multiple,
atypical nucleoli in cleaving embryos.
bibliog il Science 171:898-901 Mr 5 '71

EMERSON, Gloria
Hey, lady, what are you doing here? il por
McCalls 98:61+ Ag '71
Vietnam diary. il pors Vogue 159:74-7+ Ja 1
'72

EMERSON, Gloria—*Continued*

about

As seen by gloomy Gloria. G. Kirk. Nat R 23:426 Ap 20 '71 *

EMERSON, John D.
Outlook for energy in the United States. Bul Atom Sci 27:18-19 O '71

EMERSON, John W.
Channelization: a case study. bibliog il Science 173:325-6 Jl 23 '71

EMERSON, Ralph Waldo
Imperial self, by Q. Anderson. Review. Commentary 52:87-8 Jl '71. H. Bloom *
Reconsiderations. A. D. Wood. New Repub 166:27-9 Ja 1 '72 *

EMERSON, Roy
Sports. R. Kahn. Esquire 75:30+ Je '71 *

EMERSON, Thomas I.
Supporting an equal rights amendment. Cur 134:25-32 N '71

EMERSON electric company
Persons of Emerson electric. il por Forbes 107:52 My 15 '71

EMERY, K. O. See Meade, R. H. jt. auth.

EMERY air freight corporation
Emery introduces new garment container. R. S. Kahn. il Aviation W 95:32-3 D 13 '71
Emery posts record earnings, introduces guaranteed delivery. il Aviation W 94:30 Mr 22 '71
New tool: reinforcement for good work. il Bsns W p76-7 D 18 '71

EMIGRES
Sons of the bitter mango; Haitian political figures in the U.S. B. Thompson. Nation 213:551-4 N 29 '71

EMILIANI, Cesare
Climate cycles. il Sea Front 17:108-20 Mr '71
Depth habitats of growth stages of pelagic foraminifera. bibliog il Science 173:1122-4 S 17 '71
Last interglacial: paleotemperatures and chronology. bibliog il Science 171:571-3 F 12 '71
Paleotemperature variations across the plio-pleistocene boundary. bibliog il Science 171:60-2 Ja 8 '71

EMINENT domain
Reporter at large; house and highway. W. Balliett. New Yorker 47:40-5 D 25 '71

EMINENT domain (international law)
Expropriation: why do they do it? interviews. I. MacGregor; O. Letelier. pors Forbes 108:32-5 Jl 15 '71
See also
Latin America—Expropriation policy

EMINENT men. See Great men

EMISSION control devices (motor vehicles)
See Motor vehicles—Pollution control devices

EMLEN, Stephen Thompson
Celestial rotation: its importance in the development of migratory orientation. bibliog il Science 170:1198-201; 173:460-1 D 11 '70; Jl 30 '71

about

Celestial navigation by migrating birds. Sky & Tel 41:80 F '71 *

EMMERLING, Mary
Environments. il Mlle 73:153 Je '71

EMMETT, J. A.
Boating. See issues of Outdoor life
New boats and motors. il Outdoor Life 147:66-70+ Ja '71

EMMETT, John L.
Frontiers of laser development. bibliog Phys Today 24:24-31 Mr '71

EMORY, Ben
Ecology crisis, what you can do. il Yachting 130:56-7+ Jl '71

EMORY university, Atlanta

Yerkes primate research center
Look who's gone bananas over TV! N. Hickey. il Read Digest 98:157-8+ Ja '71
Parting shots; ape-rating the tube. il Life 70:69-70+ Mr 5 '71

EMOTIONAL maturity. See Maturity

EMOTIONAL problems of children
And now, teaching emotions. il Time 97:74 F 22 '71

EMOTIONALLY disturbed children. See Mentally ill children; Problem children

EMOTIONS
See also
Anger
Bashfulness
Emotional problems of children
Fear
Hate
Jealousy
Love
Mind and body
Temperament

EMPEROR'S fish; story. See Adams, C. H.

EMPIRE. See Imperialism

EMPIRE State building. See New York (city)—Empire State building

EMPLOYEE absenteeism. See Absenteeism

EMPLOYEE benefits. See Non-wage payments

EMPLOYEE incentives. See Incentives in industry

EMPLOYEE morale
Low spirits produce the phantom week. V. Louviere. Nations Bsns 59:13 Ja '71
See also
Incentives in industry
Job satisfaction

EMPLOYEE obsolescence. See Obsolescence

EMPLOYEE recreation. See Industrial recreation

EMPLOYEE rights. See Employees—Civil rights

EMPLOYEE rules. See Work rules

EMPLOYEE stock ownership. See Employees as stockholders

EMPLOYEE suggestions. See Suggestion systems

EMPLOYEE thefts. See Stealing

EMPLOYEE vacations. See Vacations, Employee

EMPLOYEES
Corporate underground. T. H. Ingram. Nation 213:206-12 S 13 '71
See also
Household employees
Job satisfaction
Labor turnover
Municipal employees
Office workers
Personnel management
Suggestion systems
Supervisors
Wage payment plans
also subhead Employees under various subjects, e.g. Trade unions—Employees

Civil rights
Who wants employee rights? D. W. Ewing. bibliog f il Harvard Bsns R 49:22-4+ N '71

Dismissal
Job reinstatement under section 8(a)(3) of the NLRA. L. Aspin. Mo Labor R 94:57-9 Mr '71
Suppose you lose your job... then what? il Changing T 25:31-2 Mr '71
Tips for the boss when it's time to fire. Bsns W p91 Ag 14 '71
See also
Layoff systems

Health and hygiene
Drugs and drinking in the business world; interview. H. Johnson. por U S News 70:70-3 Mr 22 '71

Leaves of absence
At Xerox: giving but not forcing. V. Louviere. Nations Bsns 59:18 D '71
Editor's page; arguments for sabbaticals. T. Benfey. Chem 44:2 S '71
Where the mouth is; social service leave plan at Xerox. Newsweek 78:82+ S 20 '71
Xerox sabbaticals. Time 98:69 S 20 '71
Xeroxing of social service. Bsns W p41 S 11 '71

Qualifications
Court's new rule on job testing. U S News 70:82-3 Ap 12 '71
Flunking job tests; black laborers in North Carolina. Time 97:53 Mr 22 '71
More of the same? Supreme court ruling on use of intelligence tests by employers. Nat R 23:352 Ap 6 '71
Stricter standards for personnel tests; Supreme court decision. Bsns W p34 Mr 20 '71

Rating
Power networks in the appraisal process. B. F. White and L. B. Barnes. bibliog f il Harvard Bsns R 49:101-9 My '71
Where they make believe they're the boss; assessment technique. il Bsns W p34-5 Ag 28 '71

Reinstatement
On reinstatement of strikers. Mo Labor R 94:62-4 bibliog(p66) N '71

Relocation
Moving time; Shell's move to Houston. L. L. Golden. Sat R 54:63 Je 12 '71
See also
Executives—Relocation

EMPLOYEES—*Continued*

Training

How union leaders view job training programs. J. E. Drotning and D. B. Lipsky. Mo Labor R 94:65-6 Ap '71

Role of on-the-job training in a clinical laboratory. W. D. White and A. Robbins. bibliog f il Mo Labor R 94:65-9 Mr '71

See also

Opportunities industrialization centers, inc.

EMPLOYEES, Recruiting of. See Recruiting of employees

EMPLOYEES as stockholders

Getting employees to put up the capital; employee stock ownership trusts. il Bsns W p86+ N 20 '71

See also

Profit sharing

EMPLOYEES loans. See Loans, Personal

EMPLOYEES magazines, handbooks, etc.

Corporate underground. T. H. Ingram. Nation 213:206-12 S 13 '71

Dissenters; corporate underground newspapers. il Newsweek 78:97-8 N 8 '71

Underground papers needle the bosses. il Bsns W p86+ O 9 '71

EMPLOYEES representation in management

Unleash the people; employee creativity; address, March 1, 1971. H. R. Sharbaugh. Vital Speeches 37:413-16 Ap 15 '71

See also

Industrial democracy

EMPLOYER-employee relations. See Industrial relations; Personnel management

EMPLOYMENT

Changes in employment and unemployment in 1970; with tables and charts. P. O. Flaim and P. M. Schwab. Mo Labor R 94:12-23 F '71

Employment effects of reduced defense spending; with tables. R. P. Oliver. bibliog Mo Labor R 94:3-11 D '71

Job vacancies in 1970. R. Konstant. Mo Labor R 94:20-1 F '71

Occupational impact of defense expenditures; with tables. R. Dempsey and D. Schmude. Mo Labor R 94:12-15 D '71

Uses of adversity. il Newsweek 77:58+ Ja 18 '71

See also

Applications for positions

College students—Employment

Forty plus clubs

Self employed

Student employment

Unemployment—United States

Woman—Employment

Working life, Length of

Statistics

Employment and unemployment, household data; tables. See issues of Monthly labor review

New federal-state occupational employment statistics program: mail questionnaire survey of employment by occupation. H. Goldstein. Mo Labor R 94:12-17 O '71

Occupational characteristics of urban workers; with tables. C. G. Gellner. bibliog Mo Labor R 94:21-32 O '71

Work experience of the population in 1970; with tables. A. M. Young and K. Michelotti. Mo Labor R 94:35-44 D '71

See also

Unemployment—Statistics

EMPLOYMENT, Supplementary. See Supplementary employment

EMPLOYMENT agencies

Executive placement firms: they got me nowhere. R. Warren. il Duns 97:59-61 Ap '71; Reply. H. Morris. 98:73 Jl '71

Newtime a-comin'. Newsweek 78:125 O 25 '71

9 big do's and don'ts for the 1971 job hunter. C. Mangel. Look 35:21-3 My 18 '71; Same abr. with title How to land the job you want. Read Digest 99:197-8+ O '71

What they do about that empty feeling; survey of temporary help services. il Nations Bsns 59:99 Ja '71

See also

Kelly services, inc.

EMPLOYMENT contracts. See Labor contracts

EMPLOYMENT discrimination. See Discrimination in employment

EMPLOYMENT interviewing

9 big do's and don'ts for the 1971 job hunter. C. Mangel. Look 35:21-3 My 18 '71; Same abr. with title How to land the job you want. Read Digest 99:197-8+ O '71

See also

Video recorders and recording—Business use

EMPLOYMENT of the aged. See Age and employment

EMPLOYMENT of the mentally ill. See Mentally ill—Employment

EMPLOYMENT systems. See Recruiting of employees

EMULSIONS

Structure of water in microemulsions: electrical, birefringence, and nuclear magnetic resonance studies. D. O. Shah and R. M. Hamlin, jr bibliog il Science 171:483-5 F 5 '71

ENAMEL and enameling

Electroformed enamels. P. Rothenberg. il Ceram Mo 19:22-5 Mr '71

Liquid enamels for background and texture. R. Berl. il Ceram Mo 19:30 N 71

Watercolor effect with enamels; direct printing with oil. M. Buffum. il Ceram Mo 19:27-9 D '71

See also

Cloisonné

ENAMELS. See Enamel and enameling

ENANTIOMERIC isomers. See Isomers and isomerism

ENCAPSULATION (electronics) See Electronic circuits—Plastic embedment

ENCAUSTIC painting

Painting with wax. S. Powell. il Design 73:39 Wint '71

ENCEPHALITIS

Culex (melanoconion) aikenii: natural vector in Panama of endemic Venezuelan encephalitis. P. Galindo and M. A. Grayson. bibliog il Science 172:594-5 My 7 '71

Subacute sclerosing panencephalitis: isolation of suppressed measles virus from lymph node biopsies. L. Horta-Barbosa and others. bibliog il Science 173:840-1 Ag 27 '71

See also

Encephalomyelitis

ENCEPHALOMYELITIS

Allergic encephalomyelitis: new form featuring polymorphonuclear leukocytes. S. Levine and R. Sowinski. bibliog il Science 171:498-9 F 5 '71

Biological activity and synthesis of an encephalitogenic determinant. R. Shapira and others. bibliog il Science 173:736-8 Ag 20 '71

Equine epidemic; Venezuelan equine encephalomyelitis. il Time 98:41 Jl 26 '71

Grim struggle with an equine killer; VEE. D. Levin. il Sports Illus 35:20-3 Ag 16 '71

Horse fever. il Newsweek 78:50-1 Jl 26 '71

Massive attack on a mystery virus. il U S News 71:77 Ag 2 '71

Specific enzymic methylation of an arginine in the experimental allergic encephalomyelitis protein from human myelin. G. S. Baldwin and P. R. Carnegie. bibliog il Science 171:579-81 F 12 '71

VEE: costliest disease break in years. C. E. Ball. il Farm J 95:20-1+ S '71

Vaccines

VEE vaccine: fortuitous spin-off from BW research. R. Gillette. Science 173:405-8 Jl 30 '71

ENCEPHALOPATHY. See Brain—Diseases

ENCHANTED piano; story. See Fernandes

ENCHILADAS. See Cookery, Mexican

ENCLOSURES, Loudspeaker. See Loud speaking apparatus—Cabinets

ENCOUNTER groups. See Group relations training

ENCYCLICALS

Anniversary of social encyclicals. America 124:529 My 22 '71

Anniversary of social encyclicals. B. L. Masse. America 124:520-1 My 15 '71

Do Humanae vitae and infallibility stand or fall together? T. A. Caffrey. America 125:66-7 Ag 7 '71

Pope Pius XI on rebuilding the social order; Rerum novarum and Quadragesimo anno. B. L. Masse. America 124:559 My 29 '71

Quadragesimo anno: forty years after. J. R. Jennings. il America 125:208-10 S 25 '71

ENCYCLOPAEDIA Britannica, inc.

Miniaturization of the book. J. Tebbel. Cur 126:46-51 F '71

21 authors file suit against Britannica. Pub W 200:30-1 Ag 9 '71

ENCYCLOPEDIA salesmen. See Canvassing

ENCYCLOPEDIAS

Blitzing the supermarket customer with books. P. A. Farrell. Pub W 200:71-2 Ag 23 '71

Consumer's guide to encyclopedias & dictionaries. il Mech Illus 67:120 Ja '71

Encyclopedias: experts pick the best of the latest. il Changing T 25:6 Ag '71

END of love is death & the end of death is love; story. See Clifton, L.
END of the duel; story. See Borges, J. L.
END of the world
How will the earth end? I. Asimov. Sci Digest 70:75-6 N '71
ENDANGERED species. See Rare animals
ENDANGERED species conservation act. See Wildlife conservation—Laws and legislation
ENDEMIC goiter. See Goiter
ENDOCRINOLOGY
See also
Pineal body
Testicles
ENDOLYMPH. See Lymph
ENDOTHELIUM. See Epithelium
ENDOTOXINS. See Toxins and antitoxins
ENDOWMENTS
Private institutions in jeopardy. Sat R 54:49 Mr 20 '71
ENDRES, Eugene
There's a tweeter in my tweeter. Hi Fi 21: 61-5 Je '71
ENDRES, M. H.
How to write for specialized magazines. Writer 84:24-5 S '71
ENDURANCE
How to increase your energy; excerpt from The energies of men; reprint from October 1961 issue. W. James. Read Digest 99:119-21 S '71
ENEA, Joseph
Fishman talks about fish; ed. by H. McCully. il por House B 113:166+ O '71
ENEMY of the people; drama. See Miller, A.
ENERGY. See Force and energy
ENERGY band theory of solids
Magnetic resonances and waves in simple metals. W. M. Walsh, jr. bibliog il Science 171:36-42 Ja 8 '71
ENERGY budget (geophysics)
Flow of energy in the biosphere. D. M. Gates. il Sci Am 225:88-92+ bibliog(p244) S '71
See also
Hydrologic cycle
ENERGY expenditure. See Bioenergetics
ENERGY industry. See Fuel industry
ENERGY levels (quantum mechanics)
Improved lamb-shift experiments. M. S. Rothenberg. bibliog Phys Today 24:20 Ag '71
Mössbauer spectroscopy. R. H. Herber. il Sci Am 225:86-95 bibliog(p 120) O '71
Photofragment spectroscopy looks at excited states. M. S. Rothenberg. bibliog il Phys Today 24:19-20 Ap '71
Saclay and Argonne see nuclear quartet states. G. B. Lubkin. il Phys Today 24: 14-15 Jl '71
ENERGY resources. See Power resources
ENFIELD, Conn.
Education
Films are in at Fermi. F. S. Gross. il Schol Teach Jr/Sr High p22-3 O '71
Kicks and flicks at Fermi. F. S. Gross. il Schol Teach Jr/Sr High p 16-17+ F 1 '71
ENFORCEMENT of law. See Law enforcement
ENGDAHL, Eric R.
Explosion effects and earthquakes in the Amchitka Island Region. bibliog il Science 173:1232-5 S 24 '71
ENGDAHL, Sylvia Louise
Changing role of science fiction in children's literature. il Horn Bk 47:449-55 O '71
ENGEL, Herbert M. and others
Belling the Berrigans. pors Cath World 213: 227-31 Ag '71
ENGEL, Randy
Whatever happened to Vietnam's other war? il Chr Cent 88:350-3 Mr 17 '71
ENGEL, Ross A.
Teacher evaluates teacher for pay differentials. Clear House 45:407-9 Mr '71
ENGEL, W. King. See Campa, J. F. jt. auth.
ENGELHARDT, Tom, and Peck, Jim
Japan: rising sun in the Pacific. il Ramp Mag 10:29-37 Ja '72
ENGELLAU, Gunnar
Accelerating Volvo's pace. G. J. Berkwitt. por Duns 97:58-9 F '71 *
ENGELS, John
Foxes; poem. Nation 212:700 My 31 '71
ENGINE turning. See Damascening
ENGINEER-Private Paul Klee misplaces an aircraft between Milbertshofen and Cambrai, March 1916; story. See Barthelme, D.

ENGINEERING
See also
Automobile engineering
Biomedical engineering
Computers—Engineering use
Study and teaching
See also
Engineering education
ENGINEERING, Medical. See Biomedical engineering
ENGINEERING colleges
Tech schools suffer as students turn off. il Bsns W p91 Ap 10 '71
See also
General motors institute, Flint, Mich.
ENGINEERING conferences. See Technical conferences
ENGINEERING education
Engineering education; ecological issues; address, February 2, 1971. M. Tribus. Vital Speeches 37:410-13 Ap 15 '71
See also
Engineering colleges
ENGINEERING societies
See also
National academy of engineering
ENGINEERING standards. See Standards, Engineering
ENGINEERING students
Tech schools suffer as students turn off. il Bsns W p91 Ap 10 '71
ENGINEERS
Accelerating obsolescence of older engineers. G. W. Dalton and P. H. Thompson. bibliog f il Harvard Bsns R 49:57-67 S '71
Engineer in the establishment. D. C. Drucker. Bul Atom Sci 27:31-4 D '71
Engineers are redesigning their own profession. J. Gooding. il Fortune 83:72-5+ Je '71
See also
Aerospace professional and technical association
Comprehensive designers, inc.
Political activities
See also
Scientists and engineers for social and political action (organization)
Supply and demand
Defense engineers: do they have special reemployment problems? B. C. Eaton. il Mo Labor R 94:52-4 Jl '71
Engineer and his work: a sociological perspective. A. Rudoff and D. Lucken. bibliog Science 172:1103-8 Je 11 '71; Discussion. 174:645 N 12 '71
Statement of Senator Edward M. Kennedy on re-employing defense scientists and engineers. E. M. Kennedy. por Bul Atom Sci 27:41-3 Mr '71
Story of a science depression. il U S News 70:24-6 Ja 25 '71
When the brains can't get work. il Bsns W p90-2+ F 13 '71
ENGINES
See also
Automobile engines
Flywheels
Gas and oil engines
Gas turbines
Heat engines
Horsepower (mechanics)
Marine engines
Motorcycle engines
Rocket engines
Steam engines
ENGLAND, Barry
Conduct unbecoming. Criticism Nat R 23:324 Mr 23 '71 *
ENGLAND, Ralph W. jr
Is the prison becoming obsolete? bibliog f il Cur Hist 61:35-9+ Jl '71
ENGLAND
See also
Americans in England
Architecture, Domestic—England
Blackpool
Carlisle
Cornwall
Country estates—England
English
Great Britain
Hunting—England
Libraries—England
London
Music festivals—England
National parks and reserves—England
Thames River

Description and travel
In England: a hunting trip for antique buffs. M. Gough. House B 113:28+ F '71

ENGLAND—*Continued*

Historic houses
See also
Literary landmarks

Literary landmarks
See Literary landmarks

Money
See Money—Great Britain

Religious institutions and affairs
See also
Methodist church in England

ENGLAND, Church of. *See* Church of England

ENGLAND and the United States
See also
Americans in England
United States—Foreign opinion—British

ENGLE, John D. Jr
Light, serious or in-between. Writers Digest 51:26-7 F '71

ENGLE, Paul
Are we losing our pioneer spirit? Read Digest 98:15-16+ Mr '71
Hong Kong blues; poem. Holiday 49:31 Jl '71
Three poems. Good H 173:260 N '71
Together; Lake; Frog; poems. McCalls 99:148 D '71

ENGLEBARDT, Stanley L.
Epidemics ahead, unless! Read Digest 99:114-18 N 71
Hospitals discover care-by-parent. il Read Digest 99:27-8+ S '71
Your mother died three years ago. il Todays Health 49:44-5+ Mr '71

ENGLISH, Margaret
Melanie is love. Look 35:37-8 Ja 12 '71
Speed: downhill all the way. il Look 35:88-9 Je 1 '71

ENGLISH
London letter. Q. Crewe. Vogue 157:96-7 My '71

ENGLISH art. *See* Art, British

ENGLISH automobiles. *See* Automobiles, Foreign

ENGLISH CHANNEL
Unjamming the Channel. il Newsweek 77:72 Ap 26 '71
See also
Channel Islands (English Channel)

ENGLISH composition. *See* English language—Composition

ENGLISH cookery. *See* Cookery, English

ENGLISH dictionaries. *See* English language—Dictionaries

ENGLISH drama
See also
London—Theater

ENGLISH furniture. *See* Furniture, English

ENGLISH grammar. *See* English language—Grammar

ENGLISH language
Language gap: must we all speak English? M. A. Tamers. Bul Atom Sci 27:38-40 Mr '71
Our native tongue, alive and well. R. MacLeish. Read Digest 98:132-5 Ja '71
See also
Slang
Vocabulary

Composition
Communication skills through self-recording. L. Smith and others. il Todays Ed 60:18-20 Ja '71
Do thirteen year olds write as well as seventeen year olds? H. B. Slotnick. il Engl J 60:1109-15 N '71
Essay grading by computer: a laboratory phenomenon? H. B. Slotnick and J. V. Knapp. bibliog f Engl J 60:75-80+ Ja '71
Family of man in an English class. P. F. Skinner. Engl J 60:220-2 F '71
Famous seventh-grade authors: building egos the lazy way. P. J. McKearn. Engl J 60:126-7 Ja '71
Grading themes: a new approach; a new dimension; tape recorded criticism. S. H. Vogler. Engl J 60:70-4+ Ja '71
Growing up absurd in a mad, mad, mad, mad world. J. Showler. Engl J 60:223-5 F '71
Implications of national assessment writing results. E. J. Farrell. Engl J 60:1116-19 N 71
Inhibited teacher; adaptation of address, November 1970. W. Kaufman. Engl J 60:382-8 Mr '71
Plagiarism and originality: some remedies. R. G. Martin. bibliog f Engl J 60:621-5+ My '71
Reading and writing exposition and argument: the skills and their relationships. M. Finder. Engl J 60:615-20 My '71

Reporting and exposition. C. Gibb. Engl J 60:251-4+ F '71
Research in the teaching of English. D. V. Gunderson. bibliog Engl J 60:792-6 S '71
Saul Steinberg and high school composition. L. Mueller. bibliog il Engl J 60:1095-100 N '71
Second R; writing of children tested by National assessment of educational progress. W. D. Boutwell. PTA Mag 65:11 F '71
Students anesthetized? Try a titillating test! M. K. Fritts. Engl J 60:264-6 F '71
Teaching writing to the non-academic student; student tutors. R. Lebda. Clear House 46:39 S '71
Term-paper hustlers. il Time 97:67 Ap 19 '71
Theme editor: English teacher's ally. G. F. Smith. Clear House 46:116-18 O '71
To sing the street: using a community film program to teach composition. H. Foley. Engl J 60:1101-8 N '71
What Volkswagen, Revlon, and Ayd's candies can tell you about writing. L. McDougall. Engl J 60:479-80 Ap '71
Writer; men who sell term papers. G. Ace. Sat R 54:3 Ag 28 '71
See also
Creative writing
Rhetoric

Courses of study
See English language—Study and teaching

Dialects
Bi-dialectalism: a special report from CAL/ERIC. A. M. Malkoc and A. H. Roberts. bibliog Engl J 60:279-88 F '71
Language and poverty, ed. by F. Williams. Review
Engl J 60:515-18 Ap '71. V. Allen
See also
Negro-English dialects

Dictionaries
American heritage dictionary: pictures at a definition; a marginal critique; with reply by W. Morris. J. B. White. il Wilson Lib Bul 45:674-80 Mr '71
Compact edition of the Oxford English dictionary. Review
Newsweek il 78:102A+ O 11 '71. W. Clemons
Consumer's guide to encyclopedias & dictionaries. il Mech Illus 67:120 Ja '71

Etymology
Anecdotes, facetiae, satire, etc.
Boycott to Zeppelin with nary a quibble. W. Zinsser. il Life 70:10 F 5 '71

Grammar
State of grammar in the state of Iowa. D. Wall Engl J 60:1127-30 N '71
See also
English language—Usage
Parts of speech

Idioms and provincialisms
See also
English language—Usage

Orthography and spelling
See Spelling

Pronunciation
Slurish. B. Hutchinson. Engl J 60:361-2 Mr '71
When everybody wins. D. Uris. Opera N 36:6-7 D 25 '71

Remedial teaching
Oral communication for the Indian student; address, April 1970. B. L. Brilhart. Engl J 60:629-32 My '71
Second vocabulary for Johnny; Milwaukee's Speech and language development program. M. P. Pfeil. il Am Ed 7:16-20 My '71

Study and teaching
Alleluia! English has risen! individual instruction. A. L. Beslin. Engl J 60:607-9 My '71
Alternative for the middle years: English for little big men. D. Dyer. Engl J 60:1091-4 N '71
Behavioral objectives. C. M. Kirkton. Engl J 60:142-50 Ja '71
Behavioral objectives and the teaching of English. P. W. Airasian. Engl J 60:495-9 Ap '71
Black English. O. Mellan; discussion. New Repub 164:34-5 Ja 16 '71
Cultural clash, crash, and cash; address, November 1970. A. Bernstein. Engl J 60:773-7 S '71

ENGLISH language—Study and teaching—
—*Continued*
Eliminating the negative in English teaching.
T. W. Hipple. Engl J 60:373-8 Mr '71
English as woodshop. M. Myers. Engl J 60:
317-25 Mr '71
English curriculum: process or product? ad-
dress, November 1970. G. E. LaRocque.
bibliog f Engl J 60:781-6 S '71
English for free; English for the hell of it;
address, November 1970. P. T. Stapleton.
Engl J 60:500-4 Ap '71
English in a sea of science; address, Novem-
ber 1970. W. D. Boutwell. Engl J 60:326-32
Mr '71
English in experimental schools. B. Leondar.
Engl J 60:748-53 S '71
English in no man's land: some suggestions
for the middle years. D. L. Burton. Engl J
60:23-30 Ja '71
Free school or chalk talk time; address,
November 1970. M. R. Graham. Engl J
60:754-9 S '71
From not so different worlds; course for non-
college-bound students. M. A. Boogaard
and E. R. Chaney. Engl J 60:226-8+ F '71
How to define the sanctity of English. A. J.
Leonard. Engl J 60:242-5 F '71
Humanistic approach to behavioral objec-
tives. H. M. Rothstein. Engl J 60:760-2
S '71
Individualizing the study of English. E. R.
Fagan. Engl J 60:236-41+ F '71
Keys to standard English; altering the speech
patterns of minority group children. R.
Caselli. Ed Digest 36:30-1 Ja '71
Language and poverty, ed. by F. Williams.
Review
Engl J 60:515-18 Ap '71. V. Allen
Linguistic gospel: a dissent. J. G. Franks.
bibliog Sch & Soc 99:98-101 F '71
Natural resources in the English curriculum.
M. Brittingham. Engl J 60:927-30 O '71
New approach: drama in the classroom. C.
D. Atkinson. Engl J 60:947-51+ O '71
New English: hot stuff or cool, man, cool?
address, November 1970. R. W. Blake. Engl
J 60:728-34 S '71
180 days: observations of an elective year.
J. E. Smith, jr. Engl J 60:229-30+ F '71
Pattern practices: we bombed in New Or-
leans. C Suhor. Engl J 60:1221-4 D '71
Raising student self-esteem for a change.
W. P. Ferris. Engl J 60:379-81 Mr '71
Research in the teaching of English. D. V.
Gunderson. bibliog Engl J 60:547-53, 792-6
Ap. S '71
Simple tools and complex learning. H. H.
Punke. Sch & Soc 99:513-14 D '71
Story of an English elective program. D. B.
Bronson. Engl J 60:1086-90 N '71
Summary of investigations relating to the
English language arts in secondary educa-
tion: 1970. N. S. Blount. bibliog Engl J 60:
633-40+ My '71
Teacher behavior and English instruction;
junior high school level. W. T. Ojala.
Clear House 45:435-8 Mr '71
Things ain't the way they used to be in the
English classroom. J. Yatvin. Engl J 60:
1080-5 N '71
This world of English. A. Tovatt and T. De-
Vries. See issues of English journal
Transactional curriculum for the transescent
learner; address, November 1970. E. L. Wil-
liams. il Engl J 60:599-602 My '71
Turning on: the selling of the present, 1970;
electronic media and the English curric-
ulum, November, 1970. B. Fillion. Engl J
60:333-8 Mr '71
Unified English: salvaging the disaffected.
E. R. Fagan. bibliog f Clear House 45:259-
64 Ja '71
Wanted: English for vocational students. E.
G. Massey. Engl J 60:116-20 Ja '71
What means this end? Some unexamined
classroom practices. R. Botts. Engl J 60:88-
92 Ja '71
Where they live; address, November 1970.
G. W. Rainey. Engl J 60:787-91 S '71
Whither an English curriculum for the seven-
ties? K. Gill. Engl J 60:447-54 Ap '71
See also
English language—Composition
English language—Grammar
English literature—Study and teaching
Journalism—Study and teaching
National council of teachers of English

Aids and devices
Teaching materials, ed. by J. R. Searles and
N. S. Blount. See issues of English journal
Using media creatively in the English class-
room. L. Brandon. Engl J 60:1231-3 D '71

Bibliography
More sources of free and inexpensive mate-
rial, comp. by J. R. Searles. Engl J 60:
797-804 S '71
Professional publications, ed. by D. Petitt.
See issues of English journal
Reading to teach: summer in professional
literature. C. M. Kirkton. Engl J 60:670-7
My '71
Reference shelf for curriculum planning
(cont) Engl J 60:142-50 Ja '71

Foreigners
Aqui estoy . . . here I am; storefront English
language center for Spanish speakers. A.
Gaber. il por Am Ed 7:18-22 Ja '71
Building a winner with well-chosen words;
teaching Latin ballplayers. T. Quinn. il
Sports Illus 34:77-8 Ap 19 '71

Syntax
Transformations, style, and the writing experience; address, November 1970. R. A. Jacobs. Engl J 60:481-4+ Ap '71

Terms and phrases
Day the iron curtain fell; W. Churchill's
speech. il por Sr Schol 98:18 Mr 8 '71
How to speak futurese. McCalls 98:41 Ag '71

Textbooks
Adventures in manipulation; appraisal of Ad-
ventures in reading, as a freshman text. B.
Christensen. Engl J 60:359-60 Mr '71

Usage
Duelist. R. Lardner. Sat R 54:6 Ja 30 '71
Limitations of language; Time essay. M. Maddocks. Time 97:36-7 Mr 8 '71
Sell-sparing usage of English; or, Why my
cat got sick in Atlanta. P. J. Reed. Engl J
60:1123-6 N '71
Word with you, Miss Thistlebottom; excerpt
from Miss Thistlebottom's hobgoblins. T.
M. Bernstein. Read Digest 98:39-40+ My
'71

ENGLISH language in Africa
New world language? a chance to mediate
the Christian message. A. Deeken. il
America 126:11-14 Ja 8 '72
ENGLISH language in Asia
New world language? a chance to mediate the
Christian message. A. Deeken. il America
126:11-14 Ja 8 '72
ENGLISH language teachers. See English
teachers
ENGLISH literature
Victorian novelists and their illustrators, by
J. R. Harvey; and The germ: a Pre-Raphae-
lite little magazine, ed. by R. S. Hosmon.
Reviews
Sat R 54:47-8 My 22 '71. R. Halsband
See also
Childrens literature—Great Britain
Publishers and publishing—Great Britain

Study and teaching
Censorship and public understanding. R. R.
Gard. bibliog Engl J 60:255-9 F '71
Dedalus speaks to Bobby Dyland; address,
November 1970. A. H. Stern. Engl J 60:610-
14 My '71
English literature for the disadvantaged;
here's how, but why? W. W. West. Engl
J 60:902-5 O '71
Performing self, by R. Poirier. Review
New Repub 164:25-6 My 1 '71. J. Seelye
Readers theatre: staging literature with mini-
mal props for maximal meaning. L. I.
Coger. il School Teach Jr/Sr High p24-5 O
'71
Theory for sequence in English. R. A. Meade.
Engl J 60:469-73 Ap '71
Three new faces of English. R. G. Lam-
bert. Engl J 60:909-12+ O '71
See also
English language—Study and teaching
ENGLISH money. See Money—Great Britain
ENGLISH opera group. See Opera—Great Brit-
ain
ENGLISH painting. See Painting, British
ENGLISH poetry
Poetry today: low profile, flatted voice. A.
T. Baker. il Time 98:61+ Jl 12 '71
ENGLISH pottery. See Pottery, English
ENGLISH silver. See Silverware
ENGLISH springer spaniel national champion
ship. See Field trials (dogs)
ENGLISH teachers
Censorship and teacher responsibility. J. F.
Symula. Engl J 60:128-31 Ja '71
English teaching: past, present, and future.
H. L. Walen. Engl J 60:1072-9 N '71

ENGLISH teachers—*Continued*
Escape from mediocrity; making English departments work. F. E. Ross. Engl J 60: 896-901 O '71
Help stamp out department chairmen. R. L. Knudson. Engl J 60:377-8 Mr '71
Scene; pressures on teachers. E. Farrell. Engl J 60:520-6 Ap '71
Sense of profession. W. A. Jenkins. Engl J 60:641-4 My '71

ENGRAVED glass. See Glass, Engraved

ENGRAVERS
  See also
Bewick, T.

ENGRAVING
  See also
Glass engraving
Wax engraving

ENGRAVING tools
Electric engravers. A. J. Hand. il Pop Sci 199:44-5 S '71

ENGRAVINGS, Rock. See Petroglyphs

ENKER, Myrna S.
Process of identity, two views. bibliog Ment Hy 55:369-74 Jl '71

ENKING, Jim
Is this the little steam engine that can? il Pop Sci 199:50+ N '71

ENLARGERS, Photographic. See Photography
—Enlargers and enlarging

ENLARGING exposure meters. See Exposure meters

ENLIGHTENMENT
Hoping against hope: the enlightened age in Hungary. G. Barany. bibliog f il Am Hist R 76:319-57 Ap '71

ENLISTMENT. See United States—Army—Recruiting and enlistment

ENNIS, John
Helicopters: unsafe at any height. il Pop Mech 136:63-7+ S '71

ENNUI. See Boredom

ENOCH Pratt free library, Baltimore
Unseen and unheard elderly; Community action program. A. S. Meyers. il Am Lib 2:793-6 S '71

ENROLLMENT, College. See Colleges and universities—Attendance

ENROLLMENT, School. See School attendance

ENSILAGE. See Silage

ENTERLINE, Joyce S.
How to live with in-laws twenty-four hours a day! il Har Yrs 11:14-15+ O '71

ENTERPRISE, Free. See Free enterprise

ENTERTAINERS
Show stoppers, 8 to 94, perform in Central park. il Aging 196:13 F '71
  See also
Actors and actresses
Beatles
Negro entertainers
  also names of entertainers, e.g. A. Cooper

ENTERTAINING
American party classics; bow to your neighbor. il Ladies Home J 88:98-107+ O '71
Bring your cookie cutter, we're having a party; with recipe. il Seventeen 30:100-1+ D '71
Coming to the aid of the party; surprise parties. House B 113:51-2 N '71
Create your own winter hospitality room. il House B 113:162-3+ O '71
Do-it-yourself parties by talented food' authorities. il House & Gard 140:50-3 Jl '71
Easy holiday hospitality; charming party givers. il Am Home 74:95-102 N '71
Entertaining; the second thirty years it gets easier; with recipes. M. Eckley and G. Plant. il McCalls 99:104-9, 114+ O '71
Festive feasting for the holidays. L. Driggs. il Har Yrs 11:36-9+ N '71
Finger food. E. Marlowe. il Am Home 74:72 N '71
Food to fit the occasion; holiday party ideas. D. Eby. il Bet Hom & Gard 49:60-70+ Ja '71
Gathering: venture. New Yorker 47:31-4 Je 26 '71
Great party giver speaks her mind. M. Evins. il por House & Gard 140:43+ N '71
How the most entertaining people entertain, and how they get away with it. il Vogue 158:78-83 N 15 '71
How to entertain when it's too hot to bother; summer parties. E. D. Craster. il Bet Hom & Gard 49:44-7+ Je '71
How to have a party in spite of everything. E. D. Craster. il Bet Hom & Gard 49:64-9 N '71

Mind-changer parties; with menus and recipes. il Seventeen 29:148-51+ O '70
Night at the movies. C. B. Roth. il Am Home 74:74+ N '71
Numbers game; how can you juggle eight plates and 16 guests? M. Wallace. il Am Home 74:56+ N '71
Party maximus. A. Penney. House & Gard 140:32+ N '71
Reel winner; making party tapes. S. Reice. il Am Home 74:58+ N '71
Secrets of a great party. il House & Gard 140:74-81 N '71
Secrets of a great party giver; with recipes. il por House & Gard 140:82-9+ N '71
Soup and bread party right in the kitchen; with recipes. il Sunset 147:82-3+ N '71
Thoughts for the hostess (cont of) Notes for the hostess. M. M. Hemingway. House & Gard 139:46 Mr '71
Today parties; just for fun. M. Wallace. il Am Home 74:48+ N '71
Unruffled hostess. N. C. Gray. Am Home 74:64-5 N '71
Your liquid assets; drinks for parties; excerpt from Complete guide to creative entertaining. House & Gard 140:130+ O '71
  See also
Balls (parties)
Caterers and catering
Christmas meals
Dinners and dining
Games
Government entertaining
Hospitality
Suppers
Table decoration
Table setting

ENTERTAINING in sales promotion
Biz Broadway $2 billion boffo. S. Blickstein. il Duns 93:46-51 Je '69

ENTOMOLOGICAL research
Know your enemy. J. McCaull. bibliog il pors Environ 13:30-9 Je '71

ENTRANCE drives. See Driveways

ENTRANCE halls. See Halls

ENTRANCE requirements, College. See Colleges and universities—Entrance requirements

ENTREMONT, Philippe
French sampler. il Hi Fi 21:32+ N '71

ENTREPRENEURS
Entrepreneurs teach others how to do it; Project Enterprise course at UCLA. il Bsns W p 124+ N 13 '71
Grass and hash business at Syracuse university. L. Kramer. il Fortune 84:102-3 S '71
Weep not for Horatio. Forbes 107:7 F 1 '71
  See also
Business enterprises
  also names of entrepreneurs, e.g. G. W. Turner

ENTROPY
Haste makes waste: pollution and entropy. H. A. Bent. bibliog il por Chem 44:6-15 O '71

ENTRY dividers. See Partitions

ENTWISTLE, O. H. Jr
What is a PTA member? por PTA Mag 66: 24-5 O '71 *

ENVIRONMENT
Defending the environment, by J. L. Sax. Review
  Natur Hist 80:103-5 F '71. G. M. Woodwell
Don't say I'll bite your ear off because some day you might mean it. R. Rodale. il Org Gard & Farm 18:34-8 F '71
Earth watch; comp. by S. Lindsay (cont) il Sat R 54:48-9 F 6 '71
Environment. See issues of Time
Environment (cont of) Environmental sciences. See issues of Science news
Environment and the quality of life. J. Lear. See issues of Saturday review
Environment yes: hysteria no. il Bet Hom & Gard 49:30 Ap; 20+ My; 28+ Je; 4+ Jl; 12+ Ag; 34+ S; 14+ O; 18+ N '71
Is man over adapting to his environment? R. Dubos. Cur 128:34-9 Ap '71
Needed, world-wide environment solutions; United auto workers and the United Nations explore pollution problems. S. Margold. il Am City 86:74+ Mr '71
Prophet of optimism; summary of statements, ed. by A. Anderson. R. Dubos. por Time 97:51 My 31 '71
S.O.S. environment; symposium. il UNESCO Courier 24:4-32 Jl '71
Time for every purpose. R. Sommer. il Natur Hist 80:24-5+ bibliog(p96) Ag '71
Vision of environment. P. L. Marks. Am Scholar 40:421-3 Sum '71

ENVIRONMENT—*Continued*
Week's watch. See occasional issues of Time
See *also*
Adaptation (biology)
Airplanes, Supersonic—Environmental effects
Ecology
Environmental movement
Man—Influence on nature
United Nations conference on the human environment

Bibliography

Literature subsequent to the environmental nova. G. Siehl. il por Library J 96:2266-70 Jl '71

Conferences

Meeting in Prague; symposium on the problems of the environment. D. N. Leff. il Environ 13:29-33 N '71
Message to our 3.5 billion neighbours on planet earth from 2,200 environmental scientists. UNESCO Courier 24:4-5 Jl '71
Pollution of Asia; report of the Conference on Asian environments. M. T. Farvar and others. bibliog il por Environ 13:10-17 O '71
See *also*
International conference on the environmental future
International youth conference on problems of the human environment

Drama

Treasure. G. F. Shea. Plays 30:76-8 Mr '71

Economic aspects

Mike Frome. M. Frome. por Am For 77:3+ Jl '71
See *also*
Pollution—Control—Economic aspects

Laws and legislation

Congressional flight on a fragile spacecraft. L. K. Lee. il Parks & Rec 6:22-4+ Mr '71
Conservationists go to court. R. D. Butcher. il Am For 77:32-5+ Je; 32-5 Jl '71 (to be cont)
Court decision jolts AEC; dawdling in implementation of the National environmental policy act. C. Holden. Science 173:799 Ag 27 '71
Courtroom shootouts; emergence of the environmental trial lawyers. J. B. Craig. Am For 77:11 Jl '71
Defending the environment, by J. L. Sax. Review
  Science 172:47-8 Ap 2 '71. H. P. Green
Environment and the bureaucracy; Hart-McGovern bill. J. L. Sax. New Repub 164:9-10 Je 19 '71
Environmental legislation: 1971 not a year for conclusive action. G. Holden. Science 174:10007-10 D 3 '71
Federal legislation in the 1960s; progress or promises? L. K. Lee. il Parks & Rec 6:10-14+ Ag '71
Hardhats, hyacinths and returnable bottles. R. W. Gibbons. Commonweal 94:324-5 Je 25 '71
Law and organic living. M. C. Goldman. Org Gard & Farm 18:104-10 D '71
Law and the environment, ed. by M. Baldwin and J. K. Page, jr. Review
  Liv Wildn 35:37-8 Spr '71. W. A. Butler
Legal strategies for environmental control. S Lawrence. Field & S 75:12+ F '71
New assertion of rights. R. Pardo. il por Am For 77:16-19+ My '71
1971 legislative session and the environment. A. Woldt. Cons 26:17+ Ag '71
Pollution and industry: pros, cons of growing fight. il U S News 71:60-2 N 22 '71
Pollution fight before the U.S. courts. J. L. Sax. il UNESCO Courier 24:20-3 Jl '71

Periodicals

Ecology, conservation, etc; ed. by B. Katz. E. Schwartz. Library J 96:3304-6 O 15 '71

Psychological aspects

Carpeting the ward: an exploratory study in environmental psychiatry. F. E. Cheek and others. bibliog Ment Hy 55:109-18 Ja '71

Study and teaching

Action program for environmental education. E. Hirst and L. Schuck. bibliog Clear House 46:203-6 D '71
Hello Ents, good-bye Aristotle; excerpts from Teaching for survival. M. Terry. Natur Hist 80:6-8+ bibliog(p84) Ja '71

Teaching and the environmental challenge; excerpts from address, June 1971. R. H. Socolow. bibliog il Phys Today 24:32-4+ D '71
See *also*
Environmental education
Nature study

ENVIRONMENT (art)

Breaking through the sound barrier; H. Jones' timesthetic projects. R. T. Coe. il Art N 70:44-5+ Sum '71
Dirty pictures. B. J. Friedman. il Esquire 75:112-17+ My '71
Earth, air, fire, and water: elements of art; Boston museum of fine arts centennial exhibition. il Design 72:37-9 Spr '71
Earthscapes, landworks and Oz. D. Hickey. il Art in Am 59:40-9 S '71
Education of the un-artist. A. Kaprow. il Art N 69:28-31+ F '71 (to be cont)
Holes without history; Earthworks and Heizer's Double negative. D. Waldman. bibliog f il Art N 70:44-8+ My '71

ENVIRONMENT (periodical)

Closing the circle; use of totally recycled paper in Environment. il Environ 13:34-7 S '71
Jaundiced eye; refusal of grant by NSF. Environ 13:53 O '71

ENVIRONMENT and pesticides. See Pesticides and the environment

ENVIRONMENT and state. See Environmental policy

ENVIRONMENT in music. See Music—Themes, Motives, etc.

ENVIRONMENTAL action groups. See Environmental associations, committees, etc.

ENVIRONMENTAL associations, committees, etc.

Back in circulation; trash-collection project of Ecology action of Florida, inc. J. G. Meyer. il Environ 13:30-3 S '71
Environmental action group. Field & S 75:24 Ja '71
Farm bureau steps up environmental crusade. D. Seim. Farm J 95:37 My '71
Garbage power! Ecology action group. M. M. McGlynn. il pors Look 35:26-30 My 4 '71
Getting started: environmental action in the community. C. C. Morrison, jr. il Cons 25:4-5 F '71
If it stinks, stop it; Long Island environmental council. J. Egan. McCalls 98:42 Mr '71
Putting PEP into fighting pollution; Pollution and environmental problems. A. Ferrara. il Org Gard & Farm 18:114-18 Mr '71
Saving Broome County's environment; groups to promote environmental quality. D. F. Newton. Cons 25:20-1 Ap '71
Where the action is: what young people have done; with discussion. il Sr Schol 98:3-5 Ap 26 '71
See *also*
Committee for environmental information
Environmental defense fund, inc.

ENVIRONMENTAL conservation, Department of. See New York (state)—Environmental conservation, Department of

ENVIRONMENTAL defense fund, inc.

DDT stopped, suit dropped; discharge of DDT from Montrose. E. P. Jones. Science 173:38 Jl 2 '71
Sue the bastards. Time 98:54+ O 18 '71

ENVIRONMENTAL education

Challenge of environmental education. J. A. Wagar. Ed Digest 36:9-12 F '71
Dow spurs a factual approach to pollution. V. Louviere. il Nations Bsns 59:16 Ag '71
E.E. needs you! C. H. Harrison. il Schol Teach Jr/Sr High p 13-17 O '71
Ecologic of nursery rhymes. J. Lear. il Sat R 54:73-6 N 6 '71
Environmental education. A. D. Roberts and O. E. Dyrli. Clear House 45:451-5 Ap '71
Environmental education as liberation. D. Stotler. Ed Digest 36:38-41 My '71
Environmental education cannot wait; with editorial comment. S. P. Marland, jr. il Am Ed 7:inside cover. 6-10 My '71
Environmental encounters; Yarmouth, Me. V. A. Schlich. il Am Ed 7:23-6 Ag '71
Feeling our way to a good environment. J. H. Cravens. il Am Ed 7:25-8 O '71
Forest rangers can spark ecology programs. Camp Mag 43:15 S '71
Making tomorrow now. M. J. Brennan. Ed Digest 36:13-15 F '71
Teacher's survival guide to environmental education resources. Schol Teach Jr/Sr High p32-4+ O '71
Update; report of the NEA Task force on environmental education. Todays Ed 60:33-48 S '71

ENVIRONMENTAL education—*Continued*
We have a long way to go; and time is running out; address, July 13, 1971. A. Godfrey. il pors Cons 26:8-14 O '71
Where do we begin? R. L. Silber. Chem 44:2 D '71
Where the action is: what young people have done; with discussion. il Sr Schol 98:3-5 Ap 26 '71
　See also
Forestry schools and education
Moving pictures in environmental education

Aids and devices
Teacher's survival guide to environmental education resources; multimedia. Schol Teach Jr/Sr High p32-3+ O '71

Bibliography
Teacher's survival guide to environmental education resources; booklets, etc. Schol Teach Jr/Sr High p40+ O '71
Teacher's survival guide to environmental education resources; paperbacks. Schol Teach Jr/Sr High p34+ O '71

ENVIRONMENTAL engineering
　See also
Life support systems (space environment)

ENVIRONMENTAL health
Case against the disaster lobby; address, January 28, 1971. T. R. Shepard, jr. il Liv Wildn 35:25-30 Sum '71
Climate and environment, what they mean to you. B. Howorth. il Consumer Bul 54:14-17 N '71
How dangerous are metals in our food and environment? Current status of metals in the environment. Good H 173:215-17 N '71
Kogai: environmental disruption in Japan. S. Tsuru. il UNESCO Courier 24:6-13 Jl '71
Mike Frome. M. Frome. Am For 77:7+ Ap '71
Sanity in research and evaluation of environmental health. H. E. Stokinger. bibliog Science 174:662-5 N 12 '71

ENVIRONMENTAL law. See Environment—Laws and legislation

ENVIRONMENTAL movement
Adversary scientists & agricultural renegades. J. Goldstein. Org Gard & Farm 18:77-80 Ap '71
After Earth week. America 124:478 My 8 '71
America you're beautiful. J. Shepherd. Look 35:33 Ja 12 '71
American institutions and ecological ideals; adaptation of address, December 29, 1969. L. Marx; discussion. Science 171:1095-6 Mr 19 '71
Back-to-nature movement a threat? letter. J. Boardman. il Phys Today 24:9 F '71; Discussion. 24:80 F; 66-8 My '71
Battle tactics for conservationists. J. N. Miller. Read Digest 98:175-80 Ja '71
Changing attitudes toward environmental problems. P. H. Abelson. Science 172:517 My 7 '71
Clean, clear summer. il Seventeen 29:98-9+ Jl '70
Clean-up mood sweeps the nation. il Life 70:30-5 Mr 5 '71
EQ action guide. il Nat Wildlife 9:32A-32D O '71
EQ and you. See occasional issues of Senior scholastic to May 10, 1971
Ecology at the supermarket; measures taken at Alexanders stores in Los Angeles. il Time 97:84 Ap 5 '71
Ecology crisis, what you can do; with editorial comment. B. Emory. il Yachting 130:33, 56-7+ Jl '71
Ecology: is it a fad? J. J. Kirk. por Camp Mag 43:5 Je '71
Ecology: what we must do now; with readers' contributions. C. Coiro. il Har Yrs 11:6-12+ Je '71
Economy & environment; the need for integrity; address, April 28, 1971. L. Wyatt. Vital Speeches 37:509-12 Je 1 '71
Ecotage. Newsweek 78:50 Ag 23 '71
Environment issues stunt airport growth. J. P. Woolsey. il Aviation W 95:46-8+ N 15 '71
Environmental action line. M. Frome. Field & S 76:34 Jl '71
Erasing grown-up vandalism. il Life 70:34 Ap 9 '71
Fellow Americans, keep out! regional isolationism. il Forbes 107:22-4+ Je 15 '71; Same abr. Read Digest 99:129-32 S '71
5 who fight pollution. C. Remsberg and B. Remsberg. pors Seventeen 30:128-9+ Ap '71
Here's how eight individuals are helping to improve our environment. B. Russell. il House & Gard 139:49+ Je '71

I would like to help; letter, with reply by P. M. Kelsey. L. Clifford. Cons 25:32-3 Je '71
Is the national parks movement anti-urban? P. Marcuse. il Parks & Rec 6:16-21+ Jl '71
Jobs that can change your world. N. A. Comer. il Mlle 73:132-4+ S '71
Junior high school people launch an unusual attack on pests and weeds. il Sunset 147:230-1 N '71
Junior vigilantes; youthful environmentalists to conduct real tests for air and water pollution. il Time 98:30 Ag 23 '71
Lesson in government. P. M. Kelsey. Cons 26:32 Ag '71
Man and environment; fighting the backlash. R. H. Gilluly. il Sci N 100:410-11 D 18 '71
New environment of the South. G. Clay. Arch Forum 133:42-5 D '70
Not nature alone. R. Neuhaus. il Harper 243:100-5 O '71; Discussion 243:6+ D '71
Our family fights pollution. J. Coggins and D.-E. Coggins il Parents Mag 46:54-5+ Mr '71
Politics of ecology, by J. Ridgeway. Review Environ 13:48-9 N '71. K. Montague and P. Montague
Renaissance; interview, ed. by H. Brandon. M. Nicholson. Sat R 54:53-4+ My 1 '71
Rescue of Elkhorn Creek. R. Herron. il Good H 172:80-1+ Mr '71
Return of Charles Lindbergh. A. Whitman. il pors N Y Times Mag p28-9+ My 23 '71; Same abr. Read Digest 99:190-2+ S '71
Santa Barbara plan; organic community garden. F. Allen. il Org Gard & Farm 18.68-71 Ja '71
Saving the crusade. P. F. Drucker. il Harper 244:66-71 Ja '72
Science and technology; an age of anxiety; address, April 30, 1971. A. H. Aymond. Vital Speeches 37:492-4 Je '71
Scouts soar with anti-litter project. Sr Schol 99:14 N 8 '71
75 ways you can help clean up the environment now. il Good H 173:199-201 S '71
Spaceship earth revisited. il Sr Schol 98:9-10 My 10 '71
Step closer to adversary centers. J. Goldstein. Org Gard & Farm 18:80-3 Jl '71
This country is on fire; interview, ed. by L. Langway. R. Nader. il por Nat Wildlife 9:17-20 Je '71
To the boondocks; litigation to federal district courts. S. J. Ungar. New Repub 165:11-12 O 2 '71
Visit with Pearl Buck; interview, ed. by C. Renshaw, jr. P. Buck. il pors Nat Wildlife 10:28-32 D '71
We blew our cool but saved a woods. il Nat Wildlife 9:32-5 Ap '71
We tried to live the EQ way. P. Feldkamp; R. Rosen. il pors Nat Wildlife 9:5-9 Ap '71
What one man can do. il Outdoor Life 147:46-7+ Je '71
Where the action is: what young people have done; with discussion. il Sr Schol 98:3-5 Ap 26 '71
Working to change the system; Public interest research groups. Mlle 73:52 S '71
Youth and the environment. See issues of Conservationist
Youth, rebellion & the environment. G. Stucker. il Nat Parks & Con Mag 45:6-9 Ap '71
　See also
Industry and the environmental movement

Anecdotes, facetiae, satire, etc.
Mad diary of a Manhattan ecologist. A. R. Roiphe. il N Y Times Mag p6+ O 17 '71; Reply with rejoinder. N. Barnes. p98 N 7 '71

Conferences
　See also
United Nations conference on the human environment

Earth week
Bench: set up during Earth week in middle of Madison avenue for two hours each day at lunchtime. New Yorker 47:29-30 My 1 '71
Earth week and beyond. il Time 97:57 My 3 '71
Earth week 1971. J. Schaeffer. il Nat Parks & Con Mag 45:17-19 Ap '71
For earth: seven days in April. Sr Schol 98:9 Mr 29 '71

Exhibitions
Ecology fair tries and misses. il Bsns W p73 N 20 '71

ENVIRONMENTAL movement—*Continued*

International aspects

International environmental problems: a taxonomy. C. S. Russell and H. H. Landsberg. bibliog Science 172:1307-14 Je 25 '71

Message to our 3.5 billion neighbours on planet earth from 2,200 environmental scientists. UNESCO Courier 24:4-5 Jl '71

Mind extinct? Unesco's work. W. McEwing. il UNESCO Courier 24:38-43 Ag '71

Pollution doesn't stop at the border. il Sr Schol 98:17-18 Mr 29 '71

Marches, rallies, etc.

Brothers run cross-country in a dash for ecology; Joel and Tony Ahstrom. il Sr Schol 99:15 O 11 '71

Alaska

Why Alaskans are upset about conservation. il U S News 71:43-5 O 4 '71

Italy

Happy mayor; ecological measures in Florence. L. Bausi. New Yorker 47:33-4 My 8 '71

Sweden

Saving Stockholm's trees. il Am For 77:8-9 Ag '71

ENVIRONMENTAL news

Eco-journalism. il Newsweek 77:43-4 F 1 '71

ENVIRONMENTAL policy

Billions to fight pollution: the President's program; excerpts from message to Congress, February 8, 1971. U S News 70:72-7 F 22 '71

Canary has fallen silent; reprint. H. E. Daly. Nat Parks & Con Mag 45:27 Je '71

Cleaner America: the war on pollution; interview. R. C. B. Morton. il por U S News 71:46-50+ O 4 '71

Cleaning of America (don't hold your breath) J. Ridgeway. Ramp Mag 9:17-18 Mr '71

Coming government moves in war against pollution; interview. W. D. Ruckelshaus. il por U S News 70:70-5 Mr 29 '71

Earth watch. S. Lindsay. See issues of Saturday review

Engineering education; ecological issues; address, February 2, 1971. M. Tribus. Vital Speeches 37:410-13 Ap 15 '71

Games with Muskie. J. Osborne. New Repub 164:15-16 F 20 '71

Getting it together. M. Frome. Field & S 76:28+ S '71

Having it both ways. Commonweal 94:27-8 Mr 19 '71

House at the crossroads. M. Frome. Field & S 76:46+ My '71

Is anybody in Washingon really listening? M. Frome. Field & S 76:38+ Ag '71

Making of a conservationist; excerpt from Who owns America? W. J. Hickel. il Sat R 54:65-7 O 2 '71

National outlook. C. H. Callison. See issues of Audubon

Needed: an about-face for the Corps of engineers. H. S. Reuss. Read Digest 99:129-32 N '71

Nixon offers large, mixed bag on environment. C. Holden. Science 171:659 F 19 '71

No more golden eggs? il Nations Bsns 59:72-6 O '71

Peace and pollution. J. B. Craig. Am For 77:12 Ag '71

Politics and pollution. Commonweal 95:195 N 26 '71

Presidential zag. M. Frome. Field & S 76:28+ N '71

President's message, February 8, 1971; excerpt. R. M. Nixon. Redbook 137:57 Jl '71

Right on, Establishment; address, October 11, 1971. M. J. Caserio. Vital Speeches 38:86-90 N 15 '71

Secrecy and elitism in science and government. R. H. Gilluly. Sci N 100:82-3 Jl 31 '71

Secrecy in pollution policy. Sci N 99:434 Je 26 '71

When a law fights a law; Mining law of 1872 vs Environmental act. B. Gilbert. il Sports Illus 34:30-2+ Ap 26 '71

When it starts to hurt; Nixon's new environmental message. Life 70:32 F 26 '71

Where are we at now? V. Cohn. Cur 125:15-19 Ja '71

See also
Conservation of resources
Environment—Laws and legislation
Man—Influence on nature
Pollution—Control
Pollution—Laws and legislation
United States—Congress—Joint committee on the environment (proposed)
United States—Council on environmental quality
United States—Environmental protection agency
United States—National industrial pollution control council

Water pollution—Control

International aspects

Environment and development: the interlocking problems; remarks, May 24, 1971. G. Bush. Dept State Bul 65:21-2 Jl 5 '71

Global pollution. J. Lear; S. Lindsay; R. N. Gardner. il Sat R 54:41-50 Ag 7 '71

International aspects of the 1971 environmental program; excerpt from message, February 8, 1971. R. M. Nixon. Dept State Bul 64:253-6 Mr 1 '71

Politics of environmental disruption. Fortune 83:69-70 Ja '71

Senator Muskie's foreign pollution policy; address to UN symposium, May 21, 1971. J. Lear. Sat R 54:20+ Je 12 '71

Trade collides with ecology. il Bsns W p72-3+ Ja 23 '71

U.N. as policeman. R. N. Gardner. Sat R 54:47-50 Ag 7 '71; Same with title Can the UN be a policeman? Cur 133:34-40 O '71

World heritage. A. W. Smith. Nat Parks & Con Mag 45:2 Ja '71

California

California's coast: the developers win. il Bsns W p21-2 N 27 '71

Cleanup battle jolts California. Bsns W p35 D 25 '71

Delaware

Coastline preserved. S. Lindsay. Sat R 54:52 Ag 7 '71

Delaware: nature over industry. il Newsweek 78:55 Jl 5 '71

Delaware's new keep out sign; law banning heavy industrial facilities from the Delaware coast. Bsns W p20-1 Jl 3 '71

Great Britain

Air power and the environmentalists. Chr Cent 88:613 My 19 '71

See also
Great Britain—Environment, Department of the

Maine

Hard test for Maine; building of oil-desulfurization plant at Penobscot Bay. Time 97:45-6 Ap 12 '71

Letter from Maine; oil and water. J. N. Cole. il Harper 243:42+ N '71

Netherlands

Cleanup collides with the GNP. il Bsns W p35 Jl 10 '71

New York (state)

Getting started: environmental action in the community. C. C. Morrison, jr. il Cons 25:4-5 F '71

Sweden

Environment in Sweden. I. Ekholm. il por Am For 77:8-9+ Ja '71

Vermont

Vermont: a small state faces up to a dilemma over development. J. Walsh. Science 173:895-7 S 3 '71

ENVIRONMENTAL policy as a campaign issue. See Campaign issues

ENVIRONMENTAL pollution. See Pollution

ENVIRONMENTAL protection act. See Environment—Laws and legislation

ENVIRONMENTAL protection administration. See United States—Environmental protection agency

ENVIRONMENTAL protection administration, New York. See New York (city)—Environmental protection administration

ENVIRONMENTAL protection agency. See United States—Environmental protection agency

ENVIRONMENTAL psychology
Find elbowroom in a crowded world. il por Bsns W p60 N 27 '71

ENVIRONMENTAL quality control. See Pollution—Control

ENVIRONMENTAL quality council. See United States—Council on environmental quality

ENVIRONMENTAL research laboratory. See Arizona. University, Tucson—Environmental research laboratory

ENVIRONMENTAL satellites. See Artificial satellites—Use in research

ENVIRONMENTAL science services administration. See United States—National oceanic and atmospheric administration

ENVIRONMENTAL sciences
Breaking down the boundaries. Sci N 100:40 Jl 17 '71

ENVY
See also
Jealousy

ENZYME allergy. See Allergy

ENZYME inhibitors. See Enzymes—Inactivation

ENZYME laundry products
Toxic factors in enzymes used in laundry products. R. Dubos. il Science 173:259-60 Jl 16 '71

ENZYMES
Acetoacetyl-coenzyme A thiolase in brain, liver, and kidney during maturation of the rat. C. Dierks-Ventling and A. L. Cone. bibliog il Science 172:380-2 Ap 23 '71
Covalent enzyme-substrate intermediates. R. M. Bell and D. E. Koshland, jr. bibliog il Science 172:1253-6 Je 18 '71
Dopamine-sensitive adenyl cyclase: possible role in synaptic transmission. J. W. Kebabian and P Greengard. bibliog il Science 174:1346-9 D 24 '71
Enzymes bound to artificial matrixes. K. Mosbach. il Sci Am 224:26-33 bibliog(p 124) Mr '71
Isolation of liver enzyme; Cytochrome P-450. Sci N 100:55 Jl 24 '71
Leucylglycinamide released from oxytocin by human uterine enzyme. R. Walter and others. bibliog il Science 173:827-9 Ag 27 '71
Linkage of genes controlling the rate of synthesis and structure of aminolevulinate dehydratase. D. L. Coleman. bibliog il Science 173:1245-6 S 24 '71
Mystery of enzymes. C. D. Hellyer. il Sci Digest 70:70-4 N '71
Regulation of enzyme activity. G. G. Hammes and C. W. Wu. bibliog il Science 172:1205-11 Je 18 '71
Reporter at large; enzymes since prehistoric times. P. Brodeur. New Yorker 46:42-8+ Ja 16 '71
Two genes, one enzyme. Sci Am 224:46 Ja '71
Urea cycle enzyme adaptation to dietary protein in primates. C. T. Nuzum and P. J. Snodgrass. bibliog il Science 172:1042-3 Je 4 '71
See also
Acetylcholinesterase
Aldolase
Asparaginase
Carbonic anhydrase
Carboxypeptidases
Cholinesterase
Coenzymes
Decarboxylase
Dehydrogenases
Esterases
Glutaminase
Histidase
Hydroxylases
Kinases
Melatonin
Neuraminidase
Oxidases
Peroxidases
Plasminogen
Polymerase
Proteinases
Synthetases
Transferases

Inactivation
Alkyl isocyanates as active site-specific inhibitors of chymotrypsin and elastase. W. E. Brown and F. Wold. bibliog il Science 174:608-10 N 5 '71

ENZYMES in detergents. See Detergents

EOCENE period. See Geology, Stratigraphic—Eocene

EOLE (satellite) See Artificial satellites, French

EPHRON, Nora
Bonnie; story. McCalls 98:74-5 Jl '71
Mush. il pors Esquire 75:89-92+ Je '71

EPIC poetry, Persian. See Persian poetry

EPICONDYLITIS
Joys of tennis elbow. il Newsweek 77:59 Je 28 '71

EPIDEMICS
New plagues of summer. il Time 98:16 Ag 2 '71
See also
Cholera
Influenza
Measles

EPILEPSY
Acetoxycycloheximide enhances audiogenic seizures in DBA/2J mice. H. D. Jameson and others. bibliog il Science 173:249-51 Jl 16 '71
Penicillin as an epileptogenic agent: effect on an isolated synapse. G. F. Ayala and others. bibliog il Science 171:915-17 Mr 5 '71
What doctors can do for epilepsy now. B. Ford. il Sci Digest 70:32-6 D '71

EPILEPTICS
Mary Litty's 25-year struggle to help epileptics. W. Cole. il pors Good H 173:48+ Jl '71
New understanding, new hope, for children with epilepsy. W. Cole. Parents Mag 46:52-3+ My '71

EPILOBIUM angustifolium. See Fireweed

EPINEPHRINE. See Adrenalin

EPIPHANY
Poets at Bethlehem. N. Braybrooke. Chr Cent 88:1497-8 D 22 '71

EPIPHYLLUMS
Epiphyllums from seed. R. James. il Horticulture 49:18-19+ Je '71

EPIPHYTES. See Air plants

EPISCOPAL church. See Protestant Episcopal church

EPISODE on a July morning; story. See Cain, E.

EPISTEMOLOGY. See Knowledge, Theory of

EPITHELIUM
Endothelial projections as revealed by scanning electron microscopy. U. Smith and others. bibliog il Science 173:925-7 S 3 '71
See also
Mucous membranes

EPOXY resins
New epoxy sealer-patcher with water washup. G. Daniels. il Pop Sci 198:100 Ja '71

EPOXY sculpture. See Plastic sculpture

EPPERSON, Aloise B.
Negro in a dime store; poem. Negro Hist Bul 34:37 F '71

EPSTEIN, Edward Jay
Reporter at large. New Yorker 46:45-6+ F 13; 125 My 8 '71
about
Mea culpa. il pors Time 97:45 Mr 8 '71

EPSTEIN, Joseph
Browsing in gangland. Commentary 53:46-55 Ja '72
Memoirs of a fraternity man. Commentary 52:59-64 Jl '71

EPSTEIN, Samuel S. and others
Eye on our defenses. bibliog il Environ 13:43-7 Ap '71

EPSTEIN-Barr virus. See Herpesvirus

EQUAL employment opportunity commission. See United States—Equal employment opportunity commission

EQUAL pay for equal work
Closing the sex gap; gains from the amendment to the Fair labor standards act of 1938. Newsweek 77:82+ Je 7 '71
Congress considers equal pay rights for academic women. D. Shapley. Science 173:215 Jl 16 '71
Dimensions of the oppression of women; address, December 5, 1970. P. J. Springen. Vital Speeches 37:265-7 F 15 '71
Sex discrimination on campus: Michigan wrestles with equal pay. D. Shapley. Science 173:214-16 Jl 16 '71

EQUAL rights amendment (proposed) See United States—Constitution—Amendments

EQUAL rights for women. See Woman—Equal rights

EQUALITY
Are the rules changing? R. Barta. America 125:341-5 O 30 '71
See also
Democracy
Race relations

EQUALITY in education. See Equalization, Educational

EQUALIZATION, Educational
For liberty and equality. N. Hill. Cur Hist 129:32-5 My '71

EQUILIBRIUM, Chemical. See Chemical equilibrium

EQUINE encephalitis. See Encephalitis

EQUINE encephalomyelitis. See Encephalomyelitis

EQUIPMENT, Municipal. See Municipal equipment
EQUIPMENT industries
See also
  Machine tool industry
EQUIPMENT leasing. See Lease and rental services
EQUITABLE life assurance society of the United States
  Artful way to win popularity on campus. il Nations Bsns 59:20 My '71
ERASMUS, Desiderius
  Erasmus, by G. Faludy. Review
    Commonweal 94:192-4 Ap 30 '71 J. Ratte •
    Sat R 54:31 Mr 13 '71. J. Pelikan •
ERDAHL, Beriyn J.
  Paint a what? Paint a bus! il Sch Arts 71:12-13 N '71
ERDMANN, Martin
  I have nothing to do with justice; with editorial comment. J. Mills. il pors Life 70:2A, 56-8+ Mr 12 '71 •
  Sanctity of robes. il por Time 98:69-70 N 22 '71 •
ERHARD, Ludwig
  Where are they now? il pors Newsweek 77:10 My 24 '71 •
ERHART, Stephen
  As the hippiest doctor almost grooved; story. Harper 242:82-4 My '71
ERIC
  Eric and the multitude. D. Dickinson. Am Lib 2:120 Ja '71
ERICAS. See Heaths (plants)
ERICKSON, Donald A.
  Devil and Catholic education. America 124: 367-71 Ap 10 '71
ERICKSON, Ellwood
  Association and the school board. pors Todays Ed 60:48-50 My '71
ERICKSON, John
  Strategic transition. il Newsweek 78:36 S 13 '71
ERICKSON, Lyle
  Sell land at auction? interview. por Suc Farm 69:10 Ag '71
ERICKSON, Ralph
  New world of the adolescent. Clear House 46:227-30 D '71
ERICSON, Edward E. jr
  Holy Mr Herbert. Chr Today 15:7-8+ S 10 '71
ERICSON, James C.
  But big for its size. il Outdoor Life 148:78-9+ Ag '71
ERICSSON, R. J. and others
  Fertilization of rabbit ova in vitro by sperm with adsorbed sendai virus. bibliog il Science 173:54-5 Jl 2 '71
ERIE, LAKE
  Lake Erie: pollution abatement, then what? J. H. Hubschman. bibliog il Science 171: 536-40 F 12 '71; Reply. S. M. Rosenblum and T. C. Hollocher. 172:1294-5 Je 25 '71
  Legend of a lake. F. Russell. il Am Heritage 22:14-23+ Ap '71
  You don't necessarily need aerobes; Rocky River, Ohio. il Am City 86:61-2 Ap '71
ERIE CANAL
  Erie Canal state park. C. Reed. il Parks & Rec 6:24-6+ S '71
ERIE CANAL state park. See New York (state)—Parks and reserves
ERIKSON, Erik
  (ed) See Lax, M. Collaboration in glass
ERIKSON, Erik Homburger
  Erik H. Erikson, by R. Coles. Review
    Sat R 54:51+ Ja 16 '71. D. Elkind •
  Process of identity, two views. M. S. Enker. bibliog Ment Hy 55:369-74 Jl '71 •
ERIKSON, Joan Mowat
  Uses of beads; excerpt from The universal bead. il Craft Horiz 31:18-21+ O '71
ERKKILA, Barbara G.
  Experiment in building a hillside kiln. il Ceram Mo 19:22-4 Ja '71
ERLANDSON, David A. and House, E. R.
  Theory and practice: why nothing seems to work. Ed Digest 37:34-7 S '71
ERLENBORN, John Neal
  Excerpt from debate, September 15, 1971. Cong Digest 50:272+ N '71
ERNANI; opera. See Verdi, G.
ERNST, Max
  Ernst at 80. D. Davis. il por Newsweek 77:92 My 10 '71 •
ERNST, Paul
  Blackout! story. Good H 173:68-9 Jl '71
  Our little girl is lost; story. Good H 172:70-1 Mr '71
ERNST, Robert C. See Rodgers, R. B. jt. auth.

EROSION
  Submarine canyon erosion: contribution of marine rock burrowers. J. E. Warme and others. bibliog il Science 173:1127-9 S 17 '71
  Why the sands aren't red; canyonlands of Utah. H. Lansford. il Sci Digest 69:61-5 My '71
  See also
  Beach erosion
  Coast changes
  Dust storms
  Solifluction
  Weathering
EROSION prevention and control
  Plants to hold soil on a slope. il Home Gard 58:46-7+ Ag '71
  See also
  Soil conservation
  Terraces (agriculture)
EROTIC literature
  See also
  Immoral literature and pictures
  Publishers and publishing—Erotic literature
EROTICA
  No recession in the skin trade. G. Astor. il Look 35:27-36 Je 29 '71
ERRINGTON, Paul Lester
  Of wilderness. Liv Wildn 34:49-51 Wint '70
ERTL, John Paul
  New test for the brain. Newsweek 78:67-8 D 13 '71 •
ERTRESVAAG, Prue
  Ivy for everyone. Good H 173:163 Jl '71
ERVIN, Samuel James, 1896-
  Excerpt from address, August 21, 1970. Cong Digest 50:11+ Ja '71
  Excerpt from newspaper column, April 1, 1971. Cong Digest 50:145 My '71
  Excerpt from remarks before the Subcommittee on constitutional rights, September 8, 1970. Cong Digest 50:233+ O '71
  Secrecy in a free society. il Nation 213:454-7 N 8 '71
  about
  Conservative libertarian. por Time 97:38-9 Mr 8 '71 •
  Drifting toward 1984. Time 97:16 Mr 29 '71 •
  Project MUM. New Repub 165:9 N 13 '71 •
  Sam Ervin and the privacy invaders. J. K. Batten. il New Repub 164:19-23 My 8 '71 •
ERVING, Julius Winfield, jr
  Back door into the big time. P. Carry. il por Sports Illus 35:26-7 N 1 '71 •
ERWIN, Frank Craig, 1920-
  Hooking horns at UT. il por Newsweek 77: 46 F 1 '71 •
  LBJification of U.T. F. Lang. Ramp Mag 10:8+ D '71 •
ERYTHROCYTES
  Erythrocyte metabolism: interaction with oxygen transport. G. J. Brewer and J. W. Eaton. bibliog il Science 171:1205-11 Mr 26 '71
  Erythrocytes: pits and vacuoles as seen with transmission and scanning electron microscopy. B. Schnitzer and others. bibliog il Science 173:251-2 Jl 16 '71
  Human red blood cells: prostaglandin E_1, epinephrine, and isoproterenol alter deformability. J. E. Allen and H. Rasmussen. bibliog il Science 174:512-14 O 29 '71
  State of water in red cells. A. K. Solomon. il Sci Am 224:88-96 F '71
ERYTHROMYCIN
  Mendelian and uniparental alterations in erythromycin binding by plastid ribosomes. L. J. Mets and L. Bogorad. bibliog il Science 174:707-9 N 12 '71
ERYTHROPOIETIC porphyria. See Porphyria
ESCAMILLO (operatic character) See Characters in opera
ESCAPE! story. See Brent, M.
ESCAPE devices (helicopters) See Helicopters —Escape devices
ESCAPES
  Great escape; J. D. Kaplan escapes prison in Mexico. por Newsweek 78:37-8 Ag 30 '71
  Great escape; Uruguay's Tupamaro jailbreak. Newsweek 78:45 S 20 '71
  More on the Kaplan caper. Time 98:15 S 20 '71
  One of the comrades is missing; K. Bley's escape from East German ship; ed. by K. Schaefer. K. Agnew il Read Digest 98:78-82 Ap '71
  Tupamaros tunnel out. il Time 98:35-6 S 20 '71
  Whirlaway; J. D. Kaplan's escape from Mexican prison. il por Time 98:27-8 Ag 30 '71
ESCAPES from death. See Survival after airplane accidents, shipwrecks, etc.

ESCHATOLOGY
See also
Second advent

ESCHERICHIA coli
Coevolution of escherichia coli and bacteriophages in chemostat culture. M. T. Horne; reply with rejoinder. M. J. B. Paynter and H. R. Bungay, 3d. bibliog Science 172:405 Ap 23 '71
DNA polymerase required for rapid repair of X-ray-induced DNA strand breaks in vivo. C. D. Town and others. bibliog il Science 172:851-4 My 21 '71
Hybrid ribosome formation from escherichia coli and chloroplast ribosome subunits. S. G. Lee and W. R. Evans. bibliog il Science 173:241-2 Jl 16 '71
Periplasmic galactose binding protein of escherichia coli. H. M. Kajckar. bibliog il Science 174:557-65 N 5 '71

ESCLARÍN, Antonio Pérez-. See Pérez-Esclarín, A.

ESENBEL, Melih
United States hails Turkish decision to ban opium poppy production. news conference, June 30, 1971. Dept State Bul 65:75-7 Jl 19 '71

ESHLEMAN, Clayton
In memoriam, Paul Blackburn; poem. Nation 213:410 O 25 '71
about
Comment. R. E. Teele. Poetry 118:176-7 Je '71 *

ESKENAZI, Gerald
Trade winds; interview, ed. by C. Amory. Sat R 54:12 Ja 30 '71

ESKIMOS
Flow of energy in a hunting society. W. B. Kemp. il Sci Am 225:104-15 S '71
I live with the Eskimos. G. Mary-Rousselière. il Nat Geog 139:188-217 F '71
Never in anger, by J. L. Briggs. Review
Natur Hist il 80:74-5 Ja '71. S. A. Freed
Way of life called Eskimo. S. Wright. il pors Am West 8:36-9 Jl '71

Antiquities
Early racial and cultural identifications in southwestern Alaska; with reply by D. E. Dumond. J. S. Aigner and others. bibliog Science 171:87-90 Ja 8 '71

Art
Eskimos tell their own story. C. Miles. il Hobbies 76:148-9+ Ag '71

Implements
Root picks. C. Miles. il Hobbies 76:150-1+ Je '71

Origin
Early racial and cultural identifications in southwestern Alaska; with reply by D. E. Dumond. J. S. Aigner and others. bibliog Science 171:87-90 Ja 8 '71

Social life and customs
Eskimo village. S. Wright. il Liv Wildn 34:3-9 Wint '70
Koviashuktok: the secret of the Eskimos' wisdom. S. Wright. il Am West 8:16-19 N '71

ESPALIERS. See Plants, Training of

ESPIONAGE
Espionage career of General Gehlen; a publishing controversy. B. A. Bannon. por Pub W 201:33-4 Ja 3 '72
Picnics and wet stuff; glossary of current spy terms. Time 98:44 O 11 '71
Plot to steal a fighter plane; excerpts from KGB. J. Barron. il Read Digest 98:69-74 F '71
See also
Secret service
Spies

ESPOSITO, Phil
Oh, brother! A pair to watch. J. Olsen. il pors Sports Illus 34:36-8+ Mr 29 '71 *
Orgy of scores. il por Newsweek 77:61 Ap 5 '71 *

ESPOSITO, Tony
Oh, brother! A pair to watch. J. Olsen. il pors Sports Illus 34:36-8+ Mr 29 '71 *

ESQUIRE (periodical)
Viking, Esquire, dropped from Calley law suit. Pub W 199:37 Ja 18 '71
See also
Business in the arts award

ESSAYS
Competitions
Winners: Writer's digest & Great books of the western world essay contest. N. Kephart. Writers Digest 51:33-4 D '71

ESSENCES and essential oils
See also
Carvone

ESSENTIALISM (education) See Education—Philosophy

ESSEX, Robert Devereux, 2d earl of
Robert, earl of Essex, by R. Lacey. Review
Sat R 54:23-4 Ag 28 '71. J. P. Kenyon *

ESSEX COUNTY, N.Y.
Microfilm system to aid law enforcement. il Am City 86:24 My '71
Reporter at large. B. Bernstein. il New Yorker 47:100+ N 27 '71

ESSLIN, Martin
TV: the challenge of the 70s: quantity plus quality; excerpts. il UNESCO Courier 24:4-7+ F '71

ESSMANN, Uwe, and Träuble, Hermann
Magnetic structure of superconductors; with biographical sketches. il Sci Am 224:14, 74-84 Mr '71

ESSO education foundation
Esso education foundation grants. Sch & Soc 99:206+ Ap '71

ESTABROOKS, G. H.
Hypnosis comes of age. il Sci Digest 69:44:50 Ap '71

ESTATE planning
When your wife is a widow, what then? il Changing T 25:6-9 Je '71
Yes, single people do need to plan their estates. il Changing T 25:33-6 F '71

ESTATES, Decedents
See also
Executors and administrators

ESTELA publishers. See Publishers and publishing—Spain

ESTENSSORO B., Hugo
Now you see a leftist, now you don't. Commonweal 93:316-18, 507+ D 25 '70, F 26 '71

ESTERASES
Adenosine 3′, 5′-monophosphate phosphodiesterase multiple molecular forms. E. Monn and R. O. Christiansen. bibliog il Science 173:540-2 Ag 6 '71
Cyclic 3′,5′-nucleotide phosphodiesterase: cytochemical localization in cerebral cortex. N. T. Florendo and others. bibliog il Science 173:745-7 Ag 20 '71
See also
Cholinesterase

ESTERS
Fatty acid ethyl esters of rhizopus arrhizus. J. L. Laseter and J. D. Weete. bibliog il Science 172:864-5 My 21 '71; Reply with rejoinder. D. H. Calam. 174:78 O 1 '71

ESTES, Rita
Houston '71: Congress city. il Parks & Rec 6:32-4+ Jl '71
Y'all come: Houston '71. il Parks & Rec 6:36-7+ Je '71

ESTHETICS. See Aesthetics

ESTROGENS
Estrogen receptor in the rabbit corpus luteum. C. Lee and others. bibliog il Science 173:1032-3 S 10 '71

ESTRUATION. See Estrus

ESTRUS
Calcium carbonate concretions: cyclic occurrence in the hamster vagina. J. J. Alleva and others. bibliog il Science 174:600-3 N 5 '71
DDT administered to neonatal rats induces persistent estrus syndrome. W. L. Heinrichs and others. bibliog il Science 173:642-3 Ag 13 '71

ETCHINGS
Exhibitions
Etcher of the id; M. Klinger. R. Hughes. il Time 98:44-5 Ag 30 '71

ETERNAL life. See Immortality

ETHACRYNIC acid
Ethacrynic acid effect on the composition of cochlear fluids. E. S. Cohn and others. bibliog il Science 171:910-11 Mr 5 '71

ETHANOL. See Alcohol

ETHICAL culture movement
Toward common ground, by H. B. Radest. Review
Commentary 51:71-6 Mr '71. M. A. Meyer; Discussion. 52:28+ Ag '71

ETHICAL drug trade. See Drug industry

ETHICAL education. See Moral education

ETHICS
Dishonest riches. Chr Today 16:25 O 22 '71
Moral rules, by B. Gert. Review
Commonweal 94:434 Ag 20 '71. J. M. Gustafson
Morality is for persons, by B. Haring. Review
Commonweal 95:284-5 D 17 '71. A. L. Schlitzer

ETHICS—*Continued*
Wilhelm Reich's theory: ethical implications. M. B. Zweig. Am Imago 28:268-86 Fall '71
See also
Advertising ethics
Business ethics
Capital punishment
Christian ethics
Conduct of life
Conscience
Courage
Duty
Journalistic ethics
Medical ethics
Moral attitudes
Moral conditions
Moral education
Police ethics
Political ethics
Puritanism
Responsibility
Sexual ethics
Situation ethics
Social ethics
Utilitarianism
Virtue
Woman—Social and moral questions
ETHICS and science. See Science and ethics
ETHIDIUM bromide. See Bromides
ETHIOPIA
Ethiopian friends; army atrocities in Eritrea; letter. New Repub 164:34 Ja 16 '71
Ethiopian perplex. B. A. Alpert. Cur Hist 60:151-6+ Mr '71
See also
Airlines—Ethiopia
Danakil
Guerrillas—Ethiopia

Politics and government
Eritrean rebellion. il Newsweek 77:34 Mr 1 '71
Shum-shir game. il Time 97:35 Mr 1 '71
ETHIOPIAN airlines. See Airlines—Ethiopia
ETHIOPIAN Orthodox church. See Ethiopic church
ETHIOPIC church
Mission to endure. il Newsweek 77:59 My 3 '71
ETHNIC citizens organizations. See Citizens associations
ETHNIC cookery. See Cookery, International
ETHNIC differences. See Ethnopsychology
ETHNIC minorities. See Minorities
ETHNOLOGICAL museums and collections
Peoples of the Pacific; ed. by M. Mead and P. McClanahan. bibliog il pors Natur Hist 80:54-7 My '71
See also
Indians of North America—Museums
ETHNOLOGY
See also
Archeology
Aryans
Culture
Ethnopsychology

New Guinea
See also
Melanesians
ETHNOPSYCHOLOGY
Why can't they be like us? by A. M. Greeley. Review
Commentary 52:82-3 Jl '71. P. L. Berger
New Yorker 47:225-6+ N 20 '71. N. Bliven
See also
Acculturation
ETHRIDGE, John
Three-cylinder sock! il Pop Mech 136:88-91 D '71
ETHYL alcohol. See Alcohol
ETHYLENE
Fate of air pollutants: removal of ethylene, sulfur dioxide, and nitrogen dioxide by soil. F. B. Abeles and others. bibliog il Science 173:914-16 S 3 '71
Fight over ethylene supplies. il Bsns W p21 D 18 '71
ETHYLENEDIAMINE tetraacetic acid
Teratogenic effects of a chelating agent and their prevention by zinc. H. Swenerton and L. S. Hurley. bibliog il Science 173:62-4 Jl 2 '71; Reply with rejoinder. R. D. Hamilton. 174:102-3 O 8 '71
ETIQUETTE
Behaving with elegance at home and abroad, by G. A. Dariaux. Review
Atlan 227:116-17 F '71. A. B. C. Whipple
How to handle anything on the menu. Bet Hom & Gard 49:107 Ap '71
[Monthly column] A. Vanderbilt. See issues of Ladies' home journal
See also
Telephone etiquette

ETNA, MOUNT
Fire on the mountain. il Newsweek 77:92-93D My 17 '71
Mount Etna turns nasty. D. J. Hamblin. il Life 70:28-30 My 28 '71
Vulcan's fiery forge. il Time 97:50 My 31 '71
ETTEN, Mary
Pinned beneath a tractor. Farm J 95:22K S '71
ETTER, Dave
Comment. L. Mueller. Poetry 117:326-8 F '71 •
ETYMOLOGY. See English language—Etymology
ETZIONI, Amitai
Need for quality filters in information systems. Science 171:133 Ja 15 '71
On academic blood tests. Science 172:1087; 174:102 Je 11, O 8 '71
On the art of university pruning. Science 172:429 Ap 30 '71
R & D processing of domestic programs. Science 171:1203 Mr 26 '71
EUCALYPTUS
Earthquakes and eucalypts in Peru. T. Cobb. il Am For 77:20-1+ S '71
EUCHARIST. See Catholic church—Eucharist; Lord's Supper
EUGENE, Ore.

Recreation
Hard lesson; drop-in youth centers. N. Murray. il Parks & Rec 6:28-31+ F '71
EUGENE Onegin; ballet. See Ballets—Criticisms
EUGENICS
Second genesis, by A. Rosenfeld. Review
Bul Atom Sci 27:47-8 Ja '71. R. Henoch
What price the perfect baby? L. R. Kass; B. Glass. Science 173:103-4 Jl 9 '71
EUGLENA
Euglena gracilis: formation of giant mitochondria. R. Calvayrac and others. bibliog il Science 173:252-4 Jl 16 '71
Internal cellular details of euglena gracilis visualized by scanning electron microscopy. H. N. Guttman. bibliog il Science 171:290-2 Ja 22 '71
EUGLOSSINE bees. See Bees
EUGSTER, Hans P.
Beginnings of experimental petrology; excerpts from address, January 1971. bibliog il Science 173:481-9 Ag 6 '71
EULA, Joe
Observations. il por Vogue 158:146 O 15 '71 •
EULER, Ulf S. von
Adrenergic neurotransmitter functions; Nobel lecture, December 12, 1970. bibliog il Science 173:202-6 Jl 16 '71
EULIE, Joseph
Meaningful tests in social studies. bibliog f Clear House 45:333-6 F '71
EUPHORBIA. See Spurges
EURASIAN watermilfoil. See Water milfoil
EUROBOND market
Hungary readies a Eurobond issue. Bsns W p27-8 Mr 6 '71
EUROCONTROL. See Air traffic control—Europe, Western
EURODOLLAR market
Banks fret over Eurodollars, brokers play the dollar game. il Bsns W p76-7+ Ap 24 '71
Eurodollar pinch pushes up rates. Bsns W p41 Je 5 '71
Eurodollars: the villain? il Bsns W p91+ S 25 '71
First step to curb the Eurodollar mart. Bsns W p35 Je 19 '71
New kind of crisis. il Newsweek 77:78 Ap 12 '71
New kind of world monetary crisis. il Newsweek 77:77+ My 10 '71
New troubles for the dollar? J. Ross-Skinner. il Duns 97:49-51 Mr '71
Nixon's expansion policy irks Europeans. il Bsns W p88-9 Mr 13 '71
Notes and comment. New Yorker 47:27-8 My 22 '71
Step to slow Eurodollar flows; with editorial comment. il Bsns W p 110-11+, 160 My 15 '71
Tighter rein on the Eurodollar. Bsns W p 17-18 My 29 '71
U.S. move to keep dollars safe at home. il Bsns W p25 Ja 16 '71
Why dollars piled up in Europe. il Bsns W p 116-17 My 15 '71
Yank banks have landed; branches in Britain and the Continent. S. G. Slappey. il Nations Bsns 59:66-71 Mr '71
EUROPA (launch vehicle) See Space vehicles—Propulsion systems

EUROPE
See also
Camping—Europe
Jews in Europe
Moving pictures—Europe
Music festivals—Europe
Religious conferences—Europe
Tourist trade—Europe

Antiquities
Carbon 14 and the prehistory of Europe. C.
Renfrew. il Sci Am 225:63-70+ bibliog
(p 120) O '71

Civilization
What did Columbus mean to Europe? S. de
Madariaga. il Américas 23:S14-15 O '71

Defenses
U.S.S.R. prepared to discuss force reductions
in Europe. Dept State Bul 64:741 Je 7 '71

Description and travel
How to cope with European culture (without
really trying) S. Mead. il Travel 135:64-9
Je '71

Economic conditions
See also
United Nations—Economic commission for
Europe

History
476-1492
Landlord and the economic revival of the
middle ages in northern Europe, 1000-1250.
R. G. Witt. bibliog f Am Hist R 76:965-88
O '71

Maps
Europe (cont) Sr Schol 99:7 O 4 '71

Politics
Fall of Europe? W. Laqueur. bibliog f Com-
mentary 53:33-40 Ja '72
Rebirth of Europe, by W. Laquer. Review
Commentary 51:96 Ap '71. A. Hartley
What they're talking about in Europe. il
Sr Schol 99:6+ O 4 '71

Population
Population explosion? emigration cause of
underpopulation. E. von Kuehnelt-Leddihn.
Nat R 23:1239 N 5 '71

Religious institutions and affairs
See also
Reformation

EUROPE, EASTERN
Day the iron curtain fell; W. Churchill's
speech. il por Sr Schol 98:18 Mr 8 '71
See also
Artificial satellites, European
Balkan Peninsula
Catholic church—Relations (diplomatic)—Eu-
rope, Eastern
Communism—Europe, Eastern
Investments, Foreign (in Europe)
Jews in Europe
Pollution—Europe, Eastern
Tourist trade—Europe, Eastern
United States—Commerce—Europe, Eastern

Commerce
Western business in eastern Europe; address, December 29, 1970. P. H. Trezise.
Dept State Bul 64:85-8 Ja 18 '71; Same
with title East-west trade: U.S. self interest. Vital Speeches 37:313-15 Mr 1 '71

Defenses
See also
Warsaw pact, 1955

Economic conditions
East Europe: the restless empire. il Time 97:
36+ Mr 29 '71
How to make it in eastern Europe. Newsweek 77:36+ Ap 5 '71

Economic policy
Why reds are turning to capitalism. il U S
News 71:61-3 N 15 '71

Foreign relations
East and west Europe: a continent divided.
A. Korbonski. Cur Hist 60:257-62+ My '71
Interested bystanders. Time 98:26 S 6 '71
United States, our NATO allies, and the
Soviet Union in an era of changing foreign
relations; address, February 19, 1971. U. A.
Johnson. Dept State Bul 64:315-21 Mr 15
'71
Germany (Federal Republic)
See Germany (Federal Republic)—Foreign
relations—Europe, Eastern

United States
See United States—Foreign relations—Europe, Eastern

Politics
East Europe, 1971; symposium. bibliog f il
Cur Hist 60:257-301+ My '71
Europe: the search for solutions; stalled
ostpolitik. il Time 97:42 Ap 26 '71
Shifts in red Europe: good news or bad?
il U S News 70:78 My 17 '71
See also
Czechoslovakia—Occupation, 1968-

Religious institutions and affairs
Mission eastern Europe: toward a new
agenda. C. C. West. Chr Cent 89:13-15 Ja 5
'72

EUROPE, WESTERN
See also
Aeronautics, Commercial—Europe, Western
Air traffic control—Europe, Western
Airplanes, Military—Europe, Western
Airports—Europe, Western
Architecture—Europe, Western
Art—Europe, Western
Banks and banking—Europe, Western
Business schools and colleges—Europe, West-
ern
Camping—Europe, Western
Children—Europe, Western
City planning—Europe, Western
Communism—Europe, Western
Evangelistic work—Europe, Western
Forests and forestry—Europe, Western
Great Britain—Economic relations—Europe,
Western
Housing projects—Europe, Western
Investments, Foreign (by Europe)
Investments, Foreign (in Europe)
Labor and laboring classes—Europe, Western
Libraries—Europe, Western
Music—Europe, Western
Music festivals—Europe, Western
Old age pensions—Europe, Western
Periodicals—Europe, Western
Postal service—Europe, Western
Railroads—Europe, Western
Restaurants—Europe, Western
Shopping and shoppers—Europe, Western
Skis and skiing—Europe, Western
Space research—Europe, Western
Tariff—Europe, Western
Tourist trade—Europe, Western
Wage-price policy—Europe, Western
Water pollution—Europe, Western
Wilderness areas—Europe, Western

Armed forces
See also
United States—Armed forces—Forces in Eu-
rope

Civilization
History
Civilisation, by K. Clark. Review
Commentary 51:111-12+ Je '71. T. K.
Rabb

Commerce
Europe's American tastes; U.S. food imports.
il Time 97:80 Mr 15 '71

Defenses
Fall of Europe? W. Laqueur. bibliog f Com-
mentary 53:33-40 Ja '72
New European defense community. F. Du-
chêne. For Affairs 50:69-82 O '71
See also
Atomic warfare—Defenses
Nato

Description and travel
Over in Dulgence: trial run of the Renais-
sance tour for the overprivileged. H. Sut-
ton. il Sat R 54:63-4+ N 6 '71
Traveling on your own in Europe. G. Bush.
il Bet Hom & Gard 49:95-101 F '71
See also
Tourist trade—Europe, Western

Economic conditions
Signs of recession in Europe. il U S News
71:29-32 N 29 '71
See also
United Nations—Economic commission for
Europe

Economic history
Unbound Prometheus, by D. S. Landes. Review
Am Hist R 76:467-74 Ap '71. R. M. Hartwell and R. Higgs; Reply. D. S. Landes.
76:1633-7 D '71

Economic integration
See also
European economic community

EUROPE, WESTERN—*Continued*
Economic policy
See also
European economic community
Economic relations
Shotgun pattern of Nixon's policies. Bsns W p30 S 4 '71
Economic union
See European economic community
Foreign relations
East and west Europe: a continent divided. A. Korbonski. Cur Hist 60:257-62+ My '71
United States, our NATO allies, and the Soviet Union in an era of changing foreign relations; address, February 19, 1971. U. A. Johnson. Dept State Bul 64:315-21 Mr 15 '71
United States
See United States—Foreign relations— Europe, Western
Industries
Profitable, but not very; with table. Bsns W p60 O 23 '71
See also
Aerospace industries—Europe, Western
Atomic power industry—Europe, Western
Automobile industry—Europe, Western
Avionics industry—Europe, Western
Computer industry—Europe, Western
Construction industry—Europe, Western
Meat industry—Europe, Western
Politics
Europe: the search for solutions; stalled ost-politik. il Time 97:42 Ap 26 '71
Letter from Europe. A. Waugh. Esquire 75: 8+ Ap; 10+ Je; 76:230 N '71
Real divisions of Europe. A. Fontaine. For Affairs 49:302-14 Ja '71
See also
Communism—Europe, Western
European federation
Union (proposed)
See European federation
EUROPE and the United States
See also
United States—Foreign opinion—European
EUROPEAN artificial satellites. See Artificial satellites, European
EUROPEAN-Asiatic airline services. See Air-lines—International services—European-Asiatic
EUROPEAN assembly of priest delegates. See Priests—Associations, institutions, etc.
EUROPEAN civil aviation conference
European group challenges U.S. supplemental influx. L. Doty. Aviation W 95:21-2 Jl 19 '71
Inter-governmental charter talks may be base for future accord. L. Doty. Aviation W 94:23 Ap 5 '71
EUROPEAN common market. See European economic community
EUROPEAN communications satellites. See Communications satellites, European
EUROPEAN congress on evangelism. See Evangelistic work—Europe, Western; Religious conferences—Europe, Western
EUROPEAN economic community
Agro-frauders. Time 97:85 My 31 '71
Altruism or cosmetics? new tariff plan. Newsweek 77:60 Ap 12 '71
Antitrusters nip a steel cartel bid. Bsns W p42 Mr 6 '71
Betrothal in Brussels; agreement by the six nations of the European common market. il Time 97:87+ F 22 '71
Bitter fruit from the EEC. H. H. Wilson. por Nations Bsns 59:42 N '71
Britain and the EEC: how strong is the technological argument? J. Walsh. Science 174:476-9 O 29 '71
Britain in Europe: undecided Harold Wilson. A. Howard. New Repub 165:8-9 Jl 10 '71
Britain: Labor's dark hour; party split over Common market. pors Newsweek 78:30+ Ag 2 '71
Britain picks Europe, impact on America. il U S News 71:85 N 8 '71
Britain stakes its future on the EEC; with editorial comment. il Bsns W p62-3+, 123 O 23 '71
Britain takes a historic decision. il Newsweek 78:51-2 N 8 '71
Britain: to market, to market; with report by William Rademaekers. il Time 98:39-40 N 1 '71

Britain's probable futures. Cur 132:53-5 S '71
British economists talk down the EEC. il Bsns W p85-6+ Ap 3 '71
Church and the Common market; British entry. T. Beeson. Chr Cent 88:396-7 Mr 31 '71
Common market: a great day for Europe. il Time 98:34+ N 8 '71
Common market: breaking out the bubbly. il Time 98:23-4 Jl 5 '71
Common market: breakthrough in Brussels. il Time 97:27-8 My 24 '71
Common market: good morning! pors Newsweek 77:29-30 My 31 '71
Common market: what if Britain says no? Time 97:26-7 Je 28 '71
Concan challenge. J. Ross-Skinner. il Duns 98:61-2+ D '71
Concan is caught in an antitrust test. Bsns W p37+ D 18 '71
Creating a European consciousness; British Parliament votes for entry. Cur 135:40-2 D '71
Critical tasks facing western Europe and the United States in a period of change and transition; address, May 13, 1971. M. J. Hillenbrand. Dept State Bul 64:743-8 Je 7 '71
Down and out in London: the Common market dilemma. A. Cockburn. il Ramp Mag 10:48-51 O '71
EEC tiptoes toward economic union. il Bsns W p78-9 F 20 '71
Engagement party; agreement to plan for economic and monetary union. Newsweek 77:72-3 F 22 '71
England: Common market. Nat R 23:1278+ N 19 '71
Europe: another step toward unity. il Newsweek 77:33+ My 24 '71
Europe: the British are coming; il pors Time 97:26+ My 31 '71
Europe: the search for solutions; showdown ahead. Time 97:45 Ap 26 '71
Fall of Europe? British entry. W. Laqueur. bibliog f Commentary 53:33-40 Ja '72
Flip flop Wilson. il Time 98:30 Ag 2 '71
For Europe, the end of the beginning; British membership. Newsweek 78:37-8 Jl 5 '71
French prospects in Europe. America 125:386 N 13 '71
Getting along with the new Europe. Life 71:36 O 1 '71
Great debate begins; on joining the Common market. il por Time 98:27 Jl 19 '71
Great debate in Britain. J. Mander. Cur 132: 51-3 S '71
If Britain goes into the Common market. G. S. Browne. il Nations Bsns 50:44-7 F '71
If Britain joins the Common market... il U S News 71:34-6 Jl 5 '71
Letter from London. M. Panter-Downes. New Yorker 47:64 Jl 3; 68-70 Ag 7; 138+ O 30; 177-80 N 13 '71
Pitchfork power; protest by farmers from Common market countries. il Time 97:32 Ap 5 '71
Politics of power; Britain's entry. T. Beeson. Chr Cent 88:993 Ag 25 '71
Price of a lie; question of Norway's joining the Common market. Time 97:38-9 Mr 15 '71
Push in Britain to join Europe. il U S News 71:76 Ag 9 '71
Reports & comment; question of Scan-dinavian membership. D. Cook. Atlan 229: 6+ Ja '72
Supermarket or superpower? A. Shub. il Harper 244:57-63 Ja '72
Trustbusters fire at a U.S. target. Bsns W p41 Mr 27 '71
U.S. welcomes British decision to enter the European community; White House state-ment; with statement by Secretary Rogers. Dept State Bul 65:589 N 22 '71
Unlocking the door; Common market and Great Britain. A. Howard. New Repub 164: 8-9 Je 5 '71
Unpopular win; British Parliament votes for entry into EEC. A. Lejeune. Nat R 23:1407 D 17 '71
Wilson agonistes. C. Brogan. Nat R 23:930+ Ag 24 '71
Yes to Europe! T. Beeson. Chr Cent 88:895 Jl 28 '71
EUROPEAN federation
Europe between the superpowers. A. Hart-ley. For Affairs 49:271-82 Ja '71
Europe on the move. P. Hebblethwaite. il America 124:169-71 F 20 '71
Is political unity Europe's next step? U S News 71:36 Jl 5 '71
Supermarket or superpower? A. Shub. il Harper 244:57-63 Ja '72

EUROPEAN federation—*Continued*
Western European unity and inter-European reconciliation; address, July 19, 1971. J. N. Irwin. Dept State Bul 65:145-50 Ag 9 '71
Yes to Europe! T. Beeson. Chr Cent 88:895 Jl 28 '71
EUROPEAN intervention in Mexico, 1861-1867. See Mexico—History—European intervention, 1861-1867
EUROPEAN launcher development organization
Disunity impedes European space effort. D. E. Fink. il Aviation W 94:46+ Mr 8 '71
ELDO pad attains operational goal. D. E. Fink. il Aviation W 96:48-50 Ja 3 '72
EUROPEAN literature
European literary scene. R. J. Clements. See issues of Saturday review
EUROPEAN migration, Intergovernmental committee for. See Intergovernmental committee for European migration
EUROPEAN organization for nuclear research
CERN: final planning begins for Europe's big machine. N. Hawkes. Science 172:653 My 14 '71
Toward asymptopia; CERN use of ISR atom smasher. il Time 99:45-6 Ja 10 '72
EUROPEAN painting. See Painting, European
EUROPEAN pension plans. See Old age pensions—Europe, Western
EUROPEAN pottery. See Pottery, European
EUROPEAN sculpture. See Sculpture, European
EUROPEAN space conference
U.S. and European space conference officials continue discussions; joint communique. Dept State Bul 64:328 Mr 15 '71
U.S. offers launch assistance to Europeans; Department announcement, November 1, 1971; with text of letter to T. Lefevre, September 1, 1971, and summary of amplifying comments. Dept State Bul 65:624-7 N 29 '71
EUROPEAN space research organization
Disunity impedes European space effort. D. E. Fink. il Aviation W 94:51-3 Mr 8 '71
Final approval of ESRO system nears. il Aviation W 95:47-8+ Ag 23 '71
Joint aerosat to be sought to avoid ICAO argument. P. J. Klass. Aviation W 94:17-18 Ap 12 '71
EUROPEAN union. See European federation
EUROPEAN war, 1914-1918

American participation
See European war, 1914-1918—United States

Chemical warfare
Mist that rolled into the trenches: chemical escalation in World war I. R. E. Cook. Bul Atom Sci 27:34-8 Ja '71

Diplomatic history
See also
European war, 1914-1918—United States

Germany
Sway of the grand saloon; excerpts. J. M. Brinnin. il Am Heritage 22:12-15 O '71

United States
Sway of the grand saloon; excerpts. J. M. Brinnin. il Am Heritage 22:12-15 O '71
Woodrow Wilson's fight for peace. T. Fleming. il por Read Digest 99:87-91 S '71
EUSTER, Gerald L.
Mental health workers: new mental hospital personnel for the seventies. bibliog Ment Hy 55:283-90 Jl '71
EUSTIS, Helen
Are you feeding your baby too much? Redbook 137:57+ O '71
EUTHANASIA
Politics of death. R. Kirk. Nat R 23:315 Mr 23 '71
When do we have the right to die? 3 case histories. P. Wilkes. il Life 72:48+ Ja 14 '72
EUTROPHICATION
Eutrophication of lake water microcosms: phosphate versus nonphosphate detergents. D. Mitchell. bibliog il Science 174:827-9 N 19 '71
Eutrophication reconsidered. Sci Am 224:50 My '71
Eutrophication, silica depletion, and predicted changes in algal quality in Lake Michigan. C. L. Schelske and E. F. Stoermer. bibliog il Science 173:423-4 Jl 30 '71
Lake Erie: pollution abatement, then what? J. H. Hubschman. bibliog il Science 171:536-40 F 12 '71; Reply. S. M. Rosenblum and T. C. Hollocher. 172:1294-5 Je 25 '71

Nutrients and eutrophication; report of meeting. G. E. Likens and others. Science 172:873-4 My 21 '71
Phosphates and nitrates in surface waters. K. E. Glines. Chem 44:25-6 Mr '71
To control algae, consider carbon. Am City 86:36 Mr '71
See also
Water bloom
EVACUATION of civilians. See World war, 1939-1945—Evacuation of civilians
EVALUATION (education) See Education—Evaluation
EVANGELICAL church
Conservative evangelicals deserve a better hearing. R. T. Hitt. por Chr Cent 88:975-7 Ag 18 '71; Discussion. 88:1144-6 S 29 '71
See also
National Negro evangelical association
EVANGELICAL congregational church in Brazil
Brazilian congregationalists convene. D. C. Hoffman. Chr Cent 88:346 Mr 17 '71
EVANGELICAL foreign missions association
Creative tension: the church-mission controversy. W. H. Fuller. Chr Today 16:33 O 22 '71
EVANGELICAL press association
EPA: looking out for the evangelicals. R. Chandler. Chr Today 15:28 Je 4 '71
EVANGELICALISM
Conservative evangelicals? L. Morris. Chr Today 16:50-1 N 19 '71
1972: year of the person? Chr Today 16:24-5 Ja 7 '72

Bibliography
Choice evangelical books of 1970. bibliog Chr Today 15:28-30 F 26 '71
EVANGELICALS, National association of. See National association of evangelicals
EVANGELISTIC work
Decisive hour for 21,000; northern California crusade. R. Chandler. il Chr Today 15:30-1 Ag 27 '71
Diverse Protestant groups plan evangelistic thrust in 1973. Chr Cent 88:1518 D 29 '71
Electronic evangelist. il por Time 97:70+ My 17 '71
Evangelism: how to get involved; excerpts from discussion. Chr Today 15:11-13 Ag 27 '71
Evangelistic imperative; proclaiming the Gospel to non-Christians. Chr Today 15:24-5 My 7 '71
Graham crusade: satanists lose to Jesus power. Chr Today 15:34 Jl 2 '71
Key 73: a continental call. D. Kucharsky. il Chr Today 16:38 N 19 '71
Key 73: on the bridge together. E. E. Plowman. Chr Today 15:32 Je 18 '71
Lesson in world-winning. S. H. Moffett. Chr Today 15:4-6 S 10 '71
New evangelism. K. Hamilton. Chr Today 15:4-7 Ja 29 '71
Not a time for timidity. Chr Today 15:38-40 Mr 12 '71
Social reform: an evangelical imperative. C. Thompson. Chr Today 15:8-12 Mr 26 '71
Taking stock of Jesus rock. E. E. Plowman. Chr Today 15:32-3 F 26 '71
Top '71 religious news: world revival. R. Chandler. Chr Today 16:40-1 Ja 7 '72
See also
Conversion
Missions
National association of evangelicals
Revivals

Europe, Western
European conference on evangelism listens to youth delegates. T. Cosmades. Chr Cent 88:1241-2+ O 20 '71
European congress: getting to know you; with editorial comment. J. J. Van Capelleveen. il Chr Today 15:39, 40-1 S 24 '71

Spain
Texans' crusade; eight-day campaign of Southern Baptist laymen. il Time 98:92 N 8 '71
EVANOFF, Vlad
Get ready to follow the blues, great battlers on light tackle. Motor B & S 127:137+ Mr '71
1970 fishing records. il Motor B & S 127:33+ F '71
Rhode Island for summer action. il Motor B & S 127:33+ Je '71
Stripers come big. il Motor B & S 127:37+ Ap '71
EVANS, Brad
Wagner lives. Nat R 23:1427-8 D 17 '71
EVANS, Christopher
Presenting the next great western movie. L. E. Sissman. Atlan 228:40+ D '71 •

EVANS, David S. and Hubbard, W. B.
Jupiter and Beta Scorpii. il por Sky & Tel 42:337-41 D '71

EVANS, Don
Segregated drama in integrated schools. Engl J 60:260-3 F '71

EVANS, E. L. and others
Kinetics of single-layer graphite oxidation: evaluation by electron microscopy. bibliog il Science 171:174-5 Ja 15 '71

EVANS, Gary W.
Biological function of copper. Chem 44:10-11 Je '71

EVANS, George Bird
Grouse and woodcock dog. il Field & S 76:126+ Jl '71
When your retriever refuses. il Field & S 75: 220+ Ap '71

EVANS, J.
J. Evans, painter. N. Savage and G. Savage. il Antiques 100:782-7 N '71 *

EVANS, J. Claude
Celebration, not sensation. Chr Cent 89:4-6 Ja 5 '72

EVANS, Jean
Town that closed its doors. il Redbook 136: 88-9+ Mr '71

EVANS, Jerome
Man who was cut out for the job; excerpt from Black coach. P. Jordan. il Sports Illus 35:90-4+ O 11 '71 *

EVANS, Larry
Chess (cont) Sports Illus 34:58-9 Je 21 '71

EVANS, Luther Harris
Month in review; retirement of Luther Evans. Wilson Lib Bul 46:128+ O '71 *

EVANS, Mary
"All my wishes end at Monticello." il Am Home 74:41-9+ Jl '71
Pewter. il Am Home 74:94-8+ Ap '71
Vieux Carré. il Am Home 74:82+ Mr '71

EVANS, Melvin H.
Governor of paradise. il pors Ebony 26:105-6+ Mr '71 *

EVANS, Phyllis P. and Bracht, N. F.
Meeting social work's challenge in community mental health. Ment Hy 55:295-7 Jl '71

EVANS, Roger
Master of the notes. Nat R 23:1316 N 19 '71

EVANS, Rowland, Jr, and Novak, R. D.
Nixonomics: how the game plan went wrong. Atlan 228:66-76+ Jl '71

EVANS, Walker
Interview; ed. by L. Katz. por Art in Am 59:82-9 Mr '71

about
Double documentary. M. R. Weiss. il Sat R 54:84 Mr 13 '71 *
Walker Evans retrospective. W. McQuade. il Life 70:12 Mr 5 '71 *

EVANS, William R. See Lee, S. G. jt. auth.

EVANS products company
Evans products cuts out the middleman. il Bsns W p70-1 Jl 31 '71

EVANSTON, Ill.
Affluent settled. S. Iker. il Time 97:17 Mr 15 '71

Recreation
Careers in recreation; high school student training program. S. Sarkisian. il Parks & Rec 6:40-1+ F '71

EVAPORATION
Evaporation retardation by monolayers: another mechanism. J. Wu. bibliog il Science 174:283-5 O 15 '71

EVE LPGA championship. See Golf—Tournaments

EVELY, Louis
Demythologizing of Louis Evely. J. L. McKenzie. Commonweal 94:307-10 Je 11 '71; Discussion. 94:370-1 Jl 23 '71 *

EVENING and continuation schools
See also
University extension

EVERDING, August
On the threshold; interview. New Yorker 47: 37-9 D 11 '71

EVEREST, MOUNT
Defeat on Everest. M. Sayle. il por Life 71: 22-9 Jl 2 '71

EVERETT, Barbara
Insectual politics. Sat R 54:68 N 20 '71

EVERETT, D. Leon
Turnabout in Houston? pors Newsweek 78: 62 S 13 '71 *

EVERGLADE kites. See Kites (birds)

EVERGLADES
Everglades. P. Caulfield. il Pop Phot 68:82-7 F '71
Everglades, by P. Caulfield. Review
Am For 77:46-7 Ja '71. M. Bush
Natur Hist 80:76-8+ Ja '71. C. R. Kirk, jr
Florida veldt. D. Butwin. il Sat R 54:39-40 F 13 '71
Imperiled Everglades. F. Ward. il Nat Geog 141:1-27 Ja '72
In Florida, where Everglades are turning dry. il U S News 70:24 My 3 '71
Wilderness waterway; through Florida's 10,000 islands. J. Martenhoff. il Yachting 130:64+ N '71
See also
Big Cypress Swamp

EVERGLADES airstrip. See Airports—Florida

EVERGLADES fire. See Fires

EVERGLADES NATIONAL PARK
Drainage, development hit Glades despite court rule. Nat Parks & Con Mag 45:34 Je '71
Fishing the Everglades. A. J. McClane. il Field & S 75:96-7+ F '71
New fishing chart opens flooded Everglades wilderness. G. X. Sand. il Field & S 76:172-4+ Je '71

EVERGREENS
See also
Christmas greens
Christmas trees
also names of evergreens, e.g. Pittosporum

EVERHART, Thomas E. and Hayes, T. L.
Scanning electron microscope; with biographical sketches. il Sci Am 226:10, 54-61+ Ja '72

EVERITT, Paulina
Lady of distinction; interview, ed. by M. S. Hare. il por Design 72:32-3 Sum '71

EVERS, Charles
Black governor for Mississippi? P. O'Neil. il pors Life 70:59-60 My 14 '71 *
Evers administration: two years of progress in Fayette. A. B. Haines. Chr Cent 88: 908-11 Jl 28 '71 *
Evers's confession. P. Goldman. por Newsweek 77:30-1 Ap 26 '71 *
Mississippi's new politics of race: the contest for governor. G. D. Gibson. Chr Cent 88:1148-9 S 29 '71 *
You gotta love me. il por Newsweek 78:22+ Ag 2 '71 *

EVERS, Mrs Medgar W.
How I rediscovered my faith in prayer. por Ladies Home J 88:106+ S '71

EVERT, Chris
Chrissie. por Newsweek 78:58 S 20 '71 *
E for Evert H. L. Masin. il por Sr Schol 99:18-19 O 18 '71 *
Happiness is six hours a day with your eye on the ball. L. Keith. il por Sports Illus 35:58-61 Jl 26 '71 *
More Joan of Arc than Shirley Temple. R. Blount. il pors Sports Illus 35:30-1 S 20 '71 *

EVERY soul is a circus; ballet. See Ballets—Criticisms

EVETT, Robert
Music (cont) Atlan 227:104-7 My; 228:96-8 Jl; 128-31 O '71
Music (cont) New Repub 164:38-40 Ja 2; 165: 28+ S 25; 22+ N 27 '71

EVIDENCE (law)
Speak, voiceprint. il Time 99:59 Ja 10 '72
Telltale bullets; case of J. L. Crowder. Time 97:53 Ap 5 '71
See also
Witnesses

EVIL. See Good and evil

EVINS, Marilyn
Great party giver speaks her mind. il por House & Gard 140:43+ N '71

about
Secrets of a great party giver. il por House & Gard 140:82-9+ N '71 *

EVLETH, Donna
Irony; poem. Good H 172:44 F '71

EVOLUTION
Amino acid composition of proteins as a product of molecular evolution. T. Ohta and M. Kimura. bibliog il Science 174:150-3 O 8 '71
Creature from the marsh; excerpt from The night country. L. Eiseley. Natur Hist 80:24+ O '71
Evolution as a scientific theory. G. Vanderkooi. Chr Today 15:13-14 My 7 '71
Symbiosis and evolution; origin of organelles. L. Margulis. il Sci Am 225:48-57 bibliog(p 120) Ag '71

EVOLUTION—*Continued*
Which way is evolution taking nature? E.
Gibbons. il Org Gard & Farm 18:116-17 O
'71
See also
Adaptation (biology)
Man—Origin and antiquity
Natural selection
Religion and science
Species
Stars—Evolution

Study and teaching
Creationism. Sci Am 224:46-7 Ja '71
EVOLUTION, Social. See Social change; Social
progress
EVSEEV, Boris
Reliability of automation versus manned
spaceflight. Space World H-8-92:31-3 Ag '71
EVSLIN, Dorothy
Husbands; excerpt from Live in. il Ladies
Home J 88:191-2+ S '71
EVTUSHENKO, Evgenii Aleksandrovich
Being famous isn't pretty; introd. to Stolen
apples, tr. by A. Kahn. Harper 243:56-8 Jl
'71
Tribute to Satchmo; poem. Harp Baz 104:
214-15 S '71
about
Sign of a thaw? il por Newsweek 78-29-30 Jl
19 '71
EWEN, David
Festival of George Gershwin. il pors Hi Fi
21:MA24-5+ Ja '71
EWERS, John C.
Crow chief's tribute to the unknown soldier.
il pors Am West 8:30-5 N '71
When red and white men met; excerpts from
address, April 1971. Am Heritage 23:107-8
D '71
EWING, David W.
Who wants corporate democracy? bibliog f
il Harvard Bsns R 49:12-14+ S '71
Who wants employee rights? bibliog f il
Harvard Bsns R 49:22-4+ N '71
EWING, Larry L. See Johnson, B. H. jt. auth.
EXAMINATION; story. See Heinemann, A.
EXAMINATION anxiety. See Anxiety
EXAMINATIONS
Case for out-of-class exams. W. S. Svoboda.
Clear House 46:231-3 D '71
See also
Educational tests and measurements
Physical examinations
EXAMINER, San Francisco. See San Fran-
cisco examiner
EXCAVATING machinery
See also
Rock drills
EXCAVATION
See also
Tunnels and tunneling
EXCAVATIONS (archeology)
Community discovers its past. D. L. Down-
ton. il PTA Mag 65:18-20 Mr '71
Search for New World man; controversial
California dig. C. Behrens. il Sci N 99:98-
100 F 6 '71
Wellfleet tavern. E. Ekholm and J. Dee-
tz. il Natur Hist 80:48-57 Ag '71
Work your science interest into your holi-
day; British science vacations. M. Roberts.
il Sci Digest 71:60-4 Ja '72
See also
Carthage, Africa
Paestum
also subhead Antiquities under names of
continents, countries, states, cities, etc.,
e.g. Turkey—Antiquities
EXCEDRIN. See Analgesics
EXCEPTIONAL children. See Children, Ex-
ceptional
EXCEPTIONAL parent (periodical)
Help for exceptional parents. Time 97:48
Je 28 '71
Help for the exceptional parent. J. Cass.
Sat R 54:39 Ag 21 '71
EXCESS profits tax
Profit controls on the way? il U S News
71:16+ S 13 '71
EXCHANGE (barter) See Barter
EXCHANGE, Foreign. See Foreign exchange
EXCHANGE, Social. See Social exchange
EXCHANGE of persons programs
Chou gives a nod to science swap. D. Shap-
ley. Science 173:616 Ag 13 '71
Community of science and the search for
peace; adaptation of address, April 26,
1971. P Doty. Science 173:998-1002 S 10 '71
Delegation of governors to visit U.S.S.R.
and Romania; Department announcement,
September 20, 1971. Dept State Bul 65:384
O 11 '71

Executive-swapping in Europe. J. Ross-
Skinner. il Duns 97:77-8+ Mr '71
From ping pong to science: cautious hope.
Sci N 99:313 My 8 '71
Uncertainties of scientific exchange; letter.
D. E. Hathaway. Science 174:1182 D 17 '71
United States and Romania agree on 1971-
72 exchanges program; remarks, Depart-
ment announcement, with text of U.S. note,
L. C. Meeker. Dept State Bul 64:126-30
Ja 25 '71
Year of the dove? possible scientific ex-
change with mainland China. D. Shapley.
Science 172:457 Ap 30 '71
EXCHANGES, Commodity. See Commodity
exchanges
EXCHANGES, Educational. See Educational ex-
changes
EXCITED states. See Energy levels (quantum
mechanics)
EX-CONVICTS. See Prisoners, Discharged
EXCRETION
See also
Feces
Urine
EXCURSION boats. See Steamships and
steamboats
EXCURSIONS
Hop aboard an excursion train. Bet Hom &
Gard 49:22+ S '71
See also
Hudson River day lines
EXCURSIONS, School. See School excursions
EXEC air, inc. See Airplane service stations
EXECUTIONS and executioners
See also
Capital punishment
EXECUTIVE ability
Myth of the well-educated manager. J. S.
Livingston. bibliog f Harvard Bsns R 49:
79-89 Ja '71; Discussion. 49:29-32+ My '71
See also
Leadership
EXECUTIVE advisory bodies
Federal advisory processes: advice and dis-
content; educational policy advisers. T. E.
Cronin and N. C. Thomas. bibliog il Sci-
ence 171:771-9 F 26 '71
Gamble; making public the advisory com-
mittee report on 2,4,5-T. T. Aaronson.
il Environ 13:20-4+ S '71
Invisible bureaucracy: advisory committees.
R. W. Dietsch. New Repub 164:19-21 F 20
'71
Scientific advisory system: some observa-
tions. M. L. Perl. bibliog Science 173:1211-
15 S 24 '71
Secrecy in pollution policy. Sci N 99:434 Je
26 '71; Reply with rejoinder. L. A. Jobe.
100:52 Jl 24 '71
2,4,5-T committee: bias untested, academy
embarrassed. N. Wade. Science 173:611 Ag
13 '71
EXECUTIVE airlines
Executive airlines files for bankruptcy. Avia-
tion W 95:30 D 20 '71
EXECUTIVE bonuses. See Bonus system
EXECUTIVE departments (United States) See
United States—Executive departments
EXECUTIVE interchange program. See United
States—President's commission on person-
nel interchange
EXECUTIVE jet aviation, inc.
Executive jet CAB filing seeks to stop Pan
Am Falcon charters. C. E. Schneider.
Aviation W 95:17 Ag 30 '71
EXECUTIVE office of elder persons. See Massa-
chusetts—Executive office of elder persons
EXECUTIVE office of the president. See United
States—Executive office of the president
EXECUTIVE placement firms. See Employ-
ment agencies
EXECUTIVE power
See also
Executive privilege (government information)
Presidents—United States—Powers and duties
EXECUTIVE privilege (government informa-
tion)
Keeping secrets. New Repub 165:7-8 S 18 '71
EXECUTIVES
Accelerated generation moves into manage-
ment. J. Gooding. il Fortune 83:100-4+ Mr
'71
Bachelor executives: the bold new minority.
G. Berkwitt. il Duns 98:44-6 D '71
Brain spa for power people at Aspen in the
Rockies. E. Carpenter. Vogue 158:62 Ag
15 '71
Buck stops here: the role of the chief execu-
tive officer. il Forbes 107:47-54+ My 15 '71

EXECUTIVES—*Continued*
Business leadership: the new breed; address, March 2, 1971. W. S. Holmes. Vital Speeches 37:424-7 My 1 '71
Businessmen still feel uncertain. il Bsns W p39-40 N 13 '71
Corporation man. by A. Jay. Review Life il 71:10 O 22 '71. R. Ardrey Newsweek il 78:94+ O 25 '71. M. A. Ruby
Dilemma of product/market management. B. C. Ames. il Harvard Bsns R 49:66-74 Mr '71
Executive trends. J. Costello. See issues of Nation's business
Executives as community volunteers. D. H. Fenn, jr. il Harvard Bsns R 49:4-6+ Mr '71
Executives in ferment. G. J. Berkwitt; reply. R. S. Travis. Duns 97:11 Ap '71
Forgotten front-line manager. G. J. Berkwitt. il Duns 98:36-9 Ag '71
Forum; problems of the manager. J. D Robertson. Duns 98:73 Ag '71
Great moments & great men of American business; symposium, ed. by S. G. Slappey. Nations Bsns 59:41-5+ Ja '71
Hats worn by a company head. V. Louviere. Nations Bsns 59:24 S '71
High cost of executive divorce. T. J. Murray. il Duns 98:52-4+ O '71
How to develop multinational executives. il pors Bsns W p88+ Je 12 '71
Information specialist: from data to dollars. J. Poindexter. il Duns 93:34-7 Je '69
Lessons of leadership. See issues of Nation's business
Make way for the new organization man. M. Hanan. il Harvard Bsns R 49:128-38 Jl '71; Reply. J. D. Hobbs. 49:19+ N '71
Men who still hang on to the reins. pors Bsns W p40+ O 2 '71
New executive elite; with editorial comment. G. J. Berkwitt. Duns 98:3, 25-7 Jl '71
New man for corporate growth; development executives. T. J. Murray. il Duns 98:47-9 N '71
New youth movement; forty- to fifty-year-old chief executives. A. A. Butkus. il Duns 98:45-7 Ag '71
Old bosses bequeath new problems; incoming chief executives. il Bsns W p50-1 Ja 1 '72
Peter Drucker attacks: our top-heavy corporations; interview, ed. by T. J. Murray. P. F. Drucker. Duns 97:38-41 Ap '71
President stands alone. H. B. Henshel. Harvard Bsns R 49:37-45 S '71
Secrets of the successful general manager. J. F. McNulty. il Nations Bsns 59:42+ My '71
Spotlight. See issues of Dun's
Swap at the top. Newsweek 79:39+ Ja 3 '72
Today's executives: how they see their jobs. il U S News 71:54-6 Jl 26 '71
Top management is getting tough. G. Berkwitt. il Duns 97:44-6 My '71
Whatever happened to the organization man? R. Levy. il Duns 98:58-9 S '71
White-collar ape; excerpts from Corporation man. A. Jay. Time 98:88 S 27 '71
Why executives hate hotels; interviews with executives, ed. by J. Perham. il Duns 98:46-9 S '71
   See also
Corporations—Directors
Leadership
Negro executives
United States—President's commission on personnel interchange
Women as executives

Applications for positions
See Applications for positions

Compensation
See Executives—Salaries, allowances, etc.

Dismissal
Plight of the fired executives. T. J. Murray. Duns 97:43-5 F '71

Employment contracts
See Labor contracts

Financial counseling services
See Financial services

Health and hygiene
See Businessmen—Health and hygiene

Health programs
New fringe: T-shirts and trunks; Xerox program. il Duns 98:79 S '71

Investment activities
Cattle feeding, and lassoed investors. il Duns 98:33-7 S '71

Political activities
See Business—Political aspects

Rating
Big new move to measure managers. G. J. Berkwitt. il Duns 98:60-2+ S '71

Recreation
Executive schuss. R. Levy. il Duns 97:66-8 Mr '71
High flyers of business. R. Levy. il Duns 97:46-8 Je '71
Paddle, the new executive sport. R. Levy. il Duns 98:49-51 O '71

Recruiting
B-school grads face a tighter market. il Bsns W p 122-3+ F 27 '71

Relocation
Trauma of the transferred executive. T. J. Murray. il Duns 97:40-3 My '71

Retirement
See Retirement

Salaries, allowances, etc.
Booby traps in executive taxes; interview, ed. by G. R. Rosen. B. Grund. por Duns 97:10-12+ F '71
Compensation cafeteria for top executives. G. W. Hettenhouse. il Harvard Bsns R 49:113-19 S '71
Devaluation needn't sour that overseas plum. Bsns W p51 D 25 '71
Executive pay: the long term is where the action is; excerpt from Seventh annual study of management compensation. R. E. Sibson. il Nations Bsns 59:29-32+ N '71
For top executives: huge raises, huge cuts. il Bsns W p58-60+ Je 19 '71
How to cope with unreasonable compensation claims. R. S. Holzman. bibliog f Harvard Bsns R 49:79-81 S '71
Maybe I'm worth $5 million a year; interview. H. S. Geneen. pors Forbes 107:186-90 My 15 '71
New executive perk: loans for options. J. Perham. il Duns 97:39-41 Je '71
Pay at the top feels the freeze. Bsns W p19 Ag 28 '71
Pay pendulum swings toward cash; with table. Bsns W p 18 Ap 3 '71
Payday. Newsweek 77:86+ Mr 15 '71
Top men demand new kinds of pay. il Bsns W p65-6 Ja 23 '71
What is the chief executive worth? with table. Forbes 107:164+ My 15 '71
Who gets the most pay; roster of 737 chief executives. Forbes 107:165+ My 15 '71
   See also
Bonus system

Sports
See Executives—Recreation

Supply and demand
Is there life after forty? S. Margetts. il Duns 98:55 D '71
Not much room at the top. il Fortune 83:66 My '71
Top executive hunts for a job. M. Durham. il pors Life 70:44-50C Mr 19 '71

Training
Executive gap. G. Olmstead. il Nations Bsns 59:67-9 D '71
Executive-swapping in Europe. J. Ross-Skinner. il Duns 97:77-8+ Mr '71
Notes on corporate man. R. Todd. il Atlan 228:83-8+ O '71
Where the boss gets an MBA on the job; Pepperdine's presidential MBA program. il Bsns W p86-7 My 8 '71

EXECUTIVES as authors
Some tips for the executive author. Bsns W p79 My 29 '71
EXECUTIVES as presidential advisers. See Presidential advisers
EXECUTIVES wives
Executive wives gaining new status. C. G. Rogers. McCalls 98:39 Ag '71
When is a wife deductible? Duns 98:63 Jl '71
EXECUTORS and administrators
How to choose the executor of your will. Suc Farm 69:12 My '71
How to pick an executor for your estate. M. Daly. Bet Hom & Gard 49:26 O '71
EXEMPTION from taxation. See Taxation, Exemption from

EXERCISE

A-Z guide to fitness. il Vogue 158:138-41 O 1 '71

All about backaches: latest advice from a specialist; interview. H. L. Feffer. il por U S News 71:74-8 S 20 '71; Same abr. Read Digest 99:203-4+ D '71

Art of aerobics. il por Time 97:60 Mr 8 '71

Art of looking beautiful; excerpts from Joan Crawford: my way of life. J. Crawford. il pors McCalls 98:55-7+ Jl '71

Bare hug treatment. il Harp Baz 104:88-9 Je '71

Be fit for life! condensation. K. Rodahl. il Read Digest 98:140-8 My '71

Beauty: how to get and keep your body great. il Mlle 73:152-3 My '71

Beauty sense and nonsense; trimming thighs. Harp Baz 104:26 Ap '71

Body battle: five models. il Seventeen 30:126-9 S '71

Exercise: the water ways. il Vogue 157:170-1 My '71

Exercises for the two of you; interview. ed. by S. Obre. B. Toomey and M. Toomey. il pors Ladies Home J 88:90-1 Ap '71

Exercises that give your face a lift. S. Lindsay. il House B 113:17-18 Ja '71

Exercising: which type is best for you? il Good H 173:225 N '71

Fitness forever. W. R. Guild. Vogue 157:172-3 My '71

Fitness program for overweight teen-agers; excerpts from The handbook of adolescence: a complete medical guide. M. J. Gersh and I. F. Litt. il Parents Mag 46:50-1+ Ag '71

For everyone bent on exercise; a survey of systems. Vogue 158:150 S 1 '71

Four-minute exercise plan: the pose that refreshes; Sanasession. Vogue 158:28 O 15 '71

Fundamentals of fitness. P. Van Wagenen. il Parents Mag 46:84-7 S; 46 O '71

GH's summer diet & exercise plan. R. H. Smithies. il Good H 173:112-14 Jl '71

Getting your hunting gear in shape. W. Davis. il Mech Illus 67:83+ Ag '71

Head start on the road to physical fitness as set forth by Larry Lorence. il Harp Baz 104:25 Jl '71

How to improve your figure in two weeks. il Redbook 136:94-7+ Mr '71

How to make your middle little. il Seventeen 29:220-1 Ag '70

How to stop dieting and start living, moving, and eating. il pors Mlle 72:126-30 Ja '71

Indoor exercises to keep you fit this winter. C. Atlas. il Mech Illus 67:53-5 D '71

Kounovsky secret of lifetime fitness; excerpt from Joy of feeling fit. il McCalls 98:72-5+ My '71

Lexercises: the shorts subject. il Vogue 157:52 Ap 1 '71

Miss Craig's face-saving exercises, by M. Craig. Review
 Vogue 157:12 Ja 15 '71

Movement: ballet exercises. E. Villella. il pors Harp Baz 104:76-7 Ap '71

Play and stay fit. F. Johnson. il Parents Mag 46:70-3 N '71

Preventing a second heart attack. il Sci Digest 69:58-9 Je '71

Princess Birgitta's royal Swedish shape-up; excerpts from Spänsta med Birgitta. Princess Birgitta. il pors Ladies Home J 88:36 Ja '71

Pulse test, new way to fitness, heart rated exercises I. E. Morehouse. il Read Digest 99:77-80 O '71

Spring shapeup for summer. C. Bartel. il Am Home 74:14+ Ap '71

Swimnastics. E. R. Charles. il Parents Mag 46:67-8+ Jl '71

T'ai Chi Ch'uan; Chinese health exercise. il Vogue 158:146-7 N 1 '71

Testament of a Samurai; tr. by M. Gallagher. Y. Mishima. il pors Sports Illus 34:24-7 Ja 11 '71

Tone up the swimming-pool way; Conrad's water exercises. C. Mitchell. il Read Digest 99:143-5 Ag '71

Travel light, travel pretty: exercise, relax. il Seventeen 30:124 Ap '71

What a wonderful beauty idea; definition, causes, and control of cellulite. Harp Baz 104:50 F; 42 Mr '71

You don't have to look old. C. Myers. Harp Baz 104:6 Jl '71
 See also
Gymnastics

EXERCISE, Yoga. See Yoga

EXERCISING equipment

Beware those quick-reducing gadgets. J. Carper. Read Digest 99:60-3 S '71

Budget exercise bike. V. Vogel. il Mech Illus 67:115 S '71

Cycle-type exercisers. il Consumer Rep 36:378-83 Je '71

Exerciser for land & sea. il Mech Illus 67:62 Ja '71

This dumbbell has a mind of its own. P. Wahl. il Pop Sci 199:63 Jl '71

EXERCISING machines. See Exercising equipment

EXHAUST control devices (motor vehicles)
 See Motor vehicles—Pollution control devices

EXHAUST gases. See Carbon monoxide

EXHAUST systems
 See also
Automobile engines—Exhaust

EXHIBITION buildings

LeBourget Paris show facilities expanded. D. E. Fink. Aviation W 96:18-19 Ja 10 '72
 See also
Chicago—McCormick Place
Pavilions

EXHIBITIONISM

Why some women prefer daring fashions. J. Brothers. Good H 173:58+ Jl '71

EXHIBITIONS

Black expo comes of age. il Ebony 27:64-8+ D '71

Doing business at the Canton trade fair. il Bsns W p41-2 O 23 '71

Jackson's expo; Black Expo trade fair. il por Newsweek 78:24 O 4 '71

1972 world travel calendar; comp. by F. Shemanski. Sat R 55:43-7 Ja 1 '72

Stampede to Canton; trade fair. il Newsweek 78:86 N 29 '71

Trading is brisk at the Canton fair. G. Ringwald. il Bsns W p76-8 O 30 '71

U.S. companies visit by proxy; Canton trade fair. Bsns W p44 D 4 '71
 See also subhead Exhibitions under various subjects, e.g. Photography—Exhibitions

EXHIBITIONS, Traveling

Historymobile. H. M. Stock. Parks & Rec 6:25+ Jl '71

National panorama of conservation. R. Pardo. il Am For 77:41 Ja '71

Paper making history from the ancient Chinese to Ben Franklin and modern times; a Library of Congress traveling exhibit. K. V. Hostick. Hobbies 75:140 F '71

EXHIBITS
 See also special types of exhibits, e.g. Library exhibits

EXILES

Rebel with a country: V. Tarsis. il Newsweek 77:6 Je 28 '71
 See also
Emigrés

EX-IM bank. See Export-Import bank of the United States of America

EXISTENCE of God. See God—Proof

EXISTENTIALISM in literature

Christ and the existential imagination. C. Miller. Chr Today 16:12+ O 22 '71

EX-NUNS, priests, etc.

First step on the outside; Next step, a non-profit corporation aids transition. R. Larsen. Chr Cent 88:538-41 Ap 28 '71

Parachuting into secularland. Chr Cent 88:575 My 5 '71

Pope Clement XV; M. Collin of Clémery, France, claimant of the papal tiara. il por Time 97:66 Mr 15 '71
 See also
Marriage of priests

EXOBIOLOGY. See Life on other planets

EXODUS house. See Narcotic addicts—Rehabilitation

EXORBITANT price; story. See Moravia, A.

EXPANDING universe. See Universe

EXPANSION, House. See Houses, Remodeled

EXPEDITIONS, Scientific. See Scientific expeditions

EXPENDITURES, Municipal. See Municipal finance

EXPENDITURES, State. See State finance

EXPENSE accounts (business)

Explain why you get up in the morning: answer to accusation of writing my regular column while traveling for government at the taxpayers' expense. W. F. Buckley, jr. Nat R 23:103 Ja 26 '71

New ruling on travel expenses. U S News 71:72 S 27 '71

EXPERIENCE (religion)
Sir Alister Hardy: science and religious experiences. D. Cohen. il por Sci Digest 70: 18-23 S '71
    See also
Conversion
EXPERIMENTAL airplanes; Experimental films; etc. See Airplanes, Experimental; Films, Experimental, etc.
EXPERIMENTAL art. See Art, Modern
EXPERIMENTAL college education. See College education, Experimental
EXPERIMENTAL design
Cloud seeding experiments: possible bias. S. M. Stigler. bibliog Science 173:850 Ag 27 '71
EXPERIMENTAL education. See Education, Experimental
EXPERIMENTAL embryology. See Embryology, Experimental
EXPERIMENTAL forests. See Forestry research
EXPERIMENTAL safety vehicles. See Automobiles, Experimental
EXPERIMENTAL schools. See Schools, Experimental
EXPERIMENTAL teacher education. See Teachers—Education
EXPERIMENTATION on man. See Medical research—Experimentation on man
EXPERTISING in art. See Art—Expertising
EXPLORATION, Underwater. See Underwater exploration
EXPLORATIONS
    See also
America—Discovery and exploration
EXPLORERS, Spanish
That August third; Columbus departs Spain in 1492. G. de Zéndegui. il Américas 23:S3-6 O '71
    See also
Vázquez de Coronado, F.
EXPLORING family school, El Cajon, Calif. See Schools, Experimental
EXPLOSIONS
Nightmare in Laurel. J. H. Winchester. il Read Digest 99:82-6 Jl '71
    See also
Coal mines and mining—Accidents and explosions
EXPLOSIONS, Tanker. See Tank ships
EXPLOSIVES
    See also
Nitroglycerin
EXPORT and import controls. See Foreign trade regulation
EXPORT controls
Kama truck project gets rolling; export license issued to Swindell-Dressler co. il Bsns W p32 Ag 14 '71
Rules ease on trade with Russia. il Bsns W p94-6 Je 12 '71
EXPORT credit
Department gives views on export finance legislation; statement, May 26, 1971. P. H. Trezise Dept State Bul 64:459-60 Mr 29 '71
EXPORT-import bank of the United States of America
Department gives views on Eximbank legislation; statement, March 9, 1971. P. H. Trezise. Dept State Bul 64:459-60 Mr 29 '71
Department gives views on export finance legislation; statement, May 26, 1971. P. H. Trezise. Dept State Bul 65:27-8 Jl 5 '71
Helping U.S. business sell more abroad; interview. H. Kearns. il por U S News 71:54-8 Jl 19 '71
LAN resists government on purchasing Soviet jets. L. Doty. Aviation W 95:28-9 S 27 '71
World bank craves a slice of Ex-Im's pie. il Bsns W p28 F 13 '71
EXPORT licenses. See Export controls
EXPORT trade
Export or die. il Forbes 108:15 S 1 '71
Have-nots and the export dilemma. R. L. Tobin. Sat R 54:16 Ag 21 '71
Increases in shipping weights of total U.S. exports and imports; tables. Aviation W 96:39 Ja 10 '72
It's time for some plain talk about trade. W. E. Swegle. Suc Farm 69:no5 L8-9 Mr '71
New view: build here and export. il Bsns W p29-30 Ja 1 '72
U.S. cotton heads overseas. il Bsns W p 142 My 15 '71
What's the future of farm exports? W. E. Swegle. il Suc Farm 69:G12-13 Ap '71
Will the green revolution ruin our export markets? W. Swegle. il Suc Farm 69:no3 B4-5 F '71

You, too, can sell abroad; projects for increasing exports. il Nations Bsns 59:84-6 S '71
Your stake in farm exports. W. E. Swegle. il Suc Farm 69:no2 B2-3 F '71
    See also subhead Commerce under names of countries, e.g. Japan—Commerce

Federal aid
Exporters scurry for the new tax break; domestic international sales corporations. Bsns W p22-3 Ja 1 '72
Tax break to boost the export drive; domestic international sales corporations. Bsns W p23 O 9 '71
EXPOSITIONS. See Exhibitions
EXPOSURE. See Photography—Exposure
EXPOSURE calculators. See Photography—Exposure
EXPOSURE meters
Ed Scully on color. E. Scully. Mod Phot 35: 53+ Jl '71
How to outwit built-in meter barriers. C. W. Kennedy. il Pop Phot 68:56+ My '71
1971 exposure meter guide; comp. by D. L. Miller. Mod Phot 35:74-5 Jl '71
Test your meter on TV. B. Bodenstein and J. Schneider. il Mod Phot 35:44 Jl '71
Through-lens meters: great, but . . . N. Goldberg. il Pop Phot 68:88-90+ My '71
View from Kramer; Sinarsix meter. A. Kramer. il Mod Phot 35:22+ Jl '71
Wolfman on printing; determining enlarging exposures with integration meters. A. Wolfman. il Mod Phot 36:70+ Ja '72

History
Camera collector; actinometers and other ingenious devices. J. Schneider. il Mod Phot 36:14+ Ja '72
L'EXPRESS (periodical) See Periodicals—France
EXPRESS companies
    See also
American express company
Wells Fargo express company
EXPRESS highways
Fight quickens over city highways. M. Smith. McCalls 99:43 D '71
Folly of our superhighway system; excerpt from Superhighway-superhoax. H. Leavitt. Read Digest 98:61-5 F '71
How the interstate changed the face of the Nation. J. Cameron. il Fortune 84:78-81+ Jl '71
I drove our first coast-to-coast interstate, the campers' expressway. D. Francis. il Pop Sci 198:78-9+ Mr '71
Interstate driving. M. Lamm. il Pop Mech 135:82-7 Je '71

Federal aid
Can we bust the highway trust? D. Hayes. il por Sat R 54:48-53 Je 5 '71; Discussion. 54:58 S 4 '71
Ecologists attack the Highway trust fund. il Bsns W p86-7 D 11 '71
Helping hand for smaller towns. il U S News 71:95 N 22 '71
Highway lobby in ambush. B. Kelley. Nation 213:496-500 N 15 '71
Highway trust fund, expressway to disaster. Audubon 73:94-5 Ja '71
Priorities or trust funds? B. Kelley and R. Hebert Nation 212:497-500 Ap 19 '71
Which direction for highway taxes? uses for highway trust fund. il Sr Schol 98:11-13 F 8 '71

Connecticut
How we resolved a highway-park conflict; Manchester, Conn. W. D. O'Neill. il Am City 86:65 Ag '71
Overlooked cloverleaf: Manchester compromise to keep recreational facilities. il Time 98:30 Ag 23 '71

Hawaii
Above Honolulu, a jungle valley with a freeway in its future: il Sunset 147:29-30 N '71

New York (state)
Rocky's road; proposed Hudson River expressway. J. L. Sax. il Am Heritage 22:78-83+ F '71

Pennsylvania
Crosstown is dead, long live the crosstown; Philadelphia's controversial expressway. M. Osborn; D. S. Brown; M. Verman. il Arch Forum 135:38-45 O '71

Texas
Parting shots: some Texas folks suggest where a hated superhighway can go. il Life 71:66-7 Ag 27 '71

EX-PRIESTS. See Ex-nuns, priests, etc.
EXPROPRIATION. See Eminent domain (international law)
EXTENSION cords. See Electric cords
EXTENSION education
  See also
  Telephone in education
  University extension
EXTERIOR mural painting and decoration. See Mural painting and decoration, Exterior
EXTERMINATION of cockroaches. See Cockroach control
EXTERMINATORS, Pest. See Pest control operators
EXTERNAL combustion engines. See Gas and oil engines
EXTINCT birds. See Birds, Extinct
EXTINCTION of animals. See Animals, Extinct
EXTORTION
  What is the business of organized crime? T. C. Schelling. bibliog f Am Scholar 40:643-53 Aut '71
  See also
  Trials (extortion)
EXTRACURRICULAR activities. See Student activities
EXTRA-marital relationships. See Sexual ethics
EXTRASENSORY perception
  Dollars may flow from the sixth sense; precognition. J. Mihalasky and others. Nations Bsns 59:64+ Ap '71
  ESP is never having to say you're psychic. J. Marks. Mlle 73:138-9+ Je '71
  Parting shots: signals from inner space. por Life 71:68 Jl 2 '71
  Party games to test your ESP; excerpts from Test your ESP. M. Ebon. il Ladies Home J 88:78+ My '71
  White tracks on the moon; report on an unofficial experiment. C. Leinster. il por Life 70:29 F 26 '71
EXTRATERRESTRIAL life. See Life on other planets
EXTRAVEHICULAR activity. See Space flight —Manned flights—Extravehicular activity
EXTRAVEHICULAR activity on the moon. See Space flight to the moon—Manned flights—Extravehicular activity
EXTREMISM. See Radicalism
EYAL-GILADI, Hefzibah. See Kochav, S. jt. auth.
EYE
  See also
  Crystalline lens
  Iris (eye)
  Optic nerve
  Optic thalamus
  Retina
  Sight
  Vitreous humor

  #### Accommodation and refraction
  Light adaptation in the rat retina: evidence for two receptor mechanisms. D. G. Green. bibliog il Science 174:598-600 N 5 '71
  Stereoscopic depth aftereffect produced without monocular cues. bibliog il Science 171:286-8 Ja 22 '71

  #### Care and hygiene
  How you can protect your children's eyes. A. J. Snider. il Sci Digest 71:68 Ja '72

  #### Diseases and hygiene
  Children's eyes. L. W. Sauer. PTA Mag 65:27-8 F '71
  When the eyes don't have it. W. A. Nolen. McCalls 99:27 N '71
  See also
  Glaucoma
  Myopia
  Strabismus

  #### Examination
  Why Jenny can't see (very much) W. Boroson. il N Y Times Mag p91+ D 5 '71; Reply. L. O. Aasen. p 15 D 26 '71

  #### Movements
  Eye-head coordination in monkeys: evidence for centrally patterned organization. E. Bizzi and others. bibliog il Science 173:452-4 Jl 30 '71
  Eye movements and visual perception. D. Noton and L. Stark. il Sci Am 224:34-43 bibliog (p 136) Je '71
  Scanpaths in eye movements during pattern perception. D. Noton and L. Stark. bibliog il Science 171:308-11 Ja 22 '71; Reply with rejoinder. H. H. Spitz. 173:753 Ag 20 '71

Superior colliculus cell responses related to eye movements in awake monkeys. R. H. Wurtz and M. E. Goldberg. bibliog il Science 171:82-4 Ja 8 '71

  #### Protection
  See also
  Eyeglasses

  #### Surgery
  New cataract surgery. A. J. Snider. Sci Digest 69:60 Ap '71
  One-day surgery for cataracts. il Bsns W p32 D 25 '71

  #### Transplantation
  Eye transplants: what's stopping them? A. J. Snider. il Sci Digest 70:70 O '71

  #### Wounds and injuries
  What to do if you get something in an eye. Good H 172:178 Je '71
EYE (animals)
  See also
  Sight (animals)
EYE (arthropods)
  See also
  Eye (insects)
EYE (crustaceans)
  Limulus lateral eye: properties of receptor units in the unexcised eye. R. B. Barlow, jr. and E. Kaplan. bibliog il Science 174:1027-9 D 3 '71
EYE (fishes)
  Receptive field mechanism in the vertebrate retina. K. I. Naka. bibliog il Science 171:691-3 F 19 '71
EYE (insects)
  Compound eyes: localization of two color receptors in the same ommatidium. M. I. Mote and T. H. Goldsmith. bibliog il Science 171:1254-5 Mr 26 '71
  Insect photoreceptor: an internal ocellus is present in sphinx moths. J. L. Eaton. bibliog il Science 173:822-3 Ag 27 '71
  On-transient of insect electroretinogram: its cellular origin. A. A. Alawi and W. L. Pak. bibliog il Science 172:1055-7 Je 4 '71
EYE banks
  Thanks for your eyes. G. Naismith. Read Digest 98:33-4+ Mr '71
EYE cups. See Eyecups
EYE donors
  Thanks for your eyes. G. Naismith. Read Digest 98:33-4+ Mr '71
EYE make-up. See Make-up
EYE movements. See Eye—Movements
EYEBROW make-up. See Make-up
EYEBROWS
  Beautiful brow. il Ladies Home J 88:26 My '71
EYECUPS
  Eye cups; collection. E. R. Plunkett. bibliog il Hobbies 76:118-19 Mr '71
EYEGLASSES
  FDA prescribes safer eyeglasses. Consumer Rep 36:526 S '71
  Facts about shatter-resistant lenses for eyeglasses. Good H 172:158-9 F '71
  See also
  Contact lenses
  Sun glasses
EYELASHES, Artificial
  About false eyelashes. il Ladies Home J 88:28 Mr '71
EYESIGHT. See Sight
EYRE, Charles F.
  Re: how segregation ended in the early seventies. Nat R 23:1303-4 N 19 '71
EYRING, Henry
  Add six years to your life. il Sci Digest 70:76-7 D '71 •
EYTON, J. Ronald
  Mini drill press for hobbyists. il Pop Mech 135:162-3 Mr '71

F

F. Jasmine Addams; musical comedy. See Musical comedies, revues, etc.—Criticisms, plots, etc.
F-14 (airplane) See Airplanes, Military—United States
FAA. See United States—Federal aviation administration
FAO. See Food and agriculture organization of the United Nations

F. A. O. Schwarz. See Schwarz, F. A. O. (firm)

FAR (federal aviation regulations) See United States—Federal aviation administration

FAS. See Federation of American scientists

FAS international, inc.
Home study school tries for better grades. il Bsns W p46-7 Ag 28 '71; Reply. M. W. Schober. p5 O 23 '71
Writing wrongs. il Time 98:70 S 20 '71

FBI. See United States—Federal bureau of investigation

FBI, Friends of the. See Friends of the FBI inc.

FBO. See Fixed base operators

FCC. See United States—Federal communications commission; Washington, D.C. Federal city college

FDA. See United States—Food and drug administration

FDIC. See Federal deposit insurance corporation

FET (field effect transistors) See Transistors

FHA. See United States—Federal housing administration

FID. See International federation for documentation

FLQ. See Front for the liberation of Quebec

FM receivers. See Radio receivers—Frequency modulation receivers

FMCS. See United States—Federal mediation and conciliation service

FNMA. See Federal national mortgage association

FNS. See Frontier nursing service

FPC. See Fish protein concentrate; United States—Federal power commission

FTA. See Future teachers of America

FTC. See United States—Federal trade commission

FABBRI, Roberto
Manta pup. il Sea Front 17:332-4 N '71

FABER, M. D.
Falstaff behind the arras. bibliog Am Imago 27:197-225 Fall '70
Othello: the justice of it pleases. bibliog Am Imago 28:228-46 Fall '71

FABIO, Rose Marie
Hi, mom, what's for lunch? See issues of Parents' magazine & better family living

FABRE, François
Beast of Gévaudan. C. H. D. Clarke. bibliog Natur Hist 80:44-51+ Ap '71 *

FABRI, Ralph
Individual realist: Luigi Lucioni. il por Am Artist 35:26-31+ O '71
Selecting the right watercolor paper. il Am Artist 35:28-32+ Ag '71

FABRIC collage. See Collage

FABRIC wall coverings. See Wall coverings

FABRICS. See Textile fabrics

FABRY'S disease. See Angiokeratoma

FABULOUS Magicians (basketball) See Basketball players

FABULOUS Miss Marie; drama. See Bullins, E.

FACE
See also
Mouth
Physiognomy

FACE exercises. See Exercise

FACE lifting. See Surgery, Plastic

FACE masks. See Masks (for the face)

FACE peeling, Chemical. See Chemosurgery

FACIAL exercises. See Exercise

FACIALS. See Skin—Care and hygiene

FACKRE, Gabriel
Going east: neomysticism and Christian faith. il Chr Cent 88:457-61 Ap 14 '71

FACSIMILE transmission
Facsimile via telephone. D. L. Heiserman. il Electr World 86:35-8 D '71

FACSIMILES of rare books. See Book rarities—Facsimiles

FACT-finding commissions. See Commissions of inquiry

FACTORIES
See also
Art in factories
Automobile factories

Design
Crisscrossed steel frame; British electronics plant. il Arch Forum 134:40-1 Ap '71
Giant fume hood; Rosenthal glass factory, Amberg, Germany. il Arch Forum 134:26-9 Ap '71

Manufacturing building for Skil corporation, Wheeling, Illinois. il Arch Rec 149:96-7 My '71
Why not build factories people can enjoy? il Arch Rec 150:91-7 Jl '71

Equipment
Mess in the factory. G. J. Berkwitt. il Duns 97:56-7+ Je '71

Location
See Location in business and industry

Pollution
Corporate polluter learns the hard way; with editorial comment. il Bsns W p52-6, 94 F 6 '71
See also
Paper mills—Pollution
Steel works—Pollution

FACTORS
Factors borrow a touch of class; acquisition by commercial banks. il Bsns W p88-9 Mr 6 '71
Talcott lends aid and wins a factor; Mill factors corp. Bsns W p 19 My 29 '71

FACTORY and trade waste. See Trade waste

FACTORY management
Anachronistic factory. W. Skinner. bibliog f il Harvard Bsns R 49:61-70 Ja '71
Mess in the factory. G. J. Berkwitt. il Duns 97:56-7+ Je '71

FACTORY produced houses. See Houses, Prefabricated

FACULTY meetings. See Teachers meetings

FADER, Daniel
Chilblains and strong tea on dark afternoons. il Library J 96:1330-2 Ap 15 '71

FADS
Jesus Christ supersell. Newsweek 78:97 N 8 '71
Radical chic is dead. S. Alsop. Read Digest 98:103-4 F '71
Time to talk of fads and fruit flies. il Bsns W p70 Ag 28 '71
See also
Food fads

FAEROE ISLANDS. See Faroe Islands

FAESSLER, Shirley
. Can I count you in? story. Atlan 229:63-9 Ja '72

FAGAN, Dennis
An, all things considered, not, realistically speaking, immodest proposal. Nat R 23:1115 O 8 '71
Your future in liberalism. Nat R 23:871 Ag 10 '71

FAGAN, Edward R.
Individualizing the study of English. Engl J 60:236-41+ F '71
Unified English: salvaging the disaffected. bibliog f Clear House 45:259-64 Ja '71

FAGER, Charles E.
Movies (title varies) (cont) Chr Cent 88:206, 389, 571-2, 756 F 10, Mr 24, My 5, Je 16 '71
Records (title varies) (cont) Chr Cent 88:302, 356, 1094 Mr 3, 17, S 15 '71
(ed) See Maddox, L. Lester Maddox: showman and radical
(ed) See Sullivan, G. A. jr. Judge George Sullivan: lawbreaker for peace

FAGERSTROM, Stan
Bugging is more fun. il Outdoor Life 147:102-3+ Ap '71
Late season largemouth. il por Field & S 76:50-1+ S '71

FAGIN, Larry
Comment. P. Schjeldahl. Poetry 117:267-9 Ja '71 *

FAHERTY, William Barnaby
Writers' conferences and literary pilgrimages. il Writers Digest 51:34-8 My '71

FAHEY, Joseph J.
Toward a theology of peace. il Cath World 213:64-8 My '71

FAHEY, Michael A.
Ecumenists meet in Dublin. America 125:141-3 S 11 '71
Hans Küng's infallible? Europe's theologians join the debate. America 124:429-31 Ap 24 '71

FAHLSTRÖM, Öyvind
Crisis game. R. Hughes. il por Time 97:64-5+ Ap 12 '71 *

FAHNESTOCK, Stephen, and Rich, Alexander
Ribosome-catalyzed polyester formation. bibliog il Science 173:340-3 Jl 23 '71

FAHY, Everett
Opening it up; interview. New Yorker 47:45-7 N 13 '71

FAILURE (psychology)
Roles, goals, and failure. W. Glasser. il Todays
Ed 60:20-1+ O '71
Winning and losing in life: a survey of
opinions about causes. H. J. Wahler. bib-
liog Ment Hy 55:91-5 Ja '71
FAILURE to assist in emergencies. See As-
sistance in emergencies
FAILURES in business. See Business failures
FAINLIGHT, Ruth
Silence; poem. New Yorker 47:28 Je 19 '71
FAIR, Charles
M. Licinius Crassus, losers; excerpt from
From the jaws of victory. il Horizon 13:
112-17 Spr '71
Trade winds; interview, ed. by C. Amory.
Sat R 54:12 Ag 14 '71
FAIR credit reporting act. See Credit—Regula-
tion
FAIRBANK, John King
Mr Nixon's rewards. por Newsweek 78:18
Jl 26 '71
Probing the Chinese mind. por U S News 71:
80-1 S 6 '71
FAIRBANKS, David N. F.
Are you shooting your hearing? il Outdoor
Life 148:57-9+ O '71
FAIRBANKS, Douglas
Doug Fairbanks: superstar of the silents.
R. Schickel. il pors Am Heritage 23:4-12+
D '71 *
FAIRBRIDGE, Rhodes W.
Sahara Desert ice cap: with biographical
sketch. il Natur Hist 80:5, 66-73 Je '71
FAIRCHILD camera and instrument corpora-
tion
Fairchild subsidiary to buy assets, resume
Swearingen production. Aviation W 95:22
N 8 '71
Manager who works with Navajos. il por
Bsns W p62 Mr 6 '71
Navajos trade hogans for air-conditioning:
Shiprock housing project. il Bsns W p 100+
O 23 '71
Recession cools Fairchild's recovery. il Bsns
W p80-1+ Ja 30 '71
Semiconductor market growth predicted. il
Aviation W 95:15 D 27 '71
FAIRCHILD Hiller corporation
Fairchild Hiller proposes giant satcom. Avia-
tion W 94:19 Mr 22 '71
FAIRFAX, James A.
Marine combat artist. il pors Ebony 26:104-
6+ My '71 *
FAIRFAX COUNTY, Va.

Housing
Fairfax County, experiment. New Repub
165:11 Jl 24 '71

Parks and reserves
We blew our cool but saved a woods: Burl-
ing tract. il Nat Wildlife 9:32-5 Ap '71
FAIRFIELD fund, Inc. See Investment trusts
FAIRHURST, William A. and East, Ben
Cloud in the big sky. il Outdoor Life 148:31-
3+ Jl '71
FAIRNESS doctrine (television) See Television
laws and regulations
FAIRS
Come to the fair. J. Beatty, jr. il Redbook
137:87-90 Jl '71
Getting together in Baltimore. Nation 213:
356-7 O 18 '71
Walk-in: when man-space becomes play-
space. H. Junker. il Vogue 157:158 Mr 1 '71
See also
Agricultural exhibitions
Bazaars, Charitable
Book fairs
Exhibitions
FAIRSERVIS, Walter A. Jr
Costumes of the East; excerpt, with bio-
graphical sketch. il Natur Hist 80:2, 28-37
N '71
FAIRY penguins. See Penguins
FAIRY plays
Snow White and Rose Red; dramatization of
a fairy tale. G. R. Creegan. Plays 30:74-6
F '71
FAIRY tales
Old and new sexual messages in fairy tales.
D. Wolkstein. il Wilson Lib Bul 46:163-6 O
'71
FAIRY terns. See Terns
FAISAL, king of Saudi Arabia. See Feisal
FAITH
Believe what you believe, excerpt from God
at large. C. Walsh. Chr Cent 88:308 Mr 10
'71
Camouflaged taboos; skepticism toward re-
ligious belief. Chr Today 15:21 Jl 2 '71

Faith for tomorrow. J. B. Healey. America
125:550-3 D 25 '71
Faith of a writer; remarks, December 2,
1971. E. B. White. Pub W 200:29 D 6 '71
How I rediscovered my faith in prayer. Mrs
M. Evers. por Ladies Home J 88:106+ S '71
Layman and his faith. L. N. Bell. See issues
of Christianity today
Survival of dogma, by A. Dulles. Review
Commonweal 95:45-7 O 8 '71. G. MacRae
See also
Hope
Trust in God
Truth
FAITH cure
Beware the commercialized faith healers. O.
K. Armstrong. Read Digest 98:179-80+ Je
'71
Miracles at Lourdes? il Newsweek 78:48-9
Ag 9 '71
My search for the Holy Grail. J. Cottrell. il
Ladies Home J 88:58+ Ap '71
See also
Medicine, Magic, mystic, etc.
FAITH healing. See Faith cure
FAKE fur. See Fur, Artificial
FAKINOS, Aris
Before the colonels. S. Rousseas. Nation 212:
729-30 Je 7 '71
FALAFEL. See Cookery, Middle Eastern
FALCO, Louis
Innovator for tomorrow. P. M. Shapiro. il
pors Dance Mag 45:62-5 F '71 *
Louis Falco co. of featured dancers, ANTA
theater, NYC. T. Borek. Dance Mag 45:
95 Ap '71 *
FALCONER, Raymond E.
Ways of the wind; with biographical sketch.
il Cons 26:22-7+, 40 D '71
FALCONRY
Clutch of the falconer. D. Amadon. il Natur
Hist 80:28-30 Mr '71
School for winged fury. J. Graham. il Sci Di-
gest 69:45-51 Mr '71
FALCONS
Clutch of the falconer. D. Amadon. il Natur
Hist 80:28-30 Mr '71
Peregrine demise. il Cons 25:33 Ap '71
FALES, D. Carver
Evolution islands. il Sci Digest 69:16-21 F
'71
FALES, Dan
Fishfinders. il Motor B & S 127:68-71+ My
'71
FALES, Edward D. Jr
How to steer clear! il Pop Mech 136:53-6+
Jl '71
10 driving tips that could save your life. il
Pop Mech 135:69-73+ Ap '71
FALK, John R.
Duck dog in the uplands. il Field & S
76:156+ S '71
Prescription for pointers. il Field & S 75:
182+ F '71
FALK, Peter
Mutt for all seasons. por Time 98:64+ D 13
'71 *
FALK, Richard A.
Why impeachment. New Repub 164:13-14 My
1 '71
about
POWs and the professor. W. F. Buckley, jr.
Nat R 23:828 Jl 27 '71 *
FALK, Ruth B.
Innovations in college mental health. Ment
Hy 55:451-5 O '71
FALKOWSKI, M. Lee
Million words of practice writing; with bio-
graphical sketch. Writer 84:23-5 Mr '71
FALL. See Autumn
FALLA, Manuel de
Falla on Wagner; tr. by F. V. Grunfeld
and J. Grunfeld. por Opera N 35:24-6 Ap 3
'71
FALLACI, Oriana
(ed) See Fonda, J. Jane Fonda: I'm coming
into focus
(ed) See Mastroianni, M. X ray of a man
FALLON, Pierre
Church leaders prick Europeans' consciences
over Pakistan tragedy. A. Woodrow. Chr
Cent 88:912 Jl 28 '71 *
FALLOUT, Radioactive. See Radioactive fall-
out
FALLOUT shelters. See Atomic bomb shelters
FALSE arrest. See Arrest
FALSE eyelashes. See Eyelashes, Artificial
FALSE faces, Indian. See Indians of North
America—Masks
FALSE teeth. See Teeth, Artificial
FALSTAFF (literary character) See Shake-
speare, W.—Characters

FALTER, Mary Elizabeth
Notes of a happy housekeeper. See issues of House & garden incorporating Living for young homemakers

FALTERMAYER, Edmund K.
Eye on the environment. Life 71:21 O 1; 20B O 29 '71
Let's break the go-to-college lockstep. Read Digest 98:154-7 F '71
What we know about marijuana, so far. il Fortune 83:96-8+ Mr '71

FAME
See also
Celebrities

FAMILY
American family; symposium; ed. by P. Coffin. il Look 35:31-40+ Ja 26 '71
Families against the city and The uses of disorder, by R. Sennett. Reviews
Commentary 51:86-90 My '71. M. Dubofsky
Family is out of fashion. A. R. Rolphe. il por N Y Times Mag p 10-11+ Ag 15 '71; Discussion. p90+ S 12; 9 O 13 '71
Family systems in the 1970's: analysis, policies, and programs; address, April 1971, with questions and answers. M. B. Sussman. bibliog f Ann Am Acad 396:40-56 Jl '71
Is the family obsolete? interviews. ed. by J. Kronenberger. Look 35:35-6 Ja 26 '71
Odd couples. J. H. Plumb. il Horizon 13:60-1 Spr '71
Preserving the species. R. Cancro. Sat R 54:50-1 Mr 6 '71
Quality living and quality learning for all Americans: promise and process; excerpts from address, May 1971. P. B. Price. PTA Mag 65:16-18+ Je '71
See also
Children
Desertion and non-support
Divorce
Eugenics
Family life
Fathers
Grandparents
Mothers
Wives

Poetry
Prayer for the great family. G. Snyder. il Look 35:54-9 Ja 26 '71

FAMILY, Size of
Hallelujah the pill? R. B. Dixon. il Trans-Action 8:44-9+ N '70
My answer to genocide. D. Gregory. il pors Ebony 26:66-70+ O '71; Discussion. 27:15-17 D '71
Should you have another baby? R. Roesch. Read Digest 98:111-13 My '71
What is the right number of children? A. Rosenfeld. il Life 71:97+ D 17 '71

FAMILY assistance plan. See Public welfare—United States

FAMILY budget. See Budget, Household

FAMILY businesses. See Family corporations

FAMILY camping. See Camping

FAMILY corporations
Caught in a closely held company. H. Smith, pseud. Duns 98:57-8 D '71
Coming in with dad; views of top executives, ed. by H. Altman. il Nations Bsns 59:58-60 Je '71
Conflicts that plague family businesses. H. Levinson. Harvard Bsns R 49:90-8 Mr '71; Reply. J. R. Biltekoff. 49:28+ Jl '71
Oedipus hex. il Time 97:71-2 Mr 22 '71

FAMILY finance. See Domestic finance

FAMILY group therapy. See Family psychotherapy

FAMILY history. See Genealogy

FAMILY law. See Domestic relations

FAMILY life
American family; symposium; ed. by P. Coffin. il Look 35:21-40+ Ja 26 '71
Family under siege; Emmethew Jackson family. W. B. Furlong. il pors Good H 172:106-7+ Ap '71
"I am a maid, and what do I know?" a Negro servant's view of a white family. R. Coles. Atlan 228:64-8 Ag '71
Lifestyle. il pors Am Home 74:12+ O '71
Little privacy is a lovely thing. D. H. Lund. il Parents Mag 46:40-1+ Je '71
My house is paper, glued with love; excerpt from Paper house. F. Mallet-Joris. il por Vogue 157:82-3 Mr 15 '71
What makes a happy family. B. Spock. il Redbook 138:60+ N '71
See also
Children
Marriage counseling
Mothers-in-law
Parent-child relationship

Anecdotes, facetiae, satire, etc.
Man next door. B. Hillis. Bet Hom & Gard 49:168 Ap '71
Ted Straight: man on the way up. W. B. Park. il Look 35:48-9 Ja 26 '71

Caricatures and cartoons
It's all in the family (cont) S. Berenstain and J. Berenstain. Good H 172:64-5 Ap; 86-7 My; 173:76-7 Ag; 72-3 D '71
Woman's way. Cissie. See issues of Today's health to June 1971

FAMILY life, Education for
See also
Parent education

FAMILY plan life insurance. See Insurance, Life—Family plan policies

FAMILY planning. See Birth control

FAMILY planning services and population research act of 1970. See Birth control—Laws and legislation

FAMILY portrait; story. See Reinbold, J.

FAMILY portraits. See Photography—Portraits

FAMILY psychotherapy
Family as patient. il Time 97:60 My 31 '71
Maybe your whole family needs a psychiatrist and you don't know it. M. Wylie. il Ladies Home J 88:110+ Mr '71

FAMILY quarrels. See Quarrels

FAMILY records
See also
Household records

FAMILY responsibility. See Responsibility

FAMILY reunions
Family reunion: our annual watering of roots. P. P. Leimbach. Farm J 95:34 Ag '71

FAMILY rooms. See Living rooms

FAMILY size. See Family, Size of

FAMILY therapy. See Family psychotherapy

FAMILY vacations. See Vacations

FAMINES
United States
Starving Kansas: the great drought and famine of 1859-60. J. G. Gambone. il Am West 8:30-5 Jl '71

FAMOUS artists schools, inc. See FAS International, inc.

FAMOUS men. See Great men

FAMOUS photographers school
Sales without mails; letter. L. E. Joy. Mod Phot 35:12+ Ap '71; Discussion. 35:125 Ap; 4 Je '71

FAMOUS women. See Women, Famous

FAMOUS writers school
Writing wrongs. il Time 98:70 S 20 '71

FAN, Kang. See Mohit, B. jt. auth.

FANALE, Fraser P. and Nash, D. B.
Potassium-uranium systematics of Apollo 11 and Apollo 12 samples: implications for lunar material history. bibliog il Science 171:282-4; 172:1167 Ja 22, Je 11 '71

FANDEL, John
Black squirrel; poem. Commonweal 93:470 F 12 '71
Invitation; poem. Commonweal 94:481 S 17 '71
Poem; I dream a poem fluent as the dawn. Commonweal 93:545 Mr 5 '71

FANG, Victor S. and others
2-Thiophenecarboxylic acid: inhibitor of bone resorption in tissue culture. bibliog il Science 172:163-5 Ap 9 '71

FANN, Al
King heroin. Criticism
Ebony il pors 26:56-8+ Je '71 •

FANNIE Mae. See Federal national mortgage association

FANNIN, Allen
Hand spinning for the 'seventies. il por Craft Horiz 31:20-5+ F '71

FANNING, James
Gardener's notes. See issues of House & garden incorporating Living for young homemakers
Ideas for street-side planting. il House & Gard 139:31+ Je '71

FANNING, Kent A. and Pilson, M. E. Q.
Interstitial silica and pH in marine sediments: some effects of sampling procedures. bibliog il Science 173:1228-31 S 24 '71

FANNING, Odom
Environment boom; excerpts from Opportunities in environmental careers. il Sat R 54:60 My 1 '71

FANON, Frantz
Fanon. H. Sutton. il por Sat R 54:16-19+ Jl 17 '71 •

FANS, Baseball. See Baseball fans
FANS, Electric. See Electric fans
FANTAR, Mhamed
  Carthage through the eyes of Greece and
    Rome. il UNESCO Courier 23:29-33 D '70
FANTASIES, Literary
  High fantasy: A wizard of Earthsea; ad-
    dress, October 1969. E. Cameron. bibliog
    f Horn Bk 47:129-38 Ap '71
  High fantasy and heroic romance; address,
    October 1969. L. Alexander. bibliog f Horn
    Bk 47:577-84 D '71
FANTASTIC architecture. See Architecture,
  Fantastic
FANTASY
    See also
  Childrens fantasies
  Fairy tales
  Games
FANTEL, Hans H.
  Case for cassettes. il Opera N 35:14-16 F 20
    '71
  Four-channel sound: where will it all end? il
    Pop Sci 199:86-8+ N '71
  4-channel stereo, here at last! il Pop Mech
    136:66-70+ Ag '71
  Sound dollar: best buys in stereo. il Opera N
    36:8-11 D 11 '71
  Wire your patio for sound. il Pop Mech
    136:142-5 Ag '71
FANTINI, Mario D.
  Rocket age, rickety curriculum? Public
    schools of choice. il PTA Mag 65:2-5 bib-
    liog(p33) Ja '71
FAR EAST
    See also
  Costume—Far East
  Food supply—Far East
  United Nations—Economic commission for
    Asia and the Far East
  United States—Armed forces—Forces in the
    Far East
  Visitors, Foreign—Far East
        Description and travel
  East is West? K. Nott. Commentary 52:65-71
    Jl '71
  Where are you, Sidney Greenstreet? D. But-
    win. il Sat R 54:76+ N 13 '71
FAR EASTERN house decoration. See House
  decoration, Oriental
FAR WEST. See West
FARBER, Ed
  Phototronics. See issues of Modern photogra-
    phy
FARBER, Manny
  Monitor. J. Kroll. por Newsweek 77:97-8 Mr
    29 '71 •
FARBER, Norma
  Carol in the straw. Chr Cent 88:1490 D 22 '71
  Job's wife; poem. Chr Cent 88:487 Ap 21 '71
  Usual news; poem. Chr Cent 89:6 Ja 5 '72
FARBER, Stephen
  Movies from behind the barricades. il Film Q
    24:24-33 Wint '70
FARBER, Viola
  Viola Farber dance company, American
    theatre lab, NYC. N. Mason. Dance Mag
    45:81 Ag '71 •
FARBERMAN, Harold
  Losers. Criticism
    Dance Mag il 45:22 Jl '71 •
    Sat R 54:16+ Ap 10 '71 •
    Sat R il por 54:50-1 Ap 24 '71 •
    Recordings. M. Mayer. Esquire 76:38 Ag '71 •
    Report:
      Losers. F. Merkling. il Opera N 35:22 My
        15 '71 •
FARBSTEIN, Mitch
  Second-guessing the Heisman. J. Newcombe.
    Life 71:12 N 26 '71 •
FARER, Tom J.
  Laws of war 25 years after Nuremberg.
    bibliog f por Int Concil 583:5-54 My '71
  Sources of United States policy in the world.
    Yale R 60:321-32 Mr '71
FARES. See subhead Fares under various sub-
  jects, e.g. Airlines—Fares
FARESE, Robert V.
  Calcium as a mediator of adrenocortico-
    trophic hormone action on adrenal protein
    synthesis. bibliog il Science 173:447-50 Jl
    30 '71
FAREWELL Roxane; story. See Stanton, W.
FARGASON, John T. Jr
  Delta prison. Am Scholar 40:667-71 Aut '71
FARGO, James C.
  In quest of Utopia. H. L. Clark. il pors Na-
    tions Bsns 59:48-9 Ja '71 •
FARKAS, Harold
  How to fall-proof your home. il Mech Illus
    68:90-1+ Ja '72

FARLEY, James A.
  Before the colors fade: the true-blue Demo-
    crat; interview, ed. by V. V. Hamilton. il
    pors Am Heritage 22:38-43+ Ag '71
  HY hall of fame; interview. il por Har Yrs
    11:22-3+ My '71
FARLEY, Jean
  Comment. N. Sullivan. Poetry 119:108 N '71 •
FARLEY, Philip Judson
  Advantages of a comprehensive nuclear test
    ban and the question of verification; state-
    ment, July 22, 1971. Dept State Bul 65:
    182-5 Ag 16 '71
FARM accounting. See Agriculture—Accounting
FARM buildings
    See also
  Barns and stables
  Granaries
  Swine houses
FARM bureau federation. See American farm
  bureau federation
FARM cooperation. See Agriculture, Coopera-
  tive
FARM corporations
  Big corporations back out of farming. J. Carl-
    son. Farm J 95:27+ Ap '71
  What's ahead for the family farm. il U S
    News 72:54-5 Ja 3 '72
FARM credit. See Agricultural credit
FARM drainage. See Drainage
FARM equipment
  Home-made and handy; photographs. See is-
    sues of Farm journal
    See also
  Agricultural machinery
  Silage handling
  Trailers
FARM finance
  Do-it-yourself budgets for big decisions. R.
    Krumme. il Suc Farm 69:28-9 My '71
  Ways to fight the dollar shrink. R. Krumme.
    Suc Farm 69:H8-9 N '71
  You can shave costs 5-10 per cent. R.
    Krumme and J. Davis. il Suc Farm 69:no3
    32-3 F '71
FARM home administration. See United States
  —Farmers home administration
FARM income. See Agriculture—Economic as-
  pects; Income
FARM labor
  Can we solve the farm labor problem? F.
    Allen. il Org Gard & Farm 18:81-7 Ap '71
  Farm help: how to find it. R. Sanders. il
    Suc Farm 69:no3 26-7 F '71
  Farm help: how to keep it. R. Sanders. il
    Suc Farm 69:no5 26-7 Mr '71
  Part time planting help. R. Krumme. il Suc
    Farm 69:no4 29 Mr '71
    See also
  American federation of labor and Congress
    of industrial organizations—United farm
    workers organizing committee
  Collective bargaining—Farm labor
  Migrant labor
FARM land contracts. See Land contracts
FARM land values. See Land values
FARM leases. See Leases
FARM life
  Farm wife stands up for Women's lib. P.
    Leimbach. il Farm J 95:28+ N '71
  Letters from farm women. See issues of
    Farm journal
  Living off the land. M. Cantwell. il Mlle 73:126
    9 Je '71
  New life on an old farm. J. A. Novak. il Org
    Gard & Farm 18:41-6 Jl '71
  Quiet falls across the plains. D. Wittner. il
    Life 70:22-31 Je 25 '71
  300 years on the same piece of land; H.
    Tuttle of Dover, N.H. il pors Life 71:44-
    53 S 17 '71
FARM lobby. See Lobbying
FARM machinery. See Agricultural machinery
FARM management
  He manages 11 farms... at age 20! J. D.
    Boyd. il Farm J 95:22 Ap '71
  He manages to pay for his farm fast. R.
    Lutz. il Suc Farm 69:L2-3 N '71
  How to get good service from your custom
    operator. T. McCartney and M. Hood. il
    Suc Farm 69:L1 Ag '71
  Management: what would it cost to..., R.
    Krumme. il Suc Farm 69:28-9 N '71
  Multiple management. R. Krumme; M. Hood.
    il Suc Farm 69:D3-5 O '71
  New farming ideas for higher yields, better
    environment. C. E Ball and G. Lorang.
    Farm J 95:28 Ag '71
  Quality animals underscore organic methods.
    C. F. Marley. Org Gard & Farm 18:75-6
    O '71

FARM management—*Continued*
Tips to keep livestock producers out of court.
Suc Farm 69:D14 O '71
See also
Agriculture—Safety devices and measures
Crop yields
Dairy farm management
Farm records
Father-son farm operating agreements
Swine farm management

FARM manure
Cow manure? B. Brinhart. il Org Gard & Farm 18:89-91 Mr '71
Horse manure and wood chips. B. E. Kappel. il Org Gard & Farm 18:49-50 Jl '71
Use manure: solve disposal problems.   Suc Farm 69:44 O '71
See also
Sewage lagoons

Handling
Dairy manure handling, what's happening. B. Eftink. Suc Farm 69:no4 D8 Mr '71
Homemade manure system for small setups. B. Eftink. il Suc Farm 69:J22 N '71
It's a manure spreader. N. Reeder. il Farm J 95:24F Ag '71
There's no more away; excerpts from address. E. P. Taiganides. Suc Farm 69:20 Ap '71

Preservation and storage
Manure bunker costs less than liquid pit. il Suc Farm 69:34 Ap '71
New pump, new system for liquid manure. N. Reeder. il Farm J 95:D9 Je '71
These farmers got cash, everybody gets a cleaner lake; Lake Mendota, Wis. B. Coffman. il Farm J 95:22E-22F Jl '71

FARM mechanization
How machinery changed the way we farm. R. Sanders. il Suc Farm 69:no2 38-9 F '71

FARM mortgages. See Mortgages
FARM odors. See Odors
FARM offices. See Offices
FARM operating agreements. See Father-son farm operating agreements

FARM ownership
What's ahead for the family farm. il U S News 72:54-5 Ja 3 '72
See also
Corporations—Agricultural operations
Land tenure

FARM prices. See Farm produce—Prices

FARM produce
See also
Surplus products, Agricultural

Advertising
Commodity promotion: are you paying your share? check off plan. L. Palmer. il Farm J 95:34-5+ F '71

Marketing
Brighter outlook for farmers; interview. C. M. Hardin. il por U S News 70:58-62 Je 29 '71
Let's keep it rolling; exports. il Farm J 95:70 Ap '71
National farmers organization to market organic crops. J. Goldstein. il Org Gard & Farm 18:79-83 D '71
What's the future of farm exports? W. E. Swegle. il Suc Farm 69:G12-13 Ap '71
Your stake in farm exports. W. E. Swegle. il Suc Farm 69:no2 B2-3 F '71
See also subhead Marketing under names of farm produce, e.g. Soybeans—Marketing

Prices
Bumper crops on the farm do their anti-inflationary bit. il Fortune 84:22 S '71
See also
Agricultural administration—United States
also subhead Prices under names of farm produce, e.g. Corn—Prices

Storage
How to store your food crops. C. F. Beck. il Org Gard & Farm 18:84-92 S '71
How to store your food crops. J. L. Harter. il Org Gard & Farm 18:42-9 Ag '71

FARM records
Little books help him farm. M. Hood. il Suc Farm 69:28-9 S '71
More tips on health records. J. G. Clark. Farm J 95:B16-17 Ap '71
Records: how to set up forms and use them; animal health record system. J. G. Clark. il Farm J 95:B17 Mr '71
Records put him in hogs. D. Seim. il Farm J 95:H8-9+ Ap '71

FARM rents
How much is an acre worth in cash rent? D. H. Doster and P. R. Robbins. il Suc Farm 69:G14 S '71

FARM safety. See Agriculture—Safety devices and measures

FARM subsidies.   See   Agricultural administration—United States

FARM tenancy
Permanent grain center on a rented farm. P. B. Jones. il Suc Farm 69:32-3 S '71
Tell your landlord but don't tell him off. M. Hood. Suc Farm 69:G16 Ap '71
See also
Farm rents
Leases
Share-cropping

FARM water supply. See Water supply, Rural

FARM women
Letters from farm women. See issues of Farm journal

FARM workers lobby. See Lobbying

FARMAR family
Farmar coat-of-arms. H. K. Eilers. il Hobbies 76:146-7+ My '71

FARMER, Charles J.
North Platte float trip. il Outdoor Life 148: 52-5+ Ag '71
Whitetails in the black. il Field & S 76:66-7+ Ag '71

FARMER, F. R.
Safety and nuclear power plants: a British view. por Bul Atom Sci 27:47-9 N '71

FARMER, Gene
(ed) See Eckstein, O. How is the economy doing?

FARMERS
If your husband is a VIP. M. Longwell. Farm J 95:40 O '71
Know your organic farmer. M. C. Goldman. il Org Gard & Farm 18:69-72 Je '71
Nixon's new push to win over farmers; "Salute to agriculture" day. il por Farm J 95:24 Je '71
Program to certify organic farmers; with list of certified California growers. F. Allen. il Org Gard & Farm 18:8013 S '71
Quiet falls across the plains; Elwood Jorgensen of Vienna, S.D. D. Wittner. il Life 70:22-31 Je 25 '71
What farmers think of family farms; national survey on big farms, programs, bargaining and credit; with editorial comment. C. W. Gifford. Farm J 95:17, 50 Je '71
Who can start farming today? M. Hood. il Suc Farm 69:no5 23-5 Mr '71
Why we like farmers so much. B. Coffman. Farm J 95:28 D '71
See also
International flying farmers (association)
Women as farmers

Retirement
You can transplant an old tree. E. Gorsline. Farm J 95:51 Mr '71

FARMERS almanac. See Almanacs

FARMERS home administration.   See   United States—Farmers home administration

FARMERS wives. See Farm women

FARMHOUSES

Designs and plans
New American farm house. il House & Gard 139:38-45 F '71

FARMHOUSES, Remodeled. See Houses, Remodeled

FARMING. See Agriculture

FARMS
Bernardo y Adela. F. Allen. il Org Gard & Farm 18:82-4+ F '71
Ever watch your farm disappear? G. Logsdon. Farm J 95:53 Mr '71
See also
Agriculture
Farm ownership
Sheep farms
Swine farms

Corporate ownership
See Corporations—Agricultural operations

FARMS, Organic
Best beef in the world. R. J. Holliday. il Org Gard & Farm 18:58-62 F '71
Complete acre, or, Keep your dream and make it real! N. W. Bubel. il Org Gard & Farm 18:40-4 Ap '71
Farm market. See issues of Organic gardening and farming
Four acres of sheer delight: a farm in southern Maine. D. Jutras. il por Org Gard & Farm 18:39-43 Ja '71

FARMS, Organic—*Continued*
Four reasons Gene Matthews chose the farm life. M. Matthews. il Org Gard & Farm 18: 78-80 Mr '71
Guru of the organic food cult. W. Greene. il pors N Y Times Mag p30-1+ Je 6 '71
New look in organic farms. M. C. Goldman. il Org Gard & Farm 18:77-80 F '71
Program to certify organic farmers; with list of certified California growers. F. Allen. il Org Gard & Farm 18:80-3 S '71
They don't try too hard. J. Cox. il Org Gard & Farm 18:46-7 My '71
2¼-acre bonanza. A. M. Loring. Org Gard & Farm 18:95-7 S '71

FARMS, Worn-out
Sad symbol of our times: an abandoned farm. K. D. Henley. il Am For 77:6-7 S '71

FARNEY, Dennis
New hope at Patuxent. il Nat Wildlife 9:44-7 O '71

FARNHAM, Katharine Gross, and Efird, C. H.
Early silversmiths and the silver trade in Georgia. il Antiques 99:380-5 Mr '71

FARNSWORTH, Dana L.
Drug scene, has it changed? il PTA Mag 66: 2-3 bibliog(p35) D '71

FAROE ISLANDS
Forgotten Faeroes. M. R. Smith. il Travel 136:38-43+ Ag '71

FARR, Roger, and Brown, V. L.
Evaluation and decision making. Ed Digest 36:40-3 Ap '71

FARR, William
Ex-reporter's privilege. Newsweek 78:42 Ag 9 '71 *

FARRAR, Straus and Giroux, inc.
Big prize; publishing rights to Solzhenitsyn's August 1914. il por Newsweek 78:55 Jl 19 '71

FARRELL, Barry
Manson jury; end of the long ordeal. il por Life 70:44-8 Ap 16 '71
Satisfactions of some memories well invested. Life 71:23 Ag 13 '71
View from the year 2000. il pors Life 70:46-8+ F 26 '71
You've come a long way, Buddy. il Life 71: 52⊥ Ag 27 '71

FARRELL, Edmund J.
Implications of national assessment writing results. Engl J 60:1116-19 N '71
Scene. Engl J 60:520-6 Ap '71

FARRELL, Patricia A.
Where is publishing heading? il Pub W 200: 40-2 S 13· 22-5 S 20 '71

FARRELL, Ray M.
Luminal art. il Sch Arts 71:18-19 O '71

FARRELL, Richard E.
Clematis, aristocrat of vines. il Home Gard 58:46-7+ F '71

FARRELL, Robert W.
Daily mirror; interview. New Yorker 47:40-2 S 25 '71

FARRINGTON, Carolyn G.
Crayon marks on the wall; story. Redbook 137:84-5 Je '71

FARRINGTON, Kip
Remembering great men and great fish; excerpt from Fishing with Hemingway and Glassell. il Field & S 75:54-5+ Ap '71

FARRIS, Nancy Pierson
Wagonload of spoiled hay changed our gardening ways. il Org Gard & Farm 18:50-2 Ag '71

FARROW, Mia
Mia comes to rest. G. Kanin. il pors McCalls 98:64-7+ Ap '71 *

FARROWING crates and pens. See Swine farrowing crates and pens

FARSON, Richard
Why good marriages fail. McCalls 99:110-11+ O '71; Same abr. Read Digest 99:131-3 D '71

FARUQUEE, Atauar
Information exchange. Wilson Lib Bul 46:290 N '71

FARVAR, M. Taghi, and others
Pollution of Asia. bibliog il por Environ 13: 10-17 O '71

FASCINATING womanhood. See Womens clubs and societies

FASCIOTT, Judi
Cardboard relief. il Sch Arts 70:46 Je '71

FASCISM
Appeal of fascism, by A. Hamilton. Review
  Nat R 23:1185-6 O 22 '71. J. Hart
  See also
National socialism

Italy
Almirante is no M-s---i--- yet. M. S. Davis. il por N Y Times Mag p27+ Je 6 '71
Europe: old feuds, fresh outbursts. il Time 97:32 F 15 '71
Fascist phenomenon. il Newsweek 77:38+ Mr 1 '71

United States
All-American friendly fascism? B. M. Gross. Cur 126:13-25 F '71
Will fascism arise in America? C. Lamont. Cur 132:11-13 S '71

FASHION
Damn those young girls! with reply by R. Drexler. G. Guinness. pors Harp Baz 105: 110-11 D '71
Face-off: a Right now debate. McCalls 98:40 Jl '71
  See also
Clothing and dress
Costume
Costume design
Hairdressing

Anecdotes, facetiae, satire, etc.
Oh! Fashion! One man's look at the preening of America. S. Blum. il Redbook 136:79+ Ap '71

FASHION designers. See Costume designers

FASHION photography. See Photography, Fashion

FASHION shows
Fashion show centennial. S. Sunderlin. il Har Yrs 11:49-51 Ag '71
People who discovered the beauty of black; Naturally shows. H. Touré. il Redbook 136:91+ Mr '71
Short and shorter; Paris shows 1971 spring collections. il Newsweek 77:86 F 8 '71

FASTENINGS
Fastening techniques. il Bet Hom & Gard 49:126 D '71
Thirty-three clever fasteners that won't let go. R. J. De Cristoforo. il Pop Sci 198:76-9 F '71
  See also
Bolts and nuts
Rivets and riveting
USM corporation

FASTING
Strictly from hunger. il Newsweek 78:122+ N 22 '71
  See also
Starvation

FASTS and feasts
  See also
Epiphany
Passover
Ramadan

FAT
Note on DDT levels in body fat. il Chem 44: 24 Je '71
  See also
Corpulence
Glycerides

FAT; story. See Carver, R.

FAT cells. See Cells

FAT content of foods. See Food—Fat content

FATHER-child relationship. See Parent-child relationship

FATHER-son corporations. See Family corporations

FATHER-son farm operating agreements
Father-son agreement for a growing hog business. R. J. Fee. il Suc Farm 69:H6 S '71

FATHER-son relationship. See Parent-child relationship

FATHER to daughter; story. See Amber, B. K.

FATHERHOOD of God. See God

FATHERS
Christian father. E. Elliot. Chr Today 15: 3-4 Je 18 '71
Father takes care of the baby. L. Weeks. il Parents Mag 46:60-1+ F '71
One man no woman ever escapes. S. Blum. Redbook 136:73+ Ap '71
  See also
Parent education

FATHERS, Unmarried
Secret wish of unwed fathers; interview, ed. by L. David. N. Littner. Seventeen 29:128-9+ O '70

FATHER'S day; drama. See Hailey, O.

FATHERS day gifts. See Gifts

FATHOMETERS. See Depth indicators

FATIGUE
  See also
Boredom
Endurance
Relaxation

FATS. See Oils and fats, Edible

FATTY acids. See Acids, Fatty

FAUBUS, Orval Eugene
Reports & comment: Arkansas. B. Herget.
Atlan 227:14+ F '71 •
FAUCETS. See Plumbing
FAUGHT, Harold F.
How science will speed your mail. E. Edelson. il Pop Sci 198:53-5+ Mr '71 •
FAULKNER, Brian
Northern Ireland: the powder keg. il por Time 97:26-32 Ap 5 '71 •
FAULKNER, Douglas
Coral; photographs. Natur Hist 80:43-7 Mr '71
Sensuous symbionts of the sea: photographs. Natur Hist 80:28-37+ Ag '71
FAULKNER, John
John Faulkner's vanishing South. R. S. Sugg, jr. il por Am Heritage 22:65-75 Ap '71
FAULTS (electric distribution) See Electric power distribution—Grounds and faults
FAULTS (geology)
Central North Atlantic plate motions over the last 40 million years. J. D. Phillips and B. P. Luyendyk; discussion. bibliog il Science 174:845-6 N 19 '71
Ground rupture in the Baldwin Hills. D. H. Hamilton and R. L. Meehan. bibliog il Science 172:333-44 Ag 23 '71
Microearthquakes in the Ahuachapan geothermal field, El Salvador, Central America. P. L. Ward and K. H. Jacob. bibliog il Science 173:328-30 Jl 23 '71
Quaking earth: what's the fault? San Andreas fault. il Sr Schol 98:14-16 Mr 1 '71
Rifting in Iceland: new geodetic data. R. W. Decker and others. bibliog il Science 173:530-3 Ag 6 '71
Same thing will happen again, only worse; San Andreas fault. il Newsweek 77:22 F 22 '71
San Andreas fault. D. L. Anderson. il Sci Am 225:52-66+ bibliog(p 136) N '71
San Fernando earthquake of 9 February 1971: pattern of faulting. D. F. Palmer and T. L. Henyey. il Science 172:712-15 My 14 '71
Science has no remedy; California quakes. il Sci N 99:126-7 F 20 '71
FAUNCE, Sarah C.
Inca baroque. il Art N 70:24-5 D '71
FAUNTROY, Walter E.
Confronting the President. il por Time 97:13-14 Ap 5 '71 •
D.C's man in the house. il por Sr Schol 98:17 Ap 19 '71 •
Little Lord. New Repub 166:12 Ja 1 '72 •
FAUST; opera. See Gounod, C. F.
FAUST counter Faust; opera. See Gessner, J.
FAUSTER, Carl U.
Louis Vaupel, master glass engraver. il por Antiques 99:696-701 My '71
FAUX, Eugene J.
Drugs, morals and family responsibilities. Ment Hy 55:260-3 Ap '71
FAVERO, M. S. and others
Pseudomonas aeruginosa: growth in distilled water from hospitals. bibliog il Science 173:836-8 Ag 27 '71
FAVIA-ARTSAY, Aida
Historical records. See issues of Hobbies
FAVISM
Favism: association with erythrocyte acid phosphatase phenotype. E. Bottini and others. bibliog il Science 171:409-11 Ja 29 '71
FAVRETTI, Rudy J.
Flowers of the colonial days. il Horticulture 49:40-1+ Ap '71
FAWCETT, Clara Hallard
Dollology. See issues of Hobbies
FAY, Leo, and Blanton, William
Rallying to the reading challenge. il PTA Mag 65:9-12 bibliog(p33) Ja '71
FAY, Lew
Important tips on rafting. il Motor B & S 128:88+ Jl '71
FAYARD, Judy
David. il pors Life 71:70-3 O 29 '71
Who can stand 32,580 seconds of Clint Eastwood? il pors Life 71:44-8 Jl 23 '71
FAYETTE, Miss.
Evers administration: two years of progress in Fayette. A. B. Haines. Chr Cent 88:908-11 Jl 28 '71
FEAL-DEIBE, Carlos
Lorca's two farces: Don Perlimplín and Don Cristóbal. bibliog Am Imago 27:358-78 Wint '70
FEAR
Breaking the fear barrier. W. H. Weiss. il Nations Bsns 59:64-5 Jl '71
Fear of failure and other handicaps; with study-discussion program, by E. Harris and D. Harris. E. D. Wagner. il PTA Mag 66:24-6+ N '71

How to help troubled children cope with fears and problems; behavior therapy. B. P. McCarthy. il Parents Mag 46:44-5+ Ag '7
See also
Anxiety
Bashfulness
Phobias
School phobia
Stage fright
FEAR; story. See Bingham, S.
FEARING, Bruce
Son of Consciousness III. Newsweek 77:78-9 Ja 25 '71 •
FEATHER, Jean
Long leather bag; dramatization of folk tale from Ireland. Plays 30:71-5 Mr '71
One wish too many; drama. Plays 30:69-73, 96 F '71
FEATHERS, David L.
New developments in camellias. il Horticulture 49:22-3+ S '71
FEATHERSTONE, Joseph
Open schools: the British and us. New Republic 165:20-5 S 11; 17-21 S 25 '71; Same abr. with title What role for open schools? Cur 134:41-51 N '71; Excerpt. Ed Digest 37:9-12 D '71
FEATURE articles. See Periodical articles
FECES
Fecal pellets; role in sedimentation of pelagic diatoms. H. J. Schrader. bibliog il Science 174:55-7 O 1 '71
FECTEAU, Richard
Two-fifths thaw. pors Time 98:8 D 27 '71 •
FEDAYEEN
Ambush at the Gate of tears; tanker attacked by Popular front for the liberation of Palestine. Time 97:33 Je 28 '71
Carrot and stick. Newsweek 78:34 Ag 23 '71
Going underground. por Time 98:45 S 27 '71
Guerrillas on the run. il Time 98:23 Ag 2 '71
My Jewish problem, and ours. S. Stern. il Ramp Mag 10:30-40 Ag '71; Discussion. 10:68-71 O '71
Withering rose; guerrilla peace poster. il Time 97:39 F 1 '71
See also
Guerrillas—Arab states
FEDERAL agencies. See United States—Executive departments
FEDERAL aid
That big government haystack. W. V. Roth, jr. il por Nations Bsns 59:64-6 F '71
See also
Government lending
Grants-in-aid
also subhead Federal aid under various subjects, e.g. Education—Federal aid; Housing—Federal aid; etc.
FEDERAL aid to science. See Research—Federal aid
FEDERAL and municipal relations
Crowded cities, empty land, and the Nixon remedy. il U S News 70:24-6 Ap 5 '71
Government renews pressure for integrated suburbs. il U S News 70:47-8 Je 28 '71
Politics of Nixon's revolution; with reply by C. DeMuth. M. W. Karmin. Cur 128:40-5 Ap '71
FEDERAL and state relations
Will revenue-sharing mean power-sharing? safeguards against discrimination. D. Lawrence. U S News 70:100 F 15 '71
FEDERAL aviation administration. See United States—Federal aviation administration
FEDERAL boat safety act, 1971. See Boats and boating—Laws and regulations
FEDERAL buildings. See Public buildings
FEDERAL bureau of investigation. See United States—Federal bureau of investigation
FEDERAL city college. See Washington, D.C.—Federal city college
FEDERAL coal mine health and safety act. See Coal mines and mining—Safety devices and measures
FEDERAL communications commission. See United States—Federal communications commission
FEDERAL contract research centers. See Research institutions
FEDERAL courts. See Courts—United States
FEDERAL debt (United States) See Debts, Public—United States
FEDERAL deposit insurance corporation
Texas does it big; case involving F. W. Sharp. Nation 213:324 O 11 '71
FEDERAL employees. See Government employees
FEDERAL fact-finding commissions. See Commissions of inquiry
FEDERAL financing bank (proposed) See Banks and banking—United States

FEDERAL government
Down the bureaucracy. M. P. Dumont. Trans-Action 7:10-12+ O '70
Government structure: inherent inability to change; address, June 21, 1971. J. J. Powers, jr. Vital Speeches 37:628-31 Ag 1 '71
Mess in Washington: how it got that way; excerpts from message to Congress, March 25, 1971. R. M. Nixon. il por U S News 70:78-80 Ap 12 '71
Real story of the Nixon revolution: government reorganization. il U S News 70:29-34 Mr 15 '71
See also
Democracy
Intergovernmental tax relations
United States—Politics and government
FEDERAL housing administration. See United States—Federal housing administration
FEDERAL housing projects. See Housing projects, Government
FEDERAL insurance administration. See United States—Federal insurance administration
FEDERAL lands. See Public lands—United States
FEDERAL mediation and conciliation service. See United States—Federal mediation and conciliation service
FEDERAL national mortgage association
Family responsibilities. il Forbes 107:34 F 15 '71
Fanny Mae's anti-consumer mortgage. Consumer Rep 36:240 Ap '71
FEDERAL parole board. See United States—Parole, Board of
FEDERAL power commission. See United States—Federal power commission
FEDERAL prison industries, inc.
Inside the prison-industrial complex. J. Castelli. Commonweal 95:124-5 N 5 '71
FEDERAL prisons. See Prisons—United States
FEDERAL reserve board. See United States—Federal reserve board
FEDERAL revenue sharing with states. See Intergovernmental tax relations
FEDERAL-state tax relations. See Intergovernmental tax relations
FEDERAL trade commission. See United States—Federal trade commission
FEDERATED department stores, inc.
Fadecut for Fedway. R. Levy. Duns 98:60 O '71
FEDERATION for authentic Lutheranism. See Lutheran church in the United States
FÉDÉRATION internationale de documentation. See International federation for documentation
FEDERATION of American scientists
Arms race: scientists question threat from Soviet military R&D. R. J. Bazell. il Science 173:707-9 Ag 20 '71
FAS: reviving lobby battles ABM, scientists' apathy. D. Shapley. Science 171:1224-7 Mr 26 '71
FEDERATION of Europe. See European federation
FEDO, Michael W.
Freelance market report: Harcourt Brace and Jovanovich trade journals. il Writers Digest 51:28-30 N '71
One idea: multiple sales. il Writers Digest 51:31 Je '71
FEDOROV, Evgraf Stepanovich
Space groups not always derivable by parallelohedra and subdivision into stereohedra. W. Nowacki. bibliog il Science 174:52-3 O 1 '71 *
FEDOROVA, Aleksandra
In the shadow of Russian tradition: interview, ed. by M. Horosko. il pors Dance Mag 45:24-8 My '71
FEDOSEEV, Anatol
Dubious defector. Newsweek 78:38+ Jl 5 '71 *
FEDWAY department stores. See Federated department stores, inc.
FEE, Rodney J.
Hog management. See issues of Successful farming
(ed) Successful hog management. il Suc Farm 69:H1 Ag; H1 O '71
FEED grinders and grinding
How to grind feed with less power. Suc Farm 69:no2 D10 F '71
FEED mills (machinery) See Feed grinders and grinding
FEED preservation and preservatives
New preservatives for high-moisture corn; acid treatment. W. Kester. Farm J 95:B20 O '71
New way to store high-moisture grain: acid treatment. W. Kester. il Farm J 95:27 N '71
FEED supplements, Antibiotic. See Antibiotic feed supplements

FEEDBACK control systems
See also
Biological control systems
FEEDER airlines. See Local service airlines
FEEDERS (birds) See Bird feeders
FEEDING, intravenous. See Intravenous feeding
FEEDING and feeding stuffs
Cattle feeding, and lassoed investors. il Duns 98:33-7 S '71
To hold down costs, try mixing feed from scratch. D. Seim. il Farm J 95:H16+ S '71
Why we must grow good beef without hormones or high-energy rations; natural feeds. R. Steffen. il Org Gard & Farm 18:61-3 Ap '71
See also
Antibiotic feed supplements
Cattle—Feeding
Cows—Feeding
Feed grinders and grinding
Feed preservation and preservatives
Forage plants
Pastures
Silage

Cookery
Are full-fat beans for you? R. J. Fee. il Suc Farm 69:D2 N '71

Testing
New ways to zero in on feed value. il Farm J 95:28-9 Ja '71

Corn
Cattle put OK on roasted corn. W. Kester. il Farm J 95:B14 S '71
New life for whole corn plant pellets. il Farm J 95:B28 S '71
Pros and cons of high-moisture corn for hogs. B. Eftink. il Suc Farm 69:H10 S '71
Wet corn cuts his gain costs 15%. J. Russell. il Farm J 95:H12+ O '71

Grain
Will processing grain for hogs pay? R. Wilmore. Farm J 95:H12+ Mr '71
See also
Feeding and feeding stuffs—Sorghum

Liquid feed
New surge in liquid supplement feeding. il Farm J 95:16-17 D '71

Manure
Recycling waste: a promising way to handle manure and cut feed costs. G. Reynolds. Farm J 95:13+ Jl '71

Medicated feed
What you must do to keep your feed additives; interview, ed. by J. A. Rohlf. C. D. Van Houweling. il por Farm J 95:22-3+ Je '71
See also
Antibiotic feed supplements

Milk
See also
Colostrum

Paper
Newsprint for dinners? C. Dawson. il McCalls 98:46 S '71
Viewpoint: what's happening to cow feeding? il Suc Farm 69:D1 My '71

Pelleted feed
Feed whole-plant soybean pellets? J. D. Boyd. il Farm J 95:B10 O '71
There are some tricks to feeding cubes. R. Borcherding. il Suc Farm 69:H12 N '71

Potatoes
Grain-fed quality beef with potato waste feed. G. Lorang. il Farm J 95:16 Ap '71

Protein supplements
New surge in liquid supplement feeding. il Farm J 95:16-17 D '71

Rye
Rye. D. Seim. Farm J 95:31 Ja '71

Sorghum
Consider sorghum as a low-cost beef ration. B. Eftink. il Suc Farm 69:B6 O '71

Soybeans
Are full-fat beans for you? R. J. Fee. il Suc Farm 69:D2 N '71
Feed whole-plant soybean pellets? J. D. Boyd. il Farm J 95:B10 O '71

Waste products
They cut cow costs with crop waste. R. Alleman. il Suc Farm 69:B18 O '71

FEEDLOTS
Clean new gas; methane from feedlot wastes.
H. L. Bohn. bibliog il Environ 13:4-9
D '71
High output with low investment. J. Davis.
il Suc Farm 69:no5 B16-17 Mr '71
How organization helped the Kissingers grow.
J. Davis. il Suc Farm 69:B12+ O '71
How teaming up can make you more competitive; cattle feedlots. W. Kester. il Farm
J 95:B6-7+ My '71
How they're financing big-time feeding. C. E.
Ball. il Farm J 95:B6-7 Mr '71
Master plan for healthier calves. W. Kester.
il Farm J 95:B6-7+ O '71
Now it's beef and mutton; DES controversy.
il Newsweek 78:85 N 8 '71
Slowdown in Southwest cattle feeding? R.
Reiman. il Suc Farm 69:H2 My '71
Special report on feeder cattle. R. Krumme
and B. Eftink. il Suc Farm 69:14-15 O '71
Where will the new fed-beef growth come?
Farm J 95:B11 My '71
Why cattle feeders didn't get back costs.
Suc Farm 69:J28 N '71
You can get federal funds to control feedlot
runoff; REAP funds. B. Eftink. il Suc Farm
69:23 O '71
FEELEY, Rich
Voyage to the Hebrides. il Yachting 129:
56-7+ Je '71
FEENY, P. P. See Whittaker, R. H. jt. auth.
FEES, Airport. See Airports—Finance
FEES, Trade union. See Trade unions—Dues,
fees, etc.
FEES, Tuition. See Colleges and universities
—Finance
FEFFER, Henry Leon
All about backaches: latest advice from a
specialist; interview. il por U S News 71:
74-8 S 20 '71; Same abr. Read Digest 99:
203-4+ D '71
FEFFER and Simons, inc.
Feffer and Simons builds up European operations. H. R. Lottman. il Pub W 200:43-4 S
13 '71
FEFFERMAN, Charles
Making waves. por Time 98:34-5 S 6 '71 *
FEGELY, Thomas D.
Planting the organic seed. il Org Gard &
Farm 18:52-3 Mr '71
FEIFFER, Jules
Carnal knowledge; excerpt from screenplay.
il Harp Baz 104:72 Jl '71
Jules Feiffer (cont) New Repub 164:30 Ja 2;
27 Ja 23; 23 F 13; 19 Mr 20; 28 Je 5;
23 Je 19; 165:25 Jl 17; 21 O 30; 21 N 27;
25 D 25 '71
FEIGEN, Sandra
Travel plot. il pors Vogue 158:136-43+ O 15 '71
FEIGIN, Grisha Isakovich
Plucking out a thorn. Newsweek 77:38+ F
15 '71 *
FEIN, Oliver. See Ehrenreich, J. jt. auth.
FEINBERG, Gerald
Survival? Yes. But in what form? Bul Atom
Sci 27:27-30 My '71

about
900-year-old beauty. N. Gittelson. Harp Baz
104:20+ Ap '71 *
FEINBERG, Karen
Growing up gifted. Ed Digest 36:44-5 Ap
'71
FEINBERG, Renee
What price professionalism? il por Library J 96:691-4 F 15 '71
FEINBLOOM, Richard I.
Is this crib necessary? il Time 98:87 N
8 '71
FEININGER, Andreas
Feininger. See issues of Modern photography
FEISAL, king of Saudi Arabia
King Faisal of Saudi Arabia visits the United
States; exchange of greetings, May 27, 1971.
Dept State Bul 64:763-4 Je 14 '71
FEKETE, Janos
Man who put Hungary into Eurobonds. por
Bsns W p52 Jl 17 '71 *
FELD, Eliot
Dance. N. Goldner. Nation 212:636-7 My 17
'71 *
Eliot Feld's American ballet company,
Brooklyn academy of music. T. Borek.
Dance Mag 45:22 Jl '71 *
FELDHUSEN, John F. See McDaniel, E. jt.
auth.
FELDKAMP, Fred
Games some people play: the tierce. Harper
244:72 Ja '72
Sloughs of secrecy. il Harper 243:79-82 D '71
Sporting scene (cont) New Yorker 47:60-72+
Ag 14 '71

FELDKAMP, Phyllis
We tried to live the EQ way. il pors Nat
Wildlife 9:6-7 Ap '71
FELDMAN, Irving
After the flight from Rockaway; poem. New
Yorker 47:96 Mr 20 '71
Air children; poem. Nation 213:471 N 8 '71
In the mental ward; poem. New Yorker
47:54 O 30 '71
Season; poem. Harper 243:18 D '71

about
Comment. W. H. Pritchard. Poetry 119:164-5
D '71 *
FELDMAN, Leonard
How to use our test reports in selecting a
speaker. il Hi Fi 21:36-42 Je '71
What makes a good stereo cartridge? Hi Fi
21:45-51 F '71
What's behind the knob? il Hi Fi 21:56-63
Jl '71
FELDMAN, Mary Ann
St Paul's summer. il por Opera N 36:18-20
S '71
FELDMAN, Morton
Give my regards to Eighth street. il por Art
in Am 59:96-9 Mr '71
FELDMAN, Nancy G.
Pride in heritage, or resentment? A sociologist analyzes library staff reaction. il Wilson Lib Bul 46:436-40 Ja '72
FELDMAN, Saul
Heightism. il Time 98:64 O 4 '71 *
FELDSPAR
See also
Anorthosite
FELENSTEIN, Walter
Fiddler on an East Berlin roof. G. R. Marek.
il Sat R 54:46-7+ F 27 '71 *
FELIDAE
Cat conference; report of International symposium on ecology, behavior and conservation of the world's cats. R. L. Eaton.
Science 174:615-16 N 5 '71
FELIX, Allen O.
Investing your money. Todays Ed 60:54-6
Ja '71
FELIX, Leon
Orleans educators association: tradition
breaker. Todays Ed 60:70 N '71
FELL, Derek
Plotting prize winning garden photographs.
il Home Gard 58:24-5 Ap '71
FELL, Joseph P.
Psychosocial analysis of sex-policing on campus; address, December 7, 1965. Ed Digest
36:38-41 Ja '71
FELLER, Robert William Andrew
Where are they now? il pors Newsweek 78:8
Ag 23 '71 *
FELLING of trees. See Tree felling
FELLINI, Federico
Current cinema. P. Gilliatt. New Yorker 47:
96+ Je 12 '71 *
Fellini's The clowns. R. Schickel. il por Life
71:9 Jl 9 '71 *
Letter from Paris; latest film. Genêt. New
Yorker 47:96-7 Mr 27 '71 *
Pierrots and Augustes. S. Kanfer. Time 97:
84 Je 21 '71 *
Riddle of The clowns. J. Lahr. il Vogue 158:
90-1 Ag 1 '71 *
Which face is Fellini? D. J. Hamblin. il pors
Life 71:58-61 Jl 30 '71 *
FELLOWSHIP of Christian athletes
Super witness. A. Taft and E. E. Plowman.
Chr Today 15:54-5 F 12 '71
FELLOWSHIP of the Spirit
Please, before I hit the ground. D. J. Benson. Chr Today 15:11-12+ S 10 '71
FELSENSTEIN, Walter
Felsenstein thing. M. Steinberg. por Hi Fi
21:MA8-9 Ag '71 *
FELSTINER, John
Neruda in translation. Yale R 61:226-51 D '71
FELT, Irving Mitchell
Sporting gesture toward innkeeping. il por
Bsns W p86 N 6 '71 *
FELT work
Flutter of felt. il House B 113:80-1+ Ja '71
FELTON, James
Temple festival gets a roof over its head.
Hi Fi 21:MA19+ N '71
FELTWORK. See Felt work
FEMALE impersonators. See Impersonators,
Female
FEMININE hygiene products. See Sanitary
napkins, tampons, etc.
FEMININE psychology. See Woman—Psychology
FEMININITY. See Woman
FEMINIST press. See Periodicals for women
FEMINISTS. See Womens liberation movement

FENCES
Behind this street screen, a private entry garden. il Sunset 146:113 Ap '71
Old grapestakes make a handsome comeback. il Sunset 146:111 Mr '71
Patterned patio screens use a mix of rough, smooth lumber. il Sunset 146:152 My '71
Screen hangs around the entry. il Sunset 147:170 S '71

FENCING coaches. See Coaches (athletics)

FENDELL, Edward I.
NASA's Captain Video. il por Time 98:12 Ag 9 '71 *

FENHOLT, Jeff
Jeff Fenholt, the star of Superstar; interview, ed. by E. Sparn. il Sr Schol 99:10-11 D 13 '71

FENHOLT, Reenie
Jeff Fenholt, the star of Superstar; interview, ed. by E. Sparn. il Sr Schol 99:10-11 D 13 '71

FENN, Charles V.
Keeping cool at ringside. il pors Nations Bsns 59:56-7 Ja '71

FENN, Dan H. Jr
Executives as community volunteers. il Harvard Bsns R 49:4-6+ Mr '71

FENN, Ellen Rebecca
Shooting your own pictures! il Writers Digest 51:28-9+ F '71

FENN, Roger C.
Achieving relevancy in nature programming. Camp Mag 43:24-5 Ap '71

FENNER, David, and Klarmann, Joseph
Power from the earth. bibliog il Environ 13:19-26+ D '71

FENSTERMACHER, Ted
Landlord of the birds. il Org Gard & Farm 18:52-3 Ap '71
This home-made cold cellar is a money saver. il Org Gard & Farm 18:48-50 D '71

FENSTERWALD, Bernard, Jr
Irregulars take the field. F. J. Cook. Nation 213:40-6 Jl 19 '71 *

FENTON, John
(ed) See Challener, R. D. Which way America? Dulles always knew

FENWICK, Daman G.
Build this low-cost winter home for your boat. il Pop Mech 136:119 N '71
How not to sell your boat. il Motor B & S 128:85-6+ O '71
Something new in winter boat cover. il Motor B & S 128:75+ O '71

FERAL dogs. See Wild dogs

FERENCY, Zolton A.
Grass roots vs. back room. S. Holtzer. por Nation 212:166-9 F 8 '71 *

FERGUSON, Eugene S.
Measurement of the man-day: with biographical sketch. il Sci Am 225:12, 96-103 O '71

FERGUSON, Lloyd Noel
Lloyd N. Ferguson: traveling salesman for chemical education. S. P. Massie. il Chem 44:13 Jl '71 *

FERGUSSON, Harvey
Taos remembered. il pors Am West 8:38-41 S '71

FERMI, Enrico
Several lives and more. J. Wilson. Bul Atom Sci 27:47-8 F '71 *

FERN pine. See Podocarpus

FERNANDES
Enchanted piano; story; tr. by J. C. Oates. Harp Baz 104:76-7 Je '71

FERNANDEZ, James W.
Zulu Zionism; with biographical sketch. il Natur Hist 80:5, 44-51 Je '71

FERNANDEZ, Maria Luisa. See Marixa

FERNANDEZ, Richard R.
Air war in Indochina: some responses. il Chr Cent 88:1404-5 D 1 '71

FERNANDEZ-MORAN, H. and others
Electron microscopy and diffraction of layered, superconducting intercalation complexes. bibliog il Science 174:498-500 O 29 '71

FERNELIUS, W. Conard
Future? Chem 44:2 Ap '71

FERNS
These ferns need little care. il Sunset 146:234 Mv '71
Unusual ferns. F. G. Foster. il Horticulture 49:36-7+ Jl '71

FERNSTROM, John D. and Wurtman, R. J.
Brain serotonin content: increase following ingestion of carbohydrate diet. bibliog il Science 174:1023-5 D 3 '71
Brain serotonin content: physiological dependence on plasma tryptophan levels. bibliog il Science 173:149-52 Jl 9 '71

FERNSWORTH, Lawrence
New tool kit for a police state. Nation 212: 721-4 Je 7 '71

FERRARA, Armand
Putting PEP into fighting pollution. il Org Gard & Farm 18:114-18 Mr '71

FERRARI (automobile) See Automobiles, Foreign

FERRÉ, Luis Alberto
Puerto Rico; address, July 27, 1971. Vital Speeches 37:741-3 O 1 '71

FERREIRA, Ricardo
Chemists' involvement in society (cont) bibliog pors Chem 44:18-20 F '71

FERRELL, Oliver P.
Direct & current. See issues of Popular electronics

FERRELL, Robert H.
Disarmament conferences: ballets at the brink. il Am Heritage 22:4-5+ F '71

FERRER, José Figueres. See Figueres Ferrer, J.

FERRER, Paul
French connection. il pors Newsweek 78:38 N 29 '71 *

FERRER, Rafael
Different drummer. K. Levin. il Art N 70: 48-51 D '71 *

FERRETS
Black-footed ferret; excerpts from Must they die? F. McNulty. il Nat Parks & Con Mag 45:9-13 My '71

FERRIES
Lingering link; Woodland ferry, Seaford, Del. R. McRoberts. il Travel 135:26 Je '71
Martini commuters; ferry from Sausalito to San Francisco. il Time 98:46 Jl 12 '71

FERRIES, Train. See Train ferries

FERRIS, Charles
Mansfield aide discusses amendment impact; interview, ed. by G. B. Lubkin. il por Phys Today 24:61-2 S '71

FERRIS, John
Ad hoc. Sat R 54:89 S 25 '71
Arf, arf, and a hearty woof. Sat R 54:6 Je 12 '71
Back in ten minutes. Sat R 55:6 Ja 8 '72
Brown suit. Sat R 54:4 Ag 14 '7)
Italy and the sandwich. Sat R 54:6 Jl 24 '71
(ed) See Hawkins, O. Osie

FERRIS, Steven H. and Pastore, Nicholas
Interocular apparent movement in depth: a motion preference effect. bibliog il Science 174:305-7 O 15 '71

FERRIS, William H.
William H. Ferris criticizes Booker T. Washington (1898); reprint from a Negro newspaper of 1898. G. P. Marks, 3d. il por Negro Hist Bul 33:162-3 N '70 *

FERRIS, William P.
Raising student self-esteem for a change. Engl J 60:379-81 Mr '71

FERRITES (magnetic materials)
Crystallography of the hexagonal ferrites. J. A. Kohn and others. bibliog il Science 172: 519-25 My 7 '71

FERRO cement boats. See Boats—Materials

FERROELECTRIC ceramics. See Electronic ceramics

FERROMAGNETISM. See Magnetism

FERRY, David
Cythera; Night-time river road; To Sally; poems. Poetry 118:31-2 Ap '71

FERTIG, Lawrence
Hysteria on the campus; address, March 2, 1971. Vital Speeches 37:454-9 My 15 '71

FERTILITY, Human
Some drugs bring babies. Sci Digest 69:17-18 Je '71

FERTILITY control. See Birth control

FERTILITY drugs
Correcting infertility without multiple births. Sci N 101:24 Ja 8 '72

FERTILITY of soils. See Soil fertility

FERTILITY vitamin. See Vitamins—Vitamin E

FERTILIZATION (in vitro)
Fertilization of rabbit ova in vitro by sperm with adsorbed sendai virus. R. J. Ericsson and others. bibliog il Science 173:54-5 Jl 2 '71
Fertilization outside womb. Sci Digest 69: 90 F '71
Obsolescent mother. E. Grossman. il Atlan 227:39-50 My '71
Test-tube baby is coming. D. M. Rorvik. il pors Look 35:83-6+ My 18 '71

FERTILIZATION of plants
Euglossine bees as long-distance pollinators of tropical plants. D. H. Janzen. bibliog il Science 171:203-5 Ja 15 '71
See also
Pollen

FERTILIZER spreaders
Ten farmer ideas that move fertilizer in a hurry. il Farm J 95:36-9 F '71

FERTILIZERS and manures
Cutting fertilizer may cost you money. il Suc Farm 69:44 Ap '71
Fertilizer nitrogen: contribution to nitrate in surface water in a Corn Belt watershed. D. H. Kohl and others. bibliog il Science 174:1331-4 D 24 '71
Fertilizer: what would it cost to... , C. E. Sommers. il Suc Farm 69:30-1 N '71
Fertilizers: liquids vs. dry. Farm J 95:30 N '71
Gardening with rock minerals. N. Bubel. Org Gard & Farm 18:69-71 O '71
Good deal, cottonseed meal. L. W. Patterson. Org Gard & Farm 18:102-3 S '71
Lawn fertilizers. il Consumer Rep 36:321-7 My '71
Look again at where to put fertilizer. R. Turner. Suc Farm 69:no3 A4 F '71
Newest findings on fertilizer runoff. B. Coffman. Farm J 95:20-2 Ag '71
Nitrogen can be applied safely on grassland. C. E. Sommers. Suc Farm 69:40 N '71
Poultry wastes; race-track manure. J. I. Rodale. il Org Gard & Farm 18:66-8 My '71
Relation of organic fertilizers to vitamins. Org Gard & Farm 18:96-8 Jl '71
Surface fertilization O.K. for no-till corn. Suc Farm 69:no2 B10 F '71
Using rock fertilizers on the farm. R. Steffen. il Org Gard & Farm 18:58-9 Mr '71
You can fertilize without harming environment. Suc Farm 69:C8 O '71
See also
Compost
Farm manure
Feeding and feeding stuffs—Manure
Humus
Liquid fertilizers and manures
Mulching
Phosphates
Sewage as fertilizer

Handling
Ten farmer ideas that move fertilizer in a hurry. il Farm J 95:36-9 F '71
Ways to save time: when fertilizing; and using chemicals. G. L. Earle. il Suc Farm 69:no4 34-7 Mr '71

Injurious effects
Effect of chemical fertilizers in water pollution. J. I. Rodale. Org Gard & Farm 18:26-8+ Ap '71
Please pass the poison. R. Stout. il Org Gard & Farm 18:36-7 Je '71

Terminology
How well do you know fertilizer terms? Suc Farm 69:no4 C18 Mr '71

FESCUE
Fescues, the hard-working grasses for home lawns. R. W. Schery. il Home Gard 58:24-5+ Mr '71

FESSENDEN, Clara L.
Tomatoes for a longer season. il Org Gard & Farm 18:62-4 Mr '71

FESTIVAL of black dance. See Dance festivals

FESTIVAL of contemporary arts. See Music festivals—Illinois

FESTIVAL of two worlds, Spoleto. See Festivals—Italy

FESTIVALS
1972 world travel calendar; comp. by F. Shemanski. Sat R 55:43-7 Ja 1 '72
See also
Carnival
Dance festivals
Drama festivals
International festival of music and drama, Edinburgh
Moving picture festivals
Music festivals
Tournaments

California
At San Francisco's Dickens fair: the spirit of Christmas past. il Sunset 147:66-7 D '71
Renaissance art faire. il Design 72:18-19 Sum '71

England
Lovely battle: Worcester's Charter festival. A. Bakshian, jr. Nat R 23:1128-9 O 8 '71

France
Communist funfest. il Time 98:48 S 27 '71

Germany (Federal Republic)
Not fit for horses; Löwenbräu beer wagons returning during Munich Oktoberfest. il Time 97:33 F 22 '71

Italy
Maggio musicale & Spoleto. W. Weaver. il Hi Fi 21:MA30-1 O '71

Michigan
See also
Holland, Mich.—Tulip time festival

Oregon
Fading roses; Portland rose festival. Nation 212:709 Je 7 '71

United States
Come to the fair. J. Beatty, jr. il Redbook 137:87-90 Jl '71
Of arms and the men we sing; with introd. note. J. Harrison; R. Drexler. il Sports Illus 34:68-72+ My 10 '71
Steam engine festivals. B. Thomas. il Travel 136:33-5 Jl '71
Summer music festivals (title varies) (cont) Hi Fi 21:MA14-16+ Mr; MA12-14 Ap '71

Virginia
Final curtain; Arabella Churchill's resignation as Norfolk Azalia queen. Nation 212:422 Ap 5 '71

Wisconsin
There's much a-brewin' in bubbly Milwaukee, summer fun! Old Milwaukee days. B. Hibbard. il Travel 135:54-7 My '71
Where is Tell? Wilhelm Tell festival. H. Kubly. il Holiday 49:48-9+ Jl '71

FESTUCA. See Fescue

FETAL hemoglobin. See Hemoglobin

FETCHIT, Stepin
Stepin Fetchit talks back; interview. ed. by J. McBride. pors Film Q 24:20-6 Sum '71

about
Whatever happened to Lincoln (Stepin Fetchit) Perry? il pors Ebony 27:202 N '71 *

FETROS, John G.
Search for a code of ethics. bibliog il Am Lib 2:743-5 Jl '71

FETTERMAN, John
People of Cumberland Gap. il Nat Geog 140:591-621 N '71

FETUS
Adult hemoglobin synthesis by reticulocytes from the human fetus at midtrimester. M. D. Hollenberg and others. bibliog il Science 174:698-702 N 12 '71
Fabry's disease: antenatal detection. R. O. Brady and others. bibliog il Science 172:174-5 Ap 9 '71
Growth hormone and fetal nutrition. Sci N 100:373-4 D 4 '71
How the fetus develops. E. B. Connell. por Redbook 137:10+ Ag '71
Sounding out the womb. J. L. Arehart. il Sci N 100:424-5 D 25 '71
Woman and the fetus: one flesh? R. C. Wahlberg. Chr Cent 88:1045-8 S 8 '71; Discussion. il 88:1450-1 D 8 '71
See also
Maternal-fetal exchange

Diseases
Diagnosis
Miracle baby of Carolyn Sinclair. J. L. Block and J. Stein. il por Good H 172:86-7+ Je '71
Prenatal diagnosis: how fast, how far? J. L. Arehart. il Sci N 100:44-5 Jl 17 '71
Prenatal diagnosis of genetic disease. T. Friedmann. il Sci Am 225:34-42 bibliog(p 136) N '71
Tay-Sachs disease: prenatal diagnosis. J. S. O'Brien and others. bibliog il Science 172:61-4 Ap 2 '71
Xeroderma pigmentosum: a rapid sensitive method for prenatal diagnosis. J. D. Regan and others. bibliog il Science 174:147-50 O 8 '71

FETUS, Effect of drugs on the
Heroin babies; going cold turkey at birth. S. Burnham. N Y Times Mag p 18-19+ Ja 9 '72

FETZ, Eberhard E. and Finocchio, D. V.
Operant conditioning of specific patterns of neural and muscular activity. bibliog il Science 174:431-5 O 22 '71

FEVER blisters. See Herpes simplex

FEW hours of sunlight; story. See Sagan, F.

FEY, Harold E.
America's most oppressed minority. il Chr Cent 88:65-8 Ja 20 '71

FEYDEAU, Georges
There's one in every marriage. Criticism Time 99:47 Ja 17 '72 *

FEYDY, Anne
How to win as a teen-age daughter; story. Vogue 158:118 S 1 '71

FFRENCH-BEYTAGH, Gonville Auble
Case against dean flawed; trial of Dean Gonville Ffrench-Beytagh. J. Squire. Chr Cent 88:1329-30 N 10 '71 *
Cut it out. por Newsweek 78:40+ Ag 16 '71 *
I won't come out alive. por Time 98:43 N 15 '71 *
South African cleric found guilty. Chr Cent 88:1343 N 17 '71 *
South African show trial. America 125:417 N 20 '71 *
South African visit reveals black anger, white apathy; with editorial comment. D. M. Parker Chr Cent 88:874, 882-3 Jl 21 '71 *
Win by losing. il por Newsweek 78:56 N 15 '71 *

FIAT (automobile) See Automobiles, Foreign

FIAT company. See Automobile industry—Italy

FIBER board
See also
Particle board

FIBER optics
Fiber optics for a tester. B. D. Hurt. il Sky & Tel 41:314-15 My '71
Genie in Poly-Optic's fiber lamps. il Bsns W p52 F 13 '71

FIBERGLASS. See Glass fabrics

FIBERGLASS boats. See Boats—Materials

FIBERS
Polymer whiskers grown from methyl 2-cyanoacrylate vapor. R. I. Smith-Johannsen. bibliog il Science 171:1246-7 Mr 26 '71
Rolls fiber interests readied for sale; carbon fibers. H. J. Coleman. Aviation W 95:17 O 25 '71
10,000 metamorphoses of plastics and synthetic fibres. G. Gregory. il UNESCO Courier 24:15-23 Je '71
See also
Sisal hemp
Textile fibers, Synthetic

FICHTER, George S.
Eighteen-hundred-and-froze-to-death. il Sci Digest 69:62-6 F '71

FICKEN, Robert W. and others
Eye marks in vertebrates: aids to vision. bibliog il Science 173:936-9 S 3 '71

FICKER, Bill
Ficker wins California cup. L. J. Kennedy. Motor B & S 127:39 Mr '71 *

FICO, Fred
International title output figures: are they really comparable? Pub W 200:pt2 187 S 27 '71

FICTION
Fiction and the figures of life. by W. H. Gass. Review
New Repub 164:22-3 Mr 20 '71. C. Bedient
Newsweek 77:86+ F 15 '71. G. Wolff
Summertime is fiction time. K. F. Kister. Library J 96:2276 Jl '71
What makes a good novel? R. P. Ashley. Engl J 60:596-8+ My '71
See also
Animals in literature
Characters in literature
Detective and mystery stories
Romanticism
Science fiction
Sex in literature
United States—History—Civil war—Fiction
War in literature

Authorship
Exclusive interview: P. G. Wodehouse; ed. by D. Bensen. P. G. Wodehouse. por Writers Digest 51:22-4+ O '71
Exclusive interview with Morris West; ed. by S. Steiner. M. West. por Writers Digest 51:30-3+ F '71
Exclusive re-visit with Evan Hunter; interview, ed. by F. Krajewski. E. Hunter. por Writers Digest 51:24-6 Ap '71
Games writers play. J. Porter. Writer 84:9-10+ D '71
How a book grows. F. E. Randall. Writer 85:11-13+ Ja '72
Involvement: action and reaction. O. Ruhen. Writer 84:16-18 F '71
Story behind the book: Wheels; interview, ed. by P. A. Farrell. A. Hailey. Pub W 200:32 O 18 '71
What to do till the novel comes. S. Jameson. Writer 84:14-15 Ap '71

Anecdotes, facetiae, satire, etc.
Found paradise. G. Keillor. New Yorker 47:32-3 S 18 '71

Bibliography
Fiction (cont) W. B. Hill. America 124:548-9, 125:430+ My 22, N 20 '71

Rounding up the new novels. il Newsweek 78:116+ O 25 '71
Roundup of recent fiction. G. Wolff; P. S. Prescot; R. A. Sokolov. il Newsweek 77:118-118B+ Ap 19 '71

Competitions
1971 short story contest. L. Reis. Writers Digest 51:31-2 O '71
1971 writing awards. Sr Schol 98:9-10 My 17 '71

Psychology
See Literature—Psychology

Technique
Confessions of the long-distance writer; family sagas. R. F. Delderfield. Writer 84:11-13 S '71
Detail makes the difference; heightening story impact. P. S. Curry. Writer 84:13-15+ N '71
Fiction technique & style: some comparisons. D. Madden. il Writers Digest 51:24-6+ Ag '71
Fiction techniques in nonfiction writing. N. B. Gerson. Writer 84:13-14+ D '71
Harbingers; storytelling in the novel. G. P. Elliott. Writer 84:9-10+ N '71
In the beginning . . . E. Ibbotson. Writer 84:9-12 Ag '71
Make it happen. R. Gatenby. Writer 84:17-19+ Ag '71
Notes on a second novel. F. Salas. Writer 84:12-15 F '71
Storytelling, old and new. E. Spencer. Writer 85:9-10+ Ja '72
Storytelling's tarnished image. M. Cowley. Sat R 54:25-7+ S 25 '71
S-t-r-e-t-c-h what you know. E. Davis. Writer 85:16-17+ Ja '72
Two-level story. V. Sneider. Writer 84:21-2 Je '71
Using an original formula. L. Duncan. Writer 84:11-12+ N '71
Viewpoint: a persuasive light; excerpt from Creating fiction from experience. P. S. Curry. Writer 84:17-18+ Mr '71
What should a novel be? adaptation of address, 1970. A. Dewlen. Writer 84:16-17 Jl '71
Where it happens; backgrounds for fiction. P. A. Whitney. Writer 85:14-15+ Ja '72
Writer's real world. S. Stevens. Writer 84:11-12+ Jl '71
Writing a first novel; symposium. Writer 84:20-3 O: 19-25 N '71
See also
Characterization
Detective and mystery stories—Technique
Dialogue
Plots (drama, novel, etc)
Short story

FICTION, Childrens. See Childrens literature
FICTION, Fantasy. See Fantasies, Literary
FICTION contests. See Fiction—Competitions
FICTION for children. See Childrens literature
FIDELIO; opera. See Beethoven, L. van

FIECHTER, Paul E.
Make a magnetic postal scale. il Pop Sci 198:108 F '71

FIEDLER, Arthur
Producer stars in DGG's first Boston Pops recording. R. D. Darrell. il por Hi Fi 20:86-7 D '70 *

FIEDLER, Leslie A.
Americans as innocents. P. S. Prescott. por Newsweek 78:76+ Ag 2 '71 *
Good bad boy and guru of American letters. C. R. Larson. por Sat R 54:27-8+ D 25 '71 *

FIEL, Maxine Lucille
Starcast. Mlle 74:132-3 Ja '72

FIELD, Carolyn
Sacred cows: the CCLD report. il por Library J 96:3445-7 O 15 '71

FIELD, David A.
National art museum of sport. il Sch Arts 70:40-3 Mr '71

FIELD, Marshall
Living with antiques. D. A. Hanks. il Antiques 100:116-19 Jl '71 *

FIELD, Michael
All manner of food; excerpts. il Ladies Home J 88:92-3+ F '71

FIELD, Nancy Dotterer
More than a space science center. il Todays Ed 60:32-3 O '71

FIELD, Pauline M. See Raisman, G. jt. auth.

FIELD and stream (periodical)
Two new shooting editors for a growing sport; S. Williams and B. Brister. M. J. O'Neill and C. Conley. pors Field & S 76:8-9 O '71

FIELD and stream fishing contest. See Fishing—Competitions
FIELD-effect meters. See Electric meters
FIELD effect transistors. See Transistors
FIELD glasses
Binoculars. il Consumer Rep 36:723-9 N '71
How to choose and use binoculars. R. Brightman. il Pop Mech 136:88-91+ S '71
Powerful glasses, sir, but are they good? P. Ryan. Sports Illus 34:73-5 Mr 8 '71
Scope that turns on and binoculars that float. C. Conley. il Field & S 76:106 Jl '71
FIELD theory (physics)
New mathematics in field theory. D. E. Thomsen. il Sci N 99:249-50 Ap 10 '71
FIELD trials (dogs)
Field trials for beagles. L. Mueller. il Field & S 75:128-30+ Ja '71
Pride of the setters; 1970 National field trial championship. L. Mueller. il Field & S 76:192+ Je '71
Shooting-dog championship; National shooting dog championship. D. M. Duffey. il Outdoor Life 147:150+ Je '71
Springer spaniel championship; English springer spaniel national championship. D. M. Duffey. il Outdoor Life 147:198+ Mr '71
FIELD trips, Conservation. See Conservation of resources—Study and teaching
FIELD trips, Educational. See School excursions
FIELD trips, Nature study. See Nature study
FIELDING, Harold
Mississippi on the Thames. il Newsweek 78:73 Ag 23 '71 *
FIELDS, Annie (Adams)
Literary lights were always bright at 148 Charles street. B. Rotundo. il pors Am Heritage 22:10-15 F '71 *
FIELDS, Howard
Parting shots; living high on a $528,471 boo-boo. il pors Life 70:78-9 Je 4 '71 *
FIELDS, James Thomas
Literary lights were always bright at 148 Charles street. B. Rotundo. il pors Am Heritage 22:10-15 F '71 *
FIELDS, W. C.
W. C. Fields & me, by C. Monti, ed. by C. Rice. Review
Newsweek il por 77:92 Je 21 '71. A. Cooper *
FIENBERG, Stephen E.
Randomization and social affairs: the 1970 draft lottery. bibliog il Science 171:255-61; 172:630+ Ja 22, My 14 '71
FIEVEZ, Paul
Torch artistry. il por Design 72:24-5 mid-Sum '71
FIFE, Daniel
Killing the goose. il Environ 13:20-2+ Ap '71
FIFE, Eric S.
American leadership in world missions. Chr Today 15:12-14 Ja 29 '71
FIFE and drum corps. See Bands (music)
FIFER, Bill
Bucket-grill barbecue cart. il Pop Sci 199:82-4 Ag '71
FIFTH committee of the General assembly. See United Nations—Administrative and budgetary committee
FIFTY books of the year exhibit. See Book exhibits
FIGHTING (psychology)
See also
Aggressiveness (psychology)
FIGHTING, Hand to hand
See also
Karate
FIGS
See also
Cookery—Fruit
FIGUERES FERRER, José
Freelance diplomacy. il por Time 97:29 Mr 8 '71 *
Terrorizing terrorists. por Time 98:33-4 D 27 '71 *
FIGURAL aftereffects
Optical illusions, how one kind can cancel out another. R. Dreistadt. il Sci Digest 69:10-14 F '71
FIGURE drawing
Harry Carmean: teacher of classical figure drawing. R. Parola. il por Am Artist 35:58-65+ Mr '71
I can't draw people. R. A. Yoder. il Sch Arts 71:16-17 N '71
FIGURES of speech
Analogy: pathway to relevance. B. M. Bivins. Engl J 60:93-6 Ja '71
See also
Metaphor
FIGURINES
See also
Bronzes

FIJI
Paradise returned: celebrating independence. E. B. Thompson. il Ebony 26:84-8+ F '71
Travel notes. R. Joseph. Esquire 72:16+ Ja '71
FILENE center. See Wolf Trap Farm Park for the performing arts
FILES, Police. See Police records
FILES and filing (documents, etc)
File it easy, find it fast. Farm J 95:37 Ja '71
Filing technical articles. H. Stratman. il por Electr World 85:58 F '71
FILES and rasps
How shop work shapes up with rotary rasps. R. J. De Cristoforo. il Pop Sci 199:96-8 Jl '71
Low-cost way to add a shaper to your shop; rotary wood rasps. H. Wicks. il Pop Mech 136:178-9 O '71
FILIBUSTERING in legislation. See United States—Congress—Senate—Rules and practice
FILING cabinets. See Cabinets (furniture)
FILION, Herve
Broken wrist, broken record. W. F. Reed. il Sports Illus 35:83-4 D 13 '71 *
Driving ambition. Newsweek 78:73 D 13 '71 *
He who laughs last. W. F. Reed. il por Sports Illus 35:26-8 S 6 '71 *
FILIPIN
Antibiotics as pesticides. il Chem 44:23 F '71
FILIPINO cookery. See Cookery, Philippine
FILIPPI, Ronald, and Rousey, C. L.
Positive carriers of violence among children: detection by speech deviations. bibliog Ment Hy 55:157-61 Ap '71
FILLETS, Fish. See Fish fillets
FILLIBEN, James J. See Rosenblatt, J. R. jt. auth.
FILLING (earthwork)
Crushing refuse down to size, compacted landfill. il Bsns W p58 F 13 '71
Dumps are signs of poor administration; using sanitary landfill in Beaumont, Tex. C. R. Cowart, jr. il Am City 86:54+ D '71
From a dump of sorts to a spot for sports; converting Brookhaven's Holtsville village into a sport city. J. Kaplan. il Sports Illus 35:52-3 Ag 23 '71
Phoenix plan at Brookhaven; conversion of landfill and waste disposal areas to park and recreational facilities. K. P. Goldbach. Cons 25:30 F '71
Skiing down a garbage pile: sanitary landfills. il Bsns W p90 N 6 '71
Solid waste demonstration programs; sanitary-landfill operations. E. F. Spitzer. il Am City 86:58-60+ Jl '71
Still another Mount Trashmore; Arlington Heights, Ill. il Am City 86:32 S '71
Up with trash. M. MacPherson. McCalls 99:33 N '71
FILLION, Bryant
Turning on: the selling of the present, 1970. Engl J 60:333-8 Mr '71
—See Burton, D. L. jt. auth.
FILLPOT, Dave
New friends, new ideas, a new direction and a new horizon. Camp Mag 43:12 Mr '71
FILM adaptations. See Moving picture adaptations
FILM audiences. See Moving picture audiences
FILM books. See Moving picture literature
FILM critics. See Critics
FILM festivals. See Moving picture festivals
FILM libraries. See Moving picture film collections
FILM propaganda. See Moving pictures—Propaganda films
FILM quarterly
Some blunt talk about money. Film Q 25:1-2 Fall '71
FILM scripts. See Moving picture scripts
FILM speeds. See Photography—Exposure
FILM strips
Screenings; filmstrips. D. L. Lembo. See occasional issues of Library journal
FILMS
Borderland of burning bubbles; role surface films play in nature's balance. D. C. Blanchard. il Sat R 55:60-3 Ja 1 '72
Surface films compacted by moving water; demarcation lines reveal film edges. C. W. McCutchen; reply. R. S. McDowell and C. W. McCutchen. bibliog Science 172:973 My 28 '71
See also
Photography—Films
Thin films
FILMS from books. See Moving picture adaptations

FILMSTRIPS. See Film strips

FILTER plants
Don't color the water black; Boonton, N.J.
F. J. Costabile and C. H. Perron. il Am Ci-
ty 86:46-7 Ja '71
FILTERS, Light. See Light filters
FILTERS and filtration
Drinking man's guide to water filters. F.
Coffee. il Mech Illus 67:86-7+ S '71
Drinking water filter; Filbrook drinking
water filter. il Consumer Bul 54:4 F '71
Invisible wall that purifies water; reverse os-
mosis filtration system. D. X. Manners. il
Sci Digest 69:70-3 Je '71
Tertiary treatment costs can be lowered;
Crane microstrainer. E. W. J. Diaper. Am
City 86:108 N '71
See also
Air filters
FILTERS and filtration (bacteriology)
Amateur scientist; experiments with a new
standard filter material that has extremely
fine pores. C. L. Stong. il Sci Am 224:118-
22 F '71
FILTERS and filtration (biological products)
Filter for the heart. il Newsweek 78:31 N 1
'71
FIMRITE, Ron
Bad case of the Short shorts. il Sports Illus
35:20-2+ Ag 9 '71
Baseball. il Sports Illus 34:62-3 My 3; 62 My
24; 68+ My 31; 54 Je 14; 35:82-4 S 13 '71
Birdbath for the Pirates. il Sports Illus 35:
20-3 O 18 '71
Buried under a sea of troubles. il Sports Illus
35:28-31 N 15 '71
Eerie September, camaraderie and the Fox
who says no. il Sports Illus 35:15-17 Ag 30
'71
For failure to give his best. il pors Sports
Illus 35:12-17 Jl 5 '71
Heading them off at the pass. il Sports Illus
35:30-2+ N 29 '71
It's all quiet on the other front. il Sports
Illus 35:23-5 S 27 '71
Three kids warm up chilly city. il Sports
Illus 34:18-21 My 17 '71
We expect them to storm the gates. il Sports
Illus 35:20-2+ S 6 '71
Week; baseball. Sports Illus 34:59 My 10; 72+
Je 7; 35:68+ S 20 '71
Well, he's that kind of guy. por Sports Illus
35:28-30+ O 4 '71
—See Mulvoy, M. jt. auth.
FINAL exam; story. See Gerber, M. J.
FINANCE
See also
Bonds
Church finance
Commerce
Credit
Depreciation
Domestic finance
Farm finance
Income
Inflation (finance)
Interest
Investment trusts
Negotiable instruments
School finance
Stock exchange
also subhead Finance under various sub-
jects, e.g. Airlines—Finance

Terminology
Language of finance: a glossary. il U S News
71:25 D 13 '71
Australia
See also
Securities—Australia

Brazil
See also
Stock exchange—Rio de Janeiro

California
See also
Taxation—California

Canada
See also
Banks and banking—Canada

France
Boondoggler's bible; accounting court's annual report. il Time 98:31 Jl 26 '71

Germany (Federal Republic)
See also
Inflation (finance)
Securities—Germany (Federal Republic)

Great Britain
See also
Budget—Great Britain

Japan
See also
Japan—Commerce
Money—Japan
Stock exchange—Tokyo

Pennsylvania
Battle over bankruptcy. il Time 98:11-12 Jl
19 '71
United States
Dollars at a discount. H. Hazlitt. Nat R
23:591-2 Je 1 '71
TRB from Washington. New Repub 164:8
F 20 '71
See also
Banks and banking—United States
Budget—United States
Debts, Public—United States
Inflation (finance)
Taxation—United States
United States—Appropriations and expendi-
tures
United States—Commission on financial struc-
ture and regulation
United States—Economic conditions
United States—Federal reserve board
United States—Monetary policy
United States—Treasury, Department of the
Wall Street
also subhead Finance under names of
cities, e.g. Palo Alto, Calif.—Finance
FINANCE, International
International competition and production;
role of the United States; address. January
14, 1971. J. Polk. Vital Speeches 37:286-8
F 15 '71
Into a time of stagflation. L. A. Mayer. il
Fortune 84:144-9 Ag '71
See also
Balance of payments
Bank for international settlements
Banks and banking, International
Eurobond market
Eurodollar market
Foreign exchange
International bank for reconstruction and
development
International finance corporation
International monetary fund
Money—International aspects
Special drawing rights
United Nations monetary and financial con-
ference
FINANCE, Local. See Local finance
FINANCE, Personal
Choose your bank carefully, then use it right.
il Changing T 25:7-10 D '71
Financial counseling: worth the price? J.
Perham. Duns 98:29-31+ Ag '71
Spending your money; questions and answers.
S. Porter. See issues of Ladies' home jour-
nal
When are you heading for real money trou-
ble? M. Daly. Bet Hom & Gard 49:26+ Je
'71
Your personal finances (cont) Todays Ed
60:54-6 Ja; 38-40 F; 60-1 Mr; 24-6 Ap; 46-7
My '71
See also
Estate planning
FINANCE, State. See State finance
FINANCE companies
See also
Factors
FINANCE corporation, Reconstruction. See Re-
construction finance corporation
FINANCIAL analysts. See Investment advisers
FINANCIAL consultants. See Financial ser-
vices
FINANCIAL counseling. See Financial services
FINANCIAL daily (newspaper) See Media gen-
eral financial daily
FINANCIAL institutions
Finance; with yardsticks of management
performance. Forbes 109:93-6 Ja 1 '72
SEC study ducks some hard questions.
Bsns W p39 Mr 13 '71
See also
Banks and banking
Investment trusts
Pension trusts
Savings and loan associations
United States—Commission on financial
structure and regulation

Investments
Sizing up the clout; SEC study of institu-
tional investors. C. Morgello. il Newsweek
77:94 Mr 22 '71
Somewhere over the rainbow. it's 1972. il
Bsns W p38 Mr 13 '71
FINANCIAL public relations. See Investor re-
lations programs

FINANCIAL ratios
Ratios of manufacturing; table; with editorial comment (cont) Duns 98:62-3+. 104 N '71
Ratios of retailing; with table. Duns 98:76-7 S '71
FINANCIAL services
Financial counseling: worth the price? J. Perham. Duns 98:29-31+ Ag '71
See also
Investment advisers
FINANCIAL statements
See also
Corporation reports
FINCH, Donald I. See Gray. W. T. jt. auth.
FINCH, Lindley
Money management; interview. por Suc Farm 69:no4 10 Mr '71
FINCH college, New York
Let 'em eat coquilles Saint-Jacques. T. Meehan; discussion. N Y Times Mag p37+ Ja 31 '71
FINCHES
See also
Indigo buntings
FINDER, Morris
Reading and writing exposition and argument: the skills and their relationships. Engl J 60:615-20 My '71
FINDER; story. See Spencer, E.
FINDLEY, Myrtle
Watercress, storehouse of vitamins and minerals. il Org Gard & Farm 18:45 Ap '71
FINDLEY, Rowe
Canyonlands: realm of rock and the far horizon. il Nat Geog 140:71-91 Jl '71
FINDSEN, Owen
Lyric brush of John Chumley. il por Am Artist 35:30-5+ Je '71
FINE, D. L. and others
Simian tumor virus isolate: demonstration of cytopathic effects in vitro. bibliog il Science 174:420-1 O 22 '71
FINE, Irene
Children welcome! il Ladies Home J 88:56 My '71
FINE, William M.
7 snares that lead men to affairs. Harp Baz 104:98-9 Ap '71
FINE arts quartet. See String quartets
FINEBERG, S. Andhil
Violence or brotherhood? A religious dilemma. il Cath World 213:17-20 Ap '71
FINEMAN, Morton
Girl on the trampoline; story. Ladies Home J 88:90-1 Jl '71
FINFOOTS (birds)
Strange bird. il Newsweek 78:108+ N 15 '71
FINGER, Seymour M.
U.N. General assembly establishes committee on procedures; statement. November 9, 1970. Dept State Bul 63:762-4 D 21 '70
FINGER LAKES
See also
Cayuga Lake
FINGER painting
Hands: inky fun with your fingers; with illustrations by B. Shein and R. Tallon. il Life 71:156-60 D 17 '71
FINGER prints. See Fingerprints
FINGERHUT, Vic
Enduring Republican minority. New Repub 165:18-20 S 11 '71
FINGERNAILS blue as flowers; drama. See Ribman, R.
FINGERPRINT pictures. See Pictures
FINGERPRINTS
Ancient impressions. il Time 97:55 Je 7 '71
Fingerprints; case of Dale B. Menard and distribution of files by the Identification division of the FBI. S. J. Ungar. New Repub 164:20-1 Je 12 '71
No more fingerprints; ruling by G. A. Gesell. New Repub 165:8 Jl 3 '71
Satellites and lasers aid fingerprint identification. Am City 86:24 N '71
FINIALS
Finial busts on eighteenth-century Philadelphia furniture. R. C. Smith. il Antiques 100:900-5 D '71
FINK, Daniel J.
Future space objectives. Aviation W 94:9 Ja 25 '71
FINK, Peter E.
Ideas on trial. America 124:202 F 27 '71
FINK, Raymond
Financing outpatient mental health care through psychiatric insurance. bibliog Ment Hy 55:143-50 Ap '71
FINK, Robert
Flying the American way. New Repub 164: 19-22 F 13 '71
Unfair air fares. New Repub 165:13-15 S 11 '71

FINK, Steven Sanford. See Sanford, S.
FINKEL, R. S.
(tr) See Singer, I. B. Peephole in the gate
FINKELSTEIN, Jerry
Our own Andromeda strain. Read Digest 99: 107-9 D '71
FINKELSTEIN, Ronnie
Confession of a biker. il Sr Schol 98:34-5 Ap 26 '71
FINKELSTEIN, Shira
We were hijacked! pors Seventeen 29:170 D '70
FINKELSTEIN memorial library, Spring Valley, N.Y.
Divorce: N.Y. style. K. Nyren. il Library J 96:2257-62 Jl '71
Spring Valley, N.Y. library secedes from system. Library J 96:909-10 Mr 15 '71
What price cooperation? W. R. Eshelman. Wilson Lib Bul 45:733 Ap '71
FINKLE, Dave, and others
DISCussions. See issues of Senior scholastic
FINKLE, Donald
Comment. M. L. Rosenthal. Poetry 119:100-1 N '71 *
FINLAND
See also
Airlines—Finland

Description and travel
Helsinki's handwriting on the wall. L. Barry. il Pop Phot 68:24+ Ap '71
In Finland, in the summer, on a lake. M. Gough. House B 113:14 Jl '71

Politics and government
Ice-bucket tempest. por Time 99:28 Ja 17 '72

Religious institutions and affairs
See also
Church and state in Finland
FINLAYSON, Eleanor
Landscaping with heaths and heathers. il Horticulture 49:41+ F '71
FINLEY, Charles O.
What if they had a world series and nobody came? L. Shecter. Look 35:22+ O 5 '71 *
FINLEY, Clarence C.
Clarence Finley's magic carpet ride. il pors Ebony 26:58-60+ F '71 *
FINLEY, Nancy
Roll a multi-colored print. il Sch Arts 71: 10-11 D '71
FINLEY, Sylvia
Washington scores Moose for snub of black librarian. il por Library J 97:11 Ja 1 '72 *
FINN, James
Catholic revolutionaries: part of the solution or part of the problem? Commonweal 94: 456-8 3 '71
Reinhold Niebuhr. Commonweal 94:324 Je 25 '71
FINNEGAN at the fair; drama. See Watts, F. B.
FINNISH baths. See Sauna
FINNISH cookery. See Cookery, Finnish
FINOCCHIO, Dom V. See Fetz, E. E. jt. auth.
FIORI, Pamela
Bed and board: Mills Hyatt house, Charleston, South Carolina. il Holiday 49:81-2 Mr '71
FIRE alarms
Build a multi-sensor alarm. C. R. Lewart. il Radio-Electr 42:58-9 N '71
Fire-alarm system guards a police station; Chicago. W. B. Buckley. il Am City 86:86+ Mr '71
Radio operated fire alarm system. B. Bernard. il Radio-Electr 42:47 D '71
FIRE ant venom. See Venom
FIRE ants. See Ants
FIRE apparatus
Firefighting: better equipment for the big ones. G. A. W. Boehm. il Pop Mech 136: 114-17+ N '71
New firefighting tool from aerospace; Jet axe. il Am City 86:22 S '71
Smaller cities bigger fire-apparatus buyers. Am City 86:46 O '71
FIRE apparatus, Motor. See Fire engines
FIRE arms. See Firearms
FIRE codes. See Fire protection—Laws and regulations
FIRE departments
See also
Fire alarms
Firemen
also subhead Fire department under names of cities, e.g. New York (city)—Fire department

FIRE engines
Air-force type fire fighter for airports; Lambert field in St Louis. il Am City 86:12 F '71
Diesel fire trucks reduce operating costs; Albuquerque, N.M. R. Kuhn. il Am City 86:36 N '71
Diesel puts new life in fire apparatus; South Charleston, W.Va. J. McConnell. il Am City 86:37 O '71
Firemen build roof for fire engine; Toledo, Ohio. il Am City 86:49 N '71
Safety shelters for fire apparatus; Baltimore fire department's protection against attacks. C. R. Warfield. il Am City 86:10 D '71
Telescoping boom moves indoors; Boston. J. M. Murphy. il Am City 86:46 Je '71

FIRE extinguishers
Consumer's guide to fire extinguishers. il Mech Illus 67:96 Ag '71
Home fire extinguishers. il Changing T 25: 37-9 F '71
How to choose and use fire extinguishers. S. J. Howard. il Pop Mech 135:116-19 Je '71

FIRE fighting. See Fire protection; Forest fire protection

FIRE ISLAND
See also
Architecture, Domestic—Fire Island
Gardens—Fire Island

FIRE making
See also
Camp fires

FIRE-police boats. See Police boats

FIRE protection
How to outmaneuver a firestorm. J. Joseph. il Todays Health 49:34-9+ S '71
20 steps to a more fire-safe home. S. Schuler. Am Home 74:90 N '71
What to do in case of fire; follow these lifesaving tips. Look 35:24 Je 29 '71
See also
Fire alarms
Fire extinguishers
Fire resisting materials
Firemen
Fireproof construction
Forest fire protection
Lightning protection
Underwriters' laboratories, inc.
also subhead Fires and fire protection under various subjects, e.g. Nursing homes —Fires and fire protection

Laws and regulations
Tougher fire safety code for skyscrapers. il Bsns W p46-7 Ag 7 '71

FIRE resistant plants. See Plants—Fire resistance

FIRE resisting materials
Space fireproofing finds wide use. Z. Strickland. il Aviation W 94:14-17 Ap 5 '71
See also
Fireproof construction

FIRE resisting textile fabrics. See Textile fabrics, Fire resisting

FIRE trucks. See Fire engines

FIRE walking
Firewalkers of Udappawa. V. Perera. Harper 242:18+ My '71

FIREARMS
Firearms. C. G. Worman. See issues of Hobbies
Getting the range. J. O'Connor. See issues of Outdoor life
Shooting. J. O'Connor. See issues of Outdoor life
Shooting; ed. by W. Page. See issues of Field & stream
See also
Revolvers
Rifles
Shotguns

Laws and regulations
Disarmament at home. Nation 211:643-4 D 21 '70
Editorial; Federal gun control act of 1968. C. Conley. Field & S 76:4 N '71
Failure of federal gun control. C. Bakal. il Sat R 54:12-15+ Jl 3 '71
Gun control and public order. Nation 212: 706-7 Je 7 '71
Handguns and homicide. America 125:135 S 11 '71
Notes and comment; Hart bill banning private ownership of handguns. New Yorker 47:40-1 N 27 '71
Politics of problems. Nation 212:770 Je 21 '71
Saturday night special and other hardware. R. Sherrill. il N Y Times Mag p 15+ O 10 '71; Discussion. p54 O 31; 16+ N 21 '71

TRB from Washington. New Repub 165:6 Jl 24 '71
TRB Washington: 24,000,000 guns. New Repub 165:6 S 18 '71

Manufacture
Little old men with files. W. Page. il Field & S 76:980-100+ Ag '71

Sights
Easy-aim sight makes it hard to miss; Weaver Qwik-Point. P. Wahl. il Pop Sci 199:56 S '71
Point-and-shoot sight puts a dot on the target. P. Wahl. il Pop Sci 198:111 F '71
Scope that turns on and binoculars that float. C. Conley. il Field & S 76:106 Jl '71
Sighting-in the rifle. J. O'Connor. il Outdoor Life 148:96+ O '71

FIREARMS industry
Saturday night special and other hardware. R. Sherrill. il N Y Times Mag p 15+ O 10 '71; Discussion. p54 O 31; 16+ N 21 '71
Those Italian shotguns. J. O'Connor. il Outdoor Life 147:124+ My '71
See also
Browning arms company

FIREFLIES
Synchrony and flash entrainment in a New Guinea firefly. F. E. Hanson and others. bibliog il Science 174:161-4 O 8 '71

FIREMEN
Get me an ax! New York city's Rescue company 1 and Engine 65. W. J. McKean. il Look 35:18-24 Je 29 '71
. . Or a firefighter? D. Smith. Read Digest 99:169-70 S '71

Training
Firemen paramedics. A. Hamilton. il Sci Digest 70:18-21 Ag '71

FIREPLACE accessories
Hi-fi? No. It's a wood locker. il Sunset 146: 142+ Je '71

FIREPLACES
Details that make the difference. W. Baldwin. House & Gard 139:10+ My '71
Prepare your fireplace now for cold weather. Good H 173:188 O '71
Products to make your job look professional; packaged fireplace. R. F. Dempewolff. il Pop Mech 135:110-11+ My '71
To use your fireplace safely. Sunset 146:109 Mr '71

FIREPROOF construction
Are our office buildings firetraps? N. A. Martin. il Duns 98:50-2+ N '71

FIREPROOFING
Space fireproofing finds wide use. Z. Strickland. il Aviation W 94:14-17 Ap 5 '71
See also
Fireproof construction

FIRES
Fiery ordeal of the Everglades. il Life 70:42-3 My 7 '71
Imperiled Everglades. F. Ward. il Nat Geog 141:1-8 Ja '72
See also
Arson
Brush fires
Chicago—Fire, October 1871
Fire protection
Forest fires
Space vehicles—Fires and fire protection
Textile fabrics, Flammable

FIRES at sea. See Ships—Fires and fire protection

FIRESTONE, Raymond Christy
Road to economic survival; address, November 15, 1971. Vital Speeches 38:155-7 D 15 '71

FIRESTORMS. See Brush fires

FIRETHORNS
Decorate with espaliered pyracantha. il Sunset 147:189 D '71

FIREWALKING. See Fire walking

FIREWEED
Nature's plastic surgeon; epilobium angustifolium. H. R. Russell. il Cons 25:17 Je '71

FIRING of employees. See Employees—Dismissal

FIRING of librarians. See Librarians—Dismissal

FIRING of library assistants. See Library assistants—Dismissal

FIRING of pottery. See Pottery—Firing

FIRMS, Architectural. See Architectural firms

FIRN caves. See Ice caves

FIRST aid in illness and injury
New techniques to help save life for accident victims. E. M. Papper. Vogue 158: 268-9+ S 1 '71
See also
Ambulances
Medicine cabinets

FIRST aid kits. See Medicine kits
FIRST amendment to the Constitution. See
United States—Constitution—Bill of rights
FIRST Boston corporation
First Boston finds the big money. il Bsns
W p64-6 Mr 6 '71
Saul details his First Boston job. por Bsns
W p86 O 23 '71
FIRST committee of the General assembly. See
United Nations—Political and security com-
mittee
FIRST good-by; story. See Perry, P.
FIRST Harlem securities corporation
Big board's first black-owned firm. por
Bsns W p78+ Mr 20 '71
Green is beautiful. il por Duns 97:68-9 Ap '71
FIRST ladies. See Presidents—United States—
Wives
FIRST national bank of Boston. See Boston—
Banks
FIRST national city bank of New York. See
New York (city)—Banks
FIRST state bank of Chicago. See Chicago—
Banks
FISCAL policy
Are you a Keynesian? W. F. Buckley, jr.
Nat R 23:162-3 F 9 '71
FISCH, Harold
Figure of the dybbuk. Commentary 51:70-5
Ap '71
FISCHBACH and Moore, inc.
Reputation too precious. il Forbes 108:46-7
N 1 '71
FISCHBECK, Frank
Gallery; photograph. Life 70:6-7 My 28 '71
Great wall comes down; photographs. Life
70:22-31 Ap 30 '71
FISCHER, Bobby
Bobby clears the board for the title. R.
Cantwell. il por Sports Illus 35:30-2+ N
8 '71 *
Bobby Fischer is a ferocious winner. B.
Darrach. il pors Life 71:50A-53 N 12 '71 *
Bobby makes his move. il pors Time 98:68+
N 8 '71 *
Computerized steamroller. il pors Time 98:54
Ag 2 '71 *
Maybe you can win them all. R. Cantwell. il
Sports Illus 35:18-19 Ag 2 '71 *
On to Moscow. Newsweek 78:80 N 8 '71 *
Parting shots. B. Darrach. il por Life 71:61
Jl 23 '71 *
Peacock vs. the wren. il pors Newsweek
78:87-8+ O 18 '71 *
Six moves toward a world championship. L.
Evans. il por Sports Illus 34:58-9 Je 21 '71 *
Strange malady called Fischer fear. H. C.
Schonberg. il pors N Y Times Mag p32-
3+ N 14 '71 *
FISCHER, Charles
How to keep African-violets blooming all
winter. il Home Gard 58:38+ O '71
FISCHER, John, 1910-
Survival U is alive and burgeoning in Green
Bay, Wisconsin. Harper 242:20+ F '71;
Same abr. with title New university for sur-
vival. Cur 128:12-18 Ap '71
FISCHER, Konrad
Art. D. McConathy. Vogue 158:68 N 1 '71 *
FISCHER, Roland
Cartography of the ecstatic and meditative
states. bibliog il Science 174:897-904 N 26
'71
FISCHER, Virlis
Storm signals over the Sawtooth. il por Am
For 77:32-5+ Ja '71
FISCHER-WILLIAMS, Barbara
Good old Guiraud. por Opera N 35:24-5 F 6
'71
On a hill in Tuscany. il Opera N 35:16-18 My
15 '71
(ed) See Baudo, S. Moving quickly
(ed) See Lance, A. Frenchman from down
under
FISCHL, Irene
Why are nurses shook-up over abortion?
Look 35:66 F 9 '71
FISCHLER, Stan
Hockey: the bloodiest game. il Look 35:32-4
F 9 '71
FISH, Frozen
See also
Shellfish, Frozen
FISH, Smoked
Fishing up a storm. H. G. Tapply. il Field
& S 76:58 S '71
FISH and wildlife service. See United States—
Fish and wildlife service
FISH as food
Fish facts, all you need to know. Bet Hom
& Gard 49:76 Mr '71
Fishman talks about fish; ed. by H. McCul-
ly. J. Enea. il por House B 113:166+ O '71

Nitrosoamines in fish. Chem 44:21-2 My '71
See also
Cookery—Fish
Fish protein concentrate
FISH culture
Farm pond revisited. W. O. McLarney. il
Org Gard & Farm 18:88-92+ N '71
Introduction to aquaculture on the organic
farm and homestead. W. O. McLarney. il
Org Gard & Farm 18:71-7 Ag '71
Jumping catfish! il Newsweek 78:90 S 27 '71
Little salmon; planted kokanee in eastern
lakes. L. J. Bashline. il Field & S 76:38 Je
'71
New trout for old waters. W. A. Flick. il
Cons 25:18-21 Je '71
Now they're herding catfish. H. Manchester.
il Read Digest 98:19-22+ Je '71
Organic gardener and farmer as a scientist.
J. H. Todd. il Org Gard & Farm 18:63-9
N '71
We must learn to walk through the water;
interest in aquaculture. R. Rodale. il Org
Gard & Farm 18:32-6 Ap '71
Wild hope from some tame Atlantic salmon;
Norwegian fish farms. C. Gammon. il Sports
Illus 35:94+ N 29 '71
See also
Shellfish culture
FISH detectors. See Detectors
FISH farming. See Fish culture
FISH fillets
Right way to fillet a fish. il Good H 172:201
Ap '71
FISH hatcheries. See Fish culture
FISH hooks. See Fishhooks
FISH ladders. See Fishways
FISH mousse. See Cookery—Fish
FISH poisons
Catch is, should you eat it? R. H. Boyle.
il Sports Illus 35:46-7 Jl 12 '71
FISH protection
See also
Fishways
FISH protein concentrate
Fish flour: protein supplement has yet to ful-
fill expectations. C. Holden. Science 173:
410-12 Jl 30 '71
FISH soups. See Chowder
FISH stories. See Fishes—Stories
FISHBEIN, Gershon
Uncle Sam's environment troika. il Nations
Bsns 59:34-6 Ap '71
FISHBEIN, William, and others
Retrograde amnesia: electroconvulsive shock
effects after termination of rapid eye move-
ment sleep deprivation. bibliog il Science
172:80-2 Ap 2 '71
FISHER, Aileen
Abe's winkin' eye; drama. Plays 30:55-64 F
'71
Sing the songs of Thanksgiving; drama; re-
print from November 1958 issue. Plays
31:69-78 N '71
FISHER, Allan C. jr
Australia's pacesetter state, Victoria. il Nat
Geog 139:218-53 F '71
FISHER, Arthur
Science newsfront. See Issues of Popular
science monthly
FISHER, Bernard, and others
Portal blood factor as the humoral agent in
liver regeneration. bibliog il Science 171:
575-7 F 12 '71
FISHER, Charles P.
Fisher vs. Lang. pors Hi Fi 21:18-19 Jl '71
FISHER, Dave
Sam Schulman, the key to the merger. il
Life 70:34 Ap 23 '71
FISHER, Geoffrey Francis, baron Fisher of
Lambeth. See Fisher of Lambeth, G. F. F.
FISHER, Isabelle
Tax reform act (cont) Dance Mag 45:83 F;
108 Ap '71
FISHER, Jonathan
Writing article queries that sell. Writer 84:
18+ Je '71
FISHER, Karen
Cashing in on fear & fantasy. Nation 213:
334-7 O 11 '71
FISHER, Louis
Hiding billions from Congress. Nation 213:
486-90 N 15 '71
FISHER, M. F. K.
Art of eating, the art of living; interview. ed.
by B. A. Bannon. il por Pub W 199:17-18 Mr
29 '71
Enclave (cont) New Yorker 46:37-41 Ja 16;
47:36-42 My 15 '71

FISHER, M. F. K.—*Continued*
Made, with love, by hand. il McCalls 98: 94-5+ S '71
Scarlet dens of Christmases past; excerpt from Among friends. McCalls 99:124-5+ D '71

about

Among friends, by M. F. K. Fisher. Review Vogue 159:122 Ja 1 '72. J. Stafford *

FISHER, Martin C.
Fishing: what it can do for your camp. il Camp Mag 43:16-17 F '71

FISHER, Mildred Ogg
Shakespeare: why ignore the comedies and the histories? Engl J 60:587-90 My '71

FISHER, W. Halder
Anatomy of inflation: 1953-1975; with biographical sketch. il Sci Am 225:12, 15-21 N '71

FISHER of Lambeth, Geoffrey Francis Fisher, baron
Open letter to Archbishop Lord Fisher of Lambeth. T. Beeson. Chr Cent 88:244-5 F 24 '71 *

FISHERIES
See also
Fish culture
Shellfish fisheries

International aspects

Canada's action on fisheries closing lines opposed by U.S.; U.S. statement. Dept State Bul 64:448 Mr 29 '71
Crisis at sea: the threat of no more fish. R. Brigham. il Life 71:60-8 D 3 '71
Fishy business; who owns the oceans? D. F. Ross. New Repub 166:19-21 Ja 1 '72
Great tuna war. Newsweek 78:28 D 27 '71
U.S. and U.S.S.R. sign addition to Atlantic fisheries agreement. Dept State Bul 64:250-1 F 22 '71
U.S. and U.S.S.R. sign agreements on Northeastern Pacific fisheries. Dept State Bul 64:460-1 Mr 29 '71
U.S. regrets Canada's extension of high seas jurisdiction; U.S. statement. Dept State Bul 64:139 F 1 '71
United States and Poland extend fisheries agreement, October 1, 1971. Dept State Bul 65:471 O 25 '71
United States and U.S.S.R. sign Atlantic fisheries agreement. Dept State Bul 64:33-5 Ja 4 '71
Why our fishing fleet is sinking. J. E. Roper. il Read Digest 99:182-6+ O '71
See also
Shellfish fisheries—International aspects

Law

See Fishery laws and legislation

Japan

Japan's salmon industry. A. Netboy. il Am For 77:32-6 D '71

Norway

Wild hope from some tame Atlantic salmon; Norwegian fish farms. C. Gammon. il Sports Illus 35:94+ N 29 '71

United States

Catch in the hatch isn't what it used to be; Provincetown, Mass. E. J. Kahn, jr. il N Y Times Mag p 12-13+ Ag 29 '71
Crisis at sea: the threat of no more fish. R. Brigham. il Life 71:60-8 D 3 '71
See also
Lobster trapping

FISHERMEN
Crisis at sea: the threat of no more fish. R. Brigham. il Life 71:60-8 D 3 '71
Nature's friend. A. S. Fick. il Cons 26:11 Ag '71
Sons of the sea goddess; the *jangadeiro* of Brazil. L. C. Brown. il Américas 23:36-7 O '71

FISHERS (animals)
What's my line? il Nat Wildlife 9:20 O '71

FISHERY laws and legislation
Canada's action on fisheries closing lines opposed by U.S.; U.S. statement. Dept State Bul 64:448 Mr 29 '71
Fishing laws; United States and Canada (cont) Field & S 75:32+ Ap '71
Fishing seasons (cont) Outdoor Life 147:50+ Ap '71
Tuna war: much ado about what? il U S News 70:40 F 15 '71
U.S. regrets Canada's extension of high seas jurisdiction; U.S. statement. Dept State Bul 64:139 F 1 '71

FISHERY products
See also
Fish protein concentrate

FISHES
Bassogigas, the fish that lives five miles deep. G. Compton. il Sci Digest 69:67 Mr '71
See also
Aquariums
Color of fishes
Electric organs in fishes
Hearing (fishes)
Nervous system—Fishes

Age

See Age (fishes)

Anatomy

Reflectors in fishes. E. Denton. il Sci Am 224:64-72 Ja '71

Eye

See Eye (fishes)

Food and feeding

What trout eat. H. G. Tapply. il Field & S 75:82 Ap '71

Habits and behavior

Chemical languages of fishes. J. H. Todd. il Sci Am 224:98-106+ My '71

Hybrids

New trout for old waters. W. A. Flick. il Cons 25:18-21 Je '71

Migration

See also
Salmon

Physiology

Light production in the luminous fishes photoblepharon and anomalops from the Banda Islands. Y. Haneda and F. I. Tsuji. bibliog il Science 173:143-5 Jl 9 '71
Light to hide by: ventral luminescence to camouflage the silhouette. J. W. Hastings. bibliog il Science 173:1016-17 S 10 '71

Research

See Ichthyological research

Stories

Exit, laughing. E. Zern. See issues of Field & stream
One for the books? C. Elliott. il Outdoor Life 147:94-5+ Ap '71

FISHES, Color of. See Color of fishes

FISHES, Effect of temperature on
Glycoproteins as biological antifreeze agents in Antarctic fishes. A. L. DeVries. bibliog il Science 172:1152-5 Je 11 '71
Temperature tolerances of some closely related tropical Atlantic and Pacific fish species. J. B. Graham. bibliog il Science 172:861-3 My 21 '71

FISHES, Insects, etc, Rain of
Crickets of Altinho. il Time 98:51 N 8 '71

FISHES, Photography of. See Photography of fishes

FISHHOOKS
When you tie one on. H. G. Tapply. il Field & S 76:62 Jl '71

FISHING
Angling theologically. J. Sams. il Field & S 76:40-1+ D '71
Boy in search of a man. il pors Life 71:65-6+ S 24 '71
Fish from the rocks! H. Bonner. il Field & S 76:64-5+ My '71
Fishing. J. Brooks. See issues of Outdoor life
Fishing; ed. by A. J. McClane. See issues of Field & stream
Fishing: what it can do for your camp. M. C. Fisher. il Camp Mag 43:16-17 F '71
Gist of it; ed. by H. Moore. See issues of Outdoor life
Lee Wulff: the complete angler; excerpt from introd. to Fishing with Lee Wulff, by E. C. Janes. A. Gingrich. por Field & S 76:50-1+ N '71
Purist; 12-year-old preparing for opening day. P. McManus. il Field & S 75:54-5+ F '71
Remembering great men and great fish; excerpt from Fishing with Hemingway and Glassell. K. Farrington. il Field & S 75:54-5+ Ap '71
Solunar tables for [month] See issues of Field & stream
Sportsman's notebook. H. G. Tapply. See issues of Field & stream
This year hang a trophy bass. J. A. Moorhouse. il Field & S 76:42-3+ Jl '71

FISHING—*Continued*
Where to go; ed. by V. T. Sparano. See issues of Outdoor life
  See also
Airplanes in hunting and fishing
Bait
Fishermen
Indians of North America—Fishing
Motor vehicles in hunting and fishing
Salt water fishing
  also Bass fishing; Bluefish fishing; and similar headings

Competitions
Catch is, should you eat it? Shinnecock swordfish tournament, Hampton Bays. R. H. Boyle. il Sports Illus 35:46-7 Jl 12 '71
Mercury monitoring highlights Long Island swordfish tournament. B. Sands. il por Cons 26:27-31 O '71
1970 winners; Field & stream fishing contest. il Field & S 75:42+ Mr; 116+ Ap '71
Plaster trout in worm heaven; National trout festival, Kalkaska, Mich. J. Harrison. il Sports Illus 34:70-2+ My 10 '71
With the sport fishermen; Hawaiian international billfish tournament. F. T. Moss. il Yachting 130:38+ O '71

Implements and appliances
Amazing airboat. J. A. Emmett. il Outdoor Life 147:20+ My '71
Build your own fishing kite. J. Samson. il Field & S 75:28+ Ap '71
Fishing tips. C. A. DeViney. il Pop Mech 135:120-1 Ap '71
Inner-tube float fishing. C. A. Deviney. il Pop Mech 136:74-5 Ag '71
New for the fisherman. il Mech Illus 67:44 N '71
Now; total fishing. S. Lievense. il Outdoor Life 147:75-7+ Ap; 58-9+ My '71
Wild rivers by air; homemade airboat. N. Asnicar. il Field & S 76:76-7+ My '71
  See also
Depth indicators
Fishing tackle

Law
  See Fishery laws and legislation

Study and teaching
Fishing schools gain in popularity; National sporting goods association fishing schools program. il Field & S 75:30+ Ap '71

Alaska
Hunting and fishing Alaska by train. G. X. Sand. il Field & S 76:156-8+ O '71

Arctic Regions
Canadian Arctic: a mecca for sportsmen. Bsns W p 121 My 15 '71

Arkansas
Don't doodlesock 'em. C. Elliott. il Outdoor Life 148:42-3+ Jl '71
Easiest trout fishing going; float trips. R. H. Reagan. il Field & S 75:56-7+ Ap '71

Australia
Barrier Reef marlin. G. W. Carmany. il Field & S 75:86+ Mr '71

Bahama Islands
Game for gourmets; stalking lobsters. J. Samson. il Field & S 75:69-70+ F '71
Hunting beneath the reef. A. W. Prince. il Field & S 75:68-9+ F '71
Thing in Hatchet Bay. R. D. Legg. il por Outdoor Life 148:80-1 S '71

California
Affair with the South Fork. V. L. Hoss. il pors Outdoor Life 148:64-7+ Ag '71
California's 800 miles of untapped fishing. L. Green. il Field & S 75:52-3+ Ja '71
Fish from the rocks! H. Bonner. il Field & S 76:64-5+ My '71
Hatch on a hot lake. M. W. Fong. il por Outdoor Life 147:68-71+ My '71
Indian summer fishing on the Trinity. il Sunset 147:58+ O '71
Jamison Loop. B. Nauheim. il por Outdoor Life 147:80-3+ Je '71
Kings of the spring. W. Curtis. il Outdoor Life 147:64-5+ Mr '71
Kings on the rocks. E. Demeter. il Field & S 75:80-1+ F '71
Limit can come quickly at Shasta. il Sunset 146:71+ My '71
Striped bass with a fly. R. Chatham. il Field & S 75:62-3+ Ap '71
Winter fishing for crab off the Tokeland pier. il Sunset 146:36+ F '71

California, Lower
Baja reverie; with reproductions of paintings by Francis Golden. il Sports Illus 34:24-9 Ja 18 '71
Baja roosterfish. J. Hardie. il Field & S 76:74-5+ Je '71

Canada
Angling and some acts of God; rainbows in British Columbia. T. McGuane. il Sports Illus 35:32-7 Ag 9 '71
Bad winds and big pike of Kesagami. D. Richey. il Outdoor Life 147:56-9+ Je '71
Bargain fishing in Manitoba. A. J. McClane. il Field & S 76:130-2+ Ag '71
Best fishing spots in Canada and. . ; symposium. il Field & S 76:82-4 +My '71
Follow that fish. D. Stair. il Field & S 75:74-5+ Ap '71
How to lure lazy pike. J. R. Sundra. il Field & S 75:80-1+ Mr '71
Jumping jacks. E. A. Bauer. il Outdoor Life 147:82-5+ Ap '71
Labrador discovery. N. Karas. il Field & S 76:58-9+ Jl '71
Lunkers of Slave Lake. J. Brooks. il Outdoor Life 147:104-6+ Mr '71
Miramichi goes public. J. Fisk. il por Outdoor Life 147:64-5+ My '71
New world record tuna. G. Gibson. il por Outdoor Life 148:49-51+ S '71
Northeast frontier. A. J. McClane. il Field & S 75:108-9+ Mr '71
Record trout lake you can drive to. E. Park. il Field & S 76:38-9+ Jl '71
Shortcut to smallmouth. S. Marking. il Field & S 76:74-5+ My '71
Speed up for muskies. R. S. Kommer. il por Outdoor Life 148:74-5+ Ag '71
Summer dog days walleye. R. A. Bartnett. il Field & S 76:82-3+ Je '71
Tullibee, the surprise fish. H. Bradshaw. il Field & S 75:80-1+ Ap '71
Uptight little island: Prince Edward Island. D. Levin. il Sports Illus 35:38-40+ O 4 '71

Colombia
Sojourn in Santa Marta. G. Gresham. il Field & S 76:48-9+ Jl '71

Connecticut
Bedlam in blue. G. Heinold. il Outdoor Life 148:76-7+ O '71
Ugly duckling. G. Heinold. il Outdoor Life 147:40+ My '71

Costa Rica
How to get hooked on tarpon. A. Spiers. il Field & S 75:54-5+ Mr '71

Ecuador
Mighty river; Humboldt Current off Ecuador. C. Elliott. il Outdoor Life 147:70-3+ Je '71

Florida
Best bass bait in the world. B. Underwood. il Outdoor Life 147:74-5+ Mr '71
Bugs and bogs and immortal bass: St Vincent Island. D. Levin. il Sports Illus 34:36-8+ F 22 '71
Catch bonefish on your own! L. Kreh. il por Field & S 76:60-1+ My '71
Doc psychs big bass. T. Weber, jr. il por Outdoor Life 147:86-8+ Je '71
Don't forget the bluegills. B. W. Dalrymple. il Outdoor Life 147:74-5+ F '71
Fish you can't forget; permit fishing. J. Brooks. il Outdoor Life 147:90-2+ My '71
Fishing the Everglades. A. J. McClane. il Field & S 75:96-7+ F '71
Florida's lunker bass king. B. Underwood. il Field & S 75:56-7+ F '71
New fishing chart opens flooded Everglades wilderness. G. X. Sand. il Field & S 76:172-4+ Je '71
New trick for crappie. C. Nansen. il Field & S 75:58-9+ Mr '71
Riddle of Miccosukee. C. Elliott. il por Outdoor Life 148:88-9+ O '71
Snook by the roadside. G. Heinold. il Outdoor Life 147:120+ F '71
Where tarpon fishing is color-coded. R. Marston. il Motor B & S 128:24+ Jl '71

Germany (Federal Republic)
Tourists, take your tackle. M. H. Garrell. il por Outdoor Life 147:78-9+ My '71

Grand Bahama Island
Bonefish behavior. A. J. McClane. il Field & S 76:102-3+ Je '71

Iceland
Witch salmon. H. Hyman. il por Field & S 76:110-13+ Jl '71

FISHING—*Continued*

Iowa

Iowa eye-opener. F. Wensel. il Outdoor Life 147:96-7+ Ap '71

Little Sioux is big on cats. H. Bradshaw. il pors Outdoor Life 148:64-6+ Jl '71

Kentucky

How the champ catches cats. G. Laycock. il Field & S 76:72-3+ My '71

Pole fishing the bass bushes. B. Holiday. il Field & S 75:66-7+ Mr '71

Kenya

Strangest bass fishing on earth. E. A. Bauer. il Field & S 75:48-9+ Ja '71

Louisiana

All you need to know about catching bass, with a fly rod. T. Nixon. il Field & S 75:72-3+ Ap '71

Maine

Barse man from Texas. B. Geagan. il Field & S 76:66-7+ N '71

Fishing up a storm. H. G. Tapply. il Field & S 76:58 S '71

Lakers along the shore; Allagash Lake. J. B. Robinson. il por Outdoor Life 147:62-3+ Je '71

Maine thing. J. Brooks. il Outdoor Life 147: 116-19+ F '71

Popping for stripers. G. Heinold. il Outdoor Life 147:180+ Ap '71

Sebago comeback. T. Janes. il Outdoor Life 147:88-9+ Ap '71

Taking smallmouths from the deep. W. Davis. il Mech Illus 67:48+ My '71

Maryland

Conowingo, Maryland's neglected bass lake. C. B. Pfeiffer. il Field & S 76:162-4+ My '71

Ice fishing in Dixie. G. H. Gillelan. il por Outdoor Life 147:36-9+ Ja '71

Potomac: smallmouth paradise. C. B. Pfeiffer. il Field & S 76:52-3+ Jl '71

Reservoir right at home. M. Caraher. il pors Outdoor Life 148:72-3+ Ag '71

Mexico

Best fishing spots in Mexico. B. Brister. il Field & S 76:85+ My '71

Mexico's madcap fish market. J. Tallon. il Outdoor Life 157:80-3+ F '71

See also
Fishing—California, Lower

Mexico, Gulf of

Grail still swims in the Yu Yum lagoon; permit fishing. C. Gammon. il Sports Illus 35:104-10+ D 6 '71

Michigan

Battle of the lakers. J. Brooks. il pors Outdoor Life 148:78-9+ N '71

Bowhunting all year. J. G. Mell. il pors Outdoor Life 147:80-3+ My '71

New ice-fishing action. J. O. Cartier. il por Outdoor Life 147:58-9+ Mr '71

Minnesota

Lakers on the breakup. B. Cary. il Outdoor Life 147:108-9+ Ap '71

Minnesota for muskies. L. J. Bashline. il Field & S 75:78-9+ Ap '71

Montana

But big for its size. J. C. Ericson. il por Outdoor Life 148:78-9+ Ag '71

Can we save Rock Creek? T. Wendelburg. il Outdoor Life 147:64-7+ F '71

Fall salmon snagging. R. F. Eggert. il Field & S 76:114+ Ag '71

My greatest trout float. P. Curtis. il Field & S 75:50-1+ Ap '71

Quiet camping and blue ribbon fishing; Rock Creek. il Sunset 147:26+ Ag '71

River named Smith. G. Laycock. il Field & S 75:50-1+ Ja '71

Those brainy browns. J. G. McCue, jr. il Field & S 75:52-3+ Ap '71

Timber vs. trout; Rock Creek, Mont. D. A. Burk. Field & S 75:12+ Ja '71

Tops in the Rockies. J. Brooks. il Outdoor Life 148:34-7+ Jl '71

Trout fishing where history happened; Missouri River. E. Park. il Field & S 76:53-5+ Je '71

Wall fish. F. G. Snook. il Outdoor Life 148: 50-1+ D '71

Nebraska

Amazing airboat. J. A. Emmett. il Outdoor Life 147:20+ My '71

Nevada

Rainbows run up to 2 pounds. il Sunset 147: 22 N '71

New Hampshire

Mountaintop trout. J. B. Robinson and H. Carroll. il Field & S 75:58-9+ Ja '71

New Jersey

Homecoming blues. H. H. Edel. il Outdoor Life 148:54-5+ Jl '71

Menhaden system. A. Reinfelder. il Field & S 75:194-7+ Ap '71

Tidewater cats. G. E. Wolfe. il Outdoor Life 148:62-3+ S '71

New Mexico

Trout agitator. E. P. Haddon. il Field & S 75:68-9+ Mr '71

New York (state)

Comeback of a heavyweight; Chautauqua muskie. C. E. Heacox. il pors Outdoor Life 148:46-9+ Jl '71

Hidden lakes of Long Island. T. Kerasote. il pors Outdoor Life 147:74-7+ My '71

Hudson River lives. R. H. Boyle. il Audubon 73:14-17+ Mr '71

Lunkers at large; public fishing at Tomhannock reservoir. A. Woldt. il Cons 25:2-3 Je '71

Montauk, small-boat paradise. A. J. Ristori. il por Field & S 75:172-5+ Mr '71

New muskie country. N. Karas. il Field & S 75:54-5+ Ja '71

New York's ice trout bonanza. A. Glowka. il Outdoor Life 148:38-9+ D '71

Return to the Roaring Kill; Catskill Mountains. P. Barrett. il Field & S 76:62-3+ My '71

Saving a fish for tomorrow. D. G. Pasko. il Cons 26:48-9+ Ag '71

Slammer blues of Oyster Bay. T. Kerasote. il pors Outdoor Life 148:58-9+ Ag '71

Some like it cold. B. Warner. il Outdoor Life 147:56-9+ F '71

North Carolina

Black bass and blue monsters. J. Brooks. il Outdoor Life 148:150-2+ O '71

Rock riot at Nags Head. K. Osborne. il pors Outdoor Life 148:56-7+ N '71

Northeastern states

News: the Northeast. T. Janes. See issues of Outdoor life

Northern Ireland

Landlocked monsters of Ireland. D. Knight. il Field & S 75:78-9+ F '71

Ohio

Go camping to catch more fish. E. A. Bauer. il por Outdoor Life 147:82-3+ Mr '71

Oregon

Klamath steelhead. B. Grant. il Field & S 76:48-9+ D '71

Late season largemouth. S. Fagerstrom. il por Field & S 76:50-1+ S '71

North Umpqua story. J. Hemingway. il Field & S 75:52-3+ F '71

Oregon trail. J. Brooks. il Outdoor Life 148: 82-5 D '71

Rogue River float. F. M. Paulson. il Field & S 76:54-7+ N '71

Panama

Acres of action; Panama's Pacific coast. M. J. Sosin. il pors Outdoor Life 147:68-71+ Mr '71

Pennsylvania

Play it again, Sam. L. J. Bashline. il Field & S 76:32-3+ D '71

Rhode Island

Casting on a sea of memories: Sakonnet Point revisited. T. McGuane. il Sports Illus 35:42-4+ S 27 '71

Rhode Island for summer action. V. Evanoff. il Motor B & S 127:33+ Je '71

Saltwater combos. G. Heinold. il Outdoor Life 147:30+ Je '71

Salvador

Big sails and marlin too. B. Warner. il Field & S 75:78-9+ Mr '71

Texas

Bluegills and blubbers. J. N. Mannix. il por Outdoor Life 147:86-8+ My '71

Fishing's newest twist or spoonfeeding bass. B. Brister. il Field & S 76:56-7+ Je '71

What our own bass tell us. B. W. Dalrymple. il pors Outdoor Life 147:52-5+ Ja '71

FISHING—*Continued*

United States

Best fishing spots in all 50 states; by 50 top outdoor writers. il Field & S 75:71-5+ F '71
How to catch big walleyes. D. Walsh, jr. il pors Outdoor Life 148:66-7+ N '71

Utah

How to fool big brown trout. H. Wixom. il Field & S 76:56-7+ My '71
Wahweap jumpoff; houseboat adventure. J. Tallon. il Outdoor Life 148:56-9+ S '71

Venezuela

Pavón paradise. A. J. McClane. il Field & S 75:49-51+ F '71

Virginia

Not a place that appeals to everyone; centuries-old millpond. E. White. il Sports Illus 34:40-2+ My 31 '71
Wilderness beach camping. P. McLain. il Field & S 76:70-1+ My '71
Winter fishing bonus. J. Brooks. il Outdoor Life 147:100-3 Ja '71

Wales

Return to the river of yesterday. C. Gammon. il Sports Illus 34:78-80+ My 24 '71

Washington (state)

Boating winter steelhead. E. Bradner. il Field & S 76:70-1+ N '71
Bugging is more fun. S. Fagerstrom. il Outdoor Life 147:102-3+ Ap '71
Go light for kings. D. H. Smith. il Field & S 75:60-1+ Mr '71
Sagebrush rainbows. E. Bradner. il Field & S 75:62-3+ F '71
Salmon fishing in America: the Indians vs. the state of Washington. P. Collier. il Ramp Mag 9:29-31+ Ap '71
Smallmouth, the fighter. J. Brooks. il Outdoor Life 147:68-9+ Je '71
Winter is the time for steelhead. L. J. Bashline. il Field & S 75:40-1+ Ja '71
Year of the giant steelhead. H. Williams. il Field & S 76:58-9+ O '71

West Indies

Fishing tropical waters. M. Rosko. il Travel 136:44-9 Ag '71

Western states

Prospecting for mountain trout. N. Strung. il Field & S 75:52-3+ Mr '71

Wisconsin

Great muskie hunt. H. Duck. il Field & S 75:58-9+ F '71
Up the down lakers. D. Otto. il por Outdoor Life 148:56-7+ Jl '71

Wyoming

Many seasons of South Pass. F. Calkins. il Field & S 76:62-3+ Ag '71
North Platte float trip. C. J. Farmer. il Outdoor Life 148:52-5+ Ag '71
Triple take at Double Lake; in Shoshone national forest. N. D. Weis. il Outdoor Life 148:66-9+ O '71
Walleye wonderlake. B. Milek. il Field & S 75:76-7+ Ap '71
Wild rivers by air; homemade airboat. N. Asnicar. il Field & S 76:76-7+ My '71
Yellowstone nobody knows. C. Nansen. il Field & S 76:44-5+ Jl '71

FISHING, Winter
Chipper-dipper and other easy-to-make ice fishing tackle. A. Glowka. il Field & S 76:16+ D '71
Ice fishing in Dixie. G. H. Gillelan. il por Outdoor Life 147:36-9+ Ja '71
Lakers on the breakup. B. Cary. il Outdoor Life 147:108-9+ Ap '71
New ice-fishing action. J. C. Cartier. il por Outdoor Life 147:58-9+ Mr '71
New York's ice trout bonanza. A. Glowka. il Outdoor Life 148:38-9+ D '71
Play it again, Sam. L. J. Bashline. il Field & S 76:32-3+ D '71
Some like it cold. B. Warner. il Outdoor Life 147:56-9+ F '71
What to feed an ice hole. H. G. Tapply. il Field & S 75:60 Ja '71
Winter fishing bonus. J. Brooks. il Outdoor Life 147:100-3 Ja '71
Winter fishing for crab off the Tokeland pier. il Sunset 146:36+ F '71

FISHING boats
Best-of-all boat; choices galore for $700. J. Peters. il Outdoor Life 147:72+ Ja '71
Fishfinders; electronic gear and especially-designed boats. D. Fales. il Motor B & S 127:68-71+ My '71

New look in fishing boats. B. McKeown. il Mech Illus 67:23-4 Ag '71
Specifying a custom sportfisherman. C. F. Sheppard. il Motor B & S 127:35 Je '71
Unique fishing boat; super sportfishing boat. J. Hardie. il por Motor B & S 128:16+ Jl '71
"Yachting" eyes a boat:
  Egg Harbor 33; fiberglass sport fisherman. J. Smith. il Yachting 129:74-5+ F '71
  DeFever offshore 38; diesel-powered trawler type. B. Crabtree. il Yachting 129:72-3+ Je '71

Design

Game fish, game boat; Striker's 44. D. Fales. il Motor B & S 128:56-9+ Ag '71
"Yachting" eyes a boat:
  Dyercraft 29. il Yachting 130:58-9+ S '71
  Mako 26, day fisherman. J. Wilson. il Yachting 129:74-5+ My '71
  Striker 44. R. Marston. il Yachting 130:68-9+ Ag '71

Equipment

With the sport fishermen; fishing chairs. F. T. Moss. il Yachting 129:39+ Ap '71
See also
Depth indicators

Testing

How to dig your own channel; Eagle 40-foot trawler yacht. P. Smyth. il Motor B & S 127:66-9+ Je '71

FISHING chairs. See Fishing boats—Equipment

FISHING flies. See Fishing lures, flies, etc.

FISHING kites. See Fishing—Implements and appliances

FISHING lines. See Fishing tackle

FISHING lures, flies, etc.
Choosing your trout flies. W. Davis. il Mech Illus 67:59+ Ap '71
Deadly anytime anywhere; wonder nymph. S. R. Slaymaker, 2d. il Field & S 76:30+ Je '71
Deadly spider. A. I. Alexander. il Field & S 76:88 Je '71
Deer hair and bluegill. T. Nixon. il Field & S 76:80-1+ My '71
Fly for all seasons; Copper nymph. E. Marsh. il Field & S 75:38+ Ap '71
Fly-tying grab bag. N. Smith. il Field & S 76:18+ Ag '71
Indispensable spinner. W. Davis. il Mech Illus 67:110+ Mr '71
Jungle cocks, trout flies, and smugglers. E. N. Layne and S. Hartgen. il Audubon 73:38-43 My '71
Lunkers on the surface. N. Smith. il Field & S 76:10 Jl '71
Most versatile fly. A. J. McClane. il Field & S 76:134-7 S '71
New slip-spoon worm; plastic worm. L. V. Abel. il Field & S 76:128-9 O '71
Performing arts. A. J. McClane. il Field & S 76:144-6+ O '71
Spin a better bass bug. N. Smith. il Field & S 76:28+ Ag '71
Twelve Pacific flies. L. Green. il Field & S 76:45-7+ S '71
Twirligigs. H. G. Tapply. il Field & S 76:72 Ag '71
Ugly duckling. G. Heinold. il Outdoor Life 147:40+ My '71

FISHING records
1970 fishing records. V. Evanoff. il Motor B & S 127:33+ F '71

FISHING rods. See Fishing tackle

FISHING tackle
Chipper-dipper and other easy-to-make ice fishing tackle. A. Glowka. il Field & S 76:16+ D '71
Fishing tropical waters. M. Rosko. il Travel 136:44-9 Ag '71
Fly-line fundamentals. A. J. McClane. il Field & S 76:110-12 My '71
Landing your fish; nets and gaffs. G. Heinold. il Outdoor Life 148:86-8 D '71
See also
Fishhooks

Storage

Triangular case for your rods. J. Hand. il Mech Illus 67:94+ My '71

FISHING tournaments. See Fishing—Competitions

FISHING with bow and arrow
Bowhunting all year. J. G. Mell. il pors Outdoor Life 147:80-3+ My '71

FISHKIN, Jim. See Robertson, I. jt. auth.

FISHMAN, Charles
Paradox; poem. Cath World 213:166 Jl '71

FISHPONDS. See Fish culture

FISHWAYS
How Scotland saved its salmon; use of fish ladders and Borland fish locks at dam. T. Holloway. il Sci Digest 69:64-7 Ap '71

FISHWICK, John Palmer
Fishwick of the Norfolk & Western. il por Forbes 107:194-5 My 15 '71 *

FISHWORMS. See Earthworms

FISK, James D.
He maps the way to success. W. Lowenberg, jr. il pors Har Yrs 11:36-9 D '71 *

FISK, James R.
Acoustic surface-wave devices. il Pop Electr 34:27-33 Mr '71

FISK, John
Miramichi goes public. il por Outdoor Life 147:64-5+ My '71
Strange white deer of New York. il Outdoor Life 148:76-7+ Ag '71

FISKE, Edward B.
Praying with the President in the White House. il N Y Times Mag p 14-15+ Ag 8 '71
Saving the earth: a challenge to our religious traditions. il Redbook 137:79+ Je '71

FISSION, Atomic. See Nuclear fission

FISSION reactors. See Nuclear reactors

FISSION-track dating. See Radioactive dating

FITCH, Robert
H. Ross Perot: America's first welfare billionaire. il pors Ramp Mag 10:42-51 N '71
How the U.S. (and Britain and Germany...) got involved in Lockheed. il Ramp Mag 10:44-6+ S '71
Jackie and Ari and Tom and George and Spiro and... il pors Ramp Mag 10:38-47+ Ja '72

FITCH, William C.
Imperatives on aging. Har Yrs 11:54-5 Ag '71

FITTIPALDI, Emerson
Fittipaldi 3200! K. Ludvigsen. il Motor T 23:52+ Ap '71 *

FITZ-GERALD, Desmond John Villiers
Irish mahogany furniture: a source for American design? il Antiques 99:568-73 Ap '71

FITZGERALD, Edmond James
Watercolor page; with biographical sketch. il por Am Artist 35:60-3+ Je '71

FITZGERALD, Francis Scott Key
Fitzgerald-Perkins papers; excerpts from Dear Max/Dear Scott; with editorial comment by A. Gingrich. pors Esquire 75:6, 106-11+ Je '71
Lo, the poor peacock; story. il por Esquire 76:154-8 S '71

about
Authority of failure; on the Riviera. R. McInerny. Commonweal 93:399-400 Ja 22 '71 *
Benjamin, Edgar, Humbert, and Jay. M. Banta. Yale R 60:532-49 Je '71 *
Crazy Sundays, by A. Latham. Review
Life 70:9 Mr 19 '71. B. Schulberg *
Nation 212:821-3 Je 28 '71. W. Hughes *
New Repub 164:29-30+ My 29 '71. J. R. Bryer *
Newsweek por 77:94-6 Ap 5 '71. G. Wolff *
Crazy Sundays, by A. Latham; Golden moment, by M. R. Stern, and Exiles from paradise, by S. Mayfield. Reviews
Sat R il por 54:39-40 Jl 24 '71 *
Exiles from paradise, by S. Mayfield. Review
Newsweek il por 78:84+ Jl 12 '71. A. Cooper *
Exiles from paradise; excerpts. S. Mayfield. il pors McCalls 98:64-5+ Jl '71 *
F. Scott Fitzgerald in his own time, ed. by M. J. Bruccoli and R. Bryer, and Dear Scott/Dear Max, ed. by J. Kuehl and R. Bryer. Reviews
Sat R 54:57-8 D 11 '71. J. F. Callahan *
Matter of measurement; the tangled relationship between Fitzgerald and Hemingway. R. Prigozy. Commonweal 95:103-6+ O 29 '71; Discussion. 95:267+ D 17 '71 *

Bibliography
Dear Scott: you're not a poor S.O.B. anymore. W. Kennedy. il Look 35:12 Ap 6 '71

FITZGERALD, George R.
To re-mythologize forgiveness. il Cath World 213:269-73 S '71

FITZGERALD, Gerald
Pilgrimage to Montreal: Alicia Alonso and Ballet nacional de Cuba. il por Dance Mag 45:8 Ag '71

FITZGERALD, Peter
Rugged run to New Guinea. il por Motor B & S 127:58-9+ F '71

FITZGERALD, R. V.
Threat to freedom. il por Library J 96:1429-30 Ap 15 '71

FITZGERALD, Scott. See Fitzgerald, F. S. K.

FITZGERALD, Thomas H.
Why motivation theory doesn't work. Harvard Bsns R 49:37-44 Jl '71

FITZGERALD, Zelda (Sayre)
Miss Ella; story. Ladies Home J 88:78-9 Ja '71

about
Exiles from paradise, by S. Mayfield. Review
Newsweek il por 78:84+ Jl 12 '71. A. Cooper *
Sat R il por 54:40 Jl 24 '71 *
Exiles from paradise; excerpts. S. Mayfield. il pors McCalls 98:64-5+ Jl '71 *

FITZGIBBON, William
Play U.S.A. Read Digest 99:17-18+ Jl '71

FITZGIBBONS, Sister Eleanor
Inferno '7-; poem. Commonweal 95:89 O 22 '71

FITZPATRICK, Char
Cranberry kites; poem. Seventeen 30:180 Ap '71

FITZPATRICK, Joseph P.
Puerto Rican migration: right place, wrong time? N. Glazer. America 125:339-41 O 30 '71 *

FITZPATRICK, Linda Rae
Don't shoot-we are your children! by J. A. Lukas. Review
Sat R il 54:34 My 1 '71. R. Cassidy*

FITZSIMMONS, Frank E.
Fitz of the teamsters. J. Lowell. Newsweek 77:76-7 Je 21 '71 *
Fitz takes the wheel and a new course. il por Bsns W p68 Jl 10 '71 *

FITZSIMONS, Godfrey
Shannon cruise. il Travel 136:40-3+ Jl '71

FIVE year plan, Russian. See Russia—Economic policy

FIXATION of nitrogen. See Nitrogen—Fixation

FIXED base operators
Beech spurs single-engine effort. C. E. Schneider. Aviation W 95:61-2 D 20 '71
Need an expert manager? Let your FBO do it. R. Blodget. il Flying 89:80-1 D '71

FIXTURES, Bathroom. See Bathroom fixtures

FLACK, Roberta
Roberta Flack: new musical messenger. P. Garland. il pors Ebony 26:54-6+ Ja '71 *

FLACKS, Richard. See Mankoff, M. jt. auth.

FLAG is up farms, inc. See Horse breeding

FLAG signals. See Signals and signaling

FLAGELLATES
See also
Euglena

FLAGG, Janice K.
CATV; new dimensions in communications. il Parks & Rec 6:30-3+ O '71

FLAGLER, J. M.
Sign off. il Look 35:74 S 7 '71
You and the big vitamin battle. il Look 35:34-6+ Je 1 '71

FLAGS
Black flag. Time 98:10 D 13 '71
Black flag in Newark. il Newsweek 78:98 D 13 '71
Gonfalons. il Sunset 147:70-3 D '71
See also
Signals and signaling

United States
Flag girl; attempt to save the burning American flag. Nation 212:710 Je 7 '71
In my opinion: we are misusing the flag. C. Steinman. por Seventeen 29:152 Jl '70
Raising the flag; uneven enforcement of desecration laws. R. W. Dietsch. New Repub 164:18-19 Je 12 '71
Supreme court and the flag; question of desecrating the flag through art. F. Graham. Art in Am 59:27 Mr '71
Symbols of flag as freedom of expression. H. F. Pilpel and K. P. Norwick. Pub W 199:31-2 Mr 29 '71
Teaching him a lesson; case of Tom Reber. Nation 213:229 S 20 '71
Why we fly the flag; It's my country, too! D. Seim; G. Logsdon. il Farm J 95:19-20 Jl '71

FLAHERTY, Doug
Raspberries; poem. Nation 212:667 My 24 '71

FLAHERTY, Joe
Geriatric memoirs of a basketballer. il Life 70:10 Ap 9 '71

FLAHERTY, Peter F.
Mayor is nobody's boy. R. Z. Hallow. il Nation 212:492-6 Ap 19 '71 *

FLAMING (cookery) See Cookery
FLAMING GORGE national recreation area.
See Recreation areas—Wyoming
FLAMMABLE textile fabrics. See Textile fabrics, Flammable
FLAN (dessert) See Custards; Tarts
FLANAGAN, Ross
Friendly persuasion in Swarthmore. C. E. Fager. Chr Cent 88:267-9 F 24 '71 *
FLANIGAN, Peter M.
Watch Peter Flanigan. G. R. Rosen. il pors Duns 98:28-31+ Jl '71 *
FLANNER, Hildegarde
Oracle; poem. Nation 213:318 O 4 '71
FLANNER, Janet
Letter from Paris. See issues of New Yorker

about

American in Paris. por Newsweek 78:104+ N 8 '71 *
FLANS. See Tarts
FLAPS, Airplane
Back to basics: flaps. P. Garrison. il Flying 88:60-4 My '71
FLASH, Edward S. jr
Macro-economics for macro-policy. bibliog f Ann Am Acad 394:46-56 Mr '71
FLASH units. See Photography—Electronic equipment
FLASHCUBES. See Electric lamps, Photoflash
FLASHERS, Emergency. See Electric lamps, Flashing
FLASHING electric lamps. See Electric lamps, Flashing
FLASHING lights. See Electric lamps, Flashing
FLASHLIGHT photography. See Photography, Flashlight
FLASHLIGHTS, Electric
Do-everything flashlights. E. F. Lindsley. il Pop Sci 199:60-2+ Jl '71
Rechargeable batteries shed brighter light; use by police of Grand Haven, Mich. R. Klempel. il Am City 86:16 Mr '71
FLASKS. See Bottles
FLATTAU, Edward
Atomic power. Sci Digest 70:15-20 O '71
Tomorrow a wasteland? Sci Digest 70:22-6 N '71
FLATWARE. See Silverware
FLAUBERT, Gustave
Flaubert the master, by E. Starkie. Review
Sat R 54:63 D 4 '71. T. Bishop *
Flaubert's Madame Bovary. S. Tomkievicz. il pors Horizon 13:114-19 Wint '71 *
Letter from Paris; new biography by J.-P. Sartre. Genêt. New Yorker 47:106+ Je 12 '71 *
FLAUTZ, John T.
What's cooking? J. Schwartz. il por Org Gard & Farm 18:126-9 Ja '71 *
FLAVIN, George
Sam Snodgrass rides again. America 124:406-7 Ap 17 '71
FLAVOR
Recuperation from illness: flavor enhancement for rats. K. F. Green and J. Garcia. bibliog il Science 173:749-51 Ag 20 '71
FLEA markets. See Markets; Paris—Markets
FLECK, James C.
Israeli kibbutz: model for religious orders? America 125:143-6 S 11 '71
Peace watch on Cyprus. America 124:587-9 Je 5 '71
FLEGENHEIMER, David
Start your vegetable seeds under lights. Home Gard 58:48 F '71
Winter gardening under lights. il Home Gard 58:30-1+ D '71
FLEISCHER, Eugene
Systems for individual study. il por Library J 96:695-8 F 15 '71
FLEISCHER, R. L. and others
Very heavy solar cosmic rays: energy spectrum and implications for lunar erosion. bibliog il Science 171:1240-2 Mr 26 '71
FLEISCHMAJER, Raul, and others
Scleroderma and the subcutaneous tissue. bibliog il Science 171:1019-21 Mr 12 '71
FLEISCHMANN, Charles
Getting to the bakery on time. H. Weigl. il pors Nations Bsns 59:90+ Ja '71 *
FLEISCHMANN distilling corporation
Getting to the bakery on time. H. Weigl. il pors Nations Bsns 59:90+ Ja '71
FLEMING, Amalia (Coutsouris) lady
Cheerful James. Nation 213:643-4 D 20 '71 *
Conspiracy of conscience. il por Time 98:53 O 11 '71 *
I accept it. por Newsweek 78:38 O 11 '71 *
Silenced lady. por Newsweek 78:36+ S 13 '71 *

FLEMING, Karl
Homecoming of Chris Mead. il pors Newsweek 77:28-9 Mr 29 '71
McCloskey: the unlikely rebel. il por Newsweek 77:19-20 My 31 '71
Troubled army brass. il Newsweek 77:21-3 My 24 '71
FLEMING, Ray
For a girl unnerved by orangutans at the zoo; poem. America 125:100 Ag 21 '71
I shall not sit by an open window; Young black man teaching Italian to middle-class white students; poems. America 124:150 F 13 '71
One on one in basketball; In the Boboli gardens; poems. Poetry 117:233-4 Ja '71
FLEMING, Richard Evelyn
Are the bears up the wrong tree? por Forbes 108:36-8 D 15 '71 *
FLEMING, Robert, and company. See London—Banks
FLEMING, Sandra J.
Carnivorous tendencies among primates. il Sci Digest 70:89-92 Ag '71
FLEMING, Shirley
At JFK center: Bernstein's Mass and Ginastera's Beatrix Cenci. il Hi Fi 21:MA10-12+ D '71
Heifetz on television. Hi Fi 21:92 Jl '71
Menuhin plays Walton, a brilliant show. Hi Fi 21:80 My '71
Passion and elegance, Kyung-Wha Chung's disc debut. Hi Fi 21:104 Ap '71
Wolf trap: something new. il Hi Fi 21:MA10+ Mr '71
FLEMING, Susan
Demise of the reluctant reader. il Schol Teach Jr/Sr High p 12-13+ Ja 11 '71
To be nobody-but-yourself. il Schol Teach Jr/Sr High p 18-19 F 1 '71
FLEMING, Theodore H.
Artibeus jamaicensis: delayed embryonic development in a neotropical bat. bibliog il Science 171:402-4 Ja 29 '71
FLEMING, Thomas James, 1927-
50 years of P.E.N. Pub W 200:pt2 184-6 S 27 '71
Lincoln's other dream. il Read Digest 98:134-9 Je '71
Surrender at Yorktown: the world turn'd upside down. il Read Digest 98:162-4+ Ja '71
Woodrow Wilson's fight for peace. il por Read Digest 99:87-91 S '71
FLEMING H. Revell company. See Revell, Fleming, H. company
FLEMINGTON, N.J.
Turntable Junction; re-creation of an early American village. B. Abel. il Travel 136:73 S '71
FLEMMING, Arthur Sherwood
Arthur Flemming: an old champion of the elderly. por Bsns W p54 N 20 '71 *
Arthur Flemming named chairman White House conference on aging. T. Schuchat. Har Yrs 11:4 Je '71 *
FLESCH, Hugo
Hugo Flesch worst seller list. Wilson Lib Bul 45:779 Ap '71 *
FLETCHER, Arthur Allen
U.S. discusses actions to combat racism and discrimination; statements, October 26 and November 3, 1971. Dept State Bul 65:628-39 N 29 '71
When industry goes south. il por Ebony 26:168-71 Ag '71

about

Watchdog for U.S. labor. A. Poinsett. il pors Ebony 26:95-100+ Ap '71 *
FLETCHER, Douglas H.
Aeration. il Parks & Rec 6:23-4+ N '71
FLETCHER, James Chipman
Fletcher to head NASA. Sci N 99:162 Mr 6 '71 *
NASA's new chief. por Newsweek 77:73 Mr 15 '71 *
Tasks pile up for NASA chief. por Bsns W p90 Mr 6 '71 *
FLETCHER, Joseph Francis, 1905-
Situation ethics in a changing situation. por Chr Cent 88:1444-6 D 8 '71
FLETCHER, Susan
Story; poem. Mlle 73:214 Ag '71
FLEVOHOF, Netherlands
Dutch Disneyland. Travel 136:27 O '71
FLEXIBLE schedules. See Schedules, School
FLICK, William A.
New trout for old waters. il Cons 25:18-21 Je '71
FLICKERS. See Woodpeckers
Der FLIEGENDE Holländer; opera. See Wagner, R.

FLIES
Housefly sex attractant. il Chem 44:22-3 D '71
Induction of microsomal oxidase in F₁ hybrids of a high and a low oxidase housefly strain. L. C. Terriere and others. bibliog il Science 171:581-3 F 12 '71
Male-producing strain of the house fly. I. C. McDonald. bibliog Science 172:489 Ap 30 '71
Ovarian maturation in stable flies: inhibition by 20-hydroxyecdysone. J. E. Wright and others. bibliog il Science 172:1247-8 Je 18 '71; Reply. F. Engelmann. 174:1041 D 3 '71
Receptive field organization of units in the first optic ganglion of diptera. D. W. Arnett. bibliog il Science 173:929-31 S 3 '71
Sex attractant pheromone of the house fly: isolation, identification and synthesis. D. A. Carlson and others. bibliog il Science 174: 76-8 O 1 '71
  See also
Blowflies
Drosophila

Resistance to control
See Insects, Injurious and beneficial—Resistance to control

FLIES, Artificial. See Fishing lures, flies, etc.

FLIGHT
He's at it again, as high as a kite. A. Verschoth. il por Sports Illus 35:60-2+ O 18 '71
Man-powered flight. P. Wahl. il Pop Sci 198: 43-5+ Ja '71
  See also
Birds—Flight
Gliding and soaring

Physiological aspects
See Aviation—Physiological aspects

FLIGHT attendants. See Airlines—Hostesses
FLIGHT fatigue. See Aviation—Physiological aspects
FLIGHT from fear; story. See White, D.
FLIGHT of insects. See Insects—Flight
FLIGHT planning. See Aviation—Safety devices and measures
FLIGHT service stations. See United States—Federal aviation administration—Flight service stations
FLIGHT simulators
Flexible simulator aids system development. Aviation W 94:100 F 8 '71
Iron birds aid DC-10, L-1011 development. R. R. Ropelewski. il Aviation W 94:36-8 Ja 25 '71
  See also
Space flight simulators
FLIGHT training. See Air pilots—Training
FLIGHT unlimited, Inc.
Flight unlimited. il pors Ebony 26:123-4+ O '71
FLINKER, Irving, and Pianko, Norman
Emerging middle school. il Clear House 46: 67-72 O '71
FLINT, Mich.
Police
  See also
Helicopters in police work
FLINT
  See also
Chert
FLINT HILLS
Last chance for the tall grass prairie. L. Payton. il Nat Wildlife 9:25-7 Ag '71
Tallgrass prairie park. A. Bohling. il Nat Parks & Con Mag 45:6-10 Mr '71
FLINT HILLS PRAIRIE NATIONAL PARK (proposed) See National parks and reserves—United States
FLINTLOCK pistols. See Pistols
FLOAT (banking) See Banks and banking—Float
FLOAT fishing. See Fishing
FLOAT trips. See River trips
FLOATING
Inner-tube float fishing. C. A. Deviney. il Pop Mech 136:74-5 Ag '71
FLOATING cities and towns. See Cities and towns, Floating
FLOATING exchange rates. See Foreign exchange
FLOATING houses. See Houseboats
FLOATING marinas. See Marinas
FLOMENHAFT, Kalman, and Langsley, D. G.
After the crisis. Ment Hy 55:473-7 O '71
FLOOD, Curt
My rebellion; excerpt from The way it is; ed. by R. Carter. il pors Sports Illus 34: 24-9 F 1 '71
  about
Curt Flood's troubles. por Newsweek 77:67 My 10 '71 *

FLOOD lighting. See Light projection
FLOOD prevention and control
City-county drainage plans come first; Houston, Tex. L. Welch. il Am City 86:70+ Ag '71
  See also
Joint Canada-United States water resource committee (proposed)
Rivers—Regulation

Canada
U.S.-Canada committee to study flooding in Pembina River basin; text of communique, October 13, 1971. Dept State Bul 65:522 N 8 '71

FLOODLIGHTING. See Light projection

FLOODS
United States
Allentown college library suffers $100,000 flood loss. Library J 96:3553-4 N 1 '71
Cave development during a catastrophic storm in the Great Valley of Virginia. D. O. Doehring and R. C. Vierbuchen. bibliog il Science 174:1327-9 D 24 '71
Near-record floods; spring flood outlook for upper Midwest. il Sci N 99:195 Mr 20 '71
Our far-flung correspondents; big rain and floods over Nelson County, Va. E. Kinkead. New Yorker 47:66+ Jl 31 '71
Western phenomenon, the origin and development of watershed research: Manti, Utah, 1889. A. Antrei. il Am West 8:42-7+ Mr '71

Vietnam (Democratic Republic)
When floods and typhoons hit North Vietnam. il U S News 71:46 N 15 '71

FLOOR care. See Floors—Maintenance and repair
FLOOR coverings
Floor is more than just a place to walk. R. Adams and L. Grundy. il House B 113: 115-25 S '71
Four ways to lay a new floor over an old one. A. Lees. il Pop Sci 198:104 Mr '71
  See also
Rugs and carpets
FLOOR machines
Scrubber-polisher. il Consumer Bul 55:25-6 Ja '72
FLOOR waxes. See Waxes
FLOORING, Plastic
Resilient flooring: how we investigate and evaluate it. il Good H 173:6 S '71
Resilient flooring: what you should know before shopping. C. S. Litsinger. il Good H 173:188-9 S '71
FLOORS
  See also
Floor coverings
Maintenance and repair
Easier kitchen-floor care. E. Taylor. il Good H 172:162 Ap '71
How to keep your floors looking splendid. R. Adams and L. Grundy. House B 113:126 S '71
How to keep your resilient floors good-looking. Sunset 147:70-1 Jl '71
How to take care of hard-surface floors. Parents Mag 46:79 Ag '71
FLORAL design. See Design, Decorative—Plant forms
FLORAL painting. See Flowers in art
FLORENCE
Music
Report:
Bartók's Bluebeard's castle, Puccini's Tabarro and Falla's Amor brujo. S. Gould. Opera N 35:31-2 F 6 '71
Cavalleria rusticana and Pagliacci. S. Gould. Opera N 35:32 F 27 '71
Politics and government
Happy mayor; interview. L. Bausi. New Yorker 47:33-4 My 8 '71
FLORENDO, Noel T. and others
Cyclic 3′,5′-nucleotide phosphodiesterase: cytochemical localization in cerebral cortex. bibliog il Science 173:745-7 Ag 20 '71
FLORENTINE art. See Art, Italian
FLORES, Edmundo
Desperation of Calcutta. Nation 212: 652-3 My 24 '71
FLORES MARINI, Carlos
City of palaces. il Américas 23:2-9 S '71
FLORIBUNDAS. See Roses
FLORICULTURE
All-season flowers. E. McDonald. il House B 113:84-5 Je '71
Flower shop in the backyard. J. Bradow. il Horticulture 49:36-8 My '71

FLORICULTURE—*Continued*
Gardener's almanac; ed. by E. Haraszty
R. E. Atkinson. il McCalls 98:30 F '71
Growing herbaceous plants from seed. P.
Swindells. il Horticulture 49:40-1+ My '71
In your greenhouse. J. U. Crockett. See issues of Horticulture
Where the new blooms start; nurseries and
plant breeders of California. E. McDonald.
il House B 113:70-2+ Mr '71
See also
Bulbs
Greenhouses
Nurseries (horticulture)
FLORIDA
Everglade state; historical events on buttons.
D. F. Brown. il Hobbies 75:129-30 Ja '71
Florida: boom! boom! boom? symposium.
il Look 35:17-28+ Ap 6 '71
See also
Airports—Florida
Architecture, Domestic—Florida
Banks and banking—Florida
Big Cypress Swamp
Birds—Florida
Conservation of resources—Florida
Ecology—Florida
Everglades
Everglades National Park
Fishing—Florida
Gardens—Florida
Justice, Administration of—Florida
Land—Florida
Marco Island
Paleobotany—Florida
Petroleum—Florida
Polk County
Prisons—Florida
Sea Islands
Tourist trade—Florida
Water pollution—Florida
Wilderness areas—Florida
Wildlife conservation—Florida

Climate
Some precipitation aspects of Florida showers and thunderstorms. W. L. Woodley and
others. bibliog il Weatherwise 24:106-13+
Je '71

Description and travel
Daytime island: Caladesi. A. Barr. il Travel
137:46-9 Ja '72
Florida: still good for retirement? N. D.
Ford. il Har Yrs 11:16-20+ Je '71
From tip to top in Florida. G. Bourke. See
issues of Travel
Gulf coast guide. G. Marston. il Yachting
130:62-3+ N '71
Redbook guide to Florida's heartland. W.
Hartley and E. Hartley. il Redbook 137:35-
42 S '71

Economic conditions
Trouble in Fantasyland. R. W. Dietsch. New
Repub 165:13-14 Jl 17 '71

Legislature
Florida fires the pork-chop gang. J. N. Miller. Read Digest 99:109-13 **Ag** '71

Parks and reserves
See also
Disney world

Politics and government
He won in a walk; L. Chiles, new senator.
F. Trippett. Look 35:46-7 Ja 12 '71
Mod. populist. il por Newsweek 79:15-16 Ja
3 '72
See also
Florida—Legislature

Population
Florida: the impact of an aging population.
il Bsns W p57 N 20 '71
Meanwhile, in Florida, no slowdown in
growth. il U S News 70:38 Je 21 '71
Wall around the Sunshine state? il Bsns W
p46-7 Jl 3 '71

Social conditions
Powder keg among the palms. W. Hedgepeth.
Look 35:33-4 Ap 6 '71
FLORIDA, STRAITS OF
Southward flow under the Florida current.
W. Düing and D. Johnson. bibliog il Science 173:428-30 Jl 30 '71
FLORIDA current. See Ocean currents
FLORIDA Derby. See Wild animal racing
FLORIDA East Coast railway
Break in Florida's nine-year strike. por Bsns
W p 18 D 25 '71

FLORIDA KEYS
Lower Keys, Florida's out islands. J. Scofield. il Nat Geog 139:72-93 Ja '71
See also
Key West, Fla.
FLORIDA land boom. See Real estate investment
FLORIDA library association
Florida LA 48th annual conference. Am Lib
2:778 S '71
FLORIDA Straits. See Florida, Straits of
FLORIDA telephone corporation
Miniwar over dividends. Time 98:24 S 20 '71
FLORIDA'S cypress gardens. See Gardens—
Florida
FLORISSANT FOSSIL BEDS NATIONAL
MONUMENT
Reporter at large; final approval. B. Roueché.
New Yorker 47:141-2+ N 13 '71
FLORY, Elisabeth De Grunne
Living with antiques. il Antiques 99:398-403
Mr '71
FLORY, Joseph
Small tree for all seasons. il Home Gard
58:30 Mr '71
FLOTATION equipment. See Boats and boating—Safety devices and measures
FLOTATION jackets. See Life preservers
FLOUNDER
See also
Cookery—Fish
FLOUNDER fishing
Spring is for flounders. O. G. Danke. il
Motor B & S 127:35+ Mr '71
FLOUR beetles
1-Pentadecene production in tribolium confusum. D. W. Von Endt and J. W. Wheeler.
bibliog Science 172:60 Ap 2 '71
FLOW meters
Magnetic flowmeter protects patients; intravenous flow control system. S. V. Jones.
il Sci Digest 71:65 Ja '72
FLOW of sewage. See Sewage flow
FLOWER, George E.
Is anybody in charge here? Ed Digest 37:1-4
D '71
FLOWER arrangements. See Flowers, Arrangement of
FLOWER boxes, planters, etc.
Add a new look to your garden with redwood planters. il Home Gard 58:42-5 Ag
'71
Coffee-can magic. L. Anthony. il Org Gard &
Farm 18:118-19 Ap '71
Different track; newest crop of indoor planters. M. Bowden il House B 113:26 Mr '71
Half barrels and a big planter are their entry garden. il Sunset 146:132 Mr '71
It's temporary, looks permanent. il Sunset
146:232 Je '71
Plants grow in baskets that are mysteriously
waterproof. il Sunset 146:166 Ap '71
Window boxes do a lot for an old building
as this Berkeley student action shows. il
Sunset 146:78-9 Mr '71
See also
Hanging baskets
FLOWER exhibits
Camellia shows in February, March. Sunset
146:174 F '71
Coming events of interest to gardeners. See
issues of Horticulture
Flowers: benefit preview opening of the third
annual Bryant park flower show. New
Yorker 47:34-5 O 16 '71
Garden events. See issues of Home garden
& flower grower to August 1971
Garden events [in month] (title varies) See
issues of Sunset
See and study wildflowers at Stinson Beach
May 1 and 2. il Sunset 146:261 My '71
FLOWER gardening. See Floriculture
FLOWER gardens. See Gardens
FLOWER painting. See Flowers in art
FLOWER pictures. See Pictures
FLOWER prints. See Flowers in art
FLOWER shows. See Flower exhibits
FLOWERING cabbage
Flowering cabbages like these in your garden this winter. il Sunset 147:102-3 O '71
FLOWERING maples
Bell flowers, color-splashed leaves; abutilons.
il Sunset 147:157 Jl '71
FLOWERING of plants. See Plants, Flowering
of
FLOWERING shrubs. See Shrubs
FLOWERING trees
Flowers in abundance from trees and shrubs.
G. Taloumis. il Home Gard 58:22-3+ Mr '71

FLOWERS
More new plants for 1971. il Horticulture 49:22-3+ F '71
Plant ideas to help make a dream garden; symposium. Home Gard 58:15-25+ D '71
Winter-spring color. il Sunset 147:257 O '71
  See also
Annuals (plants)
Buds
Bulbs
Catkins
Floriculture
Hanging baskets
Perennials
Plant conservation
Wild flowers

All America selections
See Plants—All America selections

Cut flowers
Longer life for cut flowers. L. V. Power. il Am Home 74:28+ Je '71

FLOWERS, Arrangement of
Food and flowers that make a memorable meal. C. Masson. il pors House & Gard 140:54-7 Jl '71
Gladioli in modern arrangements. A. A. Ascher. il Horticulture 49:39-40 S '71
It musn't topple, or look like it might; Japanese style. il Sunset 147:52-3 Jl '71
Little arrangements for spring. il Horticulture 49:34-5 Ap '71
Tools that can help you arrange flowers. il Sunset 147:146-7 Jl '71
Voila Vidal! Flowers with a Sassoon flair. E. McDonald. il por House B 113:102-4 N '71

FLOWERS, Dried
Preserve flowers now for year-round pleasure. Good H 173:145 Ag '71
Success in flower drying. L. Karel. il Horticulture 49:26-7 Je '71

FLOWERS, Fragrant. See Gardens, Fragrant

FLOWERS as food
  See also
Cookery—Flowers

FLOWERS in art
Embossed pictures of Samuel Dixon and his imitators. A. L. Leask. il Antiques 100:120-3 Jl '71
Eternal garden of Monsieur Redon. W. A. H. Birnie. il Read Digest 99:122-8 S '71
  See also
Design, Decorative—Plant forms

FLOWMETERS. See Flow meters

FLOYD, William Barrow
Portraits and paintings at Mount Vernon from 1754 to 1799. il Antiques 100:768-74, 894-9 N-D '71

FLU. See Influenza

FLUID dynamics
Density gradients in a rotating stratified fluid; experimental evidence for a new instability. D. J. Baker, jr. bibliog il Science 172:1029-31 Je 4 '71

FLUID injection in oil wells. See Oil field flooding

FLUIDS
  See also
Liquids

FLUIDS in plants, Motion of. See Plants, Motion of fluids in

FLUOR corporation
White elephant finds a buyer; trade of NAR plant for Fluor property. il Bsns W p28 Mr 27 '71

FLUORESCENCE
Fluorescence of the purine and pyrimidine bases of the nucleic acids in neutral aqueous solution at 300°K. M. Daniels and W. Hauswirth. bibliog il Science 171:675-7 F 19 '71
Histochemical fluorescence of raphe neurons; selective enhancement by tryptophan. G. K. Aghajanian and I. M. Asher. bibliog il Science 172:1159-61 Je 11 '71
Solvent dependence of the luminescence of N-arylaminonaphthalenesulfonates. C. J. Seliskar and L. Brand. bibliog il Science 171:799-800 F 26 '71
  See also
Fluorimetry
Mössbauer effect

FLUORESCENT antibodies. See Antibodies, Fluorescent

FLUORESCENT lamps and lighting. See Electric lamps, Fluorescent

FLUORIDES
Xenon hexafluoride: structural crystallography of tetrameric phases. R. D. Burbank and G. R. Jones. bibliog il Science 171:485-7 F 5 '71

FLUORIMETRY
X-ray fluorescence: detection of lead in wall paint. G. R. Laurer and others. bibliog il Science 172:466-8 Ap 30 '71

FLUORINE in the body
New results on dietary fluoride. L. E. Strong. il Chem 44:19-20 N '71

FLUOROCARBONS
Mix with care; interaction between PB and Freon in aerosol dispensers. J. McCaull. bibliog il Environ 13:39-42 Ja '71

FLUOROMETRIC analysis. See Fluorimetry

FLUSH tanks. See Plumbing

FLY, Claude L.
Claude Fly's seven-month nightmare. P. Friggens. il Read Digest 99:64-70 S '71 •
Free at last. Newsweek 77:56 Mr 15 '71 •

FLY ash. See Ashes

FLY casting
Fly casting simplified. C. Conley. il Field & S 76:155 My '71
Fly-rodding the blues. G. Grant. il Field & S 76:120+ Je '71
How I gave up fly fishing and became a credit to the community. J. Burgess. il Field & S 75:70-1+ Mr '71

FLY fishing. See Fly casting

FLY-line heads. See Fishing tackle

FLY tying. See Fishing lures, flies, etc.

FLYGER, Vagn. See Levin, E. Y. jt. auth.

FLYING. See Flight

FLYING boats. See Seaplanes

FLYING clubs. See Aviation clubs

FLYING D ranch. See Irvine company

FLYING Dutchman; opera. See Wagner, R.

FLYING laws. See Aviation—Laws and regulations

FLYING machines
  See also
Aeronautics—History
Autogiros
Ornithopters

FLYING saucers
Saucer diehards. il por Time 97:49 Je 28 '71
Whatever happened to UFO's? Sci N 99:435-6 Je 26 '71
Who sees flying saucers? il Sci Digest 69:34-5 F '71

FLYING Tiger line, inc.
Flying Tiger foresees 30 per cent rise in common carriage for 1971. Aviation W 94:43-4 F 1 '71
Lion's share for Flying Tigers. il Bsns W p72+ My 22 '71
Tiger reliability keyed to ground support. W. S. Hieronymus. Aviation W 95:32 O 18 '71
Tigers reduce cargo losses due to thefts. Aviation W 95:56-7 Ag 30 '71

FLYING to America; story. See Barthelme, D.

FLYNN, Arthur, and others
Mineral element correlation with adenohypophyseal-adrenal cortex function and stress. bibliog il Science 173:1035-6 S 10 '71

FLYNN, Edward J. See Spector, S. jt. auth.

FLYNN, Emily C.
Make your own dyes from plants. il Horticulture 49:43-5 S '71

FLYNN, George
How digital readouts work. il Radio-Electr 42:50-3 S '71

FLYNN, John P. See Bandler, R. jr; Chi, C. C. jt. auths.

FLYWHEELS
Lift for the auto; engine-flywheel hybrids. J. McCaull. il Environ 13:35-41 D '71

FOA, Uriel G.
Interpersonal and economic resources. bibliog il Science 171:345-51 Ja 29 '71

FOAM plastic houses. See Plastic houses

FOAM plastics. See Plastic foams

FOAM plastics in building. See Plastics in building

FOCUS gallery, San Francisco. See Photography—Galleries and museums

FOCUSING. See Photography—Focusing

FOCUSING attachment for telescopes. See Telescope—Equipment

FOEHRENBACH, Jack. See Jensen, A. C. jt. auth.

FOERSTER, Bernd
Urban serenade. il Cons 25:4-9 Je '71

FOG
New project analyzes deadly fog. Am City 86:87 F '71

FOG, Artificial
Artificial fog may make frost, fires controllable. S. V. Jones. Sci Digest 70:61 S '71

FOG navigation. See Navigation

FOGEL, Daniel Mark
Another poem on the nature of dreams and passions. Yale R 60:390-1 Mr '71

FOGEL, Jacqueline
Old furniture into art nouveau. E. Hill. il por Design 72:24-5 Sum '71 *

FOGEL, Susan Lee
(ed) See Otvös, G.   What a conductor is for

FOGERTY, John
Long as I can see the light; Commotion; Green River; songs. il Sr Schol 98:21, 23 F 15 '71

FOKINE, Michel
Les sylphides. O. Maynard. il por Dance Mag 45:43-66 D '71 *

FOKKER, Anthony Herman Gerard
Real Flying Dutchman. il por Forbes 107:40 Je 1 '71 *

FOKKER, Royal Netherlands aircraft factory.
See Airplane industry—Netherlands

FOLDES, Andor
Pianist's choice. il Hi Fi 21:24 Ja '71

FOLDES, Joseph
From here to infinity. il Pop Phot 69:90-1 Ag '71
(ed) See Kertész, A. To become a photographer

FOLDING doors. See Doors

FOLDING knives. See Knives

FOLDING of paper. See Paper work

FOLDING tables. See Tables

FOLEY, Charles
Plot the Russians muffed. Nat R 23:479-80 My 4 '71
Toward computerized warfare. Cur 132:20-3 S '71

FOLEY, Helen
To sing the street: using a community film program to teach composition. Engl J 60: 1101-8 N '71

FOLIAGE plants. See Plants, Ornamental

FOLIAR veins. See Veins (botany)

FOLK art
British folk art at Freshford manor; John Judkyn collection. J. E. Ayres. il Antiques 99:866-71 Je '71
Cornè, McIntire, and the Hersey Derby farm; Michel Cornè's painting of a Salem, Mass. country estate. N. F. Little. il Antiques 101:226-9 Ja '72
See also
Indians, Wooden

FOLK costume. See Costume

FOLK dance festivals. See Dance festivals

FOLK literature, American
American oral literature: our forgotten heritage. G. Haslam. bibliog f Engl J 60:709-23 S '71

FOLK literature, Turkish
See also
Folklore—Turkey

FOLK medicine
Kindling of hope in the disadvantaged: a study of the Afro-American healer. H. Stewart. bibliog Ment Hy 55:96-100 Ja '71

FOLK music, American
Another version of the dream; Nashville, Music city U.S.A. il Esquire 76:136-47 N '71
Country music. C. S. Wren; W. Hedgepeth; D. Halberstam. il Look 35:11-24+ Jl 13 '71
Kris Kristofferson lonely sound from Nashville; interview, ed. by E. Miller. K. Kristofferson. por Seventeen 30:130-1+ Ap '71
New music from the hills. E. Sander. Sat R 54:47 Ag 28 '71

FOLK schools, American. See John C. Campbell folk school, Brasstown, N.C.

FOLK singers. See Singers

FOLK songs
Sing to the Lord. R. Haughton. Cath World 212:230-1 F '71
See also
Sailors songs

FOLK songs, American
Country classics. C. S. Wren. il Look 35:14-21 Jl 13 '71

FOLK songs, Indian (American) See Indians of North America—Music

FOLK tales. See Folklore

FOLKES, Gordon C. and Sellers, Jerry
Water was too hard. il Am City 86:49+ Jl '71

FOLKLORE
See also
Amulets
Animal lore
Grail
Superstition
Weather lore

Jews
Figure of the dybbuk. H. Fisch. Commentary 51:70-5 Ap '71

Andros Island, Bahama Islands
Legend of the chickcharneys. S. Libby. Travel 135:15 Je '71

Turkey
Folks who tell folk tales: field collecting in Turkey. B. K. Walker. il Horn Bk 47:636-42 D '71

United States
Modest contribution to the marijuana and folklore industries. J. Fischer. Harper 242: 12+ Ap '71

FOLLICLE-stimulating hormone. See Gonadotropins

FOLLIES (architecture)
Lifestyle; Lucy the elephant in Margate, N.J. il Am Home 74:10 Jl '71

FOLLIES, musical comedy. See Musical comedies, revues, etc.—Criticisms, plots, etc.

FOLLOW the eagle; story. See Kotzwinkle, W.

FOLSOM, Franklin
Mysterious mounds at Poverty Point. il Sci Digest 69:46-8+ F '71

FOLTZ, Vivian J.
New horizons in your mailbox. il Har Yrs 11:40-1 N '71

FONDA, Jane
Jane Fonda: I'm coming into focus; interview, ed. by O. Fallaci. pors McCalls 98:122-3+ F '71
You, Jane, me fellow. G. Ace. Sat R 54:5 Je 5 '71
about
Jane Fonda, nonstop activist; with account by J. Frook. il por Life 70:50-1+ Ap 23 '71 *
Left face. New Repub 164:9 Mr 13 '71 *
Typhoon Jane. il por Time 99:71 Ja 3 '72 *
Whatever happened to Baby Jane? M. Ronan. por Sr Schol 99:36+ N 29 '71 *

FONDA, Peter
Man and the sea. il pors Vogue 158:43 Ag 1 '71 *

FONDILLER, Harvey V.
Light your movies like a pro. il Pop Phot 69:94-6 Ag '71
Try add-on optics for picture power. il Pop Phot 68:78-81+ Je '71

FONDUE pots, Electric. See Household appliances, Electric

FONDUES
Fondue for drop-in friends. il Bet Hom & Gard 49:62-3+ Ja '71
Plugged in for fondue. il McCalls 98:61 Ap '71
Wonders from the fondu pot. il Ladies Home J 88:98+ F '71

FONG, Michael W.
Hatch on a hot lake. il pors Outdoor Life 147:68-71+ My '71

FONTAINE, André
Real divisions of Europe. For Affairs 49:302-14 Ja '71

FONTAINE, Athanas Paul
Bendix plots a new course. il por Bsns W p93-4+ Jl 17 '71 *

FONTEIN, Jan
Local genius of classical Java. il Art N 70: 50-5 O '71

FONTEYN, Dame Margot
Dancing the memories. H. Saal. il por Newsweek 78:81 Ag 2 '71 *
Fonteyn: ecstasy. W. Terry. il pors Sat R 54: 43 S 4 '71 *
Passion with a put-on. J. T. Elson. il Time 98:51 Ag 2 '71 *

FOOD
Cooling off those hot-weather food myths. il Good H 173:140 Ag '71
GH poll: how satisfied are women with food and cosmetic products? Good H 172:166 F '71
See also
College students—Food
Cookery
Diet
Fasting
Fish as food
Iron in food
Nutrition
Packaged foods
Proteins
Sandwiches
School lunches
Space flight—Food problems
Vitamins

Anecdotes, facetiae, satire, etc.
My farewell to girth control. S. Levenson. il por Ladies Home J 88:116+ My '71

FOOD—*Continued*

Contamination
See Food contamination

Fat content
Growing worry over cholesterol. il Changing T 25:37-9 Jl '71
Heart-disease medics renew drive to cut down on meat, milk and eggs. G. Logsdon. Farm J 95:43 F '71
You and your heart: the real role of fats. Read Digest 99:74-7 O '71

Labeling
Advertising nutrition. New Repub 164:7-8 Mr 6 '71
Chains woo consumers with open dating. il Bsns W p48+ Ja 16 '71
Coming; food labels with nutrition facts. il Changing T 25:15-17 Ag '71
FDA seems about to abandon its opposition to truthful labeling of factory-made foods; fat ingredients. il Consumer Bul 54:24-6 Ag '71
Facts you should know about food labels; questions and answers. R. H. Smithies. il Good H 173:169-71 O '71
How fresh are our milk and eggs, and what goes into cola drinks? il Consumer Bul 54: 30-2 Ag '71
Washington's diet for food companies; nutritional labeling. il Bsns W p28 Mr 20 '71
Which do you want, good eating or good nutrition? Consumer Bul 54:19-20+ Mr '71

Marketing
Food conspiracy; buying groups. Ramp Mag 9:8 Ap '71

New sources
See Food supply—New sources

Prices
Food industry is in turmoil. il Bsns W p21 Ag 28 '71
Food outlook for 1971. Camp Mag 43:18 My '71
　See also subhead Prices under names of foods, e.g. Poultry—Prices

Ready-to-cook food
New egg products save you time and space. il Camp Mag 43:18-19 Je '71
Positives outweigh negatives for camps using convenience foods. J. A. Schwartz. il Camp Mag 43:20-2 My '71

Storage
Good housekeeping practices in camp food storage. il Camp Mag 43:18+ Ap '71
Guide to pantry-shelf storage. il Good H 172: 142 Mr '71
Nostalgia comes to the kitchen: jars and bottles with an old-time flavor. il House B 113:54 N '71
Use your refrigerator right. il Changing T 25:10-11 O '71
　See also
Farm produce—Storage

FOOD, Canned. See Canned food

FOOD, Color of. See Color of food

FOOD, Contaminated. See Food contamination

FOOD, Cost of. See Food—Prices

FOOD, Dried
Work wonders with dried soups. il Ladies Home J 89:98+ Ja '72
　See also
Potatoes, Dried

FOOD, Frozen
Be meals ahead for busy days. R. Molter. il Parents Mag 46:62-5+ Ag '71
Freeze-ahead recipes. Z. Coulson. il Good H 172:98-113 Mr '71
If your freezer stops, keep cool. il McCalls 98: 156 Mr '71
You can make one weeks or days ahead, it will wait patiently in the freezer. il Sunset 147:122-3 S '71
　See also
Freezing of food
Ice cream, ices, etc.
Vegetables, Frozen

FOOD, Organic
Are health foods worth it? D. Calloway. il McCalls 99:30 O '71
Beauty sense and nonsense. S. Lord. Harp Baz 105:124 D '71
College campus, new home for organic food. M. C. Goldman. il Org Gard & Farm 18: 86-7 Ag '71
Facts about health foods; ed. by B. Russell. C. G. King. House & Gard 140:59+ Jl '71

Guru of the organic food cult. W. Greene. il pors N Y Times Mag p30-1+ Je 6 '71
Health eaters; interviews. A. Davis and others. pors Vogue 157:167-8+ My '71
Health is busting out all over; health-food restaurants. Vogue 157:57+ F 1 '71
Join the fight against organic phonies. R. Rodale. il Org Gard & Farm 18:73-4 Je '71
Law and organic living. M. C. Goldman. Org Gard & Farm 18:104-10 D '71
Looking for the organic America. F. Allen. il Org Gard & Farm 18:39-45 Mr '71
Organic food and health (cont) J. I. Rodale. Org Gard & Farm 18:130-3 Ja; 132+ F; 128-31 Mr; 102-6+ Ap; 102-6+ My; 102-7 Je; 96-8 Jl; 88-91 Ag '71
Organic; interview with proprietor of Mother Nature & sons, ltd. A. Borov. New Yorker 47:30-2 My 22 '71
Organic shops move into the big stores. il Bsns W p76-7 Jl 10 '71
Postscript to the California growers meeting. F. Allen. Org Gard & Farm 18:75-6 Je '71
Profitable earth; merchandising of organic foods. il Time 97:90 Ap 12 '71
What makes a food organic? M. C. Goldman. il Org Gard & Farm 18:85-8 Mr '71
　See also
Cookery—Organic food

FOOD, Raw
Steak tartar: a classic, with variations. J. McCloskey. il Bet Hom & Gard 49:72 My '71

FOOD, Sensitivity to. See Food allergy

FOOD, Serving of
How to serve food at the table. il Redbook 136:86-90 F '71

FOOD, Wild
Gathering of the galloping gourmets; Nature wonder weekend. E. Gibbons. il Org Gard & Farm 18:124-6 D '71
Problem of overconversion. E. Gibbons. Org Gard & Farm 18:122-5 N '71
Sea and desert: land of wild food aplenty. E. Gibbons. por Org Gard & Farm 18:107-9+ Jl '71
Which generation gap? E. Gibbons. Org Gard & Farm 18:70+ My '71
　See also
Game
Plants, Edible

FOOD additives
Chemicals we eat, by M. A. Benarde. Review
　Consumer Bul 54:4+ S '71. B. T. Hunter
Consumer beware! by B. T. Hunter. Review
　Consumer Bul 54:4 Je '71
Food pollution. D. Zwerdling. il Ramp Mag 9:30-7+ Je '71
Heat is on chemical additives. Bsns W p83 O 23 '71
How safe is the food you buy? Good H 173: 155-7 Jl '71
Public health authority talks about food scares. E. J. Cassell. House & Gard 140: 58+ Jl '71
What are the facts about food additives? A. Q. Maisel. Read Digest 98:81-5 My '71
　See also
Diethyl pyrocarbonate
Monosodium glutamate

FOOD adulteration and inspection
　See also
Meat inspection
United States—Food and drug administration

FOOD allergy
Answers to your questions, plus cake and cookie recipes for allergy diets. R. H. Smithies. il Good H 172:178+ My '71

FOOD and agriculture organization of the United Nations
Food and population. Sci Am 225:41 O '71
Jungle, desert, icebergs, and hunger; forecast. R. L. Tobin. il Sat R 54:20 O 23 '71; Reply. N. J. Rosenberg. 54:30 N 20 '71

FOOD and drug administration. See United States—Food and drug administration

FOOD as gifts
Cook it now for holiday giving; for holiday eating. il Redbook 138:118-22+ N '71
Fancy but easy cookies as gifts. il Sunset 147:161-2 D '71
Gifts for gourmets. il House B 113:226-7 N '71
Give a new taste experience; give the makings of herbal tea. il Sunset 147:124+ D '71
Grand gift picnic. il Sunset 147:68-9 D '71
Here come the kitchen Santas. il Seventeen 30:108-9+ D '71
Presents from great cooks. J. Ellis. il House & Gard 140:88-90+ D '71

FOOTBALL—*Continued*

Buried under a sea of troubles; USC and UCLA football teams. R. Fimrite. il Sports Illus 35:28-31 N 15 '71

But Alabama poses another threat: Alabama vs Auburn. P. Putnam. il Sports Illus 35: 25-7 D 6 '71

Cheerleader could run the team; Notre Dame against Northwestern. D. Jenkins. il Sports Illus 35:26-7 S 27 '71

College football 1971. il Sports Illus 35:44-68+ S 13 '71

Conquest in Norman; Oklahoma vs. Nebraska. il Newsweek 78:52 D 6 '71

Czeslaw Marcol is no Polish joke; Hillsdale college's placekicker. J. Kaplan. il Sports Illus 35:69-70 D 6 '71

Football. See issues of New Yorker

Fumbles are planned. il Newsweek 78:76 O 25 '71

Go, you big red; Oklahoma and Nebraska head for the showdown. il Life 71:28-33 N 26 '71

Good-bye to all that rah, rah! college football. T. McClure and J. Lebow. il Look 35: 77-8+ O 5 '71

He's down. He's out. He's back. He wins! Tennessee vs Auburn. P. Putnam. il Sports Illus 35:54+ O 4 '71

Hold on, Ara, the freshmen are coming; ND freshmen vs. Mexico City Redskins. P. Putnam. il Sports Illus 35:56-7 N 1 '71

Holy Toledo! Chuck Ealey nearly lost one; University of Toledo Rockets. J. Jares. il por Sports Illus 35:64+ O 11 '71

Irish Carr moves into high gear; UCLA basketball player. C. Kirkpatrick. il por Sports Illus 34:42-4 F 1 '71

Irish stew for LSU; defeat of Notre Dame in Tiger stadium. W. F. Reed. il Sports Illus 35:26-7 N 29 '71

Ivy league Lombardi gets a Big ten jolt; B. Blackman football coach of University of Illinois. R. Blount, jr. il por Sports Illus 35:66+ O 18 '71

Jan Stenerud is no football player but he wins football games. B. Surface. il por N Y Times Mag p 10-11+ S 19 '71

King Cornhusker goes Bear hunting; Nebraska vs Alabama. D. Jenkins. il Sports Illus 35:22-4+ D 20 '71

Magic number is Sixkiller; Washington quarterback. R. Blount, jr. il por Sports Illus 35:34-7 O 4 '71

Nebraska rides high; unbeaten Cornhuskers vs Oklahoma. D. Jenkins. il Sports Illus 35:22-5 D 6 '71

No. 1 v. no. 2; Nebraska v. Oklahoma. il Time 98:76 D 6 '71

Nobody stands up to Michigan; unbeaten Wolverines. R. Blount, jr. il Sports Illus 35:60+ O 25 '71

Off like champions; Nebraska, Ohio state and Stanford. D. Jenkins. il Sports Illus 35:22-5 S 20 '71

Oh, poi, what a football team; Cornhuskers in Hawaii. R. W. Johnston. Sports Illus 35: 77-8 D 13 '71

Oklahoma wins the Wishbone war; Texas Longhorns vs. Oklahoma Sooners. D. Jenkins. il Sports Illus 35:24-7 O 18 '71

One-day season; Cornhuskers in Miami. D. Jenkins. il Sports Illus 34:10-15 Ja 11 '71

Pride in the red jersey; Alabama's Crimson Tide. P. Putnam. il Sports Illus 35:18-21 O 11 '71

Pride of Lions in cattle country; Brownwood high school lions. C. Stowers. il Sports Illus 35:38-42 N 1 '71

Pros & cons; college football preferred. H. L. Masin. il Sr Schol 99:23 O 11 '71

Saved by the itch to switch; Penn State's J. Paterno. P. Putnam. il Sports Illus 35: 24-5 O 25 '71

Somebody is going to be the turkey; Thanksgiving day with Oklahoma. D. Jenkins. il Sports Illus 35:54+ N 8 '71

Sports; R. Lilly and the Dallas Cowboys. R. Kahn. il Esquire 76:14+ D '71

This year's game of the decade; Nebraska vs Oklahoma. D. Jenkins. il Sports Illus 35:32-4+ N 22 '71

Through the Bowls darkly. P. Axthelm. il Newsweek 79:58 Ja 3 '72

Trade winds; interview. ed. by C. Amory. J. Paterno. Sat R 55:6 Ja 1 '72

Two scoring machines collide with a plink; Arizona state and Houston. P. Putnam. Sports Illus 35:61-2 S 27 '71

Underneath that 7 is an S; Auburn quarterback P. Sullivan. P. Putnam. il Sports Illus 35:67+ N 22 '71

Wedge meets the headhunters; with photographs by A. Rickerby. Life 71:32-9 D 3 '71

Week; college football. G. S. Brown. Sports Illus 35:57-9 N 1; 72+ N 15 '71

Week; college football. D. Delliquanti. Sports Illus 35:70+ D 6 '71

Week; college football. J. Jares. Sports Illus 35:62+ S 27; 56+ O 4; 68+ O 18 '71

Week; college football. L. Keith. Sports Illus 35:62+ O 25; 56+ N 8 '71

Week; college football (cont) H. Peterson. Sports Illus 35:66+ O 11 '71

Week; college football (cont) W. F. Reed. Sports Illus 35:70+ N 22 '71

What parents should know about high school football. G. P. Joyner. il Parents Mag 46:66-7+ O '71

See also

All-Star football game

Football players

Rugby football

Soccer

Accidents and injuries

New slant on the mod sod; AstroTurf, Tartan Turf and Poly-Turf. J. Underwood. il Sports Illus 35:32-4+ N 15 '71

Return of a couple of old sticks-in-the-pocket; Joe Namath of the Jets and B. B. Starr of the Packers. R. H. Boyle. il Sports Illus 35:20-1 D 13 '71

Smash thy neighbor. J. McMurtry. Atlan 229:77-80 Ja '72

Anecdotes, facetiae, satire, etc.

And the curious facts about another 'the game'; 1970 Harvard-Yale thriller. G. Plimpton. il Sports Illus 35:40-2+ N 22 '71

One woman's howling success with football's Monday nights and Saturday knights. E. Bombeck. il Todays Health 49:26-7 O '71

Finance

Grim run to fiscal daylight; college football in financial squeeze. P. Ryan. il Sports Illus 34:18-20+ F 1 '71

They call it a game, by B. Parrish. Review Time il 98:63 S 13 '71

Photographs

Wedge meets the headhunters; with editorial comment. A. Rickerby. Life 71:32-9 D 3 '71

Rules

Guide to zone defense. il Newsweek 78:76 N 29 '71

Study and teaching

My wife the fan; courses for women. Newsweek 78:73-4 N 29 '71

Teaching football widows; classes of Doris Laurini in River Grove, Ill. il Time 98:52 N 29 '71

FOOTBALL accidents. See Football—Accidents and injuries

FOOTBALL clubs

Allen's red-hot Redskins. il por Newsweek 78:54-6+ N 1 '71

Annual football roundup. L. J. Banks. il Ebony 27:172+ N '71

Beasts of Baltimore; Colts. L. L. King. il por Atlan 229:70-7 Ja '72

Biggest kick; National football league playoffs. il Time 99:56 Ja 10 '72

Booboo bowl. Time 97:67 F 1 '71

Bullet Bob v. Roger the Dodger; Super bowl game. il pors Time 99:42-5 Ja 17 '72

Call it catch-as-catch-can; O. Taylor of Kansas City Chiefs. R. H. Boyle. il por Sports Illus 35:84+ N 15 '71

Can Cowboys ride Colts? il Newsweek 77:69 Ja 18 '71

Cutting the mad duck; Detroit Lions drop A. Karras. il por Newsweek 78:101-2 S 27 '71

Eleven big mistakes; seven by Colts, four by Cowboys in Super bowl. T. Maule. il Sports Illus 34:12-17 Ja 25 '71

Getting my kicks (title varies) ed. by J. Olsen. G. Blanda. il Sports Illus 35:26-31 Jl 19; 36-8+ Jl 26; 30-6 Ag 2 '71

Goodby to the alka-seltzer and aspirin bowl; NFL the prouder. T. Maule. Sports Illus 34: 50-1 F 1 '71

Hackensack Giants. il Newsweek 78:42 S 6 '71

Heading them off at the pass; Los Angeles Rams vs San Francisco 49ers. R. Fimrite. il Sports Illus 35:30-2+ N 29 '71

Ice-cream man cometh; G. Allen, coach of the Redskins. J. Underwood. il Sports Illus 35:71-2+ O 25 '71

I'm going to punish them for last year; J. Mackey of Baltimore Colts. G. S. Brown. il pors Sports Illus 35:30-2+ Ag 30 '71

FOOTBALL clubs—*Continued*
It's how you played the game; Rams preseason defeat by the Dallas Cowboys. T. Maule. il por Sports Illus 35:24-5 Ag 16 '71
Keeping it short and sweet: Colts vs Miami Dolphins. T. Maule. il por Sports Illus 35: 14-19 D 20 '71
Kick that failed; NFL playoffs. il por Newsweek 79:46 Ja 10 '72
Late summer madness; pro football preseason games. R. H. Boyle. il Sports Illus 35:18-21 S 13 '71
Look what's afoot: G. Landry of Detroit Lions. T. Maule. il por Sports Illus 35:18-21 D 13 '71
Move to the Meadowlands: New York Giants. il Time 98:52 S 6 '71
Name of the game is O. J. Buffalo's new offense. E. Shrake. por Sports Illus 35:18-19 S 6 '71
No one's holding these Tigers: Cincinnati Bengals vs Philadelphia Eagles. T. Maule. il Sports Illus 35:28-30+ S 27 '71
No paralysis is the analysis: Pittsburg Steelers vs San Diego Chargers. T. Maule. il Sports Illus 35:26-8+ O 11 '71
On paper, Dallas is the best: Cowboys in first place in NFC's eastern division. M. Mulvoy. Sports Illus 35:30-2+ D 6 '71
Owners can be tackled, too; NFL players vs management. G. S. Brown. il Sports Illus 34:18-21 Mr 22 '71
Pro football '71: scouting reports; National football league, American football league. T. Maule. il Sports Illus 35:32-4+ S 20 '71
Purple people eaters eaten: Chicago Bears vs Minnesota Vikings. J. Underwood. il Sports Illus 35:26-7 O 4 '71
Rushing with a golden gait; San Francisco 49ers; with account by R. F. Jones. il Sports Illus 35:54-61 S 20 '71
Shuffle off in Buffalo. por Newsweek 78:83 Ag 2 '71
Sunshine Patriots. il Time 98:46 Ag 16 '71
Super bowl; Baltimore Colts vs Dallas Cowboys. R. F. Jones; M. Sharnik. il por Sports Illus 34:18-20+ Ja 18 '71
Super bowl bound. il Time 98:49 D 13 '71
Super bowl scouting reports: Dallas Cowboys, Miami Dolphins; coaches rate teams. il Life 72:32-5+ Ja 14 '72
There's no need to pity the Pats; New England Patriots. R. H. Boyle. il Sports Illus 35:30-2+ O 18 '71
They call it a game, by B. Parrish. Review Bsns W p 10-11 S 11 '71. W. G. Flanagan
They had better be super: Baltimore Colts. T. Maule. il Sports Illus 35:22-5 N 8 '71
This Polish joke is on the Browns; Denver Broncos vs Cleveland Browns. T. Maule. il Sports Illus 35:28-9 N 1 '71
This spring isn't very green; Trans-American league in Texas. T. Maule. il Sports Illus 34:65-7 My 10 '71
Whoosh and a zonk; Miami Dolphins vs Pittsburgh Steelers. T. Maule. il Sports Illus 35:24-7 N 22 '71
Witnesses for the defense; Cowboys and Colts in the Super bowl. T. Maule. il Sports Illus 34:16-18 Ja 11 '71

Organization and administration
This Joe had better be good. J. Underwood. il pors Sports Illus 35:42-4+ D 13 '71
FOOTBALL coaches. See Coaches (athletics)
FOOTBALL fans
Go, you big red: Oklahoma and Nebraska head for the showdown. il Life 71:28-33 N 26 '71
Late summer madness: pro football preseason games. R. H. Boyle. il Sports Illus 35:18-21 S 13 '71
Pigskin sex. Time 99:48 Ja 10 '72
Pigskins preceded by pâté on asphalt; Guzzling gourmets, the Viking fans. J. Kirshenbaum. il Sports Illus 35:96+ D 6 '71

Anecdotes, facetiae, satire, etc.
Parting shots; fantasy for football fans; with drawings by J. Davis. Life 70:62A-64 Ja 22 '71
FOOTBALL for children. See Sports for children
FOOTBALL players
Buried under a sea of troubles; USC and UCLA football teams. R. Fimrite. il Sports Illus 35:28-31 N 15 '71
Case for the defense; bombs, boos make job tough for defensive backfields. L. J. Banks. il Ebony 27:170-2 N '71
Cheerleader could run the team: Notre Dame against Northwestern. D. Jenkins. il Sports Illus 35:26-7 S 27 '71

Dodging the draft in Canada; U.S. college stars avoiding NFL draft. M. Mulvoy. il Sports Illus 35:8-13 Ag 23 '71
Eleven big mistakes; seven by Colts, four by Cowboys in Super bowl. T. Maule. il Sports Illus 34:12-17 Ja 25 '71
Getting my kicks (title varies) ed. by J. Olsen. G. Blanda. il Sports Illus 35:26-31 Jl 19; 36-8+ Jl 26; 30-6 Ag 2 '71
He's burning to be a success: Philadelphia Eagles linebacker. J. Underwood. il pors Sports Illus 35:90-3+ S 20 '71
How they do run on: running back of college football. D. Jenkins. il Sports Illus 35:22-5 N 1 '71
1970 H.S. football All-Americans. H. L. Masin. il Sr Schol 98:22 Mr 1 '71
On paper, Dallas is the best: Cowboys in first place in NFC's eastern division. M. Mulvoy. Sports Illus 35:30-2+ D 6 '71
One-day season; Cornhuskers in Miami. D. Jenkins. il Sports Illus 34:10-15 Ja 11 '71
Pro football '71: scouting reports; National football league, American football league. T. Maule. il Sports Illus 35:32-4+ S 20 '71
Pro football's one-man demolition squad; linebackers. B. Surface. il Read Digest 99:149-52 O '71
Rev Richardson's football farm. L. J. Banks. il pors Ebony 27:104-9 D '71
Rookies at the helm. il Time 98:76+ O 11 '71
Super All-American (cont) H. L. Masin. il Sr Schol 98:19 F 1 '71
Super bowl scouting reports: Dallas Cowboys, Miami Dolphins; coaches rate teams. il Life 72:32-5+ Ja 14 '72
They call it a game, by B. Parrish. Review Life 71:18 S 24 '71. H. H. Broun
This Polish joke on the Browns; Denver Broncos vs Cleveland Browns. T. Maule. il Sports Illus 35:28-9 N 1 '71
Time's All-America team: the pick of the pros. il Time 98:78-9 D 20 '71
Tomorrow's generals; NFL quarterback search. T. Maule. il Sports Illus 34:22-4+ F 15 '71
Wedge meets the headhunters; with photographs by A. Rickerby. Life 71:32-9 D 3 '71
Whoosh and a zonk; Miami Dolphins vs Pittsburgh Steelers. T. Maule. il Sports Illus 35:24-7 N 22 '71
See also
National football league players association
also names of football players, e.g. D. Meggyesy

Photographs
Rushing with a golden gait. il Sports Illus 35:54-61 S 20 '71

Recruiting
See Football scouting

Salaries, pensions, etc.
Annual football roundup: the year of the strike. il Ebony 26:143-7+ N '70
FOOTBALL scouting
Battle for the bodies; annual professional-football draft. il Time 97:60 F 8 '71
Buckeyes don't have it; members of Ohio state's Rose bowl team. M. Sharnik. il Sports Illus 35:30-2+ Jl 5 '71
Dodging the draft in Canada; U.S. college stars avoiding NFL draft. M. Mulvoy. il Sports Illus 35:8-13 Ag 23 '71
Draft bait. Newsweek 77:62 F 8 '71
Gary who from C. W. where? por Time 98:76 D 6 '71
Pro football '71: scouting reports; National football league, American football league. T. Maule. il Sports Illus 35:32-4+ S 20 '71
This Joe had better be good. J. Underwood. il pors Sports Illus 35:42-4+ D 13 '71
Tomorrow's generals; NFL quarterback search. T. Maule. il Sports Illus 34:22-4+ F 15 '71
FOOTBALL stadiums. See Stadiums
FOOTBALL trophies. See Trophies, Sport
FOOTE, Emerson
Population control: your child's future depends on it. por Parents Mag 46:26 Je '71
FOOTE, Nancy
Who was Sonia Sekula? with excerpts from her journals and comments. il pors Art in Am 59:73-80 S '71
FOOTE, Paul Darwin
Obituary
Phys Today por 24:73+ N '71. F. Seitz
FOOTE, Theodore P.
For the elementary teacher: time for art. il Sch Arts 71:8-9 O '71
(comp) News: people, places, events. See issues of School arts

FOOTE, Timothy
Khrushschev remembered. Harper 243:60 N '71

FOOTWEAR. See Shoes

FORAGE plants
10-ton forage yields are his challenge. J. Davis. il Suc Farm 69:no5 H8 Mr '71
See also
Alfalfa
Pastures
Soybeans

FORAKER, David
Triple-row carrots. Org Gard & Farm 1**ঃ**: 105 Ag '71

FORAKER, David, 1953?-
On the fireline. il por Seventeen 30:42+ Ag '71

FORAMINIFERA
Depth habitats of growth stages of pelagic foraminifera. C. Emiliani. bibliog il Science 173:1122-4 S 17 '71

FORAMINIFERA, Fossil
Late pleistocene paleotemperatures at Tongue of the Ocean, Bahamas. G. W. Lynts and J. B. Judd. bibliog il Science 171:1143-4 Mr 19 '71
Orbitolina, a cretaceous larger foraminifer from Flemish cap: paleoceanographic implications. B. K. Sen Gupta and A. C. Grant. bibliog il Science 173:934-6 S 3 '71
Oxygen-18 studies of recent planktonic foraminifera: comparisons of phenotypes and of test parts. A. D. Hecht and S. M. Savin; reply with rejoinder. A. W. H. Bé and J. Van Donk. bibliog il Science 173:167-9 Jl 9 '71

FORBES, Cheryl A.
Box-office religion. il Chr Today 15:36-7 Ag 27 '71
Thou shalt not copy, right? il Chr Today 15: 44 S 10 '71

FORBES, John Ripley
National wildlife federation's conservation hall of fame. il por Nat Wildlife 9:24-5 Ap '71

FORBES, Robert Elliott
Contemporary youth inherit a strange and awesome world. il Cath World 213:21-6 Ap '71

FORBIS, John
Dot to remember. il Travel 135:58-62 My '71

FORCE (violence) See Violence

FORCE and energy
Can light move objects? I. Asimov. Sci Digest 70:44-5 Jl '71
Conversion of energy. C. M. Summers. il Sci Am 225:148-60 S '71
Energy and power; symposium. il Sci Am 225:36-70+ bibliog(p244+) S '71
See also
Energy budget (geophysics)
Mass (physics)
Muscular power
Pressure

FORCED labor. See Labor, Compulsory

FORCING (plants)
For winter fragrance plant paper-whites. B. Brinhart. il Home Gard 58:32-3 D '71
Plant a little spring indoors this fall. M. Reynolds. il Horticulture 49:28-31 N '71
Start your vegetable seeds under lights. D. Flegenheimer. Home Gard 58:48 F '71
See also
Hotbeds

FORD, Arthur A.
Report from heaven. il por Newsweek *7*9:52 Ja 3 '72 *

FORD, Barbara
Industry clean-up. il Sci Digest 70:80-5 D '71
National driver survey: asleep at the wheel. il Sci Digest 70::36-43 Jl '71
Poisons in the air, what they can do to you. il Sci Digest 70:73-8+ S '71
Semites first in America? il Sci Digest 71:43-8+ Ja '72
We're fighting oil pollution with bubbles, belts and beads. il Sci Digest 69:34-9 My '71
What doctors can do for epilepsy now. il Sci Digest 70:32-6 D '71
Who will fly to Mars? il Sci Digest 70:47-52 N '71
—See Macgregor, F. C. jt. auth.

FORD, Chris W. and Dyer, F. C.
Handicapped: one of our largest minorities. America 124:284-6 Mr 20 '71

FORD, Cristina. See Ford, M. C. V. A.

FORD, David Tighe-. See Tighe-Ford, D.

FORD, Eileen
Keep-your-husband diet; excerpt from book. il por Ladies Home J 88:60+ Ja '71

FORD, Ford Madox
On Ford Madox Ford. P. Shaw. Commentary 52:79-82 S '71 *
Saddest story, by A. Mizener. Review
Nat R 23:539-40 My 18 '71. H. Kenner *
Nation 212:532-3 Ap 26 '71. G. Wickes *
New Repub 164:25-7 Ap 17 '71. A. Gordon, jr *
Sat R 54:23-5+ Ap 3 '71. J. W. Aldridge *
Swan of Avon bites chickens. W. Allen. Nation 213:22-4 Jl 5 '71 *
Unhappy giant. por Vogue 158:87 Jl '71 *

FORD, Gerald R.
Model A Ford. New Repub 164:11 F 27 '71 *

FORD, Henry, 1863-1947
First Henry Ford, by A. Jardim. Review
Time il por 97:54+ Mr 1 '71
Planetary planning; address, November 13, 1969. R. B. Fuller. Am Scholar 40:296-8 Spr '71 *

FORD, Henry, 1917-
Ford and the future. A. Butkus. il por Duns 98:29-33+ N '71 *

FORD, Jesse Hill
Continuing trial of Jesse Hill Ford. M. Frady. il pors Life 71:b0-56B+ O 29 '71 *
There'll be no jail for Jesse Ford, except the prison of his mind. L. L. King. il pors Todays Health 49:28-33+ D '71 *

FORD, Joan
Board silences "No silence" librarian. Wilson Lib Bul 46:389-90 Ja '72 *

FORD, John T.
COCU plan of union and Catholicity. Chr Cent 88:1229-32 O 20 '71

FORD, Maria Cristina Vettore Austin
Sunshine days of Cristina Ford; with interview, ed. by D. Lurie. il pors Life 70:46-52 Je 4 '71

FORD, Norman C. and Kane, J. W.
Solar power. il pors Bul Atom Sci 27:27-31 O '71

FORD, Norman D.
Buying a good car in retirement. il Har Yrs 11:6-13 O '71
Drive-in islands. bibliog il Har Yrs 11:6-13+ My '71
Flaming fall foliage. il por Har Yrs 11:6-16 Ag '71
Florida: still good for retirement? il Har Yrs 11:16-20+ Je '71
Shunpiking through Texas. il Har Yrs 11:6-13+ F '71

FORD foundation
Aid for local conservationists. S. Lindsay. Sat R 55:72-3 Ja 1 '72
Fellowships for ethnic studies. Sch & Soc 99:208+ Ap '71
Ford in their future; minority-group programs. il Newsweek 78:72 O 18 '71

FORD italiana. See Automobile industry—Italy

FORD motor company
Better idea for Detroit; Ford project to revive riverfront. il Time 98:52+ D 6 '71
Calling all Pintos. Newsweek 77:80 Ap 12 '71
Ford and the future. A. A. Butkus. il por Duns 98:29-33+ N '71
Ford and the future. il Newsweek 77:84 Mr 29 '71
Ford black flags racing. J. Brokaw. il Motor T 23:65-7+ F '71
Ford has an Asian idea. Bsns W p46 Mr 13 '71
Ford in the future? il Forbes 108:24-5 N 1 '71
Ford's Iacocca: apotheosis of a usedcar salesman. W. Serrin. il pors N Y Times Mag p8-9+ Jl 18 '71
From Philco to Ford. por Bsns W p75 O 2 '71
Jewel from the crown; Pinto-Maverick-Mustang advertising accounts. Newsweek 78: 67 Jl 19 '71
Model T for Asia? Time 97:79 Mr 8 '71
Programming of Robert McNamara. D. Halberstam. il pors Harper 242:37-40+ F '71
Three small steps to the high command. por Fortune 83:35 Ja '71

Lincoln-Mercury division
Up from Edsel. il Time 98:59 Ag 2 '71

FORD motor company, ltd.
Ford: vulnerable but not helpless. il Forbes 109:25 Ja 1 '72

FORD motorsports association. See Automobile clubs

FORD of Europe, inc.
He drives Ford through Europe. por Bsns W p76 Jl 17 '71

FORDHAM, Alfred J.
Temperature and forsythia buds. il Horticulture 49:16-17 My '71

FORD'S theatre. See Washington, D.C.—Theater

FORE-edge painting. See Book ornamentation

FORECASTING
America: where are we headed? il Sr Schol 99:6-12 S 27 '71
H. G. Wells: the man who discovered tomorrow; beginnings of futurology. J. Williamson. il pors Sat R 55:12-15 Ja 1 '72
Putting the prophets in their place; Time essay. G. Clarke. il Time 97:38-9 F 15 '71
Today and tomorrow. il Sr Schol 98:7-8 My 10 '71
What future for futurology? symposium. bibliog il UNESCO Courier 24:4-32 Ap '71
What's happened to the brain business? P. Schrag. il Sat R 54:12-15+ Ag 7 '71
World dynamics, by J. W. Forrester. Review Fortune 84:131-2 S '71. W. Bowen
See also
Agricultural forecasting
Business forecasting
Economic forecasting
Nineteen hundred and seventies
Nineteen hundred and seventy-two
Political forecasting
Prophecies
Social forecasting
Technological forecasting
Weather forecasting

FORECASTING stock prices. See Stocks— Price forecasting

FOREIGN affairs (periodical)
Brouhaha at Foreign affairs. Time 98:15-16 S 6 '71
Peace and counterpeace: from Wilson to Hitler, by H. F. Armstrong. Review Newsweek 77:86+ Je 28 '71. A. Cooper
Test for an editor. il por Newsweek 78:74 S 6 '71

FOREIGN aid. See Economic assistance, American

FOREIGN automobiles. See Automobiles, Foreign

FOREIGN bank deposits. See Bank deposits, Foreign

FOREIGN bodies (physiology)
Amazing things they find in cows. il Sci Digest 69:13-15 Je '71
Tall tail to swallow. Todays Health 49:62 Je '71

FOREIGN bondholders protective council
Bonds of oblivion; defaulted foreign bonds. R. Levy. il Duns 97:72-3 My '71

FOREIGN camp counselors. See Camp counselors

FOREIGN claims settlement commission. See United States—Foreign claims settlement commission

FOREIGN correspondents
How to get kicked out of Prague. A. Levy. il pors N Y Times Mag p28-9+ My 16 '71
Make way for the new China hands. J. Hohenberg. Sat R 55:41-2 Ja 8 '72
New times in the Far East: changing of the press guard. J. Hohenberg. il Sat R 54:91-2+ Mr 13 '71
Our woman in Peking; Italy's ANSA correspondent. por Newsweek 78:71 S 20 '71
See also
Topping, A.
Women as foreign correspondents

FOREIGN direct investments, Office of. See United States—Foreign direct investments, Office of

FOREIGN exchange
Chartless seas for foreign exchange. il Bsns W p23-4 Ag 28 '71
Deciding how far to drop the dollar. il Bsns W p59 O 9 '71
Hot dollars spark a global crisis; with editorial comment. il Bsns W p 16-17, 96 My 8 '71
How foreign controls keep out U.S. dollars. il U S News 71:17 O 4 '71
How to get a fair exchange on cash abroad. Bsns W p78 Ag 21 '71
Keep the dollar free. M. Friedman. Newsweek 78:83 D 20 '71
Learning from the monetary crisis. Fortune 83:64 Je '71
One tourist's lament: they look at our dollars as if they were germ carriers. il U S News 71:24 Ag 30 '71
Tips for travelers: don't bring cash. il Time 98:37 S 27 '71
Tourists: passing the buck. Time 98:13 Ag 30 '71
Tourists: when the buck stops. il Newsweek 78:18-19 Ag 30 '71
Travelers' guide to dollar fluctuations. Bsns W p 122 My 15 '71
Wafting through Europe on the floating dollar. I. Barmash. Harp Baz 105:101 N '71

Weeks of floating loom for currencies. il Bsns W p 19 S 4 '71
See also
Balance of payments
Eurobond market
Eurodollar market
International monetary fund

FOREIGN exchange; story. See Lepis, C. B.

FOREIGN freight forwarders. See Forwarding companies

FOREIGN funds. See Bank deposits, Foreign

FOREIGN intelligence advisory board. See United States—President's foreign intelligence advisory board

FOREIGN investments in the United States. See Investments, Foreign (in the United States)

FOREIGN languages. See Languages, Modern

FOREIGN legion. See France—Army—Foreign legion

FOREIGN licensing. See International license agreements

FOREIGN missions. See Missions

FOREIGN opinion of the United States. See United States—Foreign opinion

FOREIGN policy (periodical)
Upstart journal. il Newsweek 78:68 S 20 '71

FOREIGN service (United States) See United States—Foreign service

FOREIGN service, Women in. See Women as foreign service employees

FOREIGN sports cars. See Sports cars

FOREIGN students in Germany
American teens in Berlin; symposium. ed. by R. Hemming. il Sr Schol 98:9-10 Mr 8 '71

FOREIGN students in the United States
Far Eastern students in a big university; subcultures within a subculture. M. H. Klein and others. Bul Atom Sci 27:10+ Ja '71
Foreign students look at America. Seventeen 31:12+ Ja '72
Six royal Africans at an Indiana college. il Ebony 26:66-8+ F '71
Statistic of the month. N. A. Carlson. il Am Ed 7:inside back cover Ap '71

FOREIGN study
How teen-agers can study and travel. il Bet Hom & Gard 49:170 N '71

FOREIGN trade regulation
Antitrust & the $. Forbes 107:21 Je 15 '71
Germans press trade law change. E. H. Kolcum. il Aviation W 94:60-1+ My 31 '71
High stakes of international poker. il Time 98:22-3 S 20 '71
Tough, risky U.S. trade offensive. il Newsweek 77:81 Je 7 '71

FOREIGN travel. See Travel

FOREIGN visitors in Cuba; Foreign visitors in Morocco; etc. See Visitors, Foreign—Cuba; Visitors, Foreign—Morocco; etc.

FORENSIC chemistry. See Chemistry, Legal

FORENSIC medicine. See Medical jurisprudence

FORENSIC psychiatry
Psychiatrist in a superior court setting. E. J. Balcanoff. bibliog Ment Hy 55:45-50 Ja '71

FOREST, James
Circus of Mertons. por Commonweal 92:400-2 Ja 22 '71

FOREST conservation
Conservation: for whom? address, January 22, 1971. J. A. Zivnuska. Vital Speeches 37:304-7 Mr 1 '71; Same. il por Am For 77:8-9+ Jl '71
Mike Frome; question of the vanishing American black walnut. M. Frome. Am For 77:7+ My '71
More trees for people. E. P. Cliff. il Am For 77:16-19+ Ap '71
New forestry program; testimony before the Subcommittee on public lands of the committee on interior and insular affairs. A. W. Smith. Nat Parks & Con Mag 45:35-7 My '71
See also
Forest fire protection

FOREST fire protection
Brush fire and forest fire dangers in California are very real. What can you do? Sunset 146:272+ Ap '71
On the fireline; Wenatchee, Wash. national forest. D. Foraker. il por Seventeen 30:42+ Ag '71
Only you can prevent forest fires. il Cons 26:41 O '71
Roadblock or detour? question of cooperative federal-state funding. K. B. Pomeroy. por Am For 77:5 Jl '71
See also
Airplanes in forest fire protection

FOREST fires
Wild beast that devours the dry forests. il
Life 71:28-33 Jl 23 '71
See also
Brush fires

FOREST HILLS, N.Y. See Queens, N.Y.

FOREST history society
Forest historians to study multiple use. il
Am For 77:52 My '71

FOREST management
ABC's of even-aged management. K. P.
Davis. il Am For 77:18-21+ Ag '71
Clearcut crisis. Am For 77:11 Mr '71
Clearcut; excerpts. N. Wood. il Am West 8:
10-15+ N '71
Forest management on National wildlife re-
fuges. V. E. Carter. il Am For 77:22-5+
Ag '71
Make your woodlands work for you. E. M.
Bacon. il Camp Mag 43:13-14 Ja '71
Making trees work harder. M. Wotton. il
Am For 77:20-1+ O '71
Old gobblers and old trees. B. Towell. Am
For 77:40 Ja '71
Time for action. K. B. Pomeroy. il Am For
77:32-4+ F '71
You can have more grouse in your woods.
G. W. Gullion. il Field & S 76:60-1+ O
'71
See also
Forest conservation
Forest thinning
United States—Forest service
Western forestry center, Portland, Ore.

FOREST ownership
Who's the smartest fellow around? D. W.
Sowers, jr. il Am For 77:8+ Mr '71

FOREST planting
Trees by label; National children's forest
project backed by Hunt-Wesson foods. il
Time 98:49 N 29 '71
See also
Reforestation

FOREST products
See also
Gums and resins

FOREST products industry
Economy & environment; address, April, 28,
1971. L. Wyatt. Vital Speeches 37:509-12 Je
1 '71
Hard hit by a slump in forest products;
Canadian industry. il Bsns W p40-1 N 20
'71
See also
Boise Cascade corporation
Lumber industry
Potlatch forests, inc.
Western forestry center, Portland, Ore.
Weyerhaeuser company

Finance
Forest products; with yardsticks of management performance. il Forbes 109:178-82 Ja
1 '72

FOREST rangers
Cop image. E. G. Bowman. il Parks & Rec
6:34-6 Ja '71
Forest rangers can spark ecology programs.
Camp Mag 43:15 '71
Hassles in the park. J. Hope. il Natur Hist
80:20-3+ bibliog(p 104) My '71
Park that caught urban blight; Yosemite Na-
tional Park. E. Abbey. il Life 71:40+ S 3
'71
Watched in the wild: crime in national parks.
P. Barnes. New Repub 165:12-13 Ag 21 '71

FOREST recreation
Forest vacation. B. Thomas. il Travel 136:28-
31 Jl '71
Wreckreation in our national forests. R. B.
Ditton. il Parks & Rec 6:22-6+ Je '71

FOREST research. See Forestry research

FOREST reserves. See National forests

FOREST service (United States) See United
States—Forest service

FOREST thinning
Clearcut crisis. Am For 77:11 Mr '71
Clearcutting the National forests. M. Frome.
Field & S 76:32+ Jl '71
Crisis of our national forests; Bitterroot na-
tional forest, Mont. J. N. Miller. il Read
Digest 99:91-6 D '71
National forests in danger? a growing dis-
pute; clearcutting. il U S News 70:48-9 My
3 '71
Tumult over timbering; Forest service en-
dorsing clear cutting. Time 97:55-6 Ap 19
'71

FOREST vegetation
See also
Streamside vegetation

FORESTRY. See Forests and forestry

FORESTRY, Industrial. See Forest management

FORESTRY laws and regulations
House approves HR 8817; on to Senate. K.
B. Pomeroy. Am For 77:3 D '71
Mike Frome. M. Frome. Am For 77:7+ Mr '71

FORESTRY research
Probing the secrets of the woods; Southlands
experiment forest. H. Clepper. il Am For
77:26-9+ Ag '71
See also
International union of forestry research organizations

FORESTRY schools and education
Forestry school at age 65. D. Howlett. il por
Am For 77:14-17+ Ag '71
New era in environmental education. A. J.
Schultz and W. P. Thompson. il Am For
77:28-31+ Ap '71
See also
Washington (state). University, Seattle—
College of forest resources

FORESTRY societies
See also
American forestry association
International union of forestry research or-
ganizations

FORESTS, National. See National forests

FORESTS, Petrified. See Petrified forests

FORESTS, Private. See Forest management

FORESTS, State
Forest that was; Beall Woods, and Wegener
Woods, Mo. J. P. Jackson. il Am For 77:
20-2 Ap '71
Roadblock or detour? question of cooperative federal-state funding. K. B. Pomeroy.
por Am For 77:5 Jl '71

FORESTS, Tropical. See Forests and forestry
—Tropics

FORESTS and forestry
Forests around the world; symposium. il
Am For 77:12-32+ S '71
Let's talk about forestry; symposium. il Am
For 77:13-35+ Ag '71
See also
Forest conservation
Forest fires
Lumbering
Reforestation
Timber
Tree breeding
Tree planting

Laws and regulations
See Forestry laws and regulations

Periodicals
See also
American forests (periodical)

Study and teaching
Peace corps forestry. S. Ellis. il Am For 77:
36-8 My '71
Taos Indians train for the future. il Am
For 77:34-5 S '71
See also
Forestry schools and education

Alaska
Stump merchants; timbering Alaska's nation-
al forests. S. Roberson. Field & S 75:16+
Mr '71

Austria
Austrians call it: *landwirtschaftlichebetreid.*
H. G. Reynolds. il Am For 77:14-17+ S
'71

Brazil
D. K. Ludwig plans to harvest a jungle.
il por Bsns W p34 Jl 31 '71

California
Pygmy forest near Mendocino. il Sunset 147:
48 S '71

Europe, Western
Forest use in western Europe. D. T. Mason.
il por Am For 77:20-3+ Mr '71

Iceland
Ultima Thule. C. Peet. il Am For 77:12-15+
Je '71

Italy
Pines of Ravenna. N. T. Mirov. il Natur
Hist 80:24-6 Ja '71

Kansas
Who say trees don't grow in Kansas? J.
K. Strickler. il Am For 77:28-9 Jl '71

Oregon
Land of the trees. J. B. Craig. il Am For
77:10-11 S '71

FORESTS and forestry—*Continued*

Peru

Earthquakes and eucalypts in Peru. T. Cobb.
il Am For 77:20-1+ S '71

Southern states

Story behind the South's third forest. P.
Friggens. il Am For 77:32-5+ O '71; Same
abr. with title Biggest tree-planting job
on earth. Read Digest 99:29-30+ N '71

Texas

See also
Big Thicket

Tropics

Is Dominica's forest doomed? B. E. Weber.
il Am For 77:12-15 Jl '71

Underdeveloped areas

See Underdeveloped areas—Forests and
forestry

United States

Let's not scuttle professional forestry. B.
Towell. Am For 77:10 Mr '71
More trees for people. E. P. Cliff. il Am For
77:16-19+ Ap '71
Trees for a better environment; address, Oc-
tober 4, 1970. J. P. Campbell. por Am For
77:10+ Ja '71
Washington lookout. V. Trumbull. See issues
of American forests
See also
Lumber industry
National forests
United States—Forest service

Washington (state)

25 years later: the circle that works; Shelton working circle. C. Collins. il Am For
77:15-20+ O '71

FORET, Pierre
Outdoor pantry. Horticulture 49:27+ Ap '71
FORGERIES. See Forgery
FORGERIES, Art. See Forgery of works of
art
FORGERY
How to prevent check forgeries. Good H
173:226 N '71
See also
Musical forgeries and mystifications
FORGERY of works of art
Fakes of Hacilar. il Time 98:40 S 6 '71
Rodin drawings, true and false; exhibition at
the National gallery, Washington. J. K. T.
Varnedoe. il Art N 70:30-3+ D '71
FORGETTING. See Memory
FORGEY, Benjamin F.
Cézanne without tears. il pors Art N 70:56-
9+ Ap '71
Dance of the Chi Wara. il Art N 70:46-9+
Sum '71
FORK, Richard L.
Laser stimulation of nerve cells in aplysia.
bibliog il Science 171:907-8 Mr 5 '71
FORM (aesthetics)
See also
Natural forms
FORM, Musical. See Musical form
FORMAL dinners. See Dinners and dining
FORMAMIDE
Formamide, number 13 in outer space. il
Chem 44:27 Jl '71
Interstellar formamide. Sky & Tel 41:280 My
'71
FORMAN, James
Reparations up to date. por Time 97:51-2 My
3 '71 •
FORMAN, Milos
Milos Forman's America is like Kafka's. J.
Conaway. il pors N Y Times Mag p8-12 Ji
11 '71 •
FORMATION flying. See Aviation—Formation
flying
FORMER priests. See Ex-nuns, priests, etc.
FORMOSA. See Taiwan
FORMOSAN termites. See Termites
FORMS, blanks, etc.
See subhead Forms, blanks, etc. under
various subjects, e.g. United States—Pay
board—Forms, blanks, etc.
FORNATALE, Peter
Hey, radio, help me make it through the
night. il por Sr Schol 99:32-4 O 25 '71
FORNWALT, Russell J.
How to sell your valuables. il Har Yrs 11:
19-23 N '71
FORRESTER, Jay Wright
Secrets of a model. por Newsweek 77:73 Mr
15 '71 •
What are man's prospects? D. L. Meadows.
Cur 133:3-9 O '71 •

FORSTER, Edward Morgan
Books. G. Steiner. New Yorker 47:158+ O
9 '71 •
E. M. Forster from snobbery to love. A.
Alvarez. por Sat R 54:39-40+ O 16 '71 •
E. M. Forster, homosexuality and Christian
morality. N. Pittenger. Chr Cent 88:1468-
71 D 15 '71 •
Posthumous Forster novel to be published
by Norton. L. P. Freilicher. por Pub W 199:
45 Je 21 '71 •
Queer business. F. Kermode. Atlan 228:140-2+
N '71 •
FORSYTH, Frederick
Some very bloody critics check out the Jac-
kal. J. Bonfante. por Life 71:77 O 22 '71 •
Story behind the book: The day of the Jackal.
B. A. Bannon. pors Pub W 200:34-5 Ag
9 '71 •
FORSYTH, G. C. and Thomas, D. G.
Models for financially healthy hospitals. il
Harvard Bsns R 49:106-17 Jl '71
FORSYTH, Ralph P.
Regional blood-flow changes during 72-hour
avoidance schedules in the monkey. bib-
liog il Science 173:546-8 Ag 6 '71
FORSYTHIAS
Temperature and forsythia buds. A. J. Ford-
ham. il Horticulture 49:16-17 My '71
FORT AMSTERDAM. See Ghana—Historic
houses, etc.
FORT CHURCHILL (historic army fort) See
Nevada—Parks and reserves
FORT DETRICK, Frederick, Md. See Lab-
oratories, Government
FORT LAUDERDALE, Fla.
U.S. journal; student spring vacations. C.
Trillin. New Yorker 47:104+ My 1 '71

Description

Fort Lauderdale. S. Birmingham. il Holiday
49:60-3+ D '70
FORT MCCLELLAN. See Military posts
FORT PECK reservation. See Indians of North
America—Reservations
FORT STEELE historic park. See British Co-
lumbia—Parks and reserves
FORT WORTH. Tex.

Water supply

Readable meters make happy customers. G.
O. Muller. il Am City 86:65-6 Ja '71
FORT WORTH opera association
Report:
Douglas Moore's Ballad of Baby Doe.
O. Chism. Opera N 35:33 Ja 30 '71
FORTAS, Abe
Fortas pays his respects. por Time 97:42 Je 21
'71 •
In Washington, you just don't not return
a call from Abe Fortas. V. S. Navasky.
il pors N Y Times Mag p7+ Ag 1 '71 •
FORTIFICATION
See also
Castles
FORTNEY, Karen Dobkin
(comp) Readings on the administration of
justice in America. Cur Hist 60:362-4+ Je;
61:46+ Jl '71
FORTUNE cookies. See Cookies
FORTUNE telling
See also
Palmistry
Tarot
49ers (football club) See Football clubs
FORTY plus clubs
D.C. Forty plus group breaks records in
members, placements. Aging 198:8 Ap '71
FORUMS (discussion and debate)
Exploring books; Provo, Utah. Senior cen-
ter class. R. McDougall. il Har Yrs 11:
48-9 O '71
1971 student burgesses at colonial Williams-
burg. il Sr Schol 98:19-20 Mr 29 '71
FORWARDING companies
Forwarders ask container incentives. R. S.
Kahn. Aviation W 94:40-1 F 22 '71
From limousines to casaba melons; foreign
freight forwarders. M. V. Rosenbloom. Na-
tions Bsns 59:41 Ag '71
See also
Emery air freight corporation
FOSDICK, Harry Emerson
Unforgettable Harry Emerson Fosdick. N. R.
Campion por Read Digest 98:69-73 Ja '71 •
FOSSEY, Dian
More years with mountain gorillas. il Nat
Geog 140:574-85 O '71
FOSSIL algae; Fossil bison; etc. See Algae,
Fossil; Bison, Fossil; etc.
FOSSIL animals. See Paleontology
FOSSIL bones. See Paleontology

FOSSIL fuel combustion. See Combustion
FOSSIL fuels. See Fuel
FOSSIL man. See Man, Prehistoric
FOSSIL microorganisms. See Micropaleontology
FOSSILS. See Paleontology
FOSTER, F. Gordon
Unusual ferns. il Horticulture 49:36-7+ Jl '71
FOSTER, Frances
Will Shakespeare knew that all along. S. C. Aksel. il por Wilson Lib Bul 45:754-7 Ap '71 *
FOSTER, Gertrude B.
Seasonings from the garden. il Horticulture 49:36-7+ Ag '71
FOSTER, Irene
Where the birds live; story. Redbook 137:70 Ag '71
FOSTER, John Stuart, 1922-
Pentagon salesman. Nation 212:676 My 31 '71 *
FOSTER, Laura
Honeymoon in Hetch Hetchy. il pors Am West 8:10-15 My '71
FOSTER, Richard N.
Organize for technology transfer. bibliog il Harvard Bsns R 49:110-20 N '71
FOSTER, Wilfrid Raymond
Hunt for meteorites. il por Sci Digest 70:64-8 O '71 *
FOSTER, William S.
How to give incinerators half a chance. bibliog il Am City 86:41-3 Jl; 76+ Ag '71
Water resource leaders. il pors Am City 86:67-8 Mr '71
FOSTER botanic garden. See Honolulu—Gardens
FOSTER day care
See also
Day nurseries
FOSTER grandparent program
Adopt a grandparent plan gets good start in New Jersey. il Aging 195:12 Ja '71
FOSTER home care
See also
Adoption
FOSTER parents
Help wanted: foster mothers; ed. by J. Copland. E. Crews. il Parents Mag 46:64-5+ Mr '71
FOTO-Mem, Inc.
Missing the timing. Duns 97:69-70 Ap '71
FOUCAULD, Charles Eugène, vicomte de
Vocation in the desert. N. Braybrooke. Commonweal 94:88-9 Ap 2 '71 *
FOUCAULT, Michel
Inside mind. R. A. Sokolov. por Newsweek 77:88 Ja 25 '71 *
Order of things, by M. Foucault. Review
Nation 213:21-2 Jl 5 '71. R. Howard *
FOULING of ship bottoms. See Marine fouling
FOULKE, Adrienne
(tr) See Mallet-Joris, F. Bringing up mother
FOULKES, Nigel
Foulkes to head British airports, claims no knowledge of aviation. Aviation W 95:21 N 22 '71 *
FOUND art. See Found objects
FOUND objects
Art from a cypress swamp; cypress knees, collected by T. Gaskins. M. Hunn. il pors Design 73:4-7 Wint '71
At home: memories of a happy summer. N. Mandelbaum. il Ladies Home J 88:76+ Jl '71
Kalpa tarou; found art sculpture, Kokomo, Ind. il Design 72:29-30 mid-Sum '71
FOUNDATION garments
Answers to your questions about the new bras and girdles. V. Griffin. il Good H 172:152 Mr '71
FOUNDATIONS
ABCs of laying a firm foundation. R. Day. il Mech Illus 67:120+ My '71
See also
Shoring and underpinning
FOUNDATIONS, Charitable and educational
Amalgamation of tax-exempt foundations? R. H. Smith. Pub W 199:50 My 24 '71
Money givers, by J. C. Goulden. Review
Bsns W p8 Ap 3 '71. G. Williams
Profiles: S. R. and C. S. Mott, philanthropists. E. J. Kahn, jr. por New Yorker 47:56-8+ N 27 '71
See also names of foundations, e.g. Peabody education fund

Investments
Corporate critics gain new allies. Bsns W p29 F 13 '71

Taxation
Is the money tree withering away? il Newsweek 78:67-8 Ag 30 '71
Money givers, by J. C. Goulden. Review
Newsweek 77:80+ Ap 26 '71. J. Iams

New focus on role of foundations. il U S News 71:52 D 20 '71
Tax reform act (cont) I. Fisher. Dance Mag 45:83 F; 108 Ap '71

Denmark
Skol! Carlsberg foundation. il Forbes 108:44+ S 1 '71
FOUNDRY construction
First contract for Kama River. Bsns W p30 Ja 1 '72
FOUNDRY practice
Pewter, the humble giant. C. H. Larson. il Sch Arts 70:20-1 Mr '71
See also
Continuous casting
Metal castings
FOUNTAIN, Andy
5 who fight pollution. C. Remsberg and B. Remsberg. pors Seventeen 30:129+ Ap '71 *
FOUNTAINS
Portland's bubbling people plaza. il Am Home 74:92-3 Ap '71
There's a new wet walk in San Francisco. il Sunset 147:30-1 Ag '71
Water sculpture. il Design 73:15-16 Wint '71
FOUR-channel broadcasting. See Radio broadcasting—Stereophonic transmission
FOUR-channel sound. See Sound—Stereophonic recording and reproducing
FOUR-day week. See Hours of labor
4-H clubs
Kids who care. B. Stonebraker. Farm J 95:45 F '71
Urban 4-H. il Time 98:40 Ag 2 '71 *
FOUR last songs; ballet. See Ballets—Criticisms
FOUR on a garden; drama. See Barillet, P. and Grédy, J. P.
FOUR-poster beds. See Beds
FOUR seasons (restaurant) See New York (city)—Hotels, restaurants, etc.
FOUR wheel drive Grand prix. See Motor vehicle racing
FOUR wheel drive motor vehicles. See Motor vehicles—Four wheel drive
FOUREZ, Gerard
Contemplative life in the modern world. il Cath World 213:27-9 Ap '71
FOURNIER, Robert
Three slip trailing techniques; excerpts from Ceramic creations. il Ceram Mo 19:21-3 S '71
FOURNIER D'ALBE, E. M.
On cyclones and other natural disasters: reflections of a geophysicist. il UNESCO Courier 24:24-7 F '71
FOURTH committee of the General assembly. See United Nations—Trusteeship committee
FOURTH dimension
See also
Space and time
FOURTH of July
Honor America day. A. N. Booth. Nations Bsns 59:72 Jl '71
Old Glory; Independence day festivities. il Newsweek 78:26 Jl 5 '71
FOURTH party movement. See Political parties—United States
FOURTH street 1. See Children's periodicals (by children)
FOWLER, Leonard
Leonard Fowler ballet, Kaufmann concert hall, NYC. N. Mason. Dance Mag 45:25 Je '71
FOX, Ben
Enforcer. il por Newsweek 78:101 O 18 '71 *
FOX, Gerald S.
Grandiose transcendentalism: Horenstein and Abravanel in the Mahler Third symphony. Am Rec G 37:577+ My '71
Gustav Mahler: Das klagende lied. por Am Rec G 37:214-16+ D '70
FOX, Lucia A.
Ricardo Palma's tradiciones. il por Américas 23:31-6 Je '71
FOX, Maurice S. and Littlefield, J. W.
Reservations concerning gene therapy. Science 173:195 Jl 16 '71
FOX, Richard
Artist with nails. il pors Design 72:16-17 mid-Wint '71
FOX, Sidney W.
—and Windsor, C. R.
Synthesis of amino acids by the heating of formaldehyde and ammonia. bibliog il Science 170:984-6; 174-1040 N 27 '70, D 3 '71
about
Biology: new answers to some fundamental questions. Bsns W p42 Ja 1 '72 *

FOX, Tom
Vietnam after the election. Commonweal 95:
203-7 N 26 '71
FOX, Virgil
Recordings; Fillmore East concert. M.
Mayer. Esquire 75:62 Ja '71 •
FOX hunting
Easy fox hunting. T. M. Wunderle. il Field
& S 76:60-1+ N '71
Ounce of prevention for the banks and the
bogs: West Waterford pack. R. S. Rauch.
3d. il Sports Illus 35:48-51 N 22 '71
FOX squirrels. See Squirrels
FOXES
Another cliché, ah, bites the dust. il Life
71:80 S 17 '71
North country red. J. S. Crawford. il Out-
door Life 148:38-41+ Jl; 68-71+ Ag '71
Saga of the foiled fox. P. Darro. il Nat
Wildlife 9:62-3 O '71
See also
Fox hunting
FOXES, Photography of. See Photography of
animals
FOXHALL, William B.
Computers: tools for construction manage-
ment; excerpt from Professional construc-
tion management and project administra-
tion. Arch Rec 150:53-4 D '71
FOXHOUNDS
Special hounds. D. M. Duffey. il Outdoor
Life 148:174+ O '71
FOXWORTHY, Betty Ann
Grand American. il Holiday 49:52-6 Jl '71
FOY, Fred C.
Chairman's chair (cont) por Forbes 107:84-5
Mr 15; 108-66-7 Jl 1 '71
FOYERS. See Halls
FOYT, Anthony Joseph, 1935-
Old man of the brickyard tries again and
again and again. M. Spiegel. il por Mech
Illus 67:57-9+ My '71 •
FRAAS, Arthur P. See Lubin, M. J. jt. auth.
FRACTURE of glass. See Glass—Fracture
FRACTURES
Limb regeneration in mammals. il por Sci N
100:322-3 N 13 '71
Low charge for fractures. il Newsweek 78:
74+ N 8 '71
What if you break a bone? G. M. Knox. Bet
Hom & Gard 49:20+ Ap '71
FRACTURES (geology) See Faults (geology)
FRADIER, Georges
Tunis: a jewel of Islam. il UNESCO Cou-
rier 23:34-41 D '70
FRADY, Marshall
American innocent in the Middle East
(cont) Harper 242:65-79 Ja '71
Continuous trial of Jesse Hill Ford. il pors
Life 71:56-56B+ O 29 '71
It's all in this family, too. il Life 71:61-2+
N 19 '71
Life among the rock people. il Life 71:22-4 S
3 '71
Small victories in Americus. il Life 70:46B-
46D+ F 12 '71
Wooing of Wilbur Mills. il pors Life 71:52-
52B+ Jl 16 '71
FRAGRANT gardens. See Gardens, Fragrant
FRAIBERG, Selma
How a baby learns to love. il Redbook 137:
76+ My '71
FRAIM, John P.
Mr Fraim elected board chairman of People-
to-people program. Dept State Bul 63:752
D 21 '70 •
FRAME, George W.
They're out to save the black rhino. il Sci
Digest 70:33-8 N '71
FRAMES for pictures. See Picture frames
FRAMINGHAM, Mass.
Gardens
Our most beautiful natives; garden in the
woods. J. A. Lynch. il por Nat Wildlife 9:21-
4 Je '71
FRANCA, Celia
Image: Celia Franca and the National ballet
of Canada. O. Maynard. il por Dance Mag
45:46-55 Ap '71 •
FRANCE, Anatole
Juggler of Our Lady; dramatization. See
Hackett, W.
FRANCE, Bill
Rap 'n 'pinion. por Motor T 23:12 Mr '71
FRANCE
See also
Abortion—Laws and legislation—France
Air traffic control—France
Airplanes, Military—France
Americans in France
Ballet—France
Banks and banking—France

Canals—France
Church and state in France
Colombey-les-deux-Églises
Crime and criminals—France
Deauville
Decentralization in government—France
Education—France
Elections—France
Festivals—France
Gévaudan
Government ownership—France
Horse racing—France
Hotels, taverns, etc.—France
Illiers
Justice, Administration of—France
Labor and laboring classes—France
Loire Valley
Lourdes
Marriage customs and rites—France
Marseilles
Moving pictures—France
Music festivals—France
Opera—France
Orléans
Periodicals—France
Political clubs and associations—France
Postal service—France
Provence
Publishers and publishing—France
Puy, Le
Riviera
Schools—France
Seaside resorts—France
Shopping and shoppers—France
Space research—France
Sports—France
Strikes—France
Student demonstrations—France
Tourist trade—France
Trials—France
Visitors, Foreign—France
World war, 1939-1945—France

Antiquities
Sacred source of the Seine. S. A. Deyts. il
Sci Am 225:65-73 Jl '71

Army
Foreign legion
Whatever happened to the French foreign
legion? il U S News 71:53 Jl 19 '71

Colonies
Reports & comment: French Africa; former
colonies in black Africa. S. Meisler. Atlan
228:6+ S '71
See also
Martinique

Defenses
See also
Aeronautics, Military—France
Atomic warfare—Defenses

Description and travel
Travel notes. R. Joseph. Esquire 76:20+ Jl '71

Economic conditions
France bids to be no. 1 in Europe. il Bsns W
p88-90 Je 26 '71
France enters the enjoyable epoch. il Time
98:93-4 D 6 '71
Good life returns. il Time 97:68+ Ja 25 '71

Economic policy
French prospects in Europe. America 125:
386 N 13 '71

Economic relations
Letter from Paris; dollar crisis. Genêt. New
Yorker 47:85 My 29 '71

Foreign relations
See also
Military assistance, French

Africa
France in Africa. America 124:167-8 F 20 '71
Francophone Africa. W. H. Lewis. Cur Hist
60:142-5+ Mr '71
Reports & comment: French Africa; former
colonies in black Africa. S. Meisler. Atlan
228:6+ S '71

Germany (Federal Republic)
German-French struggle, how far will it go?
il U S News 71:35-6 D 6 '71

Pakistan
I am a paratrooper; cause of Bangla Desh.
por Newsweek 78:35-6 O 11 '71

History
See also
World war, 1939-1945—France

FRANCE—History—*Continued*

19th century

Reflections; life of A. de Custine. G. F. Kennan. New Yorker 47:46-50+ My 1 '71

Industries

See also
Aerospace industries—France
Airplane industry—France
Automobile industry—France
Avionics industry—France
Chemical industries—France
Helicopter industry—France
Munitions industries—France
Petroleum industry—France
Textile industry—France
Tire industry—France

Intellectual life

Reflections; life of A. de Custine. G. F. Kennan. New Yorker 47:46-50+ My 1 '71

Maps

Traveler's companion: a new map of France. il Nat Geog 139:832-3, sup (folded map) Je '71

Military policy

France's global strategy. M. Debré. For Affairs 49:395-406 Ap '71

National center for space studies

See also
International satellite geodesy experiment

Appropriations and expenditures

Applications satellites, launcher work to be stressed by CNES. D. E. Fink. Aviation W 94:16 Ja 18 '71

Photographs

Cartier-Bresson's France; photographs by H. Cartier-Bresson. H. Wright. Pop Phot 68:92-9 F '71

Politics and government

Honeymoon ends for France's Pompidou. il por U S News 70:70 Ap 12 '71
New European man runs France. K. Botsford. por N Y Times Mag p9+ Ag 29 '71
New mood. E. Behr. il Newsweek 77:40+ My 17 '71
Reports & comment. J. K. Glassman. Atlan 227:6+ F '71
See also
Communist party (France)
Elections—France

FRANCE (ship) See Ocean liners

FRANCES, Evan
Self-hypnosis diet. il Ladies Home J 88:52+ Je '71

FRANCHISE system
See also
International industries, inc.
Restaurants—Franchise system

Laws and legislation

Shutting the gates on area franchises. Bsns W p22 Ja 23 '71

FRANCIS of Assisi, Saint
Hippie Saint. J. Roddy. il pors Look 35:31-7 Ap 20 '71 *
Identity crisis. P. W. Schmidtchen. il pors Hobbies 76:134-6 Ap '71 *

FRANCIS, Devon
I drove our first coast-to-coast interstate, the campers' expressway. il Pop Sci 198:78-9+ Mr '71

FRANCIS, Robert
Out of the shadow. D. Young. New Repub 165:28-30 Ag 7 '71 *
Trouble with Francis, by R. Francis. Review
Sat R 54:65-6 D 4 '71. A. C. Lunn *

FRANCKE, Uta. See Nesbitt, M. jt. auth.

FRANCO, Barbara
Stoneware made by the White family in Utica, New York. il Antiques 99:872-6 Je '71

FRANCO, Francisco
Beyond Franco. il Time 98:38+ O 11 '71 *
Spain. by R. Herr. Review
New Repub 165:24+ O 2 '71. J. Walt *

FRANCO, Marjorie
No such thing as a happy marriage; story. Redbook 136:70-1 F '71
One reason why I married Henry; story. Redbook 136:67 Ja '71
Sounds of fiction. Writer 84:11-13 O '71
Uncompromising girl; story. Redbook 138:59 Ja '72

FRANCO-ENGLISH war, 1755-1763. See United States—History—French and Indian war, 1755-1763

FRANCO-German communications satellites. See Communications satellites, European

FRANCOIS, Bill
Can the press police itself? America 124:433-5 Ap 24 '71

FRANK, John P.
Hugo L. Black. New Repub 165:15-17 O 9 '71

FRANK, Judith
Write for children. il Writers Digest 51:24-5+ F '71

FRANK, Mary
Clay landscapes of Mary Frank. G. Henry. il Craft Horiz 31:18-21+ D '71 *

FRANK, Reuven
Broadcasting and the first amendment; address, November 11, 1971. Vital Speeches 38:125-7 D 1 '71

F.R.A.N.K; story. See Gilliatt, P.

FRANK Lloyd Wright school of architecture
Guardian of a great legacy; with editorial comment. L. Wainwright. il pors Life 70:3, 44-55 Je 11 '71

FRANK Merriwell; musical comedy. See Musical comedies, revues, etc.—Criticisms, plots, etc.

FRANKEL, Haskel
Criminal record. See last issue of each month of Saturday review, April 24, 1971-

FRANKEL, Max
President and press: a debate; summary. pors Time 97:53 Ap 12 '71
Revenue sharing is a counterrevolution. il N Y Times Mag p28-9+ Ap 25 '71

FRANKEL, Morris
Two-drill dentist. por Newsweek 78:72 Ag 30 '71 *

FRANKEL, Paul
Troubled oils; interview, ed. by J. Ross-Skinner. por Duns 97:85-6 Ap '71

FRANKENSTEIN, Alfred
Avant-garde music for conservatives. Hi Fi 21:68 My '71
Spring opera goes theatrical. il Hi Fi 21: MA26-7 Ag '71
Thomas triumphs as Siegfried. il Hi Fi 20: MA26+ D '70

FRANKENSTEIN, Carl
Process of identity, two views. M. S. Enker. bibliog Ment Hy 55:369-74 Jl '71 *

FRANKENTHALER, Helen
Frankenthaler as pastoral. L. Alloway. il Art N 70:66-8+ N '71 *

FRANKFORT on the Main

Airports

Frankfurt girds for another expansion. E. H. Kolcum. il Aviation W 95:55+ N 15 '71

Music

Great opera houses. E. Davidson. il Opera N 35:12-15 Mr 27 '71
Report:
Domenico Cimarosa's Il matrimonio segreto. D. Graham. Opera N 35:33 Ja 23 '71

Theater

Stage directions. S. Kauffmann. New Repub 165:24+ Jl 10 '71

FRANKFURT. See Frankfort on the Main

FRANKFURT book fair. See Book fairs

FRANKFURT opera house. See Opera houses

FRANKFURTERS
See also
Cookery—Meat

FRANKIE, Richard J. and DuBois, E. E.
Community-junior college in historical and cultural perspective. bibliog f Sch & Soc 99:45-7 Ja '71

FRANKLIN, Aretha
Aretha. C. L. Sanders. il pors Ebony 27:124-6+ D '71 *
Soul kaleidoscope: Aretha at the Fillmore. M. Lydon. il pors Ramp Mag 10:30-9 O '71 *

FRANKLIN, Benjamin
Meet Dr Franklin; excerpts. R. B. Morris. il por Am Heritage 23:80-91 D '71 *

FRANKLIN, H. Bruce
Inciting to violence. il por Time 99:41 Ja 17 '72 *
Limits of academic freedom. il por Time 97:51 Mr 15 '71 *
Pauling pickets. D. Shapley. il por Science 174:482 O 29 '71 *

FRANKLIN, J. E.
Black girl. Criticism
Nation 213:445 N 1 '71 *
New Yorker 47:76 Je 26 '71 *
Newsweek il 77:85 Je 28 '71 *

FRANKLIN, J. Ross
Colonel Herbert tried to go by the book in Vietnam: how a supersoldier was fired from his command. J. T. Wooten. il pors N Y Times Mag p 10-11+ S 5 '71 *

FRANKLIN, Jim
Armadillo man; interview. New Yorker 47:
41-2 D 11 '71
FRANKLIN, Joe
Profiles. W. Whitworth. por New Yorker 47:
44-6+ My 22 '71 •
FRANKLIN, Kenneth L.
Sky full of lines; how to read celestial co-
ordinates. il Sci Digest 70:22-9 Ag '71
FRANKLIN D. Roosevelt library, Hyde Park,
N.Y.
FDR library inquiry scores serious lapses.
Library J 96:580 F 15 '71
Probe of presidential libraries ordered. Lib-
rary J 96:2569 S 1 '71
FRANKLIN engine company
Whatever happened to the Franklin engine?
P. Garrison. il Flying 89:41 Ag '71
FRANKLIN mint
Franklin mint. il por Nations Bsns 59:74-5+
D '71
Late tape. R. Brady. Duns 98:9-10 Jl '71
Making a mint. il Newsweek 78:78 D 20 '71
Non-coin of the realm. il Time 98:58 Jl 12 '71
FRANKLIN PARK, Ill.

Parks and playgrounds
Don't guess; get answers. P. D. Elmon. il
Am City 86:110 Ag '71
FRANKLIN town. See Philadelphia—City plan-
ning
FRANKS, Jesse Gibson
Linguistic gospel: a dissent. bibliog Sch &
Soc 99:98-101 F '71
FRANSON, Paul
9 experiments with multipurpose semiconduc-
tors. il Radio-Electr 42:48-51 Ap '71
FRANZ, Maurice
Garden calendar. il Org Gard & Farm 18:
94-6+ Mr; 94-8 Ap; 74-80 My; 82-4 Je; 78-81
Ag; 104-10+ S '71
FRANZBLAU, Rose (Nadler)
Distress signals. P. S. Prescott. por News-
week 7:72 F 1 '71 •
FRANZEN, Ulrich
Franzen: four current projects. il Arch Rec
150:107-16 Jl '71 •
FRAREY, Carlyle J. and Donley, M. R.
Placements & salaries, 1970: the year that
was not what it seemed. il por Library J
96:1937-41 Je 1 '71
FRASCHETTI, Peter A.
Puppets. il Sch Arts 70:36-8 Je '71
FRASE, Robert W.
AAP spokesman testifies on postal rate in-
crease; excerpts ed. by L. Huston. Pub W
200:233 Ag 30 '71
FRASER, Alan
Drink. Mlle 73:102 O; 74:50 D '71
Wines. Mlle 72:136+ Ap; 73:30-1 S '71
FRASER, Arvonne S.
Women: the new image; address, June 3,
1971. Vital Speeches 37:599-605 Jl 15 '71
FRASER, Bruce, and Roberts, Elsa
Reply to Positive carriers of violence among
children: detection by speech deviations.
Ment Hy 55:162-4 Ap '71
FRASER, Charles
Profiles; C. Fraser and D. Brower. J. McPhee.
pors New Yorker 47:42-8+ Mr 27 '71 •
FRASER, Donald
Oiling the machinery of Congress; interview
ed. by J. Mandelstam. por Sr Schol 98:12
Mr 1 '71
FRASER, Kennedy
On and off the avenue. New Yorker 47:101-2+
Ap 3; 107-11 My 8; 60+ Jl 10; 68-9 Jl 24;
72-4 Ag 7; 123-5 N 6; 122+ N 20 '71
FRASER, Lady Antonia (Pakenham)
Bess and old Noll. pors Horizon 13:106-11 Aut
'71
FRASER, Stewart E.
Brazilian government priority projects in
education. Sch & Soc 99:364-7 O '71
Reforms for rural primary and middle schools;
introd. to text of document. Sch & Soc
99:237-8 Ap '71
FRASIER, E. Lewis
Install a three-way switch yourself? Sure
you can. il Pop Mech 136:182-4 O '71
FRATERNITIES. See College fraternities
FRATERNITY housemothers. See Housemoth-
ers
Die FRAU ohne schatten; opera. See Strauss, R.
FRAUD
America on $0 a day. A. Hoffman. il Ramp
Mag 9:48-55 F '71
Astronauts on the make; stock fraud, Texas.
K. Northcott. Ramp Mag 10:12-13 N '71
Beware the commercialized faith healers. O.
K. Armstrong. Read Digest 98:179-80+ Je '71
Big names in a Texas stock scheme; SEC
case. por Bsns W p77 Ja 23 '71

CAB to scrutinize European charters. L.
Doty. Aviation W 95:26-7 S 6 '71
Counterfeit watch racket. O. Schisgall and
D. Garr. il Pop Sci 199:54-6 D '71
Enforcer steps down; financial wheelings
and dealings of F. Sharp. Time 98:16+
O 25 '71
Fight on fraud in FHA programs. Bsns W
p39 S 25 '71
High wind in Texas; stock-fraud suit. News-
week 77:56+ F 1 '71
How to outfox the lawn gyps. L. David. il
Mech Illus 67:109-11+ My '71
I.O.U.'s of Texas are upon us; involvement
of the Houston Jesuits. America 124:139
F 13 '71
Join the fight against organic phonies. R.
Rodale. il Org Gard & Farm 18:73-4 Je '71
Multinational swindle born of tight money;
worthless flood of paper from Guernsey's
Bank of Sark. il Bsns W p46-7+ Jl 10 '71
Promoter and the crime buster; relations be-
tween F. W. Sharp and W. R. Wilson, jr.
D. Jackson. il pors Life 71:59-60+ S 24 '71
Texas does it big; case involving F. W.
Sharp. Nation 213:324 O 11 '71
See also
Advertising, Fraudulent
Forgery of works of art
Insurance—Fraudulent promotion
FRAUDULENT diplomas. See Diplomas,
Fraudulent
FRAZER, John E.
India's sacred river the Ganges. il Read Di-
gest 99:203-6+ S '71
—See Reed, D. jt. auth.
FRAZER, Phillip
Medium Chile: cinéma vérité inside the third
world. Ramp Mag 9:56-62 F '71
FRAZIER, George, 4th
Welcome back to the forties. il Esquire 76:
98-105, 108-15+ O '71
FRAZIER, Joe
I got a surprise for Clay; interview. ed. by
M. Sharnik. por Sports Illus 34:28-30+
F 22 '71
about
Ali-Frazier crunch. P. Axthelm. Vogue 157:
115 Mr 1 '71 •
Ali-Frazier fight; with editorial comment. N.
Mailer. il pors Life 70:3, 18F-19+ Mr 19
'71 •
And then there was one. il pors Time 97:35
Mr 22 '71 •
At the bell... M. Kram. il pors Sports Illus
34:18-21 Mr 8 '71 •
Battered face of a winner; Ali-Frazier fight;
photographs, with report by M. Kram.
Sports Illus 34:16-21 Mr 15 '71 •
Battle of the undefeated giants; with edi-
torial comment. T. Thompson. il pors Life
70:3, 40-9 Mr 5 '71 •
Biggest fight in history. L. J. Banks. il pors
Ebony 26:134-6+ Mr '71 •
Bull v. butterfly: a clash of champions. il
pors Time 97:63+ Mr 8 '71 •
Fight. New Yorker 47:32-5 Mr 20 '71 •
It's gonna be the champ and the tramp. T.
Maule and M. Sharnik. il pors Sports Illus
34:14-17 F 1 '71 •
Now there is one champion. il pors News-
week 77:72-6 Mr 22 '71 •
Purse snatchers. il pors Time 97:65-6 Ja 25
'71
Winner, the loser, the crowd. L. Banks. il
pors Ebony 26:132-4+ My '71 •
FRAZIER, John Linley
Environmentalist. por Time 98:14 D 13 '71 •
FREAKS (hippies) See Hippies
FRED, James A.
Different resistance decade. il Pop Electr
34:64-6 Mr '71
FREDERICK, Calvin J.
Present suicide taboo in the United States.
bibliog Ment Hy 55:178-83 Ap '71
FREDERICK, Frances
Plan now for the cherry that blooms in the
autumn. il House B 113:112 Jl '71
FREDERICK, Raymond
Swimming pool stacks away. il Pop Sci 198:
104-5+ Ap '71
FREDERICKS, Carlton, and Goodman, Her-
man
Beauty sense and nonsense; excerpt from
Low blood sugar and you. Harp Baz 104:
82 O '71
FREDERICKS, William G.
No, to revenue sharing. Nat R 23:754-7 Jl 13
'71
FREDONIA college. See New York (state).
State university—College at Fredonia
FREDRICKSON, John M. See Schwarz, D. F.
jt. auth.

FREE, John R.
Clad metals: they're moving into your home. il Pop Sci 199:12+ D '71
Cool your whole house with one window unit? il Pop Sci 198:92-4+ My '71
Electronics plays the numbers game. il Pop Sci 199:72-3 O '71
Ferroelectric ceramics, new twist with light. il Pop Sci 198:61-3 My '71
For '72, color TV goes modular and solid state. il pors Pop Sci 199:82-5 N '71
How good are those new cassette tapes? il Pop Sci 199:89+ N '71
How you'll make your own electricity in tomorrow's all-gas home. il Pop Sci 199: 46-7 Ag '71
Microelectronics shrinks the calculator. il Pop Sci 198:74-6+ Je '71
See-while-you-talk telephone service. il Pop Sci 198:65+ Mr '71
What dimouts do to your electrical equipment. il Pop Sci 198:58-9+ F '71

FREE atoms. See Atoms

FREE enterprise
American businessman; address, March 12, 1971. J. J. Riccardo. Vital Speeches 37:434-6 My 1 '71
Competitive system; to work, to preserve, to protect; address, March 25, 1971. J. M. Roche il por Vital Speeches 37:445-8 My 1 '71; Same abr. with title Let's stop blaming business! Read Digest 99:123-5 Jl '71; Excerpts. U S News 70:91-3 Ap 12 '71
Free association, free enterprise and free choice; address, November 24, 1970. H. S. Geneen. Vital Speeches 37:221-4 Ja 15 '71
Generation gap; economic illiteracy; address, December 5, 1970. D. M. Kendall. Vital Speeches 37:245-7 F 1 '71
Libertarianism: a new right credo? S. Lehr and L. Rossetto, jr. Cur 127:29-38 Mr '71
Meet Ralph Nader's most outspoken critic. pors Bsns W p58-9 Jl 24 '71
New right credo: libertarianism. S. Lehr and L. Rossetto, jr; discussion. N Y Times Mag p32 F 14 '71
Technology and society: a challenge to private enterprise; address, April 1971. I. K. MacGregor. Vital Speeches 37:525-9 Je 15 '71
Unfree nonenterprisers. F. Getlein. Chr Cent 88:461-5 Ap 14 '71
We must pull together: labor, management and government; address, June 30 1971. A. K. Davis. Vital Speeches 37:631-4 Ag 1 '71
Why reds are turning to capitalism. il U S News 71:61-3 N 15 '71
See also
Competition

Anecdotes, facetiae, satire, etc.
Two post office departments today! J. Keefauver. Nat R 23:199 F 23 '71

FREE food for school children. See School lunches

FREE-lance writing. See Authorship

FREE masons. See Freemasons

FREE press. See Freedom of the press

FREE radicals. See Radicals (chemistry)

FREE silver movement. See Silver as money

FREE speech
FTC says book ads have free speech guarantees. S. Wagner. Pub W 200:29-30 Jl 26 '71
Getting nowhere through channels; distributing dissenting materials in the army. J. V. H. Dippel. New Repub 164:13-17 My 22 '71
Speaking out in Germany. Time 97:48+ F 15 '71
Supreme court and the First amendment. R. H. Smith. Pub W 200:32 O 4 '71
Symbols of flag as freedom of expression. H. F. Pilpel and K. P. Norwick. Pub W 199: 31-2 Mr 29 '71
Television and the First amendment. F. W. Friendly. Sat R 55:46-7+ Ja 8 '72
See also
Academic freedom
Information. Freedom of
Libel and slander

FREE-stall barns. See Barns and stables

FREE stall farrowing pens. See Swine farrowing crates and pens

FREE trade and protection
Americans, go home! non-tariff protectionism; in western Europe. J. Ross-Skinner. il Duns 98:46-8+ O '71
Business and free trade. Duns 98:108 O '71
Changing basis for protectionism; address, February 24, 1971. O. R. Strackbein. Vital Speeches 37:401-4 Ap 15 '71
Free trade truths, and myths. H. S. Piquet. il Nations Bsns 59:37-8+ F '71; Reply. S. S. Cort. 59:54-7 Jl '71

Free trade v. the new protectionism; excerpts from discussion. il Time 97:90-2 My 10 '71
Free world must avoid a trade war. J. Atwater. Read Digest 99:75-9 S '71
General electric chairman Fred Borch lays it on the line; address. F. Borch. por Forbes 108:27-8+ N 15 '71
It's time for some plain talk about trade. W. E. Swegle. Suc Farm 69:no5 L8-9 Mr '71
Labor's turnabout on trade. Time 98:30 N 29 '71
One-way street; trade between U.S. and Japan. il Forbes 107:15-16 My 1 '71
Pandora's box; protectionist legislation. Commonweal 94:75-6 Ap 2 '71
Perils of the new protectionism; Time essay. G. J. Church. Time 98:26-7 D 6 '71
Protectionism in America; address, October 30, 1970. J. A. Greenwald. Dept State Bul 63:724-9 D 14 '70
Protectionism or free trade: a decision for our time; address, May 3, 1971. K. Rush. Dept State Bul 64:749-53 Je 7 '71
U.S. foreign trade: there's no need to panic; with editorial comment. S. Rose. il Fortune 84:105-6, 109-11+ Ag '71
Unions demand more jobs. il Bsns W p63-4 Jl 17 '71
World trade: a clash of wills. il Time 98: 21-2 S 20 '71
See also
Balance of trade
Export controls
Tariff

FREE verse
Principles of free verse. J. Jerome. Writers Digest 51:12+ D '71

FREED, Jack
What goes on in Harrisburg. Nation 212:464-6 Ap 12 '71

FREEDMAN, Richard
Life music review. Life 71:14 O 29 '71

FREEDMEN
Schools for the freedmen. R. D. Parmet. bibliog il Negro Hist Bul 34:128-32 O '71

FREEDOM. See Liberty

FREEDOM (theology)
Inner and outer freedom. D. L. Berry. Chr Cent 88:775-6 Je 23 '71

FREEDOM, Intellectual. See Intellectual liberty

FREEDOM in science. See Science, Freedom of

FREEDOM of information. See Information, Freedom of

FREEDOM of information act. See Information, Freedom of

FREEDOM of speech. See Free speech

FREEDOM of teaching. See Academic freedom

FREEDOM of the press
Broadcasting and the first amendment; address, November 11, 1971. R. Frank. Vital Speeches 38:125-7 D 1 '71
Case of John Peter Zenger. L. Barnett. il pors Am Heritage 29:33-41+ D '71
Free press/free people, by J. Hohenberg. Review
Bsns W p8+ Mr 20 '71. H. Brucker
Free press obligations of mass media. H. F. Pilpel and K. P. Norwick. Pub W 199:32 Mr 29 '71
Freedom of the press. Nation 213:357 O 18 '71
Harassing of CBS. Commonweal 94:206 My 7 '71
Historical confrontation. Cur 131:6-7 Jl '71
Privacy, publishing and you. H. F. Pilpel and A. U. Schwartz. Pub W 201:30-2 Ja 3 '72
Promoting of chaos: the three major catalysts; address, July 17, 1971. R. E. L. Eaton. Vital Speeches 37:687-90 S 1 '71
Reporters, subpoenas, immunity, and the Court; views of V. Blasi. R. L. Tobin. Sat R 54:63-4 D 11 '71
Repression and the press; repression and publishers. J. F. Krug and J. A. Harvey. Am Lib 2:238-9 Mr '71
Right to silence; cases of judicial inquiry into a newsman's activity, sources and unpublished materials. Time 97:53-4 Ap 12 '71
Saigon's publishing perils. il Time 98:72 O 11 '71
Supreme court and the First amendment. R. H. Smith. Pub W 200:32 O 4 '71
Those purloined papers; Pentagon papers. H. F. Pilpel and A. U. Schwartz. Pub W 200: 37 Ag 2 '71
See also
Government and the press
Information, Freedom of
Libel and slander
Newspapers

FREEDOM riders. See Negroes—Segregation, Resistance to
FREEDOM studies center
Cold-war college. Newsweek 78:95+ S 20 '71
Cold-war college. B. Rice. Nation 213:304-8 O 4 '71
Perfect timing; Cold war college. Nation 213: 4-5 Jl 5 '71
FREEDOM to know. See Information, Freedom of
FREEDOM to read. See Intellectual liberty
FREEDOM to read foundation
Freedom to read foundation. J. F. Krug and J. A. Harvey. Am Lib 2:353-4 Ap '71
FREEMAN, A. D.
Her name; poem. Sat R 54:27 D 18 '71
FREEMAN, Gaylord Augustus, 1910-
What ails the dollar. il Fortune 83:47-8+ Je '71
FREEMAN, James
Johann Simon Mayr and his friends in Aulide. bibliog f il Mus Q 57:187-210 Ap '71
FREEMAN, Jo
Growing up girlish; excerpt from Roles women play: readings towards women's liberation, ed. by M. H. Garskof. il Trans-Action 8:36-43 N '70
FREEMAN, John W.
Yerma reborn. il por Opera N 35:6-7 Je 12 '71
FREEMAN, Norman
Taking stock. il Yachting 130:66-7+ Jl '71
FREEMAN, Richard
Lifestyle. il pors Am Home 74:8 Mr '71
FREEMAN, Roland
Seeing pictures. J. Scully. il Mod Phot 35:22+ N '71 *
FREEMAN, S. David
Toward a policy of energy conservation. por Bul Atom Sci 27:8-12 O '71
FREEMAN, Sandra
Lifestyle. il pors Am Home 74:8 Mr '71
FREEMASONS
Jews and Freemasons in Europe, 1723-1939, by J. Katz. Review
Commentary 51:92-5 F '71. N. Cohn
FREEPORT, N.Y.
Ivy for everyone. P. Ertresvaag. Good H 173:163 Jl '71
FREER, Marjorie (Mueller)
Writing the career novel. Writer 84:14-16+ Mr '71
FREESE, Arthur S.
Bonanza from space. il Pop Mech 136:58-61 Jl '71
Danger in the hospital. il Pop Mech 135: 80-3 F '71
50-story firetraps. il Pop Mech 136:53-6+ Ag '71
Malaria again? il Sci Digest 70:42-6 N '71
Now: an electronic pain killer. il Pop Mech 136:68-71+ Jl '71
FREEWAY signs. See Road signs
FREEWAYS. See Express highways
FREEZE drying
Freeze-dried history; damaged documents of Godthaab, Greenland saved. il Newsweek 79:39 Ja 10 '72
FREEZERS
Compact refrigerators and a freezer. il Consumer Bul 54:18-23 N '71
FREEZING
Water drop freezing: ejection of microdroplets. R. J. Cheng; reply with rejoinder. P. V. Hobbs. bibliog il Science 173:849-50 Ag 27 '71
See also
Ice
Ice—Manufacture
FREEZING of food
How to freeze leftover poultry. Bet Hom & Gard 49:76 D '71
It's the month to rediscover the joys of fruit canning. And if you'd rather, the art of food freezing. il Sunset 147:60-5 bibliog(p 108) Jl '71
There's an art to vegetable freezing. Sunset 147:92 Ag '71
See also
Food, Frozen
FREEZING of fruits. See Freezing of food
FREEZING of vegetables. See Freezing of food
FREI, Eduardo
Second Latin American revolution. For Affairs 50:83-96 O '71
FREIBERG, Peter
Opportunity a sinistra. Commonweal 95:76-7 O 22 '71
Situation ethnics. Commonweal 94:81-3 Ap 2 '71
FREIDUS, Anne
Quest for quality, theme for 1972 convention. Camp Mag 43:7 My '71

FREIGHT airplanes. See Airplanes, Freight
FREIGHT and freightage
See also
Air freight service
Trucking
FREIGHT cars. See Railroads—Cars
FREIGHT forwarders. See Forwarding companies
FREIGHT handling
See also
Loading and unloading
FREIGHT rates. See Railroad—Rates; Shipping—Rates; Trucking—Rates
FREIGHT trains. See Railroads—Freight trains
FREIGHT travel. See Ocean travel
FREIGHT vessels. See Freighters
FREIGHTERS
Barge carriers bid for lost sea trade; Prudential-Grace lines' Lash Italia. il Time 97:78 Mr 15 '71
Barges that go to sea in ships; LASH vessels. il Bsns W p74-5 Ag 7 '71
Mini-ships bring the ocean to mid-America. il Pop Mech 135:88-9 Ap '71
Tugs reach for the ocean trade: tug-barge systems. il Bsns W p 100-1 Mr 6 '71
26-knot parking lot; the Eric K. Holzer. J. F. Pearson il Pop Mech 136:72-3 Ag '71
See also
Tank ships
FREIGHTERS, Seizure of. See Seizure of vessels and cargoes
FREILICHER, Jane
Urban pastorals. P. Schjeldahl. il Art N 69: 32-3+ F '71 *
FREIRE, Paulo
Does the shoe fit? E. Reimer. il America 124:69-70 Ja 23 '71 *
Der FREISCHUTZ; opera. See Weber, K. M. von
FREJKA, Tomas
Z.P.G. Sci Am 224:50 Ap '71 *
FRELINGER, Jeffrey A.
Maternally derived transferrin in pigeon squabs. bibliog il Science 171:1260-1 Mr 26 '71
FREMANTLE, Anne
Worlds of Ved Mehta. por Commonweal 95: 353-4 Ja 14 '72
FREMLIN, Celia
Baby sitter; story. Ladies Home J 88:118-19 Mr '71
FREMON, Suzanne S.
New ways to measure intelligence in infants. il Parents Mag 46:39-41+ Ap '71
FRENCH, Charles F.
Coin quiz. See issues of Hobbies
Numismatics. See issues of Hobbies
FRENCH, David
After the fall: what this country needs is a good counter counterculture culture. il N Y Times Mag p20-1+ O 3 '71
FRENCH, Hector
Danger; electric shock. il Sci Digest 70:66-70 Jl '71
Medical electronic equipment and hospital safety. il Pop Electr 1:32-4 Ja '72
FRENCH, Ray
I drive for money. Har Yrs 11:54 S '71
FRENCH, Roberts W.
Western wind and the complexity of poetry. Engl J 60:212-14 F '71
FRENCH academy
One woman, one vote. por Time 97:33 Ja 25 '71
FRENCH and Indian war, 1755-1763. See United States—History—French and Indian war, 1755-1763
FRENCH artificial satellites. See Artificial satellites, French
FRENCH automobiles. See Automobiles, Foreign
FRENCH CANADIAN separatist movement. See Front for the liberation of Quebec
FRENCH CANADIANS
White niggers of America, by P. Vallieres. Review
Commonweal 94:339-40 Je 25 '71. M. R. Berube
FRENCH cookery. See Cookery, French
FRENCH foreign legion. See France—Army—Foreign legion
FRENCH fried potatoes. See Cookery—Vegetables
FRENCH glass. See Glassware
FRENCH guided missiles. See Guided missiles
FRENCH house decoration. See House decoration, French
FRENCH intervention in Mexico, 1861-1867. See Mexico—History—European intervention, 1861-1867

FRENCH language
  Spreading the words. Time 97:35 My 10 '71
FRENCH language question, Belgium. See
  Belgium—Languages
FRENCH literature
  See also
  Publishers and publishing—France
FRENCH military assistance. See Military assistance, French
FRENCH opera. See Opera, French
FRENCH philosophy. See Philosophy, French
FRENCH photographers. See Photographers, French
FRENCH pottery. See Pottery, French
FRENCH quarter. See New Orleans
FRENCH radical party. See Political parties —France
FRENCH RIVIERA. See Riviera
FRENCH students
  Ralbol! Paris lycée disorders. il Time 98:46 Jl 5 '71
  See also
  Student demonstrations—France
FRENCH WEST AFRICA
  See also
  Senegal
FRENCH WEST INDIES. See West Indies, French
FRENCH wines. See Wine
FRENSDORFF, Asher, and others
  Selective stimulation of allelic expression: effect of antibodies to allotypic markers on lymphoid cells. bibliog il Science 171:391-4 Ja 29 '71
FREONS. See Fluorocarbons
FREQUENCY calibrators. See Calibrators
FREQUENCY changers
  Digital frequency dividers for any ratio. F. H. Tooker. il Electr World 86:60-2 Ag '71
FREQUENCY control
  Miniature wide-range V.L.F. tuner. N. H. Brown. il Electr World 86:61 Jl '71
FREQUENCY counters. See Counting machines and devices
FREQUENCY dividers. See Frequency changers
FREQUENCY generators. See Signal generators
FREQUENCY standards
  Low-power crystal-controlled oscillator. J. H. Wujek. il Electr World 86:69 D '71
  Piggybacking on TV waves. Bsns W p 123 S 11 '71
FRESCO, Jacques R. See Kowalski, S. jt. auth.
FRESCO painting. See Frescoes
FRESCOBALDI, Girolamo
  On Frescobaldi's chromaticism and its background. R. Jackson. bibliog f il Mus Q 57: 255-69 Ap '71
FRESCOES
  Heavenly mirrors; restored Iranian frescoes. il Vogue 158:90+ D '71
  Spoils of Paestum. M. Gendel. il Art N 70:27-31+ Sum '71
  See also
  Mural painting and decoration
FRESE, Paul F.
  Waltham butternut squash. Horticulture 49: 55 F '71
FRESH water aquariums. See Aquariums
FRESH water biology
  Life goes into hiding; pond life in winter. N. Smith. il Nat Wildlife 9:43 O '71
  See also
  Fresh water ecology
FRESH water ecology
  Hudson River lives. R. H. Boyle. il Audubon 73:14-17+ Mr '71
FRESH water mussels. See Mussels, Fresh water
FRESHMEN. See College students
FRESHNESS codes of foods. See Food—Labeling
FRESNO, Calif.
  Education
  Progress report on classroom integration. Y. Postelle. il Parents Mag 46:48-51 D '71
FRESNO state college, Fresno, Calif. See California. Fresno state college, Fresno
FREUD, Anna
  Reunion in Vienna. por Time 98:32 Ag 9 '71 *
FREUD, Lucian
  Lucian Freud; clairvoyeur. J. Russell. il Art in Am 59:104-6 Ja '71 *
FREUD, Sigmund
  FemLib case against Sigmund Freud. R. Gilman. il pors N Y Times Mag p 10-11+ Ja 31 '71; Discussion. p6+ Mr 7 '71 *

Freud's literary style: some observations. W. G. Niederland. bibliog f Am Imago 28:17-23 Spr '71 *
Passions of the mind, by I. Stone. Review
  Time il por 97:91 Ap 5 '71. B. Darrach *
FREUDIANISM. See Psychoanalysis
FREUND, Betsy
  Betsy's book bazaar. Harp Baz 104:74-5 Je; 66 Ag; 186 S; 150 O; 105:123 N; 76 D '71
FREUND, Bob, and Freund, Helen
  Maine's Mount Desert Island. il Travel 136: 34-7+ Ag '71
FREUND, Elizabeth
  Making learning real fun for blind children. il UNESCO Courier 24:28-31 My '71
FREUND, Helen. See Freund, Bob, jt. auth.
FREUND, Paul A.
  Achieving equal rights other ways. Cur 134:32-9 N '71
  Excerpt from testimony before the Senate committee on the judiciary, September 9, 1970. Cong Digest 50:23+ Ja '71
FREUND, Philip
  Two who rejected the business world; interview. il pors Fortune 83:102-3 Mr '71
FREUNDLICH, Lawrence S.
  New man in charge. P. S. Nathan. Pub W 200:29 D 20 '71 *
FREY, Donald Nelson
  Digestion and indigestion. il por Forbes 108: 35 S 1 '71 *
  He'll put snap into Bell & Howell. il por Bsns W p28+ F 20 '71 *
FREY, George T.
  Improving school-community relations. il Todays Ed 60:14-17 Ja '71
FREY, Richard
  Bridge. Sports Illus 34:76+ My 31 '71
FREY, William
  Matter of conscience. il por Newsweek 78: 127 O 25 '71 *
FRICKER, John
  Foreign accent. See occasional issues of Flying
FRIDAY, Margaret. See Carroll, F. L. jt. auth.
FRIED, Albert
  Author! Author! il por Newsweek 78:81 S 27 '71 *
FRIEDAN, Betty
  Betty Friedan's notebook. McCalls 98:32+ Je; 56+ Ag; 52+ S; 99:69+ O; 50+ N '71
  Is the family obsolete; interview, ed. by J. Kronenberger. Look 35:36 Ja 26 '71

  about
  Liberation of Betty Friedan. L. Tornabene. il McCalls 98:84-5+ My '71 *
  Mother superior to Women's lib. P. Wilkes; reply with rejoinder. L. Komisar. N Y Times Mag p44+ Ja 24 '71 *
FRIEDBERG, M. Paul
  Park power. il Parks & Rec 6:26-9+ Jl '71
FRIEDEN, Bernard, and Newman, JoAnn
  Home ownership for the poor? il Trans-Action 7:47-53 O '70
FRIEDENBERG, Edgar Z.
  High school as a focus of student unrest. bibliog f Ann Am Acad 395:117-26 My '71
  Meditations of a landed immigrant. Nation 212:656-60 My 24 '71
FRIEDENBERG, Zachary B.
  Low charge for fractures. il Newsweek 78: 74+ N 8 '71 *
FRIEDLANDER, Harold
  Art of word forms. Clear House 46:62 S '71
FRIEDMAN, Bruce Jay
  Art of autopsy. Esquire 76:96+ D '71
  Dirty pictures. il Esquire 75:112-17+ My '71
  High, wide, and handsome; story. il Esquire 76:126-7 O '71
  Lessons of the street. il Harper 243:86-8+ S '71
  Requiem for a heavy. pors Esquire 76:54-7+ Ag '71
FRIEDMAN, Eugene
  Ethan, my son. il por Newsweek 78:43 N 22 '71
FRIEDMAN, Herbert
  Single sideband for CB is now! il Pop Electr 35:25-9 Ag '71
  What makes a tape recorder professional? Hi Fi 21:50 Ag '71
FRIEDMAN, Herman
  L-Asparaginase induced immunosuppression: inhibition of bone marrow derived antibody precursor cells. bibliog il Science 174: 139-41 O 8 '71
FRIEDMAN, Irving, and Peterson, Norman
  Obsidian hydration dating applied to dating of basaltic volcanic activity. bibliog il Science 172:1028 Je 4 '71
FRIEDMAN, Lester, and Miller, J. G.
  Odor incongruity and chirality. bibliog il Science 172:1044-6 Je 4 '71

FRIEDMAN, Martin
New art action in Minneapolis. B. Rose. il
por Vogue 158:70 Ag 1 '71 *
FRIEDMAN, Meyer
Best advice: slow down! Read Digest 99:
80-2 O '71
FRIEDMAN, Milton
[Column on economic questions] See issues
of Newsweek
Paradox of doing good; excerpts from ad-
dress, June 6, 1971. Read Digest 99:189-90
O '71
about
Goodbye Milton Friedman. W. F. Buckley, jr.
Nat R 23:1010 S 10 '71 *
Milton Friedman: an oracle besieged. por
Time 97:72-3 F 1 '71 *
TRB from Washington: a policy of passivity.
New Repub 165:4 Jl 10 '71 *
FRIEDMAN, Mordecai
Crime issue. il pors Newsweek 78:32-3 N 29
'71 *
FRIEDMAN, Murray, and Binzen, Peter
Politics and parochiaid. New Repub 164:12-
15 Ja 23 '71
FRIEDMAN, Norman L.
Reflections of a sociologist in a school of
education. bibliog Sch & Soc 99:41-3 Ja '71
FRIEDMAN, Ralph
Oregon: gunning for Hatfield. Nation 212:781-
2 Je 21 '71
FRIEDMAN, Richard Emanuel
Challenge to Daley. por Time 97:14-15 Ap 5
'71 *
There's another candidate, too. il por News-
week 77:83 Ap 5 '71 *
FRIEDMAN, Roberta. See White, E. T. jt.
auth.
FRIEDMAN, Saul
Race relations is their business (cont) N Y
Times Mag p4+ F 14 '71
FRIEDMAN, Stanley P.
Farewell to Peyton Place. il por Esquire 76:
84+ D '71
FRIEDMANN, Nadav, and others
Primitive earth synthesis of nicotinic acid
derivatives. bibliog il Science 171:1026-7 Mr
12 '71
FRIEDMANN, Naomi, and others
Cyclic adenosine and guanosine monophos-
phates and glucagon: effect on liver mem-
brane potentials. bibliog il Science 171:400-
2 Ja 29 '71
FRIEDMANN, Theodore
Prenatal diagnosis of genetic disease; with
biographical sketch. il Sci Am 225:12, 34-42
bibliog(p 136) N '71
FRIEDRICH, Goetz
Behind the opera curtain. il Newsweek 78:82
D 6 '71 *
FRIEDRICH, Otto
Farewell to Peyton Place il por Esquire 76:
160-8+ D '71
I promised myself a rose garden. il McCalls
98:90-1+ Je '71
On watching Parsifal with Molly. il Esquire
75:144-8+ My '71
Reunion in Concord. il Harper 242:87-94+ My
'71
FRIEL, Janette. See Webb, W. B. jt. auth.
FRIEMAN, Richard
Richard Frieman: live as you like; with pho-
tographs. L. Drukker. Pop Phot 68:92-5 Je
'71 *
FRIEND, Judy
Rebirth of the midwife. il pors Life 71:50-5
N 19 '71 *
FRIEND of the family's; story. See Stanton, W.
FRIENDLY, Fred W.
Television. Harper 242:30-3+ Je '71
Television and the First amendment. Sat R
55:46-7+ Ja 8 '72
FRIENDS, Society of
Friendly persuasion in Swarthmore. C. E.
Fager. Chr Cent 88:267-9 F 24 '71
Friendly stewardship; British Society of
Friends. T. Beeson. Chr Cent 88:453 Ap
14 '71
See also
American Friends service committee
Churches, Friend
FRIENDS of the FBI, inc.
Friends in need. Newsweek 78:20 S 13 '71
FRIENDS of the library
Meredith Willson's legacy: program sponsored
by Friends of the North Tonawanda public
library. M. Messineo. il Am Lib 2:209-11
F '71
FRIENDS of the world council of churches.
See World council of churches
FRIENDS service committee, American. See
American Friends service committee

FRIENDSHIP
Century endorses friendship. Chr Cent 88:1403
D 1 '71
Friends as mirrors. J. Buck. Mlle 72:142-3+
F '71
What do you want from friendship? N. M.
Lobsenz. il Seventeen 30:114-15+ N '71
See also
Playmates
FRIES, Charles C.
Linguistic gospel: a dissent. J. G. Franks.
bibliog Sch & Soc 99:98-101 F '71 *
FRIGGENS, Paul
Claude Fly's seven-month nightmare. il
Read Digest 99:64-70 S '71
Colorado: the state nearest heaven. il Read
Digest 98:158-64 F '71
Grandeur and the glory of Canada's moun-
tain parks. il Read Digest 99:140-6 Jl '71
Last chance for Yellowstone. il Read Digest
98:190-2+ Mr '71
Story behind the South's third forest. il Am
For 77:32-5+ O '71; Same abr. with title
Biggest tree-planting job on earth. Read
Digest 99:29-30+ N '71
FRIGIDAIRE division. See General motors cor-
poration—Frigidaire division
FRINGE benefits. See Non-wage payments
FRISCH, Bruce H.
They live in Skylab. il Sci Digest 70:9-14 O
'71
FRISTOE, Leonard
Medicare mob. il pors Esquire 76:101 Ag '71 *
FRITILLARIES
Flowers dappled or checkered. il Sunset 147:
199 S '71
FRITTS, Martha K.
Students anesthetized? Try a titillating test!
Engl J 60:264-6 F '71
FRIZZELL, John, and Frizzell, Mildred
American stagecoaches, where are they now?
il Hobbies 76:98K-98M Ja '72
FRIZZELL, Mildred. See Frizzell, J. jt. auth.
FRIZZELL, W. D.
Poor streets cost more than good ones. il
por Am City 86:98+ Mr '71
FROEHLKE, Robert Frederick
Excerpt from testimony before the Subcom-
mittee on constitutional rights, March 2,
1971. Cong Digest 50:236+ O '71
FROG prince; drama. See Mahlmann, L. and
Jones, D. C.
FROGS
Blue frogs; rana clamitans. L. D. Uhler. il
Cons 26:4 Ag '71
Great frog war. il Sci Digest 69:29-30 Mr '71
Morphological basis for a mechanical link-
age in otolithic receptor transduction in
the frog. D. E. Hillman and E. R. Lewis.
bibliog il Science 174:416-19 O 22 '71
FROGS in art. See Animal sculpture
FROLIC, B. Michael
Visit to Peking university, what the cultural
revolution was all about. il N Y Times Mag
p29+ O 24 '71
FROME, Michael
Big lockout. Field & S 76:66-7+ O '71
Conservation. See issues of Field & stream
about
Mike Frome. See issues of American forests
to August 1971
Threats to Southern Appalachia. il Nat Parks
& Con Mag 45:6-9 Jl '71
FROMM, Erich
Therapist and theologian look at love. V. C.
Grounds. Chr Today 15:14-16 Ag 6 '71
FRONT doors. See Doors
FRONT for the liberation of Quebec
Civil justice and naked power; Quebec a
year later. B. A. Grosman. Nation 213:494-6
N 15 '71
Diplomat freed; J. R. Cross. Sr Schol 97:6-7
Ja 11 '71
Story behind the book: The revolution
script; Cross-Laporte affair, interview, ed.
by B. A. Bannon. B. Moore. por Pub W
201:42-3 Ja 3 '72
White niggers of America: the precocious
autobiography of a Quebec terrorist, by
P. Vallières. Review
Sat R por 54:29 My 8 '71. L. L. L. Golden
FRONT page of newspapers. See Newspapers
—Front page
FRONT wheel drive automobiles. See Auto-
mobiles—Front wheel drive
FRONTENIS. See Sports—Mexico
FRONTIER and pioneer life

United States
Are we losing our pioneer spirit? P. Engle.
Read Digest 98:15-16+ Mr '71
Exploitation of the American frontier; ex-
cerpts. W. R. Jacobs. Am West 8:48 My '71

FRONTIER and pioneer life—United States—
Continued
Golden dreams and silver realities; excerpts
from Gold and silver in the West. T. H.
Watkins. il Am West 8:34-43 My '71
Horses and the American frontier; excerpts
from Horses in America. F. Haines. il Am
West 8:10-15 Mr '71
Housekeeping on the early western frontier.
Antiques 99:92 Ja '71
West's gunmen. G. L. Roberts. il Am West
8:10-15+ Ja; 18-23+ Mr '71
See also
California trail
Pony express
Sons and daughters of the Soddies, inc.

Bibliography
For Old West history buffs: paperback gifts.
il Sunset 147:44-5 D '71

Childrens literature
Fine way back to our prairie past; Mrs Wild-
er's Little house series. G. McGovern. il
Life 71:12 Jl 2 '71
FRONTIER nursing service
Rebirth of the midwife. il pors Life 71:50-5
N 19 '71
FROOK, John
I suspect she wants to be Vanessa Redgrave.
il por Life 70:52D Ap 23 '71
FROSH, Maxine B.
Having wonderful time, wish I were home.
il Har Yrs 11:14-15 Jl '71
FROST, David
My mother, right or wrong. il por McCalls
98:69 My '71
about
There's no one quite like David Frost. P.
Browne. por Read Digest 98:91-5 Mr '71 *
FROST, Robert
My butterfly; poem. il Nat Wildlife 9:16-17
O '71
about
New England tradition. H. Carruth. bibliog
il Am Lib 2:944-8 O '71 *
Robert Frost: the years of triumph, 1915-
1938, by L. Thompson. Review
Commentary 52:90-4 Jl '71. D. Jacobson *
Writers Digest 51:43-7 F '71. J. Jerome *
FROST protection
Tepee frost covers. B. Wahlfeldt. il Org Gard
& Farm 18:123-4 F '71
FROST resistance in plants. See Plants—Frost
resistance
FROSTBITE yacht club regatta. See Regattas
FROUD, Stanley
Amateur scientist. il Sci Am 224:110-16 Ja
'71
FROZEN blood; Frozen food; etc. See Blood,
Frozen; Food, Frozen; etc.
FROZEN desserts. See Ice cream, ices, etc.
FROZEN ground
Digging the world's first freeze-dried tun-
nel. E. A. Zadig. il Pop Sci 198:56-7 Mr '71
Popsicle pipe, freezing the ground so you
can build on it. il Sci Digest 69:94-5 F '71
Solifluction: a model experiment. A. Higashi
and A. E. Corte. il Science 171:480-2 F 5
'71
FRUIN, A. Thomas
Waiting for that visa to China. R. Dudman.
New Repub 165:17-19 Jl 3 '71 *
FRUIT
Botany of a fruitcake. M. A. Gamble il
Horticulture 49:50-4 Mr '71
See also
Cookery—Fruit
also names of fruits, e.g. Apples

Diseases and pests
See also
Codling moths

Picking
Pluckers for the fruit that's out of reach. il
Sunset 147:264-5 O '71

Preservation
See also
Canning and preserving
FRUIT, Dried
See also
Cookery—Fruit
FRUIT, Effect of temperature on
Fruits for harsh climates. E. Cott. il Horti-
culture 49:36-7+ S '71
FRUIT bread. See Bread
FRUIT culture
Fruits for harsh climates. E. Cott. il Horti-
culture 49:36-7+ S '71
Hard times hit the peach growers. F. Allen.
il Org Gard & Farm 18:58-63 My '71
Open letter from an apple grower. M. C.
Loken. Org Gard & Farm 18:21-3 My '71
See also names of fruits, e.g. Pears

FRUIT development, Pollenless. See Parthen-
ocarpy
FRUIT drinks. See Beverages
FRUIT flies
See also
Drosophila
FRUIT industry
See also
Citrus fruit industry
FRUIT juices
See also
Lemon juice
FRUIT salads. See Salads
FRUIT trees
So sweet to eat! A. Rutherford. il Org Gard
& Farm 18:128-31 Ap '71
See also
Apple trees
FRUIT trees, Dwarf
Urban orchards. L. Grove. il Bet Hom &
Gard 49:58-9+ My '71
FRUITCAKE. See Cake
FRUITS, Citrus. See Citrus fruits
FRUMKIN, Gene
Comment. P. Schjeldahl. Poetry 117:273 Ja
'71 *
FRUSTRATION
Facing up to disappointments. J. Brothers.
il Good H 174:52+ Ja '72
FRUTKIN, Arnold W.
U.S. reviews progress in sharing benefits of
space technology; statement, July 6, 1971.
Dept State Bul 65:217-19 Ag 23 '71
FRY, C. George
Are Christian colleges worth the trouble?
Chr Today 15:6-10 F 12 '71
FRY, Edward F.
Dilemmas of the curator. il Art in Am 59:
72-7 Jl '71
NAA revision of the CAA. Art in Am 59:31-2
Mr '71
FRY, John R.
Minister who aided black gang resigns pas-
torate. Chr Cent 88:552 My 5 '71 *
FRYE, David
Deformità perfetta of Richard Nixon, Lyn-
don Johnson and other heroes. R. Bongartz.
pors Esquire 75:70-5 F '71 *
FRYE, John
Troubled oil on waters. il Sea Front 17:38-47
Ja '71
FRYE, John T.
Hand tools for the technician. il Electr
World 86:48-50+ S '71
[Monthly article on electronics] See issues
of Electronics world
Solder and soldering tools. il Electr World
85:45-8+ Je '71
Spray chemicals for servicing. il Electr World
85:39-42+ My '71
FRYING
See also
Cookery—Poultry
FRYING pans. See Skillets
FUCA, Juan de. See Juan de Fuca
FUCHS, Daniel
Is Passover Christian? il Time 97:70 Ap 12
'71 *
FUCHS, Victor R.
Differences in hourly earnings between men
and women. il Mo Labor R 94:9-15 My '71
FUCHSBERG, Jacob D.
Excerpt from address before American trial
lawyers association, March 1964. Cong Di-
gest 50:217+ Ag '71
FUCHSIAS
Fuchsias. L. Burgess. il Horticulture 49:38-
9 Jl '71
FUEL
Fossil fuels as a source of mercury pollu-
tion. O. I. Joensuu. bibliog il Science 172:
1027-8 Je 4 '71
Search for pollution-free fuel. il U S News
71:62-4 Jl 5 '71
Selenium and sulfur in a Greenland ice sheet:
relation to fossil fuel combustion. H. V.
Weiss and others. bibliog il Science 172:
261-3 Ap 16 '71
See also
Automobile engines—Fuel
Gas, Natural
Hydrogen, Liquid
Rockets—Fuel

Prices
Beginning of an understanding; adequate
fuel supplies; address, September 30, 1971.
C. H. Hardesty, jr. Vital Speeches 38:120-
2 D 1 '71
Raw materials. il Forbes 108:20-5 Ag 1 '71

FUEL cells
Black box. T. Aaronson. bibliog il Environ 13:10-18 D '71
Cell in every home? il Time 97:51 My 31 '71
How you'll make your own electricity in tomorrow's all-gas home. J. R. Free. il Pop Sci 199:46-7 Ag '71
Ideas to build on. J. H. Ingersoll. il House B 113:13 Ag '71
Little black box, power without pollution? il Sci Digest 70:18 Jl '71
FUEL conservation. See Heating; Insulation (heat)
FUEL dumping from jet airplanes. See Airplanes. Jet—Pollution
FUEL industry
Energy company: a monopoly trend in the energy markets. B. C. Netschert. il por Bul Atom Sci 27:13-17 O '71
    See also
Government investigations—Fuel industry
Petroleum industry
FUEL supply
Beginning of an understanding; adequate fuel supplies; address, September 30, 1971. C. H. Hardesty, jr. Vital Speeches 38:120-2 D 1 '71
Cold facts about the fuel shortage. Consumer Rep 36:118-21 F '71
Raw materials il Forbes 108:20-5 Ag 1 '71
Second rape of Appalachia. P. Primack. Nation 213:530-2 N 22 '71
U.S. dilemma: environment vs. power, with interview with E. E. David, jr. il U S News 71:52-6 O 18 '71
Why we have a fuel and power shortage. R. K. Bennett. Read Digest 98:74-8 Ja '71
    See also
Gas supply
FUEL systems of automobiles. See Automobile engines—Fuel feeding
FUERST, Carl F.
Indoor-outdoor. il Parks & Rec 6:30-1+ Mr '71
FUERTES, Louis Agassiz
Fuertes sampler. F. G. Marcham. il Natur Hist 80:38-43 Je '71 •
FUGARD, Athol
People are living there. Criticism
    Nation 213:605 D 6 '71 •
    Newsweek il 78:121 D 6 '71 •
FUGUE
New research on Bach's Musical offering. C. Wolff. bibliog f il Mus Q 57:379-408 Jl '71
FUHREMANN, T. W. See Lichtenstein, E. P. jt. auth.
FUJI photo film company. See Photographic apparatus and supplies industry—Japan
FUJII, Dennis
Two soldiers. J. Morgenstern. Newsweek 77:18-19 Mr 15 '71 •
FUKUDA, Takeo
Japan-U.S. cabinet committee honored by President Nixon, exchange of toasts, September 10, 1971. Dept State Bul 65:354 O 4 '71
FULBRIGHT, James William
Is America going isolationist? interview. por U S News 70:25-6 Je 28 '71
Legislator: address, February 4, 1971. Vital Speeches 37:290-4 Mr 1 '71
2,000 U.S. bases overseas: another target in Congress; excerpts from address, May 18, 1971. il por U S News 70:35 Je 21 '71
FULBRIGHT international exchange program. See Educational exchanges
FULCO, Lawrence J. See Herman, S. W. jt. auth.
FULD, Stanley H.
Born to judge. por Time 97:42-3 My 10 '71
FULFILLMENT; drama. See Murray, J.
FULLER, Bennie
Sports brighten a silent world. il pors Ebony 27:44-6+ D '71 •
FULLER, Buckminster. See Fuller, R. B.
FULLER, Claud E.
Claud E. Fuller; collector extraordinary. C. Worman. il Hobbies 76:155+ S '71 •
FULLER, F. J. and others
Computerized traffic control. il Am City 86: 109-11 O '71
FULLER, George A. company
Northrop snaps up a big-name builder. il Bsns W p 19-20 D 25 '71
FULLER, Richard Buckminster
Planetary planning; address, November 13, 1969 (cont) Am Scholar 40:285-304 Spr '71
    about
Bucky. New Yorker 47:32-3 Mr 13 '71 •
Poetics of pollution. Time 97:59 Ap 26 '71 •
View from the year 2000. B. Farrell. il pors Life 70:46-8+ F 26 '71 •

FULTON, John
Story behind the book: Bullfighting. A. H. Johnston. il pors Pub W 200:24-5 Jl 26 '71 •
FULTON, Len
Animal rising: little magazines in the sixties. il Am Lib 2:25-47 Ja '71
FULTON, Maurice
New factors in plant location. bibliog f il Harvard Bsns R 49:4-6+ My '71
FULWOOD, Charles
Battle for the South: phase two. il Ramp Mag 10:36-9 Jl '71
FUND raising
Don't be fooled by these fund-raising schemes. il Changing T 25:23-4 F '71
Fashion show centennial. S. Sunderlin. il Har Yrs 11:49-51 Ag '71
From boutique to barn sale. il Parents Mag 46:46-7+ Ag '71
Hike for Hope: organized by teens in Rochester, N.Y. M. Weider. il por Seventeen 30: 20+ Ag '71
Long hikes for money; Rochester's hike for Hope. il Life 70:42-3 My 21 '71
    See also
Bazaars, Charitable
Benefit performances
Campaign funds
FUNDY, BAY OF
    See also
Grand Manan Island
FÜNEN. See Fyn, Denmark
FUNERAL rites and ceremonies
    See also
Burial at sea
Stravinsky, I. F.—Funeral rites and ceremonies
FUNGAL genetics
Genetic restriction of energy conservation in schizophyllum. R. M. Hoffman and J. R. Raper. bibliog il Science 171:418-19 Ja 29 '71
FUNGAL mitochondria. See Mitochondria
FUNGI
Molecular structure of starch-type polysaccharides from hericium ramosum and hericium coralloides. D. A. McCracken and J. L. Dodd. bibliog Science 174:419 O 22 '71
    See also
Basidiomycetes
Lichens
Mildew
Mushrooms
Mutation (fungi)
Rusts (botany)
Truffles

    Metabolism

Fatty acid ethyl esters of rhizopus arrhizus. J. L. Laseter and J. D. Weete. bibliog il Science 172:864-5 My 21 '71; Reply with rejoinder. D. H. Calam. 174:78 O 1 '71
Genetic restriction of energy conservation in schizophyllum. R. M. Hoffman and J. R. Raper. bibliog il Science 171:418-19 Ja 29 '71

    Resistance and sensitivity

Selection of ribosomal mutants by antibiotic suppression in yeast. F. T. Bayliss and R. T. Vinopal. bibliog il Science 174:1339-41 D 24 '71
FUNGI, Effects of antibiotics on. See Fungi—Resistance and sensitivity
FUNGI, Pathogenic
Chemistry: turning an insect into a possible lifesaver; fire ant venom to fight fungi infections. il Bsns W p43 Ja 1 '72
FUNGICIDES
Pollution protection for plants; ozone protection by benomyl. il Sci Digest 69:77 Je '71
    See also
Phenylmercuric acetate
Spraying and dusting
FUNGUS diseases. See Fungi, Pathogenic
FUNK, Ben
Rainmaking comes of age. il Read Digest 98:145-9 Je '71
FUNK, Peter
It pays to increase your word power. See issues of Reader's digest
FUNK ISLAND, Newfoundland
Funk Island. F. Bruemmer. il Natur Hist 80:52-7 Je '71
FUNNIES. See Comics (books, strips, etc)
FUNNY cars. See Automobiles, Racing
FUR
    See also
Hides and skins
FUR, Artificial
Fake furs: like real and cheap. il Changing T 25:11-12 D '71

FUR bearing animals
See also
Badgers
Beavers
Fishers (animals)
Muskrats
Otters

FUR industry
Furriers wear a hunted look. il **Bsns W**
p42-4 N 20 '71

FUR seals. See Seals (animals)

FUR trade
Founders & fur traders. L. Berg. Commentary 51:77-81 My '71
New look; reprint. W. R. Jacobs. Am Heritage 22:108-9 O '71
See also
Hudson's Bay company

FURLONG, Monica
Christian television festival: making ultimate concern visual. Chr Cent 88:779-80 Je 23 '71

FURLONG, William Barry
Facing the guns of April. Todays Health 49:50-3 Ap '71
Family under siege. il pors Good H 172:106-7+ Ap '71
For the class of '71, the party's over. il N Y Times Mag p34-5+ Je 6 '71
Headache hunters meet the anxious American. il Todays Health 49:20-3+ Mr '71
How speed kills athletic careers. Todays Health 49:30-3+ F '71
It's a disease called overcommunication. il Todays Health 49:54-7+ Jl '71
What makes us tick, so mysteriously. il Todays Health 49:28-31+ My '71

FURLOW, Gayle
Composting for the new generation. il Org Gard & Farm 18:58-60 Ap '71

FURNACES
Heating: how to pay less for more comfort. il Bet Hom & Gard 49:50+ O '71
See also
Heating

FURNISHINGS, Household. See Household furnishings

FURNITURE
Discoveries from people with imaginative ideas for living. il House & Gard 139:112-13 Mr '71
Furniture that serves you four ways. R. J. De Cristoforo. il Pop Sci 199:80-2+ D '71
Furniture to sew. J. R. Cary. il Parents Mag 46:96-9 F '71
In place of tables, sofas and chairs. N. Skurka. il N Y Times Mag p74-5 Mr 21 '71
New-think furniture. il House B 113:50-5 Jl '71
On and off the avenue; good modern furniture. J. Malcolm. New Yorker 47:93-4+ Ap 10 '71
100 ideas under $100. il Bet Hom & Gard 49:8+ Jl '71
Small gestures. R. Adams. il House B 113:62-5 Jl '71
Space-saving dinette. J. Capotosto. il Mech Illus 67:65-7 Jl '71
See also
Benches
Bookcases
Buffets (furniture)
Cabinets (furniture)
Chairs
Chests
Desks
Kitchen cabinets
Kitchen furniture
Shelves
Sofas
Tables
Veneers and veneering

Care
Removing furniture scars. il McCalls 98:28 S '71
See also
Furniture polishes

Design
Inventive surprises, furniture that is shaped to fit your body. il House & Gard 139:54-5 Ja '71
On and off the avenue; housing. J. Malcolm. New Yorker 47:108+ My 15 '71
Sam Maloof. G. Loney. il por Craft Horiz 31:16-19 Ag '71

Exhibitions
Browsers still outnumber buyers; Southern furniture market. il Bsns W p25 My 1 '71

Finishing
Art of burnished gilding. il por **House & Gard** 140:124-5 O '71
Environments; fixed up finds. M. Emmerling. il Mlle 73:166-7+ S '71
From junk to joyful; refinishing. il House B 113:68-9 Ja '71
How to refinish a chair like an expert. il House & Gard 139:38 Ap '71
How to refinish a tabletop like an expert. il House & Gard 139:94 Ja '71

History
Furniture history society. C. F. Montgomery. Antiques 99:542-3 Ap '71
Queen Anne and Chippendale furniture in the Henry Francis du Pont Winterthur museum (cont) C. F. Hummel. il Antiques 99:98-107 Ja '71

Manufacture
Gardner & company of New York. K. Ames. il Antiques 100:252-5 Ag '71

Refinishing
See Furniture—Finishing

Repairing
How to renew furniture like an expert. il House & Gard 140:84 Ag '71
McCalls handywoman:
Healing your sick furniture. il McCalls 99:62 O '71

FURNITURE, American
American furniture; recent additions to the State department's collection. R. Davidson. il Antiques 100:68-70 Jl '71
Antiques; Duncan Phyfe furniture. A. Winchester. il Antiques 99:96-7 Ja '71
Bishop Hill; a colony of Swedish pietists in Illinois. R. E. Nelson. il Antiques 99:140-7 Ja '71
Cincinnati cabinet and chairmakers. 1819-1830. D. Streifthau. il Antiques 99:896-905 Je '71
Colonial revival in furniture, 1878; excerpts from Modern dwellings in town and country adapted to American wants and climate with a treatise on furniture and decoration. H. H. Holly. il Antiques 99:830+ Je '71
Final busts on eighteenth-century Philadelphia furniture. R. C. Smith. il Antiques 100:900-5 D '71
Gardner & company of New York. K. Ames. il Antiques 100:252-5 Ag '71
Old Amana furniture, by M. K. Albers. Review
Antiques il 99:908+ Je '71. K. D. Barron
On and off the avenue; collection made in Appalachia at the Handex gallery. J. Malcolm. New Yorker 47:165-6+ N 13 '71
Origins of Newport block-front furniture design. R. P. Mooz. il Antiques 99:882-6 Je '71
Queen Anne and Chippendale furniture in the Henry Francis du Pont Winterthur museum (cont) C. F. Hummel. il Antiques 99:98-107 Ja '71
Speculations on the Rhode Island block-front in 1928. W. D. Garrett. il Antiques 99:887-91 Je '71
Tennessee cabinetmakers and chairmakers through 1840. E. Beasley. il Antiques 100:612-21 O '71
Tennessee furniture and its makers. E. Beasley. il Antiques 100:425-31 S '71
Work of an anonymous Carolina cabinetmaker; colonial North Carolina. F. L. Horton. il Antiques 101:169-76 Ja '72
See also
Cabinets (furniture)
House decoration, American

FURNITURE, Arrangement of
15 great rooms and what makes them worth studying. il House B 113:74-83 Ap '71
HB's decorating scrapbook. L. B. Downs. il House B 113:63-70 Je '71
Room arrangements in the mid-eighteenth century. P. K. Thornton. il Antiques 99:556-61 Ap '71

FURNITURE, Bermudian
Bermuda's antique furniture & silver, by B. B. Hyde. Review
Antiques il 100:502-3 O '71. M. G. Fales and D. A. Fales, jr

FURNITURE, Built in
Two-faced couch is a real sleeper. D. Huff. il Pop Sci 199:106 S '71

FURNITURE, Childrens
Children's furniture & just-for-fun things. M. Kraft. il Good H 172:116-21 Mr '71
Custom-made furniture the easy way. R. Mangurian. il Pop Sci 198:94-6+ F '71

FURNITURE, Childrens—*Continued*
Her bed is the playhouse roof. il Sunset 146: 134 Je '71
Kids' lib: revolution in children's furniture. il House & Gard 139:118-19 Ap '71
Living with children. il Redbook 137:114-17 O '71
Preschooler's desk with built-in bench. il Pop Mech 136:164-5 N '71
Wheeling off to bed; giant playthings. il Life 70:64-6 Ap 30 '71
Young furniture plays it natural. il Am Home 74:92-3 S '71

FURNITURE, Convertible
For round-the-clock style and comfort: sleep sofas. il Good H 174:104-9 Ja '72

FURNITURE, English
English furniture in colonial America. M. M. Naeve. il Antiques 99:551-5 Ap '71
Final graces of the Georgian age: regency furniture. J. Gloag. il Antiques 99:574-9 Ap '71
Furniture by Giles Grendey for the Spanish trade. C. G. Gilbert. il Antiques 99:544-50 Ap '71
Holland & sons and the furniture of Osborne house. E. T. Joy. il Antiques 99:580-5 Ap '71
Honest heirs to an urbane past; 18th century English furniture, country house in Southampton. L.L. il House B 113:136-8 O '71
Some documented pieces of English furniture. L. Boynton. il Antiques 99:562-7 Ap '71

FURNITURE, Illuminated. See Furniture, Plastic

FURNITURE, Irish
Irish mahogany furniture: a source for American design? D. Fitz-Gerald. il Antiques 99: 568-73 Ap '71

FURNITURE, Modern. See Furniture

FURNITURE, Outdoor
Roll-around patio pallets. il Sunset 147:118 S '71
See also
Benches
Furniture, Summer
Parks—Equipment

FURNITURE, Paperboard
Using recycled discards, a Los Angeles couple designs furniture for here and now. il Am Home 74:12 S '71

FURNITURE, Plastic
Different track. M. Bowden. il House B 113: 14 F '71
Fantasy in plexiglas: designs by Victor Lukens. il Vogue 157:108-9 Mr 15 '71
Furniture of chemistry. il Time 98:72-3 O 25 '71
Light-ups gently glowing. S. G. Grant. il House B 113:60-3 F '71
Victor Lukens has a curvy plastic pad. J. Peter. il por Look 35:50-1 Mr 9 '71

FURNITURE, Prefabricated
Kids' lib: revolution in children's furniture. il House & Gard 139:118-19 Ap '71

FURNITURE, Summer
Come, summer, come, the sweet season. il House B 113:72-7 Je '71

FURNITURE design. See Furniture—Design

FURNITURE designers
See also
Maloof, S.

FURNITURE finishing. See Furniture—Finishing

FURNITURE history society
Furniture history society. C. F. Montgomery. Antiques 99:542-3 Ap '71

FURNITURE industry
See also
American walnut manufacturers association
Levitz furniture corporation

FURNITURE makers. See Cabinetmakers

FURNITURE polishes
Your furniture finish needs care! il Consumer Bul 54:35-7 My '71

FURNITURE rollers. See Casters, glides, etc (hardware)

FURNITURE stores
Levitz: the hot name in "instant" furniture; warehouse-showroom market. il Bsns W p90-1+ D 4 '71

FURRIERS. See Fur industry

FURSTENBERG, Frank F. jr
Public reaction to crime in the streets. il Am Scholar 40:601-10 Aut '71

FURTH, George
Twigs. Criticism
  Nation 213:604 D 6 '71 *
  New Yorker 47:112+ N 20 '71 *
  Newsweek il 78:109 N 29 '71 *
  Time 98:70 N 29 '71 *

FURTHER adventures of Brunhild; story. See Kavaler, R.

FURTWANGLER, Wilhelm
Furtwängler and America. by D. Gillis. Review
  Am Rec G por 37:660-2+ My '71. W. Botsford *

FURUTA, Kozo
Paper world of Mino. M. C. Dorst. il Craft Horiz 31:50-1 Je '71 *

FURY, Kathleen D.
Changing life of Joan Baez. il Redbook 137: 77-9+ My '71

FUSCHI, Olegna
Musical events; concert in Alice Tully Hall. New Yorker 46:105-6 F 13 '71 *

FUSES, Electric. See Electric fuses

FUSION, Nuclear. See Nuclear fusion

FUSION reactors. See Nuclear reactors

FUSSELL, B. H.
Rich, robust and rewarding: the food of Normandy. il Holiday 49:54-5+ Mr '71

FUSTER, Joaquin M. and Alexander, G. E.
Neuron activity related to short-term memory. bibliog il Science 173:652-4 Ag 13 '71

FUTCH, Ken
(ed) See Lewis, C. S. C. S. Lewis on the meaning of Christmas

FUTURE
Affluence and the world tomorrow. L. S. Wehrle. For Affairs 49:419-28 Ag '71
American future; what kind of a society do we want? H. H. Humphrey. il America 125: 476-9 D 4 '71
Can we afford tomorrow? symposium, with introd. by W. C. Stolk. il Sat R 54:35-8+ Ja 23 '71
Church eyes future shock. T. R. Haney. America 124:174-7 F 20 '71
Coming of age on earth. D. Lambert. il Nat Parks & Con Mag 45:10-16 Ap '71
Dodo didn't make it; survival and betterment. K. E. Boulding. Bul Atom Sci 27: 19-22 My '71
Future of the United States government, ed. by H. S. Perloff. Review
  Harper 243:89-91 Ag '71. J. Thompson
Future shock, by A. Toffler. Review
  Nation 212:117-20 Ja 25 '71 R. Claiborne
How to cope with Future shock; ed. by W. Kirk and A. Harris. A. Toffler. il Seventeen 30:146-7+ Mr '71
How to speak futurese. McCalls 98:41 Ag '71
Prophet of optimism; summary of statements, ed. by A. Anderson. R. Dubos. por Time 97:51 My 31 '71
Responsibility of being organic. R. Rodale. il Org Gard & Farm 18:34-8 Mr '71
View from the year 2000. B. Farrell. il pors Life 70:46-8+ F 26 '71
Youth and the future: how to avoid future shock. il por Sr Schol 98:3-6 My 10 '71
See also
Forecasting
Nineteen hundred and eighty-five
Prophecies
White House conference on the industrial world ahead (proposed)

FUTURE life
See also
Hell
Immortality
Spiritualism

FUTURE teachers of America
Youth speaks out about teachers. C. Boiarsky and N. Pedersen. il Todays Ed 60:44-6 N '71

FUTURES. See Commodity exchanges

FUTUROLOGY. See Forecasting

FYN, Denmark
Funen games. D. Butwin. il Sat R 54:54+ S 18 '71

G

GAF corporation
GAF's anchor man. por Bsns W p76 Mr 20 '71
Inside the GAF battle. N. A. Martin. il pors Duns 97:45-7 Ap '71
Milstein around the neck; proxy fight. il Forbes 107:21 Mr 15 '71
Personnel job as personal affront. Bsns W p40 Mr 13 '71

GAO. See United States—General accounting office

GARP (global atmospheric research program) See Weather research

GALBRAITH, John Kenneth—*Continued*
Self-winding industry of Switzerland. il Holiday 49:8+ F '71
Unbelievable happens in Bengal. il por N Y Times Mag p 13+ O 31 '71
—and others
Galbraith plan to promote the minorities. il N Y Times Mag p9+ Ag 22; 10+ O 10 '71; Same with title Toward greater minority employment. Cur 133:22-9 O '71

about
Against the economics grain. M. J. Ulmer. New Repub 164:28+ My 8 '71 *
Convention that went Galbraithian. il por Bsns W p 16-17 Ja 1 '72 *
Galbraith v. Lockheed. W. F. Buckley, jr. Nat R 23:888 Ag 10 '71 *
Keeping up with JKG. J. B. Burnham. Nat R 23:767-8 Jl 13 '71 *
Midnight penman returns. por Time 98:20 S 6 '71 *
Newest Nixon looks Galbraithian. il por Bsns W p37 S 25 '71 *
What the F.B.I. has on me. por Esquire 76:136-7+ D '71 *

GALE, Joseph
Broadway musical: sweet? Or turned sour? il Dance Mag 45:51-66 O '71
Rose for Miss Agnes. il pors Dance Mag 45:46-50 O '71

GALELLA, Ron
Occupation: Jackie-watcher; photographs. il pors Life 70:32-7 F 12 '71

GALICIAN poetry. See Gallegan poetry

GALINDO, Pedro, and Grayson, M. A.
Culex (melanoconion) aikenii: natural vector in Panama of endemic Venezuelan encephalitis. bibliog il Science 172:594-5 My 7 '71

GALLAGER, Scott M. See Gallager, Sheldon M. jt. auth.

GALLAGER, Sheldon M. and Gallager, Scott M.
New quickie kits for hi-fi. il Pop Mech 135:116-17 F '71

GALLAGHER, Cornelius Edward
Freedom and funding: Skinner support queried. por Sci N 100:420-1 D 25 '71 *
Misplaced zeal. New Repub 166:14 Ja 1 '72 *

GALLAGHER, Dorothy
Johnny Cash: I'm growing, I'm changing, I'm becoming. il por Redbook 137:61+ Ag '71
Teacher who chose to go to jail. il por Redbook 136:58-9+ Ja '71

GALLAGHER, Michael
Impossible beauty. il Commonweal 94:36-9 Mr 19 '71
(tr) See Mishima. Y. Testament of a Samurai

GALLAGHER, Rachel
Trustees in the news. por Parks & Rec 6:122 Ja '71 *

GALLAGHER, Ralph
Chain saw artist. M. Lincoln. il pors Design 72:4-7 mid-Sum '71 *

GALLAGHER, Terry
Youth art month really works. il Sch Arts 71:24-5 N '71

GALLAGHER, Thomas
Trouble off Bergen Point! il Read Digest 99:58-62 Ag '71

GALLANT, Mavis
Annals of justice. New Yorker 47:47-52+ Je 26 '71
In the tunnel; story. New Yorker 47:34-47 S 18 '71

GALLÉ, Émile
Let's enjoy Emile Galle's glass. L. F. Reals. il Hobbies 76:91 My '71 *

GALLEGAN poetry
Nasin cand' as prantas nasen.. ; tr. by J. F. Nims; excerpt from Sappho to Valéry: poems in translation. R. de Castro. Am Scholar 40:284 Spr '71

GALLEHER, Margie
Painting with beads. R. Wrenn. il por Design 72:8-11 Sum '71 *

GALLEN, John
Mass: successful liturgy? America 125:229 O 2 '71

GALLER, David
Alba: the furies; poem. Poetry 118:311 S '71
Hope; poem. Nation 213:374 O 18 '71

GALLERIES and museums. See Art—Galleries and museums

GALLICO, Paul
Writer's hero worship. Writer 84:12-13 Mr '71

GALLNULES
Blue Pete. H. Borland. il Audubon 73:inside cover Jl '71

GALLIVAN, Patricia S.
Movie bus. il Parks & Rec 6:37+ S '71

GALLO, Joseph
Parting shots: Unity day that split the mob. il pors Life 71:70-1 Jl 9 '71 *
What d'ya hear from the mob? P. Axthelm. il por Newsweek 78:31-2 Jl 12 '71 *

GALLO, Vincent A.
Adult learning. bibliog f Clear House 46:239-44 D '71

GALLOWAY, James V.
Military theology. L. H. Lapham. il Harper 243:73-6+ Jl '71 *

GALLUP, N.Mex.
U.S. journal: drunken Navahos. C. Trillin. New Yorker 47:108+ S 25 '71

GALLUP polls. See Public opinion polls

GALLUZZO, Tony
Movie making. See issues of Modern photography

GALNOOR, Itzhak
(ed) Social information for developing countries. bibliog f il Ann Am Acad 393:1-121 Ja '71
Social information for what? bibliog f Ann Am Acad 393:1-19 Ja '71

GALSTON, Arthur William
Biologist's view of China. Yale R 61:139-46 O '71
On the use and misuse of science. Yale R 60:458-63 Spr '71; Same with title Education of a scientific innocent: with biographical sketch. Natur Hist 80:4, 16-18+ Je '71
Science in review. See issues of Yale review
—and Signer, Ethan
Education and science in North Vietnam. bibliog Science 174:379-85 O 22 '71
—See Satter, R. L. jt. auth.

GALSWORTHY, John
Holiday feast at the Forsytes. R. A. de Groot. il Esquire 75:130-3+ Ja '71 *

GALTON, Lawrence
High blood pressure: new light on a hidden killer. Read Digest 98:65-8 Je '71
New mystery, maybe miracle drug. il N Y Times Mag p46-7+ D 5 '71

GALUB, Jack
Join the star-struck generation. il Am Home 74:32+ My '71
You can beat the high cost of living. il Parents Mag 46:64-5+ O '71

GÁLVEZ, José de, marqués de Sonora
Building of a new world: the white man's mighty effort to civilize the first Californians. D. Lavender. il Am West 8:36-41+ N '71 *

GALVIN, Hoyt R. and Asbury, Barbara
Public library building in 1971. il pors Library J 96:3968-80 D 1 '71

GALVIN, Paul V.
When his firm was auctioned, he bid. H. L. Marrs. il pors Nations Bsns 59:80-1 Ja '71 *

GALVIN, Robert W.
New picture at Motorola? A. Hershman. por Duns 93:64+ Je '69 *

GALWAY, Michael A.
Legacy of the Manhattan; with biographical sketch. il Sea Front 17:292-7, 319 S '71

GAMBLE, F. R. and others
Intercalation complexes of Lewis bases and layered sulfides: a large class of new superconductors. bibliog il Science 174:493-7 O 29 '71

GAMBLE, Mary A.
Botany of a fruitcake. il Horticulture 49:50-4 Mr '71

GAMBLERS
Reflections of a gilded cage; episode at a Las Vegas casino. R. C. Padden. Harper 242:88-91 F '71

GAMBLING
Black Mafia moves into the numbers racket. F. J. Cook. il N Y Times Mag p26-7+ Ap 4 '71
Dream machine; numbers game. il Newsweek 77:110+ Ap 19 '71
Gambling revenue tempting more states. U S News 70:80 Ja 25 '71
My problem and how I solved it: gambler husband. il Good H 172:14+ Je '71
School for gamblers; novel Nevada jobs program. L. Deni. il Ebony 27:55-6+ D '71
Sports; sports betting. R. Kahn. il Esquire 76:14+ S '71
World's best poker player. E. Shrake. il por Sports Illus 34:56-8+ Ja 25 '71
See also
Book making (betting)
Cardsharping
Casinos
Computers—Gambling use
Horse race betting
Lotteries

GAMBLING—*Continued*
Laws and regulations
Legalized gambling: is it a good bet? L.
Ross. Read Digest 99:94-8 N '71
Asia
Where the action is. Time 78:24+ Jl 19 '71
Great Britain
Gambling in Britain. J. K. Glassman. Atlan
228:23-4+ S '71
GAMBLING machines
Big jackpot in slot machines. J. Ross-Skin-
ner. il Duns 97:51-3 My '71
GAMBONE, Joseph G.
Starving Kansas. il Am West 8:30-5 Jl '71
GAMBRELL, David Henry
New day. pors Newsweek 77:33 F 15 '71 •
GAME
Early season game scouting. W. Davis. il
Mech Illus 67:81+ Jl '71
They're threatening Alaska's big game hunt-
ing. J. Rearden. il Nat Wildlife 9:21-5 F '71
See also
Cookery—Game
Hunting
Venison
GAME, Dressing of
Care of wild meat. T. Trueblood. il Field &
S 76:20+ N '71
Cut up your deer the easy way. K. Heuser.
il Field & S 76:10+ O '71
Easy way to skin a deer. H. G. Tapply. il
Field & S 76:60 D '71
Mule deer the easy way. D. L. Smith. il
Field & S 76:46+ Je '71
Right way to clean rabbits. il Field & S 76:
82+ O '71
Skin a squirrel in a minute. C. Patterson. il
Field & S 75:40 Mr '71
What to do after you shoot it. T. Trueblood.
il Field & S 76:34+ O '71
GAME birds
Small game shoot in big game land: East
Africa. R. F. Jones. Sports Illus 35:82-3+
D 6 '71
See also
Animal introduction
also names of game birds, e.g. Grouse
Food and feeding
Marijuana for the birds. J. M. Vance. il Out-
door Life 147:53-5+ Je '71
You can have more grouse in your woods.
G. W. Gullion. il Field & S 76:60-1+ O '71
GAME birds, Dressing of
Ten seconds to clean a dove. J. B. Scott.
il Field & S 76:16 S '71
GAME guns. See Shotguns
GAME laws
Don't shoot the bearded lady; Colorado's
1969 mountain-goat regulations. D. Grave-
stock. il Outdoor Life 147:60-3+ Ja '71
Editorial; no hunting allowed on Sunday. C.
Conley. Field & S 75:6 F '71
Grim reapers of the land's bounty. il Sports
Illus 35:38-40+ O 11 '71
Hunting seasons (cont) Outdoor Life 148:20+
S '71
See also
Poaching
GAME of hearts; story. See Soman, F. J.
GAME plan; story. See DeLillo, D.
GAME preserves
Try a hunting preserve? G. H. Gillelan. il
Outdoor Life 148:16+ D '71
See also
Lion country safari, inc.
GAME protection
See also
Game laws
Wildlife conservation
GAMES
Across the board in old American games. L.
Dennis. il Hobbies 76:48-9+ Ag '71
Comput-a-tutor: an educational game? il
Consumer Bul 54:40 Je '71
How about a game of Mob strategy or
Adultery? D. Rottenberg. il Todays Health
49:46-9 Ag '71
How to triumph at nim by playing safe,
and John Horton Conway's game Hacken-
bush. M. Gardner. il Sci Am 226:104-7 Ja
'72
Inventing games. J. Kuh. il Ladies Home J
88:107 Je '71
Killing in gameland; Godfather game. il News-
week 78:71 D 20 '71
Party games to test your ESP; excerpts
from Test your ESP. M. Ebon. il Ladies
Home J 88:78+ My '71

Playing President: three new political games.
Time 98:91 N 8 '71
Swinging game for executives. il Mech Illus
67:110-11 F '71
Ticktacktoe and its complications. M. Gard-
ner. il Sci Am 225:102-4 Ag '71
Tic-tac-toe you can play anywhere. M. H.
Slutz. il Pop Mech 135:153 Ap '71
World's greatest gamesman; E. Kantar. W.
Bingham. il pors Sports Illus 34:28-30+ Ja
11 '71
See also
Badminton (game)
Billiards
Cards
Chess
Childrens amusements
Courts (for games)
Croquet
Dart games
Electronic games
Parker brothers, inc.
Piñatas
Play
Puzzles
Skittles
Table tennis
History
Games children play; a study of P. Bruegel's
masterpiece. A. Eliot. il Sports Illus 34:46-
51+ Ja 11 '71
Games (young) people play. I. Opie and P.
Opie. il Horizon 13:16-17 Wint '71
GAMES, Mathematical. See Mathematical re-
creations
GAMMA globulin
Kinetic differences in unresponsiveness of
thymus and bone marrow cells. J. M.
Chiller and others. bibliog il Science 171:
813-15 F 26 '71
See also
Immunoglobulins
GAMMA rays
Cosmic antimatter and gamma rays. Sci N
100:374 D 4 '71
High energy astronomy: observations of gam-
ma radiation. W. D. Metz. Science 174:1314
D 24 '71
See also
Mössbauer effect
GAMMON, Clive
Another fine madness. il Sports Illus 35:
50-6+ S 6 '71
Charging full tilt into a bloody fray. il Sports
Illus 35:26-8+ S 13 '71
Fishing (cont) il Sports Illus 35:94+ N 29 '71
Grail still swims in the Yu Yum lagoon. il
Sports Illus 35:104-10+ D 6 '71
Man is fair game. il Sports Illus 34:74-6+
Mr 22 '71
Return to the river of yesterday. il Sports
Illus 34:78-80+ My 24 '71
Skiing. Sports Illus 35:68-71 O 4 '71
GAMON, David L.
Population growth and national development;
address, June 14, 1971. Dept State Bul 65:
172-8 Ag 16 '71
GAMOW, George
Several lives and more. J. Wilson. Bul Atom
Sci 27:47-8 F '71 •
GAMOW, Rustem Igor. See Harris, J. F. jt.
auth.
GAMSBY, Dorothea
Dorothea's story, transcribed from her ac-
count, ed. by M. A. Downie. Horn Bk 47:
192-8 Ap '71
GAMZU, Elkan, and Williams, D. R.
Classical conditioning of a complex skeletal
response. bibliog il Science 171:923-5; 173:
752-3 Mr 5, Ag 20 '71
GAN (island) See Maldive Islands
GANDELMAN, Ronald, and others
Olfactory bulb removal eliminates maternal
behavior in the mouse. bibliog il Science
171:210-11 Ja 15 '71
GANDHI, Indira (Nehru)
Not a person to be pressured; interview, ed.
by W. Stewart. por Time 99:34 Ja 3 '72
Prime Minister Gandhi of India visits the
United States; exchange of greetings,
toasts; November 4, 1971. Dept State Bul
65:615-16, 617-20 N 29 '71
Talk with Indira Gandhi; excerpts from in-
terview, ed. by E. Behr. por Newsweek
79:23 Ja 3 '72
about
Behind Mrs Gandhi's talks with Nixon. il
por U S News 71:102 N 15 '71 •
Close-up of a war's two top foes. pors U S
News 71:24 D 27 '71 •
India: a clear mandate for Mrs Gandhi. il
por Time 97:22-3 Mr 22 '71 •

GANDHI, Indira (Nehru)—about—_Continued_
Indira Gandhi is either hated or adored. D.
Moraes. il por N Y Times Mag p 10-11+
F 14 '71 •
Indira typhoon. por Newsweek 77:36-7 Mr
22 '71 •
Indira's triumph. J. D'Souza. il America 124:
400-3 Ap 17 '71 •
Losing battle. il Newsweek 78:50 N 15 '71 •
Mrs Gandhi makes her bid. il por Newsweek
77:36-7 Mr 1 '71 •
Mrs Gandhi's goal: beating old guard. J. N.
Wallace. il por U S News 70:87 Mr 8 '71 •
Of sacred cows and squint-eyed uncles. il
Time 97:27 Mr 1 '71 •
Pleader in the West; six-nation tour. il por
Time 98:45-6 N 8 '71 •
Three women leaders beset by problems. por
U S News 70:42 My 10 '71 •
Trying to cap a hot volcano. il por Time
98:32+ N 15 '71 •

GANDHI, Mohandas Karamchand
Experiments with truth. P. W. Schmidtchen.
il pors Hobbies 76:134-7 Je '71 •
Gandhi, by O. Coolidge. Review
Horn Bk 47:597 D '71. S. D. Long •
Gandhi through western eyes, by H. Alex-
ander. Review
Cath World 213:294-5 S '71. R. Aspen •
Gandhi's truth: on the origins of militant
nonviolence, by E. H. Erikson. Reviews
Am Hist R 76:1104-15 O '71. J. V. Bondu-
rant and others •
Religion and another war. Chr Cent 88:1459
D 15 '71 •

GANGES RIVER
Ganges, river of faith. J. J. Putnam. il Nat
Geog 140:445-83 O '71
India's sacred river: the Ganges. J. E.
Frazer. il Read Digest 99:203-6+ S '71

GANGLIA. See Nervous system

GANGLION cells. See Nerve cells

GANGLIOSIDOSIS. See **Nervous system—**
Diseases

GANGS
Beware the _wah ching_! il Newsweek 78:63-4
Ag 30 '71
Blackstone rangers, by R. T. Sale. Review
Sat R 55:33 Ja 8 '72. W. Kennedy
Hell's Angels 4, Breed 1. il Time 97:18-19
Mr 22 '71

GANGSTERS. See Crime and criminals—United
States

GANGULI, B. C.
Shunted aside. Time 98:33 O 25 '71 •

GANGULI, Jatindra Mohan
Opinion: on man and woman. por Mlle 73:
38+ My '71

GANNETT company
Let's all get together. por Forbes 107:42 Je
15 '71

GANNON, Edmund Joseph
Military justice. bibliog f Cur Hist 61:75-
81+ Ag '71

GANNON, Grace
Excitement in glass: making a colored glass
window. il Design 72:29-31 Sum '71

GANNON, Robert
Atomic power: what are our alternatives? il
Science Digest 70:18-23 D '71
Driving a go-cart on the moon. il pors Pop
Sci 198:70-2+ Ja '71
What are the dangers? il Sci Digest 71:36-
42 Ja '72

GANNON, Thomas M.
Baptist parking lot case. il America 125:480-1
D 4 '71
Home scene (cont) America 124:543-4 My 22
'71
Of many things. America 124:inside cover
Ja 23; 125:inside cover S 18 '71
Plato, Aristotle and neighborhood govern-
ment. America 124:288-9 Mr 20 '71
Warriors oppose the war. il America 124:
516-18 My 15 '71

GANS, Herbert J.
Challenging the work ethic. Cur 126:29-34
F '71
Demands of Consciousness II. Nation 212:
275-7 Mr 1 '71
Three ways to solve the welfare problem. il
N Y Times Mag p26-7+ Mr 7; 6+ Mr 28
'71
about
Poverty may be good for you. il Time 97:
64 Je 21 '71 •

GANTEN, Detlev, and others
Angiotensin-forming enzyme in brain tissue.
bibliog il Science 173:64-5 Jl 2 '71

GANYMEDE (satellite) See Satellites

GARAGE doors
Featherweight garage doors. il Mech Illus
68:79-81 Ja '72
How to adjust your garage door. il Bet
Hom & Gard 49:56-7 Ap '71

GARAGE sales. See Sales

GARAGE storage. See Storage in the home

GARAGES
Don't let your garage become a danger area.
Good H 172:162 F '71
Inside parking on the rise. Am City 86:48-9
O '71
Your garage can be a screened summer
room. C. Wilson. il Pop Mech 135:160-1
Ap '71
Zigzag garage; University of Montreal. il
Arch Forum 135:26-7 O '71

GARAGES (service stations) See Automobile
service stations

GARAGES, Municipal
Parking facility award winner; Binghamton,
N.Y. il Am City 86:88 Jl '71
Parking garage over a city street; Ann Ar-
bor. il Am City 86:120 My '71
Parking under a library; White Plains, N.Y.
il Am City 86:124-5 S '71

GARAGES, Underwater
Underwater car park; Geneva, Switzerland. il
Parks & Rec 6:33 My '71

GARAVENTE, Jean
Women inside China. il pors McCalls 99:79+
N '71

GARBAGE. See Refuse and refuse disposal

GARBAGE bags. See Refuse containers

GARBAGE cans. See Refuse containers

GARBAGE compactors. See **Refuse and refuse**
disposal—Apparatus

GARBAGE grinders. See Refuse grinders

GARBAGE trucks. See Refuse collection trucks

GARBO, Greta
Great Garbo: a recent footnote; with editorial comment. il pors Life 71:3, 86-7 N 12
'71 •

GARCIA, Joaquin Torres-. See Torres-Garcia,
J.

GARCIA, John. See Green, K. F. jt. auth.

GARCIA LORCA, Federico
Lorca's two farces: Don Perlimplin and
Don Cristóbal. C. Feal-Deibe. bibliog Am
Imago 27:358-78 Wint '70 •

GARD, Robert G. jr
Military and American society. For Affairs
49:698-710 Jl '71

GARD, Robert R.
Censorship and public understanding. bibliog
Engl J 60:255-9 F '71
Group instruction with the individual touch.
bibliog f Clear House 46:73-7 O '71

GARDE, Warren
Lost in an icy hell. il Outdoor Life 147:54-
5+ F '71

GARDEN, Indoor
Let's all eat the house plants. M. C. Goldman. il Org Gard & Farm 18:66-71 S '71

GARDEN apartments. See Apartment houses—
Garden apartments

GARDEN benches. See Benches

GARDEN catalogs. See Catalogs, Seed and
plant

GARDEN CITY, N.Y.
Town that closed its doors; battle against
day care center. J. Evans. il Redbook 136:
88-9+ Mr '71

GARDEN clubs
Join, or start an organic gardening club. M.
C. Goldman. il Org Gard & Farm 18:54-7
Ap '71

GARDEN contests. See Gardening—Competitions

GARDEN design
Gardens are a demanding joy. M. Sarton.
Vogue 158:52-3+ Ag 15 '71
See also
Landscape gardening

GARDEN exhibits
Coming events of interest to gardeners. See
issues of Horticulture
Garden events [in month] (title varies) See
issues of Sunset

GARDEN frauds. See Fraud

GARDEN GROVE, Calif.
Spiritual shopping center; Garden Grove
community church. il por Newsweek 78:
51 Jl 5 '71

GARDEN hose
Garden hose: friend or snake in the grass?
il Consumer Bul 54:7-9 Jl '71
How to hide your garden hose but keep it
handy. il Pop Sci 198:96 Ap '71
Stretch the life of your garden hose. il Bet
Hom & Gard 49:104 Je '71

GARDEN houses, shelters, etc.
And now, a gazebo with storage! J. Capotosto. il Mech Illus 67:91-5+ Ag '71
Bonsai house. il Sunset 146:250 Ap '71
Build this garden work center. il House B 113:112-13 My '71
Little firehouse for the backyard. C. T. Sigman. il Pop Sci 198:106-7+ Ap '71
New nature-watching house. il House & Gard 139:56-7 Je '71
Shade house means happy fuchsias. il Sunset 147:136 Ag '71
Super space for play and storage. E. McDonald. il House B 113:78-9 Ja '71
See also
Sheds
GARDEN in the woods. See Framingham, Mass.—Gardens
GARDEN lighting. See Gardens—Lighting
GARDEN literature
See also
Booksellers and bookselling—Garden literature
GARDEN ornaments
Brookgreen gardens, where sculpture and nature meet. M. D. Hodgins. il Horticulture 49:32-3+ N '71
Garden ornaments, plain and fancy. P. Hunt. il Horticulture 49:22-5 Ag '71
When art and nature meet: sculpture in your garden. A. Ogden. il House B 113:60-2+ Ag '71
See also
Sundials
GARDEN paths. See Garden walks
GARDEN pests. See Insects, Injurious and beneficial
GARDEN photography. See Photography of flowers, plants, trees, etc.
GARDEN pools
Build-it-himself, 65 feet of rapids, waterfalls, pools. il Sunset 146:158 Ap '71
Patio lotus. J. Lambeth. il Horticulture 49:30-1 Jl '71
See also
Water gardens
GARDEN power equipment. See Garden tools, equipment, and supplies
GARDEN sculpture. See Garden ornaments
GARDEN shelters. See Garden houses, shelters, etc.
GARDEN soils. See Gardening—Soil preparation
GARDEN stakes and staking
A-frame for plants. J. R. Coggins. Org Gard & Farm 18:47 Jl '71
GARDEN state ballet. See Ballet companies
GARDEN State stakes. See Horse racing
GARDEN steps
Ups and downs in the garden. il Sunset 146:92-6 Mr '71
GARDEN tillers. See Cultivators
GARDEN tools, equipment, and supplies
Design with power in mind. P. Jewell, 3d. il Horticulture 49:36-7+ F '71
Gardener's notes. J. Fanning. il House & Gard 139:178-9 Mr '71
Have you heard? See issues of Home garden & flower grower
New gadgets to save a gardener's back. il Changing T 25:11-12 F '71
See also
Compost grinders and grinding
Cultivators
Garden hose
Hedge clippers
Tractors
GARDEN tractors. See Tractors
GARDEN walks
Easy brick pathways. il Sunset 147:56-7 Ag '71
How to stabilize a woodland path. A. Taylor. il Home Gard 58:70-1 Ap '71
Paving patterns. P. Hunt. il Horticulture 49:44-7 Mr '71
GARDENER, Daniel
Bilateral symmetry and interneuronal organization in the buccal ganglia of aplysia. bibliog il Science 173:550-3 Ag 6 '71
GARDENERS
Editorial. C. B. Lees. Horticulture 49:16 Je '71
GARDENING
Build a garden you can reach! H. Knapp. il Org Gard & Farm 18:114-15 S '71
Ecology for your own backyard. M. Roche. il House & Gard 139:56-7+ Je '71
Editorial. C. B. Lees. Horticulture 49:20 Mr '71
5 easy garden ideas you can do yourself. T. Cruso. il por House & Gard 139:80-5 Ap '71

Garden calendar. See issues of Organic gardening and farming
Garden designed to be given away. J. Hudak. il House B 113:44-5 O '71
Gardener speaks his mind. W. B. Harris. See issues of House & garden incorporating Living for young homemakers
Gardener's notebook. E. McDonald. See issues of House beautiful
Gardener's notes. J. Fanning. See issues of House & garden incorporating Living for young homemakers
Greening of a gardener; adaptation of foreword to White-flower-farm garden book. W. B. Harris. il House & Gard 139:104-5+ Mr '71
[Month] in your garden. See issues of Sunset
Unexpected joys of a simple garden. J. Stafford. il Redbook 137:79+ Je '71
What to do in [month] See issues of Horticulture
White flower farm garden book, by A. Pettingill and J. Grant. Review
Life 70:10 Ap 23 '71. J. Kastner
See also
Artificial light gardening
Bulb
Catalogs, Seed and plant
Childrens gardens
City gardens
Cold frames
Colonial Williamsburg garden symposium
Container gardening
Cover crops
Cultivators
Electrohorticulture
Fertilizers and manures
Floriculture
Forcing (plants)
Frost protection
Garden clubs
Gardener
Gardens
Greenhouses
Herbs
Horticulture
Hotbeds
Indoor gardening
Landscape gardening
Lawns
Mulching
Nurseries (horticulture)
Organic gardening
Plant propagation
Plants, Potted
Pruning
Seeds
Soils
Television broadcasting—Garden programs
Tillage
Transplanting
Vegetable gardening

Bibliography
Books help make the gardener. Horticulture 49:34-5 Jl '71
Speaking of books. See issues of Home Garden & flower grower

Competitions
Again in 1971, a garden contest. Sunset 146:279 Ap '71
Enter Home garden's $2500 contest now (cont) Home Gard 58:14-15 D '71
Garden contest winners. il Sunset 146:102-8+ Ap '71
Home garden nursery contest winners. il Home Gard 58:28-30+ My; 40+ Je '71
Once again in 1971 a garden contest. Sunset 146:291 My '71
Still time to enter Sunset's 1971 garden contest. il Sunset 146:223 Je '71
Winners in the 1971 sunflower contest. il Org Gard & Farm 18:112+ D '71
Young garden prizewinners of 1970. il Sunset 146:262-3 Ap '71

Planting plans and tables
Garden guidlines, from coast to coast. See issues of Home garden & flower grower
This garden plan gives adults and children equal consideration. il Sunset 146:264 Ap '71

Soil preparation
Soil know-how: your key to beautiful plants. R. M. Carleton. il Home Gard 58:41-7+ Mr '71

California
Creating an outdoor environment where none exists. il House B 113:73-5 Mr '71

Montana
Gardening at 4,000 feet. E. Diemer. il Org Gard & Farm 18:72-3 D '71

GARDENING by children. See Childrens gardens

GARDENS
Garden of woodland paths. R. Wright. il House & Gard 140:80-5 D '71
Very personal garden of Jack and Esther Larson; dooryard herb garden. il House & Gard 139:82-5 Ja '71
Very personal garden of Mrs Albert D. Lasker: a border garden for all seasons. il House & Gard 139:62-6 F '71
Very personal garden of Mrs Enid Haupt: move-around garden that flowers wherever you put it. il House & Gard 139:58-63 Je '71
See also
Bird gardens
Childrens gardens
City gardens
Garden design
Roof gardens
Water gardens

Color
Autumn color from bulbs. J. Hudak. il Horticulture 49:38+ Ag '71
Living in a garden indoors and out; Maine houses, and garden of Mr and Mrs Henry Parish II. il House & Gard 139:86-91 Mr '71
Seven little bulb gardens you can plant on a budget! il Home Gard 58:28-31 O '71
Winter-spring color. il Sunset 147:257 O '71

Lighting
After dark; low-voltage system. il Sunset 147:80-1 N '71
Night-lighting your garden. E. McDonald. House B 113:184 My '71

Atlantic states
Great gardens on America's East coast. D. L. McFadden. il Home Gard 58:20-7+ My '71

California
Successful and flat-out gardener shares her secrets, discoveries, victories. il Sunset 146: 120-1 My '71
There is nothing much to it. il Sunset 147: 244 N '71
See also
San Francisco—Gardens

Cape Cod
Very personal garden of garden expert Thalassa Cruso. T. Cruso. il House & Gard 139:80-5 Ap '71

Connecticut
In Connecticut: a garden to visit. M. Perry. il Home Gard 58:38-9 Ap '71
Very personal garden of Harry Rogers: an easy-does-it organic garden. il House & Gard 140:64-7 Jl '71

Delaware
Winterthur in the spring. J. D. Morse. il Horticulture 49:26-7+ My '71

Fire Island
In bloom: flower garden planted by John Newfield, in Cherry Grove. New Yorker 47: 23-5 Ag 7 '71

Florida
Interlude in the tropics; Florida's cypress gardens. J. A. Pitcher. il Am For 77:28-30 D '71
See also
Tampa, Fla.—Parks and playgrounds

Georgia
Georgia's Callaway gardens. M. Perry. il Home Gard 58:39-41 F '71

Hawaii
See also
Honolulu—Gardens

Italy
Very personal garden of the Emilio Puccis. il House & Gard 140:112-15 O '71

Long Island
Very personal garden of the Richard Sears Humphreys: a blue hydrangea garden. il House & Gard 139:110-13 My '71

Louisiana
Hodges gardens. K. M. Simpson. il Horticulture 49:48-9 Mr '71

Maine
Well known gardens on the coast of Maine. D. L. McFadden. il Home Gard 58:40-3 Ap '71

Massachusetts
Garden designed to be given away. J. Hudak. il House B 113:44-5 O '71
See also
Framingham, Mass.—Gardens
Gardens—Cape Cod

Mexico
Mexican gardens. P. Clark. il Horticulture 49:26-7+ F '71
See also
New York (state)
See also
Gardens—Fire Island
New York (city)—Gardens
Rye, N.Y.—Gardens

South Carolina
Brookgreen gardens, where sculpture and nature meet. M. D. Hodgins. il Horticulture 49:32-3+ N '71
South Carolina's great iris show; Swan Lake iris gardens. Travel 135:19 Ap '71

Virginia
Virginia, where garden lovers come to look and learn. M. Perry. il Home Gard 58:26-9 Mr '71

Western states
Traveler's checklist of great West coast gardens. il Home Gard 58:16-18+ Je '71

Wisconsin
See also
Milwaukee—Mitchell park horticultural conservatory

GARDENS, Colonial
Flowers of the colonial days. R. J. Favretti. il Horticulture 49:40-1+ Ap '71

GARDENS, Fragrant
Enchanting fragrant annuals. F. C. Miller. il Horticulture 49:36-7+ Ap '71

GARDENS, Hillside
Hillside garden is built into a super raised bed. il Sunset 146:250+ My '71
Ice plant and citrus share a hillside. il Sunset 146:247 Je '71
This handsome hillside garden controls erosion and its plants offer savory help in the kitchen. il Sunset 146:246 Ap '71

GARDENS, Indoor
Real garden that is inside the house. il Sunset 146:108-11 My '71
See also
Gardens, Miniature

GARDENS, Miniature
Bottle gardens. E. McDonald. House B 113: 160 N '71
See also
Terrariums

GARDENS, Rock
See also
Plants. Rock garden

GARDENS, Watering of. See Watering of gardens, lawns, etc.

GARDENS, Wild
Wild flowers for the cultivated garden. E. S. Parcher. il Horticulture 49:32-5 Mr '71
See also
Framingham, Mass.—Gardens

GARDNER, Arthur E.
Future isn't what it used to be; adaptation of address, 1970. Pub W 199:42-5 Ja 11 '71

GARDNER, Craig
Craig's message. por Time 98:72 N 22 '71 •

GARDNER, John
Song of Grendel; story. il Esquire 76:138-9 O '71

GARDNER, John W.
How you can make big business care about the little man; ed. by J. C. G. Conniff. por Todays Health 49:17-18 D '71
Unfinished business of America. Look 35: 57 Jl 13 '71
about
Birthday for common cause. por Time 98:14 Ag 16 '71 •
Common cause. New Repub 164:5-7 Mr 20 '71 •
John W. Gardner. New Yorker 47:30-2 F 27 '71 •

GARDNER, Ken E. and Garrison, Peter
Back to basics. Flying 88:88-9 Je '71

GARDNER, Lewis
Teleguide. il Schol Teach Jr/Sr High p31 N '71

GARDNER, Marjorie
Chemistry, an interdisciplinary science. Chem 44:2 Ja '71

GARDNER, Martin
Mathematical games. See issues of Scientific American

GARDNER, Richard A.
Boys and girls book about divorce; excerpts.
il Harp Baz 104:118-21 F '71
On using anger. Harp Baz 104:64+ Jl '71
Parent and child. il N Y Times Mag p69+
N 28 '71

GARDNER, Richard Newton
U.N. as policeman. Sat R 54:47-50 Ag 7 '71;
Same with title Can the UN be a policeman? Cur 133:34-40 O '71

GARDNER, Robert
Amnesty when? New Repub 165:12-13 D 25
'71

GARFIELD, James Abram
My friend Garfield; excerpt from memoir,
with editorial comment. J. Stanley-Brown.
il pors Am Heritage 22:49-53+ Ag '71 *

GARFISHES. See Garpikes

GORGOYLISM. See Lipochondrodystrophy

GARLAND, Harry, and Melen, Roger
Add triggered sweep to your scope. il Pop
Electr 35:61-6 Jl '71
—See Melen, R. jt. auth.

GARLAND, Phyllis
Atlanta: black mecca of the South. il Ebony
26:152-7 Ag '71
Blacks challenge the airwaves. il Ebony 26:
35-8+ N '70
Roberta Flack: new musical messenger. il
pors Ebony 26:54-6+ Ja '71
Soul to soul. il Ebony 26:79-82+ Je '71
Sounds. See issues of Ebony
Taps for Satchmo. il pors Ebony 26:31-4+ S
'71
Unorthodox ministry of Leon H. Sullivan.
il pors Ebony 26:112-14+ My '71
Vibes from Verta Mae. il pors Ebony 26:
86-8+ Mr '71

GARLIC
Garlic: good for your health and bad for
the bugs! R. E. Nagrod. il Org Gard &
Farm 18:108-10 O '71
Isolation and characterization of larvicidal
principle of garlic. S. V. Amonkar and A.
Banerji. bibliog il Science 174:1343-4 D 24
'71

GARLICK, G. D. and others
Oxygen isotope ratios in eclogites from kimberlites. bibliog il Science 172:1025-7 Je 4
'71

GARLITS, Don
Big daddy's E. T. element. il por Hot Rod
24:8 N '71 *
Garlits up front. R. Guldahl, jr. il por Hot
Rod 24:52-3+ My '71 *

GARMENT cutting
Aerospace technology infusion aids apparel
industry operations; laser cutter. il Aviation W 94:48-9 Mr 29 '71
Beam; laser fabric cutter. New Yorker 47:
30-2 Mr 27 '71
Laser to cut the garment tangle. Bsns W
p46+ Mr 13 '71
Lasers for space-age tailors. il Sci Digest
70:37 O '71

GARMENT factories

Automation
Stitching shirts by tape control. Bsns W p32
Je 12 '71

GARMENT workers
See also
Clothing industry

GARMISCH-PARTENKIRCHEN
Olympic goal. Travel 136:27 S '71

GARNER, Louis E. jr
Solid state. See issues of Popular electronics

GARNISHES in cookery. See Cookery—
Garnishes

GARONE, Michael
Mike the cop studies to be Mike the nurse.
il pors Life 70:47-8+ My 14 '71 *

GARPIKES
Garfish olfactory nerve: easily accessible
source of numerous long, homogeneous,
nonmyelinated axons. D. M. Easton. bibliog il Science 172:952-5 My 28 '71

GARR, Douglas
Parachute that glides like a plane. il Pop
Sci 199:76-7+ Ag '71
—See Schisgall, O. jt. auth.

GARR, Ralph
Beep! Beep! por Time 98:43 Jl 5 '71 *
Two beeps, a cloud of dust. D. Delliquanti.
il por Sports Illus 34:58 My 10 '71 *

GARRARD, Mimi
Mimi Garrard dance theater, Henry street
settlement playhouse, NYC. L. Pastore.
Dance Mag 45:76 Jl '71 *

GARRELL, Martin H.
Tourists, take your tackle. il por Outdoor
Life 147:78-9+ My '71

GARRETT, Banning
Strange economics of the Vietnam war. il
Ramp Mag 10:34-9 N 71
Vietnam: how Nixon plans to win the war.
il por Ramp Mag 9:26-31 F '71
—See Browning, F. jt. auth.

GARRETT, George, 1929-
Story behind the book. Death of the fox. B.
A. Bannon. por Pub W 200:36-7 O 4 '71 *

GARRETT, Rodney E.
DDT: what some European countries are doing about it. il Am For 77:18-19+ S '71

GARRETT, W. E.
Pagan, on the road to Mandalay. il Nat
Geog 139:340-65 Mr '71

GARRETT, Wendell D.
Clues and footnotes. See issues of Antiques
Living with antiques. il Antiques 101:185-
92 Ja '72
Speculations on the Rhode Island block-front
in 1928. il Antiques 99:887-91 Je '71

GARRETT corporation
North American suit filed against Garrett.
Aviation W 95:20 O 25 '71

GARRIGUE, Jean
Giralda; poem. Commonweal 94:383 Jl 23 '71
On actors scribbling letters very quickly in
crucial scenes; poem. New Yorker 47:58
Ja 1 '72
On going by train to White River Junction,
Vt; poem. New Yorker 47:60 N 20 '71

GARRISON, Paul
Reporting points. Flying 88:22-3 F '71
Sky time. Flying 88:25 Ap; 24 My; 89:69 S '71

GARRISON, Peter
Back to basics (cont) il Flying 88:66-7 Mr;
60-4 My; 89:57-9 S; 56-8 O '71
Citabria in the sand. Flying 89:98 Ag '71
—See Gardner, K. E. jt. auth.

GARRISON, Robert H.
Susue Jo; story. Todays Ed 60:24-5 My '71

GARRISON, Webb B.
Care-by-parent ward: a new idea in children's hospitals. il por Parents Mag 46:34-
5+ Jl '71
Destiny and geomagnetism. il Pop Electr 35:
41-6 Jl '71
Laughter, the elusive wonder drug. il Todays Health 49:28-32 Mr '71

GARRITY, Thomas P.
Microfilm improves the revenue column. il
Am City 86:92+ My '71

GARRY, Charles R.
Mea culpa. il pors Time 97:45 Mr 8 '71 *
Reporter at large. E. J. Epstein. New Yorker 46:45-6+ F 13 '71; Reply with rejoinder.
E. Kosner. 47:125 My 8 '71 *

GARTLER, Stanley M. and others
Lesch-Nyhan syndrome: rapid detection of
heterozygotes by use of hair follicles. bibliog il Science 172:572-4 My 7 '71

GARTNER, Alan. See Riessman, F. jt. auth.

GARVER, George
Turnabout in Houston? pors Newsweek 78:62
S 13 '71 *

GARVER, Juliet
Debbie the dreamer; drama. Poetry 31:1-12,
44 D '71

GARVER, Ronald V.
Daniel's barbs and scotched reviewers; poem.
Am Lib 2:785 S '71

GARVER, Thomas H.
Balboa and the fun zone. il Art in Am 59:58-
67 S '71

GARVEY, Amy Jacques
Amy Jacques Garvey: black, beautiful & free.
B. Reed. il pors Ebony 26:45-6+ Je '71 *

GARVEY, Marcus
Amy Jacques Garvey: black, beautiful & free.
B. Reed. il pors Ebony 26:45-6+ Je '71 *

GARY, Ind.

Education
Banneker at bay. il Newsweek 77:93+ Mr 15
'71
Gary's novel school, score after a year; contract education. il U S News 71:61 O 25
'71
Gary's privately operated public school a success. il Sci N 100:246 O 9 '71
Money-back schools: unclear balance sheet.
il Time 98:78 O 11 '71
Success in Gary; performance contracting at
Banneker elementary school. Newsweek 78:
66 O 11 '71
We'll educate your kids, or your money back.
J. Star. il Look 35:56+ Je 15 '71
Will this boy's curriculum manager deserve
an apple this year? Banneker school. B.
Kaufman. il Todays Health 49:20-3 S '71

Elections
Hatcher's landslide. il por Newsweek 77:32
My 17 '71

GARY, Ind.—*Continued*

Negroes

Liberation of Gary, Indiana. E. Greer. il por Trans-Action 8:30-9+ Ja '71

Politics and government

Liberation of Gary, Indiana. E. Greer. il por Trans-Action 8:30-9+ Ja '71

GARZIO, Angelo C.

Majolica technique for stoneware. il Ceram Mo 20:19-22 Ja '72

GAS, Natural

Power without pollution? Duns 97:128 My '71

Worry over a key fuel: will there be enough? Where search for natural gas is in full swing: Louisiana's Cajun country. il U S News 71:88-90 D 13 '71

See also
Gas industry
Gas supply
Liquefied natural gas

Pipe lines

Gas now becomes an issue in the Arctic. il Bsns W p44-5 Ag 28 '71

Prices

See Gas rates

GAS and oil engines

Say, Smokey: a steam engine? rotary external combustion, low emission engine. E. F. Lindsley. il Pop Sci 199:48-9 D '71

See also
Automobile engines
Motorcycle engines
Outboard motors
Snowmobile engines
Spark plugs
Tractor engines

Cooling

Any automatic transmission can keep its cool. C. J. Baker. il Pop Sci 198:144 Ap '71

Why cooling systems must work in winter. Suc Farm 69:J18 N '71

Fuel

Should you use lead-free gas in small engines? E. F. Lindsley. il Pop Sci 199:83-5 Jl '71

Maintenance and repair

How to service small engines. M. Schultz. il Pop Mech 135:130-5 Mr; 134-9 Ap '71

GAS appliances

Fail-safe? What's that? J. Darr. il Radio-Electr 42:16+ O '71

More on fail-safe: millivolt systems. il Radio-Electr 42:16-17+ N '71

GAS as fuel

See also
Automobile engines—Fuel
Gas, Natural
Liquefied petroleum gas

GAS burners

Control

Fail-safe? What's that? J. Darr. il Radio-Electr 42:16+ O '71

More on fail-safe: millivolt systems. il Radio-Electr 42:16-17+ N '71

GAS companies

See also
El Paso natural gas company

GAS-fired barbecues. See Barbecue grills

GAS fuel cells. See Fuel cells

GAS industry

See also
Coastal states gas producing company
Distrigas corporation

Consolidations and mergers

El Paso merger heads for the hill; 1957 acquisition of Pacific Northwest pipeline corp. Bsns W p23-4 My 29 '71

Regulation

See also
United States—Federal power commission

GAS manufacture and works

See also
Coal gasification

GAS prices. See Gas rates

GAS purification

See also
Scrubbers (chemical technology)

GAS rates

Gas price rule hits a maverick. Bsns W p20 Ap 3 '71

Trying to spark a rush for gas. il Bsns W p60 My 1 '71

GAS rifles. See Rifles

GAS supply

Big gas users face a shutoff. Bsns W p20 S 4 '71

Gas: enough for present customers, but how about the new ones? il Nations Bsns 59: 31-2 Jl '71

Worry over a key fuel: will there be enough? Where search for natural gas is in full swing: Louisiana's Cajun country. il U S News 71:88-90 D 13 '71

GAS torches

Gas-lit torches around their pool. il Sunset 147:100 Jl '71

GAS turbines

Jet-turbine makers build sales power. il Bsns W p22+ Ap 3 '71

Supersonic turbines studied for 1980s. M. L. Yaffee. il Aviation W 94:68-9 My 10 '71

Williams engine designs shown, aircraft and automotive gas turbines. il Aviation W 94: 53 Ja 18 '71

GAS turbines, Aircraft. See Jet airplane engines

GAS turbines, Automotive

Time for turbines. Time 98:101 N 8 '71

Tiny 80-hp gas turbine to power compact car. J. P. Norbye. il Pop Sci 198:34 Mr '71

Williams turbine takes the road. K. Ludvigsen. il Motor T 23:30-5 N '71

GAS turbines, Marine

Boat with a turbo in its tummy. il Mech Illus 67:19 My '71

GASES

Experimental method to study Charles' law. L. McKeen. il Chem 44:27-9 F '71

See also
Atmosphere
also names of gases, e.g. Helium

Apparatus

See also
Scrubbers (chemical technology)

GASES, Asphyxiating and poisonous

Diisopropylphosphorofluoridate and Tabun: enzymatic hydrolysis and nerve function. F. C. G. Hoskin. bibliog il Science 172: 1243-5 Je 18 '71

Mist that rolled into the trenches: chemical escalation in World war I. R. E. Cook. Bul Atom Sci 27:34-8 Ja '71

See also
Carbon monoxide
Chemical and biological weapons
Mustard gas
Tear gas

GASES, Ionization of. See Ionization of gases

GASES, Liquefied

See also
Liquefied natural gas

GASES, Rare

See also
Xenon

GASES in warfare

See also
Tear gas

GASIFICATION of coal. See Coal gasification

GASKETS

Out goes the putty, here come window gaskets! J. Hand. il Pop Sci 199:137 N '71

GASKILL, Gordon

Champagne: a mood, a myth, a miracle. Read Digest 99:162-5 Ag '71

GASKIN, Stephen

I want us to get real good understanding and real good love. . ; interview, ed. by M. Cantwell and A. Gross. il pors Mlle 72:142-7+ Mr '71

GASKINS, Tom

Art from a cypress swamp. M. Hunn. il pors Design 73:4-7 Wint '71 •

GASOLINE

Consumers guide to gasoline. Mech Illus 67: 52 D '71

Those new gasolines: how to pick the right one for your car. M. Schultz. il Pop Mech 135:122-5 F '71

Additives

And for our next number; triaryl phosphate additives. S. Novick. Environ 13:24+ Je '71

Behind the hubbub over leaded gas. il Changing T 25:6-9 O '71

Chevron's pollution solution; Scott Carpenter and his F310 additive. S. Berman. Commonweal 93:546-8 Mr 5 '71

Facts about unleaded gasolines. Good H 172: 175 Mr '71

Getting the lead out. Time 97:92 My 17 '71

Lead-free, low-lead, no-lead. E. Nabb. Motor B & S 127:118+ Mr '71

Lead from automobile exhaust. R. W. Medeiros. bibliog il por Chem 44:7-9 N '71

Low-lead gas sales take off at a crawl. il Bsns W p44 Ag 21 '71

GASOLINE—Additives—*Continued*
New low-lead gasolines. Mech Illus 67:76 My '71
Pollution, the no-lead myth. D. Hill. Hot Rod 24:120-1 F '71
Rap 'n 'pinion. T. B. Tom. por Motor T 23:12 F '71
Repairing the ravages of no-lead gas. T. Tappett. il Mech Illus 67:97-9+ Ag '71
Should you use lead-free gas in small engines? E. F. Lindsley. il Pop Sci 199:83-5 Jl '71
Timetable for lead. M. H. Hyman. bibliog il Environ 13:14-23 Je '71
Warning! To owners of 2-cycle engines: use of lead-free gas. Consumer Bul 54:23 Ag '71
Will the new gasolines lick auto pollution? il Consumers Rep 36:156-9 Mr '71

Anti-knock and anti-knock mixtures
Automobile octane requirements; letter. E. J. Farkas. bibliog Science 174:545 N 5 '71

Marketing
France's Total invades the U.S. il Bsns W p34-5 Ap 24 '71

Prices
Break for drivers: gas-price wars. il U S News 70:47 Ap 19 '71
Escalating the war. Newsweek 78:90 N 15 '71

Storage
How and when to store gasoline. Suc Farm 69:B7 S '71

GASOLINE engines. See Gas and oil engines
GASOLINE stations, Airplane. See Airplane service stations
GASOLINE substitutes
See also
Automobile engines—Fuel
GASP of amazement; story. See Delattre, P.
GASPARINI, Graziano
Space, baroque and Indians. Américas 23: S18-21 Ap '71
GASPÉ PENINSULA
Gaspé: source of organically-raised foods. R. C. Adams. Org Gard & Farm 18:74-9 N '71
Go North to Gaspé. R. Bongartz. il Holiday 49:42-5 My '71
Where the whales play. E. G. Beckett. il Yachting 129:65+ F '71
GASS, William H.
Heart of the matter. G. Wolff. por Newsweek 77:86+ F 15 '71 •
GASTON, Jerry
Nuclear physics: does competition breed a monstrous game? N. Wade. Science 174:932 N 26 '71 •
GASTON de Havenon collection of African sculpture. See Art—Private collections
GASTONGUAY, Paul R.
Let's update Bible and sermon. il Cath World 213:232-5 Ag '71
GASTRIC ulcers. See Peptic ulcers
GASTRONOMY
American couple in Ireland creates a beautiful way to eat. il House & Gard 139:80-4 F '71
Art of eating, the art of living; interview, ed. by B. A. Bannon. M. F. K. Fisher. il por Pub W 199:17-18 Mr 29 '71
GASTROPODS
Belly-walkers. H. Borland. il Audubon 73: inside cover My '71
See also
Limpets
Murex
Sea slugs
Snails
GATENBY, Rosemary
Make it happen. Writer 84:17-19+ Ag '71
GATES, David M.
Flow of energy in the biosphere; with biographical sketch. il Sci Am 25:25, 88-92+ bibliog(p244) S '71
GATEWAY arch. See St Louis—Monuments, statues, etc.
GATI, Charles
Hungary: the politics of reform. Cur Hist 60:290-4+ My '71
Soviet tutelage in east Europe. bibliog f Cur Hist 61:206-9+ O '71
GATORNATIONALS. See Drag racing
GATTEGNO, Caleb
Oust ABC's, teach reading by color. C. Meyer. il McCalls 98:41-2 F '71 •
GATTEGNO method. See Reading—Study and teaching
GAUBA, Tony
Five minute dog feeder. il Design 72:33 mid-Sum '71

GAUD, William S.
Overseas private investment in today's world; address, May 3, 1971. Vital Speeches 37:566-9 Jl 1 '71
GAUDI Y CORNET, Antonio
Unfinished cathedrals. P. Schneider. il Vogue 158:96-101+ D '71 •
GAUGES. See Gages
GAUGUIN, Paul
Unforgettable self-delusion. R. Hughes. il por Time 97:56-8 Mr 22 '71 •
GAULLE, Charles de
Chatting with de Gaulle; interview, ed. by A. Malraux. por Time 97:39-40 Mr 29 '71

about
Conversations with de Gaulle; excerpt. A. Malraux. il por Esquire 76:110, 129-33+ D '71 •
Letter from Paris; with excerpts from Les Chênes qu'on abat. Genêt. New Yorker 47:98+ Ap 24 '71 •
Selling of de Gaulle. A. Tillier. il Newsweek 78:26 S 13 '71 •
Story behind the book: The day of the Jackal. B. A. Bannon. pors Pub W 200:34-5 Ag 9 '71 •

Eulogies
Tributes to General Charles de Gaulle. UN Mo Chron 7:40-2 D '70

Memorials
De Gaulle in a crystal ball. Time 98:48 N 22 '71
GAULT, Donald E. See Greeley, R. jt. auth.
GAULT, Henri, and Millau, Christian
Turning on in Paris. il Holiday 48:72-5 S '70
GAUSE, Ralph W.
Problems of pregnancy. il PTA Mag 65:24-6 Ja '71
GAUVIN, Aimé
River the loggers stole. il Audubon 73:70-6+ Jl '71
GAVAGAN, James E.
Obituary
Cons por 25:37 Ap '71
GAVIN, James M.
Everybody worries about the last 50,000 men; interview. por U S News 70:25 Ap 26 '71
Unfinished business of America. Look 35:60-1 Jl 13 '71
GAVIN, William F.
America's song of songs. il Read Digest 99:126-8 Jl '71
Confessions of a street-corner conservative. il Nat R 23:1345-7 D 3 '71
GAVRAS, Costa-. See Costa-Gavras
GAY, Bill. See Gay, F. W.
GAY, Frank W.
Letters from the invisible billionaire, with sincere regards, Howard Hughes. il por Life 70:24-8 Ja 22 '71 •
GAY liberation front. See Homosexuality
GAYE, Marvin
Motown beatitudes. por Time 98:69 O 11 '71 •
GAYLE, Margot
Defender. New Yorker 47:23-4 Ag 28 '71 •
GAYLIN, Willard
No exit. il Harper 243:86-9+ N '71
GAYNOR, Florence S.
Lady takes charge. P. Bailey. il pors Ebony 27:156-8+ N '71 •
GAZA STRIP
Carrot and stick. Newsweek 78:34 Ag 23 '71
Terror in Gaza; with report on the deaths of Marc-Daniel and Abigail Aroya. by M. Clark. il Time 98:27-8 Ag 9 '71
GAZEBOS. See Garden houses, shelters, etc.
GAZPACHO. See Soups
GEAGAN, Bill
Barse man from Texas. il Field & S 76:66-7+ N '71
GEARING
Leonardo on bearings and gears. L. Reti. il Sci Am 224:100-7+ F '71
See also
Automobiles—Gearing
Motor boats—Gearing
GEBALLE, T. H.
New superconductors; with biographical sketch. il Sci Am 225:12, 22-33 N '71
GEBEL-WILLIAMS, Gunther
Soul of the tiger. E. Hoagland. il pors Esquire 76:88-93+ Jl '71

about
Big cat with big cats. il por Time 97:67 My 24 '71 •
Gebel-Williams burning bright. R. Schickel. Harper 243:18+ Ag '71 •
Peerless potentate of pachydermia. N. F. Busch. il Read Digest 99:133-7 N '71 •

GECKOS. See Lizards

GEDDES, Andrew
Civil service jurisdiction ends for N.Y. systems. Library J 96:3713-14 N 15 '71 *

GEDNEY family
Gedney coat-of-arms. H. K. Eilers. il Hobbies 76:140-1 N '71

GEDO, John E.
Mythopoesis and psychoanalysis. bibliog Am Imago 27:329-37 Wint '70

GEES, Rudi. See MacKenzie, F. T. jt. auth.

GEESAMAN, Donald P.
Plutonium and the energy decision. por Bul Atom Sci 27:33-6 S '71

GEESE
Letter from the East. E. B. White. New Yorker 47:27-9 Jl 24 '71
Put a goose run in your garden; Embden geese. L. Hall. il Org Gard & Farm 18:56-7 Je '71

GEESE, Wild
Brant! J. Palmer. il Field & S 76:58-9+ N '71
Carnage at Sand Lake. G. Sherwood; discusion. Audubon 72:140-1 N '70; 73:103-6 Mr '71
Chow line honkers. J. Linduska. il Field & S 75:112-15+ Ja '71
Feeling like a goose. N. Buckingham. il por Outdoor Life 148:76-9+ S '71
South Dakota's golden geese. H. Bradshaw. il Outdoor Life 148:52-5+ N '71

GEEST industries, ltd.
Yes, we now have bananas. Forbes 108:38 Jl 15 '71

GEGENSCHEIN. See Counterglow

GEHLEN, Reinhard
Bormann enigma. pors Time 98:36+ S 20 '71 *
Espionage career of General Gehlen. B. A. Bannon. por Pub W 201:33-4 Ja 3 '72 *
Mixed motives. il por Newsweek 78:26+ S 13 '71 *
World gets rights to German spymaster's memoirs. Pub W 200:44 S 27 '71 *

GEHMAN, Richard
Amish are wexelin. il Holiday 49:60-3 Ap '71

GEIGER, Louis G.
Student response to faculty power. Sch & Soc 99:424-6 N '71

GEILKER, Charles D.
Mounting IC flat-packs. il Radio-Electr 42:64 Je '71

GEISERT, Stephen
Bottoms of things. il Sch Arts 71:22-3 N '71

GEISMAN, Gemma
Progress report. por Redbook 138:184 D '71

GEJVALL, T. See Löfroth, G. jt. auth.

GELATIN
Protein-metal ion binding site: determination with proton magnetic resonance spectroscopy. P. I. Rose. bibliog il Science 171:573-4 F 12 '71
See also
Agar

GELATIN desserts. See Desserts

GELATIN salads. See Salads

GELATT, Roland
Recordings. il Sat R 54:78 S 25 '71
SR goes to the movies. Sat R 54:14 Jl 17 '71

GELB, Lawrence D. and others
Heterogeneity of murine leukemia virus in vitro DNA; detection of viral DNA in mammalian cells. bibliog il Science 172:1353-5 Je 25 '71

GELB, Leslie H.
Rules of the game; summary of statement. Time 98:9 Jl 5 '71
Today's lessons from the Pentagon papers. por Life 71:34-6 S 17 '71
—and Halperin, M. H.
Diplomatic notes. il Harper 243:28-30+ N '71
What chance is reasonable in Vietnam? pors Life 71:4 Jl 16 '71

GELDZAHLER, Henry
Profiles. C. Tomkins. por New Yorker 47:58-60+ N 6 '71 *

GELL-MANN, Murray
How scientists can really help; adaptation of address, October 26, 1970. il Phys Today 24:23-5 My '71

GELLEN, Martin
Aerospace in crisis. Nation 212:232-5 F 22 '71

GELLER, Evelyn
This matter of media; address. bibliog il por Library J 96:2048-53 Je 15 '71

GELLER, Irving
Ethanol preference in the rat as a function of photoperiod. bibliog il Science 173:456-9 Jl 30 '71

GELLER, Robert
Truffaut's Wild child; another must movie? Engl J 60:778-80 S '71

GELLER, William Spence
Film collection attacked in Los Angeles County. Library J 96:771-2 Mr 1 '71; Reply. R. C. Goodwell. 96:1896-7 Je 1 '71 *
Los Angeles County PL beset on two sides. W. R. Eshelman. Wilson Lib Bul 45:816 My '71 *

GELPI, Donald L.
Religion in the age of Aquarius. il America 125:392-5 N 13 '71

GELSTHORPE, Edward
Hunt-Wesson's business. New Repub 164:8 Ap 24 '71 *

GELTMAN, Max
Arrogant cult of youth. Nat R 23:140-1 F 9 '71
Berrigans vs the United States. il Nat R 23:470-4 My 4 '71

GEMS
Questing for gems. G. S. Switzer. il Nat Geog 140:834-63 D '71
See also
Jewelry
Lapidary work
Precious stones

GENDEL, Milton
Arte povera, amore mio. il Art N 69:38-9+ F '71
Italy. Art N 70:56 My '71
Rome. Art N 70:43 Ap '71
Spoils of Paestum. il Art N 70:27-31+ Sum '71
(ed) See Getty, J. P. Interview with J. Paul Getty

GENDLIN, Frances
Palisades protest; a pattern of citizen intervention. il Bul Atom Sci 27:53-6 N '71

GENDUSA, Sam
Value of playground sculpture. il Parks & Rec 6:39+ Jl '71

GENE, Aladdin
Grateful (Al Shakir) poem. Negro Hist Bul 33:192 D '70
Wound in chains; poem. Negro Hist Bul 34:116 My '71

GENEALOGY
Freelance job idea: family histories. K. Carvell. il Writers Digest 51:30-1+ Jl '71
Genealogy; the mystery hobby. A. Schafer. il Har Yrs 11:24-5+ Ag '71
Sleuthing for ancestors. M. R. Bonebrake. il Hobbies 76:152-3+ Jl '71

GENEEN, Harold Sydney
Free association, free enterprise and free choice; address, November 24, 1970. Vital Speeches 37:221-4 Ja 15 '71
Maybe I'm worth $5 million a year; interview. pors Forbes 107:186-90 My 15 '71

about
Now it's growth from within for Harold Geneen. por Fortune 84:33 S '71 *
Options are still open. por Forbes 108:30 Ag 15 '71 *

GENERAL accounting office. See United States—General accounting office

GENERAL agreement on tariffs and trade
Bitter fruit from the EEC. H. H. Wilson. por Nations Bsns 59:42 N '71

GENERAL assembly of the Presbyterian churches in the United States (southern) See Presbyterian church in the United States (South)

GENERAL automation, inc.
Automating the jobs that others ignore. il por Bsns W p56 F 20 '71

GENERAL aviation. See Aviation

GENERAL cigar company
Winning a losing battle. il Forbes 108:50 S 15 '71

GENERAL crude oil (firm)
Late tape. R. Brady. il Duns 97:89+ Ap '71

GENERAL dynamics corporation
General dynamics. il Forbes 108:26-8+ O 15 '71
General dynamics aerospace profits drop. Aviation W 94:20 Ap 12 '71

GENERAL electric company
Borch of General electric. por Forbes 107:59-60 My 15 '71
Fred J. Borch of General electric; interview. F. J. Borch. il pors Nations Bsns 59:30-3+ F '71
GE dismissing 7,000 aircraft engine workers. Aviation W 95:20 Jl 26 '71
GE, TRW disclose aerospace financial results. il Aviation W 94:53 Mr 29 '71
GE's dream engine gets a French accent; joint development with SNECMA. il Bsns W p36 D 18 '71
General electric presents: S. Hurok. por Bsns W p22+ Jl 3 '71
L-1011 aid issue stirs aerospace. W. H. Gregory. Aviation W 94:14-16 My 17 '71

GENERAL electric company—*Continued*
SR's businessman of the year. R. L. Tobin.
por Sat R 54:55-7 Ja 23 '71
SST termination process begins; with editorial comment. Aviation W 94:9, 14-16 Mr 29 '71
Snecma selects GE as partner Aviation W 95:25 N 15 '71
Wiping out the sermon germ; employee publications. V. Louviere. Nations Bsns 59:15 Ag '71

GENERAL host corporation
He's in the market for a meatpacker. por Bsns W p70 Jl 10 '71

GENERAL information tests. See Information tests

GENERAL motors corporation
Back to Methuselah. S. Novick. il Environ 13:50-2 O '71
Biggest recall? Newsweek 78:94 O 25; 88 D 13 '71
Black director pushes reforms at GM. il pors Bsns W p100-3 Ap 10 '71
Can GM's new top team cope with the '70s? Bsns W p70-3 D 11 '71
Exit Jim Roche. por Newsweek 78:88 D 6 '71
For Roche of G.M. happiness is a 10% surcharge. W. Serrin. il pors N Y Times Mag p36-7+ S 12 '71
Full of air. P. J. Sloyan. New Repub 164: Mr 20 '71
GM switches to the inside track; selling diesel locomotives to Argentina. Bsns W p36 Ag 7 '71
GM's new boss. por Newsweek 78:72+ D 20 '71
GM's pollution man. por Bsns W p80 F 6 '71
GM's purloined letters; complaints from Chevrolet owners. il Newsweek 77:85-6 My 10 '71
How GM reacts to the pressure. il por Newsweek 77:76-7 My 24 '71
If your auto is called back—. il U S News 71:28 D 20 '71
James M. Roche of General motors; interview. J. M. Roche. il pors Nations Bsns 59: 50-4+ O '71
Job for Mr Mitchell; bus monopoly. Nation 213:69 Ag 2 '71
Largest recall. Time 98:76-7 D 13 '71
New viewpoint for General motors. J. Lear. il Sat R 54:48 Mr 6 '71
Philadelphia's banks. R. Nathan and R. Lear. New Repub 164:10+ Je 5 '71
Pierre S. du Pont and the making of the modern corporation. by A. Chandler and S. Salsbury. Review
Bsns W il por p 11 My 29 '71. W. Kroger
Profiles: S. R. and C. S. Mott. philanthropists. E. J. Kahn, jr. por New Yorker 47: 56-8+ N 27 '71
Rise of the bookkeeper: R. C. Gerstenberg. por Time 98:69-70 D 20 '71
Roche of General motors. il por Forbes 107: 48 My 15 '71

Chevrolet division
Battle but not war; interview. J. Z. DeLorean. il por Forbes 108:49 Ag 1 '71
Engineering: the car that must not fail. A B. Shuman. il Motor T 23:41-2+ F '71
Swinger tries to cure Chevrolet's ills. il pors Bsns W p60-4 S 18 '71

Frigidaire division
Chill wind at Frigidaire. Bsns W p58 Jl 31 '71
Dayton weathers a siege. Bsns W p81+ D 4 '71
No wage hikes, more jobs. U S News 71:79-80 D 6 '71

GENERAL motors institute, Flint, Mich.
Getting ready at GMI. il Ebony 26:72-4+ Je '71

GENERAL motors technical center
General motors revisited. C. Eames. il Arch Forum 134:21-8 Je '71

GENERAL practitioners. See Physicians

GENERAL reinsurance corporation
General re's finest aria. il Forbes 107:32 Je 15 '71

GENERAL services administration. See United States—General services administration

GENERAL tire and rubber company
Risking, winning and losing. il Forbes 108:16-17 S 1 '71

GENERALS
From the jaws of victory, by C. Fair. Review
New Repub 165:23-5 Ag 21 '71. R Macauley
Military theology. L. H. Lapham. il Harper 243:73-6+ Jl '71
See also
Donaldson, J. W.

GENERATION, Spontaneous. See Spontaneous generation

GENERATION gap
Gaping across the gap. P. Sullivan. bibliog il Library J 96:1767-70 My 15 '71; Reply. H. Rogers. 96:2806+ S 15 '71
Generation gap; economic illiteracy; address, December 5., 1970. D. M. Kendall. Vital Speeches 37:245-7 F 1 '71
Generation gap, education gap. C. B. Grannis. Pub W 199:36 Mr 29 '71
Generational conflict and intellectual antinomianism. S. N. Eisenstadt. bibliog f Ann Am Acad 395:68-79 My '71
If New Hampshire makes it. I. Mothner. Look 35:33-6 Ja 12 '71
Let us forge an alliance; excerpts from address, January 14, 1971. R. M. Nixon. il U S News 70:44 Ja 25 '71
Let's keep talking. R. A. McKenzie. Chr Cent 88:592-3 My 12 '71
Plugging the generation gap. D. J. Gudaitis. Clear House 45:556-7 My '71
Rock and its new role. il Sr Schol 98:5-10 My 3 '71
School gap or age gap? Sr Schol 98:14 Mr 1 '71
7 ways to bring us together. P. Hamill. Seventeen 29:266-7+ Ag '70
She's a great girl! interview. ed. by E. Miller. C. Bergen. il pors Seventeen 29:240-1+ Ag '70
Showdown at generation gap. W. L. Thomas. il Farm J 95:32-3+ Mr '71
Some ground rules for the generation gap. J. B. Kelley. America 124:457-8 My 1 '71
Sources of generational consciousness and conflict. R. S. Laufer. bibliog f Ann Am Acad 395:80-94 My '71
Train ride: three-way conversation between two commuters and boy. W. J. McLean. Look 35:37 Ja 12 '71
We encourage our youth to rebel. J. G. Wexler. por McCalls 98:63+ Ap '71
Why we ought to join our kids. E. J. Bloustein. Look 35:46-7 Ja 26 '71

Anecdotes, facetiae, satire, etc.
Ben Adam and the angel. A. Hoppe. il Read Digest 99:185-6 Ag '71
It's a wise child. J. Tierney. Nat R 23:704 Je 29 '71

GENERATIVE organs
See also
Orgasm

GENERATORS, Electric. See Electric generators

GENERATORS, Signal. See Signal generators

GENES
Increasing the multiplicity of ribosomal RNA genes in drosophila melanogaster. K. D. Tartof. bibliog il Science 171:294-7 Ja 22 '71
Silent hemoglobin alpha genes in apes: potential source of thalassemia. S. H. Boyer and others. bibliog il Science 171:182-5 Ja 15 '71
Throwing the biological clock off by altering a single gene. Sci N 100:226 O 2 '71
See also
Heredity of disease
Linkage (genetics)
Population genetics

GENESCO, inc.
Engineer in the fashion trade. Forbes 108:49 O 15 '71

GENESIS, Book of. See Bible—Old Testament —Genesis

GENESON, Kathryn
What's cooking? Org Gard & Farm 18:126-7 N '71

GENÊT, pseud. See Flanner, J.

GENET, Jean
Screens. Criticism
Nation 213:701-2 D 27 '71
Newsweek 78:58 D 20 '71 •
Time il 98:55 D 27 '71 •

GENETIC counseling
Detecting an old killer sickle-cell anemia. il Time 98:57 O 4 '71
Fighting the genetic odds. M. Steinmann. il pors Life 71:18-25 Ag 6 '71
Genetics for the community; Tay-Sachs disease and Jews in the Baltimore-Washington area. il Time 98:54 S 13 '71
Miracle baby of Carolyn Sinclair; saved from Hunter syndrome. J. L. Block and J. Stein. il por Good H 172:86-7+ Je '71
New strides in the battle against birth defects; science of genetic counseling. S. M. Spencer. Read Digest 98:159-60+ My '71

GENETIC counseling—*Continued*
Prenatal diagnosis: how fast, how far? J. L. Arehart. il Sci N 100:44-5 Jl 17 '71
Will my baby be normal? R. H. Berg. McCalls 98:52+ Ag '71

GENETIC diseases. See Heredity of disease

GENETIC engineering. See Human genetics

GENETIC polymorphism. See Polymorphism (biology)

GENETIC psychology
See also
Intelligence levels

GENETIC research
LSD and genetic damage. N. I. Dishotsky and others. bibliog il Science 172:431-40 Ap 30 '71
Man into superman; the promise and peril of the new genetics. il Time 97:33-8+ Ap 19 '71
Molecular biology: gene insertion into mammalian cells. D. Rabovsky. bibliog Science 174:933-4 N 26 '71
Of cats and men; study of Waardenburg's syndrome. Sci Am 225:50 N '71
Rabbit blood from a frog. Sci Am 225:40 D '71
Science alone is not enough. D. P. Young. il por Chem 44:14-16 N '71
Toward correction of genetic defects. Sci N 99:193-4 Mr 20 '71
Two genes, one enzyme. Sci Am 224:46 Ja '71
See also
Mutagenic substances

GENETICS
Chance and necessity, by J. Monod. Review Nation 213:568+ N 29 '71. J. H. Bryant
See also
Allelomorphism
Chemical genetics
Chromosomes
Fungal genetics
Human genetics
Insect genetics
Linkage (genetics)
Pharmacogenetics
Plant genetics
Population genetics

Conferences
Brain, genetics, and behavior. G. S. Omenn and A. G. Motulsky. Science 173:1255-6 S 24 '71

GENEVA, Switzerland
Social history
Social welfare in Calvin's Geneva; adaptation of address, December 30, 1968. R. M. Kingdon. bibliog f Am Hist R 76:50-69 F '71

GENEVA auto show. See Automobiles—Exhibitions

GENEVA conference on the peaceful uses of atomic energy. See International conference on the peaceful uses of atomic energy, 4th Geneva, 1971

GENEVA conventions
Rules of the game; conventions of 1949 applied to Vietnam. il Sr Schol 99:13-14 N 29 '71

GENICULATE body. See Optic thalamus

GENIUS
Genius: what is it? Who has it? A. Storr. Vogue 157:108+ Mr 1 '71
On trying to understand scientific genius. G. Holton. bibliog Am Scholar 41:95-110 Wint '71
Planetary planning; address, November 13, 1969. R. B. Fuller. Am Scholar 40:285-304 Spr '71

GENNARO, Joseph F. Jr
Creature revealed; with biographical sketch. il Natur Hist 80:6, 24+ Mr '71
—See Ashley, T. jt. auth.

GENOCIDE
Ethnic weapons. F. Lang. Ramp Mag 10:4 N '71

GENOTYPE and phenotype
Favism: association with erythrocyte acid phosphatase phenotype. E. Bottini and others. bibliog il Science 171:409-11 Ja 29 '71

GENRE painting
Young America. H. W. Williams, jr. il Am Heritage 22:16-32 F '71

GENSLER, Martin D.
Cuba's second Vietnam: Bolivia. Yale R 60:342-65 Mr '71

GENTELE, Göran
Man for '72; interview, ed. by F. Merkling. il pors Opera N 35:6-7 Ja 16 '71

about
Artist life. D. J. Soria. il por Hi Fi 21:MA6-7+ S '71 *
Goeran Gentele: his future & past. P. J. Smith; F. Hedman. por Hi Fi 21:MA4-5 Ap 71 *
Musical events; tomorrow is another day. W. Sargeant. New Yorker 47:83 Je 19 '71 *
New man at the Met. J. P. Boutwell. il pors N Y Times Mag p40-1+ S 12 '71; Reply with rejoinder. F. Robinson. p30 O 17 '71 *
New man at the Met. W. Weaver. il por Sat R 54:33-5+ Je 26 '71 *

GENTIANS
Gentians for the rock garden. R. Murfitt. il Horticulture 49:26-7+ O '71

GENTRY, Robert V.
Radiohalos: some unique lead isotope ratios and unknown alpha radioactivity. bibliog il Science 173:727-31 Ag 20 '71

GENUINE parts company
Middleman. il Forbes 108:62 O 1 '71

GEODES
Rock hunting in Dugway Pass. il Sunset 147:36 O '71

GEODESIC domes
Life in the round. il Time 97:40 Mr 1 '71
Our geodesic greenhouse. K. Starr. il Org Gard & Farm 18:100-1 S '71

GEODESY
Measuring the earth. L. Purrett. il Sci N 99:233 Ap 3 '71
See also
Gravity

GEOGHEGAN, J. T. and Bambrick, W. E.
Tall oil, a valuable by-product. bibliog il pors Chem 44:6-10 Ja '71

GEOGRAPHICAL distribution of animals and plants
Continental drift and the diversity of species. L. Purrett. il Sci N 100:394-5 D 11 '71
Sweepstakes route. D. Cohen. il Sci Digest 69:8-13 Mr '71
See also
Plant introduction

GEOGRAPHICAL myths
Imaginary geography: a rare map of another Great Salt Lake; dated 1703. W. M. Wiecek. il Am West 8:10-12 S '71

GEOGRAPHICAL names. See Names, Geographical

GEOGRAPHY
Did you know that. .? Sci Digest 69:81 My '71
See also
Atlases

GEOGRAPHY, Historical
Time, space, and the geographic past: a prospectus for historical geography. J. A. Jakle. bibliog f il Am Hist R 76:1084-103 O '71

GEOLOGICAL climate. See Paleoclimatology

GEOLOGICAL models
Model for plate tectonic evolution of mantle layers. W. R. Dickinson and W. C. Luth. bibliog il Science 174:400-4 O 22 '71

GEOLOGICAL research
Synthetic calcareous pseudomorphs formed from siliceous microstructures. R. I. Harker. bibliog il Science 173:235-7 Jl 16 '71

GEOLOGICAL society of America
Earth sciences; highlights of papers. Sci N 100:328 N 13 '71

GEOLOGICAL survey (United States) See United States—Geological survey

GEOLOGICAL time
See also
Paleoclimatology
Radioactive dating

GEOLOGISTS
See also names of geologists, e.g. H. Schmitt

GEOLOGY
See also
Caves
Earth—Age
Earthquakes
Faults (geology)
Geological society of America
Landslides
Ocean bottom
Petrology
Rocks—Weathering
Volcanoes

History
Schöpf, Maclure, Werner, and the earliest work on American geology. E. M. Spieker. bibliog Science 172:1333-4 Je 25 '71

GEOLOGY—*Continued*

Study and teaching
Mr Prescott's class goes wildcatting. Ed Digest 37:32-4 O '71

California
Ground rupture in the Baldwin Hills. D. H. Hamilton and R. L. Meehan. bibliog il Science 172:333-44 Ap 23 '71

Caribbean Region
Caribbean eocene volcanism and the extent of horizon A. P. H. Mattson and E. A. Pessagno, jr. bibliog il Science 174:138-9 O 8 '71

Iceland
Rifting in Iceland: new geodetic data. R. W. Decker and others. bibliog il Science 173:530-3 Ag 6 '71

Kansas
Kansas geologists and the AEC; plan to bury cannisters of nuclear wastes. il Sci N 99:161 Mr 6 '71

Radioactive salt mine. R. S. Lewis. Bul Atom Sci 27:27-31+ Je '71

Madagascar
Madagascar's paleoposition: new data from the Mozambique Channel. J. R. Heirtzler and R. H. Burroughs. bibliog il Science 174:488-90 O 29 '71

Minnesota
Lunar and terrestrial ilmenite basalt. S. S. Goldich. bibliog il Science 171:1245-6 Mr 26 '71

New Zealand
Paleomagnetic chronology of pliocene-early pleistocene climates and the plio-pleistocene boundary in New Zealand. J. P. Kennett and others. bibliog il Science 171:276-9 Ja 22 '71

Sahara Desert
Sahara Desert ice cap. R. W. Fairbridge. il Natur Hist 80:66-73 Je '71

South Africa
Sulfur isotopes in Swaziland system barites and the evolution of the earth's atmosphere. E. C. Perry. jr. and others. bibliog il Science 171:1015-16 Mr 12 '71

United States
See also
United States—Geological survey

Utah
Why the sands aren't red; canyonlands. H. Lansford. il Sci Digest 69:61-5 My '71

Vermont
Acadian orogeny: an abrupt and brief event. R. S. Naylor. bibliog il Science 172:558-60 My 7 '71

Washington (state)
Hanford revisited. S. Novick. il Environ 13:48-9 My '71

Paleomagnetic study of a reversal of the earth's magnetic field. J. R. Dunn and others. bibliog il Science 172:840-5 My 21 '71

Western states
Evolving subduction zones in the western United States, as interpreted from igneous rocks. P. W. Lipman and others. bibliog il Science 174:821-5 N 19 '71

Wisconsin
Duricrusts and deep-weathering profiles in southwestern Wisconsin. G. H. Dury and J. C. Knox. bibliog Science 174:291 O 15 '71

GEOLOGY. Stratigraphic
See also
Paleontology

Cenozoic
Evolving subduction zones in the western United States, as interpreted from igneous rocks. P. W. Lipman and others. bibliog il Science 174:821-5 N 19 '71

Paleomagnetic chronology of pliocene-early pleistocene climates and the plio-pleistocene boundary in New Zealand. J. P. Kennett and others. bibliog il Science 171:276-9 Ja 22 '71
See also
Geology, Stratigraphic—Quaternary

Cretaceous
Identifying 26 reversals during early cretaceous. Sci N 100:358 N 27 '71

Devonian
Acadian orogeny: an abrupt and brief event. R. S. Naylor. bibliog il Science 172:558-60 My 7 '71

Eocene
Caribbean eocene volcanism and the extent of horizon A. P. H. Mattson and E. A. Pessagno, jr. bibliog il Science 174:138-9 O 8 '71

Eocene volcanism and the origin of Horizon A. T. G. Gibson and K. M. Towe. bibliog il Science 172:152-4 Ap 9 '71

Ordovician
Sahara Desert ice cap. R. W. Fairbridge. il Natur Hist 80:66-73 Je '71

Pre-Cambrian
Precambrian; report of third Penrose conference of the Geological society of America. P. Cloud. Science 173:851-2+ Ag 27 '71

Sulfur isotopes in Swaziland system barites and the evolution of the earth's atmosphere. E. C. Perry, jr. and others. bibliog il Science 171:1015-16 Mr 12 '71

Quaternary
Holocene eruptions of Mauna Kea volcano, Hawaii. S. C. Porter. bibliog il Science 172:375-7 Ap 23 '71
Tertiary
See also
Geology, Stratigraphic—Eocene

GEOLOGY, Structural
Explosion effects and earthquakes in the Amchitka Island Region. E. R. Engdahl. bibliog il Science 173:1232-5 S 24 '71

Model for plate tectonic evolution of mantle layers. W. R. Dickinson and W. C. Luth. bibliog il Science 174:400-4 O 22 '71

Petrologic implications of plate tectonics; report of meeting. H. S. Yoder, jr. Science 173:464-6 Jl 30 '71

Plate tectonics in geologic history. W. R. Dickinson. bibliog il Science 174:107-13 O 8 '71

Plate tectonics: mountain building and continental geology. A. L. Hammond. Science 173:133-4 Jl 9 '71

Plate tectonics: the geophysics of the earth's surface. A. L. Hammond. bibliog Science 173:40-1 Jl 2 '71

Poetry of plate tectonics. B. C. King and G. C. P. King. Sci N 100:39 Jl 17 '71

Shaping the Alps. il Sci N 100:7 Jl 3 '71

Synthetic calcareous pseudomorphs formed from siliceous microstructures. R. I. Harker. bibliog il Science 173:235-7 Jl 16 '71

When the Pacific crustal plate reversed itself; leg 20 of the Deep sea drilling project. il Sci N 100:405 D 18 '71
See also
Faults (geology)

GEOMAGNETISM. See Magnetism, Terrestrial

GEOMETRY
Geometric fallacies: hidden errors pave the road to absurd conclusions. M. Gardner. il Sci Am 224:114-17 Ap; 116 My '71

Math tricks help you design shop projects. R. J. DeCristoforo. il Pop Sci 198:104+ My '71
See also
Polyhedrons

GEOMORPHOLOGY. See Geology, Structural

GEOPHYSICAL stations
See also
Seismological stations

GEOPHYSICISTS
See also
Geophysics as a profession

GEOPHYSICS
See also
American geophysical union
Earth—Internal structure
Earth—Radiation
Earth movements
Energy budget (geophysics)
Seismology
Solifluction

GEOPHYSICS as a profession
Opportunities in geophysics. H. R. Crane. il Phys Today 24:23-6 F '71

GEORGE III, king of Great Britain
England's Vietnam: the American revolution. R. M. Ketchum. bibliog il Am Heritage 22:6-11+ Je '71 *

George III and the mad business, by I. Macalpine and R. Hunter. Review
New Yorker 47:89-92 Je 26 '71. R. Coles *

GEORGE, B. F.
Potfuls of vegetables. Horticulture 49:40 Jl '71

GEORGE, Dan
Chief. por Newsweek 77:80 Ja 25 '71 *
Noble non-savage. por Time 97:76+ F 15 '71 *
GEORGE, David Lloyd, 1st earl Lloyd George of Dwyfor. See Lloyd George of Dwyfor, D. L. G.
GEORGE, Henry
Reconsiderations. P. Barnes. New Repub 165: 29-31 D 11 '71 *
GEORGE, Jean (Craighead)
Comeback of the canoe. Read Digest 99:193-4+ Jl '71
Diners of unlimited diversity; excerpts from Beastly inventions; with biographical sketch. il Natur Hist 80:2, 42-53 bibliog (p84) Ja '71
Mystery of the snowy owl. il Read Digest 99:219-20+ N '71
GEORGE, Kenneth F.
Grouping for motivation in mathematics. Clear House 46:81 O '71
GEORGE, Vivienne L.
Celebrating the canal's completion. il Hobbies 76:148-9 Je '71
Missouri's 150th birthday. il Hobbies 76:152-3 S '71
Most unusual post card shrine. il Hobbies 76:158-9 O '71
Panama Canal on cards. il Hobbies 76:148-9 My '71
Post card album. il Hobbies 75:158-9 Ja; 142-3 F; 76:148-9 Mr '71
Saving an American tradition. il Hobbies 76:158-9 N '71
GEORGE, LAKE
Pollution and policing; Lake George patrol. M. Crook. il Yachting 129:70+ Je '71
GEORGE A. Fuller company. See Fuller, G. A. company
GEORGE and Gilbert. See Gilbert and George
GEORGE Braziller, inc. See Braziller, George, inc.
GEORGE Eastman house of photography. See Photography—Galleries and museums
GEORGE Washington university, Washington, D.C.
Disowned: Urban law institute. New Repub 164:8-9 Ap 10 '71
GEORGETOWN university, Washington, D.C.
Nickel therapy; student counseling. il S. Mc-Bee. il McCalls 98:40 Mr '71
GEORGIA
See also
Architecture, Domestic—Georgia
Booksellers and bookselling—Georgia
Chattooga River
Cumberland Island
Gardens—Georgia
Hancock County, Ga.
Hunting—Georgia
Law—Georgia
Sea Islands

Elections
See Georgia—Politics and government

Politics and government
Lester Maddox: showman and radical; interview, by C. E. Fager. L. Maddox por Chr Cent 88:403-6 Mr 31 '71
Maddox touch. J. B. Cumming, jr. il por Newsweek 77:23 Ja 18 '71
New day. pors Newsweek 77:33 F 15 '71
New day a'coming in the South; 76th governor of Georgia elected. il por Time 97:14-20 My 31 '71
Up, uppity and away; J. Bond. J. Neary. por Esquire 75:109-11+ My '71

Race question
I say to you the time for discrimination is over; inaugural statement by J. Carter. il pors Life 70:30-1 Ja 29 '71
GEORGIA, STRAIT OF
See also
Gulf Islands
GEORGIA institute of technology, Atlanta
Filling the computer gap. J. Poindexter. por Duns 97:77-8 My '71
GEORGIA library association
Georgia history comes alive. J. Cornn. Wilson Lib Bul 46:478-9 Ja '72
GEORGIA-Pacific corporation
Brash challengers and the angry giant. il Forbes 108:30 D 15 '71
GEORGIAN architecture. See Architecture, Georgian
GEORGIEFF, K. K.
Free radical inhibitory effect of some anticancer compounds. bibliog il Science 173: 537-9 Ag 6 '71
GEOTHERMAL energy. See Steam, Natural
GEOTHERMAL power plants. See Steam power plants

GERALD, Barbara Fitz
Christening; poem. Nation 213:380 O 18 '71
GERALD, John Bart
Conventional wisdoms. il Harper 243:66-72 Jl '71
In praise of wounded men. il Harper 242: 98-100+ Ap '71
GERANIUMS
Geraniums, rewarding and easy to grow. R. Nagrod. il por Org Gard & Farm 18:119-20 Mr '71
Geraniums that mimic fruit and other fragrances. il Sunset 146:227 Je '71
Outsmarting your geraniums. T. Cruso. il McCalls 98:73+ Je '71
See also
Cookery—Flowers
GERASIMOV, Mikhail Mikhailovich
Face of Tamerlane. il por Newsweek 77:70 Mr 8 '71 *
GERASSI, John
Latin America: the left on the move. Ramp Mag 10:22-5 S '71
(ed) See Sartre, J. P. Sartre accuses the intellectuals of bad faith
GERBER, Kenneth. See Gerber, L. jt. auth.
GERBER, Leslie
Complete Bessie Smith. pors Am Rec G 37:340-2 F '71
Folk music (cont) Am Rec G 37:330-1, 784-5 Ja, Jl '71
In the pop bag. Am Rec G 37:396-7, 524-5 F, Ap '71
In two Desto albums, music by a dozen black composers. il Am Rec G 37:476-9 Ap '71
Memorable IPL release: Moszkowski. il Am Rec G 37:292-4 Ja '71
Sergei Rachmaninoff. il Am Rec G 37:438-9 Mr '71
—and Gerber, Kenneth
In the pop bag. Am Rec G 37:736-7 Je '71
GERBER, Merrill Joan
Final exam; story. Redbook 138:84-5 D '71
May I ask you who's calling? story. Ladies Home J 88:68-9 Je '71
GERDTS, William H.
Bric-a-brac still life. il Antiques 100:744-8 N '71
Marble and nudity. il Art in Am 59:60-7 My '71
GERHARDT, John. See Toyli, M. jt. auth.
GERHARDT, Lillian N.
—and others
(ed) Best books for spring 1971. il Library J 96:1780-3 My 15 '71
Best books of 1971. il Library J 96:4157-61 D 15 '71
(ed) Book review. See second issue of each month of Library journal
about
Lillian N. Gerhardt appointed SLJ editor-in-chief. por Library J 96:3423 O 15 '71 *
GERIATRICS as a profession
Wisconsin uses phone network in training title III staff workers. il Aging 203:12 S '71
GÉRICAULT, Théodore
Byron of painting. il por Newsweek 78:94-5 O 18 '71 *
Who was Théodore Géricault? L. Eitner. il Art N 70:30-5+ O '71 *
GERKEN, Eva
Byways of Europe: Wiesbaden. il Opera N 35: 20-1 My 15 '71
GERLACH, Ronald A.
Educational objectives and the new social studies. bibliog Sch & Soc 99:180-2 Mr '71
GERLING, Esther A.
Indian markets of South America. il Travel 135:42-7 F '71
GERM cells
Ovarian maturation in stable flies: inhibition by 20-hydroxyecdysone. J. E. Wright and others. bibliog il Science 172:1247-8 Je 18 '71; Reply. F. Engelmann. 1774:1041 D 3 '71
GERM free animals. See Germfree life
GERMAN authors. See Authors, German
GERMAN automobiles. See Automobiles, Foreign
GERMAN bonds. See Bonds, Government—Germany (Federal Republic)
GERMAN cookery. See Cookery, German
GERMAN foundation for developing countries
Educational materials in the third world; meeting. H. Lottman. il Pub W 200:16-18 N 22 '71
GERMAN-French communications satellites. See Communications satellites, European
GERMAN glass. See Glassware

GERMAN literature
See also
Authors, German
Childrens literature—Germany
GERMAN measles. See Rubella
GERMAN poetry

Translations into English
Eleven poems, tr. by M. Hamburger. P. Celan. Poetry 119:134-41 D '71
Love poem; tr. by M. Bullock. K. Krolow. Mlle 72:116 Mr '71
Poems: In the shape of a boar; Threadsuns; By all means; Today and tomorrow; tr. by J. Neugroschel. P. Celan. Harper 242:93 Mr '71

GERMAN refugees. See Refugees, German
GERMAN resistance movement. See Anti-Nazi movement
GERMAN-Russian war, 1941-1945. See World war, 1939-1945—Campaigns and battles—Russia
GERMAN shepherd dogs
Best of breed; army's breeding program. il Newsweek 78:68 Jl 5 '71
GERMAN scientists. See Scientists, German
GERMAN spies. See Spies
GERMAN students
Nasty shock: results of polls in West Germany. E. von Kuehnelt-Leddihn. Nat R 23:758 Jl 13 '71
GERMAN wines. See Wine
GERMANS in Pennsylvania. See Pennsylvania Germans
GERMANS in the United States
See also
Amana society
GERMANY, Charles H.
Korea-U.S. relations. Chr Cent 88:285-7 Mr 3 '71
GERMANY
See also
European war, 1914-1918—Germany
Youth movement—Germany

Army
Forgotten soldier, by G. Sajer. Review New Repub 164:28-9 F 20 '71. J. Walt

Foreign relations
Ideology and policy. L. S. Dawidowicz. Commentary 52:91-3 Ag '71

History
1918-1933
End of the Weimar republic. J. Wheeler-Bennett. For Affairs 50:351-71 Ja '72
In the twenties, by H. Kessler. Review Nat R 23:1474-5 D 31 '71. S. J. Tonsor
Psychohistorical origins of the Nazi youth cohort. P. Loewenberg. bibliog f il Am Hist R 76:1457-502 D '71

1933-1945
In Hitler's service. L. S. Dawidowicz; discussion. Commentary 51:32; Mr '71
See also
Anti-Nazi movement

Intellectual life
Germans and Jews, by G. Mosse. Review Commentary 50:94-6+ O '70. L. D. Wurgaft; Reply with rejoinder. H. M. Pachter. 51:34+ Mr '71

National socialist movement
See National socialism

Politics and government
See also
National socialism
GERMANY (Democratic Republic)
See also
Commodity control—Germany(Democratic Republic)
Elections—Germany (Democratic Republic)
Opera—Germany (Democratic Republic)
Protestant churches—Germany (Democratic Republic)
Youth—Germany (Democratic Republic)

Economic conditions
East vs. West Germany: victory for free enterprise. il U S News 70:67-8 My 10 '71

Foreign relations
See also
Berlin question, 1945-

Intellectual life
Expatriate chess on the other side of the wall. E. Shorris. il pors N Y Times Mag p30-2+ My 23 '71

Politics and government
Disciple departs. por Time 97:32+ My 17 '71
East Germany between Moscow and Bonn. R. G. Livingston. For Affairs 50:297-309 Ja '72
East Germany changes bosses. il por Newsweek 77:36-7+ My 17 '71
Merit of Ulbricht. P. Wohl. Nation 212:613 My 17 '71
Toward a triumvirate. il Time 97:36 Je 28 '71
See also
Berlin question, 1945-

Religious institutions and affairs
Worldaround. Chr Cent 88:346-7, 560, 982-3 Mr 17, My 5, Ag 18 '71
GERMANY (Federal Republic)
See also
Abortion—Laws and legislation—Germany (Federal Republic)
Air pollution—Germany (Federal Republic)
Airlines—Germany (Federal Republic)
Airplanes, Military—Germany (Federal Republic)
Americans in Germany (Federal Republic)
Astronomical observatories—Germany (Federal Republic)
Automobile industry—Germany (Federal Republic)
Automobile racing—Germany (Federal Republic)
Baden-Baden
Banks and banking—Germany (Federal Republic)
Berlin (West Berlin)
Bonds, Government—Germany (Federal Republic)
Business management and organization—Germany (Federal Republic)
Church tax—Germany (Federal Republic)
Construction industry—Germany (Federal Republic)
Crime and criminals—Germany (Federal Republic)
Dachau
Düsseldorf
Education—Germany (Federal Republic)
Festivals—Germany (Federal Republic)
Fishing—Germany (Federal Republic)
Foreign students in Germany
Frankfort on the Main
Garmisch-Partenkirchen
Hanover
Hunting—Germany (Federal Republic)
Money—Germany (Federal Republic)
Museums—Germany (Federal Republic)
Music festivals—Germany (Federal Republic)
Newspapers—Germany (Federal Republic)
Opera—Germany (Federal Republic)
Publishers and publishing—Germany (Federal Republic)
Railroads—Germany (Federal Republic)
Rothenburg
Securities—Germany (Federal Republic)
Strikes—Germany (Federal Republic)
Television broadcasting—Germany (Federal Republic)
Theater—Germany (Federal Republic)
Youth—Germany (Federal Republic)

Armed forces
Middeldorf's complaint; criticism of the Bundeswehr by its officers. Newsweek 77:42+ Ap 26 '71

Description and travel
What do you do after you've seen the cathedral in Cologne? M. M. Davis. Travel 136:72-3 Ag '71

Economic conditions
East vs. West Germany: victory for free enterprise. il U S News 70:67-8 My 10 '71
Sales and earnings gap widens. il Bsns W p36 N 27 '71
West Germany: a new kind of drive in the world. R. A. Haeger. il U S News 71:88-91 O 4 '71
West Germany: troubles overtake an economic giant. il U S News 70:17-18 My 31 '71

Economic policy
Germany's Schiller cools the boom. il Bsns W p96+ F 20 '71
Where Schiller's game plan went wrong. il por Bsns W p42+ Je 12 '71

Foreign relations
Why U.S. must stay in Europe; interview, ed. by R. Haeger. W. Brandt. il pors U S News 70:39-42+ Je 14 '71

GERMANY (Federal Republic)—Foreign relations—*Continued*

Europe, Eastern

As Willy Brandt looks east; worries for U.S.
and Germany. il por U S News 70:55-6 F
8 '71
Germany and her eastern neighbors; the sta-
bilization of peace; address, April 21, 1971.
H. Schmidt. Vital Speeches 37:459-63 My 15
'71
Hectoring Herr Brandt. New Repub 164:7-8
Ja 23 '71
Katzenjammer. E. V. Kuehnelt-Leddihn. Nat
R 23:529 My 18 '71
Willy Brandt walks a tightrope. por Read
Digest 98:96-100 Ap '71

France

See France—Foreign relations—Germany
(Federal Republic)

Germany (Democratic Republic)

East Germany between Moscow and Bonn.
R. G. Livingston. For Affairs 50:297-309
Ja '72
See also
Berlin question, 1945-

Israel

One more whirl; visit of W. Scheel. Newsweek
78:29 Jl 19 '71

Russia

See Russia—Foreign relations—Germany
(Federal Republic)

Industries

See also
Aerospace industries—Germany (Federal Re-
public)
Airplane industry—Germany (Federal Repub-
lic)
Automobile industry—Germany (Federal Re-
public)
Computer industry—Germany (Federal Re-
public)
Electric industries—Germany (Federal Re-
public)
Machine tool industry—Germany (Federal
Republic)
Photographic apparatus and supplies indus-
try—Germany (Federal Republic)

Military policy

Germany and her eastern neighbors; the stabilization of peace; address, April 21, 1971.
H. Schmidt. Vital Speeches 37:459-63 My 15
'71

Politics and government

Fourth corner. B. van Voorst. por Newsweek
77:34-5 Je 21 '71
See also
Berlin question, 1945-
Political parties—Germany (Federal Republic)

Religious institutions and affairs

Opinion press; Publik. J. Deedy. Common-
weal 95:194 N 26 '71
Visit to West Germany. Germanicus. Chr
Cent 88:1269-70 O 27 '71
See also
Catholic church in Germany (Federal Re-
public)
Church union—Germany (Federal Republic)

Treaties
Poland

Coming to terms: Polish control over former
German land. il Sr Schol 97:4 Ja 11 '71
GERMFREE isolators
Antiseptic baby; case of combined immune
deficiency. il Newsweek 78:61-2 D 20 '71
GERMFREE life
Better mouse; Charles River breeding lab-
oratories. Wilmington. Mass. il Newsweek
77:86 Mr 29 '71
Gnotobiotic animal as a tool in the study of
inflammation. M. Miyakawa and others.
Science 173:171-3 Jl 9 '71
GERMINATION
Cytokinins: permissive role in seed germina-
tion. A. A. Khan. bibliog il Science 171:
853-9 Mr 5 '71
Getting seeds to germinate. V. Tripp. Org
Gard & Farm 18:114-15 Ap '71
Identification of the germination self-inhibitor
from wheat stem rust uredospores. V.
Macko and others. bibliog Science 173:835-6
Ag 27 '71
Permeation of dry seeds with chemicals;
use of dichloromethane. H. Meyer and A.
M. Mayer. il Science 171:583 F 12 '71
See also
Dormancy (plants)
Seeds

GERONIMO, Jeffrey. See Jacklet, J. W. jt.
auth.
GERONTOLOGISTS
Ann Arbor aging placement service enters
second year. Aging 203:7 S '71
First woman gerontologist receives Kleemeier
award; excerpts from address. B. L. Neu-
garten. Aging 205:12+ N '71
GERONTOLOGY
Gerontological society research project makes
second report on research goals. Aging
200:8 Je '71
Gerontological society urged to take political
action. Aging 205:12+ N '71
See also
Institute of gerontology
GERRYMANDER
1971 gerrymander. R. W. Dietsch. New Re-
pub 164:20-2 My 29 '71
GERSCHENFELD, H. M.
Serotonin: two different inhibitory actions
on snail neurons. bibliog il Science 171:
1252-4 Mr 26 '71
GERSH, Marvin James, and Litt, I. F.
Fitness program for overweight teen-agers;
excerpts from The handbook of adoles-
cence: a complete medical guide. il Par-
ents Mag 46:50-1+ Ag '71
GERSHWIN, George
Festival of George Gershwin. D. Ewen. il pors
Hi Fi 21:MA24-5+ Ja '71 *
GERSMEHL, Glen. See Drake, J. jt. auth.
GERSON, Noel Bertram
Fiction techniques in nonfiction writing. Writ-
er 84:13-14+ D '71
GERSONI, Diane
Christmas books for '71. bibliog il Library J
96:3482-7 O 15 '71
Up for discussion. Library J 96:282-6 Ja 15 '71
GERSTACKER, Carl Allan
Carl Gerstacker of Dow chemical co; inter-
view. por Nations Bsns 59:40-5 Jl '71
GERSTEL, Judith
Faust counter Faust. il Hi Fi 21:MA26-7 My
'71
Holby's Summer and smoke hits home. il Hi
Fi 21:MA20-1 S '71
GERSTENBERG, Richard Charles
New chairman says it his way. por Bsns W
p71 D 11 '71
about
GM's new boss. por Newsweek 78:72+ D 20
'71 *
Rise of the bookkeeper. por Time 98:69-70 D
20 '71 *
GERVASI, Frank
Liberation of Gertrude Stein. il pors Sat R
54:13-14+ Ag 21 '71
GERVER, Joseph
Past as backwards movies of the future. por
Phys Today 24:40-1 Ap '71
GESCHEIDT, Alfred
Pro's secrets. il Pop Phot 68:102-5+ F '71
GESELL, Gerhard Alden
No more fingerprints. New Repub 165:8 Jl 3
'71 *
No-nonsense innovator. por Time 97:58 Ap
19 '71 *
GESNERIACEAE
How to grow gesneriads for winter bloom in-
doors. E. McDonald. il House B 113:97-9,
186-7 S '71
GESNERIADS. See Gesneriaceae
GESSNER, John
Faust counter Faust. Criticism
Hi Fi il 21:MA26-7 My '71 *
GESTURE
Mudra: Maurice Béjart's gesture. N. M.
Stoop. il pors Dance Mag 45:30-7 N '71
See also
Sign language
GETLEIN, Frank
Mad dogs and who go out in the mid-day
sun? excerpt from Playing soldier, a diatribe.
Commonweal 94:159-62 Ap 23 '71
Man who's made the most solid contribution
to the arts of any president since F.D.R.
il por N Y Times Mag p 14-16+ F 14 '71
Unfree nonenterprisers. Chr Cent 88:461-5 Ap
14 '71
GETTY, Jean Paul
I don't have to work. of course; interview,
ed. by J. Ross-Skinner. por Duns 98:42-4
N '71
Interview with J. Paul Getty; ed. by M. Gen-
del. il por Art N 70:44-5+ S '71
GETTY museum. See Los Angeles—Galleries
and museums
GETTYSBURG NATIONAL MILITARY PARK
Second battle of Gettysburg; spread of com-
mercialism. il U S News 71:66-7 O 18 '71

GETZ, Arthur
Verses from The brook by A. Tennyson; sketches. Audubon 73:10-11 Mr '71
GETZ, Howard F. and Pierce, Walter
Relating pertinence to proximity. Clear House 45:281-4 Ja '71
GÉVAUDAN, France
Best of Gévaudan. C. H. D. Clarke. bibliog Natur Hist 80:44-51+ Ap '71
GEYER, Georgie Anne
New quest for the old Russia. il Sat R 54:14-17 D 25 '71
Odyssey of Robert Williams. New Repub 164:15-17 Mr 20 '71
GEYER, Robert P.
Careers in nutrition. il por Chem 44:12-15 Ja '71
GEYSERS
Old and faithful quake warnings. il Time 98:63-4 O 18 '71
GHĀLIB, 1796?-1869
Ghazal XXXIV, translations by Aijaz Ahmad, Adrienne Rich and William Stafford. Mlle 74:50 Ja '72
GHĀLIB, Mirza. See Ghālib
GHANA
Life of Accra, the flowers of Abidjan. N. Gordimer. il Atlan 228:85-9 N '71
See also
Investments, Foreign (in Ghana)
Music festivals—Ghana

Diplomatic and consular service
Irrepressible envoy from Ghana. il pors Ebony 26:68-70+ N '70

Economic conditions
Going somewhere from the road to nowhere; U.S. companies. S. G. Slappey. il Nations Bsns 59:66-9 Je '71

Foreign relations
United States
See United States—Foreign relations—Ghana

Historic houses, etc.
Shrine to slaves; restoration of Fort Amsterdam. il Ebony 27:88-91 Ja '72

Native races
Ashanti. J. Morris. il Horizon 13:74-91 Spr '71

Politics and government
Politics and factionalism in Ghana. R. Rathbone. bibliog f Cur Hist 60:164-7+ Mr '71
al-GHAZZALI, Muhammad
As Arabs see it. J. P. O'Kane. il America 124:67-8 Ja 23 '71
GHETTO schools. See Public schools—United States
GHETTOS (slums) See Slums
GHIO, Joseph J.
Modern iris. il Horticulture 49:24-5+ Je '71
GHORMLEY, J. A. and Hochanadel, C. J.
Amorphous ice: density and reflectivity. bibliog il Science 171:62-4 Ja 8 '71
GHOSE, Subrata, and Tsang, Tung
Ordering of V^{2+}, Mn^{2+}, and Fe^{3+} ions in zoisite. $Ca_2Al_3Si_3O_{12}(OH)$ bibliog il Science 171:374-6 Ja 29 '71
GHOSE, Zulfikar
View from the observatory; poem. Poetry 118:86-7 My '71
GHOST of Hamlet's ghost; story. See Auchincloss, L.
GHOST ranch museum. See Natural history museums
GHOST towns. See Abandoned towns
GHOST wanted; drama. See Boiko. C.
GHOST writing. See Authorship—Collaboration
GHOSTS
Gazetteer of British ghosts, by P. Underwood. Review
Time 98:36+ Ag 30 '71
See also
Mediums
GHURKHAS. See Gurkhas
GIANNINI, Amadeo Peter
Largest bank was once a plank on the waterfront. A. W. Clausen. il pors Nations Bsns 59:54-5 Ja '71 •
GIANNINOTO, Frank, and associates, Inc.
Designing the silent salesman. il Nations Bsns 59:73 F '71
GIANT pandas. See Pandas
GIANT stars. See Stars. Giant
GIANTS (baseball) See Baseball clubs
GIAP, Vo-nguyen-. See Vo-nguyen-Giap
GIBB, Carson
Reporting and exposition. Engl J 60:251-4+ F '71

GIBB, Robert
Photographer discusses the dawn; poem. Esquire 76:40 D '71
GIBBERELLINS
GA_{22}: a polar gibberellin with high biological potency. B. G. Coombe. bibliog il Science 172:856-7 My 21 '71
GIBBONS, Euell
On the trail of the three sisters; with biographical sketch. Natur Hist 80:6, 14-16+ F '71
Organic nature-lover. See issues of Organic gardening and farming
about
Stalking Euell Gibbons. S. Valero. Org Gard & Farm 18:106 Jl '71 •
GIBBONS, Richard P.
Farm workers and city unions. New Repub 165:12-13 Jl 24; 33 S 11 '71
GIBBONS, Russell W.
Eggheads under the hard hats? Commonweal 94:4-5 Mr 12 '71
Hardhats, hyacinths and returnable bottles. Commonweal 94:324-5 Je 25 '71
Steel: the thaw before the freeze. Commonweal 94:444-5 S 3 '71
GIBBS, Barbara
Mother church and her wandering children. il Cath World 213:274-6 S '71
GIBBS, Richard F.
On the meaning of revolution. Nat R 23:699-700 Je 29 '71
GIBBS, Ronald J.
Mechanisms controlling world water chemistry. bibliog il Science 170:1088-90; 172:871-2 D 4 '70, My 21 '71
GIBBS, Tony
Book shelf. See issues of Motor boating & sailing
(ed) Designs & new boats (title varies) See issues of Motor boating & sailing
New boats. il Motor B & S 127:77 F '71
New designs (title varies) il Motor B & S 127:72-6 F: 98-104 Mr '71
Strange harbors. il Motor B & S 127:50-3+ My '71
GIBBS, Vernon
B.B. bringing the blues back home. pors Sr Schol 97:23-5 Ja 18 '71
GIBLETT, Eloise R. See Chen, S. H. jt. auth.
GIBNEY, Frank
Pearl Harbor in reverse. il Harper 244:49-51+ Ja '72
View from Japan. For Affairs 50:97-111 O '71
GIBRALTAR
Apes of Gibraltar: Barbary apes. B. R. MacRoberts and M. H. MacRoberts. il Natur Hist 80:38-47 Ag '71
Gibraltar: smugglers' Rock. O. Martinez. il Nation 213:17-19 Jl 5 '71
GIBRAN, Kahlil
Tales of a Levantine guru. S. Turner. il por Sat R 54:54-5+ Mr 13 '71 •
GIBSON, Althea
Lady pros seek golf glory. il pors Ebony 26:106-8+ Jl '71 •
GIBSON, Bob
Sports. R. Kahn. Esquire 76:16+ Jl '71 •
GIBSON, Frank W.
They'll never know. Flying 88:69-70 F '71
GIBSON, Glen
New world record tuna. il por Outdoor Life 148:49-51+ S '71
GIBSON, Herbert Richard
Gibson's l'il ole billion-dollar business. il pors Bsns W p60-1+ Mr 20 '71 •
GIBSON, John E.
What your dreams tell about you. Read Digest 99:21-2 O '71
GIBSON, Kenneth Allen
Urban leader; interview, ed. by L. Delpreore. por Am City 86:73-4 Jl '71
about
Following their footsteps. A. P. Bundles. il pors Seventeen 30:96-7+ Ja '71 •
Mayor Kenneth Gibson says: wherever the central cities are going, Newark is going to get there first. F. J. Cook. il N Y Times Mag p7-9+ Jl 25 '71 •
Newark a year later. A. Poinsett. il pors Ebony 27:124-6+ N '71
Newark at the brink. il por Newsweek 77:87-8 Ap 26 '71 •
GIBSON, Michael
Paris. il Art in Am 59:128-9 Mr '71
Three artists in three dimensions. il Art in Am 59:112-13 Ja '71
GIBSON, Otto Jefferson
Playwrights in residence. il por Time 98:43 Jl 26 '71

GIBSON, Richard
Detours on Africa's freedom road. Commonweal 95:172-3 N 19 '71

GIBSON, Thomas G. and Towe, K. M.
Eocene volcanism and the origin of Horizon A. bibliog il Science 172:152-4 Ap 9 '71

GIDDINGS and Lewis, inc.
Hard times is their best teacher. il Bsns W p80-1 Ag 14 '71

GIDEON and Power (rock group) See Rock groups

GIELEN, J. E. and Nebert, D. W.
Microsomal hydroxylase induction in liver cell culture by phenobarbital, polycyclic hydrocarbons, and p, p'-DDT. bibliog il Science 172:167-9 Ap 9 '71

GIELEN, Michael
Gielen's chromatic, traumatic evening. I. Kolodin. Sat R 54:85 O 30 '71 *
Music. D. Hamilton. Nation 213:413-14 O 25 '71 *
Musical events; atonality; New York Philharmonic concert in Philharmonic Hall. W. Sargeant. New Yorker 47:164 O 23 '71 *

GIELGUD, Sir John
Sir John Gielgud; interview, ed. by J. Gruen. por Vogue 158:86+ N 15 '71

GIELGUD, Maina
Brief biography. S. Goodman. pors Dance Mag 45:74-5 My '71 *

GIEMSA stain. See Stains and staining (microscopy)

GIEREK, Edward
Meeting with old mates. Time 97:31 F 8 '71 *
Patching it up. il por Newsweek 77:34 F 1 '71 *
Plan for man's needs. por Time 98:29 Jl 5 '71 *
Prices rise, Gomulka falls. il Sr Schol 97:6+ Ja 18 '71 *
Repairing a shaken regime. il por Time 97: 30-1 Ja 25 '71 *
Will it fly? il por Newsweek 78:42+ D 20 '71 *
Wooing the worker. il por Time 97:23 Mr 1 '71 *

GIESE, R. F. Jr
Hydroxyl orientation in muscovite as indicated by electrostatic energy calculations. bibliog il Science 172:263-4 Ap 16 '71

GIESECKE, Raymond H.
CPA in charge. por Bsns W p 105 F 27 '71 *

GIFFIN, Glenn
Colorado opera festival is fun. il Hi Fi 21: MA23+ O '71

GIFFORD, Beverly
New path to educational leadership. Am Ed 7:9-12 D '71

GIFFORD, Frank
Shall we rule these TV egos guilty of unnecessary roughness? S. Singer. il Todays Health 49:40-3 D '71 *
What are they doing with the sacred game of pro football? E. Shrake. pors Sports Illus 35:96-9+ O 25 '71 *

GIFT of home; story. See Oppenheimer, J.

GIFT of tongues
Pat Boone and the charismatics; interview, ed. by D. M. Lynch. P. Boone. Chr Cent 88:1167+ O 6 '71
Testing tongues; Lutheran medical center research project. D. E. Kucharsky. Chr Today 15:34-5 Je 4 '71
Truce proposal for the tongues controversy. C. H. Pinnock and G. R. Osborne. Chr Today 16:6-9 O 8 '71; Discussion. 16:17-18 N 5 '71

GIFT shops
Brattle book shop goes exotic; Ecuadorian and Galapagos Islands curio center in Boston antiquarian bookstore. P. Ingraham. Pub W 199:52 Je 28 '71
Special fixturing creates interest areas; Herald book and gift shop, Independence, Mo. il Pub W 199:59-60 Je 21 '71

GIFT wrappings. See Wrapping of packages

GIFTED children. See Children, Gifted

GIFTS
Father's day specials. P. Van Wagenen. il Parents Mag 46:18 Je '71
Grateful dad. il Esquire 75:140-1 Je '71
See also
Books as gifts
Christmas gifts
Colleges and universities—Gifts, legacies, etc.
Food as gifts
Libraries—Gifts, legacies, etc.
Plants as gifts
Wedding gifts
Wine as gifts

GIFTS for children
See also
Christmas gifts for children

GIFTS for the home
Great house gifts. il House & Gard 140:99-100 D '71
Tiny shiny treasures. H. Brown. il Am Home 74:14 D '71

GIFTS of joy; story. See Buck, P. S.

GIGNAC, Louis
Hair talk. il Mlle 73:132 Je '71

GILADI, Hefzibah Eyal-. See Eyal-Giladi, H.

GILBERG, Trond
Soviet policies in west Europe. bibliog f Cur Hist 61:198-205 O '71

GILBERT, Ben
Computerized street maintenance. il Am City 86:70-2 O '71

GILBERT, Bil
After a mountain of money. il Sports Illus 35:28-9 S 20 '71
Golf (cont) Sports Illus 34:42-3 Ja 11 '71
Here he is, ranger, and he's all yours. il Sports Illus 34:48-50+ My 17 '71
Other side of paradise. Sports Illus 34:40-8+ Ap 5 '71
Then came man and a mustard seed. il Sports Illus 35:96-9+ S 13 '71
When a law fights a law. il Sports Illus 34:30-2+ Ap 26 '71
Who sez-z-z-z man is the dominant species? il Sports Illus 34:44-6+ Je 21 '71

GILBERT, Celia
X-ray; poem. Atlan 228:76 S '71

GILBERT, Christopher G.
Furniture by Giles Grandey for the Spanish trade. il Antiques 99:544-50 Ap '71

GILBERT, Douglas L.
People are pigs. Cons 25:33 Ap '71

GILBERT, Jack J.
Ode to line vs. staff, a perspective. Duns 98: 79 O '71
about
Businessman's bard. Duns 98:3 O '71 *

GILBERT, Lawrence E.
Butterfly-plant coevolution: has passiflora adenopoda won the selectional race with heliconiine butterflies? bibliog il Science 172:585-6 My 7 '71

GILBERT, Sandra M.
Eating fish; poem. Nation 213:602 D 6 '71

GILBERT and George
Art: Gilbert and George at the Sonnabend gallery. L. Alloway. Nation 213:348 O 11 '71
Gilbert and George: human singing sculpture at the Sonnabend gallery. New Yorker 47:40-1 O 9 '71
Presenting Gilbert & George, the living sculptures. B. Reise. il pors Art N 70:62-5+ N '71 *

GILBERT and Sullivan operas
See also
Phonograph records—Operas

GILBERTS, Helen
Whistle walking. Har Yrs 11:34 My '71

GILBRETH, Frank Bunker, 1868-1924
Time out for happiness; condensation. F. B. Gilbreth, jr. il Read Digest 98:233-6+ My '71 *

GILBRETH, Frank Bunker, 1911-
Time out for happiness; condensation. il Read Digest 98:233-6+ My '71

GILBRETH, Lillian Evelyn (Moller)
Time out for happiness; condensation. F. B. Gilbreth, jr. il Read Digest 98:233-6+ My '71 *

GILDING
Rundell, Bridge and Rundell, aurifices regis. J. F. Hayward. il Antiques 99:860-5; 100: 110-15 Je-Jl '71

GILDS
European guild pewter: forms and functions. R. M. Vetter. il Antiques 101:201-8 Ja '72

GILES, Cynthia Davis
Family forum: a creative method of settling differences. il Parents Mag 46:54-5+ Ap '71

GILES, John Warren
State registration laws can trip you. Arch Rec 149:55 My '71

GILES, Louise
Planning community college resource centers. bibliog il Am Lib 2:51-4 Ja '71

GILFORD, Barbara
Recycling of the greens. il Org Gard & Farm 18:74-5 D '71

GILHOOLEY, James
On being a Catholic. J. Barthel. il pors Life 70:55-60+ Ap 30 '71 *

GILHOOLY, David
David Gilhooly. J. Arneson. il Craft Horiz 31:20-1+ Ag '71 *

GILKEY, Richard
Instructional media (cont) Clear House 45: 319-20 Ja '71

GILL, Brendan
Girls' voices; poem. New Yorker 47:48 Jl 17
'71
On refusing an invitation to dine with a
peer's son and some of the so-called beau-
tiful people; poem. New Yorker 47:81 Ag
28 '71
Profiles; C. Porter. por New Yorker 47:48-50+
S 18 '71
Regarding tradition. House & Gard 140:37-8+
Ag '71
Theatre. See issues of New Yorker
GILL, Frances McLaughlin
Studio at your doorstep. J. Scully. il Mod
Phot 35:76-9 Mr '71 *
GILL, Kent
Whither an English curriculum for the seven-
ties? Engl J 60:447-54 Ap '71
GILL, Thomas J. 3d, and others
Maternal-fetal interaction and immunolog-
ical memory. bibliog il Science 172:1346-8
Je 25 '71
GILLELAN, G. Howard
Archery. See issues of Outdoor life
Ice fishing in Dixie. il por Outdoor Life
147:36-9+ Ja '71
GILLESPIE, Charles
Don't broadcast this, but pollution can get
you fired! reprint. il Audubon 73:103-5 Ja
'71
GILLESPIE, Virginia
Training volunteer camp staff. il Camp Mag
43:16+ Ap '71
GILLETT, Richard W.
Issue of the Puerto Rican copper mines. Chr
Cent 88:857-9 Jl 14 '71
GILLETTE, Bill
Veterans' pheasant hunt. il Outdoor Life
147:64-7+ Je '71
GILLETTE, Guy
Lonely crusade of Guy Gillette. G. James. il
por McCalls 98:62-3+ Ag '71 *
GILLETTE, Jeanette L.
Chisos Mountains: an ecological island. il
Nat Parks & Con Mag 45:4-8 F '71
Mysterious Chisos. il Nat Parks & Con Mag
45:4-10 Ja '71
GILLETTE, Virginia M.
Fiction from fact. Writer 84:11-13 Ap '71
GILLETTE company
Keen drama: a razor is born; twin-blade
project. F. Morgan. il Newsweek 78:78+ O
11 '71
Losing the edge. il Forbes 108:29 Jl 15 '71
GILLHAM DAM and reservoir project (pro-
posed) See Dams
GILLIATT, Penelope
As we have learnt from Freud, there are no
jokes; story. New Yorker 47:36-43 O 2 '71
Current cinema. See issues of New Yorker.
April 3, 1971 to September 25, 1971
F.R.A.N.K; story. New Yorker 47:34-41 My 1
'71
Nobody's business; story. New Yorker 47:22-
9 Jl 3 '71
Penelope Gilliatt talks about Sunday bloody
Sunday; ed. by N. Sayre. por Vogue 158:
100-2 O 15 '71
Position of the planets; story. New Yorker
47:32-8 Ag 14 '71
about
Difficult but triumphant. il por Time 98:82-3
S 27 '71 *
Someone's in the kitchen with Maxine. M.
McKendry il por Vogue 158:66 O 15 '71 *
GILLIE, R. Bruce
Endemic goiter; with biographical sketch. il
Sci Am 224:17, 92-9+ bibliog(p 136) Je '71
GILLIES, John
Sending parable. Chr Cent 88:253-6 F 24 '71
GILLIES, S. and others
Viral RNA polymerases: electron microscopy
of reovirus reaction cores. bibliog il Science
174:694-6 N 12 '71
GILLIGAN, John Joyce
Gilligan's dilemma. por Time 98:10 D 27 '71 *
Rolling along. il por Newsweek 79:13-14 Ja
3 '72 *
GILLILAND, Elizabeth
Ceylon: the bitter harvest. Nation 212:582-
4 My 10 '71
GILLMOR, Donald M.
Crime reporting: from delirium to dialogue.
bibliog f Cur Hist 61:27-34 Jl '71
GILLMORE, Howard E.
Arizona public parks law. il Parks & Rec
6:23+ F '71
GILLS
Central and peripheral control of gill move-
ments in aplysia. I. Kupfermann and oth-
ers. bibliog il Science 174:1252-6 D 17 '71
GILMAN, Alfred G. See Seeds, N. W. jt. auth.

GILMAN, Richard
FemLib case against Sigmund Freud. il pors
N Y Times Mag p 10-11+ Ja 31 '71
Where did it all go wrong? il Life 71:48+
Ag 13 '71
about
Common and uncommon masks, by R. Gil-
man. Review
Nation 212:823-4 Je 28 '71. F. Hirsch *
GILMORE, C. P.
Look and listen. il Pop Sci 199:20 Ag; 38 S;
42+ O; 36+ N; 10 D '71
GILMORE, Clifford F.
Three North American keyboard virtuosos
give Bach a young look. il Hi Fi 21:86-7 S
'71
Total victory in the Bach revolution. il Hi
Fi 21:67-8 Jl '71
GILMORE, Frank F.
Formulating strategy in smaller companies.
bibliog f il Harvard Bsns R 49:71-81 My '71
GILMORE, Gene
Night-stick candidate. il Nation 213:397-8 O 25
'71
GILMORE, J. Herbert, Jr
Black and white gather at the river. il por
Life 71:44-6 N 5 '71 *
GILMORE, John Lewis
Easter sunrise services are for the birds.
Chr Cent 88:433-4 Ap 7 '71
Young Luther. por Chr Today 16:3-4 O 22 '71
GILMORE, Joseph L.
Reunion; story. Redbook 138:62-3 Ja '72
GILMORE, Kenneth O.
Billboards are falling! Read Digest 99:53-4+
D '71
Soviet submarines: new challenge from Cuba.
il Read Digest 98:63-7 My '71
GILSON, Estelle, and Gilson, Saul
Curiosity of history. Am Scholar 40:267-72
Spr '71
GILSON, Saul. See Gilson, E. jt. auth.
GILSVIK, Robert
Grouse: know its spots. il por Outdoor Life
148:82-3+ O '71
GILTS. See Swine
GIMBEL, Peter
Great white shark; photographs. il Life 70:
58-63 Mr 26 '71
GIMER, Richard H.
U.S. supports U.N. resolution condemning
aerial hijacking; statement. Dept State Bul
64:32 Ja 4 '71
U.S. urges support for UNRWA's efforts to
provide essential services to Palestine ref-
ugees; statement, November 23, 1970. Dept
State Bul 64:93-6 Ja 18 '71
GINASTERA, Alberto
At JFK center. S. Fleming. il Hi Fi 21:
MA11-12+ D '71 *
Beatrix Cenci. Criticism
Nation 213:285 S 27 '71 *
Sat R 54:75 S 25 '71 *
Don Rodrigo. Criticism
Hi Fi 21:MA11 Ja '71 *
GINGERBREAD houses. See Cookery, Orna-
mental
GINGERBREAD lady; drama. See Simon, N.
GINGERICH, Owen
Johannes Kepler and the Rudolphine tables.
il por Sky & Tel 42:328-33 D '71
GINGKO. See Ginkgo
GINGKO petrified forest, Wash. See Petrified
forests
GINGRICH, Arnold
Lee Wulff: the complete angler; excerpt from
introd. to Fishing with Lee Wulff, by E. C.
Janes. por Field & S 76:50-1+ N '71
Publisher's page. See issues of Esquire
GINKGO
Gingko, a petrified forest. H. D. Brown. il
Hobbies 76:144+ Ag '71
GINNIE Mae. See United States—Housing
and urban development, Department of
GINNOLD, Richard E.
ILO plan for solving the job crisis in Colom-
bia. bibliog f il Mo Labor R 94:32-40 Mr '71
GINOTT, Haim G.
Teenagers: how to drive parents sane. il To-
days Health 49:20-3 N '71
GINSBERG, Allen
Anti-war games; poem. Ramp Mag 9:40-2 My
'71
GINSBURG, Phil
Repression in Taiwan. New Repub 165:15 Jl
17 '71
GINSENG
Green gold from the forest. C. Baldwin, jr.
il Am For 77:40-3 Ap '71
Lure of ginseng. M. Smith. il McCalls 99:47
O '71
Wild ginseng: the magic root. D. J. Ander-
son. il Field & S 75:66-7+ F '71

GINZBERG, Eli
  Is hard work going out of style? interview.
    il por U S News 71:52-6 **Ag** 23 '71
GINZBURG, N. I. See Brandt, N. B. jt. auth.
GIORDANO, Daniel J.
  Daily control replaces cycle billing. il Am City
    86:109-10 **My** '71
GIORGIONE da Castelfranco
  Tempesta puzzle. R. McMullen. il Horizon 13:
    94-103 Spr '71
GIOSEFFI, Daniela
  Peace prospect; poem. Nation 212:634 **My** 17
    '71
GIOVANNI, Nikki
  Gemini, by N. Giovanni. Review
    Time por 99:63+ Ja 17 '72. M. Duffy •
GIPSY moths. See Gypsy moths
GIRAFFES
  What do you do with a drunken giraffe? il
    Sci Digest 70:14-17 D '71
GIRDLES. See Foundation garments
GIRL athletes. See Women as athletes
GIRL on the trampoline; story. See Fineman,
    M.
GIRL who ate green jelly for breakfast; story.
  See Elliston, V.
GIRL with the gold tooth; story. See Djilas,
    M.
GIRL with the harlequin glasses; story. See
    Colwin, L.
GIRLS
  Boys in your world; excerpts from The new
    Seventeen book of etiquette and young
    living. E. A. Haupt. por Seventeen 29:128-
    31+ N '70
  What boys don't know about girls, and why.
    R. Baker. il McCalls 98:49+ Je '71
  Young living; questions and answers. A.
    Wood. See issues of Seventeen
    See also
  Adolescence
  High school students
  Runaway boys and girls
  Young women
GIRLS books. See Childrens literature
GIRLS in literature. See Women in literature
GIRLS in school sports. See School athletics
GIRLS' junior championship. See Golf—
    Tournaments
GIRLS schools. See Private schools
GIRSON, Rochelle
  Friend to the displaced. il **Sat R 54:30-1+**
    D 4 '71
GITLIN, Todd
  Ellsberg and the new heroism. Commonweal
    94:447-51 S 3 '71
  Return of political poetry. Commonweal 94:
    375-80 Jl 23 '71
GITTELMAN, Martin, and Cleeman, James
  Serum magnesium differences: further evi-
    dence for discontinuity between adult and
    childhood schizophrenia. bibliog il Ment Hy
    55:492-4 O '71
GITTELSON, Natalie
  Needles and pins. See issues of Harper's
    bazaar
GITTINGS, John
  Inside China: in the wake of the cultural
    revolution. il Ramp Mag 10:10-19 Ag '71
GITTLESON, June
  Boon; interview. New Yorker 47:32-3 My 8 '71
GIULINI, Carlo Maria
  New era in Chicago (courtesy of England) H.
    Goldsmith. il por Hi Fi 21:71-2 Ja '71 •
GIVING
  Giving in U.S: now double 1960. il U S News
    70:44 Je 28 '71
  It is more blessed to give than to receive.
    M. N. Kain. il por Good H 173:48+ Ag '71
    See also
  Charities
  Corporations—Charitable contributions
GLACIAL epochs
  Are the glaciers coming back? W. R. Rob-
    inson. il Sci Digest 70:52-7 D '71
  Convection in the Antarctic ice sheet leading
    to a surge of the ice sheet and possibly to
    a new ice age. T. Hughes; reply with re-
    joinder. C. H. Harrison. bibliog il Science
    173:166 Jl 9 '71
GLACIAL geology
    See also
  Teays Valley (preglacial valley)
GLACIERS
  Mercury in a Greenland ice sheet: evidence
    of recent input by man. H. V. Weiss and
    others bibliog il Science 174:692-4 N 12 '71
  Selenium and sulfur in a Greenland ice
    sheet: relation to fossil fuel combustion.
    H. V. Weiss and others. bibliog il Science
    172:261-3 Ap 16 '71
    See also
  Glacial epochs

GLADIEUX, Bob
  Wedge-buster called Harpo by his fans; ed.
    by D. Fisher. por Life 71:41 D 3 '71
GLADIOLUS
  Glads go petite. D. E. Stebbins. il Horticul-
    ture 49:30-1+ Je '71
  Plant matched mates . . . glads and dahlias.
    B. Miles. il Horticulture 49:40-1+ Mr '71
GLADIOLUS, Arrangement of. See Flowers,
    Arrangement of
GLADSTONE, Bernard
  New money-saving materials. il Am Home
    74:62+ My '71
GLANDS
  Sea snakes: an unusual salt gland under the
    tongue. W. A. Dunson and others. bibliog
    il Science 173:437-41 Jl 30 '71
    See also
  Prostate gland
GLANDS, Ductless
    See also
  Adrenal glands
GLASER, Daniel
  From revenge to resocialization: changing
    perspectives in combating crime. Am Schol-
    ar. 40:654-61 Aut '71
GLASER, Peter Edward
  New look at the sun. il Cons 25:22-7 Je '71
GLASPHALT pavements. See Pavements, Glas-
    phalt
GLASS, Bentley. See Glass, H. B.
GLASS, H. Bentley
  Science education, process on content? ex-
    cerpt from The timely and the timeless.
    Science 171:851 Mr 5 '71
  Science: endless horizons or golden age? ad-
    dress, December 28, 1970. bibliog Science
    171:23-9; 172:111-12; 173:103-4 Ja 8, Ap 9, Jl
    9 '71
    about
  Genetic control of man. A. J. Snider. Sci
    Digest 69:56 Ap '71 •
GLASS, Malcolm
  Crux; poem. Chr Cent 88:250 F 24 '71
GLASS
  Needed: a standard for insulating glass;
    sealed insulating glass units. il Arch Rec
    149:133-6 F '71
  New glass means longer life for satellites.
    il Space World H-10-94:45 O '71
  Pitfalls and promises. H. Haessner. il Sch
    Arts 71:22-5 Ja '72
    See also
  Glassware
  Tektites
  Windows

                    Fracture
  Amateur breaks glass with a purpose: to de-
    termine the patterns of fracture. M. E.
    Meichle. il Sci Am 225:122-7 N '71
GLASS, Engraved
  Louis Vaupel, master glass engraver. C. U.
    Fauster. il por Antiques 99:696-701 My '71
GLASS, Ornamental
  Collaboration in glass; interview. ed. by
    E. Erikson. M. Lax. il Craft Horiz 31:12-
    15+ F '71
    See also
  Glass engraving
GLASS, Stained. See Glass painting and stain-
    ing
GLASS, Volcanic. See Obsidian
GLASS blowing and working
  Dale Chihuly: the fluid breath of glass. D.
    Manzella. il por Craft Horiz 31:22-6 D '71
  Lung power. il Mech Illus 67:22 My '71
    See also
  Bottles
GLASS containers
  Sweet memories: glass toy containers. D. G.
    Roberts. il Hobbies 76:98 Jl '71
GLASS engraving
  Time for recognition. P. A. Dickinson. il pors
    Har Yrs 11:36-40 Ja '71
GLASS fabrics
  Glass fabric with cotton's feel; laminate
    called Fibercoat. il Bsns W p62+ Mr 27 '71
GLASS gardens. See Gardens, Miniature
GLASS industry
  Button panel, starred loop, and diamond
    ridge. A. G. Peterson. il Hobbies 75:72-3
    Ja '71
  Collaboration in glass; Gullaskruf, Sweden;
    interview. ed. by E. Erikson. M. Lax. il
    Craft Horiz 31:12-15+ F '71
    See also
  Corning glass works
  Glass manufacture

                    Imports problem
  Glass makers get a break; anti-dumping duties
    on Japanese glass imports. Bsns W p 109+
    Ap 17 '71

GLASS manufacture
Floating glass. Sci Am 224:52 Ap '71
    See also
Glass blowing and working
GLASS mobiles. See Mobiles
GLASS painting and staining
Excitement in glass: making a colored glass
    window. G. Gannon. il Design 72:29-31 Sum
    '71
Luminous art; exhibition of stained glass at
    the Cloisters. D. Davis. il Newsweek 79:59
    Ja 3 '72
Old medium, new messages; D. Phillips of
    Cleveland. il pors Ebony 27:33-6+ D '71
Spruce up your home with real stained glass.
    W. A. Heins. il Pop Sci 198:102-3+ Ap '71
Stained glass design goes mod. R. Moore. il
    Sch Arts 71:12-13 Ja '72
Stained glass: old art, new hobby. il Chang-
    ing T 25:35-6 D '71
Stained glass windows. U. T. Overbaugh. il
    Sch Arts 71:34-5 Ja '72
Your own stained-glass window. E. F. Lind-
    sley and A. Lees. il Pop Sci 198:66-7+ My
    '71
GLASS reuse
    See also
Pavements, Glasphalt
GLASS toy containers. See Glass containers
GLASSBORO conference, 1967
LBJ's view of summit conference: disap-
    pointing. il por U S News 71:79 N 8 '71
GLASSCO, John
For Cora Lightbody, R.N; poem. Poetry 118:
    165 Je '71
            about
We had such good times. M. Cowley. New
    Repub 165:27-8 D 27 '71 *
GLASSER, Ronald J.
Lest their minds become casualties of the
    war; excerpts from 365 days. il Todays
    Health 49:50-5+ N '71
Please read this; excerpt from 365 days. Red-
    book 137:64+ Ag '71
Simpler creed; excerpt from 365 days. il Har-
    per 243:86-7 Jl '71
GLASSER, William
Roles, goals, and failure. il Todays Ed 60:
    20-1+ O '71; Same abr. Ed Digest 37:25-7
    D '71
GLASSMAN, James K.
France. Atlan 227:6+ F '71
Gambling in Britain. Atlan 228:23-4+ S '71
GLASSWARE
Actor's true identity is revealed; actress
    glass, or theatrical glass cheese dishes. F.
    Lenthall. il por Hobbies 76:50+ My '71
American historical glass:
    Administration building; the Columbian
        exposition. M. Wollett and B. Wollett.
        il Hobbies 76:98Z D '71
    Bryan plate. M. Wollett and B. Wollett.
        il Hobbies 76:99 Ja '72
    Hancock plate. M. Wollett and B. Wol-
        lett. il Hobbies 76:72 N '71
American lacy and pressed glass in the To-
    ledo museum of art. J. W. Keefe. il An-
    tiques 100:104-9 Jl '71
Better buy the dozen. A. Walker. il Am
    Home 74:78 N '71
Chain-border tray: three versions. E. Gaines.
    il Antiques 100:256-7 Ag '71
Interest grows in centennial glass-ware;
    Philadelphia centennial of 1876. S. Gores.
    il Hobbies 76:116-17+ Ja '72
Irish glass: some attributions. P. Warren. il
    Antiques 99:854-9 Je '71
Lacy hairpin in French and American glass.
    L. Innes. il Antiques 100:228-32 Ag '71
Let's enjoy Emile Galle's glass. L. F. Reals.
    il Hobbies 76:91 My '71
    See also
Bottles
Corning glass center, Corning, N.Y.
Glass, Engraved
Paperweights

Collectors and collecting
Excellence in continental glass; objects from
    Germany, Poland, and Bohemia in the
    collection of R. Von Strasser. R. G. Von
    Strasser. il Antiques 101:153-60 Ja '72

Exhibitions
Toledo glass national. il Ceram Mo 19:28 My
    '71

GLASSWARE industry. See Glass industry
GLATSTEIN, Jacob
Journey of a poet. I. Howe. Commentary
    53:75-7 Ja '72 *
GLATTHORN, Allan A.
Training teachers for excellence. il Parents
    Mag 46:68-70+ S '71

GLAUCOMA
Was Van Gogh going blind? Sci Digest 70:30
    N '71
GLAZE, Andrew
Stonewall; poem. Atlan 228:103 S '71
GLAZER, Nathan
Limits of social policy; excerpt from address,
    September 1970. Commentary 52:51-8 S '71
On being deradicalized. Commentary 50:74-
    80 O '70; 51:22-3 Ja; 25 Ap '71
Puerto Rican migration: right place, wrong
    time? America 125:339-41 O 30 '71
Role of the intellectuals; excerpt from ad-
    dress. Commentary 51:55-61 F '71
Vietnam: the case for immediate withdrawal.
    Commentary 51:33-7 My '71
When the melting pot doesn't melt. il N Y
    Times Mag p 12-13+ Ja 2 '72
GLAZES and glazing
Are lead glazes dangerous? reprint, with
    editorial comment. E. Littlefield. Ceram
    Mo 19:9, 25 Ja '71
Barium glazes. R. Behrens. Ceram Mo 19:27
    O '71
Basic matt glazes for cone 4. R. Behrens.
    Ceram Mo 19:33 D '71
Cone 6 reduction glazes. R. Behrens. il Ceram
    Mo 20:12 Ja '72
Fluoride glazes for cones 06, 4 and 6. R.
    Behrens. il Ceram Mo 19:33 S '71
Formulary of leadless glazes. R. Behrens.
    Ceram Mo 19:24+ F '71
Herbert Sanders; pioneer in porcelain crystal-
    line glazes. F. Ball. il por Ceram Mo 19:14-
    17 N '71
Nepheline syenite glazes. R. Behrens. il
    Ceram Mo 19:33 Je '71
Rosy gold glazes. R. Behrens. Ceram Mo 19:
    26+ Mr '71
Some glaze faults, and their correction. R.
    Behrens. il Ceram Mo 20:28-9 Ja '72 (to be
    cont)
Two-component glazes. R. Behrens. Ceram
    Mo 19:33 My '71
Using volumetric measurements for glazes.
    R. S. Russell. il Sch Arts 71:26-7 Ja '72
GLAZIER, Kenneth M.
Overdue. por Wilson Lib Bul 45:686-7 Mr '71
GLEASON, Herbert Wendell
Rare collection of early wilderness photog-
    raphy. il Am West 8:16-27 Jl '71
GLEN Campbell Open golf tournament. See
    Golf—Tournaments
GLENN, Morton B.
50 most asked diet questions. Ladies Home J
    88:72+ My '71; Same abr. with title What
    everyone wants to know about weight con-
    trol. Read Digest 99:54-7 Ag '71
GLENN, Tyree
Unforgettable Satchmo. il por Read Digest
    99:81-5 D '71
GLENNER, G. G. and others
Amyloid fibril proteins: proof of homology
    with immunoglobulin light chains by se-
    quence analyses. bibliog il Science 172:1150-
    1 Je 11 '71
Creation of "amyloid" fibrils from Bence
    Jones proteins in vitro. bibliog il Science
    174:712-14 N 12 '71
GLENNY, Michael
(tr) See Solzhenitsyn, A. I. Elm log; Storm
    in the mountains
GLENWOOD mission inn. See Riverside, Calif.
    —Hotels, restaurants, etc.
GLICK, David S. pseud.
Black power enclave. New Repub 164:11-12
    Ja 16 '71
GLICK, G. Wayne
Laws of men and the law of God. Chr Cent
    88:1225-9 O 20 '71
GLICK, Henry Robert
System of state and local courts. bibliog f
    Cur Hist 60:341-6 Je '71
GLICK, John Theodore
Laws of men and the law of God. G. W.
    Glick. Chr Cent 88:1225-9 O 20 '71 *
GLICK, Ted. See Glick, J. T.
GLICKSTEIN, Howard A.
Civil rights: hopes of '60s and problems of
    '70s; excerpts from testimony, August 4,
    1971. por U S News 71:25 Ag 23 '71
GLIDE memorial united Methodist church. See
    San Francisco—Churches
GLIDERS (aeronautics)
New wave in soaring. G. B. Moffat, jr. il Pop
    Sci 199:66-8+ S '71
    See also
Gliding and soaring
GLIDING and soaring
Upward miracle. W. Langewiesche. il Harper
    243:124-6+ N '71
You can watch from below, you can go for
    a ride, or you can take lessons. il Sunset
    146:44+ F '71

GLINES, C. V.
Pick up the phone and learn the earth's secrets. il Nations Bsns 59:48-51 D '71
GLIXON, David M.
SR's semiannual reference book roundup (cont) Sat R 54:39-43+ Ap 17; 44+ D 4 '71
(ed) Your literary I.Q. See issues of Saturday review
GLOAG, John
Final graces of the Georgian age: regency furniture. il Antiques 99:574-9 Ap '71
Rocking chair in Victorian England. il Antiques 99:241-4 F '71
GLOBAL atmospheric research program. See Weather research
GLOBAL rescue alarm net. See Artificial satellites—Use in rescue work
GLOBAL temperature changes
Atmospheric carbon dioxide and aerosols: effects of large increases on global climate. S. I. Rasool and S. H. Schneider. bibliog il Science 173:138-41 Jl 9 '71; Discussion. 173:982-3 S 10 '71
Atmospheric dust increase could lower earth's temperature. G. B. Lubkin. il Phys Today 24:17+ O '71
Is man changing earth's temperature? Sky & Tel 42:272 N '71
GLOBE (Boston)
They love it in Boston; or, How the Globe's book section works. B. A. Bannon. il por Pub W 199:69-70 My 31 '71
GLOBOID cell leukodystrophy. See Leukodystrophy
GLOBULAR clusters. See Stars—Clusters
GLOBULINS
　　See also
Concanavalins
Gamma globulin
Immunoglobulins
GLOMAR Challenger (ship) See Ships, Research
GLOMERULONEPHRITIS. See Kidneys—Diseases
GLOSSOLALIA. See Gift of tongues
GLOVER, Tony
America is still singing. il Sr Schol 98:36-7+ Mr 29 '71
GLOVES
Complete guide to work gloves. R. Douglas. il Mech Illus 67:86-8+ Jl '71
GLOVES, Rubber
Household gloves. il Consumer Bul 54:14-15 O '71
GLOWKA, Arthur
Hideaway hobby center. il Pop Sci 199:95 S '71
New York's ice trout bonanza. il Outdoor Life 148:38-9+ D '71
GLUCAGON
Cyclic adenosine and guanosine monophosphates and glucagon: effect on liver membrane potentials. N. Friedmann and others. bibliog il Science 171:400-2 Ja 29 '71
Immunogenicity of glucagon: determinants responsible for antibody binding and lymphocyte stimulation. G. Senyk and others. bibliog il Science 171:407-8 Ja 29 '71
GLUCK, Christoph Willibald
Orfeo ed Euridice. Criticism
Hi Fi 20:MA15 D '70 *
GLUCK, Louis
Saving the preemies. il por Newsweek 78: 71 Ag 16 '71 *
GLUCK, Louise
Undertaking; Fortress; Land's End; Magi; Archipelago; Shad-blow tree; poems. Poetry 118:63-5 My '71

about

Comment. L. Mueller. Poetry 117:324-5 F '71 *
GLUCOCORTICOIDS. See Corticosteroids
GLUCOSE
Cyclic adenosine 3', 5'-monophosphate during glucose repression in the rat liver. O. Sudilovsky and others. bibliog il Science 174:142-4 O 8 '71
GLUE
Glues and adhesives: an up-to-date use guide. Good H 172:179 Mr '71
Glues for household use. Consumer Bul 54: 35-6 F '71
　　See also
Adhesives
GLUECK, Eleanor (Touroff)
Moving toward wholesale permissiveness; interview. il por U S News 70:68-70 Ja 25 '71
GLUECK, Grace
Ivory tower versus the discotheque. il pors Art in Am 59:80-5 My '71
New York. See issues of Art in America
Power and esthetics: the trustee. il Art in Am 59:78-83 Jl '71

GLUECK, Nelson
Worthy tribute. E. M. Yamauchi. Chr Today 16:26-7 O 22 '71 *
GLUECK, Sheldon
Moving toward wholesale permissiveness; interview. il por U S News 70:68-70 Ja 25 '71
GLUNT, Ruth Reynolds
Winter on the Hudson. il Cons 26:18-19 D '71
GLUTAMIC-pyruvic transaminase. See Transferases
GLUTAMINASE
L-Glutaminase: suppression of lymphocyte blastogenic responses in vitro. E. M. Hersh and others. bibliog il Science 172:736-8 My 14 '71
GLUTATHIONE
Biphasic feeding response in a sea anemone: control by asparagine and glutathione. K. J. Lindstedt. bibliog il Science 173:333-4 Jl 23 '71
GLYCERIDES
Ethanol stimulates triglyceride synthesis by the intestine. E. A. Carter and others. bibliog il Science 174:1245-7 D 17 '71
There's more than cholesterol behind heart attacks; triglyceride problem. R. H. Berg. Look 35:51-2 F 9 '71
GLYCOGEN
Glycogen plastids in Müllerian body cells of cecropia peltata, a higher green plant. F. R. Rickson. bibliog il Science 173:344-7 Jl 23 '71
GLYCOPEPTIDES. See Peptides
GLYCOPROTEINS
Glycoproteins as biological antifreeze agents in Antarctic fishes. A. L. DeVries. bibliog il Science 172:1152-5 Je 11 '71
Glycoproteins: isolation from cell membranes with lithium diiodosalicylate. V. T. Marchesi and E. P. Andrews. bibliog il Science 174:1247-8 D 17 '71
GLYNDEBOURNE festival. See Music festivals —England
GLYNN, Edward
Faith in focus (cont) America 124:96-7, 153-4 Ja 30, F 13 '71
Overdue first word on peace and war. il America 125:396-7 N 13 '71
GLYNN, Joan
Executive mother. L. Botto. il pors Look 35: 73+ Ja 26 '71 *
GMEINER, Hermann
Father to the orphans of three continents. M. Moyal. il por Chr Cent 88:752-4 Je 16 '71 *
GNOSTICISM
Riddle of the abraxas amulets. il UNESCO Courier 24:8-9 My '71
GNOTOBIOTICS. See Germfree life
GOA
Goa, end of the line. S. Labin. Nat R 23:750-3 Jl 13 '71
GOALS, National. See United States
GOAT hunting
　　See also
Rocky Mountain goat hunting
GOATS
Notes by a new goat-keeper. N. W. Bubel. il por Org Gard & Farm 18:104-11 Mr '71
　　See also
Rocky Mountain goats
GOATS milk. See Milk, Goats
GOBA, Ronald Joseph
Marshall McLuhan and Sir Patrick Spens. Engl J 60:62-4 Ja '71
GOBAR, Alfred
Stadiums for small communities. il Parks & Rec 6:31-4+ Je '71
GOBEL, Walter, Jr
Poem for Geoff; story. Todays Ed 60:14-15 D '71
GOBIES
Who says fish can't climb trees? I. Polunin. il Nat Geog 141:84-91 Ja '72
GOBINEAU, Joseph Arthur, comte de
Aryan myth. M. D. Biddiss. il por Horizon 13:96-101 Sum '71
GOD
After the death of God the father. M. Daly. Commonweal 94:7-11 Mr 12 '71; Discussion. 94:275+ My 28 '71
Again, the mystery of God. V. P. McCorry. America 124:272-3 Mr 13 '71
God in the dock, by C. S. Lewis. Review
America 124:617-18 Je 12 '71. B. Nauer
Is God she? And so what? T. Weiss-Rosmarin. Commonweal 94:374 Jl 23 '71; Discussion. 94:467+ S 17 '71
Moses encounters the daemonic aspect of God. D. F. Zeligs. bibliog Am Imago 27: 379-91 Wint '70
New paganism. G. Meilaender, jr. il Chr Today 15:4-6 S 24 '71

GOD—*Continued*
Right answers, wrong questions. M. Blanchard. Chr Today 15:8-10 Ag 6 '71
Secular Christianity and God who acts, by R. J. Blaikie. Review
　Chr Today 15:41-2 Mr 12 '71. C. F. H. Henry
Theology confronts women's liberation. E. Woo. America 124:257-9 Mr 13 '71
　See also
Atheism
Christianity
Trinity
Trust in God
　Attributes
Limitations of God. L. McKenzie. Cath World 214:105-8 D '71
　Mercy
God merciful. V. P. McCorry. America 125: 132-4 S 4 '71
　Proof
Reviewing the proofs. G. C. Berkouwer. Chr Today 16:53-4 N 5 '71
　Transcendence
　See Transcendence of God
GOD, Grace of. See Grace (theology)
GODARD, Jean Luc
Current cinema. P. Gilliatt. New Yorker 47: 116+ My 8 '71 *
Toward a non-bourgeois camera style; excerpt from Weekend and history. B. Henderson. il Film Q 24:2-14 Wint '70 *
GODBEY, Geoffrey
Leisure: nearing the receding horizon. bibliog Parks & Rec 6:33-4+ Ag '71
GODDARD, David R. and Koons, L. C.
Intellectual freedom and the university. bibliog Science 173:607-10 Ag 13 '71
GODDARD, James Lee
Excerpt from testimony, September 16, 1969. Cong Digest 50:55+ F '71
GODDARD, Paulette
Quartet of queens. J. Barthel. il pors Life 70:62+ F 19 '71 *
GODFATHER (board game) See Games
GODFRAY, Graham
Passaging a 12-meter. il Yachting 130:60-1+ D '71
GODFREY, Aaron W.
Faculty as enemy. America 124:630-2 Je 19 '71
GODFREY, Arthur
We have a long way to go: and time is running out; address, July 13, 1971. il pors Cons 26:8-14 O '71
GODFREY, Mark, and Okamura, Akihiko
End of Lam Son 719; photographs. Life 70: 16D-28 Ap 2 '71
GODINE, David R, publisher
Young publisher, young hands keep fine printing alive. C. B. Grannis. il Pub W 199: 126-7 My 31 '71
GODMOTHERS & all that; story. See Wright, B. R.
GODOLI, Giovanni
Old Mount Etna observatory and the new. il Sky & Tel 42:20-1 Jl '71
GODS and goddesses
　See also
Mother goddesses
GODSPELL; musical comedy. See Musical comedies, revues, etc.—Criticisms, plots, etc.
GODWIN, Gail
Sorrowful woman; story. Esquire 76:75-6 Ag '71
GOEDICKE, Patricia
Looking through the window at the future; Spitfire; Love song; for the four corners; poems. Poetry 118:143-4 Je '71
GOELLER, Carl
Realities of the greeting card market. Writer 84:18-20+ D '71
GOETHE, Johann Wolfgang von
Shooting star. F. Stevenson. il Opera N 35. 24-6 Mr 27 '71 *
GOETTSCH, Roger A.
Three pottery workshops in England. il Ceram Mo 19:13-19 F '71
GOETZ, Fidel
How Penn Central lost in Liechtenstein. Bsns W p41 Mr 13 '71 *
GOETZ, Ronald
Demythologizing modern man. il Chr Cent 88:1321-5 N 10 '71
Paris must. Chr Cent 88:646 My 26 '71
GOFF, William R. See Donald, M. W. jr. jt. auth.
GOFFART, Walter
Zosimus, the first historian of Rome's fall. bibliog f Am Hist R 76:412-41 Ap '71

GOFMAN, John William
Nuclear power and ecocide: an adversary view of new technology. por Bul Atom Sci 27:28-32 S '71
　about
Fallout from the peaceful atom. P. Winslow. Nation 212:557-61 My 3 '71. Reply with rejoinder. J. A. Harris. 212:738 Je 14 '71 *
GOGERTY, Rex
Window on yesterday. il Farm J 95:42-3 Ja '71
GOGH, Vincent van
Was Van Gogh going blind? Sci Digest 70: 30 N '71
　about
Vincent van Gogh, 1880-1971. J. Rewald. il pors Art N 69:53-5+ F '71 *
GOHEEN, Robert F.
Goheen goes. Time 97:45 Ap 5 '71 *
GOINGS, Russell L. jr
Big board's first black-owned firm. por Bsns W p78+ Mr 20 '71 *
Green is beautiful. il por Duns 97:68-9 Ap '71 *
GOINS, Nellie Louise
Nitro Nellie: lady drag racer. il pors Ebony 27:63-4+ N '71 *
GOINS, Thomas
Annals of law. E. J. Kahn, jr. New Yorker 46:76-84 F 6 '71 *
GOITER
Circulating immunoglobulin M: increased concentrations in endemic and sporadic goiter. S. C. Werner and others; reply. W. T. London and R. L. Vought. Science 171:928 Mr 5 '71
Endemic goiter. R. B. Gillie. il Sci Am 224:92-9+ bibliog(p 136) Je '71
GOLD, Herbert
Death on the East side; story. Esquire 75: 140 My '71
Marriage is not enough. Vogue 157:137+ F 1 '71
On epidemic first personism. Atlan 228:85-7 Ag '71
Would you buy a used manuscript from this man? il por N Y Times Mag p 12-13+ Ja 31 '71
GOLD, Phil
Cancer breakthrough. J. Hirschy. il por Life 70:28-31 Ap 23 '71 *
GOLD, Thomas
After the final Apollo flight, says an astrophysicist, we should deploy machines, not men, in space. il N Y Times Mag p 16-17+ Ag 22 '71
GOLD, Victor
Shepherd to the wordsmith. il pors Time 98:77 O 18 '71 *
GOLD
　See also
Gold buying
Goldsmithing
　Prices
Who has the world's gold? il Time 98:25 N 8 '71
GOLD as money
Beggar my neighbor. New Repub 165:8-9 O 16 '71
Gold; Gold reserve act of 1934. M. Friedman. Newsweek 78:69 Ag 16 '71
Gold has lost its glitter. G. J. Henry. il Forbes 108:88 O 1 '71
Golden gift. Nat R 23:1100 O 8 '71
How to understand gold crisis; answers to questions. il U S News 71:21-2 S 6 '71
Is gold losing its glitter? il U S News 72:31 Ja 3 '72
Wall Street:
　Rising above the dollar. C. Morgello. il Newsweek 77:80 My 10 '71
　History
Monetary gold: to have or have not. T. Cusack. America 125:555-7 D 25 '71
GOLD buying
What's as good as gold? Gold. il Newsweek 78:86-7 D 13 '71
GOLD coins. See Coins
GOLD medal awards. See Sports foundation, inc.
GOLD mines and mining
　Canada
Survival at 70 below: it's easier these days; Klondike gold rush. B. Hildenbrand. il Todays Health 49:46-9+ F '71
　United States
Golden dreams and silver realities; excerpts from Gold and silver in the West. T. H. Watkins. il Am West 8:34-43 My '71

GOLD mines and mining—United States—
    Continued
Homestake gold: 1971; excerpts from Gold
    and silver in the West. T. H. Watkins.
    il Am West 8:24-31 S '71
Maryland's idle gold. B. Thomas. il Travel
    136:36-9 N '71
GOLD pennant marinas. See Marinas
GOLD prospecting. See Prospecting
GOLD work. See Goldsmithing
GOLDABER, Irving
    Doctor to the cities. il por Newsweek 78:36
    S 6 '71 •
GOL'DANSKII, Vitalii Iosifovich
    Science's hunt for the missing links of na-
    ture. il UNESCO Courier 24:28-31 Je '71
GOLDBACH, Kenneth P.
    Phoenix plan at Brookhaven. Cons 25:30 F
    '71
GOLDBARTH, Albert
    Survival; poem. Poetry 117:365 Mr '71
GOLDBERG, Art
    Bobby and Ericka: free at last, until next
    time. Ramp Mag 10:45-8 Ag '71
    Vietnam vets: the anti-war army. il Ramp
    Mag 10:10-17 Jl '71
GOLDBERG, Arthur
    6-4-4+: the ultimate structure. il Clear House
    46:10-14 S '71
GOLDBERG, Arthur Joseph
    India-Pakistan war. New Repub 165:7-9 D 18
    '71
GOLDBERG, Danny
    Grand Funk Railroad; pro. il Sr Schol 99:23-4
    S 27 '71
GOLDBERG, Edward D. See Bertine. K. K.
    jt. auth.
GOLDBERG, Eric
    Behind the scenes with a teenage animator;
    interview, ed. by D. Molner. il pors Schol
    Teach Jr/Sr High p 16-17 My 3 '71
GOLDBERG, Maxwell H.
    Humanities teaching and the mankind em-
    phasis Sch & Soc 99:176-8 Mr '71
GOLDBERG, Michael E. See Wurtz, R. H. jt.
    auth.
GOLDBERG, Norman
    Our stone-age cameras. il Pop Phot 68:69-73
    F '71
    Shop talk. See issues of Popular photography
GOLDBERG, Reuben Lucius. See Goldberg,
    Rube
GOLDBERG, Rube
    Rube Goldberg. J. Markow. Writers Digest
    51:46-8 Mr '71 •
    Rube Goldberg. il Design 72:10-13 Spr '71 •
GOLDBERG, Steven
    Senile society: a theory. Yale R 61:1-25 O
    '71
GOLDBERG variations; ballet. See Ballets—
    Criticisms
GOLDBERGER, Paul
    Less is more: Mies van der Rohe; less is
    a bore: Robert Venturi. il N Y Times Mag
    p34-7+ O 17 '71
    (ed) See Segal, E. W. Erich Segal's identity
    crisis
GOLDBLOOM, Maurice J.
    Two Greeces. il Commonweal 93:441-4 F 5 '71
GOLDEN, J. and Mongan, T. R.
    Sulfur dioxide emissions from power plants;
    their effect on air quality. il Science 171:
    381-3: 173:981 Ja 29. S 10 '71
GOLDEN, L. L. L.
    Public relations. See issues of Saturday
    review
GOLDEN, Morton
    Pigskin sex. Time 99:48 Ja 10 '72 •
GOLDEN, Soma. See Greene. W. jt. auth.
GOLDEN bamboo. See Bamboo
GOLDEN eagles. See Eagles
GOLDEN marmosets. See Marmosets
GOLDENBERG, Gerald J. and others
    Transport of nitrogen mustard on the trans-
    port-carrier for choline in L5178Y lympho-
    blasts. bibliog il Science 172:1148-9 Je 11 '71
GOLDENBERG, Mauricio, and Sluzki, C. E.
    Setting up a psychiatric service in a general
    hospital. bibliog Ment Hy 55:85-90 Ja '71
GOLDENSOHN, Barry
    Morning of execution; Man of words en-
    counters the circle of infinite radius whose
    center is everywhere and whose circum-
    ference is nowhere; Time and the string
    quartet domesticate Eros; poems. Poetry
    118:323-4 S '71
GOLDER, Robert M.
    CIDOC: alternatives in design and education.
    il Arch Rec 150:117-18 Jl '71
GOLDFARB, Ronald L.
    Why don't we tear down our prisons? Look
    35:45-7 Jl 27 '71

GOLDFINGER, Myron Henry
    Architect speaks his mind; interview, ed. by
    A. Stagg. por House & Gard 139:16+ Je '71
GOLDFISCHER, Sidney, and others
    Hypolipidemia in a mutant strain of acat-
    alasemic mice. bibliog il Science 173:65-6 Jl
    2 '71
GOLDFISH
    One-trial learning and biphasic time course of
    performance in the goldfish. W. H. Riege
    and A. Cherkin. bibliog il Science 172:966-8
    My 28 '71
GOLDICH, S. S.
    Lunar and terrestrial ilmenite basalt. bibliog
    il Science 171:1245-6 Mr 26 '71
GOLDMAN, Albert
    Audience as artist. Vogue 157:135-6 F 1 '71
    Can primal therapy shortcut the return to
    happiness? il por Vogue 158:270-1 S 1 '71
    Jazz meets rock; excerpt from Freakshow. il
    Atlan 227:98-101+ F '71
    Life music review (cont) Life 70:12 Mr 12;
    16 Ap 9: 14 My 28: 71:16 Jl 30 '71
    What Lenny Bruce was all about. il pors N Y
    Times Mag p 12-13+ Je 27 '71

    about
    Man in a maelstrom. J. Kroll. il por News-
    week 77:113+ My 10 '71 •
GOLDMAN, Emma
    Living my life. K. S. Lynn. New Repub
    165:26-8 N 27 '71 •
GOLDMAN, Harry L.
    Nikola Tesla's bold adventure. il por Am West
    8:4-9 Mr '71
GOLDMAN, James A.
    Cogito ergo sentio. Chem 44:4 Mr '71
    Homo loquens. Chem 44:2 Jl '71
GOLDMAN, Julie
    Two women who broke up the Beatles. pors
    McCalls 98:72-3+ Jl '71
GOLDMAN, M. C.
    College campus, new home for organic foods.
    il Org Gard & Farm 18:86-7 Ag '71
    Law and organic living. Org Gard & Farm
    18:104-10 D '71
GOLDMAN, Marshall I.
    Has the environment a future? Nation 213:
    358-61 O 18 '71
    More heat in the Soviet hothouse. bibliog f
    il Harvard Bsns R 49:4-6+ Jl '71
    Our far-flung correspondents. New Yorker
    47:58-66 Je 19 '71
GOLDMAN, Merle
    Aftermath of China's cultural revolution.
    Cur Hist 61:165-70+ S '71
GOLDMAN, Peter, and Holt, Don
    How justice works: the people vs. Donald
    Payne. il pors Newsweek 77:20-4+ Mr 8 '71
GOLDMAN, Sheldon
    American judges: their selection, tenure, va-
    riety, and quality. bibliog f il Cur Hist 61:1-
    8+ Jl '71
GOLDMAN, Sachs and company
    Heavy, heavy . . . il Forbes 108:21 Ag 15 '71
GOLDMARK, Peter Carl
    How to keep 'em down on the farm; inter-
    view. il por Forbes 108:74+ S 15 '71
GOLDNER, Nancy
    Dance (cont) Nation 212:156-7, 251-2, 348-9,
    443-5, 636-7, 731-2: 213:28-9, 91-3, 507-9,
    635-6; 214:58 F 1, 22, Mr 15, Ap 5, My 17,
    Je 7, Jl 5, Ag 2, N 15, D 13 '71, Ja 10 '72
GOLDREICH, Gloria
    Why are the trees moving? story. Ladies
    Home J 88:56 F '71
GOLDRICH, Nancy. See Dethier, V. G. jt. auth.
GOLDSCHMIDT, E. E. and others
    Auxins in citrus: a reappraisal. bibliog Sci-
    ence 174:1256-7 D 17 '71
GOLDSCHMIDT, Jean
    Pursuits; story. Atlan 227:63-6 Je '71
GOLDSCHMIDT, Walter
    Equinoxial rites of the National research
    council. Science 174:474-6 O 29 '71
GOLDSMITH, Arthur
    How to make your portfolio pay. il Pop
    Phot 68:110-11+ Je '71
GOLDSMITH, Harris
    Beethoven on records (cont) Hi Fi 21:61-2 Ja
    Beethoven violin concerto for piano. Hi Fi
    21:92 N '71
    Eighteen chamber masterpieces, gloriously
    performed. il Hi Fi 21:83-4 S '71
    Fox meets the rabbit. il pors Hi Fi 21:6-12
    My '71
    Grotesqueries by Alkan and Lewenthal. Hi
    Fi 21:86 O '71
    New era in Chicago (courtesy of England)
    il por Hi Fi 21:71-2 Ja '71
    Old masters remastered. il Hi Fi 21:71-3 Mr
    '71

GOLDSMITH, Harris—*Continued*
Rachmaninoff eruption. il Hi Fi 21:69-70 Jl '71
Serkin and Beethoven's Hammerklavier. Hi Fi 21:86 D '71
Sibelius' forgotten masterpiece. por Hi Fi 21:87 N '71

GOLDSMITH, Joel Solomon
Key to happiness; excerpts from Living the infinite way. U S News 71:108 S 20 '71

GOLDSMITH, John R. See Hexter, A. C. jt. auth.

GOLDSMITH, Oliver
She stoops to conquer. Criticism
Time il 97:69 My 17 '71 •

GOLDSMITH, Timothy H. See Mote, M. I; Zimmerman, W. F. jt. auths.

GOLDSMITHING
Gold of Coclé. R. A. Cowes. il Américas 23: S36-40 Je '71
See also
Gilding
Jewelry, Ancient

GOLDSMITHS
Rundell, Bridge and Rundell, aurifices regis. J. F. Hayward. il Antiques 99:860-5; 100: 110-15 Je-Jl '71
See also
Sanderson, R.

GOLDSTEIN, Al
No place to go but up. il pors Time 97:65 Ap 19 '71 •

GOLDSTEIN, Avram, and Judson, B. A.
Alcohol dependence and opiate dependence: lack of relationship in mice. bibliog il Science 172:290-2 Ap 16 '71

GOLDSTEIN, Donald P.
Pregnant? Find out early. Newsweek 78:68 N 29 '71 •

GOLDSTEIN, Dora B. and Pal, Nandita
Alcohol dependence produced in mice by inhalation of ethanol; grading the withdrawal reaction. bibliog il Science 172:288-90 Ap 16 '71

GOLDSTEIN, Harold
Wages of truth. il por Time 98:34 O 11 '71 •

GOLDSTEIN, Jerome
Adversary classrooms vs. strip mines. il Org Gard & Farm 18:58-61 Ag '71
Adversary scientists & agricultural renegades. Org Gard & Farm 18:77-80 Ap '71
National farmers organization to market organic crops. il Org Gard & Farm 18:79-83 D '71
Organic farmer section is reborn. il Org Gard & Farm 18:56-8 S '71
Step closer to adversary centers. Org Gard & Farm 18:80-3 Jl '71

GOLDSTEIN, Joseph
Meaning of Calley. New Repub 164:13-14 My 8 '71

GOLDSTEIN, Richard
Look at the '50s. il Mlle 74:134-5+ N '71
Movies. il Vogue 158:179 O 1 '71
Performing arts. Harper 243:32+ O '71

GOLDSTON, Eli
Books & ideas. il por Fortune 84:137+ O '71

GOLDWATER, Barry Morris, 1909-
Adequate defense posture; address, December 4, 1970. Vital Speeches 37:230-2 F 1 '71
Goldwater: Congress knew what it was doing on Vietnam; address, July 29, 1971. il por U S News 71:88-91 Ag 16 '71
Is America going isolationist? interview. por U S News 70:26-7 Je 28 '71

about
How Goldwater sees it. Nat R 23:1045-6 S 24 '71 •

GOLDWATER, Barry Morris, 1939?-
Forty thousand dollars per minute; address, March 6, 1971. Vital Speeches 37:392-4 Ap 15 '71

GOLDWATER, Leonard J.
Mercury in the environment; with biographical sketch. il Sci Am 224:12, 15-21 bibliog (p 132) My '71

GOLDWATER, Robert
Rothko's black paintings. il Art in Am 59: 58-63 Mr '71

GOLF
For want of a teeshot. . ; Japanese golf. S. Servaas. il Holiday 49:38-40+ Jl '71
My drive to be a champion. W. Bingham. il Sports Illus 35:74-7+ O 4 '71
Not infected with the conceit of infallibility; ed. by J. Underwood. S. T. Agnew. il pors Sports Illus 34:60-2+ Je 21 '71
Often bloody, but uncowed; D. Hill. M. Cope. por Sports Illus 34:50-2+ My 10 '71
Put away the putter and go for the pin. McIlvanney. il por Sports Illus 34:16-17 Je 28 '71

Sportsman of the year: L. Trevino. C. Kirkpatrick. il pors Sports Illus 35:34-9 D 20 '71
See also
Golf courses
Ladies professional golf association
Putting (golf)

Study and teaching

Vee vee the one, two . . ; Southern California high school golf program. L. D. Avance. il Parks & Rec 6:28-9+ N '71

Tournaments

Aloha for a bright young blond: T. Shaw in Hawaiian Open championship. D. Jenkins. il por Sports Illus 34:20-1 F 15 '71
And for their next number; A. Palmer and J. Nicklaus 1971 National team championship winners. M. Cope. il pors Sports Illus 35:44+ Ag 9 '71
Arnie and Sam; Westchester classic. por Newsweek 78:75 Ag 9 '71
Arnie re-arms while Lee flees; Westchester golf classic. C. Kirkpatrick. il pors Sports Illus 35:20-1 Ag 2 '71
Arnie's desert campaign; Bob Hope desert classic. Time 97:62 Mr 1 '71
Bad luck ends in a pot of gold; Sears women's world classic. W. Bingham. il por Sports Illus 34:59-60 Mr 1 '71
Dominance of the smiling bear; J. Nicklaus at the PGA. D. Jenkins. il pors Sports Illus 34:22-5 Mr 8 '71
Flailings of a zealot: G. Player in the World match play. H. McIlvanney. il por Sports Illus 35:31-3 O 18 '71
Fluttering start for a hungry Hawk; Harrelson at Little American golf classic. M. Mulvoy. por Sports Illus 35:60+ Ag 16 '71
For Jack, that beat goes on; World cup championship. D. Jenkins. il por Sports Illus 35:88-90 N 22 '71
Formful win in a most formful affair; U.S. girls' junior championship. H. Peterson. il Sports Illus 35:48+ Ag 23 '71
Game man might risk a bet; winning the grand slam: the Masters, the U.S. Open, the British Open, and the PGA. J. Nicklaus. il por Sports Illus 34:40-2+ Je 7 '71
Gentle Ben roughs up the college crowd; NCAA golf championship, Tucson national golf club. C. Kirkpatrick. il por Sports Illus 35:46-7 Jl 5 '71
Ghosts of Merion; U.S. Open golf tournament. il Sports Illus 34:32-7 Je 14 '71
Golf's biggest money winner; L. Trevino. il pors Newsweek 78:57-61 Jl 19 '71
Heads roll at head to head; Liggett & Myers inc. tournament players' division U.S. professional match play championship. D. Jenkins. il por Sports Illus 35:12-16 S 6 '71
L.A. Open dresses up in Glen's plaids. D. Jenkins. Sports Illus 34:69-70 Ja 18 '71
Lady pros seek golf glory; blacks on LPGA tour. il pors Ebony 26:106-8+ Jl '71
Look what Gary found in the cup! U.S. amateur title. J. Jares. il por Sports Illus 35:24-5 S 13 '71
Making up for the lost cup; losing the Walker cup winning the British amateur tournament. C. Kirkpatrick. il Sports Illus 34: 65-6 Je 14 '71
Meet me in St Louis, but at your own risk: Ryder cup matches. Great Britain vs U.S. G. S. Brown. il Sports Illus 35:88-90 S 27 '71
Now for the Mexican Open; L. Trevino. D. Jenkins. il por Sports Illus 35:12-15 Jl 19 '71
Old pro teaches the teachers; PGA club professional championship at Pinehurst. G. S. Brown. por Sports Illus 35:85-6 O 25 '71
Our Jack in fields of gold; Tournament of champions. D. Jenkins. il por Sports Illus 34:16-19 My 3 '71
Over the bunkers; racially mixed South African professional golf association championship. il Newsweek 78:44 D 6 '71
Poor boy makes good; 1971 Masters. il por Newsweek 77:67 Ap 26 '71
Pro who runs the tour; J. Tuthill, the PGA's tournament director. W. Bingham. il pors Sports Illus 34:52-5 Mr 15 '71
Remember the battle of Merion; U.S. Open. D. Jenkins. il pors Sports Illus 34:12-15 Je 28 '71
Sheriff Coody interrupts the showdown at Firestone; World series of golf. C. Kirkpatrick. Sports Illus 35:84+ S 20 '71
Showcase for the big names; Masters tournament. D. Jenkins. il Sports Illus 34:38-9 Ap 5 '71
Some friends of Harry Lillis; Bing Crosby national pro-amateur. D. Jenkins. il Sports Illus 34:54-5 Ja 25 '71

GOLF—Tournaments—*Continued*
Sporting scene; Masters tournament, in Augusta, Ga. H. W. Wind. New Yorker 47:95-101 My 8 '71
Sporting scene; United States Open at Merion. H. W. Wind. New Yorker 47:56-8+ Jl 17 '71
Thanks for the memory; Bob Hope desert classic. A. Wright. il pors Sports Illus 34:12-15 F 22 '71
There went the slam: Nicklaus vs Coody at Masters tournament. D. Jenkins. il por Sports Illus 34:16-19 Ap 19 '71
They never said they were perfect; U.S. amateur publinx championship. C. Kirkpatrick. il Sports Illus 35:54-5 Jl 26 '71
Triumph of Supermex; United States Open championship. il por Newsweek 78:64-5 Jl 5 '71
Two for money, one for show: J. Nicklaus, L. Trevino and A. Palmer. G. S. Brown. il pors Sports Illus 35:28-9 N 8 '71
What every well-bred rookie should know; qualifying school of the PGA's tournament players division. B. Gilbert. il Sports Illus 34:42-3 Ja 11 '71
Whoopee for the proettes; Eve LPGA championship. il por Time 97:63 Je 28 '71
Young Britons win an old cup. il Sports Illus 34:30-1 Je 7 '71

Anecdotes, facetiae, satire, etc.
Alex Karras golf classic. G. Plimpton. Harper 242:60-5 My '71
First lunar invitational. J. Updike. New Yorker 47:35-6 F 27 '71

GOLF, Miniature
Make your own miniature golf course. J. Savage. il Mech Illus 67:80-2 My '71
GOLF carts. See Motor vehicles
GOLF clubs. See Country clubs
GOLF courses
Ghosts of Merion; U.S. Open golf tournament. il Sports Illus 34:32-7 Je 14 '71
Golf and country, Champions golf club, Houston, Texas. C. Price. Holiday 49:84-5 Mr '71
Golf courses. C. E. Robinson. il Parks & Rec 6:50-1+ O '71
Other side of paradise; Augusta national golf club. B. Gilbert. Sports Illus 34:40-8+ Ap 5 '71
Sporting scene; United States Open at Merion. H. W. Wind. New Yorker 47:56-8+ Jl 17 '71

Construction and care
Make your own miniature golf course. J. Savage. il Mech Illus 67:80-2 My '71
You aren't playing the course, you're playing the designer. D. Pearson. il Esquire 75:130-5 Ap '71

Australia
Poms, butcher-birds and bogeymen. J. Underwood. il Sports Illus 35:70-3+ N 1 '71

Hawaii
Golf in Hawaii: the courses, the pars, the greens fees. il Sunset 146:54+ My '71

Ireland
Sporting scene. H. W. Wind. New Yorker 47:112-18+ Ap 3; 100+ Ap 10 '71

Japan
For want of a teeshot. . ; Japanese golf. S. Servaas. il Holiday 49:38-40+ Jl '71
GOLF fans. See Sports fans
GOLFERS
Five pros for the future. il Time 98:50 Jl 19 '71
Formful win in a most formful affair; U.S. girls' junior championship. H. Peterson. il Sports Illus 35:48+ Ag 23 '71
Game man might risk a bet; winning the grand slam: the Masters, the U.S. Open, the British Open, and the PGA. J. Nicklaus. il por Sports Illus 34:40-2+ Je 7 '71
Heads roll at head to head; Liggett & Myers inc. tournament players' division U.S. professional match play championship. D. Jenkins. il por Sports Illus 35:12-16 S 6 '71
Jones, Hogan and the rest. D. Jenkins. Sports Illus 34:37 Je 14 '71
Ladies of the links. V. Gornick. il Look 35:69-70+ My 18 '71
Poms, butcher-birds and bogeymen. J. Underwood. il Sports Illus 35:70-3+ N 1 '71
Sheriff Coody interrupts the showdown at Firestone. C. Kirkpatrick. Sports Illus 35:84+ S 20 '71
Showcase for the big names: Masters tournament. D. Jenkins. il Sports Illus 34:38-9 Ap 5 '71

They never said they were perfect; U.S. amateur publinx championship. C. Kirkpatrick. il Sports Illus 35:54-5 Jl 26 '71
What every well-bred rookie should know; qualifying school of the PGA's tournament players division. B. Gilbert. il Sports Illus 34:42-3 Ja 11 '71
See also
Ladies professional golf association
also names of golfers, e.g. L. Trevino

Anecdotes, facetiae, satire, etc.
Letter from the golf committee. W. Zinsser. il Life 70:13 Je 11 '71
Out there with slow-play Fay and play-slow Flo; women pros in Las Vegas. D. Jenkins. il Sports Illus 35:50-4+ Ag 9 '71
GOLFFING, Francis
Monologue; poem. Poetry 118:340 S '71
GOLGI apparatus
Vitamin A: concentration in the rat liver Golgi apparatus. S. E. Nyquist and others. bibliog il Science 173:939-41 S 3 '71
GOLLIN, James
Catholic church is one of the least efficient investment institutions in the world; interview. por Forbes 108:53-4+ N 1 '71
about
God's mammon. Time 98:92-3 N 8 '71 •
GOLOMB, H. M. and Bahr, G. F.
Scanning electron microscopic observations of surface structure of isolated human chromosomes. bibliog il Science 171:1024-6 Mr 12 '71
GOLOVACHOV, V.
Planet rovers of the future. Space World H-6-90:45-6 Je '71
GOMEZ, David F.
Chicanos besieged: the bloody fiesta. il Nation 212:326-8 Mr 15 '71
Chicanos: strangers in their own land. il America 124:649-52 Je 26 '71
GÓMEZ-SICRE, José
San Juan muralists. il Américas 23:2-9 Ag '71
GOMUŁKA, Władysław
Beyond the Gomulka era. A. Bromke. For Affairs 49:480-92 Ap '71 •
Iron triangle wobbles. J. K. Anderson. Nat R 23:137-9+ F 9 '71 •
Prices rise, Gomulka falls. il Sr Schol 97:6+ Ja 18 '71 •
GONADOTROPINS
Gonadotropin-releasing hormone: one polypeptide regulates secretion of luteinizing and follicle-stimulating hormones. A. V. Schally and others. bibliog il Science 173:1036-8 S 10 '71
Ornithine decarboxylase stimulation in rat ovary by luteinizing hormone. Y. Kobayashi and others. bibliog il Science 172:379-80 Ap 23 '71
Ovulation induced by synthetic luteinizing hormone-releasing hormone in the hamster. A. Arimura and others. bibliog il Science 174:511-12 O 29 '71
Sexual dimorphism in the preoptic area of the rat. G. Raisman and P. M. Field. bibliog il Science 173:731-3 Ag 20 '71
GONCHAROV, Lev, and Kunetskaia, Ludmila
Nadezhda K. Krupskaya, founder of Soviet public education. por Sch & Soc 99:235-7 Ap '71
GONERIL (literary character) See Shakespeare, W.—Characters
GONFALONS. See Flags
GONG, Joseph K.
Anemic stress as a trigger of myelogenous leukemia in rats rendered leukemia-prone by X-ray. bibliog il Science 174:833-5 N 19 '71
GONORRHEA
Clues about carriers; experiments with chimpanzees. il Newsweek 78:53 Jl 5 '71
Gonorrhea epidemic. il Newsweek 77:54 Ap 26 '71
GONZALES TORNERO, Sergio
Extinct (and hence very rare) birds of Sergio Gonzales Tornero. il Audubon 73:72-5 Ja '71 •
GONZALEZ, Arturo F. Jr
Don't blink; you'll miss the message. Nations Bsns 59:53 Jl '71
GONZALEZ, Roque
Vanishing Guarani treasures. A. Ibáñez Padilla. il Américas 23:32-5 O '71 •
GONZALEZ, Walter. See Wilcox, J. M. jt. auth.
GONZALEZ ROURA, Octavio
May revolution. il Américas 23:36-9 My '71

GOOCH, Bob
Big red of the Ozarks. il pors Outdoor Life 148:90-2+ O '71
GOOCH, Bryan N. S. and Westermark, Tory
Poet and poem: an approach to genius. Engl J 60:465-8 Ap '71
GOOD, Don L.
How good are the exotics? interview, ed. by R. Sanders. por Suc Farm 69:B2-3 Ag '71
GOOD, Paul
McManus v. the Knights of Columbus. il pors Harper 243:66-70+ S '71
GOOD, Thomas L. and Brophy, J. E.
Self-fulfilling prophecy. il Todays Ed 60:52-3 Ap '71
GOOD and evil
Fragging the beast; dehumanizing the enemy. F. H. Borsch. Chr Cent 88:720-2 Je 9 '71
Good and evil, by R. Taylor. Review
   Cath World 213:53 Ap '71. E. L. Donahue
Problem of evil. H. P. Black. Chr Today 15:9+ Ap 23 '71
   See also
Conscience
Sin
GOOD and evil in literature. See Literature and morals
GOOD Friday
Three crosses. Theophilus Protestantus. Cath World 213:243 Ag '71
GOOD housekeeping (periodical)
GH poll, the ten most admired women. il Good H 174:14+ Ja '72
GOOD king; story. See Babbitt, N.
GOOD samaritanism. See Assistance in emergencies
GOOD works (theology) See Reward (theology)
GOODALL, Jane van Lawick-. See Lawick, J. G. van
GOODALL, Rae Natalie P.
Housewife at the end of the world. il pors Nat Geog 139:130-50 Ja '71
GOODBODY and company
Riches to rags. il Newsweek 77:78+ Mr 1 '71
GOODELL, Charles Ellsworth
Happy, humble drive to dump Nixon. il pors Time 97:10-11 Je 7 '71 *
GOODFRIEND, Arthur
Dilemma of cultural propaganda: let it be. Ann Am Acad 398:104-12 N '71
GOODHEART, Barbara
Second look at the German measles vaccine. il Todays Health 49:46-7+ Mr '71
GOODHEART, Eugene
Deradicalized intellectuals. Nation 212:177-80 F 8 '71
GOODING, Judson
Accelerated generation moves into management. il Fortune 83:100-4+ Mr '71
Engineers are redesigning their own profession. il Fortune 83:72-5+ Je '71
Heinz battles for space on a worldwide shelf. il Fortune 84:76-81+ O '71
GOODLAD, John I.
What educational decisions by whom? Ed Digest 37:4-8 O '71
GOODLOE, Joseph W.
Black-operated firm; address, May 12, 1971. Vital Speeches 37:709-15 S 15 '71
GOODMAN, Allan E. See Bell, D. V. J. jt. auth.
GOODMAN, Andrew, family
But the new generation doesn't want to mind the store. S. Birmingham. il pors N Y Times Mag p 16-17+ S 26 '71
GOODMAN, Brian L.
Let's reunderstand activated sludge. bibliog il Am City 86:63-7 O '71
GOODMAN, George
B.B. King. il pors Look 35:54-7 Je 29 '71
Carrie Snodgress. pors Look 35:50-3 Ap 6 '71
Durango: Poitier meets Belafonte. il pors Look 35:56-60+ Ag 24 '71
Man needs to work. Look 35:44-5 Ja 12 '71
GOODMAN, Herman. See Fredericks, C. jt. auth.
GOODMAN, Lillian
Tutoring for credit. il Am Ed 7:26-7 Ap '71
GOODMAN, Linda
Aquarian awakening after sundown; poem. McCalls 98:115 My '71
GOODMAN, Paul
Apology for literature. Commentary 52:39-46 Jl '71
   about
Comment. M. L. Rosenthal. Poetry 119:99-100 N '71 *
GOODMAN, Robert L.
Color I.F. alignment techniques. il Radio-Electr 42:38-42 N '71

GOODMAN, Saul
Brief biography. See issues of Dance magazine
GOODMAN, Walter
Choice for thousands: heroin or methadone? il N Y Times Mag p 14-15+ Je 13 '71
Stocks without sin. il Harper 243:61-7 Ag '71
What are tomorrow's lawyers thinking today? il Redbook 136:74-5+ F '71
(ed) See Kahane, M. Rabbi Kahane says: I'd love to see the J.D.L. fold up. But
GOODMAN memorial theater. See Chicago—Theater
GOODPASTER, Andrew Jackson
Nato today; address, September 2, 1971. Vital Speeches 37:743-9 O 1 '71
GOODRICH, Benjamin Franklin
Doctor's prescription: invention and quality. W. Keener. il por Nations Bsns 59:58-9 Ja '71 *
GOODRICH, B. F, and company
Doctor's prescription: invention and quality. W. Keener. il pors Nations Bsns 59:58-9 Ja '71
Riding with radials. R. Levy. Duns 98:61-2 O '71
Top man leaps from oil to tires. por Bsns W p22-3 S 18 '71
GOODRUM, John
Alabama's magic Monday. il Travel 135:34-9+ Mr '71
North Carolina's mountain craftsmen. il Travel 135:48-51 Je '71
Now: big, quiet buses for the airlanes. il Pop Mech 135:90-3 Ap '71
See your 2-D movies in 3-D. il Pop Sci 198:50 Ja '71
GOODSTADT, Ann Ludwigsen
How many children are we entitled to have? il por Redbook 136:12+ Mr '71
GOODSTEIN, Madeline
What are scientists like? bibliog il por Chem 44:11-13 S '71
GOODSTONE, Shirley
Four seas of Israel. il Holiday 48:54-7+ N '70
GOODWIN, Leonard
Environment and the poor: toward more realistic welfare policies. bibliog f il Cur Hist 61:290-6+ N '71
GOODWIN, Richard Naradof
Social theory of Herbert Marcuse. por Atlan 227:68-70+ Je '71
GOODWIN, W. Richard
Johns-Manville tries to quicken the beat. il pors Bsns W p58-60 Ap 3 '71 *
GOODWYN, Lawrence C.
Frontier myth and southwestern literature. bibliog il Am Lib 2:161-7, 359-66 F, Ap '71
Populist dreams and Negro rights: east Texas as a case study. bibliog f il Am Hist R 76:1435-56 D '71
   about
Who is Lawrence Clark Powell? L. C. Powell. Am Lib 2:682 Jl '71 *
GOODYEAR, Frank H. Jr
Painting collection of the Rhode Island historical society. il Antiques 100:749-57 N '71
GOODYEAR blimps. See Airships
GOODYEAR tire and rubber company
Better year for Goodyear. Duns 97:73 Ap '71
This store has much to offer; Goodyear's participation in Project Transition program. Nations Bsns 59:20 My '71
GOOKIN, Ralph Burton
Good steward. il por Forbes 107:24-5+ Mr 1 '71 *
GOOLAGONG, Evonne
Another champion comes in from the Outback. J. Dunn. il pors Sports Illus 34:58-9 F 15 '71 *
Flower of the wheat fields. por Time 97:62 Mr 1 '71 *
How the daughter of an ancient race made it out of the Australian outback by hitting a tennis ball sweetly and hard. H. Gordon. il pors N Y Times Mag p 10-11+ Ag 29 '71 *
Out of the outback. il por Newsweek 78:64 Jl 5 '71 *
Singalong with Goolagong. il pors Life 71:32-3 Jl 16 '71 *
Waltz at Wimbledon. W. Bingham. il pors Sports Illus 35:14-17 Jl 12 '71 *
GOOLEY DAM (proposed) See Dams
GOOR, Amihud Y.
Salute to a great forester. T. Gill. por Am For 77:7 O '71 *
GOOSE shooting. See Geese, Wild
GORAN, Morris
Should you marry a scientist? por Chem 44:16 Ap '71

GORDIMER, Nadine
Life of Accra, the flowers of Abidjan. il Atlan 228:85-9 N '71
Why haven't you written? story. New Yorker 47:37-42 F 27 '71
GORDIS, Robert
Contention over promised land. America 124:161-2 F 20 '71
GORDON, Alex
Montego Bay. il Holiday 49:64-9+ D '70
GORDON, Arthur
Down East: the magic of the state o' Maine. il Read Digest 98:104-10 My '71
GORDON, Cyrus H.
Did Jews reach America first? il Sci Digest 70:39-40 Ag '71 •
    about
Semites first in America? B. Ford. il Sci Digest 71:43-8+ Ja '72 •
GORDON, Don
Nonperson; poem. Nation 212:283 Mr 1 '71
Refugees; poem. Nation 213:376 O 18 '71
GORDON, Ethel Edison
Well-loved wife; story. Redbook 137:155-77 Je '71
GORDON, Harry
How the daughter of an ancient race made it out of the Australian outback by hitting a tennis ball sweetly and hard. il pors N Y Times Mag p 10-11+ Ag 29 '71
GORDON, James Stewart-. See Stewart-Gordon, J.
GORDON, John
Tom Wolfe: reactionary chic. por Ramp Mag 10:58-62 Ja '72
GORDON, Max
Profiles. W. Balliett. pors New Yorker 47:50-6+ O 9 '71 •
GORDON, Ruth
Authors & editors; interview. ed. by B. A. Bannon. por Pub W 199:63-5 My 31 '71
Myself among others; excerpts. por Vogue 157:138-41 Mr 1; 102-3+ Mr 15; 126-9+ Ap 1 '71
Trade winds; interview. ed. by C. Amory. Sat R 54:8+ My 22 '71
GORDON, Thomas
For parent effectiveness: on-the-job training. R. Kramer. il N Y Times Mag p 102-3+ Mr 28 '71 •
GORDON-LAZAREFF, Hélène. See Lazareff, H. G.
GORDON research conferences
Gordon research conferences; program of meetings, 1971. A. M. Cruickshank. Science 171:1041-58+ Mr 12 '71
Gordon research conferences; winter program, 1972. A. M. Cruickshank. Science 174:730+ N 12 '71
GORDON setters. See Setters
GORE, Albert Arnold
Annals of politics. R. E. Harris. New Yorker 47:34-54 Jl 10 '71 •
End of a populist. D. Halberstam. il por Harper 242:35-45 Ja '71 •
GORE, Daniel
Faculty status for the librarians at Arbuthnot. il Am Lib 2:283-95 Mr '71
GORE, Rick
Brain priorities for touch and movement. il Life 71:56-65 N 12 '71
In search of the mind's eye. il Life 71:56+ O 22 '71
Lifeline for a man with a dying heart. il pors Life 70:51-4+ F 5 '71
GOREN, Charles Henry
Bridge. See issues of Sports illustrated
GORENSTEIN, Paul, and Tucker, Wallace
Supernova remnants; with biographical sketches. il Sci Am 225:14, 74-85 bibliog (p 122) Jl '71
—and others
X-ray structure of the Cygnus loop. bibliog il Science 172:369-72 Ap 23 '71
GORES, Joe
Writing the mystery short story. Writer 84:13-16+ Ag '71
GORES, Stan
Interest grows in centennial glass-ware. il Hobbies 76:116-17+ Ja '72
GORILLAS
Gorilla is a paper tiger. A. Rankin. il Read Digest 98:210-14+ Ap '71
More years with mountain gorillas. D. Fossey. il Nat Geog 140:574-85 O '71
    Anecdotes, facetiae, satire, etc.
Mad about the girl. S. J. Perelman. il Holiday 48:80-1 S '70
GORKIN, Michael
Trade winds; interview. ed. by C. Amory. Sat R 54:6-7 D 18 '71

GORMAN, A. L. F. and others
Photoreceptors in primitive chordates; fine structure, hyperpolarizing receptor potentials, and evolution. bibliog il Science 172:1052-4 Je 4 '71
GORMAN, Cliff
Cliff Gorman as Lenny. por Vogue 158:75 Ag 1 '71 •
GORMAN, Paul A.
Greening of International paper. A. A. Butkus. il Duns 97:36-9+ My '71 •
GORMLY, William W.
All the difference; Talbot County. il Travel 135:38-41+ My '71
GORNICK, Vivian
Ladies of the links. il Look 35:69-70+ My 18 '71
GOROKHOV, Alexei
Vertical 2. Space World H-12-96:45 D '71
GORSLINE, Ethlyn
You can transplant an old tree. Farm J 95:51 Mr '71
GORTON, John Grey
Fall of the larrikin. il pors Time 97:26 Mr 22 '71 •
Good-by John, hello Billy. il por Newsweek 77:38 Mr 22 '71 •
I did it my way. Newsweek 78:30 Ag 23 '71 •
GOSDEN, Freeman Fisher
Where are they now? pors Newsweek 78:23 N 15 '71 •
GOSH, Bobby
Mirrors of our time; interview, ed. by R. Hemming. Sr Schol 98:24-5 Ap 5 '71
GOSHEN, Charles E.
Background of today's social psychiatry. Ment Hy 55:526-32 O '71
GOSHORN, Lawrence A.
Automating the jobs that others ignore. il por Bsns W p56 F 20 '71 •
GOSPEL, Social. See Social gospel
GOSPEL according to Mark; story. See Borges, J. L.
GOSPELS. See Bible—New Testament—Gospels
GOSSENS, Salvador Allende. See Allende Gossens, S.
GOSSETT, William Thomas
Backstage power who replaces Zanuck. por Bsns W p41 Je 19 '71 •
GOSSIP
Art of gossip. Q. Crewe. Vogue 158:318-19+ S 1 '71
    See also
Rumor
GOSSIP benches. See Benches
GOTH, Andres, and others
Phosphatidylserine; selective enhancer of histamine release. bibliog il Science 173:1034-5 S 10 '71
GOTHIC architecture. See Architecture, Gothic
GOTHIC painting. See Painting, Gothic
GOTHIC revival in architecture. See Architecture, Gothic
GOTLIEB, Phyllis (Bloom)
Comment. D. Aldan. Poetry 118:37-8 Ap '71 •
GOTT, Karel
Sinatra of the East. por Newsweek 77:33-4 My 31 '71 •
GOTT, Richard
What lessons from Latin America? excerpt from Guerrilla movements in Latin America. Cur 130:55-9 Je '71
GOTT, Rodney Cleveland
Rodney C. Gott of AMF; interview. il pors Nations Bsns 59:52-4+ N '71
GOTTFRIED, Martin
Tarot: a take-over deal. il Vogue 157:84-5 F 15 '71
Theater. Vogue 157:130 Ap 15; 195 My; 158:87 Jl; 71 Ag 1; 58 Ag 15; 286 S 1 '71
When the stars fell on California. Vogue 158:87 Jl '71
GOTTFURCHT, A.
Language corner. il Chem 44:18 D '71
GOTTSCHO, Samuel Herman
Obituary
Home Gard il por 58:50-1 Ap '71
GOUCHER college, Baltimore
Goucher college teaches how-to-do-it. il Life 70:34-5 F 5 '71
GOUDGE, Elizabeth
Lost angel; story. Ladies Home J 88:98-9 D '71
GOUGEON, Jean Rene
Swing wide, sweet chariot. W. F. Reed. il Sports Illus 35:22-3 Ag 30 '71 •
GOUGH, Marion
Travel. See issues of House beautiful
GOUGH, William C. and Eastlund, B. J.
Prospects of fusion power; with biographical sketches. il Sci Am 224:12, 50-64 F '71

GOULART, João
  Brazil: all power to the generals. H. J. Steiner and D. M. Trubek. For Affairs 49:464-79 Ap '71 *
GOULD, Geoffrey
  Soul City. New Repub 165:9-11 Jl 3 '71
GOULD, Glenn
  Liszt's lament? Beethoven's bagatelle? Or Rosemary's babies? il pors Hi Fi 20:87-8+ D '70
  (ed) See Rubinstein, A. Rubinstein
GOULD, Laurence M.
  Antarctica: the world's greatest laboratory. Am Scholar 40:402-15 Sum '71
GOULD, Richard G.
  International telecommunications organizations and how they affect you. il Electr World 85:38-40+ F '71
  Report on the World administrative radio conference. Pop Electr 35:69-70+ D '71
GOULD, Shane
  Fastest splash in the West. J. Kirshenbaum. il pors Sports Illus 35:18-19 Jl 19 '71 *
GOULD, Susan
  Behind the scenes. il Hi Fi 21:16-17 Ag '71
GOULD, inc.
  Merger, factory style. por Forbes 108:54 O 1 '71
    See also
  Clevite corporation
GOULD-National batteries, inc. See Gould, inc.
GOULDEN, Joseph C.
  Guatemala: terror in silence. Nation 212:365-8 Mr 22 '71
  Phone company papers: a peek at the books. il Nation 214:37-41 Ja 10 '72
GOULET, Denis
  Helping the poor nations, or, Helping ourselves? T. Nulty and L. Nulty; G. MacEoin. Commonweal 95:138-42 N 5 '71 *
GOUNOD, Charles François
  Faust. Criticism
  New Yorker 47:119-20 O 2 '71 *
  Pathe's complete Romeo et Juliette, 1912. C. L. Osborne. il Hi Fi 21:78-9 Ap '71 *
  Records: Roméo et Juliette. D. Hamilton. Nation 212:381-2 Mr 22 '71 *
GOURDS
  Gourds make attractive bird houses. C. Hanley. il Org Gard & Farm 18:54-5 Ag '71
GOURMET clubs. See Clubs
GOURSE, Leslie
  Up the Slide. il Natur Hist 80:20-2+ N '71
GOVER, Norman
  Big textbook caper. Nation 213:468-9 N 8 '71
GOVERNMENT. See Federal government; Nationalism; Nations; Political science; Public administration
GOVERNMENT, Resistance to
  Belling the Berrigans. H. M. Engel and others. pors Cath World 213:227-31 Ag '71
  Between order and violence: the middle ground. S. Rabinove. America 125:311-12 O 23 '71
  Broils and civil commotions. H. A. Bedau. Nation 212:757-9 Je 14 '71
  Could it happen here? civil disobedience. S. Alsop. Newsweek 78:84 Jl 19 '71
  Courage. New Repub 164:14 Ja 2 '71
  Ellsberg and the new heroism. T. Gitlin. Commonweal 94:447-51 S 3 '71
  Protest and foreign policy. E. R. Cain. il Chr Cent 88:742-4 Je 16 '71
  Reflections of a jurist on civil disobedience. G. W. Crockett, jr. Am Scholar 40:584-91 Aut '71
  Walking out on the system: political strikes. V. Held. Nation 213:370-2 O 18 '71
    See also
  Insurgency
  Protests, demonstrations, etc.
  Revolutions

Russia

  Dissent in Russia: the thin wedge. il por Newsweek 77:29-34 F 1 '71
GOVERNMENT administrative efficiency. See Efficiency, Administrative
GOVERNMENT advisory boards. See Executive advisory bodies
GOVERNMENT agencies

United States

  See United States—Executive departments
GOVERNMENT and agriculture. See Agricultural administration
GOVERNMENT and art. See Art and state
GOVERNMENT and business. See Industry and state
GOVERNMENT and science. See Science and state

GOVERNMENT and technology. See Technology and state
GOVERNMENT and the press
  Blowing Henry's cover; Nixon administration use of anonymous news briefing. Nation 213:676 D 27 '71
  Busted background; Washington post breaks unwritten briefing rules. il Time 98:52-3 D 27 '71
  Clash of absolutes; Pentagon's Vietnam studies. New Repub 165:5-7 Jl 3 '71
  Counter-government and the Pentagon papers. Nat R 23:739-41 Jl 13 '71
  Court ruling on secrets: where it will lead. il U S News 71:22-4 Jl 12 '71
  Ellsberg: the battle over the right to know. il pors Time 98:6-12 Jl 5 '71
  Freedom of the press can be a matter of self-interested definition; CBS documentary Selling of the Pentagon. M. Mayer. Harper 243:40+ D '71
  Freedoms to write and read and be informed; E. Caldwell case. R. H. Smith. Pub W 200: 29 D 13 '71
  Government vs. the press; Pentagon study of the war in Vietnam. il por Newsweek 78:17-19 Jl 5 '71
  In the courts: the government vs. the press; Pentagon papers. il por Newsweek 77:27+ Je 28 '71
  Is CBS the underdog? Sedulus. New Repub 164:31-2 My 1 '71
  Legal battle over censorship. il Time 97:17-19 Je 28 '71
  Letter from Paris; reaction to recent difficulties of the New York times with the Nixon administration. Genêt. New Yorker 47:54 Jl 3 '71
  Moynihan report: after six months of benign neglect; interview, ed. by H. Brandon. D. P. Moynihan. il pors N Y Times Mag p 10-11+ Je 27 '71
  Mum's the word: how government and industry keep secrets from the people. J. Ridgeway. New Repub 165:17-19 Ag 21 '71
  Needling the networks. Nation 212:517 Ap 26 '71
  Nixon, the press and the public; interview. H. Klein. il pors U S News 71:68-70+ N 15 '71
  No censorship by government; newspaper publication of Vietnam papers. R. H. Smith. Pub W 200:57 Jl 12 '71
  Notes and comment; a possible reason for government's suit against the Times in the matter of the Pentagon papers. New Yorker 47:19 Jl 10 '71
  Our colleagues err on war secrets issue; reprint from The Detroit news, June 27, 1971. U S News 71:88+ Jl 12 '71
  Our country, right or wrong. D. Lawrence. U S News 70:76 Je 28 '71
  Paper victory: the United States v. the New York times and the Washington post. C. Rembar. Atlan 228:61-6 N '71; Reply with rejoinder. A. M. Rosenthal. 228:46+ D '71
  Papers: Pentagon papers and government dissimulation. W. F. Buckley, jr. Nat R 23: 776-7 Jl 13 '71
  Pentagon papers: a crucial legal battle erupts. il U S News 71:19 Jl 5 '71
  Pentagon papers: and freedom of the press. M. S. Hayden. Read Digest 99:133-4 S '71
  Politics of gullibility. T. M. Conrad. Commonweal 95:13-15 O 1 '71
  Presidency & the press; with editorial comment. D. P. Moynihan. Commentary 51:6-7, 41-52 Mr '71; Discussion. 52:6+ Jl '71
  Press and the cold war, by J. Aronson. Review
  Nation 212:123-4 Ja 25 '71. R. J. Walton
  Ramp Mag 9:57-60 Ap '71. S. Yurick
  Pressure on the media. Nation 212:420-1 Ap 5 '71
  Pushing the human side. Time 97:12-13 Mr 29 '71
  Reporter: a campaign to intimidate; address, April 18, 1971. J. McCaffrey. Vital Speeches 37:478-80 My 15 '71
  Reports & comment: Washington; excerpts from press briefings at the Pentagon, the State department, and the White House. E. B. Drew. Atlan 227:15+ Ap '71
  Required reading: two reports on current threats to the media. Nation 213:581 D 6 '71
  Right to publish; Supreme court's Pentagon papers decision. N. Lewin. New Repub 165:11-13 Jl 10 '71
  Secrets and security: postscript to the Pentagon papers. I. Silver. Commonweal 94:399-402 Ag 6 '71
  Security information and democracy. J. C. Hagerty. Cur 131:7-8 Jl '71
  Senate starts hearings on press freedoms. S. Wagner. Pub W 200:37 O 11 '71

GOVERNMENT and the press—*Continued*
TRB from Washington: adversaries. New Repub 165:4 Ag 7 '71
Toilet training: H. A. Kissinger's remarks on Soviet policy, on the India-Pak war. J. Osborne. New Repub 166:16-17 Ja 1 '72
Truth or consequences; controversy over anonymity of government sources. il Newsweek 78:53-4 D 27 '71
Victory for the press; Supreme court ruling on publication of the secret Pentagon history of the Vietnam war; with excerpts from opinions of 5 justices. il Newsweek 78:16-19 Jl 12 '71
When newspapers do their thing; Pentagon papers. R. L. Tobin. il Sat R 54:37-8 Jl 10 '71
    See also
Local government and the press
Nixon, R. M.—Press relations

    Anecdotes, facetiae, satire, etc.
Brinkley-Vanocur-Mudd-Reynolds conspiracy; ed. by Walter Cronkite (as told to Wm. Gavin) Nat R 23:824 Jl 27 '71

    Greece, Modern
Greek editor sums up; Athens news publisher on trial for illegal newspaper article. T. W. Pew, jr. Nation 213:654-6 D 20 '71
GOVERNMENT bonds. See Bonds, Government
GOVERNMENT book purchasing. See Purchasing, Government
GOVERNMENT buildings. See Public buildings
GOVERNMENT contracts. See Contracts, Government
GOVERNMENT crime insurance. See Insurance, Government
GOVERNMENT decentralization. See Decentralization in government
GOVERNMENT-developed inventions and patents. See Patents and government-developed inventions
GOVERNMENT documents. See Government publications
GOVERNMENT employees
    See also
American federation of state, county and municipal employees
Bureaucracy
Civil service—United States
Collective bargaining—Government employees
Conflict of interest (public office)
Negro government employees
Nepotism

    Salaries, allowances, etc.
Another U.S. pay raise: more pressure on business. il U S News 70:62-3 Ja 25 '71
Federal jobs, what they're worth now. il U S News 72:26 Ja 10 '72
New lid on biggest payroll in nation. il U S News 71:51 O 18 '71
Poor no more. Newsweek 77:75+ Je 28 '71

    Training
Education for government careers; excerpts from report. A. S. Korim. por Sch & Soc 99:328 O '71
GOVERNMENT entertaining
Big cheese at the White House: A. Jackson's inaugural celebration. il por Sr Schol 99:10-11 O 25 '71
Racing's greatest day: White House reception. il pors Hot Rod 24:30-1 D '71
GOVERNMENT guaranty of loans. See Loans. Bank—Guaranty
GOVERNMENT information
Computers and dossiers; reprint. V. Countryman. il Nation 213:134-49 Ag 30 '71
Dossier dictatorship. P. Schrag. Sat R 54:24-5 Ap 17 '71
Government easing attitude toward private enterprise in use of federal information. il Pub W 199:26-30 Ap 12 '71
Media cite increased govt. assaults on freedom of speech and press. S. Wagner. Pub W 200:28 Jl 5 '71
What moonwalk? What moon? P. Steinfels. Commonweal 93:487 F 19 '71
Your country's secrets: your right to know. A. Schlesinger, jr. Vogue 158:172-3+ O 1 '71
    See also
Executive privilege (government information)
Government and the press
Information, Freedom of
Official secrets
GOVERNMENT information services. See Information services. Government
GOVERNMENT insurance. See Insurance, Government

GOVERNMENT investigations
FBI inspection; proposal for investigation by a select Senate committee. New Repub 164:9-11 My 29 '71
Money king of Viet Nam; Senate permanent subcommittee on investigations study of army corruption. il por Time 97:19 Mr 8 '71
Secrecy and elitism in science and government. R. H. Gilluly. Sci N 100:82-3 Jl 31 '71
Who owns America? Bill to create a Special committee to investigate economic and financial concentration. Nation 212:642 My 24 '71
    See also
Commissions of inquiry
Executive privilege (government information)
United States—Congress—Joint committee to investigate the origins of the Vietnamese war (proposed)

    Advertising agencies
Madison avenue hurries to mend its fences. il Bsns W p 116 O 23 '71

    Conglomerate corporations
Celler's slingshot misses the giants. por Bsns W p44 S 11 '71

    Crime and criminals
Pay the Piranha; organized crime. V. Teresa. por Time 98:22 Ag 9 '71
Rogue's gallery; McClellan committee hears testimony of V. Teresa. por Newsweek 78:23 Ag 9 '71

    Fuel industry
FTC is staring at fuel companies. Bsns W p25 My 22 '71

    Holding companies
Unmasking corporate ownership. L. Metcalf and V. Reinemer. Nation 213:38-40 Jl 19 '71

    Independent regulatory commissions
FPC chief faces a grilling on gas. Bsns W p40+ Jl 17 '71

    Medical service
Mills decides to X-ray health care. por Bsns W p25 O 16 '71

    Public utilities
Utilities land on the hiring carpet. il Bsns W p23 N 20 '71

    Stock exchange
Hard look at why brokers fail. Bsns W p54-5 Ag 7 '71
Market structure: remodel or reform? por Bsns W p47-8 O 23 '71

    Trade unions
Years of trial for the UMW. il Bsns W p88+ F 6 '71

    Transportation
California goes after a transportation octopus. por Bsns W p54 S 25 '71

    Great Britain
British study finds Maxwell reckless at Pergamon. Pub W 200:30 Ag 9 '71
GOVERNMENT laboratories. See Laboratories, Government
GOVERNMENT lending
Uncle Sam, the banker? il Forbes 108:15-17 Ag 1 '71
    See also
Business—Federal aid
Reconstruction finance corporation
GOVERNMENT national mortgage association See United States—Housing and urban development, Department of
GOVERNMENT ownership
    See also
Railroads and state

    Algeria
New ball game; seizure of French oil and gas properties. il Newsweek 77:82 Mr 8 '71

    Chile
Nationalization in Chile. Mo Labor R 94:59 S '71
Sticking point; implications of nationalization on American companies. il Newsweek 78:38+ Jl 26 '71

    France
Satisfied stockholder; Renault automobile company. il por Forbes 107:34+ Ap 1 '71

GOVERNMENT ownership—*Continued*
Great Britain
Offer of costly salvation; Lockheed engine contract for TriStar jet. Time 97:78 Mr 15 '71
Reversing the tide of nationalization. Bsns W p30 Ja 30 '71
GOVERNMENT price control. See Price regulation by government
GOVERNMENT printing office. See United States—Government printing office
GOVERNMENT procurement. See Purchasing, Government
GOVERNMENT publications
Apollo books available. R. N. Watts, jr. Sky & Tel 43:17 Ja '72
New horizons in your mailbox; Selected U.S. government publications. V. J. Foltz. il Har Yrs 11:40-1 N '71
Publishing on the Potomac: the selling of the government. S. Wagner. Pub W 200: 28-9 Ag 9 '71
Research at Uncle Sam's bookstore. D. Stuart. Writer 84:24-5+ Jl '71
Seeing pictures; photographic gold mine in Washington, D.C. J. Scully. Mod Phot 35:12+ O '71
   See also
Consumer product information index
Security classification (government documents)
State publications

Bibliography
Congressional documents relating to foreign policy. See issues of Department of state bulletin
Publications of the Department of state. See issues of Department of state bulletin
Selected government publications. F. J. O'Hara. See issues of Wilson library bulletin
Source material; comp. by D. Wasson. See issues of Foreign affairs
GOVERNMENT purchasing. See Purchasing, Government
GOVERNMENT regulation of industry. See Industry and state
GOVERNMENT research
Federal R&D: domestic problems get new efforts but little money. A. L. Hammond. Science 171:657-8+ F 19 '71
GOVERNMENT scientists. See Scientists in government
GOVERNMENT secrets. See Official secrets
GOVERNMENT spending, Waste in. See United States—Appropriations and expenditures
GOVERNMENT spending policy
Budget deficit to top Nixon forecast. U S News 70:46 Je 21 '71
Close-up of Nixon's plan for deficit spending. il U S News 70:57-9 F 8 '71
Forty thousand dollars per minute; address, March 6, 1971. B. Goldwater, jr. Vital Speeches 37:392-4 Ap 15 '71
Nixon's spending plan for 1972. il Time 97:12 F 8 '71
Policy of self-fulfilling prophecy. il Time 97: 76-7 F 8 '71
Priorities will get you if you don't watch out. G. Will. Nat R 23:196-7 F 23 '71
Spurs to lagging recovery. il U S News 71: 13-14 Jl 5 '71
Watch on the Potomac. K. Y. Tomlinson and G. Denison. Read Digest 98:205-6 Ap '71
   See also
United States—Appropriations and expenditures
United States—Economic policy
GOVERNMENT surplus. See Surplus products
GOVERNORS
Delegation of governors to visit U.S.S.R. and Romania; Department announcement, September 20, 1971. Dept State Bul 65:384 O 11 '71
Four men for the new season: new leaders of the South. pors Time 97:18-19 My 31 '71
Governors size up the '72 election. il U S News 71:26-8 S 27 '71
Governors talk '72 politics: it looks like Muskie vs. Nixon. il U S News 70:65 Mr 8 '71
New breed? southern governors. Sr Schol 98: 17 F 8 '71
New language on inauguration day; six newly sworn Deep South governors. Time 97: 20-1 F 1 '71
Nixon in '72: views of party governors. il U S News 70:21 My 3 '71
They came looking for money; governors in Washington. H. Sidey. il Life 70:2B Mr 12 '71
   See also
Candidates, Political

GOVERNORS conference, 1970
Saying no to Nixon; problem of getting revenue sharing through Congress. il Time 97:16 Mr 8 '71
GOWDY, Curt
They hardly ever knock the product. Cyclops. por Life 71:12 Ag 13 '71 *
GOWLAND, Peter
Glamor by Gowland. il Pop Phot 68:24 Ja '71
GOWNS, Wedding. See Wedding clothes
GOWON, Yakubu
Nigeria's spectacular rebound. C. T. Rowan. Read Digest 98:156-8+ Je '71 *
GOYA Y LUCIENTES, Francisco José de
Goya's portrait of Gen Nicolas Guye. P. Muller. il Art N 70:29+ D '71 *
GRABILL, Paul
Outmiracled; poem. Chr Cent 88:969 Ag 18 '71
GRABLE, John
Allies or adversaries? High school and junior college. bibliog Clear House 46:195-9 D '71
GRACE Patricia, consort of Rainier III, prince of Monaco
H.S.H. Princess Grace of Monaco; interview, ed. by C. B. Pepper. il pors Vogue 158: 108-15 D '71
Why mothers should breast-feed their babies. por Ladies Home J 88:56+ Ag '71
   about
Parting shots: Princess Grace has a lot to say about mothers. il por Life 71:63 Jl 30 '71 *
GRACE, Karen
Redbook reader Mrs James A. Grace, an amateur who cooks like a pro. il por Redbook 136:106-12+ Ap '71 *
GRACE, W. R. and company
W. R. Grace keeps shooting for sevens. il Bsns W p 114-16 Ap 17 '71
   See also
Schwarz, F. A. O. (firm)
GRACE (theology)
Amazing grace. L. N. Bell. Chr Today 15: 38-9 S 10 '71
GRADE, Sir Lew
Top grade. por Time 98:80 O 4 '71 *
GRADE crossings. See Railroads—Crossings
GRADE teachers. See Teachers
GRADED schools. See Education—Organization by years
GRADERS (excavating machinery)
Graders take on the big drifts; Buffalo, N.Y. il Am City 86:22 Ja '71
GRADING and marking (students)
A,B,C, grades? Don't knock it! W. E. McMahon. Clear House 45:465-7 Ap '71
Bell curve has an ominous ring. G. R. Taylor. il Clear House 46:119-24 O '71
College grades; predictors of what? letter. H. C. Lindgren; discussion. Science 170:491-2; 171:232+ O 30 '70, Ja 22 '71
Differences in course grades and student ratings of teacher performance. R. G. Weigel and others. bibliog Sch & Soc 99:60-2 Ja '71
Essay grading by computer; a laboratory phenomenon? H. B. Slotnick and J. V. Knapp. bibliog f Engl J 60:75-80+ Ja '71
Grading themes: a new approach; a new dimension; tape recorded criticism. S. H. Vogler. Engl J 60:70-4+ Ja '71
I oppose testing, marking, & grading; excerpts from What do I do Monday? J. Holt. il Todays Ed 60:28-31 Mr '71
Individualized reporting. E. M. Bearg. Todays Ed 60:50 F '71
Pass-fail pitfalls. Newsweek 79:34 Ja 3 '72
Progress chart for slow learners. J. Marusek. Clear House 45:312-13 Ja '71
Why grades are argued. M. S. Marshall. Sch & Soc 99:350-3 O '71
Will pass/fail pass the test? R. H. Dalger. Todays Ed 60:24 N '71
   See also
Ability grouping in education
GRADING of meat. See Meat—Grading and standardization
GRADING of pork. See Meat—Grading and standardization
GRADUATE schools. See Colleges and universities—Graduate work
GRADUATE students
Political activities
   See also
New university conference
GRADUATE work. See Colleges and universities—Graduate work
GRADUATES, College. See College graduates

GRADUATES, High school. See High school graduates
GRADUATION addresses. See Baccalaureate addresses
GRADY, John Peter
Ambush at the courthouse. il por Time 98: 16 S 6 '71 •
GRADY, Sandy
Man the world forgot. il pors Ebony 26:154-6+ O '71
GRAETZ, Stephanie Windisch-. See Windisch-Graetz, S.
GRAF, Rudolf F. and Whalen, G. J.
Medicine chest alarm. il Mech Illus 67:106-7 Ja '71
Put a wall outlet in your car or boat. il Pop Mech 135:168-70 My '71
Tail light monitor for your car. il Radio-Electr 42:60-1 Ag '71
Tape-timing nomogram. il Radio-Electr 42: 52-3 Ag '71
—See Whalen, G. J. jt. auth.
GRAFFITI
Boston's graffiti board. C. Bratley. il Am City 86:138+ Ap '71
Graffiti, by R. Reisner. Review
Bsns W il p8 Jl 24 '71. J. A. Dierdorff
Chr Cent 88:787 Je 23 '71
People's art. R. Sommer. il Natur Hist 80: 40-5 F '71
GRAFSTEIN, Bernice
Transneuronal transfer of radioactivity in the central nervous system. bibliog il Science 172:177-9 Ap 9 '71
GRAHAM, Beardsley
Boardroom technologist. R. Levy. por Duns 98:56 Ag '71 •
GRAHAM, Benjamin
Take your dreams elsewhere; interview. por Forbes 109:89-90+ Ja 1 '72
GRAHAM, Bill
Fade-out for Fillmore. Newsweek 77:122 My 10 '71 •
Future after the Fillmores. E. Sander. Sat R 54:56 My 29 '71 •
Good-by to the Fillmores. H. Saal. il por Newsweek 78:89 Jl 12 '71 •
Goodbye to rock. M. Durham. il pors Life 70: 62-4+ My 14 '71 •
GRAHAM, Billy
Marks of the Jesus movement; excerpt from address to the European congress on evangelism. Chr Today 16:4-5 N 5 '71
Through the valley of the shadow. Read Digest 98:107-10 Ap '71
about
Biblical support. Chr Cent 88:1247 O 20 '71 •
Billy and Aimee. F. Russell. Nat R 23:716 Je 29 '71 •
Billy Graham's day; North Carolina's special commemorative program. D. Kucharsky. il por Chr Today 16:44-5 N 5 '71 •
Decisive hour for 21,000. R. Chandler. il Chr Today 15:30-1 Ag 27 '71 •
Deep in the heart of Texas. H. Lindsell. il por Chr Today 16:36-7 O 22 '71 •
Graham crusade: satanists lose to Jesus power. Chr Today 15:34 Jl 2 '71 •
New evangelical surge; with editorial comment. W. F. Willoughby. il por Chr Today 15:34. 40-1 My 21 '71 •
Reflections on a crusader. H. Lindsell. Chr Today 15:23 Jl 2 '71 •
Rev. Billy's day. J. Osborne. New Repub 165:11-13 O 30 '71 •
GRAHAM, Desmond
(ed) See Moser, E. Cool command
GRAHAM, E. H.
Over 40. . .and fired. il por Mech Illus 67:69-71+ My '71
GRAHAM, Frank, 1925-
Why we are losing the battle against pollution. il Todays Health 49:14-15 S '71
GRAHAM, Frank Porter
Three saints in politics. P. H. Douglas. Am Scholar 40:223-32 Spr '71 •
GRAHAM, Fred P.
Supreme court and the flag. Art in Am 59:27 Mr '71
GRAHAM, Helen Tredway
Obituary
Environ 13:23 Je '71. V. Brodine
GRAHAM, James A. Maxtone-. See Maxtone-Graham, J. A.
GRAHAM, James J.
Seekers after justice. P. Steinfels. Commonweal 95:150 N 12 '71 •
GRAHAM, Janet
School for winged fury. il Sci Digest 69:45-51 Mr '71
GRAHAM, Jeffrey B.
Temperature tolerances of some closely related tropical Atlantic and Pacific fish species. bibliog il Science 172:861-3 My 21 '71

GRAHAM, Katharine
Katharine Graham and how she grew. S. McBee. il pors McCalls 98:76-9+ S '71 •
GRAHAM, M. Robert
Free school or chalk talk time; address, November 1970. Engl J 60:754-9 S '71
GRAHAM, Marjorie Todd
Take time out for love. il Parents Mag 46: 42-3+ Jl '71
GRAHAM, Robert John
Adventure to antiquity. il Field & S 76:78-9+ Je '71
GRAHAM, Virginia
Virginia Graham's advice to wives; interview. ed. by M. Davidson. il por Good H 172:102-3+ My '71
GRAHAM, William Sydney
Comment. R. B. Shaw. Poetry 118:231 Jl '71 •
GRAHAM, Winston
Earring; story. Ladies Home J 88:124-5 N '71
GRAIL
My search for the Holy Grail. J. Cottrell. il Ladies Home J 88:58+ Ap '71
GRAIN
Alternatives for fighting corn blight. C. E. Sommers. il Suc Farm 69:no3 A1 F '71
See also
Cereal foods
Milo
Sorghum
Drying
Dandy drying ideas. il Suc Farm 69:34 O '71
Grading and standardization
Grain quality, what it means to you. C. E. Sommers. il Suc Farm 69:B12 S '71
Know your grain grades. C. E. Sommers. il Suc Farm 69:B5 S '71
Handling
See Grain handling
Harvesting
Hauling and handling ideas that speed up grain harvest. il Farm J 95:32-3 Jl '71
How to adjust your combine: corn, beans, grain cut field losses. P. Jones. il Suc Farm 69:26-7 Je '71
Moisture content
See also
Silage—Moisture content
Protein content
Better grain protein test is available. Suc Farm 69:D8 O '71
Standards
See Grain—Grading and standardization
Storage
New way to store high-moisture grain; acid treatment. W. Kester. il Farm J 95:27 N '71
Out of sight, out of pocket; CCC storage. Farm J 95:46 Ag '71
Your legal protection with stored grain. Suc Farm 69:no2 B12 F '71
See also
Corn—Storage
Granaries
Transportation
Shipping grain can be a nightmare. B. Coffman. Farm J 95:22L S '71
GRAIN, Stored
Diseases and pests
Be alert for storage pests in your grain. Suc Farm 69:38 O '71
GRAIN bins. See Granaries
GRAIN handling
How to handle grain at harvest. P. Jones and G. Earle. il Suc Farm 69:26-9 O '71
GRAIN in photography. See Photography—Grain
GRAIN sampling
New: an automatic grain sampler. C. F. Wilson. il Farm J 95:9 Ag '71
GRAIN surplus. See Surplus products, Agricultural
GRAINGER, Percy
Touching and toe-tingling: a salute to Percy Grainger. R. Kennedy. Am Rec G 37:295 Ja '71 •
GRAMATKY, Hardie
Watercolor page; with biographical sketch. il por Am Artist 35:38-41+ S '71
GRAMMAR, English. See English language—Grammar

GRAMONT, Nancy (Ryan) de. See De
  Gramont, N. R.
GRAMONT, Sanche de. See De Gramont, S.
GRANARIES
  Permanent grain center on a rented farm.
    P. B. Jones. il Suc Farm 69:32-3 S '71
GRANATELLI, Andy
  Mouse-milk man. il por Newsweek 77:72+
    Ap 5 '71 *
  Racer's sludge. il por Time 98:106 N 1
    '71 *
GRANBERRY, Presley
  Exotic anthuriums. Horticulture 49:18-19 D
    '71
GRAND American trapshooting tournament.
  See Amateur trapshooting association
GRAND BAHAMA ISLAND
    See also
  Fishing—Grand Bahama Island
GRAND CANYON
  There's thunder in the Canyon. N. A. Win-
    ter, jr. il Nat Wildlife 10:17-20 D '71
  Touring Grand Canyon by plane. L. Barry.
    il Pop Phot 68:36+ F '71
GRAND Funk Railroad (rock group) See Rock
  groups
GRAND HAVEN, Mich.
  Rechargeable batteries shed brighter light;
    use by police. R. Klempel. il Am City 86:16
    Mr '71
GRAND JUNCTION, Colo.
  Dear Sir: your house is built on radio-
    active uranium waste. H. P. Metzger. il
    N Y Times Mag p 14-15+ O 31 '71
  Hot sands. Newsweek 78:46 O 18 '71
  Hot town. Time 98:56 D 20 '71
GRAND Jury
  Grand jury network: how the Nixon admin-
    istration has secretly perverted a tradi-
    tional safeguard of individual rights. F. J.
    Donner and E. Cerruti. il Nation 214:5-15+
    Ja 3 '72
GRAND MANAN ISLAND
  Island in the sea. K. Scherman. il Audubon
    73:4-7 Jl '71
GRAND national roadster show. See Auto-
  mobiles—Exhbitions
GRAND opera festival, San Antonio. See Mu-
  sic festivals—Texas
GRAND prix drivers association
  Danger yes, death no. il Newsweek 77:63 Je
    7 '71
GRAND RAPIDS, Mich.

  Education
  Say it right and they will too; David Pu-
    shaw's developmental language and speech
    center. M. Lloyd. il Am Ed 7:5-7 Ja '71
GRAND TETON NATIONAL PARK
  Forgotten side of the Tetons. B. Norton. il
    Liv Wildn 35:31-4 Sum '71
La GRANDE-duchesse de Gérolstein; opera.
  See Offenbach, J.
GRANDFATHER clocks. See Clocks
GRANDFATHERS. See Grandparents
GRANDMA builds a bridge; story. See Moore,
  H. C.
GRANDMOTHERS. See Grandparents
GRANDPARENT insurance. See Insurance.
  Life—Family plan policies
GRANDPARENTS
  Are grandparents necessary? B. Spock. por
    Redbook 137:31+ Ag '71
  Generations; with photographs by M. Wald-
    man. Life 71:104-10+ D 17 '71
  Grandmothers; the delights and dilemmas.
    A. Kaplan; E. Edwards. il Har Yrs 11:39-
    41 My '71
  Grandparent king, queen, crowned at Mil-
    waukee festival. il Aging 204:13 O '71
  How young parents can get along with
    grandparents. B. Spock. Redbook 137:29+
    S '71
  Our old people: part of their lonely exile is
    their own fault. P. Wylie. il Todays Health
    49:10-11 Ag '71
  When young mothers have problems with
    grandparents. B. Spock. Redbook 137:29-30+
    O '71
  With granny & gramps at generation gap. il
    Changing T 25:24 Ap '71
    See also
  Foster grandparent program
Les GRANDS ballets canadiens. See Ballet—
  Canada
GRANEY, William
  Priests-USA and Twin circle. America 124:
    217 Mr 6 '71
GRANITE
  Lunar rock no. 12013. Sci Am 224:44-6 Ja '71
GRANT, A. C. See Sen Gupta, B. K. jt auth.
GRANT, Betsy Drake
  Authors & editors. B. A. Bannon. il por Pub
    W 200:15-17 S 27 '71 *

GRANT, Bob
  East (hunters) meets West (mule deer) il
    Field & S 76:40-1+ Jl '71
  Klamath steelhead. il Field & S 76:48-9+ D
    '71
  Now you can be a race driver, at any age.
    il Pop Mech 136:69-71+ D '71
  This car really flies. il Pop Mech 136:87
    Ag '71
GRANT, Cary
  New women in the life of Cary Grant. C.
    Mangel. il pors Look 35:58-62 F 23 '71 *
GRANT, Gardner
  Fly-rodding the blues. il Field & S 76:120+ Je
    '71
GRANT, Harold
  What I learned from my sister Mona. il por
    Seventeen 29:77 Jl '70
GRANT, James P.
  Marginal men: the global unemployment cri-
    sis. For Affairs 50:112-24 O '71
GRANT, Mary Kent
  Mystery, detective and suspense. See first
    issue of each month of Library journal
GRANT, Mona
  Bonjour, Paris! Here's Mona Grant in her
    beauty whirl. il pors Seventeen 29:112-15+
    N '70 *
GRANT, Neville
  Mercury in man. bibliog il Environ 13:2-15
    My '71
GRANT, Robert
  Full-time job. por Forbes 108:66 O 1 '71 *
GRANT, Robert T.
  School system: a look into the future. Clear
    House 45:535-7 My '71
GRANT, Taylor
  Balancing act. R. L. Shayon. Sat R 54:43 Je
    5 '71; Reply with rejoinder. L. M. C.
    Smith. 54:19 Jl 10 '71 *
GRANT, W. Vance
  Record-smashing year for American educa-
    tion. il Am Ed 7:29-31 O '71
GRANTS-in-aid
  Aid for cities and states: Nixon's latest ap-
    proach. il U S News 70:42-3 F 22 '71
  More money from Washington and who is
    getting it. il U S News 71:74-5 Jl 26 '71
  State grants-in-aid for private community
    mental health programs. H. K. Naylor.
    Ment Hy 55:190-3 Ap '71
GRANTZEVA, Tatiana
  In Paris and many other places it's Grant-
    zeva; interview, ed. by N. M. Stoop. il
    pors Dance Mag 45:26-31 Jl '71
GRANULATION tissue
  Contraction of granulation tissue in vitro:
    similarity to smooth muscle. G. Majno and
    others. bibliog il Science 173:548-50 Ag 6
    '71
GRANZOW, Edward F.
  Mickey mouse traffic-signal interconnect. il
    Am City 86:55-7 Ag '71
GRAPE industry. See Viticulture
GRAPES
  Grapes grow great in Oklahoma. L. Riotte.
    il Org Gard & Farm 18:105-6+ Ja '71
    See also
  Viticulture
  Wine making

  Diseases and pests
  Problem of mildew on grapes. F. Allen. Org
    Gard & Farm 18:92-6 Ag '71
GRAPESTAKE fences. See Fences
GRAPHIC arts
    See also
  Prints

  Collectors and collecting
  Graphic art collecting. W. E. Greening. Hob-
    bies 76:142-3 S '71
GRAPHIC methods
    See also
  Critical path analysis
  Nomography (mathematics)
GRAPHICS, Computer. See Computer graphics
GRAPHITE
  Kinetics of single-layer graphite oxidation:
    evaluation by electron microscopy. E. L.
    Evans and others. bibliog il Science 171:
    174-5 Ja 15 '71
  New materials science of carbon and graph-
    ite; report of meeting. G. L. Montet. Sci-
    ence 172:87 Ap 2 '71
GRAPHOLOGY
  Composer calls. S. Jenkins. il Opera N 35:6-7
    F 20 '71
  Hand of a man going his own way. A. Kan-
    fer. il Life 70:27 Ja 22 '71
  How to analyze your child's handwriting; ex-
    cerpt from Handwriting. H. O. Teltscher.
    Ladies Home J 88:92+ Mr '71

GRASS, Artificial. See Turf, Artificial
GRASS harp; musical comedy. See Musical comedies, revues. etc.—Criticisms, plots, etc.
GRASS lands. See Prairies
GRASS mats. See Rugs and carpets
GRASSES
Better name for sea oats is bamboo grass. il Sunset 146:127 Ja '71
Experts' choice of lawn grasses. Changing T 25:47 S '71
Top turfgrasses. R. W. Schery. il Horticulture 49:22-3+ Ap '71
Turf management interactions. J. Madison. il Parks & Rec 6:32-5 S '71
    See also
Alfalfa
Fescue
Hay
Lawns
Sod
GRASSHOPPERS
2,5-Dichlorophenol (from ingested herbicide?) in defensive secretion of grasshopper. T. Eisner and others. bibliog il Science 172:277-8 Ap 16 '71
Flight orientation in locusts. J. M. Camhi. il Sci Am 225:74-81 bibliog(p 120) Ag '71
Grasshopper chemical factories, 2,5-dichlorophenol from 2,4-D in defensive secretions. R. H. Gilluly. il Sci N 99:406 Je 12 '71
Handling hoppers: live bait. N. Smith. il Field & S 76:50 Je '71
GRASSIE, Frank
Who says bankers aren't friendly? por Forbes 107:15-16 F 1 '71 *
GRASSLAND ecology. See Prairie ecology
GRASSLAND ecosystems. See Prairie ecology
GRASSLAND farming. See Stock ranges
GRASSLANDS. See Prairies
GRATEFUL dead (rock group) See Rock groups
GRATERS. See Kitchen utensils
GRATITUDE
Word gratitude.V.P. McCorry. America 125: inside back cover O 2 '71
    See also
Thanksgiving
GRAVEL, Mike
Breach of decorum. Newsweek 78:21 Jl 19 '71 *
Late late show. il por Newsweek 78:29-30 Jl 12 '71 *
GRAVELY, Samuel L. Jr
Black admiral signals new look for U.S. navy. L. J. Banks. il pors Ebony 26:72-4+ S '71 *
First black admiral. Negro Hist Bul 34:117 My '71 *
GRAVEREAUX, Daniel
How important is stylus overhang? il Hi Fi 21:52-3 F '71
GRAVES, Charles M.
Three-pool city. il Parks & Rec 6:34-5+ Mr '71
GRAVES, Dorothy
Adolescent grievances at school. il PTA Mag 66:26-8 bibliog(p36) O '71
Coping with "I won't". il PTA Mag 65:12-14 bibliog(p34) Ap '71
How not to embarrass your children. il PTA Mag 66:28-30 bibliog(p35) S '71
GRAVES, Douglas R.
Douglas Graves: painter with charcoal. D. C. Hines. il por Am Artist 35:58-63+ N '71 *
GRAVES, Elizabeth Minot
Children's books: highlights of the Spring. il Commonweal 94:263-6 My 21 '71
Selected list of children's books (cont) il Commonweal 94:266-71; 95:185-91 My 21, N 19 '71
Year of the witch. Commonweal 95:179-82 N 19 '71
GRAVES, Ginny
Discovery in Johnson County. il Am Lib 2:204-6 F '71
Don't buy it, beg it. Sch Arts 70:42-3 Ap '71
GRAVES, Robert
Green-sailed vessel; poem. New Yorker 47:46 Mr 20 '71
Song: reconciliation. Atlan 228:110 S '71
Strangeness; poem. Ladies Home J 88:111 Je '71
Two poems: Defeat of time; Gorgon mask. Mlle 74:70 N '71
    about
Poems 1968-1970, by R. Graves. Review Time por 98:84-5+ D 13 '71. T. E. Kalem *

GRAVES. See Cemeteries
GRAVESTOCK, Dan
Don't shoot the bearded lady. il Outdoor Life 147:60-3+ Ja '71
GRAVESTONE rubbings. See Rubbings
GRAVESTONES. See Sepulchral monuments
GRAVITATION
Finding a better value for G. J. W. Beams. bibliog il Phys Today 24:34-40 My '71
Perpetual motor of the universe. S. Khabarov. Space World H-8-92:38-9 Ag '71
    See also
Gravity waves
Relativity (physics)
Weightlessness
GRAVITATIONAL mass. See Mass (physics)
GRAVITY
Gravity measured at the Apollo 14 landing site. R. L. Nance. bibliog il Science 174:1022-3 D 3 '71
Lunar gravity analysis from long-term effects. A. S. Liu and P. A. Laing. bibliog il Science 173:1017-20 S 10 '71
Most mysterious force in the universe. R. Schiller. Read Digest 99:152-5 Jl '71

Measurement

Finding a better value for G. J. W. Beams. bibliog il Phys Today 24:34-40 My '71
Measuring gravity. Newsweek 77:91-2 My 24 '71

Physiological effects

Bilateral symmetry in chick embryo determination by gravity. S. Kochav and H. Eyal-Giladi. bibliog il Science 171:1027-9 Mr 12 '71
GRAVITY waves
Detection of gravitational waves. J. Weber. il Sci Am 224:22-9 bibliog (p 132) My '71
Laser earth-strain gauge to search for gravity waves. M. S. Rothenberg. bibliog il Phys Today 24:19-20 Je '71
Starquakes: have they been observed? L. C. Green. il Sky & Tel 41:76-9 F '71
GRAVY. See Sauces
GRAY, Betty MacMorran
Economics of sex bias. Nation 212:742-4 Je 14 '71
GRAY, Elisha, 2d
What business has to do about consumerism. Look 35:68+ Mr 9 '71
GRAY, Francine du Plessix. See Du Plessix, F
GRAY, Harry Jack
Another Litton manager wants to run his own show. il por Fortune 84:33 N '71 *
New engine man. por Time 98:98 O 11 '71 *
United aircraft picks a savvy outsider. por Bsns W p29-30 O 2 '71 *
GRAY, Jane, and Boucot, A. J.
Early Silurian spore tetrads from New York: earliest New World evidence for vascular plants? bibliog il Science 173:918-21 S 3 '71
GRAY, John Delbert
Held back at home, expanding abroad. por Bsns W p31 Ja 1 '72 *
GRAY, Lee Learner
AASA's nonacademic academy. Am Ed 7:21-4 O '71
GRAY, Lois. See Corwin, R. D. jt. auth.
GRAY, R. and others
Vitamin D metabolism: the role of kidney tissue. bibliog il Science 172:1232-4 Je 18 '71
GRAY, Thomas M.
Daley news. New Repub 164:16-18 Ap 3; 165:32-3 Jl 10 '71
GRAY, Walter
Classical nature of Schubert's lieder. bibliog f Mus Q 57:62-72 Ja '71
GRAY, Walter, Jr
ALA asked to investigate Oklahoma County firing. pors Library J 96:3075+ O 1 '71 *
GRAY, William S.
One who came back: a cancer patient's story. il por Newsweek 77:86-7 F 22 '71
GRAY, William T. and Finch, D. I.
How accurately can temperature be measured? il Phys Today 24:32-40 S '71
GRAY whales. See Whales
GRAYLING fishing
Everyone loves a grayling. J. Brooks. il Outdoor Life 148:86-8+ Ag '71
GRAYSON, Charles Jackson, 1923-
Bootstrap teaching. il Time 98:82 N 15 '71 *
Grayson sees no letup soon. il por Bsns W p22 D 25 '71 *
New controllers, and new doubts. il pors Newsweek 78:67-9 N 1 '71 *
Take charge price czar. por Time 98:19 D 20 '71 *

GRAYSON, George W. Jr
Peru's military populism. bibliog f Cur Hist
60:71-7+ F '71

GRAYSON, Margaret A. See Galindo, P. jt.
auth.

GRAZIANO, Rocky
Art of Rock. D. Davis. il por Newsweek 77:
64+ F 22 '71 •

GRAZING
Double mileage from pasture; supplemental
corn-salt ration. W. Waltner and E. Walt-
ner. il Suc Farm 69:A8 N '71
Grazing association works in the corn belt.
J. Davis. il Suc Farm 69:32-3 My '71
Grazing ecosystem in the Serengeti. R. H. V
Bell. il Sci Am 225:86-93 Jl '71
$250 net an acre from alfalfa pasture. G.
Lorang. il Farm J 95:28+ My '71
See also
Pastures
Stock ranges

GRAZING lands. See Stock ranges

GREAT Atlantic and Pacific tea company
Operation Breadbasket campaigns against
A&P at the national level. A. Simon. Chr
Cent 88:349-50 Mr 17 '71
Red ink at the A&P. Time 99:21 Ja 17 '72
Renewing A&P. por Bsns W p68 F 20 '71
Sit-in at A&P was no tea party; Operation
Breadbasket il Bsns W p21 F 6 '71
Will they find the flair at A&P? il Fortune
83:29 Ap '71

GREAT BARRIER REEF
Australia: a quiet place to fossick. F. Riley.
il Sat R 54:52-3+ O 23 '71
Christmas with corals. G. Durrell. House &
Gard 140:70-1+ D '71

GREAT BRITAIN
See also
Aged—Great Britain
Airlines—Great Britain
Architecture, Domestic—Great Britain
Archives—Great Britain
Art—Great Britain
Automobile racing—Great Britain
Ballet—Great Britain
Banks and banking—Great Britain
Booksellers and bookselling—Great Britain
Bridges—Great Britain
Budget—Great Britain
Business consolidations and mergers—Great
Britain
Canals—Great Britain
Censorship—Great Britain
Children—Great Britain
Childrens literature—Great Britain
Church and social problems—Great Britain
Church union—Great Britain
Colleges and universities—Great Britain
Crime and criminals—Great Britain
Education—Great Britain
Environmental policy—Great Britain
Gambling—Great Britain
Government investigations—Great Britain
Government ownership—Great Britain
Hotels, taverns, etc.—Great Britain
Housing—Great Britain
Hunting—Great Britain
Immigration and emigration—Great Britain
Industrial relations—Great Britain
Industry and state—Great Britain
Justice, Administration of—Great Britain
Labor laws and legislation—Great Britain
Libraries—Great Britain
Money—Great Britain
Moving picture industry—Great Britain
Moving pictures—Great Britain
Museums—Great Britain
Narcotic laws—Great Britain
Newspapers—Great Britain
Opera—Great Britain
Periodicals—Great Britain
Physics—Great Britain
Police—Great Britain
Prisons—Great Britain
Public opinion
Publishers and publishing—Great Britain
Railroads and state—Great Britain
Religious conferences—Great Britain
Restaurants—Great Britain
School libraries—Great Britain
Science—Great Britain
Science and state—Great Britain
Security classification (government docu-
ments)—Great Britain
Shopping and shoppers—Great Britain
Strikes—Great Britain
Taxation—Great Britain
Television broadcasting—Great Britain
Television industry—Great Britain
Terrorism—Great Britain
Theological seminaries—Great Britain

Armed forces
How two allies fare with volunteers. il U S
News 70:35 Mr 1 '71

Forces in Germany
See also
Great Britain—Army—Forces in Germany

Army
Brigade of guards—Uniforms
Save that tiger, not that yak. il Time 98:
46 N 22 '71

Brigade of Gurkhas
They're changing the guard at Buckingham
palace. il Life 71:70-1 D 10 '71

Forces in Germany
Man is fair game. C. Gammon. il Sports Illus
34:74-6+ Mr 22 '71

Forces in Northern Ireland
Men on the spot. A. Deming. il Newsweek
78:29-30 S 6 '71

Atomic energy authority
Safety and nuclear power plants: a British
view. F. R. Farmer. por Bul Atom Sci 27:
47-9 N '71

British airports authority
Charters force revised airport standards. H.
J. Coleman. il Aviation W 95:113+ N 15
'71
Foulkes to head British airports, claims no
knowledge of aviation. Aviation W 95:21
N 22 '71

Census
Day in the life; childrens' accounts of census
day, April 25, 1971, to be preserved. H.
R. Mayes. Sat R 54:10+ N 6 '71

Church history
Father of English history: Venerable Bede.
P. W. Schmidtchen. il por Hobbies 75:134-
6+ Ja '71

Colonies
See also
Anguilla (island)
Bermuda
Gibraltar
Malta

Commerce
Export decline seen. Aviation W 95:21 O 25
'71
See also
Crown agents for oversea governments and
administrations
European economic community

Defenses
See also
Atomic warfare—Defenses

Economic conditions
Down and out in London: the Common
market dilemma. A. Cockburn. il Ramp
Mag 10:48-51 O '71
Insolvency of Rolls-Royce. America 124:195
F 27 '71
International monetary system: a possible
reform; address, September 28, 1971. A.
Barber. Vital Speeches 38:61-3 N 1 '71
Running out of sea room. il Time 97:38 Mr
15 '71
Way of life. il Newsweek 77:48+ Mr 15 '71
See also
Unemployment—Great Britain

Economic policy
Can Heath hold the line? C. Brogan. Nat R
23:634+ Je 15 '71
Europe: the British are coming? il pors Time
97:26+ My 31 '71
Heath tries industrial Darwinism. il por Bsns
W p41-2 Mr 20 '71
Lesson for the United States? Time 98:57
Ag 2 '71
Letter from London (cont) M. Panter-Downes.
New Yorker 47:113-15 Ap 17 '71
Mr Heath sticks to his guns. A. Lejeune. Nat
R 23:366 Ap 6 '71
Skipper Heath watches tack of pilot Nixon.
B. J. Masse. America 125:250 O 9 '71
Time of trial in Britain: make or break for
Tories. il U S News 70:76-7 My 17 '71
Where is Britain heading? interview, ed. by
J. Fromm. E. Heath. por Read Digest 98:
115-18 Mr '71
See also
Budget—Great Britain
Taxation—Great Britain
Wage-price policy—Great Britain

GREAT BRITAIN—*Continued*

Economic relations
See also
European economic community

Europe, Western
Britain's probable futures. Cur 132:53-5 S '71
Europe; the search for solutions; showdown ahead. Time 97:45 Ap 26 '71
Great debate in Britain. J. Mander. Cur 132: 51-3 S '71

Rhodesia
Embargo's end. Fortune 83:41 Ap '71

Environment, Department of the
Conversation with Britain's environmental chief; interview. ed. by S. Lindsay. P. Walker. il por Sat R 55:64+ Ja 1 '72

Foreign opinion
London letter. H. R. Mayes. Sat R 54:8+ O 9 '71

Foreign relations
Douglas-Home's oceanic policy; questioning the sale of arms to South Africa. N. A. Sims. por(p481) Chr Cent 88:490-3 Ap 21 '71
Royal navy and the Ethiopian crisis of 1935-36. A. Marder; reply with rejoinder. A. Clayton and H. P. Willmott. Am Hist R 76:1257-8 O '71

Arab states
Persian Gulf: after the British raj. D. Holden. il For Affairs 49:721-35 Jl '71

Europe, Western
Time out of joint. G. W. Ball. Newsweek 77: 54 Je 14 '71

Far East
Shanghai crisis of 1932: the basis of British policy. C. Thorne; reply. G. B. Ostrower. Am Hist R 76:1265-7 O '71

Ireland
Long-range forecast; John Lynch-Edward Heath talks. il Newsweek 78:45-6 S 20 '71
Vietnam and Ulster. Nation 213:227 S 20 '71

Rhodesia
Break in the deadlock. il Time 98:50 O 4 '71

Russia
How Russia spies: a new game; case of Oleg Lyalin and expulsions. il por Newsweek 78: 31-2+ O 11 '71
To Russia without love; mass ouster of spies. il Newsweek 78:43 O 4 '71

South Africa
Douglas-Home's oceanic policy; questioning the sale of arms to South Africa. N. A. Sims. por(p481) Chr Cent 88:490-3 Ap 21 '71

Spain
See also
Gibraltar

United States
See United States—Foreign relations—Great Britain

History
17th century
Placing a name. H. R. Mayes. Sat R 54:5 Ag 7 '71

Restoration, 1660-1688
World of Samuel Pepys, esqre; with supplement: eight-page panorama of London. J. Kenyon. il Horizon 13:57-71 Sum '71

18th century
Curiosity of history; similarity of 18th century England and 20th century United States. E. Gilson and S. Gilson. Am Scholar 40:267-72 Spr '71

1760-1789
See also
United States—History—Revolution

South African war, 1899-1902
See South African war, 1899-1902

20th century
Run it down the flagpole, by B. Levin. Review
Atlan 227:96+ Mr '71. F. Kermode

Edwardian period, 1901-1910
The Edwardians; with an essay by H. Nicolson. J. H. Plumb. il Horizon 13:18-41 Aut '71

History, Naval
Royal navy and the Ethiopian crisis of 1935 36. A. Marder; reply with rejoinder. A. Clayton and H. P. Willnott. Am Hist R 76:1257-8 O '71

Industries
Britain stakes its future on the EEC; with editorial comment. il Bsns W p62-3+, 128 O 23 '71
Harried industry tightens its belt. il Bsns W p52 F 27 '71
New beat in the heart of Britain; with reproductions of paintings by N. Solovioff. Fortune 83:98-105 Ja '71
See also
Aerospace industries—Great Britain
Atomic power industry—Great Britain
Automobile industry—Great Britain
Beecham group, ltd.
Helicopter industry—Great Britain
Imperial chemical industries, ltd.
Liquor industry—Great Britain
Motorcycle industry
Office equipment industry—Great Britain
Rank-Xerox. ltd.
Wool industry

Intellectual life
See also
Great Britain—Popular culture

Kings and rulers
See also
Elizabeth II, queen of Great Britain
Great Britain—Royal family
Mary, queen of Scots
Prerogative, Royal

Labor policy
See also
Labor laws and legislation—Great Britain

Military policy
British strategy continues focus on NATO. H. J. Coleman. il Aviation W 94:32-3 Mr 8 '71

Moral conditions
Ethics: 1970 style; address, November 11, 1970. J. Heenan. Vital Speeches 37:294-8 Mr 1 '71
Full frontal absurdity. T. Beeson. Chr Cent 88:1221 O 20 '71
Lighting moral darkness. J. D. Douglas. Chr Today 16:42 O 22 '71

Politics and government
Conservatism's new British accent. R. Ball. il Fortune 83:80-3+ Ap '71
Dismal toryism. T. Beeson. Chr Cent 88:93-4 Ja 27 '71
Downhill to Dutschke. R. Williams. Nation 212:210-12 F 15 '71
Has Britain got a chance? B. Wicker. Commonweal 95:220-1 D 3 '71
Personal record. by H. Wilson. Review
New Repub 165:23-6 D 4 '71. A. Howard
Radical of 10 Downing street. A. Lewis. il pors N Y Times Mag p36-8+ Mr 14 '71
See also
Labor party (Great Britain)

Popular culture
Snobberies of the left: abusive articles about Blackpool. P. Worsthorne. Nat R 23:76 Ja 26 '71
See also
Great Britain—Census

Population
See also
Great Britain—Census

Prime ministers
See also
Heath. E. R. G.
Palmerston, H. J. T. 3d viscount
Wilson, Harold

Race question
Discrimination in British industry. T. Beeson. il Chr Cent 88:1156 O 6 '71
Press and race. Chr Cent 88:1515 D 29 '71

Religious institutions and affairs
British Methodist leader warns that the church may disappear. Chr Cent 88:947 Ag 11 '71
Forbidden worship? house churches of Britain. T. Beeson. Chr Cent 88:1042 S 8 '71
See also
Baptists in Great Britain
Catholic church in Great Britain

Royal family
Raises for royalty. il Time 98:34 D 27 '71

GREAT BRITAIN—*Continued*

Social conditions

Has Britain got a chance? B. Wicker. Commonweal 95:220-1 D 3 '71

History

The Edwardians; with an essay by H. Nicolson. J. H. Plumb. il Horizon 13:18-41 Aut '71

Social life and customs

Day in the life; childrens' accounts of census day, April 25, 1971, to be preserved. H. R. Mayes. Sat R 54:10+ N 6 '71

Technology, Ministry of

Britain: successor to Mintech loses jurisdiction over research. N. Hawkes. Science 173: 34-6 Jl 2 '71

Vital statistics

See also
Great Britain—Census

GREAT DISMAL SWAMP. See Dismal Swamp

GREAT feeling; story. See Rogers, M.

GREAT GULL ISLAND

Early warning of the terns. H. Hays and R. W. Risebrough. il Natur Hist 80:38-47 N '71

GREAT LAKES

Fresh look at fresh water; future planning for the Great Lakes basin. A. Limburg. il Motor B & S 127:10-12+ Ap '71

Ship canals and aquatic ecosystems. W. I. Aron and S. H. Smith. bibliog il Science 174:13-17 O 1 '71

See also
Erie, Lake
Michigan, Lake
Ontario, Lake
Superior, Lake

GREAT LAKES REGION

See also
Water pollution—Great Lakes Region

GREAT LAKES shipping. See Inland water transportation

GREAT men

Great men; interview. W. Lippmann. Commonweal 95:122 N 5 '71

History's love stories: down heartthrob lane with Kleenex and camera. D. Kaye. il Sat R 54:38-9+ Mr 13 '71

Silence, gentlemen, please: prominent personages who have nothing to say. T. Beeson. Chr Cent 89:6-7 Ja 5 '72

10 greatest men of American business, as you picked them. il Nations Bsns 59:44-6+ Mr '71

See also
Celebrities
Genius
Leadership
Negro celebrities

GREAT MIAMI RIVER

Valley's their business. R. W. Brenberger. il Am For 77:44-6+ My '71

GREAT Northern railway

John F. Stevens: pathfinder for western railroads. E. Clark. bibliog il pors Am West 8:28-33+ My '71

GREAT PLAINS

Dust bowl 1971. il Newsweek 77:32-3 Ap 26 '71

Ocean of grass. P. M. Tilden. il Nat Parks & Con Mag 45:4-5 Mr '71

See also
Agriculture—Great Plains

GREAT pyramid. See Pyramids

GREAT SANTEE swamp, S.C. See Marshes

GREAT SMOKY MOUNTAINS

See also
Great Smoky Mountains National Park

GREAT SMOKY MOUNTAINS NATIONAL PARK

To meet spring halfway. J. Keats. il Holiday 49:66-9+ Ap '71

GREAT society. See United States—Social policy

GREAT Western united corporation

Bitter lessons. por Forbes 108:52 N 15 '71

Nice piece of desert: Cochiti Lake, a fraud in the recreational city business. R. A. Jones. il Nation 213:616-26 D 13 '71

GREAT WHITE SANDS. See White Sands National Monument

GREATEST treasure; drama. See Winther, B.

GRECAR, Rudy

Four-year wait. il por Outdoor Life 147:84-5+ Je '71

GRÉDY, Jean Pierre. See Barillet, P. jt. auth.

GREECE, Ancient

See also
Mycenae

History

Carthage through the eyes of Greece and Rome. M. Fantar. il UNESCO Courier 23: 29-33 D '70

Peloponnesian war, 431-404 B.C.

Looking back on a golden age, the relevancy of history; address, November 10, 1971. P. MacKendrick. Vital Speeches 38:188-92 Ja 1 '72

GREECE, Modern

See also
Aegean Islands
Athens, Greece
Communism—Greece, Modern
Publishers and publishing—Greece, Modern
Investments, Foreign (in Greece)
Military assistance, American—Greece, Modern
Political prisoners—Greece, Modern
Publishers and publishing—Greece, Modern
Villages—Greece, Modern
Women—Greece, Modern

Air force

Greeks seek to modernize tactical fleet. E. H. Kolcum. il Aviation W 95:20-1 D 20 '71

U.S., France vie for Greek facility award. E. H. Kolcum. Aviation W 95:21-2 D 13 '71

Economic conditions

Letter from Athens. A. Bailey. New Yorker 47:130+ N 20 '71

Foreign relations

See also
Cyprus

United States

See United States—Foreign relations—Greece, Modern

Industries

See also
Airplane industry—Greece, Modern

Politics and government

And then there was one. Time 98:30 S 6 '71

Cheerful James; the Greek political situation as viewed by conservative J. Burnham. Nation 213:643-4 D 20 '71

Greece: immune to criticism? il Newsweek 78:33-4 Ag 16 '71

Jackie and Ari and Tom and George and Spiro and... R. Fitch. il pors Ramp Mag 10:38-47+ Ja '72

Lame defense of a deadly dictatorship; M. Hillenbrand's testimony before a Council of Europe's committee. Chr Cent 88:680 Je 2 '71

Letter from Athens. A. Bailey. New Yorker 47:130+ N 20 '71

Letter from Greece. J. Burnham. Nat R 23: 1169-70 O 22 '71

Melina Mercouri: I was born Greek; interview, ed. by J. Oringer. M. Mercouri. pors Ramp Mag 10:48-51 Ja '72

Permanency of colonels. Nation 212:549 My 3 '71

There's the Greece of Greeks and there's the tourists' Greece. A. Sotiris. il N Y Times Mag p 12-14+ Jl 25 '71

Two Greeces. M. Goldbloom. il Commonweal 93:441-4 F 5 '71

See also
Communism—Greece, Modern

Social life and customs

Only on Sundays. M. Schein. il Natur Hist 80:52-61 Ap '71

There's the Greece of Greeks and there's the tourists' Greece. A. Sotiris. il N Y Times Mag p 12-14+ Jl 25 '71

GREED. See Avarice

GREEK cookery. See Cookery, Greek

GREEK frescoes. See Frescoes

GREEK islands. See Aegean Islands

GREEK manuscripts. See Manuscripts, Greek

GREEK mythology. See Mythology, Greek

GREEK orthodox church. See Orthodox Eastern church

GREEKS

To understand Greece, go to Lia. N. Gage. il pors N Y Times Mag p 16-17+ Ja 31 '71; Reply with rejoinder. S. Bartzokis. p92 Mr 7 '71

GREELEY, Andrew M.

After the synod. America 125:424-6 N 20 '71

For a black vice president in 1972. il N Y Times Mag p28+ S 19 '71

GREELEY, Andrew M.—*Continued*
Last of the American Irish fade away. il N Y Times Mag p32-3+ Mr 14 '71
Take heart from the heartland. New Repub 163:16-19 D 12 '70; 164:43 Ja 2 '71
—and Sheatsley, P. B.
Attitudes toward racial integration; with biographical sketches. il Sci Am 225:10, 13-19 biblio(p 120) D '71

GREELEY, Arthur W.
In the service: a Christmas story. il por Am For 77:10-11+ D '71

GREELEY, Ronald
Lunar Hadley Rille: considerations of its origin. bibliog il Science 172:722-5 My 14 '71
—and Gault, D. E.
Endogenetic craters interpreted from crater counts on the inner wall of Copernicus. bibliog il Science 171:477-9 F 5 '71

GREEN, Alan
Book business. See last issue of each month of Saturday review

GREEN, Daniel G.
Light adaptation in the rat retina: evidence for two receptor mechanisms. bibliog il Science 174:598-600 N 5 '71

GREEN, Ernest
Looking back; interview. New Yorker 47:30-2 My 8 '71

GREEN, H. Gordon
Boy's best teacher. Read Digest 98:187-8 Je '71

GREEN, H. W. 2d, and others
Allende meteorite: a high-voltage electron petrographic study. bibliog il Science 172: 936-9 My 28 '71

GREEN, Kenneth F. and Garcia, John
Recuperation from illness: flavor enhancement for rats. bibliog il Science 173:749-51 Ag 20 '71

GREEN, L. M.
Hey, pastor! Chr Cent 88:126-8 Ja 27 '71

GREEN, Larry
California's 800 miles of untapped fishing. il Field & S 75:52-3+ Ja '71
Imminent death of San Francisco Bay. il Field & S 75:10+ Ap '71
Twelve Pacific flies. il Field & S 75:45-7+ S '71

GREEN, Louis C.
Starquakes: have they been observed? il Sky & Tel 41:76-9 F '71

GREEN, Mark J.
Growing up in America. New Repub 165:14-17 S 18 '71

GREEN, Marshall
Assistant Secretary Green and Assistant Secretary Trezise interviewed for Japanese national television; February 26, 1971. Dept State Bul 64:449-54 Mr 29 '71
Challenge of constructive cooperation in east Asia; address, October 4, 1971. Dept State Bul 65:459-62 O 25 '71
Nixon doctrine: a progress report; address, January 19, 1971. Dept State Bul 64:161-5 F 8 '71
Security assistance programs in east Asia; statement, May 4, 1971. Dept State Bul 64: 714-19 My 31 '71
U.S. and Japan: broadening bonds of understanding; address, October 27, 1971. Dept State Bul 65:623-4 N 29 '71
U.S. national security and assistance to East Asia; statement, November 30, 1970. Dept State Bul 63:756-62 D 21 '70

GREEN, Maurice R. and others
Interactional problems between mental health professionals and non-psychiatric physicians. bibliog Ment Hy 55:206-13 Ap '71

GREEN, Morris B. Jr
Extra fine papier-mâché mix. il Sch Arts 71:26-7 N '71
Santa and the summer rotisserie. il Design 73:24-7 Wint '71

GREEN, Philip
Obligations of American social scientists. bibliog f Ann Am Acad 394:13-27 Mr '71

GREEN, Robert A.
Under way with the USPS. See issues of Motor boating & sailing beginning April 1971

GREEN, Teddy
My first last rites; excerpt from High stick; ed. by A. Hirshberg. il Sports Illus 35: 90-3+ N 15 '71

GREEN, W. L.
Underwater fish finder. il Pop Electr 35:48-9+ Ag '71

GREEN BAY campus. See Wisconsin. University—Green Bay campus

GREEN Beret force. See United States—Army —Special forces

GREEN manuring
See also
Cover crops

GREEN MOUNTAINS
Profile for posterity: saving the skylines of Vermont. F. A. Young. il Nat Parks & Con Mag 45:20-4 F '71

GREEN revolution. See Underdeveloped areas —Agriculture

GREEN RIVER
Green River: use it or lose it? V. Huser. il Am For 77:20-3+ Je '71

GREENAWAY, Kate
Kate Greenaway. G. N. Brett. il Hobbies 76: 76+ D '71 *

GREENBERG, Al
Technology of the ski. il Esquire 76:202-7 D '71

GREENBERG, Daniel S.
Scientists as politicians. Cur 128:19-24 Ap '71

GREENBERG, Emanuel
Blend in the flavor of summer. il House B 113:128+ My '71

GREENBERG, Idaz. See Greenberg, J. jt. auth.

GREENBERG, Jerrold
Blues for Nechaiev; poem. Nation 212:535 Ap 26 '71

GREENBERG, Jerry, and Greenberg, Idaz
Buck Island: underwater jewel. il Nat Geog 139:674-83 My '71

GREENBERG, Judith Anne
Chain saw; poem. Nation 213:342 O 11 '71

GREENBERG, Stanley R.
Pueblo. Criticism
  Life il 70:17 Ap 16 '71 *
  Sat R 54:63-4 Mr 27 '71 *

GREENBLATT, Milton
Overcrowding and mental illness. A. J. Snider. Sci Digest 69:57-8 Ap '71 *

GREENBURG, Dan
Day of the Lhasa Apso; story. New Yorker 47:43-6 O 23 '71
Dear (name of magazine) New Yorker 47:43 Ap 24 '71

GREENE, Bob
Up on two wheels. See issues of Hot rod

GREENE, David H.
That enquiring man, John Synge. Nation 213:150-2 Ag 30 '71

GREENE, Felix
More heat than light. J. Gilbert. New Repub 164:35 My 29 '71 *

GREENE, Graham
Greenes of Berkhamsted; excerpt from A sort of life. il Esquire 76:126-9+ S '71
On becoming a Catholic; excerpt from A sort of life. Commonweal 94:451-3 S 3 '71

about
Books. L. E. Sissman. New Yorker 47:126-7+ O 2 '71 *
Greene-ing of America. R. McInerny. Commonweal 95:59-61 O 15 '71 *
Greene-ing of Graham Greene. W. Sheed. por Life 71:10 S 24 '71 *
Growing up as Greene. C. Hughes. il por America 125:230-2 O 2 '71 *
Ice in the heart. P. S. Prescott. por Newsweek 78:94+ S 20 '71 *
In the gloomy country of Graham Greene's heart. A. Alvarez. por Sat R 54:33-5+ S 25 '71 *
Let us all now be thankful for Mr Greene's deadly boredom. W. Kennedy. Look 35:64 O 19 '71 *
Man without. T. Foote. por Time 98:94 S 27 '71 *
Nihilism of boredom. C. Bedient. New Repub 165:23-4 O 2 '71 *
Peripatetic reviewer. E. Weeks. Atlan 228: 132 O '71 *
Sort of life, by G. Greene. Review
  Commonweal 95:113-14 O 29 '71. J. Finn *

GREENE, Holley D. 3d
Shopping centers, boon or bust? Pub W 199: 54-5 F 1; 70-1 F 8 '71

GREENE, Luther
Chrysanthemums in Japan. il Horticulture 49:26+ N '71

GREENE, Nathanael
Men of the Revolution. R. M. Ketchum. por Am Heritage 23:48-9 D '71 *

GREENE, Ron
Greeneing of U NO who—or do you? L. Keith. por Sports Illus 34:58-9 Mr 15 '71 *

GREENE, Wade
Guru of the organic food cult. il pors N Y Times Mag p30-1+ Je 6 '71
—and Golden, Soma
Luddites were not all wrong. il por N Y Times Mag p40-2+ N 21 '71

GREENE, William Cornell
Instant millionaire: Colonel W. C. Greene in fact and folklore. C. L. Sonnichsen. bibliog il pors Am West 8:4-9+ N '71 *

GREENE COUNTY, Ala.
Black power enclave. D. S. Glick. New Repub 164:11-12 Ja 16 '71
Greene County, Ala: change comes to the courthouse. J. Kane. il Time 97:21 F 1 '71
Judgment on the judge. New Repub 164:11-12 Ja 30 '71

GREENFELD, Josh
(ed) See Bergen, C. Candy Bergen: what can you say about a sleeping beauty?

GREENFIELD, Edward
Behind the scenes. See issues of High fidelity and Musical America
Midsummer marriage. il pors Am Rec G 37: 696-8+ Je '71
Proms, Aldeburgh, Glyndebourne. Hi Fi 21: MA29-30 D '71
Tippett's Knot garden, Britten's Owen Wingrave. il Hi Fi 21:MA30-1 Ag '71

GREENFIELD, Jeff
Member of the first TV generation looks back. il N Y Times Mag p8-11 Jl 4 '71
Performing arts. Harper 244:16-18+ Ja '72

GREENGARD, Paul. See Kebabian, J. W. jt. auth.

GREENHORN endurance run. See Motorcycle racing

GREENHOUSE, Gerald A. and others
Sea urchin embryos are permeable to actinomycin. bibliog il Science 171:686-9 F 19 '71

GREENHOUSE, Linda J.
At the Talk center, they talk of drugs. il N Y Times Mag p67-9+ F 21 '71
—See Moser, M. jt. auth.

GREENHOUSES
Active back-yard plastic greenhouse. M. Holck, jr. il Org Gard & Farm 18:46-50 N '71
Building a hobby greenhouse. D. J. Cotter. il Horticulture 49:42-5 My '71
Greenhouses. il Parks & Rec 6:38+ My '71
Greenhouses unlimited. T. N. Asa. il Org Gard & Farm 18:63 F '71
Grow cut flowers in your greenhouse. C. H. Potter. il Horticulture 49:18-19+ N '71
Growing alpines under glass. J. P. Osborne. il Horticulture 49:34-5 F '71
Home greenhouses. J. A. Eaton. See issues of Home garden & flower grower
In your greenhouse. J. U. Crockett. See issues of Horticulture
My mother's greenhouse. T. Anderson. Org Gard & Farm 18:105-7 O '71
Mystery of the one-way heat trap. I. Asimov. Sci Digest 69:82-3 My '71
Our geodesic greenhouse. K. Starr. il Org Gard & Farm 18:100-1 S '71
Our winter greenhouse. C. Wolstenholme. il Org Gard & Farm 18:103-4 N '71
12 month gardening under glass. il Home Gard 58:22-7 O '71
You gain more than space when you add greenhouse bays. L. Walker and others. il Pop Sci 198:90-3 Ap '71
See also
Cold frames
Hotbeds
Milwaukee—Mitchell park horticultural conservatory

GREENING, W. E.
Graphic art collecting. Hobbies 76:142-3 S '71

GREENLAND Ice sheet. See Glaciers

GREENLEAF, Dorothy. See Greenleaf, W. jt. auth.

GREENLEAF, Wayne, and **Greenleaf, Dorothy**
Effects on treatment of summarizing psychiatric records of chronic hospitalized patients. Ment Hy 55:407-9 Jl '71

GREENLEE, Lyman E.
VHF frequency converter. il Pop Electr 35: 52-3+ D '71

GREENLER, Robert G.
Infrared rainbow. bibliog il Science 173:1231 S 24 '71

GREENLIEF, Francis S.
Our most serious problem; interview. il por U S News 71:62-3 N 8 '71

GREENOUGH, Horatio
Horatio Greenough in the classic mold. T. B. Brumbaugh. il por Antiques 99:252-6 F '71 *

GREENOUGH, Richard
Unesco fellowships for study abroad. Sch & Soc 99:442-3 N '71

GREENOUGH, William B. 3d. See Hirschhorn, N. jt. auth.

GREENS, Edible
What's cooking?
Spring treats, Chinese Style. J. W. Holm. il Org Gard & Farm 18:98-101 My '71
Surprises in the green patch. Org Gard & Farm 18:132-3 Mr '71

What's for salad? Dandelion greens. il Sunset 146:196 My '71
See also
Purslane
Salads
Water cress

GREENSBORO, N.C.

Recreation
Try mobile recreation units. O. T. Hester. il Am City 86:70+ F '71

Water supply
Multipurpose water program. T. Z. Osborne and R. E. Shaw. il Am City 86:95+ Ap '71

GREENSPAN, Bud
Man who blew a Derby. il por Sports Illus 34:40-2+ My 17 '71

GREENWALD, Joseph A.
Protectionism in America; address, October 30, 1970. Dept State Bul 63:724-9 D 14 '70

GREENWAY, Hugh D. S.
Laos. Atlan 228:6+ Jl '71

GREENWICH, Conn.

Architecture
Greenwich, Conn; American can headquarters. il Arch Forum 134:28-35 Ja '71
Greenwich high school. il Arch Rec 150:133-8 N '71

GREENWICH VILLAGE, New York. See New York (city)—Greenwich Village

GREENWOOD, J. Michael. See Sirota, D. jt. auth.

GREENWOOD, S.C.

Sanitary affairs
1700-foot outfall laid in one day. C. A. Bell. il Am City 86:66-7 S '71

GREER, Edward
Liberation of Gary, Indiana. il por Trans-Action 8:30-9+ Ja '71

GREER, Frank, and **Katz, Paula**
People's peace treaty. Mlle 73:234 My '71

GREER, Germaine
Authors & editors; interview, ed. by L. P. Freilicher. por Pub W 199:13-14 My 10 '71
Female eunuch; excerpt. il McCalls 98:92-3+ Mr '71
Germaine Greer; interview, ed. by K. Tynan. il pors Vogue 159:68-71 Ja 1 '72
My Mailer problem. por Esquire 76:90-3+ S '71

about
Female eunuch. por Newsweek 77:48 Mr 22 '71 *
Saucy feminist. J. Bonfante. il pors Life 70: 30-3 My 7 '71 *
Selling of a feminist. C. Dreifus. Nation 212:728-9 Je 7 '71 *
Sex and the super-groupie. por Time 97:75 Ap 12 '71 *
Vain servile bores are we. K. Tynan. por Vogue 157:131 Ap 15 '71 *

GREER, Gordon G.
Education. Bet Hom & Gard 49:16+ Ap '71

GREET, Cabell
Where is Prof. Greet? J. C. Ottinger. Nat R 23:943 Ag 24 '71 *

GREETING cards
Earn greeting card money selling promotion ideas. H. J. Chadwick. il Writers Digest 51:22-3+ Ag '71
Packaged sentiment. R. Rhodes. il Harper 243:61-6 D '71
Realities of the greeting card market; outlook for the greeting card freelance writer in the seventies. C. Goeller. Writer 84:18-20+ D '71
UNICEF greeting cards. il UNESCO Courier 24:33 N '71
See also
Booksellers and bookselling—Greeting cards
Christmas cards
Valentines

GREETINGS. See Salutations

GREGG, Duane L.
Cars. See issues of Better homes and gardens
—and **Lidster, D. M.**
Good news. See issues of Better homes and gardens

GREGG, Gordon
Solid-state probe thermometer. il Electr World 85:70-1 Mr '71

GREGG, Russell T. and **Knezevich, S. J.**
Man we call superintendent. Ed Digest 37: 21-3 O '71

GREGOR, Arthur
Gift of the firebird; Addressed to the firebird; poems. Poetry 118:145-6 Je '71
Wilderness child; poem. New Yorker 47:48 O 9 '71

GREGORIAN chants. See Chants (Gregorian, plain, etc)

GREGORY, André
Alice in Wonderland; dramatization of story by L. Carroll. Criticism
Nat R 23:155-6 F 9 '71 *

GREGORY, Dick
And I ain't just whistlin' Dixie. il por Ebony 26:149-50 Ag '71
My answer to genocide. il pors Ebony 26: 66-70+ O '71

GREGORY, Gene
Magic of modern chemistry. il UNESCO Courier 24:4-23 biblfog(p27) Je '71
Tale of the trail. il Nat R 23:701-2+ Je 29 '71
Time for change in Hanoi? Nat R 23:427+ Ap 20 '71

GREGORY, George
Medicine learned how to save Katie Peck. D. Zimmerman. il por Todays Health 49: 20-3+ D '71 *

GREGORY, Stewart
Living with antiques. J. Lipman. il Antiques 99:112-21 Ja '71 *

GREGORY, Susan A.
Criteria for selecting supervising teachers. il Clear House 46:178-82 N '71

GREGORY family
Bringing themselves up. M. Gross. il pors Good H 173:42-4+ S '71

GREHAN, Farrell
Long light of midnight. photographs. Life 71:42-9 Jl 30 '71
Parting shots. il Life 70:73-4+ My 21 '71
Six wild havens to explore; photographs. il Life 71:52-9 S 3 '71

GREINER, Charles F.
Are you listening to or talking at? Todays Ed 60:38-9 N '71

GRENADA
Real life Grenada. G. Cotler. il Holiday 48: 45+ N '70

GRENADINES (islands)
Bareboating in the Grenadines. E. Horan. il Yachting 130:56-7+ N '71
See also
Beguia (island)

GRENIER, Carlotta
How people really travel; interview. il por Vogue 157:120 Ap 15 '71

GRESHAM, Grits
Sojourn in Santa Marta. il Field & S 76:48-9+ Jl '71

GREVE, P. A.
Chemical wastes in the sea: new forms of marine pollution. biblog il Science 173: 1021-2 S 10 '71

GREY, Anthony
Hostage in Peking, by A. Grey. Review
Sat R 54:27 Je 26 '71. H. Schwartz *
Hostage in Peking, condensation. il Read Digest 98:181-8+ Ja '71

GREY WALTER, William
They've found a wish switch in your brain. D. Lampe. por Pop Sci 198:30+ Ja '71 *

GREYHOUND corporation
Greyhound puts on weight. il Fortune 83: 230 My '71
His Greyhound goes to Phoenix. Bsns W p59 Jl 3 '71
With several ways to go, he chose up. R. F. Shaffer. il pors Nations Bsns 59:60-1 Ja '71

GREYHOUND racing. See Dog racing

GREYHOUNDS
Training
See Dogs—Training

GREYSER, Stephen A. and Reece, B. B.
Businessmen look hard at advertising. biblog f il Harvard Bsns R 49:18-20+ My '71

GRID-dip meters. See Electric meters

GRIDDLE cakes
Cheerful breakfasts: pineapple pancakes, Kumquat waffles. il Sunset 146:241 Ap '71
Double duty pancakes. il Farm J 95:40 Je '71
Flaming desserts, an introduction; crêpes. Sunset 146:140+ F '71
How to make Russian-Jewish cheese blintzes. il Sunset 146:195 Je '71
Just add caviar; palacsinta; and buck-wheat blini. R. A. Sokolov. il N Y Times Mag p22 D 26 '71
Just strawberries in a pancake. il Sunset 146:176 Je '71
Spicy cornmeal pancakes. il Sunset 146:130 F '71
They're still the way to start the day; sour cream pancakes. il N Y Times Mag p72 S 26 '71

GRIDDLES, Electric. See Household appliances, Electric

GRIDER, J. Kenneth
Christmas method. Christmas meaning. Chr Today 16:6-8 D 3 '71

GRIDIRON club. See Washington, D.C.—Clubs

GRIEB, Donald L.
Mitchell park conservatory. J. MacQuarrie. il Horticulture 49:34-5+ S '71 *

GRIEDER, Terence
Divided world of Miguel Covarrubias. il Américas 23:19-24 My '71

GRIEF. See Bereavement

GRIEF; story. See Stewart, N.

GRIEGER, Scott
Three reconnoitering artists. J. Livingston. il Art in Am 59:114-17 My '71 *

GRIER, Harry
Shoot fish in a barrel. il Pop Phot 68:72-3+ Ap '71

GRIESE, Bob
Bullet Bob v. Roger the Dodger. il pors Time 99:42-5 Ja 17 '72 *

GRIESSMAN, B. Eugene, and Argow, K. A.
Jobs in the southern forests. il Am For 77: 42-3+ Ja '71

GRIEVANCE man, Official. See Ombudsman

GRIEVANCE procedures
Employee rights under an agreement: a current evaluation. B. Aaron. biblog Mo Labor R 94:52-6 Ag '71
Legalism in U.S. industrial relations. D. V. Brown. Mo Labor R 94:51-3 Mr '71

GRIFFEN, Agnes M.
Libraries and hunger. il Library J 96:3287-91 O 15 '71

GRIFFIN, Frank L. Jr
Changes ahead in pension plans; interview. por U S News 70:88-92 Ap 5 '71

GRIFFIN, Jasper Walter
Jogger; poem. Chr Cent 88:1017 S 1 '71

GRIFFIN, John
This must be the place! il Sat R 54:54+ O 23 '71

GRIFFIN, Kelly Jean
Child can do it. il Design 73:8-9 Wint '71

GRIFFIN, Olva R.
Compost piles. il Org Gard & Farm 18:47-9 Je '71
Making money with leaves. il Org Gard & Farm 18:42-3 My '71

GRIFFIN, Richard B.
Our Catholic enemies. Commonweal 94:402-4 Ag 6 '71

GRIFFIN, Susan
Rape: the all-American crime. il Ramp Mag 10:26-35 S '71

GRIFFIN, William B.
On the beach; a stroll through a seaside nursery. il Audubon 73:33-5 My '71

GRIFFITH, Belver C. and others
Informal contacts in science: a probabilistic model for communication processes. biblog il Science 173:164-6 Jl 9 '71

GRIFFITH, David Wark
Griffith, film's old master. il por Newsweek 77:87-8+ Mr 8 '71 *

GRIFFITH, F. H.
Old mechanical banks. See issues of Hobbies

GRIFFITH, Francis
Pitfalls a guidance counselor should avoid. Clear House 46:105 O '71

GRIFFITH, Robert
Liberal capitulation. New Repub 165:23 O 9 '71

GRIFFITH, Winthrop
Daring educational experiment: the one-room schoolhouse. il N Y Times Mag p 14-16+ My 30 '71
Taos Indians have a small generation gap. il N Y Times Mag p26-7+ F 21 '71

GRIFFITHS, Martha (Wright)
Excerpt from testimony before the Subcommittee on constitutional amendments, May 5, 1970. Cong Digest 50:16+ Ja '71
Set stage for new equal rights battle. S. B. Conroy. por McCalls 98:37 My '71 *

GRIGSON, Geoffrey
Oculi; Chapel; No sprinkling of bright weeds; Pawlonia; Après la chasse; Myth enacted; Hill of the bees; Return to Florence; poems. Poetry 119:28-33 O '71

GRILIKHES, Alexandra
Antonioni poem. Am Scholar 40:700 Aut '71

GRILL cookery. See Barbecue cookery

GRILLS, Barbecue. See Barbecue grills

GRIMES COUNTY, Tex.
Populist dreams and Negro rights: east Texas as a case study. L. C. Goodwyn. biblog f il Am Hist R 76:1435-56 D '71

GRIMM, Willard T.
That old urge is back again. il Bsns W p26 O 16 '71 *

GRIMOND, John
Rhodesia. Atlan 228:24+ O '71
GRINDAL, Gracia
For the Sunday school superintendent with love and hope; poem. Chr Cent 88:880 Jl 21 '71
GRINDING machines
Bench grinders. il Consumer Rep 36:618-21 O '71
Build this pedestal grinder for $40. R. S. Hedin. il Pop Mech 136:144-5 N '71
Hobby hand grinders. il Consumer Rep 36: 615-17 O '71
See also
Compost grinders and grinding
GRINDING wheel dressers. See Dressers (tools)
GRINDING wheels
Grinding wheel for cutting costs; Emrald wheel. il Bsns W p 104 D 4 '71
GRINSPOON, Lester
Marijuana: who smokes it, and why; excerpt from Marihuana reconsidered. Mlle 73:180-1+ My '71
GRISEZ, Germain
Making the ethical case against abortion. pors Time 97:70 Mr 29 '71 *
GRISSOM, Betty
Capsule fire flares up again. il pors Life 71: 24-9 S 17 '71 *
GRITS. See Corn grits
GRIZZLY bear hunting. See Bear hunting
GRIZZLY bears. See Bears
GROBMAN, Arnold B.
Bipolarity on the campus. Science 174:457 O 29 '71
GROCERY store chains. See Supermarkets
GROCERY stores. See Food stores
GROCERY trade
See also
Great Atlantic and Pacific tea company
Pierce, S. S, company
Supermarkets
GROEBLI, René
Gallery; photograph. Life 71:8-9 O 15 '71
GROENE, Gordon, and Groene, Janet
Make your water tank from wood. il Motor B & S 128:74-8 Ag '71
—See Groene, J. jt. auth.
GROENE, Janet, and Groene, Gordon
Bimini: island in the stream. il Motor B & S 127:54+ Je '71
—See Groene, G. jt. auth.
GROENING, Homer
One last impossible shot at fame. il Sports Illus 35:56-8+ D 6 '71
GROLIER, Inc.
FTC takes new tack on door-to-door book sales. S. Wagner. Pub W 200:29 Jl 26 '71
GROMAN, Janice
Brief biography. S. Goodman. pors Dance Mag 45:68-9 Jl '71 *
GROMYKO, Andrei Andreevich
Foreign policy and the United Nations; address, October 4, 1971. Vital Speeches 38: 38-45 N 1 '71
Our foreign policy; address, April 6, 1971 Vital Speeches 37:427-30 My 1 '71
U.S. and U.S.S.R. sign agreements to reduce risk of nuclear war; remarks, September 30, 1971. Dept State Bul 65:400 O 18 '71
GROPPI, James Edward
Groppi quits black movement, calls for black-white coalition. Chr Cent 88:970 Ag 18 '71 *
Groppi's worth. J. Deedy. Commonweal 95: 194 N 26 '71 *
GROSKINSKY, Henry
Brain; photographs. Life 71:57-65+ N 12 '71
Movie palaces; photographs. Life 70:44-51 F 19 '71
Saving Savannah; photographs. Life 70:48-55+ My 7 '71
GROSMAN, Brian A.
Civil justice and naked power. Nation 213: 494-6 N 15 '71
GROSS, Alex
National art workers community. Art in Am 59:23 S '71
Toward a community of artists. Am Artist 35:5 Je '71
GROSS, Amy
Chewing your way to health, sexual vitality, peace. Mlle 72:184-5+ Ap '71
Let George do it. Mlle 73:160-1+ O '71
Santa Cruz mystique. il Mlle 74:102-3+ Ja '72
(ed) See Skinner, B. F. Nice new world of B. F. Skinner
GROSS, Beatrice, and Gross, Ronald
Radical school reform. Sch & Soc 99:28-9 Ja '71
GROSS, Bertram M.
All-American friendly fascism? Cur 126:13-25 F '71

GROSS, Daniel R.
Great sisal scheme; with biographical sketch. il Natur Hist 80:8, 48-55 Mr '71
GROSS, Franklin S.
Films are in at Fermi. il School Teach Jr/Sr High p22-3 O '71
Kicks and flicks at Fermi. il Schol Teach Jr/Sr High p 16-17+ F 1 '71
Teleguide. il Schol Teach Jr/Sr High p 15 D '71
GROSS, H. R.
Not only red tape, but millions for a lot of claptrap; excerpts. il por U S News 71:30-1 Jl 19 '71
GROSS, Leonard
Introducing: the supernurse. McCalls 98:75+ Mr '71
Woodstock discovers Washington. Who? George Washington. il Look 35:30+ Ag 24 '71
(ed) See Perenchio, A. G. In this corner Jerry Perenchio
GROSS, Ludwik
Where are they now? il pors Newsweek 77: 10 F 22 '71 *
GROSS, Marthe
Bringing themselves up. il pors Good H 173: 42-4+ S '71
GROSS, Nelson
Recent activities in international drug control; statement, October 27, 1971. Dept State Bul 65:600-4 N 22 '71
GROSS, Robert A.
Lieutenant Calley's army. il Esquire 76:154-8+ O '71
GROSS, Ronald. See Gross, B. jt. auth.
GROSS national product
Economy: fair and warmer, so far. il Newsweek 77:71-2 Ap 26 '71
Economy: our deceptive growth dividend. J. R. Meyer. il Sat R 54:44-5 Ja 23 '71
GNP does matter. J. Darmstadter. il Bul Atom Sci 27:46-8 D '71
Making progress slowly. Time 97:90 Ap 26 '71
$100 billion in growth: a startling forecast. il Time 98:20 O 4 '71
1065 and all that. por Time 97:83 F 22 '71
Springtime euphoria. P. A. Samuelson. Newsweek 77:90 My 10 '71
Toward comprehensive measurement of prices. A. D. Searle. bibliog f il Mo Labor R 94:9-22 Mr '71
Trillion-dollar economy: the real meaning. il U S News 70:18-19 F 8 '71
GROSSBERG, Sidney E. and Morahan, P. S.
Repression of interferon action: induced dedifferentiation of embryonic cells. bibliog il Science 171:77-9 Ja 8 '71
GROSSER, Maurice
Art. Nation 212:222 F 15 '71
GROSSER, Morton
Little light on the subject; use of lasers in art and entertainment. Atlan 227:92-6 Je '71
GROSSMAN, Alan H.
China & the U.S.: the twain shall meet. il Harper 243:86-8+ O '71
GROSSMAN, Edward
Obsolescent mother. il Atlan 227:39-50 My '71
GROSSMAN, Morton I. See Barbezat, G. O. jt. auth.
GROSSMANN, Mary Ann
Museum for fun and learning. il Am Ed 7:24-5 My '71
GROSVENOR, Verta Mae
Vibes from Verta Mae. P. Garland. il pors Ebony 26:86-8+ Mr '71 *
GROS VENTRE wilderness area (proposed)
See Wilderness areas—Wyoming
GROTHAUS, Emily A. and others
Human lymphocyte antigen reactivity modified by neuraminidase. bibliog il Science 173:542-4 Ag 6 '71
GROTON, Conn, public library
Go-for-broke in Groton. J. T. Carey. il por Library J 96:1684-5 My 15 '71
Groton censors win: trustees back down. Library J 96:1318 Ap 15 '71
Nevergreen in Groton: special news analysis. S. C. Scott. il pors Wilson Lib Bul 45:818-20+ My '71
GROTOWSKI, Jerzy
Grotowski and Schechner: the servitudes of freedom. T. Hoffman. il Art in Am 59:74-81 Mr '71 *
GROUND covers. See Cover plants
GROUND effect machines. See Air cushion vehicles
GROUND squirrels
Annual biological clocks. E. T. Pengelley and S. J. Asmundson. il Sci Am 224:72-9 Ap '71
GROUND stations (communications satellites)
See Communications satellites—Ground stations

GROUND transportation, High speed. See
Transportation, High speed
GROUND water. See Water, Underground
GROUNDCOVERS. See Cover plants
GROUNDING (electricity) See Electric currents—Grounding
GROUNDS, Vernon C.
Therapist and theologian look at love. Chr Today 15:14-16 Ag 6 '71
GROUP buying. See Purchasing, Cooperative
GROUP conflict. See Social conflict
GROUP counseling
See also
Group psychotherapy
GROUP health cooperative of Puget Sound
Health care in Seattle. P. Barnes. New Repub 165:12-13 D 18 '71
GROUP instruction
Group instruction with the individual touch. R. R. Gard. bibliog f Clear House 46:73-7 O '71
GROUP leadership. See Leadership
GROUP living. See Collective settlements
GROUP marriage counseling. See Marriage counseling
GROUP of ten (organization)
Gloomy prelude to the IMF meeting; with editorial comment. il Bsns W p20, 96 S 18 '71
Group of 10 begins to bargain. Bsns W p26 D 4 '71
Group of ten ministerial meeting held at Washington; text of communique, September 26, 1971. Dept State Bul 65:458 O 25 '71
Money; the dangers of the U.S. hard line. il por Time 98:34-5 S 27 '71
Repairing Humpty Dumpty. Newsweek 78:74 S 20 '71
Solving a crisis: John Connally superstar; Rome meeting. il por Newsweek 78:85-6+ D 13 '71
Tough talk and an ominous deadline. il por Newsweek 78:82-4 S 27 '71
U.S. taking a hard line on dollar. trade. il U S News 71:70-1 S 27 '71
GROUP psychology. See Groups (sociology)
GROUP psychotherapy
Family centered project in a state mental hospital. M. E. Elder and P. E. Weinberger. bibliog il Ment Hy 55:337-43 Jl '71
Report on a consciousness-raising group. il Mlle 73:80-1+ Jl '71
Structured approach to group marriage counseling. T. A. McClellan and D. R. Stieper. bibliog Ment Hy 55:77-84 Ja '71
See also
Family psychotherapy
GROUP relations training
Big Vic; operator of Institute of human abilities More Houses. C. H. Simonds. Nat R 23:1471 D 31 '71
Carl Rogers on encounter groups, by C. Rogers. Review
Commonweal 95:136+ N 5 '71. C. A. Weber
Critique of sensitivity training. M. K. Reimer. bibliog Sch & Soc 99:356-7 O '71
Encounter games: a dangerous new trend. B. Wysor. Harp Baz 104:60-1 Je '71
Encounter groupers up against the wall. B. L. Maliver; discussion. N Y Times Mag p53 F 7 '71
Encounter groups: a dangerous game? B. L. Maliver. Cur 126:3-12 F '71
Further view on laboratory education. K. G. Van Auken, jr. Mo Labor R 94:63-5 Mr '71
Human relations training for camp staff members. C. B. Rotman and C. S. Clayman. il Camp Mag 43:10+ Ap '71
I became a bum to understand their problems; societal sensitivity program. S Bacon il pors Sci Digest 69:40-7 My '71
Notes on corporate man. R. Todd. il Atlan 228:83-8+ O '71
Sensitivity education. S. M. Corey and E. K. Corey. Ed Digest 36:23-5 Mr '71
Sensitivity: new awareness of yourself; with editorial comment. C. Coiro; E. Moir; J. A. Bolch. il Har Yrs 11:6-10+ Mr '71
Sensitivity training; Raymond school project, Chicago R. L. Jerrems. Ed Digest 37:26-9 O '71
Sharing and caring; microlabs. E. Hunter. Todays Ed 60:73 S: 60 O '71
Teacher and the T-group: NTL's Center for the development of educational leadership. C. H. Harrison. il Schol Teach Jr/Sr High p6-7+ F 1 '71

Caricatures and cartoons
Casualties of sensitivity. J. Noonan. il Cath World 212:316-17 Mr '71
GROUPE Boussac. See Textile industry—France

Le GROUPE express. See Publishers and publishing—France
GROUPIES
Prey to charisma; The Groupies. C. E. Fager. Chr Cent 88:356 Mr 17 '71
GROUPING by ability. See Ability grouping in education
GROUPS (sociology)
Catalytic agent for effective planning; coordinator's role. J. C. Chambers and others. il Harvard Bsns R 49:110-19 Ja '71
Effects of fallout shelter confinement on mental health. M. P. Beussee and others. Ment Hy 55:121-3 Ja '71
New tribalism; an attempt by minorities to preserve a cultural identity. Nation 214:36-7 Ja 10 '72
GROUSE
Facts about the grouse cycle. K. Davis. il Field & S 76:38+ S '71
GROUSE shooting
Glorious Twelfth. S. Williams. il Field & S 76:98-100+ N '71
Grouse behind the iron curtain. H. Jensen. il Outdoor Life 147:86-7+ Ap '71
Grouse in the West. T. Trueblood. il Field & S 76:20+ S '71
Grouse: know its spots. R. Gilsvik. il por Outdoor Life 148:82-3+ O '71
Indians were only first. K. C. Schuyler. il Field & S 76:52-3+ S '71
Paddy's grouse. N. Riley. il Outdoor Life 148:80-3+ Ag '71
See also
Ptarmigan shooting
GROVE, Edward R.
Making of a medal. il Am Artist 36:20-5+ Ja '72
GROVE press, inc.
Grove press, New York city. il Arch Rec 149:102-3 Ja '71
GROWING up; story. See Dunovan, C.
GROWTH
Depth habitats of growth stages of pelagic foraminifera. C. Emiliani. bibliog il Science 173:1122-4 S 17 '71
Fish otoliths: daily growth layers and periodical patterns. G. Pannella. bibliog il Science 173:1124-7 S 17 '71
Temporal synergism of corticosterone and prolactin controlling gonadal growth in sparrows. A. H. Meier and others. bibliog il Science 173:1240-2 S 24 '71
See also
Regeneration (biology)
Stature
GROWTH (plants)
Maximizing tree growth. C. E. Whitcomb. Horticulture 49:44-5+ Ap '71
Motion-induced inhibition of elongation and induction of dormancy in liquidambar. P. L. Neel and R. W. Harris. bibliog il Science 173:58-9 Jl 2 '71; Reply. R. Turgeon and J. A. Webb. 174:961-2 N 26 '71
Shaken trees. il Time 98:42 S 6 '71
See also
Electrohorticulture
GROWTH, Economic. See Economic development
GROWTH funds. See Investment trusts
GROWTH inhibiting substances
Inhibition of normal growth by chronic administration of Δ-9-tetrahydocannabinol. F. J. Manning and others. bibliog il Science 174:424-6 O 22 '71
See also
Methotrexate
GROWTH inhibiting substances (plants)
See also
Abscisic acid
Maleic hydrazide
GROWTH of children. See Children—Growth and development
GROWTH of cities and towns. See Cities and towns—Growth
GROWTH promoting substances
Growth effects of vanadium in the rat. K. Schwarz and D. B. Milne. bibliog il Science 174:426-8 O 22 '71
See also
Pituitary hormones
GROWTH promoting substances (plants)
See also
Gibberellins
Morphactins
GRUBB, L. Edward
Hard-liner gets Inco's no. 1 slot. por Bsns W p68 N 13 '71
GRUBER, Michael
Great ocean sweepstakes. il Sea Front 17:146-59 My '71
Lancers of the reef. il Sea Front 17:30-7 Ja '71
Tank on the bottom of the sea. il Sea Front 17:26-9 Ja '71

GRUBER, Murray
Welfare-industrial complex. Nation 212:808-11 Je 28 '71
GRUEBY, William H.
Grueby art pottery. R. W. Blasberg. il Antiques 100:246-9 Ap '71 *
GRUEBY faience and tile company. See Pottery industry
GRUEN, John
Dance. Vogue 157:73 Mr 15 '71
Do you mind critics calling you cheap, decadent, sensationalistic, gimmicky, vulgar, overinflated, megalomaniacal? il por N Y Times Mag p 14-16+ Ja 2 '72
Greedy underground. Vogue 157:136 F 1 '71
(ed) See Bernstein, L. Leonard Bernstein
(ed) See Gielgud, J. Sir John Gielgud
(ed) See Richardson, R. Sir Ralph Richardson
GRUENBERG, Selma
Carry a big stick and print with it. il Sch Arts 70:22-3 F '71
GRUENING, Ernest
Man who let down the side. Nation 213:378-9 O 18 '71
about
Early dove. Nation 212:261 Mr 1 '71 *
GRUENINGER, Walter F.
Phonograph records. See issues of Consumer bulletin
GRUMBACH, Doris
Greening of the laity. Commonweal 94:372-3 Jl 23 '71
Living through the revolution. Commonweal 93:412-13 Ja 29 '71
Sexual revolution, would you believe? Commonweal 94:180-1 Ap 30 '71
GRUMER, H.-D. See Lott, J. A. jt. auth.
GRUMMAN corporation
Cost overrun threatens Grumman. Bsns W p37 Ap 10 '71
Grumman's F-14 draws more flak. il Bsns W p25 O 9 '71
Grumman's whipsaw? F-14 contract. il Forbes 108:32-3 D 15 '71
Up, up, up; F-14 cost overrun. il Newsweek 77:80+ Je 14 '71
What Grumman has learned from Lockheed. il Bsns W p74-5 Je 12 '71
GRUND, Benjamin
Booby traps in executive taxes; interview, ed. by G. R. Rosen. por Duns 97:10-12+ F '71
GRUNDER, H. A. and others
Acceleration of heavy ions at the bevatron. il Science 174:1128-9 D 10 '71
GRUNDIG, Max
His ad produced an heir apparent. il por Bsns W p70 O 9 '71 *
GRUNFELD, Frederic V.
Echoes of the Aryans. il Horizon 13:102-4 Sum '71
How to choose a royal bride. il por Horizon 13:118-19 Spr '71
Johann Sebastian Bach. il por Horizon 13:58-65 Wint '71
Most gifted human being that has ever been born. il pors Horizon 13:96-103 Aut '71
(tr) See Falla, M. de. Falla on Wagner
GRUNFELD, Jacoba
(tr) See Falla, M. de. Falla on Wagner
GRUNION
See also
Cookery—Fish
GUADALAJARA, Mexico
Fiesta dining in Guadalajara. M. Woodward. il Travel 135:63 Mr '71
Mexico: a haven for disabled vets. L. Robinson. il Ebony 27:31-4+ Ja '72
GUADELOUPE (islands)
See also
Architecture, Domestic—Guadeloupe (islands)
GUALTIERI, Antonio R.
Resurrection as God's historical deed. Chr Cent 88:432 Ap 7 '71
GUAM
Appealing flight interruption and some trans-Pacific options. il Sunset 146:65-6 Je '71
GUANOSINE monophosphate
Cyclic adenosine and guanosine monophosphates and glucagon: effect on liver membrane potentials. N. Friedman and others. bibliog il Science 171:400-2 Ja 29 '71
GUANTANAMO naval base. See Navy yards and naval stations
GUARANI Indians. See Indians of South America
GUARANTEED annual income
Guaranteed annual income: a hope and question mark. A. Sheahen. America 125:503-7 D 11 '71
Welfare bill boomerang: bonus for working less; study findings of Alfred Teller and Dorothy Teller. il Nations Bsns 59:62-5 S '71

GUARANTEED income. See Guaranteed annual income
GUARANTY. See Warranty
GUARANTY of loans. See Loans, Bank—Guaranty
GUARD dogs. See Watchdogs
GUARD rails. See Roads—Safety guards
GUARDIAN and ward
Protective arms of the law. K. Donelson and I. Donelson. Har Yrs 11:15-17 Mr '71
Willing your child. F. Sabin. Ladies Home J 88:194 My '71
GUARDS
Guard you hire may be dangerous; Rand study. Bsns W p25-6 D 4 '71
Rent-a-cop boom. il Newsweek 79:43-4 Ja 10 '72
GUARDS, Prison. See Prisons—Officials and employees
GUARDS, Saw. See Machinery—Safety devices and measures
GUARE, John
House of blue leaves. Criticism
Nation 212:285-6 Mr 1 '71 *
New Yorker 47:90 F 20 '71 *
Sat R 54:10 Mr 20 '71 *
GUARNERI string quartet. See String quartets
GUATEMALA
See also
Church and state in Guatemala
Guerrillas—Guatemala
Nutrition problems—Guatemala
Police—Guatemala
Terrorism—Guatemala
Water supply—Guatemala

Politics and government
Guatemala: terror in silence. J. C. Goulden. Nation 212:365-8 Mr 22 '71
Guatemala's right-wing terror. A. Portes. il Nation 214:47-8 Ja 10 '72
Inside a state of siege: legalized murder in Guatemala. S. Bodenheimer. il Ramp Mag 9:50-2 Je '71
GUBERNATORIAL elections. See Elections—United States
GUBRIUM, Jaber F.
Self-conceptions of mental health among the aged. bibliog Ment Hy 55:398-403 Jl '71
GUCCIONE, Robert
Prodigal son makes it big. il por Forbes 107:19 Mr 1 '71 *
GUDAITIS, Donald J.
Plugging the generation gap. Clear House 45:556-7 My '71
GUENTHER, George C.
Ready to police safety practices. Bsns W p101 Mr 27 '71 *
GUERARD, Edmund R.
Diversification can solve many camp problems. il Camp Mag 43:10-11 N '71
La GUERRA; opera. See Rossellini, R.
GUERRILLA warfare
Anarchist cookbook, by W. Powell. Review
Newsweek 77:98 Ap 12 '71
Can urban guerrilla warfare succeed? H. Tinker. Cur 129:52-7 My '71
Myth of the guerrilla, by J. B. Bell. Review
Sat R 54:36-8 D 25 '71. E. Capouya
GUERRILLAS
NLF epoch. J. Burnham. Nat R 23:418 Ap 20 '71
Tactics of terror: where reds will strike next; interview, ed. by J. Fromm. B. Crozier. il por U S News 70:75-8 Mr 1 '71
Trade in troublemaking. il Time 97:28+ My 10 '71

Africa
Visit with African liberation front leaders. C. Rogers. Chr Cent 88:1099 S 22 '71

Arab states
Giving the commandos a hand. L. Jenkins. il Newsweek 78:34-5 Jl 26 '71
This is a hijacking! condensation. J. A. Elten. il Read Digest 99:213-17+ Jl '71
We were hijacked! teen travelers in Jordanian desert and Amman. S. Finkelstein and P. Burt. pors Seventeen 29:170 D '70
See also
Fedayeen
Guerrillas—Lebanon

Bolivia
Cuba's second Vietnam; Bolivia. M. D. Gensler. Yale R 60:342-65 Mr '71

Burma
Buddha vs. General. M. Parker. il Newsweek 77:40+ Mr 22 '71

GUERRILLAS—*Continued*

Canada

See also
Front for the liberation of Quebec

Ceylon

Civil war in Ceylon. T. Deutscher. il Ramp Mag 10:26-9 Jl '71

Chad

Day the rebels attacked; ed. by O. Brooks. E. M. Ochoa. il pors Outdoor Life 147:44-7+ Ja '71

Chile

Chile's Che Guevara? Miristas' Comandante Pepe or G. J. Liendo. N. Ossa. Nat R 23: 307-8 Mr 23 '71

Ethiopia

Eritrean rebellion. il Newsweek 77:34 Mr 1 '71
Shum-shir game. il Time 97:35 Mr 1 '71

Guatemala

When the blood began to run. il por Time 97:33 Mr 22 '71

India

Future of guerrilla warfare. H. Tinker; E. Haubold. Cur 129:52-60 My '71

Jordan

Hussein routs the guerrillas. il U S News 71:23 Ag 2 '71
Showdown season in the Middle East. il por Newsweek 78:35-7 Ag 2 '71
See also
Fedayeen

Latin America

Guerrilla movements in Latin America, by R. Gott. Review
New Repub 164:29-30 My 22 '71. V. Free-hafer
What lessons from Latin America; excerpt from Guerrilla movements in Latin America. R. Gott. Cur 130:55-9 Je '71

Lebanon

Lebanon: the politics of survival. J. B. Wolf. bibliog f Cur Hist 62:30-4+ Ja '72

Mexico

Plot the Russians muffed. C. Foley. Nat R 23:479-80 My 4 '71
Soviet plot to destroy Mexico; excerpt from KGB. J. Barron. il Read Digest 99:227-32+ N '71
Troubles on the Via Pacifica. il Time 97:23-4 Ap 19 '71

Middle East

Death at the Gate of Hope. il Time 98:17 Jl 19 '71
See also
Guerrillas—Arab states
Guerrillas—Lebanon

Northern Ireland

As open war rages in Northern Ireland. il U S News 71:36-7 Ag 23 '71

Oman

Oil and revolution in the Persian Gulf. F. Halliday. il Ramp Mag 9:52-4 Ap '71

Pakistan

Bengal: the time of revenge. A. de Borch-grave. il Newsweek 78:46+ N 22 '71
Bengalis strike back. il Newsweek 78:36 Jl 19 '71
Eyewitness in East Pakistan: an occupied, conquered territory. il U S News 71:44 Ag 23 '71
Hunting for Mukti Bahini behind the lines. J. Saar. il Life 71:32-4 D 10 '71

Philippines

Marcos and the Communists. J. de Herrerra. il America 126:6-10 Ja 8 '72

Thailand

Counterinsurgency's proving ground. M. T. Klare. Nation 212:527-31 Ap 26 '71

Turkey

Hard times. il Newsweek 77:47+ Je 14 '71
Tempting target; Israeli diplomat E. Elrom. Time 97:37 My 31 '71

Uruguay

Back in action; seizure of G. H. S. Jackson. Newsweek 77:34+ Ja 18 '71
Claude Fly's seven-month nightmare. P. Friggens. il Read Digest 99:64-70 S '71

Great escape; Tupamaro jailbreak. Newsweek 78:45 S 20 '71
Tupamaros tunnel out. il Time 98:35-6 S 20 '71
GUESS, Earl E.
One man's fight. il pors Outdoor Life 147:4+ F '71
GUEST, Barbara
Jeanne Reynal. il Craft Horiz 31:40-3 Je '71
GUEST houses
Guest in the garden; the Bruce Colens' guest-house-in-a-garden in North Hollywood. il House B 113:56-9 Mr '71
GUEST, Keen and Nettlefolds, ltd.
Old ironmonger gets new muscle. il Bsns W p66+ S 25 '71
GUEST rooms
Checking out the guest room. W. Baldwin. House & Gard 139:8+ Je '71
From attic corner to child-sized guest-room. M. Hass. il House B 113:54 My '71
Making the best-dressed guest room list. C. Kriebel. il Harp Baz 104:36-7 Jl '71
Suffering summering houseguests. J. Stafford. Vogue 158:112 Ag 15 '71
Tuck a bedroom into a closet. K. Fanelli. il Pop Sci 199:96 S '71
GUEST speakers. See Public speaking
GUESTS
That was the weekend that was. Vogue 157: 116-17 Je '71
See also
Entertaining
Hospitality
GUGGENHEIM, Solomon R, museum, New York. See Solomon R. Guggenheim museum, New York
GUICCIOLI, Teresa (Gamba) contessa
Lovers; excerpt from The nympho and other maniacs. I. Wallace. pors Ladies Home J 88:132-3 F '71 *
GUIDANCE. See Personnel service in education; Vocational guidance
GUIDE books. See Guidebooks
GUIDEBOOKS
Bibliography
Discover America in 1972; comp. by S. S. Benson. il Américas 23:40-3 O '71
GUIDED missile bases
Construction wages burden arms talks; slowdown in building third Safeguard site. Bsns W p28 Ag 14 '71
GUIDED missile industries
Italian guided missile firm has international ambitions. Aviation W 94:191 My 31 '71
See also
Lockheed missiles and space company
GUIDED missiles
Chinese ICBM's next? Sr Schol 98:6-7 Ap 5 '71
Digging the silos; China's missile program. Time 97:22 Mr 8 '71
Foreign technology sought in missile work; Japanese defense agency. Aviation W 95: 63 N 1 '71
Growing threat: Soviet Union's new military hardware. C. Brownlow and B. Miller. Aviation W 95:12-15 O 4 '71
Maneuvering missile re-entry vehicle studied. Aviation W 94:17 Je 28 '71
Missile myths. H. Scoville, jr. New Repub 165:17-19 O 2; 19-20 O 9 '71; Reply with rejoinder. J. R. Rumbaugh. 165:32-3 D 25 '71
Our four-star military mess; with editorial comment. G. P. Hunt. il Life 70:3, 50-2+ Je 18 '71
Shocks and shivers; Russia-U.S. spiral. New Repub 165:7-8 O 30 '71
Soviets continue stress on tactical air. il Aviation W 94:27-8 Mr 8 '71
Soviets deploy new, larger ICBM. C. Brownlow. il Aviation W 94:16-17 Mr 15 '71
Soviets stressing offensive mix of strategic arms for which U.S. has little defense. C. Brownlow and B. Miller. il Aviation W 95: 36-40 O 11 '71
U.S. looks at a French missile; radar-guided Crotale. il Bsns W p78 Ja 23 '71
USAF unit seeks integrator role; Aeronautical systems division. M. L. Yaffee. Aviation W 94:14-15 My 10 '71
See also
MIRV

Animal pilots

See Animals, War use of

Defenses

ABCs of ABM. P. J. Ognibene. Commonweal 94:31-4 Mr 19 '71
ABCs of ABMs. G. W. Rathjens. Bul Atom Sci 27:14-16 Mr '71
ABM critics taken to task; Safeguard program. R. Halstead. Nat R 23:1299 N 19 '71

GUIDED missiles—Defenses—*Continued*
ABM debate: learned society split by old grievance. N. Wade. Science 174:276-7 O 15 '71
Congress may force Safeguard changes. D. C. Winston. Aviation W 94:18-19 Ap 26 '71
Deterrence through defense. C. Benson. il Nat R 23:251-9 Mr 9 '71; Discussion. 23:240, 342+, 356-7 Mr 9, Ap 6 '71
Is the ABM moral? An argument for the affirmative. E. S. Boylan. Commonweal 94:303-6 Je 11 '71; Discussion 94:418-19+ Ag 20 '71
Judgment; ORSA ABM debate. Sci Am 225: 48 N '71
Lobbying against the ABM, 1967-1970; adaptation of address, September, 1970. T. A. Halsted. il Bul Atom Sci 27:23-8 Ap '71
Notes on the new isolationists; ABM and Cooper-Church amendment. J. Clotfelter. Bul Atom Sci 27:37 F '71
Our strategic-arms advantage is fading fast. C. J. V. Murphy. Read Digest 98:94-8 F '71
Ready to give on arms control; with editorial comment. il Bsns W p86, 136 Mr 13 '71
Stop now. Commonweal 93:483-4 F 19 '71
Time dimension of military forces; address, May 14, 1971. J. C. Meyer. Vital Speeches 37:518-21 Je 15 '71
See also
Ballistic missile early warning system

Design
French study advanced IRBMs. D. E. Fink. il Aviation W 95:52-6 Ag 30 '71
New target missile keyed to flexibility; BATS missile. il Aviation W 94:69-71 Je 14 '71

Ethical aspects
See Atomic warfare—Ethical aspects

Launching from airplanes
Missile that aborted: Skybolt. il Newsweek 78:7 D 27 '71
SRAM may exceed performance goals. C. Brownlow. Aviation W 94:22-3 Je 21 '71

Launching from ships
Closing a gap in missiles; Harpoon. il Bsns W p96 Je 26 '71
USSR improves cruise missile capabilities. C. Brownlow and B. Miller. il Aviation W 95: 38-43 N 8 '71

Launching sites
See Guided missile bases

Propulsion systems
Thiokol chosen as second source SRAM rocket motor supplier. Aviation W 95:19 N 29 '71

Specifications
Leading international missiles; tables (cont) Aviation W 94:72-3 Mr 8 '71
U.S. & Canadian drones and target missiles (title varies) tables (cont) Aviation W 94: 89 Mr 8 '71
U.S. missiles; tables (cont) Aviation W 94: 63-4 Mr 8 '71
USSR missiles; tables (cont) Aviation W 94: 71 Mr 8 '71

Testing
Freeze on missile testing. J. Lederberg. Bul Atom Sci 27:4-6+ Mr '71
New facility to reduce R&D costs; army missile command's advanced simulation facility. M. L. Yaffee. il Aviation W 95: 44-6 Jl 19 '71

GUIDES
Fly El Elijah! clergyman as tour conductor. A. R. Stees. Chr Cent 88:1471-2 D 15 '71
How good will your next guided hunt be? R. R. Lyons. il Field & S 76:45+ N '71
How to choose an outfitter. J. O'Connor. il Outdoor Life 148:49-51+ Ag '71
Summer diplomat, U.S.A: guide for G. Yogtiba of Ghana and S. Nganoubara of Burundi. A. Adams. por Seventeen 29:270-1+ Ag '70
Your future in the past: retirees as guides and craft demonstrators. W. Hoffer. il Har Yrs 11:39-42 Jl '71
See also
Mountaineering
National park personnel
GUIDES, Taped. See Tape recordings
GUILD, Ben
Ghosts of the Wrangells. il Outdoor Life 147: 78-81+ Ap '71
GUILD, Warren R.
Fitness forever Vogue 157:172-3 My '71
GUILDS. See Gilds
GUILLERMO, Gelacio
Pan de sal; poem. Poetry 118:208 Jl '71

GUILLERY, R. W. and others
Mutants with abnormal visual pathways: an explanation of anomalous geniculate laminae. bibliog il Science 174:831-2 N 19 '71
GUILLORY, Ferrell
New Orleans schools ten years later. America 125:93-5 Ag 21 '71
GUILT, Plea of. See Pleas (criminal procedure)
GUINEA
La bizarrérie in Guinea; conspiracy plot. America 124:107 F 6 '71
Blood rites; judgments on invaders. Newsweek 77:36 F 8 '71
See also
United Nations—Guinea

Native races
Baga and the inscrutable Nimba. L. Bangoura. bibliog il Negro Hist Bul 34:30-2 F '71
GUINEA, PORTUGUESE. See Portuguese Guinea
GUINNESS, Dolores
Swans and cygnets: three generations of beautiful Guinnesses; photographs. C. Beaton. Vogue 157:60-1 Ja 15 '71 *
GUINNESS, Gloria
Damn those young girls! por Harp Baz 105: 110 D '71
Sex appeal 1971. Harp Baz 104:196-7 S '71
about
Swans and cygnets: three generations of beautiful Guinnesses; photographs. C. Beaton. Vogue 157:60-1 Ja 15 '71 *
GUIRAUD, Ernest
Good old Guiraud. B. Fischer-Williams. por Opera N 35:24-5 F 6 '71 *
GULATI, Jagdish, and Jones, A. W.
Cooperative control of potassium accumulation by ouabain in vascular smooth muscle. bibliog il Science 172:1348-50 Je 25 '71
GULBENK, Roupen M.
Living with antiques. il Antiques 100:602-5 O '71 *
GULDAHL, Ralph, Jr
Supernaturals. il Hot Rod 24:36-41 F '71
GULF American corporation
Peddling the great West. T. W. Pew, jr. il Sat R 54:48-51 S 4 '71
GULF and Western Industries, Inc.
Conglomerateur comes back. por Bsns W p67 D 18 '71
Roughneck from Bologna. por Bsns W p43 Je 5 '71
GULF ISLANDS
Exploring the border islands. il Sunset 147: 44-51 Jl '71
GULF OF CALIFORNIA. See California, Gulf of
GULF OF TONKIN incident, 1964. See Tonkin Gulf incident, 1964
GULF oil corporation
Curse of too much. il Forbes 107:33 Ap 1 '71
Gulf oil kneels to church wishes. Bsns W p39 F 27 '71
Wall Street beat. R. Brady. Duns 97:81-2 F '71
GULF resources and chemical corporation
Something out of nothing. il Forbes 107:40 Je 15 '71
GULF STREAM
Gulf Stream and middle Atlantic bight: complex thermal structure as seen from an environmental satellite. P. K. Rao and others. il Science 173:529-30 Ag 6 '71
GULLION, Gordon W.
You can have more grouse in your woods. il Field & S 76:60-1+ O '71
GULLS
Case of the missing gulls; littered shoreline of Traverse City. il Time 97:52 Je 28 '71
GUM nebula. See Nebulae
GUMERMAN, George J. and Lyons, T. R.
Archeological methodology and remote sensing. bibliog il Science 172:126-32 Ap 9 '71
GUMM, George H.
Sex education: time for appraisal. Clear House 46:110-11 O '71
GUMPERT, David
ILGWU: the old age of a union. Nation 212: 716-19 Je 7 '71
GUMPERZ, Julian
Voice of experience; interview. por Forbes 107:46+ Mr 1 '71 *
GUMPILIL, David
Just in from the Outback. J. Downs. il pors Life 71:72-4 S 17 '71 *
GUMS (anatomy)
Diseases
See also
Periodontia

GUMS and resins
Tall oil, a valuable by-product. J. T. Geoghegan and W. E. Bambrick. bibliog il pors Chem 44:6-10 Ja '71
GUN control legislation. See Firearms—Laws and regulations
GUN play; drama. See Udoff, Y.
GUN racks
Let your gun rack work year round. L. A. Wilke. il Pop Mech 135:114 F '71
GUN sights. See Firearms—Sights
GUNBY, Phil
(ed) Medical briefs. See issues of Today's health to July 1971
GUNDERSON, Doris V.
Research in the teaching of English. bibliog Engl J 60:547-53, 792-6 Ap, S '71
GUNITE
We tried gunite to repair spalled curbs; Manchester, Conn. W. D. O'Neill. il Am City 86:69 Ja '71
GUNKHOLING. See Cruising
GUNN, Barbara A.
Toward a national policy on aging. address, May 15, 1971. Vital Speeches 37:597-9 Jl 15 '71
GUNN, Hartford, Jr
PBS, NET and the FBI. il Newsweek 78:127 O 18 '71
GUNNERY ranges. See Bombing and gunnery ranges
GUNS (small arms) See Firearms; Pistols; Revolvers
GUNS in the closet; story. See Yglesias, J.
GUNSMITHING
Little old men with files. W. Page. il Field & S 76:98-100+ Ag '71
GUNSTON Hall. See Virginia—Historic houses, etc.
GUNTHER, Max
Wives who run away. il Ladies Home J 88: 6+ F '71
GUPTON, James A. Jr
Build an electronic darkroom temperature monitor. il Radio-Electr 42:40-2 F '71
Build R-E's photo densitometer. il Radio-Electr 42:48-51 My '71
GURFEIN, Murray Irwin
In the courts: the government vs. the press. il por Newsweek 77:27+ Je 28 '71 *
GURIN, Samuel, and Carr, W. E.
Chemoreception in nassarius obsoletus: the role of specific stimulatory proteins. bibliog il Science 174:293-5 O 15 '71
GURKHAS
See also
Great Britain—Army—Brigade of Gurkhas
GURNEY, A. R. Jr
Scenes from American life. Criticism
New Yorker 47:95-7 Ap 3 '71 *
GURNEY, Dan
Dan Gurney on snowmobiles; interview. ed. by G. Reiger. il pors Pop Mech 136:148-50+ O '71
Drivin' with Dan; questions and answers. See issues of Popular mechanics
I'm retiring from driving, but I'll never quit racing! interview. il pors Pop Mech 135:86-9+ Mr '71
GURR, Betty A.
Doing your own thing. il Sch Arts 70:34-6 Mr '71
GUSFIELD, Joseph R.
Student protest and university response. bibliog f Ann Am Acad 395:26-38 My '71
GUSSINYER ALFONSO, Jordi
Metro monuments. il Américas 23:13-19 Ap '71
GUSSOW, Mel
(ed) See Pinter, H. Conversation [pause] with Harold Pinter
GUSTAFSON, Donald H.
New perspectives on aging. Cur 132:40-2 S '71
GUSTAFSON, E. Donald
What is college publishing all about? Pub W 200:63-4 N 15 '71
GUSTAFSON, Faith
How much in a word? poem. Seventeen 29:170 Ag '70
GUSTAVUS, Alaska
Hooked on Gustavus. D. Butwin. il por Sat R 54:46-7 Jl 24 '71
GUTENBERG, Arthur W.
U.S.-Japanese textile squabble: is it economics? Is it politics? or did our industry goof? interview. por Forbes 108:22-3 O 15 '71
GUTENBERG, Johann
Johannes Gutenberg, where are you? P. A. Farrell. il Pub W 199:48-9 Ap 26 '71 *
GUTENBERG museum, Mainz
Johannes Gutenberg, where are you? P. A. Farrell. il Pub W 199:48-9 Ap 26 '71

GUTERMUTH, Clinton Raymond
Man called Pink: citizen of the year; adaptation of address, February 25, 1971. H. Clepper. por Am For 77:3+ My '71 *
GUTH, Francis
Conversation food. il House & Gard 139: 85-91 F '71
GUTH, Hans P.
Behavioral objectives and the teaching of English. P. W. Airasian. Engl J 60:495-9 Ap '71 *
GUTHEIM, Frederick
Architecture. Nation 213:190 S 6 '71
GUTHMAN, Edwin O.
Into the breach at Bobby's side. J. Canan. il Bsns W p 16+ Je 19 '71 *
GUTHRIE, Ramon
Comment. W. H. Pritchard. Poetry 119:162 D '71 *
Epic for a bad century. A. Laing. Nation 212:213-16 F 15 '71 *
Inner world where poets wander. J. Kessler. Sat R 54:39 O 2 '71 *
GUTHRIE, Rita
Create creativity. il Sch Arts 71:28-30 S '71
GUTHRIE, William Lane
Mike Frome. M. Frome. Am For 77:7+ F '71 *
GUTIÉRREZ, José Angel
U.S. journal: Crystal City, Tex. E. Hahn. New Yorker 47:102+ Ap 17 '71 *
GUTIERREZ CANTU, Xavier
Latin America: a U.S. news orphan. il America 124:290-1 Mr 20 '71
GUTKIND, Lee Alan
Little agony, a little ecstasy. il por Sports Illus 35:36-8+ S 27 '71
GUTMAN, Robert W.
Obviously produced with loving care: from London: Die zauberflöte. il Am Rec G 37: 472-4 Ap '71
GUTTERS
Clean and open 5000 catchbasins in ninety days; New York city. il Am City 86:58 Ja '71
Cleaning
$4.31 vs. $34 per basin; Denver. il Am City 86:38 Ap '71
GUTTMAN, Helene N.
Internal cellular details of euglena gracilis visualized by scanning electron microscopy. bibliog il Science 171:290-2 Ja 22 '71
GUTTMAN, Louis
Social problem indicators. bibliog f il Ann Am Acad 393:40-6 Ja '71
GUYANT, Tom
Little boy taught me . . . il Nat Wildlife 10: 13-15 D '71
GWATHMEY, Charles
Architect speaks his mind; interview. por House & Gard 139:20+ Mr '71
Art of architecture. il Art in Am 59:92-7 Ja '71
about
All-year vacation house: a surge of space. A. Stagg. il House & Gard 139:114-21 Mr '71 *
GYMNASIUMS
Prep school athletics building; Phillips Exeter academy, Exeter, N.H. il Arch Rec 149:97-106 Je '71
Sports showcase; Japan dental college gym. Tokyo. il Arch Forum 135:42-5 Jl '71
GYMNASTICS
In sporting shape: two top gyms, two approaches to fitness; for men. il Vogue 157: 113 My '71
See also
Acrobats and acrobatism
Exercise
GYNECOLOGY
Gynecology: yesterday and today. E. B. Connell. Redbook 137:14+ Jl '71
GYÖRGYI, Albert Szent-. See Szent-Györgyi, A.
GYPSIES
European gypsy leaders ask for recognition. Chr Cent 88:519 Ap 28 '71
GYPSIES in Ireland
Portrait of tinkers. B. MacMahon. il Natur Hist 80:24-35+ D '71
GYPSY moths
Gypsy moth backlash. P. R. Ehrlich and J. P. Holdren. il Sat R 54:71 O 2 '71
Gypsy moth runs wild. B. C. Kilvert, Jr. il Home Gard 58:28-9+ Ag '71
Inchworm caper; dispute over the use of insecticide to battle gypsy moth and worms. il Newsweek 77:95 Je 7 '71
It's time to stop the gypsy moth, sanely. V. Zaffiro. il Org Gard & Farm 18:59-63 O '71

GYPSY moths—*Continued*
Moths 65, USDA O N. Wade. Science 174:41
O 1 '71
Plague of moths. il Time 98:48 Jl 26 '71
Report on gypsy moths. il Chem 44:23 S '71
GYROCOPTERS. See Autogiros
GYROSCOPES
Navaid uses electrostatic gyros. B. Miller. il
Aviation W 94:49-50 Mr 22 '71
Vibrating wire, new twist in gyros. R. Mac-
Dhai. il Pop Sci 198:49 Ja '71
GYROSCOPIC instruments
See also
Inertial guidance systems

H

HEW. See United States—Health, education
and welfare, Department of
HIAS. See United HIAS service, inc.
HISC. See United States—Congress—House—
Internal security, Committee on
H. J. Heinz company. See Heinz, H. J, com-
pany
HUD. See United States—Housing and urban
development, Department of
HAACK, Robert William
Haack steps down. Time 98:106 N 1 '71 •
Leaving the big board. il Fortune 83:145-6
Ja '71 •
Quitting the club. por Newsweek 78:72+ N 1
'71 •
HAACKE, Hans
Art; cancellation of exhibition at the Gug-
genheim. L. Alloway. Nation 213:93-4 Ag
2 '71 •
Artists vs. museums; Haacke-Guggenheim af-
fair. E. C. Baker. Art N 70:25+ My '71;
Discussion 70:21+ S '71 •
HAAK, John R.
Goal determination; address, August 1970.
bibliog il Library J 96:1573-8 My 1 '71
HAAK, Ronald O.
Co-opting the oppressors: the case of the
Japanese-Americans. il Trans-Action 7:23-
31 O '70
HAAR, Charles M.
Alternative 11: an urban development bank.
Cur 128:50-2 Ap '71
HAAS, Ernst
Henri Cartier Bresson: a lyrical view of
life. il Mod Phot 35:88-97+ N '71
HABASH, George
Going underground. por Time 98:45 S 27 '71 •
HABASHI, Fathi
Ida Noddack. 75 & element 75. bibliog il por
Chem 44:14-15 F '71
HABEAS corpus
Stretch points of liberty. A. Dershowitz. Na-
tion 212:329-34 Mr 15 '71
HABER, Deborah
Hollywood tennis does socko biz. il Sports
Illus 34:42-4+ Mr 8 '71
HABER, George
Dream super 8 outfit. il por Pop Phot 68:
114+ F '71
HABER, Leo
Run, Dick, run! Sat R 54:6 Je 12 '71
HABIB, Philip Charles
[Plenary session] on Viet-Nam held at Paris.
See issues of Department of state bulletin.
August 23, 1971-
HABITS
How to break habits that make you unhappy;
excerpt from The will to happiness. A. A.
Hutschnecker. il Ladies Home J 88:134+
F '71
How to teach your child good habits; be-
havior therapy. A. Lake. il Redbook 137:
74+ Je '71
HABITS, Nervous. See Nervous habits
HABITS of animals. See Animals—Habits and
behavior
HACALA, Joseph R. and Kakalec, J. M.
Court breaks new social ground in housing
policy. America 124:228-30, 590-1 Mr 6, Je 5
'71
HACH, V. and McDonald, E. C.
Diethylamide of thujic acid: a potent repell-
ent of aedes aegypti. bibliog il Science 174:
144-5 O 8 '71
HACHETTE (firm) See Publishers and publish-
ing—France
HACHTEN, Harva
Kitchen safari; excerpts. il Ladies Home J
88:140-1+ Mr '71

HACKETT, Alice Payne
Hardcover best sellers of 1970: the year of
the love story. il Pub W 199:34-7 F 8 '71
HACKETT, Blanche
Legs are coming back. il Am For 77:5+ S '71
HACKETT, Bobby
Musical events; Cape Cod notes. W. Balliett.
New Yorker 47:75 Ag 28 '71 •
HACKETT, Earle
Ecologic of nursery rhymes. J. Lear. il Sat
R 54:73-6 N 6 '71 •
HACKETT, Francis
Kilkenny boy. H. B. Hough. New Repub 164:
26-7 F 6 '71 •
HACKETT, Walter
Juggler of Our Lady; dramatization of a story
by A. France. Plays 31:89-94 D '71
HACKLER, Rhoda E. A. See Rainwater, D. T.
jt. auth.
HACKSAW blades. See Saws
HACKSAWS. See Saws
HACKWORTH, David H.
Let's get out; summary of interview, ed. by
K. Buckley and N. Proffitt. por Newsweek
78:34 Jl 5 '71
HADDON, E. P.
Trout agitator. il Field & S 75:68-9+ Mr '71
HADEISHI, T. and McLaughlin, R. D.
Hyperfine Zeeman effect atomic absorption
spectrometer for mercury. bibliog il Science
174:404-7 O 22 '71
HADJ. See Pilgrimages to Mecca
HADLEY, Mac E. See Vesely, D. L. jt. auth.
HADLEY, Walter C.
Boats by Purdy. il Yachting 130:68-9+ N '71
HADLEY, William H.
Money man. M. Mayer. por Opera N 35:28-9
Ap 3 '71 •
HADRONS. See Particles (nuclear physics)
HAEMANTHUS. See Blood lilies
HAENSEL, Vladimir, and Burwell, R. L. Jr
Catalysis; with biographical sketches. il Sci
Am 225:10, 46-58 D '71
HAERER, Deane N.
Summer school outdoors. il Todays Ed 60:
18-19 F '71
HAESSNER, Helen
Pitfalls and promises. il Sch Arts 71:22-5
Ja '72
HAFELE, Joseph C.
Question of time. il pors Time 98:63 O 18 '71 •
HAFIF, Herbert
Excerpt from letter in Los Angeles times.
October 10, 1970. Cong Digest 50:223 Ag
'71
HAFNER, Stefan S. See Dundon, R. W. jt.
auth.
HAFTER, R. P.
Smoldering resentment in French Canada. Cur
132:46-50 S '71
HAGA, Kinzo
I sell Japanese steel. N. A. Martin. por Duns
97:49-50+ Je '71 •
HAGANS, Orville R.
On time. See issues of Hobbies
HAGEDORN, George G.
1971 outlook; address, March 21, 1971. Vital
Speeches 37:376-9 Ap 1 '71
HAGEL, Raymond Charles
New look at educational publishing; inter-
view. Pub W 200:27-8 D 13 '71
HAGEN, David
On the table; poem. Commonweal 95:202 N
26 '71
HAGEN, Dorothy
Sendak sampler; interview, ed. by A. DeMir-
jian, jr. il Pub W 200:37-9 D 6 '71
HAGEN, Johann Georg
J. G. Hagen and his cosmic clouds. J. Ash-
brook. bibliog il por Sky & Tel 42:215-16
16 O '71 •
HAGEN, Uta
Don't call me madam! interview, ed. by G.
Loney. il por Opera N 335:6-7 Ja 23 '71
HAGERTY, James C.
Security information and democracy. Cur
131:7-8 Jl '71
HAGFISH
Immunity of the hagfish. D. S. Linthicum. il
Sea Front 17:17-22 Ja '71
HAGGARD, Merle
Merle Haggard. P. Hemphill. por Atlan 228:
98-103 S '71 •
Merle Haggard. C. S. Wren. il pors Look 35:
36-8+ Jl 13 '71 •
HAGGERTY, Patrick Eugene
Productivity; industry isn't the only place
where it's a problem; interview. il por
Forbes 107:43-5 F 1 '71
Shift to the production of services. Science
173:679 Ag 20 '71

HAGGIN, Bernard H.
New records in review. See issues of Yale review

HAGGIN, Joseph H. S.
Adsorption. il Chem 44:6-9 Ap '71

HAGUE, The
International court of justice
See International court of justice. The Hague

HAGUE peace conferences
Anecdotes, facetiae, satire, etc.
Mr Dooley on The Hague conference, 1907. F. P. Dunne. Am Heritage 22:6 F '71

HAHM, Pyong Choon
Korea and the emerging Asian power balance. For Affairs 50:339-50 Ja '72

HAHN, Emily
Reporter at large. New Yorker 47:46-8+ Ap 17; 46-60+ Ap 24; 54-6+ D 11 '71

HAHN, Vera D.
American treasury: New Orleans. il Am Home 74:72-81 Mr '71
Decorating newsletter. See issues of American home
Old Salem: a Moravian memoir. il Am Home 74:28+ D '71

HAHN, Walter
Changing school patterns in West Germany. bibliog Clear House 45:300-4 Ja '71

HAHN, William E. and Laird, C. D.
Transcription of nonrepeated DNA in mouse brain. bibliog il Science 173:158-61 Jl 9 '71

HAIDER, Donald H.
Governors and mayors view the poverty program. bibliog f Cur Hist 61:273-8+ N '71

HAIKU
Haiku: ancient poetry for today's ecology. G. Randorf. il Cons 26:8-13 D '71

HAIL
Birth of a hailstone. il Chem 44:18-19 Ap '71
Hailstones. C. Knight and N. Knight. il Sci Am 224:96-103 Ap '71
Search for a way to suppress hail. K. Frazier. il Sci N 99:200-2 Mr 20 '71

HAILEY, Arthur
Story behind the book: Wheels; interview. ed. by P. A. Farrell. Pub W 200:32 O 18 '71
Wheels; condensation of novel. Good H 173: 87-91 S; 96-9 O; 118-19 N '71

HAILEY, Oliver
Father's day. Criticism
Sat R 54:22 Ap 3 '71 •
Time il 97:67 Mr 29 '71 •

HAINES, Aubrey B.
Evers administration: two years of progress in Fayette. Chr Cent 88:908-11 Jl 28 '71

HAINES, Francis
Horses and the American frontier; excerpts From Horses in America. il Am West 8:10-15 Mr '71

HAIR
Blond comes in many colors. il McCalls 98: 96-9+ F '71
Keep this under your hat; the long-haired hard hat. K. Fleming. il Newsweek 78: 30-1 Jl 26 '71
10 most common hair myths. Good H 173: 187 O '71
What brunettes have that blondes don't. il Harp Baz 104:122-3 F '71
Why your hair may be curly. Good H 172: 182 Mr '71
See also
Baldness
Beards
Hairdressing
Wigs

Anecdotes, facetiae, satire, etc.
Short note on long hair. R. Armour. Sat R 54:4 Je 19 '71

Care
Beauty: how to stop killing your hair; and your scalp. il Mlle 74:122-5 Ja '72
Bits and pieces about all sorts of hair and its care. Mlle 73:126-7 Jl '71
Common-sense guide to hair. il Ladies Home J 88:90-1+ F '71
Cosmic conditioning of hair. X. Pové. See issues of Harper's bazaar
Don Lee cures hair ills. D. Lee. por Harp Baz 104:44 F '71
Great hair: it's a matter of conditioning. C. Bartel. il Am Home 74:16 F '71
Hair arts. G. Briand. il por Harp Baz 104:41 F '71
Hair care or careless hair: the case for conditioners. S. Lindsay. il House B 113: 22+ S '71
Hair conditioning: the rites of spring. il Redbook 136:82-3+ Ap '71

Hair: cut, color, and condition. P. Van Wagenen. il Parents Mag 46:137-9 N '71
Hair talk: about cut and health. L. Gignac. il Mlle 73:132 Je '71
Hairdressers tell you how to go six weeks without them. il Vogue 157:76-81 Ja 15 '71
Right ways to use hair-care products. Good H 174:143 Ja '72

Dyeing and bleaching
All you need to know about hair color. il Mlle 73:124-5 Jl '71
Easy streaking. C. Bartel. il Am Home 74: 14+ S '71
Henna: should she or shouldn't she? Vogue 157:43 Mr 1 '71
Instant youth the new real-life haircolorings. il Vogue 158:108-11 Jl '71

Transplantation
Hair transplants are there to stay. B. Ford. il Sci Digest 69:35-6 My '71

HAIR; musical comedy. See Musical comedies, revues, etc.—Criticisms, plots, etc.

HAIR (botany) See Trichomes

HAIR bleaching. See Hair—Dyeing and bleaching

HAIR clippers
Clippers for hairy heads, and beards? il Consumer Bul 54:10-12 S '71

HAIR cutting. See Haircutting

HAIR dressing. See Hairdressing

HAIR dryers
Hair dryers. il Consumer Rep 37:33-8 Ja '72
Project: you, electric beauty. il Ladies Home J 88:47 Ja '71

HAIR mass. See Mass (music)

HAIR pieces. See Wigs

HAIR stylists. See Beauty operators

HAIR styles. See Hairdressing

HAIRCUTTING
Cut & care; interview. A. Lintermans. il por Mlle 73:130-1 Jl '71
How to get the haircut you want. il pors Redbook 136:82-5+ F '71
Parting shots; about face! Fix hairnets! Forward march! il Life 70:76 Je 18 '71
Scissors superstar! P. McGregor. W. J. Parente. il Sr Schol 99:42+ S 27 '71
What I learned from my sister Mona; blunt cut. H. Grant. il por Seventeen 29:77 Jl '70
You've gotta take a chance. il Mlle 72:121-3 Mr '71

HAIRDOS. See Hairdressing

HAIRDRESSING
Ancient African look becomes new look in Paris. il Ebony 26:121-2+ Je '71
Beautiful holiday hairdos for the family. T. Pavlik. il Good H 173:74-5 D '71
Beautifully simple summer hairdos. T. Pavlik. il Good H 172:116-19 Je '71
Beyond the Afro. il Time 98:72 O 25 '71
Bonjour, Paris! Here's Mona Grant in her beauty whirl. il pors Seventeen 29:112-15+ N '70
Courts and long hair. il Sr Schol 98:6-9 Ap 26 '71
Cut and care. il Mlle 73:128-9 Jl '71
Easy pretty head; wigs, coiffures; the shortest, kindest cut. il Vogue 157:110-15 Ap 1 '71
For four young women: new beauty with a positive point of view. il Good H 172:206-9 F '71
Great hairdo for everyone. il Mlle 74:148-51 N '71
Hair is darting in all directions. il Seventeen 30:228-35+ Ag '71
Hair talk; interview with California haircutter; ed. by N. Bertin. C. White. pors Mlle 73:208-9 My '71
Hair talk: Mlle treats model Jean White to a new cut, new health. il Mlle 73:130-1 Je '71
Hair today, gone tomorrow. K. Perutz. Seventeen 30:160+ Mr '71
Help! What'll I do? Too thick, too thin, too sallow, too pale. il Mlle 73:151-9 O '71
Long hair: new things to do with it. il Mlle 72:134-7 F '71
Long hair, the new, soft shape. S. Obre. il Ladies Home J 88:136-9 My '71
Mr Bruce takes permanents. il Harp Baz 104: 46 F '71
New classic, continuing classics. il Seventeen 29:222-5+ Ag '70
Nite brites: how you shine is up to you. il Seventeen 30:100-5 O '71
Simple secrets of today's free and easy hair. il Redbook 137:116-19+ S '71
Splitting hair; men's styles. il Newsweek 79: 42 Ja 3 '72

HAIRDRESSING—*Continued*
Summer hair strategy. il McCalls 98:86-9+ Je
'71
23 new hairdos, exciting young makeup
looks. T. Pavlik. il Good H 173:100-11+ O
'71
23 romantic hairdos; radiant new makeup
looks. il Good H 172:94-105 **Ap** '71
Wet heads: hair that goes wet to dry, beautifully. il Mlle 73:156-9 My '71
What I learned from my sister Colleen. M.
Corby. il por Seventeen 29:78 Jl '70

History
Cuts and curls and other shear delights. il
Sr Schol 98:10-12 Ap 26 '71
HAIRPIECES. See Wigs
HAIRSTYLISTS. See Beauty operators
HAITI
Darkness in Haiti. R. D. Crassweller. For
Affairs 49:315-29 Ja '71
Enter Mama Doc. il por Time 97:41 F 22
'71
Intimations of mortality. por Time 97:36 Ja
25 '71

Politics and government
Breaking the spell. il por **Time 97:33-4**
My 3 '71
Haiti, by R. I. Rothberg and C. K. Clague.
Review
Sat R 54:44 Mr 27 '71. H. Lavine
Haiti without Papa Doc; new faces, but more
of the same. il por U S News 70:39 **My 3**
'71
Jean-Claude Duvalier; I will continue the
revolution with my father's fierce energy;
with editorial comment. il pors **Life 70:3,**
34-6 My 7 '71
Pooh-Bah. il Time 98:53-4 O 11 '71
President for life dies. il por Newsweek 77:
40+ My 3 '71
Relevance of black power in Haiti. C. W.
Thomas. New Repub 164:11-13 Je 19 '71
Sons of the bitter mango; Haitian political
figures in the U.S. B. Thompson. Nation
213:551-4 N 29 '71

Social conditions
Known evil; Haiti of Papa Doc. E. Peer.
por Newsweek 77:39+ Ap 26 '71
HAITIAN emigrés. See Emigrés
HAITIANS in the United States
New York's Haitians: working, waiting,
watching Bébé Doc. M. W. Lear. il N Y
Times Mag p22-3+ O 10 '71; Reply. G. Ju-
melle. p 16+ O 24 '71
El HAJJ Malik; drama. See Davidson, N. R. jr.
HALABY, Najeeb E.
Trader as diplomat, address, October 20,
1971. Vital Speeches 38:145-8 D 15 '71

about
Pan American: carriers in crisis. por Time
98:84 O 25 '71 •
Why Pan Am doesn't have a new president.
pors Bsns W p 120-2 N 13 '71 •
HALASZ, Gyula. See Brassaï
HALAWA, Fayez
Yassin, my son. Criticism
Time il 97:39 Ap 5 '71 •
HALBERSTAM, David
End of a populist. il por Harper 242:35-45 Ja
'71
Fairest dark horse of them all. il pors Mc-
Calls 99:102-3+ N '71
Hank Williams remembered. Look 35:42 Jl 13
'71
Programming of Robert McNamara. il pors
Harper 242:37-40+ F; 8+ My '71
War of continuing illusions. Cur 128:3-4 Ap
'71
HALBERSTAM, Michael Joseph
Doctor's new dilemma: will I be sued? il
N Y Times Mag p8-9+ F 14 '71
I've never been healthy a day in my life. il
Todays Health 49:34-9+ N '71
HALBIG, Peter L.
Stay for the ending. il Outdoor Life 147:76-9+
F '71
HALBREICH, Susan T.
(comp) Children's paperbacks (cont) Library
J 96:297-9 Ja 15 '71
HALDEMAN, Harry Robbins
Nixon's Haldeman; power is proximity. C.
S. Wren. il pors Look 35:15-19 **Ag 24** '71 •
HALE, Bob
Some lessons on dying. il por Chr Cent 88:
1076-9 S 15 '71
HALE, Dennis
How reformers bombed in New Haven. Com-
monweal 94:473-7; 95:143, 215 S 17, N 5, 26
'71

HALE, Irlene W.
Black culture: a reading program develops
better understanding. Clear House 45:269-72
Ja '71
HALE, Robert
Pastoral prayer. Chr Cent 88:100 Ja 27 '71
Trust; poem. Cath World 213:129 Je '71
HALE, Robert D.
Censorship: what a bookseller can do about
it. Pub W 200:26-7 Jl 26 '71
HALEAKALA NATIONAL PARK
Hawaii's Seven pools. il Sunset 146:40-5 Ja
'71
HALEIWA, Hawaii
Hawaii's yesterday, just an hour from Hono-
lulu. il Sunset 147:23 S '71
HALEY, Gail E.
Caldecott award acceptance; address, June
21,1971. il Horn Bk 47:363-8 Ag '71
Newbery/Caldecott awards; excerpts from
addresses ed. by P. Bragg. Pub W 200:28 S
6 '71

about
Gail E. Haley. A. Arnold. por Horn Bk 47:
369-72 Ag '71 •
Viking and Atheneum authors are 1970 New-
bery and Caldecott winners. L. Russ. il
pors Pub W 199:116-18 F 22 '71 •
HALKIN, Hillel
Building Jerusalem. Commentary 52:59-66 S
'71
HALL, Alice J.
Climb up Cone crater. il Nat Geog 140:136-
48 Jl '71
HALL, Ben
Movie palaces; photographs. Life 70:44-51
F 19 '71
HALL, Christopher
Water. bibliog il por Chem 44:6-10 S '71
HALL, Clarence W.
Must our churches finance revolution? Read
Digest 99:95-100 O '71
They take vacations for humanity. il Read
Digest 98:45-6+ Ap '71
Which way the World council of churches?
Read Digest 99:177-8+ N '71
HALL, Claude Temple
When families fight pollution. il Parents Mag
46:76-7+ N '71
HALL, Clem M.
Arts and humanities in the library: a guide
for federal aid to libraries. il Am Lib 2:
201-2 F '71
HALL, Conrad
Conrad Hall: an interview; ed. by M. Shed-
lin. il Film Q 24:2-11 Spr '71
HALL, Donald
Writing poems. Writer 84:19-21 F '71
HALL, Donald Joyce
What's a nice firm like yours doing in a place
like this? il pors Nations Bsns 59:62-3 Ja
'71
HALL, E. Raymond
Tallgrass Prairie National Park. il Am For
77:16-21 D '71
HALL, Floyd D.
Different crisis; excerpts from address, Feb-
ruary 1971. Aviation W 94:9 Mr 1 '71
Freedom and enterprise; address, February
24, 1971. Vital Speeches 37:430-4 My 1 '71
HALL, Frances
Interchange; poem. America 125:100 Ag 21
'71
HALL, Graham M.
College racing. Yachting 130:168 N '71
Post time for college sailing. il Yachting 129:
66-7+ Mr '71
Racing clinic. See issues of Yachting
64th Chicago-Mackinac. Yachting 130:43+ S
'71
HALL, J. Floyd. See Punke, H. H. jt. auth.
HALL, Jack W.
Rebel in paradise. Nation 212:196-7 F 15 '71 •
HALL, Joyce Clyde
What's a nice firm like yours doing in a place
like this? D. J. Hall. il pors Nations Bsns
59:62-3 Ja '71 •
HALL, Judy
Beginning teacher; interview. il por Todays
Ed 60:54-9 S '71
HALL, Leonard Wood
Where are they now? il pors Newsweek 79:
7 Ja 10 '72 •
HALL, Lloyd Augustus
Lloyd A. Hall: the time has come. S. P.
Massie. por Chem 44:21 Mr '71 •
HALL, Louise
Put a goose run in your garden. il Org Gard
& Farm 18:56-7 Je '71
HALL, Marjory
Molly meets the general; drama. Plays 30
47-54, 64 F '71
Pilgrim rebel; drama. Plays 31:13-24 N '71

HALL, Mary Bowen
Help save our heritage. il Har Yrs 11:38-40 O '71
Painting with petals. il Design 72:36 Spr '71

HALL, Ray
Security, safety: two sides of the coin. bibliog il Parks & Rec 6:22+ D '71

HALL, Ridgway M. jr
Cutting off aid to expropriators. New Repub 165:15-17 O 2 '71
Legal services, inc. New Repub 164:24-5 My 29 '71

HALL, Robert
Pedaling to Shangri-la. il Cons 26:5-7 D '71

HALL, William Stanley
Obituary
Pub W 200:39 O 11 '71

HALL marks
Early silversmiths and the silver trade in Georgia; with check list of Georgia marks. K. G. Farnham and C. H. Efird. il Antiques 99:380-5 Mr '71
Mobile silversmiths and jewelers 1820-1867; with check list of Mobile silversmiths. S. A. Smith. il Antiques 99:407-11 Mr '71

HALL of fame, Baseball. See National baseball hall of fame and museum

HALL of peoples of the Pacific. See American museum of natural history, New York

HALLE, Louis J.
After Vietnam, another witchhunt? il N Y Times Mag p36-8+ Je 6 '71
Language of statesmen. il Sat R 54:30-1 O 16 '71

HALLECK, Seymour Leon
Psychiatric reappraisal; excerpts from The politics of therapy. Cur 131:43-50 Jl '71

Les **HALLES** market. See Paris—Markets

HALLETT, Garth L.
Plain meaning of abortion. America 124:632-3 Je 19 '71

HALLEY, Edmond
Edmond Halley at St Helena. J. Ashbrook; reply. W. G. Tatham. Sky & Tel 41:280 My '71 *

HALLIDAY, E. M.
Sphairistiké, anyone? il Am Heritage 22: 48-59 Je '71

HALLIDAY, Fred
Egypt moves west. por Ramp Mag 10:41-4 Ag '71
Oil and revolution in the Persian Gulf. il Ramp Mag 9:52-4 Ap '71
Once and future shah. Ramp Mag 10:18+ N '71

HALLIE, Philip Paul
Raskolnikov, the Scholar, and fresh air. Am Scholar 40:579-82 Aut '71

HALLMARK cards, inc.
Packaged sentiment. R. Rhodes. il Harper 243:61-6 D '7
What's a nice firm like yours doing in a place like this? D. J. Hall. il pors Nations Bsns 59:62-3 Ja '71

HALLMARKS. See Hall marks

HALLORAN, Art
Oklahoma's new wilderness. il Liv Wildn 35: 9-12 Spr '71

HALLORAN, Richard T.
Politics of suicide. por Commonweal 94:34-6 Mr 19 '71

HALLOW, Ralph Z.
Mayor is nobody's boy. il Nation 212:492-6 Ap 19 '71

HALLOWEEN
Halloween adventures, some cautions. Sunset 147:150 O '71
Halloween safety guide for trick-or-treaters. il Parents Mag 46:20 O '71
Pumpkin fever; Sycamore, Ill. T. Bennett. il Travel 136:46-7 S '71

Drama
Broken broomstick. H. L. Miller. Plays 31: 67-71 O '71
Ghost wanted. C. Boiko. Plays 31:17-26, 36 O '71
Rosy-cheeked ghost. B. G Blaine. Plays 31: 52-6 O '71
Trick or treat for UNICEF. C. Boiko. Plays 31:57-62 O '71

HALLOWEEN masks. See Masks (for the face)

HALLOWELL, H. Thomas, 1908-
SPS: trouble at the top. A. A. Butkus. por Duns 97:72 Mr '71 *

HALLS
Highways of the house: halls and hallways. W. Baldwin. House & Gard 139:8+ Mr '71
Make a grand entry. R. Campotosto. il Pop Mech 135:144-7+ Mr '71
Space saving American talent: halls into rooms. il House & Gard 139:74-7 F '71

HALLS of fame
Where fame is not fleeting. D. B. Warnick. il Travel 136:44-7+ O '71
See also
Sports halls of fame

HALLUCINATION and illusion producing plants
Further conversations with Don Juan; excerpt from A separate reality. C. Castaneda. il Esquire 75:75-89+ Mr '71; Discussion. 75:14 My '71
Separate reality, by C. Castaneda. Review Commonweal 94:482 S 17 '71. J. Grange Life 70:20 My 14 '71. B. Darrach Natur Hist il 80:74-6+ Je '71. W. Madsen and C. Madsen

HALLUCINATIONS and illusions
Cartography of the ecstatic and meditative states. R. Fischer. bibliog il Science 174: 897-904 N 26 '71

HALLUCINOGENIC drugs
Chemistry of madness. R. Campbell. il Life 71:66-8+ N 26 '71
Drugs of habit & the drugs of belief; with editorial comment. S. McCracken. bibliog f Commentary 51:4. 42-52 Je '71
Trip before dying; pain relief through use of mind-effecting drugs. il Newsweek 78:67 N 29 '71
See also
LSD
THC

HALMAN, Talât Sait
Turkish culture. New Yorker 47:46-7 N 20 '71 *

HALOID company. See Xerox corporation

HALOPERIDOL
Finding partial solutions. il Sci N 99:331-2 My 15 '71

HALOS (meteorology)
Comets: production mechanisms of hydroxyl and hydrogen halos. A. H. Delsemme. bibliog Science 172:1126-7 Je 11 '71
Mirrors on Mars. V. Komarov. Space World H-12-96:42 D '71

HALOS (mineralogy)
Giant radioactive halos. Chem 44:21 Ja '71
Radiohalos: some unique lead isotope ratios and unknown alpha radioactivity. R. V. Gentry. bibliog il Science 173:727-31 Ag 20 '71

HALPER, Albert
Personal memoir. L. Berg. Commentary 51: 98+ Ap '71 *

HALPERIN, Morton H.
President and the military. For Affairs 50: 310-24 Ja '72
Rules of the game; summary of statement. Time 98:9 Jl 5 '71
—See Gelb, L. H. jt. auth.

HALPERN, Bruce P. and Tapper, D. N.
Taste stimuli: quality coding time. bibliog il Science 171:1256-8 Mr 26 '71

HALPERN, Daniel
Traveling on credit; poem. Sat R 54:31 Ja 23 '71

HALPRIN, Ann
Raw dance. D. Davis. il por Newsweek 78:137 N 22 '71 *
World of dance: performance at City center. W. Terry. il Sat R 54:70 D 4 '71 *

HALPRIN, Daria
On location; interview. ed. by E. Miller. por Seventeen 30:52 O '71

HALSTEAD, Roger
ABM critics taken to task. Nat R 23:1299 N 19 '71

HALSTED, Thomas A.
Lobbying against the ABM, 1967-1970; adaptation of address, September, 1970. il Bul Atom Sci 27:23-8 Ap '71

HALVERSTADT, Hal
Ron Nagle. il Craft Horiz 31:34 Je '71

HAM, Fred
Up on two wheels. B. Green. il pors Hot Rod 24:138+ Je '71 *

HAM
Special on meat: how to buy ham. L. Wing. il Good H 173:160 D '71
See also
Cookery—Meat

HAMACHEK, Don E.
Briefing for parents: how to get your child to listen to you and how to listen to your child. bibliog il Todays Ed 60:33-48 Ap '71

HAMAN, Gene
Back-yard float trip. il Pop Mech 136:92-4+ Jl '71

HAMBLETON, William W.
Radioactive salt mine; comment. Bul Atom Sci 27:31 Je '71

HAMBLETONIAN race. See Harness racing

HAMBLIN, Dora Jane
Hot wheels Italian style. il Sports Illus 35:
24-9 Ag 30 '71
Italy tries to maroon some Mafiosi. il Life
70:34-6 Je 18 '71
Mount Etna turns nasty. il Life 70:28-30 My
28 '71
Which face is Fellini? il pors Life 71:58-61
Jl 30 '71

HAMBRO, Edvard Isak
Human rights day, 10 December 1970, message. UN Mo Chron 7:1 D '70

HAMBURG
Music
Report:
Carmen, Regina Resnik's first directorial
effort. J. H. Sutcliffe. il Opera N 36:26
S '71
Lucia di Lammermoor with Joan Suther-
land. J. H. Sutcliffe. Opera N 35:31 Ap
17 '71
Star rises out of Jacob, by Paul Burkhard.
J. H. Sutcliffe. il Opera N 35:30 F 6 '71

Theater
Stage directions. S. Kauffmann. New Repub 165:34 Jl 10 '71

HAMBURG, Wis.
Unique lab: the little red schoolhouse. H.
M. Kinnear. il Am For 77:26-7+ N '71

HAMBURGER, Michael
Travelling IV: poem. Poetry 119:94-7 N '71
(tr) See Celan, P. Eleven poems

about
Comment. M. L. Rosenthal. Poetry 119:103-4
N '71 •

HAMBURGER, Philip
Reporter at large. New Yorker 47:106+ Je 5
'71

HAMBURGER. See Beef; Cookery—Meat

HAMEED, F. Abdel-. See Abdel-Hameed, F.

HAMELN, Glückel von
Glückel von Hameln: Bertha Pappenheim's
idealized ancestor. G. H. Pollock. bibliog
Am Imago 28:216-27 Fall '71 •

HAMER, Philip May
Obituary
Am Hist R 76:1640-2 D '71. L. H. Butter-
field

HAMILL, Pete
Disintegration of a folk hero. por Harp Baz
104:104-5 My '71
New American western: on writing Doc. il
Harp Baz 104:71+ Jl '71
7 ways to bring us together. Seventeen 29:
266-7+ Ag '70

HAMILL, Robert H.
Abortion: a campus chaplain's reply to his
colleagues. Chr Cent 88:957-8 Ag 11 '71

HAMILTON, Andrew, 1676?-1741
Case of John Peter Zenger. L. Barnett. il
pors Am Heritage 23:36-41+ D '71 •

HAMILTON, Andrew Jackson
Bubonic plague: it's still around but under
control. il Sci Digest 69:9-13 My '71
Firemen paramedics. il Sci Digest 70:18-21
Ag '71
Glomar Challenger drills deep-sea peephole
into earth's past. il Pop Sci 198:58-60+ My
'71
Is one-day hernia repair for real? Todays
Health 49:52-4 Mr '71

HAMILTON, David
Carter's Concerto for orchestra, a gripping
musical experience. Hi Fi 21:82 Mr '71
DGG in Boston. il Hi Fi 20:85-6 D '70
Fantasy world of Pierrot lunaire. il Hi Fi
21:70-1 Jl '71
Fresh view of Pelleas. por Hi Fi 21:63-4 F
'71
ISCM's forty-fifth forum. Hi Fi 21:MA27-8 S
'71
Karajan's Meistersinger. il Hi Fi 21:80-1
D '71
Music. See issues of Nation
Over 400 Schubert songs: Fischer-Dieskau and
Gerald Moore. il Hi Fi 21:74-5 Ja '71
Parsifal at Bayreuth. il Hi Fi 21:85-6 N
'71
Records (cont) Nation 211:670; 212:381-2, 573,
701-2; 213:510, 633-4; 214:62 D 21 '70, Mr 22,
My 3, 31, N 15, D 13 '71, Ja 10 '72
Solid bass. por Hi Fi 21:64-5 My '71
Toy pianos, musical saws and a great vocal
tour de force. Hi Fi 21:78 Ag '71
Tragedy of Father Amelia. il Hi Fi 21:69-70
Je '71
Weber's English opera in German. Hi Fi
21:108 O '71

HAMILTON, Douglas H. and Meehan, R. L.
Group rupture in the Baldwin Hills. bibliog
il Science 172:333-44 Ap 23 '71

HAMILTON, Fanchon
Camp staff members, just as campers, need
individual guidance; excerpts from address.
il Camp Mag 43:8-9 Ap '71

HAMILTON, Floyd
Medicare mob. il pors Esquire 76:98 Ag '71 •

HAMILTON, Iain Douglas-. See Douglas-
Hamilton, I.

HAMILTON, Jack (editor)
Looking TV straight in the eye. il Look 35:
17 S 7 '71

HAMILTON, Joseph, family
Here's to you, Mrs Hamilton; with report
by J. Downs. il pors Life 70:92-5+ My 14
'71

HAMILTON, Kenneth
New evangelism. Chr Today 15:4-7 Ja 29
'71

HAMILTON, Peter Goodwill
Yankee pedaler. S. Kelly. il pors Hot Rod
24:66-8 Jl '71 •

HAMILTON, Robert L. and others
Cholestasis: lamellar structure of the abnormal human serum lipoprotein. bibliog
il Science 172:475-8 Ap 30 '71

HAMILTON, Virginia Van Der Veer
(ed) See Farley, J. A. Before the colors
fade: the true-blue Democrat

HAMILTON, William
Authors at work; drawings. Horizon 13:112-
13 Wint '71

HAMILTON college, Clinton, N.Y.
Latin America's antinomy; conference. J.
Villaverde. il Américas 22:2-10 N '70

HAMILTON watch company
Defense dept. makes a timely purchase. il
Bsns W p27 Ag 14 '71

HAMLET evaluation system. See Vietnamese
war, 1957-   —Pacification programs

HAMLIN, Roy M. jr. See Shah, D. O. jt. auth.

HAMMEL, Lisa
Home (cont) N Y Times Mag p40-1 Ag 8 '71

HAMMER, Armand
Overstaying his time? por Forbes 108:31-2 N
15 '71 •
Yet he retired 14 years ago. por Bsns W p79
D 18 '71 •

HAMMER, Donald A.
Durable snapping turtle; with biographical
sketch. il Natur Hist 80:5, 58-65 Je '71

HAMMER, Louis
Comment. L. Mueller. Poetry 117:329 F '71 •

HAMMER, Max
Reflections on one's own death as a peak
experience. Ment Hy 55:264-5 Ap '71

HAMMER films. See Moving picture industry—
Great Britain

HAMMERFEST, Norway
Top of the world. J. H. Winchester. il Travel
136:55-9 Ag '71

HAMMERMILL paper company
Hammermill urges you. Nation 212:485 Ap 19
'71
Marketing change that meant everyone won.
R. D. DeVitt. il pors Nations Bsns 59:64-5
Ja '71

HAMMES, Gordon G. and Wu, C. W.
Regulation of enzyme activity. bibliog il
Science 172:1205-11 Je 18 '71

HAMMOND, Geoffrey F.
Adventure on a shoestring. il Motor B & S
127:70-5 Mr '71
Scuttlebutt. See issues of Motor boating &
sailing
Watersports. See issues of Motor boating
& sailing to July 1971

HAMMOND, Jeff. See Hammond, G. F.

HAMMOND, John
Discoverer. por Newsweek 77:92 Mr 29 '71 •

HAMMOND, Kenneth R.
Computer graphics as an aid to learning.
bibliog il Science 172:903-8 My 28 '71

HAMMOND, Robert C.
Making book at Turnagain. il Outdoor Life
148:60-1+ S '71

HAMMOND, inc
Map-making at Hammond. A. DeMirjian, jr.
il Pub W 200:69-76 S 13 '71

HAMPF, Fred E. See Pierson, G. jt. auth.

HAMPSHIRE, Stuart
Ascent towards freedom. P. Caws. New Repub 165:24-5+ O 23 '71 •

HAMPSHIRE, Susan
At home in Paris with Susan Hampshire. G.
Perint. Harp Baz 104:70 My '71 •
Susan Hampshire. H. Ehrlich. il pors Look
35:28-31 F 23 '71 •

HAMPSHIRE college
Heaven at Hampshire. il Time 97:44 Ap 5
'71
Two schools innovate to stay in the black. il
Bsns W p 100-2 O 30 '71

HAMPTON, Christopher
Philanthropist. Criticism
America 124:540 My 22 '71 •
Nation 212:442 Ap 5 '71 •
New Yorker 47:83 Mr 27 '71 •
Newsweek 77:109 Mr 29 '71
Sat R 54:22 Ap 3 '71 •
Time 97:67 Mr 29 '71 •
HAMPTON, James
Tinfoil tribute to God. il Chr Today 15:21
Ag 27 '71 •
HAMPTON, Robert Edward
New labor policies in the Civil service; interview il por Nations Bsns 59:70-2+ Je '71
HAMPTON, Ruth
From stream bed to strawberries. il Org Gard
& Farm 18:44-6 F '71
HAMPTON-Preston house. See Columbia, S.C.
—Historic houses, sites, etc.
HAMS (radio) See Radio operators, Amateur
HAMSTERS
Calcium carbonate concretions: cyclic occurrence in the hamster vagina. J. J. Alleva and others. bibliog il Science 174:600-3 N 5 '71
Latent meiotic anomalies related to an ancestral exposure to a mutagenic agent. K. S. Lavappa and G. Yerganian. bibliog il Science 172:171-4 Ap 9 '71
Ovulation induced by synthetic luteinizing hormone-releasing hormone in the hamster. A. Arimura and others. bibliog il Science 174:511-12 O 29 '71
HAMTRAMCK, Mich.
Don't laugh at Hamtramck; most impoverished city in the nation. por Newsweek 77:95-6 My 17 '71
Hamtramck: waiting for Pilsudski; financial troubles. D. Smith. Nation 214:41-3 Ja 10 '72
Renewal or removal? ruling on housing for blacks. Newsweek 78:79 D 6 '71

Education
Let's hear it from Hamtramck; St Ladislaus high school. il Sr Schol 98:18-19 Ap 19 '71
HAMTRAMCK, Mich, public library
Librarian takes a stand: case of M. E. Hutto. por Am Lib 2:435-7 My '71
HANAN, Mack
Make way for the new organization man. il Harvard Bsns R 49:128-38 Jl '71
HANCHETT, George D.
Build R-E's 4-channel IC power amplifier. il Radio-Electr 42:37-40 O '71
HANCHEY, Penelope. See Wheeler, H. jt. auth.
HANCOCK, Herbie
Study; interview. New Yorker 47:29 Je 12 '71
HANCOCK COUNTY, Ga.
Hancock county; black takeover of power. New Repub 164:8-9 Mr 6 '71
HAND, Holly
Inspiration; story. Mlle 73:304 Ag '71
HAND, Jackson
Homemade storage devices for recycling rubbish. il Pop Sci 198:94-5+ Je '71
How to build a contemporary pedestal table. il Pop Mech 135:162-4 Ap '71
How to find those hidden storage spaces. il Mech Illus 67:95-6+ F '71
How to get an honest move. il Mech Illus 67:67-8+ Je '71
Low-cost air conditioners. il Mech Illus 67:94-5+ Jl '71
Tall, slim and showy. il Pop Mech 136:142-3 N '71
Triangular case for your rods. il Mech Illus 67:94+ My '71
Tripods are up to new tricks. il Pop Mech 135:140-3+ Mr '71
HAND
Give your hands a beauty break. C. Bartel. il Am Home 74:16+ O '71
Hands-make a show of them. il McCalls 98:82-5 Mr '71
Hands that speak volumes. il Harp Baz 104:74-5 Ap '71
Pamper your hands & feet. T. Pavlik. il Good H 173:104-5 Ag '71
Working with your hands. A. A. Hutschnecker. Vogue 158:114+ Jl '71
See also
Palmistry
HAND ball. See Handball
HAND care. See Hand
HAND luggage. See Luggage
HAND railings
Wood safeguards to keep children away from the glass. il Sunset 147:104-5 N '71
HAND saws. See Saws
HAND tools. See Tools

HAND washing
Wash your hands, damn it! W. E. Homan. il N Y Times Mag p82-3+ Mr 7 '71; Discussion. p61-2 Ap 11 '71
HAND weaving. See Weaving
HANDBAGS
Male bag. il Newsweek 77:94-94A Mr 1 '71
See also
Purses
HANDBALL
In Europe they call this handball. il Life 71:45-6+ O 8 '71
HANDBOOKS
See also subhead Handbooks, manuals, etc. under various subjects, e.g. Airplanes
—Handbooks, manuals, etc.
HANDEDNESS. See Left- and right-handedness
HANDEL, Georg Friedrich
Ariodante. Criticism
Hi Fi 21:MA12 D '71 •
Nation 213:349 O 11 '71 •
Carole Bogard: a revelation. S. Lincoln. Am Rec G 37:722-3 Je '71 •
Fisher vs. Lang. C. P. Fisher; P. H. Lang. por Hi Fi 21:18-19 Jl '71 •
Handel at half mast; Orlando. R. Jacobson. Sat R 54:51 Je 26 '71 •
Magnificent baroque opera. P. H. Lang. Hi Fi 21:65-7 F '71 •
Music for the season. J. Diether. il Am Rec G 37:204-8 D '70 •
Report:
Ariodante concert performance in Carnegie Hall. R. D. Daniels. Opera N 35:24 My 15 '71 •
Roland rides again. F. Merkling. il Opera N 35:14-15 Ja 23 '71 •
Tamerlane and Julius Caesar. H. Weinstock. Sat R 54:79 Mr 27 '71 •
HANDEL society of New York
Musical events; concert performance in Carnegie Hall of Handel's opera, Orlando. W. Sargeant. New Yorker 46:90 Ja 30 '71
Musical events; concert performance of Handel's Ariodante. W. Sargeant. New Yorker 47:119 Ap 17 '71
Report:
Ariodante concert performance in Carnegie Hall. R. D. Daniels. Opera N 35:24 My 15 '71 •
Handel's Orlando at Carnegie Hall. F. Merkling. Opera N 35:32-3 Mr 6 '71 •
Roland rides again: Handel's Orlando in Carnegie Hall. F. Merkling. il Opera N 35:14-15 Ja 23 '71
HANDELL, Albert
Inner universe of Albert Handell. H. Meredith-Owens. il por Am Artist 35:60-6+ Ap '71 •
HANDICAPPED
Hostility to the handicapped. il Time 98:67 D 20 '71
Mimi. H. R. Shapiro. il Look 35:18-25 Mr 23 '71
See also
Amputees
Blind
Children, Handicapped
Deaf-mutes
Mentally handicapped
Paralytics
Parents of the handicapped
Recreation for the handicapped

Employment
Handicapped: one of our largest minorities. C. W. Ford and F. C. Dyer. America 124:284-6 Mr 20 '71; Reply. W. P. McCahill. America 124:581 Je 5 '71
Vocational rehabilitation of the older handicapped worker. S. Olshansky. Ment Hy 55:507-10 O '71

Rehabilitation
See Rehabilitation
HANDICAPPED, Apparatus for the
He brings them back to life. R. Tunley. il por Read Digest 98:193-4+ Ap '71
See also
Wheelchairs
HANDICAPPED children. See Children, Handicapped
HANDICRAFT
Bazaar: dozens of ingenious things to make. M. B. Smith. il Bet Hom & Gard 49:70-3 S '71
Crafting in style. D. L. Brightbill and E. de Villeneuve. il Am Home 74:106-9+ N '71
Do it yourself; ideas for household furnishings. il Vogue 158:34 Jl '71
Gifts you can make. il Mlle 74:154-7 N '71
Lure of working with your hands. il House & Gard 139:73-9 Ap '71

HANDICRAFT—*Continued*
Make-it-yourself holiday gifts. H. Alpert. il
Har Yrs 11:24-33 D '71
Projects '71; comp. by A. Wiglama .il House
B 113:67-81+ Jn '71
Your future in the past; retirees as guides
and craft demonstrators. W. Hoffer. il Har
Yrs 11:39-42 Jl '71
See also
Arts and crafts
Christmas projects
Craftsmanship
Easter eggs
Felt work
Jewelry making
Lapidary work
Patchwork
HANDKE, Peter
My foot my tutor. Criticism
Newsweek il 77:122-3 My 10 '71 •
Self-accusation. Criticism
Newsweek 77:122-3 My 10 '71 •
HANDLER, Philip
Exaggeration: the other pollution peril;
interview. pors Nation Bsns 59:30-3 Ap '71
Federal government and the scientific com-
munity; address, December 26, 1970. bibliog
Science 171:144-51 Ja 15 '71
Handler's dissent explained. Science 172:792
My 21 '71
In defense of science; address, May 26, 1971.
Vital Speeches 37:715-20 S 15 '71; Excerpt.
Science 172:1320 Je 25 '71
Science in America: we're still in first place,
but—; interview. il pors U S News 70:30-4
Ja 18 '71
about
Handler dissents on NSF budget. C. Holden.
Science 172:247 Ap 16 '71 •
HANDLES
How to customize your hunting-knife handle.
M. Burch. il Pop Mech 136:110-12 D '71
HANDLEY Page aircraft, ltd. See JetStream
aircraft, ltd.
HANDLIN, David
Venetian notes: experiencing the city. Am
Scholar 41:65-78 Wint '71
HANDLIN, Oscar
History: a discipline in crisis? adaptation of
address, December 1970. Am Scholar 40:447-
65 Sum '71
HANDMADE paper. See Paper making
HANDMAN, Wynn
Broadway breakthrough. J. Kroll. il por
Newsweek 79:48-9 Ja 3 '72 •
HANDS in art
Painter of hands; work of E. Kingman. D.
Suro. il Américas 23:37-40 Je '71
HANDSAWS. See Saws
HANDWORK. See Handicraft
HANDWRITING. See Penmanship
HANDWRITING analysis. See Graphology
HANEDA, Yata, and Tsuji, F. I.
Light production in the luminous fishes
photoblepharon and anomalops from the
Banda Islands. bibliog il Science 173:143-5
Jl 9 '71
HANESWORTH, Gil
Gold medal awards. il Parks & Rec 6:27-30+
Ap '71
HANEY, Thomas R.
Church eyes future shock. America 124:174-
7 F 20 '71
HANFF, Helene
Letter from cloud nine. il Read Digest 99:
87-91 Ag '71
HANFORD works, Richland, Wash.
Hanford reactors down but not out. P. M.
Boffey. Science 171:555 F 12 '71
Hanford revisited. S. Novick. il Environ 13:
48-9 My '71
HANG ten funny car 500. See Drag racing
HANGARS
Giant steel hangars' cantilevered roofs will
each shelter four jumbo planes. M. Villecco.
il Arch Forum 134:58-61 Ja '71
New carousel hangar shown. il Aviation W
94:55 Mr 29 '71
HANGING baskets
Hanging baskets. B. Wahlfeldt. Org Gard &
Farm 18:114-15 O '71
Victoria's hanging baskets. R. Baird. il Horti-
culture 49:24 Jl '71
HANGING electric lamps. See Lighting fix-
tures
HANGING of pictures. See Pictures, Hanging
of
HANGINGS, Wall. See Wall hangings
HANGOVER cures. See Alcohol—Physiological
effects

HANIMEX, ltd. See Photographic apparatus
and supplies industry—Australia
HANKE, Jeannette J.
Filmmaking: some experiences with the gifted.
Engl J 60:121-5 Ja '71
HANKS, David A.
Living with antiques. il Antiques 100:116-
19 Jl '71
HANKS, Nancy
In support of freedom; adaptation of ad-
dress, February 17, 1971. il Parks & Rec
6:44-5+ Ag '71
Making faces across the gulf. Science 173:
479 Ag 6 '71
Willingly to school. il PTA Mag 65:18-21
Ap '71
HANLEY, Catherine
Gourds make attractive bird houses. il Org
Gard & Farm 18:54-5 Ag '71
HANLEY, Edward James
Crisis of costs: address, January 24, 1971.
Vital Speeches 37:298-301 Mr 1 '71
HANNA, William John
Student protest in independent Black Africa.
bibliog f il Ann Am Acad 395:171-83 My '71
HANNAH, John Alfred
Foreign assistance and the U.S. national in-
terest; statement, October 30, 1971. Dept
State Bul 65:577-9 N 22 '71
Institutional problems in the developing coun-
tries; address, February 15, 1971. Dept State
Bul 64:297-301 Mr 8 '71
Misconceptions and outmoded conceptions
about foreign aid; address, July 21, 1971.
Dept State Bul 65:152-5 Ag 9 '71
HANNAN, Dennis J.
Student poet power. Engl J 60:913-20 O '71
HANNAY, James Ballantyne
Man-made diamonds, who really made them
first? R. Davids. il Sci Digest 69:88-90
Ap '71
HANNEMAN, Ralph
Pedal power. il Parks & Rec 6:28-33 Ja '71
HANNES, Jack D.
Camera maker aims at the U.S. il por Bsns
W p66 My 15 '71 •
HANNIGAN, Thomas A.
Excerpt from statement, November 4, 1971.
Cong Digest 50:299+ D '71
HANO, Arnold
Awakening of the Chicanos. il Seventeen
30:148-9+ Mr '71
Billie Jean King: this is not a good life.
Redbook 137:86+ O '71
Incredible ordeal of Chad Calland, M.D. il por
Redbook 137:94+ S '71
HANOVER, Germany
IBM project short-circuits; projected plant in
Hanover. il Bsns W p40 Ag 21 '71
HANRAHAN, Edward V.
Clearing the slate. il Newsweek 79:14 Ja 3
'72 •
Daley on the defensive. por Time 99:24+ Ja
3 '72 •
Hanrahan indictment. il por Time 98:49-50 S
6 '71 •
Indicted prosecutor. New Repub 165:9-10 S
11 '71 •
Mayor Daley's way with justice. J. R.
Waltz. il Nation 213:460-8 N 8 '71 •
Panther ghost. il por Newsweek 78:20+ S 6
'71 •
Panther raid coverup. J. W. Singer and
T. J. Dolan. New Repub 165:21-3 Jl 24 '71 •
HANSBERRY, Lorraine
Les blancs. Criticism
Commonweal 93:397 Ja 22 '71 •
From a time of racial hope. Cyclops. il Life
72:14 Ja 14 '72 •
HANSEL and Gretel; opera. See Humperdinck,
E.
HANSEN, Alvin Harvey
Where are they now? pors Newsweek 77:12
F 8 '71 •
HANSEN, Dale P.
It's fishing season for the great grizzly
bears of Alaska; photographs. Audubon
73:14-17 Jl '71
HANSEN, James E. and Arking, Albert
Clouds of Venus: evidence for their nature.
bibliog il Science 171:669-72 F 19 '71
HANSEN, Søren
Story behind the book: The little red school-
book. L. P. Freilicher. pors Pub W 200:
32-3 D 13 '71 •
HANSEN'S disease. See Leprosy and lepers
HANSLICK, Eduard
Dvořák's relations with Brahms and Hans-
lick. J. Clapham. pors Mus Q 57:241-54 Ap
'71 •
HANSON, Dick
Across the editor's desk. See issues of Suc-
cessful farming

HANSON, Frank E. and others
Synchrony and flash entrainment in a New Guinea firefly. bibliog il Science 174: 161-4 O 8 '71
HANSON, Kenneth O.
Poem on history. Nation 212:790 Je 21 '71
HANSON, Kitty
High price of weddings; excerpt from For richer, for poorer. Read Digest 98:99-102 F '71
HANSON, Robert P. and others
Susceptibility of mink to sheep scrapie. bibliog il Science 172:859-61 My 21 '71
HANSON, Timothy
Researching the parables. P. Steinfels. Commonweal 94:230 My 14 '71 *
HANSON, Wallace
Between the dark and the daylight. il Pop Phot 68:86-8+ Je '71
Color processing: anywhere, anytime. il Pop Phot 69:90-1+ Jl '71
Day the silver runs out... il Pop Phot 68: 61-3+ Mr '71
Hold what you've got! il Pop Phot 69:83-5 O '71
HANSON, Warren H.
Attica: the hostages' story. il N Y Times Mag p 18-19+ O 31 '71; Same abr. with title Attica revisited. Nat R 23:1274 N 19 '71; Reply with rejoinder. A. O. Eve. N Y Times Mag p 18 N 28 '71
HANSSEN, E. Tandberg-. See Tandberg-Hanssen, E.
HANTULA, James
Social education: is it Zing, Zang, or Zong? bibliog Clear House 46:40-3 S '71
HAPGOOD, Marilyn
Open classroom: protect it from its friends. il Sat R 54:66-9+ S 18 '71
HAPPENINGS (art)
Art; Gilbert and George at the Sonnabend gallery. L. Alloway. Nation 213:348 O 11 '71
Gilbert and George: human singing sculpture at the Sonnabend gallery. New Yorker 47:40-1 O 9 '71
Presenting Gilbert & George, the living sculptures. R. Reise. il pors Art N 70:62-5+ N '71
HAPPINESS
See also
Joy
HAPPY ending; story. See Maloney, R.
HAPPY life; story. See Holland, B.
HARA, K. and Schonhorn, H.
Preparation of high-crystallinity polyethylene at low pressures. bibliog il Science 172:562-4 My 7 '71
HARADA, Kaoru, and others
Evidence for compounds hydrolyzable to amino acids in aqueous extracts of Apollo 11 and Apollo 12 lunar fines. bibliog il Science 173:433-5 Jl 30 '71
HARAKIRI
Politics of suicide; Mishima's seppuku. R. T. Halloran. por Commonweal 94:34-6 Mr 19 '71
Samurai protest. por Sr Schol 97:6 Ja 11 '71
HARAMURA, Hiroshi. See Kushiro, I. jt. auth.
HARASZTY, Eszter
(ed) See Atkinson, R. E. Gardener's almanac
HARAYDA, Janice
Bright ideas for this year's Europe-bound. il Mlle 72:106-7+ Mr '71
New look in Heidiland. Sat R 54:34 Ag 28 '71
HARBERT, Mary Ann
Two-fifths thaw. pors Time 98:8 D 27 '71 *
HARBIN, Edward
Poaching; poem. Nation 213:669 D 20 '71
HARBOR police. See Police boats
HARBORS
See also
Marinas
also subhead Harbor under names of cities, e.g. Marseilles—Harbor
HARBOUR, Dave
Fundamentals of deer stalking. il Field & S 76:42-3+ Ag '71
HARCLEROAD, Fred H. and others
Developing state colleges and universities: current status and future roles. Sch & Soc 99:157-60 Mr '71
HARCOURT, Hastings
New breed, new ideas, new taxes. A. Wright. il pors Sports Illus 34:48-53 Je 7 '71 *
HARCOURT Brace Jovanovich, inc.
Adelle Davis celebrates 25 years with Harcourt; interview, ed. by L. P. Freilicher. A. Davis. il por Pub W 199:56 Je 21 '71
HARD-core unemployed
See also
Cope program
National alliance of businessmen

HARD of hearing. See Deafness
HARDENING of the arteries. See Arteriosclerosis
HARDER, Howard Charles
Company that fled New York. il por Newsweek 78:97-8 O 18 '71 *
HARDER, Ray
Living ship; memories of the great schooner Vega. il Yachting 130:62-3+ D '71
HARDESTY, Charles Howard, 1922-
Beginning of an understanding; address, September 30, 1971. Vital Speeches 38:120-2 D 1 '71
HARDIE, Dee
Special gifts of Christmas. il House & Gard 140:86+ D '71
HARDIE, Jim
Baja roosterfish. il Field & S 76:74-5+ Je '71
Unique fishing boat. il por Motor B & S 128:16+ Jl '71
HARDIE, R. H. and Krebs, M. E.
Finding sidereal time. il Sky & Tel 41:288-9 My '71
HARDIMAN, Arthur A.
Start your corn indoors. il Org Gard & Farm 18:83 My '71
HARDIN, Clifford Morris
Brighter outlook for farmers. interview. il por U S News 70:58-62 Je 28 '71
Future of farming. il pors Nations Bsns 59: 34-7+ Ag '71
about
Agricultural mission to Turkey to be led by Secretary Hardin; White House announcement, September 28, 1971. Dept State Bul 65:413-14 O 18 '71 *
HARDIN, Garrett
Nobody ever dies of overpopulation. Science 171:527 F 12 '71
Survival of nations and civilization. bibliog Science 172:1297; 174:1078 Je 25. D 10 '71
To trouble a star; the cost of intervention in nature. Bul Atom Sci 26:17-20 Ja '70; 27:4 Ap '71
HARDING, Bruce C.
New research source: archives branches. bibliog il Am Lib 2:306-7 Mr '71
HARDING, Warren
Because it's nowhere. H. Peterson. il pors Sports Illus 34:76-8+ My 3 '71 *
HARDWARE
See also
Bolts and nuts
Casters, glides, etc (hardware)
Fastenings
Nails
HARDWARE Industry
Nuts and bolts are in a bind. il Bsns W p 104+ Ap 17 '71
HARDWICK, Elizabeth
Books (cont) il Vogue 158:90-1 S 15; 62 N 1 '71
Ties women cannot shake, and have. por Vogue 157:86-7 Je '71
HARDWICK, Lillian Mann
We grow our strawberries in huge strawberry boxes. il Org Gard & Farm 18:48-9 F '71
HARDY, Sir Alister
Sir Alister Hardy: science and religious experiences. D. Cohen. il por Sci Digest 70: 18-23 S '71 *
HARDY, Melissa A.
Books by young writers. por Seventeen 30: 14 Ja '71
HARDY, Ark.
Treasures of the Ozarks. A. J. Runsick. il por Travel 136:50-4 Ag '71
HARE, David
Slag. Criticism
Nation 212:315 Mr 8 '71 *
New Repub 164:32 Mr 13 '71 *
New Yorker 47:68-9 Mr 6 '71 *
HARE, Denise
Film. il Craft Horiz 31:7 Ap; 10+ Je; 10+ Ag; 10+ O; 10+ D '71
Photography as media. il Craft Horiz 31:14-17+ D '71
HARE, Julia. See Hare, N. jt. auth.
HARE, Mary Salisbury
(ed) See Everitt, P. Lady of distinction.
HARE, Nathan, and Hare, Julia
Black women 1970. il Trans-Action 8:65-8+ N '70
HARE, P. E. See Wehmiller, J. jt. auth.
HARE, the hippo, and the elephant; drama. See Thane, A.
HAREM
Secrets of the harem; Topkapi palace. il Time 98:34 S 13 '71

HART, Philip A.
Case for no-fault auto insurance. por Pop Sci 198:56+ Ja '71
Excerpts from remarks, February 24, 1971. Cong Digest 50:176+ Je '71
about
Notes and comment. New Yorker 47:40-1 N 27 '71 •

HART-McGovern bill. See Environment—Laws and legislation

HART Schaffner and Marx (firm)
Held back at home, expanding abroad. por Bsns W p31 Ja 1 '71

HARTE, Ben
Theatre on film and tape. il Am Lib 2:1065-8 N '71

HARTER, James L.
How to store your food crops. il Org Gard & Farm 18:42-9 Ag '71

HARTFORD, Bill
Daytona 500: big year for the little guys? il Pop Mech 135:66-9 F '71

HARTFORD, Huntington
Free advice. por Forbes 107:56 Ap 1 '71 •

HARTFORD, John
John Hartford, sloppy aristocrat. G. Lees. por Hi Fi 21:22+ Ag '71 •

HARTFORD, Conn.
One man's peace corps; Revitalization corps. por Time 98:12 Jl 19 '71

Historic houses, etc.
Antiquarian & landmarks society, inc. of Connecticut: Butler-McCook homestead. il Antiques 100:342 S '71

Music
See also
Hartford symphony orchestra

HARTFORD, Wis.
S.M.E.L.L.S. v. smells; offensive odors from beet-processing plant. Time 98:84 N 22 '71

HARTFORD symphony orchestra
Musical events; Mahler's Eighth symphony. W. Sargeant. New Yorker 47:111 My 1 '71

HARTGEN, Stephen. See Layne, E. N. jt. auth.

HARTKE, Vance
Excerpt from address, February 9, 1971. Cong Digest 50:109+ Ap '71

HARTLEY, Anthony
Europe between the superpowers. For Affairs 49:271-82 Ja '71
Impossibility of dropping out. il Horizon 13:104-5 Aut '71

HARTLEY, Ellen
Mayan mystery of the Onima caves. il Sci Digest 69:9-13 Ap '71
Recycled water il Sci Digest 70:82-6 N '71
—See Hartley, W. B. jt. auth.

HARTLEY, William B.
Article writing today. Writer 84:14-16+ S '71
—and Hartley, Ellen
Can land be developed without wrecking nature? il Sci Digest 71:73-8 Ja '72
Her home is a sanctuary for injured wildlife. il pors Good H 173:78+ O '71
Insect explosion. il Sci Digest 69:26-31 F '71
Redbook guide to America's Heritage trails (cont) il Redbook 136:87-94 Ap '71
Redbook guide to Florida's heartland. il Redbook 137:35-42 S '71
Special gift of Mary Perkins. il por Seventeen 30:110+ D '71

HARTMAN, Albert E.
Lathe-powered band sander. il Pop Sci 198:110 Je '71

HARTMAN, Chester W.
Urban field service. Arch Forum 135:50-3 S '71

HARTMAN, Geoffrey
Mariner's song. Yale R 61:253 D '71

HARTMAN, Philip E. and others
Hycanthone: a frameshift mutagen. bibliog il Science 172:1058-60 Je 4 '71

HARTNETT, Ken
US as slumlord. New Repub 165:11-13 D 11 '71

HARTOG, Joseph
Transcultural aspects of community psychiatry. bibliog Ment Hy 55:35-44 Ja '71

HARTS, William W. Jr
One way to connect on the Continent. Bsns W p35 Jl 31 '71 •

HARTUNG, Philip T.
Screen. Commonweal 93:447-8; 94:15, 112, 238-9, 310-11, 428, 480-1; 95:88 F 5, Mr 12, Ap 9, My 14, Je 11, Ag 20, S 17, O 22 '71

HARTWELL, Robert M.
Historical analogism, public policy, and social science in eleventh- and twelfth-century China. bibliog f il Am Hist R 76:690-727 Je '71

HARTWICK college, Oneonta, N.Y.
Library
Hartwick serves blind. C. Wolf and J. Miller. il Am Lib 2:1193-4 D '71

HARTZOG, George Benjamin, 1920-
Profiles. J. McPhee. por New Yorker 47:45-8+ S 11 '71 •

HARVARD, Pauline
Unarmored; poem. Ladies Home J 88:162 Jl '71

HARVARD medical school. See Harvard university—Medical school

HARVARD university
Free speech movement; charges against participants in the Sanders theater affair. il Newsweek 77:73 Ap 12 '71
Harvard: new president's task to unify, preside over change. T. P. Southwick. Science 171:264-6 Ja 22 '71
Harvard picks a president. il por Newsweek 77:70-2 Ja 18 '71
Harvard picks a president; with interview, ed. by E. Kern. D. C. Bok. il pors Life 70:34-6 Ja 22 '71
Harvard's quiet man. il por Time 97:60-1 Ja 25 '71
President's chair; troubles of Harvard's early presidents. J. T. Bethell. il Am Heritage 23:110 D '71
Program given notice; pioneering program on technology and society to be phased out. J. Walsh. Science 173:219 Jl 16 '71

Graduate school of design
Urban field service. C. W. Hartman. Arch Forum 135:50-3 S '71

Law school
Harvard law revisited. M. Kasindorf. il Newsweek 77:52+ My 24 '71

Medical school
Boston hospital dispute: Harvard rectifies expansionist policies. R. J. Bazell. il Science 171:358-61 Ja 29 '71

HARVEST labor. See Farm labor

HARVEST years (periodical)
Ten years old, still growing! il Har Yrs 11:2, 14 Mr '71

HARVESTER ants. See Ants

HARVESTING
Odds for good harvest weather. C. E. Sommers. il Suc Farm 69:A8 O '71
See also
Corn—Harvesting
Threshing
Vegetables—Harvesting

HARVESTING machinery
How fast can you harvest? P. B. Jones. il Suc Farm 69:25 Je '71
How to adjust your combine: corn, beans, grain cut field losses. P. Jones. il Suc Farm 69:26-7 Je '71
Ideas that keep the combine moving. il Farm J 95:16-17 S '71

Leasing and renting
Farmers hit the combine trail. il Suc Farm 69:M10 Ag '71

HARVESTMEN
Defense of phalangid: liquid repellent administered by leg dabbing. T. Eisner and others. bibliog il Science 173:650-2 Ag 13 '71
Giving ants the brush-off; chemical repellent of vonones. il Chem 44:19 N '71

HARVEY, Everett
Same old song. Harper 243:56 Ag '71

HARVEY, Harold
Obituary
Pop Phot 69:48 Jl '71. M. Komroff

HARVEY, James
Stage. Commonweal 94:239-40 My 14 '71

HARVEY, James A.
James A. Harvey, librarian for intellectual freedom. il pors Wilson Lib Bul 45:740-1 Ap '71 •
—See Krug, J. F. jt. auth.

HARVEY, Paul
(ed) See Lenin, V. I. Prescription for revolution

HARVEY, Tad
Warning: tsunamis! il Pop Sci 199:62-4+ D '71

HARVEY, William Hope
Coin Harvey. O. Stephens. il por Am West 8:4-9 S '71 •

HARWERTH, R. S. and Sperling, H. G.
Prolonged color blindness induced by intense spectral lights in rhesus monkeys. bibliog il Science 174:520-3 O 29 '71
—See Sperling, H. G. jt. auth.

HARWOOD, Michael
Black mayonnaise at the bottom of Jamaica
Bay. il N Y Times Mag p9-11+ F 7 '71
We are killing the sea around us. il N Y
Times Mag p34-5+ O 24 '71
HASBRO industries, inc.
Toy maker builds on a TV name. il por
Bsns W p 116+ Mr 13 '71
HASEGAWA, Jack K.
Saul Alinsky in Japan. Chr Cent 88:1306-8
N 3 '71
HASEGAWA, Norishige
Japan's free-trader. N. Martin. por Duns
98:55-6 Ag '71 *
HASELTINE, William
Automated air war. New Repub 165:15-17
O 16 '71
—and Westing, A. H.
Wasteland. New Repub 165:13-15 O 30 '71
HASHISH. See Marijuana
HASKELL, Molly
J.C. superstar enterprises, inc. il Sat R 54:
65-7+ O 30 '71
Television. Vogue 157:158 Ap 1 '71
HASKETT, Thomas R.
Multi-set TV-FM systems for the home. il
Electr World 85:32-5+ Ap '71
HASKEW, Laurence D.
Bridging the parent-teacher-student gap;
excerpts from address, 1971. il PTA Mag
65:8-11 Ap '71
HASKINS, Caryl P.
Science and policy for a new decade. bib-
liog f For Affairs 49:237-70 Ja '71
HASLAM, Gerald
American oral literature: our forgotten heri-
tage. bibliog f Engl J 60:709-23 S '71
HASLER, Richard A.
Our Puritan heritage. Chr Today 15:23-4 F
26 '71
HASS, Mary
From attic corner to child-sized guestroom.
il House B 113:54 My '71
HASSALL, Don R. See Wright, J. D. jt.
auth.
HASSAN II, king of Morocco
Arab friend of U.S. fights to stay in power.
il por U S News 72:67-8 Ja 3 '72 *
Coup that failed. por Newsweek 78:26 Jl 19
'71 *
Hassan's last hurrah? il por Newsweek 78:
46+ D 6 '71 *
Meaning to U.S. of uprising in Morocco.
por U S News 71:50 Jl 26 '71 *
Morocco: bloody birthday. il por Time 98:16
Jl 19 '71 *
Promises, promises. Newsweek 78:37 Ag 16
'71 *
Slaughter at the summer palace. W. Wynn.
Time 98:27 Jl 26 '71 *
Vengeance of King Hassan. il por Newsweek
78:33-4 Jl 26 '71 *
HASSE, Eileen M.
We started our own co-op. il Har Yrs 11:
14-15 Ap '71
HASSE, Johann Adolph
Dear Saxon. R. Berges. por Opera N 35:6-7
Mr 20 '71 *
Music to my ears. I. Kolodin. Sat R 54:42 Ap
3 '71 *
Report:
Olimpiade. F. Merkling. Opera N 35:22 My
15 '71 *
Two by Hasse: Clairon's L'Olimpiade, Bar-
nard's Gentleman. P. J. Smith. Hi Fi 21:
MA27 Je '71 *
HASSENFELD, Stephen
Toy maker builds on a TV name. il por
Bsns W p 116+ Mr 13 '71 *
HASSLER, Paula J.
How to make money in your spare time.
Ladies Home J 88:82 Jl '71
HASTINGS, J. Woodland
Light to hide by: ventral luminescence to
camouflage the silhouette. bibliog il Sci-
ence 173:1016-17 S 10 '71
HASTINGS, Sally
Mini-armature. il Sch Arts 70:12-13 Je '71
HASTINGS house publishers, inc.
Hastings house is 35: high standards and a
touch of nostalgia. M. R. Kraner. il Pub W
200:12-14 N 29 '71
HASWELL, Anthony
On the track: Railpax vobiscum. D. Butwin.
por Sat R 54:80-3 Ja 23 '71 *
HATCH, Francis W.
Maine grandmother; poem. Sat R 54:24 F 20
'71
So long, think; poem. Sat R 54:19 Mr 13 '71
Wardrobe note for the rural retiree; poem.
Sat R 54:67 D 4 '71

HATCH, Robert
Bout of Thackeray. Nation 212:309-11 Mr 8 '71
Films. See issues of Nation
HATCHER, Richard Gordon
Hatcher's landslide. il por Newsweek 77:32
My 17 '71 *
Liberation of Gary, Indiana. E. Greer. il
por Trans-Action 8:30-9+ Ja '71 *
HATCHERIES. See Fish culture
HATE
In defense of hatred. Time 97:45 F 1 '71
HATFIELD, Ceil
You're not Mrs Hatfield... B. Lindeman.
pors Todays Health 49:25-7+ F '71 *
HATFIELD, Mark Odom
Excerpt from address, January 28, 1971. Cong
Digest 50:146+ My '71

about

News from home. il por Newsweek 78:21 Jl
19 '71 *
Oregon: gunning for Hatfield. R. Friedman.
Nation 212:781-2 Je 21 '71 *
Politics and conscience. por Time 98:80 S 27
'71 *
HATFIELD-McGovern amendment. See Viet-
namese war, 1957- —American troop with-
drawals
HATHAWAY, Lodene Brown
Prophecy; poem. Chr Cent 88:1491 D 22 '71
Recollection; poem. Chr Cent 88:1256 O 27
'71
Self-revelation; poem. Chr Cent 88:1319 N 10
'71
HATRED. See Hate
HATS
Bonnet that's wonderful good. J. Milligan.
il Holiday 49:18 Ap '71
Brim goes its own way; soft, floppy hat. il
Sunset 146:134+ My '71
Gift for the chef of the house. il Sunset 146:
109 Je '71
Hard hat for a hard guy. R. Starnes. Field &
S 76:8+ My '71
Leather hat for the seventies. il Sunset 147:
48-9 Ag '71
On and off the avenue. K. Fraser. New York-
er 47:123-5 N 6 '71
HATTERER, Lawrence J.
What makes a homosexual? McCalls 98:32+
Jl '71: Same abr. Read Digest 99:71-4 S '71
—and Hatterer, M. S.
What parents should know about homosex-
uality. il PTA Mag 65:69 Je '71
HATTERER, Myra S. See Hatterer, L. J. jt.
auth.
HATTERSLEY, Ralph
Hattersley class. See issues of Popular
photography
HATTIS, Phyllis
Ingres in Rome. il Art N 70:26-9+ My '71
HATTORI company. See Watch industry—Ja-
pan
HAUBOLD, Erhard
What future for India's Naxalites? Cur 129:
57-61 My '71
HAUCK, Allan
Scientific stamps and coins. il Sci Digest
70:84 S; 88 O; 78-9 N; 79 D '71; 71:89 Ja
'72
HAUGHEY, John C.
Buddhist role in South Vietnam. il America
125:259-62 O 9 '71
Church and state in Cambodia. il America
125:279-81 O 16 '71
Commune: child of the 1970's. America 124:
254-6 Mr 13 '71
Dateline: Pakistan, East and West. il Amer-
ica 125:365-7 N 6 '71
From proclamation to dialogue: a new pro-
file for Christians. America 124:483-5 My 8
'71
NFPC's celibacy stand. America 124:341-3, 441-
2 Ap 3, My 1 '71
Pakistani relief: compound of hope and trag-
edy. il America 125:420-3 N 20 '71
Papal exhortation to religious. America 125:
34 Jl 24 '71
Priest-bishop relations: American perspective.
America 124:518-20 My 15 '71
Religion and politics in Anwar el Sadat.
America 124:605 Je 12 '71
HAUGHTON, Daniel Jeremiah
Lockheed's unflappable boss. por Bsns W p65
F 13 '71 *
Salvage of the Lockheed 1011. H. B. Meyers.
il por Fortune 83:66-71+ Je '71 *
TriStar engine may be U.S.-made; with
commentary. il por Bsns W p42-3 Mr 13
'71 *
HAUGHTON, James G.
Chicago hires a black top doc. il pors Ebony
26:76-8+ Ap '71 *

HAUGHTON, Rosemary
New meaning of marriage. il Read Digest 98:79-81 Ja '71
Signs of the times. See issues of Catholic world
HAUNTED houses. See Ghosts
HAUNTING of Hathaway house; drama. See Murray, J.
HAUPERT, John S.
Iran. il Focus 21:1-8 Ja '71
HAUPT, Alexander Lehmann-. See Lehmann-Haupt, A.
HAUPT, Enid A.
Boys in your world; excerpts from The new Seventeen book of etiquette and young living. por Seventeen 29:128-31+ N '70
Manners of the road; excerpt from The new Seventeen book of etiquette and young living. Seventeen 30:146 N '71

about

Very personal garden of Mrs Enid Haupt: move-around garden that flowers wherever you put it. il House & Gard 139:58-63 Je '71 *
HAUSER, Bengamin Gayelord
Gayelord Hauser: for my toast, I want butter. Vogue 158:24 Jl '71 *
HAUSER, Ernest O.
Mary, mother of Christ. il Read Digest 99: 168-72 D '71
HAUSER, Gayelord. See Hauser, B. G.
HAUSER, Jerald
Calling; poem. America 125:559 D 25 '71
HAUSER, Jon
What kind of kitchen? The cook decides, says this designer; interview, ed. by S. Nirenberg. House B 113:44-5 S '71
HAUSER, Philip M.
Census of 1970; with biographical sketch. il Sci Am 225:14, 17-25 bibliog(p 122) Jl '71 '71
HAUSER, W. L.
Business for the birds. O. Henry. il pors Har Yrs 11:19-22 Ag '71 *
HAUSWALD, Don, family
Lifestyle. il Am Home 74:12+ N '71
HAUSWIRTH, William. See Daniels, M. jt. auth.
HAVANA

Description

Alicia Alonso, the flower of Cuba; diary of a trip to Havana. M. Horosko. il pors Dance Mag 45:43-58 Ag '71
Having at a ball in new Havana. J. Kirshenbaum. il Sports Illus 35:18-21 Ag 30 '71
HAVASU LAKE
See also
Lake Havasu City, Ariz.
HAVEMANN, Ernest
Marriage's eight money traps. Read Digest 99:91-4 O '71
Second marriages. il Ladies Home J 88:106+ My '71
HAVENON, Gaston de, collection of African sculpture. See Art—Private collections
HAVENS, Richie
Rock family affair. il por Life 71:54-5 S 24 '71 *
HAVER, June. See MacMurray, J. H.
HAVERSTOCK, Mary Sayre
Meet the armored spoof. il Nat Wildlife 10: 52-5 D '71
HAVIGHURST, Robert J.
Extent and significance of suicide among American Indians today. bibliog il Ment Hy 55:174-7 Ap '71
Reorganization of education in metropolitan areas. Ed Digest 36:5-8 My '71
HAVILAND, Virginia
Second golden age? In a time of flood? adaptation of address, October 1970. Horn Bk 47:409-19 Ag '71
HAVNER, Vance
Repentance as a church priority. Chr Today 15:12+ Mr 12 '71
HAWAII
See also
Aged—Hawaii
Banks and banking—Hawaii
Botany—Hawaii
Cost of living—Hawaii
Education—Hawaii
Express highways——Hawaii
Golf courses—Hawaii
Haleakala National Park
Haleiwa
Honolulu
Honolulu academy of arts
Maui (island)
Mauna Kea
Mauna Loa

Missions—Hawaii
Molokai (island)
Music festivals—Hawaii
National parks and reserves—Hawaii
Pollution—Hawaii
Temples—Hawaii
Tourist trade—Hawaii
Wildlife sanctuaries—Hawaii

Capitol

Lighting dramatizes a new state capitol. il Am City 86:104 Ag '71

Description and travel

Hawaii. E. Welke. il Bet Hom & Gard 49: 163-8+ N '71
Hawaii, the aloha state. B. Clark. il Read Digest 98:146-52 Ja '71

Economic conditions

Hawaii at the crossroads, a boom runs into trouble. il U S News 71:68-70 N 22 '71
Hawaii's impossible choice; jobs and progress vs. beauty and ecology. il Forbes 108:31-4 Ag 15 '71
How dock strike is hurting Hawaii. U S News 71:94-5 O 4 '71
See also
Cost of living—Hawaii

Parks and reserves

Just 12 miles from Waikiki for hikes, picnics, overnights; Keaiwa Heiau state park. il Sunset 147:36+ Ag '71

Social conditions

Elderly have problems even in Hawaii. il Aging 203:13 S '71
HAWAII beaches. See Beaches
HAWAII craftsmen annual. See Arts and crafts —Exhibitions
HAWAII VOLCANOES NATIONAL PARK
Fire rivers and fire falls in Hawaii. il Sunset 147:50-3 S '71
Flower island in the lava. il Sunset 416:57 Mr '71
Hawaii's lava forests. R. Nickerson. il Am For 77:16-19 Ja '71
HAWAIIAN ISLANDS national wildlife refuge. See Wildlife sanctuaries—Hawaii
HAWAIIAN Open tournament. See Golf—Tournaments
HAWAIIAN seals. See Seals (animals)
HAWK, Ernest M.
It takes two for dialogue. Chr Cent 88:1418-20 D 1 '71
HAWK, Howard
Rio lobotomy. W. S. Pechter. Commentary 51:87-8 Je '71 *
HAWK and the mules; story. See Merwin, W. S.
HAWKES, Alex Drum
Luscious fruit. il House & Gard 139:127-8+ My '71
HAWKING. See Falconry
HAWKINS, Augustus Freeman
Excerpts from remarks, September 15, 1971. Cong Digest 50:279+ N '71
HAWKINS, Erick
Erick Hawkins dance company, ANTA theatre, NYC. N. Mason. Dance Mag 45:89 My '71 *
World of dance. W. Terry. il Sat R 54:30 Ap 10 '71 *
HAWKINS, Nancy
Painting with fingerprints. il por Design 72: 20-1 Sum '71
HAWKINS, Osie Penman, 1913-
Osie; interview, ed. by J. Ferris. il por Opera N 35:30-1 Ja 16 '71
HAWKINS, W. Lincoln
Behind "number, please" the story of W. Lincoln Hawkins. S. P. Massie. il por Chem 44:16 O '71 *
HAWKINS, William J.
Action at your fingertips. il Pop Sci 198:96-7+ Mr '71
HAWKINS, William R.
New camp transportation policy. il Camp Mag 43:15-16 My '71
HAWKS, Howard Winchester
Hawk. il por Newsweek 77:96+ F 8 '71 *
HAWKS, Richard L.
Crazy about carrots! il Home Gard 58:34-5 My '71
HAWKS
See also
Falcons
Kites (birds)
HAWKS (basketball team) See Basketball teams

HAWLEY, John K.
Can automotive air pollution be curbed?
il Cons 25:9-12 Ap; 10-12 Je '71
HAWN, Goldie
Goldie Hawn. J. Wilkie. il pors Good H 172:
54-6+ My '71 *
HAY, Edwards
Eye in the sky. il Am For 77:20-3 Ja '71
Smog: the tree killer. il Am For 77:8-10+
O '71
HAY, John
Place to live in; poem. Am Scholar 41:133
Wint '71
HAY, Raymond A.
No. 2 at Xerox. por Bsns W p76 Mr 20 '71 *
HAY
Hay bales: an answer to pond weeds? R. Mar-
tin. Org Gard & Farm 18:70-1 N '71
HAY fever
God bless you! Some tips for hayfever suf-
ferers. Bsns W p79-80 Je 12 '71
HAY handling
Small-time hay-making. N. Bubel and M.
Bubel. il Org Gard & Farm 18:98-101 Ag
'71
HAY making. See Hay handling
HAY mulch. See Mulching
HAY stackers
Easiest way yet to winter a cow herd. D. K.
O'Brien. il Farm J 95:B16-17 S '71
HAYAKAWA Samuel Ichiyé
College presidents and students; interview.
Mlle 73:244+ Ag '71
Most precious gift a father can give to his
son; ed. by S. O'Quin. il por Todays Health
49:21-3 Je '71
HAYASHI, Izuo. See Panish, M. B. jt. auth.
HAYDÉE, Marcia
Team. W. Terry. il pors Sat R 54:42 Je 5 '71 *
HAYDEN, Julie
Touch of nature; story. New Yorker 47:
30-5 Ag 21 '71
HAYDEN, Martin S.
Pentagon papers: and freedom of the press.
Read Digest 99:133-4 S '71
HAYDEN, Melissa
Miss Hayden, ballerina. W. Terry. por Sat R
54:45 F 13 '71 *
HAYDEN, Stone, inc.
Case of the Hayden, Stone letter. C. J.
Loomis. Fortune 83:143+ Mr '71
Unbelievable last months of Hayden, Stone.
C. J. Loomis. il Fortune 83:114-16+ Ja '71
HAYDN, Franz Joseph
Beethoven's contrapuntal studies with Haydn.
A. Mann. bibliog f il Mus Q 56:711-26 O
'70
Eighteen chamber masterpieces gloriously
performed. H. Goldsmith. il Hi Fi 21:83-4 S
'71 *
Unique pleasures of Haydn's 107 symphonies.
R. C. Marsh. il Hi Fi 21:75-6 Ap '71 *
HAYDN, Johann Michael
Other Haydn. H. C. R. Landon. Hi Fi 21:100
D '71 *
HAYDOCK family
Haydock coat-of-arms. H. K. Eilers. il Hob-
bies 75:146-7 Ja '71
HAYES, Denis
Can we bust the Highway trust? il por Sat
R 54:48-53 Je 5 '71
HAYES, Isaac
Black Moses. por Time 98:55 D 20 '71 *
HAYES, John R.
Research, teaching, and faculty fate. bibliog
il Science 172:227-30 Ap 16 '71
HAYES, Joseph
Authors & editors. D. N. Mount. por Pub W
200:13-15 O 18 '71 *
Is anyone listening? Criticism
Sat R 54:38 F 20 '71 *
HAYES, Mary Jane
Streak of adventure. il por Yachting 129:
54-5+ Mr '71
HAYES, Melvin L.
Principals' profile of big-city high schools.
Sch & Soc 99:253-4 Ap '71
HAYES, Ralph E.
Turning novel cuts into short stories. il Writ-
ers Digest 51:28-9+ Jl '71
HAYES, Samuel L. 3d
Investment banking: power structure in
flux. bibliog f il Harvard Bsns R 49:136-52
Mr '71
HAYES, Thomas L. See Everhart, T. E. jt.
auth.
HAYES, Wayne Woodrow
Leader of men. il por Newsweek 78:52+ D
6 '71 *
HAYES, Woody. See Hayes, W. W.
HAYNES, John
Philosopher of madness; photographs. Life
71:86-90 O 8 '71

HAYNES, Lincoln. See Roberts, M. jt. auth.
HAYNES, Marques
Basketball's black entrepreneur. A. S. Young.
il pors Ebony 26:96-8+ Mr '71 *
HAYNSWORTH, Clement Furman, 1912-
Haynsworth court rejects Hodgin appeal;
with editorial comment. Library J 96:573,
577 F 15 '71 *
HAYS, H. R.
Ready for retirement; poem. Nation 213:222 S
13 '71
HAYS, Helen, and Risebrough, R. W.
Early warning of the terns; with biograph-
ical sketches. il Natur Hist 80:3-4, 38-47
N '71
HAYSTACK Mountain school of crafts, Deer
Isle, Me.
Portfolio: coming of age at Haystack. F. B.
Merritt. il Ceram Mo 19:19-26 Je '71
HAYWARD, John F.
Rundell, Bridge and Rundell, aurifices regis.
il Antiques 99:860-5; 100:110-15 Je-Jl '71
HAYWARD, Calif.
Office rentals pay for half of new city hall.
il Am City 86:40 Mr '71
HAYWOOD, Spencer
Anybody else care to bid for Spencer Hay-
wood? P. Carry. il por Sports Illus 34:52-3
Ja 25 '71 *
Who owns Haywood? por Newsweek 77:79
F 15 '71 *
HAZARDOUS substances

Disposal in the ocean
Chemical wastes in the sea: new forms of
marine pollution. P. A. Greve. bibliog il
Science 173:1021-2 S 10 '71

Transportation
See also
Chemicals—Transportation
HAZEL, Robert
Eyeless in Indiana; poem. Esquire 76:312 D
'71
about
Poet come in glory. A. Planz. Nation 212:
410-11 Mr 29 '71 *
HAZELTON, Nika Standen
Corporate gift giving. Nat R 23:992+ S 10
'71
Delectations. See issues of National review
Hamburger: America's sweetheart; excerpt
from Hamburger. il Ladies Home J 88:88-9+
Ja '71
HAZELTON, Roger
Truth in theology. il Chr Cent 88:772-4 Je 23
'71
HAZLITT, Henry
Dollars at a discount. Nat R 23:591-2 Je 1
'71
Nobody wins at leapfrog. Nat R 23:83-5+ Ja
26 '71
HAZZARD, Shirley
Statue and the bust; story. McCalls 98:32 Ag
'71
HEACOX, Cecil E.
Comeback of a heavyweight. il pors Outdoor
Life 148:46-9+ Jl '71
HEAD, Ivan L.
Foreign policy of the new Canada. For Af-
fairs 50:237-52 Ja '72
HEAD
See also
Baldness
HEADACHE
Beauty sense and nonsense. B. Benjamin.
Harp Baz 104:20 My '71
Doctors teach migraine control. M. Mercer.
McCalls 99:31 N '71
Fortification illusions of migraines. W. Rich-
ards. il Sci Am 224:88-94+ bibliog(p 132) My
'71
Headache hunters meet the anxious Ameri-
can. W. B. Furlong. il Todays Health
49:20-3+ Mr '71
Headaches and Alice in Wonderland: mi-
graine. il Chem 44:4-5 S '71
HEADBOARDS. See Beds
HEADERS. See Automobile engines—Exhaust
HEADGEAR
See also
Hats
Millinery
HEADLEY, Dorothy
Mental health movement meets women's lib;
interview. Ment Hy 55:1-9 Ja '71
HEADLIGHTS, Automobile. See Automobiles—
Lighting
HEADPHONES
Hi-fi product report: Sharpe model 7 stereo
phones. il Electr World 85:13 F '71
Hi-fi product report: Sharpe SC-3 stereo head-
phone adapter. il Electr World 86:14 N '71

HEADPHONES—*Continued*
Hirsch-Houck lab tests stereo headphones. J. D. Hirsch. il Electr World 86:39-42 O '71
Pick & choose among stereo headphones. J. Steele. il Pop Electr 34:44-7+ Ap '71
Stereo headphones. il Consumer Bul 54:34-6 N '71

HEADS (automobile engines) See Automobile engines—Cylinders

HEADS of departments
Chairman: where does he fit in? W. R. Beck and D. S. Rosenberger. Clear House 46:48-51 S '71

HEADS of state
Hail to the chiefs, are they human? Sr Schol 99:24 O 4 '71

HEALEY, John B.
Faith for tomorrow. America 125:550-3 D 25 '71
Why older priests need the Synod. America 125:210-13 S 25 '71

HEALTH
Family doctors' health guide. D. Schultz. Ladies Home J 88:34+ Ag '71
Family health. G. M. Knox. See issues of Better homes and gardens
Health and beauty from the sea, by M. Castle. Review
House B 113:9 Jl '71. S. Lindsay
Health matters. PTA Mag 66:22 N '71
How healthy is your sport? G. M. Knox. Bet Hom & Gard 49:10+ My '71
Ignorance about health. il Time 99:67 Ja 17 '72
Today's health news. See issues of Today's health
Your health (cont) Todays Ed 60:51-2 F; 71-2 N '71
See also
Diet
Exercise
Longevity
Men—Health and hygiene
Nutrition
Public health
Woman—Health and hygiene

Periodicals
See also
Prevention (periodical)
HEALTH and weather. See Weather—Mental and physiological effects
HEALTH centers. See Health facilities
HEALTH clinics. See Health facilities
HEALTH clubs
There's the rub; massage parlors. il Newsweek 77:62 Ap 26 '71
HEALTH costs. See Medical service. Cost of
HEALTH, education and welfare, Department of. See United States—Health, education and welfare, Department of
HEALTH examinations. See Physical examinations
HEALTH facilities
Building types study. il Arch Rec 149:135-50 Mr '71
Doctor who practices what he preaches; work in a roadhouse clinic. S. Streshinsky. il por Redbook 138:78+ N '71
Health facilities. il Arch Forum 134:30-47 Je '71
Neighborhood center: newest public health remedy. H. Bims. il Ebony 26:124-6+ N '70
Neighborhood health centers, bringing more care to needy. il U S News 71:62-4 D 27 '71
Shapers of the future: the need for doctors; address. November 29, 1970. W. C. Bornemeier. Vital Speeches 37:315-18 Mr 1 '71
Superclinic, science-fiction structure takes the pain out of medical treatment. N. Schaffer. il Arch Forum 135:30-5 N '71
U.S. journal: Imperial County, Calif; doctors' views on the Clinica de salubridad de campesinos. C. Trillin. New Yorker 46:83-9 F 13 '71
See also
Hospitals
Mental health centers
HEALTH fads. See Medical delusions
HEALTH food stores. See Food stores
HEALTH foods. See Food, Organic; Food fads
HEALTH insurance. See Insurance, Health
HEALTH physics. See Radioactivity—Physiological effects
HEALTH resorts, watering places, etc.
His and hers super spa; La Costa, Calif. il pors Vogue 157:174-7 My '71
Maine Chance; Arizona desert resort. Vogue 157:12+ F 15 '71

Spa check: Florida's Palm-aire. his-and-hers spa. Vogue 158:16 S 15 '71
Where the rich grow young; Renaissance; spa of the Balmoral hotel, Nassau. L. Tornabene. il Ladies Home J 89:86-7+ Ja '72
See also
Baden-Baden
Seaside resorts
HEALTH sciences centre, McMaster university. See McMaster university, Hamilton, Ontario
HEALTH service. See Medical service
HEALTH services industry, Committee on the. See United States—Health services industry, Committee on the
HEALTH workers
Nonprofessionalization of the war on mental illness. D. C. Marler. Ment Hy 55:291-4 Jl '71
Professional's nonprofessional experience: suggestions for supervisors. T. L. Woods. Ment Hy 55:298-302 Jl '71

Training
Mental health workers: new mental hospital personnel for the seventies. G. L. Euster. bibliog Ment Hy 55:283-90 Jl '71
HEALTH workers, Volunteer
Coordinating a volunteer program. V. D. Pettinelli. Ment Hy 55:516-18 O '71
HEALY, Eugene
Bookmobiles: a somewhat closer look. il Am Lib 2:72-8 Ja '71
HEALY, John E. 2d
Inflationary woes of the construction industry after the wage price freeze; address, August 1971. Vital Speeches 37:762-5 O 1 '71
HEANEY, Seamus
Aubade; poem. New Yorker 47:47 N 27 '71
Home; poem. New Yorker 47:48 My 1 '71
HEARING
Are you shooting your hearing? D. N. F. Fairbanks. il Outdoor Life 148:57-9+ O '71
Auditory backward inhibition in concert halls. G. Von Békésy. bibliog il Science 171:529-36 F 12 '71
Ears and hearing. M. Hugunin. Todays Ed 60:51-2 F '71
Patients hear during surgery? A. J. Snider. Sci Digest 69:57 F '71
See also
Deafness
Ear
Echolocation (physiology)

Testing
Safeguard your baby's sense of hearing. M. I. Sims. il Parents Mag 46:62-3+ N '71
HEARING; story. See Weesner, T.
HEARING (birds)
How owls spot their prey. il Sci Digest 70:81-2 Jl '71
HEARING (fishes)
Can fish hear? J. Palmer. il Field & S 76:29+ D '71
HEARING (insects)
Periodical cicada: sound production and hearing. J. A. Simmons and others. il Science 171:212-13 Ja 15 '71
HEARING aids
Hearing aids; with Veterans administration ratings. il Consumer Rep 36:310-20 My '71
1971 hearing aid selections by the Veterans administration. il Consumer Bul 54:31-2 My '71
Veterans administration reveals results of tests on hearing aids. T. Schuchat. il Har Yrs 11:56-8 Mr '71
What about hearing aids? Next month. Consumer Rep 36:193-4 Ap '71
HEARING loss. See Deafness
HEARN, Chick
TV talk. F. Deford. Sports Illus 34:14 Mr 29 '71 *
HEARON, Shelby
Small expectations; story. Redbook 138:127-49 Ja '72
HEARST, James
Farmer's bride; poem. Commonweal 95:85 O 22 '71
HEARST, William Randolph, 1863-1951
Onward and upward with the arts. P. Kael. por New Yorker 47:43-52+ F 20; 44-50+ F 27 '71 *
HEARST San Simeon state historical monument. See California—Parks and reserves

HEART

Abnormities and deformities

Joshua's tomorrows; transposition of the great vessels; with editorial comment. il Redbook 137:84-5+. 164 O '71

Sex differences in I.Q. pattern of children with congenital heart defects. M. P. Honzik and others. bibliog il Science 174:1042-4 D 3 '71

Analysis and chemistry

Thyroxine: conversion to triiodothyronine by isolated perfused rat heart. J. L. Rabinowitz and E. S. Hercker. bibliog Science 173:1242-3 S 24 '71

Diseases

Dynamite heart; overexposure to nitroglycerin by ammunition plant workers. il Time 98:41 Jl 12 '71

Magnetocardiography of direct currents: S-T segment and baseline shifts during experimental myocardial infarction. D. Cohen and others. bibliog il Science 172:1329-33 Je 25 '71

What women should know about heart attacks; excerpt from Heart attack: you don't have to die. C. Barnard. il por Ladies Home J 89:92-3+ Ja '72
See also
Cardiacs

Diagnosis

Image analysis: application to automated medical diagnosis; rheumatic heart disease. A. L. Hammond. il Science 174:1011-12 D 3 '71
See also
Cardiography

Mortality

American way of death. Sci Am 224:44-5 My '71

Nutritional aspects

Cardiac rate regulated by nutritional factor in young rats. M. A. Hofer. bibliog il Science 172:1039-41 Je 4 '71

Five new diets to save your heart. Look 35:53-4 F 9 '71

Growing worry over cholesterol. il Changing T 25:37-9 Jl '71

Heart-disease epidemic; ways to cut the toll. U S News 71:94-5 N 29 '71

New reports on changing diet to lower heart disease risks. il Good H 172:180-1 Mr '71

On vitamin C, cholesterol, and heart attack. il Chem 44:24-5 Je '71

Plain talk about your diet and heart attacks; excerpt from The family guide to better food and health. R. Deutsch. Bet Hom & Gard 49:4+ Ag '71

You and your heart: the real role of fats. Read Digest 99:74-7 O '71

Prevention

Best advice: slow down! M. Friedman. Read Digest 99:80-2 O '71

Framingham study. Trans-Action 8:6 N '70

Heart-disease medics renew drive to cut down on meat, milk and eggs. G. Logsdon. Farm J 95:43 F '71

How to guard your husband's heart (and your own) D. Schultz. Ladies Home J 88: 36+ Ag '71

Preventing a second heart attack. il Sci Digest 69:58-9 Je '71

There's more than cholesterol behind heart attacks; triglyceride problem. R. H. Berg. il Look 35:51-2 F 9 '71

Muscle

Maintenance of resting potential in anoxic guinea pig ventricular muscle: electrogenic sodium pumping. T. F. McDonald and D. P. MacLeod. bibliog il Science 172:570-2 My 7 '71

Surgery

Lifeline for a man with a dying heart; bypass grafting. R. Gore. il pors Life 70:51-4+ F 5 '71

Old hearts, new plumbing. il por Time 97:51-2 My 10 '71

Saving the heart; vein grafts from leg to bypass atherosclerotic deposits. il Newsweek 78:50 Jl 26 '71

Terry and the parents; alternative to blood transfusion. il Newsweek 77:43 Ja 18 '71

Transplantation

Barnard touch; heart and lungs given to A. Herbert. por Newsweek 78:62-3 Ag 9 '71

Barnard's bullet; heart and lungs given to A. Herbert. por Time 98:37 Ag 9 '71

Spectacular that failed; heart-lung recipient Adrian Herbert. Time 98:46 Ag 30 '71

Transplant slump. il por Newsweek 77:69 My 17 '71

World's leading heart transplant sets super pace. L. J. Banks. il pors Ebony 26:106-8+ Ap '71

Year they changed hearts; excerpt from Hearts, with editorial comment. T. Thompson. il Life 71:3, 56-56B+ S 17 '71

HEART beat

Cardiac activity preparatory to overt and covert behavior. G. E. Schwartz and J. D. Higgins. bibliog il Science 173:1144-6 S 17 '71

Cardiac rate regulated by nutritional factor in young rats. M. A. Hofer. bibliog il Science 172:1039-41 Je 4 '71

Home remedy; chest thump for restoring normal rhythm in cases of ventricular tachycardia. Sci Am 224:47 F '71

Marihuana: standardized smoke administration and dose effect curves on heart rate in humans P. F. Renault and others. bibliog il Science 174:589-91 N 5 '71

Preavoidance blood pressure elevations accompanied by heart rate decreases in the dog. D. E. Anderson and J. V. Brady. bibliog il Science 172:595-7 My 7 '71
See also
Pacemaker, Artificial (heart)

HEART defects. See Heart—Abnormities and deformities

HEART muscle. See Heart—Muscle

HEART of a child; story. See Hillyer, L.

HEART patients. See Cardiacs

HEART pumps. See Hearts, Artificial

HEART rate. See Heart beat

HEART rated exercises. See Exercise

HEARTS, Artificial

Assist for an ailing heart; heart pumps. il por Time 98:52 Ag 23 '71
See also
Blood—Circulation, Artificial

Filters

See Filters and filtration (biological products)

HEAT

See also
Waste heat

Measurement

See also
Pyrometers and pyrometry

Physiological effects

See also
Heatstroke

HEAT, Specific. See Specific heat

HEAT, Waste. See Waste heat

HEAT engines

Amateur scientist; some delightful engines driven by the heating of rubber bands. P. B. Archibald. il Sci Am 224:118-22 Ap '71

Amazing hot-gas engine powers clean-air bus; Stirling external-combustion engine. D. Scott. il Pop Sci 198:54-6 Je '71

HEAT exchangers

New rotary heat exchanger; it doubles cooling efficiency. E. F. Lindsley. il Pop Sci 198:46+ Mr '71

HEAT lamps. See Electric torches

HEAT pipes. See Heat transmission

HEAT resistant materials

See also
Space vehicles—Materials

HEAT sinks. See Heat transmission

HEAT stroke. See Heatstroke

HEAT transmission

Heat pipes for semiconductor cooling. D. L. Heiserman. il Electr World 85:37-9 Je '71

Hot spots and heat sinks. J. Darr. il Radio-Electr 42:69-70+ O '71
See also
Heat exchangers

HEATERS

Happiness is a warm shop. R. Capotosto. il Mech Illus 67:97-9+ D '71

Heating and insulating the home. il Consumer Rep 36:595-9 O '71

HEATH, Aloise Buckley

Before you say no. Nat R 23:1459-60 D 31 '71

HEATH, Edward Richard George

Prime Minister Heath of the United Kingdom visits Washington; exchange of greetings, toasts. December 17, 1970. Dept State Bul 64:56-60 Ja 11 '71

Where is Britain heading? interview, ed. by J. Fromm. por Read Digest 98:115-18 Mr '71

HEATH, Edward Richard George—*Continued*
about

Britain stages a technological retreat. il
Bsns W p 114-15 Mr 13 '71 *
Can Heath hold the line? C. Brogan. Nat R
23:634+ Je 15 '71 *
Common market: good morning! pors News-
week 77:29-30 My 31 '71 *
Commonwealth on collision course. il News-
week 77:35 Ja 25 '71 *
Conservatism's new British accent. R. Ball. il
Fortune 83:80-3+ Ap '71 *
Europe: the British are coming? il pors Time
97:26+ My 31 '71 *
Great debate begins; on joining the Common
market. il por Time 98:27 Jl 19 '71 *
Heath tries industrial Darwinism. il por
Bsns W p41-2 Mr 20 '71 *
Radical of 10 Downing street. A. Lewis.
il pors N Y Times Mag p36-8+ Mr 14 '71 *
Sailor Ted's sinking shipyards; or, All's
not bonny on Clyde. il por Time 98:31 Ag
16 '71 *
Steering the ship of state. H. McIlvanney.
il por Sports Illus 35:44-6 Ag 23 '71 *
Unlocking the door. A. Howard. New Repub
164:8-9 Je 5 '71 *
Way of life. il Newsweek 77:48+ Mr 15 '71 *
HEATH, Frank
Nostalgia shock. Sat R 54:18 My 29 '71
HEATH, Fred
Switching regulator power supply. il Electr
World 86:43-4+ O '71
HEATH, G. Louis
Counterculture at Kickapoo Creek. bibliog Sch
& Soc 99:247-50 Ap '71
HEATH, Gordon, pseud.
Despair in Russia. Read Digest 98:125-8 Je
'71
HEATH, Percy, 1923-
Profiles. W. Balliett. New Yorker 47:62-4+
N 20 '71 *
HEATH, Ted. See Heath, E. R. G.
HEATHERS
Landscaping with heaths and heathers. E.
Finlayson. il Horticulture 49:41+ F '71
HEATHROW International airport. See London
—Airports
HEATHS (plants)
Landscaping with heaths and heathers. E.
Finlayson. il Horticulture 49:41+ F '71
HEATING
Can you cut your fuel bill in half? F. Coffee.
il Mech Illus 67:132-3+ N '71
Hot tips on heating your home. R. Rejnis.
Read Digest 99:21-2 N '71
How to keep your heating system humming.
R. G. Cook. il Good H 173:238 N '71
Save on heating bills. Consumer Bul 54:23-
4 F '71
See also
Furnaces
Gas burners
HEATING equipment
See also
Furnaces
Radiators
HEATSTROKE
Hippocrates, thermal stress, and stroke
mortality, 1966. L. A. Helfand and C.
Bridger. il Weatherwise 24:100-4 Je '71
HEAVY-ion accelerators. See Accelerators
(electrons, etc)
HEAVYWEIGHT boxers. See Boxers
HEBBLETHWAITE, Peter
Europe on the move. il America 124:169-71
F 20 '71
HEBER, Rick
Earlier head start. Sci N 100:24 Jl 10 '71 *
HEBERT, Bliss
Two for the desert; interview, ed. by F. B.
St Clair. por Opera N 35:15 Je 12 '71
HEBERT, Richard. See Kelley, B. jt. auth.
HEBREW Immigration aid society. See United
HIAS service, inc.
HEBREW inscriptions. See Inscriptions, He-
brew
HEBREW language
See also
Yiddish language
HEBREW literature
See also
Jewish literature
HEBRIDES
Voyage to the Hebrides. R. Feeley. il Yacht-
ing 129:56-7+ Je '71
HECHLER, Ken
TVA ravages the land. Nat Parks & Con
Mag 45:15-16 Jl '71; Same. Cur 132:35-9 S
'71

HECHT, Alan D. and Savin, S. M.
Oxygen-18 studies of recent planktonic for-
aminifera: comparisons of phenotypes and
of test parts. bibliog il Science 170:69-71;
173:168-9 O 2 '70, Jl 9 '71
HECHT, Anthony
Autumnal; poem. Harper 242:79 Ap '71
Green: an epistle; poem. New Yorker 47:38-9
My 22 '71
HECHT, George J.
100 million American children: a rededication
on our forty-fifth anniversary. por Parents
Mag 46:44 O '71
HECHT, James L.
Matter of life or death. Parks & Rec 6:39-
40+ Mr '71
about
Postscript to tragedy: a father's crusade. M.
Cohen. il Redbook 137:76-7+ Je '71 *
HECHT, Roger
What one survivor said; poem. Nation 212:
316 Mr 8 '71
HECKELMANN, Charles N.
Six functions of dialogue in fiction. Writers
Digest 51:24-7 Je '71
HECKMAN, Harry H. and others
Fragmentation of nitrogen-14 nuclei at 2.1
Gev per nucleon. il Science 174:1130-1 D 10
'71
HECKMAN, J. R. and others
Trout leukocytes: growth in oxygenated
cultures. bibliog Science 173:246 Jl 16 '71
HECKSCHER, Morrison H.
Form and frame: new thoughts on the
American easy chair. il Antiques 100:886-
93 D '71
HEDDA Gabler; drama. See Ibsen, H.
HEDGE clippers
Electric hedge trimmers. il Consumer Rep
36:288-92 My '71
HEDGEPETH, William
Cape Kennedy. Look 35:48 Ja 12 '71
Commune way keeps spreading because:
maybe it'll be different here. il Look 35:63
6+ Mr 23 '71
Powder keg among the palms. Look 35:33-4
Ap 6 '71
Superstars, poets, pickers, prophets. il Look
35:28-30+ Jl 13 '71
HEDGES
Pruning
See Pruning
HEDGING
Deflating a theory. C. Morgello. il Newsweek
78:72 Jl 12 '71
Harvest from a new commodity contract:
Chicago mercantile exchange's milo cam-
paign. il Bsns W p70+ S 18 '71
Hedge-fund miseries. Fortune 83:269-70 My
'71
Hedges for the prudent man. J. A. Livingston.
il Sat R 54:19-20+ Mr 6 '71
How Michigan farmers made money on the
futures market; hedging workshops. Suc
Farm 69:14 N '71
How to hedge the freeze. R. Stovall. il
Forbes 108:86-7 O 1 '71
Smart money is hedging its bet. il Bsns W
p21-2 O 30 '71
HEDIN, Robert S.
Build this pedestal grinder for $40. il Pop
Mech 136:144-5 N '71
Salvaged motor makes a handy shop sander.
il Pop Mech 136:172+ D '71
HEDRICH, Vivian
Seattle's concentration on careers. Ed Digest
37:34-7 N '71
Seattle's concentration on careers. il Am Ed
7:12-15 Jl '71
HEEBNER, A. Gilbert
Holding back the cost push. por Nations
Bsns 59:25 F '71
HEELS (shoes) See Shoes
HEENAN, John Carmel, cardinal
Ethics: 1970 style; address, November 11.
1970. Vital Speeches 37:294-8 Mr 1 '71
HEESACKER, Frank L.
Small school can be a good school. Ed Digest
36:12-15 Ja '71
HEEZEN, Bruce C. and Hollister, C. D.
Deep, deep sea floor; excerpt from The face
of the deep; with biographical sketches. il
Natur Hist 80:6-7, 30-3 bibliog (p 104) My
'71
HEFLEY, James C. and Hefley, Marti
One parent, better than none. il Todays
Health 49:33-5+ Mr '71
HEFLEY, Marti. See Hefley, J. C. jt. auth.
HEFNER, Hugh Marston
Forbes interview. por Forbes 107:21 Mr 1 '71
about
Can you bare it? il por Forbes 107:17-20 Mr
1 '71 *

HEGEL, Georg Wilhelm Friedrich
Boyg and the sphinx in Ibsen's theatre. B. Johnston. Yale R 60:366-82 Mr '71 *

HEGER, Herbert K.
Educational change and pedagogical validity. bibliog Clear House 45:563-7 My '71

HEIDELBAUER, Frank A.
There's a picture window in my muskrat house. il por Nat Wildlife 9:44-6 Ag '71

HEIDNER, Elizabeth G. and others
Subunit structure of aldolase. bibliog il Science 171:677-80 F 19 '71

HEIFERS
Crossbred heifers, new source of breeding stock. B. Eftink. il Suc Farm 69:no3 D21 F '71
Get more calves: breed heifers to calve at two years of age. il Suc Farm 69:B6-7 Ag '71
Wanted: dairymen who won't milk; heifer raisers. il Farm J 95:16-17 Jl '71
See also
Calving

Feeding
See Cattle—Feeding

HEIFETZ, Jascha
Heifetz on television. S. Fleming. Hi Fi 21: 92 Jl '71 *
Music's most distant star; with discography. I. Kolodin. il pors Sat R 54:45-7 Ap 24 '71 *

HEIGHT of man. See Stature

HEIKAL, Mohammed Hassanein
Man to see. Newsweek 77:37 F 1 '71 *
Second most important man in Egypt, and possibly the world's most powerful journalist. E. R. F. Sheehan. il pors N Y Times Mag p 12-13+ Ag 22 '71 *

HEIKKILA, Richard, and Cohen, Gerald
Inhibition of biogenic amine uptake by hydrogen peroxide: a mechanism for toxic effects of 6-hydroxydopamine. bibliog il Science 172:1257-8 Je 18 '71

HEILBRONER, Robert Louis
Benign neglect in the United States. il Trans-Action 7:15-22 O '70
Phase II of the capitalist system. il N Y Times Mag p30-1+ N 28 '71

HEILMAN, Joan Rattner. See Symonds, M. jt. auth.

HEIMAN, Grover
Business: a look ahead. See issues of Nation's business

HEIMER, Lennart
Pathways in the brain; with biographical sketch. il Sci Am 225:14, 48-57+ Jl '71

HEINEMANN, Arthur
Examination: story. Redbook 136:60-1 Ja '71

HEINES, Sister Virginia
Markers for chromatography. il por Chem 44: 25 N '71

HEINIG, Jean. See Roper, B. W. jt. auth.

HEINOLD, George
Elk: sultans of the Rockies. il Sci Digest 69: 22-6 My '71
Salt water. See issues of Outdoor life

HEINRICH, Milt
Animal parade. il Sch Arts 71:22-3 O '71
Not-so-still life. il Sch Arts 71:20-1 N '71

HEINRICHS, W. L. and others
DDT administered to neonatal rats induces persistent estrus syndrome. bibliog il Science 173:642-3 Ag 13 '71

HEINS, Ethel L.
(comp) American children's books for teachers in England. Horn Bk 47:630-5 D '71

HEINS, Marjorie
Los siete de la raza. il Ramp Mag 9:19-26 Mr; 10:50 Jl '71

HEINS, Paul, and others
(comp) Booklist (title varies) See issues of Horn book magazine

HEINS, William A.
Spruce up your home with real stained glass. il Pop Sci 198:102-3+ Ap '71

HEINZ, Henry John, 1844-1919
Hero with blemishes. por Forbes 107:31 Mr 1 '71 *

HEINZ, H. J, company
Good steward. il Forbes 107:24-5+ Mr 1 '71
Heinz battles for space on a worldwide shelf. J. Gooding. il Fortune 84:76-81+ O '71
Irish wunderkind joins U.S. Heinz. il por Bsns W p57-8 S 11 '71

HEINZ, J. P.
In defense of the sweet science. il Sports Illus 35:70-4+ Ag 16 '71

HEINZ Hall for the performing arts, Pittsburgh
Recycled centers. il Time 98:50 D 27 '71

HEIPLE, Clark
Figures of clay and plaster. il Sch Arts 71: 28-9 O '71

HEIRLOOMS
What a priceless possession is heritage. J. Breen. Read Digest 98:172-4 Ja '71

HEIRTZLER, J. R. and Burroughs, R. H.
Madagascar's paleoposition: new data from the Mozambique Channel. bibliog il Science 174:488-90 O 29 '71

HEISENBERG, Werner
Books. J. Bernstein. New Yorker 47:123-31 Je 5; 135-6 O 9 '71 *
Encounters and conversations during the growth of quantum mechanics. P. Morrison. Sci Am 224:127-8 My '71 *
Indeterminate but ordered. M. Lebowitz. Nation 212:280+ Mr 1 '71 *

HEISERMAN, David L.
Automatic railroad-car identification. il Electr World 86:46-7 S '71
Electronic image tubes in astronomy. il Electr World 86:34-5 N '71
Electronic typesetting. il Electr World 86: 35-7+ Ag '71
Facsimile via telephone. il Electr World 86: 35-8 D '71
Heat pipes for semiconductor cooling. il Electr World 85:37-9 Je '71
How to watch the moon hide a star. il Pop Sci 198:122+ F '71
Opportunity awareness; questions and answers. See issues of Popular electronics
Optical character recognition. il Electr World 85:43-4+ Ap '71
Optical communications with semiconductor light sources. il Electr World 86:20-2 D '71
Scanning electron microscopes. il Electr World 85:42-4+ F '71

HEISMAN memorial trophy. See Trophies, Sport

HEITZ, Dottie
G-R-A-double N-Y. S. Elder. pors Har Yrs 11:14-15 S '71 *

HEIZER, Michael
Holes without history. D. Waldman. bibliog f il Art N 70:44-8+ My '71 *

HEKKER Gerard
Christian life communities. 1971. America 125:150-1 S 11 '71

HEKLA, MOUNT
Hellfire. S. Thorarinsson. il Natur Hist 80: 58-63 Ag '71

HELD, John, 1889-1958
Cartoonist's bite. D. Davis. il Newsweek 77: 106-7 My 24 '71 *

HELD, Richard, and Shattuck, S. R.
Color- and edge-sensitive channels in the human visual system: tuning for orientation. bibliog il Science 174:314-16 O 15 '71

HELD, Virginia
Walking out on the system; political strikes. Nation 213:370-2 O 18 '71

HELFAND, L. A. and Bridger, C.
Hippocrates, thermal stress, and stroke mortality. 1966. il Weatherwise 24:100-4 Je '71

HELGELAND, Glenn B.
How to see America and never leave home. il Nat Wildlife 9:46-9 Ap '71

HELGOLAND underwater laboratory. See Underwater laboratories

HELICOPTER industry

Imports problem
Importation of Soviet Ka-26 helicopter may be blocked. C. E. Schneider. Aviation W 95:59-60 Ag 30 '71

France
French spur civil helicopter sales effort. il Aviation W 94:126+ My 31 '71

Great Britain
WG.13 helicopter civil market predicted. il Aviation W 94:116-18 My 31 '71

Italy
Agusta expanding U.S. licensing. E. H. Kolcum. il Aviation W 94:46-9 F 1 '71

United States
U.S. helicopters facing export market struggle. il Aviation W 94:160 Mr 8 '71
See also
United aircraft corporation—Sikorsky aircraft division

HELICOPTERS
Helicopters: onward and upward. J. Fricker. il Flying 89:42-4 Ag '71
Super lift from supercopters. F. K. Coffee. il Mech Illus 68:50-1+ Ja '72
See also
Autogiros
Heliports

Accidents
Helicopters: unsafe at any height. J. Ennis. il Pop Mech 136:63-7+ S '71

HELICOPTERS—*Continued*

Airworthiness
See Helicopters—Standards

Armaments
New SeaCobra arms control developed. K.
J. Stein. il Aviation W 95:40-3 Ag 9 '71

Blades
See Helicopters—Rotors

Certification
See Helicopters—Standards

Design
Subsidy sought for compound helicopter. il
Aviation W 94:125 My 31 '71
V-12 has civil military missions. D. C. Wins-
ton. il Aviation W 94:14-19 Je 7 '71
WG.13 helicopter civil market predicted. il
Aviation W 94:116-18 My 31 '71

Equipment
See also
Helicopters—Radar equipment
Helicopters—Radio equipment

Escape devices
Helicopters: unsafe at any height. J. Ennis.
il Pop Mech 136:63-7+ S '71

History
Early whirlybird. il por Newsweek 77:16 Mr
15 '71

Landing
Army buys tactical landing system. il Pop
Electr 1:51 Ja '72

Materials
Wide use of composites planned for HLH.
W. S. Hieronymus. Aviation W 95:43 Ag
30 '71

Military use
Bell stresses equipped prototype.   E. J.
Bulban. il Aviation W 95:44-7 O 11 '71
Blackhawk exhibits speed, agility. D. A.
Brown. il Aviation W 94:38-43 F 15 '71
Five key machines in Laos. il Life 70:30-1 Mr
12 '71
From first to last; role of helicopters in
Vietnam. il Newsweek 78:26 D 27 '71
Helicopter war; Laotian campaign. il News-
week 77:39-40+ Mr 15 '71
Helicopters: unsafe at any height. J. Ennis.
il Pop Mech 136:63-7+ S '71
Killing is our business and business is good.
il Time 97:24-5 Mr 22 '71
Navy planning Sea Knight modifications.
Aviation W 95:42 D 13 '71
Navy seeks modified CH-53 for crane. W. H.
Gregory. il Aviation W 95:46-7+ S 27 '71
Rough time for the choppers; service in the
Laos operation. il Time 97:25 F 22 '71
Saigon's choppers: a crash waiting to hap-
pen; problem of maintenance. E. Behr. il
Newsweek 77:35 Mr 29 '71
UH-2C shows Lamps gear. il Aviation W 94:
20 My 24 '71
Vertol wins heavy lift helicopter. il Aviation
W 94:21 My 17 '71
See also
Helicopters—Armaments

Noise
Army, Hughes demonstrate OH-6 modified
into quiet helicopter. R. R. Ropelewski.
Aviation W 94:15 Mr 1 '71

Photographs
Mil V-12 gets postflight test. Aviation W 94:
18-19 Je 28 '71
New French helicopters. Aviation W 94:54 Je
7 '71
Soviets unveil Mi-12 heavy lift helicopter.
Aviation W 94:36-7 My 31 '71

Radar equipment
Radar evaluated on rotor blade. il Aviation
W 95:51 S 6 '71

Radio equipment
Army tests helicopter satcom use. il Aviation
W 94:39-41 Mr 15 '71

Records
See Aviation records

Rotors
New rotor blade tests ahead of schedule. W.
H. Gregory. il Aviation W 95:37-8 N 22 '71
New rotors quiet OH-6. il Aviation W 94:21
Ap 19 '71
Rotor head change initiated in AH-56. Avia-
tion W 94:22 My 17 '71

Safety devices and measures
See also
Helicopters—Escape devices

Specifications
Leading international rotary-wing aircraft;
tables (cont) Aviation W 94:77 Mr 8 '71
U.S. rotary-wing aircraft; tables (cont)
Aviation W 94:76 Mr 8 '71

Standards
Helicopters: unsafe at any height. J. Ennis.
il Pop Mech 136:63-7+ S '71

Television apparatus
See Television apparatus on aircraft

Testing
Aviation week pilot report:
Blackhawk exhibits speed, agility. D. A.
Brown. il Aviation W 94:38-43 F 15 '71
Puma exhibits fixed-wing traits. R. R.
Ropelewski. il Aviation W 94:44-7 Mr
22 '71
Enstrom F28A. R. Blodget. il Flying 90:
66-9 Ja '72
Mi flies McCulloch's new hoppercopter! W.
Thoms. il Mech Illus 67:60-1+ My '71
Pilot report:
Vought Alouette III. R. Blodget. il Flying
89:58-61 D '71

HELICOPTERS, Ambulance
Helicopter-ambulance inaugurated; Denver.
il Am City 86:138 Je '71
HELICOPTERS, Government
I think I'll try the White House; use of pres-
idential helicopter. T. Armbrister. il Read
Digest 98:71-5 My '71
HELICOPTERS, Military. See Helicopters—Mil-
itary use
HELICOPTERS, Municipal
Los Angeles builds separate helicopter facil-
ity. J. Purko. il Am City 86:97 Je '71
HELICOPTERS in building
Sikorsky sells first commercial S-64E. Avia-
tion W 96:21 Ja 3 '72
HELICOPTERS in lumbering
S-64E utilized in logging tests. R. G. O'Lone.
il Aviation W 95:54-5+ O 25 '71
HELICOPTERS in medical service
See also
Helicopters, Ambulance
HELICOPTERS in police work
Chopper coppers; Chicago crime-fighters. il
Ebony 26:78-80+ Jl '71
Helicopter patrol fights crime; Flint, Mich.
J. Jones. il Am City 86:108-9 Ag '71
Police helicopters offered by Hughes. il Avia-
tion W 95:47 N 22 '71
HELIOLUX. See Astronomical instruments
HÉLION, Jean
Realism is alive and well and living in Paris.
S. Lewis. il Art N 70:34-7+ Sum '71 •
HELIOTHIS. See Bollworms
HELIPORTS
Roof heliport keyed to 21st century; facility
atop new U.S. steel headquarters in Pitts-
burgh. il Aviation W 95:50-1 O 18 '71
HELIUM
Great balloondoggle. Time 97:76+ Je 7 '71
Helium: should it be conserved? il Sci N
99:261-2 Ap 17 '71
Lifetime of heliumlike metastable ions mea-
sured. J. T. Scott. bibliog Phys Today 24:
19 Mr '71
HELIUM, Liquid
See also
Superfluidity
HELL
Sorrows of hell. C. D. Linton. Chr Today
16:12-14 N 19 '71
HELLEINER, Mary
Androsaces in the garden. il Horticulture 49:
32 Jl '71
HELLENIC air force. See Greece, Modern—
Air force
HELLER, Alfred. See Volkman, P. H. jt.
auth.
HELLER, Ben, collection. See Art—Private
collections
HELLER, Erich
Literature and political responsibility. Com-
mentary 52:47-54 Jl '71
HELLER, Walter Wolfgang
Economic growth and ecology: an economist's
view. bibliog Mo Labor R 94:14-21 N '71
HELLER, Warren G.
V.T.V.M. battery eliminator. il Electr World
85:72 Ap '71
HELLER-Aller company
Blowing in the wind. Newsweek 77:78-9 Je
21 '71

HELLMAN, Geoffrey T.
Profiles; L. Edel. por New Yorker 47:43-6+
Mr 13 '71
Profiles; F. T. P. Plimpton. por New Yorker
47:61-2+ D 4 '71
HELLMAN, Peter
Stealing cars is a growth industry. il pors
N Y Times Mag p7+ Je 20 '71
HELL'S Angels. See Gangs
HELLS CANYON DAM. See Dams
HELLSTRÖM, Ingegerd
Cancer and transplants. il pors Newsweek 77:
98 My 10 '71 *
HELLSTRÖM, Karl
Cancer and transplants. il pors Newsweek 77:
98 My 10 '71 *
HELLYER, Clement David
Mystery of enzymes. il Sci Digest 70:70-4
N '71
HELLYER, Dave
Southern California market letter. Writers
Digest 51:28-30+ My '71
HELLYER, David
Shhh: new noiseless alloys will make it easy
on your ears. il Pop Sci 199:38+ Jl '71
HELM, Everett
Biennale 1970 fails to excite. Hi Fi 20:
MA27 D '70
Opera house crisis. il Hi Fi 21:MA26+ S '71
200 years of B. Schott's söhne. il por Hi Fi
21:55-60 Ja '71
HELMAN, Sandy I. and Miller, D. A.
In vitro techniques for avoiding edge dam-
age in studies of frog skin. bibliog il Sci-
ence 173:146-8 Jl 9 '71
HELMETS
How to choose a crash helmet. C. R. Self.
ir. il Mech Illus 67:59-61+ S '71
Up on two wheels; Bell Star helmet. B.
Greene. il Hot Rod 24:124+ Jl '71
See also
Astronauts—Clothing
HELMS, Richard McGarrah
Global intelligence; address, April 14, 1971.
Vital Speeches 37:450-4 My 15 '71; Excerpts.
il por U S News 70:84-6 Ap 26 '71
about
CIA on CIA. New Repub 164:10 My 1 '71 *
Congress and the CIA. Nation 213:548-9 N 29
'71 *
Cool pro who runs the CIA. il por Newsweek
78:30-1 N 22 '71 *
H-L-S of the C.I.A. B. Welles. il pors N Y
Times Mag p34-5+ Ap 18 '71 *
It won't wash. Nation 212:546-7 My 3 '71 *
Middle East: dead but not buried. pors Time
98:23 Jl 12 '71 *
Spy versus spy. New Repub 165:10 N 20 '71 *
Tale of two travelers. il pors Newsweek 78:
37-8 Jl 12 '71 *
Why the shake-up in intelligence. por U S
News 71:40-1 N 22 '71 *
HELMSLEY, Harry Brakmann
Gamble on Manhattan. il por Time 97:92 My
17 '71 *
HELMUTH, Larry
Ceramic sculpture from wheel-thrown parts.
il Ceram Mo 19:22-5 My '71
Throwing the covered pot. il Ceram Mo 19:
26-9 N '71
HELOISE
Farewell to Heloise. M. Lukas. il Cath World
213:174-7 Jl '71 *
HELPING behavior
Is altruism dead? R. J. Trotter. Sci N 99:
387 Je 5 '71
They throw money away on purpose; experi-
ments in the social psychology of pro-social
behavior. S. Bacon. il Sci Digest 69:39-44 F
'71
HELPMATE; story. See Shyer, M. F.
HELSINKI
Description
Helsinki's handwriting on the wall. L. Barry.
il Pop Phot 68:24+ Ap '71
Music
Night at the (Finnish) opera. G. Loney. il
Hi Fi 21:MA26-7 Ja '71
HELTON, Lyn
Love that lights the last days of a brave
young mother. M. Michaelson. il pors To-
days Health 49:48-53+ D '71 *
HELTZER, Harry
Heltzer of 3M. il por Forbes 107:62 My 15 '71 *
HELWIG, Carl
Innovation: what's it all about? bibliog
Clear House 46:82-5 O '71

HEMAGGLUTINATION inhibition test. See
Blood—Testing
HEMENWAY, Arthur
For all seasons. il Yachting 129:54-5+ My '71
Special report: Northwest yachting. il Yacht-
ing 129:51+ My '71
HEMEROCALLIS. See Day lilies
HEMES
Chemically induced porphyria: increased
microsomal heme turnover after treatment
with allylisopropylacetamide. U. A. Meyer
and H. S. Marver. bibliog il Science 171:
64-6 Ja 8 '71 *
Stereochemistry of hemes and other metallo-
porphyrins. J. L. Hoard. bibliog il Science
174:1295-302 D 24 '71
HEMINGWAY, Ernest
African journal. il Sports Illus 35:42-52+ D 20
'71
about
Critical menagerie in The short happy life of
Francis Macomber. T. L. Gaillard, jr. Engl
J 60:31-5 Ja '71 *
Jack Hemingway remembers his father; ed.
by J. Hess. J. Hemingway. il pors Nat Wildlife 9:12-15 F '71 *
Matter of measurement; the tangled relation-
ship between Fitzgerald and Hemingway.
R. Prigozy. Commonweal 95:103-6+ O 29
'71; Discussion. 95:267+ D 17 '71 *
Remembering great men and great fish; ex-
cerpt from Fishing with Hemingway and
Glassell. K. Farrington. il Field & S 75:
54-5+ Ap '71 *
Turning the Keys. D. Butwin. il Sat R 54:
38-40 F 27 '71 *
HEMINGWAY, Jack
Jack Hemingway remembers his father; ed.
by J. Hess. il pors Nat Wildlife 9:12-15 F
'71
North Umpqua story. il Field & S 75:52-3+
F '71
Will we let the pink and silver warrior die?
il pors Nat Wildlife 9:34-7 Ag '71
HEMINGWAY, Mary (Welsh)
African journal; with introd. by R. Cave. E.
Hemingway. il Sports Illus 35:40-52+ D 20
'71 *
HEMINGWAY, Mary Moon
Thoughts for the hostess (cont of) Notes
for the hostess. House & Gard 139:46 Mr
'71
HEMINGWAY, Nicola
Sailing without water. il Motor B & S 127:40+
Je '71
HEMLOCK
Trees of the totem culture; excerpts from
Edge of a continent. D. G. Kelley. il Am
West 8:18-21+ My '71
HEMMING, Roy
If it's Thursday and La valse, this must be
Wuppertal. il Sr Schol 98:18 My 10 '71
—and others
DIScussions. See issues of Senior scholastic
HEMODIALYSIS. See Kidneys, Artificial
HEMOGLOBIN
Adult hemoglobin synthesis by reticulocytes
from the human fetus at midtrimester. M.
D. Hollenberg and others. bibliog il Sci-
ence 174:698-702 N 12 '71
Conformational equilibria in spin-labeled
hemoglobin. W. J. Deal and others. bibliog
il Science 171:1147-9 Mr 19 '71
Differences in the interaction of 2,3-diphos-
phoglycerate with certain mammalian hemo-
globins. H. F. Bunn. bibliog il Science 172:
1049-50 Je 4 '71
Profile of hemoglobin. il Chem 44:22 Ap '71
Specialization of rabbit reticulocyte transfer
RNA content for hemoglobin synthesis. D.
W. E. Smith and A. L. McNamara. bibliog
il Science 171:577-9 F 12 '71; Correction.
171:1040 Mr 12 '71
State of water in red cells. A. K. Solomon.
il Sci Am 224:88-96 F '71
See also
Porphyria
HEMOGLOBIN polymorphism. See Polymorph-
ism (biology)
HEMOPHILIA
Breakthrough for bleeders if they can afford
it. A. J. Snider. il Sci Digest 70:55-6 Ag '71
Factor VIII detection by hemagglutination
inhibition: hemophilia A and von Wille-
brand's disease. D. P. Stites and others.
bibliog il Science 171:196-7 Ja 15 '71
No wheelchair for Steven; case of a hemo-
philic child. A. Silberman. il Good H 173:
99+ N '71
HEMORRHAGE
See also
Nosebleed

HEMP
Botany and chemistry of cannabis, ed. by
C. R. B. Joyce and S. H. Curry. Review
Sci Am 225:238+ S '71. P. Morrison
Don't let your hemp weed go to pot. G. W.
Wormley. il Farm J 95:40-1+ F '71
Eradicate marijuana. E. L. Knake. il Suc
Farm 69:no3 W20 F '71
See also
Marijuana
Sisal hemp

HEMPHILL, F. E. and others
Lead suppression of mouse resistance to salmonella typhimurium. bibliog il Science 172:
1031-2 Je 4 '71

HEMPHILL, Paul
Growing up in Birmingham. il N Y Times
Mag p42-3+ S 12 '71
Merle Haggard. por Atlan 228:98-103 S '71

HENAHAN, Donal
Berio's anguished trinity. Hi Fi 21:78 Mr '71
Component maker meets record company: the
AR/DDG contemporary music project. Hi Fi
21:96-7 F '71
Delian delight. por Hi Fi 21:77 Ap '71
He reminds me of me at that age, says
Leonard Bernstein. il pors N Y Times Mag
p36-8+ O 24 '71
Schubert, transcendental amateur. il por Hi
Fi 21:71-2 Je '71

HENDERSON, Bill, and others
Great cost cutback. Camp Mag 43:8-10 N '71

HENDERSON, Brian
Toward a non-bourgeois camera style; excerpt from Weekend and history. il Film Q
24:2-14 Wint '70
Two types of film theory. Film Q 24:33-42 Spr
'71

HENDERSON, Everett S.
Oriental poppies. il Horticulture 49:22-3 J
'71
Perennials for early bloom. il Horticulture
49:38-41 N '71

HENDERSON, Hazel
Toward managing social conflict. bibliog f
Harvard Bsns R 49:82-90 My '71

HENDERSON, Oran K.
End of the affair. por Newsweek 78:18-19 D
27 '71 *
Lies about My Lai. Time 98:25 N 29 '71 *

HENDERSON, Robert
Wanderers; story. New Yorker 47:48-55 N 27
'71

HENDERSON, Upton B.
Mallards by the numbers. il Outdoor Life
147:48-9+ Ja '71
HENDERSON trial. See Courts martial and
courts of inquiry
HENDERSON verdict. See Courts martial and
courts of inquiry—Verdicts

HENDIN, Herbert
Psychoanalyst looks at student revolutionaries. il N Y Times Mag p 16-17+ Ja 17;
59 F 21 '71

HENDON, William S.
Rating a neighborhood park. il Am City 86:
70-1 Ap '71

HENDRIX, Jimi
Janis and Jimi, op. posth. W. Bender. pors
Time 97:76 F 15 '71 *
Music. M. Josephson. il pors Art in Am 59:
96-7 S '71 *

HENKES, Robert
How and why of classroom art. il Design
72:21-3 mid-Sum '71
Right philosophy. Design 72:38-9 mid-Wint
'71
Why parents can't understand Johnny's picture. il Sch Arts 71:18-21 S '71
Why we can't understand art. il Design 72:
16-19 Spr '71

HENLE, Faye
Get ready in November to give in December.
Harp Baz 105:130-1 N '71

HENLEY, Arthur
Muggers of the mind. il Todays Health 49:
38-41+ F '71

HENLEY, Keith D.
Sad symbol of our times: an abandoned
farm. il Am For 77:6-7 S '71

HENNEDY, Hugh L.
Shakespeare on screen. il Commonweal 95:
134-5 N 5 '71

HENNESEY, James
Right of sanctuary: then and now. America
125:482-3 D 4 '71

HENRI, Raymond
How God spent his summer; poem. Harper
244:87 Ja '72

HENRICO COUNTY, Va.
Gabriel insurrection of 1800. W. J. Kimball.
bibliog Negro Hist Bul 34:153-6 N '71

HENRIKSEN, Thomas H.
Black is beautiful: an old idea. bibliog il
Negro Hist Bul 34:150-2 N '71

HENRIOT, Peter J.
Nixon's NEP and the developing world. il
America 125:448-50 N 27 '71

HENRY, Ann
Ann of Mount Angel abbey. L. Robinson. il
pors Ebony 26:29-30+ F '71 *

HENRY, Carl F. H.
Finding a new stride. Chr Today 15:29-30
Jl 2 '71
Introduction to theology. Chr Today 15:25-6
Je 4 '71
Prophetic hope. Chr Today 15:40-1 S 10 '71
Question of identity. Chr Today 15:30 Ag 6
'71
Rationale for the Christian college. Chr To-
day 15:7-8+ My 21 '71

HENRY, E. William
Trade winds. C. Amory. Sat R 54:10-11 Jl 3
'71 *

HENRY, George J.
Overseas commentary. See first issue of
each month of Forbes

HENRY, Gerrit
Clay landscapes of Mary Frank. il Craft
Horiz 31:18-21+ D '71

HENRY, J. L. See Calaresu, F. R. jt. auth.

HENRY, Louis H.
Caring for our aged poor. New Repub 164:17-
22 My 22 '71

HENRY, Mary Roblee
Christmas traveler: Provence. Mlle 74:144-5+
D '71

HENRY, Nicholas L.
Hardin Craig: professor. Am Scholar 40:305-8
Spr '71

HENRY, Omer
Business for the birds. il pors Har Yrs 11:
19-22 Ag '71
Interviewing for trade journals. Writer 84:
22-5 F '71

HENRY Francis du Pont Winterthur museum
Paintings in the Winterthur collection. J. A.
H. Sweeney. il Antiques 100:758-67 N '71
Print collection at Winterthur. N. E. Rich-
ards. il Antiques 100:586-90. 734-9 O-N '71
Queen Anne and Chippendale furniture in
the Henry Francis du Pont Winterthur
museum (cont) C. F. Hummel. il Antiques
99:98-107 Ja '71
HENRY Oscar One Bull (Sioux chief) See One
Bull
HENRY Regnery company. See Regnery, Hen-
ry, company
HENRY W. Coe state park. See California—
Parks and reserves

HENSHEL, Harry B.
President stands alone. Harvard Bsns R 49:
37-45 S '71

HENSLEY, Glenn S.
Trailing your mini-yacht. il Yachting 130:
60-1+ Ag '71

HENSLEY, Stuart Knox
Health market gets a new giant. il por
Bsns W p38-9+ F 20 '71 *

HENSON, Kenneth T.
Application of science principles to teaching.
bibliog Clear House 46:143-6 N '71
Improving courses in methods of teaching.
bibliog Sch & Soc 99:413-15 N '71

HENTOFF, Nat
Using drugs in classrooms. Cur 126:40-5 F '71
Why students want their constitutional
rights. il Sat R 54:60-3+ My 22 '71; Same
abr. bibliog Ed Digest 37:39-42 O '71

HENYEY, T. L. See Palmer, D. F. jt. auth.

HENZE, Hans Werner
Current chronicle; tr. by L. Wallach. W.
Becker-Carsten. Mus Q 57:314-17 Ap '71 *

HEPATITIS
Annals of medicine; epidemic of the infectious form of viral hepatitis from eating
contaminated glazed and iced pastry. B.
Roueché. New Yorker 47:72-81+ Ag 21 '71
Gift of blood; excerpt from The gift relationship. R. Titmuss. il Trans-Action 8:18-26+
Ja '71
More insurance against hepatitis; hemag-
gutination inhibition test for serum hepatitis. il Bsns W p 116+ Ap 10 '71

Vaccines
Breakthrough in curbing a baffling virus. il
U S News 70:100-1 Ap 5 '71
Breakthrough on hepatitis. por Newsweek
77:97-8 Ap 5 '71
Developing a vaccine; serum hepatitis. Sci
N 99:211 Mr 27 '71
Help against hepatitis. Time 97:75 Ap 5 '71
Next: a hepatitis vaccine? A. J. Snider. Sci
Digest 69:58-9 Ap '71

HEPATITIS viruses
Production of hemadsorption-negative areas
by serums containing Australia antigen.
D. H. Carver and D. S. Y. Seto. bibliog il
Science 172:1265-7 Je 18 '71

HEPATOLENTICULAR degeneration
Ned's legacy. F. Miller. il Read Digest 98: 42-6 Ja '71
HEPBURN, Audrey
Audrey Hepburn Dotti and her family; interview, ed. by C. B. Pepper. il pors Vogue 157:94-101+ Ap 1 '71
HEPBURN, Katharine
He-she chemistry of Katherine Hepburn and Spencer Tracy; excerpts from Tracy and Hepburn. G. Kanin. il pors Vogue 158: 142-3+ N 1 '71 •
Tracy and Hepburn. by G. Kanin. Review Sat R pors 55:29+ Ja 8 '72. R. Hector •
HERALD, New York
Herald: new Sunday newspaper. New Yorker 47:38-40 O 9 '71
HERALDRY
At the sign of the crest. H. K. Eilers. See issues of Hobbies
HERB teas. See Tea
HERBACEOUS peonies. See Peonies
HERBARTIANISM. See Education—Philosophy
HERBER, R. H.
Mössbauer spectroscopy; with biographical sketch. il Sci Am 225:12, 86-95 bibliog(p 120) O '71
HERBERG, Will
Limits of pluralism. Nat R 23:198-9 F 23 '71
HERBERS, John
What makes Proxmire run. il pors N Y Times Mag p28-9+ Ap 4 '71
HERBERT, Adrian
Barnard touch. por Newsweek 78:62-3 Ag 9 '71 •
Barnard's bullet. por Time 98:37 Ag 9 '71 •
HERBERT, Anthony Bernard
Colonel Herbert tried to go by the book in Vietnam: how a supersoldier was fired from his command. J. T. Wooten. il pors N Y Times Mag p 10-11+ S 5 '71; Discussion. p97 S 26 '71 •
Colonel Herbert v. the army. il por Time 98:24+ N 22 '71 •
Compounding the tragedy. Time 97:16 Mr 22 '71 •
Good soldiers. L. K. Truscott. 4th. Nation 213:517 N 22 '71 •
Importance of Col Herbert. Nat R 23:1454+ D 31 '71 •
Is this justice? M. McGrory. America 125: 337 O 30 '71 •
Maverick. por Newsweek 78:40 N 22 '71 •
More atrocities. por Newsweek 77:26 Mr 22 '71 •
Notes and comment; news coverage of firing. New Yorker 47:35 O 23 '71 •
HERBERT, Dorothy
Talent unlimited. il por Design 72:26-8 Sum '71
HERBERT, George
Holy Mr Herbert. E. E. Ericson. jr. Chr Today 15·7-8+ S 10 '71 •
HERBERT, Jay
Books and records to give for Christmas. House & Gard 140:38+ D '71
HERBICIDE assessment commission. See American association for the advancement of science
HERBICIDE metabolism in insects. See Insects—Metabolism
HERBICIDE metabolism in soils. See Soil metabolism
HERBICIDES
Controlling weeds in groundcovers. A. Bing. il Horticulture 49:20-3 Je '71
Critics weigh EPA herbicide report, find it wanting; 2,4,5-T controversy. C. Holden. Science 173:312 Jl 23 '71
Decision on 2,4,5-T: leaked reports compel regulatory responsibility. N. Wade. Science 173:610-12+ Ag 13 '71; Discussion. 174:545-7 N 5 '71
Destruction of Indochina; report of Stanford biology study group. il Bul Atom Sci 27:36-40 My '71
Gamble; making public the advisory committee report on 2,4,5-T. T. Aaronson. il Environ 13:20-4+ S '71
Herbicides in Vietnam: violating the laws, starving our allies. C.-G. McDaniel. Chr Cent 88:195-7 F 10 '71
Newest developments in herbicides. C. E. Sommers. Suc Farm 69:F4 Ap '71
Starvation as a policy; report of the Science-herbicide assessment commission. P. R. Ehrlich and J. P. Holdren. Sat R 54:91 D 4 '71
Striking the balance; TVA use of 2,4-D to control Eurasian watermilfoil. E. Hirst. and H. Bank. bibliog il Environ 13:34-41 N '71

Use of herbicides in Viet-Nam to be phased out; White House announcement, December 26, 1970. Dept State Bul 64:77 Ja 18 '71
Weed control for soybeans. Suc Farm 69:no3 W4 F '71
Weed control in corn. Suc Farm 69:no3 42+ F '71
See also
Maleic hydrazide
Propanil

Injurious effects
Difficulty of evaluating the toxicity and teratogenicity of 2,4,5-T from existing animal experiments. T. D. Sterling. bibliog Science 174:1358-9 D 24 '71

Residues
Photodecomposition of chlorinated dibenzo-p-dioxins. D. G. Crosby and others. bibliog il Science 173:748-9 Ag 20 '71
HERBICIDES as defoliants. See Defoliation
HERBS
Cooking with herbs & spices; excerpts. C. Claiborne. il por Ladies Home J 88:84+ Je '71
Growing herbs indoors. E. Taylor. il Good H 172:166 Mr '71
Hanging herb pot near the kitchen. il Sunset 146:212 Je '71
Herb chart for health and beauty and fun. il Mlle 72:166-9 Mr '71
Herb secrets of famous cooks; with recipes. il House & Gard 139:87+ Ja '71
How to grow herbs indoors. il House & Gard 139:86 Ja '71
Many herbs in small space. il Sunset 147:246 N '71
Mints to plant now. Good H 172:190 My '71
Out of the herb garden. E. Alston. il Look 35:52-3 Ag 10 '71
Seasonings from the garden. G. B. Foster. il Horticulture 49:36-7+ Ag '71
This handsome hillside garden controls erosion and its plants offer savory help in the kitchen. il Sunset 146:246 Ap '71
Training herbs. C. Stewart. il Horticulture 49:28+ Mr '71
Very personal garden of Jack and Esther Larson; dooryard herb garden. il House & Gard 139:82-5 Ja '71
See also
Coriander
Garlic
Ginseng
Parsley
HERBST, Derral
Disjunct foliar veins in Hawaiian euphorbias. bibliog il Science 171:1247-8 Mr 26 '71
HERCKER, Eileen S. See Rabinowitz, J. L. jt. auth.
HERDER and Herder, Inc.
From sacred to sensational. Chr Cent 88:239 F 17 '71
HERE is Einbaum; story. See Morris, W.
HEREDITARY angioneurotic edema. See Edema
HEREDITY
Biology of behavior. R. J. Williams. Sat R 54:17-19+ Ja 30 '71
Intelligence and race. W. F. Bodmer and L. L. Cavalli-Sforza; discussion. Sci Am 224: 6-8 Ja '71
See also
Clones (biology)
Eugenics
Evolution
Linkage (genetics)
Population genetics
Prenatal influences
HEREDITY of disease
Clinical aspects of inherited disorders; report of meeting. W. H. Finley and S. C. Finley. Science 173:1167-8 S 17 '71
Myths about your health and heredity. G. M. Knox. Bet Hom & Gard 49:14+ Je '71
Prenatal diagnosis of genetic disease. T. Friedmann. il Sci Am 225:34-42 bibliog (p 136) N '71
See also
Amaurotic family idiocy
Angiokeratoma
Hemophilia
Huntington's chorea
Metabolism, Disorders of
Porphyria
HERESY
No more heresy. il Time 97:57 F 15 '71
HERGET, Barlow
Arkansas. Atlan 227:14+ F '71
HERHOLD, Robert M.
Vietnam veteran speaks out against continuing the war. Chr Cent 88:833-5 Jl 7 '71
(ed) See Brown, R. M. Bob Brown: reluctant radical

HERICIUM. See Fungi
HERING, Doris
  Joffrey journey. il Dance Mag 46:30-5 Ja '72
  Why Ohio? il Dance Mag 45:47-62 S '71
HERING, Millicent B.
  Drug dilemma. bibliog il por Library J 96:
  593-6 F 15 '71
HERITAGE trails. See United States—Description and travel
HERITAGE Village. See Southbury, Conn.
HÉRITIER, Jean L'. See L'Héritier, J.
HERLIHY, James Leo
  Trade winds; interview, ed. by C .Amory. Sat
  R 54:10 My 29 '71
HERMAN, Shelby W. and Fulco, L. J.
  Changes in productivity and unit labor costs:
  a yearly review. il Mo Labor R 94:3-8 My
  '71
HERMAN, Sheldon. See Klein, R. jt. auth.
HERMAN, Yvonne
  Arctic paleo-oceanography in late cenozoic
  time. bibliog Science 169:474-7; 174:963 Jl
  31 '70. N 26 '71
HERMITAGE (historic house) See Tennessee
  —Historic houses, etc.
HERMITS
  Noah John Rondeau: Adirondack hermit, by
  M. C. DeSormo. Review
    Liv Wildn por 35:42-4 Spr '71. W. K. Verner
HERN, Warren M.
  Biological tyranny. New Repub 164:15-17 F 27
  '71
HERNANDEZ, Amalia
  Doña Amalia's at it again. D. Hering. il por
  Dance Mag 45:47-9 Je '71 *
HERNANDEZ, Arturo D.
  Tortoise; story. Américas 23:25-7 Ja '71
HERNANDEZ, Miguel
  To smile with the joyful sadness of the olive
  tree; poem, tr. by T. Baland. New Repub
  165:23 N 27 '71
HERNANDEZ, Rosa
  Aqui estoy. . .here I am. A. Gaber. il por
  Am Ed 7:18-22 Ja '71 *
HERNDON, James
  Way you're spozed to teach. R. Gross. il por
  Life 70:14 Ap 23 '71 *
HERNDON, James Dennis
  Judgment on the judge. New Repub 164:
  11-12 Ja 30 '71 *
HERNIA
  Is one-day hernia repair for real? A. Hamilton. Todays Health 49:52-4 Mr '71; Reply.
  A. W. Ulin. 49:60 Ag '71
HERO worship
  Youth's heroes have no haloes. C. Quigley.
  Todays Ed 60:28-9 F '71; Same abr. Ed
  Digest 36:46-8 Ap '71
HERODOTUS
  Herodotus: observer of sexual psychopathology. C. P. Rosenbaum and R. Rossi. bibliog Am Imago 28:71-8 Spr '71
HEROES
  Baker's dozen of heroic vitalists; address,
  June 4, 1971. H. G. Baker. Vital Speeches
  37:586-92 Jl 15 '71
  Experiments with truth. P. W. Schmidtchen.
  il pors Hobbies 76:134-7 Je '71
  Of war and heroes. il Time 97:12 Je 14 '71
    See also
  Hero worship
  Mythology
HEROIN
  America's battle against the white death! il
  Newsweek 77:41-3 Mr 29 '71
  Finding partial solutions. il Sci N 99:331-2
  My 15 '71
  GI's other enemy: heroin. il Newsweek 77:
  26+ My 24 '71
  Heroin plague: what can be done? with report by M. Kasindorf. il Newsweek 78:27-
  32 Jl 5 '71
  Heroin shooting war; situation in Detroit. il
  Time 97:18 Je 21 '71
  Heroin: the source of supply. E. Marshall.
  New Repub 165:23-5 Jl 24 '71
  Indochina's heroin traffic. il por Newsweek
  78:15 Jl 19 '71
  Narcotic antagonists: new methods to treat
  heroin addiction. A. L. Hammond. Science
  173:503-6 Ag 6 '71
  New math of addiction; addict population estimates: Washington, D.C. Time 98:54+ S
  13 '71
  Our most dangerous epidemic. R. H. Steele.
  il por Nations Bsns 59:46-8 Jl '71
  Smell of death; heroin malignancy in New
  York. S. Alsop. Newsweek 77:76 F 1 '71
HEROIN babies. See Fetus, Effect of drugs
  on the
HEROIN smuggling. See Smuggling

HEROINES in literature. See Characters in
  literature; Women in literature
HERPES simplex
  Cure for cold sores? il Time 98:41 Jl 12 '71
  Lurking enemy of beauty: how to cope with
  it. il Vogue 157:164-5 My '71
  New cold sore treatment. A. J. Snider. Sci
  Digest 70:73 O '71
  New light on cold sores. il Newsweek 78:81
  Jl 12 '71
HERPES simplex virus
  Interaction of rheumatoid factor with infectious herpes simplex virus-antibody complexes. W. K. Ashe and others. bibliog il
  Science 172:176-7 Ap 9 '71
  Latent herpes simplex virus in spinal ganglia
  of mice. J. G. Stevens and M. L. Cook.
  bibliog il Science 173:843-5 Ag 27 '71
HERPESVIRUS
  Acute lymphocytic leukemia in owl monkeys
  inoculated with herpesvirus saimiri. L. V.
  Meléndez and others. bibliog il Science
  171:1161-3 Mr 19 '71
  Herpesvirus antigens on cell membranes detected by centrifugation of membrane-antibody complexes. B. Roizman and P. G.
  Spear. bibliog il Science 171:298-300 Ja 22
  '71
  Herpesvirus type 2 isolated from cervical tumor cells grown in tissue culture. L. Aurelian and others. bibliog il Science 174:704-7
  N 12 '71
  Nonencapsidated infectious DNA of adeno-satellite virus in cells coinfected with herpesvirus. D. W. Boucher and others. bibliog il Science 173:1243-5 S 24 '71
  On the track of a cancer suspect: Epstein-Barr virus. il Fortune 84:225 N '71
HERPESVIRUS infections
  Genital herpesvirus hominis type 2 infection:
  an experimental model in cebus monkeys.
  A. J. Nahmias and others. bibliog Science
  171:297-8 Ja 22 '71
HERRERRA, Jose de
  Marcos and the Communists. il America 126:
  6-10 Ja 8 '72
HERRICK, Neal Q. and Quinn, R. P.
  Working conditions survey as a source of
  social indicators. il Mo Labor R 94:15-24
  Ap '71
HERRIGEL, Eugen
  Zen in the art of archery: a bridge to the
  East. C. Edwards. America 125:31 Jl 24
  '71 *
HERRNSTEIN, Richard Julius
  I.Q. il Atlan 228:43-58+ S; 110 D '71
    about
  Creeping meritocracy? por Newsweek 78:57
  Ag 23 '71 *
  Is equality bad for you? il Time 98:33 Ag 23
  '71 *
HERRON, Ron
  Rescue of Elkhorn Creek. il Good H 172:80-
  1+ Mr '71
HERSCHBERGER, Ruth
  Comment. H. Witt. Poetry 118:43-4 Ap '71
HERSCHMAN, Arthur
  Keeping up with what's going on in physics.
  bibliog il Phys Today 24:23-9 N '71
HERSEY, John
  Informal notes, taken on reading John Hersey on Yale. R. Moses. Nat R 23:142-4+ F 9
  '71 *
HERSH, Evan M. and others
  L-Glutaminase: suppresion of lymphocyte
  blastogenic responses in vitro. bibliog il
  Science 172:736-8 My 14 '71
HERSH, Seymour M.
  Reporter at large. New Yorker 47:101-2+ O
  9 '71
HERSHEY, Lenore
  (ed) See Loren, S. Sophia: serenely female
HERST, Herman, Jr
  Stamps. See issues of Hobbies
    about
  Absolutely stuck on stamps. R. H. Boyle.
  il por Sports Illus 35 :32-7 Ag 23 '71 *
HERTER, Christian A. Jr.
  U.S. discusses priorities for the 1972 U.N.
  conference on the human environment;
  statements, September 16 and 24, 1971. Dept
  State Bul 65:530-1, 534-6 N 8 '71
HERTER'S, Inc.
  Jungle cocks, trout flies, and smugglers. E.
  N. Layne and S. Hartgen. il Audubon 73:
  38-43 My '71
HERTZ corporation
  McCahill vs Hertz (Chevrolet) vs Avis
  (Plymouth) il Mech Illus 67:56-8+ Jl '71
HERTZBERG, Hendrik
  (ed) Centrality of the cat. il Esquire 75:66-9
  F '71

HERZ, Marcelle
Dream came true. G. A. Broten and G. R. Twardokens. il Parks & Rec 6:111+ Ja '71 *
HERZ, Michael J. See Peeke, H. V. S. jt. auth.
HERZBERG, Elleen
Chase for classic cars. il Duns 98:65-6 Jl '71
Empty skyscarper. il Duns 97:75-6 F '71
Making book on the Dow. por Duns 97:75-6 Je '71
HERZBERG, Gerhard
Emigré Nobelists. il por Newsweek 78:106+ N 15 '71 *
Gifted refugees. pors Time 98:45 N 15 '71 *
1971 Nobel prizes in science. por Chem 45:22 Ja '72 *
Nobel prize for chemistry: Herzberg and molecular spectroscopy. A. E. Douglas. por Science 174:672-3 N 12 '71 *
Nobel prizes: physics to Gabor, chemistry to Herzberg. G. B. Lubkin. bibliog pors Phys Today 24:69-71 D '71 *
Work in holography, molecular structure net Nobel prizes. Sci N 100:309 N 6 '71 *
HERZOG, Ray E.
TV service and safety. il Electr World 85: 30-1 F '71
Vocation profile: the TV product-service technician. il por Electr World 85:40-1 Je '71
HESBURGH, Theodore Martin
College presidents and students: interview. Mlle 73:244-5+ Ag '71
Mr Secretary: please reconsider; letter to George Romney. America 124:238-9 Mr 6 '71

about
Mellowing of a president. il por Time 97:67 F 15 '71 *
HESHMATI, Leota B.
Abdul and the Caliph's treasure; dramatization of story. Plays 31:63-5, 68 N '71
Old man minds his wife; dramatization of an English ballad. Plays 31:63-6 O '71
HESS, Eliot
Points of view; photographs. Mod Phot 36: 120-1 Ja '72
HESS, George J.
Lessons from the squall. il Yachting 129:64+ Je '71
HESS, Rudolf
Last prisoner at Spandau. G. A. Craig. Atlan 228:90-2 Ag '71 *
HESS, Stephen
Notes from the cavern. J. Osborne. New Repub 165:13-14 D 4 '71 *
HESS, Thomas B.
Barnett Newman: American artist; excerpts from an essay. Vogue 158:124-5 N 1 '71
HESSE, Eva
Eva Hesse: the circle. L. R. Lippard. il Art in Am 59:68-73 My '71
HESSE, Hermann
Hesse on peace; excerpt from If the war goes on, tr. by R. Mannheim. Mlle 72:76-7 Ja '71
Life story briefly told; excerpt from Autobiographical writings, tr. by D. Lindley. il Mlle 74:152-3+ N '71

about
Siddhartha. F. Trippett. il Look 35:46-54+ F 23 '71 *
HESSIAN state theater, Wiesbaden. See Opera houses
HESTER, Oka T.
Try mobile recreation units. il Am City 86: 70+ F '71
HETCH HETCHY VALLEY
Honeymoon in Hetch Hetchy. L. Foster. il pors Am West 8:10-15 My '71
HETCH HETCHY water supply project
Honeymoon in Hetch Hetchy; question of reservoir. L. Foster. il pors Am West 8:10-15 My '71
HETER, Christian A, Jr
U.S. initiatives for the 1972 U.N. conference on the human environment; statement February 9, 1971. Dept State Bul 64:334-9 Mr 15 '71
HETEROCHROMATIN. See Chromatin
HETEROPLOIDY. See Chromosomes
HETTENHOUSE, George W.
Compensation cafeteria for top executives. il Harvard Bsns R 49:113-19 S '71
HEUBLEIN, inc.
Riding high on a Moscow mule. J. G. Martin. il pors Nations Bsns 59:66-7 Ja '71
HEUMANN, Judy
She fought to teach. E. Blaustein. il pors Good H 173:56+ S '71 *
HEUSER, Ken
What's happening to our deer? il Field & S 76:56-7+ O '71

HEUSSENSTAMM, F. K.
Analysis of a high school underground paper. Ed Digest 36:53-4 Ja '71
Bumper stickers and the cops. il Trans-Action 8:32-3 F '71
HEUVEL, E. P. J. van den, and Conti, P. S.
Time scales for lithium depletion and rotational braking in solar-type main-sequence stars. bibliog il Science 171:895-6 Mr 5 '71
HEUVEL, Emile van
China's new mood; relaxation, self-confidence. il N Y Times Mag p 10-11+ Jl 25 '71
HEVER, Robert
Who says a man can't iron? il Good H 173: 42+ Ag '71
HEWES, Henry
(comp) Summer repertory schedule, 1971. Sat R 54:43 Je 26 '71
Theater. See issues of Saturday review
Theater in '71. il Sat R 54:14-19 Je 12 '71
HEWITT, Jean
Food (cont) il N Y Times Mag p57 F 28; 89+ Mr 28; 56 Ap 11; 63 My 9; 36 Jl 18; 49 Ag 22; 34 Ag 29; 79 O 10; 79 N 14; 105+ D 5 '71
HEXACHLOROPHENE
Danger in baby soap? Time 98:57 D 20 '71
Disinfectant may be dangerous. A. J. Snider. Sci Digest 71:71 Ja '72
Hexachlorophene: FDA temporizes on brain-damaging chemical. N. Wade. Science 174: 805-7 N 19 '71
HEXTER, Alfred C. and Goldsmith, J. R.
Carbon monoxide: association of community air pollution with mortality. bibliog il Science 172:265-7; 173:576+ Ap 16, Ag 13 '71
HEXTER, J. H.
Doing history. bibliog f Commentary 51:53-62 Je '71
HEYEN, William
Return; Snapper; poems. Poetry 118:27-8 Ap '71
Swan; poem. Poetry 119:150 D '71

about
Comment. J. T. Irwin. Poetry 118:352-3 S '71 *
HEYERDAHL, Thor
Trade winds; interview, ed. by C. Amory. Sat R 54:12+ O 9 '71
Voyage of Ra II. il pors Nat Geog 139:44-71 Ja '71
Voyages of Ra; condensed from The Ra expeditions. il por Read Digest 99:187-90+ Ag '71

about
Thor Heyerdahl's paper boat, plowing a filthy ocean. G. Moore. il por Life 71:81 S 24 '71 *
HEYLMAN, Katherine M.
No bargain for Frances. bibliog il por Library J 96:3433-8 O 15 '71
HEYM, Stefan
Expatriate chess on the other side of the wall. E. Shorris. il pors N Y Times Mag p38+ My 23 '71 *
HEYMAN, Wayne
Choosing the right plugs. il Motor B & S 127:97+ Ap '71
HEYNS, Roger William
Diplomatic lobbyist. Newsweek 78:46 Ag 2 '71 *
HEYWARD, Frank
Elephants are hard on trees. il Am For 77:24-7+ Je '71
HIATT, Peter. See Davis, C. H. jt. auth.
HIATT, Suzanne Radley
Uncorinthian Philadelphians. T. W. Moore. por Chr Cent 88:930-1 Ag 4 '71 *
HIAWATHA national forest, Mich. See National forests
HIBACHI cookery. See Barbecue cookery
HIBBARD, Bill
There's much a-brewin', in bubbly Milwaukee. Summer fun! il Travel 135:54-7 My '71
HIBBARD, Ginnie
Redbook beauty report. il Redbook 138:84-7+ Ja '72 *
HIBBEN, Frank Cummings
Easy chair; species being saved by transplantation to the American Southwest. J. Fischer. Harper 243:16+ O '71 *
HIBERNATION
Annual biological clocks. E. T. Pengelley and S. J. Asmundson. il Sci Am 224:72-9 Ap '71
HIBISCUS
Hibiscus, carefree exotic. Org Gard & Farm 18:100-1 Ap '71
HICCUPS
Sugar-cursed hiccups. il Newsweek 79:66 Ja 10 '72

HICKE, Bill
These major-leaguers succeeded in spite of
. . . E. Kiester. il pors Todays Health 49:
51 O '71 *

HICKEL, Walter Joseph
Making of a conservationist; excerpt from
Who owns America? il Sat R 54:65-7 O 2
'71

about

Exit Secretary Hickel, enter Secretary Mor-
ton. Audubon 73:94 Ja '71 *
Goodbye, Mr Hickel. M. Frome. Field & S
75:46+ F '71 *
TRB from Washington: kind regards; no re-
grets. New Repub 165:6 O 2 '71 *
Wally Hickel revisited. il por Time 98:56 O 4
'71 *
We were wrong! J. B. Craig. Am For 77:11
F '71 *
Who owns America? by W. J. Hickel. Re-
view
Nation 213:378-9 O 18 '71. E. Gruening *
Will Wally Hickel ever come home? with
travel notes. R. Joseph. il por Esquire 76:
12, 91-7 Ag '71 *

HICKEY, Dave
Earthscapes, landworks and Oz. il Art in Am
59:40-9 S '71

HICKEY, Gerald
Departing words. Newsweek 77:37 My 3 '71 *

HICKEY, Nell
Look who's gone bananas over TV! il Read
Digest 98:157-8+ Ja '71

HICKEY, Thomas
Social life space of nuns in the seventies;
address, April 1970. il Cath World 212:292-
6 Mr '71

HICKMAN, Kenneth, and White, Ian
Modified superheating of purified water.
bibliog il Science 172:718-22 My 14 '71

HICKMAN, Martha Whitmore
World to share; story. Good H 172:90-1 Mr
'71

HICKS, David
Decorating with fabrics; excerpt from Da-
vid Hicks on decoration—with fabrics. il
McCalls 98:80-7 S '71

HICKS, Douglas L.
Bargain basement habitat; Sublimnos. il Pop
Mech 135:104-7+ Ap '71

HICKS, Louise (Day)
Running back into the past; with reports by
J. Pekkanen and R. Brigham. il pors Life
71:32-4+ O 29 '71 *

HICKS, Mabel
Nihilist; poem. Chr Cent 88:213 F 17 '71

HICKS, Sheila
Sheila Hicks at Rabat. B. Werther. il por
Craft Horiz 31:30-3 Je '71 *

HIDALGO, Francisco
Cityscapes; photographs. Pop Phot 68:74-9
Ap '71

HIDES and skins
Adventures in the skin trade. F. W. King. il
Natur Hist 80:8-10+ bibliog(p 104) My '71
See also
Tanning

HIEMENZ, Jack
Musician of the month (cont) Hi Fi 21:
MA4-5 Ja; MA4-5 D '71
Taping Le rossignol for television. il Hi Fi
21:71-3 N '71

HIEROGLYPHICS, Maya. See Mayas—Writing

**HIEROPHANTIC theater. See Theater, Experi-
mental**

HI-FI shelves. See Shelves

**HI-FI systems. See High fidelity sound sys-
tems**

HIGASHI, Akira, and Corte, A. E.
Solifluction: a model experiment. il Science
171:480-2 F 5 '71

HIGBY, Richard L.
Harvesting sunflowers, the right tool for
the right job. il Org Gard & Farm 18:68-9
Ap '71

HIGDON, Hal
Jogger power, memoirs of a fitness buff;
excerpt from On the run from dogs and
people. il Todays Health 49:50-2+ F '71
When sports figures turn author; jocks and
their ghosts. il Sat R 54:48-9+ Ag 14 '71 *

HIGGINS, Alice
Horse shows (cont) Sports Illus 35:95+ N 22
'71
Modern pentathlon. Sports Illus 35:80 O 25
'71

HIGGINS, Chester
Black stars do 'give a damn'. il Ebony 26:
44-6+ S '71
The Temptations. il Ebony 26:64-8+ Ap '71

HIGGINS, J. David, and others
Shock-elicited pain and its reduction by concurrent tactile stimulation. bibliog il Science 172:866-7 My 21 '71
—See Schwartz, G. E. jt. auth.

HIGGINS, James
Drinan's Bay state volunteers. Nation 211:
648-52 D 21 '70
Union and campus: talking together. Nation
213:171-4 S 6 '71

HIGGINS, Jim, and Higgins, S. R.
Run away to sea, with the whole family. il
Todays Health 49:36-9 Mr '71

HIGGINS, Judith
Biographies they can read. il Library J 96:
1431-2 Ap 15 '71
Everybody into the pool. il por Library J 96:
2842-5 S 15 '71
—and Stellwag, August
Mini reference library: 21 paperbacks. il pors
Library J 96:245-7 Ja 15 '71

**HIGGINS, Shirley Rose. See Higgins, J. jt.
auth.**

HIGH blood pressure. See Hypertension

**HIGH commissioner for refugees. See United
Nations—High commissioner for refugees**

HIGH energy physics. See Nuclear physics

HIGH fidelity amplifiers. See Amplifiers

HIGH fidelity and Musical America (periodical)
High fidelity moves into its second genera-
tion. A. Rich. il Hi Fi 21:57+ Ap '71
Story of an idea. R. Long. il Hi Fi 21:46-56
Ap '71

HIGH fidelity shows. See Audio fairs

HIGH fidelity sound systems
And don't forget the old products. F. R.
White. il Fi Hi 21:62-4 O '71
Audio. I. Berger. Sat R 54:49+ Jl 31 '71
Equipment in the news. See issues of High
fidelity and Musical America
Fancy new shapes in hi-fi. S. M. Gallager.
il Pop Mech 136:48-9 D '71
Fi, W., F. Rickenbacker. Nat R 23:209-10
F 23 '71
Look and listen. C. P. Gilmore. il Pop
Sci 199:20 Ag; 38 S; 42+ O; 36+ N; 10 D '71
New equipment reports. See issues of High
fidelity and Musical America
New products for 1972. il Hi Fi 21:50-2+
O '71
OK! What is high fidelity? J. G. Holt. Pop
Electr 35:71+ Jl '71
Portable sound systems for performers. D.
L. Patten. il Electr World 86:27-9+ Ag:
38-40 S '71
6 ways to improve your hi-fi system. M.
Mandl. il Radio-Electr 42:54-6 Mr '71
See also
KLH research and development corporation
Stereophonic sound systems

Cabinets

3-way hi-fi cabinet: a lot of looks for little
money. J. Hand. il Pop Mech 136:129-31 S
'71

Control

How to control your hi-fi from any room
in the house. E. Walters. il Pop Mech
136:132-7 O '71
Low-distortion hi-fi volume expander. R.
Wilt. il Electr World 85:54-5 Je '71

History

High fidelity moves into its second gener-
ation. A. Rich. il Hi Fi 21:57+ Ap '71
Story of an idea. R. Long. il Hi Fi 21:46-56
Ap '71

Noise

Stereo scene; Dolby noise-reduction system.
J. G. Holt. il Pop Electr 34:71+ F '71
Tape-noise reducer at a reduced price; Model
101 noise reduction unit. Consumer Rep
36:338-9 Je '71

**HIGH fidelity speakers. See Loud speaking ap-
paratus**

**HIGH ground; or, Look, ma, I'm explicating;
story. See De Vries, P.**

HIGH jumping. See Jumping

HIGH pressure (science)
Superconductivity at high pressure. N. B.
Brandt and N. I. Ginzburg. il Sci Am 224:
83-8+ Ap '71

HIGH school athletics. See School athletics

HIGH school boys. See Boys

HIGH school buildings. See School buildings

HIGH school counselors. See Student counselors

**HIGH school drama. See College and school
drama**

HIGH school dropouts. See Dropouts

HIGH school football. See Football

HIGH school football players. See Football players
HIGH school girls. See Girls
HIGH school graduates
Employment of high school graduates and dropouts. A. M. Young. il Mo Labor R 94: 33-8 My '71
High school class faces the future. il Ebony 26:74-6+ Ag '71
Reunion in Concord. O. Friedrich. il Harper 242:87-94+ My '71
Statistic of the month. N. A. Carlson. il Am Ed 7:45 Ag '71
HIGH school journalism. See College and school journalism
HIGH school libraries

Periodical collections
See   School libraries—Periodical collections
HIGH school of performing arts. See New York (city)—Education
HIGH school publications.   See College and school journalism
HIGH school student militants. See Student militants
HIGH school student opinion. See Student opinion
HIGH school students
Class reunions: dare we? M. Adams. il Har Yrs 11:28-9 S '71
Escrow college: high school students study at community colleges. P. Parker. bibliog il Clear House 45:439-43 Mr '71
Getting high on high school; new alternatives. K. Branan. il Schol Teach Jr/Sr High p 12-14+ F 1 '71
How is women's liberation doing in the high schools? S. Edmiston. Seventeen 30:48+ Ap '71
Love project. A. Lorrance. il Todays Ed 60: 60-2 S '71
School-age mothers go to classes. J. W. Martin. Ed Digest 36:44-5 Ja '71
Talking it over; questions and answers. Sr Schol 98:20 Ap 19; 19 My 3 '71
Time to fail; a time to succeed. C. Easton. il Parents Mag 46:44-5+ D '71
See also
High school graduates
Scholastic research center
School management and organization—Student participation
Self government in education
also headings beginning Student
Attitudes
See Students—Attitudes
Cheating
See Cheating in school work
Civil rights
See Students—Civil rights
Clothing
See Clothing and dress—Students
Dating
See Dating
Demonstrations
See Student demonstrations
Employment
See Student employment
Political activities
Yes was a big word at Reavis; Don Depa and the school tax referendum for high school in Burbank. Ill. Sr Schol 99:3 O 11 '71
Reading
Black culture: a reading program develops better understanding. I. W. Hale. Clear House 45:269-72 Ja '71
Individualized reading program. A. Gosney. Clear House 45:272 Ja '71
HIGH school students, Married. See Teen-age marriage
HIGH school students, Mentally superior
Presidential scholars: the spectacular achievers. S. Hunt. il Am Ed 7:29-31 Je '71
HIGH school students, Negro. See Negro students
HIGH school students and smoking. See Smoking and youth
HIGH school students and war
What's a POW-MIA, and what are high school students doing about it? il Sr Schol 99:8-12 N 29 '71
HIGH school students as teachers aides. See Teachers aides

HIGH school students as tutors. See Tutors and tutoring
HIGH school underground press. See College and school journalism
HIGH schools
High schools, too, have a crime problem. il U S News 71:26 N 22 '71
Principals' profile of big-city high schools. M. L. Hayes. Sch & Soc 99:253-4 Ap '71
What makes a good comprehensive high school? W. C. Malone. Clear House 46:3-5 S '71
What's going on in schools & colleges. See every other issue of Changing times
See also
Education, Secondary
Negro schools
Trade schools
Curriculum
College admissions policies. R. W. Young. Ed Digest 36:19-21 Ja '71
Need for an upgrading program. C. Savitzky. Clear House 46:154 N '71
Open curriculum; student-planned programs. M. L. Patton. il Schol Teach Jr/Sr High p20-3 S '71
Room design and curriculum planning. C. Rash. il Ceram Mo 19:30-1 S '71
Students lay it on the line. C. H. Harrison. il Schol Teach Jr/Sr High p8+ Ap 5 '71
Trends in state-level curriculum requirements. R. L. Cox and E. M. Ramer. Clear House 45:309-11 Ja '71
Urban affairs, right on; social studies course in Dayton, Ohio high schools. W. L. Bombeck. il Todays Ed 60:38-9 O '71
See also
Elective system in education
Independent study
Schedules, School
Departments
Chairman: where does he fit in? W. R. Beck and D. S. Rosenberger. Clear House 46: 48-51 S '71
Desegregation
See Public schools—Desegregation
Security measures
Battlefield communique; high school security measures. Time 98:52 Ag 16 '71
HIGH SIERRAS. See Sierra Nevada Mountains
HIGH speed ground transport systems. See Transportation, High speed
HIGH speed transportation. See Transportation, High speed
HIGH, wide, and handsome; story. See Friedman, B. J.
HIGHAM, C. F. W. and Leach, B. F.
Early center of bovine husbandry in southeast Asia. bibliog il Science 172:54-6 Ap 2 '71
HIGHER education. See College education; Junior colleges
HIGHER education act, 1965. See Colleges and universities—Federal aid
HIGHET, Gilbert
Venice revisited. il Horizon 13:54-7 Wint '71
about
Explorations, by G. Highet. Review
Sat R 54:31 S 4 '71. J. M. Roos •
HIGHLAND boy; story. See Norris, L.
HIGHLAND PARK, Mich.
Is the revolt starting? commuter traffic problem. Sci N 100:107 Ag 14 '71
Finance
Highland Park's yes. E. R. Wujcik. Am City 86:92+ Jl '71
HIGHLANDS of Scotland
Highlands of Scotland. J. D. Lockie. il Natur Hist 80:68-81 F '71
Spring in the Scottish Highlands. J. A. Carrier. il Travel 135:40-5 Mr '71
HIGHSMITH, Robert F. and Kline, D. L.
Kidney: primary source of plasminogen after acute depletion in the cat. bibliog il Science 174:141-2 O 8 '71
HIGHTOWER, John B.
Man on the spot. por Newsweek 77:82 Ja 25 '71 •
New man out. por Time 99:38 Ja 17 '72 •
HIGHWAY, Pan American. See Pan American highway
HIGHWAY accidents. See Traffic accidents
HIGHWAY action coalition
Ecologists attack the Highway trust fund. il Bsns W p86-7 D 11 '71
HIGHWAY beautification. See Roadside improvement

HIGHWAY engineering
Street construction & maintenance. See is-
sues of American city
See also
Roads—Safety guards
HIGHWAY interchanges. See Roads—Inter-
changes and intersections
HIGHWAY lighting. See Roads—Lighting
HIGHWAY location. See Roads—Location
HIGHWAY planting. See Roadside improve-
ment
HIGHWAY research board. See National re-
search council—Highway research board
HIGHWAY safety. See Traffic safety
HIGHWAY signs. See Road signs
HIGHWAY trust fund. See Express highways—
Federal aid
HIGHWAY users federation for safety and
mobility. See Pressure groups
HIGHWAYS. See Express highways; Roads
HIGLEY, John R.
Guzzler cottontails. il por Outdoor Life 148:
62-3+ Jl '71
HIJACKING of airplanes. See Airplane hijack-
ing
HIJACKING of ships. See Ship hijacking
HIKING. See Walking
HIKING boots. See Shoes
HILDEBRAND, Joel H.
Motions of molecules in liquids: viscosity
and diffusivity. bibliog il Science 174:490-3
O 29 '71
HILDEBRAND, Mark
Building-block design brings modular flexi-
bility to anywhere living. il Am Home
74:68 Ag '71
HILDEBRAND, Norb
New physical assessment & conditioning
program for sportsmen. il Field & S 76:66-
71+ Je '71
HILDEBRAND, R. Paul
Katherine by Anya Seton for high school sen-
iors. Engl J 60:746-7+ S '71
HILDENBRAND, Barbara
Nature. Sports Illus 35:72 O 4 '71
Survival at 70 below: it's easier these days.
il Todays Health 49:46-9+ F '71
HILGARD, Ernest
Who can be hypnotized. pors Newsweek 77:
68-9 Je 14 '71 *
HILGARD, Josephine
Who can be hypnotized. pors Newsweek 77:
68-9 Je 14 '71 *
HILKE, Jürgen
Burying an epoch of ecumenical politics. Chr
Cent 88:493-5 Ap 21 '71
HILL, Aaron
Blasting off at curr-like booksellers, in 1709
yet; excerpt. Pub W 199:43 Mr 29 '71
HILL, Charles H.
Teachers as change agents. bibliog Clear
House 45:424-8 Mr '71
HILL, Dave
David Hill's bitter pill. Newsweek 77:74 Je 14
'71 *
Often bloody, but uncowed. M. Cope. por
Sports Illus 34:50-2+ My 10 '71 *
HILL, Dean
Auto shop series carburetors. il Hot Rod
24:90-3 O '71
Pollution. Hot Rod 24:120-1 F '71
HILL, Ed
Old furniture into art nouveau. il por Design
72:24-5 Sum '71
HILL, Gladwin
Pristine preserves or popcorn playgrounds?
il Sat R 55:40-1+ Ja 1 '72
HILL, Henry Aaron
Henry A. Hill: the second mile. S. P. Massie.
por Chem 44:11 Ja '71 *
HILL, Herbert
Black workers & unemployment; address,
July 8, 1971. Vital Speeches 37:658-62 Ag 15
'71
HILL, James Jerome
John F. Stevens: pathfinder for western rail-
roads. E. Clark. bibliog il pors Am West 8:
28-33+ My '71 *
HILL, Jeanne
Lesson of the fire flowers. il Read Digest 99:
119-22 Ag '71
HILL, Joseph, pseud.
Being Meany to Nixon. Commonweal 95:268-9
D 17 '71
HILL, Lewis
Apples are ready! il Org Gard & Farm 18:
62-5 S '71
HILL, Morton A.
Insider's attack on obscenity report. por U S
News 70:78 F 22 '71

HILL, Norman
For liberty and equality. Cur 129:32-5 My '71
Growing phenomenon of the journalism re-
view. il Sat R 54:59-60 S 11 '71
HILL, Ray
Carry your boat to the water in a bag. il
por Pop Sci 198:118-20+ Ap '71
4 cylinders, 4 carbs, 4 strokes, and 500cc of
action. il Pop Sci 199:53 D '71
Garbage into gold. il Pop Sci 199:40 N '71
Having fun in wild white water. il Pop Sci
198:72-3 Je '71
Two-wheel-drive toughies. il Pop Sci 199:69
S '71
HILL, Richard Devereux
Oldest bank's newest innovator. por Bsns W
p 112 S 11 '71 *
HILL, Tom
Tom Hill: the American artist in Mexico;
with biographical sketch. il por Am Artist
35:56-61 F '71
HILL, William B.
Fiction (cont) America 124:548-9. 125:430+
My 22, N 20 '71
HILL family
To the brink and beyond. M. Kram. il Sports
Illus 35:48-52+ Jl 12 '71
HILLARD, James M.
Right of center. Wilson Lib Bul 46:229, 405
N '71, Ja '72
HILLEMAN, Maurice R. and Tytell, A. A.
Inductor of interferon; with biographical
sketches. il Sci Am 225:14, 26-31 Jl '71
HILLENBRAND, Barry
Strangulation of Fresno state. Commonweal
94:136-8 Ap 16 '71
HILLENBRAND, Martin Joseph
Critical tasks facing western Europe and
the United States in a period of change and
transition; address, May 13, 1971. Dept
State Bul 64:743-8 Je 7 '71
NATO and United States security interests;
statement, October 14, 1971. Dept State
Bul 65:518-21 N 8 '71

about

Lame defense of a deadly dictatorship. Chr
Cent 88:680 Je 2 '71 *
HILLIARD, Edward Hobbs, 1922-1970
Obituary
Liv Wildn por 34:4 Aut '70
HILLIARD, William Arthur
From token to the top. il por Time 97:65
My 17 '71 *
HILLIER, James
Reliability physics; address, April 1, 1971. Vi-
tal Speeches 37:474-7 My 15 '71
HILLIS, Burton
Man next door. Bet Hom & Gard 49:168 Ap
'71
HILLIS, Richard K.
Photo draw. il Design 72:24-7 Spr '71
Television as idea. il Design 73:8-10 Fall '71
HILLMAN, D. E. and Lewis, E. R.
Morphological basis for a mechanical linkage
in otolithic receptor transduction in the
frog. bibliog il Science 174:416-19 O 22 '71
HILLMAN, Richard H.
How to redeploy assets. il Harvard Bsns R
49:95-103 N '71
HILLS, J. I. See Russell, G. F. jt. auth.
HILLSIDE architecture
Exposed pilings support eight-level wood
frame house. il Arch Rec 150:135-8 S '71
Graham house, Fairfield County, Conn. il
Arch Rec 149:64-5 mid-My '71
House which enhances its site. il Arch Rec
149:119-22 F '71
Real cliffhanger. il Arch Forum 134:62-5
Ja '71
What a wonderful space to be in; Belvedere
Island, Calif. il Sunset 147:80-1 O '71
HILLSIDE gardens. See Gardens, Hillside
HILLYARD, Kay
Come fly with me; poem. il Har Yrs 11:34-7
O '71
Come walk with me; poem (cont) il Har
Yrs 11:18-19 Ja; 22-4 Mr; 26-9 Ap; 30-3
Je; 30-3 Ag '71
Count your blessings; poem. Har Yrs 11:30-3
N '71
New-fashioned picnic; poem. Har Yrs 11:24-7
Jl '71
Solitude; poem. il Har Yrs 11:30-3 S '71
Today: a good yesterday tomorrow. Har Yrs
11:39-40 Mr; 56-7 O '71
Today: let's give thanks. il Har Yrs 11:42-3
N '71
What is a valentine? poem. Har Yrs 11:26
F '71
Your Harvest years almanac for 1971. Har
Yrs 11:23-9 Ja '71

HILLYARD, Steven A. and others
Evoked potential correlates of auditory signal detection. bibliog il Science 172:1357-60 Je 25 '71

HILLYER, Laurie
Heart of a child; story. Good H 172:96-7 My '71

HILTON, Alison
When the renaissance came to Russia. bibliog il Art N 70:34-9+ D '71

HILTON, Barron
Hilton's coup in Las Vegas. por Bsns W p34 Jl 17 '71 *

HILTON HEAD ISLAND
Palmetto dunes golf villas. il Arch Rec 149: 96-8 mid-My '71
Showdown at Hilton Head. il Bsns W p 102 Ap 17 '71
Southern comfort for the seventies; Hilton Head, S.C. J. Y. Dickinson. il Holiday 49:70-4 Mr '71

HIMALAYAS
See also
Everest, Mount

HIMMELFARB, Milton
Never again! Commentary 52:73-6 Ag '71
Plague of children. Commentary 51:37-43 Ap; 52:20+ S '71

HIMMLER, Heinrich
Unsuccessful adolescence of Heinrich Himmler. P. Loewenberg. bibliog f Am Hist R 76:612-41 Je '71; Reply with rejoinder. G. W. F. Hallgarten. 76:1267-70 O '71 *

HINCHMAN, Jane
Day they gave hamsters away; story. Redbook 137:94-5 O '71

HINDE, R. A. and Spencer-Booth, Yvette
Effects of brief separation from mother on rhesus monkeys. bibliog il Science 173:111-18 Jl 9 '71

HINDU KUSH
Echoes of the Aryans. F. V. Grunfeld. il Horizon 13:102-4 Sum '71

HINDU-Muslim relations. See Islam—Relations
—Hinduism

HINE, Alvaro Cardona-. See Cardona-Hine, A.

HINE, Daryl
Nomad exquisite. Poetry 119:171-2 D '71

HINER, N. Ray
Herbartians, history, and moral education. Ed Digest 37:51-3 N '71

HINES, Diane Casella
Douglas Graves; painter with charcoal. il por Am Artist 35:58-63+ N '71
Robert Kulicke; painter, designer, craftsman. il Am Artist 35:38-43+ Ap '71
Seymour Pearlstein. il por Am Artist 35:62-7+ F '71

HINES, Jerome
Hines variety. G. Fitzgerald. il por Opera N 36:6 D 11 '71 *

HINKEMEYER, Michael T.
Diffusion of innovations. Clear House 45: 429-34 Mr '71

HINKLEY, E. D. and Kelley, P. L.
Detection of air pollutants with tunable diode lasers. bibliog il Science 171:635-9 F 19 '71

HINRICHS, Marie A.
Doctor, I have a question; questions and answers. See issues of Harvest years

HINTON, Harold C.
Sino-Soviet relations in the Brezhnev era. bibliog f Cur Hist 61:135-41+ S '71

HIP culture. See Counter culture

HIPPIE communes. See Collective settlements

HIPPIES
Decline of flower power. P. C. Rule. America 124:141-5 F 13 '71
Don't shoot—we are your children! by J. A. Lukas. Review
Sat R Il 54:34 My 1 '71. R. Cassidy
Fat Tuesday; Mardi gras and the hippies in New Orleans. il Newsweek 77:57 Mr 8 '71
Goa: an addendum; hashish trail at Katmandu, Nepal; letter to the editor. J. S. Mason. Nat R 23:1255 N 5 '71
Goa, end of the line; hashish trail at Kalengute. S. Labin. Nat R 23:750-3 Jl 13 '71
Hassles in the park. J. Hope. il Natur Hist 80:20-3+ bibliog (p 104) My '71
Hippies have rights; California supreme court strikes down ordinance against sitting on lawns. Nation 212:324-5 Mr 15 '71
Life and death of Atlanta's hip strip. J. T. Wooten. il N Y Times Mag p34-5+ Mr 14 '71
U.S. journal: Arroyo Seco, N.Mex. C. Trillin. New Yorker 47:104+ S 18 '71
See also
Counter culture

Anecdotes, facetiae, satire, etc.
Grandma visits her hippies. G. Natchez. il N Y Times Mag p74+ D 5 '71; Reply. S. Koren. p28 Ja 9 '72
It's a wise child. J. D. Tierney. Nat R 23:704 Je 29 '71

Caricatures and cartoons
When a hippie marries. Todays Health 49:63-4 Je '71

Political activities
Anecdotes, facetiae, satire, etc.
How Henry J. Littlefinger licked the hippies' scheme to take over the country by tossing pot in postage stamp glue. J. Keefauver. Nat R 23:1180+ O 22 '71

Religion
Gulf spanned at Calvary. Chr Today 15:21 Ja 29 '71
Jesus and the star system. D. Donnelly. America 125:350-2 O 30 '71
Jesus festivals. A. Eggebroten. Chr Today 15:38-40 Ag 6 '71
Jesus now: hogwash and holy water. J. Nolan. il Ramp Mag 10:20-6 Ag '71
Jesus people. il Newsweek 77:97 Mr 22 '71
Jesus presses are rolling; underground newspapers. E. E. Plowman. il Chr Today 15: 38 Ap 9 '71
New rebel cry: Jesus is coming! il Time 97:56-63 Je 21 '71; Same abr. with title Jesus revolution. Read Digest 99:135-8 D '71
Pacific Northwest: revival in the underground; street Christians in Spokane, Wash. E. E. Plowman. Chr Today 15:34-5 Ja 29 '71
Straights meet streets; TV documentary on Children of God encampment in Thurber, Tex. E. E. Plowman. Chr Today 15:35 Ja 29 '71
We need their faith! N. V. Peale. Read Digest 99:138-41 D '71

HIPPLE, Theodore W.
Eliminating the negative in English teaching. Engl J 60:373-8 Mr '71

HIPPOCAMPUS (brain) See Cerebral cortex

HIPPOCRATES
Hippocrates, thermal stress, and stroke mortality, 1966. L. A. Helfand and C. Bridger. il Weatherwise 24:100-4 Je '71 *

HIPPOCRATIC oath. See Oaths

HIRAOKA, Kimitake. See Mishima, Y. pseud.

HIRDMAN, Sven
Weapons in the deep sea. bibliog il Environ 13:28-42 Ap '71

HIRN, Doris D.
Feeding horses properly. il Camp Mag 43:32 My '71

HIROHITO, emperor of Japan
President Nixon and Emperor Hirohito of Japan meet in Alaska; exchange of greetings. September 26, 1971. Dept State Bul 65:398 O 18 '71
about
As Nixon and Hirohito meet; can allies heal a split? pors U S News 71:35-6 S 27 '71 *
Bad trip. il por Newsweek 78:58+ O 18 '71 *
Emperor who meets the President today. T. Oka. il pors N Y Times Mag p44-5+ S 26 '71 *
Hirohito keeps things simple. il pors Newsweek 78:34-5 O 4 '71 *
Hirohito of Japan, was he a war criminal? por U S News 71:76-7 D 13 '71 *
Hirohito: the first gentleman. il pors Time 98:35 O 4 '71 *
Is Hirohito the war's real villain? il por Time 98:43-4 O 4 '71 *
Japan's imperial conspiracy. by D. Bergamini. Review
Bsns W por p 15 D 4 '71. G. Ringwald *
Life por 71:11 O 15 '71. C. Elliott *
Sat R 54:48-9 O 16 '71. R. Halloran *
Japan's imperial conspiracy; interview. ed. by A. H. Johnston. D. Bergamini. il por Pub W 200:26-7 O 4 '71 *
Some airport diplomacy for the Emperor of Japan. S. Chang. il por Life 71:77 S 17 '71 *
What Japan expects of the emperor. il pors U S News 71:37 S 27 '71 *

HIROSHIMA
Hiroshima: beauty from fused rubble. T. Benfey. il Chem 44:2-3 N '71
Unmentioned victims; American P.O.W.s. il Time 98:30 Ag 9 '71

HIRSCH, Julian D.
EW lab report: volt-ohm milliammeters. il
Electr World 85:34-8 Mr '71
EW lab tests new Dolby-ized cassette decks. il
Electr World 85:25-8+ Mr '71
Hirsch-Houck lab tests automatic turntables.
il Electr World 85:27-30+ Je '71
Hirsch-Houck lab tests stereo headphones.
il Electr World 86:39-42 O '71
Noise filters in hi-fi amplifiers. il Electr
World 85:44+ Je '71
Solid-state V.O.M.'s. il Electr World 85:
39-42+ Ap '71
Status report on four-channel stereo. il
Electr World 86:13-14 Ag '71
HIRSCH, Maurice, baron de
Moses of the new world, by S. J. Lee. Review
Sat R 54:68-9 Ja 23 '71. P. Kresh
HIRSCH, Moritz, baron. See Hirsch, Maurice,
baron de
HIRSCHBERG, J. Cotter
Psychiatrists helping young mommas understand baby; interview, ed. by P. A. Farrell.
il pors Pub W 122:38-9 Je 28 '71
HIRSCHFELD, Corson
Barking lizard; with biographical sketch. il
Natur Hist 80:4, 60-3 Ja '71
**HIRSCHHORN, Norbert, and Greenough, W.
B. 3d**
Cholera; with biographical sketches. il Sci
Am 225:13, 15-21 Ag '71
HIRSCHMAN, Shalom Z.
Inhibitors of DNA polymerases of murine
leukemia viruses: activity of ethidium
bromide. bibliog il Science 173:441-3 Jl 30
'71
HIRSCHOWITZ, Ralph G.
Mental health consultation to schools. Ment
Hy 55:237-41 Ap '71
HIRSCHY, Jill
Cancer breakthrough. il por Life 70:28-31
Ap 23 '71
HIRSHBERG, Al
(ed) See Green, T. My first last rites
HIRST, Eric, and Bank, Harvey
Striking the balance. bibliog il Environ 13:
34-41 N '71
—and Schuck, Linda
Action program for environmental education. bibliog Clear House 46:203-6 D '71
HISPANO-American art. See Art, Latin American
HISPANO-American fiction. See Latin American fiction
HISS, Alger
Alger Hiss case revisited. A. Weinstein. Am
Scholar 41:121-32 Wint '71 *
Hiss again. W. F. Buckley, jr. Nat R 23:
1374 D 3 '71 *
HISS, Anthony
Postcards from the Hudson. il New Yorker
47:54-65 N 13 '71
HISTAMINE
Brain histamine: rapid apparent turnover altered by restraint and cold stress. K. M.
Taylor and S. H. Snyder. bibliog il Science
172:1037-9 Je 4 '71
Histamine augments leukocyte adenosine
3',5'-monophosphate and blocks antigenic
histamine release. H. R. Bourne and others. bibliog il Science 173:743-5 Ap 20 '71
Nuclear localization of histamine in neonatal
rat brain. A. B. Young and others. bibliog
il Science 173:247-9 Jl 16 '71
Phosphatidylserine: selective enhancer of
histamine release. A. Goth and others. bibliog il Science 173:1034-5 S 10 '71
HISTIDASE
Histidase activity in cultivated human
amniotic fluid cells. S. B. Melancon and
others. bibliog il Science 173:627-8 Ag 13
'71
HISTIDINE
Crystal structure L-N-acetylhistidine monohydrate: an open and closed case. T. J.
Kistenmacher and R. E. Marsh. bibliog il
Science 172:945-6 My 28 '71
Two more possibilities; arthritis treatment.
Sci N 99:44+ Ja 16 '71
HISTOCOMPATIBILITY. See Immunological
tolerance
HISTORIANS
Doing history. J. H. Hexter. bibliog f Commentary 51:53-62 Je '71
HISTORIANS, American
History: a discipline in crisis? adaptation of
address, December 1970. O. Handlin. Am
Scholar 40:447-65 Sum '71
See also
Nevins, A.
HISTORIANS, Greek
See also
Herodotus

HISTORIC houses, sites, etc.
Historic houses, landmarks, and museums.
See issues of Antiques
Spring and the traveler: in search of a romantic world; symposium. il Sat R 54:37-
42+ Mr 13 '71
See also
Houses, Restored
also subhead Historic houses, etc. under
names of countries, states, cities, etc, e.g.
Lima, Peru—Historic houses, etc.
Conservation and restoration
See Architecture—Conservation and restoration
HISTORIC sites. See Historic houses, sites, etc.
HISTORICAL change. See Change
HISTORICAL fiction
See also
Fiction—Technique
also subhead Fiction under historical
events, e.g. United States—History—Civil
war—Fiction
HISTORICAL letters. See Letters
HISTORICAL museums
This museum is mainly for kids; Historical
center, Columbus, Ohio. il Arch Rec 150:85-
90 Jl '71
HISTORICAL research
Doing history. J. H. Hexter. bibliog f Commentary 51:53-62 Je '71
HISTORICAL societies
See also
American historical association
Rhode Island historical society
HISTORIOGRAPHY. See History—Historiography
HISTORY
Looking back on a golden age, the relevancy
of history; address, November 10, 1971. P.
MacKendrick. Vital Speeches 38:188-92 Ja
1 '72
See also
Church history
Civilization
Current events
Revolutions
also subheads Antiquities; Foreign relations; History; Politics and government under names of countries, states, etc. e.g.
United States—History; also subhead History under various subjects, e.g. Electricity
—History
Bibliography
History. V. A. Lapomarda. America 125:435-6
N 20 '71
History. H. J. Sievers. America 124:546-7 My
22 '71
Historiography
History: a discipline in crisis? adaptation of
address, December 1970. O. Handlin. Am
Scholar 40:447-65 Sum '71
See also
China—History—Historiography
Rome—History—Historiography
Philosophy
See also
Civilization—Philosophy
Sources
See also
Archives
Oral history
Study and teaching
Story of mankind; produced by sophomores
at Thorp high school, Wis. il Sr Schol 99:
24-5 N 29 '71
See also
United States—History—Study and teaching
Textbooks
See also
World history—Textbooks
HISTORY, Ancient
See also
Greece, Ancient—History
Rome—History
HISTORY, Hypothetical
See also
Church history, Hypothetical
HISTORY, Modern
Explorations in crisis: papers on international history, by W. L. Langer. Review
Am Hist R 76:119-26 F '71. P. Paret
HISTORY and geography. See Geography, Historical
HITCH hiking. See Hitchhiking
HITCHCOCK, Alfred Joseph
On suspense and mystery. il Harp Baz 104:70
Jl '71
about
Current cinema. P. Gilliatt. New Yorker 47:
91-4 S 11 '71 *

HITCHCOCK, James
Aggiornamento has failed; excerpt from The decline and fall of radical Catholicism. Commonweal 94:231-5 My 14 '71
Short course in the three types of radical professors. il N Y Times Mag p30-1+ F 21 '71; Discussion. p80 Mr 21 '71
What really happened in the 1960's? America 124:449-53 My 1 '71
Women's liberation: tending toward idolatry. il Chr Cent 88:1104-7 S 22 '71

HITCHHIKING
Hitching a ride across America. R. Brook. il pors Life 71:36-43 Ag 27 '71
Meditations on a hitchhiking ticket. D. Anderson. il Nat R 23:1069-70 S 24 '71

HITCHHIKING, Air. See Air travel

HITLER, Adolf
Bidding for Adolf. il pors Time 97:29 Ap 19 '71 *
Law and order, said Hitler, or, did he? J. Remak. por Commonweal 94:429-32 Ag 20 '71 *

Anecdotes, facetiae, satire, etc.
Schmeed memoirs. W. Allen. New Yorker 47:36-7 Ap 17 '71

HITLER youth movement. See Youth movement—Germany

HITT, Russell T.
Conservative evangelicals deserve a better hearing. por Chr Cent 88:975-7 Ag 18 '71

HITTIG, Edwin
Shoot portraits with a single light. il Pop Mech 135:130-1 Ap '71

HITTMAN, Fred
Hittman's other folly. J. Poindexter. por Duns 97:59 F '71 *

HITTMAN associates, inc.
Hittman's other folly. J. Poindexter. por Duns 97:59 F '71

HIVES (urticaria)
Cold that can kill; cold urticaria. il Newsweek 78:52 D 27 '71

HJELLMING, R. M. and Wade, C. M.
Radio stars. bibliog il Science 173:1087-92 S 17 '71

HO, Rita
Ion-exchange fable. il Chem 44:26 S '71

HOAG, Jessie Faith
God is like that; poem. Chr Today 15:14 My 7 '71

HOAGLAND, Edward
Hailing the elusory mountain lion. New Yorker 47:26-33 Ag 7 '71
Of cows and Cambodia. Atlan 228:33-9 Jl '71
Portland freight run. Atlan 227:26+ F '71
Soul of the tiger. il pors Esquire 76:88-93+ Jl '71
Two clowns. il Life 70:70A Ap 23 '71
War in the woods; excerpt from The courage of turtles. Harper 242:96-103 F '71

about
Very busy life. G. Wolff. por Newsweek 77:73 Ja 18 '71 *

HOARD, J. L.
Stereochemistry of hemes and other metalloporphyrins. bibliog il Science 174:1295-302 D 24 '71

HOAXES
Author! Author! A. Fried's History of the modern age. il por Newsweek 78:81 S 27 '71
Buckley papers. Newsweek 78:21-2 Ag 2 '71
Buckley's prank. por Time 98:43 Ag 2 '71
Call to defeat H.R. 6142; letter. K. J. Sitewell. Sat R 54:21 Ap 3 '71
Decline and fall of congressman Day; an April fools joke. Sat R 54:18+ My 8 '71
Everybody is up in arms; documentary film of Alaskan polar bear hunt. D. Connelly. il Sports Illus 34:32-4+ Ap 5 '71
Midnight penman returns; A history of the modern age. por Time 98:20 S 6 '71
National review papers. W. F. Buckley, jr. Nat R 23:850 Ag 10 '71
Notes & asides: press comments on the Buckley papers. ed. by W. F. Buckley, jr. Nat R 23:852-4 Ag 10 '71
Papillon papers (yesterday's Pentagon papers?) Sr Schol 99:5 S 20 '71
Schmeercase affair. Chem 44:3-4 Je '71
Secret papers they didn't publish; documents leaked to National review. Nat R 23:798-811 Jl 27 '71; Discussion. 23:904, 915-18, 975-6 Ag 24-S 10 '71
See also
Musical forgeries and mystifications

HOBBIES
Hobbies are my hobby. L. Kleist. il Har Yrs 11:32-3 O '71
See also
Art, Amateur
Collectors and collecting

Bibliography
Books reviewed. See issues of Hobbies

HOBBS, Sam H.
Add 1% for esthetics. il Am City 86:107-8+ S '71

HOBGOOD, Clarence E.
Plowshares into swords. T. W. Moore. il Chr Cent 88:294+ Mr 3 '71 *

HOCHANADEL, C. J. See Ghormley, J. A. jt. auth.

HOBSON, J. Allan. See McCarley, R. W. jt. auth.

HO-chi-Minh
Poets and leaders. R. Whittemore. New Repub 165:27-8 Ag 7 '71; Reply. Huynh Sanh Thong. 165:32 S 18 '71

HOCHMAN, Sandra
Millionairess; story; excerpt from Walking papers. Harp Baz 104:124-5 Ag '71
Notes of an eccentric. il Harp Baz 104:78+ S '71
On changing doctors; story. Harp Baz 105:122-3 N '71
Originality in others. il por Harp Baz 105:106 D '71

HOCHSCHILD, Arlie
American woman: another idol of social science. il Trans-Action 8:12-14 N '70

HOCHSTEIN, Rollie
When the paychecks stopped. il Good H 173:108-9+ S '71
—See Sugarman, D. A. jt. auth.

HOCKER, Mel
Decline of nudism. T. Tyler. il por Time 98:58-9 Jl 19 '71 *

HOCKEY
America first, B.U. foremost: NCAA championship. M. Mulvoy. Sports Illus 34:48 Mr 29 '71
Hockey time, and the kids go crazy. J. G. Hubbell. il Read Digest 99:67-70+ D '71
New awakening in Orr land: little league mania. M. Maddocks. il Sports Illus 35:32-7 O 11 '71

Accidents and injuries
Hockey: the bloodiest game. S. Fischler. il Look 35:32-4 F 9 '71
My first last rites; excerpt from High stick; ed. by A. Hirshberg. T. Green. il Sports Illus 35:90-3+ N 15 '71

HOCKEY fans. See Sports fans

HOCKEY players
Brief reign of the lordly Bruins; Canadiens vs Bruins. M. Mulvoy. il Sports Illus 34:14-19 Ap 26 '71
Icemen you'd love to hate. P. Jordan. il Sports Illus 35:86-9+ D 13 '71
It takes two to win the cup; New York Rangers in neck-and-neck race with Boston. M. Mulvoy. il Sports Illus 34:40-1 Ja 11 '71
My first last rites; excerpt from High stick; ed. by A. Hirshberg. T. Green. il Sports Illus 35:90-3+ N 15 '71
Poor broken Wings; Detroit Red Wings. M. Mulvoy. il Sports Illus 34:10-13 Ja 18 '71
TNT on ice. H. L. Masin. il Sr Schol 99:20-1 N 15 '71
See also
Hockey teams
Howe, G.
Kahn, R.
Orr, B.
Sanderson, D.

Photographs
Cold cold heart of hockey. T. Triolo. il Sports Illus 34:24-31 Ja 25 '71

Salaries, pensions, etc.
Hockey is here with dollars up and fists down. M. Mulvoy. il Sports Illus 35:36-40+ O 18 '71
Orr effect. T. Dowling. il Atlan 227:62-8 Ap '71

HOCKEY teams
Banned in Boston, knighted in Montreal; interview. ed. by J. Olsen. K. Dryden. il Sports Illus 35:45-6+ O 18 '71
Bobby Boston doesn't own. M. Mulvoy. il por Sports Illus 35:60+ N 1 '71
Brief reign of the lordly Bruins; Canadiens vs Bruins. M. Mulvoy. il Sports Illus 34:14-19 Ap 26 '71
Four-story goalie. il por Newsweek 77:62 My 17 '71

HOCKEY teams—*Continued*
Get mad and win; Chicago's Black Hawks vs. Canadiens. il Newsweek 77:86-7 My 31 '71
Here come the big, good Bruins. M. Mulvoy. Sports Illus 34:72 Ap 5 '71
Hockey fanatics; New York Rangers. J. Greenfield. Harper 244:16-18+ Ja '72
Hockey is here with dollars up and fists down. M. Mulvoy. il Sports Illus 35:36-40+ O 18 '71
Icehouse gang. il Time 97:60+ Ap 19 '71
Icy love-in for Vic, Jean and Rod; New York Rangers. M. Mulvoy. il Sports Illus 34:22-3 My 3 '71
It takes two to win the cup; New York Rangers in neck-and-neck race with Boston. M. Mulvoy. il Sports Illus 34:40-1 Ja 11 '71
Loitering in this Park is forbidden: B. Park of New York Rangers. M. Mulvoy. il por Sports Illus 35:26-7 N 8 '71
Minnies who are no moochers; goalies of Minnesota North Stars. M. Mulvoy. il pors Sports Illus 35:28-9 N 22 '71
Montreal serves one up, extra Dryden: Montreal Canadiens vs Chicago Black Hawks. M. Mulvoy. il Sports Illus 35:80+ N 15 '71
My first last rites; excerpt from High stick; ed. by A. Hirshberg. T. Green. il Sports Illus 35:90-3+ N 15 '71
North Stars are the greatest; Stanley cup playoffs. M. Mulvoy. Sports Illus 34:60-1 My 10 '71
Oh, brother! A pair to watch: Boston's Phil vs Chicago's Tony. J. Olsen. il pors Sports Illus 34:36-8+ Mr 29 '71
Old custom at customs; Stanley cup and Montreal Canadiens. M. Mulvoy. il Sports Illus 34:74-5 My 31 '71
Orgy of scores; Boston Bruins. il por Newsweek 77:61 Ap 5 '71
Orr effect; Boston Bruins. T. Dowling. il Atlan 227:62-8 Ap '71
Poor broken Wings; Detroit Red Wings. M. Mulvoy. il Sports Illus 34:10-13 Ja 18 '71
Quiet man; B. Nevin. il por Newsweek 77:67-8 Ap 26 '71
TNT on ice. H. L. Masin. il Sr School 99:20-1 N 15 '71
This is Orr country, Orr is it? Boston Bruins vs Montreal Canadiens in Stanley cup series. M. Mulvoy. il Sports Illus 34:20-1 Ap 19 '71
To pick a golden flower; Montreal Canadiens' G. Lafleur. M. Mulvoy. il pors Sports Illus 34:34-6 Mr 1 '71
HOCKMAN, Charles H. and others
Electroencephalographic and behavioral alterations produced by Δ²-tetrahydrocannabinol. biblilog il Science 172:968-70 My 28 '71
HOD carriers union. *See* International hod carriers', building and common laborers' union of America
HODDER, Edwin
Producing an A-V facility that suits the client. il Arch Rec 150:127-8 Jl '71
HODEIR, André
Hodeir on Finnegan's wake. I. Kolodin. Sat R 54:53 Ja 30 '71 *
HODENFIELD, G. K.
English channels. PTA Mag 65:32-3 F '71
HODGE, Anne Garner
There are no peas like snow peas! il Org Gard & Farm 18:62-4 D '71
HODGE, Harold
Gomer is tops in the tepee. G. Curry. por Sports Illus 35:51 Jl 26 '71 *
HODGE, Ronald J.
Some British snap for a fastener maker. por Bsns W p42 Mr 20 '71 *
HODGES gardens. *See* Gardens—Louisiana
HODGIN, Ellis
Haynsworth court rejects Hodgin appeal; with editorial comment. Library J 96:573, 577 F 15 '71 *
HODGINKSON, Marian
Justice: Turkish style. Cath World 213:144-5 Je '71
HODGINS, Maibelle Dickey
Brookgreen gardens, where sculpture and nature meet. il Horticulture 49:32-3+ N '71
HODGKIN'S disease
Cancer: a detective story; cases among the 1954 graduates of Albany high school. il Newsweek 77:59-60 Je 28 '71
Cancer and viruses: need for caution. il Sci N 100:185-6 S 18 '71
Fatal links? Albany, N.Y. study. Time 97:57 Je 28 '71
Little night music: the curvature of the earth. L. E. Sissman. Atlan 229:18+ Ja '72
One who came back: a cancer patient's story. W. S. Gray. il por Newsweek 77:86-7 F 22 '71
Pushing for a total cure. Sci N 99:263-4 Ap 17 '71

HODGKINSON, Marian
On the hot line. il Har Yrs 11:48-50 N '71
HODGSON, Anthony M. and Dill, W .R.
Programmed case: the misfired missive; Dashman case (cont) Harvard Bsns R 49:140-2+ Ja '71
HODGSON, Edward S.
Invasion of sharks; with biographical sketch. il Natur Hist 80:4, 92-101 D '71
HODGSON, James D.
Any cure for big strikes? interview. il pors U S News 71:68-72 N 29 '71
Collective bargaining; address, February 24, 1971. Vital Speeches 37:382-4 Ap 1 '71
Construction industry; address, January 20, 1971. Vital Speeches 37:258-60 F 15 '71
Preparing youth for reality; address, October 29, 1971. Vital Speeches 38:166-8 Ja 1 '72

about

Bat in Mr Nixon's hand. il por Newsweek 77:75 Mr 1 '71 *
HODGSON, Moira
Quick and easy raw food cookbook; excerpts. il Ladies Home J 88:80-1+ Ag '71
HOEKENGA, Earl N.
Making small shipments pay their way. por Bsns W p82-4 Jl 17 '71 *
HOEM, Jean C.
Music and the environment. il Cons 25:2-4 Ap '71
HOFE, G. Douglas, Jr
American trails, rediscovered. il Parks & Rec 6:41-8 Mr '71
HOFER, Myron A.
Cardiac rate regulated by nutritional factor in young rats. bibliog il Science 172:1039-41 Je 4 '71
HOFF, Darrel
An experiment to measure the earth's orbital velocity. il Sky & Tel 43:9-10 Ja '72
HOFF, Jacobus Henricus van't
Beginnings of experimental petrology; excerpts from address, January 1971. H. F. Eugster. bibliog il Science 173:481-9 Ag 6 '71
HOFF, Katherine
Survival training: bonus for life. bibliog il Schol Teach Jr/Sr High p 18-19+ O '71
HOFFA, James Riddle
Hoffa and the witness; Hoffa-Partin affair. T. Bethell. Nation 212:678-9 My 31 '71 *
Hoffa home free. por Time 99:29 Ja 3 '72 *
Hoffa stay in jail may change teamsters. U S News 70:82 Ap 12 '71 *
Hoffa steps down, for now. il por Time 97:22 Je 14 '71 *
Hoffa strikes out. por Newsweek 78:72 Ag 30 '71 *
Hoffa's exit opens new doors. il por Bsns W p77 Je 12 '71 *
Hoffa's hard time. por Newsweek 77:78+ Ap 12 '71 *
Mr Hoffa regrets. por Newsweek 77:86 Je 14 '71 *
Parting shots; top guy at Lewisburg. por Life 70:73 Je 18 '71 *
Teamsters reassess Hoffa's chances. il por Bsns W p52+ Ap 17 '71 *
What the 'Little Fellow' says to the teamsters is what counts. A. H. Raskin. il pors N Y Times Mag p 12-13+ My 30 '71 *
HOFFER, Eric
Thoughts of Eric Hoffer, including: 'absolute faith corrupts absolutely'. il N Y Times Mag p24-5+ Ap 25 '71; Same abr. with title Reflections on a waterfront man. por Read Digest 99:133-5 Ag '71

about

Bear and the hummingbird. J. Seelye. New Repub 164:28-31 Je 19 '71 *
Whose country? R. Berman. Nat R 23:765+ Jl 13 '71 *
HOFFER, William R.
Your future in the past. il Har Yrs 11:39-42 Jl '71
HOFFMAN, Abbie
America on $0 a day. il Ramp Mag 9:48-55 F '71
Yo-yo power! il por Esquire 76:106-7+ O '71

about

Court of his peers. Time 98:59 O 4 '71 *
Straight word on Abbie Hoffman's hair. R. Vaughan. por Life 71:77 O 22 '71 *
HOFFMAN, Daniel
Comanches; Stone; Blood; Poem: arriving at last; poems. Poetry 119:17-19 O '71

about

Comment. R. B. Shaw. Poetry 118:231-2 Jl '71 *

HOFFMAN, Elizabeth
If you're an Aries. bibliog il Library J 96:241-4 Ja 15 '71
HOFFMAN, Jill
Riverside park; poem. New Yorker 47:57 Jl 10 '71
HOFFMAN, Julius J.
Some off-bench opinions from Judge Julius Hoffman: interview. ed. by B. Dunn. il por Life 72:69 Ja 14 '72
HOFFMAN, Lisa
Sunday shopping spree. il Har Yrs 11:44-5 F '71
HOFFMAN, Paul
End of liberalism. Nation 212:457-61 Ap 12 '71
HOFFMAN, Paul Gray
Hoffman's decade of aid. por Time 99:31 Ja 17 '72 •
HOFFMAN, Robert
Your state aviation director. Flying 88:S1-4+ My '71
HOFFMAN, Robert M. and Dutton, R. W.
Genetic restriction of energy conservation in schizophyllum. bibliog il Science 171:418-19 Ja 29 '71
HOFFMAN, Theodore
Grotowski and Schechner: the servitudes of freedom. il Art in Am 59:74-81 Mr '71
HOFFMANN, Ernst Theodor Amadeus
Musical events. W. Sargeant. New Yorker 47: 158+ D 11 '71 •
HOFFMANN, M. and Dutton, R. W.
Immune response restoration with macrophage culture supernatants. bibliog il Science 172:1047-8 Je 4 '71
HOFFMANN, Rita
Main street; 1971. il Mlle 73:124-5+ Je '71
HOFFMANN, Stanley
Vietnam and western Europe. New Repub 164:18-23 Ja 30 '71
HOFFMANN-LaRoche, F, and company
Secret life of Hoffmann-LaRoche. R. Ball il Fortune 84:130-5+ Ag '71
HOFFMANN-La Roche, inc.
See also
Roche institute of molecular biology
HOFFMEISTER, John Edward
Earthquake at sea. il Sea Front 17:288-91 S '71
HOFMANN, Anton
Ah, freedom! Forbes 108:36+ Jl 15 '71 •
HOFMANN, Hans
Where vitality rests in abstract art. G. Rose. il Vogue 157:156 Mr 1 '71 •
HOFMANN, Josef
New tales of Josef Hofmann. R. Jacobson. il por Sat R 54:50 Ag 28 '71 •
Very first release, from RCA Victrola, of 1935-1938 recordings by Josef Hofmann. R. Kammerer. il por Am Rec G 37:480-1 Ap '71 •
HOFSTADTER, Richard
Richard Hofstadter, 1916-1970. A. Kazin. Am Scholar 40:397-401 Sum '71 •
HOFSTRA university, Hempstead, N.Y.
Young explorers start out; Hofstra university's child development center. il Parents Mag 46:38-9 Je '71
HOG cholera
We have hog cholera under control! R. Wilmore. Farm J 95:H17 Ap '71
HOG contracts. See Contracts, Agricultural
HOG feeders. See Swine self feeders
HOG houses. See Swine houses
HOG trailers. See Trailers
HOGAN, Clarence Lester
Technological change; address, October 20, 1971. Vital Speeches 38:139-42 D 15 '71
HOGAN, Donald
Catholic edge on revolution. Harper 244:72-80 Ja '72
HOGAN, John Vincent Lawless
How New York's pioneer classical station has fallen upon sorry Times. C. Briefer. il pors Hi Fi 21:74-9 S '71 •
HOGAN, Patrick
Three reconnoitering artists. J. Livingston. il Art in Am 59:114-17 My '71 •
HOGARTH, William
Hogarth, by R. Paulson. Review
    Atlan 229:92-5 Ja '72. L. Kronenberger •
    Sat R il por 54:31-4 D 18 '71. R. Halsband •
Low life in the grand manner. C. L. Markmann. Nation 212:789-90 Je 21 '71 •
Music and theater in Hogarth. M. F. Klinger. bibliog f il Mus Q 57:409-26 Jl '71 •
Two Hogarth exhibitions; National gallery of art, Washington, D.C. il Antiques 99:310+ Mr '71 •

HOGG, Tony
How to drive like a millionaire. il Esquire 76: 142-5+ D '71
Now that America has decided to buy the small car... Esquire 75:68+ Je '71
HOGNESS, John Rusten
Hogness to head NAS medical unit. C. Holden. Science 172:355 Ap 23 '71 •
HOGS. See Swine
HOGUE, Larry
Education in Mississippi: Leflore County. il Am Lib 2:985-6 O '71
HOHENBERG, John
Can a good journalist be a good citizen? il Sat R 54:87-8+ N 13 '71
Commencement for journalists. Sat R 54: 57-8+ Je 12 '71
Free press on trial; excerpt from Free press, free people, the best cause. Cur 130:40-7 Je '71
Make way for the new China hands. Sat R 55:41-2 Ja 8 '72
New times in the Far East; changing of the press guard. il Sat R 54:91-2+ Mr 13 '71
Twenty-five years of the API. il Sat R 54: 72-3+ D 11 '71
HOHENEMSER, Kurt H.
Aircraft in the balance. bibliog il Environ 13: 42-9 D '71
HOHENSEE, W. H.
Deer liver on a stick. il Outdoor Life 148:84 N '71
HOIBY, Lee
Lee Hoiby, Tennessee Williams. S. Fleming. pors Hi Fi 21:MA16+ Jl '71 •
St Paul's summer. M. A. Feldman. il por Opera N 36:18-20 S '71 •
Summer and smoke. Criticism
    Hi Fi il 21:MA20-1 S '71 •
    Opera N il por 36:18-20 S '71 •
HOISTING machinery
See also
Winches
HOKE COUNTY, N.C.
Army snow job; D. Middleton's story on the army's Nation-building program. W. L. Robb. New Repub 165:15-17 D 11 '71
HOKIN, Edwin E.
Fabricating growth. Fortune 83:138 Je '71 •
HOKKAIDO (island)
Hokkaido; Japan's frontier wonderland. L. Stowe. il Read Digest 99:138-44 N '71
Pre-Olympic swing through the soy sauce and Coca-Cola signs. W. Johnson. il Sports Illus 35:58-64 N 15 '71
HOLBERT, J. C.
Let up on quality and beef's in big trouble; interview. ed. by W. Kester. il pors Farm J 95:B6-8+ N '71
HOLBROOK, Hal
Irony of a succès de'Emmy. Cyclops. Life 70:11 Je 18 '71 •
HOLCK, Manfred, Jr
Active back-yard plastic greenhouse. il Org Gard & Farm 18:46-50 N '71
HOLDEN, David
Persian Gulf: after the British raj. il For Affairs 49:721-35 Jl '71
HOLDEN, Donald
Apprenticeships for graphic designers. Am Artist 35:56-8 My '71
HOLDER, Ernest
Coal sculpture. J. McCaughey. il Design 72: 14-15 Spr '71 •
HOLDER, Fred W.
Channel electron multipliers. il Electr World 86:30-1+ D '71
Electronic bartender. il Electr World 85:31 Je '71
What's new in car electronics. il Radio-Electr 42:33-6 Ap '71
HOLDER, William G. See Siuru, W. D. jt. auth.
HOLDERLIN; drama. See Weiss, P.
HOLDING companies
See also
Bank holding companies
Boston company
CNA financial corporation
Government   investigations—Holding   companies
Greyhound corporation
INA corporation
Reynolds, R. J. industries, inc.
Southern company

Belgium
Belgium's Lambert deepens its U.S. stake. il Bsns W p80-4 N 6 '71

Italy
Bastogi takeover smells of success. Bsns W p40-1 O 16 '71

HOLDING devices (machine work)
This die holder makes thread cutting easy.
A. M. Barkey. il Pop Mech 135:155 F '71
See also
Chucks
Clamps
Jigs
Vises

HOLDING tanks. See Boats—Sanitation

HOLDREN, John P. See Ehrlich, P. R. jt.
auth.

HOLFORD, D. J.
Russia's MiG-23: unbeatable? with excerpt
from Thud ridge by Jack Broughton. il
Pop Mech 136:90-4 N '71

HOLIDAY, Bob
Pole fishing the bass bushes. il Field & S 75:
66-7+ Mr '71

HOLIDAY (periodical)
On Holiday. il por Newsweek 77:60 Ja 25 '71

HOLIDAY parties. See Entertaining

HOLIDAYS
Agreeable disagreement; Business day. Na-
tions Bsns 59:16 Ja '71
For the elementary teacher: holiday stereo-
types. V. J. Popolizio. il Sch Arts 71:8-9 S
'71
Holiday for blacks; Kwanza. il Time 99:73
Ja 10 '72
Three day week ends boost business. il U S
News 71:64 N 8 '71
See also
Vacations
also names of holidays, e.g. Memorial
day

HOLIDAYS with pay. See Vacations, Employee

HOLLAND, Barbara
Happy life; story. Redbook 136:56-7 Ja '71

HOLLAND, Cecelia
American thing: a view of southern California. Mlle 72:207+ Ap '71

HOLLAND, Gerald
Lunches with Luce. por Atlan 227:54-6+ My
'71

HOLLAND, Kenneth
Education, population, and the quality of life
in Latin America. Sch & Soc 99:439-42 N '71

HOLLAND, Robert G.
Year of the bus. Nat R 23:475+ My 4 '71

HOLLAND, Mich.
Tulip time festival
Tiptoe through the tulips; Tulip festival. il
Holiday 49:46-7 My '71

HOLLANDER, John
Alaska brown bear; poem. New Yorker 46:42
F 13 '71
End of a Munich meeting; poem. New Yorker 47:26 Jl 3 '71
His master's voice; poem. New Yorker 47:
42 Ag 14 '71
Music volute; poem. Harper 242:86 My '71
String player in the shack; Long and the
short of it; Two slices of Sequoia; Hall
of ocean life; Sunday A.M. not in Manhattan; As the sparks fly upward; Another
firefly; Kinds of kindling; poems. Poetry
118:264-9 Ag '71
White noise; poem. New Yorker 47:36 My
29 '71

HÖLLDOBLER, Bert
Communication between ants and their
guests; with biographical sketch. il Sci Am
224:14, 86-93 Mr '71
Homing in the harvester ant pogonomyrmex
badius. bibliog il Science 171:1149-51 Mr 19
'71

HOLLENBERG, Morley D. and others
Adult hemoglobin synthesis by reticulocytes
from the human fetus at midtrimester.
bibliog il Science 174:698-702 N 12 '71

HOLLERING contests. See Competitions

HOLLIDAY, Cyrus Kurtz
Man who met the longhorns with a railroad.
J. S. Reed. il por Nations Bsns 59:50-1 Ja
'71 *

HOLLIDAY, Richard J.
Best beef in the world. il Org Gard & Farm
18:58-62 F '71

HOLLINGS, Ernest Frederick
Reality of American hunger. Nation 212:518-
21 Ap 26 '71
about
Education of a conservative. R. Sherrill.
Nation 213:105-10 Ag 16 '71 *

HOLLINGSWORTH, J. Rogers
U.S. should cut loose. Nation 212:390-4 Mr
29 '71

HOLLISTER, Charles D. See Heezen, B. C.
jt. auth.

HOLLISTER, Frederic F.
15,000 wrecks in the Great Lakes await
adventure and treasure hunters. Motor
B & S 127:202 Mr '71

HOLLISTER, Leo E.
Marihuana in man: three years later. bibliog
Science 172:21-9 Ap 2 '71

HOLLISTER, William G.
Combating the drug peril. il PTA Mag 65:2-5
bibliog(p36) Mr '71

HOLLO, Anselm
Comment. P. Schjeldahl. Poetry 117:264-6 Ja
'71 *

HOLLORAN, Richard
What curbs on government surveillance? Cur
129:10-12 My '71

HOLLOWAY, Bruce Keener
Survival as a free country depends on modern
weapons; interview. il por U S News 71:
52-5 D 27 '71

HOLLOWAY, John
Poem for breakfast. Esquire 75:83 Ap '71
about
Comment. J. T. Irwin. Poetry 118:352 S '71 *

HOLLOWAY, Trevor
How Scotland saved its salmon. il Sci Digest
69:64-7 Ap '71

HOLLSTEIN, Elsa
Artists and artisans. il Américas 22:25-9 N
'70

HOLLY
American holly. R. B. Clark. il Horticulture
49:22-3 D '71
See also
Cassena

HOLLYWOOD, Calif.
Sunset over the fable factory. C. Champlin.
il Sat R 54:52+ Mr 13 '71

Education
Hollywood community adult school. E.
Blangsted. il Sch Arts 70:36-7 F '71

Industries
See also
Moving picture industry—United States

HOLLYWOOD, Fla.
Daily control replaces cycle billing. D. J.
Giordano. il Am City 86:109-10 My '71

HOLLYWOOD bowl
Mini-marathon at Hollywood bowl: J. S.
Bach, Mozart, and Ives. K. Monson. Hi Fi
21:MA26 D '71

HOLM, Don
(ed) See Moon, D. Ordeal on Mount Hood

HOLM, Jane Wang
What's cooking? il Org Gard & Farm 18:98-
101 My '71

HOLMES, Ann P. Craig-. See Craig-Holmes,
A. P.

HOLMES, Chris
Committee documents flagrant inequities in
British rent acts. Chr Cent 88:885-6 Jl
21 '71

HOLMES, Jay
Mercury is heavier than you think. il Esquire
76:135-9+ My '71

HOLMES, Marjorie
Plea for privacy. il PTA Mag 65:10-12 Mr '71

HOLMES, Oliver Wendell, 1841-1935
Story behind the book: Holmes Devise
fund's history of U.S. Supreme court. R.
H. Smith. il Pub W 200:20 N 1 '71 *

HOLMES, Sherlock, stories. See Doyle, A. C.

HOLMES, Walter Stephen, 1919-
Business leadership; address, March 2, 1971.
Vital Speeches 37:424-7 My 1 '71

HOLOBINKO, Paul. See Rasmussen, F. A. jt.
auth.

HOLOCAUST literature. See Jewish literature

HOLOCENE period. See Geology, Stratigraphic
—Quaternary

HOLOGRAMS. See Holography

HOLOGRAPHIC data storage. See Information
storage and retrieval systems

HOLOGRAPHY
Amateur scientist; how to ensure a good
hologram and how to build an unusual
kind of barometer. L. D. Dickson. il Sci Am
225:110-11 Jl '71
Crystal stores holograms. il Radio-Electr 42:
2+ O '71
Emigré Nobelists. il por Newsweek 78:106+
N 15 '71
Getting the whole picture from holography.
L. Lessing. il Fortune 84:110-14+ S '71
Gifted refugees. pors Time 98:45 N 15 '71
Hand-held holography camera seen as new
industrial, medical tool. il Space World H-
11-95:49-50 N '71
Holography. D. Gabor and others. bibliog il
Science 173:11-23 Jl 2 '71

HOLOGRAPHY—Continued
Holography in your living room. S. V. Jones. il Sci Digest 69:90 Mr '71
Make holograms at home, at a budget price. R. M. Benrey. il Pop Sci 198:84-6 Ja '71
Making holograms from sound waves. S. V. Jones. il Sci Digest 69:60 My '71
1971 Nobel prizes in science. por Chem 45:22 Ja '72
Nobel prize for physics: Gabor and holography. W. E. Kock. bibliog por Science 174:674-5 N 12 '71
Nobel prizes: physics to Gabor, chemistry to Herzberg. G. B. Lubkin. bibliog pors Phys Today 24:69-71 D '71
See also
Holotron corporation
HOLOTRON corporation
Little colossus of holography. il Bsns W p 122-3 S 11 '71
HOLSENDOLPH, Ernest
Black colleges are worth saving. il Fortune 84-104-7+ O '71
Tale of two universities. il Fortune 83:104-8+ F '71
HOLST, Gustav
Herrmann's Holst: warmly recommended. J. Diether. Am Rec G 37:372 F '71 *
Music to my ears: concert performance of The planets. I. Kolodin. Sat R 54:19 D 11 '71 *
HOLT, Don. See Goldman, P. jt. auth.
HOLT, J. Gordon
15 things we do know about phono cartridges. il Pop Electr 34:25-30 Je '71
Stereo scene (cont) il Pop Electr 34:71+ F; 71+ Mr '71
HOLT, John Caldwell
Big Bird, meet Dick and Jane: a critique of Sesame street. Atlan 227:72-4+ My '71
I oppose testing, marking, & grading: excerpts from What do I do Monday? il Todays Ed 60:28-31 Mr '71
about
Sesame under attack. il pors Newsweek 77:52 My 24 '71 *
HOLTON, A. Linwood
Governor's dilemma. il por Newsweek 77:69 F 15 '71 *
Linwood Holton of Virginia. por Time 97:18 My 31 '71 *
HOLTON, Gerald
On trying to understand scientific genius. bibliog Am Scholar 41:95-110 Wint '71
HOLTON, Samuel M.
Education in the changing South. Ed Digest 36:5-8 Ja '71
HOLTZ, David, and Beauchamp, J. L.
Xenon as a nucleophile in gas-phase displacement reactions: formation of the methyl xenonium ion. bibliog il Science 173:1237-8 S 24 '71
HOLTZER, Susan
Grass roots vs. back room. por Nation 212:166-9 F 8 '71
HOLTZMAN, Eric, and others
Stimulation-dependent alterations in peroxidase uptake at lobster neuromuscular junctions. bibliog il Science 173:733-6 Ap 20 '71
HOLWAY, John
Before you could say Jackie Robinson. il Look 35:46-50 Jl 13 '71
HOLWEG, Arthur
Our wildflowers. il Cons 26:14-16 Ag '71
HOLWERK, David
Dusty death in Kentucky. il Nation 211:657-9 D 21 '70
HOLY Child is everywhere; story. See Wahtera, J.
HOLY Shroud
Were you there when they photographed my Lord? K. E. Meyer. il Esquire 76:72-4+ Ag '71
HOLY Spirit
Experience of the Spirit. V. P. McCorry. America 124:580-inside back cover My 29 '71
Holy Spirit and these days. A. H. Leitch. Chr Today 15:14-16 My 21 '71
See also
Trinity
HOLZER, Rusty
Someone's in the kitchen with Maxime. M. McKendry. il pors Vogue 159:34 Ja 1 '72 *
HOLZMAN, Robert S.
How to cope with unreasonable compensation claims. bibliog f Harvard Bsns R 49:79-81 S '71
HOMAGE to the San Francisco YMCA; story. See Brautigan, R.

HOMAN, William E.
Parent and child. il N Y Times Mag p82-3+ Mr 7; 75+ Je 6 '71
HOME, Alexander Frederick Douglas-Home, 14th earl of. See Douglas-Home, A. F.
HOME
Home: today's most provocative four-letter word. P. Williams. Mlle 74:124-5+ D '71
See also
Family
Family life
Fathers
HOME accidents. See Accidents
HOME and the school. See School and the home
HOME aquariums. See Aquariums
HOME building. See House construction
HOME building industry. See Construction industry
HOME building materials. See Building materials
HOME buying. See House buying
HOME decoration. See House decoration
HOME economics
Ask Rufus; questions and answers. R. Cartwright. See issues of Mechanix illustrated
Clean book; excerpt from Nobody said you had to eat off the floor. C. G. Eisen. Ladies Home J 88:135-7 Jl '71
50 tips that can save you time in the kitchen. Good H 174:137-8 Ja '72
How much does he do around the house? il Changing T 25:41 Ap '71
Keeping house with Emily Taylor. E. Taylor. See issues of Good housekeeping
New freedom of domestic bliss. il Vogue 157:70-83+ Je '71
Notes of a happy housekeeper. M. E. Falter. See issues of House & garden incorporating Living for young homemakers
Wintry wisdom. il Ladies Home J 89:60+ Ja '72
Women's lib; liberation from drudgery. R. Haughton. Cath World 212:287-8 Mr '71
See also
Budget, Household
Computers—Home economics use
Cookery
Domestic finance
Food
Household employees
Storage in the home

Study and teaching
Male role in home economics. L. G. Baker, jr. Ed Digest 37:48-9 D '71
See also
Cookery—Study and teaching
HOME equipment. See Household appliances
HOME files. See Files and filing (documents, etc)
HOME fire protection. See Fire protection
HOME from the war; story. See Ledecky, B.
HOME furnishings. See Household furnishings
HOME garden and flower grower garden contest. See Gardening—Competitions
HOME garden contest. See Gardening—Competitions
HOME garden photography contest. See Photography—Competitions
HOME grounds
Lesson in dividing outdoor space, between generations. il Sunset 146:162 Ap '71
See also
Lawns
HOME improvements. See Houses—Maintenance and repair
HOME industries. See Cottage industries
HOME insurance. See Insurance—All risk policies
HOME is for sharing; story. See Bloom, R.
HOME labor
See also
Cottage industries
HOME life. See Family life
HOME made furniture. See Furniture
HOME mechanics. See Mechanics, Household
HOME morale. See Family life
HOME movies. See Moving pictures, Amateur
HOME offices. See Offices
HOME ownership
Home ownership for the poor? B. Frieden and J. Newman. il Trans-Action 7:47-53 O '70
See also
American homeowners association
Apartment houses—Cooperative ownership
Mortgages

HOME remedies. See Medicines, Patent, proprietary, etc.
HOME repairs. See Houses—Maintenance and repair
HOME safes. See Safes
HOME safety devices and measures. See Safety devices and measures
HOME selling. See House selling
HOME sewing. See Sewing
HOME sites. See Building sites
HOME storage. See Storage in the home
HOME study courses. See Correspondence schools and courses
HOME-swapping vacations. See Vacations
HOME-team; story. See Klein, E.
HOME visitations. See School and the home
HOME waste disposal appliances. See Refuse and refuse disposal—Apparatus
HOME weather stations. See Meteorological stations
HOME workshops. See Workshops
HOMECOMING; drama. See Pinter, H.
HOMELESS, The
Shame of the cities; conditions in welfare hotels in New York. il Newsweek 77:24-5 F 8 '71
HOMEMAKERS. See Housewives
HOMEMAKING. See Home economics
HOMEOWNER policies. See Insurance—All risk policies
HOMEOWNERS emergency services, Inc.
And others tap a household market. il Bsns W p25-6 Mr 27 '71
HOMER
Ulysses complex. L. P. R. Santiago. bibliog il Am Imago 28:158-86 Sum '71 *
HOMES, Institutional
Credences of summer; boy's home on a farm. R. Rhodes. il Harper 243:57-60 Ag '71
House in place of home; residence for underprivileged children. il Arch Forum 134:56-7 My '71
Mental hygiene influences in children's institutions: organization and technology for treatment. J. K. Whittaker. bibliog Ment Hy 55:444-50 O '71
See also
Nursing homes
Old age homes
HOMES for the aged. See Old age homes
HOMESICKNESS. See Nostalgia
HOMESTAKE mine. See Gold mines and mining—United States
HOMESTEADS
21st-century homestead. J. H. Todd. il Org Gard & Farm 18:57-61 D '71
HOMIDIUM bromide. See Bromides
HOMING instinct. See Orientation
HOMING pigeons. See Pigeon post
HOMINIDS. See Man, Prehistoric
HOMOSASSA SPRINGS, Fla.

Parks and playgrounds
Otter-proof bulkheading. E. W. Jones. il Parks & Rec 6:43-4+ My '71
HOMOSEXUALITY
Adopting a lover. Time 98:50 S 6 '71
Authors & editors; interview, ed. by B. A. Bannon. M. Miller. por Pub W 200:17-18 O 4 '71
E. M. Forster, homosexuality and Christian morality. N. Pittenger. Chr Cent 88:1468-71 D 15 '71
Gay church. il Time 98:39 Ag 23 '71
Gay is: SRRT Task force on gay liberation at ALA conference. il Wilson Lib Bul 46:17 S '71
Homosexual chemistry. Newsweek 77:54-5 Ap 26 '71
Homosexual couple: Jack Baker and Michael McConnell. J. Star. il Look 35:69-71 Ja 26 '71
Homosexual minister? por Newsweek 77:114 Je 14 '71
Homosexuality, Aquinas, and the church. J. A. McCaffrey. por Cath World 213:183-6 Jl '71
Homosexuality in the seventies. J. A. McCaffrey. il Cath World 213:121-5 Je '71
Homosexuality; letter to the editor. W. E. Glover. Am Lib 2:925 O '71
Homosexuals in revolt; with report by M. Durham. il Life 71:62-72 D 31 '71
Militant homosexual; gay liberation movement. il Newsweek 78:45-8 Ag 23 '71
Minn. court rules library may deny homosexual post; James M. McConnell case. il Library J 96:4046+ D 15 '71

Out of the closet: a gay manifesto. A. Young. il Ramp Mag 10:52-9 N '71
To accept homosexuals. Chr Cent 88:275 Mr 3 '71; Discussion. 88:497-500 Ap 21 '71
What it means to be a homosexual. M. Miller. il pors N Y Times Mag p9-11+ Ja 17 '71; Discussion. p 14+ F 21; 67+ O 10 '71
What makes a homosexual? L. J. Hatterer. McCalls 98:32+ Jl '71; Same abr. Read Digest 99:71-4 S '71
What parents should know about homosexuality. L. J. Hatterer and M. S. Hatterer. il PTA Mag 65:6-9 Je '71
See also
Church work with homosexuals
Lesbianism
HOMOSEXUALITY in literature
Books; E. M. Forster's Maurice. New Yorker 47:158+ O 9 '71
Sexual heretics, ed. by B. Reade. Review New Repub 164:30-1 F 27 '71. S. Weintraub
HONAN, William H.
Playing chicken over the Mediterranean. il Read Digest 98:77-81 Mr '71
Will he say: help me finish what my brothers began? il pors N Y Times Mag p27+ N 28 '71
HONDA (automobile) See Automobiles, Foreign
HONDURAS

Foreign relations
United States
See United States—Foreign relations—Honduras
HONECKER, Erich
East Germany changes bosses. il por Newsweek 77:36-7+ My 17 '71 *
New broom in East Germany. il por Newsweek 78:55+ N 22 '71 *
Russians' new man in East Berlin. il por Time 97:32 My 17 '71 *
Toward a triumvirate. il por Time 97:36 Je 28 '71 *
HONESTY
They throw money away on purpose; experiments in the social psychology of prosocial behavior. S. Bacon. il Sci Digest 69:39-44 F '71
See also
Sincerity
HONEY, Joel B.
Dr Strange cop. por Newsweek 78:28 N 29 '71 *
HONEY bees. See Bees
HONEYCOMB worms. See Annelids
HONEYMOON
Honeymoon is alive in 1971. S. Cuneo. Mlle 72:114-15+ Ja '71
Planning a honeymoon. il Mlle 72:48-9 Ja '71
HONEYWELL, Inc.
Challenging the jolly gray giant; Honeywell competes with IBM. il Time 99:62-3 Ja 3 '72
Heat's on at Honeywell. R. Levy. il Duns 93:44-5+ Je '69
Honeywell builds on the GE line. Bsns W p30 F 20 '71
Progress report. il Forbes 108:53 O 15 '71
HONGISTO, Richard
New-breed cop. New Repub 165:7 D 4 '71 *
Sheriff of San Francisco. Nation 213:518 N 22 '71
HONG KONG
See also
Airports—Hong Kong
Americans in Hong Kong
Libraries—Hong Kong
Periodicals—Hong Kong

Commerce
See also
Jardine, Matheson and company, ltd.

Description
Glory returns to Fragrant Harbor. R. Joseph. il pors Esquire 75:87-93 Ap '71
Saturday's child Hong Kong. J. Judge. il Nat Geog 140:540-73 O '71

Economic conditions
View from red China's border. E. Sparn. il Sr Schol 99:9 S 20 '71

Foreign relations
China (People's Republic)
See China (People's Republic)—Foreign Relations—Hong Kong

Industries
See also
Hong Kong—Economic conditions

Parks and playgrounds
Sculpture parks: can they work? P. Selinger. il Parks & Rec 6:38-9+ F '71

HONNOREZ, José. See Bonatti, E. jt. auth.

HONOLULU

Gardens

Holy days and holidays this month in Honolulu; Foster botanic garden. il Sunset 147:29 D '71

It was the queen's own garden; Liliuokalani garden. il Sunset 146:88 My '71

Historic houses, etc.

Look back into Honolulu's past. il Sunset 146:45 Je '71

Silver from Iolani palace, Honolulu. D. T. Rainwater and R. E. A. Hackler. il Antiques 99:271-7 F '71

History

Mad Jack and the missionaries. L. McKee. il pors Am Heritage 22:30-7+ Ap '71

Music

Report:
Tosca and Der fliegende Holländer. W. Aguiar, jr. il Opera N 35:30 Ap 10 '71

Parks and playgrounds

Bird watching in Honolulu; Paradise park. il Sunset 146:35-6 My '71

Police

Hawaiian bank gets behind the badge; recruiting campaign. V. Louviere. il Nations Bsns 59:15 Jl '71

HONOLULU academy of arts

Honolulu museum that's part garden; Alice Cooke Spalding house. il Sunset 146:58+ Ap '71

HONOR

Question of honor. A. Sherman. il Read Digest 98:77-80 My '71

HONOR America day. See Fourth of July

HONORARY degrees. See Degrees, Honorary

HONZIK, Marjorie P. and others

Sex differences in I.Q. pattern of children with congenital heart defects. bibliog il Science 174:1043-4 D 3 '71

HOOD, Caroline

Opening door. L. L. L. Golden. Sat R 54:47-8 Jl 10 '71 *

HOOD, Edwin M.

Transport technology; address, February 4, 1971. Vital Speeches 37:309-11 Mr 1 '71

HOOD, Graham

American silver: the seventeenth century; excerpt from American silver: a history of style, 1650-1900. il Antiques 100:576-9 O '71

HOOD, James R.

Taking over the OEO. Nation 213:646-9 D 20 '71

HOOD, Joan H.

Norwegian craft revitalized. il por Design 72:40-1 mid-Sum '71

HOOD, Joseph F.

All the daring young men. il Am West 8:10-15+ Jl '71

HOOD, Loyd

Bax seat. G. Baxter. il por Flying 89:24-5 Ag '71 *

HOOK, Ernest B. and Kim, Dong-soo

Height and antisocial behavior in XY and XYY boys. il Science 172:284-6 Ap 16 '71

HOOK, Sidney

Books & ideas. por Fortune 83:140-1 F '71

HOOK, Thom

How to turn your attic into a movie theater. il Mech Illus 67:90-2 Mr '71

Tips from a pro on hanging kitchen cabinets. il Mech Illus 67:92-3+ Jl '71

HOOKER, Ronald

First hurrah for hizzoner. age 19. il por Life 71:77 N 19 '71 *

HOOPER, L. O.

Market comment. See issues of Forbes

HOOPER, Patricia

Desert; poem. Poetry 119:25 O '71

HOOPES, Townsend

How to set a date for getting out of Vietnam. il N Y Times Mag p20-1+ My 9 '71

President is the problem. New Repub 164:23-7 Mr 6 '71

HOOPS

Build this water hoop for the fun of it. il Pop Mech 136:128 S '71

HOOTON, Burt

Dropout with a big future. R. Fimrite. por Sports Illus 34:68+ My 31 '71 *

They're out of their classes. J. Jares. pors Sports Illus 34:51 Je 28 '71 *

HOOVER, Arlie J.

Naturalism: philosophical smuggler. Chr Today 15:12-14 Jl 2 '71

HOOVER, John Edgar

Bugging Hoover. Time 97:17-18 Ap 26 '71 *

Bugging J. Edgar Hoover. por Time 97:15-16 Ap 19 '71 *

FBI today:
Case for effective control. H. H. Wilson. Nation 212:169-72 F 8 '71; Same. Cur 128:53-8 Ap '71 *

Heresy of John F. Shaw: a purloined letter; with editorial comment. J. F. Shaw. Nation 212:172-7 F 8 '71 *

FBI's Hoover: what fight is all about. il por U S News 70:89 Ap 19 '71 *

File on J. Edgar Hoover. il pors Time 98:14-16 O 25 '71

G-man under fire; with report by T. Wicker. il pors Life 70:39-45 Ap 9 '71 *

Heat on Hoover. Sr Schol 98:17 My 10 '71 *

Hoover-Berrigan-Wills. Nat R 23:578 Je 1 '71 *

Hoover: sacred and profane. Nat R 23:461 My 4 '71 *

Hoover under fire. por Newsweek 78:50 O 25 '71 *

Hoover's FBI: time for a change? il pors Newsweek 77:28-32+ My 10 '71 *

Hoover's woes. por Newsweek 77:39 Ap 12 '71 *

Metamorphosis of a hawk: why an ex-navy hero from Tennessee attacked J. Edgar Hoover. R. Wool. il pors N Y Times Mag p22-3+ Ap 25 '71 *

Not quite invulnerable. Nation 212:164 F 8 '71 *

Of Hoover and Clark. por Time 97:16-17 My 3 '71 *

Public justice v. J. Edgar Hoover. W. F. Buckley, jr. Nat R 23:1322 N 19 '71 *

Sacred no longer. Nation 212:483-4 Ap 19 '71 *

Save-Hoover drive. Nation 213:5-6 Jl 5 '71 *

Schenley chapter. H. Messick. il Nation 212:428-31 Ap 5 '71; Reply. W. H. Ferry. 212:514 Ap 26 '71 *

Sovereign FBI. Nation 212:514-15 Ap 26 '71 *

Who's retiring? il por Newsweek 79:19 Ja 10 '72 *

HOOVER, Kathleen O'Donnell

Despot of French opera. il por Opera N 35:6-11 Mr 6 '71

HOPE, A. D.

Comment. J. McGann. Poetry 118:223-7 Jl '71

HOPE, Adrian

Brain. il Life 71:42-59 O 1 '71

HOPE, Bob

Bob Hope: the road gets rougher. J. Barthel. il pors Life 70:48-50+ Ja 29 '71 *

HOPE, Frank L. jr

Building entirely new cities. Cur 125:30-2 Ja '71

HOPE, Jack

Hassles in the park; with biographical sketch. il Natur Hist 80:6, 20-3+ bibliog (p 104) My '71

A man, a boat, a river, a dream. il por Audubon 73:80-7 Mr '71

HOPE, Marjorie, and Young, James

Great nuclear debate: are our newborn babies' lives in danger? Redbook 138:16+ Ja '72

HOPE, Norman V.

Jesus the realist: I am...the truth. Chr Today 15:10-12 My 7 '71

HOPE

Future theology: hope or suffering? Hope and the future of man conference. D. J. Turner. Chr Today 16:42+ N 5 '71

Rebirth: out of our troubles, hope. J. Shepherd. Look 35:15 Ja 12 '71

Weekend of hope: Hope and the future of man. L. J. O'Donovan. America 125:319-21 O 23 '71

What kind of hope is adequate? H. R. Dymale. Chr Today 15:9-10 Je 18 '71

HOPE (ship) See Hospital ships

HOPE diamond. See Diamonds

HOPI Indians

Bad day at Black Mesa. P. Barnes. New Repub 165:23-4 Jl 17 '71

Murder of the southwest. A. M. Josephy, jr. il Audubon 73:52-67 Jl '71

HOPKINS, Henry

Dennis Hopper's America. il Art in Am 59:86-91 My '71

HOPKINS, Jerry

Hidden life of Elvis Presley; excerpt from Elvis. il pors Look 35:33-8+ My 4; 41-4+ My 18 '71

HOPKINS, Joseph Martin

Examining his Worldwide church of God. Chr Today 16:6-9 D 17 '71

HOPPE, Art

Ben Adam and the angel. il Read Digest 99:185-6 Ag '71

HOPPER, Dennis
Dennis Hopper makes The last movie, in Peru; interview, ed. by E. Miller. il pors Seventeen 29:92-3+ Jl '70

about
Current cinema. P. Kael. New Yorker 47: 152-4 O 9 '71 *
Dennis Hopper's America. H. Hopkins. il Art in Am 59:86-91 My '71 *
Our local correspondents. J. Stevenson. New Yorker 47:116+ N 13 '71 *

HOPPER, Edward
Art. L. Alloway. Nation 213:221-2 S 13 '71 *
Edward Hopper, and the melancholy of Robinson Crusoe. L. Campbell. il Art N 70:36-9+ O '71 *
Edward Hopper, by L. Goodrich. Review
Commentary 53:94-5+ Ja '72. J. Hollander *
Life il 71:8 N 12 '71. S. Terkel *
Edward Hopper; greatest American realist of the 20th century. B. Rose. il Vogue 158:284-5 S 1 '71 *
Hopper bequest at the Whitney. B. O'Doherty. il Art in Am 59:68-72 S '71 *
Light and loneliness. A. T. Baker. il por Time 98:74-5 S 27 '71 *
Master's legacy. D. Davis. il por Newsweek 78:98-9 S 27 '71 *
World of Edward Hopper. J. R. Mellow. il por(p 1) N Y Times Mag p 14-16+ S 5 '71 *

HOPPER joints. See Joints (carpentry)
HORAN, Ellen
Cruising yachtsman. il Yachting 130:44 S '71
With the racing classes. See issues of Yachting
HORD, Charles W. See Barth, C. A. jt. auth.
HORDERN, William. See Cone. J. H. jt. auth.
HORGAN, John
Ireland's great kidnap plot. Commonweal 93: 439 F 5 '71
HORGAN, Paul
Whitewater; story. Ladies Home J 88:109-16 Ja '71
HORIZON house. See Narcotic addicts—Rehabilitation
HORMAN, Charles
Looking for a different approach to sadism. il Commonweal 95:281-3 D 17 '71
HORMEL, George A, and company
Management from the great beyond. il Forbes 107:44 Ap 1 '71
HORMONES
How hormones act on cells. Sci N 101:7 Ja 1 '72
Lennart Nilsson explores the crystalline world of hormones; photographs. Life 70:6-9 Ap 23 '71
Primary structure of the human chorionic somatomammotropin (HCS) molecule. C. H. Li. bibliog il Science 173:56-8 Jl 2 '71
Serum parathyroid hormone in X-linked hypophosphatemia. C. Arnaud and others. bibliog il Science 173:845-7 Ag 27 '71
Telemetered recording of hormone effects on hippocampal neurons. D. W. Pfaff and others. bibliog il Science 172:394-5 Ap 23 '71
Toward birth control by peptides; synthetic hypothalamic hormone. LH-RH/FSH-RH. por Sci N 100:37 Jl 17 '71
See also
ACTH
Adrenalin
Ecdysone
Glucagon
Juvenile hormone
Melanotropin
Oxytocin
Pheromones
Pituitary hormones
Prostaglandins
Stilbestrols
Thyroxine
HORMONES, Plant
See also
Abscisic acid
Auxins
Kinins
HORMONES, Sex
EEG responses in regularly menstruating women and in amenorrheic women treated with ovarian hormones. W. Vogel and others. bibliog il Science 172:388-91 Ap 23 '71
Prenatal sex hormone levels; a possible link to intelligence. il Sci N 101:8 Ja 1 '72
See also
Estrogens
Gonadotropins
Testosterone
HORN, Huston
Harness racing. Sports Illus 35:64 N 1 '71

HORN, John L. and Knott, P. D.
Activist youth of the 1960's: summary and prognosis. bibliog il Science 171:977-85 Mr 12 '71
HORN, Roger
Divine right of kings: academic status. il Am Lib 2:626-9 Je '71
HORN, Stanley F.
Hermitage, home of Andrew Jackson. il Antiques 100:413-17 S '71
HORN, Yannis
Greek editor sums up. T. W. Pew, jr. Nation 213:654-6 D 20 '71 *
HORN, Yvonne
Your growing years. il Har Yrs 11:16-19 Jl '71
HORN, Zoia
Anachronisms of another day. W. R. Eshelman. Wilson Lib Bul 45:719 Ap '71 *
HORN, CAPE
Cape Horn; voyage of the sailing ship, British Isles. E. Bunster. il Américas 23:2 11 Mr '71
HORNADAY, William Temple
National wildlife federation's conservation hall of fame. J. R. Forbes. il por Nat Wildlife 9:24-5 Ap '71 *
HORNBLOWER, Horatio (literary character)
See Characters in literature
HORNBOOKS
Hornbook, an invitation to learning. E. Shaffer. il Horn Bk 47:85-91 F '71
HORNBY, Lesley. See Twiggy (model)
HORNE, David
How did Amanda get into this? Pub W 199: 41 Ja 11 '71
HORNE, M. T.
Coevolution of escherichia coli and bacteriophages in chemostat culture. bibliog il Science 168:992-3; 172:405 My 22 '70, Ap 23 '71
HORNE, Marilyn
Marilyn Horne becomes a prima donna. M. Mayer. il pors N Y Times Mag p 14-15+ Ja 17 '71 *
HORNET bookstore, Sacramento state college. See College bookstores
HORNSTEIN, Harvey A.
They throw money away on purpose. S. Bacon. il Sci Digest 69:39-44 F '71
HORNY, Karen
Building Northwestern's Core. il por Library J 96:1580-3 My 1 '71
HOROSCOPE. See Astrology
HOROSKO, Marian
Alicia Alonso, the flower of Cuba. il pors Dance Mag 45:43-58 Ag '71
Tap, tapping and tappers. il Dance Mag 45: 32-7 O '71
(ed) See Doubrovska, F. In the shadow of Russian tradition
(ed) See Doubrovska, F. Pierre Vladimiroff
(ed) See Fedorova, A. In the shadow of Russian tradition
HOROVITZ, Israel
Acrobats. Criticism
Nation 212:314 Mr 8 '71 *
New Yorker 47:82-4 F 27 '71 *
Line. Criticism
Nation 212:314 Mr 8 '71 *
New Yorker 47:82-4 F 27 '71 *
Time 97:67 Mr 1 '71 *
HOROWITZ, Al
Chess corner. See issues of Saturday review
HOROWITZ, David
Making of America's China policy. il Ramp Mag 10:40-7 O '71
Revolutionary karma vs. revolutionary politics. il Ramp Mag 9:27-33 Mr '71
HOROWITZ, Irving Louis
Rock and rebellion. il Commonweal 93:466-9 F 12 '71
Schism between action and doctrine. Cur 135: 43-52 D '71
HOROWITZ, Mannie
Designing solid-state stereo amplifiers (title varies) See issues of Radio-electronics
HOROWITZ, Norman H.
Search for life on Mars: where we stand today. il Bul Atom Sci 27:13-17 N '71
HORROR films. See Moving pictures—Horror films
HORS d'œuvres. See Appetizers
HORSE auctions. See Auctions
HORSE breeding
New breed, new ideas, new taxes; California breeders of thoroughbred horses. A. Wright. il pors Sports Illus 34:48-53 Je 7 '71
HORSE power. See Horsepower (mechanics)

HORSE race betting
Bookie rates off-track betting; ed. by J. Lebow. Barney the Bookie. il Look 35:46+ Ag 10 '71
Can a computer beat the horses. J. Morgan. il Look 35:33 Je 1 '71
Games some people play: the tierce. F. Feldkamp. Harper 244:72 Ja '72
I got the horse right, where? OTB patrons. P. Putnam. il Sports Illus 34:22-4+ Ap 19 '71
It's money in the bank: J. Banks, British bookie. T. Maule. il por Sports Illus 35: 36-8+ N 29 '71
Never sell the horses short; ed. by F. Deford. il Sports Illus 35:87-9+ O 18 '71
Putting the case to Howie the horse; ed. by W. Tower. E. B. Ryan. il por Sports Illus 34:26-9 Je 28 '71
Sports; horse racing. R. Kahn. Esquire 76: 24+ O '71
Tiercé king. il por Newsweek 78:48-50 D 27 '71
What, no horses? New York's OTB. il Newsweek 77:73+ Ap 19 '71
You know me and horses. Al. il Time 97:10 Ap 19 '71
See also
Off-track betting corporation, New York
HORSE racing
After a mountain of money; quarter-horse racing. B. Gilbert. il Sports Illus 35:28-9 S 20 '71
¡Arriba! Canonero does it again; at the Preakness. W. Tower. il Sports Illus 34: 22-5 My 24 '71
Call it the survival of the fittest: not necessarily the best. W. Tower. Sports Illus 35: 68 N 8 '71
Conscious challenge to Hoist The Flag. W. Tower. il Sports Illus 34:53 Mr 29 '71
Executioner by a head; Flamingo stakes. il Newsweek 77:70 Mr 15 '71
Gunner makes history; Canonero II winning Kentucky Derby. il Time 97:61 My 10 '71
Happy story ends; Canonero's quest for the Triple crown at Belmont. W. Tower. il Sports Illus 34:18-21 Je 14 '71
He has them over a barrel; jockey L. Pincay. W. Tower. por Sports Illus 35:76+ D 6 '71
It may be adios to Canonero; Preakness at Pimlico. W. Tower. il Sports Illus 34:80+ My 17 '71
LJ proves thoroughbreds are color-blind. G. Jones. il pors Ebony 26:100-2+ N '70
Last year's crop of misses is starting to hit; thoroughbred colts. W. Tower. il Sports Illus 34:50-1 F 15 '71
Making passes at girls who take classics; five-year-old Shuvee at the 44th running of the Whitney stakes at Saratoga. W. Tower. il Sports Illus 35:68-9 Ag 16 '71
Missing data unavailable; Venezuela's Canonero II. W. Tower. il Sports Illus 34:18-21 My 10 '71
Muddy picture of young colts; Saratoga's Hopeful stakes. W. Tower. il Sports Illus 35:40 S 6 '71
New York derby. il Newsweek 77:61 My 17 '71
On the fence about winning; His Majesty. W. Tower. il Sports Illus 34:54 Mr 1 '71
One more blur in a confusion Derby; no favorite for Kentucky Derby. W. Tower. il Sports Illus 34:20-1 Ap 26 '71
People's horse; Belmont stakes. il Newsweek 77:74 Je 14 '71
Race track. A. Minor. See issues of New Yorker
Son of the Axe chops 'em; Executioner winner of Flamingo stakes. W. Tower. il Sports Illus 34:22-3 Mr 15 '71
Sunday races, with kids accommodated; Delaware park. M. R. Werner. il Sports Illus 34:69-70 Je 14 '71
They're all running after The Flag; Hoist The Flag. W. Tower. il Sports Illus 34:28-31 Ap 5 '71
Thoroughbred can of worms; 1 1/4-mile race for 3-year-olds at Saratoga. W. Tower. Sports Illus 35:53-4 Ag 30 '71
Tip on a lost race. C. Winfrey. il pors Harper 242:64-70 Je '71
Unconscious, List and Twist; Kentucky Derby. W. Tower. il Sports Illus 34:32-3 My 3 '71
Year of Cañonero; winner of Kentucky Derby and the Preakness. il Time 97:67 Je 14 '71
You can't blame a girl for trying; Garden State stakes for 2-year-olds. W. Tower. il Sports Illus 35:30-1 N 22 '71
See also
Harness racing
Jockeys
Race tracks

Accidents and injuries
Pretenders to the crown; Hoist The Flag's likely successors. W. Tower. il Sports Illus 34:26-9 Ap 12 '71

France
Showing them a thing or two; Prix de l'Arc de triomphe. W. Tower. il Sports Illus 35: 81-2 O 11 '71
Sporting scene; Deauville. F. Feldkamp. New Yorker 47:60-72+ Ag 14 '71

Great Britain
Down to earth in Britain; photographs by Gerry Cranham; account by J. Lawrence. il Sports Illus 34:22-9 F 8 '71
HORSE shows
Blues for an Orange redhead; National horse show at Madison Square Garden. A. Higgins. il Sports Illus 35:95+ N 22 '71
See also
Rodeos
HORSE sleeping sickness. See Encephalomyelitis
HORSE surgery. See Veterinary surgery
HORSE trails. See Trails
HORSE trainers
See also
Arias, J.
Baldwin, R.
Campo, J.
Neloy, E.
HORSE training
Staking a claim for big John. T. Maule. por Sports Illus 34:34-6+ My 3 '71
HORSEBACK trips
Going west to West Virginia. L. W. Swift and R. W. Swift. il pors Am For 77:16-19 Mr '71
Horses and riders: a galloping growth. W. L. Rohde. il Cons 25:13+ Ap '71
Twenty-five hundred miles on horseback; from Mexico to Canada. B. Murray. il pors Life 71:60-6+ S 3 '71
HORSEMANSHIP
See also
Horseback trips
Polo
Rodeos
HORSEPOWER (mechanics)
Portable computer tests engines in the field. il Am City 86:73 S '71
HORSES
Fight to save wild horses. il Time 98:48-51 Jl 12 '71
Good-by to the wild horse? excerpt from America's last wild horses. H. Ryden. il Read Digest 98:227-30+ My '71
Horses and the American frontier; excerpts from Horses in America. F. Haines. il Am West 8:10-15 Mr '71
Mustang controversy. R. H. Gilliuly. il Sci N 99:219-20 Mr 27 '71
On the track of the West's wild horses. H. Ryden. il Nat Geog 139:94-109 Ja '71
Threat to the free spirit: the question of the mustang's future. A. Amaral. il Am West 8:13-17+ S '71
Urban pollution: many long years ago. J. A. Tarr. il Am Heritage 22:65-9+ O '71
Wild horse, worth saving? A. Amaral. il Nat Parks & Con Mag 45:21-4 Mr '71
See also
Race horses
Diseases and pests
See also
Encephalomyelitis

Feeding
Feeding horses properly; nutritional needs of camp horses. D. D. Hirn. il Camp Mag 43:32 My '71
HORSES, Surgery on. See Veterinary surgery
HORSES as carriers of infection. See Animals as carriers of infection
HORSES in art
Bronze horses of Marilyn Newmark. M. Malmstrom. il por Am Artist 35:28-33+ Ap '71
HORSESHOE nails. See Nails
HORSESHOE trivets. See Trivets
HORTA-BARBOSA, Luiz, and others
Subacute sclerosing panencephalitis: isolation of suppressed measles virus from lymph node biopsies. bibliog il Science 173:840-1 Ag 27 '71
HORTICULTURAL societies
Members' news. See issues of Horticulture to August 1971
See also
Massachusetts horticultural society

HORTICULTURE
See also
Electrohorticulture
Nurseries (horticulture)

Bibliography
Book reviews. See issues of Horticulture

History
Flowers of the colonial days. R. J. Favretti. il Horticulture 49:40-1+ Ap '71

HORTICULTURE (periodical)
Garden club yearbook contest winners (cont) Horticulture 49:46-7 Jl; 45-6 O '71

HORTON, Barbara
Olympic adventure: ridge of the wild goats. il Nat Parks & Con Mag 45:30-4 My '71

HORTON, Frank L.
Work of an anonymous Carolina cabinetmaker. il Antiques 101:169-76 Ja '72

HORVATH, Ian
Brief biography. S. Goodman. pors Dance Mag 45:66-7 S '71 •

HORVITZ, Diana Frank. See Sloane, R. B. jt. auth.

HORWITZ, Carey. See Stokvis, I. E. jt. comp.

HORWITZ, Herbert R.
British crime prevention. Am Scholar 40:677-85 Aut '71

HORWITZ, Susan B. and others
Chemosterilant action of anthramycin: a proposed mechanism. bibliog il Science 174: 159-61 O 8 '71

HOSE
See also
Garden hose

HOSE, Garden. See Garden hose

HOSE reels. See Reels

HOSIERY
Panty hose: see how they run. A. Chamberlin. McCalls 98:24+ Mr '71
Panty hose: why they're better now. J. Van Leeuwen. il Good H 172:136 My '71
Sheer madness. il Time 97:88 Ap 12 '71
Socks & ties. il Mech Illus 68:82 Ja '72

HOSIERY industry
Multinational monarch of pantyhose; Schulte and Dieckhoff GmbH. il Bsns W p50-1 Ap 17 '71

HOSKIN, Francis C. G.
Diisopropylphosphorofluoridate and Tabun: enzymatic hydrolysis and nerve function. bibliog il Science 172:1243-5 Je 18 '71

HOSKINS, Katherine
Baucis and Philemon; I think I must be dying; poems. Poetry 118:92-3 My '71

HOSPITAL administrators
See also
Gaynor, F. S.

HOSPITAL beds
It's not cloud 9, it's superbed! air-fluidized bed. J. Pickerell. il Pop Mech 135:80-1 My '71

HOSPITAL care
Last-ditch fight for life; Respiratory intensive care unit at Massachusetts general. E. M. Wylie. il Good H 172:98-9+ My '71
Who shall die? intensive-care unit creating new problems. E. Clark. il Newsweek 77: 49-50 My 24 '71
See also
Children—Hospital care
Computers—Medical use

Cost
End of hospital shortage: why the turnaround. il U S News 71:72-4 S 6 '71

HOSPITAL chains. See Hospitals

HOSPITAL of the University of Pennsylvania. See Pennsylvania. University. Philadelphia —Hospital

HOSPITAL ombudsman. See Ombudsman

HOSPITAL patients. See Sick, The

HOSPITAL records. See Medical records

HOSPITAL service, Cost of. See Hospital care—Cost

HOSPITAL ships
Hike for Hope: organized by teens in Rochester, N.Y. M. Weider. il por Seventeen 30:20+ Ag '71
17th annual Mr Travel award: crew and staff of the S.S. Hope. il Travel 136:54-7 Jl '71

HOSPITAL supplies. See Hospitals—Equipment and supplies

HOSPITAL visiting. See Hospitals—Visitors

HOSPITALITY
Having wonderful time, wish I were home. M. B. Frosh. il Har Yrs 11:14-15 Jl '71
See also
Entertaining

HOSPITALIZATION insurance. See Insurance, Hospitalization

HOSPITALS
See also
Computers—Hospital use
Hospital care
Hospital ships
Nursing homes

Accounting
Models for financially healthy hospitals. G. C. Forsyth and D. G. Thomas. il Harvard Bsns R 49:106-17 Jl '71

Administration
Hospitals are learning to share. L. DeView. McCalls 98:48 F '71
New blood for tired hospitals. R. G. Wasyluka; reply with rejoinder. R. A. Malt. Harvard Bsns R 49:32+ Ja '71
Physician's role in hospital management. A. Robbins. Mo Labor R 94:60-2 Ap '71

Architecture
Building types study. il Arch Rec 150:139-50 S '71
Cincinnati, Ohio; Bethesda hospital north. il Arch Forum 134:40-1 Je '71
Creating consolidated clinical techniques spaces for an expanding role in health care. S. Clibbon and M. L. Sachs. bibliog il Arch Rec 149:105-12 F '71
Evolution of nursing space planning for efficient operation. M. L. Bobrow. il Arch Rec 150:151-4 S '71
Natick, Mass; Leonard Morse hospital. il Arch Forum 134:42-5 Je '71
Search for flexibility in hospital design: a perspective on the work of Clibbon and Sachs. G. Best and J. Weeks. Arch Rec 150: 66+ S '71
Technology; North Central Bronx hospital. il Arch Forum 134:56-9 Je '71
Valley general hospital, Renton, Washington. il Arch Rec 149:98-9 Ja '71

Electric equipment
Danger in the hospital. A. S. Freese. il Pop Mech 135:80-3 F '71
Leakage current & electrical shock P. B Jarrett. Pop Electr 34:46 Mr '71
Medical electronic equipment and hospital safety. H. French. il Pop Electr 1:32-4 Ja '72
Ralph Nader's most shocking exposé. R. Nader. il Ladies Home J 88:98+ Mr '71

Emergency services
Curing the emergency room. il Time 98:94-5 N 22 '71
I never dreamed medicine would be like this! first day in the emergency room. il pors Todays Health 49:40-5 O '71
Needed: more help for accident victims. J. R. Miller. Read Digest 98:83-7 Ja '71
Trauma treatment; the Illinois plan. il Newsweek 78:80-1 N 1 '71

Equipment and supplies
Case of bottled death; contaminated intravenous-feeding bottles. il Newsweek 77:57 Mr 29 '71
Food and drug administration: is protecting lives the priority? contaminated IV feeding bottles. R. J. Bazell. Science 172:41-3 Ap 2 '71; Reply with rejoinder. C. C. Edwards. 173:379 Jl 30 '71
Magnetic flowmeter protects patients; intravenous flow control system. S. V. Jones. il Sci Digest 71:65 Ja '72
Robot orderlies; Amscars. il Newsweek 78: 44 S 6 '71
System of coordinated containers, frames and carts for hospitals. il Arch Rec 150:159-61 S '71
Tainted products. Newsweek 78:45 Ag 2 '71
Thriving market in turn-key hospitals. il Bsns W p37 O 9 '71
See also
American hospital supply corporation
Bard. C. R. inc.
Hospital beds
Medical instruments and apparatus

Finance
Profit boost for hospitals: chain operators. il Bsns W p96+ O 2 '71
What controls mean to medical care. Bsns W p38-9 Ja 1 '72
See also
Hospitals—Accounting

Hygiene
Annals of medicine; outbreak of salmonella cubana at Massachusetts general hospital caused by contaminated carmine dye. B. Roueché. New Yorker 47:66-72+ S 4 '71

HOSPITALS—Hygiene—*Continued*
Case of bottled death; contaminated intravenous-feeding bottles. il Newsweek 77:57 Mr 29 '71
Pseudomonas aeruginosa: growth in distilled water from hospitals. M. S. Favero and others. bibliog il Science 173:836-8 Ag 27 '71

Management and regulation
See Hospitals—Administration

Outpatient service
See also
Hospitals, Psychiatric—Outpatient service

Psychiatric service
Setting up a psychiatric service in a general hospital. M. Goldenberg and C. E. Sluzki. bibliog Ment Hy 55:85-90 Ja '71

Staff
Recognition, negotiation, and work stoppages in hospitals. D. D. Pointer and H. Graham. bibliog il Mo Labor R 94:54-8 My '71
See also
Hospitals, Psychiatric—Staff
Strikes—United States—Hospital employees

Visitors
Up the wall. E. Bombeck. il Good H 173:43-4+ N '71

Argentina
Setting up a psychiatric service in a general hospital. M. Goldenberg and C. E. Sluzki. bibliog Ment Hy 55:85-90 Ja '71

Cambodia
Compassion pace; World vision hospital. Chr Today 16:33 N 5 '71

Underdeveloped areas
See Underdeveloped areas—Hospitals

United States
America's 10 best hospitals. R. C. Smith. il Todays Health 49:24-9+ N '71
End of hospital shortage: why the turnaround. il U S News 71:72-4 S 6 '71
Not what Catholic hospitals ordered. R. A. McCormick. America 125:510-13 D 11 '71
See also
Negroes—Hospitals
United States—Veterans administration hospitals
also subhead Hospitals under names of cities, e.g. Chicago—Hospitals

HOSPITALS, Military
See also
United States—Veterans administration hospitals

HOSPITALS, Psychiatric
Asylums' effect on mental health. A. J. Snider. Sci Digest 69:69 My '71
Government of Doctor Caligari: Soviet mental hospitals; address, December 3, 1971. B. D. Wolfe. Nat R 23:1461-2 D 31 '71
Mental hospitals and the winds of change. W. R. Bartz and others. Ment Hy 55:266-9 Ap '71
New right to treatment; Tuscaloosa's Bryce hospital. il Time 97:52+ Ap 5 '71
Observations in a mental hospital: a sociological perspective. S. S. Robin. bibliog Ment Hy 55:253-9 Ap '71
Psychotherapy in a public mental hospital. W. B. Simon and J. E. Wood, jr. bibliog Ment Hy 55:221-4 Ap '71
Therapeutic community. R. Almond. il Sci Am 224:34-42 bibliog(p 124) Mr '71
Your mother died three years ago; aged in state mental hospitals. S. L. Engelbardt. il Todays Health 49:44-5+ Mr '71

Administration
State mental hospital in transition: an approach to the study of mental hospital decentralization. L. Rowitz and L. Levy. bibliog Ment Hy 55:68-76 Ja '71

Outpatient service
After the crisis; Family treatment unit at Colorado psychiatric hospital. K. Flomenhaft and D. G. Langsley. Ment Hy 55:473-7 O '71
Supportive outpatient treatment. C. P. Rosenbaum. bibliog Ment Hy 55:225-7 Ap '71

Rehabilitation centers
Gateways to outside; New York state's mental hospital system. il Arch Forum 133:26-41 D '70

Staff
Nonprofessionalization of the war on mental illness. D. C. Marler. Ment Hy 55:291-4 Jl '71
Staff-patient interaction, race and patient behavior on a psychiatric ward. C. O. Turner and G. Spivack. bibliog Ment Hy 55:499-503 O '71

Training
Mental health workers: new mental hospital personnel for the seventies. G. L. Euster. bibliog Ment Hy 55:283-90 Jl '71

HOSPITALS, Rural
Demise of rural medicine; address, February 20, 1971. B. L. McCullough. Vital Speeches 37:517-18 Je 15 '71

HOSS, Virgil L.
Affair with the South Fork. il pors Outdoor Life 148:647+ Ag '71

HOSTAGES
Hostage in Peking; condensation. A. Grey. il Read Digest 98:181-8+ Ja '71
We were hijacked! teen travelers in Jordanian desert and Amman. S. Finkelstein; P. Burt. pors Seventeen 29:170 D '70

HOSTESSES. See Hospitality

HOSTESSES, Air. See Airlines—Hostesses

HOSTICK, King V.
Autographs. See issues of Hobbies

HOSTILITY (psychology)
Valentine for our times; where has love gone? S. Levine. il Todays Health 49:22-4 F '71
See also
Anger

HOT air engines. See Automobile engines

HOT line (Washington and Moscow)
Intelsat system proposed for new Washington-Moscow hotline link. K. Johnsen. Aviation W 95:22 S 27 '71
U.S. may lease Molniya station for hotline link from contractor. Aviation W 95:17 O 11 '71

HOT owl (periodical)
For, about and by kids. il Time 97:46-7 Ja 25 '71

HOT peppers. See Peppers

HOT rod (periodical)
Editorially speaking; Rod & custom magazine to be combined with Hot rod. D. Evans. Hot Rod 24:6 Je '71
1970 Street rod of the year award presentation. il Hot Rod 24:114-15 O '71
1971 Street rod of the year poll. il Hot Rod 24:26-9 D '71

HOT rod clubs. See Automobile clubs

HOT rods. See Automobiles, Remodeled

HOT water heating. See Heating

HOT water supply
See also
Water heaters

HOTALING, Ed
Herculaneum at Malibu. il Art N 70:40-3+ S '71

HOTBEDS
Mini hotbed and propagating frame. R. E. Wester and W. R. Parker. il Horticulture 49:42-3 Mr '71

HOTEL architecture. See Hotels, taverns, etc.

HOTEL charges. See Hotels, taverns, etc.—Rates

HOTEL decoration
Bouquet of happy colorings by David Hicks. il House B 113:60-1 Jl '71

HOTELS, taverns, etc.
Hotel headliners. See issues of Travel
Lapidus' pornography of comfort. M. Josephson. il Art in Am 59:108-9 Mr '71
Three greatest hotels in the world; plus some great alternatives; with travel notes. R. Joseph. il Esquire 76:12, 130-5+ O '71
Weekend travelers; there's a small hotel. il Mlle 73:184-7 S '71
See also
Hotel decoration
also subhead Hotels, restaurants, etc. under names of cities, e.g. Mexico (city)—Hotels, restaurants, etc.

Designs and plans
Building types study; with introd. by M. F. Schmertz. il Arch Rec 150:95-112 N '71

Employees
Wages and tips in restaurants and hotels; with tables and a chart. C. M. O'Connor. Mo Labor R 94:47-51 Jl '71

Rates
Phantom charges that haunt hotels; class actions for refunds. Bsns W p40-1 D 25 '71

HOTELS, taverns, etc.—*Continued*

Reservation systems

Travel notes; hotel representation. R. Joseph. Esquire 75:76+ Je '71

Services

Films check in to motel rooms. il Bsns W p79 O 9 '71

Motel Bijou; experiment with TV cartridges for closed-circuit showings of moving pictures in motel rooms. il Newsweek 78:43 Ag 9 '71

Social aspects

Eroticism of hotels. Q. Crewe. il Vogue 157: 101 Ap 15 '71

Africa, East

East Africa's tourist boom begins. il Fortune 83:84-91 Je '71

Caribbean Region

Chill wind nips island hotels. il Bsns W p 17 Ap 3 '71

Denmark

Fairy-tale atmosphere of Danish inns. P. Brooks. il Holiday 49:60-1+ F '71

France

Chateaux of France. G. Trotta. il Harp Baz 104:34-5 Ag '71

Have you never lived in a castle? M. Gough. House B 113:14-15+ Ja '71

Great Britain

Britain's international innkeeper; Trust houses forte. il Forbes 107:28-9 My 1 '71

Troubled hotel chain is ripe for takeover; Trust houses Forte, ltd. Bsns W p40-1 O 30 '71

Puerto Rico

Puerto Rico now. D. Messinesi. Vogue 157:121 Ja 15 '71

Slovakia

High hopes in the Slovak uplands. H. Sutton. il Sat R 54:31-2 Je 19 '71

United States

Big-city hotels in a fight for survival. il U S News 71:54-6 N 1 '71

End of an era; Edgewater Gulf, Miss. closed. il Newsweek 77:118-19 Je 7 '71

Grand old resort hotels. il Life 71:42-51 Jl 16 '71

Great homes away from home: Mohonk mountain house. J. Egan. il Am Home 74: 42+ O '71

Hotel occupancy is springing back. il Bsns W p53 Ja 1 '72

Inns for all seasons; New England. P. Brooks. il Holiday 48:82-3+ S '70

There are too many rooms at the inn. il Bsns W p60-2 Je 12 '71

Those hidden hotel charges. Consumer Rep 36:368 Je '71

Why executives hate hotels; interviews with executives. ed. by J. Perham. il Duns 98:46-9 S '71

Why we joined the inn group. T. Hunt. il Travel 135:62-4+ Ap '71

See also

Marriott corporation

also subhead Hotels, restaurants, etc. under names of cities, e.g. New York (city) —Hotels, restaurants, etc.

HOTELS, taverns, etc, Prefabricated. See Buildings, Prefabricated

HOTTELET, Richard C.

What new role for the People's Republic of China? il Sat R 54:27-30 S 18 '71

HOTTLEMAN, Girard D.

Performance contracting is a hoax! Ed Digest 37:1-4 S '71

HOUCK, John C. and others

Lymphocyte DNA synthesis inhibition. bibliog il Science 173:1139-41 S 17 '71

HOUGH, Joseph C. Jr

Church alive and changing. il Chr Cent 89: 8-12 Ja 5 '72

HOUNDS

Are you up on hounds? questions and answers. D. Du Bois. Outdoor Life 147:188-9 Mr '71

Cat hounds. D. M. Duffey. il Outdoor Life 148:142-4+ N '71

Coon hound bear dogs. L. Mueller. il por Field & S 76:164+ Ag '71

Ounce of prevention for the banks and the bogs: West Waterford pack. R. S. Rauch, 3d. il Sports Illus 35:48-51 N 22 '71

What is the Plott hound? D. M. Duffey. il Outdoor Life 148:116+ Jl '71

See also

Foxhounds

HOUPHOUET-BOIGNY, Félix

Sages of Abidjan. il Time 97:82 Mr 15 '71 •

HOURIET, Robert

Authors & editors; interview. ed. by D. N. Mount. por Pub W 200:33-5 S 13 '71

Trade winds; interview. ed. by C. Amory. Sat R 54:18+ S 18 '71

HOURS, Books of

Authors & editors: Braziller reproduction of Catherine of Cleves; interview. ed. by A. H. Johnston. G. Braziller. Pub W 200:17-19 O 11 '71

HOURS of business. See Business hours

HOURS of labor

And now, the four-day week. Duns 97:93 Je '71

As 4-day week spreads, it meets some doubters. il U S News 70:49-50 My 17 '71

Auto union, Chrysler study 4-day week. U S News 70:55 F 1 '71

Can the four-day week work? comments by members of Dun's presidents' panel; ed. by N. A. Martin. Duns 98:39-40+ Jl '71; Reply. K. E. Wheeler. 98:99 S '71

Coming soon: the three-day weekend, every week. V. Bernstein. il Redbook 138:77+ Ja '72

Four-day week, and productivity. Duns 98: 84 Jl '71

Four-day week gets more play. Bsns W p33 Jl 17 '71

4-day work week and what to do about it. il Mech Illus 67:50-1 Jl '71

Hours and earnings, private nonagricultural payrolls; tables. See issues of Monthly labor review

How four-day workweek is catching on. il U S News 70:41-3 Mr 8 '71; Same abr. with title Make way for the shorter workweek. Read Digest 98:108-10 Je '71

Insurance sells itself on the shorter week. Bsns W p52 S 4 '71

Lady's law vanishes. Nations Bsns 59:62 D '71

Limits on pay for 4-day week. U S News 71: 92 S 27 '71

Look at the 4-day workweek. J. N. Hedges. bibliog Mo Labor R 94:33-7 O '71

On the way to a four-day week. il Time 97: 69 Mr 1 '71

Pick your hours; experiment in Germany. Time 98:68 Jl 19 '71

Research summaries. See issues of Monthly labor review

Spreading four-day week. il Newsweek 78: 63-4 Ag 23 '71

Thank God it's Thursday! Coming soon? The four-day week. G. Samuels. il N Y Times Mag p32-3+ My 16 '71

Thank God it's Thursday? four-day work week. Time 97:71 F 1 '71

Trends in labor and leisure; with tables. G. H. Moore and J. N. Hedges. bibliog Mo Labor R 94:3-11 F '71

Two views of 4-day workweek. U S News 70:57 My 3 '71

UAW will ask government aid for 4-day week. Aviation W 94:22 Mr 29 '71

Why the work week pattern is changing. il Bsns W p 108-9 Mr 13 '71

See also

Overtime

Staggered hours

HOUSE, Ernest R. See Erlandson. D. A. jt. auth.

HOUSE, J. E. Jr

Beryllium. il por Chem 44:10-13 D '71

Negative hydrogen. il por Chem 44:8-11 Mr '71

HOUSE; story. See Benchley, N.

HOUSE; story. See Calisher, H.

HOUSE appropriations committee. See United States—Congress—House—Appropriations, Committee on

HOUSE boats. See Houseboats

HOUSE building industry. See Construction industry

HOUSE building materials. See Building materials

HOUSE buying

Build your own first mortgage; off-site removal. M. Bicknell. Har Yrs 11:34-5 Je '71

Homes for young couples who can't afford castles. A. M. Watkins. il Redbook 138: 86-7+ N '71

House buying: the cost of closing the deal. il Changing T 25:15-17 N '71

House hunting with a Polaroid. B. Berger. il Mech Illus 68:86 Ja '72

Houses: the year of the big buy. il Time 97: 75-6 Mr 29 '71

Housing squeeze. Bet Hom & Gard 49:12 S '71

HOUSE buying—*Continued*
In shopping for an older house, consider the approach of the professional house inspector. Sunset 147:86-7 S '71
Ten most common mistakes in buying a house. Bet Hom & Gard 49:46+ S '71
  See also
House selling
Mortgages
HOUSE call services. See Medical service
HOUSE caravans. See Caravans
HOUSE cleaning
Indoor ecology; cleaning up from basement to attic to closets. M. A. Rodgers. Good H 172:33-4+ Je '71
HOUSE construction
Building a house? 20 tips that save time and your back. R. F. Dempewolff. il Pop Mech 135:112-15 My '71
Comeback for housing; builders see a boom year. il U S News 70:37-9 F 1 '71
Homes: new and remodeled; Emily Anne Smith's building career. M. Kraft. il por Good H 172:140-7+ Ap '71
How to use prefab methods to build your own home. R. Day. il Mech Illus 67:87-92+ Je '71
Well-built house; how they built the computer house. il House B 113:104-6 F '71
  See also special kinds of house construction, e.g. Metal houses
HOUSE decoration
Beauty all around you. il House & Gard 139:86-107+ My '71
Big effects in small space; with paint, wallpaper, fabric and mirrors. P. Rumely. il Bet Hom & Gard 49:48-59 F '71
Candice Bergen and her California house. C. Bergen. il pors Vogue 157:74-9+ Je '71
Decorating newsletter. V. D. Hahn. See issues of American home
Decorating Q's & A's (cont of) Decorating clinic. See issues of American home
Decorating: the fun phase. V. D. Hahn. il Am Home 74:70 My '71
Decorating with fabrics; excerpt from David Hicks on decoration—with fabrics. D. Hicks. il McCalls 98:80-7 S '71
Decorating zest American style: denim & bandanas. il House & Gard 140:62-5 Ag '71
Decorator speaks his mind. W. Baldwin. See issues of House & garden incorporating Living for young homemakers
Everything in one enormous room. il House & Gard 140:102-11 O '71
50 decorating ideas for problem rooms. Am Home 74:69 F '71
Fifty pieces of furniture and how you can decorate with them in marvelous new ways. il House & Gard 140:86-99 O '71
Fresh ideas for more livable living. M. Kraft. il Good H 173:142-9 O '71
From Manhattan brownstone...to San Francisco Bay. H. Brown; N. C. Gray. il pors Am Home 74:98-101+ My '71
Gaslight classic; Greenwich Village town house. R. Reif. il N Y Times Mag p54-5 F 28 '71
Glassed-in personal showcase. il House B 113:40-4 Ja '71
Gloomy Victorian lights up. R. Fitzgerald. il House B 113:52-6 Ja '71
House for children and dog and adults. N. Skurka. il N Y Times Mag p94-5 Ap 4 '71
House of the year: decorated by American home. V. D. Hahn. il Am Home 74:87-97 O '71
How to be an expert with pattern. W. Baldwin. House & Gard 140:8+ O '71
How to shop a model room. L. B. Downs. il House B 113:16+ O '71
Ideas: yours and ours. il Seventeen 30:82-3 Ja '71
Immediate style: 5 rooms for today. L. Grundy. il House B 113:139-45 O '71
Living in styles: eclectic. il Redbook 137:110-13+ My '71
Living in styles: turn-of-the-century. il Redbook 136:122-6 Mr '71
Loveliest rooms I've ever seen. C. Conger. House & Gard 140:38+ O '71
Lure of working with your hands. il House & Gard 139:73-9 Ap '71
Make yours a better home. N. Seney and J. Pinkham. il Bet Hom & Gard 49:42-57 My '71
Making of a personal mood. N. Schram. il House B 113:146-7 O '71
New American farm house. il House & Gard 139:38-45 F '71
New house in a new town: great idea for a growing family. il Good H 173:146-53+ N '71
New house with a past; Paul Lynde's home in Hollywood. il House B 113:38-41 Ag '71

Notes to help you decorate-it-yourself; questions and answers. P. Corbin. House & Gard 139:40+ Ap; 24 My; 140:52+ S; 70 O '71
Room for all reasons. il McCalls 99:98-101 N '71
Sew your own decorator flourishes. il House B 113:69-78 bibliog(p 127) Ag '71
Super naturals. N. Mandelbaum. il Ladies Home J 89:88-91 Ja '72
Tiny bit of French perfection; Southampton, N.Y. L. Grundy. il House B 113:34-9 Ja '71
Touch of nostalgia. N. Skurka. il N Y Times Mag p 19 Jl 4 '71
Touch-up decorating. M. Gough. House B 113:98+ Ap '71
Truly sensuous house; Victorian townhouse. S. G. Lewin. il House B 113:118-21 N '71
20 no-cost ways to make your home more beautiful. V. D. Hahn. Am Home 74:48+ Ap '71
Two worlds; East meets West in an old New England water mill. il House B 113:116-17 N '71
Victorian valentine. N. Skurka. il N Y Times Mag p86-7 O 24 '71
Villa for active Americans; French Riviera. W. Baldwin. il House & Gard 139:48-55 F '71
  See also
Apartments
Christmas decorations
Clocks
Color in house decoration
Curtains and draperies
Display of antiques, art objects, etc.
Electric lamps
Furniture, Arrangement of
Halls
Household furnishings
Interior decorators
Laundries
Lighting, Architectural and decorative
Mirrors
Painting, Industrial and practical
Paper-hanging
Pictures, Hanging of
Plants in house decoration
Rooms
Rugs and carpets
Shelves
Slip covers
Studios
Telephone centers, nooks, etc.
Wall coverings
Walls
Windows
  also names of rooms, e.g. Bathrooms

Anecdotes, facetiae, satire, etc.
We did it: a moat, waterfall and bridge in my living room. L. Ayer. il House B 113:24+ Ap '71

HOUSE decoration, American
On and off the avenue. J. Malcolm. New Yorker 46:96+ F 13 '71
HOUSE decoration, French
Green world in an open-air house; old farmhouse given the charm of a French mill. il House & Gard 139:86-91 Je '71
HOUSE decoration, Mediterranean
Living in styles: Mediterranean. il Redbook 136:95-9+ F '71
HOUSE decoration, Oriental
Living in styles: the Far East. il Redbook 136:102-5+ Ap '71
HOUSE expansion. See Houses, Remodeled
HOUSE flies. See Flies
HOUSE guests. See Guests
HOUSE heating. See Heating
HOUSE insulation. See Insulation (heat)
HOUSE internal security committee. See United States—Congress—House—Internal security, Committee on
HOUSE mothers. See Housemothers
HOUSE moving. See Moving of structures, etc.
HOUSE of blue leaves; drama. See Guare, J.
HOUSE of Schott. See Music publishing
HOUSE organs
  See also
Employees magazines, handbooks, etc.
HOUSE paint. See Paint
HOUSE painting
Mr Darling paints his dream house. S. Darling. il pors Life 70:66-9 Je 25 '71
Notes to help you decorate it yourself. P. Corbin. House & Gard 139:40+ Ap '71
Painting the house is easier, inside and out. il Changing T 25:19-21 Mr '71

HOUSE painting, interior. See Painting. Industrial and practical

HOUSE plans. See Architecture, Domestic—Designs and plans

HOUSE plants
Houseplant how-to. il Bet Hom & Gard 49: 132 O; 180 N; 12 D '71
How to grow fruiting plants indoors in pots. E. McDonald. House B 113:151 D '71
How to grow houseplants 15 stories high. L. V. Power. il Am Home 74:46-7+ F '71
How to have your own personal garden indoors. il House & Gard 140:114-15+ S '71
Humidify for healthier house plants. B. Thompson. Home Gard 58:74-5 Ap '71
Multiplying your houseplants. K. S. Taylor. il Horticulture 49:30-3 F '71
Right ways to care for houseplants. il Good H 172:176-7 Mr '71
Uncommon bulbs for indoors L. Cutak. il Horticulture 49:32-6 O '71
Your garden indoors. F. S. David. See issues of Home garden & flower grower
　　See also
African violets
Anthuriums
Artificial light gardening
Aspidistra
Bromeliads
Cactus
Coleus
Gesneriaceae
Ivy
Poinsettias
Watering of plants

HOUSE prices. See Housing—Costs

HOUSE protection
　　See also
Burglary protection

HOUSE purchasing. See House buying

HOUSE rules committee. See United States—Congress—House—Rules, Committee on

HOUSE selling
Elegy for an old home. L. Osborn. il Har Yrs 11:30-1+ O '71
How to make an (almost) trouble-free transfer. J. Ingersoll. House B 113:24-5 Ja '71

HOUSE-swapping vacations. See Vacations

HOUSE to house selling. See Canvassing

HOUSE wiring. See Electric wire and wiring

HOUSEBOATS
Cheerful water noises, a deck for sitting, no lawn to cut, it's the river life. il Sunset 146: 94-5 Je '71
Escape on a houseboat, it's a fun way of life. J. Roe. il Pop Sci 199:78-9+ Ag '71
Honeymoon on a houseboat. G. Reiger. il Pop Mech 135:102-5+ F '71
House boat anchors life for Mr and Mrs Barend Van Gerbig, 2d. il pors Vogue 157: 112-15 Ap 15 '71
Houseboat that sails. E. B. Benjamin. il Yachting 130:55+ Jl '71
Life on the Hudson. il Mech Illus 67:62 S '71
New bargain houseboats. B. McKeown. il Mech Illus 67:40 Ap '71
Off-season cruising in a Shasta Lake houseboat. il Sunset 147:34+ N '71
Try the joys of houseboating. il Changing T 25:11-13 Je '71
Very special houseboat. T. Gibbs. il Motor B & S 127:98-9 Mr '71
Wahweap jumpoff; houseboat adventure. J. Tallon. il Outdoor Life 148:56-9+ S '71
Wave of floating houses. il Life 71:70+ S 3 '71
Why don't they call them homeboats? R. Williamson. il Motor B & S 127:66-9+ Mr '71
Yachting eyes a boat; the Cruise-a-home 40. il Yachting 130:62-3+ O '71

Automobile trailer combination
Boating in a breadbox. G. W. Reiger. il Pop Mech 135:102-5 Je '71
Livin' is easy on a boat-camper. J. Roe and D. D. Vigren. il Pop Sci 199:80-2 Jl '71
Trailers that float. B. W. Dalrymple.il pors Outdoor Life 147:84-6+ Mr '71

Design
House yacht comes of age. il Motor B & S 128:68-73 O '71

Handling
Tips for houseboat pilots. F. M. Paulson. il Field & S 76:158-60+ Je '71

Testing
Well-used houseboat; Pacemaker's 35-ft. Drift-R-Cruz. P. Smyth. il Motor B & S 128:64-7+ O '71

HOUSEFLIES. See Flies

HOUSEHOLD, Geoffrey
Books. L. E. Sissman. New Yorker 47:125-9 My 1 '71 •

HOUSEHOLD accidents. See Accidents

HOUSEHOLD accounts. See Domestic finance

HOUSEHOLD appliances
Exciting new products. C. Bilski. See issues of Popular mechanics
400 best designed products for the home. il Bet Hom & Gard 49:22+ Ja '71
Guide to compact appliances. C. Kilvert. il Mech Illus 68:98-100+ Ja '72
Standard-sizes chart. Am Home 74:76 My '71
What you should know about buying home appliances. Redbook 137:76+ S '71
　　See also
Gas appliances
Kitchen utensils

HOUSEHOLD appliances, Electric
American ingenuity: problem-solvers for your kitchen. il House & Gard 139:70-3 F '71
Appliances: try thinking small. A. F. Rush. il McCalls 99:94-7 O '71
Blender magic for kitchen lib. J. M. Bauer. il Am Home 74:64+ O '71
Buying a major appliance? avoid these post-purchase problems. J. Keely. il Good H 172:166+ My '71
Egg cookers. il Consumer Bul 54:17-18 Mr '71
Electric fondue pots. il Consumer Bul 54: 15-19 D '71
Electric griddles. il Consumer Rep 36:656-9 N '71
Electric knife sharpeners. il Consumer Rep 36:175 Mr '71
Four appliances that make anyone an expert cook. J. Mees. il Good H 173:102-3 Ag '71
400 best designed products for the home. il Bet Hom & Gard 49:22+ Ja '71
Make the most of your blender. Bet Hom & Gard 49:110 Ap '71
New adventures in applianceland. N. Craig. il House B 113:68-9 Jl '71
New kitchen switched on to all-appliance cooking. il House & Gard 139:120-2 Ap '71
Notes for the corporate nomad: moving electrically. il Fortune 84:82-3 Ag '71
Outdoor appliances: handle with care. Bet Hom & Gard 49:82 Je '71
Plugged-in circuit; with recipes. il Seventeen 30:260-5+ Ag '71
Red sweeps in. A. Walker. il Am Home 74: 54-5 Jl '71
Truly instant heating element: wok. L. Buckwalter. il Mech Illus 67:90-1+ Ja '71
What dimouts do to your electrical equipment. J. R. Free. il Pop Sci 198:58-9+ F '71
What to look for in major appliances. Bet Hom & Gard 49:98-9 D '71
Work wonders with blenders; with recipes. il Ladies Home J 88:148+ My '71
　　See also names of electric household appliances, e.g. Washing machines

Maintenance and repair
Appliance clinic; questions and answers. P. Mann. See issues of Popular mechanics. September 1971-
Appliance repairs anyone can make. L. Buckwalter. il Mech Illus 67:98-101+ O '71
Home appliance electronics. J. Darr. See issues of Radio-electronics
How to prevent appliance breakdowns. E. Powell. il Pop Sci 199:86-7+ Jl '71

Noise
Pitch for the noiseless home. il Bsns W p87-8 My 22 '71

Safety devices and measures
How to protect your appliances when power is reduced. Good H 172:175 Je '71

HOUSEHOLD appliances industry
Appliance sales blow hot and cold. il Bsns W p37-8 Je 5 '71
　　See also
General motors corporation—Frigidaire division
Rubbermaid, inc.
Silo, inc.

Wages and hours
No wage hikes, more jobs. U S News 71:79-80 D 6 '71

Italy
For appliances. la dolce vita is just a memory. il Bsns W p32 Ag 28 '71

HOUSEHOLD brushes. See Brushes

HOUSEHOLD budget. See Budget. Household

HOUSEHOLD cleaning preparations. See Cleaning compositions

HOUSEHOLD employees
How to find and keep a maid. F. M. Eckman. Ladies Home J 88:70+ My '71
"I am a maid, and what do I know?" a Negro servant's views of a white family. R. Coles. Atlan 228:64-8 Ag '71
See also
Housekeepers
National committee on household employment

Wages and hours
Notes for the corporate nomad: scarcer household help. Fortune 83:44-5 F '71
HOUSEHOLD expenses. See Domestic finance
HOUSEHOLD furnishings
Beautiful bath accessories: you can make. M. B. Smith. il Bet Hom & Gard 49:50-3 Ag '71
Decorating newsletter. V. D. Hahn. See issues of American home
Discoveries from people with imaginative ideas for living. il House & Gard 139:112-13 Mr '71
Discoveries: living machines. il House & Gard 139:94-7 Ap '71
400 best designed products for the home. Bet Hom & Gard 49:22+ Ja '71
How to make small rooms work better. D. Popplestone and M. B. Smith. il Bet Hom & Gard 49:66-71 O '71
Living in styles, contemporary. il Redbook 136:74-7+ Ja '71
Living with children:
  The kitchen. il Redbook 137:122-5+ S '71
  The living room-family room. il Redbook 138:109-11+ N '71
  Master bedroom. il Redbook 138:88-91 Ja '72
New designs to tempt your talent. il House & Gard 139:78-9 F '71
New room: no furniture; cubes and platforms to replace furniture. il Time 97:60+ Ap 26 '71
On and off the avenue. J. Malcolm. New Yorker 46:96+ F 13 '71
100 ideas under $100. il Bet Hom & Gard 49:8+ Jl '71
Party makers. A. Walker. il Am Home 74:103-5 N '71
17 ways to recycle a room; new life for your bedroom. il Seventeen 30:138-41 S '71
Take-home decorating zest. il House & Gard 139:108-11 Ap '71
Wrap your house in summer inside and out. il House & Gard 139:64-5, 68-9, 72-3 Je '71
See also
Christmas gifts for the home
Color in house decoration
Electric lamps
HOUSEHOLD furnishings, Moving of. See Moving
HOUSEHOLD furnishings industry
Grand Rapids tries to copy Detroit; Debut '72 promotional blitz. il Bsns W p23 S 18 '71
HOUSEHOLD furnishings moving companies. See Moving and storage companies
HOUSEHOLD mechanics. See Mechanics, Household
HOUSEHOLD odors. See Odors
HOUSEHOLD records
Keep your records safe and handy. il Changing T 26:34-5 Ja '72
What everyone must know about family records. Good H 174:144 Ja '72
Which records should your family keep? F. Casey. il Mech Illus 68:46-7+ Ja '72
HOUSEHOLD waterproof gloves. See Gloves, Rubber
HOUSEKEEPERS
My most unforgettable character. C. Gaffron. Read Digest 98:105-9 F '71
HOUSEKEEPING. See Home economics
HOUSEMOTHERS
Pick the fraternity housemother. il Life 70:81-4 Ap 16 '71
HOUSER, George M.
Polaroid approach to South Africa. Chr Cent 88:249-52 F 24 '71
HOUSES
See also
Architecture, Domestic
Doll houses
Storage in the home
Summer homes

Air conditioning
See Air conditioning

Location
See Building sites

Maintenance and repair
Help about the house; questions and answers. See issues of American home
Homeowners' clinic; questions and answers, W. C. Lammey. See issues of Popular mechanics
6 easy home repairs. il Mech Illus 67:80-2 Ag '71

Prices
See Housing—Costs
HOUSES, Concrete. See Concrete houses
HOUSES, Foam plastic. See Plastic houses
HOUSES, Historic. See Historic houses, sites, etc.
HOUSES, Metal. See Metal houses
HOUSES, Paperboard. See Paperboard houses
HOUSES, Plastic. See Plastic houses
HOUSES, Prefabricated
Creative systems in housing; address, December 28, 1970. J. Stulman. Vital Speeches 37:241-5 F 1 '71
Factory-built homes are gaining, but—. il U S News 71:70-1 O 11 '71
Four levels for living in the treetops; M. Goldfinger house. il House & Gard 139:76-81 Je '71
Heart of the house; Service support module. M. K. Spencer. il Am Home 74:40+ My '71
Homes from the factory. il Mech Illus 67:112+ Mr '71
Houses from kits. il Mech Illus 67:108-9 D '71
Houses: the year of the big buy. il Time 97:75-6 Mr 29 '71
Instant (almost) vacation house; molded fiberglas house from Finland. N. Skurka. il N Y Times Mag p32 S 5 '71
Instant living cubes; modular housing. il McCalls 98:41 My '71
LTV subsidiary builds homes. il Aviation W 94:41 My 17 '71
Many moods of modular: American home's House of the year. B. Plumb. il pors Am Home 74:76+ O '71
Molded house you can buy in any color you want. il House & Gard 140:98-9 S '71
New house in a new town: great idea for a growing family. M. Kraft. il Good H 173:146-53+ N '71
Packaged house; house designed by W. Feierbach. il House B 113:29-33 Jl '71
Prefabs set pace in the housing boom. il U S News 70:74 Ap 26 '71
Quiet gamble on a steel house. il Bsns W p 108 F 27 '71
$20,000 prefab for a 3-bedroom family. B. Plumb. il Am Home 74:46-7+ Ag '71
See also
Mobile homes

Transportation
Modules look for a cheaper ride. il Bsns W p22-3 My 22 '71
HOUSES, Remodeled
Andrew Wyeth kind of house. N. Skurka. il N Y Times Mag p42-3 Jl 25 '71
At home in a barn: Bridgehampton. N. Skurka. il N Y Times Mag p90-1 N 7 '71
Barn mystique; 150-year-old dairy barn. N. Skurka. il N Y Times Mag p84-6 Ap 18 '71
Barn with a spirit all its own. S. G. Lewin. il House B 113:86-9 My '71
Basics of expanding any room. B. Duggan. il Mech Illus 67:115-17+ Ja '71
Buy an old house and fix it up? il Changing T 25:31-4 My '71
Cantilever: a good word for more living space. R. P. Stevenson. il Pop Sci 198:94-5 Ap '71
Country living from the 1790's. il Am Home 74:52-3 Jl '71
Debutante look for a depressed dowager: Ansley park, Atlanta. J. H. Ingersoll. il House B 113:78-85 My '71
Design students change a family's lifestyle. J. H. Ingersoll. il House B 113:68+ S '71
Exciting face-lifts:
  Double-decker wing. il House & Gard 139:114-15 My '71
  Inside lift for light. il House & Gard 139:118-19 My '71
  Skylit duplex out back. il House & Gard 139:116-17 My '71
Far cry from hay and horses; 19th-century barn/carriage house. il House B 113:90-1 My '71
Great barn reconstructed. il House & Gard 139:57+ Ja '71
Heckschers remodel. R. Reif. il N Y Times Mag p78-9 My 2 '71
Home improvement guide. il Am Home 74:47-8+ My '71

HOUSES, Remodeled—*Continued*
Homes: new and remodeled. M. Kraft. il por Good H 172:140-7+ Ap '71
How to make a major addition to your home. M. Pieronek. il Mech Illus 67:103-7 Ap '71
How to turn your attic into a movie theater T. Hook. il Mech Illus 67:90-2 Mr '71
Improve your home; symposium. il Pop Sci 198:90-110+ Ap '71
Living through a remodeling. Bet Hom & Gard 49:8 My '71
Living with antiques; Stewart Gregory's Connecticut barn. J. Lipman. il Antiques 99: 112-21 Ja '71
Make yours a better home. N. Seney and J. Pinkham. il Bet Hom & Gard 49:42-57 My '71
New pavers, new patio and deck, it's their fourth remodel. il Sunset 146:84-5 Ap '71
Old inn opened up the outdoors indoors. il House & Gard 139:56+ Ja '71
Old Texas farmhouse restored for a family of five. il House & Gard 140:68-71 Ag '71
On stuffing a mushroom; rearranging a house. N. S. Hazelton. Nat R 23:149 F 9 '71
Poetry of gentle color. N. Schram. il House B 113:90-3 S '71
Remodeled garage beside Long Island's waters. L. Grundy. il House B 113:70-4 F '71
Remodeling. M. Kraft. il Good H 172:110-18+ F '71
Remodeling a brownstone in Brooklyn. R. Kirsch. il House B 113:70 My '71
Remodeling: 8 ways to reduce costs and still get what you want. House B 113:48+ My '71
Remodeling '71. il Am Home 74:83-97 My '71
Rescuing a homestead from the wrath of time. E. McDonald. il House B 113:98-9 My '71
Room at the top; Philadelphia four-room house. L. Hammel. il N Y Times Mag p40-1 Ag 8 '71
Step by step an old tract house begins a more spacious new life. il Sunset 146:88-9 Mr '71
Take an old mill; 18th-century French mill. N. Skurka. il N Y Times Mag p68-9 Je 13 '71
Tuscan restoration. N. Skurka. il N Y Times Mag p80-1 N 28 '71
We added on and saved, so can you! R. F. Dempewolff. il Pop Mech 135:104-9+ My '71
We did it:
One room schoolhouse. K. Dickinson. il House B 113:56 S '71
1794 farmhouse. S. Peterson. il House B 113:58 S '71
Treasurehouse of fine old woodwork. B. Elliott. il House B 113:60 S '71
Windmill house rebuilt for family weekends; Newport Harbor, R.I. il House & Gard 140:72-5 Ag '71
Would you believe this was once a garage? H. Wicks. il Pop Mech 136:138-41+ S '71

Bibliography
Remodeling ideas by the book. House B 113: 62 S '71

HOUSES, Restored
Three young families put new life in historic houses. il House & Gard 140:52-9 Ag '71

HOUSES, Seashore. See Beach architecture

HOUSES, Steel. See Steel houses

HOUSES of heaven; story. See Loeser, K.

HOUSEWARES. See Household appliances

HOUSEWIVES
Being a housewife. D. Reuben. McCalls 99:55 D '71
Don't be ashamed to call yourself housewife! interview, ed. by J. C. G. Conniff. E. I. Agnew. il pors Todays Health 49: 20-3+ Jl '71
Housewives and the drug habit. C. D. Chambers and D. Schultz. il Ladies Home J 88:66+ D '71
See also
Home economics
Mothers

HOUSEWORK. See Home economics

HOUSING
Housing. il Arch Forum 134:21-51 My '71
See also
Aged—Housing
College students—Housing
Discrimination in housing
Slums

Costs
Homes for young couples who can't afford castles. A. M. Watkins. il Redbook 138: 86-7+ N '71

How builders, buyers, renters will fare under Phase 2; convention of the National association of real estate boards. il U S News 71:53-4 N 29 '71
Planning to buy a house? Word from mortgage bankers. il U S News 71:79-81 O 25 '71

Desegregation
As the blacks move in, the ethnics move out; Cleveland's East side. P. Wilkes. il por N Y Times Mag p9-11+ Ja 24 '71
Court breaks new social ground in housing policy; Philadelphia court decision. J. R. Hacala and J. M. Kakalec. America 124: 228-30 Mr 6 '71; Reply with rejoinder. G. Cavanaugh. 124:589-91 Je 5 '71
Government renews pressure for integrated suburbs. il U S News 70:47-8 Je 28 '71
Statement in black and white; President Nixon's position on housing integration. J. C. Rosapepe. Commonweal 94:421-2 Ag 20 '71

Anecdotes, facetiae, satire, etc.
Re: how segregation ended in the early seventies. C. F. Eyre. Nat R 23:1303-4 N 19 '71

Federal aid
Are big cities worth saving? interview. G. S. Sternlieb. il por U S News 71:42-6+ Jl 26 '71
Black humor of housing. R. Sherrill. Nation 212:397-402 Mr 29 '71
Court breaks new social ground in housing policy; Philadelphia court decision. J. R. Hacala and J. M. Kakalec. America 124: 228-30 Mr 6 '71
Home ownership for the poor? B. Frieden and J. Newman. il Trans-Action 7:47-53 O '70
Housing and the public sector. M. Harrington. Arch Forum 134:32-3 My '71; Reply with rejoinder. B. P. Hayden. 135:15 Jl '71
Housing: is Washington cooling off on federal aid? il U S News 70:47-8 Je 7 '71
Stroke of the pen; proposal for open low-cost housing. A. Simon. Commonweal 93: 391-5 Ja 22 '71
TRB from Washington; broken promises. New Repub 164:6 Mr 13 '71
US as slumlord. K. Hartnett. New Repub 165: 11-13 D 11 '71
What it will take to bring cities back to life; interview. D. Rockefeller. il por U S News 70:50-2+ Je 7 '71
Why so many mortgages are being foreclosed. il U S News 72:25-6 Ja 3 '72
Why Uncle Sam is pulling back his dollars from healthful housing programs for the poor. R. Sherrill. il Todays Health 49:16- 19+ Jl '71
See also
Housing projects, Government
New cities and towns—Federal aid

Finance
See Housing finance

Management
See Housing management

Social aspects
Why Uncle Sam is pulling back his dollars from healthful housing programs for the poor. R. Sherrill. il Todays Health 49:16- 19+ Jl '71

California
Surplus threatens California's market. il Bsns W p46-7 O 23 '71

Great Britain
Committee documents flagrant inequities in British rent acts. C. Holmes. Chr Cent 88: 885-6 Jl 21 '71

Singapore
Public housing and urban renewal. Y. M. Yeung. bibliog il Focus 21:9-12 Ap '71

United States
Another boom year for builders. il Bsns W p52-3 Ja 1 '72
Building snaps back with a bang. il Bsns W p34-5 Ap 10 '71
Building types study; with introd. by J. D. Morgan. il Arch Rec 150:123-38 O '71
Creative systems in housing; address, December 28, 1970. J. Stulman. Vital Speeches 37:241-5 F 1 '71
Housing: a boom that goes on and on. il U S News 71:51-2 N 15 '71
Housing boom starts off cautiously. il Bsns W p70+ F 6 '71
Housing gets closer to the ceiling. il Fortune 84:22 O '71

HOUSING—United States—*Continued*
Housing outlook: a turn, perhaps, to more house per house. il Fortune 83:20 Ap '71
New big boom in housing. il U S News 70:20-2 Mr 8 '71
Stroke of the pen; proposal for open low-cost housing. A. Simon. Commonweal 93: 391-5 Ja 22 '71
  See also
Construction industry
Housing—Federal aid
Housing, Rural
Housing finance
Housing projects, Government
Negroes—Housing
United States—Federal housing administration
United States—Housing and urban development, Department of
  also subhead Housing under names of cities, e.g. Chicago—Housing
HOUSING, Cooperative
  See also
Apartment houses—Cooperative ownership
HOUSING, Discrimination in. See Discrimination in housing
HOUSING, Prefabricated
Equipotential space, by R. Severino. Review Arch Forum 134:8+ Je '71. M. Brill
HOUSING, Rural
Scandal of rural housing. C. L. Cochran. Arch Forum 134:52-5 Mr '71
HOUSING and urban development, Department of. See United States—Housing and urban development, Department of
HOUSING finance
Housing's boom is alive and well. il Bsns W p61 S 4 '71
  See also
Federal national mortgage association
Housing—Federal aid
Mortgages
United States—Federal housing administration
HOUSING laws and legislation
  See also
Building laws and regulations
Rent laws
HOUSING management
Wanted: more professional managers. il U S News 71:40 Ag 2 '71
HOUSING projects
Building types study. il Arch Rec 149:115-38 Ap '71
C. Fraser's Sea Pines plantation, S.C. J. McPhee. New Yorker 47:42-8+ Mr 27 '71
Chicago, Ill; Woodlawn gardens. E. P. Berkeley. il Arch Forum 134:38-41 My '71
Leslie salt all but gives up; Redwood shores project. il Bsns W p22 N 27 '71
Navajos trade hogans for air-conditioning; Shiprock housing project. il Bsns W p 100+ O 23 '71
New York, N.Y; the East River project. il Arch Forum 134:42-5 My '71
Technology; Operation Breakthrough. M. Villecco. il Arch Forum 134:58-62 My '71
Tulsa, Okla; Center plaza. il Arch Forum 134: 28-31 My '71
  See also
Apartment houses

Relocation of tenants
Patients' views on relocation; reactions of psychiatric patients to urban renewal. P. Sifneos. Ment Hy 55:495-8 O '71

Site planning
Cluster houses. N. Seney. il Bet Hom & Gard 49:64-7 F '71
Islandia, Alameda, Calif. il Arch Rec 149:90-1 mid-My '71
Palmetto dunes golf villas, Hilton Head Island, S.C. il Arch Rec 149:96-8 mid-My '71
Pre-sited houses; Echo hill, Amherst, Mass. S. Mead. il Bet Hom & Gard 49:48-9 Je '71
Warren gardens inc, Roxbury, Mass. il Arch Rec 149:86-7 mid-My '71

Europe, Western
Levittown spreads across the Continent. Bsns W p52 N 6 '71
HOUSING projects, Government
Equal housing: Nixon defines his policy; excerpts from statement, June 11, 1971. R. M. Nixon. il U S News 70:72 Je 21 '71
FHA housing used to fleece poor; 235-program suspended. P. S. Templin. America 124:83 Ja 30 '71
Gauntlet for the poor; Supreme court decision. Nation 212:611 My 17 '71

Mr Secretary: please reconsider; letter to George Romney. T. M. Hesburgh. America 124:238-9 Mr 6 '71
Neighborhood veto: a ruling on housing; Supreme court decision. il U S News 70:38 My 10 '71
Shift in policy on housing? low-cost housing in the suburbs. il U S News 70:63 Ap 5 '71
Tragedy of Pruitt-Igoe; St Louis. il Time 98:38 D 27 '71
Urban development corporation housing for Utica, New York. il Arch Rec 150:110-11 Jl '71
Where the tenants have a say in the plans; Sursum corda development. il Bsns W p 132+ S 11 '71
  See also
National tenants organization
New York (state)—Urban development corporation
HOUSMAN, Alfred Edward
Poet's duty. B. Bendow. Nation 212:469-71 Ap 12 '71 *
HOUSTON, Douglas B.
Ecosystems of national parks. bibliog Science 172:648-51 My 14 '71
HOUSTON, Penelope
(ed) See Kubrick, S. Kubrick country
HOUSTON, Sam, pseud.
Oil slick on the Potomac. Commonweal 93: 436-8 F 5 '71
HOUSTON, Walter Scott
Deep-sky wonders. See issues of Sky and telescope
HOUSTON, Tex.
New no. 1 city in the southwest. il Bsns W p82-4+ Je 12 '71

Air pollution
Ill wind in Houston. Newsweek 78:78 Jl 26 '71

Airports
Driverless automated trains improve air passenger mobility. il Am City 86:109-10 Ap '71

Banks
Founder; Sharpstown state bank failure. il por Time 97:18+ F 15 '71
Widening impact of a Texas scandal; closing of Sharpstown state bank. por Bsns W p22 Ja 30 '71

Chapels
Art and faith in Houston; Rothko chapel. il por Newsweek 77:63 Mr 15 '71
Art; Rothko paintings in chapel at Texas medical center. L. Alloway. Nation 212:349-50 Mr 15 '71
Can art be used? Dedication of Rothko chapel. T. B. Hess. Art N 70:33 Ap '71
Celebration of genius at the Rothko chapel. il Vogue 157:109-11 Mr 1 '71
Maximum of poignancy; Rothko chapel. K. Kuh. por Sat R 54:52+ Ap 17 '71
Rothko memorial chapel for universal celebration. T. W. Moore. il Chr Cent 88:435-6 Ap 7 '71

Description
Businessman's guide to Houston. Bsns W p75 My 22 '71
Houston '71: Congress city. R. Estes. il Parks & Rec 6:32-4+ Jl '71
Y'all come; Houston '71. R. Estes. il Parks & Rec 6:36-7+ Je '71

Economic conditions
Houston is where they're moving. C. G. Burck. il Fortune 83:91-7 F '71

Education, Board of
Turnabout in Houston? pors Newsweek 78: 62 S 13 '71

Music
At the corner of Glory avenue and Hallelujah street; concert of white gospel music at Jones Hall. W. C. Martin. Harper 244: 95-9 Ja '72
  See also
Houston grand opera association

Politics and government
Houston: the terrorists. il Newsweek 77:54+ My 3 '71

Recreation
Fenceless pool in congress city. W. G. Sheibe. il Parks & Rec 6:32 Mr '71

Sanitary affairs
City-county drainage plans come first. L. Welch. il Am City 86:70+ Ag '71
HOUSTON Astros (baseball) See Baseball clubs

HOUSTON grand opera association
Report:
Aida. A. Holmes. il Opera N 35:30 Mr 27 '71
Carl Orff's Moon (Maria Pelikan's English version) and Pagliacci. A. Holmes. il Opera N 35:32 F 20 '71
Carmen. A. Holmes. Opera N 36:38 D 25 '71

HOUT, Albert P.
Little human happiness; excerpt from The lion. por Read Digest 99:121-2 O '71

HOVERCRAFT. See Air cushion vehicles

HOVING, Thomas Pearsall Field
Ivory tower versus the discotheque. G. Glueck. il pors Art in Am 59:80-5 My '71 *

HOW, Mrs G. E. P.
Robert Sanderson in England. il Antiques 99: 718-19 My '71

HOW are you? Don't tell me; story. See Smith, L.

HOW mothers came to be; drama. See Boiko, C.

HOW my father was murdered; story. See Oates, J. C.

HOW the other half loves; drama. See Ayckbourn, A.

HOW to win as a teen-age daughter; story. See Feydy, A.

HOWAR, Barbara
For adults only. il por Newsweek 77:93 Ap 12 '71 *
What the F.B.I. has on me. por Esquire 76:138-9+ D '71 *

HOWARD, Alvin W. See Howard, J. R. jt. auth

HOWARD, Anthony
[Report from Britain] (title varies) (cont) New Repub 164:8-9 Je 5; 165:8-9 Jl 10; 10-11 O 23; 13-14 N 13 '71

HOWARD, Dick
Confession was within the logic of Stalinism. Commonweal 93:550+ Mr 5 '71

HOWARD, Sir Ebenezer
Sir Ebenezer Howard and the town planning movement, by D. MacFadyen. Review
New Repub 164:30-1 My 22 '71. C. Whitman *

HOWARD, Edward N.
Toward PPBS in the public library. bibliog il Am Lib 2:386-93 Ap '71

HOWARD, Frances Minturn
Owl in science museum; Signals; Antelope, royal gardens, Athens; poems. Poetry 118: 321-2 S '71

HOWARD, Harry N.
Jordan in turmoil. bibliog f Cur Hist 62:14-19+ Ja '72

HOWARD, Helen L.
Nurnberg stove; dramatization of story by L. De La Ramée. Plays 31:35-43 D '71

HOWARD, Jack
Into China with ball and paddle. il por Newsweek 77:18-19 Ap 26 '71

HOWARD, Jane
Earth mother to the foodists. il pors Life 71: 67-8+ O 22 '71
Family business is wrecked by the poison. il pors Life 71:28-9 S 10 '71
Groovy Christians of Rye, N.Y. il Life 70:78-82+ My 14 '71
Herman Wouk surfaces again. il pors Life 71:53-4+ N 26 '71
Is Women's lib a dirty word in Milwaukee? il Life 71:46-51 Ag 27 '71
Parting shots: the diary of a polluter. Life 70:71-2 Ap 23 '71
Quiet, please! Please. il Life 71:75-6+ D 3 '71

HOWARD, John Addison
Any future for private colleges? interview. il por U S News 71:43-6 S 6 '71
Detoxifying the liberal arts; address, September 8, 1971. Vital Speeches 38:27-31 O 15 '71

HOWARD, John P.
How to solve the police crisis; interview. ed. by G. M. Chamberlain. pors Am City 86: 94-5+ S; 88+ O;106-8 N '71

HOWARD, John R. and Howard, A. W.
Mail-order Ph.D.'s. Ed Digest 37:32-3 S '71

HOWARD, Lore
Better look at budgets. il Library J 96:1081-2 Mr 15 '71

HOWARD, Pamela
Ms and the journalism of Women's lib. il Sat R 55:43-5+ Ja 8 '72

HOWARD, Richard
Beginning, a middle, and an ode to terminus. Poetry 119:34-9 O '71
Natural death; poem. Craft Horiz 31:31-8 O '71
Presenting a watch; poem. New Yorker 46: 28 Ja 30 '71

HOWARD, Steven J.
How to choose and use fire extinguishers. il Pop Mech 135:116-19 Je '71

HOWARD, Thomas
On evil in art. Chr Today 16:4-5 D 17 '71

HOWARD-JONES, Norman
Origins of hypodermic medication; with biographical sketch. il por Sci Am 224:13, 96-102 bibliog(p 122) Ja '71

HOWARD COUNTY, Md.

Education
Our middle schools give the kids a break. J. Di Virgilio. il Todays Ed 60:30-2 Ja '71

HOWARD university, Washington, D.C.
Metamorphosis of Howard university. A. Poinsett. il Ebony 27:110-12+ D '71

Library
William Dean Cunningham, university librarian. il pors Wilson Lib Bul 46:236-7 N '71

HOWARTH, Herbert
Discords in the music of time. Commentary 53:70-5 Ja '72

HOWATCH, Susan
Penmarric; condensation of novel. McCalls 98:121-32 My; 123-30 Je '71
Road to a best seller. Writer 84:11-12 D '71

HOWE, Darrell
Wheeling off to bed. il Life 70:64-6 Ap 30 '71 *

HOWE, Fanny
Ireland revisited. Atlan 227:113-16 F '71

about
Comment. F. MacShane. Poetry 118:299-300 Ag '71 *

HOWE, Florence
Sexual stereotypes start early; excerpt from address. il Sat R 54:76-7+ O 16 '71

HOWE, Gordon
Durable hero. il por Newsweek 78:59 S 20 '71 *

HOWE, Harold, 2d
Anatomy of a revolution. il Sat R 54:84-8+ N 20 '71

HOWE, Irving
Ballet for the man who enjoys Wallace Stevens. Harper 242:102-6+ My '71
Books. See occasional issues of Harper's magazine
City in literature. Commentary 51:61-8 My '71
Journey of a poet. Commentary 53:75-7 Ja '72
Literary criticism and literary radicals. Am Scholar 41:113-20 Wint '71

HOWE, John E.
Record snowstorms and problems of snow measurement on Mount Washington. il Weatherwise 23:280-2 D '70

HOWE, Leland W.
Team-it: an instructional strategy. Clear House 45:444-6 Mr '71

HOWELL, Barbara
Indonesia's Suharto seeks vote of confidence in July 3 parliamentary election. Chr Cent 88:802-3 Je 30 '71

HOWELL, Leon
Little error that grew. Cur 131:63-4 Jl '71
Relief to East Pakistan: a political dilemma. il Chr Cent 88:1135-7 S 29 '71
Will of the people in Pakistan: is Eastern independence the answer? Chr Cent 88:595-9 My 12 '71

HOWELL, Thomas R.
What a place to lay an egg! il Nat Geog 140:414-19 S '71

HOWELLS, William Dean
William Dean Howells, by K. S. Lynn. Review
Harper 242:94-8 Je '71. J. Thompson *
New Repub 165:23-6 Jl 3 '71. J. Seelye *
Sat R il por 54:24 Ag 21 '71. L. Edel *

HOWES, Barbara
Returning to Store Bay; poem. Am Scholar 40:642 Aut '71

HOWES, Helen Claire
In Denmark the future holds promise. il Har Yrs 11:36-8 My '71
Most costly dinner service. il Design 72:14-15 mid-Wint '71

HOWES, Robert G.
Neon noise; poem. Cath World 212:258 F '71
Our thing: some further reflections on space ship earth. Cath World 213:169-73 Jl '71
Space ship earth! poem. Cath World 213:193 Jl '71

HOWLAND, Carol
Charming charter on the Thames. il Motor B & S 128:60-1+ Jl '71

HOWLAND, Joseph E.
Sod creates instant park. il Parks & Rec 6:27+ N '71
HOWLAND, William S.
Unforgettable Ralph McGill. por Read Digest 99:63-7 Ag '71
HOWLETT, Duncan
Forestry school at age 65. il por Am For 77: 14-17+ Ag '71
HOWLING, Frieda O.
Creativity with textile paint. il Sch Arts 70:18-19 Mr '71
HOWORTH, Beckett
Climate and environment, what they mean to you. il Consumer Bul 54:14-17 N '71
HOYEM, Andrew
Circumambulation of Mt Tamalpais; Of a ruined Roman sculpture; While in waiting; Up in the air; Filtres; 512 cubic furlongs; poems. Poetry 117:289-95 F '71
HOYER, Linda Grace
Arabian beauty; story; excerpt from Enchantment. McCalls 98:56 F '71

about
Authors & editors. B. A. Bannon. por Pub W 199:31-2 F 1 '71 *
HOYT, Hayes Blake
Pet news. Ladies Home J 88:62+ Jl '71
HOYT, J. W.
Pink urchin of the deep sea; with biographical sketch. il por Sea Front 17:140-5, 191 My '71
HOYT, Robert G.
Baffled bishops. il Harper 243:76-81 O '71

about
Catholic editor fired. J. S. Tinney. Chr Today 15:35-6 Je 4 '71 *
Hoyt on bishops. J. Deedy. Commonweal 95:26 O 8 '71 *
HRUZA, Karel
Tormenter in Prague. America 124:528 My 22 '71 *
HSU, Francis, bp
Hong Kong Catholics. Commonweal 94:23 Mr 12 '71
HSU, Tao-chiuh
Dr Hsu's frozen zoo. Time 98:57 D 6 '71 *
HSU, Yu-chih
Bridging a gap. por Sci N 99:278 Ap 24 '71 *
HU, James Wei
Activity change as the cause of apparent aversiveness during prolonged hypothalamic stimulation. bibliog il Science 172:84-5 Ap 2 '71
HU, Shih
Hu Shih and the Chinese renaissance, by J. B. Grieder. Review
Chr Cent 88:912-13 Jl 28 '71. A. C. Yu *
HUANG, Hua
Chinese ambassador. il por Newsweek 78: 15 Ag 2 '71 *
Mao's new America watcher. por Time 97:27 Je 21 '71
New face from China. il pors Life 71:38-9 N 19 '71 *
Now red China has a watchtower over U.S. il pors U S News 71:67-9 S 13 '71 *
Sudden celebrities. il por Time 98:43 O 18 '71 *
HUANG-ti, emperor of China. See Ch'in Shih-huang-ti
HUAYLAS, Callejón de
From disaster to development. P. L. Doughty. il Américas 23:25-35 My '71
HUBBARD, Alfred H.
Who is Al Hubbard? W. Overend. Nat R 23: 589+ Je 1 '71 *
HUBBARD, David Graham
Bringing skyjackers down to earth. Time 98: 64-5 O 4 '71 *
HUBBARD, Elbert
Commune in East Aurora. R. L. Beisner. il pors Am Heritage 22:72-7+ F '71 *
HUBBARD, Jake T.
Americans as guerrilla fighters: Robert Rogers and his rangers. il por Am Heritage 22:81-6 Ag '71
HUBBARD, William B. See Evans, D. S. jt. auth.
HUBBELL, John G.
Hockey time, and the kids go crazy. il Read Digest 99:67-70+ D '71
HUBBERT, Marion King
Energy resources of the earth; with biographical sketch. il Sci Am 225:25, 60-70 bibliog(p244) S '71
HUBER, Gary
Bucking the system. J. Morgenstern. il pors Newsweek 79:65 Ja 10 '72 *
HUBER, Joe
Married students vs. married dropouts. Ed Digest 36:42-3 Ja '71

HUBER, Paul, 1910-1971
Obituary
Phys Today por 24:71-2 Je '71. W. Haeberli
HUBSCHMAN, Jerry H.
Lake Erie: pollution abatement, then what? bibliog il Science 171:536-40 F 12 '71
HUCKLEBERRIES
Huckleberries, anyone? J. R. Coggins. il Org Gard & Farm 18:64-5 F '71
HUCKLEBERRY Finn; drama. See DuBois, G.
HUCKLEBERRY Finn; opera. See Overton, H.
HUDAK, Joseph
Autumn color from bulbs. il Horticulture 49: 38+ Ag '71
Garden designed to be given away. il House B 113:44-5 O '71
HUDDLE, John
Interrogation of prisoner Bung by Mister Hawkins and Sergeant Tree; story. Esquire 75:128-9 Ja '71
HUDGINS, H. C. Jr
Locker searches and the law. Todays Ed 60:30-2 N '71
HUDNALL, Margaret S.
Dearest Meg. Good H 174:12 Ja '72
HUDSON, Deanna
Guinea pigs and goals. Library J 96:2456-7 Ag '71
HUDSON, John
Put away the putter and go for the pin. H. McIlvanney. il por Sports Illus 34:16-17 Je 28 '71 *
HUDSON, Lou
He's a Lou-Lou! H. L. Masin. il por Sr Schol 98:20 Mr 22 '71 *
HUDSON, Peggy
Television. See issues of Senior scholastic
HUDSON, Roy L.
Strybing arboretum and botanical garden. il Horticulture 49:36-7+ Je '71
HUDSON RIVER
Hudson River lives. R. H. Boyle. il Audubon 73:14-17+ Mr '71
Law that could clean up our rivers. J. N. Miller. Read Digest 98:31-2+ My '71
My dirty stream; words and music. P. Seeger. Audubon 73:85-6 Mr '71
Sea chanties & marlinspikes; life aboard the ecology-inspired Clearwater. D. Kasanof. il Motor B & S 127:88-9+ Mr '71
Upper Hudson: whitewater or washwater? L. Pringle. il Audubon 73:88+ Mr '71
Winter on the Hudson. R. R. Glunt. il Cons 26:18-19 D '71

Photographs
Hudson, a journey from wilderness whitewater to megalopolis murk. R. Perron. Audubon 73:25-40 Mr '71
HUDSON RIVER day lines
All ashore: final trip for Alexander Hamilton, last of the Hudson River sidewheelers. il Am Heritage 23:109 D '71
Postcards from the Hudson; farewell to the Alexander Hamilton. A. Hiss. il New Yorker 47:54-65 N 13 '71
HUDSON RIVER expressway (proposed) See Express highways—New York (state)
HUDSON RIVER school. See Painting, American
HUDSON RIVER sloops. See Sloops
HUDSON RIVER VALLEY
Irving and the misty valley. C. Carmer. il Sat R 54:41+ Mr 13 '71
HUDSON'S BAY company

Anecdotes, facetiae, satire, etc.
Dissertation on the beaver; excerpts from The great fur opera. K. Dobbs. il Natur Hist 80:8+ Je '71
HUEBENER, Theodore
History as taught through East German textbooks. Sch & Soc 99:56-9 Ja '71
HUEBNER, David
Cardboard supports for clay structures. il Ceram Mo 19:14-16 D '71
HUEBNER, Robert Joseph
C particle: a unified theory of cancer. L. Edson. il por N Y Times Mag p28-9+ Mr 7 '71 *
HUEHN, Arnold H.
Shrubbery light you can make for $3. il Pop Mech 136:180 O '71
HUERTAS, F. See Linares, J. jt. auth.
HUFF, Betty Tracy
Last of the Ghastleys; drama. Plays 30:1-12 F '71
Tessie, the tea bag maker; drama. Plays 30: 13-24, 58 My '71

HUFF, Darrell
European camping, a big travel bargain. il Pop Sci 198:76-8+ My '71
How to install a skylight. il Pop Sci 198:130 Ap '71
Two-faced couch is a real sleeper. il Pop Sci 199:106 S '71

HUFF, William H. and Brown, N. B.
Price indexes for 1971; Serials services. il Library J 96:2274-5 Jl '71

HUFFMAN, Diane
Unscheduled voyage. il Yachting 130:55+ Ag '71

HUFFNAGLE, Norman P.
El panel driver. il Pop Electr 34:43-8 My '71

HUFFSTUTLER, S. A.
Sound of trumpets; story. Har Yrs 11:26-9 O '71

HUGDAHL, Norma
Norwegian craft revitalized. J. H. Hood. il por Design 72:40-1 mid-Sum '71 •

HUGGINS, Ericka
Black Panther thrust in American revolution. R. Chrisman. il Sat R 54:35-8 Jl 24 '71 •
Freed in New Haven. pors Time 97:12-13 Je 7 '71 •
Trials of the system. por Newsweek 77:27-8 Je 7 '71 •

HUGHES, Carroll J.
Financial aid for the small city. Am City 86:136+ S '71

HUGHES, Catharine R.
Broadway and the British. il Cath World 212:313-15 Mr '71
Decline and fall of the Broadway musical. America 124:124-5 F 6 '71
Growing up as Greene. il por America 125:230-2 O 2 '71
Ibsen? Yes, Ibsen. America 124:318-19 Mr 27 '71
Is there an audience in the house? America 124:151-3 F 13 '71
Theatre. See issues of America

HUGHES, Chuck
What killed Chuck Hughes. Newsweek 78:74 N 8 '71 •

HUGHES, Clarence
Underground newspaper, what's it all about? bibliog Clear House 46:155-7 N '71
—See McGreal, T. L. jt. auth.

HUGHES, Edward
Hussein: monarch in the middle. il por Read Digest 98:175-6+ Mr '71
On the holy road to Mecca. il Read Digest 99:27-8+ O '71

HUGHES, Eileen Lanouette
Fight for baby Lenore. il pors Ladies Home J 88:58+ S '71

HUGHES, Emmet John
Politics of the sixties: from the new frontier to the new revolution. il N Y Times Mag p24-5+ Ap 4; 12+ Ap 25 '71

HUGHES, Glyn
Comment. J. Martin. Poetry 118:344-5 S '71 •

HUGHES, Harold Everett
Hard drugs in the military. New Repub 164:17-18 Je 12 '71

about
Enter Harris, exit Hughes. il por Newsweek 78:28 Jl 26 '71 •
First casualty. por Time 98:20-1 Jl 26 '71 •
For God and country: the presidential candidacy of Harold Hughes. P. R. Wieck. New Repub 164:19-24 My 15 '71 •
Hughes withdraws. New Repub 165:11 Jl 24 '71 •
One for O'Brien. New Repub 165:9-10 O 23 '71 •

HUGHES, Herman S.
Yukio Mishima: genius or madman? il America 125:262-4 O 9 '71

HUGHES, Howard Robard
All the Hughes that's fit to print. W. Turner. Esquire 76:64-7+ Jl '71 •
Cable TV: turn on, tune in, rip off. F. Browning. il Ramp Mag 9:32-8 Ap '71 •
High rollers shoot for power in Las Vegas. T. O'Hanlon. il por Fortune 83:36-7 Ja '71 •
Letters from the invisible billionaire, with sincere regards, Howard Hughes; with editorial comment, and handwriting analysis by A. Kanfer. il por Life 70:2A, 24-8 Ja 22 '71 •
Life without Hughes. K. Fleming. Newsweek 78:88+ N 8 '71 •
Waiting for Hughes. Newsweek 78:92+ S 13 '71 •
What happened to Howard Hughes. B. F. Schemmer. il por Look 35:21-5 Je 1 '71 •

HUGHES, Jean Peters. See Peters, J.

HUGHES, John
Out of the cloister. il por Newsweek 78:51 Ag 23 '71 •

HUGHES, John Henry
Schenley chapter. H. Messick. il Nation 212:428-31 Ap 5 '71 •

HUGHES, John Jay
On eating our cake and having it too. Cath World 213:83-6 My '71

HUGHES, John W.
Humanism and the Orphic voice. il por Sat R 54:31-3 My 22 '71

HUGHES, Laura
We're losing our sense of humor. por Seventeen 29:216 O '70

HUGHES, Mabel W.
Obituary
PTA Mag por 65:17 F '71

HUGHES, Mary Gray
Judge; story. Atlan 228:74-6+ N '71

HUGHES, Robert
Anatomy of a minotaur. il pors Time 98:68-78 N 1 '71
Letter from the publisher. il por Time 98:11 N 1 '71 •

HUGHES, T.
Convection in the Antarctic ice sheet leading to a surge of the ice sheet and possibly to a new ice age. bibliog il Science 170:630-3; 173:166 N 6 '70, Jl 9 '71

HUGHES, Ted
Crow paints himself into a Chinese mural; poem. New Yorker 46:38 Ja 23 '71

about
Crow, by T. Hughes. Review
Commonweal 94:483-4 S 17 '71. B. Wallenstein •
Inner world where poets wander. J. Kessler. Sat R 54:39+ O 2 '71 •
Tree and the bird. J. Kroll. pors Newsweek 77:114-114A Ap 12 '71 •

HUGHES aircraft company
Aerospace technology infusion aids apparel industry operations; laser cutter. il Aviation W 94:48-9 Mr 29 '71

HUGHES tool company
High rollers shoot for power in Las Vegas. T. O'Hanlon. il por Fortune 83:36-7 Ja '71
Silver boom that frizzled; Hughes rush to buy Nevada mines. il Bsns W p42 O 16 '71

HUGO, Richard F.
Comment. R. Howard. Poetry 119:35-6 O '71 •

HUGUNIN, Mary
Ears and hearing. Todays Ed 60:51-2 F '71

HUINKER, Dave
Selection pointers from a pro. il Suc Farm 69:H2-3 O '71

HULAN, Richard H.
Music in Tennessee. il Antiques 100:418-19 S '71
Tennessee textiles. il Antiques 100:386-9 S '71

HULL, Cordell
Exhibit of Cordell Hull manuscripts at Library of Congress. K. V. Hostick. Hobbies 76:151+ D '71 •

HULL, Jerome Webster
Public concerns of private enterprise; address, February 3, 1971. Vital Speeches 37:367-70 Ap 1 '71

HULL, Raymond
How to promote your book on radio and TV interviews. il Writers Digest 51:28-30+ Ag '71

HULLS (naval architecture)
Concrete hull is not a boat. R. Koci. Motor B & S 127:54+ F '71
New breed of offshore fishermen; new stable center-console designs. G. W. Reiger. il Pop Mech 135:104-7 Mr '71
Seaworthy Seamaster. G. W. Reiger. il Pop Mech 136:96-9 Jl '71
Speedboat for rough seas; Sea Knife, with supercritical hull. il Bsns W p64 O 16 '71
Surfing or seakindliness? F. Bilek. il Yachting 130:64-5+ Jl '71
Truth about hull design; interviews with four designers. ed. by E. H. Arctander. pors Pop Sci 198:81-3+ F '71

HULM, John K. and others
Superconducting magnets. bibliog il Phys Today 24:48-53+ Ag '71

HULSEY, Ralph
Wheeled refuse containers please every one. il Am City 86:113 S '71

HUMAN behavior. See Behavior (psychology)

HUMAN beings. See Man

HUMAN body. See Body, Human

HUMAN chorionic somatomammotropin. See Hormones

HUMAN development month. See Special days, weeks, and months

HUMAN environment, United Nations conference on the. See United Nations conference on the human environment

HUMAN events (newspaper)
Right way. Newsweek 78:75 S 6 '71
HUMAN fertility. See Fertility, Human
HUMAN figure in art
Sculpture of Bruno Lucchesi. M. Malmstrom.
il por Am Artist 35:32-4+ O '71
See also
Figure drawing
Hands in art
Human figure in photography
Nude in art
Women in art
HUMAN figure in photography
Figure in motion. W. G. Larson. il Mod Phot
35:78-81 Ap '71
Nude as nature; D. Ornitz. J. Scully. il Mod
Phot 34:76-9 N '70
HUMAN genetics
Anxiety about genetic engineering. P. H.
Abelson. Science 173:285 Jl 23 '71
Body: from baby hatcheries to Xeroxing
human beings. il Time 97:37-8+ Ap 19 '71
Gene therapy: another possibility; polyoma
pseudovirion system. Sci N 100:291 O 30 '71
Genetic control of man. A. J. Snider. Sci
Digest 69:56 Ap '71
Genetic engineering. J. J. Nagle. il Bul Atom
Sci 27:43-5 D '71
Genetic engineering: myth or reality? J. L.
Arehart. il Sci N 100:152-3 Ag 28 '71
Genetics: a friendly virus. il Newsweek 78:
109 O 25 '71
Mapping of human chromosomes. V. A. Mc-
Kusick. il Sci Am 224:104-13 Ap '71
Mini-people, inc? H. Manchester. Sat R 54:6+
O 16 '71
Reservations concerning gene therapy. M. S.
Fox and J. W. Littlefield. Science 173:195
Jl 16 '71
Transfer of bacterial genes to human cells.
Sci N 100:276 O 23 '71
Transplanting a gene. il Time 98:59 O 25 '71
See also
Genetic counseling
Heredity of disease
Population genetics
HUMAN growth hormone. See Pituitary hor-
mones
HUMAN information processing
Control of short-term memory. R. C. Atkin-
son and R. M. Shiffrin. il Sci Am 225:82-90
bibliog(p 120) Ag '71
Decision and stress, by D. E. Broadbent.
Review
Science 174:683-4 N 12 '71. R. W. Pew
HUMAN milk. See Milk, Human
HUMAN race. See Man
HUMAN relations
After the fall: what this country needs is
a good counter counterculture culture. D.
French. il N Y Times Mag p20-1+ O 3
'71; Discussion. p26 O 24; 98 N 7; 22+ N
21 '71
Love project. A. Lorrance. il Todays Ed 60:
60-2 S '71
See everything, do everything, feel nothing.
N. Cousins. Sat R 54:31 Ja 23 '71
Tools of our tools; dehumanization of Ameri-
can life; address, August 14, 1971. J. H.
Adamson. Vital Speeches 37:720-3 S 15 '71
See also
Bores (persons)
Brotherhood of man
Friendship
Group relations training
Helping behavior
Loneliness
Love
Marriage
Personal space
Popularity
Prejudice
Race relations
Sex relations
Social exchange
Youth-adult relationship
HUMAN relations day (proposed)
Human relations day. Negro Hist Bul 33:170 N
'70
HUMAN resources school, Albertson, N.Y. See
Special classes and special schools
HUMAN rights. See Civil rights
HUMAN rights, Universal declaration of. See
Universal declaration of human rights
HUMAN rights commission of the United
Nations. See United Nations—Commission
on human rights
HUMAN rights day and week
Bill of rights day, Human rights day; proc-
lamation. R. M. Nixon. Dept State Bul 63:
774 D 28 '70
Human rights day, 10 December 1970; text of
messages. E. Hambro; Thant. UN Mo Chron
7:1-11 D '70

HUMAN sacrifice. See Sacrifice, Human
HUMAN sweat. See Perspiration
HUMANAE vitae. See Encyclicals
HUMANISM
Humanists. V. Cronin. il Horizon 13:80-103
Wint '71
HUMANISTIC education. See Liberal education
HUMANISTIC psychology. See Psychology
HUMANISTIC studies, Aspen institute for. See
Aspen institute for humanistic studies
HUMANITIES
See also
Liberal education
Science and the humanities
Study and teaching
Adventures in the multi-disciplinary world
of the arts and humanities. N. C. Polos. il
Sch Arts 71:34-5 S '71
Creativity in the humanities class; program
at Booker T. Washington high school, At-
lanta. J. H. Whatley. il Todays Ed 60:10-
12+ D '71
Humanities in the library: the role of the
National endowment for the humanities;
symposium, ed. by R. G. Swartz. il por
Wilson Lib Bul 46:426-45 Ja '72
Humanities teaching and the mankind em-
phasis. M. H. Goldberg. Sch & Soc 99:176-8
Mr '71
Aids and devices
Multi-media approach to humanities. N.
Montemuro. Engl J 60:1228-30 D '71
HUMANITIES and science. See Science and
the humanities
HUMBARD, Rex
Edifice rex: grubstaking the Gospel. por Chr
Today 16:42-3 O 8 '71 *
Electronic evangelist. il por Time 97:70+ My
17 '71 *
HUMBLE oil and refining company
Striking it big, the unorthodox way. T. D.
Barrow. il pors Nations Bsns 59:68-9 Ja '71
HUMBOLDT, Tenn.
There'll be no jail for Jesse Ford, except
the prison of his mind. L. L. King. il pors
Todays Health 49:28-33+ D '71
HUMBOLDT national forest. See National
forests
HUME, James B.
Wells, Fargo's Jekyll and Hyde. R. H. Dillon.
il por Am West 8:28-33+ Mr '71
HUME family
Hume coat-of-arms. H. K. Eilers. il Hobbies
76:146-7+ Ap '71
HUMES, Barbara. See Humes, Bill, jt. auth.
HUMES, Bill, and Humes, Barbara
Lamb, the meat deluxe. Org Gard & Farm
18:102-4 Ag '71
HUMES, Harry
Spring horses; poem. Nation 213:700 D 27 '71
HUMIDIFIERS
Happiness is a humidified home. F. K.
Coffee. il Mech Illus 67:118-19+ Ja '71
Room humidifiers. il Consumer Rep 36:106-12
F '71
HUMIDITY
See also
Plants, Effect of humidity on
HUMILITY
Humility, anybody? V. P. McCorry. America
125:104-inside back cover Ag 21 '71
HUMMEL, Charles F.
Queen Anne and Chippendale furniture in
the Henry Francis du Pont Winterthur mu-
seum (cont) il Antiques 99:98-107 Ja '71
HUMMERSTONE, Robert G.
President's other friend. il pors Life 70:55-
6+ Mr 5 '71
HUMMING
Anecdotes, facetiae, satire, etc.
Hummmming. G. Ace. Sat R 54:6 Ag 14 '71
HUMMINGBIRDS
Hummingbirds. L. Schroeder. il Horticulture
49:28-9+ S '71
Time, energy, and territoriality of the anna
hummingbird (calypte anna) F. G. Stiles.
bibliog il Science 173:818-21 Ag 27 '71
HUMOR
Advice to the laughlorn. G. Ace. Sat R 54:10
Ja 23 '71
Heard any new (old) jokes lately? D. Car-
linsky. il Seventeen 30:114-15 O '71
Markets for gagmen. J. Markow. Writers
Digest 51:38-41 Ag '71
Sense in humor; excerpt from Laughter and
liberation. H. Mindess. Sat R 54:10-12 Ag
21 '71

HUMOR—*Continued*
We're losing our sense of humor. L. Hughes.
  por Seventeen 29:216 O '70
  See also
Comedy
Laughter
Phonograph records—Humorous records
Puns and punning
Radio broadcasting—Humor
  also subhead Anecdotes, facetiae, satire,
  etc. under various subjects, e.g. Children
  —Anecdotes, facetiae, satire, etc.

HUMOR, American
Mark Twain and journalistic humor today;
  address, November 1970. J. B. McCullough.
  Engl J 60:591-5 My '71

HUMOR, Pictorial
Gallery: subtle humor in Paris by R. Dois-
  neau. il Life 71:8-9 N 5 '71
  See also
Caricatures and cartoons
Comics (books, strips, etc)

HUMORISTS

Anecdotes, facetiae, satire, etc.
Spiro and the Buchwald blues. W. O'Toole.
  Commonweal 93:465 F 12 '71

HUMPBACK whales. See Whales

HUMPERDINCK, Engelbert
Hansel and Gretel. Criticism
  New Yorker 47:60 Ja 1 '72 *
  Opera N il 36:15-18 D 25 '71 *
  Opera N il 36:19-22 D 25 '71 *

HUMPHREY, Cliff
Garbage power! M. M. McGlynn. il por Look
  35:26-30 My 4 '71 *

HUMPHREY, Hubert Horatio, 1911-
American future: what kind of a society do
  we want? il America 125:476-9 D 4 '71
Peace of mind. por Look 35:29-30 Jl 27 '71
What my students taught me; ed. by J. C.
  G. Conniff. il por Todays Health 49:20-3+
  Ag '71
Will the appeal still be there? interview.
  por Nations Bsns 59:64-5 N '71

about
HHH: walking a political tightrope. por Newsweek 78:23 D 6 '71 *
Humphrey sets sail. New Repub 164:7-8 Je 12
  '71 *
No. 1 and no. 2 for the Democrats. il pors
  Time 99:16-17 Ja 17 '72 *
Odyssey of Hubert Humphrey. por Time 98:
  18-19 D 6 '71 *
Old faithful. il por Newsweek 77:20-1 Ap 5
  '71 *
20-20 hindsight; Vietnamese war stance; with
  excerpts from address to Georgetown university undergraduates. New Repub 164:8-9
  Ap 17 '71*

HUMPHREY, Richard
CB and the coast guard. il Pop Electr 35:42-
  4 S '71
Communications scene. Pop Electr 1:52-3 Ja
  '72
Mystery of the musical motor. Motor B & S
  128:69+ S '71
Portable radar becomes a reality. il Pop
  Electr 35:67-8+ Jl '71

HUMPHREYS, Lloyd Girton
NSF aide resigns over budget. Sci N 100:186
  S 18 '71 *
NSF official resigns protesting science educa-
  tion cuts. N. Wade. por Science 173:1109 S
  17 '71 *

HUMPHREYS, Tom. See Emerson, C. P. jr.
  jt. auth.

HUMPHRIES, Rolfe
Comment. J. T. Irwin. Poetry 118:351 S '71 *

HUMPSTONE, Charles Cheney
Pollution: precedent and prospect. For Affairs
  50:325-38 Ja '72

HUMUS
Keeping the earth in good health. W. B.
  Harris. House & Gard 139:40+ Je '71
Leaf plug sparks tree growth. M. Roach. Org
  Gard & Farm 18:43 O '71

HUNCHES. See Intuition

HUNEWILL, Stanley
How I make artificial insemination work. il
  por Suc Farm 69:no3 D5-7 F '71

HUNGARY
Hungary: changing homeland of a tough,
  romantic people. B. McDowell. il Nat Geog
  139:443-83 Ap '71
  See also
Bonds, Government—Hungary
Investments, Foreign (in Hungary)
Transylvania

Economic policy
Hungary: the politics of reform. C. Gati. Cur
  Hist 60:290-4+ My '71
Taking the initiative in Hungary. il News-
  week 77:36+ Ap 5 '71

Politics and government
Hungary: the politics of reform. C. Gati. Cur
  Hist 60:290-4+ My '71

Social history
Hoping against hope: the enlightened age in
  Hungary. G. Barany. bibliog f il Am Hist
  R 76:319-57 Ap '71

HUNGER
  See also
Appetite

HUNN, Max
Art from a cypress swamp. il pors Design
  73:4-7 Wint '71

HUNT, Andrew
Raisin; poem. New Yorker 47:138 Ap 10 '71

HUNT, Elsie D.
How I found therapy in thistles. Farm J 95:
  44 My '71

HUNT, George Pinney
Our four-star military mess. il Life 70:50-2+
  Je 18 '71

HUNT, Ira Augustus
Military theology. L. H. Lapham. il Harper
  243:73-6+ Jl '71 *

HUNT, Morton M.
Letter from Long Island Sound. New Yorker
  47:62+ Ag 28 '71
Special sex education survey. il Seventeen
  29:94-7+ Jl '70

HUNT, Peter
Garden ornaments, plain and fancy. il Horti-
  culture 49:22-5 Ag '71
Paving patterns. il Horticulture 49:44-7 Mr '71

HUNT, Ron
Ron Hunt is some soft touch. P. Carry.
  Sports Illus 35:42 Ag 2 '71 *

HUNT, Scott
Presidential scholars: the spectacular achievers. il Am Ed 7:29-31 Je '71

HUNT, Todd
Why we joined the inn group. il Travel 135:
  62-4+ Ap '71

HUNT commission. See United States—Commission on financial structure and regulation

HUNT-Wesson foods, Inc.
Hunt-Wesson's business; pledge to hire draft
  resisters and anti-war veterans. New Repub 164:8 Ap 24 '71
Trees by label; National children's forest
  project. il Time 98:49 N 29 '71

HUNTER, Beatrice Trum
Ice cream. il Consumer Bul 54:26-9 O '71
Nitrosamines: a universal cancer-causing
  chemical? il Consumer Bul 54:25 Mr '71
Upsetting facts about our diet. il Consumer
  Bul 54:4+ Jl '71

HUNTER, Elizabeth
Interaction briefs. Todays Ed 60:73 S; 60
  O '71

HUNTER, Evan
Exclusive re-visit with Evan Hunter; interview, ed. by F. Krajewski. por Writers Digest 51:24-6 Ap '71

HUNTER, Neale
Working group 7. Commonweal 93:60-1; 94:
  23 O 16 '70, Mr 12 '71

HUNTER, Robert E.
In defense of foreign aid. New Repub 165:
  18-20 N 20 '71
Troops, trade and diplomacy. il Nation 212:
  776-80 Je 21 '71

HUNTER, Sam
Jean Dubuffet's landscape for trolls and
  ogres. il pors Vogue 157:62-5+ Ja 15 '71

HUNTER, Wilbur Harvey
New painting by Alfred Jacob Miller. il
  Antiques 101:221-5 Ja '72

HUNTER syndrome. See Lipochondrodystrophy

HUNTERS
Thanks to the hunter! R. Stack. Nat Wildlife 9:17 O '71

HUNTING
Boom in exciting big game. B. W. Dalrymple.
  il Field & S 75:70-1+ Ap '71
Editorial. C. Conley. Field & S 76:4 S '71
Gist of it; ed. by H. Moore. See issues of
  Outdoor life
How to buy and use maps to improve your
  hunting. E. Park. il Field & S 76:68-9+ O
  '71
Hunter. M. Frome. Field & S 76:42+ Je '71
Hunters and conservationists share goals;
  official policy toward hunting. il Nat Wild-
  life 9:18-19 O '71

HUNTING—*Continued*

Sportsman's notebook. H. G. Tapply. See issues of Field & stream

Strange ways of bullets. W. Davis. il Mech Illus 67:82+ F '71

Where to go; ed. by V. T. Sparano. See issues of Outdoor life

See also
Airplanes in hunting and fishing
Falconry
Game
Game. Dressing of
Hunting with bow and arrow
Poaching
Whaling
also Moose hunting; Deer hunting; and similar headings

Accidents and injuries

Hunting accident report for 1970. B. E. Burgin. il Cons 26:9 Ag '71

Nightmare. G. O'Brien. il Outdoor Life 148: 57+ Ag '71

Bibliography

All about game and how to hunt it. H. Bradshaw and V. Bradshaw. il Field & S 76:68-71+ Ag '71

Equipment and supplies
See Hunting outfits

Ethical aspects

Case for the lung shot. B. Milek. Field & S 76:44-5+ Ag '71

Gang that could shoot straight. W. Davis. il Mech Illus 67:40+ S '71

Grim reapers of the land's bounty. J. Harrison. il Sports Illus 35:38-40+ O 11 '71

The hunting ethic. H. E. Doig. il Cons 26: 15-16 O '71

To place the shot. J. O'Connor. il Outdoor Life 147:90+ Ja '71

History

Man, the hunter; australopithecine. J. Pfeiffer. il Horizon 13:28-33 Spr '71

Safety devices and measures

Magnum boner. C. Elliott. il Outdoor Life 147:88 My '71

Africa

Airweight battery. W. Page. il Field & S 75: 86-9 Ja '71

On the horns of a dilemma; big-game trophy competition. V. Kraft. Sports Illus 34:69-70 Ap 26 '71

Rifles in Africa. J. O'Connor. il Outdoor Life 147:90+ F '71

Safari in the seventies. J. O'Connor. il Outdoor Life 147:55-7+ Mr '71

Africa, East

African journal; with introd. by R. Cave. E. Hemingway. il Sports Illus 35:40-52+ D 20 '71

Small game shoot in big game land. R. F. Jones. Sports Illus 35:82-3+ D 6 '71

Alabama

Team turkey. C. Elliott. il por Outdoor Life 147:66-7+ Mr '71

Alaska

Alaska's agony; illegal hunting. B. East. il Outdoor Life 147:33-5+ Ja '71

Best hunting spots in Canada and Alaska; symposium. il Field & S 76:61+ Ag '71

Brown bear the hard way. B. Brister. il Field & S 76:30-1+ D '71

Everybody is up in arms; documentary film hoax. D. Connelly. il Sports Illus 34:32-4+ Ap 5 '71

Ghosts of the Wrangells. B. Guild. il Outdoor Life 147:78-81+ Ap '71

Hunting and fishing Alaska by train. G. X. Sand. il Field & S 76:156-8+ O '71

Ptarmigan. B. Brister. il Field & S 76:36-7+ S '71

Snowshoes in the wind. R. L. Tucker. il pors Outdoor Life 148:58-9+ N '71

They're threatening Alaska's big game hunting. J. Rearden. il Nat Wildlife 9:21-5 F '71

Trouble ahead for Alaska's big bears. W. Page. il Field & S 75:60-1+ F '71

Arctic Regions

Canadian Arctic: a mecca for sportsmen. Bsns W p 121 My 15 '71

Arizona

Grand Canyon ram. L. A. Keim. il Outdoor Life 148:58-9+ D '71

Arkansas

Feeling like a goose. N. Buckingham. il por Outdoor Life 148:76-9+ S '71

Austria

Hat and the sprig. P. Barrett. il Outdoor Life 148:50-3+ Jl '71

California

Blacktails for beginners. E. Paradzinski. il Field & S 76:52-3+ O '71

Guzzler cottontails. J. R. Higley. il por Outdoor Life 148:62-3+ Jl '71

How to bag bandtails. W. Curtis. il Field & S 76:54-5+ S '71

Canada

Best hunting spots in Canada and Alaska; symposium. il Field & S 76:58-60+ Ag '71

Bulls of Barriere. W. N. Roach. il pors Outdoor Life 148:84-7+ O; 80-3+ N; 54-7+ D '71

Chow line honkers. J. Linduska. il Field & S 75:112-15+ Ja '71

Cougar does attack. D. D. Ellis. il Outdoor Life 148:64-7+ S '71

Drive-in caribou: province of Saskatchewan. S. Netherby. il Field & S 76:164-6+ N '71

Encounter with a cougar. S. Udall. il Field & S 76:64-5+ N '71

I never want a bigger moose. D. Revoir. il Outdoor Life 147:60-1+ Je '71

I wanted it wild. W. N. Roach. il pors Outdoor Life 148:84-7+ O '71 (to be cont)

Indians were only first. K. C. Schuyler. il Field & S 76:52-3+ S '71

Killing buffalo to save buffalo. W. Davis. il Mech Illus 67:86+ O '71

Land of the blue wolf; British Columbia. W. Page. il Field & S 76:54-5+ Ag '71

Leader of the band; Stone ram hunting. R. A. Lubeck. il pors Outdoor Life 147:72-3+ Mr '71

Lookout grizzly. A. Money. il por Outdoor Life 148:60-3+ O '71

Making book at Turnagain. R. C. Hammond. il Outdoor Life 148:60-1+ S '71

Mixed bag for bear hunters. R. Elman. il Field & S 75:46-7+ Ja '71

Nightmare. G. O'Brien. il Outdoor Life 148: 57+ Ag '71

Pterrible ptemperature ptarmigan. N. Karas. il Field & S 75:64-5+ Mr '71

Stay for the ending; record moose and caribou. P. L. Halbig. il Outdoor Life 147:76-9+ F '71

Top of the world. L. L. Eddy. il Outdoor Life 148:42-5+ D '71

Chad

Day the rebels attacked; ed. by O. Brooks. E. M. Ochoa. il pors Outdoor Life 147: 44-7+ Ja '71

Colorado

Don't shoot the bearded lady. D. Gravestock. il Outdoor Life 147:60-3+ Ja '71

Lion of a lifetime. L. Bamford. il Field & S 76:64-5+ Ag '71

Secret of the Rock. J. Wootters. il Outdoor Life 147:60-1+ F '71

Veterans' pheasant hunt. B. Gillette. il Outdoor Life 147:64-7+ Je '71

England

How the English hunt rabbits. F. Taylor. il pors Field & S 75:84-5+ Mr '71

Georgia

Bobwhite leftovers. C. Elliott. il Outdoor Life 148:40-1+ D '71

Germany (Federal Republic)

Man is fair game. C. Gammon. il Sports Illus 34:74-6+ Mr 22 '71

Great Britain

Pheasant shooting in Britain. A. Oglesby. il Field & S 76:42-3+ D '71

Idaho

Lost in an icy hell. W. Garde. il Outdoor Life 147:54-5+ F '71

Illinois

Easy fox hunting. T. M. Wunderle. il Field & S 76:60-1+ N '71

Indiana

Bunnies by barometer. J. Parry. il Field & S 76:34-5+ S '71

Challenge of the chuck. H. C. Corley. il Outdoor Life 147:80-1+ Mr '71

Iowa

Walking a coyote track. R. Byerly. il Outdoor Life 147:50-1+ Ja '71

HUNTING—*Continued*

Ireland

Ounce of prevention for the banks and the bogs: West Waterford pack. R. S. Rauch. 3d. il Sports Illus 35:48-51 N 22 '71

Paddy's grouse. N. Riley. il **Outdoor Life** 148:80-3+ Ag '71

Uproar is the name of the game: Irish woodcock hunting. N. Riley. il Outdoor Life 147:76-9+ Mr '71

Kentucky

Cottontail hunting, eastern style. C. Nansen. il Field & S 76:54-5+ O '71

Maine

Spring bear down east. L. Dietz il Field & S 75:56-7+ Mr '71

Tolling bells for the Maine timberdoodle. R. F. Jones. il Sports Illus 35:74+ N 8 '71

Maryland

Foggy float for squirrel. L. Kreh. il Field & S 75:32-3+ Ja '71

Massachusetts

Madcap of the swamps; snowshoe rabbit. D. Knight. il Field & S 76:46-7+ N '71

Michigan

Lean and angry bear; black bear. C. T. Johnson. il Outdoor Life 147:84-5+ My '71

Man's errand. R. L. Johnson, jr. il Outdoor Life 147:104-7+ Ap '71

Stalk your buck to his hideaway. L. A. Anderson. il Field & S 76:34-5+ D '71

Whitetails have their faults. L. A. Anderson. il Field & S 76:62-3+ Je '71

Minnesota

Grouse: know its spots. R. Gilsvik. il por Outdoor Life 148:82-3+ O '71

Hunt silently: by canoe. N. Nelson, jr. il pors Outdoor Life 148:72-5+ N '71

Mississippi

Mr Bob is full of beans. B. H. Brady. il Outdoor Life 147:72-3+ F '71

Putt, putt, and gone. B. Warner. il por Field & S 75:82-3+ Mr '71

Missouri

Big red of the Ozarks. B. Gooch. il pors Outdoor Life 148:90-2+ O '71

Breadbasket bobwhites. J. M. Vance. il Field & S 76:72-3+ N '71

Crows like wildfire. J. O. Cartier. il Outdoor Life 147:42-3+ Ja '71

Nothing like doves. J. O. Cartier. il Outdoor Life 148:70-1+ S '71

Phantom of record; white-antlered buck. J. A. Brunk. il por Outdoor Life 148:49-51+ N '71

Montana

Are you tough enough to hunt big game? H. Rate. il Field & S 76:50-3+ Ag '71

Beginner on elk. H. K. Cox. il Field & S 76:46-7+ Ag '71

Deer for my pains. J. O. Cartier. il pors Outdoor Life 148:76-7+ N '71

Guide was a dude. H. Rate. il Field & S 76:32-3+ S '71

Northerns are in. N. Strung. il Field & S 76:52-3+ N '71

Nebraska

Mallards by the numbers. U. B. Henderson. il Outdoor Life 147:48-9+ Ja '71

New Jersey

Brant! J. Palmer. il Field & S 76:58-9+ N '71

New Mexico

Big elk come high and hard. D. Knight. il pors Outdoor Life 148:68-71+ N '71

Happy hunting ground; Jicarilla Apache reservation. K. Campbell. il pors Outdoor Life 148:72-5+ O '71

New York (state)

Bobcat paradise. D. J. Anderson. il Field & S 76:68-9+ N '71

Hunting accident report for 1970. B. E. Burgin. il Cons 26:9 Ag '71

Northeastern states

News: the Northeast. T. Janes. See issues of Outdoor life

Norway

Set guns kill polar bears, and it's legal! B. East. il Outdoor Life 147:58-9 Ja '71

Ohio

Bulls of the midnight pond. E. A. Bauer. il Outdoor Life 147:78-9+ Je '71

Changing pheasant. E. A. Bauer. il Outdoor Life 148:60-3+ N '71

Four-year wait; white tail buck. R. Grecar. il por Outdoor Life 147:84-5+ Je '71

Free-for-all ducks. E. A. Bauer. il Outdoor Life 148:34-7+ D '71

Strategy for whitetails. E. A. Bauer. il Outdoor Life 148:52-5+ S '71

Pennsylvania

Boat-in bucks. J. Bashline. il Field & S 76:48-9+ O '71

Of space, time and deer. D. J. Anderson. il Field & S 76:48-9+ N '71

Russia

Grouse behind the iron curtain. H. Jensen. il Outdoor Life 147:86-7+ Ap '71

Scotland

Glorious Twelfth. S. Williams. il Field & S 76:98-100+ N '71

South Dakota

Can you really see deer? J. Palmer. il Field & S 76:31+ S '71

South Dakota's golden geese. H. Bradshaw. il Outdoor Life 148:52-5+ N '71

Where raccoons come tough. H. Bradshaw. il Field & S 75:56-7+ Ja '71

Spain

Call of the cuckoo. W. Page. il Field & S 76:50-1+ Jl '71

Tennessee

Dove shooter's fever. C. Vinson. il Outdoor Life 148:52-3+ D '71

Ghost of Shelby forest. D. Johnson. il Outdoor Life 147:72+ My '71

Texas

Bobwhite is no gentleman anymore! B. Brister. il Field & S 75:34-5+ Ja '71

Eye for deer. B. W. Dalrymple. il Outdoor Life 149:30-3+ D '71

Sheep that is a goat; aoudad, or Barbary sheep. W. Page. il Field & S 76:76-7+ Je '71

Trophies to order; fee hunting for foreign game. J. O'Connor. il Outdoor Life 147:40-1+ Ja '71

Turkeys talk in Texas. B. W. Dalrymple. il Outdoor Life 147:98-101+ Ap '71

United States

Best fall hunting places in the United States; symposium. il Field & S 76:39-44+ S '71

Special hunting issue. il Field & S 76:41-55+ Ag '71

Utah

Cat in Pace Canyon. M. R. James. il Outdoor Life 147:56-7+ Ja '71

East (hunters) meets West (mule deer) B. Grant. il Field & S. 76:40-1+ Jl '71

Vermont

Float trip for crows. J. B. Robinson. il pors Outdoor Life 147:66-7+ My '71

Vermont bear hunt. T. A. Chadwick. il por Outdoor Life 148:64-5+ N '71

Western states

Grouse in the West. T. Trueblood. il Field & S 76:20+ S '71

Wyoming

Double take: deer and antelope. J. R. Olt. il pors Outdoor Life 148:72-5+ S '71

Elk paid me off. R. W. Charlton. il pors Outdoor Life 148:60-3+ Ag '71

Many seasons of South Pass. F. Calkins. il Field & S 76:62-3+ Ag '71

Sheep hunting is an art. J. O'Connor. il Outdoor Life 147:68-71+ F '71

Whitetails in the black. C. J. Farmer. il Field & S 76:66-7+ Ag '71

HUNTING creek. See Potomac River

HUNTING dogs

Dogs. D. M. Duffey. See issues of Outdoor life

Greatest hunting dog you'd never guess. B. Dalrymple. il Field & S 76:48-9+ S '71

Hair of the dog. D. M. Duffey. il Outdoor Life 148:165-6+ S '71

Popular dogs. D. M. Duffey. il Outdoor Life 147:120+ Ja '71

See also

Bird dogs

Foxhounds

Hounds

HUNTING guides. See Guides
HUNTING in art
Sassanian royal hunt. il UNESCO Courier 24:34-8 O '71
HUNTING knives. See Bowie knives
HUNTING laws. See Game laws
HUNTING licenses. See Licenses
HUNTING outfits
Action for shooters: five new-product reports. P. Wahl. il Pop Sci 199:48-9 Jl '71
Getting your hunting gear in shape. W. Davis. il Mech Illus 67:83+ Ag '71
See also
Archery—Equipment
Hunting—Safety devices and measures
HUNTING preserves. See Game preserves
HUNTING rifles. See Rifles
HUNTING spaniels. See Spaniels
HUNTING trophies
On the horns of a dilemma; big-game trophy competition. V. Kraft. Sports Illus 34:69-70 Ap 26 '71
Trophies to order; fee hunting for foreign game in the U.S. J. O'Connor. il Outdoor Life 147:40-1+ Ja '71
HUNTING with bow and arrow
Archery. G. H. Gillelan. See issues of Outdoor life
Best method for you. G. H. Gillelan. il Outdoor Life 148:32+ S '71
Challenge of the chuck. H. C. Corley. il Outdoor Life 147:80-1+ Mr '71
Double-season hunter. G. H. Gillelan. il Outdoor Life 148:28+ O '71
Expert ingredients. G. H. Gillelan. il Outdoor Life 148:20+ N '71
Four outstanding American bowhunters: Field & stream interviews. Field & S 76:58-9+ Je '71
Four-year wait; white tail buck. R. Grecar. il por Outdoor Life 147:84-5+ Je '71
How bowhunters get that way. G. H. Gillelan. il Outdoor Life 147:44+ Je '71
Hunt the off hours. G. H. Gillelan. il Outdoor Life 148:24+ Ag '71
Indians were only first. G. C. Schuyler. il Field & S 76:52-3+ S '71
Lion of a lifetime. L. Bamford. il Field & S 76:64-5+ Ag '71
Profit from every bowhunt. G. H. Gillelan. il Outdoor Life 148:86+ Jl '71
Shots I remember. G. H. Gillelan. il Outdoor Life 147:32+ F '71
Stay for the ending; record moose and caribou. P. L. Halbig. il Outdoor Life 157-76-9+ F '71
Timetable for bowhunters. J. Palmer. il Field & S 76:46-7+ Jl '71
Top of the world. L. L. Eddy. il Outdoor Life 148:42-5+ D '71
See also
Archery
HUNTINGTON, Roger
1972 Detroit model review. il Consumer Bul 54:7-12 O '71
Those little 4-cylinder engines: can you have durability and performance? il Pop Mech 135:94-7+ Ap '71
Why you should hop up your ignition. il Pop Mech 136:128-31+ O '71
HUNTINGTON, Samuel P.
Vietnam: how Nixon plans to win the war. B. Garrett. il por Ramp Mag 9:26-31 F '71 *
HUNTINGTON'S chorea
Must they sacrifice today because of threatened tomorrows? A. Harmetz. il Todays Health 49:44-7+ N '71
HUNTLEY, Chet
For Chet Huntley. few worries over a herd of elk. R. Woodbury. il por Life 71:81 O 15 '71 *
HUQ, Naim Ali
Huq's rebellion. M. J. Kubic. il por Newsweek 77:50 My 10 '71 *
HURD, John G.
Undiplomatic behavior. il por Newsweek 78: 35 Jl 26 '71 *
HURD, L. E. and others
Stability and diversity at three trophic levels in terrestrial successional ecosystems. bibliog il Science 173:1134-6 S 17 '71
HURD family
Hurd coat-of-arms. H. K. Ellers. il Hobbies 76:138-9+ O '71
HURDLE racing
Jump ahead of extinction: steeplechasing. F. Deford. il Sports Illus 35:36-8+ N 8 '71
Last hurrah of a gallant sport: steeplechasing in South Carolina. W. Tower. il Sports Illus 35:22-5 N 29 '71
Not a dry foot in the house; NCAA steeplechase. A. Verschoth. il por Sports Illus 34: 84-5 Je 7 '71

HURLBURT, Allan S. See Osborne, G. S. jt. auth.
HURLBURT, Allen
Norman Rockwell's 78th spring. il pors Look 35:26-30 Je 1 '71
HURLER syndrome. See Lipochondrodystrophy
HURLEY, Lucille S. See Swenerton, H. jt. auth.
HUROK, Sol
General electric presents: S. Hurok. por Bsns W p22+ Jl 3 '71 *
HURRICANE control. See Hurricane protection
HURRICANE ISLAND outward bound school. See Outward bound schools
HURRICANE models. See Meteorological models
HURRICANE protection
How to subdue a hurricane; Project Stormfury I. Purrett. il Sci N 100:128-9 Ag 21 '71
Pacifying Ginger. il Time 98:61 O 11 '71
Storm stalkers; Project Stormfury seed the storms. M. Gosnell. il Newsweek 78:62-3 S 20 '71
HURRICANES
Force 12; genesis of a hurricane. J. McCollam. il Yachting 130:60-1+ O '71
Hurricane Celia damage in Corpus Christi, Tex, libraries. il Am Lib 2:138 F '71
Hurricane season of 1970. L. G. Pardue. bibliog il Weatherwise 24:24-33+ F '71
Tropical analysis program of the National hurricane center. C. W. Wise and R. H. Simpson. bibliog il Weatherwise 24:164-73 Ag '71
See also
Hurricane protection
HURST, Charles G.
Intellectual black power. il por Time 98:50+ Ag 16 '71 *
Monument to blackness. il por Newsweek 78:46-7 Ag 2 '71 *
HURST, Janet
Dark figure; poem. Negro Hist Bul 34:58 Mr '71
HURST rescue tool. See Life saving equipment
HURWITCH, Robert Arnold
United States policy toward Cuba: statement, September 16, 1971. Dept State Bul 65:391-5 O 11 '71
HURWITZ, Al
What children tell us through their art. il PTA Mag 65:24-5 My '71
HUSAIN, Liaquat, and others
Ages of crystalline rocks from Fra Mauro. bibliog il Science 173:1235-6 S 24 '71
HUSAIN, Waqif
Frontal analysis in chromatography. il por Chem 44:25 D '71
HUSAK, Gustav
People dissolved. il por Time 97:18 Je 7 '71 *
HUSBAND and wife. See Husbands; Marriage
HUSBANDS
Do strong, silent men make good husbands? J. Brothers. il Good H 173:66+ S '71
How much does he do around the house? il Changing T 25:41 Ap '71
Husbands; excerpt from Live in. D. Evslin. il Ladies Home J 88:191-2+ S '71
Husbands who are married to their jobs. B. Wysor. il Ladies Home J 88:65+ F '71
I am a househusband but call me mister. S. C. Brown, jr. il por Redbook 137:80+ My '71
I was ashamed of my husband. il Good H 173:14+ O '71
Nagging husband. il Good H 173:50+ N '71
Swapping family roles; role-swapping experiment by couples in Norway. il Time 98:72+ N 22 '71
Why won't some husbands talk to their wives? T. I. Rubin. Ladies Home J 88:28 Jl '71
See also
Marriage
Marriage counseling
Separation (law)
Wives
HUSE, Edgar F. and Beer, Michael
Eclectic approach to organizational development. il Harvard Bsns R 49:103-12 S '71
HUSER, Verne
Behind the Sleeping Indian; the Gros Ventre wilderness. il Liv Wildn 35:4-8 Spr '71
Green River: use it or lose it? il Am For 77: 20-3+ Je '71
Rocky Mountain National Park. il Nat Parks & Cong Mag 45:4-9 Ag '71
Who needs the Clark's Fork Canyon road? il Am For 77:24-7 D '71
HUSKING, Corn. See Corn husking
HUSKING bees. See Corn husking

HUSSEIN, king of Jordon
Jordon's Hussein: things will work out; statements. por Time 98:27 Jl 5 '71

about

Hussein: monarch in the middle. E. Hughes. il por Read Digest 98:175-6+ Mr '71 *
Thrust and parry. Newsweek 77:36-7 Ja 25 '71 *
HUTCHES (furniture) See Cabinets (furniture)
HUTCHINSON, Bonnie
Slurish. Engl J 60:361-2 Mr '71
HUTCHINSON, Larry
Flash! Famous novelist OD's on coffee! Sr Schol 98:36 My 17 '71
Playing the hits like the heavies. il Sr Schol 98:24+ Ap 26 '71
Stage fright. il Sr Schol 98:29 F 15 '71
HUTCHISON, Albert. Jr
Domestic architecture in Middle Tennessee. il Antiques 100:402-7 S '71
HUTCHISON, Ira J. Jr
Sweet bird of youth. il Parks & Rec 6:46-7+ O '71
HUTCHISON, William R.
Cultural strain and Protestant liberalism. bibliog f il Am Hist R 76:386-411. 1632-3 Ap. D '71
HUTSCHNECKER, Arnold A.
How to break habits that make you unhappy; excerpt from The will to happiness. il Ladies Home J 88:134+ F '71
Tension: the everyday threat to American women, and what to do about it. Vogue 157:120-1+ Je '71
Working with your hands. Vogue 158:114+ Jl '71
HUTTERITE Brethren
Hutterite hassle. L. Tarr. Chr Today 15:36 Ag 6 '71
HUTTO, Charles
My Lai: a question of orders. il pors Time 97:24 Ja 25 '71 *
HUTTO, Henry
Dies irae; poem. Chr Cent 88:614 My 19 '71
I preached Franciscanly; poem. Chr Cent 88:62 Ja 20 '71
HUTTO, Mildred E.
Librarian takes a stand. por Am Lib 2:435-7 My '71 *
HUTTON, Betty
Quartet of queens. J. Barthel. il pors Life 70:64+ F 19 '71 *
HUTTON, Lauren
How people really travel; interview. il por Vogue 157:116-17 Ap 15 '71
HUTTON, Winfield
Yankees in Valhalla. il Opera N 35:8-11 Mr 20 '71
HUTTUNEN, Matti O. See Díaz, J.-L. jt. auth.
HUXLEY, Aldous
Poems of a prosaist. J. Wain. New Repub 165:27-8 S 11 '71 *
HUXTABLE, Ada Louise
Lyndon Baines Johnson library; reprint. il Am Lib 2:669-71 Jl '71
HUYCK, Dorothy Boyle
Telling it like it is, or was. il Am For 77:16-19+ Je: 24-7 Jl '71 (to be cont)
Trails: so who needs them? il Am For 77:22-4+ O '71
HYADES. See Stars—Clusters
HYALINE membrane disease
Medicine learned how to save Katie Peck. D. Zimmerman. il por Todays Health 49:20-3+ D '71
HYAMS, Ben
Arts of this century. il Hi Fi 21:MA24-5 O '71
HYBRID corn. See Corn—Hybrids
HYBRIDIZATION
From fink to fowl, in research; Michigan state university studies on cross-breeding. J. Marks. Suc Farm 69:D7 Je '71
See also
Plant breeding
Tree breeding
also subhead Hybrids under various subjects, e.g. Corn—Hybrids
HYCANTHONE
Hycanthone: a frameshift mutagen. P. E. Hartman and others. bibliog il Science 172:1058-60 Je 4 '71; Reply. E. Hirschberg and I. B. Weinstein. 174:1147-8 D 10 '71
Hycanthone resistance: development in schistosoma mansoni. S. H. Rogers and E. Bueding. bibliog il Science 172:1057-8 Je 4 '71
HYDE, Arnout, Jr
West Virginia; photographs. Nat Wildlife 10:56-63 D '71

HYDE, Joe
Trick or *truite*: here comes Joe Hyde. R. H. Boyle. il por Sports Illus 35:44-6+ N 8 '71 *
HYDE PARK, N.Y.
See also
Franklin D. Roosevelt library
HYDRANGEAS
Very personal garden of the Richard Sears Humphreys: a blue hydrangea garden. il House & Gard 139:110-13 My '71
HYDRAULIC aerial lifts. See Cranes, derricks, etc.
HYDRAULIC engineering
See also
Channels (hydraulic engineering)
Dams
Flood prevention and control
HYDRAULIC jackhammer. See Hydraulic tools
HYDRAULIC tools
Hydraulic jackhammer breaks the noise barrier. E. F. Lindsley. il Pop Sci 199:32 N '71
HYDRIDES
Negative hydrogen. J. E. House, jr. il por Chem 44:8-11 Mr '71
HYDROCARBONS
Aromatic hydrocarbons in the Murchison meteorite. K. L. Pering and C. Ponnamperuma. bibliog il Science 173:237-9 Jl 16 '71
Primordial oil slick. Sci Digest 71:57-8 Ja '72
Ubiquitous hydrocarbons. G. A. Mills. bibliog il por Chem 44:8-13 F; 12-17 Mr '71
What is petroleum? M. B. Blumer. Environ 13:10 Mr '71
HYDROCORTISONE
Hydrocortisone-mediated increase of norepinephrine uptake by brain slices. J. W. Maas and M. Mednieks. bibliog il Science 171:178-9 Ja 15 '71
HYDRODYNAMICS
See also
Drops
Fluid dynamics
Magnetohydrodynamics
Waves
HYDROELECTRIC plants
He'll develop Quebec's TVA; James Bay Hydroelectric project. por Bsns W p56 N 27 '71
One million kilowatts from a mountain cave; Northfield Mountain pumped storage hydroelectric project. M. Walker. il Pop Mech 136:104-5 N '71

Pollution

Blue Ridge dams: the pollution dilution approach. R. E. Janssen. il Nat Parks & Con Mag 45:14-15+ Ag '71
HYDROELECTRIC power
How they'll pump energy from the sea; experiments under way off St Croix, Virgin Islands. W. S. Bacon. il Pop Sci 198:38 Mr '71
HYDROGEN
Making hydrogen a metal. il Sci N 99:231 Ap 3 '71
Metallic hydrogen. L. E. Strong. Chem 44:24 D '71

Isotopes

See also
Deuterium
HYDROGEN, Liquid
Liquid hydrogen as a fuel for the future. L. W. Jones. bibliog il Science 174:367-70 O 22 '71
Liquid hydrogen as a motor fuel. il Chem 45:26 Ja '72
HYDROGEN bonds. See Chemical bonds
HYDROGEN halos. See Halos (meteorology)
HYDROGEN ion concentration
See also
Buffer solutions
Soil acidity
HYDROGEN peroxide
Inhibition of biogenic amine uptake by hydrogen peroxide: a mechanism for toxic effects of 6-hydroxydopamine. R. Heikkila and G. Cohen. bibliog il Science 172:1257-8 Je 18 '71
HYDROLOGIC cycle
Recycling: an old idea with new significance. R. Andrus and S. P. Mathur. il Cons 25:28-31 Je '71
This watery planet; excerpt from Water and life. R. Platt. il Audubon 73:4-9 Mr '71
Water rules the world. A. R. Chalfant. bibliog il Nat Wildlife 9:38-41 Ag '71
Waterwise. A. Rango. il Weatherwise 24:68-73 Ap '71
HYDROLOGIC research
See also
Airplanes in hydrologic research
Watersheds—Research

HYDROLYSIS
Glycerinated muscle fibers: relation between isometric tension and adenosine triphosphate hydrolysis. W. J. Bowen and L. Mandelkern. bibliog il Science 173:239-40 Jl 16 '71
p-Nitrophenyl phosphate hydrolysis and calcium ion transport in fragmented sarcoplasmic reticulum. G. Inesi. bibliog il Science 171:901-3 Mr 5 '71

HYDROPLANE racing
She does a lot for a Little. H. D. Whall. il por Sports Illus 35:24-5 O 4 '71
Thunderboating; Madison, Ind. regatta. B. Thomas. il Travel 136:31-3 Jl '71

HYDROPORTS. See Seaplane bases

HYDROTHERAPY
Water: great therapy for what ails you. P. Corbin. il House & Gard 139:90-1+ My '71

HYDROXYCHOLECALCIFEROL. See Vitamins —Vitamin D

HYDROXYDOPAMINE. See Dopamine

HYDROXYECDYSONE. See Ecdysone

HYDROXYINDOLEACETIC acid
Origin of 5-hydroxyindoleacetic acid in the spinal fluid. M. Bulat and B. Živković. bibliog il Science 173:738-40 Ag 20 '71

HYDROXYL
Hydroxyl in two other galaxies. il Sci N 100:54 Jl 24 '71
Hydoxyl orientation in muscovite as indicated by electrostatic energy calculations. R. F. Giese, jr. bibliog il Science 172:263-4 Ap 16 '71
Universal radicals. Sci Am 225:80 S '71

HYDROXYLASES
Decrease in adrenal tyrosine hydroxylase and increase in norepinephrine synthesis in rats given L-dopa. W. Dairman and S. Udenfriend. bibliog il Science 171:1022-4 Mr 12 '71
Effects of long-term reserpine treatment on brain tyrosine hydroxylase and behaviorial activity. D. S. Segal and others. bibliog il Science 173:847-9 Ag 27 '71
Microsomal hydroxylase induction in liver cell cuture by phenobarbital, polycyclic hydrocarbons, and p,p'-DDT. J. E. Gielen and D. W. Nebert. bibliog il Science 172:167-9 Ap 9 '71
Perinatal undernutrition: accumulation of catecholamines in rat brain. W. J. Shoemaker and R. J. Wurtman. bibliog il Science 171:1017-19 Mr 12 '71
Proportional release of norepinephrine and dopamine-β-hydroxylase from sympathetic nerves. R. M. Weinshilboum and others. bibliog il Science 174:1349-51 D 24 '71
Serum dopamine-β-hydrolylase; decrease after chemical sympathectomy. R. Weinshilboum and J. Axelrod. bibliog il Science 173:931-4 S 3 '71

HYDROXYLATION
Collagen polypeptides: normal release from polysomes in the absence of proline hydroxylation. E. Lazarides and L. N. Lukens. bibliog il Science 173:723-5 Ag 20 '71

HYDROXYPYRUVATE. See Pyruvates

HYDROXYTRYPTAMINE. See Serotonin

HYGIENE
See also
Baths
Hand washing
Health
Men—Health and hygiene
Water pollution
Woman—Health and hygiene

HYMAN, Hal
Witch salmon. il por Field & S 76:110-13+ Jl '71

HYMAN, Joe
Bid for power in Yorkshire wool. por Bsns W p55 Je 19 '71 •

HYMAN, M. H.
Timetable for lead. bibliog il Environ 13:14-23 Je '71

HYMAN, Sylvia
Raku beads. il Ceram Mo 19:28-30 O '71

HYMNALS. See Hymns

HYMNS
New Canadian hymnal brings Anglican-UCC union a step closer. G. Lane. Chr Cent 89: 18-19 Ja 5 '72
See also
Church music

HYMOFF, Edward
Technology vs. guerrillas. il Bul Atom Sci 27:27-30 N '71

HYNEK, Josef Allen
Saucer diehards. il por Time 97:49 Je 28 '71 •

HYPERICUM coris. See St John's wort

HYPERKINESIS
Case of Ritalin: drugs for hyperactive children. A. F. Charles. New Repub 165:17-19 O 23 '71
Drugs and the hyperactive syndrome. Am Ed 7:14 Je '71
Drugs for children; the Omaha program and resulting involvement. H. Vinnedge. New Repub 164:13-15 Mr 13 '71; Discussion. 164: 28-9 Ap 10; 37-8 Ap 17 '71
Hyperactive engineering. V. Krauch. il Am Ed 7:12-13+ Je '71
Hyperactivity and learning problems: implications for teachers. B. K. Keogh. Ed Digest 37:45-7 D '71
Nonstop Timmy, our two-year-old terror. L. Copeland. il por Redbook 137:38+ O '71
Panel sanctions amphetamines for hyperkinetic children. R. J. Bazell. Science 171: 1223 Mr 26 '71
Photic responses in hyperkinesis of childhood. T. Shetty. bibliog Science 174:1356-7 D 24 '71
Pills for classroom peace? E. T. Ladd. Ed Digest 36:1-4 F '71
Using drugs in classrooms. N. Hentoff. Cur 126:40-5 F '71

HYPERONS
Experiments with 25-GeV hyperon beam at Brookhaven. Phys Today 24:20 D '71

HYPEROXALURIA
Hyperoxaluria in L-glyceric aciduria: possible pathogenic mechanism; effect of hydroxypyruvate. H. F. Williams and L. H. Smith, jr. bibliog il Science 171:390-1 Ja 29 '71

HYPERSONIC airplanes. See Airplanes, Supersonic

HYPERSPACE
See also
Space and time

HYPERTENSION
Decreased systolic blood pressure through operant conditioning techniques in patients with essential hypertension. H. Benson and others bibliog il Science 173:740-2 Ag 20 '71
High blood pressure during pregnancy; ed. by E. Jacobs. C. I. Bryans, jr. Redbook 136: 20+ F '71
High blood pressure: new light on a hidden killer. L. Galton. Read Digest 98:65-8 Je '71
Hypertension of renal origin: evidence for two different mechanisms. H. R. Brunner and J. D. Kirshman. bibliog il Science 174: 1344-6 D 24 '71
Intelligence and blood pressure in the aged. F. Wilkie and E. Eisdorfer. bibliog il Science 172:959-62 My 28 '71

HYPNOANALYSIS. See Hypnotism—Therapeutic use

HYPNOPAEDIA. See Sleep learning

HYPNOTICS
Synergy of ethanol and a natural soporific—gamma hydroxybutyrate. E. R. McCabe and others. bibliog il Science 171:404-6 Ja 29 '71

HYPNOTISM
Hypnosis comes of age. G. H. Estabrooks. il Sci Digest 69:44-50 Ap '71
Truth about hypnosis. S. Lord. Harp Baz 104:80 Jl '71
Who can be hypnotized? pors Newsweek 77:68-9 Je '71

Therapeutic use

Can hypnosis help you? L. David. il Seventeen 30:94-5+ Jl '71
How hypnotism helped solve a lifelong weight problem. N. Lobsenz. il pors Good H 173:116-17+ O '71
Self-hypnosis diet. E. Frances. il Ladies Home J 88:52+ Je '71

HYPOCHONDRIA
Hypochondriacs bug doctors. A. J. Snider. il Sci Digest 70:51 Jl '71
I've never been healthy a day in my life. M. Halberstam. il Today's Health 49:34-9+ N '71

HYPODERMIC injections. See Injections, Hypodermic

HYPOGEUSIA. See Taste

HYPOGLYCEMIA. See Blood sugar

HYPOPHOSPHATEMIA. See Metabolism, Disorders of

HYPOTHALAMUS
Activity change as the cause of apparent aversiveness during prolonged hypothalamic stimulation. J. W. Hu; J. Mendelson. bibliog il Science 172:84-6 Ap 2 '71
Electrical activity of the hypothalamus: effects of intraventricular catecholamines. R. J. Weiner and others. bibliog il Science 171:411-12 Ja 29 '71

HYPOTHALAMUS—*Continued*
Habituation of electrically induced readiness to gnaw. R. E. Cain and others. bibliog il Science 173:262-4 Jl 16 '71
Lateral hypothalamus: reevaluation of function in motivated feeding behavior. L. D. Devenport and S. Balagura. bibliog il Science 172:744-6 My 14 '71
Neural pathways associated with hypothalamically elicited attack behavior in cats. C. C. Chi and J. P. Flynn. bibliog il Science 171:703-6 F 19 '71
Norepinephrine: reversal of anorexia in rats with lateral hypothalamic damage. B. D. Berger and others. bibliog il Science 172: 281-4 Ap 16 '71
Sensory neglect produced by lateral hypothalamic damage. J. F. Marshall and others. bibliog il Science 174:523-5 O 29 '71
Thyrotropin-releasing hormone: biosynthesis by rat hypothalamic fragments in vitro. M. Mitnick and S. Reichlin. bibliog il Science 172:1241-3 Je 18 '71
Visual patterned reflex present during hypothalamically elicited attack. R. Bandler, jr. and J. P. Flynn. bibliog il Science 171:817-18 F 26 '71; Reply. A. Trehub. 173:1041 S 10 '71
HYPOTHERMIA
Freezing aids brain surgery. A. J. Snider. Sci Digest 70:58-9 S '71
HYPOTHETICAL church history. See Church history, Hypothetical
HYSTERECTOMY. See Uterus—Surgery

I

I-129. See Iodine—Isotopes
IAEA. See International atomic energy agency
IA-ECOSOC. See Inter-American economic and social council
IAF. See International astronautical federation
IAM. See International association of machinists and aerospace workers
I. A. O'Shaughnessy auditorium, St Paul. See Concert halls
IATA. See International air transport association
I ain't playin, I'm hurtin; story. See Bambara, T. C.
I am Elijah Thrush; story. See Purdy, J.
IBA. See Investment bankers association of America
IBEC. See International basic economy corporation
IBM. See International business machines corporation
IBP. See International biological program
IC industries, inc.
Acquisition week for IC industries. Bsns W p38 S 25 '71
ICAO. See International civil aviation organization
ICBM (intercontinental ballistic missiles) See Guided missiles
ICC. See United States—Interstate commerce commission
ICEM. See Intergovernmental committee for European migration
ICI. See Imperial chemical industries, ltd.
IDS. See Investors diversified services, inc.
IEU. See International union of electrical, radio and machine workers
I. F. Stone's bi-weekly
End of the Stone age. por Time 98:52 D 20 '71
Izzy slows down. il Newsweek 78:84 D 20 '71
Old new lefty. il por Time 97:47 F 8 '71
IFA. See Independent farmers alliance
IFAMA. See Interdenominational foreign mission association
IFC. See American library association—Intellectual freedom committee
IFCO. See Interreligious foundation for community organization
IFI (Istituto finanziario industriale) See Holding companies—Italy
IFLA. See International federation of library associations
IFR flying. See Aviation—Instrument flying
IGFA. See International game fish association
IHC, Inc.
Case of the Hayden Stone letter. C. J. Loomis. Fortune 83:143+ Mr '71

I have heard the mermaids singing; story. See Jensen, E.
ILA. See Illinois library association; International longshoremen's association
ILGWU. See International ladies' garment workers' union
ILO. See International labor organization
ILS (instrument landing system) See Airplanes —Landing
ILTF. See International lawn tennis federation
ILWU. See International longshoremen's and warehousemen's union
IMC. See Instructional materials centers
IMF. See International monetary fund
IMP (interplanetary monitoring platform) See Artificial satellites—Astronomical use
INA corporation
Inside-outside. il Forbes 108:51 O 1 '71
IOS. See Investors overseas services, ltd.
IPSA. See Independent postal system of America
IQ. See Intelligence quotient
IQ tests. See Intelligence tests
IRA. See Irish republican army
IRBM (intermediate range ballistic missiles) See Guided missiles
IRRI. See International rice research institute
IRS. See United States—Internal revenue service
ISCM. See International society for contemporary music
ISIS (international satellite for ionospheric studies) See Artificial satellites, Canadian
ISR (intersecting storage rings) See Accelerators (electrons, etc)
ITA (initial teaching alphabet) See Alphabet
ITACS (integrated tactical air control system) See Airplanes, Military—Radio equipment
ITT. See International telephone and telegraph corporation
ITT Continental baking company
Admen burn over baker's bow to FTC. Bsns W p25-6 Jl 10 '71
End to puffery? FTC charges. il Newsweek 77:88-9 Mr 29 '71
Mea culpa, sort of; Profile bread's TV ad. Newsweek 78:98 S 27 '71
ITU. See International telecommunication union; International typographical union
IUFRO. See International union of forestry research organizations
IVCF. See Inter-varsity Christian fellowship
I want to see my mother; story. See Delston, E.
I went to the rocks; story. See Dalton, S.
IACOCCA, Lee Anthony. See Iacocca, Lido Anthony
IACOCCA, Lido Anthony
What you will pay for safer cars of future; interview. il por U S News 70:32-6 Mr 8 '71
about
Ford's Iacocca: apotheosis of a used-car salesman. W. Serrin. il pors N Y Times Mag p8-9+ Jl 18 '71 •
Three small steps to the high command. por Fortune 83:35 Ja '71 •
IANNI, Francis A. J.
Managing the unmanageable; address. July 13, 1971. Vital Speeches 37:683-7 S 1 '71
IANNONE, Ronald V.
Programmed unhappiness: when will schools of education make teaching a relevant act? bibliog Clear House 46:102-5 O '71
IASHIN, Lev Ivanovich
Honor the Octopus. il por Newsweek 77: 75-6 Je 14 '71 •
IATROPHYSICAL school
Iatrochemistry; tr. by R. S. Oesper. F. Szabadvary. il por Chem 44:18-20 Je '71
IBANEZ, Carlos
Carlos Ibanez company, Kaufman concert hall, NYC. L. Pastore. Dance Mag 45:79 Jl '71 •
IBANEZ, J. D. and others
Possible prebiotic condensation of mononucleotides by cyanamide. bibliog il Science 173:444-6 Jl 30 '71
IBÁÑEZ PADILLA, Alberto
Vanishing Guarani treasures. il Américas 23:32-5 O '71
IBBOTSON, Eva
In the beginning... Writer 84:9-12 Ag '71
Joyful noises; story. il Redbook 138:80-1 D '71
Love as she is spoken; story. Ladies Home J 88:126 My '71
IBEX hunting
Call of the cuckoo. W. Page. il Field & S 76: 50-1+ Jl '71

IBISES
200,000 ibis live here. il Sci Digest 70:27 N '71
IBIZA (island)
Ibiza is in, and wants out. il Newsweek 78: 26-7 Jl 19 '71
IBSEN, Henrik
Enemy of the people; adaptation. See Miller, A.

about

Boyg and the sphinx in Ibsen's theatre. B. Johnston. Yale R 60:366-82 Mr '71 *
Doll's house. Criticism
America 124:318-19 Mr 27 '71 *
Life 70:10 Mr 12 '71 *
Nation 212:154-6 F 1 '71 *
New Repub 164:24+ Mr 13 '71 *
New Yorker 46:66-7 Ja 23 '71
Newsweek 77:66-7 Mr 1 '71 *
Time il 97:48 Ja 25 '71 *
Vogue 157:114+ Mr 1 '71 *
Hedda Gabler. Criticism
America 124:318-19 Mr 27 '71 *
Life 70:10 Mr 12 '71 *
Nation 212:314 Mr 8 '71 *
New Repub 164:24+ Mr 13 '71 *
New Yorker 47:84-5 F 27 '71 *
Newsweek 77:66-7 Mr 1 '71 *
Time 97:67 Mr 1 '71 *
Ibsen. by M. Meyer. Review
Newsweek por 78:82 Ag 16 '71 *
Time il por 98:84+ S 13 '71. B. Darrach *
Ibsen: the shy giant. E. Le Gallienne. il por Sat R 54:23-6+ Ag 14 '71 *
Ibsen's Nora and ours. J. Richardson. Commentary 52:77-80 Jl '71 *
Master builder. Criticism
New Repub 165:24+ N 6 '71
New Yorker 47:103-4 O 30 '71
Not Women's lib. J. Finn. New Repub 165: 22-3 O 23 '71 *
ICARIAN communism. See Communism—France—History
ICE
Amorphous ice: density and reflectivity. J. A. Ghormley and C. J. Hochanadel. bibliog il Science 171:62-4 Ja 8 '71
Ice nucleation by coprecipitated silver iodide and silver bromide. B. Vonnegut and H. Chessin. bibliog il Science 174:945-6 N 26 '71
Solution of eight-vertex model excites critical-point theorists. G. B. Lubkin. bibliog il Phys Today 24:17+ S '71
See also
Glaciers

Manufacture

How ice makers work, what to do if they don't. E. Powell. il Pop Sci 198:87-9+ Je '71
Ice—making and keeping it. J. Hart. il Yachting 129:70+ Ap '71

Polar Regions

Ice and the breaker. G. R. Boling. il Sea Front 17:363-71 N '71
Shifting world of Arctic sea ice. L. Purrett. il Sci N 100:80-1 Jl 31 '71
ICE ages. See Glacial epochs
ICE breaking operations
Lakes shippers chip out a longer season. il Bsns W p50-1 F 13 '71
ICE breaking vessels
Ice and the breaker. C. R. Boling. il Sea Front 17:363-71 N '71
ICE calorimetry. See Calorimeters and calorimetry
ICE caves
Summit firn caves, Mount Rainier, Washington. E. P. Kiver and M. D. Mumma. bibliog il Science 173:320-2 Jl 23 '71
ICE cream, ices, etc.
Big scoop in ice cream. il Bsns W p73 Ag 28 '71
Big scream for ice cream. E. Alston. il Look 35:52-5 Jl 13 '71
Complete ice cream cookbook. L. S. Pappas. il House & Gard 140·127-8+ S '71
Fast and fancy ice cream desserts. il Bet Hom & Gard 49:67-8 Je '71
Freeze that pleases; Baskin-Robbins California-based franchise chain. il Time 97:76+ Je 21 '71
Homemade ice cream. E. W. Manning. il Farm J 95:38-9 Ag '71
Homemade ice cream; with recipes. F. M. Crawford. il Am Home 74:58-9+ Jl '71
Ice cream cake you make ahead. il Sunset 146:224 Ap '71
Ice cream; what happened to grandma's holiday treat. B. T. Hunter Consumer Bul 54:26-9 O '71

King of desserts: ice cream and sauces. H. McCully. il House B 113:66-7+ Ag '71
Pumpkin ice cream. il Sunset 147:184 N '71
Refreshing ices use fruit wines. Sunset 147: 107 Ag '71
Thirty-one flavors: Baskin-Robbins chain. New Yorker 47:19-20 Jl 10 '71
ICE cream industry. See Ice cream, ices, etc.
ICE cream man; story. See Carroll, R.
ICE cream parlors
Frozen nostalgia. il Newsweek 78:53 Jl 26 '71
ICE cream sauces. See Sauces
ICE crystals
See also
Snow crystals
ICE cycles. See Ice vehicles
ICE fishing. See Fishing, Winter
ICE hazards in aviation. See Airplanes—Ice protection
ICE hockey. See Hockey
ICE making. See Ice—Manufacture
ICE racing, Automobile. See Automobile racing
ICE removal. See Snow and ice removal
ICE sheets. See Glaciers
ICE skates. See Skates
ICE skating rinks. See Skating rinks
ICE storms
Distribution of icing in the Northeast's ice storm of 26-27 December 1969. S. F. Ackley and K. Itagaki. bibliog il Weatherwise 23:274-9 D '70
ICE vehicles
For a slick ride, try an ice cycle. E. F. Lindsley. il Pop Sci 198:121 Ja '71
ICEBREAKERS. See Ice breaking vessels
ICELAND
See also
Airlines—Iceland
Childrens literature—Iceland
Fishing—Iceland
Forests and forestry—Iceland
Geology—Iceland
Reykjavik

Description and travel

In the land of vodka and coke. D. Butwin. il Sat R 54:32-4 Ag 28 '71
Long light of midnight. il Life 71:42-9 Jl 30 '71

Industries

See also
Chemical industries—Iceland
ICELANDIC airlines. See Airlines—Iceland
ICELANDIC poetry
See also
Eddas

Translations into English

Elder Edda, a selection; tr. by P. B. Taylor and W. H. Auden. Review
Poetry 117:341-4 F '71. G. Johnston
ICES. See Ice cream, ices, etc.
ICHINOHE, Saeko
Saeko Ichinohe and company, the Cubiculo, NYC. L. Pastore. Dance Mag 45:82 S '71 *
ICHTHYOLOGICAL research
Breeding carp with fewer bones. il Sci Digest 69:91-3 F '71
ICONS project. See Isotopes
IDAHO
See also
Booksellers and bookselling—Idaho
Coeur d'Alene Lake
Salmon River
Wilderness areas—Idaho

Parks and reserves

He's rolling down one of the world's tallest sand dunes; Bruneau dunes state park. il Sunset 146:57 Ap '71
IDEAL states. See Utopias
IDEALISM in literature. See Romanticism
IDEAS in business
See also
Suggestion systems
IDENTIFICATION
Just call him 181213 3 1234 5; proposal by West German government. il Time 98:28 Jl 12 '71
One for all; one-number system. Nations Bsns 59:22 O '71
See also
Fingerprints
Voiceprints
also subhead Identification under various subjects, e.g. Trees—Identification

IDENTITY (psychology)
Identity crisis in black Americans visiting West Africa. A. A. Messer. bibliog Ment Hy 55:375-81 Jl '71
Process of identity, two views. M. S. Enker. bibliog Ment Hy 55:369-74 Jl '71

IDEOLOGY, Sex role. See Sex role

IDUARTE, Andrés
Books. N. Bliven. New Yorker 47:85-7 Jl 17 '71 *

IDYLL, Clarence P.
Crab that shakes hands. il Nat Geog 139:254-71 F '71
Harvest of plankton; excerpt from The sea against hunger. il Sea Front 17:258-67 S '71
Harvest of seaweed; excerpt from The sea against hunger. il Sea Front 17:342-8 N '71
Mercury and fish. il Sea Front 17:230-40 Jl '71

IFSHIN, David
Young Ifshin objects. W. F. Buckley, jr. Nat R 23:496 My 4 '71 *

IGNATIUS of Loyola, Saint. See Loyola, Ignatius of, Saint

IGNATOW, David
Comment. R. B. Shaw. Poetry 118:228-9 '71 *
Living; poem. Am Lib 2:1049 N '71
Two poets. R. Knudson. il pors Am Lib 2:1048 N '71 *

IGNEOUS rocks. See Rocks, Igneous

IGNITION
See also
Automobile engines—Ignition

IGNITION devices. See Automobile engines—Ignition; Marine engines—Ignition

IKARD, Frank Neville
Criticism, policy and reality; address, May 28, 1971. Vital Speeches 37:625-8 Ag 1 '71

IKEDA, Patricia
Reflections; poem. Sr Schol 98:8 My 17 '71

IKKO
Ikko: tradition meets a modern eye: photographs. Pop Phot 68:80-5 Ap '71

ILION, N.Y.
Decorative panels solve tank-location problem. il Am City 86:14 My '71

ILL. See Sick, The

ILLEGAL radio stations. See Radio stations, Illegal

ILLEGITIMACY
Amer-Asian children in Vietnam. D. Luce. Chr Cent 88:996-7 Ag 25 '71; Discussion. 88:1181-2 O 6 '71
See also
Fathers, Unmarried
Mothers, Unmarried

ILLIAC computers. See Computers

ILLICH, Ivan D.
Alternative to schooling. il Sat R 54:44-8+ Je 19 '71; Same abr. with title For disestablishment of the school. Cur 131:24-34 Jl '71
Education: a consumer commodity and a pseudo-religion; adaptation of address, 1971. Chr Cent 88:1464-8 D 15 '71
about
Dangers in de-schooling. T. Beeson. Chr Cent 88:1341 N 17 '71 *
Should schools be abolished? por Time 97:33 Je 7 '71 *

ILLIERS, France
A la recherche de Marcel Proust; hamlet of Illiers, renamed itself Illiers-Combray. il por Time 98:30+ Jl 5 '71

ILLIERS-COMBRAY. See Illiers, France

ILLIG, Joyce E.
Paperback bag. Seventeen 29:66+ N '70

ILLINOIS
See also
Agriculture—Illinois
Architecture, Domestic—Illinois
Booksellers and bookselling—Illinois
Camps—Illinois
Chicago River
Colleges and universities—Illinois
Courts—Illinois
Crime and criminals—Illinois
Education—Illinois
Hunting—Illinois
Justice. Administration of—Illinois
Libraries—Illinois
Music festivals—Illinois
Politics, Corruption in—Illinois
State aid to education—Illinois
Water supply—Illinois

Description and travel
Other Illinois. R. Sullivan. il Travel 135:56-61 Ap '71

Politics and government
Illinois gerrymander. Nation 213:323-4 O 11 '71
Journey of 1,000 miles; gubernatorial candidate, D. Walker. por Newsweek 78:45 N 8 '71
Slatemakers. il Newsweek 78:29-30 D 20 '71
See also
Politics, Corruption in—Illinois

Vigilance committees
See Vigilance committees

ILLINOIS library association
Task analysis study in Illinois: phase I of a cooperative project; ALA progress report. T. M. Brown. Am Lib 2:312-14 Mr '71

ILLINOIS. University
Integrity group seminars; graduate study. il Sch & Soc 99:333 O '71
New music festival at U. of Illinois. B. Johnson. il Hi Fi 21:MA28-9 Ag '71
Within and without the circle of faith; end of Illinois plan. D. B. Larson. il Chr Cent 88:1172-4 O 6 '71; Reply. R. B. Garrison. 88:1430 D 1 '71

Graduate school of library science
Robert B. Downs retires; with tribute by H. Goldhor. por Wilson Lib Bul 45:920-1 Je '71

Libraries
More than a house of books: undergraduate library. K. Rugen. il Am Lib 2:876-81 S '71

ILLITERACY
Illiteracy in the United States. W. V. Grant. il Am Ed 7:inside back cover Je '71
International literacy day awards. Sch & Soc 99:9+ Ja '71
Mind awakening; Unesco's work in education. W. McEwing. il UNESCO Courier 24:16-20 Ag '71
Toward world literacy; excerpts from address, September 8, 1970. Thant. por Sch & Soc 99:282-3 Sum '71
World drive at crucial point. Sch & Soc 99:461 D '71
Iran
Education corps. G. Soffer. il Focus 21:9-12 Ja '71

ILLUMINATION of books and manuscripts
Gottingen model book. A. DeMirjian, jr. il Pub W 200:44 D 6 '71
Luminous messenger; exhibit at New York's Pierpont Morgan library. R. Hughes. il Time 97:64-5 My 3 '71
See also
Hours, Books of

ILLUSION and hallucination producing plants. See Hallucination and illusion producing plants

ILLUSIONS, Optical. See Optical illusions

ILLUSIONS and hallucinations. See Hallucinations and illusions

ILLUSTRATED annual reports. See Corporation reports

ILLUSTRATED books
Story of Wheaties boxtops and other good books. M. Mann. il Pop Phot 68:17+ Je '71
See also
Picture books

ILLUSTRATION of books and periodicals
American heritage dictionary: pictures at a definition; a marginal critique; with reply by W. Morris. J. B. White. il Wilson Lib Bul 45:674-80 Mr '70
Are illustrators obsolete? S. W. Little. il Sat R 54:40-4 Jl 10 '71
Art vs. adventitious circumstances. W. Chappell. il Horn Bk 47:456-61 O '71
Book that never was, by J. R. Dunlap. Review Pub W il 200:45-6 D 6 '71. C. B. Grannis
Introduction to pictures by Maurice Sendak. M. Sendak. il Pub W 200:40 D 6 '71
John Sloan as an illustrator. E. J. Bullard. il Am Artist 35:52+ O '71
Ken Dallison: the education of an illustrator. N. Meglin. il por Am Artist 35:24-9+ N '71
Portfolio of Robert Byrd. D. Klemin. il por Am Artist 35:54-9 Je '71
Seeing pictures; magazine trends. J. Scully. il Mod Phot 34:10+ D '70
Sendak sampler; interview, ed. by A. DeMirjian, jr. M. Sendak; D. Hagen. il Pub W 200:37-9 D 6 '71
Splendor of iridescence; the making of H. Simon's new book. il Pub W 199:35-8 Mr 22 '71
Warhol as illustrator: early manipulations of the mundane. J. Masheck. bibliog il Art in Am 59:54-9 My '71
See also
Bible—Pictures, illustrations, etc.
Picture books for children

ILLUSTRATORS
Are illustrators obsolete? S. W. Little. il Sat R 54:40-4 Jl 10 '71
Illustrator in the courtroom: Hal Ashmead. M. Schaefer. il por Am Artists 36:30-5+ Ja '72
See also
Byrd, R.
Chwast, S.
Dallison, K.
Johnson, P C
Keats, E. J.
Kent, R.
McCall, R. T.
Saris, A
Sloan, J.
Wyeth, N. C.

ILMENITE
Lunar and terrestrial ilmenite basalt. S. S. Goldich. bibliog il Science 171:1245-6 Mr 26 '71

IMAGE amplifiers. See Image intensifiers
IMAGE converters
See also
Image intensifiers
IMAGE intensifiers
Bright idea; dye-laser image amplifier. Sci Am 224:50 My '71
Electronic image tubes in astronomy. D. L. Heiserman. il Electr World 86:34-5 N '71
IMAGES: story. See Oppenheimer, J.
IMAGINARY church history. See Church history, Hypothetical
IMAGINARY numbers. See Numbers, Complex
IMAGINATION
NCTE presidential address: imagination and the health of everyman; November 1970. J. E. Miller, jr. Engl J 60:189-98 F '71
See also
Creation (literary, artistic, etc)
Creative ability
IMAI, Ryukichi
Japan and the world of SALT. por Bul Atom Sci 27:13-16 D '71
IMHOFF, Rhoda
Art open lab. il Sch Arts 70:38-40 F '71
IMIDES
See also
Cycloheximide
IMITATION in literature
Writer's real world. S. Stevens. Writer 84:11-12+ Jl '71
IMITATION in music
Schubert's Beethoven. E. T. Cone. bibliog f il Mus Q 56:779-93 O '70
IMMATURITY, Emotional. See Maturity
IMMIGRANTS in Canada
Canada's other U.S. emigrants. J. C. Jones. il Newsweek 77:38+ My 24 '71
IMMIGRANTS in the United States
I love America. J. Atkins. Read Digest 98:187-8 Mr '71
See also
Cubans in the United States
IMMIGRATION and emigration
See also
Alien labor

Arab states
Brain drain from the Arab world; adaptation of address, December 22, 1969. M. S. Adiseshiah. Sch & Soc 99:367-9 O '71

Canada
See also
Immigrants in Canada

Cuba
See also
Cubans in the United States

Europe
See also
Intergovernmental committee for European migration

Europe, Western
Real divisions of Europe. A. Fontaine. For Affairs 49:302-14 Ja '71

Great Britain
Civis Britannicus non sum; new immigration bill. il Time 97:28-9 Mr 8 '71
See also
Deportation

Israel
Few who got out. il Time 97:35 F 8 '71
Not-so-lost tribe; Black Israelites turned away. il Newsweek 78:61 O 18 '71

Russia
Plucking out a thorn; exit visa for G. I. Feigin Newsweek 77:38+ F 15 '71
Suddenly I became Jewish; case of Alla Rusinek. il Newsweek 77:70 Ap 19 '71

United States
Canada's other U.S. emigrants. J. C. Jones. il Newsweek 77:38+ My 24 '71
Generations; with photographs by M. Waldman. Life 71:104-10+ D 17 '71
Government and private agency partnership in refugee assistance programs; address, March 14, 1971. F. L. Kellogg. Dept State Bul 64:576-8 My 3 '71
New Americans: where they're coming from. il U S News 70:12-14 Je 14 '71
Victimizing the third world; immigration of professionals from developing countries to the U.S. Nation 214:2 Ja 3 '72
See also
Intergovernmental committee for European migration

IMMITT, Salvatore J.
Opening up the classroom. Engl J 60:505-7 Ap '71
IMMORAL literature and pictures
Aesthetics of pornography, by P. Michelson.
Review
America 124:487 My 8 '71. P. C. Rule
Commonweal 94:240-2 My 14 '71. J. P. Sisk
New Repub 164:30+ My 15 '71. J. Yardley
New Yorker 47:84-6 Ag 28 '71. G. Steiner
Alien porn; new Russian books. il Newsweek 78:50+ N 22 '71
Danger: smut. J. N. Bell. Good H 172:85+ Ap '71
Facts versus fears: why should we worry about pornography? W. C. Wilson. bibliog f Ann Am Acad 397:105-17 S '71
From Denmark, with love; English publication of The little red schoolbook. H. R. Mayes. Sat R 54:8-9 Jl 3 '71
Hard cores and soft. P. S. Prescott. Newsweek 77:113-14 Mr 15 '71
Let's put the smut merchants out of business. W. M. Blount. il Nations Bsns 59:34-6+ S '71
Pornography collection; excerpts from Magazine selection. B. Katz. bibliog il Library J 96:4060-6 D 15 '71
Pornography, ho-hum. C. H. Simonds. Nat R 23:705 Je 29 '71
Pornography, obscenity and the case for censorship. I. Kristol. il N Y Times Mag p24-5+ Mr 28 '71; Discussion. p 14+ Ap 18, 21 Ap 25; 79 My 9 '71
Pornography revisited: where to draw the line; Time essay. R. Brine. il Time 97:64-5 Ap 5 '71
Pornography: what can we do to protect our kids? G. Greer. Bet Hom & Gard 49:16+ D '71
Sex biz. L. E. Sissman. Atlan 228:24+ Ag '71
Smut era, on the decline? il U S News 71:43-5 O 18 '71
Smut: the Mafia's newest racket; with editorial comment. G. Denison. Read Digest 99:11-12, 157-60 D '71
Speaking of sex and so forth. M. Ward. America 124:613-15 Je 12 '71
What sex offenders say about pornography. G. D. Shultz. Read Digest 99:53-7 Jl '71
What's happening to American morals; symposium. U S News 70:68-74 Ja 25 '71
See also
Booksellers and bookselling—Immoral literature and pictures
Censorship
Obscenity (law)
Sex in literature
United States—Commission on obscenity and pornography
IMMORTALITY
Finality; survival after death. V. P. McCorry. America 125:188-inside back cover S 18 '71
Hell of a question. J. E. Kokjohn; reply with rejoinder. S. Stopa. Commonweal 93:503 F 19 '71
No myth here; resurrection after death. V. P. McCorry. America 125:inside back cover O 30 '71
Something to look forward to. V. P. McCorry. America 124:inside back cover My 1 '71
IMMROTH, John Phillip
I'm a media freak! Library J 96:1935-6 Je 1 '71
IMMUNE response. See Immunological tolerance
IMMUNITY
Epidemics ahead, unless! S. L. Englebardt. Read Digest 99:114-18 N '71
Lead suppression of mouse resistance to salmonella typhimurium. F. E. Hemphill and others. bibliog il Science 172:1031-2 Je 4 '71

IMMUNITY—*Continued*
Plasmodium berghei: enhanced protective immunity after vaccination of white rats born of immune mothers. R. S. Desowitz. bibliog il Science 172:1151-2 Je 11 '71
See also
Agglutination
Antigens and antibodies
Complements (immunity)
Immunochemistry
Inoculation
Vaccination
Vaccines

Conferences
Immune complexes and disease. S. Loebl. Science 173:754+ Ag 20 '71

IMMUNOASSAY. See Biological assay

IMMUNOCHEMISTRY
Immunochemical detection of minor bases in nucleic acids. D. L. Sawicki and others. bibliog il Science 174:70-2 O 1 '71

IMMUNOFLUORESCENCE. See Antibodies, Fluorescent

IMMUNOGLOBULINS
Amyloid fibril proteins: proof of homology with immunoglobulin light chains by sequence analyses. G. G. Glenner and others. bibliog il Science 172:1150-1 Je 11 '71
Deletions in immunoglobulin polypeptide chains as evidence for breakage and repair in DNA. O. Smithies and others. bibliog il Science 172:574-7 My 7 '71
Immunoglobulin M and secretory immunoglobulin A: presence of a common polypeptide chain different from light chains. J. Mestecky and others. bibliog il Science 171:1163-5 Mr 19 '71
Immunoglobulin production by human lymphocytoid lines and clones: absence of genic exclusion. A. D. Bloom and others. bibliog il Science 172:382-3 Ap 23 '71
Interaction of rheumatoid factor with infectious herpes simplex virus-antibody complexes. W. K. Ashe and others. bibliog il Science 172:176-7 Ap 9 '71
Quantitative aspects of plasma membrane-associated immunoglobulin in clones of diploid human lymphocytes. R. A. Lerner and others. bibliog il Science 173:60-2 Jl 2 '71
Structure of the hinge region of the mu heavy chain of human IgM immunoglobulins. C. Paul and others. bibliog il Science 172:69-72 Ap 2 '71
Variation and homology in the mu and gamma heavy chains of human immunoglobulins. A. Shimizu and others. bibliog il Science 173:629-33 Ag 13 '71

IMMUNOLOGIC deficiency syndromes. See Deficiency diseases

IMMUNOLOGICAL tolerance
Autoimmune murine thyroiditis relation to histocompatibility (H-2) type. A. O. Vladutiu and N. R. Rose. bibliog il Science 174:1137-9 D 10 '71
Gestation, aging and cancer. il Sci N 100:107-8 Ag 14 '71
Immune response restoration with macrophage culture supernatants. M. Hoffmann and R. W. Dutton. bibliog il Science 172:1047-8 Je 4 '71
Immunocompetent cells among mouse thymocytes: a minor population. E. Leckband and E. A. Boyse. bibliog il Science 172:1258-60 Je 18 '71
Kinetic differences in unresponsiveness of thymus and bone marrow cells. J. M. Chiller and others. bibliog il Science 171:813-15 F 26 '71
Lymph node cells: their differential capacity to induce tolerance of heart and skin homografts in rats. C. F. Barker and others. bibliog il Science 172:1050-2 Je 4 '71
Lymphocyte stimulation: selective destruction of cells during blastogenic response to transplantation antigens. S. Salmon and others. bibliog il Science 172:490-2 Ap 30 '71
Maternal-fetal interaction and immunological memory. T. J. Gill, 3d. and others. bibliog il Science 172:1346-8 Je 25 '71
New discoveries about how immunity works. M. Steinmann. il Life 70:54 My 28 '71
Specificity of allogeneic cell recognition by human lymphocytes in vitro. D. C. Zoschke and F. H. Bach. bibliog il Science 172:1350-2 Je 25 '71
See also
Antilymphocytic serum

IMMUNOLOGY
See also
Immunological tolerance

IMMUNOSUPPRESSIVE agents
See also
Antilymphocytic serum
Asparaginase
Concanavalins
Glutaminase
Methotrexate

IMMUNOTHERAPY of cancer. See Cancer—Therapy

IMPEACHMENTS
Why impeachment; case against Mr Nixon. R. A. Falk. New Repub 164:13-14 My 1 '71

IMPEDANCE testers. See Testing instruments

IMPERIAL chemical industries, ltd.
Arrival of enemy no. 1. por Fortune 83:65 My '71
What Atlas has that ICI wants. Bsns W p33 Ap 24 '71

IMPERIAL COUNTY, Calif.
U.S. journal: doctors' views on the Clinical de salubridad de campesinos. C. Trillin. New Yorker 46:83-9 F 13 '71

IMPERIALISM
Enemy, by F. Greene. Review
New Repub 164:35 My 29 '71. J. Gilbert
Mad dogs and who go out in the mid-day sun? excerpt from Playing soldier, a diatribe. F. Getlein. Commonweal 94:159-62 Ap 23 '71
New American imperialism?
Does the U.S. economy require it? S. M. Miller and others. Cur 125:42-50 Ja '71
Logic of imperialism. H. Magdoff. Cur 125:51-63 Ja '71
On war and greed in the second century B.C; economic motives of Roman imperialism. W. V. Harris. bibliog f Am Hist R 76:1371-85 D '71

IMPERSONATORS, Female
Charles Pierce: female impersonator as culture hero(ine) J. Stewart. il pors Ramp Mag 10:60-3 O '71

IMPLEMENTS, utensils, etc.
See also
Indians of North America—Implements
Kitchen utensils
Stone implements and weapons

IMPORT and export controls. See Foreign trade regulation

IMPORT tax. See Tariff

IMPORTS
Firsts from mainland China; wicker baskets. N. C. Gray. il Home 74:30+ N '71
Hot buys. Newsweek 78:54 S 6 '71
Import surcharge jolts the retailers. il Bsns W p68 Ag 21 '71
Import thaw is no help to Scotch; Japan. il Bsns W p51 Jl 17 '71
Increases in shipping weights of total U.S. exports and imports; tables. Aviation W 96:39 Ja 10 '72
Lifelines for import victims. il Nations Bsns 59:28+ Je '71
Made in China. il Newsweek 78:73 N 29 '71
See also
Books—Importation
Dumping (commercial policy)
Helicopter industry—Imports problem
Meat industry—Imports problem
Pier 1 imports, inc
Shoe industry—Imports problem
Steel industry—Imports problem
Sugar industry—Imports problem
Textile industry—Imports problem

IMPOSTORS and imposture
See also
Fraud

IMPRESARIOS
Goodbye to rock; B. Graham gets out of rock concert business. M. Durham. il pors Life 70:62-4+ My 14 '71
See also
Edgley, M.

IMPRESSIONISM (art)
Prophet of light; musée Marmottan and the Monet bequest. R. Hughes. il Time 98:54-5 Jl 19 '71
Sunday afternoon on the Island of La Grande Jatte. R. McMullen. il por Horizon 13:82-95 Sum '71

IMPRISONMENT of children. See Children—Imprisonment

IMURA, Nobumasa, and others
Chemical methylation of inorganic mercury with methylcobalamin, a vitamin B_{12} analog. bibliog il Science 172:1248-9 Je 18 '71

IN New England; drama. See Bullins, E.

IN-service training of employees. See Employees—Training

IN the men's room of the sixteenth century; story. See DeLillo, D.

IN the tunnel; story. See Gallant, M.

IN Utica; story. See Bumpus, J.

INAUGURATION day. See Inaugurations

INAUGURATIONS
Big cheese at the White House: A. Jackson's inaugural celebration. il por Sr Schol 99:10-11 O 25 '71
See also
Kennedy, J. F.—Inaugural address

INBAU, Fred E. and Carrington, F. G.
Case for the so-called hard line approach to crime. bibliog f Ann Am Acad 397:19-27 S '71

INBOARD motor boats. See Motor boats
INBOARD motors. See Motor boat engines
INBORN errors of metabolism. See Metabolism, Disorders of
INCANDESCENT electric lamps. See Electric lamps. Incandescent

INCARNATION
Mystery of the manger. Chr Today 16:30 D 3 '71

INCAS
East of the Andes; Incas' *montaña* campaigns. J. Rawls. il Américas 23:15-24 Ag '71

INCENTIVES in industry
New tool: reinforcement for good work. il Bsns W p76-7 D 18 '71
See also
Bonus system
Profit sharing
Wage payment plans

INCIDENTAL music. See Music, Incidental
INCINERATORS. See Refuse incinerators
INCLINOMETERS. See Measuring instruments
INCO. See International nickel company of Canada

INCOME
Affluence spreading over U.S; findings of a new study. il U S News 71:28-9 D 6 '71
Blue-collar/white-collar pay trends: earnings and family income; with tables. R. L. Stein and J. N. Hedges. bibliog il Mo Labor R 94:13-24 Je '71
5 ways to figure farm income. Suc Farm 69:no5 12 Mr '71
How blue-collar workers are doing; a new study. U S News 70:58+ My 10 '71
How much is your job really worth? with tables. I. Mothner. il Look 35:60-3 Ap 20 '71
Mr Nixon's reactionary revolution. M. Harrington. Commonweal 95:199-202 N 26 '71
Not so affluent society. il Life 70:42 My 14 '71
People are getting richer. il U S News 71:35 S 20 '71
Personal income; tables. See occasional issues of Business week
Phase two: will it work? For whom? D. Deitch. Nation 213:678-82 D 27 '71
See also
Gross national product
Guaranteed annual income
Minimum wage
Purchasing power
Retirement income
Salaries
Wealth, Distribution of

INCOME policy. See Wage-price policy

INCOME tax
Auditing
See Tax auditing

Deductions
Better than revenue sharing; tax credits. M. J. Ulmer. New Repub 164:16-19 F 13 '71; Same abr. with title Alternative 1: tax credits. Cur 128:46-50 Ap '71
Bigger deductions: a tax break with broad effects. il U S News 72:51-2 Ja 3 '72
14 ways you can legally cut your taxes; interview, ed. by J. R. Moskin, M. M. Caplin. Look 35:15-17 Mr 23 '71
How to avoid income-tax troubles. D. Wharton. Read Digest 98:105-7 Mr '71
How to make your taxes into a one-evening job. il Mech Illus 67:60-1+ Ap '71
If your tax return is questioned: case histories, what to expect; with interview with R. W. Thrower. il U S News 70:23-6 Je 14 '71
Income tax law changes that save you money. il Good H 172:184 Mr '71
On stimulating the gift of blood. W. Bevan. Science 173:583 Ag 13 '71
Senate considers House changes in retirement income tax credit. Har Yrs 11:4 Ag '71
Tax angles on dependents. il Changing T 26:22-3 Ja '72
Tax angles on medical expenses. il Changing T 25:33-4 D '71

Tax checklist. Writers Digest 51:21 Ap '71
Tax credits for education; proposal of Catholic bishops. America 125:474-5 D 4 '71
Tax tips for the good old summertime. Suc Farm 69:23 Je '71
There is still time to get expert tax help. Bsns W p 101 F 27 '71
Ways to save on '71 taxes. U S News 71:47-50 N 15 '71
When is a wife deductible? Duns 98:63 Jl '71
You may save on taxes if you act right now. M. Daly. Bet Hom & Gard 49:18+ D '71
See also
Amortization deductions
Expense accounts (business)
Tax planning

Forms
See Tax forms

Poetry
In April when it's tax time. Pub W 199:27 Ap 5 '71

Returns
See Tax returns

Ireland
Artists and Irish taxes. Art in Am 59:23 My '71

United States
Ahead, a shift away from property taxes. il U S News 71:93-4 D 6 '71
Heat builds for a tax cut: a look at the chances. il U S News 70:52-4 Je 28 '71
How to save on income tax: latest changes. il U S News 70:49-51 Mr 22 '71
Income tax information for teachers. Todays Ed 60:38-40 F '71
Tax calendar for '71: dates you need to watch. U S News 70:73 Ja 18 '71
Tax cuts a step nearer: who gets the breaks. il U S News 71:56-8 O 4 '71
Tax relief that Congress planned. il U S News 71:27 D 13 '71
What's your tax problem. (Cont) il Changing T 25:41-2 F; 11-12 Mr; 19-20 Ap '71
See also
Excess profits tax
Tax evasion
Tax returns

INCOME tax, Municipal
Should a city tax commuters? il Changing T 25:45-6 Ag '71

INCOME tax, State
More states put the bite on incomes. il Bsns W p86+ Ag 14 '71

INCOMPARABLE Max; drama. See Lawrence, J. and Lee R. E.

INCORPORATED farms. See Farm corporations

INCURABLES
When do we have the right to die? 3 case histories. P. Wilkes. il Life 72:48+ Ja 14 '72

INDECENT assault
See also
Child molesters

INDEPENDENCE day. See Fourth of July

INDEPENDENCE NATIONAL HISTORICAL PARK
Independence National Historical Park. J. C. Milley. il Antiques 100:99-103 Jl '71

INDEPENDENT farmers alliance
Fed-up NFO'ers form IFA. B. Coffman. Farm J 95:48 Ap '71

INDEPENDENT postal system of America
Private mail service tries for first class. il Bsns W p38 D 11 '71

INDEPENDENT regulatory commissions
Agency shuffle starts drawing fire. Bsns W p25 F 13 '71
New plan for regulating industry. il U S News 70:44-5 F 22 '71
Who'll regulate the regulators? Nations Bsns 59:18 Jl '71
See also
Government investigations—Independent regulatory commissions
United States—President's advisory council on executive organization

INDEPENDENT study
Independent study, a plan for all pupils. J. P. Casey. Clear House 46:173-7 N '71
Library-university. L. Shores. Sch & Soc 99:163-6 Mr '71
Rationale for independent study degree programs. W. J. Driscoll. bibliog Sch & Soc 99:411-13 N '71
Teaching black studies with independent study. il Negro Hist Bul 34:4-5 Ja '71

INDEPENDENT television authority. See Television broadcasting—Great Britain

INDETERMINATE sentence
Kind and usual punishment in California.
J. Mitford. il Atlan 227:45-52 Mr '71; Discussion. 227:34+ My '71

INDEX numbers (economics)
Forbes index. See issues of Forbes
See also
Price indexes

INDEXES
See also
Cumulative book index

INDEXING
$1,000 misunderstanding: UM's index to its Dissertation abstracts international; with reply by R. F. Asleson. R. L. Scott. Wilson Lib Bul 46:73-7 S '71
Selective dissemination and indexing of scientific information. J. H. Schneider. bibliog il Science 173:300-8 Jl 23 '71
See also
Computers—Indexing use

INDEXING (machine work)
Add an indexing attachment to your lathe.
W. E. Burton. il Pop Mech 135:170-6 Mr '71

INDIA
Pakistan: what never gets said. P. Deutschman. Nation 213:457-60 N 8 '71
See also
Art—India
Atomic power—India
Calcutta
Colleges and universities—India
Economic assistance in India
Elections—India
Guerrillas
Investments, Foreign (in India)
Kashmir
Medical service—India
Moving pictures—India
Paleontology—India
Political campaigns—India
Political crimes and offenses—India
Political parties—India
Prohibition—India
Rites and ceremonies—India
Science—India
Sikkim
Wildlife conservation—India

Air force
Indian air power isolates Pakistani forces in east. il Aviation W 95:15-16 D 13 '71

Armed forces
My classmate the enemy; top officers. il Newsweek 78:38 D 20 '71

Boundaries
See also
Sino-Indian border dispute, 1957-

Defenses
Equal hatred, unequal odds. il Newsweek 78:40 D 13 '71

Description and travel
How people really travel; interview. C. Grenier. il por Vogue 157:120 Ap 15 '71
Instant India. R. H. Peck. il Travel 136:28-35+ S '71

Economic conditions
Buoyant economy in a bitter war. il Bsns W p58-9 D 18 '71
Growth with social justice: India today; address, November 6, 1970. L. K. Jha. Vital Speeches 37:218-21 Ja 15 '71
India's endless troubles, and why they worry U.S. il U S News 71:86-9 N 8 '71

Foreign relations
Behind Mrs Gandhi's talks with Nixon. il por U S News 71:102 N 15 '71
Pleader in the West; six-nation tour of I. Gandhi. il por Time 98:45-6 N 8 '71

Pakistan
Blackouts and border battles. il Time 98:41-2 N 22 '71
Hindus vs. Moslems: conflict that goes back 450 years. il U S News 71:12-13 D 20 '71
India and Pakistan: poised for war. il Time 98:28+ D 6 '71
India-Pakistan: powder keg with a lighted fuse. il U S News 71:41 N 1 '71
India vs. Pakistan: is this the next war? il U S News 71:42-4 Ag 23 '71
Most fearful consequence. il Time 98:28-9 Jl 5 '71
Nehru's plan for peace. S. S. Harrison. New Repub 164:17-22 Je 19 '71
Not if, but when. il Time 98:38 N 29 '71
Smell of war. il Newsweek 78:39 N 1 '71
Still another war. Commonweal 95:219-20 D 3 '71

Talk with India's Prime Minister Gandhi; excerpts from interview, ed. by E. Klein. por Newsweek 78:53 N 15 '71
Trying to cap a hot volcano; I. Gandhi's Washington visit. il por Time 98:32+ N 15 '71
War in Bengal: India attacks; with reports by A. de Borchgrave and T. Clifton. il Newsweek 78:30+ D 6 '71
War waiting to happen; with report by M. Parker and interview with Y. Khan. il Newsweek 78:52-3 N 8 '71
Why India and Pakistan are at it again. U S News 71:21-2 D 6 '71
Why India won't risk peace. il Newsweek 78:38+ D 6 '71
See also
India-Pakistan war, 1971

Russia
See Russia—Foreign relations—India

United States
See United States—Foreign relations—India

Politics and government
Indira Gandhi is either hated or adored. D. Moraes. il por N Y Times Mag p 10-11+ F 14 '71
Indira's triumph. J. D'Souza. il America 124:400-3 Ap 17 '71
See also
Communist party (India)
Elections—India

Religious institutions and affairs
Ganges, river of faith. J. J. Putnam. il Nat Geog 140:445-83 O '71

Social life and customs
Chronicles of wasted time. M. Muggeridge. il pors Esquire 76:128-31+ N '71

Treaties
Russia
See Russia—Treaties—India
INDIA-Pakistan dispute. See Kashmir
INDIA-Pakistan war, 1971
Anguished birth of Bangladesh. il Life 71:2-5 D 31 '71
Another war in Asia: who's to blame? S. Dring. il Newsweek 78:34-8 D 20 '71
Bangladesh: out of war, a nation is born. il Time 98:20-2+ D 20 '71
Buoyant economy in a bitter war. il Bsns W p58-9 D 18 '71
Choice of wars. P. Steinfels. Commonweal 95:319+ Ja 7 '72
Choosing sides in the subcontinent. il Newsweek 78:18-19 D 20 '71
Crisis and parity; policies of Russia and the U.S. Z. Brzezinski. Newsweek 79:26 Ja 3 '72
In Pakistan, now it's war; with report on the Mukti Bahini, by J. Saar. il Life 71:30-4 D 10 '71
India and Pakistan, on the road to all-out war. il U S News 71:47 D 13 '71
India and Pakistan: over the edge. il Time 98:23-5 D 13 '71
India: easy victory, uneasy peace. il Time 98:28-30+ D 27 '71
India-Pakistan war. A. J. Goldberg. New Repub 165:7-9 D 18 '71
India vs. Pakistan. il Sr Schol 99:16-17+ D 13 '71
India vs. Pakistan: the war nobody wanted; questions and answers. il Sr Schol 99:14-15 Ja 10 '72
Involve ourselves in India? W. F. Buckley, jr. Nat R 23:1487 D 31 '71
Late show at the U.N; discussion in the Security council. Nation 213:642 D 20 '71
Letter from West Bengal. V. Mehta. New Yorker 47:166+ D 11 '71
Leverage fallacy; influence of U.S. aid to Pakistan. Nation 213:611-12 D 13 '71
Notes and comment. New Yorker 47:37 D 11 '71
Pakistan and India go to war. il Newsweek 78:39-40 D 13 '71
Pan Am, Pakistan airlines hurt by war. J. P. Woolsey. Aviation W 96:24 Ja 3 '72
Peril of picking a loser: Dacca's last days. il Newsweek 78:22-3+ D 27 '71
Picking up the pieces; U.S. policy. New Repub 166:7-9 Ja 1 '72
Protracted conflict; with editorial comment. J. Burnham. Nat R 23:1450-1, 1458 D 31 '71
Reporters at war. il Newsweek 78:85 D 20 '71
Stakes in the subcontinent. R. Hotz. Aviation W 955:9 D 13 '71

INDIA-Pakistan war, 1971—*Continued*
Toilet training; H. A. Kissinger's remarks on Soviet policy. J. Osborne. New Repub 166:16-17 Ja 1 '72
War in Asia; why India spurned U.S. peace efforts. il U S News 71:11-14 D 20 '71
War nobody stopped. V. G. Kiernan; R. Sobhan; V. P. Nanda. il Nation 213:682-91 D 27 '71
War on the subcontinent. il Nat R 23:1392 D 17 '71
We know how the Persians felt; surrender of Dacca. D. Coggin. il Time 98:31 D 27 '71
See also
Pakistan—Air force

Reconstruction
Painful adjustment. il Time 99:28-9 Ja 10 '72
INDIAN affairs, Bureau of. See United States —Indian affairs, Bureau of
INDIAN arrow points. See Arrowheads
INDIAN arts and crafts. See Indians of North America—Industries
INDIAN baskets. See Indians of North America—Basket making
INDIAN burial grounds. See Cemeteries
INDIAN-Chinese border dispute, 1957-. See Sino-Indian border dispute, 1957-
INDIAN clothing. See Indians of North America—Costume and adornment
INDIAN communications satellites. See Communications satellites, Indian (East Indian)
INDIAN cookery (East Indian) See Cookery, Indian (East Indian)
INDIAN dancing (East Indian) See Dancing, Indian (East Indian)
INDIAN Head, Inc.
Riskless options? Duns 97:71 Je '71
INDIAN languages. See Indians of North America—Languages
INDIAN masks. See Indians of North America —Masks
INDIAN meal moths. See Moths
INDIAN mounds. See Mounds and mound builders
INDIAN moving picture actors and actresses. See Moving picture actors and actresses
INDIAN OCEAN
New hotspot for big black marlin. J. C. Chapralis. il Field & S 76:84+ Je '71
Red star over the Indian Ocean. A. Harrigan. Nat R 23:421-3 Ap 20 '71
U.S. national security policy and the Indian Ocean area; statement, July 28, 1971. R. I. Spiers. Dept State Bul 65:199-203 Ag 23 '71
See also
Aldabra Island
Maldive Islands
INDIAN-Pakistan war, 1971. See India-Pakistan war, 1971
INDIAN poetry. See Indians of North America —Poetry
INDIAN reservations. See Indians of North America—Reservations
INDIAN tobacco pipes. See Tobacco pipes
INDIAN youth. See Indians of North America— Youth
INDIANA
See also
Architecture, Domestic—Indiana
Crawford County
Education—Indiana
Hunting—Indiana
Libraries—Indiana
Prisons—Indiana
Recreation areas—Indiana
Unemployment—Indiana
INDIANA Standard. See Standard oil company (Indiana)
INDIANA, University, Bloomington
What the fans came to see is what they got; Hoosier' fourth NCAA swimming and diving championship. W. F. Reed, jr. Sports Illus 34:77-9 Ap 5 '71
INDIANAPOLIS

Education
Programed tutor; Programed tutorial reading project in Indianapolis public schools. J. White. il Am Ed 7:18-21 D '71

Galleries and museums
New home for the arts; Indianapolis museum of art. il Design 72:22-6 mid-Wint '71

Police department
Computerized police communications. il Am City 86:32 My '71

Politics and government
Self-help and the cities. il pors Nations Bsns 59:22-6 Je '71

Sanitary affairs
Put speed and control in your snow fighting program. il Am City 86:37 D '71

Street traffic
Low-cost computer halves driving time. C. A. Venable. il Am City 86:37 D '71
INDIANAPOLIS automobile races. See Automobile racing
INDIANAPOLIS 500. See Automobile racing
INDIANAPOLIS museum of art. See Indianapolis—Galleries and museums
INDIANS
See also
Paleo-Indians

Agriculture
See also
Chinampas

Art
See also
Eskimos—Art
Indians of Central America—Art
Indians of North America—Art
Petroglyphs

Education
See also
Indians of North America—Education

Industries
See also
Beadwork
INDIANS (baseball) See Baseball clubs
INDIANS, Treatment of
About Indians, by Indians; quotations. il Sr Schol 99:2-7 D 6 '71
American thing: white society is breaking down around us; interview, ed. by P. Collier. V. Deloria, jr. Mlle 72:202-4+ Ap '71
America's most oppressed minority. H. E. Fey. il Chr Cent 88:65-8 Ja 20 '71
Bury my heart at Wounded Knee, by D. Brown. Review
Newsweek il 77:69 F 1 '71. G. Wolff
Custer myth. A. M. Josephy, jr. il por Life 71:48-52+ Jl 2 '71
Four Indian kings in London; journey of Mohawk sachems led by P. Schuyler in 1709-10. M. Bishop. il Am Heritage 23:62-5 D '71
Trial of Coronado. W. J. Buchanan. il Américas 23:28-38 Ja '71
When red and white men met; excerpts from address, April 1971. J. C. Ewers. Am Heritage 23:107-8 D '71
Wounded knee and My Lai. Chr Cent 88:59 Ja 20 '71
INDIANS, Wooden
Chain saw artist; cigar store Indian. M. Lincoln. il pors Design 72:4-7 mid-Sum '71
INDIANS in art
Colorful Southwest of R. Brownell McGrew. F. Whitaker. il Am Artist 35:72-9+ Mr '71
Paul Kane's frontier; sketches among the Indians of North America, 1845-1848. J. R. Harper. Antiques 99:391-7 Mr '71
INDIANS in literature
Guidelines for evaluation of Indian materials for adults. J. S. Smith. Am Lib 2:610-11 Je '71
Hi, ho, Silver and all that. D. Broderick. bibliog il Library J 96:2852-3 S 15 '71
Plight of the native American. R. Mickinock. il por Library J 96:2848-51 S 15 '71
INDIANS of Alaska. See Indians of North America—Alaska
INDIANS of Brazil. See Indians of South America—Brazil
INDIANS of Central America
Pre-Columbian America: Mesoamerica; symposium. il Américas 23:S1-40 Je '71
Surviving a guided tour of America; Choco tribal chief, guest of U.S. il Life 70:73 Je 18 '71
Visit to the San Blas Indians takes you backward in time; Cuna Indians. G. Skinner. il Yachting 129:66-7+ F '71

Antiquities
Pre-Columbian America: Mesoamerica; symposium. il Américas 23:S1-40 Je '71
See also
Copán, Honduras
Sculpture, Pre-Columbian

Art
Newest ancient art. J. H. Kay. il Américas 23:S16-21 Je '71

Culture
Architecture, sculpture, environment. F. L. Phelps. il Américas 23:S12-15 Je '71

INDIANS of Central America—*Continued*
Religion and mythology
Persistence of smalltown saints; cults of King San Pascual and San Simón. J. Luján Muñoz. il Américas 23:10-15 My '71

Writing
See also
Mayas—Writing
INDIANS of Chile. See Indians of South America—Chile
INDIANS of Mexico
See also
Aztecs
Mayas
Yaqui Indians
Antiquities
See Mexico—Antiquities
Religion and mythology
Mesa del Nayar's strange Holy week; Cora Indians celebration. G. Aldana E. il por Nat Geog 139:780-95 Je '71
INDIANS of North America
Extent and significance of suicide among American Indians today. R. J. Havighurst. bibliog il Ment Hy 55:174-7 Ap '71
Our Indian heritage; with editorial comment. il Life 71:5, 38-47 Jl 2 '71
See also
Crow Indians
Eskimos
Hopi Indians
Iroquois Indians
Navaho Indians
Pueblo Indians
Taos Indians
Ute Indians
Yahi Indians
Antiquities
Indian relics. C. Miles. See issues of Hobbies
See also
Louisiana—Antiquities
New York (state)—Antiquities
Utah—Antiquities
Wyoming—Antiquities
Art
First Americans as artists. K. Kuh. il Sat R 54:44-5 S 4 '71
Make it a vacation in Indian crafts country. M. Gough. House B 113:30-2 Je '71
New vitality rekindles proud fires of the past. L. K. New. House B 113:38-9+ Je '71
Surprising riches of Indian art. il Life 71:60-5 Jl 2 '71
Tribes in the gallery; exhibition at Manhattan's Whitney museum. R. Hughes. il Time 98:78 D 6 '71
200 years of North American Indian art. R. Drexler. bibliog il Craft Horiz 31:30-9+ D '71
See also
Totem poles
Basket making
Notes on Indian basketry. C. Miles. il Hobbies 76:146-7+ D '71
Civil rights
Indians and sociologists: science or exploitation? R. J. Trotter. Sci N 100:234 O 2 '71
Civilization
See Indians of North America—Culture
Costume and adornment
Indian summer; real Indian gear with report by D. Antum. il Mlle 73:114-19. 182 Je '71
Painting artifacts. C. Miles. il Hobbies 76:144-5+ Ja '72
Tools and clothing of the Indian. C. Miles. il Hobbies 76:146-7 O '71
Culture
American Indian culture: promises, problems, and possibilities; classroom study. A. L. Stensland. bibliog Engl J 60:1195-200 D '71
Cultural conflict in urban Indians. J. Ablon. bibliog Ment Hy 55:199-205 Ap '71
New vitality rekindles proud fires of the past. L. K. New. House B 113:38-9+ Je '71
Vision beyond time and place. N. S. Momaday. il Life 71:66-7 Jl 2 '71
Dances
Make it a vacation in Indian crafts country. M. Gough. House B 113:30-2 Je '71
Economic conditions
Indian in the city; effects of relocation. il Newsweek 77:94+ Je 14 '71

Education
Blazing a new trail; recommendations of the National study of American Indian education. S. Boyer. Sat R 54:53 Ja 16 '71
Cultivating student teachers in the Yakima Valley; Center for the study of migrant and Indian education, Central Washington state college. C. H. Potter. il Am Ed 7:27-31 My '71
ED funds for Indians misused charges NAACP. Library J 96:1413 Ap 15 '71
IBM computer for Navajo language textbooks. il Sch & Soc 99:468-9 D '71
Oral communication for the Indian student; address, April 1970. B. L. Brilhart. Engl J 60:629-32 My '71
Red power in Maine; TRIBE high school for Indian dropouts. Newsweek 77:55 My 31 '71
Smooth path at Rough Rock. R. Tunley. il Am Ed 7:15-20 Mr '71
Fishing
Salmon fishing in America: the Indians vs. the state of Washington. P. Collier. il Ramp Mag 9:29-31+ Ap '71
Government relations
American thing: white society is breaking down around us; interview, ed. by P. Collier. V. Deloria, jr. Mlle 72:202-4+ Ap '71
America's most oppressed minority. H. E. Fey. il Chr Cent 88:65-8 Ja 20 '71
Anomie at Alcatraz; report. W. Marmon. il Time 97:21 Ap 12 '71
Indian in the city; effects of relocation. il Newsweek 77:94+ Je 14 '71
Salmon fishing in America: the Indians vs. the state of Washington. P. Collier. il Ramp Mag 9:29-31+ Ap '71
See also
Indians of North America—Land tenure
Indians of North America—Reservations
Indians of North America—Treaties
United States—Indian affairs, Bureau of
History
American history: a native American view. Library J 96:678+ F 15 '71
Building a new world: the white man's mighty effort to civilize the first Californians. D. Lavender. il Am West 8:36-41+ N '71
Four Indian kings in London; journey of Mohawk sachems lead by P. Schuyler in 1709-10. M. Bishop. il Am Heritage 23:62-5 D '71
Implements
Adventure to antiquity. R. J. Graham. il Field & S 76:78-9+ Je '71
Dance basket; Indians' bow. C. Miles. il Hobbies 76:146-8 S '71
Painting artifacts. C. Miles. il Hobbies 76:144-5+ Ja '72
Root picks; Mat creaser. C. Miles. il Hobbies 76:150-1+ Je '71
Tobacco among the Karuks. C. Miles. il Hobbies 76:146-7+ N '71
Tools and clothing of the Indian. C. Miles. il Hobbies 76:146-7 O '71
See also
Arrowheads
Industries
Crafts of the Indian. M. Gough. il House B 113:37-62+ Je '71
Making it on your own, Navajo-style. il Nations Bsns 59:19 My '71
See also
Indians of North America—Basket making
Land tenure
Battle for Blue Lake. D. O. Collins. il Am West 8:32-7 S '71
Cherokee tragedy, by T. Wilkins. Review Sat R 54:50 F 13 '71. R. D. Fogelson
U.S. journal: Tesuque, N.M. C. Trillin. New Yorker 47:93-7 D 18 '71
Languages
See also
Navaho language
Study and teaching
Indian teens agree, take Cree and see; Senior youthview. L. V. MacLean. il Sr Schol 99:8-9 D 6 '71
Libraries
Indian library aides and a librarian friend. il Wilson Lib Bul 46:324-5 D '71
Anecdotes, facetiae, satire, etc.
Quo jure? advertising for suitable librarian to serve American Indians without discriminating. B. E. Richardson. il Am Lib 2:304-5 Mr '71

INDIANS of North America—*Continued*

Masks

False faces; exhibition at New York's Whitney museum, 200 years of North American Indian art. D. Davis. il Newsweek 78:79 N 29 '71

Missions

Indian uprising, five years later; dispute between the Catholic church and the Isleta Indians. P. Reyes. il Chr Cent 88:80+ Ja 20 '71

Museums

If you wonder about the Utes. il Sunset 147:8 Ag '71

Music

Magic world, ed. by W. Brandon. Review Pub W il 199:42-3 Je 21 '71. A. H. Johnston

Photographs

Gallery; Indian portraits by J. K. Dixon. Life 71:10-11 Jl 2 '71

Poetry

Magic world, ed. by W. Brandon. Review Pub W il 199:42-3 Je 21 '71. A. H. Johnston

Psychology

Cultural conflict in urban Indians. J. Ablon. bibliog Ment Hy 55:199-205 Ap '71

Religion and mythology

Indian uprising, five years later; dispute between the Catholic church and the Isleta reservation? G. P. Noble. Chr Cent 88:78-80 Ja 20 '71
Our Indian heritage; with editorial comment. il Life 71:5, 38-47 Jl 2 '71
See also
Totem poles

Relocation

See Indians of North America—Government relations

Reservations

Epilogue: twenty years after the Little Bighorn. R. M. Utley. il Am Heritage 22:40-1 Je '71
Ganado project: any change for the Navajo reservation? G. P. Noble. Chr Cent 88:78-80 Ja 20 '71; Discussion. 88:320-2, 537-8 Mr 10, Ap 28 '71
How 114 washing machines came to the Crow reservation; excerpt from The death of the Great Spirit. E. Shorris. Atlan 227:73-7 F '71
Navajos trade hogans for air-conditioning; Shiprock housing project. il Bsns W p 100+ O 23 '71
Notes on a Fort Peck pamphlet. C. Miles. Hobbies 75:152-3 Ja '71
Trinkets for the Navajos. P. Barnes. New Repub 165:15-16 Jl 3 '71
We like us: attitudes of the mental health staff toward other agencies on the Navajo reservation. L. S. Schoenfeld and others. Ment Hy 55:171-3 Ap '71

Sculpture

See also
Totem poles

Songs

See Indians of North America—Music

Treaties

U.S. journal: Tesuque, N.M. C. Trillin. New Yorker 47:93-7 D 18 '71

Treatment

See Indians, Treatment of

Wars

Custer myth. A. M. Josephy, jr. il por Life 71:48-52+ Jl 2 '71
Navajo roundup by L. Kelly. Review Am West 8:49 Jl '71. R. H. Dillon
See also
Little Big Horn, Battle of the, 1876
United States—History—French and Indian war, 1755-1763

Youth

Indian teens tell it like it isn't; interviews, ed. by E. Sparn. il Sr Schol 98:18-19 Mr 1 '71

Alaska

Natives may win one: great Alaskan real-estate deal. T. M. Brown. il N Y Times Mag p42-3+ O 17 '71

INDIANS of North America in art. See Indians in art

INDIANS of North America in literature. See Indians in literature

INDIANS of Peru. See Indians of South America—Peru

INDIANS of South America
Lola; last surviving Ona Indian in Tierra del Fuego. A. M. Chapman. il Natur Hist 80:32-41 Mr '71

Antiquities

Vanishing Guarani treasures. A. Ibáñez Padilla. il Américas 23:32-5 O '71

Commerce

Indian markets of South America. E. A. Gerling. il Travel 135:42-7 F '71

Brazil

Brazil protects her Cinta Largas. W. J. Von Puttkamer. il Nat Geog 140:420-44 S '71
Stone age or twentieth century. H. B. Ryan. il Américas 23:19-24 S '71

Chile

This land or death; Mapuche Indians seize farms. Newsweek 77:41-2 F 15 '71

Peru

Titicaca, abode of the sun. L. Marden. il Nat Geog 139:272-94 F '71
See also
Incas

INDICATORS, Proximity warning. See Proximity warning indicators

INDIGO buntings
Celestial navigation by migrating birds. Sky & Tel 41:80 F '71
Celestial rotation: its importance in the development of migratory orientation. S. T. Emlen; reply with rejoinder. E. G. F. Sauer. bibliog Science 173:459-61 Jl 30 '71

INDIVIDUAL and society
Addiction as a necessity and opportunity; address, April 20, 1970. E. H. Land. Science 171:151-3 Ja 15 '71
Senile society; a theory. S. Goldberg. Yale R 61:1-25 O '71
To speak of certainties. B. W. Overstreet. il PTA Mag 66:21-3 O '71

INDIVIDUAL and state
Does the shoe fit? a background piece on the silent majority. E. Reimer. il America 124:69-70 Ja 23 '71
Notes and comment. New Yorker 47:29-30 F 27 '71; Same with title Prologue to a war with China? Cur 128:8-11 Ap '71

INDIVIDUAL differences
See also
Sex differences

INDIVIDUAL instruction
Alleluia! English has risen! A. L. Beslin. Engl J 60:607-9 My '71
How do I get them to go home? C. Rudder. Ed Digest 36:32-4 Mr '71
Individualized instruction. M. McQueen. Ed Digest 36:25-8 Ap '71
Individualizing the study of English. E. R. Fagan. Engl J 60:236-41+ F '71
Multimedia classroom; Project SPOKE, Norton, Mass. D. C. Steffen. il Am Ed 7:28-30 Ag '71
School for the 70's an immodest proposal. M. C. Olson. Clear House 45:488-92 Ap '71
Wide open for learning; Project SOLVE; schools without walls in New Hampshire. R. C. Wing and P. H. Mack. Ed Digest 36:19-21 F '71

INDIVIDUAL labor contracts. See Labor contracts

INDIVIDUAL liberty. See Liberty

INDIVIDUALISM
Hannibal for president. G. W. Johnson. Am Scholar 41:29-39 Wint '71
Politics of authenticity, by M. Berman. Review Commonweal 94:362-4 Jl 9 '71. L. Kriegel
See also
Individual and state

INDIVIDUALITY
Biology of behavior. R. J. Williams. Sat R 54:17-19+ Ja 30 '71
To speak of certainties. B. W. Overstreet. il PTA Mag 66:21-3 O '71
See also
Personality
Self
Temperament

INDIVIGLIA, Salvatore
Watercolor page; with biographical sketch. il Am Artist 35:34-7+ Ag '71

INDO-ARYAN languages
Echoes of the Aryans. F. V. Grunfeld. il Horizon 13:102-4 Sum '71

INDO-ARYANS. See Aryans

INDOCHINA
Whither Indochina? D. J. Duncanson. Cur
Hist 61:345-9+ D '71
  See also
Ecology—Indochina
Laos
Vietnamese war, 1957-
INDOCHINA, FRENCH

History
Civil war, 1946-1954
U.S. offered A-bombs at Dienbienphu. Avia-
tion W 95:53 Ag 30 '71
Vietnam and the American revolution. D.
V. J. Bell and A. E. Goodman. Yale R 61:
26-34 O '71

Civil war, 1946-1954—Press reports
Vietnam: how the press went along; excerpt
from Communication in international politics, ed. by R. L. Merritt. S. Welch. Nation 213:327-30 O 11 '71; Discussion. 213:
418, 450 N 1-8 '71

**INDO-EUROPEAN languages. See Aryan lan-
guages**
INDO-EUROPEANS. See Aryans
**INDO-GERMANIC languages. See Aryan lan-
guages**
INDONESIA
Indonesia: transition to stability? D. B. H.
  **Denoon. bibliog f il Cur Hist 61:332-8+ D
'71**
  See also
Arts and crafts—Indonesia
Astronomical observatories—Indonesia
Bali
Investments, Foreign (in Indonesia)
Java
Libraries—Indonesia
Natural resources—Indonesia
Petroleum—Indonesia
Political campaigns—Indonesia
Political parties—Indonesia
Villages—Indonesia

Description and travel
  See also
Java—Description and travel

Economic conditions
Indonesia: new hope for 120 million people.
  W. S. Merick. il U S News 70:80-1 My 24
'71
Indonesia: things look up. T. Clifton and J.
  Williams. il Newsweek 78:41-3 Jl 12 '71
Population crisis and economic development.
  W. Withington. bibliog il Focus 21:9-12 My
'71

Industries
Indonesia. W. Withington. bibliog il Focus
21:1-9 My '71
  See also
Indonesia—Economic conditions

Native races
Peoples of the Pacific; ed. by M. Mead and
  P. McClanahan. bibliog il pors Natur Hist
80:50-1 My '71

Politics and government
Indonesia: new hope for 120 million people.
  W. S. Merick. il U S News 70:80-1 My 24 '71
  See also
Elections—Indonesia
Political parties—Indonesia

Population
Population crisis and economic development.
  W. Withington. bibliog il Focus 21:9-12
My '71
INDONESIAN art. See Art, Indonesian
**INDONESIAN cookery. See Cookery, Indone-
sian**
INDOOR gardening
Indoor planting adventures for children. il
  Sunset 146:164-5 F '71
Your garden indoors. F. S. David. See issues
  of Home garden & flower grower
  See also
Artificial light gardening
Greenhouses
House plants
INDOOR gardens. See Gardens, Indoor
INDOOR plants. See House plants
INDUCTION coils
Air-core coil nomogram. J. E. McAlister. il
  Electr World 86:45 S '71
All about inductors. F. J. Waters. il Radio-
  Electr 42:51-4 N '71
Induction coil. G. Shiers. il Sci Am 224:80-7
  My '71
  See also
Tesla coils

**INDUSTRIAL advertising. See Advertising, In-
dustrial**
**INDUSTRIAL agreements. See Trade agree-
ments**
INDUSTRIAL alcohol. See Alcohol, Denatured
**INDUSTRIAL arbitration. See Arbitration, In-
dustrial**
INDUSTRIAL arts
Goucher college teaches how-to-do-it. il Life
  70:34-5 F 5 '71
INDUSTRIAL buildings
  See also
Electric plants
Factories

Designs and plans
Building type study. il Arch Rec 150:91-106
  Jl '71
Industrial buildings. il Arch Forum 134:19-41
  Ap '71
Three industrial buildings; Brockton water
  filtration plant, Monarch machine tool co.
  and Pepperell spring water co. il Arch Rec
  149:123-32 F '71
**INDUSTRIAL chaplains. See Chaplains, Indust-
rial**
**INDUSTRIAL chemistry. See Chemistry, Tech-
nical**
INDUSTRIAL chemists. See Chemists
INDUSTRIAL demobilization
Bills introduced to reorient research to so-
  cial goals. D. C. Winston. Aviation W 94:
  21 F 22 '71
Conversion pains. Newsweek 77:76-7 Mr 1 '71
Conversion: the new management game; ad-
  dress, January 21, 1971. A. J. Kelley. Vital
  Speeches 37:318-20 Mr 1 '71
Reader's guide to the warfare state. D.
  Shearer. bibliog Ramp Mag 9:55-9 Je '71
Reorganizing the lines of power. D. Shearer.
  Nation 212:618-23 My 17 '71
Thorny shifts in priorities. Sci N 99:128 F 20
  '71
INDUSTRIAL democracy
After the revolution,by R. A. Dahl. Review
  Nation 213:117-21 Ag 16 '71. G. T. Gitlin
INDUSTRIAL design. See Design, Industrial
**INDUSTRIAL diamonds. See Diamonds, Indus-
trial**
INDUSTRIAL diseases. See Diseases, Industrial
**INDUSTRIAL diversification. See Diversifica-
tion in industry**
INDUSTRIAL education
  See also
Vocational education
**INDUSTRIAL efficiency. See Efficiency, Indus-
trial**
**INDUSTRIAL equality. See Woman—Equal
rights**
INDUSTRIAL equipment
  See also
Factories—Equipment
INDUSTRIAL equipment industry
  See also
Midland-Ross corporation

Finance
Industrial equipment; with yardsticks of
  management performance. il Forbes 109:
  162-4 Ja 1 '72
INDUSTRIAL exhibitions. See Exhibitions
INDUSTRIAL expansion
  See also
Capital investments
**INDUSTRIAL forestry. See Forest manage-
ment**
**INDUSTRIAL laboratories. See Research lab-
oratories**
**INDUSTRIAL location. See Location in busi-
ness and industry**
INDUSTRIAL management and organization
  See also
Assembly line methods
Business management and organization
Collective bargaining
Communication in management
Executives—Training
Factory management
Industrial relations
Labor productivity
Obsolescence
Personnel management

Italy
Why labor gives Olivetti peace in times of
  strife. il Bsns W p38 Je 26 '71
INDUSTRIAL museums
Industrial museums: history on parade. Na-
  tions Bsns 59:22 Ap '71
**INDUSTRIAL musicals. See Entertaining in
sales promotion**

INDUSTRIAL pensions. See Pensions

INDUSTRIAL psychology. See Psychology, Industrial

INDUSTRIAL recreation
At play in the fields of the company; employees at Texas Instruments. P. O'Neil. il Life 71:26-9+ S 3 '71

INDUSTRIAL relations
Developments in industrial relations. See issues of Monthly labor review
Significant decisions in labor cases. See issues of Monthly labor review
Stabilization of labor relations? address. April 1971, with questions and answers. N. W. Chamberlain. Ann Am Acad 396:79-89 Jl '71
Unfair practices and arbitration. bibliog Mo Labor R 94:64-6 N '71
We must pull together: labor, management and government; address, June 30, 1971. A. K. Davis. Vital Speeches 37:631-4 Ag 1 '71
Won't you come back, John Lewis? il Forbes 108:59-60 O 1 '71
See also
Arbitration, Industrial
Collective bargaining
Communication in management
Employees representation in management
Grievance procedures
Industrial democracy
Layoff systems
Personnel management
Trade agreements
United States—Labor policy
United States—National labor relations board

Study and teaching
Labor-management: a potent teaching unit. T. J. Watman. Clear House 45:493-5 Ap '71

Great Britain
Violence, threats halt Heathrow flights. Aviation W 95:30 N 8 '71

Italy
See also
Industrial management and organization—Italy

Japan
Behind Japan's huge boosts in output. il U S News 71:28 O 4 '71

Latin America
Rising worry in South America: flare-up of worker unrest. il U S News 70:67-8 Je 28 '71

INDUSTRIAL relations research association
IRRA conference papers; excerpts. Mo Labor R 94:51-62 Mr; 60-4 Ap '71

INDUSTRIAL research
Applying science to industry: why America falls behind; excerpts from address, December 2, 1970. M. Tribus. por U S News 70:35-6 Ja 18 '71
Bringing the laboratory down to earth. D. Cordtz. il Fortune 83:106-8+ Ja '71
Lead in the air: industry weight on Academy panel challenged. R. Gillette. Science 174: 800-2 N 19 '71
Nixon's new economic policy: hints of a resurgence for R&D. N. Wade. Science 173: 794-6 Ag 27 '71
Now it's a technology gap that threatens America. il U S News 70:22-4 Je 7 '71
Squeeze hurts lab spending. il Bsns W p94 My 8 '71
See also
Operations research
Research laboratories
Technology transfer

INDUSTRIAL safety
Occupational safety and health loans: an advance look for small businessmen. Nations Bsns 59:20 O '71
System safety spreads into industry. il Bsns W p57+ Jl 17 '71

Laws and regulations
For employers and workers: answers on safety regulations. il U S News 70:63-6 Je 14 '71
Ready to police safety practices. Bsns W p 101 Mr 27 '71
Safety law without bite. Bsns W p73 Ap 24 '71

INDUSTRIAL security measures. See Industry—Security measures

INDUSTRIAL statistics
See also
Employment—Statistics
Input-output analysis

INDUSTRIAL trusts. See Trusts, Industrial

INDUSTRIAL waste. See Trade waste

INDUSTRIAL waste disposal. See Trade waste disposal

INDUSTRIAL water supply. See Water supply, Industrial

INDUSTRIAL workers. See Labor and laboring classes

INDUSTRIALIZATION
See also
Underdeveloped areas

INDUSTRIALIZED buildings. See Buildings, Prefabricated

INDUSTRIES, Service. See Service industries

INDUSTRY
See also
Big business
Location in business and industry
Water supply, Industrial

Location
See Location in business and industry

Security measures
Crime in the office building. J. Perham. il Duns 98:29-33 O '71

Sign language
See Sign language

Social aspects
Trends; with editorial comment. il Parks & Rec 6:26-57+ My '71

INDUSTRY and state
Antipopulists. J. Ridgeway. Ramp Mag 10: 6+ D '71
Coming of the managed economy. G. R. Rosen. il Duns 98:27-9+ D '71
Cutting down on lost causes. H. P. Patterson. il pors Nations Bsns 59:60-3 F '71
Lead in the air: industry weight on Academy panel challenged. R. Gillette. Science 174: 800-2 N 19 '71
Mum's the word: how government and industry keep secrets from the people. J. Ridgeway. New Repub 165:17-19 Ag 21 '71
New industrial state, by J. K. Galbraith. Review
New Repub 165:38-40 O 16 '71. S. Lazarus
Sat R 54:40+ O 2 '71. R. Eisner
Nixon's new keep-them-guessing policy. Time 97:70 F 1 '71
Phase II of the capitalist system. R. L. Heilbroner. il N Y Times Mag p30-1+ N 28 '71
Roll-call of colonels that industry hires. il Bsns W p20 N 27 '71
Truce talk; question of government regulation. L. L. Golden. Sat R 54:98 Mr 13 '71
Washington desk. G. R. Rosen. See issues of Duns
Washington's corporate ambassadors. G. R. Rosen. il Duns 97:48-50+ Ap '71
We must pull together: labor, management and government; address June 30, 1971. A. K. Davis. Vital Speeches 37:631-4 Ag 1 '71
Welfare-industrial complex. M. Gruber. Nation 212:808-11 Je 28 '71
See also
Business—Federal aid
Electric utilities—Regulation
Free enterprise
Government ownership
Military-industrial complex
Railroads and state
Stock exchange—Regulation
Strikes—United States—Government intervention
Transportation—Laws and regulations
Trusts, Industrial
United States—Federal trade commission
United States—Interstate commerce commission
United States—Labor policy
United States—President's commission on personnel interchange

Great Britain
Heath tries industrial Darwinism. il por Bsns p41-2 Mr 20 '71

Italy
$7.2-billion spur for petrochemicals; state-inspired investment plan. il Bsns W p26 D 25 '71
Sick companies spur a rescue action. il Bsns W p34 F 6 '71

Yugoslavia
See also
Yugoslavia—Labor policy

INDUSTRY and the arts. See The Arts and industry

INDUSTRY and the environmental movement
Champions of conservation; Portland general electric co. Nation 213:389-90 O 25 '71
Ecology contest aimed at business; ecotage contest. Bsns W p40 Ap 17 '71
Environmental advertising: a question of integrity; CEP report. Sci N 100:356 N 27 '71
Financing environmental improvements. A. M Ruskin. il Am City 86:70+ N '71
Hardhats, hyacinths and returnable bottles. R. W. Gibbons. Commonweal 94:324-5 Je 25 '71
Industrial pollution: the high cost of prosperity. Bet Hom & Gard 49:34+ S '71
Industrialist looks at pollution. H. D. Doan. il por Chem 44:13-15 Ap '71
Next big industry: environmental improvement. J. B. Quinn. il Harvard Bsns R 49:120-4+ S '71
No more golden eggs? il Nations Bsns 59:72-6 O '71
Pollution and industry: pros, cons of growing fight. il U S News 71:60-2 N 22 '71
Right on, Establishment, address, October 11, 1971. M. J. Caserio. Vital Speeches 38:86-90 N 15 '71
Steel industry and pollution. J. D. Phelan. il Parks & Rec 6:20-2+ S '71
Wait a minute; address, July 15, 1971. M. H. Stans. Vital Speeches 37:690-3 S 1 '71
Wall Street:
Price of virtue. C. Morgello. Newsweek 77:84-5 My 24 '71
What has business done? A. Rothenberg. Look 35:23 My 4 '71
Where pollution control is slowing industrial growth il U S News 71:47-50 Ag 23 '71
See also
Paper industry

INDYK, Henry W.
Lawns. New Yorker 47:27-9 S 18 '71

INERTIAL guidance systems
Area-inertial aid tests planned. P. J. Klass. il Aviation W 94:50-1+ F 1 '71
Brain that tells a 747 where to go! Carousel IV. L. Morgan. il por Pop Mech 136:108-11+ O '71
Corporate inertial navigation use grows. K. J. Stein. il Aviation W 95:70-2 S 20 '71
Inertial navaid features new multisensors. B. Miller. il Aviation W 95:44-6 D 13 '71
JAL studies retrofit of DC-8s. Aviation W 95:85 N 1 '71
Navaid uses electrostatic gyros. B. Miller. il Aviation W 94:49-50 Mr 22 '71
Navy test rapid-reaction Navaid; Cains navigation system. B. Miller. il Aviation W 94:62-4 Je 14 '71

INESI, Giuseppe
p-Nitrophenyl phosphate hydrolysis and calcium ion transport in fragmented sarcoplasmic reticulum. bibliog il Science 171:901-3 Mr 5 '71

INEZ, Colette
Old woman and the war; poem. Nation 213:542 N 22 '71

INFALLIBILITY. See Catholic church—Infallibility

INFALLIBILITY, Papal. See Popes—Infallibility

INFANCY of animals. See Animals, Infancy of

INFANT feeding. See Infants—Nutrition

INFANT intelligence tests. See Intelligence tests

INFANT learning. See Infants—Growth and development

INFANT mortality
Giving more of our infants the lives they deserve. T. Berland. il Todays Health 49:16-19+ Ag '71
Great nuclear debate: are our newborn babies' lives in danger? M. Hope and J. Young. Redbook 138:16+ Ja '72
Health effects from radiation; address, July 14, 1971. E. J. Sternglass. bibliog Vital Speeches 37:699-703 S 1 '71

INFANTE, Juan José Díaz. See Díaz Infante, J. J.

INFANTILE paralysis. See Poliomyelitis

INFANTS
See also
Adoption
Play

Accidents
See Accidents

Care and hygiene
Difficult baby is born that way. B. W. Wyden. il N Y Times Mag p67+ Mr 21 '71; Discussion. p60-1 Ap 11 '71
Launching healthy children; symposium. il Life 71:61+ D 17 '71

Skinnerian innovation: baby in a box. il pors Time 98:51 S 20 '71
Toilet training the easy way. M. A. Wessel. il Parents Mag 46:36-7+ Je '71
With granny & gramps at generation gap. il Changing T 25:24 Ap '71
See also
Baby sitters
Child welfare
Children—Care and hygiene
Colic
Infant mortality
Infants—Nutrition
Infants, Premature

Clothing
See also
Diapers, Infants

Food
See Infants food

Growth and development
Are there too many sights and sounds in your baby's world? T. B. Brazelton and M. Main. il Redbook 137:91+ S '71
Awesome power of human love; excerpt from The humanization of man. A. Montagu. Read Digest 99:103-5 Jl '71
Baby steps out. H. B. Pryor and M. C. Martin. il Parents Mag 46:40-1+ D '71
Earlier head start. Sci N 100:24 Jl 10 '71
How a baby learns to love. S. Fraiberg. il Redbook 137:76+ My '71
How to improve your child's ability to learn. Good H 173:190-1 O '71
Infant responses to impending collision: optical and real. W. Ball and E. Tronick. bibliog il Science 171:818-20 F 26 '71
Launching healthy children; symposium. il Life 71:61+ D 17 '71
New ways to measure intelligence in infants. S. S. Fremon. il Parents Mag 46:39-41+ Ap '71
Object in the world of the infant. T. G. R. Bower. il Sci Am 225:30-8 bibliog(p 120) O '71
Space perception in early infancy: perception within a common auditory-visual space. E. Aronson and S. Rosenbloom. bibliog il Science 172:1161-3 Je 11 '71
Speech perception in infants. P. D. Eimas and others. bibliog il Science 171:303-6 Ja 22 '71
Terrible, wonderful twos. C. Lang. il Parents Mag 46:54-5+ O '71
Tip-offs on personality traits; with study-discussion program, by M. M. Conant. L. Morgan. bibliog il PTA Mag 66:22-4+, 34 S '71
Understanding baby talk. W. Petschek. il McCalls 98:46 S '71
See also
Child study

Language
See Children—Language

Law
See Children—Law

Nutrition
Are you feeding your baby too much? H. Eustis. Redbook 137:87+ O '71
Child is being beaten; the effects of hunger; address, March 21, 1971. B. Pasamanick. Vital Speeches 37:465-72 My 15 '71
See also
Breast feeding
Infants food
Milk, Human

Sight
See Sight

INFANTS, Cost of. See Domestic finance

INFANTS, Deformed. See Deformities

INFANTS, Newborn
What childbirth drugs can do to your child. T. B. Brazelton. il por Redbook 136:65+ F '71

Diseases
Antiseptic baby; case of combined immune deficiency. il Newsweek 78:61-2 D 20 '71

Hospital care
See Children—Hospital care

INFANTS, Photography of. See Photography of children

INFANTS, Premature
New hope for high-risk babies. B. Eisenpreis. il Parents Mag 46:42-3+ Ag '71
Saving the preemies: respiratory distress syndrome. il por Newsweek 78:71 Ag 16 '71
What if your baby is born prematurely? il Changing T 25:18-20 My '71

INFANTS, Travel with. See Travel with children

INFANTS food
Baby food: a good-sense guide. il Good H 172:6 Mr '71
INFANTS supplies
See also
Cribs (beds)
INFANTS walkers. See Walkers, Infants
INFECTIOUS hepatitis. See Hepatitis
INFIELD, Glenn B.
Disaster at Bari; excerpts. il por Am Heritage 22:60-4+ O '71
INFLAMMABLE textile fabrics. See Textile fabrics, Flammable
INFLAMMATION
Gnotobiotic animal as a tool in the study of inflammation. M. Miyakawa and others. Science 173:171-3 Jl 9 '71
INFLATABLE boats. See Boats and boating
INFLATABLE structures. See Air-supported structures
INFLATION (finance)
Anatomy of inflation: 1953-1975. W. H. Fisher. il Sci Am 225:15-21 N '71
Applied Nixonomics; inflation/unemployment seesaw. M. J. Ulmer. New Repub 164:15-18 Ap 24 '71
As Europe's bankers see inflation. il U S News 70:15 Je 28 '71
Bitchy society will be an inflationary society, and other responses to a questionnaire. E. L. Dale, jr. il N Y Times Mag p 18-19+ S 26 '71
Businessmen want to break the spiral. il Bsns W p20-1 Ag 7 '71
Case for an incomes policy, now; address, April 23, 1971. E. S. Adams. Vital Speeches 37:546-9 Jl 1 '71
Control of inflation and recession; address, April 1971, with questions and answers. F. W. Schiff. Ann Am Acad 396:90-104 Jl '71
Coping with inflation: what readers report. il Changing T 25:35-9 Ag '71
Depression: the only cure? reprint from 1957 issue. D. Lawrence. U S News 70:104 My 10 '71
Economic torture? il por Forbes 107:50 F 1 '71
Europe feels symptoms of 'stagflation'. il Newsweek 77:78-9+ My 10 '71
Hot Springs: inflation on their minds. Bsns W p48 My 15 '71
How to control inflation: a three-stage formula; excerpt from address, January 20, 1971. R. H. Larry. por U S News 70:72-4 F 8 '71
How to stop inflation: stop raising wages. E. L. Dale, jr. il Look 35:64+ F 23 '71
I am now a Keynesian; President Nixon. Nation 212:99-100 Ja 25 '71
Inflation, incomes policy and all that. B. L. Masse. America 124:398 Ap 17 '71
Inflation looks stubborn to business; with editorial comment. il Bsns W p26-7, 104 My 1 '71
Inflation scores on the game plan. il Newsweek 78:59-60 Ag 16 '71
Inflation, threat of another round. il U S News 70:13-15 Je 28 '71
Inflation versus unemployment: another view of the trade-off. S. S. Wallack. bibliog Mo Labor R 94:49-54 N '71
Inflation versus unemployment: the worsening trade-off; excerpt from Changing labor markets and inflation. G. L. Perry. il Mo Labor R 94:68-71 F '71
Inflation's impact on consumer behavior and attitudes; a little inflation tolerable; address, January 14, 1971. G. Katona. Vital Speeches 37:263-5 F 15 '71
Is the recession over? interview. L. Olsen. Read Digest 99:123-6 Ag '71
Is there hope for collective bargaining? the inflation threat; address, May 7, 1971. R. H. Larry. Vital Speeches 37:537-40 Je 15 '71
Jobs, inflation: what Nixon's top economist expects; excerpts from statement before the Joint economic committee, July 8, 1971. P. W. McCracken. il por U S News 71:57-9 Jl 26 '71
Kicking the inflation habit. Life 71:30 Ag 13 '71
Labor law reform: essential to fight inflation. J. G. Tower. por Nations Bsns 59:42-5 D '71
Manpower approach to the unemployment-inflation dilemma. C. C. Holt and others. Mo Labor R 94:51-4 My '71
Need for legislation; union power and inflation; address, April 26, 1971. C. M. Brooks. Vital Speeches 37:563-6 Jl 1 '71

1971: the year of the consumer? with reports by M. Friedman; P. A. Samuelson; H. C. Wallich. il Newsweek 77:55-6+ F 15 '71
Nixon-Burns battle? R. Lekachman. Duns 97:9 F '71
Nixonomics. J. Fischer. Harper 243:10+ N '71
Nixonomics: how the game plan went wrong. R. Evans, jr. and R. D. Novak. Atlan 228:66-76+ Jl '71
Now, about our cover and the change in the dollar. il Sr Schol 98:14-15 Ap 5 '71
Readers tell how inflation hits them. il Changing T 25:21-3 S '71
Road to 1976. B. W. Zumeta. por Nations Bsns 59:32 Ag '71
Showdown fight over inflation. il Time 98:64-70 Ag 16 '71
Social cost of curbing inflation. B. L. Masse. America 124:644 Je 26 '71
Squeeze-freeze dilemma; address, January 20, 1971. R. H. Larry. Vital Speeches 37:253-6 F 1 '71; Excerpts. por U S News 70:72-4 F 8 '71
Strategy for winding down inflation. R. V. Roosa. il Fortune 84:70-3+ S '71
TRB from Washington; views of A. Burns. New Repub 164:6 Ap 17 '71
Tax cuts and easier credit: how Britain is trying to pep up its economy. il U S News 71:33 Ag 2 '71
That old spiral. Newsweek 77:80 Je 14 '71
Union power and the new inflation. G. Burck. il Fortune 83:65-9+ F '71; Same abr. with title High cost of wage inflation. Read Digest 98:139-43 Ap '71
Unions: scapegoat for inflation. A. Reynolds. Nat R 23:1463-4+ D 31 '71
Use LIFO to offset inflation. R. M. Copeland and others. bibliog f il Harvard Bsns R 49:91-100 My '71; Discussion. 49:35+ S '71
Ways to fight the dollar shrink. R. Krumme. Suc Farm 69:H8-9 N '71
West Germany: troubles overtake an economic giant. il U S News 70:17-18 My 31 '71
What inflation is costing Americans. il U S News 70:23-5 My 17 '71
Where is the dollar going? R. Lekachman; J. A. Livingston; C. C. Brown. il Sat R 54:15-20+ Mr 6 '71
Who's fooling with it? P. A. Samuelson. il Look 35:59-61 Ap 20 '71
World inflation and the international payments system; address, January 14, 1971. P. A. Volcker. Dept State Bul 64:212-18 F 15 '71
See also
Currency question
INFLUENCE of literature. See Literature, Influence of
INFLUENCE of music. See Music, Influence of
INFLUENZA
Vaccines
They can't do much if the flu strikes. il Bsns W p26 N 27 '71
INFORMAL education. See Open plan schools
INFORMATION, Freedom of
Alternative to schooling. I. D. Illich. il Sat R 54:44-8+ Je 19 '71; Same abr. with title For disestablishment of the school. Cur 131:24-34 Jl '71
Gamble; making public the advisory committee report on 2,4,5-T. T. Aaronson. il Environ 13:20-4+ S '71
Getting the goods on the government. J. Miller. New Repub 165:13-15 D 11 '71
Media cite increased govt. assaults on freedom of speech and press. S. Wagner. Pub W 200:28 Jl 5 '71
Politics of gullibility. T. M. Conrad. Commonweal 95:13-15 O 1 '71
Public information act; with text. M. J. Kerbec; discussion. Library J 96:1175-6 Ap 1 '71
Right to know; Laos campaign and the Frazier-Ali fight. R. L. Tobin. Sat R 54:41-2 Ap 10 '71
Secrecy and elitism in science and government. R. H. Gilluly. Sci N 100:82-3 Jl 31 '71
See also
Executive privilege (government information)
Freedom of the press
Government and the press
Government information
Intellectual liberty
Journalistic ethics
Science, Freedom of
Security classification (government documents)
INFORMATION display systems
Digital Japan; use of digital readout devices in commonly used equipment. M. Mann. il Pop Electr 35:50 Ag '71
See also
Aeronautic instruments—Display systems

INFORMATION industry association
Government easing attitude toward private enterprise in use of federal information. il Pub W 199:26-30 Ap 12 '71
Gutenberg vs. McLuhan, round three. R. E. Bye. Library J 96:1585 My 1 '71; Reply. J. Norton. 96:1651 My 15 '71
INFORMATION processing, Human. See Human information processing
INFORMATION services
Dial for abortion. il Time 97:64 Mr 15 '71
See also
Agriculture—Information services
Airlines—Information services
Information industry association
Science—Information services
INFORMATION services, Government
Federal government as a source of data. C. Taeuber. bibliog f Ann Am Acad 394:114-24 Mr '71
Pick up the phone and learn the earth's secrets. C. V. Glines. il Nations Bsns 59:48-51 D '71
This month's feature: controversy over federal data banks. Cong Digest 50:225-56 O '71
What curbs on government surveillance? R. Holloran. Cur 129:10-12 My '71
See also
Consumer product information index
INFORMATION storage and retrieval systems
Crystals and data storage; holographic data storage. il Chem 44:22 S '71
Databank society: can we cope? R. Malik. Cur 129:6-10 My '71
ISR in Europe in July: the Cranfield conference; report. B. M. Woods. Wilson Lib Bul 46:107 S '71
Information science and computer basics, by R. K. Mitchell. Review
Library J 96:2746 S 15 '71. P. Atherton; Reply. R. K. Mitchell. 96:3702-3 N 15 '71
Need for quality filters in information systems. A. Etzioni. Science 171:133 Ja 15 '71
See also
Computer programming
Electronic data processing
Information services. Government
Libraries—Automation
Microfilm records
Microforms
Science
Selective dissemination and indexing of scientific information. J. H. Schneider. bibliog il Science 173:300-8 Jl 23 '71
INFORMATION systems, Management
Perils of data systems. il Bsns W p62-3+ Je 5 '71
Problems in planning the information system; computer-based information systems. F. W. McFarlan. il Harvard Bsns R 49:75-89 Mr '71
See also
Television in business
INFORMATION tests
Changing times quiz (cont) Changing T. 25:42 Ap; 47 Ag '71
Educators' quiz. M. Rosenberg. See issues of Education digest
[Electronics quiz] (cont) R. P. Balin. il Pop Electr 34:50+ Mr '71
End-term review test (cont) il Sr Schol 97:21-2 Ja 18; 98:21-2 My 17 '71
Family quiz game. C. Levine. See issues of Parents' magazine & better family living
How color sensitive are you? H. Aach. House & Gard 140:10-11+ S '71
I'll bet you don't know this one or do you? Test yourself. E. A. Zadig. il Motor B & S 127:62-5 F '71
Midterm review test (cont) il Sr Schol 98:23-4 Mr 22; 99:24 N 15 '71
Play U.S.A; family game of questions about the 50 states. W. Fitzgibbon. Read Digest 99:17-18+ Jl '71
Quiz. J. Daugherty and M. Daugherty. See issues of Science digest
Quizzing the collegians; The college bowl quiz book. W. Zinsser. Life 70:14 My 7 '71
What do you want for Christmas? M. Reznikoff and G. Domino. Ladies Home J 88:62+ D '71
What is it? identifying common woods. J. A. Starkey. il Am For 77:44-5 Je '71
Who laid the egg? quiz. il Nat Wildlife 9:12-15+ Ap '71
Who was Richard Nixon's running mate in 1960? a quiz on who did what, where, when, and to whom in the sixties. il Esquire 76:146-53 D '71
Your literary I.Q; ed. by D. M. Glixon. See issues of Saturday review

INFORMATION theory
Energy and information. M. Tribus and E. C. McIrvine. il Sci Am 225:179-84+ bibliog (p244+) S '71
See also
Human information processing
INFORMERS (law)
Berrigan informer; B. F. Douglas. il pors Time 97:20 F 1 '71
How to grab the brain child; charges of conspiring to kidnap H. Kissinger. il pors Time 97:15-16 My 10 '71
Money pays off; Secret witness program of Detroit news. il Time 97:65 My 17 '71
Privacy and the third-party bug; case of James White. N. Lewin. New Repub 164:12-17 Ap 17 '71
Pushers pushed; drive against drug pushers in Tampa, Fla. il Newsweek 78:60 Ag 9 '71
Real conspiracy; use of informers by the FBI in political cases. Nation 212:101 Ja 25 '71
Secret witness: new weapon against crime; Detroit News program. J. Stewart-Gordon. il Read Digest 99:190-1+ N '71
Tampa turns in its pushers. C. Whitehorn. McCalls 99:32 N '71
INFRARED detectors. See Detectors, Infrared
INFRARED photography. See Photography, Infrared
INFRARED rainbow. See Rainbow
INFRARED rays
Industrial use
Infrared peeling of fruits and vegetables. Chem 44:25-6 Jl '71
Measurement use
Infrared exploration, new light on the environment. J. Lear. il Sat R 54:53-7 Ap 3 '71
INFRARED receptors. See Nervous system—Reptiles
INFRARED spectrum. See Spectrum, Infrared
INFRASONIC waves. See Sound waves
INGE, J. L. and others
New map of Mars from planetary patrol photographs. il Sky & Tel 41:336-9 Je '71
INGERSOLL, John E.
U.S. urges stronger multilateral commitments to narcotics control; statement, October 1, 1971. Dept State Bul 65:523-9 N 8 '71
INGERSOLL, John H.
Ideas to build on. See issues of House beautiful
Perspectives. il House B 113:20+ F '71
Security for your home; more urgent than ever. House B 113:62+ N '71
Well-built house. See issues of House beautiful
INGERSOLL-Rand company
Won't you come back, John Lewis? il Forbes 108:59-60 O 1 '71
INGHAM, M. F.
Spectrum of the airglow; with biographical sketch. il Sci Am 226:10, 78-85 Ja '72
INGLEWOOD, Calif.
Simple test for telephone courtesy. D. Taylor. il Am City 86:134+ My '71
INGLIS, David Rittenhouse
Nuclear energy and the Malthusian dilemma. Bul Atom Sci 27:14-18 F; 39-41 Je '71
INGRAHAM, Bob
World on a string. il Har Yrs 11:35-6 Mr '71
INGRAHAM, Hollis S.
Parent's guide to childhood illness. il Parents Mag 46:54-5 N '71
INGRAM, Timothy H.
Corporate underground. Nation 213:206-12 S 13 '71
Students sign a peace treaty. Nation 211:646-8 D 21 '70
INGRES, Jean Auguste Dominique
Classicist's tic. D. Davis. il Newsweek 77:107 My 24 '71 *
Ingres in Rome. P. Hattis. il Art N 70:26-9+ My '71 *
Ingres's landscape drawings. il Antiques 99:174+ F '71 *
Probity in Rome. R. Hughes. il Time 97:53 Ja 25 '71 *
INHERITANCE
See also
Estate planning
Reversion (law)
Wills
INHERITANCE (biology) See Heredity
INHERITANCE of disease. See Heredity of disease
INHIBITION of enzymes. See Enzymes—Inactivation
INITIAL teaching alphabet. See Alphabet
INITIATIVE and referendum. See Referendum

INJECTIONS
   See also
Inoculation
INJECTIONS, Hypodermic
   Controlling pain at the gate; dorsal column stimulation and saline injection. Sci N 100:7 Jl 3 '71
   Origins of hypodermic medication. N. Howard-Jones. il por Sci Am 224:96-102 bibliog(p 122) Ja '71
INJURIES
   See also
Traumatism
INJURIES from sports. See Sports—Accidents and injuries
INJURIOUS insects. See Insects, Injurious and beneficial
INK blot test. See Personality tests
INLAND homes corporation. See IHC, inc.
INLAND navigation
   See also
Boats—Towing
Canals
Waterways
INLAND steel company
   Facing the future in a troubled industry. il Fortune 84:13 Jl '71
INLAND water transportation
   Lakes shippers chip out a longer season. il Bsns W p50-1 F 13 '71
   Litton jumps ship on the Great Lakes. il Bsns W p44-5 S 11 '71
INLAND waterways. See Waterways
INMAN, Robert E. and others
   Soil: a natural sink for carbon monoxide. bibliog il Science 172:1229-31 Je 18 '71
INNER City; musical comedy. See Musical comedies, revues, etc.—Criticisms, plots, etc.
INNER tube floating. See Floating
INNES, Lowell
   Lacy hairpin in French and American glass. il Antiques 100:228-32 Ag '71
INNOVATION, Technological. See Technological change
INNOVATIONS in education. See Educational innovations
INNS. See Hotels, taverns, etc.
INOCULATION
   Current pediatric immunization procedures. L. W. Sauer. il PTA Mag 65:25-6 Mr '71
   Inoculations every child needs. il Good H 173:203 S '71
   See also
Immunity
Vaccination
INOUYE, Daniel Ken
   Does anyone want to visit the U.S.A? H. Sutton. il Sat R 55:36-7+ Ja 1 '72 *
INPUT-output analysis
   Anatomy of inflation: 1953-1975. W. H. Fisher il Sci Am 225:15-21 N '71
   Input-output: management's newest tool. G. J. Berkwitt. il Duns 97:57-8 Mr '71
INQUIRY teaching. See Teaching
INSANE
   Legal status, laws, etc.
   See Mental health laws
INSANE, Criminal and dangerous
   See also
Forensic psychiatry
INSANITY
   See also
Mental illness
Psychoses
   Jurisprudence
   See also
Forensic psychiatry
INSCRIPTIONS
   See also
Graffiti
Petroglyphs
INSCRIPTIONS, Cuneiform. See Cuneiform inscriptions
INSCRIPTIONS, Hebrew
   Did Jews reach America first? il Sci Digest 70:39-40 Ag '71
INSCRIPTIONS, Maya. See Mayas—Writing
INSECT baits and repellents
   Diethylamide of thujic acid: a potent repellent of aedes aegypti. V. Hach and E. C. McDonald. bibliog il Science 174:144-5 O 8 '71
INSECT communication
   Attack by pheromone. Sci Am 225:45 Jl '71
   Chemical communication and propaganda in slave-maker ants. F. E. Regnier and E. O. Wilson. bibliog il Science 172:267-9 Ap 16 '71
   Communication between ants and their guests. B. Hölldobler. il Sci Am 224:86-93 Mr '71

INSECT control
   Big schemes for little ants; fire ants. A. Wolff. il Audubon 73:120-4 Mr '71
   Control of agricultural pests. P. H. Abelson. Science 171:437 F 5 '71
   Inchworm caper; dispute over the use of insecticide to battle gypsy moth and worms. il Newsweek 77:95 Je 7 '71
   Organic soil keeps the insects away. R. Rodale. il Org Gard & Farm 18:28-32 Je '71
   Scientists map strategy on How you'll fight future pest outbreaks; National academy of sciences symposium. il Farm J 95:22H Jl '71
   Sensible ways to get rid of bugs and weeds. Changing T 25:31-3 Ag '71
   Weed and insect control guide; symposium. ed. by C. E. Sommers. il Suc Farm 69:no3 39-42+ F '71
   See also
Cockroach control
Insecticides
Mosquito control
Pest control operators
Spraying and dusting

   Biological control
   Back into the future. D. Pelzer. il Cons 26: 32-3 D '71
   Biological control of vectors; report of meeting. M. Laird. Science 171:590+ F 12 '71
   Fighting insects with insects. il Chem 44:3 Jl '71
   Getting the bugs out of organic farming. M. C. Goldman. il Org Gard & Farm 18: 77-84 Ja '71
   Infectious cure. K. P. Shea. il Environ 13: 43-5 Ja '71
   Insect control by genetic manipulation of natural populations. M. J. Whitten. bibliog il Science 171:682-4 F 19 '71
   Insect explosion: how science is fighting back without insecticides. W. Hartley and E. Hartley. il Sci Digest 69:26-31 Jl '71
   Insects that can make your garden grow better. il Good H 173:159 Jl '71
   It's time to stop the gypsy moth, sanely. V. Zaffiro. il Org Gard & Farm 18:59-63 O '71
   Know your enemy. J. McCaull. bibliog il pors Environ 13:30-9 Je '71
   New weapon in the war on insects; hormone sprays. il Bsns W p94+ N 13 '71
   Old weapons are best. K. P. Shea. bibliog il Environ 13:40-9 Je '71
   Termite Mary; Formosan termites. Newsweek 78:111-12 N 15 '71
   There's a bird in the frog house! C. C. Stewart. il Org Gard & Farm 18:70-1 D '71
   Using yesterday's ways to stop today's bugs! M. C. Goldman. il Org Gard & Farm 18:52-7 Jl '71
   See also
Sterility in insects
INSECT control of weeds. See Weed control —Biological control
INSECT flight. See Insects—Flight
INSECT genetics
   Genetic control of an insect neuronal network. D. R. Bentley. bibliog il Science 174: 1139-41 D 10 '71
   Insect control by genetic manipulation of natural populations. M. J. Whitten. bibliog il Science 171:682-4 F 19 '71
INSECT pests. See Insects, Injurious and beneficial
INSECT repellents. See Insect baits and repellents
INSECT resistance of plants. See Plants—Disease and pest resistance
INSECT sex attractants
   Housefly sex attractant. il Chem 44:22-3 D '71
   Hydrocarbon sex pheromone in tiger moths (arctiidae) W. L. Roelofs and R. T. Cardé. bibliog il Science 171:684-6 F 19 '71
   Sex attractant of the codling moth: characterization with electroantennogram technique. W. Roelofs and others. bibliog il Science 174:297-9 O 15 '71
   Sex attractant pheromone of the house fly: isolation, identification and synthesis. D. A. Carlson and others. bibliog il Science 174: 76-8 O 1 '71
   Sex pheromone of the almond moth and the Indian meal moth: cis-9, trans-12-tetradecadienyl acetate. Y. Kuwahara and others. bibliog Science 171:801-2 F 26 '71
   Sex pheromone specificity and taxonomy of budworm moths (choristoneura) C. J. Sanders. bibliog il Science 171:911-13 Mr 5 '71
   Sex stimulant and attractant in the Indian meal moth and in the almond moth. U. E. Brady and others. bibliog il Science 171: 802-4 F 26 '71

INSECT societies
Social insects; report of meeting. E. O. Wilson. Science 172:406 Ap 23 '71
INSECT sounds
Genetic control of an insect neuronal network; cricket singing. D. R. Bentley. bibliog il Science 174:1139-41 D 10 '71
Periodical cicada: mechanism of sound production. K. H. Reid. bibliog il Science 172:949-51 My 28 '71
Periodical cicada: sound production and hearing. J. A. Simmons and others. il Science 171:212-13 Ja 15 '71
INSECT traps
Bug trap you can make. P. F. Dexter. il Pop Sci 199:106 Ag '71
INSECT viruses. See Viruses, Insect
INSECTICIDES
Carbonic anhydrase interaction with DDT, DDE, and dieldrin. Y. Pocker and others. bibliog il Science 174:1336-9 D 24 '71
Corn insect controls for '71. Suc Farm 69:no3 W24 F '71
Eradicate them one more time; fire ant eradication program. G. Laycock. Field & S 76:46-7+ D '71
How poisonous are corn rootworm insecticides? W. L. Gojmerac. il Suc Farm 69:no3 W32 F '71
Mirex and the fire ant: decline in fortunes of perfect pesticide. D. Shapley. il Science 172:358-60 Ap 23 '71
Non-hazardous cockroach control; utilizing Drione. E. H. Paisley. il Am City 86:60-1 Ja '71
Systemics. W. H. Youngman. il Horticulture 49:18-19+ Jl '71
      See also
Aldrin
DDT (insecticide)
Filipin
Pyrethrins

                    Injurious effects
DDT substitute; carbaryl. L. C. T. Nisbet and D. Miner. bibliog il Environ 13:10-17 Jl '71
Eye on our defenses; MDP synergists in insecticides. S. S. Epstein and others. bibliog il Environ 13:43-7 Ap '71
Melancholy addiction of Ol'King Cotton. R. Van Den Bosch. il Natur Hist 80:86-91 bibliog(p 120) D '71
Mix with care. J. McCaull. bibliog il Environ 13:39-42 Ja '71

                        Residues
      See also
DDT (insecticide)—Residues
INSECTICIDES, Resistance to. See Insects, Injurious and beneficial—Resistance to control
INSECTIVORA
      See also
Shrews
INSECTIVOROUS plants
      See also
Sundews
INSECTS
Who sez-z-z-z man is the dominant species? R. Gilbert. il Sports Illus 34:44-6+ Je 21 '71
      See also
Hearing (insects)
Insect sounds
Nervous system—Insects
Parasites—Insects
Photography of insects
      also names of insects, e.g. Bees

                        Control
      See Insect control

                    Development
Blowflies: alteration of adult taste responses by chemicals present during development. V. G. Dethier and N. Goldrich. bibliog il Science 173:242-4 Jl 16 '71
Silkworm bombyx mori L: nature of diapause factor. H. Sonobe and E. Ohnishi. bibliog il Science 174:835-8 N 19 '71

                          Eyes
      See Eye (insects)

                         Flight
Flight orientation in locusts. J. M. Camhi. il Sci Am 225:74-81 bibliog (p 120) Ag '71

                   Food and feeding
Butterfly feeding on lycopsid. M. C. Singer and others. bibliog il Science 172:1341-2 Je 25 '71
Detoxication enzymes in the guts of caterpillars: an evolutionary answer to plant defenses? R. L. Krieger and others. bibliog il Science 172:579-81 My 7 '71

Keep beneficial bugs in your garden, feed them! Home Gard 58:17 Ag '71
Micromurderers. N. Smith. il Nat Wildlife 9:19 Ag '71

                 Habits and behavior
      See also
Insect communication
Insect societies

                      Host plants
      See Insects—Food and feeding

                      Metabolism
2,5-Dichlorophenol (from ingested herbicide?) in defensive secretion of grasshopper. T. Eisner and others. bibliog il Science 172:277-8 Ap 16 '71
Grasshopper chemical factories, 2,5-dichlorophenol from 2,4-D in defensive secretions. R. H. Gilluly. il Sci N 99:406 Je 12 '71

                      Orientation
      See Orientation

                 Protective equipment
      See Defense mechanisms (biology)
INSECTS, Injurious and beneficial
How to get insects identified. Suc Farm 69:G32 Ap '71
How to identify insect strangers. bibliog il Sunset 147:141 Jl '71
Keep beneficial bugs in your garden, feed them! Home Gard 58:17 Ag '71
Know your enemy better. Suc Farm 69:no5 D6 Mr '71
      See also
Weed control—Biological control
      also names of insects, e.g. Bollworms;
      also subhead Diseases and pests under names of crops, trees, plants, etc, e.g. Corn —Diseases and pests

                  Biological control
      See Insect control—Biological control

                        Control
      See Insect control

                 Resistance to control
Activity to an NADPH-dependent nitroreductase in houseflies. E. P. Lichtenstein and T. W. Fuhremann. bibliog il Science 172:589-91 My 7 '71
Induction of microsomal oxidase in F_1 hybrids of a high and a low oxidase housefly strain. L. C. Terriere and others. bibliog il Science 171:581-3 F 12 '71
INSECTS, Predatory
Micromurderers. N. Smith. il Nat Wildlife 9:19 Ag '71
INSECTS, Rain of. See Fishes, insects, etc, Rain of
INSECTS, Sound production by. See Insect sounds
INSECTS as carriers of infection
Biological control of vectors; report of meeting. M. Laird. Science 171:590+ F 12 '71
      See also
Lice
Mosquitoes as carriers of infection
Ticks as carriers of infection
INSEMINATION, Artificial. See Artificial insemination
INSERVICE teacher education. See Teachers—Education in service
INSERVICE training of school administrators. See School superintendents and principals —Education in service
INSIDE passage
Cruise to Alaska, so many choices. il Sunset 146:16+ Ap '71
INSOMNIA
New help for nonsleepers. T. J. Rakstis. il Todays Health 49:16-19+ S '71
R for depression. Newsweek 78:61 Ag 30 '71
INSPECTION of automobiles. See Automobiles —Inspection
INSPECTION of banks. See Bank examination
INSPIRATION
      See also
Creation (literary, artistic, etc)
INSPIRATION; story. See Hand, H.
INSPIRATIONISTS
      See also
Amana society
INSTALMENT contracts
Consumer protection; proposed Federal trade commission regulation. New Repub 164:9-10 F 6 '71
      See also
Land contracts

INSTALMENT plan
Financing your used car. Motor T 23:114 Je '71
What you should know before buying on credit. Good H 173:162 Jl '71
INSTANT mashed potatoes. See Potatoes, Dried
INSTANT replay. See Video recorders and recording
INSTINCT
See also
Habits
Self preservation
INSTITUTE for American strategy
See also
Freedom studies center
INSTITUTE for communications research. See Stanford university, Palo Alto, Calif.—Institute for communications research
INSTITUTE for policy studies
Thinking of positive power. G. Willis. il Esquire 75:98-101+ Mr '71
INSTITUTE of ecology
Man and environment: fighting the backlash. R. H. Gilluly. il Sci N 100:410-11 D 18 '71
INSTITUTE of gerontology
Ann Arbor aging Placement service enters second year. Aging 203:7 S '71
INSTITUTE of life insurance, New York
Alerting management; Trend analysis program. L. L. L. Golden. Sat R 54:70 S 11 '71
INSTITUTE of medicine
Institute of medicine. I. Page. Science 172: 635 My 14 '71
Institute of medicine: board-spectrum prescription. J. Walsh. Science 174:929+ N 26 '71
NAS institute of medicine: what role will it play? J. L. Arehart. Sci N 100:380-1 D 4 '71
INSTITUTE of student opinion. See Scholastic research center
INSTITUTES, Library. See Library institutes and workshops
INSTITUTIONAL accounting
Program budgeting works in nonprofit institutions. R. K. Macleod. Harvard Bsns R 49:46-56 S '71
INSTITUTIONAL homes. See Homes, Institutional
INSTITUTIONS, Nonprofit
Can nonprofit organizations be well managed? address, February 18, 1971. R. N. Anthony. Vital Speeches 37:442-5 My 1 '71
Jeopardy of private institutions. A. Pifer. Ed Digest 36:34-7 My '71
Accounting
See Institutional accounting
INSTITUTIONS, Research. See Research institutions
INSTITUTIONS, Social. See Social institutions
INSTRUCTIONAL materials. See Teaching—Aids and devices
INSTRUCTIONAL materials centers
Experimental models for school library media education. R. N. Case. bibliog il por Library J 96:4151-6 D 15 '71
Libraries look to the state agency. M. F. K. Johnson. bibliog il Am Lib 2:736-9 Jl '71
Media fragments and ALA. A. B. Martin. il Library J 96:1339 Ap 15 '71
Planning community college resource centers. L. Giles. bibliog il Am Lib 2:51-4 Ja '71
Santa's workshop for teachers; Learning centers project and the Teacher center at Durham elementary school, Philadelphia. A. Silberman. il Am Ed 7:3-8 D '71
Systems for individual study. E. Fleischer. il por Library J 96:695-8 F 15 '71
Who should do what in the media center. R. N. Case. por Wilson Lib Bul 45:852-5 My '71
INSTRUCTORS, College. See College professors and instructors
INSTRUMENT boards (airplanes) See Airplanes—Instrument boards
INSTRUMENT flying. See Aviation—Instrument flying
INSTRUMENT landing. See Airplanes—Landing
INSTRUMENTAL music
See also
Chamber music
Military music
Piano music
INSTRUMENTS
See also
Scientific apparatus and instruments
INSTRUMENTS, Drawing. See Drawing instruments

INSTRUMENTS, Testing. See Testing instruments
INSULATED jugs. See Thermos containers
INSULATION (electric)
Neat packaging for power lines; gas insulation. il Bsns W p58 Mr 20 '71
See also
Dielectrics
INSULATION (heat)
Heating and insulating the home. il Consumer Rep 36:595-9 O '71
If your house is under-insulated. Sunset 147: 108 N '71
Insulation: a federal case; FHA standards. A. J. Maher. Am Home 74:68-9 O '71
You can't make a power plant look like a tree, or, Waste not, want not. W. F. Wagner, jr. Arch Rec 150:9-10 N '71
INSULIN
Insulin and microtubules in rat adipocytes. D. Soifer and others. bibliog il Science 172:269-71 Ap 16 '71
Methamphetamine-induced insulin release. E. M. McMahon and others. bibliog il Science 174:66-8 O 1 '71
INSURANCE
Insurance crisis: risks without takers. il Newsweek 77:80+ Mr 22 '71
Insurance man; claims and cancellations. G. Ace. Sat R 54:6 O 9 '71
See also
Estate planning
Investment trusts—Insurance
Risk (insurance)
Adjustment of claims
Understanding insurance; insurance claims. R. Simpson. Har Yrs 11:34-5 S '71
Advertising
Violent sell; advertising campaign for violence indemnity policy. Time il 98:100-1 N 8 '71
All risk policies
Insurance: time to update your homeowner policy. Bsns W p86 O 30 '71
Claims
See Insurance—Adjustment of claims
Fraudulent promotion
Health trap. il Newsweek 78:62+ Ag 2 '71
Legal costs
See Insurance, Litigation
Policies
Understanding insurance; questions and answers. R. Simpson. Har Yrs 11:40-1 Ap; 34-5 S '71
Why insurance is so hard to get. L. Velie. Read Digest 98:83-8 Ap '71
Reinsurance
See also
United States—Federal insurance administration
INSURANCE, Agricultural
Insure your corn against blight? F. Bailey, jr. Suc Farm 69:no2 A6 F '71
INSURANCE, Automobile
Aid to motorists: insurance changes ahead. il U S News 70:26-8 Mr 15 '71
Are you liable for your child's driving accidents? Bet Hom & Gard 49:34+ O '71
Case for/against no-fault auto insurance. P. A. Hart; P. S. Wise. Pop Sci 198:56-7+ Ja '71
Drive for cheaper auto insurance; with report on no-fault insurance in Saskatchewan and Puerto Rico. U S News 71:22-4 Jl 26 '71
How to buy auto insurance today. il Changing T 25:6-11 Jl '71
Insurance reform: good plan on the wrong road. Consumer Rep 36:295 My '71
Insurance: the road to reform. Consumer Rep 36:223-6 Ap '71
Is no-fault insurance the answer? il U S News 72:27-9 Ja 3 '72
More auto insurance for less money. D. L. Gregg. Bet Hom Gard 49:6 Je '71
New facts on auto insurance. L. David. Mech Illus 67:66 Ap '71
No-fault auto insurance: what is it? F. J. Naffziger. America 124:627-30 Je 19 '71; Reply. C. S. Abood. 125:1 Jl 10 '71
No-fault auto insurance: what you should know. M. Daly. il Bet Hom & Gard 49:84-5+ N '71
No fault default. S. Lazarus. New Repub 164:21-3 Ap 17 '71
No-fault plans hit more potholes. Bsns W p44 My 15 '71
No-fault wins its case; with editorial comment. il Bsns W p74, 80 Jl 31 '71

INSURANCE, Automobile—*Continued*
Reputable snoops; Meisner case. Nation 213:
131-2 Ag 30 '71
Spiral's end? il Newsweek 78:65-6 Ag 23 '71
This month's feature: the no-fault auto in-
surance controversy. Cong Digest 50:162-92
Je '71
Timid step toward reform. il por Time 97:
82+ Mr 29 '71
Toward blameless collisions? C. Meyer. Mc-
Calls 99:45 D '71
Toward the socialization of injury. P. Van-
derwicken. il Fortune 84:160-3+ N '71
Traffic gets heavy for auto insurers; Italy's
new law. il Bsns W p54-5 Je 19 '71
Want to save money on auto insurance?
Bet Hom & Gard 49:94 Jl '71
Weak push toward no-fault. Bsns W p30+ Mr
27 '71
What to do if your auto insurance is not re-
newed. il Good H 173:148 Ag '71
See also
Allstate insurance company
State farm mutual automobile insurance com-
pany

INSURANCE, Aviation
See also
Airlines—Insurance

INSURANCE, Burglary
Write your own camera theft policy. E. Mey-
ers. il Pop Phot 68:60+ My '71
See also
Insurance, Government

INSURANCE, Business
Avoid losses through risk management. F. X.
McCahill, jr. Harvard Bsns R 49:57-65 My
'71

INSURANCE, Casualty
See also
Insurance, Automobile
Insurance, Disaster
Insurance, Earthquake

INSURANCE, Credit
See also
Insurance, Mortgage guaranty

INSURANCE, Disaster
Disaster insurance. R. Krumme. Suc Farm
69:no5 N1-3+ Mr '71

INSURANCE, Earthquake
California tallies an earthquake's cost. il
Bsns W p24 F 13 '71

INSURANCE, Fire
See also
Arson

INSURANCE, Government
Crime insurance hard to get? U.S. aid is on
the way. il U S News 70:18-19 Ja 18 '71
If crime makes insurance hard to get; federal crime insurance. Changing T 25:6 D
'71
See also
United States—Federal insurance administration

INSURANCE, Health
See also
Insurance—Fraudulent promotion
Insurance, Hospitalization
Insurance, Mental health

United States
Coming battle over health care; proposals
before Congress. il Nations Bsns 59:26-8
N '71
Debate on national health insurance. Amer-
ica 124:222 Mr 6 '71
Economics of health care. J. Ridgeway. il
Ramp Mag 10:8-9 S '71
Health care for everybody; how various
plans would work. il U S News 70:36-8
My 3 '71
Health care: supply, demand and politics. il
Time 97:86-8+ Je 7 '71
Health insurance. H. C. Wallich. por News-
week 78:57 Ag 9 '71
Health insurance: battle focuses on Nixon
and Kennedy schemes. R. J. Bazell. il Sci-
ence 171:783-5 F 26 '71
Health insurance for older people. il Changing
T 25:21-3 Ag '71
Health service: is the next step socialism?
address, November 19, 1970. T. J. Watson,
jr. Vital Speeches 37:249-51 F 1 '71
Mr Nixon's health-care plan. il Newsweek
77:20-1 Mr 1 '71
National health insurance. J. Ehrenreich and
O. Fein. Cur 129:24-31 My '71
National health insurance, do we need it?
What kind? At what cost? A. Q. Maisel.
Read Digest 98:86-90 F '71
Nixon's blueprint for a national health pro-
gram. il U S News 70:69 Mr 1 '71
Our sick medical system; the Kennedy and
Nixon proposals. Life 70:4 Mr 5 '71
Political doctors argue health care; Nixon
vs. Kennedy. Bsns W p99 F 27 '71

Politics of health care. Time 98:41 Jl 5 '71
Prepaid health care: the way it works,
what's being planned. il U S News 70:
76-7 Mr 29 '71
President proposes health policy for 70's in
message to Congress. Aging 198:7 Ap '71
Presidential prescription for health. il Time
97:11-12 Mr 1 '71
President's message on medical care; excerpts from message to Congress, February
18, 1971, R. M. Nixon. il U S News 70:70-
4 Mr 1 '71
Push is on for added federal health aids. il
U S News 70:35-6 F 8 '71
Quality of mercy, by S. Greenberg. Review
Bsns W p6 Mr 13 '71. R. Fein
Should chiropractors be paid with your tax
dollars? A. Q. Maisel. Read Digest 99:76-
81 Jl '71
TRB from Washington; Nixon-Kennedy pro-
posals. New Repub 164:8 F 27 '71
Thunder in the AMA. il por Newsweek 78:
52-3 Jl 5 '71
To your health; Nixon-Kennedy-AMA pro-
posals. J. Osborne. New Repub 164:12-14
Mr 6 '71
Will health beat Nixon in '72? J. Castelli.
Commonweal 94:108-12 Ap 9 '71
Writing the prescription for health care;
proposals before Congress. D. W. Petten-
gill. Harvard Bsns R 49:37-43 N '71
See also
Group health cooperative of Puget Sound
Medicare

INSURANCE, Hospitalization
Aid for Blue cross in Nixon's plan. il Bsns W
p94-6 F 27 '71
Blue Cross. J. Ridgeway. Ramp Mag 9:4+
My '71
Getting something for the money: Pennsyl-
vania's Blue cross. R. DeWolf. Nation 213:
435-6 N 1 '71
Inside critic; Blue cross plan. il Forbes 107:
48 F 15 '71

INSURANCE, Liability
See also
Insurance, Automobile

INSURANCE, Life
How much life insurance do you need? il
Changing T 26:37-40 Ja '72
Ways life insurance benefits are paid. il
Good H 173:226 N '71
What if you're turned down for life insurance?
Bet Hom & Gard 49:4+ My '71

Family plan policies
Grandparent insurance. S. N. Scherer. il Har
Yrs 11:46-7 D '71
Quick guide to life insurance. L. David. il
Mech Illus 67:75-7+ Ja '71

Policies
Caveat emptor on campus; selling policies to
students on credit. il Consumer Rep 37:
50-1 Ja '72
Fat policy; premiums based on weight of
policy holder. il Time 98:103 N 22 '71
Life insurance: now you can spot the low-
cost policies. il Changing T 25:6-10 Mr '71;
Discussion. 25:48 My; 47 Je '71
What kind of life insurance should you buy?
il Changing T 25:7-10 S '71

Policy settlement
Here's how to collect on life insurance. R.
Krumme. il Suc Farm 69:12 Je '71
What to do with your life insurance when
you retire. il Changing T 25:37-9 My '71

INSURANCE, Litigation
Now group insurance pays the lawyer; prepaid legal plans. il Bsns W p58+ Jl 10 '71

INSURANCE, Mental health
Financing outpatient mental health care
through psychiatric insurance. R. Fink.
bibliog Ment Hy 55:143-50 Ap '71

INSURANCE, Mortgage guaranty
Karl the magic man. il por Time 99:60 Ja
17 '72

INSURANCE, Property
Insurers get burned on ghetto policies. il
Bsns W p38 N 6 '71
See also
Insurance, Government
Insurance, Mortgage guaranty

INSURANCE, Psychiatric. See Insurance, Mental health

INSURANCE, Social
See also
Insurance, Health
Insurance, Unemployment
Old age pensions
Pensions
Social security taxes

INSURANCE, Social—*Continued*
United States
Automatic increases, $12,000 social security tax base urged. Aging 199:10+ My '71
Chiselers and social security. L. W. Raymond. Cath World 214:117-19 D '71
House passes social security, medicare, welfare changes. Har Yrs 11:4-5 Jl '71
New thoughts on social security. R. W. Dietsch. New Repub 165:13-15 N 27 '71
Nixon approves 10% social security rise for 26 million; checks go out in June. Aging 198:3 Ap '71
Overhauling welfare, social security: the latest plan. il U S News 70:49-50 My 24 '71
Plan to guarantee income: chances now. il U S News 71:52 Jl 5 '71
Plan to liberalize social security. U S News 70:84 Ap 19 '71
Social security. R. M. Ball. Todays Ed 60:24-6 Ap '71
Social security benefits: how much higher? il U S News 70:38-9 Mr 29 '71
Social security to increase benefits. T. Schuchat. Har Yrs 11:4-5 F '71
What are your new social security benefits? M. Daly. il Bet Hom & Gard 49:6+ N '71
Your social security: how to protect it. il Changing T 25:29-30 O '71
See also
Insurance, Health—United States
Insurance, Unemployment—United States
Social security taxes
United States—Social security administration
INSURANCE, Theft. See Insurance, Burglary
INSURANCE, Unemployment

California
Hairy jobless are shorn of benefits. il Bsns W p34 Jl 24 '71
United States
Jobless reach for record benefits. il Bsns W p35-6 Ap 10 '71
Measuring total and state insured unemployment; with tables and charts. G. P. Green. bibliog Mo Labor R 94:37-48 Je '71
Reminder on unemployment benefits. Changing T 25:6 S '71
Status report on state unemployment insurance laws; with tables. J. A. Hickey. Mo Labor R 94:22-30 Ja '71
Unemployment insurance and employment service operations; tables. See issues of Monthly labor review
INSURANCE, Workmens compensation
Compromise agreements as a means of work injury settlement. S. B. Barton. bibliog il Mo Labor R 94:51-3 S '71
INSURANCE advertising. See Insurance—Advertising
INSURANCE companies
Putting insurers' feet to the fire; Pennsylvania's insurance commissioner. il Bsns W p32 Mr 27 '71
See also
Aetna life and casualty company
American national insurance company
Chubb and son, inc.
Equitable life assurance society of the United States
General reinsurance corporation
Institute of life insurance, New York
Kemper insurance group
National bankers life insurance company
North Carolina mutual life insurance company
Overseas private investment corporation
State farm mutual automobile insurance company
State mutual life assurance company of America
Directories
50 largest life-insurance companies. Fortune 83:194-5 My '71

Mutual fund operations
Odd couple. il Forbes 108:83-4 O 15 '71

Regulation
Health economics; R. M. Nixon's health message. F. Land and J. Ridgeway. Ramp Mag 9:7 Je '71
INSURANCE policies. See Insurance—Policies
INSURGENCY
Camelot revisited; study of ethical aspects of assistance to counterinsurgency efforts. Sci Am 224:45-6+ My '71
Theory and fallacies of counterinsurgency. E. Ahmad. il Nation 213:70-85 Ag 2 '71; Reply. L. G. Wolf. 213:162+ S '71
INSURRECTIONS. See Revolutions
INTAKE manifolds. See Manifolds

INTEGRATED circuit testers. See Testing instruments
INTEGRATED circuits. See Electronic circuits, Integrated
INTEGRATED tactical air control system. See Airplanes, Military—Radio equipment
INTEGRATION, Agricultural. See Contracts, Agricultural
INTEGRATION, Racial. See United States—Race question
INTEGRATION of public schools. See Public schools—Desegregation
INTELLECT
Mind: from memory pills to electronic pleasures beyond sex. il Time 97:45-7 Ap 19 '71
See also
Genius
Intelligence
Nutritional aspects
Perinatal undernutrition: accumulation of catecholamines in rat brain. W. J. Shoemaker and R. J. Wurtman. bibliog il Science 171:1017-19 Mr 12 '71
INTELLECTUAL cooperation
See also
United States—Cultural relations
INTELLECTUAL development of children. See Children—Growth and development
INTELLECTUAL development of infants. See Infants—Growth and development
INTELLECTUAL liberty
Freedom to read: attacks & defense; AAP general meeting. il Pub W 200:30-2 O 11 '71
Gathering of the forces of repression: forecast for the 1970s. J. F. Krug and J. A. Harvey. Am Lib 2:238-40 Mr '71
Threats to intellectual freedom; address, June 1971. E. T. Moore. il por Library J 96:3563-7 N 1 '71; Same abr. with title Rise of a new censorship? Cur 135:3-8 D '71
See also
Academic freedom
American library association—Intellectual freedom committee
Libraries and intellectual liberty
Science, Freedom of
INTELLECTUAL life
Authenticity and the modern unconscious. L. Trilling. Commentary 52:39-50 S '71
See also
Enlightenment
also subhead Intellectual life under names of countries, states, cities, e.g. Boston—Intellectual life
INTELLECTUALS
Cooling of the intellectuals; the case of Commentary and the New York review of books. P. Steinfels. Commonweal 94:255-61 My 21 '71; Discussion. 94:365-7, 418 Jl 9, Ag 20 '71
Despair in Russia. G. Heath. Read Digest 98:125-8 Je '71
Revolt of the thinking class. R. Taagepera. Nation 212:681-4 My 31 '71
INTELLIGENCE
Prenatal sex hormone levels: a possible link to intelligence. il Sci N 101:8 Ja 1 '72
See also
Age and intelligence
INTELLIGENCE, Artificial. See Artificial intelligence
INTELLIGENCE levels
Intellectual development of children from interracial matings. L. Willerman and others; discussion. bibliog il Science 172:8+ Ap 2 '71
Intelligence and race. W. F. Bodmer and L. L. Cavalli-Sforza; discussion. Sci Am 224:6-8 Ja; 46 F '71
Intelligence: genetic or environmental? Sci N 100:167 S 11 '71
Race and I.Q. excerpts from Race and psychology. O. Klineberg. il UNESCO Courier 24:4-9+ N '71
See also
Intelligence tests
Negroes
Is intelligence racial? H. Simmons. il por Newsweek 77:69-70 My 10 '71
Nurturing intelligence; influence of ghetto environment on IQ's. il Time 99:56 Ja 3 '72
Parent education and cultural inheritance. D. Tanner and L. N. Tanner. bibliog Sch & Soc 99:21-4 Ja '71
Women
Conversation pit stop. D. Newman and R. Benton. Mlle 72:28+ Ja '71
Man talk; get smart. D. Newman and R. Benton. Mlle 73:116 My '71
INTELLIGENCE quotient
Creeping meritocracy? por Newsweek 78:57 Ag 23 '71
Exploding the myth of I.Q. D. Klein. il Parents Mag 46:52-3+ O '71

INTELLIGENCE quotient—*Continued*
I.Q. R. Herrnstein. il Atlan 228:43-58+ S
'71; Discussion. 228:101-4+ D '71
I.Q. argument. by H. J. Eysenck. Review
Commonweal 95:42-5 O 8 '71. A. F. D'Ad-
amo, jr
Intelligence and race. W. F. Bodmer and
L. L. Cavalli-Sforza; discussion. Sci Am
224:6-8 Ja '71
Intelligence quotient pattern over age: com-
parisons among siblings and parent-child
pairs. R. B. McCall; reply. F. Weizmann.
bibliog Science 171:589 F 12 '71
Is equality bad for you? il Time 98:33 Ag 23
'71
Magical aura of the IQ; excerpt from address.
J. Kagan. il Sat R 54:92-3 D 4 '71
Race and I.Q. excerpts from Race and psy-
chology. O. Klineberg. il UNESCO Cour-
ier 24:4-9+ N '71
Race, social class, and IQ. S. Scarr-Salapa-
tek. bibliog il Science 174:1285-95 D 24 '71
Sex differences in I.Q. pattern of children
with congenital heart defects. M. P. Hon-
zik and others. bibliog il Science 174:1042-4
D 3 '71
Unknowns in the IQ equation. S. Scarr-Sala-
patek. bibliog Science 174:1223-8 D 17 '71
INTELLIGENCE service
See also
Secret service

Egypt
One big fishbowl. il Newsweek 77:44+ Je 14
'71

United States
Dossier dictatorship. P. Schrag. Sat R 54:
24-5 Ap 17 '71
Drifting toward 1984; hearing of Subcom-
mittee on constitutional rights into the ex-
tent of government surveillance of citizens.
Time 97:16 Mr 29 '71
Growing alarm over official snooping. il U S
News 70:38-41 F 22 '71
Has big brother got your number? il Sr
Schol 98:12-16 Mr 29 '71
How the U.S. army spies on citizens. il
por Life 70:20-7 Mr 26 '71
Invisible intruders; army's justification for
collection of domestic political information.
P. Schrag. Sat R 54:20-1 Ja 30 '71
Loophole spying; question of army snooping
and destruction of files. New Repub 165:7-
8 D 25 '71
On being monitored. J. R. Waltz. Nation 212:
113-14 Ja 25 '71
Project MUM; army snooping. New Repub
165:9 N 13 '71
Sam Ervin and the privacy invaders. J. K.
Batten. il New Repub 164:19-23 My 8 '71
Sniffing out the super-snoopers. C. Rabb.
Commonweal 94:126-7 Ap 16 '71
Spy versus spy; the President's new reor-
ganization order. New Repub 165:10 N 20
'71
U.S. foreign intelligence community re-
organized by President Nixon; White
House announcement, November 5, 1971.
Dept State Bul 65:658-9 D 6 '71
Why the shake-up in intelligence. por U S
News 71:40-1 N 22 '71
See also
United States—Central intelligence agency
INTELLIGENCE tests
I.Q. R. Herrnstein. il Atlan 228:43-58+ S
'71; Discussion. 228:101-4+ D '71
IQ test: education's bugaboo. A. C. Pepin.
bibliog Clear House 45:278-80 Ja '71
Magical aura of the IQ; excerpt from address.
J. Kagan. il Sat R 54:92-3 D 4 '71
New test for the brain. Newsweek 78:67-8 D
13 '71
New ways to measure intelligence in infants.
S. S. Fremon. il Parents Mag 46:39-41+
Ap '71
Tests that destroy. il Newsweek 78:97 S 20
'71
What IQ tests really reveal. il Good H 173:
202 S '71
What price I.Q. tests? il UNESCO Courier
24:10-11 N '71
See also
Aptitude tests
Intelligence quotient
Prediction of scholastic success
INTELSAT. See International telecommunica-
tions satellite consortium
INTENSIFIERS, Image. See Image intensifiers
INTENSIVE care nurseries. See Children—
Hospital care
INTENSIVE care units. See Hospital care
INTERACTION analysis in education. See
Teachers and students

INTER-AMERICAN children's institute
Inter-American children's institute; Elizabeth
S. Enochs contest prizes. Américas 23:43 Ap
'71
INTER-AMERICAN committee on the Alliance
for progress. See Alliance for progress
INTER-AMERICAN conferences
Formal beginnings. il Américas 23:S11-12 Ja
'71
INTER-AMERICAN council for education,
science, and culture
Experts meet on educational development. il
Américas 23:45 S '71
New inter-American effort; excerpt from ad-
dress, February 8, 1971. G. Plaza. Améri-
cas 23:1 Mr '71
Problem of youth; CIECC resolution. Américas
23:1 My '71
INTER-AMERICAN economic and social coun-
cil
IA-ECOSOC speaks out on surtax. Améri-
cas 23:44 O '71
Inter-American cooperative action. F.
Domínguez. il Américas 23:16-18 My '71
Inter-American economic and social council
meets at Panama City; statements, Sep-
tember 13 and 15, 1971. N. Samuels; C. A.
Meyer. Dept State Bul 65:379-84 O 11 '71
INTER-AMERICAN highway. See Pan Ameri-
can highway
INTER-AMERICAN music festival, Washing-
ton, D.C.
Fifth Inter-American music festival. Américas
23:46 Ap '71
Inter-American festival; gimmickry abounds,
but Teatro Colon opera visit cheers all.
G. Lafay. il Hi Fi 21:MA22-3 Ag '71
Opera and sonic collage: fifth Inter-Amer-
ican music festival. I. Lowens. il Américas
23:10-14 Ag '71
South American way; Inter-American music
festival. il Newsweek 77:49 My 31 '71
INTER-AMERICAN relations
Dream that became a reality; ed. by G. de
Zendegui. il Américas 23:S1-16 Ja '71
Latin America: a U.S. news orphan. X.
Gutierrez Cantu. il America 124:290-1 Mr
20 '71
Our nonpolicy toward Latin America. S. Lin-
owitz. por Life 70:4 Je 18 '71
Western hemisphere ambassadors honored by
President Nixon; toast at White House
dinner, April 6, 1971. Dept State Bul 64:
581-3 My 3 '71
See also
Alliance for progress
Organization of American states
Pan American day and week
INTERCELLULAR junctions. See Junctions
(physiology)
INTERCHANGES (highway engineering) See
Roads—Interchanges and intersections
INTERCITY transportation. See Transporta-
tion—United States
INTERCO, inc.
Doing the wrong thing successfully. Forbes
108:39 O 1 '71
INTERCOLLEGIATE rowing association
championships. See Rowing
INTERCOMMUNICATING systems
Instant paging-intercom system. H. Levin.
il Radio-Electr 43:61 Ja '72
Wired home intercoms. il Consumer Rep 36:
734-6 N '71
See also
Television, Closed circuit
INTERCOMMUNION. See Lords Supper
INTERCOMMUNITY action, inc. See Citizens
associations
INTERCOMMUNITY cooperation
City-county drainage plans come first; Hous-
ton, Tex. L. Welch. il Am City 86:70+ Ag
'71
Good neighbor policy; sister city, Kobe,
Japan donates food to hungry people of
Seattle. Nation 214:4 Ja 3 '72
INTERCONNECTION of power systems. See
Electric plants—Interconnection
INTERCONTINENTAL ballistic missiles. See
Guided missiles
INTERCOSMOS (satellite) See Artificial satel-
lites, European
INTERCULTURAL education
Cultural evaluation of contemporary educa-
tional innovations. S. I. Miller. bibliog Sch
& Soc 99:507-8+ D '71
INTERCULTURAL relations. See Cultural re-
lations
INTERCUTTING of moving pictures. See Mov-
ing pictures—Editing
INTERDENOMINATIONAL cooperation. See
Religious cooperation

INTERDENOMINATIONAL foreign mission association
Creative tension: the church-mission controversy. W. H. Fuller. Chr Today 16:33 O 22 '71

INTERDISCIPLINARY teaching. See Teaching

INTEREST
Arthur Burns explains policy on dividends, interest rates; excerpts from testimony before the Senate committee on banking, housing and urban affairs, November 2, 1971. A. F. Burns. por U S News 71:91-2 N 15 '71
Bankers try more markdowns. Bsns W p 17 Ja 23 '71
Banks prod demand with a new rate cut. Bsns W p21-2 F 20 '71
Battle brewing over interest on charge accounts. Pub W 199:42 Mr 29 '71
Big money question. C. Morgello. il Newsweek 77:80 Je 28 '71
Big payoffs for savers coming to an end. il U S News 70:72-3 Ap 5 '71
Borrowers shrug at prime rate cut. il Bsns W p24 Ja 16 '71
Bunting's bet. por Time 97:72 Je 28 '71
Connally warning on interest rates. U S News 71:58 Ag 16 '71
Controls ahead on interest rates? il U S News 71:104-6 S 20 '71
Drop in interest rates for consumer. U S News 70:80 Ja 25 '71
Fear of inflation rules the markets. il Bsns W p37-8 Jl 17 '71
Free fall. Time 98:30+ N 22 '71
Gainers and losers as money gets cheaper. il U S News 70:58-9 F 1 '71
Good news for borrowers: easing of interest rates. il U S News 70:95-9 Mr 15 '71
Highest interest; lowest risks. M. T. Bloom. il Har Yrs 11:30-2 My '71; Same abr. with title How to get the most out of your savings. Read Digest 98:211-12+ My '71
How far will the Fed go? Duns 93:116 Je '69
How to manage high-priced money. M. Hood. il Suc Farm 69:no3 23 F '71
Inevitable boost to 6%. Bsns W p 19 Jl 10 '71
Interest rate outlook. F. H. Schott. por Nations Bsns 59:73 D '71
Interest rates: a possible bind, a possible way out. il Fortune 83:34 My '71
Interest rates: a troublesome rise. il Time 97:68 Je 7 '71
Interest rates keep tumbling. Bsns W p41-2 N 13 '71
Long and short of the Fed's problem; money rates. il Bsns W p26-7 Mr 20 '71
Monetary outlook: a little tightening. il Bsns W p 15-16 Ja 1 '72
Money, tight or easy? M. Friedman. il Newsweek 77:80 Mr 1 '71
More interest-rate cuts in offing? U S News 70:74 Ja 18 '71
Now the Fed can work more freely. il Bsns W p51 Ag 28 '71
Peril point in interest rates. Fortune 83:17-18 Je '71
Plain talk about interest. J. P. Baughman. por Nations Bsns 59:96 Ja '71
Prime dilemma for the bankers; with editorial comment. il Bsns W p34. 126 Je 19 '71
Rate change draws cautious approval; Citibank's floating prime rate. il Bsns W p25 O 30 '71
Rush to repay. Time 97:80 Mr 29 '71
Surprising turns in Operation Twist; long-term interest rates. Bsns W p32 My 1 '71
Those interesting new interest rates. il Fortune 83:145 Ja '71
Tight money returning: effect on borrowers. il U S News 71:44-6 Ag 9 '71
Where interest rates are headed now. il U S News 71:97-100 N 8 '71
Why it's costing more to borrow money. il U S News 71:42-3 Jl 5 '71
See also
Instalment plan
Savings deposits—Interest
United States—Interest and dividends, Committee on

INTEREST and dividends, Committee on. See United States—Interest and dividends, Committee on

INTERFAITH cooperation. See Religious cooperation

INTERFERENCE, Electric. See Electric interference

INTERFERENCE, Radio. See Radio interference

INTERFERENCE, Television. See Television interference

INTERFEROMETRY
Evidence for internal structure in quasars. Sci N 99:245 Ap 10 '71
Focusing on the stars. Newsweek 77:92+ My 3 '71

Joint Soviet-American radio interferometry. K. I. Kellermann. il Sky & Tel 42:132-3 S '71
Quasars: millisecond-of-arc structure revealed by very-long-baseline interferometry. C. A. Knight and others. bibliog il Science 172:52-4 Ap 2 '71
Quasars revisited: rapid time variations observed via very-long-baseline interferometry. A. R. Whitney and others. bibliog il Science 173:225-30 Jl 16 '71
Stanford's high-resolution radio interferometer. R. N. Bracewell and others. il pors Sky & Tel 42:4-9 Jl '71

INTERFERON
Induction of interferon. M. R. Hilleman and A. A. Tytell. il Sci Am 225:26-31 Jl '71
Interferon action: inhibition of vesicular stomatitis virus RNA synthesis induced by virion-bound polymerase. P. I. Marcus and others. bibliog il Science 174:593-8 N 5 '71
Repression of interferon action: induced differentiation of embryonic cells. S. E. Grossberg and P. S. Morahan. bibliog il Science 171:77-9 Ja 8 '71

INTERGOVERNMENTAL   committee   for European migration
United States delegation named to ICEM council meeting; Department of state announcement, November 26, 1971. Dept State Bul 65:714 D 20 '71

INTERGOVERNMENTAL fiscal relations
Alternative 11: an urban development bank. C. M. Haar. Cur 128:50-2 Ap '71
See also
Grants-in-aid
Intergovernmental tax relations

INTERGOVERNMENTAL tax relations
Aid for cities and states: Nixon's latest approach. il U S News 70:42-3 F 22 '71
Better than revenue sharing. M. J. Ulmer. New Repub 164:16-19 F 13 '71; Same abr. with title Alternative 1: tax credits. Cur 128:46-50 Ap '71
Can Nixon bail out the states? il U S News 70:17-18 Ja 25 '71
Case for revenue sharing. I. Ross. Read Digest 98:77-81 Je '71
Congress: quarrel over sharing. il Time 97: 18 Je 14 '71
Constitutional blackmail; threat of convention to push revenue-sharing plan. New Repub 164:10 Mr 6 '71
Crowded cities, empty land, and the Nixon remedy. il U S News 70:24-6 Ap 5 '71
Doubts expressed about revenue sharing. Am City 86:16 N '71
Drummers for the revolution; reform programs for revenue sharing, executive reorganization and welfare. il Time 97:13 F 8 '71
Forty thousand dollars per minute; address, March 6, 1971. B. Goldwater, jr. Vital Speeches 37:392-4 Ap 15 '71
Hard sell by the White House; revenue sharing. il por Newsweek 77:20 F 8 '71
How to bail out the states; general revenue sharing. il Newsweek 77:25-6 F 15 '71
How will you spend the money? il Farm J 95:58 My '71
Letter from Washington. R. H. Rovere. New Yorker 47:108+ F 20 '71
Limitations of revenue sharing. M. J. Ulmer. bibliog f Ann Am Acad 397:48-59 S '71
Mayors' complaint; revenue-sharing. Newsweek 77:53 F 22 '71
Mayors' revolt; voyage to Washington to press support for President Nixon's revenue-sharing plan. il Newsweek 77:94 My 24 '71
Nixon spells out revenue sharing. U S News 70:55-6 F 15 '71
Nixon's new American revolution: revenue sharing. Sr Schol 98:2-7 Mr 15 '71
Nixon's new federalism: is it the answer? M. S. Stewart. Cur Hist 61:279-83+ N '71
Nixon's share-the-wealth-plan. il por Newsweek 77:15-16 Ja 18 '71
No strings (?) revenue sharing. Am City 86: 8 Ag '71
No, to revenue sharing. W. G. Fredericks. Nat R 23:754-7 Jl 13 '71
Politics of Nixon's revolution; with reply by C. DeMuth. M. W. Karmin. Cur 128:40-5 Ap '71
President Nixon's proposals for welfare reform and revenue-sharing; excerpts from messages to Congress, 1969. Cur Hist 61:297-9+ N '71
Pros and cons of revenue sharing. J. Steele. il Time 97:18-19 F 1 '71
Real story of revenue sharing. il U S News 70:41-3 Mr 1 '71
Real story of the Nixon revolution. il U S News 70:29-34 Mr 15 '71

INTERGOVERNMENTAL tax relations—*Cont.*
Revenue sharing. W. F. Buckley, jr. Nat R 23:390-1 Ap 6 '71
Revenue sharing. H. C. Wallich. Newsweek 77:79 F 22 '71
Revenue sharing: chance in Congress. U S News 70:40 F 8 '71
Revenue sharing: deception and semantics. P. S. Templin. America 124:193 F 27 '71
Revenue sharing faces a bloody battle. il Bsns W p68 Ja 30 '71
Revenue sharing is a counterrevolution. M. Frankel. il N Y Times Mag p28-9+ Ap 25 '71
Revenue sharing is not enough. Fortune 83:59-60 F '71
Revenue sharing: myths and alternatives. Chr Cent 88:309-10 Mr 10 '71
Revenue sharing: slicing the pie. il U S News 70:86-7 My 3 '71
Revenue sharing, solution or band-aid? Am City 86:8 F '71
Revenue sharing that works. New Repub 164:7-8 My 29 '71
Revolution or reversal? revenue sharing. J. Osborne. New Repub 164:15-16 F 6 '71
Saying no to Nixon; problem of getting revenue sharing through Congress. il Time 97:16 Mr 8 '71
Selling the revolution; revenue sharing. J. Osborne. New Repub 164:7-8 Mr 20 '71
Sharing loaves and fishes; R. Nixon's recommendations for revenue sharing. il por Time 97:15-16 F 15 '71
Some dangers in federal revenue-sharing. R. H. Smith. Pub W 199:38 Mr 1 '71
Some pros and cons on revenue sharing. B. L. Masse. America 124:200-2 F 27 '71
Splitting the take; President Nixon's State of the Union speech, questions and answers. il Life 70:28 F 5 '71
State of the Union. il por Newsweek 77:15-17 F 1 '71
They came looking for money; governors in Washington. H. Sidey. il Life 70:2B Mr 12 '71
This month's feature: the controversy over revenue sharing. Cong Digest 50:99-128 Ap '71
Through the Mills; hearings on R. M. Nixon's revenue sharing plan. il por Newsweek 77:28-9 Je 14 '71
We're having second thoughts; concept of shared revenue. Parks & Rec 6:15 Jl '71
What's new? revenue-sharing. New Repub 164:13 F 6 '71

INTERIOR, Department of. See United States —Interior. Department of

INTERIOR and insular affairs, Committee on. See United States—Congress—House—Interior and insular affairs, Committee on

INTERIOR decoration
Record interiors of 1971. il Arch Rec 149:85-104 Ja '71
6 interiors. il Arch Rec 150:93-104 Ag '71
See also
Airplane decoration
Hotel decoration
House decoration
Stores

INTERIOR decorators
How to choose an interior designer. C. L. Crane. Am Home 74:72+ My '71

INTERIOR designers. See Interior decorators

INTER-LEAGUE exhibition games. See Basketball teams

INTERLIBRARY communication
Better look at budgets; cooperation to improve media programs in schools. L. Howard. il Library J 96:1081-2 Mr 15 '71
Library urban info network scheme explained to NYLA; summary of statement, 1971. T. Costello. por Library J 96:3707 N 15 '71
N.Y. union spokesmen oppose state plan. Library J 96:154 Ja 15 '71
Systems and networks: the state library role. C. A. Nelson and A. H. Nelson. bibliog il Am Lib 2:883-7 S '71

INTERMARRIAGE of races
Black/white dating; with result of national poll. J. Downs. il Life 70:56-67 My 28 '71
Marriage in black and white, by J. R. Washington, jr. Review
Chr Cent 88:755-6 Je 16 '71. G. Clanton

History
Intermarriage in history. il Negro Hist Bul 34:100-2 My '71

INTERMARRIAGE of races in the Bible. See Marriage in the Bible

INTERMARRIAGES, Religious. See Marriages, Mixed

INTERMEDIA performances. See Performing arts

INTERMEDIATE range ballistic missiles. See Guided missiles

INTERMISSIONS
See also
Opera—Intermissions

INTERNAL combustion engines. See Automobile engines; Gas and oil engines

INTERNAL revenue service. See United States —Internal revenue service

INTERNAL security
Liberal capitulation; origins of Title II of the Internal security act of 1950. R. Griffith. New Repub 165:23 O 9 '71
Never again? move in Congress to repeal Title II of McCarran act. il Newsweek 77:22+ Ap 5 '71
New tool kit for a police state; bills before Congress. L. Fernsworth. Nation 212:721-4 Je 7 '71; Reply. S. E. Crane. 212:770+ Je 21 '71
Secretary Rogers' news conference of July 1; the duty of the executive branch to protect the national security. W. P. Rogers. Dept State Bul 65:78-82 Jl 19 '71
Secrets and security; postscript to the Pentagon papers. I. Silver. Commonweal 94:399-402 Ag 6 '71
Security: highways and byways. F. J. Donner. Nation 212:182-5 F 8 '71
Toward a new definition of national security. I. J. Winn. Bul Atom Sci 27:35-7 Mr '71
See also
Insurgency
Subversive activities

INTERNAL security, Committee on. See United States—Congress—House—Internal security, Committee on

INTERNAL security, Subcommittee on. See United States—Congress—Judiciary, Committee on the—Internal security, Subcommittee on

INTERNAL security division. See United States—Justice, Department of—Internal security division

INTERNAL structure of the moon. See Moon —Internal structure

INTERNATIONAL air transport association
Carriers fear stifling of IATA bargaining. L. Doty. Aviation W 95:23-4 Jl 5 '71
European youth fare directives intensify IATA-government rifts. Aviation W 94:30 Je 14 '71
Europeans ponder charter limits. L. Doty. Aviation W 94:27-8 My 24 '71
Faith in IATA fare mechanism slipping. L. Doty. Aviation W 95:26-7 O 11 '71
Fares, charters draw IATA focus. L. Doty. Aviation W 95:16-17 N 15 '71
Government edicts guide agenda for IATA. L. Doty. il Aviation W 94:28-9 Je 28 '71
IATA meeting role shift emerges. L. Doty. Aviation W 95:23-4 N 29 '71
IATA members aim at charters. R. S. Kahn. Aviation W 95:22-5 Ag 2 '71
IATA moves to curb container losses. Aviation W 94:24 Mr 1 '71
IATA parley to weigh freight increases. E. H. Kolcum. Aviation W 94:29 My 10 '71
IATA threatens action in court to stop mandatory UHF aerosat. E. H. Kolcum. Aviation W 95:24 Jl 5 '71
IATA urged to restructure cargo tariffs. Aviation W 95:26 D 6 '71
Lufthansa forces IATA into experiment. E. H. Kolcum. Aviation W 95:26 S 20 '71
More North Atlantic talks to dominate IATA parley. E. H. Kolcum. Aviation W 95:27-8 S 6 '71
New parley seeks Atlantic fare pact. Aviation W 95:27 N 1 '71
Passenger, cargo surcharges set to offset new navigation fees. E. H. Kolcum. Aviation W 94:27 Ja 25 '71
Perspective on IATA. R. Hotz. Aviation W 95:9 D 6 '71
Price of victory in the air fare war. il Bsns W p84 O 2 '71
Red Baron strikes again. Time 98:49 Ag 23 '71
Some flags defy IATA authority; with editorial comment. L. Doty. Aviation W 95:9, 27-8 N 22 '71
Supplementals bracing for IATA action. R. G. O'Lone. Aviation W 95:20-1 Jl 19 '71
Transatlantic open rate expected as IATA fare talks hit impasse. Aviation W 95:27 N 8 '71
Uncertain sky. il Time 98:58-9 S 6 '71
Youth fare battle hits government level. Aviation W 94:26 Je 21 '71

INTERNATIONAL association of art critics
International art critics' conference. M. Amaya. il Art in Am 59:130-1 Ja '71

INTERNATIONAL association of machinists and aerospace workers
Aircraft unions hold their fire. il Bsns W p 118 My 15 '71
Airlines, Administration face first test on wage portion of Phase 2. Aviation W 95: 26 N 29 '71
Negotiating with a hard-hit industry. Bsns W p98 Mr 6'71

INTERNATIONAL astronautical federation
Satellite environment application highlights IAF Brussels congress. E. H. Kolcum. Aviation W 95:23 S 27 '71

INTERNATIONAL atomic energy agency
General conference of the International atomic energy agency holds 15th session at Vienna; statement, September 22, 1971. G. T. Seaborg. Dept State Bul 65:419-24 O 18 '71
IAEA and non-proliferation of a nuclear black market. D. Shapley. Science 172:144 Ap 9 '71
    See also
International centre for theoretical physics. Trieste, Italy

INTERNATIONAL Azalea festival. See Festivals—Virginia

INTERNATIONAL balance of payments. See Balance of payments

INTERNATIONAL bank for reconstruction and development
Basic problems of development: the World bank; address, September 27, 1971. R. S. McNamara. Vital Speeches 38:17-21 O 15 '71
Boards of governors of the IMF and IBRD meet at Washington; statement, September 30, 1971. J. B. Connally. Dept State Bul 64:453-7 O 25 '71
World bank craves a slice of Ex-Im's pie. il Bsns W p28 F 13 '71

INTERNATIONAL banking. See Banks and banking, International

INTERNATIONAL basic economy corporation
Do-gooders. il Newsweek 77:77-8 Je 21 '71
Turn public problems to private account. R. C. Rockefeller. Harvard Bsns R 49:131-8 Ja '71

INTERNATIONAL bienniale of tapestry. See Tapestry—Exhibitions

INTERNATIONAL biological program
Biome approach in ecology. Sci N 99:247-8 Ap 10 '71

INTERNATIONAL book year, 1972
Congress passes IBY resolution. S. Wagner. Pub W 201:34-5 Ja 3 '72
IBY: first genuine international publishing since the middle ages. H. R. Lottman. il Pub W 200:pt2 148-9 S 27 '71
International book year, 1972. Sch & Soc 99: 79 F '71
International book year: what's the point. C. B. Grannis. Pub W 201:39 Ja 3 '72
U.S.A.: countdown for IBY. S. Wagner. il Pub W 200:pt2 150-1 S 27 '71

INTERNATIONAL boundary and water commission (United States and Mexico)
U.S. and Mexico extend agreement on Colorado River salinity; Department announcement. Dept State Bul 63:732 D 14 '70

INTERNATIONAL brotherhood of teamsters, chauffeurs, warehousemen and helpers of America
Fitz of the teamsters. J. Lowell. Newsweek 77:76-7 Je 21 '71
Fitz takes the wheel and a new course. il por Bsns W p68 Jl 10 '71
Hoffa stay in jail may change teamsters. U S News 70:82 Ap 12 '71
Hoffa steps down, for now. il por Time 97:22 Je 14 '71
Hoffa's exit opens new doors. il por Bsns W p77 Je 12 '71
International brotherhood of teamsters convention. M. H. Cimini. Mo Labor R 94:54-5 S '71
Social climbing. il Newsweek 78:70 Jl 19 '71
Teamsters reassess Hoffa's chances. il por Bsns W p52+ Ap 17 '71
What the 'Little Fellow' says to the teamsters is what counts. A. H. Raskin. il pors N Y Times Mag p 12-13+ My 30 '71; Correction. p20 Je 13 '71
    See also
Alliance for labor action

INTERNATIONAL business machines corporation
Business under the freeze: a top executive's appraisal; interview. T. V. Learson. il por U S News 71:36-9 S 13 '71
Eames and the mythic monster; exhibition at IBM display center. K. Kuh. il Sat R 54:34+ My 29 '71
Greetings; interview. T. V. Learson. por Forbes 108:46 Ag 1 '71

IBM. il Forbes 108:18-22 S 1 '71
IBM: a corporate United Nations? il Forbes 109:26-7 Ja 1 '72
IBM in Boca Raton: Breuer builds on Florida's flood plain. il Arch Rec 149:113-18 F '71
IBM project short-circuits; projected plant in Hanover. il Bsns W p40 Ag 21 '71
IBM's new team. il Newsweek 78:68 Jl 12 '71
IBM's price war hurts the independents. Bsns W p53-4+ D 18 '71
IBM's quiet aid for college blacks. il Bsns W p28 D 18 '71
Learson at IBM's helm. il por Time 98:55 Jl 12 '71
Mountainous defense by IBM. Bsns W p26+ D 18 '71
New hand on the tiller at I.B.M. il por Fortune 84:33 Ag '71
Watson dynasty ends at IBM. Bsns W p20 Jl 3 '71
When IBM gets a flat. C. Morgello. il Newsweek 78:60 Jl 26 '71

INTERNATIONAL cartels. See Trusts, Industrial—International trusts

INTERNATIONAL catamaran challenge trophy. See Catamaran racing

INTERNATIONAL catechetical congress. See Religious conferences—Italy

INTERNATIONAL centre for theoretical physics, Trieste, Italy
Trieste: world rendezvous for physicists. D. Behrman. il UNESCO Courier 24:12-16+ My '71
Winter college format. J. Ziman. Science 171: 352-4 Ja 29 '71

INTERNATIONAL chemical and nuclear corporation
Serbian boy builds his dream castle in the drug business; M. Panic. P. Siekman. il por Fortune 83:94-7+ Ja '71

INTERNATIONAL civil aviation organization
India institutes proceedings in international court concerning jurisdiction of ICAO council. UN Mo Chron 8:89-90 O '71
Joint aerosat to be sought to avoid ICAO argument. P. J. Klass. Aviation W 94:17-18 Ap 12 '71
President appoints Mrs Dillon to ICAO council. Dept State Bul 65:639 N 29 '71

INTERNATIONAL code of zoological nomenclature. See Zoology—Nomenclature

INTERNATIONAL code signals. See Signals and signaling

INTERNATIONAL coffee agreement
1968 international coffee agreement at the halfway mark; address, February 1, 1971. J. L. Katz. Dept State Bul 64:260-3 Mr 1 '71
Sixth annual report on the International coffee agreement transmitted to the Congress; letter of transmittal; with text of report and Secretary Rogers' letter. R. M. Nixon. il Dept State Bul 64:584-91 My 3 '71

INTERNATIONAL commission of enquiry into United States crimes in Indochina
Tainted tribunal. Newsweek 78:47 Jl 5 '71

INTERNATIONAL competition. See Competition, International

INTERNATIONAL computers, ltd.
Russians look west for computers. Bsns W p34-5 F 6 '71

INTERNATIONAL conference on leisure and gerontology. See Aging, Conferences on

INTERNATIONAL conference on the environmental future
Has the environment a future? M. I. Goldman. Nation 213:358-61 O 18 '71

INTERNATIONAL conference on the peaceful uses of atomic energy, 4th Geneva, 1971
Peaceful uses of atomic energy. UN Mo Chron 8:83-5 O '71

INTERNATIONAL conference on the problems of the human environment. See United Nations conference on the human environment

INTERNATIONAL conferences
Behind Nixon's 5 meetings with allies; with pictogram. il U S News 71:19-23 D 13 '71
Breakthrough on Berlin? Time 98:26-7 Ag 16 '71
Calendar of international conferences. See issues of Department of state bulletin
Guess who's coming to dinner; forthcoming summit meetings. il Newsweek 78:20 D 6 '71
Meetings are the message; forthcoming summits. il por Time 98:7 D 20 '71
Nixon: a fresh burst of summitry; series of summit meetings to come. il pors Time 98: 14-15 D 6 '71
President Nixon to hold meeting with allied leaders; announcements, November 1971. Dept State Bul 65:703 D 20 '71

INTERNATIONAL conferences—*Continued*
Talk and travel; coming consultations of the President with chief executives of France, Portugal, Great Britain, West Germany, Canada and Japan. J. Osborne. New Repub 165:9-11 D 11 '71
Two cheers for summit diplomacy. W. P. Bundy. Newsweek 78:29 D 27 '71
View from the summit; views of statesmen. il Newsweek 78:21 O 25 '71
Warming up; R. M. Nixon's pre-summit meetings. il Newsweek 78:22 D 20 '71
See also
Economic conferences
also names of conferences, e.g. International youth conference on problems of the human environment
INTERNATIONAL controls corporation
Cornfeld's colonels try an IOS revolt. il Bsns W p25-6 Je 26 '71
INTERNATIONAL cookery. See Cookery, International
INTERNATIONAL cooperation
Community of the developed nations. Z. Brzezinski. Newsweek 77:40 F 1 '71
Development of institutions to meet the world population crisis; address, March 12, 1971. P. P. Claxton, jr. Dept State Bul 65:165-72 Ag 16 '71
See also
Astronomy—International aspects
Banks and banking, International
Cultural relations
International organization
Nato
Science—International aspects
Space research—International aspects
United Nations
INTERNATIONAL copyright. See Copyright
INTERNATIONAL copyright information center. See UNESCO—International copyright information center
INTERNATIONAL corporations. See Corporations, International
INTERNATIONAL council of scientific unions

Committee on space research
Physical sciences. Sci N 100:25 Jl 10 '71

Special committee on problems of the environment
To a planetary tomorrow; first general assembly. J. Lear. Sat R 54:63-4 O 2 '71
INTERNATIONAL court of justice, The Hague
Communiqués relating to Namibia. UN Mo Chron 8:22-3 F '71
India institutes proceedings in international court concerning jurisdiction of ICAO council. UN Mo Chron 8:89-90 O '71
Request for advisory opinion relating to Namibia. UN Mo Chron 8:22-4 Mr; 42-3 Ap; 73 Je '71
U.N. General assembly calls for study to further the work of the International court of justice; U.S. statements; with text of resolution. J. K. Javits; H. Reis. Dept State Bul 64:116-24 Ja 25 '71
INTERNATIONAL criminal police organization
Interpol: behind the scenes in world war against crime. il U S News 70:96-7 F 15 '71
INTERNATIONAL day for the elimination of racial discrimination
International day for elimination of racial discrimination; with statements. UN Mo Chron 8:6-11 Ap '71
INTERNATIONAL development corporation (proposed)
Plan to streamline. Time 97:16 My 3 '71 ,
INTERNATIONAL documents
See also
International federation for documentation
INTERNATIONAL economic integration
See also
European economic community
INTERNATIONAL economic relations. See Economic relations
INTERNATIONAL education
See also
Education—International cooperation
INTERNATIONAL educational exchanges. See Educational exchanges
INTERNATIONAL electric vehicle exhibition. See Motor vehicles—Exhibitions
INTERNATIONAL federation for documentation
FID and IFLA: a coming together; meeting in Brussels. J. P. Danton. Wilson Lib Bul 45:928-9 Je '71
INTERNATIONAL federation of library associations
Demonstration at IFLA for Reizia Palatnik. il por Wilson Lib Bul 46:391 Ja '72
FID and IFLA: a coming together; meeting in Brussels. J. P. Danton. Wilson Lib Bul 45:928-9 Je '71

IFLA in Liverpool: return of the native. M. P. Barnett. Wilson Lib Bul 46:469-70 Ja '72
Liebaers on libraries and the 37th session of IFLA in Liverpool. H. Liebaers. il Wilson Lib Bul 45:950-1 Je '71
Organization of the library profession: 37th IFLA. M. A. Gelfand. il Wilson Lib Bul 46:470-2 Ja '72
INTERNATIONAL fellowship of evangelical students. See Student Christian movements
INTERNATIONAL festival of music and drama, Edinburgh
Art without a border, but with a fringe. H. Hewes. Sat R 54:14+ O 2 '71
Report:
Walküre. J. W. Stedman and G. McElroy. Opera N 36:28 N '71
Three operas by Janacek: Prague national theater. F. Stevenson. il Hi Fi 20:MA28-9 D '70
INTERNATIONAL finance. See Finance, International
INTERNATIONAL finance corporation
Overseas private investment in today's world; the place of the I.F.C; address, May 3, 1971. W. S. Gaud. Vital Speeches 37:566-9 Jl 1 '71
INTERNATIONAL flying farmers (association)
Flying farmers. G. Baxter. il Flying 90:20 Ja '72
INTERNATIONAL foodservice systems, inc.
Doughnuts to dollars. il por Time 98:58-9 Ag 9 '71
INTERNATIONAL game fish association
IGFA rules and records. G. Heinold. il Outdoor Life 148:150+ S '71
INTERNATIONAL harvester company
America first; interview. W. E. Callahan. il Forbes 108:43 Ag 1 '71
Harvester puts pizazz into light trucks. il Bsns W p 134+ N 13 '71
INTERNATIONAL hod carriers', building and common laborers' union of America
Building with the Buffalo boys. il Time 98:21-2 Ag 30 '71
INTERNATIONAL industries, inc.
Flip-flop of the flapjack king. por Bsns W p20 Ap 24 '71
INTERNATIONAL institute for peace and conflict research. See Stockholm international peace research institute
INTERNATIONAL iron and steel institute
Steel's outlook continues gray. il Bsns W p29-30 O 16 '71
INTERNATIONAL joint commission (United States and Canada)
IJC completes report on pollution of the lower Great Lakes; statement, with Department announcement. W. P. Rogers. Dept State Bul 64:203-5 F 15 '71
INTERNATIONAL junior pairs championship. See Bridge tournaments
INTERNATIONAL labor organization
ILO plan for solving the job crisis in Colombia. R. E. Ginnold. bibliog f il Mo Labor R 94:32-40 Mr '71
International labor in crisis. For Affairs 49:519-32 Ap '71
Seamen and modernization of merchant shipping: 55th International (maritime) labor conference. Geneva, Switzerland. J. P. Goldberg. Mo Labor R 94:49-54 F '71
Tripartism reaffirmed by the 1971 International labor conference. J. P. Goldberg. Mo Labor R 94:30-7 S '71
INTERNATIONAL ladies' garment workers' union
ILGWU: the old age of a union. Nation 212:716-19 Je 7 '71
INTERNATIONAL law
Hostile international propaganda and international law. J. B. Whitton. bibliog f Ann Am Acad 398:14-25 N '71
See also
Geneva conventions
International court of justice, The Hague
Intervention (international law)
Nuremberg trials
Space law
Territorial waters
United Nations—Charter
United States—State, Department of—Advisory panel on international law
War, Laws of
INTERNATIONAL lawn tennis federation
Rhubarb divides the tennis world; ILTF vs. WCT on open tennis. Bsns W p34 Ag 14 '71
INTERNATIONAL license agreements
Agusta expanding U.S. licensing. E. H. Kolcum. il Aviation W 94:46-9 F 1 '71
Data general's coup in minicomputers. il Bsns W p54 Je 19 '71

INTERNATIONAL license agreements—*Cont.*
Russia sells its knowhow; wrapped in red tape. il Bsns W p59-60 My 8 '71
South Africa gains fighter pact. Aviation W 95:19 Jl 5 '71

INTERNATIONAL longshoremen's and warehousemen's union
All-coasts strike threatens the docks. il Bsns W p 14-15 Jl 24 '71
Dockers form a common front. il Bsns W p55 N 6 '71
Harry Bridges veers right. por Bsns W p50 My 1 '71
Hopeful sign from the Pacific docks. il Bsns W p66-7 S 4 '71
ILWU won't freeze. M. E. Leary. Nation 213: 174-6 S 6 '71
International longshoremen's and warehousemen's union. A. A. Belman. Mo Labor R 94:60-2 Ag '71
Nixon will use no hooks on dockers. il Bsns W p66 Mr 20 '71

INTERNATIONAL longshoremen's association
All-coasts strike threatens the docks. il Bsns W p 14-15 Jl 24 '71
Dockers form a common front. il Bsns W p55 N 6 '71
International longshoremen's association convention. A. A. Belman. Mo Labor R 94:72 O '71

INTERNATIONAL Miami conference on communication arts. See Photographic conferences

INTERNATIONAL monetary fund
Boards of governors of the IMF and IBRD meet at Washington; statement. September 30, 1971. J. B. Connally. Dept State Bul 65:453-7 O 25 '71
Changing the world's money. il Time 98:21-4 O 4 '71
Connally's high-stakes poker game. il por Newsweek 78:20-1 O 11 '71
Deadlock over the dollar; with editorial comment. il Bsns W p82-6+, 144 S 25 '71
Deciding how far to drop the dollar. il Bsns W p59 O 9 '71
IMF board of governors adopts resolution on monetary system; text of resolution, October 1, 1971. Dept State Bul 65:457-8 O 25 '71
IMF: running scared and making gains. il Bsns W p21-2 O 2 '71
International financial institutions bill signed into law; statement, December 30, 1970. R. M. Nixon. Dept State Bul 64:113-14 Ja 25 '71
International monetary system: a possible reform; address, September 28, 1971. A. Barber. Vital Speeches 38:61-3 N 1 '71
Money: a move toward disarmament. il por Time 98:26 O 11 '71
Reporter at large; annual meeting. J. Brooks. New Yorker 47:117-18+ O 23 '71
See also
Group of ten (organization)
Special drawing rights

INTERNATIONAL nickel company of Canada
Hard-liner gets Inco's no. 1 slot. por Bsns W p68 N 13 '71

INTERNATIONAL organization
Amchitka and tribalism. N. Cousins. Sat R 54:30 S 25 '71
Building the city of man, by W. W. Wagar. Review
Sat R 54:57-8 N 6 '71. R. J. Barnet
World in re-birth? D. Mattern. il Cath World 213:139-43 Je '71

INTERNATIONAL organizations, Regional
New balance of power in Asia and the Pacific. H. Bull. For Affairs 49:669-81 Jl '71

INTERNATIONAL paper company
Greening of International paper. A. A. Butkus. il por Duns 97:36-9+ My '71
Probing the secrets of the woods; Southlands experiment forest. H. Clepper. il Am For 77:26-9+ Ag '71

INTERNATIONAL peace academy
Curriculum for peace. H. Taylor. Sat R 54: 22-3 S 4 '71

INTERNATIONAL peace research institute, Stockholm. See Stockholm international peace research institute

INTERNATIONAL PEN club. See PEN club

INTERNATIONAL petroleum company
Revolutionary nationalism in Peru. M. Niedergang. For Affairs 49:454-63 Ap '71

INTERNATIONAL press institute
World press and the teaching of journalism; Helsinki convention. J. Tebbel. il Sat R 54: 64-5+ S 11 '71

INTERNATIONAL propaganda. See Propaganda, International

INTERNATIONAL psycho-analytical association
Congress of Vienna. il Newsweek 78:62 Ag 9 '71
Reunion in Vienna; main theme at the International psycho-analytical association's meeting. por Time 98:32 Ag 9 '71

INTERNATIONAL publishers association
Rebirth of activity: International publishing associations. H. R. Lottman. il Pub W 200:pt2 156-7 S 27 '71

INTERNATIONAL publishing corporation
U.K. science press: New scientist absorbs sibling Science journal. M. Butler. Science 171:157-60 Ja 15 '71

INTERNATIONAL relations
Foreign policy and the United Nations. W. P. Rogers; A. A. Gromyko; M. Schumann. Vital Speeches 38:34-49 N 1 '71
How not to negotiate with the Russians. H. M. Jackson. por Nations Bsns 59:52+ Ap '71
International propaganda and statecraft. B. Wedge. il Ann Am Acad 398:36-43 N '71
Not war but anarchy. Z. Brzezinski. Newsweek 77:47 Ap 5 '71
President Nixon's news conference of June 1, 1971. R. M. Nixon. Dept State Bul 64: 789-93 Je 21 '71
Six scenarios for 1980. W. Laqueur. il N Y Times Mag p8-9+ D 19 '71
U.S. & world affairs annual. il Sr Schol 99: 2-22+ O 4 '71
Wane and wax of isolationism. Chr Cent 88:1315 N 10 '71
Who can make peace now in Asia? D. Lawrence. U S News 71:92 D 20 '71
See also
Agriculture—International aspects
Arbitration, International
Balance of power
Church and international relations
Council on foreign relations
Disarmament
Europe—Politics
Imperialism
International commission of enquiry into United States crimes in Indochina
International conferences
International court of justice, The Hague
International law
International organization
International security
Interparliamentary union
Intervention (international law)
Language and languages—International aspects
Munitions
Peace
Propaganda, International
Radio broadcasting—International aspects
Tariff
United Nations
War
World politics
also subhead Foreign relations under names of countries, e.g. Japan—Foreign relations

Anecdotes, facetiae, satire, etc.

What in the world! G. Ace. Sat R 54:4 Jl 3 '71

Bibliography

Recent books on international relations; comp. by J. G. Stoessinger. See issues of Foreign affairs
Source material; comp. by D. Wasson. See issues of Foreign affairs
World scene (cont) V. S. Kearney. America 124:544-5; 125:428-30 My 22, N 20 '71

Periodicals

Magazines; ed. by B. Katz. Library J 96: 4077-8 D 15 '71

Psychological aspects

Psychological factors in international persuasion. Y. Tanaka. bibliog f Ann Am Acad 398:50-60 N '71

INTERNATIONAL rescue committee
Friend to the displaced. R. Girson. il Sat R 54:30-1+ D 4 '71

INTERNATIONAL rice research institute
Revolution in rice. A. Cutshall. il Focus 21: 10-12 Mr '71

INTERNATIONAL satellite geodesy experiment
ISAGEX. Sky & Tel 41:83 F '71

INTERNATIONAL security
Declaration on the strengthening of international security. L. N. Kutakov. UN Mo Chron 8:88-101 Je '71
SALT and international security; excerpt from statement. Bul Atom Sci 27:17-19 D '71
What does security mean today? M. D. Shulman. For Affairs 49:607-18 Jl '71
See also
International organization
Peace
United Nations—Security council
United Nations—Special committee on peace-keeping operations
INTERNATIONAL settlements, Bank for. See Bank for international settlements
INTERNATIONAL shoe company. See Interco, inc.
INTERNATIONAL shooting union. See Shooting—Competitions
INTERNATIONAL social cooperation. See International cooperation
INTERNATIONAL socialist congress. See Socialist international congress, Helsinki, 1971
INTERNATIONAL society for contemporary music
Depressing uniformity of the avant-garde. H. C. Schonberg. Harper 243:103-4 S '71
ISCM's forty-fifth forum. D. Hamilton. il Hi Fi 21:MA27-8 S '71
Music. D. Hamilton. Nation 213:123-4 Ag 16 '71
INTERNATIONAL society of sugar cane technologists
Sugar daddies; question of expulsion of Cuban delegates. Newsweek 78:54+ N 8 '71
INTERNATIONAL summer school on disarmament and arms control
School for disarmament. UNESCO Courier 24:37 Mr '71
INTERNATIONAL telecommunication union
International telecommunications organizations and how they affect you. R. G. Gould. il Electr World 85:38-40+ F '71
INTERNATIONAL telecommunications satellite consortium
Compromises permit Intelsat agreement. K. Johnsen. Aviation W 94:38 My 31 '71
Definitive Intelsat agreements signed at Washington; background information with remarks by Secretary Rogers. Dept State Bul 65:303-4 S 20 '71
Growing, reorganized Intelsat ponders new satellite series. il Aviation W 95:32-4 Ag 23 '71
Intelsat conference resumes at Washington; Department announcement, with remarks by Acting Secretary Irwin, April 14, 1971. Dept State Bul 64:569-73 My 3 '71
Intelsat IV. il Space World H-4-88:5-9 Ap '71
Intelsat system proposed for new Washington-Moscow hotline link. K. Johnsen. Aviation W 95:22 S 27 '71
Permanent charter for Intelsat. S. E. Doyle. Dept State Bul 65:415-18 O 18 '71
President Nixon hails agreement on permanent Intelsat charter; remarks, May 21, 1971. R. M. Nixon. Dept State Bul 64:817-18 Je 28 '71
13 nations approve new Intelsat charter. Aviation W 95:18 O 18 '71
U.S. offers launch assistance to Europeans; Department announcement, November 1, 1971; with text of letter to T. Lefevre, September 1, 1971, and summary of amplifying comments. Dept State Bul 65:624-7 N 29 '71
U.S.-U.K. fight over services stalls permanent Intelsat accord. K. Johnsen. Aviation W 94:19 My 17 '71
INTERNATIONAL telephone and telegraph corporation
Cooling crusade? Newsweek 78:62+ Ag 16 '71
ITT's bigger push in Europe. il por Time 98:70+ D 20 '71
Now it's growth from within for Harold Geneen. por Fortune 84:33 S '71
Trimming a colossus. Time 98:72 Ag 16 '71
Two ways to do it. il Forbes 109:24-5 Ja 1 '72
What ITT gave up to keep the best of the lot. Bsns W p61 Ag 7 '71
See also
Levitt and sons, inc.
INTERNATIONAL television. See Television broadcasting—International aspects
INTERNATIONAL track meet. See Track athletics
INTERNATIONAL trade. See Commerce
INTERNATIONAL trade regulation. See Foreign trade regulation

INTERNATIONAL traffic in arms. See Munitions
INTERNATIONAL travel. See Travel
INTERNATIONAL trusteeships
See also
United Nations—Trusteeship council
INTERNATIONAL trusts. See Trusts, Industrial—International trusts
INTERNATIONAL typographical union
Lost strike goes on and on; ITU strike against Toronto's three daily newspapers. Bsns W p90+ F 6 '71
INTERNATIONAL union of electrical, radio and machine workers
Chill wind at Frigidaire. Bsns W p58 Jl 31 '71
Japanese face suit for dumping TV sets. Bsns W p68 Mr 20 '71
INTERNATIONAL union of forestry research organizations
World forest research congress. K. B. Pomeroy. il Am For 77:32-5 Ag '71
INTERNATIONAL utilities corporation
See also
Ryder truck lines, inc.
INTERNATIONAL volunteer service. See Volunteer service, International
INTERNATIONAL whaling commission
Does the whale's magnitude diminish?—Will he perish? growing list of endangered species. S. McVay. il Bul Atom Sci 27:38-41 F '71
International whaling commission meets at Washington; address, with text of Commission statement; June 21, 1971. U. A. Johnson. Dept State Bul 65:116-19 Jl 26 '71
Whales; a skirmish won, but what about the war? S. McVay. il Nat Parks & Con Mag 45:14-15+ F '71
INTERNATIONAL wheat agreement
International wheat agreement, 1971, transmitted to the Senate; message. R. M. Nixon. Dept State Bul 65:66 Jl 12 '71
INTERNATIONAL year for action to combat racism and racial discrimination, 1971
International year for action to combat racism and racial discrimination. UN Mo Chron 8:5-6 Ap '71
International year for action to combat racism and racial discrimination, 1971; message, March 21, 1971. Thant. UN Mo Chron 8:1-ii Mr '71
International year for action to combat racism and racial discrimination; statement. L. McIntyre. UN Mo Chron 8:1 Ja '71
INTERNATIONAL youth conference on problems of the human environment
We, the young; excerpts from final report. Environ 13:15 O '71
INTERNMENT camps. See Concentration camps
INTERPARLIAMENTARY union
Wayward bus; 59th assembly. A. de Borchgrave. Newsweek 78:46+ S 20 '71
INTERPERSONAL relations. See Human relations
INTERPLANETARY monitoring platform. See Artificial satellites—Astronomical use
INTERPLANETARY rockets. See Rockets, Interplanetary
INTERPOL. See International criminal police organization
INTERPRETER; story. See Walker, T.
INTERPRETERS. See Translators
INTERPUBLIC group of companies, inc.
Late tape. R. Brady. Duns 97:10 Je '71
INTERRACIAL adoption. See Adoption
INTERRACIAL cooperation
One man's peace corps; Revitalization corps, Hartford, Conn. por Time 98:12 Jl 19 '71
Scouting blazes a trail into the ghetto. il Life 70:38-42 Je 4 '71
Small victories in Americus; children's reactions. M. Frady. il Life 70:46B-46D+ F 12 '71
Some hate, some hope. J. DeMuth. Commonweal 94:84-6 Ap 2 '71
Strange alliance; NAACP helping striking timber haulers. Newsweek 78:48 N 8 '71
INTERRACIAL marriages. See Intermarriage of races
INTERRACIAL relations. Race relations
INTERRELIGIOUS foundation for community organization
IFCO asks churches to use funds for minority empowerment. Chr Cent 88:398 Mr 31 '71
IFCO plans campaign against apartheid in southern Africa. Chr Cent 88:874 Jl 21 '71
IFCO resumes allocations with grants of $437,336. Chr Cent 88:683 Je 2 '71
Third image of the church. Chr Cent 88:1252 O 27 '71

INTERROGATION of prisoner Bung by Mister Hawkins and Sergeant Tree; story. See Huddle, D.
INTERSECTIONS (highway engineering) See Roads—Interchanges and intersections
INTERSPECIES competition. See Struggle for existence
INTERSTATE commerce
See also
United States—Interstate commerce commission
INTERSTATE highway system. See Express highways
INTERSTELLAR communication
Interstellar communications: what are the prospects. L. G. Lawrence. il Electr World 86:34-5+ O '71
Is anybody out there? J. P. Wiley, jr. il Natur Hist 80:42-3 D '71
Is anybody out there sending. il Sci N 100: 223-4 O 2 '71
Soviet-American conference urges search for other worlds. C. Holden. Science 174:130-1 O 8 '71

Anecdotes, facetiae, satire, etc.
Is anyone there? J. Ciardi. Sat R 54:27 N 20 '71
INTERSTELLAR matter. See Matter, Interstellar
INTER-VARSITY Christian fellowship
Evangelical students at Urbana '70: zeal and social passion. W. R. Wineke. Chr Cent 88:226-7 F 17 '71
Urbana '70: evangelical student power; with editorial comment. D. Tinder. il Chr Today 15:20, 29-30 Ja 29 '71
INTERVENTION (international law)
After neo-isolationism, what? L. P. Bloomfield. Bul Atom Sci 27:9-13 Ap '71
Misuse of power. H. S. Commager. New Repub 164:17-21 Ap 17 '71
INTERVIEWING
Interviewing for trade journal articles. M. Tyson. il Writers Digest 51:25-7 Jl '71
Interviewing for trade journals. O. Henry. Writer 84:22-5 F '71
See also
Employment interviewing
INTESTINES
Ethanol stimulates triglyceride synthesis by the intestine. E. A. Carter and others. bibliog il Science 174:1245-7 D 17 '71
I am Joe's intestine. J. D. Ratcliff. il Read Digest 99:75-8 Ag '71
Intestinal secretion: stimulation by peptides. G. O. Barbezat and M. I. Grossman. bibliog il Science 174:422-4 O 22 '71
Unstirred water layers in intestine: rate determinant of fatty acid absorption from micellar solutions. F. A. Wilson and others. bibliog il Science 174:1031-3 D 3 '71
See also
Hernia

Diseases
Diverticulosis: a disease that strikes after 40. il Changing T 25:45-7 Ap '71
See also
Constipation
INTIMACY; story. See Maloney, R.
INTO your tent I'll creep; story. See DeVries, P.
INTOLERANCE. See Prejudice; Toleration
INTOURIST. See Travel agencies and agents
INTRACOASTAL WATERWAY
History hopping down the I.C.W. G. Merrill. bibliog il Motor B & S 128:50-1+ S '71
Waterway to the south; Norfolk-Miami inland waterway. J. A. Emmett. il Outdoor Life 148:42+ O '71
INTRAUTERINE diagnosis. See Fetus—Diseases—Diagnosis
INTRAVENOUS feeding
Total intravenous feeding. Sci Am 224:51-2 My '71
INTRAVENOUS-feeding bottles. See Hospitals —Equipment and supplies
INTRUDER alarms. See Burglar alarms
INTUITION
Woman's intuition; symposium. Vogue 158: 60-1+ S 15 '71
INTUITION of duration. See Time perception
INVALIDS. See Sick, The
INVASION of Russia. See World war, 1939-1945—Campaigns and battles—Russia
INVENTIONS
Just patented. See issues of Popular mechanics
Me: an inventor? J. Davison. il Har Yrs 11: 51-3 O '71

New ideas from the inventors. See issues of Popular science monthly
Weird, wild and wonderful; ideas from the International patents exposition. S. M. Gallager. il Pop Mech 135:98-103 Mr '71
World showcase for inventors. D. Scott. il Pop Sci 199:48-9 Ag '71
See also
Patents
Patents and government-developed inventions
INVENTORIES
Industrial production will get a lift from inventories. il Fortune 84:22 N '71
Inventory outlook: a turn to the plus side. il Fortune 83:38 My '71
Still going slow on inventories. il Bsns W p42 Je 5 '71
See also
Booksellers and bookselling—Stock
INVENTORS
Geniuses down on the farm. W. Kester and G. Logsdon. il Farm J 95:20-1+ Je '71
See also
Inventions
Lear, W. P.
Tesla, N.
INVERNESS, Miss.
Devastation in the Delta. R. Rein. il Time 97: 17 Mr 8 '71
INVERSION of atmospheric temperature. See Temperature inversions
INVERTERS, Electric. See Electric current inverters
INVESTMENT. See Investments
INVESTMENT advisers
Cake for the masses; competition for the small investor's business. Forbes 108:22-3 O 1 '71
Disciple. por Forbes 107:41-2 F 1 '71
Investment individualist. R. Brady. il pors Duns 93:105-6 Je '69
Man on the ground floor; Eurofinance. pors Forbes 107:37-9 Ja 15 '71
Wall Street ignores the money crisis. il Bsns W p 106+ My 15 '71
Why security analysts irk management. il Bsns W p96-7 N 6 '71
See also
Schroder, Naess and Thomas (firm)
INVESTMENT bankers association of America
Looking to the public; annual convention. C. Morgello. il Newsweek 78:91 D 13 '71
INVESTMENT banking
Investment banking: power structure in flux. S. L. Hayes, 3d. bibliog f il Harvard Bsns R 49:136-52 Mr '71
See also
Cogan, Berlind, Weill and Levitt, inc.
First Boston corporation
Goldman, Sachs and company
Merrill Lynch, Pierce, Fenner and Smith, inc.
INVESTMENT clubs
Investment clubs: how they stood the crunch. il Changing T 25:25-7 My '71
Money club; B&C investment club, for Buy and cry. M. Gunther. McCalls 98:44 Jl '71
INVESTMENT companies. See Investment trusts
INVESTMENT counselors. See Investment advisers
INVESTMENT tax credit
Business looks warily at the tax credit. il Bsns W p78-9 O 2 '71
Domestic business aircraft boost seen in investment tax credit. C. E. Schneider. Aviation W 95:20 Ag 23 '71
Everybody is edgy about Phase two. il Newsweek 78:60-1 O 4 '71
Good news: investment credit is back. R. Krumme. Suc Farm 69:9 O '71
Great tax debate. il Time 98:36-7 S 27 '71
Measured portion of economic stimulus. il Bsns W p24-5 Ag 21 '71
Sale in Macy's basement? il Forbes 108:63 O 15 '71
Tax cuts a step nearer: who gets the breaks. il U S News 71:56-8 O 4 '71
Threat of the booming leasing business. il Bsns W p42+ S 4 '71
Tire makers get a breather. il Bsns W p20-1 Ag 28 '71
INVESTMENT trusts
Conscience money. il Time 98:100 N 22 '71
Contrarian; views of J. Neff of the Windsor fund. R. Brady. por Duns 97:100A-100B Mr '71
Court frowns on favors to funds. Bsns W p26 Je 12 '71
Custodians; mutual fund management contracts. Newsweek 78:67+ Ag 2 '71
Disenchanted investors bypass the funds. il Bsns W p 116 N 13 '71
Fund operators rush into bonds. il Bsns W p57 Jl 24 '71

INVESTMENTS, Foreign (in Algeria)
New ball game; seizure of French oil and gas properties. il Newsweek 77:82 Mr 8 '71

INVESTMENTS, Foreign (in Argentina)
Investors shy from a shaky economy. il Bsns W p31 S 4 '71

INVESTMENTS, Foreign (in Belgium)
Belgian boom goes on. G. R. Rosen. il Duns 98:81-2+ S '71

INVESTMENTS, Foreign (in Brazil)
After the miracle. Nation 213:645-6 D 20 '71
D. K. Ludwig plans to harvest a jungle. il por Bsns W p34 Jl 31 '71
Export list grows and grows. il Bsns W p46 Je 12 '71
New Yanquis; Japanese investments. il Newsweek 78:62-3 Jl 5 '71

INVESTMENTS, Foreign (in Canada)
Cold wind from Canada, the Gray report. E. Cowan. Nation 213:613-16 D 13 '71
Future of American investment; address, October 8, 1971. G. A. Regan. Vital Speeches 38:92-6 N 15 '71
Our northern neighbor. G. J. Henry. Forbes 108:65 Jl 1 '71
U.S. corporation in Canada. M. Reid. por Nations Bsns 59:87 Ap '71

INVESTMENTS, Foreign (in Chile)
Copper crisis. Newsweek 78:77 O 11 '71
Copper pays the price of nationalism. il Bsns W p38+ Ag 21 '71

INVESTMENTS, Foreign (in Communist countries)
Nobody here but us Marxists? il Forbes 108:48+ Jl 15 '71

INVESTMENTS, Foreign (in Europe)
Americans, go home! non-tariff protectionism. J. Ross-Skinner. il Duns 98:46-8+ O '71
Going 50-50 in east Europe; east-west deals. il Bsns W p41+ Ja 16 '71
Levittown spreads across the Continent. Bsns W p52 N 6 '71
Man on the ground floor; Eurofinance. por Forbes 107:37-9 Ja 15 '71
What the move means to U.S. companies; expansion of the Common market. Bsns W p67 O 23 '71

INVESTMENTS, Foreign (in Ghana)
Going somewhere from the road to nowhere; U.S. companies. S. G. Slappey. il Nations Bsns 59:66-9 Je '71

INVESTMENTS, Foreign (in Greece)
U.S. France vie for Greek facility award. E. H. Kolcum. Aviation W 95:21-2 D 13 '71

INVESTMENTS, Foreign (in Hungary)
Nobody here but us Marxists? il Forbes 108:48+ Jl 15 '71

INVESTMENTS, Foreign (in India)
U.S. companies get caught in a crossfire. il Bsns W p25 D 25 '71

INVESTMENTS, Foreign (in Indonesia)
First fruits. il Time 98:100+ N 22 '71
Slim pickings for U.S. lumbermen. il Bsns W p48+ N 6 '71

INVESTMENTS, Foreign (in Japan)
Doing business in Japan, address, October 19, 1971. D. L. Williams. Vital Speeches 38:76-80 N 15 '71
Fast-food stands sprout on the Ginza. il Bsns W p41 O 16 '71
Odd shape that sold Japan; Tetra pak containers. il Bsns W p30-1 Ja 30 '71
Price of success; Coke and Pepsi. Newsweek 78:88+ D 6 '71
Street's pipeline to Japanese stocks. il Bsns W p66+ My 29 '71

INVESTMENTS, Foreign (in Latin America)
Latin America slams the door. P. Lernoux. Nation 213:271-5 S 27 '71
Latin American investment. H. C. Wallich. Newsweek 78:94 D 13 '71
New woes for U.S. companies in Latin America. il U S News 70:80-2 Ap 26 '71
Why invest in Latin America? S. M. Linowitz. il Harvard Bsns R 49:120-30 Ja '71; Reply. R. L. Drake. 49:30-1 Jl '71

INVESTMENTS, Foreign (in Luxembourg)
Strength through weakness. il Time 98:59-60 Ag 9 '71

INVESTMENTS, Foreign (in Northern Ireland)
Gun-shy investors stay away. il Bsns W p84-5 D 4 '71
Land of hope and despair. il Forbes 108:26-7 N 1 '71

INVESTMENTS, Foreign (in Peru)
No love for the Yanqui dollar. por Bsns W p62 My 15 '71

INVESTMENTS, Foreign (in Rumania)
Open window to the West chills Russia. il Bsns W p57 S 11 '71

INVESTMENTS, Foreign (in Russia)
First contract for Kama River. Bsns W p30 Ja 1 '72
Picking up where Mack left off; Kama plant. il Bsns W p42-3 S 25 '71

INVESTMENTS, Foreign (in Singapore)
Letter from Singapore; American investments. B. Weisberg. Nation 214:51-2 Ja 10 '72

INVESTMENTS, Foreign (in South Africa)
Dilemma for the American corporation. America 124:586 Je 5 '71
Dilemma of foreign investment in South Africa; remarks, April 30, 1971. R. S. Smith. Dept State Bul 64:825-7 Je 28 '71
Polaroid approach to South Africa. G. M. Houser. Chr Cent 88:249-52 F 24 '71
Polaroid stays put. il Newsweek 79:50+ Ja 10 '72
Question in South Africa. America 124:623 Je 19 '71
U.S. business in South Africa. il Newsweek 77:80+ Mr 29 '71
U.S. firms bestirred. America 125:2-3 Jl 10 '71

INVESTMENTS, Foreign (in Taiwan)
Fading rose. Newsweek 78:88+ O 25 '71
On the ropes but no K.O. il Bsns W p48 N 6 '71
Taiwan's strategy for survival. L. Kraar. il Fortune 84:124-31+ N '71
Where Nixon's Peking visit casts a chill. il Bsns W p32-3 Jl 24 '71

INVESTMENTS, Foreign (in the Dominican Republic)
Place in the sun; Punta Cana club. il Forbes 108:21 O 15 '71

INVESTMENTS, Foreign (in the United States)
Big foreign stake in U.S. industry. E. J. Tracy. il Fortune 84:118-23 Ag '71
Culture shokku in Texas. Time 98:103-4 N 22 '71
Europeans get back in the game. Bsns W p30-1 D 11 '71
How about it, gnomes? Nat R 23:576 Je 1 '71
New discovery of America. il Nations Bsns 59:78-81 O '71
Old World looks closer at Wall Street. Bsns W p50-1 Jl 17 '71
Whose grass is greener? interview. N. K. Siegel. por Forbes 108:54+ N 15 '71

INVESTMENTS, Foreign (in underdeveloped areas)
New rules for investing in the LDC's. il Newsweek 78:80-2 S 20 '71
Overseas private investment in today's world; the place of the I.F.C; address, May 3, 1971. W. S. Gaud. Vital Speeches 37:566-9 Jl 1 '71
Pick a spot. pors Forbes 108:57-8+ D 15 '71

INVESTMENTS, Foreign (in Uruguay)
Yankees do business under fire. il Bsns W p42 D 4 '71

INVESTMENTS, Foreign (in Vietnam [Republic])
There's a Toyota in their future? J. Ridgeway. il Ramp Mag 10:40-1 N '71
U.S. investors eye a postwar Vietnam. il Bsns W p28 D 25 '71

INVESTOR relations programs
Crucial role of investor relations. R. H. Savage; reply. C. L. Anders. Harvard Bsns R 49:163-7 Mr '71

INVESTORS. See Stockholders

INVESTORS diversified services, Inc.
Minneapolis money machine; with interviews with J. A. Murray and J. P. Vervoort, ed. by R. J. Flaherty. il por Forbes 108:42+ S 15 '71

INVESTORS overseas services, ltd.
Cornfeld's colonels try an IOS revolt. Bsns W p25-6 Je 26 '71
Cornfeld's farewell. Newsweek 77:52+ F 1 '71
Do you sincerely want to be rich? by C. Raw and others. Review
Bsns W il p 15 Ag 14 '71. G. Williams
Sat R 54:32+ S 4 '71. S. W. Clements

INVITATIONS
So you're invited to the wedding. Changing T 25:16 Je '71

INVOLVEMENT corps
Corps that cares. B. Falconer. McCalls 99:44 D '71

IO (satellite) See Satellites

IOCHROMA
Plant collector's corner: cherubs' bugles and Miss Mason's nerine. il Sunset 147:150-1 Jl '71

IODIDES
See also
Silver iodide

IODINE

Isotopes

Iodine-129 in terrestrial ores. B. Srinivasan and others. bibliog il Science 173:327-8 Jl 23 '71

Seventeen million years; half-life of iodine-129. S. Novick. bibliog il Environ 13:42-7 N '71

IODODEOXYURIDINE

Murine leukemia virus: high-frequency activation in vitro by 5-iododeoxyuridine and 5-bromodeoxyuridine. D. R. Lowy and others. bibliog il Science 174:155-6 O 8 '71

IOLANI palace. See Honolulu—Historic houses, etc.

ION binding. See Chemical bonds

ION exchange

Anecdotes, facetiae, satire, etc.

Ion-exchange fable. R. Ho. il Chem 44:26 S '71

IONESCO, Eugène

Eugène Ionesco and his remarkable irreducibility. W. Kennedy. Look 35:36 Jl 27 '71 *

Grand master of the absurd amid the pachyderms. A. Alvarez. por Sat R 54:27-9+ S 4 '71 *

Letter from Paris; new member of the Académie française. Genêt. New Yorker 47:117 Mr 13 '71

IONIAN ISLANDS

See also

Corfu (island)

IONIZATION of gases

Gum nebula: a new kind of astronomical object. S. P. Maran and others. bibliog il Phys Today 24:42-7 S '71

IONIZED air. See Air, Ionized

IONOSPHERE. See Atmosphere, Upper

IONOSPHERIC research. See Atmospheric research

IONS

Clustering of sulfur dioxide and water vapor about oxonium and nitric oxide ions. A. W. Castleman, jr. and others. bibliog il Science 173:1025-6 S '10 '71

See also

Cations

Metal ions

Beams

Accelerating heavy ions in the Bevatron. D. E. Thomsen. il Sci N 100:266-8 O 16 '71

Heavy ion acceleration; symposium. bibliog il Science 174:1121-34 D 10 '71

Two accelerators switch to nitrogen ions. M. S. Rothenberg. Phys Today 24:18-19 D '71

Physiological effects

Prediction of the spatial distribution of cell survival in heavy ion beams. K. G. Vosburgh. bibliog il Science 174:1125-7 D 10 '71

Spatial distribution of biological effect in a 3.9-Gev nitrogen ion beam. P. Todd and others. bibliog il Science 174:1127-8 D 10 '71

IOWA

In the sticks. L. Lafore. il Harper 243:108-9+ O '71

See also

Crime and criminals—Iowa

Fishing—Iowa

Hunting—Iowa

Music festivals—Iowa

IOWA library association

Iowa council ends sub to Berkeley barb. Library J 96:4048-50 D 15 '71

Of note; seventy-eighth annual conference. Am Lib 2:1134 D '71

IOWA state traveling library, Des Moines

Iowa council ends sub to Berkeley barb. Library J 96:4048-50 D 15 '71

Iowa library wins permission to purchase Hair tape. Library J 97:21-2 Ja 1 '72

IRAN

Iran: cultural crossroads for 2,500 years; symposium. bibliog il UNESCO Courier 24:4-46 O '71

Leadership role for Iran in the Persian Gulf? A. T. Schulz. bibliog f il Cur Hist 62:25-30+ Ja '72

See also

Americans in Iran

Arts and crafts—Iran

Book industries—Iran

Colleges and universities—Iran

Illiteracy—Iran

Natural resources—Iran

Railroads—Iran

Science—Iran

Visitors, Foreign—Iran

Anniversaries, etc.

Bash of bashes. il Newsweek 78:61+ S 27 '71

Big bash at Persepolis. Nation 213:421-2 N 1 '71

Confessions of a religious junketeer. H. A. Jack. Chr Cent 88:1448-9 D 8 '71

Fête for a king. il Vogue 158:62 O 15 '71

Iran: ceremonies and celebrations. il Art in Am 59:110-11 S '71

Iran: the show of shows. il Time 98:32-3 O 25 '71

Iran's birthday party. L. Jenkins. il Newsweek 78:58-3 O 25 '71

Party at Persepolis; with editorial comment. il Life 71:3, 34-6+ O 15 '71

Shah's princely party; with report by W. A. McWhirter and photographs by P. Boulat and others. Life 71:42-30 O 29 '71

2,500th birthday of Iran. il Life 71:58-9 D 31 '71

Antiquities

Another ancient civilization; ruins at Tepe Yahya. il Chem 44:24-5 Mr '71

Clues to an unknown civilization; Tepe Yahya mound. il Sci Digest 69:78-9 Mr '71

Early city in Iran; Tepe Yahyā excavation. C. C. Lamberg-Karlovsky and M. Lamberg-Karlovsky. il Sci Am 224:102-11 bibliog(p 136) Je '71

See also

Persepolis

Bibliography

UNESCO bookshelf on Iran. UNESCO Courier-24:46 O '71

Politics and government

Iran. J. S. Haupert. il Focus 21:1-8 Ja '71

Iran: let the world take note. L. Jenkins. il por Newsweek 78:42+ O 11 '71

Once and future shah. F. Halliday. Ramp Mag 10:18+ N '71

IRANIAN civilization. See Civilization, Iranian

IRANIAN cookery. See Cookery, Iranian

IRANIAN frescoes. See Frescoes

IRANIAN pottery. See Pottery, Iranian

IRAQ

Antiquities

Shanidar: the first flower people, by R. S. Solecki. Review

Natur Hist il 80:82-6 Ag '71. C. L. Brace

Politics and government

Iraq under Baathist rule. R. E. Thoman. bibliog f Cur Hist 62:31-7+ Ja '72

IRELAND, Charles Thomas, 1921-

CBS gets an expert in diversification. por Bsns W p22 S 18 '71 *

IRELAND

American couple in Ireland creates a beautiful way to eat. il House & Gard 139:80-4 F '71

Divided Ireland: a modern nation on the move. J. Rockwell. il Chr Cent 88:265-7 F 24 '71

See also

Airlines—Ireland

Aran Islands

Birth control—Ireland

Canals—Ireland

Dublin

Education—Ireland

Golf courses—Ireland

Gypsies in Ireland

Hunting—Ireland

Income tax—Ireland

Limerick

Music festivals—Ireland

Northern Ireland

Public opinion—Ireland

Shannon River

Stone age—Ireland

Antiquities

Ireland of the spirits. J. Vachon. il Look 35:42-9 Mr 23 '71

Description and travel

Erin a la cart; tour in Irish tinker's cart. E. H. Urban. il Travel 135:52-4 F '71

Ireland—phase II: Kerry, Killarney and the west. M. Gough. House B 113:26+ S '71

Ireland revisited. F. Howe. Atlan 227:113-16 F '71

Economic conditions

High hope in the South. il Time 98:85 O 25 '71

Foreign relations

United States

See United States—Foreign relations—Ireland

IRELAND—*Continued*

History

In the shadow of the gunmen. il Time 99:30-4+ Ja 10 '72
Like ghosts crying out. Time 98:20 Ag 23 '71

Politics and government

Ireland's great kidnap plot. J. Horgan. Commonweal 93:439 F 5 '71
Ireland's rocky road to pluralism. T. P. O'Mahony. il America 124:513-16 My 15 '71
Master of the tightrope act; J. Lynch. por Time 98:30 S 20 '71
See also
Northern Ireland—Politics and government

Religious institutions and affairs

Focus on Ireland, a land where faith matters. P. Elmen. Chr Cent 88:170+ F 3 '71
See also
Protestant churches in Ireland

IRIDIUM
Oxygen-carrying iridium complexes: kinetics, mechanism, and thermodynamics. L. Vaska and others. bibliog il Science 174:587-9 N 5 '71

IRION, Mary Jean
Notes made during a sermon at Oxford; poem. Chr Cent 88:103 Ja 27 '71
Post-Christian cross; poem. Chr Cent 88:402 Mr 31 '71

IRIS (eye)
Cholinergic sensitivity: normal variability as a function of stimulus background. L. Z. Bito and others. bibliog il Science 172:583-5 My 7 '71

IRIS gardens, South Carolina. See Gardens—South Carolina

IRISES
Big bargain in bulbs, the beautiful Dutch iris. B. Brinhart. il Home Gard 58:38-9 D '71
Iris: beautiful, but hard to discourage. R. J. Wyndham. il Org Gard & Farm 18:60-2 N '71
Iris caper. E. Reed. Har Yrs 11:18 Ap '71
Iris in the landscape. H. B. Aul. il Horticulture 49:28-9+ My '71
Modern iris. J. J. Ghio. il Horticulture 49:24-5+ Je '71
Pick of the iris. M. Price. il Home Gard 58:24-5+ Je '71
Trailing the wild iris. D. E. Rose. il Horticulture 49:48-9 My '71

IRISH AMERICANS
Last of the American Irish fade away. A. M. Greeley. il N Y Times Mag p32-3+ Mr 14 '71; Discussion. p 102-3 Ap 4 '71
Ourselves alone: Irish exiles in Brooklyn. W. Alfred. il por Atlan 227:53-8 Mr '71

IRISH furniture. See Furniture, Irish

IRISH glass. See Glassware

IRISH in the United States
See also
Irish Americans

IRISH poetry

Translations into English

Two poems: Jim Larkin; The versemaker's wish; tr. by U. O'Connor. B. Behan. Atlan 227:67 Je '71

IRISH republican army
Acceptable violence? il Time 98:32+ D 27 '71
Appalling crime; slaying of British soldiers. il Time 97:32-3 Mr 22 '71
As open war rages in Northern Ireland. il U S News 71:36-7 Ag 23 '71
Dublin conversation: do you support the I.R.A.? W. Sheed. il N Y Times Mag p32-3+ O 24 '71
Fatal error. il Time 98:32 S 13 '71
In the shadow of the gunmen. il Time 99:30-4+ Ja 10 '72
Ireland's odd men out. il Newsweek 78:56-8 O 18 '71
Keepers of the flame; women of the IRA. il Newsweek 78:33-4 N 29 '71
Last gasp for Irish terrorists? il U S News 72:39 Ja 3 '72
Murder of Santa Claus. il Time 98:40 D 20 '71
NLF epoch. J. Burnham. Nat R 23:418 Ap 20 '71
Northern Ireland: violent jubilee. il Time 98:18-21 Ag 23 '71
Portrait gallery of Provisionals: Sean Macstiofáin, Ruarí Ó Bradaigh and Joe Cahill. pors Time 99:39 Ja 10 '72
Red and the green: the divided I.R.A. A. Carthew. il N Y Times Mag p22-3+ Mr 28 '71

Return to tar and feathers. il Time 97:33 Ja 25 '71
Ulster: bloody Dodge City. Time 98:46+ N 22 '71
Ulster: in the green hell. M. Kupfer. il Newsweek 77:42+ Ap 5 '71
War of attrition. il Time 99:42 Ja 3 '72
We will stop at nothing. por Newsweek 78:46 S 20 '71

IRISH setters. See Setters

IRISH unification question
See also
Irish republican army

IRON age
In the footsteps of ancient man; Archaeology research center in Lejre, Denmark. J. Zimmerman. il Chem 44:16-17 F '71

IRON curtain. See Europe, Eastern

IRON Hail (Sioux chief)
Echoes of the Little Bighorn. D. H. Miller. il pors Am Heritage 22:37-9 Je '71 *

IRON in diet
Getting the iron you need. R. H. Smithies. il Good H 173:199-200+ N '71

IRON in food
Are you getting enough iron in your diet? with chart. R. H. Smithies and H. P. Schoenberg. Good H 172:184 F '71

IRON in the body
Iron- and riboflavin-dependent metabolism of a monoamine in the rat in vivo. A. L. Symes and others. bibliog il Science 174:153-5 O 8 '71

IRON kettles. See Kettles

IRON meteorites. See Meteorites

IRON mines and mining

Brazil

Mining becomes big business. il Bsns W p51 S 25 '71

Sweden

Project management, Swedish style; LKAB system. P. Jonason. Harvard Bsns R 49:104-9 N '71

IRON ores
See also
Ilmenite

Transportation

Dual-purpose ships build a business; combination ore-oil carriers. il Bsns W p60-2 D 18 '71

IRON porphyrins. See Porphyrins

IRON rust. See Corrosion and anticorrosives

IRON silicates
See also
Olivine

IRON stands. See Trivets

IRONDEQUOIT BAY. See Ontario, Lake

IRONING
How to iron less and enjoy it more; questions and answers. Redbook 136:57+ Mr '71

Anecdotes, facetiae, satire, etc.

Who says a man can't iron? R. Hever. il Good H 173:42+ Ag '71

IRONS, Electric. See Electric irons

IRONWORK
Talent unlimited; work of B. Scarbrough. D. Herbert. il por Design 72:26-8 Sum '71
You can make this chair for $15. W. C. Leckey. il Pop Mech 136:152-4+ Jl '71

IROQUOIS Indians
From Northeast woods; corn husk, quill & birchbark. il House B 113:50-3 Je '71
Iroquois confederacy. J. A. Tuck. il Sci Am 224:32-42 F '71

IROQUOIS rehabilitation center. See Narcotic addicts—Rehabilitation

IRRADIATION
Chromosome lesions produced with an argon laser microbeam without dye sensitization. M. W. Berns and others. bibliog il Science 171:903-5 Mr 5 '71
Cyclic adenosine monophosphate in brain areas: microwave irradiation as a means of tissue fixation. M. J. Schmidt and others. bibliog il Science 173:1142-3 S 17 '71
See also
Sewage purification—Radioactive treatment

IRRIGATION
See also
Arid regions
Dry farming

Abu Dhabi

Arid land agriculture: Shaikh up in Arizona research. R. J. Bazell. il Science 171:989-90 Mr 12 '71

IRRIGATION—*Continued*

Arizona

Wildlife versus irrigation; phreatophyte removal. R. H. Gilluly. il Sci N 99:184-5 Mr 13 '71

California

Game never stops: subsidies to California cotton growers. G. L. Baker. il Nation 213: 114-16 Ag 16 '71

Water, water for the wealthy; Imperial Valley. P. Barnes. New Repub 164:9-10+ My 8 '71

Egypt

See also
Aswan High Dam

Kansas

928 pounds of beef an acre. C. Peterson, jr. il Suc Farm 69:B4 Ag '71

Texas

High Plains irrigation in trouble. Suc Farm 69:no3 47 F '71

Western states

Matter of opinion: reclamation. W. W. Porter. Am West 8:48 Ja '71; Discussion. 8: 48+ Jl '71

IRRIGATION farming

Tow line is inexpensive. R. Krumme. il Suc Farm 69:M6 Ag '71

IRRIGATION machinery

Center pivot requires low labor. R. Krumme. il Suc Farm 69:no5 D1 Mr '71

IRVIN, Robert W.

We unveil the 1972 cars. il Mech Illus 67:52-4+ Jl '71

about

Motor monk. il por Newsweek 78:54 D 27 '71 *

IRVINE, Reed J.

Selling of the Selling of the Pentagon. Nat R 23:855-7+ Ag 10 '71

IRVINE, Sadie

Sadie Irvine letters: a further note on the production of Newcomb pottery; excerpts from letters, ed. by R. W. Blasberg. il Antiques 100:250-1 Ag '71

IRVINE company

Clouds in the big sky; locked gates bar hunters and fishermen from public lands. W. A. Fairhurst and B. East. il Outdoor Life 148:31-3+ Jl '71

Irvine ranch fights regulation. por Bsns W p57-8 Jl 3 '71

IRVING, Blanche M.

Burnt cabin cienaga; poem. Liv Wildn 35:31 Spr '71

IRVING, Clive

Sight & sound. See issues of McCall's

IRVING, Washington

Heart that would not hold, by J. Johnston. Review

Sat R 54:36 Ag 14 '71. N. H. Pearson *

Irving and the misty valley. C. Carmer. il Sat R 54:41+ Mr 13 '71 *

IRWIN, James B.

Apollo 15: three views of the moon. Read Digest 99:74-6 N '71

about

High-flying crew for Apollo. por Time 98:39 Ag 2 '71 *

Mission into the moon's past. E. Driscoll. il pors Sci N 100:28-30 Jl 10 '71 *

Moon witness. E. E. Plowman. Chr Today 15:35 Ag 27 '71 *

See also

Space flight to the moon—Manned flights—Apollo 15 flight

IRWIN, John Nichol, 1913-

Foreign assistance program to meet the conditions of the seventies; statement, June 11, 1971. il Dept State Bul 65:23-7 Jl 5 '71

Intelsat conference resumes at Washington; remarks, April 14, 1971. Dept State Bul 64: 572-3 My 3 '71

New approaches to international security assistance; statement, February 2, 1971. il Dept State Bul 64:221-7 F 22 '71

OAS foreign ministers discuss coastal state fisheries question; statement, February 1, 1971. Dept State Bul 64:247-8 F 22 '71

Strengthened and revitalized foreign aid program; statement, April 27, 1971. Dept State Bul 64:657-64 My 24 '71

Viet-Nam: ending U.S. involvement in the war; statement, May 3, 1971. Dept State Bul 64:711-14 My 31 '71

Western European unity and inter-European reconciliation; address, July 19, 1971. Dept State Bul 65:145-50 Ag 9 '71

IRWIN, John T.

Four practitioners. Poetry 118:351-3 S '71

IRWIN, Theodore

So people won't stare. il Todays Health 49: 28-9 F '71

IS anyone listening? drama. See Hayes, J.

ISAAC, Glynn Ll. and others

Archeological traces of early hominid activities, east of Lake Rudolf, Kenya. bibliog il Science 173:1129-34 S 17 '71

ISAAC, Heinrich

Reviews of records. R. Cross. Mus Q 57:524-7 Jl '71 *

ISAAC, Rhys

Order and growth, authority and meaning in colonial New England. Am Hist R 76: 728-37 Je '71

ISAGEX. See International satellite geodesy experiment

ISBELL, Harold

For David, going to bed; poem. Commonweal 94:89 Ap 2 '71

ISCHEMIA. See Blood—Circulation, Disorders of

ISELIN, John Jay

Iselin goes from H&R to educational TV. Pub W 199:30 Mr 22 '71 *

ISHI (Indian)

Last stone age American; excerpt from The first American. C. W. Ceram. il pors Am Heritage 22:14-19+ Ag '71 *

ISHII, Momoko

Virginia Lee Burton's trip to Japan. il Horn Bk 47:147-56 Ap '71

ISLAM

See also

Mosques
Panislamism
Pilgrimages to Mecca
Ramadan

Relations

Hinduism

Hindu and Moslem: the gospel of hate. il Time 98:32-3 D 6 '71

Religion and another war. Chr Cent 88:1459 D 15 '71

ISLAM and Christianity. See Christianity and other religions

ISLAMIC countries

See also

Arab states

ISLANDS

Adopt an island; Lovell's island in Boston harbor. L. D. Harris. il Am For 77:4-5 My '71

Drive-in islands; Canadian and United States islands. N. D. Ford. bibliog il Har Yrs 11: 6-13+ My '71

Island: the ultimate dream place. il Holiday 48:66-7 S '70

Islands. P. Smyth. il Motor B & S 127:49 Je '71

See also

Coral reefs and islands

[also names of islands, e.g. Aruba (island)]

ISLANDS, Artificial. See Artificial islands

ISLANDS of the Pacific

Bed and board at Aggie Grey's. R. Trumbull. il Sat R 54:60-1+ O 23 '71

See also

Cruising—Islands of the Pacific
Guam
Norfolk Island
Oceania

ISLA VISTA, Calif.

California's Isla Vista: From anathema to dialogue; Student service center. N. Cousins. Sat R 54:22-4 Je 5 '71

ISOCYANATES

Alkyl isocyanates as active site-specific inhibitors of chymotrypsin and elastase. W. E. Brown and F. Wold. bibliog il Science 174:608-10 N 5 '71

ISOLATION chambers

Womb with a view; isolation sphere. il Time 98:44 Jl 5 '71

ISOLATIONISM (United States) See United States—Foreign relations

ISOLATORS, Germfree. See Germfree isolators

ISOMERS and isomerism

Asymmetry, its importance to the action and metabolism of abscisic acid. E. Sondheimer and others. bibliog il Science 174:829-31 N 19 '71

Left- and right-handed odors. Sci Am 225: 46 Ag '71

Odor differences between enantiomeric isomers. G. F. Russell and J. I. Hills. bibliog il Science 172:1043-4 Je 4 '71

Odor incongruity and chirality. L. Friedman and J. G. Miller. bibliog il Science 172:1044-6 Je 4 '71

ISOMERS and isomerism—_Continued_
Probability distribution of enantiomorphous forms in spontaneous generation of optically active substances. R. E. Pincock and others. bibliog il Science 174:1018-20 D **3** '71
Shape isomers and the double-humped barrier. D. D. Clark. bibliog il Phys Today 24:23-31 D '71

ISOPRINOSINE
Cure for the cold? T. J. Murray. il **Duns** 97:64 Je '71
Virus killer. Time 97:68 Ap 26 '71

ISOTOPE separation
Laser-induced reaction separates **isotopes.** bibliog Phys Today 24:19 Ap '71

ISOTOPES
Safe isotopes; icons, isotopes of carbon, oxygen, nitrogen and sulfur. il Newsweek 78:49-50 Ag 2 '71
See also subhead Isotopes under names of chemical elements, e.g. Uranium—Isotopes

ISOTOPIC power generators
Safe nuclear experiments with Minigenerator. S. V. Jones. il Sci Digest 70:65 Jl '71
See also
Space vehicles—Atomic power plants

ISRAEL
American innocent in the Middle East. M. Frady. Harper 242:65-79 Ja '71
In Israel: an air of peace, not war. il U S News 72:23-4 Ja 3 '72
Mood of relaxation; report. M. Levin. il Time 98:28 Ag 16 '71
See also
Airlines—Israel
Christians in Israel
Collective settlements—Israel
Education—Israel
Immigration and emigration—Israel
Jerusalem
Labor and laboring classes—Israel
Marriage law—Israel
Military assistance, American—Israel
Morale, National—Israel
Poor—Israel
Protests, demonstrations, etc.—Israel
Public opinion—Israel
Publishers and publishing—Israel
Purchasing, Military—Israel
Red Sea
Religious conferences—Israel
Russia—Foreign relations—Israel
Seaside resorts—Israel
Shipping—Israel
Sinai (peninsula)
United Nations—Israel
United Nations—Special committee to investigate Israeli practices affecting the human rights of the population of the occupied territories
Youth—Israel
Zionism

Bibliography
David and the Philistines: Israel's fight for survival. D. Schoenbrun. il Sat R 54:21-5 F 6 '71

Boundaries
Bulldozers carve out Israel's new frontiers. M. Orshefsky. il Life 70:32-4 Mr 12 '71
Half a hope. New Repub 164:7 Mr 6 '71
Israel: does geography matter? por Newsweek 77:37-8 Mr 29 '71
Talk with Golda Meir; interview. ed. by A. De Borchgrave. G. Meir. il por Newsweek 77:66-7+ Mr 8 '71

Commerce
Superfluous boycott; effect of boycott by Arab countries. il Time 98:17-18 Jl 19 '71

Description and travel
Look at Israel. M. Decter. Commentary 51:38-42 My '71
This is Israel? R. Joseph. il Esquire 75:114-21 Mr '71

Economic conditions
Middle East: Israel's other war. il Time 97:30+ Je 21 '71
Travel notes. R. Joseph. Esquire 75:24+ Mr '71

Foreign relations
Germany (Federal Republic)
See Germany (Federal Republic)—Foreign relations—Israel
Russia
See Russia—Foreign relations—Israel
United States
See United States—Foreign relations—Israel

History
2 chronicles 37. R. Nathan. Sat R 54:20 My **8** '71

Industries
See also
Airplane industry—Israel

Politics and government
Communist parties of Israel. W. A. Brannigan. Nation 213:398-401 O 25 '71
On to the political wars. il por Time 98:44+ N 22 '71

Social conditions
Israeli youth: the coming explosion. J. R. Moskin. il Look 35:20-4+ Je 15 '71
Middle East: Israel's other war. il Time 97:30+ Je 21 '71
Social problem indicators. L. Guttman. bibliog f il Ann Am Acad 393:40-6 Ja '71

Social history
Israel's power elite. R. Rosenzweig and G. Tamarin; reply with rejoinder. I. Kugler. Trans-Action 8:4 Ja '71

ISRAEL-Arab relations. See Jewish-Arab relations

ISRAELI-Arab war, 1967-
American innocent in the Middle East. M. Frady. Harper 242:65-79 Ja '71
As the flash point nears. S. Alsop. Newsweek 77:80 Ja 18 '71

Aerial operations
Foxbats again evade Israeli intercept. il Aviation W 95:17 N 15 '71
Sparring along the canal. Newsweek 78:46 S 27 '71

Peace and mediation
American policy toward the Middle East; address, January 10, 1971. P. T. Hart. Vital Speeches 37:370-4 Ap 1 '71
American pressures on Israel. J. B. Sheerin. Cath World 213:59-60 My '71
As U. S. presses for peace in Mideast. il U S News 70:17 Mr 29 '71
Assistant Secretary Sisco interviewed on Face the Nation program, February 14, 1971. J. J. Sisco. Dept State Bul 64:291-6 Mr 8 '71
Détente in the Mideast. T. Theodoracopulos. Nat R 23:312+ Mr 23 '71
Fantasy of reconciliation in the Middle East. A. R. Eckardt. bibliog il por Chr Cent 88:1198-202 O 13 '71
Fleeting opportunity. N. Safran. Nation 212:425-8 Ap 5 '71
Fluid and evolving situation in the Middle East; address, November 6, 1970. J. J. Sisco. Dept State Bul 63:748-51 D 21 '70
Four wise men; African leaders on peace mission to Israel. il por Time 98:38 N 15 '71
Four wise men; OAU presidents in Tel Aviv. Newsweek 78:42 N 15 '71
Half a hope. New Repub 164:7 Mr 6 '71
How Israel feels about war and peace; Time-Louis Harris poll. il Time 97:31-2 Ap 12 '71
Inching closer to peace. il Time 97:22-3 Mr 8 '71
Israel: does geography matter? por Newsweek 77:37-8 Mr 29 '71
Israelis' views, site by site, on conquered lands. il U S News 70:82 Mr 15 '71
Israel's quest for security. B. Reich. bibliog f Cur Hist 62:1-5+ Ja '72
Jarring in Jerusalem. il por Newsweek 77:32-3 Ja 18 '71
Last chance for peace in the Mideast. C. Yost. por Life 70:4 Ap 9 '71
Masada complex. S. Alsop. Newsweek 78:92 Jl 12 '71
Middle East: a new momentum; with interview with A. Sadat. ed. by A. de Borchgrave. il pors Newsweek 77:39-41 F 22 '71
Middle East: cease-fire in the balance. il Time 97:30 F 8 '71
Middle East: dead but not buried. pors Time 98:23 Jl 12 '71
Mideast: back from the brink. il por Newsweek 77:37-8 F 15 '71
Mideast: in Israel's court. Newsweek 77:47-8 Mr 15 '71
Mideast troika. Nat R 23:462 My 4 '71
Need for patience. Nation 212:388 Mr 29 '71
Negotiation de facto. Nat R 23:414 Ap 20 '71
One more whirl. il Newsweek 78:27+ Jl 19 '71
Peace is more important than real estate; interview. ed. by J. M. Roots. D. Ben Gurion. il por Sat R 54:14-16 Ap 3 '71
Peace with Israel. America 124:279 Mr 20 '71

ISRAELI-Arab war, 1967- —Peace and mediation—*Continued*
Plan for the Sinai: something less than peace in return for something less than total withdrawal. A. Rubinstein. il N Y Times Mag p 12-13+ Ja 17 '71
Pondering peace. M. Elkins. il Newsweek 77: 59-60 Ap 12 '71
Power of positive thinking. Newsweek 77: 33-4 Mr 1 '71
Price of reconciliation. W. G. Oxtoby; A. R. Eckardt. bibliog il pors Chr Cent 88:1192-202 O 13 '71
Reports and comment: Suez. G. G. Stevens. Atlan 228:16-19 Jl '71
Sadat: we are now back to square one; interview. ed. by A. de Borchgrave. A. Sadat. il pors Newsweek 78:43-4+ D 13 '71
Secretary Rogers discusses a Middle East peace plan. W. P. Rogers. Cur Hist 62: 44+ Ja '72
Secretary Rogers discusses Middle East and southeast Asia in interview on CBS Morning news; January 15, 1971. W. P. Rogers. Dept State Bul 64:133-6 F 1 '71
Secretary Rogers' news conference of March 16, 1971. W. P. Rogers. Dept State Bul 64: 478-86 Ap 5 '71
Small blessings; activities in Gunnar Jarring's office. il Newsweek 77:36 F 1 '71
Strain between friends. il Time 97:24 Mr 29 '71
Talk with Golda Meir; interview. ed. by A. De Borchgrave. G. Meir. il por Newsweek 77:66-7+ Mr 8 '71
Talk with Yigal Allon. H. Krosney. il Nation 212:550-2 My 3 '71
Tenacity and trouble. il Time 97:32+ Mr 15 '71
Thirty days more. Time 97:33-4 F 15 '71
Thrust and parry. Newsweek 77:36-7 Ja 25 '71
Uncorking the Suez. G. Owens and S. A. Blumberg. Nation 211:656-7 D 21 '70
Whatever became of quiet diplomacy? B. Pilkington. Commonweal 94:53-4 Mr 26 '71
Why the Israelis are being difficult. A. Rubinstein. il N Y Times Mag p32-3+ Ap 18 '71
Worries of April. Time 97:22+ Ap 19 '71
Yassin. my son. Time 97:39 Ap 5 '71
Year of peace and decision. il Time 98:27+ Ag 16 '71

Personal narratives
Trade winds; interview. ed. by C. Amory. M. Tsur. Sat R 54:12-13 Ap 3 '71

Public opinion
Reports and comment: Israel. F. Lewis. Atlan 227:14+ Je '71

Russian participation
Living on the brink of war. A. Kucherov. il U S News 70:78-82 Mr 15 '71
ISRAELI technical assistance. See Technical assistance, Israeli
ISRAELIS
American innocent in the Middle East. M. Frady. Harper 242:65-79 Ja '71
Israelis and Jews, by S. N. Herman. Review Commentary 53:84-6 Ja '72. M. Sklare
Israelis, by A. Elon. Review Atlan 228:106-9 S '71. J. Kraft Commentary 52:85-6 S '71. R. Alter
Travel notes. R. Joseph. Esquire 75:24+ Mr '71
Why the Israelis are being difficult. A. Rubinstein. il N Y Times Mag p32-3+ Ap 18 '71
ISTANBUL
Galleries and museums
Secrets of the harem; Topkapi palace. il Time 98:34 S 13 '71
Music
Holocaust on the Golden Horn: Istanbul culture center. C. E. Adelsen. il Opera N 35: 14-16 Ja 30 '71
ISTANBUL culture center
Fires and fire protection
See Opera houses—Fires and fire protection
ISTHMUS of Panama. See Panama, Isthmus of
ISTITUTO finanziario industriale. See Holding companies—Italy
ITAGAKI, K. See Ackley. S. F. jt. auth.
ITALIAN-AMERICAN civil rights league
Family man: J. Colombo. Nation 212:454 Ap 12 '71
How one family stamped out the M----. il pors Newsweek 77:22-3 Ap 5 '71

It's Joe! They got Joe! il por Newsweek 78:30-1 Jl 12 '71
Mafia: back to the bad old days? il pors Time 98:14-18+ Jl 12 '71
Mafia tries a new tune; with report by E. Harvey. T. Buckley. il Harper 243:46-7+ Ag '71
Night for Colombo. il por Time 97:16 Ap 5 '71
ITALIAN art. See Art, Italian
ITALIAN artificial satellites. See Artificial satellites, Italian
ITALIAN communications satellites. See Communications satellites, Italian
ITALIAN cookery. See Cookery, Italian
ITALIAN designers. See Designers
ITALIAN majolica. See Majolica
ITALIAN music. See Music, Italian
ITALIAN opera. See Opera, Italian
ITALIAN painting. See Painting, Italian
ITALIAN poetry
Translations into English
After a flight; poem; tr. by L. Rebav. E. Montale. Am Scholar 40:416-20 Sum '71
ITALIAN social movement. See Political parties—Italy
ITALIAN wines. See Wine
ITALO-ETHIOPIAN war, 1935-1936
Royal navy and the Ethiopian crisis of 1935-36. A. Marder; reply with rejoinder. A. Clayton and H. P. Willmott. Am Hist R 76:1257-8 O '71
ITALY
See also
Aeronautics, Military—Italy
Air traffic control—Italy
Americans in Italy
Architecture. Domestic—Italy
Arts and crafts—Italy
Astronomical observatories—Italy
Automobile racing—Italy
Bari
Bologna
Booksellers and bookselling—Italy
Business consolidations and mergers—Italy
Child welfare—Italy
Crime and criminals—Italy
Education—Italy
Elba (island)
Elections—Italy
Environmental movement—Italy
Gardens—Italy
Holding companies—Italy
Industrial management and organization—Italy
Industry and state—Italy
Justice, Administration of—Italy
Music—Italy
Music festivals—Italy
Political parties—Italy
Politics. Corruption in—Italy
Pollution—Italy
Publishers and publishing—Italy
Ravenna
Religious conferences—Italy
Shipping—Italy
Strikes—Italy
Television broadcasting—Italy
Tourist trade—Italy
Trials—Italy
Water pollution—Italy
Anecdotes, facetiae, satire, etc.
Letter from Europe. A. Burgess. Am Scholar 41:139-42 Wint '71
Antiquities
See also
Paestum
Pompeii
Description and travel
Annual enchantment: hill-town hopping. H. A. Kline. il Travel 135:40-5+ Je '71
Down at the heel. H. Sutton. il Sat R 54:56-8 S 25 '71
Journey from Rome to Florence. S. McIlhany. il Am Artist 35:22-3+ F; 66-71 Mr '71
Economic conditions
At the brink of recession. il Bsns W p34 My 8 '71
Italy: a key ally fighting off chaos. il U S News 71:74-5 Ag 16 '71
Italy's current political crisis. W. E. Greening. Chr Cent 88:477-8 Ap 14 '71
Theology and economy in Italy. T. Beeson. Chr Cent 88:1252-3 O 27 '71
Fascist movement
See Fascism—Italy

ITALY—*Continued*

Foreign relations
United States
   See United States—Foreign relations—Italy

Industries
Lady magnate of Milan; owner of Beni immobili Italia. il por Time 97:73 Je 7 '71
   See also
Aerospace industries—Italy
Airplane industry—Italy
Automobile industry—Italy
Chemical industries—Italy
Drug industry—Italy
Electric industries—Italy
Helicopter industry—Italy
Household appliances industry—Italy
Olivetti
Publishers and publishing—Italy

Politics and government
Can Italian democracy survive? J. Navone. Commonweal 95:323-5 Ja 7 '72
Ecce Leone. il por Newsweek 79:27 Ja 10 '72
Italian colonels? J. Burnham. Nat R 23:1223 N 5 '71
Italy: a key ally fighting off chaos. il U S News 71:74-5 Ag 16 '71
Italy's current political crisis. W. E. Greening. Chr Cent 88:477-8 Ap 14 '71
Trying to take wing. por Time 97:28+ F 22 '71
   See also
Communist party (Italy)
Elections—Italy
Fascism—Italy
Political parties—Italy

Religious institutions and affairs
Il Regno firings protested by Italian intellectuals. Chr Cent 88:1408 D 1 '71
   See also
Catholic church in Italy

Social conditions
Revolution, Italian style. J. Whitmore. il Newsweek 78:33+ Ag 9 '71
ITALY in art
   See also
Venice in art
ITO, Yoichiro, and Bowman, R. L.
Countercurrent chromatography with flow-through coil planet centrifuge. bibliog il Science 173:420-2 Jl 30 '71
ITSKOVITZ, Harold D. and Odya, Charles
Intrarenal formation of angiotensin I. bibliog il Science 174:58 O 1 '71
IVES, Charles Edward
Memos. il Hi Fi 21:66-72 O '71
   about
Gunther Schuller, a very right man to interpret Ives. P. L. Miller. Am Rec G 37:353 F '71 •
House of many mansions: the songs of Charles Ives and the American experience. P. L. Miller. Am Rec G 37:563+ My '71 •
IVES, Ronald L.
Rugged auto emergency flasher. il Pop Electr 34:67-9+ My '71
IVIZA (island) See Ibiza (island)
IVORY-billed woodpeckers. See Woodpeckers
IVORY COAST
Life of Accra, the flowers of Abidjan. N. Gordimer. il Atlan 228:85-9 N '71
New Riviera? il Newsweek 77:83-4 Je 14 '71
Sages of Abidjan. il Time 97:82 Mr 15 '71
IVY
Perfect potted partners. T. Cruso. il McCalls 98:28+ Jl '71
IVY poisoning. See Poison ivy
IZARD, Anne R.
Children's librarians 'n 1970; address. bibliog il Am Lib 2:973-6 O '71
IZMIR. See Smyrna, Turkey

J

J, pseud.
How sensuous are you? il Ladies Home J 88:74+ F '71
J. C. Bradford and company. See Bradford, J. C. and company
J. C. Penney company. See Penney, J. C. company

JCA. See Japan-California association
J. DAVID LEE DAM. See Dams
J. LYONS and company, ltd. See Lyons, J, and company, ltd.
J. P. Stevens and company. See Stevens, J. P. and company
JA'BARI, Mohammed Ali
Third way. il por Time 98:33 S 13 '71 •
JABBAR, Kareem Abdul-. See Abdul-Jabbar, K.
JABBUR, S. J. and others
Visual and auditory inputs into the cuneate nucleus. bibliog il Science 174:1146-7 D 10 '71
JACK, Homer A.
America responds to Pakistan. Chr Cent 88:1137-8 S 29 '71
Confessions of a religious junketeer. Chr Cent 88:1448-9 D 8 '71
JACK Eckerd corporation. See Eckerd, Jack, corporation
JACK knives. See Knives
JACKETS. See Clothing and dress—Sports clothes; Coats
JACKHAMMERS, Hydraulic. See Hydraulic tools
JACKLET, Jon W. and Geronimo, Jeffrey
Circadian rhythm: population of interacting neurons. bibliog il Science 174:299-302 O 15 '71
JACKMAN, William E. See Leinbach, C. jt. auth.
JACKS
Buy an auto jack that won't let you down. il Changing T 25:43-4 Ap '71
JACKSON, Adline
Family under siege. W. B. Furlong. il pors Good H 172:106-7+ Ap '71 •
JACKSON, Andrew
Big cheese at the White House. il por Sr Schol 99:10-11 O 25 '71 •

Homes
Hermitage, home of Andrew Jackson. S. F. Horn. il Antiques 100:413-17 S '71
JACKSON, Anne
I like having a husband, but I don't want to be a wife; interview, ed. by S. Nirenberg. il por House B 113:35+ O '71
JACKSON, Barbara (Ward) lady. See Ward, B.
JACKSON, Bruce
Prison: the new academy. il Nation 213:584-9 D 6 '71
JACKSON, Charles B.
Tektite unlocks secrets from the ocean's floor. il Nat Wildlife 9:50-5 Ap '71
JACKSON, Donald
Cloud comes to Quibbletown. il Life 71:72-4+ D 10 '71
Confessions of the winter soldiers. il Life 71:22-7 Jl 9 '71
Promoter and the crime buster. il pors Life 71:59-60+ S 24 '71
Reviewing our public land use policies. Cur 127:24-8 Mr '71
JACKSON, Frederick S. Jr
Black capitalism: a study of struggle. il por Bsns W p96-8+ Ja 16 '71 •
JACKSON, Geoffrey Holt Seymour
Back in action. Newsweek 77:34+ Ja 18 '71 •
JACKSON, George
Death in San Quentin. il por Time 98:17-18 S 6 '71 •
Dialogue with my Soledad son. L. Jackson. il pors Ebony 27:72-4+ N '71 •
George Jackson radicalizes the brothers in Soledad and San Quentin. T. Szulc. il pors N Y Times Mag p 10-11+ Ag 1 '71 •
Getting to the core; T. Wicker's views. pors Time 98:63 S 20 '71 •
Jackson's legacy. il Newsweek 78:17-18 S 13 '71 •
Pistol in the Afro wig. Nat R 23:970+ S 10 '71 •
San Quentin massacre. il por Newsweek 78:29 Ag 30 '71 •
Sifting the facts about George Jackson. il por Sr Schol 99:15-16 O 18 '71 •
Soledad brother: the prison letters of G. Jackson. Review
   Commonweal 94:65-7 Mr 26 '71. D. G. Shockley •
What about the other five? G. Kirk. Nat R 23:1058 S 24 '71 •
What happened at San Quentin. il Newsweek 78:18-20 S 6 '71 •
JACKSON, Glenda
On location; interview, ed. by E. Miller. il pors Seventeen 30:38+ D '71
Reluctant Oscars; interview, ed. by C. Irving. pors McCalls 98:12+ Jl '71

JACKSON, Glenda—*Continued*

about

Reign of Glenda Jackson. por Vogue 157:
 159 Ap 1 '71 *
Talented Mrs Hodges. il pors Time 97:53-4
 Ap 26 '71 *
JACKSON, Henry Martin
How not to negotiate with the Russians. por
 Nations Bsns 59:52+ Ap '71
New western star? interview. por Nations
 Bsns 59:66-7 N '71
Strategic balance; address, April 15, 1971.
 Vital Speeches 37:482-5 Je '71

about

Another President Jackson? P. R. Wieck. New
 Repub 165:17-21 S 18 '71 *
Candidacy of Senator Jackson. J. Connelly.
 por Nation 213:490-3 N 15 '71 *
Democrats' liberal hawk on Capitol hill. por
 Time 97:14 Mr 22 '71 *
Enter Jackson. Cato. Nat R 23:522 My 18 '71 *
From out of the West. Nat R 23:912-13 Ag
 24 '71 *
Jackson: a hawk eying the White House?
 por U S News 70:43 Mr 22 '71 *
Jackson and the big lie. P. Steinfels. Com-
 monweal 94:446 S 3 '71 *
Jackson's splash. New Repub 165:13 S 25 '71 *
Nixon's accomplice. Nation 213:485-6 N 15
 '71 *
Rites of spring. Nation 212:387-8 Mr 29 '71 *
Scoop. por Newsweek 77:30+ F 15 '71 *
Scoop and the Democrats. por Newsweek
 78:18-19 N 29 '71 *
Scoop declares. Time 98:18 N 15 '71 *
Scoop goes public. por Time 98:22 N 22 '71 *
Scoop Jackson: an alternative for cautious
 Democrats. C. S. Wren. il pors Look 35:19-
 21 S 21 '71 *
Scoop on candidate Jackson. il pors News-
 week 78:24-5 O 11 '71 *
Scratch. Newsweek 78:32 D 13 '71 *
Senator Scoop Jackson: Pentagon populist.
 F. Browning. por Ramp Mag 10:54-7 Ja '72 *
Will the real majority stand up for Scoop
 Jackson? R. J. Whalen. il pors N Y Times
 Mag p 13+ O 3 '71 *
JACKSON, James P.
Forest that was. il Am For 77:20-2 Ap '71
JACKSON, Jeremy B. C. and others
Recent brachiopod-coralline sponge commu-
 nities and their paleoecological significance.
 bibliog il Science 173:623-5 Ag 13 '71
JACKSON, Jesse L.
Unfinished business of America. Look 35:
 59:60 Jl 13 '71

about

Jackson pushes on. il por Time 99:30 Ja 3
 '72 *
Jackson's expo. il por Newsweek 78:24 O 4
 '71 *
Jesse Jackson quits SCLC after being sus-
 pended. Chr Cent 88:1488 D 22 '71 *
Rev Jesse Jackson a new kind of black cat.
 E. Dunbar. il pors Look 35:16-20 O 5 '71 *
Split in SCLC. il por Newsweek 78:27-8 D 20
 '71 *
JACKSON, John F.
Read on: the magic is in the books. il Am
 Lib 2:210-11 F '71
JACKSON, Lawrence W.
Your dog: Dr Jekyll and Mr Hyde. il Cons 26:
 30-1 D '71
JACKSON, Lester
Dialogue with my Soledad son. il pors Ebony
 27:72-4+ N '71
JACKSON, Mary
Let's make foreign language study more rele-
 vant. il Todays Ed 60:18-20 Mr '71
JACKSON, Milt
Profiles. W. Balliett. New Yorker 47:62-4+
 N 20 '71 *
JACKSON, Neta
Our commune in suburbia. il por Redbook
 138:44+ Ja '72
JACKSON, Roland
On Frescobaldi's chromaticism and its back-
 ground. bibliog f il Mus Q 57:255-69 Ap '71
JACKSON, Roy P.
Air transport goals; excerpts from address.
 Aviation W 94:9 My 24 '71
JACKSON, Samuel C.
Homecoming for Sam Jackson. il pors Ebony
 26:60-1+ Jl '71 *
JACKSON, Shirley
Jackson's The witch: a satanic gem. R. L.
 Kelly. Engl J 60:1204-8 D '71 *
JACKSON, Stewart
Stewart Jackson: instant pro? with photo-
 graphs. B. Nemser. por Pop Phot 69:102-5
 O '71 *

JACKSON, Miss.

Education

Progress in Jackson. E. Clift. il Newsweek 78:
 34 S 20 '71

Race question

Swimming pools: black and white. America
 124:645 Je 26 '71
JACKSON Five. See Rock groups
JACKSON state college, Jackson, Miss.
Jackson state a year after. S. Lesher. il N Y
 Times Mag p24-5+ Mr 21 '71
Jackson state becalmed. S. Lesher. il News-
 week 77:69 Mr 1 '71
JACKSONVILLE, Fla.
Centralize your fleet for economy's sake. S.
 Pearson. il por Am City 86:88+ Je '71
Cure for city blight, the Jacksonville story:
 merger of city and county governments;
 And a look at three other areawide govern-
 ments. il U S News 72:34-6 Ja 3 '72

Negroes

Jacksonville: so different you can hardly believe it. J. Fischer. Harper 243:20-2+ Jl '71

Politics and government

Jacksonville: so different you can hardly be-
 lieve it. J. Fischer. Harper 243:20-2+ Jl '71
JACOB, Klaus H. See Ward, P. L. jt. auth.
JACOBS, Arthur
On teaching critics. Hi Fi 21:MA19+ Ag '71
JACOBS, Evelyn
(ed) See Bryans, C. I. jr. High blood pres-
 sure during pregnancy
JACOBS, Frederic. See Orth, C. D. 3, jt. auth.
JACOBS, Hayes B.
New York market letter. See issues of Writ-
 er's digest
JACOBS, Jay
Books. See issues of Art in America
JACOBS, Paul
Precautions are being taken by those who
 know. Atlan 227:45-56 F; 34 Ap; 36 My; 36
 Je '71
JACOBS, Roderick A.
Transformations, style, and the writing ex-
 perience; address, November 1970. Engl J
 60:481-4+ Ap '71
JACOBS, Wilbur R.
Exploitation of the American frontier; ex-
 cerpts. Am West 8:48 My '71
New look; reprint. Am Heritage 22:108-9 O
 '71
JACOB'S Pillow dance festival. See Dance fes-
 tivals
JACOBSEN, Anita
Twenty years ago in the dollology depart-
 ment of hobbies; reprint. Hobbies 75:44 F
 '71
JACOBSEN, Josephine
Three poets. Poetry 118:166-9 Je '71
JACOBSON, Barbara
Day after Christmas; poem. Chr Today 16:9
 D 17 '71
JACOBSON, Betty
Women's work: a job description. il Li-
 brary J 96:2596 S 1 '71
JACOBSON, Frank, and others
Negotiations and beyond. Todays Ed 60:63
 F '71
JACOBSON, Robert
Britten's prodigal. Sat R 54:57 My 29 '71
Day with de Larrocha. il pors Sat R 54:68-9+
 O 30 '71
(comp) Mirror of the word. il Sat R 54:46-7
 My 29 '71
Recordings. Sat R 54:58 F 27; 58 Ap 24;
 51 Je 26; 50 Ag 28; 77 S 25; 80 N 27 '71
JACOBSON, Sol
Faculty collective bargaining at the City
 university of New York. Sch & Soc 99:
 346-9 O '71
JACOBY, Susan
Russian book publishing: inexorably wedded
 to censorship. il Pub W 200:pt2 169-71 S 27
 '71
Soviet schooling: a quiet revolution. il Sat R
 54:43-5+ Jl 17 '71; Same abr. Ed Digest 37:
 17-20 D '71
Who raises Russia's children? il Sat R 54:
 40-3+ Ag 21 '71
JAFFE, Bernard M. and others
Radioimmunoassay for prostaglandins. bibliog
 il Science 171:494-6 F 5 '71
JAFFE, Daniel
Poetry quarterly. il Sat R 54:31-3+ Ap 3
 '71
JAFFE, Ellen
There's no movie like an old movie. Seven-
 teen 31:135 Ja '72

JAFFE, Frederick S.
Toward the reduction of unwanted pregnancy; adaptation of address. January 21, 1971. bibliog il Science 174:119-27 O 8 '71
JAFFE, Jerome H.
New public enemy no. 1; R. M. Nixon's program. il por Time 97:20+ Je 28 '71 •
War on drugs. il pors Newsweek 77:32+ Je 28 '71 •
JAFFE, Leonard D.
Blowing of lunar soil by Apollo 12: Surveyor 3 evidence. bibliog il Science 171:798-9 F 26 '71
JAFFRY, Jacques
Cooking lesson. See issues of American home
about
This month in American home. F. R. Smith. por Am Home 74:8 O '71 •
JAGGER, Mick
Apocalypse at Altamont. R. Schickel. por Life 70:12 Ja 29 '71 •
Pagan event. pors Newsweek 77:36 My 24 '71 •
JAGUAR (automobile) See Automobiles, Foreign
JAGUAR (sports car) See Sports cars
JAHN, Friedrich
Fortune from fowl fare. por Time 98:80+ N 15 '71 •
JAHN, Mike
(comp) Cheap thrills. il Esquire 76:68-71 Ag '71
If you think it's groovy to rap. you're shucking. il N Y Times Mag p28-9+ Je 6 '71
JAIL detention of children. See Children—Imprisonment
JAIL libraries. See Prison libraries
JAILS. See Prisons
JAKLE, John A.
Time, space, and the geographic past: a prospectus for historical geography. bibliog f il Am Hist R 76:1084-103 O '71
JAL, N.Mex.
Hospitals
Profiles: E. L. Schmidt, the only doctor. B. Roueché. il por New Yorker 47:30-40 Ja 1 '72
JALLOW, Raymond
Companies in bondage to debt. por Nations Bsns 59:77 Je '71
JAM. See Jelly, jam, etc.
JAMAICA
Shopping in Jamaica's two straw markets. il Sunset 147:58 N '71
See also
Montego Bay

Economic conditions
About bananas; relations between Jamaica and Fyffes, Haslemere group report. T. Beeson. Chr Cent 88:148-9 F 3 '71

Historic houses, etc.
Travel: Rose hall. restored Georgian great house. M. Gough. il House B 113:185+ My '71
JAMAICA BAY
Academy panel kicks over traces: study of consequences of new runways in Jamaica Bay. C. Holden. Science 171:781 F 26 '71
JAMAICA BAY wildlife refuge. See Wildlife sanctuaries—New York (state)
JAMES, Bernard J. See Beaumont, R. A. jt. auth.
JAMES, Eric
Can the Church of England be renewed? Chr Cent 88:313-15 Mr 10 '71
JAMES, Gregory
Lonely crusade of Guy Gillette. il por McCalls 98:62-3+ Ag '71
JAMES, Henry
Profiles; L. Edel. G. T. Hellman. por New Yorker 47:43-6+ Mr 13 '71 •
JAMES, Jesse
Life, times and treacherous death of Jesse James. by F. Triplett. Review
Am West por 8:50 Mr '71. L. Foster •
JAMES, Lloyd L.
Ground tires reduce pavement cracking. il Am City 86:64-5+ F '71
JAMES, M. R.
Cat in Pace Canyon. il Outdoor Life 147:56-7+ Ja '71
JAMES, Ronald R.
When you negotiate with municipal labor unions. Am City 86:140-2 Je '71
JAMES, Rosa
Epiphyllums from seed. il Horticulture 49:18-19+ Je '71
JAMES, Thomas
Reasons; poem. Poetry 117:308 F '71

JAMES, Vernon L.
Care-by parent ward: a new idea in children's hospitals. W. Garrison. il por Parents Mag 46:34-5+ Jl '71 •
JAMES, William
How to increase your energy; excerpt from The energies of men; reprint from October 1961 issue. Read Digest 99:119-21 S '71
about
The medium had the message: Mrs Piper and the professors; excerpts from Here, Mr Splitfoot. R. Somerlott. il pors Am Heritage 22:33-7+ F '71 •
Varieties of religious experience. R. Coles. New Repub 165:28-31 O 2 '71 •
JAMES BAY hydroelectric project. See Hydroelectric plants
JAMES RIVER
Answer the ecologists; Richmond's pollution abatement program. P. D. Eimon. il Am City 86:118+ O '71
JAMES Talcott, inc. See Talcott, James, inc.
JAMESON, H. D. and others
Acetoxycycloheximide enhances audiogenic seizures in DBA/2J mice. bibliog il Science 173:249-51 Jl 16 '71
JAMESON, Storm
What to do till the novel comes. Writer 84:14-15 Ap '71
about
Neglected presence. S. Maloff. New Repub 164:25-6 Mr 13 '71 •
JAMESTOWN, Va.
Labor problem at Jamestown. 1607-18. E. S. Morgan. bibliog f il Am Hist R 76:595-611 Je '71
JAMIESON, John Kenneth
Truce talk. L. L. L. Golden. Sat R 54:98 Mr 13 '71
JANÁČEK, Leoš
Makropoulos affair. Criticism
Hi Fi il 21:MA16+ F '71 •
Nation 213:254 S 20 '71 •
Music to my ears; performance of works by the Little orchestra society. I. Kolodin. Sat R 54:24 Ap 24 '71 •
Musical events; Little orchestra society program in Alice Tully Hall. W. Sargeant. New Yorker 47:116 Ap 17 '71 •
JANDA, J.
Of prophets and prophecy; poem. Cath World 212:288 Mr '71
Sioux town in march; poem. America 124:340 Ap 3 '71
JANES, Kelly
Shepherdess; poem. Chr Cent 88:1285 N 3 '71
JANES, Ted
(ed) News: the Northeast. See issues of Outdoor life
Sebago comeback. il Outdoor Life 147:88-9+ Ap '71
JANEWAY, Eliot
They love me in Terre Haute. por Forbes 107:45-6 Je 15 '71 •
JANEWAY, Elizabeth
End of the world is coming. Atlan 228:87-90 Ag '71
In praise of middle age. McCalls 99:112+ O '71
JANICKI, Ralph H. and Kinter, W. B.
DDT: disrupted osmoregulatory events in the intestine of the eel anguilla rostrata adapted to seawater. bibliog il Science 173:1146-8 S 17 '71
JANNASCH, Holger W. and others
Microbial degradation of organic matter in the deep sea. bibliog il Science 171:672-5 F 19 '71
JANOS, Leo
Georgia O'Keeffe at eighty-four. il por Atlan 228:114-17 D '71
JANOV, Arthur
Can primal therapy shortcut the return to happiness? A. Goldman. il por Vogue 158:270-1 S 1 '71 •
Primal screamer. il por Newsweek 77:97 Ap 12 '71 •
JANSON, Dora Jane
From slave to siren. il Art N 70:49-53 My '71
JANSONISTS
See also
Bishop Hill, Ill.
JANSSEN, Peter A.
Education vouchers. Ed Digest 36:5-8 Mr '71
JANSSEN, Raymond E.
Blue Ridge dams: the pollution dilution approach. il Nat Parks & Con Mag 45:14-17 Ag '71
JANTZEN, Steve
Teleguide. Sr Schol Teach ed 99:4 Ja 10 '72

JANZEN, D. H.
Euglossine bees as long-distance pollinators
of tropical plants. bibliog il Science 171:
203-5 Ja 15 '71

JAPAN
Digital Japan; use of digital readout devices
in commonly used equipment. M. Mann. il
Pop Electr 35:50 Ag '71
Japan, 1971; symposium. bibliog f il Cur
Hist 60:193-236+ Ap '71
See also
Aeronautics, Commerical—Japan
Airlines—Japan
Airplanes, Military—Japan
Americans in Japan
Baseball—Japan
Birth control—Japan
Business management and organization—Ja-
pan
Business schools and colleges—Japan
Crime and criminals—Japan
Education—Japan
Golf courses—Japan
Hokkaido (island)
Investments, Foreign (by Japan)
Investments, Foreign (in Japan)
Kurashiki
Kyoto
Labor and laboring classes—Japan
Medicine—Japan
Money—Japan
Moving pictures—Japan
Natural resources—Japan
Newspapers—Japan
Okinawa
Photography—Japan
Physics—Japan
Pollution—Japan
Protests, demonstrations, etc.—Japan
Publishers and publishing—Japan
Railroads—Japan
Research—Japan
Ryukyu Islands
Sapporo
Shipping—Japan
Space research—Japan
Student demonstrations—Japan
Supermarkets—Japan
Theater—Japan
Tourist trade—Japan
United   States—Armed   forces—Forces   in
Japan
United States—Commerce—Japan
United States—Trade missions—Japan
Visitors, Foreign—Japan
Women—Japan
World war, 1939-1945—Japan

Air force
New hardware planned for Japan defense.
il Aviation W 95:47-8+ N 1 '71

Armed forces
Japan's self-defense force wins a skirmish
with the past. T. Oka. il por N Y Times
Mag p 12-13+ F 28 '71

Civilization
Educational and cultural trends in Japan
today. W. S. Morton. Cur Hist 60:213-17
Ap '71

Commerce
After the blow, Japan picks up the pieces.
il Bsns W p60-1 Ag 28 '71
Bidding up shrimp. il Time 99:63 Ja 3 '72
Business around the world. U S News 71:63-4
S 13 '71
Japan, inc: winning the most important bat-
tle. il Time 97:84-9 My 10 '71
Japanese boom. il Newsweek 77:63-4 F 15 '71
Japanese face suit for dumping TV sets. Bsns
W p68 Mr 20 '71
Japan's executives turn to diplomacy. il Bsns
W p36-7 My 22 '71
Letter from Tokyo. J. Kraft. New Yorker 47:
140-2+ D 11 '71
Next target: Europe. il Forbes 108:20-1 D 15
'71
Pacific trade challenge; address, March 15,
1971. N. Ushiba. Vital Speeches 37:390-2 Ap
15 '71
Pearl Harbor in reverse. F. Gibney. il Harper
244:49-51+ Ja '72
Trade drops off as yen moves up. Bsns W p51-
2 S 25 '71
Yen for revaluation. Time 97:69-70 Je 7 '71
See also
Japan-California association
Joint United States-Japan committee on trade
and economic affairs

United States
See United States—Commerce—Japan

Constitution
Story of Article 9. il Newsweek 78:38+ O 4
'71

Defenses
Japan plans air defense net expansion. il
Aviation W 95:54-5+ N 1 '71
Nukes for Nippon? il Time 98:28+ Jl 26 '71
Prospect of Japanese rearmament. M. K.
Yiu. bibliog f il Cur Hist 60:231-6 Ap '71
See also
Japan—Air force

Description and travel
Japan: the land of the re-rising sun. R. Ter-
rill. il Atlan 227:78-82+ Mr '71
Japanese Gothic: Ako castle. L. Namioka. il
Travel 136:52-7 N '71

Economic conditions
Changing trade policy in Japan; address,
November 1, 1971. N. Ochi. Vital Speeches
38:102-5 D 1 '71
Emerging Japanese superstate, by H. Kahn.
Review
Sat R 54:64-6 Ja 23 '71. H. Rosovsky
Japan: adjusting to the Nixon snokku. il
Time 98:34+ O 4 '71
Japan and the continental giants. M. E.
Weinstein. bibliog f Cur Hist 60:193-9+ Ap
'71
Japan revisited. P. A. Samuelson. News-
week 78:101 N 15 '71
Japan will have to slow down. N. Kiucki.
Fortune 83:98-9+ F '71
Japan's drive to pass U.S. as top industrial
power. il U S News 70:60-3 Ap 26 '71
Japan's growth economy; joy and anguish.
S. B. Levine. bibliog f Cur Hist 60:218-24+
Ap '71
Kicking the growth cult. Time 98:56-7 D 27
'71
Letter from Tokyo. J. Kraft. New Yorker 47:
140-2+ D 11 '71
See also
Japan—Industries
Money—Japan

Economic relations
China; Sino-Japanese relations. H. Yu. Chr
Cent 88:414 Mr 31 '71
Japan and southeast Asia in the 1970's K.
Wakaizumi. il Cur Hist 60:200-6+ Ap '71
Japan looks to the 1970's: an economic super-
power; address, September 16, 1971. N.
Ushiba. Vital Speeches 38:11-13 O 15 '71
Japan: rising sun in the Pacific. T. Engel-
hardt and J. Peck. il Ramp Mag 10:29-37
Ja '72
Japan's economic relations with Asia. K.
Taira. bibliog f Cur Hist 60:225-30+ Ap '71
Why U.S. must stay in Asia; interview. H.
Kahn. il pors U S News 70:60-4 F 8 '71
See also
Joint United States-Japan committee on trade
and economic affairs

United States
See United States—Economic relations—
Japan

Emperors and empresses
See also
Hirohito, emperor of Japan

Foreign relations
Japan and the continental giants. M. E.
Weinstein. bibliog f Cur Hist 60:193-9+ Ap
'71
Japan: into a colder world. Time 98:25-6 S
6 '71
Japan: on Nixon's China bandwagon. il por
Newsweek 78:29 Ag 9 '71

China (People's Republic)
See China (People's Republic)—Foreign
relations—Japan

United States
See United States—Foreign relations—
Japan

History
See also
Russian-Japanese war, 1904-1905

Industries
Japan, inc: winning the most important bat-
tle. il Time 97:84-9 My 10 '71
What we can learn from Japan. E. Goldston.
il por Fortune 84:137+ O '71
See also
Aerospace industries—Japan
Airplane industry—Japan
Automobile industry—Japan
Avionics industry—Japan
Chemical industries—Japan
Coffee industry—Japan
Computer industry—Japan
Cosmetics industry—Japan

JAPAN—Industries—See also—*Continued*
Electric industries—Japan
Fisheries—Japan
Japan—Commerce
Japan—Economic conditions
Liquor industry—Japan
Machinery industry
Mitsubishi
Paper industry—Japan
Photographic apparatus and supplies industry—Japan
Steel industry—Japan
Television apparatus industry—Japan
Textile industry—Japan
Watch industry—Japan

Military policy
Japan's fall from grace. Nation 213:420-1 N 1 '71
See also
Japan—Defenses

Nationalism
Politics of suicide; Mishima's seppuku. R. T. Halloran. por Commonweal 94:34-6 Mr 19 '71

Politics and government
Japan: a time of decision. il Newsweek 78:32-4 O 4 '71
See also
Political parties—Japan

Population
How many people? Sci Am 225:43-4 Jl '71

Religious institutions and affairs
See also
United church of Christ in Japan

Social conditions
Saul Alinsky in Japan. J. K. Hasegawa. Chr Cent 88:1306-8 N 3 '71
See also
Women—Japan

Treaties
United States
See United States—Treaties—Japan

JAPAN air lines. See Airlines—Japan
JAPAN and China (People's Republic) See China (People's Republic) and Japan
JAPAN-California association
Some Japanese yield on the yen. il Bsns W p22 O 2 '71
JAPAN house gallery. See New York (city)—Galleries and museums
JAPAN-United States conference on natural resources. See Natural resources—Conferences
JAPAN-United States cooperative medical science committee. See Medical research—International cooperation
JAPAN-United States ministerial conference on environmental pollution. See Pollution—Control—Conferences
JAPANESE airways. See Airways
JAPANESE AMERICANS
Co-opting the oppressors: the case of the Japanese-Americans. R. O. Haak. il Trans-Action 7:23-31 O '70
San Jose's new mayor. Nation 212:549 My 3 '71
Success story: outwhiting the whites. il Newsweek 77:24-5 Je 21 '71
JAPANESE anemones. See Anemones
JAPANESE art. See Art, Japanese
JAPANESE automobiles. See Automobiles, Foreign
JAPANESE brokers. See Brokers
JAPANESE businessmen. See Businessmen
JAPANESE castles. See Castles
JAPANESE economic assistance. See Economic assistance, Japanese
JAPANESE flower arrangements. See Flowers, Arrangement of
JAPANESE guided missiles. See Guided missiles
JAPANESE In New York. See Japanese in the United States
JAPANESE In the United States
Culture *shokku* in Texas. Time 98:103-4 N 22 '71
Japanization of New York. D. Butwin. il Sat R 54:63-5 N 27 '71
See also
Japanese Americans
JAPANESE International aerospace show. See Aviation—Exhibitions
JAPANESE legends. See Legends, Japanese
JAPANESE newspapers. See Newspapers—Japan

JAPANESE painting. See Painting, Japanese
JAPANESE peonies. See Peonies
JAPANESE poetry
See also
Haiku
JAPANESE prints. See Prints
JAPANESE quails. See Quails
JAPANESE screen painting. See Painting, Japanese
JAPANESE stockholders meetings. See Stockholders meetings
JAPANESE students
See also
Student demonstrations—Japan
Student militants—Japan
JAPANESE tourists. See Travelers
JAPONICAS. See Camellias
JARDINE, Don
Richard Lack's atelier system of training painters. il por Am Artist 35:48-53+ Je '71
JARDINE, James W.
Computer assures pinpoint water control. il Am City 86:82+ S '71
JARDINE, Matheson and company, ltd.
Old China hands who know how to live with the new Asia. A. T. Demaree. il Fortune 84:132-5+ N '71
JARES, Joe
And, in a prettier part of the forest . . . il por Sports Illus 35:16-17 S 6 '71
Baseball. Sports Illus 35:51 Je 28; 35:42-3 Ag 30 '71
Bowling. il Sports Illus 35:92+ O 25 '71
Camille goes under again. il Sports Illus 34:14-17 F 15 '71
Close one at last. il Sports Illus 34:24-7 Ap 5 '71
College basketball (cont) il Sports Illus 34:56-7 Ja 18; 46-7 F 22; 65-6 Mr 8 '71
College football. Sports Illus 35:64+ O 11 '71
Look what Gary found in the cup! il por Sports Illus 35:24-5 S 13 '71
Perennial problem. il Sports Illus 34:12-17 Mr 22 '71
Volleyball. il Sports Illus 34:72+ My 17 '71
We have a neurotic in the backfield, doctor. il pors Sports Illus 34:30-4 Ja 18 '71
Week; baseball. Sports Illus 34:62+ Ap 26; 63-4 My 3; 35:51-2 Jl 26 '71
Week; college basketball (cont) Sports Illus 34:59-60 Mr 15 '71
Week; college football. Sports Illus 35:62+ S 27; 56+ O 4; 68+ O 19 '71
Winner takes $50,000 loser, $1 million. il por Sports Illus 35:28-9 D 6 '71
JARGON
Escaping escaping gas; art jargon. M. Batterberry and A. Batterberry. il Harp Baz 104:71 Ag '71
See also
Slang
JARMAN, Franklin Maxey
Engineer in the fashion trade. Forbes 108:49 O 15 '71 •
JAROSEWICH, Eugene. See Olsen, E. jt. auth.
JARRETT, Paul B.
Leakage current & electrical shock. Pop Electr 34:46 Mr '71
JARRING, Gunnar
Jarring in Jerusalem. il por Newsweek 77:32-3 Ja 18 '71 •
JARVIS, Jane
In the mood for baseball. R. Cantwell. il Sports Illus 34:54-6+ Je 7 '71 •
JASON, Hilliard
Student pilot. Flying 88:118 Je; 89:120 Ag; 24 O '71
JASPAN, Norman
Why employes steal; interview. il por U S News 70:78-82 My 3 '71; Same abr. Read Digest 99:83-6 S '71
JASPER, Herbert H. and Tessier, Jacques
Acetylcholine liberation from cerebral cortex during paradoxical (REM) sleep. bibliog il Science 172:601-2 My 7 '71
JASTROW, Robert
Man in space or chip in space? il N Y Times Mag p 14-15+ Ja 31 '71
JAUNDICE, Infectious. See Hepatitis
JAVA
Java: Eden in transition. K. MacLeish. il Nat Geog 139:1-43 Ja '71
Population crisis and economic development. W. Withington. bibliog il Focus 21:9-12 My '71
Description and travel
Java, Bali: the exotic isles. M. Litton. il Holiday 49:42-7+ Jl '71

JAVITS, Jacob Koppel
U.N. General assembly calls for study to further the work of the International court of justice; statements, October 29 and December 15, 1970. Dept State Bul 64:116-23 Ja 25 '71
Women's lib in Congress. Esquire 76:76+ O '71

about

Four Nobelists zap senator. N. Wade. Science 173:1114 S 17 '71 •
Questions for Senator Javits. W. F. Buckley, jr. Nat R 23:330 Mr 23 '71 *

JAY, Alexander
Lindsay papers. Nat R 23:990 S 10 '71

JAY, Antony
White-collar ape; excerpts from Corporation man. Time 98:88 S 27 '71

about

Genesis. il por Forbes 107:198-201 My 15 '71 •

JAYCEES. See United States Jaycees (organization)

JAYESS; story. See Boles, P. D.

JAZZ music
Black nationalism and the revolution in music, by F. Kofsky. Review
Ramp Mag 9:54-7 Mr '71. R. Young
Jazz meets rock; excerpt from Freakshow. A. Goldman. il Atlan 227:98-101+ F '71
Musical events; Cape Cod notes: B. Hackett, D. McKenna and M. Marcus. W. Balliett. New Yorker 47:75+ Ag 28 '71
Reporter at large; C. Mingus. W. Balliett. New Yorker 47:42-4+ My 29 '71
Saints preserved; Preservation hall concerts. K. R. Zimmermann. Nat R 23:882 Ag 10 '71
See also
Phonograph records—Jazz music
Rock music (songs, etc)

History

Scanning the history of jazz. L. Armstrong. pors Esquire 76:184-7+ D '71

Study and teaching

Jazz goes to college. il Time 97:67 Je 7 '71

JAZZ musicians
Jazz meets rock; excerpt from Freakshow. A. Goldman. il Atlan 227:98-101+ F '71
See also
Armstrong. L.
King, R. B.

JAZZ quartets
See also
Modern jazz quartet

JAZZNITE; drama. See Jones, W.

JEALOUSY
Doctor Rubin. T. I. Rubin. por Ladies Home J 88:78 Mr '71
Oh jealous love. S. G. Streshinsky. il Parents Mag 46:39-41+ Ag '71

JEANES, William, memorial library. See William Jeanes memorial library, Whitemarsh Township, Lafayette Hill, Pa.

JEANNERET, Marsh
Marsh Jeanneret: businesslike but not in business; excerpts from address, May 15, 1971. Pub W 199:21-3 Je 14 '71

JEANS, Kit
C&O Canal: our newest national park. il Am For 77:24-7 Ap '71
Try woodland camping, family style. il Parents Mag 46:44-5+ Je '71

JEANS. See Clothing and dress—Sports clothes

JEEP automobiles
Land-Rover: is it really indestructible? D. Lampe. il Pop Mech 135:44+ Mr '71
1972 Jeep: gettin' more guts. C. Koch. il Motor T 23:84-6 D '71
PM owners report: Jeep Universal. M. Lamm. il Pop Mech 136:58-61 Ag '71

JEFFERS, Le Roy
Gleason: presenting a rare collection of early wilderness photography; excerpts from The call of the mountains. il Am West 8:16-27 Jl '71

JEFFERS, Robert A.
Poor of God and the black Christian in America. il Cath World 213:126-9 Je '71

JEFFERSON, Eva
Eva Jefferson: young voice of change. H. H. King. il pors Ebony 26:71-4+ Ja '71 •

JEFFERSON, Thomas
"All my wishes end at Monticello." M. Evans. il Am Home 74:41-9+ Jl '71 •
Historical confrontation. Cur 131:6-7 Jl '71 •
Thomas Jefferson and Maria Cosway. C. B. Van Pelt. il pors Am Heritage 22:22-5+ Ag '71 •

JEFFERSON national expansion memorial. See St Louis—Monuments, statues, etc.

JEFFREY, Dorothy
How I handle our farm accounting. por Suc Farm 69:10 O '71

JEHOVAH'S Witnesses
Terry and the parents; alternative to blood transfusion. il Newsweek 77:43 Ja 18 '71

JELLICO, John
Dane Clark: adobe landscapes in acrylic and watercolor. il por Am Artist 35:52-7+ Ap '71

JELLINEK, George
Before their time. il Opera N 36:32-4 D 25 '71

JELLINEK, Hedy D.
Guide to European music festivals, 1971. Sat R 54:68-9 Mr 27 '71
(comp) Music festivals USA, Summer 1971. Sat R 54:40-2 Je 26 '71

JELLY, jam, etc.
ABC's of jam, jelly, preserves. il Am Home 74:76 Jl '71
Country fair. il Ladies Home J 88:77+ S '71
Making jams and jellies. il Redbook 137:114-15+ My '71
New Polaner's rated low in CU jam session. Consumer Rep 36:135-6 Mr '71
Take a jelly quiz. Bet Hom & Gard 49:70 Ag '71
Thoughts for the hostess: recipes. M. M. Hemingway. House & Gard 140:36+ S '71

JELLYFISH
Hazard of the ocean. H. M. Farkas. Mech Illus 67:22 Ag '71
How to cope with a jellyfish sting. il Sunset 146:79 My '71
Jack in jellyfish. il Sea Front 17:349 N '71

JENCKS, Christopher
Vouching for education; letter to editor. Commonweal 94:44-6 Mr 19 '71

about

Trouble with vouchers. M. R. Berube. Commonweal 93:414-17 Ja 29 '71; Discussion. 94:27+ Mr 19 '71 •

JENKINS, Dan
Aloha for a bright young blond. il por Sports Illus 34:20-1 F 15 '71
Cheerleader could run the team. il Sports Illus 35:26-7 S 27 '71
College football (cont) il Sports Illus 35:54+ N 8 '71
Dominance of the smiling bear. il pors Sports Illus 34:22-5 Mr 8 '71
Golf (cont) Sports Illus 34:69-70 Ja 18; 54-5 Ja 25; 35:88-90 N 22 '71
Heads roll at head to head. il por Sports Illus 35:12-16 S 6 '71
How they do run on. il Sports Illus 35:22-5 N 1 '71
In the footsteps of Knute. il Sports Illus 35:44-51 S 13 '71
Jones, Hogan and the rest. Sports Illus 34:37 Je 14 '71
King Cornhusker goes Bear hunting. il Sports Illus 35:22-4+ D 20 '71
Nebraska rides high. il Sports Illus 35:22-5 D 6 '71
Now for the Mexican Open. il por Sports Illus 35:12-15 Jl 19 '71
Off like champions. il Sports Illus 35:22-5 S 20 '71
Oklahoma wins the Wishbone war. il Sports Illus 35:24-7 O 18 '71
One-day season. il Sports Illus 34:10-15 Ja 11 '71
Our Jack in fields of gold. il por Sports Illus 34:16-19 My 3 '71
Out there with slow-play Fay and play-slow Flo. il Sports Illus 35:50-4+ Ag 9 '71
Remember the battle of Merion. il pors Sports Illus 34:12-15 Je 28 '71
Showcase for the big names. il Sports Illus 34:38-9 Ap 5 '71
There went the slam. il por Sports Illus 34:16-19 Ap 19 '71
This year's game of the decade. il Sports Illus 35:32-4+ N 22 '71

JENKINS, Ellen
Wanderlust; poem. Seventeen 30:132 Jl '71

JENKINS, Ferguson
Invisible man. por Newsweek 78:43 S 6 '71 •

JENKINS, Gary
Painting with fingerprints. N. Hawkins. il por Design 72:20-1 Sum '71 •

JENKINS, Harold R.
ABC's of PPB. bibliog il por Library J 96:3089-93 O 1 '71

JENKINS, Roy Harris
Britain: Labor's dark hour. pors Newsweek 78:30+ Ag 2 '71 •
Labour pains. A. Howard. New Repub 165:13-14 N 13 '71 •
Rebel vindicated. Time 98:45-6 N 22 '71 •

JENKINS, Speight, Jr
Dream of love. il Opera N 36:24-5 D 18 '71
Meeting of minds. il pors Opera N 35:6-9 Ap 17 '71
(ed) See Arroyo, M. Real Martina
(ed) See Bonazzi, E. Two for the desert
JENKINS, William A.
Sense of profession. Engl J 60:641-4 My '71
JENKS, Jeremy C.
Disciple. por Forbes 107:41-2 F 1 '71 •
JENNIE; story. See Martin, R. G.
JENNINGS, James R.
Quadragesimo anno: forty years after. il America 125:208-10 S 25 '71
JENNINGS, Jo Ann
Enlivening the publications class. Todays Ed 60:33 F '71
JENNINGS, Robert E.
Student activism: a perspective and strategy. Clear House 46:86-90 O '71
JENSEN, Albert C.
Land birds at sea. il Sea Front 17:48-56 Ja '71
—and Foehrenbach, Jack
Testing for mercury in New York's marine fish and shellfish. il Cons 26:31-3 O '71
JENSEN, Arthur Robert
Is intelligence racial? H. Simmons. il por Newsweek 77:69-70 My 10 '71
JENSEN, Eileen
I have heard the mermaids singing; story. Redbook 137:71-2 Ag '71
JENSEN, Gorden D.
Day care centers in Europe: a focus on consequences for mental health. Ment Hy 55: 425-32 O '71
JENSEN, Holger
Grouse behind the iron curtain. il Outdoor Life 147:86-7+ Ap '71
JENSEN, Jerry
Wheels are spinning. il pors Design 73:16-17 Fall '71 •
JENSEN, Jesper
Story behind the book: The little red schoolbook. L. P. Freilicher. pors Pub W 200:32-3 D 13 '71 •
JENSEN, Oliver
Fight for the Queen; or, Two cheers for Congress. il Am Heritage 22:4-7+ Ap '71
Weekender's companion. il Horizon 13:105-12 Sum '71
JENSEN, Orville. See Palmer, G. jt. auth.
JENSEN, Tony
Obituary
Phys Today por 24:70-1 S '71. A. J. Heeger and others
JENSEN, William B.
Caricature and the chemist. bibliog il Chem 44:6-9 D '71
JEREZ, Francisco, pseud.
Bolivia: prayers before a coup. Commonweal 94:469-70 S 17 '71
JERMANN, Thomas C.
Zero population growth, do we need it now? America 124:538-40 My 22 '71
JEROME, Judson
Poetry: how and why. See issues of Writer's digest
JERRARD, Margot
Very small shipwreck; story. Redbook 138: 92-3 N '71
JERREMS, Raymond L.
Sensitivity training. Ed Digest 37:26-9 O '71
JERSEY CITY, N.J.

Politics and government
Jersey City Catholics break with machine. Chr Cent 88:1287 N 3 '71
JERUSALEM
Awakening in the Old City. C. Irving. McCalls 99:28+ D '71
British prelate suggests new plan for control of Jerusalem. Cur Cath 18:794 Je 30 '71
Peace of Jerusalem; with editorial comment. H. Siegman. il Chr Cent 88:1191, 1203-5 O 13 '71
Resurrection land. D. Baker. Chr Today 15: 40 Ap 9 '71
U.S. reiterates position on Jerusalem; statement, with text of resolution, September 25, 1971. G. Bush. Dept State Bul 65:469-70 O 25 '71

Antiquities
Rite of crucifixion. il Newsweek 77:52-3 Ja 18 '71

City planning
Building Jerusalem. H. Halkin. Commentary 52:59-66 S '71
Full speed ahead and damn the aesthetics. il Time 97:21-2 Mr 1 '71
Judaizing Jerusalem. il Newsweek 77:41 Ja 25 '71
Planning for Jerusalem; report on international conference. R. Meier. il Arch Forum 134:56-7 Ap '71

Holy places
Jerusalem and the holy places: a Christian viewpoint. J. Kritzeck and J. L. Ryan. Chr Cent 88:1205-6+ O 13 '71

Politics and government
Building a new Jerusalem. S. L. Davidson. il Time 98:35-6 D 27 '71
Security council calls upon Israel to rescind measures affecting status of Jerusalem; with text of resolution. UN Mo Chron 8:3-30 O '71

Riots
Jewish Black Panthers. il Newsweek 77:33 My 31 '71
JERUSALEM; drama. See Gaines, F.
JERUSALEM artichokes
Jerusalem artichoke, year-round vegetable. G. L'Allemand. il Org Gard & Farm 18:52-3 My '71
JERUSALEM conference on Biblical prophecy.
See Religious conferences—Israel
JERUSALEM international book fair. See Book fairs
JESSEN, Ruth
Bad luck ends in a pot of gold. W. Bingham. il por Sports Illus 34:59-60 Mr 1 '71 •
JESSUP, Philip C.
Berlin blockade and the use of the United Nations. bibliog f For Affairs 50:163-73 O '71
JESUITS
Ecumenists meet in Dublin; Fourth international congress of Jesuit ecumenists. M. A. Fahey. America 125:141-3 S 11 '71
I.O.U.'s of Texas are upon us; involvement of the Houston Jesuits. America 124:139 F 13 '71
In Dublin's fair city, the Jesuits Fourth international congress of Jesuit ecumenists. J. R. Nelson. Chr Cent 88:1072-3 S 15 '71
New Jesuits, by G. Riemer. Review
America 124:293-4 Mr 20 '71
Cath World 213:157 Je '71. H. T. Camel
Commonweal 94:174 Ap 23 '71. J. L'Heureux
Questions for globe-trotting general; interview, with editorial comment. P. Arrupe. il America 125:inside cover, 55-8 Ag 7 '71

Education
Keeping schools democratic. America 124:397-8 Ap 17 '71
JESUS CHRIST
Christology without Jesusolatry. R. Kysar; discussion. Chr Cent 87:1201, 1287; 88:375-7 O 7, 28 '70, Mr 24 '71
Cosmological Christology. T. Organ. Chr Cent 88:1293-5 N 3 '71
Historical notes on the (in)comparable Christ. E. M. Yamauchi. il Chr Today 16:7-11 O 22 '71
In what sense is Christ unique? J. A. T. Robinson; discussion. Chr Cent 87:1569; 88:19, 194-5 D 30 '70, Ja 6, F 10 '71
Jesus and nationalism. J. W. Oliver. Today 15:18-19 Ap 9 '71
Jesus and our search for security. G. O'Collins. il America 124:237-8 Mr 6 '71
Many things to many men. Time 97:60 Je 21 '71
Was Jesus married? by W. E. Phipps. Review
Chr Cent 88:299 Mr 3 '71. J. G. Gibbs
Witness of the Baptists. V. P. McCorry. America 126:inside back cover Ja 8 '72
See also
Holy Shroud
Sacred Heart, Devotion to
Second advent

Art
Artists portray a black Christ. il Ebony 26: 176-8+ Ap '71
Color of the Lord. il Negro Hist Bul 33:187 D '70

Atonement
See Atonement

Beatitudes
See Beatitudes

Birth
See Jesus Christ—Nativity

Crucifixion
Historical notes on the trial and crucifixion of Jesus Christ. E. M. Yamauchi. Chr Today 15:6-11 Ap 9 '71
No more cross? G. O'Collins. America 124: 320 Mr 27 '71
Offense of the cross. Chr Today 15:24 Mr 26 '71

Drama
See also
Passion plays

JESUS CHRIST—*Continued*

Forty days in the wilderness
See Jesus Christ—Temptation

Humanity
D. H. Lawrence's appraisal of Jesus. W.
E. Phipps. Chr Cent 88:521-4 Ap 28 '71
Discussion. 88:861-2, 1365-6 Jl 14, N 17 '71
Faith for tomorrow. J. B. Healey. America
125:550-3 D 25 '71

Incarnation
See Incarnation

Jewish interpretations
Jesus and Israel, by J. Isaac. Review
Commentary 52:92-5 S '71

Kingdom
Royal one. V. P. McCorry. America 125:413
N 13 '71

Music
See Jesus Christ in music

Nativity
Coming of Jesus; excerpt from The story
Bible. P. S. Buck. Ladies Home J 88:83+
D '71
First Christmas. P. L. Maier. Redbook
138:65+ D '71
Poets at Bethlehem. N. Braybrooke. Chr Cent
88:1497-8 D 22 '71
Why keep on celebrating Christmas? J. Blen-
kinsopp. Commonweal 95:302-3 D 24 '71
See also
Christmas
Incarnation
Magi
Mary, Virgin

Parables
Researching the parables. P. Steinfels. Commonweal 94:230 My 14 '71

Passion
Passion as school. V. P. McCorry. America
124:355-6 Ap 3 '71

Poetry
Passion of the women. R. Spargur. Chr Cent
88:429-30 Ap 7 '71; Discussion. 88:737, 756-7
Je 16 '71
See also
Christmas poetry

Resurrection and ascension
Easter people. V. P. McCorry. America 124:
392-inside back cover Ap 10 '71
Empty tomb: does it matter? G. O'Collins.
America 124:345 Ap 3 '71
Jesus is alive! Chr Today 15:28 Ap 9 '71
Man alive! L. N. Bell. Chr Today 15:32-3
Ap 9 '71
Resurrection as God's historical deed. A. R.
Gualtieri. Chr Cent 88:432 Ap 7 '71; Dis-
cussion. 88:760-2, 1026-7 Je 16, S 1 '71
Resurrection of Jesus of Nazareth, by W.
Marxsen. Review
Chr Today 15:24 Jl 2 '71. D. P. Fuller
See also
Easter

Second advent
See Second advent

Teachings
Jesus the realist: I am... the truth. N. V.
Hope. Chr Today 15:10-12 My 7 '71

Temptation
Strange happening. V. P. McCorry. America
124:216-17 F 27 '71

Trial
Historical notes on the trial and crucifixion
of Jesus Christ. E. M. Yamauchi. Chr To-
day 15:6-11 Ap 9 '71
Plea of innocence; theory of H. Cohn. il
por Newsweek 77:96+ Mr 15 '71
Trial and death of Jesus, by H. Cohn. Review
Chr Today 15:22+ S 10 '71. E. M. Ya-
mauchi
Sat R 54:22+ Je 19 '71. E. Rivkin

JESUS CHRIST in literature
Christ and the existential imagination. C.
Miller. Chr Today 16:12+ O 22 '71
D. H. Lawrence's appraisal of Jesus. W.
E. Phipps. Chr Cent 88:521-4 Ap 28 '71;
Discussion. 88:861-2, 1365-6 Jl 14, N 17 '71

JESUS CHRIST in music
Jesus Christ superstar: electric age messiah.
C. Edwards. Cath World 213:217-21 Ag '71
JESUS Christ superstar; rock opera. See
Webber, A. L.

JESUS freaks. See Hippies—Religion
JESUS on Honshu; story. See Updike, J.
JET airplane engines
Advanced M45H versions aimed at STOL air-
craft. il Aviation W 94:158-61 My 31 '71
Airbus CF6 production plans resolved. il
Aviation W 94:93+ My 31 '71
Continued engine market shrinkage seen.
M. L. Yaffee. il Aviation W 96:40-1 Ja 3 '72
French goal is broader engine capability.
Aviation W 94:162 My 31 '71
GE's dream engine gets a French accent;
joint development with SNECMA. il Bsns
W p36 D 18 '71
Lockheed study shows RB.211 operating costs
above rivals. R. R. Ropelewski. il Avia-
tion W 94:29-30 Je 7 '71
Lockheed, U.K. stymied on RB.211. J. P.
Woolsey. Aviation W 94:23-5 Mr 15 '71
RB.211 deadline extended for negotiation. H.
J. Coleman. Aviation W 94:23-4 Mr 1 '71
RB.211 hangs on fate of L-1011. Aviation W
94:24 Je 7 '71
RB.211 support withdrawal stirs airline
doubts on British orders. Aviation W 94:
35-6 F 15 '71
Rolls, Pratt & Whitney agree on joint
Pegasus development. Aviation W 95:24 N
1 '71
Turbofan alternative proposed for SST en-
gine. H. D. Watkins. il Aviation W 94:17
Mr 22 '71
U.S. pact gives Germans right to produce
own F-4 engines. Aviation W 95:20 S 20 '71

Air intakes
Engine inlet change designed for reduced 747
noise levels. il Aviation W 94:28 My 10 '71
Refinement of Concorde inlet design continues. il Aviation W 94:62-4 F 8 '71

Control
Microcircuits trim control size, weight; Concorde engine and intake controls. Aviation W 94:106 F 8 '71

Design
Airlines evaluate modification to eliminate
jet fuel dumping. Aviation W 94:26 F 1 '71
Economics of noise rules studied. M. L.
Yaffee. il Aviation W 94:40-2 Ap 12 '71
F101 engine keyed to milestone concept. M.
L. Yaffee. il Aviation W 95:32-4 Ag 9 '71
GE drops SST engine afterburner. Aviation W
94:26 F 15 '71
Hybrid fighter engine designed; continuous
bleed turbojet. M. L. Yaffee. il Aviation
W 95:40-2 S 6 '71
Larzac designers seek markets in U.S. il
Aviation W 94:152-3 My 31 '71
Olympus 593 reaches initial Mach 2 cruise
speed goal; afterburning turbojet Concorde
propulsion system. il Aviation W 94:54-5+
F 8 '71
RB.211 thrust near design goal. Aviation W
94:25 Ap 26 '71
SST engine, wing changes weighed. R. G.
O'Lone. il Aviation W 94:36-8 Mr 15 '71
Supersonic turbines studied for 1980s. M. L.
Yaffee. il Aviation W 94:68-9 My 10 '71
Uprated versions of CF6 developed; with
table. M. L. Yaffee. il Aviation W 95:36-8
Ag 2 '71

Exhaust
Modification of United JT8Ds on schedule.
R. G. O'Lone. il Aviation W 94:27-8 Ap 26
'71
Reduction of stratospheric ozone by nitrogen
oxide catalysts from supersonic transport
exhaust. H. Johnston. bibliog il Science
173:517-22 Ag 6 '71
See also
Airplanes—Pollution control devices
Airplanes, Jet—Pollution

Failure
Afterburner failure slows 001 Concorde. Aviation W 94:22 Je 7 '71

Manufacture
Rolls assembles production RB. 211 engines.
il Aviation W 95:38-9 O 4 '71
TriStar engine may be U.S.-made; with
commentary. il por Bsns W p42-3 Mr 13
'71

Mounting
Redesign of C-5A pylons studied; cause of
fatigue cracks disputed. Aviation W 95:19
N 8 '71

Specifications
Leading international gas turbines; tables.
Aviation W 94:78-9 Mr 8 '71
U.S. gas turbine engines; tables. Aviation W
94:80-1 Mr 8 '71

JET airplane engines—*Continued*

Testing

Astafan test-flown on Hawk Commander. il Aviation W 94:212-15 My 31 '71

Optical system analyzes engines. B. M. Elson. il Aviation W 94:48-9+ Mr 1 '71

Tests of L-1011 continuing. Aviation W 94:26 F 22 '71

Thrust reversers

Fan jet Falcon thrust reverser certification expected in July. Aviation W 94:73 Je 14 '71

JT8D-15 afterbody design has dual role; rear engine silencer/reverser system. il Aviation W 94:156-7 My 31 '71

Major drag reduction sought with nozzle. il Aviation W 94:69-70+ F 8 '71

JET airplanes. See Airplanes, Jet

JET axe. See Fire apparatus

JET boats. See Boats, Jet

JET capital corporation

Control of Texas international gained by Jet capital group. J. P. Woolsey. Aviation W 95:27 D 20 '71

JET cargo planes. See Airplanes, Freight

JET fuel dumping. See Airplanes, Jet—Pollution

JET propulsion

USAF propulsion interests detailed. M. L. Yaffee. Aviation W 94:54-7 Mr 1 '71

JET transports. See Airplanes, Jet

JETSTREAM aircraft, ltd.

JetStream turboprop production restarted by British company. Aviation W 94:19 My 24 '71

JEWEL boxes, cases, etc.

Mini chest for jewelry. T. H. Jones. il Mech Illus 67:100-2+ Ag '71

JEWEL chests. See Jewel boxes, cases, etc.

JEWEL companies, inc.

See also

Osco drug, inc.

JEWELERS

Mobile silversmiths and jewelers 1820-1867; with check list of Mobile silversmiths. S. A. smith. il Antiques 99:407-11 Mr '71

JEWELER'S saws. See Saws

JEWELL, Pliny, 3d

Design with power in mind. il Horticulture 49:36-7+ F '71

JEWELRY

Copper foil jewelry. J. D. Kain. il Sch Arts 71:8-9 Ja '72

Electronic jewelry. V. Ward. il Sch Arts 71:16-19 Ja '72

Impressed clay jewelry. J. F. Warwick. il Sch Arts 71:16-17 S '71

Jewelry of Marci Zelmanoff. R. Lusker. il Craft Horiz 31:16-19 F '71

Sea gems; creations by Marguerite and Hugh Stix. J. A. Segal. il Look 35:40-3 Jl 27 '71

See also

Diamonds

Gems

Goldsmithing

Collectors and collecting

Grandmother's jewel box. G. Klewans. il Hobbies 76:92 My '71

Exhibitions

From slave to siren; exhibition of 19th-century jewelry at Duke university. D. J. Janson. il Art N 70:49-53 My '71

JEWELRY, Ancient

Golden links to the bronze age; display at the Museum of fine arts, Boston. E. Vermeule. il Horizon 13:50-3 Wint '71

JEWELRY boxes, cases, etc.

Jewelry box for your queen. T. H. Jones. il Pop Mech 136:124-7+ Jl '71

JEWELRY crosses. See Cross and crosses

JEWELRY in opera

All that glisters. R. Kerr. il Opera N 35:6-7 Ap 10 '71

JEWELRY making

Copper foil jewelry. J. D. Kain. il Sch Arts 71:8-9 Ja '72

Fun jewelry. K. Berl. il Ceram Mo 19:29 Ja; 27 Ap '71

Horseshoe nail jewelry. O. Johnson. il Sch Arts 70:26-8 F '71

Make your own jewelry; macramé jewelry. il Redbook 137:84-5+ My '71

Stained glass jewelry. il Design 72:40 Sum '71

Your inexperience won't show; brass and bead chokers. il Sunset 147:116+ N '71

JEWELS. See Gems; Jewelry

JEWISH-Arab relations

As Arabs see it. J. P. O'Kane. il America 124:67-8 Ja 23 '71; Reply. R. Gordis. 124:161-2 F 20 '71

Four ways to break the Arab-Israeli stalemate. M. J. Kubic. il Newsweek 78:31 Ag 9 '71

Israel vs. the Arabs. il Sr Schol 99:16-17 D 13 '71

Martin Buber: friend of the court. D. J. Moore. il America 124:231-4 Mr 6 '71; Reply. J. M. Oesterreicher. 124:301 Mr 27 '71

Middle East: frozen. Nat R 23:1100 O 8 '71

Mideast: unstable as water. Time 98:21 Ag 2 '71

My Jewish problem, and ours. S. Stern. il Ramp Mag 10:30-40 Ag '71; Discussion. 10:68-71 O '71

Permanent war; symposium, discussion. Trans-Action 8:4+ N '70

Talk with Golda Meir; interview, ed. by M. Clark. G. Meir. por Time 98:29 Ag '30 '71

See also

Israeli-Arab war, 1967- —Peace and mediation

United Nations—Israel

JEWISH art. See Art, Jewish

JEWISH cookery. See Cookery, Jewish

JEWISH daily forward

Worthy editor. . ; excerpts from A bintel brief; sixty years of letters from the Lower East side to the Jewish daily forward, ed. by I. Metzker. Commentary 51:53-62 Mr '71

JEWISH defense league

Armed summer camp. il Time 98:21 Ag 30 '71

Bully tactics. il Newsweek 77:34 Ja 18 '71

Curbing the J.D.L. il Time 97:21 My 24 '71

Foulmouthed diplomacy. Life 70:28 Ja 29 '71

Kahane's commandos. il por Newsweek 77:29+ Ja 25 '71

Kibitzers. Newsweek 78:29 Jl 19 '71

Never again. Chr Today 15:40 Ap 9 '71

New tension between Russia and U.S; anti-Russian violence. il U S News 70:20-1 Ja 25 '71

Private Jewish war on Russia. il por Time 97:18+ Ja 25 '71

Rabbi Kahane says: I'd love to see the J.D.L. fold up. But; interview, ed. by W. Goodman. M Kahane. il pors N Y Times Mag p32-3+ N 21 '71

Violence is not un-Jewish. il Newsweek 77:32-3 Ja 25 '71

JEWISH education. See Jews—Education

JEWISH folklore. See Folklore—Jews

JEWISH-gentile marriages. See Marriages, Mixed

JEWISH intellectuals. See Intellectuals

JEWISH literature

Holocaust literature: today's burning bush. H. J. Cargas. il America 125:458-9 N 27 '71

Story behind the book: Jewish classical series. D. G. Maryles. Pub W 200:32-3 D 20 '71

See also

Yiddish literature

JEWISH militants

Revolutionism & the Jews. W. Laqueur; R. Alter; N. Glazer. bibliog f Commentary 51:38-61 F '71; Discussion 51:8-10+ Je '71

See also

Jewish defense league

JEWISH-Moslem marriages. See Marriages, Mixed

JEWISH mysticism. See Mysticism—Judaism

JEWISH newspapers

See also

Jewish daily forward

JEWISH parochial schools. See Jews—Education

JEWISH periodicals

See also

Commentary (periodical)

JEWISH philosophy. See Philosophy, Jewish

JEWISH question. See Anti-Semitism

JEWISH refugees. See Refugees, Jewish

JEWISH sects

New Covenanters of Qumran. S. Talmon. il Sci Am 225:72-81 bibliog(p 136) N '71

See also

Reconstructionist Judaism

JEWISH students

How Jewish quotas began. S. Steinberg. Commentary 52:67-76 S '71; Discussion 53:16+ Ja '72

JEWISH studies

Research resources in Jewish studies. Sch & Soc 99:17 Ja '71

JEWISH women

Mother Portnoy's complaints. P. Bart. il Trans-Action 8:69-74 N '70

JHABVALA, R. Prawer
Rose petals; story. New Yorker 47:24-32 Jl 10 '71
Two more under the Indian sun; story. New Yorker 47:34-41 My 29 '71

JI, Maharaj. See Balyogeshwar (Indian guru)

JIGS
Clamp-on bandsaw jig produces perfect circles. G. Gaston. il Pop Mech 136:160 D '71
Ingenious jig for a table saw. R. J. De Cristoforo. il Mech Illus 67:102-4+ Mr '71
Jig pivots for edge doweling. A. Lees. il Pop Sci 199:32 Jl '71
Make this supersafe pusher jig. R. K. Wallace. il Pop Mech 136:188-9 N '71

JIGSAWS
Straight-line cutting with a jigsaw? Yep! R. Capotosto. il Pop Sci 199:22 Ag '71

JIM Walter corporation. See Walter, Jim, corporation

JOAN; musical comedy. See Musical comedies, revues, etc.—Criticisms, plots, etc.

JOANIS, John W.
Corporate utopia: RFD? Nations Bsns 59:90 O '71
Focus on the future; address, January 28, 1971. Vital Speeches 37:275-9 F 15 '71

JOANNA'S peaceable kingdom; story. See Moulton, E.

JOB, Book of. See Bible—Old Testament—Job

JOB aptitude tests. See Aptitude tests

JOB discrimination. See Discrimination in employment

JOB enrichment. See Job satisfaction

JOB hopping. See Labor turnover

JOB hunting. See Applications for positions

JOB interviews. See Employment interviewing

JOB performance. See Employees—Rating

JOB satisfaction
Blue-collar blues. il Newsweek 77:80+ My 17 '71
Challenging the work ethic. H. J. Gans. Cur 126:29-34 F '71
Discontented blue-collar workers; a case study. H. L. Sheppard. il Mo Labor R 94:25-32 Ap '71
Overcoming union opposition to job enrichment. M. S. Myers. bibliog f il Harvard Bsns R 49:37-49 My '71
Productivity: the blue collar blues; address, February 9, 1971. J. M. Rosow. Vital Speeches 37:488-91 Je 1 '71
Unleash the people; employee creativity; address, March 1, 1971. H. R. Sharbaugh. Vital Speeches 37:413-16 Ap 15 '71
Work satisfaction and teacher mobility. R. G. Davison. bibliog Clear House 45:265-8 Ja '71

JOB sharing. See Part time employment

JOB training. See Vocational education

JOBBERS
See also
Book wholesalers

JOBE, Jeff
He's at it again, as high as a kite. A. Verschoth. il por Sports Illus 35:60-2+ O 18 '71 *

JOBS. See Employment; Occupations

JOCKEYS
Sports; horse racing. R. Kahn. Esquire 76:24+ O '71
See also
Avila. G.
Durousseau, L. J.
Shoemaker, W
Women as jockeys

JOENSUU, Oiva I.
Fossil fuels as a source of mercury pollution. bibliog il Science 172:1027-8 Je 4 '71

JOFFE, Sy
Heady dreams at University computing. il por Bsns W p54-5+ My 1 '71 *

JOFFREY ballet. See City center Joffrey ballet

JOGGING
Jogger power, memoirs of a fitness buff; excerpt from On the run from dogs and people. H. Higdon. il Todays Health 49:50-2+ F '71

JOHANNSEN, R. I. Smith-. See Smith-Johannsen, R. I.

JOHANSEN, John M.
Toward a new slang. R. Hughes. il por Time 97:68-9 My 31 '71 *

JOHANSEN, Robert C.
Of politics and prophecy: student activism today. il Chr Cent 88:219-23 F 17 '71

JOHANSSON, Bertram B.
Whisking the garbage. il Sat R 54:40-3 Jl 3 '71

JOHN, Saint, the Baptist
Witness of the Baptist. V. P. McCorry. America 126:inside back cover Ja 8 '72

JOHN XXIII, pope
Improbable triumvirate: Khrushchev, Kennedy, and Pope John. N. Cousins. pors Sat R 54:24-35 O 30 '71 *

JOHN, Elton
New minstrels. pors Harp Baz 104:59 Je '71 *
Rock family affair. il por Life 71:48-9 S 24 '71 *

JOHN, Gospel of. See Bible—New Testament—Gospels—John

JOHN C. Campbell folk school, Brasstown, N.C.
Appalachian folk school. J. M. Ramsay. il Nat Parks & Con Mag 45:22-4 Jl '71

JOHN F. Kennedy center for the performing arts, Washington, D.C.
Against odds, it came off well. C. J. McNaspy. il America 125:228-9 O 2 '71
American ballet theatre & Kennedy, the center. L. Lerman. il Mlle 73:182-3+ S '71
Ariodante, vintage Handel at JFK center. P. J. Smith. Hi Fi 21:MA12 D '71
Artist life. D. J. Soria. il Hi Fi 21:MA6-8+ D '71
Arts center debut: more controversy. il U S News 71:73 S 20 '71
Capital gets some culture. A. Cross. il Am For 77:14-19 N '71
Capital glitter; opening of a performing arts center. R. D. Daniels. il Opera N 36:8-11 S '71
Celebration of the spirit; first concerts at Kennedy center. H. Saal. il por Newsweek 78:29-30+ S 20 '71
Close-up of Kennedy center. il U S News 71:48-50 S 13 '71
Countdown for Kennedy. I. Kolodin. il Sat R 54:37-9+ Jl 31 '71
Cultural crown for the Capital. il Sr Schol 99:20 S 27 '71
Cultural crown for the Nation's capital. il U S News 7038-40 Mr 8 '71
Curtain up. il Newsweek 78:109-10 S 13 '71
Dream realized. J. Onassis. por Ladies Home J 88:113+ S '71
Enter aesthetic populism. H. C. Schonberg. Harper 243:130+ D '71
Fireworks and champagne; gala debut. il Life 70:26-33 Je 11 '71
Government and the arts, again. Nat R 23:1103 O 8 '71
Grand night in a superbunker. il Time 98:40-40C S 20 '71
JFK center for the performing arts. B. Belt. il Hi Fi 21:52-7 S '71
JFK rip-off. il Newsweek 78:37 D 13 '71
Julius Rudel: Washington's music man. J. Roddy. por Look 35:38 S 21 '71
Kennedy center. il Américas 23:15-18 S '71
Kennedy center. R. Evett. New Repub 165:28+ S 25 '71
Kennedy center preview. Newsweek 77:49-50 My 31 '71
Let them eat stubs; blind-seat troubles. il Newsweek 78:27 O 11 '71
Memorial on the Potomac; opening night. K. Auchincloss. il Newsweek 78:22-9 S 20 '71
Music; first performances at Kennedy center. D. Hamilton. Nation 213:284-5 S 27 '71
Music; presentation of Handel's Ariodante at Kennedy center. D. Hamilton. Nation 213:349 O 11 '71
New monuments. R. Hughes. il Time 98:66-7 S 13 '71
Not to be missed: inaugural 1971-1972 season. G. Trotta. il Harp Baz 104:188-9 S '71
Opening of a vast showplace. il Life 71:30-2 S 17 '71
Report:
Handel's Ariodante. R. D. Daniels. Opera N 36:26 N '71
Leonard Bernstein's mass. S. Jenkins. il Opera N 36:20-1 O '71
Washington: a gala to remember. il Time 97:12 Je 7 '71

JOHN F. Kennedy international airport. See New York (city)—Airports

JOHN F. Kennedy library, Cambridge, Mass.
Kennedy non-papers. C. Roberts. il Newsweek 78:24 Ag 9 '71

JOHN F. Kennedy space center. See United States—John F. Kennedy space center

JOHN Fitzgerald Kennedy college, Wahoo, Neb.
J.F.K. college won't die. J. Star. Look 35:47 Ja 12 '71

JOHN Wiley and sons, inc. See Wiley, John, and sons, inc.

JOHNNY Horizon. See Advertising characters

JOHNS, Betty
Obituary
Chr Cent 88:873 Jl 21 '71

JOHNS, Jasper
Art: exhibition of Map based on Buckminster Fuller's Dymaxion airocean world at the Museum of modern art. L. Alloway. Nation 213:541-2 N 22 '71
Imago mundi. D. Shapiro. il Art N 70:40-1+ O '71 •
Treasure Map. il Newsweek 77:89 F 15 '71 •

JOHNS, R. L.
Toward equity in school finance. Am Ed 7:3-6 N '71

JOHNS, Ruth Elizabeth. See Johns, B.

JOHNS-MANVILLE corporation
Johns-Manville tries to quicken the beat. il pors Bsns W p58-60 Ap 3 '71
Rebuilding Johns-Manville. A. Hershman. Duns 97:77 My '71

JOHNSON, A. Benjamin, Jr
Criminal law with a Johnson touch. A. Peters. il pors Ebony 26:93-4+ F '71 •

JOHNSON, A. Myron, and others
C1 inhibitor: evidence for decreased hepatic synthesis in hererditary angioneurotic edema. bibliog il Science 173:553-4 Ag 6 '71

JOHNSON, Alex
Alex and the angry Angels. il por Time 97: 64 Je 28 '71 •
Alex on the bench. il por Newsweek 77:53-4 Je 21 '71 •
For failure to give his best. R. Fimrite. il pors Sports Illus 35:12-17 Jl 5 '71 •

JOHNSON, Ben
New music festival at U. of Illinois. il Hi Fi 21:MA28-9 Ag '71

JOHNSON, Ben, 1920-
Two screen cowboys talk about the reel West & the real West; interview, ed. by M. Ronan. il pors Sr Schol 99:11 D 6 '71

JOHNSON, Benjamin
Style; interview. New Yorker 47:34-5 Ap 24 '71

JOHNSON, Betsey
Clothes are just clothes. il Newsweek 77:77 Mr 29 '71 •

JOHNSON, Bryan H. and Ewing, L. L.
Follicle-stimulating hormone and the regulation of testosterone secretion in rabbit testes. bibliog il Science 173:635-7 Ag 13 '71

JOHNSON, Bushrod Rust
Yankee Quaker Confederate general, by C. M. Cummings. Review
Sat R 54:39 My 22 '71 •

JOHNSON, Carl T.
Lean and angry bear. il Outdoor Life 147:84-5+ My '71

JOHNSON, Charles E.
Mössbauer spectroscopy and biophysics. bibliog il Phys Today 24:35-40 F '71

JOHNSON, Charles Y. and others
Magnetoglow: a new geophysical resource. bibliog il Science 171:379-81 Ja 29 '71

JOHNSON, Charlotte Buel
Mirrors, motors and motion. il Sch Arts 70: 34-5 F '71

JOHNSON, Christopher H.
Communism and the working class before Marx: the Icarian experience. bibliog f il Am Hist R 76:642-89 Je '71

JOHNSON, Claudia Alta (Taylor)
Welcome to the LBJ library. il Read Digest 99:205-8+ Jl '71
about
Portrait of a lady. D. Rabinowitz. Commentary 51:108+ Je '71 •
Wife-power. D. McConathy. por Vogue 157: 110-11+ Je '71 •

JOHNSON, Dale
Ghost of Shelby forest. il Outdoor Life 147: 72+ My '71

JOHNSON, Don M. and Peterson, Dale
Canteen forms adapted from stones. il Ceram Mo 19:30-2 Ap '71

JOHNSON, Donald. See Düing. W. jt. auth.

JOHNSON, Eileen D.
High-altitude gardening, a success story. il Org Gard & Farm 18:54-5 My '71

JOHNSON, Elaine L.
Young printmakers in Latin America. il Art in Am 59:116-17 Ja '71

JOHNSON, Eldon Lee
Survival and after: the outlook for higher education; excerpts from From riot to reason. Todays Ed 60:65-7 S '71

JOHNSON, Elizabeth, 1911-
Margaret Sidney vs Harriet Lothrop: address, October 8, 1970. bibliog Horn Bk 47:139-46; 313-20 Ap, Je '71

JOHNSON, Eric V.
Rare escape from DDT. il Cons 25:2-3 F '71

JOHNSON, Frederick
Play and stay fit. il Parents Mag 46:70-3 N '71

JOHNSON, George Washington
In justice to George Washington Johnson. J. Walsh. il pors Hobbies 75:37-9+ Ja; 37+ F '71

JOHNSON, Gerald W.
Hannibal for president. Am Scholar 41:29-39 Wint '71

JOHNSON, Harold
Requiem for a grandfather. il por Newsweek 77:74-5 Ap 12 '71

JOHNSON, Harry
Drugs and drinking in the business world; interview. por U S News 70:70-3 Mr 22 '71

JOHNSON, Haynes
S.S.T. duel at Mach 3. il Todays Health 49: 17-21 F '71

JOHNSON, J. Stewart
New antiques: art deco and modernism. il Antiques 101:230-6 Ja '72

JOHNSON, J. W.
How to turn your unwanted possessions into money. il Mech Illus 67:57-8+ D '71

JOHNSON, James, Jr
Hell in the factory. il por Time 97:39 Je 7 '71 •

JOHNSON, James A. See Radebaugh, B. F. jt. auth.

JOHNSON, James L.
This plane for hire. il por Time 97:80+ Mr 29 '71 •

JOHNSON, Jerome
Colombo. por Time 98:13 Jl 19 '71 •
It's Joe! They got Joe! il por Newsweek 78: 30-1 Jl 12 '71 •
Mafia: back to the bad old days? il pors Time 98:14-18+ Jl 12 '71 •

JOHNSON, John E. Jr
He writes, he directs, he produces. P. Hudson. por Sr Schol 98:22 Mr 22 '71 •

JOHNSON, John H.
Five major myths of black business; address. il Ebony 27:156-7 D '71

JOHNSON, Joy (Duvall)
Ten teenage troubles. il PTA Mag 65:2-4 bibliog(p35) Ap '71

JOHNSON, Kenneth R.
Teacher attitudes toward nonstandard Negro dialect. Ed Digest 36:45-8 My '71

JOHNSON, Kimbell
Plain talk on employee fitness; excerpt. Cong Digest 50:252+ O '71

JOHNSON, Lady Bird. See Johnson, C. A. T.

JOHNSON, Lefty. See Johnson, Benjamin

JOHNSON, Lester
Johnson's men; exhibition at Martha Jackson gallery. H. Rosenberg. New Yorker 47:117-20 Mr 27 '71 •

JOHNSON, Lyndon Baines
From LBJ: some warnings about today's America; address, November 15, 1971. il por U S News 71:92-3 N 29 '71
about
As Lyndon Johnson sees it. il por Newsweek 77:22+ Je 28 '71 •
Down home in the happy kingdom of L.B.J. H. Sidey. il pors Life 70:44-52 My 21 '71 •
Jigsaw puzzle of history; adaptation of address. J. P. Roche. il por N Y Times Mag p 14-15+ Ja 24 '71; Reply with rejoinder. R. Hilsman. p59+ F 21 '71 •
LBJ: he who gets slapped. G. Wills. Harper 244:92-4 Ja '72 •
LBJ in retirement. il pors U S News 70:71-3 Ap 12 '71 •
LBJ looks back. W. F. Buckley, jr. Nat R 23:1323 N 19 '71 •
LBJ of TV. W. L. O'Neill New Repub 165: 28-30 N 13 '71 •
LBJ reconsidered. E. V. Rostow. por Esquire 75:118-19+ Ap '71
LBJ revisited. Chr Cent 88:1286 N 3 '71 •
LBJification of U.T. F. Lang. Ramp Mag 10:8+ D '71 •
LBJ's best friend: the love story of a man & his dog. L. J. Nugent. il pors Ladies Home J 88:77-9+ Ap '71 •
LBJ's story: 5 critical decisions on Vietnam. il pors U S News 71:77-80 N 8 '71 •
LBJ's view of the LBJ years. il pors Newsweek 78:22+ N 1 '71 •
Lyndon's uncandid memoirs; with views of H. Sidey. pors Time 98:19-20 N 8 '71 •
Parting shots; sitting back and savoring every delicious moment. por Life 70:80 Je 4 '71 •
Seeing things through for JFK. J. K. Galbraith. il pors Sat R 54:37-8+ N 6 '71 •
Some pages not in L.B.J.'s book. H. Sidey. Life 71:4 N 5 '71 •
Vantage point. by L. B. Johnson. Review Life il por 71:13 N 12 '71. A. Schlesinger, jr •
Was Lyndon Johnson a liar? S. Alsop. Newsweek 78:80 Jl 5 '71 •

JOHNSON, Lyndon Baines—about—*Continued*
When the war might have ended; excerpt from The labour government, 1964-70. H. Wilson. il pors Life 70:54B-56+ My 21 '71 •
With Cheops in Texas. J. Osborne. New Repub 164:9-10 Je 5 '71 •
See also
Glassboro conference, 1967
JOHNSON, Lyndon Baines, library. See Lyndon Baines Johnson library, Austin, Tex.
JOHNSON, Margaret F.
Agazzari's Eumelio, a dramma pastorale. bibliog f il Mus Q 57:491-505 Jl '71
JOHNSON, Mendel
New cruising sailboats; suddenly everybody's in the act. il Motor B & S 128: 48-51+ O '71
When storm warnings go up! il Motor B & S 128:8+ S '71
JOHNSON, Neil
Low-voltage remote power control. il Pop Electr 35:69-70+ Jl '71
JOHNSON, Nicholas
Is television messing with your mind? Vogue 158:92 Jl '71
Life party. New Repub 164:21-3 Ap 10 '71
Rx for children's television. PTA Mag 66: 21-4 D '71
Test pattern for living. il por Sat R 54:12-15+ My 29 '71
about
Two bites of the apple. R. L. Shayon. New Repub 165:22+ D 11 '71 •
JOHNSON, Oliver
Horseshoe nail jewelry. il Sch Arts 70:26-8 F '71
JOHNSON, Philip Cortelyou
Art under glass. il Vogue 158:102-5 Ag 15 '71 •
Medical illustration: Philip C. Johnson. H. Meredith-Owens. il Am Artist 35:50-5+ D '71 •
Sculpture under glass. J. M. Dixon. il Arch Forum 133:22-5 D '70
JOHNSON, Pyke, Jr
Re incarnation; poem. Sat R 54:13 Ap 17 '71
JOHNSON, Ralph L. Jr
Man's errand. il Outdoor Life 147:104-7+ Ap '71
JOHNSON, Ray
Masterpiece in the mail? C. Troy. il McCalls 98:44 Ag '71 •
JOHNSON, Raymond E.
See what's coming in pesticide regulation; interview, ed. by F. Bailey. Suc Farm 69:7 Ap '71
JOHNSON, Robert Wood, foundation. See Robert Wood Johnson foundation
JOHNSON, Rodney W.
Spiritual implications of exploring the moon. Chr Today 16:4-6 Ja 7 '72
JOHNSON, Ronald V.
Power of the press. Nation 211:645 D 21 '70 •
JOHNSON, Ross G. and Sheridan, J. D.
Junctions between cancer cells in culture: ultrastructure and permeability. bibliog il Science 174:717-19 N 12 '71
JOHNSON, Samuel
Samuel Johnson and the life of writing, by P. Fussell. Review
Nation 212:601-3 My 10 '71. W. Allen •
JOHNSON, Sheila K.
Christmas card syndrome. il N Y Times Mag p38-9+ D 5 '71
Sociology of Christmas cards. Trans-Action 8:27-9 Ja '71
JOHNSON, Stella
All bankers don't have to be stodgy old men. il pors Ebony 26:58+ S '71 •
JOHNSON, U. Alexis
International whaling commission meets at Washington; address, June 21, 1971. Dept State Bul 65:116-19 Jl 26 '71
Role of police forces in a changing world; address, August 13, 1971. Dept State Bul 65:280-3 S 13 '71
Trends in United States-Japan relations; address, October 18, 1971. Dept State Bul 65:513-17 N 8 '71
United States, our NATO allies, and the Soviet Union in an era of changing foreign relations; address, February 19, 1971. Dept State Bul 64:315-21 Mr 15 '71
JOHNSON, Valerie Miner
Maple leaves among the ivy. Commonweal 95:35-7 O 8 '71
JOHNSON, Virginia E.
Sex questions people don't ask and should; interview, ed. by L. Kent. il pors Vogue 158:88-91 Ag 15 '71
—See Masters, W. H. jt. auth.
JOHNSON, William
As smooth as silk in Sapporo. il Sports Illus 34:16-19 F 22 '71
Greatest athlete in Yates Center, Kansas. il pors Sports Illus 35:26-31 Ag 9 '71

It's one for fun in tomorrow's sun. il Sports Illus 34:39-41 F 1 '71
Legal license to steal the stars. il Sports Illus 34:34-6+ Ap 12 '71
Phantoms of the snow. il Sports Illus 34:54-6+ F 8 '71
Pre-Olympic swing through the soy sauce and Coca-Cola signs. il Sports Illus 35:58-64 N 15 '71
Win one and they give you the ax. il Sports Illus 34:24-6+ Mr 1 '71
JOHNSON C. Smith university, Charlotte, N.C.
South from Fordham. il por Bsns W p91 Mr 20 '71
JOHNSON COUNTY, Kan, library
Discovery in Johnson County. G. Graves. il Am Lib 2:204-6 F '71
JOHNSON publishing company
Why minority publishing? ed. by B. Chambers. il pors Pub W 199:47 Mr 15 '71
JOHNSON-Sea-Link (research submarine) See Submarine research vehicles
JOHNSON service company
Consistent capitalist. M. F. Brdlik. il por Duns 93:65+ Je '69
JOHNSTON, Albert H.
New gift and art books; with portfolio. Pub W 200:43-62 Ag 23 '71
JOHNSTON, Brian
Boyg and the sphinx in Ibsen's theatre. Yale R 60:366-82 Mr '71
JOHNSTON, Edward E.
Trust Territory of the Pacific Islands; statement, May 26, 1971. Dept State Bul 65:209-17 Ag 23 '71
JOHNSTON, George
Wild apples; Indoors; Self-portrait; Pride of ownership; poems. Poetry 118:139-40 Je '71
JOHNSTON, Harold
Reduction of stratospheric ozone by nitrogen oxide catalysts from supersonic transport exhaust. bibliog il Science 173:517-22 Ag 6 '71
JOHNSTON, Jill
Opinion: a lesbian and a homosexual on female sexuality. Mlle 74:76 N '71
JOHNSTON, Richard W.
Black Bart and the mechanical marlin. il por Sports Illus 35:34-8 Ag 16 '71
College football. Sports Illus 35:77-8 D 13 '71
Conservation. Sports Illus 35:86+ S 13 '71
Playground divided. il por Sports Illus 35: 78-81+ N 8 '71
Surfing. il Sports Illus 35:102-3 D 6 '71
JOHNSTON, Velma
Fight to save wild horses. il Time 98:48-51 Jl 12 '71 •
JOHNSTON, William
Superthinking: an introduction to Christian Zen, excerpt from Christian Zen. America 125:28-30 Jl 24 '71
JOHNSTONE, L. Craig
Ecocide and the Geneva protocol. For Affairs 49:711-20 Jl '71
JOINERY
How to build a table the Chinese way. D. Warren. il por Pop Sci 199:104-6+ N '71
JOINT adventures
Bally who? Melville joint venture. Forbes 108:32-3 N 15 '71
Cooking big deals with Russia. il Bsns W p28-9 D 4 '71
GE's dream engine gets a French accent; joint development with SNECMA. il Bsns W p36 D 18 '71
Going 50-50 in east Europe; east-west deals. il Bsns W p41+ Ja 16 '71
Long wait; Deere & co. joint venture with Italy's Fiat, S.p.A. il Forbes 108:55-6 D 1 '71
Marriage, Swedish-American style; RTE-ASEA. il Forbes 107:50 F 15 '71
Partners in profits, and losses. il Duns 98: 67-8 O '71
Rockwell Parsons fails to connect; steam turbine-generator venture. Bsns W p31-2 Ag 14 '71
Texans make it big in the city; Burston & Texas commerce bank, ltd. Bsns W p33 My 29 '71
See also
Distrigas corporation
JOINT Canada-United States water resource committee (proposed)
U.S.-Canada committee to study flooding in Pembina River basin; text of communique, October 13, 1971. Dept State Bul 65:522 N 8 '71
JOINT committee on atomic energy. See United States—Congress—Joint committee on atomic energy

JOINT committee on society, development and peace
Churches and the oppressed; the WCC and the Vatican. W. Triggs. Chr Cent 88:484 Ap 21 '71
Warfare on the ecumenical frontier. Chr Cent 88:713 Je 9 '71
JOINT committee on the environment (proposed) See United States—Congress—Joint committee on the environment (proposed)
JOINT congressional committee to investigate the origins of the Vietnamese war (proposed) See United States—Joint congressional committee to investigate the origins of the Vietnamese war (proposed)
JOINT economic committee. See United States —Congress—Joint economic committee
JOINT United States-Canadian committee on trade and economic affairs
U.S.-Canadian economic committee meets at Ottawa; statement with text of joint communique, November 25, 1970. W. P. Rogers. Dept State Bul 63:730-2 D 14 '70
JOINT United States—Japan committee on trade and economic affairs
Japan-U.S. cabinet committee honored by President Nixon, exchange of toasts, September 10, 1971. R. M. Nixon; T. Fukuda. Dept State Bul 65:353-4 O 4 '71
Joint Japan-U.S. committee on trade and economic affairs holds eighth meeting at Washington; remarks, September 9, with text of communique, September 10, 1971. W. P. Rogers. Dept State Bul 65:346-53 O 4 '71
JOINT ventures. See Joint adventures
JOINTERS (woodworking machinery)
Bonus shop tricks you can do with a jointer. R. J. De Cristoforo. il Pop Sci 199:100-2+ D '71
JOINTS
Why knuckles crack. il Time 98:45 Ag 16 '71
Diseases
See also
Arthritis
JOINTS (carpentry)
Easy route to perfect hopper joints. R. J. De Cristoforo. il Pop Sci 199:108-11 N '71
New variations on the old mortise and tenon. R. J. De Cristoforo. il Pop Sci 199:100-2 O '71
You can make professional-fitting dowel joints. D. Warren and H. Wicks. il Pop Mech 136:114-17 Ag '71
JOKES. See Humor
JOLLEY, Thomas Glenn
Reporter without a country. por Sr Schol 99:16-17 Ja 10 '72 •
JOLLY, Cynthia
Tchaikovsky at home. il por Opera N 35:10-15 My 15 '71
JOLSON, Alfred J.
Church-state countdown in Rhodesia. America 124:481-3 My 8 '71
JONAS, Eugen
Birth control by astrology; excerpt from Psychic discoveries behind the iron curtain. S. Ostrander and L. Schroeder. Harp Baz 104:104-5 F '71 •
JONAS, Frank H.
Matter of opinion: Mormonism's Negro policy. Am West 8:48 N '71
JONAS, Gerald
Reporter at large. New Yorker 47:92+ Mr 13; 99-104+ Mr 20 '71
Song, with burden; poem. Sat R 54:88 Mr 13 '71
JONAS, Louis Paul
Hands that see. W. Trimm. por Cons 25:16 Je '71 •
JONASON, Per
Project management, Swedish style. Harvard Bsns R 49:104-9 N '71
JONES, Allan W. See Gulati, J. jt. auth.
JONES, Ann Haydon
Women lobbers. il pors Newsweek 77:90-1 My 3 '71 •
JONES, Antony Charles Robert Armstrong-, 1st earl of Snowdon. See Snowdon, A. C. R. A.-J.
JONES, Bobby. See Jones, R. T. jr
JONES, Charles M. See Da Costa, C. P. jt. auth.
JONES, Clara Stanton
Detroit's top librarian. il pors Ebony 27: 115-16+ N '71
about
Emancipated librarian. L. DeView. por McCalls 98:46 Ap '71 •

JONES, Clifford A.
Delaying the game. il por Time 99:58-9 Ja 10 '72 •
JONES, David Cadwalader
Magic mushrooms; drama. Plays 30:63-5 Ap '71
—See Mahlmann, L. jt. auth.
JONES, Derek
Public ministry in a London suburb. Chr Cent 88:1309-10 N 3 '71
JONES, Donald J. Lloyd-. See Lloyd-Jones, D. J.
JONES, Sir Edward Coley Burne-. See Burne-Jones. E. C.
JONES, Edward W.
Otter-proof bulkheading. il Parks & Rec 6: 43-4+ My '71
JONES, Fletcher
New breed, new ideas, new taxes. A. Wright. il pors Sports Illus 34:48-53 Je 7 '71 •
JONES, G. R. See Burbank, R. D. jt. auth.
JONES, G. William
Eroticism and the art of film; address, 1970. il Library J 96:3809-10 N 15 '71
JONES, Gordon
LJ proves thoroughbreds are color-blind. il pors Ebony 26:100-2+ N '70
JONES, Harold D.
Memo to the building committee. Library J 96:1579 My 1 '71
JONES, Howard
Breaking through the sound barrier. R. T. Coe. il Art N 70:44-5+ Sum '71 •
JONES, J. Raymond
Where are they now? il pors Newsweek 77:20 Je 7 '71 •
JONES, Jack
Top drivers make the grade. il Am Ed 7:34-40 N '71
JONES, James, 1921-
Harry Gallagher's Paris revolution; story; excerpt from The merry month of May. Esquire 75:73-81 Ja '71
Scenes from the almost revolution; story; excerpt from The merry month of May. Harper 242:78-80 F '71
about
Twosomes and threesomes in gray Paree. J. W. Aldridge. Sat R 54:23-6 F 13 '71 •
JONES, James Earl
Wounded animal. T. E. Kalem. por Time 97: 75 Ap 26 '71 •
JONES, James H.
Financial hero in New Orleans. il por Bsns W p80 S 18 '71 •
JONES, Jesse Holman
Professional SOB. por Forbes 108:16 Ag 1 '71 •
JONES, Karl P.
Roses as shrubs. il Horticulture 49:38-40 O '71
JONES, Lawrence W.
Liquid hydrogen as a fuel for the future. bibliog il Science 174:367-70 O 22 '71
JONES, LeRoi
Black (art) drama is the same as black life. il Ebony 26:74-6+ F '71
JONES, Loyal
Appalachia. il Todays Ed 60:54-5 Ap '71
JONES, Marie
Indian library aides and a librarian friend. il Wilson Lib Bul 46:324-5 D '71 •
JONES, Norah E.
Undergraduate library, for undergraduates! address, 1970. il por Wilson Lib Bul 45:584-90 F '71
JONES, Norman Howard-. See Howard-Jones, N.
JONES, Orville E.
What are today's college-age counselors really like? excerpts from address. il por Camp Mag 43:11-12+ Ja '71
JONES, Peaches
Hollywood stunt girl. W. P. Burrell. il pors Ebony 27:147-8+ D '71 •
JONES, Phil B.
Machinery management. See issues of Successful farming
JONES, Richard L. and others
Host-seeking stimulant for parasite of corn earworm; isolation, identification, and synthesis. bibliog il Science 173:842-3 Ag 27 '71
JONES, Robert
Preacher poem. Chr Cent 88:591 My 12 '71
JONES, Robert A.
Nice piece of desert. il Nation 213:616-26 D 13 '71
JONES, Robert F.
¡Ay chihuahua! What a race. il por Sports Illus 34:20-1 F 8 '71
Can-do Scot in the Can-Am. il por Sports Illus 35:22-3 Jl 5 '71

JONES, Robert F.—*Continued*
Fast last fling for an old girl. il Sports Illus 34:16-21 Mr 29 '71
Harvey on the lam. por Sports Illus 35:55-6+ Ag 23 '71
Hoist a bottle to leadfoot U. il por Sports Illus 35:26-7 S 20 '71
Hunting (cont) Sports Illus 35:74+ N 8; 82-3+ D 6 '71
Johnny Lightning drives through the wreckage. il por Sports Illus 34:26-9 Je 7 '71
Just one more for the road, s'il vous plait. il Sports Illus 35:26-8+ O 25 '71
Lift a pint to the king, luv. il por Sports Illus 35:14-17 Jl 26 '71
Motor sports (cont) Sports Illus 34:56 F 22; 35:48-9 Jl 5; 73+ O 11 '71
Peter, Peter, Donohue beater. il por Sports Illus 34:34-6+ My 24 '71
Prime of Mr John Brodie. por Sports Illus 35:62-6 S 20 '71
Real choosy about the Doozy. il Sports Illus 34:22-5 My 10 '71
Slide-rule boys at Indy. il pors Sports Illus 34:32-4+ My 31 '71
Something new in the solar system. il Sports Illus 34:12-19 Je 21 '71
Super bowl. il por Sports Illus 34:18+ Ja 18 '71
To kill a memory that still hurts. il por Sports Illus 34:18-21 Ja 11 '71
White magic in a noble black land. il Sports Illus 35:48-57 Ag 2 '71
JONES, Robert R.
Winterized dining hall provides for 11 different functions. il Camp Mag 43:13 S '71
JONES, Robert Tyre, 1902-1971
Golfer of the golden era. il por Newsweek 78:48 D 27 '71 •
JONES, Shirley
Shirley Jones: her struggle for family success. B. Davidson. il pors Good H 173:30-2+ Ag '71 •
JONES, Stacy V.
Inventions. See issues of Science digest
JONES, Thad
Whoops of joy. il por Time 97:73 Mr 15 '71 •
JONES, Thomas B. and others
Dielectric siphons. bibliog il Science 174:1232-3 D 17 '71
JONES, Tom H.
Jewelry box for your queen. il Pop Mech 136:124-7+ Jl '71
Mini chest for jewelry. il Mech Illus 67:100-2+ Ag '71
JONES, W. D.
Medicare mob. il pors Esquire 76:100 Ag '71 •
JONES, Walter
Jazznite. Criticism
New Yorker 47:96 My 1 '71 •
JONES and Laughlin steel corporation
Conscience of a steel worker. B. Ehrenreich and J. Ehrenreich. il Nation 213:268-71 S 27 '71
Waiting for tenure at Jones & Laughlin. por Bsns W p20 Ja 23 '71
JONESBORO, Tenn.
History in towns. M. D. Eberling. il Antiques 100:420-4 S '71
JONG, Erica Mann
Climbing you; Universal explicator; Wives of Mafiosi; Man who can only paint death; Seminar; poems. Poetry 118:201-5 Jl '71
Seventeen warnings in search of a feminist poem. Nation 212:444 Ap 5 '71
Where it begins; Narcissus, photographer; Touch; Books; poems. Poetry 117:309-13 F '71
JONQUILS. See Narcissus
JONSSON, Olof
White tracks on the moon. C. Leinster. il por Life 70:29 F 26 '71 •
JOPLIN, Janis
Janis and Jimi, op. posth. W. Bender. pors Time 97:76 F 15 '71 •
Music. M. Josephson. il pors Art in Am 59:96-7 S '71 •
Rock, etc. E. Willis. New Yorker 47:81-2 Ag 14 '71 •
JOPLIN, Scott
King of rag. H. Saal. il por Newsweek 78:97-8 N 1 '71 •
Piano rags by Scott Joplin. por Am Rec G 37:354-5 F '71 •
JORDAN, Chuck
Motor trend interview. il pors Motor T 23:88+ Jl '71
JORDAN, Eileen Herbert
Beautiful, beautiful me; story. Ladies Home J 89:78-9 Ja '72
2312-35-989 where did you go? story. Ladies Home J 88:106 N '71

JORDAN, Joan
Working women and the equal rights amendment. Trans-Action 8:16+ N '70
JORDAN, Pat
Clutch of odd birds. il Sports Illus 35:56-60+ Ag 30 '71
College basketball. Sports Illus 34:50 Mr 1 '71
Icemen you'd love to hate. il Sports Illus 35:86-9+ D 13 '71
Man who was cut out for the job; excerpt from Black coach. il Sports Illus 35:90-4+ O 11 '71
Old hand with a prospect. il Sports Illus 34:72-6+ Je 14 '71
JORDAN, Porter
Cast off! story. Har Yrs 11:14-15 My '71
JORDAN, Raphael
Freak out; poem. Cath World 213:29 Ap '71
JORDAN, Robert Paul
Oklahoma, the adventurous one. il Nat Geog 140:149-89 Ag '71
JORDAN, Vernon E. Jr
Black people and labor unions; address, November 22, 1971. Vital Speeches 38:171-4 Ja 1 '72
about
Man at the bridge. por Time 97:25 Je 28 '71 •
JORDAN
Jordan in turmoil. H. N. Howard. bibliog f Cur Hist 62:14-19+ Ja '72

Politics and government
Black day in Cairo; assassination of W. Tal. il Newsweek 78:50 D 13 '71
Guerrillas on the run. il Time 98:23 Ag 2 '71
Jordan's Hussein: things will work out; statements. Hussein. por Time 98:27 Jl 5 '71
JORDEN, Bill
Bill Jorden: the real and exotic New York. il Pop Phot 69:78-81 Jl '71 •
JORIS, Françoise Mallet-. See Mallet-Joris, F.
JORSTAD, Erling
Greening of revival: the Jesus revolution and other signs. il Cath World 213:265-8 S '71
JOSEPH, James
De-shocking solutions to electric kisses. il Todays Health 49:14 F '71
How to outmaneuver a firestorm. il Todays Health 49:34-9+ S '71
JOSEPH, Richard
Four oarsmen of the epochal trips. il Esquire 75:82-3+ F '71
Glory returns to Fragrant Harbor. il pors Esquire 75:87-93 Ag '71
This is Israel? il Esquire 75:114-21 Mr '71
Travel notes. See issues of Esquire
Six of the healthiest vacation spots in the U.S.A. il Todays Health 49:24-7+ Je '71
JOSEPH E. Seagram and sons. See Seagram, Joseph E, and sons
JOSEPH P. Kennedy, Jr. foundation
Kennedy's clinical Camelot. J. R. Nelson. Chr Cent 88:1351-2 N 17 '71
JOSEPH Regenstein library. See Chicago. University—Libraries
JOSEPH White Bull (Sioux chief) See White Bull
JOSEPH White Cow Bull (Sioux Indian) See White Cow Bull
JOSÉPHINE, consort of Napoleon I, emperor of the French
From Martinique to Malmaison. M. Simons. il por Sat R 54:49-50+ Mr 13 '71 •
JOSEPHS, Lois S.
Electives in the English high school program: drama and flexibility. bibliog Engl J 60:246-50 F '71
JOSEPHSON, Barney
Profiles. W. Balliett. pors New Yorker 47:50-6+ O 9 '71 •
JOSEPHSON, Mary
Architecture. il Art in Am 59:108-9 Mr '71
Music. il pors Art in Am 59:96-7 S '71
Warhol: the medium as cultural artifact. bibliog il Art in Am 59:40-6 My '71
JOSEPHSON effect. See Superconductivity
JOSEPHY, Alvin M. Jr
Custer myth. il por Life 71:48-52+ Jl 2 '71
Murder of the Southwest. il Audubon 73:52:69 Jl '71
JOSEY, E. J.
Coddling segregation. por Library J 96:1778-9 My 15 '71
Faculty status for librarians; address, November 7, 1970. bibliog por Library J 96:1333-6 Ap 15 '71
Statement on the IFC report. por Library J 96:2828-31 S 15 '71
JOSHUA trees. See Yucca

JOSQUIN Deprès. See Deprès, J.
JOULE effect engines. See Heat engines
JOURARD, Sidney M. and Whitman, Ardis
Fear that cheats us of love. Redbook 137:82-3+ O '71

JOURNALISM
Freelance job idea: school public relations. W. Voncannon. il Writers Digest 52:20-1 Ja '72
See also
College and school journalism
Crime and the press
Environmental news
Foreign correspondents
Freedom of the press
Interviewing
Journalistic ethics
News
Newspaper court reporting
Newspapers
Reporters and reporting
Television broadcasting—News
Women as journalists

Authorship
On epidemic first personism. H. Gold. Atlan 228:85-7 Ag '71
One idea: multiple sales. M. W. Fedo. il Writers Digest 51:31 Je '71
What the city desk uses. N. Melnick. il Writers Digest 52:22-3+ Ja '72

Periodicals
Growing phenomenon of the Journalism review. N. Hill. il Sat R 54:59-60 S 11 '71
Journalism's in-house critics. il Time 98:74 D 6 '71
New voices of newsmen: local journalism reviews. D. Rose. il Nation 214:43-6 Ja 10 '72
See also
More (periodical)

Study and teaching
Enlivening the publications class. J. A. Jennings. Todays Ed 60:33 F '71
Journalism education, a matter of coexistence. M. L. Stein. Sat R 54:71-3 O 9 '71
World press and the teaching of journalism. J. Tebbel. il Sat R 54:64-5+ S 11 '71

Japan
See also
Newspapers—Japan

United States
Our troubled press, ed. by J. Boylan and A. Balk. Review
New Repub 165:25-7 N 6 '71. R. Whittemore
Presidency & the press; with editorial comment. D. P. Moynihan. Commentary 51:6-7, 41-52 Mr '71; Discussion. 52:6+ Jl '71
What we don't know will hurt us. R. L. Tobin. Sat R 54:85-6 N 13 '71
See also
Newspapers—United States
Periodicals—United States

JOURNALISM, Religious
Lugubrious economics of religious journalism. Chr Cent 88:212 F 17 '71

JOURNALISM as a profession
Commencement for journalists. J. Hohenberg. Sat R 54:57-8+ Je 12 '71

JOURNALISTIC ethics
Again the Pentagon papers. Time 98:30 Jl 19 '71
Can the press police itself? B. Francois. America 124:433-5 Ap 24 '71
Ethical considerations in public relations; the government and the press; address, April 2, 1971. J. Miller. Vital Speeches 37:421-4 My 1 '71
New voices of newsmen: local journalism reviews. D. Rose. il Nation 214:43-6 Ja 10 '72
See also
Confidential communications—Press
Crime and the press

JOURNALISTIC photography. See Photography, Journalistic

JOURNALISTS
Anderson's brass ring. il por Time 99:34 Ja 17 '72
Can a good journalist be a good citizen? J. Hohenberg. il Sat R 54:87-8+ N 13 '71
Journalistic ideal; excerpts from statement, May 1971. C. Sanz de Santamaria. Américas 23:1 Je '71

Radicalism and the young journalist. W. E. Porter. il Sat R 54:65-6 D 11 '71
See also
Foreign correspondents
International press institute
National press club
Negro journalists
War correspondents
Women as journalists
also names of journalists, e.g. E. Cochrane

JOURNALS. See Periodicals
JOURNALS, Personal. See Diaries
JOUSTING. See Tournaments
JOVA, Joseph John
OAS foreign ministers discuss coastal state fisheries question; statement, January 27, 1971. Dept State Bul 64:245-7 F 22 '71
Review of the progress and problems of the Organization of American states; statement, July 26, 1971. bibliog f il Dept State Bul 65:284-93 S 13 '71
U.S. calls for joint solutions to western hemisphere problems; statement, April 29, 1971. Dept State Bul 64:783-6 Je 14 '71

JOVANOVICH, William
Tumult of talk. Am Scholar 41:40-9 Wint '71
Universal Xerox life compiler machine. Am Scholar 40:249-55 Spr '71

JOWITT, Deborah
Dance. il Art in Am 59:102-3 My '71
Post-Judson dance. il Art in Am 59:81-7 S '71

JOY, Art F.
Dial-a-bison. il Parks & Rec 6:118-19+ Ja '71

JOY, Edward T.
Holland & sons and the furniture of Osborne house. il Antiques 99:580-5 Ap '71

JOY
Joy? Why? V. P. McCorry. America 125:496 D 4 '71

JOYCE, James
Auditory experience in Joyce's Portrait. R. Tarbox. bibliog Am Imago 27:301-28 Wint '70

JOYCE Kilmer memorial forest. See National forests

JOYFUL noises; story. See Ibbotson, E.

JOYNER, Glenn P.
What parents should know about high school football. il Parents Mag 46:66-7+ O '71

JOYNER, James A.
Photo print dryer you can build for peanuts. il Pop Mech 135:120-1 F '71

JUAN Carlos, prince of Spain
Prince Juan Carlos of Spain visits the United States; exchange of greetings and toasts. Dept State Bul 64:236-9 F 22 '71

about
Behind the visit of Spain's future king. il por U S News 70:86 F 8 '71
A Borbón in Washington. il por Time 97:24 F 8 '71
Crown for Juan Carlos? Time 98:21 Ag 23 '71

JUAN, Don, 1891-
Further conversations with Don Juan; excerpt from A separate reality. C. Castaneda. il Esquire 75:75-89+ Mr '71; Discussion. 75:14 My '71
Separate reality, by C. Castaneda. Review
Commonweal 94:482 S 17 '71. J. Grange

JUAN de Fuca
Old man of the western sea. K. C. Tessendorf. il Américas 23:25-32 S '71

JUAN DE FUCA STRAIT
Old man of the western sea; Juan de Fuca. K. C. Tessendorf. il Américas 23:25-32 S '71

JUAN Muraña; story. See Borges, J. L.

JUDAICA. See Jewish studies

JUDAISM
Catholics, Jews and Israel. J. B. Sheerin. Cath World 213:115-16 Je '71; Discussion. 214-5, 101 O, D '71
Paganism-Christianity-Judaism, by M. Brod. Review
Commentary 51:85-6 My '71. A. A. Cohen
Sound of the shofar. il por Time 98:69 O 4 '71
Turning on to Jeshua; Messianic Judaism. E. E. Plowman. il Chr Today 16:33-4 D 17 '71
See also
Circumcision
Jesus Christ—Jewish interpretations
Jews
Mysticism—Judaism
Passover
Philosophy, Jewish
Reconstructionist Judaism
Tradition (Judaism)

JUDAISM—*Continued*
Study and teaching
Jewish studies course via TV; City university of New York. Sch & Soc 99:402 N '71
See also
Jewish studies
JUDAISM and Christianity. See Christianity and other religions
JUDD, A. E.
Are modern military radars infallible? il Pop Electr 35:45-51 S '71
JUDD, Donald
Don Judd's less is more art. B. Rose. il Vogue 158:88 Jl '71 *
Exquisite minimalist. R. Hughes. il por Time 97:68-9+ My 24 '71 *
JUDD, Henry A.
What to do before the restorationist comes. il Antiques 101:209-16 Ja '72
JUDD, James B. See Lynts, G. W. jt. auth.
JUDGE, Anthony J. N.
Information systems and inter-organizational space. bibliog f Ann Am Acad 393:47-64 Ja '71
JUDGE, Joseph
New Orleans and her river. il Nat Georg 139:151-87 F '71
Saturday's child Hong Kong. il Nat Geog 140:540-7 O '71
Zulus: black nation in a land of apartheid. il Nat Geog 140:738-51 D '71
JUDGE; story. See Hughes, M. G.
JUDGES
Square's night behind bars; Nevada graduate course for judges. P. E. Wilson. por Nation 212:200-6 F 15 '71
Turnabout trials; competence, propriety and qualifications questioned. il por Time 98:44-5 Jl 19 '71
Your honors, you're under arrest; Reno course for judges. il Time 98:50 S 6 '71
See also
Negro judges
United States—Supreme court
Women as judges

Appointment, qualifications, tenure, etc.
American judges: their selection, tenure, variety and quality. S. Goldman. bibliog f il Cur Hist 61:1-8+ Jl '71
British, French and American systems of justice compared. B. C. Canon. bibliog f Cur Hist 61:97-104+ Ag '71
JUDGING of photographs. See Photography—Criticism, interpretation, etc.
JUDGMENT day
Day of the Lord. V. P. McCorry. America 125:383-4 N 6 '71
See also
Second advent
JUDGMENTS
See also
Indeterminate sentence
JUDICIARY. See Judges
JUDSON, Barbara A. See Goldstein, A. jt. auth.
JUETTNER, Walter R.
Piloting contests. il Motor B & S 128:54-5+ Ag '71
28 ways to stretch your boating buck. Motor B & S 127:114-15+ Mr '71
JUGO, Miguel de Unamuno y. See Unamuno y Jugo, M. de
JUGOSLAVIA. See Yugoslavia
JUGS
Handbuilt puzzle jugs. R. F. Eilenberger. il Ceram Mo 19:26-9 S '71
JUGS, insulated. See Thermos containers
JUHASZ, Ferenc
Comment. J. Atlas. Poetry 119:50 O '71 *
JUILLIARD American opera center. See Lincoln Center for the performing arts, New York—Juilliard school
JUILLIARD school. See Lincoln center for the performing arts, New York—Juilliard school
JUILLIARD string quartet. See String quartets
JULESZ, Bela. See Blakemore, C. jt. auth.
JULIEN, Claude
Long night's journey into day; reprint. Nation 212:431-4 Ap 5 '71
JULLIAN, Philippe
Olga the wild. il pors Vogue 158:154-9+ O 1 '71
JULLIEN, Claude Francois
(ed) See Küng, H. Christianity with a human face

JUMPING
She gets her back up; D. Brill. A. Verschoth. por Sports Illus 34:52-3 F 22 '71
JUMPING spiders. See Spiders
JUNCTIONS (physiology)
Junctions between cancer cells in culture: ultrastructure and permeability. R. G. Johnson and J. D. Sheridan. bibliog il Science 174:717-19 N 12 '71
See also
Neuromuscular junctions
JUNE, Orrin Wickersham
Living with antiques. il Antiques 100:438-41 S '71
JUNEAU, Alaska
Alaska's past and sourdough waffles. il Sunset 146:69 Je '71
JUNG, Walter G.
IC potpourri. il Radio-Electr 43:68-9 Ja '72
IC power supplies. il Radio-Electr 42:58-9 Ag; 69-70+ S '71
Inside linear IC's. il Radio-Electr 42:60-1 N; 50-1 D '71
Potpourri of IC applications. il Radio-Electr 42:58-60 Je '71
Power supplies using the uA723. il Radio-Electr 42:49-50 Jl '71
JUNGER, Theresa
Pinhole camera. il Sch Arts 71:14-15 D '71
JUNGK, Robert
Breakthrough to tomorrow. UNESCO Courier 24:9-17 Ap '71
JUNGLE fowls
Jungle cocks, trout flies, and smugglers. E. N. Layne and S. Hartgen. il Audubon 73:38-43 My '71
JUNIOR achievement companies
Mini-businesses of junior achievement. A. Steinberg. Read Digest 98:19-22+ My '71
JUNIOR baseball. See Baseball
JUNIOR college buildings. See College architecture
JUNIOR college libraries. See College libraries
JUNIOR colleges
Allies or adversaries? High school and junior college. J. Grable. bibliog Clear House 46:195-9 D '71
Areas of concern for comprehensive community colleges. M. K. Reimer. bibliog f Sch & Soc 99:47-9 Ja '71
Education for government careers; excerpts from report. A. S. Korim. por Sch & Soc 99:328 O '71
Escrow college: high school students study at community colleges. P. Parker. bibliog il Clear House 45:439-43 Mr '71
Here's what junior-college faculties think. Todays Ed 60:67-8 Mr '71
Occupational education and black students. il Sch & Soc 99:76-7 F '71
Planning community college resource centers. L. Giles bibliog il Am Lib 2:51-4 Ja '71
St Louis' educational supermarket. N. P. Salus. il Am Ed 7:24-8 Mr '71
See also
Catholic junior colleges

History
Community-junior college in historical and cultural perspective. R. J. Frankie and E. E. DuBois. bibliog f Sch & Soc 99:45-7 Ja '71
JUNIOR high school library catalog
Junior high school library catalog. 2d ed. Review
Library J 96:2856 S 15 '71. J. Higgins; Reply. B. Plucker. 96:2808-9 S 15 '71
JUNIOR high school teachers. See Teachers
JUNIOR high schools
See also
Middle schools
Curriculum
Learning to cope in Prince Georges County; new course on Teen-agers' rights and responsibilities for all eighth-graders. B. L. Collier. il Sat R 54:64-5+ My 22 '71
JUNIPER
Red cedar. C. E. Lewis. il Horticulture 49:18-19+ My '71
Trees of the totem culture; excerpts from Edge of a continent. D. G. Kelley. il Am West 8:18-21+ My '71
JUNKER, Howard
Walk-in: when man-space becomes play-space. il Vogue 157:158 Mr 1 '71
JUNKINS, Donald
Uncle Harry: shooting partridge, 1941; poem. Atlan 229:38 Ja '72

JUNKS
Chinese junks. W. Menard. il Sea Front 17: 322-31 N '71

JUPITER (planet)
How it is on Jupiter. il Chem 45:24-5 Ja '72
See also
Space flight to Jupiter

Atmosphere
Casting some (star) light on Jupiter's atmosphere. D. E. Thomsen. il Sci N 99:267-8 Ap 17 '71
Explaining a Jovian mystery; Jupiter's great red spot. Time 98:50-1 Jl 5 '71
Jupiter, an unidentified feature in the 5-micron spectrum of the north equatorial belt. G. Münch and G. Neugebauer. bibliog il Science 174:940-1 N 26 '71
Jupiter's atmosphere and an eclipse of Ganymede. il Sky & Tel 41:151-2 Mr '71

Observations
Lunar and planetary laboratory studies of Jupiter. G. P. Kuiper. il por Sky & Tel 43: 4-8 Ja '72 (to be cont)
Observations of new major disturbances on Jupiter. il Sky & Tel 42:176-80 S '71
Star is stillborn; University of Texas findings. Newsweek 78:49 Ag 2 '71
When you wish upon a Jupiter. Sci N 100: 261 O 16 '71

Satellites
See Satellites

JURENAS, Albert C.
Free school. Clear House 45:418 Mr '71

JURIES, Art
Jurying: science, art, or gamble? H. J. Brennan. por Ceram Mo 19:31-2 O '71

JURISPRUDENCE
See also
Sociological jurisprudence

JURISPRUDENCE, Medical. See Medical jurisprudence

JURKOWSKI, John
Scenario; story. New Yorker 47:40-5 Ap 17 '71

JURY, Mark
GI's Vietnam photo book; excerpt from The Vietnam photo book. il Look 35:22-6+ S 21 '71

JURY
American jury system. M. J. Bloomstein. Cur Hist 60:357-61+ Je '71
Case for trial by jury. J. M. Murtagh. America 125:309-11 O 23 '71
Civil juries lose a decision; abolishing jury trials in civil suits. Nations Bsns 59:24 My '71
Jury system reform. A. S. Nanes. bibliog f Cur Hist 61:92-6+ Ag '71
Life among the Manson jurors. il Time 97:42+ Ap 12 '71
Manson jury: end of the long ordeal. H. Farrell. il por Life 70:44-8 Ap 16 '71
Now: mini-juries. Sr Schol 98:5 Ap 5 '71
Sequestering sanity. New Repub 164:14 F 20 '71
This month's feature: the question of revising the jury system. Cong Digest 50:193-224 Ag '71
See also
Grand jury

JUST, Cassia
Reins in Spain; Le Monde interview; excerpts. Commonweal 93:386 Ja 22 '71

JUST, Ward S.
Three Washington stories. Atlan 228:65-8+ D '71

JUST call me honey; story. See Bahr, E.-J.

JUSTICE, Administration of
See also
Bail
Courts
Criminal law
Criminal procedure
Jury
Preventive detention
Probation
Searches and seizures
Speedy trial

Alabama
Judge Branch of Greene County. il pors Ebony 26:82-5 Ag '71

Alaska
Cop and the lion. Time 98:43 D 27 '71

California
Ex-reporter's privilege; case of W. Farr. Newsweek 78:42 Ag 9 '71
Miranda extended; case of B. B. Burton. Time 99:58 Ja 10 '72

Florida
By the sea of confusion; problems over new speedy-trial deadlines. Time 98:80 N 8 '71
Eye-opener for Will; W. Varn's quest to clear clients. por Newsweek 78:19-20 D 27 '71

France
Annals of justice; G. Russier case in Marseille. M. Gallant. New Yorker 47:47-52+ Je 26 '71

Great Britain
Justice British style: lessons U.S. lawyers see. il U S News 71:36-7 Ag 2 '71
Our troubled courts; comparison with British system. D. Napley. il Nations Bsns 59:76-81 My '71

Illinois
Panther raid coverup. J. W. Singer and T. J. Dolan. New Repub 165:21-3 Jl 24 '71
Retroactive justice. Time 98:38 D 13 '71
See also
Courts—Illinois

Italy
Insufficient evidence. Time 97:44 Ap 12 '71
Justice, Italian style. il por Time 97:52 Ap 5 '71

New York (state)
Wayward winners; Wayward minor statute declared unconstitutional. Time 99:59 Ja 10 '72

Ohio
Citizens battle for justice; Kent state shootings by Ohio national guard; with editorial comment. P. Davies. Nation 213:547-8, 557-9 N 29 '71

Pennsylvania
Criminal law with a Johnson touch. A. Peters. il pors Ebony 26:93-4+ F '71

Southern states
Black judges in the South. il por Ebony 26:31-4+ Mr '71
See also
Justice, Administration of—Alabama

United States
American justice at work; symposium. bibliog f Cur Hist 61:1-39+ Jl '71
American system of justice; symposium. Cur Hist 60:321-61 Je '71
Attica: time to think. C. Rogers. Chr Cent 88:1286 N 3 '71
Balance sheet on justice. Nation 213:166 S 6 '71
Chief justice looks at crime and the courts; interview. W. E. Burger. por Read Digest 98:113-16 Ap '71
Crimes without victims. A. B. Smith and H. Pollack. Sat R 54:27-9 D 4 '71
Defense never rests, by F. L. Bailey. Review
Bsns W il p 16+ D 11 '71. J. Patterson
Grand jury network; how the Nixon administration has secretly perverted a traditional safeguard of individual rights. F. J. Donner and E. Cerruti. il Nation 214:5-15+ Ja 3 '72
Improving justice in America; symposium. bibliog f Cur Hist 61:65-104+ Ag '71
Jam-up: crisis in our criminal courts. J. Star. il Look 35:32-4+ Mr 23 '71
Justice and the Panthers. Life 70:4 My 28 '71
Justice on trial; with account by P. Goldman and D. Holt. il Newsweek 77:16-24+ Mr 8 '71
Legal services: reform in the seventies; address, April 15, 1971. R. Taft, jr. Vital Speeches 37:615-18 Ag 1 '71
Neither truth nor victory; freeing of Edgar Smith. il por Time 98:51 D 20 '71
Our creaking courts; interview. W. E. Burger. por Read Digest 98:217-19+ My '71
Our troubled courts: two views. P. B. Kurland; D. Napley. il Nations Bsns 59:76-81 My '71
President Nixon on the American judiciary; excerpts from address, March 12, 1971. R. M. Nixon. Cur Hist 60:365-7 Je '71
Push to streamline the courts. il Bsns W p46-7 D 4 '71
Sanctity of robes. il por Time 98:69-70 N 22 '71
Sentencing on review; new limitation on the sentencing power of trial judges. Time 98:80 N 8 '71
Slow justice is inadequate justice; interview. W. E. Burger. il por Forbes 108:21-3 Jl 1 '71
Speeding up justice; president's plan. il U S News 70:37 Mr 22 '71

JUSTICE, Administration of—United States
—*Continued*
State of the federal judiciary; address, August 10, 1970. W. E. Burger. Forbes 108: 15-18 Jl 1 '71
See also
Courts—United States
Courts martial and courts of inquiry
Jury
Pleas (criminal procedure)
Sacco-Vanzetti case
Trials—United States
United States—Justice, Department of
Youth—Law
Bibliography
Neglected values locked into the law. S. Hyman. Sat R 54:19-22 Ag 7 '71
Readings on the administration of justice in America. K. D. Fortney. Cur Hist 60:362-4+ Je; 61:46+ Jl '71
JUSTICE, Department of. See United States—Justice, Department of
JUSTICE and politics
Judging the Chicago trial. A. M. Bickel; discussion. Commentary 51:10+ My '71
JUSTICES, Supreme court. See United States—Supreme court
JUTRAS, Denice
Four acres of sheer delight. il por Org Gard & Farm 18:39-43 Ja '71
JUVENILE courts
See also
Juvenile delinquency
JUVENILE delinquency
Band-aid or vision? comparison of 1947 radio documentary with television documentary. R. L. Shayon. Sat R 54:51 My 22 '71
Height and antisocial behavior in XY and XYY boys. E. B. Hook and D. S. Kim. bibliog il Science 172:284-6 Ap 16 '71
Rat packs of New York. S. Stevens. il N Y Times Mag p28-9+ N 28 '71; Discussion. p 14 D 26 '71
Reading disability, tendency toward delinquency? W. H. Miller and E Windhauser. bibliog Clear House 46:183-7 N '71
Should parents be punished for their children's misdeeds? GH poll. il Good H 173:40+ Jl '71
Toward juvenile justice; address. July 12. 1971. B Bayh. Am Scholar 40:662-6 Aut '71
When children break the law; Parental responsibility ordinances. M. A. Rodgers. Good H 173:67+ Jl '71
Youth in trouble. bibliog il Todays Ed 60:31-2+ S; 53-4 O; 49-50+ N; 26-8 D '71
See also
Gangs
Narcotics and youth
Problem children
Rehabilitation of juvenile delinquents

Prevention
Delinquency: its prevention rests upon the academic community. F. I. Closson. bibliog Clear House 45:290-3 Ja '71
Is curfew the cure? il Newsweek 78:36+ S 6 '71
JUVENILE hormone
Juvenile hormone induces vitellogenin synthesis in the monarch butterfly. M. L. Pan and G. R. Wyatt. bibliog il Science 174:503-5 O 29 '71
New weapon in the war on insects; hormone sprays. il Bsns W p94+ N 13 '71
JUVENILE literature. See Childrens literature
JUXTAGLOMERULAR apparatus. See Kidneys

K

K mesons. See Mesons
KGB. See Secret service—Russia
KGIL (radio station) See Radio stations
KKK. See Ku Klux klan
KLH research and development corporation
Ah, freedom! Forbes 108:36+ Jl 15 '71
KLM (airline) See Airlines—Netherlands
KTXT-TV. See Television stations, Educational
KABACK, Michael Melvin
Jewish disease. il por Newsweek 77:39 My 31 '71 •
KABECK, Claudine
How to stop dieting and start living, moving, and eating. il pors Mlle 72:126-30 Ja '71 •

KABUKI
Wakashu Kabuki dance theater, Kaufmann concert hall, NYU. T. Borek. Dance Mag 45:76 Je '71
KACEN, Norma M. See Robbins, L. R. jt. auth.
KACHATUROFF, Grace
Student involvement in social studies through simulation. Clear House 45:541-4 My '71
KADDAFI, Muammar. See Qaddafi, M.
KAEL, Pauline
Current cinema. See issues of New Yorker to March 27, 1971; October 2, 1971-
Onward and upward with the arts. por New Yorker 47:43-52+ F 20; 44-50+ F 27 '71
about
Authors & editors. D. N. Mount. por Pub W 199:31-2 My 24 '71 •
Movie studies: read all about it. R. Schickel. Harper 242:24+ Mr '71 •
Raising Kael. H. Alpert. il por Sat R 54: 48-9+ Ap 24 '71 •
el KAFI, Jelal
Carthage must not be destroyed. il UNESCO Courier 23:4-8 D '70
KAFIR lilies. See Clivias
KAFIRISTAN. See Nuristan
KAFIRS (Nuristan) See Nuristan—Native races
KAGAN, Jerome
Magical aura of the IQ; excerpt from address. il Sat R 54:92-3 D 4 '71
KAGAN, Norman
Return of The Emperor Jones. il Negro Hist Bul 45:160-2 N '71
KAHANE, Meir D.
Rabbi Kahane says: I'd love to see the J.D.L. fold up. But; interview, ed. by W. Goodman. il pors N Y Times Mag p32-3+ N 21 '71
about
Cries from the heart. Newsweek 77:70+ Mr 8 '71 •
Kahane's commandos. il por Newsweek 77: 29+ Ja 25 '71 •
Private Jewish war on Russia. il por Time 97:18+ Ja 25 '71 •
Violence is not un-Jewish. il Newsweek 77: 32-3 Ja 25 '71 •
KAHIN, George McT.
Negotiations: the view from Hanoi. New Repub 165:13-16 N 6 '71
One-third of a nation uprooted. New Repub 165:19-21 Ag 7 '71
(ed) See Suvanna Phouma. Future of Laos
KAHL, M. Philip
Courtship of storks; with biographical sketch. il Natur Hist 80:2, 36-45 O '71
KAHN, Agha Mohammed Yahya. See Yahya Kahn, A. M.
KAHN, Alan
Pickwick buyer urges best seller list for West coast; interview, ed. by B. A. Bannon. Pub W 199:51-2 Je 28 '71
KAHN, Anthony
(tr) See Evtushenko, E. A. Being famous isn't pretty
KAHN, Ely Jacques, 1916-
Annals of law. New Yorker 46:76-84 F 6 '71
Catch in the hatch isn't what it used to be. il N Y Times Mag p 12-13+ Ag 29 '71
Profiles: J. U. Monro. New Yorker 47:43-8+ Ap 10 '71
Profiles; S. R. and C. S. Mott, philanthropists. por New Yorker 47:56-8+ N 27 '71
Reporter at large. New Yorker 47:98+ D 18 '71
KAHN, Ephraim
No-nonsense report on mercury in fish. Redbook 137:80+ My '71
KAHN, Herman
Herman Kahn thinks about the thinkable: most of the traditional causes of war have disappeared; interview, ed. by G. R. Urban; excerpt from Can we survive our future? il por N Y Times Mag p 12-13+ Je 20 '71
Why U.S. must stay in Asia; interview. il pors U S News 70:60-4 F 8 '71
KAHN, Irving B.
His voice is still loud above the static. por Bsns W p46+ Je 26 '71 •
Scandal clouds the CATV picture. il Bsns W p88 N 6 '71 •
KAHN, Larry
Puns in the sports world. Chem 44:31 Je '71
KAHN, Louis Isadore
More than just a volume. J. M. Dixon. il Arch Forum 134:20-5 Ap '71 •
KAHN, Morley
Uncover extra stereo channels. il Hi Fi 21:43-6 Je '71

KAHN, Roger
Sports. See issues of Esquire

KAIBAB TRAIL. See National parks and reserves—Trails

KAIN, Jay D.
Copper foil jewelry. il Sch Arts 71:8-9 Ja '72

KAIN, Mildred Nelson
It is more blessed to give than to receive. il por Good H 173:48+ Ag '71

KAINZ, Howard P.
Mary the paradox. il Chr Cent 88:1020-2 S 1 '71

KAISER, Edgar Fosburgh, 1908-
Kaiser of Kaiser industries. il pors Forbes 107:68 My 15 '71 •

KAISER, Elmer R.
What about incinerators, Professor? interview, ed. by B. Foster. pors Am City 86: 70+ D '71

KAISER, Robert Blair
What happened to a teacher who touched kids. il Look 35:64-8 Ag 10 '71

KAISER industries corporation
Kaiser industries searches for a new mix. il Bsns W p76-8 Ap 10 '71
Kaiser of Kaiser industries. il pors Forbes 107:68 My 15 '71
Kaiser's crunch. il Forbes 107:67-8 Mr 15 '71

KAISER resources, ltd. See Kaiser steel corporation

KAISER steel corporation
How Kaiser dug a hole for itself; Kaiser resources, Elkview operation. il Bsns W p98+ Je 19 '71
Kaiser calls for help; Japanese deal with Kaiser resources. Fortune 83:43-4 F '71

KAITZ, Hyman B.
Hyman B. Kaitz wins second annual Lawrence R. Klein award. Mo Labor R 94:2 Je '71 •

KAKALEC, Joseph M. See Hacala, J. R. jt. auth.

KALB, Marvin, and Abel, Elie
From Roots of involvement; excerpt. Sat R 54:33 Mr 27 '71

KALCKAR, Herman M.
Periplasmic galactose binding protein of escherichia coli. bibliog il Science 174:557-65 N 5 '71

KALEM, T. E.
Letter from the publisher. H. Luce. por Time 98:10 N 29 '71

KALIL, Ronald E. and others
Anomalous retinal pathways in the Siamese cat: an inadequate substrate for normal binocular vision. bibliog il Science 174: 302-5 O 15 '71

KALINGA prize
Letter from Lincoln:
Development and the Kalinga prize. Aurum. Bul Atom Sci 27:24+ Mr '71

KALISCH, Philip A.
Appeal for public school archives. Clear House 45:562 My '71

KALISH, Richard A.
Social values and the elderly. Ment Hy 55:51-4 Ja '71

KALLAB, Valeriana, and Aggarwala, Narinder
(eds) Issues before the 26th General assembly. bibliog f il Int Concil 584:1-222 S '71

KALLEN, Horace Meyer
Covenant of the different, by the different, for the different; with excerpts from What I believe and why, maybe. M. R. Konvitz. Sat R 54:19-20 Jl 31 '71 •

KALLIS, Stephen A. Jr
Leapfrogging the SST. Nat R 23:419-20 Ap 20 '71

KALMAN, Paul
That itchy ivy league. il Field & S 76:54-5+ Jl '71

KAMA RIVER foundry construction, Russia. See Foundry construction

KAMB, Barclay
Hydrogen-bond stereochemistry and anomalous water. bibliog il Science 172:231-42 Ap 16 '71

KAMMERER, Rafael
Super great recordings of the century: Backhaus. por Am Rec G 37:430-1 Mr '71
Very first release, from RCA Victrola, of 1935-1938 recordings by Josef Hofmann. il por Am Rec G 37:480-1 Ap '71

KANE, Art
Our Indian heritage; photographs. Life 71: 38-47 Jl 2 '71

KANE, J. Herbert
Closing doors: fact and fiction; excerpt from The Christian mission: problems and prospects. Chr Today 16:6-10 N 19 '71

KANE, James B.
Adjust your compass. il Motor B & S 127:80+ Je '71

KANE, Joseph W. See Ford, N. C. jt. auth.

KANE, Martin
Assessment of black is best. il Sports Illus 34:72-6+ Ja 18 '71

KANE, Michael B.
Minorities: what textbooks don't say; excerpt from Minorities in textbooks. Cur 129:13-16 My '71

KANE, Paul
Paul Kane, painter of North American Indians; international exhibition. S. B. Sherrill. il Antiques 99:788 Je '71 •
Paul Kane's frontier, by P. Kane; ed. by J. R. Harper. Review
Am West 8:49 S '71. D. G. Pike •
Antiques 99:391-7 Mr '71

KANE, Robert S.
Travel bazaar. il Harp Baz 104:26+ Je; 72+ O '71

KANE, William J.
Renewing A&P. por Bsns W p68 F 20 '71 •

KANEGIS, Arthur, and Richards, Lindsay
Budget gives the game away. Nation 213:337-40 O 11 '71

KANFER, Alfred
Hand of a man going his own way. il Life 70:27 Ja 22 '71

KANFER, Allen
Laying on of hands; poem. Harper 244:87 Ja '72
Now is the time; poem. Harper 243:18 D '71

KANIN, Garson
He-she chemistry of Katherine Hepburn and Spencer Tracy; excerpts from Tracy and Hepburn. il pors Vogue 158:142-3+ N 1 '71
Mia comes to rest. il pors McCalls 98:64-7+ Ap '71
Trade winds; interview, ed. by C. Amory. Sat R 54:6+ N 20 '71

KANN, Peter R. and Lescaze, Lee
East Pakistan. Atlan 228:26+ D '71

KANNAN, Seshadri
Plasmalemma: the seat of dual mechanisms of ion absorption in chlorella pyrenoidosa. bibliog il Science 173:927-9 S 3 '71

KANNY, Mark
Music from Marlboro. il por Am Rec G 37: 282-7 Ja '71
Winter dreams, the newest and best. Am Rec G 37:592+ My '71

KANOWITZ, Leo
Women before the law. McCalls 98:43 My; 40 Je; 42 Ag; 45 S; 99:38 N '71

KANSAS
See also
Flint Hills
Forests and forestry—Kansas
Geology—Kansas
Irrigation—Kansas
National parks and reserves—Kansas

History
Starving Kansas: the great drought and famine of 1859-60. J. G. Gambone. il Am West 8:30-5 Jl '71

KANSAS CITY, Mo.
Municipal safety program that works. M. D. Calkins. il Am City 86:67-8 Ag '71

Airports
How to plan regionally for a regional airport. W. G. Roeseler. il Am City 86:70+ Mr '71
Kansas City will test gate arrival plan. D. C. Winston. il Aviation W 95:104-5+ N 15 '71

Metropolitan districts
How to plan regionally for a regional airport. W. G. Roeseler. il Am City 86:70+ Mr '71

Music
Wrenching rock opera, Jesus Christ superstar. il Life 70:20B-26 My 28 '71

Police department
Police task force analyses future needs. Am City 86:33 My '71

Street traffic
Computerized signal settings speed traffic flow. Am City 86:126 Ap '71

KANSAS CITY Chiefs (football club) See Football clubs

KANSAS CITY Royals (baseball) See Baseball clubs

KANSAS CITY Royals baseball academy. See Baseball—Study and teaching

KANSAS state university, Manhattan
Kansas state U: whatever happened to good
old State U? D. Shapley. Science 174:803-5
N 19 '71
U.S. journal: Manhattan and Atchison, Kan;
the Maes family. C. Trillin. New Yorker
47:90-5 Je 12 '71
KANT, Immanuel
Categorical imperative. P. W. Schmidtchen.
il por Hobbies 76:134-6+ S '71 •
KANTAR, Eddie
World's greatest gamesman. W. Bingham.
il pors Sports Illus 34:28-30+ Ja 11 '71 •
KANTEN. See Agar
KANTOR, Alfred
Story behind the book; interview, ed. by
D. G. Maryles. Pub W 200:28-9 O 25 '71
KANTROWITZ, Adrian
Assist for an ailing heart. il por Time 98:
52 Ag 23 '71 •
KANTROWITZ, Arthur
Relevance of space; adaptation of address,
October 1970. il Bul Atom Sci 27:32-3 Ap
'71
KAO, Henry Y.
This country is a reality; interview. por
U S News 71:24 N 8 '71
KAOLINITE
Kaolinite: synthesis at room temperature. J.
Linares and F. Huertas. bibliog il Science
171:896-7 Mr 5 '71
KAON. See Mesons
KAPELL, William
Blazing virtuosity and intellect of William
Kapell. M. N. Kanny. por Am Rec G 37:
303+ Ja '71 •
KAPLA, Anne
Should grandmas be quarantined? Har Yrs
11:39-40 My '71
KAPLAN, Barbara. See Resnik, S. jt. auth.
KAPLAN, Ehud. See Barlow, R. B. jr. jt.
auth.
KAPLAN, Jim
College football. il Sports Illus 35:69-70 D 6
'71
Design for sport. Sports Illus 35:52-3 Ag 23
'71
KAPLAN, Joan
Soviet Jews. New Repub 165:18-21 D 25 '71
KAPLAN, Joel David
Great escape. por Newsweek 78:38 Ag 30 '71 •
More on the Kaplan caper. Time 98:15 S 20
'71 •
Whirlaway. il por Time 98:27-8 Ag 30 '71 •
KAPLAN, Johanna
Loss of memory is only temporary; story.
Harper 242:94-8 Mr '71
Scenes from a special classroom. Commen-
tary 51:69-76 My '71
KAPLAN, John
Prohibition of marijuana. New Repub 163:11-
12 N 21 '70; 164:42-3 Ja 2 '71
Vindication of John Bricker. Nat R 23:1413-14
D 17 '71
KAPLAN, L.
Build R-E's 4-channel IC preamp. il Radio-
Electr 42:41-5 O '71
KAPLAN, Milton A.
Fire; poem. Am Scholar 40:218 Spr '71
Function of stanzaic form. bibliog f Engl J
60:47-53 Ja '71
Outside reading belongs inside. Ed Digest
37:41-3 S '71
KAPLAN, Mordecai Menahem
Reconstructionism in American Jewish life,
by C. S. Liebman. Review
Commentary 51:74-6 Mr '71. M. A. Meyer;
Discussion. 52:28+ Ag '71 •
KAPLAN, Morris
Obituary
Consumer Rep por 36:647 N '71
KAPLAN, Samuel
Balkanization of suburbia. il Harper 243:72-4
O '71
KAPP, Bruce S. and Schneider, A. M.
Selective recovery from retrograde amnesia
produced by hippocampal spreading depres-
sion. bibliog il Science 173:1149-51 S 17 '71
KAPPEL, Bonnie E.
Horse manure and wood chips. il Org Gard
& Farm 18:49-50 Jl '71
KAPROW, Allan
Education of the un-artist. il Art N 69:
28-31+ F '71 (to be cont)
KAPUSINSKI, Albert T.
Future of poverty. il America 125:346-9 O
30 '71
KARAJAN, Herbert von
Karajan invades East Germany. P. Moor. il
pors Hi Fi 21:20+ Ap '71 •
Letter from Paris; Verdi's Requiem per-
formed by the Orchestra de Paris. Genêt.
New Yorker 47:70 Jl 10 '71 •

KARAMOJONG (native race) See Uganda—
Native races
KARAS, Nicholas
How to outfit for a wilderness canoe trip. il
Pop Mech 135:100-3 Ap '71
Labrador discovery. il Field & S 76:58-9+ Jl
'71
New muskie country. il Field & S 75:54-5+
Ja '71
Pterrible ptemperature ptarmigan. il Field &
S 75:64-5+ Mr '71
KARATE
Face to face with a karate black belt; Shar-
on Yardley of Knoxville, Tenn. il Seven-
teen 29:55 O '70
KAREL, Leonard
Success in flower drying. il Horticulture 49:
26-7 Je '71
KARL, Jean
Bringing Chicken Licken up to date. por
Pub W 199:81-3 F 22 '71
KARL, Max H.
Karl the magic man. il por Time 99:60 Ja
17 '72 •
KARLEN, Arno
Moody woman called Superior; excerpts from
Superior: portrait of a living lake. il Nat
Wildlife 9:43-7 F '71
KARLOVSKY, C. C. Lamberg-. See Lamberg-
Karlovsky, C. C.
KARLOVSKY, Martha Lamberg-. See Lam-
berg-Karlovsky, M.
KARMIN, Monroe W.
Politics of Nixon's revolution. Cur 128:40-2
Ap '71
KARNALI. See Nepal
KARON, Myron. See Benedict, W. F. jt. auth.
KARP, Irwin
Downgrading the protection of international
copyright. Pub W 200:pt2 143-7 S 27 '71
KARP, Walter
Feminine utopia. il Horizon 13:4-13 Spr '71
KARPEL, Craig
Craig Karpel's list. Esquire 75:122+ My '71
KARRAS, Alex
Cutting the mad duck. il por Newsweek 78:
101-2 S 27 '71 •
Lion at large. por Time 98:49 D 27 '71 •
KARSCH, Carl G.
Karsch kloseups. Am For 77:6-7 Ag '71
KARSH, Yousuf
Five portraits; excerpt from Faces of our
time. il Sat R 54:13-15 Ag 28 '71
Trade winds; interview, ed. by C. Amory.
Sat R 54:14+ O 16 '71
KARTH, Joseph Edward
On revitalizing space. Space World H-11-95:
32 N '71
KARUK Indians. See Indians of North America
KASANOF, David
Sea chanties & marlinspikes. il Motor B & S
127:88-9+ Mr '71
What's up down there? il Motor B & S 128:
46-9 bibliog(p53) Jl '71
KASER, Thomas
Hilo reads with aloha spirit. il Am Ed 7:16-
20 Ap '71
KASHMIR
Nehru's plan for peace. S. S. Harrison. New
Repub 164:17-22 Je 19 '71
KASPAREK, Robert B.
Harpers Ferry: arsenal of awareness. il Nat
Parks & Con Mag 45:22-6 Ja '71
KASPER, Charles B. See Kubinski, H. jt.
auth.
KASS, Leon R.
Death as an event: a commentary on Robert
Morison; adaptation of address, December
29, 1970. bibliog Science 173:698-702 Ag 20
'71
New biology: what price relieving man's es-
tate? bibliog Science 174:779-88 N 19 '71
KASSEL, Germany
Music
Report:
Das Rheingold. J. H. Sutcliffe. il Opera
N 35:31 F 6 '71
KASUBA, Aleksandra
Last year in Ireland: pre-history recalled to
life. Craft Horiz 31:5+ Ag '71
about
On and off the avenue. J. Malcolm. New
Yorker 47:115-17 S 25 '71 •
Self in chambered space. M. Shorr. il Craft
Horiz 31:26-9+ Ag '71 •
KATEB, George
Toward a wordless world. Atlan 228:122-5
O '71
KATHMANDU. See Katmandu, Nepal

KATMAI, MOUNT
Alaska's valley of death. G. X. Sand. il Sci Digest 69:24-9 Ap '71
KATMAI NATIONAL MONUMENT
Alaska's valley of death. G. X. Sand. il Sci Digest 69:24-9 Ap '71
KATMANDU, Nepal
Goa: an addendum; hashish trail; letter to the editor. J. S. Mason. Nat R 23:1255 N 5 '71

KATONA, George
Inflations impact on consumer behavior and attitudes; address. January 14, 1971. Vital Speeches 37:263-5 F 15 '71

about

Consumer is still scared. por Forbes 107:46 F 1 '71•
KATZ, Alex
Alex Katz and the tactics of representation. D. Antin. il Art N 70:44-7+ Ap '71 •
Art; exhibition of works at the Wadsworth atheneum, Hartford. L. Alloway. Nation 213:605-6 D 6 '71 •
KATZ, Sir Bernard
Quantal mechanism of neural transmitter release; Nobel lecture, December 12, 1970. bibliog il Science 173:123-6 Jl 9 '71
KATZ, Bill
(ed) Magazines. See issues of Library journal Pornography collection; excerpts from Magazine selection. bibliog il Library J 96:4060-6 D 15 '71
KATZ, Fred
No one roots for Goliath. il Todays Health 49:24-9 S '71
Winter survival. il Todays Health 49:44-7+ D '71
KATZ, Julius Louis
Department discusses Sugar act extension before Senate committee; statement, June 16, 1971. Dept State Bul 65:89-91 Jl 19 '71
Department gives views on sugar legislation; address, May 6, 1971. Dept State Bul 64:778-82 Je 14 '71
1968 international coffee agreement at the halfway mark; address, February 1, 1971. Dept State Bul 64:260-3 Mr 1 '71
KATZ, Leon
Dracula: Sabbat; dramatization of novel by B. Stoker. Criticism
Sat R 54:17 My 15 '71 •
KATZ, Leslie
(ed) See Evans, W. Interview
KATZ, Menke
Doll; poem. Atlan 227:84 F '71
KATZ, Milton
Decision-making in the production of power; with biographical sketch. Sci Am 225:32, 191-2+ bibliog(p246) S '71

about

Technology and the law. Sci Am 224:45-6 F '71 •
KATZ, Paula. See Greer, F. jt. auth.
KATZ, Phyllis B.
(ed) Family clinic. See issues of Parents' magazine & better family living
KATZ, Rob
Which computer, the minicomputer? il Electr World 86:23-5+ O '71
KATZMAN, Allen
Walking to Bethlehem; poem. Nation 212:406 Mr 29 '71
KATZMAN, Howard, and Libby, W. F.
Sintered diamond compacts with a cobalt binder. bibliog il Science 172:1132-4 Je 11 '71
KAUAI NATIONAL PARK (proposed) See National parks and reserves—United States
KAUFFMAN, Mark
Sport is a double exposure: photographs. Sports Illus 35:98-107 D 20 '71
KAUFFMANN, Stanley
Album of older women. Harper 242:67-8+ My '71
From Germany. New Repub 165:24+ Jl 10; 26+ Jl 24 '71
From Paris New Repub 165:26+ Ag 7 '71
Middling ages: notes on some American film directors. Yale R 60:626-40 Je '71
Theater. See occasional issues of New republic
KAUFMAN, Alicia. See Bay Laurel, A. pseud.
KAUFMAN, Arnold Saul
Seekers after justice. P. Steinfels. Commonweal 95:150 N 12 '71 •
KAUFMAN, Bel
Will this boy's curriculum manager deserve an apple this year? il Todays Health 49:20-3 S '71

KAUFMAN, Elaine
Elaine: her restaurant, her famous friends. il por Vogue 157:88-9+ Je '71 •
KAUFMAN, Max
Working model of a 70-inch telescope. il por Sky & Tel 42:170-3 S '71
KAUFMAN, Richard F.
Double-talk bookkeeping; military budget. Nation 213:429-32 N 1 '71
KAUFMAN, Wallace
Inhibited teacher; adaptation of address, November 1970. Engl J 60:382-8 Mr '71
KAUN, David E. and Lentz, William
Occupational migration, discrimination, and the central city labor force. bibliog Mo Labor R 94:57-61 D '71
KAVALER, Lucy
How your body adapts to cold; excerpt from Freezing point: cold as a matter of life and death. Read Digest 98:125-8 Ja '71
KAVALER, Rebecca
Further adventures of Brunhild; story. Yale R 61:35-56 O '71
KAVAN, Anna
Edge of panic; story. Vogue 158:75-7 O 1 '71
KAVANAGH, P. J.
Occasional birds; poem. New Yorker 47:46 Ap 10 '71
KAVANAUGH, James
Trade winds; interview, ed. by C. Amory. Sat R 54:10+ Je 26 '71

about

Neglected prophecy of James Kavanaugh. E. C. Kennedy. por Commonweal 94:287-8 My 28 '71 •
—See Shostrom, E. L. jt. auth.
KAVANAUGH, John Francis
Death theme in natural cinema. America 125:122-3 S 4 '71
KAY, Connie
Profiles. W. Balliett. New Yorker 47:62-4+ N 20 '71 •
KAY, Jane Holtz
Boston's public library: a keeper with many keys. il Art in Am 59:78-81 Ja '71
Newest ancient art. il Américas 23:S16-21 Je '71
Way of seeing. Writer 84:24-6 My '71
KAYAKS
Having fun in wild white water. R. Hill. il Pop Sci 198:72-3 Je '71
KAYE, Dena
History's love stories: down heartthrob lane with Kleenex and camera. il Sat R 54:38-9+ Mr 13 '71
Student travelers should. . . il Sat R 54:63 F 20 '71
KAYE, Hilary
Ham actors in furs and feathers. il Sci Digest 71:30-4 Ja '72
KAZAK rugs. See Rugs and carpets, Oriental
KAZANTZAKIS, Nikos
My entire soul is a cry. J. Blenkinsopp. Commonweal 93:514-18 F 26 '71; Reply. G. W. Polley, jr. 94:155+ Ap 23 '71 •
KAZIN, Alfred
Books (cont) Vogue 157:72-3 Mr 15; 158 My '71; 159:16 Ja 1 '72
Gedaliah. Atlan 227:68-71 My '71
Girl from the Village. Atlan 227:57-63 F '71
Joan Didion: portrait of a professional. Harper 243:112-14+ D '71
Midtown and the Village. il Harper 242:82-9 Ja '71
Oates. il por Harper 243:78-82 Ag '71
Pilgrimage of Walker Percy. Harper 242:81-6 Je '71
Prince, American style. il Vogue 157:132-3+ F 1 '71
Professors are too sophisticated. Sat R 54:23-4+ My 22 '71
Return of the '30's, sweet and sharp. il Vogue 157:55 Ja 15 '71
Richard Hofstadter, 1916-1970. Am Scholar 40:397-401 Sum '71
War novel: from Mailer to Vonnegut. Sat R 54:13-15+ F 6 '71
KAZIN, Charles
Gedaliah. A. Kazin. Atlan 227:68-71 My '71 •
KCHESSINSKA, Mathilde
Kchessinska at ninety-nine. O. Maynard. il pors Dance Mag 45:22-4 N '71 •
KEAIWA Heiau state park. See Hawaii—Parks and reserves
KEAN, Gerald
Best friend; story. Seventeen 30:120-1 N '71
Day he met the girl who asked all the right questions; story. Ladies Home J 88:124-5 S '71
Toolshed; story. Seventeen 30:218-19 Ag '71
KEANE, Bil. See Bombeck, E. jt. auth.

KEANE, John T.
Wilderness act as Congress intended. il Am
For 77:40-3+ F '71
KEAR, Vern A.
Sons and daughters of the Soddies. J. Rob-
ertson. il Har Yrs 11:20 Jl '71 •
KEARNEY, Vincent S.
World scene (cont) America 124:544-5. 125:
428-30 My 22. N 20 '71
KEARNS, Charles Maxwell, 1915-
Aerospace and the common good; excerpts
from address, January 1971. Aviation W
94:9 Ja 18 '71
KEARNS, Henry
Helping U.S. business sell more abroad; in-
terview. il por U S News 71:54-8 Jl 19 '71
KEATING, Charles H. Jr.
Report that shocked the Nation. Read Digest
98:37-41 Ja '71
KEATING, Richard
Question of time. il pors Time 98:63 O 18 '71 •
KEATS, Ezra Jack
Christmas message; story. Redbook 138:73 D
'71
              about
Gentle world of Ezra Jack Keats. E. Perry.
il por Am Artist 35:48-53+ S '71 •
KEATS, John
Philadelphia, a triumph over time. il Holiday
49:42-7+ Ap '71
To meet spring halfway. il Holiday 49:66-
9+ Ap '71
KEATS, Sheila
Current chronicle. il Mus Q 57:141-8 Ja '71
KEAVENEY, Sydney Starr
Pictures. bibliog Wilson Lib Bul 46:310-11
D '71
KEBABIAN, John W. and Greengard, Paul
Dopamine-sensitive adenyl cyclase: possible
role in synaptic transmission. bibliog il
Science 174:1346-9 D 24 '71
KECHI TOWNSHIP, Kan.
Big performance from a little loader. C. Bur-
dette. il Am City 86:20 Ja '71
KEE, Alistair
God without God? J. A. T. Robinson. Chr
Cent 88:1379-82 N 24 '71 •
KEEFAUVER, John
How Henry J. Littlefinger licked the hip-
pies' scheme to take over the country by
tossing pot in postage stamp glue. Nat R
23:1180+ O 22 '71
KEEFE, Carolyn
To Bathsheba; poem. Chr Cent 88:1522 D
29 '71
KEEFE, John W.
American lacy and pressed glass in the
Toledo museum of art. il Antiques 100:104-
9 Jl '71
KEEGAN, Francis W. and MacLean, J. A.
Elementary school volunteers. Todays Ed 60:
55 O '71
KEELER, Ruby
Ruby Keeler is alive and tapping. L. Botto. il
pors Look 35:70-4 F 9 '71 •
KEEN, Geraldine
Expensive nineteenth century. Art in Am 59:
29 S '71
KEENE, Chris
Recordings. M. Mayer. Esquire 75:58 My '71 •
KEENER, Jefferson Ward
Doctor's prescription: invention and quality.
il pors Nations Bsns 59:58-9 Ja '71
KEENER, Ward. See Keener, J. W.
KEENLEYSIDE, Hugh L.
What's wrong at the United Nations. Sat R
54:11-13+ Je 19 '71
KEEP America beautiful day
Soaring with the scouts. W. E. Towell. il
Am For 77:38-9+ Je '71
KEESE, Parton
Waterskiing champions and tvros. il Motor
B & S 127:86-7+ Mr '71
KEFAUVER, Estes
Kefauver, by J. B. Gorman. Review
Newsweek 11 por 78:92+ N 1 '71. W.
Clemons •
Sat R 55:29+ Ja 1 '72. R. Griffith •
KEHAYA, Dorothea
Gallery; photographs. Life 71:8-9 O 8 '71
KEHRER, Harold H. See Toksöz, M. N. jt.
auth.
KEHRLI, Gerald V.
As common as chewing gum. il Time 97:14-
15 Mr 1 '71 •
Up in smoke. por Newsweek 77:25-6 Mr 1
'71 •
KEIDEL, Albert
Restorations experts speak their minds;
interview. House & Gard 140:6+ Ag '71
KEIKOBAD (operatic character) See Charac-
ters in opera

KEILLOR, Garrison
Found paradise. New Yorker 47:32-3 S 18 '71
How are the legs, Sam? New Yorker 46:24-5
Ja 30 '71
New baseball. New Yorker 47:35 My 15 '71
Re the tower project. New Yorker 47:25
Ag 28 '71
Sex tips. New Yorker 47:31 Ag 14 '71
U.S. still on top, says rest of world. New
Yorker 47:35 O 2 '71
KEIM, Levi A.
Grand Canyon ram. il Outdoor Life 148:58-9+
D '71
KEITH, John L.
Non-destructive transistor tester. il Pop
Electr 34:47-9 Mr '71
KEITH, Larry
Baseball (cont) Sports Illus 34:52 Je 21;
35:40 Ag 9 '71
College basketball. il Sports Illus 34:48 F 15;
58-9 Mr 15 '71
Tennis. il Sports Illus 35:58-61 Jl 26; 73 S 27
'71
Week; college basketball. Sports Illus 35:84+
N 29 '71
Week; college football. Sports Illus 35:62+
O 25; 56+ N 8 '71
KEITHLEY, George
Donner party; poems; excerpts. il Harper 243:
65-72+ N '71
KEKKONEN, Urho Kaleva
Ice-bucket tempest. por Time 99:28 Ja 17
'72 •
KELDYSH, Mstislav
Luna 16's trophies; excerpts from address,
October 28, 1970. Space World H-6-90:18-19
Je '71
KELLER, George C.
College & careers. il Seventeen 30:23+ S
'71
—See Boyer, E. L. jt. auth.
KELLER, Marcia
East Palo Alto federal library project. il
Am Lib 2:631-5 Je '71
KELLERMAN, Sally
Barge is sailing along. por Time 97:40 Mr 8
'71 •
New-found fame for Hot Lips. il pors Life
70:58-61 F 5 '71 •
KELLERMANN, K. I.
Joint Soviet-American radio interferometry.
il Sky & Tel 42:132-3 S '71
KELLEY, Albert Joseph
Conversion; address, January 21, 1971. Vital
Speeches 37:318-20 Mr 1 '71
KELLEY, Ben
Highway lobby in ambush. Nation 213:496-
500 N 15 '71
—and Hebert, Richard
Priorities or trust funds? Nation 212:497-500
Ap 19 '71
KELLEY, Charles F.
Fires and explosions. Yachting 130:66+ Ag
'71
More electrical power. il Yachting 130:62+ Jl
'71
KELLEY, Clarence M.
How to solve the police crisis; interview,
ed. by G. M. Chamberlain. pors Am City
86:94-5+ S; 88+ O; 106-8 N '71
KELLEY, Dean M.
Un-service station. Chr Cent 88:799-801 Je 30
'71
KELLEY, Don Greame
Trees of the totem culture; excerpts from
Edge of a continent. il Am West 8:18-21+
My '71
KELLEY, James B.
Some ground rules for the generation gap.
America 124:457-8 My 1 '71
KELLEY, Larry L.
New horizons for WEA. Todays Ed 60:76 S
'71
KELLEY, P. L. See Hinkley, E. D. jt auth.
KELLEY, Reeve Spencer
Gift; poem. Sat R 54:23 Ap 17 '71
Poems are made by gods like me; poem. Sat
R 54:30 My 8 '71
KELLEY, Roger Timothy
Excerpt from testimony before the Senate
armed services committee, February 2, 1971.
Cong Digest 50:158 My '71
KELLEY, William N. See McDonald, J. A.
jt. auth.
KELLOGG, Francis Leonard
Government and private agency partnership
in refugee assistance programs; address,
March 14, 1971. Dept State Bul 64:576-8 My
3 '71
KELLOGG, James Crane, 1915-
Specialist speaks; interview. pors Forbes
107:49-50 Mr 15 '71

KELLSTADT, Charles H.
Charles Kellstadt of General development corp; interview. por Nations Bsns 59:38-41+ Je '71
KELLY, Bernard M. bp
American bishop blasts hierarchy on Vietnam silence, quits post. Chr Cent 88:794 Je 30 '71 •
Bishops in the dock. por Newsweek 77:62 Je 28 '71 •
Bishops under attack. il por Time 97:58 Je 29 '71 •
KELLY, Eddie
Wimpy tackles an ex-tiger. J. Morgan. il pors Sports Illus 34:52-3 F 8 '71 •
KELLY, Ellsworth
Kelly, collage and color. D. Waldman. bibliog il Art N 70:44-7+ D '71 •
KELLY, Eugene T. and Turano, J. P.
Variable scheduling. il Clear House 45:365-8 F '71
KELLY, Frank K.
Is anybody ready for peace? Sat R 54:16+ Ag 7 '71
KELLY, George A.
Brooklyn's little giant of Catholic education. America 125:312-14 O 23 '71
KELLY, George W.
Wild flowers in the mountains. il Horticulture 49:26-9 Ag '71
KELLY, Grace. See Grace Patricia, consort of Rainier III, prince of Monaco
KELLY, Hal
Aquarod. il Mech Illus 67:66-70+ Mr '71
Build the Scottish schooner. il Mech Illus 67:42-7+ Ag '71
Build Tom's Quacker. il Mech Illus 67:70-2 N '71
Home study center. il Mech Illus 67:112-14 S '71
KELLY, Jack
Jack Kelly speaks out on shamateurism. Sports Illus 34:34-5 My 10 '71

about

No bird, no plane, just Superjack. J. Underwood. il pors Sports Illus 34:32-5+ My 10 '71 •
KELLY, James R.
New Roman church: a modest proposal. Commonweal 95:222-6 D 3 '71
KELLY, Mervin J.
Obituary
Phys Today 24:71 Je '71. W. Haeberli
KELLY, Richard
Cultivation of borrelia hermsi. bibliog il Science 173:443-4 Jl 30 '71
KELLY, Robert
Comment. D. Wakoski. Poetry 118:355-7 S '71 •
KELLY, Robert L.
Jackson's The witch: a satanic gem. Engl J 60:1204-8 D '71
KELLY, Steve
Roundy-round corner. See issues of Hot rod
KELLY, Tom
Bye-bye, baby boom. il Nations Bsns 59:52-5 D '71
KELLY, Virginia
Oh, my that Nellie Bly! por Read Digest 99:33-4+ D '71
KELLY, Walt
Parting shots: Walt Kelly canines with a little extra bite. Life 71:61 Ag 13 '71 •
KELLY, William Russell
Distress call changed the temporary help industry. T. E. Adderley. il pors Nations Bsns 59:70-1 Ja '71 •
KELLY services, Inc.
Distress call changed the temporary help industry. T. E. Adderley. il pors Nations Bsns 59:70-1 Ja '71
KELMAN, Steven J.
Sweden's liberated men and women. New Repub 164:21-3 Mr 13 '71
KELP
Underwater battle; southern California's Pacific coastline. G. T. Bowden. il Parks & Rec 6:22-4 Jl '71
KELSEY, Paul M.
Lesson in government. Cons 26:32 Ag '71
Long, slow job. il Cons 25:32-3 Je '71
KEMBLE, Penn
Rediscovering American labor. Commentary 51:45-52 Ap; 52:22-3 Ag '71
KEMP, Jerrold E.
Better way to show the way. Ed Digest 37:52-3 O '71
KEMP, William B.
Flow of energy in a hunting society; with biographical sketch. il Sci Am 225:25, 104-15 S '71
KEMPE, Carl, collection. See Art—Private collections

KEMPER insurance group
Control without ownership; Kemper family. Forbes 107:43 F 15 '71
Cutting companies' and society's losses; public service films. V. Louviere. il Nations Bsns 59:14 Ja '71
KEMPFF, Wilhelm
Schubert, transcendental amateur. D. Henahan. il por Hi Fi 21:71-2 Je '71 •
KEMPTON, Murray
Murrow's legatees. il Hi Fi 21:63-4 My '71
KENDALL, Donald McIntosh
Generation gap; address, December 5, 1970. Vital Speeches 37:245-7 F 1 '71

about

Nixon's inner circle of businessmen. il por Bsns W p52-3+ Jl 31 '71 •
KENDALL, Elaine
Invisible suburbs; excerpts from The happy mediocrity. il Horizon 13:104-11 Wint '71
KENDALL, Henry W. and Panofsky, W. K. H.
Structure of the proton and the neutron; with biographical sketches. il Sci Am 224:16, 60-6+ Je '71
KENDALL, R. Elliott
Rhodesia: a crucial issue for the Christian conscience. Chr Cent 88:1086-8 S 15 '71
KENDALL, Willmoore
Book burners: Virginia Kirkus service summary of Contra mundum. Nat R 23:687-8 Je 29 '71 •
Difficult, singular and legendary. L. P. S. De Alvarez. Nat R 23:935-6 Ag 24 '71 •
KENDALL company
Boston grudge fight may lead to a merger. il por Bsns W p58+ N 6 '71
KENISTON, Kenneth
Liberal antecedents of the revolt; excerpt from Youth and dissent. Cur 134:3-20 N '71
—and Lerner, Michael
Campus characteristics and campus unrest. bibliog f il Ann Am Acad 395:39-53 My '71
Selected references on student protest. Ann Am Acad 395:184-94 My '71

about

Keniston's kids. J. K. Footlick. il por Newsweek 78:62+ N 1 '71 •
KENNAN, George Frost
Hazardous courses in southern Africa. For Affairs 49:218-36 Ja '71; Same abr. with title What policies toward southern Africa? Cur 127:50-63 Mr '71
Reflections. New Yorker 47:46-50+ My 1 '71

about

Footbridge into the quagmire. C. Phillips. New Repub 165:13-15 Jl 24 '71 •
KENNEBEC RIVER
River the loggers stole. A. Gauvin. il Audubon 73:70-6+ Jl '71
KENNEBECK, Edwin
Not guilty of what? Black Panthers in New York city. il Nation 213:296-304 O 4 '71
KENNECOTT copper corporation
Copper counts the cost of clean air. il Bsns W p 104 Jl 17 '71
How Kennecott got hooked with Catch-22. R. Loving, jr. il Fortune 84:98-101+ S '71
KENNEDY, Cora Wright
Tools & techniques. See issues of Popular photography
KENNEDY, David Johnston
Centennial city; paintings. il por Am Heritage 23:17-32 D '71

about

Centennial city. E. P. Richardson. il por Am Heritage 23:17-32 D '71 •
KENNEDY, Edward Moore
Administration's policy defies understanding; war in Asia, address, December 7, 1971. por U S News 71:68-9 D 20 '71
Indochina: a slaughter of innocents. Nation 212:806-8 Je 28 '71
Mounting tragedy of East Bengal. Cur 135:53-62 D '71
Pakistan refugee; address, August 26, 1971. Vital Speeches 37:738-41 O 1 '71
Statement of Senator Edward M. Kennedy on re-employing defense scientists and engineers. por Bul Atom Sci 27:41-3 Mr '71

about

Another Kennedy on Cuba. Chr Cent 88:1254 O 27 '71 •
Cloud on the Kennedy horizon. pors U S News 70:18 F 1 '71 •
Future of Ted Kennedy as politicians see it. il por U S News 70:38-9 F 8 '71 •

KENNEDY, Edward Moore—about—*Continued*
Kennedy and McElroy differ. C. Holden.
  Science 174:573 N 5 '71 *
Kennedy on Fifth avenue. New Yorker 47:
  47-9 D 4 '71 *
Kennedy's comeback. will he or won't he?
  W. Rogers. il pors Look 35:13-20+ Ag 10
  '71 *
Kennedy's searing trip through Pakistani
  grief. il por Life 71:26-9 Ag 27 '71 *
Memo from Richard Scammon; standing
  with voters. R. Scammon. il Newsweek 78:
  41 O 25 '71 *
Non-candidacy of Edward Moore Kennedy;
  A Time election survey. il pors Time 98:16-
  20+ N 29 '71 *
Off the deep end; views on the troubles of
  Northern Ireland. Time 98:48 N 1 '71 *
TRB from Washington: noncandidate Ken-
  nedy. New Repub 164:4 Je 5 '71 *
Talk with Kennedy. por Time 97:13 Mr 1
  '71 *
Ted Kennedy: his triumphs and tragedies;
  excerpts. L. David. por Ladies Home J
  89:77+ Ja '72 *
Teddy and the Democrats. por Newsweek 77:
  22 Je 21 '71 *
Teddy: will he or won't he? il pors News-
  week 78:37-8 N 15 '71 *
Teddy's scenario. Nat R 23:1337-8 D 3 '71 *
Tortoise and the hare. il por Newsweek 77:
  18-20 F 1 '71 *
What Kennedy is up to. il pors U S News 70:
  20-2+ My 24 '71 *
What would Teddy do? S. Alsop. Newsweek
  78:112 N 29 '71 *
Whip lash. por Sr Schol 98:6 F 15 '71 *
Will he say: help me finish what my brothers
  began? W. H. Honan. il pors N Y Times
  Mag p27+ N 28 '71 *

KENNEDY, Elizabeth
Baby bubble sequel. il por Ladies Home J
  88:56+ O '71

KENNEDY, Ethel (Skakel)
Ethel & Andy. M. Cheshire. il pors Ladies
  Home J 88:86+ O '71 *

KENNEDY, Eugene C.
Neglected prophecy of James Kavanaugh.
  por Commonweal 94:287-8 My 28 '71

KENNEDY, Gerald, bp
Anti-COCU but pro-ecumenism. Chr Cent
  88:985-6 Ag 18 '71

KENNEDY, James F.
Sound-operated light controllers. il Electr
  World 86:39 N '71

KENNEDY, Jane
Singular woman. A. Snyder. pors McCalls 98:
  43 Je '71 *

KENNEDY, Joan (Bennett)
Non-candidate's wife. por Time 98:23 N 29
  '71 *

KENNEDY, John Fitzgerald, 1917-1963
Improbable triumvirate: Khrushchev, Kennedy, and Pope John. N. Cousins. pors
  Sat R 54:24-35 O 30 '71 *
Jigsaw puzzle of history; adaptation of address. J. P. Roche. il por N Y Times Mag
  p 14-15+ Ja 24 '71; Discussion. p4 F 14;
  59+ F 21; 12 Mr 14 '71
Kennedy years: what endures? K. Auchincloss. il pors Newsweek 77:20-2 F 1 '71 *
LBJ looks back. W. F. Buckley, jr. Nat R
  23:1323 N 19 '71 *
Mark Twain & John F. Kennedy. C. Clemens.
  il Hobbies 76:138-9 Mr '71 *

Assassination
  See also
Committee to investigate assassinations

Inaugural address
JFK, bitter memories of a cold day. G.
  Clarke. New Repub 164:13-15 Ja 16 '71

Statues, portraits, etc.
Kennedy portraits: White House portraits by
  Aaron Shikler. pors U S News 70:88 F 15
  '71

KENNEDY, John Fitzgerald, family
Painting of a legend. A. Shikler. il pors
  McCalls 98:76-81+ Mr '71

KENNEDY, John F. library. See John F. Kennedy library, Cambridge, Mass.

KENNEDY, Joseph P. jr. foundation. See Joseph P. Kennedy. jr. foundation

KENNEDY, Joseph Patrick, family
My 8 years as the Kennedys' private nurse;
  ed. by M. Cheshire. R. Dallas. il por Ladies
  Home J 88:77+ F; 106+ Mr '71

KENNEDY, Kathleen
Kathleen Kennedy; interview, ed. by B.
  Kevles. por Seventeen 29:160-1+ S '70

KENNEDY, Lois J.
Congressional cup. il Motor B & S 127:37+
  Mr '71
Ficker wins California cup. Motor B & S 127:
  39 Mr '71
Outboard world championship: Havasu, too
  hot for the pros. il Motor B & S 127:28-30+
  F '71
West is best in the test. il Motor B & S
  127:30-1+ Je '71

KENNEDY, Mary
Even a flower; poem. Cath World 213:273
  S '71

KENNEDY, Robert Francis, 1925-1968
Kennedy justice, by V. S. Navasky. Review
  Bsns W il por p 13 O 9 '71. D. B.
  Moskowitz *
  Commentary 53:82-4 Ja '72. J. Q. Wilson *
  Nat R 23:1312-13 N 19 '71. G. F. Will *
  New Repub 165:26+ O 9 '71. J. J. Fried *

Assassination
R.F.K. must die! by R. B. Kaiser. Review
  America 124:156+ F 13 '71. J. F. Drane
  See also
Committee to investigate assassinations

Funeral rites and ceremonies
American journey; interviews, ed. by J.
  Stein and G. Plimpton. Review
  Cath World 213:95-6 My '71. R. J. Meister
  New Yorker 46:108-11 F 13 '71. L. E.
  Sissman

KENNEDY, Rose (Fitzgerald)
Family-power all the way; interview, ed. by
  A. Talmey. por Vogue 157:84-5+ Je '71

about
Keeping up with Rose Kennedy at 81. L.
  Bergquist. il por McCalls 98:92-3+ S '71 *
Rose, by G. Cameron. Review
  Life 70:10 Je 18 '71. B. Darrach *
Rose; excerpts. G. Cameron. il pors Ladies
  Home J 88:87-9+ Jl; 67-9+ Ag '71 *

KENNEDY, Ted. See Kennedy, E. M.

KENNEDY family
Kennedys emerge for an opening. il pors
  Life 71:86 D 31 '71

KENNEDY, CAPE
Cape Kennedy. W. Hedgepeth. Look 35:48
  Ja 12 '71
  See also
United States—John F. Kennedy space center

KENNEDY center for the performing arts,
  Washington, D.C. See John F. Kennedy
  center for the performing arts, Washington,
  D.C.

KENNEDY international airport. See New
  York (city)—Airports

KENNEDY international awards. See Joseph
  P. Kennedy, jr. foundation

KENNEDY library. See John F. Kennedy library, Cambridge, Mass.

KENNEDY space center. See United States—
  John F. Kennedy space center

KENNELS
In short, nothing is too good for Butch. il
  Life 71:92-3 N 26 '71
Jupiter's run and doghouse are built into the
  hill. il Sunset 146:90 F '71

KENNER, Hugh
Epilogue: the dead-letter office. il Art in Am
  59:104-11 Jl '71
Reviewer's choice. il Life 71:8 D 10 '71

KENNETT, James P. and others
Paleomagnetic chronology of pliocene-early
  pleistocene climates and the plio-pleisto-
  cene boundary in New Zealand. bibliog il
  Science 171:276-9 Ja 22 '71
—See Watkins, N. D. jt. auth.

KENNEY, Brigitte L. and Norwood, F. W.
CATV: visual library service. bibliog il Am
  Lib 2:723-6 Jl '71

KENNEY, Frances Marie (Burke)
I guess I'm a gung-ho mother; interview,
  ed. by A. Hollister. il por Life 70:48 F 5 '71

KENNEY, James E.
Coming of the cosmocorp. il America 125:450-
  2 N 27 '71

KENNY, Herbert Andrew
They love it in Boston; or, How the Globe's
  book section works. B. A. Bannon. il por
  Pub W 199:69-70 My 31 '71 *

KENSINGTON rune stone
Stone of contention. il Sr Schol 99:2 S 27 '71

KENT, Leticia
(ed) See Johnson, V. E. Sex questions people
  don't ask and should
(ed) See Mailer, N. Rape of the moon
(ed) See Masters, W. A. Sex questions people
  don't ask and should
(ed) See Pauling, L. Doctor Linus Pauling
  talks about vitamin C. and. . .

KESSLER, Harry Klemens Ulrich, graf von
Do you suffer from déjà vu? S. J. Tonsor.
Nat R 23:1474-5 D 31 '71
In the twenties: the diaries of Harry Kessler,
tr. by C. Kessler. Review
Newsweek por 78:81 Ag 30 '71. S. K.
Oberbeck *
KESSLER, Jane W.
Steps toward self control. il PTA Mag 65:
14-16 bibliog(p32) Ja '71
KESSLER, Jascha
Inner world where poets wander. Sat R 54:
39+ O 2 '71
KESSLER, Sydney
It is a near light portending; poem. Sat R
54:29 S 25 '71
KESWICK family
Keswicks keep it all in the family. A. T.
Demaree. il Fortune 84:135 N '71
KETCHES. See Sailing vessels
KETCHIKAN, Alaska
Taking the cure in Ketchikan. D. Butwin.
il Sat R 54:38-40 Jl 17 '71
KETCHUM, Richard M.
England's Vietnam: the American revolution.
bibliog il Am Heritage 22:6-11+ Je '71
Men of the Revolution. por Am Heritage
22:20-1 Ag; 20-1 O; 23:48-9 D '71
KETTENTANZ; ballet. See Ballets—Criticism
KETTERING, Ohio
Government center instead of city hall. il
Am City 86:65 Je '71
KETTLES
Cast-iron cooking vessels. J. D. Tyler. il
Antiques 100:217-21 Ag '71
Electric water kettles. il Consumer Bul 54:34-
6 O '71
KETTNER, Irene
Printing with tiles. il Ceram Mo 19:30-1 D '71
KEUTER, Cliff
Cliff Keuter dance company, the Cubiculo,
NYC. N. Mason. Dance Mag 45:77 Jl '71 *
KEVLES, Barbara H.
(ed) When I was 17; interviews. pors Seven-
teen 30:130-1+ O '71
(ed) See Kennedy, K. Kathleen Kennedy
KEVORKIAN, Jack
Mercury in human tissues shows 50-year
decline. Sci N 100:278-9 O 23 '71 *
KEY, Mary Ritchie
Role of male and female in children's books,
dispelling all doubt. bibliog il por Wilson
Lib Bul 46:167-76 O '71
KEY cases, holders, etc.
Novel type of key case. il Consumer Bul 54:
38-9 My '71
KEY holders. See Key cases, holders, etc.
KEY 73 central committee. See Evangelistic
work
KEY WEST, Fla.
Key West, to have and have not. F. Trippett.
Look 35:44-5 Ap 6 '71
Turning the Keys. D. Butwin. il Sat R 54:
38-40 F 27 '71
KEYES, Paul W.
Prayer by the Statue of liberty. il Read
Digest 99:84-5 O '71
KEYNES, John Maynard Keynes, 1st baron
Are you a Keynesian? W. F. Buckley, jr.
Nat R 23:162-3 F 9 '71 *
KEYS, FLORIDA. See Florida Keys
KEYSERLING, Mary Dublin
Excerpt from testimony before the Senate
committee on the judiciary, September 11,
1970. Cong Digest 50:27+ Ja '71
KHABAROV, Stanislav
Perpetual motor of the universe. Space World
H-8-92:38-9 Ag '71
KHACHIKIAN, Edward E. and Weedman, D.
W.
Byurakan observatory in Soviet Armenia.
il Sky & Tel 41:217-19 Ap '71
KHAIRALLAH, Philip A. See Robertson, A. L.
jr. jt. auth.
KHAMA, Sir Seretse
Africa and America: the seventies; address,
March 1971. Vital Speeches 37:679-83 S 1
'71
KHAMSIN (wind) See Winds
KHAN, Agha Mohammed Yahya. See Yahya
Khan, A. M.
KHAN, Aijaz A. and Baur, W. H.
Eight-membered cyclosilicate rings in muirite.
bibliog il Science 173:916-18 S 3 '71
KHAN, Anwar A.
Cytokinins: permissive role in seed germina-
tion. bibliog il Science 171:853-9 Mr 5 '71
KHARE, Bishun N. See Sagan, C. jt. auth.
KHERDIAN, David
Over hills into Berkshire pines; poem. Na-
tion 212:762 Je 14 '71
KHMER ballet. See Ballet—Cambodia

KHOMAN, Thanat. See Thanat Khoman
KHRUSHCHEV, Nikita Sergeevich
All war can prove is how stupid we are; ex-
cerpt from letter, August 1963. Sat R 54:35
O 30 '71
Straight from the bear's mouth. Nat R 23:
70-1 Ja 26 '71
                    about
Burial of an unperson. il pors Sr Schol 99:
16-17 O 11 '71 *
Detective story; controversy over Khrush-
chev remembers. il por Newsweek 77:36+
F 8 '71 *
Improbable triumvirate: Khrushchev, Ken-
nedy, and Pope John. N. Cousins. pors
Sat R 54:24-35 O 30 '71 *
Khrushchev memoirs. N. Cousins. Sat R 54:
20-1 Mr 13 '71 *
Khrushchev remembered. T. Foote. Harper
243:60 N '71 *
Kremlin scoop? Sr Schol 97:7-8 Ja 18 '71 *
Obituary
   Newsweek il pors 78:40-1+ S 20 '71
   Time il pors 98:27-9 S 20 '71
Proletarian ruler. T. Frankel. Commentary
51:96+ Je '71 *
Quiet passing of Nikita Khrushchev. R. Chel-
minski. il Life 71:40 S 24 '71 *
Second death of a Soviet leader. il por
Life 71:12-13 D 31 '71 *
Soviet public relations. Nation 213:259 S 27
'71 *
Technological fraud; authenticity of the
memoirs. T. Szamuely. Nat R 23:201-3 F
23 '71 *

Visit to the United States, 1959
Day Khrushchev visited the establishment.
J. K. Galbraith. pors Harper 242:72-5 F
'71; Reply with rejoinder. H. J. Szold.
242:11 Ap '71 *
KIASAT, Ahmad, and Chambliss, C. R.
Observatory-planetarium at Kutztown, Penn-
sylvania. il Sky & Tel 42:76-7 Ag '71
KIBBEE, Robert J.
Fresh face for CUNY. por Newsweek 78:76
Ag 9 '71 *
New chancellor of CUNY. por Sch & Soc 99:
398 N '71 *
KIBBUTZ. See Collective settlements—Israel
KICKBOXING. See Boxing
KIDD, Charles V. See Wolfle, D. jt. auth.
KIDD, Isaac C. Jr
Look at U.S.-Soviet rivalry in the Medi-
terranean; interview. il por U S News 71:
110-11 N 15 '71
KIDD, James
Psychical research society awarded funds
to prove soul's existence. Chr Cent 88:
947 Ag 11 '71 *
Soul searching. Newsweek 77:65 F 8 '71 *
KIDDE, Walter, and company
Walter Kidde's stormy voyage with U.S.
lines. W. S. Rukeyser. il Fortune 84:82-5+
Jl '71
KIDERA, Ed
Transmission they said wouldn't work. E. F.
Lindsley. il Pop Sci 198:112-13 Ap '71 *
KIDNAPPING
Almost-perfect kidnaping; abduction of ten-
year-old Kenneth Young. J. P. Blank.
Read Digest 98:140-4 Je '71
Back in action: seizure of G. H. S. Jackson
by Uruguay's Tupamaros. Newsweek 77:34+
Ja 18 '71
Claude Fly's seven-month nightmare. P.
Friggens. il Read Digest 99:64-70 S '71
Convention on terrorism transmitted to the
Senate; message, may 11, 1971. R. M.
Nixon. Dept State Bul 65:28 Jl 5 '71
83 hours till dawn; excerpts. G. Miller and
B. Mackle. il pors Ladies Home J 88:197-
204 My; 70-1+ Je '71; Same abr. Read Di-
gest 99:235-41+ D '71
Getting tough; kidnaping of 4 U.S. airmen
in Turkey. il Newsweek 77:53-4 Mr 15 '71
Story behind the book: the revolution script;
Cross-Laporte affair, interview, ed. by B.
A. Bannon. B. Moore. por Pub W 201:42-3
Ja 3 '72
Tempting target; Israeli diplomat E. Elrom.
Time 97:37 My 31 '71
Third special session of the OAS general
assembly adopts measures on kidnaping
and terrorism; statements, with text of
convention and resolution. W. P. Rogers.
Dept State Bul 64:228-34 F 22 '71
   See also
Ransom

   Anecdotes, facetiae, satire, etc.
Day they stole the Agnew. P. Steinfels.
Commonweal 93:390+ Ja 22 '71

KIDNEY donors
Family that raised the art of living to its
noblest form. D. Snell. il Todays Health
49:20-5+ O '71
Kidney transplant donor tensions. Sci Digest
69:56-7 Je '71
Rejection in the family. il Newsweek 77:
64-5 Mr 1 '71

KIDNEYS
Intrarenal formation of angiotensin I. H. D.
Itskovitz and C. Odya. bibliog il Science
174:58 O 1 '71
Kidney: primary source of plasminogen after
acute depletion in the cat. R. F. Highsmith
and D. L. Kline. bibliog il Science 174:141-2
O 8 '71
Renin secretion: an anatomical basis for
tubular control; juxtaglomerular apparatus. L. Barajas. bibliog il Science 172:485-7
Ap 30 '71
Sugar transport: effect of temperature on
concentrative uptake of α-methylglucoside
by kidney cortex slices. P. McNamara and
others. bibliog il Science 172:1033-4 Je 4
'71
Vitamin D metabolism: the role of kidney
tissue. R. Gray and others. bibliog il Science 172:1232-4 Je 18 '71
See also
Urine

Diseases
I can't take any more; dialysis treatment
for polycystic kidney disease. il por Newsweek 78:51-2 Jl 26 '71
Incredible ordeal of Chad Calland, M.D;
glomerulonephritis. A. Hano. il por Redbook 137:94+ S '71
What every woman should know about a common urinary-tract infection: bacteriuria.
Good H 173:147 Ag '71

Transplantation
Heart of the matter. Trans-Action 8:17 Ja
'71
Kidney in time; case of C. Salamensky. il
por Newsweek 78:45 Ag 2 '71
See also
Kidney donors

KIDNEYS, Artificial
Burgeoning business in artificial kidneys. N.
A. Martin. il Duns 98:81+ O '71
Coating the charcoal; improved kidney dialy-
sis. il Sci N 100:138 Ag 28 '71
Heart of the matter. Trans-Action 8:17 Ja '71
I can't take any more; dialysis treatment
for polycystic kidney disease. il por News-
week 78:51-2 Jl 26 '71
Survival for $25,000. il Time 98:57 D 20 '71

KIDS (periodical)
For, about and by kids. il Time 97:46-7 Ja
25 '71
Kids' answer to Dick and Jane. il Life 70:
59-60 Ja 29 '71

KIEFFABER, Lois M. See Peterson, A. W. jt.
auth.

KIEL
Music
Report:
Isang Yun's Spirit love. J. H. Sutcliffe.
il Opera N 36:27 S '71

KIELBASO, J. James. See Koelling, M. K. jt
auth.

KIELLOR, Garrison
Lowliest bush a purple sage would be. New
Yorker 47:35 Mr 6 '71

KIENAST quintuplets. See Quintuplets

KIENHOLZ, Edward
Horror show. il Newsweek 78:65 Ag 9 '71 •

KIERNAN, V. G.
Great powers wash their hands. il Nation 213:
682-6 D 27 '71

KIERSTEAD, David L.
Calibrating digital voltmeters. il Electr World
85:36+ Je '71

KIESTER, Edwin, Jr
Ombudsman: new BMOC. il Todays Health
49:34-7 Ap '71
These major-leaguers succeeded in spite
of... il pors Todays Health 49:46-51 O '71
Ugly truths about today's beauty aids. il
Todays Health 49:16-20+ Je '71

KIGOSHI, Kunihiko
Alpha-recoil thorium-234: dissolution into
water and the uranium-234/uranium-238
disequilibrium in nature. bibliog il Science
173:47-8 Jl 2 '71

KIKUTAKE, Kiyonori
Cities on the sea? J. Lear. il Sat R 54:80-
6+ D 4 '71 •

KILBORN, Jean
Dainty miniature daffodils. il Horticulture
49:28-9+ Ap '71

KILBURN, F. C.
Contact lenses that are easy on the eyes.
il Mech Illus 68:84-5+ Ja '72
Facts on financing an RV. il Mech Illus 67:
58-9+ Ag '71

KILCOYNE, Colm
Untangling the Irish question. il America
125:140-1 S 11 '71

KILEY, Laura
Hands; poem. Seventeen 31:91 Ja '72

KILLACKEY, H. and Diamond, I. T.
Visual attention in the tree shrew: an ablation study of the striate and extrastriate
visual cortex. bibliog il Science 171:696-9
F 19 '71

KILLER whales. See Whales

KILLIAN, Charles
Wilberforce university. bibliog il por Negro
Hist Bul 34:83-7 Ap '71

KILLIFISHES
Desert pupfish. J. H. Brown. il Sci Am 225:
104-10 N '71
Rare pupfish transplanted. Cons 25:33 F '71

KILLING, Mercy. See Euthanasia

KILLING of animals. See Hunting—Ethical
aspects

KILLINGSWORTH, Charles C.
Emergency disputes and public policy. Mo Labor R 94:42-5 Ag '71

KILLY, Jean Claude
Lights, camera! Here comes Oscar candi-
date Jean-Claude. C. Gammon. il por
Sports Illus 35:68-71 O 4 '71 •

KILNS
Experiment in building a hillside kiln. B. G.
Erkkila. il Ceram Mo 19:22-4 Ja '71
Workshop: kiln building with space age ma-
terials. F. Colson. il Craft Horiz 30:46-5
Ag '70; reply with rejoinder. C. Nitchie.
31:8 Ag '71

KILPATRICK, James Jackson
High court: where now? il Nat R 23:1287-91
N 19 '71
In Guinea: stuff and nonsense. Nat R 23:81-2
Ja 26 '71

KILVERT, B. Cory, Jr
Furor over mower safety. il Mech Illus 67:
84-5+ Ag '71
Guide to compact appliances. il Mech Illus
68:98-100+ Ja '72
Gypsy moth runs wild. il Home Gard 58:28-
9+ Ag '71

KIM, Chin
Librarians and copyright legislation: the historical background. bibliog il Am Lib 2:
615-22 Je '71

KIM, Dong-soo. See Hook, E. B. jt. auth.

KIM, Sangduk. See Paik, W. K. jt. auth.

KIMBALL, Roland B.
Educational philosophy and behavioral ob-
jectives. bibliog il Clear House 45:496-500
Ap '71

KIMBALL, William J.
Gabriel insurrection of 1800. bibliog Negro
Hist Bul 34:153-6 N '71

KIMERLITE. See Peridotite

KIMBERLY-Clark corporation
Last hurrah. il Forbes 108:24-5 O 15 '71

KIMURA, Motoo. See Ohta, T. jt. auth.

KINARD, Epsie
Address book. See issues of House beautiful up
to December 1971

KINASES
Adenosine 3',5'-monophosphate-dependent pro-
tein kinase of cultured mammalian cells.
M. I. Klein and M. H. Makman. bibliog
Science 172:863-4 My 21 '71

KINDERGARTEN
Happy classroom home. C. Winterton and
J. Winterton. Todays Ed 60:69 S '71
See also
Nursery schools

KINDERGARTEN teachers. See Teachers

KINDSVATTER, Richard, and Tosi, D. J.
Assistant principal: a job in limbo. bibliog
Clear House 45:456-64 Ap '71

KINETIC art
Mirrors, motors and motion; exhibition for
children at the Albright-Knox art gallery,
Buffalo. C. B. Johnson. il Sch Arts 70:34-5
F '71

KING, Billie Jean (Moffitt)
Billie Jean King goes for the net profits. R.
Woodbury. il por Life 71:77 N 19 '71 •
Billie Jean King: this is not a good life.
A. Hano. Redbook 137:86+ O '71 •
More Joan of Arc than Shirley Temple. R.
Blount. il pors Sports Illus 35:30-1 S 20
'71 •
Old lady of tennis. L. Foster. il McCalls 98:41
Jl '71 •
Women lobbers. il pors Newsweek 77:90-1
My 3 '71 •

KING, Blues Boy. See King, R. B.
KING, Bruce
Certification: an educational necessity. il
Dance Mag 45:71-3 Je '71
KING, Charles Glen
Facts about health foods; ed. by B. Russell.
House & Gard 140:59+ Jl '71
Warning: you can take too much vitamin C.
McCalls 98:65 Mr '71
KING, Clyde Clayton
Old man. L. L. King. Harper 242:80-9 Ap '71;
Same abr. il Read Digest 99:100-4 Ag '71 *
KING, Coretta (Scott)
Finally, I've begun to live again; ed. by C. L.
Sanders. il pors Ebony 26:172-6+ N '70

about

Growing strength of Coretta King. A. Walker.
Redbook 137:96-7+ S '71 *
KING, David
Veterans' march to Boston. New Repub 164:
11-13 Je 12 '71
KING, F. Wayne
Adventures in the skin trade; with biograph-
ical sketch. il Natur Hist 80:6, 8-10+ bib-
liog (p 104) My '71
KING, Helen H.
Black woman and Women's lib. il Ebony 26:
68-70+ Mr '71
Eva Jefferson: young voice of change. il pors
Ebony 26:71-4+ Ja '71
Soul of Christmas; story. Ebony 27:172-6 D '71
KING, Ivan R.
Dynamics of star clusters. il Sky & Tel 41:
139-43 Mr '71
KING, Joan
Color now with Europe; story. Redbook 136:
66 Ja '71
KING, John McCandish
Oilman King loses his spread. il Bsns W
p 19 Ap 3 '71 *
Penury without tears. il por Time 99:59-60
Ja 17 '72
KING, Larry L.
Beasts of Baltimore. il pors Atlan 229:70-7
Ja '72
Old man. Harper 242:80-9 Ap '71; Same abr.
il Read Digest 99:100-4 Ag '71
Playboy's literary ego-trip. Pub W 200:17-18
N 1 '71
Road to power in Congress. Harper 242:39-
42+ Je '71
There'll be no jail for Jesse Ford, except
the prison of his mind. il pors Todays
Health 49:28-33+ D '71
KING, Lawrence T.
Governor Reagan's private war. Commonweal
94:358-9 Jl 9 '71
KING, Martin Luther, 1929-1968
I have a dream; excerpts from address, 1963.
il por Sr Schol 98:2 Mr 22 '71

Assassination

Frame-up, by H. Weisberg. Review
Sat R 54:23-4 Ap 10 '71. F. J. Cook
See also
Committee to investigate assassinations
KING, Maxine Joyce. See King, M.
KING, Maxwell
Violence to reform to apathy. Nation 213:325-
7 O 11 '71
KING, Micki
Queen of the divers is King. W. F. Reed.
il por Sports Illus 35:31-3 Ag 16 '71 *
KING, Muriel
Coordinated patient care: a consultant's
view. Ment Hy 55:461-6 O '71
Evaluation and treatment of suicide-prone
youth. bibliog Ment Hy 55:344-50 Jl '71
KING, Nancy Williams, and others
Behavioral sensitivity to microwave irradia-
tion. bibliog il Science 172:398-401 Ap 23 '71
KING, Riley B.
B.B. bringing the blues back home. V. Gibbs.
pors Sr Schol 97:23-5 Ja 18 '71 *
B.B. King. G. Goodman. il pors Look 35:54-7
Je 29 '71 *
KING, Robert H.
Pipeline rehabilitation proved better, cheap-
er. il por Am City 86:80+ O '71
KING, Ruth G.
Rescue squad. il Har Yrs 11:28-9 N '71
KING, Wallace
Beginning teacher; interview. il por Todays
Ed 60:54-9 S '71
KING, Yolanda Denise
Martin Luther King's daughter: people expect
me to be a saint; interview, ed. by M.
Jablow. il pors Seventeen 31:92-3+ Ja '72
KING COUNTY library system, Seattle
Libraries and hunger. A. M. Griffen. il Li-
brary J 96:3287-91 O 15 '71

KING crabs
Crab that shakes hands. C. P. Idyll. il Nat
Geog 139:254-71 F '71
KING features syndicate. See Newspapers—
Syndicate service
KING heroin; drama. See Fann, A.
KING James Bible. See Bible—Versions
KING Lear; drama. See Shakespeare, W.—
Plays
KING resources company
Oilman King loses his spread. il Bsns W
p 19 Ap 3 '71
Two likely buyers for King oil funds. Bsns
W p32 Mr 20 '71
KING salmon fishing. See Salmon fishing
KINGDOM of God
Community. V. P. McCorry. America 124:
551-2 My 22 '71
Politics of the kingdom of God. R. Stone.
Chr Cent 88:337-40 Mr 17 '71
See also
Jesus Christ—Kingdom

Biblical teaching

Dreams of a third age. H. O. J. Brown. Chr
Today 15:3-5 Jl 16 '71
KINGDON, Robert M.
Social welfare in Calvin's Geneva; adapta-
tion of address, December 30, 1968. bibliog f
Am Hist R 76:50-69 F '71
KINGMAN, Eduardo
Painter of hands. D. Suro. il Americas 23:
37-40 Je '71 *
KINGMAN, Lee
Search for children's books in Iceland. il
Horn Bk 47:462-9 O '71
KINGS and rulers
How inflation hits pomp and circumstance.
il U S News 70:54+ Je 21 '71
See also
Divine right of kings
KING'S valentine tarts; drama. See Watts,
F. B.
KINGSWELL, Joseph Attard
One vote. New Yorker 47:43-4 N 6 '71 *
KININS
Cytokinins: permissive role in seed germina-
tion. A. A. Khan. bibliog il Science 171:
853-9 Mr 5 '71
KINKEAD, Eugene
Our far-flung correspondents. New Yorker
47:66+ Jl 31 '71
Thoreau and the endless beach. il Sat R 54:
40+ Mr 13 '71
KINNEAR, H. M.
Unique lab: the little red schoolhouse. il Am
For 77:26-7+ N '71
KINNELL, Galway
Path toward the high valley; poem. New
Yorker 47:38 Ap 17 '71
KINNEY national service, inc.
Kinney chooses the quick over the dead. il
Bsns W p38-9+ Jl 3 '71
KINNICK, B. Jo
Day I kissed Anton Chekhov; story. Todays
Ed 60:26-7 My '71
KINO, Eusebio Francisco
On Father Kino's trail. W. T. LeViness. il
por Américas 22:30-5 N '70 *
KINSLEY, Michael E.
My life and hard times with Nader's raiders.
il Seventeen 30:148-9+ S '71
(ed) See McConnell, E. Face to face with a
female Senate page
KINSTLER, Everett Raymond
Using reference materials to paint portraits;
excerpts from Painting portraits. il por Am
Artist 35:30-8 My '71
KINTER, William B. See Janicki, R. H. jt.
auth.
KIPLING, Rudyard
Mark Twain & Rudyard Kipling. C. Clemens.
Hobbies 76:151 S '71 *
KIPNIS, Alexander
Solid bass. D. Hamilton. por Hi Fi 21:64-5
My '71 *
KIPPHARDT, Heinar
Stage directions. S. Kauffmann. New Repub
165:24+ Jl 10 '71 *
KIRBY, F. E.
Beethoven's Pastoral symphony as a Sin-
fonia caracteristica. bibliog f il Mus Q 56:
605-23 O '70
KIRBY, Thomas B. and Robinson, J. C.
Dust storm observations from New Mexico.
il Sky & Tel 42:264-5 N '71
KIRCHER, Donald Peter
Whatever happened to Singer? il por Forbes
108:31-3 Ag 1 '71 *
KIRCHNER, Leon
Musician of the month. J. Hiemenz. por Hi
Fi 21:MA4-5 Ja '71 *

KIRK, Donald
Who wants to be the last American killed in Vietnam? il N Y Times Mag p9+ S 19 '71
Why they call Lon Nol the mayor of Pnompenh. il N Y Times Mag p26-7+ Je 27 '71

about

Army at sea. Nation 213:291-2 O 4 '71 *

KIRK, Gerry
As seen by gloomy Gloria. Nat R 23:426 Ap 20 '71
What about the other five? Nat R 23:1058 S 24 '71

KIRK, John J.
Ecology: is it a fad? por Camp Mag 43:5 Je '71
Incredible journey. por Camp Mag 43:5 F '71

KIRK, Malcolm S.
Travel bazaar. Harp Baz 104:20+ Jl '71

KIRK, Russell
From the academy. See issues of National review

KIRK, Ruth
Place to stretch your soul. il Nat Wildlife 9: 42-7 Je '71

KIRK, Will
(ed) See Toffler, A. How to cope with Future shock

KIRKENDALE, Warren
New roads to old ideas in Beethoven's Missa solemnis. bibliog f il Mus Q 56:665-701 O '70

KIRKLAND, Gelsey
Dance; interview. ed. by E. Miller. por Seventeen 30:138 Ag '71
What I learned from my sister Johnna. il por Seventeen 29:79 Jl '70

about

Brief biography. S. Goodman. pors Dance Mag 45:80-1 D '71 *

KIRKLAND, Joseph Lane
Mr Inside at the AFL-CIO. por Newsweek 78:50 S 6 '71 *

KIRKMAN, Henry N.
Kinetic path of genes undergoing selection. bibliog il Science 174:68-70 O 1 '71

KIRKPATRICK, Curry
Arnie re-arms while Lee flees. il pors Sports Illus 35:20-1 Ag 2 '71
Big one who stayed. il por Sports Illus 35: 46-50 N 29 '71
Closest thing to being born. il Sports Illus 34:60-4+ F 22 '71
College basketball (cont) Sports Illus 34:42-4 F 1; 42-5 F 8; 35:65-6 D 13 '71
Crazy cat and his curious Warriors. il Sports Illus 34:32-6 Ja 25 '71
Far out in middle America. il Sports Illus 34: 20-1 Mr 1 '71
Golf (cont) Sports Illus 34:65-6 Je 14; 35:46-7 Jl 5; 54-5 Jl 26; 84+ S 20 '71
Just forget UCLA, the man said. il Sports Illus 34:22-5 Mr 29 '71
Sportsman of the year. il pors Sports Illus 35:34-9 D 20 '71
Week; college basketball. Sports Illus 34:38-9 Ja 11 '71
Young Britons win an old cup. il Sports Illus 34:30-1 Je 7 '71

KIRKPATRICK, Lyman B. Jr
Former CIA executive defends its operations. por U S News 71:81-2+ O 11 '71

KIRKPATRICK, Miles W.
More consumer action by the FTC; interview. pors Nations Bsns 59:38-40 Ja '71

KIRKTON, Carole Masley
Behavioral objectives. Engl J 60:142-50 Ja '71
Class discussion and the craft of questioning. bibliog Engl J 60:408-13+ Mr '71
Media literacy: focus on film. bibliog Engl J 60:831-8 S '71
Play's the thing: theater and dramatic arts in secondary schools. bibliog Engl J 60:533-9 Ap '71
Reading to teach: summer in professional literature. Engl J 60:670-7 My '71

KIRKUS bulletin (periodical)
Book burners: Virginia Kirkus service summary of Contra mundum by W. Kendall. Nat R 23:687-8 Je 29 '71

KIRSCH, Rita
Remodeling a brownstone in Brooklyn. il House B 113:70 My '71

KIRSCHEN, Étienne Sadi
Pick a spot. pors Forbes 108:57-8+ O 15 '71 *

KIRSHENBAUM, Jerry
And here, to bring you the play by play. il Sports Illus 35:32-5+ S 13 '71
Basketball. il Sports Illus 34:76+ Je 7 '71
Bats and busts, size-15 sneakers and a dead bird. il Sports Illus 34:62-6+ Je 28 '71

Fastest splash in the West. il pors Sports Illus 35:18-19 Jl 17 '71
Having at a ball in new Havana. il Sports Illus 35:18-21 Ag 30 '71
Horse racing. Sports Illus 35:79+ S 27 '71
Let me make one thing clear. il Sports Illus 34:34-6+ Je 7 '71
Our enemy gets the 'ook. pors Sports Illus 34:26-7 Mr 29 '71
Pro football. il Sports Illus 36:96+ D 6 '71
Rodeo. Sports Illus 35:85+ D 20 '71
Sport's $5 million payday. il por Sports Illus 34:20-3 Ja 25 '71
Working at a life of leisure. il Sports Illus 34:52-6+ F 1 '71

KIRSHMAN, J. Dianne. See Brunner, H. R. jt. auth.

KIRSTEIN, Lincoln
Art books of 1970 (cont) Nation 211:663-4+ D 21 '70

KIRSTEN, Dorothy
Kirsten on Puccini; interview. ed. by J. Rockwell. il por Opera N 35:21-3 Mr 6 '71

KIRTLEY, David W.
Reef-building worms; with biographical sketch. il Sea Front 17:102-7, 127 Mr '71

KIRWAN, John D.
Everything under control; poem. Nat R 23: 1050 S 24 '71
Lysistrata rides again; poem. Nat R 23:1105 O 8 '71

KISH, Frances
Only the family knows. Har Yrs 11:42 D '71

KISS before midnight; story. See Ledbetter, E.

KISSEL, Maryanne M.
Marionette project. il Sch Arts 70:14-15 Je '71

KISSEL, Peter
Son of the Axe chops 'em. W. Tower. il Sports Illus 34:22-3 Mr 15 '71 *

KISSIMMEE, Fla.
What hath Disney wrought? H. Ehrlich. il Look 35:26-8+ Ap 6 '71

KISSINGER, Henry Alfred
President Nixon's planned visits to China and the U.S.S.R. discussed by presidential assistant Kissinger; transcript of news conference, November 30, 1971. Dept State Bul 65:705-14 D 20 '71

about

Evening with Henry; speaker at conference sponsored by Project Runnymede at MIT's Endicott house. D. Shearer. il Nation 212: 296-9 Mr 8 '71 *
In search of Kissinger. J. Kraft. por Harper 242:54-61 Ja '71 *
Key man exploring a summit in Peking. il por U S News 71:26 N 1 '71 *
Kissinger and Rogers. J. Osborne. New Repub 164:13-15 Mr 27 '71 *
Kissinger tilt. Time 99:15 Ja 17 '72 *
Kissinger's role. Nation 212:357 Mr 22 '71 *
Logic of defection. Nat R 23:301 Mr 23 '71 *
Making of a new China hand. il por Newsweek 78:52 O 18 '71 *
More about Kissinger. New Repub 164:13-14 Ap 3 '71 *
Predominance of Kissinger. Time 97:13 Mr 8 '71 *
Rise of Henry Kissinger. D. Landau. il por Ramp Mag 10:36-44 D '71 *
Road to Peking; or, How does this Kissinger do it? B. L. Collier. il pors N Y Times Mag p34-5+ N 14 '71 *
Toilet training; remarks on Soviet policy. J. Osborne. New Repub 166:16-17 Ja 1 '72 *
Uses of Kissinger. Nat R 23:351-2 Ap 6 '71 *
Vietnam: how Nixon plans to win the war. B. Garrett. il por Ramp Mag 9:26-31 F '71 *
Who's in charge here. il H. Sidey. Life 71: 4 D 10 '71 *
Who's secretary of state? il pors Newsweek 77:26-7 Mr 15 '71 *
Why Nixon is relatively good. E. Snow. il por Time 98:13 Ag 2 '71 *

Visits to China
(People's Republic) 1971
Blazing the trail to Peking. il U S News 71:17 Ag 2 '71
Diplomatic notes. L. H. Gelb and M. H. Halperin. il Harper 243:28-30+ N '71
Kissinger in Peking (cont) il por Newsweek 78:40 N 1 '71
Kissinger's mission to China: a close-up. por U S News 71:53 Jl 26 '71
Letter from Hong Kong. R. Shaplen. New Yorker 47:58-60+ Jl 31 '71
Nixon: I will go to China. il pors Newsweek 78:16-21 Jl 26 '71
Peking's other face. K. Baarslag. Nat R 23: 991+ S 10 '71

KISSINGER, Henry Alfred—Visits to China
(People's Republic) 1971—*Continued*
Round-trip ticket to Peking. il por News-
week 78:61-2 O 18 '71
Secret of Lincoln's sitting room. H. Sidey.
Life 71:6 Jl 30 '71
Secret voyage of Henry K. il por Time 98:13
Jl 26 '71
With Kissinger in China. il pors Life 71:
32-3 N 12 '71
KISSINGER kidnap plot. See Conspiracy
KISTENMACHER, Thomas J. and Marsh, R. E.
Crystal structure of L-N-acetylhistidine mono-
hydrate: an open and closed case. bibliog
il Science 172:945-6 My 28 '71
KISTER, Kenneth F.
Viewpoint. Library J 96:173, 935, 1687, 2276,
2745, 3735 Ja 15, Mr 15, Jl, S 15, N 15 '71
KISTIAKOWSKY, George B.
After the Pentagon papers: talk with Kistia-
kowsky, Wiesner; interview. ed. by E. Lan-
ger. pors Science 174:923-8 N 26 '71
KIT amplifiers. See Amplifiers
KITCHEN cabinets
Push-button cupboard. il House & Gard 140:
68-9 Jl '71
Spices and herbs, a home of their own. il
Sunset 146:121 Ap '71
Tips from a pro on hanging kitchen cabinets.
T. Hook. il Mech Illus 67:92-3+ Jl '71
KITCHEN carpets. See Rugs and carpets
KITCHEN cutlery. See Cutlery
KITCHEN furniture
Island saves steps. S. K. Stone. il Farm J 95:
50 My '71
Place for flour, sugar, spices: a place for
mixing and kneading. il Sunset 146:128
Je '71
This kitchen's crossroads is a mapletopped
island. il Sunset 146:164 Ap '71
Traffic center in a busy kitchen. il Sunset
146:138 Je '71
See also
Kitchen cabinets
KITCHEN garbage grinders. See Refuse grind-
ers
KITCHEN gardening. See Vegetable garden-
ing, Home
KITCHEN ranges. See Stoves
KITCHEN scissors. See Scissors and shears
KITCHEN storage. See Storage in the home
KITCHEN thermometers. See Thermometers,
Cooking
KITCHEN timers. See Timing devices
KITCHEN utensils
About cookware. il Redbook 137:118-19 O '71
Chinese wok cookery. il Bet Hom & Gard
49:116 O '71
Chinese wok for crisper vegetables. K.
McReynolds. il Org Gard & Farm 18:
127-9 D '71
Cooking with a wok: which wok and what
other tools? il Sunset 146:154 F '71
Egg aids. il Bet Hom & Gard 49:77 D '71
Fisherman's luck: cooking fish. A. F. Rush.
il McCalls 98:58+ S '71
Flourishes with food; tools for the good
cook's workshop. il McCalls 98:58+ My '71
How much technology in the kitchen? J. Cox.
il Org Gard & Farm 18:100-4 Ja '71
Kitchen shower, after 25 years? S. Lindsay
and S. Nirenberg. il House B 113:30+ My
'71
Know your pots and pans. J. R. Cary. il
Parents Mag 46:94-6 S '71
Perfect omelet every time. il McCalls 99:
76+ O '71
Shopping for your kitchen in Honolulu. il
Sunset 146:86-7 Je '71
Shopping for your kitchen in Manhattan. il
Sunset 147:66+ N '71
Those colorful cookware finishes. il Good H
172:6 Ap '71
Tools and rules for meat roasting. il Bet
Hom & Gard 49:114+ Ap '71
22 great kitchen buys from 60¢. H. Brown. il
Am Home 74:44-5 Ag '71
Very special cookware. il Redbook 138:116-17+
N '71
Western kitchen. See issues of Sunset
What's cooking is black and white. il McCalls
99:86-7 D '71
Wood you love to touch. J. M. Bauer. il Am
Home 74:60+ O '71
Your choice in graters. il Sunset 147:93-4
S '71
See also
Cookery—Measurements
Kettles
Popeil brothers, inc.
Skillets

Care
Cleaning a cast iron pot in camp. il Sunset
146:34 Ap '71

KITCHEN ware. See Kitchen utensils
KITCHENS
Adobe and tile give her kitchen a Mexican
flavor. il Sunset 147:110 O '71
Airy kitchen for a mountaintop. il House B
113:78 Jl '71
Country kitchen in a city apartment; New
York, N. Craig. il House B 113:92-3 F '71
Designing a kitchen that works. M. David-
son. il Ladies Home J 88:84+ Mr '71
Dozen great ideas in my kitchen. L. Widman.
il Farm J 95:76-7 F '71
Farm kitchen is a gathering place. il Sunset
147:104 D '71
For computer-age cooks. N. Craig. il House B
113:38 F '71
Four best kitchen plans. M. K. Spencer. Am
Home 74:60 My '71
4 great kitchens with ideas you can use.
S. Mead. il Bet Hom & Gard 49:86-91 N
'71
4 kitchens a cook could covet. N. Craig. il
House B 113:100-9 S '71
Great new kitchen life; kitchens you'd love
to live in. il House & Gard 140:36-47 Jl '71
How to run a kitchen. Redbook 138:36+ Ja '72
Inside kitchen, flooded with sky light. il
Sunset 147:64-5 Ag '71
Introducing the Galloping gourmet and his
personal test kitchen. J. Kelly. il pors
Good H 172:113-15 Je '71
Kitchen hung in a hall. M. K. Spencer. il Am
Home 74:92+ Mr '71
Kitchens: 3 private views. M. Davidson. il
pors Ladies Home J 88:21+ Je '71
Living with children:
The kitchen. il Redbook 137:122-5+ S
'71
New kitchen switched on to all-appliance
cooking. il House & Gard 139:120-2 Ap '71
New life for an old kitchen. il Good H 174:
97-9+ Ja '72
Our new super kitchen. il House & Gard
139:36-41 Ja '71
Putting walls to work in a corridor kitchen.
M. K. Spencer. il Am Home 74:70-1+ Mr
'71
Remodeled farmhouse kitchen. J. R. Cary. il
Parents Mag 46:74-7 Ap '71
Stylish function in a talk-as-you-work kit-
chen. il House B 113:72 N '71
Taste for graphics; Los Angeles display
kitchen. il House B 113:88-9 Mr '71
Tradition and timesavers, now side by side.
N. Craig. il House B 113:130-1 N '71
Under old beams, an all-new kitchen. N.
Craig. il House B 113:122-5 My '71
Up-to-the-minute kitchen with practicality-
plus. il Good H 172:122-4 Mr '71
What kind of kitchen? The cook decides,
says this designer; interview. ed. by S.
Nirenberg. J. Hauser. House B 113:44-5
S '71
KITES
He's at it again, as high as a kite. A. Ver-
schoth il por Sports Illus 35:60-2+ O 18 '71
Kites. il Design 72:36-7 Sum '71
Proper way to fly a kite. Good H 173:194 O
'71
Taking a flyer; delta-wing kites. il Time
98:46 D 20 '71
World on a string. B. Ingraham. il Har Yrs
11:35-6 Mr '71
KITES (birds)
Swallowtails of Royal Palm; with photographs
by M. Wright, R. Green and N. Reed. Au-
dubon 73:40-9 Ja '71
KITES, Fishing. See Fishing—Implements and
appliances
KITS, Medicine. See Medicine kits
KITT, Eartha
C'est si bon. por Newsweek 78:61-2 N 22 '71 •
KITTENS. See Cats
KITTIKACHORN, Thanom
Coup that wasn't. Newsweek 78:38+ N 29
'71 •
Same old crowd. il por Time 98:39 N 29 '71 •
KITTREDGE, William
Underground river; story. Atlan 227:87-8 Mr
'71
KIUCHI, Nobutane
Japan will have to slow down. Fortune 83:
98-9+ F '71
KIVER, Eugene P. and Mumma, M. D.
Summit firn caves, Mount Rainier, Washing-
ton. bibliog il Science 173:320-2 Jl 23 '71
KIWI berries. See Yangtaos
KIZER, Carolyn
Food of love; Heart's limbo; poems. Poetry
118:71-3 My '71
KIZER, George A.
Religion and education: cooperation or con-
flict? bibliog Sch & Soc 99:152-6 Mr '71

KLAPPERT, Peter
Invention of the telephone; poem. New Yorker
47:32 Je 19 '71
Mail at your new address; poem. Atlan 228:45
Jl '71
KLARE, Michael T.
Counterinsurgency's proving ground. Nation
212:527-31 Ap 26 '71
KLARMANN, Joseph. See Fenner, D. jt. auth.
KLASS, Philip J.
Spies above. il Time 98:20+ Ag 30 '71 •
KLASSEN, Elmer Theodore
To get things done. Newsweek 78:78 D 20
'71 •
KLEBANOFF, Lewis Bernard
Help for the exceptional parent. J. Cass.
Sat R 54:39 Ag 21 '71 •
KLEIN, Anne
Year of the lion. M. Palmer. McCalls 99:49
O '71 •
KLEIN, David
Dangerous fallacy of the accident-prone
child. il Parents Mag 46:78-9+ N '71
Exploding the myth of I.Q. il Parents Mag
46:52-3+ O '71
KLEIN, David R.
Reaction of reindeer to obstructions and dis-
turbances. bibliog il Science 173:393-8 Jl
30 '71
KLEIN, Elinor
Home-team; story. Harp Baz 104:116-17 My
'71
KLEIN, Herbert George
Nixon, the press and the public; interview.
il pors U S News 71:68-70+ N 15 '71
KLEIN, Jerry
Carry me back to Chicago; story. Redbook
138:60-1 Ja '72
KLEIN, Lawrence R, award. See Lawrence R.
Klein award
KLEIN, Marjorie H. and others
Far Eastern students in a big university.
subcultures within a subculture. Bul Atom
Sci 27:10+ Ja '71
KLEIN, Monroe I. and Makman, M. H.
Adenosine 3',5'-monophosphate-dependent pro-
tein kinase of cultured mammalian cells.
bibliog Science 172:863-4 My 21 '71
KLEIN, Oskar
Arguments concerning relativity and cosmol-
ogy. bibliog il Science 171:339-45 Ja 29 '71
KLEIN, Ronald, and Herman, Sheldon
Precautions with alkyl mercury. Science 172:
872 My 21 '71
KLEIN, Sardl
Ham on wry. R. Hattersley. il Pop Phot 68:
110-13 Ja '71 •
KLEIN, Stanley
Havoc in your household. il Sci Digest 69:14-
19 My '71
Lawn mowers & other killers. il Nation 212:
402-4 Mr 2 '71
KLEINDIENST, Richard G.
Honesty in politics. W. Pincus. New Repub
165:9-10+ D 4 '71 •
Man to follow Mitchell. por Newsweek 79:
12-13 Ja 3 '72 •
KLEINSMITH, Lewis J. See Dokas, L. A.
jt. auth.
KLEIST, Lucille
Hobbies are my hobby. il Har Yrs 11:32-3 O
'71
KLEMESRUD, Judy
Disciples of Sappho, updated. il N Y Times
Mag p38-9+ Mr 28 '71
KLEMIN, Diana
Panorama of children's book design. il Pub W
199:56-8+ F 1 '71
Portfolio of Robert Byrd. il por Am Artist
35:54-9 Je '71
KLEMPERER, Otto
Comic Klemperer. E. Greenfield. por Hi Fi
21:10-12 Je '71 •
KLEPPE, Thomas S.
Bigger help to small business? interview. il
por Nations Bsns 59:26-30 My '71
KLEWANS, Georgine
Bird on Nellie's hat. il Har Yrs 11:14-15 Ja
'71
Grandmother's jewel box. il Hobbies 76:92
My '71
KLINE, Daniel L. See Highsmith, R. F. jt.
auth.
KLINE, Hester Ann
Annual enchantment: hill-town hopping. il
Travel 135:40-5+ Je '71
Grow-and-cut your own Christmas trees. il
pors Har Yrs 11:46-9 Ja '71
It's time to think Christmas. il Home Gard
58:41 D '71
KLINE, Lloyd W.
Changing expectations in the doctorate. Sch
& Soc 99:93-4 F '71

KLINEBERG, Otto
Race and I.Q. excerpts from Race and
psychology. il UNESCO Courier 24:4-9+
N '71
KLINGEBIEL, Ute I. See Plimmer, J. R. jt.
auth.
KLINGER, Georgette
Face maintenance. il Harp Baz 104:36 Mr '71
about
Good-earth way to glow. il pors Mlle 72:170-
3 Mr '71 •
KLINGER, Mary F.
Music and theater in Hogarth. bibliog f il
Mus Q 57:409-26 Jl '71
KLINGER, Max
Etcher of the id. R. Hughes. il Time 98:44-5
Ag 30 '71 •
KLITGAARD, Robert E.
Dual labor market and manpower policy.
bibliog Mo Labor R 94:45-8 N '71
KLOBUCHAR, Jim
Ordeal on Beartooth Mountain. il Pop Mech
136:84-9+ N '71
KLONDIKE gold rush. See Gold mines and
mining—Canada
KLOSS, Henry
Ah, freedom! Forbes 108:36+ Jl 15 '71 •
KLUETMEIER, Heinz
Gallery: photographs. Life 70:4-5 F 26 '71
KLUGE, John Werner
Metromedia. il por Forbes 107:19-20 Ap 1
'71 •
KLUGE, P. F.
Ann-Margret, suddenly blooming. il pors
Life 71:30-5 Ag 6 '71
Detective Egan's new assignment. il pors
Life 71:85-6+ D 10 '71
Memorable song for our times. il pors Life
72:44A-44B Ja 14 '72
Micronesia: America's troubled island ward.
il Read Digest 99:161-4 D '71
KNAP, Jerome J.
Play versus discipline. il Field & S 76:184+
My '71
KNAPP, Howard
Build a garden you can reach! il Org Gard
& Farm 18:114-15 S '71
KNAPP, John V. See Slotnick, H. B. jt. auth.
KNAPP commission. See Commissions of in-
quiry
KNAPSACKS
To get a load on your back. il Sunset 147:
90-1 O '71
KNAUER, Virginia Harrington (Wright)
How you can make big business care about
the little man; ed. by J. C. G. Conniff.
por Todays Health 49:18 D '71
Report for shoppers; interview. por U S
News 71:53-4 Ag 30 '71
KNEBEL, Fletcher
Cop named Joe. il Look 35:15-19 Jl 27 '71
Skyjacker; with excerpt from The skyjacker,
by David G. Hubbard. il Look 35:22-6 F 9
'71
KNEE
Knee's the thing. E. Sheppard. Harp Baz
104:134-5 Ap '71
KNEELAND, Douglas E.
From tin can on wheels to the mobile home.
il N Y Times Mag p 18-19+ My 9 '71
KNEF, Hildegard
Authors & editors. L. P. Freilicher. por Pub
W 200:39-41 Jl 12 '71 •
Bitter goddess. A. Cooper. por Newsweek 78:
73 Jl 5 '71 •
Hildegard rides again. M. Orshefsky. il pors
Life 71:36-7 Jl 23 '71 •
KNEIP, Richard Francis
Governor proposes program. il por Am Lib
2:1032-3 N '71 •
KNEZEVICH, Stephen J. See Gregg, R. T. jt.
auth.
KNICKERBOCKER, Suzy, pseud. See Mehle, A.
KNICKS (basketball team) See Basketball
teams
KNIDOS excavations. See Turkey—Antiquities
KNIEVEL, Evel
Evel Knievel. New Yorker 47:22-6 Jl 24 '71 •
I'm going to jump a mile anyway. R. F.
Jones. il por Sports Illus 35:48-9 Jl 5 '71 •
KNIFE handles. See Handles
KNIFE sharpeners, Electric. See Household
appliances, Electric
KNIGHT, Arthur
Film. il Sat R 54:40-1 Jl 31 '71
SR goes to the movies. See issues of Satur-
day review
KNIGHT, Charles, and Knight, Nancy
Hailstones; with biographical sketches. il Sci
Am 224:14. 96-103 Ap '71

KNIGHT, Cook
Piper Cherokee Flite Liner. il Flying 88:42-4+
My '71
KNIGHT, Curtis A. and others
Quasars: millisecond-of-arc structure re-
vealed by very-long-baseline interferome-
try. bibliog il Science 172:52-4 Ap 2 '71
KNIGHT, Doug
Big elk come high and hard. il pors Out-
door Life 148:68-71+ N '71
Landlocked monsters of Ireland. il Field & S
75:78-9+ F '71
Madcap of the swamps. il Field & S 76:46-7+
N '71
KNIGHT, Leavitt A. Jr
How to relax without pills. Read Digest 98:
139-41 F '71
KNIGHT, Nancy. See Knight, C. jt. auth.
KNIGHT, Pamela
Design for sport (cont) Sports Illus 35:66-7
N 8 '71
KNIGHT, Wallace E.
Three poems; In the old camp; Sailing; Paths.
Atlan 228:65 Jl '71
KNIGHTS and knighthood
See also
Tournaments
KNIGHTS of Columbus
McManus v. the Knights of Columbus. P.
Good. il pors Harper 243:66-70+ S '71
KNIPSCHER, Gerard
Human touch: Gerard Knipscher. J. Vander-
wall. il por Am Artist 35:38-43+ D '71 •
KNISLEY, Joseph L. Jr
Watershed recreation without water. il
Parks & Rec 6:27 Ja '71
KNIT goods
Glossary of knits to help you shop and sew.
S. Christensen. il Good H 172:186 Mr '71
Knits: something new in menswear. Chang-
ing T 25:19-20 S '71
What well-knit men will wear. il Bsns W
p89 Ja 23 '71
KNITTING
Redbook guide. il Redbook 137:104-12 O '71
KNITWEAR. See Knit goods
KNIVES
Consumer's guide to pocket knives. il Mech
Illus 67:73 Je '71
Diamond knives. il Chem 44:20-1 Ja '71
Redbook guide to cutlery. il Redbook 137:97-
100 My '71
See also
Bowie knives
KNOPF, Terry Ann
Doesn't anyone care about Cairo? Common-
weal 93:510-12 F 26 '71
KNORR, Donald J. See Weintraub, A. E. jt.
auth.
KNOTS. See Macramé
KNOTS and splices
8-strand eye splice. T. Bottomley. il Motor B
& S 128:73 Ag '71
KNOTT, James Proctor
Untold delights of Duluth; address, January
27, 1871, ed. by D. G. McCullough. il por
Am Heritage 22:76-80 Je '71
KNOTT, Paul D. See Horn, J. L. jt. auth.
KNOTTING. See Macramé
KNOTWEEDS
Long blooming, well behaved polygonum
ground cover. il Sunset 146:228-9 Je '71
KNOWLEDGE
New role for foundations courses in teacher
education. J. W. Wagener. Ed Digest 36:
29-31 Mr '71
See also
Information, Freedom of
Intuition
KNOWLEDGE, Sociology of
Crises and knowledge. J. Schmandt. Science
174:231 O 15 '71
KNOWLEDGE, Theory of
Insights and illusions of philosophy, by J.
Piaget. Review
Nation 212:792-4 Je 21 '71. M. Lebowitz
Knowing isn't everything. J. Smith. America
124:286-8 Mr 20 '71
KNOWLES, Asa S.
Changes in the traditional concepts of higher
education. Sch & Soc 99:405-9 N '71
President's view of campus unrest. Sch &
Soc 99:81-4 F '71
KNOWLES, John H.
Higher education and the nation's health.
Science 171:337 Ja 29 '71
about
Quest for a silver unicorn. E. Kern. il pors
Life 70:58+ Je 4 '71 •
KNOWLES, Laurence W.
Student rights find a friend in court(s) Ed
Digest 36:15-17 My '71

KNOX, Gerald M.
Education. Bet Hom & Gard 49:26+ S; 6+ O;
56+ N '71
Family health. See issues of Better homes
and gardens
KNOX, Kevin
Whoosh goes the Wasco whiz. G. Curry il por
Sports Illus 34:66+ My 3 '71 •
KNOX, William T.
Cable television; with biographical sketch.
il Sci Am 225:12, 22-9 O '71
KNOXVILLE and Knox County, Tenn, public
library
Knoxville, Tenn: five levels in a block. il
Library J 96:3982 D 1 '71
KNUCKLE joints. See Joints
KNUDSEN, Semon Emil
Bunkie Knudsen redesigns White motor. il
por Bsns W p44+ O 30 '71 •
Knudsen returns in a White truck. por Bsns
W p22-3 My 1 '71 •
KNUDSON, Richard L.
Help stamp out department chairmen. Engl
J 60:377-8 Mr '71
KNUDSON, Rozanne
Censor's horoscope. il Am Lib 2:180-5 F '71
Two poets. il pors Am Lib 2:1045-6+ N '71
KOANGA; opera. See Delius, F.
KOBAL, John
(comp) Not quite ready when you are, C.B.
Esquire 75:86 Ap '71
KOBAYASHI, Yutaka, and others
Ornithine decarboxylase stimulation in rat
ovary by luteinizing hormone. bibliog il
Science 172:379-80 Ap 23 '71
KOCH, Charles R.
NFO takes on the world. Farm J 95:50 F '71
KOCH, Edward I.
Excerpt from testimony before the Subcom-
mittee on constitutional rights, February
23, 1971. Cong Digest 50:237+ O '71
about
Travelling office. New Yorker 47:30-3 O 2
'71 •
KOCH, Herman William
Current physics information. bibliog il Sci-
ence 174:918-22 N 26 '71
On physics and employment of physicists in
1970. bibliog il Phys Today 24:23-7 Je '71
about
Prospects for physics support continue to
deteriorate. M. S. Rothenberg. il por Phys
Today 24:91-2 Ja '71 •
KOCH, Kenneth
Rhapsode from cinci. P. Carroll. Poetry 119:
104-6 N '71 •
KOCHAV, Shimshon, and Eyal-Giladi, Hefzibah
Bilateral symmetry in chick embryo deter-
mination by gravity. bibliog il Science 171:
1027-9 Mr 12 '71
KOCHEN, Joseph. See Roth, E. F. jr, jt. auth.
KOCI, Robert
Concrete hull is not a boat. Motor B & S
127:54+ F '71
KOCSIS, John D.
Mardi gras time in high school. il Sch Arts
71:22-3 S '71
KODAK company. See Eastman Kodak company
KODAK international newspaper snapshot
awards. See Photography—Competitions
KODAK teenage movie contest. See Moving
picture photography—Competitions
KODÁLY, Zoltán
Zoltán Kodály, by L. Eösze. Review
Am Rec G 37:675 My '71. G. Jellinek •
KOEHLER, Margaret H.
Making of a seashore: Cape Cod. il Travel
136:60-7 Ag '71
KOEHLER, Mathilde
Echoes; poem. Seventeen 30:80 Ja '71
KOELLING, Melvin K. and Kielbaso, J. J.
Christmas trees in America. il Horticulture
49:24-7+ D '71
KOENIG, Bob
Freelance market: TV news and features. il
Writers Digest 51:28-30 Je '71
KOENIG, Gea. See Koenig, H. jt. auth.
KOENIG, H. P.
Nova Scotia. il Travel 135:28-37+ My '71
KOENIG, Helmut, and Koenig, Gea
Country cousin to the sport of kings. il
Travel 135:34-9 Je '71
Unique Martinique. il Travel 136:28-33 Ag
'71
KOENIG, John
Washington's retreat: Barbados. il Travel 136:
70-4 Jl '71
KOENIG, Louis W.
President needs new kinds of power. bibliog
f Ann Am Acad 397:71-82 S '71

KOEPPE, David E. See Miller, R. J. jt. auth.
KOESTLER, Arthur
Marrakech. Atlan 228:6+ D '71
KOETHE, John
Boston (cont) Art N 70:18+ Sum '71
KOETTER, Fred
Many moods of modular. B. Plumb. il pors
Am Home 74:76+ O '71 •
KOFLER, Karl
Turnabout trials. il por Time 98:44-5 Jl 19
'71 •
KOGA, Toyoki
Theory versus practicality. por Phys Today
24:40-1 Ap '71
KOGAN, Herman
Story behind the book. L. P. Frelicher. il
Pub W 200:36-7 O 25 '71 •
KOHAK, Erazin V.
Maoism in east Europe? Commonweal 95:
275-7 D 17 '71
KOHL, Daniel H. and others
Fertilizer nitrogen: contribution to nitrate
in surface water in a Corn Belt watershed.
bibliog il Science 174:1331-4 D 24 '71
KOHLBERG, Lawrence
Toward moral maturity. il por Time 97:48
Je 28 '71 •
KOHLRABI
Kohlrabi and beets grow in the same row.
Org Gard & Farm 18:62-3 Ag '71
Kohlrabi and chard: two early and easy
vegetables. J. G. Bowman. il por Org Gard
& Farm 18:56-7 F '71
What kohlrabi is is peculiar. il Sunset 147:
130 Ag '71
KOHN, Howard
Civil war in Cairo, Ill: a dispatch from the
front. il Ramp Mag 9:46-51 Ap '71
KOHN, J. A. and others
Crystallography of the hexagonal ferrites.
bibliog il Science 172:519-25 My 7 '71
KOJIS, T. Robert
Switch off. Flying 89:60+ Jl '71
KOK, Bessel. See Radmer, R. jt. auth.
KOKANEE. See Salmon
KOKJOHN, Joseph E.
Hell of a question. Commonweal 93:367-70, 503
Ja 15, F 19 '71
KOLBE, Maximilian
Honors beyond bitterness. Chr Cent 88:1283
N 3 '71 •
KOLBE, Robert
(ed) See Seller, A. Arthur Seller by design
KOLINS, Bill
London notebook (cont) Pub W 199:34 Mr
1; 25-6 My 17; 50-1 Je 28; 200:pt2 163-5 S 27
'71
KOLKO, Gabriel
Illusion of withdrawal. New Repub 165:19-21
O 2 '71
Oiling the escalator: an economic incentive
for winning the war? New Repub 164:18-20
Mr 13 '71
KOLLAS, Joseph E.
How to really hang a picture. il Design 72:
40-1 mid-Wint '71
KOLODIN, Irving
A is for abacus. il Sat R 54:66-7 Mr 27 '71
Countdown for Kennedy. il Sat R 54:37-9+
Jl 31 '71
Man and the machine. Sat R 54:45 My 29 '71
Music to my ears. See issues of Saturday
review
Music's most distant star. il pors Sat R
54:45-7 Ap 24 '71
Recordings in review. See issues of Saturday
review
Recordings reports: miscellaneous LPs. See
issues of Saturday review
KOLTON, Paul
Market structure: remodel or reform? por
Bsns W p47-8 O 23 '71 •
KOMAROV, Victor
Mirrors on Mars. Space World H-12-96:42 D
'71
KOMATSU manufacturing company. See Ma-
chinery industry
KOMISAR, Lucy
Feminist manifesto: excerpt from address
Read Digest 97:105-8 Ag '71
KOMMER, Ronald S.
Speed up for muskies. il por Outdoor Life
148:74-5+ Ag '71
KOMODO dragons. See Lizards
KOMORNY, Annie
Four poems. Good H 173:177 D '71
You haven't changed a bit! poem. Good H
172:132 Mr '71
KOMOSKI, P. Kenneth
Untested textbooks. il Time 97:33 Je 7 '71 •
KONIGSBERG, Harold
Gorilla cowed his keepers; with editorial com-
ment. D. Walsh. il pors Life 70:3, 42-8+
Je 25 '71 •

KONIGSBURG, Elaine (Lobl)
Eliot Miles does not wish you a Merry
Christmas because; story. Redbook 138:78 D
'71
KONISHI, T. and Slepian, J.
Summating potential with electrical stimula-
tion of crossed olivocochlear bundles. bib-
liog il Science 172:483-4 Ap 30 '71
KONKEL, Carl R.
Importance of space exploration. Space World
H-4-88:44-5 Ap '71
KONRAD, Klaus. See Wolff, K. jt. auth.
KOOB, C. Albert
Catholic educators face new options. Amer-
ica 124:366 Ap 10 '71
Undiscussed alternatives. America 125:168-70
S 18 '71
KOONS, Linda C. See Goddard, D. R. jt.
auth.
KOONTZ, Dean R.
Always an open door for the paperback
category novel. il Writers Digest 52:24-6+
Ja '72
KOONTZ, Elizabeth Duncan
New priorities and old prejudices. Todays
Ed 60:25-6 Mr '71; Same abr. Ed Digest 36:
32-3 My '71
KOPECKY, Gini
Pet journal. Ladies Home J 88:68 O '71
KOPKIND, Andrew
Hard times. See issues of Ramparts
I wanna hold your head: John Lennon after
the fall. pors Ramp Mag 9:18-19+ Ap '71
—and Ridgeway, James
Mental health industry: this way lies mad-
ness. il Ramp Mag 9:38-44 F '71
KORALL, Burt
Jimmy Webb. Sat R 54:76 S 25 '71
Mingus on Mingus. Sat R 54:42 Jl 31 '71
Pop. Sat R 54:59 D 25 '71
KORBONSKI, Andrzej
East and west Europe: a continent divided.
Cur Hist 60:257-62+ My '71
KOREA
Foreign relations
Korea and the emerging Asian power balance.
P. C. Hahm. For Affairs 50:339-50 Ja '72
Union (proposed)
Dawning hope for reunion. T. I. Moon. Chr
Cent 88:1360-1 N 17 '71
Korea-U.S. relations. C. H. Germany. Chr
Cent 88:285-7 Mr 3 '71
Korean unification: problems and prospects.
T. I. Moon. Chr Cent 88:72-3 Ja 20 '71
KOREA (People's Republic)
See also
United Nations—Korea (People's Republic)
KOREA (Republic)
See also
Student demonstrations—Korea (Republic)
United Nations—Korea (Republic)
United States—Armed forces—Forces in Korea
Economic conditions
Booming South Korea: Park gets go-ahead
for another 4 years. il U S News 70:75-6 My
10 '71
Foreign relations
Imaginary emergency. Time 98:39-40 D 20 '71
United States
See United States—Foreign relations—
Korea (Republic)
Politics and government
See also
Elections—Korea (Republic)
KOREA (Republic)-United States air agree-
ment. See Aviation—International aspects
KOREAN armistice. See Korean war, 1950-1953
—Peace and mediation
KOREAN cookery. See Cookery, Korean
KOREAN war, 1950-1953
American participation
Korean decision, by G. D. Paige. Review
Trans-Action 8:93-6 N '70. D. S. McClellan
Peace and mediation
POW's in Korea: choosing sides. il Sr Schol
99:15-16 N 29 '71
Prisoners and prisons
POW's in Korea: choosing sides. il Sr Schol
99:15-16 N 29 '71
KOREN, Ed
Postcards from the Hudson: drawings. New
Yorker 47:54-65 N 13 '71
KORIM, Andrew S.
Education for government careers; excerpts
from report. por Sch & Soc 99:328 O '71

KORJUS, Miliza
Korjus and Martini on LP. A. Favia-Artsay. pors Hobbies 76:35-6+ S '71 *
Miliza Korjus. A. Favia-Artsay. por Hobbies 76:35-6+ Je '71 *

KORTENAAR, Henry ten
Go. and synod no more. Commonweal 95:196-7 N 26 '71
Might the synod surprise? Commonweal 95:4-5 O 1 '71
Synod of small expectations. Commonweal 94:28-9 Mr 19 '71
Trying to undo the Council. Commonweal 94:348-9 Jl 9 '71

KORVETTE, E. J, Inc. See Arlen realty and development corporation

KOSCOT Interplanetary, Inc.
Fast-buck gospel; enterprises of G. W. Turner. il por Time 98:76+ N 29 '71

KOSHLAND, Daniel Edward, 1920-. See Bell, R. M. jt. auth.

KOSINSKI, Jerzy Nikodem
Trade winds; interview, ed. by C. Amory. Sat R 54:16-17 Ap 17 '71

about
Author & editors. D. N. Mount. por Pub W 199:13-16 Ap 26 '71 *
Fabrication of a culture hero. J. W. Aldridge. Sat R 54:25-7 Ap 24 '71 *
Who here doesn't know how good Kosinski is? W. Kennedy. il Look 35:12 Ap 20 '71 *

KOSKI, George
En route to your grave; poem. Nation 213:602 D 6 '71

KOSSOFF, Evelyn
Evaluating college professors by scientific methods. Am Scholar 41:79-93 Wint '71

KOSTELANETZ, Richard
Nick the knife; or, The life of a football doctor. il pors N Y Times Mag p 12-13+ D 19 '71

KOSTER, Samuel W.
Justice for the general. Newsweek 77:21 F 8 '71 *
Star is lost. por Time 97:13 My 31 '71 *

KOSTOF, Spiro
Soleri's arcology: a new design for the city? il Art in Am 59:90-5 Mr '71

KOSYGIN, Aleksei Nikolaevich
Feathers and foie gras; visit to Cuba. il pors Newsweek 78:54 N 8 '71 *
My friend Trudeau. il por Time 98:51 N 1 '71 *
Soother in Havana. il pors Time 98:40+ N 8 '71 *
Suitor next door. il por Newsweek 78:33 N 1 '71 *
Unlikeliest Indian since Coolidge; attendance at Indian ceremony wearing feather headdress. il pors Life 71:38-9 N 5 '71 *
See also
Glassboro conference, 1967

KOTLER, Philip, and Levy, S. J.
Demarketing, yes demarketing. il Harvard Bsns R 49:74-80 N '71

KOTLOWITZ, Robert
Catching Lenny. il pors N Y Times Mag p6-7+ D 19 '71

KOTRE, John N.
Church as inkblot. America 124:196-200 F 27 '71

KOTZWINKLE, William
Follow the eagle; story. Redbook 136:86 Ap '71
Love story; story. Redbook 138:86-7 D '71
Most incredible meal; story. Mlle 72:154-5 Mr '71

KOUHOUPT, Rudy
You can make this model steam tractor. il Pop Mech 135:94-7+ F '71

KOUNOVSKY, Nicholas
Kounovsky secret of lifetime fitness; excerpt from Joy of feeling fit. il McCalls 98:72-5+ My '71 *

KOURILSKY, Marilyn
Anatomy of a dead lecture. il Clear House 46:20-6 S '71

KOVACH, Bill
Nixon's too left-wing for William Loeb. il por N Y Times Mag p 14+ D 12 '71

KOVAL, Alexander
Soviet space research programme. Space World H-6-90:9-11 Je '71

KOVAL, Ivan
What is Mars like? il Space World H-8-92:40-1 Ag '71

KOVAL, John
Clergy under stress. Newsweek 77:58 Ja 25 '71 *

KOWALSKI, Steven, and Fresco, J. R.
Preparation of highly labeled [³²P] nucleic acids from yeast; isolation of denaturable leucine acceptor transfer RNA. bibliog il Science 172:384-5 Ap 23 '71
—and others
Nucleotide sequence of the denaturable leucine transfer RNA from yeast. bibliog il Science 172:385-7 Ap 23 '71

KOZLOFF, Max
Esthetic valence of cubism. il Art N 70:34-7+ Ap '71
Under the corporate wing. il Art in Am 59:92-9 Jl '71

KOZLOV, Vasilii Ivanovich
Open letter to the Kremlin; reprint. America 124:346-8 Ap 3 '71

KOZOLL, Charles E. See Murphy, M. K. jt. auth.

KRAAR, Louis
Taiwan's strategy for survival. il Fortune 84:124-31+ N '71
Wealth and power of the overseas Chinese. il Fortune 83:78-81+ Mr '71

KRABBE'S disease. See Leukodystrophy

KRADO, Jono
Confrontation; poem Chr Cent 88:334 Mr 17 '71

KRAEMER, Paul M. and others
DNA constancy in heteroploidy and the stem line theory of tumors. bibliog il Science 174:714-17 N 12 '71

KRAFT, Joseph
In search of Kissinger. por Harper 242:54-61 Ja '71
Letter from Cairo. il New Yorker 47:76+ S 18 '71
Letter from Moscow. New Yorker 47:64+ My 29 '71
Letter from Santiago. New Yorker 46:80-9 Ja 30 '71
Letter from Tokyo. New Yorker 47:140-2+ D 11 '71
Reports & comment: Washington. Atlan 227:6+ Je '71
Those Arabists in the State department. il N Y Times Mag p38-9+ N 7 '71

KRAFT, Ken, and Kraft, Pat
Useful onion. il Horticulture 49:38-9+ F '71

KRAFT, Leo
Music of George Perle. bibliog f il Mus Q 57:444-65 Jl '71

KRAFT, Pat. See Kraft, K. jt. auth.

KRAFT, Virginia
Hunting. Sports Illus 34:69-70 Ap 26 '71

KRAFT, William
Rather delightfully wild, the music of William Kraft. D. W. Moore. Am Rec G 37:570 My '71 *

KRAFTCO corporation
Say cheese! Forbes 108:24-5 O 15 '71

KRAHULIK, Henrietta M.
Wanted. Todays Ed 60:20-1 Ap '71

KRAJEWSKA, Estera, and Shugar, D.
Photochemical transformation of 5-alkyl-uracis and their nucleosides. bibliog il Science 173:435-7 Jl 30 '71

KRAJEWSKI, Fran
(ed) See Hunter, E. Exclusive re-visit with Evan Hunter

KRAKATOA (island)
Krakatoa, the killer wave. J. D. Truby. il Sea Front 17:130-9 My '71

KRAM, Mark
At the bell... il pors Sports Illus 34:18-21 Mr 8 '71
Boxing (cont) Sports Illus 35:74+ S 27 '71
Do yuh hear that whistle down the line? il Sports Illus 35:106-10+ N 29 '71
Encounter with an athlete. il pors Sports Illus 35:92-4+ S 27 '71
Everyone will remember what happened. Sports Illus 34:21 Mr 15 '71
To the brink and beyond. il Sports Illus 35:48-52+ Jl 12 '71
about
Letter from the publisher. J. R. Munro. il por Sports Illus 35:5 N 29 '71 *

KRAMER, Arthur
View from Kramer. See issues of Modern photography

KRAMER, Hilton
Cubist epoch. il Art in Am 59:51-7 Mr '71

KRAMER, Jack
Bromeliads. il Horticulture 49:24-7 Mr '71

KRAMER, Larry
Grass and hash business at Syracuse university. il Fortune 84:102-3 S '71

KRAMER, Orin S.
Death of the American ethic. Yale R 61:69-75 O '71

KRAMER, Rita
Parent and child (cont) il N Y Times Mag p 102-3+ Mr 28; 85+ Ap 4 '71
Revolution in our adoption laws. il Parents Mag 46:37-9+ D '71
KRAMER, Robert
Ice-man cometh no more. J. R. MacBean. il Film Q 24:26-33 Sum '71
KRANS, Olof
Bishop Hill; a colony of Swedish pietists in Illinois. R. E. Nelson. il Antiques 99:140-7 Ja '71 •
KRASHNA, Dick
College presidents and students; interview. Mlle 73:373-5 Ag '71
KRASNE, Sally, and others
Freezing and melting of lipid bilayers and the mode of action of nonactin, valino-mycin, and gramicidin. bibliog il Science 174:412-15 O 22 '71
KRASNODAR airport. See Airports—Russia
KRATSCH, Gerald
Snowthrowers: winter fun machines. il Pop Mech 136:50+ N '71
KRAUCH, Velma
Hyperactive engineering. il Am Ed 7:12-13+ Je '71
KRAUS, H. P. (firm) See Booksellers and bookselling—Book rarities
KRAUS, Karl
Offenbach. . .and other Germans. J. Rock-well. por Opera N 35:24-5 Ap 10 '71 •
KRAUS, Richard
Economics of leisure today. bibliog Parks & Rec 6:62-6+ Ag '71
—See Cosgrove, F. A. jt. auth.
KRAUSE, Allison
Behind the headlines with a witness from Kent state. Seventeen 29:156+ Ag '70 •
KRAUSE, Charles A.
New university conference. New Repub 164: 17-18 Mr 20 '71
KRAUSS, Ruth
Comment. P. Schjeldahl. Poetry 117:272 Ja '71
KRAUSS, William A.
What is the best bargain in Europe? Maybe Cadaqués in Spain. il Holiday 49:74-6+ F '71
KRAUSSER, Frank
Do we need 4-channel stereo? il Electr World 86:42-4 Ag '71
KRAUT, Joseph
Nature's way. il por Time 98:64-5 N 29 '71 •
KRAVITZ, Harvey
Pediatrician's view about bedtime stories. Todays Health 49:33 S '71
KREBS, Albert V. Jr
On the road in Mississippi. Cath World 212: 297-300 Mr '71
KREBS, M. E. See Hardie, R. H. jt. auth.
KREH, Lefty
Catch bonefish on your own! il por Field & S 76:60-1+ My '71
Duck hunting tips. il por Pop Mech 136:113 D '71
Foggy float for squirrel. il Field & S 75:32-3+ Ja '71
KREH, William R.
How science helps combat fliers escape over enemy territory. il Sci Digest 69:16-19 Mr '71
KREIGH, Helen
Overdue. por Wilson Lib Bul 46:360-1+ D '71
We're counting them in! il Am Lib 2:208-9 F '71
KREISKY, Bruno
Ball rolls left. Time 98:43 O 25 '71 •
KRESSEL, Trudy
Pioneer in Peru. J. Reibstein. il pors Dance Mag 45:68-9 F '71 •
KRETCHMER, Jerome
Running for mayor on a garbage truck. G. Lichtenstein. il pors N Y Times Mag p30-1+ Ap 25 '71 •
KRETTEK, Germaine, and Cooke, E. D.
ALA Washington notes. See issues of Wil-son library bulletin
KRETZ, Thomas
Doors and enterings; poem. Chr Cent 88:491 Ap 21 '71
Yes, but not too long; poem. Chr Cent 88: 366 Mr 24 '71
KREUN, Ruby
Our permanent strawberry bed. il Org Gard & Farm 18:46-8 F '71
KREUZER, L. B. and Patel, C. K. N.
Nitric oxide air pollution: detection by opto-acoustic spectroscopy. bibliog il Science 173:45-7 Jl 2 '71
KREYCHE, Gerald F.
Academe and its models. Sch & Soc 99:410 N '71
On the death of college. Sch & Soc 99:223-4 Ap '71

KREYE, Audrea
Electroformed enamels. P. Rothenberg. il Ceram Mo 19:22-5 Mr '71
KRIEBEL, Charles
His bazaar. See issues of Harper's bazaar
Living in luxury with Sister Parish. il por Harp Baz 105:134 D '71
One-room living with Billy Baldwin. il por Harp Baz 105:146 N '71
KRIEGER, Robert I. and others
Detoxication enzymes in the guts of cater-pillars: an evolutionary answer to plant defenses? bibliog il Science 172:579-81 My 7 '71
KRIEGHBAUM, Hillier
Op-ed page revisited. il Sat R 54:91-3 N 13 '71
KRINSKY, Carol Herselle
Albrecht Dürer, 1471-1971. il Art N 70:22-6+ Sum '71
KRIPS, Josef
Becoming a conductor. Opera N 35:14-15 Mr 20 '71
KRISHNA MENON, Vengalil Krishnan
Where are they now? il pors Newsweek 78: 16-17 D 6 '71
KRISHNAMURTI, Jiddu
Durable-avatar. por Time 97:63 Je 7 '71 •
KRISHNASWAMI, S. and others
Olivines: revelation of tracks of charged par-ticles. bibliog il Science 174:287-91 O 15 '71
KRISLOV, Joseph
NLRB petitions that are dismissed or with-drawn. il Mo Labor R 94:71-2 Je '71
KRISS, Ronald P.
Consummate professional. por Time 98:74+ D 6 '71 •
New man at the Review. il Newsweek 78:70 D 6 '71 •
Report to the readers. N. H. Charney. por Sat R 54:20-1 D 25 '71 •
KRISTENSEN, Thorkil
Adult education and economic planning as weapons against unemployment. Sch & Soc 99:232-4 Ap '71
KRISTOFFERSON, Kris
Kris Kristofferson lonely sound from Nash-ville; interview, ed. by E. Miller. por Sev-enteen 30:130-1+ Ap '71

about

New minstrels. pors Harp Baz 104:57 Je '71 •
Pilgrim's progress. P. Axthelm. por News-week 77:105-6 My 24 '71 •
Superstars, poets pickers, prophets. W. Hedgepeth. por Look 35:30+ Jl 13 '71 •
KRISTOL, Irving
Books & ideas (cont) il Fortune 84:173-4 Ag; 183+ N '71
Foolish American ism: utopianism. il N Y Times Mag p31+ N 14 '71
Pornography, obscenity and the case for cen-sorship. il N Y Times Mag p24-5+ Mr 28 '71
Welfare: the best of intentions, the worst of results. Atlan 228:45-7 Ag '71
KRITTER, Ronald
Pile of books; poem. Commonweal 95:280 D 17 '71
KRITZECK, James, and Ryan, J. L.
Jerusalem all but lost; holy places: a Christian viewpoint. Chr Cent 88:1205-6+ O 13 '71
KRIWANEK, Franz
Where and how to find clay; excerpts from Keramos; the teaching of pottery. il Ceram Mo 19:16-19 Ja '71

about

Franz Kriwanek. R. Wolverton and M. Wol-verton. il por Ceram Mo 19:13-15 Ja '71 •
KRLEZA, Miroslav
Stones with the raised hands. il UNESCO Courier 24:17-22 My '71
KROCH'S and Brentano's. See Booksellers and bookselling—Illinois
KROCK, Arthur
Times' loss, history's gain. J. Chamberlain. Nat R 23:656-7 Je 15 '71 •
Where are they now? il pors Newsweek 77: 16 My 3 '71 •
KROEBER, Alfred Louis
Last stone age American; excerpt from The first American. C. W. Ceram. il pors Am Heritage 22:14-19+ Ag '71 •
Persistent cultural systems. E. H. Spicer. bib-liog Science 174:795-800 N 19 '71 •
KROL, John Joseph, cardinal
For the bishops, a non-agenda. J. Over-brook. Commonweal 95:148-9 N 12 '71 •
Krol era. por Time 98:66 N 29 '71 •

KROLL, Ernest
Beer joint alley; poem. New Repub 164:36 Ap 17 '71
Two views of Sunday; poem. Nation 213:602 D 6 '71
KROLL, Jack
Movies. il Art in Am 59:114-15 Mr '71
KROLOW, Karl
Love poem; tr. by M. Bullock. Mlle 72:116 Mr '71
KROMMER, Judith
Kites; A feeling; Hymn to modern candor; poems. Harper 243:81 S '71
KRONENBERGER, John
Cable: shape of things to come? il Look 35:66 S 7 '71
(ed) Is the family obsolete? Look 35:35-6 Ja 26 '71
Kids play outside every day. il Look 35:38-41+ Ap 6 '71
KRONENBERGER, Louis
Broadway's banner years. Atlan 227:101-2+ My '71
KRONENTHAL, Syd
Can you make it into a park? il Am City 86:115-16 S '71
KROSNEY, Herbert
Talk with Yigal Allon. il Nation 212:550-2 My 3 '71
KRUG, Judith F. and Harvey, J. A.
Intellectual freedom. See issues of American libraries
—See Delzell, R. F. jt. auth.
KRUGER, Jannie
M*A*S*H*E*D. Newsweek 77:45-6 F 22 '71 *
KRUGMAN, Saul
Breakthrough on hepatitis. por Newsweek 77:97-8 Ap 5 '71 *
KRUMME, Richard
Money management. See issues of Successful farming
KRUPSKAΓA, Nadezhda Konstantinovna
Nadezhda K. Krupskaya, founder of Soviet public education. L. Goncharov and L. Kunetskaΐa. por Sch & Soc 99:235-7 Ap '71 *
KRUSZYNSKI, Eugene
Urban teachers for urban youth. bibliog Sch & Soc 99:511-13 D '71
KRUTCH, Joseph Wood
Canyonlands. il Audubon 73:32-51 Jl '71
KU KLUX klan
And I ain't just whistlin' Dixie. D. Gregory. il por Ebony 26:149-50 Ag '71
White terror, by A. W. Trelease. Review New Repub 165:30 Jl 17 '71
KUBEK, Tony
TV talk. F. Deford. Sports Illus 34:10 Je 28 '71 *
KUBELIK, Rafael
Kubelik speaks; interview. ed. by J. H. Sutcliffe. por Opera N 36:6-7 S '71

about
Music man for the Met. Time 97:69 Je 21 '71 *
KUBIN, Alfred
Possessed by dybbuks. R. Hughes. il Time 97:68+ F 8 '71 *
KUBINSKI, H. and Kasper, C. B.
Carcinogen and microsomal membrane interactions: changes in membrane density and ability to bind nucleic acids. bibliog il Science 171:201-3 Ja 15 '71
KUBLY, Herbert
Where is Tell? il Holiday 49:48-9+ Jl '71
KUBRICK, Stanley
Kubrick country; interview. ed. by P. Houston. por Sat R 54:42-4 D 25 '71

about
Current cinema. P. Kael. New Yorker 47:50-3 Ja 1 '72 *
Kubrick: degrees of madness. il por Time 98:80-5 D 20 '71 *
Kubrick's brilliant vision. P. D. Zimmerman. il por Newsweek 79:28-33 Ja 3 '72 *
Milk-plus and ultra-violence. H. Alpert. il Sat R 54:40-1+ D 25 '71 *
KUCHARSKY, David
Careers with Christian impact. Chr Today 15:11-14+ S 24 '71
KUCHOWICZ, Bronislaw
Transastronomy at the Dubna conference. Sky & Tel 41:358 Je '71
KUEHL, Linda
Dazzle-dust: a Wolfe in chic clothing. pors Commonweal 94:212-16 My 7 '71
(ed) See Ouologuem, Y. Yambo Ouologuem on violence, truth and black history
KUEHN, Harold
Soybeans' newest ambassador; interview. ed. by B. Coffman. il Farm J 95:35 O '71

KUEHNELT-LEDDIHN, Erik Maria, ritter von
Arab world in turmoil. Nat R 23:993 S 10 '71
Europe's Tibet; Switzerland, a military democracy. il Cath World 214:120-3 D '71
Geolatry, topolatry and chronolatry. Cath World 212:237-9 F '71
Letter from Spain. Nat R 23:134 F 9 '71
Nasty shock. Nat R 23:758 Jl 13 '71
Population explosion? Nat R 23:1239 N 5 '71
Soviet victories. Nat R 23:1415 D 17 '71
KUENSTLER, Frank
Poem: Walking my old haunts. Nation 212:121 Ja 25 '71
KUH, Joyce
How to make money in your spare time. See occasional issues of Ladies' home journal
KUH, Katharine
Fine arts. See issues of Saturday review
Roots of Turkish art. il Sat R 54:20-6+ N 20 '71
KUHN, Edward, Jr
Trade winds; interview. ed. by C. Amory. Sat R 54:16-17 S 4 '71
KUHN, Harold B.
Legacy of Niebuhr. Chr Today 15:23 Je 18 '71
Prospect of carbon-copy humans. Chr Today 15:11-12+ Ap 9 '71
KUHN, P. M. and others
Water vapor: stratospheric injection by thunderstorms. bibliog il Science 174:1319-21 D 24 '71
KUHN, Warren B.
UCSD: the new central library. il Am Lib 2:168-73 F '71
KUIPER, Gerard P.
Lunar and planetary laboratory studies of Jupiter. il por Sky & Tel 43:4-8 Ja '72 (to be cont)
KULICKE, Robert
Robert Kulicke: painter, designer, craftsman. D. Hines. il Am Artist 35:38-43+ Ap '71 *
KULKARNI, Maya
Shakuntala, 92nd street Y, NYC. M. Marks. Dance Mag 45:78 Jl '71 *
KULLESEID, Eleanor
What records should you give to children? il Hi Fi 20:79-83 D '70
KUMIN, Maxine (Winokur)
Faint-hearted suicide; poem. Atlan 228:84 Ag '71
Running away together; poem. New Yorker 47:38 S 4 '71
Saying goodbye; poem. New Repub 165:24 D 11 '71
Song for seven parts of the body; Eternal lover; poems. Poetry 119:12-16 O '71
KUNETSKAΓA, Ludmila. See Goncharov, L. jt. auth.
KUNETT, Rudolph
Riding high on a Moscow mule. J. G. Martin. il pors Nations Bsns 59:66-7 Ja '71 *
KÜNG, Hans
Christianity with a human face; interview. ed. by C. F. Jullien. Commonweal 94:106-7 Ap 9 '71
Hans Küng replies to Gregory Baum. Commonweal 94:326-30 Je 25 '71
Why I am staying in the church. il America 124:281-3 Mr 20 '71

about
Alternative: indefectibility. E. H. Brill. New Repub 164:27-8 My 15 '71 *
Do Humanae vitae and infallibility stand or fall together? T. A. Caffrey. America 125:66-7 Ag 7 '71 *
Follow-up on the Küng-Rahner feud. Chr Cent 88:997-1000 Ag 25 '71 *
Hans Kung et al. J. Deedy. Commonweal 95:98 O 29 '71 *
Hans Küng, papal gadfly. Chr Today 15:27-8 Ap 23 '71 *
Has Küng opened the dikes? J. B. Sheerin. Cath World 213:3-4 Ap '71 *
Infallibility beyond polemics. G. Baum. Commonweal 94:103-4 Ap 9 '71 *
Infallibility fight. pors Newsweek 77:57 Ja 25 '71 *
Küng and Rahner: dueling over infallibility. B. Van Voorst. por Chr Cent 88:617-22 My 19 '71 *
Küng: no fixed point. Chr Today 15:21-2 Jl 2 '71 *
Kung on infallibility. C. Davis. Commonweal 93:445-7 F 5 '71; Correction. 93:555 Mr 5 '71; Reply. F. Simons. 94:295 My 28 '71 *
Küng-Rahner debate. G. C. Berkouwer. Chr Today 15:45-6 My 7 '71 *
Question of infallibility. por Time 97:54+ Ap 5 '71 *
Return of the hero. P. Steinfels. Commonweal 95:198 N 26 '71 *
Symposium on Hans Küng's Infallible? an inquiry. A. Dulles; M. A. Fahey; G. A. Lindbeck America 124:427-33 Ap 24 '71 *

KUNITZ, Stanley
Magic curtain; poem. New Yorker 46:34 F 6 '71

about
Tree and the bird. J. Kroll. pors Newsweek 77:114-114A Ap 12 '71 *

KUNSTLER, William Moses
Bobby Seale's birthday cake. J. A. Lukas. il por N Y Times Mag p42+ O 31 '71 *
Kunstler. W. F. Buckley, jr. Nat R 23:1258 N 5 '71 *
Will Mr William Kunstler please step down. J. W. Bishop, jr. il pors Esquire 75:115-17+ Ap '71 *
William Kunstler for the defense, of himself. T. Moore. por Life 71:77 O 1 '71 *

KUNZ, Marji
Stewardesses. il Ladies Home J 88:58 My '71

KUPFERMANN, Irving, and others
Central and peripheral control of gill movements in aplysia. bibliog il Science 174:1252-6 D 17 '71

KURASHIKI, Japan
Way out west in Kurashiki. D. Butwin. il Sat R 54:42+ O 23 '71

KURLAND, Philip B.
Our troubled courts. il Nations Bsns 59:76-81 My '71

KURLFINKE, Dianne
New Cannery Row. il Travel 136:62-7 O '71

KURTZMAN, Harvey
@&%$#!! or, Takin' the lid off the id. il Esquire 75:128-36 Je '71

KUSHIRO, Ikuo, and Haramura, Hiroshi
Major element variation and possible source materials of Apollo 12 crystalline rocks. bibliog il Science 171:1235-7 Mr 26 '71

KUTAKOV, L. N.
Declaration on the strengthening of international security. UN Mo Chron 8:88-101 Je '71

KUTTNER, Robert L.
Chile is not Cuba, or is it? Commonweal 94:405-7 Ag 6 '71
Rebel Republican. Commonweal 94:380-2 Jl 23 '71

KUWAHARA, Y. and others
Sex pheromone of the almond moth and the Indian meal moth; cis-9, trans-12-tetradecadienyl acetate. bibliog Science 171:801-2 F 26 '71

KUWAIT
See also
Petroleum—Kuwait

KUZMA, Greg
Fish; poem. New Yorker 47:50 D 11 '71
Pelican; Map; Nightfall; Midnight; After midnight in a small town; poems. Poetry 118:151-5 Je '71
Poetry; old forms are like birdhouses; Turning off the TV. Poetry 119:125-6 D '71
Sleepwalker; poem. New Yorker 47:41 O 16 '71

about
Comment. S. Dobyns. Poetry 117:394 Mr '71 *

KUZNETS, Simon Smith
Nobel and competent. por Time 98:88 O 25 '71 *
Nobel prize for economics: Kuznets and economic growth. M. Abramovitz. bibliog por Science 174:481-3 O 29 '71 *
What brought Kuznets his Nobel. por Bsns W p88 O 23 '71 *

KUZNETSOV, Anatolii Vasil'evich
Emerging A. Kuznetsov. H. R. Mayes; discussion. Sat R 54:59-62 Ja 23; 27-9 Mr 27 '71 *

KVARACEUS, William C.
Reading: failure and delinquency. bibliog Todays Ed 60:53-4 O '71

KY, Nguyen-cao-. See Nguyen-cao-Ky

KY, Nguyen-cao-, Mme. See Nguyen-cao-Ky, Mme

KYD, Thomas
Spanish tragedy. Criticism
Am Imago 28:247-67 Fall '71 *

KYODAN. See United church of Christ in Japan

KYOTO, Japan
Kyoto mon amour. D. Butwin. il Sat R 54:38-9+ My 8 '71

L

L-dopa. See Dopa
LAD. See American library association—Library administration division
LAN-Chile (airline) See Airlines—Chile
LAPL. See Los Angeles public library

LASH (lighter aboard ship) vessels. See Freighters
LC headings. See Subject headings
L. E. Myers company. See Myers, L. E, company
LEAA. See United States—Justice, Department of—Law enforcement assistance administration
LED (light-emitting diodes) See Diodes
LFE corporation
Defense contractor goes civilian. il pors Bsns W p74-5 Mr 6 '71
LIFO (last in, first out) See Corporations—Accounting
LKAB (Luossavaara-Kirunavaara AB) See Iron mines and mining—Sweden
LMSC. See Lockheed missiles and space company
LNG. See Liquefied natural gas
LPG. See Liquefied petroleum gas
LPGA. See Ladies professional golf association
LPGA tournament. See Golf—Tournaments
LSCA (Library services and construction act) See Library laws and legislation
LSD
LSD and DNA; dispute over effects. il Sci N 100:74 Jl 31 '71
LSD and genetic damage. N. I. Dishotsky and others. bibliog il Science 172:431-40 Ap 30 '71
[³H]Lysergic acid diethylamide: cellular autoradiographic localization in rat brain. I. M. Diab and others. bibliog il Science 173:1022-4 S 10 '71
Persistent increase in brain serotonin turnover after chronic administration of LSD in the rat. J.-L. Díaz and M. O. Huttunen. bibliog il Science 174:62-4 O 1 '71
LSI (large-scale integration) See Electronic circuits, Integrated
LTP. See American library association—Library technology program
LTV. See Ling-Temco-Vought, inc.
LTV aerospace corporation. See Ling-Temco-Vought, inc.
LABARRE, Harriet
Plastic surgery. il Ladies Home J 88:102+ My '71
Sexually sensible woman. Ladies Home J 88:50+ Ag '71
LABELING machines
Mini label-mate. il Consumer Bul 54:39-40 Je '71
Moving plastic writes. D. Williamson. Sat R 54:19 Mr 13 '71
LABELS
Bumper stickers and the cops; effect of Black Panther stickers. F. K. Heussenstamm. il Trans-Action 8:32-3 F '71
Orange-crate art; display at New York's Whitney museum of American art. J. L. Phillips. il Look 35:50-1 Ag 10 '71
Revealing bumper stickers. il Mech Illus 67:50-1 Ap '71
What the new oil-can markings mean. D. L. Gregg. Bet Hom & Gard 49:96 Je '71
See also
Commercial products, Certification of
Food—Labeling
Unit pricing
Wine labels
LABIN, Suzanne
Goa, end of the line. Nat R 23:750-3 Jl 13 '71
LABOR (obstetrics) See Childbirth
LABOR, Compulsory
Civilian forced labor in Ba Chuc minefields. A. Shimkin. Chr Cent 88:297-8 Mr 3 '71
LABOR, Department of. See United States—Labor, Department of
LABOR, Migrant. See Migrant labor
LABOR absenteeism. See Absenteeism
LABOR and laboring classes
Foreign labor briefs. See issues of Monthly labor review
See also
Alien labor
Hours of labor
Job satisfaction
Middle classes
Woman—Employment
Work
also headings. beginning Industrial; also subhead Employees under various subjects, e.g. Airlines—Employees; also classes of laborers, e.g. Coal miners

Bibliography
Book reviews and notes. See issues of Monthly labor review

LABOR and laboring classes—*Continued*

Education

Educational attainment of workers. March 1971; with tables. W. V. Deutermann. bibliog il Mo Labor R 94:30-5 N '71

Labor market twist, 1964-69; with charts. D. F. Johnston. bibliog f Mo Labor R 94: 26-36 Jl '71

Non-wage payments
See Non-wage payments

Statistics

Comparing employment shifts in 10 industrialized countries. C. Sorrentino. il Mo Labor R 94:3-11 O '71

Current labor statistics. See issues of Monthly labor review

See also
United States—Labor statistics, Bureau of

Wages
See Wages

Canada
See also
Collective bargaining—Canada

Chile

Chilean rural labor in the nineteenth century. A. J. Bauer. bibliog f il Am Hist R 76:1059-83 O '71

Europe, Western

European slave market; immigrant worker. T. Beeson. il Chr Cent 88:1372-3 N 24 '71

France

Letter from Paris. Genêt. New Yorker 47: 106 Je 12 '71
See also
Strikes—France

History

Communism and the working class before Marx: the Icarian experience. C. H. Johnson. bibliog f il Am Hist R 6:642-89 Je '71

Great Britain
See also
Labor laws and legislation—Great Britain
London—Labor and laboring classes
Strikes—Great Britain

Israel

Homemade rebellion. il Time 98:30 O 25 '71

Japan

Myth of Japan's cheap labor. U S News 72: 48-9 Ja 10 '72

Therapy by dummies; self-control room used by Japanese workers. il Time 98:60-1 O 18 '71

Latin America

Latin America's employment problem. W. C. Thiesenhusen. bibliog il Science 171:868-74 Mr 5 '71

Rising worry in South America; flare-up of worker unrest. il U S News 70:67-8 Je 28 '71

Poland

Blue-collar revolution? J. Burnham. Nat R 23:261 Mr 9 '71

Patching it up. K. Huszar. il por Newsweek 77:34 F 1 '71

Wooing the worker. il por Time 97:23 Mr 1 '71

Russia
See also
Russia—Labor policy

Spain
See also
Trade unions—Spain

United States

Blue-collar/white-collar pay trends; symposium. bibliog il Mo Labor R 94:3-36 Je '71

Blue-collar winter of discontent. B. L. Masse. America 125:447 N 27 '71

Challenging the work ethic. H. J. Gans. Cur 126:29-34 F '71

Discontented blue-collar workers; a case study. H. L. Sheppard. il Mo Labor R 94: 25-32 Ap '71

Further look at the blue-collar blues. P. Henle. Mo Labor R 94:40 N '71

Has the blue-collar worker's position worsened? excerpt from Blue-collar workers. S. A. Levitan and R. Taggart, 3d. bibliog Mo Labor R 94:23-9 S '71

How blue-collar workers are doing: a new study. U S News 70:58+ My 10 '71

Labor and the economy in 1970. R. W. Fisher. bibliog il Mo Labor R 94:3-13 Ja '71

Labor month in review. See issues of Monthly labor review

Labor's new style. B. J. Widick. Nation 212:358-60 Mr 22 '71

Overriding issue. Time 78:18-19 Jl 26 '71

Pay board meets, and disputes begin. il U S News 71:37-9 N 8 '71

Plight of the ethnics. P. J. Riga. il Cath World 212:289-91 Mr '71

Work experience of the population in 1969. H. V. Hayghe. bibliog il Mo Labor R 94: 45-52 Ja '71

Work in America; symposium. il Atlan 228: 60-8+ O '71

Working-class majority; end of the myth of the middle class majority. A. Levison. il Nation 213:626-8 D 13 '71
See also
American federation of labor and Congress of industrial organizations
Child labor—United States
Contracts, Government—Labor problems
Labor laws and legislation—United States
Labor supply—United States
Migrant labor
Negroes—Economic conditions
Poor—United States
Strikes—United States
Trade unions—United States
United States—Labor, Department of
Wages—United States

History

Labor problem at Jamestown, 1607-18. E. S. Morgan. bibliog f il Am Hist R 76:595-611 Je '71

Political activities
See Trade unions—Political activities

Yugoslavia

Helping to decide in Yugoslavia. il por Newsweek 77:39-40 Ap 5 '71

LABOR and public welfare, Committee on. See United States—Congress—Senate—Labor and public welfare, Committee on

LABOR conferences
See also
International labor organization

LABOR contracts

Job termination without trauma; executives contracts. Duns 98:59 Ag '71

No-strike contract. H. C. Wallich. Newsweek 77:76 Ja 25 '71

Prehire agreements in construction. bibliog Mo Labor R 94:66-8 O '71

When to use employment contracts. P. Meyer. Harvard Bsns R 49:70-3 N '71

LABOR cost

Changes in productivity and unit labor costs: a yearly review. S. W. Herman and L. J. Fulco. il Mo Labor R 94:3-8 My '71

Crisis of costs: address, January 24, 1971. E. J. Hanley. Vital Speeches 37:298-301 Mr 1 '71

Holding back the cost push. A. G. Heebner. por Nations Bsns 59:25 F '71

Productivity: seeking that old magic. il Time 98:56-7 Ag 2 '71

Striking out the wage gap. il Time 98:77-8 D 13 '71

Unit labor costs in eleven countries; with tables and charts. A. Neef. Mo Labor R 94:3-12 Ag '71
See also
Collective bargaining
Non-wage payments

LABOR disputes
See also
Arbitration, Industrial
Grievance procedures
Strikes
United States—Federal mediation and conciliation service
United States—National labor relations board

LABOR ethics

Socking it to a rough union; E. Lassitter sues Fort Lauderdale operating engineers. il Time 98:42-3 D 27 '71

LABOR in politics. See Trade unions—Political activities

LABOR laws and legislation
See also
Hours of labor
Insurance, Workmens compensation
Work rules

Great Britain

Cure for labor abuses? Industrial relations bill. il Nations Bsns 59:80-3 Ap '71

United States

Changes in state labor laws in 1970. S. Weissbrodt. bibliog il Mo Labor R 94:14-21 Ja '71

High-court rulings: labor wins 1 of 3. U S News 71:90-1 D 20 '71

LABOR laws and legislation—United States
—*Continued*
How to curb union power. J. Davenport. il
Fortune 84:52+ Jl '71
Is the right to strike a right to injure the
innocent? D. Lawrence. U S News 71:92
S 13 '71
Job reinstatement under section 8(a)(3) of
the NLRA. L. Aspin. Mo Labor R 94:57-9
Mr '71
Labor law reform: essential to fight infla-
tion. J. G. Tower. por Nations Bsns 59:
42-5 D '71
NLRB remedies for unfair labor practices. J.
H. Fanning. bibliog f Mo Labor R 94:53-7
Mr '71
New try at curbing transportation strikes.
Bsns W p 116 Je 19 '71
Right defendant; suit against President Nixon
and other government officials for not com-
plying with Employment act of 1946. Nation
213:100-1 Ag 16 '71
Significant decisions in labor cases. See is-
sues of Monthly labor review
Strike-legislation showdown expected; trans-
portation industries. U S News 70:58 Ja 18
'71
See also
Child labor laws and legislation—United
States
Insurance, Unemployment—United States
Minimum wage—United States
Social legislation—United States

Taft-Hartley law
Emergency disputes and public policy. C. C.
Killingsworth. Mo Labor R 94:42-5 Ag '71
LABOR leaders. See Trade unions—Officials
LABOR lobby. See Lobbying
LABOR-management relations. See Industrial
relations
LABOR mobility
Comparing employment shifts in 10 indus-
trialized countries. C. Sorrentino. il Mo
Labor R 94:3-11 O '71
European slave market; immigrant worker. T.
Beeson. il Chr Cent 88:1372-3 N 24 '71
LABOR officials. See Trade unions—Officials
LABOR output. See Labor productivity
LABOR party (Great Britain)
Bit of a muddle. Newsweek 78:34+ N 29 '71
Britain in Europe: undecided Harold Wilson.
A. Howard. New Repub 165:8-9 Jl 10 '71
Britain: Labor's dark hour; party split over
Common market. pors Newsweek 78:30+
Ag 2 '71
Labour pains. A. Howard. New Repub 165:13-
14 N 13 '71
Letter from London; opposition to entering
Europe. M. Panter-Downes. New Yorker 47:
177-80 N 13 '71
Saying no to Europe. A. Howard. New Repub
165:10-11 O 23 '71
See also
Trades union congress
LABOR productivity
Blue-collar/white-collar pay trends: compen-
sation per man-hour and take-home pay.
J. Alterman. bibliog il Mo labor R 94:25-34
Je '71
Changes in productivity and unit labor costs:
a yearly review. S. W. Herman and L. J.
Fulco. il Mo Labor R 94:3-8 My '71
City hall discovers productivity. D. Cordtz.
il Fortune 84:92-6+ O '71
Four-day week, and productivity. Duns 98:84
Jl '71
Golden rule: productivity. il Newsweek 78:
31-2 O 18 '71
Holding back the cost push. A. G. Heebner.
por Nations Bsns 59:25 F '71
Labor chills talks about productivity. il Bsns
W p29-30 Ag 14 '71
Limits of productivity. il Time 98:24 N 15
'71
Lower productivity threatens growth. il Bsns
W p36-7 Ja 1 '72
Output per man-hour in selected industries.
A. S. Herman. il Mo Labor R 94:59-60 O
'71
Poor performance in productivity. il Fortune
83:18 Ap '71
Productivity in the petroleum pipelines in-
dustry. C. S. Fehd. il Mo Labor R 94:46-8
Ap '71
Productivity: industry isn't the only place
where it's a problem; interview. P. E. Hag-
gerty. il por Forbes 107:43-5 F 1 '71
Productivity is the sticking point. il Bsns W
p 17-19 Jl 10 '71
Productivity: seeking that old magic. il Time
98:56-7 Ag 2 '71
Productivity: tables. See issues of Monthly
labor review

Productivity: the blue collar blues; address.
February 9, 1971. J. M. Rosow. Vital
Speeches 37:488-91 Je 1 '71
Productivity: weak link in our economy. G.
F. Bloom. bibliog f Harvard Bsns R 49:4-
6+ Ja '71; Discussion. 49:31-2+ Jl '71
Proving the case for a price hike. il Bsns W
p34+ D 4 '71
Road to economic survival; address. Novem-
ber 15, 1971. R. C. Firestone. Vital Speech-
es 38:155-7 D 15 '71
Spotlight on productivity: why it's a key to
U.S. problems. il U S News 71:25-8 O 4 '71
Steelworkers set out to rescue steel. il Bsns
W p58-9 D 11 '71
Work rules: the main barrier to produc-
tivity. il Bsns W p54-5 Ag 28 '71
LABOR racketeering. See Racketeering
LABOR relations. See Industrial relations
LABOR relations board, National. See United
States—National labor relations board
LABOR statistics, Bureau of. See United States
—Labor statistics, Bureau of
LABOR supply
See also
College graduates—Employment
Labor mobility
Manpower
Unemployment
Working life, length of

United States
Construction manpower needs by 1980. W. F.
Hahn. bibliog f il Mo Labor R 94:12-18
Jl '71
Dual labor market and manpower policy. R.
E. Klitgaard. bibliog Mo Labor R 94:45-8
N '71
Unutilized manpower in poverty areas of 6
U.S. cities; with tables. H. J. Hilaski.
bibliog Mo Labor R 94:45-52 D '71
LABOR turnover
Job-hopping and MBA. J. A. De Pasquale
and R. A. Lange. il Harvard Bsns R 49:4-8+
N '71
Labor turnover rates (title varies) tables.
See issues of Monthly labor review
LABOR unions. See Trade unions
LABORATORIES
See also
Aeronautic laboratories
Medical laboratories
Research laboratories
Underwater laboratories

Architecture
Fortresses for science. il Life 70:74-9 Ap 16 '71
Longer white line; Estee Lauder labora-
tories, Melville, N.Y. il Arch Forum 134:
30-1 Ap '71
LABORATORIES, Government
Cancer researchers finally get Ft Detrick.
Sci N 100·278 O 23 '71
Fort Detrick: a top laboratory is threatened
with extinction. P. M. Boffey. Science 171:
262-4 Ja 22 '71
Ft. Detrick's uncertain fate. Sci N 99:64 Ja
23 '71
Germ war lab salvaged. C. Holden. Science
174:387 O 22 '71
Pine Bluff saved, Detrick critical. P. M. Bof-
fey. Science 171:462 F 5 '71
See also
Argonne national laboratory
Patuxent wildlife research center
United States—Air force—Aero propulsion
laboratory
United States—Arnold engineering develop-
ment center
United States—National institutes of health
—Rocky Mountain laboratory
United States—Transportation, Department of
—Transportation systems center
LABORATORY animals
Rush to raise animals for labs. il Bsns W
p 146+ My 16 '71
See also
Animals—Treatment
Germfree life
Vivisection
also names of laboratory animals, e.g.
Chimpanzees
LABORATORY architecture. See Laboratories
—Architecture
LABORATORY for electronics, Inc. See LFE
corporation
LABORATORY method
Laboratory approach to elementary mathe-
matics. E. Deans. il Todays Ed 60:20-2 F
'71
LABORDE, Harold
Tahiti to Rarotonga. il Yachting 129:56+ F '71

LABOUISSE, Henry Richardson
For the world's children. UNICEF at 25. il UN Mo Chron 8:48-60 Ap '71

LABRADOR SEA
It's a different kind of cruising; heading north from Newfoundland. M. Wiley. il Yachting 129:58-9+ F '71

LABYRINTH (ear)
Fish otoliths; daily growth layers and periodical patterns. G. Pannella. bibliog il Science 173:1124-7 S 17 '71
Summating potential with electrical stimulation of crossed olivocochlear bundles. T. Konishi and J. Slepian. bibliog il Science 172:483-4 Ap 30 '71

LACHENBRUCH, David
Looking ahead. See issues of Radio-electronics

LACHMAN, Seymour P.
Students' rights and responsibilities: the New York city experience. PTA Mag 65:14-17 bibliog(p33) My '71
—and Bresnick, David
Educational ombudsman for New York city? bibliog f Sch & Soc 99:168-70 Mr '71

LACK, Richard F.
Richard Lack's atelier system of training painters. D. Jardine. il por Am Artist 35: 48-53+ Je '71 *

LACKNER, J. A.
Build a Spanish-style lamp the easy way. il Pop Mech 136:166-7 O '71

LACLOCHE, Arabella
Arabella Lacloche cooks Italian. M. McKendry. il por Vogue 158:108+ O 1 '71 *

LACOMBE, Charles
Mayan mystery of the Onima caves. E. Hartley. il Sci Digest 69:9-13 Ap '71 *

LA COSTA, Calif. See Health resorts, watering places, etc.

LACOSTE, Michel Conil-. See Conil-Lacoste. M.

LACQUER and lacquering
Lacquer of the West: the history of a craft and an industry, by H. Huth. Review
Antiques il 100:722+ N '71. R. Davidson

LACROSSE
Big Red votes itself no. 1; Cornell national champion. P. Carry. il Sports Illus 34:58-9 Je 14 '71

LACTONES
See also
Butyrolactone

LACY, Dan
[Copyright] quagmire. Sat R 54:24-8 N 27 '71

LACY, Edward A.
Giant billboard antennas for space-age radars. il Pop Electr 35:44-7+ D '71

LACY glass. See Glassware

LADA, Igor V. Bestuzhev-. See Bestuzhev-Lada, I. V.

LADA-MOCARSKI, Valerian
Obituary
Craft Horiz por 31:4 D '71. M. Lyon

LA-dah-dah-dah-dum; story. See Rogin, G.

LA DANY, Louis
China as it is today. America 125:87-8 Ag 21 '71

LADD, Bruce C. Jr
Copyright protection of recordings favored by Department. Dept State Bul 65:67 Jl 12 '71

LADD, Edward T.
Pills for classroom peace? Ed Digest 36:1-4 F '71

LADDERS
Make these steel ladders for your equipment. G. L. Earle. il Suc Farm 69:no3 B1 F '71

LADER, Lawrence
Guide to abortion laws in the United States. il Redbook 137:51-8 Je '71

LADIES' home journal
Power of a woman; Ladies home journal delegation at Paris. il Ladies Home J 88: 46+ Jl '71

LADIES professional golf association
Lady pros seek golf glory; blacks on LPGA tour. il pors Ebony 26:106-8+ Jl '71
Whoopee for the proettes. il por Time 97:63 Je 28 '71

LADIES professional golf association tournament. See Golf—Tournaments

LADINSKY, Jack
Lawyer manpower in the criminal justice system. bibliog f Cur Hist 61:9-12+ Jl '71

LADOF, Nina Sydney
Censorship: the tip and the iceberg. il Am Lib 2:309-10 Mr '71

LADY Audley's secret; musical comedy. See Musical comedies, revues, etc.—Criticisms, plots, etc.

LADY-slippers. See Ladys slippers

LADY who stole trees; story. See Stephens, M.

LADYBIRDS
Using yesterday's ways to stop today's bugs! M. C. Goldman. il Org Gard & Farm 18:52-7 Jl '71

LADYBUGS. See Ladybirds

LADYS slippers
Luck with cypripediums. E. M. Woodford. il Horticulture 49:33+ Jl '71

LAETRILE
Debate over Laetrile. il Time 97:80 Ap 12 '71

LA FARGE, Henry A.
Second incarnation of Ben Heller. il Art N 70:38-9+ Ap '71

LA FARGE, Oliver
Indian man. by D. McNickle. Review
Sat R 54:32+ O 23 '71. J. A. Clifton *

LAFAY, Gloria
Inter-American festival; gimmickry abounds, but Teatro Colon opera visit cheers all. il Hi Fi 21:MA22-3 Ag '71

LA FAY, Howard
Carnival in Trinidad. il Nat Geog 140:690-701 N '71
Leningrad. il Nat Geog 139:636-73 My '71
Uganda: Africa's uneasy heartland. il Nat Geog 140:708-35 N '71

LAFAYETTE, La.
Mirrored skylight; Natural history museum and planetarium center for environment studies. il Arch Forum 135:28-31 S '71

LAFFER, Arthur
1065 and all that. por Time 97:83 F 22 '71 *

LAFLEUR, Guy
To pick a golden flower. M. Mulvoy. il pors Sports Illus 34:34-6 Mr 1 '71 *

LAFORE, Laurence Davis
In the sticks. il Harper 243:108-9+ O '71

LAGMANOVICH, David
Sur: 40 years. il pors Américas 23:10-14 S '71

LA GREGGA, Frank
What it really costs to maintain a swimming pool. il Mech Illus 67:63 Ag '71

LAHAINA, Hawaii
Lahaina charter. T. Culbertson and T. Culbertson, 3d. il Yachting 129:52-3+ Mr '71

LAHR, John
Riddle of The clowns. il Vogue 158:90-1 Ag 1 '71
Television. Vogue 157:116 Mr 15 '71

LAIDLAW, Angus
They fly forward into the past, colorfully. il Mech Illus 67:59-61 Jl '71

LAINEZ, Diego
Ecumenical "if". C. J. McNaspy. il America 124:655-6 Je 26 '71 *

LAING, Philip A. See Liu, A. S. jt. auth.

LAING, Ronald David
New look at the meaning of reality. R. H. Gilluly. il por Sci N 99:335-7 My 15 '71 *
Philosopher of madness. il pors Life 71:86-90 O 8 '71 *
Truth which dares not speak its name. R. Schickel. Harper 242:104-8 Ap '71; Reply with rejoinder. L. Redler. 243:10 Jl '71 *

LAIRD, Carlton W. and Scott, John
How street sweepers perform today. il Am City 86:58-62 Mr '71

LAIRD, Charles D. See Hahn, W. E. jt. auth.

LAIRD, Melvin R.
Continuing U.S. efforts on behalf of prisoners of war and missing in southeast Asia; remarks, September 28, 1971. Dept State Bul 65:448-50 O 25 '71
Foreign assistance and the U.S. national interest; news conference, November 1, 1971. Dept State Bul 65:579-83 N 22 '71
More balanced sharing of the burdens of security; statement, November 25, 1970. Dept State Bul 63:753-6 D 21 '70
U.S. strategy beyond Vietnam; interview. il por U S News 70:27-30+ My 17 '71

about
Big bad bear. New Repub 164:9 Mr 27 '71 *
Delicacy of being Laird. il por Time 97:18 Ap 26 '71 *
For the defense: Melvin R. Laird. C. J. V. Murphy. por Read Digest 99:49-53 Ag '71 *
Laird plans Pentagon management changes. Aviation W 94:17 Mr 15 '71 *
Melvin Laird and CBS. Sedulus. New Repub 165:29-30 Jl 10 '71; Reply. K. D. Tiven. 165:33 Jl 24 '71 *
Political pro who runs Defense. J. Duscha. il pors N Y Times Mag p 18-19+ Je 13 '71 *
Political theatricals. Nation 212:194 F 15 '71 *

LAISSEZ faire. See Free enterprise

LAITY
Church-sponsored renewal; Lay witness renewal mission. M. Parrish. Chr Today 15: 35 Ag 6 '71
Church's mission: let the laity do it. J. E. Wagner. Chr Today 15:21 S 10 '71
Who's listening to lay people? NCC project. Chr Cent 88:943 Ag 11 '71

Catholic church
Catholic lay group seeks world parley of Christians; National association of laity. Chr Today 15:37 Ag 6 '71
Greening of the laity; National association of laity. D. Grumbach. Commonweal 94:372-3 Jl 23 '71
Permanent diaconate. G. S. Sloyan; C. J. Armbruster; J. J. Begley. Commonweal 94: 56-64 Mr 26 '71; Discussion. 94:227+ My 14 '71
See also
National council of Catholic laity

LAKE, Alice
How to teach your child good habits. il Redbook 137:74+ Je '71
Keeping up with the quints. il Good H 173: 96-9+ S '71
One woman's walk for peace. il pors Good H 173:70-1+ Jl '71
Questions you ask most about birth control. Seventeen 30:84-5+ Ja '71
Quints go into action. il pors Good H 172: 72-7+ Mr '71
Rape: the unmentionable crime. Good H 173: 104-5+ N '71
What you can do now to fight pollution. il Redbook 137:56-7+ Jl '71

LAKE, Peyton M.
About Vietnamization. Nat R 23:761 Jl 13 '71

LAKE CHARLES, La.
Good-time Charlie's Lake. Travel 136:27 Ag '71

LAKE ERIE opera theater
Report:
Cosí fan tutte. R. Finn. Opera N 35:32 Ja 30 '71

LAKE HAVASU CITY, Ariz.
Only in America: London bridge opened. il Newsweek 78:125 O 25 '71

LAKE MANYARA NATIONAL PARK. See National parks and reserves—Tanzania

LAKE of the woods; drama. See Tesich, S.

LAKE ONTARIO; Lake Tahoe; etc. See Ontario, Lake; Tahoe, Lake; etc.

LAKE park, Yorba Linda, Calif. See Mobile home parks

LAKE SHASTA. See Shasta Lake

LAKE trout fishing. See Trout fishing

LAKERS (basketball team) See Basketball teams

LAKES
In what different ways are lakes formed? Sci Digest 70:83 O '71
See also
Great Lakes
Water pollution

Temperature
Now: total fishing:
Blueprint for success. S. Lievense. il por Outdoor Life 147:58-9+ My '71
Neglected tool, thermometer. S. Lievense. il Outdoor Life 147:75-7+ Ap '71
State's thermal profile; temperature of New York's waters. D. H. Shafer. il Cons 25: 31-2 F '71

Florida
Aeration saves a lake. D. H. Fletcher. il Parks & Rec 6:23-4+ N '71

New Mexico
Battle for Blue Lake. D. O. Collines. il Am West 8:32-7 S '71

LAKES, Artificial
Fall and rise of sewage salvage; use of reclaimed water for Santee Lakes. W. Marx. il Bul Atom Sci 27:10-15 My '71
Indiana's new lakes. B. Thomas. il Travel 135:48-51+ F '71
See also
Powell, Lake
Reservoirs

LAKES, Imaginary. See Geographical myths

LAKES, rivers, etc.

Clearing
See Clearing of lakes, rivers, etc.

LAKOFF, Sanford A.
Knowledge, power, and Democratic theory. bibliog f Ann Am Acad 394:4-12 Mr '71

L'ALLEMAND, Gordon
Jerusalem artichoke, year-round vegetable. il Org Gard & Farm 18:52-3 My '71
New way to bigger, tastier strawberries. il Home Gard 58:60-1 Mr '71

LAMANCE, Thomas
Mistaken identity; poem. Good H 172:206 F '71

LAMAR, Dwight
Good times come to Cajun country. W. F. Reed. il por Sports Illus 35:20-1 D 20 '71 •

LAMAR, Paul
On Bluefish Beach; poem. Yale R 61:252 D '71

LAMAR, South Carolina
On the overturning of two school buses in Lamar, S.C. W. F. McIlwain. il Esquire 75:98-103+ Ja '71

LAMAZE method. See Childbirth

LAMB, Lady Caroline (Ponsonby)
Lovers; excerpt from The nympho and other maniacs. I. Wallace. pors Ladies Home J 88:131-2 F '71 •

LAMB (meat)
Lamb, the meat deluxe. B. Humes and B. Humes. Org Gard & Farm 18:102-4 Ag '71
See also
Cookery—Meat

LAMB shift. See Energy levels (quantum mechanics)

LAMBDIN, Bethany B. See Bacot, H. P. jt. auth.

LAMBERG-KARLOVSKY, C. C. and Lamberg-Karlovsky, Martha
Early city in Iran; with biographical sketches. il Sci Am 224:17, 102-11 bibliog(p 136) Je '71

LAMBERG-KARLOVSKY, Martha. See Lamberg-Karlovsky, C. C. jt. auth.

LAMBERT, Byron C.
On avoiding work. Chr Today 15:7-8 Ag 27 '71

LAMBERT, Darwin
(ed) Exploring earthman's world with Darwin Lambert. See issues of National parks & conservation magazine

LAMBERT, Richard David
(ed) America's most challenging objectives. bibliog f Am Am Acad 396:1-114 Jl '71

LAMBERT, Robert G.
Three new faces of English. Engl J 60:909-12+ O '71

LAMBERT, Sam M.
After all. Todays Ed 60:64 My '71
From Moscow to Irkutsk to Leningrad; interview. il pors Todays Ed 60:36-40 D '71

LAMBERT company. See Holding companies —Belgium

LAMBERT field airport. See St Louis—Airports

LAMBETH, Benjamin S.
Moscow and the missile race. bibliog f Cur Hist 61:215-21+ O '71

LAMBETH, Julie
Patio lotus. il Horticulture 49:30-1 Jl '71

LAMBUTH, David, and others
Words: how to use them effectively; excerpt from The golden book on writing. Writers Digest 51:35-7 Ag '71

LAMKIN, Burton E.
Toward a federal strategy in library training; address, January 15, 1971. pors Am Lib 2: 496-9 My '71

LAMM, Michael
'71s: pickups that pamper. il Pop Mech 135: 98-101+ F '71

LAMM, Richard D.
Is bigger also better? New Repub 164:17-19 Je 5 '71

LAMMEY, W. Clyde
Give your garden that final touch. il Nat Wildlife 9:17 Ag '71
Homeowners' clinic; questions and answers. See issues of Popular mechanics

LAMONT, Corliss
Will fascism arise in America? Cur 132:11-13 S '71

LAMOTT, Kenneth
San Quentin story: the prisons are getting a tougher class of convicts. il por N Y Times Mag p28-9+ My 2 '71

LAMP bulbs. See Electric lamps, Incandescent

LAMP shades
It's not a Tiffany, but it's yours. il Sunset 147:103 Jl '71
Paper cup galaxy. B. Schlitt. il Design 72: 31-2 Mid-Sum '71

LAMPARTER, William C.
Book making trends for the 21st century; excerpts from address, 1971. il Pub W 200: 38+ N 1 '71

LAMPE, David
Land-Rover: is it really indestructible? il Pop Mech 135:44+ Mr '71
They've found a wish switch in your brain. por Pop Sci 198:30+ Ja '71

LAMPS
See also
Electric lamps

LAMPSHADES. See Lamp shades

LANCASTER, Burt
Burt force. por Time 97:97 Ap 26 '71

LANCASTER, Donald E.
Build a digi-viewer. il Pop Electr 34:41-6 Mr '71
Build the psych-tone. il Pop Electr 34:25-35 F '71
Can you beat tic-tac-tronix? il Radio-Electr 42:32-5+ D '71

LANCASTER COUNTY, Pa, library, Lancaster
ABC's of PPB; planning-programming-budgeting. H. R. Jenkins. bibliog il por Library J 96:3089-93 O 1 '71

LANCE, Albert
Frenchman from Down Under; interview, ed. by B. Fischer-Williams. por Opera N 35:16 Mr 13 '71

LANCHBERY, John Arthur
Potpourri for Beatrix Potter. R. D. Darrell. il Hi Fi 21:98 O '71 •

LAND, Edwin Herbert
Addiction as a necessity and opportunity; address, April 20, 1970. Science 171:151-3 Ja 15 '71

LAND, Herman W.
How a parent can reach his child about drugs. il Todays Health 49:42-5 Ag '71

LAND, Irene Ellen (Stokvis) See Stokvis, I. E.

LAND
See also
Clearing of land
Land utilization
Reclamation of land
Regional planning
Soils
Wetlands

Clearing
See Clearing of land

Prices
See Land values

Subdivision
Now a land rush in the West as city folks stake claims. il U S News 71:32-5 Jl 19 '71
Peddling God's country; wilderness project. Calif. R. Rapoport. il por Sports Illus 35:68-9 N 1 '71
Peddling the great West. T. W. Pew, Jr. il Sat R 54:48-51 S 4 '71

Taxation
See Property tax

California
Peddling God's country; wilderness project. R. Rapoport. il por Sports Illus 35:68-9 N 1 '71
Rescuing California; survey by R. Nader. P. Barnes. New Repub 165:12-13 S 18 '71

Colorado
Saving the slopes; land boom. il Time 99:62 Ja 10 '72

Florida
Can land be developed without wrecking nature? W. Hartley and E. Hartley. il Sci Digest 71:73-8 Ja '72
Land speculators play Disney's money machine. il Bsns W p80+ S 11 '71

Poland
Poles reclaim wasteland. S. Lindsay. Sat R 54:63 Ap 3 '71

United States
See also
Public lands—United States

Vietnam
Land war. E. W. Pfeiffer; A. H. Westing. il pors Environ 13:2-15 N '71
Wasteland. W. Haseltine and A. H. Westing. New Repub 165:13-15 O 30 '71

Western states
Now a land rush in the West as city folks stake claims. il U S News 71:32-5 Jl 19 '71
Peddling the great West. T. W. Pew, Jr. il Sat R 54:48-51 S 4 '71

LAND-atmosphere interaction. See Soil-atmosphere interaction

LAND auctions. See Auctions

LAND buying. See Real estate investment

LAND clearing. See Clearing of land

LAND contracts
Buying on contract: good or bad deal? il Suc Farm 69:G5-7 S '71

LAND drainage. See Drainage

LAND fills. See Filling (earthwork)

LAND grant colleges
See also
Kansas state university, Manhattan

LAND management, Bureau of. See United States—Land management, Bureau of

LAND planning. See Land utilization

LAND reclamation. See Reclamation of land

LAND reform. See Land tenure

LAND-Rovers. See Jeep automobiles

LAND slides. See Landslides

LAND speculation. See Real estate investment

LAND subdivision. See Land—Subdivision

LAND tenure

Alaska
Bush power wins Alaska land claims. por Bsns W p23 D 18 '71
Great Alaskan inconsistency. W. E. Towell. Am For 77:46-7 S '71
Letter from Alaska: plan or plunder for the American Arctic? R. B. Weeden il Liv Wildn 35:35-40 Sum '71
Natives may win one: the great Alaskan real-estate deal. T. M. Brown. il N Y Times Mag p42-3+ O 17 '71
Second purchase; federal government compensates Eskimos, Aleuts and Indians. Time 98:11 D 27 '71
Unfreezing Alaska. P. Barnes. New Repub 165:15-17 S 11 '71
Who owns the Slope? Newsweek 78:93+ O 18 '71

Brazil
Trickle of justice in Brazil. F. B. Morris. por Chr Cent 88:1353-4+ N 17 '71

Chile
Land grab; illegal seizure of farms by peasants. J. Barnes. il Newsweek 77:37+ F 1 '71
This land or death; Mapuche Indians seize farms. Newsweek 77:41-2 F 15 '71

Latin America
Latin America's employment problem. W. C. Thiesenhusen. bibliog il Science 171:868-74 Mr 5 '71

United States
Bombing forests; dispute between Indians and Mexican-Americans over the ownership of Carson national forest. J. Rowen. New Repub 164:12 Mr 6 '71
Land reform. P. Barnes. New Repub 164:19-23 Je 5; 21-4 Je 12; 13-17 Je 19 '71; Reply. R. L. Bard. 165:32 Ag 21 '71
Living on the land; ruling on the residency requirement of the 1902 Reclamation act. New Repub 165:7 D 11 '71
Nader land mine; report on California. Newsweek 78:54+ S 6 '71
Water, water for the wealthy; California's Imperial Valley. P. Barnes. New Repub 164:9-10+ My 8 '71

Vietnam (Republic)
Tuyet Mai's dream place. il por Newsweek 77:25 Ja 18 '71

LAND titles
Nice piece of real estate: J. Y. Limantour's claim to most of San Francisco. R. Reinhardt. il Am Heritage 23:42-7+ D '71
Untapped revenue source; land-title search. T. Wheelan. il Am City 86:79+ My '71

LAND utilization
Bad scene at Mike horse mine. J. N. Miller. Read Digest 98:75-9 F '71
Can land be developed without wrecking nature? W. Hartley and E. Hartley. il Sci Digest 71:73-8 Ja '72
Land; making room for tomorrow. J. Lear. Sat R 54:45-8 Mr 6 '71
Leadership on land. Sci N 99:112 F 13 '71
Living space; EQ index. il Nat Wildlife 9:33 O '71
Mojave Desert; a treasure in trouble. E. Selby and M. Selby. il Nat Wildlife 9:52-7 O '71; Same abr. with title Trouble in the Mojave. Read Digest 99:45-8+ O '71
Progress toward points of no return; excerpts from letter, August 17, 1970. T. M. Edison. Liv Wildn 34:52-3 Wint '70

LAND utilization—*Continued*
Saving the slopes; land boom. il Time 99: 62 Ja 10 '72
Vital step on land use. Time 97:54 F 8 '71
See also
City planning
Soil conservation
Suburbs
LAND values
What is the land market doing? M. Hood. il Suc Farm 69:G10 S '71
See also
Real property—Valuation
LANDAU, Alice
From blossoms, birds, butterflies. il por Américas 22:36-7 N '70
LANDAU, David
Rise of Henry Kissinger. il por Ramp Mag 10:36-44 D '71
LANDAU, Genevieve Millet
Peril of overpopulation: our greatest threat. por Parents Mag 46:56 N '71
LANDAU, Robert
Worlds beyond the dust. il Newsweek 77:89 Ja 25 '71 *
LANDERS, Ann, pseud.
What to tell your daughter about Women's lib; questions and answers, ed. by T. Langleben. il pors Todays Health 49:52-5+ O '71
LANDFILLS. See Filling (earthwork)
LANDGREN, Marchal E.
Thomas Couture, painter and teacher of painters; with editorial comment. il Antiques 99:772, 877-81 Je '71
LANDING gear, Airplane. See Airplanes—Landing gear
LANDING sites
Moon
See Moon—Surface
LANDING systems for space vehicles. See Space vehicles—Landing systems
LANDLORD and tenant
Committee documents flagrant inequities in British rent acts. C. Holmes. Chr Cent 88:885-6 Jl 21 '71
Housing abandonment. Arch Forum 134:42-5 Ap '71
Last and leased. D. Sanford. New Repub 165:17-20 S 4 '71
Leases are still too lopsided. Changing T 25: 17 Ap '71
See also
Farm tenancy
National tenants organization
LANDMARKS, Literary. See Literary landmarks
LANDOLFI, Tommaso
Fable; story, tr. by R. Rosenthal. Mlle 73: 112-13 Je '71
LANDON, H. C. Robbins
Other Haydn. Hi Fi 21:100 D '71
LANDRIEU, Maurice E. See Landrieu, Moon
LANDRIEU, Moon
Moon over New Orleans. por Newsweek 77: 94 Je 14 '71 *
LANDRITH, Harold F.
Prescription for junior college dropouts. bibliog Sch & Soc 99:49-51 Ja '71
LANDRY, Greg
Look what's afoot. T. Maule. il por Sports Illus 35:18-21 D 13 '71 *
LANDSBERG, Hans H. See Russell, C. S. jt. auth.
LANDSBERG, Helmut E.
Man-made climatic changes. bibliog il Science 170:1265-74; 173:462 D 18 '70, Jl 30 '71
LANDSCAPE architecture
Civilizing American cities, ed. by S. B. Sutton. Review
Arch Forum 135:8+ O '71. H. H. Reed
Design with power in mind. P. Jewell, 3d. il Horticulture 49:36-7+ F '71
LANDSCAPE design. See Landscape architecture
LANDSCAPE gardening
Cool it with trees. A. U. Smith. il Horticulture 49:18-21 Ag '71
Creating an outdoor environment where none exists; planned gardens in California. il House B 113:73-5 Mr '71
Iris in the landscape. H. B. Aul. il Horticulture 49:28-9+ My '71
Landscaping a little at a time. H. Mason. il Bet Hom & Gard 49:64-9 S '71
Landscaping with heaths and heathers. E. Finlayson. il Horticulture 49:41+ F '71
Planting for privacy. il Sunset 147:198-9 D '71
Planting ideas for side yards. il Sunset 147: 161 Jl '71

Relaxing solutions for landscaping problems. H. Mason. il Bet Hom & Gard 49: 46-55 Mr '71
Summer and spring show, and a water view. il Sunset 147:142-3 Jl '71
Trees left in place, wild grasses just mowed. il Sunset 147:120-1 N '71
Using wood in the garden; redwood projects. il Home Gard 58:74-5 F '71
Very personal garden of the Emilio Puccis. il House & Gard 140:112-15 O '71
See also
City gardens
Cover plants
Garden pools
Garden steps
Gardens
Gardens, Hillside
Golf courses
Landscape architecture
Lawns
Municipal improvement
Outdoor rooms
Parks
Roadside improvement
LANDSCAPE painting
Grand opera and the small still voice. B. Novak. il Art in Am 59:64-73 Mr '71
LANDSCAPE photography. See Photography—Landscapes
LANDSCAPE protection
Land: making room for tomorrow. J. Lear. Sat R 54:45-8 Mr 6 '71
Superjet airports run into trouble. il U S News 70:30-2 Mr 22 '71
Visual pollution: our junked-up landscape? Bet Hom & Gard 49:4+ Jl '71
See also
Conservation of resources
Environmental movement
Regional planning
Roadside improvement
Wilderness areas

Pennsylvania
Second battle of Gettysburg: spread of commercialism. il U S News 71:66-7 O 18 '71

Vermont
Profile for posterity: saving the skylines of Vermont. F. A. Young. il Nat Parks & Con Mag 45:20-4 F '71

Virginia
Little sturm und drang at Hunting creek. J. Sax. il Esquire 75:84-8+ F '71
LANDSCAPES
Exhibitions
See Art—Exhibitions
LANDSLIDES
Town that disappeared: Saint-Jean Vianney. J. P. Blank. il Read Digest 99:86-90 D '71
What do you know about earthflows & landslides? quiz. J. Daugherty and M. Daugherty. il Sci Digest 69:58-9+ My '71
LANDY, Joachim
Night prayer; poem. Chr Cent 88:66 Ja 20 '71
LANE, William
News; poem. Nation 212:766 Je 14 '71
LANE Bryant, inc.
Eartha M. M. White, 94, daughter of slave, gets Lane Bryant award. il por Aging 198: 11 Ap '71
Late tape. R. Brady. Duns 97:9-10 My '71
LANES, Selma G.
Child-sized primers for survival. il Life 71: 44+ D 17 '71
Communes: a firsthand report on a controversial new life style. il Parents Mag 46: 61-3+ O '71
Open school: an experiment in learning through joy. il Parents Mag 46:56-9 S '71
Tales young readers cherish. il Parents Mag 46:50-1+ My '71
LANG, Cynthia
Terrible, wonderful twos. il Parents Mag 46:54-5+ O '71
LANG, Daniel
Reporter at large (cont) New Yorker 46: 52-61 Ja 9; 47:35-40+ S 4 '71
LANG, Frances
(ed) Hard times: war crimes. il Ramp Mag 9:12+ F '71
Mormon empire. il Ramp Mag 10:36-43 S '71
Women in Congress. il Ramp Mag 9:10+ My '71
LANG, Jean McKinney
When a lady cruises solo. il por Yachting 130:56-7+ S '71
LANG, Martin A.
Catechetics, theology and religious education. America 125:39-41 Jl 24 '71

LANG, Paul Henry
Beethoven on records. Hi Fi 20:49-50+ D '70
Fisher vs. Lang. pors Hi Fi 21:19 Jl '71
Karajan's Mozart. il Hi Fi 21:82 O '71
Magnificent baroque opera. Hi Fi 21:65-7 F
'71

LANG, Pearl, dance company. See Pearl Lang
dance company

LANGDON, Harry
Current cinema. P. Gilliatt. New Yorker 47:
130+ Ap 24 '71 *

LANGE, Jean R.
In Britain they grow flowers. il Har Yrs
11:35-6 My '71

LANGE, Oliver, pseud.
Trade winds; interview, ed. by C. Amory.
Sat R 54:12 My 1 '71

LANGE, Richard A. See De Pasquale, J. A.
jt. auth.

LANGER, Arthur M. and others
Inorganic particles in cigars and cigar
smoke. bibliog il Science 174:585-7 N 5 '71

LANGER, Elinor
(ed) See Kistiakowsky, G. After the Pentagon papers: talk with Kistiakowsky,
Wiesner
(ed) See Wiesner, J. After the Pentagon
papers: talk with Kistiakowsky, Wiesner

LANGER, Richard W. pseud.
Almost certain way to grow a practically
perfect avocado plant; excerpt from The
after-dinner gardening book. Redbook 136:
86+ Mr '71
Brunei. il Travel 136:32-9+ O '71

LANGEWIESCHE, Wolfgang
Bubbles: newest thing in building! il Read
Digest 99:39-40+ Ag '71
Upward miracle. il Harper 243:124-6+ N '71

LANGHAM, Michael
Guthrie theater reborn. H. Hewes. il por Sat
R 54:52-3 D 25 '71 *

LANGLEBEN, Tina
(ed) See Landers, A. What to tell your
daughter about Women's lib

LANGLOIS, Henri
Savior of old movies. R. Chelminski. il pors
Life 71:45-6+ D 10 '71 *
Talk of the town. New Yorker 47:43-4 O 30
'71 *

LANGSLEY, Donald G. See Flomenhaft, K.
jt. auth.

LANGSTAFF, Nancy
Recommended recordings (cont) Horn Bk 47:
322 Je '71

LANGTON, Daniel J.
Fresh air; poem. Am Scholar 41:94 Wint '71

LANGUAGE, Drum. See Drum language

LANGUAGE, Universal
See also
Language and languages—International
aspects

LANGUAGE and culture
Order of things, by M. Foucault. Review
New Repub 164:28+ Mr 27 '71. P. Caws

LANGUAGE and languages
Chomsky is difficult to please. . . I. Shenker.
il por Horizon 13:104-9 Spr '71
Language in America. by C. Laird. Review
Nation 213:89-90 Ag 2 '71. R. L. Chap-
man
Onward and upward with the arts; linguis-
tics: N. Chomsky's theory of transforma-
tional grammar. V. Mehta. il New Yorker
47:44-8+ My 8 '71
To describe it all, growl softly. W. J. Rey-
nolds. Engl J 60:267-9 F '71
Tumult of talk. W. Jovanovich. Am Scholar
41:40-9 Wint '71
See also
Communication
Metaphor
Rhetoric
Semantics
Speech

International aspects
Language gap: must we all speak English?
M. A. Tamers. Bul Atom Sci 27:38-40 Mr
'71
Year of world minority language groups;
proclamation. R. M. Nixon. Dept State Bul
65:304 S 20 '71

Religious aspects
See Religion and language

Study and teaching
See also
Languages, Modern—Study and teaching

LANGUAGE and religion. See Religion and language

LANGUAGE development. See Children—Language

LANGUAGE laboratories
Why language labs fail and why they succeed. J. M. Cordts. Ed Digest 37:30-1 O
'71

LANGUAGE of animals. See Animal communication

LANGUAGES, Mixed
See also
Pidgin English

LANGUAGES, Modern

Study and teaching
Foreign languages: how pertinent? R. A.
Pillet. Ed Digest 37:54-6 O '71
Learning languages; modern language apti-
tude test. Fortune 83:42 Mr '71
Let's make foreign language study more
relevant. M. Jackson. il Todays Ed 60:
18-20 Mr '71
Teaching foreign languages: need for accord.
K. L. Peckham. Clear House 45:523 My '71
See also
Language laboratories

LANGUAGES, Secret
Only the family knows. F. Kish. Har Yrs
11:42 D '71

LANGWAY, Lynn
(ed) See Nader, R. This country is on fire

LANIER, Hal
These major-leaguers succeeded in spite
of. . . E. Kiester. il pors Todays Health
49:48-9 O '71 *

LANIER, Robin S.
From two channels to four, with a little
bit o' pluck. il Hi Fi 21:78-81 N '71

LANING, Edward
Spoon River revisited. il por Am Heritage 22:
14-17+ Je '71

LANNING, Robert
Amphibian; poem. Commonweal 94:144 Ap 16
'71

LANSBURY, Angela
Prime of Miss Angela Lansbury. C. Irving.
por McCalls 99:12+ O '71 *

LANSDALE, Edward G.
Lansdale's secret war. il por Newsweek 78:
16 Jl 19 '71 *

LANSFORD, Henry
Why the sands aren't red. il Sci Digest 69:61-
5 My '71

LANSING, Mich.

Lighting
Street lighting, a growth service. il Am City
86:110 Mr '71

LANSKY, Meyer
Browsing in gangland; with editorial comment. J. Epstein. Commentary 53:4+, 46-
55 Ja '72 *
Crime issue. il pors Newsweek 78:32-3 N 29
'71 *

LANTERNS
See also
Electric lanterns

LANUSSE, Alejandro A.
Magic in the Pink House. por Time 97:34+
Ap 5 '71 *

LANZAROTE
Return to Lanzarote. F. R. Buckley. Nat
R 23:883 Ag 10 '71

LAOS
Indochina: blunting a buildup. il Time 97:29-
30 F 8 '71
Laos: the contest of wills; excerpt from The
contest of wills. A. J. Dommen. bibliog f
Cur Hist 61:350-6+ D '71
Reports & comment. H. D. S. Greenway. At-
lan 228:6+ Jl '71
See also
Laotian campaign
United States—Armed forces—Forces in Laos

Foreign relations

China (People's Republic)
See China (People's Republic)—Foreign
relations—Laos

United States
See United States—Foreign relations—
Laos

Native races
Meo culpa. New Repub 164:11-12 Ap 10 '71

Neutrality
Future of Laos; interview, ed. by G. M.
Kahin. Souvanna Phouma. New Repub
165:15-16 Jl 24 '71

Politics and government
Two brothers vying for control of Laos. pors
U S News 70:71 F 22 '71

LARROCHA, Alicia de
Day with de Larrocha. R. Jacobson. il pors Sat R 54:68-9+ O 30 '71 *
With a brain in each of her fingers. Alicia de Larrocha. por Am Rec G 37:420-1 Mr '71 *

LARRY, R. Heath
House divided; address, October 4, 1971. Vital Speeches 38:58-61 N 1 '71
How to control inflation: a three-stage formula; excerpt from address, January 20, 1971. por U S News 70:72-4 F 8 '71
Is there hope for collective bargaining? address, May 7, 1971. Vital Speeches 37:537-40 Je 15 '71
Squeeze-freeze dilemma; address, January 20, 1971. Vital Speeches 37:253-6 F 1 '71; Excerpts. por U S News 70:72-4 F 8 '71

about
Man who speaks for steel. por Bsns W p 18 Jl 10 '71 *
Trying to avoid an unwanted strike. il pors Time 97:77-8 My 24 '71 *

LARSEN, Bent
Computerized steamroller. il pors Time 98:54 Ag 2 '71 *

LARSEN, Jack Lenor
Great change in living values. por House & Gard 140:100-1+ O '71
Greatest craft show on earth. Craft Horiz 31:23+ O '71

about
Jack Lenor Larsen in Boston. L. Salmon. il Craft Horiz 31:14-23 Ap '71 *
Thoughts on Jack Lenor Larsen and the textile horizon. E. Rossbach. il por Craft Horiz 31:12-13 Ap '71 *

LARSEN, Rebecca
First step on the outside. Chr Cent 88:538-41 Ap 28 '71

LARSEN, Roy E.
Old soldier. pors Forbes 107:56 F 15 '71 *

LARSEN, Thor
Polar bear: lonely nomad of the North. il Nat Geog 139:574-90 Ap '71

LARSON, Alan
EDP keeps tabs on wife supporters. il Am City 86:82 My '71

LARSON, Carl
Ethnic weapons. F. Lang. Ramp Mag 10:4 N '71 *

LARSON, Carl H.
Pewter, the humble giant. il Sch Arts 70:20-1 Mr '71

LARSON, Charles R.
Africa's past: another version. Nation 212:697-9 My 31 '71

LARSON, Dale B.
Within and without the circle of faith. il Chr Cent 88:1172-4 O 6 '71

LARSON, Julie
Tyrone and Julie Larson. T. Shafer. il pors Ceram Mo 19:14-16 Ap '71 *

LARSON, Margaret P.
Living lab for high school students. il Todays Ed 60:22-4 Mr '71

LARSON, R. L.
Wastewater treatment lures industry. il Am City 86:74 N '71

LARSON, Robert
China: open door to what? Chr Today 15:3-5 Ag 27 '71

LARSON, Stephen M.
Bosscha observatory in Indonesia. il Sky & Tel 42:70-1 Ag '71
—and Minton, R. B.
Some high-resolution photographs of Mars. il Sky & Tel 42:260-2 N '71

LARSON, Tyrone
Tyrone and Julie Larson. T. Shafer. il pors Ceram Mo 19:14-16 Ap '71 *

LARSON, William G.
Figure in motion. il Mod Phot 35:78-81 Ap '71

LA RUE, Linda J. M.
Black liberation and Women's lib. il Trans-Action 8:59-64 N '70

LARVAE
See also
Caterpillars
Insects—Development

LASAGA, Antonio C. and others
Primordial oil slick. bibliog il Science 174:53-5 O 1 '71

LASAGNA, John B.
Make your MBO pragmatic. il Harvard Bsns R 49:64-9 N '71

LASATER, Tom
Lasater ranch: applied range ecology. F. T. Colbert. il Nat Parks & Con Mag 45:18-20 Mr '71 *

LASEK, Raymond J. and Dower, W. J.
Aplysia californica: analysis of nuclear DNA in individual nuclei of giant neurons. bibliog il Science 172:278-80 Ap 16 '71

LASER communication systems. See Light communication systems

LASER photography. ~~See Lasers—Photographic use~~

LASERS
Already dozens of civilian uses for the laser. il U S News 71:86-7 O 18 '71
Amateur scientist; a carbon dioxide laser is constructed by a high school student in California. J. Levatter. il Sci Am 225:218-20+ S '71
Ball stands still in the air; demonstrating radiation pressure with laser beams. il Sci N 100:309-10 N 6 '71
Basic laser experiments. il Radio-Electr 42:77 Je; 62 Ag '71
Bright idea; dye-laser image amplifier. Sci Am 224:50 My '71
Color it anything; first continuous tunable dye laser. A. Fisher. il Pop Sci 198:40 Ap '71
Continuous dye laser yields tunable putput. G. B. Lubkin. il Phys Today 24:19-21 Ja '71
Detection of air pollutants with tunable diode lasers. E. D. Hinkley and P. L. Kelley. bibliog il Science 171:635-9 F 19 '71
Exciting product of the excited atom. J. S. Butz, jr. il Nations Bsns 59:78-82 S '71
Fusion by laser. M. J. Lubin and A. P. Fraas. il Sci Am 224:21-33 Je '71
Hydrogen laser holds record for short wavelength. G. B. Lubkin. il Phys Today 24:22 Ja '71
Laser (cont) W. F. Van Pelt and others. il Radio-Electr 42:43-5 F; 61-3 Mr; 69-70 My '71 (to be cont)
Laser earth-strain gauge to search for gravity waves. M. S. Rothenberg. bibliog il Phys Today 24:19-20 Je '71
Laser may be ready for the big time. Bsns W p54-5+ S 18 '71
Lasers; annual instrumentation issue; symposium. bibliog il Phys Today 24:23-31+ Mr '71
Lasers measure air pollution. S. Lindsay. il Sat R 54:52 Ag 7 '71
Little light on the subject; use of lasers in art and entertainment. M. Grosser. Atlan 227:92-6 Je '71
Measuring the earth. L. Purrett. il Sci N 99:233 Ap 3 '71
New class of diode lasers. M. B. Panish and L. Hayashi. il Sci Am 225:32-40 bibliog (p 122) Jl '71
New danger in the sky: warning aircraft to keep clear of laser experiment sites. il Time 97:56 Mr 15 '71
New laser attracts broad interest; transverse excitation atmospheric pressure lasers. P. J. Klass. il Aviation W 95:48-51 Jl 19 '71
Simple technique produces photon echoes and optical nutation. G. B. Lubkin. Phys Today 24:17+ D '71
Solid-state laser for the experimenter. F. M. Mims. il Pop Electr 35:46-9+ O '71
Superficial laser. Sci Am 225:49-50 N '71
Ultrafast laser pulses. A. J. DeMaria and others. bibliog il Phys Today 24:19-26 Jl '71
Understanding solid-state lasers. F. M. Mims. il Pop Electr 35:35-7+ O '71

Astronomical use
Focusing on the stars. Newsweek 77:92+ My 3 '71

Biological use
Laser stimulation of nerve cells in aplysia. R. L. Fork. bibliog il Science 171:907-8 Mr 5 '71

Industrial use
Aerospace technology infusion aids apparel industry operations; laser cutter. il Aviation W 94:48-9 Mr 29 '71
Beam; laser fabric cutter. New Yorker 47:30-2 Mr 27 '71
Cutting cloth by laser. il Time 97:71 Mr 22 '71
Laser to cut the garment tangle. Bsns W p46+ Mr 13 '71
Lasers for space-age tailors. il Sci Digest 70:37 O '71

Medical use
Take a dead man's eyes; determining the time of death. Newsweek 77:42 F 1 '71

Military use
DOD to coordinate laser-weapon efforts. P. J. Klass. Aviation W 95:24 N 8 '71
Lasers aid delivery of weapons. B. Miller. il Aviation W 94:48-53 My 3 '71

LASERS—Military use—*Continued*
Next U.S. superweapon: the Pentagon's light ray. il U S News 71:85-7 O 18 '71
Weapon delivery aid flexibility sought. B. Miller. il Aviation W 94:75-6+ My 10 '71

Photographic use
Is science an art? with photographs. I. Dryer. Pop Phot 69:71-3 Ag '71
See also
Holography

Physiological effects
Chromosome lesions produced with an argon laser microbeam without dye sensitization. M. W. Berns and others. bibliog il Science 171:903-5 Mr 5 '71

Standards
Laser may face new barriers. Bsns W p30 O 2 '71

LASETER, John L. and Weete, J. D.
Fatty acid ethyl esters of rhizopus arrhizus. bibliog il Science 172:864-5; 174:78 My 21, O 1 '71

LASH, Joseph P.
Eleanor; excerpt from Eleanor and Franklin. il pors McCalls 99:92-3+ O '71

LASIEWSKI, Robert C. See Ohmart, R. D. jt. auth.

LASKER, Mrs Albert D.
In very small personal ways, all of us can make our towns more beautiful. il House & Gard 139:67+ F '71

LASKER, Mary
Behind the cancer campaign. R. Bazell. il Ramp Mag 10:28-34 D '71 *

LASKER awards. See Albert and Mary Lasker foundation

LASS, Abraham H. and Wilson, E. S.
Freedom: booby trap for students; excerpt from The college student's handbook. Todays Ed 60:27-8 Ap '71; Same abr. Ed Digest 37:30-1 S '71

LASSERS, Willard J.
Death takes a holiday. Trans-Action 8:10+ Ja '71

LASSITER, Luther
Wimpy tackles an ex-tiger. J. Morgan. il pors Sports Illus 34:52-3 F 8 '71 *

LASSON, Kenneth
Two workers. il Atlan 228:74-82 O '71

LAST, Martin
Rudy Perez, in whose hands. il pors Dance Mag 45:28-31+ Je '71

LAST Don Juan; story. See Madocs, R.

LAST Judgment. See Judgment day

LAST of the Ghastleys; drama. See Huff, B. T.

LAST sandcastle; story. See Leland, J.

LAS VEGAS, Nev.

Hotels, restaurants, etc.
See also
Casinos

LATE bloomer; story. See Robinson, V.

LATENESS. See Tardiness

LATENT life. See Cryptobiosis

LATEX paint. See Paint

LATHAM, Aaron. See Latham, J. A.

LATHAM, Gary V. and others
Moonquakes. bibliog il Science 174:687-92 N 12 '71

LATHAM, John Aaron
Lardners: a writing dynasty. il N Y Times Mag p 10-11+ Ag 22 '71

LATHES
Add a limit switch to your lathe carriage. A. Volz. il Pop Mech 135:162 F '71
Add this sander table to your faceplate lathe. C. W. Ball. il Pop Mech 136:143 Jl '71
Carriage chuck mount for your lathe. W. E. Burton. il Pop Mech 136:60 N '71
Lathe attachment duplicates woodturnings. W. C. Leckey. il Pop Mech 136:196 O '71
Lathe ball-turning attachment. W. E. Burton. il Pop Mech 136:138-42 Jl '71
Midget metal lathe: modeler's friend. P. McCafferty. il Pop Sci 199:64 O '71
See also
Turning

LATIN AMERICA
Latin America today and tomorrow; excerpts. G. Plaza. il Américas 23:41-3 Je '71

Latin America's antinomy; conference at Clinton, N.Y. J. Villaverde. il Américas 22:2-10 N '70
See also
Architecture—Latin America
Arts and crafts—Latin America
Automobile industry—Latin America
Birds—Latin America
Birth control—Latin America
Catholic church in Latin America
Church and social problems—Latin America
Church and state in Latin America
Colleges and universities—Latin America—History
Communism—Latin America
Cruising—Latin America
Economic assistance in Latin America
Guerrillas—Latin America
Industrial relations—Latin America
Investments, Foreign (in Latin America)
Land tenure—Latin America
Missions—Latin America
Petroleum—Latin America
Purchasing, Military—Latin America
Religious conferences—Latin America
United States—Economic relations—Latin America
United States—Foreign relations—Latin America
Visitors, Foreign—Latin America

Bibliography
New series on Latin America. Wilson Lib Bul 45:530 F '71

Civilization
Colonial art; symposium, ed. by G. de Zéndegui. il Américas 23:S1-24 Ap '71

Commerce
IA-ECOSOC speaks out on surtax. Américas 23:44 O '71
U.S. trade policy and Latin America; statement, July 12, 1971. D. Szabo. Dept State Bul 65:239-46 Ag 30 '71

Description and travel
By freighter to the Inca. A. Buchsbaum. il Américas 23:18-24 O '71

Economic conditions
Colonialism lives in South America. E. K. Culhane. il America 125:67-9 Ag 7 '71; Reply. A. Shea. 125:301 O 23 '71
Marxist label pasted on wrong bottle; study of inter-American development efforts by Organization of American states. B. L. Masse. America 125:137 S 11 '71
Neocolonialism in Latin America; excerpt from Revolution next door. G. MacEoin. bibliog Chr Cent 88:685-97 Je 2 '71
Next development decade; excerpts from address. G. Plaza. Américas 23:42 Ja '71
Sustaining a meaningful commitment to Latin American development; statement, August 4, 1971. C. A. Meyer. Dept State Bul 65:236-8 Ag 30 '71
U.S. calls for joint solutions to western hemisphere problems; statement, April 29, 1971. J. J. Jova. Dept State Bul 64:783-6 Je 14 '71
U.S. policy toward a changing Latin America; adaptation of address, January 29, 1971. S. Weintraub. Dept State Bul 64:550-4 Ap 26 '71
See also
Labor and laboring classes—Latin America
United Nations—Economic commission for Latin America

Economic policy
Second Latin American revolution. E. Frei. For Affairs 50:83-96 O '71

Economic relations
United States
See United States—Economic relations—Latin America

Expropriation policy
Learning to live with expropriation. il Bsns W p34-5 Jl 10 '71

Foreign opinion
American
Latin America: a U.S. news orphan. X. Gutierrez Cantu. il America 124:290-1 Mr 20 '71

History
Wars of independence, 1806-1830
May revolution; Buenos Aires uprising, May 25, 1810. O. González Roura. il Américas 23:36-9 My '71

LAVIN, Mary
Trastevere; story. New Yorker 47:43-51 D 11 '71

LAW, John
Scoundrel who invented credit. M. Bishop. por Horizon 13:110-11 Spr '71 •

LAW, Stephen L.
Methyl mercury and inorganic mercury collection by a selective chelating resin. bibliog il Science 174:285-7 O 15 '71

LAW
See also
Appellate procedure
Children—Law
Civil rights
Copyright
Criminal law
Habeas corpus
International law
Jury
Justice, Administration of
Lawyers
Military law
Rule of law
Wills
Woman—Legal status, laws, etc.
also Law on special subjects, e.g. Game laws; Television laws and regulations

Practice
See also
Malpractice

Sociology
See Sociological jurisprudence

Study and teaching
Teaching about law. A. Elson and M. Elson. Todays Ed 60:61-2 Ap '71
They lay the law on kids, and kids love it! il Changing T 25:25-8 S '71

Georgia
Purity in Atlanta; new anti-lewdness statute. New Repub 165:9 Jl 24 '71

Southwestern states
Frontier law and order, by P. D. Jordan. Review
Am West 8:49 Ja '71. R. Trennert

United States
Family legal matters (cont) L. M. Brown. Bet Hom & Gard 49:100 My '71
How fair a fair trial can you get today? state juvenile laws. il Sr Schol 99:2-5+ N 8 '71
With justice for some, ed. by B. Wasserstein and M. J. Green. Review
Nation 213:502-4 N 15 '71. C. Garry
See also
American bar association
Courts—United States
Justice, Administration of—United States
Law enforcement
Legislation—United States
Negroes—Legal status, laws, etc.
Teachers—Legal status, laws, etc.
United States—Constitution
Wage-price policy—Legal aspects

LAW, Sunday. See Sunday legislation
LAW and Christianity. See Religion and law
LAW and mental illness. See Mental health laws
LAW and religion. See Religion and law
LAW and sex. See Sex and law
LAW and society. See Rule of law; Sociological jurisprudence

LAW enforcement
Case for the so-called hard line approach to crime. F. E. Inbau and F. G. Carrington. bibliog f Ann Am Acad 397:19-27 S '71
Crimes without victims. A. B. Smith and H. Pollack. Sat R 54:27-9 D 4 '71
Federal law enforcement in America. J. T. Elliff. Cur Hist 60:335-40+ Je '71
Plea from the President. Newsweek 77:24 Mr 22 '71
President Nixon's new look at justice. il Time 97:13 Mr 22 '71
Social change and the police. P. V. Murphy. Am Scholar 40:686-90 Aut '71
Victimless crime; findings of the San Francisco committee on crime. New Repub 165:9 Jl 3 '71
See also
Law—United States
United States—Justice, Department of—Law enforcement assistance administration

Anecdotes, facetiae, satire, etc.
Lawful disorder. Chr Cent 88:963 Ag 11 '71

History
Development of local and state law enforcement. V. W. Peterson. bibliog f Cur Hist 60:327-34 Je '71
Frontier law and order, by P. D. Jordan. Review
Am West 8:49 Ja '71. R. Trennert

LAW enforcement assistance administration.
See United States—Justice, Department of—Law enforcement assistance administration

LAW making. See Legislation
LAW partnership
See also
Mudge, Rose, Guthrie and Alexander (firm)

LAW schools
See also
Harvard university—Law school

LAW societies
See also
American bar association

LAW students
Harvard law revisited. M. Kasindorf. il Newsweek 77:52+ My 24 '71
Lawyer's choice; prosperity or public interest. il Forbes 107:42-3 Ap 1 '71
Streetcar strategists; University of Detroit law school students earning course credits for services to the poor. il Time 98:28+ Ag 23 '71
Teaching survival in the sales jungle. R. R. Morris. il Am Ed 7:28-31 Ap '71
What are tomorrow's lawyers thinking today? W. Goodman. il Redbook 136:74-5+ F '71

LAWFORD, Valentine
House of Grace, countess of Dudley, in Nassau. Vogue 157:142+ Mr 1 '71
Jungle jewel box. il por Vogue 157:112-19+ F 15 '71
Mr and Mrs Gardner Cowles's New York apartment. il Vogue 158:180-7+ O 1 '71

LAWICK, Jane (Goodall) baroness van
Authors & editors; interview, ed. by L. P. Freilicher. il por Pub W 200:7-9 N 22 '71
Jane of the apes; excerpt from In the shadow of man. il por Ladies Home J 88: 78+ O '71
about
Hairy mirror. B. Darrach. il por Time 98:104+ N 8 '71 •

LAWICK-GOODALL, Jane, baroness van. See Lawick, J. G. van

LAWLER, Justus George
Educational technocrat. Commonweal 95: 343-7 Ja 14 '72

LAWLESS, James G. and others
Amino acids indigenous to the Murray meteorite. bibliog il Science 173:626-7 Ag 13 '71

LAWLESSNESS
Could it happen here? civil disobedience. S. Alsop. Newsweek 78:84 Jl 19 '71
Roots of lawlessness. H. S. Commager. por Sat R 54:17-19+ F 13 '71

LAWLOR, Francis X.
Lawlor on the line. il por Newsweek 78:54 S 13 '71 •

LAWN bowling. See Bowling
LAWN fertilizers. See Fertilizers and manures
LAWN mowers
Battery-operated reel lawn mower; Black & Decker cordless. il Consumer Bul 54:37 Ag '71
Battery-powered reel lawn mower. il Consumer Rep 36:268 My '71
Electricity solved my mowing problem. B. Black. il Home Gard 58:38-9 Ag '71
New mowers; they're safer, and easier to use, too. E. F. Lindsley. il Pop Sci 198: 98-101 Mr '71
Now: an electric rider for silent mowing. E. F. Lindsley. il Pop Sci 199:16+ S '71
Patents reflect trends. il Parks & Rec 6:28-9 My '71
'71 riders: new style, speed, and safety. E. F. Lindsley. il Pop Sci 198:84-6+ Je '71
Super mowers. D. Demske. il Mech Illus 67: 142-5 Mr '71
Supersafe rotary mower; it's bladeless. E. F. Lindsley. il Pop Sci 198:69 Ap '71
Thrifty man's guide to lawnmowers. D. Demske. il Mech Illus 67:94+ Je '71

Safety devices and measures
Furor over mower safety. B. C. Kilvert, jr. il Mech Illus 67:84-5+ Ag '71
Lawn mowers & other killers. S. Klein. il Nation 212:402-4 Mr 29 '71

LAWN sprinklers. See Sprinklers

LAWN tools, equipment, and supplies
Make a bagger for your fall leaves. J. Hand.
il Pop Sci 199:156 O '71
Vacuum sweeper replaces rakes and brooms.
il Am City 86:44 O '71
LAWNS
Fescues, the hard-working grasses for home
lawns. R. W. Schery. il Home Gard 58:
24-5+ Mr '71
Getting your lawn in shape for winter. il
Home Gard 58:34-5 O '71
How to make your lawn grow green. W. B.
Harris. House & Gard 139:46+ My '71
Keeping on top of your lawn. T. Cruso. Mc-
Calls 98:48+ Ag '71
Lawn renovation, the modern way. R. W.
Schery. il Home Gard 58:38-9+ My '71
Lawns. H. W. Indyk. New Yorker 47:27-9 S 18
'71
Planning a zoysia lawn. R. L. Bergman. il
Home Gard 58:60+ F '71
Starting a lawn from scratch. il Bet Hom &
Gard 49:144 Ap '71
Turf management interactions. J. Madison. il
Parks & Rec 6:32-5 S '71
Yes, you can grow grass in the shade. il
Changing T 25:37-8 Ap '71
See also
Grasses
LAWNS, Artificial. See Turf, Artificial
LAWNS, Watering of. See Watering of gardens,
lawns, etc.
LAWRENCE, Chester H.
4-channel stereo synthesizer. il Radio-Electr
42:71-3 Mr '71
R-E builds Heath AR-1500 stereo receiver. il
Radio-Electr 42:36-8 D '71
LAWRENCE, David Herbert
D. H. Lawrence's appraisal of Jesus. W. E.
Phipps. Chr Cent 88:521-4 Ap 28 '71; Dis-
cussion. 88:1365-6 N 17 '71 *
Taos remembered. H. Fergusson. il pors Am
West 8:38-41 S '71 *
LAWRENCE, Jerome, and Lee, R. E.
Incomparable Max. Criticism
America 125:427 N 20 '71
New Yorker 47:101 O 30 '71
Time 98:95 N 1 '71 *
Night Thoreau spent in jail. Criticism
Life il 70:17 Ap 16 '71 *
LAWRENCE, John
Rider's life. Sports Illus 34:29 F 8 '71
LAWRENCE, L. George
Animal guidance systems. il Electr World
86:27-9+ D '71
Experimental electro-culture. il Pop Electr
34:66-70+ F '71
Instrumentation balloons carry electronic
payloads. il Electr World 86:13-15 D '71
Interstellar communications: what are the
prospects. il Electr World 86:34-5+ O '71
More experiments in electroculture. bibliog il
Pop Electr 34:63-8+ Je '71
Plants have feelings, too. . . il Org Gard &
Farm 18:64-7 Ap '71
LAWRENCE, Robert
Recordings. Sat R 54:57 Ja 30; 83 O 30 '71
LAWRENCE, Steve
Legal strategies for environmental control.
Field & S 75:12+ F '71
LAWRENCE, Thomas Edward
Vocation in the desert. N. Braybrooke. Com-
monweal 94:88-9 Ap 2 '71 *
LAWRENCE R. Klein award
Hyman B. Kaitz wins second annual Law-
rence R. Klein award. Mo Labor R 94:2 Je
'71
LAWRENCE radiation laboratory, Berkeley,
Calif. See California. University—Lawrence
radiation laboratories
LAWRENSON, Helen
Feminine mistake. il Esquire 75:82-5+ Ja '71
Mamma mia, that'sa some musical meatball!
il Esquire 76:94-7+ Jl '71
Weekend with Chief Michael Butler and his
inner tribe. il Esquire 76:165-8+ N '71
LAWS of war. See War, Laws of
LAWSON, Francis R.
Know your enemy. J. McCaull. bibliog il
pors Environ 13:30-9 Je '71 *
LAWSON, Judy
Winning is the only thing: International 14
class team racing series. il Yachting 130:
64-5+ Ag '71
LAWSON, Simpson
Towns for the urban and rural poor. Cur 125:
35-41 Ja '71
LAWSON McGhee library, Knoxville, Tenn.
See Knoxville and Knox County, Tenn,
public library
LAWSUITS. See Actions and defenses
LAWYERS
Advocate. D. Rainowitz. Commentary 51:69-
71 Mr '71

Angry young lawyers. P. Vanderwicken. il
Fortune 84:74-7+ S '71
F. Lee Bailey's strangest murder case; Coppolino case; excerpts from The defense
never rests; ed. by H. Aronson. F. L.
Bailey. il por Ladies Home J 88:122-3+ N
'71
F. Lee Bailey's The defense never rests;
excerpt from The defense never rests; ed.
by H. Aronson. F. L. Bailey. il pors Ladies
Home J 88:93-5+ O '71 (to be cont)
Gilt-edged profession. il Forbes 108:30-4+ S
15 '71
Lawyer manpower in the criminal justice sys-
tem. J. Ladinsky. bibliog f Cur Hist 61:9-
12+ Jl '71
Legal problems? It pays to shop for your
lawyer. Bsns W p73-4 D 18 '71
Role of the lawyer; the new consumerism; ad-
dress, February 8, 1971. B. S. Rosenthal.
Vital Speeches 37:407-10 Ap 15 '71
Standardizing bar exams. Newsweek 78:116 N
22 '71
Unruly lawyers are menace; excerpts from
address, May 18, 1971. W. E. Burger. por
U S News 70:83 My 31 '71; Same. Cur Hist
61:111+ Ag '71
Using a lawyer for a personal-injury claim.
L. M. Brown. Bet Hom & Gard 49:12+ Ap
'71
Where have all the lawyers gone? corporation
lawyers. Duns 98:75-6+ N '71
See also
American bar association
Malpractice
Metzger, M. H.
National bar association (Negro)
Negro lawyers
Volunteer lawyers for the arts

Public relations
Respect for the law and lawyers; in an age
of unrest; address, February 6, 1971. P.
Lesly. Vital Speeches 37:301-4 Mr 1 '71
LAWYERS military defense committee
At war with the army; McLemore case. il
Time 97:48 F 8 '71
LAX, Michael
Collaboration in glass; interview. ed. by E.
Erikson. il Craft Horiz 31:12-15+ F '71
LAYCOCK, George
Eradicate them one more time. Field & S
76:46-7+ D '71
For American profit and Japanese steel,
they're tearing down the Canadian Rock-
ies. il Audubon 73:77-84 Ja '71
How the champ catches cats. il Field & S
76:72-3+ My '71
River named Smith. il Field & S 75:50-1+ Ja
'71
LAYING up of boats. See Boats—Storage
LAYMEN. See Laity
LAYNE, Elizabeth N. and Hartgen, Stephen
Jungle cocks, trout flies, and smugglers. il
Audubon 73:38-43 My '71
LAYOFF systems
Case of the borderline black. T. V. Purcell.
il Harvard Bsns R 49:128-30+ N '71
How companies deal with cutback jitters.
Bsns W p88 Ap 24 '71
Layoff and recall provisions in major agree-
ments. W. L. Tillery. il Mo Labor R 94:
41-6 Jl '71
RB.211 problem spurs Rolls layoff study.
Aviation W 94:24 Mr 15 '71
LAZARD, Naomi
Looking for Itsy; poem. New Yorker 47:42 S
18 '71
LAZAREFF, Hélène Gordon
Grande mademoiselle Chanel. il por Harp
Baz 104:160-1 Mr '71
LAZAREVICH, Gordana
Neapolitan intermezzo and its influence on
the symphonic idiom. bibliog f il Mus Q
57:294-313 Ap '71
LAZARIDES, Elias, and Lukens, L. N.
Collagen polypeptides: normal release from
polysomes in the absence of proline hydro-
xylation. bibliog il Science 173:723-5 Ag 20
'71
LAZARUS, Dick
Bit about anchoring. il Yachting 129:69+
Ap '71
LAZARUS, Simon
No-fault default. New Repub 164:21-3 Ap 17
'71
Who's the boss? New Repub 164:22-3 My 29;
32 Je 19 '71
LAZO, Mario
Straight from the bear's mouth. Nat R 23:
70-1 Ja 26 '71
LEACH, B. F. See Higham, C. F. W. jt. auth.

LEACH, Josephine
Study of Chinua Achebe's Things fall apart in mid-America. Engl J 60:1052-6 N '71

LEACOCK, Eleanor
At play in African villages. il Natur Hist 80:60-5 D '71

LEAD
Lead, the Clydesdale workhorse in space. il Space World H-4-88:16-19 Ap '71
Screening for lead in pottery. Chem 44:24 S '71
See also
Plants. Effect of lead on

Isotopes
Radiohalos: some unique lead isotope ratios and unknown alpha radioactivity. R. V. Gentry. bibliog il Science 173:727-31 Ag 20 '71

LEAD additives. See Gasoline—Additives

LEAD alloys
Case of the flowing roof; lead roof of Washington national cathedral. C. P. Saylor. il Chem 44:19-20 D '71

LEAD in the air. See Air pollution

LEAD in the body
Lead suppression of mouse resistance to salmonella typhimurium. F. E. Hemphill and others. bibliog il Science 172:1031-2 Je 4 '71

LEAD paint. See Paint

LEAD pencils. See Pencils

LEAD poisoning
Air of poverty. P. P. Craig and E. Berlin. bibliog il Environ 13:2-9 Je '71
Dangerous pottery removed from market. Consumer Rep 36:302 My '71
Develop new screening test for lead poisoning. il Todays Health 49:71 Ap '71
Don't chew your pencil. Sci Digest 70:29 N '71
Half step forward. D. T. Magidson. il Environ 13:10-13 Je '71
Health programs: slum children suffer because of low funding. R. J. Bazell. il Science 172:921-5 My 28 '71
Lead in pencils, but not in the lead. Consumer Rep 36:646-8 N '71
Lead in pottery. il Chem 44:23-4 S '71
Lead poisoning. J. J. Chisolm, jr. il Sci Am 224:15-23 bibliog(p 130) F '71
Lead poisoning combating the threat from the air. R. J. Bazell. Science 174:574-6 N 5 '71
Lead poisoning; risks for pencil chewers? J. Pichirallo. Science 173:509-10 Ag 6 '71
Lead poisoning: zoo animals may be the first victims; study of Bronx and Staten Island zoo. R. J. Bazell. Science 173:130-1 Jl 9 '71
Lead, the inexcusable pollutant. P. P. Craig. il Sat R 54:68-70+ O 2 '71; Reply. P. B. Hammond. 54:96+ D 4 '71
Metallic menaces in the environment. G. Bylinsky. il Fortune 83:110-13+ Ja '71
Murder by neglect. Commonweal 94:371 Jl 23 '71
Pencil chewers beware. Chem 44:5 N '71
Which way will you be lead? letters. Natur Hist 80:6-7 D '71
Will the FDA get the lead out? J. A. Page. Commonweal 95:246-7 D 10 '71

LEADED gasoline. See Gasoline—Additives

LEADERSHIP
Administrative revolution, by G. E. Berkley. Review
Bsns W p21+ Je 5 '71. W. R. Dill
Baker's dozen of heroic vitalists; address, June 4, 1971. H. G. Baker. Vital Speeches 37:586-92 Jl 15 '71
Catalytic agent for effective planning; coordinator's role. J. C. Chambers and others. il Harvard Bsns R 49:110-19 Ja '71
Conflict: new emphasis in leadership. A. Saville. Clear House 46:52-5 S '71
From the jaws of victory, by C. Fair. Review
New Repub 165:23-5 Ag 21 '71. R. Macauley
If your husband is a VIP. M. Longwell. Farm J 95:40 O '71
Our critical shortage of leadership. A. J. Reichley. li Fortune 84:88-93+ S '71
President stands alone. H. B. Henshel. Harvard Bsns R 49:37-45 S '71
Principal as a change agent. L. E. Annese. bibliog Clear House 45:273-7 Ja '71
Public policy making; why the churches strike out; moral leadership. V. C. Blum. America 124:224-8 Mr 6 '71; Discussion. 124:348-9 Ap 3 '71
Sounds of executive silence. N. A. Adler. il Harvard Bsns R 49:100-5 Jl '71; Discussion. 49:21+ N '71

Where have all the leaders gone? B. Brower. il Life 71:68-9+ O 8 '71
See also
Christian leadership
Elite (social sciences)
Negro leadership

LEAF cutting bees. See Bees

LEAF cuttings. See Plant propagation

LEAF gatherers
See also
Lawn tools, equipment, and supplies

LEAF mold (humus) See Humus

LEAF movements. See Plants—Irritability and movements

LEAF mulch. See Mulching

LEAFHOPPERS
Stop alfalfa leafhopper damage. Suc Farm 69:B12 Je '71

LEAFLETS. See Pamphlets

LEAGUE of American writers
See also
Congress of American writers

LEAGUE of New York theatres, inc.
Theater; effect of the limited gross contract. H. Hewes. Sat R 54:76 Ja 23 '71

LEAGUE of the Iroquois. See Iroquois Indians

LEAHY, Donald J.
Death in the code room. por Newsweek 78:38-9 S 13 '71 *

LEAKEY, Louis Seymour Bazett
Once more into the past. il por Sci N 100:259 O 16 '71 *

LEAKEY, Richard E. F.
Australopithecus, a long-armed short-legged, knuckle-walker. Sci N 100:357 N 27 '71 *
Two distinct hominids? por Sci N 99:398 Je 12 '71 *

LEAKS in sewer pipes. See Sewer pipes—Leakage

LEAMER, Laurence
Eccles no. 6. il Harper 243:100-2+ D '71

LEAN, David
Movie audiences don't change; interview, ed. by M. Ronan. por Sr Schol 98:18 F 15 '71

LEAP year
Now, the leap second. Time 98:54 D 27 '71

LEAR, John
Environment and the quality of life. See Issues of Saturday review
Environment repair: the U.S. army engineers' new assignment. il Sat R 54:47-52 My 1 '71

LEAR, Martha Weinman
New York's Haitians: working, waiting, watching Bébé Doc. il N Y Times Mag p22-3+ O 10 '71

LEAR, Norman
Meet Archie Bunker and the man who created All in the family; interview. ed. by P. Hudson. il pors Sr Schol 99:6-7+ O 25 '71
TV: speaking about the unspeakable. il por Newsweek 78:52-4+ N 29 '71 *

LEAR, Robert. See Nathan, R. jt. auth.

LEAR, William Powell
Bill Lear: inventor of the impossible. R. Schiller. por Read Digest 99:148-52 Ag '71 *
Damn the smog, full steam ahead! Forbes 107:36 F 1 '71 *
Lear: the steam king? K. Ludvigsen. il pors Motor T 23:30-2+ F '71 *

LEARNED institutions and societies
See also
Scientific societies

LEARNING, Psychology of
Forget you are a teacher. C. Rogers. Ed Digest 37:17-19 N '71
Head start for logic. Sci N 100:124 Ag 21 '71
Informative feedback: an educational controversy. W. Baller and E. Lower. bibliog Sch & Soc 99:417-19 N '71
Latent talent: the anagram a parent can solve. B. Nikitin. il UNESCO Courier 24:28-32 F '71
Miracle of learning. B. W. Overstreet. il PTA Mag 66:6-8 D '71
To be nobody-but-yourself. S. Fleming. il Schol Teach Jr/Sr High p 18-19 F 1 '71 *
Why some bright children have trouble in school. S. Chess. il Parents Mag 46:42-3+ My '71
See also
Animal learning
Comprehension
Conditioned responses
Memory
Psychology, Educational
Recall (psychology)
Sleep learning

LEARNING, Psychology of—Continued

Emotional aspects

Curriculum is the self; affective development. H. Morgan. Ed Digest 36:19-22 Mr '71

Emotional emphasis in education; laboratory for confluent education, and the Center for humanistic education. Sch & Soc 99:78-9 F '71

I get a very different feeling in that class; affective education in Philadelphia schools. K. Branan. il Schol Teach Jr/Sr High p8-10 My 3 '71; Same abr. Ed Digest 37:9-11 S '71

Sharing and caring; microlabs. E. Hunter. Todays Ed 60:73 S '71

LEARNING and scholarship
See also
Culture
Humanities

LEARNING centers. See Instructional materials centers

LEARNING centers, Business. See Business education

LEARNING disabilities. See Children, Exceptional; Minimal brain dysfunction

LEARNING materials. See Teaching—Aids and devices

LEARNING theory. See Learning, Psychology of

LEARSON, Thomas Vincent
Business under the freeze: a top executive's appraisal; interview. il por U S News 71:36-9 S 13 '71

Greetings; interview. por Forbes 108:46 Ag 1 '71

about

Learson at IBM's helm. il por Time 98:55 Jl 12 '71 •

New hand on the tiller at I.B.M. il por Fortune 84:33 Ag '71 •

Successor. pors Forbes 108:19 S 1 '71 •

LEARY, Daniel J.
Why not-ers and what they are reading. il Cath World 212:240-4 F '71

LEARY, Mary Ellen
California's mad mix. Nation 212:685-7 My 31 '71

Democratic new guard. Nation 212:302-5 Mr 8 '71

ILWU won't freeze. Nation 213:174-6 S 6 '71

LEAS, Susan E.
Richard III, Shakespeare, and history. bibliog Engl J 60:1214-16+ D '71

LEASCO data processing equipment corporation
How's that again? por Forbes 107:14-15 Ja 15 '71

LEASE-a-plane international. See Airplanes—Leasing and renting

LEASE and rental services
Airlines wary of accounting change for leased equipment. W. H. Gregory. Aviation W 95:25-6 O 25 '71

Threat to the booming leasing business. il Bsns W p42+ S 4 '71

You can rent almost anything these days. il Changing T 25:35-6 N '71
See also
Agricultural machinery—Leasing and renting
Airplanes—Leasing and renting
Automobiles—Leasing and renting
Boats—Leasing and renting
Motor trucks—Leasing and renting
Recreational vehicles—Leasing and renting

LEASES
There's no such thing as a 50-50 lease. F. J. Reiss. il Suc Farm 69:D20 O '71
See also
Landlord and tenant
Oil and gas leases

LEASK, Ada Longfield
Embossed pictures of Samuel Dixon and his imitators. il Antiques 100:120-3 Jl '71

LEATHER
Keep leather alive. B. E. Kappel. Field & S 76:84+ Ag '71

Long live leather. Harp Baz 104:129 Ag '71
See also
Tanning

LEATHER belts. See Belts

LEATHER cleaning. See Cleaning

LEATHER substitutes
Leather's shoes prove tough to fill. Bsns W p28-9 O 30 '71

Requiem for a polymer; Corfam. Time 97:82 Mr 29 '71

LEATHER work
Leatherworking tips. il Mlle 73:163 Jl '71

LEATHERBURY, Leven C.
For the elementary teacher: your art program. il Sch Arts 71:6-7 N '71

LEAVES
Leaves: nature's autumn dividend. W. F. Bowers. il Org Gard & Farm 18:44-5 O '71

On not knowing the trees by their leaves. E. A. Menninger. il Am For 77:12-15 D '71
See also
Buds
Defoliation
Veins (botany)

LEAVES of absence
See also
Employees—Leaves of absence

LEAVITT, H. Douglas
Certification. Parks & Rec 6:123+ Ja '71

LEAVITT, Helen
Folly of our superhighway system; excerpt from Superhighway-superhoax. Read Digest 98:61-5 F '71

LEAVITT, Thomas W.
Beleaguered director. il Art in Am 59:66-71 Jl '71

LEAWOOD, Kan.
Affluent bedroom. C. Clark. il Time 97:16 Mr 15 '71

LEBANON
See also
Air freight service—Lebanon
Guerrillas—Lebanon

Antiquities

Deer buried in ancient ritual. il Sci Digest 70:64 Ag '71

Man from Sarepta. il Sci Digest 70:68-9 N '71

Politics and government

Lebanon: the politics of survival. J. B. Wolf. bibliog f Cur Hist 62:20-4+ Ja '72

LEBANON COUNTY
Lebanon Valley. D. J. Del Marcelle. il Travel 136:64-7 D '71

LEBARRON, Suzanne
Revelations and Robert's rules. Library J 96: 2457 Ag '71

LEBEDEV, Vîacheslav
Earth's orange neighbor. Space World H-12-96:40 D '71

LEBLANC, John F.
Pedagogy in elementary mathematics education. Ed Digest 36:24-6 Ja '71

LE BOEUF, Burney J.
Aggression of the breeding bulls; with biographical sketch. il Natur Hist 80:10, 82-94 F '71

—See Peterson, R. S. jt. auth.

LEBOW, Jared
Advice from a pediatrician. il Look 35:64 Je 1 '71

Girl has to suffer. il Look 35:60-2+ Je 29 '71

Nice story about boxing. il pors Look 35: 64-7 Ag 24 '71

—See McClure, T. jt. auth.

LEBRUN, Rico
Thoughts on drawing; excerpts. Am Artist 35: 4 Mr '71

LECHE, Hans Gunnar
Swedish psychiatry today; adaptation of address; July 1969. Ment Hy 55:404-6 Jl '71

LECITHIN
Binding of DDT to lecithin. I. J. Tinsley and others. bibliog il Science 174:145-7 O 8 '71

LECKBAND, E. and Boyse, E. A.
Immunocompetent cells among mouse thymocytes: a minor population. bibliog il Science 172:1258-60 Je 18 '71

LECKERTS, Steve
All about Dolby. il Radio-Electr 42:38-40 Je '71

LECKY, Robert S.
Clergy and laymen: broadening the concern. Commonweal 94:468 S 17 '71

LE CLAIR, Henry
Small town incinerator. il Am City 86:63-4 My '71

LE CORBEILLER, Clare
Design sources of early China trade porcelain. il Antiques 101:161-8 Ja '72

LECTURE halls. See Auditoriums

LECTURE method in teaching
Anatomy of a dead lecture. M. Kourilsky. il Clear House 46:20-6 S '71

LECTURES and lecturing
Bantam books launches its lecture bureau. Pub W 200:19 N 1 '71

Lecture notes. R. Schickel. il Harper 243:30+ D '71
See also
Lecture method in teaching

LEDBETTER, Bedford G.
Tales of sea floor soundings; with biographical sketch. il Sea Front 17:274-84, 319 S '71

LEDBETTER, Eve
Kiss before midnight; story. Good H 174: 78-9 Ja '72

LEDDIHN, Erik Maria, ritter von Kuehnelt-. See Kuehnelt-Leddihn, E. M. von

LEDECKY, Berta
Home from the war; story. Redbook 137:106-7 S '71
Special day; story. Redbook 137:77-8 Ag '71
Visit home; story. Redbook 136:115 Mr '71

LEDERBERG, Joshua
Freeze on missile testing. Bul Atom Sci 27:4-6+ Mr '71
Need for technological assessment. Cur 128:24-8 Ap '71
Squaring an infinite circle: radiobiology and the value of life. Bul Atom Sci 27:43-5 S '71

LEDERER, Esther Pauline (Friedman) See Landers, A. pseud.

LEDERLE, John W.
Public higher education in Massachusetts. il Sch & Soc 99:51-4 Ja '71

LEDERLE laboratories
New antibiotic finally gets born; Minocin. il Bsns W p56+ O 16 '71

LE Duan
Impact in Hanoi. R. Critchfield. Nation 213:102-5 Ag 16 '71 *

LEDUC, Violette
Mad in pursuit, by V. Leduc. Review
Sat R 54:47 S 18 '71. A. Balakian *
My mother: a masterpiece cut adrift; excerpts from Mad in pursuit. Vogue 158:97 Jl '71

LEE, Al
Going whoring; Federal reserve bank of New York; poems. Poetry 117:248-50 Ja '71

LEE, Albert
Prized art of bonsai. bibliog il Har Yrs 11:18-21 F '71

LEE, Bennie, and Lewis, Don
Making double-spouted pots on the wheel. il Ceram Mo 20:23-5 Ja '72

LEE, Calvin
Quest for a silver unicorn. E. Kern. il pors Life 70:66-8 Je 4 '71 *

LEE, Carleton L.
Black Americana studies. Negro Hist Bul 34:114-15 My '71

LEE, Chester M.
Learning from the moon. il Todays Ed 60:50-2 Ja '71

LEE, Chin O. See Armstrong, W. M. jt. auth.

LEE, Chung, and others
Estrogen receptor in the rabbit corpus luteum. bibliog il Science 173:1032-3 S 10 '71

LEE, Don
Don Lee cures hair ills. por Harp Baz 104:44 F '71

LEE, Don L.
Why minority publishing? ed. by B. Chambers. il pors Pub W 199:45-6 Mr 15 '71 *

LEE, Donald T.
Recovery, inc: aid in the transition from hospital to community. bibliog Ment Hy 55:194-8 Ap '71

LEE, Felicia
Skiing. il Sports Illus 34:50-1 Ja 25 '71

LEE, James A.
Behavioral theory vs. reality. bibliog f Harvard Bsns R 49:20-2+ Mr '71

LEE, Kuan-yew
Lee cracks down. por Newsweek 77:49 Je 7 '71 *
Press lord without portfolio. Time 97:71 My 31 '71 *

LEE, Laurie
Morocco: more than a place, a world. Mlle 73:148-54+ Je '71

LEE, Linda K.
Congressional flight on a fragile spacecraft. il Parks & Rec 6:22-4+ Mr '71
Federal legislation in the 1960s. il Parks & Rec 6:10-14+ Ag '71

LEE, Raymond Eliot
Living through the blitz. S. K. Oberbeck. por Newsweek 78:105-105A+ N 29 '71 *

LEE, Robert Edwin. See Lawrence, J. jt. auth.

LEE, Sally
College presidents and students; interview. Mlle 73:350-1 Ag '71

LEE, Sherman Emery
Ivory tower versus the discotheque. G. Glueck. il pors Art in Am 59:80-5 My '71 *

LEE, Stan
Shazam! Here comes Captain Relevant. S. Braun. il por N Y Times Mag p32-3+ My 2 '71 *

LEE, Stanley H.
Throwing the large plate. il por Ceram Mo 19:18-20 S '71

LEE, Sung Gue, and Evans, W. R.
Hybrid ribosome formation from escherichia coli and chloroplast ribosome sub-units. bibliog il Science 173:241-2 Jl 16 '71

LEE, Tsung-dao
Weak interaction: puzzle of the fourth force. D. E. Thomsen. il por Sci N 100:252-3 O 9 '71 *

LEE, Virginia, and Claiborne, Craig
Cook-as-you-go Chinese lunch. il pors House & Gard 140:52-3+ Jl '71

LEECHES
Leech-repellent property of eastern red-spotted newts, notophthalmus viridescens. F. H. Pough. bibliog il Science 174:1144-6 D 10 '71

LEEDOM, Joanne
Linking up through LINKS. il Am Ed 7:31-2 Ag '71

LEEDS, Albert Ripley
? pollution of the water supply of—; 1887 lawsuit against industries polluting the Passaic River. il Chem 44:19-20 Ap '71 *

LEEKS
See also
Cookery—Vegetables

LEES, Carlton B.
Editorial. Horticulture 49:20 Mr '71

LEES, Gene
Great recordings of the decade:
Pops. il Hi Fi 21:69-71 Ap '71
Lees side. See issues of High fidelity and Musical America
Sinatra: that certain style. por Sat R 54:45+ Ag 28 '71

LEEWARD ISLANDS
Otterworldliness; St Eustatius, Saba, and St Barthélemy. D. Butwin. il Sat R 54:48-50 Ap 17 '71
Reefing through the Leewards. W. D. Teague. il Yachting 130:52-3+ N '71

LEFEBRE, Jorge
Jorge Lefebre and Oedipus Rex, his Afro-Cuban-ancient Greek ballet; interview. ed. by N. M. Stoop. il por Dance Mag 45:38-42 Ag '71

LEFEVRE, Paul
Remote U.H.F.-TV signal-seeking system. il Electr World 86:66-7 Jl '71

LEFF, David N.
Meeting in Prague. il Environ 13:29-33 N '71

LEFF, Deborah
Lady is a tiger. il Seventeen 29:124-5+ O '70

LEFFEL, David A.
David A. Leffel: 20th century old master. D. Cochrane. il por Am Artist 35:20-5 O '71 *

LEFKOWITZ, Dave
Profiles. W. Whitworth. New Yorker 47:38-42+ D 18 '71 *

LEFKOWITZ, Louis J.
Excerpt from testimony, September 16, 1969. Cong Digest 50:52-3+ F '71

LEFLORE COUNTY, Miss.

Education
Education in Mississippi: Leflore County. L. Hogue. il Am Lib 2:985-6 O '71

LEFT and right (political science) See Right and left (political science)

LEFT- and right-handedness
Boon: The left hand, small store; interview. J. Gittleson. New Yorker 47:32-3 My 8 '71
Making life easier for lefties. J. F. Pearson. il Pop Mech 135:66-7 Je '71
On telling left from right. M. C. Corballis and I. L. Beale. il Sci Am 224:96-104 bibliog(124) Mr '71

LEFT wing (politics) See Right and left (political science)

LEFTON, Leon
Mechanic turns artist. F. Worth. il por Design 72:11 mid-Sum '71 *

LEFTOVERS. See Cookery—Leftovers

LEG
See also
Knee

Diseases
Why leg pains? K. Anderson. il Har Yrs 11:46-8 Ag '71

LEG exercises. See Exercise

LEGAL aid
Governor Reagan's private war; California rural legal assistance. L. T. King. Commonweal 94:358-9 Jl 9 '71
Legal services, inc; proposed National legal services corporation. R. M. Hall, jr. New Repub 164:24-5 My 29 '71
Poor betrayed; refunding the California rural legal assistance program. J. Osborne. New Repub 164:13-15 F 13 '71
Reagan model: veto of California rural legal assistance. M. E. Leary. Nation 212:134-5 F 1 '71
Reagan versus the poverty lawyers. P. Barnes. New Repub 164:15-17 Ja 23 '71; Reply. L. C. Battle. 164:33 F 13 '71
Reagan's legal aid. R. B. Taylor. Nation 212:645 My 24 '71

LEGAL aid—*Continued*
Showdown with Reagan; funding California
rural legal assistance, inc. J. Osborne. New
Repub 165:9-11 Jl 10 '71
War on the poor? OEO grant for the Cali-
fornia rural legal assistance program ve-
toed by state. il Newsweek 77:18-19 Ja 18
'71
Well-deserved boot; OEC inquiry into R. Rea-
gan's charges against CRLA. Nation 213:
37 Jl 19 '71
  See also
Lawyers military defense committee
LEGAL aid societies
  See also
Volunteer lawyers for the arts
LEGAL costs insurance. See Insurance, Litiga-
tion
LEGAL medicine. See Medical jurisprudence
LEGAL profession. See Lawyers
LEGAL services program. See United States—
Economic opportunity, Office of
LE GALLIENNE, Eva
Ibsen: the shy giant. il por Sat R 54:23-6+
Ag 14 '71
LE GASTELOIS, Alphonse
Hermit of Les Ecréhous. il por Time 98:
32 D 13 '71 *
LEGENDS
  See also
Folklore
Grail
Mythology
LEGENDS, Japanese
Forgotten inlet; Waiting Port, Madama But-
terfly's vigil. M. D. Morris. il Opera N 35:
22-3 Ap 17 '71
LÉGER, Fernand
Léger taking the edge off the cube. B. Rose.
Vogue 157:161 Ap 1 '71 *
LEGG, Roger D.
Thing in Hatchet Bay. il pors Outdoor Life
148:80-1 S '71
LEGGE, Nancy
Opinion: the Potter's house; a coffeehouse
church. por Mlle 73:66+ S '71
LEGGETT, Gene
Homosexual minister? por Newsweek 77:114
Je 14 '71 *
LEGGETT, Robert Louis
How to bring them all home. Nation 212:
394-7 Mr 29 '71
Nixon's objective in Paris. Nation 213:610 D
13 '71
LEGGETT, William
Baseball (cont) il Sports Illus 35:40 Jl 5; 58
Ag 16; 38-9 Ag 23; 85-6 O 11 '71
Beware of the cliff dwellers. il Sports Illus
34:22-4+ Je 21 '71
Experiment in drugs at Santa Anita. il Sports
Illus 34:18-19 Ja 25 '71
$40 million body shuffle. il Sports Illus 35:22-
3 D 13 '71
In Greek it's Los Angeles. il Sports Illus
34:22-4+ Mr 22 '71
It's that time again. il Sports Illus 35:12-15
Ag 30 '71
Just who is knocking out whom? il Sports
Illus 35:20-3 S 27 '71
Riot act changes the scene. il Sports Illus 34:
20-1 My 3 '71
Some kind of a comeback. il Sports Illus 35:18-
23 O 25 '71
Tightening-up at the Fens. il Sports Illus
34:26-8+ My 24 '71
Year of the player. il Sports Illus 34:52-4+
Ap 12 '71
LEGION, American. See American legion
LEGISLATION
  See also
Referendum
Massachusetts
Vox pop; citizen-filed bills. Newsweek 79:
20 Ja 10 '72
United States
Appraising the legislatures. il Time 97:16-17
F 15 '71
Good-by look. il Newsweek 78:16-17 Ag 16
'71
How not to legislate. D. Lawrence. U S News
71:68 D 27 '71
Laws may have missed. U S News 70:77
Ja 18; 71:13 D 27 '71
Nixon and Congress; score card on '71 ses-
sion. il U S News 71:16-18 D 27 '71
While the mice are away; extending the use
of pocket veto. New Repub 164:9 Mr 13 '71
Your congressman: myth and reality. il Sr
Schol 98:9-11 Mr 1 '71
  See also
Consumer protection—Laws and legislation
Library laws and legislation
Social legislation—United States
United States—Supreme court

LEGISLATIVE bodies
  See also
Caucus
Parliamentary practice
United States
  See also
State legislatures
United States—Congress
LEGISLATURES, State. See State legislatures
LEGLER, Philip
Letters; poem. Nation 212:471 Ap 12 '71
LE GUIN, Ursula Kroeber
High fantasy: A wizard of Earthsea; ad-
dress, October 1969. E. Cameron. bibliog
f Horn Bk 47:129-38 Ap '71 *
LEGUMES
  See also
Beans
Peas
Soybeans
LEHMAN, David
This unmentionable feeling; Goodbye in-
structions; Goodnight poem; poems. Po-
etry 118:88-90 My '71
LEHMAN, Herbert Henry
Three saints in politics. P. H. Douglas. Am
Scholar 40:223-32 Spr '71 *
LEHMAN, Robert, collection. See Art—Private
collections
LEHMAN CAVES NATIONAL MONUMENT
If you plan to cross Nevada in sweltering
August, here's the great place to cool off.
il Sunset 147:44-7 Ag '71
LEHMAN collection. See Art—Private collec-
tions
LEHMANN, Walter Xavier
Doctor, what about marijuana? interview.
Read Digest 98:169-70+ Ap '71
LEHMANN-HAUPT, Alexander
Wall-eyed glancing; poem. Esquire 76:14 N
'71
LEHNER, Francis
First communion; poem. Cath World 212:
311 Mr '71
LEHR, Stan, and Rossetto, Louis, jr
Libertarianism: a new right credo? Cur 127:
29-38 Mr '71
LEIBENGUTH, Charla
Films on drug abuse; with filmography. il
Am Lib 2:483-7 My '71
Road to nowhere; drug abuse. il Library J
96:587-92 F 15 '71
LEIBOWITZ, Samuel Simon
Where are they now? il pors Newsweek 77:8
Mr 8 '71 *
LEICHTLING, Jerry
3 nice times. por Sr Schol 98:32 My 17 '71
LEIGHTON, Lauren G.
(tr) See Chukovskiĭ, K. I. Confessions of an
old story-teller
LEIGHTON, Robert B.
Panel discussions: is there any hope? il
Phys Today 24:30-4 Ap '71
LEIMBACH, Patricia P.
Family reunion: our annual watering of
roots. Farm J 95:34 Ag '71
Farm wife stands up for Women's lib. il
Farm J 95:28+ N '71
LEINBACH, Chapin, and Jackman, W. E.
Naysayers never die; excerpt from Down
the centuries with the prophets. Aviation W
94:9 Mr 22 '71
LEINSTER, Colin
Veteran comes home, to limbo. il pors Life
70:28-38 Ap 16 '71
White tracks on the moon. il por Life 70:
29 F 26 '71
LEIS, Leonard E.
Computer brings big dividends to small-
city administration. il por Am City 86:
97-8 My '71
LEISENRING, Edward Barnes, jr
Coal king from Philly. por Forbes 108:29-30
S 1 '71 *
LEISER, Dorothy
Lot's wife; poem. Chr Cent 88:1134 S 29 '71
LEISER, Wayne
Apollo 15; poem. Chr Cent 88:1222 O 20 '71
Translation; poem. Chr Cent 88:157 F 3 '71
LEISURE
Ecological man and leisure man. D. Robin-
son and D. Clayton. Parks & Rec 6:81-2
Ag '71
Leisure & education; with yardsticks of
management performance. il Forbes 109:
174+ Ja 1 '72
Leisure: nearing the receding horizon. G.
Godbey. bibliog Parks & Rec 6:33-4 Ag '71
Time for rewards. P. A. Dickinson. il Har
Yrs 11:36-40 Ja; 41-8 Mr; 45-53 Jl; 48-
51 D '71
Time, work and leisure today. G. J. Dahl.
Chr Cent 88:185-9 F 10 '71

LEISURE—*Continued*
Trends in labor and leisure; with tables. G. H. Moore and J. N. Hedges. bibliog Mo Labor R 94:3-11 F '71
See also
Recreation
Time. Use of
LEISURE group, Inc.
Frantic days of a leisure empire. il Bsns W p27 O 9 '71
LEITCH, Addison H.
Holy Spirit and these days. Chr Today 15: 14-16 My 21 '71
Ten years in the wrong direction. Chr Today 15:55-6 S 10 '71
LEIVA, Guillermo Cabrera. See Cabrera Leiva, G.
LEJEUNE, Anthony
Letter from London (cont) Nat R 23:366, 1110+, 1407 Ap 6, O 8, D 17 '71
LEKACHMAN, Robert
Economy. See issues of Dun's to October 1971
Training a pleasant demon. il Sat R 54:15-18 Mr 6 '71
LELAND, Jeremy
Last sandcastle; story. Mlle 73:162-3 O '71
LELAND, Mich.
Midwest fishtown. B. Schill and B. Schill. il Yachting 130:56-7 D '71
LELCHUK, Alan
(ed) See Roth, P. On satirizing presidents
LE LIONNAIS, François
What future for futurology? UNESCO Courier 24:4-6 Ap '71
LELOIR, Luis F.
Two decades of research on the biosynthesis of saccharides; Nobel lecture, December 11, 1970. bibliog il Science 172:1299-303 Je 25 '71
LELYVELD, Joseph
Chancellor Harvey Scribner: the most powerful man in the school system, on paper. il pors N Y Times Mag p30-1+ Mr 21 '71
Dear Mr President, the P.O.W. families. il N Y Times Mag p 14-15+ O 3 '71
Status of the movement: the energy levels are low. il pors N Y Times Mag p36-7+ N 7 '71; Reply with rejoinder. R. A. Falk. p 14+ N 28 '71
LEMAIRE, William H.
Artistic greatness of China. il Design 72:14-15 mid-Sum '71
LEMAN, A. D.
Fastest way to boost litter size. Farm J 95: H12 S '71
LEMAY, Harding
American classic. P. S. Prescott. por Newsweek 77:106 My 3 '71 •
Authors & editors. B. A. Bannon. por Pub W 199:13-14 Ap 19 '71 •
LEMAY, Pete. See Lemay, H.
LEMBERGER, Louis, and others
Delta-9-tetrahydrocannabinol: metabolism and disposition in long-term marihuana smokers. bibliog il Science 173:72-4 Jl 2 '71
LEMBO, Diana L.
Screenings: filmstrips. See occasional issues of Library journal
LEMIEUX, Charles P. Jr
How the ball bounces. il por Newsweek 77: 71-2 My 3 '71 •
LEMKOWITZ, Florence
Scandinavian spectacular. il Schol Teach Jr/ Sr High p6-8 Mr 8 '71
LEMMART, James
One good scare. Flying 89:60-1 S '71
LEMON, Edgar
—and others
Sun's work in a cornfield. bibliog il Science 174:371-8 O 22 '71

about
SPAM: a computer views a cornfield. il Sci N 100:292-3 O 30 '71 •
LEMON juice
Beauty: fresh lemon twists. S. Obre. il Ladies Home J 88:48+ Je '71
LEMONDS, Ron
Interview. por Suc Farm 69:no5 10 Mr '71
LE MONE, Evelyn
Records for teachers. Dance Mag 45:94-5 Ap; 98+ O '71; 46:90 Ja '72
LEMOV, Michael
Whatever happened to Product safety? New Repub 164:12-13 Ap 3 '71
LEMP, Robert J.
How to handle three-foot winter rye. il Org Gard & Farm 18:110-11 Je '71
LENDLE, H. G.
Strawberries show-me style. il Org Gard & Farm 18:48-50 My '71
Sunflowers needn't be yellow. il Org Gard & Farm 18:70-1 Ap '71
LENGTH of life. See Longevity

LENGTH of skirts. See Clothing and dress
LENGTH of working life. See Working life, Length of
LENIN, Vladimir Il'ich
Prescription for revolution; excerpts, ed. by P. Harvey. Read Digest 98:93-4 Ja '71

about
Lenin's childhood, by I. Deutscher. Review Nation 212:342-5 Mr 15 '71. L. Menashe •

Tomb
Mummy of Red Square. F. Russell. Nat R 23:865-6 Ag 10 '71
LENINGRAD
Leningrad, Russia's window on the West. H. La Fay. il Nat Geog 139:636-73 My '71

Description
In Russia, a problem of rubles. L. Barry. il Pop Phot 68:36+ My '71

Music
Behind the scenes. V. D. Yurchenkov. Hi Fi 21:12+ Je '71
LENNON, John
Lennon: the working-class hero turns red; interview, ed. by R. Blackburn and T. Ali. pors Ramp Mag 10:43-9 Jl '71

about
Beatledammerung. il por Time 97:55 Ja 25 '71 •
Confessions of a Beatle. H. Saal. il por Newsweek 77:50-1 Ja 18 '71 •
George and John. E. Willis. New Yorker 47: 96-7 F 27 '71 •
I wanna hold your head: John Lennon after the fall. A. Kopkind. pors Ramp Mag 9: 18-19+ Ap '71 •
John Lennon's almanac. W. F. Buckley, jr. Nat R 23:391 Ap 6 '71 •
Settling down. C. H. Simonds. Nat R 23:145 F 9 '71 •
Two women who broke up the Beatles. J. Goldman. pors McCalls 98:72-3+ Jl '71 •
LENNY; drama. See Barry, J.
LENORD, Susan
Way it is with girls; story. Ladies Home J 88:80-1 F '71
LENOX, Mass.

Music
See also
Lenox arts center
LENOX arts center, Lenox, Mass.
Lenox arts center; festival in the Berkshires. R. Vincent. Hi Fi 21:MA18 N '71
LENS adapters. See Photography—Apparatus and supplies
LENS of the eye. See Crystalline lens
LENSES
Making an 8-inch refractor objective. R. G. Quade; R. E. Cox. il Sky & Tel 41:243-9 Ap '71
See also
Contact lenses
Eyeglasses
LENSES, Photographic
...And from Nikon: a lens that focuses for you. il Pop Mech 136:43 S '71
Can lens coloration affect your pictures. B. Sherman. il Mod Phot 35:74-5+ Mr '71
From here to infinity; compact lens kit. J. Foldes. il Pop Phot 69:90-1 Ag '71
How good a lens can you use? N. Goldberg. il Pop Phot 68:88-91+ Mr '71
Keppler on the SLR; buying telephoto lenses. H. Keppler. il Mod Phot 35:8+ Ag '71
Keppler on the slr; great lens multicoating race. H. Keppler. il Mod Phot 35:12+ Je '71
Last look at Photokina '70. B. Schwalberg. il Pop Phot 68:75+ F '71
Lens that focuses itself. A. J. Hand. il Pop Sci 199:85 Ag '71
1970-71 interchangeable lens list; comp. by D. L. Miller. Mod Phot 34:88-95+ N '70
1971-72 interchangeable lens list; comp. by D. L. Miller. Mod Phot 35:82-94+ O '71
Photo expo 71. H. Birnbaum. il Pop Phot 69: 82+ Ag '71
Phototronics; Nikon's auto focusing lens. E. Farber. il Mod Phot 35:48 S '71
Projector lenses compared. il Mod Phot 35: 92-5 Je '71
Pupillary problems: more data for close-up photography. B. Schwalberg. il Pop Phot 69: 28+ O '71
Techniques tomorrow; fast mirror lenses. B. Sherman. Mod Phot 35:56+ Ja '71

LENSES, Photographic—*Continued*
Techniques tomorrow; multilayer lens coatings. B. Sherman. il Mod Phot 35:43-4+ My '71
Techniques tomorrow; new glasses for telephoto lenses. B. Sherman. Mod Phot 35: 58+ O '71
Techniques tomorrow; Nikon autofocus system. B. Sherman. il Mod Phot 35:32+ S '71
Techniques tomorrow; super multi-coating. B. Sherman. il Mod Phot 35:50+ D '71
Tele fun with minus lenses. J. H. Robinson. il Mod Phot 35:22+ Ag '71
2400mm f/12 for 2¼ and 35mm SLR! H. Maersk-Moller. il Mod Phot 35:94-5+ Ag '71
View from Kramer; Apochromatic lenses. A. Kramer. Mod Phot 35:37-8 Ja '71
Want a lens with a propeller? A. Kramer. il Mod Phot 35:145+ Je '71
Wild lens puts swings and tilts in your SLR. A. J. Hand. il Pop Sci 198:16 Ap '71
You've never had it so good! N. Goldberg. il Pop Phot 68:75-7+ Je '71
Zooming in on those non-zoom lenses. N. Rothschild. il Pop Phot 69:18+ Ag '71

Care
Let's talk dirty; protecting lenses from dust. N. Goldberg. il Pop Phot 68:56+ F '71
Techniques tomorrow; lens damage. B. Sherman. Mod Phot 35:124+ Mr '71
Your photographic electronics and optics; keeping them in shape. N. Goldberg. il Pop Phot 68:70-1+ Mr '71

Testing
Family plan; how Popular photography tests lenses. N. Goldberg. il Pop Phot 68:106-9+ My '71
How to test your lenses. il Mod Phot 34:131-2 D '70
Keppler on the SLR. H. Keppler. il Mod Phot 35:12+ Mr '71
Lab report:
Four Takumars. N. Goldberg. il Pop Phot 68:110-11+ My '71
Leitz lenses. N. Goldberg. il Pop Phot 69: 100-1+ S '71
Modern tests:
Questar. il Mod Phot 35:97-8 Ag '71
Test your lenses the modern way. D. L. Miller. il Mod Phot 35:21-2 D '71

LENT, Blair
How the sun and the moon got into a film. il Horn Bk 47:589-96 D '71

LENT, Charles M.
Metachronal limb movements by artemia salina: synchrony of male and female during coupling. bibliog il Science 173:1247-8 S 24 '71

LENT
Jewish Lent; rabbis leading Christians in observing Lent. Chr Cent 88:331 Mr 17 '71
Lent and ecology; program of self-denial. America 124:222-3 Mr 6 '71
Lenten reading suggestions (cont) America 124:181-8 F 20 '71

LENTHALL, Franklyn
Actor's true identity is revealed. por Hobbies 76:50+ My '71

LENTILS
See also
Cookery—Vegetables

LENTZ, Thomas L.
Nerve trophic function: in vitro assay of effects of nerve tissue on muscle cholinesterase activity. bibliog il Science 171:187-9 Ja 15 '71

LENTZ, William. See Kaun, D. E. jt. auth.

LENZ, Siegfried
Authors & editors. H. R. Lottman. por Pub W 200:5-6 N 29 '71 *

LEO, John
Timetable of a bloodbath. Commonweal 95: 6-7 O 1 '71

LEONARD, Alan J.
How to define the sanctity of English. Engl J 60:242-5 F '71

LEONARD, C. M. See Norgren, R. jt. auth.

LEONARD, Charles E.
Sailing blind. il Yachting 130:62-3+ Ag '71

LEONARD, Diana
Every time Diana kisses Joe goodbye it could be their last embrace. M. Michaelson. il pors Todays Health 49:37-41+ Ag '71 *

LEONARD, Eugene, and others
MINERVA: a participatory technology system. il Bul Atom Sci 27:4-12 N '71

LEONARD, J. Joseph
Slouching toward Didion. Sat R 54:4 Ag 14 '71

LEONARD, James F.
Geneva disarmament conference agrees on draft text of bacteriological weapons convention; statement, September 28, 1971. Dept State Bul 65:504-8 N 1 '71
U.S. and U.S.S.R. table draft biological weapons convention at Geneva disarmament conference; statement, August 5, 1970. Dept State Bul 65:221-4 Ag 30 '71
U.S. states views on conventional arms restraints; statement, August 26, 1971. Dept State Bul 65:309-15 S 20 '71

LEONARD, Jerris
How to combat crime. pors U S News 71:35 8 O 11 '71

LEONARD, Joe
Every time Diana kisses Joe goodbye. M. Michaelson. il pors Todays Health 49:37-41+ Ag '71 *
Hoist a bottle to leadfoot U. R. F. Jones. il por Sports Illus 35:26-7 S 20 '71 *

LEONARD, John
Life TV review (cont) il Life 70:12 Ja 22; 12-13 F 5; 16 F 19; 18 Mr 5; 10 Mr 19 '71

about
Changing Times. por Newsweek 77:59 Ap 5 '71 *

LEONARD, Michael
Arranger arrives. G. Lees. por Hi Fi 21:90-1 My '71 *

LEONARDO da Vinci
Leonardo on bearings and gears. L. Reti. il Sci Am 224:100-7+ F '71 *

LEONCAVALLO, Ruggiero
Pagliacci. Criticism
Opera N 35:17-20 F 13 '71 *

LEONDAR, Barbara
English in experimental schools. Engl J 60: 748-53 S '71

LEONE, Giovanni
Ecce Leone. il por Newsweek 79:27 Ja 10 '72 *

LEONIAN, Phillip
Don't tell the girls how pretty they are; photographs. Sports Illus 34:28-32 Mr 29 '71

LEONIDS. See Meteors

LEOPARDS
Imperiled phantom of Asian peaks. G. B. Schaller. il Nat Geog 140:702-7 N '71
See also
Cheetahs

Photographs
See Animals—Photographs

LEOPOLD, Carolyn
School librarians: are we for real? excerpts. il por Library J 96:1424-8 Ap 15 '71

LEOPOLD, Michael
Los Angeles. Art N 69:12 F; 70:14 Mr '71

LEPAGE, Marc
Movie making; interview, ed. by T. Galluzzo. Mod Phot 35:38+ Jl '71

LE PAN, Douglas
Stragglers; Song in October; Double; Hysterica passio; poems. Poetry 119:1-5 O '71

LEPERS. See Leprosy and lepers

LEPIDOPTERA
See also
Moths

LEPIS, Cabrini B.
Foreign exchange; story. Cath World 213: 240-2 Ag '71

LEPLEY, Derward, 1924-
Transplant trepidation. R. Chandler. Chr Today 15:32 Ag 6 '71 *

LEPROSY and lepers
Unforgettable Stanley Stein. L. G. Blochman. il por Read Digest 98:88-92 Je '71

LEPROSY research
Armadillo helps. Sci N 100:138 Ag 28 '71

LEPTOSPIROSIS
Leptospirosis epizootic among California sea lions. N. A. Vedros and others. bibliog il Science 172:1250-1 Je 18 '71

Vaccines
New lepto vaccine. Farm J 95:30 Jl '71

LE PUY en Velay. See Puy, Le, France

LERMAN, Leo
Catch up with. See issues of Mademoiselle
Scene/seen. See issues of Mademoiselle

LERNER, Daniel
Is international persuasion sociologically feasible? bibliog f Ann Am Acad 398:44-9 N '71

LERNER, Gerda
Women's rights and American feminism. Am Scholar 40:235-48 Spr '71

LERNER, Max
Are we really coming apart? Cur 132:3-5 S
'71
Culture of machine living. il UNESCO Cou-
rier 24:23-7 My '71
LERNER, Michael. See Keniston, K. jt. auth.
LERNER, Michael P.
May day: anatomy of the movement. il Ramp
Mag 10:18-25+ Jl '71
LERNER, Richard A. and others
Quantitative aspects of plasma membrane-
associated immunoglobulin in clones of
diploid human lymphocytes. bibliog il Sci-
ence 173:60-2 Jl 2 '71
LERNOUX, Penny
Antarctica. il Travel 136:40-5+ S '71
Latin America slams the door. Nation 213:
271-5 S 27 '71
LESBIANISM
Disciples of Sappho, updated. J. Klemesrud.
il N Y Times Mag p38-9+ Mr 28 '71; Dis-
cussion. p5+ Ag 11; 79 My 9 '71
When women love other women: a frank
discussion of female homosexuality. il
Redbook 138:84-5+ N '71
LESCH-Nyhan syndrome
Lesch-Nyhan syndrome: altered kinetic prop-
erties of mutant enzyme. J. A. McDonald
and W. N. Kelley. bibliog il Science 171:
689-91 F 19 '71
Lesch-Nyhan syndrome: rapid detection of
heterozygotes by use of hair follicles. S.
M. Gartler and others. bibliog il Science
172:572-4 My 7 '71
LESCAZE, Lee. See Kann, P. R. jt. auth.
LESH, Jack
Hooked on Gustavus. D. Butwin. il por Sat
R 54:46-7 Jl 24 '71 *
LESHER, Stephan
Calley case re-examined. S. Lesher. il pors
N Y Times Mag p6-7+ Jl 11 '71
Jackson state a year after. il N Y Times
Mag p24-5+ Mr 21 '71
Who knows what frustrations lurk in the
hearts of X million Americans. il por N Y
Times Mag p9+ Ja 2 '72
LESLIE, Jacques
John Tunney, Kennedy's friend in Muskie's
corner. il pors N Y Times Mag p4-5+ D 26
'71
LESLIE effect simulator. See Organ, Elec-
tronic—Equipment
LESLIE salt company
Leslie salt all but gives up; Redwood shores
project. il Bsns W p22 N 27 '71
LESLY, Philip
Neglected science of mass communication;
address, November 11, 1971. Vital Speeches
38:117-20 D 1 '71
Respect for the law and lawyers; address,
February 6, 1971. Vital Speeches 37:301-4
Mr 1 '71
LESNEY products, ltd.
Great auto race. il Forbes 107:28+ F 15 '71
LESSER, M. L.
Wives are for cruising with. il Motor B & S
128:108-11 S '71
LESSER, Milton
Where's the money: hard cover or paperback?
il Writers Digest 51:28-30+ S '71
LESSING, Doris May
Ancient way to new freedom. Vogue 158:98+
Jl '71
about
Toward a more human world. B. DeMott.
por Sat R 54:25-7+ Mr 13 '71 *
White bird of truth. por Time 97:80 Mr 8 '71 *
LESSING, Erich
Story behind the book: Jesus: history and
culture of the New Testament; photo-
graphs. Pub W 201:29 Ja 3 '72
LESSING, Lawrence
Getting the whole picture from holography.
il Fortune 84:110-14+ S '71
Senseless war on science. il Fortune 83:88-
91+ Mr '71
Stand by for the cartridge TV explosion. il
Fortune 83:80-3+ Je '71
about
In defense of science. Time 97:56 Mr 8 '71 *
LESSINGER, Leon M.
It's time for accountability in education. il
Nations Bsns 59:54-7 Ag '71
LESSON plans
Plan books are a waste of time! R. Dawe.
Todays Ed 60:49 S '71; Discussion. 60:55-
6 D '71
LESTER, Janice K.
Ten years younger in ten minutes. il Har Yrs
11:34 F '71

LESTER, Richard I.
Britain's university of the second chance. il
Am Ed 7:7-11 Ag '71
LESTOURGEON, Wallace M. and Rusch, H. P.
Nuclear acidic protein changes during dif-
ferentiation in physarum polycephalum.
bibliog il Science 174:1233-6 D 17 '71
LETELIER, Orlando
Expropriation: why do they do it? interview.
pors Forbes 108:33-5 Jl 15 '71
LETTER to the world, ballet. See Ballets—
Criticisms
LETTER writing

Anecdotes, facetiae, satire, etc.
What enormous problems a man can cause
himself by answering his mail! C. Trillin.
il N Y Times Mag p30-1+ My 2 '71
LETTERS
Doors of the past. S. B. Saunders. Hobbies
76:147 Ja '72
First letter from the New World; with text
of Christopher Columbus' letter. M. A.
Lubin. il Américas 23:2-12 Ap '71
Letter from cloud nine. H. Hanff. il Read
Digest 99:87-91 Ag '71
LETTERS from servicemen
See also
Vietnamese war, 1957- —Personal narratives
LETTERS to congressmen. See Lobbying
LETTERS to the editor. See Newspapers—Let-
ters to the editor; Periodicals—Letters
to the editor
LETTUCE
Bibb lettuce, a very big return on a small
investment. L. W. Patterson. il Org Gard
& Farm 18:102+ O '71
LETTUCE boycott. See Boycotts
LÉTURMY, Michel
Thousand and one nights or the secret of
Scheherazade. il UNESCO Courier 24:40-3 O
'71
LEUCINE
Marine sediments: dating by the racemization
of amino acids. J. L. Bada and others; re-
ply with rejoinder. M. C. McKenna. Science
172:503 Ap 30 '71
LEUKEMIA
Acute lymphocytic leukemia in owl monkeys
inoculated with herpesvirus saimiri. L. V.
Meléndez and others. bibliog il Science 171:
1161-3 Mr 19 '71
Anemic stress as a trigger of myelogenous
leukemia in rats rendered leukemia-prone
by X-ray. J. K. Gong. bibliog il Science
174:833-5 N 19 '71
Detection of an antigen associated with
acute leukemia. D. L. Mann and others.
bibliog il Science 174:1136-7 D 10 '71
God tempers the wind. S. Alsop. por Newsweek 78:84 Ag 30; 76 S 6 '71
Radiation and leukemia rates; letter. E. L.
Saenger and others. bibliog Science 171:
1096+ Mr 19 '71; Reply. E. B. Lewis. 174:
454 O 29 '71
...Rather than scream. F. Brainard. il pors
Todays Health 49:32-7 Je '71

Therapy
Can leukemia be cured? J. H. Burchenal. il
Parents Mag 46:68-9+ N '71
LEUKEMIA cells. See Cancer cells
LEUKEMIA viruses
Heterogeneity of murine leukemia virus in
vitro DNA; detection of viral DNA in mammalian cells. L. D. Gelb and others. bibliog il Science 172:1353-5 Je 25 '71
Induction of murine C-type viruses from clonal lines of virus-free BALB/3T3 cells. S.
A. Aaronson and others. bibliog il Science
174:157-9 O 8 '71
Inhibitors of DNA polymerases of murine
leukemia viruses: activity of ethidium
bromide. S. Z. Hirschman. bibliog il Science 173:441-3 Jl 30 '71
Murine leukemia virus: high-frequency activation in vitro by 5-iododeoxyuridine and
5-bromodeoxyuridine. D. R. Lowy and others. bibliog il Science 174:155-6 O 8 '71
LEUKOCYTES
Allergic encephalomyelitis: new form featuring polymorphonuclear leukocytes. S. Levine and R. Sowinski. bibliog il Science 171:
498-9 F 5 '71
Cells capable of colony formation in the peripheral blood of man. K. B. McCredie and
others. bibliog il Science 171:293-4 Ja 22 '71
Cyclic urinary leukopoietic activity in gray
collie dogs. D. C. Dale and others. bibliog
il Science 173:152-3 Jl 9 '71

LEUKOCYTES—*Continued*
Histamine augments leukocyte adenosine 3',5'-monophosphate and blocks antigenic histamine release. H. R. Bourne and others. bibliog il Science 173:743-5 Ag 20 '71
Trout leukocytes: growth in oxygenated cultures. J. R. Heckman and others. bibliog Science 173:246 Jl 16 '71

LEUKODYSTROPHY
Correction of abnormal cerebroside sulfate metabolism in cultured metachromatic leukodystrophy fibroblasts. M. T. Porter and others. bibliog il Science 172:1263-5 Je 18 '71
Krabbe's globoid cell leukodystrophy: deficiency of galactocerebrosidase in serum, leukocytes, and fibroblasts. Y. Suzuki and K. Suzuki. bibliog il Science 171:73-5 Ja 8 '71

LEVANT, Lorna
(ed) See Warfield, S. Return engagement

LEVATTER, Jeffrey
Carbon dioxide laser is constructed by a high school student in California. il Sci Am 225:218-20+ S '71

LE VAUDREUIL, France. See New cities and towns

LEVENDOSKY, Charles
Comment. F. MacShane. Poetry 118:295-6 Ag '71 •

LEVENSON, Sam
My farewell to girth control. il por Ladies Home J 88:116+ My '71

LEVENSPIEL, Octave
Osmotic pump, an unusual timer and how to enhance contrast in astronomical photographs. il Sci Am 225:100 D '71

LEVENSTEIN, Phyllis
Are toys passé? il PTA Mag 66:16-18 N '71

LEVENTRITT award
Run for the money; 27th Leventritt international competition. il Newsweek 77:105 My 24 '71

LEVERTON, Ruth M.
Facts about nutrition. Todays Ed 60:71-2 N '71

LEVERTOV, Denise
Comment. B. Quinn. Poetry 118:97-8 My '71 •
Magistral strokes and first steps. P. Zweig. Nation 212:794-5 Je 21 '71 •

LEVI, Albert William
Humanism and survival. Sat R 54:32 My 15 '71

LEVI Strauss and company. See Strauss, Levi, and company

LEVIN, Alan Jay
Art for the self-contained classroom. il Sch Arts 71:10-11 S '71

LEVIN, Dan
Badminton. Sports Illus 35:82-4 N 22 '71
Baseball. Sports Illus 35:40 Jl 19 '71
Bugs and bogs and immortal bass. il Sports Illus 34:36-8+ F 22 '71
Grim struggle with an equine killer. il Sports Illus 35:20-3 Ag 16 '71
Looking for kicks and a few bucks, too. il pors Sports Illus 34:38-40+ Ap 26 '71
Rugby (cont) il Sports Illus 35:73-4 D 13 '71
Sailing (cont) il Sports Illus 35:88+ D 6 '71
She takes a long swim off a short pier. por Sports Illus 35:38-40+ D 6 '71
Uptight little island il Sports Illus 35:38-40+ O 4 '71

LEVIN, Ephraim Y. and Flyger, Vagn
Uroporphyrinogen III cosynthetase activity in the fox squirrel (sciurus niger) bibliog il Science 174:59-60 O 1 '71

LEVIN, Herman
Instant paging-intercom system. il Radio-Electr 43:61 Ja '72

LEVIN, Kim
Different drummer. il Art N 70:48-51 D '71

LEVIN, Martin
(ed) Phoenix nest. See issues of Saturday review

LEVIN, Ruth
Seeds; story. Ladies Home J 88:80 My '71

LEVINE, Barry
Behind the headlines with a witness from Kent state. Seventeen 29:156+ Ag '70 •

LEVINE, Carol
Family quiz game. See issues of Parents' magazine & better family living
When alcoholism is a family problem. Parents Mag 46:74-6+ F '71

LEVINE, Charles A.
How not to fly the Atlantic; excerpts from Oceans, Poles and airmen. R. Montague. il pors Am Heritage 22:42-7+ Ap '71 •

LEVINE, David
Deformità perfetta of Richard Nixon, Lyndon Johnson and other heroes. R. Bongartz. pors Esquire 75:70-5 F '71 •
Double vision of David Levine. P. A. Dreyfus. il por Am Artist 35:34-9+ N '71 •

Traditional revolutionists. il por Newsweek 77:84 My 3 '71 •

LEVINE, F. S.
Troubled romance of little Mary Mass and speedy Edward Energy. il Chem 44:32 My '71

LEVINE, Frank
Reply; poem. Negro Hist Bul 34:36 F '71

LEVINE, Frank M.
The seventies, years of challenge. il Camp Mag 43:8-10 F '71

LEVINE, James
Total immersion. il por Newsweek 78:74 Ag 23 '71 •
Wunderkind; interview, ed. by A. M. Lingg. por Opera N 36:12 D 11 '71

LEVINE, Philip
Alone; Way down; Here; poems. Poetry 118:136-8 Je '71
Breath; poem. New Yorker 47:40 S 11 '71
Dark rings; poem. New Yorker 47:54 O 9 '71
Letters for the dead; poem. Poetry 119:79-90 N '71

LEVINE, Richard M.
End of the politics of pleasure. por Harper 242:45-8+ Ap '71

LEVINE, Seymour
Stress and behavior; with biographical sketch. il Sci Am 224:12, 26-31 bibliog (p 122) Ja '71
—and Sowinski, Richard
Allergic encephalomyelitis: new form featuring polymorphonuclear leukocytes. bibliog il Science 171:498-9 F 5 '71

LEVINE, Solomon B.
Japan's growth economy: joy and anguish. bibliog f Cur Hist 60:218-24+ Ap '71

LEVINE, Suzanne
Valentine for our times: where has love gone? il Todays Health 49:22-4 F '71

LEVINESS, W. Thetford
On Father Kino's trail. il por Américas 22:30-5 N '70

LEVINGSTON shipbuilding company
Late tape. R. Brady. Duns 98:10 Jl '71

LEVINSON, Arthur
Making book on the Dow. E. Herzberg. por Duns 97:75-6 Je '71 •

LEVINSON, Harry
Conflicts that plague family businesses. Harvard Bsns R 49:90-8 Mr '71

LEVISON, Andrew
Working-class majority. il Nation 213:626-8 D 13 '71

LEVITAN, Herbert. See Barker, J. L. jt. auth.

LEVITAN, Sar A. and Marwick, David
Mounting and insurmountable welfare problem. Cur Hist 61:261-5+ N '71
—and Taggart, Robert, 3d
Has the blue-collar worker's position worsened? excerpt from Blue-collar workers. bibliog Mo Labor R 94:23-9 S '71

LEVITIN, Sonia
What's good for the gifted is good for everyone. il Parents Mag 46:62-3+ S '71

LEVITT, Leonard
She. il por Esquire 76:87-9+ O '71

LEVITT and sons, inc.
Development and decay; Palm Coast development, Florida. il Time 97:52+ Je 28 '71
New city in a hurry; Palm Coast, Fla. R. Levy. por Duns 97:63 Je '71
Over the wall at Levitt. por Bsns W p36 My 8 '71

LEVITZ furniture corporation
Levitz: the hot name in "instant" furniture; warehouse-showroom market. il Bsns W p90-1+ D 4 '71

LEVY, Alan
Ezra Pound's voice of silence. il pors N Y Times Mag p 14-15+ Ja 9 '72
How long will the winter last? il Seventeen 30:250-1+ Ag '71
How to get kicked out of Prague. il pors N Y Times Mag p28-9+ My 16 '71
On Audenstrasse, in the autumn of the age of anxiety. pors N Y Times Mag p 10-11+ Ag 8 '71
Understanding Vladimir Nabokov. il pors N Y Times Mag p20-2+ O 31 '71

LEVY, H. 2d
Normal atmosphere: large radical and formaldehyde concentrations predicted. bibliog il Science 173:141-3 Jl 9 '71

LEVY, H. M. See Paolino, R. M. jt. auth.

LEVY, Howard Brett
Where are they now? il pors Newsweek 77:18 Ap 12 '71 •

LEVY, Kenneth
Lux de luce: the origin of an Italian sequence. bibliog f il Mus Q 57:40-61 Ja '71

LEVY, Leo. See Rowitz, L. jt. auth.

LEVY, Natalie
Frapped fun: putting your hobbies on ice. il Har Yrs 11:30-3 Ja '71
Instant souvenirs. il Har Yrs 11:45-9 S '71
School for sailors. il Har Yrs 11:30-4 Jl '71
Snug Harbor, where the only tide is yule. il Motor B & S 127:16+ Je '71

LEVY, Phyllis
(comp) Audiovisual guide. Library J 96: 1443-4+, 3824-6+ Ap 15, N 15 '71

LEVY, Sidney J. See Kotler, P. jt. auth.

LEVY, Walter James
Oil power. For Affairs 49:652-68 Jl '71

LEWART, C. R.
Build a multi-sensor alarm. il Radio-Electr 42:58-9 N '71

LEWENSTEIN, Eileen
Marianne de Trey: Shinners Bridge pottery. il pors Ceram Mo 19:14-17 S '71

LEWIN, Arie Y. and Duchan, Linda
Women in academia. bibliog Science 173: 892-5 S 3 '71

LEWIN, Nathan
Facts about wiretapping. New Repub 165: 16-17 N 20 '71
Privacy and the third-party bug. New Republic 164:12-17 Ap 17 '71
Right to publish. New Repub 165:11-13 Jl 10 '71
Sometime eighteen-year-old vote. New Republic 164:21-2 Ja 2 '71
Splintering in the Supreme court. New Repub 164:13-15 F 27 '71

LEWIS, Anthony
Notes on being at home and abroad. il Atlan 227:58-62 Je '71
Radical of 10 Downing street. il pors N Y Times Mag p36-8+ Mr 14 '71

about

Under two hats. por Newsweek 78:52+ Jl 19 '71 *

LEWIS, Boyd
Syndicates and how they grew. il Sat R 54:67-9 D 11 '71

LEWIS, Charles A.
Flowers on Avenue D. il Horticulture 49:30-1+ Ag '71

LEWIS, Clarence E.
Red cedar. il Horticulture 49:18-19+ My '71

LEWIS, Clive Staples
On moving with the times; excerpt from God in the dock. Chr Today 15:4-6 Mr 12; 13-15 Mr 26 '71

about

C. S. Lewis: apostle to the imagination. D. Downing. por Chr Today 16:10-12 O 8 '71 *
C. S. Lewis on the meaning of Christmas; excerpts from Mere Christianity by C. S. Lewis, ed. by K. Futch. Chr Today 16: 10+ D 17 '71
God in the dock, by C. S. Lewis. Review America 124:617-18 Je 12 '71. B. Nauer *
Three Brightest Christians. S. M. Smith. Nat R 23:545+ My 18 '71 *

LEWIS, Don. See Lee, B. jt. auth.

LEWIS, Dorothea J. See Coulter, O. W. jt. auth.

LEWIS, Dorothy Otnow, and Backes, Ruth
Intuition does not come naturally. Vogue 158:60 S 15 '71

LEWIS, E. R. See Hillman, D. E. jt. auth.

LEWIS, Flora
Education of a senator. por Atlan 228:55-64 D '71
Reports and comment: Israel. Atlan 227:14+ Je '71
Reports and comment: Prague. Atlan 228: 14-16+ Ag '71
U.S. and Indochina. Atlan 227:6+ Mr '71

LEWIS, George Q.
Selling the comedy bit. il Writers Digest 51: 31 S '71

LEWIS, Irving J.
Government investment in health care; with biographical sketch. il Sci Am 224:14, 17-25 bibliog(p 130) Ap '71

LEWIS, Jean Battey
Capital dance with Potomac setting. il Dance Mag 45:24-5 S '71

LEWIS, Joe
Looking for kicks and a few bucks, too. D. Levin. il pors Sports Illus 34:38-40+ Ap 26 '71 *

LEWIS, John
Sowing the seeds of power. il pors Ebony 26:104-8+ O '71 *

LEWIS, John, 1920-
Profiles. W. Balliett. New Yorker 47:62-4+ N 20 '71 *

LEWIS, John Llewellyn
Ghost of John L. por Newsweek 77:86+ My 10 '71 *

LEWIS, John S.
Satellites of the outer planets: thermal models. bibliog il Science 172:1127-8 Je 11 '71

LEWIS, Joseph Anthony. See Lewis, Anthony

LEWIS, Meriwether
See also
Lewis and Clark expedition

LEWIS, Mort R.
Lincoln's favorite stories. il por Read Digest 98:151-3 F '71

LEWIS, Oscar
Obituary
Trans-Action 8:48 F '71. I. L. Horowitz

LEWIS, Richard S.
End of Apollo: end of an era. il Bul Atom Sci 27:26-8 Ja '71
Radioactive salt mine. Bul Atom Sci 27:27-31+ Je '71
Requiem for the scientist-astronauts. Bul Atom Sci 27:17-18 My '71

LEWIS, Robert Alexander
Heartbreak; poem. Ladies Home J 88:111 N '71

LEWIS, Robert F.
Low-cost 10.7-MHz signal generator. il Pop Electr 34:61-3+ Mr '71

LEWIS, Roger
Amtrak: the need for a hard sell. il Bsns W p 19 My 8 '71 *
Amtrak's one-way ticket to the dole. il Newsweek 78:69 D 20 '71 *

LEWIS, Stanley
Realism is alive and well and living in Paris. il Art N 70:34-7+ Sum '71

LEWIS, Thomas
Reflections from the pig farm. Commonweal 74:499-500 S 24 '71

LEWIS, W. Bennett, and Marko, A. M.
Seeking a convergent view: the unfinished detective story. pors Bul Atom Sci 27: 50-2 N '71

LEWIS, Walter H. and others
Multiple genotypes in individuals of Claytonia virginica. bibliog il Science 172:564-5 My 7 '71

LEWIS, William H.
Francophone Africa. Cur Hist 60:142-5+ Mr '71

LEWIS, Wyndham
Obscured genius. M. Montgomery. Nat R 23: 876-8 Ag 10 '71 *
Wyndham Lewis, paintings and drawings, by W. Michel. Review
Commonweal 95:304+ D 24 '71. T. Materer *

LEWIS and Clark expedition
This nation never saw a black man before. D. Zochert. il por Am Heritage 22:8-9 F '71

LEWISBURG federal penitentiary. See Prisons
—Pennsylvania

LEWISOHN, Leif
Christmas medley; poem. Good H 173:38 D '71

LEWITZKY, Bella
Bella Lewitzky dance company, Brooklyn academy of music. M. Marks. Dance Mag 45:87 D '71 *
Dance. N. Goldner. Nation 213:507-9 N 15 '71 *

LEXAN. See Plastics

LEXINGTON, Mass.

Protests, demonstrations, etc.

Veterans' march to Boston. D. King. il New Repub 164:11-13 Je 12 '71

LEXINGTON, Battle of, 1775
Voices of Lexington and Concord; eyewitness accounts; excerpts from Voices of 1776, comp. by R. Wheeler. il Am Heritage 22:8 13+ Ap '71

LEYLAND motor corporation. See British Leyland motor corporation

LEYS, Robert
What's your corporate image? Nations Bsns 59:61 S '71

L'HÉRITIER, Jean
Johannes Lheritier. H. C. Slim. il Mus Q 57: 149-55 Ja '71 *

LI, Choh Hao
—and others
Primary structure of the human chorionic somatomammotropin (HCS) molecule. bibliog il Science 173:56-8 Jl 2 '71

about

Diligence and luck pay off. il por Sci N 99: 41-2 Ja 16 '71 *
Human growth hormone. il por Newsweek 77:38+ Ja 18 '71 *
Revising the sequence. por Sci N 99:230 Ap 3 '71 *

LIABILITY (law)
Are you liable for your child's driving accidents? Bet Hom & Gard 49:34+ O '71
Cost of cremating your household goods. Consumer Rep 36:336-7 Je '71

LIABILITY (law)—*Continued*
Stars in his eyes; case of Texaco advertising. il Time 97:59-60 F 22 '71
Toward the socialization of injury. P. Vanderwicken. il Fortune 84:160-3+ N '71
See also
Torts

LIAMS, Thomas M.
National libraries of Latin Europe. il Am Lib 2:1081-5 N '71

LIBBY, Steve
Legend of the chickcharneys. Travel 135:15 Je '71

LIBBY, Willard Frank
Promising catalyst for auto exhaust. il Science 171:499-500 F 5 '71

about
Nobel prize winner teaches freshmen. il por Sch & Soc 99:395-6 N '71 •
—See Katzman, H. jt. auth.

LIBEL and slander
Strange case of libel; suits against newspapers and magazines. S. G. Blackman. Sat R 54:48-9+ Ap 10 '71
Truths and untruths. H. F. Pilpel and A. U. Schwartz. Pub W 200:38 Ag 2 '71

LIBERAL education
Contemporary crisis of humanistic studies: education or propaganda? H. Neumann. Sch & Soc 99:178-80 Mr '71
Detoxifying the liberal arts; address, September 8, 1971. J. A. Howard. Vital Speeches 38:27-31 O 15 '71
See also
Humanities

LIBERALISM
Hysteria on the campus; who is responsible? address, March 2, 1971. L. Fertig. Vital Speeches 37:454-9 My 15 '71
Let 'em eat cake; private schools for children of United States liberals. Nat R 23:1398-9 D 17 '71
Nixon agonistes, by G. Wills. Review Commentary 51:85-8 F '71 M. Cunliffe
Your future in liberalism. D. Fagan. Nat R 23:871 Ag 10 '71
See also
Conservatism

LIBERALISM (theology) See Modernism

LIBERATION. See Liberty

LIBERATION front of Quebec. See Front for the liberation of Quebec

LIBERIA
Back to Africa: a history of Sierra Leone and Liberia, by R. West, and Liberia: black Africa in microcosm, by C. M. Wilson. Reviews
Sat R 54:41-2 My 15 '71. C. Miller
Liberia: end of the Tubman era. H. J. Massaquoi. il por Ebony 26:46-8+ O '71
Passing of Uncle Shad. por Newsweek 78:33 Ag 2 '71
Patriarch yields the reins. il por Time 98:30-1 Ag 2 '71
See also
Monrovia

LIBERMAN, Alexander
Beauty in our time; reprint of May 1961 article. Vogue 158:115-16 O 1 '71

about
Sprezzature in steel. R. Hughes. il por Time 97:76 Ap 26 '71 •
Vogue for the new. pors Newsweek 77:54-5 My 31 '71 •

LIBERTY
Between order and violence: the middle ground; attitudes toward civil liberties. S. Rabinove. America 125:311-12 O 23 '71
Conditions of freedom revisited. J. V. Schall. Commonweal 95:9-13 O 1 '71
Crack in the bell. Chr Today 15:20 Jl 2 '71
Democracy, by C. Cohen. Review Nation 213:213-15 S 13 '71. R. Sampson
Escapes from freedom; universities' effort to help people; address, May 22, 1971. R. W. Lyman. Vital Speeches 37:757-9 O 1 '71
Skinner's utopia: panacea, or path to hell? il pors Time 98:47-52+ S 20 '71
Uses of liberation. N. Cousins. Sat R 54:33 Jl 24 '71
See also
Civil rights
Democracy
Free speech
Freedom of the press
Intellectual liberty
Liberalism

LIBERTY (periodical)
New life for Liberty. Time 97:47 F 8 '71
Return home; Liberty revived. S. J. Adamo. America 125:235-6 O 2 '71

LIBERTY lobby (organization)
Willis Carto. C. H. Simonds. il por Nat R 23:978-89 S 10 '71

LIBERTY lumber company
Salvaging New York harbor debris. G. Pierson and F. E. Hampf. il Cons 26:2-3 Ag '71

LIBERTY of the press. See Freedom of the press

LIBHART, Henry Miller
John Jay Libhart, nineteenth-century American eclectic. il Antiques 100:778-81 N '71

LIBHART, John Jay
John Jay Libhart, nineteenth-century American eclectic. H. M. Libhart. il Antiques 100:778-81 N '71 •

LIBIA. See Libya

LIBIEN, Lois
Try a babysitting co-op. il Parents Mag 46:32-3+ Jl '71

LIBRAIRIE Hachette. See Publishers and publishing—France

LIBRARIANS
Consciousness I, II, III: using Charles Reich's The greening of America for sorting out our colleagues. K. Nyren. Library J 96:429 F 1 '71
If you're an Aries; an astrological guide for librarians. E. Hoffman. bibliog il Library J 96:241-4 Ja 15 '71
Library front-liners. See issues of Wilson library bulletin
Library jobs: out of the stacks into the streets; the librarian as activist. A. M. Cunningham. il Mlle 74:168-9+ N '71
Library life in Middle America; Cornhuskers. A. Plotnik. il Wilson Lib Bul 46:412-25 Ja '72
What has to be said: a personal statement; librarian drops 6,000 miles out. A. Sable. il Wilson Lib Bul 46:338-47 D '71
See also
Childrens librarians
College librarians
Library assistants
Negro librarians
School librarians

Anecdotes, facetiae, satire, etc.
Captain Catalog; comic strip (cont) il Wilson Lib Bul 45:764-8 Ap '71
Hooper strikes back; revenge for Esquire ad from American motors. K. Nyren. il Library J 96:171 Ja 15 '71
Lolling it up; proposed new division: Little old lady librarians of ALA; letter to the editor. J. E. Everson. Am Lib 2:1039 N '71
Women's work: a job description B. Jacobson. il Library J 96:2596 S 1 '71

Dismissal
ALA asked to investigate Oklahoma County firing. pors Library J 96:3075+ O 1 '71
Bite your tongue: censorship controversy as grounds for resignation or firing and due process rights. J. F. Krug and J. A. Harvey. Am Lib 2:1213-14 D '71
FCC librarians association to launch investigation. Library J 97:16+ Ja 1 '72
Haynsworth court rejects Hodgin appeal; with editorial comment. Library J 96:573, 577 F 15 '71
Librarian takes a stand: Hamtramck, Mich. case of M. E. Hutto. por Am Lib 2:435-7 My '71
Oklahoma City-County library fires Betty Lou Townley. Library J 96:2417+ Ag '71

Education
See Library schools and education; School librarians—Education

Placement
See Librarians—Selection and appointment

Poetry
These unsparked flints, these uncut gravestone brides. R. Bradbury. il por Wilson Lib Bul 45:842-3 My '71

Qualifications
See also
School librarians—Qualifications

Anecdotes, facetiae, satire, etc.
Quo jure? advertising for suitable librarian to serve American Indians without discriminating. B. E. Richardson. il Am Lib 2:304-5 Mr '71

LIBRARIANS—*Continued*

Recruiting

Hold-back advocacy: recruitment of minorities; letter to the editor. E. M. Smith. Am Lib 2:784 S '71
Parity now: report on the Preconference on recruitment of minorities. S. Havens. Library J 96:2452 Ag '71

Salaries

ALA salary survey: personal members. il Am Lib 2:409-17 Ap '71
Average salary is $12,044. W. R. Eshelman. Wilson Lib Bul 45:639 Mr '71
Overdue; taking issue with the issues: salary and status of women. J. T. Carey. bibliog por Wilson Lib Bul 45:593-4 F '71; Discussion. 45:780-1 Ap '71
Placements & salaries, 1970: the year that was not what it seemed. C. J. Frarey and M. R. Donley. il por Library J 96:1937-41 Je 1 '71
Survey of library salaries as reflected in classified ads: September 1969 and September 1970; ALA report. il Am Lib 2:118-19 Ja '71
See also
College librarians—Salaries

Selection and appointment

How cold is the job market? P. Barber. Am Lib 2:1129 D '71
Job crisis; letter to the editor. P. B. Mangla. Library J 96:1305 Ap 15 '71
Job crisis; letter to the editor. D. Tudor. Library J 96:2024 Je 15 '71
Placements & salaries, 1970: the year that was not what it seemed. C. J. Frarey and M. R. Donley. il por Library J 96:1937-41 Je 1 '71

Anecdotes, facetiae, satire, etc.

Quo jure? advertising for suitable librarian to serve American Indians without discriminating. B. E. Richardson. il Am Lib 2:304-5 Mr '71

Supply and demand

How cold is the job market? P. Barber. Am Lib 2:1129 D '71
I'm glad you asked that: policy on library education and manpower; questions and answers. L. Asheim. Am Lib 2:597-9 Je '71; Reply. P. B. Hanna. 2:1144-5 D '71
Job catalog. A. M. Cunningham. Mlle 74:169+ N '71
Job crisis; letter to the editor. P. B. Mangla. Library J 96:1305 Ap 15 '71
Job crisis; letter to the editor. D. Tudor. Library J 96:2024 Je 15 '71
See also
Librarians—Recruiting
School librarians—Supply and demand

Anecdotes, facetiae, satire, etc.

Spiro and the recession. K. Nyren. il Library J 96:2467 Ag '71

Tenure

See also
College librarians—Tenure

Trade unions

See Librarians unions
LIBRARIANS, Professional ethics for
Code of ethics for librarians; reprint. Am Lib 2:746 Jl '71
Search for a code of ethics. J. G. Fetros. bibliog il Am Lib 2:743-5 Jl '71
LIBRARIANS unions
Library union prospects aired at Rutgers. il Library J 96:1662+ My 15 '71
N.Y. union spokesmen oppose state plan. Library J 96:154 Ja 15 '71
NYPL employee group opposes agency shop pact. il Library J 96:4044-5 D 15 '71
OE library agency aide heads resurgent union. Library J 96:578 F 15 '71
Personnel work: third force? K. Nyren. Library J 96:767 Mr 1 '71
LIBRARIANSHIP
Aware. D. Dickinson. il Am Lib 2:120-1, 214, 318-19, 422, 537-8, 641-2, 756-7 Ja-Jl '71
Aware. A. R. Schiller. Am Lib 2:895, 1008-9, 1105, 1215-16 S-D '71
Booktrucking about town. Wilson Lib Bul 46:117+, 213-14+ O-N '71
Constancy with change; letters to the editor. R. L. Harris. Am Lib 2:924 O '71
Frontier of faith, geography of joy: a librarian's testament. P. Willey. il pors Wilson Lib Bul 45:858-63 My '71; Discussion. 45:856-7; 46:43-4 My, S '71

Future is up to you; address, June 25, 1971. K. Doms. por Am Lib 2:987-90 O '71
Let it all hang out. S. Berman. il Library J 96:2054-8 Je 15 '71; Discussion. 96:2561 S 1 '71
Librarianship as a way of life. M. M. Finch. Am Lib 2:346-7 Ap '71; Reply. S. Lundberg. 2:574-5 Je '71
Library front-liners. See issues of Wilson library bulletin
Library jobs: out of the stacks into the streets; the librarian as activist. A. M. Cunningham. il Mlle 74:168-9+ N '71
On the beach at Marmaroneck; costs increasing, services decreasing. K. Nyren. Library J 96:2243 Jl '71
Overdue; librarian and the AV specialist: less talk of either/or, more of both. C. K. Silver. por Wilson Lib Bul 46:461+ Ja '72
Proper study of librarianship; address, February 1971. F. A. Sharr. il por Library J 96:3727-30 N 15 '71
Textbooks, propaganda, and librarians. A. J. Dyson. bibliog il por Wilson Lib Bul 46:260-7 N '71

Anecdotes, facetiae, satire, etc.

Editor's choice: snippets from libraryland inspired by the opening of a Florida branch of fantasyland. il Am Lib 2:1043 N '71
Jane Pirnie's puzzler. J. Pirnie. Wilson Lib Bul 45:778-9 Ap '71
LJ's annual awards. J. Berry, 3d. and others. Library J 96:4043 D 15 '71
Solution to Pirnie's April puzzler. J. Pirnie. il Wilson Lib Bul 45:831+ My '71
LIBRARIANSHIP as a profession
Ghost of the hairy Javelin. J. Osborn. il Am Lib 2:747-9 Jl '71
Healthy anger: women's role. H. Lowenthal. bibliog il Library J 96:2597-9 S 1 '71
I'm glad you asked that: policy on library education and manpower; questions and answers. L. Asheim. Am Lib 2:597-9 Je '71; Reply. P. B. Hanna. 2:1144-5 D '71
Librarian and/or citizen? G. Dunbar. por Library J 97:42-3 Ja 1 '72
Melvil! Thou shouldst be living: women's library careers. L. N. Gerhardt. Library J 96:2567 S 1 '71
One librarian? letter to the editor. M. McFadden. Am Lib 2:687-8 Jl '71
Overdue; a student to Dallas speaks out on ALA, with editorial comment. D. R. Dowell. il Wilson Lib Bul 46:27, 79-80 S '71
Overdue; taking issue with the issues: salary and status of women. J. T. Carey. bibliog por Wilson Lib Bul 45:593-4 F '71; Discussion. 45:780-1 Ap '71
Professionalism in ALA; letter to the editor. J. T. Thomas. Am Lib 2:1139 D '71
Professionalism: school librarianship in Maryland; letter to the editor. M. W. Stoer. Library J 96:1062-3 Mr 15 '71
Report on women in librarianship. A. R. Schiller. Am Lib 2:1215-16 D '71
Sic 'em II: women as leaders in librarianship; letter to the editor. S. Shepherd. Am Lib 2:1140-1 D '71
Students to Dallas; symposium. Library J 96:2454-7 Ag '71
Task analysis study in Illinois: phase I of a cooperative project; ALA progress report. T. M. Brown. Am Lib 2:312-14 Mr '71
Units of loyalty. J. Berry. Library J 96:2413 Ag '71
LIBRARIES
Against the dogmatists: a sceptical view of libraries. D. Gore; discussion. Am Lib 2:16, 147-8, 343-4 Ja-F, Ap '71
See also
Books and reading
College libraries
Librarians
Presidential libraries
Prison libraries
Research libraries
School libraries

Acquisitions

Central ordering and processing; excerpts from Melcher on acquisition. D. Melcher. Am Lib 2:704-8 Jl '71
See also
College libraries—Acquisitions

Administration

See Library administration

Advertising

See Library publicity

Architecture

See Library architecture

LIBRARIES—*Continued*

Art collections
See also
Libraries—Print collections

Audio-visual materials
See Libraries and audio-visual materials

Automation
Along the academic way. E. Mason. il por Library J 96:1671-6 My 15 '71; Discussion. bibliog 96:1657, 2408-9, 3277-82, 3699 My 15, Ag, O 15, N 15 '71

Cataloging, processing, and automation; excerpts from Melcher on acquisition. D. Melcher. Am Lib 2:701-13 Jl '71; Discussion. 2:927-8 O '71

Coin-op digital computer tried at Monterey pl. Library J 96:4051 D 15 '71

Library services well-suited to automation; technical services at Los Angeles public library. A. Sklar. il Am City 86:79 D '71

Little boxes; book storage by Randtriever, that locates and delivers books in seconds, automatically. D. Dickinson. Am Lib 2:422 Ap '71; Reply. M. Cart. 2:575-6 Je '71

MARC: what is it? machine readable cataloging. M. Chisholm. Ed Digest 36:42-4 My '71

SDI is for people. Selective dissemination of information in small Indiana public libraries. C. H. Davis and P. Hiatt. bibliog il por Library J 96:3573-5 N 1 '71

Stamping automation in and out. Wilson Lib Bul 45:925 Je '71

When some library systems fail: is it the system, or the librarian? address, June 1971. I. A. Warheit. por Wilson Lib Bul 46:52-8 S '71

See also
Information storage and retrieval systems

Anecdotes, facetiae, satire, etc.
Hooper in love. K. Nyren. Library J 96:803 Mr 1 '71

Book discarding
Overdue; laundry slips and primary documentation, sorting and discarding. K. M. Glazier. por Wilson Lib Bul 45:686-7 Mr '71

Book mutilation
See Books—Mutilation, defacement, etc.

Book selection
See Book selection

Branch architecture
See Library architecture

Censorship
Aftershocks in L.A: film censorship case. Library J 96:1185 Ap 1 '71

Bite your tongue; censorship controversy as grounds for resignation or firing and due process rights. J. F. Krug and J. A. Harvey. Am Lib 2:1213-14 D '71

Censorship. E. J. Gaines; J. T. Carey. il pors Library J 96:1681-5 My 15 '71; Discussion. 96:2410-11 Ag '71

Censorship in Coldwater; letter to the editor. R. H. Rosichan. Library J 96:3256 O 15 '71

Censorship? letter to the editor. Library J 96:3056 O 1 '71

Censorship: reevaluated. D. Broderick. bibliog Library J 96:3816 N 15 '71

Censorship: the tip and the iceberg. N. S. Ladof. il Am Lib 2:309-10 Mr '71

Decision in Tulsa: an issue of censorship. A. B. Martin. il Am Lib 2:370-4 Ap '71

Demonstration at IFLA for Reizia Palatnik. il por Wilson Lib Bul 46:391 Ja '72

Film collection attacked in Los Angeles County. Library J 96:771-2 Mr 1 '71; Reply. R. C. Goodwell. 96:1896-7 Je 1 '71

Groton censors win; trustees back down. Library J 96:1318 Ap 15 '71

Groton, Conn. library board rejects Carey ouster. Library J 96:2251-2 Jl '71

Iowa council ends sub to Berkeley barb. Library J 96:4048-50 D 15 '71

Iowa library wins permission to purchase Hair tape. Library J 97:21-2 Ja 1 '72

Military libraries: a defense; letter to the editor. B. E. Stevens. Library J 96:4041 D 15 '71

More important things? censorship at Minneapolis public library; letter to the editor. G. Dunbar. Library J 96:2241 Jl '71

NCOP report, Queens case, debated at NYLA. il Library J 96:3796-7 N 15 '71

Nevergreen in Groton: special news analysis. S. C. Scott. il pors Wilson Lib Bul 45:818-20+ My '71

Pornography collection; excerpts from Magazine selection. B. Katz. bibliog il Library J 96:4060-6 D 15 '71

Rhode Island librarians meet censorship fan: Reverend Mr Ennio Cugini. Library J 96:2249 Jl '71

Vigilante of the month; censoring Grove press. W. R. Eshelman. Wilson Lib Bul 46:225 N '71

When under pressure. J. F. Krug and J. A. Harvey. Am Lib 2:1107-8 N '71

See also
American library association—Intellectual freedom committee
American library association—Office for intellectual freedom
Open and closed shelves
School libraries—Censorship

Anecdotes, facetiae, satire, etc.
Censor's horoscope. R. Knudson. il Am Lib 2:180-5 F '71

Childrens rooms
See Libraries, Childrens

Circulation, loans, etc.
Information exchange; Read and return collection of multiple copies of popular books at Orange public library. M. H. Scilken. il Wilson Lib Bul 46:104-5 S '71

Library almanac; Central Kansas library system's service by mail. D. Johnson. il Am Lib 2:1194-5 D '71

Cooperative service
See Library cooperation

Equipment and supplies
See Library furniture and equipment

Federal aid
Arts and humanities in the library: a guide for federal aid to libraries. C. M. Hall. il Am Lib 2:201-2 F '71

East Palo Alto federal library project; branch of San Mateo County library. Belmont, Calif. M. Keller. il Am Lib 2:631-5 Je '71

Financing discrimination; services to the disadvantaged. E. Geller; discussion. Library J 96:219, 671 Ja 15, F 15 '71

HEA amendments. G. Krettek and E. D. Cooke. Wilson Lib Bul 45:798-9 Ap '71

Hearings continue on 72 OE funds. G. Krettek and E. D. Cooke. Wilson Lib Bul 45:1005 Je '71

House action on '72 education funds; administration proposals. G. Krettek and E. D. Cooke. Wilson Lib Bul 45:896+ My '71

Humanities in the library: the role of the National endowment for the humanities; symposium, ed. by R. G. Swartz. il por Wilson Lib Bul 46:426-45 Ja '72

Libraries emphasized in Emergency employment act. G. Krettek and E. D. Cooke. Am Lib 2:1071-2 N '71

Libraries look to the state agency. E. Greenaway. il Am Lib 2:735-6 Jl '71

Office of the director, Washington office. G. Krettek and E. D. Cooke. il Am Lib 2:275-8, 378-81, 490-2 Mr-My '71

Pentagon vs. libraries. J. Berry. Library J 96:1179 Ap 1, 71; Reply. G. Palandri. 96:1895 Je 1 '71

What NEH has done for libraries, and how it can help yours. W. B. Edgerton. il por Wilson Lib Bul 46:427-30 Ja '72

See also
College libraries—Federal aid
School libraries—Federal aid

Film programs
See Libraries and moving pictures

Finance
Budget cut contested by Vigo library board. Library J 96:3548 N 1 '71

Change in budgetary thinking: PPBS; address, June 1971. W. Summers. bibliog il Am Lib 2:1174-80 D '71

Fiscal happiness. R. Bartnofsky. il Wilson Lib Bul 45:826 My '71

Job crisis; letter to the editor. P. B. Mangla. Library J 96:1305 Ap 15 '71

Job crisis; letter to the editor. D. Tudor. Library J 96:2024 Je 15 '71

Library wins tax referendum; St Charles County library, Mo. il Am Lib 2:559 Je '71

1969 tax reform act hurting libraries. Library J 96:1553-4 My 1 '71

Nixon freeze. K. Nyren. Library J 96:2713 S 15 '71

On the beach at Marmaroneck; costs increasing, services decreasing. K. Nyren. Library J 96:2243 Jl '71

LIBRARIES—Finance—*Continued*

Public libraries: on the skids? J. Eisner. bibliog Library J 96:3094-5 O 1 '71

Puppies are signs of spring; librarians and publishers: price picture. K. Nyren. Library J 96:1309 Ap 15 '71

Some hope in Syracuse. W. R. Eshelman. Wilson Lib Bul 46:7 S '71

Spring, National library week, and an observer come to small-town library, U.S.A. (W.Va.); or, Seed money, grass-roots, and the greening of the American library dream. A. Plotnik. il Wilson Lib Bul 45:932-40 Je '71

Syracuse public library faces budget disaster. Library J 96:2029-30 Je 15 '71

Three branch closings announced by Detroit P.L. Library J 96:3547-8 N 1 '71

To answer the taxpayer: duplication of library service for children by public and school libraries. J. Berry. Library J 96: 2027 Je 15 '71

See also
Libraries—Federal aid
Libraries—Statistics
School libraries—Finance

Anecdotes, facetiae, satire, etc.
Spiro and the recession. K. Nyren. il Library J 96:2467 Ag '71

Furniture
See Library furniture and equipment

Gifts, legacies, etc.
Statement of policy regarding gifts and bequests to libraries; reprint. Am Lib 2:721 Jl '71

Hours of opening
Libraries in their Sunday best: a survey; report. A. DeCamps. Wilson Lib Bul 45: 728 Ap '71

Instruction in use
Library orientation in the college and university. V. V. Melum. bibliog il por Wilson Lib Bul 46:59-66 S '71
See also
School libraries—Instruction in use

Intermediate departments
See also
Libraries—Services to young people

International aspects
International issue; symposium. bibliog il Wilson Lib Bul 45:928-9, 950-82 Je '71

Legislation
See Library laws and legislation

Management
See Library administration

Map collections
See also
School libraries—Map collections

Moving picture collections
See Moving picture film collections

Organization
See Library administration

Paperback books
On the management and use of paperbacks in libraries; address, 1970. W. H. Kaiser; reply. A. Gordon. Library J 96:425-6 F 1 '71

Periodical collections
Information exchange; serials: free gift and exchange programs. D. J. Coombs. il Wilson Lib Bul 45:1010-11 Je '71
See also
School libraries—Periodical collections

Phonograph and phonograph records
Classic recordings for a song; discography of historic reissues. J. R. Douglas. il por Library J 96:597-607 F 15 '71

Picture collections
Dust from old photographs; Oklahoma state exhibit. il Am Lib 2:556-7 Je '71

Pictures. S. S. Keaveney. bibliog Wilson Lib Bul 46:310-11 D '71

Poetry
Admonition: smoking; by a working man. il Wilson Lib Bul 45:776 Ap '71

Print collections
Boston's public library: a keeper with many keys. J. H. Kay. il Art in Am 59:78-81 Ja '71
See also
New York public library—Print collection

Public relations
Albuquerque's free-wheeling library. L. Waugh and J. Waugh. il Am Ed 7:33-5 Ag '71

Information exchange; how to prepare a community calendar. A. Farquhee. Wilson Lib Bul 46:290 N '71

Information exchange; Read and return collection of multiple copies of popular books at Orange public library. M. H. Scilken. il Wilson Lib Bul 46:104-5 S '71

Two percent for P.R. A. B. Martin. il Library J 96:4073 D 15 '71

Reference work
Instant classification: improving service in research libraries. D. A. Diefenbach. por Library J 96:801-2 Mr 1 '71; Discussion. 96: 1547 My 1 '71
See also
College libraries—Reference work
Reference books

Reports
See Library reports

Security measures
See Library protection systems

Services to aged
Minot serves aged. M. Kuehn. il Am Lib 2: 1198 D '71

Public library service to the aging; ASD special report. G. M. Casey. il Am Lib 2: 999-1004 O '71

Rhode Island project: book reviews by older citizens. J. Drickhamer. bibliog il por Library J 96:2737-43 S 15 '71

Unseen and unheard elderly; Community action program of Baltimore's Enoch Pratt free library. A. S. Meyers. il Am Lib 2:793-6 S '71

Services to blind
Walter L. Smith: blind librarian for the blind. il pors Wilson Lib Bul 45:838-9 My '71

World will never be so small again; a Thanksgiving story from a blind reader. R. Russell. il Wilson Lib Bul 46:238-45 N '71
See also
College libraries—Services to blind

Services to children
Discovery in Johnson County. C. Graves. il Am Lib 2:204-6 F '71

Future of children's service discussed in Finger Lakes. Library J 96:1068 Mr 15 '71

Is CCLD all that bad? patterns of children's library service in New York state. M. R. Sive. il por Library J 96:3442-5 O 15 '71

Letter to the editor; thin books vs. thick books. B. K. Walker. Horn Bk 47:558-9 O '71

Pilot program on alternatives in children's service to test school library recommendation in CCLD report. il Library J 96:223-5+ Ja 15 '71

Pox on both their houses; CCLD report on services to children. D. Broderick. Library J 96:3448-9 O 15 '71

Run twice as fast: service to children; New York city. H. R. Sattley. bibliog il Am Lib 2:845-9 S '71

To answer the taxpayer: duplication of library service for children by public and school libraries. J. Berry. Library J 96: 2027 Je 15 '71

Where will all the children go? service in New York state. J. G. Burke. bibliog il Am Lib 2:56-61 Ja '71; Discussion. 2:448-9, 601-4, 783-4 My-Je. S '71

Services to mentally handicapped children
Our hidden children: need for services to institutionalized, incarcerated, and incapacitated children. L. N. Gerhardt. Library J 96:3421 O 15 '71

Services to prisons
Prison escape; Connecticut department of correction paperback book fair, conducted and sponsored by the Connecticut state library. E. W. Strain. il por Library J 96: 169-70 Ja 15 '71

Publishers and prisoners; letter to the editor. O. W. Walter. Library J 96:1306-7 Ap 15 '71

LIBRARIES—*Continued*

Services to schools
See Libraries and schools

Services to socially handicapped
Coping with COPES on LSD; services to disadvantaged at ALA meeting. E. Geller. il Library J 96:2825-9 S 15 '71
Day care and NYPL: Washington Heights branch Discovery room. il Library J 96:4136-7 D 15 '71
Financing discrimination. E. Geller; discussion. Library J 96:219, 671 Ja 15, F 15 '71
Jumping the eighteenth century barrier: Carnegie West library part of the Cleveland public library; letter to the editor. F. Stein. Am Lib 2:1146 D '71
Model cities community information center; Free library of Philadelphia. R. J. Luce. Am Lib 2:206-7 F '71
Our hidden children: need for services to institutionalized, incarcerated, and incapacitated children. L. N. Gerhardt. Library J 96:3421 O 15 '71
Philadelphia free wheeler on-the street service. il Library J 96:4138-9 D 15 '71

Services to young people
Creative writing: the inner eye; publication of Lincoln Heights branch of the Los Angeles public library. J. L. Buelna. il Wilson Lib Bul 45:750-3 Ap '71
Monster movies? S. Vaughn. il Library J 96:3439-41 O 15 '71
We're counting them in! young adults program for the Daniel Boone regional library. H. Kreigh. il Am Lib 2:208-9 F '71
See also
Libraries and students

Special collections
See also
College libraries—Special collections
Libraries—Picture collections

Standards
Emergence of evaluation. A. R. Schiller. Am Lib 2:1105 N '71
On the development of libraries and information centers. G. Salton; discussion. Library J 96:421-2. 1175 F 1, Ap 1 '71
See also
Libraries, State—Standards

Statistics
Library statistics: a century plus. F. L. Schick. Am Lib 2:727-31 Jl '71
Public library building in 1971. H. Galvin and B. Asbury. il pors Library J 96:3968-80 D 1 '71

Tape recordings
Tips on cassette tapes offered to libraries. Library J 96:4050-1 D 15 '71

Technical processes
Cataloging, processing, and automation: excerpts from Melcher on acquisition. D. Melcher. Am Lib 2:701-13 Jl '71; Discussion. 2:927-8 O '71

Trustees, boards, committees, etc.
Go-for-broke in Groton. J. T. Carey. il por Library J 96:1684-5 My 15 '71
Governing authority; opposition by trustees to reciprocal borrowing and use of libraries. J. Berry. Library J 96:3541 N 1 '71
Groton censors win: trustees back down. Library J 96:1318 Ap 15 '71
Groton, Conn. library board rejects Carey ouster. Library J 96:2251-2 Jl '71
Nevergreen in Groton: special news analysis. S. C. Scott. il pors Wilson Lib Bul 45:818-20+ My '71
Urban library trustees form new association. Library J 96:2245 Jl '71

Volunteer workers
Cooperation, volunteers. K. Nyren. Library J 96:3059 O 1 '71
Guidelines for using volunteers in libraries; ALA report. bibliog Am Lib 2:407-8 Ap '71

Alaska
Frontier of faith, geography of joy: a librarian's testament. P. Willey. il pors Wilson Lib Bul 45:858-63 My '71; Discussion. 45:856-7; 46:43-4 My S '71

Arizona
See also
Arizona library association
Tucson, Ariz, public library

Arkansas
See also
Arkansas library association

California
See also
Alameda County, Calif, library, Hayward
Los Angeles—Libraries
Los Angeles County public library
Los Angeles public library
Monterey, Calif, public library
Ontario, Calif, public library
Pasadena, Calif, public library
San Francisco public library
San Mateo County, Calif, free library, Belmont

Canada
Information Canada plan opposed by librarians. Library J 96:434+ F 1 '71
See also
Canadian library association
Toronto public library

China
World's most evil man; book burning in third century B.C. in China. P. W. Schmidtchen. il Hobbies 76:134-6+ Mr '71

China (People's Republic)
Libraries in the People's Republic of China since 1949. J. T. Ma. bibliog il por Wilson Lib Bul 45:970-5 Je '71

Colorado
See also
Boulder, Colo, public library
Colorado library association
Denver public library

Connecticut
See also
Connecticut state library, Hartford
Groton, Conn, public library

England
Easy reading in Redcar; new library of Redcar, England. D. Roessler. il Arch Forum 135:48-51 N '71

Europe, Western
National libraries of Latin Europe. T. M. Liams. il Am Lib 2:1081-5 N '71

Florida
See also
Central Florida regional library, Ocala

France
See also
Paris—Libraries

Georgia
See also
Georgia library association

Great Britain
British library world, 1971. B. Usherwood. il por Wilson Lib Bul 45:952-61 Je '71
See also
Libraries—England
Library association

Hong Kong
Serving the Pearl of the Orient. W. Deakyne. il por Wilson Lib Bul 45:966-9 Je '71

Illinois
Illinois suburban systems face reciprocal borrowing. Library J 96:2248 Jl '71; Reply. Mrs D. D. Baron. 96:3536+ N 1 '71
See also
Chicago public library
Northbrook, Ill, public library

Indiana
SDI is for people: Selective dissemination of information in small public libraries. C. H. Davis and P. Hiatt. bibliog il por Library J 96:3573-5 N 1 '71
See also
Marion, Ind. public library
Vigo County, Ind, public library, Terre Haute

Indonesia
Persistence of Indonesian libraries. D. Scott. bibliog il Wilson Lib Bul 45:976-82 Je '71

Iowa
See also
Iowa library association

Kansas
See also
Central Kansas library system, Great Bend
Johnson County, Kan, library

LIBRARIES—*Continued*

Kentucky
New library service: newsletter which lists and abstracts bills of interest to Kentucky. A. R. Schiller. Am Lib 2:1106 N '71

Maryland
See also
Enoch Pratt free library. Baltimore

Massachusetts
See also
John F. Kennedy library, Cambridge
Massachusetts—Library extension. Bureau of

Michigan
See also
Coldwater, Mich. public library
Detroit public library
Hamtramck, Mich. public library

Minnesota
See also
Minneapolis public library

Missouri
See also
Daniel Boone regional library, Columbia
St Charles County, Mo. library, St Charles

Nebraska
Library life in Middle America; Cornhuskers. A. Plotnik. il Wilson Lib Bul 46:412-25 Ja '72

Nevada
See also
Clark County, Nev. library, Las Vegas

New Jersey
Library union prospects aired at Rutgers. il Library J 96:1662+ My 15 '71
See also
Burlington County, N.J. library, Mount Holly
New Jersey library association
Orange, N.J. public library
Wanaque, N.J. free public library

New Mexico
See also
Albuquerque, N.Mex.—Libraries

New York (state)
Divorce: N.Y. style; situation in Rockland County. K. Nyren. il Library J 96:2257-62 Jl '71
Major New York County LA critical of state plan; criticism by Suffolk County library association. Library J 96:908 Mr 15 '71
N.Y. union spokesmen oppose state plan. Library J 96:154 Ja 15 '71
See also
East Hampton, N.Y. free library
Franklin D. Roosevelt library, Hyde Park
Monroe County library system, Rochester
New York library association
New York public library
New York state library, Albany
North Tonawanda, N.Y. public library
Queens borough public library
Shelter Rock public library, Albertson
Syracuse, N.Y. public library
Wantagh, N.Y. public library

North Dakota
See also
Minot, N.D. public library

Ohio
Dump scholarship program? One state decides; report. P. A. Agriesti. Wilson Lib Bul 45:733+ Ap '71
See also
Cleveland public library
Ohio library association
Ohio state library, Columbus
Toledo-Lucas County, Ohio, public library

Oklahoma
See also
Oklahoma City-County library

Ontario
See also
Ontario library association
Toronto public library

Pennsylvania
See also
Lancaster County, Pa. library, Lancaster
Pennsylvania library association
Philadelphia—Libraries
Philadelphia free library
Pittsburgh—Libraries
Southampton, Pa. free library

Rhode Island
Rhode Island project: book reviews by older citizens. J. Drickhamer. bibliog il por Library J 96:2737-43 S 15 '71
See also
Newport, R.I. public library

Southern states
Statement on the IFC report. E. J. Josey. por Library J 96:2828-31 S 15 '71

Tennessee
See also
Knoxville and Knox County, Tenn. public library

Texas
See also
Dallas public library
Lyndon Baines Johnson library, Austin
Nicholson memorial library, Garland

United States
Average director of a large public library. R. K. Maloney. il por Library J 96:443-5 F 1 '71
Aware. D. Dickinson. il Am Lib 2:120-1, 214, 318-19, 422, 537-8, 641-2, 756-7 Ja-Jl '71
Aware. A. R. Schiller. Am Lib 2:895, 1008-9, 1105, 1215-16 S-D '71
Christmas & note cards produced by libraries. R. Bartnofsky. il Wilson Lib Bul 46:248-55 N '71
Looking back in angst. W. R. Eshelman. Wilson Lib Bul 46:51 S '71
News report, 1971; change in libraries and librarianship. K. Nyren. il Library J 97:29-36 Ja 1 '72
Nontraditions: meeting the need. A. B. Martin. Library J 96:3299 O 15 '71
Owed to the public library. L. Conger. Writer 84:7-8 N '71
Public library: future shock. A. B. Martin. Library J 96:2469 Ag '71
This matter of media; address. E. Geller. bibliog il por Library J 96:2048-53 Je 15 '71
See also
Friends of the library
Indians of North America—Libraries
Libraries—Statistics
Libraries, Regional
Libraries and state
Library surveys
National library week
School libraries
Special libraries association

Virginia
See also
Arlington, Va.—Libraries

Wales
See also
Wales—National library

Washington (state)
See also
King County library system, Seattle
Timberland regional library, Olympia

West Virginia
Spring, National library week, and an observer come to small-town library, U.S.A. (W.Va); or, Seed money, grass-roots, and the greening of the American library dream. A. Plotnik. il Wilson Lib Bul 45:932-40 Je '71

LIBRARIES, Army. See United States—Army—Libraries

LIBRARIES, Childrens
Media programming for children; address, 1970. S. Stroner. il Library J 96:3811-13 N 15 '71
See also
Libraries—Services to children

LIBRARIES, Church
Church libraries: unrecognized resources. J. L. White. il Am Lib 2:397-9 Ap '71

LIBRARIES, County
See also
Alameda County, Calif. library, Hayward
Johnson County, Kan. library
Los Angeles County public library
Monroe County library system, Rochester, N.Y.

LIBRARIES, Institution
See also
Prison libraries

LIBRARIES, Instruction in use of. See Libraries—Instruction in use

LIBRARIES, Moving picture. See Moving picture film collections

LIBRARIES, National
National libraries of Latin Europe. T. M. Liams. il Am Lib 2:1081-5 N '71
See also
Wales—National library

LIBRARIES, Negroes. See Libraries and Negroes

LIBRARIES, Prison. See Prison libraries

LIBRARIES, Regional
Library systems: tough times ahead? K. R. Shaffer. il por Library J 96:2263-5 Jl '71; Reply. J. A. Ruef. 97:7 Ja 1 '72

LIBRARIES, School. See School libraries

LIBRARIES, Special
Libraries look to the state agency. R. M. White. bibliog il Am Lib 2:741-2 Jl '71
    See also
Research libraries
Special libraries association

LIBRARIES, State
Libraries look to the state agency; symposium. bibliog il Am Lib 2:735-42 Jl '71
Library leadership and the state library agency. S. G. Prentiss. il Am Lib 2:186-91 F '71
Systems and networks: the state library role. C. A. Nelson and A. H. Nelson. bibliog il Am Lib 2:883-7 S '71
    See also
Iowa state traveling library, Des Moines
New York state library, Albany
Ohio state library, Columbus

        Standards
State library standards, revised: a critique. F. W. Summers. Library J 96:1191-2 Ap 1 '71

LIBRARIES, Traveling
    See also
Bookmobiles
Iowa state traveling library, Des Moines

LIBRARIES, University. See College libraries

LIBRARIES and art
Roundup of art action in libraryland. il Wilson Lib Bul 45:758-62 Ap '71

LIBRARIES and audio-visual materials
AV task force survey report. C. W. Stone; discussion. Am Lib 1:44-5; 2:149-50 Ja '70, F '71
Media fragments and ALA. A. B. Martin. il Library J 96:1339 Ap 15 '71
Media programming for children; address, 1970. S. Stroner. il Library J 96:3811-13 N 15 '71
Monroe County library system issues audio-visual plan. Library J 96:3270 O 15 '71
This matter of media; address. E. Geller. bibliog il por Library J 96:2048-53 Je 15 '71
    See also
School libraries and audio-visual materials

LIBRARIES and authors
Two poets: with poems and with photographs by R. Basso. R. Knudson. il Am Lib 2:1045-9 N '71

LIBRARIES and booksellers
    See also
Bookselling in libraries

LIBRARIES and communication. See Interlibrary communication

LIBRARIES and drama
Will Shakespeare knew that all along; actress F. Foster's visit to library of George Westinghouse vocational and technical high school, Brooklyn. S. C. Aksel. il por Wilson Lib Bul 45:754-7 Ap '71

LIBRARIES and educational technology, Bureau of. See United States—Education, Office of—Libraries and educational technology, Bureau of

LIBRARIES and intellectual liberty
Commentary. Am Lib 2:14-15 Ja '71
Defending the defenders of intellectual freedom; ed. by J. F. Krug and J. A. Harvey. D. Berninghausen. bibliog Am Lib 2:18-21 Ja '71
Dogma of absolute truth. J. E. Krug and J. A. Harvey. Am Lib 2:638-40 Je '71
Editor's choice; to be professional: police officer in William Steig's Sylvester and the magic pebble. J. G. Burke. il Am Lib 2:159 F '71
Hide before you're hunted? K. F. Kister. Library J 96:173 Ja 15 '71
Jerry Rubin's Do it! still in the Philadelphia free library. il Am Lib 2:137 F '71
Knights and windmills. W. Brahm. il Library J 96:3096-8 O 1 '71; Discussion. 96:3701-2, 3927; 97:4-5 N 15-D 1 '71, Ja 1 '72
Library record snooping: more thumbs down. Library J 96:1182 Ap 1 '71
Overdue; Sambo and Sylvester. D. MacCann. Wilson Lib Bul 45:880-1 My '71; Discussion. 46:43 S '71
Ox of a different color; Sylvester and the magic pebble; Little Black Sambo. J. F. Krug and J. A. Harvey. Am Lib 2:532-4 My '71

Poor old Sylvester and the magic pebble. Am Lib 2:226 Mr '71
Repression in libraries. J. F. Krug and J. A. Harvey. Am Lib 2:239-40 Mr '71
Threat to freedom: Sylvester and the magic pebble in Toledo. R. V. Fitzgerald. il por Library J 96:1429-30 Ap 15 '71
    See also
American library association—Intellectual freedom committee
Freedom to read foundation

        Anecdotes, facetiae, satire, etc.
Smith/Jones. D. DeCamp; reply. P. M. Kasprzak. Library J 96:902 Mr 15 '71
Spiro and the goddess of love. K. Nyren. il Library J 96:3098-9 O 1 '71

LIBRARIES and mentally handicapped children. See Libraries—Services to mentally handicapped children

LIBRARIES and moving pictures
Aftershocks in L.A: film censorship case. Library J 96:1185 Ap 1 '71
McLaren film festival; Boulder, Colo. public library program. J. Heckel. il Am Lib 2:1195-7 D '71
Monster movies? S. Vaughn. il Library J 96:3439-41 O 15 '71
    See also
Libraries and audio-visual materials
School libraries and audio-visual materials

LIBRARIES and Negroes
Crisis in library education; urban information specialist project at University of Maryland School of library and information services. M. L. Bundy. il por Library J 96:797-800 Mr 1 '71; Discussion. 96:1895 Je 1 '71
Curious counsels. E. Geller. Library J 96:2811 S 15 '71; Discussion. 96:4129-32 D 15 '71
Dope that users can't find. K. Scarich and M. Trumpeter. pors Wilson Lib Bul 46:256-9 N '71
East Palo Alto federal library project; branch of San Mateo County library, Belmont, Calif. M. Keller. il Am Lib 2:631-5 Je '71
Overdue; staffing inner-city libraries: black or white, or black and white? J. R. Wright. por Wilson Lib Bul 45:987 Je '71
Some of my best friends; letter to the editor. V. M. Puryear. Am Lib 2:233 Mr '71
Statement on the IFC report. E. J. Josey. por Library J 96:2828-31 S 15 '71
Unseen and unheard elderly; Community action program of Baltimore's Enoch Pratt free library. A. S. Meyers. il Am Lib 2:793-6 S '71
    See also
School libraries and Negroes

LIBRARIES and publishers
End of the alliance? J. Berry. Library J 97:9 Ja 1 '72
Librarians scrutinize publishers' catalogs. Pub W 200:51-3 N 15 '71
Puppies are signs of spring: price picture. K. Nyren. Library J 96:1309 Ap 15 '71
    See also
College libraries and publishers

LIBRARIES and readers
Community and library: some possible futures. T. Childers. bibliog il por Library J 96:2727-30 S 15 '71
Library services casebook; symposium. il Am Lib 2:1191-8 D '71
Public library casebook; symposium. il Am Lib 2:204-11 F '71
Roundup of art action in libraryland. il Wilson Lib Bul 45:758-62 Ap '71
SDI is for people: Selective dissemination of information in small Indiana public libraries. C. H. Davis and P. Hiatt. bibliog il pors Library J 96:3573-5 N 1 '71
Why libraries? letter to the editor. H. J. Ettelt. Library J 96:2240 Jl '71; Discussion. 96:2709 S 15 '71

        Anecdotes, facetiae, satire, etc.
Phantom of the library; reprint. N. Blei. il Am Lib 2:367-9 Ap '71

LIBRARIES and research
Independent study & library use; North Carolina Wesleyan college, letter to the editor. A. W. Stewart. Am Lib 2:17 Ja '71
New research source: archives branches. B. C. Harding. bibliog il Am Lib 2:306-7 Mr '71
Reading before writing. R. Unrau. Writer 84:25 D '71

LIBRARIES and schools
Educationists and librarians; NYLA conference. J. Berry. Library J 96:153 Ja 15 '71
Is CCLD all that bad? patterns of children's library service in New York state. M. R. Sive. il por Library J 96:3442-5 O 15 '71
NYLA 77th annual conference, November 1970. il Am Lib 2:5-6 Ja '71
Pilot program on alternatives in children's service to test school library recommendation in CCLD report. il Library J 96:223-5+ Ja 15 '71
Pox on both their houses; CCLD report on services to children. D. Broderick. Library J 96:3448-9 O 15 '71
Run twice as fast: service to children; New York city. H. R. Sattley. bibliog il Am Lib 2:345-9 S '71
Sacred cows: the CCLD report; New York findings and Philadelphia schools. C. Field. il por Library J 96:3445-7 O 15 '71
Sadistic hogwash: editorial leaning toward the importance of school libraries over public libraries; letter to the editor. C. W. Field. Library J 96:1059 Mr 15 '71
Where will all the children go? service in New York state. J. G. Burke. bibliog il Am Lib 2:56-61 Ja '71; Discussion. 2:448-9, 601-4, 783-4 My-Je, S '71
See also
School libraries

LIBRARIES and social and economic problems
Equal employment opportunity: affirmative action plans for libraries; ALA report. il Am Lib 2:977-83 O '71
Libraries and hunger; King County library system, Seattle. A. M. Griffen. il Library J 96:3287-91 O 15 '71
Library education and the public library. G. Garrison; discussion. Library J 95:3855; 96: 5, 570 N 15 '70, Ja 1, F 15 '71
News report, 1971; change in libraries and librarianship. K. Nyren. il Library J 97:29-36 Ja 1 '72
Proper study of librarianship; address, February 1971. F. A. Sharr. il por Library J 96:3727-30 N 15 '71
See also
American library association—Social responsibilities round table
Libraries—Services to socially handicapped
Libraries and Negroes
School libraries and social and economic problems

LIBRARIES and state
Civil service jurisdiction ends for N.Y. systems. Library J 96:3713-14 N 15 '71
Information Canada plan opposed by librarians. Library J 96:434+ F 1 '71
Library leadership and the state library agency. S. G. Prentiss. il Am Lib 2:186-91 F '71
New library service: newsletter which lists and abstracts bills interesting to Kentucky and its State planning office. A. R. Schiller. Am Lib 2:1106 N '71
See also
Libraries—Federal aid

LIBRARIES and students
Gaping across the gap. P. Sullivan. bibliog il Library J 96:1767-70 My 15 '71; Reply. H. Rogers. 96:2806+ S 15 '71
Philadelphia project: decrease in students' use of public and school libraries between 4th and 12th grades. J. Q. Benford. il por Library J 96:2041-7 Je 15 '71
See also
Libraries—Services to young people

LIBRARIES and television
CATV: visual library service. B. L. Kenney and F. W. Norwood. bibliog il Am Lib 2:723-6 Jl '71
Get into CATV picture, ALA urges libraries. Library J 96:3709-10 N 15 '71

LIBRARIES and the arts
Working with foundations: how to start a local arts council. D. J. Sager. bibliog il Wilson Lib Bul 45:744-9 Ap '71

LIBRARIES and the Cambodian-Vietnamese conflict. See Libraries and the Vietnamese war

LIBRARIES and the public. See Libraries—Public relations

LIBRARIES and the Vietnamese war
Moratorium history committee; UCLA. R. Trager. il Am Lib 2:1157-60 D '71
Recommend for purchase: three books on Vietnam; letters to the editor. G. Gostas. Am Lib 2:1038 N '71
Reconstitution for peace and relevancy; Library school at the University of California at Berkeley and the 1970 crisis in southeast Asia. C. MacLeod. il pors Library J 96: 1192-6 Ap 1 '71

LIBRARIES and theater. See Libraries and drama

LIBRARIES and unemployment. See Libraries and social and economic problems

LIBRARIES and war
See also
Libraries and the Vietnamese war

LIBRARIES in literature
How, instead of being educated in college, I was graduated from libraries; or, Thoughts from a chap who landed on the moon in 1932; address, with questions and answers. R. Bradbury. il por Wilson Lib Bul 45:842-51 My '71

LIBRARY administration
ABC's of PPB; planning-programming-budgeting at Lancaster County library. H. R. Jenkins. bibliog il por Library J 96:3089-93 O 1 '71
Average director of a large public library. R. K. Maloney. il por Library J 96:443-5 F 1 '71
Coop administrators: poor change agents. Library J 96:1554 My 1 '71
Decision making; excerpts. K. R. Shaffer. il por Library J 96:1677-80 My 15 '71; Discussion. 96:2409-10, 2710-11 Ag, S 15 '71
Library leadership and the state library agency. S. G. Prentiss. il Am Lib 2:186-91 F '71
On the development of libraries and information centers. G. Salton; discussion. Library J 96:421-2, 1175 F 1, Ap 1 '71
Personnel work: third force? K. Nyren. Library J 96:767 Mr 1 '71
Report on women in librarianship. A. R. Schiller. Am Lib 2:1215-16 D '71
Sic 'em II: women as leaders in librarianship; letter to the editor. S. Shepherd. Am Lib 2: 1140-1 D '71
Toward PPBS in the public library; planning-programming-budgeting system at Vigo County public library. E. N. Howard. bibliog il Am Lib 2:386-93 Ap '71
See also
Librarians—Selection and appointment
Libraries—Trustees, boards, committees, etc.
School libraries—Supervisors and supervision

LIBRARY administration division of ALA. See American library association—Library administration division

LIBRARY and museum of the performing arts. See Lincoln Center for the performing arts, New York—Library and museum of the performing arts

LIBRARY architecture
Aalto's second American building: an abbey library for a hillside in Oregon; Mount Angel abbey library, St Benedict, Ore. il Arch Rec 149:111-16 My '71
Architectural issue (cont) il Library J 96: 3947-89 D 1 '71
Books in the suburbs; branch library, San Lorenzo, Calif. il Arch Forum 135:46-7 N '71
Bricks and mortar. See occasional issues of Library journal
British university library buildings. E. B. Stanford. bibliog il por Library J 96:4067-71 D 15 '71
Easy reading in Redcar; new library of Redcar, England. D. Roessler. il Arch Forum 135:48-51 N '71
Library designed for intensive community use; Brighton branch library, Brighton, Mass. il Arch Rec 149:109-14 Ap '71
Lyndon Baines Johnson library; reprint. A. L. Huxtable. il Am Lib 2:669-71 Jl '71
Making of a civic space; Columbus, Ind. J. Baker. il Arch Forum 135:40-5 N '71
More than a house of books: University of Illinois undergraduate library. K. Rugen. il Am Lib 2:876-81 S '71
Planning community college resource centers. L. Giles. bibliog il Am Lib 2:51-4 Ja '71
Toronto's new library stalled by disagreement. Library J 96:1316 Ap 15 '71
UCSD: the new central library. W. B. Kuhn. il Am Lib 2:168-73 F '71
Ubibliotheca: the spiral library, by G. Ottewell. Review
Am Lib il 2:120 Ja '71. D. Dickinson

LIBRARY assistants
Equal employment opportunity: affirmative action plans for libraries; ALA report. il Am Lib 2:977-83 O '71
Task analysis study in Illinois: phase I of a cooperative project; ALA progress report. T. M. Brown. Am Lib 2:312-14 Mr '71

Dismissal
Black caucus charges Mumford evades ALA probe of LC. il Library J 97:14+ Ja 1 '72
Fauntroy to introduce bill on discrimination at LC. Library J 96:3262 O 15 '71

LIBRARY assistants—Dismissal—*Continued*
Protests end at LC: Congress may probe charges. Library J 96:3061-4+ O 1 '71
Thirteen fired by Library of Congress: protesting black staff members. Library J 96: 2415-16 Ag '71

Education

I'm glad you asked that: policy on library education and manpower; questions and answers. L. Asheim. Am Lib 2:597-9 Je '71; Reply. P. B. Hanna. 2:1144-5 D '71
What every librarian should know about library technical assistants. M. C. Rudnik. bibliog il por Wilson Lib Bul 46:67-72 S '71

Training

Criteria for programs to prepare library/media technical assistants; LED policy statement. il Am Lib 2:1059-63 N '71
DCLA new careers program reports good progress; project of District of Columbia public library. il Library J 96:2034-6 Je 15 '71

LIBRARY association
Theme: expanding librarianship; Blackpool conference. G. A. Marco. il Wilson Lib Bul 46:472-5 Ja '72

LIBRARY associations
Viewpoint. A. B. Martin. il Library J 96:609 F 15 '71
See also names of library associations, e.g. Ontario library association

LIBRARY bill of rights
Excerpts from the revised Program of action in support of the Library bill of rights. Am Lib 2:264 Mr '71
Proceedings and findings pertaining to a request for action submitted by Robert E. Scott, under the Program of action in support of the Library bill of rights; ALA report. Am Lib 2:316-17 Mr '71

LIBRARY boards. See Libraries—Trustees, boards, committees, etc.
LIBRARY budgets. See Libraries—Finance
LIBRARY buildings. See Library architecture
LIBRARY bulletins. See Library publications
LIBRARY censorship. See Libraries—Censorship
LIBRARY classification. See Classification
LIBRARY conferences
Calendar. See issues of Library journal
Conference questions. L. N. Gerhardt. Library J 96:3793 N 15 '71
ISR in Europe in July: the Cranfield conference; report. B. M. Woods. Wilson Lib Bul 46:107 S '71
Meetings (title varies) See issues of Wilson library bulletin
See also
Conference of eastern college librarians

LIBRARY cooperation
Central ordering and processing; excerpts from Melcher on acquisition. D. Melcher. Am Lib 2:704-8 Jl '71
Coop administrators: poor change agents. Library J 96:1554 My 1 '71
Governing authority; influence of trustees. J. Berry. Library J 96:3541 N 1 '71
Illinois suburban systems face reciprocal borrowing. Library J 96:2248 Jl '71; Reply. Mrs D. D. Baron. 96:3536+ N 1 '71
Information exchange; serials: free gift and exchange programs. D. J. Coombs. Wilson Lib Bul 45:1010-11 Je '71
Libraries look to the state agency; symposium. bibliog il Am Lib 2:735-42 Jl '71
Libraries look to the state agency: the academic library. A. L. McNeal. bibliog il Am Lib 2:739-41 Jl '71
Library systems: tough times ahead? K. R. Shaffer. il por Library J 96:2263-5 Jl '71; Reply. J. A. Ruef. 97:7 Ja 1 '72
On the development of libraries and information centers. G. Salton; discussion. Library J 96:421-2, 1175 F 1, Ap 1 '71
Toronto's new library stalled by disagreement. Library J 96:1316 Ap 15 '71
See also
Interlibrary communication

LIBRARY discipline. See Library administration
LIBRARY education. See Library schools and education
LIBRARY employees. See Library assistants
LIBRARY equipment. See Library furniture and equipment
LIBRARY exhibits
Booth-hopping in big D. il Library J 96: 2461 Ag '71
Does it pay to exhibit? R. E. Bye. Library J 96:2605 S 1 '71

LIBRARY display. See issues of Wilson library bulletin
LIBRARY extension
See also
Bookmobiles
Libraries, Regional
LIBRARY finance. See Libraries—Finance
LIBRARY furniture and equipment
Buyers' guide; ed. by T. W. McConkey. See (usually) first issue of each month of Library journal
Little boxes: book storage by Randtriever, that locates and delivers books in seconds, automatically. D. Dickinson. Am Lib 2:422 Ap '71; Reply. M. Cart. 2:575-6 Je '71
Purchasing guide 1971; ed. by T. W. McConkey. Library J 96:1207 Ap 1 '71
LIBRARY gifts. See Libraries—Gifts, legacies, etc.
LIBRARY institutes and workshops
LAPL racism workshop reaction to SLJ feature; excerpts from report on the institute sent to SLJ by B. Tate. Library J 96:1752+ My 15 '71
Library training: education programs sponsored by other sources for school, youth, and children's librarians. Library J 96:1414 Ap 15 '71
Meetings (title varies) See Issues of Wilson library bulletin
LIBRARY instruction. See Libraries—Instruction in use
LIBRARY journal
Columnists mail: mixed bag; letters to LJ and the author. K. F. Kister. Library J 96:3735 N 15 '71
LIBRARY law and legislation
ALA Washington notes. G. Krettek and E. D. Cooke. See issues of Wilson library bulletin
LSCA signed as Congress adjourns. Am Lib 2:175-6 F '71
Librarians and copyright legislation: the historical background. C. Kim. bibliog il Am Lib 2:615-22 Je '71
Library services and construction act. il Am Ed 7:28-9 D '71
Library services law survives end of Congress. Pub W 199:35 Ja 18 '71
See also
United States—National commission on libraries and information science
LIBRARY loans. See Libraries—Circulation, loans, etc.
LIBRARY management. See Library administration
LIBRARY of Congress. See United States—Library of Congress
LIBRARY of Congress catalog cards. See Catalog cards
LIBRARY of Congress subject headings. See Subject headings
LIBRARY orientation. See Libraries—Instruction in use
LIBRARY patrons. See Libraries and readers
LIBRARY personnel. See Librarians; Library assistants
LIBRARY programs, Division of. See United States—Education, Office of—Libraries and educational technology, Bureau of—Library programs, Division of
LIBRARY promotion. See Libraries and publishers
LIBRARY protection systems
Barriers to and barriers of library security. R. A. Schefrin. bibliog il por Wilson Lib Bul 45:870-8 My '71
Magnetized plate said to cut library thefts. Pub W 199:47 Je 21 '71
LIBRARY publications
Library almanac: Central Kansas library system's Library almanac and reader's friend. D. Johnson. il Am Lib 2:1194-5 D '71
LIBRARY publicity
Meredith Willson's legacy: program sponsored by Friends of the North Tonawanda public library. A. Messineo. il Am Lib 2: 209-11 F '71
See also
National library week
LIBRARY reports
Read on: the magic is in the books; tarot card theme for Manchester library's annual report. J. F. Jackson. il Am Lib 2:210-11 F '71

Anecdotes, facetiae, satire, etc.

Editor's choice: confidential, confidential; annual report. Credence state university. Am Lib 2:1149 D '71
LIBRARY research. See Library science—Research
LIBRARY revenue. See Libraries—Finance

LIBRARY scholarships. See Library science—
Scholarships and fellowships

LIBRARY schools and education
Beyond full-time faculties; imaginative use
of part-time instructors. P. S. Breivik. bib-
liog il por Library J 96:1197-9 Ap 1 '71
Continuing education.   il Am Lib 2:1217-19
D '71
Crisis in library education; urban informa-
tion specialist project at University of
Maryland School of library and information
services. M. L. Bundy. il por Library J 96:
797-800 Mr 1 '71; Discussion. 96:1895 Je 1 '71
Graduate library school programs accredited
by the American library association. Am
Lib 2:1091-2 N '71
I'm a media freak! the use of new media in
the teaching of library school courses. J. P.
Immroth. Library J 96:1935-6 Je 1 '71
Library-college land: a puzzlement. K. F.
Kister. Library J 96:935 Mr 15 '71
Library education and the public library. G.
Garrison; discussion. Library J 95:3855,
4079; 96:5, 570 N 15-D 1 '70. Ja 1, F 15 '71
Library science as liberal education; letter
to the editor. C. A. Elliott. Am Lib 2:236-
7 Mr '71
Meetings (title varies) See issues of Wilson
library bulletin
Out of the ivory tower. A. B. Martin. il Li-
brary J 96:2060 Je 15 '71
Overdue; a student to Dallas speaks out on
ALA, with editorial comment. D. R.
Dowell. il Wilson Lib Bul 46:27, 79-80 S
'71
Revised standards for accreditation; ALA
tentative draft. Am Lib 2:959-63 O '71
Sixth year study and the academic librarian.
M. L. Dimmock. bibliog por Library J 96:
2731-3 S 15 '71
Students to Dallas; symposium. Library J
96:2454-7 Ag '71
Toward a federal strategy in library train-
ing; address, January 15, 1971. B. E. Lam-
kin. pors Am Lib 2:496-9 My '71
Training for the trade. A. M. Cummingham.
Mlle 74:169+ N '71
See also
Association of American library schools
Library assistants—Education
School librarians—Education
also names of library schools, e.g. Illinois.
University—Graduate school of library sci-
ence
Anecdotes, facetiae, satire, etc.
Wind in the Winchells; or, Mr Toad goes to
library school. K. F. Kister. Library J 96:
1687 My 15 '71

LIBRARY science
See also
Cataloging
Librarianship
Bibliography
Professional reading. See issues of Library
journal
Publications checklist. See issues of Amer-
ican libraries
Periodicals
See also
American libraries (periodical)
Library journal
Research
Emergence of evaluation. A. R. Schiller. Am
Lib 2:1105 N '71
What it is all about, or might be. A. R.
Schiller. Am Lib 2:895 S '71
Scholarships and fellowships
Dump scholarship program? One state de-
cides; Ohio's scholarship program; report.
P. A. Agriesti. Wilson Lib Bul 45:733+ Ap
'71
Toward a federal strategy in library train-
ing; address, January 15, 1971. B. E. Lam-
kin. pors Am Lib 2:496-9 My '71
Study and teaching
See also
Library schools and education

LIBRARY science literature
Press and the grapevine. J. Berry. Library
J 96:3705 N 15 '71

LIBRARY service to the socially handicapped.
See Libraries—Services to socially handicapped

LIBRARY services and construction act. See
Libraries—Federal aid

LIBRARY staffs
See also
Librarians unions

LIBRARY standards. See College libraries—
Standards; Libraries—Standards

LIBRARY statistics. See Libraries—Statistics

LIBRARY surveys
ALA salary survey: personal members. il
Am Lib 2:409-17 Ap '71
Along the academic way; with editorial
comment. E. Mason. il por Library J 96:
1657, 1671-6 My 15 '71; Discussion. 96:2408-
9 Ag '71
Average director of a large public library.
R. K. Maloney. il por Library J 96:443-5 F 1
'71
Libraries in their Sunday best: a survey;
report. A. DeCamps. Wilson Lib Bul 45:
728 Ap '71
Philadelphia project: decrease in students'
use of public and school libraries between
4th and 12th grades. J. Q. Benford. il por
Library J 96:2041-7 Je 15 '71
Placements & salaries, 1970: the year that
was not what it seemed. C. J. Frarey and
M. R. Donley. il por Library J 96:1937-41
Je 1 '71
Survey of library salaries as reflected in classified ads: September 1969 and September
1970; ALA report. il Am Lib 2:118-19 Ja '71

LIBRARY technology program. See American
library association—Library technology program

LIBRARY trustees. See Libraries—Trustees, boards, committees, etc.

LIBRARY week. See National library week

LIBRARY workers. See Librarians; Library assistants

LIBRARY workshops. See Library institutes
and workshops

LIBRETTISTS
See also
Libretto

LIBRETTO
Aida's creator: Auguste Mariette. S. J. Lon-
don. il por Hi Fi 21:52-6 Ag '71
Magic flute. Masonic opera, by J. Chailley.
Review
Am Rec G por 37:636-8 My '71. R. W.
Gutman

LIBY, Shirley
Enriching the elementary art program. il
por Sch Arts 71:14-15 S '71

LIBYA
See also
Airlines—Libya
Arab. Republics, Federation of
Petroleum industry—Libya
Foreign relations
Gaddafi to the rescue. por Time 99:27-8
Ja 17 '72
Libya's Qaddafi: candidate for Arab world's
strong man. por U S News 71:77 Ag 23 '71
Nationalism
Oil-rich country with an uncertain future.
il U S News 70:86-8 Je 7 '71
Politics and government
Libya: the enfant terrible. il por Time 98:22
Ag 2 '71
Oil-rich country with an uncertain future. il
U S News 70:86-8 Je 7 '71
Oil-rich Libya, is revolution turning sour?
il U S News 71:43-4 D 20 '71
Rich young rebel. por Newsweek 78:38-9 Ag
30 '71

LIBYAN Arab airlines. See Airlines—Libya

LICE
Lousy state of affairs; crab and body lice
epidemic. il Newsweek 78:66-7 S 20 '71

LICENSE agreements, International. See International license agreements

LICENSE plates, Automobile. See Automobiles
—License plates

LICENSES
Licensing: for cars and babies. B. M. Rus-
sett; discussion. Bul Atom Sci 27:2-3 My
'71
Nonresident license gouge; hunting license.
J. O'Connor. il Outdoor Life 148:27-9+ D '71
Safari in the seventies. J. O'Connor. il Out-
door Life 147:55-7+ Mr '71
See also
Automobile drivers—Licenses
Television service shops—Licenses

LICENSES, Export. See Export controls

LICENSES, Radio. See Radio laws and regulations

LICENSES, Television.   See Television laws
and regulations

LICENSING of patents. See Patents—Licensing

LICHENS
Lichens and air pollution. I. M. Brodo. il
Cons 26:22-6 Ag '71
Photographs
What bird's nests are these? A. B. Burn-
and. il Nat Wildlife 9:24 Ag '71

LICHFIELD, Thomas Patrick John Anson, 5th earl of
Earl of Lichfield presents: instant elegance. I. Bauer. il pors Look 35:78-80 Mr 23 '71 •

LICHT, Jennifer
Rodchenko, practicing constructivist. bibliog il por Art N 70:60-3+ Ap '71

LICHTENBERG, Georg Christoph
Low life in the grand manner. C. L. Markmann. Nation 212:789-90 Je 21 '71 •

LICHTENBERG, Paul
Game is over. il Forbes 107:52 Je 1 '71 •

LICHTENSTEIN, E. P. and Fuhremann, T. W.
Activity of an NADPH-dependent nitroreductase in houseflies. bibliog il Science 172:589-91 My 7 '71

LICHTENSTEIN, Grace
Running for mayor on a garbage truck. il pors N Y Times Mag p30-1+ Ap 25 '71

LICHTENSTEIN, Roy
Glass of fashion and the mold of form. E. C. Baker. il Art N 70:40-1+ Ap '71 •

LICHTHEIM, George
Modern master. N. Birnbaum. Commentary 52:72-7 Jl '71 •

LICHTMAN, Robert
Family photography as a sacrament; photographs. Pop Phot 68:106-9 Je '71

LIDDELL HART, Sir Basil Henry
Illusion of victory; excerpt from Why don't we learn from history. il Harper 243:20-1 S '71

about
Thinking about the thinkable. R. Walters. Nation 212:725-6 Je 7 '71 •

LIDDY, James
Comment. W. H. Pritchard. Poetry 119:159-60 D '71 •

LIDOCAINE hydrochloride
Oxidative N-dealkylation: a mannich intermediate in the formation of a new metabolite of lidocaine in man. G. D. Breck and W. F. Trager. bibliog il Science 173:544-6 Ag 6 '71

LIDSTER, Douglas M.
Pets. See occasional issues of Better homes and gardens
—See Gregg, D. L. jt. auth.

LIE detectors
See also
Polygraph

LIEBAERS, Herman
Liebaers on libraries and the 37th session of IFLA in Liverpool. il Wilson Lib Bul 45:950-1 Je '71

LIEBENBERG, Jeromee
Not a dry foot in the house; NCAA steeplechase. A. Verschoth. il por Sports Illus 34:84-5 Je 7 '71

LIEBER, Charles S. See Rubin, E. jt. auth.

LIEBERMAN, Annette
Mrs Lieberman of Baltimore. J. Corry. por Harper 242:92-5 F '71; Discussion. 242:10 Ap '71 •

LIEBERMAN, Joseph A.
Ionizing-radiation standards for population exposure; adaptation of address, July 1971. il Phys Today 24:32-8 N '71

LIEBERMAN, Laurence
Inside the gyroscope; poem. Sat R 54:23 S 4 '71
Three poems: Whelk hunter in the staghorns; Killing of daddy; Song of the thrush. Yale R 60:562-7 Je '71

LIEBERMAN, Myron
New business on the urban frontier communities. Sat R 54:20 My 15 '71
Professors, unite! Harper 243:61-4+ O; 14 D '71; Same abr. Cur 135:27-35 D '71

LIEBERMANN, Rolf
Opera buffa. Newsweek 78:74 Ag 9 '71 •

LIEBES, Dorothy
Dorothy Liebes: her approach to design and weaving. il Am Artist 35:44-9+ Ap '71 •

LIEBHERR, Hans
Liebherr digs the U.S. market. por Bsns W p40 Je 26 '71 •

LIEBMAN, Arthur
Student activism in Mexico. bibliog f Ann Am Acad 395:159-70 My '71

LIEBSON, Malvina
Businessmen's expectations (cont) il Duns 97:117 Mr; 98:109 S '71

LIECHTENSTEIN
See also
Woman suffrage—Liechtenstein

LIENDO, Gregorio José
Chile's Che Guevara? N. Ossa. Nat R 23:307-8 Mr 23 '71 •

LIEPMAN, Peter. See Welsh, P. M. jt. auth.

LIEVENSE, Stan
Now: total fishing. il Outdoor Life 147:75-7+ Ap; 58-9+ My '71

LIFE
Boundaries, by R. J. Lifton. Review Sat R 54:28-9+ F 20 '71. E. Capouya
See also
Conduct of life
Death

LIFE (biology)
Chance and necessity, by J. Monod. Review Atlan 228:125-30 N '71. G. Stent
See also
Cryptobiosis

Origin
Possible pattern for origin of life. Space World H-9-93:47-8 S '71
Primordial oil slick. A. C. Lasaga and others. bibliog il Science 174:53-5 O 1 '71

LIFE (periodical)
Are you personally afraid of crime? Readers speak out. il Life 72:28-31 Ja 14 '72
Bicentennial photography contest. Life 71:20D-21 Jl '71
Life in the dark. L. Lockwood. Nation 213:66 Ag 2 '71
Life's smaller span. Newsweek 78:69 D 6 '71
Margaret Bourke-White; with editorial comment. il pors Life 71:3, 34+ S 10 '71
Scrutability in Life; treatments of Chou En-lai. Nat R 23:974 S 10 '71
35 years ago in Life. il Life 72:22-4+ Ja 14 '72
We're looking for a picture that speaks to us; contest for amateurs only. R. Graves. il Life 70:3 Ap 2 '71
Winners of the Life 1971 contest. il Life 71:35-52+ Jl 9 '71

LIFE, Latent. See Cryptobiosis

LIFE, Length of. See Longevity

LIFE adjustment education. See Progressive education

LIFE and times of J. Walter Smintheus; drama. See White, E.

LIFE expectancy. See Longevity

LIFE extension. See Longevity

LIFE in other worlds. See Life on other planets

LIFE insurance. See Insurance, Life

LIFE insurance companies. See Insurance companies

LIFE jackets. See Life preservers

LIFE on Mars
How we'll search for life on Mars. G. A. Soffen and J. S. Martin, jr. il Pop Sci 198:51-3+ F '71
Mariner seeks clues to Martian life forms. W. S. Hieronymus. il Aviation W 95:49-50 N 8 '71
Organic production on Mars. Sci N 99:210 Mr 27 '71
Primitive life on Mars? Space World H-7-91:32 Jl '71
Search for life on Mars: where we stand today. N. H. Horowitz. il Bul Atom Sci 27:13-17 N '71
Toward a universal biology: the search for life on Mars. D. E. Thomsen. il Sci N 100:64-5 Jl 24 '71
Unified procedure for the detection of life on Mars. R. Radmer and B. Kok. bibliog il Science 174:233-9 O 15 '71

LIFE on other planets
Applied exobiology. J. M. Prytz. Space World H-11-95:34-5 N '71
Gold mine in the sky. Newsweek 77:56+ Ap 26 '71
Is there life on Mars, or beyond? il Time 98:50-2+ D 13 '71
Nature's way. il por Time 98:64-5 N 29 '71
See also
Interstellar communication
Life on Mars

LIFE preservers
Flotation jacket. il Yachting 129:60-1+ Ap '71
See also
Life saving equipment

LIFE saving equipment
Hurst rescue tool. il Motor T 23:82-3 S '71
Lifesaver; Hurst rescue tool. il Mech Illus 67:140 O '71
See also
Life preservers

History
Staying afloat in the patent office. M. Sherwood. il Am West 8:16-17 My '71

LIFE support systems (space environment)
News from the world of space exploration; water electrolysis for life support systems. Space World H-8-92:46 Ag '71
See also
Space vehicles—Cabin atmospheres

LIFE support systems (space environment)
—*Continued*

Testing

Space station life support experiment. il
Space World H-3-87:7-9 Mr '71

LIFE support systems (submarine environment)
Neon for deep diving. il Sci N 100:139 Ag 28
'71

One mile down. Sci Am 225:44 O '71

LIFE, wonderful life! story. See Morris, E.

LIFT (aerodynamics)
See also
Flaps, Airplane

LIFTING bodies. See Space vehicles—Landing
systems

LIFTON, Robert Jay
Beyond atrocity; excerpt from introd. to
Crimes of war. Sat R 54:23-5+ Mr 27 '71;
Same abr. with title Reflections on Hiro-
shima and beyond. Cur 130:48-54 Je '71

LIFTS, Aerial. See Cranes, derricks, etc.

LIGETI, György
Music to my ears; performance of Concerto
for cello and orchestra by the New York
philharmonic. I. Kolodin. Sat R 54:24+ N
13 '71 •

LIGHT
Can light move objects? I. Asimov. Sci Digest
70:44-5 Jl '71
How much do you know about the physics
of light? quiz. J. Daugherty and M. Daug-
erty. il Sci Digest 69:86-7+ Je '71
See also
Aberration (optics)
Airglow
Fluorescence
Lasers
Photochemistry
Photography—Light
Photons
Polarization (light)
Raman effect
Reflection (optics)
Sunlight

Physiological effects

Human circadian rhythms in continuous
darkness: entrainment by social cues. J.
Aschoff and others. bibliog il Science 171:
213-15 Ja 15 '71
Irreversible effects of visible light on the
retina: role of vitamin A. W. K. Noell
and R. Albrecht. bibliog il Science 172:76-
80 Ap 2 '71
Prolonged color blindness induced by intense
spectral lights in rhesus monkeys. R. S.
Harwerth and H. G. Sperling. bibliog il Science 174:520-3 O 29 '71
Vitamin A deficiency effect on retina: dependence on light. W. K. Noell and others.
bibliog il Science 172:72-6 Ap 2 '71
See also
Photoperiodism

Pressure
See Pressure

LIGHT, Photography of. See Photography of
light

LIGHT adaptation. See Eye—Accommodation
and refraction

LIGHT amplification by stimulated emission
of radiation. See Lasers

LIGHT amplifiers. See Lasers

LIGHT bulbs. See Electric lamps, Incandescent

LIGHT bulbs in art. See Electric lamps
(incandescent) in art

LIGHT communication systems
Laser communications: off to a bright start.
il Bsns W p55 S 18 '71
Laser data link demonstrations delayed. B.
Miller. il Aviation W 96:51-3 Ja 3 '72
Laser studied for satcom relay use. B.
Miller. il Aviation W 94:36-8 Mr 29 '71
Optical communications research progress. S.
E. Miller; reply with rejoinder. D. Weiner.
Science 174:1045 D 3 '71
Optical communications with semiconductor
light sources. D. L. Heiserman. il Electr
World 86:20-2 D '71
Walkie-talkie flashlight: Light telephone. P.
Wahl. il Pop Sci 199:61 D '71

LIGHT displays. See Stroboscopic lighting

LIGHT-emitting diodes. See Diodes

LIGHT filters
Acetate & gelatin filter guide. N. Rothschild.
il Pop Phot 69:70-1+ Jl '71

LIGHT in art
See also
Chiaroscuro
Electric lamps (incandescent) in art

LIGHT intensification. See Image intensifiers

LIGHT meters. See Exposure meters

LIGHT-operated remote switches. See Electric
switches

LIGHT particles. See Photons

LIGHT poles. See Street lighting fixtures

LIGHT production in animals and plants. See
Bioluminescence

LIGHT projection
Lighting dramatizes a new state capitol:
Hawaii. il Am City 86:104 Ag '71

LIGHT shows

Apparatus

Lights! Music! Action! automated light
show. il Radio-Electr 42:50-2 Ag '71

LIGHT standards. See Street lighting fixtures

LIGHTER aboard ship vessels. See Freighters

LIGHTHOUSES
Lonely light, Piedras Blancas. il Sunset 147:
31 S '71

LIGHTING
See also
Electric lighting
Skylights
Stroboscopic lighting
also subhead Lighting under various sub-
jects, e.g. Photography—Lighting

Competitions

Women's clubs win street lighting awards:
Charleston, W.Va. il Am City 86:80 F '71

LIGHTING, Architectural and decorative
Enlarge your rooms with light. R. M. Benrey. il Pop Sci 199:98-9+ S '71
Good footcandles for better quality lighting.
il Arch Rec 149:129-32 Ja '71
Light coming up from below. il Sunset 146:
138 My '71
New methods for evaluating lighting systems.
il Arch Rec 150:139-44 O '71
Overhead lights ride on a track. il Sunset
146:73 Ja '71

LIGHTING, Christmas. See Christmas decorations

LIGHTING, Outdoor
Game not called because of darkness. H.
Wicks. il Pop Mech 136:137-9 Ag '71
If you need a light for your fish pond, or
anywhere else outdoors. il Redbook 137:
91-3 Jl '71
Lighting for beauty and for service. il Parks
& Rec 6:41+ My '71
Outdoor lighting. See issues of American
city
Shrubbery light you can make for $3. A. H.
Huehn. il Pop Mech 136:180 O '71
See also
Christmas decorations, Outdoor
Light projection
Street lighting fixtures
also subhead Lighting under various sub-
jects, e.g. Gardens—Lighting; *also* under
names of cities, e.g. San Francisco—
Lighting

Competitions
See Lighting—Competitions

LIGHTING fixtures
Fluorescent droplight. E. C. Wade. il Mech
Illus 67:100+ Ja '71
New fixtures lessen reading glare: Per-
cepta. il Arch Forum 133:53 D '70
Telescoping wood rings turn into lamp; hang-
ing lamps. R. Capotosto. il Pop Sci 199:109-
10+ O '71
See also
Street lighting fixtures

LIGHTING fixtures, Outdoor. See Lighting,
Outdoor

LIGHTING of cities. See Street lighting

LIGHTNING
Ball lightning controversy. il Chem 44:22-3
Je '71
Lightning: observations by satellite. il Sci
N 100:142 Ag 28 '71
Nuclear theory of ball lightning. Chem 44:25-6
F '71
Some striking facts about lightning. il Na-
tions Bsns 59:76 O '71
What is ball lightning? M. A. Uman. il Sci
Digest 70:21-5 O '71
See also
Aviation—Lightning hazards
Boats and boating—Lightning hazards
Thunderstorms

LIGHTNING protection
Charge no sportsman needs, lightning haz-
ards. B. Hildenbrand. Sports Illus 35:72
O 4 '71

Lightning and color TV sets. E. Cunningham.
il Radio-Electr 42:48 Jl '71

LIGHTNING protection—*Continued*
Lightning and you; excerpts from Understanding lightning. M. A. Uman. il Sci Digest 70:45-8+ S '71
  See also
Boats and boating—Lightning hazards
LIGHTS, Traffic. See Traffic signals
LIKE fireflies in August; story. See Deasy, M.
LILACS
How lilacs and other plants time their blooming. J. M. Caprio. Horticulture 49:26-7+ S '71
LILIENSTEIN, Saul
Harford theater is a group effort. G. Ostrove. il Hi Fi 21:MA20-2 N '71 *
LILIENTHAL, Alfred Morton
Israel quagmire; address, December 3, 1970. Vital Speeches 37:206-9 Ja 15 '71
LILIENTHAL, David Eli
Agents of the new empire. M. Windmiller. Nation 212:592-6 My 10 '71 *
Liberal's testament. S. K. Oberbeck. por Newsweek 77:103A-104 My 24 '71 *
LILIES
New rage for lilies. L. V. Power. il Am Home 74:56+ O 8 '71
Taming of the lily. W. B. Harris. House & Gard 140:30+ S '71
  See also
Blood lilies
Calla lilies
Day lilies
Fritillaries
Spear lilies
LILIES, Kafir. See Clivias
LILIUOKALANI garden. See Honolulu—Gardens
LILLY, Eli, and company
Eli Lilly; weakness behind the facade. il Forbes 107:26-8+ Ap 15 '71
Train trip that was a turning point. H. F. DeBoest. il pors Nations Bsns 59:72-3 Ja '71
LILLY, Josiah Kirby
Train trip that was a turning point. H. F. DeBoest. il pors Nations Bsns 59:72-3 Ja '71 *
LILLY, Othelia
Everywoman after every war; poem. Commonweal 94:87 Ap 2 '71
For those with ears; poem. Chr Cent 88:1158 O 6 '71
If only; poem. Chr Cent 88: 646 My 26 '71
LILLY, Robert
Sports. R. Kahn. il Esquire 76:14+ D '71 *
LILLY family
Lillys; fighting the 20th century. il Forbes 107:31+ Ap 15 '71
LIMA, Frank
Demitasse; poem. Sat R 54:34 Je 12 '71
Scorpio rising; poem. Sat R 54:53 My 22 '71
LIMA, Peru
    Historic houses, etc.
Peruvian problem in historic preservation: Lima home of Dr and Mrs Pedro G. Beltrán. W. M. Whitehill. il Antiques 99:720-4 My '71
LIMANTOUR, Joseph Yves
Nice piece of real estate. R. Reinhardt. il Am Heritage 23:42-7+ D '71 *
LIMB regeneration. See Regeneration (biology)
LIMBACHER, James L.
On the record: Words. See issues of Library journal
Recordings. See occasional issues of Library journal
LIMBIC system
Brain priorities for touch and movement. R. Gore. il Life 71:62-3 N 12 '71
LIMBURG, Al
Fresh look at fresh water. il Motor B & S 127:10-12+ Ap '71
Keeping your head above water. il Motor B & S 128:83-5 Jl '71
LIMERICK, Ireland
Discover Ireland on a walk in Limerick. Sunset 147:49-50 N '71
LIMITATION of arms. See Disarmament
LIMITATION of population. See Birth control
LIMITED partnership
New popularity for limited partnerships. il Bsns W p88+ D 11 '71
Partners in profits, and losses. il Duns 98:67-8 O '71
LIMMER, Eleanor
When mother goes away. il Parents Mag 46: 42-3+ D '71
LIMNOLOGY
  See also
Eutrophication

LIMPETS
Opal precipitation by marine gastropods (mollusca) H. A. Lowenstam. bibliog il Science 171:487-90 F 5 '71
LIMULUS eye. See Eye (crustaceans)
LIN, Piao
China: the fall of Mao's heir. il por Time 98: 35-6 N 22 '71 *
Clues to fight for power in red China. il pors U S News 71:29 N 22 '71 *
LINAC. See Accelerators (electrons, etc)
LINARES, J. and Huertas, F.
Kaolinite; synthesis at room temperature. bibliog Science 171:896-7 Mr 5 '71
LINCOLN, Abraham
Lincoln's favorite stories. M. R. Lewis. il por Read Digest 98:151-3 F '71 *
Roots of lawlessness. H. S. Commager. por Sat R 54:17-19+ F 13 '71 *

    Anecdotes, facetiae, satire, etc.
Abraham Lincoln: lawyer, statesman, and golf nut. T. Meehan. New Yorker 47:35-5 Ag 28 '71

    Bibliography
Lincolniana in 1970; related Civil war activities. B. E. Wheeler. il Hobbies 75:116-21 F '71

    Drama
Abe's winkin' eye. A. Fisher. Plays 30:55-64 F '71

    Religion
Lincoln's almost chosen people. T. H. Clancy. il por America 124:145-7 F 13 '71
LINCOLN, Marshall
Chain saw artist. il pors Design 72:4-7 mid-Sum '71
Photographer's test meter. il Radio-Electr 42: 59-61 O '71
Star gazing the easy way. il Pop Sci 199· 122+ O '71
LINCOLN, Mary (Todd)
Lincolniana in 1970. B. E. Wheeler. il Hobbies 75:116-21 F '71 *
LINCOLN, Stoddard
Great master of sonata form: the real Muzio Clementi. il pors Am Rec G 37:228-34 D '70
In tender memory, what the *lobgesang* means to me. il por Am Rec G 37:412-16 Mr '71
LINCOLN, Neb.
^3 cities, innovative reporting. il Am City 86: 132+ Je '71
LINCOLN Center for the performing arts, New York

    Juilliard school
Juilliard dance ensemble, the Juilliard theatre, NYC. J. Anderson. Dance Mag 46:29 Ja '72
Mozart's Tito at the Juilliard. I. Kolodin. Sat R 54:38 F 6 '71
Music to my ears; Juilliard orchestra performs in Alice Tully Hall. I. Kolodin. Sat R 54:25 D 18 '71
Music to my ears; presentation of L. Farberman's opera, The losers, by the American opera center. I. Kolodin. Sat R 54:16+ Ap 10 '71
Musical events; presentation of H. Overton's Huckleberry Finn at the Juilliard theatre. W. Sargeant. New Yorker 47:57 My 29 '71
Realism at the Juilliard; presentation of L. Farberman's opera, The losers. I. Kolodin. il por Sat R 54:50-1 Ap 24 '71
Report:
Hall Overton's Huckleberry Finn. F. Merkling. Opera N 36:22 S '71
Losers. F. Merkling. il Opera N 35:22 My 15 '71
Mozart's La clemenza di Tito. S. Jenkins. il Opera N 35:32 Mr 6 '71

    Library and museum of the performing arts
Theatre on film and tape. B. Harte. il Am Lib 2:1065-8 N '71

    Opera house
Grand night for drinking; onstage and off, spirits flow freely at the Met. R. Zachary. il Opera N 35:26-8 F 13 '71

    Vivian Beaumont theater
Crossroads at Lincoln rep; controversy over the Beaumont and Forum theaters. J. Kroll. il Newsweek 78:121 D 6 '71
Drama at Lincoln Center; future of the Forum and the Beaumont. S. Kauffman. New Repub 165:20+ O 23 '71; Reply with rejoinder. D. Schary. 165:29-30 N 27 '71
Tale of two centers; take over of the Vivian Beaumont theater by City center. il Newsweek 77:45 F 1 '71

LINCOLN-Mercury division. See Ford motor company—Lincoln-Mercury division

LINCOLN park. See Chicago—Parks and playgrounds

LINCOLN university, Oxford, Pa.
Lincoln university in the nineteenth century. D. A. Peters. bibliog Negro Hist Bul 34: 80-2 Ap '71

LIND, Jenny
Elusive Jenny Lind record. H. Birdoff. il por Hobbies 75:35-6+ F '71 •
More souvenirs of Jenny Lind. F. Cavanah. il Hobbies 75:138-40+ Ja '71 •

LINDBECK, Assar
New-left economics. P. A. Samuelson. Newsweek 78:94 D 6 '71 •

LINDBECK, George A.
Hans Küng's infallible? A Protestant perspective. America 124:431-3 Ap 24 '71

LINDBERG, Olga
On the trail of old sundials. il Sci Digest 70: 69-72 S '71

LINDBERGH, Charles Augustus, 1902-
Way of wildness. Read Digest 99:90-3 N '71

about

Lone Eagle. L. Berg. Commentary 51:95-8 F '71; Reply with rejoinder. I. M. Engel. 52:30 Jl '71 •
Return of Charles Lindbergh. A. Whitman. il pors N Y Times Mag p28-9+ My 23 '71; Same abr Read Digest 99:190-2+ S '71 •
Travels with Charlie. E. Needham. il por Esquire 75:90-1+ Mr '71 •

LINDBERGH flight. See Aviation—Transatlantic flights

LINDBLAD, Lois
Voyagers; poem. Nation 213:438 N 1 '71

LINDEMAN, Bard
Noel Charron's courage alone makes him the toughest kid on the block. il Todays Health 49:46-51 S '71
Will somebody please welcome this hero home? il pors Todays Health 49:54-6+ Je '71
You're not Mrs Hatfield... pors Todays Health 49:25-7+ F '71

LINDEMAN, Jack
Migrant work; poem. Nation 213:30 Jl 5 '71
Sour; poem. Commonweal 95:154 N 12 '71

LINDEN, Eugene
Demoralization of an army: fragging and other withdrawal symptoms. il Sat R 55: 12-17+ Ja 8 '72

LINDER collection of the works and drawings of Beatrix Potter. See National book league

LINDLEY, Denver
(tr) See Hesse, H. Life story briefly told

LINDOP, Patricia J. and Rotblat, Joseph
Radiation pollution of the environment. il por Bul Atom Sci 27:17-24 S '71

LINDSAY, John Vliet
Chartering national cities. Cur 131:9-11 Jl '71
For a new policy balance. For Affairs 50:1-14 O '71
John Lindsay looks at the church; interview, ed. by T. Early. Chr Cent 88:400-3 Mr 31 '71
National goals: survival is the issue. il Sat R 54:46-8 Ja 23 '71

about

All-purpose Lindsay comment. J. Aylward. Sat R 54:4 D 25 '71 •
Around city hall (cont) A. Logan. New Yorker 46:77-80+ Ja 16; 47:142+ Mr 20; 117-24 My 15; 79-82 Je 26; 64-70 Ag 21; 105-12 O 30; 50+ D 25 '71 •
Bloodied Lindsay. Time 99:29 Ja 3 '72 •
Challenger from city hall. il por Newsweek 79:14 Ja 10 '72 •
Changing priorities; article in Foreign affairs magazine. Newsweek 78:64 S 27 '71 •
City as sandbox; or, Now we know what John Lindsay does. Nat R 23:1339-40 D 3 '71 •
Conversion of John Lindsay. il pors Time 98:7-9 Ag 23 '71 •
Democrat Lindsay. New Repub 165:10 Ag 21; 10 S 4 '71 •
Democrat Lindsay: getting set for '72. por US News 71:68 Ag 23 '71 •
Exit Lindsay. W. F. Buckley, jr. Nat R 23: 1010-11 S 10 '71 •
Fairest dark horse of them all. D. Halberstam. il pors McCalls 99:102-3+ N '71 •
Lindsay: a switch in time? il pors Newsweek 78:15-16+ Ag 23 '71 •
Lindsay and 1972. Nation 212:291-2 Mr 8 '71 •
Lindsay, Aurelio & co. hit the road. F. Trippet. il pors N Y Times Mag p36-7+ N 21 '71

Lindsay balloons. por Time 97:15-16 Mr 8 '71 •
Lindsay choice now: to preach or to run. T. H. White. il por Life 71:66-7 Ag 20 '71 •
Lindsay goes west. il por Time 98:22 O 11 '71 •
Lindsay on the road. il por Newsweek 78:25-6 O 11 '71 •
Lindsay talk. il por Newsweek 77:22-3 Mr 1 '71 •
Lindsay the Democrat. Nation 213:130 Ag 30 '71 •
Mayor doth protest. por Newsweek 78:27-8 Jl 26 '71 •
Mayor Lindsay's hot summer starts early. il por Bsns W p28-9 Je 12 '71 •
Off and running for '72. il pors Time 99:11-12 Ja 10 '72 •
Rockefeller and Lindsay feud. R. Reeves. pors Life 70:54-6 Je 25 '71 •
Two John Lindsays. D. K. Shipler. New Repub 164:16-20 My 1 '71; Reply with rejoinder. M. D. Glass. 164:33-4 Je 26 '71 •
What should Lindsay do? P. Steinfels. Commonweal 93:542 Mr 5 '71 •

Anecdotes, facetiae, satire, etc.

Lindsay papers. A. Jay. Nat R 23:990 S 10 '71

LINDSAY, Sally
Cleanup man Maurice Strong. il por Sat R 54:43-7 Ag 7 '71
Earth watch. See issues of Saturday review

LINDSAY, Seton
Beauty & the bath. See issues of House beautiful

LINDSBORG, Kan.
Post card album: little Sweden on the plains. V. L. George. il Hobbies 76:148-9 Mr '71

LINDSTEDT, K. June
Biphasic feeding response in a sea anemone: control by asparagine and glutathione. bibliog il Science 173:333-4 Jl 23 '71

LINDUSKA, Joe
Chow line honkers. il Field & S 75:112-15+ Ja '71

LINE, Les
Snowmobiles: love 'em or hate 'em. Nat Wildlife 10:21-2 D '71
They're still not safe. il Audubon 73:12-13 Jl '71

LINE; drama. See Horovitz, I.

LINEAR accelerators. See Accelerators (electrons, etc)

LINEAR integrated circuits. See Electronic circuits, Integrated

LINEAWEAVER, Thomas H. 3d
Hotbloods. il Sea Front 17:66-71 Mr '71

LINEBACKERS See Football players

LINEHAN, Edward J.
Norway: land of the generous sea. il Nat Geog 140:1-43 Jl '71

LINEHAN, John P.
LP-gas aids longer camp seasons. Camp Mag 43:16 N '71

LINEN, Household
Buying the best bed linens. il Good H 174: 130 Ja '72
Prints that bloom in the night. il House B 113:114-17 My '71
See also
Pillow cases
Table linen

LINERS. See Ocean liners

LING, James Joseph
Back at the old stand. il por Newsweek 78: 79-80 N 1 '71 •
How Ling engineered a new beginning. il por Bsns W p76-7 My 29 '71 •
Ling tries old tricks at a new stand. por Bsns W p72+ O 30 '71 •
Rival offer stymies Ling's Okonite bid. Bsns W p30+ Mr 6 '71 •
Will Jimmy Ling do it again? A. A. Butkus. il por Duns 98:38-42+ S '71 •

LING-Temco-Vought, inc.
LTV aerospace reports gains in commercial diversification. E. J. Bulban. il Aviation W 94:66 My 10 '71
LTV begins sale of Braniff holdings. Aviation W 94:27 Mr 22 '71
LTV nine-month loss declines. Aviation W 95:57 N 8 '71
LTV resurrects a Ling game plan. Bsns W p30-1 Mr 20 '71
LTV studies entry in Corvette program. Aviation W 94:221 My 31 '71
LTV wins a plum in airport transit. il Bsns W p39 Jl 17 '71
Revaluation. Forbes 107:38 Je 1 '71
Rival offer stymies Ling's Okonite bid. Bsns W p30+ Mr 6 '71
Vought helicopter benefits from tie to Aerospatiale. E. J. Bulban. il Aviation W 94: 132-3 My 31 '71

LING-Temco-Vought, inc.—*Continued*
Vought to build airport transit system. E. J. Bulban. il Aviation W 95:16-17 Jl 19 '71
Will Jimmy Ling do it again? A. A. Butkus. il por Duns 98:38-42+ S '71
LINGG, Ann M.
Pied Piper. il pors Opera N 36:10-14 D 25 '71
(ed) See Deiber, P. E. Alsatian
(ed) See Levine, J. Wunderkind
LINGUISTIC analysis. See Analysis (philosophy)
LINGUISTICS. See Language and languages
LINHART, C. I.
Try a city-school park program. il Am City 86:82-3 Mr '71
LINKAGE (genetics)
Linkage of genes controlling the rate of synthesis and structure of aminolevulinate dehydratase. D. L. Coleman. bibliog il Science 173:1245-6 S 24 '71
LINKLETTER, Art
Don't legalize marijuana; excerpts from address, May 1971. PTA Mag 65:15 Je '71
Drug abuse; address, September 14, 1971. Vital Speeches 38:22-5 O 15 '71
How schools can fight drug abuse. Ed Digest 37:17-20 O '71
Kids and drugs; address, May 1971. il PTA Mag 66:2-5 S; 2-5 O '71
LINNANE, George W.
Surf fishing with a 4-wheel drive. il Pop Mech 135:106-7+ F '71
LINO, Hector V. Jr
Look into blackness. por Sr Schol 98:10-11+ Mr 22 '71
LINOLEUM block printing
Color linocuts. M. Panchal. il Sch Arts 71:12-13 D '71
Erwin Schachner makes a linocut. E. Schachner. il por Am Artist 35:40-5 N '71
Tapestries: a versatile approach; linoleum block printing and creative stitchery. B. Culley. il Sch Arts 71:10-11 Ja '72
LINOWES, David F.
Government agencies are failing our people; address, June 29, 1971. Vital Speeches 37:759-62 O 1 '71
about
Productive approach to social programs. V. Louviere. Nations Bsns 59:23 S '71 *
LINOWITZ, Sol Myron
Our nonpolicy toward Latin America. por Life 70:4 Je 18 '71
Why invest in Latin America? il Harvard Bsn R 49:120-30 Ja '71
LINTERMANS, Aurélien
Cut & care; interview. il por Mlle 73:130-1 Jl '71
LINTHICUM, D. Scott
Immunity of the hagfish; with biographical sketch. il por Sea Front 17:17-22, 63 Ja '71
LINTON, Calvin D.
Literary style in religious writing. Chr Today 15:5-6+ Je 18; 8-12 Jl 2 '71
Sorrows of hell. Chr Today 16:12-14 N 19 '71
LINTON, Henry
Test capacitors fast. il Radio-Electr 42:60-1 D '71
LINVILLE brothers
Two beauties and a Beast; Jack and Jim Linville and a boat called Beast. H. D. Whall. Sports Illus 34:43 Je 21 '71
LION country safari, inc.
King of the jungle. T. J. Murray. il por Duns 98:59-60 N '71
LION hunting
African journal; with introd. by R. Cave. E. Hemingway. il Sports Illus 35:40-52+ D 20 '71
LIONS
Freeing the big cats. W. Nussey and H. Reuter. il pors Sci Digest 69:46-8 Je '71
Send them back alive; export to Africa from wild-game park, Château de Thoiry, France. Time 97:40+ Je 14 '71
Wiring the king for sound. il Sci Digest 71:25-7 Ja '72
LIONS, Mountain. See Pumas
LIPCHITZ, Jacques
Visit with Jacques Lipchitz; interview, ed. by L. Arking. il pors Atlan 227:68-77 Mr '71
LIPEZ, Richard
Our busy and versatile literary sun. Sat R 54:18 Ag 7 '71
LIPIDS
Conductance changes produced by acetylcholine in lipidic membranes containing a proteolipid from electrophorus. M. Parisi and others. bibliog il Science 172:56-7 Ap 2 '71

Freezing and melting of lipid bilayers and the mode of action of nonactin, valinomycin, and gramicidin. S. Krasne and others. bibliog il Science 174:412-15 O 22 '71
Molecular biology of synaptic receptors. E. de Robertis. bibliog il Science 171:963-71 Mr 12 '71
See also
Lipoproteins
Phosphatides
LIPMAN, Jean
(comp) Casual comparisons. il Art in Am 59:68-71 Ja '71
Living with antiques. il Antiques 99:112-21 Ja '71
LIPMAN, Peter W. and others
Evolving subduction zones in the western United States, as interpreted from igneous rocks. bibliog il Science 174:821-5 N 19 '71
LIPMAN-BLUMEN, Jean
How ideology shapes women's lives; with biographical sketch. il Sci Am 226:10, 34-42 Ja '72
LIPMANN, Fritz
Attempts to map a process evolution of peptide biosynthesis. bibliog il Science 173:875-84 S 3 '71
LIPPMANN, Walter
Great men; interview. Commonweal 95:122 N 5 '71
World we're in; excerpts from interview, ed. by R. Steel. New Repub 165:18-23 N 13 '71
LIPOCHONDRODYSTROPHY
Fighting the genetic odds; Cheryl Storm, victim of Hurler's disease. M. Steinmann. il pors Life 71:18-25 Ag 6 '71
Miracle baby of Carolyn Sinclair; saved from Hunter syndrome. J. L. Block and J. Stein. il por Good H 172:86-7+ Je '71
LIPOPROTEINS
Cholestasis: lamellar structure of the abnormal human serum lipoprotein. R. L. Hamilton and others. bibliog il Science 172:475-8 Ap 30 '71
Compositional relatedness between histocompatibility antigens and human serum lipoproteins. K. Berg. bibliog il Science 172:1136-8 Je 11 '71
LIPPARD, Lucy R.
Eva Hesse: the circle. il Art in Am 59:68-73 My '71
Sexual politics, art style. Art in Am 59:19-20 S '71
(ed) See Smith, T. Tony Smith: talk about sculpture
LIPPOLD, Olof
Physiological tremor; with biographical sketch. il Sci Am 224:14, 65-73 Mr '71
LIPS to lips; story. See Nabokov. V.
LIPSCOMB, James
Ultimate predator. il Sports Illus 35:22-6+ Ag 23 '71
LIPSET, Seymour Martin
Polls and protests; excerpt from They would rather be left, by S. M. Lipset and G. Schaflander. For Affairs 49:548-55 Ap '71
Socialism of fools: the new left calls it anti-Zionism. il N Y Times Mag p6-7+ Ja 3; 39 Ja 31; 16+ Mr 14 '71
about
More podunks than Harvards. por Newsweek 77:62-3 F 22 '71 *
LIPSKY, Michael
Social scientists and the riot commission. bibliog f Ann Am Acad 394:72-83 Mr '71
LIPSTICK
Mouth: a colorful comeback. S. Obre. il Ladies Home J 88:72-3 Ag '71
LIPSYTE, Robert
I don't have to be what you want me to be, says Muhammad Ali. il pors N Y Times Mag p24-5+ Mr 7 '71
LIPTON, Dean
Wildlife ranching. Sci Digest 70:76-9 Ag '71
LIPTON, Herbert. See Strum, I. E. jt. auth.
LIPTON, Morris Abraham
Violence is a part of the times; interview. por U S News 70:73-4 Ja 25 '71
LIPTON, Norman C.
Harold Lloyd. il por Pop Phot 69:50+ Ag '71
LIPTON, Peggy
Can two TV beauties survive TV? interview, ed. by R. Meryman. il pors Life 70:54-6 Ja 22 '71
LIPTON, Seymour
Lipton's code. H. Rosenstein. il Art N 70:46-7+ Mr '71 *
LIQUEFIED natural gas
First rumblings of a world boom. il Bsns W p32 Ap 3 '71
See also
Distrigas corporation

LIQUEFIED petroleum gas
LPG in your RV; butane, propane, or bottled gas. B. Behme. il Field & S 76:142-4 Ag '71
See also
Automobile engines—Fuel

LIQUEURS
Labyrinth of liqueurs. R. J. Misch. il House B 113:72-3+ D '71

LIQUID assets. See Liquidity (economics)

LIQUID enamels. See Enamel and enameling

LIQUID feed. See Feeding and feeding stuffs —Liquid feed

LIQUID fertilizers and manures
Liquid manure as plant food. il Sunset 146:242 My '71
What to do 'til the compost comes; liquid manure. R. Young. Org Gard & Farm 18: 51-3 D '71

LIQUID hydrogen. See Hydrogen, Liquid

LIQUID manures. See Liquid fertilizers and manures

LIQUIDAMBARS
Motion-induced inhibition of elongation and induction of dormancy in liquidambar. P. L. Neel and R. W. Harris. bibliog il Science 173:58-9 Jl 2 '71

LIQUIDATION
Why Barton toasts its liquidation. il Bsns W p45 S 11 '71

LIQUIDITY (economics)
Watershed of the American economy. D. Deitch. Nation 213:198-202 S 13 '71; Reply with rejoinder. J. Yuccas. 213:386+ O 25 '71

LIQUIDITY, International
See also
Special drawing rights

LIQUIDS
Motions of molecules in liquids: viscosity and diffusivity. J. H. Hildebrand. bibliog il Science 174:490-3 O 29 '71
See also
Emulsions

Diffusion
See Diffusion

LIQUIFIED petroleum gas. See Liquefied petroleum gas

LIQUOR habit. See Alchoholism

LIQUOR industry
Billion-dollar gamble in whisky; promoting light whiskey. il Time 97:84-5 Ap 12 '71
Distillers serve up new brands. il Bsns W p80-2 Mr 6 '71
Liquor store: Grand plaza on Flatbush avenue in Brooklyn. New Yorker 47:20-3 Ag 28 '71
See also
American distilling company
Barton brands, inc.
Distilleries
Heublein, inc.
National distillers and chemical corporation
Seagram, Joseph E. and sons

Great Britain
Scotch makers play it straight; boom in malt whiskey. il Bsns W p33 Ag 28 '71

Japan
Import thaw is no help to Scotch. il Bsns W p51 Jl 17 '71

LIQUOR problem
See also
Alcohol—Physiological effects
Alcoholism

LIQUOR traffic
Great Britain
See also
Bars and barrooms

LIQUORI, Marty
All easterners aren't effete. P. Putnam. il por Sports Illus 34:64+ Mr 22 '71 •
Dream comes true. P. Putnam. il pors Sports Illus 34:18-21 My 24 '71 •
Happy runners. il pors Newsweek 77:86 My 31 '71 •
Match-up for Munich. il pors Time 97:66-7 My 31 '71 •

LIQUORS
Drinks; six summer quenchers. M. Emmerling. il Mlle 73:153 Je '71
See also
Alcohol
Brandy
Cocktails
Liqueurs
Rum
Whiskey
Wine

Bibliography
Bottle in the book. G. Henle. House B 113: 124 Ap '71

LISBON, Portugal
Description
Instant Portugal. P. J. Martineau. il Holiday 49:47+ F '71

Music
Report:
Darius Milhaud's Médée and Ravel's Heure espagnole. F. Teixeira Direito. Opera N 35:33 Mr 27 '71

LISI, Virna
Beauty in a classic way. pors Vogue 158: 66-7 Ag 1 '71 •

LISS, Alan, and Maniloff, Jack
Isolation of mycoplasmatales viruses and characterization of MVL1, MVL52 and MVG51. bibliog il Science 173:725-7 Ag 20 '71

LIST, John E.
Ballroom murders. il por Newsweek 78:30+ D 20 '71 •

LISTEN for the whisperer; story. See Whitney, P. A.

LISTENING devices, Electronic. See Electronics in criminal investigation, espionage, etc.

LISTER, C. R. B.
Tectonic movement in the Chile trench. bibliog il Science 173:719-22 Ag 20 '71

LISTER, Merle
Merle Lister dance company, the Cubiculo, NYC. T. Borek. Dance Mag 45:100 Ap '71

LISTER, R. P.
Bat; poem. Atlan 228:111 O '71

LISTON, Charles. See Liston, S.

LISTON, James M.
Great new ideas for motor camping. il Pop Mech 135:147-8+ My '71

LISTON, Sonny
Requiem for a heavy. B. J. Friedman. pors Esquire 76:54-7+ Ag '71 •

LISZT, Franz
Music to my ears; performance of the Dante symphony by New York philharmonic. I. Kolodin. Sat R 54:68 N 6 '71 •
Music to my ears; performance of The legend of St Elizabeth. I. Kolodin. Sat R 54:38+ O 16 '71 •
Musical events; A symphony to Dante's Divine comedy performed by New York philharmonic in Philharmonic Hall. W. Sargeant. New Yorker 47:147 O 30 '71 •
Musical events; oratorio The legend of St Elizabeth performed by New York philharmonic in Philharmonic Hall. W. Sargeant. New Yorker 47:133 O 9 '71 •
What a prince ought to be: two books. D. Dubal. il pors Am Rec G 37:606-9 My '71 •

LITCHFIELD, Minn.
One form for all tax receipts. H. T. Curtis. il Am City 86:62 Ja '71

LITERACY. See Illiteracy

LITERARY agents
Literary agent's notebook. P. R. Reynolds. Writer 84:15-17+ D '71
Man in the middle; excerpts from The middle man. P. R. Reynolds. por Pub W 200: 21-3 O 18 '71
Scandinavia's lively literary agents. P. Nathan. Pub W 200:pt2 175-6 S 27 '71
Should you really have an agent? Writer 84:13-15 Jl '71; Discussion. 84:3-5 S; 5 O; 5 N '71

LITERARY censorship. See Censorship

LITERARY characters. See Characters in literature

LITERARY clubs
See also
PEN club

LITERARY collaboration. See Authorship—Collaboration

LITERARY contests. See Literature—Competitions

LITERARY criticism
Dickens the novelist, by F. R. Leavis and Q. D. Leavis. Review
Commonweal 94:337-9 Je 25 '71. B. Wicker
Fiction and the figures of life, by W. H. Gass. Review
Nation 212:374-6 Mr 22 '71. B. Gross
Literary criticism and literary radicals. I. Howe. Am Scholar 41:113-20 Wint '71
Repentance and a stand. N. Podhoretz. Commentary 52:4 Jl '71
Romance and realism, by C. Caudwell. Review
Nation 212:761-2 Je 14 '71. C. Molesworth
Seventh thing; writer's need for a thick skin. L. Conger. Writer 85:6-8 Ja '72
See also
Book reviewers and reviewing
Book reviews
Poetry—History and criticism

LITERARY fantasies. See Fantasies, Literary

LITERARY hoaxes. See Hoaxes

LITERARY landmarks
Profiles; the Pines, Putney, home of A. C. Swinburne and T. Watts-Dunton. M. Panter-Downes. il New Yorker 46:40-4+ Ja 23; 31-43 Ja 30; 40-6+ F 6 '71
Turning the Keys; E. Hemingway's house. D. Butwin. il Sat R 54:38-40 F 27 '71

LITERARY periodicals. See Literature—Periodicals

LITERARY piracy. See Copyright—Unauthorized reprints

LITERARY prizes
Contests & awards. See issues of Writer's digest
Literary prizes and awards, 1970. Pub W 199:54-7 F 8 '71
Prize offers and awards. Writer 84:44-6 Ap '71
Prizes and awards. See issues of Publishers' weekly
Sarah O'Loughlin Foley award; with winning poem by R. Siegel. America 124:594 Je 5 '71
See also
Anisfield-Wolf awards
Carey-Thomas award
Mystery writers of America, inc.
National book awards
National institute of arts and letters
Newbery medal
Science fiction writers of America

LITERARY property. See Copyright

LITERARY research
Research at Uncle Sam's bookstore. D. Stuart. Writer 84:24-5+ Jl '71
Tell it like it was, exactly; excerpt from One way to write your novel. D. Winfield. il Writers Digest 51:34-6 F '71
Writer's serendipity. R. Mathison. Writers Digest 51:27 Ap '71

LITERARY style. See Style, Literary

LITERATURE
Apology for literature. P. Goodman. Commentary 52:39-46 Jl '71
Your literary I.Q; ed. by D. M. Glixon. See issues of Saturday review
See also
Animals in literature
Authorship
Best sellers
Bible—Literary character
Biography
Censorship
Characters in literature
Childrens literature
Fiction
Folklore
Humanism
Immoral literature and pictures
Indians in literature
Literary criticism
Romanticism
Sex role in literature
Sound in literature
Supernatural in literature
Symbolism in literature
also national literatures, e.g. English literature; also literature of special subjects, e.g. Religious literature

Appreciation and interpretation
See also
Poetry—Appreciation

Competitions
Contests & awards. See issues of Writer's digest
1971 Writer's digest writing contest winners. Writers Digest 51:31-3+ O '71
Prize offers and awards. Writer 84:44-6 Ap '71
Winners: Writer's digest & Great books of the western world essay contest. N. Kephart. Writers Digest 51:33-4 D '71
Write on; excerpts from winning entries in the 1971 Scholastic writing awards. il Sr Schol 98:17-18 My 17 '71
See also
Fiction—Competitions
Poetry—Competitions

Local color
See Local color in literature

Moral and religious aspects
See Literature and morals

Periodicals
Anima rising: little magazines in the sixties. L. Fulton. il Am Lib 2:25-47 Ja '71; Discussion. 2:345 Ap '71; Library J 96:1949 Je 1 '71

English little mags; ed. by B. Katz. Library J 96:1588-90 My 1 '71
Writer's demotion to solid-citizen status; American little magazines. J. W. Aldridge. il Sat R 54:35-6+ S 18 '71
See also
Dial (periodical)
New American review

Prizes
See Literary prizes

Psychology
Reference notebook: Principles of psychology. B. R. Bugelski. Writers Digest 51:31-2 N '71

Study and teaching
Analogy: pathway to relevance. B. M. Bivins. Engl J 60:93-6 Ja '71
Critical thinking in the English classroom. J. P. Madison. bibliog Engl J 60:1133-40+ N '71
Literature and society's values; address, November 1970. D. T. Turner. bibliog f Engl J 60:577-86 My '71
Literature in a technological age: maintaining the wonder. L. Woolf. Engl J 60:1217-20+ D '71
Literature in the ghetto school. S. Bachner. Clear House 46:147-50 N '71
Literature program for students; student choice of books read. M. W. Amend and others. Engl J 60:65-9 Ja '71
Look at Solzhenitsyn. M. Mayne. Engl J 60:205-7 F '71
New climate for personal responses to literature in the classroom. C. R. Cooper. Engl J 60:1063-71 N '71
Outside reading belongs inside. M. A. Kaplan. Ed Digest 37:41-3 S '71
Soft sell; introducing new books to commercial high school students. F. Cole. Engl J 60:931-2 O '71
Study of Chinua Achebe's Things fall apart in mid-America. J. Leach. Engl J 60:1052-6 N '71
Taste and aftertaste; address, November 1970. D. A. Sohn. Engl J 60:369-72 Mr '71
Term paper alternative; paper comparing two works. M. H. Murray. Clear House 45:447-8 Mr '71
Themes in A separate peace. C. L. Thompson. Clear House 46:188-9 N '71
Whatever happened to insights? R. A. Meade. bibliog f Engl J 60:1234-7 D '71
Witnessing; or, The myth of the global village. B. R. Tanner. Engl J 60:740-5 S '71
See also
American literature—Study and teaching
English language—Study and teaching
English literature—Study and teaching
Short story—Study and teaching

Aids and devices
War in literature and film: a guided independent project. H. D. Nadig, jr. Engl J 60:906-8+ O '71

Technique
How & where to find biographical information. C. MacLeod. il Writers Digest 52:28-30 Ja '72
See also
Fiction—Technique

Themes
Always an open door for the paperback category novel. D. R. Koontz. il Writers Digest 52:24-6+ Ja '72
Authors & editors: New centurions; interview, ed. by J. Weisman. J. Wambaugh. por Pub W 200:33-5 Ag 23 '71
City in literature. I. Howe. Commentary 51:61-8 My '71
End of the world is coming; anti-utopian novels. E. Janeway. Atlan 228:87-90 Ag '71
Look back on anger; Time essay. M. Maddocks. il Time 98:40 Ag 16 '71
Machine as God; spectacle of the locomotive. J. Jerome. Writers Digest 51:12+ My '71
Rebel-victim: past and present. B. J. Lundblad. Engl J 60:763-6 S '71
Wild prayer of longing: poetry and the sacred, by N. A. Scott, jr Review Sat R 54:33+ My 22 '71. W. Heyen
See also
Animals in literature
Childrens literature—Themes
Clergy in literature
Drama—Themes
Dreams in literature
Homosexuality in literature
Jesus Christ in literature
Love in literature

LITERATURE—Themes—See also—*Continued*
Mythology in literature
New England in literature
Religion in literature
Science fiction—Themes
Sex in literature
Social isolation in literature
South in literature
Southwest in literature
War in literature
LITERATURE, Childrens. See Childrens literature
LITERATURE, Immoral. See Immoral literature and pictures
LITERATURE, Influence of
Goats, moors, and Harley Street. L. Conger. Writer 84:7-8 Je '71
Literature and crisis; excerpts from address. R. P. Warren. PTA Mag 65:35-7 Ja '71
Literature and society's values; address, November 1970. D. T. Turner. bibliog f Engl J 60:577-86 My '71
Our need for perspective. M. Self. bibliog f Engl J 60:603-6 My '71
Siddhartha; craze for works of H. Hesse. F. Trippett. il Look 35:46-54+ F 23 '71
LITERATURE, Photographic. See Photographic literature
LITERATURE, Psychology of. See Literature—Psychology
LITERATURE, Regional
See also
New England in literature
Southwest in literature
LITERATURE and morals
Moral features of seven poets. M. McCloskey. Poetry 118:98-102 My '71
On evil in art. T. Howard. Chr Today 16:4-5 D 17 '71
Poetry and preaching. J. Jerome. il Writers Digest 51:19-21 Jl '71
LITERATURE and politics
Literature and political responsibility: apropos the Letters of Thomas Mann. E. Heller. Commentary 52:47-54 Jl '71
LITERATURE and psychoanalysis. See Psychoanalysis and literature
LITERATURE and science
Science and the profession of literature. G. P. Elliott. Atlan 228:105-7+ O '71
See also
Science fiction
LITERATURE and society
Poetry of new community. J. Jerome. Writers Digest 51:18-19 Ag '71
LITERATURE and war. See War and literature
LITERATURE as a profession. See Authorship
LITERATURE classification, Decimal. See Classification, Decimal
LITHIUM
Lithium: the lightest metal. B. L. Weand. il por Chem 44:10-12 Jl '71
Time scales for lithium depletion and rotational braking in solar-type main-sequence stars. E. P. J. van den Heuvel and P. Conti. bibliog il Science 171:895-6 Mr 5 '71
LITHIUM diiodosalicylate. See Salicylates
LITHIUM in the body
Rubidium and lithium: opposite effects on amine-mediated excitement. B. J. Carroll and P. T. Sharp. bibliog il Science 172:1355-7 Je 25 '71
LITHOGRAPHS
Prang prints. il Hobbies 76:116 D '71
LITHOGRAPHY
Lithography 1800-1850, by M. Twyman. Review
Pub W 199:62 F 1 '71
Tamarind lithography workshop (title varies) cont) M. N. Tabak. il Craft Horiz 31:34-7+ F '71
LITIGATION. See Actions and defenses
LITIGATION insurance. See Insurance, Litigation
LITT, Iris F. See Gersh, M. J. jt. auth.
LITTER. See Refuse and refuse disposal
LITTLE, Arthur D, Inc.
A. D. Little's general takes full command. il Bsns W p24 N 27 '71
LITTLE, Bernie
She does a lot for a Little. H. D. Whall. il por Sports Illus 35:24-5 O 4 '71 *
LITTLE, David
On the ethics of principle. por Chr Cent 88:1441-4 D 8 '71
LITTLE, Lester K.
Pride goes before avarice: social change and the vices in Latin Christendom. bibliog f il Am Hist R 76:16-49 F '71
LITTLE, Nina Fletcher
Corné, McIntire, and the Hersey Derby farm. il Antiques 101:226-9 Ja '72

LITTLE, Royal
Don't let your brain go down the drain. il pors Fortune 84:164-8+ N '71
about
Royal Little's second career. por Bsns W p42 Je 26 '71 *
LITTLE, Stuart W.
Are illustrators obsolete? il Sat R 54:40-4 Jl 10 '71
Books in communications. See issues of Saturday review
Madison avenue. Sat R 54:59+ Je 12; 76 D 11 '71
What happened at Harper's. il por Sat R 54:43-7+ Ap 10 '71
What is black and white and the tenth largest industry in the country? Sat R 54:54-5 F 13 '71
LITTLE American golf classic. See Golf—Tournaments
LITTLE BIG HORN, Battle of the, 1876
Echoes of the Little Bighorn. D. H. Miller. il pors Am Heritage 22:28-39 Je; 108 O '71
LITTLE, Brown and company
Khrushchev memoirs. N. Cousins. Sat R 54:20-1 Mr 13 '71
LITTLE brown jug (race) See Harness racing
LITTLE leagues
Establishing a harmonious relationship between recreation departments and organized youth leagues. W. D. Martin. il Parks & Rec 6:42-3+ Jl '71
Parting shots: Sharon Poole, girl star, gets the little league thumb. il Life 71:64 Jl 23 '71
LITTLE magazines. See Literature—Periodicals
LITTLE orchestra society, New York
Music to my ears: all-Janáček program in Alice Tully hall. I. Kolodin. Sat R 54:24 Ap 24 '71
Musical events: Janáček program in Alice Tully Hall. W. Sargeant. New Yorker 47:116+ Ap 17 '71
Report:
Magda Olivero in Poulenc's La voix humaine. R. D. Daniels. il Opera N 36:30-1 D 18 '71
LITTLE players theater company. See Puppets and puppet plays
LITTLE ROCK, Ark.
Education
Looking back; interview. E. Green. New Yorker 47:30-2 My 8 '71
LITTLEFIELD, Edgar
Are lead glazes dangerous? reprint. Ceram Mo 19:25 Ja '71
LITTLEFIELD, John W. See Fox, M. S. jt. auth.
LITTNER, Ner
Secret wish of unwed fathers; interview, ed. by L. David. Seventeen 29:128-9+ O '70
LITTON, Martin
Java, Bali: the exotic isles. il Holiday 49:42-7+ Jl '71
Rip-roaring river. il Holiday 49:50-3 My '71
LITTON industries, inc.
Advanced sensors used to survey Algeria. il Aviation W 94:42 Mr 15 '71
Litton jumps ship on the Great Lakes. il Bsns W p44-5 S 11 '71
Litton: seasick. il Forbes 108:17-18 D 15 '71
LITTY, Mary
Mary Litty's 25-year struggle to help epileptics. W. Cole. il pors Good H 173:48+ Jl '71 *
LITURGICAL language
Liturgical English. R. Haughton. il Cath World 213:215-16 Ag '71
LITURGIES
Some notes on liturgy. J. Nilssen. il Chr Cent 88:924-7 Ag 4 '71
See also
Catholic church—Liturgy and ritual
LIU, Anthony S. and Laing, P. A.
Lunar gravity analysis from long-term effects. bibliog il Science 173:1017-20 S 10 '71
LIU, Shao-chi
Aftermath of the cultural revolution. E. Snow. New Repub 164:18-21 Ap 10 '71 *
LIUBIMOV, Gherman
Shock waves of cosmic rays. Space World H-12-96:46-7 D '71
LIVE bait. See Bait
LIVER
Cyclic adenosine 3',5'-monophosphate during glucose repression in the rat liver. O. Sudilovsky and others. bibliog il Science 174:142-4 O 8 '71

LIVER—*Continued*

Diseases

See also
Hepatitis

LIVER as food
Food from afar; pâté en brioche. il Bet Hom
& Gard 49:84 Mr '71
See also
Cookery—Meat

LIVER enzymes. See Enzymes

LIVER regeneration. See Regeneration (biology)

LIVERMORE, Ann
Rousseau, Beaumarchais, and Figaro. bibliog f il Mus Q 57:466-90 Jl '71

LIVESTOCK
See also
Stock ranges
Swine

Diseases and pests

See also
Anthrax

Marketing

Feeders spell out marketing demands. W.
Kester. Farm J 95:B7 Ag '71

Prices

How to predict livestock prices. Suc Farm
69:no2 51-5 F '71

LIVESTOCK, Cooling of
How to keep your dairy herd cool. B. Eftink.
il Suc Farm 69:B18 Je '71

LIVESTOCK, Weight and measurements of
See also
Cattle, Weight and measurements of

LIVESTOCK trailers. See Trailers

LIVESTOCK waste disposal. See Farm manure—Handling

LIVING. See Conduct of life

LIVING, Standard of. See Standard of living

LIVING conditions. See Standard of living

LIVING rooms
How to live in your living room. W. Bald-
win. House & Gard 139:8+ Ja '71
Living room-family room. il Redbook 138:109-
11+ N '71
Opposites with a mutual attraction. il House
B 113:50-1 Ja '71
Subdividing a family room. il Bet Hom &
Gard 49:122 D '71

LIVING rooms, Outdoor. See Outdoor rooms

LIVINGSTON, A. D.
Sawyer takes the pot anytime. il Sports Illus
35:41-2+ N 15 '71
Watering holes offer bonus dove hunting.
il Field & S 76:56-7+ S '71

LIVINGSTON, David
Right defendant. Nation 213:100-1 Ag 16 '71 •

LIVINGSTON, J. A.
Hedges for the prudent man. il Sat R 54:19-
20+ Mr 6 '71

LIVINGSTON, J. Sterling
Myth of the well-educated manager. bibliog
f Harvard Bsns R 49:79-89 Ja '71

LIVINGSTON, James C.
Ecological challenge to Christian ethics. il
Chr Cent 88:1409-12 D 1 '71

LIVINGSTON, Jane
Los Angeles. il Art in Am 59:114-17 My '71
West coast report (cont) Art in Am 59:124-7
Ja '71

LIVINGSTON, Myra Cohn
I still would plant my little apple-tree; ex-
cerpts from address, June 1970. bibliog f
Horn Bk 47:75-84 F '71

LIVINGSTON, Robert Gerald
East Germany between Moscow and Bonn.
For Affairs 50:297-309 Ja '72

LIZARDS
Barking lizard; tokay gecko. C. Hirschfeld.
il Natur Hist 80:60-3 Ja '71
Geckoes: Australia's quick change artists. il
Sci Digest 70:86 S '71
Notes and comment: geckos as protection
against cockroaches. New Yorker 46:19-20
Ja 30 '71
We lived with dragons; Komodo dragons;
ed. by W. Hartley and E. Hartley. W.
Auffenberg. il Sci Digest 70:32-8 Ag '71

LLOYD, Harold
Harold Lloyd. N. C. Lipton. il por Pop Phot
69:50+ Ag '71 •
Obituary
Newsweek por 77:110 Mr 22 '71. P. D.
Zimmerman

LLOYD, Mike
Say it right and they will too. il Am Ed 7:
5-7 Ja '71

LLOYD, William Bross, Jr
Switzerland: absent host to the United Nations. Bul Atom Sci 27:42-3 Ja '71

LLOYD GEORGE, David, 1st earl Lloyd
George of Dwyfor. See Lloyd George of
Dwyfor, D. L. G.

LLOYD GEORGE of Dwyfor, David Lloyd
George, 1st earl
Lloyd George, by F. Stevenson. Review
Newsweek il por 79:62 Ja 10 '72. W.
Clemons •

LLOYD-JONES, Donald J.
Plane that broke the profit barrier. il por
Nations Bsns 59:44-5 Ja '71

LO, the poor peacock; story. See Fitzgerald,
F. S.

LOADERS (machines)
Big performance from a little loader; Kechi
Township, Kan. C. Burdette. il Am City
86:20 Ja '71

LOADING and unloading
Back to basics: weight and balance. P. Gar-
rison. Flying 88:66-7 Mr '71
How to cartop a boat without suffering a
hernia; boat loaders. G. Reiger. il Pop
Mech 135:122-3 Ap '71
Loading of cars shown in 747F. il Aviation
W 95:31 S 6 '71
See also
Automobiles—Loading
Loaders (machines)

LOADING chutes for cattle. See Cattle handling equipment

LOADING machines. See Loaders (machines)

LOAN associations. See Savings and loan associations

LOANS
See also
Credit
Government lending
Interest
Mortgages
Reconstruction finance corporation
Student loans

LOANS, Bank
Banks prod demand with a new rate cut.
Bsns W p21-2 F 20 '71
Banks still scrape for borrowers. il Bsns W
p21 Ap 3 '71
Begging for borrowers. il Time 97:71 F 1 '71
Money for sale; First national city bank.
por Forbes 107:49-50 Ap 1 '71
Money management; interview. B. L. Finch.
por Suc Farm 69:no4 10 Mr '71
Quality of credit is strained. il Bsns W p70-
2+ Je 26 '71
Softening the blow on electronics row; loan
fund for unemployed. V. Louviere. Nations
Bsns 59:17 Je '71
Who says bankers aren't friendly? loan to
purchase Beck's shoe and handbag opera-
tion. por Forbes 107:15-16 F 1 '71
Why it's costing more to borrow money. il
U S News 71:42-3 Jl 5 '71

Guaranty

Administration loan bill contains few limita-
tions. Aviation W 94:16 My 17 '71
Congress delays on loan guarantee bill.
J. P. Woolsey. Aviation W 95:20-1 Ag 2 '71
Depression fear carries loan bill. Aviation W
95:24-5 Ag 9 '71
Future aerospace funding studied. J. P. Wool-
sey. Aviation W 94:14-15 Je 21 '71
House unit supports Senate loan bill. Avi-
ation W 95:16-17 Jl 26 '71
Lift for Lockheed. il Time 98:70+ Ag 16 '71
Loan guarantee expansion sought. D. C. Win-
ston. Aviation W 94:14-15 My 24 '71
Lockheed squeak. il Newsweek 78:65+ Ag
16 '71
Uncle Sam, the banker? il Forbes 108:15-
17 Ag 1 '71

LOANS, Foreign
See also
Export-import bank of the United States
of America

LOANS, Government. See Government lending

LOANS, Mortgage. See Mortgages

LOANS, Personal
Lend money to a friend, and stay friendly.
Changing T 25:34 Ag '71
Loans for out-of-work scientists proposed.
G. B. Lubkin. Phys Today 24:61+ My '71
Longer auto loans but no enthusiasm. il
Bsns W p22 Ag 7 '71
Meet the need; East Palo Alto's program for
needy food stamp purchasers. New Repub
164:11 Mr 6 '71
New executive perk: loans for options. J.
Perham. il Duns 97:39-41 Je '71

LOANS to employees. See Loans, Personal

LOBBYING
Around city hall; attempts by citizens to influence local legislation. A. Logan. New Yorker 47:105-12 O 30 '71
Blue cross lobby. J. Ridgeway. Ramp Mag 10:17 Ja '72
Cutting down on lost causes. H. P. Patterson. il pors Nations Bsns 59:60-3 F '71
Do dairymen want this? W. E. Swegle. il Suc Farm 69:A2 Je '71
Farm workers and city unions. R. P. Gibbons. New Repub 165:12-13 Jl 24 '71; Reply with rejoinder. G. Grant. 165:32-3 S 11 '71
Growing church lobby in Washington, by J. L. Adams. Review
    Chr Cent 88:76-7 Ja 20 '71. J. M. Swomley, jr
If you want to write your congressman. Good H 172:194 My '71
Lockheed workers lobby for the loan. Bsns W p 16 Jl 3 '71
Milking the consumer. M. Allen and J. Schnittker. New Repub 165:17-18 Jl 17 '71
New round for the SST. Newsweek 77:81-2 Mr 8 '71
Prestige lobbying; lawyers peace lobby. New Repub 164:7 Je 19 '71
Profit motive and the public interest: Wright Patman vs. the bankers. W. Shapiro. il Ramp Mag 9:16-20 My '71
S.S.T. duel at Mach 3. H. Johnson. il Todays Health 49:17-21 F '71
Where labor gets its political muscle. G. Denison. Read Digest 98:98-101 Je '71
    See also
Common cause (political organization)
Federation of American scientists
Lobbyists
Pressure groups
LOBBYISTS
Church lobby in spotlight, a look at how it operates. il U S News 71:53-5 N 22 '71
Lobbying Congress; the President's lobbyists. J. Osborne. New Repub 165:9-10 D 18 '71
Washington's corporate ambassadors. G. R. Rosen. il Duns 97:48-50+ Ap '71
LOBDELL, Jared C.
Scenes from Houston. Nat R 23:1111+ O 8 '71
LOBEL, Anita
Authors & editors. P. Bragg. por Pub W 199: 11-13 My 17 '71 •
LOBEL, Arnold
Authors & editors. P. Bragg. por Pub W 199: 11-13 My 17 '71 •
LOBENTHAL, Joseph S. jr
What to do if your child gets arrested. Harp Baz 104:174-5 S '71
LOBOS, Heitor Villa-. See Villa-Lobos, H.
LOBSENZ, Norman M.
How divorced young mothers learn to stand alone. il Redbook 138:83+ N '71
How hypnotism helped solve a lifelong weight problem. il pors Good H 173:116-17+ O '71
What do you want from friendship? il Seventeen 30:114-15+ N '71
What parents should know about punishing their children. il Redbook 138:64-5+ Ja '72
LOBSTER fisheries. See Shellfish fisheries
LOBSTER trapping
Letter from Cape Cod: a lobsterman needs a good memory and an abiding love of the sea. J. Adkins. Harper 243:48+ O '71
LOBSTERS
High price of lobsters; affected by oil pollution. il Newsweek 78:62 N 29 '71
Migrations and growth of deep-sea lobsters, homarus americanus. R. A. Cooper and J. R. Uzmann. bibliog il Science 171:288-90 Ja 22 '71
Oil-eating lobsters. Sci Digest 70:25 D '71
    See also
Cookery—Shellfish
LOCAL color in literature
Artist and his country. E. O'Brien. por Vogue 158:232-3+ S 1 '71
LOCAL conservation commissions. See Conservation commissions, Municipal
LOCAL 1199 of the Drug and hospital employees union. See Drug and hospital employees union (local 1199)
LOCAL finance
State and local governments: more cash flowing. il Fortune 83:20 Mr '71
    See also
Municipal finance
LOCAL government
Balkanization of suburbia. S. Kaplan. il Harper 243:72-4 O '71
Why local reform is a businessman's concern. W. G. Colman. il Nations Bsns 59:70-1 Jl '71
    See also
City manager plan
Decentralization in government

Metropolitan government
Municipal government
LOCAL government and the press
News access isn't only a Washington problem. M. L. Stein. il Sat R 54:50-1+ Ag 14 '71
LOCAL income tax. See Income tax, Municipal
LOCAL service airlines
New pressures face local carriers. L. Doty. Aviation W 94:22-3 Mr 1 '71
Poor relations; regional airlines. il Forbes 108:85 S 15 '71
    See also
Air taxi service
Executive airlines
Pacific Southwest airlines
Southwest airlines company
Texas international airlines

Federal aid
CAB studies increased payments to local carriers despite budget. H. D. Watkins. il Aviation W 94:23 F 8 '71
Locals predict rising subsidy need. J. P. Woolsey. Aviation W 95:26-7 N 15 '71

Traffic
California commuter market growth seen. W. S. Hieronymus. Aviation W 95:35-6 S 27 '71
Local service traffic grows substantially. J. P. Woolsey. Aviation W 94:30 F 22 '71
LOCAL taxation
Grass-roots taxes: no cause for cheer. il U S News 71:58 O 18 '71
How tax bills compare, city by city. il Changing T 25:14-15 Je '71
3rd layer of income taxes: cities, counties pile it on. il U S News 70:42-3 Ap 12 '71
    See also
Income tax, Municipal
Libraries—Finance
LOCAL transit
Aerospace crowds into mass transit; Pittsburgh's annual International conference on urban transportation. il Bsns W p20-1 S 18 '71
Case for free transit. R. A. Aleshire. Cur 135:19-22 D '71
New push for public transportation. il Bsns W p74 My 15 '71
Personal rapid transit. S. Lindsay. Sat R 54:94-5 D 4 '71
Personal rapid transit. P. Wahl. il Pop Sci 199:73-7+ N '71
Rapid transit makes progress in an uphill fight. il U S News 71:82-3 D 6 '71
Technology; Transeat, a transit system. il Arch Forum 135:46-7 O '71
    See also
Citizens' committee on public transportation
Motor bus lines
Motor buses
    also subhead Transit systems under names of cities, e.g. Atlanta—Transit systems
Federal aid
Can $30 billion buy a better ride? il Newsweek 77:48 Ja 18 '71
Which direction for highway taxes? uses for highway trust fund. il Sr Schol 98:11-13 F 8 '71
Finance
Troubles of mass transit. il U S News 70:28-30 Ap 26 '71
LOCALIZATION of brain functions. See Brain —Localization of functions
LOCATION in business and industry
Big-city banks follow people to the suburbs. il U S News 70:78-9 Mr 29 '71
Company that fled New York. il por Newsweek 78:97-8 O 18 '71
Corporate utopia: RFD? J. W. Joanis. Nations Bsns 59:90 O '71
Delaware: nature over industry. il Newsweek 78:55 Jl 5 '71
Delaware's choice. Time 98:51 Jl 12 '71
Delaware's new keep out sign; law banning heavy industrial facilities from the Delaware coast. Bsns W p 20-1 Jl 3 '71
Far from the madding crowd? reversing the exodus to suburbia. il Forbes 107:28-9 Ja 15 '71
Fellow Americans, keep out! regional isolationism. il Forbes 107:22-4+ Je 15 '71; Same abr. Read Digest 99:129-32 S '71
Hard test for Maine; building of oil-desulfurization plant at Penobscot Bay. Time 97:45-6 Ap 12 '71
Lease guarantees help small firms obtain prime locations. Nations Bsns 59:20 D '71
Matchmaking with industry. il Nations Bsns 59:66-8+ O '71

LOCATION in business and industry—*Cont.*
New factors in plant location. M. Fulton. bibliog f il Harvard Bsns R 49:4-6+ My '71
Offices in the suburbs. il Time 97:53 F 8 '71
Pioneering in South Carolina. il Time 97:67+ F 22 '71
Roadblocks in the trek to suburbia. il Bsns W p60 Ap 17 '71
Suburbs have to open their gates. L. Davidoff and others. il N Y Times Mag p40-4+ N 7 '71
When a big company moves next door. Bsns W p87 Mr 20 '71
Why companies are fleeing the cities. il Time 97:86-8 Ap 26 '71
Will the suburbs beckon? il Ebony 26:112-13 Jl '71

See also
Atomic power plants—Location
Electric plants—Location
Petroleum refineries—Location
Power plants—Location
LOCATION of airports. See Airports—Location
LOCATIONS, Moving picture. See Moving pictures—Setting and scenery
LOCH NESS monster
Work your science interest into your holiday; British science vacations. M. Roberts. il Sci Digest 71:60-4 Ja '72
LOCHER, David
Christmas eve: San Xavier del Bac; poem. America 125:558 D 25 '71
LOCKARD, Duane
Blood on the coal. Nation 212:207 F 15 '71
LOCKE, Robert Wynter
Has the education industry lost its nerve? il Sat R 54:42-4+ Ja 16 '71
LOCKERS
Locker searches and the law. H. C. Hudgins, jr. Todays Ed 60:30-2 N '71
LOCKHEED aircraft corporation
Administration nearing decision on L-1011 guarantees request. Aviation W 94:27 My 3 '71
Aftermath of Lockheed's defeat. Bsns W p22-3 F 6 '71
Against a Lockheed precedent. Time 97:75-6 Je 21 '71
Bankers trust? New Repub 164:10-11 Je 26 '71
Break for Lockheed. il Newsweek 78:56 Jl 26 '71
British reduce funding for Lockheed L-1011. Aviation W 95:17 O 25 '71
C-5A: postmortem of a mess. B. Rice. Look 35:80-1 My 18 '71
C-5A+L-1011=Lockheed's financial crisis: what price Lockheed? B. Rice. il N Y Times Mag p24-5+ My 9 '71
Carriers, banks queried in L-1011 accord J. P. Woolsey. Aviation W 94:22-3 Ap 5 '71
Case for helping Lockheed; with editorial comment. il Bsns W p41-2, 160 My 15 '71
Chances dim for loan guarantees as Senate Lockheed hearings end. J. P. Woolsey. Aviation W 94:30 Je 28 '71
Closer to a deal: to save the TriStar. Bsns W p37 Ap 10 '71
Collapse of Rolls-Royce adds to Lockheed's woes. il U S News 70:98 F 15 '71
Congress delays on loan program bill. J. P. Woolsey. Aviation W 95:20-1 Ag 2 '71
Delta signs letter for 5 DC-10s as RB.211 engine talks reopen. J. P. Woolsey. Aviation W 94:25-6 Mr 22 '71
Depression fear carries loan bill. Aviation W 95:24-5 Ag 9 '71
Do losers have to pay up? Nat R 23:686 Je 29 '71
Down to the wire at Lockheed. il Fortune 84:34 Ag '71
Even the Douglas trijet is in trouble. il Bsns W p62-3 Jl 31 '71
Galbraith v. Lockheed. W. F. Buckley, jr. Nat R 23:888 Ag 10 '71
Give Lockheed a second chance. Fortune 83:63-4 Je '71
Help wanted sign back at Lockheed; Lockheed-California co. Bsns W p24 My 29 '71
Highfliers. Nation 212:260-1 Mr 1 '71
House unit supports Senate loan bill. Aviation W 95:16-17 Jl 26 '71
How the U.S. (and Britain and Germany...) got involved in Lockheed. R. Fitch. il Ramp Mag 10:44-6+ S '71
In Burbank and Derby, they wait. il Newsweek 78:52 Ag 9 '71
Inch for Lockheed. Newsweek 77:66+ My 24 '71
Insistence on guarantees proves stumbling block to L-1011 effort. J. P. Woolsey. Aviation W 94:24-5 Ap 26 '71

Knock for Lockheed; Senate banking committee hearings. il Newsweek 77:71-2 Je 21 '71
L-1011 aid issue stirs aerospace. W. H. Gregory. Aviation W 94:14-16 My 17 '71
L-1011 pacts signed with lenders, airlines. Aviation W 95:31 S 20 '71
L-1011 subcontractors wary of committing new funds. Aviation W 94:16 My 17 '71
Lift for Lockheed. il Time 98:70+ Ag 16 '71
Lift for Lockheed? Newsweek 77:78 My 17 '71
Loan board quickens Lockheed talk pace. J. P. Woolsey. Aviation W 95:25 S 6 '71
Loan guarantee problems mount. Aviation W 94:27 Je 7 '71
Lockheed. Newsweek 77:63-4 My 31 '71
Lockheed: a forecast that may never fly. Bsns W p30 Je 12 '71
Lockheed accepts $200-million C-5 loss. il Aviation W 94:20-1 F 8 '71
Lockheed bailout battle. Time 98:57 Ag 9 '71
Lockheed, British reopen talks on future of RB.211 for TriStar. Aviation W 94:185 Mr 8 '71
Lockheed dole; opposition by Business council delegates. New Repub 164:15 My 29 '71
Lockheed earns $8.3 million for first quarter. Aviation W 94:28 Je 14 '71
Lockheed employe; letter. J. M. Buckley. Aviation W 95:62 Jl 5 '71
Lockheed maintains L-1011 test program. Aviation W 94:25 Mr 1 '71
Lockheed research aims at 50% attenuation in turbofan noise. il Aviation W 95:54-5 Jl 19 '71
Lockheed rolls out an antisub jet; S-3A. Bsns W p36-7 N 6 '71
Lockheed sale of Ventura aimed at small business work. Aviation W 94:84 My 10 '71
Lockheed says guarantee means saving U.S. jobs, investments. J. P. Woolsey. il Aviation W 94:15-16 My 24 '71
Lockheed says no cost overrun on the C-5A. Newsweek 77:66 Ja 18 '71
Lockheed seeks L-1011 plan. Aviation W 94:34-5 F 15 '71
Lockheed squeak. il Newsweek 78:65+ Ag 16 '71
Lockheed still faces airlines negotiations. Aviation W 95:25 Ag 9 '71
Lockheed stirs up the ghost of RFC. Bsns W p23 Je 26 '71
Lockheed study shows RB.211 operating costs above rivals. R. P. Ropelewski. il Aviation W 94:29-30 Je 7 '71
Lockheed, U.K. stymied on RB.211. J. P. Woolsey. Aviation W 94:23-5 Mr 15 '71
Lockheed: wing and a prayer. il Newsweek 78:51-3 Ag 9 '71
Lockheed workers lobby for the loan. Bsns W p 16 Jl 3 '71
Lockheed's fate if it loses in Congress. Bsns W p33-4 Je 19 '71
Lockheed's last chance. Newsweek 77:74+ F 22 '71
Lockheed's life and hard times. J. Yudken. il Ramp Mag 10:47-9 S '71
Lockheed's ray of hope. Newsweek 77:78 Mr 15 '71
Lockheed's rough ride with Rolls-Royce. il Time 97:68-9 F 15 '71
Lockheed's search for survival. il Bsns W p64-8 F 13 '71
Lockheed's trijet market begins to crumble. il Bsns W p 17 Jl 24 '71
Longer-range L-1011 offered. Aviation W 95:29 Ag 30 '71
New life for TriStar. il Time 97:90+ My 17 '71
Nixon to ask Lockheed loan guarantees. il Aviation W 94:26-7 My 10 '71
No early decision expected on RB.211. Aviation W 94:19 Ap 19 '71
Offer of costly salvation; Lockheed engine contract for TriStar jet. Time 97:78 Mr 15 '71
On the skids: Rolls goes bankrupt. il Sr Schol 98:14-15 Mr 8 '71
Pentagon power. New Repub 164:7-8 F 6 '71
Perils of Lockheed. Newsweek 77:76 Mr 1 '71
RB.211 talks still inconclusive as L-1011 resumes flight test. Aviation W 94:22 Ap 12 '71
Rescuing Lockheed: easier said than done. il U S News 71:42 Ag 16 '71
Rolls-Royce: the trap of technological pride. il Time 97:84+ F 22 '71
Salvage of the Lockheed 1011. H. B. Meyers. il por Fortune 83:66-71+ Je '71
Senate unit approves loan plan; Lockheed still facing obstacles. J. P. Woolsey. Aviation W 95:25-6 Jl 19 '71
Shedding the albatross. Newsweek 77:76+ My 3 '71

LOCKHEED aircraft corporation—*Continued*
Should Lockheed be saved? il **Time 97**:78-9 My 31 '71
Time continues critical factor to Lockheed loan guarantees. **Aviation W 94**:15-16 Je 21 '71
Too big to fall? **Nation 212**:644 My 24 '71
TriStar engine may be U.S.-made; with commentary. il por **Bsns W** p42-3 Mr 13 '71
TriStar: the cost of buying American. **Bsns W** p29 Mr 20 '71
U.K. government officials join Lockheed-Rolls talks in U.S. J. E. Woolsey. **Aviation W 94**:26 Mr 29 '71
What? Me worry? **Newsweek 77**:86+ Je 14 '71
Why the drive to bail out businesses in trouble. il **U S News 70**:41-4 My 24 '71
LOCKHEED-California company. See Lockheed aircraft corporation
LOCKHEED missiles and space company
Lockheed cashes in on a winner. il **Bsns W** p64+ Ag 7 '71
Lockheed leads team of 16 firms on satcom demonstration model. K. Johnsen. **Aviation W 95**:21 N 1 '71
See also
MCI Lockheed satellite corporation
LOCKIE, James D.
Highlands of Scotland; with biographical sketch il **Natur Hist 80**:68-81 F '71
LOCKOUTS
Western Europe: the luxury strikes; Sweden's big lockout. il **Time 97**:24+ Mr 8 '71
LOCKS (hydraulic engineering)
Who's afraid of the big bad locks. G. P. Manning. il **Motor B & S 128**:52-3+ Ag '71
LOCKS and keys
Door locks. il **Consumer Rep 36**:93-103 F '71
Electronic combination lock. J. A. Nunley. il **Pop Electr 35**:51-3+ Ag '71
How electronics can lock power tools. R. M. Benrey. il **Pop Sci 199**:98-9+ D '71
Identi-lock: electronic security for your home. W. J. Hawkins il **Pop Sci 199**:63 Jl '71
Padlocks. il **Consumer Rep 36**:146-8 Mr '71
Proof lock offers low security at high price. il **Consumer Rep 37**:4 Ja '72
Push-button lock changer; Omni-key. **Bsns W** p94 N 27 '71
LOCKWOOD, Lee
How the kidnap conspiracy was hatched. il pors **Life 70**:24-30 My 21 '71
Life in the dark. **Nation 213**:66 Ag 2 '71
LOCKWOOD, Lewis
Beethoven's unfinished piano concerto of 1815: sources and problems. bibliog f il **Mus Q 56**:624-46 O '70
LOCOMOTIVE simulators. See Simulators
LOCOMOTIVES

Collectors and collecting

My husband, the locomotive tycoon. S. Wright. il **Read Digest 99**:159-60+ N '71

Whistles

Whistle talk. A. P. S. Sweet. il **Am Heritage 22**:108-9 Ag '71
LOCOMOTIVES in poetry. See Literature—Themes
LOCUSTS. See Grasshoppers
LOCUSTS, Seventeen year. See Cicadas
LODGE, Henry Cabot, 1902-
Commission on the 25th anniversary of the United Nations submits final report to President Nixon; excerpt from report; with letter of transmittal. **Dept State Bul 65**:128 Ag 2 '71
LODGE, Robert A.
Instant wilderness. il por **Parks & Rec 6**:19-22+ F '71
LOEB, Gerald
Investment individualists. R. Brady. il pors **Duns 93**:105-6 Je '69 •
LOEB, William
Nixon's too left-wing for William Loeb. B. Kovach. il por **N Y Times Mag** p 14+ D 12 '71 •
LOEB, Rhoades and company
Whistle-blowing on Wall Street. D. McClintick. **New Repub 165**:20-5 S 4 '71
LOEBL, Suzanne. See Margolis, A. J. jt. auth.
LOENGARD, John
Gallery; photographs. **Life 70**:4-7 F 5; **71**:6-9 Ag 6; 8-9 N 19 '71

about

Top pro prints them his way. J. Scully. il **Mod Phot 35**:68-77 F '71 •
LOESER, Katinka
Houses of heaven; story. **New Yorker 47**:35-40 Ap 3 '71

LOEVINGER, Lee
How to succeed in business without being tried; address, May 4, 1971. **Vital Speeches 37**:529-34 Je 15 '71
LOEWENBERG, Peter
Psychohistorical origins of the Nazi youth cohort. bibliog f il **Am Hist R 76**:1457-502 D '71
Unsuccessful adolescence of Heinrich Himmler. bibliog f **Am Hist R 76**:612-41, 1270 Je-O '71
LOEWINSOHN, Ron
Comment. J. Atlas. **Poetry 119**:49 O '71 •
LOEWS corporation
How the Tisches run their little store. C. G. Burck. il por **Fortune 83**:158-61+ My '71
LÖFROTH, G. and Gejvall, T.
Diethyl pyrocarbonate: formation of urethan in treated beverages. bibliog il **Science 174**:1248-50 D 17 '71
LOFT buildings
Loft world of Lowell Nesbitt. il **Vogue 158**:8, 118-19 Ag 1 '71
See also
Artists studios
LOFTON, John
Pretrial crime news: to curb or not to curb? **Cur Hist 61**:71-4+ Ag '71
LOFTON, John D. Jr
Monday master. por **Time 98**:48 S 13 '71 •
LOGAN, Andy
Around city hall (cont) **New Yorker 46**:77-80+ Ja 16; **47**:142+ Mr 20; 117-24 My 15; 79-82 Je 26; 64-70 Ag 21; 105-12 O 30; 50+ D 25 '71
LOGAN, Elizabeth D.
Fun masks to make for Halloween. il **Good H 173**:33 O '71
LOGAN John
Scattered craft. J. Galassi. **Poetry 118**:292-4 Ag '71 •
LOGAN, Waverly
Cops as pushers. il **Time 98**:17-18 N 8 '71 •
LOGGING railroads. See Railroads, Logging
LOGIC
See also
Dilemma
LOGIC, Symbolic and mathematical
New models of the real-number line. L. A. Steen. il **Sci Am 225**:92-9 Ag '71
Unsolved problems in arithmetic. H. DeLong. il **Sci Am 224**:50-60 bibliog(p 124) Mr '71
LOGIC circuits
CMOS logic: low powered and versatile. J. H. Wujek, jr. il **Electr World 85**:42-3+ Je '71
Equivalency in RTL circuits. F. H. Tooker. il **Pop Electr 34**:49-53+ F; 39-46 Je '71
Logic terms quiz. W. R. Shippee. **Electr World 86**:8+ N '71
Novel counter, decoder, readout. F. H. Tooker. il **Electr World 86**:40-2 D '71
Product gallery: IC logic design program. il **Pop Electr 34**:78-80 Je '71
Triggering logic circuits. J. E. McAlister. il **Electr World 85**:29+ Mr '71
Troubleshooting reed-relay logic. D. Blacklock. il **Radio-Electr 42**:39-42 D '71
Unusual, but useful, digital circuits. F. H. Tooker. il **Electr World 85**:36-7+ Ap '71
Waveshaping with logic gates. J. E. McAlister. il **Electr World 85**:38+ Ap '71
LOGS (nautical instruments)
Simple chip log. J. C. Lupton. il **Motor B & S 128**:86-7 Jl '71
LOGUE, Christopher
Gone ladies; poem. **Vogue 157**:112 Mr 1 '71
LOGUE, Edward J.
Piecing the political pie. il **Sat R 54**:27-9+ My 15 '71
LOHRMANN, R. and Orgel, L. E.
Urea-inorganic phosphate mixtures as prebiotic phosphorylating agents. bibliog il **Science 171**:490-4 F 5 '71
LOIRE VALLEY
France for loving couples: nests along the Loire. C. Proulx and I. Keown. il **Sat R 54**:58-9+ Mr 13 '71
LOKEN, M. Christian
Open letter from an apple grower. **Org Gard & Farm 18**:21-3 My '71
LOLICH, Mickey
Fat record made to thin applause. R. Fimrite. il por **Sports Illus 35**:82-4 S 13 '71 •
LOMAX, Louis Emanuel
Obituary
Negro Hist Bul por **33**:170 N '70
LOMBARD, George F. F.
Relativism in organizations. bibliog f **Harvard Bsns R 49**:55-65 Mr '71

LON Nol
Change of guard. il Newsweek 77:36 F 22 '71 *
Partial paralysis. il por Time 97:30+ My 3 '71 *
Return of Lon Nol. N. Proffitt. Newsweek 77:46-7 Ap 26 '71 *

LONDON, Artur Gerard
Confession was within the logic of Stalinism. D. Howard. Commonweal 93:550+ Mr 5 '71 *

LONDON, George
Speaking of records. Hi Fi 21:22+ My '71

LONDON, S. J.
Aida's creator: Auguste Mariette. il por Hi Fi 21:52-6 Ag '71

LONDON
Chelsea, London's haven of individualists. J. Cerruti. il Nat Geog 141:28-55 Ja '72

Air raids
London war notes 1939-1945, by M. Panter-Downes. Review
 Life 71:11 O 29 '71. C. P. Snow

Airports
Beware the Londoners; protests against Wing project. il Newsweek 77:74 F 15 '71
Bulldoze history? proposal to build an airport in the Stewkley area. Sr Schol 98:15 Mr 15 '71
Environmental reasons cited in London third airport choice. H. J. Coleman. Aviation W 94:28 My 3 '71
Violence, threats halt Heathrow flights. Aviation W 95:30 N 8 '71

American colony
See Americans in England

Architecture
See also
London—Buildings

Art
London. J. Russell. See issues of Art news

Banks
Are the bears up the wrong tree? Robert Fleming & co. por Forbes 108:36-8 D 15 '71
New U.S. bankers abroad. J. Ross-Skinner. Duns 97:51-2+ F '71
Texans make it big in the city; Burston & Texas commerce bank, ltd. Bsns W p33 My 29 '71

Buildings
Empty skyscraper; Centrepoint office building. E. Herzberg. il Duns 97:75-6 F '71

Churches
See also
London—St Paul's cathedral

Clubs
New blue, true blue. il Forbes 107:44 Mr 15 '71

Covent Garden
25 years of Covent Garden. B. Fischer-Williams. Opera N 36:34 D 18 '71
 See also
Royal opera, Great Britain

Crime
Red-faced league; bank heist overheard on ham radio. il Time 98:47 S 27 '71

Finance
Tips on purchasing from the British. R. G. Wessells. il Am City 86:90+ Mr '71

Galleries and museums
Letter from London; entrance fee. M. Panter-Downes. New Yorker 47:102 F 27 '71

Historic houses, etc.
Profiles; the Pines, Putney, home of A. C. Swinburne and T. Watts-Dunton. M. Panter-Downes. il New Yorker 46:40-4+ Ja 23; 31-43 Ja 30; 40-6+ F 6 '71

Hotels, restaurants, etc.
Memo from London. G. Perint. Harp Baz 104:40 Ap '71
Pushing burgers. il por Newsweek 78:67 O 4 '71

Labor and laboring classes
Unknown Mayhew, by E. Yeo and E. P. Thompson. Review
 Commentary 52:93-6 Ag '71. G. Himmelfarb

Music
Behind the scenes. E. Greenfield. See issues of High fidelity and Musical America
Behind the scenes. R. Wimbush. il Hi Fi 21:17-18 Ag '71

Proms, Aldeburgh, Glyndebourne. E. Greenfield. Hi Fi 21:MA29-30 D '71
 See also
Royal opera, Great Britain
Sadler's Wells opera

Newspapers
 See also
Sunday times, London

Police
Profiles: P. R. Sawyer, police constable. J. Bainbridge. por New Yorker 47:40-50+ Ag 14 '71

St Paul's cathedral
Save St Paul's. il Newsweek 78:70 D 13 '71

Schools
See Schools—England

Social life and customs
Weekend in London. A. Waugh. Nat R 23:200+ F 23 '71
 History
World of Samuel Pepys, esqre; with supplement eight-page panorama of London. J. Kenyon. il Horizon 13:57-71 Sum '71

Theater
British bundle. H. Hewes. il Sat R 54:20+ S 11 '71
Broadway and the British. C. Hughes. il Cath World 212:313-15 Mr '71
Decline of the West end. H. Spurling. il Art in Am 59:108-9 My '71
Letter from London; production of The philanthropist, by Christopher Hampton. M. Panter-Downes. New Yorker 47:103 F 27 '71
Mississippi on the Thames. il Newsweek 78:73 Ag 23 '71
Pick of the London season. C. Porterfield. Time 98:48-9 Ag 30 '71
Samuel Phelps and Sadler's Wells theatre, by S. S. Allen. Review
 Sat R il 54:28 Jl 3 '71. B. Grebanier
Theatre. H. Clurman. Nation 213:282+ S 27 '71
Theatre; new plays. H. Clurman. Nation 213:61-2 Jl 19 '71
Two on the isle; New York and London prices. H. R. Mayes. Sat R 54:6-7 Je 5 '71

LONDON festival. See Music festivals—England

LONDON silver. See Silverware

LONE, Salim
Indians of East Africa. New Repub 165:10-11 S 4 '71

LONE scouts of America. See Boy scouts

LONELINESS
Everyone feels lonely sometimes. T. I. Rubin. Ladies Home J 88:88 My '71
Kris Kristofferson lonely sound from Nashville; interview, ed. by E. Miller, K. Kristofferson. por Seventeen 30:130-1+ Ap '71
Loneliness in old age. I. M. Burnside. bibliog Ment Hy 55:391-7 Jl '71

LONEY, Glenn M.
Byways of Europe: Copenhagen. il Opera N 35:29 F 13 '71
Night at the (Finnish) opera. il Hi Fi 21:MA26-7 Ja '71
Sam Maloof. il por Craft Horiz 31:16-19 Ag '71
(ed) See Butler, J. All the strange things: John Butler on opera choreography among other kinds of dance
(ed) See Hagen, U. Don't call me madam!
(ed) See Shane, R. Lulu

LONG, Augustus C.
Texaco's Long steps aside again. Bsns W p36 D 11 '71 *

LONG, Bruce E.
Guide for the supervising teacher. Clear House 46:151-4 N '71

LONG, Edna Margaret
Answer; poem. Chr Cent 88:714 Je 9 '71
Night writers; poem. Horn Bk 47:71 F '71

LONG, Franklin A.
Interdisciplinary problem-oriented research in the university. Science 171:961 Mr 12 '71

LONG, Huey Pierce
Huey Long, by T. H. Williams. Review
 Trans-Action 8:54-6 Ja '71. A. P. Sindler *

LONG, Robert
Color of sound. Hi Fi 21:54-9+ Mr '71
Four-channel discs, 1971. il Hi Fi 21:64 Jl '71
Instant quadriphony. il Hi Fi 21:42-3 S '71
Stereo stocking stuffers, for under $23. il Hi Fi 21:66-70 D '71
Story of an idea. il Hi Fi 21:46-56 Ap '71

LONG, Russell Billiu
Welfare costs: sky-high or down to earth?
interview. il por Nations Bsns 59:50-2+ My
'71
LONG BEACH, Calif.
Albatross queen; Queen Mary project. il
Newsweek 77:80+ Mr 15 '71
**LONG day's journey into night; drama. See
O'Neill, E. G.**
LONG ISLAND
Long Island's ocean beaches. C. J. Schu-
berth. il Sea Front 17:350-62 N '71
See also
Architecture, Domestic—Long Island
Birds—Long Island
Gardens—Long Island
Jamaica Bay
Montauk Point
Nassau County
LONG ISLAND environmental council. See
Environmental associations, committees,
etc.
LONG ISLAND SOUND
Letter from Long Island Sound. M. Hunt.
New Yorker 47:62+ Ag 28 '71
See also
Great Gull Island
Marine pollution—Long Island Sound
LONG leather bag; drama. See Feather, J.
LONGE, Robert C.
Notes. Todays Ed 60:40 Mr '71
LONGEVITY
Formula for longevity. A. J. Snider il Sci Di-
gest 70:55-6 N '71
900-year-old beauty; Prometheus project. N.
Gittelson. Harp Baz 104:20+ Ap '71
Why they live to be 100, or even older, in
Abkhasia. S. Benet. il N Y Times Mag p3+
D 26 '71
See also
Centenarians
Middle age
Old age
Rejuvenation
Working life, Length of
LONGLEY, Michael
Symbolic landscapes. B. Quinn. Poetry 118:
289-90 Ag '71 *
LONGMONT, Colo.
Plastic tape warns contractors. il Am City 86:
122 Je '71
LONGSHOREMEN
See also
Collective bargaining—Maritime workers
International longshoremen's and warehouse-
men's union
International longshoremen's association
Strikes—United States—Maritime workers
LONGYEAR, Rey M.
Beethoven and romantic irony. bibliog f il
Mus Q 56:647-64 O '70
LONHEIM, Dale M.
City camping calls for coordination. Camp
Mag 43:20-1 Ap '71
LONSDALE, Dame Kathleen, and Sutor, D. J.
Uric acid dihydrate in bird urine. bibliog il
Science 172:958-9 My 28 '71
LOOK (periodical)
Death of a magazine. Commonweal 95:99-100
O 29 '71
Death of Look. N. Cousins. Sat R 54:26-7
O 2 '71; Same with title What killed Look?
U S News 71:104+ O 11 '71
End of Look. R. H. Smith. Pub W 200:46
S 27 '71
Last Look. il Newsweek 78:78 S 27 '71
Last Look. por Time 98:55 S 27 '71
Look suspends publication after 34 years. Pub
W 200:42-3 S 27 '71
Teacher of the year 1971: M. M. Stringfellow.
W. J. McKean. il pors Look 35:51-4 My 4
'71
Who killed cock robin? Nat R 23:1102-3 O
8 '71
See also
All-America cities
LOOKOUT MOUNTAIN
Lookout Mountain. G. Ripple. il Travel 135:
47-9 My '71
LOOMIS, Carol J.
Lesson of the credit crisis. il Fortune 83:
141-3+ My '71 *
One story the Wall Street journal won't
print. il Fortune 84:140-3+ Ag '71
Unbelievable last months of Hayden, Stone.
il Fortune 83:114-16+ Ja '71
LOOMIS, Philip Albert, 1915-
Making it official. por Forbes 108:68 O 1
'71 *
LOOMIS, W. F.
Rickets; with biographical sketch. il Sci Am
223:10, 76-82+ bibliog(p 140) D '70; 224:6
F '71

LOOMIS, William G.
Vocational (career) education. il Am Ed 7:
3-5 Mr '71
LOOPERS
Inchworm caper; dispute over the use of in-
secticide to battle gypsy moth and worms.
il Newsweek 77:95 Je 7 '71
LOOTING. See Pillage
LOPEZ, Barry
What you need to know before you buy
4-wheel drive. il Pop Sci 198:76-7+ Mr '71
LORCA, Federico Garcia. See Garcia Lorca, F.
LORD, Shirley
Heady stuff. il Harp Baz 105:84-5 N '71
Skin peel before & after. il Harp Baz 104:
112-13 O '71
**LORD Chugger of Cheer; story. See Saroyan,
W.**
LORDS Supper
Consensual progress for the sacrament of
reconciliation. Chr Cent 88:149 F 3 '71
Ecumenical accord; Church of England and
the Roman Catholic church agree on
Eucharistic doctrine. il Newsweek 79:47
Ja 10 '72
Liturgy for a divided household. A. P. Ware.
Chr Cent 88:496-7 Ap 21 '71; Discussion. 88:
730 Je 9 '71
Mass accord; agreement on doctrine of
eucharist between Roman Catholic church
and Church of England. Time 99:44 Ja 10
'72
Six certainties about the Lord's Supper. G. W.
Bromiley. Chr Today 15:5-8 Jl 16 '71
LOREN, Sophia
Sophia; serenely female; interview. ed. by L.
Hershey. pors Ladies Home J 88:48+ Ja '71
LORENCE, Larry
Head start on the road to physical fitness.
il Harp Baz 104:25 Jl '71 *
LORENGAR, Pilar
Recordings. M. Mayer. il Esquire 76:40+ O
'71 *
LORENZ, Paul Francis
He drives Ford through Europe. por Bsns W
p76 Jl 17 '71 *
LORENZEN, Fred
Motor trend interview. il pors Motor T 23:
26+ Je '71
LORING, A. M.
2¼-acre bonanza. Org Gard & Farm 18:
95-7 S '71
LORR, John S.
Making of a trademark. il Design 72:34-5 Sum
'71
LORRANCE, Arleen
Love project. il Todays Ed 60:60-2 S '71
LOS ANGELES
Defending Los Angeles. il Time 98:41 Ag 9 '71
Television guards a power plant. R. K. Mor-
ten. il Am City 86:42+ S '71

Air pollution
Carbon monoxide: association of community
air pollution with mortality. A. C. Hexter
and J. R. Goldsmith. bibliog il Science 172:
265-7 Ap 16 '71; Discussion. 173:576+ Ag
13 '71
Greetings from Los Angeles. I. J. Winn. il
Natur Hist 80:12-14+ bibliog(p 108) O '71
Lethal blanket: Los Angeles smog. Nation
213:388-9 O 25 '71
NOx is the next pollutant to go. Bsns W
p 108+ Mr 6 '71

Airports
High cost of noise; removing the people. il
Newsweek 78:55 Ag 2 '71
Los Angeles builds separate helicopter fa-
cility; Van Nuys municipal airport. J.
Purko. il Am City 86:97 Je '71
New L.A. airport development slowed. Avia-
tion W 95:23 Jl 26 '71
Traffic growth, noise wrack Los Angeles air-
port planning. R. R. Ropelewski. il Avia-
tion W 95:74-5+ N 15 '71

Architecture
Los Angeles, by R. Banham. Review
Newsweek il 78:82 Ag 23 '71. D. Davis
Los Angeles the architecture of four ecolo-
gies, by R. Banham. Review
Arch Forum il 135:10+ N '71. J. S. Mar-
golies

Art
Los Angeles. M. Leopold. Art N 69:12 F;
70:14 Mr '71
Los Angeles. J. Livingston. il Art in Am
59:114-17 My '71
Los Angeles, 1971. E. C. Baker. il Art N
70:27-39 S '71
Onward and upward with the arts; exhibition: the Cubist epoch at the County museum of art. F. Steegmuller. New Yorker
46:70-5 Ja 23 '71
View from the Coast. il Time 97:58-9 F 1 '71

LOS ANGELES—*Continued*

Buildings
Office glut hits Los Angeles. il Bsns W p43 S 11 '71

Churches
Church losses: in the wake of the quake. Chr Today 15:44+ Mr 12 '71

Description
Businessman's guide to Los Angeles. Bsns W p81 D 11 '71

Earthquake, 1971
After the quake: the psychic tremors still shake people up. S. O'Quin. il Todays Health 49:20-2+ My '71
Aftershock; children emotionally traumatized. il Newsweek 77:76 Mr 8 '71
California tallies an earthquake's cost. il Bsns W p24 F 13 '71
California's quake disaster, and a look at the future; with interview with C. F. Richter. il U S News 70:34-6 F 22 '71
Church losses: in the wake of the quake. Chr Today 15:44+ Mr 12 '71
Close look at the quake's toll. il U S News 70:44 Mr 1 '71
Earthquake in L.A: damage and a lesson. il Library J 96:906-7 Mr 15 '71
Earthquake jitters. il Time 97:59 Mr 8 '71
Forewarned. Sci Am 224:48-9 Ap '71
Important lessons learned from the big California earthquake. Good H 172:171 Je '71
Lessons from the quake. Sci N 99:211-12 Mr 27 '71
Los Angeles: when the earth quaked. il Newsweek 77:19-23 F 22 '71
No news was bad news: continuous information about Los Angeles earthquake from KNBC only. P. Hudson. Sr Schol 98:22 Mr 15 '71
Quaking earth: what's the fault? San Andreas fault. il Sr Schol 98:14-16 Mr 1 '71
San Fernando earthquake of 9 February 1971: pattern of faulting. D. F. Palmer and T. L. Henyey. il Science 172:712-15 My 14 '71
San Fernando earthquake study: NRC panel sees premonitory lessons. R. Gillette and J. Walsh. Science 172:140-3 Ap 9 '71
Science has no remedy. il Sci N 99:126-7 F 20 '71
Terror in Los Angeles. il Time 97:20-2 F 22 '71
Veteran California librarians on Los Angeles quake. il Am Lib 2:227 Mr '71

Economic conditions
Watts report: no progress. il Bsns W p70+ Ag 14 '71

Galleries and museums
Herculaneum at Malibu; J. Paul Getty's new museum. E. Hotaling il Art N 70:40-3+ S '71

Harbor
Rebirth of a harbor. il Newsweek 77:88 Ap 26 '71

Hotels, restaurants, etc.
Health is busting out all over; health-food restaurants. Vogue 157:57+ F 1 '71

Industries
Watts report: no progress. il Bsns W p70+ Ag 14 '71

Libraries
Earthquake in L.A: damage and a lesson. il Library J 96:906-7 Mr 15 '71
Veteran California librarians on Los Angeles quake. il Am Lib 2:227 Mr '71
See also
Los Angeles public library

Music
Behind the scenes. K. Monson. Hi Fi 21:22 S '71
Mini-marathon at Hollywood bowl; J. S. Bach, Mozart, and Ives. K. Monson. Hi Fi 21:MA26 D '71
See also
Los Angeles philharmonic orchestra

Parks and playgrounds
Giant mountain park for Los Angeles? il Sunset 146:60-3 F '71

Police
Chief; E. M. Davis. por Newsweek 77:31-2 Ap 26 '71
Hard-liner; federal grand jury indictments. por Newsweek 77:37 Mr 15 '71

Police department
Authors & editors; interview, ed. by J. Weisman. J. Wambaugh. por Pub W 200: 33-5 Ag 23 '71
Training police sergeants in early warning signs of emotional upset. R. J. Sokol and M. Reiser. bibliog Ment Hy 55:303-7 Jl '71

Public health
Firemen paramedics. A. Hamilton. il Sci Digest 70:18-21 Ag '71

Public library
See Los Angeles public library

Publishers and publishing
See Publishers and publishing—California

Recreation and parks, Department of
New boy's baseball policy for Los Angeles. J. C. Barr. il Parks & Rec 6:35+ Je '71
Now if the Frederickson revolt would only spread; reprint. Parks & Rec 6:17 Ja '71

Riots
Chicanos besieged: the bloody fiesta. D. F. Gomez. il Nation 212:326-8 Mr 15 '71
Machismo riot. il Newsweek 77:34 F 15 '71

Strikes
See also
Strikes—United States—Teachers

Theater
Off Broadway; the James Joyce memorial liquid theatre performed at the Guggenheim museum by the Company theatre. E. Oliver. New Yorker 47:101-2 O 16 '71
Up from Othello in Los Angeles; Centre theatre group. W. I. Scobie. Nat R 23:714-15 Je 29 '71

Transportation
Wayward ways of Watts bus lines. il Bsns W p40 S 25 '71

LOS ANGELES COUNTY, Calif.

Coroners office
Inside Los Angeles: the coroner's report; T. T. Noguchi. M. Boas il por Ramp Mag 10:30-5 Jl '71

LOS ANGELES COUNTY public library
Aftershocks in L.A: film censorship case. Library J 96:1185 Ap 1 '71
Film collection attacked in Los Angeles County. Library J 96:771-2 Mr 1 '71; Reply. R. C. Goodwell. 96:1896-7 Je 1 '71
Los Angeles County PL beset on two sides. W. R. Eshelman. Wilson Lib Bul 45:816 My '71

LOS ANGELES International airport. See Los Angeles—Airports

LOS ANGELES Lakers (basketball team) See Basketball teams

LOS ANGELES music festival. See Music festivals—California

LOS ANGELES philharmonic orchestra
Politics at the Philharmonic: selections by audience vote. Time 98:81 N 1 '71

LOS ANGELES public library
LAPL racism workshop reaction to SLJ feature; excerpts from report on the institute sent to SLJ by B. Tate. Library J 96:1752+ My 15 '71
Library services well-suited to automation. A. Sklar. il Am City 86:79 D '71

Branches
Creative writing: the inner eye; publication of Lincoln Heights branch. J. L. Buelna. il Wilson Lib Bul 45:750-3 Ap '71

LOS ANGELES Rams (football club) See Football clubs

LOS ANGELES times
Chandler's change of heart. Time 97:46 Je 28 '71
Heir apparent; R. J. Donovan. Newsweek 78: 74 S 6 '71
Magic million. Newsweek 77:64 Je 14 '71
New edition in Los Angeles. Bsns W p27 N 20 '71

LOSERS; opera. See Farberman, H.

LOSEY, Joseph
Current cinema. P. Gilliatt. New Yorker 47: 55-7 Jl 31 '71 *
Losey situation. Sat R 54:42 Ag 14 '71 *
Two by Losey. il por Time 98:63-4 Ag 9 '71 *

LOS GATOS, Calif.
With useful land but little money, with energy and 14 weekend days; park construction. il Sunset 147:68-9 S '71

LOSING. See Failure (psychology)

LOSS of memory is only temporary; story. See Kaplan. J.

LOST angel; story. See Goudge. E.

LOST children. See Missing persons

LOST cities. See Cities and towns, Ruined, extinct, etc.

LOST continent. See Atlantis

LOST persons. See Missing persons

LOT, Choice by. See Choice by lot

LOTHROP, Harriet Mulford (Stone)
Margaret Sidney vs. Harriet Lothrop; address, October 8, 1970. E. Johnson. bibliog Horn Bk 47:139-46 Ap; 313-20 Je '71

LOTT, John A. and Grümmer, H.-D.
Clinical chemistry laboratory. il por Chem 44:6-9 Je '71

LOTTERIES
About Reader's digest sweepstakes. Read Digest 98:151-2 Mr '71
Legalized gambling: is it a good bet? I. Ross. Read Digest 99:94-8 N '71
Lottery fever is highly contagious; New Jersey. il Bsns W p45 Mr 13 '71
Numbers game; state lotteries. il Newsweek 78:18 S 13 '71
When states turn to lotteries to hold down taxes. il U S News 70:37-9 My 24 '71

LOTTERY, Draft. See Military service, Compulsory

LOTTMAN, Eileen
Ads in paperbacks; are they necessary? Pub W 200:14-16 N 1 '71

LOTTMAN, Herbert R.
European scene. See issues of Publishers' weekly
(tr) See Singer, I. B. Cabalist of East Broadway

LOTUS
Patio lotus. J. Lambeth. il Horticulture 49: 30-1 Jl '71

LOTUS (sports car) See Sports cars

LOTUS; story. See Buchan, P.

LOTZ, Kurt
Sturm und drang at VW. Newsweek 78:89 S 13 '71 *
Troubled giant. por Time 98:86-7 S 27 '71 *
VW drops the driver. il Bsns W p34 S 18 '71 *

LOUCYE Gordy Wakefield scholarship
Sterling ball funds ghetto scholarships. il Ebony 26:72-4+ Jl '71

LOUD speaking apparatus
Case for the single woofer. D. B. Weems. il Pop Electr 34:33-5+ My '71
Choosing a speaker system. J. G. Holt. il Pop Electr 35:66-8 D '71
Colossal woofer. D. B. Weems. il Pop Electr 34:47-53 Je '71
Electrostat that isn't; tweeters. I. Berger. il Sat R 54:76 Mr 27 '71
Get the most from your speakers; questions and answers. R. Allison. Hi Fi 21:48-50 Je '71
Hi-fi speakers for reverberant sound. D. Davis. il Electr World 85:30-1+ Ap '71
Pipe speaker system; use with electronic organs and similar instruments. J. R. Smith. il Electr World 86:24-6 D '71
Portable sound systems for performers. D. L. Patten. il Electr World 86:38-40 S '71
Speakers for PA. B. Raventos. il Radio-Electr 42:52-4 My '71
Wire your patio for sound. H. Fantel. il Pop Mech 136:142-5 Ag '71

Cabinets
Continental speaker system. D. B. Weems. il Pop Electr 35:41-7 Ag '71
Labyrinth speakers for hi-fi. D. B. Weems. il Pop Electr 1:40-5 Ja '72

Testing
Hi-fi product report:
Acoustic research AR-6 speaker. il Electr World 85:12+ Ap '71
Kenwood KL-5060 speaker system. il Electr World 85:12-13 F '71
Wharfedale W-35 speaker system. il Electr World 86:9-10 S '71
How to use our test reports in selecting a speaker. L. Feldman. il Hi Fi 21:36-42 Je '71

LOUDON, Harry
Nice story about boxing. J. Lebow. il pors Look 35:64-7 Ag 24 '71 *

LOUIS XI, king of France
Louis XI, by P. M. Kendall. Review
Newsweek il 77:90+ F 8 '71. P. S. Prescott *

LOUIS XVII, of France
Lost dauphin of France. C. H. Fawcett. Hobbies 76:45+ Ag '71 *

LOUIS, Arthur M.
It's Moody versus Moody in the struggle for American national. il por Fortune 83:108-12+ Mr '71
Labor can make or break the stabilization program. il Fortune 84:140-3+ N '71
Ross Perot moves in on Wall Street. il por Fortune 84:90-3+ Jl '71

LOUIS, Murray
Nikolais and Louis: a new space. T. Tobias. il pors Dance Mag 45:46-54 F '71 *

LOUIS, Victor
Russia's conspicuous consumer. J. Axelbank. il por Newsweek 78:38 Jl 12 '71 *
Tale of two travelers. il pors Newsweek 78: 37-8 Jl 12 '71 *
Would you buy a used manuscript from this man? H. Gold. il por N Y Times Mag p 12-13+ Ja 31 '71 *

LOUIS-Nikolais dance theater lab. See Dance institutes and workshops

LOUISE; opera. See Charpentier, G.

LOUISELL, David W.
Rationales for feticide. Cath World 212:318-19 Mr '71

LOUISIANA
See also
Architecture, Domestic—Louisiana
Fishing—Louisiana
Gardens—Louisiana
Music festivals—Louisiana
Negro schools—Louisiana

Antiquities
Mysterious mounds at Poverty Point. F. Folsom. il Sci Digest 69:46-8+ F '71

LOUISIANA state university, Baton Rouge
Gumbo in the soup; yearbook. il Newsweek 77:77 Je 14 '71

LOUISIANA superdome. See Stadiums

LOUISVILLE
Education
How Louisville put it all together. S. Moorefield. il Am Ed 7:30-4 D '71

Housing
Towns for the urban and rural poor. S. Lawson. Cur 125:35-41 Ja '71

Music
See also
Kentucky opera association

Streets
Systems approach to street sweeping. E. D. Alston. il Am City 86:91-2+ N '71

LOUNGES (rooms)
See also
Student lounges

LOURDES, France
Miracles at Lourdes? il Newsweek 78:48-9 Ag 9 '71

LOUSE. See Lice

LOUVIERE, Vernon
Panorama of the nation's business. See issues of Nation's business

LOUVRE, Paris
France's palace of the arts. H. L. Cooke, jr. il Nat Geog 139:796-831 Je '71
Letter from Paris; Ingres's Le Bain Turc at the Pavillon de flore. Genét. New Yorker 47:130 My 15 '71

LOVE, Bob
Cinderellas of the superstars. L. J. Banks. il pors Ebony 27:70-3 Ja '72 *

LOVE, Iris Cornelia
American good looks. por Vogue 157:169 F 1 '71
about
Archeological find named Iris Love. E. Stevens. il pors N Y Times Mag p32-4+ Mr 7 '71; Discussion. p 16+ Ap 4 '71 *
When Love came to Cnidus. Cyclops. il Life 70:18 Je 11 '71 *

LOVE
Fighting words: American women are lousy lovers. S. Rattazzi. Vogue 158:91+ Jl '71
How a baby learns to love. S. Fraiberg. il Redbook 137:76+ My '71
Love, by R. Haughton. Review
Cath World 213:100-1 My '71. F.N. Julien
Many faces of love. D. A. Sugarman and R. Hochstein. il Seventeen 29:112-13+ D '70
Teaching lovingness to children. B. Spock. il Redbook 137:26+ Jl '71
Therapist and theologian look at love. V. C. Grounds. Chr Today 15:14-16 Ag 6 '71
Will liberalized sex kill romantic love? J. Brothers. il Good H 172:62+ Je '71

LOVE—*Continued*
Youngsters' need to love; with study-discussion program, by M. M. Conant. S. F. Ward. bibliog il PTA Mag 66:12-14. 33 D '71
See also
Courtship
Jealousy
Marriage
LOVE (theology)
Church needs Christian lovers, not oedipal boys; ordination sermon. G. A. Benson. Chr Cent 88:101-4 Ja 27 '71
Large order; demands of Christian love. V. P. McCorry. America 124:188-inside back cover F 20 '71
LOVE, Maternal
Awesome power of human love; excerpt from The humanization of man. A. Montagu. Read Digest 99:103-5 Jl '71
See Spot and his monkey mother. il Life 70:71-2 Ap 16 '71
Take time out for love. M. T. Graham. il Parents Mag 46:42-3 Jl '71
Understanding baby talk. W. Petschek. il Mc-Calls 98:46 S '71
What makes a super-mother? Selfishness. J. Poppy. il pors Look 35:20-7+ Ag 24 '71
LOVE as she is spoken; story. See Ibbotson, E.
LOVE: first lessons; story. See Updike, J.
LOVE in literature
Fiction technique & style: some comparisons. D. Madden. il Writers Digest 51:24-6+ Ag '71
Love story; runaway hit; why? M. Cousins. il Vogue 157:130-2+ Mr 1 '71
LOVE is catching; story. See McGinnis, L. S.
LOVE is the most fun you can have in the world without laughing; story. See Aguallo, F.
LOVE me, love my children; musical comedy. See Musical comedies, revues, etc.—Criticisms, plots, etc.
LOVE potions. See Aphrodisiacs
LOVE story; story. See Kotzwinkle, W.
LOVE triangle; story. See Posner, R.
LOVELACE, Richard
Shape of the coming renewal. il Chr Cent 88:1164-7 O 6 '71
LOVELADY, Steve
Design for learning. il Todays Ed 60:54-6 F '71
LOVELL, James A. 1928-
Astronauts on the make. K. Northcott. Ramp Mag 10:12-13 N '71 *
LOVELY ladies, kind gentlemen; musical comedy. See Musical comedies, revues, etc.—Criticisms, plots, etc.
LOVERS; opera. See Barber, S.
LOVE'S seasoning; story. See McKimmey, J.
LOVING, Rush, Jr
Guarded optimism at the top. il Fortune 83:168-9+ My '71
How Kennecott got hooked with Catch-22. il Fortune 84:98-101+ S '71
LOW, Abraham Adolf
Recovery, inc: aid in the transition from hospital to community. D. T. Lee. bibliog Ment Hy 55:194-8 Ap '71 *
LOW, Jacqueline
Music to the gourmet's ears. Puget Sound. il Holiday 49:70-1+ Ap '71
LOW, Malcolm
Ah, freedom! Forbes 108:36+ Jl 15 '71 *
LOW cholesterol diet. See Diet
LOW cost housing. See Housing
LOW fat diet. See Diet
LOW temperature physics. See Low temperatures
LOW temperatures
Experiments in cryogenics. E. A. Arrigoni. bibliog il por Chem 44:23-6 O '71
Isaac Asimov explains; low temperature of space. I. Asimov. Sci Digest 69:76-7 F '71
Physics at low temperatures; symposium. bibliog il Phys Today 24:23-8+ Ag '71
See also
Superfluidity
LOWE, C. Marshall
Psychology of social control. bibliog Ment Hy 55:124-9 Ja '71
LOWELL, C. Stanley
Will churches give up their colleges? Ed Digest 37:24-5 O '71
LOWELL, Frederick K.
Segregation comes to Columbia. Nat R 23:1236 N 5 '71
LOWELL, Robert
Comment. W. H. Pritchard. Poetry 119:166-9 D '71 *
Reading Robert Lowell. D. Bromwich. Commentary 52:78-83 Ag '71 *

LOWENBERG, William, Jr
He maps the way to success. il pors Har Yrs 11:36-9 D '71
LÖWENBRAU brewery. See Breweries
LOWENFELS, Walter
On reading the Journal of geophysical research; poem. Nation 212:542 Ap 26 '71
LOWENHEIM, Francis L.
FDR library inquiry scores serious lapses. Library J 96:580 F 15 '71 *
LOWENS, Irving
Opera and sonic collage. il Américas 23:10-14 Ag '71
LOWENSTAM, Heinz A.
Opal precipitation by marine gastropods (mollusca) bibliog il Science 171:487-90 F 5 '71
LOWENSTEIN, Allard Kenneth
Dump Nixon campaign. Look 35:80 Je 1 '71
about
Critics of Richard Nixon. W. F. Buckley, jr. Nat R 23:496-7 My 4 '71 *
Man to watch. por Newsweek 78:21-2 Ag 23 '71 *
LOWENSTEIN, Jack G.
Steins and other drinking vessels pictured on stamps. il Hobbies 76:89-92 Jl '71
LOWENSTEIN, John, and Tornheim, Keith
Ammonia production in muscle: the purine nucleotide cycle. bibliog il Science 171:397-400 Ja 29 '71
LOWENTHAL, Helen
Healthy anger. bibliog il Library J 96:2597-9 S 1 '71
LOWENTHAL, Max
Obituary
Nation 212:741 Je 14 '71
LOWENTHAL, Richard
Return of Stalin's mustache on a higher level. il N Y Times Mag p26-7+ Mr 28 '71
Russia and China: controlled conflict. For Affairs 49:507-18 Ap '71
LOWER, Earl. See Baller, W. jt. auth.
LOWER CALIFORNIA. See California, Lower
LOWERY, David
Back to basics. il Flying 90:50-1+ Ja '72
LOWESTOFT ware, Oriental. See Pottery, Chinese
LOWINSKY, Edward Elias
New York: a week of Josquin. S. T. Sommer. il Hi Fi 21:MA14-15 O '71 *
LOWREY, Anna Mary. See Case, R. N. jt. auth.
LOWRY, Judith
Go granny go! il pors Life 71:83-4 O 8 '71 *
LOWY, D. R. and others
Murine leukemia virus: high-frequency activation in vitro by 5-iododeoxyuridine and 5-bromodeoxyuridine. bibliog il Science 174:155-6 O 8 '71
LOY, Myrna
Quartet of queens. J. Barthel. il pors Life 70:66+ F 19 '71 *
LOYAL order of Moose. See Moose, Loyal order of
LOYALTY, Oaths of
In my opinion; we should abolish the Pledge of allegiance! M. Berg. Seventeen 30:62 S '71
To the flag; with reminiscence by F. Russell. N. Brandt. il Am Heritage 22:72-5+ Je '71
LOYD, F. Glen
Food stamp pirates take their cut. il Todays Health 49:23-4+ Ap '71
Lady of the mountain. il por Todays Health 49:37 F '71
Today's health news. Todays Health 49:7-8 Jl; 7-8 Ag '71
LOYD, Sam
Advertising premiums to beguile the mind; classics by Sam Loyd, master puzzle-poser. M. Gardner. il Sci Am 225:114-16+ N '71 *
LOYOLA, Ignatius of, Saint
Ignatius Loyola: a soldier-saint? T. H. Clancy. America 125:317-18 O 23 '71 *
LUBBOCK, Michael R.
Canada looks southward. il Américas 23:2-8 Ja '71
LUBBOCK Christian college, Lubbock, Tex.
General and the Christian college: where was the dissent? D. M. Lynch. Chr Cent 88:724-6 Je 9 '71
LUBECK, Robert A.
Leader of the band. il pors Outdoor Life 147:72-3+ Mr '71
LUBELL, Samuel
18-year-old vote could beat Nixon in '72. il Look 35:64+ Jl 13 '71
LUBETZKY, Seymour
1976 minus 6...5... il por Library J 96:450-1 F 1 '71

LUBIN, A. Harold, and others
Sex and population differences in the incidence of a plasma cholinesterase variant. bibliog il Science 173:161-4 Jl 9 '71
LUBIN, Maurice A.
First letter from the New World. il Américas 23:2-12 Ap '71
LUBIN, Moshe J. and Fraas, A. P.
Fusion by laser; with biographical sketches. il Sci Am 224:16, 21-33 Je '71
LUBKA, Nancy
Day care centers: our top child-health priority. il Parents Mag 46:64-5+ N '71
LUBKIN, Gloria B.
Women in physics. il por Phys Today 24:23-7 Ap '71
LUBOLD, Joyce Kissock
It pays to increase your worry power. Read Digest 98:116-18 F '71
LUBOVITCH, Lar
Dance. N. Goldner. Nation 213::635-6 D 13 '71 *
Energetic angels; productions at Stage city. W. Terry. il Sat R 54:18 D 11 '71 *
Lar Lubovitch and company, N.Y. Shakespeare festival public theater. D. Hering. Dance Mag 45:76 Jl '71 *
LUBRICANTS. See Lubrication and lubricants
LUBRICATION and lubricants
Consumer's guide to motor oils. il Mech Illus 67:82 Ap '71
Guide to household lubrication. il Bet Hom & Gard 49:110-11 My '71
New super oils for your car. R. Potter. il por Pop Sci 198:45-7 Je '71
Under the hood. F. W. Miller. bibliog il por Chem 44:12-14 Je '71
What the new oil-can markings mean. D. L. Gregg. Bet Hom & Gard 49:96 Je '71
See also
Automobiles—Lubrication
Motor boats—Lubrication

Additives
Additive mystique. E. Nabb. il Motor B & S 127:98+ F '71
Racer's sludge; questioning the value of STP. il por Time 98:106 N 1 '71
STP: does your car really need it? Consumer Rep 36:422 Jl '71
LUBRIZOL corporation
When there's no reason to diversify. il Bsns W p38-9 Jl 31 '71
LUCAL, John A.
United Nations and the Holy See. il America 123:315-17; 124:179-80 O 24 '70, F 20 '71
LUCAS, Christopher
Macao: city of money and mystery. il Read Digest 98:127-31 F '71
LUCAS, George
Man of the future. il por Newsweek 77:50+ My 31 '71
LUCAS, Kay
Lament for the camphor tree. il Am For 77: 34-6 Ap '71
LUCCHESI, Bruno
Sculpture of Bruno Lucchesi. M. Malmstrom. il por Am Artist 35:32-4+ O '71 *
LUCE, Clare (Boothe)
Abortion: the Catholic presentation. America 124:62 Ja 23 '71 *
Clare Boothe Luce, by S. Shadegg. Review Nat R il 23:660-2 Je 15 '71. E. McDowell *
Where are they now? pors Newsweek 78:10 Ag 16 '71 *
LUCE, Don
Amer-Asian children in Vietnam. Chr Cent 88:996-7 Ag 25 '71
about
Let politics live in Vietnam. Chr Cent 88: 711 Je 9 '71 *
LUCE, Gay Gaer
Biological clocks; adapted from Biological rhythms in psychiatry and medicine. il Todays Ed 60:40-2+ O '71
Body time; excerpt (title varies) Vogue 158: 156-7+ N 1; 132-3+ N 15 '71
—and Peper, Erik
Mind over body, mind over mind. il N Y Times Mag p34-5+ S 12 '71
LUCE, Henry Robinson
Harry Luce and the Russian century. J. Chamberlain. Nat R 23:524-5+ My 18 '71 *
Lunches with Luce. G. Holland. por Atlan 227:54-6+ My '71 *
LUCE, Robert J.
Model cities community information center. Am Lib 2:206-7 F '71
LUCIA di Lammermoor; opera. See Donizetti, G.
LUCIANO, Dale
(ed) See Lumet, S. Long day's journey into night

LUCIENTES, Francisco José de Goya y. See Goya y Lucientes, F. J. de
LUCINA, Sister Mary. See Mary Lucina, Sister
LUCIONI, Luigi
Individual realist: Luigi Lucioni. R. Fabri. il por Am Artist 35:26-31+ O '71 *
LUCKEN, Dorothy. See Rudoff, A. jt. auth.
LUCKY breweries, inc.
Brewer goes on the austerity wagon. il por Bsns W p37-8 N 6 '71
LUCRETIUS
Atomic theory in the ancient world. il Chem 44:17-18 Ap '71 *
LUDLUM, David M.
Snowfall season of 1969-1970. il Weatherwise 24:18-23+ F '71
LUDVIGSEN, Karl E.
Lear: the steam king? il pors Motor T 23: 30-2+ F '71
(ed) See Amon, C. A. Chris Amon on Can-Am
LUDWIG, Christa
Singer's choice. Hi Fi 21:27 Jl '71
about
Music to my ears: performance in Beethoven's Fidelio. I. Kolodin. Sat R 54:24 Mr 13 '71 *
LUDWIG, Daniel K.
D. K. Ludwig plans to harvest a jungle. il por Bsns W p34 Jl 31 '71 *
LUDWIG, Leopold
Self-made maestro; interview, ed. by C. J. Luten. il por Opera N 35:27 Ap 3 '71
LUECKE, Richard Henry
Urban training, English style. Chr Cent 88:1348-51 N 17 '71
LUEHRS, Armin F.
Organized camping looks to 1971. por Camp Mag 43:4 Mr '71
LUFF, Christopher. See Norris, L. jt. auth.
LUFTHANSA. See Airlines—Germany (Federal Republic)
LUGAR, Richard G.
Self-help and the cities. il pors Nations Bsns 59:22-6 Je '71 *
LUGGAGE
Molded luggage. il Consumer Rep 36:137-42 Mr '71
Unconventional piece of luggage: Permatic suitcase. il Consumer Rep 36:464 Ag '71
What to wear where, and how to carry it. Holiday 49:103 F '71
See also
Knapsacks
Packing of luggage
LUGGAGE handling, Airline. See Airlines—Luggage handling
LUHAN, Mabel Dodge
Taos remembered. H. Fergusson. il pors Am West 8:38-41 S '71 *
LUIS, Earlene
How not to teach English in high school. Ed Digest 36:32-3 Ja '71
LUISA Miller; opera. See Verdi, G.
LUJÁN MUÑOZ, Jorge
Persistence of smalltown saints. il Américas 23:10-15 My '71
LUKÁCS, György
George Lukács, by G. Lichtheim. Review Commentary 52:72-7 Jl '71. N. Birnbaum *
Pure essence of totalitarianism. T. Szamuely. il Nat R 23:595-6 Je 1 '71 *
Quest for Christa T, by C. Wolf. Review Sat R 54:31-2 My 8 '71. P. Moscoso-Góngora *
LUKACS, John Adalbert
America may be in its last phase of adolescence. il N Y Times Mag p48+ D 5 '71
LUKAS, J. Anthony
After the Pentagon papers, a month in the new life of Daniel Ellsberg. il por N Y Times Mag p29+ D 12 '71
As American as a McDonald's hamburger on the Fourth of July. il N Y Times Mag p4-5+ Jl 4 '71; Same abr. with title America's hamburger king. Read Digest 99:137-41 O '71
Bad day at Cairo, Ill. il N Y Times Mag p22-3+ F 21 '71
Bobby Seale's birthday cake. il por N Y Times Mag p42+ O 31 '71
Council on foreign relations, is it a club? Seminar? Presidium? Invisible government? il N Y Times Mag p34-5+ N 21 '71'
How Mel Allen started a lifelong love affair. il N Y Times Mag p38-9+ S 12 '71
Plaint of the Virgin Islands: we have been encroached on, invaded, engulfed. il N Y Times Mag p30-1+ Ap 18 '71
Roy. il pors Esquire 75:122-6+ Mr '71

LUNAR photography. See Space photography
LUNAR receiving laboratory. See United States
—Manned spacecraft center—Lunar receiving laboratory
LUNAR research. See Moon
LUNAR rocks
  Analysis
    See Lunar geology
LUNAR roving vehicle. See Lunar vehicles
LUNAR science conference. See Moon—Conferences
LUNAR seismology. See Seismology
LUNAR vehicles
  Apollo 15's moon buggy. G. Alexander. il Newsweek 77:92 My 17 '71
  Data bonus expected from Lunokhod 1. il Aviation W 94:15 Ja 18 '71
  Driving a go-cart on the moon. R. Gannon. il pors Pop Sci 198:70-2+ Ja '71
  First manned rover on moon. Z. Strickland. il Aviation W 95:13-17 Ag 9 '71
  Golf cart to cruise on the moon; Lunar roving vehicle. il Life 70:70-4 Je 11 '71
  Letter from the space center; Apollo 15 Lunar roving vehicle, or moon car. H. S. F. Cooper, jr. New Yorker 47:40-2+ Jl 17 '71
  Lunar rover and its navigation system. il Space World H-7-91:44-5 Jl '71
  Lunar rover program spurred. R. G. O'Lone. il Aviation W 94:49-51 F 15 '71
  Lunar roving vehicle. il Space World H-12-96:12-25 D '71
  Lunar roving vehicle. R. N. Watts, jr. il Sky & Tel 42:14-15 Jl '71
  Lunokhod finishes lunar mission; Soviets plan redesigned vehicle. Aviation W 94:16 Mr 1 '71
  Lunokhod 1, thirty-five days of work on the moon. Space World H-5-89:35-9 My '71
  Moon mobile debut on Apollo 15. E. Driscoll. il Sci N 99:404-5 Je 12 '71
  Moon: traveling on wheels. Y. Marinin. il Space World H-4-88:25-7 Ap '71
  Planet rovers of the future. V. Golovachov. Space World H-6-90:45-6 Je '71
  Rover revs up for a moon ride. il Bsns W p73 Ja 16 '71
  Roving the moon. il Time 98:44+ Jl 26 '71
  Something new this time: a dune buggy. il U S News 71:20 Ag 2 '71
  Soviet lunar rover; Lunokhod. R. N. Watts, jr. il Sky & Tel 41:155-7 Mr '71
  Soviet self-propelled lunar space chariot; interview, ed. by Boris Koltovoi. Space World H-4-88:34-6 Ap '71
  Unmanned lunar rovers planned by Soviets for nonstop operation. il Aviation W 94:23 Ja 25 '71
  We ride the moon car! B. Wennerstrom. il Mech Illus 67:37-8+ Ag '71
  We're going motoring on the moon. W. Von Braun. il Pop Sci 199:50-3+ Jl '71

  Cost
  Lunar rovers cost $38.1 million. Aviation W 95:18 Ag 2 '71
  Design
  Lunar rover ready for moon drive. Z. Strickland. il Aviation W 94:42-5 My 24 '71
  Lunokhod, Venus 7 features disclosed. il Aviation W 94:22-3 F 22 '71
  Testing
  Lunar roving vehicle tested with LM. il Aviation W 94:20-1 Mr 22 '71
  Tires
    See Tires, Rubber
LUNCHEONS
    See also
  Brunches
LUNCHES
  Dieter's news; with recipes. il Seventeen 29:166-7+ S '70
  Hi, mom, what's for lunch? R. M. Fabio; J. Morales. See issues of Parents' magazine & better family living
    See also
  School lunches
LUNCHES, School. See School lunches
LUNCHROOMS, Roadside
  Parting shots: Life's great diners. il Life 70:68-72 Ap 30 '71
LUND, Arline
  Teaching migrant children. Todays Ed 60:49-51 O '71
LUND, Doris Herold
  Little privacy is a lovely thing. il Parents Mag 46:40-1+ Je '71
LUND, Jennifer S. See Lund, R. D. jt. auth.

LUND, R. D. and Lund, J. S.
  Synaptic adjustment after deafferentation of the superior colliculus of the rat. bibliog il Science 171:804-7 F 26 '71
LUND, Robert
  Detroit listening post. See issues of Popular mechanic
  What ever happened to air bags? il Pop Mech 135:63-5+ F '71
LUNDBLAD, Bonnie Jo
  Rebel-victim: past and present. Engl J 60:763-6 S '71
LUNDQUIST, Robert
  In the soft cheek of clay; poem. Nation 213:345 O 11 '71
LUNG adenomas. See Tumors
LUNG cancer. See Cancer
LUNGS
  Cigarette smoking: objective evidence for lung damage in teen-agers. J. E. Seely and others. bibliog il Science 172:741-3 My 14 '71
  Diseases
  Pulmonary compliance: alteration during infection. N. L. Somerson and others. bibliog il Science 171:66-8 Ja 8 '71
    See also
  Pneumonia
  Tuberculosis
  Dust diseases
  Asbestos, useful but deadly. il Sci Digest 69:16-17 Je '71
  Black lung: dispute about diagnosis of miners' ailment. J. Pichirallo. Science 174:132-4 O 8 '71
  Cotton-mill killer. R. Nader. Nation 212:335-7 Mr 15 '71
  Department of amplification: relationship between asbestos, lung cancer and mesothelioma. P. Brodeur. New Yorker 47:147-51+ O 23 '71
  Dusty death in Kentucky; black-lung runaround. D. Holwerk. il Nation 211:657-9 D 21 '70
  Hidden dangers in the air we breathe. Consumer Bul 54:29-30 S '71
  Miner's plight; black lung. Sci N 100:141 Ag 28 '71
  Public meanness; suit to eliminate X-ray as test of black lung. Nation 213:261 S 27 '71
  Subverting the black lung law. J. DeMuth. America 125:530-2 D 18 '71
  Technology; danger of asbestos. M. Villecco. il Arch Forum 133:50-2 D '70
  Transplantation
  Barnard touch; heart and lungs given to A. Herbert. por Newsweek 78:62-3 Ag 9 '71
  Barnard's bullet; heart and lungs given to A. Herbert. por Time 98:37 Ag 9 '71
  Spectacular that failed; heart-lung recipient Adrian Herbert. Time 98:46 Ag 30 '71
LUNGWORMS
  Animal health: lungworms still a problem for hogmen. il Suc Farm 69:H14 Ag '71
LUNN, Sir Arnold
  Humbug for beginners. Nat R 23:1292 N 19 '71
LUNOKHOD (moon vehicle) See Lunar vehicles
LUNS, Joseph Marie Antoine Hubert
  Diplomat in stocking feet. por Time 97:37 Je 14 '71 *
LUOSSAVAARA-Kiirunavaara AB. See Iron mines and mining—Sweden
LUPINES
  Lupins. A. V. Pike. il Horticulture 49:39+ My '71
LUPOFF, Dick
  Music. Ramp Mag 10:61 S '71
  Records. il Ramp Mag 10:65-6 O; 67-8 N; 63-5 D '71; 64-6 Ja '72
LUPTON, James C.
  Simple chip log. il Motor B & S 128:86-7 Jl '71
LURIE, Abraham, and Ron, Harold
  Self-help in an aftercare socialization program. bibliog il Ment Hy 55:467-72 O '71
LURIE, Diane
  (ed) See Ford, M. C. V. A. Sunshine days of Cristina Ford
LURIE, Morris
  Cardplayers; story. New Yorker 47:35-6 D 18 '71
LURIE, Sidney B.
  Market outlook. See issues of Forbes
LUSCHER, Charles W.
  Attitudes toward conservation in the Soviet Union. il Liv Wildn 34:13-19 Aut '70
LUSCOMB, Florence
  Miss Luscomb takes a stand. por Time 97:20 Ap 26 '71 *

LUSKER, Ronald
Jewelry of Marci Zelmanoff. il Craft Horiz 31:16-19 F '71
LUSTED, Lee Browning
Signal detectability and medical decision-making. bibliog il Science 171:1217-19 Mr 26 '71
LUTE
Musical events; second recital in series: A renaissance of lute song in Alice Tully Hall. W. Sargeant. New Yorker 47:98-9 N 27 '71
LUTEINIZING hormone. See Gonadotropins
LUTEN, C. J.
Limited edition: twenty discsful of Toscaniniana. il Am Rec G 37:744-5+ Jl '71
Mozart of the boulevards. Opera N 35:24-5 Ja 23 '71
LUTEN, Daniel B.
Economic geography of energy; with biographical sketch. il Sci Am 225:28+, 164-71+ S '71
LUTH, W. C. See Dickinson, W. R. jt. auth.
LUTHER, Martin
Luther: his life and times, by R. Friedenthal. Review
Commonweal 94:192-4 Ap 30 '71. J. Ratte •
My conscience is bound by the word of God; address, April 7, 1971. C. L. Manschreck. bibliog Vital Speeches 37:540-4 Je 15 '71 •
Young Luther. J. L. Gilmore. por Chr Today 16:3-4 O 22 '71
LUTHERAN church in America. See Lutheran church in the United States
LUTHERAN church in the United States
Cold and cruel; W. F. Wolbrecht dismissal. Chr Cent 88:1102 S 22 '71
Conservative fallout. R. Chandler. Chr Today 15:42-3 S 24 '71
Keeping the wolf from Good Shepherd's door; Wisconsin Evangelical Lutheran synod E. E. Plowman. Chr Today 15:38 My 7 '71
Last days of the late, great synod of Missouri. J. W. Montgomery. Chr Today 15:56-7 Ap 9 '71
Libertyville for Lutherans; Federation for authentic Lutheranism. Chr Today 16:41 D 3 '71
Lutheran church—Missouri synod: dynamic tensions of sect and church. J. E. Adams. Chr Cent 88:1058+ S 8 '71
Lutherans to the right; divided Missouri synod. il por Newsweek 78:64-5 Jl 12 '71
Missouri waltz: whose tunes? with editorial comment. R. Chandler. Chr Today 15:24, 31-2 Ag 6 '71
New Lutheran church born; Federation for authentic Lutheranism. Chr Cent 88:1343 N 17 '71
1971 called year of indecision. Chr Cent 88:1190 O 13 '71
Politics of piety; Lutheran church-Missouri synod convention in Milwaukee. il Time 98:42-3 Jl 26 '71
Sent to reconcile; excerpt from report to Missouri synod. J. A. O. Preus. Chr Today 15:16-18+ S 10 '71
See also
Concordia theological seminary, St Louis
LUTHERANS in the United States
Lutheran fellowship. Chr Today 15:46+ F 26 '71
Lutherans: a matching plan. Chr Today 15:44 S 10 '71
LUTOSLAWSKI, Witold
Lutoslawski comes to town. B. Murray. il por Hi Fi 21:MA24 S '71 •
LUTTERS, Valerie
Man who played with dolls; story. Mlle 73:305 Ag '71
LUTZ, Ron
(ed) Soybean management guide. il Suc Farm 69:SB3-5+ N '71
LUX, H. D.
Ammonium and chloride extrusion: hyperpolarizing synaptic inhibition in spinal motoneuron. bibliog il Science 173:555-7 Ag 6 '71
LUXEMBOURG
See also
Investments, Foreign (in Luxembourg)
LUXEMBURG, Rosa
Rosa Luxemburg. P. A. Samuelson. Newsweek 78:99 O 25 '71 •
LUZERNE COUNTY, Pa.
Microfilm improves the revenue column. T. P. Garrity. il Am City 86:92+ My '71
LUZON
Footloose on Luzon. C. Pepper. il Travel 137:40-5+ Ja '72
LY Aurigae. See Stars, Eclipsing binary
LYALIN, Oleg
How Russia spies: a new game. il por Newsweek 78:31-2+ O 11 '71 •

LYCÉES. See Education—France
LYDON, Michael
Second coming of Bo Diddley. il pors Ramp Mag 9:21-31 My '71
Soul kaleidoscope: Aretha at the Fillmore. il pors Ramp Mag 10:30-9 O '71
LYKES, June
Economy-minded Waco chooses high-strength steel. il Am City 86:58-9 My '71
LYKKEN, Louis
Chemical control of pests. bibliog il por Chem 44:18-21 Jl '71
LYMAN, Richard Wall
Escapes from freedom; address, May 22, 1971. Vital Speeches 37:757-9 O 1 '71
LYMAN LAKE state park. See Arizona—Parks and reserves
LYMPH
Ethacrynic acid effect on the composition of cochlear fluids. E. S. Cohn and others. bibliog il Science 171:910-11 Mr 5 '71
LYMPH nodes. See Lymphatic system
LYMPHATIC system
Lymph node cells: their differential capacity to induce tolerance of heart and skin homografts in rats. C. F. Barker and others. bibliog il Science 172:1050-2 Je 4 '71

Diseases

See also
Hodgkin's disease
LYMPHOCYTES
Human lymphocyte antigen reactivity modified by neuraminidase. E. A. Grothaus and others. bibliog il Science 173:542-4 Ag 6 '71
Quantitative aspects of plasma membrane-associated immunoglobulin in clones of diploid human lymphocytes. R. A. Lerner and others. bibliog il Science 173:60-2 Jl 2 '71
Specificity of allogeneic cell recognition by human lymphocytes in vitro. D. C. Zoschke and F. H. Bach. bibliog il Science 172:1350-2 Je 25 '71
Theta-bearing and complement-receptor lymphocytes are distinct populations of cells. C. Bianco and V. Nussenzweig. bibliog il Science 173:154-6 Jl 9 '71
Tumor immunity: tumor suppression in vivo initiated by soluble products of specifically stimulated lymphocytes. I. D. Bernstein and others. bibliog il Science 172:729-31 My 14 '71
LYMPHOCYTIC choriomeningitis virus. See Viruses
LYMPHOCYTIC leukemia. See Leukemia
LYMPHOID cells. See Tumor cells
LYMPHOMA cells. See Tumor cells
LYNCH, Audry
Local history: a beginner's gold mine. Writer 84:26 F '71
LYNCH, Dudley Morton
General and the Christian college: where was the dissent? Chr Cent 88:724-6 Je 9 '71
North Phoenix's corporate ministry: a question mark. Chr Cent 88:562-3+ My 5 '71
(ed) See Boone, P. Pat Boone and the charismatics
LYNCH, Gail
Untitled; poem. Mlle 73:306 Ag '71
LYNCH, John
Prime Minister of Ireland visits Washington; exchange of greetings. Dept State Bul 64:508-9 Ap 12 '71

about

Ireland's great kidnap plot. J. Horgan. Commonweal 93:439 F 5 '71 •
Master of the tightrope act. por Time 98:30 S 20 '71 •
LYNCH, John A.
Our most beautiful natives. il por Wildlife 9:21-4 Je '71
LYNCH, John Roy
Hundred years of history. G. A. Sewell. bibliog il pors Negro Hist Bul 34:78-9 Ap '71 •
LYNCH, Mary Jo
RSD and ASD: getting it all together. bibliog Am Lib 2:501-3 My '71
LYNCH, Richard J.
Molding history. il por Har Yrs 11:41-3 Ag '71
LYNCHBURG, Tenn.
Flying visit. R. L. Collins. il Flying 88:108-9 Je '71
LYND, Staughton, 1929-
Organizing the new politics: a proposal. Ramp Mag 10:14-15+ D '71
LYNDON Baines Johnson library, Austin, Tex.
In praise of a monument to Lyndon B. Johnson; with introd. by M. F. Schmertz. il Arch Rec 150:113-20 N '71
L.B.J. library. il Times 97:20 My 17 '71

LYNDON Baines Johnson library, Austin, Tex.
—*Continued*
LBJ's library sets new style. il U S News
  70:36-8 Je 7 '71
Lyndon Baines Johnson library; reprint. A.
  L. Huxtable. il Am Lib 2:669-71 Jl '71
Lyndon gets his library. N. C. Chriss. Na-
  tion 212:710-12 Je 7 '71
New monuments. R. Hughes. il Time 98:66-7
  S 13 '71
Place to put the papers, all 31 million pages
  of them. il por Life 70:50-1 My 21 '71
Remembering LBJ. il Newsweek 77:25 My 24
  '71
Welcome to the LBJ library. C. A. Johnson.
  il Read Digest 99:205-8+ Jl '71
With Cheops in Texas; dedication. J. Os-
  borne. New Repub 164:9-10 Je 5 '71
LYNE, Phil
And they laid it on the Lyne at the O. C.
  corral. J. Kirshenbaum. il por Sports Illus
  35:85+ D 20 '71 *
LYNES, Russell
State of taste (cont) por Art in Am 59:19
  Ja '71
LYNN, Nicholas
Mexico's new stars. il Travel 137:28-33+
  Ja '72
Nepal: Shangri-la in the seventies. il Travel
  135:28-35+ F '71
Portals to West Africa. il Travel 136:40-5+
  D '71
LYNN, Mass.
              Sanitary affairs
Revised refuse procedure cuts budget more
  than 25%. D. L. Phillips. il por Am City
  86:66-9 Ap '71
LYNTS, George W. and Judd, J. B.
Late pleistocene paleotemperatures at Tongue
  of the Ocean, Bahamas. bibliog il Science
  171:1143-4 Mr 19 '71
LYONS, Augusta Wallace
Dig for buried treasure. Writer 84:15-17 Je '71
LYONS, D. L.
Liberation of Mrs Howard Hughes. il pors
  Ladies Home J 88:112+ Mr '71
LYONS, Gene M.
President and his experts. bibliog f Ann Am
  Acad 394:36-45 Mr '71
(ed) Social science and the federal govern-
  ment. bibliog f Ann Am Acad 394:1-128 Mr
  '71
LYONS, J. and company, ltd.
Goodbye, Victoria! il Forbes 107:33+ F 1
  '71
**LYONS, Thomas R. See Gumerman, G. J. jt.
  auth.**
LYRIC opera of Chicago
Birth of an ensemble: Chicago's lyric opera.
  G. McElroy. il Opera N 36:16-18 O '71
New Rosenkavalier tops lyric season. R. C.
  Marsh. il Hi Fi 21:MA30-1 F '71
Report:
  Bluebeard's castle, Gianni Schicchi, and
    Madama Butterfly. C. Cassidy. il Opera
    N 35:32 Ja 16 '71
  Don Carlo and Das Rheingold. G.
    McElroy and J. Stedman. il Opera N
    36:36-7 D 25 '71
  Rigoletto, Tosca, and Werther. G. Mc-
    Elroy and J. Stedman. Opera N 36:26-
    7 D 11 '71
  Rossini's Semiramide. S. Jenkins. il
    Opera N 36:24 N '71
LYRICS. See Music. Popular (songs, etc)
LYSENKO, Trofim Denisovich
Lysenko affair, by D. Joravsky. Review.
  Science 172:929-30 My 28 '71. F. C. Bar-
  ghoorn *
LYSERGIC acid diethylamide. See LSD
LYTTON, E. Bulwer-. See Bulwer-Lytton, E.
LYUBIMOV, Gherman. See Lfubimov, G.

M

**MAC. See United States—Military airlift com-
  mand**
MAO (monoamine oxidase) See Oxidases
**MBAs. See Business schools and colleges—
  Graduates**
MBD. See Minimal brain dysfunction
**MBO (management by objectives) See Busi-
  ness management and organization**
**MBTA. See Massachusetts Bay transportation
  authority**
**MCHR.   See Medical committee for human
  rights**

**MCI. See Microwave communications, inc;
  Module communities, inc.**
MCI Lockheed satellite corporation
MCI Lockheed foresees network savings. K.
  Johnsen. Aviation W 95:17 N 22 '71
**MCLS. See Monroe County library system,
  Rochester, N.Y.**
**MDP compounds. See Methylenedioxyphenyl
  compounds**
**MESBIC (minority enterprise small business
  investment companies) See Small business
  investment companies**
MG (automobile) See Automobiles, Foreign
MGIC investment corporation
Karl the magic man. il por Time 99:60 Ja 17
  '72
MHD. See Magnetohydrodynamics
MIRV. See Mirv
**MIT. See Massachusetts institute of technolo-
  gy, Cambridge**
MS (periodical)
Feminist forum. Newsweek 78:104 N 8 '71
For the liberated female. il Time 98:52 D
  20 '71
Ms and the journalism of Women's lib.
  P. Howard. il Sat R 55:43-5+ Ja 8 '72
Ms Gloria Steinem creates a new magazine
  Ms. B. Goldsmith. Harp Baz 105:34 D '71
MSG. See Monosodium glutamate
**MSH (melanophore-stimulating hormone) See
  Melanotropin**
**MSI (Italian social movement) See Political
  parties—Italy**
**MSS (methylprednisolone sodium succinate)
  See Methylprednisolone**
MTV (multi-terrain vehicles) See Motor vehicles
MA, John T.
Libraries in the People's Republic of China
  since 1949. bibliog il por Wilson Lib Bul
  45:970-5 Je '71
MAAS, James W. and Mednieks, Maija
Hydrocortisone-mediated increase of nore-
  pinephrine uptake by brain slices. bibliog
  il Science 171:178-9 Ja 15 '71
MAAZEL, Lorin
Maazel to the N.P.O. T. Heinitz. Sat R
  54:59 F 27 '71 *
New maestro for Cleveland. por Time 98:69
  O 11 '71 *
MCADAM, Dale W. and Whitaker, H. A.
Language production: electroencephalographic
  localization in the normal human brain.
  bibliog il Science 172:499-502; 174:1360-1 Ap
  30, D 24 '71
MCAFEE, Donald A. and others
Adenosine 3',5'-monophosphate in nervous
  tissue: increase associated with synaptic
  transmission. bibliog il Science 171:1156-8
  Mr 19 '71
MCALISTER, Sister Elizabeth
Sister Elizabeth McAlister; interview. ed. by
  H. J. Cargas. por Commonweal 95:63-6 O 15
  '71
                   about
How about it, Sister? Nat R 23:516-17 My 18
  '71 *
How the kidnap conspiracy was hatched. L.
  Lockwood. il pors Life 70:26-30 My 21 '71 *
How to grab the brain child. il pors Time 97:
  15-16 My 10 '71 *
Study in contrasts; various reactions to Har-
  risburg indictments. J. Deedy. Commonweal
  93:434 F 5 '71 *
Talk with Sister Elizabeth. R. Anson. pors
  Time 97:14 Ja 25 '71 *
MCALISTER, James
He takes off, he takes it in. P. Putnam. il
  pors Sports Illus 34:26-8+ My 17 '71 *
This one was for James. P. F. Putnam. il
  Sports Illus 34:54-6 Je 28 '71 *
Who flunked? il por Newsweek 78:83-4 Ag 2
  '71 *
MCALISTER, James E.
Air-core coil nomogram. il Electr World
  86:45 S '71
Nomogram for power in switching transis-
  tors. il Electr World 86:44-5 N '71 *
Nomograms aid capacitance calculations. il
  Electr World 85:27+ F '71
Triggering logic circuits. il Electr World 85:
  29+ Mr '71
Waveshaping with logic gates. il Electr
  World 85:38+ Ap '71
MCALLASTER, Elva
Professional; poem. Chr Cent 88:94 Ja 27 '71
MCALLISTER, Jim
Eastern music festival: new concepts. il Hi
  Fi 21:MA18-19 O '71
MCALLISTER, Wilma
Day my whole class dyed. il Sch Arts 70:18-19
  Je '71

MACAO
Macao: city of money and mystery. C. Lucas.
il Read Digest 98:127-31 F '71
MACARONI
Ham and egg spaghetti; with recipe. il
Seventeen 30:134-5 N '71
Thank you, Marco Polo: spaghetti with an-
chovy and clam sauce. il N Y Times Mag
p 106 S 12 '71
See also
Noodles
MACARTHUR, Douglas
MacArthur, ed. by L. S. Wittner. Review
Nat R il 23:1241-2 N 5 '71. A. Bakshian,
jr. •
Presentation: record album called MacAr-
thur's legacy presented to Mrs MacArthur.
New Yorker 47:24-5 Jl 17 '71 •
MACARTHUR, Jean (Faircloth)
Presentation: record album called Mac-
Arthur's legacy presented to Mrs MacAr-
thur. New Yorker 47:24-5 Jl 17 '71 •
MCATEER, John F.
Library as a teaching asset. Clear House 45:
510-12 Ap '71
MCBAIN, Ed, pseud. See Hunter, E.
MACBEAN, James Roy
Ice-man cometh no more. il Film Q 24:26-33
Sum '71
See you at Mao: Goddard's revolutionary
British sounds. il Film Q 24:15-23 Wint '70
MCBEE, Susanna
Katharine Graham and how she grew. il pors
McCalls 98:76-9+ S '71
You've got to get them involved. il por Mc-
Calls 98:28+ My '71
MACBETH, Jerome R.
Portraits by Ralph E. W. Earl. il Antiques
100:390-3 S '71
MACBETH; drama. See Shakespeare W.—Plays
MCBRIDE, Joseph
(ed) See Fetchit, S. Stepin Fetchit talks
back
MCBRIDE, Patricia
Balanchine's girls: the making of a style.
A. Croce. Harper 242:30+ Ap '71 •
MCBRIDE, Robert M.
Historic sites in Tennessee. il Antiques 100:
394-401 S '71
MCBRIEN, Richard P.
Whatever happened to theology? Common-
weal 94:129-33 Ap 16 '71
MCCABE, E. R. and others
Synergy and ethanol and natural soporific—
gamma hydroxybutyrate. bibliog il Science
171:404-6 Ja 29 '71
MCCAFFERTY, Don
Dallas Cowboys. il Life 72:32-3+ Ja 14 '72
MCCAFFREY, Joseph
Reporter; address. April 18, 1971. Vital
Speeches 37:478-80 My 15 '71
MCCAFFREY, Joseph A.
Homosexuality, Aquinas, and the church.
Cath World 213:183-6 Jl '71
Homosexuality in the seventies. il Cath
World 213:121-5 Je '71
MCCAFFREY, Patrick J.
Black and white in Baltimore. Nation 211:
652-3 D 21 '70
MCCAHILL, F. X. Jr
Avoid losses through risk management. Har-
vard Bsns R 49:57-65 My '71
MCCAHILL, Tom
Mail for McCahill. See issues of Mechanix
illustrated
Tom McCahill tests (title varies) See issues
of Mechanix illustrated
about
Tom McCahill 25 years later. B. Beason. il
pors Mech Illus 67:53-6+ F '71 •
MCCAIN, John Sidney, 1911-
Collective security in Asia; address. August
31, 1971. Vital Speeches 37:749-57 O 1 '71
MCCALEB, Claude B.
Campus bookselling: a complete service.
Pub W 199:30-1 Ja 18 '71
MCCALL, Robert T.
Robert McCall, illustrator. P. A. Dreyfus. il
por Am Artist 35:80-5+ Mr '71 •
MCCALL, Thomas D.
Urban neighborhood influences on high school
administration. bibliog Sch & Soc 99:172-4
Mr '71
MCCALL, Thomas Lawson
Oregon: gunning for Hatfield. R. Fried-
man. Nation 212:781-2 Je 21 '71 •
MCCALL publishing company
Norton Simon to sell McCall book to CRM.
Pub W 200:51 Jl 12 '71
MCCALLION, Edna
Women of Belfast. il America 125:453-6 N
27 '71

MACCALLUM, Robert
Treat septic-tank wastes separately. il Am
City 86:48-9 Ja '71
MCCANN, Cecile
Community of crafts; Redwood Mountain. il
Craft Horiz 31:37+ Ap '71
MACCANN, Donnarae
Overdue. Wilson Lib Bul 45:880-1 My '71
MCCANN, Peter J.
Rock. Nat R 23:156-7 F 9 '71
MCCARLEY, Robert W. and Hobson, J. A.
Single neuron activity in cat gigantocellular
tegmental field: selectivity of discharge and
desynchronized sleep. bibliog il Science 174:
1250-2 D 17 '71
MCCARRAN act. See Internal security
MCCARTEN, John
Irish sketches (cont) New Yorker 47:131-4
My 8; 190+ N 20 '71
MCCARTHY, Barbara Powell
How to help troubled children cope with
fears and problems. il Parents Mag 46:44-
5+ Ag '71
MCCARTHY, Clem
Man who blew a Derby. B. Greenspan. il por
Sports Illus 34:40-2+ My 17 '71 •
MCCARTHY, Colman
Working stiffs. New Repub 165:13-15 S 4 '71
MCCARTHY, Esther
Passage through Botswana. Commonweal
95:131-2 N 5 '71
Rhodesia: the church hesitant. Commonweal
93:460-1 F 12 '71
MCCARTHY, Eugene Joseph
Kind word for the military. por Life 70:38
Mr 5 '71
Mylai conversation; poem. New Repub 165:
27 Jl 24 '71
Pentagon papers. New Repub 165:14-17 Jl 10
'71
Vote of confidence. Nation 212:423-5 Ap 5 '71
What to do about the economy. New Repub
165:16-18 Ag 7 '71
about
Candidate McCarthy. New Repub 165:8-9 N
13 '71 •
Gene lives. por Newsweek 78:40+ N 8 '71 •
I'll be around. New Repub 164:10 Ja 23 '71 •
McCarthy in '72. P. R. Wieck. New Repub
165:13-16 Ag 7 '71 •
Poetics, not politics, a day in class with Prof
Eugene McCarthy. E. Merriam. il por N Y
Times Mag p6+ O 24 '71 •
MCCARTHY, Joseph Raymond
Nightmare decade, by F. J. Cook. Review
Sat R 54:47+ S 18 '71. F. Darwin •
Shabby demagogue. P. S. Prescott. por News-
week 77:106+ Je 14 '71 •
TRB from Washington: the spook. New Re-
pub 165:6 Ag 21 '71 •
MCCARTHY, Mary
Authors & editors; interview. por Pub W
200:19-21 Jl 26 '71
Underpinning of birds of America; an inter-
view ed. by P. Ress. por Harp Baz 104:92-3
Je '71
about
Books: Mary McCarthy's latest. D. Mc-
Conathy. il por Vogue 158:90 Jl '71 •
Egalitarian snobs. J. W. Aldridge. Sat R 54:
21-4 My 8 '71 •
Miss McCarthy's obit to nature. M. Mad-
docks. por Life 70:12 My 21 '71 •
MCCARTHY, Paddy
My most admired man. L. Wainwright. il
por Life 72:10 Ja 14 '72 •
MCCARTNEY, Linda (Eastman)
Two women who broke up the Beatles. J.
Goldman. pors McCalls 98:72-3+ Jl '71 •
MCCARTNEY, Paul
Paul McCartney on the Beatle breakup; inter-
view, ed. by R. Meryman. il pors Life 70:
52-4+ Ap 16 '71
about
Two women who broke up the Beatles. J.
Goldman. pors McCalls 98:72-3+ Jl '71 •
MCCARTNEY, Susan
Gallery; photographs. Life 70:6-9 Je 4 '71
Susan McCartney's faces of New York; pho-
tographs. Pop Phot 68:89-91 Je '71
MCCARTY, Charles P.
Mayor for all seasons. il por Newsweek 77:59
F 8 '71 •
MCCARTY, Theodore M.
Making music. il Parks & Rec 6:25-6+ Ap '71
MCCAUGHEY, Jon
Coal sculpture. il Design 72:14-15 Spr '71
MCCAUGHEY, Patrick
Where paleface meets redskin. il Art N 70:30-
3+ My '71

MCCAULL, Julian
    Building a shorter life. bibliog f il Environ
        13:2-15+ S '71
    Know your enemy. bibliog il pors Environ 13:
        30-9 Je '71
    Lift for the auto. il Environ 13:35-41 D '71
    Mix with care. bibliog il Environ 13:39-42
        Ja '71
    Questions for an old friend. bibliog il En-
        viron 13:2-9 Jl '71
MCCLANAHAN, Ed
    Famous people I have known. Esquire 75:
        86-91+ Ja '71
MCCLANAHAN, Preston. See Mead, M. jt.
        auth.
MCCLANE, A. J.
    (ed) Fishing. See issues of Field & stream
MCCLEARY, Elliott H.
    Disney builds the clean, green world of to-
        morrow. il Pop Mech 136:94-9+ O '71
    Nursery schools: a primer for parents. il
        Ladies Home J 88:74+ N '71
    To protect yourself against air pollution.
        Read Digest 99:41-2 S '71
    Will 10,000,000 people ruin all this? il Nat
        Wildlife 9:5-9 Je '71
MCCLELLAN, John Little
    Notes and comment; excerpts from letter to
        the editor. New Yorker 47:39-40 N 27 '71
MCCLELLAN, Thomas A. and Stieper, D. R.
    Structured approach to group marriage
        counseling. bibliog Ment Hy 55:77-84 Ja '71
MCCLELLAN, FORT. See Military posts
MCCLELLAN committee. See United States—
    Congress—Senate—Government operations.
    Committee on—Investigations, Permanent
    subcommittee on
MCCLELLAN-Kerr Arkansas River naviga-
    tion system. See Arkansas River Waterway
MCCLELLAND and Stewart (firm) See Pub-
    lishers and publishing—Canada
MCCLINTICK, David
    Whistle-blowing on Wall Street. New Repub
        165:20-5 S 4 '71
MCCLINTOCK. Michael, and others
    Talking to ourselves. bibliog f il Environ 13:
        16-19+ S '71
MCCLINTOCK, Robert
    Ortega y Gasset: the partly faithful professor;
        excerpt from Man and his circumstances;
        Ortega as educator. bibliog Sch & Soc 99:
        304-15 Sum '71
MCCLINTOCK, Robert, 1909-
    Development of nationalism and the nation-
        alism of development; address, February
        18, 1971. Dept State Bul 64:522-8 Ap 19 '71
MCCLOSKEY, Mark
    Moral features of seven poets. Poetry 118:
        98-102 My '71
MCCLOSKEY, Michael
    Energy crisis; address, June 15, 1971. Vital
        Speeches 37:621-5 Ag 1 '71
MCCLOSKEY, Paul N. 1927-
    Challenger within. por Time 97:16-17 Ap 26
        '71 *
    Early birds. il por Newsweek 78:17-18 Ag 2
        '71 *
    Happy, humble drive to dump Nixon. il pors
        Time 97:10-11 Je 7 '71 *
    Into the breach. J. Deedy. Commonweal 94:
        298 Je 11 '71 *
    Is McCloskey the McCarthy of '72? R. W.
        Apple, jr. il pors N Y Times Mag p28-9+
        Ap 18 '71 *
    Looking ahead: McCloskey. Nat R 23:792 Jl
        27 '71 *
    McCloskey: the unlikely rebel. K. Fleming.
        il por Newsweek 77:19-20 My 31 '71 *
    McCloskey's rebellion. Nation 212:484-5 Ap 19
        '71 *
    Maverick. por Newsweek 77:52+ Mr 8 '71 *
    Mr McCloskey v. Nixon. W. F. Buckley, jr.
        Nat R 23:722 Je 29 '71 *
    President dumping. P. R. Wieck. New Repub
        164:11-14 Ap 24 '71 *
    Rebel Republican. R. Kuttner. Commonweal
        94:380-2 Jl 23 '71 *
    Reports & comment: Washington. E. Drew.
        Atlan 227:6+ My '71 *
    Vietnam war is immoral. il pors Life 70:28B-
        29 My 7 '71 *
MCCLOUD, Paul. See Cawelti, G. jt. auth.
MCCLUGGAGE, Denise
    How to buy a used car. Am Home 74:52+ Ap
        '71
    On parking. Am Home 74:42+ Mr '71
    Sauna experience: discover how life can
        be beautiful at 200° F. Am Home 74:40+
        F '71
    Woman driver. Am Home 74:40+ Je; 60+ S;
        48+ O; 42+ N '71
MCCLURE, Greg
    Swinging with the swingers. il por Newsweek
        77:99 Je 21 '71 *

MCCLURE, John
    Igor Fyodorovitch Stravinsky. por Hi Fi 21:
        20 Jl '71
MCCLURE. Robert Baird
    First nonordained moderator returns to medi-
        cal missions. Chr Cent 88:64 Ja 20 '71 *
MCCLURE, Samuel Sydney
    Syndicates and how they grew. B. Lewis.
        il Sat R 54:67-9 D 11 '71 *
MCCLURE, Tim, and Lebow, Jared
    Good-bye to all that rah, rah! il Look 35:
        77-8+ O 5 '71
MCCOLLAM, Jim
    Anatomy of a squall. il Yachting 129:64-5+ Ap
        '71
    Force 12. il Yachting 130:60-1+ O '71
MCCOLOUGH, Charles Peter
    Advantage of starting young. por Forbes 108:
        32-3 Jl 1 '71 *
MCCOMB, Miss.
    'South of freedom' 1971. C. T. Rowan. il
        pors Ebony 26:134-9 Ag '71
MCCOMBE, Leonard
    Terriers; photographs. Life 70:38-45 F 12 '71
        about
    Improving on Miss America. R. Graves. il
        Life 71:3 Jl 16 '71 *
MCCONATHY, Dale
    Art. il Vogue 157:127 Ap 15; 158:89+ S 15;
        68 N 1 '71
    Books. il por Vogue 158:90 Jl '71
    Theatre. il Vogue 157:154-5 My '71
    Wife-power. por Vogue 157:110-11+ Je '71
MCCONKEY, Thomas W.
    (ed) Buyers' guide. See (usually) first issue
        of each month of Library journal
    (ed) Purchasing guide 1971. Library J 96:1207
        Ap 1 '71
MCCONNELL, Ellen
    Face to face with a female Senate page;
        ed. by M. E. Kinsley. por Seventeen 30:52
        N '71
MCCONNELL, James M.
    Minn. court rules library may deny homo-
        sexual post. il Library J 96:4046+ D 15
        '71 *
MACCONNELL, John G. and Silverstein, R. M.
    Chemical ecology. il pors Chem 44:6-9 Jl '71
MACCONOMY, Alma Deane
    They were the spirit of the summit. il Nat
        Wildlife 9:40-2 F '71
MCCORD, Howard
    Solitude; poem. Nation 212:572 My 3 '71
MCCORD, James I. and others
    Financing theological education. Chr Cent 88:
        106-7 Ja 27 '71
MCCORD, Thomas B. See Adams, J. B. jt.
        auth.
MCCORMACK, Mark H.
    Men behind the men who make money in
        sports. P. Axthelm. il Vogue 157:186-7+ My
        '71 *
MCCORMACK Mike
    Mike McCormack: a potential Mr Science
        comes to Congress. D. Shapley. il por
        Science 173:408-10 Jl 30 '71
MCCORMICK, Gerald
    New life for an old ball game. il Sports Illus
        35:36-41 Jl 12 '71
MCCORMICK, John
    Bullfighting. il Sports Illus 35:56-7 Jl 26 '71
    On offering the bull his body. il pors Sports
        Illus 34:26-8+ Je 14 '71
MCCORMICK, Ken
    Hows and whys of writers' conferences. Writ-
        er 84:27-8 My '71
MCCORMICK, Richard A.
    Not what Catholic hospitals ordered. Amer-
        ica 125:510-13 D 11 '71
MCCORMICK, Robert Rutherford
    No more frater trafic. Time 97:47 Ja 25 '71 *
MCCORMICK, Robert V.
    Acorns at seven. il Field & S 76:48-9+ Ag
        '71
MCCORMICK Place, Chicago. See Chicago—
    McCormick Place
MCCORRY, Vincent P.
    Word. See issues of America
MCCOY, Charles Brelsford
    How should business respond to its critics?
        address, May 7, 1971. por U S News 70:65-7
        My 31 '71
    How to cope with critics. por Nations Bsns
        59:24 S '71
        about
    Changing chemistry of du Pont. A. A. But-
        kus. por Duns 97:35-7+ Ap '71 *
MCCOY, Dorothy
    Electrified term papers. Engl J 60:107-10 Ja
        '71

MCCRACKEN, D. A. and Dodd, J. L.
Molecular structure of starch-type poly-saccharides from hericium ramosum and hericium coralloides. bibliog Science 174: 419 O 22 '71

MCCRACKEN, James, and Warfield, Sandra
Tale of two singers; excerpts from the diary of a husband-and-wife team. pors Opera N 35:8-11 F 27 '71

MCCRACKEN, Paul Winston
Basis for progress; address, November 30, 1971. Vital Speeches 38:137-9 D 15 '71
Jobs, inflation: what Nixon's top economist expects; excerpts from statement before the Joint economic committee, July 8, 1971. il por U S News 71:57-9 Jl 26 '71
Prospects for 1972 are now markedly improved; interview. il pors U S News 71:48-52 Ag 30 '71

about
McCracken bows out. il por Newsweek 78: 96 D 6 '71 *

MCCRACKEN, Samuel
Drugs of habit & the drugs of belief. bibliog f Commentary 51:43-52 Je '71
Liberal draws the line. il Nat R 23:1402-6 D 17 '71
Schools in trouble. il Parents Mag 46:57-9+ F '71

MCCREDIE, Kenneth B. and others
Cells capable of colony formation in the peripheral blood of man. bibliog il Science 171: 293-4 Ja 22 '71

MCCRORY corporation
Meshulam Riklis: the power, the profit and the glory. il Forbes 107:24-6+ Mr 15 '71

MCCUE, George
Architecture. il Art in Am 59:96-7 My; 98-9 S '71

MCCUE, James G. Jr
Those brainy browns. il Field & S 75:52-3+ Ap '71

MCCULLEN, Audry. See Burns, R. H. jt. auth.

MCCULLERS, Carson (Smith)
Like that; Breath from the sky; Instant of the hour after; stories; excerpt from Mortgaged heart, ed. by M. G. Smith. il Redbook 137:91-3+ O '71

about
Girl named Carson. M. G. Smith. il pors Redbook 137:90-1+ O '71 *

MCCULLOCH, Robert Paxton
Cities of the desert. il por Newsweek 78: 54+ Ag 9 '71 *

MCCULLOUGH, Bill L.
Demise of rural medicine; address, February 20, 1971. Vital Speeches 37:517-18 Je 15 '71

MCCULLOUGH, David G.
A man, a plan, a canal, Panama! il pors Am Heritage 22:64-71+ Je '71
(ed) See Knott, J. P. Untold delights of Duluth

MCCULLOUGH, Edith L.
AMIGOS: a friendly title for a new teacher education program. Clear House 45:476-9 Ap '71

MCCULLOUGH, Frances
First winner picked for Roger Klein Young editors' award. B. A. Bannon. il por Pub W 199:22-3 Ap 26 '71 *

MCCULLOUGH, J. Robert
Keep that stored water fresh. il por Am City 86:63-5 Ap '71

MCCULLOUGH, Joseph B.
Mark Twain and journalistic humor today; address, November 1970. Engl J 60:591-5 My '71

MCCULLOUGH, Robert F.
Look down and rediscover the ever-changing seascape. il Pop Phot 68:92-5 Mr '71

MCCULLY, Helen
Cooking: why the experts succeed; excerpts from Cooking with Helen McCully beside you. il Ladies Home J 88:100+ Ap '71
Nobody ever tells you these things. See issues of House beautiful

MCDANIEL, Charles-Gene
Accelerating protons and social reform. Chr Cent 88:1032-4 S 1 '71
Ghetto nightmare. Chr Cent 89:15-16 Ja 5 '72

MCDANIEL, Ernest, and Feldhusen, J. F.
College teaching effectiveness. Todays Ed 60: 27 Mr '71

MCDANIEL, Joseph C.
Persimmons. il Horticulture 49:32-3+ S '71

MCDERMOTT, Frank
Cultural policy: a modern dilemma. il UNESCO Courier 24:4-17 Ja '71

MCDERMOTT, Patrick P.
New "encyclical" on social justice. por Chr Cent 88:748-51 Je 16 '71
Round II; peace movement vs. Vietnamization il Cath World 213:6-12 Ap '71
SST, end product of Consciousness II. America 124:171-4 F 20 '71

MCDERMOTT, Stephen W.
Bosman's follies. il pors Dance Mag 45:32-7 My '71
From the wonderful folk who gave you the Swan queen: rock-ballet as synthesis of forms. il Dance Mag 45:38-45+ O '71
On supering with the Stuttgart. il Dance Mag 45:50-7 Je '71

MACDHAI, Rob
Vibrating wire, new twist in gyros. il Pop Sci 198:49 Ja '71

MACDONALD, Don
How to save a pile of money when you buy a new car. il Mech Illus 68:39-41+ Ja '72

MCDONALD, Elvin
Gardener's notebook. See issues of House beautiful
—and Power, L. V.
Automated lawn; excerpt from The low-upkeep book of lawns and landscape. il Am Home 74:24+ Jl '71

MCDONALD, Ian C.
Male-producing strain of the house fly. bibliog il Science 172:489 Ap 30 '71

MCDONALD, Jack H.
Excerpt from address, January 29, 1971. Cong Digest 50:124+ Ap '71

MACDONALD, James B. and Wolfson, B. J.
Case against behavioral objectives. Ed Digest 36:22-5 F '71

MCDONALD, James Edward
Obituary
Phys Today 24:71 S '71

MCDONALD, John
Oil and the environment: the view from Maine. il Fortune 83:84-9+ Ap '71

MCDONALD, John A. and Kelley, W. N.
Lesch-Nyhan syndrome: altered kinetic properties of mutant enzyme. bibliog il Science 171:689-91 F 19 '71

MCDONALD, John Kennely
Taking proteins apart. D. E. Thomsen. il por Sci N 101:14-15 Ja 1 '72 *

MCDONALD, Robert
Epilogue to Z, an Athenian tragedy. New Repub 164:25 Je 12 '71

MCDONALD, Robert Emmett
Tougher Univac? A. A. Butkus. por Duns 97:58 F '71 *

MACDONALD, Ross, pseud.
Art of murder. R. A. Sokolov. il por Newsweek 77:101-2+ Mr 22 '71 *
Authors & editors. B. A. Bannon. por Pub W 200:19-20 Ag 9 '71 *
Detective story. R. Schickel. Commentary 52:96+ S '71 *
Ross Macdonald: the prince in the poorhouse. B. Cook. por Cath World 214:27-30 O '71 *

MCDONALD, T. F. and MacLeod, D. P.
Maintenance of resting potential in anoxic guinea pig ventricular muscle: electrogenic sodium pumping. bibliog il Science 172:570-2 My 7 '71

MCDONALD, Virginia
Almost-perfect house plant. il Org Gard & Farm 18:54-6 D '71

MCDONALD'S corporation
As American as a McDonald's hamburger on the Fourth of July. J. A. Lukas. il N Y Times Mag p4-5+ Jl 4 '71; Same abr. with title America's hamburger king. Read Digest 99:137-41 O '71; Reply. R. J. McDonald. N Y Times Mag p70 S 19 '71
Beef against big Mac. Time 98:43 D 27 '71
McDonald's is their kind of place. V. Louviere. il Nations Bsns 59:20 Mr '71

MCDONNELL, Kilian
Ecumenism: who cares? Commonweal 95:55-9 O 15 '71

MCDONNELL Douglas corporation
Aerospace unions pick a target. Bsns W p84 O 9 '71
Boeing's earnings up, McDonnell Douglas' dip. Aviation W 95:14 Ag 2 '71
DC-10 orders reported at 238. Aviation W 94:19 F 8 '71
Douglas launches a real estate rocket. il Bsns W p25-6 O 9 '71
Even the Douglas trijet is in trouble. il Bsns W p62-3 Jl 31 '71
Long-term loan sought for DC-10 by McDonnell Douglas. Aviation W 94:55 My 17 '71
McDonnell Douglas forms STOL group. Aviation W 95:19 O 11 '71
McDonnell Douglas reports DC-10 charges. il Aviation W 94:45 Ap 5 '71

MCDONNELL Douglas corporation—*Cont.*
McDonnell Douglas studies DC-11 to challenge A-300B airbus. Aviation W 95:27 O 4 '71
No dancing, please. il Forbes 107:23 Ap 15 '71
Unions threaten Douglas shutdown. Aviation W 95:21 O 11 '71

MCDONOUGH, Bernard Patrick
Do-it-yourself man from Parkersburg, West Virginia. I. Ross. il pors Fortune 84:98-102+ Jl '71 •

MACDOUGALL, D.
Deep sea drilling: age and composition of an Atlantic basaltic intrusion. bibliog il Science 171:1244-5 Mr 26 '71

MCDOUGALL, Lois
What Volkswagen, Revlon, and Ayd's candies can tell you about writing. Engl J 60:479-80 Ap '71

MCDOUGALL, Robert
Exploring books. il Har Yrs 11:48-9 O '71

MCDOWELL, Bart
Hungary: changing homeland of a tough, romantic people. il Nat Geog 139:443-83 Ap '71

MCDOWELL, L. A.
Odor-prevention insurance. il Am City 86:54+ F '71

MCDOWELL, Malcolm
New stars, the new films. B. Goldsmith. por Harp Baz 105:70 D '71 •

MACDOWELL colony. See Authors colonies

MCDUFFIE, Bruce
Mercury monitoring highlights Long Island swordfish tournament. B. Sands. il por Cons 26:27-31 O '71 •

MCEACHERN, John
High adventure in high latitudes. il por Motor B & S 128:70-3+ S '71

MCEACHERN, Margaret
****ing is no longer a dirty word. il Todays Health 49:24-7 Mr '71

MCELHINNY, Michael W.
Geomagnetic reversals during the phanerozoic. bibliog il Science 172:157-9 Ap 9 '71

MCELIN, Thomas W.
Hysterectomy; ed. by H. Touré. Redbook 137:48+ My '71

MCELROY, George
Birth of an ensemble. il Opera N 36:16-18 O '71
—See Stedman, J. W. jt. auth.

MCELROY, William David
Kennedy and McElroy differ. C. Holden. Science 174:573 N 5 '71 •
McElroy leaving NSF. por Sci N 100:54-5 Jl 24 '71 •
McElroy will leave NSF. R. Gillette. Science 173:310 Jl 23 '71 •

MACEOIN, Gary
Latin America: who is to blame? il Commonweal 94:331-6 Je 25 '71
Neocolonialism in Latin America; excerpt from Revolution next door. bibliog Chr Cent 88:685-97 Je 2 '71
(ed) Unequal in the sight of God; interviews. il McCalls 98:78-9+ Je '71
Writing on the wall: Colonnese go home. Commonweal 94:492-3 S 24 '71

MCEWING, Wayne
Seasons of the mind. il por UNESCO Courier 24:9-58 Ag '71
25 years of Unesco viewed by a student of 25. E. Naraghi. il UNESCO Courier 24:6-7 Ag '71 •

MACEY, Joan Mary
Painting with a brayer. il Sch Arts 71:8 D '71

MCFADDEN, Dorothy Loa
Great gardens on America's East coast. il Home Gard 58:20-7+ My '71
Well known gardens on the coast of Maine il Home Gard 58:40-3 Ap '71

MCFADDEN, Sister Therese Dolores
Emily Dickinson: a poet for the now generation. Engl J 60:462-4 Ap '71

MCFALL, Russell Whitney
Getting the message at Western union. A. A. Butkus. il por Duns 98:39-42 O '71 •

MCFARLAN, F. Warren
Problems in planning the information system. il Harvard Bsns R 49:75-89 Mr '71

MACFARQUHAR, Roderick
Barriers to a deal between U.S. and red China; interview. il por U S News 70:30-2 My 3 '71

MCFERRAN, Douglass D.
Cult of Jacques Ellul. America 124:122-4 F 6 '71
New magic. Commonweal 94:477-80 S 17 '71

MCGAHAN, Jerry
Condor, soaring spirit of the Andes. il por Nat Geog 139:684-709 My '71

MCGANN, Jerome
Australia Felix. Poetry 118:223-7 Jl '71

MCGEE, Frank
Hugh Downs to Frank McGee: the big switch on the Today show; interview, ed. by R. Ballad. pors Look 35:13-15 O 5 '71
Television; interview, ed. by P. Hudson. pors Sr Schol 99:19 Ja 10 '72

MCGEE, Leo
Early efforts towards educating the black adult. bibliog Negro Hist Bul 34:88-90 Ap '71

MCGEE, Richard K.
Suicide prevention programs and mental health associations. bibliog Ment Hy 55:60-7 Ja '71

MCGEE, Robert T.
Accountable leadership. Clear House 46:170-2 N '71

MCGHAN, Barry
Student movement: where do you stand? bibliog f Clear House 46:91-5 O '71

MCGHEE, Bernice
Black coed at Armed forces college. il pors Ebony 26:108-10+ N '70 •

MCGILL, Ralph
Unforgettable Ralph McGill. W. S. Howland. por Read Digest 99:63-7 Ag '71 •

MCGILL, William James
New tensions on campus. por Life 71:55 O 8 '71
What lies ahead for our universities; address, February 16, 1971. Vital Speeches 37:337-40 Mr 15 '71; Same. Sch & Soc 99:337-41 O '71

MCGINNIS, Lila Sprague
Love is catching: story. il Good H 173:84-5 Ag '71

MACGLASHAN, David
Paperback is king at Eisenhower college. il Pub W 199:31-2 My 10 '71

MCGLYNN, Margaret M.
Garbage power! il por Look 35:26-30 My 4 '71

MCGOUGH, Elizabeth
Add a studio/sitting room. il Mech Illus 67:118-20+ O '71
Building a backyard basketball court. il Mech Illus 67:102+ O '71
Extend your swimming season with sun power. il Mech Illus 67:98-9 S '71

MCGOVERN, George Stanley
Can George do it? interview. por Nations Bsns 59:68-9 N '71
Fine way back to our prairie past. il Life 71:12 Jl 2 '71

about

After twenty years; proposal of recognition of red China. Nation 212:164-5 F 8 '71 •
Audacity of George McGovern. New Repub 164:7-8 Ja 30 '71 •
Brave man chooses. Chr Cent 88:243 F 24 '71 •
Can a good man win? Nation 212:100-1 Ja 25 '71 •
Early birds. Newsweek 78:18+ Ag 2 '71 •
Is he really serious about becoming president? Yes. L. C. DuBois. il pors N Y Times Mag p26-7+ My 2 '71 •
Is McGovern a stalking horse? il por Time 98:19-20 Ag 9 '71 •
Is McGovern credible? S. Alsop. Newsweek 77:92 Ja 25 '71 •
Later George, not now. New Repub 164:5-6 My 8 '71 •
Let George do it? J. F. Richard. Commonweal 94:11-15 Mr 12 '71 •
McGovern in South Dakota. P. Schrag. Atlan 228:6-9 O '71 •
McGovern *redux*. il por Time 98:9 D 27 '71 •
McGovern: the meaning. Nat R 23:124+ F 9 '71
McGovern: the tortoise of '72. il pors Newsweek 78:16-17 D 27 '71 •
McGovern's campaign. P. R. Wieck. New Repub 165:15-20 O 30 '71 •
McGovern's spark. por Time 97:21-2 Ja 25 '71 •
Notes and comment. New Yorker 46:27 F 13 '71 •
Our local correspondents. J. Stevenson. New Yorker 47:47-9 Ja 1 '72 •
Strategy of McGovern's team. por U S News 70:29 Ja 25 '71 •
TRB from Washington. New Repub 164:6 Ja 30 '71 •
Two to make ready. por Newsweek 77:25 F 1 '71 •

MCGOVERN, Robert
For Dan Berrigan; poem. Nation 212:220 F 15 '71
Up on the housetop; poem. Chr Cent 88:1490 D 22 '71

MCGOVERN-Hatfield amendment. See Vietnamese war, 1957- —American troop withdrawals

MCGRADY, Patrick M. Jr
Youth pill. il Ladies Home J 88:72-4+ Jl '71

MCGRANAHAN, Donald V.
Analysis of socio-economic development through a system of indicators. bibliog f il Ann Am Acad 393:65-81 Ja '71

MCGRATH, Lee Parr, and Scobey, Joan
What is a pet? excerpts. Good H 173:90-1 Jl '71

MCGRATH, Thomas
Comment. J. Atlas. Poetry 119:47-8 O '71 *

MACGRAW, Ali
Is there a new now? interview. ed. by M. Ronan. por Sr Schol 98:3+ F 15 '71

about

Ali: life story. G. Carro. il pors Ladies Home J 88:86-9+ F '71 *

MCGRAW-Edison company
CPA in charge. por Bsns W p 105 F 27 '71

MCGRAW-Hill, Inc.
Countdown? il Forbes 107:24-5 Ap 15 '71
McGraw-Hill's move to Sixth avenue includes plans for mammoth bookstore. P. A. Farrell. il Pub W 200:52-4 S 13 '71

MCGREAL, Thomas L. and Hughes, Clarence
Operating in the school job market. Clear House 45:397-403 Mr '71

MACGREGOR, Frances C. and Ford, Barbara
Other face of plastic surgery: the disappointed patient. Sci Digest 69:16-20 Ap '71

MACGREGOR, Ian Kinloch
Expropriation: why do they do it? interview. pors Forbes 108:32-3 Jl 15 '71
Technology and society: address, April 1971. Vital Speeches 37:525-9 Je 15 '71

MCGREGOR, Mary
Lines in praise of Farmington; poem. Seventeen 29:170 Ag '70

MCGREGOR, Paul
Scissors superstar! W. J. Parente. il Sr Schol 99:42+ S 27 '71 *

MCGREW, R. Brownell
Colorful Southwest of R. Brownell McGrew. F. Whitaker. il Am Artist 35:72-9+ Mr '71 *

MCGRORY, Mary
Washington front. See issues of America

MCGUANE, Thomas
Angling and some acts of God. il Sports Illus 35:32-7 Ag 9 '71
Casting on a sea of memories. il Sports Illus 35:42-4+ S 27 '71
Riders on the brink. il Sports Illus 34:46-51 My 3 '71

MCGUIRE, Al
McGuire's Marquette. il por Newsweek 77: 96-7 Mr 1 '71 *

MCGUIRE, Robert F.
Adventure playgrounds. il Parks & Rec 6: 30-2 N '71

MACHADO, China
China paradox. il por Harp Baz 104:68-9 Ap '71 *

MACHAN, Cathy. See Reeder, N. jt. auth.

MCHARG, Ian L.
Man; planetary disease; address, March 10, 1971. Vital Speeches 37:634-40 Ag 1 '71

MACHINE billing. See Billing

MACHINE shop practice
See also
Centering
Indexing (machine work)

MACHINE theory
On cellular automata, self-reproduction, the Garden of Eden and the game, life. M. Gardner. il Sci Am 224:112-17 F '71
On winding down. W. Zinsser. il Life 70:4 My 21 '71
Turing game and the question it presents: can a computer think? M. Gardner. il Sci Am 224:120-2 bibliog(p 136) Je '71

MACHINE tool industry
Toolmakers get a boost from GE. Bsns W p31 N 6 '71
Toolmakers' mission to Moscow. il Bsns W p24-5 Mr 20 '71
Trading with Russia gets down to hardware. il Bsns W p95 Je 12 '71
Trouble in tools. il Time 98:106 N 1 '71
See also
Cincinnati milacron, inc.

Finance

Machine tools: waiting for the year after next. il Bsns W p46-7 D 25 '71
Slowdown that is hard to shake off. il Bsns W p 18-19 Ja 30 '71
Toolmakers write more orders. il Bsns W p20-1 Jl 31 '71

Securities

For machine tools, 1972 is the year. il Bsns W p53+ S 4 '71

Germany (Federal Republic)

Germany's new edge may soon be dulled. il Bsns W p25 Mr 20 '71

MACHINE tools
See also
Chucks
Files and rasps
Grinding machines
Jigs
Planing machines
Vises

MACHINE translating
Translation by computer; letter. H. W. Sinaiko. Science 174:1182+ D 17 '71

MACHINE work
See also
Indexing (machine work)

MACHINERY
See also
Belting
Construction machinery
Gearing
Pumping machinery
Woodworking machinery

Safety devices and measures

See-through saw guard is always in place. G. Daniels. il Pop Sci 198:106 Je '71

Stands

Big band-saw table; jack-of-many-jobs. R. J. DeCristoforo. il Pop Sci 198:96-8 Ja '71

MACHINERY, Automatic
See also
Automation

MACHINERY and civilization. See Technology and civilization

MACHINERY in agriculture. See Agricultural machinery

MACHINERY industry
Japanese bulldozers invade U.S. market; Komatsu mfg. co. il Bsns W p48-9 Ja 23 '71
Technology and manpower in nonelectrical machinery. L. T. O'Carroll. bibliog il Mo Labor R 94:56-62 Je '71
See also
Machine tool industry

MACHINISTS union. See International association of machinists and aerospace workers

MCHUGH, Heather
Because you are made of the same possibilities; poem. Mlle 73:214 Ag '71

MCHUGH, James T.
Population growth and public policy. il America 125:368-9+ N 6 '71

MCILHANY, Sterling
Journey from Rome to Florence. il Am Artist 35:22-3+ F; 66-71 Mr '71

MCILVANNEY, Hugh
But the south shall rise again (and again!) il Sports Illus 34:22-5 My 17 '71
Fighting carpenter from Scotland. il pors Sports Illus 34:30-2+ F 8 '71
Golf. Sports Illus 35:81-3 O 18 '71
Put away the putter and go for the pin. il por Sports Illus 34:16-17 Je 28 '71
Revival of an old rock festival. il Sports Illus 35:18-19 Ag 9 '71
Sailing. Sports Illus 35:44-6 Ag 23 '71
Soccer. Sports Illus 35:64-5 O 4 '71

MCILWAIN, William Franklin, 1925-
Farewell to alcohol. il Atlan 229:29-35 Ja '72
On the overturning of two school buses in Lamar, S.C. il Esquire 75:98-103+ Ja '71
Performing arts. Harper 243:22+ S '71

MCINERNY, Ralph
Authority of failure. Commonweal 93:399-400 Ja 22 '71
Big secret. Writer 84:9-11 F '71
Greene-ing of America. Commonweal 95:59-61 O 15 '71
MF. Commonweal 94:290-1 My 28 '71

MCINNES, William Charles
Win one, lose one: the Supreme court. America 125:170-3 S 18 '71

MCINTIRE, Carl
Degree decree. Chr Today 15:45 F 12 '71 *
Forecast for Shelton: a few degrees warmer? R. Chandler. Chr Today 15:42 Mr 26 '71 *
It rained on McIntire's victory parade. E. E. Plowman. il por Chr Today 15:30-2 Je 4 '71 *
McIntire: on the gateway to the stars. W. Willoughby. Chr Today 15:30-1 Ja 29 '71 *
McIntire on the way. Chr Cent 88:175 F 3 '71 *
McIntire's mélange. E. E. Plowman. Chr Today 15:36 My 7 '71 *
Tycoons in the temple. E. E. Plowman. Chr Today 16:56-7 O 8 '71 *

MCINTOSH, Charles
Trade magazines: the largest market. Writer 84:22-4 Ag '71
MCINTYRE, Sir Laurence
International year for action to combat racism and racial discrimination; statement. UN Mo Chron 8:1 Ja '71
MCIRVINE, Edward C. See Tribus, M. jt. auth.
MACK, Charles S.
Excerpt from testimony, April 13, 1970. Cong Digest 50:45+ F '71
MACK, Herbert. See Cook, A. jt. auth.
MACK, Patricia H. See Wing, R. C. jt. auth.
MACK trucks, Inc.
Big breakthrough in East-West trade; with editorial comment. il Bsns W p84-8, 126 Je 19 '71
Break for the bulldog. il Newsweek 78:68-9 Ag 23 '71
Bulldog and the bear. Newsweek 77:80 Je 28 '71
Picking up where Mack left off; Kama plant. il Bsns W p42-3 S 25 '71
MCKAY, David, company
Market for book manuscripts. E. Rawson. Writer 84:18-19 Jl '71
MCKAY, David S. and others
Lunar metallic particle, mini-moon; an interpretation. bibliog il Science 171:479-80 F 5 '71
MACKAY, Tann
France's new Riviera. il Travel 135:28-33 Je '71
MACKAYE, Benton
Long, long trail awinding. P. Whitley. il por Am For 77:16-18+ F '71 *
MCKEAN, William J.
Get me an ax! il Look 35:18-24 Je 29 '71
Longhair hard hat. Look 35:38+ Ja 12 '71
Train ride. Look 35:37 Ja 12 '71
MCKEARN, Patricia John
Famous seventh-grade authors: building egos the lazy way. Engl J 60:126-7 Ja '71
MCKECHNIE, Donna
Choreographer's dream. C. Zadan. il pors Dance Mag 45:71-3+ O '71 *
MCKEE, Gladys
Anthem for aunts; poem. Good H 172:170 F '71
MCKEE, Linda
Mad Jack and the missionaries. il pors Am Heritage 22:30-7+ Ap '71
MCKEEN, Laurence W.
Experimental method to study Charles' law. il Chem 44:27-9 F '71
MACKENDRICK, Paul Lachlan
Looking back on a golden age, address, November 10, 1971. Vital Speeches 38:188-92 Ja 1 '72
MCKENDRY, Maxime
Food gazette. See issues of Vogue
MCKENNA, Dave
Musical events: Cape Cod notes. W. Balliett. New Yorker 47:77-8 Ag 28 '71 *
MCKENNA, Siobhan
Off Broadway; Here are ladies. E. Oliver. New Yorker 47:68-9 Mr 6 '71 *
Saints of the word. T. E. Kalem. por Time 97:48 Mr 8 '71 *
MCKENNA, William Edward
Technicolor: red to black. T. J. Murray. por Duns 98:70+ S '71 *
MACKENZIE, Charles S.
Justification by faith in the seventies. Chr Today 15:6-7 S 24 '71
MACKENZIE, Fred T. and Gees, Rudi
Quartz synthesis at earth-surface conditions. bibliog il Science 173:533-5 Ag 6 '71
MCKENZIE, John Lawrence
Demythologizing of Louis Evely. Commonweal 94:307-10, 370-1 Je 11, Jl 23 '71
MCKENZIE, Leon
Limitations of God. Cath World 214:105-8 D '71
MCKENZIE, Robert A.
Let's keep talking. Chr Cent 88:592-3 My 12 '71
MACKENZIE, William
Rogue Elk. il por Newsweek 78:70 D 13 '71 *
MACKENZIE VALLEY pipeline (proposed) See Petroleum—Pipe lines
MCKEOWN, Bill
Boats & boating. See issues of Mechanix illustrated
Lost at sea, and what to do about it. il Mech Illus 67:72+ Jl '71
Maine to Mexico in a camper, without getting out. il pors Mech Illus 67:89-91+ Ap '71
MCKEOWN, Tom
Spoon; Looking forward; poems. Sat R 54:63 O 16 '71
Strange formations; poem. New Yorker 47:156 N 6 '71

MCKERN, Sharon S.
They're digging up witch lore in Salem. il Sci Digest 69:27-8+ My '71
—and McKern, T. W.
Ape artists: what they tell us about origins of human tool use. il Sci Digest 70:28-33 O '71
MCKERN, Thomas W. See McKern, S. S. jt. auth.
MACKEY, John
I'm going to punish them for last year. G. S. Brown. il pors Sports Illus 35:30-2+ Ag 30 '71 *
MACKEY, William Wellington
Behold! Cometh the Vanderkellans. Criticism New Yorker 47:67-8 Ap 10 '71 *
MCKIM, Mead and White (firm)
Classical walk: tour of buildings designed by S. White. New Yorker 47:47-8 N 20 '71
MCKIMMEY, James
Love's seasoning; story. Good H 173:110-11 S '71
Second chance; story. Good H 172:94-5 Mr '71
MACKINAC race. See Yacht racing
MCKINLEY, Larry
In glass; poem. Seventeen 30:81 Ja '71
MCKINLEY, William
My last words concerning the controversial McKinley record. J. Walsh. il pors Hobbies 76:37-8+ O: 37-8+ N '71 *
MCKINLEY NATIONAL PARK. See Mount McKinley National Park
MCKINNEY, George Wesley, 1922-
Now generation; address, June 15, 1971. Vital Speeches 37:665-9 Ag 15 '71
MACKINTOSH, Malcolm
Era of negotiations with Russia? interview, ed. by J. Fromm. Read Digest 98:57-61 Ja '71
MCKISSICK, Floyd Bixler
Soul City. G. Gould. New Repub 165:9-11 Jl 3 '71 *
MACKLE, Barbara. See Miller, G. jt. auth.
MACKLE, Barbara Jane, case. See Kidnapping
MACKO, V. and others
Identification of the germination self-inhibitor from wheat stem rust uredo-spores. bibliog Science 173:835-6 Ag 27 '71
MCKUEN, Rod
Trade winds; interview, ed. by C. Amory. Sat R 55:18 Ja 8 '72
When I was nine; poem; excerpt from And to each season. Ladies Home J 88:96-7 D '71

about

Mush. N. Ephron. il pors Esquire 75:89-92+ Je '71 *
Poet and paradox. por Ladies Home J 88:122 D '71 *
Says Rod McKuen: it doesn't matter who you love or how you love, but that you love! W. Murray. il pors N Y Times Mag p32-4+ Ap 4 '71 *
MCKUSICK, Victor A.
Mapping of human chromosomes; with biographical sketch. il Sci Am 224:14, 104-13 Ap '71
MCLAIN, John
Developing flexible all-year schools. Ed Digest 36:12-14 My '71
MCLAIN, Pete
Wilderness beach camping. il Field & S 76:70-1+ My '71
MACLAINE, Shirley
Is the family obsolete; interview, ed. by J. Kronenberger. Look 35:35 Ja 26 '71
Trade winds; interview, ed. by C. Amory. Sat R 54:8 F 6 '71

about

Diversification of Shirley MacLaine. H. Alpert. il pors Sat R 54:43-5+ F 27 '71 *
MACLAREN, George
Windsor chair in Nova Scotia. il Antiques 100:124-7 Jl '71
MCLAREN, Richard Wellington
McLaren's march to the sea; interview. pors Forbes 109:129+ Ja 1 '72

about

Antitrust: change at the top, but no change in policy. il por U S News 71:29-30 D 20 '71 *
Busting a trust buster. por Newsweek 78:76+ D 20 '71 *
Fallout from McLaren's fast exit. por Bsns W p31 D 11 '71 *
McLaren out. Time 98:75 D 20 '71 *

MCLARNEY, William O.
Farm pond revisited. il Org Gard & Farm 18:88-92+ N '71
Introduction to aquaculture on the organic farm and homestead. il Org Gard & Farm 18:71-7 Ag '71
Raising crayfish in the farm pond. Org Gard & Farm 18:84-5+ D '71

MCLAUGHLIN, John J.
White House padre. por Newsweek 78:27 Jl 26 '71 •

MCLAUGHLIN, Leo Plowden
South from Fordham. il por Bsns W p91 Mr 20 '71 •

MCLAUGHLIN, R. D. See Hadeishi, T. jt. auth.

MACLEAN, Alistair
Ho-hum life of the man from Navarone. por Life 71:91 N 26 '71 •

MCLEAN, Don
Memorable song for our times. P. F. Kluge. il pors Life 72:44A-44B+ Ja 14 '72 •
Montage of loss; American pie. por Time 99: 55 Ja 3 '72 •
Only yesterday. S. K. Oberbeck. por Newsweek 78:64+ O 20 '71 •

MACLEAN, Jean Ann. See Keegan, F. W. jt. auth.

MCLEAN, Michael D.
Nature's chaperones. il Am For 77:32-4 N '71

MACLEISH, Archibald
Cottonwoods astir. Sat R 54:40-1 N 13 '71
Scratch; dramatization of The devil and Daniel Webster by S. V. Benét. Criticism
New Yorker 47:102 My 15 '71 •
Newsweek il 77:96 My 17 '71 •
Sat R 54:55 My 29 '71 •

MACLEISH, Kenneth
Help for Philippine tribes in trouble. il pors Nat Geog 140:220-55 Ag '71
Java: Eden in transition. il Nat Geog 139:1-43 Ja '71
Quebec: French city in an Anglo-Saxon world. il Nat Geog 139:416-42 Mr '71

MACLEISH, Roderick
Our native tongue, alive and well. Read Digest 98:132-5 Ja '71
Washington's capital crime-stopper. Read Digest 98:53-4+ My '71

MCLELLAN, Joseph
Change of mood at CICOP. Commonweal 93: 508-10 F 26 '71
Statistics of crisis. Commonweal 93:421-3 Ja 29 '71

MCLEMORE, Gerald D.
At war with the army. il por Time 97:48 F 8 '71 •

MCLENDON, James
Operate your own wire service for a dime. Writers Digest 51:35 N '71

MCLENDON, Winzola
Nixons nobody knows. il McCalls 98:76-83+ My '71
Private world of Judy Agnew. il pors McCalls 98:102-7 F '71
Trade winds; interview, ed. by C. Amory. Sat R 54:6+ Ja 16 '71
(ed) See Mitchell, M. I went to London to visit the queen!
—and Smith, S. F.
Recipe for a Washington dinner party. il pors Ladies Home J 88:110+ My '71

MACLEOD, Celeste
How & where to find biographical information. il Writers Digest 52:28-30 Ja '72
Reconstitution for peace and relevancy. il pors Library J 96:1192-6 Ap 1 '71

MACLEOD, Colin, and Minners, H. A.
International cooperation in science. Science 173:1085 S 17 '71

MACLEOD, Don P. See McDonald, T. F. jt. auth.

MACLEOD, Myron R.
Obituary
Am City 86:26 Ap '71

MACLEOD, Roderick K.
Program budgeting works in nonprofit institutions. il Harvard Bsns R 49:46-56 S '71

MCLUHAN, Herbert Marshall
Obiter dicta; letter. Atlan 228:38-40 O '71

about
Inquest on McLuhan. G. Woodcock. Nation 213:437-9 N 1 '71 •
New English: hot stuff or cool, man, cool? address. November 1970. R. W. Blake. Engl J 60:728-34 S '71 •

MCLUHAN, Marshall. See McLuhan, H. M.

MCLURE, Gail T. and others
Sex discrimination in schools. Todays Ed 60:33-5 N '71

MACLURE, William
Schöpf, Maclure, Werner, and the earliest work on American geology. E. M. Spieker. bibliog Science 172:1333-4 Je 25 '71 •

MCMAHON, Allan
Trade winds; interview, ed. by C. Amory. Sat R 54:12-13 Jl 31 '71

MACMAHON, Bryan
Portrait of tinkers; with biographical sketch. il Natur Hist 80:2, 24-35+ D '71

MCMAHON, Edward M. and others
Methamphetamine-induced insulin release. bibliog il Science 174:66-8 O 1 '71

MCMAHON, Thomas A.
Rowing: a similarity analysis. bibliog il Science 173:349-51 Jl 23 '71

MCMAHON, William
Fall of the larrikin. il pors Time 97:26 Mr 22 '71 •
Good-by John, hello Billy. il por Newsweek 77:38 Mr 22 '71 •
Just a passing glance. il Time 98:34 N 15 '71 •
Prime Minister McMahon of Australia meets with President Nixon; remarks, November 2, 1971. R. M. Nixon. Dept State Bul 65: 646 D 6 '71 •
What's wrong with Australia? M. Parker. il por Newsweek 79:24-6 Ja 3 '72 •

MCMAHON, William E.
A,B,C, grades? Don't knock it! Clear House 45:465-7 Ap '71

MCMANUS, Martin J.
Canon law: justice by variety. America 125: 257-9 O 9 '71

MCMANUS, Patrick F.
Backyard safari. il Field & S 76:60-1+ Je '71
Big trip. il Field & S 76:64-5+ O '71
Misery kit. il Field & S 76:68-9+ My '71
Purist. il Field & S 75:54-5+ F '71

MCMANUS, Robert
McManus v. the Knights of Columbus. P. Good. il pors Harper 243:66-70+ S '71 •

MCMASTER university, Hamilton, Ontario
Hamilton, Ontario; Health sciences centre. J. M. Dixon. il Arch Forum 134:30-5 Je '71

MCMILLAN, Calvin
Photoperiod evidence in the introduction of xanthium (cocklebur) to Australia. bibliog il Science 171:1029-31 Mr 12 '71

MCMILLAN, James Bryan
Busing judge. por Time 97:40 My 3 '71 •

MCMILLAN, Jeff
House that built grandpa. il Har Yrs 11:39 Ap '71

MCMILLAN, John Lanneau
Close call. por Newsweek 77:27-8 F 15 '71 •
Warning for the chairmen. il por Time 97:17 F 15 '71 •

MCMINNVILLE, Tenn.
'South of freedom' 1971. C. T. Rowan. il pors Ebony 26:134-9 Ag '71

MCMULLEN, Roy
Painters' painting: cubism. il Am Scholar 40:432-46 Sum '71
Questions and answers. il Hi Fi 21:MA28+ My '71
Sunday afternoon on the Island of La Grande Jatte. il por Horizon 13:82-95 Sum '71
Tempesta puzzle. il Horizon 13:94-103 Spr '71

MACMURRAY, Fred
Magic of a good marriage; ed. by C. Schroeder. J. H. MacMurray. il pors Good H 173:94-5+ O '71 •

MACMURRAY, June Haver
Magic of a good marriage; ed. by C. Schroeder. il pors Good H 173:94-5+ O '71

MCMURRAY, Marjorie C.
Batik: a short cut. il por Sch Arts 70:20-1 Ap '71

MCMURRIN, Sterling M.
What are the hallmarks of innovation? address, October 26, 1971. Vital Speeches 38: 115-17 D 1 '71

MCMURTRY, John
Smash thy neighbor. Atlan 229:77-80 Ja '72

MCNALLY, Terrence
Where has Tommy Flowers gone? Criticism
Nation 213:410-11 O 25 '71 •
New Yorker 47:101 O 16 '71 •
Newsweek il 78:108 O 18 '71 •
Time il 98:80 O 18 '71 •

MCNAMARA, A. C. Jr
Predicting ballast noise from H.I.D. lighting systems. il Arch Rec 149:139-42 My '71

MCNAMARA, Anne L. See Smith, D. W. E. jt. auth.

MCNAMARA, James F.
Statistics: a vital educational tool; adaptation of address. Clear House 45:558-61 My '71

MCNAMARA, Pamela, and others
Sugar transport: effect of temperature on concentrative uptake of α-methylglucoside by kidney cortex slices. bibliog il Science 172:1033-4 Je 4 '71

MCNAMARA, Robert Strange
Basic problems of development; address, September 27, 1971. Vital Speeches 38:17-21 O 15 '71

about

How much is enough, by A. C. Enthoven and K. W. Smith. Review
 Nation 212:629 My 17 '71. R. F. Kaufman •
McNamara and the Pentagon: limits of the management view. J. Walsh. Science 172:1008-9+ Je 4 '71 •
McNamara. by H. L. Trewhitt. Review
 Bsns W por p 16+ Jl 17 '71. H. Cheshire •
 Newsweek il por 78:66-7 Ag 9 '71. R. C. Christopher •
Particular tragedy of Robert McNamara. por Time 98:21 Jl 5 '71 •
Programming of Robert McNamara. D. Halberstam. il pors Harper 242:37-40+ F '71; Discussion. 242:6+ Ap; 8+ My '71 •
Robert McNamara revisited. H. L. Trewhitt. por Newsweek 78:17-18 Ag 16 '71 •

MCNAMEE, Gil
BARC and the consumer. bibliog il **Library J** 96:3292-4 O 15 '71

MCNAMEE, Thomas
Louise leaning over the water; poem. Yale R 60:392 Mr '71

MCNARRY, L. R. and O'Farrell, S.
Students reveal negative attitudes toward technology. Science 172:1060-1 Je 4 '71

MCNASPY, Clement J.
Against odds, it came off well. il America 125:228-9 O 2 '71
Ecumenical "if" il America 124:655-6 Je 26 '71
Fine arts. America 124:263; 125:95-6, 376-7; 126:21-2 Mr 13, Ag 21, N 6 '71, Ja 8 '72

MCNEE, Patrick
Patrick Macnee is the best dressed man in the world. I. Bauer. il pors Look 35:50-3 O 5 '71 •

MCNEELY, Richard. See Schwartz, R. jt. auth.

MACNEISH, Richard S.
Early man in the Andes; with biographical sketch. il Sci Am 224:13, 36-46 Ap '71

MACNICHOL, Edward Ford, 1918-
Two cultures note. J. Walsh. Science 174: 128-9 O 8 '71 •

MCNULTY, Faith
Black-footed ferret; excerpts from Must they die? il Nat Parks & Con Mag 45:9-13 My '71
War on wildlife. il Nat Parks & Con Mag 45:11-17 Mr '71

MCNULTY, Henry P.
Champagne: psychological magic. House & Gard 139:79+ My '71
Cognac: to put the cook in good spirits. House & Gard 140:126+ S '71
Drinks that bloom with fruit and flowers. House & Gard 140:76 Ag '71

MCNULTY, James F.
Secrets of the successful general manager. il Nations Bsns 59:42+ My '71

MACOMBER, William Butts, 1921-
Diplomacy for the seventies: a program of management reform for the Department of state; letter of transmittal. November 20, 1970. Dept State Bul 63:775 D 28 '70

MACON COUNTY, Ala.
Rough justice; police arrested. por Newsweek 77:25 Mr 1 '71

MCPHEE, John
Profiles; G. Hartzog. por New Yorker 47:45-8+ S 11 '71
Profiles; C. Park and D. Brower. por New Yorker 47:42-8+ Mr 20; 42-8+ Mr 27: 41-4+ Ap 3 '71

MCPHERSON, Aimee Semple
Billy and Aimee. F. Russell. Nat R 23:716 Je 29 '71 •
Storming heaven, by L. Thomas. Review
 Chr Cent 88:322 Mr 10 '71. D. Klass •
Theology of joy. S. Darst. Nation 213:440+ N 1 '71 •

MCPHERSON, Sandra
Coin; poem. Nation 213:445 N 1 '71
Community; War surplus store; Triolets; poems. Poetry 118:94-6 My '71
Peddler; poem. Nation 213:602 D 6 '71

about

Scattered craft. J. Galassi. Poetry 118:291-2 Ag '71 •

MCQUADE, Lawrence C.
Doing business with China; address, November 1, 1971. Vital Speeches 38:151-5 D 15 '71

MCQUADE, Walter
Computer in perspective. il Life 70:12 Ap 30 '71
Embattled prince of Fiat. il pors Fortune 84:124-6+ Ag '71

High style disrupts the men's wear industry. il Fortune 83:70-2+ F '71
Momentary community for a mobile era. il Life 71:8 Jl 23 '71
Walker Evans retrospective. il Life 70:12 Mr 5 '71

MACQUARIE ISLAND
Macquarie Island. D. Braxton. il Sea Front 17:224-9 Jl '71

MCQUEEN, Mildred
Individualized instruction. Ed Digest 36:25-8 Ap '71

MCQUEEN, Noel. See Hark, M. jt. auth.

MCQUEEN, Steve
Harvey on the lam. R. F. Jones. por Sports Illus 35:55-6+ Ag 23 '71 •
Le Mans. E. Seidler. il por Motor T 23:94+ Je '71 •

MACRAMÉ
Knotty but nice. il Time 97:50 My 17 '71
Macramé. D. Mellach. il Todays Health 49:28-31 O '71
Macrame-not as knotty as it looks. M. B. Smith. il Bet Hom & Gard 49:60-1+ F '71
Macrame ties country in knots. McCalls 98:43 Ap '71
Make your own jewelry. il Redbook 137:84-5+ My '71
One square knot after another; macramé belt. il Sunset 146:83-4+ F '71

MCREYNOLDS, Karman
I call my cold frame indispensable. il por Org Gard & Farm 18:53-5 O '71
What's cooking? il Org Gard & Farm 18:127-9 D '71

MACROBERTS, Barbara R. and MacRoberts, M. H.
Apes of Gibraltar; with biographical sketches. il Natur Hist 80:4, 38-47 Ag '71

MACROBERTS, Michael H. See MacRoberts, B. R. jt. auth.

MCROBERTS, Rufus
Lingering link. il Travel 135:26 Je '71

MACROBIOTIC diet. See Diet

MACROCYCLIC compounds. See Cyclic compounds

MACROPHAGES
Immune response restoration with macrophage culture supernatants. M. Hoffmann and R. W. Dutton. bibliog il Science 172:1047-8 Je 4 '71

MACSHANE, Frank
Range of six. Poetry 118:295-301 Ag '71

MCVAY, Scott
Can leviathan long endure so wide a chase? with biographical sketch. il Natur Hist 80:2, 36-41+ Ja '71
Day at the Ayukaua whaling station. il Nat Parks & Con Mag 45:16-18 F '71
Does the whale's magnitude diminish?—Will he perish? il Bul Atom Sci 27:38-41 F '71
Whales: a skirmish won, but what about the war? il Nat Parks & Con Mag 45:14-15+ F '71
—See Payne, R. S. jt. auth.

MCWHIRTER, William A.
American family arrives in Paris. il Life 70:59-60+ Je 25 '71
Grand rerun for Charlie Chaplan. il pors Life 71:93-6 D 3 '71
We all meet at the club for lunch. Life 71:30 O 29 '71
Will there be a Concorde in our future? il Life 70:86+ My 28 '71
(ed) See Eckstein, O. Expert views the freeze and the future

MCWILLIAMS, Carey
Book marks. Nation 213:345-6+, 700-1 O 11, D 27 '71

MCWILLIAMS, Wilson Carey
Path to Peking. Commonweal 94:397-8 Ag 6 '71

MACY, R. H. and company
Macy's opens bargain bookshop in the underground. P. A. Farrell. Pub W 200:40 Jl 26 '71
Value store that grew and grew. E. L. Molloy. il por Nations Bsns 59:74-5 Ja '71

MAD dog blues; drama. See Shepard, S.

MADAGASCAR
Big frame-up; imprisonment of vice-president and expulsion of the U.S. ambassador. il por Newsweek 78:44+ Jl 5 '71
See also
Geology—Madagascar

   Foreign relations

    United States

 See United States—Foreign relations—Madagascar

MADAGASCAR periwinkle. See Periwinkles

MADAME Butterfly; opera. See Puccini, G.

MADARIAGA, Salvador de
What did Columbus mean to Europe? il
Américas 23:S14-15 O '71

MADDEN, Carl H.
Mixing politics and economics. por Nations
Bsns 59:40+ Mr '71

MADDEN, David
Fiction technique & style: some comparisons. il Writers Digest 51:24-6+ Ag '71

MADDEN, Richard B.
Potlatch's oil man. por Bsns W p79 Ap 17
'71 *

MADDOCKS, Melvin
Have Americans gone mad? Cur 125:5-9 Ja
'71
Life book review (cont) Life 70:6-7 F 12;
8-9 Ap 2; 8-9 My 7; 12 My 21; 14-15 Je 25
'71; 72:17 Ja 14 '72
New awakening in Orr land. il Sports Illus
35:32-7 O 11 '71
Proust: a prophet remembered. Atlan 228:
92-5 Jl '71

MADDOX, Everette H.
Shades mountain; poem. New Yorker 47:48
O 30 '71

MADDOX, Jerald C.
Beaufort wind scale; photographs. Art in Am
59:90-1 Ja '71

MADDOX, Lester G.
Lester Maddox: showman and radical; interview, ed. by C. E. Fager. por Chr Cent
88:403-6 Mr 31 '71

about

Maddox touch. J. B. Cumming, jr. il por
Newsweek 77:23 Ja 18 '71 *

MADEIRA, Jean
Strauss and the low voice. por Opera N 35:27
F 27 '71

MADELEINE, Sister
Boquen monastery: growing seeds in tired
soil. Chr Cent 88:431 Ap 7 '71

MADEMOISELLE (periodical)
Mlle award winners: 7 women who know the
answers. il Mlle 74:66-8 Ja '72
Young women of the year. il Mlle 72:61-3+ Ja
'71

MADERNA, Bruno
Artist life. D. J. Soria. il por Hi Fi 21:MA4-6
Je '71 *

MADIGOSKY, W. M.
Polywater or sodium acetate? bibliog il Science 172:264-5 Ap 16 '71

MADISON, James
James Madison, by R. Ketcham. Review
Nat R 23:709-10 Je 29 '71. V. Miller *

MADISON, John
Turf management interactions. il Parks &
Rec 6:32-5 S '71

MADISON, John P.
Critical thinking in the English classroom.
bibliog Engl J 60:1133-40+ N '71

MADISON, Wis.

Education

Library books for leftover class time; art
reading tables at Monona public schools.
J. W. Stewig. bibliog il por Wilson Lib
Bul 45:681-4 Mr '71; Correction. 45:836 My
'71

Recreation

Give youth a volunteering chance: Saturday morning recreation program for handicapped children. C. M. Anderson. il Parks
& Rec 6:44-5 O '71

Sanitary affairs

Grinding refuse is no experiment. E. J.
Duszynski. il Am City 86:61-3 S '71

MADOCS, Rita
Baby sitter who didn't love children; story.
Redbook 137:75-6 Ag '71
Last Don Juan; story. Ladies Home J 88:78
S '71
Must have a sense of humor; story. Ladies
Home J 88:32 Je '71

MADONNAS. See Mary, Virgin—Art

MADSEN, C. R.
Thirty-year hike. il Har Yrs 11:24-6 Je '71

MADSEN, Roy P.
Wax engraving technique of Roy P. Madsen.
P. Whitaker. il Am Artist 35:50-5 My '71 *

MADSON, John
It's a good ol' place: Uncle Sam's mini-park.
il Audubon 73:30-5 Ja '71

MADURA (island)
Population crisis and economic development.
W. Withington. bibliog il Focus 21:9-12 My
'71

MADURODAM, The Hague. See Models of
cities, towns, etc.

MAERSK-MOLLER, Hans
2400mm f/12 for 2¼ and 35mm SLR! il Mod
Phot 35:94-5+ Ag '71

MAERTENS, Norbert W.
Who's afraid of modern math? il Parents
Mag 46:54+ Ag '71

MAFFEI galaxies. See Galaxies

MAFFIT, James S.
Actor's true identity is revealed. F. Lenthall. il pors Hobbies 76:50+ My '71 *

MAFIA
Age of touchiness; Time essay. M. Maddocks. il Time 97:21 My 10 '71
Building with the Buffalo boys. il Time 98:
21-2 Ag 30 '71
Capo who went public. Time 98:16-17 Jl 12
'71
Chronicle of bloodletting. il Time 98:21 Jl
12 '71
Comeuppance for Newark's unholy alliance. J.
Reedy. il Read Digest 98:113-17 Ja '71
Death of a mob family; R. Patriarca. T.
Renner. Read Digest 98:175-6+ My '71
Dying out. P. S. Nathan. il Pub W 200:53
Ag 2 '71
Honor thy father, by G. Talese. Review
Sat R il 54:25 Ag 28 '71. A. Green
Honor thy father; excerpts. G. Talese. il
pors Esquire 76:45-53+ Ag; 116-21+ S;
140-7+ O '71
How one family stamped out the M----. il
pors Newsweek 77:22-3 Ap 5 '71
How organized crime invades the home. N.
Gage. il Good H 173:68-9+ Ag '71
Italy tries to maroon some Mañosi. D. J.
Hamblin. il Life 70:34-6 Je 18 '71
Mafia: back to the bad old days? il pors
Time 98:14-18+ Jl 12 '71
Mafia is not an equal opportunity employer,
by N. Gage. Review
Sat R il 54:49 O 9 '71. F. J. Cook
Mafia tries a new tune; with report by E.
Harvey. T. Buckley. il Harper 243:46-7+
Ag '71
Mob's grip on New Jersey. W. Schulz. Read
Digest 98:111-15 F '71
Night for Colombo. il por Time 97:16 Ap 5 '71
Parting shots: Unity day that split the mob.
il pors Life 71:70-1 Jl 9 '71
Police, the press & the legend; call it Mafia.
E. Ruffini. il Nation 213:520-4 N 22 '71
Smut: the Mafia's newest racket; with editorial comment. D. Denison. Read Digest
99:11-12, 157-60 D '71
Unsinkable Mafia; parliamentary report,
Italy. il Newsweek 78:35+ Jl 26 '71
What d'ya hear from the mob? P. Axthelm.
il por Newsweek 78:31-2 Jl 12 '71

MAGAZINE advertising. See Advertising, Magazine

MAGAZINE art. See Illustration of books and
periodicals

MAGAZINE publishing. See Publishers and
publishing—Periodicals

MAGAZINE stands, racks, etc.
Make a closet-door magazine rack. D. Huff.
il Pop Sci 199:97 S '71
Simple magazine rack with the modern look.
K. Wells. il Pop Mech 136:168-9 N '71

MAGAZINES. See Periodicals

MAGDOFF, Harry
Logic of imperialism. Cur 125:51-63 Ja '71

MAGEE, James J.
Jews and the early church. Cath World 214:
113-16 D '71

MAGEE, Malcolm
South African violence, black or white? Commonweal 93:388-9 Ja 22 '71

MAGEE, Ruchell
No exit. il pors Newsweek 78:26-7 Ag 9 '71 *

MAGEE, Stephen Pat
Man with the figures. il por Fortune 84:138
N '71 *

MAGGIO musicale fiorentino. See Music festivals—Italy

MAGI
Epiphany counterpoint. V. P. McCorry.
America 125:inside back cover D 25 '71

MAGIC
New magic. D. McFerran. Commonweal 94:
477-80 S 17 '71; Reply. R. Woods. 95:219+
D 3 '71
See also
Children as magicians
Witchcraft

MAGIC and Christianity. See Christianity and
magic

MAGIC chef, inc.
Right product at the right time. il Forbes
108:34-5 D 15 '71

MAGIC flute; opera. See Mozart, J. C. W. A.

MAGIC lady; story. See Ross, I.

MAGIC mask; story. See Moray, A.

MAGIC mushrooms; drama. See Jones, D. C.
MAGID, Nora L.
Booknotes. Commonweal 93:471+ F 12 '71
Canadian club. Commonweal 95:327-30 Ja 7 '72
MAGIDSON, Daniel T.
Half step forward. il Environ 13:10-13 Je '71
MAGISTRO, Charles F.
Abortion and the pluralist society. il Nat R 23:476-8+ My 4 '71
MAGLIĆ, Bogdan
Split in the A₂ meson. Sci N 99:314 My 8 '71 *
MAGNAVOX company
New game? Forbes 108:24-5 Jl 1 '71
Wider spectrum at Magnavox. por Bsns W p 112 Mr 13 '71
MAGNESIUM
Magnesium. J. D. Navratil. bibliog il por Chem 44:6-10 My '71
MAGNETIC bubbles. See Domain structure
MAGNETIC domains. See Domain structure
MAGNETIC fields
Magnetic structure of superconductors. U. Essmann and H. Träuble. il Sci Am 224:74-84 Mr '71
  See also
Magnetic resonance

Physiological effects
How the heavens influence our lives. M. Cohen. il Todays Health 49:16-19 O '71
Magnetic reversals and biological extinctions. L. Purrett. il Sci N 100:300-1 O 30 '71

MAGNETIC fields (cosmic physics)
Analyzing the periodicity in the sun's magnetism. il Sci N 100:358 N 27 '71
Geometry of the coronal magnetic field. M. D. Altschuler. il Sky & Tel 41:146-50 Mr '71
Magnetism of the moon. P. Dyal and C. W. Parkin. il Sci Am 225:62-73 bibliog(p 120) Ag '71
Permanent lunar surface magnetism and its deflection of the solar wind. A. Barnes and others. bibliog il Science 172:716-18 My 14 '71
Possible fossil lunar magnetism inferred from satellite data. J. D. Mihalov and others. bibliog il Science 171:892-5 Mr 5 '71
Rotating solar magnetic dipole observed from 1926-1968. J. M. Wilcox and W. Gonzalez. bibliog il Science 174:820-1 N 19 '71
Solar prominences and their magnetic fields. E. Tandberg-Hanssen. il Sky & Tel 42:72-5, 142-5 Ag-S '71
Whole body response of the moon to electromagnetic induction by the solar wind. C. P. Sonett and others. bibliog il Science 172:256-8 Ap 16 '71

MAGNETIC materials
  See also
Ferrites (magnetic materials)
Magnets
MAGNETIC memory (computers) See Memory devices (computers)
MAGNETIC poles. See Magnetism, Terrestrial
MAGNETIC recorders and recording
Cassette or cartridge: which tape machine for you? W. G. Salm. il Pop Mech 135:72-5+ F '71
Cassette tape recorders. il Consumer Rep 36:279-83 My '71
Cheerful earfuls. il Seventeen 29:136-9 S '70
Harman-Kardon cassette deck. il Pop Electr 35:80-1 O '71
Higher-fi goes into cassettes. il Bsns W p44 Jl 3 '71
It's all on tape! C. S. Litsinger. il Good H 173:154+ D '71
Look what they've done with the lowly cassette! W. G. Salm. il Pop Mech 136:100-5+ D '71
New deck, new tape, new high in cassette hi-fi; Sony's TC-160 cassette deck. J. R. Free. il Pop Sci 199:85 Ag '71
Reel winner; making party tapes. S. Reice. il Am Home 74:58+ N '71
Tape-timing nomogram. R. F. Graf and G. J. Whalen. il Radio-Electr 42:52-3 Ag '71
What makes a tape recorder professional? H. Friedman. Hi Fi 21:50 Ag '71
  See also
Ampex corporation
Phonograph records—Recording
Tape recordings

Educational use
Electronic creativity in the elementary classroom. A. D. Modugno. il Todays Ed 60:62-4 Mr '71
Grading themes: a new approach; a new dimension. S. H. Vogler. Engl J 60:70-4+ Ja '71

Equipment
Attenuator for smoother recordings. J. Chamkis. il Radio-Electr 42:96-7 S '71
Novel stereo recording meter. il Radio-Electr 42:84 Ag '71
Speaker monitor for your tape recorder. F. Blechman. il Radio-Electr 42:45+ N '71

Maintenance and repair
Factory adjustments and maladjustments. J. G. Holt. il Pop Electr 35:84-6 S '71
Setting up a tape recorder. J. G. Holt. il Pop Electr 35:67-70 O '71
Stereo cassettes, the electronic side: programmed instruction. L. Allen. il Radio-Electr 42:39-43 Mr '71

Noise
Hi-fi product report; Advent advocate model 101 noise-reduction unit. il Electr World 85:14+ Mr '71
Out goes the tape hiss with new Dolby unit. I. Berger. il Pop Sci 198:20 F '71
Stereo scene; Dolby noise-reduction system. J. G. Holt. il Pop Electr 34:71+ F '71

Stereophonic recorders
From two channels to four, with a little bit o' pluck. R. S. Lanier. il Hi Fi 21:78-81 N '71
Magnecord 2001 tape deck. il Pop Electr 35:78-80 S '71
Stereo cassettes, the mechanical side: programmed text. L. Allen. il Radio-Electr 42:37-40 Ap '71

Testing
EW lab tests new Dolby-ized cassette decks. J. D. Hirsch. il Electr World 85:25-8+ Mr '71
Hi-fi product report; KLH model 41 tape deck. il Electr World 86:6-7 Jl '71

Unauthorized recording
$100-million market in bootleg tapes. il Bsns W p 132+ My 15 '71
Sound advice; bootleg tapes. R. Angus. Mod Phot 35:134 Je '71

Visual recording
  See Video recorders and recording
MAGNETIC resonance
Magnetic resonances and waves in simple metals. W. M. Walsh. jr. bibliog il Science 171:36-42 Ja 8 '71
Ordering of V²⁺, Mn²⁺, and Fe²⁺ ions in zoisite, Ca₂Al₃Si₃O₁₂(OH) use of EPR technique. S. Ghose and T. Tsang. bibliog il Science 171:374-6 Ja 29 '71; Reply. D. R. Hutton and others. 174:1259 D 17 '71
Protein-metal ion binding site: determination with proton magnetic resonance spectroscopy. P. I. Rose. bibliog il Science 171:573-4 F 12 '71
  See also
Nuclear magnetic resonance
MAGNETIC tape
Getting the most from your tape cassettes. M. Mandl. il Radio-Electr 42:51-3 Jl '71
How good are those new cassette tapes? J. R. Free. il Pop Sci 199:89+ N '71
Tape up to date. L. Zide. il Hi Fi 21:43-7 Ag '71
  See also
Data tapes
Tape recordings
MAGNETIC tape players
Cassette or cartridge: which tape machine for you? W. G. Salm. il Pop Mech 135:72-5+ F '71
Equipment report; Toyo CH-702 tape player. il Radio-Electr 42:26 O '71
Nine cassettes to show off and test your tape playback system. R. D. Darrell. Hi Fi 21:48-9 Ag '71
PS buyer's guide to cassette players; with table. il Pop Sci 199:90-3 N '71
Product test reports; Lafayette RK-48 2/4-channel cartridge tape player and Toyo CH-702 2/4-channel cartridge tape player system. il Pop Electr 1:76-8 Ja '72
  See also
Advertising mediums—Magnetic tape players
MAGNETIC trains. See Air cushion vehicles
MAGNETISM
Magnetism and local molecular field; Nobel lecture, 1970. L. Néel. bibliog il Science 174:985-92 D 3 '71
Magnetism as a tool in biology. D. E. Thomsen. il Sci N 99:117-18 F 13 '71
Mechanism for producing magnetic remanence in meteorites and lunar samples by cosmic-ray exposure. R. F. Butler and A. V. Cox. bibliog il Science 172:939-41 My 28 '71

MAGNETISM—*Continued*
One-dimensional antiferromagnets. G. B.
Lubkin. bibliog Phys Today 24:19-20 Mr
'71
See also
Electromagnetism
Magnets
Physiological effects
See Magnetic fields—Physiological effects
MAGNETISM, Terrestrial
Comets did it. Time 98:40+ S 6 '71
Destiny and geomagnetism. W. Garrison. il
Pop Electr 35:41-6 Jl '71
Following the trail of a magnetic reversal.
il Sci N 99:366 My 29 '71
Geomagnetic reversals during the phanerozoic.
M. W. McElhinny. bibliog il Science 172:
157-9 Ap 9 '71
Identifying 26 reversals during early cre-
taceous. Sci N 100:358 N 27 '71
Pacific geomagnetic secular variation. R. R.
Doell and A. Cox. bibliog il Science 171:
248-54 Ja 22 '71
Paleomagnetic chronology of pliocene-early
pleistocene climates and the plio-pleistocene boundary in New Zealand. J. P. Kennett and others. bibliog il Science 171:276-
9 Ja 22 '71
Paleomagnetic study of a reversal of the
earth's magnetic field. J. R. Dunn and
others. bibliog il Science 172:840-5 My 21
'71
Seven-year itch; correlation between the
earth's wobble and earthquakes. il Newsweek 78:54-5 Ag 30 '71
When the North Pole goes south. L. Purrett.
il Sci N 99:251-3 Ap 10 '71
MAGNETOCARDIOGRAPHY. See Cardiography
MAGNETOGLOW. See Earth—Radiation
MAGNETOHYDRODYNAMICS
MHD for electrical power: Interior grant
gives boost. Sci N 100:204 S 25 '71
MAGNETO-OPTICS
Polarized light from white-dwarf star. G. B.
Lubkin. bibliog il Phys Today 24:19-20 Ja
'71
MAGNETOSPHERE. See Atmosphere, Upper
MAGNETS
1000 GeV with superconducting magnets at
Batavia? M. S. Rothenberg. il Phys To-
day 24:19-20 My '71
Pulsating world of magnetics. I. Geller. il
Duns 93:75-6+ Je '69
Superconducting magnets. J. K. Hulm and
others. bibliog il Phys Today 24:48-53+
Ag '71
MAGNIFIERS
Small magnifier with built-in lighted scales;
the Flash magnifier. il Consumer Bul 55:27
Ja '72
MAGNIFYING glasses. See Magnifiers
MAGNOLIA
See also
Michelia
MAGOON, Bob
True love at first contusion. C. Phinizy. il
por Sports Illus 34:52-4 Mr 22 '71 *
MAGRUDER, William M.
Aerospace industry; address, February 1,
1971. Vital Speeches 37:359-63 Ap 1 '71
For the SST: why the U.S. needs it; inter-
view. il por U S News 70:68 Mr 15 '71
about
Magruder in White House: SST man plans
new technology take-off. D. Shapley. por
Science 174:386-8 O 22 '71 *
$1-billion monthly cost foreseen to apply
technology to social ills. Aviation W 95:46
N 29 '71 *
MAGUIRE, Daniel C.
End of a battle. il por Time 98:38 Ag 23 '71 *
MAGUIRE, Francis
Exposed to light; poem. Chr Today 16:6 Ja
7 '72
MAGUIRE, John W.
Political technique in school bond and millage
elections. bibliog Sch & Soc 99:514-15 D
'71
MAHAN, Larry
Best damn cowboy in the world. J. Stewart-
Gordon. il Read Digest 99:215-16+ S '71 *
MAHAN, Paul E.
Grow more cucumbers, use less space. il
Org Gard & Farm 18:51 My '71
MAHARAJ Ji. See Balyogeshwar (Indian guru)
MAHER, Arthur J.
Easy backyard living. Am Home 74:32+ Je
'71
Insulation: a federal case. Am Home 74:
68-9 O '71

MAHEU, René
Educational aid for the Palestine refugees.
UNESCO Courier 24:38-9 Mr '71
Youth of the world, youth of Unesco.
UNESCO Courier 24:4-5 Ag '71
MAHEU, Robert A.
High rollers shoot for power in Las Vegas.
T. O'Hanlon. il Fortune 83:36-7 Ja '71 *
Letters from the invisible billionaire, with
sincere regards, Howard Hughes. il por
Life 70:24-8 Ja 22 '71 *
MAHGOUB, Abdel Khalek
Black eye for Moscow. il por Newsweek 78:
30+ Ag 9 '71 *
MAHIGEL, E. Louis, and Stone, G. P.
How card hustlers make the game. bibliog
(p8) il Trans-Action 8:40-5 Ja '71
MAHLER, Gustav
Georg Solti's first Chicago recordings. J.
Diether. il Am Rec G 37:346-9 F '71 *
Grandoise transcendentalism: Horenstein
and Abravanel in the Mahler Third sym-
phony. G. S. Fox. Am Rec G 37:577+ My
'71 *
Gustav Mahler: Das klagende lied. G. S. Fox.
por Am Rec G 37:214-16+ D '70 *
Mahler's symphonies, the best complete set.
R. C. Marsh. Hi Fi 21:83-4 N '71 *
Musical events; Eighth symphony performed
by Hartford symphony orchestra. W. Sar-
geant. New Yorker 47:111 My 1 '71 *
On London: Solti the Hungarian. R. C. Marsh.
Hi Fi 21:72-3 Ja '71 *
MAHLMANN, Lewis, and Jones, D. C.
Frog prince; dramatization of Grimm's
fairy tale. Plays 30:66-72 My '71
MAHOGANY, Mountain. See Mountain ma-
hogany
MAHONEY, David Joseph, 1923-
Moving in; interview. New Yorker 47:28-9 My
29 '71
MAHONEY, John
Winter soldiering in Detroit. Commonweal
93:540-1 Mr 5 '71
MAIAKOVSKII, Vladimir Vladimirovich
Life of Mayakovsky, by W. Woroszylski. Re-
view
Nation 212:597-9 My 10 '71. G. Daniels *
New Repub 164:25-7 Ap 3 '71. R. Whitte-
more *
Newsweek il por 77:94-5 F 22 '71. G.
Wolff *
Vogue il por 157:72-3 Mr 15 '71. A.
Kazin *
MAIDS (servants) See Household employees
MAIER, Art
Congressional hearings: a trap for business-
men? il Duns 97:44-6+ Mr '71
MAIER, Henry W.
Duel in Milwaukee; feud between mayor and
newspaper editor. por Time 99:50 Ja 3 '72 *
Milwaukee's Mayor Maier. il por Newsweek
78:71 Ag 23 '71 *
MAIER, Paul L.
First Christmas. Redbook 138:65+ D '71
MAIL advertising. See Advertising, Direct mail
MAIL boxes. See Mailboxes
MAIL order business
Ready to mail: National mail order merchan-
dise show. New Yorker 47:29-31 My 29 '71
See also
Herter's, inc.
Postal service—Unordered merchandise
Sears, Roebuck and company
MAIL service. See Postal service
MAILBOXES
Countryside sculpture. il Design 72:16-20
mid-Sum '71
MAILER, Norman
Ali-Frazier fight. il pors Life 70:18F-19+ Mr
19 '71
Authors & editors; interview, ed. by B. A.
Bannon. por Pub W 199:177-9 Ja 25 '71
Prisoner of sex. bibliog f il por(p4) Harper
242:41-6+ Mr '71
Rape of the moon; interview, ed. by L. Kent.
Vogue 157:134-5 F 1 '71
about
Mailer lights another fire. D. N. Mount.
Pub W 199:55 F 15 '71 *
Mailer mystique. S. K. Oberbeck. il por
Newsweek 77:56 F 22 '71 *
Mailer opening. New Yorker 47:33 O 2 '71 *
My Mailer problem. G. Greer. por Esquire 76:
90-3+ S '71 *
Norman Mailer: devil in the fire. N. Gittel-
son. Harp Baz 104:14+ Jl '71 *
Norman Mailer meets the Butch Brigade. J.
Greenway. Nat R 23:815 Jl 27 '71 *
Perfect absurd figure of a mighty, absurd
crusade. J. W. Aldridge. il por Sat R 54:
45-6+ N 13 '71 *

MAILER, Norman—about—*Continued*
Stars and celebrities. R. Schickel. Commentary 52:61-5 Ag '71 •
Ups and downs of Mailer. R. Poirier. New Repub 164:23-6 Ja 23 '71 •
With Norman Mailer at the sex circus. V. S. Pritchett; J. C. Oates. Atlan 228:40-5 Jl '71 •
Women's lib; Mailer v. Millett. il por Time 97:71 F 22 '71 •

MAILING lists
AAP seminar focuses on direct mail. P. A. Farrell. Pub W 200:16-17 N 29 '71
Direct-mail ads will get more direct. il Bsns W p84+ N 27 '71

MAIN, Mary. See Brazelton, T. B. jt. auth.

MAINBOCHER
Mainbocher; great gentleman of fashion. il Harp Baz 104:70-3 Je '71 •

MAINE
Letter from the East. E. B. White. New Yorker 47:35-7 Mr 27 '71
Snowshoe country. V. N. DeFelice. il Am For 77:20-3+ F '71
    See also
Acadia National Park
Cliff Island
Environmental policy—Maine
Fishing—Maine
Gardens—Maine
Hunting—Maine
Kennebec River
Mount Desert Island
Skis and skiing—Maine

Description and travel
Along the Maine line. R. W. Brace. il Travel 136:64+ N '71
Down East: the magic of the state o' Maine. A. Gordon. il Read Digest 98:104-10 My '71

Industries
    See also
Petroleum industry—Maine

MAINE CHANCE, Ariz. See Health resorts, watering places, etc.

MAINES, Patrick D.
Unselling of the Vietnam war. il Nat R 23:858-9 Ag 10 '71

MAINZ
    See also
Gutenberg museum

MAIORANO, Robert
Brief biography. S. Goodman. pors Dance Mag 45:58-9 Je '71 •

MAISEL, Albert Q.
Controversy over breast cancer. Read Digest 99:151-6 D '71
National health insurance, do we need it? What kind? At what cost? Read Digest 98:86-90 F '71
Should chiropractors be paid with your tax dollars? Read Digest 99:76-81 Jl '71
What are the facts about food additives? Read Digest 98:81-5 My '71

MAISEL, Louis, 2d
Stretch camps' responsibility to include disadvantaged. Camp Mag 43:8-10 Mr '71

MAITLAND, Elizabeth (Murray) duchess of Lauderdale. See Lauderdale, E. M. M.

MAIZE. See Corn

MAIZE dwarf mosaic. See Viruses. Plant

MAJNO, G. and others
Contraction of granulation tissue in vitro; similarity to smooth muscle. bibliog il Science 173:548-50 Ag 6 '71

MAJOLICA
Italian majolica plate. il Ceram Mo 20:13 Ja '72
Majolica technique for stoneware. A. C. Garzio. il Ceram Mo 20:19-22 Ja '72
Pottery in Manises; Moorish-influenced majolica of southern Spain. T. Shafer and Y. Shafer. il Ceram Mo 20:14-18 Ja '72

MAJOR, Clarence
Comment. F. MacShane. Poetry 118:297-8 Ag '71 •

MAJOR appliance consumer action panel. See Consumer protection

MAJOR league baseball players association
My rebellion; excerpt from The way it is; ed. by R. Carter. C. Flood. il pors Sports Illus 34:24-9 F 1 '71
Who says baseball is like ballet? il Forbes 107:24-6+ Ap 1 '71

MAJORITIES
That elusive political majority. A. J. Reichley. il por Fortune 83:68-73+ Mr '71

MAKARIOS III, abp
Reports & comment. E. Drew. Atlan 228:6+ N '71 •

MAKAROVA, Dina
Beyond Giselle? il pors Dance Mag 46:46-55 Ja '72

MAKAROVA, Natalya
Beyond Giselle? D. Makarova. il pors Dance Mag 46:46-55 Ja '72

    about
And if you're a good girl, I'll take you to a Makarova rehearsal. T. Tobias. il pors Dance Mag 45:38-43 My '71 •
Beauty in a classic way. pors Vogue 158:68-9 Ag 1 '71 •
Dance. N. Goldner. Nation 212:156-7 F 1 '71 •
Lovely new swan alights; photographs. M. Waldman. Life 70:38-43 Ja 22 '71 •
Makarova: a marvel. W. Terry. il pors Sat R 54:77+ Ja 23 '71 •

MAKE-it-yourself furniture. See Furniture

MAKE-up
Adrien Arpel instructs in make-up. il Harp Baz 104:30 Ap '71
Beautiful brow. il Ladies Home J 88:26 My '71
Beauty bulletin; the newsy makeup colors and how to use them. il Good H 174:100-3 Ja '72
Beauty sense and nonsense. Harp Baz 104:68 S '71
Beauty tips for a rainy day T.. Pavlik. il Good H 172:14-15 Mr '71
Beauty view: Maria says. .; eye make-up. il Seventeen 29:188 S '70
Everybody's doing the shimmer; night make-up. il Vogue 158:144-5 N 1 '71
Expressive eye. C. Bartel. il Am Home 74:14+ Mr '71
Eyes: color's the key. S. Obre. il Ladies Home J 88:112-15 O '71
Face battle. il Seventeen 30:130-1 S '71
Find your best makeup look. T. Pavlik. il Good H 173:142-3+ N '71
For four young women: new beauty with a positive point of view. il Good H 172:106-9 F '71
Give your eyes a second look. il Redbook 138:94-7 N '71
Help! What'll I do? Too thick, too thin, too sallow, too pale. il Mlle 73:151-9 O '71
How to be divine all over. il Mlle 74:118-20 Ja '72
How to do eyes now! il Seventeen 30:228-9 Ag '71
Keep your eye on color; a pot of gloss, a fingertip and a shining new world of beauty. J. Birken. il por Vogue 158:120-3 N 15 '71
Look who's coming to town; experts demonstrate the look for spring '71. S. Obre. il Ladies Home J 88:120-3 Mr '71
Make up for a tan with makeup. il McCalls 98:66-9 Jl '71
Makeup shakeup. il Vogue 157:116-17 Ap 1 '71
Makeup that makes them say wow! il McCalls 99:88-91 D '71
New beauty looks for fall. il Seventeen 29:122-5 S '70
New face saving salon; P. Manzoni of Elizabeth Arden. pors Harp Baz 104:28 Ap '71
Nite brites: how you shine is up to you. il Seventeen 30:100-5 O '71
Nostalgia revives the romantic look. C. Bartel. il Am Home 74:14+ N '71
Put on a colorful face. il Time 98:46 S 20 '71
Stir up a colorquake. il Seventeen 29:114-17 O '70
There's more than one way to look at your face. il Redbook 137:96-9+ O '71
Things my sister taught me. L. Dey. il por Seventeen 29:76 Jl '70
3 new makeup plans timed for the busy woman. T. Pavlik. il Good H 172:122-3 My '71
Trading beauty tips/tricks with two Newcombers. il Mlle 73:206 My '71
23 new hairdos, exciting young makeup looks. T. Pavlik. il Good H 173:100-11+ O '71
23 romantic hairdos; radiant new makeup looks. il Good H 172:94-105 Ap '71
What will be the next face in the looking glass? R. Warfield. House & Gard 139:16+ Ja '71
    See also
Beauty, Personal

MAKENS, James C.
Paper and beer cans win. il Am City 86:53 Ja '71

MAKINODAN, Takashi
Shot of youth for the ills of age. il por Bsns W p60+ N 20 '71 •

MAKLAI, Nikolai Nikolaevich Miklukha-. See Miklukha-Maklai, N. N.

MAKMAN, Maynard H. See Klein, M. I. jt. auth.

MAKONDE sculpture. See Sculpture, African
MAKROPOULOS affair; opera. See Janáček, L.
MALAGASY. See Madagascar
MALARIA
Blood and malaria; donation of blood by drug addicts. Time 97:62+ Mr 15 '71
Malaria again? A. S. Freese. il Sci Digest 70:42-6 N '71
Malaria resistance: artificial induction with a partially purified plasmodial fraction. L. E. D'Antonio and others; reply with rejoinder. R. T. Cook and M. Aikawa. bibliog Science 171:1175-6 Mr 19 '71
MALARIAL parasites. See Plasmodium (parasite)
MALAWI
Killing of Hastings Banda; spying for the free world in the Peace corps. P. Theroux. Esquire 76:22+ D '71

Foreign relations

South Africa

See South Africa—Foreign relations—Malawi

MALAYSIA
See also
Singapore
MALCOLM, Andrew H.
Sex goes to college. il Todays Health 49:26-9 Ap '71
MALCOLM, Janet
On and off the avenue (cont) New Yorker 46:96+ F 13; 47:93-4+ Ap 10; 118+ My 1; 108+ My 15; 46-52 Jl 3; 59-62 S 4; 111-15 S 18; 115-17 S 25; 165-6+ N 13 '71
MALCOLM X community college. See Chicago city college—Malcolm X campus
MALDIVE ISLANDS
Island of not having; Gan, British refueling base in the Indian Ocean. J. Blashill. il Time 97:40 My 17 '71
MALE coiffure. See Hairdressing
MALE nurses. See Nurses and nursing
MALE teachers. See Teachers
MALEIC hydrazide
Chemical hedge trimmer; cancer-inducing element in Science hedge-trim. il Consumer Bul 54:19+ My '71
MALEK, Frederick Vincent
Administration talent search: alternatives to the buddy system. N. Wade. por Science 173:1216-18 S 24 '71 *
MALENBAUM, Wilfred
Progress in health: what index of what progress? bibliog f il Ann Am Acad 393:109-21 Ja '71
MALEY, Arthur F.
Fishing, at the swimming pool. il Parks & Rec 6:112-15 Ja '71
MALFATTI. See Cookery, Italian
MALIK, Adam
United Nations day 24 October 1971; message. UN Mo Chron 8:i-ii O '71
MALIK, Rex
Databank society; can we cope? Cur 129:6-10 My '71
MALINA, Joseph F. jr, and Smith, M. L.
How much refuse in your city? il Am City 86:64-6 Mr '71
MALINA, Judith
This is theater. por Newsweek 78:40 Ag 16 '71 *
MALING, Reginald
He brings them back to life. R. Tunley. il por Read Digest 98:193-4+ Ap '71 *
MALINOWSKI, W. R.
Toward a change in the international distribution of shipping activity. bibliog f Int Concil 582:66-79 Mr '71
MALIPONTE, Adriana
Little lion; interview, ed. by G. Fitzgerald. il por Opera M 36:13 D 11 '71
MALIVER, Bruce L.
Encounter groupers up against the wall. il N Y Times Mag p4-5+ Ja 3; 53 F 7 '71
Encounter groups: a dangerous game? Cur 126:3-12 F '71
MALKIEL, Burton G. and Quandt, R. E.
Moral issues in investment policy. bibliog f Harvard Bsns R 49:37-47 Mr '71
MALKIN, Lawrence
Practical politician at the Fed. il por Fortune 83:148-51+ My '71
MALKO, George
When you're in Banff, man, you're in Nelson Eddy country! il Holiday 48:70-1 S '70
MALKOC, Anna Maria, and Roberts, A. H.
Bi-dialectalism: a special report from CAL/ERIC. bibliog Engl J 60:279-88 F '71

MALLALIEU, H. B.
Confrontation with a stork; Berkshire landscape; Bow in the attic; Line to Roy Fuller; poems. Poetry 117:381-4 Mr '71
MALLARD; story. See Norris, L.
MALLARD ducks. See Ducks, Wild
MALLE, Louis
Current cinema. P. Kael. New Yorker 47:139-46 O 23 '71 *
MALLECZEWEN, Friedrich Percyval Reck-. See Reck-Malleczewen, F. P.
MALLET-JORIS, Françoise
Bringing up mother; interview, tr. by A. Foukle. Vogue 158:68+ O 1 '71
My house is paper, glued with love; excerpt from Paper house. il por Vogue 157:82-3 Mr 15 '71
MALLORY, Elizabeth
Gifts of the spirit. por PTA Mag 66:11 D '71
How we stand. PTA Mag 66:15 N '71
Inaugural; remarks, May 26, 1971. por PTA Mag 66:16-17 S '71
Membership proclamation. PTA Mag 66:9 O '71
MALLS, Shopping. See Shopping malls
MALLY, E. Louise
Moon rock; poem. Nation 213:94 Ag 2 '71
MALMQVIST, N. G. D.
Poetry of Chairman Mao. por Sat R 54:29-30 N 27 '71
MALMSTROM, Margit
Bronze horses of Marilyn Newmark. il por Am Artist 35:28-33+ Ap '71
Sculpture of Bruno Lucchesi. il por Am Artist 35:32-4+ O '71
MALNUTRITION. See Infants—Nutrition; Nutrition problems
MALOFF, Saul
Edward Dahlberg: pariah. por Commonweal 93:497-9 F 19 '71
Stormbird of the working class. Commonweal 95:226-9 D 3 '71
Waiting for the voice to crack. New Repub 164:33-5 My 8 '71
MALONE, John I. and others
Galactose toxicity in the chick: hyperosmolality. bibliog il Science 174:952-4 N 26 '71
MALONE, Thomas P.
Do-it-yourself encounter. Time 97:64 Je 21 '71 *
MALONE, Wayne C.
What makes a good comprehensive high school? Clear House 46:3-5 S '71
MALONEY, Elbert S.
H.O.229: new tables for an old task. il Motor B & S 127:102+ F '71
Notices to boatmen. Motor B & S 128:96+ Jl '71
MALONEY, George A.
And now, the Yoga retreat. America 124:591-3 Je '71
Ukrainians on the march. por Cath World 214:109-12 D '71
MALONEY, Ralph
Happy ending; story. Atlan 228:93-7 S '71
Intimacy; story. Atlan 227:78-82 F '71
MALONEY, Ruth Kay
Average director of a large public library. il por Library J 96:443-5 F 1 '71
MALOOF, Sam
Sam Maloof. G. Loney. il por Craft Horiz 31:16-19 Ag '71 *
MALOZEMOFF, Plato
From shotguns to rifles. por Forbes 107:48+ Je 15 '71 *
MALPRACTICE
Doctor's new dilemma: will I be sued? M. J. Halberstam. il N Y Times Mag p8-9+ F 14 '71
Medical lawsuits can kill you. il Sci Digest 69:58 Mr '71
People suing their lawyers, a growing trend. il U S News 70:30-2 Je 7 '71
Suing the doctor: a rising problem. il U S News 70:70-2 Mr 8 '71
MALRAUX, André
Conversations with de Gaulle; excerpt. il por Esquire 76:110, 129-33+ D '71

about

History's witness: Malraux at 70. por Time 98:40+ N 15 '71 *
I am a paratrooper. por Newsweek 78:35-6 O 11 '71 *
Letter from Paris; with excerpts from Les Chênes qu'on abat. Genêt. New Yorker 47:98+ Ap 24 '71 *
Malraux; by P. Galante. Review
    Atlan 227:86+ Je '71. D. Brogan *
(ed) See Gaulle, C. de. Chatting with de Gaulle

MALT whiskey. See Whiskey

MALTA
Cross Maltese. il por Time 98:26 Jl 19 '71
Deadline Dom. il Time 99:29 Ja 10 '72
Gaddafi to the rescue. por Time 99:27-8 Ja 17 '72
Of many things; need for improved communication within the church. D. R. Campion. America 124:inside cover Je 5 '71
Pulling up stakes? Newsweek 79:27+ Ja 10 '72

See also
Catholic church in Malta
Elections—Malta

Politics and government
See also
Elections—Malta

Religious institutions and affairs
See also
Church and state in Malta

MALTBY, Richard, jr
Sporting words. Harp Baz 104:146 My '71

MALTHUSIANISM
Nuclear energy and the Malthusian dilemma. D. R. Inglis. Bul Atom Sci 27:14-18 F '71; Reply with rejoinder. A. M. Weinberg. 27: 3+ Je '71

MAMBAS. See Snakes

MAMMALS
How much do you know about mammals? quiz. J. Daugherty and M. Daugherty. il Sci Digest 69:72-3+ Ap '71
Mammalian scent marking. K. Ralls. bibliog il Science 171:443-9 F 5 '71

See also
Embryology—Mammals
Felidae
Marine mammals
Photography of mammals
Primates

MAMMAPLASTY. See Surgery, Plastic

MAMMARY cancer. See Cancer

MAN
Chance and necessity, by J. Monod. Review
Atlan 228:125-30 N '71. G. Stent
Ecological man and leisure man. D. Robinson and D. Clayton. bibliog Parks & Rec 6:81-2 Ag '71
Humanities teaching and the mankind emphasis. M. H. Goldberg. Sch & Soc 99:176-8 Mr '71
Letter from a devout agnostic. F. Zubryd. America 124:486 My 8 '71
Man-child, by D. Jonas and D. Klein. Review
Nation 212:661-2 My 24 '71. A. Karlen
Natural man. il Cons 26:2 O '71
Perfectibility of man, by J. Passmore. Review
Sat R 54:64 S 4 '71. W. Arnold
Science and our understanding of ourselves. L. L. Whyte. Bul Atom Sci 27:32-3 Mr '71
Sunflower forest; excerpts from The invisible pyramid. L. Eiseley. il Nat Wildlife 9:42-5 Ap '71
What are people for? man, fate and Kurt Vonnegut. E. W. Ranly. il por Commonweal 94:207-11 My 7 '71
What have we learned? Where are we going? M. Mead. por Redbook 137:12-13+ O '71
Why we fear witches. M. Mead. Redbook 138:49+ N '71

See also
Civilization
Evolution
History
Human relations
Humanism
Longevity
Psychology
Woman

Influence of environment
Coping with future shock; excerpt from Future shock. A. Toffler. Read Digest 99: 81-6 Ag '71
Environment and man, by R. H. Wagner. Review
Am For 77:42+ S '71. M. Bush
Exploring earthman's world with Darwin Lambert. D. Lambert. See issues of National parks and Conservation magazine
Man in his setting. B. W. Overstreet. il PTA Mag 66:10-12 N '71
Morals and measurements. D. Munby. il Commonweal 95:271-5 D 17 '71
See also
Environmental health
Weather—Mental and physiological effects

Influence on nature
Christianity and the environmental crisis; interview; with editorial comment. C. H. Reidel. Chr Today 15:4-8, 26-7 Ap 23 '71
Decision making in the biological field; address, October 24, 1971. J. Mayer. Vital Speeches 38:174-9 Ja 1 '72
Despairing optimist. R. Dubos. Am Scholar 40:208+ Spr '71
Dominion of man, by J. Black. Review
Environ 13:46-7 Ja '71. J. W. Bennett
Ecological challenge to Christian ethics. J. C. Livingston. il Chr Cent 88:1409-12 D 1 '71
Editorial; television show Say good-bye. C. Conley. Field & S 75:6 Ap; 76:4 My '71
Environment and man, by R. H. Wagner. Review
Am For 77:42+ S '71. M. Bush
Environment: preparing for the crunch; findings and recommendations of the Study of critical environmental problems. C. L. Wilson. il Sat R 54:42-3+ Ja 23 '71
Exploring earthman's world with Darwin Lambert. D. Lambert. See issues of National parks & Conservation magazine
Global circulation of atmospheric pollutants. R. E. Newell. il Sci Am 224:32-42 Ja '71
Global ecological problems: tragedy of the commons. Sci N 100:244 O 9 '71
Invisible pyramid, by L. Eiseley. Review
Nation 212:312-14 Mr 8 '71. H. Fruchtbaum
Man and meaning; excerpts from address, November 1970. G. Wald. por Sr Schol Teach ed 97:4 Ja 11 '71
Man-made climatic changes. H. E. Landsberg; reply with rejoinder. A. N. Dingle. bibliog il Science 173:461-2 Jl 30 '71
Man; planetary disease; address, March 10, 1971. I. McHarg. Vital Speeches 37:634-40 Ag 1 '71
Man's impact on climate: what is ahead? SMIC international study. il Sci N 100:73 Jl 31 '71
Man's impact on the global environment. Review
Environ 13:48-9 Mr '71. J. McCaull
Negative animal. P. R. Ehrlich and J. P. Holdren. Sat R 54:58-9 Je 5 '71
One culture. L. Morris. Chr Today 15:55-6 My 21 '71
One-inch journey; excerpt from The unforeseen wilderness. W. Berry. il Audubon 73: 4-11 My '71
Proud to be human—here we stand: a singular species. B. W. Overstreet. il PTA Mag 66:6-8 S '71
Question for the (ice) ages; effects of aerosols in the atmosphere. Sci N 100:39 Jl 17 '71
Science alone is not enough. D. P. Young. il por Chem 44:14-16 N '71
Survival? Yes, But in what form? G. Feinberg. Bul Atom Sci 27:27-30 My '71
To trouble a star; the cost of intervention in nature. G. Hardin; reply with rejoinder. R. B. Coffman. Bul Atom Sci 27:2-4 Ap '71
What are man's prospects? Club of Rome's project. D. L. Meadows. Cur 133:3-9 O '71
See also
Environmental policy
Pollution
United Nations conference on the human environment

Migrations
Early racial and cultural identifications in southwestern Alaska; with reply by D. E. Dumond. J. S. Aigner and others. bibliog Science 171:87-90 Ja 8 '71

Origin and antiquity
Once more into the past: planned expedition by L. S. B. Leakey. il por Sci N 100:259 O 16 '71
Population genetics and human origins. R. B. Eckhardt. il Sci Am 226:94-103 Ja '72
See also
Archeology
Man, Prehistoric
Neanderthal race

Periodicity
See Biology—Periodicity

Survival
Humanism and survival. A. W. Levi. Sat R 54:32 My 15 '71
Man; planetary disease; address, March 10, 1971. I. McHarg. Vital Speeches 37:634-40 Ag 1 '71
Not nature alone. R. Neuhaus. il Harper 243:100-5 O '71; Discussion. 243:6+ D '71

MAN—Survival—*Continued*

People problem, by D. Fraser. Review
New Repub 164:26-8 My 22 '71. J. Gilbert
Psychiatry and the survival of man. J. Marmor. Sat R 54:18-19+ My 22 '71
Science and society symposium: prospects for survival. K. E. Boulding; R. S. Berry; G. Feinberg. Bul Atom Sci 27:19-30 My '71
This endangered planet, by R. A. Falk. Review
New Repub 164:34-5 My 15 '71. C. G. Bolte

MAN (theology)

Appeal of Buddhism: a Christian perspective. D. K. Swearer. il Chr Cent 88:1289-93 N 3 '71
Demythologizing modern man. R. Goetz. il Chr Cent 88:1321-5 N 10 '71
Future theology: hope or suffering? Hope and the future of man conference. D. J. Turner. Chr Today 16:42+ N 5 '71
Man as an image of the Trinity. A. Deeken. il Cath World 214:9-13 O '71
Primitivism or technocracy: must we choose? D. J. Elwood. il Chr Cent 88:1413-18 D 1 '71
Weekend of hope; Hope and the future of man. L. J. O'Donovan. America 125:319-21 O 23 '71

MAN, Erect position of. See Posture

MAN, Prehistoric

Antiquity of Australopithecus. Sci Am 224:52 Ap '71
Australopithecus, a long-armed short-legged, knuckle-walker. Sci N 100:357 N 27 '71
Humans before man; Australopithecus africanus. Sci Am 224:46-7 Mr '71
Man of Tautavel. il Newsweek 78:78+ O 25 '71
Man, the hunter; australopithecines. J. Pfeiffer. il Horizon 13:28-33 Spr '71
More complete view of man's ancestors; Australopithecus. il Sci N 99:141 F 27 '71
Oldest Frenchman; Pyrenees fossils. Sci Am 225:42 D '71
Search for New World man; controversial California dig. C. Behrens. il Sci N 99:98-100 F 6 '71
Strange, unfinished saga of Peking man. H. L. Shapiro. il Natur Hist 80:8-10+ N '71
Two distinct hominids? homo and australopithecus. por Sci N 99:398 Je 12 '71
See also
Cave drawings and paintings
Man—Origin and antiquity
Neanderthal race
Paleo-Indians
Stone implements and weapons

MAN, Primitive
See also
Society, Primitive

MAN, Size of. See Body size

MAN amplifiers

Science's eye on the universe; head-coupled television systems. R. E. Packer. il Sci Digest 69:67-72 F '71

MAN and nature. See Man—Influence on nature

MAN in the museum; story. See Panter, C.

MAN-made diamonds. See Diamonds, Artificial

MAN of the year distinguished service award. See American forestry association

MAN-powered airplanes. See Airplanes, Light

MAN who came home; story. See Bittle, C.

MAN who played with dolls; story. See Lutters, V.

MAN with a soul; story. See Moffett, C.

MANAGEMENT
See also
Business management and organization
Farm management
Housing management
Wildlife management

MANAGEMENT and budget, Office of. See United States—Management and budget, Office of

MANAGEMENT conferences. See Business meetings

MANAGEMENT consultants. See Business consultants

MANAGEMENT information systems. See Information systems, Management

MANAGEMENT of children. See Children—Management and training

MANAGEMENT of factories, shops, etc. See Factory management

MANAGER plan, City. See City manager plan

MANCHESTER, Harland
Mini-people, inc? Sat R 54:6+ O 16 '71
Now they're herding catfish. il Read Digest 98:19-22+ Je '71

MANCHESTER, Conn.
We tried gunite to repair spalled curbs. W. D. O'Neill. il Am City 86:69 Ja '71

Parks and playgrounds
How we resolved a highway-park conflict. W. D. O'Neill. il Am City 86:65 Ag '71

MANCHESTER, Conn, public library
Read on: the magic is in the books; tarot card theme for annual report. J. F. Jackson. il Am Lib 2:210-11 F '71

MANCHESTER, N.H.
Newspapers
See also
Manchester union leader

MANCHESTER college, North Manchester, Ind.
Home is down the road. W. Dunbar. il Americas 23:32-6 Mr '71

MANCHESTER union leader
Nixon's too left-wing for William Loeb. B. Kovach. il por N Y Times Mag p 14+ D 12 '71

MANDELBAUM, Bernard, and Ratner, V. M.
Who are the addicted? excerpt from The high holy day message of the Jewish theological seminary of America. Read Digest 98:137-8 Ja '71

MANDELBAUM, Nathan
Day of the tray. il Ladies Home J 88:130-3 My '71
One man's private alphabet. il Ladies Home J 88:126-7 Mr '71
Super naturals. il Ladies Home J 89:88-91 Ja '72

MANDELKERN, L. See Bowen, W. J. jt. auth.

MANDEL'SHTAM, Nadezhda
Poems over power. O. Carlisle. il por Vogue 157:58-9+ Ja 15 '71 *

MANDEL'SHTAM, Osip Emil'evich
Hope against hope, by N. Mandelstam. Review
Newsweek 77:100+ Mr 29 '71. S. K. Oberbeck *
Ramp Mag pors 10:55-8 S '71. T. Deutscher
Poems over power. O. Carlisle. il por Vogue 157:58-9+ Ja 15 '71 *

MANDEL'SHTAM, Sergel
Lunokhod 1 on the expansion of the universe. Space World H-4-88:46 Ap '71

MANDELSTAM, Janet
Africa: frontier for summer study. il Schol Teach Jr/Sr High p 17-19 Ja 11 '71

MANDER, John
Great debate in Britain. Cur 132:51-3 S '71

MANDL, Matthew
Getting the most from your tape cassettes. il Radio-Electr 42:51-3 Jl '71
6 easy projects for beginners. il Radio-Electr 42:60-2 Ap '71
6 ways to improve your hi-fi system. il Radio-Electr 42:54-6 Mr '71

MANDLE, Joan D.
Women's liberation: humanizing rather than polarizing. bibliog f Ann Am Acad 397:118-28 S '71

MANELOVEG, Herbert D.
Madison avenue; TV announcements to woo young men to the proposed all-volunteer army. Sat R 54:49+ My 8 '71

MANGAKIS, George
Letter in a bottle. il Atlan 228:53-9 O '71

MANGANESE
See also
Water supply—Manganese content

MANGEL, Charles
Healthy body? il Look 35:61-2 Je 1 '71
How to make a criminal out of a child. il Look 35:49+ Je 29 '71
9 big do's and don'ts for the 1971 job hunter. Look 35:21-3 My 18 '71; Same abr. with title How to land the job you want. Read Digest 99:197-8+ O '71

MANGERS, Dennis H.
Education in the grapes of wrath. Ed Digest 36:16-18 F '71

MANGIERI, Adolph A.
Build the charge now. il Pop Electr 34:53+ Ap '71

MANGURIAN, Robert
Custom-made furniture the easy way. il Pop Sci 198:94-6+ F '71

MANHATTAN. See New York (city)

MANHATTAN school of music
American festival orchestra goes to Italy. J. Strasser. il Hi Fi 21:MA10-11 F '71
Musical events; performances of Rossellini's La guerra and Busoni's Arlecchino. W. Sargeant. New Yorker 47:93-4 Mr 27 '71

MANHATTAN school of music—*Continued*
Report:
    Arlecchino. F. Stevenson. Opera N 35:
        22 My 15 '71
    Jules Massenet's Cinderella. H. E. Phil-
        lips. Opera N 36:22-3 S '71
    Mozart's Magic flute. R. D. Daniels.
        Opera N 35:31 Ja 30 '71
MANHATTANVILLE college of the Sacred
    heart, Purchase, N.Y.
    Department of amplification: W. F. Buckley
        on Blaine amendment. E. McCormack. New
        Yorker 47:121-3 D 18 '71
MANHEIM, Michael Philip
    Winter surfing in Rhode Island. il Travel
        136:52-5 D '71
MANIAGO, Cesare
    Minnies who are no moochers. M. Mulvoy. il
        pors Sports Illus 35:28-9 N 22 '71 *
MANIATES, Maria Rika
    Musical mannerism: effeteness or virility? ex-
        cerpts from address. bibliog f Mus Q 57:270-
        93 Ap '71
MANIC-depressive psychoses. See Psychoses
MANICOTTI. See Cookery, Italian
MANICURING
    See also
    Nails (anatomy)
MANIFOLDS
    Auto shop series: manifolds. J. McFarland.
        il Hot Rod 24:62-5 N '71
    Clean and mean; Dual port manifold. S.
        Green. il Hot Rod 24:58 O '71
    Dual-port 360. il Hot Rod 24:112-13 Mr '71
    Exterminator. J. Dianna. il Hot Rod 24:80-1
        N '71
    More domination. J. Dianna. il Hot Rod 24:
        138 Ag '71
    Punch for Pintos. S. Green. il Hot Rod 24:
        64 My '71
    Strictly for stocks. J. Dianna. il Hot Rod
        24:76 S '71
    Tarantula: single four-barrel manifold. J.
        Dianna. il Hot Rod 24:108-9 Mr '71
    Vrod progress report. J. Thawley. il Hot
        Rod 24:110-11 S '71
MANIGAULT, Earl
    For now the answer is not in the Stars. P.
        Carry. il por Sports Illus 35:74+ S 20 '71 *
MANILOFF, Jack. See Liss, A. jt. auth.
MANIN, Gregg
    Rain; poem. Seventeen 30:108 Ag '71
MANINGS, Muriel
    Modern dance in Cuba; foothold with a fu-
        ture. il Dance Mag 45:59-63 Ag '71
MANISES, Spain
    Pottery in Manises; Moorish-influenced ma-
        jolica of southern Spain. T. Shafer and
        Y. Shafer. il Ceram Mo 20:14-18 Ja '72
MANKER, Don
    Quotes; poem. Good H 172:170 F '71
MANKIEWICZ, Herman J.
    Onward and upward with the arts. P. Kael.
        por New Yorker 47:46-52+ F 20; 44-50+
        F 27 '71 *
MANKOFF, Milton, and Flacks, Richard
    Changing social base of the American stu-
        dent movement. bibliog f il Ann Am Acad
        395:54-67 My '71
MANLEY, John F.
    Rise of Congress in foreign policy-making.
        bibliog f il Ann Am Acad 397:60-70 S '71
MANLEY, Merlin
    Antidote: when teaching sours. Ed Digest
        36:46-8 Ja '71
MANN, Alfred
    Beethoven's contrapuntal studies with
        Haydn. bibliog f il Mus Q 56:711-26 O '70
MANN, Dean L. and others
    Detection of an antigen associated with
        acute leukemia. bibliog il Science 174:1136-
        7 D 10 '71
MANN, Horace
    Father of American public education. P. W.
        Schmidtchen. il Hobbies 76:135-6+ N '71 *
MANN, Jack
    Baseball's odd couple meets the wild bunch.
        il pors Look 35:71-2+ My 4 '71
        about
    Mann on the run. il por Newsweek 78:50-1
        Ag 23 '71 *
MANN, Jim
    Ballew raid. New Repub 165:12-13 S 11 '71
MANN, Margery
    View from the Bay. See issues of Popular
        photography
MANN, Murray Gell-. See Gell-Mann, M.
MANN, Paul
    Appliance clinic; questions and answers.
        See issues of Popular mechanics, Sep-
        tember 1971-

MANN, Thomas
    Letters of Thomas Mann to Henry Walter
        Brann; tr. by H. W. Brann. Am Scholar
        40:256-65 Spr '71
        about
    Decadence and morbidity, a certain weak-
        ness, a certain comfort. J. Meyers. Com-
        monweal 94:113-14 Ap 9 '71 *
    Last artist. G. Wolff. il por Newsweek 77:
        90 Mr 8 '71 *
    Letters of Thomas Mann, ed. by R. Winston
        and C. Winston. Review
        New Repub 164:28-30 Ap 3 '71. D. Little-
        john *
        Time il pors 97:94+ F 22 '71. M. Duffy *
    Literature and political responsibility: apropos
        the Letters of Thomas Mann. E. Heller.
        Commentary 52:47-54 Jl '71 *
    Mann's letters. J. Thompson. Harper 242:
        90-2 Ja '71 *
MANNE, Henry G.
    Meet Ralph Nader's most outspoken critic.
        pors Bsns W p58-9 Jl 24 '71 *
MANNED orbiting space station. See Space
    stations
MANNED space flights. See Space flight—
    Manned flights
MANNED spacecraft center. See United States
    —Manned spacecraft center
MANNEQUINS. See Models (persons)
MANNERS, David X.
    Invisible wall that purifies water. il Sci Di-
        gest 69:70-3 Je '71
MANNERS, Ian R.
    Desert and the sown: an ecological appraisal
        of the Middle East. bibliog il Focus 22:1-8
        O '71
    Political dimension: colonialism to nation-
        alism in the Middle East. bibliog Focus 22:
        6-8 S '71
MANNERS and customs
    Fashionable body; excerpt from The un-
        fashionable human body. B. Rudofsky. il
        Horizon 13:56-65 Aut '71
        See also
    Bees (cooperative gatherings)
    Clothing and dress
    Costume
    Dating
    Hairdressing
    Rites and ceremonies
    Taboo
    Tipping
MANNERS and customs in literature. See
    Local color in literature
MANNES, Marya
    How men will benefit from the women's
        power revolution. il PTA Mag 65:6-8 Ja
        '71
    MacDowell colony. il por Pub W 199:32-4
        My 17 '71
        about
    Out of my time, by M. Mannes. Review
        Sat R 54:50-2 N 20 '71. P. MacManus *
MANNHEIM, L. Andrew
    Think you get sharper pictures by stopping
        down, eh? Well, you don't! il Mod Phot 35:
        84-7+ N '71
MANNHEIM, Ralph
    (tr) See Hesse, H. Hesse on peace
MANNING, Elise W.
    Holiday heirloom recipes. il Farm J 95:
        36-7+ D '71
MANNING, Frederick J. and others
    Inhibition of normal growth by chronic ad-
        ministration of Δ-9-tetrahydrocannabinol.
        bibliog il Science 174:424-6 O 22 '71
MANNING, Gordon P.
    Easy-to-make automatic windshield washer.
        il Motor B & S 127:89 Je '71
    Gunkholing on Lake Champlain. il Motor
        B & S 128:50-1 Ag '71
    Who's afraid of the big bad locks. il Motor
        B & S 128:52-3+ Ag '71
MANNIX, Daniel
    For use on giants not turkeys. il Sports Illus
        34:44-6+ Je 14 '71
MANNIX, James N.
    Bluegills and blubbers. il por Outdoor Life
        147:86-8+ My '71
MANO, D. Keith
    Cannibalism in the Episcopal church. Nat R
        23:867+ Ag 10 '71
MANPOWER
    Manpower approach to the unemployment-
        inflation dilemma. C. C. Holt and others.
        Mo Labor R 94:51-4 My '71
        See also
    Labor supply—United States
MANPOWER, Muscular. See Muscular power
MANPOWER and education. See Education
    and manpower

MANSCHRECK, Clyde L.
My conscience is bound by the word of God; address, April 17, 1971. bibliog Vital Speeches 37:540-4 Je 15 '71

MANSFIELD, Michael Joseph
From the Democrats: a reply to Nixon; excerpts from interview. por U S News 70: 37 F 8 '71
Is America going isolationist? interview. por U S News 70:24-5 Je 28 '71
New economic program; address, September 14, 1971. Vital Speeches 38:4-7 O 15 '71
Nixon doctrine; address, March 29, 1971. Vital Speeches 37:418-21 My 1 '71
Size-up of President Nixon; interview. il pors U S News 71:56-61 D 6 '71

about

Foreign policy: Mansfield's rebellion. il por Newsweek 77:18-19 My 24 '71 •
Mansfield ruckus. Nation 212:675-6 My 31 '71 •
Mission-oriented R&D. R. W. Nichols. bibliog Science 172:29-37 Ap 2 '71 •
NATO troops. New Repub 164:11 My 29 '71 •
Who would ever have thought it? demand for troop withdrawal. M. McGrory. America 124:585 Je 5 '71 •

MANSFIELD, La.
Where Vida Blue grew. J. Lebow. il pors Look 35:73-6+ S 21 '71

MANSINHA, L. See Smylie, D. E. jt. auth.

MANSON, Charles
Charlie and the devil; excerpt from The family. E. Sanders. il por Esquire 76:105-12+ N '71 •
Family: the story of Charles Manson's dune-buggy attack battalion, by E. Sanders. Review
  Nat R 23:1311-12 N 19 '71. C. H. Simonds •
Manson convicted. Nat R 23:128-9 F 9 '71 •

MANSON, Charles, trial. See Trials (murder)

MANTAS. See Rays (fishes)

MANTEGNA, Andrea
Mantegna's Judith in Washington. L. Steinberg. il Art N 70:42-3 N '71 •

MANTI, Utah
Western phenomenon, the origin and development of watershed research. A. Antrei. il Am West 8:42-7+ Mr '71

MANTIS, Praying. See Praying mantis

MANTLE, Mickey
Sports. R. Kahn. Esquire 75:16+ My '71 •

MANTUA industrial development corporation
Black capitalism: a study of struggle. il Bsns W p96-8+ Ja 16 '71
Businessmen go to the ghetto to learn. il pors Bsns W p 102+ Je 19 '71

MANUEL, Oliver K. See Boulos, M. S. jt. auth.

MANUFACTURED houses. See Houses, Prefabricated

MANUFACTURERS Hanover trust company. See New York (city)—Banks

MANUFACTURES

Statistics

Labor turnover rates (title varies) tables. See issues of Monthly labor review
Ratios of manufacturing; table; with editorial comment (cont) Duns 98:62-3+, 104 N '71

MANURE as feed. See Feeding and feeding stuffs—Manure

MANURE bunkers. See Farm manure—Preservation and storage

MANURE handling. See Farm manure—Handling

MANURE odors. See Odors

MANURES. See Farm manure; Fertilizers and manures

MANURES, Liquid. See Liquid fertilizers and manures

MANUSCRIPTS
When you send your manuscript to an editor. Writer 84:20-1 Ag '71
See also
Beethoven, L. van—Manuscripts
Eliot, Thomas Stearns—Manuscripts
Illumination of books and manuscripts
Music—Manuscripts

Conservation and restoration

Freeze-dried history; damaged documents of Godthaab, Greenland saved by freeze-drying. il Newsweek 79:39 Ja 10 '72

MANUSCRIPTS, Coptic (papyri)
Coptic voices from the past; Nag Hammadi codices. H. Brabyn. il UNESCO Courier 24:11 My '71

Early Christian manuscripts from the sands of the Nile; Nag Hammadi codices. J. M. Robinson. il UNESCO Courier 24:4-8+ My '71

MANUSCRIPTS, Greek
Plato parchment; earliest known Plato text in codex. il Sci Digest 70:62-3 Ag '71
Scrap of parchment; second century A.D. Plato text. il Chem 44:3 My '71

MANUSCRIPTS, Hebrew
See also
Dead Sea scrolls

MANUSCRIPTS, Illumination of. See Illumination of books and manuscripts

MANUSCRIPTS, Medieval
Lure of medieval documents. W. Rodger. il Hobbies 76:150-3 N '71

MANZANITAS. See Bearberries

MANZELLA, David
Dale Chihuly: the fluid breath of glass. il por Craft Horiz 31:22-6 D '71

MANZONI, Pablo
New face saving salon. pors Harp Baz 104: 28 Ap '71 •

MAO, Tse-tung
Aftermath of China's cultural revolution. M. Goldman. Cur Hist 61:165-70+ S '71 •
Aftermath of the cultural revolution. E. Snow. New Repub 164:18-21 Ap 10 '71 •
Alive and well in Peking. il por Time 98:40 O 18 '71 •
Conversation with Mao Tse-tung. E. Snow. il por Life 70:46-8 Ap 30 '71 •
Mao's attempt to remake man. il por Time 98:24-5 Jl 12 '71 •
Mao's long march. C. Barnett. il pors Horizon 13:72-9 Wint '71 •
Poetry of Chairman Mao. N. G. D. Malmqvist. por Sat R 54:29-30 N 27 '71 •
Round-trip ticket to Peking. il por Newsweek 78:51-2 O 18 '71 •

MAOISM. See Communism—China (People's Republic)

MAP making. See Cartography; Mapping, Aerial

MAP reading
How to buy and use maps to improve your hunting. E. Park. il Field & S 76:68-9+ O '71

MAPLES, Flowering. See Flowering maples

MAPLEWOOD, N.J.
Have you tried platform tennis? W. D. Carew. il Am City 86:22 Jl '71
How to compost leaves. R. Walter. il por Am City 86:115-17 Je '71

MAPPING, Aerial
Sharper eyes seek the world's resources. il Bsns W p54-5 N 27 '71

Equipment

Advanced sensors used to survey Algeria. il Aviation W 94:42 Mr 15 '71

MAPS
See also
Atlases
Cartography
Map reading
Municipal maps
Orienteering (sport)
School libraries—Map collections
Topographic maps
  also subhead Maps under names of countries, states, cities, e.g. France—Maps

MAPS, Assyro Babylonian
Babylonian map. H. B. Moore. il Sea Front 17:23-5 Ja '71

MAPS, Babylonian. See Maps, Assyro-Babylonian

MAPS, Decorative
Art: exhibition of Map based on Buckminster Fuller's Dymaxion airocean world at the Museum of modern art. L. Alloway. Nation 213:541-2 N 22 '71

MAPS, Imaginary. See Geographical myths

MAPUCHE Indians. See Indians of South America—Chile

MARAN, Meredith
Chamisa road with Paul & Meredith. by P. Steiner and M. Maran. Review
  Sat R 54:27 Jl 31 '71. J. Luria •

MARAN, Stephen P.
Gum nebula; with biographical sketch. il Sci Am 225:10, 20-9 bibliog(p 120) D '71
—and others
Gum nebula: a new kind of astronomical object. bibliog il Phys Today 24:42-7 S '71
—See Thomas, R. J. jt. auth.

MARASHIO, Paul
Moving toward a new direction. Clear House 46:252-3 D '71
Proposal for helping the beginning teacher. Clear House 45:419-21 Mr '71

MARATECK, Jacob
Blow struck for the revolution; tr. by S.
Wincelberg. Commentary 53:62-6 Ja '72
MARATHON oil company
Getting more oil from an oil field; Mara-
flood recovery process. il Bsns W p 108
Mr 6 '71
Running Marathon's miniature airline. V.
Louvière. Nations Bsns 59:18 O '71
MARATHON running. See Running
MARBLE, Artificial
How to work with Corian. R. J. De Cristo-
foro. il Pop Sci 198:105-7+ Mr '71
MARCHAM, F. G.
Fuertes sampler; with biographical sketch.
il Natur Hist 80:4-5, 38-43 Je '71
MARCHESI, V. T. and Andrews, E. P.
Glycoproteins: isolation from cell membranes
with lithium diiodosalicylate. bibliog il Sci-
ence 174:1247-8 D 17 '71
MARCHETTI, Victor
Former staff officer criticizes CIA activities;
interview, ed. by E. K. Delong. il por U S
News 71:78-80 O 11 '71
MARCKS, Gerhard
Gerhard Marcks, the form of nature.   A.
Werner. il por Am Artist 35:32-7+ D '71 *
MARCO ISLAND
Can land be developed without wrecking na-
ture? W. Hartley and E. Hartley. il Sci
Digest 71:73-8 Ja '72
MARCO Polo club
Marco Polo's mixer; Hong King westerners
meet with officials of the People's Republic
of China. por Time 99:41 Ja 10 '72
MARCOL, Chester
Czeslaw Marcol is no Polish joke. il Sports
Illus 35:69-70 D 6 '71 *
MARCONA corporation
Dual-purpose ships build a business. il
Bsns W p60-2 D 18 '71
MARCOS, Ferdinand E.
Binding up the wounds. Time 98:44 N 23 '71 *
Engulfed in strife: Philippines' Marcos. il
por U S News 70:56 Mr 29 '71 *
Marcos and the Communists. J. de Herrerra.
il America 126:6-10 Ja 8 '72 *
Prescription for revolution. il por Time 97:
38 Ap 12 '71 *
MARCOU, Thomas J.
Our colossal carrots. il Org Gard & Farm
18:50-1 Ap '71
MARCREST-Pacific company
He custom-builds light steel beams. il Bsns
W p92 Je 26 '71
MARCUS, Irwin
Hubert Harrison: Negro advocate. bibliog
por Negro Hist Bul 34:18-19 Ja '71
MARCUS, James Lewis
Percentage of the take, by W. Goodman.
Review
Bsns W p8 F 20 '71. J. Patterson *
Commentary 51:95-6 My '71. R. Starr *
Life 70:10 F 26 '71. F. J. Cook *
MARCUS, Leonard
Four-channel discs, 1904. il Hi Fi 21:65 Jl '71
MARCUS, Marie
Musical events; Cape Cod notes. W. Balliett.
New Yorker 47:78 Ag 28 '71 *
MARCUS, Philip I. and others
Interferon action: inhibition of vesicular
stomatitis virus RNA synthesis induced by
virion-bound polymerase. bibliog il Science
174:593-8 N 5 '71
MARCUS, Ruth
Small wonders. See issues of Good house-
keeping to June 1971
MARCUSE, Herbert
Dear Angela; letter. Ramp Mag 9:22 F '71

about

Contra Marcuse, by E. Vivas. Review
Nat R 23:997-8 S 10 '71. H. Caton *
Social theory of Herbert Marcuse. R. Good-
win. por Atlan 227:68-70+ Je '71 *
MARCUSE, Peter
Is the national parks movement anti-urban?
il Parks & Rec 6:16-21+ Jl '71
Rise of tenant organizations. Nation 213:50-3
Jl 19 '71
MARDEN, Luis
Ama, sea nymphs of Japan. il Nat Geog 140:
122-35 Jl '71
Exquisite orchids. il Nat Geog 139:484-513 Ap
'71
Titicaca, abode of the sun. il Nat Geog 139:
272-94 F '71
MARDER, Arthur
Royal navy and the Ethiopian crisis of 1935-
36. bibliog f Am Hist R 75:1327-56; 76:1258
Je '70-O '71
MARDI gras. See Carnival

MARDIAN, Robert Charles
Internal security makes a comeback. F. Lang.
il Ramp Mag 10:10+ Ja '72 *
Red squad. il por Newsweek 77:17-18 My 31
'71 *
Tough new man at Justice. por Time 97:53
F 1 '71 *
MAREK, George R.
Applause. il Opera N 36:6-7 D 18 '71
Fiddler on an East Berlin roof. il Sat R 54:
46-7+ F 27 '71
Will the real W.A.M. please stand? pors
Opera N 35:24-7 Mr 20 '71
MAREK, Kurt Wilhelm.   See Ceram, C. W.
pseud.
MARES, Vaclav E.
Czechoslovakia three springs later. bibliog
f Cur Hist 60:282-9+ My '71
MARGARET Mary Murtha, Sister. See Murtha,
M. M.
MARGATE CITY, N.J.
Lifestyle; Lucy the elephant. il Am Home 74:
10 Jl '71
MARGETTS, Susan
Executive ledger. il Duns 98:55 D '71
MARGOLD, Stella
Needed, world-wide environment solutions.
il Am City 86:74+ Mr '71
MARGOLIES, John Samuel
Pap art. il pors Time 98:90 N 1 '71 *
MARGOLIN, Malcolm
Now scientists are breeding super trees. il
Sci Digest 69:40-4 Mr '71
MARGOLIS, Alan J. and Loebl, Suzanne
Guide for women. Redbook 136:26 Ja '71
MARGOLIS, Art
Symptom: no color. il Radio-Electr 42:23-5
D '71
MARGOLIS, Gary
Consider yourself; poem. Am Scholar 40:690
Aut '71
MARGULIES, Herbert F.
Four-party race? Commentary 51:75-6 Ap '71
MARGULIS, Lynn
Symbiosis and evolution; with biographical
sketch. il Sci Am 225:13, 48-57 bibliog(p 120)
Ag '71
MARIA Stuarda; opera. See Donizetti, G.
MARIAH, Paul
Concordances with Dali; poem. Poetry 118:
66-70 My '71
MARIE; story. See Woiwode, L.
MARIELLE
Memory's vault; poem. Negro Hist Bul
33:169 N '70
MARIETTA, Ohio
Corporate polluter learns the hard way; with
editorial comment. il Bsns W p52-6, 94 F
6 '71
MARIETTE, Auguste
Aida's creator: Auguste Mariette. S. J. Lon-
don. il por Hi Fi 21:52-6 Ag '71 *
MARIHUANA. See Marijuana
MARIJUANA
Are you growing marijuana without knowing
it? J. B. Sutter. il Home Gard 58:42+ F
'71
As common as chewing gum; problem in
Vietnam. il Time 97:14-15 Mr 1 '71
Botany and chemistry of cannabis, ed. by
C. R. B. Joyce and S. H. Curry. Review
Sci Am 225:238+ S '71. P. Morrison
Can we counteract the cult of marijuana?
M. Moser and L. Greenhouse. Parents Mag
46:40-1+ Jl '71
Cerebral atrophy in marijuana smokers.
Sci N 100:406 D 18 '71
Continuing battle over pot. il Sci N 99:277
Ap 24 '71
Delta-9-tetrahydrocannabinol: metabolism and
disposition in long-term marihuana smok-
ers. L. Lemberger and others. bibliog il
Science 173:72-4 Jl 2 '71
Doctor, what about marijuana? interview.
W. X. Lehmann. Read Digest 98:169-70+
Ap '71
Don't legalize marijuana; excerpts from ad-
dress, May 1971. A. Linkletter. PTA Mag
65:15 Je '71
Drug scene, has it changed? with study-
discussion program, by C. Smallenburg and
H. Smallenburg. D. H. Powelson. bibliog
il PTA Mag 66:3-4, 34-5 D '71
Drugs of habit & the drugs of belief; with
editorial comment. S. McCracken. bibliog
f Commentary 51:4, 43-52 Je '71
First year: few surprises. Sci N 99:114 F 13
'71
Goa: an addendum; hashish trail at Kat-
mandu, Nepal; letter to the editor. J. S.
Mason. Nat R 23:1255 N 5 '71
Goa, end of the line; hashish trail at Kalengute. S. Labin. Nat R 23:750-3 Jl 13 '71

MARIJUANA—_Continued_

How a parent can reach his child about drugs. H. W. Land. il Todays Health 49: 42-5 Ag '71

Latest findings on marijuana. il U S News 70:26-7 F 1 '71

Latest medical facts about marijuana. Good H 172:185-6 My '71

Make marijuana laws easier? Most young people say no; Scholastic's National institute of student opinion. Sr Schol 99:7 N 29 '71

Marihuana and memory: acquisition or retrieval? E. L. Abel. bibliog il Science 173: 1038-40 S 10 '71

Marihuana components: effects of smoking on Δ⁹-tetrahydrocannabinol and cannabidiol. F. Mikeš and P. G. Waser. bibliog il Science 172:1158-9 Je 11 '71

Marijuana experts: findings of study by William T. Moore and Harold Kolansky. New Repub 164:7-8 Je 5 '71

Marijuana harmful? The dispute goes on. il U S News 70:68 My 31 '71

Marihuana: identification of cannabinoids by centrifugal chromatography. D. G. Petcoff and others. bibliog il Science 173:824-6 Ag 27 '71

Marihuana in man: three years later. L. E. Hollister. bibliog Science 172:21-9 Ap 2 '71

Marijuana is for the birds. J. M. Vance. il Outdoor Life 147:53-5+ Je '71

Marijuana reconsidered, by L. Grinspoon. Review
Nat R 23:597+ Je 1 '71. S. K. Oberbeck Sat R 54:29-30 My 22 '71. W. Abruzzi

Marihuana: standardized smoke administration and dose effect curves on heart rate in humans. P. F. Renault and others. bibliog il Science 174:589-91 N 5 '71

Marijuana: who smokes it, and why; excerpt from Marihuana reconsidered. L. Grinspoon. Mlle 73:180-1+ My '71; Discussion. 73:353 Ag '71

More controversy about pot. Time 97:65 My 31 '71

My view of drug use, and drug abuse. B. Spock. Redbook 136:29+ Ap '71

New view on pot. il Time 97:45-6 My 3 '71

Of pot and rats. Time 98:71 S 27 '71

Polemics of pot. il Newsweek 77:109 My 3 '71

Pot report: still inconclusive. Time 97:46 F 15 '71

Pot: your kids will encounter it, so be prepared. Bsns W p87 D 4 '71

Preventing drug abuse in children. B. Spock. bibliog Redbook 137:36+ My '71

Prohibition of marijuana. J. Kaplan; reply with rejoinder. F. A. Bartimo. New Repub 164:42-3 Ja 2 '71

Psychiatrist and his daughter talk frankly about marijuana; interview, ed. by A. Bramson. M. Yolles; S. F. Yolles. pors Seventeen 29:134-5+ O '70

Psychiatrists comment on pot. A. J. Snider. Sci Digest 69:72 My '71

Questioning the legal status. Sci N 99:349 My 22 '71

Search for data on marijuana. il Bsns W p50+ D 4 '71

Spotlight on pot. Sr Schol 98:16-17 Mr 1 '71

Uses of marijuana, by S. H. Snyder. Review Science 174:935-6 N 26 '71. M. Jarvik

We know too little about marijuana; questions and answers. A. S. Norris. Sci Digest 69:78-81 F '71

What we have forgotten about pot, a pharmacologist's history: cannabis sativa. S. H. Snyder; reply with rejoinder. D. H. Milman. N Y Times Mag p6 Ja 17 '71

What we know about marijuana, so far. E. K. Faltermayer. il Fortune 83:96-8+ Mr '71

Who is smoking pot? A. J. Snider. Sci Digest 71:69 Ja '72

See also
THC

MARIN, John

Marin on Marin; excerpts from John Marin. por Vogue 157:80-1 F 15 '71

about

Fugues in space. R. Hughes. il por Time 97: 62-3 F 22 '71 *

Where paleface meets redskin. P. McCaughey. il Art N 70:30-3+ My '71 *

MARIN COUNTY, Calif.

Architecture

Frank Lloyd Wright's Hall of justice. R. Montgomery. il Arch Forum 133:54-9 D '70

MARIN headlands state park. See California—Parks and reserves

MARINARO, Ed

Big red machine. il Time 98:52 N 15 '71 *

Diamond in the ivy. por Newsweek 78:80 N 8 '71 *

MARINAS

Cleveland's floating marina. il Parks & Rec 6:30 My '71

Fresh look at fresh water; future planning for the Great Lakes basin. A. Limburg. il Motor B & S 127:10-12+ Ap '71

Gale-tested marina; Cleveland. R. H. Anderson and F. W. Reusswig. il Am City 86: 130+ Ap '71

Golden chain; Gold pennant marinas. B. Crabtree. il Yachting 129:98+ My '71

Letter from Long Island Sound. M. Hunt. New Yorker 47:62+ Ag 28 '71

See also
Anchorage

MARINE, Gene

One dammed thing after another. il Nat Parks & Con Mag 45:14-19 My '71

MARINE accidents. See Shipwrecks

MARINE archeology. See Archeology, Submarine

MARINE architects. See Naval architects

MARINE biology

See also
Benthos
Fresh water biology
Marine ecology
Marine fauna
Marine fouling
Marine microbiology
Marine sediments
Plankton

MARINE charts. See Nautical charts

MARINE corps. See United States—Marine corps

MARINE ecology

Consequences of a sea-level canal. R. H. Gilluly. il Sci N 99:52-3 Ja 16 '71

Gulf weed communities of south Florida. T. W. Thompson. il Sea Front 17:95-101 Mr '71

Man and marine ecology: crisis in the estuaries. Sci N 100:293 O 30 '71

Need for immediate action; testimony before the U.S. Senate commerce subcommittee. J. Y. Cousteau. Cur 135:36-9 D '71

Sea-level canal: how the academy's voice was muted. P. M. Boffey. Science 171:355-6+ Ja 29 '71

Sea snakes are coming. W. A. Dunson. il Natur Hist 80:52-61 N '71

Ship canals and aquatic ecosystems. W. I. Aron and S. H. Smith. bibliog il Science 174:13-20 O 1 '71

Tektite unlocks secrets from the ocean's floor. C. B. Jackson. il Nat Wildlife 9:50-5 Ap '71

Underwater battle; southern California's Pacific coastline. G. T. Bowden. il Parks & Rec 6:22-4 Jl '71

MARINE engines

Alternator and voltage regulator. C. Miller. il Motor B & S 128:76+ O '71

Dual-pump cooling. C. Miller. il Motor B & S 128:67 S '71

Marine engines. E. Nabb. See issues of Motor boating & sailing to July 1971

Radical and the practical. E. Nabb. Motor B & S 127:113+ Ap '71

Vee drive: an old idea that's newer than tomorrow. E. Nabb. il Motor B & S 128:68+ Ag '71

See also
Gas turbines, Marine
Motor boat engines
Outboard motors

Ignition

Hotter ignition for your boat's engine. C. Miller. il Motor B & S 128:74+ Jl '71

Lubrication

See Motor boats—Lubrication

Maintenance and repair

Be prepared! C. Miller. Motor B & S 127:78-9+ My '71

Cast-iron breeze; auxiliary engines. C. Miller. il Motor B & S 127:78-9+ Je '71

Noise

Mystery of the musical motor. R. Humphrey. Motor B & S 128:69+ S '71

Starting

See Motor boats—Starting

MARINE fauna

Deepstar explores the ocean floor. R. Church. il por Nat Geog 139:110-29 Ja '71

MARINE fauna—*Continued*
Other reef; sand flats adjacent to coral reefs.
P. L. Colin. il Sea Front 17:160-70 My '71
Purple wind. W. Zeiller and G. Compton. il
Sea Front 17:372-7 N '71
Sea life's chemical senses. Sci N 100:186 S 18
'71
Sensuous symbionts of the sea. L. Thomas.
il Natur Hist 80:28-37+ bibliog(p96) Ag '71
Tektite II: science's window on the sea. J.
G. Vanderwalker. il por Nat Geog 140:256-
89 Ag '71
What's up down there? D. Kasanof. il Motor
B & S 128:46-99 bibliog(p58) Jl '71
　See also
Barnacles
Foraminifera
Marine mammals
Octopus
Plankton
Sea anemones
Sea snakes
Shrimps
Sponges
Starfishes
Tunicates
Zoanthus

MARINE fires. See Ships—Fires and fire pro-
tection
MARINE flora
What's up down there? D. Kasanof. il Motor
B & S 128:46-9 bibliog(p58) Jl '71
　See also
Diatoms
Plankton
Seaweed

MARINE fouling
Barnacles and grasses are a pain on the bot-
tom. E. A. Zadig. Motor B & S 127:90-1+
Je '71
Barnacles and hormones. D. Tighe-Ford. il
Sea Front 17:243-50 Jl '71

MARINE gas turbines. See Gas turbines, Ma-
rine
MARINE lumber. See Lumber
MARINE mammals
Hotbloods. T. H. Lineaweaver, 3d. il Sea
Front 17:66-71 Mr '71
　See also
Dolphins (mammals)
Whales

MARINE microbiology
Alvin's lunches. Time 97:56 Mr 8 '71
Deep sea as a food refrigerator. il Chem 44:
25 My '71
Microbial degradation of organic matter in
the deep sea. H. W. Jannasch and others.
bibliog il Science 171:672-5 F 19 '71

MARINE mineral resources
　See also
Ocean mining

MARINE navigation. See Navigation
MARINE paint. See Paint

MARINE painting
John Stobart, marine artist. L. Chmelik. il
por Am Artist 35:46-51+ N '71
Robert Davis: painter of the sea. A. R.
Bloeme. il por Am Artist 35:50-5 F '71
Robert Salmon: painter of ship and shore.
J. Wilmerding. il Antiques 99:257-61 F '71
Watercolor page: Edmond J. Fitzgerald. E.
J. Fitzgerald. il por Am Artist 35:60-3+ Je
'71

MARINE parks and reserves
Progress in marine parks. J. E. Randall.
il Sea Front 17:2-16 Ja '71
　See also
Buck Island Reef National Monument

MARINE plants. See Marine flora
MARINE pollution
Dying oceans, poisoned seas; views presented
at United Nations symposium on the en-
vironment. J. Cousteau and J. Piccard.
Time 98:74+ N 8 '71
Growing worry, dirty oceans and waterways.
il U S News 71:61 N 1 '71
Marine pollution. P. H. Abelson. Science
171:21 Ja 8 '71
Marine pollution, potential for catastrophe.
O. Schachter and D. Serwer. UN Mo Chron
8:28-49 Mr '71
Need for immediate action; testimony before
the U.S. Senate commerce subcommittee.
J. Y. Cousteau. Cur 135:36-9 D '71
Thor Heyerdahl's paper boat, plowing a
filthy ocean. G. Moore. il por Life 71:81
S 24 '71
We are killing the sea around us. M. Har-
wood. il N Y Times Mag p34-5+ O 24 '71
　See also
Mercury pollution of rivers, lakes, etc.
Oil pollution of rivers, harbors, etc.
Waste disposal in the ocean

Laws and legislation
　See Water pollution—Laws and legisla-
tion
Long Island Sound
Spread oil on the Sound's troubled waters
and you'll be in hot water with the chief.
S. Singer. il pors Todays Health 49:35-9+
O '71
North Sea
Chemical wastes in the sea: new forms of
marine pollution. P. A. Greve. bibliog il
Science 173:1021-2 S 10 '71
Pacific coast
DDT residues: distribution of concentrations
in emerita analoga (stimpson) along coast-
al California. R. Burnett. bibliog il Science
174:606-8 N 5 '71
When families fight pollution; volunteer ven-
ture to save wildlife of San Francisco Bay.
C. T. Hall. il Parents Mag 46:76-7+ N '71

MARINE radio telephone. See Radio telephone
on ships, boats, etc.
MARINE refrigerators. See Refrigeration on
boats
MARINE resources
How they'll pump energy from the sea; ex-
periments under way off St Croix, Virgin
Islands. W. S. Bacon. il Pop Sci 198:38
Mr '71
We must learn to walk through the water;
interest in aquaculture. R. Rodale. il Org
Gard & Farm 18:32-6 Ap '71

MARINE sediments
Antarctic bottom water: major change in
velocity during the late Cenozoic between
Australia and Antarctica. N. D. Watkins
and J. P. Kennett. bibliog il Science 173:
813-18 Ag 27 '71
Eocene volcanism and the origin of Horizon A. T. C. Gibson and K. M. Towe.
bibliog il Science 172:152-4 Ap 9 '71
Fecal pellets; role in sedimentation of pelagic diatoms. H. J. Schrader. bibliog il
Science 174:55-7 O 1 '71
Interstitial silica and pH in marine sediments: some effects of sampling procedures.
K. A. Fanning and M. E. Q. Pilson. bibliog
il Science 173:1228-31 S 24 '71
Magnesium-iron replacement in clay minerals
in anoxic marine sediments. J. I. Drever.
bibliog il Science 172:1334-6 Je 25 '71
Marine sediments: dating by the racemization of amino acids. J. L. Bada and others; reply with rejoinder. M. C. McKenna.
Science 172:503 Ap 30 '71
Racemization of amino acids in marine sediments. J. Wehmiller and P. E. Hare. bibliog
il Science 173:907-11 S 3 '71
Where plate meets plate; leg 18 of the Deep
sea drilling project. il Sci N 100:90 Ag 7 '71

MARINE service
　See also
Signals and signaling
MARINE sextants. See Sextants
MARINE snails. See Snails
MARINE spark plugs. See Spark plugs
MARINE toilets. See Boats—Toilet facilities
MARINE weapons. See Weapons systems
MARINE worms
　See also
Annelids
Arrowworms
MARINE zoology. See Marine fauna
MARINER spacecraft. See Space probes
MARINI, Carlos Flores. See Flores Marini, C.
MARININ, Yuri
Cold food diet is becoming a thing of the
past in outer space. Space World H-12-96:
44 D '71
Moon: traveling on wheels. il Space World
H-4-88:25-7 Ap '71
MARION, Ind.
Water supply
Old records and new technology find a water
supply. P. J. Satterthwaite. il Am City 86:
68+ S '71
MARION, Ind. public library
Library services casebook. M. G. Ballard. il
Am Lib 2:1191-2 D '71
MARIONETTES. See Puppets and puppet
plays
MARITIME fruit carriers company. See Ship-
ping—Israel
MARITIME law
　See also
Boats and boating—Laws and regulations
Territorial waters
United Nations conference on the law of the
sea, 1973

MARITIME meteorology. See Meteorology, Maritime

MARITIME workers
See also
Collective bargaining—Maritime workers
Strikes—United States—Maritime workers

MARIXA
Marixa. J. Opalak. il Design 73:40-1 Fall '71 *

MARK, Norman
Television. New Repub 165:24+ D 25 '71

MARK, Gospel of. See Bible—New Testament —Mark

MARK Twain, pseud. See Clemens, S. L.

MARK (money) See Money—Germany (Federal Republic)

MARKESBERY, William R. See Lapham, L. W. jt. auth.

MARKET research
What makes the new consumer buy. il Bsns W p52-8 Ap 24 '71

MARKET surveys
See also
Consumer surveys

MARKETING
Cracking down on pyramid plans. il Bsns W p 104+ D 11 '71
Demarketing, yes, demarketing. P. Kotler and S. J. Levy. il Harvard Bsns R 49:74-80 N '71
Dilemma of product/market management. B. C. Ames. il Harvard Bsns R 49:66-74 Mr '71
See also
Advertising
Booksellers and bookselling
Chain stores
Computers—Marketing use
Consumers
Mail order business
Merchandising
Negro market
Old age market
Roadside marketing
Salesmen and salesmanship
Samples (merchandising)
Supermarkets
Youth market
also subhead Marketing under various subjects, e.g. Steel—Marketing

Direct selling
See also
Canvassing

MARKETING, Cooperative
Coordination without contracts does work; swine marketing. J. Russell. il Farm J 95:H10+ Mr '71
NFO's new floor price contract. Farm J 95:29 S '71
See also
Cooperative associations

MARKETS
Alabama's magic Monday. J. Goodrum. il Travel 135:34-9+ Mr '71
Europe's flea markets. N. Beare. il Travel 135:36-41 Ap '71
They swap & talk & sell. il Mech Illus 67:6 D '71
See also subhead Markets under names of cities, e.g. Paris—Markets

MARKETS, Black. See Black markets

MARKETS, Outdoor. See Street trades

MARKETS for authors. See Authors and publishers

MARKHAM, Lois A.
Teleguide. il Sr Schol Teach ed 99:7 N 15 '71

MARKHAM, W. Kent
Build this two-man sub for $400. il Pop Mech 135:94-7+ Je '71

MARKING, Syl
Shortcut to smallmouth. il Field & S 76:74-5+ My '71

MARKING (students) See Grading and marking (students)

MARKINGS of animals. See Color of animals

MARKMANN, Charles Lam
Low life in the grand manner. Nation 212: 789-90 Je 21 '71

MARKO, A. M. See Lewis, W. B. jt. auth.

MARKOFF, Richard
How to tell when you're going crazy. il Mech Illus 67:60-2+ Mr '71

MARKOVA, Dame Alicia
Markova on mime. W. Terry. il pors Sat R 54:40-1 Ag 28 '71 *

MARKOVITS, Andrew S.
What you should have in your medicine chest. il Mech Illus 67:48-9 Ja '71

MARKOW, Jack
Cartoonist Q's. See issues of Writer's digest

MARKOWSKI, Robert
Gassing up the VIPs. R. Levy. por Duns 98:60 Jl '71 *

MARKS, George P. 3d
William H. Ferris criticizes Booker T. Washington (1898); reprint from a Negro newspaper of 1898. il por Negro Hist Bul 33:162-3 N '70

MARKS, Jane
American thing: grooving on your heritage? or assimilation? Mlle 72:205-6+ Ap '71
Counter culture: groupthink or liberation? Mlle 72:166-7+ F '71
Dance. Vogue 157:157 My '71
ESP is never having to say you're psychic. Mlle 73:138-9+ Je '71
Women in rock. Vogue 157:112 Mr 1 '71

MARKS, Peter L.
Vision of environment. Am Scholar 40:421-31 Sum '71

MARKS, S. J.
Night friends; poem. New Yorker 47:52 D 4 '71

MARKSMANSHIP. See Shooting

MARKSON, Ralph
Lightning and the plastic airplane. Flying 89:6 Jl '71

MARLAND, Sidney Percy, 1914-
Career education. il Todays Ed 60:22-5 O '71
Career education: a new job for the schools; interview, ed. by M. K. Murphy. Schol Teach Jr/Sr High p4-5 D '71
Career education now; address, January 23, 1971. Vital Speeches 37:334-7 Mr 15 '71; Same abr. Ed Digest 36:9-11 My '71
Condition of education in the Nation. Am Ed 7:3-5 Ap '71
Education's rigged lottery; address, October 12, 1971. Vital Speeches 38:122-5 D 1 '71
Environmental education cannot wait. il Am Ed 7:6-10 My '71
Marland on career education: questions and answers. pors Am Ed 7:25-8 N '71
New ideas for better schools; interview. il por U S News 71:80-5 N 1 '71
Quoting Marland; excerpts from speeches and writings. por Am Ed 7:3-4 Ja '71
Toward parental support of a national institute of education. por Parents Mag 46:42 S '71
about
Models in career education. W. D. Boutwell. PTA Mag 66:9 S '71 *
New U.S. commissioner of education. por Sch & Soc 99:205 Ap '71 *
Nixon administration aims at federal education programs. Pub W 199:36 Ja 18 '71 *

MARLBORO festival of music. See Music festivals—Vermont

MARLER, Don C.
Nonprofessionalization of the war on mental illness. Ment Hy 55:291-4 Jl '71

MARLEY, C. F.
Quality animals underscore organic methods. Org Gard & Farm 1:75-6 O '71

MARLEY, Doone
Travel bazaar. Harp Baz 104:64+ Mr '71

MARLEY, Harold P.
Child body count; poem. Chr Cent 88:310 Mr 10 '71

MARLEY, William P.
Sedentary camper syndrome. por Camp Mag 43:14 My '71

MARLIN fishing
Barrier Reef marlin. G. W. Carmany. il Field & S 75:86+ Mr '71
Better way to master marlin. V. Dunaway. il Field & S 76:66-7+ My '71
Big sails and marlin too. B. Warner. il Field & S 75:78-9+ Mr '71
Black Bart and the mechanical marlin. R. W. Johnston. il por Sports Illus 35:34-8 Ag 16 '71
Marlin are for learning. D. Fales. il Motor B & S 127:36-7+ My '71
Mighty river; Humboldt Current off Ecuador. C. Elliott. il Outdoor Life 147:70-3+ Je '71
New hotspot for big black marlin; Bazaruto Islands in the Indian Ocean. J. C. Chapralis. il Field & S 76:84+ Je '71
Remembering great men and great fish; excerpt from Fishing with Hemingway and Glassell. K. Farrington. il Field & S 75: 54-5+ Ap '71

MARLOR, Clark S.
John Barnard Whittaker, Brooklyn artist. il Antiques 100:775-7 N '71

MARLOWE, Eleanor
Finger food. il Am Home 74:72 N '71

MARLOWE, Stephen, pseud. See Lesser, M.

MARMOR, Judd
Psychiatry and the survival of man. Sat R 54:18-19+ My 22 '71

MARMOSETS
Rescuing the golden marmosets. K. Severin. il Sci Digest 70:46-8 D '71

MARMOTTAN musee. See Paris—Galleries and museums

MAROON, Fred
Story behind the book: Courage and hesitation. A. H. Johnston. il por Pub W 200:22-3 O 25 '71 *

MAROV, Mikhail
Venus: what we know about this planet. Space World H-6-90:33-4 Je '71

MARQUETTE university, Milwaukee, Wis.
Crazy cat and his curious Warriors; Marquette Warriors. C. Kirkpatrick. il Sports Illus 34:32-6 Ja 25 '71

MARR, David G.
United States in Vietnam: a study in futility. Ann Am Acad 397:11-18 S '71

MARRA, Vito
How not to fly a localizer. Flying 88:73 Mr '71

MARRAKESH
Reports & comment. A. Koestler. Atlan 228:6+ D '71

MARRIAGE
Advice to married couples. W. H. Masters and V. E. Johnson. il Redbook 137:92-3+ S '71
Can this marriage be saved? ed. by D. C. Disney. See issues of Ladies' home journal
Couple-speak: happy marriage. A. Sarris; M. H. Sarris. pors Vogue 157:106-7+ Je '71
Did you marry the right man? quiz; excerpt from Between man and woman. E. L. Shostrom and J. Kavanaugh. Ladies Home J 88:100+ Mr '71
Exercises to wake up your marriage. il Ladies Home J 88:90+ N '71
50/50 marriage: is this what women want? S. North. il Look 35:57-61 O 5 '71
Hallelujah the pill? R. B. Dixon. il Trans-Action 8:44-9+ N '70
Happy marriage, is it real? D. B. Thompson. Vogue 158:117+ N 1 '71
How we met and why we married. S. Blum. il Redbook 136:62-3+ Ja '71
In my opinion; marriage and motherhood aren't for everyone. B. Wagner. por Seventeen 30:166 Jl '71
Is marriage going out of style? E. Sheppard. il Harp Baz 104:168-9 O '71
Is your marriage a fighting affair? il Changing T 25:25-7 F '71
Magic of a good marriage; ed. by C. Schroeder. J. H. MacMurray. il pors Good H 173:94-5+ O '71
Making marriage more sensuous. J. Brothers. Good H 172:22+ F '71
Marriage. J. Cook. il Ladies Home J 88:192+ S '71
Marriage is not enough. H. Gold. Vogue 157:137+ F 1 '71
Must marriage cheat today's young women? P. E. Slater. il Redbook 136:66-7+ F '71
New meaning of marriage. R. Haughton. il Read Digest 98:79-81 Ja '71
Off the pig. D. Newman and R. Benton. Mlle 72:144 Ap '71
Opinion: on marriage. R. Ryder. Mlle 72:17+ Ja '71
Politics of marriage: a delicate balance. V. Cadden. il Redbook 137:55+ Jl '71
Raising your child to have a good marriage. B. Spock. Redbook 137:29+ Je '71
Rebuilding marital fidelity. H. Wildeboer. Chr Today 15:19 Je 18 '71
Speaking of sex and so forth. M. Ward. America 124:613-15 Je 12 '71
Tested ways of saving your marriage; excerpt from The adventure of being a wife. R. S. Peale. Read Digest 99:72-5 Jl '71
Virginia Graham's advice to wives; interview. ed. by M. Davidson. V. Graham. il por Good H 172:109 3+ My '71
Why get married? H. Alpert. Har Yrs 11:6-10+ Ap '71
Why good marriages fail. R. Farson. McCalls 99:110-11+ O '71; Same abr. Read Digest 99:131-3 D '71
See also
Celibacy
Desertion and non-support
Divorce
Eugenics
Family
Husbands
Intermarriage of races
Polygamy
Remarriage
Sex relations
Sexual ethics
Teen-age marriage
Weddings
Wives

Annulment (canon law)
When the courts don't work. J. T. Catoir. America 125:254-7 O 9 '71

Church of England
Welcome report; Marriage, divorce and the church. T. Beeson. Chr Cent 88:517-18 Ap 28 '71

Handbooks, manuals, etc.
Good-bye to the plain brown wrapper; sex manuals. M. Seligson. il McCalls 98:Mr '71
Intelligent woman's guide to sex manuals. L. Roxon. il Mlle 73:118-19+ Jl '71

Statistics
Marriage game; findings of Bureau of the census survey. Time 98:51 O 25 '71

United States
See Marriage

MARRIAGE, Companionate
Companionate marriage, by B. B. Lindsey and W. Evans. Review
New Repub 165:35-6 N 20 '71. D. Grumbach

MARRIAGE counseling
Can this marriage be saved? ed. by D. C. Disney. See issues of Ladies' home journal
Marital counseling. R. B. Sloane and D. F. Horvitz. bibliog Ment Hy 55:534-7 O '71
Structured approach to group marriage counseling. T. A. McClellan and D. R. Stieper. bibliog Ment Hy 55:77-84 Ja '71

MARRIAGE customs and rites
Just say yes, he'll do the rest; marrying Mayor R. Bouvet of Novel. il Time 97:21 Je 7 '71
Pagan event; M. Jagger of Rolling Stones observing strictest forms in wedding proceedings. pors Newsweek 77:36 My 24 '71
See also
Weddings

Russia
Love and marriage, Russian-style. L. Barry. il Pop Phot 68:26+ Je '71

MARRIAGE in the Bible
Interracial marriage and the Bible. H. O. Thompson. bibliog il Negro Hist Bul 34:103-6 My '71

MARRIAGE law
See also
Remarriage
Separation (law)

Israel
Israel's leaders score rabbinate's strict marriage rulings. Chr Cent 88:519 Ap 28 '71

United States
Renewable marriage; bill before Maryland legislature. Time 97:43 Mr 15 '71

Zambia
Zambian women recommend reform in marriage laws. O. Eby. Chr Cent 88:112-14 S 22 '71

MARRIAGE manuals. See Marriage—Handbooks, manuals, etc.

MARRIAGE of priests
East vs. west. il por Newsweek 78:52-3 Ag 30 '71
End of a battle. il por Time 98:38 Ag 23 '71
Just plain Bob. il por Time 97:73 Ap 26 '71
Of many things; case of Fr Duryea. D. R. Campion. America 124:469 My 8 '71
On eating our cake and having it too. J. J. Hughes. Cath World 213:83-6 My '71
Priests vs. bishops. Newsweek 77:97 Ap 26 '71
Secret family of Father Duryea. J. N. Bell. il pors Good H 173:80-1+ Ag '71

MARRIAGE tribunal. See Ecclesiastical courts

MARRIAGES, Mixed
Ecumenical then; Lutheran film The ecumenical now. T. W. Moore. Chr Cent 88:192-3 F 10 '71
Marriage Israeli style; Jews and Moslems. Newsweek 77:59 Je 21 '71
Mixed marriage feelings; CCAR and Jewish-gentile marriages. Newsweek 78:52 Jl 5 '71
Two faiths and one love. M. Rosenbaum. il por Redbook 138:33-4+ D '71

MARRIED women
Braining of maternity. R. Haughton. Cath
World 213:263-4 S '71
See also
Mothers

Education
See Education of women

Employment
Analysis of Michigan's experience with work
incentives; mothers receiving AFDC grants.
G. L. Appel and R. E. Schlenker. bibliog
il Mo Labor R 94:15-22 S '71
Child-care centers, working mothers, fathers
who stay home. B. Bettelheim. Ladies Home
J 88:37 +My '71
Children of women in the labor force; with
tables. E. Waldman and K. R. Gover.
bibliog f Mo Labor R 94:19-25 Jl '71
Executive mother: J. Glynn. L. Botto. il
pors Look 35:73+ Ja 26 '71
Happy returns; working mothers. S. Obre
and T. Owett. il Ladies Home J 88:116-
23 S '71
How on earth do working wives manage?
il Changing T 25:7-10 N '71
If you want to resume a full-time job. il
Good H 172:187 My '71
Liberated mothers. M. Bouma. Chr Today
15:4-6 My 7 '71
Marital and family characteristics of work-
ers, March 1970. E. Waldman and A. M.
Young. il Mo Labor R 94:46-50 Mr '71
Newtime a-comin Newsweek 78:125 O 25 '71
Woman's place is on the job. il Time 98:56
Jl 26 '71
Working woman. L. C. Pogrebin. por Ladies
Home J 88:46+ Je; 54+ Ag; 62+ S '71
See also
Part time employment

Law
See Woman—Legal status, laws, etc.

MARRIOTT, John Willard, 1900-
J. Willard Marriott sr. of Mariott corp; in-
terview. il pors Nations Bsns 59:60-5 Mr
'71
MARRIOTT corporation
J. Willard Marriott sr. of Mariott corp; in-
terview. J. W. Marriott. il pors Nations
Bsns 59:60-5 Mr '71
Marriott story. il Forbes 107:20-5 F 1 '71
MARRIOTT, the marine; story. See Styron, W.
MARRON, Dyanne
Chen Chi: the way of the heart. il por Am
Artist 36:40-5 Ja '72
MARROW
L-Asparaginase induced immunosuppression;
inhibition of bone marrow derived anti-
body precursor cells. H. Friedman. bibliog
il Science 174:139-41 O 8 '71

Transplantation
Alternative to false teeth? il Time 98:57 O 4
'71
Bone marrow transplantation. C. C. Congdon.
bibliog il Science 171:1116-24 Mr 19 '71
Gift of life from a big sister; bone marrow
transplant; with report by M. Steinmann.
il Life 70:32-6+ My 28 '71
MARRS, Homer L.
When his firm was auctioned, he bid. il
pors Nations Bsns 59:80-1 Ja '71
MARS, Forrest
Man from Mars. A. A. Butkus. il por Duns
97:41-2+ F '71 •
MARS (planet)
Earth's orange neighbor. V. Lebedev. Space
World H-12-96:40 D '71
In orbit around Mars: into the second week;
Mariner 9 data. il Sci N 100:355 N 27 '71
Is there life on Mars, or beyond? il Time 98:
50-2+ D 13 '71
Mariner finds equatorial bulges on Mars. W.
S. Hieronymus. Aviation W 95:20 D 6 '71
Mariner ultraviolet spectrometer: topography
and polar cap. C. A. Barth and C. W.
Hord. bibliog il Science 173:197-201 Jl 16 '71
Mars anthology; symposium. il Sky & Tel
42:259-65+ N '71
Mars' closest approach. J. Stokley. il Sci N
100:66 Jl 24 '71
Mars is nearing earth. M. Y. Qutub. bibliog
il Space World H-7-91:4-10 Jl '71
Mars occultation roundup. il Sky & Tel 42:
48-51 Jl '71
1971 apparition of Mars. il Sky & Tel 41:
123-4 F '71
Recent Martian studies. il Sky & Tel 41:267+
My '71

What is Mars like? I. Koval. il Space World
H-8-92:40-1 Ag '71
See also
Life on Mars
Space flight to Mars
Space vehicles—Landing systems—Mars

Atmosphere
Area of Mars believed perpetually dusty.
W. S. Hieronymus. il Aviation W 95:22-3
D 20 '71
Mars: has nitrogen escaped? R. T. Brink-
mann. bibliog il Science 174:944-5 N 26 '71

Maps
Mariners' 1969 closeup of Mars. C. A. Cross.
il Sky & Tel 42:16-17 Jl '71
Mars chart for the Mariner flights. G. De
Vaucouleurs. il Sky & Tel 41:283-7 My '71
New map of Mars from planetary patrol pho-
tographs. J. L. Inge and others. il Sky &
Tel 41:336-9 Je '71

Observations
Dust storm observations from New Mexico.
T. B. Kirby and J. C. Robinson. il Sky &
Tel 42:264-5 N '71
How you can see the biggest show in the
solar system; retrograde movement. C. P.
Gilmore and D. Heiserman. il Pop Sci 199:
92-3+ Jl '71
Martian weather forecast. Sky & Tel 42:206
O '71
Martian yellow clouds, past and future. C.
F. Capen. il Sky & Tel 41:117-20 F '71
Stormy weather on Mars. il Sci N 100:245
O 9 '71
Telescopic observations of Mars in 1971. G.
De Vaucouleurs. il Sky & Tel 42:134-5,
263-4; 43:20-1 S, N '71, Ja '72
This is the year to see Mars. T. D. Nichol-
son. il Natur Hist 80:34-5 Je '71

Photographs
Portfolio of amateurs' Mars photographs.
Sky & Tel 42:310-14 N '71
Some high-resolution photographs of Mars.
S. M. Larson and R. B. Minton. il Sky &
Tel 42:260-2 N '71

Photographs from space
Mariner photos show earth-like craters. Avi-
ation W 95:18-19 D 13 '71
Mariners' 1969 closeup of Mars. C. A. Cross.
il Sky & Tel 42:16-17 Jl '71
Red flag on Mars; Mariner 9's pictures. il
Newsweek 78:67 D 13 '71
Three spacecraft study the red planet. il
Sky & Tel 43:14-17 Ja '72
View from Mariner. Time 98:82-3 D 6 '71

Radiation
Scientists get new look at Mars; infrared
light radiations. Space World H-11-95:46+
N '71

Satellites
See Satellites

Surface
Dust storm dims early data from Mariner. il
Aviation W 95:24-6 N 22 '71
Mapping the topography of Mars with radar.
Sci N 100:277 O 23 '71
Mariner 9 shows some clearing on Mars. W.
S. Hieronymus. il Aviation W 95:17-18 N 29
'71
Mars missions: the saga continues. il Sci N
100:387-8 D 11 '71
Mars radar observations, a preliminary re-
port. G. S. Downs and others. bibliog il
Science 174:1324-7 D 24 '71
Mars revisited; Mariner photographs. Sci Am
224:50+ Ag '71
Martian craters and a scarp as seen by
radar. G. H. Pettengill and others. bibliog
il Science 174:1321-4 D 24 '71
No men on Mars, but a surprise anyway. il
U S News 71:46 N 29 '71
Orbital view of a Martian dust storm. il Sci
N 100:339-40 N 20 '71
Ripply landscape on Mars, believe it or not.
il Sci N 101:24 Ja 8 '72
Storms of Mars. il Newsweek 78:65 S 13 '71
Super hurricanes on Mars? Space World H-
11-95:37 N '71
MARS, Inc.
Man from Mars. A. A. Butkus. il por Duns
97:41-2+ F '71
MARSEILLES
Harbor
Oil needs inspire a new Europort. il Bsns W
p53 Ap 10 '71
MARSH, Diane
Should the new TV writer go to Hollywood?
ed. by N. Vogel. por Writers Digest 51:
33-5+ Je '71

MARSH, Ed
Fly for all seasons. il Field & S 75:38+ Ap '71

MARSH, Othniel C.
Professor Cope vs. Professor Marsh. J. Penick. il pors Am Heritage 22:4-13+ Ag '71 *

MARSH, Raymond Eugene
Obituary
Am For 77:2 Ag '71. J. B. Craig

MARSH, Richard E. See Kistenmacher, T. J. jt auth

MARSH, Robert C.
Greatest orchestra in the world. Hi Fi 21:82 Je '71
Mahler's symphonies, the best complete set. Hi Fi 21:83-4 N '71
New Rosenkavalier tops lyric season. il Hi Fi 21:MA30-1 F '71
On London: Solti the Hungarian. Hi Fi 21:72-3 Ja '71
Solti is special. por Hi Fi 21:MA26-7 Ap '71
Unique pleasures of Haydn's 107 symphonies. il Hi Fi 21:75-6 Ap '71

MARSH, Stewart
We left them laughing. il Har Yrs 11:24-5 S '71

MARSH, Tracy H.
Great men in American history honored in sulphides or cameo encrustations. il Hobbies 75:116-17 Ja '71

MARSH and McLennan, inc.
Broader base for Marsh & McLennan. il Bsns W p55+ Mr 13 '71

MARSH ecology
What's happening to our salt water marshes? with study-discussion program, by J. A. Weeks. J. J. Spagnoli. il Cons 25:22-3+ Ap '71

MARSH hares. See Muskrats

MARSH plants
Some salt water marsh plants of New York. il Cons 25:24-5 Ap '71

MARSHALL, Anthony D.
Big-frame-up. il por Newsweek 78:44+ Jl 5 '71 *

MARSHALL, Carlton D.
On call for crises. D. Robinson. il por Good H 172:92-3+ Mr '71 *

MARSHALL, Catherine (Wood)
Catherine Marshall's A man called Peter; 20th anniversary edition. L. P. Freilicher and B. A. Bannon. por Pub W 200:36-7 O 18 '71 *

MARSHALL, Eliot
Heroin: the source of supply. New Repub 165:23-5 Jl 24 '71

MARSHALL, George
Bob Marshall and the Alaska Arctic wilderness. bibliog f por Liv Wildn 34:29-32 Aut '70

MARSHALL, H. C.
Buttons; summary of address. il Hobbies 76:128-30 Ag; 129-30 S; 129-30 O '71

MARSHALL, Joe
Howard Cosell is just another pretty face. il por Esquire 76:93-7+ O '71
Pro football. Sports Illus 35:100+ N 29 '71

MARSHALL, John F. and others
Sensory neglect produced by lateral hypothalamic damage. bibliog il Science 174:523-5 O 29 '71

MARSHALL, Karen
To "stay" with tax-supported love. il Am Ed 7:6-10 Ap '71

MARSHALL, Lenore
Nuclear sword of Damocles. Liv Wildn 35:17-19 Spr '71
Obituary
Sat R 54:29 O 9 '71. N. Cousins

MARSHALL, Max S.
Curse of courses. Sch & Soc 99:32-5 Ja '71; Same abr. Ed Digest 36:37-9 Ap '71
Involved in the relevant. Sch & Soc 99:89-90 F '71
Why grades are argued. Sch & Soc 99:350-3 O '71

MARSHALL, Peter
Catherine Marshall's A man called Peter; 20th anniversary edition. L. P. Freilicher and B. A. Bannon. por Pub W 200:36-7 O 18 '71 *

MARSHALL, Robert
Universe of the wilderness is vanishing; reprint from April, 1937 issue of Nature magazine. il por Liv Wildn 35:8-14 Sum '71
about
Bob Marshall and the Alaska Arctic wilderness. G. Marshall. bibliog f por Liv Wildn 34:29-32 Aut '70 *
To jump three thousand years. S. Wright. il por Am West 8:24-7 Mr '71 *

MARSHALL, Roger
Conversation at Chu Lai hospital; excerpt from letter. Chr Cent 88:237-8 F 17 '71

MARSHALL, Roy K.
Rambling through the [month] skies. See issues of Sky and telescope

MARSHALL, Wayne. See Young, A. jt. auth.

MARSHES
Death hovers over Santeeland; South Carolina public service authority vs the forces of conservation. J. Rutherfoord. Field & S 76:124+ Je '71
See also
Big Cypress Swamp
Dismal Swamp

MARSHES, Tide
What's happening to our salt water marshes? with study-discussion program, by J. A. Weeks. J. J. Spagnoli. il Cons 25:22-3+ Ap '71

MARSHMALLOWS
See also
Cookery—Marshmallows

MARSTON, Gordon
Gulf coast guide. il Yachting 130:62-3+ N '71

MARSTON, R. M.
24 easy-to-build burglar alarms. il Radio-Electr 42:23-6 Je; 38-41 Jl; 46-9 Ag; 54-7 S '71
2 safety aid projects for your car. il Radio-Electr 42:44-7 Ap '71

MARSTON, Red
SORC re-match. Motor B & S 127:35+ F '71
Where tarpon fishing is color-coded. il Motor B & S 128:24+ Jl '71
"Yachting" eyes a boat. il Yachting 129:72-3+ Mr '71

MARSTON, Susan
9 midnight snacks you'll want to lose sleep over. il Todays Health 49:48-50 Je '71

MARSUPIALS
See also
Tasmanian devils

MARSZALEK, John F. Jr
Black cadet at West Point. il pors Am Heritage 22:30-7+ Ag '71

MARTENHOFF, Jim
How to figure your planing speed from hull and horsepower. il Pop Mech 135:120-1 Mr '71
Starting procedure. il Yachting 129:66-7+ My '71
Wilderness waterway. il Yachting 130:64+ N '71

MARTENS, Anne Coulter
Age of precarious; drama. Plays 30:35-42 My '71
Thirteen: drama, reprint from October 1956 issue. Plays 30:55-64 Mr '71

MARTENS, C. R. See Shurr, G. G. jt. auth.

MARTENS, H. H. See Whitnack, G. C. jt. auth.

MARTENS, Wilfred
Portraits of the preacher in American fiction. Chr Today 16:12-13 D 3 '71

MARTHA Graham and dance company
Dance: Every soul is a circus, Letter to the world and Deaths and entrances. J. Maskey. il Hi Fi 21:MA6-7 Ja '71

MARTI, Jill
Mascots of war. il Ramp Mag 10:52-3 Ja '72

MARTÍ, Jorge L.
Influence of French thought. il Américas 23:S9-12 Ag '71

MARTIAL, Saint
Early trope repertory of Saint Martial de Limoges, by P. Evans. Review
Mus Q bibliog f 57:519-23 Jl '71. A. E. Planchart *

MARTIAN halos. See Halos (meteorology)

MARTIN, Alex
How to overrun Czechoslovakia il Nat R 23:1408-11+ D 17 '71

MARTIN, Allie Beth
Decision in Tulsa: an issue of censorship. il Am Lib 2:370-4 Ap '71
Viewpoint. il Library J 96:609, 1339, 2060, 2469, 3299, 4073 F 15, Ap 15, Je 15, Ag, O 15, D 15 '71

MARTIN, Billy
Billy the kid as peacemaker. R. Fimrite. il por Sports Illus 34:18-19 Je 28 '71 *

MARTIN, Carter
Flannery O'Connor and fundamental poverty; address, November 1970. Engl J 60:458-61 Ap '71

MARTIN, Charles
East Sixty-fifth; Work in progress; After; Sonnet: my paradise; my urban pastoral; poems. Poetry 118:162-4 Je '71

MARTIN, Charles M.
China: future of the university. Bul Atom Sci 27:11-15 Ja '71

MARY, Virgin—*Continued*
Perfect victory: assumption of the Blessed
Virgin. V. P. McCorry. America 125:77
Ag 7 '71
So glad to see you; Mary's visit to Elizabeth.
V. P. McCorry. America 125:525 D 11 '71

Art

Black Madonna and child. il Negro Hist Bul
33:184-7 D '70
MARY, Virgin, in art. See Mary, Virgin—Art
MARY, queen of Scots
Hapless queen of Scots. R. D. Daniels. il
pors Opera N 36:10-15 N '71 *
MARY Chrysantha Rudnik, Sister. See Rudnik,
M. C.
MARY Ellen, Sister
Interim at the apartment house; poem. Com-
monweal 95:178 N 19 '71
MARY Lucina, Sister
Picnic; poem. Horn Bk 47:146 Ap '71
MARY Poppins (literary character) See Cha-
racters in literature
MARY Stuart, queen of the Scots. See Mary,
queen of Scots
MARY-ROUSSELIÈRE, Guy
I live with the Eskimos. il Nat Geog 139:188-
217 F '71
MARY Imogene Bassett hospital. See Coopers-
town, N.Y.—Hospitals
MARY Lou's Mass; ballet. See Ballets—
Criticisms
MARY Stuart; drama. See Schiller, J. C. F.
von
MARYANNA Childs, Sister. See Childs, M.
MARYLAND
See also
Architecture, Domestic—Maryland
Carroll County
Chesapeake Bay
Education—Maryland
Fishing—Maryland
Hunting—Maryland
School libraries—Maryland
Talbot County

Marriage law

See Marriage law—United States

**National capital park and planning
commission**

Land acquisition: unique procedures. W. W.
Kershow. il Parks & Rec 6:14-17+ N '71

Parks and reserves

Land acquisition: unique procedures. W. W.
Kershow. il Parks & Rec 6:14-17+ N '71
MARYLAND academy of sciences, Baltimore
Events of 1972 in the Graphic time table.
il Sky & Tel 43:33-5 Ja '72
MARYLAND mine. See Gold mines and mining
—United States
MARYLAND. University, College Park

**School of library and information
services**

Crisis in library education; urban informa-
tion specialist project. M. L. Bundy. il por
Library J 96:797-800 Mr 1 '71; Discussion.
96:1895 Je 1 '71
MASAI (native race) See Africa—Native races;
Kenya—Native races
MASCAGNI, Pietro
Cavalleria rusticana. Criticism
Opera N il 35:17-20 F 13 '71 *
MASCOUTAH, Ill.
Middle America; center of population. il News-
week 77:37 My 10 '71
MASCULINITY (psychology)
Machismo mystique. S. J. Perelman. il Mc-
Calls 98:88-9+ F '71
MASELLO, Robert
Placebo; story Seventeen 30:88-9 Ja '71
MASHECK, Joseph
Warhol as illustrator: early manipulations of
the mundane. bibliog il Art in Am 59:54-9
My '71
MASIN, Herman L.
Knights before Christmas; poem. Sr Schol
99:26 D 13 '71
Sports. See issues of Senior scholastic
MASKED ball; opera. See Verdi, G.
MASKEY, Jacqueline
Dance. See issues of High fidelity and Musical
America
MASKING creams. See Cosmetics
MASKS (for the face)
Face coverings; exhibition at the Museum
of contemporary crafts. il Sch Arts 70:21-8
Je '71
Fun masks to make for Halloween. E. D.
Logan. il Good H 173:33 O '71

God has given you one face, and you make
yourselves another. B. Rudofsky. il Hori-
zon 13:72-9 Sum '71
Look who will be knocking at your door. il
Sunset 147:98-9 O '71
Mardi gras time in high school. J. D. Kocsis.
il Sch Arts 71:22-3 S '71
Mask; children art projects. L. J. Miller.
il Design 72:18-19 mid-Wint '71
New faces of 1971. il Esquire 75:92-5 Mr '71
See also
Indians of North America—Masks
MASKS (plays)
God has given you one face, and you make
yourselves another. B. Rudofsky. il Horizon
13:72-9 Sum '71
MASON, Brian
Lunar rocks; with biographical sketch. il Sci
Am 225:12, 45-58 bibliog(p 120) O '71
MASON, David T.
Forest use in western Europe. il por Am For
77:20-3+ Mr '71
MASON, Ellsworth
Along the academic way. il por Library J
96:1671-6, 3699 My 15, N 15 '71
MASON, Raymond, 1922-
Where have all the eggplants gone? il Art
N 70:72-4+ N '71
MASONRY
See also
Foundations
MASONS (secret order) See Freemasons
MASS
Let's update Bible and sermon. P. R. Gas-
tonguay. il Cath World 213:232-5 Ag '71
New defenders of the old mass; reprint. D.
Brown. Nat R 23:1235 N 5 '71
Where else but Britain? preserve the Latin
mass. J. Deedy. Commonweal 94:466 S 17
'71
See also
Liturgical language
MASS (music)
Bernstein-Ginastera premieres at Kennedy
center. I. Kolodin. il Sat R 54:74-5 S 25 '71
Bernstein's Mass: no word from the Lord.
C. A. Forbes. il Chr Today 16:40-1 O 8 '71
Bernstein's Mass opens Kennedy center. C.
J. McNaspy; J. Gallen. il America 125:228-
9 O 2 '71
Celebration of the spirit; first performance
of L. Bernstein's Mass. H. Saal. il por
Newsweek 78:29-30+ S 20 '71
Mass for everyone, maybe; Bernstein's Mass.
W. Bender. il Time 98:41-3 S 20 '71
Media is the mass; L. Bernstein's new Mass.
R. Thibodeau. Commonweal 95:17-18 O 1
'71
Music; L. Bernstein's Mass. D. Hamilton.
Nation 213:317-18 O 4 '71
New roads to old ideas in Beethoven's Missa
solemnis. W. Kirkendale. bibliog f il Mus Q
56:665-701 O '70
Troubadours for God; Hair mass at Manhat-
tan's Cathedral of St John the Divine. il
Time 97:46+ My 24 '71
Western wind masses; Tudor church music.
N. Davison. bibliog f il Mus Q 57:427-43
Jl '71
MASS (physics)
Does the mass of an object increase with
time? Sci N 100:203 S 25 '71
MASS communication. See Mass media
MASS culture. See Popular culture
MASS media
Down with media! Time essay. H. Grunwald.
il Time 97:56-7 Je 7 '71
Look at the news; Senior youthview. il Sr
Schol 99:13 O 18 '71
Mass media and mass culture. F. McDermott.
il UNESCO Courier 24:15-17 Ja '71
Need better news coverage? San Diego
County, Calif. il Am City 86:80 S '71
News: how straight? How slanted? il Sr Schol
99:5-9 O 18 '71
Of budgets & media. P. Steinfels. Common-
weal 94:30 Mr 19 '71
Politics of gullibility. T. M. Conrad. Com-
monweal 95:13-15 O 1 '71
Who makes history? J. Burnham. Nat R
23:1286 N 19 '71
World boom in TV and publishing. Sch & Soc
99:265-9 Sum '71
See also
Environmental news
Moving pictures
Newspapers
Television broadcasting

International aspects

Propaganda through the printed media in the
developing countries. Y. V. L. Rao. bibliog
f Ann Am Acad 398:93-103 N '71

MASS media—*Continued*

Psychological aspects

It's a disease called overcommunication; overdramatization of bad news. W. B. Furlong. il Todays Health 49:54-7+ Jl '71

Social aspects

Information machines. by B. H. Bagdikian. Review

New Repub 164:27-8 My 1 '71. J. Zukosky

Mass media: its place in your world; address, February 11, 1971. J. K. Sisk. Vital Speeches 37:404-7 Ap 15 '71

New sensorium: the new student. R. Pratte. Sch & Soc 99:160-3 Mr '71

What did you say? address, July 17, 1971. W. A. Nail. Vital Speeches 37:723-6 S 15 '71

You are what you see. America 126:5 Ja 8 '72

MASS media in education

New English: hot stuff or cool, man, cool? address, November 1970. R. W. Blake. Engl J 60:728-34 S '71

Taste and aftertaste; address, November 1970. D. A. Sohn. Engl J 60:369-72 Mr '71

Turning on: the selling of the present, 1970; electronic media and the English curriculum, November, 1970. B. Fillion. Engl J 60:333-8 Mr '71

MASS media in religion

Catch-up leadership; Vatican's pastoral instruction on public communications. Commonweal 94:323 Je 25 '71

Church and communications; pastoral instruction on the means of social communication. America 124:622 Je 19 '71

Secrecy; Vatican's instruction on communications. S. J. Adamo. America 124:638 Je 19 '71

MASS murder. See Murder

MASS spectrometry

Unified procedure for the detection of life on Mars. R. Radmer and B. Kok. bibliog il Science 174:233-9 O 15 '71

MASS transit. See Local transit

MASSACHUSETTS

See also

Booksellers and bookselling—Massachusetts

Cape Ann

Cape Cod

Colleges and universities—Massachusetts

Colleges and universities, State—Massachusetts

Gardens—Massachusetts

Hunting—Massachusetts

Legislation—Massachusetts

Publishers and publishing—Massachusetts

Unemployment—Massachusetts

Executive office of elder affairs

Massachusetts creates new elder affairs executive office. il Aging 195:11 Ja '71

Historic houses, etc.

Crown and Eagle mills. il Arch Forum 135:62-5 Jl '71

Library extension, Bureau of

Mass. state library agency blisters regional systems. Library J 96:3268 O 15 '71

Politics and government

Drinan's Bay state volunteers. J. Higgins. Nation 211:648-52 D 21 '70

Three, four, many parties? Nat R 23:357 Ap 6 '71

MASSACHUSETTS Bay transportation authority

Boston's transit system hits the skids. il Bsns W p62+ Ja 16 '71

300 new buses. Am City 86:57 N '71

MASSACHUSETTS general hospital, Boston. See Boston—Hospitals

MASSACHUSETTS horticultural society

Hub box: growing things. C. B. Lees. il Horticulture 40:30-1+ Mr '71

MASSACHUSETTS institute of technology, Cambridge

Environment: preparing for the crunch; findings and recommendations of the Study of critical environmental problems. C. L. Wilson. il Sat R 54:42-3+ Ja 23 '71

M.I.T.: Wiesner to succeed Johnson in presidency, office restructured. J. Walsh. Science 171:987-9 Mr 12 '71

New team at MIT. il por Newsweek 77:93 Mr 15 '71

Transition at M.I.T. por Time 97:51-2 Mr 15 '71

Visitors ask M.I.T. faculty to renounce military research. T. P. Southwick. Science 171:156 Ja 15 '71; Reply. L. Grodzins. 172:214+ Ap 16 '71

What are man's prospects? Club of Rome's project. D. L. Meadows. Cur 133:3-9 O '71

MASSACHUSETTS. University, Amherst

Mandate for change; report by R. C. Wood. il por Newsweek 79:34 Ja 3 '72

MASSAGE

Body: a woman's own environment. il Vogue 157:104-5 Ap 1 '71

Massage. il Harp Baz 104:70-1 Ap '71

Rubbing the right way. R. Atcheson. Holiday 49:22+ D '70

MASSAGE parlors. See Health clubs

MASSAQUOI, Hans J.

Liberia: end of the Tubman era. il por Ebony 26:46-8+ O '71

MASSARI, Lea

What she promises, she gives. por Vogue 158:71 Ag 1 '71 •

MASSE, Benjamin Louis

Rich, poor and in between. America 124:120-2 F 6 '71

Social front. See issues of America

Some pros and cons on revenue sharing. America 124:200-2 F 27 '71

Thoughts on leaving the America staff. America 125:25 Jl 24 '71

about

Of many things; retirement. D. R. Campion. America 125:inside cover Jl 24 '71; Discussion. 125:133 S 11 '71 •

MASSELL, Sam, 1927-

Liberal mayor's advice to blacks: think white; excerpts from address, October 6, 1971. por U S News 71:94-5 N 1 '71

about

Win for Mayor Sam. por Newsweek 78:76+ D 6 '71 •

MASSENET, Jules

Average sensual man. M. Cooper. il por Opera N 35:6-11 Mr 27 '71 •

Manon à la Sills. R. Jacobson. Sat R 54:58 Ap 24 '71 •

Massenet. by J. Harding. Review

Opera N 36:6 N '71. M. E. Peltz •

Sills and Gedda star in an ideal Manon. G. Movshon. il Hi Fi 21:72-3 Je '71 •

Werther. Criticism

New Yorker 47:94 F 27 '71. •

Opera N il 35:6-11 Mr 27 '71 •

Opera N il 35:17-20 Mr 27 '71 •

Sat R 54:43 Mr 6 '71 •

Sat R 54:43 Ap 3 '71 •

MASSEY, Ellen Gray

Wanted: English for vocational students. Engl J 60:116-20 Ja '71

MASSEY-Ferguson, ltd.

Back to the drawing board? il Forbes 108:37-8 Ag 15 '71

MASSIE, Robert K.

Nicholas and Alexandra; interview. il Vogue 158:112-13+ N 15 '71

MASSIE, Robert L.

Death by degrees. Esquire 75:179-80 Ap '71

MASSIE, Samuel P.

Behind "number, please" the story of W. Lincoln Hawkins. il por Chem 44:16 O '71

Henry A. Hill: the second mile. por Chem 44:11 Ja '71

Lloyd A. Hall: the time has come. por Chem 44:21 Mr '71

Lloyd N. Ferguson: traveling salesman for chemical education. il Chem 44:13 Jl '71

Story of Lloyd M. Cooke. il Chem 44:11 My '71

MASSIE, Tom, case. See Trials (murder)

MASSINGHAM, Harold

Agnes Cassilda Adams; poem. New Yorker 47:44 Mr 13 '71

MASSON, Charles

Food and flowers that make a memorable meal. il pors House & Gard 140:54-7 Jl '71

MASSON, Walter

Turnips, encore vegetables for double harvests. il Org Gard & Farm 18:112-13 Mr '71

MASSOW, Rosalind

Ski-tour trails. il Seventeen 30:141 D '71

MASTECTOMY. See Breast—Surgery

MASTER builder; drama. See Ibsen, H.

MASTERMAN, Sir John

Double-cross system. por Newsweek 78:58+ N 22 '71 •

MASTERPIECES

Prices

See Art—Prices

MASTERS, Charles O.
American waterlilies. il Horticulture 49:26-9
Jl '71
MASTERS, Edgar Lee
Spoon River revisited. E. Laning. il por Am
Heritage 22:14-17+ Je '71 *
MASTERS, William Howell
My mother, right or wrong. il por McCalls
98:71 My '71
Sex questions people don't ask and should;
interview, ed. by L. Kent. il pors Vogue
158:88-91 Ag 15 '71
—and Johson, V. E.
Advice to married couples. il Redbook 137:
92-3+ S '71
Advice to young women; questions and an-
swers. il Redbook 138:78-9+ Ja '72
Doctor William H. Masters and Virginia E.
Johnson: advice on married love. Redbook
137:75+ My '71; Same abr. with title Real
role of love in marriage. Read Digest 99:
127-32 Ag '71
MASTERS golf tournament. See Golf—Tourna-
ments
MASTITIS
Management suggestions to control mastitis.
Suc Farm 69:no2 D5 F '71
Mastitis research needs a tune-up. Farm J
95:D7 Je '71
MASTROIANNI, Marcello
X ray of a man; ed. by O. Fallaci. il McCalls
98:88-9+ S '71
MASTS and rigging
Booms; excerpt from Winning. J. Oakeley. il
Yachting 130:82+ N '71
Jib sheets and mast pullers. G. Hall. il
Yachting 130:35+ D '71
Non-mysteries of tuning. P. Smyth. il Motor
B & S 127:116+ Ap '71
Rod rigging: racer's leading edge. S. V. War-
ing. Motor B & S 127:77+ My '71
Sails and rigging. J. Duffett. Motor B & S
127:101 Ap '71
Sails, spars & rigging. See issues of Motor
boating & sailing to June 1971
See also
Sails
MATADORS. See Bullfighters
MATAK, Sisowath Sirik. See Sirik Matak, S.
MATCHETT, William H.
Person to person; poem. New Yorker 47:46
O 2 '71
MATEER, Samuel A.
Two Christmas stories. il Chr Today 16:5-7
D 3 '71
MATERIALS
See also
Building materials
Lunar materials
Raw materials
MATERIALS centers. See Instructional ma-
terials centers
MATERIALS handling
See also
Grain handling
MATERNAL behavior. See Mothers
MATERNAL behavior in animals. See Animals
—Habits and behavior
MATERNAL deprivation
Effects of brief separation from mother on
rhesus monkeys. R. A. Hinde and Y. Spen-
cer-Booth. bibliog il Science 173:111-18 Jl
9 '71
Separating mother and child. Sci N 100:
40 Jl 17 '71
When mother goes away; how young children
learn to cope with separations. E. Limmer.
il Parents Mag 46:42-3+ D '71
MATERNAL effect. See Prenatal influences
MATERNAL-fetal exchange
Maternal-fetal interaction and immunological
memory. T. J. Gill, 3d. and others. bibliog
il Science 172:1346-8 Je 25 '71
Plasmodium berghei: enhanced protective im-
munity after vaccination of white rats born
of immune mothers. R. S. Desowitz. bib-
liog il Science 172:1151-2 Je 11 '71
MATERNAL love. See Love, Maternal
MATERNITY benefits
Employers review maternity plans. C. G.
Rogers. il McCalls 99:45 O '71
MATERNITY clothes. See Clothing and dress—
Maternity clothes
MATHEMATICAL instruments
See also
Slide rule
MATHEMATICAL logic. See Logic, Symbolic
and mathematical
MATHEMATICAL models
Secrets of a model. por Newsweek 77:73 Mr
15 '71
See also
Machine theory

MATHEMATICAL recreations
Mathematical games. M. Gardner. See issues
of Scientific American
MATHEMATICAL statistics
See also
Regression analysis
MATHEMATICS
See also
Arithmetic
Combinations
Computers—Mathematical use
Logic, Symbolic and mathematical
Mathematical recreations
Permutations

Problems, exercises, etc.
Longest root; square root of 2 to more than
one million places. il por Time 98:59+ O 25
'71
Study and teaching
Grouping for motivation in mathematics. K.
F. George. Clear House 46:81 O '71
Laboratory approach to elementary mathe-
matics. E. Deans. il Todays Ed 60:20-2 F
'71
See also
Arithmetic—Study and teaching
Statistics—Study and teaching
MATHEMATICS teachers

Education
Pedagogy in elementary mathematics educa-
tion. J. F. LeBlanc. Ed Digest 36:24-6 Ja
'71
MATHER, Kirtley F.
Harlow Shapley, man of the world. Am
Scholar 40:475-81 Sum '71
MATHER, Stephen T, training center. See
United States—National park service
MATHER family
Mathers, by R. Middlekauff. Review
Sat R 54:30 Jl 10 '71. N. Pettit
MATHESON, William
Approach to special collections. il Am Lib
2:1151-6 D '71
MATHEWS, Carol
Big step backward. il Nation 213:593-5 D 6 '71
MATHEWS, David. See Mathews, F. D.
MATHEWS, Forrest David
New beat in the heart of Dixie. P. Schrag. il
por Sat R 54:42-5+ Mr 20 '71 *
MATHEWS, James
Just plane flat; photographs. J. Dreyfus.
Mod Phot 34:80-1 N '70 *
MATHEWS, John
Game plan for a youth conference. Nation
212:627-8 My 17 '71
Jailed with the Mayday tribe. Nation 212:646-
8 My 24 '71
MATHEWSON, Joseph
Right out of their league. Sports Illus 34:62-
4 Ap 5 '71
MATHIEU, Bill
Today's unwritten pop music. Writers Di-
gest 51:25 N '71
MATHISON, Richard R.
Writer's serendipity. Writers Digest 51:27 Ap
'71
MATHUR, S. P. See Andrus, R. jt. auth.
MATILLA, Alfredo
Casals. il pors Américas 23:5-9 My '71
MATO GROSSO, Brazil
Story behind the book: Mato Grosso. A. H.
Johnston. il Pub W 200:26-7 N 8 '71
MATOS, Luis Palés. See Palés Matos, L.
MATRIX management. See Business manage-
ment and organization
MATS. See Rugs and carpets
MATSON, Randy
No practice makes almost perfect. P. Put-
nam. il por Sports Illus 34:18-19 F 8 '71 *
MATSUMURA, Fumio, and others
Phenylmercuric acetate: metabolic conversion
by microorganisms. bibliog il Science 173:
49-51 Jl 2 '71
MATSUSHITA, Konosuke
Konosuke Matsushita of Matsushita electric;
interview. pors Nations Bsns 59:32-7 Ja '71
MATSUSHITA electric industrial company. See
Electric industries—Japan
MATT glazes. See Glazes and glazing
MATTA, Gordon
Alchemist and the phenomenologist. C.
Nemser. bibliog il Art in Am 59:100-3 Mr
'71 *
MATTEL, Inc.
Has Mattel lost its magic? T. J. Murray.
il Duns 98:40-3 Ag '71

MATTER
  See also
  Atoms
  Critical point
  Force and energy
  Mass (physics)
MATTER, Interstellar
  Chemistry between the stars. Sci N 99:382 Je 5 '71
  Cosmic antimatter and gamma rays. Sci N 100:374 D 4 '71
  Distant molecules. Time 98:47 Jl 26 '71
  Does annihilation power quasars? J. T. Scott. il Phys Today 24:32 F '71
  Formamide, number 13 in outer space. il Chem 44:27 Jl '71
  Gold mine in the sky. Newsweek 77:56+ Ap 26 '71
  How protein-like compounds could evolve in space. Sci N 100:323 N 13 '71
  Hydroxyl in two other galaxies. il Sci N 100:54 Jl 24 '71
  Ingredients for life in outer space. R. Amidei. bibliog il Sci Digest 70:24-9 S '71
  Interstellar formamide. Sky & Tel 41:280 My '71
  Interstellar molecules and dense clouds. D. M. Rank and others. bibliog il Science 174:1083-101 D 10 '71
  Mercury in stellar atmospheres. il Sky & Tel 41:278 My '71
  Molecules in space: our galaxy and beyond. Chem 44:20 N '71
  More interstellar compounds. il Sky & Tel 42:84 Ag '71
  New look at the galaxy. D. E. Thomsen. il Sci N 100:378-9 D 4 '71
  Two more molecules in space; cyanoacetylene and formic acid. Chem 44:24 Ja '71
  Universal radicals. Sci Am 225:80 S '71
MATTERN, Douglas
  World in re-birth? il Cath World 213:139-43 Je '71
MATTHAU, Walter
  Triumph of a one-man trio. S. Kanfer. il pors Time 97:86+ My 24 '71 *
  What the OTB bettor can learn from Walter Matthau. T. Meehan. il pors N Y Times Mag p6-7+ Jl 4 '71 *
MATTHEW, Gospel of. See Bible—New Testament—Matthew
MATTHEWS, Douglas
  College degrees have got to go! Mlle 72:120-1+ Ja '71
MATTHEWS, Jack
  Three poems: Movies on a summer night; Rocks and stones; The wall. Am Scholar 40:623 Aut '71
MATTHEWS, Leonard Sarver
  Guilty until proven innocent; address, April 15, 1971. Vital Speeches 37:505-9 Je 1 '71
MATTHEWS, Les
  Mr One-Two-Five Street; interview. New Yorker 47:30-1 S 18 '71
MATTHEWS, Marybeth
  Four reasons Gene Matthews chose the farm life. il Org Gard & Farm 18:78-80 Mr '71
MATTHEWS, Mildred Shapley
  ᵃAsteroid conference in Tucson. il Sky & Tel 42:22-4 Jl '71
MATTHEWS, Samuel W.
  Antarctica's nearer side. il Nat Geog 140:622-55 N '71
MATTHEWS, T. S.
  To Atalanta; poem. Atlan 227:102 Ap '71
MATTHEWS, William
  Discovery; poem. Nation 212:604 My 10 '71
      about
  Comment. F. D. Reeve. Poetry 118:237-8 Jl '71 *
MATTHEWS, Winton E.
  Dewey 18: a preview and a report to the profession. il por Wilson Lib Bul 45:572-7 F '71
MATTHIAS, Bernd T.
  Search for high-temperature superconductors. bibliog il Phys Today 24:23-8 Ag '71
MATTHIAS, John
  And then he spoke of the language itself; poem. Nation 213:503 N 15 '71
MATTHIESSEN, Peter
  And God created great whales; excerpt from Blue meridian. il Read Digest 98:117-21 Ap '71
  In the blue mist; excerpts from Blue meridian. il Audubon 73:4-12 Ja '71
  Waiting for the last whales. il Esquire 75:64-5+ F '71
MATTIL, Edward
  Handcrafts and the teacher. il Design 72:36-9 mid-Sum '71
MATTLAGE, Louise
  Dance drama: Mayan sacrifice. il Dance Mag 45:20-2 My '71

MATTO GROSSO. See Mato Grosso, Brazil
MATTSON, Peter H. and Pessagno, E. A. Jr
  Caribbean eocene volcanism and the extent of horizon A. bibliog il Science 174:138-9 O 8 '71
MATURITY
  Behavior modified? behavior modification therapy. E. Canning. il Sci Digest 70:26-31 Jl '71
MATURITY, Sexual. See Puberty
MATZ, Mary Jane
  He and Lenor. il pors Opera N 35:11-13 F 13 '71
  Let there be light. il pors Opera N 35:8-11 Ap 3 '71
MATZER, John, Jr
  Parking problems in residential areas. il Am City 86:68 Jl '71
MATZO balls. See Cookery, Jewish
MAUCHLY, John William
  Little known creators of the computer. J. Costello. il pors Nations Bsns 59:56-62 D '71 *
MAUER, Irving, and others
  Acetylsalicylic acid: no chromosome damage in human leukocytes. bibliog il Science 169:198-201; 171:829-30 Jl 10 '70, F 26 '71
MAUI (island)
  Maui, where old Hawaii still lives. K. F. Weaver. il Nat Geog 139:514-43 Ap '71
  New sun-place in Hawaii: Kaanapali. D. Messinesi. Vogue 159:30-1 Ja 1 '72
      See also
  Haleakala National Park
MAULDIN, Bill
  My confrontation with General Patton; excerpt from The brass ring. il pors Life 71:50-2+ Ag 6 '71
      about
  Compelled to irritate. G. A. Harrison. New Repub 165:26-7 D 25 '71 *
  Up front at Fort Carson with Willie and Joe and Bill. R. Graves. pors Life 70:2A F 5 '71 *
MAULDIN, William Henry. See Mauldin, B.
MAULE, Tex
  Bigger and better than ever. il Sports Illus 35:32-4+ S 20 '71
  Eleven big mistakes. il Sports Illus 34:12-17 Ja 25 '71
  End of a beautiful friendship. il por Sports Illus 35:10-11 Ag 2 '71
  Got to look good to Allah. il pors Sports Illus 35:28-9 N 29 '71
  He has heavy things on his mind. il por Sports Illus 35:24-6 Jl 26 '71
  It's how you played the game. il por Sports Illus 35:24-5 Ag 16 '71
  It's money in the bank. il por Sports Illus 35:36-8+ N 29 '71
  Keeping it short and sweet. il por Sports Illus 35:14-19 D 20 '71
  Look what's afoot. il por Sports Illus 35:18-21 D 13 '71
  No one's holding these Tigers. il Sports Illus 35:28-30+ S 27 '71
  No paralysis is the analysis. Sports Illus 35:26-8+ O 11 '71
  Staking a claim for big John. por Sports Illus 34:34-6+ My 3 '71
  They had better be super. il Sports Illus 35:22-5 N 8 '71
  This Polish joke is on the Browns. il Sports Illus 35:28-9 N 1 '71
  Tomorrow's generals. il Sports Illus 34:22-4+ F 15 '71
  Whoosh and a zonk. il Sports Illus 35:24-7 N 22 '71
  Witnesses for the defense. il Sports Illus 34:16-18 Ja 11 '71
  —and Sharnik, Morton
  It's gonna be the champ and the tramp. il pors Sports Illus 34:14-17 F 1 '71
MAUNA KEA
  Holocene eruptions of Mauna Kea volcano, Hawaii. S. C. Porter. bibliog il Science 172:375-7 Ap 23 '71
MAUNA LOA
  Solar radiation: absence of air pollution trends at Mauna Loa. H. T. Ellis and R. F. Pueschel. bibliog il Science 172:845-6 My 21 '71
MAUPASSANT, Guy de
  Necklace; dramatization. See Olfson, L.
MAUPIN, Armistead, Jr
  Ten vets who went back. Nat R 23:1465-7 D 31 '71
MAURA, Sister
  Fall of a kingdom; poem. America 124:150 F 13 '71
  Freedom; poem. Cath World 214:112 D '71
  On having a conference with a student; poem. Commonweal 95:34 O 8 '71

MAURY, Lowndes
Eclecticism is always satisfying: Lowndes
Maury A. Cohn. Am Rec G 37:585 My '71 *
MAUSOLEUMS. See Tombs
MAX Levinson gerontological policy institute.
See Brandeis university. Waltham, Mass.
MAX-MÜLLER, Friedrich. See Müller, F. M
MAXAM, June
Sizzling snow. il Har Yrs 11:32-3 F '71
MAXIMILIAN, emperor of Mexico
Cactus throne, by R. O'Connor. Review
Nat R 23:322-4 Mr 23 '71. A. Bakshian, jr
MAXSON, Gloria
Pedagogue; poem. Chr Cent 88:1465 D 15 '71
Worshiper; poem Chr Cent 88:1340 N 17 '71
MAXTONE-GRAHAM, James A.
England's New Forest. il Am For 77:22-5+ S
'71
Winds that blow the earth. il Am For 77:12-
15+ Mr '71
MAXWELL, C. G.
Tree that is not a tree. il Am For 77:4-5 Mr
'71
MAXWELL, Henry O.
Automatic tint controls for everyone. il
Radio-Electr 43:53-6+ Ja '72
MAXWELL, Lucien Bonaparte
Midas of New Mexico. H. Chapman and T.
Chapman. bibliog il pors Am West 8:4-9+
Ja '71 *
MAXWELL, Robert
British study finds Maxwell reckless at Per-
gamon. Pub W 200:30 Ag 9 '71 *
Peace at Pergamon;. Robert Maxwell returns
to board. Pub W 199:38-9 My 17 '71 *
MAXWELL, William
Ancestors, by W. Maxwell. Review
Commonweal 95:262-3 D 10 '71. F. J. Bar-
ry *
Books. B. Gill. New Yorker 47:88-91 Ag 21
'71 *
MAY, Edgar
Drugs without crime. Harper 243:60-5 Jl '71
MAY, Rollo
Too much sex, too little joy? excerpt from
Love and will. Read Digest 98:68-70 My '71

about

Love and will and Rollo May. D. Dempsey.
il pors N Y Times Mag p28-9+ Mr 28 '71;
Reply. R. May. p 100 Ap 18 '71 *
MAY, William F.
Return to cave and candle? il Nations Bsns
59:81-3 N '71
MAY flies
Three flies for trout. A. J. McClane. il Field
& S 75:98-100+ Ja '71
MAY I ask you who's calling? story. See
Gerber, M. J.
MAYAKOVSKY, Vladimir Vladimirovich. See
Maiakovskiĭ, V. V.
MAYAS
Dance drama: Mayan sacrifice. L. Mattlage.
il Dance Mag 45:20-2 My '71
Mayan nutrition, then and now. Chem 44:
23-4 Jl '71
Why did the pre-Columbian Maya civiliza-
tion collapse? report of meeting. G. R.
Willey and D. B. Shimkin. Science 173:
656+ Ag 13 '71

Writing

Maya hieroglyphic study. il Américas 23:46
My '71
Mayan mystery of the Onima caves. E. Hart-
ley. il Sci Digest 69:9-13 Ap '71
MAYDAY (signal) See Signals and signaling
MAYER, A. M. See Meyer, H. jt. auth.
MAYER, Albert
Architecture with inner meaning, notes to-
ward a definition of urban design. il Arch
Forum 135:60-3 N '71
MAYER, David J. and others
Analgesia from electrical stimulation in the
brainstem of the rat. bibliog il Science 174:
1351-4 D 24 '71
MAYER, George Louis
At last, les Huguenots. il por Am Rec G 37:
484-7 Ap '71
Recordings. Sat R 54:79 N 27 '71
MAYER, Jean
Decision making in the biological field; ad-
dress, October 24, 1971. Vital Speeches 38:
174-9 Ja 1 '72
Let's put women in their place like, for in-
stance, city hall. McCalls 98:74+ F '71
We are ignorant about nutrition; excerpts
from comment to the press. McCalls 98:78
F '71
MAYER, Lawrence A.
Capital goods may get a growing share.
il Fortune 83:96-9+ Je '71

Into a time of stagflation. il Fortune 84:144-9
Ag '71
New questions about the U.S. population. il
Fortune 83:80-5+ F '71
MAYER, Martin
Freedom of the press can be a matter of
self-interested definition. Harper 243:40+
D '71
How will television feel after it gives up
smoking? il Fortune 83:86-9+ Ja '71
Marilyn Horne becomes a prima donna. il pors
N Y Times Mag p 14-15+ Ja 17 '71
Martin Mayer's list. Esquire 75:122+ My '71
Money man. por Opera N 35:28-9 Ap 3 '71
Recordings. See issues of Esquire
MAYER, Meinrad
Shore theater. il Holiday 49:36-7 Jl '71
MAYER, Milton
Onward as to war? a report from Prague.
Chr Cent 88:1316-19 N 10 '71
MAYER, Parm
Mother of the bride; poem. Good H 172:218
Je '71
MAYER, Ralph
Ralph Mayer's technical question & answer
page. See issues of American artist
MAYERS, Kathleen S. and others
Development of polysensory responses in as-
sociation cortex of kitten. bibliog il Sci-
ence 171:1038-40 Mr 12 '71
MAYES, Herbert R.
London letter (cont) Sat R 54:28-9 Mr 27;
6-7 Je 5; 8-9 Jl 3; 5 Ag 7; 14-15 S 4; 8+ O
9; 10+ N 6; 10+ D 4 '71
MAYFIELD, Sara
Exiles from paradise; excerpts. il pors Mc-
Calls 98:64-5+ Jl '71
MAYFLIES. See May flies
MAYHALL, Jane
Nightmares; poem. Nation 212:734 Je 7 '71

about

Comment. H. Witt. Poetry 118:44-5 Ap '71 *
MAYHEW, Henry
Unknown Mayhew, by E. Yeo and E. P.
Thompson. Review
Commentary 52:93-6 Ag '71. G. Himmel-
farb *
MAYHEW, Lewis Baltzell
Neighboring black and white colleges. Ed
Digest 37:29-31 N '71
MAYLATH, Ronald E.
Water, water everywhere. il Cons 25:14-17+
Ap '71
MAYNARD, Harry E.
Experiment with 4-channel stereo. il Radio-
Electr 42:33-8 Mr '71
4-channel sound today. il por Radio-Electr
42:33-6 O '71
MAYNARD, Joyce
Country music; story. Seventeen 31:88-9 Ja '72
MAYNARD, Olga
Idea, image and purpose: ballet in Canada
today. il Dance Mag 45:32-65+ Ap '71
Les sylphides. il por Dance Mag 45:43-66 D '71
MAYNARD, Richard
Classroom cinema. bibliog Schol Teach Jr/Sr
High p29+ S; 28+ O; 22 N '71; 18-20 Ja '72
El Exigente meets the Pepsi generation; com-
mercials in the curriculum. il Schol Teach
Jr/Sr High p 12-14 My 3 '71
MAYNE, Melba
Look at Solzhenitsyn. Engl J 60:205-7 F '71
MAYO, Sheila
African gift. Chr Cent 88:252-3 F 24 '71
MAYORAL candidates. See Candidates, Po-
litical
MAYORS
City woes: easing a bit, mayors say. il U S
News 70:32 Je 28 '71
First hurrah for hizzoner, age 19; R. Hooker
as mayor. il por Life 71:77 N 19 '71
Who should run your town? Maybe you. il
Changing T 25:39-42 N '71
See also
United States conference of mayors
MAYR, Ernst, and others
Stability in zoological nomenclature. Science
174:1041-2 D 3 '71
MAYR, Johann Simon. See Mayr, S.
MAYR, Simone
Johann Simon Mayr and his Ifigenia in
Aulide. J. Freeman. bibliog f il Mus Q 57:
187-210 Ap '71 *
Medea á la Mayr. R. Lawrence. Sat R 54:57
Ja 30 '71 *
MAYS, Benjamin Elijah
Doctor Benjamin E. Mays. il pors Ebony
26:88-92+ Jl '71 *
MAYS, Willie
Age of Willie Mays. P. Schrag. il pors Sat R
54:15-17+ My 8 '71 *
Annual baseball roundup: the last of the big
bats. il pors Ebony 26:92-4+ Je '71 *

MAYSLES, Albert
Death theme in natural cinema. J. F. Kavanaugh. America 125:122-3 S 4 '71 *
MAZDA (automobile) See Automobiles, Foreign
MAZER, Gwen. See Capron, M. jt. auth.
MAZEWSKI, Aloysius A.
U.S. gives views on question of Namibia; statement, November 16, 1970. Dept State Bul 64:101-3 Ja 18 '71
MAZIE, David M. See Rowan, C. T. jt. auth.
MAZLISH, Bruce
Are we ready for an American Lenin? il Horizon 13:48-55 Aut '71
MAZRUI, Ali A.
Learning the three T's in school. UNESCO Courier 24:28-30+ N '71
MAZURSKY, Paul
Current cinema. P. Kael. New Yorker 46: 62-5 Ja 9 '71 *
MAZZARO, Jerome
Ransom's new selected poems. Poetry 117: 275-6 Ja '71
MAZZO, Kay
Oh Kay. H. Saal. por Newsweek 77:99-100 F 22 '71 *
ME nobody knows; musical comedy. See Musical comedies, revues, etc.—Criticisms, plots, etc.
MEACHAM, Carl E.
Separate but better. New Repub 165:10-11 O 9 '71
MEACHAM, Stewart
Reporter at large. G. Jonas. New Yorker 47: 99-104+ Mr 20 '71 *
MEAD, Chris
Homecoming of Chris Mead. K. Fleming. il pors Newsweek 77:28-9 Mr 29 '71 *
MEAD, Margaret
Drugs & us. Harp Baz 104:130-1+ Mr '71
Is the family obsolete; interview, ed. by J. Kronenberger. Look 35:36 Ja 26 '71
Margaret Mead views education today. Ed Digest 37:5-8 D '71
[Monthly column] See issues of Redbook
Rap on race; excerpts. pors McCalls 98:84-5+ Je '71
Rap on race; how James Baldwin and I talked a book. il por Redbook 137:70-2+ S '71
—and McClanahan, Preston
(eds) Peoples of the Pacific. bibliog il pors Natur Hist 80:34-70 My '71

about
Following their footsteps. S. Latz. il pors Seventeen 30:94-5+ Ja '71 *
How Margaret Mead and James Baldwin got together for A rap on race. B. A. Bannon. pors Pub W 199:104-5 My 31 '71 *
Muffled voices. G. Wolff. pors Newsweek 77:100+ My 24 '71 *
MEAD, Shepherd
How to cope with European culture (without really trying) il Travel 135:64-9 Je '71
MEAD corporation
Late tape. R. Brady. Duns 97:106 Mr '71
MEADE, Marion
Politics of day care. Commonweal 94:133-5 Ap 16 '71
MEADE, Richard A.
Theory for sequence in English. Engl J 60: 469-73 Ap '71
Whatever happened to insights? bibliog f Engl J 60:1234-7 D '71
MEADE, Robert H. and Emery, K. O.
Sea level as affected by river runoff, eastern United States. bibliog il Science 173:425-8 Jl 30 '71
MEADE, Tom
Meade in Italy. G. Borgeson. il por Motor T 23:66+ Ap '71 *
MEADLO, Paul David
My Lai: a question of orders. il pors Time 97:24 Ja 25 '71
MEADMORE, Clement
Solid man. R. Hughes. il por Time 97:66 Ap 5 '71 *
MEADOR, Melba
Bringing Job into the twentieth century. Engl J 60:921-3 O '71
MEADOWS, Dennis L.
What are man's prospects? Cur 133:3-9 O '71
MEADOWS, Milo Martin, Jr
Attitudes and values: ingredients of good teaching. Clear House 45:377-9 F '71
MEALS
Day of the tray. N. Mandelbaum. il Ladies Home J 88:130-3 My '71
Food and flowers that make a memorable meal. C. Masson. il pors House & Gard 140:54-7 Jl '71

Keep cool cooking. D. Eby and N. Hopkins. il Bet Hom & Gard 49:64-9 Jl '71
Oven meals that won't bruise the budget; with menus and recipes. D. Eby. il Bet Hom & Gard 49:72-8 F '71
See also
Breakfasts
Buffet meals
Christmas meals
Cookery
Diet
Dinners and dining
Entertaining
Food
Menus
Outdoor meals
Snacks
Suppers
Thanksgiving dinners
Wedding meals
MEALS on wheels. See Aged—Nutrition
MEANLEY, Brooke
Dismal Swamp; its flora and fauna. il Liv Wildn 34:34+ Wint '70
MEANY, George
Code of fair practises; address, June 16, 1971. Vital Speeches 37:618-21 Ag 1 '71
Meany puts the heat on; excerpts from interview, ed. by T. Joyce. pors Newsweek 78:48-9 S 6 '71
Meany's idea for wage controls after the freeze; excerpts from interview. por U S News 71:58-61 S 13 '71

about
Angry unions aim for a deal with Nixon. il por Bsns W p52-5+ Ag 28 '71 *
Battle of Bal Harbour. Time 98:16 D 6 '71 *
Being Meany to Nixon. J. Hill. Commonweal 95:268-9 D 17 '71 *
Complicated desires of George Meany. Nat R 23:1044 S 24 '71 *
For George Meany, life begins at 77. H. Sidey. Life 71:4 N 19 '71 *
George Meany: fight over the freeze. il pors Newsweek 78:46+ S 6 '71 *
Jockeying for Meany's job begins. il por Bsns W p64+ D 18 '71 *
Labor's disturbing challenge. pors Time 98: 29 N 29 '71 *
Living with the Pay board, strategy of big unions. il U S News 71:59-60 N 29 '71 *
Mr. Meany's big cigar. Nation 213:194 S 13 '71 *
Mr Nixon knows what he can do. il pors Newsweek 78:16-18 N 29 '71 *
Nix on Nixon. il Newsweek 78:60 Ag 23 '71 *
Nixon and labor widen the breach. por Bsns W p 18-19 N 27 '71 *
Nixon: we have an obligation to the next generation; address, November 19, 1971. R. M. Nixon. por U S News 71:87-90 D 6 '71; Excerpts. 71:87 N 29 '71 *
Nixon's freeze and the mood of labor. il por Time 98:9-15 S 6 '71 *
Phase II planners; close to consensus. il Bsns W p 17-19 S 18 '71 *
Plumber who delivers. il por Time 98:10-11 S 6 '71 *
Show biz in Miami. Nation 213:578-9 D 6 '71 *
TRB from Washington. New Repub 165:6 S 11 '71 *
MEASEL, Wes, and Crawford, L. L.
School children and book selection. il pors Am Lib 2:955-7 O '71
MEASLES
Measles: the new rash. Newsweek 77:65 Mr 1 '71
MEASLES, German. See Rubella
MEASLES in cattle
Beef measles: what they are, what you can do to control 'em. J. G. Clark. il Farm J 95:B24 O '71
MEASLES virus
Subacute sclerosing panencephalitis: isolation of suppressed measles virus from lymph node biopsies. L. Horta-Barbosa and others. bibliog il Science 173:840-1 Ag 27 '71
MEASUREMENT
See also
Cookery—Measurements
Geodesy
Surfaces—Measurement
MEASURING instruments
Make you own inclinometer. J. Dillon. il Motor B & S 128:68 S '71
See also
Calipers
Micrometers
MEASURING utensils, Household. See Cookery—Measurements
MEASURING worms. See Loopers

MEAT
See also
Beef
Carving (meat, etc)
Cookery—Meat
Ham
Meat inspection

Grading and standardization
Don't lower beef quality! H. J. Tuma. Farm
  J 95:B10 Mr '71
Grades of meat: what they mean. il Environ
  13:48 Jl '71
New approach to branded pork. R. Wilmore.
  Farm J 95:H16 N '71
You can make your meat dollar go further. il
  Changing T 26:13-15 Ja '72

Preservation
Two-hour jerky. N. Weis and J. Howard. il
  Field & S 76:30 O '71

Prices
Good news for meat buyers. il U S News
  70:29 Ja 18 '71
Great new ways to cut food costs. M. Hap-
  pel. il Ladies Home J 88:132-7+ S '71
How much will the price spurt hurt? beef.
  Farm J 95:B19 Ap '71
Pricecast. See issues of Farm journal

MEAT, Frozen
Frozen breaded veal "steaks". il Consumer
  Rep 36:336 Je '71
What about frozen hamburgers? Consumer
  Rep 36:482-3 Ag '71

MEAT, Synthetic. See Food substitutes

MEAT cutting
Simple tricks to boning meat. M. Happel. il
  Ladies Home J 88:134-5+ S '71
  See also
Game, Dressing of

MEAT eating by animals. See Animals—Food
  and feeding

MEAT industry
Who will run the pork industry? National
  symposium on vertical coordination in the
  pork industry, Purdue university. J. Rus-
  sell. Farm J 95:34+ Je '71
  See also
Armour and company
Cattle industry
Hormel. George A, and company
Meat—Prices
Meat, Frozen
Meat inspection

Advertising
Grassroots promotion moves pork, and pork
  producers, too. J. Russell. il Farm J 95:
  H14-15 My '71
Push pork with style; National pork queen
  Marilyn Bidner. B. Coffman. il Farm J
  95:H8-9 Mr '71
Say mister, want to sign up for a free ham?
  D. Seim. Farm J 95:H24 S '71

Imports problem
Pork imports: how big a threat to your
  market? J. Russell. il Farm J 95:H9+ O
  '71

Laws and legislation
  See also
Meat inspection

Argentina
Survival race may be going to Swift. il Bshs
  W p40 O 16 '71

Europe, Western
Your pork-producing competition in Europe.
  R. Wilmore. il Farm J 95:H10-11+ O '71

MEAT inspection
Nader's newest raid for tougher meat inspection; with editorial comment. J. Carlson. Farm J 95:13+. 42 S '71
What you'd better know about the meat you
  are buying. J. Snyder. il Todays Health 49:
  37-9+ D '71

MEAT loaf, pies, etc. See Cookery—Meat

MEAT prices. See Meat—Prices

MEAT sauce. See Sauces

MEAT substitutes. See Food substitutes

MEAT thermometers. See Thermometers, Cooking

MEATBALLS. See Cookery—Meat

MEATLESS meals. See Vegetarianism

MECCA
  See also
Pilgrimages to Mecca

MECCA, Pilgrimages to. See Pilgrimages to
  Mecca

MECH, Dave
Can you match them up? il Outdoor Life
  147:176-7+ Ap '71

MECH, L. David
Where the wolves are and how they stand;
  with biographical sketch. Natur Hist 89:6,
  26-9 Ap '71

MECHANICAL drawing
  See also
Drawing instruments

MECHANICAL engineering
  See also
Computers—Engineering use

MECHANICS
  See also
Force and energy
Horsepower (mechanics)

MECHANICS (persons)
  See also
Automobile mechanics (persons)

MECHANICS, Celestial
Apples in a spacecraft. H. Alfvén. bibliog il
  Science 173:522-5 Ag 6 '71
Energy in the universe. F. J. Dyson. il Sci
  Am 225:50-9 S '71

MECHANICS, Household
Ask Rufus; questions and answers. R. Cart-
  wright. See issues of Mechanix illustrated
Don't call the repairman yet. il Changing T
  25:43-4 D '71
40 great hints to save you time and money.
  il Pop Mech 136:171-6 O '71
McCalls handywoman:
  Curing your sick vacuum cleaner. il Mc-
    Calls 98:52 Jl '71
  Electrical first aid. il McCalls 98:114 Je '71
  Healing your sick furniture. il McCalls
    99:62 O '71
  Know your housepower. McCalls 98:143
    My '71
  No more leaky faucets. il McCalls 98:
    28 Ag '71
  Removing furniture scars. il McCalls 98:
    28 S '71
McCall's handywoman. il McCalls 98:182 F;
  156 Mr; 48 Ap '71
Solving home problems. See issues of Pop-
  ular mechanics
20 household headaches you can solve your-
  self. il Bet Hom & Gard 49:26+ N '71
  See also
Plumbing

MECHANIZATION, Agricultural. See Farm
  mechanization

MECHLING, Thomas B.
Marts of trade. J. Brooks. New Yorker 47:
  138+ O 9 '71 *

**MECKLENBURGER, James A. and Wilson,
  J. A.**
Learning C.O.D: can the schools buy suc-
  cess? il Sat R 54:62-5+ S 18 '71; Same abr.
  Ed Digest 37:1-4 N '71

MECOM, John W.
Mecom's rescue plan. por Bsns W p77 Jl 17
  '71 *

MECOM, John W. Jr
Signal helps itself and bails out Mecom.
  il Bsns W p20 D 25 '71 *

MEDAL of freedom
President presents Medal of freedom to NATO
  Secretary General Brosio; remarks and re-
  sponse, September 29, 1971. R. M. Nixon;
  M. Brosio. Dept State Bul 65:487-8 N 1
  '71

MEDALS
Making of a medal; processes involved in pro-
  ducing an art medal. E. R. Grove. il Am
  Artist 36:20-5+ Ja '72
Medals. C. French. il Hobbies 76:132+ N '71
Non-coin of the realm. il Time 98:58 Jl 12 '71
  See also
Franklin mint
  also names of medals, e.g. National medal
  of science

Collectors and collecting
Making a mint; commemorative medals. il
  Newsweek 78:78 D 20 '71
Medals and proof sets. C. French. Hobbies
  76:132 O '71

MEDAWAR, Sir Peter Brian
For a better world. Vogue 159:64-5 Ja 1 '72

MEDEIROS, Robert W.
Lead from automobile exhaust. bibliog il por
  Chem 44:7-9 N '71
Smog formation simplified. bibliog il por Chem
  45:16-18 Ja '72

MEDFORD, Charles F. See Casey, W. L. jr. jt.
  auth.

MEDFORD, Ore.
Put more green in the park maintenance
  budget. M. A. Starr. il Am City 86:81+
  My '71

MEDIA general, inc.
Down the river. D. C. Berliner. Nation 213: 292-3 O 4 '71; Discussion. 213:482+ N 15 '71
Stock-market racing form. por Time 98:48+ S 13 '71

MEDIA general financial daily
Space-age newspaper. il Newsweek 78:72 Ag 16 '71

MEDIAN barriers. See Roads—Safety guards

MEDIATION, arbitration and inquiry, Staff committee on. See American library association—Mediation, arbitration and inquiry, Staff committee on

MEDICAID. See Medical service, State

MEDICAL assistance programs, inc.
They take vacations for humanity. C. W. Hall. il Read Digest 98:45-6+ Ap '71

MEDICAL assistants. See Medical workers

MEDICAL care. See Medical service

MEDICAL care of the aged. See Aged—Medical care

MEDICAL clinics. See Health facilities

MEDICAL colleges
   See also
California college of podiatric medicine, San Francisco, Calif.
Harvard university—Medical school
Medical education
Miami. University, Coral Gables, Fla.—School of medicine
Stanford university—School of medicine

   Curriculum
Projected changes in medical school curriculum. D. Stetten, jr. bibliog il Science 174:1303-6 D 24 '71

   Federal aid
Health manpower: buying off the care crisis. Sci N 100:421-2 D 25 '71

MEDICAL committee for human rights
Health radicals: crusade to shift medical power to the people. R. J. Bazell. il Science 173:506-9 Ag 6 '71

MEDICAL consultants
   See also
Psychiatric consultants

MEDICAL corps. See United States—Army—Medical corps

MEDICAL delusions
Vitamin C mania. P. O'Neil. il por Life 71:55-6+ Jl 9 '71

MEDICAL education
Doctor shortage, what's being done; armed forces medical school. il U S News 71:67 N 22 '71
Doktor. dottore. docteur; Americans studying in foreign schools. il Newsweek 78:95 N 22 '71
Higher educaton and the nation's health. J. H. Knowles. Science 171:337 Ja 29 '71
Medical and dental education for the health care crisis. il Sch & Soc 99:71-4 F '71
Medical education: Carnegie panel urges expansion, acceleration. J. Walsh; discussion. Science 171:846 Mr 5 '71
Peace, health, and the doctor. J. Lear. Sat R 54:33-5+ Ap 17 '71
Shapers of the future: the need for doctors; address. November 29, 1970. W. C. Bornemeier. Vital Speeches 37:315-18 Mr 1 '71
   See also
Medical colleges

   Federal aid
Health manpower training: funding levels at issue. J. Walsh. il Science 174:1003-5 D 3 '71

MEDICAL electronics
Controlling pain at the gate; dorsal column stimulation and saline injection. Sci N 100:7 Jl 3 '71
Jamming the pain waves. Newsweek 77:97 Ap 5 '71
Medical spin-offs from the space program. W. Von Braun. il Pop Sci 198:62-4 Mr '71
Now: an electronic pain killer; dorsal column stimulator. A. S. Freese. il Pop Mech 136: 68-71+ Jl '71
Radio signal relieves pain. A. J. Snider. Sci Digest 71:69 Ja '72
   See also
Computers—Medical use

MEDICAL engineering. See Biomedical engineering

MEDICAL ethics
Betrayal of trust: General medical council's decision on the Browne case in England. T. Beeson. Chr Cent 88:420-1 Ap 7 '71
Ethical issues in biomedicine: choices on everyone's conscience; ed. by R. J. Trotter. il Sci N 100:275-6 O 23 '71

Ethics in biomedicine: a call for action. Sci N 100:294 O 30 '71
From Hippocrates to Senate Res. 75. R. J. Trotter. Sci N 100:377 D 4 '71
New biology: what price relieving man's estate? L. R. Kass. bibliog Science 174:779-88 N 19 '71
Not what Catholic hospitals ordered; ethical directives. R. A. McCormick. America 125: 510-13 D 11 '71
Patient as person: explorations in medical ethics, by Ramsey. Review
   Cath World 213:152-3 Je '71. P. R. Gastonguay
R for medical ethics: an injection of compassion. J. R. Greisch. Chr Today 16:41-2 N 5 '71
Right to life: who is to decide? J. L. Arehart. il Sci N 100:298-300 O 30 '71
Spirit: who will make the choices of life and death? il Time 97:48+ Ap 19 '71
   See also
Embryology, Experimental—Moral and religious aspects

MEDICAL examinations. See Physical examinations

MEDICAL fakers. See Quacks and quackery

MEDICAL fees. See Medical service, Cost of

MEDICAL history. See Medicine—History

MEDICAL hypnosis. See Hypnotism—Therapeutic use

MEDICAL illustration
Delicate art of illustrating the brain; work of F. Armitage. R. Graves. il por Life 71:3 O 22 '71
Medical illustration: Philip C. Johnson. H. Meredith-Owens. il Am Artist 35:50-5+ D '71

MEDICAL instruments and apparatus
Mechanical medics. il Time 97:66 Ap 26 '71
   See also
Hospitals—Equipment and supplies
Medical electronics

   Standards
Danger in the hospital. A. S. Freese. il Pop Mech 135:80-3 F '71
Leakage current & electrical shock. P. B. Jarrett. Pop Electr 34:46 Mr '71
Product testing for medical devices. Consumer Rep 36:468 Ag '71

MEDICAL insurance. See Insurance, Health

MEDICAL jurisprudence
Crime doctors; forensic pathology. il Newsweek 78:67-8 O 11 '71
   See also
Forensic psychiatry

MEDICAL laboratories
Clinical chemistry laboratory. J. A. Lott and H.-D. Grümer. il por Chem 44:6-9 Je '71
Role of on-the-job training in a clinical laboratory. W. D. White and A. Robbins. bibliog f il Mo Labor R 94:65-9 Mr '71

MEDICAL library association
Medical library association: a lively annual meeting. Library J 96:3073 O 1 '71
Treating a 70-year-old for professionitis; annual meeting. A. Plotnik; J. S. Rauch. il Wilson Lib Bul 46:36-9 S '71

MEDICAL linacs. See Accelerators (electrons, etc)—Medical use

MEDICAL literature
   See also
Pharmacopoeias

MEDICAL news
Medical briefs; ed. by P. Gunby. See issues of Today's health to July 1971
Scientists and the press: cancer scare story that wasn't. N. Wade. Science 174:679-80 N 12 '71
Today's health news. See issues of Today's health

MEDICAL practice. See Medicine—Practice

MEDICAL radiology. See Radiology, Medical

MEDICAL records
Effects on treatment of summarizing psychiatric records of chronic hospitalized patients. W. Greenleaf and D. Greenleaf. Ment Hy 55:407-9 Jl '71
   See also
Computers—Medical use

MEDICAL relief work
   See also
Direct relief foundation
Medical assistance programs, inc.

   Peru
Doctorcito, don't let them abandon us. D. Rennie. il por Todays Health 49:23-4+ My '71

MEDICAL workers—*Continued*
Training
Bucking the system, program under Dr Huber at Boston city hospital. J. Morgenstern. il pors Newsweek 79:65 Ja 10 '72
Helping out the doctor; Medex program recruiting former military medics. il Time 97:42 Mr 29 '71
Introducing: the supernurse; nurse-practitioners as physicians assistants. L. Gross. McCalls 98:75+ Mr '71

MEDICARE
Automatic increases, $12,000 social security tax base urged. Aging 199:10+ My '71
Caring for our aged poor. L. H. Henry. New Repub 164:17-22 My 22 '71
Economics of health care. J. Ridgeway. Il Ramp Mag 10:8-9 S '71
Health insurance for older people. il Changing T 25:21-3 Ag '71
House passes social security, medicare, welfare changes. Har Yrs 11:4-5 Jl '71
Medicare premium up from $5.30 to $5.60 monthly, starting July 1. T. Schuchat. Har Yrs 11:4 F '71
National health insurance debate signals shakeup in medicare law. Har Yrs 11:4 Ap '71
Should chiropractors be paid with your tax dollars? A. Q. Maisel. Read Digest 99:76-81 Jl '71

MEDICATED feed. See Feeding and feeding stuffs—Medicated feed

MEDICINE
Keep up with medicine. B. Yuncker. See issues of Good housekeeping
Medical sciences. See occasional issues of Science news
Medicine today. D. R. Zimmerman. See issues of Ladies' home journal
News from the world of medicine. See issues of Reader's digest
See also
Acupuncture
Atomic medicine
Biomedical engineering
Folk medicine
Health
Iatrophysical school
Medical research
Prescriptions
Quacks and quackery
Space medicine
Surgery
Bibliography
Books to come (cont) Library J 96:867-8+, 2383-5+, 3647+ Mr 1, Jl, N 1 '71

Emblems and symbols
See Symbolism in medicine

History
Origins of hypodermic medication. N. Howard-Jones. il por Sci Am 224:96-102 bibliog (p 122) Ja '71
See also
Hippocrates
Bibliography
History of medicine: a bookshelf for the public library. B. Waserman and M. Waserman. il pors Library J 97:37-41 Ja 1 '72

Practice
Doctor for Vinton County: plight of a country doctor. il Time 98:82 N 1 '71
New type of doctor emerges. il Time 98:61-2+ N 8 '71
See also
Malpractice
Medical ethics
Medical service
Physicians and patients

Study and teaching
See also
Medical colleges
Medical education
Medical students

China (People's Republic)
See also
Acupuncture

Japan
Western alchemy symbols in a Japanese medical work; translation of 18th century Dutch pharmacopoeia. T. Benfey. bibliog il Chem 44:14-18 S '71

United States
Gerber report. by A. Gerber. Review
Life por 70:15 Ap 23 '71. M. Halberstam

Looking at medicine (cont) W. C. Alvarez. Look 35:18 F 23; 12-13 Je 29; 54 Ag 24 '71
See also
Institute of medicine
MEDICINE, Adolescent. See Youth—Health and hygiene
MEDICINE, Atomic. See Atomic medicine
MEDICINE, Greek and Roman
See also
Hippocrates
MEDICINE, Magic, mystic, etc.
Bizarre rites of the cobra shrine; saving snake bite victims. K. Severin. il Sci Digest 69:52-5 Mr '71
MEDICINE, Military
See also
Vietnamese war, 1957- —Medical and sanitary affairs
World war, 1939-1945—Medical and sanitary affairs
MEDICINE, Popular
See also
Chiropractors
Folk medicine
MEDICINE, Preventive
See also
Heart—Diseases—Prevention
MEDICINE, Primitive
See also
Medicine men
MEDICINE, Veterinary. See Veterinary medicine
MEDICINE and religion
Not what Catholic hospitals ordered; ethical directives. R. A. McCormick. America 125: 510-13 D 11 '71
MEDICINE and sports. See Sports medicine
MEDICINE bottles. See Bottles
MEDICINE cabinets
Medicine chest alarm. R. Graf and G. J. Whalen. il Mech Illus 67:106-7 Ja '71
What you should have in your medicine chest; over the counter drugs. A. S. Markovits. il Mech Illus 67:48-9 Ja '71
MEDICINE dolls. See Medicine men
MEDICINE kits
Tips for your home and family; travel first aid kit. Today's Health 49:67 Ap '71
MEDICINE men
Medicine dolls and primitive peoples. K. Severin. il Sci Digest 69:65-9 Je '71
Of babalawos and shamans. M. Pines. McCalls 98:43 Ag '71
Under the power of the Gran Gadu; Bush Negro witchcraft. L. C. Whiton. il Natur Hist 80:14-16+ Ag '71
MEDICINES. See Drugs
MEDICINES, Patent, proprietary, etc.
Bottles, flasks and Dr Dyott, by H. McKearin. Review
Antiques il 100:196+ Ag '71. E. Gaines
Cough-remedy caution. Time 97:45 F 15 '71
Sweet extract of hokum. G. Carson. il pors Am Heritage 22:18-27+ Je '71
What you should have in your medicine chest; over the counter drugs. A. S. Markovits. il Mech Illus 67:48-9 Ja '71
MEDICS. See Medical workers
MEDIEVAL manuscripts. See Manuscripts, Medieval
MEDINA, Ernest L.
My God, don't go to pieces. il Newsweek 77: 24-5 Mr 22 '71
about
Captain who commanded Lieutenant Calley. T. Buckley. il por N Y Times Mag p8-9+ Je 20 '71 *
Lies about My Lai. Time 98:25 N 29 '71 *
Medina's turn. il por Newsweek 78:22+ Ag 23 '71 *
My Lai: a question of orders. il pors Time 97:24 Ja 25 '71*
One is lying. por Time 97:16 Mr 22 '71 *
Postscript to the Medina trial. K. Reich. Nation 213:433-5 N 1 '71 *
MEDINA trial. See Courts martial and courts of inquiry
MEDINILLA
Magnificent medinilla; kapa-kapa. L. Cabalquinto and J. Pancho. il Horticulture 49: 46-7 F '71
MEDITATION
Cartography of the ecstatic and meditative states. R. Fischer. bibliog il Science 174: 897-904 N 26 '71
Involvement. P. B. Price. PTA Mag 65:13 Ja '71
Key to happiness; excerpts from Living the infinite way. J. S. Goldsmith. U S News 71:108 S 20 '71

MEDITATION—*Continued*
Mind over drugs. il Time 98:51 O 25 '71
Superthinking; an introduction to Christian Zen; excerpt from Christian Zen. W. Johnston. America 125:28 Jl 24 '71
Time for contemplation. P. A. Dickinson. il Har Yrs 11:48-51 D '71

MEDITERRANEAN house decoration. See House decoration, Mediterranean

MEDITERRANEAN REGION
Playing chicken over the Mediterranean. W. H. Honan. il Read Digest 98:77-81 Mr '71
See also
Malta
Petroleum—Mediterranean Region

History
Adventures of Hanno the navigator. il UNESCO Courier 23:14-16 D '70

MEDITERRANEAN Sea
Dead sea II. R. Starnes. il Field & S 76:8+ Jl '71
Deep-water archeology. W. Bascom. bibliog il Science 174:261-9 O 15 '71
Is the Mediterranean dying? J. Cornwell? il N Y Times Mag p24-5+ F 21 '71
Salvaging ancient ships; Alcoa Seaprobe. il Newsweek 78:84 N 22 '71
Soviet thrust in the Mediterranean; Black Sea fleet and Sixth fleet. il Time 97:27-8 Je 28 '71
See also
Aegean Islands
Corsica
Suez Canal

MEDIUMS
The medium had the message: Mrs Piper and the professors; excerpts from Here, Mr Splitfoot. R. Somerlott. il pors Am Heritage 22:33-7+ F '71
See also
Spiritualism

MEDNIEKS, Maija. See Maas, J. W. jt. auth.

MEDVEDEV, Roi Aleksandrovich
—See Medvedev, Z. A. jt. auth.

about
Dissent in the USSR. A. Astrachan. Commentary 53:86-7+ Ja '72 *
New indictment of Stalin. Time 98:42 N 1 '71 *
Question of madness, by R. Medvedev. Review
Sat R pors 54:35-7 N 20 '71. S. Jacoby *

MEDVEDEV, Zhores Aleksandrovich
—and Medvedev, R. A.
Question of madness; excerpt. il pors N Y Times Mag p34-5+ N 7 '71

about
Dissent in the USSR. A. Astrachan. Commentary 53:86-7+ Ja '72 *
Medvedev papers, by Z. A. Medvedev, and A question of madness, by Z. A. Medvedev and R. A. Medvedev. Reviews
Sat R pors 54:35-7 N 20 '71. S. Jacoby *
Psychoadaptation; or, How to handle dissenters. por Time 98:44-5 S 27 '71 *
Science censored. D. Shapley. Science 174: 273 O 15 '71 *

MEDWAY, Pat
Two-by-four tomatoes. Org Gard & Farm 18: 28-9 My '71

MEEHAN, Richard L. See Hamilton, D. H. jt. auth.

MEEHAN, Thomas
Abraham Lincoln: lawyer, statesman, and golf nut. New Yorker 47:33-5 Ag 28 '71
Carter Burden question. il pors N Y Times Mag p33+ N 7 '71
Cruise director on the Titanic. il pors N Y Times Mag p 10-11+ Ja 8 '72
If someone says his work is art, it's art. il Horizon 13:4-15 Aut '71
Let 'em eat coquilles Saint-Jacques. il N Y Times Mag p6-7+ D 27 '70; 37+ Ja 31 '71
What the OTB bettor can learn from Walter Matthau. il pors N Y Times Mag p6-7+ Jl 4 '71
Where have all the orange blossoms gone? Mlle 72:113+ Ja '71
Yale faculty makes the scene. il N Y Times Mag p 12-13+ F 7; 16+ Mr 7 '71

MEEK, Charles R.
No outside help wanted. il Am City 86:79 Mr '71

MEEK, George
First General assembly. il Américas 23:2-7 Je '71

MEEKER, Edward Warren
Assisting artists in Edison cylinders. J. Walsh. por Hobbies 76:37-8 Ap '71 (to be cont) *

MEEKER, John J.
How my garden soil grew and grew. il Org Gard & Farm 18:39-43 F '71
Put the world in your garden. Org Gard & Farm 18:33-7 N '71

MEEKER, Leonard Carpenter
United States and Romania agree on 1971-72 exchanges program; remarks, November 27, 1970. Dept State Bul 64:126 Ja 25 '71

MEERSMAN, William F.
Optional celibacy; letter to editor. Commonweal 94:487 S 17 '71

MEESE, William Giles
Detroit Edison's profit-minded boss. por Bsns W p74 O 2 '71 *

MEETINGHOUSES, Friend. See Churches, Friend

MEETINGS
Types of meetings defined; reprint. Writers Digest 51:27 My '71
See also
Business meetings
Conventions
Sales conventions
Stockholders meetings

MEEUS, Jean
Some bright visual binary stars (cont) il Sky & Tel 41:88-92 F '71

MEFISTOFELE; opera. See Boito, A.

MEGGYESY, Dave
Sports; disillusioned professional football players. J. Scott. Ramp Mag 10:68-70 N '71 *

MEGLIN, Nick
Anthony Saris: variations on angel's theme. il Am Artist 35:22-5 D '71
Ken Dallison: the education of an illustrator. il por Am Artist 35:24-9+ N '71

MEHLE, Aileen
Suzy: dare to be different. pors Vogue 157: 104-5 Je '71

MEHLHOFF, Tom
Veterinarian. C. See. il Atlan 228:95-8+ O '71 *

MEHR, Sandy. See Ehrlich, A. jt. auth.

MEHTA, Ved
Department of amplification. New Yorker 47: 121-4 Mr 13 '71
Letter from West Bengal. New Yorker 47: 166+ D 11 '71
Onward and upward with the arts. il New Yorker 47:44-8+ My 8 '71
about
Worlds of Ved Mehta. A. Fremantle. por Commonweal 95:353-4 Ja 14 '72 *

MEHTA, Zubin
Music to my ears; Bruckner à la Mehta. I. Kolodin. Sat R 54:43 Mr 6 '71 *

MEICHLE, Michael E.
Amateur breaks glass with a purpose: to determine the patterns of fracture. il Sci Am 225:122-7 N '71

MEIER, Albert H. and others
Temporal synergism of corticosterone and prolactin controlling gonadal growth in sparrows. bibliog il Science 173:1240-2 S 24 '71

MEIER, Donna
Driftwood zoo. il Design 72:20-1 Spr '71
Popsicle sticks build a church. il Design 72: 36-7 mid-Wint '71

MEIER, Richard
Planning for Jerusalem. il Arch Forum 134: 56-7 Ap '71

MEILACH, Dona Z.
Macramé. il Todays Health 49:28-31 O '71

MEILAENDER, Gilbert, Jr
New paganism. il Chr Today 15:4-6 S 24 '71

MEINEL, Aden Baker, and Meinel, M. P.
Is it time for a new look at solar energy? il pors Bul Atom Sci 27:32-7 O '71

MEINEL, Marjorie Pettit. See Meinel, A. B. jt. auth.

MEINERT, Herb
Should the new TV writer go to Hollywood? ed. by N. Vogel. por Writers Digest 51:32-3 Je '71

MEINHOF, Ulrike Marie
Most dangerous lady. il por Newsweek 78:43-4 D 6 '71 *

MEINKE, Peter
Dear reader; poem. New Repub 165:27 Ag 7 '71
This is a poem to my son Peter. New Repub 165:26 D 25 '71
Vegetables; poem. New Repub 164:25 Ap 10 '71
Words; poem. New Repub 164:39 Ja 2 '71
World is spindled on two poles; poem. Chr Cent 88:286 Mr 3 '71

MEIR, Golda
Talk with Golda Meir; interview, ed. by M. Clark. por Time 98:29 Ag 30 '71
Talk with Golda Meir; interview, ed. by A. De Borchgrave. il por Newsweek 77:66-7+ Mr 8 '71
        about
Golda Meir: Israel's tough grandmother-prime minister. D. Reed. por Read Digest 99:109-13 Jl '71 *
Israel: does geography matter? por Newsweek 77:37-8 Mr 29 '71 *
Mrs Meir: a phantom smile? il por Newsweek 78:42 D 13 '71 *
Three women leaders beset by problems. por U S News 70:42 My 10 '71 *
MEISENBERG, Sheldon
Making money work. See issues of Harvest years
MEISLER, Stanley
Congo. Atlan 227:26+ Mr '71
French Africa. Atlan 228:6+ S '71
Ten years of fratricide. il Nation 213:582-4 D 6 '71
MEKONG development project. See United Nations—Economic commission for Asia and the Far East
MEKONG RIVER DELTA
Quislings: the new meaning. Nation 212:804 Je 28 '71
Where peace is returning in Vietnam; interview. J. P. Vann. il por U S News 70:29-31 My 31 '71
MELADY, Thomas Patrick
United Nations faces the next twenty-five years. il Cath World 213:189-93 Jl '71
MELAMED, Monte
Most camps need better garbage disposal facilities. il Camp Mag 43:25-6 My '71
MELANCON, Serge B. and others
Histidase activity in cultivated human amniotic fluid cells. bibliog il Science 173:627-8 Ag 13 '71
MELANDRI, Bruno A. and others
Interchangeability of phosphorylation coupling factors in photosynthetic and respiratory energy conversion. bibliog il Science 174:514-16 O 29 '71
MELANESIANS
Peoples of the Pacific; ed. by M. Mead and P. McClanahan. bibliog il pors Natur Hist 80:44-7 My '71
Waiting for that Cargo. il Time 98:23-4 Jl 19 '71
        See also
New Hebrides—Native races
MELANIN
Melanin pigmentation: an in vivo model for studies of melanosome kinetics within keratinocytes. K. Wolff and K. Konrad. bibliog il Science 174:1034-5 D 3 '71
MELANOPHORE-stimulating hormone. See Melanotropin
MELANOPHORES
Calcium requirement for melanophore-stimulating hormone action on melanophores. D. L. Vesely and M. E. Hadley. bibliog il Science 173:923-5 S 3 '71
MELANOTROPIN
Calcium requirement for melanophore-stimulating hormone action on melanophores. D. L. Vesely and M. E. Hadley. bibliog il Science 173:923-5 S 3 '71
MELATONIN
Melatonin and abnormal movements induced by L-dopa in mice. G. C. Cotzias and others. bibliog il Science 173:450-2 Jl 30 '71
Melatonin: effect on punished and non-punished operant behavior of the pigeon. R. I. Schoenfeld. bibliog il Science 171:1258-60 Mr 26 '71
MELBOURNE, Caroline (Ponsonby) Lamb, viscountess. See Lamb, C. P.
MELBOURNE, Australia
        Music
Report:
    Bohème. A. L. Hoffman. il Opera N 35: 31 Ap 17 '71
Today and yesterday in musical Melbourne. I. Kolodin. il Sat R 54:20 Jl 10 '71
MELCHER, Daniel
Cataloging, processing, and automation; excerpts from Melcher on acquisition. Am Lib 2:701-13 Jl '71
MELEN, Roger, and Garland, Harry
Build the fil-oscillator. il Pop Electr 34:58-62 My '71
—See Garland, H. jt. auth.
MELÉNDEZ, L. V. and others
Acute lymphocytic leukemia in owl monkeys inoculated with herpesvirus saimiri. bibliog il Science 171:1161-3 Mr 19 '71

MELHEM, D. H.
Dogbaby; poem. Nation 212:568 My 3 '71
MELIKIAN-CHIRVANI, Assadullah Souren
Romance of Varghe and Golshah. il UNESCO Courier 24:27-9 O '71
MELL, Jack G.
Bowhunting all year. il pors Outdoor Life 147:80-3+ My '71
MELLEN, Joan
Fascism in the contemporary film. il Film Q 24:2-19 Sum '71
MELLMAN, William J. See Tedesco, T. A. jt. auth.
MELLON, Bruce, collection. See Art—Private collections
MELLONIE, David M. H.
Thick as pea soup; valuable tips from Europe on coping with fog. il Motor B & S 127:66-7 My '71
MELLOW, James R.
World of Edward Hopper. il por(p 1) N Y Times Mag p 14-16+ S 5 '71
MELMAN, Seymour
After the military-industrial complex? adaptation of address, 1969. Bul Atom Sci 27:7-9 Mr '71
All the muscle at one-third the cost. Sat R 54:26-7+ O 9 '71
U.S. technology looking for a better mousetrap; interview. ed. by R. Nash. il pors Forbes 108:36-8+ N 15 '71
MELNICK, Norman
What the city desk uses. il Writers Digest 52:22-3+ Ja '72
MELODY
Neapolitan intermezzo and its influence on the symphonic idiom. G. Lazarevich. bibliog f il Mus Q 57:304-10 Ap '71
MELONS
        See also
Cookery—Fruit
MELTON, Bill
Secret weapon of the Sox. L. Keith. por Sports Illus 35:40 Ag 9 '71 *
MELUM, Verna V.
Library orientation in the college and university. bibliog il por Wilson Lib Bul 46:59-66 S '71
MELVILLE, Herman
Moby Dick: dramatization. See Aranson, J.
MELVILLE, Marjorie
Catholic revolutionaries: part of the solution or part of the problem? J. Finn. Commonweal 94:456-8 S 3 '71 *
MELVILLE, Sam
Letters from Attica and elsewhere; with introduction. il por Ramp Mag 10:45-50 D '71
MELVILLE, Thomas
Catholic revolutionaries: part of the solution or part of the problem? J. Finn. Commonweal 94:456-8 S 3 '71 *
MELVILLE PENINSULA
From the world of Tomasik Nutarareak. B. Skovbo. il Natur Hist 80:28-35 Ja '71
MELVILLE shoe corporation
Bally who? joint venture. Forbes 108:32-3 N 15 '71
MELVIN, A. Gordon
Natural history. See issues of Hobbies
MELVIN, Stuart
Kent state agan? il Todays Health 49:30-3 Ap '71
MEMBERS of Congress for peace through law
Fighter programs hit by Proxmire group. D. C. Winston. Aviation W 94:17-18 My 17 '71
MEMBRANE filters. See Filters and filtration (bacteriology)
MEMBRANE lipids. See Lipids
MEMBRANE transport system. See Biological transport
MEMBRANES (biology)
Carcinogen and microsomal membrane interactions: changes in membrane density and ability to bind nucleic acids. H. Kubinski and C. B. Kasper. bibliog il Science 171:201-3 Ja 15 '71
Cyclic adenosine and guanosine monophosphates and glucagon: effect on liver membrane potentials. N. Friedmann and others. bibliog il Science 171:400-2 Ja 29 '71
Freezing and melting of lipid bilayers and the mode of action of nonactin, valinomycin, and gramicidin. S. Krasne and others. bibliog il Science 174:412-15 O 22 '71
Glycoproteins: isolation from cell membranes with lithium diiodosalicylate. V. T. Marchesi and E. P. Andrews. bibliog il Science 174:1247-8 D 17 '71
Plasmalemma: the seat of dual mechanisms of ion absorption in chlorella pyrenoidosa. S. Kannan. bibliog il Science 173:927-9 S 3 '71

MEMBRANES (biology)—*Continued*
Reversal potential for an electrophysiological event generated by conductance changes: mathematical analysis. J. E. Brown and others. bibliog Science 174:318 O 15 '71
State of water in red cells. A. K. Solomon. il Sci Am 224:88-96 F '71
Theoretical and experimental basis for a specific countertransport system in membranes. E. L. Cussler and others. bibliog il Science 172:377-9 Ap 23 '71
See also
Blood-brain barrier
Epithelium
Mucous membranes

MEMBRANES (technology)
Invisible wall that purifies water; reverse osmosis filtration system. D. X. Manners. il Sci Digest 69:70-3 Je '71
Membrane filters purify water. il Am City 86:24 F '71
Steady-state sieving across membranes. E. H. Bresler and others. bibliog il Science 172:858-9 My 21 '71

MEMORIAL day
Old vets; Decoration day in New England. R. M. Dewey. il Am Heritage 22:54-7+ Ap '71

MEMORIAL embroidery. See Embroidery

MEMORIAL sculpture. See Sepulchral monuments

MEMORIAL to the martyrs of deportation. See Paris—Monuments, statues, etc.

MEMORIALS
See also
Crazy Horse (Sioux Indian)—Statues, portraits, etc.
Gaulle, C. de—Memorials
Monuments
Roosevelt, F. D.—Memorials
War memorials

MEMORY
Caudate nucleus stimulation retroactively impairs complex maze learning in the rat. H. V. S. Peeke and M. J. Herz. bibliog il Science 173:80-2 Jl 2 '71
Chemical transfer of learning. Chem 44:22-3 My '71
Cholinergic synapse and the site of memory. J. A. Deutsch. bibliog il Science 174:788-94 N 19 '71
Control of short-term memory. R. C. Atkinson and R. M. Shiffrin. il Sci Am 225:82-90 bibliog(p 120) Ag '71
Cycloheximide: its effects on activity are dissociable from its effects on memory. D. S. Segal and others. bibliog il Science 172:82-4 Ap 2 '71
Forgetting: trace erosion or retrieval failure? R. M. Shiffrin; reply with rejoinder. G. Slaybaugh and others. Science 173:1040-1 S 10 '71
Learning and memory transfer: more experimental evidence. Sci N 100:308 N 6 '71
Loci of memory. Sci Am 225:48-9 N '71
Marihuana and memory; acquisition or retrieval? E. L. Abel. bibliog il Science 173:1038-40 S 10 '71
Memory chemical isolated; scotophobin. Sci Digest 69:81-2 Ap '71
Mind: from memory pills to electronic pleasures beyond sex. il Time 97:45-7 Ap 19 '71
Mystery of memory. W. Bradbury. il Life 71:66+ N 12 '71
Neuron activity related to short-term memory. J. M. Fuster and G. E. Alexander. bibliog il Science 173:652-4 Ag 13 '71
Norepinephrine biosynthesis inhibition: effects on memory in mice. C. T. Randt and others. bibliog il Science 172:498-9 Ap 30 '71
One-trial learning and biphasic time course of performance in the goldfish. W. H. Riege and A. Cherkin. bibliog il Science 172:966-8 My 28 '71
See also
Amnesia
Past, The
Recall (psychology)
Recognition (psychology)
Reminiscence

Anecdotes, facetiae, satire, etc.
Forgetting to remember. E. Bombeck. il Good H 172:38+ My '71

MEMORY devices (computers)
Chip memories go peripheral; semiconductor storage unit. Bsns W p 120 Mr 13 '71
Easier way to tap mass data; compact tape cartridge mass-memory system. il Bsns W p94 N 27 '71
Little chips invade the memory market. G. Bylinsky. il Fortune 83:100-4+ Ap '71
Magnetic bubbles. A. H. Bobeck and H. E. D. Scovil. il Sci Am 224:78-90 Je '71

Magnetic world of bubble domains. D. E. Thomsen. il Sci N 99:318-19 My 8 '71
Memorizing more on tape; Terabit memory. il Bsns W p65 Ap 17 '71

MEMPHIS, Tenn.

Architecture
Luther towers in Memphis: the MLS concept is one of the most sophisticated to date. il Arch Rec 149:122-3 Ap '71

Description
Reports & comment. J. Conaway. Atlan 228:24+ N '71
Steamin' up the river; redbud time in blues town. D. Butwin. il Sat R 54:36-8 My 29 '71
Step by step through Memphis. R. Deardorff. il Travel 136:48-53+ S '71

Economic conditions
Wide-awake time down South. il Nations Bsns 59:54-9 F '71

Historic houses, etc.
Victorian mansions in Memphis. T. B. Morton. il Antiques 100:408-12 S '71

Negroes
Bad day in Memphis; the only major southern city to have a major racial incident this year. N. C. Chriss. Nation 213:653-4 D 20 '71
Memphis: how assassination changed a city in three years. il U S News 70:66-8 Ap 5 '71

Parks and playgrounds
Showdown in the park; conservationists' action over building U.S. highway through Overton park. Time 97:44 Mr 15 '71

MEN
See also
Boys
Christmas gifts for men
Cookery by men
Fathers
Great men
Husbands
Mens liberation movement
Needlepoint by men
Sewing by men
Sex differences
Single men

Clothing
See Clothing and dress—Men

Health and hygiene
New physical assessment & conditioning program for sportsmen from the research of Dr Bruno Balke and associates. N. Hildebrand. il Field & S 76:66-71+ Je '71
Statistics show that women usually outlive men. T. I. Rubin. Ladies Home J 88:34 Ja '71; Same abr. with title What wives can do to help. Read Digest 98:76-7 Ap '71
Testament of a Samurai; tr. by M. Gallagher. Y. Mishima. il pors Sports Illus 34:24-7 Ja 11 '71
See also
Climacteric
Health clubs

Legal status, laws, etc.
Men have their day in court, too. L. Kanowitz. McCalls 98:40 Je '71

Psychology
Here comes your 19th nervous breakdown. D. Newman and R. Benton. Mlle 73:90 S '71
Life and loves of the American beach bum. P. S. Catling. Vogue 158:52-3+ Ag 15 '71
Man talk; as you desire me. D. Newman and R. Benton. Mlle 73:48 Je '71
Rape: the all-American crime. S. Griffin. il Ramp Mag 10:26-35 S '71

MEN, Short. See Stature

MEN and women. See Women and men

MEN teachers. See Teachers

MENAGERIES
Southern California animal parks get you close to lions, elephants, bears. il Sunset 146:90-3 Je '71

MENARCHE. See Puberty

MENARD, Wilmon
Chinese junks; with biographical sketch. il Sea Front 17:322-31, 383 N '71

MENCHER, Alan G.
On the social deployment of science. il Bul Atom Sci 27:34-8 D '71

MENCKEN, Henry Louis
H. L. Mencken, by D. C. Stenerson. Review Sat R 54:54-5 O 30 '71. C. Fadiman *
What enormous problems a man can cause himself by answering his mail! C. Trillin. il N Y Times Mag p30-1+ My 2 '71 *

MENDELEEV, Dmitrii Ivanovich
Chemists' involvement in society. R. Ferreira. bibliog pors Chem 44:18 F '71 *
That chart on the laboratory wall. G. Teterin and C. Terlon. il pors UNESCO Courier 24:24-7+ Je '71 *

MENDELL, J. R. and others
Duchenne muscular dystrophy: functional ischemia reproduces its characteristic lesions. bibliog il Science 172:1143-5 Je 11 '71

MENDELSOHN, Nathan K.
Nice piece of desert. R. A. Jones. il Nation 213:616-26 D 13 '71 *

MENDELSON, Joseph
Activity change as the cause of apparent aversiveness during prolonged hypothalamic stimulation. bibliog il Science 172: 85-6 Ap 2 '71

MENDELSON, Martin
Oscillator neurons in crustacean ganglia. bibliog il Science 171:1170-3 Mr 19 '71

MENDELSSOHN, Felix
In tender memory, what the lobgesang means to me. S. Lincoln. il por Am Rec G 37: 412-16 Mr '71 *
MENDELSSOHN symphony; ballet. See Ballets
—Criticisms

MENDOTA, Ill.
Time was village museum. J. L. Stoutenburgh. il Hobbies 76:142-3+ Ag '71

MENDOTA, LAKE
These farmers got cash, everybody gets a cleaner lake. B. Coffman. il Farm J 95:22E-22F Jl '71

MENEN, Aubrey
Rome's glorious garden. il Holiday 49:34-9+ My '71
St Peter's. il Nat Geog 140:864-79 D '71

MENGELING, Marvin E.
Ray Bradbury's Dandelion wine: themes, sources, and style. bibliog f Engl J 60:877-87 O '71

MENGER, Matthias
Into the breach. J. Deedy. Commonweal 94: 298 Je 11 '71 *

MENHADEN fishing
Menhaden system. A. Reinfelder. il Field & S 75:194-7+ Ap '71

MENKUS, Belden
Evangelical responsibility in public education. Chr Today 15:10-12 F 12 '71

MENNINGER, Edwin A.
On not knowing the trees by their leaves. il Am For 77:12-15 D '71

MENNONITE central committee
Alternative service locates in Appalachia. J. DeMuth. il America 125:374-5 N 6 '71

MENNONITES
Amish schools today. J. Wittmer. Sch & Soc 99:227-30 Ap '71
Amish win important Court decision; question of compulsory school attendance. Chr Cent 88:95 Ja 27 '71
Mennonite mandates. Chr Today 15:47 S 24 '71
Mennonites shift priorities as conservatives gain strength. M. Shelly. Chr Cent 88:1089-90 S 15 '71
Other Illinois. R. Sullivan. il Travel 135:59-60 Ap '71
Using the Amish? Chr Today 16:26-7 Ja 7 '72

MENON, Narayana
India's performing arts center. D. J. Soria. il por Hi Fi 21:MA6-7+ Mr '71 *

MENON, Vengalil Krishnan Krishna. See Krishna Menon, V. K.

MENOPAUSE
You can stop worrying about menopause. D. M. Rorvik. McCalls 99:102-3+ O '71
See also
Climacteric

MENOTTI, Gian Carlo
Diary of two deadlines. F. Rizzo. Opera N 35:26-8 Mr 13 '71 *
Most important man. Criticism
New Yorker 47:132 Mr 20 '71 *
Newsweek il 77:92+ Mr 29 '71
Sat R 54:16 Mr 27 '71 *
Time il 97:59 Mr 22 '71 *
Original-cast Amahl. P. L. Miller. Am Rec G 37:208 D '70 *

MENS clothes. See Clothing and dress—Men
MENS hairdressing. See Hairdressing
MENS hats. See Hats

MENS liberation movement
And now, men's liberation. il Time 97:54 My 10 '71
Opinion: the goodness of men's groups. W. Schlesinger. Mlle 73:36+ O '71
You've come a long way, Buddy. B. Farrell. il Life 71:52+ Ag 27 '71

MENS shirts. See Shirts
MENS shoes. See Shoes
MENS underwear. See Underwear

MENSTRUATION
EEG responses in regularly menstruating women and in amenorrheic women treated with ovarian hormones. W. Vogel and others. bibliog il Science 172:388-91 Ap 23 '71
Disorders
Menstrual problems: causes and treatment. Good H 172:195 My '71
MENSTRUATION, Cessation of. See Menopause

MENSWEAR industry. See Clothing industry
MENTAL ability. See Intelligence
MENTAL deficiency
See also
Mentally handicapped
MENTAL depression. See Depression, Mental
MENTAL development of children. See Children—Growth and development
MENTAL development of infants. See Infants—Growth and development
MENTAL health. See Mental hygiene
MENTAL health, National association for. See National association for mental health, inc.
MENTAL health associations
See also
National association for mental health, inc.
MENTAL health centers
Citizens' corporations as true community mental retardation and mental health centers; Intercommunity action, inc. R. C. Stephanos. Ment Hy 55:410-12 Jl '71
Community mental health centers: growing movement seeks identity. C. Holden. Science 174:1110-13 D 10 '71
Community mental health centers: storefront therapy and more. C. Holden. Science 174: 1219-21 D 17 '71
Counselor is a housewife; Southern California counseling center. B. Vachon. McCalls 98:44 S '71
Mental health industry: this way lies madness. A. Kopkind and J. Ridgeway. il Ramp Mag 9:38-44 F '71
Police: ally or enemy of the comprehensive community mental health center? H. G. Whittington. bibliog Ment Hy 55:55-9 Ja '71
Problems in developing a community-based research component for a mental health center. D. L. Ellison and others. bibliog Ment Hy 55:312-17 Jl '71
Psychiatry comes of age. G. W. Weinstein. il Parents Mag 46:66-7+ N '71

MENTAL health counselors
Counselor is a housewife. B. Vachon. McCalls 98:44 S '71
When clergymen help the mentally ill. Good H 172:174 Je '71
MENTAL health insurance. See Insurance, Mental health
MENTAL health laws
Normality is a square circle or a four-sided triangle; views of T. Szasz. M. Scarf. il pors N Y Times Mag p 16-17+ O 3 '71; Discussion. p6+ N 14 '71

MENTAL health service
Coordinated patient care: a consultant's view. M. King. Ment Hy 55:461-6 O '71
Evaluating the quality of mental health services: criteria for rapid informal judgement. J. Zusman. Ment Hy 55:478-86 O '71
Innovations in college mental health. R. B. Falk. Ment Hy 55:451-5 O '71
Meeting social work's challenge in community mental health. P. P. Evans and N. F. Bracht. Ment Hy 55:295-7 Jl '71
Model cities program as a field placement for graduate students in mental health nursing. J. A. Collins. Ment Hy 55:308-11 Jl '71
Theoretical models in community mental health. R. A. Pasewark and M. W. Rardin. bibliog Ment Hy 55:358-64 Jl '71
We like us: attitudes of the mental health staff toward other agencies on the Navajo reservation. L. S. Schoenfeld and others. Ment Hy 55:171-3 Ap '71
Finance
State grants-in-aid for private community mental health programs. H. K. Naylor. il Ment Hy 55:190-3 Ap '71

MENTAL health service, Cost of
Effective low cost aftercare. A. C. David.
bibliog Ment Hy 55:351-7 Jl '71
Financing outpatient mental health care
through psychiatric insurance. R. Fink. bib-
liog Ment Hy 55:143-50 Ap '71
MENTAL health workers. See Health workers
MENTAL health workers, Volunteer. See
Health workers, Volunteer
MENTAL hospital attendants. See Hospitals,
Psychiatric—Staff
MENTAL hospitals. See Hospitals, Psychiatric
MENTAL hygiene
Does the way our food is grown affect our
mental well-being? bibliog Org Gard &
Farm 18:102-6+ My '71
Mental health movement meets women's lib;
interview. E. Tobach; N. Shainess; D.
Headley. Ment Hy 55:1-9 Ja '71
Mental health of our children: we must con-
serve our most precious natural resource.
B. S. Brown. por Parents Mag 46:24 Jl '71
Mental hygiene influences in children's in-
stitutions: organization and technology for
treatment. J. K. Whittaker. bibliog Ment
Hy 55:444-50 O '71
Self-conceptions of mental health among the
aged. J. F. Gubrium. bibliog Ment Hy 55:
398-403 Jl '71
Winning and losing in life: a survey of opin-
ions about causes. H. J. Wahler. bibliog
Ment Hy 55:91-5 Ja '71
See also
Adjustment, Social
Boredom
Child psychiatry
College students—Adjustment
College students—Health and hygiene
Fear
Mental health service
Police—Health and hygiene
Psychiatric social work
Psychotherapy
School children—Adjustment
Social psychiatry
Teachers—Health and hygiene
Worry
Youth—Health and hygiene

Bibliography
Book reviews. See issues of Mental hygiene

Research
See Psychiatric research
MENTAL illness
Attitudes of teachers and the public toward
mental illness. W. K. Bentz and others.
bibliog il Ment Hy 55:324-30 Jl '71
How to tell when you're going crazy. R.
Markoff. il Mech Illus 67:60-2+ Mr '71
Normality is a square circle or a four-sided
triangle; views of T. Szasz. M. Scarf. il
pors N Y Times Mag p 16-17+ O 3 '71;
Discussion. p6+ N 14 '71
See also
Mental hygiene
Psychoses
Schizophrenia

Research
See Psychiatric research

Social aspects
Conceptions of mental illness by patients
and normals. R. M. Weinstein and N. Q.
Brill. bibliog il Ment Hy 55:101-8 Ja '71

Therapy
See also
Psychotherapy
MENTAL illness and law. See Mental health
laws
MENTAL tests. See Intelligence tests
MENTAL types. See Typology (psychology)
MENTALLY handicapped
Nurturing intelligence: influence of ghetto en-
vironment on IQ's. il Time 99:56 Ja 3 '72
MENTALLY handicapped children
See also
Mentally ill children
Slow learning children

Education
Jacksonville builds for its exceptional children. il Arch Rec 149:130-1 My '71
Rights for the retarded; decision of federal
court in Philadelphia. il Time 98:52+ O
25 '71
Teaching the mentally retarded; Central cooperative school, Parish, La. N. Roberts.
il Sat R 54:70-1+ S 18 '71
See also
Libraries—Services to mentally handicapped
children
Slow learning children—Education

MENTALLY ill
Community caretakers as mental health casefinders. J. Mueller and others. Ment Hy 55:
214-18 Ap '71
Occupation, income and mental hospitalization. W. A. Rushing. bibliog il Ment Hy 55:
248-52 Ap '71
Patient's views on relocation; reactions of
psychiatric patients to urban renewal. P.
Sifneos. Ment Hy 55:495-8 O '71
Personality descriptions of mental health
center patients for use as pre-therapy information. R. A. Apostal. Ment Hy 55:
119-20 Ja '71
See also
Church work with the handicapped

Care and treatment
Coordinated patient care: a consultant's view.
M. King. Ment Hy 55:461-6 O '71
Effects on treatment of summarizing psy-
chiatric records of chronic hospitalized pa-
tients. W. Greenleaf and D. Greenleaf.
Ment Hy 55:407-9 Jl '71
New right to treatment; Tuscaloosa's Bryce
hospital. il Time 97:52+ Ap 5 '71
Staff-patient interaction, race and patient
behavior on a psychiatric ward. C. O.
Turner and G. Spivack. bibliog Ment Hy
55:499-503 O '71
See also
Hospitals—Psychiatric service
Hospitals, Psychiatric

Employment
Who employs the mentally restored and why?
C. A. Burden. Ment Hy 55:487-91 O '71

Legal status, laws, etc.
See Mental health laws

Rehabilitation
Countering defeatism in psychiatric vocation-
al placement. I. E. Sturm and H. Lipton.
bibliog Ment Hy 55:230-3 Ap '71
See also
Group psychotherapy
Mentally ill—Employment
Recovery, inc.
Schizophrenics—Rehabilitation

Sexual behavior
Some implications of sexual activity for men-
tal illness. G. H. Rozan and others. bibliog
Ment Hy 55:318-23 Jl '71
MENTALLY ill children
Mental health consultation to schools. R. G.
Hirschowitz. Ment Hy 55:237-41 Ap '71
See also
Child psychiatry
MENTALLY retarded. See Mentally handi-
capped
MENTALLY retarded children. See Mentally
handicapped children
MENTALLY superior high school students.
See High school students, Mentally superior
MENTHADIENONE. See Carvone
MENTLER, Sandor
Improved vehicular intrusion alarm. il Electr
World 86:38-9 Ag '71
MENUHIN, Hephzibah
Ladies' week in the world of music. I. Kolo-
din. Sat R 54:44 F 13 '71 *
MENUHIN, Jeremy
Menuhin & Menuhin. D. J. Soria. pors Hi
Fi 21:MA4-5+ My '71 *
MENUHIN, Yehudi
Menuhin & Menuhin. D. J. Soria. pors Hi
Fi 21:MA4-5+ My '71 *
Musical events. W. Sargeant. New Yorker
47:93-4 Mr 27 '71 *
MENUS
Barefoot in the kitchen; excerpts. M. Wal-
lace. il Am Home 74:64-72+ Je '71
Forty-eight-hour feast; good plans make
good weekends. M. McKendry. Vogue 158:
40 Ag 1 '71
How to read a menu. C. Schwalberg. il Travel
135:63-5 F '71
[Month] menus; with recipes. See issues of
Sunset
Poppy Cannon's meal-a-day menus. P. Can-
non. See issues of Ladies' home journal
See also
Camp cookery
Dinners and dining
Meals
Thanksgiving dinners
MEOS (native race) See Laos—Native races
MERCADANTE, Saverio
Merits of Mercadante. W. Weaver. Hi Fi 21:
MA29-30 My '71 *
MERCEDES Benz (automobile) See Auto-
mobiles, Foreign

MERCER, Asa
Mercer girls. S. C. Shulsinger. il por Am West 8:28-9 Jl '71 *
MERCER, Joan Bodger
Innocence is a cop-out. il Wilson Lib Bul 46:144-6 O '71
MERCER, Marilyn
Remember? il McCalls 99:90-1 O '71
MERCHANDISING
Riding the coattails of Mickey Mouse; with editorial comment. il Bsns W p72-3+, 103 S 11 '71
Rise of the conglomerchant. R. Tillman. il Harvard Bsns R 49:44-51 N '71
See also
Samples (merchandising)
Stores
Television broadcasting—Merchandising tie-in
MERCHANT, W. Moelwyn
Breaking the code; poem. Poetry 119:11 O '71
MERCHANT marine
See also
Shipping—International aspects

Norway
See also
Shipping—Norway

United States
Jobs at sea. il Changing T 25:45-7 My '71
Transport technology: moving ahead; address, February 4, 1971. E. M. Hood. Vital Speeches 37:309-11 Mr 1 '71
U.S. merchant fleet: it's still hard aground. il U S News 71:82-3 S 6 '71
See also
Freighters
MERCIER, Jeanne Y.
(ed) See Segal, E. W. Erich Segal's last last interview
MERCIER, Vivian
Critic, review thyself. Nation 213:662-4 D 20 '71
MERCOURI, Melina
First man I ever loved; excerpt from I was born Greek. il McCalls 98:86-7 Ag '71
Melina Mercouri: I was born Greek; interview, ed. by J. Oringer. pors Ramp Mag 10:48-51 Ja '72
MERCURY
Fossil fuels as a source of mercury pollution. O. I. Joensuu. bibliog il Science 172:1027-8 Je 4 '71
Mercury in the air. bibliog il Environ 13: 24+ My '71
Mercury in the environment. L. J. Goldwater. il Sci Am 224:15-21 bibliog(p 132) My '71
Mercury in the environment: natural and human factors. A. L. Hammond. Science 171:788-9 F 26 '71
Methyl mercury and inorganic mercury collection by a selective chelating resin. S. L. Law. bibliog il Science 174:285-7 O 15 '71
Surface-related mercury in lunar samples G. W. Reed and others. bibliog il Science 172:258-61 Ap 16 '71
Weight watchers, beware! il Newsweek 77: 91 Ja 25 '71
MERCURY (planet)
Infrared thermal studies of Mercury's dark side. Sky & Tel 41:79 F '71
MERCURY compounds
Chemical methylation of inorganic mercury with methylcobalamin, a vitamin B12 analog. N. Imura and others. bibliog il Science 172:1248-9 Je 18 '71
Precautions with alkyl mercury. R. Klein and S. Herman. Science 172:872 My 21 '71; Reply. G. F. Wright. 174:771 N 19 '71
See also
Phenylmercuric acetate
MERCURY in the body
Eggshell thinning in Japanese quail fed mercuric chloride. G. S. Stoewsand and others. bibliog il Science 173:1030-1 S 10 '71
Hyperfine Zeeman effect atomic absorption spectrometer for mercury. T. Hadeishi and R. D. McLaughlin. bibliog il Science 174: 404-7 O 22 '71
Mastodon had a mercury problem, too. il Sci Digest 70:28-9 N '71
Mercury in human tissues shows 50-year decline. Sci N 100:278-9 O 23 '71
Mercury in man. N. Grant. bibliog il Environ 13:2-15 My '71
MERCURY mines and mining
Mercury mining goes down the hole. il Bsns W p86 Jl 10 '71
MERCURY poisoning
Japanese mercury crackdown; court settlement of pollution case. S. Lindsay. Sat R 54:95 D 4 '71
Mercury, by K. Montague and P. Montague. Review
Environ 13:52 D '71. T. Aaronson

Mercury: how much are we eating? P. Montague and K. Montague. Sat R 54:50-5 F 6 '71
Mercury in man. N. Grant. bibliog il Environ 13:2-15 My '71
Mercury menace; contamination of fish. Newsweek 77:47 My 31 '71
Mercury: no need for hysteria; questions and answers. il Life 70:32-3 Ja 29 '71
No-nonsense report on mercury in fish. E. Kahn. Redbook 137:80+ My '71
Organic mercury identified as the cause of poisoning in humans and hogs. A. Curley and others. bibliog il Science 172:65-7 Ap 2 '71
Quiet heroism of Dorothy Nichols. L. David. il pors Good H 172:114-15+ Ap '71
MERCURY pollution of rivers, lakes, etc.
Catastrophe brewing in quiet waters. E. Chaney. il Nat Wildlife 9:4-7 Ag '71
Catch is, should you eat it? R. H. Boyle. il Sports Illus 35:46-7 Jl 12 '71
Mad hatter disease: mercury poisoning. G. Compton. il Sci Digest 69:61-6 Mr '71
Mercury: a grave threat to human life. il Consumer Bul 54:32-4 Mr '71
Mercury and fish. C. F. Idyll. il Sea Front 17:230-40 Jl '71
Mercury: how much are we eating? P. Montague and K. Montague. Sat R 54:50-5 F 6 '71
Mercury in a Greenland ice sheet: evidence of recent input by man. H. V. Weiss and others. bibliog il Science 174:692-4 N 12 '71
Mercury in fish: a slippery question. Sr Schol 98:7 F 8 '71
Mercury in the environment. T. Aaronson. il Environ 13:16-23 My '71
Mercury in the environment. L. J. Goldwater. il Sci Am 224:15-21 bibliog(p 132) My '71
Mercury is heavier than you think. J. Holmes. il Esquire 75:135-9+ My '71
Mercury monitoring highlights Long Island swordfish tournament. B. Sands. il por Cons 26:27-31 O '71
Mercury: no need for hysteria; questions and answers. il Life 70:32-3 Ja 29 '71; Same abr. with title Tuna fish and swordfish: are they safe to eat? Read Digest 98:93-5 Ap '71
Mercury pollution: new studies show a lot of work must still be done. R. H. Gilluly. il Sci N 100:156 Ag 28 '71
No-nonsense report on mercury in fish. E. Kahn. Redbook 137:80+ My '71
Residues of total mercury and methylmercuric salts in lake trout as a function of age. C. A. Bache and others. bibliog il Science 172:951-2 My 28 '71
Testing for mercury in New York's marine fish and shellfish. A. C. Jensen and J. Foehrenbach. il Cons 26:31-3 O '71
Truth about mercury. J. Van Coevering. Field & S 76:14+ My '71
MERCY
Mercy and severity: Christ acknowledges human weakness. V. P. McCorry. America 124:328-9 Mr 27 '71
See also
God—Mercy
MERCY killing. See Euthanasia
MEREDITH, Don
Shall we rule these TV egos guilty of unnecessary roughness? S. Singer. il Todays Health 49:40-3 D '71 *
What are they doing with the sacred game of pro football? E. Shrake. pors Sports Illus 35:96-9+ O 25 '71 *
MEREDITH, William
Mild-spoken citizen finally writes to the White House; poem. Sat R 54:31 N 27 '71

about
Comment. R. B. Shaw. Poetry 118:233 Jl '71 *
MEREDITH-OWENS, Heather
Inner universe of Albert Handell. il por Am Artist 35:60-6+ Ap '71
Medical illustration: Philip C. Johnson. il Am Artist 35:50-5+ D '71
MERGERS. See Business consolidations and mergers
MERHIGE, Robert Reynold, 1919-
Scandal in Virginia. il Newsweek 78:39 N 15 '71 *
MÉRIMÉE, Prosper
Prosper Mérimée, by A. W. Raitt. Review Nation 212:537-8 Ap 26 '71. J. Barzun *
MERINGUE
Magic meringue. il Redbook 137:98-9+ Ag '71
MERION golf course. See Golf courses
MERIT for leadership awards. See American city (periodical)
MERIT pay. See Teachers—Salaries, allowances, etc.

MERIT system (civil service) See Civil service
MERIT system, Teachers. See Teachers—
  Promotion
MERIWETHER, Delano
  Champion of the armchair athletes. R. H.
    Boyle. il pors Sports Illus 34:20-2+ F 22
    '71 *
  Doctor Meriwether saga. por Time 98:40 Jl
    12 '71 *
  Hey, I can beat those guys; S. Treadwell.
    il por Sports Illus 34:14-15 Ja 18 '71 *
  Meet Dr. Meriwether. il por Newsweek 77:
    62 F 8 '71 *
MERKLE, Donald R.
  Furnace and the tower: a new look at the
    symbols in Native son. Engl J 60:735-9 S
    '71
MERKLING, Frank
  (ed) See Crosby, J. O. Pilgrim's progress
MERLINO, Stefano, and Sartori, Franco
  Ammonioborite: new borate polyion and its
    structure. bibliog il Science 171:377-9 Ja 29
    '71
MERLISS, R. R.
  Talc-treated rice and Japanese stomach
    cancer. bibliog il Science 173:1141-2 S 17 '71
MERMAN, Ethel
  Ethel Merman: queen of Broadway. L. Den-
    nis. Read Digest 98:112-16 Je '71 *
MEROLA opera program. See San Francisco
  opera company
MERRIAM, Eve
  I hear America ringing; poem. N Y Times
    Mag p6+ My 2 '71
  Poetics, not politics, a day in class with
    Prof Eugene McCarthy. il por N Y Times
    Mag p6+ O 24 '71
MERRIAM, Lawrence C. Jr
  Parks of the upper Paraná. Nat Parks & Con
    Mag 45:27 Ag '71
  Return to wilderness. il Nat Parks & Con
    Mag 45:28-31 Je '71
MERRICK, David
  Road runner no.1. H. L. Masin. por Sr Schol
    98:22 Ap 19 '71 *
MERRIL, Carl R.
  Transfer of bacterial genes to human cells.
    Sci N 100:276 O 23 '71 *
MERRILL, Dina
  How Dina does it. N. Gittelson. Harp Baz
    104:46+ S '71 *
MERRILL, Eugene H.
  Who are today's true prophets? Chr Today
    15:8-10+ Mr 12 '71
MERRILL, Grayson
  History hopping down the I.C.W. bibliog il
    Motor B & S 128:50-1+ S '71
MERRILL, Herbert
  Sing of spring; poem. Good H 172:171 My '71
MERRILL, James
  Another April; Seaside doorway, summer
    dawn; Banks of a stream where creatures
    bathe; Black mesa; Komboloi; Desert mo-
    tel with frog amulet; Flèche d'or; poems.
    Poetry 118:1-7 Ap '71
  Pieces of history; poem. Harper 242:42 My '71
  Through the fire screen. F. D. Reeve. Poetry
    117:388-91 Mr '71 *
MERRILL Lynch, Pierce, Fenner and Smith,
  inc.
  Biggest goes public. Bsns W p37 Ap 17 '71
  Going public. il Newsweek 78:59+ Jl 5 '71
  Making out. Forbes 108:36-7 D 1 '71
  New money for Merrill Lynch. Time 97:90
    Ap 26 '71
  Thundering herd; leads investment banking
    field. il Time 99:58 Ja 17 '72
MERRITT, Brison B.
  Wee world in pictures. S. Parvin. il por
    Hobbies 76:146-7 Ag '71 *
MERRITT, Francis S.
  Portfolio: coming of age at Haystack. il
    Ceram Mo 19:19-26 Je '71
MERRITT, Richard L.
  (ed) See Welch, S. Vietnam: how the press
    went along
MERRY, Edwin D.
  Tree planter; poem. Am For 77:48 Ja '71
MERRY Christmas, Mary Kay; story. See
  Amft, M. J.
MERRY wives of Windsor; drama. See Shakes-
  peare, W.—Plays
MERSZEI, Zoltan
  Dow Europe's man for all countries. por
    Bsns W p79 Ap 17 '71 *
MERTES, J. D. and others
  Living library. il pors Parks & Rec 6:34-5+
    O '71
MERTON, Robert K. See Zuckerman, H. jt.
  auth.
MERTON, Thomas
  Circus of Mertons. J. Forest. por Common-
    weal 93:400-2 Ja 22 '71 *

MERWIN, W. S.
  Door; poem. Atlan 227:82 F '71
  Hawk and the mules; story. New Yorker 47:
    52-3 N 13 '71
  Malayan figures; poem. Poetry 118:16-19 Ap
    '71
  Seven poems: Door; Way ahead; Mist;
    Bread; One time; Division; Horses. New
    Yorker 47:44 Ap 24 '71
  Three stories: First moon; Devil's pig; The
    taste. New Yorker 47:33 Jl 10 '71
  Unwritten poem. New Yorker 47:36 F 20 '71
MERYMAN, Harold Thayer
  Frozen blood. il por Newsweek 78:47 S 13
    '71 *
MERYMAN, Richard
  I live at the edge of a very strange coun-
    try. il pors Life 71:60-60B+ O 15 '71
  Parting shots: Satchmo, the greatest of all,
    is gone. il pors Life 71:70-1 Jl 16 '71
  When the funniest writer in America tried to
    be serious. pors Life 70:60B-60D+ My 7 '71
  (ed) See McCartney, P. Paul McCartney on
    the Beatle breakup
MESELSON, Matthew S.
  Tear gas in Vietnam and the return of poison
    gas. Bul Atom Sci 27:17-19 Mr '71
MESIC, Michael
  Bookends. Poetry 117:277-80 Ja '71
MESKILL, Thomas J.
  Reaganism in Connecticut. J. Quinn. New
    Repub 164:17 My 29 '71 *
MESONS
  Cosmic-ray muon flux and the W particle. G.
    B. Lubkin. Phys Today 24:17-18 N '71
  How does the muon differ from the electron?
    M. L. Perl. bibliog il Phys Today 24:34-5+
    Jl '71
  Is the A_2 meson split? Two experiments say
    no. H. L. Davis. il Phys Today 24:18 Ap
    '71
  LAMPF meson factory calls for beam-time
    proposals. J. T. Scott. il Phys Today 24:
    19-20 F '71
  Latest work on the A_2 meson sees no split.
    G. B. Lubkin. Phys Today 24:16 Jl '71
  Long-lived kaon shows no 2-muon decay. G.
    B. Lubkin. Phys Today 24:13-14 Jl '71
  Split in the A_2 meson. Sci N 99:314 My 8 '71
MESOTHELIOMA
  Department of amplification: relationship be-
    tween asbestosis, lung cancer. P. Brodeur.
    New Yorker 47:147-51+ O 23 '71
MESOZOIC period. See Paleontology—Mesozoic
MESPLÉ, Mady
  Flair for precision; interview, ed. by D. Ste-
    vens. por Opera N 35:11 Mr 13 '71
MESSER, Alfred A.
  Identity crisis in black Americans visiting
    West Africa. bibliog Ment Hy 55:375-81
    Jl '71
MESSERER, Asaf
  Classes in classical ballet; excerpt, tr. by
    O. Briansky. il pors Dance Mag 46:40-5 Ja
    '72 (to be cont)
MESSIAEN, Olivier
  Crucifix of sugar. R. Evett. Atlan 227:104-7
    My '71 *
MESSIANIC Judaism. See Judaism
MESSICK, Hank
  Schenley chapter. il Nation 212:428-31 Ap 5
    '71
MESSICK, Tom
  Art from a tatting shuttle. il Design 73:34-6
    Fall '71
MESSINEO, Anthony
  Meredith Willson's legacy. il Am Lib 2:209-
    11 F '71
MESSINESI, Despina
  Travel. Vogue 158:130 Ag 1; 111+ Ag 15;
    16 O 15 '71; 159:30-1 Ja 1 '72
MESSINGER, Edwin A.
  Balsa. il Am For 77:38-9 Ap '71
MESTECKY, Jiri, and others
  Immunoglobulin M and secretory immuno-
    globulin A: presence of a common poly-
    peptide chain different from light chains.
    bibliog il Science 171:1163-5 Mr 19 '71
MESTER, Jorge
  Recordings. M. Mayer. Esquire 75:14 Mr '71
MESTROVIC, Matthew M.
  Balkanization in Titoland. Commonweal 94:
    252-3 My 21 '71
METABOLISM
  Ascorbate sulfate: a urinary metabolite of
    ascorbic acid in man. E. M. Baker. 3d. and
    others. bibliog il Science 173:826-7 Ag 27
    '71
  Erythrocyte metabolism: interaction with
    oxygen transport. G. J. Brewer and J. W.
    Eaton. bibliog il Science 171:1205-11 Mr 26
    '71

METABOLISM—*Continued*
Iron- and riboflavin-dependent metabolism of a monoamine in the rat in vivo. A. L. Symes and others. bibliog il Science 174: 153-5 O 8 '71
Vitamin B₁₂. T. C. Stadtman. bibliog il Science 171:859-67 Mr 5 '71
Vitamin D metabolism: the role of kidney tissue. R. Gray and others. bibliog il Science 12:1232-4 Je 18 '71
   See also
Bioenergetics
Brain—Metabolism
Carbohydrate metabolism
Drugs—Metabolism
Galactose metabolism
Insects—Metabolism
Microorganisms—Metabolism
Plants—Metabolism

METABOLISM, Disorders of
Acetoxycycloheximide enhances audiogenic seizures in DBA/2J mice. H. D. Jameson and others. bibliog il Science 173:249-51 Jl 16 '71
Serum parathyroid hormone in X-linked hypophosphatemia. C. Arnaud and others. bibliog il Science 173:845-7 Ag 27 '71
   See also
Amyloidosis
Angiokeratoma
Galactosemia
Goiter
Hepatolenticular degeneration
Hyperoxaluria
Lesch-Nyhan syndrome
Leukodystrophy
Lipochondrodystrophy
Porphyria

METABOLISM in soils. See Soil metabolism
METACHROMATIC leukodystrophy. See Leukodystrophy

METAL castings
Titanium castings studied by USAF. W. S. Hieronymus. il Aviation W 95:52-4 Jl 19 '71
   See also
Continuous casting

METAL cleaning
Build a sonic cleaner. H. Pallatz. il Radio-Electr 42:46 D '71
   See also
Sand blast

METAL coating
Spray good-bye to friction! Xylan, low-friction/high-release coating. R. J. De Cristoforo. il Pop Sci 199:104 Ag '71
   See also
Teflon

METAL coloring
   See also
Gilding

METAL cutting
   See also
Cutting machines

METAL detection. See Metal detectors

METAL detectors
Beginner's metal detector. C. Conley. il Field & S 76:148 Ag '71
Buried treasure, hot new hobby for RVers. F. Coffee. il Mech Illus 67:100-2+ S '71
Treasure hunter's guide to metal detectors. J. Davis. il Pop Sci 198:82-3+ Je '71
Underground survey meter and metal locator. H. Pallatz. il Pop Electr 35:63-5 Ag '71

METAL houses
Metal housing: new way to build your next home. J. Hand. il Pop Sci 199:58-61+ O '71

METAL industry
Finance
Metal markets: area of weakness. il U S News 70:12 Je 21 '71
Metals; with yardsticks of management performance. il Forbes 109:101-2+ Ja 1 '72

METAL ions
Metal ion control of chemical reactions. D. H. Busch. bibliog il Science 171:241-8 Ja 22 '71
Ordering of V²⁺, Mn²⁺, and Fe²⁺ ions in zoisite, Ca₂Al₃Si₃O₁₂(OH) S. Ghose and T. Tsang. bibliog il Science 171:374-6 Ja 29 '71; Reply. D. R. Hutton and others. 174: 1259 D 17 '71

METAL locators. See Metal detectors

METAL poisoning
How dangerous are metals in our food and environment? Current status of metals in the environment. Good H 173:215-17 N '71
Metals in the air. H. A. Schroeder. bibliog il por Environ 13:18-24+ O '71

METAL rolling. See Rolling (metal work)

METAL sculpture
Don't throw away that can. R. Wrenn. il Design 72:28-9 Spr '71
Experiments in self-expression. M. N. Steinhauser. il Sch Arts 70:24-6 Ap '71
Sprezzature in steel. R. Hughes. il por Time 97:76 Ap 26 '71
Torch artistry; works of R. Newman. P. Fievez. il por Design 72:24-5 mid-Sum '71

METAL turning lathes. See Lathes

METAL work
Soviet metalworking progress continues. il Aviation W 95:46-8 Jl 26 '71
   See also
Art metal work
Ironwork
Tube bending
Projects
Winter workshop: paper safe for photographers; spotting tool for machinists. K. Wells; R. Corwin. il Pop Sci 199:90 D '71

METAL working industries
Experimental survey of occupations in metalworking; with table. G. T. Silvestri. Mo Labor R 94:18-20 O '71

METAL working machinery
Maximat VIO: one-tool machine shop. J. Burroughs. il Pop Mech 136:146-8+ Ag '71
Two English tools for the metalshop; kit-built milling machine and hand-powered metal shaper. P. McCafferty. il Pop Sci 198: 90-1 Ja '71

METALIOUS, Grace
Farewell to Peyton Place. O. Friedrich. il por Esquire 76:160-8+ D '71 *

METALLIC pollution. See Pollution

METALLOORGANIC compounds. See Organometallic compounds

METALLURGY
   See also
Case hardening
Physical metallurgy

METALS
   See also
Alkali metals
Alloys
Precious metals
   See also names of metals, e.g. Lead
Detection
See Metal detectors
Heat treatment
   See also
Case hardening
Prices
Metals find a price loophole. il Bsns W p21-2 Ag 28 '71
Testing
Cracks: the rodder's invisible enemy! Magnaflux method. J. Thawley. il Hot Rod 24: 118-19 Jl '71
Toxicology
See Metal poisoning

METALS, Clad
Clad metals: they're moving into your home. J. R. Free. il Pop Sci 199:12+ D '71

METALS, Effect of radiation on
Radiation-induced swelling of stainless steel P. G. Shewmon. bibliog il Science 173:987-91 S 10 '71

METALS, Nonferrous
Metals; with yardsticks of management performance. il Forbes 109:101-2+ Ja 1 '72
Prices
Nonferrous metals start to live a little. il Bsns W p39 Je 5 '71
Nonferrous prices: no silver lining. il Bsns W p29 Ja 16 '71

METALS in the body
Weighty evidence against heavy metals. il Bsns W p46-8 F 20 '71

METALWORK. See Metal work

METAMORPHOSES; drama. See Weinstein, A.

METAPHOR
Creativity, poetic language, and the computer. M. Borroff. Yale R 60:481-513 Je '71

METCALF, Lee
Invisible senator. R. Sherrill. por Nation 212: 584-9 My 10 '71 *
—and Reinemer, Vic
Unmasking corporate ownership. Nation 213: 38-40 Jl 19 '71

METEORITES
Allende meteorite: a high-voltage electron petrographic study. H. W. Green, 2d. and others. bibliog il Science 172:936-9 My 28 '71
Amino acid analyses of the Murchison and Allende carbonaceous chondrites. J. R. Cronin and C. B. Moore. bibliog il Science 172:1327-9 Je 25 '71

METEORITES—_Continued_
Amino acids from outer space. il Chem 44: 24 F '71
Amino acids in both moon and meteorite. G. B. Lubkin. bibliog il Phys Today 24:17-19 F '71
Amino acids indigenous to the Murray meteorite. J. G. Lawless and others. bibliog il **Science 173:626-7 Ag 13 '71**
Aromatic hydrocarbons in the Murchison meteorite. K. L. Pering and C. Ponnamperuma. bibliog il Science 173:237-9 Jl 16 '71
Chondrules: first occurrence in an iron meteorite. E. Olsen and E. Jarosewich. bibliog il Science 174:583-5 N 5 '71
Episode in early American astronomy: the Weston meteorite. J. Ashbrook. bibliog por Sky & Tel 41:223+ Ap '71
Extraterrestrial amino acids. Sci N 99:435 Je 26 '71
Finnish meteorite studied. **Sky & Tel 43:10** Ja '72
Hunt for meteorites. W. R. Foster. il por Sci Digest 70:64-8 O '71
Life beyond the earth? Sci Digest 69:31 Mr '71
Mechanism for producing magnetic remanence in meteorites and lunar samples by cosmic-ray exposure. R. F. Butler and A. V. Cox. bibliog il Science 172:939-41 My 28 '71
More evidence for life in space. il Sci Digest 70:30-1 S '71
Origin in space; Murchison amino acids. **Sci N 99:195 Mr 20 '71**
Plutonium-244: confirmation as an extinct radioactivity. E. C. Alexander, jr. and others. bibliog il Science 172:837-40 My 21 '71
Possible pattern for origin of life. Space World H-9-93:47-8 S '71
Protostuff; Allende meteorite. Sci Am 225: 46 Ag '71
Wethersfield, Connecticut, meteorite. il **Sky & Tel 41:346+ Je '71**
Xenon record of extinct radioactivities in the earth. M. S. Boulos and O. K. Manuel. bibliog il Science 174:1334-6 D 24 '71
   See also
Tektites

METEOROLOGICAL instruments
Home weather station. il Mech Illus 67:106-7 F '71
Weather, whether you like it or not. il Consumer Bul 55:28-32 Ja '72
   See also
Anemometers
Barometers
Transmissometers

METEOROLOGICAL models
DOT using mathematical models to study SST climate effects. Aviation W 94:42 Ja 25 '71
Global meteorology: numerical models of the atmosphere. A. L. Hammond. Science 174: 393-5 O 22 '71
Three dimensional particle trajectories in a model hurricane. R. A. Anthes and others. il Weatherwise 24:174-8 Ag '71

METEOROLOGICAL optics
   See also
Airglow
Atmospheric transparency
Atmospheric turbidity
Halos (meteorology)
Rainbow

METEOROLOGICAL research
   See also
Artificial satellites—Meteorological use
Rain making
Weather control
Weather research
World meteorological organization

METEOROLOGICAL stations
Homemade weather station. J. A. Weeks. il Cons 26:48+ D '71

METEOROLOGY
   See also
American meteorological society
Atmosphere, Upper
Atmospheric nucleation
Atmospheric pressure
Auroras
Climate
Clouds
Evaporation
Floods
Hail
Radio in meteorology
Rain and rainfall
Rainbow
Rivers—Temperature
Snow
Soil-atmosphere interaction
Storms
Sun and meteorology

Television in meteorology
Thunderstorms
Tornadoes
United States—National weather service
Weather
Weather forecasting
Weathering
Winds
World meteorological organization

   Bibliography
Selective bibliography in meteorology. il Weatherwise 24:208-26 O '71

METEOROLOGY, Aeronautic
Secret of the sequence report. M. R. Bryan. Flying 89:70-1+ N '71

METEOROLOGY, Agricultural
Sun's work in a cornfield. E. Lemon and others. bibliog il Science 174:371-8 O 22 '71
U.S. and Soviets to share data on Mars missions. Sci N 100:291-2 O 30 '71

METEOROLOGY, Maritime
Anatomy of a squall. J. McCollam. il Yachting 129:64-5+ Ap '71
Real sea; wave forecasting; excerpt from **The sea in motion. F. G. W. Smith. il Sea Front 17:298-311 S '71**

METEORS
Leonids in November. il **Sky & Tel 43:57-8** Ja '72
Notes from Perseid observers. il Sky & Tel 42:246-7 O '71
Possible new meteor radiant. P. A. Koning. il Sky & Tel 41:316-17 My '71
Quadrantids in 1971. il **Sky & Tel 41:188 Mr '71**

METER reading
Readable meters make happy customers; Fort Worth, Tex. G. O. Muller. il Am City 86:65-6 Ja '71
Small size is no excuse; Perkasie, Pa. D. K. Price. il por Am City 86:60-2 My '71

METERS
Use a VOM as a dwell meter. H. Zave. il Radio-Electr 42:75 Ag '71
   See also
Dwell meters
Electric meters
Exposure meters
Flow meters
Micrometers
Parking meters
Photographic meters
Voltmeters

METHADONE
Choice for thousands: heroin or methadone? W. Goodman. il N Y Times Mag p 14-15+ Je 13 '71; Reply. R. Bayer. p20 Jl 25 '71
Heroin plague: what can be done? with report by M. Kasindorf. il Newsweek 78:27 32 Jl 5 '71
Improving on methadone. **Time 97:74 Je 14 '71**
New hope in fight against drugs; with interview with G. E. Davidson. il U S News 71: 39-44 S 27 '71
Pittsburgh narcotics addicts find hope in the methadone method. il Ebony 26:48-50+ N '70
Trying to hlep the GI addicts; Palo Alto VA hospital program; with editorial comment. il Life 71:3, 20-7 Jl 23 '71

METHAMPHETAMINE. See Amphetamines

METHANE
Clean new gas; methane from feedlot wastes. H. L. Bohn. bibliog il Environ 13:4-9 D '71

METHODIST church
   See also
Methodist world conference

METHODIST church in Bolivia
U.S. students held hostage. M. Arias. Chr Cent 88:1179-80 O 6 '71

METHODIST church in England
Expulsion of an outsider; R. Billington. T. Beeson. Chr Cent 88:849 Jl 14 '71
   See also
Church union—Great Britain

METHODIST church in the United States
Wesleyan vigor; meeting of the Wesleyan theological society. D. W. Dayton. Chr Today 16:45 D 3 '71
   See also
United Methodist church

METHODIST church of Great Britain. See Methodist church in England

METHODIST Episcopal church, African. See African Methodist Episcopal church

METHODIST publishing house
Court ruling may limit religious publishers' tax-exempt status. Chr Cent 88:1489 D 22 '71

METHODIST world conference
Family reunion: Methodists at Denver. B. Thompson. Chr Cent 88:1158 O 6 '71
World Methodists: revival in '75? W. Willoughby. **Chr Today 15:45 S 10 '71**

METS, Laurens J. and Bogorad, Lawrence
Mendelian and uniparental alterations in erythromycin binding by plastid ribosomes. bibliog il Science 174:707-9 N 12 '71

METS (baseball) See Baseball clubs

METZ, Christian
Old Amana furniture. by M. K. Albers. Review
Antiques il 99:908+ Je '71. K. D. Barron *

METZ, William D.
High energy astronomy: observations of gamma radiation. Science 174:1314 D 24 '71

METZGER, Daniel
Transistor and FET curve tracer. il Electr World 86:52-4 Ag '71

METZGER, H. Peter
Dear Sir: your house is built on radioactive uranium waste. il N Y Times Mag p 14-15+ O 31 '71

METZGER, Michael H.
From D.A. to dope lawyer. N. Pileggi. il pors N Y Times Mag p34-5+ My 16 '71 *

METZGER, Peter. See Metzger, H. P.

METZLER, Jacqueline. See Shepard, R. N. jt. auth.

MEUDT, Edna
Trees for tomorrow; poem. Am For 77:56 Ap '71

MEXICAN abelias. See Abelias

MEXICAN AMERICAN literature
Collection for la raza. K. Revelle. il por Library J 96:3719-26 N 15 '71
See also
Booksellers and bookselling—Mexican American literature

MEXICAN AMERICAN students
Awakening of the Chicanos. A. Hano. il Seventeen 30:148-9+ Mr '71
Quiet minority speaks out; Senior youthview. Sr Schol 99:12-13 Ja 10 '72
U.S. journal: Crystal City, Tex. C. Trillin. New Yorker 47:102+ Ap 17 '71

MEXICAN AMERICANS
Bishops for Chicanos. America 124:556 My 29 '71
Chicano sensibility. R. Blauner. Trans-Action 8:51-6+ F '71
Chicano workers, Rio Grande farmers agree to meet. N. D. Phillips. Chr Cent 88:84-6 Ja 20 '71
Chicanos besieged: the bloody fiesta. D. F. Gomez. il Nation 212:326-8 Mr 15 '71
Chicanos campaign for a better deal. il Bsns W p48-53 My 29 '71
Chicanos: strangers in their own land. D. F. Gomez. il America 124:649-52 Je 26 '71; Discussion. 125:77, 247 Ag 21, O 9 '71
Machismo riot; flare-up in East Los Angeles's barrio. il Newsweek 77:34 F 15 '71
Old-fashioned U.S. success story; R. A. Banuelos and P. V. Sanchez. il pors U S News 71:80 O 4 '71
La raza: the race for equality. bibliog il Sr Schol 99:4-9 Ja 10 '72
To die standing: Cesar Chavez and the Chicanos. J. G. Dunne. por Atlan 227:39-45 Je '71; Reply with rejoinder. J. Angell. 228:36 S '71
See also
Spanish speaking students

Education
Education in the grapes of wrath; problems of an elementary school principal. D. H. Mangers. Ed Digest 36:16-18 F '71
Schools for Mexican-Americans: between two cultures. P. D. Ortego. il Sat R 54:62-4+ Ap 17 '71

MEXICAN cookery. See Cookery, Mexican

MEXICAN literature
See also
Mexican American literature

MEXICAN national institute of anthropology and history. See Mexico—National institute of anthropology and history

MEXICAN students
See also
Student militants—Mexico

MEXICAN war, 1845-1848. See United States—History—War with Mexico, 1845-1848

MEXICANOS. See Mexican Americans

MEXICANS in the United States
Why wetbacks are so hard to control. U S News 71:50 O 18 '71
See also
Mexican Americans

MEXICO
One way to see Mexicans and Mexico close up is to make a tour by bus. il Sunset 147:54-5 O '71
See also
Acapulco
Ballet—Mexico
California, Lower
Cities and towns—Mexico
Coasts—Mexico
Copper mines and mining—Mexico
Cruising—Mexico
Fishing—Mexico
Gardens—Mexico
Guadalajara
Guerrillas—Mexico
Motor vehicle racing—Mexico
Puerto Vallarta
Radio broadcasting—Mexico
Russians in Mexico
San Blas
San Luis Potosi
San Miguel De Allende
Sonoran Desert
Sports—Mexico
Student militants—Mexico
Yucatan

Antiquities
Metro monuments; salvage archaeology of Mexico-Tenochtitlán. J. Gussinyer Alfonso. il Américas 23:13-19 Ap '71
Obsidian trade at San Lorenzo Tenochtitlan. Mexico. R. H. Cobean and others. bibliog il Science 174:666-71 N 12 '71
Olmec: America's first civilization. M. Stirling. il Américas 23:S23-31 Je '71
Shadow of the Olmecs. M. D. Coe. il Horizon 13:66-75 Aut '71

Boundaries
U.S.-Mexico boundary treaty transmitted to the Senate; President's letter of transmittal with Secretary Rogers' report of March 22, 1971. R. M. Nixon. il Dept State Bul 64:674-8 My 24 '71

Description and travel
Adventure on a shoestring; exploring La Media Luna Lake. G. F. Hammond. il Motor B & S 127:70-5 Mr '71
Many faces of Mexico. D. Dunlop. il Nat Wildlife 10:44-7 D '71
Their Mexico, your Mexico, my Mexico. E. Motoviloff. il Schol Teach Jr/Sr High p 12-15 Mr 8 '71

Economic conditions
Who's making it in Mexico? M. J. Ulmer. New Repub 165:21-3 S 25 '71

Foreign relations
Russia
See Russia—Foreign relations—Mexico

Frontier troubles
To 1910
Henry A. Crabb, filibuster or colonizer? Sonora expedition in 1857. J. A. Stout. il pors Am West 8:4-9 My '71

History
1821-1861
See also
Mexico—Frontier troubles—To 1910

European intervention, 1861-1867
Cactus throne, by R. O'Connor. Review
Nat R 23:322-4 Mr 23 '71. A. Bashian, jr

1867-1910
Instant millionaire: Colonel W. C. Greene in fact and folklore. C. L. Sonnichsen. bibliog il pors Am West 8:4-9+ N '71

1910-1946
Niño: child of the Mexican revolution. by A. Iduarte. Review
New Yorker 47:85-7 Jl 17 '71. N. Bliven

American punitive expedition, 1916
See United States—History—Punitive expedition to Mexico, 1916

Industries
See also
Photographic apparatus and supplies industry—Mexico

National institute of anthropology and history
Anthropology and history prizes. Américas 23:45 Mr '71

MEXICO—*Continued*

Politics and government

Mexico at the crossroads. M. C. Needler. Cur Hist 60:65-70+ F '71

Showing them who's boss. il por Time 97:38 Je 28 '71

MEXICO (city)

Description

Mexican festival of sounds and sights. L. Barry. il Pop Phot 68:32+ Mr '71

Historic houses, etc.

City of palaces. C. F. Marini. il Américas 23:2-9 S '71

Hotels, restaurants, etc.

Eating high, in Mexico city. Q Crewe. Vogue 157:52-3 Je '71

Riots

Fearsome Falcons. il Time 97:33 Je 21 '71

Subways

In Mexico don't miss the new metro. il Sunset 146:41 Mr '71

Mexican Metro. il Travel 135:52-5 Je '71

Transit systems

See also

Mexico (city)—Subways

MEXICO, GULF OF

Montreal to Tampico; ed. by G. F. Hammond. J. Desjardins. il por Motor B & S 127:56-9+ My; 61-3+ Je '71

See also

Fishing—Mexico, Gulf of

MEXICO-Tenochtitlán excavations. See Mexico—Antiquities

MEYE, Robert P.

Mark's special Easter emphasis. Chr Today 15:4-6 Mr 26 '71

MEYER, Charles A.

Department comments on policy toward Chile; statement, October 15, 1971. Dept State Bul 65:498-500 N 1 '71

Inter-American economic and social council meets at Panama City; statement, September 15, 1971. Dept State Bul 65:382-4 O 11 '71

Sustaining a meaningful commitment to Latin American development; statement, August 4, 1971. Dept State Bul 65:236-8 Ag 30 '71

U.S. policy toward Latin America: where we stand today; address, October 25, 1971. Dept State Bul 65:559-64 N 15 '71; Same. Vital Speeches 38:109-12 D 1 '71

MEYER, Daniel

Build the five forty power amplifier. il Pop Electr 34:49-53+ My '71

Digital thermometer module for the digital measurements lab. il Pop Electr 34:69-71+ Je '71

Plastic tiger audio power amplifier. il Pop Electr 35:27-34+ O '71

Ultimate decimal counter. il Pop Electr 34:45-8+ F '71

MEYER, Frank S.

Principles and heresies. See occasional issues of National review

MEYER, Hanna, and Mayer, A. M.

Permeation of dry seeds with chemicals: use of dichloromethane. il Science 171:583 F 12 '71

MEYER, Hans

He types portraits. il pors Design 73:20-3 Wint '71

MEYER, John Charles

Peacetime air force of the seventies; address, September 29, 1971. Vital Speeches 38:56-8 N 1 '71

Time dimension of military forces; address, May 14, 1971. Vital Speeches 37:518-21 Je 15 '71

MEYER, John R.

Economy: our deceptive growth dividend. il Sat R 54:44-5 Ja 23 '71

MEYER, Joseph

Big brother; crime deterrent transponder system. R. Barkan. il Ramp Mag 10:10+ S '71 •

MEYER, Judith G.

Back in circulation. il Environ 13:30-3 S '71

MEYER, Karl E.

Were you there when they photographed my Lord? il Esquire 76:72-4+ Ag '71

MEYER, Olga Alberta (Caracciolo) baroness de

Olga the wild. P. Jullian. il pors Vogue 158:154-9+ O 1 '71 •

MEYER, Pearl

When to use employment contracts. Harvard Bsns R 49:70-3 N '71

MEYER, Robert H.

Dylan Thomas: the experience, the picture, and the message. bibliog f Engl J 60:199-204 F '71

MEYER, Robert L.

Hard-liner por Newsweek 77:37 Mr 15 '71 •

MEYER, Susan E.

Footnotes; new editor. por Am Artist 35:6 Mr '71 •

(ed) See Clements, G. How Geoffrey Clements photographs fine art

MEYER, Tony

Nothing surprises him. B. Coffman. il por Farm J 95:H18-19 S '71

MEYER, Urs A. and Marver, H. S.

Chemically induced porphyria: increased microsomal heme turnover after treatment with allylisopropylacetamide. bibliog il Science 171:64-6 Ja 8 '71

MEYERBEER, Giacomo

At last, les Huguenots. G. L. Mayer. il por Am Rec G 37:484-7 Ap '71 •

Meyerbeer's bloody machine. P. G. Davis. por Hi Fi 21:73-4 Ja '71 •

MEYERLE, George

Build a four-channel stereo. decoder. il Pop Electr 35:52-3+ Jl '71

Professional intruder; fire alarm. il Pop Electr 35:61-5 D '71

MEYERS, Arthur S.

Unseen and unheard elderly. il Am Lib 2:793-6 S '71

MEYERS, Edward

Protechniques. See issues of Popular photography

MEYERS, Harold B.

Salvage of the Lockheed 1011. il por Fortune 83:66-71+ Je '71

MEYERS, Jeffrey

Decadence and morbidity, a certain weakness, a certain comfort. Commonweal 94:113-14 Ap 9 '71

MEYERS, Judith, and Barber, Raymond

McNamara, media and you. bibliog il Library J 96:1079-81, 1743+ Mr 15, My 15 '71

MEYNELL, Sir Francis

Nonesuch press; excerpts from My lives. il Pub W 200:78+ S 13 '71

MEZEY, Robert

I have lived under Orion all my life; poem. Nation 212:694 My 31 '71

about

Comment. F. MacShane. Poetry 118:300-1 Ag '71 •

MIAMI, Fla.

Foreign population

How the immigrants made it in Miami. il Bsns W p88-9 My 1 '71

Miami: the Cuban flavor. A. Burt. il Nation 212:299-302 Mr 8 '71; Reply with rejoinder. J. D. Garst. 212:450 Ap 12 '71

Intellectual life

Down among the sheltering palms. W. Alderson. il Opera N 35:6-10 Mr 13 '71

Music

Down among the sheltering palms. W. Alderson. il Opera N 35:6-10 Mr 13 '71

Festival of George Gershwin. D. Ewen. il pors Hi Fi 21:MA24-5+ Ja '71

Opera guild of Greater Miami 1941-71. Opera N 35:17 Mr 13 '71

Place in the sun. F. Stevenson. il por Opera N 35:12-13 Mr 13 '71

MIAMI BEACH, Fla.

Police department

Police patrol boats cut crime, save lives. il Am City 86:33 Jl '71

MIAMI Dolphins (football club) See Football clubs

MIAMI RIVER (Ohio) See Great Miami River

MIAMI, University, Coral Gables, Fla.

Bookstore

See College bookstores

School of medicine

Alleviating the shortage of physicians. W. J. Harrington and others. bibliog il Science 172:1109-11 Je 11 '71; Discussion. 174:979-80 D 3 '71

MIAMI university, Oxford, Ohio

Dissent vs. disruption. Sch & Soc 99:7-8 Ja '71

MICA

Hydroxyl orientation in muscovite as indicated by electrostatic energy calculations. R. F. Giese, jr. bibliog il Science 172:263-4 Ap 16 '71

MICE
Activity of Δ⁸-andΔ⁹-tetrahydrocannabinol and related compounds in the mouse. H. D. Christensen and others. bibliog il Science 172:165-7 Ap 9 '71
Alcohol dependence produced in mice by inhalation of ethanol: grading the withdrawal reaction. D. B. Goldstein and N. Pal. bibliog il Science 172:288-90 Ap 16 '71
Autoimmune murine thyroiditis relation to histocompatibility (H-2) type. A. O. Vladutiu and N. R. Rose. bibliog il Science 174:1137-9 D 10 '71
Linkage groups II and XII of the mouse: cytological localization by fluorochrome staining. M. Nesbitt and U. Francke. bibliog il Science 174:60-2 O 1 '71
Olfactory bulb removal eliminates maternal behavior in the mouse. R. Gandelman and others. bibliog il Science 171:210-11 Ja 15 '71
Parthenogenesis: does it occur spontaneously in mice? W. K. Whitten. bibliog Science 171:406-7 Ja 29 '71

MICE, White footed
This dairy queen offers 24 hours service! il Nat Wildlife 9:42-3 Ag '71

MICHAEL, Richard P. and others
Pheromones: isolation of male sex attractants from a female primate. bibliog il Science 172:964-6 My 28 '71

MICHAELS, James W.
Light touch of acid. por Forbes 108:7 Jl 15 '71

MICHAELSON, Michael G.
Failure of American medicine. Am Scholar 39:694; 40:325-6 Aut '70, Spr '71
Sickle cell anemia: an interesting pathology. il Ramp Mag 10:52-8 O '71

MICHAELSON, Mike
Bounty hunter wore sneakers. il Todays Health 49:41-3+ Ap '71
Every time Diana kisses Joe goodbye, it could be their last embrace. il pors Todays Health 49:37-41+ Ag '71
Love that lights the last days of a brave young mother. il pors Todays Health 49:48-53+ D '71
Queasy rider. il Todays Health 49:44-7+ Je '71
Toys that bring joy and challenge. il Todays Health 49:34-6+ D '71
Wyoming's war on deadly strep. il Todays Health 49:40-3+ Mr '71

MICHALS, Duane
Sequence; interview. New Yorker 46:27-8 Ja 16 '71
about
Seeing pictures. J. Scully. il Mod Phot 35:22+ F '71 *
Sequential approach to photography. J. Deschin. por Pop Phot 68:22+ Mr '71 *

MICHAUX, Henri
Henri Michaux: an urbane anxiety. M. Gibson. il Art in Am 59:128-9 Mr '71

MICHELIA
Strong, musky fragrance, big bursts of white flowers, and February is its month. il Sunset 146:172 F '71

MICHELIN and company. See Tire industry —France

MICHELINO Molinari da Besozzo. See Besozzo. M. M. da

MICHELMAN, William
Seal of confession. America 124: 218 Mr 6 '71 *

MICHELSON, Peter
Bringing the war home. il New Repub 164:21-5 F 27 '71

MICHENER, James Albert
James Michener speaks out; excerpts from remarks at press conference, April 27, 1971. por Pub W 199:17-18 My 10 '71
Kent state: what happened and why; condensation. il Read Digest 98:57-63+ Mr; 217-20+ Ap '71
Lament for Pakistan. il N Y Times Mag p 11-13+ Ja 9 '72
One and a half cheers for progress. il N Y Times Mag p9+ S 5 '71; Same abr. Read Digest 99:209+ D '71
Peace of mind. por Look 35:22 Jl 27 '71
about
Trade winds. C. Amory. Sat R 54:12-13 My 15 '71 *
What the F.B.I. has on me. por Esquire 76:134-5+ D '71 *

MICHIE, Allan A.
Brain drain and development. Sch & Soc 99:102-3 F '71

MICHIGAN
See also
Banks and banking—Michigan
Fishing—Michigan
Hunting—Michigan
School laws and legislation—Michigan
State aid to education—Michigan

Politics and government
Grass roots vs. back room; liberal democrats. S. Holtzer. por Nation 212:166-9 F 8 '71

MICHIGAN, LAKE
Cruising Lake Michigan. J. Roe. il por Yachting 130:58-9+ Jl '71
Eutrophication, silica depletion, and predicted changes in algal quality in Lake Michigan. C. L. Schelske and E. F. Stoermer. bibliog il Science 173:423-4 Jl 30 '71

MICHIGAN. University, Ann Arbor
Michigan war research charged. R. J. Bazell. Science 171:656 F 19 '71
Sex discrimination on campus: Michigan wrestles with equal pay. D. Shapley. Science 173:214-16 Jl 16 '71
See also
Institute of gerontology

Conference on aging
See Aging, Conferences on

MICKINOCK, Rey
Plight of the native American. il por Library J 96:2848-51 S 15 '71

MICKLO, Anne Marie
Women is losers. il Sr Schol 98:22-3+ Ap 26 '71

MICOSSI, Anita Lynn
Conversion to Women's lib. il Trans-Action 8:82-90 N '70

MICROBIAL degradation. See Degradation (biology)

MICROBIOLOGY
See also
Marine microbiology

MICROELECTRONIC soldering. See Solder and soldering

MICROELECTRONICS
See also
Electronic circuits, Integrated

MICROEMULSIONS. See Emulsions

MICROFICHE. See Microforms

MICROFICHE records. See Microfilm records

MICROFILM records
On-the-spot credit checker; constantly updated credit information on microfiche. il Bsns W p78 O 9 '71
See also
County records on microfilm
Police records on microfilm
State records on microfilm

MICROFILMS
Bigger things are seen for microfilm. V. Louviere. Nations Bsns 59:20 Mr '71
Do-it-yourself microfilming; Micrographic technology's combination camera-processor. il Bsns W p70 Mr 20 '71
Microfilm looks for a booming market. Bsns W p23 My 29 '71
See also
Periodicals on microfilm
University microfilms, inc.

MICROFORMS
Micrographics: a growing industry; exhibition in Washington. J. Tebbel. Sat R 54:48-50 Jl 10 '71
Miniaturization of the book. J. Tebbel. Cur 126:46-51 F '71
See also
Publishers and publishing—Microforms

MICROGRAPHICS. See Microforms

MICROIRRADIATION. See Irradiation

MICROMETERS
Everything you always wanted to know about the micrometer. B. Berger. il Mech Illus 67:95-7+ S '71

MICRONESIA
Americanization of Micronesia: paradise lost. S. Murray. il Ramp Mag 9:35-7+ F '71
Keys to the Pacific. H. W. Baldwin. Read Digest 99:164-5 D '71
Micronesia: America's troubled island ward. P. F. Kluge. il Read Digest 99:161-4 D '71
Reporter at large. E. J. Kahn, jr. New Yorker 47:98+ D 18 '71
See also
Education—Micronesia
Trust Territory of the Pacific Islands

Description and travel
Micronesia. il Sunset 147:42-4 O '71

MICRONESIANS
Peoples of the Pacific; ed. by M. Mead and
P. McClanahan. bibliog il pors Natur Hist
80:43 My '71
Reporter at large. E. J. Kahn, jr. New York-
er 47:89+ D 18 '71

MICROORGANISMS
See also
Plankton
Viruses

Metabolism

Phenylmercuric acetate: metabolic conversion
by microorganisms. F. Matsumura and others. bibliog il Science 173:49-51 Jl 2 '71

MICROPALEONTOLOGY
Oldest fossils. E. S. Barghoorn. il Sci Am 224:
30-42 bibliog(p 132) My '71
See also
Spores (botany), Fossil

MICROPHONES
Build a VOX gain rider; voice-controlled
mike. D. W. Beaty. il Pop Electr 34:58-62
Je '71
Portable sound systems for performers. D.
L. Patten. il Electr World 86:27-9+ Ag '71

MICROPHONES in criminal investigation, espionage, etc. See Electronics in criminal
investigation, espionage, etc.

MICROPHOTOGRAPHY
See also
Microfilms
Microforms

MICROSCOPE and microscopy
Molecular microscopy: fundamental limita-
tions. J. R. Breedlove, jr. and G. T. Tram-
mell; reply. E. H. Jacobsen and others.
bibliog Science 173:751-2 Ag 20 '71
See also
Electron microscope and microscopy
Microscopic sections
Photomicrography
Stains and staining (microscopy)

MICROSCOPIC sections
Three-dimensional structure identified from
single sections; adaptation of address, August 1971. H. Elias. bibliog il Science 174:
993-1000 D 3 '71

MICRO-social learning center. See Vineland,
N.J.—Education

MICROTEACHING. See Teachers—Education in
service

MICROTUBULES. See Cells

MICROWAVE communications, inc.
Goeken tunes up his microwave net. il Bsns
W p28-9 O 16 '71
See also
MCI Lockheed satellite corporation

MICROWAVE data transmission systems. See
Data transmission systems

MICROWAVE irradiation. See Irradiation

MICROWAVE ovens. See Electronic ovens

MICROWAVE radio communications. See Radio
communication, Short wave

MICROWAVE radiometers. See Radiometers

MICROWAVES
See also
Traveling wave tubes

Physiological effects

Behavioral sensitivity to microwave irradiation. N. W. King and others. bibliog il Science 172:398-401 Ap 23 '71
Microwave absorption by normal and tumor
cells. S. J. Webb and A. D. Booth. bibliog il Science 174:72-4 O 1 '71

MIDAS-international corporation
Family fight to control Midas. il Bsns W
p40+ Ap 17 '71

MID-ATLANTIC ridge. See Ocean bottom

MIDDELDORF, Eike
Middeldorf's complaint. Newsweek 77:42+ Ap
26 '71 •

MIDDENDORF, J. W. print collection. See
Prints—Collectors and collecting

MIDDLE age
Disarmed at middle age. A. Chayes. Atlan
228:72-3 N '71
I'm glad I'm a middle-aged sex object. J.
Rivers. por McCalls 99:78+ O '71
In praise of middle age. E. Janeway. Mc-
Calls 99:112+ O '71
Lively challenge of middle life. K. L. Wood-
ward. McCalls 99:81+ O '71
Middle-aged declaration of independence. L.
E. Sissman. Atlan 227:26+ Ap '71
This glorious feeling! Could it be middle
age? M. Drury. il Ladies Home J 88:84+
My '71

Anecdotes, facetiae, satire, etc.

Standing in the wind. M. J. Arlen. il McCalls
99:54+ O '71

Psychology

How to cope with those middle-age blues.
M. Symonds and J. R. Hellman. Read Digest 99:101-4 N '71

Sexual behavior

Sex and middle age. D. Reuben. il McCalls
99:64+ O '71

MIDDLE aged workers. See Age and employment

MIDDLE ages
Pride goes before the avarice: social change
and the vices in Latin Christendom. L. K.
Little. bibliog f il Am Hist R 76:16-49 F
'71
Yves Renouard and the economic history of
the middle ages. D. Herlihy. Am Hist
R 76:127-31 F '71
See also
Church history—Middle ages
Manuscripts, Medieval

History

See also
Economic history—Medieval
Europe—History—476-1492

MIDDLE class Americans. See Americans

MIDDLE classes
Blueing of America. P. L. Berger and B. Ber-
ger. New Repub 164:20-3 Ap 3 '71; Same.
Cur 131:56-62 Jl '71
Saul Alinsky in Japan. J. K. Hasegawa. Chr
Cent 88:1306-8 N 3 '71
Shafting of Mr Average. S. Alsop. News-
week 77:132 Ap 19 '71
Soul in suburbia; dilemma of the black mid-
dle class. O. Coombs. il Harper 244:24-6+
Ja '72

MIDDLE EAST
See also
Armenia
Central treaty organization
Cities and towns—Middle East
Ecology—Middle East
Guerrillas—Middle East
Iran
Jordan
Petroleum—Middle East
Petroleum industry—Middle East
Suez Canal
Syria
United Nations—Middle East
United Nations relief and works agency for
Palestine refugees in the Near East

Antiquities

Near Eastern archaeology in the twentieth
century: essays in honor of Nelson Glueck,
ed. by J. A. Sanders. Review
Chr Today 16:26-7 O 22 '71. E. M.
Yamauchi

Defenses

Balancing act. New Repub 165:8 D 4 '71

Economic conditions

Challenge of change: petroleum and planning
in the Middle East. J. A. Bill. bibliog il
Focus 22:1-5 S '71
Middle East: the makings of a boom. il Bsns
W p86-7 Ap 10 '71

Foreign relations

United States

See United States—Foreign relations—
Middle East

Maps

Africa & Middle East. Sr Schol 99:11 O 4 '71

Nationalism

Political dimension: colonialism to nationalism in the Middle East. I. R. Manners.
bibliog Focus 22:6-8 S '71

Politics

Desert battle and a deadline. il Time 98:17
Ag 23 '71
Gasoline by an open fire. il Time 98:29-30 O
25 '71
Israel: the weakness is here. S. Alsop.
Newsweek 78:64 D 27 '71
Little victories. il Newsweek 78:44 D 20 '71
Middle East: a case of jitters. il por Time
98:36-7 D 6 '71
Middle East, 1972; symposium. bibliog f Cur
Hist 62:1-43+ Ja '72
New dangers in Mideast; key questions and
answers. il U S News 71:40-2 D 6 '71
Political dimension: colonialism to national-
ism in the Middle East. I. R. Manners.
bibliog Focus 22:6-8 S '71
Rancorous road to peace. il Time 98:31 D 13
'71

MIDDLE EAST—Politics—*Continued*
Sadat rattles his saber. por Newsweek 78:
40+ D 6 '71
What they're talking about in the Middle
East & Africa. il Sr Schol 99:10 O 4 '71
Year of debacle? il Time 99:40 Ja 3 '72
See also
Arab states—Politics
Jewish-Arab relations

Population
Cities of the Middle East and their problems.
R. S. Harrison. bibliog il Focus 22:1-8 N '71
MIDDLE EAST crisis. See Israeli-Arab war,
1967-
MIDDLE EAST treaty organization. See Central
treaty organization
MIDDLE EASTERN cookery. See Cookery,
Middle Eastern
MIDDLE FORK RIVER, Idaho. See Salmon
River
MIDDLE schools
Emerging middle school. I. Flinker and N.
Pianko. il Clear House 46:67-72 O '71
Middle school reform in Italy. G. L. Williams.
bibliog f Clear House 46:245-9 D '71
Middle school requires some direction. J.
Bondi. Clear House 45:568 My '71
Middle school, specially trained teachers are
vital to its success. S. Clarke. bibliog f
Clear House 46:218-22 D '71
Our middle schools give the kids a break;
Howard County, Md. J. Di Virgilio. il To-
days Ed 60:30-2 Ja '71
What's the score on: middle schools? W. M.
Alexander Todays Ed 60:67 N '71
MIDDLE WEST
See also
Camping—Middle Western states
MIDDLETON, Drew
Army snow job. W. L. Robb. New Repub
165:15-17 D 11 '71 •
MIDDLETON, R. Hunter
Middleton's type designs viewed in retro-
spect. il Pub W 200:50 O 4 '71
MIDDLETON, Robert G.
TV antenna accessories. il Radio-Electr 42:
33-5+ S '71
Using the right probes. il Radio-Electr 42:23-
5+ Ag '71
MIDGES
Uncoupling cell junctions in a glandular
epithelium by depolarizing current. S. J.
Socolar and A. L. Politoff. bibliog il Sci-
ence 172:492-4 Ap 30 '71
MIDGETTE, Willard F.
Portrait of the artist as a portrait of the
artist. D. Rosand. il por Art N 70:32-5+
Mr '71 •
MIDISKIRTS. See Clothing and dress
MIDLAND, Mich.
Company town calls for nuclear power now. il
Bsns W p34 Ja 1 '72
MIDLAND-Ross corporation
All or nothing? Forbes 108:22-3 Ag 15 '71
MIDSUMMER marriage; opera. See Tippett, M.
MIDSUMMER night's dream; drama. See
Shakespeare, W.—Plays
MIDWAY airport. See Chicago—Airports
MIDWEST beef cattle conference. See Agricul-
tural conferences
MIDWEST stock exchange, Chicago. See
Stock exchange—Chicago
MIDWIVES
Rebirth of the midwife. il pors Life 71:50-5
N 19 '71
MIDWOOD, Barton
Fiction. Esquire 75:64+ Ja; 50+ F; 52 Mr;
30+ Ap; 52+ My; 50+ Je; 76:63+ O '71
Riddle; story. Esquire 75:108-11 Mr '71
MIEULI, Franklin
Will Franklin Mieuli spoil success? F. De-
ford. il pors Sports Illus 34:62-4+ F 15 '71 •
MIG airplanes. See Airplanes, Military—Russia
MIGDOLL, Herbert
Astarte; a portfolio of photographers. Hori-
zon 13:19-26 Spr '71
MIGRAINE. See Headache
MIGRANT children

Education
See Children of migrant laborers—Educa-
tion
MIGRANT labor
Company that helps migrants; Coke's Minute
maid groves. il Bsns W p61 Mr 6 '71
Down on the farm; hearings of Senate sub-
committee on migratory labor in California.
Nation 214:3 Ja 3 '72
Place in the sun for the migrant; Coca-Cola's
housing project. il Nations Bsns 59:70-3 S
'71

So shall ye reap, by H. Anderson and J.
London. Review
America 124:416+ Ap 17 '71. M. Day
See also
American federation of labor and Congress
of industrial organizations—United farm
workers organizing committee
Children of migrant laborers
MIGRANT laborers, Children of. See Children
of migrant laborers
MIGRATION, Internal
Is California's people boom over? Meanwhile,
in Florida, no slowdown in growth. il U S
News 70:37-8 Je 21 '71
Occupational migration, discrimination, and
the central city labor force; with tables.
D. E. Kaun and W. Lentz. bibliog Mo Labor
R 94:57-61 D '71
One county's loss is another's gain. Na-
tions Bsns 59:79 N '71
See also
Cities and towns—Growth
Labor mobility
Negroes—Migration
MIGRATION from farms
Quiet falls across the plains. D. Wittner. il
Life 70:22-31 Je 25 '71
MIGRATION of animals. See Animals—Migra-
tion
MIGRATION of birds. See Birds—Migration
MIGRATION of Negroes. See Negroes—Migra-
tion
MIGRATION of teachers. See Teachers—Mi-
gration
MIHALASKY, John, and others
Dollars may flow from the sixth sense. Na-
tions Bsns 59:64+ Ap '71
MIHALOV, J. D. and others
Possible fossil lunar magnetism inferred from
satellite data. bibliog il Science 171:892-5
Mr 5 '71
MIKEŠ, František, and Waser, P. G.
Marihuana components; effects of smoking
on ▲9-tetrahydrocannabinol and cannabi-
diol. bibliog il Science 172:1158-9 Je 11 '71
MIKLOS, Laszlo D. See Miklos, M. O. jt. auth
MIKLOS, Mary Oellerich, and Miklos, L. D.
Student council: useful or useless? Ed Digest
36:47-9 Mr '71
MIKLUKHA-MAKLAI, Nikolai Nikolaevich
19th century champion of anti-racism in New
Guinea; excerpts from diaries, correspon-
dence and other papers, ed. by N. A. Buti-
nov. il por UNESCO Courier 24:24-7 N '71
MIKULSKI, Barbara
Growing up ethnic means learning who you
are. Redbook 137:86+ O '71
MIKVA, Abner J.
Illinois gerrymander. Nation 213:323-4 O 11
'71
MILAN, Italy
Report:
Verdi's I vespri Siciliani and L'Elisir
d'amore. P. Elvins. il Opera N 35:32-3
Ja 23 '71

Architecture
Milan; Chase Manhattan bank headquarters.
il Arch Forum 134:36-9 Ja '71

Art
Arte povera. amore mio; conceptual and eco-
logical art. M. Gendel. il Art N 69:38-9+
F '71

La Scala
Report:
Berg's Wozzeck. P. Elvins. il Opera N
35:27 My 15 '71
Donizetti's Maria Stuarda at La Scala. P.
Elvins. Opera N 35:26 Je 12 '71
I Puritani. P. Elvins. Opera N 35:30 Ap
17 '71

Music
Report:
Mussorgsky's Khovanschchina. P. Elvins.
il Opera N 35:31 Mr 6 '71
Parsifal and Samson et Dalila at La
Scala. P. Elvins. il Opera N 35:30 Mr 20
'71
Il Trovatore. P. Elvins. Opera N 35:33
F 13 '71
See also
Milan, Italy—La Scala
MILDEW
Problem of mildew on grapes. F. Allen. Org
Gard & Farm 18:92-6 Ag '71
MILEK, Bob
Case for the lung shot. il Field & S 76:44-
5+ Ag '71
Walleye wonderlake. il Field & S 75:76-7+
Ap '71
MILES, Bebe
Plant matched mates... glads and dahlias.
il Horticulture 49:40-1+ Mr '71

MILES, Betty
Harmful lessons little girls learn in school. il
Redbook 136:86-7+ Mr '71

MILES, Buddy
Buddy Miles: going thru changes. L. J. Banks.
il pors Ebony 27:74-6+ D '71 •

MILES, Charles
Indian relics. See issues of Hobbies

MILES, Dick
Exterminating a ping-pong pest. il Sports
Illus 34:30-5 Je 28 '71
They still swing a mean paddle. il Sports Illus
34:32-3 Ap 12 '71

MILES, Maebyn L.
Ready to drive? il Parents Mag 46:44+ Jl '71

MILES college, Birmingham, Ala.
Profiles: J. U. Monro, white director of
freshman studies. E. J. Kahn, jr. New
Yorker 47:43-8+ Ap 10 '71

MILFORD, N.H.
If New Hampshire makes it. I. Mothner.
Look 35:33-6 Ja 12 '71

MILHORAT, Thomas H. and others
Cerebrospinal fluid production by the choroid
plexus and brain. bibliog il Science 173:
330-2 Jl 23 '71

MILINAIRE, Caterine
Home birth: a feast of joy. il por Vogue 159:
72-3+ Ja 1 '72
Pacific crossing. il pors Vogue 158:194+ O 1
'71

MILITANT students. See Student militants
MILITARY airlift command. See United States
—Military airlift command
MILITARY architecture
See also
Barracks
MILITARY art and science
See also
Computers—Military use
Guerrilla warfare
Guerrillas
Strategy
War
MILITARY assistance, Algerian
Giving the commandos a hand. L. Jenkins. il
Newsweek 78:34-5 Jl 26 '71
MILITARY assistance, American
Arms and the Congress. New Repub 165:7-9
Ag 21 '71
Development aid and security assistance in
the Near East and South Asia; statement,
July 14, 1971. R. P. Davies. Dept State
Bul 65:204-8 Ag 23 '71
Double-talk bookkeeping; military budget. R.
F. Kaufman. Nation 213:429-32 N 1 '71
Farewell to foreign aid; address, October 29,
1971. F. Church. Vital Speeches 38:66-73 N
15 '71; Same abr. New Repub 165:14-17
N 13 '71; Reply. R. E. Hunter. 165:18-20
N 20 '71
Flybys and superspies; Middle East power
balance. Time 98:25 Jl 26 '71
Foreign aid: end of an era? il U S News 71:
20-2 N 15 '71
Foreign aid: the dawn of a new era; list
the Senate tore up. il Newsweek 78:40-1
N 15 '71
Military assistance; statistics. New Repub
165:10 Jl 24 '71
More balanced sharing of the burdens of
security; statement, November 25, 1970.
M. R. Laird. Dept State Bul 63:753-6 D
21 '70
Mysterious mushiness; Winston Churchill's
view on American power vs. Soviet power.
S. Alsop. Newsweek 77:88 My 31 '71
NATO force modernization aided. D. E. Fink.
Aviation W 95:14 D 20 '71
New approaches to international security as-
sistance; statement, February 2, 1971. J.
N. Irwin. il Dept State Bul 64:221-7 F 22 '71
New muscle in arms; sales to Latin Amer-
ica. il Time 98:57-8 Jl 12 '71
No one is in charge; Joint economic sub-
committee hearings. Newsweek 77:16-17
Ja 18 '71
Peace and stability in the Middle East and
Asia; statement, December 8, 1970. W. P.
Rogers. Dept State Bul 64:61-7 Ja 11 '71
Revived aid. New Repub 165:11-12 N 20 '71
Runaway enterprise. B. D. Nossiter. Nation
212:135-7 F 1 '71
Scrub it up, don't wipe it out: Senate debate.
New Repub 165:5-7 N 13 '71
Self-help and the search for peace; state-
ment, November 25, 1970. W. P. Rogers.
Dept State Bul 63:713-17 D 14 '70
Senate votes $1.5 billion arms aid. D. C.
Winston. Aviation W 95:14 N 22 '71

Supplemental assistance and basic U.S. pol-
icies in the Middle East and East Asia.
W. P. Rogers. Dept State Bul 64:19-26 Ja
4 '71
U.S. national security and assistance to
East Asia; statement, November 30, 1970.
M. Green. Dept State Bul 63:756-62 D 21
'70

Asia
Five major blunders by the U.S. in Asia. C.
Bowles. il por Sat R 54:28-31 N 6 '71
Security assistance programs in East Asia;
statement, May 4, 1971. M. Green. Dept
State Bul 64:714-19 My 31 '71

Asia, Southeastern
Getting Thieu through '72. New Repub 165:5-
6 N 27 '71
Where it hurts. Nation 214:35-6 Ja 10 '72

Cambodia
Instant replay. Newsweek 78:49 O 18 '71

Greece, Modern
Greece: immune to criticism? il Newsweek
78:33-4 Ag 16 '71
Greek drama. W. F. Buckley, jr. Nat R
23:949 Ag 24 '71

Israel
Erosion of U.S. military strength: can there
be peace without power? address, July 14,
1971. J. L. Buckley. Vital Speeches 37:
642-4 Ag 15 '71
Mideast: the Phantom 'No'. il por Newsweek
78:31-2 N 29 '71
On the spot. il Newsweek 78:59 O 25 '71

Pakistan
Arms harvest; west Pakistan. Nation 212:
803-4 Je 28 '71
Arms peddling. New Repub 165:8 O 23 '71
Lengthening shadow of war. America 125:
414-15 N 20 '71
Leverage fallacy; influence of U.S. aid to
Pakistan. Nation 213:611-12 D 13 '71
Pakistan. F. Lang. Ramp Mag 10:17+ S '71
Passage of arms. Newsweek 78:47 Jl 5 '71
Sins of commission. New Repub 165:10-11
Jl 24 '71

Vietnam (Republic)
Gross immorality; Senate vote on the Cooper-
Church amendment. S. Alsop. Newsweek 78:
122 N 8 '71
Struggle for the democratic soul; views of
democratic presidential aspirants. S. Alsop.
Newsweek 77:120 Je 7 '71

MILITARY assistance, Chinese
Russia and red China, the ways they serve
their clients; backing of India and Pakistan. U S News 71:14 D 20 '71

MILITARY assistance, French
French arms invasion. J. Ross-Skinner. il
Duns 98:48-50+ Ag '71

MILITARY assistance, Russian
Flybys and superspies; Middle East power
balance. Time 98:25 Jl 26 '71
Moscow's arms aid to Egypt; 4.5 billions since
1967. il U S News 70:29 Ap 12 '71
Russia and red China, the ways they serve
their clients; backing of India and Pakistan. U S News 71:14 D 20 '71
Soviet Viet Nam; activities in the Sudan.
il Time 97:30+ Mr 1 '71

Egypt
Latest gifts from Russia; MIG-21s to Egypt.
Time 97:40 Ap 26 '71
On the spot. il Newsweek 78:59 O 25 '71
Sadat: we are now back to square one; inter-
view, ed. by A. de Borchgrave. A. Sadat.
il pors Newsweek 78:43-4+ D 13 '71
Soviets spur arms flow to Egypt; with edi-
torial comment. E. H. Kolcum. il Avia-
tion W 94:9, 14-16 Ap 19 '71
Strategic stakes. R. Hotz. Aviation W 94:9
Ap 26 '71
World's hottest plane? advanced jet fighters
to Egypt. il Newsweek 77:39 Ap 26 '71

MILITARY astronautics. See Space flight—Mil-
itary use
MILITARY atrocities. See War crimes
MILITARY avionics. See Airplanes, Military—
Electronic equipment
MILITARY barracks. See Barracks
MILITARY bases
Keys to the Pacific: Micronesia. H. W. Bald-
win. Read Digest 99:164-5 D '71
2,000 U.S. bases overseas: another target in
Congress; excerpts from address, May 18,
1971. J. W. Fulbright. il por U S News 70:
35 Je 21 '71
See also
Air bases
Okinawa

MILITARY budget. See United States—Armed forces—Appropriations and expenditures
MILITARY chaplains. See Chaplains. Military
MILITARY chaplains association. See Chaplains. Military
MILITARY-civilian relations. See United States—Armed forces—Relations with civilians
MILITARY communications satellites. See Communications satellites—Military use
MILITARY discipline. See Discipline, Military
MILITARY doctors. See Physicians
MILITARY draft. See Military service, Compulsory

MILITARY education
    See also
Military schools

United States
    See also
United States military academy, West Point
MILITARY electronics. See Electronics—Military use
MILITARY exchanges. See United States Armed forces—Post exchanges
MILITARY expenditures. See Armed forces—Appropriations and expenditures; United States—Armed forces—Appropriations and expenditures

MILITARY history
    See also subhead History, Military under names of countries, e.g. United States—History, Military

MILITARY-industrial complex
After the military-industrial complex? adaptation of address, 1969. S. Melman. Bul Atom Sci 27:7-9 Mr '71
Military establishment, by A. Yarmolinsky. Review
    Bul Atom Sci 27:38 Je '71. H. Scoville, jr
    Bsns W p6 F 6 '71. J. E. Pluenneke
Military-industrial complexities. C. Wolf, jr. Bul Atom Sci 27:19-22 F '71; Discussion. 27:2-3 Je '71
Toward a military welfare state? N. Cousins. Sat R 54:26-7 Mr 27 '71
War profiteers. by R. F. Kaufman. Review Nation 213:535-6 N 22 '71. R. Sherrill

MILITARY intelligence
    See also
Spies

MILITARY law
Military justice. E. J. Gannon. bibliog f Cur Hist 61:75-81+ Ag '71
    See also
Courts martial and courts of inquiry
Discipline, Military
Military service, Compulsory

MILITARY life
Military goes mod. Read Digest 98:100-4 Mr '71
Willie and Joe visit the new U.S. army; Fort Carson, Colo. il Life 70:207 F 5 '71

MILITARY manpower. See United States—Armed forces

MILITARY markets
    See also
United States—Armed forces—Post exchanges

MILITARY morale. See United States—Armed forces—Morale; United States—Army—Morale

MILITARY museums
    See also
Aeronautic museums

MILITARY music
Beethoven's septet, Opus 20; an arrangement for military band. M. Schwager. bibliog f il Mus Q 56:727-41 O '70

MILITARY officers, Retired. See Retired military personnel

MILITARY policy
    See also
United States—Military policy

MILITARY post schools, American
America's most far-flung school system; United States dependents schools, European area. A. D. Olson. il Am Ed 7:12-15 Ag '71; Same abr. Ed Digest 37:32-4 D '71

MILITARY posts
Race rumblings at McClellan. Time 98:24 N 29 '71
Willie and Joe visit the new U.S. army; Fort Carson, Colo. il Life 70:20-7 F 5 '71

Libraries
    See United States—Army—Libraries
MILITARY psychiatry. See Psychiatry, Military
MILITARY purchasing. See Purchasing, Military
MILITARY radar. See Radar—Military use

MILITARY reconnaissance
    See also
Aerial reconnaissance
MILITARY recreation. See United States—Armed forces—Recreation

MILITARY research
Arms race: scientists question threat from Soviet military R&D. R. J. Bazell. il Science 173:707-9 Ag 20 '71
    See also
Aeronautic research
Colleges and universities—Research

Federal aid
Defense operation procurement. RDT&E and construction; tables. Aviation W 94:14-15 F 1 '71
Mission-oriented R&D. R. W. Nichols. bibliog Science 172:29-37 Ap 2 '71

Russia
Soviets sustain military research growth. D. C. Winston. Aviation W 94:23 Ap 12 '71
MILITARY schools
No more parades; military academies battling for survival. il Time 98:35 S 6 '71
    See also
Sandhurst, Royal military college
United States military academy, West Point
MILITARY secrets. See Defense information, Classified

MILITARY service, Compulsory
As draft is renewed; interview. C. Tarr. il por U S News 71:30-2 O 4 '71
Big drop coming in draft calls. il U S News 71:34 D 27 '71
Caught in the draft; Senate vote. Newsweek 77:27 Je 7 '71
Crucial days for the draft, and not only in Congress. U S News 71:51 Jl 12 '71
Draft continues. Nation 213:290 O 4 '71
Draft extended. Sr Schol 98:15-16 My 3 '71
Draft extended: two more years of greetings. Sr Schol 99:14 O 25 '71
Draft gap; extension bill. Newsweek 78:35 Jl 12 '71
Draft goes on. Commonweal 95-76 O 22 '71
Draft wheels keep turning. il U S News 71:31 Jl 26 '71
Draftmanship; Senate votes. Newsweek 78:40+ S 27 '71
Draft's end: sooner than expected? il U S News 72:54 Ja 10 '72
Dumping the draft; USCC testimony. Commonweal 94:52 Mr 26 '71
Greetings' man; with interview, ed. by M. Byers. il pors Life 70:57-8 Je 11 '71
How Congress should change the draft; interview. C. W. Tarr. il pors U S News 70:28-32 F 1 '71
In the draft. New Repub 165:9-10 O 9 '71
Latest word for draft-age youths. il U S News 71:82 S 27 '71
More of the same: Draft extension bill. Nat R 23:1098 O 8 '71
National service: worse than the draft; report on idea of Universal national service. J. Castelli. Chr Cent 88:315-16 Mr 10 '71
New direction for the draft? Sr Schol 98:11 Mr 15 '71
New rules for draft-age youths. il U S News 71:54 N 15 '71
Once more. Greetings. il Time 98:17 O 4 '71
Parents' guide to the new draft. D. Suttler. il Ladies Home J 88:56+ D '71
Question of legitimacy; compromise draft bill. Newsweek 78:23 Ag 9 '71
Randomization and social affairs: the 1970 draft lottery. S. E. Fienberg. bibliog il Science 171:255-61 Ja 22 '71; Reply with rejoinder. C. J. Scheirer. 172:630+ My 14 '71
Randomization and the draft lottery; with tables. J. R. Rosenblatt and J. J. Filliben. bibliog Science 171:306-8 Ja 22 '71
Replacing the draft. J. B. Bingham. New Repub 164:17-21 Ja 16 '71; Reply with rejoinder. B. A. Sheridan. 164:33-4 F 13 '71
Setting a date; Senate debate draft extension bill. il Newsweek 78:25 Jl 5 '71
Somebody has to give; stalemated bill to extend the draft. Newsweek 78:21 Jl 19 '71
Uncle Sam still wants you, kid. J. R. Moskin. Look 35:21-2 F 23 '71
Vietnam roulette; the draft lottery. P. J. Ognibene. Commonweal 94:236-8 My 14 '71
Winds of change in the draft; interview. C. W. Tarr. il pors Nations Bsns 59:48-50+ F '71
With draft call-ups halted; the outlook. il U S News 71:72-3 Ag 16 '71
Without draft, can national guard survive? with interview. il U S News 71:61-3 N 8 '71
    See also
Conscientious objectors

MILITARY service, Compulsory—*Continued*

Deferments and exemptions

Congress, the draft and seminarians. America 124:330 Ap 3 '71

Millions who avoided the draft. il U S News 70:33 Mr 1 '71

Pearly gates amendment and congressional images of church and ministry; question of draft exemption for ministerial students. P. Deats, jr. Chr Cent 88:486-7 Ap 21 '71

Time to draft the clergy. P. J. Riga. America 125:456-7 N 27 '71

Draft resisters

Agony and amnesty. H. Barnette. il Chr Cent 88:1133-4 S 29 '71

America's sad young exiles; draft evaders and deserters in Canada. K. Fleming. il Newsweek 77:28-30 F 15 '71

Amnesty. Commonweal 95:339-40 Ja 14 '72

Amnesty when? Vietnam war resisters and deserters. R. Gardner. New Repub 165:12-13 D 25 '71

Canadian Christians primed for ministry to U.S. draft refugees. C. de Mestral. Chr Cent 88:73 Ja 20 '71

Draft resister talks about his future. D. Miller. McCalls 98:42 F '71

If draft dodgers come home. il U S News 71:34 D 6 '71

If this be treason, by F. Stevens. Review Nation 212:662-3 My 24 '71. W. O'Rourke

Lonely crusade of Guy Gillette. G. James. il por McCalls 98:62-3+ Ag '71

Men who cannot come home. il Time 99:15 Ja 10 '72

New exiles, by R. N. Williams. Review Nation 212:762-3 Je 14 '71. K. Widmer

Pros and cons of granting amnesty. il Time 99:16-17 Ja 10 '72

Reporter without a country; T. G. Jolley. por Sr Schol 99:16-17 Ja 10 '72

Vietnam amnesty; a proposal to the President. J. Reston, jr. New Repub 165:21-2 O 9 '71

MILITARY service, Voluntary

Climate's all wrong. W. W. Yale. Nat R 23:651-2+ Je 15 '71

Do we need an army? S. Alsop. Newsweek 77:112 Mr 29 '71

Dodge to end the draft. P. J. Ognibene. il Nation 212:467-8 Ap 12 '71

How two allies fare with volunteers: Britain and Canada. il U S News 70:35 Mr 1 '71

If U.S. tries an all-volunteer army; survey of military experts. il U S News 70:32-4 Mr 1 '71

Showdown on the volunteer army. T. H. Clancy. America 124:647-8 Je 26 '71

This month's feature: Congress & an all-volunteer armed force. Cong Digest 50:130-60 My '71

Voluntary service; letter to editor. D. J. Eberly. Chr Cent 88:757 Je 16 '71

MILITARY strategy. See Strategy

MILITARY supplies
See also
United States—Armed forces—Equipment and supplies

MILITARY tanks. See Tanks, Military

MILITARY training

On the army and the age. R. Martin. Nat R 23:590 Je 1 '71

Onward Christian soliders: dehumanization and the military chaplain. R. E. Klitgaard; discussion. Chr Cent 87:1569; 88:467-8, 956-7 D 30 '70, Ap 14, Ag 11 '71

Ounce of prevention: army course on laws of land warfare. il Newsweek 77:30+ Ap 19 '71

What army is doing to prevent another My Lai. il U S News 70:24-5 Ap 12 '71
See also
Bayonet practice
Military schools
United States—Reserve officers training corps

MILITARY transport airplanes. See Airplanes, Military transport

MILITARY trials. See Courts martial and courts of inquiry

MILITARY uniforms. See Uniforms, Military

MILK

One drink everyone needs. D. Calloway. McCalls 98:18 Ag '71

Who needs yogurt? And other facts about milk. D. Calloway. McCalls 98:30 S '71
See also
Colostrum
Cookery—Milk

Bacteriology

That count is not a farce; leucocyte count. Farm J 95:D12 Je '71

Prices

Milking the consumer. M. Allen and J. Schnittker. New Repub 165:17-18 Jl 17 '71

Production

He smashed the all-time record. D. Braun. il Farm J 95:D4 Je '71

MILK, Acidophilus
See also
Yogurt

MILK, Goats

Notes by a new goat-keeper. N. W. Bubel. il por Org Gard & Farm 18:104-11 Mr '71

MILK, Human

Milk bank thrives; Mothers' milk bank of San Francisco. B. Falconer. il McCalls 99:50 O '71
See also
Breast feeding

MILK, Synthetic. See Milk substitutes

MILK industry
See also
Borden, inc.

MILK juggers. See Milk plants

MILK plants

Ideas from Pennsylvania milk juggers; with editorial comment. il Suc Farm 69:D1-3 S '71

MILK processing plants. See Milk plants

MILK production. See Milk—Production

MILK substitutes

Now it's chemical milk. Sci Digest 71:22-3 Ja '72

MILKING machines

Milker with an automatic shift. D. Braun. il Farm J 95:36 Ja '71

MILKING parlors

Equipment

These gates bring in the cows. il Farm J 95:23 Mr '71

MILKY way

New look at the galaxy. D. E. Thomsen. il Sci N 100:378-9 D 4 '71

MILL, Harriet (Hardy) Taylor

Justice and Harriet Taylor. V. Held. Nation 213:405-6 O 25 '71 •

MILL, John Stuart

Justice and Harriet Taylor. V. Held. Nation 213:405-6 O 25 '71 •

MILL factors corporation. See Factors

MILLAR, Kenneth. See Macdonald, R. pseud.

MILLAR, Ronald

Abelard and Heloise; dramatization of Peter Abelard, by H. Waddell. Criticism
America 124:640-1 My 22 '71 •
Cath World 213:174-7 Jl '71 •
New Yorker 47:93 Mr 20 '71 •
Newsweek il 77:115 Mr 22 '71 •
Time il 97:41 Mr 22 '71 •

MILLAU, Christian. See Gault, H. jt. auth.

MILLENSON, Michael

In my opinion. por Seventeen 30:160 D '71

MILLER, Alexander B.

How to call your convertibles. Harvard Bsns R 49:66-70 My '71

MILLER, Alfred Jacob

New painting by Alfred Jacob Miller. W. H. Hunter. il Antiques 101:221-5 Ja '72 •

MILLER, Arthur

Enemy of the people; adaptation of play by H. Ibsen. Criticism
Nation 212:411-13 Mr 29 '71 •
New Yorker 47:93 Mr 20 '71 •
Newsweek 77:114 Mr 22 '71 •
Time il 97:41 Mr 22 '71 •

MILLER, Arthur Selwyn

Nixon's N.E.P. & the Constitution. il Nation 213:293-6 O 4 '71

MILLER, Bart

Black Bart and the mechanical marlin. R. W. Johnston. il por Sports Illus 35:34-8 Ag 16 '71 •

MILLER, Calvin

Christ and the existential imagination. Chr Today 16:12+ O 22 '71

Ministering in a death-oriented culture. Chr Today 16:10-12 N 19 '71

St Paul and the liberated woman. Chr Today 15:13-14 Ag 6 '71

MILLER, Catherine Lanham

Hospital holiday; excerpt from How to say yes to life. il Good H 173:68-9+ D '71

MILLER, Conrad

Cast-iron breeze. il Motor B & S 127:78-9+ Je '71

Marine engines. il Motor B & S 128:74+ Jl '71

Your boat's electric motors. il Motor B & S 127:80-2+ F '71

MILLER, David
Draft resister talks about his future. McCalls 98:42 F '71
MILLER, David A. See Helman, S. I. jt. auth.
MILLER, David Humphreys
Echoes of the Little Bighorn. il pors Am Heritage 22:28-39 Je; 108 O '71
MILLER, Edwin
Close-up (cont of) Spotlight! See issues of Seventeen, April 1971-
MILLER, Eugene
Investing is a family decision. il PTA Mag 65:22-4 F '71
MILLER, F. W.
Under the hood. bibliog il por Chem 44:12-14 Je '71
MILLER, Fern Christian
Enchanting fragrant annuals. il Horticulture 49:36-7+ Ap '71
MILLER, Floyd
Ned's legacy. il Read Digest 98:42-6 Ja '71
MILLER, Francis Pickens
Launcher of 50 ships. A. Howard. New Repub 165:24+ O 30 '71
MILLER, Gary E.
Superior cruising. il Motor B & S 127:62-5+ My '71
MILLER, Gene, and Mackie, Barbara
83 hours till dawn; excerpts. il pors Ladies Home J 88:197-204 My; 70-1+ Je '71; Same abr. Read Digest 99:235-41+ D '71
MILLER, George William
Textron goes its own way. il Forbes 108:58 S 15 '71 *
MILLER, Hannah
Feature films for children. bibliog il por Wilson Lib Bul 45:560-71 F '71
Why children's films are not rated R. il Wilson Lib Bul 46:183-4 O '71
MILLER, Harold C. and Cudkowicz, Gustavo
Density gradient separation of marrow cells restricted for antibody class. bibliog il Science 171:913-15 Mr 5 '71
Density gradient separation of marrow precursor cells restricted for antibody specificity. bibliog il Science 173:156-8 Jl 9 '71
MILLER, Harry G.
American history: innovating or enervating? il Clear House 45:483-7 Ap '71
MILLER, Helen Louise
Broken broomstick; drama. Plays 31:67-71 O '71
Cupid on the loose; drama; reprint from February 1955 issue. Plays 30:31-8 F '71
Rabbit's foot; drama. Plays 30:9-18 Ap '71
What makes it tick? drama; reprint from November 1952 issue. Plays 31:25-36 N '71
MILLER, Henry
Picasso at 90. il pors Life 71:52-4 O 29 '71

about

Henry Miller: rebel-clown at eighty. B. De-Mott. il pors Sat R 54:29-32 D 11 '71 *
MILLER, J. Irwin
Changing priorities: hard choices, new price tags. il Sat R 54:36-7+ Ja 23 '71

about

Miller of Cummins engine. il por Forbes 107:50-1 My 15 '71 *
MILLER, J. Jefferson, 2d
English yellow-glazed earthenware from the Eleanor and Jack L. Leon collection. il Antiques 100:93-8, 236-40 Jl-Ag '71
MILLER, Jack
Brewer goes on the austerity wagon. il por Bsns W p37-8 N 6 '71 *
MILLER, Jack Richard
Ethical considerations in public relations; address. April 2, 1971. Vital Speeches 37:421-4 My 1 '71
MILLER, Jacqueline D.
My brother's keeper, my brother's friend. il por Redbook 137:42+ Je '71
MILLER, James E. Jr
NCTE and politics. Engl J 60:508-9 Ap '71
NCTE presidential address: imagination and the health of everyman; November 1970. Engl J 60:189-98 F '71
MILLER, James M. and Zahniser, D. V.
Antacid analysis. bibliog il pors Chem 44:28 Jl '71
MILLER, James Nathan
Bad scene at Mike horse mine. Read Digest 98:75-9 F '71
Battle tactics for conservationists. Read Digest 98:175-80 Ja '71
Crisis of our national forests. il Read Digest 99:91-6 D '71
Florida fires the pork-chop gang. Read Digest 99:109-13 Ag '71
Law that could clean up our rivers. Read Digest 98:31-2+ My '71

Needed: a bill of rights for our rivers. Read Digest 99:161-2+ Jl '71
Water and wilderness: the melody of Minnesota. il Read Digest 99:92-7 Ag '71
What happens after busing starts. Read Digest 99:86-90 O '71
MILLER, James R.
Needed: more help for accident victims. Read Digest 98:83-7 Ja '71
MILLER, Jason
Veil; Call; Tenement sky; Web; Gate; poems. Poetry 117:235-9 Ja '71
MILLER, John C.
Star-studded show. il Motor B & S 128:54-5 bibliog(p58) Jl '71
MILLER, John G. See Friedman, L. jt. auth.
MILLER, Joseph A. See Pearson, A. D. jt. auth.
MILLER, Judith
Getting the goods on the government. New Repub 165:13-15 D 11 '71
MILLER, Mrs Lawrence K.
Cottages and castles in English ceramics. il Antiques 99:122-6 Ja '71 *
MILLER, Louis J.
Contemporary scene in creative expression. il Sch Arts 70:16-17 Ap '71
Creating a construction or assemblage. il Sch Arts 71:36-7 O '71
Drawing on tracing cloth. il Design 72:22-3 Spr '71
Mask. il Design 72:18-19 mid-Wint '71
Projects from plaster. il Design 72:34-5 mid-Sum '71
Pyrography and plywood. il Design 73:27 Fall '71
Shell painting. il Design 72:40 Spr '71
MILLER, Marraine
Small-seeded sunflowers for sunshine on the wing. il Org Gard & Farm 18:72-6 Ap '71
MILLER, Mary Britton. See Bolton, I. pseud.
MILLER, Merle
Authors & editors; interview, ed. by B. A. Bannon. por Pub W 200:17-18 O 4 '71
What it means to be a homosexual. il pors N Y Times Mag p9-11+ Ja 17; 67+ O 10 '71
MILLER, Mike
Alaska's Tongass suit: the exercise at Juneau. il Am For 77:28-31+ Mr '71
Fight for the trees in the Tongass. il Am For 77:16-19 Jl '71
Triple play. il Travel 136:74-5 Ag '71
MILLER, Mitzi Perry-. See Perry-Miller, M.
MILLER, Norman C.
Getting rid of the seniority system. Cur 126:26-8 F '71
MILLER, O. J. and others
Human thymidine kinase gene locus: assignment to chromosome 17 in a hybrid of man and mouse cells. bibliog il Science 173:244-5 Jl 16 '71
MILLER, Paul
Let's all get together. por Forbes 107:42 Je 15 '71 *
MILLER, Philip L.
Archive explosion. Opera N 35:28-9 Ja 23 '71
London's Anna Bolena. il Am Rec G 37:276-9 Ja '71
MILLER, Raymond J. and Koeppe, D. E.
Southern corn leaf blight: susceptible and resistant mitochondria. bibliog il Science 173:67-9 Jl 2 '71
MILLER, Robert L.
Wild bears in the Catskills. il Cons 26:3-4 D '71
MILLER, Ronald
Ag class in the sky. Ed Digest 36:32-3 Ap '71
MILLER, S. E.
Optical communications research progress. bibliog il Science 170:685-95; 174:1045 N 13 '70, D 3 '71
MILLER, S. M. and others
New American imperialism? Cur 125:42-70 Ja '71
MILLER, Steven I.
Cultural evaluation of contemporary educational innovations. bibliog Sch & Soc 99:507-8+ D '71
MILLER, Stuart
Millerite. J. Seelye. New Repub 165:37-8 O 16 '71 *
MILLER, Timothy
Drug bust in Kansas. Chr Cent 88:332-3 Mr 17 '71
MILLER, W. H. and others
Cyclic adenosine monophosphate: function in photoreceptors. bibliog il Science 174:295-7 O 15 '71
MILLER, William C.
Light touch. il Todays Ed 60:21 Ja '71

MILLER, Wilma H. and Windhauser, Eileen
Reading disability, tendency toward delinquency? bibliog Clear House 46:183-7 N '71

MILLETT, Kate
Day in the life of Kate Millett; interview, ed. by S. Edmiston. por Mlle 72:138-9+ F '71

about

Prisoner of sex. N. Mailer. bibliog f il por(p4) Harper 242:45-6+ Mr '71 *
Women's lib: Mailer v. Millett. il pors Time 97:71 F 22 '71 *

MILLEY, John Calvin
Independence National Historical Park. il Antiques 100:99-103 Jl '71

MILLIAMMETERS. See Ammeters

MILLIGAN, Jane
Bonnet that's wonderful good. il Holiday 49:18 Ap '71
Jacket fit for a tiger. Holiday 49:30 Jl '71

MILLIKEN, William E.
Why I don't smoke pot. Read Digest 99:147-8 O '71

MILLINERY
See also
Hats

MILLIONAIRESS; story. See Hochman, S.

MILLS, Charles Wright
Taking it big: a memoir of C. Wright Mills. D. Wakefield. il Atlan 228:65-71 S '71 *

MILLS, Ernest M.
Travel guidelines. il Consumer Bul 54:38-40 Jl '71

MILLS, G. Alex
Ubiquitous hydrocarbons. bibliog il por Chem 44:8-13 F; 12-17 Mr '71

MILLS, James
I have nothing to do with justice. il pors Life 70:56-8+ Mr 12 '71
Waiting for a riot. il Life 71:30-5 O 1 '71

MILLS, James R.
Locking up the Tenney files. Nation 213:10-11 Jl 5 '71

MILLS, Joan
It's spring? il Read Digest 98:97-9 Mr '71

MILLS, Ralph J. Jr
Pig, and several poets. Poetry 117:331-8 F '71

MILLS, Wilbur Daigh
Mills: cut taxes, curb wages, prices; excerpts from address, July 16, 1971. por U S News 71:73 Jl 26 '71
Tax cuts, social security, welfare reform; interview. il pors U S News 70:42-4+ Mr 15 '71
What chance has an Arkansas traveler? interview. por Nations Bsns 59:70-1 N '71
—and others
Outlook for the President's tax plans; interviews. pors U S News 71:19-20 S 6 '71

about

Candidate Mills ballyhoos his expertise. il por Bsns W p60+ S 11 '71 *
Double whammy. por Forbes 108:26 Jl 1 '71 *
Eyeball to eyeball, Congress blinked. il Time 98:11-12 D 13 '71 *
Hard sell by the White House. il por Newsweek 77:20 F 8 '71 *
Mills decides to X-ray health care. por Bsns W p25 O 16 '71 *
Mills has the ways and means. por Newsweek 77:26-7 F 15 '71 *
Most powerful man in Congress. I. Ross. por Read Digest 98:101-5 Ja '71 *
Nixon and Mills bill. il por Time 98:22 Jl F '71 *
Nixon v. Mills: showdown on trade policy. por Time 97:70-1 Mr 22 '71 *
Reports & comment: Washington. M. Seeger. Atlan 228:6+ Ag '71 *
Republic of Wilbur Mills. H. Sidey. por Life 70:4 F 19 '71 *
Through the Mills. il por Newsweek 77:28-9 Je 14 '71 *
Ways & means tackles three hot issues. il por Bsns W p72-5 My 8 '71 *
Wilbur Mills: aiming for the White House? por U S News 70:39 Je 7 '71 *
Wilbur Mills' noncandidacy. P. R. Wieck. New Repub 165:17-19 Jl 24 '71 *
Wooing of Wilbur Mills. M. Frady. il pors Life 71:52-52B+ Jl 16 '71 *

MILLS Hyatt house. See Charleston, S.C.—Hotels, restaurants, etc.

MILLSAP, Lucille
Ubiquitous book report. Ed Digest 36:52-4 F '71

MILNE, David B. See Schwarz, K. jt. auth.

MILNE, Robert Scott
Great day in Moosonee. il Seventeen 29:130 Jl '70

MILNER, Doris
Women in the wilderness; supplementary essay. por Liv Wildn 34:49-50 Aut '70

MILNER, Joe W.
Why the East chose revolution. Nat R 23: 530-1 My 18 '71

MILNES, Sherrill
Role in hand. por Opera N 36:12-14 O '71

about

Big baritone. H. Saal. por Newsweek 77:67-8 Mr 1 '71 *

MILO
Harvest from a new commodity contract. il Bsns W p70+ S 18 '71

Marketing

Selling tips: wheat, milo. M. S. Turner. il Suc Farm 69:34 Je '71

MILO silage. See Silage

MILPITAS, Calif.

Parks and playgrounds

Adventure playgrounds; Milpitas thinks they can work in America. R. F. McGuire. il Parks & Rec 6:30-2 N '71

MILSTEIN, Seymour
Inside the GAF battle. N. A. Martin. il pors Duns 97:45-7 Ap '71 *
Personnel job as personal affront. Bsns W p40 Mr 13 '71 *

MILTON, John P.
Nameless valleys, shining mountains; excerpts. il Liv Wildn 34:10-17 Wint '70

MILTON, Nerissa Long
Questions from a six-year old; poem. Negro Hist Bul 34:20 Ja '71
She sang a tribute to Charlotte Wesley Holloman; poem. Negro Hist Bul 34:20 Ja '71

MILWAUKEE

Description

There's much a-brewin' in bubbly Milwaukee. Summer fun! B. Hibbard. il Travel 135:54-7 My '71

Education

Can slum children learn? University of Wisconsin infant education center project. S. P. Strickland. il Am Ed 7:3-7 Jl '71
Second vocabulary for Johnny. M. P. Pfeil. il Am Ed 7:16-20 My '71

Mitchell park horticultural conservatory

Mitchell park conservatory. J. MacQuarrie. il Horticulture 49:34-5+ S '71

Social conditions

Is Women's lib a dirty word in Milwaukee? J. Howard. il Life 71:46-51 Ag 27 '71

MILWAUKEE art center
In the Midwest. R. Berenson. Nat R 23:94-5 Ja 26 '71

MILWAUKEE art institute. See Milwaukee art center

MILWAUKEE Bucks (basketball team) See Basketball teams

MIME
Meeting of the mimes, the Cubiculo, NYC. R. Philp. Dance Mag 45:95 O '71
See also
Pantomime

MIMEOGRAPH
Craft of mimeography; book publishing. C. Moore. il por Craft Horiz 31:30-3 F '71

MIMS, Forrest M. 3d
Solid-state laser for the experimenter. il Pop Electr 35:46-9+ O '71
Understanding solid-state lasers. il Pop Electr 35:35-7+ O '71

MINARCIN, Pat
What riot? il Newsweek 78:82 N 1 '71 *

MIND. See Intellect

MIND, Peace of. See Peace of mind

MIND-altering drugs. See Hallucinogenic drugs

MIND and body
Freedom of the mind and other essays, by S. Hampshire. Review
New Repub 165:24-5+ O 23 '71 P Caws
Skin shows emotional problems. A. J. Snider. il Sci Digest 69:59-60 Ap '71
See also
Consciousness
Faith cure
Hypnotism
Meditation
Mental hygiene
New Thought
Psychology, Physiological
Self

MINDANAO

Race question

See Philippines—Race question

MINDESS, Harvey
Sense in humor; excerpt from Laughter and liberation. Sat R 54:10-12 Ag 21 '71

MINDSZENTY, Jozsef, cardinal
Cardinal Mindszenty departs U.S. embassy at Budapest. Dept State Bul 65:405 O 18 '71 *
Cardinal Mindszenty gains freedom after 15 years. il pors Sr Schol 99:15-16 O 25 '71 *
Chapter is closed. il por Newsweek 78:36 O 11 '71 *
End of a private cold war. Time 98:63 O 11 '71 *
Heaviest cross. Chr Cent 88:1187 O 13 '71 *
Mindszenty as symbol. America 125:387 N 13 '71 *
Mindszenty moves to Vienna. Chr Cent 88:1320 N 10 '71 *
Mindszenty settlement. Commonweal 95:51-2 O 15 '71 *
Of many things. D. R. Campion. America 125:246 O 9 '71 *
Styles in martyrdom. J. T. Elson. il Time 98:62 O 11 '71 *

MINE accidents and explosions
See also
Coal mines and mining—Accidents and explosions
Coal mines and mining—Safety devices and measures

MINER, Dallas. See Nisbet, I. C. T. jt. auth.

MINER, Marilyn
Finky cows I have known. il por Farm J 95:D7-8 D '71

MINERAL fertilizers. See Fertilizers and manures

MINERAL King recreation area (proposed) See Recreation areas—California

MINERAL waters
See also
Water, Bottled

MINERAL WELLS, Tex.
Return of a native. L. Robinson. il pors Ebony 26:120-5 Ag '71

MINERALOGY
See also
Crystallography
Halos (mineralogy)
Meteorites
Soils—Mineral content

MINERALS in diet
See also
Iron in diet

MINERALS in sea water. See Sea water
MINERALS in soils. See Soils—Mineral content
MINERALS in the body
See also
Copper in the body
Trace elements

MINERS
See also
Coal miners
United mine workers of America

MINERVA system
MINERVA: a participatory technology system. E. Leonard and others. il Bul Atom Sci 27:4-12 N '71

MINES and mineral resources
See also
Coal mines and mining
Mercury mines and mining
Oil shales
Raw materials
Salt

Australia
Australia: opals are a girl's best friend; black opals. N. Morgan. il Sat R 54:50-1+ O 23 '71

Canada
See also
Coal mines and mining—Canada

Columbia
See also
Emerald mines and mining

Mexico
See also
Copper mines and mining—Mexico

United States
Loci of conflict and compromise; preservation and consumption; address, December 5, 1970. R. A. Brown. Vital Speeches 37:247-9 F 1 '71
Minerals; EQ index. il Nat Wildlife 9:36 O '71
See also
Coal mines and mining—United States
Gold mines and mining—United States
Silver mines and mining—United States

Venezuela
See also
Diamond mines and mining

MINETA, Norman Y.
San Jose's new major. Nation 212:549 My 3 '71 *

MINGUS, Charles
Agonies of a mongrel. J. Yardley. New Repub 165:29 Jl 3 '71 *
Man with a bass. G. Wolff. por Newsweek 77:110 My 17 '71 *
Mingus on Mingus. B. Korall. Sat R 54:42 Jl 31 '71 *
Reporter at large. W. Balliett. New Yorker 47:42-4+ My 29 '71 *

MINGUS dancers; ballets. See Ballets— Criticisms

MINH, Duong-van-. See Duong-van-Minh
MINH, Ho-chi-. See Ho-chi-Minh
MINIATURE cameras. See Cameras
MINIATURE churches. See Church models
MINIATURE cities. See Models of cities, towns, etc.
MINIATURE computers. See Computers— Miniaturization
MINIATURE electronic calculators. See Calculating machines, Electronic
MINIATURE electronic equipment
See also
Computers—Miniaturization
MINIATURE gardens. See Gardens, Miniature
MINIATURE golf. See Golf, Miniature
MINIATURE objects
European miniatures. S. Parvin. il Hobbies 76:142+ Ja '72
Miniaturia. S. A. Parvin. See issues of Hobbies
Quilting party. S. Parvin. il Hobbies 76:144+ O '71
Wee world in pictures. S. Parvin. il por Hobbies 76:146-7 Ag '71
See also
Doll houses
Models of cities, towns, etc.
MINIATURE trees. See Trees, Dwarf
MINIBIKES. See Bicycles; Motorcycles
MINIBUS lines. See Motor bus lines
MINICARS. See Automobiles, Compact
MINICARS, inc.
Inside the Minicar think tank. il Motor T 23:78+ Jl '71
MINICHIELLO airplane hijacking trial. See Trials—Italy
MINICOMPUTERS. See Computers—Miniaturization
MINIMAL brain dysfunction
Hyperactivity and learning problems; implications for teachers. B. K. Keogh. Ed Digest 37:45-7 D '71
Psychologist and minimal brain dysfunction: ten steps to maximum incompetence. L. J. Aronson. Ment Hy 55:523-5 O '71

MINIMUM wage
United States
High noon for Pucinski. Nat R 23:577-8 Je 1 '71
Making more jobs for young Americans. il Nations Bsns 59:88-90 S '71
Two-tier system for minimum wages. Bsns W p46 My 15 '71
When minimum wage means no wage at all. il Bsns W p82+ My 15 '71

MINING engineering
See also
Strip mining

MINING industry and finance
Australia
Mining crash felt round the world; collapse of Mineral securities, ltd. il Bsns W p23-4 F 20 '71
Mexico
See also
Copper mines and mining—Mexico
United States
See also
Newmont mining corporation

MINING towns
See also
Tonopah, Nev.

MINK, Patsy (Takemoto)
Excerpt from remarks, February 10, 1971. Cong Digest 50:119+ Ap '71

MINKS
Susceptibility of mink to sheep scrapie. R. P. Hanson and others. bibliog il Science 172:859-61 My 21 '71

MINNEAPOLIS
City planning
Walk in the sky. Newsweek 77:73-4 F 15 '71

MINNEAPOLIS—*Continued*
Description
Minneapolis/St Paul: living and working in the Twin Cities. M. Cunningham. Mlle 73:152+ S '71
Galleries and museums
See also
Minneapolis institute of arts
Libraries
See also
Minneapolis public library
Music
See also
Center opera company, Minneapolis
Politics and government
Life under Stenvig. C. Roberts. il por Newsweek 77:37-8 Je 14 '71
Streets
Color-coded street name signs. il Am City 86: 114 Mr '71
Theater
Guthrie theater reborn; productions of Cyrano de Bergerac; The taming of the shrew; The diary of a scoundrel. H. Hewes. il por Sat R 54:52-3 D 25 '71
Walker art center
See Walker art center
MINNEAPOLIS center opera company. See Center opera company, Minneapolis
MINNEAPOLIS institute of arts
In the Midwest. R. Berenson. Nat R 23:94-5 Ja 26 '71
MINNEAPOLIS public library
Moderation in Minneapolis. E. J. Gaines. il pors Library J 96:1681-3 My 15 '71
More important things? censorship; letter to the editor. G. Dunbar. Library J 96:2241 Jl '71
Branches
Minneapolis: a teepee for Nokomis. il Library J 96:3984 D 1 '71
MINNERS, Howard A. See MacLeod, C. jt. auth.
MINNESOTA
See also
Camps—Minnesota
Fishing—Minnesota
Geology—Minnesota
Hunting—Minnesota
Wilderness areas—Minnesota
Antiquities
See also
Kensington rune stone
Description and travel
Water and wilderness: the melody of Minnesota. J. N. Miller. il Read Digest 99: 92-7 Ag '71
MINNESOTA dance theatre. See Dance companies
MINNESOTA education association
Establishing a standards board. R. Dittes. Todays Ed 60:23 D '71
MINNESOTA mining and manufacturing company
Heltzer of 3M. il por Forbes 107:62 My 15 '71
MINNESOTA North Stars (hockey team) See Hockey teams
MINNESOTA. University, Minneapolis
Battle of the yield tables. il Forbes 107:62 Mr 15 '71
MINNESOTA Vikings (football club) See Football clubs
MINNEY, R. J.
George Bernard Shaw's vegetarian recipes. il por Harp Baz 104:151-3 O '71
MINNOWS
Minnows a different way. J. J. Hudock. il Field & S 76:10+ D '71
MINOCIN. See Tetracyclines
MINOFF, Lee
Yellow submarine passenger list; letter. N Y Times Mag p3 Jl 4 '71
MINOR. Audax, pseud.
Race track. See issues of New Yorker
MINOR, Pearl
Poem for Christmas. Chr Cent 88:1491 D 22 '71
MINOR leagues. See Baseball clubs
MINORITIES
Age of touchiness; Time essay. M. Maddocks. il Time 97:21 My 10 '71
Ethnic minority groups: source of regional instability; Cambodian minorities. P. A. Poole. il Focus 21:9-12 F '71

Fellowships for ethnic studies; new program of Ford foundation. Sch & Soc 99:208+ Ap '71
Growing up ethnic means learning who you are. B. Mikulski. Redbook 137:86+ O '71
Interracial books: background of a challenge; activities of Council on interracial books for children. B. Chambers. il Pub W 200:23-9 O 11 '71
Minorities in social studies textbooks. Negro Hist Bul 33:166-7 N '70
Minorities still underrepresented. Sat R 54: 52-3 Je 19 '71
Minorities: what textbooks don't say; excerpt from Minorities in textbooks. M. B. Kane. Cur 129:13-16 My '71
Minority publishing: bringing the record up to date; findings and plans of Council on interracial books for children. B. Chambers. Pub W 201:27 Ja 3 '72
Minority publishing fund proposed at conference. Library J 96:2030 Je 15 '71
NAACP unit issues new multi-racial history syllabus. Negro Hist Bul 33:167 N '70
NCTE issues criteria to combat racism and bias in texts. Library J 96:1070 Mr 15 '71
Nation killers: the Soviet deportation of nationalists, by R. Conquest. Review Nat R 23:483-4 My 4 '71. F. Russell
New tribalism; an attempt by minorities to preserve a cultural identity. Nation 214:36-7 Ja 10 '72
On minority materials: school librarians move. R. H. Smith. Pub W 199:61 F 8 '71
75 million Americans: a profile. il U S News 71:32 Ag 9 '71
Situation ethnics; new ethnic community organizations. P. Freiberg. Commonweal 94:81-3 Ap 2 '71
Unhappy Americans: who they are, what they want. il U S News 70:90-4+ Ap 19 '71
What do you want from NEA? symposium. il Todays Ed 60:26-9+ Ja '71
White ethnic. M. Novak. il Harper 243:44-6+ S '71; Discussion. 243:6 N; 14-15 D '71
Why minority publishing? ed. by B. Chambers. il pors Pub W 199:35-50 Mr 15 '71
See also
Intercultural education
Bibliography
The scene. L. Ruth. Engl J 60:656-63 My '71
Education
Ford in their future. il Newsweek 78:72 O 18 '71
Employment
Hold-back advocacy: recruitment of minorities; letter to the editor. E. M. Smith. Am Lib 2:784 S '71
Parity now! report on the Preconference on recruitment of minorities. S. Havens. Library J 96:2452 Ag '71
MINORITIES in textbooks. See Textbooks
MINORITY enterprise small business investment companies. See Small business investment companies
MINORITY manpower, Office of. See Association of American publishers—Office of minority manpower
MINORS (law) See Children—Law; Youth—Law
MINOT, N.D. public library
Minot serves aged. M. Kuehn. il Am Lib 2:1198 D '71
MINT 400 race. See Motor vehicle racing
MINTOFF, Dom
Cross Maltese. il por Time 98:26 Jl 19 '71 *
Deadline Dom. il Time 99:29 Ja 10 '72 *
MINTON, R. B. See Larson, S. M. jt. auth.
MINTS
See also
Franklin mint
MINTS, Private
See also
Franklin mint
MINTZ, Edward N.
Celebrity spotlight. See issues of Travel
MINTZ, Morton
Story behind the book: America, inc. S. Wagner. il Pub W 200:60-1 N 15 '71 *
MINUDRI, Regina
(ed) Adult books for young adults. See second issue of each month of Library journal
MIOCENE period. See Paleontology—Miocene
MIRABELLA, Grace
Vogue for the new. pors Newsweek 77:54-5 My 31 '71 *
MIRACLE, June
Ganyard doll house. il Hobbies 76:141+ S '71

MIRACLE fruit
Ghana's miracle berry; from synsepalum dulcificum. Newsweek 77:97 Je 21 '71
MIRACLES
See also
Faith cure
MIRACLES (rock group) See Rock groups
MIRACULOUS mandarin; ballet. See Ballets—Criticisms
MIREX. See Insecticides
MIROV, Nicholas T.
Pines of Ravenna; with biographical sketch. il Natur Hist 80:2, 24-6 Ja '71
MIRROR, New York (newspaper) See New York mirror
MIRROR lenses. See Lenses, Photographic
MIRRORS
Decorating magic with mirrors. M. Kraft. il Good H 173:128-33 S '71
$45 worth of beauty and convenience you can build for $21; wall-hung pier set. R. Capotosto. il Pop Mech 135:134-7 Je '71
Magic mirror. R. Adams and others. il House B 113:57-66 Ja '71
Mirror that won't shatter or break. il Consumer Rep 36:134-5 Mr '71
MIRRORS, Automobile. See Automobiles—Equipment
MIRRORS for telescopes
Stock removal in mirror making. R. E. Cox. il Sky & Tel 42:174-5 S '71

Testing
Fiber optics for a tester. B. D. Hurt. il Sky & Tel 41:314-15 My '71
MIRV
Best chance; ban on MIRV. Sci Am 224:44 Mr '71
Latest red scare. H. Scoville, jr. New Repub 164:16-19 My 15 '71
Myth of arms control and disarmament. B. M. Becker. Bul Atom Sci 27:5-8+ Ap '71
Roots of the strategic arms race: ambiguity and ignorance. W. K. H. Panofsky. Bul Atom Sci 27:15-20 Je '71
MISCARRIAGE. See Abortion
MISCEGENATION. See Intermarriage of races
MISCH, Robert Jay
Labyrinth of liqueurs. il House B 113:72-3+ D '71
Light whiskey. House B 113:114 S '71
MISHAN, Ezra J.
Luddites were not all wrong. W. Greene and S. Golden. il por N Y Times Mag p40-2+ N 21 '71 *
MISHIMA, Yukio, pseud.
Testament of a Samurai; tr. by M. Gallagher. il pors Sports Illus 34:24-7 Ja 11 '71
Yukio Mishima: genius or madman? H. S. Hughes. il America 125:262-4 O 9 '71

about
Impossible beauty. M. Gallagher. il Commonweal 94:36-9 Mr 19 '71 *
Japan's self-defense force wins a skirmish with the past. T. Oka. il por N Y Times Mag p 12-13+ F 28 '71 *
Mishima's legacy. il Newsweek 77:34 F 8 '71
Politics of suicide. R. T. Halloran. por Commonweal 94:34-6 Mr 19 '71 *
Samurai protest. por Sr Schol 97:6 Ja 11 '71 *
MISPRONUNCIATION. See English language—Pronunciation
MISREPRESENTATION. See Fraud
MISS America contests. See Beauty contests
MISS Ella; story. See Fitzgerald. Z. S.
MISS Teen-age America contests. See Beauty contests
MISS Witherspoon regrets; story. See Bahr, E.-J
MISSILE bases. See Guided missile bases
MISSILE command, Army. See United States—Army—Materiel command
MISSILE firing installations. See Bombing and gunnery ranges
MISSILES, Guided. See Guided missiles
MISSING persons

Search and rescue operations
Child is lost, and found; Kevin Dye. il por Time 98:22 Ag 9 '71
Hunt for a boy who didn't want to be found; Kevin Dye. il pors Life 71:38-9 Ag 6 '71
Wild child; Kevin Dye. il Newsweek 78:25 Ag 9 '71
MISSING ships
Vanishing ships. P. Brock. Mech Illus 67:22+ O '71
MISSION control (space flight) See United States—Manned spacecraft center

MISSION inn. See Riverside, Calif.—Hotels, restaurants, etc.
MISSION of the church
Burying the Gospel. D. G. Bloesch. Chr Today 15:8-11 S 24; 16:12-14 O 8 '71
Careful plan; Law of God through the church. V. P. McCorry. America 124:inside back cover Ja 23 '71
Cause and effect. L. N. Bell. Chr Today 15:18-19 Jl 2 '71
Chicago ecumenism: changes in style and agenda. R. L. Rogers. il Chr Cent 88:626-31 My 19 '71
Church's mission: let the laity do it. J. E. Wagner. Chr Today 15:21 S 10 '71
Invincible weapons; victory through Christian love. L. N. Bell. Chr Today 16:34-5 N 5 '71
Justification by faith in the seventies. C. S. MacKenzie. Chr Today 15:6-7 S 24 '71
Liberation of men and nations; role of the Catholic church in Latin America. America 125:53-4 Ag 7 '71
New henotheism. Chr Cent 88:307 Mr 10 '71
New politics for Christians; address. R. Tucci. America 125:112-16 S 4 '71
Not bread alone. L. N. Bell. Chr Today 16:22-3 N 19 '71
Those church pronouncements! L. N. Bell. Chr Today 15:38-9 F 12 '71
Un-service station. D. M. Kelley. Chr Cent 88:799-801 Je 30 '71
See also
Church and the world
MISSIONARIES
Dacca departure: most missionaries flee. R. Chandler. Chr Today 16:41 Ja 7 '72
Missionaries: Christ for a changing world. il Time 97:90+ F 22 '71
Missionary retreat. il Chr Today 16:26-7 N 19 '71
Missions today. S. F. Rowen. Chr Today 15:24-6 Je 18 '71
See also
Children of missionaries
Missions
MISSIONARY conferences
Urbana '70: evangelical student power; with editorial comment. D. Tinder. il Chr Today 15:20, 29-30 Ja 29 '71
MISSIONS
American leadership in world missions. E. S. Fife. Chr Today 15:12-14 Ja 29 '71
Closing doors: fact and fiction; excerpt from The Christian mission: problems and prospects. J. H. Kane. Chr Today 16:6-10 N 19 '71
Creative tension: the church-mission controversy. W. H. Fuller. Chr Today 16:33 O 22 '71
Evangelical students at Urbana '70; zeal and social passion. W. R. Wineke. Chr Cent 88:226-7 F 17 '71
Missions and mammon: what leaders are saying. D. Kucharsky. Chr Today 16:43-4 D 3 '7
See also
Evangelistic work
Missionaries

California
See California—Missions

China
Recollections of a cultural imperialist (j.g.) J. C. Thomson, jr. Atlan 228:35-9 Ag '71

China (People's Republic)
China; mission study for 1969-70. H. Yu. Chr Cent 88:1398 N 24 '71
China: open door to what? R. Larson. Chr Today 15:3-5 Ag 27 '71
China records project at Yale. R. P. Morris. Chr Cent 88:832-3 Jl 7 '71

Hawaii
Mad Jack and the missionaries. L. McKee. il pors Am Heritage 22:30-7+ Ap '71

Latin America
Colombian seminar: whose mission? R. Chandler. Chr Today 15:35 My 7 '71
What price liberation? attack on missionary work at symposium financed by the World council of churches. Chr Today 16:30 O 8 '71

Mozambique
Shedding the protector. America 124:622 Je 19 '71
See also
Catholic church—Missions

Nigeria
Nigerian expropriation. W. H. Fuller. Chr Today 15:38-9 My 7 '71

MISSIONS to Jews
See also
American board of missions to the Jews

MISSISSIPPI
See also
Architecture, Domestic—Mississippi
Hunting—Mississippi
Leflore County
Negroes—Mississippi
Prisons—Mississippi
School libraries—Mississippi

Description and travel
Mississippi tour. R. L. Collins. il **Flying 89:** 72-5 N '71

Historic homes, etc.
Mississippi's ante-bellum itinerary. J. Cortese. il Travel 135:28-33 Mr '71

Politics and government
Black election defeat in Mississippi: why and what next? G. D. Gibson. Chr Cent 88:1525-6 D 29 '71
Black governor for Mississippi? P. O'Neil. il **pors Life 70:59-60 My 14 '71**
Black politics. New Repub 165:13 Jl 17 '71
Black setback in Mississippi. il Time 98: 17-18 N 15 '71
Eulogies and evasions; Democratic party groups. R. Sherrill. Nation 212:197-200 F 15 '71
If not Charles Evers, who? interviews, ed. by R. Branson. J. Swann; C. Sullivan. Chr Cent 88:906-8 Jl 28 '71
Mississippi's new politics of race: the contest for governor. G. D. Gibson. Chr Cent 88: 1148-9 S 29 '71
Sowing the seeds of power; J. Bond and J. Lewis seek voters. il pors Ebony 26:104-8+ O '71
Swan's song: Democratic gubernatorial primary. Newsweek 78:20+ Ag 16 '71
You gotta love me; gubernatorial primary campaign of C. Evers. il por Newsweek 78:22+ Ag 2 '71

MISSISSIPPI cookery. See Cookery, American
MISSISSIPPI RIVER
Life on the Mississippi: 1971 style. il U S News 71:68 S 20 '71

MISSOURI
Missouri's 150th birthday. V. L. George. il Hobbies 76:152-3 S '71
See also
Architecture, Domestic—Missouri
Blackwater River
Booksellers and bookselling—Missouri
Hunting—Missouri

MISSOURI RIVER
Great Lakes of the Missouri. C. L. Cadieux. il Yachting 129:58-9+ Je '71
That dammed Missouri River. G. Young. il Nat Geog 140:374-413 S '71

MISSOURI. University, Columbia
Missouri's freedom of information center. M. L. Stein. il Sat R 54:93-4+ Mr 13 '71
Tenure investigation; library administration division's report concerning non-renewal of contracts of five librarians; discussion. Am Lib 2:150-2 F '71

MR Barr; story. See Welke, H. C.
MR Esteban; musical comedy. See Musical comedies, revues, etc.—Criticisms, plots, etc.
MR Lawrence; story. See Munson, G.
MR Staal; story. See Reinbold, J. S.
MR Stevenson, sir; story. See Adarkar, V.
MR Travel award
17th annual Mr Travel award: crew and staff of the S.S. Hope. il Travel 136:54-7 Jl '71
MISTRAL, Gabriela
Disburdened; excerpt from Selected poems, tr. by D. Dana. Mlle 72:20 Ja '71

about
In the true language of a woman; with poem. F. Alegria. Sat R 54:25-6 Jl 17 '71 *
Woman from the high Andes: memories and a tribute; with three poems. A. H. Johnston. il Pub W 200:22-3 Jl 5 '71 *

MITCHELL, Albert
Looping for whitetail. il Field & S 76:50-1+ O '71
MITCHELL, Arthur
Choreographic partners; interview. New Yorker 47:28-30 My 22 '71

about
Black ballet can be beautiful. W. Terry. il por Sat R 54:48-9 F 27 '71 *
Doing the thing you do best. J. T. Elson. il Time 97:59-60 Mr 22 '71 *

MITCHELL, Blythe C. See Robertson, G. J. jt. auth.
MITCHELL, Carleton
Diving cruise to Horse Shoe reef. il Yachting 130:58-60+ N '71
Down the Mexican coast. il Motor B & S 128: 52-5+ O '71
Fair wind for Montego Bay. il Sports Illus 34:46-8+ My 24 '71
It's the little things that count. il Motor B & S 127:66-71+ Ap '71
Northland memory (cont) il Yachting 129: 60-1+ F '71
Yacht chartering. il Holiday 48:44+ N '70
Yacht with a taste for haste. il Sports Illus 34:38-44 F 15 '71
MITCHELL, Curtis
Tone up the swimming-pool way. il Read Digest 99:143-5 Ag '71
Your best weapon against overweight. Read Digest 99:94-6 Jl '71
MITCHELL, Dee
Eutrophication of lake water microcosms: phosphate versus nonphosphate detergents. bibliog il Science 174:827-9 N 19 '71
MITCHELL, Don
Heavy snow and cheerless rhetoric in the mountains of Colorado. Harper 243:24-6 Ag '71
MITCHELL, Edgar D.
Parting shots; signals from inner space. por Life 71:68 Jl 2 '71 *
White tracks on the moon. il por Life 70:26-9 F 26 '71 *
See also
Space flight to the moon—Manned flights—Apollo 14 flight
MITCHELL, Henry H. and O'Neal E. S.
Tale of two cities. Chr Cent 88:156-8 F 3 '71
MITCHELL, John Newton
Where war against crime is being won; interview. il pors U S News 70:38-42 Mr 22 '71

about
Authors & editors; imaginary interview about The vertical smile. por Pub W 200:193-6 Ag 30 '71 *
Balance sheet on justice. Nation 213:166 S 6 '71 *
Chosen two. J. Osborne. New Repub 165: 12-13 N 6 '71 *
Mitchell magic. il por Newsweek 78:37 N 8 '71 *
No. 1 in Cabinet, and in controversy. il pors U S News 71:58-9 Ag 2 '71 *
Overruling Mitchell. Time 97:58-9 Ap 19 '71 *
Politics of problems. Nation 212:770 Je 21 '71 *
Ripping off the FBI. por Time 97:15 Ap 5 '71 *
TRB from Washington. New Repub 164:4 My 22 '71 *
That's always the way it is for John Mitchell. M. S. Forbes. por Forbes 108:16 O 1 '71 *
Who's in charge here. H. Sidey. il Life 71:4 D 10 '71 *
MITCHELL, Martha (Beall)
I went to London to visit the queen! ed. by W. McLendon. por Ladies Home J 88: 82+ N '71
Martha Mitchell: people I'd love to phone. il por Ladies Home J 88:68+ Jl '71
MITCHELL, Paul
How to get the haircut you want. il pors Redbook 136:82-5+ F '71 *
MITCHELL, Sue
Most heartbreaking race I ever sailed. il por Yachting 129:35+ Je '71
MITCHELL, William LeRoy
Motor trend interview. il pors Motor T 23: 88+ Jl '71
MITCHELL, William R.
Disciple; poem. Chr Cent 88:875 Jl 21 '71
MITCHELL park horticultural conservatory. See Milwaukee—Mitchell park horticultural conservatory
MITER boxes, gages, etc.
Miter board with locking cams. R. Wortham. il Pop Sci 199:139 S '71
MITFORD, Jessica
Kind and usual punishment in California. il Atlan 227:45-52 Mr '71
MITGANG, Herbert
At war with the Stars and stripes. il Am Heritage 22:58-64+ Ap '71
Portrait of a protester. New Repub 164:14-15 My 8 '71
MITNICK, MaryAnn, and Reichlin, Seymour
Thyrotropin-releasing hormone: biosynthesis by rat hypothalamic fragments in vitro. bibliog il Science 172:1241-3 Je 18 '71

MODULAR coordination (architecture) See Buildings, Prefabricated
MODULAR houses. See Houses, Prefabricated
MODULAR schedules. See Schedules, School
MODULE communities, inc.
Technology, first U.S. systems-built highrise; Futura in Yonkers, N.Y. M. Villecco. il Arch Forum 135:68-70 N '71
MOE, Daniel
Cantata of peace premiered at church music meeting. Chr Cent 88:1018 S 1 '71 *
MOEBIUS, William
Comment. F. MacShane. Poetry 118:298 Ag '71 *
MOELLENBERG, Wayne P.
Distinguishing fact from fiction in social crises. bibliog Sch & Soc 99:420-4 N '71
MOELLER, Georgia B.
Parent-student-teacher triangle. il Todays Ed 60:40-1 N '71
MOFFAT, Alex W.
One man's boat. il Yachting 129:63+ Mr '71
MOFFAT, George B. jr
New wave in soaring. il Pop Sci 199:66-8+ S '71
MOFFATT, Dorothy
Confession; poem. Ladies Home J 88:200 Mr '71
MOFFETT, Cleveland
Man with a soul; story. Redbook 136:98 Mr '71
MOFFETT, Kenworth
Jack Bush; illusions of transparency. il por Art N 70:42-5 Mr '71
Noland vertical. il Art N 70:48-9+ O '71
MOFFETT, Samuel Hugh
Lesson in world-winning. Chr Today 15:4-6 S 10 '71
MOFFETT, Toby
Story behind the author; interview. ed. by E. Lottman. por Pub W 200:28-9 N 22 '71
MOFFITT, John
Meditation; poem. America 125:559 D 25 '71
(comp) Undergraduate poems. America 124: 510-11 My 15 '71
MOFFORD, Juliet Haines
Gravestone rubbings in New England. il Travel 135:52-5 Mr '71
Tent for rent on an island in the sun. il Schol Teach Jr/Sr High p26-7+ F 1 '71
—See Mofford, T. jt. auth.
MOFFORD, Thomas, and Mofford, J. H.
Improvisational techniques. bibliog il School Teach Jr/Sr High p 14-16 Ja '72
MOGUL, Philip H. and Portnoy, S. B.
Analyzing metallic mixtures. il pors Chem 44:27-9 Mr '71
MOHAMMED
Mohammed: the prophet armed. S. De Gramont. il Horizon 13:18-23 Sum '71 *
MOHAMMED Reza Pahlevi, shah of Iran
Iran: let the world take note. L. Jenkins. il por Newsweek 78:42+ O 11 '71 *
Once and future shah. F. Halliday. Ramp Mag 10:18+ N '71 *
Shah of Iran: king and revolutionary. il por U S News 71:88 O 18 '71 *
Shah's princely party; with report by W. A. McWhirter and photographs by P. Boulat and others. Life 71:22-30 O 29 '71 *
MOHAMMEDANISM and Christianity. See Christianity and other religions
MOHAN, M. S. See Rechnitz, G. A. jt. auth.
MOHAWK Indians
Four Indian kings in London. M. Bishop. il Am Heritage 23:62-5 D '71
MOHIT, Behzad, and Fan, Kang
Hybrid cell line from a cloned immunoglobulin-producing mouse myeloma and a non-producing mouse lymphoma. bibliog il Science 171:75-7 Ja 8 '71
MOHLER, Orren C. See Wehinger, P. A. jt. auth.
MOHOLY-NAGY, Sibyl
Obituary
Arch Forum 134:29 Je '71. P. Rudolph
MOHONK mountain house. See Hotels, taverns, etc.—United States
MOIR, Elsie
Some thoughts on an encounter weekend. Har Yrs 11:9 Mr '71
MOISTURE
See also
Evaporation
Soil moisture
Water vapor
MOISTURE content of wood. See Wood—Moisture content
MOISTURE detectors. See Detectors
MOISTURIZERS. See Cosmetics

MOJAVE DESERT
Mojave Desert; a treasure in trouble. E. Selby and M. Selby. il Nat Wildlife 9:52-7 O '71; Same abr. with title Trouble in the Mojave. Read Digest 99:45-8+ O '71
MOLDED salads. See Salads
MOLDING, Plaster. See Plaster work (craft)
MOLDS (botany)
See also
Mildew
Slime molds
MOLDS (for ceramic products)
Impromptu plates molded on a carved base. R. F. Eilenberger. il Ceram Mo 19:27-9 Mr '71
Slab-built cylinders from improvised molds. P. Rothenberg. il Ceram Mo 19:34-5 My '71
MOLE, Arthur
I didn't raise my boy to be an eyebrow. il Life 71:82-3 S 24 '71 *
MOLECULAR binding energy. See Chemical bonds
MOLECULAR biology
Chance and necessity, by J. Monod. Review Atlan 228:125-30 N '71. G. Stent
See also
Chemical genetics
Roche institute of molecular biology
Conferences
Enzyme control and macromolecular assembly. H. Neurath and others. Science 172: 185-6+ Ap 9 '71
MOLECULAR evolution. See Evolution
MOLECULAR microscopy. See Microscope and microscopy
MOLECULAR models
Solution of eight-vertex model excites critical-point theorists. G. B. Lubkin. bibliog il Phys Today 24:17+ S '71
MOLECULAR rotation
See also
Isomers and isomerism
MOLECULAR sieving. See Adsorption
MOLECULAR spectroscopy. See Spectrum analysis
MOLECULES
Gold mine in the sky. Newsweek 77:56+ Ap 26 '71
See also
Polymers
Models
See Molecular models
MOLECULES, interstellar. See Matter, Interstellar
MOLESTERS, Child. See Child molesters
MOLESWORTH, Charles
Walk in the city; poem. Poetry 118:77 My '71
MOLETTE, Barbara. See Molette, C. jt. auth.
MOLETTE, Carlton, and Molette, Barbara
Rosalee Pritchett. Criticism
New Yorker 46:56-7 Ja 30 '71 *
MOLIÈRE, Jean Baptiste Poquelin
School for wives; drama; adapted by P. T. Nolan. Plays 31:85-96 N '71
School for wives (L'école des femmes) tr. by R. Wilbur. Criticism
Nation 212:315 Mr 8 '71 *
New Repub 164:24 My 8 '71 *
New Yorker 47:82 F 27 '71 *
Sat R 54:21 Mr 6 '71 *
Time 97:67 Mr 1 '71 *
MOLINARO, Leo A.
Truths and consequences for older cities. il Sat R 54:30-1+ My 15 '71
MOLLENKOTT, Virginia Ramey
Up from ignorance: awareness-training and racism. Chr Today 15:6-8 Mr 26 '71
MOLLER, Hans Maersk-. See Maersk-Moller, H.
MOLLI, Jeanne. See Avedon, L. jt. auth.
MOLLOY, Ernest Lawrence
Value store that grew and grew. il por Nations Bsns 59:74-5 Ja '71
MOLLOY, Eugene J.
Brooklyn's little giant of Catholic education. G. A. Kelly. America 125:312-14 O 23 '71 *
MOLLUSKS
Great discovery: monoplacophora. A. G. Melvin. il Hobbies 76:146-7 Ja '72 (to be cont)
See also
Limpets
Murex
Mussels, Fresh water
Nautilus
Nervous system—Mollusks
Oysters
Sea slugs
Snails

MOLNER, Don
A-V clinic; questions and answers (cont) Schol Teach Jr/Sr High p25 F 1; 38 Mr 8; 23 Ap 5; 46 S; 58 O; 21 N '71
A-V roundup (cont) il Schol Teach Jr/Sr High p22 F 1 '71
Processing film, no muss, no fuss. il Schol Teach Jr/Sr High p28-9 Mr 8 '71
(ed) See Goldberg, E. Behind the scenes with a teenage animator

MOLOKAI (island)
Molokai: still the lonely island. H. Sutton. il Holiday 48:14-17 S '70

MOLONY, Joseph P.
Steel imports; address, February 3, 1971. Vital Speeches 37:307-9 Mr 1 '71

MOLSON, Wash.

Historic houses, etc.
See Washington (state)—Historic houses, etc.

MOLTMANN, Jürgen
What kind of hope is adequate? H. R. Dymale. Chr Today 15:9-10 Je 18 '71 •

MOLTON, Warren Lane
Pornogram; poem. Chr Cent 88:1344 N 17 '71

MOMADAY, N. Scott
Vision beyond time and place. il Life 71:66-7 Jl 2 '71

MOMMY, mommy; story. See Debbi, M.

MONACO
See also
Automobile racing—Monaco

Economic conditions
Turnaround for Monte Carlo? with interview with Prince Rainier, ed. by A. Jones. il Forbes 108:64+ S 15 '71

Royal family
Reigning family of Monaco; photographs by Snowdon. Vogue 158:109-15 D '71

MONACO Grand prix. See Automobile racing —Monaco

MONARCH, Mont.

Education
Daring educational experiment: the one-room schoolhouse. W. Griffith. il N Y Times Mag p 14-16+ My 30 '71

MONARCH butterflies. See Butterflies

MONARCHS. See Kings and rulers

MONASTERIES
Boquen monastery: growing seeds in tired soil. Sister Madeleine. Chr Cent 88:431 Ap 7 '71
Wordly religious community; Bavaria's Casteller Ring. G. Weckman; reply. P. Johnson. Chr Cent 88:194 F 10 '71
See also
Abbeys
Montserrat, Spain

MONASTICISM
New charter for monasticism, ed. by J. Moffitt. Review
America 124:210 F 27 '71. T. Berry
Chr Cent 88:808 Je 30 '71. R. Weber and E. Samanns
See also
Contemplative orders

MONBERG, Helene C.
Washington lookout. il Am For 77:3-9+ Je '71

MONDADORI, Arnoldo
Obituary
Pub W 199:43 Je 28 '71

MONDADORI, Arnoldo, editore. See Publishers and publishing—Italy

MONDALE, Walter Frederick
Mondale of Minnesota. R. Coles. New Repub 165:21-3 D 25 '71 •

MONDRIAAN, Pieter Cornelis
Art; exhibition at the Solomon R. Guggenheim museum. L. Alloway. Nation 213: 412-13 O 25 '71 •
Art world: retrospective exhibition at the Guggenheim museum. H. Rosenberg. New Yorker 47:201-4+ N 20 '71 •
Centennial of a Dutch master. il Life 71: 42-7 N 19 '71 •
Center of reality; exhibition at the Guggenheim museum. K. Kuh. il Sat R 54:62-3 O 30 '71 •
Making the gallery scene. B. Wasserman. il Sch Arts 71:28-31 N '71 •
Mondrian: less is more art. B. Rose. Vogue 158:169 D '71 •
P.M. at 100. C. R. Baldwin. il Art N 70: 26-8+ D '71 •
Pursuit of the square. R. Hughes. il por Time 98:88-90 N 8 '71 •
Red, the yellow, the blue. D. Davis. il pors Newsweek 78:90-3 O 18 '71 •

MONELL, Lucinda
Orly; story. Seventeen 30:90-1 Ja '71

MONET, Claude
Letter from Paris; exhibition of impressionist pictures in the Marmottan museum. Genêt. New Yorker 47:71-2 Jl 10 '71 •
Prophet of light. R. Hughes. il Time 98:54-5 Jl 19 '71 •
Unfinished cathedrals. P. Schneider. il Vogue 158:96-101+ D '71 •

MONETARY conference, Bretton Woods. See United Nations monetary and financial conference

MONETARY fund. See International monetary fund

MONETARY policy
See also
Currency question
Fiscal policy

MONEY, Anton
Lookout grizzly. il por Outdoor Life 148: 60-3+ O '71

MONEY, John W.
Prenatal sex hormone levels: a possible link to intelligence. il Sci N 101:8 Ja 1 '72 •

MONEY
Controlled currency. C. French. Hobbies 76: 132+ D '71
See also
Checks
Coins
Credit
Foreign exchange
Gold as money
Inflation (finance)
Interest
Liquidity (economics)

International aspects
Advantages of the unthinkable; results of currency realignment. il Time 98:24+ D 27 '71
After the crisis. il Newsweek 77:71+ My 24 '71
Alternatives to economic nationalism. il Time 97:78+ My 24 '71
As latest money crisis fades, the problems that remain. il U S News 70:11-12 My 24 '71
Asiadollar? Forbes 108:26-7 N 1 '71
Battered dollar. il Time 98:58 Ag 9 '71
Beggar my neighbor. New Repub 165:8-9 O 16 '71
Breakthrough in world's money tangle: what's proposed. il U S News 71:24-6 D 13 '71
Changing the rules. Time 97:78+ Je 21 '71
Changing the world's money. il Time 98:21-4 O 4 '71
Devaluation economics. P. A. Samuelson. Newsweek 78:69 Ag 23 '71
Devaluation jitters. Time 98:50 Ag 23 '71
Dollar: a power play unfolds. il Time 98:14+ Ag 30 '71
Dollar abroad: on its own. Newsweek 78: 59-60 Ag 23 '71
Dollar crises. P. A. Samuelson. Newsweek 77:69 My 31 '71
Dollar crisis: floating toward reform? il Time 97:85-6+ My 17 '71
Dollar game. H. C. Wallich. il Newsweek 78: 86 S 20 '71
Dollar goes begging. il Newsweek 77:75-7 My 17 '71
Dollar survives still another crisis. il U S News 70:82-4 Ap 19 '71
Dollar under attack abroad: impact on U.S. il U S News 70:9-10 My 24 '71
Dollars at a discount. H. Hazlitt. Nat R 23: 591-2 Je 1 '71
End is in sight for the money crisis. il Bsns W p29-30 D 11 '71
Facing facts; yen floated. il Newsweek 78: 32-3 S 6 '71
Floating together? Eurocurrencies and the dollar. il Newsweek 78:69-70 Jl 19 '71
Forthcoming devaluation of the dollar. il Time 98:18-20 D 13 '71
Game is over. il por Forbes 107:52 Je 1 '71
Group of ten ministerial meeting held at Washington: text of communique, September 26, 1971. Dept State Bul 65:458 O 25 '71
Hardening lines. il Newsweek 78:61 O 4 '71
High price of national pride. R. Lekachman. Duns 98:13 Jl '71
Hints of a deal. Time 98:26 D 6 '71
Hot dollars spark a global crisis; with editorial comment. il Bsns W p 16-17, 96 My 8 '71
How foreign bankers size up the dollar. A. Zanker. il U S News 70:48-50 Je 14 '71
Keep the dollar free. M. Friedman. Newsweek 78:83 D 20 '71
Letter from the Azores. T. Szulc. New Yorker 47:54-8 Ja 1 '72

MONEY—International aspects—*Continued*
Monetary gold: to have or have not. T. Cusack. America 125:555-7 D 25 '71
Monetary peace by Christmas? il Newsweek 78:85-6 D 6 '71
More equal system; monetary realignment. il Time 99:60-1 Ja 3 '72
More things change; effects of import surtax. J. Burnham. Nat R 23:977 S 10 '71
Mutual responsibility for maintaining a stable monetary system; address, May 28, 1971. J. B. Connally. Dept State Bul 65:42-6 Jl 12 '71; Excerpts with title Tough talk to U.S. allies on trade, defense. U S News 70:51-3 Je 14 '71
New monetary system for the 1980's, the spirit of Bretton Woods; address, December 3, 1971. D. C. Platten. Vital Speeches 38:179-82 Ja 1 '72
New system for world's money: the hard bargaining starts. il U S News 71:62-4 S 6 '71
New view: build here and export. il Bsns W p29-30 Ja 1 '72
New warning signs for the dollar. Nat R 23:186-7 F 23 '71
Nixon's dollar and the foreign fallout. il Time 98:56-7 S 6 '71
Now that money crisis is over, effects on business. il U S News 72:11-13 Ja 3 '72
Now the yen is floating, too. il Newsweek 78:52+ S 6 '71
Problems devaluation will not solve. il Bsns W p 18-19 D 18 '71
Remember the dollar? the reaction abroad. il Sr Schol 99:15-16 S 27 '71
Restoring self-respect to the dollar. G. W. Ball. Newsweek 78:33 S 6 '71
Rising stakes for a new system. Bsns W p21-2 O 9 '71
Road ahead. H. C. Wallich. Newsweek 79:39 Ja 3 '72
Saga of the dollar. New Repub 164:7 My 22 '71; Reply with rejoinder. B. McCrea. 165: 32-3 Jl 3 '71
Search for equity. il Time 98:74 S 13 '71
Shaky dollar. P. A. Samuelson. Newsweek 77:106 Ap 19 '71
Solving a crisis: John Connally superstar. il por Newsweek 78:85-6+ D 13 '71
Soviet gold. Nation 212:677-8 My 31 '71
Step to slow Eurodollar flows; with editorial comment. il Bsns W p 110-11+, 160 My 15 '71
System torn down must be rebuilt. il Bsns W p26-7 Ag 21 '71
Talk with Europe's top banker; interview. ed. by B. van Voorst. H. J. Abs. por Newsweek 77:72-3 F 22 '71
Tough talk and an ominous deadline. il por Newsweek 78:82-4 S 27 '71
Tough talk to U.S. allies on trade, defense; excerpts from address, May 28, 1971. J. B. Connally. il pors U S News 70:51-3 Je 14 '71
U.S. gains an edge. il Bsns W p 14-16 D 25 '71
U.S. taking a hard line on dollar, trade. il U S News 71:70-1 S 27 '71
What ails the dollar. G. Freeman. il Fortune 83:47-8+ Je '71
What next for the dollar? C. A. Cerami. Nations Bsns 59:66-9 Ag '71
What's ahead for the dollar. il U S News 71:22-4 Ag 30 '71
World downgrades the dollar. il Bsns W p24-5 Ag 14 '71
See also
Currency question
Eurodollar market
Gold as money
International monetary fund
Special drawing rights
United Nations monetary and financial conference

England
See Money—Great Britain

Germany (Federal Republic)
D-mark makes the markets jumpy. il Bsns W p26 Jl 31 '71
Mark crisis; hypothetical dialogue. M. Friedman. Newsweek 77:72 My 24 '71

Great Britain
Britain: lament for a lost currency. Time 97: 27 Mr 1 '71
Britain's good-bye to shillings. Sunset 146: 62 Mr '71
Letter from London; decimal-currency. M. Panter-Downes. New Yorker 47:101 F 27 '71
Notes and suggestions; explanation of English currency. H. R. Mayes. Sat R 54:8 O 9 '71

Profitable path to decimalization. Bsns W p31+ Ja 23 '71
Tens situation. Sr Schol 98:7-8 F 15 '71
Think decimal! Great Britain switching to a decimal currency system. il Time 97:32+ F 15 '71

Japan
Facing facts. il Newsweek 78:32-3 S 6 '71
Now the yen is floating, too. il Newsweek 78:52+ S 6 '71
Some Japanese yield on the yen. il Bsns W p22 O 2 '71
Yen for revaluation. Time 97:69-70 Je 7 '71

United States
Alas, poor dollar! Nat R 23:1450 D 31 '71
Dollars and diplomacy: a new reality; dollar devaluation. il Time 98:7 D 27 '71
Growth rate bedevils the Fed. il Bsns W p25 Je 12 '71
New dollar. il U S News 71:9-10 D 27 '71
New dollar prevails; devaluation. il Newsweek 78:12-14 D 27 '71
New dollar, what devaluation means; questions and answers. il U S News 71:11-12 D 27 '71
Now that money crisis is over, effects on business. il U S News 72:11-13 Ja 3 '72
Problems devaluation will not solve. il Bsns W p 18-19 D 18 '71
Quiet triumph of devaluation. il Time 98: 22-3 D 27 '71

MONEY management. See Budget, Household; Domestic finance
MONEY raising campaigns. See Fund raising
MONEY rates. See Interest
MONGAN, T. R. See Golden, J. jt. auth.
MONJAN, Andrew A. and others
Cerebellar hypoplasia in neonatal rats caused by lymphocytic choriomeningitis virus. bibliog il Science 171:194-6 Ja 15 '71
MONK, Edwin
Anti-roll devices. il Yachting 129:64-5+ Mr '71
MONK, Meredith
Vessel, an opera epic by Meredith Monk and The house, NYC. D. Hering. Dance Mag 46:24-5 Ja '72
MONK seals. See Seals (animals)
MONKEY business; drama. See Boiko, C.
MONKEYS
Acute lymphocytic leukemia in owl monkeys inoculated with herpesvirus saimiri. L. V. Meléndez and others. bibliog il Science 171: 1161-3 Mr 19 '71
Aflatoxin P_1: a new aflatoxin metabolite in monkeys. J. Dalezios and others. bibliog il Science 171:584-5 F 12 '71
Apes of Gibraltar: Barbary apes. B. R. MacRoberts and M. H. MacRoberts. il Natur Hist 80:38-47 Ag '71
Contours and contrast: responses of monkey lateral geniculate nucleus cells to luminance and color figures. R. L. De Valois and F. L. Pease. bibliog il Science 171:694-6 F 19 '71
Developmental behaviors: delayed appearance in monkeys asphyxiated at birth. J. A. Sechzer and others. bibliog il Science 171: 1173-5 Mr 19 '71
Effects of brief separation from mother on rhesus monkeys. R. A. Hinde and Y. Spencer-Booth. bibliog il Science 173:111-18 Jl 9 '71
Eye-head coordination in monkeys: evidence for centrally patterned organization. E. Bizzi and others. bibliog il Science 173:452-4 Jl 30 '71
Genital herpesvirus hominis type 2 infection: an experimental model in cebus monkeys. A. J. Nahmias and others. bibliog Science 171:297-8 Ja 22 '71
Hemoglobin polymorphism. M. H. Crawford. Science 171:706 F 19 '71
Knowing noses. Sci Am 225:76+ S '71
Monkeys at play. S. J. Suomi and H. F. Harlow. il Natur Hist 80:72-7 D '71
Operant conditioning of specific patterns of neural and muscular activity. E. E. Fetz and D. V. Finocchio. bibliog il Science 174: 431-5 O 22 '71
Pheromones: isolation of male sex attractants from a female primate. R. P. Michael and others. bibliog il Science 172:964-6 My 28 '71
Prolonged color blindness induced by intense spectral lights in rhesus monkeys. R. S. Harwerth and H. G. Sperling. bibliog il Science 174:520-3 O 29 '71
Recovery of function after serial ablation of prefrontal cortex in the rhesus monkey. J. Rosen and others. bibliog il Science 173: 353-6 Jl 23 '71

MONKEYS—*Continued*
Separating mother and child. Sci N 100:
40 Jl 17 '71
Social behavior of monkeys selectively de-
pleted of monoamines. D. E. Redmond, jr.
and others. bibliog il Science 174:428-31 O
22 '71
Superior colliculus cell responses related to
eye movements in awake monkeys. R. H.
Wurtz and M. E. Goldberg. bibliog il Sci-
ence 171:82-4 Ja 8 '71
See also
Apes
Baboons
Chimpanzees
Marmosets
MONKEYS in literature. See Animals in lit-
erature
MONN, Eirik, and Christiansen, R. O.
Adenosine 3',5'-monophosphate phosphodies-
terase multiple molecular forms. bibliog il
Science 173:540-2 Ag 6 '71
MONOAMINE oxidase. See Oxidases
MONOAMINES. See Amines
MONOD, Jacques
Just a game of chance? por Newsweek 77:
99 Ap 26 '71 *
MONOLOGUES
Off Broadway; S. McKenna's Here are ladies.
E. Oliver. New Yorker 47:68-9 Mr 6 '71
Saints of the word; S. McKenna's one-woman
show. Here are ladies. T. E. Kalem.
por Time 97:48 Mr 8 '71
MONONGAHELA national forest, W.Va. See
National forests
MONONUCLEOTIDES. See Nucleotides
MONOPLACOPHORA. See Mollusks
MONOPOLIES
See also
Competition
Patents—Licensing
Trusts, Industrial
MONORAIL railroads. See Railroads, Single
rail
MONOSODIUM glutamate
Monosodium glutamate: absence of hypothal-
amic lesions after ingestion by newborn
primates. W. A. Reynolds and others. bib-
liog il Science 172:1342-4 Je 25 '71
Monosodium glutamate lack of effects on
brain and reproductive function in rats.
N. J. Adamo and A. Ratner; reply with
rejoinder. J. W. Olney. bibliog Science 172:
294 Ap 16 '71
MONOTONY
See also
Boredom
MONRO, John Usher
Profiles. E. J. Kahn, jr. New Yorker 47:
43-8+ Ap 10 '71 *
MONROE, Bill
Captive medium; address. November 23, 1970.
Vital Speeches 37:267-70 F 15 '71
MONROE, Earl
Bully for the Bullets. il por Newsweek 77:91
My 3 '71 *
MONROE, Jay Randolph
Abacus, American style. J. Sheridan. il pors
Nations Bsns 59:76-7 Ja '71 *
MONROE, Marilyn
Gallery; young Marilyn Monroe before the
wave; photographs. W. Burnside. pors Life
71:6-7 Jl 23 '71 *
MONROE, Mich.
Computer brings big dividends to small-city
administration. L. E. Leis. il por Am City
86:97-8 My '71
MONROE calculating machine company
Abacus, American style. J. Sheridan. il pors
Nations Bsns 59:76-7 Ja '71
MONROE COUNTY library system, Rochester,
N.Y.
Monroe County library system issues audio-
visual plan. Library J 96:3270 O 15 '71
MONROE COUNTY water authority, N.Y.
Computer bills, pays, operates. il Am City
86:22 O '71
MONROVIA, Liberia
Liberian lady wears three hats; E. A.
Sandimanie. E. B. Thompson. il pors Ebony
27:54-6+ Ja '72
MONSALVAT. See Montserrat, Spain
MONSANTO company
Dealing with a disaster. C. H. Sommer. il
pors Nations Bsns 59:78-9 Ja '71
PCB's: leaks of toxic substances raises issue
of effects, regulation. J. Pichirallo. Science
173:899-902 S 3 '71
MONSARRAT, Nicholas
Breaking in, breaking out, by N. Monsarrat.
Review
America 125:520 D 11 '71. J. V. McDon-
nell *

MONSER, George J.
Build a mini-pyramidal UHF TV antenna.
il Pop Electr 35:40-3 D '71
MONSON, Karen
Behind the scenes. Hi Fi 21:22 S '71
Cal Arts: freedom is the password; no grades,
no exams. il Hi Fi 21:MA10-12 Je '71
Mini-marathon at Hollywood bowl. Hi Fi
21:MA26 D '71
Ojai: music for the minority. il Hi Fi 21:
MA22-3 S '71
School of hard knocks. il Opera N 36:8-9 N '71
MONSTERS
See also
Sea serpent
MONTAGNARDS
People of sorrow. il Newsweek 77:61 My
10 '71
MONTAGNES, Ian
Publishing the pre-shrunk; reprint. il Pub
W 200:13-15 N 22 '71
MONTAGU, Ashley
Awesome power of human love; excerpt from
The humanization of man. Read Digest 99:
103-5 Jl '71
MONTAGUE, Joel B. jr
Comprehensive school under fire in Britain.
bibliog Clear House 46:44-7 S '71; Same
abr. with title British comprehensive school
under fire. Ed Digest 37:52-4 D '71
MONTAGUE, Katherine. See Montague, P. jt.
auth.
MONTAGUE, Peter, and Montague, Katherine
Great caterpillar war and the ecopolitics of
pesticides. il Audubon 73:50-8 Ja '71
Mercury; how much are we eating? il Sat R
54:50-5 F 6 '71
MONTAGUE, Richard
How not to fly the Atlantic; excerpts from
Oceans, Poles and airmen. il pors Am
Heritage 22:42-7+ Ap '71
MONTALE, Eugenio
After a flight; poem; tr. by L. Rebay. Am
Scholar 40:416-20 Sum '71
MONTALVA, Eduardo Frei
Latin America, no longer a U.S. sphere of
influence; interview. il por U S News 71:
77-80 D 20 '71
MONTANA
See also
Conservation of resources—Montana
Fishing—Montana
Gardening—Montana
Hunting—Montana
National bison range
Paleobotany—Montana
Paleontology—Montana
Wilderness areas—Montana

History
See also
Little Big Horn, Battle of the, 1876
MONTANO, Rocco
Dante and Virgil. Yale R 60:550-61 Je '71
MONTAUK POINT
Riding the New York range. D. Butwin. il
Sat R 54:69-70+ N 20 '71
MONTCLAIR, Calif.
Minibikes and motorbikes only; Motorbike
park. L. M. Wasserman. il Am City 86:
100 Ag '71
MONTECATINI-Edison. See Chemical indus-
tries—Italy
MONTEGO BAY, Jamaica
Montego Bay. A. Gordon. il Holiday 49:64-9+
D '70
MONTEMURO, Norma
Multi-media approach to humanities. Engl J
60:1228-30 D '71
MONTEPARO, Joseph Michael
Cop named Joe. F. Knebel. il Look 35:15-19
Jl 27 '71 *
MONTEREY, Calif.
New Cannery Row. D. Kurlinke. il Travel
136:62-7 O '71
Old Cannery Row is an ever-changing show.
il Sunset 147:94-5 O '71
MONTEREY, Calif, public library
Coin-op digital computer tried at Monterey
P.L. Library J 96:4051 D 15 '71
MONTEREY BAY, Calif.

Education
Negotiations and beyond; Monterey Bay
teachers association. F. Jacobson and
others. Todays Ed 60:63 F '71
MONTERO, Homero Martinez-. See Martinez-
Montero, H.
MONTERROSO, Augusto
Chameleon who ended up not knowing what
to turn; story, excerpt from The black
sheep. Harper 243:95 Jl '71
Two fables: Recurrent savior; Black sheep.
il Harper 243:71 Ag '71

MONTGOMERY, Charles F.
Furniture history society. Antiques 99:542-3 Ap '71
Living with antiques. W. D. Garrett. il Antiques 101:185-92 Ja '72 *
MONTGOMERY, Charlotte
Speaker for the house. See issues of Good housekeeping
MONTGOMERY, John Warwick
Ark fever. Chr Today 15:38-9 Jl 2; 15 Ag 27 '71
MONTGOMERY, Robert
Subject to fits. Criticism
America 124:409 Ap 17 '71 *
New Repub 164:28-30 Mr 6 '71 *
New Yorker 47:84 F 27 '71 *
Newsweek 77:66 Mr 1 '71 *
MONTGOMERY, Roger
Elastic office building. il Arch Forum 135:54-7 S '71
MONTGOMERY, Ruth
Report from heaven. il por Newsweek 79:52 Ja 3 '72 *
MONTGOMERY, Ala.

Negroes
In Montgomery; with photographs by M. Sleet, jr. G. Brooks. Ebony 26:42-8 Ag '71
Whatever happened to Mrs Rosa Parks? bus boycott. il pors Ebony 26:180-1 Ag '71
MONTGOMERY COUNTY, Ohio

Parks and reserves
Land acquisition: a county's responsibility. J. Raderstorf. Parks & Rec 6:41+ Jl '71
MONTHS
See also
November
MONTI, Carlotta
His last chickadee. A. Cooper. il por Newsweek 77:92 Je 21 '71 *
MONTICELLO (historic house)
"All my wishes end at Monticello." M. Evans. il Am Home 74:41-9+ Jl '71
MONTOR, Karel
Cheating in high school. Sch & Soc 99:96-8 F '71
MONTOYA, Joseph M.
Excerpt from statement, January 22, 1970. Cong Digest 50:44+ F '71
MONTREAL

Climate
Montreal's great snowstorm of '69. M. E. H. Trueman. il Weatherwise 23:270-3 D '70

Description
Europe in Canada's front yard; old Montreal. A. Bester. il Holiday 49:40-1 My '71
MONTREAL Canadiens (hockey team) See Hockey teams
MONTROSE chemical division. See Baldwin-Montrose chemical company
MONTSERRAT, Spain
Montserrat; prototype of Wagner's Monsalvat; with photographs by E. Davidson. Opera N 35:14-16 Ap 3 '71
MONUMENTS
Mark of man. W. Hedgepeth. il Look 35:58-63 Ja 12 '71
See also
Crazy Horse (Sioux Indian)—Statues, portraits, etc.
Pyramids
Sepulchral monuments
War memorials
also subhead Monuments, statues, etc. under names of cities, e.g. Paris—Monuments, statues, etc.
MOOD, Alexander M.
Another approach to higher education. Ed Digest 37:13-16 D '71
MOODY, William Lewis, 1865-1954
It's Moody versus Moody in the struggle for American national. A. M. Louis. il por Fortune 83:108-12+ Mr '71 *
MOODY, William Lewis, family
It's Moody versus Moody in the struggle for American national A. M. Louis. il por Fortune 83:108-12+ Mr '71 *
MOOG, Florence
Women, students, and tenure. Science 174:983 D 3 '71
MOON, Dale
Ordeal on Mount Hood; ed. by D. Holm. il pors Nat Wildlife 9:36-9 Je '71
MOON
Moon as transmitter. Newsweek 78:83-4 N 22 '71
Sun, moon, and planets this month. R. C. Victor. See issues of Sky and telescope

Surprising moon. R. Hotz. Aviation W 95:7 O 25 '71
Velikovsky controversy. Chem 44:17 O '71
Was the moon originally cold? H. C. Urey. bibliog Science 172:403-5 Ap 23 '71
See also
Eclipses, Lunar
Lunar geology
Occultations
Space flight to the moon
Tides

Age
Dating of moon samples: pitfalls and paradoxes. E. Driscoll. Sci N 101:12-14 Ja 1 '72
Of time and the moon. G. W. Wetherill. bibliog il Science 173:383-92 Jl 30 '71

Anecdotes, facetiae, satire, etc.
First lunar invitational. J. Updike. New Yorker 47:35-6 F 27 '71

Conferences
At the moon conference: consensus and conflict. il Sci N 99:61-2 Ja 23 '71
Lunar sciences; second annual Lunar science conference. Sci N 99:65 Ja 23 '71
Moon origin controversy continues; second annual Lunar science conference. Z. Strickland. Aviation W 94:50-1+ Ja 25 '71
Mysteries remain. il Newsweek 77:63-4 F 1 '71

Exploration
Learning from the moon. C. M. Lee. il Todays Ed 60:50-2 Ja '71
See also
Space flight to the moon—Manned flights—Extravehicular activity

Equipment
Apollo 17 to probe for lunar water; surface electrical properties experiment. W. H. Gregory. il Aviation W 95:12-15 O 18 '71
On the moon with Apollo 15. G. Simmons. il Space World H-10-94:19-35 O '71

Internal structure
Apollo 17 to probe for lunar water. W. H. Gregory. il Aviation W 95:12-15 O 18 '71
Early lunar interior believed molten. Aviation W 95:73 D 20 '71
Moon's interior. Sci N 100:167-8 S 11 '71
Possible observation of water vapor on the moon. Sci N 100:277 O 23 '71
Water on the moon. Newsweek 78:78 O 25 '71
Water vapor could speed base on moon. Aviation W 95:15 O 25 '71
Wet moon? Time 98:59 O 25 '71

Legal aspects
See Space law
Mass
Isaac Asimov explains; what are the mascons on the moon? I. Asimov. Sci Digest 69:72-3 Mr '71
More light on mascons. Sci N 99:232 Ap 3 '71

Observations
Some very thin lunar crescents. J. Ashbrook. bibliog il Sky & Tel 42:78-9 Ag '71

Photographs
Apollo 14 photos detail Fra Mauro terrain. Aviation W 94:14-19 F 22 '71
Apollo 15 crew, rover widen lunar horizons. Aviation W 95:14-21 Ag 16 '71
Apollo 15 photos show lunar landscapes. Aviation W 95:34-7 S 6 '71
Apollo 15 pictorial. J. A. Ashbrook. Sky & Tel 42:192-201 O '71
Apollo 15 television from the moon. il Sky & Tel 42:136-8 S '71
Astronauts, rover reap geologic harvest. Aviation W 95:52A-52H Ag 23 '71
Lunar horizons shown in panoramic views. Aviation W 95:48-9 S 13 '71
Two lunar scenes from Apollo 14. Sky & Tel 41:356-7 Je '71

Photographs from space
High-altitude photos pick out LM on moon. Aviation W 95:48-9 O 18 '71
Lunar features seen from orbit. Aviation W 95:18-19 S 6 '71
Lunar photos reveal new details. W. H. Gregory. il Aviation W 95:66-73 D 20 '71
Orbital photos detail cinder cone area. Aviation W 95:14-15 D 6 '71

Radiation
See Moon—Temperature and radiation

MOON—*Continued*

Surface

Apollo 15 landing site. Space World T-2-86: 45 F '71

Blowing of lunar soil by Apollo 12: Surveyor 3 evidence. L. D. Jaffe. bibliog il Science 171:798-9 F 26 '71

Changing the lunar image. il Time 97:42 Ja 25 '71

Choosing the last two lunar landing sites. il Sci N 99:397-8 Je 12 '71

Endogenetic craters interpreted from crater counts on the inner wall of Copernicus. R. Greeley and D. E. Gault. bibliog il Science 171:477-9 F 5 '71

Far side: study of contrast. E. Driscoll. il Sci N 100:194-5 S 18 '71

Fra Mauro craters: more answers to riddle of universe? il U S News 70:31 F 15 '71

Layered moon. il Sci Am 225:74 S '71

Lunar Hadley Rille: considerations of its origin. R. Greeley. bibliog il Science 172:722-5 My 14 '71

Lunar photos reveal new details. W. H. Gregory. il Aviation W 95:66-73 D 20 '71

Man's return to the moon; second attempt at Fra Mauro Region. E. Driscoll. il Sci N 99:66-7 Ja 23 '71

Stunning scenes from a desolate moonscape. il Time 98:26-7 Ag 23 '71

Very heavy solar cosmic rays: energy spectrum and implications for lunar erosion. R. L. Fleischer and others. bibliog il Science 171:1240-2 Mr 26 '71

Temperature and radiation

Moonglow. Sci Am 226:47 Ja '72

MOON rocks. See Lunar geology

MOON vehicles. See Lunar vehicles

MOONCHILDREN; drama. See Weller, M.

MOONEY, Carol
Ode to living; poem. Seventeen 31:91 Ja '72

MOONEY, Elina
Elina Mooney dances, the Cubiculo, NYC. M. Marks. Dance Mag 45:79 Jl '71 *

MOONLIGHTING. See Supplementary employment

MOONMOBILES. See Lunar vehicles

MOONQUAKES. See Seismology

MOOR, Paul
Behind the scenes. il pors Hi Fi 21:20+ Ap '71

Color TV from a video disc. Sat R 54:73 S 25 '71

Regina Resnik's Carmen. il Hi Fi 21:MA28-9 O '71

MOORE, Anne Carroll
Art vs. adventitious circumstances. W. Chappell. il Horn Bk 47:456-61 O '71 *

MOORE, Arch Alfred, 1923-
Break for West Virginia. W. E. Chilton. 3d. Nation 213:390-2 O 25 '71 *

States' biggest problems; interview. il pors Nations Bsns 59:26-9 D '71 *

MOORE, Brian
Story behind the book: The revolution script; interview. ed. by B. A. Bannon. por Pub W 201:42-3 Ja 3 '72

MOORE, C. L.
De-wrapping the spinnaker. il Yachting 129: 65+ Je '71

MOORE, Carleton B. See Cronin, J. R. jt. auth.

MOORE, Claire
Craft of mimeography. il por Craft Horiz 31: 30-3 F '71

MOORE, Dan H.
Progress on breast cancer. il por Newsweek 77:129 Ap 19 '71 *

MOORE, David W.
Pablo Casals: a tribute. por Am Rec G 37: 280-1 Ja '71

MOORE, Donald J.
Martin Buber: friend of the court. il America 124:231-4 Mr 6 '71

MOORE, Edward H.
Repairing your fiberglass boat. il Cons 25: 48-9 Ap '71

MOORE, Everett T.
Threats to intellectual freedom: address, June 1971. il por Library J 96:3563-7 N 1 '71; Same abr. with title Rise of new censorship? Cur 135:3-8 D '71

MOORE, Gabriel
Grits. Sat R 54:56 O 9 '71

MOORE, Gerald C.
Thirty hours plus thirty years. Am Artist 35:5 O '71

MOORE, Helen C.
Grandma builds a bridge; story. Har Yrs 11: 14-15 F '71

MOORE, Henry
(ed) Gist of it. See issues of Outdoor life

MOORE, Henry Spencer
Moore in multiple view. il Sat R 54:44-5 Ap 3 '71 *

MOORE, Hilary B.
Babylonian map. il Sea Front 17:23-5 Ja '71

MOORE, James R.
Sex and the supernatural. Chr Today 15:7-8+ My 7 '71

MOORE, Kenneth E. See Von Voigtlander, P. F. jt. auth.

MOORE, Kenny
One of the pleasures of my life. Sports Illus 35:53 N 1 '71

MOORE, Marianne
Ladies of the Dial; excerpt from Eloquent April. M. Cane. Am Scholar 40:316-21 Spr '71 *

MOORE, Melba
Peach Melba. H. Saal. por Newsweek 77:94 Je 28 '71 *

People are talking about . . . por Vogue 158: 106-7 O 15 '71 *

MOORE, Richard
Revelation; poem. Nation 212:158 F 1 '71

MOORE, Richard E. and Scheuer, P. J.
Palytoxin: a new marine toxin from a coelenterate. bibliog il Science 172:495-8 Ap 30 '71

MOORE, Rosanna
Poetry and paint. il Sch Arts 70:16-17 Je '71

Stained glass design goes mod. il Sch Arts 71:12-13 Ja '72

MOORE, Ruth
Record in the rocks. il Audubon 73:13-29 Ja '71

MOORE, Trevor Wyatt
Art (cont) Chr Cent 88:233-4, 864-5 F 17, Jl 14 '71

Ecumenical then. Chr Cent 88:192-3 F 10 '71

Records. Chr Cent 88:390 Mr 24; 785-6 Je 23 '71

Uncorinthian Philadelphians. por Chr Cent 88:930-1 Ag 4 '71

MOORE, William C.
If Giap were a U.S. general. por U S News 70:35 My 3 '71

Reason for confidence in Cambodia. por U S News 70:20-1 F 8 '71

MOORE, William Harreld
We're broke, he told the workers. We need your help. M. Smith. il pors Life 71:69-70+ S 24 '71 *

MOORE, Winston E.
My cure for prison riots: end prison racism. il pors Ebony 27:84-6+ D '71

MOORE-BETTY, Maurice
Cooking lesson with Maurice Moore-Betty. il pors House & Gard 140:74-5+ Jl '71 *

Maurice Moore-Betty, a pro at the stove. M. McKendry. il por Vogue 158:54+ N 15 '71 *

MOORE corporation
True to form. il Forbes 108:39 O 15 '71

MOOREFIELD, Story
How Louisville put it all together. il Am Ed 7:30-4 D '71

MOOREHEAD, Alan
Peripatetic reviewer. E. Weeks. Atlan 227: 102 Ap '71 *

MOORER, Thomas Hinman
Budget aspects and national security; address, December 10, 1970. Vital Speeches 37:194-7 Ja 15 '71

What next in Indo-China; interview. il por U S News 70:44-8 Ap 5 '71

MOORHOUSE, James A.
This year hang a trophy bass. il Field & S 76:42-3+ Jl '71

MOORING of boats. See Anchorage

MOOSE, Loyal order of
Washington scores Moose for snub of black librarian; S. Finley from Timberland regional library. il por Library J 97: 11 Ja 1 '72

MOOSE hunting
Bulls of Barriere. W. N. Roach. il pors Outdoor Life 148:84-7+ O; 80-3+ N: 54-7+ D '71

I never want a bigger moose. D. Revoir. il Outdoor Life 147:60-1+ Je '71

I wanted it wild. W. N. Roach. il pors Outdoor Life 148:84-7+ O '71 (to be cont)

Stay for the ending. P. L. Halbig. il Outdoor Life 157:76-9+ F '71

MOOSONEE, Ontario
Great day in Moosonee. R. S. Milne. il Seventeen 29:130 Jl '70

MOOZ, R. Peter
Origins of Newport block-front furniture design. il Antiques 99:882-6 Je '71

MORAES, Dom
Indira Gandhi is either hated or adored. il por N Y Times Mag p 10-11+ F 14 '71

MORAHAN, Page S. See Grossberg, S. E. jt. auth.

MORAL attitudes
Is virginity outmoded? D. A. Sugarman and R. Hochstein. il Seventeen 30:120-1+ O '71
Living in a valueless world. Chr Today 16: 30-1 N 5 '71
Pride goes before avarice; social change and the vices in Latin Christendom. L. K. Little. bibliog f il Am Hist R 76:16-49 F '71

MORAL conditions
Situation ethics in a changing situation. J. Fletcher. por Chr Cent 88:1444-6 D 8 '71
See also
Moving pictures—Moral aspects

MORAL education
Attitudes and values: ingredients of good teaching. M. M. Meadows, jr. Clear House 45:377-9 F '71
Early concepts of morality; with study-discussion program. by E. Harris and D. Harris. G. Wile. bibliog il PTA Mag 66: 25-7+, 33-4 D '71
Herbartians, history, and moral education. N. R. Hiner. Ed Digest 37:51-3 N '71
Toward moral maturity; teaching ethics in the reformatory. il por Time 97:48 Je 28 '71
Why is crime now a worldwide epidemic? D. Lawrence. U S News 71:84 S 6 '71

MORAL leadership. See Leadership
MORAL obligation. See Duty
MORAL philosophy. See Ethics
MORAL theology. See Christian ethics; Theology
MORAL values. See Worth

MORALE
Can teacher unrest be averted? C. O'Connor. Clear House 45:308 Ja '71
See also
Discipline, Military
Employee morale
United States—Armed forces—Morale
United States—Army—Morale

MORALE, National

Egypt
Today's Egypt: war-weary with no peace in sight. J. Law. il U S News 70:30-1 My 24 '71

Israel
Israel: problems of "peace." J. Law. il U S News 70:11 Je 14 '71
Living on the brink of war. A. Kucherov. il U S News 70:78-82 Mr 15 '71

United States
Can we regain the spirit of '76? W. E. Swegle. Suc Farm 69:A4 O '71
Drugs and defeatism; U.S. decadence; excerpts from remarks, July 6, 1971. R. M. Nixon. il por U S News 71:37 Jl 19 '71
Longing for Armageddon. L. H. Lapham. il Harper 243:10+ Ag '71
Mood of America: wait-and-see optimism. il U S News 71:50-5 S 6 '71
Question. Nation 212:258-9 Mr 1 '71
Rebirth: Americans moving on; symposium. Look 35:33-8+ Ja 12 '71
Solid base of national support. il Bsns W p 17-18 Ag 28 '71
U.S. identity crisis. P. A. Samuelson. Newsweek 77:81 Je 21 '71

Vietnam (Democratic Republic)
Answers to a mystery: why North Vietnam fights on. il U S News 71:40-1 Ag 9 '71

MORALES, Jane
Hi, mom, what's for lunch? See Issues of Parents' magazine & better family living

MORALITY. See Ethics
MORALS and literature. See Literature and morals

MORAN, Gabriel
Catechetics, R.I.P. Commonweal 93:299-302, 411+ D 18 '70, Ja 29 '71
Religious education-community. America 124: 86-9 Ja 30 '71

MORAN, H. Fernández-. See Fernández-Morán, H.

MORAN, Thomas P.
Artificial, intelligent architecture: computers in design. bibliog f il Arch Rec 149:129-34 Mr '71

MORANDI, Giorgio
Letter from Paris; exhibition at the Musée d'art moderne. Genêt. New Yorker 47:95-6 Mr 27 '71 *

MORANDI, Riccardo
Morandi's bridges. il Arch Forum 135:48-53 O '71 *

MORASH, Tai
ACA accreditation through a revised standards visitation program. Camp Mag 43: 19-20 Ja '71

MORATH, Inge
How people really travel; interview. il por Vogue 157:118 Ap 15 '71

MORAVIA, Alberto
Exorbitant price; story. Ladies Home J 89:80-1 Ja '72
Wardrobe; story. Harp Baz 104:134-5 O '71

MORAVIANS
Old Salem: a Moravian memoir. V. D. Hahn. il Am Home 74:28+ D '71
Peaceful people. M. Evans. il Am Home 74: 44-9+ D '71

MORAY, Ann
Magic mask; story. il Redbook 138:71-3 D '71

MORE, Sir Thomas, Saint
More's Utopia: confessional modes. D. Bleich. bibliog f Am Imago 28:24-52 Spr '71 *

MORE (periodical)
Promising More. il Newsweek 77:64 Je 14 '71

MORE like a friend; story See Amft, M. J.

MORE to love; story. See Deal, B. H.

MOREA, Douglas
Listening to Pearl; poem. New Yorker 47:52 S 25 '71

MOREAU, David
Jet lag: how time-zone changes can shake up travellers' health. Vogue 157:102+ Ap 15 '71
Once-a-month birth-control pill. Vogue 158: 95 Ag 1 '71

MOREHOUSE, Laurence E.
Pulse test, new way to fitness. il Read Digest 99:77-80 O '71

MOREHOUSE college, Atlanta, Ga.
Doctor Benjamin E. Mays. il pors Ebony 26: 88-92+ Jl '71

MOREL, Emery B. See Bauer, E. O. jr, jt. auth.

MORENA, Bianca Teresa Perez-. See Perez-Morena, B. T.

MORENO DIAZ, María Eugenia (Rojas)
La capitana. il pors Time 98:43-4+ D 6 '71 *

MOREV, Fyodor
How the Vostok spaceship was developed. il Space World H-8-92:26-7 Ag '71

MORGAN, Aubrey Niel
Collection of Swansea and Nantgarw porcelain. il Antiques 100:596-601 O '71

MORGAN, Barbara
Barbara Morgan: one of America's great photographers reflects a decade of dance, 1935-1945. D. Hering. il por Dance Mag 45: 43-56 Jl '71 *

MORGAN, Berry
Passing; story New Yorker 47:44-6 Je 26 '71

MORGAN, Charles Eugene, Jr
Charley Morgan speaks up; interview. ed. by G. F. Hammond. il por Motor B & S 127: 58-60+ Je '71
about
Dynamic growth companies. il por Nations Bsns 59:76-8 Ap '71 *

MORGAN, Corinne
Corinne Morgan. J. Walsh. il por Hobbies 76:37-8+ Jl; 37-8+ Ag; 37-8+ S '71 *

MORGAN, Edmund S.
Labor problem at Jamestown, 1607-18. bibliog f il Am Hist R 76:595-611 Je '71

MORGAN, Harry
Curriculum is the self. Ed Digest 36:19-22 Mr '71

MORGAN, Henry
Mr Sullivan discusses the stock market (with apologies to Mr Arbuthnot) Sat R 54:4 Ja 23 '71

MORGAN, James
Can a computer beat the horses? il Look 35: 33 Je 1 '71
Guaniamo diamond miner is nobody's best friend. il Atlan 227:56-61 Ap '71
Pool. Sports Illus 34:52-3 F 8 '71

MORGAN, John W. and others
Glazed lunar rocks: origin by impact. bibliog il Science 172:556-8 My 7 '71

MORGAN, Karl Z.
Never do harm. bibliog il Environ 13:28-38 Ja '71

MORGAN, Len
Brain that tells a 747 where to go! il por Pop Mech 136:108-11+ O '71

MORGAN, Leslie
Tip-offs on personality traits. il PTA Mag 66:22-4+ bibliog (p34) S '71

MORGAN, Nell
Australia: opals are a girl's best friend. il Sat R 54:50-1+ O 23 '71
Baja California. il Holiday 48:48-51+ N '70

MORGAN, Robert
Chestnut; poem. Nation 212:732 Je 7 '71
Sound of our speaking. Nation 213:188-90
S 6 '71
MORGAN, Robert P.
Masterwork by Boulez. por Hi Fi 21:70-1
Ag '71
Pianistic culminations. por Hi Fi 21:20 Je '71
Three North American keyboard virtuosos
give Bach a young look. il Hi Fi 21:86 S
'71
MORGAN, William Jason
Hot spots and crust motion. Sci N 99:180
Mr 13 '71 *
MORGAN guaranty trust company
What would J.P. do now? il Forbes 107:18-19
My 1 '71
MORGAN yacht corporation
Dynamic growth companies. il por Nations
Bsns 59:76-8 Ap '71
MORGANTOWN, W.Va.
New rapid transit systems tested; proto-
type computer-controlled system. M. L.
Yaffee. il Aviation W 95:44-6+ N 8 '71
Personal rapid transit. S. Lindsay. Sat R 54:
94-5 D 4 '71
MORGELLO, Clem
Wall Street. See issues of Newsweek
MORGENSTERN, Joseph
[Column] See every other issue of News-
week
New face of adoption. il Newsweek 78:
66-8+ S 13 '71
What hath Disney wrought! il Newsweek
78:38-43+ O 18 '71
MORGENTHAU, Hans Joachim
Agreement on Berlin. New Repub 165:16-18 D
25 '71
Changes and chances in American-Soviet
relations. For Affairs 49:429-41 Ap '71
Show of support. New Repub 164:10-11 Mr
13 '71
What price victory? New Repub 164:21-3 F
20 '71; Same abr. with title Will we use our
nuclear option? Cur 128:4-8 Ap '71
MORHANGE, Charles Henri Valentin. See Al-
kan. C. H. V.
MORI, Tom
Japanese royalties: two points of views. Pub
W 199:17-18 My 3 '71
MORIN, Edgar
One right way to write and think? B. De-
Mott. Am Scholar 41:53-62 Wint '71 *
MORINI, Simona
Breast sculpture. il Vogue 157:82-5+ Ja 15 '71
Face-lifts; excerpt from Body sculpture. il
Vogue 158:114-17+ S 15 '71
New aid to plastic surgery: silicone. il Vogue
157:84-7+ Mr 15 '71
MORISON, Robert S.
Death: process or event? adaptation of ad-
dress, December 29, 1970. bibliog Science
173:694-8 Ag 20 '71
MORISON, Stanley
Stanley Morison. by J. Moran. Review
Pub W 201:51-2 Ja 3 '72 *
MORLEY, Olive J.
Robin Hood and the Gentle knight; drama-
tization of a legend. Plays 30:45-54 Mr '71
Sherlock Holmes and the second stain;
dramatization of story by A. C. Doyle.
Plays 31:72, 83-96 O '71
MORMONS and Mormonism
Busy like the bees. il Forbes 107:24-5 F 1 '71
Mormon empire. F. Lang. il Ramp Mag 10:
36-43 S '71
Mormon trails in the Midwest. S. Murdock.
il Travel 137:58-63+ Ja '72
Race, evolution and Mormonism. C. W.
Quaintance. Chr Cent 88:586-9 My 12 '71
Urban shadows fall on sunny Salt Lake City.
H. Waters. il Newsweek 77:102+ Mr 15 '71
See also
Polygamy
MORMONS and Mormonism, Negro
Matter of opinion: Mormonism's Negro poli-
cy. F. H. Jonas. Am West 8:48 N '71
MOROCCAN dancing. See Dancing, Moroccan
MOROCCO
Arab friend of U.S. fights to stay in power.
il por U S News 72:67-8 Ja 3 '72
Morocco: land of the farthest west. T. J.
Abercrombie. il Nat Geog 139:834-65 Je '71
See also
Arabs in Morocco
Automobile touring—Morocco
Marrakesh
Tangier
Textile industry—Morocco
Visitors, Foreign—Morocco
Women—Morocco
Description and travel
Getting & moving around Morocco; with re-
port by L. Lee. Mlle 73:90, 148-54+ Je '71

Politics and government
Coup that failed. por Newsweek 78:26 Jl 19
'71
Hassan's last hurrah? il por Newsweek 78:
46+ D 6 '71
Meaning to U.S. of uprising in Morocco.
por U S News 71:50 Jl 26 '71
Morocco: bloody birthday; attempted coup. il
por Time 98:16 Jl 19 '71
Morocco: the cracked facade. il Time 98:
26-8 Jl 26 '71
Promises, promises. Newsweek 78:37 Ag 16
'71
Vengeance of King Hassan. il por Newsweek
78:33-4 Jl 26 '71
Social life and customs
See also
Women—Morocco
MORPHACTINS
Morphactin-induced parthenocarpy in the
cucumber. R. W. Robinson and others.
bibliog il Science 171:1251 Mr 26 '71
MORPHINE
Disposition of morphine in man. S. Spector
and E. S. Vesell. bibliog il Science 174:
421-2 O 22 '71
Morphine tolerance and dependence induced
by intraventricular injection. E. Eidelberg
and C. A. Barstow. bibliog il Science 174:
74-6 O 1 '71
Narcotic tolerance and dependence: lack of
relationship with serotonin turnover in
the brain. D. L. Cheney and others. bibliog il Science 171:1169-70 Mr 19 '71
MORPHOGENESIS
Microfilaments in cellular and developmental
processes. N. K. Wessells and others. bibliog il Science 171:135-43 Ja 15 '71; Reply.
with rejoinder. R. D. Estensen and others.
173:356-9 Jl 23 '71
MORRELL, Lenore K. and Salamy, J. G.
Hemispheric asymmetry of electrocortical
responses to speech stimuli. bibliog il
Science 174:164-6 O 8 '71
MORRELL, Marc
Supreme court and the flag. F. Graham.
Art in Am 59:27 Mr '71 *
MORRILL, George P.
Best white friend black Americans ever had.
il por Read Digest 99:169-70+ Jl '71
MORRIS, Byron F.
Petroleum: tar quantities floating in the
northwestern Atlantic taken with a new
quantitative neuston net. bibliog il Science
173:430-2 Jl 30 '71
MORRIS, Daniel Luzon
Stress collisions and constants. il por Chem
44:10-12 Ap; 15-19 My; 15-17 Je '71
MORRIS, Edita
Life wonderful life! story. Redbook 137:157-79
S '71
MORRIS, Frank E.
Overhaul urged for municipal bonds; excerpts
from address, January 18, 1971. por U S
News 70:59-60 F 1 '71
MORRIS, Fred B.
Trickle of justice in Brazil. por Chr Cent
88:1353-4+ N 17 '71
MORRIS, George B.
Ford weighing aid for strikers; excerpts from
address, June 3, 1971. U S News 70:88 Je
21 '71
MORRIS, Gouverneur
Charles Willson Peale's portrait of Robert
and Gouverneur Morris. C. C. Sellers. il
pors Antiques 99:404-6 Mr '71 *
MORRIS, Ivan
Up the cerebral cortex. il Esquire 75:92-5
Ja '71
MORRIS, James, 1926-
Ashanti. il Horizon 13:74-91 Spr '71
Most African country in Africa. il Holiday
49:50-3+ Mr '71
Mozambique. il Holiday 48:46-51+ S '70
What is an Arab? il Horizon 13:4-17 Sum '71
MORRIS, John E.
Accountability: watchword for the 70's.
bibliog Clear House 45:323-8 F '71
MORRIS, John L.
Interview: guidelines for making it a more
effective hiring device. il Clear House 46:35-9
S '71
MORRIS, John N.
Comment. R. Howard. Poetry 119:34-5 O '71 *
Quiet life; Life beside this one; That sum-
mer; poems. Poetry 118:336-7 S '71
MORRIS, June Wood
Rape of the moon; poem. Negro Hist Bul
33:169 N '70
MORRIS, Leon
Luke the theologian. Chr Today 15:39 Ag
27 '71

MORRIS, M. D.
Forgotten inlet. il Opera N 35:22-3 Ap 17 '71
MORRIS, Mary Louise
Dolls of Old Salem. il Hobbies 76:42+ Jl '71
MORRIS, Norval
Reform: it must come; interview, ed. by J.
Pekkanen. il por Life 71:36 S 24 '71
MORRIS, Raymond P.
China records project at Yale. Chr Cent 88:
832-3 Jl 7 '71
MORRIS, Richard B.
Meet Dr Franklin; excerpts. il por Am Heritage 23:80-91 D '71
MORRIS, Robert, 1734-1806
Charles Willson Peale's portrait of Robert
and Gouverneur Morris. C. C. Sellers. il
pors Antiques 99:404-6 Mr '71 *
MORRIS, Robert K.
Literary community. Nation 212:695-6 My 31
'71
MORRIS, Roger R.
Teaching survival in the sales jungle. il Am
Ed 7:28-31 Ap '71
MORRIS, William
White's time, not White space, was wasteful; reply to J. B. White. Wilson Lib Bul
45:679-80 Mr '71
MORRIS, William, 1834-1896
Book that never was, by J. R. Dunlap. Review
Pub W il 200:45-6 D 6 '71. C. B. Grannis *
MORRIS, Willie
Authors & editors. D. N. Mount. por Pub W
199:15-16 Je 14 '71 *
Boy's home town makes good R. Z. Sheppard. por Time 97:93 My 10 '71 *
Coup at Harper's. por Newsweek 77:64 Mr
15 '71 *
Hang-up at Harper's. pors Time 97:41 Mr 15
'71 *
Morris quits at Harper's; cites severe disagreements. Pub W 199:51 Mr 15 '71 *
What happened at Harper's. S. Little. il por
Sat R 54:43-7+ Ap 10 '71; Reply. N. Mailer.
54:56 Je 12 '71 *
You can go home again. G. Wolff. Newsweek
77:110+ My 1 0'71 *
MORRIS, Wright
Here is Einbaum; story. New Yorker 47:35-
41 Je 26 '71
    about
Remembrance of cranks past. il por Time 98:
88-9 O 18 '71 *
MORRIS (automobile) See Automobiles, Foreign
MORRISON, Charles C. Jr
Getting started: environmental action in the
community. il Cons 25:4-5 F '71
MORRISON, David
R for an age-old dilemma: should I take
this job for life? il Schol Teach Jr/Sr High
p24-5+ S '71
MORRISON, Donald E.
From Moscow to Irkutsk to Leningrad; interview. il pors Todays Ed 60:36-40 D '71
Meet NEA president Donald Morrison; interview. pors Todays Ed 60:50-3 S '71
MORRISON, Donald E. family
Meet the Morrisons. pors Todays Ed 60:31
O '71
MORRISON, Gordon
Beans and more beans. il Horticulture 49:
34-5+ My '71
MORRISON, Philip
—and Morrison, Phylis
Books about science for the younger reader:
an annual Christmas survey. Sci Am 225:
106-15 D '71
    about
Teaching physics in the corridors. H. L. Davis. Phys Today 24:88 Ag '71 *
MORRISON, Phylis. See Morrison, Philip jt.
auth.
MORRISON, Toni
What the black woman thinks about Women's lib. il N Y Times Mag p 14-15+ Ag
22 '71
MORRISON, Van
New minstrels. pors Harp Baz 104:56 Je '71 *
MORROW, Everett Frederic
Whatever happened to E. Frederic Morrow?
il pors Ebony 27:182 D '71 *
MORROW, Susan
Tomorrow is too late; story. Good H 172:76-
7 Je '71
MORSE, John D.
Winterthur in the spring. il Horticulture 49:
26-7+ My '71
MORSE, Wayne Lyman
Young in heart. Nation 213:357-8 O 18 '71 *

MORTALITY
American way of death. Sci Am 226:50 Ja '72
    See also
Death
Heart—Diseases—Mortality
Infant mortality
MORTENSEN, William
Pictorialism. E. Scully. il Mod Phot 35:94-9
Ja '71 *
MORTGAGE guaranty insurance. See Insurance, Mortgage guaranty
MORTGAGES
Ahead, easier ways to finance home purchases. il U S News 71:59-61 D 27 '71
And builders get more to build on. il Bsns W
p 17 Ja 23 '71
Can we prevent another bust? il Forbes 109:
114-15 Ja 1 '72
Credit act cools mortgage men. Bsns W p84
My 22 '71
Fanny Mae's anti-consumer mortgage. Consumer Rep 36:240 Ap '71
Farm mortgage of the future? Variable interest rate loans. G. Reynolds. Farm J 95:
24G Ag '71
Financing a restoration. B. Russell. House &
Gard 140:10+ Ag '71
House: the year of the big buy. il Time
97:75-6 Mr 29 '71
Housing abandonment. Arch Forum 134:42-5
Ap '71
How three kinds of mortgages compare. il
Changing T 25:41-3 Ag '71
How to pay less for a home loan. il Changing
T 25:22-4 Mr '71
Is now a good time for you to refinance?
farm mortgages. Suc Farm 69:B12 Je '71
Why so many mortgages are being foreclosed.
il U S News 72:25-6 Ja 3 '72
    See also
Federal national mortgage association
Insurance, Mortgage guaranty
Land contracts
United States—Farmers home administration
United States—Federal housing administration
MORTISE and tenon joints. See Joints (carpentry)
MORTON, A. W.
Third annual Chapman award. il por Motor
B & S 127:12 Ap '71 *
MORTON, Craig
Super bowl. R. F. Jones. il por Sports Illus
34:18+ Ja 18 '71 *
MORTON, Eugene S.
Nest predation affecting the breeding season
of the clay-colored robin, a tropical song
bird. bibliog il Science 171:920-1 Mr 5 '71
MORTON, Frederic
Bohemia, such as it is, on the West side.
il N Y Times Mag p22-3+ My 9 '71
MORTON, Keith
Potter's trip. Ceram Mo 19:32 S '71
MORTON, Peter
Pushing burgers. il por Newsweek 78:67 O 4
'71 *
MORTON, Rogers Clark Ballard
Cleaner America: the war on pollution; interview. il por U S News 71:46-50+ 0 4
'71
    about
Blow to the pipeline. Newsweek 77:81 Mr 1
'71 *
Exit Secretary Hickel, enter Secretary Morton. Audubon 73:94 Ja '71 *
Morton questions pipeline project; with editorial comment. Liv Wildn 35:2, 45 Spr '71 *
Rogers C. B. Morton. il pors Parks & Rec
6:30-1 S '71 *
Search for alternatives. Sci N 99:143 F 27
'71 *
MORTON, Terry B.
Victorian mansions in Memphis. il Antiques
100:408-12 S '71
MORTON, Thomas H. and Del Dolori, M. P.
Electives program in a small high school?
It works! Engl J 60:952-6 O '71
MORTON, W. Scott
Educational and cultural trends in Japan
today. Cur Hist 60:213-17 Ap '71
MORTUARY art. See Sepulchral monuments
MORTUARY sculpture. See Sepulchral monuments
MOSAIC diseases
Wheat disease to look for; wheat streak
mosaic. C. E. Sommers. Suc Farm 69:40 S
'71
MOSAICS
Child can do it; mosaic coffee table. K. J.
Griffin. il Design 73:8-9 Wint '71
In the courtyard with an art student. D.
Allen. il Sch Arts 70:18-19 Ap '71

MOSAICS—*Continued*
Jeanne Reynal. B. Guest. il Craft Horiz 31:40-3 Je '71
Lasting piece of art. I. B. Ormen. il Sch Arts 71:28-9 Ja '72
MOSBACH, Klaus
Enzymes bound to artificial matrixes; with biographical sketch. il Sci Am 224:14, 26-33 bibliog(p 124) Mr '71
MOSBACHER, Emil, 1922-
Savvy skipper of protocol. N. F. Busch. por Read Digest 99:161-5 O '71 *
MOSCONA, A. A.
Embryonic and neoplastic cell surfaces: availability of receptors for concanavalin A and wheat germ agglutinin. bibliog il Science 171:905-7; 173:265 Mr 5, Jl 16 '71
MOSCOW

Education
Two schools in Moscow. Sat R 54:45 Jl 17 '71

Music
Close look at the Tchaikovsky competition. L. Effenbach. Hi Fi 20:MA22-3+ D '70

Photographs
Can this be Moscow? J. Launois. Fortune 83:90-3 Ap '71

Street traffic
Electronics in Moscow's streets. il Am City 86:106 Ag '71
MOSCOW circus. See Circus
MOSCOW film festival. See Moving picture festivals
MOSELEY, Henry Nottidge
Notes by a naturalist on the Challenger; excerpts. il Natur Hist 80:76-80 O '71
MOSELEY, Spencer Dumaresq
Executive jungle? il por Forbes 107:60 F 15 '71 *
MOSER, Don
Lament for some companions of my youth. il Life 70:46-8+ Ja 22 '71
MOSER, Edda
Cool command; interview, ed. by D. Graham. por Opera N 35:16 Mr 20 '71
MOSER, Marvin, and Greenhouse, L. J.
Can we counteract the cult of marijuana? Parents Mag 46:40-1+ Jl '71
MOSES
Moses encounters the daemonic aspect of God. D. F. Zeligs. bibliog Am Imago 27:379-91 Wint '70
MOSES, Ed
View from the Coast. il pors Time 97:58-9 F 1 '71 *
MOSES, Richard B.
CANACONDA? por Library J 96:915-17 Mr 15 '71
Meeting. Am Lib 2:244-5 Mr '71
MOSES, Robert, 1888-
Informal notes, taken on reading John Hersey on Yale. Nat R 23:142-4+ F 9 '71
Stretching outdoor recreation. il por Cons 26:28-9 D '71
MOSES and Aaron; opera. See Schönberg, A.
MOSHER, Loren R.
Schizophrenia. il Todays Ed 60:14-17 Mr '71
MOSHER, T. Edward
Inside the revolutionary left. Read Digest 99:53-7 S '71
MOSKIN, J. Robert
Israeli youth: the coming explosion. il Look 35:20-4+ Je 15 '71
Uncle Sam still wants you, kid. Look 35:21-3 F 23 '71
(ed) See Ellsberg, D. Ellsberg talks
MOSLEM-Jewish marriages. See Marriages, Mixed
MOSLEY, Jean Bell
Bucket of clear, cool spring water. il Read Digest 98:89-92 Ap '71
MOSQUES
Sacred art in Persian culture. S. H. Nasr. il UNESCO Courier 24:16-25 O '71
MOSQUITO control
Isolation and characterization of larvicidal principle of garlic. S. V. Amonkar and A. Banerji. bibliog il Science 174:1343-4 D 24 '71
MOSQUITO repellents. See Insect baits and repellents
MOSQUITOES
Immortality; excerpts from Mosquito safari. C. B. Worth. il Audubon 73:28-31 Jl '71
Linkage group-chromosome correlation in culex tritaeniorhynchus. R. H. Baker and others. bibliog il Science 171:585-7 F 12 '71

Extermination
See Mosquito control

MOSQUITOES as carriers of infection
Culex (melanoconion) aikenii: natural vector in Panama of endemic Venezuelan encephalitis. P. Galindo and M. A. Grayson. bibliog il Science 172:594-5 My 7 '71
MOSS, Frank T.
With the sport fishermen. See issues of Yachting
MOSS, Howard
Bay days; poem. New Yorker 47:30 Ag 28 '71
Cold-water flats; poem. Esquire 75:139 Je '71
Hansel and Gretel; poem. Harper 242:79 Ap '71
Magic affinities; poem. Poetry 118:74-6 My '71
Refrigerator; poem. New Yorker 47:36 S 18 '71
Sawdust; poem. New Yorker 47:34 Jl 24 '71
Three winter poems. New Yorker 47:46 F 20 '71
MOSS, James N.
Change and self-determination at Ganado. Chr Cent 88:321-2 Mr 10 '71
MOSS, John Hardie
World's best poker player. E. Shrake. il por Sports Illus 34:56-8+ Ja 25 '71 *
MOSS, Joy. See Muskopf, A. jt. auth.
MOSS, Laurence I.
Taxing U.S. polluters; excerpt from testimony before the Joint economic committee of Congress. Sat R 54:51 Ag 7 '71
MOSS, Marquita
Late Liz; metamorphosis of a rich alcoholic. Chr Today 16:34-5 O 22 '71
MOSS, Spanish. See Spanish moss
MÖSSBAUER effect
Mössbauer spectroscopy. R. H. Herber. il Sci Am 225:86-95 bibliog(p 120) O '71
Mössbauer spectroscopy and biophysics. C. E. Johnson. bibliog il Phys Today 24:35-40 F '71
MOSSES
See also
Lichens
MOSSMAN, James
Volcano. il Travel 136:46-7+ N '71
MOST, Bruce
Carpathians: better walnuts for the Midwest. il Org Gard & Farm 18:56-9 N '71
MOST, Harry. See Yoeli, M. jt. auth.
MOST important man; opera. See Menotti, G. C.
MOST incredible meal; story. See Kotzwinkle, W.
MOSTEL, Zero
Zero in; interview, ed. by S. Jenkins. por Opera N 35:14-15 F 13 '71
MOSZKOWSKI, Moritz
Memorable IPL release: Moszkowski. L. Gerber. il Am Rec G 37:292-4 Ja '71 *
Moszkowski's splashy piano concerto. R. W. Schaaf. Hi Fi 21:86+ Ja '71 *
MOTE, Michael I. and Goldsmith, T. H.
Compound eyes: localization of two color receptors in the same ommatidium. bibliog il Science 171:1254-5 Mr 26 '71
MOTH orchids. See Orchids
MOTHBALL fleet; story. See Barthelme, D.
MOTHER-child relationship. See Parent-child relationship
MOTHER earth; revue. See Musical comedies, revues, etc.—Criticisms, plots, etc.
MOTHER goddesses
Venus of Valdivia. F. Samaniego Salazar. il Américas 23:25-31 Mr '71
MOTHER Goose
Rimes de la Mère Oie; French text; excerpts. O. De Kay, jr. il Horizon 13:120 Wint '71
Story behind the book: Mother Goose gets the French treatment; interview ed. by P. Bragg. O. De Kay, jr. il Pub W 200:18-19 D 13 '71
MOTHER love. See Love, Maternal
MOTHER of us all; opera. See Thomson, V.
MOTHER participation in school activities. See Volunteer workers in education
MOTHERHOOD. See Mothers
MOTHERS
How divorced young mothers learn to stand alone. N. M. Lobsenz. il Redbook 138:83+ N '71
How many raindrops in the world? S. Streshinsky. il Redbook 136:53+ Ja '71
In my opinion; marriage and motherhood aren't for everyone. B. Wagner. por Seventeen 30:166 Jl '71
Motherhood still essential. A. J. Snider. Sci Digest 69:58 F '71
My mother, right or wrong; symposium, ed. by J. Campbell. il McCalls 98:69-71+ My '71
Parting shots: Princess Grace has a lot to say about mothers. il por Life 71:63 Jl 30 '71

MOTHERS—*Continued*
Redbook beauty report; Ginnie Hibbard. il
Redbook 138:84-7+ Ja '72
Young mother's story. See issues of Redbook
See also
Childbirth
Foster parents
Love, Maternal
Maternal deprivation
Parent education
Stepparents

Employment

See Married women—Employment
MOTHERS, Jewish. See Jewish women
MOTHERS, Unmarried
Help for high school mothers; Citrus high,
Azusa, Calif. program. R. Woodbury. il
Life 70:34-41 Ap 2 '71
Opinion: on when a single girl becomes preg-
nant. R. Pierce. Mlle 72:36+ Mr '71
Single motherhood. il Time 98:48 S 6 '71
MOTHERS and daughters. See Parent-child
relationship
MOTHERS-in-law
How to live with in-laws twenty-four hours
a day! J. S. Enterline. il Har Yrs 11:14-15+
O '71
MOTHERS milk. See Human milk
MOTHNER, Ira
Few kind words for parents. Look 35:50 Ja
26 '71
How much is your job really worth? il Look
35:60-3 Ap 20 '71
If New Hampshire makes it. Look 35:33-6
Ja 12 '71
Junkie in the house. il Look 35:38-9 Ja 26
'71
Summer power! Canada gives youth its head,
and bread. il Look 35:48-53 Ag 24 '71
—See Astor, G. jt. auth.
MOTHS
Hydrocarbon sex pheromone in tiger moths
(arctiidae) W. L. Roelofs and R. T. Cardé.
bibliog il Science 171:684-6 F 19 '71
Insect photoreceptor: an internal ocellus is
present in sphinx moths. J. L. Eaton. bib-
liog il Science 173:822-3 Ag 27 '71
Sex pheromone of the almond moth and the
Indian meal moth: cis-9, trans-12-tetrade-
cadienyl acetate. Y .Kuwahara and others.
bibliog Science 171:801-2 F 26 '71
Sex pheromone specificity and taxonomy
of budworm moths (choristoneura) C. J.
Sanders. bibliog il Science 171:911-13 Mr 5
'71
Sex stimulant and attractant in the
Indian meal moth and in the almond moth.
U. E. Brady and others. bibliog il Science
171:802-4 F 26 '71
See also
Codling moths
Gypsy moths
MOTHS, Photography of. See Photography of
insects
MOTION
See also
Force and energy
MOTION of fluids in plants. See Plants, Motion
of fluids in
MOTION perception
Stereoscopic depth movement: two eyes less
sensitive than one. C. W. Tyler. bibliog il
Science 174:958-61 N 26 '71
MOTION pictures. See Moving pictures
MOTION sickness
Cause and treatment of motion sickness.
Good H 172:176 Je '71
MOTIONS of the stars. See Stars—Motion
MOTIVATION (education)
Airplane as a teaching tool. T. Taylor. Fly-
ing 89:54-6 D '71
Motivation: the key to changing educational
times. G. Murphy. Ed Digest 36:39-42 Mr
'71
Practical reading course for the slow learner
in high school. B. Ashton. il Engl J 60:97-
101 Ja '71
Relating pertinence to proximity. H. G. Getz
and W. Pierce. Clear House 45:281-4 Ja
'71
MOTIVATION (psychology)
How to tell whether you're in the right job.
S. Bacon. il Mech Illus 67:39-41+ Ag '71
Why motivation theory doesn't work. T.
H. Fitzgerald. Harvard Bsns R 49:37-44
Jl '71
See also
Reward (psychology)

MOTOR boat engines
Buy a jet for your jon; Otterbine jet pro-
pulsion unit. I. E. Prall. il Pop Mech 136:
109 S '71
See also
Gas turbines, Marine
Outboard motors

Fuel

Lead-free, low-lead, no-lead. E. Nabb. Motor
B & S 127:118+ Mr '71

Maintenance and repairs

Inboard engine. C. Miller. il Motor B & S
127:96-7 Ap '71
Power train maintenance, controls main-
tenance. C. Miller. il Motor B & S 127:98-9
Ap '71
MOTOR boat racing
All-American racing team. M. Crook. il
Yachting 129:68-9+ Mr '71
Bahamas 500. G. F. Hammond. il Motor B &
S 128:42-5+ Ag '71
Dragboats better than sex. M. Harris. il por
Motor B & S 127:30-2+ Mr '71
Duel of delicate mechanisms; Outboard
world championship. il Time 98:49 D 13
'71
Hennessy Grand prix: confessions of a timid
boatman. G. F. Hammond. il Motor B & S
128:46-7+ S '71
Hop, skip and kerplunk: powerboat racing;
photographs by Eric Schweikardt; report by
H. D. Whall. Sports Illus 35:30-5 S 6 '71
Month in yachting. See issues of Yachting
More power to you. M. Crook. See issues of
Yachting
Outboard world championship: Havasu, too
hot for the pros. L. Kennedy. il Motor B
& S 127:28-30+ F '71
True love at first contusion; powerboat rac-
ing. C. Phinizy. il por Sports Illus 34:52-4
Mr 22 '71
Up on the props and out ahead; Bahamas 500.
H. D. Whall. il por Sports Illus 34:24-5 Je 14
'71
See also
American power boat association
Motor boat speed records

Accidents

Driver falls into drink as Home Brew spills;
Southland sweepstakes regatta. il Motor
B & S 127:33 My '71
MOTOR boat speed records
Records, wet and dry. E. Crimmin. il Hot Rod
24:120-1 Je '71
MOTOR boating and sailing (periodical)
Third annual Chapman award. il por Motor
B & S 127:12 Ap '71
MOTOR boats
Build the Scottish schooner. H. Kelly. il
Mech Illus 67:42-7+ Ag '71
HYDRA/CYCLE: jet ride on the water. R.
Gannon. il Pop Sci 198:93+ F '71
In the old days she ran full of rum; rum-
running boat called The Cigarette. H. D.
Whall. il Sports Illus 35:34-5 S 6 '71
New boats and motors J. A. Emmett. il
Outdoor Life 147:66-70+ Ja '71
Single-screw handling: it's easier than you
think. F. C. Clark, jr. il Motor B & S 128:
62-3+ Jl '71
Three new hot ones: off the drawing board,
into the swim. J. Roe il Pop Sci 198:62-3+
Je '71
Wake surfing is for anywhere; Bertram
Pop-Top camper. G. Reiger. il Pop Mech
135:112-14 Mr '71
Water toys. il Pop Mech 135:122-3 Mr '71
See also
Cruisers (pleasure boats)
Fishing boats
Outboard motor boats

Design

Small boat with a big plan: Larson Shark
1800. D. Fales. il Motor B & S 128:56-9+
S '71

Electric equipment

Anatomy of a powerboat; electrical wiring
and battery charging. J. West. il Yachting
129:70-1+ F '71

Equipment

Yachting's boat show (cont) il Yachting
129:206-11 F '71

Finance

See Boats—Finance

Gearing

Modern reverse gear. E. H. Nabb. il Yachting
130:52+ S '71

MOTOR boats—*Continued*

Lubrication

Additive mystique. E. Nabb. il Motor B & S 127:98+ F '71

Noise

See also
Cruisers (pleasure boats)—Noise

Pollution

Pollution and policing; Lake George patrol. M. Crook. il Yachting 129:70+ Je '71
See also
Cruisers (pleasure boats)—Pollution

Speed

How to figure your planing speed from hull and horsepower. J. Martenhoff. il Pop Mech 135:120-1 Mr '71
We go 100 mph on the water! B. McKeown. il Mech Illus 67:83+ My '71

Starting

Starting procedure. J. Martenhoff. il Yachting 129:66-7+ My '71

Testing

Try before you buy. E. Nabb. Motor B & S 127:74-5 Ap '71
We go 100 mph on the water! B. McKeown. il Mech Illus 67:83+ My '71

Toilet facilities

See Boats—Toilet facilities
MOTOR boats, Outboard. See Outboard motor boats
MOTOR bus accidents. See Traffic accidents
MOTOR bus lines
Minibuses buck city traffic. il Bsns W p66+ O 30 '71
See also
Blue and white bus company
Cheetah charter bus service company
Greyhound corporation

Nigeria

Haring after Greyhound; Midwest line. il Newsweek 78:58 S 6 '71
MOTOR bus travel
One way to see Mexicans and Mexico close up is to make a tour by bus. il Sunset 147:54-5 O '71
MOTOR buses
Job for Mr Mitchell; General motors bus monopoly. Nation 213:69 Ag 2 '71

Pollution

Bus system combats pollution; New York city. il Am City 86:130 Je '71
MOTOR buses, Steam
Law-abiding, steam-powered bus. il Bsns W p25 N 27 '71
Steambus a-coming. S. Lindsay. il Sat R 54:86 N 6 '71
MOTOR camping. See Camping
MOTOR cycle racing. See Motorcycle racing
MOTOR cycles. See Motorcycles
MOTOR fuels
Liquid hydrogen as a fuel for the future. L. W. Jones. bibliog il Science 174:367-70 O 22 '71
Liquid hydrogen as a motor fuel. il Chem 45:26 Ja '72
See also
Automobile engines—Fuel

Taxation

Higher taxes or facility shortage face aviation interests. C. E. Schneider. il Aviation W 94:56-9+ Ap 26 '71
MOTOR homes. See Campers and coaches, Truck
MOTOR oils. See Lubrication and lubricants
MOTOR responses
Eye-head coordination in monkeys: evidence for centrally patterned organization. E. Bizzi and others. bibliog il Science 173:452-4 Jl 30 '71
MOTOR trend (periodical)
Marking time; Motor trend combined with Sports car graphic. E. Dahlquist. Motor T 23:6 Je '71
MOTOR trend awards
Cars of the year: a new and expanded program. il Motor T 23:86-8 N '71
1971 car of the year; Chevrolet Vega 2300. il Motor T 23:38-47 F '71
MOTOR trend 500. See Automobile racing

MOTOR truck drivers
Ethan, my son; case of 10-year-old boy killed by truck in Beverly Hills. il por Newsweek 78:43 N 22 '71
See also
Strikes—United States—Truck drivers

Training

Top drivers make the grade; Transportation opportunity program in Los Angeles. J. Jones. il Am Ed 7:34-40 N '71
MOTOR truck engines
See also
Motor vehicles—Pollution control devices
MOTOR truck industry
Trucks for fun roll into high. il Bsns W p43 N 13 '71
See also
International harvester company
Mack trucks, inc.
White motor corporation
MOTOR truck lines
See also
Associated truck lines
Ryder truck lines, inc.
Smith's transfer corporation
Yellow transit freight lines, inc.
MOTOR trucks
Big enough; expressway accidents involving big trucks. Nation 213:4 Jl 5 '71
Chevy builds 'em tough; pickup truck modifications. J. Thawley. il Hot Rod 24:122-5 My '71
Fine art of mating a camper and pickup. J. Copeland. il Pop Sci 198:74-5+ Mr '71
How to match your truck and camper. J. Parry. il Pop Mech 135:166D+ My '71
Machinery management (cont of) Truck and car news. P. B. Jones. See issues of Successful farming
1972 light truck story. il Mech Illus 67:62+ D '71
'71s: pickups that pamper. M. Lamm. il Pop Mech 135:98-101+ F '71

Axles

Tag axle: one more for the road. J. Copeland. il Pop Sci 199:52 O '71

Control

Saab-Scania builds a robot truck; dump truck. il Pop Sci 199:56 S '71

Laws and regulations

Unsafe trucks can kill you! F. A. Tinker. il Pop Mech 135:63-7+ My '71

Leasing and renting

Has one-way truck rental hit a dead end? il Bsns W p44+ Mr 27 '71
How to move yourself. J. De Marco. il Mech Illus 67:74-5+ F '71
Sure, you can do your moving yourself. il Changing T 25:35-7 S '71
See also
Ryder system, inc.

Maintenance and repair

Taking care of a pickup. T. Tappett. il Mech Illus 67:106-7+ Je '71

Testing

Just a little truckin'; Datsun and Toyota pickups. S. Green. il Hot Rod 24:50-2 Jl '71
Roller derby special: Hollywood haulers vs Tokyo rough riders. J. Brokaw. il Motor T 23:42-6 My '71

Transmission

Automatic transmissions help snow plowing. il Am City 86:22 Ja '71
MOTOR trucks, Municipal
See also
Refuse collection trucks
MOTOR trucks, Remodeled
Tomato of independence. R. Guldahl, jr. il Hot Rod 24:86-9 O '71
West coast vans. S. Green. il Hot Rod 24:82-6 Ag '71
MOTOR vehicle fleets, Municipal
Centralize your fleet for economy's sake; Jacksonville, Fla. S. Pearson. il por Am City 86:88+ Je '71
MOTOR vehicle racing
Baby prix for buggies; National four wheel drive Grand prix. il Mech Illus 67:44-5 Jl '71
Drive ya buggy. J. Thawley See issues of Hot rod to May 1971
Dust racing: the Mint 400. il Life 70:70-4 My 14 '71
4WD GP; four drive Grand Prix. R. Guldahl, jr. il Hot Rod 24:44-5 Jl '71

MOTOR vehicle racing—*Continued*
Mint-flavored desert. S. Green. il Hot Rod 24:60-2 Je '71
Vehicles and environmental responsibility; the role of off-road vehicles. B. Behme. il Field & S 75:142-4+ Ap '71

Mexico
Back from Baja. W. R. C. Shedenhelm. il Motor T 23:50-1 F '71
Beating the Baja. E. Ingalls. il Hot Rod 24:120-2 S '71

MOTOR vehicles
Golf cart that heels. il Mech Illus 67:97 O '71
MTV: off-road fun code. il Hot Rod 24:68 N '71
See also
Automobiles
Dune buggies
Ice vehicles
Jeep automobiles
Lunar vehicles
Recreational vehicles
Snowmobiles and snowmobiling

Exhibitions
Great voltage war; International electric vehicle symposium and exposition. il Newsweek 78:101+ N 22 '71

Four wheel drive
Brute: 2-cycle engine with 4-wheel drive. J. Davis. il Pop Sci 198:24 Ap '71
Haflinger 4WD goes anywhere, with more. J. P. Norbye. il Pop Sci 198:55 My '71
What you need to know before you buy 4-wheel drive. B. Lopez. il Pop Sci 198:76-7+ Mr '71
See also
Station wagons—Four wheel drive

Fuel
See Motor fuels

Laws and regulations
See also
Motor trucks—Laws and regulations

License plates
See also
Motor vehicles—Registration

Pollution control devices
Catalyst that may really curb pollution. il Bsns W p24 D 18 '71
Keep your emission control system working. M. Schultz. il Pop Mech 136:138-41+ N '71
Pollution device ready for '74 autos: PTX exhaust purifier. il Am City 86:46-7 N '71
Take care of these new car-truck features. Suc Farm 69:34 Ag '71

Radar equipment
Driving blind; AVOID systems for airport vehicles. Sci Am 226:52 Ja '72

Registration
Illinois microfilms its wheel book. il Am City 86:73-4 Ap '71

MOTOR vehicles, Amphibious
New look at ATV's. B. Behme. il Field & S 76:136-8 O '71
Now! Second generation ATVs. il Mech Illus 67:89-91 S '71
Taking care of an ATV. il Mech Illus 67:98-9+ Ap '71

Laws and regulations
Let's harness those go-anywhere machines. Bet Hom & Gard 49:8-9 Ja '71

Purchasing
How to buy a fun machine. B. Behme. il Field & S 75:94-6 Ja '71

MOTOR vehicles, Electric

Exhibitions
See Motor vehicles—Exhibitions

MOTOR vehicles, Municipal
See also
Motor vehicle fleets, Municipal
Tractors, Municipal

MOTOR vehicles in hunting and fishing
Surf fishing with a 4-wheel drive. G. W. Linnane. il Pop Mech 135:106-7+ F '71

MOTORBIKES. See Motorcycles
MOTORBOATS. See Motor boats
MOTORCYCLE engines
Stinger without the ouch; Hooker Headers' new tuned expansion chamber. il Hot Rod 24:108 N '71

MOTORCYCLE gangs. See Gangs
MOTORCYCLE helmets. See Helmets

MOTORCYCLE industry
Cycle maker tries to avoid a spill; Birmingham small arms co. Bsns W p60 N 13 '71
Leather jackets & kinetic art; Slegers-Forbes retail motorcycle sales and service dealer in Whippany, N.J. il Forbes 108:11 D 1 '71

MOTORCYCLE jumping. See Motorcycling—Stunt cycling
MOTORCYCLE racing
Acrobats on tricycles; cycle-sidecar combination for racing. il Mech Illus 67:76 N '71
Big, bright vaarroom for a large, fast buck; SRO audience in Manhattan. P. Ryan. il Sports Illus 34:48+ F 8 '71
Harvey on the lam; S. McQueen, racing enthusiast. R. F. Jones. por Sports Illus 35:55-6+ Ag 23 '71
Laugh-in trophy trial; motorcycling press corps takes to the saddle. T. Murphy. il Hot Rod 24:124 Mr '71
Riders on the brink. T. McGuane. il Sports Illus 34:46-51 My 3 '71
Something new in the solar system. R. F. Jones. il Sports Illus 34:12-19 Je 21 '71
Up on two wheels; Bonneville national speed trials; with table. B. Greene. il Hot Rod 24:142-7 N '71
Up on two wheels; Greenhorn endurance run. B. Greene. il Hot Rod 24:130+ Ag '71

History
Up on two wheels; setting of 24-hour record in 1937. B. Green. il pors Hot Rod 24:138+ Je '71

MOTORCYCLE riding. See Motorcycling
MOTORCYCLES
Better Bultaco. T. Murphy. il Hot Rod 24:134-5 O '71
Big mini; Benelli 180cc Volcano. B. Greene. il Hot Rod 24:124-5 Je '71
Bike for every trail. B. Greene. il Hot Rod 24:116-19 Ap '71
4 cylinders, 4 carbs, 4 strokes, and 500cc of action; Honda CB-500. R. Hill. il Pop Sci 199:53 D '71
Harley's little goat. B. Greene. il Hot Rod 24:58-9 My '71
In-between bikes. J. Davis and R. Hill. il Pop Sci 199:86-8 Ag '71
Maxi-craze for minibikes. il Life 70:58-61 Ja 22 '71
Mini kit with foldaway handlebars. E. F. Lindsley. il Pop Sci 199:64-5 O '71
Minicycle: a whole new breed of bike! E. H. Arctander. il Pop Mech 136:140-3 O '71
Mod monster: 1,200cc and no fat; Harley-Davidson Super Glide. J. Davis. il Pop Sci 198:61 Je '71
Montesa Cota. T. Murphy. il Hot Rod 24:124-5 F '71
New motorbikes. T. Barber. Mech Illus 67:47 Ja '71
New trail bike from Heath. il Mech Illus 67:110 D '71
New vintage motorcycle; 650cc Russian Ural. J. Davis. il Pop Sci 199:14 Jl '71
Ossa makes it. B. Greene. il Hot Rod 24:126-7 S '71
Our man's bag is a minibike. J. Davis. il Pop Sci 198:110 F '71
QA-50: a go-go mini for the back trails. J. Davis. il Pop Sci 198:79 Ap '71
Storm warning: the Fury is coming. B. Greene. il Hot Rod 24:110-11 Mr '71
Sturdy mini for the trail: Suzuki Trailhopper. J. Davis. il Pop Sci 198:31 Je '71
Suzuki's big splash. D. Boller. il Hot Rod 24:92-3 D '71
Suzuki's Sunday punch; 185cc Sierra. B. Greene. il Hot Rod 24:122-3 Ag '71
Take a better look at minibikes. il Changing T 25:31-2 Ap '71
Three-cylinder sock! Kawasaki 350-S2. J. Ethridge. il Pop Mech 136:88-91 D '71
Trail bike that comes in pieces. E. F. Lindsley. il Pop Sci 199:61 Ag '71
Trail bikes you can build from kits. S. M. Gallager. il Pop Mech 136:80-5 D '71
Trick with a twin; Yamaha 250. B. Greene. il Hot Rod 24:106-7 N '71
250cc+250cc=one of the best buys in motorcycling; Suzuki T-500R. J. Davis. il Pop Sci 199:68 N '71
Two-wheel-drive toughies. R. Hill. il Pop Sci 199:69 S '71
Up on two wheels. B. Greene. See issues of Hot rod
Yamaha mini Enduro: the trail bike to beat. J. Davis. il Pop Sci 198:36 Ja '71
See also
Motorcycling

MOTORCYCLES—*Continued*

Design

Sissy bars will be lower this year. T. Wolfe.
il Esquire 75:60-3+ F '71
Un-easy rider. R. Saxe. il Sr Schol 99:32+
N 29 '71

Maintenance and repair

Tire balancing from a can. J. Davis. il Pop
Sci 198:53 Je '71

Protection against theft

Build a $5 vehicle alarm system. H. Phillips.
il Radio-Electr 42:35-6 N '71

Safety devices and measures

Should your youngster ride a motorcycle?
D. McCluggage. il Am Home 74:60 S '71

Seats

Add a tag-along seat to your cycle. L.
House. il Pop Mech 136:20 Jl '71

Standards

Up on two wheels; standardization of motorcycle controls. B. Greene. il Hot Rod 24:138-
40 F; 132+ My '71

Testing

500; Honda Four. B. Greene. il Hot Rod
24:88-9 Jl '71

Transportation

How to tote your motobike. J. Davis. il Pop
Sci 198:108 Mr '71

MOTORCYCLES, Electric

Two-wheel nonpolluting commuting. il Mech
Illus 67:60 N '71

MOTORCYCLING

Guide to safe motorcycling; AAA booklet. il
Consumer Bul 54:4 Ag '71
Hey, mister, is my bike okay? M. Spiegel.
il Sr Schol 98:26-7+ Mr 29 '71
Minibikes and motorbikes only; Montclair,
Calif. Motorbike park. L. M. Wasserman.
il Am City 86:100 Ag '71
Motorcycling mania: new magazine market
report. C. R. Self, jr. il Writers Digest
51:24-6+ Mr '71
Myth of the motorcycle hog; Time essay. R.
Hughes. il Time 97:74 F 8 '71
Night riders; Crotona motorcycle club's
midnight road run. il Hot Rod 24:142-3
Ap '71
Trail riding, a route to happy days. J. Davis.
il Pop Sci 198:96-7 Je '71
Up on two wheels; regulation of off-road
cycling. B. Greene. il Hot Rod 24:130+ Ap
'71
Woman behind the man. M. Boyle. il Har
Yrs 11:22-3 Ap '71
See also
Motorcycle racing

Stunt cycling

I'm going to jump a mile anyway; E. Knievel. R. F. Jones. il por Sports Illus 35:48-
9 Jl 5 '71

MOTOROLA, Inc.

Assembly line message comes in loud and
clear. V. Louviere. il Nations Bsns 59:
22 N '71
Motorola creates a more demanding job. il
Bsns W p32 S 4 '71
New picture at Motorola? A. Hershman. por
Duns 93:64+ Te '69
When his firm was auctioned, he bid. H. L.
Marrs. il pors Nations Bsns 59:80-1 Ja '71

MOTORS. See Electric motors; Outboard motors

MOTORS, Rocket. See Rocket engines

MOTORSAILERS. See Cruisers (pleasure boats)

MOTOVILOFF, Ellen

Their Mexico, your Mexico, my Mexico. il
Schol Teach Jr/Sr High p 12-15 Mr 8
'71

MOTT, Charles Stewart

Profiles. E. J. Kahn, jr. por New Yorker 47:
56-8+ N 27 '71

MOTT, Michael

Recent developments in British poetry. Poetry 118:102-14 My '71

MOTT, Stewart Rawlings

Profiles. E. J. Kahn, jr. por New Yorker 47:
56-8+ N 27 '71 •

MOTT foundation. See Foundations, Charitable
and educational

MOTTA, Dick

Beware, little big man is here. F. Deford.
por Sports Illus 35:46-7+ O 25 '71 •

MOTULSKY, Arno G. See Murray, R. F. jr.
jt. auth.

MOTY, Eleanor

Workshop: photofabrication. bibliog f il
Craft Horiz 31:12-17 Je '71

MOTZKUS, John E.

Accountability and the Reverend Dogwood.
Todays Ed 60:57 Mr '71

MOULTON, Elizabeth

Joanna's peaceable kingdom; story. Redbook
137:68-9 Jl '71

MOUND, Milton

What can one man do? il pors Forbes 107:
17-18 F 15 '71 •

MOUNDS and mound builders

Mysterious mounds at Poverty Point. F.
Folsom. il Sci Digest 69:46-8+ F '71

MOUNT, Douglas

If you have hidden talent and like to eat,
have we got an expense account for you!
Esquire 76:214-15+ D '71

MOUNT ANGEL abbey, St Benedict, Ore. See
Abbeys

MOUNT ARARAT; Mount Rainier; etc. See
Ararat, Mount; Rainier, Mount; etc.

MOUNT DESERT ISLAND

Maine's Mount Desert Island. B. Freund and
H. Freund. il Travel 136:34-7+ Ag '71
See also
Acadia National Park

MOUNT MCKINLEY NATIONAL PARK

National park that has nothing. C. Nansen.
il Field & S 76:53-5+ My '71

MOUNT RAINIER NATIONAL PARK

Hike to visit marmots. il Sunset 147:34+ Jl
'71
Story of a mountain. A. D. Martinson. il
Am West 8:34-41 Mr '71

MOUNT VERNON (historic house)

Portraits and paintings at Mount Vernon
from 1754 to 1799. W. B. Floyd. il Antiques 100:768-74, 894-9 N-D '71

**MOUNT VERNON Junior college, Washington,
D.C.**

Chapel in the dell. il Arch Forum 134:56-9 Mr
'71

MOUNTAIN (rock group) See Rock groups

MOUNTAIN bisons. See Buffaloes

MOUNTAIN building. See Geology, Structural

MOUNTAIN climbing. See Mountaineering

MOUNTAIN ecology

Chisos Mountains: an ecological island. J.
Gillette. il Nat Parks & Con Mag 45:4-8
F '71
See also
Alpine flora

MOUNTAIN goat hunting. See Rocky Mountain
goat hunting

MOUNTAIN goats. See Goats

MOUNTAIN lion hunting. See Puma hunting

MOUNTAIN lions. See Pumas

MOUNTAIN mahogany

Birchleaf mountain mahogany. il Sunset 147:
266 O '71

MOUNTAIN plants. See Alpine flora

MOUNTAIN rescues. See Rescue work

MOUNTAIN sculpture

See also
Crazy Horse (Sioux Indian)—Statues, portraits, etc.

MOUNTAIN sheep

That desert-sheep case; Swanson charged
and sentenced. il Outdoor Life 148:8 N '71
This animal walks up walls; desert bighorn.
R. Murphy. il Nat Wildlife 9:16-18 Ap '71

Protection

See Animals—Protection

MOUNTAIN sheep hunting

Are you tough enough to hunt big game?
H. Rate. il Field & S 76:50-3+ Ag '71
Bighorns' last stand. il Newsweek 77:108+ Mr
15 '71
Ghosts of the Wrangells. B. Guild. il Outdoor
Life 147:78-81+ Ap '71
Good guys, bad guys and the bighorn. E.
Zern. il por Sports Illus 34:20-2+ Je 28 '71
Grand Canyon ram. L. A. Keim. il Outdoor
Life 148:58-9+ D '71
Leader of the band; Stone ram hunting.
R. A. Lubeck. il pors Outdoor Life 147:72-
3+ Mr '71
Making book at Turnagain. R. C. Hammond.
il Outdoor Life 148:60-1+ S '71
Notes on the sheep rifle. J. O'Connor. il Out-
door Life 148:64+ D '71
Sheep hunting is an art. J. O'Connor. il
Outdoor Life 147:68-71+ F '71
Sheep that is a goat; aoudad, or Barbary
sheep. W. Page. il Field & S 76:76-7+ Je '71

MOUNTAIN soaring. See Gliding and soaring

MOUNTAIN whites (southern states) See
Mountaineers (southern states)

MOUNTAINEERING
Because it's nowhere; El Capitan climb. H.
Peterson. il pors Sports Illus 34:76-8+ My
3 '71
Inch by inch up El Capitan. D. Caldwell. il
Read Digest 98:64-9 Mr '71
Lady of the mountain; El Capitan climb. F.
G. Loyd. il por Todays Health 49:37 F '71
Life among the rock people. M. Frady. il
Life 71:22-4 S 3 '71
This is a vacation? climbing the Mountains
of the Moon. N. Ellena. il por Todays
Health 49:34-6+ F '71
See also
Everest, Mount
Kenya, Mount

Accidents
Ordeal on Mount Hood; ed. by D. Holm. D.
Moon. il pors Nat Wildlife 9:36-9 Je '71
Ordeal on Mt Kenya. L. Elliott. il Read
Digest 99:92-7 S '71
Report at large; Alpine accidents and res-
cues. J. Bernstein. New Yorker 47:118-32+
O 30 '71

Anecdotes, facetiae, satire, etc
Himalayan trek or treat. J. Bruce. il Sports
Illus 34:86-8+ Je 7 '71
Up the Slide; being the grueling account
of the ascending wiles of Sly Sy and Burt
the Body. L. Gourse. il Natur Hist 80:
20-2+ N '71

MOUNTAINEERS (southern states)
Domain of sorts; excerpt from Children of
crisis: migrants, sharecroppers and moun-
taineers. R. Coles. il Harper 243:116-18+
N '71
Mountaineers in the affluent society. H. M.
Caudill. il Nat Parks & Con Mag 45:17-21
Jl '71
People of Cumberland Gap. J. Fetterman. il
Nat Geog 140:591-621 N '71
Southern highlands; a short history. il Nat
Parks & Con Mag 45:4 Jl '71

MOUNTAINS
See also
Watersheds

MOUNTAINS, Undersea. See Ocean bottom

MOUNTAINS in art
See also
Adirondack Mountains in art

MOUNTAINS OF THE MOON. See Ruwenzori
Mountains

MOUNTING of automobile engines. See Automobile engines—Mounting

MOUNTINGS, Telescope. See Telescope mountings

MOUNTZOURES, H. L.
Rich people are happier than poor; healthy,
happier than sick; young, happier than
old; story. New Yorker 47:45-50 O 30 '71

MOURNING becomes Electra; drama. See
O'Neill, E. G.

MOURNING dove shooting
Dove dog. R. Starnes. Field & S 75:8+ Ap
'71
Dove shooter's fever. C. Vinson. il Outdoor
Life 148:52-3+ D '71
Nothing like doves. J. O. Cartier. il Out-
door Life 148:70-1+ S '71
Watering holes offer bonus dove hunting.
A. D. Livingston. il Field & S 76:56-7+
S '71

MOUSETRAPS
Woodman's mouse trap. A. Holland. il Outdoor Life 147:159 F '71

MOUSSAKA. See Cookery, Middle Eastern

MOUSSORGSKY, Modest Petrovich. See Musorgskii, M. P.

MOUTH
Make the most of your smile. P. Van Wagenen. il Parents Mag 46:36 F '71

MOVABLE room dividers. See Partitions,
Movable

MOVEMENT, Notation of. See Dance notation

MOVEMENT, Psychology of
See also
Motion perception

MOVEMENT of cells. See Cells—Motility

MOVIE bus. See Moving picture theaters,
Traveling

MOVIE critics. See Critics

MOVIE shorts. See Moving pictures—Short
subject films

MOVIMENTO sociale italiano (political party)
See Political parties—Italy

MOVING
Easing the trauma of moving. Bsns W p 101
Mr 13 '71
Has one-way truck rental hit a dead end?
il Bsns W p44+ Mr 27 '71
How to get an honest move. J. Hand. il Mech
Illus 67:67-8+ Je '71
How to move yourself. J. De Marco. il Mech
Illus 67:74-5+ F '71
Moving made easy. G. W. Weinstein. il
Parents Mag 46:70-1+ F '71
Sure, you can do your moving yourself. il
Changing T 25:35-7 S '71
Taking the terror out of moving. A. F.
Rush. il McCalls 98:102-3+ Mr '71
When moving men show their worst side.
Bsns W p86 Ag 21 '71
See also
Airplanes in moving
Moving and storage companies

Anecdotes, facetiae, satire, etc.
Moving made easy. E. Bombeck. il Good H
173:80+ S '71

MOVING and storage companies
Cost of cremating your household goods.
Consumer Rep 36:336-7 Je '71
For the moving man, the hurdles multiply.
il Bsns W p80+ Ag 21 '71

MOVING of structures, etc.
Build your own first mortgage; off-site re-
moval. M. Bicknell. Har Yrs 11:34-5 Je '71
We did it; moving and rebuilding of Seward
house; ed. by R. D. Shelley. L. L. R.
Owens. il House B 113:118-19 O '71
See also
Houses, Prefabricated—Transportation

MOVING of trees. See Tree planting

MOVING picture acting
Reluctant Oscars; interviews, ed. by C. Irv-
ing. G. C. Scott; G. Jackson. pors Mc-
Calls 98:12+ Jl '71

MOVING picture actors and actresses
Beauty & the bath; influence of Hollywood
stars on makeup, fashions, and hairstyles.
S. Lindsay. il House B 113:14+ Mr '71
Bits and pieces; character actors. G. Weales.
Sat R 54:67+ Mr 27 '71
Carrie Snodgress. G. Goodman. pors Look
35:50-3 Ap 6 '71
Close-up (cont of) Spotlight! E. Miller. See
issues of Seventeen, April 1971-
Current cinema; notes on new actors, new
movies. P. Kael. New Yorker 47:168-73
D 4 '71
Films; the old stars. J. Brackman. Esquire
75:44+ Ja '71
Hollywood (hot) dog days. il Time 98:46 Ag 23
'71
Hollywood tennis does socko biz. D. Haber.
il Sports Illus 34:42-4+ Mr 8 '71
Noble non-savage; Chief D. George. por
Time 97:76+ F 15 '71
Quartet of queens. J. Barthel. il pors Life
70:60-2+ F 19 '71
Stars and celebrities. R. Schickel. Commen-
tary 52:61-5 Ag '71
See also
Academy awards (moving pictures)
Children as actors
Screen actors' guild
also names of moving picture actors
and actresses, e.g. J. Arness

MOVING picture adaptations
Love story; it's required. B. F. Dick. Nat R
23:771 Jl 13 '71
Medium is the motivation; movies, TV and
paperbacks. K. Cremonini. il Schol Teach
Jr/Sr High p 12-14 Ap 5 '71
Rights and permissions. P. S. Nathan. See
issues of Publisher's weekly
What's happening to Ernest Tidyman's Shaft
on the way to the screen. B. A. Bannon.
il Pub W 199:22-3 Ap 19 '71

MOVING picture audiences
Movie audiences don't change; interview,
ed. by M. Ronan. D. Lean. por Sr Schol
98:18 F 15 '71
Why we go to the movies. M. Mead. Redbook
136:48+ Mr '71

MOVING picture authorship
Onward and upward with the arts; producing
Citizen Kane. P. Kael. por New Yorker 47:
43-52+ F 20; 44-50+ F 27 '71

MOVING picture awards
See also
Academy awards (moving pictures)

MOVING picture cameras
Coming: color movies from black-and-white
film! camera for use with electronic video
recording process. S. M. Gallager. il Pop
Mech 135:76-8 My '71
Dream super 8 outfit; symposium. il Pop
Phot 68:114-16 F '71
F/1.2 at 1/28 sec. on ASA 160 for movies?
E. Scully. il Mod Phot 35:8+ N '71

MOVING picture cameras—*Continued*
Movie equipment close-up:
Canon DS-8. il Mod Phot 35:28 Ap '71
Honeywell Elmo super filmatic 103T. il
Mod Phot 35:130 D '71
Sankyo super CME 660. il **Mod Phot 35:**
136+ Je '71
Movie equipment close-up. il Mod Phot 35:
22+ Ja; 135 Mr '71
Now: dim-light movies without movie lights.
E. H. Ortner. il Pop Sci 199:154 O '71
Photo expo 71. L. Brown. il Pop Phot 69:
81+ Ag '71
Super 8 movie cameras. il Consumer Rep
36:227-36 Ap '71
This super-8 camera packs 200 feet of film.
A. Fisher. il Pop Sci 198:125 Ap '71
What's new? Look! il Mod Phot 35:63-78 Ja
'71

Sound equipment

Has super 8 sound come of age? T. Galluzzo.
Mod Phot 35:100-1+ Ja '71
Super 8 sound-movie systems. il Consumer
Rep 36:550-3 S '71
MOVING picture cartoons. See Moving pic-
tures—Animated cartoons
MOVING picture censorship
Edited for television. Time 97:60-1 Mr 1
'71
King Kong was a dirty old man. il **Esquire**
76:146-9 S '71
See also
Moving pictures—Moral aspects
MOVING picture collections. See Moving pic-
ture film collections
MOVING picture criticism
Movie studies: real all about it. R. Schickel.
Harper 242:24+ Mr '71; Discussion. 242:10+
My '71
Movies into film, by J. Simon. Review
Nation 212:278-80 Mr 1 '71. B. Bendow
Pains of love; views of J. Valenti. por
Newsweek 77:74 F 1 '71
See also
Moving picture plays—Criticisms, plots, etc.
MOVING picture critics. See Critics
MOVING picture directors
Cinema in the sixties; with filmography. C.
T. Samuels. il Am Lib 2:461-73 My '71
Hollywood's new wave. R. Sklar. il Ramp
Mag 10:60-6 N '71
Middling ages: notes on some American
film directors. S. Kauffmann. Yale R 60:
626-40 Je '71
Not to be missed; film directors. G. Trotta.
il Harp Baz 104:140-1 My '71
See also
Altman, R.
Antonioni, M.
Bergman, I.
Bogdanovich, P.
Capra, F.
Cassavetes, J.
Costa-Gavras
Fellini, F.
Forman, M.
Hitchcock, A. J.
Kubrick, S.
Maysles, A.
Mazursky, P.
Peckinpah, S.
Polanski, R.
Rohmer, E.
Russell, K.
Schlesinger, J
Van Peebles, M.
Wise, R.
Women as moving picture directors
MOVING picture distributors. See Moving pic-
tures—Distribution
MOVING picture editing. See Moving pictures
—Editing
MOVING picture festivals
Dubious bonanza; New York film festival.
H. Alpert. Sat R 54:80 O 30 '71
Festival; New York film festival. il Time
98:86-7 O 18 '71
Hollywood has its filmex. A. Knight. Sat
R 54:14 N 20 '71
Movie making. T. Galluzzo. Mod Phot 35:
47 N '71
Movies in the round; New York festival.
P. D. Zimmerman. il por Newsweek 78:
108+ O 18 '71
So long at the fair; New York film festival.
P. T. Hartung. Commonweal 95:279-80 D
17 '71
U.S. declines to participate in Moscow film
festival. Dept State Bul 64:705 My 31 '71
MOVING picture film collections
Collecting classic films; with filmography.
P. J. Bukalski. il Am Lib 2:475-9 My '71
Film collection attacked in Los Angeles
County. Library J 96:771-2 Mr 1 '71; Reply.
R. C. Goodwell. 96:1896-7 Je 1 '71

Movie making; sources for free films and
outlets to show your own. T. Galluzzo.
Mod Phot 35:47 N '71
New York's new anthology film archives.
B. Rose. il Vogue 158:70 N 1 '71
Savior of old movies: H. Langlois of
Cinémathèque Française, Paris. R. Chel-
minski. il pors Life 71:45-6+ D 10 '71
MOVING picture film cutting. See Moving pic-
tures—Editing
MOVING picture films
Movie making; the new Ektachrome 160. T.
Galluzzo. Mod Phot 36:20+ Ja '72
MOVING picture industry
See also
Moving picture production and direction
Ross, Dick, and associates (firm)

Finance

Can Quaker Oats rescue Hollywood? M. A.
Callahan. America 125:121-2 S 4 '71
Cinema, corporate style. il Time 98:76+ S
13 '71
New money in movies; corporate invest-
ments, with interview with M. Palevsky.
A. Hershman. il Duns 97:33-6 F '71

Great Britain

Rise of the house of Hammer. il **Time 98:**
66+ D 6 '71

United States

Booknotes: these, these our players. N. L.
Magid. Commonweal 93:471+ F 12 '71
Cinema, corporate style. il Time 98:76+ S
13 '71
Hollywood: fewer stars, more profits. il U S
News 70:48-50 Ja 18 '71
Hollywood (hot) dog days. il Time 98:46 Ag 23
'71
Hollywood's new wave. R. Sklar. il Ramp
Mag 10:60-6 N '71
New Mexico steals the movie scene. il
Bsns W p92+ Ag 21 '71
Nostalgia: sentimental craze for the past;
symposium. il Life 70:39-56+ F 19 '71
What about the movies? Hollywood break-
down. P. S. Nathan. Pub W 199:53 Je 28
'71
Wit and wisdom of Hollywood. by M. Wilk.
Review
Vogue 158:286 S 1 '71. A. Talmey
See also
Metro-Goldwyn-Mayer, inc.
Screen actors' guild
Twentieth century-Fox film corporation
MOVING picture literature
Recent film writing; a survey. E. Callenbach.
bibliog Film Q 24:11-32 Spr '71
MOVING picture locations. See Moving pic-
tures—Setting and scenery
MOVING picture photography
Conrad Hall: an interview; ed. by M. Shedlin.
C. Hall. il Film Q 24:2-11 Spr '71
Dolly or zoom? They ain't the same. T.
Galluzzo. il Mod Phot 35:84-5 Mr '71
How to shoot from the hip. D. Sutherland.
il Pop Phot 69:102-3+ S '71
Long day's journey into night; interview;
ed. by D. Luciano. S. Lumet. il Film Q 25:
20-9 Fall '71
Movie making. T. Galluzzo. See issues of
Modern photography
Rarely is the medium well done; overuse of
zoom and pan. D. Sutherland. il Pop Phot
69:102-3+ Jl '71
Seeing pictures; the switch from stills to
movies. J. Scully. il Mod Phot 35:18+
Jl '71
See also
Moving pictures. Amateur
Travel photography

Apparatus and supplies

Easy movies. il Esquire 76:78-83 Ag '71;
Reply. B. Brown. 76:73 N '71

Bibliography

Movie making. T. Galluzzo. Mod Phot 35:42+
S '71

Competitions

Movie making; Kodak teenage movie award
winners. T. Galluzzo. Mod Phot 35:36+
Ap '71

Films
See Moving picture films

Focusing

Rubber focus is a stretched-out story; Pathé
and other universal focus systems. N. Goldberg. il Pop Phot 68:48+ Mr '71

Lighting

Light your movies like a pro. H. V. Fondiller.
il Pop Phot 68:96-7+ Je '71

MOVING picture photography—Lighting—*Cont.*
Movie making. T. Galluzzo. il Mod Phot 35:
18+ My '71
Movies; minimum exposure, maximum impact! T. Galluzzo. il Mod Phot 35:82-3+
S '71

MOVING picture photography, Journalistic.
See Photography, Journalistic

MOVING picture photography, Trick
Movie making; distorted images. T. Galluzzo.
il Mod Phot 34:38+ D '70
Wildi's wild pinwheels; filming amusement
parks through patterned glass. E. Wildi.
il Pop Phot 68:96-7+ Je '71

MOVING picture photography in criminal investigation, espionage, etc. See Photography
in criminal investigation, espionage, etc.

MOVING picture plays
See also
Moving picture adaptations
Moving pictures
Television broadcasting—Moving pictures

Criticisms, plots, etc.
Aesthete at the movies. A. Sarris. Commentary 51:81-4 F '71
Close-up (cont of) Spotlight! E. Miller. See
issues of Seventeen, April 1971–
Critics vote. Newsweek 79:59 Ja 10 '72
Current cinema. P. Gilliatt. See issues of
New Yorker, April 3, 1971 to September
25, 1971
Current cinema. P. Kael. See issues of New
Yorker to March 27, 1971; October 2, 1971–
Depreciated dozen; ten best movies C. L.
Westerbeck, jr. Commonweal 93:495-6 F 19
'71
Family movie guide; ed. by J. Ripp. See issues
of Parents' magazine & better family living
Film chronicle (title varies) Nat R 23:381-2,
489-90, 662, 822-3, 941, 1191-2, 1250, 1368,
1479-80 Ap 6, My 4, Je 15, Jl 27, Ag 24, O
22-N 5, D 3, 31 '71
J. Brackman. See issues of Esquire
Films. M. Ronan. See issues of Senior scholastic
Films. M. Walsh. See issues of America
Films; year's best. J. Brackman. Esquire 75:
88+ My '71
Going on about town. See issues of New
Yorker
Last look at 1971's movies. P. D. Zimmerman.
il Newsweek 79:33 Ja 3 '72
Life movie review. R. Schickel. See issues
of Life
Look at the movies. G. Shalit. See occasional
issues of Look to October 19, 1971
Motion picture previews (cont) B. Sanjek.
il PTA Mag 65:38-40 Ja '71
Motion picture previews. E. Whitehorn. See
issues of PTA magazine
Movie report. C. Terry. See issues of Good
housekeeping
Movies. See issues of Consumer reports
Movies. See issues of Newsweek
Movies. D. Denby. See issues of Atlantic
Movies. J. Kroll. il Art in Am 59:114-15 Mr
'71
Movies (title varies) See occasional issues of
Christian century continuing New Christian
Movies; successes of 1971. R. Schickel. il
Life 71:20 D 31 '71
Negative space, by M. Farber. Review
Vogue 157:156+ My '71. B. Rose
New movies. F. Somers. See issues of Redbook
Ratings of current motion pictures. See
issues of Consumer bulletin
Reflections on movies. H. Clurman. Harper
242:30+ My '71
SR goes to the movies. H. Alpert; A. Knight.
See issues of Saturday review
Screen. C. L. Westerbeck, jr. See issues of
Commonweal
Short notices. See issues of Film quarterly
Sight & sound. C. Irving. See issues of McCall's
What movies try to sell us; flimflam vision
of the world. L. Lapham. il Harper 243:
106-8+ N '71
What's happening. G. Shalit. See issues of
Ladies' home journal

Single works
Adrift
Chr Cent 88:955 Ag 11 '71
Alex in wonderland
Commentary 51:79 Ap '71
New Yorker 46:62-4 Ja 9 '71
Anderson tapes
Commonweal 94:408 Ag 6 '71
Newsweek 78:82 Jl 12 '71
Sat R 54:12 Jl 10 '71
Time il 98:69-70 Jl 19 '71

Andromeda strain
America 124:354 Ap 3 '71
Atlan 227:97-8 My 29 '71
Commonweal 94:190-1 Ap 30 '71
Holiday 49:10 My '71
Newsweek il 77:98 Mr 29 '71
Sat R 54:52 Ap 3 '71
Sr Schol il 98:22-3 Ap 5 '71
Vogue 157:160 Ap 1 '71

Bananas
America 124:619 Je 12 '71
Atlan 228:92-4 Ag '71
Look il 35:80 Je 15 '71
New Repub 164:24+ My 22 '71
New Yorker 47:127-9 My 15 '71
Newsweek il 77:102 My 17 '71

Barren lives. See Vidas secas, page 769

Bed and board
America 124:128 F 6 '71
Chr Cent 88:809 Je 30 '71
Commentary 51:89 Je '71
Nat R 23:662 Je 15 '71
Nation 212:284 Mr 1 '71
New Repub 164:24 F 13 '71
New Yorker 46:89 F 6 '71
Newsweek il 77:79 Ja 25 '71
Sat R 54:84 Ja 23 '71
Time il 97:82 F 8 '71
Vogue il 157:75 Mr 15 '71

Bed and domicile
Commonweal 94:64-5 Mr 26 '71

Bedknobs and broomsticks
New Yorker 47:138-9 D 11 '71

Beguiled
Commonweal 94:310-11 Je 11 '71
Newsweek il 77:126 Ap 19 '71
Time 97:94 Ap 12 '71

Big Jake
Time 97:85 Je 21 '71

Billy Jack
Chr Cent 88:1213-14 O 13 '71
New Yorker 47:148+ N 27 '71
Newsweek il 78:76 Ag 30 '71

Black Jesus
Sat R 54:30 S 11 '71

Black Peter
Newsweek 78:75 Ag 2 '71

Blackmail
New Yorker 47:92-3 S 11 '71

Bless the beasts & children
Newsweek il 78:67 S 6 '71
Sat R 54:25 O 23 '71

Born to win
New Yorker 47:170-2 D 4 '71
Newsweek 78:118+ N 15 '71
Time il 98:109-10 N 1 '71

Le boucher
Time il 99:55-6 Ja 17 '72

Boy friend
Commonweal 95:326 Ja 7
Newsweek il 78:61-2 D 27 '71
Time il 98:82-3+ D 20 '71

Brewster McCloud
Commonweal 93:470 F 12 '71
Esquire 75:28+ Ap '71
New Repub 164:28+ Ja 2 '71
New Yorker 46:64 Ja 9 '71

Brother John
Sr Schol 98:18 Mr 22 '71

Buttercup chain
Time 97:99 My 10 '71

C.C. and company
Chr Cent 88:389 Mr 24 '71

Carnal knowledge
America 125:48 Jl 24 '71
Atlan 228:144+ N '71
Chr Cent 88:1364-5 N 17 '71
Commentary 52:26+ S '71
Commonweal 94:453 S 3 '71
Esquire 76:45-6+ O '71
Life il 71:12 Ag 6 '71
Nat R 23:1192 O 22 '71
New Repub 165:22+ Ag 21 '71
New Yorker 47:43-4 Jl 3 '71
Newsweek 78:9 Ag 2 '71
Newsweek il 78:71 Jl 5 '71
Sat R il 54:18 Jl 3 '71
Time 98:66-7 Jl 5 '71
Vogue 158:60 Ag 15 '71

Celebration at Big Sur
Sat R 54:44 My 1 '71

Cisco pike
Newsweek il 78:119-20 N 22 '71
Time il 98:102 D 6 '71

Citizen Kane
Commonweal 94:286-7 My 28 '71
New Yorker 47:44-50+ F 27 '71

MOVING picture plays—Criticisms, plots, etc.—
  Single works—*Continued*
  Claire's knee
    America 124:244 Mr 6 '71
    Commentary 52:84-6 Ag '71
    Commonweal 94:112 Ap 9 '71
    Esquire 75:36+ Je '71
    Nat R 23:823 Jl 27 '71
    Nation 212:317-18 Mr 8 '71
    New Repub 164:20+ Mr 20 '71
    New Yorker 47:136+ Mr 20 '71
    Newsweek 77:89-90 Mr 1 '71
    Sat R 54:14 F 20 '71
    Time il 97:93 Ap 12 '71
    Vogue 157:159 My '71
  Clockwork orange
    Commonweal 95:351-2 Ja 14 '72
    Nation 214:28 Ja 3 '72
    New Repub 166:22+ Ja 1 '72
    New Yorker 47:50-3 Ja 1 '72
    Newsweek il 79:28-33 Ja 3 '72
    Sat R il 54:40-1+ D 25 '71
    Time il 98:80-1+ D 20 '71
    Time il 98:59 D 27 '71
  Clowns
    Commonweal 94:501-2 S 24 '71
    Film Q 25:53-5 Fall '71
    Holiday 49:12 Jl '71
    Life il 71:9 Jl 9 '71
    Nat R 23:1191 O 22 '71
    Nation 212:828-9 Je 28 '71
    New Repub 165:22+ Jl 3 '71
    New Yorker 47:96+ Je 12 '71
    Newsweek 77:86 Je 21 '71
    Time il 97:84 Je 21 '71
    Vogue il 158:90-1 Ag 1 '71
  Cold turkey
    America 124:619 Je 12 '71
    Holiday 49:12 My '71
    New Repub 164:22+ Ap 24 '71
    Newsweek 77:136 Ap 19 '71
    Time 97:89 My 3 '71
  La collectionneuse
    Commonweal 94:310 Je 11 '71
    Commonweal 94:336-7 Je 25 '71
    Nation 212:574 My 3 '71
    New Repub 164:26+ My 29 '71
    New Yorker 47:119 My 8 '71
    Newsweek il 77:100-1 My 3 '71
    Time il 97:100+ My 17 '71
    Vogue 158:89 Jl '71
  Confession
    America 124:158+ F 13 '71
    Atlan 227:122-5 F '71
    Chr Cent 88:571-2 My 5 '71
    Commonweal 93:548-9 Mr 5 '71
    Film Q il 24:54-6 Sum '71
    Holiday 49:20+ F '71
    Sr Schol 98:21 F 8 '71
    Vogue 157:54 Ja 15 '71
  Conformist
    Esquire 76:42 Ag '71
    Film Q il 24:2-19 Sum '71
    Life il 70:18 Ap 16 '71
    Nat R 23:1191 O 22 '71
    Nation 212:446 Ap 5 '71
    New Repub 164:24 Ap 10 '71
    New Yorker 47:118 Mr 13 '71
    New Yorker 47:99 Mr 27 '71
    Newsweek il 77:92 Ap 5 '71
    Sat R 54:40 Ap 10 '71
    Time il 97:86 Ap 5 '71
  Cop
    Nation 212:765 Je 14 '71
  Cromwell
    Chr Cent 88:234-5 F 17 '71
    Sr Schol il 97:22 Ja 11 '71
  The crook
    New Yorker 47:85-6 Je 26 '71
    Newsweek 77:106 Je 7 '71
  Crucified lovers
    Film Q il 25:15-19 Fall '71
  Cry uncle
    Time il 98:76 S 20 '71
  Damned
    Film Q il 24:2-19 Sum '71
  Dancing lady
    New Yorker 47:93-4 S 11 '71
  Daughters of darkness
    New Yorker 47:69 Je 19 '71
  Dead of summer
    Look 35:67 My 18 '71
  Death in Venice
    America 125:17 Jl 10 '71
    Atlan 228:111-13 S '71
    Chr Cent 89:22 Ja 5 '72
    Commonweal 94:501-2 S 24 '71
    Film Q il 25:41-7 Fall '71
    Holiday 49:10 Jl '71
    Nat R 23:941 Ag 24 '71
    Nation 212:829 Je 28 '71
    New Yorker 47:114-15 Ap 17 '71
    New Yorker 47:85 Je 26 '71
    Newsweek il 77:90 Je 28 '71
    Sat R 54:28 Je 19 '71
    Time 98:66 Jl 5 '71

Début
    Nation 213:411-12 O 25 '71
    New Yorker 47:143-4 O 23 '71
  Decameron
    Commonweal 95:158 N 12 '71
  Deep end
    New Repub 165:22 S 18 '71
    New Yorker 47:56-7 S 4 '71
    Newsweek il 78:80-1 Ag 23 '71
    Sat R 54:48 Ag 28 '71
    Time 98:61 S 6 '71
  Desperate characters
    America 125:293 O 16 '71
    Chr Cent 88:1529 D 29 '71
    Commonweal 95:89 O 22 '71
    Nation 213:381 O 18 '71
    New Repub 165:24+ S 25 '71
    New Yorker 47:101-4 S 25 '71
    Newsweek il 78:109 S 27 '71
    Sat R 54:14 S 18 '71
  Devils
    America 125:127 S 4 '71
    Chr Cent 88:1299-300 N 3 '71
    Commonweal 95:16-17 O 1 '71
    Life il 71:12 S 24 '71
    Nat R 23:1250 N 5 '71
    New Repub 165:26+ S 11 '71
    New Yorker 47:58+ Jl 24 '71
    Newsweek il 78:71 Jl 26 '71
    Sat R 54:50 Jl 31 '71
    Time il 98:50 Jl 26 '71
    Vogue il 158:88-9 S 15 '71
  Diamonds are forever
    Commonweal 95:325 Ja 7 '72
    Newsweek il 78:61 D 27 '71
    Sat R 55:22 Ja 1 '72
    Time il 99:50 Ja 10 '72
  Diary of a chambermaid
    Film Q il 24:48-51 Wint '70
  Dirty Harry
    Newsweek il 79:59 Ja 10 '72
    Time il 99:66 Ja 3 '72
  Doc
    America 125:153 S 11 '71
    Commonweal 95:88 O 22 '71
    Life il 71:15 S 17 '71
    New Repub 165:33 S 4 '71
    New Yorker 47:60+ Ag 21 '71
    Newsweek 78:76 Ag 30 '71
    Sat R 54:26 S 4 '71
    Time 98:52 Ag 30 '71
  Doctors' wives
    Life il 70:7 F 26 '71
    New Yorker 47:89 Mr 13 '71
    Newsweek 77:82 F 15 '71
    Time il 97:65 F 15 '71
  Dodeskaden
    Film Q 24:63 Sum '71
    Nation 213:446 N 1 '71

    Commonweal 95:325-6 Ja 7 '72
    Sat R 55:22 Ja 1 '72
    Time 98:58-9 D 27 '71
  Drive, he said
    Commentary 52:32+ S '71
    Esquire 76:82+ S '71
    New Yorker 47:55-6 Jl 10 '71
    Newsweek 77:86+ Je 21 '71
    Ramp Mag 10:51-4 S '71
    Time il 97:85 Je 21 '71
  Dusty and Sweets McGee
    Newsweek 78:72 Jl 26 '71
    Sat R 54:47 Je 26 '71
    Sr Schol il 99:30+ S 27 '71
    Time il 98:62 Ag 2 '71
  Eagle in a cage
    Newsweek 78:62 D 27 '71
  L'enfant sauvage
    Engl J 60:778-80 S '71
    Film Q il 24:42-5 Spr '71
  Escape from the Planet of the apes
    New Yorker 47:102-4 Je 5 '71
  Evel Knievel
    Time il 98:55 Ag 16 '71
  Fat city
    Look il 35:88-90 O 19 '71
  Une femme douce
    Am Scholar 40:309-15 Spr '71
    Commonweal 94:428 Ag 20 '71
    Nation 212:796 Je 21 '71
    New Repub 164:28 Je 26 '71
    New Yorker 47:79 My 29 '71
    Newsweek 77:106 Je 7 '71
  Fiddler on the roof
    Life il 71:87-90 D 3 '71
    Life il 71:16 D 10 '71
    New Repub 165:28 N 20 '71
    New Yorker 47:133-9 N 13 '71
    Newsweek il 78-114+ N 15 '71
    Sat R 54:30 N 13 '71
    Sr Schol 99:20 D 13 '71
    Time il 98:107+ N 22 '71
  Figures in a landscape
    New Yorker 47:55-7 Jl 31 '71
    Sat R 54:42 Ag 14 '71
    Time 98:63 Ag 9 '71

MOVING picture plays—Criticisms, plots, etc.—
  Single works—*Continued*
  Five easy pieces
    Chr Cent 88:357-8 Mr 17 '71
    Chr Cent 88:593-4 My 12 '71
    Harper 242:113-14 My '71
    Holiday 49:30+ D '70
  Flap
    New Repub 164:22 Ja 23 '71
  Flight of the doves
    America 124:435-6 Ap 24 '71
    Sr Schol 98:21 My 3 '71
  Fools' parade
    America 125:235 O 2 '71
    Life il 70:20 Je 11 '71
  Fortune and men's eyes
    America 125:235 O 2 '71
    Newsweek 78:72 Jl 5 '71
  French connection
    America 125:321 O 23 '71
    Commonweal 95:301 D 24 '71
    Life il 71:13 N 19 '71
    New Repub 165:22 O 30 '71
    New Yorker 47:114 O 30 '71
    Sat R 54:70 N 6 '71
    Sr Schol il 99:20 Ja 10 '72
    Time il 98:109 N 1 '71
  Friends
    America 124:491-2 My 8 '71
    Time il 97:99 My 10 '71
  Le gai savoir
    Film Q 25:51-3 Fall '71
  Gang that couldn't shoot straight
    Time 99:55 Ja 10 '72
  Garden of delights
    America 124:209 F 27 '71
    Commonweal 94:15 Mr 12 '71
    Film Q il 24:2-19 Sum '71
    Life il 70:12 Mr 19 '71
    Nation 212:318 Mr 8 '71
    New Repub 164:24+ Ap 3 '71
    New Yorker 47:90 Mr 13 '71
    Newsweek il 77:92+ Mr 1 '71
    Sat R 54:22 F 27 '71
  Garden of the Finzi-Continis
    New Yorker 47:48+ D 18 '71
    Newsweek 79:58 Ja 10 '72
    Sat R 55:19 Ja 8 '72
    Time 99:54 Ja 17 '72
  Geo. Washington
    Look il 35:30+ Ag 24 '71
  Get Carter
    Life il 70:6 F 26 '71
    Look 35:66 My 18 '71
    New Repub 164:24 Ap 3 '71
    Sat R 54:42 F 13 '71
    Time il 97:77 Mr 22 '71
  Gimme shelter
    Chr Cent 88:756 Je 16 '71
  Gladiators
    Newsweek 78:120+ N 15 '71
  Glen and Randa
    Newsweek 77:106 Je 7 '71
  Go-between
    Commonweal 94:480-1 S 17 '71
    Life il 71:10 O 1 '71
    Nat R 23:1368 D 3 '71
    Nation 213:316-17 O 4 '71
    New Repub 165:26+ S 11 '71
    New Yorker 47:55-7 Jl 31 '71
    Newsweek il 78:76 Ag 16 '71
    Sat R 54:42 Ag 14 '71
    Sr Schol il 99:20 O 18 '71
    Time 98:63 Ag 9 '71
    Vogue il 158:88 S 15 '71
  Going home
    New Yorker 47:173 D 4 '71
    Newsweek 78:111 D 6 '71
    Time il 98:61 D 13 '71
  Great white hope
    Film Q 24:56-7 Spr '71
  Grissom gang
    America 124:595 Je 5 '71
  Guess what we learned in school today!
    Chr Cent 88:985 Ag 18 '71
  Gunfight
    Sat R 54:54 Je 12 '71
  Happy birthday, Wanda June
    Newsweek 78:87 D 20 '71
    Sat R 54:60 D 11 '71
    Time il 98:61-2 D 13 '71
  Hired hand
    Commonweal 95:88 O 22 '71
    Life il 71:15 S 17 '71
    New Repub 165:26+ S 4 '71
    New Yorker 47:62-3 Ag 21 '71
    Newsweek il 78:75 Ag 2 '71
    Sat R 54:31 Ag 7 '71
    Time 98:62 Ag 2 '71
  Hoa binh
    America 125:152 S 11 '71
    Commonweal 95:61 O 15 '71
    Nation 213:316 O 4 '71
    New Yorker 47:69-70 S 18 '71
    Newsweek 78:66+ S 6 '71
    Sat R 54:30 S 11 '71
    Sr Schol il 99:20 O 18 '71
    Time il 98:83+ S 13 '71

  Horsemen
    Time il 98:55+ Ag 16 '71
  Hospital
    Newsweek 78:88 D 20 '71
    Time 99:50+ Ja 10 '72
  House that dripped blood
    Sr Schol 98:30 My 17 '71
  Husbands
    Commonweal 93:469 F 12 '71
    Esquire 75:38 F '71
    Harp Baz 104:34+ F '71
    Look il 35:29 F 7 '71
    Vogue 157:88-9 F 15 '71
  I love my wife
    Commonweal 93:448 F 5 '71
    New Repub 164:28 Ja 2 '71
    Vogue 157:88 F 15 '71
  I never sang for my father
    Chr Cent 88:665 My 26 '71
    Film Q 24:57-8 Spr '71
    Holiday 48:22+ S '70
  I walk the line
    Esquire 75:44+ Ja '71
  Ice
    Film Q il 24:26-33 Sum '71
  In the name of the father
    Commonweal 95:159 N 12 '71
  In the summertime
    Commonweal 95:158 N 12 '71
    Nation 213:445-6 N 1 '71
  Investigation of a citizen above suspicion
    America 124:160 F 13 '71
    Film Q il 24:2-19 Sum '71
    New Repub 164:22 Ja 23 '71
  Is there sex after death?
    New Yorker 47:188-90 N 6 '71
  It only happens to others
    Commonweal 95:256 D 10 '71
  Jennifer on my mind
    Sat R 54:73 N 27 '71
    Time 98:56 N 29 '71
  Joe Hill
    Life il 71:8 N 26 '71
    Newsweek il 78:89 N 1 '71
    Sr Schol 99:20-1 Ja 10 '72
    Time il 98:103+ N 8 '71
    Vogue 159:33 Ja 1 '72
  Johnny got his gun
    America 125:126-7 S 4 '71
    Commonweal 95:62 O 15 '71
    New Yorker 47:65-7 Ag 7 '71
    Newsweek il 78:70+ Ag 9 '71
    Sat R 54:48 Ag 28 '71
    Time il 98:52 Ag 30 '71
  Julius Caesar
    Look il por 35:31 Mr 9 '71
  Kidnapped
    Time il 99:54-5 Ja 17 '72
  King Lear
    Nation 213:574 N 29 '71
    New Yorker 47:135-6 D 11 '71
    Newsweek 78:101 N 29 '71
    Sat R 54:18 D 4 '71
    Time 98:54-5 N 29 '71
  Klute
    Atlan 228:144 N '71
    Chr Cent 88:1143-4 S 29 '71
    Commonweal 94:407-8 Ag 6 '71
    Film Q 25:55-6 Fall '71
    Life 71:14 Jl 30 '71
    New Repub 165:22 S 18 '71
    New Yorker 47:42-3 Jl 3 '71
    Time il 98:44 Jl 12 '71
    Vogue 158:60-1 Ag 15 '71
  Kotch
    America 125:321 O 23 '71
    Time il 98:81 O 11 '71
  Lady in the car with glasses and a gun
    America 124:98 Ja 30 '71
    Time il 97:50 Ja 25 '71
  Last movie
    Atlan 228:130-3 D '71
    Nat R 23:1368 D 3 '71
    New Repub 165:22+ O 30 '71
    New Yorker 47:152-4 O 9 '71
    Newsweek il 78:114-15 O 18 '71
    Sat R 54:63 O 16 '71
    Time il 98:87+ O 18 '71
  Last picture show
    Atlan 228:130-3 D '71
    Commentary 53:79-80 Ja '72
    Commonweal 95:132-3 N 5 '71
    Commonweal 95:348-50 Ja 14 '72
    Life il 71:14 O 15 '71
    Nation 213:411-12 O 25 '71
    New Repub 165:18+ O 16 '71
    New Yorker 47:145-7+ O 9 '71
    Newsweek il 78:57 O 11 '71
    Sat R 54:63 O 16 '71
    Time 98:80 O 11 '71
    Vogue 158:170 N 1 '71
  Last run
    Newsweek il 78:79 Jl 19 '71
    Sat R 54:50 Jl 31 '71
    Time il 98:51 Jl 26 '71

MOVING picture plays—Criticisms, plots, etc.—
Single works—*Continued*
Last valley
America 124:128 F 6 '71
New Yorker 46:90 F 13 '71
Newsweek 77:94+ F 8 '71
Time 97:85 Mr 15 '71
Late Liz
Chr Today 16:34-5 O 22 '71
Let's scare Jessica to death
Sat R 54:71 S 25 '71
Time 98:74 S 20 '71
Little big man
America 124:97 Ja 30 '71
Atlan 227:106+ Mr '71
Commentary 51:80-1 Ap '71
Commonweal 93:447 F 5 '71
Esquire 75:70 Mr '71
Film Q il 25:30-3 Fall '71
Nat R 23:381 Ap 6 '71
Sr Schol 98:20-1 Mr 1 '71
Little murders
America 124:292 Mr 20 '71
Atlan 227:98-9+ Ap '71
Commentary 52:24+ S '71
Commonweal 94:453-4 S 3 '71
Life il 70:10 F 12 '71
Nat R 23:662 Je 15 '71
New Repub 164:24+ F 6 '71
New Yorker 47:92+ Mr 6 '71
Newsweek il 77:82 F 15 '71
Sat R 54:44 F 6 '71
Sr Schol il 98:22 Ap 19 '71
Time il 97:54 F 22 '71
Little theatre of Jean Renoir
Film Q 24:51-4 Spr '71
Lodger
New Yorker 47:92-3 S 11 '71
Long ago, tomorrow
America 125:321 O 23 '71
Commonweal 95:89 O 22 '71
Life 71:14 N 5 '71
New Yorker 47:183-4+ N 6 '71
Time 98:90 O 25 '71
Long way back
Chr Today 15:50 My 21 '71
Love machine
America 125:126-7 S 4 '71
Newsweek 78:76+ Ag 16 '71
Time 98:52 Ag 30 '71
Vogue il 158:178-9 O 1 '71
Love story
America 124:97-8 Ja 30 '71
Atlan 227:108-9 Mr '71
Commonweal 93:447 F 5 '71
Commonweal 94:40 Mr 19 '71
Esquire 75:26+ Ap '71
New Repub 164:28 Ja 2 '71
Newsweek 77:10-11 F 1 '71
Vogue 157:89 F 15 '71
Vogue il 157:130-2+ Mr 1 '71
Macbeth
Nation 214:28 Ja 3 '72
New Repub 166:32 Ja 1 '72
Newsweek il 79:59 Ja 10 '72
Time il 97:45 Ja 25 '71
Time il 99:55 Ja 10 '72
McCabe & Mrs Miller
America 125:153 S 11 '71
Atlan 228:109-11 S '71
Chr Cent 88:1274 O 27 '71
Commonweal 94:408 Ag 6 '71
Life il 71:15 S 17 '71
Look il 35:44 Ag 10 '71
Nat R 23:1191 O 22 '71
New Repub 165:33 S 4 '71
New Yorker 47:40-2 Jl 3 '71
Newsweek 78:9 Ag 2 '71
Newsweek il 78:71-2 Jl 5 '71
Sat R 54:31 Ag 7 '71
Time 98:51 Jl 26 '71
Mad dogs and Englishmen
Sat R 54:44 My 1 '71
Time il 97:70 Ap 19 '71
Made for each other
New Yorker 47:59-60+ D 25 '71
Time il 98:58 D 27 '71
Maidstone
Nation 213:540-1 N 22 '71
New Yorker 47:33 O 2 '71
Newsweek il 78:90 O 4 '71
Time il 98:97-8+ N 15 '71
Make a face
Sat R 54:14 S 18 '71
Making it
Time 97:99 My 10 '71
Man and boy
Ebony 26:42-4+ Ap '71
Man called Sledge
Sat R 54:21 Mr 20 '71
Man in the wilderness
New Yorker 47:136-8 D 11 '71
Le Mans
Sr Schol 99:21 S 20 '71
Time il 98:45 Jl 12 '71

Marriage of a young stockbroker
Commonweal 95:88 O 22 '71
New Repub 165:32 S 18 '71
Newsweek il 78:104+ S 13 '71
Time il 98:61 S 6 '71
Mary, queen of Scots
Time il 99:50 Ja 10 '72
M*A*S*H
Commonweal 93:469 F 12 '71
Medea
Newsweek il 78:104 S 13 '71
Opera N 36:43 D 25 '71
Melody
America 124:436 Ap 24 '71
Holiday 49:6 My '71
Newsweek il 77:113+ Ap 12 '71
Sr Schol 98:21 My 3 '71
Time il 97:99 My 10 '71
Mephisto waltz
Time il 97:89 My 3 '71
Midnight cowboy
Sat R 54:14 Jl 17 '71
Mind of Mr Soames
Redbook 136:48+ Mr '71
Minnie and Moskowitz
Nation 214:27 Ja 3 '72
Newsweek 78:62 D 27 '71
Sat R 55:19 Ja 8 '72
Time il 98:58 D 27 '71
Murmur of the heart
Commonweal 95:208 N 26 '71
Life 71:16 N 12 '71
Nation 213:446 N 1 '71
New Repub 165:24+ N 13 '71
New Yorker 47:139-43 O 23 '71
Time il 98:89+ O 25 '71
Vogue 158:170 N 1 '71
Murphy's war
America 125:17 Jl 10 '71
Life 71:14 Jl 16 '71
Sat R 54:51 Jl 24 '71
Sr Schol 98:30 My 17 '71
Time 98:51 Jl 26 '71
Music lovers
America 124:209 F 27 '71
Life 70:12-13 F 5 '71
New Yorker 46:76-9 Ja 30 '71
Newsweek il 77:94 F 8 '71
Opera N il 35:33 F 27 '71
Sat R 54:36 Ja 30 '71
Time il 97:82-3 F 8 '71
My night at Maud's
Commentary 52:84-6 Ag '71
My uncle
New Yorker 47:58+ Ag 28 '71
Myra Breckinridge
Film Q 24:61-2 Wint '70
New leaf
America 124:354 Ap 3 '71
Commonweal 94:262 My 21 '71
New Repub 164:37 Mr 27 '71
New Yorker 47:140 Mr 20 '71
Newsweek 77:112 Mr 22 '71
Sat R 54:50 Mr 27 '71
Sr Schol 98:21 My 3 '71
Time il 97:85 Mr 29 '71
Nicholas and Alexandra
Life 72:14 Ja 14 '72
New Yorker 47:58 D 25 '71
Newsweek il 78:87-8 D 20 '71
Night of the living dead
Newsweek il 78:118+ N 8 '71
Night visitor
Look il 35:84 F 23 '71
Sat R 54:22 F 27 '71
The nun
Chr Cent 88:1299 N 3 '71
New Yorker 47:54 Jl 17 '71
Omega man
Time 98:61 S 6 '71
One day in the life of Ivan Denisovich
America 124:595 Je 5 '71
Life 70:12 Je 25 '71
Nation 212:730-1 Je 7 '71
New Repub 164:24 Je 19 '71
New Yorker 47:71-2 My 22 '71
Newsweek 77:97 My 24 '71
Time il 97:86 My 31 '71
Organization
America 125:353 O 30 '71
Sat R 54:70 N 6 '71
Panic in Needle park
Esquire 76:74+ S '71
New Repub 164:28+ Je 26 '71
Newsweek 78:76 Ag 2 '71
Sat R 54:47 Je 26 '71
Sr Schol il 99:30+ S 27 '71
Time 98:62 Ag 2 '71
People next door
Sat R 54:50 Mr 27 '71
Performance
Art in Am 59:114-15 Mr '71
Play Misty for me
Newsweek 78:120 N 22 '71
Sat R 54:73 N 27 '71

MOVING picture plays—Criticisms, plots, etc.—
Single works—*Continued*
Plaza suite
America 124:579 My 29 '71
Atlan 228:92-3 Ag '71
New Yorker 47:129 My 15 '71
Newsweek 77:97 My 24 '71
Sat R 54:50 My 22 '71
Time 97:86 My 24 '71
Vogue 158:79 Jl 8 '71
Pretty maids all in a row
Commonweal 94:239 My 14 '71
Time il 97:100 My 10 '71
Priest's wife
America 124:292 Mr 20 '71
Commonweal 94:239 My 14 '71
New Repub 164:24 Ap 3 '71
Newsweek 77:110+ Mr 15 '71
Sat R 54:21 Mr 20 '71
Time il 97:85 Mr 15 '71
Private life of Sherlock Holmes
Film Q il 24:45-8 Spr '71
Projectionist
Life 70:7 F 26 '71
Nation 212:381 Mr 22 '71
Promise at dawn
Holiday 49:24+ F '71
Life il 70:7 F 26 '71
New Yorker 46:89-92 F 6 '71
Newsweek 77:75 F 1 '71
Sat R 54:42 F 13 '71
Time il 97:82 F 8 '71
Punishment park
Newsweek il 78:120+ N 15 '71
Sat R 54:25 O 23 '71
Pursuit of happiness
Nat R 23:662 Je 15 '71
Newsweek 77:110B Mr 15 '71
Puzzle of a downfall child
New Yorker 46:90+ F 13 '71
Newsweek 77:92-3 F 22 '71
Sat R 54:84 Ja 23 '71
Time 97:64 F 15 '71
Quiet place in the country
Holiday 48:14+ N '70
Rabbit, run
Vogue 157:139 F 1 '71
Raid on Rommel
Newsweek 77:105 My 17 '71
Railway children
Life il 71:12 D 3 '71
Time il 98:97 N 15 '71
Ramparts of clay
Commonweal 94:86 Ap 2 '71
Film Q 24:64+ Sum '71
Nation 212:284 Mr 1 '71
New Repub 164:35 F 27 '71
Newsweek 77:90+ Mr 1 '71
Sat R 54:14 F 20 '71
Time il 97:54 F 22 '71
Vogue 157:162 Ap 1 '71
Reckoning
Life il 70:6-7 F 26 '71
New Repub 164:24+ F 13 '71
Newsweek il 77:75 F 1 '71
Time il 97:64 F 15 '71
Red sky at morning
America 124:579-80 My 29 '71
Chr Cent 88:1066 S 8 '71
Newsweek il 77:54 My 31 '71
Sat R 54:18 My 15 '71
Sr Schol 98:30 My 17 '71
Red tent
America 125:153 S 11 '71
Sat R 54:15 Ag 21 '71
Sr Schol il 99:20 S 20 '71
Time il 98:58 Ag 16 '71
Right on!
New Yorker 47:135-6 Ap 10 '71
Time il 97:98 My 10 '71
Rio Lobo
Commentary 51:87-8 Je '71
Time il 97:85+ Mr 15 '71
Romance of a horse thief
Sr Schol 99:17 N 8 '71
Ryan's daughter
Sr Schol il 98:20-1 F 1 '71
Sacco & Vanzetti
America 125:405 N 13 '71
Life 71:8 N 26 '71
Nat R 23:1479-80 D 31 '71
New Repub 165:18+ O 16 '71
Newsweek il 78:89 N 1 '71
Sat R il 54:53-4 O 9 '71
Sr Schol 99:17 N 8 '71
Vogue 159:33 Ja 1 '72
See no evil
Commonweal 95:88-9 O 22 '71
New Yorker 47:69 S 18 '71
Newsweek 78:89 S 20 '71
Sat R 54:71 S 25 '71
Time il 98:74 S 20 '71
Separate peace
Sr Schol il 99:22 N 15 '71
Seven minutes
Newsweek 78:72 Ag 9 '71

Severed head
Commonweal 94:239 My 14 '71
Life 70:14 Mr 5 '71
Nat R 23:822-3 Jl 27 '71
New Repub 164:24 Ap 3 '71
Newsweek il 78:113 Ap 12 '71
Time 97:98 Ap 26 '71
Shaft
America 125:48 Jl 24 '71
New Yorker 47:67 Ag 7 '71
Newsweek 78:80 Jl 19 '71
Time il 98:51 Jl 26 '71
Skezag
Newsweek 77:102+ My 17 '71
Time 97:98 My 10 '71
Skin game
America 125:353 O 30 '71
Life il 71:12 O 29 '71
New Yorker 47:154+ O 9 '71
Socrates
Newsweek il 78:112 D 6 '71
Sometimes a great notion
Time il 98:60 D 13 '71
Song of Norway
Sr Schol 98:21 Mr 8 '71
Souffle au coeur
New Yorker 47:130+ My 15 '71
Speed is of the essence
Look il 35:88-9 Je 1 '71
Sporting club
New Yorker 47:89-90 Mr 13 '71
Sat R 54:80 Mr 13 '71
Star spangled girl
Time il 99:54 Ja 17 '72
Steagle
New Repub 165:22+ O 2 '71
Newsweek il 78:90+ O 4 '71
Sat R 54:18 O 2 '71
Straw dogs
Newsweek il 78:87 D 20 '71
Sat R 54:22 D 18 '71
Time il 98:84-5+ D 20 '71
Struggle in Italy
Film Q 25:56 Fall '71
Such good friends
Time 99:50+ Ja 10 '72
Sudden terror
America 124:436 Ap 24 '71
Summer of '42
America 124:492-3 My 8 '71
Atlan 228:98-9 Jl '71
Chr Cent 88:1066 S 8 '71
Commonweal 94:261 My 21 '71
Esquire 76:48 Jl '71
New Repub 164:26+ My 29 '71
Newsweek il 77:91 Ap 26 '71
Time 97:99 My 10 '71
Sunday bloody Sunday
America 125:292-3 O 16 '71
Chr Cent 88:1529-30 D 29 '71
Commonweal 95:207 N 26 '71
Life il 71:16 O 8 '71
Nation 213:382 O 18 '71
New Repub 165:24+ O 9 '71
New Yorker 47:93-7 O 2 '71
Newsweek il 78:106+ S 27 '71
Sat R il 54:71 S 25 '71
Time il 98:82 S 27 '71
Vogue 158:102 O 15 '71
Sweet Sweetback's baadasssss song
Ebony il 26:106-8+ S '71
Life 71:61 Ag 13 '71
Nation 212:669-70 My 24 '71
New Yorker 47:68 Je 19 '71
Newsweek 77:116+ My 10 '71
Time il 98:47 Ag 16 '71
THX 1138
Atlan 227:98-9 My 29 '71
Commonweal 94:191 Ap 30 '71
Film Q 24:inside back cover Sum '71
Nat R 23:662 Je 15 '71
New Repub 164:24+ Ap 10 '71
Newsweek il 77:98 Mr 29 '71
Newsweek il 77:50+ My 31 '71
Sat R 54:52 Ap 3 '71
Sr Schol il 98:19 My 10 '71
Time il 97:85+ Mr 29 '71
T. R. Baskin
New Yorker 47:144-6 O 23 '71
Newsweek 78:89-90 N 1 '71
Sat R 54:70 N 6 '71
Time 98:109 N 1 '71
Taking off
Chr Cent 88:1093 S 15 '71
Commonweal 94:262-3 My 21 '71
Life 70:12 Ap 2 '71
Nat R 23:823 Jl 27 '71
Nation 212:508-9 Ap 19 '71
New Repub 164:22 Ap 24 '71
New Yorker 47:107-9 Ap 3 '71
Newsweek il 77:92+ Ap 5 '71
Time il 97:86 Ap 5 '71
Tam Lin
Sat R 54:73 N 27 '71

MOVING picture plays—Criticisms, plots, etc.—
  Single works—*Continued*
  10 Rillington place
    America 124:619 Je 12 '71
    Commonweal 94:359-60 Jl 9 '71
    New Repub 164:24 Je 19 '71
    New Yorker 47:72-3 My 22 '71
    Newsweek il 77:97+ My 24 '71
    Sat R 54:40 My 8 '71
    Sr Schol 98:30 My 17 '71
  Tender moment
    Sat R 54:22 F 27 '71
  There was a crooked man
    New Repub 164:33-4 Ja 23 '71
    New Yorker 46:65 Ja 9 '71
    Time 97:50 Ja 25 '71
  There's a girl in my soup
    Commonweal 93:448 F 5 '71
  They might be giants
    Holiday 49:12 Jl '71
    Newsweek 77:113B Ap 12 '71
    Sat R 54:40 My 8 '71
    Sr Schol 98:21 My 3 '71
    Time il 97:98+ Ap 26 '71
  This man must die
    Commonweal 94:64 Mr 26 '71
  Three lives
    Newsweek 78:119 N 8 '71
  El topo
    Commonweal 95:301 D **24** '71
    Esquire 75:34+ Je '71
    Nation 213:540 N 22 '71
    New Yorker 46:212+ N **20** '71
    Newsweek 78:119 N 22 '71
    Time il 97:77 Je 28 '71
  The touch
    America 125:119-20 S 4 '71
    Commonweal 95:37-8 O 8 '71
    Life il 71:12 S 10 '71
    New Repub 165:35 Ag 21 '71
    New Yorker 47:57-8 Jl 24 '71
    Newsweek il 78:70 Jl 26 '71
    Sat R 54:50 Jl 31 '71
    Time il 98:50-1 Jl 26 '71
    Vogue 158:287 S 1 '71
  Tristana
    Chr Cent 88:301-2 Mr 3 '71
    Commentary 51:76-8 Mr '71
    Film Q il 24:52-5 Wint '70
  Trojan women
    New Repub 165:24 N 13 '71
    New Yorker 47:155-6+ O 16 '71
  200 motels
    Time il 98:55 N 29 '71
  Two-lane blacktop
    Commentary 53:78-9 Ja '72
    New Yorker 47:55 Jl 10 '71
    Newsweek il 78:72 Jl **5** '71
    Sat R 54:14 Jl 17 '71
    Time il 98:44 Jl 12 '71
  Unman, Wittering and Zigo
    Time 98:51 Jl 26 '71
  Valdez is coming
    Time 97:97 Ap 26 '71
  Very curious girl
    Chr Cent 88:261-2 F 24 '71
    Newsweek 77:94 F 8 '71
  Vidas secas
    Film Q il 24:49-50 Spr '71
  Villain
    Time 97:83 Je 14 '71
  Virgin and the gipsy
    Chr Cent 88:168-9 F 3 '71
  Vladimir and Rosa
    New Repub 164:24+ My 1 '71
    New Yorker 47:116+ My 8 '71
    Newsweek il 77:116 My 10 '71
  W.R. mysteries of the organism
    New Repub 165:28+ N 20 '71
    Newsweek il 78:90+ N 1 '71
  Walkabout
    America 125:48 Jl 24 '71
    Chr Cent 88:1029-30 **S** 1 **'71**
    Esquire 76:42 Ag '71
    Life il 70:16 Je 4 '71
    New Repub 165:34 Jl 3 '71
    New Yorker 47:55 Jl 10 '71
    Sat R 54:12 Je 5 '71
    Time il 97:77 Je 28 '71
  Wanda
    Commonweal 94:87 Ap 2 '71
    Film Q 25:49-51 Fall '71
    Nation 212:381 Mr 22 '71
    New Repub 164:24+ Mr 27 '71
    New Yorker 47:138-40 Mr 20 '71
    Sat R 54:80 Mr 13 '71
    Time 97:77 Mr 22 '71
  Waterloo
    America 124:390-2 Ap 10 '71
    Commonweal 94:238 My 14 '71
    Nat R 23:489-90 My 4 '71
    New Repub 164:24+ Je 19 '71
    New Yorker 47:130+ Ap 10 '71
    Newsweek il 77:126 Ap 19 '71
    Sat R 54:53 Ap 17 '71
    Sr Schol 98:21 My 3 '71
    Time il 97:70 Ap 19 '71

  Where's poppa?
    Film Q 24:60-3 Sum '71
  Who is Harry Kellerman and why is he
  saying those terrible things about me?
    Look il por 35:39 Jl 27 '71
    New Repub 165:22+ S 18 '71
    New Yorker 47:56-7 Jl 10 '71
    Newsweek 77:90+ Je 28 '71
    Sat R 54:18 Jl 3 '71
  Wild child. See L'enfant sauvage, page 765
  Wild rovers
    America 125:17 Jl 10 '71
    Sat R 54:12 Jl 10 '71
    Time 98:51 Jl 26 '71
  Willard
    Life 71:11 Ag 27 '71
    New Yorker 47:65 Ag 7 '71
    Time 98:51 Jl 26 '71
    Time il 98:47 Ag 23 '71
  Willy Wonka and the chocolate factory
    Look il 35:35 Ag 24 '71
  Wings
    Life il 71:22 O 22 '71
    New Yorker 47:104-6 S 25 '71
  WUSA
    Film Q 24:58 Spr '71
    Holiday 48:16-17+ N '70
  Wuthering Heights
    America 124:244 Mr 6 '71
    Newsweek il 77:110 Mr 15 '71
    Sat R 54:40 Ja 16 '71
    Sr Schol il 98:18-19 Mr 15 '71
    Time il 97:79+ Mr 1 '71
  Zachariah
    Chr Cent 88:508 Ap 21 '71
    Nat R 23:662 Je 15 '71
    Sr Schol il 98:20 Mr 8 '71
  Zeppelin
    Sr Schol 98:21 My 3 '71

Themes

See Moving pictures—Themes

MOVING picture production and direction
  Around the bend in eighty days. S. J. Perelman. New Yorker 47:22-4 Ja 1 '72 (to be cont)
  Breaking through, selling out, dropping dead, by W. Bayer. Review
    Newsweek 78:101-101A N **29** '71. P. D. Zimmerman
  Dennis Hopper makes The last movie, in Peru; interview, ed. by E. Miller. D. Hopper. il pors Seventeen 29:92-3+ Jl '70
  Diary of a dead Bavarian; three days with Dalton Trumbo. J. Zinnamon; reply. W. Heffley. Esquire 75:22+ Mr '71
  Difficulties of Little big man. L. Braudy. il Film Q 25:30-3 Fall '71
  Durango: Poitier meets Belafonte; Buck and the preacher. G. Goodman. il pors Look 35:56-60+ Ag 24 '71
  Eric Rohmer: an interview; tr. by G. Petrie. E. Rohmer. il Film Q 24:34-51 Sum '71
  Grab the goat and ride, Omar! filming of The horsemen. R. H. Boyle. il Sports Illus 34:58-61 My 17 '71
  How the sun and the moon got into a film; making of Why the sun and the moon live in the sky. B. Lent. il Horn Bk 47:589-96 D '71
  I live at the edge of a very strange country; with comments by I. Bergman and others. R. Meryman. il pors Life 71:60-60B+ O 15 '71
  Kubrick country; interview, ed. by P. Houston. S. Kubrick. por Sat R 54:42-4 D 25 '71
  Lights, camera! Here comes Oscar candidate Jean-Claude; filming of The great ski caper. C. Gammon. il pors Sports Illus 35:68-71 O 4 '71
  Long day's journey into night; interview, ed. by D. Luciano. S. Lumet. il Film Q 25:20-9 Fall '71
  Love calls the tune; filming Fiddler on the roof. E. Miller il Seventeen 30:144-5+ S '71
  Making of Fat city; craft beats art by a T.K.O. L. Shecter. il Look 35:88-90 O 19 '71
  Making of The godfather; sort of a home movie. N. Pileggi. il N Y Times Mag p7+ Ag 15 '71; Reply. C. Conrad. p70 S 19 '71
  Man and boy. L. Robinson. il pors Ebony 26:42-4+ Ap '71
  On actors & directors. J. Cassavetes. Harp Baz 104:72 Jl '71
  On closed sets. R. Brooks. il Harp Baz 104:66-7 Jl '71
  On directors and technicians. A. Penn. Harp Baz 104:65 Jl '71
  Onward and upward with the arts; producing Citizen Kane. P. Kael. por New Yorker 47:43-52+ F 20; 44-50+ F 27 '71
  Our local correspondents; afternoons with Hopper. J. Stevenson. New Yorker 47:116+ N **13 '71**

MOVING picture production and direction—
Continued
Polish imposition; shooting of Macbeth. K.
Tynan. pors Esquire 76:122-5+ S '71
Shooting The godfather. il Newsweek 77:89
Je 28 '71
Spiffy musical spoof: The boy friend. E. Mil-
ler. il Seventeen 30:90-1+ D '71
Stars and celebrities; N. Mailer's Maidstone.
R. Schickel. Commentary 52:61-5 Ag '71
Tea with Twiggy; interview. N. Davies;
Twiggy. New Yorker 47:30-1 D 18 '71
That self-sufficient thing; C. Eastwood as
a director. il pors Time 98:66 D 6 '71
Toward a non-bourgeois camera style; ex-
cerpt from Weekend and history. B. Hen-
derson. il Film Q 24:2-14 Wint '70
Warhol as filmmaker. D. Bourdon. il Art in
Am 59:48-53 My '71
What's behind those beautiful blue eyes?
interview, ed. by E. Miller. P. Newman.
Seventeen 29:124-5+ N '70
Which face is Fellini? D. J. Hamblin. il pors
Life 71:58-61 Jl 30 '71
Woodstock discovers Washington. Who?
George Washington. L. Gross. il Look 35:
30+ Ag 24 '71
See also
Moving picture directors
Moving pictures—Setting and scenery

Study and teaching

Filming poetry; Max Cameron high school.
British Columbia. T. Barker. il Schol
Teach Jr/Sr High p 10-11 Ap 5 '71
Filmmaking in the classroom. L. Bastian. il
Sch Arts 70:10-11 Je '71
Filmmaking; some experiences with the
gifted. J. J. Hanke. Engl J 60:121-5 Ja '71
High school newsreels; Redmond, Wash. J.
A. Newman. il Schol Teach Jr/Sr High
p22-3 Mr 8 '71
Movie making; Columbia university film
school; interview, ed. by T. Galluzzo. M.
Le Page. Mod Phot 35:38+ Jl '71
Movie making; Ecole nationale supérieure de
la photographie, cinématographie et de la
télévision. T. Galluzzo. il Mod Phot 35:62+
Je '71
Story of mankind; produced by sophomores
at Thorp high school. Wis. il Sr Schol 99:
24-5 N 29 '71
MOVING picture projectors
Now it's instant color movies! self-develop-
ing projector. S. M. Gallagher. il Pop Mech
136:90-1 O '71
Photo expo 71. L. Brown. il Pop Phot 69:
81+ Ag '71
See your 2-D movies in 3-D; Invision pro-
jector system. J. Goodrum. il Pop Sci
198:50 Ja '71
Update: movie projectors. il Consumer Rep
36:237-8 Ap '71
MOVING picture scripts
Carnal knowledge; excerpt from screenplay.
J. Feiffer. il Harp Baz 104:72 Jl '71
Last rites for a young marriage; excerpts
from a screenplay. E. O'Brien. Vogue 158:
92-3 Jl '71
New American western; on writing Doc. P.
Hamill. il Harp Baz 104:71+ Jl '71
MOVING picture serials. See Moving pictures
—Serial films
MOVING picture sets. See Moving pictures—
Setting and scenery
MOVING picture societies
See also
American film institute
MOVING picture sound recording
Don't just add a sound-track: fuse it. R.
Pinney. il Pop Phot 68:47+ My '71
Dull lenses and low-fi. il Pop Phot 68:46+
Ap '71
Friends of The boy friend. D. Hamilton. Hi
Fi 21:17+ S '71
Movie making; history of sound in the
movies. T. Galluzzo. Mod Phot 35:48+ Ja
'71
Screen's third dimension. R. Pinney. il Pop
Phot 68:56+ Mr '71
MOVING picture studios
What about the movies? Hollywood break-
down. P. S. Nathan. Pub W 199:53 Je 28 '71
MOVING picture theaters
Back to the Bijou; restoration of Penn the-
atre. Pittsburgh. A. Velis. il Opera N 36:
12-14 S '71
Cashing in on vintage flicks. il Bsns W p25
D 18 '71

Movie palaces. il Life 70:44-51 F 19 '71
NATO is a house o'weenies; meeting of
National association of theater owners. il
Time 98:79 N 8 '71
See also
New York (city)—Radio City music hall

Finance

But where are the profits? il Forbes 108:37+
Jl 1 '71

Management

Six for the show; young film buffs turn
theater managers; Rushford, Minn. il Seven-
teen 30:106 Ja '71
MOVING picture theaters, Traveling
Movie bus; Syracuse, N.Y. P. S. Gallivan.
il Parks & Rec 6:37+ S '71
MOVING pictures
Cinema in the sixties; with filmography. C.
T. Samuels. il Am Lib 2:461-73 My '71
Current cinema; notes on new actors, new
movies. P. Kael. New Yorker 47:168-73 D
4 '71
Films; symposium. il Harp Baz 104:65-72+
Jl '71
Not quite ready when you are. C.B; movie
goofs; comp. by J. Kobal. Esquire 75:86
Ap '71
Screenings: 16mm (cont) Library J 96:1789.
2861 My 15. S 15 '71
There's no movie like an old movie. E. Jaffe.
Seventeen 31:135 Ja '72
See also
Academy awards (moving pictures)
Negroes in moving pictures
Realism in moving pictures
Shakespeare, W.—Moving pictures
Television broadcasting—Moving pictures
Women in moving pictures
also headings beginning Moving picture

Animated cartoons

Behind the scenes with a teenage animator;
interview, ed. by D. Molner. E. Goldberg.
il pors Schol Teach Jr/Sr High p 16-17
My 3 '7
See also
Disney, Walt, productions

Criticisms, plots, etc.
Aristocats
Time il 97:51 Ja 25 '71
Phantom tollbooth
Time il 97:76 Mr 22 '71
Shinbone Alley
New Yorker 47:98-9 Ap 17 '71
Why the sun and the moon live in the sky
Horn Bk il 47:589-96 D '71

Art films

Film. D. Hare. il Craft Horiz 31:7 Ap; 10+
Je; 10+ Ag; 10+ O '71

Audiences

See Moving picture audiences

Bibliography

Books. Film Q 25:57-63 Fall '71

Biographical films

Film lives of great composers. H. C. Schonberg. Harper 242:110+ Ap '71

Censorship

See Moving picture censorship

Children, Effect on

See Moving pictures and children

Classification

Booed in Boston ditto in Detroit. P. C. Rule.
America 125:404 N 13 '71
Church film agencies withdraw support of
rating system. Chr Cent 88:683 Je 2 '71
Film ratings flunk out. T. Thompson. il
Life 71:50B+ Ag 20 '71
Film ratings: 1934 revisited; with editorial
comment. P. C. Rule. America 124:557-8,
570-2 My 29 '71
Films. J. Brackman. Esquire 76:114+ D '71
G for go? M. Ronan. il Sr Schol 98:20-1 My
3 '71
In defense of the voluntary film rating pro-
gram. J. Valenti. il Harp Baz 104:68-9 Jl '71
Less pornography, more fun wanted in the
movies. Consumer Bul 54:13-14 Ag '71
New problems with "X" films. America 125:
528-9 D 18 '71
Rating the rating system. il Time 97:72-3
My 31 '71

MOVING pictures—*Continued*

Collectors and collecting

Collecting film-art. B. Rose. il Vogue 157: 74 Mr 15 '71

Savior of old movies: H. Langlois. R. Chelminski. il pors Life 71:45-6+ D 10 '71
See also
Moving picture film collections

Dance films

Beatrix Potter rides again. il Life 70:54-7 F 12 '71

Movie carousel. il Dance Mag 45:74-7 O '71

Criticisms, plots, etc.

Peter Rabbit and Tales of Beatrix Potter
America 125:235 O 2 '71
Dance Mag il 45:20-1 Jl '71
Life il 70:54-7 F 12 '71
Look il 35:32-5 Jl 27 '71
New Yorker 47:86-8 Je 26 '71
Newsweek il 78:80 Jl 19 '71
Sat R 54:82 S 18 '71
Time 98:67 Jl 5 '71

Detective and mystery films

Detective Egan's new assignment. P. F. Kluge. il pors Life 71:85-6+ D 10 '71

My Laura and Otto's. V. Caspary. il Sat R 54:36-7 Je 26 '71

On suspense and mystery. A. Hitchcock. il Harp Baz 104:70 Jl '71

Distribution

Right on with Rugoff. H. Alpert. il por Sat R 54:61-3+ S 25 '71

Documentary films

Everybody is up in arms; documentary film hoax. D. Connelly. il Sports Illus 34:32-4+ Ap 5 '71

Film reviews. See issues of Mental hygiene

Radical scavenging; interview. ed. by B. Weiner. E. De Antonio. il por Film Q 25: 3-15 Fall '71
See also
Moving pictures—Short subject films
Moving pictures in environmental education
Moving pictures in narcotics education
Moving pictures in sex instruction

Criticisms, plots, etc.

African elephant
Look il 35:74 O 19 '71

Blue water, white death
Chr Cent 88:1118 S 22 '71
Time il 97:86 My 31 '71

Body
Sat R 54:44 Mr 6 '71

British sounds. See See you at Mao, below

Carry it on
Chr Cent 88:206 F 10 '71

Le chagrin et la pitié. See Sorrow and the pity, below

Derby
America 124:619 Je 12 '71
Look il 35:71 Je 29 '71
New Repub 164:24+ My 22 '71
New Yorker 47:129 My 15 '71
Sat R 54:54 My 29 '71

Elvis, that's the way it is
Commonweal 93:448 F 5 '71
Sat R 54:48 Ja 30 '71

Gimme shelter
America 125:122-3 S 4 '71
Film Q il 24:56-60 Sum '71
Life 70:12 Ja 29 '71
Nat R 23:381-2 Ap 6 '71
New Repub 164:28 Ja 2 '71
Sat R il 54:48-9 Ja 30 '71
Vogue il 157:86-7 F 15 '71

Groupies
Sat R 54:50 Ja 30 '71

Hellstrom chronicle
Commonweal 94:382-3 Jl 23 '71
New Yorker 47:54 Jl 17 '71
Newsweek 78:9 Ag 2 '71
Newsweek il 78:82 Jl 12 '71
Sat R 54:51 Jl 24 '71

La hora de los hornos. See Hour of the furnaces, below

Hour of the furnaces
New Repub 164:26+ F 27 '71
New Yorker 47:95-7 Mr 6 '71
Newsweek 77:93A Mr 1 '71

Millhouse
Nat R 23:1368 D 3 '71
Nation 213:382 O 18 '71
New Repub 165:32 O 2 '71
Newsweek 78:121 N 15 '71
Time 98:87 O 18 '71

Monterey pop
Sat R 54:48 Ja 30 '71

Murder of Fred Hampton
Newsweek il 78:81 Ag 23 '71

On any Sunday
Hot Rod il 24:126-7 Je '71
Newsweek il 78:79 Ag 16 '71
Sr Schol il 99:18 O 11 '71
Time il 98:55 Ag 16 '71

Saturday morning
Atlan 228:99-101 Jl '71
New Repub 164:24+ My 1 '71
New Yorker 47:121-2 My 8 '71
Sat R 54:54 My 29 '71
Time il 97:89 My 3 '71

See you at Mao
Film Q il 24:15-23 Wint '70

Sorrow and the pity
Nation 213:477 N 8 '71
New Yorker 47:134-5 My 15 '71
Newsweek il 78:60+ O 25 '71

Sweet Toronto
Sat R il 54:49 Ja 30 '71

Three lives
Commonweal 95:257 D 10 '71

The woman's film
Film Q 25:48-9 Fall '71

Woodstock
Film Q 24:54-6 Spr '71

Editing

Moving making; sequential photography. T. Galluzzo. il Mod Phot 35:32+ D '71

Two types of film theory. B. Henderson. Film Q 24:33-42 Spr '71
See also
Moving pictures—Sound editing

Educational aspects
See Moving pictures in education

Educational films
See Moving pictures in education

Escapist films
See Moving pictures—Themes

History

Moving making; history of sound in the movies T. Galluzzo. Mod Phot 35:48+ Ja '71

Bibliography
Books. Film Q 25:58-63 Fall '71

Horror films

Cheap thrills; comp. by M. Jahn. il Esquire 76:68-71 Ag '71

Horror films: big fall film boom. R. Goldstein. il Vogue 158:179 O 1 '71

Monster movies? S. Vaughn. il Library J 96:3439-41 O 15 '71

Meteorological films

Educational film program of the American meteorological society; with list of films. M. Toyli and J. Gerhardt. Weatherwise 24: 228-9+ O '71

Moral aspects

Current cinema; violence in El Topo. P. Kael. New Yorker 47:212+ N 20 '71

Doing violence. C. T. Samuels. Am Scholar 40:695-700 Aut '71

Ice-man cometh no more: R. Kramer's violent film about revolution. J. R. MacBean. il Film Q 24:26-33 Sum '71

Losing it at the movies. D. Brudnoy; reply. R. Corliss. Nat R 23:101 Ja 26 '71

No joy in Peckville; problems of theater owner Nick Angeli, jr. J. Morgenstern. Newsweek 77:17 Je 7 '71

Our misanthropic movies. D. Denby. Atlan 228:144+ N '71

Please, less violence. A. Knight. Sat R 54:22 D 18 '71

Violence forsworn. P. S. Nathan. Pub W 199: 27 Je 21 '71
See also
Moving pictures—Classification
National Catholic office for motion pictures
Sex in moving pictures

Musical films

Busby Berkeley's girls glitter again. H. Wingo. il por Life 70:42-3 F 19 '71

Fidelio. R. Zachary. Opera N 35:29 My 15 '71

Love calls the tune; filming Fiddler on the roof. E. Miller. il Seventeen 30:144-5+ S '71

News films
See Newsreels

MOVING pictures—*Continued*

Periodicals
See also
Film quarterly

Political films
Fascism in the contemporary film. J. Mellen. il Film Q 24:2-19 Sum '71
Radical scavenging; interview, ed. by B. Weiner. E. De Antonio. il por Film Q 25: 3-15 Fall '71

Propaganda films
International film and television propaganda: campaigns of assistance. B. Rubin. bibliog f il Ann Am Acad 398:81-92 N '71

Religious films
See also
Ross, Dick, and associates (firm)

Renting
Night at the movies. C. B. Roth. il Am Home 74:74+ N '71

Romantic films
See Moving pictures—Themes

Science fiction films
Technical dilemma; operation of robots by legless men in film by D. Trumbul. il Esquire 76:130-5 S '71

Science films
Films of the week. See issues of Science news
Films: Wondering about things. G. Pimentel. il Chem 44:26-7 N '71
See also
Moving pictures—Meteorological films

Serial films
Les vampires; serial made in 1915-1916 by Louis Feuillade. E. Mandel. Film Q 24:56-60 Wint '70

Setting and scenery
Around the bend in eighty days. S. J. Perelman. New Yorker 47:22-4 Ja 1 '72
Current cinema; New York-made movies. P. Kael. New Yorker 47:113-16 O 30 '71
Love calls the tune; filming Fiddler on the roof. E. Miller. il Seventeen 30:144-5+ S '71

Sex films
See Sex in moving pictures

Short subject films
Women, wives, film-makers; interview, ed. by B. Richardson. G. Nelson; D. Wiley. il Film Q 25:34-40 Fall '71

Silent films
Collecting classic films; with filmography. P. J. Bukalski. il Am Lib 2:475-9 My '71
Current cinema; Channel 13-WNET series; The silent years. P. Kael. New Yorker 47:183 N 6 '71
Doug Fairbanks: superstar of the silents. R. Schickel. il pors Am Heritage 23:4-12+ D '71
Silents weren't just voiceless talkies. R. Schickel. il N Y Times Mag p32-3+ N 28 '71

Social aspects
What movies try to sell us; flimflam vision of the world. L. Lapham. il Harper 243: 106-8+ N '71

Sound editing
Movie making; Handiola system. T. Galluzzo. il Mod Phot 35:52+ Mr '71

Sound recording
See Moving picture sound recording

Special effects
Violence bag. il Newsweek 78:110-110A+ D 13 '71

Sports films
Le Mans. E. Seidler. il por Motor T 23:94+ Je '71

Study and teaching
Filmmaking and social criticism. L. Bastian. il Sch Arts 71:38-9 D '71
Films are in at Fermi; Enfield, Conn. F. S. Gross. il Schol Teach Jr/Sr High p22-3 O '71
Grooving with film. H. Stonesifer. il Har Yrs 11:6-8 S '71
Kicks and flicks at Fermi; Enfield, Conn. il Schol Teach Jr/Sr High p 16-17+ F 1 '71
Media literacy: focus on film. C. M. Kirkton. bibliog Engl J 60:831-8 S '71
See also
Moving picture production and direction—Study and teaching

Suspense films
See Moving pictures—Detective and mystery films

Themes
Bergman's odyssey. R. E. Lauder. America 125:119-20 S 4 '71
Current cinema; New York-made movies. P. Kael. New Yorker 47:113-16 O 30 '71
Death theme in natural cinema; Maysles' cinematic theory. J. F. Kavanaugh. America 125:122-3 S 4 '71
Drug movies: turn-ons or turn-offs? M. Ronan. il Sr Schol 99:30+ S 27 '71
Enough to make you cry. C. Irving. il McCalls 98:14+ Ap '71
Exile of pirates & princes; escapist films. T. S. Reck. Commonweal 95:155-8 N 12 '71
Last of the schlockmeisters; movies for the teen age audience. R. Ebert. il pors Esquire 76:152-5+ N '71
Love stories. C. T. Samuels. Am Scholar 41: 134-8 W!nt '71
Now at your local theater: a new kind of shoot-'em up; dope operas. B. Darrach. il Life 71:82-3 N 5 '71
Pains of love; views of J. Valenti. por Newsweek 77:74 F 1 '71
Virgin again; return to romance. J. Morgenstern. Newsweek 77:10-11 F 1 '71
See also
Jews in moving pictures
Youth in moving pictures

Anecdotes, facetiae, satire, etc.
Parting shots: films that will offend nobody. il Life 70:62A-62B Ap 2 '71

Westerns
It don't hurt much, ma'am; gunfight myths of western fiction and film. J. S. Packer. il Am Heritage 22:66-9 F '71
Two screen cowboys talk about the reel West & the real West; interviews, ed. by M. Ronan. J. Wayne; B. Johnson. il pors Sr Schol 99:10-11 D 6 '71

Chile
Medium Chile: cinéma vérité inside the third world. P. Frazer. Ramp Mag 9:56-62 F '71

Europe
Fascism in the contemporary film. J. Mellen. il Film Q 24:2-19 Sum '71

France
Eric Rohmer: an interview; tr. by G. Petrie. E. Rohmer. il Film Q 24:34-41 Sum '71

Great Britain
Current cinema; A. Hitchock. P. Gilliatt. New Yorker 47:91-4 S 11 '71

India
From Madras: a view of the southern film. S. H. Rudolph. Yale R 60:468-80 Mr '71

Japan
Crucified lovers of Mizoguchi. J. Belton. il Film Q 25:15-19 Fall '71
Sinerama in Osaka. Time 97:62 Mr 22 '71
Those *longeurs* in Japanese films. B. Wolf. Nation 213:152-4 Ag 30 '71

United States
Cashing in on vintage flicks. il Bsns W p25 D 18 '7'
Fascism in the contemporary film. J. Mellen. il Film Q 24:12-19 Sum '71
See also
American film institute
Moving picture industry—United States

MOVING pictures, Amateur
Good home movie is not necessarily well made. D. Sutherland. il Pop Phot 69:122-3+ O '71
Make a movie from your family album. R. Pinney. il Pop Phot 68:112-13 Je '71
Why don't we make more movies? N. Rothschild. Pop Phot 68:18+ Mr '71

Sound effects
Sound sets the stage. R. Pinney. il Pop Phot 69:47+ S '71

MOVING pictures, Childrens. See Moving pictures for children
MOVING pictures, English. See Moving pictures—Great Britain
MOVING pictures, Experimental
Women, wives, film-makers; interview, ed. by B. Richardson. G. Nelson; D. Wiley. il Film Q 25:34-40 Fall '71
Yoko Lennon's latest film has a cast of 200-flies. E. Washington. il por Life 71:61 Ag 6 '71

MOVING pictures, Musical. See Moving pictures—Musical films
MOVING pictures, Realism in. See Realism in moving pictures
MOVING pictures, Silent. See Moving pictures—Silent films
MOVING pictures and children
What every parent needs to know about movies and isn't told. R. Kramer. il N Y Times Mag p85+ Ap 4 '71; Reply. J. Valenti. p95 My 2 '71
See also
Moving pictures—Moral aspects
Moving pictures for children
MOVING pictures and libraries. See Libraries and moving pictures
MOVING pictures and morals. See Moving pictures—Moral aspects
MOVING pictures and television
Current cinema; Channel 13-WNET series: The silent years. P. Kael. New Yorker 47: 183 N 6 '71
Medium is the motivation; movies, TV and paperbacks. K. Cremonini. il Schol Teach Jr/Sr High p 12-14 Ap 5 '71
MOVING pictures and youth
I hate Love story! And other remarks about movies; symposium, ed. by E. Miller. il Seventeen 30:108-9+ Jl '71
Love story: it's required. B. F. Dick. Nat R 23:771 Jl 13 '71
Movies from behind the barricades; student protest movies. S. Farber. il Film Q 24:24-33 Wint '70
MOVING pictures for children
Children; production of films designed especially for children. M. Walsh. America 124:435-6 Ap 24 '71
Family movie guide; ed. by J. Ripp. See issues of Parents' magazine & better family living
Feature films for children; with lists of companies and film festivals. H. Miller. bibliog il por Wilson Lib Bul 45:560-71 F '71
Why children's films are not rated R. H. Miller. il Wilson Lib Bul 46:183-4 O '71
MOVING pictures in education
Baseball, film. and poetry. R. W. Reising. Clear House 45:317-18 Ja '71
Better way to show the way. J. E. Kemp. Ed Digest 37:52-3 O '71
Classroom cinema. R. Maynard. bibliog Schol Teach Jr/Sr High p29+ S; 28+ O; 22 N '71; 18-20 Ja '72
Eroticism and the art of film; address, 1970. G. W. Jones. il Library J 96:3809-10 N 15 '71
Film stimuli, an approach to creative writing. P. Dauterman and R. Stahl. Engl J 60:1120-2 N '71
Moral dilemma, a teaching unit for slow learners. R. G. Brown. Engl J 60:924-6+ O '71
Movie's the message! P. A. O'Keefe. Engl J 60:957-9 O '71
Screenings: 8mm (cont) A. Cohen. Library J 96:2860-1 3454 S 15, O 15 '71
To sing the street; using a community film program to teach film composition. H. Foley. Engl J 60:1101-8 N '71
See also
Libraries and moving pictures
Moving pictures—Study and teaching
Moving pictures in environmental education
Moving pictures in sex instruction
MOVING pictures in environmental education
Teacher's survival guide to environmental education resources. Schol Teach Jr/Sr High p38-9+ O '71
MOVING pictures in hotel rooms. See Hotels, taverns, etc.—Services
MOVING pictures in narcotics education
Cutting companies' and society's losses. V. Louviere. il Nations Bens 59:14 Ja '71
Drug film fallacies exposed in report. il Library J 96:3264-6 O 15 '71
Films on drug abuse; with filmography. C. Leibenguth. il Am Lib 2:483-7 My '71
MOVING pictures in psychotherapy
Film reviews. See issues of Mental hygiene
MOVING pictures in science
See also
Moving pictures—Science films
MOVING pictures in sex instruction
Sex education on film; with list of film and filmstrip references. il pors Wilson Lib Bul 46:177-82 O '71
MOVSHON, George
Caramoor's Dido and Aeneas. il Hi Fi 21: MA21+ O '71
Double-barreled Donizetti. por Hi Fi 20:90+ D '70
Festival retains its glamor. Hi Fi 21:MA28-9 N '71

History brought to life. il Hi Fi 21:77-8 O '71
Met season opens with Don Carlo. il Hi Fi 21:MA15+ D '71
Milestone Aida. por Hi Fi 21:57-8 Ag '71
Peg board: meet Jack field. il Hi Fi 20:70-4 D '70
Sills and Gedda star in an ideal Manon. il Hi Fi 21:72-3 Je '71
Wonder of the age. il Hi Fi 21:84-5 S '71
MOWING machines
See also
Lawn mowers
MOWRER, O. Hobart
Integrity group seminars. il Sch & Soc 99: 333 O '71 *
MOYAL, Maurice
Father to the orphans of three continents. il por Chr Cent 88:752-4 Je 16 '71
MOYERS, Bill D.
Vietnam: what is left of conscience? Sat R 54:20-1 F 13 '71
MOYNIHAN, Daniel Patrick
Case for the President's plan; ed. by G. Wierzynski. por Time 97:23 F 8 '71
Moynihan at the UN. Nat R 23:1322-3 N 19 '71
Moynihan report: after six months of benign neglect; interview, ed. by H. Brandon. il pors N Y Times Mag p 10-11+ Je 27 '71
Pat Moynihan on welfare; interview, ed. by F. Morgan. por Newsweek 77:26 F 8 '71
Presidency & the press. Commentary 51:41-52 Mr; 52:6+ Jl '71
President and press: a debate; summary. pors Time 97:53 Ap 12 '71
United States discusses report of UNHCR; statement, November 17, 1971. Dept State Bul 65:716-17 D 20 '71

about

Education of Pat Moynihan. Nat R 23:742+ Jl 13 '71 *
Halfway to where? J. Osborne. New Repub 164:18-10 Ja 2 '71 *
Kennedy-Nixon man. por Newsweek 77:23-4 My 31 '71 *
Moynihan on Nixon. W. F. Buckley. jr. Nat R 23:102-3 Ja 26 '71 *
Moynihan writes again. Time 97:16 Ap 19 '71 *
Updating the Moynihan report. Sci N 99:384 Je 5 '71 *
MOZAMBIQUE
Mozambique. J. Morris. il Holiday 48:46-51+ S '70
See also
Missions—Mozambique
Periodicals—Mozambique

Race question
Berman too much! concerning review of periodical Mozambique revolution. Library J 96:1305-6 Ap 15 '71; Discussion. 96:2022-3, 2562+ Je 15, S 1 '71
MOZART, Johann Chrysostom Wolfgang Amadeus
La clemenza di Tito. Criticism
Sat R 54:38 F 6 '71 *
Colin Davis on Figaro. G. L. Mayer. Sat R 54:79 N 27 '71 *
Cosi fan tutte. Criticism
Sat R 54:24 N 13 '71 *
Don Giovanni. Criticism
New Yorker 47:83 Je 19 '71 *
Opera N il 35:17-20 Mr 20 '71 *
Sat R 54:42-3 Ap 3 '71 *
Eighteen chamber masterpieces, gloriously performed. H. Goldsmith. il Hi Fi 21:83-4 S '71 *
Karajan's Mozart. P. H. Lang. il Hi Fi 21: 82 O '71 *
Magic flute (Die zauberflöte) Criticism
New Yorker 47:86 S 4 '71 *
Magic flute. Masonic opera, by J. Chailley. Review
Am Rec G por 37:636-8 My '71. R. W. Gutman*
Most gifted human being that has ever been born. F. V. Grunfeld. il pors Horizon 13: 96-103 Aut '71 *
Multum in parvo, Marlboro Mozart. M. N. Kanny. il Am Rec G 37:287-8 Ja '71 *
Music to my ears; performance of Davidde penitente by the New York philharmonic. I. Kolodin. Sat R 54:68 N 6 '71 *
Obviously produced with loving care: from London: die zauberflöte. R. W. Gutman. il Am Rec G 37:472-4 Ap '71 *
One of the great Mozart piano records. L. Gerber. Am Rec G 37:320 Ja '71 *
Steal for the modest price asked. Am Rec G 37:378 F '71 *
Will the real W. A. M. please stand? G. R. Marek. pors Opera N 35:24-7 Mr 20 '71 *

MOZART festivals. See Music festivals—New York (state)

MOZLEY, Ann
Change in Argonne national laboratory: a case study. bibliog Science 174:30-8 O 1 '71

MOZZI, Leonard
When will they ever learn. Camp Mag 43:28 F '71

MPHAHLELE, Ezekiel
Books. J. Updike. New Yorker 47:187-8+ N 13 '71 •

MUCHMORE, Marguerite C.
Farewell to the Glenwood mission inn. il Hobbies 76:156+ Ja '72

MUCOSA. See Mucous membranes

MUCOUS membranes
Why the stomach does not digest itself. H. W. Davenport. il Sci Am 226:86-93 bibliog (p 122) Ja '72

MUDD, Henry T.
Reexamination of trustee responsibility; address, March 17, 1971. Vital Speeches 37:472-4 My 15 '71

MUDFISHES. See Gobies

MUDGE, Rose, Guthrie and Alexander (firm)
Spoils of politics? M. K. Udall to investigate why the President's former law firm might have received preferential treatment. Newsweek 78:53-4 Ag 9 '71

MUDSKIPPERS. See Gobies

MUEHLNER, Egon E.
Amateur scientist. il Sci Am 225:111-14 Jl '71

MUELLER, Andrew J.
(comp) CB troubleshooter's casebook. See issues of Radio-electronics to April 1971
Troubleshooting CB transceivers. il Radio-Electr 42:47-50 Je '71

MUELLER, Jeanne, and others
Community caretakers as mental health casefinders. Ment Hy 55:214-18 Ap '71

MUELLER, Larry
Coon hound bear dogs. il por Field & S 76:164+ Ag '71
Field trials for beagles. il Field & S 75:128-30+ Ja '71
Irish luck improved. il Field & S 76:168-70+ O '71
Master's plan for springers. il Field & S 76:178-80+ N '71
Pride of the setters. il Field & S 76:192+ Je '71
Your dog talks back. il Field & S 75:196-8+ Mr '71

MUELLER, Lavonne
Saul Steinberg and high school composition. bibliog il Engl J 60:1095-100 N '71

MUELLER, Lisel
Versions of reality. Poetry 117:322-30 F '71

MUENCH, David
It's about too late for Tahoe; photographs. Audubon 73:46-62+ My '71

MUFFLERS. See Automobile engines—Mufflers

MUFFOLETTO, Anna
Books in the field: cookery. bibliog il por Wilson Lib Bul 45:653-63 Mr '71

MUGGERIDGE, Malcolm
Books. See issues of Esquire
Chronicles of wasted time. il pors Esquire 76:94-9+ S; 128-31+ N '71

about
Unsafe revolution? P. O'Donovan. New Repub 165:35-6 O 16 '71 •

MUGGING (crime) See Assault and battery

MUGHO pine. See Pine

MUHAMMAD Ali. See Clay, C.

MUIRITE. See Barium silicates

MUJIBUR Rahman
Awakening of a people. L. Jenkins. il Newsweek 77:52+ Ap 12 '71
East Pakistan: joy Bangla; joy Jesu. P. Parshall. Chr Today 15:34 Ap 23 '71 •
Jinnah's fading dream. il por Time 97:31 Mr 15 '71 •
Mujib on trial. il por Newsweek 78:28 Ag 23 '71 •
Mujib's road from prison to power. il por Time 99:22-5 Ja 17 '72 •
Mujib's secret trial. il Time 98:16+ Ag 23 '71 •
Political tidal wave that struck East Pakistan. P. Durdin. il por N Y Times Mag p24-5+ My 2 '71 •
Raise your hands and join me. por Time 97:19 Ap 5 '71 •

MUKTI Bahini (freedom fighters) See Guerrillas—Pakistan

MULAS, Ugo
Artful camera of Ugo Mulas. M. R. Weiss. il pors Sat R 54:44-5 Je 12 '71 •

MULATAS ISLANDS
San Blas: untrammeled islands off Panama. C. C. Rodman. Harp Baz 104:60+ Ap '71
Visit to the San Blas Indians takes you backward in time; Cuna Indians. G. Skinner. il Yachting 129:66-7+ F '71

MULATTOES
Intellectual development of children from interracial matings. L. Willerman and others; discussion. bibliog il Science 172:8+ Ap 2 '71

MULCAHY, David L.
Correlation between gametophytic and sporophytic characteristics in zea mays L. bibliog il Science 171:1155-6 Mr 19 '71

MULCHERS. See Compost grinders and grinding

MULCHING
How helpful is black plastic? il Sunset 146:276-7 My '71
How to handle three-foot winter rye. R. J. Lemp. il Org Gard & Farm 18:110-11 Je '71
Mrs Markle's mulch. D. Huber. McCalls 99:34 N '71
Mulch will help your garden grow. il Changing T 25:43-4 My '71
New way to bigger, tastier strawberries. G. L'Allemand. il Home Gard 58:60-1 Mr '71
Organic leftovers as soil improvers. il Sunset 146:218-20 Je '71
Please pass the poison. R. Stout. il Org Gard & Farm 18:36-9 Je '71
Recycling of the greens. B. Gilford. il Org Gard & Farm 18:74-5 D '71
Rock mulch under a tree. il Sunset 147:235 N '71
This year garden with leaves. M. Franz. il Org Gard & Farm 18:35-42 O '71
Tricks with leaves. C. C. Stewart. il Org Gard & Farm 18:46-8 O '71
Turning over an old leaf. T. Cruso. il McCalls 99:66+ N '71
Wagonload of spoiled hay changed our gardening ways. N. P. Farris. il Org Gard & Farm 18:50-2 Ag '71
What to do 'til the compost comes; liquid manure. R. Young. Org Gard & Farm 18:51-3 D '71
Wood chips hold our garden together. N. W. Bubel. il por Org Gard & Farm 18:38-41 N '71
Wool-gathering produces two-pound tomatoes. M. Roach. il Org Gard & Farm 18:70-2 Mr '71

MULE dear hunting. See Deer hunting

MULHERIN, Kathy
Five-foot shelf for women's lib. Commonweal 94:90-2 Ap 2 '71

MULKERN, Louis J.
Fundamenals of the economy; address, November 1, 1971. Vital Speeches 38:148-51 D 15 '71

MULL, Walter V.
Framed! il Flying 89:78-9+ N '71

MULLEN, Anne
America's vagabond ambassadors; interview, ed. by D. Butwin. il por Sat R 54:59-62+ F 20 '71

MULLER, Adrian H. and son
Charon's toll; securities auctions. por Forbes 107:25-6 My 1 '71

MULLER, Bill
Safe and lovable toys. B. Baer. il por Am Home 74:94-5+ S '71 •

MULLER, D. G. and others
Sex attractant in a brown alga: chemical structure. bibliog il Science 171:815-17 F 26 '71

MULLER, Dan. See Demsch, B. jt. auth.

MULLER, Friedrich Max
Aryan myth. M. D. Biddiss. il por Horizon 13:96-101 Sum '71 •

MULLER, G. H.
Shah vs. bureaucrats. Nation 212:240-3 F 22 '71

MULLER, George O.
Readable meters make happy customers. il Am City 86:65-6 Ja '71

MULLER, Kal
Social climbing in the New Hebrides; with biographical sketch. il Natur Hist 80:4, 66-75 O '71
Taboos and magic rule Namba lives. il por Nat Geog 141:56-83 Ja '72

MULLER, Max. See Müller, F. M.

MULLER, Paul Herman
Deadly dust; the unhappy history of DDT. K. S. Davis. il pors Am Heritage 22:44-7+ F '71 •

MULLER, Priscilla
Goya's portrait of Gen Nicolas Guye. il Art N 70:29+ D '71

MULLER, Roderick J. N.
Pollen, a key to the history of the earth. bibliog il Sci Digest 70:19-23 Jl '71
MULLER, Trinidad V.
Summer school: a time for imagination. Clear House 45:422-3 Mr '71
MULLIGAN, Elizabeth
(ed) See Cummings, S. How Ngoc-Lan became Melissa
MULLIGAN, Robert, jr
City hall. New Repub 164:10-11 My 15 '71
MULLIN, Chris
8:00 p.m. from Moscow to Peking is dead on time. il por N Y Times Mag p40-1+ D 5 '71
MULLIN, Willard
Disappearing, inch by inch. il por Time 97:46 Ja 25 '71 *
MULLINS, Edward
Gardening with birds. il Horticulture 49:38-40 Je '71
MULTI-DISCIPLINARY teaching. See Teaching
MULTILEVEL houses. See Architecture, Domestic
MULTILINGUALISM

Anecdotes, facetiae, satire, etc.
Travel; a little language is a dangerous thing. M. Gough. House B 113:20+ Ap '71
MULTI-MEDIA performances. See Performing arts
MULTINATIONAL corporations. See Corporations, International
MULTIPLE, independently targeted, re-entry vehicle. See Mirv
MULTIPLE art
Art: give multiples. A. Batterberry and M. Batterberry. il Harp Baz 105:72-3 D '71
MULTIPLE exposure photography. See Photography, Trick
MULTIPLE input network for evaluating reactions, votes, and attitudes. See MINERVA system
MULTIPLE jobholding. See Supplementary employment
MULTIPLE sclerosis. See Sclerosis, Multiple
MULTIPLEX radio broadcasting. See Radio broadcasting—Multiplex system
MULTIPLEX system in telecommunication. See Telecommunication—Multiplex system
MULTIPURPOSE furniture. See Furniture
MULTISPECTRAL analysis. See Spectrum analysis
MULTI-terrain vehicles. See Motor vehicles
MULTIVIBRATORS
Waveshaping with logic gates. J. E. McAlister. il Electr World 85:38+ Ap '71
MULVOY, Mark
Aesop is the official scorer. il por Sports Illus 35:18-19 Jl 26 '71
Baseball. Sports Illus 35:42-3 Jl 12 '71
Brief reign of the lordly Bruins. il Sports Illus 34:14-19 Ap 26 '71
Dodging the draft in Canada. il Sports Illus 35:8-13 Ag 23 '71
Golf (cont) Sports Illus 34:86-7 Ap 12; 35:60+ Ag 16 '71
Hockey (cont) Sports Illus 34:40-1 Ja 11; 48 Mr 29; 72 Ap 5; 60-1 My 10; 74-5 My 31; 35:60+ N 1; 80+ N 15 '71
Hockey is here with dollars up and fists down. il Sports Illus 35:36-40+ O 18 '71
Icy love-in for Vic, Jean and Rod. il Sports Illus 34:22-3 My 3 '71
Loitering in this Park is forbidden. il por Sports Illus 35:26-7 N 8 '71
Minnies who are no moochers. il pors Sports Illus 35:28-9 N 22 '71
On paper, Dallas is the best. il Sports Illus 35:30-2+ D 6 '71
Poor broken Wings. il Sports Illus 34:10-13 Ja 18 '71
This is Orr country. Orr is it? il Sports Illus 34:20-1 Ap 19 '71
To pick a golden flower. il pors Sports Illus 34:34-6 Mr 1 '71
Week; baseball. Sports Illus 34:54+ Je 14; 52-3 Je 21; 35:40+ Jl 5 '71
—and Fimrite, Ron
Show me the way to go home. il pors Sports Illus 35:16-17 Jl 19 '71
MUMFORD, Lewis
Enemy within. por Forbes 108:46 N 15 '71
MUMMA, Gordon
On the off-beat. A. Rich. il Hi Fi 21:MA9+ F '71 *
MUMMA, Martin D. See Kiver, E. P. jt. auth.
MUMMERS theater, Oklahoma City. See Oklahoma City—Theater

MUMMIES
Mummy yummies: X-rays find treasure. Sr Schol 98:7 F 15 '71
Probing the New Kingdom pharaohs with X-rays. il Sci N 100:245 O 9 71
What a well-dressed mummy wears. il Sci Digest 69:80-1 Ap '71
MUMS. See Chrysanthemums
MUNBY, Denys
Morals and measurements. il Commonweal 95:271-5 D 17 '71
MUNCH, G. and Neugebauer, G.
Jupiter: an unidentified feature in the 5-micron spectrum of the north equatorial belt. bibliog il Science 174:940-1 N 26 '71
MUNCIE, Ind.

Air pollution
Air pollution and street lights don't mix. il Am City 86:108 Mr '71

Lighting
Air pollution and street lights don't mix. il Am City 86:108 Mr '71
MUNDELL, William D.
Gallery; photographs. Life 70:8-9 Mr 5 '71

about
Craftsman of vanishing Vermont. por Life 70:10 Mr 5 '71 *
Green mountain poet. M. W. Andrews. il pors Am For 77:24-7 F '71 *
MUNDLE, Rob
Rough one. il Yachting 130:56+ Ag '71
MUNDT, Karl Earl
Mundt's empty chair. New Repub 165:8 D 4 '71 *
MUNICH
Schwabing: Germany's Greenwich Village. G. Colter. il Holiday 49:62-3+ F '71

Music
Report:
Alban Berg's Wozzeck. H. E. Reed. il Opera N 35:30-1 Ja 23 '71
Lohengrin. H. E. Reed. il Opera N 35:30-1 Ap 17 '71
Die schweigsame frau, Paisiello's Re Teodoro. Simon Boccanegra, Salome and Mozart's Clemenza di Tito. H. Reed. Opera N 36:26-7 O '71
Smetana's Bartered bride. H. Reed. Opera N 36:33 D 18 '71
Shostakovich's the Nose sparkles in Munich. R. S. Brown. Hi Fi 21:MA25 Je '71
MUNICH festival. See Music festivals—Germany (Federal Republic)
MUNICIPAL accounting

See also
Billing
MUNICIPAL administration. See Municipal government
MUNICIPAL advertising
Municipal public relations (cont of) City tells its story; ed. by P. D. Eimon. See issues of American city
MUNICIPAL and federal relations. See Federal and municipal relations
MUNICIPAL and state relations. See State and municipal relations
MUNICIPAL annexation. See Annexation (municipal government)
MUNICIPAL art. See Art, Municipal
MUNICIPAL art society of New York
Surprises: program of guided tours. New Yorker 47:38-9 O 23 '71
MUNICIPAL bonds
How to invest, tax free! il Suc Farm 69:12 Ag '71
Misdeal in municipals? A. Hershman. il Duns 98:37-9+ D '71
Municipal finance. See issues of American city
New ways to sell municipal bonds. Bsns W p32 Ja 16 '71
Overhaul urged for municipal bonds. F. E. Morris. por U S News 70:59-60 F 1 '71
Second chance in tax-exempts. A. Hershman. il Duns 98:32-4+ Ag '71
Some new municipal concerns. il Fortune 83:129-31 F '71
MUNICIPAL buildings
Abandoned vehicles couldn't wait; Baltimore. il Am City 86:16 Ap '71
Make it show leadership; municipal justice and fire station complex; Chandler, Ariz. G. D. Christy. il Am City 86:83 Mr '71
Municipal buildings award winners. il Am City 86:35 Ap '71

MUNICIPAL buildings—*Continued*
Super-roundhouse for public works; Southfield, Mich. A. F. Wilusz. il Am City 86: 84+ Ag '71
See also
City halls
Municipal centers

MUNICIPAL centers
Scottsdale's new civic center. il Arch Rec 149:119-24 Mr '71
Theaters framing a square; Birmingham, Ala. il Arch Forum 134:44-7 Mr '71

MUNICIPAL communication systems
Instant communication; West Covina, Calif. W. Vanettes. il Am City 86:130+ My '71

MUNICIPAL conservation commissions. See Conservation commissions, Municipal

MUNICIPAL contracts
Computerized total-cost bidding; Palo Alto Calif. J. W. Wear. il Am City 86:60-1 F '71
Omit the general contractor; how to save construction costs. G. Smith. il Am City 86:77 N '71

MUNICIPAL cooperation. See Intercommunity cooperation

MUNICIPAL corporations
Legal notes and decisions prepared by National institute of municipal law officers. See issues of American city

MUNICIPAL dumps
See also
Filling (earthwork)
Refuse and refuse disposal

MUNICIPAL employees
Municipal monopoly. E. S. Savas. il Harper 243:55-60 D '71
See also
Park employees
Strikes—United States—Municipal employees

Pensions
Growing burden on taxpayers; public-employe pensions. il U S News 71:24-6 Jl 19 '71
Hidden cost that may break the cities. il Nations Bsns 59:30-3 S '71

Salaries, allowances, etc.
Comparing municipal salaries with industry and federal pay; with tables. S. H. Perloff. Mo Labor R 94:46-50 O '71
Vulnerable public sector. Nation 212:133-4 F 1 '71

Transportation
Employee bus service; traveling between city hall and other government buildings. il Am City 86:112 O '71

MUNICIPAL engineering
See also
Drainage

MUNICIPAL equipment
Chicago moves from truck cranes to backhoe-loaders. J. T. Mattucci. il Am City 86: 38 Mr '71
New products and processes. See issues of American city
Run machines on a profit-or-loss basis; Denver, Colo. R. A. Phillips. il Am City 86: 84+ N '71
See also
Loaders (machines)
Snow removal equipment, Municipal
Street cleaning apparatus
Tractors, Municipal

MUNICIPAL finance
Financial aid for the small city. C. J. Hughes. Am City 86:136+ S '71
Municipal finance. See issues of American city
Sinking cities. New Repub 164:11 F 27 '71
State and local government spending in 1975; with tables and charts. T. F. Fleming, jr. bibliog Mo Labor R 94:19-28 Ag '71
Untapped revenue source: land-title search. T. Wheelan. il Am City 86:79+ My '71
Wage-price freeze on water, wastewater construction. G. R. Boyce. Am City 86:29 N '71
Why cities are going broke; interview. D. Netzer. il por U S News 70:30-3 F 22 '71
See also
Local taxation
Purchasing, Municipal
also subhead Finance under names of cities, e.g. New York (city)—Finance

Federal aid
See Federal and municipal relations
MUNICIPAL garages. See Garages, Municipal

MUNICIPAL government
For new national cities. Cur 131:9-15 Jl '71
Municipal public relations (cont of) City tells its story; ed. by P. D. Eimon. See issues of American city
No more saviors. Nat R 23:1047 S 24 '71
Thomas Jefferson, won't you please come home? address, April 1971, with questions and answers. L. N. Cutler. bibliog f Ann Am Acad 396:25-39 Jl '71
See also
Annexation (municipal government)
City manager plan
Computers—Municipal use
Mayors
Metropolitan government
Municipal officers
Municipal services
National league of cities
Purchasing, Municipal
also subhead Politics and government under names of cities, e.g. Chicago—Politics and government

Public relations
Don't guess; get answers; Franklin Park, Ill. P. D. Eimon. il Am City 86:110 Ag '71

United States
See Municipal government

MUNICIPAL improvement
Don't guess; get answers; Franklin Park, Ill P. D. Eimon. il Am City 86:110 Ag '71
In very small personal ways, all of us can make our towns more beautiful. Mrs A. D. Lasker. il House & Gard 139:67+ F '71
Ivy for everyone. P. Ertresvaag. Good H 173:163 Jl '71
M.I.T. professor challenges garden clubs. J. Clarkson. Horticulture 49:32-5 Je '71
Urban wilderness; excerpt from CEQ report. il Sat R 54:52-5 S 4 '71
You have to make reservoirs look good; Spokane, Wash. R. E. Saty. il Am City 86:58-9 Ag '71
See also
All-America cities
Art, Municipal
City planning
Cleaning of cities, towns, etc.
Parks
Playgrounds
Smoke prevention
Urban renewal
also subhead Municipal improvement under names of cities, e.g. Cincinnati—Municipal improvement

MUNICIPAL incinerators. See Refuse incinerators

MUNICIPAL income tax. See Income tax, Municipal

MUNICIPAL maps
City maps that work; Westminster, Colo. H. B. Browning. il Am City 86:74-5 Je '71

MUNICIPAL marinas. See Marinas

MUNICIPAL officers
Who should run your town? Maybe you. il Changing T 25:39-42 N '71
See also
City managers
Mayors
Negro municipal officers
Women as municipal officers

MUNICIPAL ordinances
Legal notes and decisions prepared by National institute of municipal law officers. See issues of American city
When children break the law; Parental responsibility ordinances. M. A. Rodgers. Good H 173:67+ Jl '71

MUNICIPAL publications

Bibliography
Book reviews and reports. See issues of American city

MUNICIPAL purchasing. See Purchasing, Municipal

MUNICIPAL records on microfilm
See also
Police records on microfilm

MUNICIPAL revenue. See Local taxation

MUNICIPAL services
Are city services breaking down? il U S News 70:26-8 My 24 '71
City hall discovers productivity. D. Cordtz. il Fortune 84:92-6+ O '71
Municipal monopoly. E. S. Savas. il Harper 243:55-60 D '71

MUNICIPAL stadiums. See Stadiums

MUNICIPAL-state fiscal relations. See Intergovernmental fiscal relations

MUNICIPAL swimming pools. See Swimming pools, Municipal

MUNICIPAL taxation. See Local taxation
MUNICIPAL tractors. See Tractors, Municipal
MUNICIPAL transportation. See Urban transportation
MUNITIONS
Arms race. H. C. Wallich. Newsweek 78:69 Jl 19 '71
Merchants of death; SIPRI study of the international trade in arms. Sci Am 226:44-5 Ja '72
  See also
Weapons
Weapons systems
MUNITIONS industries
Famine years for the arms makers. G. Burck. il Fortune 83:162-7+ My '71
War profiteers, by R. F. Kaufman. Review Nation 213:535-6 N 22 '71. R. Sherrill
France
French arms invasion. J. Ross-Skinner. il Duns 98:48-50+ Ag '71
United States
  See also
Firearms industry
MUNNELLY, Robert J.
Is it time to break the silence on violence? Ed Digest 36:16-18 Ap '71
MUÑOZ, Jorge Luján. See Luján Muñoz, J.
MUÑOZ REYES, Jorge
Biography of a lake. il Américas 23:11-16 Ja '71
MUNSON, Genevieve
Mr Lawrence; story. Seventeen 29:126-7 D '70
MUNSON, Russell
Duster; photographs. Flying 88:49-56 F '71
MUNVES, R. Peter
Peddler. il por Time 97:66 Je 28 '71 •
MUNZIG, Horst
Death of an elephant; photographs. Life 70:60-5 F 26 '71
MUONS. See Mesons
MURAL painting and decoration
Blowup; photographic reproduction of D. Rivera's dream of a Sunday afternoon in the grove at the New York cultural center. D. Davis. il por Newsweek 78:77 Jl 5 '71
Designing a class mural. M. Acosta. il Design 72:32-3 Spr '71
Raku murals of Paul Rayar. P. Rothenberg. il Ceram Mo 19:14-15 Je '71
Wall that changes with the seasons. R. Capotosto. il Mech Illus 67:104-5 D '71
  See also
Cave drawings and paintings
Mosaics
Stencil work
MURAL painting and decoration, Exterior
Adair plaques adorn new Rockford library. il Ceram Mo 20:26-7 Ja '72
Canvas 33 stories high; Arlen building, New York. D. Davis. Newsweek 78:65-6 Ag 9 '71
Dear Editor: mural painting by students in Hebron, Ind. J. Seemann. il Sch Arts 71:47 D '71
Green is for coolness. yellow for good auspices. F. A. Zimmer. il Natur Hist 80:54-9 Ja '71
Paint a what? Paint a bus! B. J. Erdahl. il Sch Arts 71:12-13 N '71
Paint-in. J. H. Ross. il Sch Arts 70:49 My '71
San Juan muralists. J. Gómez-Sicre. il Américas 23:2-9 Ag '71
Walls belong to the people; photographs by Elihu Blotnick. Ramp Mag 9:30-2 Mr '71
MURATA, Steve
Now Eddie Smith has a better chance of getting his Rhodes scholarship. il Todays Health 49:54-6 D '71
MURCHISON, William, jr
Dr Spock for president. Nat R 23:1470 D 31 '71
MURCHISON meteorite. See Meteorites
MURDER
Anatomy of a murder suspect; Yuba City, Calif. il por Time 97:24 Je 14 '71
Ballroom murders; the J. List family. il por Newsweek 78:30+ D 20 '71
California's sub-subculture; mass murders reported at Yuba City, Calif. Nation 212:740 Je 14 '71
Charlie and the devil; excerpts from The Family. E. Sanders. il por Esquire 76:105-12+ N '71
Corona in court. por Newsweek 77:37 Je 14 '71
Death in the orchards; Yuba City, Calif. il por Time 97:14 Je 7 '71

F. Lee Bailey's strangest murder case; Coppolino case; excerpt from The defense never rests; ed. by H. Aronson. F. L. Bailey. il por Ladies Home J 88:122-3+ N '71
F. Lee Bailey's The defense never rests; Sheppard case; excerpt from The defense never rests; ed. by A. Aronson. F. L. Bailey. il pors Ladies Home J 88:93-5+ O '71
Grisly harvest of the orchard; mass murder in Yuba City. il por Life 70:38-9 Je 11 '71
Incident at Tragedy Springs; an unsolved mystery of the California trail. F. Egan. il Am West 8:36-9 Ja '71
Massacre at Yuba City. il por Newsweek 77:28-9 Je 7 '71
Mourning the police. il Time 97:8 Je 7 '71
New York ten; murdered policemen. G. Astor. il N Y Times Mag p32-5 D 12 '71
Rosemary's babies; case of Patrick Michael Newell. il Newsweek 78:22 Jl 19 '71
Senseless killing; high school graduate J. Collier of Drew, Miss. por Time 97:13-14 Je 7 '71
Suddenly, this summer; murder of two New York cops. il Newsweek 77:29 Je 7 '71
U.S. journal: Center Junction, Iowa; Jim, Tex. and the one-armed man. C. Trillin. New Yorker 47:100-2+ F 20 '71
What language do you speak? wording in reports of police killings in New York. J. Burnham. Nat R 23:633 Je 15 '71
  See also
Capital punishment
Euthanasia
Trials (murder)
MURDER trials. See Trials (murder)
MURDERERS. See Murder
MURDEROUS angels; drama. See O'Brien, C. C.
MURDICK, Olin J.
Return to the marketplace. il America 124:565-7 My 29 '71
MURDOCH, Keith Rupert
New boy on Fleet Street. il por Newsweek 77:97 My 10 '71 •
MURDOCK, Carolyn (Sheldon)
Time for living. il Liv Wildn 35:13-16 Spr '71
MURDOCK, Ray
Garbageman, ed. by K. Lasson. il Atlan 228:78-82 O '71
MURDOCK, Steve
Mormon trails in the Midwest. il Travel 137:58-63+ Ja '72
MUREX
Tyrian purple. J. P. Robinson, jr. il Sea Front 17:76-82 Mr '71
MURFEE, Patty T.
History in towns. il Antiques 100:914-18 D '71
MURFITT, Rex
Gentians for the rock garden. il Horticulture 49:26-7+ O '71
MURIE, Margaret E.
Bright journey in East Africa. il Liv Wildn 34:38-43 Aut '70
MURIE-Broome awards. See Wilderness society
MURINE leukemia virus. See Leukemia viruses
MURPHY, Audie
Parting shots; buddy's tribute to Audie Murphy. B. Mauldin. il por Life 70:77 Je 11 '71 •
To hell and not quite back. por Time 97:27 Je 14 '71 •
MURPHY, Burt
Shot in the dark. il Pop Mech 136:108-11 Jl '71
Wrap a ring light around your lens. il Pop Mech 135:84-7+ F '71
MURPHY, C. F. associates
Design in the Miesian tradition: the current work of C. F. Murphy associates. il Arch Rec 149:95-106 My '71
MURPHY, Calvin
Little big man. il por Time 97:66 F 1 '71 •
San Diego's Calvin Murphy: pro basketball's tiny giant. il pors Ebony 26:38-40+ F '71 •
MURPHY, Charles J. V.
For the defense: Melvin R. Laird. por Read Digest 99:49-53 Ag '71
Our strategic-arms advantage is fading fast. Read Digest 98:94-8 F '71
What is behind red China's smile? Read Digest 99:69-73 O '71
MURPHY, Charles M.
Celebrating infallibility; letter to the editor. Commonweal 94:51+ Mr 26 '71
MURPHY, Diana
Birdless skies; poem. Seventeen 30:80 Ja '71
MURPHY, Sister Ellen
Fireflies; poem. Commonweal 94:87 Ap 2 '71

MURPHY, Francis X.
Strait jacket for the mystical body. America
124:611-13 Je 12 '71
Third roman synod. America 124:454-6 My 1
'71

MURPHY, Frederick V. and Yount, D. E.
Photons as hadrons; with biographical
sketches. il Sci Am 225:14, 94-104 bibliog
(p 122) Jl '71

MURPHY, Gardner
Motivation: the key to changing educational
times. Ed Digest 36:39-42 Mr '71

MURPHY, Gerald
Living well is the best revenge, by C. Tom-
kins. Review
Newsweek il 78:72 Jl 19 '71. P. S. Pre-
scott *
Time pors 98:70 Jl 19 '71. M. Duffy *

MURPHY, James L.
Maize from an Adena mound in Athens
County, Ohio. bibliog il Science 171:897-8
Mr 5 '71

MURPHY, John
U.W: an old established firm. il Am For
77:28-31+ O '71

MURPHY, Joseph
College presidents and students; interview.
Mlle 73:246-7+ Ag '71

MURPHY, Leonard. See Oliver, J. jt. auth.

MURPHY, Mary Kay
(ed) Career education: a new job for the
schools; interview. il por Sch Teach Jr/
Sr High p4-7 D '71
Diary of the year-round school. il Schol
Teach Jr/Sr High p 16-19 N '71
—and Kozoll, C. E.
Don't let this go to waste. il Am Ed 7:6-9
Mr '71

MURPHY, Michael C.
Running Marathon's miniature airline. V.
Louvière. Nations Bsns 59:18 O '71 *

MURPHY, Patrick V.
Social change and the police. Am Scholar 40:
686-90 Aut '71

about

Murphy among the meat-eaters. T. Buckley.
il pors N Y Times Mag p 10-11+ D 19 '71*
Of many things; Murphy and command responsibility. T. M. Gannon. America 125:
inside cover S 18 '71 *
Police. New Repub 164:6 Je 19 '71 *
Taking dirty money. il por Time 98:20 S 13
'71 *

MURPHY, Reg
Trade winds; interview, ed. by C. Amory.
Sat R 54:16 Je 5 '71

MURPHY, Richard
Saint Gormgall's well; Little hunger; Corn-
crake; Gallows riddle; poems. Poetry 118:
333-5 S '71

MURPHY, Richard W.
Hunting for America. Harper 242:16-18+ Je
'71
Natural history of the young. Atlan 229:36-8
Ja '72
On breathing and other ills. Harper 242:22+
My '71

MURPHY, Robert
This animal walks up walls. il Nat Wildlife
9:16-18 Ap '71

MURPHY, Sara
Living well is the best revenge, by C. Tom-
kins. Review
Newsweek il 78:72 Jl 19 '71. P. S. Pre-
scott *
Time pors 98:70 Jl 19 '71. M. Duffy *

MURPHY, Seamus
Seamus Murphy dance company, the Clark
center for the performing arts. L. Pastore.
Dance Mag 45:82 Ag '71 *

MURPHY, Timothy
Four poems: Wind; Prologue; Together with
the devil; On first glancing at Warren's
promises. Yale R 61:76-9 O '71

MURRAH, Charles R.
How to get on top of your job. il Nations
Bsns 59:68-9 S '71

MURRAY, Albert Lee
South to a very old place, by A. Murray. Re-
view
Time por 99:65 Ja 10 '72. R. Z. Sheppard *

MURRAY, Andrew W. and others
Adenosine 3′,5′-monophosphate phosphodiesterase in the growth medium of physarum
polycephalum. bibliog il Science 171:496-8
F 5 '71

MURRAY, Bain
Lutoslawski comes to town. il por Hi Fi 21:
MA24 S '71

MURRAY, Barry
Twenty-five hundred miles on horseback.
il pors Life 71:60-6+ S 3 '71

MURRAY, David J.
Federation of Nigeria. Cur Hist 60:157-63+
Mr '71

MURRAY, James A.
Minneapolis money machine; interview, ed.
by R. J. Flaherty. il por Forbes 108:43-4+ S
15 '71

MURRAY, John
Case for two spies; drama. Plays 30:25-34,
58 My '71
Come to the fair! drama. Plays 30:1-12, 42
My '71
Customs caper; drama. Plays 30:1-13 Mr '71
Fulfillment; drama. Plays 30:19-28 Ap '71
Haunting of Hathaway house; drama. Plays
31:1-12, 56 N '71
One in a million; drama. Plays 30:21-9, 46 F
'71

MURRAY, Michael
Stage. Commonweal 93:525; 94:166-7 F 26, Ap
23 '71

MURRAY, Michael H.
Term paper alternative. Clear House 45:447-8
Mr '71

MURRAY, Neil
Hard lesson. il Parks & Rec 6:28-31+ F '71

MURRAY, Philip
T'ang; Confessions of philosopher Ting;
poems. Poetry 118:125-35 Je '71

MURRAY, Raymond C.
Salt; with biographical sketch. il Natur Hist
80:2-3, 46-53 O '71

MURRAY, Robert F. Jr, and Motulsky, A. G.
Developmental variation in the isoenzymes of
human liver and gastric alcohol dehydrogenase. bibliog il Science 171:71-3 Ja 8 '71

MURRAY, Steve
Americanization of Micronesia: paradise lost.
il Ramp Mag 9:35-7+ F '71

MURRAY, Thomas M.
Private mail service tries for first class. il
Bsns W D38 D 11 '71

MURRAY, William
Says Rod McKuen: it doesn't matter who
you love or how you love, but that you
love! il pors N Y Times Mag p32-4+ Ap 4
'71

MURRAY, Utah

Parks and playgrounds

Fences are out in Murray city park. L. C.
Cushing. il Parks & Rec 6:30-1+ Jl '71

* **MURROW, Edward R.**
Prime time, by A. Kendrick. Review
Trans-Action 7:57-9 O '70. A. A. Stern *

MURTAGH, John Martin
Case for trial by jury. America 125:309-11 O
23 '71

MURTHA, Sister Margaret Mary
Nun who refused to divulge information jailed
again. Chr Cent 88:970 Ag 18 '71 *
Religious and the right to secrecy. America
125:82-3 Ag 21 '71 *

MUS, David
Evening walk; some years later; poem.
Poetry 118:270-5 Ag '71
Wall; poem. Poetry 117:251-7 Ja '71

MUSCAT and Oman. See Oman

MUSCLE
Ammonia production in muscle: the purine
nucleotide cycle. J. Lowenstein and K.
Tornheim. bibliog il Science 171:397-400 Ja
29 '71
Angiotensin II: rapid localization in nuclei
of smooth and cardiac muscle. A. L. Robertson, jr. and P. A. Khairallah. bibliog
il Science 172:1138-9 Je 11 '71
Cooperative control of potassium accumulation by ouabain in vascular smooth muscle.
J. Gulati and A. W. Jones. bibliog il Science
172:1348-50 Je 25 '71
Glycerinated muscle fibers: relation between
isometric tension and adenosine triphosphate hydrolysis. W. J. Bowen and L.
Mandelkern. bibliog il Science 173:239-40
Jl 16 '71
Mammalian motor units: physiological-histochemical correlation in three types in cat
gastrocnemius. R. E. Burke and others.
bibliog il Science 174:709-12 N 12 '71
p-Nitrophenyl phosphate hydrolysis and calcium ion transport in fragmented sarcoplasmic reticulum. G. Inesi. bibliog il Science 171:901-3 Mr 5 '71
Physiological tremor. O. Lippold. il Sci Am
224:65-73 Mr '71
Sodium and potassium activities in normal
and sodium-rich frog skeletal muscle. W.
M. Armstrong and C. O. Lee. bibliog il Science 171:413-15 Ja 29 '71
Striated muscle fibers: facilitation of contraction at short lengths by caffeine. R.
Rüdel and S. R. Taylor. bibliog il Science
172:387-8 Ap 23 '71

MUSCLE—*Continued*
Strontium accumulation by sarcoplasmic reticulum and mitchondria in vascular smooth muscle. A. V. Somlyo and A. P. Somlyo. bibliog il Science 174:855-8 N 26 '71
See also
Heart—Muscle
Neuromuscular junctions
MUSCLE fibers. See Muscle
MUSCLE power. See Muscular power
MUSCLES
See also
Muscular power
Diseases
See also
Dystrophy, Muscular
Myasthenia gravis
MUSCOVITE. See Mica
MUSCULAR dystrophy. See Dystrophy, Muscular
MUSCULAR power
Measurement of the man-day. E. S. Ferguson. il Sci Am 225:96-103 O '71
MUSEUM directors
Beleaguered director. T. W. Leavitt. il Art in Am 59:66-71 Jl '71
Dilemmas of the curator. E. F. Fry. il Art in Am 59:72-7 Jl '71
Man on the spot; J. Hightower of the Museum of modern art, New York. por Newsweek 77:82 Ja 25 '71
MUSEUM of African art. See Washington, D.C.—Galleries and museums
MUSEUM of art of Carnegie institute. See Carnegie institute, Pittsburgh
MUSEUM of contemporary crafts, New York
Seeing pictures; Photo media. J. Scully. Mod Phot 36:11+ Ja '72
MUSEUM of fine arts, Boston. See Boston museum of fine arts
MUSEUM of modern art, New York
Adversary proceeding; The artist as adversary show. D. Davis. il Newsweek 78:81 Jl 19 '71
Man on the spot. por Newsweek 77:82 Ja 25 '71
New man out; J. Hightower leaves. por Time 99:38 Ja 17 '72
Walking out on MOMA. il Newsweek 78:53 Ag 30 '71
MUSEUM of natural history. See American museum of natural history, New York
MUSEUM of sport. See New York (city)—Galleries and museums
MUSEUM of the city of New York
Drugs; exhibition. New Yorker 47:31-2 Mr 13 '71
Run to the mindblower; Drug scene exhibition. N. Gittelson. Harp Baz 104:6 Je '71
MUSEUM of the sea, Long Beach, Calif. See Museums
MUSEUM trustees. See Art—Galleries and museums—Trustees, boards, committees, etc.
MUSEUM villages. See Villages, Restored
MUSEUM workers
See also
Strikes—United States—Museum workers
MUSEUMS
Museum world. J. L. Stoughtenburgh. See issues of Hobbies
Rather large vessel in Long Beach invites you to come aboard; Queen Mary. il Sunset 147:38-9 S '71
Time was village museum. J. L. Stoutenburgh. il Hobbies 76:142-3+ Ag '71
See also
Aeronautic museums
Art—Galleries and museums
Circus world museum. Baraboo, Wis.
College art galleries and museums
Ethnological museums and collections
Indians of North America—Museums
Industrial museums
Natural history museums
Naval museums
Open-air museums
Photography—Galleries and museums
Science museums
also subhead Galleries and museums under names of cities, e.g. London—Galleries and museums
Architecture
Art under glass; P. Johnson's sculpture gallery. il Vogue 158:102-5 Ag 15 '71
Florida museum uses earth forms boldly; Florida state museum, Gainesville. il Arch Rec 150:121-6 S '71
Museums for learning. il Arch Forum 135:19-39 S '71

Sculpture under glass; Philip Johnson's personal sculpture collection. J. M. Dixon. il Arch Forum 133:22-5 D '70
This museum is mainly for kids; Historical center, Columbus, Ohio. il Arch Rec 150:85-90 Jl '71
Finance
London; debate on entrance fees. J. Russell. Art N 69:56-7 F '71
Work with children
Museum for fun and learning; St Paul public schools volunteer services program and the Minnesota museum of art. M. A. Grossmann. il Am Ed 7:24-5 My '71
Germany (Federal Republic)
Hellmut-Kienzle clock and watch museum, Black Forest, Germany (cont) O. R. Hagans. il Hobbies 75:125-6 Ja; 126 F '71
Great Britain
London; debate on entrance fees. J. Russell. Art N 69:56-7 F '71
MUSEUMS and Negroes
Museums; art for who's sake? B. Schwartz. il Ramp Mag 9:38-49 Je '71
MUSEUMS and schools
Metropolitan museum of art pioneers in the classroom. il Harp Baz 104:74 My '71
Schools where education comes alive. G. W. Weinstein. il Parents Mag 46:33-5+ Je '71
See also
Museums—Work with children
MUSGRAVE, Clifford
Uppark, Sussex. il Antiques 99:848-53 Je '71
MUSHROOMS
What do you know about mushrooms? quiz. J. Daugherty and M. Daugherty. bibliog il Sci Digest 70:86-7+ D '71
See also
Truffles
MUSIC
Artist life. D. J. Soria. See issues of High fidelity and Musical America
Beyond the avant garde. E. Siegmeister. il Hi Fi 21:MA13-14+ D '71
Depressing uniformity of the avant-garde. H. C. Schonberg. Harper 243:103-4 S '71
Here & there. See issues of High fidelity and Musical America
Paths to modern music, by L. Davies. Review
New Yorker 47:59 Ja 1 '72. W. Sargeant
Shaking up the musical establishment. R. Hemming. il Sr Schol 99:18 N 15 '71
See also
Band music
Chamber music
Church music
Composition (music)
Computers—Musical use
Concertos
Imitation in music
Jesus Christ in music
Melody
Metronomes
Military music
Negro music
Opera
Piano music
Radio broadcasting—Music
Television broadcasting—Music
also headings beginning Musical
Analysis, Interpretation, etc.
Dream of love, in Tristan und Isolde. S. Jenkins. il Opera N 36:24-5 D 18 '71
Operas—Criticisms, plots, etc.
Appreciation
Growing up with music: from crib to combo. E. McDonald. House B 113:56-7 O '71
Mirrors of our time; interview, ed. by R. Hemming. Sr Schol 98:19 My 17 '71
Music and the environment. J. C. Hoem. il Cons 25:2-4 Ap '71
Records I don't want to live without. A. Rich. Redbook 137:95+ S '71
Trash. R. Evett. New Repub 165:22+ N 27 '71
See also
Opera—Appreciation
Bibliography
Book reviews. P. J. Smith. See issues of High fidelity and Musical America
Musical events. W. Sargeant. New Yorker 46:79-80 Ja 9 '71

MUSIC—Bibliography—*Continued*
Quarterly book-list. J. Newsom. See issues
of Musical quarterly
Reviews of books. See issues of Musical quar-
terly
See also
Music literature

Competitions

Close look at the Tchaikovsky competition.
L. Effenbach. Hi Fi 20:MA22-3+ D '70
Making music; Chicago's summer youth mu-
sic competition. T. M. McCarty. il Parks
& Rec 6:25-6+ Ap '71
See also
Leventritt award

Economic aspects

Is anybody listening? the concert business.
H. C. Schonberg. Harper 242:111-12 F '71

History and criticism

Asian concepts and twentieth-century wes-
tern composers. W. C. Chou. bibliog f il
Mus Q 57:211-29 Ap '71
Classical style: Haydn, Mozart, Beethoven,
by C. Rosen. Review
Nation 213:596-8 D 6 '71. R. Lilienfeld
Emerging triadic tonality in the fifteenth
century. D. M. Randel. bibliog f il Mus Q
57:73-86 Ja '71
Music and the nausea delle cose cotidiane.
D. Burrows. bibliog f il Mus Q 57:230:10 Ap
'71
Should music be played wrong? C. Rosen. il
Hi Fi 21:54-8 My '71
See also
Classicism in music
Opera—History and criticism

Instruction and study

See also
Music students
Rochester, N.Y. University—Eastman school
of music

Interpretation

See Music—Analysis, interpretation, etc.

Manuscripts

Schubert: discoveries of the last decade.
M. J. E. Brown. bibliog f il por Mus Q
57:351-78 Jl '71
See also
Beethoven, L. van—Manuscripts

Philosophy and aesthetics

Musical mannerism: effeteness or virility?
excerpts from address. M. R. Maniates.
bibliog f Mus Q 57:270-93 Ap '71
Rock and rebellion, from modern jazz to
hard rock, a sociological view. I. L. Horo-
witz. il Commonweal 93:466-9 F 12 '71
See also
Classicism in music
Romanticism in music
Style, Musical

Psychology

See also
Music, Influence of
Music and color

Themes, motives, etc.

Music and the environment. J. C. Hoem.
il Cons 25:2-4 Ap '71

Theory

See also
Musical form
Tonality
Twelve-tone system

Australia

How Australians learn their ABCs. I Kolodin.
Sat R 54:48 Jl 24 '71
Mix that goes into Australia's melting pot.
I. Kolodin. Sat R 54:32 Ag 7 '71
See also
Adelaide, Australia—Music
Canberra, Australia—Music
Melbourne, Australia—Music
Opera—Australia

Austria

See also
Music, Austrian
Salzburg festival

Canada

Toronto, a new Nashville? G. Lees. Hi Fi 21:
102 Je '71

Czechoslovakia

See also
Prague—Music

Denmark

See also
Copenhagen—Music

Europe, Western

Journey to judgment, an audiomusical tour
of Europe. L. Marcus. Hi Fi 21:4+ D '71

France

See also
Opera—France
Paris—Music

Germany (Democratic Republic)

See also
Berlin (East Berlin)—Music
Opera—Germany (Democratic Republic)

Germany (Federal Republic)

See also
Berlin (West Berlin)—Music
Hamburg—Music
Kiel—Music
Munich—Music
Opera—Germany (Federal Republic)
Stuttgart, Germany—Music
Wiesbaden, Germany—Music

Great Britain

See also
Opera—Great Britain

Greece, Modern

See also
Athens, Greece—Music

Italy

See also
Florence—Music
Milan, Italy—Music
Music, Italian
Naples—Music
Siena, Italy—Music
Verona, Italy—Music

Louisiana

See also
Shreveport, La.—Music

Russia

See also
Leningrad—Music

Scotland

See also
Edinburgh—Music

Spain

See also
Music festivals—Spain

Sweden

See also
Opera—Sweden

Switzerland

See also
Zurich—Music

Turkey

See also
Istanbul—Music

United States

Current chronicle. See issues of Musical
quarterly
Music in Tennessee. R. H. Hulan. il Antiques
100:418-19 S '71
See also
Jazz music
Music, American
also subhead Music under names of
cities, e.g. New York (city)—Music

History and criticism

Those were the days; through the pages of
High fidelity, Musical America, and Bill-
board. Hi Fi 21:36 O; 48 N; 36 D '71
MUSIC, American
American music since 1910, by V. Thomson.
Review
Sat R 54:82-3 S 25 '71. O. Daniel
Classic Cole Porter. L. Smit. il por Sat R
54:48-9+ D 25 '71
See also
Folk music, American
Jazz music
Music—United States
MUSIC, Asian
Asian concepts and twentieth-century west-
ern composers. W. C. Chou. bibliog f il Mus
Q 57:211-29 Ap '71
MUSIC, Austrian
Musical events; works of the decadence peri-
od by the Philharmonic. W. Sargeant. New
Yorker 47:102 Ap 24 '71
MUSIC, Chamber. See Chamber music
MUSIC, Church. See Church music
MUSIC, Czech
See also
Dvořák, A.

MUSIC, Electronic
Electronic creativity in the elementary classroom. A. D. Modugno. il Todays Ed 60:62-4 Mr '71
   See also
Phonograph records—Electronic music

MUSIC, French
   See also
Opera, French

MUSIC, Imitation in. See Imitation in music

MUSIC, Incidental
Music and theater in Hogarth. M. F. Klinger. bibliog f il Mus Q 57:409-26 Jl '71

MUSIC, Influence of
Music is music. G. Lees. Hi Fi 21:32 O '71

MUSIC, Italian
Music and the nausea delle cose cotidiane. Burrows. bibliog f il Mus Q 57:230-40 Ap '71
   See also
Phonograph records—Italian music

MUSIC, Latin American
Music. See issues of Américas

MUSIC, Military. See Military music

MUSIC, Modern. See Music

MUSIC, Negro. See Negro music

MUSIC, Oriental
   See also
Music, Asian

MUSIC, Popular (songs, etc)
Have a Coke, world; commercial jingle becomes a popular hit. Newsweek 79:47 Ja 3 '72
Jimmy L. Webb; interview. J. L. Webb. New Yorker 46:24-5 Ja 9 '71
Mirrors of our time; interview, ed. by R. Hemming. B. Gosh. Sr Schol 98:24-5 Ap 5 '71
Songs to live by; lyrics of D. Previn. por Time 98:84+ D 6 '71
   See also
Blues (songs, etc)
Phonograph records—Music, Popular (songs, etc)
Rock music (songs, etc)

MUSIC, Primitive
   See also
Drum language

MUSIC, Russian
   See also
Composers, Russian

MUSIC, Theatrical. See Music, Incidental

MUSIC, Twelve-tone. See Twelve-tone system

MUSIC and children. See Children and music

MUSIC and color
Color of sound. R. Long. Hi Fi 21:54-9 Mr '71

MUSIC and politics
Musician as activist. W. Zakariasen. il Hi Fi 21:50-5 Jl '71

MUSIC and religion. See Religion and music

MUSIC and romanticism. See Romanticism in music

MUSIC and society
Future after the Fillmores; rock and society. E. Sander. Sat R 54:56 My 29 '71
Revolt into style, by G. Melly. Review
   Sat R il 54:31-3 N 20 '71. E. Dowling

MUSIC at Long Verney; story. See Warner, S. T.

MUSIC boxes
Magic music boxes. il Life 70:62-5 Mr 19 '71

MUSIC conference, American. See American music conference

MUSIC conferences
NOA, COS conferences. R. Mercer. Opera N 36:41 D 25 '71
   See also
Music educators national conference

MUSIC educators national conference
Music for all ages. Sch & Soc 99:138+ Mr '71

MUSIC festivals
World as summer festival. il Newsweek 78:79-9 Jl 5 '71
   See also
Bach festivals
Inter-American music festival, Washington, D.C.

Austria
Report:
   Herbert von Karajan's Salzburg Easter festival Fidelio. J. H. Sutcliffe. il Opera 35:24 Je 12 '71
Vienna is a state of mind. R. Commanday. il Hi Fi 21:MA26-7 O '71
   See also
Salzburg festival

California
Contempo '71, calm and becalmed, twentieth-century music at Los Angeles Philharmonic. M. Bernheimer. il Hi Fi 21:MA24-5 Ag '71
Grand musical experience in Carmel starting July 16; Bach festival. il Sunset 147:27-8 Jl '71
Ojai: music for the minority. K. Monson. il Hi Fi 21:MA22-3 S '71

Colorado
Colorado opera festival is fun. G. Giffin. il Hi Fi 21:MA23+ O '71

England
ISCM's forty-fifth forum. D. Hamilton. Hi Fi 21:MA27-8 S '71
Proms, Aldeburgh, Glyndebourne. E. Greenfield. Hi Fi 21:MA29-30 D '71

Europe
Guide to European music festivals, 1971. H. D. Jellinek. Sat R 54:68-9 Mr 27 '71
Music. D. Hamilton. Nation 213:123-4 Ag 16 '71

Europe, Western
Summer evenings (cont) Opera N 35:33-4 Ap 3 '71
Where to hear music in Europe. il Hi Fi 21:MA20-1 Je '71

France
Music of the East at Royan. H. L. De La Grange. Sat R 54:38 Je 26 '71
Report:
   Die zauberflöte and world premiere of Beatris de Planissolas by Jacques Charpentier at Aix-en-Provence. D. Stevens. Opera N 36:27-8 O '71

Germany (Federal Republic)
Current chronicle; Berlin festival; tr. by L. Wallach. W. Becker-Carsten Mus Q 57:314-17 Ap '71
Operatic impass: Bayreuth and Munich festivals. P. G. Davis. il Hi Fi 21:MA26-7 N '71
Report:
   Aribert Reimann's Melusine. J. H. Sutcliffe. Opera N 36:29 S '71
   See also
Bayreuth festival

Ghana
Soul to soul. P. Garland. il Ebony 26:79-82+ Je '71

Hawaii
Arts of this century; Hawaii's Festival of the arts of this century. B. Hyams. il Hi Fi 21:MA24-5 O '71

Illinois
Making music; Chicago's summer youth music competition. T. M. McCarty. il Parks & Rec 6:25-6+ Ap '71
New music festival at U. of Illinois. B. Johnson. il Hi Fi 21:MA28-9 Ag '71

Iowa
Stephens auditorium houses new Iowa festival: Ames international orchestra festival. il Hi Fi 21:MA17 O '71

Ireland
Report:
   Bizet's Pêcheurs de perles; Puccini's Rondine and Mozart's Re pastore. W. H. A. Williams. Opera N 36:39-40 D 25 '71

Italy
American festival orchestra goes to Italy. J. Strasser. il Hi Fi 21:MA10-11 F '71
Biennale 1970 fails to excite: Venice music biennale. E. Helm. Hi Fi 20:MA27 D '70
Maggio musicale & Spoleto. W. Weaver. il Hi Fi 21:MA30-1 O '71
Report:
   Maggio musicale. W. Weaver. Opera N 36:27-9 S '71

Latin America
Summer evenings (cont) Opera N 35:33-4 Ap 3 '71

Louisiana
Parting shots: perhaps the last of the rock festival fiascos. il Life 71:72 Jl 9 '71
Rip-off; rock festival, on the banks of Atchafalaya River. il Newsweek 78:32+ Jl 12 '71

New York (state)
Caramoor's Dido and Aeneas. G. Movshon. il Hi Fi 21:MA21+ O '71
Composers theater presents a provocative May festival. A. Derhen. Hi Fi 21:MA14 Ag '71

MUSIC festivals—New York (state)—Cont.
In my opinion; there'll never be another
Woodstock. A. Sideman. por Seventeen 29:
390 Ag '70
Mostly Mozart festival; concerts at Philhar-
monic Hall. Hi Fi 21:MA12 N '71
Report:
Caramoor festival. F. Merkling. Opera N
36:24 S '71

North Carolina
Eastern music festival; new concepts. J.
McAllister. il Hi Fi 21:MA18-19 O '71

Pennsylvania
Temple festival gets a roof over its head.
J. Felton. Hi Fi 21:MA19+ N '71

Puerto Rico
Casals. A. Matilla. il pors Américas 23:5-9
My '71

Rhode Island
Musical events; Newport notes. W. Balliett.
New Yorker 47:76+ Jl 17 '71
Newport, the third of July. R. Crystal. il Hi
Fi 21:62-5 D '71

Scotland
See also
International festival of music and drama,
Edinburgh

Spain
Third music festival of the Americas and
Spain. il Américas 23:45 Ap '71

Texas
Report:
Tristan und Isolde, Otello, Fledermaus
and La Bohème in San Antonio. R. Pincus. Opera N 35:22 Je 12 '71

United States
Festivals: rock moving indoors, to theatres
and auditoriums. il Sr Schol 98:10-11 My 3
'71
Music festivals USA, Summer 1971; comp. by
H. D. Jellinek. Sat R 54:40-2 Je 26 '71
Sounds in the streets. il Newsweek 78:48 Ag
16 '71
Summer evenings (cont) Opera N 35:33-4 Ap
3 '71
Summer music festivals (title varies) (cont)
Hi Fi 21:MA14-16+ Mr; MA12-14 Ap '71
U.S. calendar. See issues of Opera news
published during opera season
See also
Inter-American music festival, Washington,
D.C.

Vermont
Music from Marlboro. M. Kanny. il por Am
Rec G 37:282-7 Ja '71
Musical events; Music from Marlboro series,
in Alice Tully Hall. W. Sargeant. New
Yorker 47:114 F 20 '71
MUSIC for children
See also
Phonograph records—Childrens records
MUSIC halls (variety theaters, etc)
See also
New York (city)—Radio City music hall
MUSIC in religion. See Religion and music
MUSIC in the home
See also
Music rooms and equipment
MUSIC libraries
See also
Libraries—Phonograph and phonograph
records
MUSIC literature
Journalists of rock. E. Sander. bibliog f il
Sat R 54:47+ Jl 31 '71
MUSIC of color. See Music and color
MUSIC on television. See Television broadcast-
ing—Music
MUSIC pavilions
Technology; orchestral performing spaces. il
Arch Forum 134:64-5 Mr '71
MUSIC publishing
200 years of B. Schott's söhne; Beethoven's
last publisher. E. Helm. il por Hi Fi 21:55-
60 Ja '71
MUSIC research. See Musicology
MUSIC rooms and equipment
They built a soundproof room for family
jam sessions. il Sunset 147:112+ O '71
MUSIC schools
On a hill in Tuscany; Accademia musicale
Chigiana, Siena, Italy. B. Fischer-Williams.
il Opera N 35:16-18 My 15 '71

Yale's summer school. R. Browne. il Hi Fi 21:
MA12-14 My '71
See also
California institute of the arts, Valencia, Calif.
Manhattan school of music
New England conservatory of music, Boston
North Carolina school of the arts, Winston-
Salem
Rochester, N.Y. University—Eastman school
of music
MUSIC shells. See Orchestra shells
MUSIC students
Summer experience; summer training cen-
ters. M. Abravanel. il por Hi Fi 21:MA12-
13 F '71
MUSIC writing. See Composition (music)
MUSICAL appreciation. See Music—Apprecia-
tion
MUSICAL arrangement
Arranger arrives. G. Lees. por Hi Fi 21:90-1
My '71
MUSICAL boxes. See Music boxes
MUSICAL comedies, revues, etc.
Nostalgia. il Life 71:30 D 31 '71
See also
Musical comedy, revue, etc.
Phonograph records—Musical comedies, re-
vues, etc.
Ziegfeld follies

Criticisms, plots, etc.
Aint supposed to die a natural death
Nation 213:476-7 N 8 '71
New Yorker 47:101-2 O 30 '71
Newsweek il 78:85-6 N 1 '71
Sat R 54:10+ N 13 '71
Time il 98:95 N 1 '71
Applause
Commentary 51:79-80 F '71
Ari
New Yorker 46:66 Ja 23 '71
Blind junkie
New Yorker 47:54 S 4 '71
Company
Commentary 51:79 F '71
Croesus and the witch
New Yorker 47:54 S 4 '71
Day in the life of just about everyone
New Yorker 47:96 Mr 20 '71
Earl of Ruston
New Yorker 47:102+ My 15 '71
F. Jasmine Addams
America 125:427 N 20 '71
New Yorker 47:115-16 N 6 '71
Follies
America 124:615 Je 12 '71
Commonweal 94:239-40 My 14 '71
Dance Mag 45:81-2 Je '71
Nat R 23:1129-30 O 8 '71
Nation 212:509-10 Ap 19 '71
New Repub 164:24+ My 8 '71
New Yorker 47:67 Ap 10 '71
Newsweek il 77:121 Ap 12 '71
Sat R 54:16+ My 1 '71
Time il 97:78 Ap 12 '71
Time il 97:70-4 My 3 '71
Vogue il 157:154-5 My '71
Frank Merriwell
New Yorker 47:94 My 1 '71
Godspell
America 125:516-17 D 11 '71
Chr Cent 88:938 Ag 4 '71
Chr Today il 15:36-7 Ag 27 '71
New Yorker 47:56 My 29 '71
Grass harp
America 125:427 N 20 '71
New Yorker 47:66 N 13 '71
Hair
Engl J 60:626-8 My '71
Inner city
Nation 214:61 Ja 10 '72
Joan
New Yorker 47:101 D 11 '71
Lady Audley's secret
Sat R 54:33 Ag 7 '71
Love me, love my children
New Yorker 47:66+ N 13 '71
Lovely ladies, kind gentlemen
New Yorker 46:51 Ja 9 '71
Me nobody knows
Commonweal 93:396 Ja 22 '71
Schol Teach Jr/Sr High il p 18-19 F 1 '71
Mr Esteban
New Yorker 47:54 S 4 '71
Mother earth
Nat R 23:1481 D 31 '71
No, no, Nanette
Life il 70:40-1 F 19 '71
Nat R 23:440 Ap 20 '71
New Yorker 46:54 Ja 30 '71
Newsweek il 77:73-4 F 1 '71
Sat R 54:62+ F 6 '71
Sat R 54:14 Ap 24 '71
Time il 97:76 F 1 '71

MUSICAL comedies, revues, etc.—Criticisms, plots, etc.—*Continued*

On the town
America 125:428 N 20 '71
Nation 213:538-9 N 22 '71
New Yorker 47:115 N 6 '71
Newsweek il 78:106 N 15 '71
Time il 98:51 N 15 '71

Proposition
New Yorker 47:97 Ap 3 '71

Rothschilds
America 124:125 F 6 '71

Selling of the president
Look il 35:52-3 S 7 '71
Newsweek 77:121 Ap 12 '71

70, girls, 70
America 124:615-16 Je 12 '71
Dance Mag 45:81-2 Je '71
Nation 212:570-1 My 3 '71
New Yorker 47:93-4 Ap 24 '71

Show me
Chr Today il 15:50-1 My 21 '71

Six
New Yorker 47:95 Ap 24 '71

Soon
New Yorker 46:66 Ja 23 '71

To live another summer, to pass another winter
Time 98:95 N 1 '71

Two by two
America 124:124-5 F 6 '71
Commentary 51:80 F '71
Commonweal 93:397 Ja 22 '71

Two gentlemen of Verona
America 125:534-5 D 18 '71
Nation 213:668 D 20 '71
New Yorker 47:101 D 11 '71
Newsweek 78:114 D 13 '71
Sat R 55:38 Ja 8 '72
Sat R 54:18 Ag 21 '71
Time il 98:48 D 13 '71
Vogue il 158:124 D '71

Wedding of Iphigenia plus Iphigenia in concert
Nation 214:28-9 Ja 3 '72
New Yorker 47:57 D 25 '71

MUSICAL comedy, revue, etc.
Box-office religion; return to religious themes. C. A. Forbes. il Chr Today 15:36-7 Ag 27 '71
Broadway musical: sweet? Or turned sour? J. Gale. il Dance Mag 45:51-66 O '71
Decline and fall of the Broadway musical. C. R. Hughes. America 124:124-5 F 6 '71
Goings on about town. See issues of New Yorker
Musical wastes. J. Richardson. Commentary 51:78-80 F '71
Musicals that were playful, irresponsible and blissfully irrelevant. W. Kerr. il N Y Times Mag p 14-15+ Ap 11 '71; Reply. J. Papp. p 12+ My 23 '71
Two for the show; D. McKechnie and G. Nelson. C. Zadan. il Dance Mag 45:67-73+ O '71

MUSICAL comedy dancing. See Dancing
MUSICAL comedy production. See Theatrical production and direction
MUSICAL composition. See Composition (music)
MUSICAL conferences. See Music conferences
MUSICAL criticism
On teaching critics; the how and the why. A. Jacobs. Hi Fi 21:MA19+ Ag '71
MUSICAL education
See also
Children and music
Music—Appreciation
MUSICAL families
See also
Bach family
MUSICAL festivals. See Music festivals
MUSICAL films. See Moving pictures—Musical films
MUSICAL forgeries and mystifications
Liszt's lament? Beethoven's Bagatelle? Or Rosemary's babies? recording of R. Brown. G. Gould. il pors Hi Fi 20:87-8+ D '70
Supernatural symphonies; excerpt from Unfinished symphonies. R. Brown. il por Ladies Home J 88:92+ S '71
MUSICAL form
Neapolitan intermezzo and its influence on the symphonic idiom. G. Lazarevich. bibliog f il Mus Q 57:294-313 Ap '71
See also
Concertos
Fugue
MUSICAL instruments
See also names of musical instruments, e.g. Autoharp

MUSICAL instruments, Electronic
Build digisyntone-new music synthesizer. F. Maynard; reply. G. Moline. Radio-Electr 42:18 Mr '71
Build the psych-tone; melody synthesizer. D. Lancaster. il Pop Electr 34:25-35 F '71
Digital music maker. B. Carlquist. il Electr World 85:60 Ap '71
Drummer boy; electronic rhythm section. J. S. Simonton, jr. il Pop Electr 35:25-35+ Jl '71; Correction. 35:100-1 O '71
See also
Organ, Electronic

Equipment
Build a timbre gate; envelope generator for great new sounds. C. Anderton. il Pop Electr 34:29-35 Ap '71
MUSICAL instruments, Mechanical
See also
Music boxes
MUSICAL intervals and scales
See also
Twelve-tone system
MUSICAL literature. See Music literature
MUSICAL pitch
Here's the pitch. Newsweek 78:73 Ag 9 '71
How high was G? H. Pleasants. Opera N 35:24-5 F 20 '71
Pitch game; trying to adopt the international standard. il Time 98:46-7 Ag 9 '71
MUSICAL prodigies. See Children as musicians
MUSICAL research. See Musicology
MUSICAL societies
See also
American music conference
Handel society of New York
MUSICAL style. See Style, Musical
MUSICAL taste. See Music—Appreciation; Music—Philosophy and aesthetics
MUSICIANS
Artist life. D. J. Soria. See issues of High Fidelity and Musical America
Debuts & reappearances; New York concerts. See issues of High fidelity and Musical America
Here & there. See issues of High fidelity and Musical America
Musical whirl; photographs. See issues of High fidelity and Musical America
Young artists, 1971; photographs. Hi Fi 21: MA10-14 Jl '71
See also
Children as musicians
Composers
Narcotics and musicians
Singers
Street musicians
Women as musicians
MUSICIANS, American
See also names of American musicians, e.g. V. Thomson
MUSICIANS, Austrian
See also
Brendel, A.
Mozart, J. C. W. A.
MUSICIANS, English
See also
Ogdon, J.
MUSICIANS, German
See also
Bach, J. S
Furtwängler, W.
MUSICIANS, Russian
See also
Rostropovich, M.
MUSICOLOGY
New research on Bach's Musical offering. C. Wolff. bibliog f il Mus Q 57:379-408 Jl '71
MUSKELLUNGE fishing
Comeback of a heavyweight; Chautauqua muskie. C. E. Heacox. il pors Outdoor Life 148:46-9+ Jl '71
Great muskie hunt. H. Duck. il Field & S 75: 58-9+ F '71
Minnesota for muskies. L. J. Bashline. il Field & S 75:78-9+ Ap '71
New muskie country. N. Karas. il Field & S 75:54-5+ Ja '71
Speed up for muskies. R. S. Kommer. il por Outdoor Life 148:74-5+ Ag '71
MUSKIE, Edmund Sixtus
As Maine goes . . . (?) interview. por Nations Bsns 59:72+ N '71
Is America going isolationist? interview. por U S News 70:30-1 Je 28 '71
Muskie: maintaining momentum; interview. ed. by D. Fischer. Time 99:17 Ja 17 '72
Muskie on the issues; interview. Fortune 83: 79+ Je '71

MUSKIE, Edmund Sixtus—*Continued*
about
Baby grand tour. il pors Newsweek 77:19 Ja 18 '71 •
Bandwagon gambit. pors Newsweek 78:22+ D 20 '71 •
Democratic roller-coaster. Cato. Nat R 23: 468 My 4 '71 •
Democrats in '72: Muskie and the Teddy boys. J. Ridgeway. Ramp Mag 10:3-4+ Ag '71 •
Ed Muskie asks you to trust him; with editorial comment. B. Brower. il pors Life 71:3, 58-60+ N 5 '71 •
Facing up to the indecisiveness issue. por Time 97:15 My 3 '71 •
Front runner. il por Newsweek 78:17-18 Jl 19 '71 •
Games with Muskie. J. Osborne. New Repub 164:15-16 F 20 '71 •
Has Muskie got it? A. Alsop. il Newsweek 78:98 S 20 '71 •
Making of a front runner. il Newsweek 79:13-14+ Ja 10 '72 •
Manager for Muskie. pors Time 97:13 Mr 1 '71 •
Muskie, by T. Lippman, jr. and D. C. Hansen. Review
    New Repub 164:32 F 27 '71. G. Johnson •
Muskie campaign. P. R. Wieck. New Repub 165:15-20 N 27 '71 •
Muskie on withdrawal. New Repub 164:14 F 20 '71 •
Muskie: the longest journey begins. il pors Time 98:14-19 S 13 '71 •
Muskie's problem is how to keep being himself. A. J. Reichley. il por Fortune 83:76-9+ Je '71 •
Muskie's strategy for winning '72 nomination. il pors U S News 70:46-7 Ja 18 '71 •
Nixon tries to follow Muskie's cleanup act. Bsns W p21-2 F 6 '71 •
No. 1 and no. 2 for the Democrats. il pors Time 99:16-17 Ja 17 '72 •
Polish connection; Ohio Gov Gilligan's endorsement. il por Time 99:24 Ja 3 '72 •
Remaking of Muskie. J. F. Richard. por Nation 212:235-40 F 22 '71 •
Reports & comment: Washington; the Muskie problem. J. Kraft. Atlan 227:6+ Je '71 •
Revenue sharing that works. New Repub 164:7-8 My 29 '71 •
Rolling along. il por Newsweek 79:13-14 Ja 3 '72 •
Senator Muskie's foreign pollution policy; address to UN symposium, May 21, 1971. J. Lear. Sat R 54:20+ Je 12 '71 •
Senator Muskie's gaffe. W. F. Buckley, jr. Nat R 23:1198 O 22 '71 •
Sneak preview; West coast swing. R. Stout. il pors Newsweek 78:19-20 S 20 '71 •
TRB from Washington. New Repub 164:6 Ja 30 '71 •
Temper, temper. Newsweek 77:25-6 Mr 29 '71 •
Undeclared campaign. por Time 98:12 S 20 '71 •

MUSKIE fishing. See Muskellunge fishing
MUSKOPF, Allan, and Moss, Joy
Integrated day workshop. Ed Digest 36:26-8 My '71
MUSKRATS
Even muskrats believe in life insurance. J. D. Scott. il Nat Wildlife 9:58-61 O '71
MUSLIM-Hindu relations. See Islam—Relations—Hinduism
MUSLIMS
    See also
Pilgrimages to Mecca
MUSLIMS in India
    See also
Islam—Relations—Hinduism
MUSLIMS in Pakistan
Dateline: Pakistan. East and West. J. C. Haughey. il America 125:365-7 N 6 '71
MUSORGSKII, Modest Petrovich
Boris Godunov. Criticism
    New Yorker 47:86-7 My 29 '71 •
MUSSELS, Fresh water
Pearl hunting in Scotland. il Sci Digest 69: 21-3 Ap '71
MUSSOLINI, Benito
Duce! by R. Collier. Review
    Sat R il por 54:50 N 20 '71. G. Gersh •
MUST have sense of humor; story. See Madocs, R.
MUSTANGS. See Horses
MUSTARD gas
Disaster at Bari; excerpts. G. Infield. il por Am Heritage 22:60-4+ O '71
    See also
Nitrogen mustards
MUSTARD plants. See Cruciferae

MUTAGENIC substances
Hycanthone: a frameshift mutagen. P. E. Hartman and others. bibliog il Science 172:1058-60 Je 4 '71; Reply. E. Hirschberg and I. B. Weinstein. 174:1147-8 D 10 '71
Latent meiotic anomalies related to an ancestral exposure to a mutagenic agent. K. S. Lavappa and G. Yerganian. bibliog il Science 172:171-4 Ap 9 '71
Mutagenicity of chemicals and drugs. M. Harris. Science 171:51-2 Ja 8 '71
    See also
Nitrogen mustards
MUTATION (biology)
Hypolipidemia in a mutant strain of acatalasemic mice. S. Goldfischer and others. bibliog il Science 173:65-6 Jl 2 '71
Mutants with abnormal visual pathways: an explanation of anomalous geniculate laminae. R. W. Guillery and others. bibliog il Science 174:831-2 N 19 '71
New class of purine mutants of Chinese hamster ovary cells. M. W. Taylor and others. bibliog il Science 172:162-3 Ap 9 '71
MUTATION (botany)
Induced mutations in plants. B. Sigurbjörnson. il Sci Am 224:86-95 bibliog(p 122) Ja '71
    See also
Mutation (fungi)
MUTATION (fungi)
Selection of ribosomal mutants by antibiotic suppression in yeast. F. T. Bayliss and R. T. Vinepal. bibliog il Science 174:1339-41 D 24 '71
MUTATIONS; ballet. See Ballets—Criticisms
MUTCHMOR, J. R.
Canada: a troubled nation. Chr Cent 88:189-92 F 10 '71
MUTESA II, king of Buganda
King Freddie comes home. il por Time 97:37 Ap 12 '71 •
MUTILATION of books. See Books—Mutilation, defacement, etc.
MUTUAL funds. See Investment trusts
MY cousin from Tycho; drama. See Boiko, C.
MY foot my tutor; drama. See Handke, P.
MY LAI massacre. See Vietnamese war, 1957—Atrocities—My Lai massacre
MYASTHENIA gravis
Kinetics of acetylcholine synthesis and hydrolysis in myasthenia gravis. R. N. Rosenberg and others. bibliog il Science 173:644-5 Ag 13 '71
MYCENAE
    Photographs
House of Atreus. F. Stevenson. Opera N 35: 14-16 F 27 '71
MYCOBACTERIUM
Immunotherapy of cancer: regression of tumors after intralesional injection of living mycobacterium bovis. B. Zbar and T. Tanaka. bibliog il Science 172:271-3 Ap 16 '71
Suppression of urethan-induced lung adenomas in mice treated with trehalose-6,6-dimycolate (cord factor) and living bacillus Calmette Guérin. A. Bekierkunst and others. bibliog il Science 174:1240-2 D 17 '71
MYCOPLASMA
Pulmonary compliance: alteration during infection. N. L. Somerson and others. bibliog il Science 171:66-8 Ja 8 '71
MYCOPLASMATALES viruses. See Viruses
MYCORHIZA
Mycorrhizal enhancement of water transport in soybean. G. R. Safir and others. bibliog il Science 172:581-3 My 7 '71
MYDANS, Carl
Businessmen who weather the winter in Nanyang. il Fortune 83:82-7 Mr '71
Gallery; photographs. Life 70:4-6A Je 25 '71
MYELIN. See Nerve cells
MYELOMA cells. See Tumor cells
MYER, Charles R.
Towing techniques. il Motor B & S 128: 14+ Ag '71
MYERHOFF, Barbara G.
Revolution as a trip: symbol and paradox; address, 1970. bibliog f Ann Am Acad 395: 105-16 My '71
MYERS, Carmel
You don't have to look old. Harp Baz 104:6 Jl '71
MYERS, Henry R.
Extending the nuclear-test ban; with biographical sketch. il Sci Am 226:10, 13-23 bibliog(p 122) Ja '72
MYERS, Jack
Wing to root; We never talk; Trap; Invention of mushrooms; poems. Poetry 119:148-9 D '71

MYERS, Joel N. and Cahir, J. J.
Weather business. bibliog il **Weatherwise 24:**
64-7+ Ap '71
MYERS, John Bernard
Exercises in taste. il Craft Horiz 30:50-3 My;
7 Ag '70; 31:6-7 F '71
Puppets: The little players. il Craft Horiz
31:27-9+ D '71
MYERS, Kent E.
Teaching: an educational adventure. bibliog
Clear House 46:131-5 N '71
MYERS, L. E. company
Late tape. R. Brady. Duns 97:105 Mr '71
MYERS, M. Scott
Overcoming union opposition to job enrich-
ment. bibliog f il **Harvard Bsns R 49:**37-49
My '71
MYERS, Miles
English as woodshop. Engl J 60:317-25 Mr
'71
MYERSON, Bess
As Bess weighs in Frank says so long. il
pors Life 71:56-7 D 31 '71 *
Consumer champion lays down with the law;
with editorial comment. H. Wingo. il pors
Life 71:322-9 Jl 16 '71 *
MYERSON, Michael
(ed) See Davis, A. Angela Davis in prison
MYLAI massacre. See Vietnamese war, 1957-
—Atrocities—My Lai massacre
MYOCARDIAL infarction. See Heart—Diseases
MYOPIA
Close work and nearsightedness. A. J. Snider.
Sci Digest 69:55 F '71
MYRA
Poem; Unshielded by collective power. Na-
tion 212:119 Ja 25 '71
MYRDAL, Gunnar. See Myrdal, K. G.
MYRDAL, Karl Gunnar
Are the developing countries really develop-
ing? adaptation of address, August 23, 1970.
il Bul Atom Sci 27:5-8 Ja '71
Gunnar Myrdal talks about troubles in Utopia;
interview, ed. by S. G. Slappey. il por
Nations Bsns 59:44-5+ Ap '71
Need for internal reform; excerpts from ad-
dress, June 1971. por Sch & Soc 99:325 O '71
MYRIOPHYLLUM. See Water milfoil
MYRTLE, James F. and Norman, A. W.
Vitamin D: a cholecalciferol metabolite highly
active in promoting intestinal calcium trans-
port. bibliog il Science 171:79-82 Ja 8 '71
MYSLENSKI, Skip. See Putnam, P. jt. auth.
MYSTERY stories. See Detective and mystery
stories
MYSTERY story writers, American. See Nov-
elists, American
MYSTERY writers of America, inc.
MWA lists Edgar awards nominees. Pub W
199:59 Ap 12 '71
MYSTICISM
Durable-avatar; Krishnamurti. por Time 97:
63 Je 7 '71
Going east: neomysticism and Christian
faith. G. Fackre. il Chr Cent 88:457-61
Ap 14 '71
Judaism
Rebirth of Jewish mysticism. D. Singer. il
Commonweal 93:492-5 F 19 '71
Mohammedanism
See also
Sufism
MYSTICISM in literature
Siddhartha; craze for works of H. Hesse. F.
Trippett. il Look 35:46-54+ F 23 '71
MYTHOLOGY
Abuse of myth. J. Castelli. il Cath World 213:
88-92 My '71
Classic hero in a new mythology; Chronicles
of Prydain. M. Carr. il Horn Bk 47:508-
13 O '71
Need for new myths; views of J. Camp-
bell. G. Clarke. il por Time 99:50-1 Ja 17
'72
MYTHOLOGY, Assyro-Babylonian
Astarte phenomenon. K. Cavander. il Horizon
13:14-18+ Spr '71
MYTHOLOGY, Greek
Many faces of Orpheus. M. Springer. Opera
N 35:16 Ja 23 '71
MYTHOLOGY, Indian (American Indian) See
Indians of North America—Religion and
mythology
MYTHOLOGY in literature
Mythopoesis and psychoanalysis. J. E. Gedo.
bibliog Am Imago 27:329-37 Wint '70
MYTHS. See Mythology
MZIMA SPRINGS
Mzima. Kenya's spring of life. J. Root and
A. Root. il pors Nat Geog 140:350-73 S
'71

N

N-radiography. See Radiography
NAA. See New art association
NAACP. See National association for the ad-
vancement of colored people
NAAF. See National association for air freight,
inc.
NAB. See National alliance of businessmen
NACC. See New York (state)—Narcotic ad-
diction control commission
NACCC. See National association of citizens
crime commissions
NACS. See National association of college
stores
NAE. See National academy of engineering;
National association of evangelicals
NAEP. See National assessment of educational
progress
NAES. See National association of ecumenical
staff
NAIA (National association of intercollegiate
athletics tournament. See Basketball tour-
naments
NAMH. See National association for mental
health, inc.
NASA. See United States—National aeronau-
tics and space administration
NASA communications network. See United
States—National aeronautics and space ad-
ministration—Communications network
NASDAQ (National association of securities
dealers automated quotation) system. See
Computers—Investment use
NASUA. See National association of state units
on aging
NATO. See National association of theater
owners; Nato
NAWC. See National art workers community
NBA. See National basketball association; Na-
tional book awards
NBAA. See National business aircraft asso-
ciation
NBC. See National book committee
NBER. See National bureau of economic re-
search
NBS. See United States—Standards, Nation-
al bureau of
NCAA. See National collegiate athletic asso-
ciation
NCAA golf championship. See Golf—Tourna-
ments
NCARB. See National council of architectural
registration boards
NCBA. See National caucus on the black aged
NCBC. See National committee of Black church-
men
NCC. See National council of churches
NCCL. See National council of Catholic laity
NCEA. See National Catholic educational as-
sociation
NCOA. See National council on the aging
NCOMP. See National Catholic office for mo-
tion pictures
NCSC. See National council of senior citizens,
inc.
NCSS. See National council for the social stud-
ies
NCTE. See National council of teachers of
English
NEA. See National education association; Na-
tional electronic associations
NEH (National endowment for the humanities)
See United States—National foundation on
the arts and the humanities
NERVA (nuclear engine for rocket vehicle ap-
plication) See Rockets, Atomic powered
NET. See National educational television net-
work
NFO. See National farmers organization
NFPC. See National federation of priests'
councils
NHRA Springnationals. See Drag racing
NHRA Winternationals. See Drag racing
NIESR. See National institute of economic
and social research, London
NIH. See United States—National institutes
of health
NIMH. See United States—National institute of
mental health
NINDS. See United States—National institute
of neurological diseases and stroke
NISO (National institute of student opinion)
See Scholastic research center
NJLA. See New Jersey library association

NAGY, Ivan
Ivan Nagy: Albrecht and others. O. Maynard. il pors Dance Mag 45:38-46 S '71 •
NAGY, Sibyl Moholy-. See Moholy-Nagy, S.
NAHMIAS, A. J. and others
Genital herpesvirus hominis type 2 infection: an experimental model in cebus monkeys. bibliog Science 171:297-8 Ja 22 '71
NAIDEN, James
Face; poem. Poetry 118:29 Ap '71
Good omen? Poetry 118:46-7 Ap '71
NAIL, William A.
What did you say? address, July 17, 1971 Vital Speeches 37:723-6 S 15 '71
NAILS
Ask Rufus; making square cut nails. R. Cartwright. Mech Illus 67:108 Je '71
Horseshoe nail jewelry. O. Johnson. il Sch Arts 70:26-8 F '71
NAILS (anatomy)
Give your hands a beauty break. C. Bartel. il Am Home 74:16+ O '71
How to beat the broken nail. S. Lindsay. House B 113:70 O '71
NAIPAUL, V. S.
One out of many; story. Atlan 227:71-8 Ap '71
NAISBITT, Noel
What school reformers want. il PTA Mag 66:6-8+ N '71
NAISMITH, Grace
Thanks for your eyes. Read Digest 98:33-4+ Mr '71
NAJARI Levons' old country advice to the young Americans on how to live with a snake; story. See Saroyan, W.
NAKA, Ken-ichi
Receptive field mechanism in the vertebrate retina. bibliog Science 171:691-3 F 19 '71
NAKAUCHI, Isao
Mao in the supermarket. il por Time 97:74 Je 28 '71 •
NAKEDNESS. See Nudism; Nudity
NAMATH, Joe Willie
My mother, right or wrong. McCalls 98:110 My '71
about
Achilles' knee. Sports Illus 35:11 Ag 16 '71 •
Night they wiped the smile off Namath's knee. D. Anderson. il por Life 71:65 Ag 20 '71 •
Too late for Joe; ed. by M. Kane. Sports Illus 34:9 Je 21 '71 •
NAMBAS. See New Hebrides—Native races
NAMES, Geographical
American place names, by G. R. Stewart. Review
Harper 242:22-3+ Ja '71. J. Hollander
New Repub 164:26-8 F 13 '71. J. Seelye
See also
Street names
NAMES, Personal
Appellations. M. L. Stohlman. Sat R 54:4+ Ja 23 '71
Happy birthday, 73/1970; name Che not accepted by registrar in Erding, West Germany. il Time 97:39 F 1 '71
See also
Baseball players—Names

Anecdotes, facetiae, satire, etc.
My backward youth. R. Armour. Sat R 54:4-5 Ag 28 '71
NAMES of animals. See Zoology—Nomenclature
NAMES of baseball players. See Baseball players—Names
NAMES of birds. See Birds—Nomenclature
NAMES of streets. See Street names
NAMIBIA
Clinging to the land of thirst. il Time 98:31 Jl 5 '71
Holding on tight; with report by P. Younghusband. il Newsweek 78:43-4 Jl 5 '71
See also
United Nations—Namibia
United Nations council for Namibia
NAMIER, Sir Lewis Bernstein
Arts of memory. G. Steiner. New Yorker 47:61-3 Ja 1 '72 •
NAMIOKA, Lensey
Japanese Gothic. il Travel 136:52-7 N '71
NANCE, Richard L.
Gravity measured at the Apollo 14 landing site. bibliog il Science 174:1022-3 D 3 '71
NANDA, Krish
Will India go nuclear? il Bul Atom Sci 27:39-41 D '71
NANDA, Ved P.
Bangla Desh: from genocide toward statehood. Nation 213:690-1 D 27 '71

NANES, Allan S.
Jury system reform. bibliog f Cur Hist 61:92-6+ Ag '71
NANEY, William
I have never kissed you; poem. Ladies Home J 88:105 S '71
NANNIES. See Nursemaids
NANSEN, Charles
Cottontail hunting, eastern style. il Field & S 76:54-5+ O '71
National park that has nothing. il Field & S 76:53-5+ My '71
New trick for crappie. il Field & S 75:58-9+ Mr '71
Yellowstone nobody knows. il Field & S 76:44-5+ Jl '71
NANTAHALA national forest. See National forests
NANTGARW porcelain. See Pottery, Welsh
NAPA VALLEY
Miracle of the vine. J. D. Weaver. il Holiday 49:64-5+ Ap '71
Tradition and technology blend nicely in the Napa Valley. il Fortune 84:83-7. S '71
NAPIER, Arch
Surfing. il Sports Illus 34:80+ Ap 5 '71
NAPLES

Music

Report:
Das Rheingold, and Saverio Mercadante's Elisa e Claudio. E. Tellini. Opera N 35:30 Mr 13 '71
Il Trovatore and Cavalleria rusticana. E. Tellini. Opera N 35:30 Ap 17 '71
Verdi's Attila, and Puccini's Madama Butterfly. E. Tellini. Opera N 35:33 F 13 '71
NAPLEY, David
Our troubled courts. il Nations Bsns 59:76-81 My '71
NAPOLES, José
Everything's rosy with Jose. R. H. Boyle. il pors Sports Illus 34:22-3 Je 14 '71 •
NARAGHI, Ehsan
25 years of Unesco viewed by a student of 25. il UNESCO Courier 24:6-7 Ag '71
NARCISSUS
Dainty miniature daffodils. J. Kilborn. il Horticulture 49:28-9+ Ap '71
For a spring look in winter, try bulbs in pebbles il Sunset 147:252 O '71
For winter fragrance plant paper-whites. B. Brinhart. il Home Gard 58:32-3 D '71
Growing daffodils and tulips in kitchen pots and pans. il Sunset 147:237-8 N '71
Irish sketches; crossbreeding daffodils by Mrs Lionel Richardson of Prospect house, Waterford, Ireland. J. McCarten. New York 47:131-4 My 8 '71
NARCO avionics (firm)
Narco catches up. A. Trammell. il Flying 88:65-8 Je '71
NARCOLEPSY
National driver survey: asleep at the wheel. B. Ford. il Sci Digest 70:36-43 Jl '71
NARCOTIC addiction control commission of New York state. See New York (state) —Narcotic addiction control commission
NARCOTIC addicts
Heroin babies; going cold turkey at birth. S. Burnham. N Y Times Mag p 18-19+ Ja 9 '72
Heroin plague: what can be done? with report by M. Kasindorf. il Newsweek 78:27-32 Jl 5 '71
New math of addiction. Time 98:54+ S 13 '71
Our most dangerous epidemic. R. H. Steele. il por Nations Bsns 59:46-8 Jl '71
Some drugs bring babies. Sci Digest 69:17-18 Je '71
See also
Heroin
Narcotics and crime

Rehabilitation

Addict treatment programs. A. L. Hammond. Science 173:504 Ag 6 '71
Addiction, the counter-culture; therapy at Exodus house. M. Proctor. Nation 212:623-7 My 17 '71
Anti-drug program that works; Smarteens. J. B. Shuman. Read Digest 98:139-42 Mr '71
Drugs without crime. E. May. Harper 243:60-5 Jl '71
Heroin and the black community. V. E. Taylor. Am Scholar 40:691-4 Aut '71
Hope and help for narcotics addicts; Iroquois rehabilitation center. A. S. Fick. il Cons 26:28-9 Ag '71
Hope from Horizon house. T. J. O'Connell. il America 125:282-5 O 16 '71

NARCOTIC addicts—Rehabilitation—*Continued*
House on 92nd street; institute of applied psychotherapy and other centers. il Newsweek 78:115 N 22 '71
How 10 cities fight drugs. G. Astor and I. Mothner. Look 35:73-4+ F 23 '71
Marathon therapy and changes in attitude toward treatment and behavior ratings. B. Crowther and P. M. Pantleo. bibliog Ment Hy 55:165-70 Ap '71
New public enemy no. 1; R. M. Nixon's program. il por Time 97:20+ Je 28 '71
Now the navy. il Newsweek 78:25 Ag 23 '71
Rehabilitating addicts; program outlined by President Nixon. America 124:625 Je 19 '71
Return from the drug scene; Narcotics addicts rehabilitation center organization, Atlantic City, organized by J. Brooks. il pors Ebony 26:50+ S '71
Trying to help the GI addicts; Palo Alto VA hospital program; with editorial comment. il Life 71:3, 20-7 Jl 23 '71
Vera: cleaning of Bethesda fountain, in Central park and other rehabilitation projects of the Pioneer messenger service. New Yorker 47:39-41 D 11 '71
War on drugs; R. M. Nixon's program. il pors Newsweek 77:32+ Je 28 '71
See also
Methadone
United States—Drug abuse prevention, Special action office for (proposed)
United States—Veterans administration hospitals—Drug treatment centers

NARCOTIC antagonists
Fighting drug addiction with drugs. il Bsns W p58+ F 27 '71
Industry's pledge: an antidrug drug. Bsns W p85 S 18 '71
Narcotic antagonists: new methods to treat heroin addiction. A. L. Hammond. Science 173:503-6 Ag 6 '71
See also
Methadone

NARCOTIC habit
Decline in hard drug use. America 125:388 N 13 '71
Our own Andromeda strain. J. Finkelstein. Read Digest 99:107-9 D '71
See also
Heroin
Narcotics and youth

NARCOTIC habit in drama. See Drama—Themes

NARCOTIC habit in moving pictures. See Moving pictures—Themes

NARCOTIC laws
Department discusses international aspects of President Nixon's drug control program; statement, July 8, 1971. H. R. Wellman. Dept State Bul 65:157-60 Ag 9 '71
International aspects of drug abuse control; address, April 16, 1971. H. R. Wellman. il Dept State Bul 64:639-47 My 17 '71
Make marijuana laws easier? Most young people say no; Scholastic's National institute of student opinion. Sr Schol 99:7 N 29 '71
Normality is a square circle of a four-sided triangle; views of T. Szasz. M. Scarf. il pors N Y Times Mag p 16-17+ O 3 '71; Discussion. p6+ N 14 '71
U.S. urges stronger multilateral commitments to narcotics control; statement, October 1, 1971. J. E. Ingersoll. Dept State Bul 65:523-9 N 8 '71

France
Combating la drug scene, in France. L. Christiaens. America 125:286-7 O 16 '71

Great Britain
Wide open British drug scene. J. Dimbleby. New Repub 164:15-16 Ap 3 '71

NARCOTIC smuggling. See Smuggling

NARCOTIC trade. See Narcotics, Control of

NARCOTIC traffic. See Narcotics, Control of

NARCOTICS
Alcohol dependence and opiate dependence: lack of relationship in mice. A. Goldstein and B. A. Judson. bibliog il Science 172:290-2 Ap 16 '71
See also
Cocaine
Drugs
Heroin
Morphine
Opium trade
United Nations—Commission on narcotic drugs

NARCOTICS, Control of
America's battle against the white death. il Newsweek 77:41-3 Mr 29 '71
Chicago's black vigilantes; anti-drug Afro-American group attack team. il Newsweek 78:75+ S 27 '71
City killer. S. Alsop. Newsweek 77:104 F 8 '71

Combating la drug scene, in France. L. Christiaens. America 125:286-7 O 16 '71
Convention on psychotropic drugs transmitted to the Senate; President Nixon's message with Secretary Rogers' report. R. M. Nixon; W. P. Rogers. Dept State Bul 65:140-2 Ag 2 '71
Drive at heart of the drug problem. U S News 70:61 Mr 8 '71
Drug abuse: a challenge to U.S.-Turkish cooperation in the seventies; address, December 14, 1970. H. R. Wellman. Dept State Bul 64:140-6 F 1 '71
From D.A. to dope lawyer; M. Metzger of San Francisco. N. Pileggi. il pors N Y Times Mag p34-5+ My 16 '71
Golden arm of the law: narcotics squad. W. P. Brown. Nation 213:392-7 O 25 '71
Heroin shooting war; situation in Detroit. il Time 97:18 Je 21 '71
Heroin: the source of supply. E. Marshall. New Repub 165:23-5 Jl 24 '71
How two influential fathers turned family drug tragedies into a triumph for the public. R. Sullivan. il Todays Health 49:42-5 My '71
International drug trade: poppy to pusher. il Sr Schol 98:11-3 My 17 '71
Introduction to flash; Harlem drug dealer. R. Woodley. il Esquire 75:79-83 Ap '71; Same abr. with title Drug scene; excerpt from Dealer: portrait of a cocaine agent. Read Digest 99:103-7 Jl '71
Let's halt heroin at the source; eighty percent originates from Turkey. W. Schulz. Read Digest 98:97-101 My '71
Opium: sweeping the sands. Nation 213:421 N 1 '71
Planning group on drug problems established by U.S. and Thailand; joint statement. Dept State Bul 65:279 S 13 '71
President calls for comprehensive drug control program; message to Congress, June 17, 1971. R. M. Nixon. Dept State Bul 65:58-66 Jl 12 '71
Pushers pushed; drive against drug pushers in Tampa, Fla. il Newsweek 78:60 Ag 9 '71
Recent activities in international drug control; statement, October 27, 1971. N. Gross. Dept State Bul 65:600-4 N 22 '71
Tampa turns in its pushers. C. Whitehorn. McCalls 99:32 N '71
Travelers warned of penalties for drug violations abroad; Department announcement. Dept State Bul 65:56-7 Jl 12 '71
U.S. and Thailand sign memorandum of understanding on international narcotics control; remarks, with text of memorandum, September 28, 1971. W. P. Rogers; Thanat Khoman. Dept State Bul 65:411-13 O 18 '71
U.S. urges stronger U.N. efforts in narcotics control; statement, May 3, 1971. G. Bush. Dept State Bul 64:769-71 Je 14 '71
See also
Narcotic laws
United Nations—Commission on narcotic drugs
United Nations fund for drug abuse control (proposed)
United States—Cabinet committee on international narcotics control

NARCOTICS addicts rehabilitation center organization, Atlantic City, N.J. See Narcotic addicts—Rehabilitation

NARCOTICS agents. See Narcotics, Control of

NARCOTICS and athletes. See Doping in sports

NARCOTICS and crime
Cops can't find the pusher. K. S. Christianson. Nation 213:562-4 N 29 '71
Golden arm of the law: narcotics squad. W. P. Brown. Nation 213:392-7 O 25 '71

NARCOTICS and musicians
In rock, it's a bad, mad world; J. and L. Taylor. A. Goldman. pors Life 70:12 Mr 12 '71

NARCOTICS and service men
Another sort of H-bomb; heroin scandal in South Viet Nam. il Time 97:21-2 Ap 19 '71
As common as chewing gum; problem in Vietnam. il Time 97:14-15 Mr 1 '71
Catch in amnesty. S. A. Simon. Nation 213:308-9 O 4 '71
Coming home with a habit. W. K. Wyant, jr. Nation 213:7-10 Jl 5 '71
Drug problem; new moves by the White House. U S News 70:63 Je 28 '71
Dzu story. por Time 98:18+ Jl 19 '71
G.I.'s and O.J.'s in Vietnam. N. E. Zinberg. il N Y Times Mag p37+ D 5 '71
GI's other enemy: heroin. il Newsweek 77:26+ My 24 '71
Hard drugs in the military. H. F. Hughes. New Repub 164:17-18 Je 12 '71; Reply. J. S. Monagan. 164:35 Je 26 '71

NASHVILLE, Tenn.
New sound in Nashville; battle over Vanderbilt university's plans for expansion. il Newsweek 78:105 O 11 '71

Architecture
Keys to growth: quality, cost control and service. il Arch Rec 149:67-70 **Ap '71**
Nineteenth-century public buildings in Nashville. A. Senkevitch, jr. il Antiques 100:222-7 Ag '71

Economic conditions
Nashville thrives on a city-county merger. il Bsns W p 133-4+ S 25 '71

Education
CATV story in Nashville. S. Smith and R. W. Bogen. Todays Ed 60:57-8 N '71

Metropolitan district
Nashville thrives on a city-county merger. il Bsns W p 133-4+ S 25 '71

Music
Another version of the dream; Nashville. Music city U.S.A. il Esquire 76:136-47 N '71
Current chronicle. R. L. Weaver. il Mus Q 57:317-22 Ap '71
Grand ole opry. W. Hedgepeth. il Look 35:22-4+ Jl 13 '71

NASR, Seyyed Hossein
Sacred art in Persian culture. il UNESCO Courier 24:16-20 O '71

NASSARIUS obsoletus. See Snails

NASSAU COUNTY, N.Y.
Trial courts in urban politics, by K. M. Dolbeare. Review
Trans-Action 8:96+ N '70. W. K. Muir, jr

NASSAU library system
Civil service jurisdiction ends for N.Y. systems. Library J 96:3713-14 N 15 '71

NASSER, Gamal Abdel
Arab Socialist union; address, June 10, 1971. A. Sadat. Vital Speeches 37:580-3 Jl 15 '71 •
Doubleday acquires English rights to Nasser memoir. Pub W 200:233-4 Ag 30 '71 •
Mixed motives; Heikal memoirs. il por Newsweek 78:26+ S 13 '71 •

NAST, Thomas
Life and death of Thomas Nast; excerpts from Thomas Nast's Christmas drawings for the human race. T. N. St Hill. il pors Am Heritage 22:81-96 O '71

NASTURTIUMS
See also
Cookery—Flowers

NAT Turner's insurrection. See Southampton insurrection, 1831

NATCHEZ, Gladys
Grandma visits her hippies. il N Y Times Mag p74+ D 5 '71

NATHAN, George Jean
Broadway's banner years. L. Kronenberger. Atlan 227:101-2+ **My '71** •

NATHAN, Jason R.
Price planners pay for secrecy. il Bsns W p28 Je 26 '71 •

NATHAN, Leonard
Comment. P. Schjeldahl. Poetry 117:271 Ja '71 •

NATHAN, Norman, and Berger, Allen
Building blocks of poetry. Engl J 60:42-6 Ja '71

NATHAN, Paul S.
Rights and permissions. See issues of Publishers' weekly

NATHAN, Robert
2 chronicles 37. Sat R 54:20 My 8 '71

NATHAN, Robert Roy
Youth, dollars, and development. Sat R 54:24-5+ My 1 '71

NATHAN, Ronald, and Lear, Robert
Philadelphia's banks. New Repub 164:10+ Je 5 '71

NATHAN, Simon
Simon says. See issues of Popular photography

NATION (periodical)
Books by Nation contributors. C. McWilliams. Nation 212:538+ Ap 26 '71
Books by Nation contributors. C. McWilliams. Nation 213:121-2 Ag 16 '71

NATIONAL academy of engineering
NAE names new members. Science 172:356 Ap 23 '71

NATIONAL academy of sciences
Ivory tower is under siege; adaptation of address, December 1970. S. L. Udall. Audubon 73:118-19 Mr '71
NAS elects new members. Science 172:540 My 7 '71

Nader to sponsor study of Academy. Sci N 99:247 Ap 10 '71
National academy of sciences: awkward moments at the meeting. J. Walsh. Science 172:539-42 My 7 '71
New visibility at the NAS. Sci N 99:299 My 1 '71
Optimism and population; NAS report. Sci Am 225:40 O '71
Sea-level canal: how the academy's voice was muted. P. M. Boffey. Science 171:355-6+ Ja 29 '71
Second NAS member resigns. N. Wade. Science 174:931 N 26 '71
See also
Institute of medicine
National research council

NATIONAL accelerator laboratory
Accelerating protons and social reform. C.-G. McDaniel. Chr Cent 88:1032-4 S 1 '71
Accelerator at Batavia: the next step in high energy physics. A. L. Hammond. Science 171:362-4 Ja 29 '71
Batavia's ferret. il Time 98:66 O 4 '71
Decelerated accelerator; wet magnet problem. Sci Am 226:46-7 Ja '72
New pride of the prairie: Batavia accelerator. il Time 98:50 Jl 5 '71
1000 GeV with superconducting magnets at Batavia? M. S. Rothenberg. il Phys Today 24:19-20 My '71
Problems at Batavia: delays for high energy physics. A. L. Hammond. Science 174:1222 D 17 '71

NATIONAL advertising review board
Admen set up their own watchdog. Bsns W p56 Je 12 '71

NATIONAL advisory commission on civil disorders. See United States—National advisory commission on civil disorders

NATIONAL aeronautics and space administration. See United States—National aeronautics and space administration

NATIONAL airlines, inc.
Airline's ad encounters some turbulence. il Life 71:75-6 O 29 '71
American, National drop 13 DC-10 transport options. Aviation W 94:21 My 10 '71
Miami-London carriers vary cabin service. H. D. Watkins. Aviation W 95:29-30 N 29 '71
National on the offensive. il Newsweek 78:96+ N 15 '71

NATIONAL alliance of businessmen
Business fights the social ills; in a recession. il Bsns W p51-4+ Mr 6 '71

NATIONAL archives. See United States—National archives

NATIONAL archives and records service. See United States—General services administration—National archives and records service

NATIONAL arctic wildlife range. See Wildlife sanctuaries—Alaska

NATIONAL art museum of sport. See New York (city)—Galleries and museums

NATIONAL art workers community
National art workers community. A. Gross. Art in Am 59:23 S '71
Toward a community of artists. A. Gross. Am Artist 35:5 Je '71

NATIONAL assessment of educational progress
National assessment moves ahead. Todays Ed 60:45 F '71
What we are learning from the National assessment. E. L. Norris. il Am Ed 7:18-23 Jl '71

NATIONAL association for air freight, inc.
Second business at our airports: theft. D. Walsh. il Life 70:16-23 F 12 '71

NATIONAL association for mental health, inc.
NAMH position statement on:
Marriage counselors. Ment Hy 55:533-7 O '71
Pastoral counseling. Ment Hy 55:538-43 O '71
Right to treatment. Ment Hy 55:270-4 Ap '71
Therapeutic abortions, suicide prevention and homosexuality. Ment Hy 55:130-2 Ja '71
Principles for mental health provisions in national health insurance; adopted by Board of directors, June 19, 1971. Ment Hy 55:544-5 O '71
Suicide prevention programs and mental health associations. R. K. McGee. bibliog Ment Hy 55:60-7 Ja '71

NATIONAL association for the advancement of colored people
All together now! our goal of full equality; address, July 5, 1971. S. G. Spottswood. Vital Speeches 37:662-5 Ag 15 '71
Curious counsels. E. Geller. Library J 96:2811 S 15 '71; Discussion. 96:4129-32 D 15 '71

NATIONAL association for the advancement of colored people—*Continued*
ED funds for Indians misused charges NAACP. Library J 96:1413 Ap 15 '71
Legal defense fund after 30 years. A. B. Haines. Chr Cent 88:508-10 Ap 21 '71
NAACP unit issues new multi-racial history syllabus. Negro Hist Bul 33:167 N '70
Peace feelers. Newsweek 78:22 Jl 19 '71

NATIONAL association of business economists
Boom on the way? Top experts size up the outlook. il U S News 71:21-4 O 11 '71

NATIONAL association of citizens crime commissions
Citizens' war on crime. il U S News 71:23-5 D 20 '71

NATIONAL association of college stores
NACS convention hits doldrums. P. A. Farrell and L. P. Freilicher. il Pub W 199:44-5+ My 17 '71
1970 in review. il Pub W 199:48-9 F 8 '71

NATIONAL association of ecumenical staff
New name, new links. Chr Cent 88:873 Jl 21 '71

NATIONAL association of evangelicals
NAE: new marching orders? W. Willoughby. Chr Today 15:37 My 7 '71
New evangelical surge; with editorial comment. W. F. Willoughby. il por Chr Today 15:34, 40-1 My 21 '71

NATIONAL association of intercollegiate athletics
Most conventional win for the Thorobreds; Kentucky state in NAIA finals. S. Treadwell. il Sports Illus 34:58+ Mr 22 '71

NATIONAL association of laity. See Laity—Catholic church

NATIONAL association of manufacturers
Pollution teleconference. Sat R 54:44-5 Jl 3 '71

NATIONAL association of railroad passengers
On the track: Railpax vobiscum. D. Butwin. por Sat R 54:80-3 Ja 23 '71

NATIONAL association of securities dealers, inc.
New way to trade. C. Morgello. il Newsweek 77:93 Je 7 '71
Present and future shock. Time 97:87 F 22 '71
Tussle over automatic OTC trading. il Bsns W p72+ Ja 30 '71

NATIONAL association of state boating law administrators
Report from an all-important NASBLA meeting. D. Fales. Motor B & S 127:10-11 F '71

NATIONAL association of state units on aging
NASUA meets, elects officers. Aging 195:6 Ja '71

NATIONAL association of theater owners
NATO is a house o'weenies. il Time 98:79 N 8 '71

NATIONAL atlas of the United States. See Atlases

NATIONAL Audubon society
Eight new directors chosen by National Audubon society. il Audubon 73:91 Ja '71
Nine action priorities for Audubon chapters, members. Audubon 73:95 Ja '71
See also
Audubon nature camps

NATIONAL automobile dealers association
Gloom stalks a dealers' meeting. il Bsns W p 18 Ja 23 '71

NATIONAL ballet of Canada
Image: Celia Franca and the National ballet of Canada. O. Maynard. il por Dance Mag 45:46-55 Ap '71

NATIONAL ballet of Cuba. See Ballet nacional de Cuba

NATIONAL bankers life insurance company
Astronauts on the make; stock fraud, Texas. K. Northcott. Ramp Mag 10:12-13 N '71
Big names in a Texas stock scheme; SEC case. por Bsns W p77 Ja 23 '71
Widening impact of a Texas scandal; closing of Sharpstown state bank. Bsns W p22 Ja 30 '71

NATIONAL Baptist convention, USA, inc. See Baptists in the United States

NATIONAL bar association (Negro)
Black judges; meeting in Atlanta to establish Judicial council. il Time 98:28 Ag 23 '71

NATIONAL baseball hall of fame and museum
Hollow ring to fame. por Ebony 26:124-5 Ap '71

NATIONAL basketball association
Basketball's super bowl; proposed merger of NBA-ABA. Newsweek 77:65 My 24 '71
Dribbling on the verge of the merge; basketball leagues, the NBA and the ABA. F. Deford. Sports Illus 35:42 Ag 9 '71
Hey, look, ma! Only one hand; Bucks champions of NBA. P. Carry. il Sports Illus 34:26-8+ My 10 '71

Instant millionaires from the basketball war; with account by D. Fisher. il Life 70:32-4 Ap 23 '71
Meanwhile, back at the merge; NBA vs. ABA. P. Carry. il Sports Illus 34:68+ My 24 '71
Who owns Haywood? por Newsweek 77:79 F 15 '71

NATIONAL bison range
In Montana you can drive through buffalo territory. il Sunset 147:31 Jl '71

NATIONAL black economic development conference
Reparations up to date. por Time 97:51-2 My 3 '71

NATIONAL black political fund
Clifford Alexander, chief, black political fund. Negro Hist Bul 33:171 N '70

NATIONAL boat show. See Boats—Exhibitions

NATIONAL book awards
Children's literature award announced by NBA jury. il Library J 96:1067 Mr 15 '71
NBA awards. il Newsweek 77:113 Mr 15 '71
NBA winner stresses seriousness of fantasy. Library J 96:1412-13 Ap 15 '71
National book award finalists named. Pub W 199:54 F 15 '71
National book awards Brouhaha and three ways to cool it. B. A. Bannon. Pub W 199:122-3 F 22 '71
National book awards, 1971. il Am Lib 2:438-9 My '71
National book awards: nominees released. Library J 96:774-6 Mr 1 '71
National book awards presented as controversy drones on. il Pub W 199:50 Mr 8 '71
1971 National book awards: summary of news conference, panel discussion and acceptance speeches. il Library J 96:1248-9 Ap 1 '71
Trade winds; Spring author panel. C. Amory. Sat R 54:16 Mr 20 '71
22nd National book awards. Wilson Lib Bul 45:720 Ap '71
Why do they do it? The NBA rides again. il Pub W 199:16-28 Mr 22 '71

NATIONAL book committee
Book committee elects Stevens, honors E. B. White. il Pub W 200:34 D 20 '71
NLW office arranges regional workshops. Pub W 200:28 S 20 '71
1970 in review. il Pub W 199:47 F 8 '71

NATIONAL book league
Linder collection of the works and drawings of Beatrix Potter. K. Clark. il Horn Bk 47:554-5 O '71

NATIONAL broadcasting company
Chancellor on his own; NBC nightly news. il por Newsweek 78:71 Ag 2 '71
Iron Chancellor. por Time 98:55 Ag 2 '71

NATIONAL budget. See Budget—United States

NATIONAL bureau of economic research
Now it's official: there was a slump. Bsns W p 16 My 29 '71

NATIONAL bureau of standards. See United States—Standards, National bureau of

NATIONAL business aircraft association
Good business. R. B. Parke. Flying 89:46 O '71
NBAA eases membership rules to strengthen influence, finances. Aviation W 95:52 O 4 '71

NATIONAL can corporation
Hefty lightweight. il Forbes 107:30 My 1 '71

NATIONAL cancer institute. See United States—National cancer institute

NATIONAL capital region planning. See Washington, D.C.—City planning

NATIONAL cash register company
Dayton weathers a siege. Bsns W p81+ D 4 '71

NATIONAL cathedral. See Washington, D.C.—Churches

NATIONAL Catholic educational association
Advance report: U.S. Catholic schools, 1970-71; excerpt. America 124:371-2 Ap 10 '71
Statistics of crisis; NCEA survey. J. McLellan. Commonweal 93:421-3 Ja 29 '71

NATIONAL Catholic office for motion pictures
Film ratings: 1934 revisited; with editorial comment. P. C. Rule. America 124:557-8, 570-2 My 29 '71

NATIONAL Catholic reporter
Appealing appeal; National Catholic reporter. S. J. Adamo. America 124:76 Ja 23 '71
Cartoonist Noonan urges boycott of National Catholic reporter. Chr Cent 88:740 Je 16 '71
Catholic editor fired. J. S. Tinney. Chr Today 15:35-6 Je 4 '71
Changeover. S. J. Adamo. America 125:47-8 Jl 24 '71
Hoyt dismissed as editor of Catholic weekly. Chr Cent 88:615 My 19 '71
NCR and the future. J. Deedy. Commonweal 93:538 Mr 5 '71

NATIONAL caucus on the black aged
New organization urges actions to aid black
aged. Aging 196:10 F '71
Why a National caucus on the black aged?
C. Coiro. il Har Yrs 11:12-18 N '71
NATIONAL center for space studies. See
France—National center for space studies
NATIONAL centre for the performing arts,
Bombay. See Bombay—National centre for
the performing arts
NATIONAL championship drag races. See Drag
racing
NATIONAL characteristics
Understand your overseas work force; with
folded charts. D. Sirota and J. M. Green-
wood. il Harvard Bsns R 49:53-60 Ja '71
NATIONAL characteristics, American; Na-
tional characteristics Israeli; etc. See
Americans; Israelis; etc.
NATIONAL characteristics in literature. See
Local color in literature.
NATIONAL cherry blossom festival. See
Washington, D.C.—National cherry blossom
festival
NATIONAL childrens book week. See Book
week
NATIONAL collegiate athletic association
All easterners aren't effete; NCAA indoor
championships in Detroit. P. Putnam. il
por Sports Illus 34:64+ Mr 22 '71
Ho, ho, ho went the jolly white giant; R.
Wanamaker 1970 NCAA decathlon cham-
pion. W. F. Reed. il por Sports Illus 34:
20-1 Je 21 '71
It's the Hoosier title wave; Indiana swim-
ming team at NCAA competitions. W. F.
Reed. il Sports Illus 34:28-30+ Mr 22 '71
NATIONAL commission on libraries and infor-
mation science. See United States—Nation-
al commission on libraries and information
science
NATIONAL commission on product safety. See
United States—National commission on prod-
uct safety
NATIONAL commission on teacher education
and professional standards
Governance is integral to accountability. L.
Williams. Todays Ed 60:59-60 Ap '71
NATIONAL commission on the causes and
prevention of violence. See United States—
National commission on the causes and pre-
vention of violence
NATIONAL committee for support of the pub-
lic schools
Public and its schools; reshaped NCSPS. J.
Cass. Sat R 54:61+ S 18 '71
NATIONAL committee of Black churchmen
Black manifesto revisited. G. S. Wilmore, jr.
Chr Cent 88:452-3 Ap 14 '71
Black power struggle. Chr Today 16:43 Ja 7
'72
NCBC: retooling for economic liberation. C.
Rogers. Chr Cent 88:1406-7 D 1 '71
NATIONAL committee on household employ-
ment
Farewell to Dinah: first national conference.
il Newsweek 78:67 Ag 2 '71
NATIONAL conference of Catholic bishops
Aftermath of Detroit. America 124:501-2 My
15 '71
Appeal to the bishops. Commonweal 94:155-6
Ap 23 '71
Backlash and the bishops. W. Wallace. Com-
monweal 94:253-4 My 21 '71
Bishops and just war. M. Bordelon. Amer-
ica 126:17-19 Ja 8 '72
Bishops and poverty; Campaign for human
development. J. Deedy. Commonweal 95:218
D 3 '71
Bishops at bay. il Time 97:69 My 10 '71
Bishops call for educational tax credits, end
to war. Chr Cent 88:1407 D 1 '71
Bishops in Detroit. Commonweal 94:251 My
21 '71
Bishops move; resolution on the Indochina
war. Newsweek 78:48 N 29 '71
Bishops open meetings, close pulpits. R.
Chandler. Chr Today 16:42 D 3 '71
Bishop's study: war no more. R. Chandler.
Chr Today 16:35-6 D 17 '71
For the bishops, a non-agenda. J. Over-
brook. Commonweal 95:148-9 N 12 '71
Krol era. por Time 98:66 N 29 '71
Priest is as a priest does. K. L. Woodward.
il Newsweek 77:74-5 My 10 '71
Priestly problems. R. Chandler. Chr Today
15:44-5 My 21 '71
Synod and the study; NORC study of the
American priesthood. Commonweal 94:205-6
My 7 '71
Tightening their cinctures; with editorial
comment. J. Overbrook. Commonweal 95:
243, 245-6 D 10 '71
NATIONAL conference of Catholic charities
Help poor fight oppression. Catholic con-
ferees told. Chr Cent 88:1223 O 20 '71

NATIONAL conference on composting and
waste recycling
National conference on composting, waste
recycling will be held May 20-21, 1971 in
Denver. Org Gard & Farm 18:50-1 Mr '71
NATIONAL conference on social welfare
Welfare-industrial complex. M. Gruber. Na-
tion 212:808-11 Je 28 '71
NATIONAL congress for recreation and parks.
See Congress for recreation and parks
NATIONAL congress of parents and teachers
How we stand. E. Mallory. PTA Mag 66:15
N '71
Inaugural; remarks, May 26, 1971. E. Mallory.
por PTA Mag 66:16-17 S '71
PTA people of the month. pors PTA Mag 66:
16-17 D '71
NATIONAL consumers' union. See Consumer
protection
NATIONAL conventions (political)
National conventions, where and when.
U S News 71:25 Ag 2 '71
Will courts decide makeup of '72 conven-
tions? il U S News 71:74-6 O 18 '71
NATIONAL conventions, Democratic
Back to Chicago? New Repub 164:15 F 20 '71
Democrats in '72; questions before the
O'Hara commission. New Repub 164:13 Ja
2 '71
Democrats open the door. S. C. Brightman.
Nation 212:552-5 My 3 '71
Democrats: trying for party reform. il Time
98:17-19 D 6 '71
Dilemma of the lesser Democrats. K. Bode.
New Repub 165:14-16 D 25 '71
Round 1 to the regulars; choosing a chair-
man of Credentials committee. il por Time
98:13 O 25 '71
Those damned rules. Nation 213:420 N 1 '71
Why a black man should run. H. Romaine.
Nation 213:264-8 S 27 '71
NATIONAL conventions, Republican
Commuter's convention site. il Newsweek
78:18 Ag 2 '71
President picks a place: San Diego, Calif.
il Time 98:15-16 Ag 2 '71
San Diego backs into a smoke-filled room;
bid for 1972 Republican convention. il Bsns
W p23 Jl 10 '71
NATIONAL council distributive workers of
America. See Distributive workers of
America, National council of
NATIONAL council for the social studies
NCSS debates human condition in 50th meet-
ing; with summaries of addresses and ex-
cerpts from addresses by B. Ward and G.
Wald. il Sr Schol Teach ed 97:1-4 Ja 11 '71
NATIONAL council of architectural registration
boards
New look at registration and licensing. E. K.
Thompson. Arch Rec 150:9-10 S '71
NATIONAL council of Catholic laity
New NCCL faces prompt challenge. T.
Schick. il America 125:483-4 D 4 '71
NATIONAL council of churches
Bid to quiet NCC turned back; with editorial
comment. D. Kucharsky. Chr Today 15:
35, 44-5 F 12 '71
Colombian seminar: whose mission? R.
Chandler. Chr Today 15:35 My 7 '71
Conciliarism in America. Chr Cent 88:1125 S
29 '71
More power to the NCC! Chr Cent 88:179 F
10 '71
NCC: a rare rebuff. D. Kucharsky. Chr To-
day 15:34-5 Jl 2 '71
NCC on the boardwalk. A. Geyer. Chr Cent
88:791-2 Je 30 '71
NCC: upbeat in New Orleans. A. Geyer. Chr
Cent 88:1100 S 22 '71
New Orleans compromise. D. Kucharsky. Chr
Today 16:44+ O 8 '71
So long to SOHAM. Chr Cent 88:1223 O 20
'71
Who's listening to lay people? NCC project.
Chr Cent 88:943 Ag 11 '71

Corporate information center
Pacifist portfolios? investments in companies
with defense contracts. il Time 99:52 Ja 17
'72

NATIONAL council of senior citizens, inc.
NCSC re-elects Cruikshank, urges WHCOA
every 3 years. il por Aging 201:9-10 Jl '71
NATIONAL council of teachers of English
NCTE and politics. J. E. Miller, jr. Engl J
60:508-9 Ap '71
NCTE counciletter. R. A. Bennett. Engl J
60:1131-2 N '71
NCTE issues criteria to combat racism and
bias in texts. Library J 96:1070 Mr 15 '71
NCTE; 1971; address, November 1970. R. A.
Bennett. Engl J 60:455-7 Ap '71

NATIONAL council of teachers of English
—*Continued*
New guidelines against racism in textbooks.
R. H. Smith; reply. R. F. Hogan. Pub W
199:32-3 F 1 '71
Preliminary program; 61st annual meeting.
Engl J 60:963-1002 O '71
NATIONAL council of the Metropolitan opera
association. See Metropolitan opera nation-
al council
NATIONAL council on the aging
Imperatives on aging. W. C. Fitch. Har Yrs
11:54-5 Ag '71
Organizations meet with NCOA, discuss pos-
sible action roles. il Aging 199:8 My '71
See also
National institute of senior centers
NATIONAL dairy products corporation. See
Kraftco corporation
NATIONAL dance company of Morocco. See
Dancing, Moroccan
NATIONAL debt (United States) See Debts,
Public—United States
NATIONAL defense
See also subhead Defenses under names
of countries, e.g. United States—Defenses
NATIONAL democratic party. See Political
parties—Germany (Federal Republic)
NATIONAL distillers and chemical corporation
Accident-prone. il Forbes 107:36+ My 1 '71
NATIONAL distribution services, inc.
Eastern forms logistics concern. Aviation W
95:65 S 27 '71
NATIONAL education association
After all: NEA and integration. Todays Ed
60:80 N '71
Are myths about misses amiss? Report says
yes. il Sr Schol 99:12-13 O 25 '71
Con con; constitutional convention. P. M.
Connelly. Todays Ed 60:57 My '71
Meet NEA president Donald Morrison; inter-
view. D. Morrison. pors Todays Ed 60:50-3
S '71
NEA candidates to be voted on in Detroit.
il Todays Ed 60:52-3 My '71
NEA special services. See issues of Today's
education
NEA's concerns in the new Congress. Todays
Ed 60:33 Ja '71
Proposed amendments to the NEA bylaws.
Todays Ed 60:74-9 Ap '71
Target; NEA's report. Schools for the '70's
and beyond. H. J. Langer. Sat R 54:75 F 20
'71
Update; report of the NEA Task force on
environmental education. Todays Ed 60:
33-48 S '71
What do you want from NEA? symposium.
il por Todays Ed 60:26-9+ Ja '71
See also
National commission on teacher education
and professional standards
National training laboratories

**Association for educational communi-
cation and technology**
Librarians & AECT. E. Geller. il Library J
96:1749, 1771-4+ My 15 '71; Discussion. 96:
2805-6 S 15 '71
NATIONAL educational finance project. See
School finance
NATIONAL educational television network
Current cinema; Channel 13-WNET series:
The silent years. P. Kael. New Yorker 47:
183 N 6 '71
Great scissors debate. R. L. Shayon. Sat R
54:68 D 4 '71
Musical events; NET opera theatre broad-
cast of Offenbach's Tales of Hoffmann. W.
Sargeant. New Yorker 47:158+ D 11 '71
Musical events; NET opera theatre produc-
tion, Monteverdi's Orfeo. W. Sargeant. New
Yorker 46:90 Ja 30 '71
New lift for the weary tube. C. Irving. il Mc-
Calls 98:14+ My '71
PBS, NET and the FBI. il Newsweek 78:127
O 18 '71
Taping Le rossignol for television. J.
Hiemenz. il Hi Fi 21:71-3 N '71
NATIONAL electronic associations
NEA state association presidents. Electr
World 86:55 Ag '71
NATIONAL endowment for the humanities.
See United States—National foundation on
the arts and the humanities
NATIONAL evangelical congress of Australia.
See Religious conferences—Australia
NATIONAL farm bureau federation. See Amer-
ican farm bureau federation
NATIONAL farmers organization
NFO takes on the world. C. Koch. Farm J
95:50 F '71
NFO's new floor price contract. Farm J 95:
29 S '71
Why farmers "forget" their farm organiza-
tion dues; ed. by B. Coffman. Farm J 95:
22C Jl '71

NATIONAL federation of Christian life com-
munities
Christian life communities, 1971. G. Hekker.
America 125:150-1 S 11 '71
NATIONAL federation of priests' councils
Catholic priests federation urges broad church
reforms. Chr Cent 88:39-8 Mr 31 '71
NFPC's celibacy stand. J. C. Haughey. Amer-
ica 124:341-3 Ap 3 '71; Discussion. 124:441-
2 My 1 '71
Priest power in Baltimore. J. J. Egan. Com-
monweal 94:101-2 Ap 9 '71
NATIONAL field trials. See Field trials (dogs)
NATIONAL flying farmers association. See
International flying farmers (association)
NATIONAL folk ballet of Korea. See Dancing,
Korean
NATIONAL football league
Battle for the bodies. il Time 97:60 F 8 '71
Goodby to the alka-seltzer and aspirin bowl;
NFL the prouder. T. Maule. Sports Illus
34:50-1 F 1 '71
How to win while losing; playoff system.
Newsweek 79:58-9 Ja 3 '72
NATIONAL football league players association
Owners can be tackled, too; NFL players
vs management. G. S. Brown. il Sports Il-
lus 34:18-21 Mr 22 '71
NATIONAL forest service. See United States
—Forest service
NATIONAL forests
Across the canal & into the trees. M. Frome.
Field & S 75:46+ Ap '71
Alaska's Tongass suit: the exercise at Juneau.
M. Miller. il Am For 77:28-31+ Mr '71
Big Scrub makes the grade: Ocala national
forest. C. E. Randall. il Am For 77:28-31+
N '71
Bitter tea in the Bitterroot. J. B. Craig. Am
For 77:10 F '71
Clearcutting the National forests; misuse
and abuse of public lands. M. Frome. Field
& S 76:32+ Jl '71
Crisis of our national forests; Bitterroot
national forest, Mont. J. N. Miller. il Read
Digest 99:91-6 D '71
Fight for the trees in the Tongass. M. Mil-
ler. il Am For 77:16-19 Jl '71
Hiawatha national forest by the big-sea-
water. C. E. Randall. il Am For 77:32-5+
Mr '71
If you plan to cross Nevada in sweltering
August, here's the great place to cool off;
Wheeler Peak scenic area in Humboldt
national forest. il Sunset 147:44-7 Ag '71
Mike Frome; Bolle report on timber cutting
in Bitterroot national forest. M. Frome.
Am For 77:5+ Ja '71
Mining the national forests; findings of the
Bolle committee on the Bitterroot national
forest. D. A. Burk. il Nation 212:110-13 Ja
25 '71
Montana versus the mining companies; new
awakening or impractical idealism? R. H.
Gilluly. il Sci N 100:235-7 O 2 '71
Montana's select committee; studying man-
agement practices on the Bitterroot na-
tional forest. J. B. Craig. il por Am For
77:35-7+ F '71
National forests in danger? a growing dis-
pute; clearcutting. il U S News 70:48-9
My 3 '71
New Hampshire's Great Gulf, a wilderness
area in trouble; White Mountain national
forest. J. H. Cravens. il Am For 77:30-2+
S '71
On the fireline; Wenatchee, Wash, national
forest. D. Foraker. il por Seventeen 30:42+
Ag '71
President's Quetico-Superior committee. Liv
Wildn 34:54-8 Wint '70
Regional forester bites the bullet; land man-
agement practices in the Bitterroot nation-
al forest. N. M. Rahm. il por Am For 77:
38-9+ F '71
Senator looks at forestry; Monongahela na-
tional forest, W.Va. J. Randolph. il por Am
For 77:12-15+ Ja '71
Stump merchants; timbering Alaska's nation-
al forests. S. Roberson. Field & S 75:16+
Mr '71
Superior forest. C. E. Randall. il Am For 77:
26-7+ S '71
Timber mining: accusation or prospect? R.
W. Behan. il Am For 77:4-6+ N '71
Warning: the chain saw cometh; Tongass
national forest. P. Brooks. il Atlan 228:95-
9 D '71
See also
National parks and reserves—United States

NATIONAL forests—*Continued*

Roads

Across the canal & into the trees. M. Frome. Field & S 75:46+ Ap '71

Death row; Joyce Kilmer's forest; Nantahala national forest. G. Laycock. Audubon 73:107 Ja '71

Who needs the Clark's Fork Canyon road? Shoshone national forest. V. Huser. il Am For 77:24-7 D '71

Wreckreation in our national forests. R. B. Ditton. il Parks & Rec 6:22-6+ Je '71

NATIONAL foundation for higher education (proposed) See United States—National foundation for higher education (proposed)

NATIONAL foundation on the arts and the humanities. See United States—National foundation on the arts and the humanities

NATIONAL gallery of art, Washington, D.C.
Auguste Rodin affair. K. Kuh. il Sat R 54: 22-3 D 25 '71
New monument; extension of gallery. il Time 97:83 My 17 '71

NATIONAL geographic magazine
Photo education; annual seminar for staff photographers. E. Scully. Mod Phot 35:48+ My '71

NATIONAL geographic society
Mississippi odyssey begins 1971-72 series of special publications. M. M. Payne. il Nat Geog 139:882-6 Je '71

NATIONAL goals. See United States

NATIONAL guard (United States) See United States—National guard

NATIONAL health insurance. See Insurance, Health

NATIONAL health; or, Nurse Norton's affair; drama. See Nichols. P

NATIONAL highway traffic safety administration. See United States—National highway traffic safety administration

NATIONAL holidays. See Holidays

NATIONAL holiness association. See Christian holiness association

NATIONAL horse snow. See Horse shows

NATIONAL hot rod association
NHRA then and now; with introd. by Wally Parks. il Hot Rod 24:62-3 Jl '71

NATIONAL hurricane center. See United States—National weather service

NATIONAL industrial pollution control council. See United States—National industrial pollution control council

NATIONAL institute of arts and letters
Holding the fort on Audubon Terrace. M. Cowley. il Sat R 54:17+ Ap 3 '71

NATIONAL institute of economic and social research, London
Vindication of a British think tank. Bsns W p76-7 S 4 '71

NATIONAL institute of education (proposed) See United States—National institute of education (proposed)

NATIONAL institute of mental health. See United States—National institute of mental health

NATIONAL institute of neurological diseases and stroke. See United States—National institute of neurological diseases and stroke

NATIONAL institute of senior centers
NCOA senior center institute founded: Leo Laks named head. Aging 199:9 My '71

NATIONAL institute of student opinion. See Scholastic research center

NATIONAL institutes of health. See United States—National institutes of health

NATIONAL jousting championship. See Tournaments

NATIONAL labor relations board. See United States—National labor relations board

NATIONAL lead company. See NL industries, inc.

NATIONAL league of cities
Self-help and the cities. il pors Nations Bsns 59:22-6 Je '71

NATIONAL libraries. See Libraries, National

NATIONAL library week
NLW office arranges regional workshops. Pub W 200:28-9 S 20 '71
NLW poster protest: letters to the editor. il Library J 96:760, 1548 Mr 1, My 1 '71
Spring, National library week, and an observer come to small-town library, U.S.A. (W.Va); or, Seed money, grass-roots, and the greening of the American library dream. A. Plotnik. il Wilson Lib Bul 45:932-40 Je '71

NATIONAL library week poster. See Posters

NATIONAL livestock feeders association
Big man for a big job; O. Bredthauer. W. Kester. pors Farm J 95:B-5 My '71
Livestock feeders ask expanded market service. Farm J 95:B15 Ap '71

NATIONAL medal of science
National medal of science winners. Science 171:464 F 5 '71

NATIONAL minorities. See Minorities

NATIONAL monuments
See also names of national monuments, e.g. Katmai National Monument

NATIONAL morale. See Morale, National

NATIONAL municipal league
See also
All-America cities

NATIONAL Negro evangelical association
NNEA: important crossroads. V. W. Murray. Chr Today 15:37 My 7 '71

NATIONAL ocean survey. See United States—National ocean survey

NATIONAL oceanic and atmospheric administration. See United States—National oceanic and atmospheric administration

NATIONAL opera association
NOA, COS conferences. R. Mercer. Opera N 36:41 D 25 '71

NATIONAL opinion research center
Attitudes toward racial integration. A. M. Greeley and P. B. Sheatsley. il Sci Am 225:13-19 bibliog(p 120) D '71

NATIONAL panorama of conservation action. See Exhibitions, Traveling

NATIONAL parents and teachers association. See National congress of parents and teachers

NATIONAL park personnel
Telling it like it is, or was. D. B. Huyck. il Am For 77:16-19+ Je '71

NATIONAL park safety. See National parks and reserves—United States—Safety devices and measures

NATIONAL park service (United States) See United States—National park service

NATIONAL parks and conservation association
Report of the president and general counsel, May 20, 1971. A. W. Smith. Nat Parks & Con Mag 45:23-6 My '71

NATIONAL parks and reserves
See also
Marine parks and reserves
Wilderness areas

Africa, East
Elephants are hard on trees. F. Heyward. il Am For 77:24-7+ Je '71

Alaska
See also
Katmai National Monument
Mount McKinley National Park

California
See also
Pinnacles National Monument
Point Reyes National Seashore
Redwood National Park
Yosemite National Park

Canada
Grandeur and the glory of Canada's mountain parks. P. Friggens. il Read Digest 99: 140-6 Jl '71
North to Canada's grand mountain parks. il Sunset 146:74-9 Je '71
Telling it like it is, or was. D. B. Huyck. il Am For 77:16-19+ Je; 24-7 Jl '71
See also
Algonquin Provincial Park

Colorado
See also
Rocky Mountain National Park

England
England's New Forest. J. A. Maxtone-Graham. il Am For 77:22-5+ S '71
National parks in England and Wales. R. Eagle. il Liv Wildn 34:33-7 Aut '70

Florida
See also
Everglades National Park

Hawaii
Do Hawaiian parks double as goat hunting preserves. Nat Parks & Con Mag 45:32-3 Je '71
See also
Haleakala National Park
Hawaii Volcanoes National Park

Maine
See also
Acadia National Park

Maryland
See also
Chesapeake and Ohio Canal National Historical Park

NATIONAL parks and reserves—*Continued*

Massachusetts
See also
Cape Cod National Seashore

Nevada
See also
Lehman Caves National Monument

New Mexico
See also
Carlsbad Caverns National Park
White Sands National Monument

Oklahoma
See also
Platt National Park

Pennsylvania
See also
Gettysburg National military park
Independence National Historical Park

South Dakota
See als
Wind Cave National Park

Tanzania
Close in among the elephants; Lake Manyara National Park; with editorial comment. I. Douglas-Hamilton. il Life 71:1, 40-8 Ag 6 '71

Texas
See also
Big Bend National Park

United States
Congressional flight on a fragile spacecraft. L. K. Lee. il Parks & Rec 6:22-4+ Mr '71
Ecosystems of national parks. D. B. Houston. bibliog Science 172:648-51 My 14 '71
Human injury inflicted by grizzly bears. S. Herrero; discussion. Science 171:431-3 F 5 '71
Is the national parks movement anti-urban? P. Marcuse. il Parks & Rec 6:16-21+ Jl '71
Kauai, nature's paradise. G. A. Randorf. il Liv Wildn 35:20-3 Spr '71
Last chance for the tall grass prairie; push to create a national park in the Flint Hills area. L. Payton. il Nat Wildlife 9:25-7 Ag '71
Matter of life or death. J. L. Hecht. Parks & Rec 6:39-40+ Mr '71
National parks and conservation association; report of the president and general counsel, May 20, 1971. A. W. Smith. Nat Parks & Con Mag 45:23-6 My '71
National parks are concentrations of photo fun. F. Rohr. il Travel 135:75-7 My '71
Parks. A. W. Smith. Nat Parks & Con Mag 45:2+ My '71
Parks under siege. Newsweek 78:47 Jl 19 '71
Pristine preserves or popcorn playgrounds? G. Hill. il Sat R 55:40-1+ Ja 1 '72
Tallgrass Prairie National Park. E. R. Hall. il Am For 77:16-21 D '71
Tallgrass prairie park. A. Bohling. il Nat Parks & Con Mag 45:6-10 Mr '71
Teen travel talk. il Seventeen 29:58 Ag '70
Telling it like it is, or was. D. B. Huyck. il Am For 77:16-19+ Je '71 (to be cont)
Who's minding the store? Parks & Rec 6:27 O '71
Why not sell the national parks? E. Dolan. Nat R 23:362-5 Ap 6 '71
Youth camp safety act. A. Ribicoff. por Parks & Rec 6:23+ S '71
See also
United States—National park service
also names of national parks and reserves, e.g. Great Smokey Mountains National Park

Roads
See also
National forests—Roads

Safety devices and measures
Postscript to tragedy: a father's crusade. M. Cohen. il Redbook 137:76-7+ Je '71

Trails
Kaibab Trail is open again. il Sunset 146:36 Je '71
Out trail. E. A. Shead. Nat Parks & Con Mag 45:11 Ja '71

Utah
See also
Arches National Monument
Canyonlands National Park

Virginia
See also
Wolf Trap Farm Park for the performing arts

Wales
National parks in England and Wales. R. Eagle. il Liv Wildn 34:33-7 Aut '70

Washington (state)
See also
Mount Rainier National Park
North Cascades National Park
Olympic National Park

Wyoming
See also
Grand Teton National Park
Yellowstone National Park

NATIONAL planning

United States
See United States—Social policy
NATIONAL playwrights conference. See Authors conferences
NATIONAL press club
Breakfast with Budge. Newsweek 78:64-5 Jl 26 '71
Open sesame! women journalists. S. McBee. McCalls 98:45 Jl '71
NATIONAL program for educational leadership
New path to educational leadership. B. Gifford. Am Ed 7:9-12 D '71
NATIONAL railroad passenger corporation
All set now: new service for rail passengers. U S News 70:79 F 8 '71
Amtrak: the need for a hard sell. il Bsns W p 19 My 8 '71
Amtrak's one-way ticket to the dole. il Newsweek 78:69 D 20 '71
Astro or Castro. Nation 212:485-6 Ap 19 '71
Bickering starts on the Railpax line. Bsns W p37 Ap 17 '71
Coming: a new era for train buffs. il U S News 70:29 My 3 '71
Controversial travel plan. il U S News 70:56-7 Ap 5 '71
Future of passenger trains; interview. B. F. Biaggini. il por U S News 72:44-8 Ja 3 '72
How to run a railroad: Amtrak learns the hard way. il U S News 71:42-4 Ag 30 '71
Is 1971 your year to discover or rediscover the railroad adventure? il Sunset 146:100-5 My '71
Off the rails. New Repub 164:9 Ap 10 '71
On the track: Railpax vobiscum. D. Butwin. por Sat R 54:80-3 Ja 23 '71
Over the mountains with Amtrak. Sunset 147:70+ N '71
Rail trends spur airline concern. H. D. Watkins. Aviation W 95:26-7 N 1 '71
Railroads by Railpax. il Sr School 98:15-16 Ap 19 '71
That lonesome road. il Forbes 108:34-5 N 15 '71
NATIONAL reading council. See United States—National reading council
NATIONAL recreation and park association
Crash funding won't do it! C. M. Pendleton, jr. il Parks & Rec 6:39-41+ Ap '71
Dwight F. Rettie to head NRPA. por Parks & Rec 6:13 S '71
NRPA news. See issues of Parks & recreation
Trustees in the news. por Parks & Rec 6:122 Ja '71
See also
Congress for recreation and parks
NATIONAL recreation vehicle exposition. See Recreational vehicles—Exhibitions
NATIONAL register of scientific and technical personnel
Manpower: federal register of scientists discontinued. R. Gillette. Science 174:42-4 O 1 '71
Parting look at the National register. S. Barisch. il Phys Today 24:40-3+ O '71
NATIONAL research council
Equinoxial rites of the National research council. W. Goldschmidt. Science 174:474-6 O 29 '71
NRC auto emissions study: scope too limited? Sci N 100:224 O 2 '71
National research council: and how it got that way. J. Walsh. Science 172:242-6 Ap 16 '71
National research council: answering the right questions? J. Walsh. Science 172:353-7 Ap 23 '71
San Fernando earthquake study: NRC panel sees premonitory lessons. R. Gillette and J. Walsh. Science 172:140-3 Ap 9 '71

Highway research board
Transportation. Sci N 99:82 Ja 30 '71
NATIONAL responsibility. See Responsibility

NATIONAL review (periodical)
Buckley papers; W. F. Buckley's hoax.
  Newsweek 78:21-2 Ag 2 '71
Buckley's prank. por Time 98:43 Ag 2 '71
National review papers. W. F. Buckley, jr.
  Nat R 23:850 Ag 10 '71
Notes & asides: press comments on the
  Buckley papers, ed. by W. F. Buckley, jr.
  Nat R 23:852-4 Ag 10 '71
Opinion on the campus; analysis of, and com-
  mentary on questions and responses of
  poll. il Nat R 23:635-50 Je 15 '71
Ten years in the wrong direction. A. H.
  Leitch. Chr Today 15:55-6 S 10 '71
Week's journal. W. F. Buckley, jr. New
  Yorker 47:36-43+ Ag 21; 36-42+ Ag 28 '71
NATIONAL safety council
National safety council's accident-prevention
  checklist. il Parents Mag 46:52 N '71
NATIONAL school lunch program. See School
  lunches
NATIONAL science board. See United States
  —National science board
NATIONAL science foundation. See United
  States—National science foundation
NATIONAL security. See Internal security
NATIONAL security council. See United States
  —National security council
NATIONAL service, Non-military. See Service,
  Compulsory non-military
NATIONAL shooting dog championship. See
  Field trials (dogs)
NATIONAL ski patrol system
National ski patrol. H. A. Berkman. il Cons
  26:20-1 D '71
NATIONAL socialism
Diary of a man in despair, by F. P. Reck-
  Malleczewen. Review
  New Yorker 46:92-5 Ja 30 '71. R. Coles
German dictatorship, by K. D. Bracher. Re-
  view
  Commonweal 95:355-7 Ja 14 '72. J. Ratte
  Nat R 23:600-1 Je 1 '71. F. Oppenheimer
  Nation 212:151-2 F 1 '71. C. L. Markmann
Ideology and policy. L. S. Dawidowicz. Com-
  mentary 52:91-3 Ag '71
In Hitler's service. L. S. Dawidowicz; dis-
  cussion. Commentary 51:32+ Mr '71
Psychohistorical origins of the Nazi youth
  cohort. P. Loewenberg. bibliog f il Am
  Hist R 76:1457-502 D '71

Anecdotes, facetiae, satire, etc.
Schmeed memoirs. W. Allen. New Yorker
  47:36-7 Ap 17 '71
NATIONAL songs

United States
See also
Star spangled banner (song)
NATIONAL sporting goods association fishing
  schools program. See Fishing—Study and
  teaching
NATIONAL standard company
In the eye of the storm; production of radial-
  type wire. il Forbes 108:64 D 1 '71
NATIONAL starch and chemical corporation
Specialized profits. A. A. Butkus. por Duns
  98:48-9 D '71
NATIONAL steel corporation
See also
Stran-steel corporation
NATIONAL street rod association. See Auto-
  mobile clubs
NATIONAL student marketing corporation
Funny money game, by A. Tobias. Review
  Bsns W p8 D 25 '71. J. Madrick
NATIONAL tenants organization
Rise of tenant organizations. P. Marcuse.
  Nation 213:50-3 Jl 19 '71
NATIONAL therapeutic recreation society
Therapeutic recreation; charts. il Parks &
  Rec 6:57-61 Ag '71
NATIONAL tourism resources review com-
  mission. See United States—National tour-
  ism resources review commission
NATIONAL training laboratories
Teacher and the T-group; NTL's Center for
  the development of educational leadership.
  C. H. Harrison. il Schol Teach Jr/Sr High
  p6-7+ F 1 '71
NATIONAL trust for historic preservation
New era in preservation. H. B. Byrd. il Nat
  Parks & Con Mag 45:21-2+ My '71
Now, historic homes for rent. il U S News
  70:34-6 Mr 22 '71
Saving old buildings, and money, too. il Na-
  tions Bsns 59:49 Je '71
NATIONAL urban coalition. See Urban coali-
  tion (organization)

NATIONAL urban league
America mourns Whitney M. Young jr; with
  editorial comment. S. Booker. il pors Ebony
  26:31-4+, 144 My '71
King of bridge. por Time 97:20 Mr 22 '71
Man at the bridge. por Time 97:25 Je 28 '71
Whitney Young: he was a doer. il por News-
  week 77:29 Mr 22 '71
Whitney Young's open society; address, April
  1971, with questions and answers. H. R.
  Sims. Ann Am Acad 396:70-8 Jl '71
NATIONAL weather service. See United States
  —National weather service
NATIONAL welfare rights organization
We're gonna get angry; annual convention.
  Newsweek 78:26 Ag 9 '71
NATIONAL wildlife (periodical)
Forgive us our trespasses. il Nat Wildlife 9:
  16 Je '71
NATIONAL wildlife federation
Death hovers over Santeeland; South Car-
  olina public service authority vs the forces
  of conservation. J. Rutherfoord. Field &
  S 76:124+ Je '71
1971 EQ index. il Nat Wildlife 9:25-40 O '71
They were the spirit of the summit. A. D.
  MacConomy. il Nat Wildlife 9:40-2 F '71
War against pollution rages on; 35th an-
  nual convention. il Nat Wildlife 9:34-5 Je
  '71
NATIONAL wildlife refuge system. See Wild-
  life sanctuaries
NATIONAL women's political caucus
Never underestimate... il Newsweek 78:29
  Jl 26 '71
Women's Political caucus: what it is, what
  it wants. il U S News 71:67-8 Ag 16 '71
NATIONALISM
Development of nationalism and the national-
  ism of development; address, February 18,
  1971. R. McClintock. Dept State Bul 64:522-
  8 Ap 19 '71
Does a bell toll for the nation-state? J. V.
  Schall. il America 125:59-63 Ag 7 '71
Jesus and nationalism. J. W. Oliver. Chr To-
  day 15:18-19 Ap 9 '71
See also subhead Nationalism under
  names of continents, countries, etc. e.g.
  Libya—Nationalism; also under groups of
  people, e.g. Jews—Nationalism
NATIONALIZATION of industry. See Govern-
  ment ownership
NATIONS
Facts & figures of nations & states: tables
  (cont) Sr Schol 99:15-18 O 4 '71
NATIVE races
See also subhead Native races under
  names of countries, continents, etc. e.g.
  Philippines—Native races
NATIVITY of Christ. See Jesus Christ—Na-
  tivity
NATO
Foreign policy: Mansfield's rebellion. il por
  Newsweek 77:18-19 My 24 '71
Letter from Washington. R. S. Rovere. New
  Yorker 47:122+ Je 5 '71
NATO seeks Phase 3 satellite proposals.
  Aviation W 95:58 Ag 23 '71
NATO seeks to revitalize defenses. D. E.
  Fink. Aviation W 94:55-6 Mr 22 '71
Nato today; the Russian threat; address,
  September 2, 1971. A. J. Goodpaster.
  Vital Speeches 37:743-9 O 1 '71
New economic program: western Europe;
  address, September 14, 1971. M. Mansfield.
  Vital Speeches 38:4-7 O 15 '71
North Atlantic council meets at Lisbon;
  text of final communique, June 4, 1971.
  Dept State Bul 64:819-21 Je 28 '71
North Atlantic council ministerial meeting
  held at Brussels; Secretary Rogers' arrival
  statement, December 2, 1970 and message
  from President Nixon; with text of com-
  munique and annex. W. P. Rogers; R. M.
  Nixon. Dept State Bul 64:1-6 Ja 4 '71
Our permanent interests in Europe; address,
  December 1, 1971; with questions and
  answers. W. P. Rogers. Dept State Bul 65:
  693-702 D 20 '71
Pros and cons of NATO troop withdrawal.
  il Time 97:18 My 24 '71
Quakes, science and NATO. Sci N 99:383-4 Je
  5 '71
Secretary gratified at decision of Senate on
  NATO forces; statement, May 15, 1971.
  W. P. Rogers. Dept State Bul 64:740-1 Je
  7 '71
Secretary Rogers interviewed on Meet the
  press; program, May 16, 1971. W. P. Rogers. Dept State Bul 64:734-40 Je 7 '71
Secretary Rogers pays tribute to the NATO
  alliance; excerpt from remarks, December
  10, 1970. W. P. Rogers. Dept State Bul 64:6-
  7 Ja 4 '71

NATO—*Continued*
  Soviet threat to NATO's northern flank. il
    Time 98:39 O 18 '71
  United States, our NATO allies, and the So-
    viet Union in an era of changing foreign
    relations; address, February 19, 1971. U.
    A. Johnson. Dept State Bul 64:315-27 Mr 15
    '71
  Weapons training center for Crete urged; air
    weapons training center to complement
    NATO missile firing installation. il Avia-
    tion W 96:62-3 Ja 10 '72
  Western explorer heads for Moscow; mission
    of M. Brosio. il por Time 98:38+ O 18 '71

Armed forces

  Great trip-wire delusion; American presence.
    A. Cranston. Sat R 54:14 Je 19 '71
  Mansfield ruckus. Nation 212:675-6 My 31 '71
  NATO: a taste of Soviet wine; meeting in
    Lisbon to discuss mutual and balanced force
    reductions. il Time 97:16-17 Je 7 '71
  NATO and United States security interests;
    statement, October 14, 1971. M. J. Hillen-
    brand. Dept State Bul 65:518-21 N 8 '71
  NATO force modernization aided. D. E. Fink.
    Aviation W 95:14 D 20 '71
  NATO talks about talks; annual meeting. il
    Newsweek 77:42 Je 14 '71
  NATO: the bargaining begins; troop-reduc-
    tion talks. il Time 97:32+ Je 14 '71
  NATO troops; Senate rejection of Mansfield
    resolution. New Repub 164:11 My 29 '71
  Old warriors rally round. H. Sidey. Life 70:4
    Je 11 '71
  Sledgehammer; lobby to reduce America's
    troop commitments. il Newsweek 77:16-17
    My 31 '71
  Still a bumpy road to detente; mutual and
    balanced force reductions. A. de Borch-
    grave. il Newsweek 78:28 S 6 '71
  Troop balance: NATO vs. Warsaw pact. il
    Newsweek 77:27+ My 31 '71
  Who would ever have thought it? M. Mans-
    field's demand for troop withdrawal. M.
    McGrory. America 124:585 Je 5 '71
  Why U.S. forces will stay in Europe. il U S
    News 70:20 My 31 '71

Committee on the challenges of modern society

  Mr Train named to NATO committee on the
    challenges of modern society; White House
    announcement. Dept State Bul 64:197 F
    15 '71

NATURAL areas. See Wilderness areas
NATURAL childbirth. See Childbirth
NATURAL cosmetics. See Cosmetics
NATURAL disaster warning system. See
    United States—National weather service
NATURAL feeds. See Feeding and feeding
    stuffs
NATURAL forms
  Go now and look for beauty; excerpt from
    The seeing eye. V. B. Scheffer. il Nat
    Wildlife 9:8-12 Ag '71
    See also
  Found objects
NATURAL gas. See Gas, Natural
NATURAL gas industry. See Gas industry
NATURAL history
  Naturalist at large. See issues of Natural
    history
    See also
  Nature study

Study and teaching

    See also
  Nature study
NATURAL history museums
  Museum joins the forest service; Ghost ranch
    museum, Abiquiu, N.Mex. F. A. Tinker. il
    por Am For 77:32-5 My '71
    See also
  American museum of natural history, New
    York
NATURAL resources
  Tomorrow a wasteland? E. Flattau. Sci
    Digest 70:22-6 N '71
    See also
  Conservation of resources
  Power resources
  Raw materials
  United Nations—Committee on natural re-
    sources
  Water supply
  Wildlife conservation

Bibliography

  Reading about resources. M. Bush. See is-
    sues of American forests

Conferences

  Sixth Natural resources conference held by
    United States and Japan; joint communi-
    que, September 3, 1971. Dept State Bul
    65:334-5 S 27 '71

Alaska

    See also
  Conservation of resources—Alaska

Cambodia

  Cambodia. W. A. Withington. bibliog il
    Focus 21:1-9 F '71

Canada

  Recent resource development. G. S. Tomkins.
    il Focus 21:8-12 Je '71

Indonesia

  First fruits. il Time 98:100+ N 22 '71
  Indonesia. W. Withington. bibliog il Focus
    21:1-9 My '71

Iran

  Iran. J. S. Haupert. il Focus 21:1-8 Ja '71

Japan

  Scramble for supplies. Time 97:80+ Mr 15 '71

Philippines

  Philippines. A. Cutshall. bibliog il Focus 21:
    1-9 Mr '71

Singapore

  Singapore. Y. M. Yeung. bibliog il Focus 21:
    1-8 Ap '71

United States

  Washington lookout. V. Trumbull. See issues
    of American forests
    See also
  Water supply—United States

Vietnam (Democratic Republic)

  Vietnam. il Focus 22:1-8 D '71

Vietnam (Republic)

  Vietnam. il Focus 22:1-8 D '71
NATURAL selection
  Fitting discrete probability distributions to
    evolutionary events. T. Uzzell and K. W.
    Corbin. bibliog il Science 172:1089-96 Je 11
    '71
    See also
  Struggle for existence
NATURAL steam. See Steam, Natural
NATURALISM (philosophy)
  Naturalism: philosophical smuggler. A. J.
    Hoover. Chr Today 15:12-14 Jl 2 '71
NATURALISTS
  Naturalist at large. See issues of Natural
    history
NATURE
  After the gold rush. C. Reich and D. Carroll.
    3d. Nat Parks & Con Mag 45:4-5 Ap '71
  Water, man, and nature, a portrait of the
    web of life; with photographs by E. Braun.
    D. Cavagnaro. il Am West 8:18-29 Ja '71
    See also
  Man—Influence on nature
  Outdoor life
  Smithsonian institution—Center for short-
    lived phenomena
  Wildlife
  Winter

Bibliography

  Books in review. See issues of Natural his-
    tory

Photographs

  Karsch kloseups. C. G. Karsch. Am For 77:
    6-7 Ag '71
  Nature's jewels. J. H. Carmichael, jr. Am
    For 77:44-5 Ja '71
  Nature's jewels. E. Cooper. Am For 77:44-5
    Mr '71
  Nature's jewels. D. M. Small. Am For 77:44-5
    F '71

Poetry

  Haiku: ancient poetry for today's ecology.
    G. Randorf. il Cons 26:8-13 D '71
NATURE (aesthetics)
  Alas for him who never sees; excerpt from
    address. W. A. Stevens. Read Digest
    99:103-4 O '71
  Alchemist and the phenomenologist. C.
    Nemser. bibliog il Art in Am 59:100-3 Mr '71
  Go now and look for beauty; excerpt from
    The seeing eye. V. B. Scheffer. il Nat
    Wildlife 9:8-12 Ag '71
NATURE and man. See Man—Influence on na-
    ture
NATURE centers
  Schylkill Valley nature center. B. Newbold.
    il Parks & Rec 6:14-18+ F '71

NATURE conservation
Endangered species. il Nat Parks & Con
Mag 45:25-8 Jl '71
NATURE forms. See Natural forms
NATURE in art
Conservationists find contemporary interest
in Bewick prints. P. Standard. il Pub W
199:60-2 Mr 8 '71
See also
Flowers in art
Landscape painting
NATURE in literature
See also
Animals in literature
NATURE in music. See Music—Themes, motives, etc.
NATURE in poetry
Poet's workshop. F. Trefethen. Writer 84:
20-3 S '71
NATURE of man. See Man
NATURE photography
Capturing captivating autumn's colorful contrasts. F. Rohr. il Travel 136:70-2 N '71
Everglades. P. Caulfield. il Pop Phot 68:82-7
F '71
For better outdoor pictures. T. Trueblood.
il Field & S 76:20+ Ag '71
Gallery: David Cavagnaro photograph of a
spider web and a glacial lake. Life 71:8-9
Jl 16 '71
Getting close to Mother Nature. F. Rohr.
Travel 135:74-6 Ap '71
Go now and look for beauty; excerpt from
The seeing eye. V. B. Scheffer. il Nat
Wildlife 9:8-12 Ag '71
See also
Photography—Landscapes
Photography of animals
Photography of birds
Photography of fishes
Photography of flowers, plants, trees, etc.
Photography of reptiles
NATURE prints. See Nature in art
NATURE protection. See Nature conservation
NATURE study
Achieving relevancy in nature programing.
R. C. Fenn. Camp Mag 43:24-5 Ap '71
Learning at the zoo; Phoenix zoo's children's
natural history and art program. F. J.
Turkowski. il Parks & Rec 6:25-6 N '71
Taking the classroom outdoors. B. Thomas.
il Parents Mag 46:48-9+ Ap '71
They were the spirit of the summit; plans for
two conservation summits in 1971 for members of National wildlife federation. A. D.
MacConomy. il Nat Wildlife 9:40-2 F '71
Unique lab: the little red schoolhouse. H. M.
Kinnear. il Am For 77:26-7+ N '71
Walk, look and learn. G. Randorf. il Cons
25:6-8 Ap '71
See also
Audubon nature camps
Camping—Educational aspects
Childrens gardens
Natural history museums
Nature centers
Outdoor education
NATURE trails. See Trails
NATURE trails for the blind. See Trails
NATURE writers. See Authors
NATZLER, Gertrud (Amon) See Natzler, O.
jt. artist
NATZLER, Otto, and Natzler, G. A.
Natzler retrospective exhibition. il Ceram
Mo 19:14-15 O '71 *
NAUGHTON, James M.
How the 2d best-informed man in the White
House briefs the 2d worst-informed group
in Washington. il pors N Y Times Mag p9+
My 30 '71
NAUGHTON, Patience Jarvis
We love you, pass it on . . . we love you, pass
it on . . ; story. Ladies Home J 88:78-9 F '71
NAUHEIM, Bob
Jamison Loop. il por Outdoor Life 147:80-3+
Je '71
NAUMAN, Bruce
Man of parts. D. Davis. il Newsweek 77:
70 Mr 1 '71 *
NAUSEA
See also
Motion sickness
NAUTICAL astronomy
See also
Navigation
NAUTICAL charts
How to read a marine chart. J. Roe. il Pop
Sci 198:86+ F '71
Notices to boatmen. See issues of Motor
boating & sailing
Strange harbors. T. Gibbs. il Motor B & S
127:50-3+ My '71

NAUTICAL education
See also
Training ships
NAUTICAL instruments
See also
Compass
Sextants
NAUTICAL tables. See Navigation—Tables
NAUTILUS
Sentimental mollusk: Chambered nautilus. A.
G. Melvin. il Hobbies 76:158-9 Ag '71
NAUVOO, Ill.
Mormon trails in the Midwest. S. Murdock. il
Travel 137:58-63+ Ja '72
NAVAHO Indians
Murder of the Southwest. A. M. Josephy,
jr. il Audubon 73:52-67 Jl '71
Navajo roundup, by L. Kelly. Review
Am West 8:49 Jl '71. R. H. Dillon
U.S. journal: Gallup, N.Mex; drunkenness.
C. Trillin. New Yorker 47:108+ S 25 '71
NAVAHO language

Study and teaching
IBM computer for Navajo language textbooks. il Sch & Soc 99:468-9 D '71
NAVAHO war, 1865. See Indians of North
America—Wars
NAVAJO Indian reservation. See Indians of
North America—Reservations
NAVAJO Indians. See Navaho Indians
NAVAL architects
Great yacht designers:
Clinton Crane. B. Robinson. il por Yachting 129:72+ F '71
Philip L. Rhodes. B. Robinson. il por
Yachting 129:66-7+ Je '71
NAVAL architecture
See also
Hulls (naval architecture)
Warships
Yachts—Design
NAVAL art and science
See also
Signals and signaling
NAVAL bases. See Navy yards and naval stations
NAVAL maneuvers
Culebran protest: what of the navy's peace
treaty with the islanders? S. Bliss. Chr
Cent 88:262-4 F 24 '71
Operation Rescue Culebra: islanders halt U.S.
navy; Operation Springboard. S. Bliss. Chr
Cent 88:235-7 F 17 '71
NAVAL museums
Kon Tiki, the Fram, and ancient Viking
ships in Oslo. il Sunset 146:42+ Ap '71
NAVAL power. See Sea power
NAVAL radio communication. See Radio communication, Naval
NAVAL stations. See Navy yards and naval
stations
NAVAL uniforms. See Uniforms, Naval
NAVASKY, Victor S.
In Washington, you just don't not return a
call from Abe Fortas. il pors N Y Times
Mag p7+ Ag 1 '71
NAVIES
See also
Sea power
NAVIGATION
Common-sense navigation. J. A. Emmett.
il Outdoor Life 147:38+ Je '71
Navigating by the stars. E. N. Wasserman.
il Yachting 129:62-3+ Ap '71
Strange harbors. T. Gibbs. il Motor B & S
127:50-3+ My '71
Techniques of eyeball navigation. J. Hart. il
Yachting 130:65+ N '71
Thick as pea soup: valuable tips from Europe
on coping with fog. D. M. H. Mellonie. il
Motor B & S 127:66-7 My '71
See also
Boats and boating
Compass
Nautical charts
Pilot guides
Radio in navigation
Sailing
Seamanship
Sextants
Signals and signaling
Television in navigation
United States power squadrons, inc.
Waterways
Yachts and yachting

Aids and devices
Speed curves. J. West. il Yachting 130:58-9+
Ag '71
See also
Radio in navigation
Television in navigation

NAVIGATION—*Continued*

Competitions
By the mark. B. Crabtree. See issues of Yachting
Control points. B. Crabtree. See issues of Yachting to June 1971
Navigation contest. J. D. Rowe. il Motor B & S 127:78+ M- '71
Piloting contests. W. R. Juettner. il Motor B & S 128:54-5+ Ag '71

History
Sailing by Caravel; age of discovery. F. Romero. il Américas 23:S7-10 O '71

Study and teaching
Tankers in the Alps: a school for skippers. R. Dyment. il Sea Front 17:72-5 Mr '71

Tables
H.O.229: new tables for an old task; sight reduction tables for marine navigation. il Motor B & S 127:102+ F '71

NAVIGATION (space flight)
How Apollo spacecraft find their way to the moon. il Space World H-5-89:16-22 My '71

NAVIGATION, Aerial
See also
Radio in aviation

Aids and devices
Eastern receives certification for R-Nav. il Aviation W 94:29-30 My 24 '71
New navaid system tested on 747. K. J. Stein. il Aviation W 95:49-51 Jl 5 '71
Safer, cheaper way to fly planes; area navigation. il Bsns W p62+ Ap 24 '71
System versus area navigation. R. L. Collins. il Flying 88:41-5 Mr '71
See also
Inertial guidance systems

NAVIGATION satellites. See Artificial satellites—Navigational use

NAVIS, Maida
One woman's war against poverty. C. Remsberg and B. Remsberg. il por Good H 173: 91+ O '71 •

NAVONE, John
Can Italian democracy survive? Commonweal 95:323-5 Ja 7 '72

NAVRATIL, James D.
Magnesium. bibliog il por Chem 44:6-10 My '71

NAVY yards and naval stations
East of Suez: start of a big base for U.S? British island of Diego Garcia in the Indian Ocean. il U S News 70:36 Ap 19 '71
Missiles in Cuba, 1970; Cienfuegos submarine base. G. H. Quester. For Affairs 49:493-506 Ap '71
New understanding: Soviet base on Cuba. Newsweek 77:33-4 Ja 18 '71
Soviet moves highlight Guantanamo role. C. Brownlow. il Aviation W 94:16-17 Ja 25 '71
U.S. navy stakes out the Indian Ocean: proposed base on Diego Garcia. il Bsns W p66 Mr 27 '71
U.S. to transfer Sangley Point naval station to the Philippines. Dept State Bul 64:60 Ja 11 '71

NAXALITES (organization) See Communist party (India)

NAYLOR, H. Kelly
State grants-in-aid for private community mental health programs. il Ment Hy 55:190-3 Ap '71

NAYLOR, Richard S.
Acadian orogeny: an abrupt and brief event. bibliog il Science 172:558-60 My 7 '71

NAZARÉ, Portugal
Nazaré: the fishing village that refuses to change. il Holiday 49:50-5 O '71

NAZISM. See National socialism

NDONGMO, Albert, bp
Africa's dangerous precedent: sentencing Catholic bishops. O. Okite. Chr Today 15: 45-6 F 26 '71 •
Bishop in the dock. America 124:60 Ja 23 '71 •

NE reveillez pas madame; drama. See Anouilh, J.

NEAL, Dorothy Patricia
Telephone operator. ed. by K. Lasson. il Atlan 228:74-8 O '71

NEAL, Fred Warner
Leaf from Metternich. Nation 213:162-4 S 6 '71

NEAL, G.
New squelch for CB receiver. il Radio-Electr 42:37 N '71

NEAL, Harry Edward
Writing & selling the nonfiction book. Writers Digest 51:28-31 Ap '71

NEALE Watson academic publications. See Watson. Neale. academic publications

NEANDERTHAL race
Deer buried in ancient ritual. il Sci Digest 70:64 Ag '71
Neanderthals had rickets. il Sci Digest 69: 35-6 F '71
Shanidar, by R. S. Solecki; Face finder, by M. M. Gerasimov. Reviews
Sci Am 225:234+ S '71. P. Morrison
Shanidar: the first flower people, by R. S. Solecki. Review
Natur Hist il 80:82-6 Ag '71. C. L. Brace
Upgrading Neanderthal man; discovery in cave near village of Shanidar in Iraqi Kurdistan. il Time 97:75 My 17 '71

NEARING, Erwin M.
County land-records support local development. il Am City 86:103 My '71

NEARING, Scott
Why not try it? P. Caws. New Repub 164:25-6 My 15 '71 •

NEARSIGHTEDNESS. See Myopia

NEARY, John
Hello, energy: goodbye, big sky. il Life 70:61-4+ Ap 16 '71
Looking for ourselves in the news of '71. il pors Life 71:74-6+ D 31 '71
Lost men of Muldoon Canyon. il pors Life 70:50D-50F+ Mr 19 '71
President wants firm law enforcement. il pors Life 70:32-9 My 14 '71
Up, uppity and away. por Esquire 75:109-11+ My '71

NEBERT, D. W. See Gielen, J. E. jt. auth.

NEBOLSINE, Arcadi
Death of an artist. Commonweal 94:167-8 Ap 23 '71

NEBRASKA
See also
Fishing—Nebraska
Hunting—Nebraska

NEBULA awards. See Science fiction writers of America

NEBULAE
Blast that lit the sky; gum nebula. il Sci N 99:113 F 13 '71
Gum nebula. B. J. Bok. il por Sky & Tel 42: 64-9 Ag '71
Gum nebula. S. P. Maran. il Sci Am 225:20-9 bibliog(p 120) D '71
Gum nebula: a new kind of astronomical object. S. P. Maran and others. bibliog il Phys Today 24:42-7 S '71
Is the Gum nebula the ghost of an exploding supernova? G. B. Lubkin. il Phys Today 24: 17-19 Mr '71
Nature of pulsars. J. P. Ostriker. il Sci Am 224:48-60 Ja '71
Soft X-rays from the Cygnus loop: interpretation. W. H. Tucker. bibliog il Science 172: 372-4 Ap 23 '71
Study of a reflection nebula: Cederblad 201. il Sky & Tel 42:334 D '71
Supernova remnants. P. Gorenstein and W. Tucker. il Sci Am 225:74-85 bibliog(p 122) Jl '71
X-ray structure of the Cygnus loop. P. Gorenstein and others. bibliog il Science 172:369-72 Ap 23 '71

NECKLACE; drama. See Olfson, L.

NECKTIES
Socks & ties. il Mech Illus 68:82 Ja '72

NEDERLANDS dans theater. See Netherlands dance theater

NEE, Thomas R.
Educational usages of the computer. Clear House 46:63-4 S '71

NEEDHAM, Edgar H.
Larry Burrows: a photographer's own story. il pors Pop Phot 69:98-9+ Jl '71
Travels with Charlie. il por Esquire 75:90-1+ Mr '71

NEEDHAM, James Joseph
Restructuring the securities industry: address, May 17, 1971. Vital Speeches 37:549-52 Jl 1 '71

NEEDHAM, Joseph
Science and civilisation in China, by J. Needham. Review
Sci Am il 226:113-18 Ja '72. N. Sivin •

NEEDLEMAN, Jacob
Winds from the East. Commonweal 94:188-90 Ap 30 '71

NEEDLEPOINT
Stitch a flowered headboard. M. Gough. il House B 113:76-7 Ja '71

NEEDLEPOINT by men
Man that needle! with editorial comment. il Life 70:3, 80-3 My 28 '71

NEEDLER, Martin C.
Mexico at the crossroads. Cur Hist 60:65-70+ F '71
New directions for our Latin American policy. Yale R 60:333-41 Mr '71

NEEDLEWORK
Keep yourself in stitches. il McCalls 98:100-1+ F '71
Needlework; needlepoint, embroidery, and crewelwork. il Redbook 136:82-91 Ja '71
Room for self-expression. il McCalls 98:72-7 Ap '71
Stitch a gift for someone special. il McCalls 99:80-5 N '71
Stitch yourself a memory. il McCalls 98:94-5+ Mr '71
See also
Crocheting
Embroidery
Quilts
Samplers
Sewing
Tapestries

NEEL, Alice
Art; exhibition at Moore college of art, Philadelphia. M. Grosser. Nation 212:222 F 15 '71 •

NÉEL, Louis Eugène Félix
Magnetism and local molecular field; Nobel lecture, 1970. bibliog il Science 174:985-92 D 3 '71

NEEL, P. L. and Harris, R. W.
Motion-induced inhibition of elongation and induction of dormancy in liquidambar. bibliog il Science 173:58-9 Jl 2 '71

NEER, Andrew C.
Go total communications. il Am City 86:117-18+ Ap '71

NEFF, Hildegarde. See Knef, H.

NEFF, John
Contrarian. R. Brady. por Duns 97:100A-100B Mr '71 •

NEGATIVE color films. See Photography—Films

NEGATIVE income tax
Welfare reform: a persistent quest. W. J. Cohen. Cur Hist 61:257-60+ N '71

NEGATIVES, Photographic. See Photography—Negatives

NEGLIGENCE
See also
Liability (law)
Torts

NEGOTIABLE instruments
Row over commercial-paper ratings. Fortune 83:274 My '71 •
See also
Checks

NEGOTIATION
Doctor to the cities; I. Goldaber. il por Newsweek 78:36 S 6 '71

NEGOTIATION, International. See Arbitration, International; International relations

NEGRO (term)
What's in a name. C. G. Woodson. Negro Hist Bul 34:28-9 F '71

NEGRO actors and actresses
See also
Fetchit, S.
Negroes in moving pictures
Pace, J.
Poitier, S.
Roundtree, R.

NEGRO admirals
See also
Gravely, S. L. jr

NEGRO air pilots
Charles King and his magnificent flying machine; gyrocopter Midnight Mover. il Ebony 27:94-6+ N '71

NEGRO ambassadors
Irrepressible envoy from Ghana. il pors Ebony 26:68-70+ N '70

NEGRO American visitors in Africa. See Visitors, Foreign—Africa

NEGRO architects
Architecture's new wave. il Ebony 26:33-6+ Je '71

NEGRO art. See Art, Negro (American)

NEGRO artists
See also
Bearden, R.
Fairfax, J. A.

NEGRO associations. See Negroes—Clubs, societies, etc.

NEGRO athletes
Assessment of black is best. M. Kane. il Sports Illus 34:72-6+ Ja 18 '71
Black athlete in the golden age of sports (title varies) (cont) A. S. Young. il Ebony 26:44-6+ Ja; 96-8+ Mr; 139-42+ Ap '71
See also
Baseball players
also names of Negro athletes, e.g. A. Gibson

NEGRO authors
See also
Baldwin, J.
Du Bois, W. E. B.
Fanon, F.
Novelists, Negro
Wright, R.

NEGRO authors and publishers
Separate and, eventually, maybe equal? R. H. Smith. Pub W 200:46 Ag 2 '71
Story behind the book: If they come in the morning, by A. Davis and other writers, published by Third press. R. H. Smith. por Pub W 200:52-3 N 15 '71

NEGRO automobile dealers. See Automobile dealers

NEGRO bachelors. See Single men

NEGRO baseball players. See Baseball players

NEGRO basketball players. See Basketball players

NEGRO boys. See Negro youth

NEGRO businessmen
Crowning blow. il Newsweek 78:68+ O 4 '71
Five major myths of black business; address. J. H. Johnson. il Ebony 27:156-7 D '71
See also
Black capitalism
Negro executives

NEGRO celebrities
100 most influential black Americans. il Ebony 26:33-6+ Ap '71

NEGRO children
Feeling one's way across the chasm; city kids in day camp. W. Service. il Sports Illus 35:62-4+ Jl 26 '71
Ghetto nightmare. C.-G. McDaniel. Chr Cent 89:15-16 Ja 5 '72

Management and training
Wanted: a Dr Spock for black mothers. J. Dann. il por N Y Times Mag p78-80+ Ap 18 '71

NEGRO children in literature
Lessons in leadership D. Broderick. il Library J 96:699-701 F 15 '71
Overdue; Sambo and Sylvester. D. MacCann. Wilson Lib Bul 45:880-1 My '71; Discussion. 46:43 S '71

NEGRO childrens literature. See Childrens literature

NEGRO church. See Negroes—Religion

NEGRO clergy
Dr King's legacy: a gospel of freedom. C. Rogers. Chr Cent 88:148 F 3 '71
See also
National committee of Black churchmen

NEGRO clubs. See Negroes—Clubs, societies, etc.

NEGRO college professors and instructors
Emancipation of black scholars; excerpt from The Bonds: an American family. R. M. Williams. il Sat R 54:54-6+ D 18 '71

NEGRO colleges and universities
Beauty, and the beat; halftime entertainment. il Ebony 27:83-7 Ja '72
Black colleges are worth saving. E. Holsendolph. il Fortune 84:104-7+ O '71
Ford in their future. il Newsweek 78:72 O 18 '71
Neighboring black and white colleges. L. B. Mayhew. Ed Digest 37:29-31 N '71
Separate but better. C. E. Meacham. New Repub 165:10-11 O 9 '71
Separate but better; report findings of the Carnegie commission on higher education. il Time 97:56 Mr 1 '71
To be black and equal; report by the Race relations information center. Sat R 54:49 Ag 21 '71
Up from isolation; report findings of the Carnegie commission on higher education. Newsweek 77:68-9 Mr 1 '71
Up from isolation; report from the Carnegie commission on higher education. Sat R 54:48 Mr 20 '71
Why black colleges need help. il Bsns W p91-2 Mr 20 '71
See also
Alcorn agricultural and mechanical college, Lorman, Miss.
Chicago city college—Malcolm X campus
Howard university, Washington, D.C.
Jackson state college, Jackson, Miss.
Johnson C. Smith university. Charlotte, N.C.
Lincoln university, Oxford, Pa.
Miles college, Birmingham, Ala.
Morehouse college, Atlanta, Ga.
Wilberforce university, Wilberforce, Ohio

NEGRO colleges and universities—*Continued*
Curriculum
Metamorphosis of Howard university. A. Poinsett. il Ebony 27:110-12+ D '71
Federal aid
AoA makes $329,990 training grants to six black colleges. Aging 203:4 S '71
NEGRO comedians
See also
Wilson, F.
NEGRO companies
Black Expo in Chicago. il Time 98:22-3 O 11 '71
Black-operated firm: the men, markets & myths; address, May 12, 1971. J. W. Goodloe. Vital Speeches 37:709-15 S 15 '71
Steps we must take: training, economic development and togetherness; address, July 6, 1971. L. H. Sullivan. Vital Speeches 37:676-9 S 1 '71
See also
Black capitalism
Blue and white bus company
Cheetah charter bus service company
Daniels and Bell (firm)
First Harlem securities corporation
Mantua industrial development corporation
Watts manufacturing company
NEGRO composers
See also
Joplin, S.
NEGRO conductors. See Conductors (music)
NEGRO conferences
See also
National black economic development conference
NEGRO congressmen
Black caucus. il Newsweek 77:23-4 Mr 1 '71
Black caucus. S. Booker. il Ebony 26:100-2+ S '71
Black lawmakers in Congress. il Ebony 26:115-18+ F '71
Black politics: new way to overcome; with report by R. Scammon. il Newsweek 77:30-4+ Je 7 '71
Black study. J. Osborne. New Repub 164:11-12 Mr 13 '71
Old order changeth. . . pors Ebony 26:116-17 Ja '71
NEGRO cooperatives. See Cooperative associations
NEGRO corporate directors. See Corporations—Directors
NEGRO dancers
See also
Ailey. A.
NEGRO dialect. See Negro-English dialects
NEGRO drama
Black (art) drama is the same as black life. L. Jones. il Ebony 26:74-6+ F '71
Black militant drama. G. R. Adams. bibliog f Am Imago 28:107-28 Sum '71
King heroin; Harlem play on destructive effects of dope addiction in the black community. il Ebony 26:56-8+ Je '71
NEGRO economists
Do black economists have a special role. il Bsns W p98-9+ Jl 17 '71
NEGRO education. See Negroes—Education
NEGRO educators
Casualties of progress; effect of desegregation in the South. Sat R 54:53 Ja 16 '71
See also
Carroll. T.
Woodson, C. G.
NEGRO-English dialects
Black children, black speech: attitudes toward Black English. D. Z. Seymour. Commonweal 95:175-8 N 19 '71; Discussion. 95:339+ Ja 14 '72
Black English. O. Mellan; discussion. New Repub 164:34-5 Ja 16 '71
Teacher attitudes toward nonstandard Negro dialect. K. R. Johnson. Ed Digest 36:45-8 My '71
NEGRO entertainers
Black stars do 'give a damn'. C. Higgins. il Ebony 26:44-6+ S '71
See also
Henry, A.
NEGRO executives
See also
Finley, C. C.
Training
Developing a resource: the black executive; Consortium for graduate study in business for blacks. il Nations Bsns 59:66-9 Jl '71
NEGRO family life. See Negroes—Social conditions

NEGRO fashion shows. See Fashion shows
NEGRO fiction
Politics and the black novel. J. H. Bryant. Nation 213:660-2 D 20 '71
NEGRO government employees
Uncle Sam's own black bias. il Bsns W p36-7 Ag 28 '71
Housing
Housing black workers; implications of relocating federal facilities. R. Cassidy. New Repub 165:16-17 Jl 17 '71
NEGRO hairdressing. See Hairdressing
NEGRO high school graduates. See High school graduates
NEGRO historians
See also
Du Bois, W. E. B.
NEGRO history. See Negroes—History
NEGRO history bulletin
Bulletin: a concept of education. T. D. Perry. Negro Hist Bul 34:124-6 O '71
NEGRO history week
Black history, plus. . . il Ebony 26:100-1 F '71
Current history; observances in various states and cities. Negro Hist Bul 34:90-4 Ap '71
Negro history week, 1971. por Negro Hist Bul 34:59 Mr '71
NEGRO holidays. See Holidays
NEGRO hospitals. See Negroes—Hospitals
NEGRO institutions. See Negroes—Clubs, societies, etc.
NEGRO Jews. See Jews, Negro
NEGRO journalism. See Negro press
NEGRO journalists
From token to the top; Oregonian's Negro city editor. il por Time 97:65 My 17 '71
NEGRO judges
Black judges in the South. il por Ebony 26:31-4+ Mr '71
Black judges; meeting in Atlanta to establish Judicial council. il Time 98:28 Ag 23 '71
See also
Branch, W. M.
NEGRO labor. See Negroes—Employment
NEGRO lawyers
Blacks and the law. R. P. Alexander. por Negro Hist Bul 34:109-13 My '71
Law & order; address, August 4, 1971. H. O. Reed. Vital Speeches 37:730-6 S 15 '71
See also
Allen, M. B.
Johnson, A. B. jr
National bar association (Negro)
NEGRO leadership
Black politics takes a different turn. il U S News 71:57-60 S 20 '71
History
Black pioneer period. L. Bennett, jr. il Ebony 26:56-8+ N '70
NEGRO liberation flag. See Flags
NEGRO librarians
Black bias charges pressed at Library of Congress. Library J 96:2032 Je 15 '71
Black librarians' caucus formed in Queens, N.Y. Library J 96:3555-6 N 1 '71
Southern integration: writing off the black librarian. P. Schuman. il Library J 96:1775-7 My 15 '71
Washington scores Moose for snub of black librarian; S. Finley from Timberland regional library. il por Library J 97:11 Ja 1 '72
See also
Jones. C. S.
Libraries and Negroes
NEGRO literature
Book reviews. See issues of Negro history bulletin
Ebony book shelf. See issues of Ebony
Harlem renaissance, by N. I. Huggins. Review
Nation 213:501-2 N 15 '71. C. R. Larson
Some of my best friends; letter to the editor. V. M. Puryear. Am Lib 2:233 Mr '71
See also
Negro drama
Negro fiction
Negro poetry
Publishers and publishing—Negro literature
Bibliography
Brothers crying out for more access to life. A. Kazin. il Sat R 54:33-5 O 2 '71

NEGRO literature—*Continued*

Study and teaching

Black literature and the English curriculum. J. Perry. Engl J 60:1057-62 N '71

Black literature and the non-black teacher of black students. R. Bizot. Engl J 60:889-95 O '71

Black literature revisited: Sonny's blues. E. R. Ognibene. Engl J 60:36-7 Ja '71

NEGRO market

Airlines focus on special interest groups. W. H. Gregory. il Aviation W 95:32-4 Ag 2 '71

Military exchanges think black. il Ebony 26:54-6+ Jl '71

NEGRO mayors

See also

Butler, N. A.

Evers, C.

Gibson, K. A.

Widener, W.

NEGRO middle class. See Middle classes

NEGRO migration. See Negroes—Migration

NEGRO militants

Battle for the South: phase two; Junta of militant organizations in Florida. C. Fulwood. il Ramp Mag 10:36-9 Jl '71

Black liberation and Women's lib. L. J. M. La Rue. il Trans-Action 8:59-64 N '70

Radical chic & mau-mauing the flak catchers, by T. Wolfe. Review

Harper 242:104-9 F '71. I. Howe

Right on toward a new black pluralism. K. Prager. il Time 97:13-14 F 22 '71

Violent harvest for black militants; Rap Brown's capture boosts the toll. il pors Life 71:41-2 O 29 '71

See also

Black Panther party

NEGRO Mormons. See Mormons and Mormonism, Negro

NEGRO municipal officers

Black takeover of U.S. cities? A. Poinsett. il Ebony 26:76-9+ N '70

NEGRO music

Back to the Apollo; soul acts at Harlem theatre. New Yorker 46:24-6 Ja 23 '71

Black nationalism and the revolution in music, by F. Kofsky. Review

Ramp Mag 9:54-7 Mr '71. R. Young

Soul to soul; music festival in Ghana. P. Garland. il Ebony 26:79-82+ Je '71

See also

Jazz music

Phonograph records—Negro music

NEGRO musicians

See also

Armstrong, L.

Davis, M.

Ellington, D.

King, R. B.

Miles, B.

Scott, H.

Watts, A.

NEGRO newspaper editors. See Negro journalists

NEGRO newspapers. See Negro press

NEGRO novelists. See Novelists, Negro

NEGRO opera singers

Black performer; from the minstrels to the Met. G. Shirley. il Opera N 35:6-13 Ja 30 '71

Opening doors in music. B. J. Novak. il Negro Hist Bul 34:10-14 Ja '71

NEGRO organizations. See Negroes—Clubs, societies, etc.

NEGRO periodicals

See also

Black world (periodical)

Negro history bulletin

NEGRO physicians

See also

Williams, D. H.

NEGRO poetry

Poems. Negro Hist Bul 34:20 Ja '71

Poems. L. M. Carter; M. Christian. Negro Hist Bul 34:157 N '71

NEGRO poets

See also

Clem, C.

Giovanni, N.

NEGRO police

Black cop: a man caught in the middle. il Newsweek 78:19-20 Ag 16 '71

Chopper coppers; Chicago crime-fighters. il Ebony 26:78-80+ Jl '71

Dilemma of the black policeman. A. Poinsett. il Ebony 26:122-4+ My '71

Lonely struggle of the black cop. T. Armbrister. Read Digest 98:123-7 Mr '71

NEGRO political candidates. See Candidates, Political

NEGRO press

Mr One-Two-Five Street; column in Amsterdam news; interview. L. Matthews. New Yorker 47:30-1 S 18 '71

Paper to say ouch; New York's Amsterdam news. Newsweek 77:98 My 10 '71

NEGRO prisoners

Dialogue with my Soledad son. L. Jackson. il pors Ebony 27:72-4+ N '71

Heroin and the black community. V. E. Taylor. Am Scholar 40:691-4 Aut '71

Library service for prisons aim of new organizations. Library J 97:20 Ja 1 '72

Treatment

See Prisoners—Treatment

NEGRO private schools. See Private schools, Negro

NEGRO public officers

Black elected officials in the United States. Negro Hist Bul 33:168 N '70

Black politics in the South. H. Walton, jr. il Ebony 26:140-3 Ag '71

Black power enclave, Greene County, Ala. D. S. Glick. New Repub 164:11-12 Ja 16 '71

For a black vice president in 1972. A. M. Greeley. il N Y Times Mag p28+ S 19 '71; Discussion. p8+ O 17 '71

NEGRO publishers and publishing

Book publishing a racist club? B. Chambers. il Pub W 199:40-4 F 1 '71; Same abr. Cur 129:16-22 My '71; Reply. L. Hill. Pub W 199:13-14 Mr 29 '71

Minority publishing fund proposed at conference. Library J 96:2030 Je 15 '71

Venture capital for minority publishers? R. H. Smith. Pub W 199:35 Ap 5 '71; Same abr. with title Another chance for publishing. Cur 129:22-3 My '71

Why minority publishing? ed. by B. Chambers. il pors Pub W 199:35-50 Mr 15 '71

NEGRO race

See also

Negroes—Nationalism

NEGRO reporters

Black reporter and his problems. M. L. Stein. il Sat R 54:58-60 F 13 '71

NEGRO rock groups. See Rock groups

NEGRO schools

See also

Private schools, Negro

Louisiana

High school class faces the future. il Ebony 26:74-6+ Ag '71

NEGRO scientists

See also

Hall, L. A.

Hill, H. A.

NEGRO seamen

Negro maritime worker and the sea. P. Olsen. bibliog il Negro Hist Bul 34:38-41 F '71

NEGRO sharecroppers. See Share-cropping

NEGRO singers

See also

Anderson, I. M.

Flack, R.

Franklin, A.

Gaye, M.

Havens, R.

Pride, C.

Shirley, G.

Turner, I.

Turner, T.

NEGRO societies. See Negroes—Clubs, societies, etc.

NEGRO songs

See also

Blues (songs, etc)

NEGRO student militants

Roy. J. A. Lukas. il pors Esquire 75:122-6+ Mr '71

NEGRO students

Black professor says: colleges are skipping over competent blacks to admit authentic ghetto types. T. Sowell; discussion. N Y Times Mag p6+ Ja 24 '71

Loneliness of being black; senior year at an integrated school. L. Williams. il Seventeen 30:118+ Jl '71

Mau-mauing at Penn state. H. Caton. Nat R 23:428 Ap 20 '71

What can I do about racism? K. Branan. Schol Teach Jr/Sr High p26+ S '71

See also

High school graduates

Negro student militants

NEGRO students, Women

Princeton chose me. J. Robinson. il por Redbook 136:68-9+ F '71

NEGRO stunt women. See Stunt women

NEGRO surgeons
  See also
Williams, D. H.
NEGRO teachers
  See also
Negro college professors and instructors
NEGRO theater. See Theater, Negro
NEGRO towns and settlements
  See also
Soul City, N.C.
NEGRO universities. See Negro colleges and universities
NEGRO veterans
Black veteran: battle on the home front. H. Bims. il Ebony 27:35-8+ N '71
Mexico: a haven for disabled vets. L. Robinson. il Ebony 27:31-4+ Ja '72
NEGRO vice-presidents. See Negro public officers
NEGRO-white intermarriage. See Intermarriage of races
NEGRO-white relations. See Race relations
NEGRO women
Belles of the South. il Ebony 26:158-62 Ag '71
Black woman and Women's lib. H. H. King. il Ebony 26:68-70+ Mr '71
Black women 1970. N. Hare and J. Hare. il Trans-Action 8:65-8+ N '70
I can't call you my sister yet; interview, ed. by M. Cantwell. D. Pitman. por Mlle 73:182-3+ My '71
What the black woman thinks about Women's lib. T. Morrison. il N Y Times Mag p 14-15+ Ag 22 '71; Discussion. p26 S 5 '71
  See also
Single women

Employment

  See also
Negro women—Occupations

Occupations

New careers for the new woman. il Ebony 26:31-4+ Jl '71
NEGRO women, Famous. See Negro celebrities
NEGRO women as bankers. See Women as bankers
NEGRO women as executives. See Women as executives
NEGRO women celebrities. See Negro celebrities
NEGRO women in television. See Women in television
NEGRO youth
Look into blackness; 20-year-old Afro-American's summer trip to Africa. H. V. Lino, jr. por Sr Schol 98:10-11+ Mr 22 '71
When the cops pick up a black kid. Trans-Action 8:6+ N '70
  See also
Negro students
NEGROES
Black is beautiful: an old idea. T. H. Henriksen. bibliog il Negro Hist Bul 34:150-2 N '71
Blacks in America. il Sr Schol 98:2-11+ Mr 22 '71
Coming of the black ghetto-state. E. C. Smith. Yale R 61:161-82 D '71
Current history. See issues of Negro history bulletin
Identity crisis in black Americans visiting West Africa. A. A. Messer. bibliog Ment Hy 55:375-81 Jl '71
100 most influential black Americans. il Ebony 26:33-6+ Ap '71
Term of trials; report on events of 1971. S. Morris. il Ebony 27:92-7 Ja '72
What's in a name. C. G. Woodson. Negro Hist Bul 34:28-9 F '71
  See also
Black capitalism
Black power
Freedmen
Interracial cooperation
National association for the advancement of colored people
National urban league
Negro history week
Negro market
Race relations
Slavery—United States
Suburbs—Negroes
Universal Negro improvement association
  also subhead Negroes under names of cities, e.g. Chicago—Negroes

Civil rights

Annual progress report: black coalitions bring gains at the polls. il Ebony 26:94-9 Ja '71
Birmingham revisited. F. L. Shuttlesworth. il pors Ebony 26:114-18 Ag '71
Black caucus urges goals. Negro Hist Bul 34:118 My '71

Blacks and Mr Nixon. New Repub 164:5-6 Je 5 '71
Blacks and the law. R. P. Alexander. por Negro Hist Bul 34:109-13 My '71
Civil rights: a new approach. il U S News 71:26-9 Ag 23 '71
Civil rights: hopes of '60s and problems of '70s; excerpts from testimony before House subcommittee, August 4, 1971. H. A. Glickstein. por U S News 71:25 Ag 23 '71
Double hypocritical standards; record of the administration. Nation 212:709 Je 7 '71
Everybody out of the pool; ruling for Jackson, Miss. Newsweek 77:36 Je 28 '71
Looking upward. il Ebony 26:172-3 Ag '71
Man's home, a man's castle, by K. G. Weinberg. Review
  New Repub 165:26-7 O 30 '71. R. Margolis • Old order changeth. . . pors Ebony 26:116-17 Ja '71
Right on toward a new black pluralism. K. Prager. il Time 97:13-14 F 22 '71
'South of freedom' 1971. C. T. Rowan. il pors Ebony 26:134-9 Ag '71
TRB from Washington: R. Nixon's alienation from the blacks. New Repub 164:8 F 13 '71
Unforgettable Ralph McGill. W. S. Howland. por Read Digest 99:63-7 Ag '71
Whitney Young's open society; address, April 1971, with questions and answers. H. R. Sims. Ann Am Acad 396:70-8 Jl '71
  See also
A. Philip Randolph institute
Black power
Race relations

History

Black pioneer period. L. Bennett, jr. il Ebony 26:56-8+ N '70
Omaha De Porres club. J. H. Smith. bibliog Negro Hist Bul 33:194-9 D '70

Clubs, societies, etc.

Businessmen go to the ghetto to learn; Young great society. il pors Bsns W p 102+ Je 19 '71
Omaha De Porres club. J. H. Smith. bibliog Negro Hist Bul 33:194-9 D '70
  See also
Black academy of arts and letters
National association for the advancement of colored people

Finance

Time for giving. il Ebony 26:126-7 Je '71

Crime

As the blacks move in. the ethnics move out; Cleveland's East side. P. Wilkes. il por N Y Times Mag p9-11+ Ja 24 '71

Culture

  Study and teaching
  See also
Afro-American studies

Economic conditions

Black couples catching up? il Sr Schol 98:16 Mr 22 '71
Black lag. Time 98:16 Ag 9 '71
Black people and labor unions; address, November 22, 1971. V. E. Jordan, jr. Vital Speeches 38:171-4 Ja 1 '72
Differentials and overlaps in annual earnings of blacks and whites; with tables. A. Strasser. bibliog Mo Labor R 94:16-26 D '71
Fringe benefits for black citizens. il Ebony 26:182-3 O '71
Negroes' economic gains in 10 years. il U S News 71:30-1 Ag 23 '71
Soul in suburbia; dilemma of the middle class. O. Coombs. il Harper 244:24-6+ Ja '72
Where blacks are moving, and moving up. il U S News 70:24-6 Mr 1 '71
White paper; race and poverty. il Newsweek 77:18-19 My 31 '71
  See also
Black capitalism
Black power
Negroes—Migration

Education

Black Ph.D's; reply. J. J. Jackson. Trans-Action 7:60 O '70
Bulletin: a concept of education. T. D. Perry. Negro Hist Bul 34:124-6 O '71
Following through in Macon County. J. Reed. il Am Ed 7:7-12 N '71
Occupational education and black students; community colleges. il Sch & Soc 99:76-7 F '71
Paradox without promise: a dream deferred; address; April 21, 1971. F. A. Rodgers. Vital Speeches 37:521-5 Je 15 '71

NEGROES—Education—*Continued*
Predicting college success of the education-
ally disadvantaged; adaptation of address.
June 1970. J. C. Stanley. bibliog Science
171:640-7 F 19 '71; Discussion.   173:1079;
174:1278-9 S 17, D 24 '71
 See also
Howard university, Washington, D.C.
Negro colleges and universities
Private schools, Negro
Public schools—Desegregation
Socially handicapped children—Education
United Negro college fund

History
Early efforts toward educating the black
adult. L. McGee. bibliog Negro Hist Bul
34:88-90 Ap '71
Schools for the freedmen. R. D. Parmet.
bibliog il Negro Hist Bul 34:128-32 O '71

Employment
Black workers & unemployment: court orders
must be policed; address, July 8, 1971. H.
Hill. Vital Speeches 37:658-62 Ag 15 '71
Hell in the factory; verdict in J. Johnson
case, Detroit. il por Time 97:39 Je 7 '71
Man needs to work, Thomas Henry White,
chair-car attendant. G. Goodman. Look 35:
44-5 Ja 12 '71
Philadelphia plan is valid. Mo Labor R 94:
64-6 S '71
School for gamblers; novel Nevada jobs pro-
gram. L. Deni. il Ebony 27:55-6+ D '71
When industry goes South. A. A. Fletcher.
il por Ebony 26:168-71 Ag '71
 See also
Discrimination in employment
Negro government employees
Opportunities industrialization centers, inc.

Health and hygiene
 See also
Anemia
Negroes—Hospitals

History
Gabriel insurrection of 1800. W. J. Kimball.
bibliog Negro Hist Bul 34:153-6 N '71
Making of black America (cont) L. Bennett,
jr. il Ebony 26:56-8+ N '70; 44-6+ F '71
Negro maritime worker and the sea. P. Ol-
sen. bibliog Negro Hist Bul 34:38-41 F '71
Populist dreams and Negro rights: east Tex-
as as a case study; Grimes County, Tex. L.
C. Goodwyn. bibliog f il Am Hist R 76:
1435-56 D '71
 See also
Southampton insurrection, 1831

Study and teaching
Missing chapter in American history. V.
Block. il Parents Mag 46:64-5+ S '71
Struggle for the inclusion of Negro history
in our text-books: a California experi-
ence; address, October 24, 1970. M. M.
Dymally. Negro Hist Bul 33:188-91 D '70
 See also
Afro-American studies

Hospitals
Provident hospital: historic Chicago hospital struggles to survive. il por Ebony 26:
64-6+ Je '71

Housing
Fixing the odds in Black Jack; zoning con-
troversy. il Time 97:19-20 Ap 26 '71
On breaking the black impasse; resettling
low-income families. R. M. Christenson. il
Chr Cent 88:902-6 Jl 28 '71
TRB from Washington: broken promises.
New Repub 164:6 Mr 13 '71
 See also
Discrimination in housing
Housing—Desegregation
Negro government employees—Housing

Intelligence
 See Intelligence levels—Negroes

Language
 See Negro-English dialects

Legal status, laws, etc.
Blacks and the law. R. P. Alexander. por Ne-
gro Hist Bul 34:109-13 My '71
Law & order; address, August 4, 1971. H. O.
Reed. Vital Speeches 37:730-6 S 15 '71
Southern justice for blacks. K. S. Tollett. il
por Ebony 26:58-60+ O '71

Libraries
 See Libraries and Negroes

Migration
Chickenbone special, by D. E. Walls. Review
 New Repub 164:28-9 My 22 '71. G. W.
 Johnson
It's good to be home again. il Ebony 26:66-71
 Ag '71
Official figures on Negro trek to cities. il
 U S News 71:42 Jl 19 '71
Where blacks are moving, and moving up. il
 U S News 70:24-6 Mr 1 '71
Where the blacks are. il Newsweek 77:53 F
 22 '71
Will the suburbs beckon? il Ebony 26:112-13
 Jl '71

Nationalism
Are American blacks natives? J. Burnham.
 Nat R 23:133 F 9 '71
Coming of the black ghetto-state. E. C.
 Smith. Yale R 61:161-82 D '71
Search for black identity in East Africa. C.
 Rogers. Chr Cent 88:1124 S 29 '71; Reply. H.
 H. Mitchell. 88:1357 N 17 '71
Support for Angela Davis; letter to the
 editor. J. English. Library J 96:903 Mr 15
 '71
 See also
Black power

History
Rhetoric of ante-bellum black separatism. R.
 C. Dick. bibliog il Negro Hist Bul 34:133-7
 O '71

Occupations
Speaking of people. See issues of Ebony

Politics and suffrage
 See Negroes and politics

Psychology
Black suicide, by H. Hendin. Review
 Atlan 227:108-10+ F '71. J. Updike
Question every black parent asks: what shall
 I tell my child? A. F. Poussaint and J. P.
 Comer. il Redbook 136:64-5+ Ja '71

Religion
Black Baptists condemn racial separation.
 Chr Today 16:51-2 O 8 '71
Black Catholic caucus; joint convention of
 the National black Catholic clergy caucus
 and the National black Catholic lay cau-
 cus. America 125:107 S 4 '71
Black origins of the Pentecostal movement.
 J. S. Tinney. Chr Today 16:4-6 O 8 '71; Dis-
 cussion 16:31+ N 19 '71
Black theology of James Cone. R. Ruether.
 por Cath World 214:18-20 O '71
New society is born; Study of black religion.
 Chr Cent 88:1342 N 17 '71
Pan-Africanism and the black church; a
 search for solidarity. C. Rogers. il Chr Cent
 88:1345-7 N 17 '71
Poor of God and the black Christian in
 America. R. A. Jeffers. il Cath World 213:
 126-9 Je '71
Quest for a black theology, by J. J. Gar-
 diner and D. Roberts and The search for
 common ground, by H. Thurman. Reviews
 Commonweal 95:93-4 O 22 '71. E. Wright
Tale of two cities. H. H. Mitchell and E. S.
 O'Neal. Chr Cent 88:156-8 F 3 '71; Reply.
 C. D. Tripp. 88:379+ Mr 24 '71
 See also
African Methodist Episcopal church
Mormons and Mormonism, Negro
National committee of Black churchmen
National Negro evangelical association

Bibliography
Black churchmen speak out. J. S. Tinney.
 Chr Today 15:30+ S 24 '71

Reparations
Black manifesto revisited. G. S. Wilmore,
 jr. Chr Cent 88:452-3 Ap 14 '71
 See also
National black economic development con-
ference

Segregation
One step forward, one step back. Time 97:25
 Je 28 '71
 See also
Libraries and Negroes
Public schools—Desegregation
Segregation in education

Segregation, Resistance to
Freedom riders on their trip to equality. il
 Sr Schol 98:15 Mr 22 '71
Whatever happened to Mrs Rosa Parks?
 Montgomery bus boycott. il pors Ebony 26:
 180-1 Ag '71

Sexual behavior
 See Sexual behavior

NEGROES—*Continued*

Social conditions

Are the rules changing? R. Barta. **America** 125:341-5 O 30 '71

Critical look. il Ebony 26:110-11 Mr '71

Family matter; study by Robert B. Hill. il Newsweek 78:26 Ag 9 '71

Journey through black America; condensation of Odyssey; journey through black America; with editorial comment. E. Selby and M. Selby. Read Digest 99:11-13, 223-8+ S '71

My answer to genocide. D. Gregory. il **pors** Ebony 26:66-70+ O '71; Discussion. 27:15-17 D '71

Negroes' economic gains in 10 years. il **U S** News 71:30-1 Ag 23 '71

On breaking the black impasse; resettling, low-income families. R. M. Christenson. il Chr Cent 88:902-6 Jl 28 '71

Policeman complains; interview. ed. by R. Coles; excerpt from Middle Americans. il N Y Times Mag p 11+ Je 13 '71; Reply. F C. Hughes. p2+ Jl 11 '71

Unchanged South. J. E. White, jr. il Ebony 26:126-8+ Ag '71

Updating the Moynihan report. Sci N 99:384 Je 5 '71

Social history

Revolution in a technological society; address, October 22, 1970. S. D. Proctor. **por** Negro Hist Bul 34:6-9 Ja '71

Social life and customs

Memo to a young black, from an older one. G. B. Nesbitt. Negro Hist Bul 34:127 O '71

Societies

See Negroes—Clubs, societies, etc.

Statistics

New profile of U.S. latest from census. il U S News 70:24-5 Mr 15 '71

Trade union membership

See Trade unions—Negro membership

Alabama

See also
Montgomery, Ala.—Negroes

Georgia

See also
Atlanta—Negroes

Mississippi

Battle of the Republic; raid on members of the Republic of New Africa movement. il Newsweek 78:27 Ag 30 '71

Eudora Welty's world in the '30s; excerpts from One time, one place. E. Welty. il Mlle 73:162-5+ S '71

One time, one place, by E. Welty. Review New Yorker 47:66-8 D 25 '71. B. Gill

Northern states

See also
Cleveland—Negroes
New York (city)—Harlem

South Carolina

Victoria Delee, in her own words; interview. ed. by C. Trillin. V. Delee. New Yorker 47:86+ Mr 27 '71

Southern states

Been down home so long it looks like up to me. J. B. Cumming, jr. il Esquire 76:84-90+ Ag '71

Black voices of the South; symposium. il Ebony 26:50-4 Ag '71

Family assistance. L. M. Salamon. New Repub 164:17-18 F 20 '71

Looking upward. il Ebony 26:172-3 Ag '71

Old illusions and new Souths; with editorial comment. L. Bennett, jr. il Ebony 26:33, 35-8+ Ag '71

Some hate, some hope. J. DeMuth. Commonweal 94:84-6 Ap 2 '71

Some progress, more myth. R. W. Dietsch. Nation 212:615-18 My 17 '71

Southern justice for blacks. K. S. Tollett. il **por** Ebony 26:58-60+ O '71

White voices of the South; symposium. il Ebony 26:164-7 Ag '71

NEGROES, Catholic. See Catholic church—Negroes

NEGROES, Discrimination against. See Race discrimination

NEGROES, Famous. See Negro celebrities

NEGROES and Jews. See Jews and Negroes

NEGROES and libraries. See Libraries and Negroes

NEGROES and museums. See Museums and Negroes

NEGROES and politics

Annual progress report; black coalitions bring gains at the polls. il Ebony 26:94-9 Ja '71

Another "historic" meeting; concerning interview of black congressmen with President Nixon. Nation 212:452 Ap 12 '71

Black Expo in Chicago. il Time 98:22-3 O 11 '71

Black politics in the new South. C. C. Douglas. il Ebony 26:27-30+ Ja '71

Black politics in the South. H. Walton, jr. il Ebony 26:140-3 Ag '71

Black politics; new way to overcome; with report by R. Scammon. il Newsweek 77:30-4+ Je 7 '71

Black politics takes a different turn. il U S News 71:57-60 S 20 '71

Black takeover of U.S. cities? A. Poinsett. il Ebony 26:76-9+ N '70

Black voters wield power. America 125:23 Jl 24 '71

Blacks, Democrats and the '72 convention. K. Bode. New Repub 165:11-15 O 16 '71

Election notes. Nat R 23:1276+ N 19 '71

Greene County, Ala; change comes to the courthouse. J. Kane. il Time 97:21 F 1 '71

Hancock County; black takeover of power. New Repub 164:8-9 Mr 6 '71

In search of a black strategy. **por** Time 98:9-10 D 20 '71

On the Chisholm campaign trail. P. R. Wieck. New Repub 165:16-18 D 4 '71

Vote mobilization for the 1970s. il **por** Ebony 26:84-6 Jl '71

Why a black man should run. H. Romaine. Nation 213:264-8 S 27 '71

See also
Black power
National black political fund
Negro public officers

NEGROES and television. See Television broadcasting and Negroes

NEGROES in Africa

Back to Africa; a history of Sierra Leone and Liberia, by R. West, and Liberia; black Africa in microcosm, by C. M. Wilson. Reviews
Sat R 54:41-2 My 15 '71. C. Miller

See also
South Africa—Race question

NEGROES in art

Paint it black; exhibition at Rice university, Houston. D. McConathy. il Vogue 157:127 Ap 15 '71

Sanguinary saga; Some American history exhibition. T. W. Moore. il Chr Cent 88:864-5 Jl 14 '71

NEGROES in business. See Negro businessmen

NEGROES in children's literature

Book publishing; a racist club? B. Chambers. il Pub W 199:40-4 F 1 '71; Same abr. Cur 129:16-22 My '71

Interracial books; background of a challenge; activities of Council on interracial books for children. B. Chambers. il Pub W 200:23-9 O 11 '71

Minority publishing; bringing the record up to date; findings and plans of Council on interracial books for children. B. Chambers. Pub W 201:27 Ja 3 '72

Ox of a different color; Sylvester and the magic pebble; Little Black Sambo. J. F. Krug and J. A. Harvey. Am Lib 2:532-4 My '71

NEGROES in Latin America

See also
Latin America—Race question

NEGROES in literature

Book reviews. See issues of Negro history bulletin

Ebony book shelf. See issues of Ebony

See also
Negroes in childrens literature

NEGROES in moving pictures

Black movie boom. il Newsweek 78:66 S 6 '71

Return of The Emperor Jones. N. Kagan. il Negro Hist Bul 34:160-2 N '71

Stepin Fetchit talks back; interview. ed. by J. McBride. S. Fetchit. pors Film Q 24:20-6 Sum '71

NEGROES in South Africa

See also
South Africa—Race question

NEGROES in South America

See also
Negroes in Surinam

NEGROES in Surinam

Under the power of the Gran Gadu; Bush Negro witchcraft. L. C. Whiton. il **Natur** Hist 80:14-16+ Ag '71

NEGROES in the Caribbean Region
Palm tree revolt. H. Sutton. il Sat R 54:
15-19+ F 27 '71
NEGROES in the United States army. See
United States—Army—Negroes
NEGROES in the West Indies
Black nationalism: a growing worry in the
Caribbean. C. Migdail. il U S News 70:
52-4 Mr 29 '71
NEGROES in trade unions. See Trade unions—
Negro membership
NEHRU, Jawaharlal
Nehru's plan for peace. S. S. Harrison. New
Repub 164:17-22 Je 19 '71 •
NEIGHBORHOOD fairs. See Fairs
NEIGHBORHOOD health centers. See Health
facilities
NEIGHBORS; story. See Carver, R.
NEIMAN, Earl
Earl Neiman: a great artist. G. Baum. il
Cath World 213:69-74 My '71 •
NEIMAN, Joseph C.
New frontiersmen in religious education.
America 124:378-80 Ap 10 '71
NELOY, Eddie
Obituary
Newsweek il por 77:63+ Je 7 '71
NELSON, A. G.
Audio amplifiers quiz. Electr World 85:41 F
'71
NELSON, Anne H. See Nelson, C. A. jt. auth.
NELSON, Charles A. and Nelson, A. H.
Systems and networks: the state library role.
bibliog il Am Lib 2:883-7 S '71
NELSON, Gaylord Anton
Against: what's wrong with the SST; inter-
view. il por U S News 70:69 Mr 15 '71
Stop killing our oceans. Read Digest 98:132-6
F '71
NELSON, Gene
Brand new life. C. Zadan. il pors Dance Mag
45:67-70 O '71 •
NELSON, George
Design, technology, and the pursuit of ug-
liness; excerpt from The synthetic garden.
il Sat R 54:22-5+ O 2 '71
NELSON, Gunvor
Women, wives, film-makers; interview. ed.
by B. Richardson. il Film Q 25:34-40 Fall '71
NELSON, J. Robert
Kennedy's clinical Camelot. Chr Cent 88:1351-
2 N 17 '71
Stringfellow-Towne indictment. Chr Cent 88:
60-1 Ja 20 '71
Toward ecumenical convergence. por Chr
Cent 88:972-4 Ag 18 '71
NELSON, Janet
Shooing out myths about footwear. il To-
days Health 49:32-4 My '71
NELSON, Lowry
School dropout problem in Cuba. Sch & Soc
99:234-5 Ap '71
NELSON, Norbert
Lighting problems and solutions; excerpts
from Photographing your product. il Ceram
Mo 19:22-3 O '71
NELSON, Norm, Jr
Hunt silently by canoe. il pors Outdoor Life
148:72-5+ N '71
NELSON, Owen N. See Shane, H. G. jt. auth.
NELSON, Ozzie, family
Happy, happy, happy Nelsons. S. Davidson.
il pors Esquire 75:97-101+ Je '71; Reply.
O. Nelson. 76:22 Ag '71
NELSON, Ronald E.
Bishop Hill; a colony of Swedish pietists in
Illinois. il Antiques 99:140-7 Ja '71
NELSON, Theodore F.
We're failing to teach effective talking. To-
days Ed 60:43 O '71
NELSON COUNTY, Va.
Our far-flung correspondents; big rain and
floods. E. Kinkead. New Yorker 47:66+ Jl 31
'71
NELUMBO. See Lotus
NEMATODES
See also
Lungworms
NEMEROV, Howard
Beginner's guide; Druidic rimes; Poet as
eagle scout; Threshold; Snowflakes;
Memory of my friend; Creation myth on
a Moebius strip; poems. Poetry 119:6-10
O '71
Rent in the screen; poem. New Yorker 47:
36 D 18 '71
NEMSER, Cindy
Alchemist and the phenomenologist. bibliog
il Art in Am 59:100-3 Mr '71

NEODESHA, Kan.
Always leave 'em smiling; Twin Rivers in-
dustrial park. il Newsweek 79:36-7 Ja 3 '72
Saving a small town. L. L. L. Golden. Sat R
54:94 N 13 '71
NEO-FASCISM. See Fascism
NEO-GOTHIC architecture. See Architecture,
Gothic
NEO-ISOLATIONISM. See United States—For-
eign relations
NEOLITHIC period. See Stone age
NEOMYSTICISM. See Mysticism
NEON in the body
Neon for deep diving. il Sci N 100:139 Ag
28 '71
NEPAL
Karnali, roadless world of western Nepal. L.
M. Bishop and B. C. Bishop. il Nat Geog
140:656-89 N '71
See also
Katmandu
Visitors, Foreign—Nepal

Description and travel

Nepal: a violent crescendo of mountains. L.
Van Der Post. il Holiday 48:56-7+ S '70
Nepal: Shangri-la in the seventies. N. Lynn.
il Travel 135:28-35+ F '71
NEPOTISM
Coming in with dad; view of top executives.
ed. by H. Altman. il Nations Bsns 59:58-
60 Je '71
Congress: a family business. J. Volz. Nation
212:819-20 Je 28 '71
Professor and his wife; anti-nepotism
rules. L. Kanowitz. McCalls 98:42 Ag '71
NERINES
Plant collector's corner: cherubs' bugles and
Miss Mason's nerine. il Sunset 147:150-1 Jl
'71
NERKEN, Ira
Unselling the war. il Newsweek 77:69 Je 21
'71 •
NERUDA, Pablo
Four poems: Falling; Enemy; On the road;
Song with landscape and a river; tr. by
B. Belitt. New Yorker 47:54 N 20 '71
Prize for a Chilean poet; with sampling of
poems. por Time 98:47-8 N 1 '71

about

Neruda in translation. J. Felstiner. Yale R
61:226-51 D '71 •
Neruda laureate. R. J. Clements. por Sat R
54:50-1 N 13 '71 •
Nobel prize at Isla Negra. J Felstiner. New
Repub 165:29-30 D 25 '71 •
NERVA engine. See Rockets, Atomic powered
NERVE cells
Cyclic adenosine monophosphate and nore-
pinephrine: effects on transmembrane prop-
erties of cerebellar Purkinje cells. G. R.
Siggins and others. bibliog il Science 174:
192-4 Ja 15 '71; Reply with rejoinder. 174:
1257-9 D 17 '71
Extracellular recordings from human retinal
ganglion cells. G. W. Weinstein and others.
bibliog il Science 171:1021-2 Mr 12 '71
Giant brain cells in mollusks. A. O. D.
Willows. il Sci Am 224:68-75 F '71
Histochemical and functional correlations in
anterior horn neurons of the cat spinal-cord.
J. F. Campa and W. K. Engel. bibliog il
Science 171:198-9 Ja 15 '71
Histochemical fluorescence of raphe neurons:
selective enhancement by tryptophan. G.
K. Aghajanian and I. M. Asher. bibliog
il Science 172:1159-61 Je 11 '71
Laser stimulation of nerve cells in aplysia.
R. L. Fork. bibliog il Science 171:907-8
Mr 5 '71
Nerve trophic function: in vitro assay of ef-
fects of nerve tissue on muscle cholinester-
ase activity. T. L. Lentz. bibliog il Science
171:187-9 Ja 15 '71
Neuron; workings of the brain; with reports
by E. Kern and R. Gore. il Life 71:42-56+
O 22 '71
Oscillator neurons in crustacean ganglia.
M. Mendelson. bibliog il Science 171:1170-3
Mr 19 '71
Pathways in the brain. L. Heimer. il Sci Am
225:48-57+ Jl '71
Receptive field mechanism in the vertebrate
retina. K. I. Naka. bibliog il Science 171:
691-3 F 19 '71
Recurrent excitation of secondary olfactory
neurons: a possible mechanism for signal
amplification. R. A. Nicoll. bibliog il Science 171:824-6 F 26 '71
Serotonin: two different inhibitory actions on
snail neurons. H. M. Gerschenfeld. bibliog
il Science 171:1252-4 Mr 26 '71

NERVE cells—*Continued*

Sex difference in the number of sympathetic neurons in the spinal cord of the cat. F. R. Calaresu and J. L. Henry. bibliog il Science 173:343-4 Jl 23 '71

Single neuron activity in cat gigantocellular tegmental field: selectivity of discharge in desynchronized sleep. bibliog il Science 174:1250-2 D 17 '71

Somatosensory system: organizational hierarchy from single units in monkey area 5. F. H. Duffy and J. L. Burchfiel. bibliog il Science 172:273-5 Ap 16 '71

Specific enzymic methylation of an arginine in the experimental allergic encephalomyelitis protein from human myelin. G. S. Baldwin and P. R. Carnegie. bibliog il Science 171:579-81 F 12 '71

Supraoptic neurosecretory cells: adrenergic and cholinergic sensitivity. J. L. Barker and others. bibliog il Science 171:208-10 Ja 15 '71

Supraoptic neurosecretory cells: autonomic modulation. J. L. Barker and others. bibliog il Science 171:206-7 Ja 15 '71

Transneuronal transfer of radioactivity in the central nervous system. B. Grafstein. bibliog il Science 172:177-9 Ap 9 '71
See also
Electrophysiology

NERVE conduction. See Electrophysiology

NERVE gases. See Gases, Asphyxiating and poisonous

NERVE regeneration. See Regeneration (biology)

NERVES
See also
Electrophysiology
Neuromuscular junctions
Olfactory nerves
Optic nerve
Synapses

Transplantation

Transplanted precursors of nerve cells: their fate in the cerebellums of young rats. G. D. Das and J. Altman. bibliog il Science 173:637-8 Ag 13 '71

NERVO, Amado

Council's homage to the memory of Amado Nervo. por Américas 22:38 N '70 •

NERVOUS habits

Those irritating habits. J. Brothers. por Good H 172:46+ Ap '71

NERVOUS system

Preganglionic stimulation increases calcium uptake by sympathetic ganglia. M. P. Blaustein. bibliog il Science 172:391-3 Ap 23 '71

Somatosensory system: organizational hierarchy from single units in monkey area 5. F. H. Duffy and J. L. Burchfiel. bibliog il Science 172:273-5 Ap 16 '71
See also
Biological control systems
Brain
Cerebral cortex
Chemoreceptivity
Electrophysiology
Minimal brain dysfunction
Receptors, Neural
Synapses
Tremor

Amphibia

Morphological basis for a mechanical linkage in otolithic receptor transduction in the frog. D. E. Hillman and E. R. Lewis. bibliog il Science 174:416-19 O 22 '71

Crustaceans

Neuronal circuit mediating escape responses in crayfish. R. S. Zucker and others. bibliog il Science 173:645-50 Ag 13 '71

Oscillator neurons in crustacean ganglia. M. Mendelson. bibliog il Science 171:1170-3 Mr 19 '71

Stimulation-dependent alterations in peroxidase uptake at lobster neuromuscular junctions. E. Holtzman and others. bibliog il Science 173:733-6 Ag 20 '71

Synaptic facilitation: long-term neuromuscular facilitation in crustaceans. R. G. Sherman and H. L. Atwood. bibliog il Science 171:1248-50 Mr 26 '71

Synaptic transmission in the crayfish: increased release of transmitter substance by bacterial endotoxin. I. Parnas and others. bibliog il Science 171:1153-5 Mr 19 '71

Diseases

Latent herpes simplex virus in spinal ganglia of mice. J. G. Stevens and M. L. Cook. bibliog il Science 173:843-5 Ag 27 '71

Neuronal GM$_1$ gangliosidosis in a Siamese cat with β-galactosidase deficiency. H. J. Baker, jr. and others. bibliog il Science 174:838-9 N 19 '71
See also
Amaurotic family idiocy
Brain—Diseases
Huntington's chorea
Lesch-Nyhan syndrome
Sclerosis, Multiple

Fishes

Connections of the nurse shark's telencephalon. S. O. E. Ebbesson and D. M. Schroeder. bibliog il Science 173:254-6 Jl 16 '71

Garfish olfactory nerve: easily accessible source of numerous long, homogeneous, nonmyelinated axons. D. M. Easton. bibliog il Science 172:952-5 My 28 '71

Insects

Flight orientation in locusts. J. M. Camhi. il Sci Am 225:74-81 bibliog(p 120) Ag '71

Genetic control of an insect neuronal network. D. R. Bentley. bibliog il Science 174:1139-41 D 10 '71

Neural regeneration: delayed formation of central contacts by insect sensory cells. J. S. Edwards and J. Palka. bibliog il Science 172:591-4 My 7 '71

Receptive field organization of units in the first optic ganglion of diptera. D. W. Arnett. bibliog il Science 173:929-31 S 3 '71

Uncoupling cell junctions in a glandular epithelium by depolarizing current. S. J. Socolar and A. L. Politoff. bibliog il Science 172:492-4 Ap 30 '71

Mollusks

Aplysia californica: analysis of nuclear DNA in individual nuclei of giant neurons. R. J. Lasek and W. J. Dower. bibliog il Science 172:278-80 Ap 16 '71

Bilateral symmetry and interneuronal organization in the buccal ganglia of aplysia. D. Gardener. bibliog il Science 173:550-3 Ag 6 '71

Central and peripheral control of gill movements in aplysia. I. Kupfermann and others. bibliog il Science 174:1252-6 D 17 '71

Circadian rhythm: population of interacting neurons. J. W. Jacklet and J. Geronimo. bibliog il Science 174:299-302 O 15 '71

Cyclic adenosine monophosphate: function in photoreceptors. W. H. Miller and others. bibliog il Science 174:295-7 O 15 '71

Giant brain cells in mollusks A. O. D. Willows. il Sci Am 224:68-75 F '71

Laser stimulation of nerve cells in aplysia. R. L. Fork. bibliog il Science 171:907-8 Mr 5 '71

Salicylate: effect on membrane permeability of molluscan neurons. J. L. Barker and H. Levitan. bibliog il Science 172:1245-7 Je 18 '71

Serotonin: two different inhibitory actions on snail neurons. H. M. Gerschenfeld. bibliog il Science 171:1252-4 Mr 26 '71

Reptiles

Snake infrared receptors: thermal or photochemical mechanism? J. F. Harris and R. I. Gamow. bibliog il Science 172:1252-3 Je 18 '71

Surgery

Serum dopamine-β-hydroxylase: decrease after chemical sympathectomy. R. Weinshilboum and J. Axelrod. bibliog il Science 173:931-4 S 3 '71

NERVOUS tension. See Stress (physiology)

NERVOUSNESS
See also
Stage fright

NES, David Gulick

Israel: the 51st state? Cur 131:16-17 Jl '71

NESBITT, Elizabeth

Early record; address, October 30, 1970. bibliog f Horn Bk 47:268-74 Je '71

NESBITT, George B.

Memo to a young black, from an older one. Negro Hist Bul 34:127 O '71

NESBITT, Muriel, and Francke, Uta

Linkage groups II and XII of the mouse: cytological localization by fluorochrome staining. bibliog il Science 174:60-2 O 1 '71

NESTLÉ company

Merger breeds fears of monopoly. Bsns W p54 F 27 '71

NESTS

Where a bird nests. W. A. H. Birnie. il Read Digest 98:150-5 Je '71

You can get killed shooting birds' eggs. H. H. Harrison. il Nat Wildlife 9:10-15 Ap '71

NETBOY, Anthony
Japan's salmon industry. il Am For 77:32-6 D '71
Vicissitudes of the Pacific salmon. il Sea Front 17:83-93 Mr '71
NETHERBY, Steve
Canoe-camping the Adirondacks. il Field & S 76:56-7+ Jl '71
Drive-in caribou. il Field & S 76:164-6+ N '71
NETHERLANDS
See also
Airplanes, Military—Netherlands
Airlines—Netherlands
Booksellers and bookselling—Netherlands
Environmental policy—Netherlands
Flevohof
Restaurants—Netherlands
Visitors, Foreign—Netherlands

Description and travel
Holiday in Holland; cruising the canals and rivers. J. Smith. il Yachting 129:62-3+ F '71
Source Hollandaise. H. Sutton. Sat R 54:34+ Ap 24 '71

Economic conditions
Placid Holland boils over. B. Van Voorst. Newsweek 77:53+ My 10 '71

Industries
See also
Airplane industry—Netherlands
Electric industries—Netherlands

Politics and government
Placid Holland biols over. B. Van Voorst. il Newsweek 77:53+ My 10 '71

Religious institutions and affairs
Peace week in the Netherlands. H. Biersteker. Chr Cent 88:1330+ N 10 '71
See also
Catholic church in the Netherlands
Church and state in the Netherlands
NETHERLANDS dance theater
Dutch mutations; interview, ed. by G. Loney. G. Tetley. il Dance Mag 45:55-9 F '71
Netherlands dance theater, Auditorium theater, Chicago, Ill. A. Barzel. Dance Mag 45:79 Je '71
NETHERLANDS WEST INDIES
See also
Aruba (island)
NETO, Antônio Delfim. See Delfim Neto, A.
NETSCHERT, Bruce C.
Energy company: a monopoly trend in the energy markets. il por Bul Atom Sci 27:13-17 O '71
NETTLETON, A. E, company
Adventures in the skin trade. F. W. King. il Natur Hist 80:8-10+ bibliog(p 104) My '71
NETWORK analysis (planning) See Critical path analysis
NETZER, Dick
Why cities are going broke; interview. il por U S News 70:30-3 F 22 '71
NEUE Heimat companies. See Construction industry—Germany (Federal Republic)
NEUFELD, John
Thought, not necessarily the deed: sex in some of today's juvenile novels. il Wilson Lib Bul 46:147-52 O '71
NEUGARTEN, Bernice L.
First woman gerontologist receives Kleemeier award; excerpts from address. Aging 205:12+ N '71
NEUGEBAUER, G. See Münch, G. jt. auth.
NEUGROSCHEL, Joachim
(tr) See Celan, P. In the shape of a boar; Thread-suns; By all means; Today and tomorrow
NEUHAUS, Richard John
Not nature alone. il Harper 243:100-5 O; 6+ D '71
NEUMANN, Carl John
Red-hot new pistol in Rebel land. C. Kirkpatrick. il pors Sports Illus 34:42-5 F 8 '71 *
NEUMANN, Harry
Contemporary crisis of humanistic studies: education or propaganda? Sch & Soc 99: 178-80 Mr '71
NEUMARKT, Paul
Amos Tutuola: emerging African literature. bibliog Am Imago 28:129-45 Sum '71
NEURAMINIDASE
Human lymphocyte antigen reactivity modified by neuraminidase. E. A. Grothaus and others. bibliog il Science 173:542-4 Ag 6 '71
NEUROBIOLOGY

Conferences
Brain, genetics, and behavior. G. S. Omenn and A. G. Motulsky. Science 173:1255-6 S 24 '71

NEUROCHEMISTRY
Adenosine 3',5'-monophosphate in nervous tissue: increase associated with synaptic transmission. D. A. McAfee and others. bibliog il Science 171:1156-8 Mr 19 '71
[³H]adenosine triphosphate: release during stimulation of enteric nerves. C. Su and others. bibliog il Science 173:336-8 Jl 23 '71
Adrenergic neurotransmitter functions; Nobel lecture, December 12, 1970. U. S. von Euler. bibliog il Science 173:202-6 Jl 16 '71
Dopamine-sensitive adenyl cyclase: possible role in synaptic transmission. J. W. Kebabian and P. Greengard. bibliog il Science 174:1346-9 D 24 '71
Molecular biology of synaptic receptors. E. de Robertis. bibliog il Science 171:963-71 Mr 12 '71
Noradrenaline: fate and control of its biosynthesis; Nobel lecture, December 12, 1970. J. Axelrod. bibliog il Science 173:598-606 Ag 13 '71
Possible etiology of schizophrenia: progressive damage to the noradrenergic reward system by 6-hydroxydopamine. L. Stein and C. D. Wise. bibliog il Science 171:1032-6 Mr 12 '71
Preganglionic stimulation increases calcium uptake by sympathetic ganglia. M. P. Blaustein. bibliog il Science 172:391-3 Ap 23 '71
Proportional release of norepinephrine and dopamine-β-hydroxylase from sympathetic nerves. R. M. Weinshilboum and others. bibliog il Science 174:1349-51 D 24 '71
Receptors: localization and specificity of binding of serotonin in the central nervous system. S. G. A. Alivisatos and others. bibliog il Science 171:809-12 F 26 '71
See also
Brain—Analysis and chemistry

Conferences
Histochemistry of nervous transmission. R. L. Hunter. Science 172:295 Ap 16 '71
NEUROLOGY
See also
Developmental neurology
NEUROMUSCULAR junctions
Developing neuromuscular junctions: first signs of chemical transmission during formation in tissue culture. N. Robbins and T. Yonezawa. bibliog il Science 172: 395-8 Ap 23 '71
Quantal mechanism of neural transmitter release; Nobel lecture, December 12, 1970. B. Katz. bibliog il Science 173:123-6 Jl 9 '71
Stimulation-dependent alterations in peroxidase uptake at lobster neuromuscular junctions. E. Holtzman and others. bibliog il Science 173:733-6 Ag 20 '71
NEURONS. See Nerve cells
NEURORECEPTORS. See Receptors, Neural
NEUROSECRETORY cells. See Nerve cells
NEUROSES
Neurosis: just a bad habit? il Time 98:41 Ag 2 '71
See also
Depression, Mental
Phobias
NEUROTOXINS. See Toxins and antitoxins
NEUTRALITY
See also
Intervention (international law)
Switzerland—Neutrality
NEUTRINOS
Mystery of the missing neutrinos. D. E. Thomsen. il Sci N 100:210-11 S 25 '71
Neutrino astronomy: probing the sun's interior. G. L. Wick. il Science 173:1011-12 S 10 '71
NEUTRON radiography. See Radiography
NEUTRON stars
Neutron stars vs. black holes. D. E. Thomsen. il Sci N 99:151-2 F 27 '71
Possible neutron star; Ara XR-1. Sky & Tel 43:12-13 Ja '72
Solid stars. M. A Ruderman il Sci Am 224: 24-31 F '71
Starquakes: have they been observed? L. C. Green. il Sky & Tel 41:76-9 F '71
Stellar old age: neutron stars and pulsars. A. L. Hammond. Science 171:1133-4 Mr 19 '71
X-ray blackbody: a neutron star? il Sci N 100:290 O 30 '71
NEUTRONS
Structure of the proton and the neutron. H. W. Kendall and W. K. H. Panofsky. il Sci Am 224:60-6+ Je '71

Beams
Visual phenomena noted by human subjects on exposure to neutrons of energies less than 25 million electron volts. T. F. Budinger and others. bibliog il Science 172: 868-70 My 21 '71

NEVADA
See also
Fishing—Nevada
Lehman Caves National Monument
Prisons—Nevada
Tahoe, Lake
Water pollution—Nevada

Parks and reserves
Half a day north from Las Vegas; Cathedral Gorge state park. il Sunset 147:24 Ag '71
It's 11 gravel miles to these ovens; Ward charcoal ovens historic state monument. il Sunset 146:58 Je '71
It's lonesome at Fort Churchill. il Sunset 147:32 O '71
Picnic with a Comstock millionaire. il Sunset 147:41 O '71

NEVELSON, Louise
I don't want to waste time, says Louise Nevelson at 70. R. Bongartz. il pors N Y Times Mag p 12-13+ Ja 24 '71 *

NEVILLE, Phoebe
Phoebe Neville, Judson memorial church. NYC. P. G. Richmond. Dance Mag 45:72 F '71 *

NEVIN, Bob
Quiet man. il por Newsweek 77:67-8 Ap 26 '71 *

NEVIN, John J.
Zenith tunes in on a new president. por Bsns W p24 My 22 '71 *

NEVINS, Allan
Nevins papers and library at Columbia. Sch & Soc 99:462-3 D '71 *
Obituary
Am Heritage por 22:2-3 Je '71. B. Catton
Sat R 54:24 Mr 20 '71. A. Whitman

NEW, Lloyd Kiva
New vitality rekindles proud fires of the past. House B 113:38-9+ Je '71

NEW American review
Literary community. R. K. Morris. Nation 212:695-6 My 31 '71

NEW art association
NAA revision of the CAA. E. F. Fry. Art in Am 59:31-2 Mr '71.

NEW BRITAIN, Conn.
Lighting
Does your city die at night? il Am City 86:72 Ja '71

NEW BRUNSWICK, Canada
See also
Education—New Brunswick
Grand Manan Island

NEW business enterprises. See Business enterprises

NEW cities and towns
Barrio Gaudí; Reus, Spain. J. M. Carandell. il Arch Forum 134:22-7 My '71
Big move to new towns. E. Carruth. il Fortune 84:94-7+ S '71
Cities or towns to live in; symposium. Cur 125:30-41 Ja '71
Columbia and the new cities, by G. Breckenfeld. Review
Commonweal 94:506-7 S 24 '71. S. Goldstein
New Repub 165:31-2 S 4 '71. G. Gappert
Don't oversell new towns. W. L. Slayton. Am City 86:8 My '71
Housing and the public sector. M. Harrington. Arch Forum 134:32-3 My '71; Reply with rejoinder. B. P. Hayden. 135:15 Jl '71
New business from new towns? M. Apgar, 4th. il Harvard Bsns R 49:90-109 Ja '71
New business on the urban frontier communities; symposium, ed. by M. Lieberman. il Sat R 54:20-31+ My 15 '71
New cities in the countryside. G. Logsdon and J. Carlson. il Farm J 95:34-5+ Mr '71
New city in a hurry; Palm Coast, Fla. R. Levy. por Duns 97:63 Je '71
New towns 73 years later. W. Von Eckhardt. il Sat R 54:61 F 6 '71
New towns, urban rehabilitation; the predevelopment costs; address, February 16, 1971. D. Rockefeller. Vital Speeches 37:354-7 Ap 1 '71
Nice piece of desert; Cochiti Lake, a fraud in the recreational city business. R. A. Jones. il Nation 213:616-26 D 13 '71
Race is on for new towns. Bsns W p 130+ Mr 13 '71
Sir Ebenezer Howard and the town planning movement, by D. MacFadyen. Review
New Repub 164:30-1 My 22 '71. C. Whitman
U.S. gets its first walled city; Sugar Creek, Tex. electronically fortified. il Bsns W p28 Mr 6 '71

Le Vaudreuil: French experiment in urbanism without tears. C. Holden. il Science 174:39-42 O 1 '71
What America can learn from Britain's new towns. il U S News 71:61-3 S 20 '71
What it will take to bring cities back to life. D. Rockefeller. il por U S News 70:50-2+ Je 7 '71
See also
California City, Calif.
Columbia, Md.
Lake Havasu City, Ariz.
Radburn, N.J.
Soul City, N.C.

Federal aid
More millions for new cities, towns. il U S News 70:45 Ja 18 '71
Starving new communities. New Repub 164:9 My 29 '71

Finance
Private investment and the public weal. A. Downes. il Sat R 54:24-6+ My 15 '71

NEW Covenanters (sect) See Jewish sects

NEW education. See Education, Experimental

NEW ENGLAND
Six gems of New England; a photographic tribute. Holiday 49:48-51 Ap '71
See also
Architecture, Domestic—New England
Churches—New England

Description and travel
Flaming fall foliage. N. D. Ford. il por Har Yrs 11:6-16 Ag '71
New England. S. Cuneo. il Mlle 72:244-6 Ap '71

History
Colonial period
Order and growth, authority and meaning in colonial New England. R. Isaac. Am Hist R 76:728-37 Je '71
See also
Puritans

Hotels, taverns, etc.
See Hotels, taverns, etc.—United States

Intellectual life
New England tradition. H. Carruth. bibliog il Am Lib 2:690-700, 938-48 Jl, O '71

Social history
Order and growth, authority and meaning in colonial New England. R. Isaac. Am Hist R 76:728-37 Je '71

NEW ENGLAND book festival. See Book fairs

NEW ENGLAND book show. See Book exhibits

NEW ENGLAND conservatory of music, Boston
Oldest school. Q. Eaton. il Opera N 35:12-16 Ap 17 '71

NEW ENGLAND dance theatre. See Dance companies

NEW ENGLAND in literature
New England tradition. H. Carruth. bibliog il Am Lib 2:690-700, 938-48 Jl, O '71

NEW ENGLAND library association
Of note; annual conference. J. L. Nash. il Am Lib 2:1136-7 D '71

NEW ENGLAND Patriots (football club) See Football clubs

NEW ENGLAND poets. See Poets, American

NEW ENGLAND witchcraft. See Witchcraft

NEW ENGLANDERS
If New Hampshire makes it. I. Mothner. Look 35:33-6 Ja 12 '71

NEW Forest. See National parks and reserves —England

NEW GLARUS, Wis.
Where is Tell? Wilhelm Tell festival. H. Kubly. il Holiday 49:48-9+ Jl '71

NEW GUINEA
Description and travel
New Guinea. M. Kirk. il Harp Baz 104:20+ Jl '71

History
19th century champion of anti-racism in New Guinea; excerpts from diaries, correspondence and other papers, ed. by N. A. Butinov. N. N. Miklukha-Maklai. il por UNESCO Courier 24:24-7 N '71

Native races
Flow of energy in an agricultural society; Tsembaga tribe. R. A. Rappaport. il Sci Am 225:116-22+ bibliog(p244) S '71
Peoples of the Pacific; ed. by M. Mead and P. McClanahan. bibliog il pors Natur Hist 80:46-7 My '71

NEW HAMPSHIRE
See also
Architecture, Domestic—New Hampshire
Camps—New Hampshire
Education—New Hampshire

NEW HAMPSHIRE. University, Durham
Meet the press. il por Newsweek 78:84 Ag 23 '71

NEW HAVEN, Conn.
Low-cost tunnel renovation. il Am City 86:14 F '71

City planning
Model city, by F. Powledge. Review
Arch Forum 134:71 Ap '71. V. Scully
Nation 212:663-4 My 24 '71. S. Kaplan

Politics and government
How reformers bombed in New Haven. D.
Hale. Commonweal 94:473-7 S 17 '71; Reply
with rejoinder. E. Switzer. 95:195+ N 26 '71

Social conditions
How reformers bombed in New Haven. D.
Hale. Commonweal 94:473-7 S 17 '71; Reply
with rejoinder. E. Switzer. 95:195+ N 26 '71

NEW HAVEN oil slicks. See Oil pollution of rivers, harbors, etc.

NEW HEBRIDES
This must be the place! J. Griffin. il Sat R 54:54+ O 23 '71
See also
Rites and ceremonies—New Hebrides

Native races
Taboos and magic rule Namba lives. K. Muller. il por Nat Geog 141:56-83 Ja '72

NEW JERSEY
See also
Agriculture—New Jersey
Architecture, Domestic—New Jersey
Bergen County
Colleges and universities, State—New Jersey
Conservation of resources—New Jersey
Fishing—New Jersey
Hunting—New Jersey
Libraries—New Jersey
Passaic River
Politics, Corruption in—New Jersey
Port of New York authority
Prisons—New Jersey
Regional planning—New Jersey
School libraries—New Jersey
Transportation—New Jersey
Vigilance committees—New Jersey

Parks and reserves
Instant wilderness; Oswego River trip
through the Wharton tract. R. A. Lodge.
il por Parks & Rec 6:19-22+ F '71

Politics and government
See also
Politics, Corruption in—New Jersey

NEW JERSEY library association
NJLA cuts ALA support: COPES' tight budget cited. Library J 96:3934-5 D 1 '71

NEW JERSEY lottery. See Lotteries

NEW JERSEY standard oil company. See
Standard oil company (New Jersey)

NEW JERSEY symphony orchestra
Musical events; concert at Carnegie Hall. W.
Sargeant. New Yorker 47:186-8 N 20 '71

NEW left (politics) See Right and left (political science)

NEW life; story. See Plagemann, B.

NEW MARKET, Battle of, 1864
V.M.I. remembers; the Battle of New Market
annual re-enactment. il Time 97:24 My 24 '71

NEW MEXICO
See also
Fishing—New Mexico
Hunting—New Mexico
Pueblo Indians
White Sands National Monument

Description and travel
New Mexico nuggets. F. A. Tinker. il Travel 136:36-9+ S '71

History
Midas of New Mexico. H. Chapman and T.
Chapman. bibliog il pors Am West 8:4-9+ Ja '71

Land tenure
See Land tenure—United States

NEW ORLEANS
Fat Tuesday; Mardi gras and the hippies.
il Newsweek 77:57 Mr 8 '71
New Orleans and her river. J. Judge. il Nat
Geog 139:151-87 F '71

Stroll through New Orleans. M. Evans; V.
D. Hahn. Am Home 74:54+ Mr '71
Vieux Carré. M. Evans. il Am Home 74:82+ Mr '71

Architecture
American treasury: New Orleans. V. D.
Hahn. il Am Home 74:72-81 Mr '71
New Orleans architecture: the lower garden
district, by S. Wilson, jr. and B. Lemann.
Review
Antiques il 101:255-6 Ja '72. J. G. Guthrie, jr
New Orleans' Vieux Carré. G. McCue. il Art
in Am 59:96-7 My '71

Description
New Orleans: a top spot in the fall. Bsns W p81 S 18 '71
New Orleans: step by step through the crescent city. R. Deardorff. il Travel 135:36-41 F '71
Vacation getaways. F. Shemanski. il Schol
Teach Jr/Sr High p20 My 3 '71

Education
New Orleans schools ten years later. F.
Guillory. America 125:93-5 Ag 21 '71
Orleans educators association: tradition breaker. L. Felix. Todays Ed 60:70 N '71
Pattern practices: we bombed in New Orleans. C. Suhor. Engl J 60:1221-4 D '71

Hotels, restaurants, etc.
Gourmet in New Orleans. G. M. Semmes.
Holiday 49:20 Mr '71

Mayors
Moon over New Orleans. por Newsweek 77:94 Je 14 '71

Music
Saints preserved; Preservation hall concerts.
K. R. Zimmermann. Nat R 23:882 Ag 10 '71
See also
New Orleans opera house association

Sanitary affairs
High-performance incinerator. J. Cassreino
and others. il Am City 86:54-7 Ja '71

Social life and customs
E. J. Bellocq: storeyville portraits. by L.
Friedlander and J. Szarkowski. Review
Commonweal 94:409-10 Ag 6 '71. S. Cohen

NEW ORLEANS Mardi gras. See Carnival

NEW ORLEANS opera house association
Report:
Salome. J. Belsom. Opera N 35:24 My 15 '71

NEW ORLEANS stadium. See Stadiums

NEW Philharmonia orchestra
Maazel to the N.P.O. T. Heinitz. Sat R 54:59 F 27 '71

NEW products. See Products, New

NEW republic (periodical)
Midtown and the Village. A. Kazin. il Harper 242:82-9 Ja '71

NEW right (politics) See Right and left (political science)

NEW RIVER
Blue Ridge dams: the pollution dilution approach. R. E. Janssen. il Nat Parks & Con
Mag 45:14-17 Ag '71

NEW step (organization) See Ex-nuns, priests, etc.

NEW stock issues. See Stocks

NEW Thought
Key to happiness; excerpts from Living the
infinite way. J. S. Goldsmith. U S News
71:108 S 20 '71

NEW towns. See New cities and towns

NEW university conference
New university conference. C. A. Krause.
New Repub 164:17-18 Mr 20 '71

NEW Vibrations (folk music) See Rock music (songs, etc)

NEW World. See America

NEW World man. See Man, Prehistoric

NEW YEAR
Happy New Year! with recipes. N. Hazelton. Nat R 23:1480-1 D 31 '71
New Year's prayer; excerpt from issue of
January 2, 1942. D. Lawrence. U S News
72:80+ Ja 10 '72

NEW YEARS parties. See Entertaining

NEW YEARS resolutions
Me I'm going to be. J. Viorst. il Redbook
138:66-7+ Ja '72
Resolutions, anyone? P. Bracken. il Read Digest 98:129-31 Ja '71

NEW YORK (city)

Bohemia, such as it is, on the West side. F. Morton. il N Y Times Mag p22-3+ My 9 '71

Parting shots; appalling homecoming to New York. F. Grehan. il Life 70:73-4+ My 21 '71

Summer glimpses. New Yorker 47:24-6 Jl 31 '71

Walking my dog on the West side. J. Yglesias. il Esquire 75:120-3 Je '71

Who owns New York? il Forbes 107:24-6+ Je 1 '71
See also
Port of New York authority
Staten Island

Airports

Academy panel kicks over traces; study of consequences of new runways in Jamaica Bay. C. Holden. Science 171:781 F 26 '71

IFR DCA to JFK; flight log. R. Peterson. il Flying 89:88-92 O '71

Kennedy airport seeks travel delay cuts. K. J. Stein. Aviation W 94:36 Je 28 '71

Master pitchman for a jetport. il por Bsns W p60 Mr 27 '71

Le Monde restaurant, TWA terminal, John F. Kennedy airport. il Arch Rec 149:86-7 Ja '71

New aviation growth blocked at New York. Aviation W 95:31 O 4 '71

New York city studies hydroport usage. R. S. Kahn. il Aviation W 95:29-30 S 20 '71

Pavilion at Kennedy; the National airlines terminal at New York's JFK airport. il Arch Forum 135:18-25 O '71

Stewart expansion stirs mixed reaction. R. S. Kahn. Aviation W 95:28-9 Jl 19 '71

Study group opposes Kennedy expansion. Aviation W 94:27 F 22 '71

Architecture

Bright new life the third time around; Manhattan limestone house. S. G. Lewin. il House B 113:102-7 My '71

Last cast iron. C. Robinson. il Arch Forum 135:46-9 S '71

Manhattan safari. K. Simmon. il Natur Hist 80:72-7 My '71
See also
Brooklyn—Architecture
New York (city)—Buildings
New York (city)—Empire State building

Art

Art world (cont) H. Rosenberg. New Yorker 46:71-5 Ja 30; 47:73-7 Mr 6; 117-20 Mr 27; 102-5 My 8; 101-5 Je 12; 201-4+ N 20 '71; 43-6 Ja 1 '72

Give my regards to Eighth street. M. Feldman. il por Art in Am 59:96-9 Mr '71

Potpourri. R. Berenson. Nat R 23:1367 D 3 '71
See also
New York (city)—Galleries and museums

Banks

Bank that makes up for lost time; Manufacturers Hanover. il Bsns W p58-61 Ja 16 '71

Big push on the Swiss banks; First national city bank of New York. J. Ross-Skinner. il Duns 98:46-8 Jl '71

How Citibank gets the job done; computer operations. il Bsns W p 106+ Je 5 '71

How it feels to be Naderized; report on First national city bank of New York. J. Tompkins. il por Time 98:63-4 Jl 5 '71

Money for sale; First national city bank. por Forbes 107:49-50 Ap 1 '71

Rate change draws cautious approval; Citibank's floating prime rate. il Bsns W p25 O 30 '71
See also
Morgan guaranty trust company

Bookstores

See Booksellers and bookselling—New York (state)

Bridges

TV monitors a bridge; Verrazano-Narrows bridge. il Am City 86:76-7 Ja '71

Budget

See New York (city)—Finance

Buildings

Classical walk; tour of buildings designed by S. White. New Yorker 47:47-8 N 20 '71

New York hangs out the for-rent sign; surplus of office space. E. Carruth. il Fortune 83:86-90+ F '71

Office space goes begging in New York. il U S News 70:50-1 F 1 '71

Penn Central: now the family jewels; forthcoming sale of real-estate. il Newsweek 77:79 Je 14 '71

Carnegie Hall

Music to my ears; all-Brahms recital on behalf of Student fund. I. Kolodin. Sat R 54:27 N 13 '71

Churches

New York crime and the religious sector. T. Early. Chr Cent 88:977-8 Ag 18 '71

Real thing; All nite soul at St Peter's Lutheran church. M. E. Marty. Chr Cent 88:1311 N 3 '71
See also
New York (city)—St John the Divine, Cathedral of

City center of music and drama

See City center of music and drama, inc.

City planning

New set of rules to reshape New York; incentive zoning. il Bsns W p70-2 F 13 '71

New town in town; Battery Park city. il Newsweek 78:40+ Jl 19 '71
See also
Regional plan association

City university

See New York (city). City university

Clubs

See also
Salmagundi club

Commissions of inquiry

See Commissions of inquiry

Community centers

Clinton youth and family center. il Arch Rec 149:107-10 Je '71

Consumer affairs, Department of

Consumer champion lays down the law; with editorial comment. H. Wingo. il pors Life 71:3, 22-9 Jl 16 '71

Courts

I have nothing to do with justice; M. Erdmann; the guilty always win, with editorial comment. J. Mills. il pors Life 70:2A, 56-8+ Mr 12 '71

Two John Lindsays. D. K. Shipler. New Repub 164:16-20 My 1 '71; Reply with rejoinder. M. D. Glass. 164:33-4 Je 26 '71

Crime

Fortress on 78th street; with account by K. Thorsen, editorial comment and questionnaire. il Life 71:3, 26-36 N 19; 3 D 10 '71

Lessons of the street. B. J. Friedman. il Harper 243:86-8+ S '71

New York crime and the religious sector; church burglaries. T. Early. Chr Cent 88:977-8 Ag 18 '71

Rat packs of New York. S. Stevens. il N Y Times Mag p28-9+ N 28 '71; Discussion. p 14 D 26 '71

Stealing cars is a growth industry. P. Hellman. il pors N Y Times Mag p7+ Je 20 '71
See also
Mafia

Anecdotes, facetiae, satire, etc.

An, all things considered, not, realistically speaking, immodest proposal. D. Fagan. Nat R 23:1115 O 8 '71

Description

Rediscovery of New York city; 80-mile canoe trip over New York waterfront. C. Phinizy. il Sports Illus 35:98-101+ N 22 '71

Economic conditions

Decline and decline of New York. R. Starr. il N Y Times Mag p31+ N 21 '71; Discussion. p 18+ D 12; 2+ D 19 '71

National goals; survival is the issue. J. V. Lindsay. il Sat R 54:46-8 Ja 23 '71

New York city goes out in a rowboat. il Time 97:13-15 Je 21 '71

Education

Battlefield communique; high school security measures. Time 98:52 Ag 16 '71

Brooklyn's little giant of Catholic education; Msgr. Molloy. G. A. Kelly. America 125:312-14 O 23 '71

Chancellor Harvey Scribner; the most powerful man in the school system, on paper. J. Lelyveld. il pors N Y Times Mag p30-1+ Mr 21 '71

College bound; a study in success. B. Bard. il Parents Mag 46:66-7+ S '71

Educational ombudsman for New York city? S. P. Lachman and D. Bresnick. bibliog f Sch & Soc 99:168-70 Mr '71

NEW YORK (city)—Education—*Continued*
Help for girls in trouble. B. Shanas. Parents
    Mag 46:42-3+ Je '71
Mini high; Haaren high school. il Newsweek
    78:55 O 4 '71
New York's mini-schools. D. Divoky. Sat R
    54:60-1+ D 18 '71
Oasis in East Harlem; East Harlem block
    schools day care centers. J. Black. il Sat R
    54:52-3+ F 20 '71
Open school: an experiment in learning
    through joy. S. G. Lanes. il Parents Mag
    46:56-9 S '71
Talk of the town: bazaar to prevent cutting
    back rehabilitation programs of Livingston
    school. New Yorker 47:41-3 O 30 '71
What price professionalism? High school of
    performing arts. R. Feinberg. il por Library
    J 96:691-4 F 15 '71
    See also
Brooklyn—Education
New York (city), City university
Private schools. Negro

Education, Board of
Students' rights and responsibilities: the New
    York city experience; with text of resolu-
    tion; study-discussion program by C. Smal-
    lenburg and H. Smallenburg. S. P. Lach-
    man. bibliog il PTA Mag 65:14-17, 33 My '71

Empire State building
Empire State building. W. McQuade. il Life
    71:20 D 10 '71
Points of view. J. Greenberg. il Mod Phot
    36:120-1 Ja '72

Employees
    See also
New York (city)—Strikes

Environmental protection administration
Running for mayor on a garbage truck; J.
    Kretchmer. G. Lichtenstein. il pors N Y
    Times Mag p30-1+ Ap 25 '71

Finance
City hall discovers productivity. D. Cordtz.
    il Fortune 84:92-6+ O '71
City-sponsored health research eludes New
    York budget ax. R. J. Bazell. Science 173:
    1108-10 S 17 '71
Limited liability. il Time 97:17 My 3 '71
Lindsay's threat. Newsweek 77:59 My 3 '71
New York city goes out in a rowboat. il
    Time 97:13-15 Je 21 '71
Passed: 1971-72 operating budget. New York-
    er 47:19-21 Jl 3 '71
    See also
New York (city)—Taxation

Fire department
Company for dinner? Engine 310, Ladder
    174, Brooklyn, that is. K. V. Brown. il
    pors Todays Health 49:46-9+ My '71
Get me an ax! Rescue company 1 and Engine
    65. W. J. McKean. il Look 35:18-24 Je 29 '71

Foreign population
Japanization of New York. D. Butwin. il
    Sat R 54:63-5 N 27 '71
    See also
Puerto Ricans in the United States

Fountains
    See Fountains

Galleries and museums
Art; downtown galleries. L. Alloway. Nation
    213:348 O 11 '71
Art; the Tanager, a cooperative gallery. L.
    Alloway. Nation 214:29-30 Ja 3 '72
Gallery-hopping in New York. D. Davis. il
    Newsweek 78:36-7 D 27 '71
National art museum of sport. D. A. Field.
    il Sch Arts 70:40-3 Mr '71
New museum; Japan house gallery. S. B.
    Sherrill. il Antiques 100:286 S '71
New York. G. Glueck. See issues of Art in
    America
Reviews and previews. See issues of Art
    news
Underneath the archness; SoHo art commu-
    nity. J. Ashbery. Art N 70:29 N '71
    See also
American museum of natural history
Metropolitan museum of art
Museum of contemporary crafts
Museum of modern art
Museum of the city of New York
Solomon R. Guggenheim museum
Whitney museum of American art

Gardens
Flowers on Avenue D. C. A. Lewis. il
    Horticulture 49:30-1+ Ag '71
    See also
Brooklyn botanic garden
New York botanical garden

Greenwich Village
Greenwich Village: help! il Newsweek 78:70
    Ag 16 '71

Harbor
Salvaging New York harbor debris. G. Pier-
    son and F. E. Hampf. il Cons 26:2-3 Ag '71

Harlem
Black Mafia moves into the numbers racket.
    F. J. Cook. il N Y Times Mag p26-7+ Ap 4
    '71
Introduction to flash; Harlem drug dealer.
    R. Woodley. il Esquire 75:79-83 Ap '71;
    Same abr. with title Drug scene; excerpt
    from Dealer; portrait of a cocaine agent.
    Read Digest 99:103-7 D '71
Mr One-Two-Five Street; column in Amster-
    dam news; interview. L. Matthews. New
    Yorker 47:30-1 S 18 '71
Oasis in East Harlem; East Harlem block
    schools day care centers. J. Black. il Sat R
    54:52-3+ F 20 '71
Urban health and environment: a new ap-
    proach; East Harlem environmental exten-
    sion service. R. J. Bazell. Science 174:1005-
    6 D 3 '71

Historic houses, etc.
Defender: Mrs M. Gayle. New Yorker 47:
    23-4 Ag 28 '71

History
New York is worth twenty Richmonds. N.
    Brandt. il Am Heritage 22:74-80+ O '71

Hospitals
Lady takes charge; new hospital director
    brings sensitive medical care to Harlem's
    needy. P. Bailey. il pors Ebony 27:156-8+
    N '71
Report on the abortion capital of the coun-
    try. S. Edminston. il N Y Times Mag p 10-
    11+ Ap 11 '71; Discussion. p80 My 9 '71

Hotels, restaurants, etc.
From quick lunch to quick millions; Riese
    chain. il Bsns W p 126 O 23 '71
Gamble on Manhattan; opening of Park lane
    hotel. il por Time 97:92 My 17 '71
Goings on about town. See issues of New
    Yorker
Lunch of a lifetime; visit to the Four seasons
    restaurant, with recipes. il Seventeen 30:
    92-3+ Ja '71
Luncheonette: Marty's luncheonette on
    Sherman avenue. New Yorker 47:26-8 Ag
    14 '71
Où est la cuisine d'antan? desperate help sit-
    uation in restaurants. N. Hazelton. Nat R
    23:1366 D 3 '71
Reward: lunch at the Fondue pot. New
    Yorker 47:33 Ap 17 '71
Stars eat out: singers' guide to New York
    restaurants. Q. Eaton. il Opera N 35:12-16
    Mr 6 '71
Talk of the town; party at new Bengali
    restaurant. New Yorker 47:24-5 D 25 '71
Thebouidienne: fish and rice dish at the
    African chef in Harlem; interview. W.
    Werner. New Yorker 47:44-5 N 6 '71
    See also
Bars and barrooms
Night clubs

Housing
Mock trial: Housing crimes trial, conceived
    by the Metropolitan council on housing and
    staged by community organizations. New
    Yorker 46:22-4 Ja 9 '71
New York, N.Y; the East River project. il
    Arch Forum 134:42-5 My '71
Roofs or ceilings. M. Friedman. Newsweek
    77:92 Mr 22 '71
Stuyvesant town USA, by A. Simon. Review
    Commonweal 93:403-4 Ja 22 '71. R. J. Neu-
    haus
    See also
East Side house settlement, inc.
Queens, N.Y.—Housing
Rent laws

Industries
Far from the madding crowd? reversing the
    exodus to suburbia. il Forbes 107:28-9 Ja 15
    '71

NEW YORK (city)—Continued

Libraries

Library urban info network scheme explained to NYLA; summary of statement, 1971. T. Costello. por Library J 96:3707 N 15 '71

Run twice as fast: service to children. H. R. Sattley. bibliog il Am Lib 2:845-9 S '71

See also
Brooklyn public library
New York public library
Queens borough public library

Mayors

See also
Lindsay, J. V.

Metropolitan district

See also
Regional plan association

Metropolitan museum of art

See Metropolitan museum of art

Moral conditions

See also
New York (city)—Crime
Prostitution

Municipal art society

See Municipal art society of New York

Music

Audiences, what's happened to them? F. Taylor. Hi Fi 20:MA10-12+ D '70

Behind the scenes. P. G. Davis. Hi Fi 21:22 D '71

Boulez and new breezes; concerts in Philharmonic Hall. A. Satz. por Hi Fi 21:MA 12+ Ag '71

Current chronicle; Henze conducting American symphony orchestra. S. Keats. il Mus Q 57:141-8 Ja '71

Debuts & reappearances. See issues of High fidelity and Musical America

Music (cont) D. Hamilton. Nation 212:157-8, 315-17, 445-6, 637-8; 213:156-7, 254, 443-4, 670 F 1, Mr 8, Ap 5, My 17, Ag 30, S 20, N 1, D 20 '71

Music to my ears. I. Kolodin. See issues of Saturday review

Musical events. W. Sargeant. See issues of New Yorker

New York: a week of Josquin. S. T. Sommer. il Hi Fi 21:MA14-15 O '71

Report:
Jesus Christ superstar. F. Merkling. il Opera N 36:30 D 18 '71
Puccini's original version of Madama Butterfly. H. E. Phillips. Opera N 35:29 Mr 13 '71
Survival of St Joan, a medieval rock opera by Hank and Gary Ruffin. S. Jenkins. il Opera N 35:31 Mr 27 '71

Three musical gatherings: Theatre 80 St Marks opening; Harlem jazz music center, inc. open house; street festival on Lenox avenue. New Yorker 47:32-3 S 11 '71

See also
Little orchestra society, New York
New York city opera company
New York philharmonic-symphony orchestra
New York pro musica antiqua (organization)

Negroes

Annals of law; false arrest of black T. Goins by Bronx police on narcotics charge. E. J. Kahn, jr. New Yorker 46:76-84 F 6 '71

Newspapers

Around city hall; pressroom. A. Logan. New Yorker 47:50+ D 25 '71

Daily will try where others failed; new New York afternoon newspaper. por Bsns W p27-8 O 16 '71

New dailies whistle past the graveyard; New York daily mirror and the New York American. il Bsns W p22+ Ja 23 '71

See also
Herald. New York
New York mirror
New York times
Village voice (newspaper)

Noise

Visible noise; Project Quiet City. S. Lindsay. Sat R 54:54 Mr 6 '71

Office buildings

See New York (city)—Buildings

Parks and playgrounds

Day in the life of Riverside park. G. Drummond. America 125:265 O 9 '71

Demonstration: protest against subway in Central park New Yorker 47:21-2 S 4 '71

Flowers; benefit preview opening of the third annual Bryant park flower show. New Yorker 47:34-5 O 16 '71

New vest-pocket park; Greenacre park. S. Lindsay. il Sat R 54:94 D 4 '71

Zoo friends; benefit party at Central park zoo. New Yorker 47:32-4 Je 5 '71

See also
New York (city)—Police department—Central park precinct

Photographs

Bill Jorden: the real and exotic New York. il Pop Phot 69:78-81 Jl '71

Bruce Davidson: East 100th street. M. Edelson. il Pop Phot 69:110-17+ O '71

New York city in the nineteenth century; exhibit of photographs at the New York historical society. S. B. Sherrill. Antiques 99:14+ Ja '71

Parting shots; appalling homecoming to New York. F. Grehan. il Life 70:73-4+ My 21 '71

Police

Annals of law; false arrest of black T. Goins by Bronx police on narcotics charge. E. J. Kahn, jr. New Yorker 46:76-84 F 6 '71

Bad connection; non-criminal charges against E. Egan. il por Newsweek 78:28 N 29 '71

Cops as pushers; findings of Knapp commission. Time 98:17-18 N 8 '71

Cops on the take; Knapp commission hearings. il por Newsweek 78:48+ N 1 '71

Crusader; F. Serpico's testimony on corruption. por Newsweek 77:24 My 31 '71

Guarding the guardians: hearings by Knapp commission. il por Time 98:22+ N 1 '71

Knapp commission didn't know it couldn't be done. B. Davidson. il N Y Times Mag p 16-17+ Ja 9 '72

Knapp trap. il Newsweek 79:16 Ja 3 '72

Mourning the police. il Time 97:8 Je 7 '71

Murphy among the meat-eaters. T. Buckley. il por N Y Times Mag p 10-11+ D 19 '71

New York ten; murdered policemen. G. Astor. il N Y Times Mag p32-5 D 12 '71

New York: the cops return. il Newsweek 77:47-8 F 1 '71

New York's rotten apples; report of the Knapp commission. Newsweek 78:78-9 Jl 12 '71

Policing the police. Newsweek 78:41 S 6 '71

Red-handed men in blue; Knapp commission hearings. il Newsweek 78:77-8 N 8 '71

Suddenly, this summer. il Newsweek 77:29 Je 7 '71

Taking dirty money. il por Time 98:20 S 13 '71

TV in helicopter aids New York police. K. J. Stein. il Aviation W 95:42-5 Ag 2 '71

Up against the cops; Knapp commission on corruption. il por Time 97:52+ My 31 '71

What language do you speak? wording in reports of police killings. J. Burnham. Nat R 23:633 Je 15 '71

Police department

Bureau of special services

BOSS is watching. C. Dreifus. il Nation 212:102-8 Ja 25 '71

Central Park precinct

Auxiliary; interview. E. Abramowitz. New Yorker 47:28-30 D 18 '71

Police strike

See Strikes—United States—Police

Politics and government

Around city hall (cont) A. Logan. New Yorker 46:77-80+ Ja 16; 47:142+ Mr 20; 117-24 My 15; 79-82 Je 26; 64-70 Ag 21; 105-12 O 30; 50+ D 25 '71

Carter Burden question. T. Meehan. il por N Y Times Mag p33+ N 7 '71; Discussion. p6+ N 28 '71

City as sandbox; or, Now we know what John Lindsay does. Nat R 23:1339-40 D 3 '71

Conversion of John Lindsay. il por Time 98:7-9 Ag 23 '71

Fellows: program to train college students. New Yorker 46:28-30 Ja 16 '71

Lindsay: a switch in time? il por Newsweek 78:15-16+ Ag 23 '71

Saving cities from abuse. Cur 131:14-15 Jl '71

Should New York city be the 51st state? il Time 97:14-15 Je 21 '71; Same with title City states versus national cities. Cur 131:11-14 Jl '71

Stalking of the president; R. Aurelio. R. Wool. il Esquire 76:85-7+ Jl '71

NEW YORK (city)—Politics and government
—*Continued*
Statehood for cities: the impossible dream.
R. Reeves. Sat R 54:18-21 S 4 '71
Travelling office; how E. I. Koch meets his
constituents. New Yorker 47:30-3 O 2 '71
Two John Lindsays. D. K. Shipler. New Re-
pub 164:16-20 My 1 '71; Reply with rejoin-
der. M. D. Glass. 164:33-4 Je 26 '71
Up drawbridges. il Newsweek 77:47-8 Je 21
'71

Anecdotes, facetiae, satire, etc.
Lindsay papers. A. Jay. Nat R 23:990 S 10 '71
Metropolitan comics; comic strip. J. Steven-
son. New Yorker 47:36-9 Jl 17 '71

Poor
See also
New York (city)—Public welfare

Prisons and reformatories
Waiting for a riot. J. Mills. il Life 71:30-5 O
1 '71

Protests, demonstrations, etc.
Demonstration: protest against subway in
Central park. New Yorker 47:21-2 S 4 '71

Public health
Cause and effect; decline in birthrate with
new abortion law. Sci Am 225:42 O '71
Dog fight; anti-dog-pollution crusader. il
Newsweek 77:95 Ap 12 '71
Smell of death; heroin malignancy. S. Alsop.
Newsweek 77:76 F 1 '71
Urban health and environment: a new ap-
proach; East Harlem environmental exten-
sion service. R. J. Bazell. Science 174:1005-
6 D 3 '71

Public welfare
Back-to-work movement. il Newsweek 78:
23 Ag 16 '71
Headless horseman rides again. P. Steinfels. Commonweal 95:54 O 15 '71
Shame of the cities; conditions in welfare
hotels. il Newsweek 77:24-5 F 8 '71
Where welfare was reformed. il U S News
71:16 Ag 9 '71

Radio City music hall
One and only Radio City music hall. G. Cotler.
il Holiday 49:78-9+ D '70
Trouble in paradise. il Newsweek 78:113-14+
O 25 '71

Recreation
See also
New York (city)—Parks and playgrounds

Religious institutions and affairs
Cannibalism in the Episcopal church; 1971
New York Episcopal convention. D. K.
Mano. Nat R 23:867+ Ag 10 '71
See also
Council of churches of the city of New York

Restaurants
See New York (city)—Hotels, restaurants,
etc.

St John the Divine, Cathedral of
Troubadours for God; Hair mass. il Time
97:46+ My 24 '71

Sanitary affairs
Clean and open 5000 catchbasins in ninety
days. il Am City 86:58 Ja '71
Pneumatic street cleaning? il Am City 86:
26 F '71
See also
New York (city)—Environmental protection
administration

Schools
See New York (city)—Education

Shops
See New York (city)—Stores

Social conditions
See also
New York (city)—Harlem

Social history
Egalitarian myth and the American social
reality: wealth, mobility, and equality in
the era of the common man. E. Pessen.
bibliog f il Am Hist R 76:989-1034 O '71

Social life and customs
Everything is everything: costume ball. New
Yorker 47:23 Je 19 '71
Talk of the town; party for Henri Langlois.
New Yorker 47:43-4 O 30 '71
Three gatherings: Otto Preminger's announce-
ment, of motion-picture rights to Foxway;
inspection of new apartment of Mr and
Mrs Gardner Cowles; cast party of No, no,
Nanette. New Yorker 46:22-3 Ja 30 '71

Three gatherings: rock group Black Sab-
bath; party in sculpture garden of the
Museum of modern art, and party for the
Queens district leaders and George Mc-
Govern. New Yorker 47:22-3 Ag 21 '71
See also
Night clubs

Social work
See also
East Side house settlement. inc.

SoHo
Last studios. il Time 98:52-6 Jl 5 '71
Underneath the archness; SoHo art commu-
nity. J. Ashbery. Art N 70:29 N '71

Stations
Grandeur that was Penn station; drawings.
N. Schneider. Arch Forum 133:60-2 D '70

Stock exchange
See Stock exchange—New York (city)

Stores
Boon: The left hand, small store; interview.
J. Gittleson. New Yorker 47:32-3 My 8 '71
Broadway-Hale makes it to Fifth avenue; to
acquire Bergdorf Goodman. il Bsns W p68
Ap 3 '71
But the new generation doesn't want to
mind the store; Bergdorf Goodman. S. Bir-
mingham. il pors N Y Times Mag p 16-17+
S 26 '71
Liquor store: Grand plaza on Flatbush
avenue in Brooklyn. New Yorker 47:20-3
Ag 28 '71
Shopping for your kitchen in Manhattan. il
Sunset 147:66+ N '71
See also
Macy, R. H, and company
Schwarz, F. A. O. (firm)

Street traffic
New patterns for a metropolis; midtown
Manhattan. S. Van Ginkel and B. Van Gin-
kel. il Arch Forum 135:28-33 O '71
Traffic; interview. D. H. Elliott. New Yorker
47:29-30 S 18 '71

Streets
That homey touch; series of articles on West
85th street for New York times. Time 98:
77 O 18 '71

Strikes
Dissenting opinion. Nation 212:772 Je 21 '71
Mayor Lindsay's hot summer starts early. il
por Bsns W p28-9 Je 12 '71
New York city crisis: even worse ahead?
walkouts by city employees. il U S News
70:26 Je 21 '71
Strike: bridge tenders, and other city work-
ers. New Yorker 47:19-21 Je 19 '71
Up drawbridges. il Newsweek 77:47-8 Je 2 '71
See also
Strikes—United States—Police
Strikes—United States—Teachers

Subways
Hearing: Second avenue subway. New Yorker 47:39-40 S 25 '71
Paying for the transit tab. Cur 135:22-5 D
'71

Taxation
New York: slipping. Newsweek 77:53 Mr 22
'71

Theater
Back to the Apollo; soul acts at Harlem the-
atre. New Yorker 46:24-6 Ja 23 '71
Beyond coteries; the Public theater. il por
Time 98:71 N 15 '71
Broadway and the British. C. Hughes. il
Cath World 212:313-15 Mr '71
Broadway breakthrough; opening of the
American place theatre. J. Kroll. il por
Newsweek 79:48-9 Ja 3 '72
Close-up (cont of) Spotlight! E. Miller. See
issues of Seventeen, April 1971-
Fabulous invalid's new symptoms. Time 98:
66-7 O 25 '71
Goings on about town. See issues of New
Yorker
Gold rush to Golgotha; Jesus Christ super-
star at Mark Hellinger theater. il Time
98:64-8+ O 25 '71
Is there an audience in the house? C. R.
Hughes. America 124:151-3 F 13 '71
Onstage for the new season. il Newsweek 78:
64-5 S 20 '71
Pick of the summer. T. E. Kalem. il Time 98:
42 Jl 19 '71
Public fights for life; J. Papp's public the-
ater. il por Newsweek 77:113-14 Mr 22 '71
Public theater. E. P. Berkeley. il Arch Forum
134:48-51 Mr '71

NEW YORK (city)—Theater—*Continued*
Public theater; New York Shakespeare festival public theater. L. Lerman. il por Mlle 73:133-7 Je '71
See Broadway shows at half price. il Changing T 25:6 F '71
Singing in the sun; Lincoln Center street theater festival. J. Kroll. il Newsweek 78: 73 S 6 '71
Spotlight! (cont as) Close-up. E. Miller. See issues of Seventeen
Tarot: a take-over deal; Ridiculous theatrical company. M. Gottfried. il Vogue 157:84-5 F 15 '71
Theater. See issues of Newsweek
Theater; effect of the limited gross contract. H. Hewes. Sat R 54:76 Ja 23 '71
Theater in '71. H. Hewes. il Sat R 54:14-19 Je 12 '71
Tonight at 7:30. il Newsweek 77:78-9 Ja 18 '71
Two on the isle; New York and London prices. H. R. Mayes. Sat R 54:6-7 Je 5 '71
What's happening. G. Shalit. See issues of Ladies home journal
See also
New York drama critics circle
New York Shakespeare festival

Traffic problem
See New York (city)—Street traffic

Transit systems
See also
Metropolitan transportation authority
New York (city)—Subways

Transportation
See also
New York (city)—Subways

Water supply
Fluoridation. New Yorker 46:21-2 Ja 9 '71

World trade center
Battle over a TV antenna. il Bsns W p27 N 20 '71
Colossus nobody seems to love. il Bsns W p50-1 Ap 3 '71
Dampers blunt the wind's force on tall buildings; World trade center. il Arch Rec 150: 155-8 S '71
Topping out the world's tallest building. R. Gannon. il Pop Sci 198:82-3+ My '71

Zoological park
See New York zoological park

NEW YORK (city). City university
Community relations for special programs in higher education; SEEK program. R. D. Wilkinson. Sch & Soc 99:170-2 Mr '71
Continuing education; SEEK program. B. Foster. Am Lib 2:776-7 S '71
Faculty collective bargaining at the City university of New York. S. Jacobson. Sch & Soc 99:346-9 O '71
Fresh face for CUNY; chancellor Kibbee. por Newsweek 78:76 Ag 9 '71
Jewish studies course via TV; City university of New York. Sch & Soc 99:402 N '71
New chancellor of CUNY. por Sch & Soc 99: 398 N '71
Open admissions: a mixed report. il Time 98:50+ N 29 '71
Report card on open admissions: remedial work recommended. S. Resnik and B. Kaplan. il N Y Times Mag p26-8+ My 9 '71; Discussion. p21+ Je 6 '71

Brooklyn college
College credits for life experiences. Sch & Soc 99:271-2 Sum '71

University graduate school
University cheesecake; interview with manager of Graduate center cafeteria. E. Brasesco. New Yorker 47:32-4 Mr 27 '71

NEW YORK (state)
See also
Adirondack Mountains
Architecture—New York (state)
Architecture, Domestic—New York (state)
Booksellers and bookselling—New York (state)
Broome County
Camping—New York (state)
Cattaraugus Creek
Cayuga Lake
Courts—New York (state)
Education—New York (state)
Environmental policy—New York (state)
Erie Canal
Essex County
Express highways—New York (state)
Fishing—New York (state)
George, Lake

Hudson River
Hudson River Valley
Hunting—New York (state)
Jamaica Bay
Justice, Administration of—New York (state)
Libraries—New York (state)
Long Island
Music festivals—New York (state)
Paleobotany—New York (state)
Politics, Corruption in—New York (state)
Prisons—New York (state)
Public welfare—New York (state)
Regional planning—New York (state)
School libraries—New York (state)
Staten Island
Water supply—New York (state)
Wildlife sanctuaries—New York (state)

Antiquities
Iroquois confederacy. J. A. Tuck. il Sci Am 224:32-42 F '71

Description and travel
Tour New York by air. S. Wilkinson. il Flying 89:S12-16 Ag '71

Education, Department of
Commissioner's committee on library development
Is CCLD all that bad? patterns of children's library service. M. R. Sive. il por Library J 96:3442-5 O 15 '71
Pox on both their houses; CCLD report on services to children. D. Broderick. Library J 96:3448-9 O 15 '71
Sacred cows: the CCLD report; New York findings and Philadelphia schools. C. Field. il por Library J 96:3445-7 O 15 '71

Elections
See New York (state)—Politics and government

Environmental conservation, Department of
First year. H. L. Diamond. Cons 25:1 Je '71

Finance
Limited liability. il Time 97:17 My 3 '71

Legislature
Joint committee on crime, its causes, control and effect on society
Schenley chapter. H. Messick. il Nation 212: 428-31 Ap 5 '71

Mental hygiene, Department of
State research budget; letter. J. Zubin. Science 173:380 Jl 30 '71

Metropolitan transportation authority
See Metropolitan transportation authority

Narcotic addiction control commission
Hope and help for narcotics addicts; Iroquois rehabilitation center. A. S. Fick. il Cons 26:28-9 Ag '71

Parks and reserves
Adirondack park agency. H. L. Diamond. il Parks & Rec 6:14-17+ D '71
Adirondack park study; reprint of summary of report. il Liv Wildn 35:34-6 Spr '71
Bear Mountain's Christmas festival. S. Traiman. il Parks & Rec 6:24-6 F '71
Erie Canal state park. C. Reed. il Parks & Rec 6:24-6+ S '71
Future of the Adirondack park; recommendations of Temporary study commission and summary of report. il Cons 25:10-29 F '71
Park power; Harlem River Bronx state park. M. P. Friedberg. il Parks & Rec 6:26-9+ Jl '71

Politics and government
Crisis facing key states: what Reagan, Rockefeller are doing. pors U S News 70: 41-2 My 17 '71
End of liberalism; New York state. P. Hoffman. Nation 212:457-61 Ap 12 '71
Notes and comment; fate of the transportation bond issue. New Yorker 47:44-5 N 13 '71

Urban development corporation
Economic/political systems; UDC housing projects. il Arch Rec 149:124-31 Ap '71
Piecing the political pie. E. J. Logue. il Sat R 54:27-9+ My 15 '71
Turnkey housing. Am City 86:78 D '71

NEW YORK (state). Downstate medical center, Brooklyn
Danger in the hospital; department for equipment testing and maintenance. A. S. Freese. il Pop Mech 135:80-3 F '71
Healer for Downstate. por Time 98:40-1 D 13 '71

NEW YORK (state). State university
Building types study; State university construction fund; with editorial comment. M. F. Schmertz. il Arch Rec 149:55-6. 105-28 Ja '71
College without a campus. Time 97:56+ Mr 1 '71

College at Fredonia
Fredonia's athletic center: legible design in steel by Richard Meier. il Arch Rec 150: 105-8 Ag '71

College at Old Westbury
Autopsy on Old Westbury. T. Powers. il Harper 243:52-3+ S '71

College at Oneonta
Contour dorms. il Arch Forum 133:8 D '70

Downstate medical center, Brooklyn
See New York (state). Downstate medical center, Brooklyn

Stony Brook campus
Made for walking; student union at Stony Brook. il Arch Forum 135:58-61 Jl '71
NEW YORK Amsterdam news. See Negro press
NEW YORK antiques fair. See Antiques—Exhibitions
NEW YORK botanical garden
Garden evening; annual members' evening. New Yorker 47:27-8 Ap 3 '71
NEW YORK city ballet
Balanchine's girls: the making of a style. A. Croce. Harper 242:30+ Ap '71
Ceremony of joy. H. Saal. il Newsweek 77: 115 My 17 '71
Dance; interview, ed. by E. Miller. G. Kirkland. por Seventeen 30:138 Ag '71
Dance; Suite no. 3. J. Maskey. Hi Fi 21: MA18-19 Mr '71
Dance; The Goldberg variations and Octandre. J. Maskey. il Hi Fi 21:MA10-11 O '71
Musical events:
Goldberg variations. W. Sargeant. New Yorker 47:120-1 Je 5 '71
Kodály dances, La sonnambula and Suite No. 3. W. Sargeant. New Yorker 46:107 F 13 '71
Scotch symphony, Four last songs, and Concerto for two solo pianos. W. Sargeant. New Yorker 46:91 Ja 30 '71
New York city ballet, New York state theater. M. Marks. Dance Mag 45:24+ Jl '71
People watching at the New York city ballet. D. Hering. il Dance Mag 45:24-7 F '71
Something's up, or down. M. Marks. il Dance Mag 45:76+ Ag '71
World of dance; production of Nutcracker and Suite no. 3. W. Terry. il Sat R 54:35 Ja 16 '71
World of dance; trio of new ballets. W. Terry. Sat R 54:45 F 13 '71
NEW YORK city council of churches. See Council of churches of the city of New York
NEW YORK city in art
Urban pastorals; J. Freilicher's paintings. P. Schjeldahl. il Art N 69:32-3+ F '71
NEW YORK city off-track betting corporation. See Off-track betting corporation, New York
NEW YORK city opera company
Beverly Sills; the fastest voice alive. il pors Time 98:74-6+ N 22 '71
John Stewart; Britten's Albert Herring at City opera. J. Hiemenz. por Hi Fi 21:MA18-19 D '71
King of the May; B. Britten's Albert Herring. il Opera N 36:16-17 S '71
Musical events:
Bizet's Carmen. New Yorker 47:167-8 O 16 '71
Britten's Albert Herring and Verdi's La Traviata. W. Sargeant. New Yorker 47: 118-20 S 25 '71
G. Charpentier's Louise and Donizetti's Roberto Devereux. W. Sargeant. New Yorker 47:127 Mr 13 '71
G. Rossini's La Cenerentola. W. Sargeant. New Yorker 47:94 F 27 '71
Menotti's most important man. W. Sargeant. New Yorker 47:132 Mr 20 '71
Performance of Verdi's Un ballo in maschera. W. Sargeant. New Yorker 47: 110 Ap 3 '71

New York city opera. (cont) il Hi Fi 20: MA16+ D '70; 21:MA10-11 Ja; MA16+ F; MA16+ Je; MA17 Jl; MA16-17 D '71
Profiles; B. Sills. W. Sargeant. New Yorker 47:42-6+ Mr 6 '71
Report:
Albert Herring. F. Merkling. il Opera N 36:23 N '71
Un ballo in maschera. S. Jenkins. Opera N 35:29 Ap 17 '71
Carlisle Floyd's Susannah. S. Jenkins. il Opera N 36:31 D 18 '71
Carmen. F. Merkling. il Opera N 36:25-6 D 11 '71
Così fan tutte. R. D. Daniels. Opera N 36:23 N '71
Gian Carlo Menotti's The most important man. J. W. Freeman. il Opera N 35:29 Ap 17 '71
Louise. S. Jenkins. il Opera N 35:30 Ap 3 '71
NEW YORK city poets. See Poets, American
NEW YORK city police strike. See Strikes—United States—Police
NEW YORK city summer dance festival. See Dance festivals
NEW YORK city transit authority. See Metropolitan transportation authority
NEW YORK cotton exchange. See Commodity exchanges
NEW YORK dance festival. See Dance festivals
NEW YORK drama critics circle
New York drama critics circle choices, 1971. Sat R 54:15 Je 12 '71
NEW YORK film festival. See Moving picture festivals
NEW YORK Giants (football club) See Football clubs
NEW YORK Knickerbockers (basketball team) See Basketball teams
NEW YORK library association
Disenfranchised: school librarians at NYLA. Library J 96:3797-8 N 15 '71
Educationists and librarians; NYLA conference. J. Berry. Library J 96:153 Ja 15 '71
NCOP report, Queens case, debated at NYLA. il Library J 96:3796-7 N 15 '71
NYLA 77th annual conference, November 1970. il Am Lib 2:5-6 Ja. '71
New issues surface at NYLA discussion. Library J 96:3712-13 N 15 '71
Of note; annual conference. M. E. Martignoni. il Am Lib 2:1136-7 D '71
Survival politics for libraries; NYLA conference. W. R. Eshelman. Wilson Lib Bul 46:217-18+ N '71
NEW YORK mirror
Daily mirror; interview. R. W. Farrell. New Yorker 47:40-2 S 25 '71
NEW YORK philharmonic-symphony orchestra
Boulez at the Philharmonic; Berg-Schoenberg-Webern program. I. Kolodin. Sat R 54:18 My 1 '71
Boulez to the attack. H. Saal. il pors Newsweek 78:86-8+ O 11 '71
Gielen's chromatic, traumatic evening. I. Kolodin. Sat R 54:85 O 30 '71
Music to my ears; concert conducted by M. T. Thomas. I. Kolodin. Sat R 54:75 N 20 '71
Music to my ears; concert performance of The planets by G. Holst. I. Kolodin. Sat R 54:19 D 11 '71
Music to my ears; first programs under direction of P. Boulez. I. Kolodin. Sat R 54:20 O 9 '71
Music to my ears; In memoriam, Igor Stravinsky. I. Kolodin. Sat R 54:19 My 15 '71
Music to my ears; performance of Concerto for cello and orchestra, by G. Ligeti. I. Kolodin. Sat R 54:24+ N 13 '71
Music to my ears; performance of Mozart's Davidde penitente, and Liszt's Dante symphony. I. Kolodin. Sat R 54:68 N 6 '71
Music to my ears; performances of Liszt's The legend of St Elizabeth and The politics of harmony. I. Kolodin. Sat R 54:38+ O 16 '71
Music to my ears; program devoted to works of Mendelssohn, Goehr and Beethoven. I. Kolodin. Sat R 54:14 Ja 16 '71
Musical events:
Atonality; concert in Philharmonic Hall. W. Sargeant. New Yorker 47:164 O 23 '71
Concerts in Philharmonic Hall. W. Sargeant. New Yorker 47:111 Ap 3; 159 N 6 '71
F. Liszt's oratorio The legend of St Elizabeth in Philharmonic Hall. W. Sargeant. New Yorker 47:133 O 9 '71

NEW YORK philharmonic-symphony orchestra
—*Continued*
Musical events—*Continued*
F. Liszt's symphony to Dante's Divine
comedy. W. Sargeant. New Yorker
47:147 O 30 '71
Opening concerts in Philharmonic Hall.
W. Sargeant. New Yorker 47:120-1 O 2
'71
Program devoted to works of the Aus-
trian decadence. W. Sargeant. New
Yorker 47:102 Ap 24 '71
Venice promenade concert. W. Sargeant.
New Yorker 47:58 My 29 '71
NEW YORK port authority. See Port of New
York authority
NEW YORK pro musica antiqua (organization)
Prince of music; concert of works by Jos-
quin. H. Saal. il Newsweek 78:77 N 15 '71
NEW YORK public library
Government and libraries cooperate. D. Dick-
inson. Am Lib 2:214 F '71
NYPL employee group opposes agency shop
pact. il Library J 96:4044-5 D 15 '71
  See also
Lincoln Center for the performing arts, New
York—Library and museum of the perform-
ing arts

Branches
Day care and NYPL: Washington Heights
branch Discovery room. il Library J 96:
4136-7 D 15 '71

Print collection
Worth a thousand words. K. Kuh. il Sat R
54:52-3 Mr 27 '71

Science and technology division
Outstanding science library to close. R. J.
Bazell. Science 174:133 O 8 '71
NEW YORK racing association
Chairman; New York racing association; in-
terview. A. G. Vanderbilt. New Yorker 47:
33-5 Ap 17 '71
NEW YORK Rangers (hockey team) See Hock-
ey teams
NEW YORK review of books (periodical)
Case of the New York review. D. H. Wrong;
discussion. Commentary 51:8+ Mr '71
Cooling of the intellectuals. P. Steinfels.
Commonweal 94:255-61 My 21 '71; Discus-
sion. 94:365-7 Jl 9 '71
NEW YORK Shakespeare festival
Going bumpety bump on the rocky road
to love; production of Two gentlemen of
Verona. H. Hewes. Sat R 54:18 Ag 21 '71
On the town; production of Two gentlemen
of Verona. J. Kroll. il Newsweek 78:75 Ag
16 '71
Pitchman for free (and freewheeling) thea-
ter; J. Papp. R. Bongartz. il pors N Y
Times Mag p 12-13+ Ag 15 '71
NEW YORK state library, Albany
History of the New York state library, by
C. R. Roseberry. Review
  Wilson Lib Bul 45:536 F '71
NEW YORK state library association. See
New York library association
NEW YORK stock exchange. See Stock ex-
change—New York (city)
NEW YORK taxicabs. See Taxicabs
NEW YORK telephone company
Guided tour of the balance sheet. F. Cerra.
il Nation 212:562-4 My 3 '71
NEW YORK theatres, League of. See League
of New York theatres, inc.
NEW YORK theological seminary
Open seminary. il Newsweek 77:65 F 8 '71
NEW YORK times
Again the Pentagon papers. Time 98:30 Jl 19
'71
Another failure in communication. H. L.
Davis. Phys Today 24:88 D '71
Breach of security. S. Alsop. Newsweek 77:
99 Je 28 '71
Costs and competition shake the Times.
Bsns W p62 D 11 '71
Court allows publication of Pentagon study;
Bantam to publish N.Y. times version. il
Pub W 200:51 Jl 12 '71
DNA double helix; photo sends controversy
spiraling. B. Nelson. il Science 173:800-1 Ag
27 '71; Reply. G. W. Stroke. 174:1078 D 10
'71
Day in the life of the New York times, by
R. Adler. Review
  Nation 213:406-8 O 25 '71
Extra nickel's worth; Op-Ed page. il pors
Time 97:36 Je 21 '71
Food beat; interview. R. A. Sokolov. New
Yorker 47:20-2 Ag 21 '71
Government vs. the press; Pentagon study
of the war in Vietnam. il por Newsweek 78:
17-19 Jl 5 '71
Great sense of elation; offer of Pentagon
study. il Newsweek 77:25-6 Je 28 '71

Hard times at the Times. Time 98:58 N 29
'71
I have in my hand a photostatic copy of. . .
Nat R 23:685-6 Je 29 '71
In the courts; the government vs. the press;
Pentagon papers. il Newsweek 77:27+ Je
28 '71
Justice Blackmun's dissent. W. F. Buckley,
jr. Nat R 23:828-9 Jl 27 '71
Legal battle over censorship. il Time 97:17-19
Je 28 '71
Letter from Paris; reaction to recent diffi-
culties of the New York times with the
Nixon administration. Genêt. New Yorker
47:54 Jl 3 '71
Ms Muddle. Newsweek 78:70 D 6 '71
Miniaturization of the book. J. Tebbel. Cur
126:46-51 F '71
1984; closer than we'd thought? publication
of Vietnam papers. Pub W 199:45 Je 28 '71
Notes and comment; Pentagon papers. New
Yorker 47:19 Jl 10 '71
Our colleagues err on war secrets issue; re-
print from The Detroit news, June 27, 1971.
U S News 71:88+ Jl 12 '71
Pentagon papers; did the public win or lose?
questions and answers. Sr Schol 99:4-5 S 20
'71
Pentagon papers; the decision to publish and
the painful lessons. Life 71:6 Jl 2 '71
Press wins and presses roll. il Time 98:10-12
Jl 12 '71
Project X; publishing the Pentagon's secret
record of U.S. involvement in Viet Nam.
il por Time 97:45-6 Je 28 '71
Right to publish; Supreme court's Pentagon
papers decision. N. Lewin. New Repub 165:
11-13 Jl 10 '71
Secret decisions that altered the Vietnam
war; storm over leaked documents. il U S
News 70:21-3 Je 28 '71
Serving their times; blows at the old new
right. Nat R 23:186 F 23 '71
So you want to be an obit writer. A. Whit-
man. Sat R 54:70-1 D 11 '71
TRB from Washington; Pentagon papers.
New Repub 164:6 Je 26 '71
That homey touch, series of articles on West
85th street. Time 98:77 O 18 '71
Times v. its law firm; Pentagon papers case.
Time 98:42 Ag 2 '71
Times, Vietnam and security. Nat R 23:792
Jl 27 '71
Victory for the press; Supreme court ruling
on publication of the secret Pentagon his-
tory of the Vietnam war; with excerpts
from opinions of 5 justices. il Newsweek
78:16-19 Jl 12 '71
When newspapers do their thing; Pentagon
papers. R. L. Tobin. il Sat R 54:37-8 Jl 10
'71
Would you have done what the Times did?
Time 98:39 Jl 5 '71

Anecdotes, facetiae, satire, etc.
Through history with the Times; headlines
for historical incidents. il Am Heritage 22:
112 F '71
NEW YORK times book review
Changing Times. por Newsweek 77:59 Ap 5 '71
NEW YORK times company
Its business is much more than the news.
il por Bsns W p75-6 Je 26 '71
NEW YORK wines. See Wine
NEW YORK zoological park
Tell me that U Mishmi, Gracie; a pair of
takins at the Bronx zoo. C. Trillin. il Life
71:18 N 5 '71
NEW YORKER (periodical)
New Yorker lists at this season some books
by its contributors published during the
year (cont) New Yorker 47:164-5 D 11 '71
NEW YORKERS
Eleven o'clock; Tuesday, January 12, 1971;
an ordinary morning for celebrities of New
York. New Yorker 46:26-7 Ja 23 '71
Fortress on 78th street; with account by K.
Thorsen, editorial comment and question-
naire. il Life 71:3, 26-36 N 19; 3 D 10 '71
Gallery; New York faces photographed by S.
McCartney. Life 70:6-9 Je 4 '71
Laundromat; Apthorp self-service. New
Yorker 47:30-2 F 20 '71
Liquor store; Grand plaza on Flatbush
avenue in Brooklyn. New Yorker 47:20-3
Ag 28 '71
Luncheonette; Marty's luncheonette on Sher-
man avenue. New Yorker 47:26-8 Ag 14
'71
Summer glimpses. New Yorker 47:24-6 Jl 31
'71
Surviving in New York. P. Steinfels. Com-
monweal 93:513 F 26 '71

NEW YORKERS—*Continued*

Susan McCartney's faces of New York; photographs. K. Poli. Pop Phot 68:89-91 Je '71

Telephone call. New Yorker 47:30-1 Mr 6 '71

Three gatherings: Otto Preminger's announcement, of motion-picture rights to Foxway; inspection of new apartment of Mr and Mrs Gardner Cowles; cast party of No, no, Nanette. New Yorker 46:22-3 Ja 30 '71

Three gatherings: rock group Black Sabbath; party in sculpture garden of the Museum of modern art, and party for the Queens district leaders and George McGovern. New Yorker 47:22-3 Ag 21 '71

Three musical gatherings: Theatre 80 St Marks opening; Harlem jazz music center, inc. open house; street festival on Lenox avenue. New Yorker 47:32-3 S 11 '71

U.S. journal: Manhattan; bicycle riding. C. Trillin. New Yorker 47:120+ O 9 '71

NEW ZEALAND

See also

Astronomical observatories—New Zealand

Church union—New Zealand

Geology—New Zealand

Queenstown

Royal astronomical society of New Zealand

Description and travel

New Zealand's bountiful South Island. P. Benchley. il Nat Geog 141:92-123 Ja '72

Why New Zealand isn't Australia. il Sat R 54:46-8 O 23 '71

Religious institutions and affairs

Worldaround. Chr Cent 88:1032 S 1 '71

NEW ZEALAND spinach. See Spinach

NEWARK, N.J.

Airports

Newark expansion to add 83 gates. il Aviation W 95:64 N 15 '71

City planning

Newark: bellwether city. E. P. Berkeley. il Arch Forum 135:40-5 S '71

Crime

Comeuppance for Newark's unholy alliance. J. Reddy. il Read Digest 98:113-17 Ja '71

Education

Black flag. Time 98:10 D 13 '71

Black flag in Newark. il Newsweek 78:98 D 13 '71

Mayor Kenneth Gibson says: wherever the central cities are going, Newark is going to get there first. F. J. Cooke. il N Y Times Mag p7-9+ Jl 25 '71; Reply. F. A. Fiorito. p27 Ag 15 '71

Newark's parent-powered school; Springfield avenue community school. L. Rich. il Am Ed 7:35-9 D '71

Education, Board of

Bored of education? No, sir! teenage Larry Hamm. Sr Schol 99:3 S 20 '71

Music

Report:

Giordano's Fedora. D. Nichelson. il Opera N 36:38 D 25 '71

Hansel and Gretel. R. Zachary. Opera N 35:33 F 20 '71

Police

Mayor Kenneth Gibson says: wherever the central cities are going, Newark is going to get there first. F. J. Cook. il N Y Times Mag p7-9+ Jl 25 '71

Police department

Cop for all seasons: D. Toma. il pors Newsweek 78:40 Jl 19 '71

Politics and government

Newark a year later. A. Poinsett. il pors Ebony 27:124-6+ N '71

Newark at the brink. il por Newsweek 77:87-8 Ap 26 '71

Urban leader; interview, ed. by L. Delpreore. K. Gibson. por Am City 86:73-4 Jl '71

Race question

It would not be fun. S. Alsop. Newsweek 77:116 My 17 '71

School board

See Newark, N.J.—Education, Board of

Social conditions

Mayor Kenneth Gibson says: wherever the central cities are going, Newark is going to get there first. F. J. Cook. il N Y Times Mag p7-9+ Jl 25 '71; Discussion. p27 Ag 15 '71

Strikes

See also

Strikes—United States—Teachers

Theater

Black (art) drama is the same as black life. L. Jones. il Ebony 26:74-6+ F '71

NEWARK-Elizabeth transportation complex. See Transportation—New Jersey

NEWARK news

Down the river. D. C. Berliner. Nation 213:292-3 O 4 '71; Discussion. 213:482+ N 15 '71

NEWBERY medal

Newbery award acceptance; address, June 21, 1971. B. Byars. il Horn Bk 47:354-8 Ag '71

Newbery-Caldecott awards. il Library J 96:1094 Mr 15 '71

Newbery/Caldecott awards; excerpts from addresses, ed. by P. Bragg. G. Haley; B. Byars. Pub W 200:28 S 6 '71

Newerbery? L. N. Gerhardt. Library J 96:4135 D 15 '71

Viking and Atheneum authors are 1970 Newbery and Caldecott winners. L. Russ. il pors Pub W 199:116-18 F 22 '71

Anecdotes, facetiae, satire, etc.

Up for discussion; a modest proposal for the very first worst children's book award ever. L. N. Gerhardt. Library J 96:1136-7 Mr 15 '71

Up for discussion; Finn Pin picked & Budd Button popped. L. N. Gerhardt. Library J 96:1525 Ap 15 '71

NEWBOLD, Bill

Schuylkill Valley nature center. il Parks & Rec 6:14-18+ F '71

NEWBORN, Jud

Plath; poem. Nation 214:62 Ja 10 '72

NEWBORN infants. See Infants, Newborn

NEWBURGH, N.Y.

Twilight of the booster. J. Morgenstern. Newsweek 78-9 Jl 5 '71

NEWCOMB college. See Tulane university, New Orleans—Newcomb college

NEWCOMB pottery. See Pottery, American

NEWCOMBE, Jack

End of a company town. il Life 70:36-45 Mr 26 '71

NEWCOMBE, John

Waltz at Wimbledon. W. Bingham. il pors Sports Illus 35:14-17 Jl 12 '71 *

NEWELL, Homer

Matter of perspective. Science 172:331 Ap 23 '71

NEWELL, Reginald E.

Global circulation of atmospheric pollutants; with biographical sketch. il Sci Am 224:12, 32-42 Ja '71

NEWFIELD, Jack

Shafting of Mr Average. S. Alsop. Newsweek 77:132 Ap 19 '71 *

Textbook for everyone. S. W. Little. Sat R 54:66 S 11 '71 *

NEWFOUNDLAND

See also

Funk Island

NEWHALL, Scott

Father leaves home. por Time 97:53-4 F 15 '71 *

NEWLANDS, Don

Testing for athletic talent. il Look 35:67 Je 1 '71

NEWMAN, Barbara. See Stockton, P. D. H. jt. auth.

NEWMAN, Barnett

Around Barnett Newman; interviews with, and statements from 12 painters and sculptors; ed. by J. Siegel. il pors Art N 70:42-7+ O '71 *

Art world. H. Rosenberg. New Yorker 47:43-6 Ja 1 '72 *

Barnett Newman, American artist; with excerpts from essay by J. Hess. il pors Vogue 158:122-9 N 1 '71 *

Can art be used? dedication of Rothko chapel. T. B. Hess. Art N 70:33 Ap '71 *

Celebration of genius at the Rothko chapel. il Vogue 157:109 Mr 1 '71 *

Pursuit of the sublime. R. Hughes. il por Time 98:66-9 O 18 '71 *

Red, the yellow, the blue. D. Davis. il pors Newsweek 78:90-3 O 18 '71 *

NEWMAN, David, and Benton, Robert

From hot panting to hotpants. il Mlle 73:82-3+ Jl '71

Man talk. See issues of Mademoiselle

NEWMAN, Gloria

Gloria Newman dance theater. Downey theater, Downey, Calif. V. H. Swisher. Dance Mag 45:85-6 D '71 *

NEWMAN, James E.
Climatic changes: some evidence and implications. il Weatherwise 24:56-62 Ap '71
NEWMAN, Joan A.
High school newsreels. il Schol Teach Jr/Sr High p22-3 Mr 8 '71
NEWMAN, JoAnn. See Frieden. B. jt. auth.
NEWMAN, Montgomery
Oilman; story. New Yorker 47:120-2 S 18 '71
NEWMAN, Paul
What's behind those beautiful blue eyes? interview, ed. by E. Miller. por Seventeen 29:124-5+ N 70
about
Lee Marvin and Paul Newman. C. Bergen. pors Vogue 158:146-7+ O 1 '71 *
Mr & Mrs Paul Newman. M. Davidson. il pors Good H 173:84-7+ Jl '71 *
NEWMAN, Peter C.
Thawing of Canada. il Sat R 54:15-18+ Mr 13 '71
NEWMAN, Ros
Torch artistry. P. Fievez. il por Design 72: 24-5 mid-Sum '71 *
NEWMAN, Simon M.
ASIS: information science in motion. il Wilson Lib Bul 46:475-7 Ja '72
NEWMARK, Marilyn
Bronze horses of Marilyn Newmark. M. Malmstrom. il por Am Artist 35:28-33+ Ap '71 *
NEWMONT mining corporation
From shotguns to rifles. por Forbes 107:48+ Je 15 '71
NEWPORT, R.I.

History
Growing up in Newport; excerpts from Alpha omega. W. T. Scott. il Am Heritage 22:54-7+ Ag '71
NEWPORT, R.I, Jazz festival. See Music festivals—Rhode Island
NEWPORT, R.I, public library
Newport librarian resigns; cites lack of funds. Library J 96:3080 O 1 '71
NEWPORT furniture. See Furniture, American
NEWPORT NEWS, Va.

Education
Newport News education association. B. J. DeHoff. Todays Ed 60:58 O '71
NEWS
Looking for ourselves in the news of '71. J. Neary. il pors Life 71:74-6+ D 31 '71
New windows on the world; reading newspapers and journals from abroad. T. H. Barton. Harvard Bsns R 49:136-8+ S '71
Top editor's view: why press is under fire; excerpts from address, April 14, 1971. N. Noyes. U S News 70:94-5 Ap 26 '71
Vulnerable media: dependence on advertising. Nation 212:195 F 15 '71
See also
Current events
Foreign correspondents
Government and the press
Journalism
Medical news
Radio broadcasting—News
Religious news
Reporters and reporting
Science news
Television broadcasting—News
NEWS; story. See Spencer, S.
NEWS agencies
See also
Community news service
Newspapers—Syndicate service
Reuters news service
NEWS broadcasts. See Radio broadcasting—News; Television broadcasting—News
NEWS commentators. See Television broadcasting—News
NEWS films. See Newsreels
NEWS media. See Mass media
NEWS photographers
See also
Burrows, L
Smith, W. S.
Vietnamese war, 1957-   —War correspondents and photographers
NEWS photographs. See Current events—Photographs
NEWSBOYS
Changing American newsboy. J. Tebbel. il Sat R 54:56-8 F 13 '71
NEWSCASTERS. See Television broadcasting—News
NEWSDAY (newspaper)
Even on Sunday. il Newsweek 78:108-9 N 8 '71
Return of muckraking; target: the President of the U.S. il Time 98:76-7 O 25 '71

NEWSOM, David D.
African issues at the U.N; address, September 21, 1971. Vital Speeches 38:14-17 O 15 '71; Same. Dept State Bul 65:373-8 O 11 '71
Assistant Secretary Newsom reports to Congress on his visit to southern Africa; statement, December 3, 1970. Dept State Bul 64:27-9 Ja 4 '71
Department reviews U.S. position on Southern Rhodesia; statement, July 7, 1971. Dept State Bul 65:111-15 Jl 26 '71
North Africa: lessons from the past and future directions; address, November 18, 1971. Dept State Bul 65:677-83 D 13 '71
U.S. and North Africa; address, November 18, 1971. Vital Speeches 38:162-6 Ja 1 '72
United States options in southern Africa; address, December 8, 1970. Dept State Bul 64:80-4 Ja 18 '71
NEWSOM, Jon
Quarterly book-list. See issues of Musical quarterly
NEWSPAPER advertising. See Advertising, Newspaper
NEWSPAPER and periodical wholesalers
See also
Association for the promotion of the international circulation of the press
NEWSPAPER columnists. See Journalists
NEWSPAPER columns. See Newspapers—Sections, columns, etc.
NEWSPAPER correspondents.   See Reporters and reporting
NEWSPAPER court reporting
Crime reporting: from delirium to dialogue. D. M. Gillmor. bibliog f Cur Hist 61:27-34+ Jl '71
Sheppard v. Maxwell, 1966. Cur Hist 61: 106-10+ Ag '71
NEWSPAPER ethics. See Journalistic ethics
NEWSPAPER postal rates

United States
See Postal rates—United States
NEWSPAPER publishers and publishing
What is black and white and the tenth largest industry in the country? S. W. Little. Sat R 54:54-5 F 13 '71
See also
Gannett company
Media general, inc.
NEWSPAPER reporters. See Reporters and reporting
NEWSPAPERS
See also
Advertising, Newspaper
Caricatures and cartoons
Freedom of the press
International press institute
Journalism
News
Newsboys
Reporters and reporting
also names of newspapers, e.g. Stars and stripes (newspaper)

Bibliography
Another list, oh God! But a list as good as anyone else's list; with additional lists by C. Karpel and M. Mayer. Esquire 75: 120-2+ My '71

Columns
See Newspapers—Sections, columns, etc.

Consolidations and mergers
Let's all get together; acquisition policy of the Gannett co. por Forbes 107:42 Je 15 '71

Crime reporting
See Crime and the press

Front page
What tomorrow's front page will look like. J. Tebbel. il Sat R 54:50-2 My 8 '71

History
When it wasn't news. Sr Schol 99:12 O 18 '71

Letters to the editor
Correspondence course; letters to the editor of the Times of London. H. R. Mayes. Sat R 54:10+ D 4 '71
Extra nickel's worth; Op-Ed page. il pors Time 97:36 Je 21 '71
Letter to the editor; a veteran in Viet-Nam on racial labels of blood. Negro Hist Bul 33:164 N '70
Letters to the world's editors; comp. by N. G. Balint. See issues of Saturday review
Letters you write to the editor. R. L. Tobin. Sat R 54:43-4 Ag 14 '71

NEWSPAPERS—*Continued*

Political news
See also
Government and the press

Prices
From penny press to premium press. R. L. Tobin. il Sat R 54:51-2 F 13 '71

Readers
Do they read? Catholic transcript survey. S. J. Adamo. America 124:493-4 My 8 '71

Sections, columns, etc.
Cruise director on the Titanic; A. Buchwald's column. T. Meehan. il pors N Y Times Mag p 10-11+ Ja 2 '72
Dream assignment; R. J. Donovan's reports based on interviews. por Time 98:58 N 29 '71
Food beat: New York times; interview. R. A. Sokolov. New Yorker 47:20-2 Ag 21 '71
Op-ed page revisited. H. Krieghbaum. il Sat R 54:91-3 N 13 '71
Socrates of the ironing board; E. Bombeck. B. Dunn. il pors Life 71:66+ O 1 '71
They love it in Boston; or, How the Globe's book section works. B. A. Bannon. il por Pub W 199:69-70 My 31 '71
13 questions on becoming a syndicated columnist. H. Bottel. Writers Digest 51:32-4 Ap '71
See also
Newspapers——Syndicate service

Anecdotes, facetiae, satire, etc.
Miss Buttonworth wed to family's relief; society page and coverage of weddings. J. Mathewson. Look 35:9 Ag 24 '71

Social aspects
Free press on trial; excerpt from Free press, free people, the best cause. J. Hohenberg. Cur 130:40-7 Je '71

Syndicate service
King features syndicate. J. Markow. Writers Digest 51:18-19 My '71
Syndicates and how they grew. B. Lewis. il Sat R 54:67-9 D 11 '71

Travel news
Sunday travel page markets. R. Arnold. Writers Digest 51:31+ My '71

Womens pages
What's wrong with the woman's page? R. L. Tobin. il Sat R 54:57-8 S 11 '71

Canada
See also
Toronto—Newspapers

Egypt
Man to see; editor of Al Ahram. Newsweek 77:37 F 1 '71
Second most important man in Egypt, and possibly the world's most powerful journalist. E. R. F. Sheehan. il pors N Y Times Mag p 12-13+ Ag 22 '71

Europe, Western
New windows on the world; reading newspapers and journals from abroad. T. H. Barton. Harvard Bsns R 49:136-8+ S '71

France
See also
Paris—Newspapers

Germany (Federal Republic)
West Germany's adversary press. M. L. Stein. Sat R 54:47-8 My 8 '71

Great Britain
Can the press police itself? British press council. B. Francois. America 124:433-5 Ap 24 '71
Failure on Fleet Street. il Time 97:72 My 10 '71
New boy on Fleet Street. il por Newsweek 77:87 My 10 '71
Press and race. Chr Cent 88:1515 D 29 '71
See also
Sunday times, London

Japan
How we bombed Tokyo's press. A. Axelbank. Nation 213:205-6 S 13 '71
Sob sisters; advice columns. B. Krisher. il Newsweek 77:50+ Je 7 '71

Singapore
Lee cracks down. por Newsweek 77:49 Je 7 '71

United States
Can the press police itself? B. Francois. America 124:433-5 Ap 24 '71
Everything changes even the newsroom. M. L. Stein. Sat R 54:45-6+ Jl 10 '71
New journalism. J. Ridgeway. bibliog il Am Lib 2:585-92 Je '71
See also
Negro press
also names of newspapers, e.g. Christian science monitor (newspaper); *also* subhead Newspapers under names of cities, e.g. New York (city)—Newspapers

Foreign language press
See also
Jewish daily forward

NEWSPAPERS, Student. See College and school journalism

NEWSPAPERS and politics
Dilemma; editors involved in political action. S. J. Adamo. America 124:572 My 29 '71
Later George, not now; nonrecognition of candidates. New Repub 164:5-6 My 8 '71
Press, president & Pentagon. P. Steinfels. Commonweal 94:78 Ap 2 '71

NEWSREELS
Eyes and ears of the world. J. Tebbel. il Sat R 54:60-2 Je 12 '71

NEWSTRAND, Clyde F.
Drinkable sewage? il Mech Illus 67:148-9 N '71

NEWSWEEK (periodical)
Doubt about Newsweek tribute; Catholics in public office. B. L. Masse. America 125: 361 N 6 '71
Ted Slate, special librarian. il pors Wilson Lib Bul 46:138-9 O '71

NEWSWRITERS. See Reporters and reporting

NEWTIME, Inc. See Employment agencies

NEWTON, David F.
Saving Broome County's environment. Cons 25:20-1 Ap '71

NEWTON, Huey P.
Black Panther thrust in American revolution. R. Chrisman. il Sat R 54:35-8 Jl 24 '71
Hung jury for Huey. por Time 98:11 Ag 23 '71 •

NEWTON, Sir Isaac
First Newtonian. R. A. Wells. bibliog il por Sky & Tel 42:342-4 D '71 •

NEWTON, Niles Anne
Emotional changes during pregnancy. Redbook 138:10+ D '71

NEWTS
Leech-repellent property of eastern red-spotted newts, notophalmus viridescens. F. H. Pough. bibliog il Science 174:1144-6 D 10 '71

NG, K. Y. and others
Dopamine: stimulation-induced release from central neurons. bibliog il Science 172:487-9 Ap 30 '71

NGANOUBARA, Sylvain
Summer diplomat, U.S.A. A. Adams. por Seventeen 29:270-1+ Ag '70 •

NGHI, Nguyen-vinh-. See Nguyen-vinh-Nghi

NGO-cong-Duc
Trials of Ngo Cong Duc. il por Time 98:24-5 S 6 '71 •
Two men who didn't make; with editorial comment. il pors Life 71:24-5, 32 S 10 '71 •

NGO-dinh-Diem
Plot against Diem, as told by Pentagon papers; with interview with F. E. Nolting, jr. por U S News 71:66-70 Jl 26 '71 •
Round two: what the new documents show. il por Time 98:15-16 Jl 5 '71 •

NGO Dzu
Dzu story. por Time 98:18+ Jl 19 '71 •
Indochina's heroin traffic. il por Newsweek 78:15 Jl 19 '71 •

NGUGI, James
Independence of Africa and cultural decolonization. il UNESCO Courier 24:25-6+ Ja '71

NGUYEN-cao-Ky
Two voices in a one-man race; excerpts from interview. pors Time 98:34 S 20 '71
about
And then there were two. Time 98:29 Ag 16 '71 •
Generals. New Repub 165:8-9 S 4 '71 •
Is this written in the stars? See it through with Nguyen van Thieu. T. Buckley. il pors N Y Times Mag p 14-15+ S 26 '71 •
Letter from Saigon. R. Shaplen. New Yorker 47:96+ S 11 '71 •
No Ky and a big win? por Newsweek 78:30 Ag 16 '71 •

NGUYEN-cao-Ky—about—*Continued*
Off and running. il por Newsweek 77:37 My
    3 '71 *
South Viet Nam: two against Thieu. il pors
    Time 98:22+ Jl 26 '71 *
Spectral presence. il por **Time 98:22 Ag 23**
    '71 *
Still a Thieu-way race in South Viet Nam.
    il por Time 98:23-4 Ag 30 '71 *
That other presidential election. il por Time
    97:31-2 Je 14 '71 *
NGUYEN-cao-Ky, Mme
Tuyet Mai's dream place. il por Newsweek
    77:25 Ja 18 '71 *
NGUYEN-truong-Con
Vietnamese student; letter. D. Truong. New
    Repub 165:31 Jl 3 '71 *
NGUYEN-van-Thieu
Two voices in a one-man race; excerpts from
    interview. pors Time 98:33 S 20 '71

about
Aftermath of a victory. il por Newsweek 77:
    42+ Ap 12 '71 *
And then there was one. il Newsweek 78:41
    S 13 '71 *
Controversy over Thieu's one-man victory.
    por Sr Schol 99:14-15 N 8 '71 *
Democracy and government. Nat R 23:1280 N
    19 '71 *
For Thieu, biggest test still ahead. il por U S
    News 71:20 O 4 '71 *
Hollow triumph? Newsweek 78:49 O 11 '71 *
Is this written in the stars? See it through
    with Nguyen van Thieu. T. Buckley. il
    pors N Y Times Mag p 14-15+ S 26 '71 *
Letter from Saigon. R. Shaplen. New Yorker
    47:96+ S 11 '71*
Letter from Vietnam. R. Shaplen. New York-
    er 47:77-8+ N 13 '71 *
Mood turns violent. il Time 98:46 S 27 '71 *
Mudslingers. il por **Newsweek 78:38 Ag 2**
    '71 *
New strong man in Asia? por U S News
    71:72 O 18 '71 *
No Ky and a big win? por Newsweek 78:30
    Ag 16 '71 *
Non-contest. J. Larsen. il por Time 98:30 O
    4 '71 *
Power play. il por Newsweek 77:26 Je 21 '71 *
Puppet pulls the strings. K. Buckley. il
    Newsweek 78:25 O 4 '71 *
South Viet Nam: no longer a choice. il por
    Time 98:23-4 S 13 '71 *
South Viet Nam: two against Thieu. il pors
    Time 98:22+ Jl 26 '71 *
Thieu and democracy. W. F. Buckley, jr.
    Nat R 23:1136 O 8 '71 *
Thieu's election in context. Nat R 23:1162+
    O 22 '71 *
Vietnam after the election: is Thieu losing
    his Catholic support? T. Fox. Commonweal
    95:203-7 N 26 '71 *
War: edge of an abyss. il por Time 97:24+
    Ap 12 '71 *
NGUYEN-vinh-Nghi
Parting shots; it has been a very long war
    in Vietnam. il por Life 70:80 Je 11 '71 *
NHAM. Tran-tuan-. See Tran-tuan-Nham
NIACIN. See Nicotinic acid
NIAGARA ballet. See Ballet companies
NIAGARA FALLS
To the brink and beyond; in a barrel. M.
    Kram. il Sports Illus 35:48-52+ Jl 12 '71
NICE book festival. See Book fairs
NICHOLAS II, emperor of Russia
Nicholas and Alexandra; interview. R. K.
    Massie. il Vogue 158:112-13+ N 15 '71 *
NICHOLAS, Gerardus
Entrance, twilight, and dark life of the cave;
    with biographical sketch. il Natur Hist 80:
    6, 30-5 bibliog(p 84) Ap '71
NICHOLAS, Hunter
Bucking the system. J. Morgenstern. il pors
    Newsweek 79:65 Ja 10 '72 *
NICHOLAS, James A.
Nick the knife; or, The life of a football
    doctor. R. Kostelanetz. il pors N Y Times
    Mag p 12-13+ D 19 '71 *
NICHOLS, Bill
Screen. Commonweal 94:64-5 Mr 26 '71
NICHOLS, Dorothy
Quiet heroism of Dorothy Nichols. L. David.
    il pors Good H 172:114-15+ Ap '71 *
NICHOLS, Jeannette
There's so much and you're missing most
    of it; poem. Yale R 60:568 Je '71
NICHOLS, Neal K.
NEA of Shawnee Mission. Todays Ed 60:
    54 My '71

NICHOLS, Peter, 1927?-
National health; or, Nurse Norton's affair.
    Criticism
    Cath World 212:314-15 Mr '71 *
NICHOLS, Robert
Address to the smaller animals; poem. Na-
    tion 212:566 My 3 '71
After Labor day; poem. Nation 213:118 Ag
    16 '71
Cadmium red color; poem. Nation 212:382 Mr
    22 '71
Jasper's day off; poem. Nation 212:473 Ap 12
    '71
Poem: I dreamed I caught an owl in an old
    coat. Nation 212:760 Je 14 '71
Poem: I have keys on my ring. Nation 212:
    412 Mr 29 '71
Songs and other songs. Nation 212:254 F 22 '71
NICHOLS, Rodney Wayson
Mission-oriented R & D. bibliog Science 172:
    29-37 Ap 2 '71
NICHOLSON, Elmer Lyle
CNA chooses a chief and loses a top V-P.
    il por Bsns W p35 Jl 17 '71 *
NICHOLSON, Jack
Jack Nicholson looks east. J. Stewart. il
    pors Ramp Mag 10:51-4 S '71 *
NICHOLSON, Margaret
Copyright, fair use, permissions. Writer Di-
    gest 51:22-3 N '71
NICHOLSON, Mary Ann
Washington's paper army; drama. Plays 30:
    65-8, 96 F '71
NICHOLSON, Max
Renaissance; interview, ed. by H. Brandon.
    Sat R 54:53-4+ My 1 '71
NICHOLSON, Thomas D.
Celestial events. See issues of Natural his-
    tory
NICHOLSON memorial library, Garland, Tex.
    Garland, Texas: growing like sixty. il Li-
    brary J 96:3983 D 1 '71
NICKEL, Lawrence S.
Understanding complex waveforms. il Electr
    World 86:68-9 Jl '71
NICKEL cadmium batteries. See Storage bat-
    teries
NICKEL industry
                    Canada
Canadian nickel cries ouch. il Bsns W p26-7
    O 9 '71
    See also
International nickel company of Canada
NICKERSON, Roy
Hawaii's lava forests. il Am For 77:16-19 Ja
    '71
NICKLAUS, Jack
Game man might risk a bet. il por Sports
    Illus 34:40-2+ Je 7 '71

about
And for their next number. M. Cope. il pors
    Sports Illus 35:44+ Ag 9 '71 *
Dominance of the smiling bear. D. Jenkins. il
    pors Sports Illus 34:22-5 Mr 8 '71 *
For Jack, that beat goes on. D. Jenkins.
    il por Sports Illus 35:88-90 N 22 '71 *
Our Jack in fields of gold. D. Jenkins. il
    por Sports Illus 34:16-19 My 3 '71 *
Remember the battle of Merion. D. Jenkins.
    il pors Sports Illus 34:12-15 Je 28 '71 *
Two for money, one for show. G. S. Brown. il
    pors Sports Illus 35:28-9 N 8 '71 *
NICOLA, J. D.
Editors' editor. S. J. Adamo. America 124:
    154 F 13 '71 *
NICOLL, R. A.
Recurrent excitation of secondary olfactory
    neurons: a possible mechanism for signal
    amplification. bibliog il Science 171:824-6
    F 26 '71
NICOLSON, Harold
Weekending; or, Why we cannot forgive the
    Edwardians; reprint of 1929 essay. il Hori-
    zon 13:30-1 Aut '71
NICOTINIC acid
Primitive earth synthesis of nicotinic acid
    derivatives. N. Friedmann and others. bib-
    liog il Science 171:1026-7 Mr 12 '71
NIEBUHR, Reinhold
Niebuhr in the Century; excerpts. por Chr
    Cent 88:736-7 Je 16 '71

about
Death of a Christian realist. por Time 97:56+
    Je 14 '71 *
Legacy of Niebuhr. H. B. Kuhn. Chr Today
    15:23 Je 18 '71 *
Narrow path: Reinhold Niebuhr (1892-1971)
    B. H. Smith. America 125:63-5 Ag 7 '71 *

NIEBUHR, Reinhold—about—*Continued*
Obituary
America 124:inside cover Je 12 '71. D. R.
Campion
Chr Cent 88:735 Je 16 '71
Commonweal 94:324 Je 25 '71. J. Finn
Nat R 23:690-1 Je 29 '71. W. Herberg
Newsweek por 77:113 Je 14 '71
Pub W 199:33 Je 14 '71
Of many things; A. Schlesinger's tribute.
T. H. Stahel and D. R. Campion. America
125:inside cover N 20 '71 •
NIEDECKER, Lorine
Comment. P. Schjeldahl. Poetry 117:269-70
Ja '71 •
NIEDERGANG, Marcel
Revolutionary nationalism in Peru. For Affairs 49:454-63 Ap '71
NIEDERLAND, William G.
Freud's literary style: some observations.
bibliog f Am Imago 28:17-23 Spr '71
NIELSEN, Brian
Racing and rapping. Library J 96:2456 Ag
'71
NIELSEN, Knut Schmidt-. See Schmidt-Nielsen, K.
NIERENBERG, Gerard I.
With understanding, confidence, and help,
intuition can be improved. Vogue 158:61+
S 15 '71
about
Piggybacking. P. S. Nathan. por Pub W
200:23 Jl 26 '71 •
NIETZSCHE, Friedrich Wilhelm
Nietzsche's madness: tragic wisdom. C. P.
Ellerman. bibliog Am Imago 27:338-57
Wint '70 •
NIGERIA
Nigeria's spectacular rebound. C. T. Rowan.
Read Digest 98:156-8+ Je '71
See also
Children—Nigeria
Missions—Nigeria
Motor bus lines—Nigeria

Antiquities
Two blacks discover lost African world. S.
Booker. il Ebony 27:47-8+ N '71

Civil war, 1967-1970
Reflections on the Nigerian civil war, by R.
Uwechue. Review
Sat R 54:28 Ja 16 '71. S. Jervis

Reconstruction
No news and good news from Nigeria. Chr
Cent 88:1222 O 20 '71
Recovery after Biafra. il Time 99:40-1 Ja
10 '72

Economic conditions
Federation of Nigeria. D. J. Murray. Cur Hist
60:157-63+ Mr '71

Politics and government
Federation of Nigeria. D. J. Murray. Cur Hist
60:157-63+ Mr '71
NIGHSWONGER, Carl
Some lessons on dying. B. Hale. il por Chr
Cent 88:1076-9 S 15 '71 •
NIGHT boating. See Boats and boating
NIGHT clubs
Profiles; M. Gordon and B. Josephson; night
club owners. W. Balliett. pors New Yorker
47:50-6+ O 9 '71
Reaching the groovy ones: Jesus nightclub;
Hollywood's Right On. Chr Today 15:37-8
Ag 6 '71
France
Turning on in Paris. H. Gault and C. Millau.
il Holiday 48:72-5 S '70
NIGHT Enoch slept downstairs by the fire;
story. See Sillitoe, A.
NIGHT flying. See Aviation—Night flying
NIGHT in the cemetery; story. See Chekhov,
A.
NIGHT out; story. See Alvarez, A.
NIGHT out; story. See Walker, T.
NIGHT photography. See Photography, Night
NIGHT sky. See Sky
NIGHT Thoreau spent in jail; drama. See Lawrence, J. and Lee, R. E.
NIGHTCLUBS. See Night clubs
NIGHTGOWNS, pajamas, etc.
Pick the coziest sleepwear for the whole
family. il Good H 172:168 F '71
NIGHTINGALE, E. M.
Truth about Croesus; drama. Plays 31:63,
79-83 N '71
The NIGHTINGALE (opera) See Television
operas

NIHILISM (philosophy)
Nietzsche's madness: tragic wisdom. C. P.
Ellerman. bibliog Am Imago 27:338-57
Wint '70
NIJINSKY, Waslaw
Bejart's Nijinsky: Clown of God; tr. by N.
M. Stoop. M. F. Christout. il Dance Mag
45:34-41 D '71 •
NIJINSKY: Clown of God; ballet. See Ballets
—Criticisms
NIKITIN, Boris
Latent talent: the anagram a parent can solve.
il UNESCO Courier 24:28-32 F '71
NIKOLAIEFF, George
How teachers feel about tenure. Schol
Teach Jr/Sr High p2 D '71
One town's hot & cold views of the freeze.
il Sr Schol 99:11-13 O 11 '71
NIKOLAIS, Alwin
Nikolais and Louis: a new space. T. Tobias.
il pors Dance Mag 45:46-54 F '71 •
NIKOLAIS, Alwin, dance company. See Alwin
Nikolais dance company
NILE RIVER
See also
Aswan High Dam
NILSSEN, Jerome
Some notes on liturgy. il Chr Cent 88:924-7
Ag 4 '71
NILSSON, Lennart
Brain; photographs. Life 71:44-59 O 1; 42-
56+ O 22 '71 (to be cont)
Gallery; photographs. Life 70:6-9 Ap 23 '71
about
Photographing the brain as no one ever has.
R. Graves. il por Life 71:3 O 1 '71 •
NIM (game) See Games
NIMANGI ceremony. See Rites and ceremonies
—New Hebrides
NIMBUS satellites. See Artificial satellites—
Meteorological use
NIMEIRY, Jaafar. See Nimieri, G. M.
el NIMIERI, Gaafar Mohamed
Revenge in the Sudan. il por Time 98:26-7
Ag 9 '71 •
Showdown season in the Middle East. il por
Newsweek 78:34-5 Ag 2 '71 •
NIMS, John Frederick
(tr) See Castro, R. de Nasin cand' as prantas nasen. . .
NIN, Anaïs
Anaïs Nin on women; interview, ed. by J.
Oringer. il Ramp Mag 9:43-5 My '71
Anaïs Nin talks about being a woman. por
Vogue 158:98-9+ O 15 '71
about
Novel of her life. D. Stern. Nation 213:570-2
N 29 '71 •
911 (telephone number) See Telephone numbers
NINETEEN hundred and twenties
Cosier sports. E. Sheppard. Harp Baz 104:
142-3 My '71
NINETEEN hundred and thirties
Eudora Welty's world in the '30s; excerpts
from One time, one place. E. Welty. il
Mlle 73:162-5+ S '71
NINETEEN hundred and thirty-seven
35 years ago in Life. il Life 72:22-4+ Ja 14
'72
NINETEEN hundred and forties
Play it again, Sam Bogie, Harry, Wendell,
Claude. B. Brower. il Esquire 76:120-1+ N
'71
Welcome back to the forties. G. Frazier. il
Esquire 76:98-105, 108-15+ O '71
NINETEEN hundred and fifties
Look at the '50s. R. Goldstein. il Mlle 74:
134-5+ N '71
NINETEEN hundred and sixties
Politics of the sixties: from the new frontier to the new revolution. E. J. Hughes.
il N Y Times Mag p24-5+ Ap 4 '71; Reply
with rejoinder. S. Alsop. p4+ Ap 25 '71
Sensibility in the 70's; excerpt from The
disjunction of culture and social structure.
D. Bell. Commentary 51:63-73 Je '71
What really happened in the 1960's? J. Hitchcock. America 124:449-53 My 1 '71
Who was Richard Nixon's running mate in
1960? a quiz on who did what, where, when,
and to whom in the sixties. il Esquire 76:
146-53 D '71
NINETEEN hundred and seventies
Hidden promise of the 1970s. Time 97:70-1 F
15 '71
Let's take a look into the 1970's. E. F.
Schmidt. por Camp Mag 43:4 Ja '71
Looking back on the seventies: notes toward a
cultural history. B. DeMott. Atlan 227:59-64
Mr '71

NINTEEN hundred and seventies—*Continued*
Mlle's next word: where it is now. Mlle 72: 57-60 Ja '71
Surprising seventies. P. F. Drucker. il Harper 243:35-9 Jl '71; Same abr. Read Digest 99: 49-52 S '71; Same with title What surprises, if any, for the seventies? Cur 134:56-64 N '71; Discussion. Harper 243:6-8 S '71
Twenty-one theses; a radical perspective on the '70s. A. I. Waskow. Commonweal 93: 463-5 F 12 '71

NINETEEN hundred and seventy

Anecdotes, facetiae, satire, etc.
Esquire's dubious achievement awards for 1970. il Esquire 75:104-13 Ja '71

NINETEEN hundred and seventy-one
Images '71; photographs. Time 99:20-3 Ja 3 '72
Some cartoons of 1971. il Nation 214:16-17 Ja 3 '72
Year in pictures 1971. il Life 71:2-16+ D 31 '71
1971 Gigi looks at sex; story. See Calisher, H.

NINETEEN hundred and seventy-two
Changes to expect in new year. U S News 72:11 Ja 10 '72
Great year coming? P. A. Samuelson. Newsweek 78:45 D 27 '71
In deference to Pope Gregory. G. W. Ball. Newsweek 79:32 Ja 10 '72
1972: our new year of grace. America 126:1 Ja 8 '72
Outlook, '72. il U S News 72:12-14+ Ja 10 '72

NINETEEN hundred and seventy-six
Unfinished business of America; views of prominent Americans. il Look 35:56-7+ Jl 13 '71

NINETEEN hundred and eighty-five
Look at the great economy of 1985. il Bsns W p84-5 D 18 '71

NINETEEN hundred and ninety-one
Where will we be 20 years from now? M. H. Stans por Nations Bsns 59:26-8 F '71

NIRENBERG, Sue
Perspectives. il House B 113:46-8 S; 35+ O '71

NISBET, Ian C. T. and Miner, Dallas
DDT substitute. bibliog il Environ 13:10-17 Jl '71

NISBET, Robert A.
Deluge of humanitarianism in the American university; excerpt from Degradation of the academic dogma. Sch & Soc 99:241-4+ Ap '71
Epistle to the Americans. Commentary 50: 40-5 D '70: 51:34 Ap '71
Future of the university; excerpt from address, February 1970. Commentary 51:62-71 F '71
Nisbet: reversing the degradation of scholarship; excerpts from address; May 16, 1971. Pub W 199:24-5 Je 14 '71

NISEI. See Japanese Americans

NISKA, Maralin
Recordings. M. Mayer. Esquire 75:30 F '71

about
Musician of the month. O. Howard. pors Hi Fi 21:MA6-7 F '71 *

NISSEN, Robert J.
Providing for electronic signal distribution. il Arch Rec 150:125-7 Jl '71

NITRATES
See also
Water supply—Nitrogen content

NITRILOTRIACETIC acid
NTA in detergents. il Chem 44:21-3 Ja '71
Phosphates make a sudsy comeback. Bsns W p25 S 18 '71
Return of the phosphates. Time 98:90 S 27 '71

NITRITES
Environmental nitroso compounds: reaction of nitrite with creatine and creatinine. M. C. Archer and others. bibliog il Science 174: 1341-3 D 24 '71

NITROGEN
See also
Water supply—Nitrogen content

Fixation
Extending symbiotic nitrogen fixation to increase man's food supply: report of meeting. D. A. Phillips and others. Science 174: 169-71 O 8 '71
Nitrogen, phosphorus, and eutrophication in the coastal marine environment. J. H. Ryther and W. M. Dunstan. bibliog il Science 171:1008-13 Mr 12 '71

NITROGEN content of soils. See Soils—Nitrogen content

NITROGEN dioxide. See Nitrogen oxides

NITROGEN fixation. See Nitrogen—Fixation

NITROGEN mustards
Transport of nitrogen mustard on the transport-carrier for choline in L5178Y lymphoblasts. G. J. Goldenberg and others. bibliog il Science 172:1148-9 Je 11 '71

NITROGEN oxides
Making tubes for NO$_2$—N$_2$O$_4$ equilibrium reaction. E. C. Sutton. il por Chem 45:28 Ja '72
NOx is the next pollutant to go. Bsns W p 108+ Mr 6 '71

NITROGEN tetroxide. See Nitrogen oxides

NITROGLYCERIN
Dynamite heart; overexposure to nitroglycerin by ammunition plant workers. il Time 98:41 Jl 12 '71

NITROPHENOLS. See Phenols

NITROSAMINES
Nitrosamines: a universal cancer-causing chemical? B. T. Hunter. il Consumer Bul 54:25 Mr '71
Nitrosoamines in fish. Chem 44:21-2 My '71

NITROSO compounds
Environmental nitroso compounds; reaction of of nitrite with creatine and creatinine. M. C. Archer and others. bibliog il Science 174:1341-3 D 24 '71

NIXIE tubes. See Electron tubes

NIXON, Alan Charles
Chemists pick Nixon. R. Gillette. Science 174:1309 D 24 '71 •

NIXON, Colin
Honeymoon; poem. Chr Cent 88:62 Ja 20 '71
Soho encounter; poem. Chr Cent 88:612 My 19 '71

NIXON, Patricia (Ryan)
Caring for others creates the spirit of a nation; interview. il pors U S News 71: 54-7 Ag 2 '71; Same abr. with title First lady, first volunteer. Read Digest 99:125-8 N '71
Christmas at the White House. il House & Gard 140:62-9 D '71

about
African queen for a week. il pors Time 99: 12-14 Ja 17 '72 •
Fellow traveler; visit to West Africa. il por Newsweek 79:19 Ja 10 '72 •
Pat into the fray. il por Time 98:15 D 6 '71 •
Real Pat Nixon. J. West. il pors Good H 172: 66-71+ F '71; Same abr. with title Pat Nixon: as she is. Read Digest 98:129-33 Ap '71 •

NIXON, Richard Milhous
Agreement with Japan on reversion of Okinawa transmitted to the Senate; message, September 21, 1971. Dept State Bul 65:431-3 O 18 '71
Ambassador Bruce resigns as head of U.S. delegation to Paris talks; with exchange of letters, July 28, 1971. Dept State Bul 65:180 Ag 16 '71
American strength: the keystone of peace; address, May 29, 1971. Dept State Bul 64: 813-15 Je 28 '71
Annual report on foreign assistance program transmitted to Congress; letter of transmittal, February 18, 1971. Dept State Bul 64: 301-2 Mr 8 '71
Annual report on World weather program transmitted to Congress; letter of transmittal, April 15, 1971. Dept State Bul 64:625 My 10 '71
As Nixon looks beyond the freeze; remarks, September 23, 1971. il por U S News 71:77-9 O 4 '71
Budget message of the President; excerpts. Dept State Bul 64:239-41 F 22 '71
Changing U.S. role in the world; address February 25, 1971. il U S News 70:49-52 Mr 8 '71; Same with title Redefinition of the United States role in the world. Dept State Bul 64:305-10 Mr 15 '71; Excerpt. Cur Hist 61:357-8+ D '71
Continuing U.S. efforts on behalf of prisoners of war and missing in southeast Asia; remarks, September 28, 1971. Dept State Bul 65:447 O 25 '71
Convention on terrorism transmitted to the Senate; message, May 11, 1971. Dept State Bul 65:28 Jl 5 '71
Death of President Tubman of Liberia; statement, July 26, 1971. Dept State Bul 65:180 Ag 16 '71
Drugs and defeatism; U.S. decadence; excerpts from remarks, July 6, 1971. il por U S News 71:37 Jl 19 '71
Equal housing: Nixon defines his policy; excerpts from statement, June 11, 1971. il U S News 70:72 Je 21 '71

NIXON, Richard Milhous—*Continued*
President requests additional funds for south Asian relief; statement, October 1, 1971. Dept State Bul 65:444 O 25 '71
President Tito of Yugoslavia visits the United States; exchange of greetings, toasts, October 28, 1971. Dept State Bul 65:590, 591-2 N 22 '71
President urges nursing home reforms, hints action by U.S; excerpts from address, June 25, 1971. Aging 201:5+ Jl '71
President welcomes South Viet-Nam's initiative on prisoners of war, statement, April 14, 1971. Dept State Bul 64:568 My 3 '71
President's economic policy in his own words; address, August 15, 1971. por U S News 71:62-5 Ag 30 '71; Same with title Challenge of peace. Dept State Bul 65:253-6 S 6 '71; Same with title New economic policy. Vital Speeches 37:674-6 S 1 '71
President's message on medical care; excerpts from message to Congress, February 18, 1971. il U S News 70:70-4 Mr 1 '71
President's own appraisal of the Laos operation; excerpt from interview, March 22, 1971. il por U S News 70:17 Ap 5 '71
Prime Minister Colombo of Italy visits the United States; exchange of greetings, toasts, February 18, 1971. Dept State Bul 64:329-33 Mr 15 '71
Prime Minister Gandhi of India visits the United States; exchange of greetings, toasts; November 4, 1971. Dept State Bul 65:615, 616-17 N 29 '71
Prime Minister Heath of the United Kingdom visits Washington; exchange of greetings, toasts, December 17, 1970. Dept State Bul 64:56-8 Ja 11 '71
Prime Minister McMahon of Australia meets with President Nixon; remarks, November 2, 1971. Dept State Bul 65:646 D 6 '71
Prime Minister of Ireland visits Washington; exchange of greetings. Dept State Bul 64:508 Ap 12 '71
Prince Juan Carlos of Spain visits the United States; exchange of greetings and toasts. Dept State Bul 64:236-8 F 22 '71
Private world of Richard Nixon; interview, ed. by J. Schecter. il pors Time 99:18-19 Ja 3 '72
Purpose of America's power; address, March 12, 1971. Dept State Bul 64:487-9 Ap 5 '71; Excerpts. Cur Hist 60:365-7 Je '71
Reform of the U.S. foreign assistance program: message to Congress, April 21, 1971 Dept State Bul 64:614-25 My 10 '71
Report on educational and cultural exchange program sent to Congress; message, August 5, 1971. Dept State Bul 65:250 Ag 30 '71
Report on trade agreements program transmitted to the Congress; message, December 30, 1970. Dept State Bul 64:114-15 Ja 25 '71
Report on trade agreements program transmitted to the Congress; message, December 1, 1971. Dept State Bul 65:714-15 D 20 '71
Role of the Supreme court; Nixon gives his criteria; address, October 21, 1971. por U S News 71:62-3 N 1 '71
Significant development: address, May 20, 1971. por U S News 70:19 My 31 '71
Sound limitations on armaments urged by President Nixon; message, February 23, 1971. Dept State Bul 64:310-11 Mr 15 '71
State of the Union; address, January 22, 1971. il pors U S News 70:66-70 F 1 '71; Same. Vital Speeches 37:226-30 F 1 '71
Strong economy and a strong national defense; address, August 19, 1971. Dept State Bul 65:273-6 S 13 '71
Top challenge now: ending the missile race; excerpts from message to Congress, February 25, 1971. il U S News 70:53-4 Mr 8 '71 Cur Hist 60:302 My '71
U.S. continues disaster relief to Pakistan; statement, January 4, 1971. Dept State Bul 64:138 F 1 '71
U.S. foreign policy for the 1970's building for peace. report to the Congress; February 25, 1971. Dept State Bul 64:341-432 Mr 22 '71
U.S.-Mexico boundary treaty transmitted to the Senate; President's letter of transmittal. il Dept State Bul 64:674-5 My 24 '71
U.S. Panama, and Colombia to build link to Pan American highway; statement, May 6, 1971. Dept State Bul 64:673 My 24 '71
U.S. participation in the U.N. during 1970; text of letter, September 20, 1971. Dept State Bul 65:502-3 N 1 '71
United States hails Turkish decision to ban opium poppy production; statement and remarks, June 30, 1971. Dept State Bul 65:74-5 Jl 19 '71

Vienna convention on the law of treaties transmitted to the Senate; message, November 22, 1971. Dept State Bul 65:684 D 13 '71
Welfare vs. jobs. President sees a threat to America; excerpts from address, April 19, 1971. U S News 70:67 My 3 '71
We've broken the ice with Communist China; excerpts from news conference, April 29, 1971. por U S News 70:27 My 10 '71
What U.S. needs to do now: the President's size-up; message to Congress, September 9, 1971. il por U S News 71:31-4 S 20 '71; Same with title President Nixon asks congressional support for new economic program. Dept State Bul 65:362-6 O 4 '71; Same with title Wage price freeze. Vital Speeches 37:706-9 S 15 '71
White House conversation: the President and Howard K. Smith; excerpts from TV interview, March 22, 1971. Dept State Bul 64:497-506 Ap 12 '71
Wilsonian principle after half a century; remarks, February 18, 1971. Dept State Bul 64:312-14 Mr 15 '71
World and U.S. problems, address; July 6, 1971. Vital Speeches 37:611-15 Ag 1 '71; Excerpts. U S News 71:46-7 Ag 2 '71; Dept State Bul 65:93-7 Jl 26 '71
Would U.S. support an invasion of North Vietnam? President's news conference, March 4, 1971. il por U S News 70:41 Mr 15 '71; Same. Dept State Bul 64:433-9 Mr 29 '71

about

Again, a new Nixon. il por Newsweek 77:15-16 Ja 25 '71 *
All set for the fourth act. H. Sidey. il por Life 71:41 D 31 '71 *
Another "historic" meeting. Nation 212:452 Ap 12 '71 *
Another route to peace. Nation 213:546-7 N 29 '71 *
As Nixon and Hirohito meet, can allies heal a split? pors U S News 71:35-6 S 27 '71 *
Austin story. J. Osborne. New Repub 165:13-15 Ag 21 '71 *
Battle lines drawn for '72 election; union, White House showdown. il por U S News 71:11-13 D 6 '71 *
Battle of Bal Harbour. Time 98:16 D 6 '71 *
Best way to run for president. il por Newsweek 78:26-7 N 22 '71 *
Black study. J. Osborne. New Repub 164:11-12 Mr 13 '71 *
Blockbuster three? S. Alsop. Newsweek 78:112 S 13 '71 *
Budgeting toward a new prosperity. il por Newsweek 77:68-70 F 8 '71 *
Candidate with the built-in edge. il por Newsweek 78:21-2 D 13 '71 *
The catch. Nation 212:98 Ja 25 '71 *
Catholic strategy: remarks at Knights of Columbus banquet il por Newsweek 78:52 Ag 30 '71 *
Chance to bargain on Vietnam. Life 71:34 Jl 23 '71 *
Chosen two. J. Osborne. New Repub 165:12-13 N 6 '71 *
Clifford interview. Nation 213:133 Ag 30 '71 *
Coddled criminal; interventions in the Calley case. New Repub 164:10-11 Ap 17 '71 *
Declaration: suspension of support by twelve conservative spokesmen. Nat R 23:842 Ag 10 '71; Discussion. 23:908-9 Ag 24 '71 *
De-Vietnamization of America. Fortune 83:133-4 My '71 *
Disenchanted. il Newsweek 78:35+ N 8 '71 *
Down, George! Alabama visit. New Repub 164:7 Je 5 '71 *
Drive to beat inflation, and Democrats; Blurry banner for Phase II; program presented October 7, 1971. il por Time 98:10-12+ O 18 '71 *
Dump Nixon campaign. D. W. Riegle, jr; A. K. Lowenstien. Look 35:79-80 Je 1 '71 *
Eaton on Nixon. Nation 213:229 S 20 '71 *
Elmer Bobst tells his Nixon story. E. H. Bobst. por Bsns W p54-5 Jl 31 '71 *
First planks in Nixon's 1972 platform. Bsns W p 14-15 Ja 1 '72 *
Four-year itch. H. Sidey. Life 71:4 N 26 '71 *
Games with Muskie. J. Osborne. New Repub 164:15-16 F 20 '71 *
Guess who's coming to dinner; forthcoming summit meetings. il Newsweek 78:20 D 6 '71 *
Halfway to where? views of D. P. Moynihan. J. Osborne. New Repub 164:18-19 Ja 2 '71 *
Happy in his work. H. Hubbard. il pors Newsweek 78:23 O 11 '71 *
Impeachment? G. W. Johnson. New Repub 164:14-15 Ap 10 '71 *

NIXON, Richard Milhous—about—*Continued*
Inside the White House 1971; excerpts from
Courage and hesitation. A. Drury. il pors
Look 35:32-42+ O 19 '71 *
Is it safe to trust Washington? Newsweek
78:25 S 13 '71 *
Keynesian Nixon gets passing marks. il Bsns
W p 15-16 F 6 '71 *
Kingdom come on Pennsylvania avenue. H.
Sidey. Life 70:28 F 26 '71 *
Labor's disturbing challenge. pors Time 98:29
N 29 '7'
Let a million voters bloom. M. Novak. Com-
monweal 94:79-81 Ap 2 '71; Discussion. 94:
205+ My 7 '71 *
Letter from Washington (cont) R. H. Rovere.
New Yorker 46:85-90 Ja 23; 47:155-8 O 23;
157-61 N 13; 82+ D 18 '71 *
Looking forward to the harvest. H. Sidey.
Life 70:8 Je 25 '71 *
Man who's made the most solid contribution
to the arts of any president since F.D.R.
F. Getlein. il por N Y Times Mag p 14-16+
F 14 '71; Reply. M. R. Rogers. p36 Mr 28
'71 *
Mathematics of '72. S. Alsop. Newsweek 78:
132 N 15 '71 *
Meet the President. Nation 212:386 Mr 29
'71 *
Meetings are the message. il por Time 98:
7 D 20 '71 *
Mr McCloskey v. Nixon. W. F. Buckley, jr.
Nat R 23:722 Je 29 '71 *
Mr Nixon knows what he can do. il pors
Newsweek 78:16-18 N 29 '71 *
Mr Nixon's course? F. S. Meyer. Nat R 23:86
Ja 26 '71 *
Moynihan on Nixon. W. F. Buckley, jr. Nat
R 23:102-3 Ja 26 '71 *
Moynihan report: after six months of be-
nign neglect; interview, ed. by H. Bran-
don. D. P. Moynihan. il pors N Y Times
Mag p 10-11+ Je 27 '71 *
Nix on Nixon. il Newsweek 78:60 Ag 23 '71 *
Nixon: a fresh burst of summitry. il pors
Time 98:14-15 D 6 '71 *
Nixon and labor widen the breach. por Bsns
W p 18-19 N 27 '71 *
Nixon at mid-term. Sr Schol 97:10-19 Ja 18
'71 *
Nixon-Connally arrangement. R. J. Whalen.
por Harper 243:29-33+ Ag '71 *
Nixon: determined to make a difference;
Time magazine Man of the year. il pors
Time 99:10-13+ Ja 3 '72 *
Nixon economics. P. A. Samuelson. News-
week 78:70 Ag 2 '71 *
Nixon: how vulnerable? Nation 213:387-8 O
25 '71 *
Nixon in the White House. by R. Evans and
R. Novak. Review
Bsns W p 13+ O 23 '71 *
Nat R 23:1307+ N 19 '71. W. A. Rusher *
Nixon of the O.P.A. M. Viorst. pors N Y
Times Mag p70+ O 3 '71 *
Nixon offers large, mixed bag on environment.
C. Holden. Science 171:659 F 19 '71 *
Nixon on energy. R. E. Lapp. New Repub
164:14-15 Je 26 '71 *
Nixon: opening moves. Nat R 23:1337 D 3
'71 *
Nixon: power for peace. il por Newsweek 77:
22-3 Mr '71 *
Nixon '71: a vintage year. il pors Newsweek
79:10-11 Ja 3 '72 *
Nixon tightrope. J. M. Burns. il pors Life
70:48B-48D+ Ap 2 '71 *
Nixon tries the treatment. il pors Newsweek
78:18-19 S 20 '71 *
Nixon year III: the year of the presidential
hat. Life 70:30-1 Ja 22 '71; Reply. G.
Romney. 70:62A F 5 '71 *
Nixonomics: how the game plan went wrong.
R. Evans, jr. and R. D. Novak. Atlan 228:
66-76+ Jl '71 *
Nixon's chances in 1972. il por U S News
71:16-18 Jl 5 '71 *
Nixon's chances in '72, as top Republicans
see them. il U S News 71:37-9 Ag 9 '71 *
Nixon's economic bombshell; with editorial
comment and interview with O. Eckstein.
H. Sidey. il por Life 71:4, 20-5 Ag 27 '71 *
Nixon's four-point do-nothing plan. il pors
Newsweek 78:67 Jl 12 '71 *
Nixon's frozen, floating dollar. il Newsweek
78:10-21 Ag 30 '71 *
Nixon's grand design for recovery. il por
Time 98:4-14+ Ag 30 '71 *
Nixon's hop, skip and yule; Christmastide
schedule. il Newsweek 78:15 D 27 '71 *
Nixon's inner circle of businessmen. il por
Bsns W p52-3+ Jl 31 '71 *
Nixon's N.E.P. Chr Cent 88:992 Ag 25 '71 *
Nixon's new push to win over farmers. il por
Farm J 95:24 Je '71 *

Nixon's objective in Paris. R. L. Leggett.
Nation 213:610 D 13 '71 *
Nixon's odd view of the Court. Life 71:36
N 5 '71 *
Nixons of the O.P.A. M. Kranzberg. N Y
Times Mag p 115 N 14 '71 *
Nixon's secret strategy. R. Reeves. Harper
243:96-8 D '71 *
Nixon's share-the-wealth plan. il por News-
week 77:15-16 Ja 18 '71 *
Notes and comment (cont) New Yorker 47:
31-3 Ap 17 '71 *
On the road. J. Osborne. New Repub 165:11-
12 O 9 '71 *
100,000 homeward bound. il Sr Schol 98:13-14
Ap 26 '71 *
Patience of Mr Nixon. W. F. Buckley, jr. Nat
R 23:669 Je 15 '71 *
Phase two: living with controls. il pors News-
week 78:26-32 O 18 '71 *
Praggy Dick. J. Osborne. New Repub 165:14-
15 S 25 '71 *
Presidency. il por Time 97:12-13 Mr 29; 13
Ap 5 '71 *
President. See occasional issues of News-
week *
President at midpassage. M. Elfin. il pors
Newsweek 77:21-2+ Ja 25 '71; Reply. E.
Richardson. 77:16-17 F 1 '71 *
President is the problem. T. Hoopes. New Re-
pub 164:23-7 Mr 6 '71 *
President makes a costly bargain. Bsns W
p 104 O 16 '71; Reply. P. M. Flanigan.
p5 O 23 '71 *
President out on a limb. S. Alsop. il News-
week 77:116 Mr 22 '71 *
Presidential trek: prelude to '72. por U S
News 71:29 Ag 30 '71 *
President's double finesse. S. Alsop. News-
week 77:98 Mr 1 '71 *
President's other friend; R. H. Abplanalp.
R. G. Hummerstone. il pors Life 70:55-6+
Mr 5 '71 *
President's problem. Nation 212:162-3 F 8
'71 *
Racing's greatest day; White House recep-
tion. il pors Hot Rod 24:30-1 D '71 *
Rekindling the spirit of '76. H. Sidey. il por
Life 71:4 Ag 13 '71 *
Rev. Billy's day. J. Osborne. New Repub
165:11-13 O 30 '71 *
Richard Nixon on the cuff-link trail; trip to
Alabama. il pors Newsweek 77:26-7 Je 7
'71 *
Say it isn't so, Mr President. W. F. Buck-
ley, jr. il pors N Y Times Mag p8-9+ Ag
1 '71 *
School busing: confusing ends and means.
America 125:82 Ag 21 '71 *
'72 preview: two issues, one candidate. il
por Newsweek 78:15-16 Ag 16 '71 *
Sharing loaves and fishes. il por Time 97:15-
16 F 15 '71 *
Shooting at the bluebirds of happiness. il
pors Time 98:17-18 Ag 9 '71 *
Show biz in Miami. Nation 213:578-9 D 6 '71 *
Showdown with Reagan. J. Osborne. New
Repub 165:9-11 Jl 10 '71 *
Size-up of President Nixon; interview. M.
J. Mansfield. il pors U S News 71:56-61
D 6 '71 *
Southern strategy, by R. Murphy and H.
Gulliver. Review
Sat R 54:28 Ag 7 '71. R. D. Behn *
State of the Union, state of the President.
il pors Time 97:10-11 Ja 25 '71 *
Statement in black and white. J. C. Rosa-
pepe. Commonweal 94:421-2 Ag 20 '71 *
Steady as you go. M. Friedman. Newsweek
78:62 Jl 26 '71 *
Story behind the book: Courage and hesita-
tion. A. H. Johnston. il por Pub W 200:
22-3 O '71 *
Suburban snobbery. New Repub 164:7-9 Je
26 '71 *
Suburban strategy. il Newsweek 77:19 Je 21
'71 *
TRB from Washington. See occasional issues
of New republic *
Talk and travel. J. Osborne. New Repub
165:9-11 D 11 '71 *
Teeth in Phase two. il por Newsweek 78:84+
S 27 '71 *
That elusive political majority. A. J. Reich-
ley. il por Fortune 83:68-73+ Mr '71 *
Thirsting to get into China. H. Sidey. Life
70:4 Ap 30 '71 *
Thunder in the AMA. il por Newsweek 78:
52-3 Jl 5 '71 *
'Tis the season to be nasty. H. Sidey. il Life
71:4 D 3 '71 *
Trouble with secrets. J. Osborne. New Re-
pub 165:11-12 Jl 3 '71 *
Truth and busing. J. Osborne. New Repub
165:11-12 S 11 '71 *

NIXON, Richard Milhous—about—*Continued*
Turnabout. J. Osborne. New Repub 165:11-13 S 4 '71 *
Two Nixons. P. A. Samuelson. Newsweek 77:84 F 8 '71 *
Waning game plan. R. Lekachman. Duns 98:13 Ag '71
Wanted: the first president brave enough to lose a war. R. Shnayerson. Harper 243:12+ S '71 *
Watch on the Potomac. il por Time 97:72+ My 10 '71 *
We can't until 1973. New Repub 164:7-8 Mr 13 '71 *
What would you do? S. Alsop. Newsweek 77:92 F 15 '71 *
When it starts to hurt. Life 70:32 F 26 '71 *
White House: the President in motion. il pors Time 98:18-19 O 11 '71 *
Why impeachment. R. A. Falk. New Repub 164:13-14 My 1 '71 *
Why Nixon is relatively good. E. Snow. il por Time 98:13 Ag 2 '71 *
With Cheops in Texas. J. Osborne. New Repub 164:9-10 Je 5 '71 *

Health
Latest on Nixon's health. il pors U S News 72:27 Ja 10 '72

Homes
Other White Houses of President Nixon. il U S News 71:29-31 S 6 '71

Memorials
Anecdotes, facetiae, satire, etc.
Richard M. Nixon library. E. Sorel. il Atlan 227:85-92 F '71

Messages
Drug abuse control: policy turns toward rehabilitation. J. Walsh. Science 173:32-4 Jl 2 '71
Energy: President asks $3 billion for breeder reactor, fuel studies. R. Gillette. Science 172:1114-16 Je 11 '71
Health economics. F. Land and J. Ridgeway. Ramp Mag 9:6-7 Je '71
New prosperity: hard sell begins. il por U S News 71:21 S 20 '71
No energy to waste; special message on energy policy. J. Lear. Sat R 54:37-9 Jl 3 '71
Policy and performance; foreign policy message. New Repub 164:5-6 Mr 6 '71
Policy in midstream; State of the world message. W. P. Bundy. Newsweek 77:73 Mr 8 '71
President's consumer message. Consumer Rep 36:293-5 My '71
Rescue operation; aid for higher education and repackaged consumer message. il Newsweek 77:52 Mr 8 '71
State of the world. il por Newsweek 77:65 Mr 8 '71
To your health. J. Osborne. New Repub 164:12 14 Mr 6 '71
War on drugs. il pors Newsweek 77:32+ Je 28 '71

Press conferences
Art of follow-up. Nation 212:739 Je 14 '71
Indochina: the new optimism. il por Newsweek 77:18-19 Mr 1 '71
Mayday! Mayday! on Washington's Mayday arrests. il Newsweek 77:27-8 Je 14 '71
Notes from a nightmare; televised conversation, January 4, 1971. J. Osborne. New Repub 164:9-11 Ja 16 '71
Of many things; President Nixon's January 4 TV encounter. T. M. Gannon. America 124:inside cover Ja 23 '71
President defends a policy and a man; televised press conference, March 4, 1971. il pors Time 97:13 Mr 15 '71
TRB from Washington; evading the press. New Repub 164:4 Ap 24 '71
Talk show; January 4, 1971. Newsweek 77:16 Ja 18 '71

Anecdotes, facetiae, satire, etc.
If you were president. G. Ace. Sat R 54:8 Ja 30 '71

Press relations
How the 2d best-informed man in the White House briefs the 2d worst-informed group in Washington. J. M. Naughton. il pors N Y Times Mag p9+ My 30 '71
Meet the press. il por Newsweek 77:29 Ap 26 '71
Needling the press. Nation 212:386-7 Mr 29 '71
No complaint department. New Repub 164:10 Ap 10 '71
President and press: a debate; summary. D. Moynihan; M. Frankel. pors Time 97:53 Ap 12 '71

Recruiting the opposition. por Time 97:65 Ap 19 '71
TRB from Washington: poor Richard's bad press. New Repub 165:4 D 4 '71
TV: delusions of infallibility; address, March 30, 1971. A. Capp. Vital Speeches 37:477-8 My 15 '71
This is the White House calling. H. Sidey. Life 70:2B Ap 2 '71

Anecdotes, facetiae, satire, etc.
TRB from Washington. New Repub 164:6 Ap 3 '71

Public relations
Bad news from the pollsters. H. Sidey. il Life 70:2B Mr 19 '71
Blacks and Mr Nixon. New Repub 164:5-6 Je 5 '71
Bleak week for Richard Nixon. il por Newsweek 77:18-19 Ap 5 '71
Bring us together; Nixon as President and partisan. il pors Sr Schol 97:16-17 Ja 18 '71
Crisis of confidence. R. Lekachman. Duns 97:9 Ap '71
Don't they know we're getting out? H. Sidey. il por Life 70:2 F 12 '71; Same abr. Read Digest 98:131-2 My '71
Heady days of presidential power. H. Sidey. il Life 71:4 O 22 '71
Hunkered down for the last act. H. Sidey. il Life 70:4 Ap 16 '71
Kent state in '72. Nation 213:612-13 D 13 '71
Latest poll, Nixon leads four top Democrats. U S News 71:64 D 20 '71
Lieutenant Calley and the President. Life 70:40 Ap 16 '71
Mr Nixon: the jury is still out. il por Newsweek 77:25-6 Mr 15 '71
Monologue: prime time. Nation 212:420 Ap 5 '71
Personal approach; TV and radio interviews. il Newsweek 77:24 Mr 29 '71
Pushing the human side. Time 97:12-13 Mr 29 '71
Right wing v. Nixon. il Time 98:12-13 Ag 16 '71
Second thoughts about Calley. Newsweek 77:29-30 Ap 19 '71
TRB from Washington; alienation from the blacks. New Repub 164:8 Jl 3 '71
This is the White House calling. H. Sidey. Life 70:2B Ap 2 '71
Thunderclap politics. Nation 213:164 S 6 '71
Time for truth. S. Alsop. Newsweek 77:124 Ap 12 '71
Wedding present. Nation 212:805 Je 28 '71
Week that was: possibility of re-election. Nation 213:674 D 27 '71
What are the sleepers. S. Alsop. Newsweek 77:100 Je 21 '71
White House conversation: the President and Howard K. Smith; excerpts from TV interview, March 22, 1971. R. M. Nixon. Dept State Bul 64:497-506 Ap 12 '71
Zanesville: the mood of the president makers. R. Stout. il Newsweek 77:31 Mr 15 '71

Relations with Congress
Coming battle between President and Congress. il pors Time 97:12-14+ F 1 '71
Congress is nicer than Nixon expected. Bsns W p 15-16 Jl 24 '71
Erosion of confidence; congressional opposition to the war. Nation 212:323-4 Mr 15 '71
Is 1972 here already? D. Lawrence. U S News 71:92 Ag 16 '71
Let's be the movers this time. H. Sidey. il por Life 70:2B F 5 '71
Lobbying Congress. J. Osborne. New Repub 165:9-10 D 18 '71
Nitty-gritty time. J. Osborne. New Repub 164:10-11 Ap 24 '71
Nixon and Congress: a look at the record. Sr Schol 97:10-13 Ja 18 '71
Nixon and Congress, score card on '71 session. il U S News 71:16-18 D 27 '71
President vs. Congress. America 124:279-80 Mr 20 '71
President vs. Congress: the right to know. H. J. Sievers. America 124:193 F 27 '71
President vs. Congress: toll of divided government. il pors U S News 71:16-18+ Jl 12 '71
President vs. the 92nd Congress. il Newsweek 77:16-18+ Ja 25 '71
Problems of divided government: Nixon vs. Congress. il U S News 70:15-16 Mr 22 '71
Shooting Santa Claus. J. Osborne. New Repub 165:10-12 D 25 '71

NIXON, Richard Milhous—*Continued*

Religion
National prayer breakfast: powerful audience. R. Chandler. Chr Today 15:40+ F 26 '71
Praying with the President in the White House. E. B. Friske. il N Y Times Mag p 14-15+ Ag 8 '71

Speeches, addresses, etc.
Captain and the President; A. Daniel's letter to the President in contrast to the President's TV address of April 7. Nation 212:482-3 Ap 19 '71
Nixon on Vietnam: more of the same; television address, April 7, 1971. il por Newsweek 77:26-7 Ap 19 '71
Nixon's stunning turnabout; televised address, August 15, 1971. por Newsweek 78:14-15 Ag 23 '71
Putting off the poor; Labor day speech. New Repub 165:10 S 18 '71
What Nixon didn't say; televised statement on U.S. involvement in Vietnamese war. New Repub 164:7-8 Ap 17 '71

Anecdotes, facetiae, satire, etc.
TRB from Washington: swift solution; use of small, tactical, nuclear weapons in Laos. New Repub 164:4 Mr 20 '71

State of the Union message, January 22, 1971
Dark night. Commonweal 93:459-60 F 12 '71
End the long, dark night. Sr Schol 98:14 F 8 '71
Nixon behind the scenes. E. Richardson. Newsweek 77:16-17 F 1 '71
Nixon revolution: promise and performance. il pors Time 97:10-12 F 1 '71
President and the State of the Union. America 124:111 F 6 '71
Promises, promises. New Repub 164:11-12 F 13 '71
Reports & comment: Washington. E. B. Drew. Atlan 227:6+ Ap '71 *
Revolution or reversal? J. Osborne. New Repub 164:15-16 F 6 '71
Selling the revolution. J. Osborne. New Repub 164:7-8 Mr 20 '71
Splitting the take. il Life 70:28 F 5 '71
State of the Union. Nat R 23:124 F 9 '71 *
State of the Union. il por Newsweek 77:15-17 F 1 '71
TRB from Washington. New Repub 164:6 F 6 '71
What's new? New Repub 164:13 F 6 '71

Visit to China (People's Republic) 1972
After Saigon, Peking ahead. il por Time 98: 31-2 O 18
Agenda in Peking. New Repub 165:5-7 Ag 7 '71
Breakthrough with China: the meaning. il por U S News 71:13-14 Jl 26 '71
China will talk from a position of strength; with editorial comment. E. Snow. il pors Life 71:20-1, 22-7 Jl 30 '71
Cow kicked Nelly. S. Alsop. Newsweek 78:84 Ag 16 '71
Hazards along the road to Peking. il Time 98:11-13 Ag 2 '71
How about a panda or two? Nation 213:100 Ag 16 '71
It takes two to tango. America 125:50 Ag 7 '71
Leadership and aid. J. Osborne. New Repub 165:11-13 N 13 '71
Leapfrogging the Paris talks. il Newsweek 78:22 Jl 26 '71
Letter from Hong Kong. R. Shaplen. New Yorker 47:58-60+ Jl 31 '71
Letter from Washington. R. H. Rovere. New Yorker 47:77-80 Ag 7 '71
Long, bumpy road to Peking. Newsweek 78: 14-15 Ag 2 '71
Marco Nixon. Chr Cent 88:898 Jl 28 '71
Mr Nixon's rewards. J. K. Fairbank. por Newsweek 78:18 Jl 26 '71
Nixon and Chou: the hard work begins; with report on story behind the invitation. il U S News 71:15-17 Ag 2 '71
Nixon: I will go to China. il pors Newsweek 78:16-21 Jl 26 '71
Nixon sets his goal: a journey for peace; address, July 15, 1971. R. M. Nixon. U S News 71:14 July 26, '71; Same. Dept State Bul 65:121 Ag 2 '71; Same with title United States—Peoples Republic of China. Vital Speeches 37:610 Ag 1 '71; Same with title President's visit to China. Cur Hist 61: 178 S '71

Nixon speaks out: China, prices, controls; news conference, August 4 1971. R. M. Nixon. por U S News 71:76-80 Ag 16 '71
Nixon's China visit: good fortune or misfortune cookie? il Sr Schol 99:10-11 S 20 '71
Nixon's coup: to Peking for peace. il pors Time 98:11-12+ Jl 26 '71
Nixon's too left-wing for William Loeb. B. Kovach. il por N Y Times Mag p 14+ D 12 '71
Notes and comment. New Yorker 47:41 N 6 '71
On to China. il Newsweek 78:22 D 13 '71 *
Packing the trunks for China. G. W. Ball. il Newsweek 78:53+ S 27 '71
Peace in our time. F. S. Meyer. Nat R 23:873 Ag 10 '71
Peking spectacular. Nation 213:66-7 Ag 2 '71
President Nixon's China trip. W. J. Richardson. il America 125:84-7 Ag 21 '71
President Nixon's planned visits to China and the U.S.S.R. discussed by presidential assistant Kissinger; transcript of news conference, November 30, 1971; with introd. by R. L. Ziegler. H. A. Kissinger. Dept State Bul 65:705-14 D 20 '71 *
President's Peking trip. W. P. Bundy. Newsweek 78:37 Ag 2 '71
Secret of Lincoln's sitting room. H. Sidey. Life 71:6 Jl 30 '71
Strange, strange bedfellows. il por Ebony 26: 142-3 S '71
Substance and style. Z. Brzezinski. por Newsweek 78:41 Ag 9 '71
Summitry. Nat R 23:1214+ N 5 '71
TRB from Washington: the spook; J. McCarthy. New Repub 165:6 Ag 21 '71
Twain shall meet. Nat R 23:845-7 Ag 10 '71
World and U.S. problems; address, July 6, 1971. Vital Speeches 37:611-15 Ag 1 '71; Excerpts. U S News 71:46-7 Ag 2 '71
Young Conservative looks at Nixon and China. R. Brookhiser. por Nat R 23:1056+ S 24 '71

Visit to Russia, 1972 (proposed)
From Peking to Moscow to San Diego. il por Newsweek 78:20-1 O 25 '71
In his own words: why Nixon is going to Moscow; news conference, October 12, 1971. R. M. Nixon. il por U S News 71:102-3 O 25 '71; Excerpts. Dept State Bul 65:473-7 N 1 '71
Summitry. Nat R 23:1214+ N 5 '71
Summitry: from Peking to Moscow. il pors Time 98:10-12 O 25 '71
Why Nixon is going to Moscow. il por U S News 71:19-21 O 25 '71

Visit to the Azores, 1971
Letter from the Azores. T. Szulc. New Yorker 47:54-8 Ja 1 '72

NIXON, Richard Milhous, family
First family; excerpts from interview. R. M. Nixon. il pors U S News 70:29 Mr 22 '71
Nixons nobody knows. W. McLendon. il McCalls 98:76-83+ My '71
White House Christmas, 1971, photo report. U S News 71:40-1 D 27 '71

NIXON, Tom
All you need to know about catching bass, with a fly rod. il Field & S 75:72-3+ Ap '71
Deer hair and bluegill. il Field & S 76:80-1+ My '71

NIXON, Tricia
Note:
For material after June 12, 1971, see Cox, Tricia (Nixon)
Alice was a tough character; statements, ed. by B. Angelo. Time 97:16 Je 14 '71
Father and the bride: interview, ed. by A. Coffin. il pors Look 35:74-9 Je 15 '71
Tricia Nixon: my wedding; interview, ed. by L. B. Robb. il pors Ladies Home J 88:64-7+ Je '71

about
Behind the main event. il pors Life 70:40-9 Je 18 '71 *
June wedding in the White House. il pors Time 97:11-12 Mr 29 '71 *
Love story. il pors Newsweek 77:24-5 Mr 29 '71 *
Mr Cox takes a June bride. il pors Time 97:16 Je 21 '71 *
Simple spectacular at the White House. il pors Time 97:13-17 Je 14 '71 *
Tricia got her rose garden. M. Seligson. il pors Life 70:32-5 Je 25 '71 *
Tricia Nixon's romance with Ed Cox. il pors Life 70:18-23 Ja 22 '71 *
Wedding in the garden. il pors Newsweek 77:20-1 Je 21 '71 *

NIXON, Tricia—about—*Continued*
What kind of a man has Tricia married? S. B. Conroy. pors Good H 173:14-16+ Jl '71 *
When Tricia Nixon marries—. il por U S News 70:54 Je 14 '71 *
White House wedding. il pors Newsweek 77: 30-4 Je 14 '71 *
NO-fault auto insurance. See Insurance, Automobile
NO-load mutual funds. See Investment trusts
NO more tears; story. See Drury, A.
NO, no, Nanette; musical comedy. See Musical comedies, revues, etc.—Criticisms, plots, etc.
NO such thing as a happy marriage; story. See Franco, M.
NOAH'S ark
Ark fever. J. W. Montgomery. Chr Today 15:38-9 Jl 2 '71; Reply with rejoinder. R. A. Lenton. 15:15 Ag 27 '71
Arkeology 1971. J. W. Montgomery. Chr Today 16:50-1 Ja 7 '72
NOAKES, David
France's great teacher is honored. il por Hi Fi 21:MA22-3 D '71
(tr) See Boulez, P. Style or idea?
NOBEL, Alfred Bernhard
Nobel prizes. D. Robinson. il Todays Ed 60:16-19 Ap '71 *
Who wins the Nobel prize in literature? A. DeMirjian, jr. il Pub W 200:pt2 152-5 S 27 '71 *
NOBEL foundation
Swing to equities builds Nobel funds. il Bsns W p64 D 11 '71
NOBEL prizes
Brandt and the peace prize; Nominator. Nation 213:452-3 N 8 '71
Does economics deserve a Nobel prize? M. Hudson; reply. M. P. Murray. Commonweal 93:387 Ja 22 '71
Embarrassing award. Time 98:30+ S 13 '71
Emigré Nobelists. il por Newsweek 78:106+ N 15 '71
Gifted refugees; science winners. pors Time 98:45 N 15 '71
Neruda laureate. R. J. Clements. por Sat R 54:50-1 N 13 '71
1970 Nobel prizes in science. Chem 44:19-20 Ja '71
1971 Nobel prize for physiology or medicine. I. H. Pastan. por Science 174:392-3 O 22 '71
1971 Nobel prizes in science. por Chem 45: 22-3 Ja '72
Nobel and competent; economics award. por Time 98:88 O 25 '71
Nobel prize at Isla Negra; literature prize awarded. P. Neruda. J. Felstiner. New Repub 165:29-30 D 25 '71
Nobel prize for chemistry: Herzberg and molecular spectroscopy. A. E. Douglas. por Science 174:672-3 N 12 '71
Nobel prize for economics: Kuznets and economic growth. M. Abramovitz. biblog por Science 174:481-3 O 29 '71
Nobel prize for physics: Gabor and holography. W. E. Kock. biblog por Science 174:674-5 N 12 '71
Nobel prizes. Sci Am 225:38-40 D '71
Nobel prizes. D. Robinson. il Todays Ed 60:16-19 Ap '71
Nobel prizes: physics to Gabor, chemistry to Herzberg. G. B. Lubkin. biblog pors Phys Today 24:69-71 D '71
Nobelist in Nashville; research in cyclic AMP. por Newsweek 78:109-10 O 25 '71
Prize for a Chilean poet. por Time 98:47-8 N 1 '71
Prize for a German peacemaker. il por Time 98:48 N 1 '71
Prize for a good neighbor; peace prize awarded to W. Brandt. Newsweek 78:35+ N 1 '71
Second messenger; prize in medicine and physiology. por Time 98:63 O 25 '71
Sutherland's cyclic AMP work brings him 1971 Nobel prize. por Sci N 100:278 O 23 '71
What brought Kuznets his Nobel. por Bsns W p88 O 23 '71
Who wins the Nobel prize in literature? A. DeMirjian, jr. il Pub W 200:pt2 152-5 S 27 '71

Anecdotes, facetiae, satire, etc.
Great race: virus find awakens hope for sufferers; Wagonband theory of nobelogenesis. N. Wade. Science 174:1112 D 10 '71
NOBLE, Donald R.
James Fenimore Cooper and the environment. il por Cons 26:3-7 O '71
NOBLE, Galie P.
Ganado project: any change for the Navajo reservation? Chr Cent 88:78-80, 320-2, 537-8 Ja 20, Mr 10, Ap 28 '71

NOBLE, Joseph V.
Drugs. New Yorker 47:31-2 Mr 13 '71 *
NOBODY'S business; story. See Gilliatt, P.
NOCHLIN, Linda
Museums and radicals: a history of emergencies. biblog il Art in Am 59:26-39 Jl '71
NODDACK, Ida Eva (Tacke)
Ida Noddack, 75 & element 75. F. Habashi. biblog il por Chem 44:14-15 F '71 *
NOELL, Werner K. and Albrecht, R.
Irreversible effects of visible light on the retina: role of vitamin A. biblog il Science 172:76-80 Ap 2 '71
—and others
Vitamin A deficiency effect on retina: dependence on light. biblog il Science 172:72-6 Ap 2 '71
NOFZIGER, Fred D.
Backpacking. il Travel 136:62-7+ S '71
Don't run over the train. il Travel 135:70-3 Je '71
NOGUCHI, Thomas T.
Art of autopsy. B. J. Friedman. Esquire 76: 96+ D '71 *
Inside Los Angeles: the coroner's report. M. Boas. il por Ramp Mag 10:30-5 Jl '71 *
NOGUÉS, Germinal
Silent tour of Buenos Aires. il Américas 23: 24-31 O '71
NOISE
Reporter at large; house and highway. W. Balliett. New Yorker 47:40-5 D 25 '71
See also
Household appliances, Electric—Noise
Silence

Psychological effects
Next sound you hear may be just too much. il Changing T 25:33-5 Mr '71
Noise an emerging hazard. V. A. D'Aprile. il Cons 25:29-32 Ap '71
Psychology and noise pollution. Sci N 101: 6-7 Ja 1 '72
NOISE, Electronic. See Electronic noise
NOISE control
Noise in the home: a growing health menace. il Good H 173:142-3 Ag '71
Noise pollution: what can we do about all that racket? il Bet Hom & Gard 49:18+ N '71
Silence is golden; noise-suppression industry. G. Berkwitt. il Duns 98:61-2+ Ag '71
Sound control for a new attic or basement room. Sunset 147:114 S '71
They're finally doing something to end the din. R. Starnes. Field & S 76:8+ N '71
Tyranny of noise. Chr Cent 88:1155 O 6 '71; Reply. H. A. Robinson. 88:1429 D 1 '71
See also
Chicago—Noise
Electronics in noise control
New York (city)—Noise

Laws and legislation
Acoustical retrofit bill stirs controversy. Aviation W 94:26 Ap 26 '71
Congress considers noise control bill. Aviation W 95:23 Jl 19 '71
FAA noise paper may ask JT8D retrofit program. J. P. Woolsey. Aviation W 95:23-4 O 18 '71
Industrial noise curtain widens. Bsns W p88 My 22 '71
Make your noise-ordinance realistic. Am City 86:67 O '71
Proposed New York anti-noise bill could ban several aircraft. Aviation W 94:23 Ja 18 '71
NOISE prevention. See Noise control
NOISE-reduction systems. See High fidelity sound systems—Noise
NOISELESS alloys. See Alloys
NOL, Lon. See Lon Nol
NOLAN, J. E.
Tree farm and how it grew. il por Nations Bsns 59:94-5 Ja '71
NOLAN, James
Jesus now: hogwash and holy water. il Ramp Mag 10:20-6 Ag '71
NOLAN, Paul T.
School for wives; adaptation. See Molière, J. B. P.
Who's compatible? drama. Plays 31:27-35 O '71
NOLAND, Kenneth
Noland vertical. K. Moffett. il Art N 70:48-9+ O '71 *
NOLEN, William A.
Doctor's world. McCalls 98:20 Je; 20 Jl; 30 Ag; 6 S; 99:20 O; 27 N; 32+ D '71
Mistakes surgeons make most often. Vogue 158:92-3 Ag 1 '71

NOLEN, William A.—*Continued*
Operation women fear most. McCalls 98:52+ Ap '71
Why we must see our doctors in a new light. il Todays Health 49:70-1 D '71
NOLL, Bink
Blank room; Gathering watercress; poems. Poetry 118:338-9 S '71
NOLTING, Frederick Ernest, 1911-
Plot against Diem: shameful and disastrous; interview. il por U S News 71:67-70 Jl 26 '71
NOMENCLATURE. See subhead Nomenclature under various subjects, e.g. Birds—Nomenclature
NOMINATION expenditures. See Campaign funds
NOMINATIONS for office
  See also
  Primaries
NOMOGRAPHY (mathematics)
Air-core nomogram. J. E. McAlister. il Electr World 86:45 S '71
How to figure your planing speed from hull and horsepower. J. Martenhoff. il Pop Mech 135:120-1 Mr '71
Nomogram for power in switching transistors. J. E. McAlister. il Electr World 86:44-5 N '71
Nomograms aid capacitance calculations. J. E. McAlister. il Electr World 85:27+ F '71
Tape-timing nomogram. R. F. Graf and G. J. Walen. il Radio-Electr 42:52-3 Ag '71
Zener diode voltage-regulator nomograms. C. W. Young. il Electr World 86:32-3+ Jl '71
NONBOOK materials, Cataloging of. See Cataloging
NONCOMMERCIAL television. See Television broadcasting, Noncommercial
NONESUCH press
Nonesuch press; excerpts from My lives. F. Meynell. il Pub W 200:78+ S 13 '71
NONFERROUS metals. See Metals, Nonferrous
NON-GOVERNMENTAL organizations of the United Nations. See United Nations—Nongovernmental organizations
NONGRADED classes. See Ungraded classes
NONINTERVENTION. See Intervention (international law)
NONLINEAR optics
X-ray parametic conversion: two photons for one; use of beryllium crystal. M. S. Rothenberg. Phys Today 24:17+ Ap '71
NON-MILITARY compulsory service. See Service, Compulsory non-military
NON NOK THA excavations. See Thailand—Antiquities
NONPROFIT institutions. See Institutions, Nonprofit
NONPROFIT organizations. See Institutions, Nonprofit
NON-PROLIFERATION treaty. See Atomic weapons—International control
NONRETURNABLE bottles. See Bottles
NONSENSE verse
  See also
  Mother Goose
NONTE, George C. Jr
Is there really an all-around rifle? il Pop Mech 136:106-8+ S '71
Something really new in revolvers. il Pop Mech 136:107 Ag '71
NONVERBAL communication. See Communication, Nonverbal
NONVIOLENCE
Christian nonviolent workshop. J. Pisani. Cath World 214:31-4 O '71
Payne pamphlet: violence, non-violence and human rights. T. Beeson. Chr Cent 88:793 Je 30 '71
NON-WAGE payments
Ferment in fringes. J. Perham. il Duns 98:34-6 D '71
Fringe benefits of urban workers; with tables. L. L. Petermann. bibliog Mo Labor R 94:41-4 N '71
Growth of private welfare plans. B. L. Masse. America 124:110 F 6 '71
How much is your job really worth? with tables. I. Mothner. il Look 35:60-3 Ap 20 '71
Industry's untold multibillion-dollar story. il Nations Bsns 59:62-4 My '71
What workers are getting on top of big pay raises. il U S News 70:56-7 Ja 18 '71
  See also
  Bonus system
  Profit sharing
NOODLES
Good and cheap; homemade noodles. J. Hewitt. il N Y times Mag p57 F 28 '71
NOONAN, John T. 1926-
Making the ethical case against abortion. pors Time 97:70 Mr 29 '71 •

NOONAN, Joseph
Anybody for the priesthood? cartoons. Cath World 214:35-6 O '71
Call out the guard! cartoons. Cath World 212:264 F '71
Casualties of sensitivity. il Cath World 212:316-17 Mr '71
Meanwhile, back at the polarized parish; cartoons. Cath World 213:93-4 My '71
Peace march; cartoons. Cath World 213:287 S '71
NOQUEIRA, Ronaldo
Economic torture? il por Forbes 107:50 F 1 '71 •
NORA (literary character) See Characters in literature
NORADRENALINE. See Norepinephrine
NORBECK, Edward
Man at play. il Natur Hist 80:48-53 D '71
NORBYE, Jan P.
View down the road. il Pop Sci 199:14 O; 54 N; 36 D '71
NORDAIR oy. See Airlines—Finland
NOREPINEPHRINE
Cyclic adenosine monophosphate and norepinephrine: effects on transmembrane properties of cerebellar Purkinje cells. G. R. Siggins and others. bibliog il Science 171-192-4 Ja 15 '71; Reply with rejoinder. 174:1257-9 D 17 '71
Decrease in adrenal tyrosine hydroxylase and increase in norepinephrine synthesis in rats given L-dopa. W. Dairman and S. Udenfriend. bibliog il Science 171:1022-4 Mr 12 '71
Hydrocortisone-mediated increase of norepinephrine uptake by brain slices. J. W. Maas and M. Mednieks. bibliog il Science 171:178-9 Ja 15 '71
Noradrenaline: fate and control of its biosynthesis; Nobel lecture, December 12, 1970. J. Axelrod. bibliog il Science 173:598-606 Ag 13 '71
Norepinephrine biosynthesis inhibition: effects on memory in mice. C. T. Randt and others. bibliog il Science 172:498-9 Ap 30 '71
Norepinephrine pools in rat brain: differences in turnover rates and pathways of metabolism. J. J. Schildkraut and others. bibliog il Science 172:587-9 My 7 '71
Norepinephrine: reversal of anorexia in rats with lateral hypothalamic damage. B. D. Berger and others. bibliog il Science 172:281-4 Ap 16 '71
Norepinephrine stimulated increase of cyclic AMP levels in developing mouse brain cell cultures. N. W. Seeds and A. G. Gilman. bibliog il Science 174:292 O 15 '71
Proportional release of norepinephrine and dopamine-β-hydroxylase from sympathetic nerves. R. M. Weinshilboum and others. bibliog il Science 174:1349-51 D 24 '71
NORFOLK, Va.
  City planning
Show and sell with slides and sound. il Am City 86:126+ S '71
NORFOLK and Western railway
Fishwick of the Norfolk & Western. il por Forbes 107:194-5 My 15 '71
NORFOLK ISLAND
Dot to remember. J. Forbis. il Travel 135:58-62 My '71
NORFOLK-Miami inland waterway. See Intracoastal Waterway
NORGREN, R. and Leonard, C. M.
Taste pathways in rat brainstem. bibliog il Science 173:1136-9 S 17 '71
NORM, Social. See Social norm
NORMA; opera. See Bellini, V.
NORMAN, Anthony W. and others
1,25-dihydroxycholecalciferol: identification of the proposed active form of vitamin D₃ in the intestine. bibliog il Science 173:51-4 Jl 2 '71
—See Myrtle, J. F. jt. auth.
NORMAN, David L.
Excerpt from testimony, March 3, 1971. Cong Digest 50:278+ N '71
NORODOM Sihanouk, king of Cambodia (abdicated 1955)
Sihanouk in exile; excerpts from interview, ed. by S. Cohen. Newsweek 78:47+ D 20 '71
With Sihanouk in Peking; interview, ed. by A. Casella. Nation 212:305-8 Mr 8 '71
NORRIS, Albert S.
We know too little about marijuana; questions and answers. Sci Digest 69:78-81 F '71
NORRIS, Eleanor L.
What we are learning from the National assessment. il Am Ed 7:18-23 Jl '71

NORRIS, Hoke
Most beautiful time of the year. il Nat Wild-
life 9:4-9 O '71
NORRIS, Karen Drury
Shut up, teacher! excerpt from Getting the
teacher to shut up. Todays Ed 60:46 N '71
NORRIS, Leslie, and Luff, Christopher
Can we do business with China? interview,
ed. by J. Ross-Skinner. il Duns 97:14-16+
Je '71
NORRIS, Leslie, 1921-
Highland boy; story. Atlan 227:52-3 Je '71
Mallard; story. il Esquire 75:106-7+ F '71
Mountains polecats pheasants; poem. New
Yorker 47:56 D 4 '71
Waxwings; story. Atlan 227:93-5 F '71
NORTH, Charles
For you; Poem: Now that I am seeing my-
self as a totally different person; poems.
Poetry 119:20-1 O '71
NORTH, Sandie
50/50 marriage: is this what women want?
il Look 35:57-61 O 5 '71
NORTH, William D.
ALA seeks broad support on copyright; ex-
cerpts from address, ed. by G. Krettek and
E. D. Cooke. Am Lib 2:1182-5 D '71
NORTH AFRICAN cookery. See Cookery, North
African
NORTH AMERICAN air defense command
Alert that wasn't. Sr Schol 98:14 Mr 15 '71
Impish alert. Newsweek 77:46 Mr 1 '71
Warning system that failed. U S News 70:28
Mr 8 '71
NORTH AMERICAN chemicals corporation
Past stains a detergent maker. il Bsns W
p28-9 Mr 20 '71
NORTH AMERICAN conference on labor sta-
tistics
Policymaking and the role of labor statistics;
excerpts from some of the papers present-
ed. il Mo Labor R 94:38-43 S '71
NORTH AMERICAN Indians. See Indians of
North America
NORTH AMERICAN Rockwell corporation
Another challenge for Pay board. U S News
71:90 D 20 '71
Another opening; B-1 program. il Newsweek
78:90+ N 15 '71
Capsule fire flares up again: a widow's law-
suit and an engineer's story about the
Apollo disaster. il pors Life 71:24-9 S 17 '71
Collins radio finds a friend with money. il
Bsns W p 111-12 Je 19 '71
Collins, Rockwell explore affiliation. Avi-
ation W 94:20 My 24 '71
North American earnings rise; Northrop re-
ports profit drop. Aviation W 95:20 N 22
'71
North American Rockwell, Collins reach ac-
cord. Aviation W 94:27 Je 7 '71
North American suit filed against Garrett.
Aviation W 95:20 O 25 '71
Rockwell Parsons fails to connect; steam
turbine-generator venture. Bsns W p31-2 Ag
14 '71
Shuttle engine awarded to Rocketdyne. Avi-
ation W 95:12 Jl 19 '71
White elephant finds a buyer; trade of NAR
plant for Fluor property. il Bsns W p28
Mr 27 '71
NORTH ATLANTIC council. See Nato
NORTH ATLANTIC treaty organization. See
Nato
NORTH by Northwest adventures, inc.
Idea from below nowhere; P. Bellesen and
his youth organization. E. Crimmin. il por
Motor B & S 127:12+ My '71
NORTH CAROLINA
See also
Chattooga River
Dismal Swamp
Fishing—North Carolina
Great Smoky Mountains National Park
Hoke County
Music festivals—North Carolina
New River
Outer Banks (islands)
Public health—North Carolina
Skis and skiing—North Carolina

Description and travel
New winter trails: North Carolina. R. B.
Satterwhite. il Travel 136:28-33+ D '71
NORTH CAROLINA arts and crafts. See Arts
and crafts—United States
NORTH CAROLINA Continentals. See
United States—History—Revolution—Amer-
ican forces
NORTH CAROLINA mutual life insurance com-
pany
Black-operated firm: the men, markets &
myth. address, May 12, 1971. J. W. Good-
loe. Vital Speeches 37:709-15 S 15 '71

NORTH CAROLINA school of the arts, Wins-
ton-Salem
Student makes music in Siena. K. Wilson.
il Hi Fi 21:MA10-11 Ap '71
NORTH CAROLINA Wesleyan college, Rocky
Mount
Independent study & library use; letter to
the editor. A. W. Stewart. Am Lib 2:17 Ja
'71
NORTH CASCADES NATIONAL PARK
Cooperation, mountain style; North Cas-
cades reconnaissance task force. G. W.
Pelton. il Parks & Rec 6:34-5 N '71
NORTH CASCADES wilderness area. See
Wilderness areas—Washington (state)
NORTH central airlines
Fleet, route matching aid North central. H.
D. Watkins. il Aviation W 94:45+ My 31
'71
North central earnings remain consistent.
H. D. Watkins. il Aviation W 94:32-8 My
24 '71
NORTH DAKOTA
See also
Education—North Dakota
Paleontology—North Dakota
NORTH DAKOTA. University, Grand Forks
Promise of change in North Dakota; pro-
grams of the New school for behavioral
studies in education. H. S. Resnik. il Sat
R 54:67-9+ Ap 17 '71
NORTH KINGSTOWN, R.I.

Education
Linking up through LINKS; Laymen in
North Kingstown schools, R.I. J. Lee-
dom. il Am Ed 7:31-2 Ag '71
NORTH MANCHESTER, Ind.
Home is down the road. W. Dunbar. il Amér-
icas 23:32-6 Mr '71
NORTH MANKATO, Minn.
Tour, talk, tell and build. il Am City 86:
116+ Mr '71
NORTH MICHIGAN avenue. See Chicago—
Streets
NORTH POLE, Magnetic. See Magnetism,
Terrestrial
NORTH RIVER. See Hudson River
NORTH SEA
See also
Marine pollution—North Sea
Petroleum—North Sea Region
NORTH side cooperative ministry
SISS mischief; testimony against NSCM. Chr
Cent 88:365-6 Mr 24 '71
NORTH Stars (hockey team) See Hockey
teams
NORTH TONAWANDA, N.Y, public library
Meredith Willson's legacy: program sponsored
by Friends of the library. M. Messineo. il
Am Lib 2:209-11 F '71
NORTHBROOK, Ill, public library
Vigilante of the month; censoring Grove
press. W. R. Eshelman. Wilson Lib Bul
46:225 N '71
NORTHCOTT, Kaye
Astronauts on the make. Ramp Mag 10:12-13
N '71
NORTHEAST airlines, inc.
Eastern, Delta court Northeast. Aviation W
94:27 Mr 22 '71
Northeast airlines' family fare plan rejected
by CAB. Aviation W 94:30 Je 7 '71
Northwest-Northeast link hangs on Miami-
Los Angeles authority. J. P. Woolsey. Avia-
tion W 94:26-7 Ja 25 '71
NORTHEAST corridor project. See Transpor-
tation, High speed
NORTHEAST petroleum industries
Tempting of a small town. R. Vaughan. il
Life 71:50-1+ Jl 30 '71; Same abr. Read
Digest 99:207-8+ O '71
NORTHEAST regional ballet festival. See
Dance festivals
NORTHEASTERN states
See also
Fishing—Northeastern states
Hunting—Northeastern states
Skis and skiing—Northeastern states
NORTHERN IRELAND
See also
Belfast
Children—Northern Ireland
Civil rights—Northern Ireland
Community service—Northern Ireland
Concentration camps—Northern Ireland
Fishing—Northern Ireland
Great Britain—Army—Forces in Northern
Ireland
Guerrillas—Northern Ireland
Investments, Foreign (in Northern Ireland)
Political prisoners—Northern Ireland
Women—Northern Ireland

NORTHERN IRELAND—*Continued*

Economic conditions

High hope in the South. il Time 98:85 O 25 '71

Politics and government

Appalling crime; slaying of British soldiers. il Time 97:32-3 Mr 22 '71

As open war rages in Northern Ireland. il U S News 71:36-7 Ag 23 '71

Battle of the Boyne II. J. Wyatt. Commonweal 94:162-5 Ap 23 '71

Behind the spiraling violence in Ireland. il U S News 70:58 F 22 '71

British Vietnam. J. Burnham. Nat R 23: 919 Ag 24 '71

Catholic vs. Protestants. il Sr Schol 99:16-18 D 13 '71

Deadly stalemate. Time 98:26+ S 6 '71

Deepening agony of a conflict where almost no one is a bystander. il Life 71:52-3 D 31 '71

Fatal error. il Time 98:32 S 13 '71

Gallery; farewell for a new Irish martyr. il Life 71:2-3 Ag 27 '71

Gun-shy investors stay away. il Bsns W p84-5 D 4 '71

Hazards of journalism; charges against foreign journalists. Nation 212:773 Je 21 '71

In the shadow of the gunmen. il Time 99: 30-4+ Ja 10 '72

Internal affairs; Senator Kennedy's suggestion that an American statesman act as mediator. Nation 213:676-7 D 27 '71

Is there an Irish solution? America 124: 168 F 20 '71

Long-range forecast; John Lynch-Edward Heath talks. il Newsweek 78:45-6 S 20 '71

Massive wedge. Time 98:47 S 27 '71

Needs of Northern Ireland. Chr Cent 88:454 Ap 14 '71

No jollification. A. Deming. il Newsweek 78: 27 D 27 '71

Northern Ireland: Britain's Vietnam? il U S News 71:52 S 20 '71

Northern Ireland: deepening bitterness. il Time 98:24 Ag 30 '71

Northern Ireland: the powder keg. il por Time 97:26-32 Ap 5 '71

Northern Ireland: violent jubilee. il Time 98: 18-21 Ag 23 '71

Of many things; conflicts in Northern Ireland. D. R. Campion. America 125:384 N 13 '71

Of many things; Irish question. D. R. Campion. America 125:inside cover O 23 '71

Of many things; political resolution of the troubled Irish situation. D. R. Campion. America 125:524 D 18 '71

Off the deep end; views of E. Kennedy. Time 98:48 N 1 '71

Orange bullies & British Tories. A. Boyd. il Nation 212:521-4 Ap 26 '71

Orange enigma. Chr Today 15:22-3 Ag 6 '71; Discussion. 15:17-18 S 24; 16:38 D 17 '71

People lost in hate. L. Wainwright. il Life 71:20-5 Ag 20 '71

Stormont and Saigon. Nation 213:165 S 6 '71

Stormont on Britain's back. A. Boyd. Nation 213:560-2 N 29 '71

Terrible days in Northern Ireland. il Newsweek 78:28-30 Ag 23 '71

To restore confidence. T. Beeson. Chr Cent 88:1284 N 3 '71

Ulster: a kind of plague. A. Boyd. Nation 213:176-8 S 6 '71

Ulster: a note of realism; Harold Wilson's proposal for the unification of Ireland. Nation 213:612 D 13 '71

Ulster: must the riots go on forever? J. Laurence. il Cath World 214:14-17 O '71

Ulster: normally abnormal. J. D. Douglas. Chr Today 15:38-9 Je 18 '71

Ulster: steering toward civil war? il Time 98: 29-30 S 20 '71

Ulster stew. New Repub 165:9 S 4 '71

Untangling the Irish question; with editorial comment. C. Kilcoyne. il America 125:138, 140-1 S 11 '71

Vicious circle. Newsweek 78:37 Ag 30 '71

Vietnam on the Irish Sea. A. Lejeune. Nat R 23:110+ O 8 '71; Discussion. 23:1210+, 1270 N 5-19 '71

Religious institutions and affairs

Focus on Ireland, a land where faith matters. P. Elmen. Chr Cent 88:170+ F 3 '71

Ulster: must the riots go on forever? J. Laurence. il Cath World 214:14-17 O '71

Riots

Shoot on sight. Newsweek 77:46 Je 7 '71

Ulster: the children of violence; with excerpts from essays by children. il Newsweek 77:46-50+ Ap 19 '71

NORTHERN lights. See Auroras

NORTHFIELD MOUNTAIN pumped storage hydroelectric project. See Hydroelectric plants

NORTHROP corporation

North American earnings rise; Northrop reports profit drop; with table. Aviation W 95:20 N 22 '71

Northrop puts on a show to sell Cobras. il Bsns W p71 S 4 '71

Northrop seeks aid abroad for fighter. B. Miller. il Aviation W 94:20-1 F 1 '71

Northrop snaps up a big-name builder. il Bsns W p 19-20 D 25 '71

NORTHWEST

Description and travel

Northwest. D. Wagoner. Mlle 72:246+ Ap '71

Special report: Northwest yachting; symposium. il Yachting 129:50-61+ My '71

Politics

History

Puget Sound's war within a war; fight for political power in the mid-nineteenth century. I. Doig. il Am West 8:22-7 My '71

NORTHWEST, CANADIAN

See also

British Columbia

NORTHWEST airlines, inc.

Hijacker parachutes from Northwest 727. Aviation W 95:22 D 6 '71

Lower altitude. Forbes 107:18-19 My 1 '71

New landing method aimed at reduction in approach noise. W. S. Hieronymus. il Aviation W 94:46-7 Mr 1 '71

Northwest-Northeast link hangs on Miami-Los Angeles authority. J. P. Woolsey. Aviation W 94:26-7 Ja 25 '71

Northwest plant to retain cost control. H. D. Watkins. il Aviation W 94:34-5 Je 14 '71

Strike, new competition test Northwest. H. D. Watkins. il Aviation W 94:32-4 Je 7 '71

NORTHWEST TERRITORIES, Canada

See also

Melville Peninsula

NORTHWESTERN steel and wire company

Profits and paternalism. il Forbes 108:24-5 Ag 15 '71

NORTHWESTERN university, Evanston, Ill.

Eva Jefferson: young voice of change. H. H. King. il pors Ebony 26:71-4+ Ja '71

Northwestern university; goings-on at NU. A. Ehrlich and S. Mehr. Mlle 72:60 Mr '71

Searching for the perfect university president with editorial comment. W. G. Bennis. il Atlan 227:4, 39-44+ Ap '71; Discussion. 227:32-5 Je '71

Libraries

Building Northwestern's Core: noncirculating duplicate collection aimed particularly at the undergraduate. K. Horny. il por Library J 96:1580-3 My 1 '71

NORTON, Boyd

Forgotten side of the Tetons. il Liv Wildn 35:31-4 Sum '71

NORTON, Eleanor Holmes

When I was 17; interview, ed. by B. Kevles. pors Seventeen 30:130+ O '71

about

I hope I'm not a token. C. Dreifus. por McCalls 99:51 O '71 *

NORTON, M. Scott

Current problems of the school superintendent. il Clear House 46:15-19 S '71

NORTON, Thomas French

Lure of dark water. il Motor B & S 128: 54-5+ S '71

NORTON, Mass.

Education

Multimedia classroom; Project SPOKE. D. C. Steffen. il Am Ed 7:28-30 Ag '71

NORTON company

Norton aligns its top jobs with its markets. il Bsns W p80-2 Ag 7 '71

NORTON Simon, inc. See Simon, Norton, inc.

NORWALK, Conn.

Street traffic

Too many political traffic signals. L. M. Rodgers. il Am City 86:69 F '71

NORWAY

Norway: land of the generous sea. E. J. Linehan. il Nat Geog 140:1-43 Jl '71

See also

Arts and crafts—Norway

Colleges and universities—Norway

Hammerfest

Hunting—Norway

Shipping—Norway

NORWAY—*Continued*

Defenses

Soviet threat to NATO's northern flank. il
Time 98:39 O 18 '71

Politics and government

Indiscreet traveler. Newsweek 77:50+ Mr 15
'71
Price of a lie. Time 97:38-9 Mr 15 '71

Religious institutions and affairs
See also
Church and state in Norway

NORWEGIAN cookery. See Cookery, Norwegian

NORWICK, Kenneth P. See Pilpel, H. F. jt.
auth.

NORWOOD, Christopher
Southern stamp strategy. Commonweal 94:
455-6 S 3 '71

NORWOOD, Frank W. See Kenney, B. L. jt.
auth.

NORWOOD, James M. G.
Tarot takeoff, a new game that strips off
psychic layers. Vogue 157:85+ F 15 '71

NOSEBLEED
Some nosebleeds are serious. il Changing T
25:41 D '71

NOSEDA, Lydia Rosa
Lorenzo Dominguez. il Américas 23:33-7 Ap
'71

NOSHPITZ, Joseph D.
Quiet ones, the noisy ones. il Todays Ed
60:24-7 S '71; Same abr. Ed Digest 37:
45-7 N '71

NOSS, Luther
Reviews of records. Mus Q 57:163-6 Ja '71

NOSSITER, Bernard Daniel
Runaway enterprise. Nation 212:135-7 F 1 '71
What's good for oil and no one else. New
Repub 164:17-18 F 6 '71

NOSTALGIA
Cosier sports. E. Sheppard. Harp Baz 104:
142-3 My '71
Home is where it used to be. L. Wain-
wright. Life 70:77-8 F 19 '71
I got a letter! help for campers' home-
sickness. E. Bristol. il PTA Mag 65:26-7
Ap '71
Meaning of nostalgia; Time essay. G. Clarke.
il Time 97:77 My 3 '71
Nostalgia shock. F. Heath. Sat R 54:18 My
29 '71
Nostalgia: who says it's only for over-30's?
D. Carlinsky. il Seventeen 30:114-15+ Jl
'71
Poets are remembering it well. J. F. Cotter.
America 125:514-16 D 11 '71
Remember? M. Mercer. il McCalls 99:90-1
O '71

NOTABLE books council. See American library
association—Adult services division

NOTABLES. See Celebrities

NOTE taking
Make a note to take some notes. il Changing T 25:28 My '71

NOTEBOOKS
Best selling novelist tells why she keeps a
notebook; excerpt from Slouching towards
Bethlehem. J. Didion. il por Writers Digest 51:26-7+ D '71

NOTES: what I think pudding says; story. See
Deck, J.

NOTON, David, and Stark, Lawrence
Eye movements and visual perception; with
biographical sketches. il Sci Am 224:16, 34-
43 bibliog(p 136) Je '71
Scanpaths in eye movements during pattern
perception. bibliog il Science 171:308-11; 173:
753 Ja 22, Ag 20 '71

NOTRE DAME, Ind. University
Hold on, Ara, the freshmen are coming;
ND freshmen vs. Mexico City Redskins. P.
Putnam. il Sports Illus 35:56-7 N 1 '71
Mellowing of a president. il por Time 97:67 F
15 '71

NOTROM, Henry B.
Boatowner's guide to repair compounds. il
Pop Mech 135:106-9 Je '71
How to get your snowmobile ready for snow.
il Pop Mech 136:122-5 N '71

NOTT, Kathleen
East is West? Commentary 52:65-71 Jl '71

NOTTERMAN, J. M. and others
Perception of changes in certain exteroceptive stimuli. bibliog il Science 173:1206-
11 S 24 '71

NOVA SCOTIA
See also
Oak Island

Description and travel

No chicken counting; Nova Scotia cruise. T.
Sturges. il Yachting 129:68-9+ My '71
Nova Scotia. H. P. Koenig. il Travel 135:28-
37+ My '71

NOVAE. See Stars, New

NOVAK, Barbara
Grand opera and the small still voice. bibliog il Art in Am 59:64-73 Mr '71

NOVAK, Benjamin J.
Opening doors in music. il Negro Hist Bul
34:10-14 Ja '71

NOVAK, Jane A.
New life on an old farm. il Org Gard & Farm
18:41-6 Jl '71

NOVAK, Michael
Battle hymn of Lt Calley and the Republic.
Commonweal 94:183-6 Ap 30 '71
Let a million voters bloom. Commonweal
94:79-81 Ap 2 '71
Religion in higher education. Commonweal
93:395-6 Ja 22 '71
White ethnic. il Harper 243:4-6+ S; 6 N
'71

NOVAK, Robert D. See Evans, R. jr. jt. auth.

NOVELISTS
First novelists; spring-summer-fall, 1971;
statements by the writers, ed. by I. E.
Stokvis. il Library J 96:505-11, 2118-21,
3164-8 F 1, Je 15, O 1 '71

NOVELISTS, American
On the road to Manderley. M. Duffy. il Time
97:95+ Ap 12 '71
Seven who do the whodunits. il Newsweek 77:
102-3 Mr 22 '71
See also
Bellow, S.
Cather, W. S.
Davies, R.
Kerouac, J.
McCarthy, M.
McCullers, C. S.
Macdonald, R. pseud.
Metalious, G.
Nabokov, V.
Oates, J. C.
Slesinger, T.
Stowe, H. E. B.
Wharton, E. N. J.

NOVELISTS, British. See Novelists, English

NOVELISTS, Canadian
See also
Callaghan, M. E.

NOVELISTS, English
On the road to Manderley. M. Duffy. il Time
97:95+ Ap 12 '71
See also
Burgess, A. pseud.
Forster, E. M.
Forsyth, F.
Thirkell, A. M.
Wodehouse, P. G.

NOVELISTS, French
See also
Prévost, A. F.

NOVELISTS, Japanese
See also
Mishima, Y. pseud.

NOVELISTS, Negro
Politics and the black novel. J. H. Bryant.
Nation 212:436-8 Ap 5 '71

NOVELISTS, Polish
See also
Kosinski, J. N.

NOVELISTS, Scottish
See also
MacLean, A.

NOVELS. See Fiction

NOVEMBER
Novembrist manifesto. L. E. Sissman. Atlan
228:48+ N '71

NOVICK, Robert E.
Rats and how your students can fight them.
il Todays Ed 60:26-8 O '71

NOVICK, Sheldon
Seventeen million years. bibliog il Environ
13:42-7 N '71

NOVY, John
John Novy, third generation potter. D. H.
Sweetman. il por Ceram Mo 19:13 Mr '71

NOW ain't it just a wonder? story. See De
France, E.

NOWACKI, W.
Space groups not always derivable by parallelohedra and subdivision into stereohedra.
bibliog il Science 174:52-3 O 1 '71

NOXON, John F. See Clark, I. D. jt. auth.

NOYCE, Gaylord B.
Expansive man and the church of the '70s.
Chr Cent 88:1377-9 N 24 '71

NUCLEOPROTEINS
Hybrid ribosome formation from escherichia coli and chloroplast ribosome subunits. S. G. Lee and W. R. Evans. bibliog il Science 173:241-2 Jl 16 '71
Mendelian and uniparental alterations in erythromycin binding by plastid ribosomes. L. J. Mets and L. Bogorad. bibliog il Science 174:707-9 N 12 '71
Ribosome-catalyzed polyester formation. S. Fahnestock and A. Rich. bibliog il Science 173:340-3 Jl 23 '71
See also
Interferon

NUCLEOSIDES
Crystal structure of a naturally occurring dinucleoside monophosphate: uridylyl (3',5') adenosine hemihydrate. J. Rubin and others. bibliog il Science 174:1020-2 D 3 '71
Enzymatic modification of transfer RNA. D. Söll. bibliog il Science 173:293-9 Jl 23 '71
Molecular conformation of dihydrouridine: puckered base nucleoside of transfer RNA. M. Sundaralingam and others. bibliog il Science 172:725-7 My 14 '71
Urea-inorganic phosphate mixtures as prebiotic phosphorylating agents. R. Lohrmann and L. E. Orgel. bibliog il Science 171:490-4 F 5 '71

NUCLEOTIDE phosphodiesterase. See Esterases

NUCLEOTIDES
Ammonia production in muscle: the purine nucleotide cycle. J. Lowenstein and K. Tornheim. bibliog il Science 171:397-400 Ja 29 '71
Nucleotide sequence of the denaturable leucine transfer RNA from yeast. S. Kowalski and others. bibliog il Science 172:385-7 Ap 23 '71
Possible prebiotic condensation of mononucleotides by cyanamide. J. D. Ibanez and others. bibliog il Science 173:444-6 Jl 30 '71
Release of nuclear DNA template restrictions by specific polyribonucleotides. D. G. Brown and D. S. Coffey. bibliog il Science 171:176-8 Ja 15 '71
See also
Adenosine monophosphate
Adenosine triphosphate
Guanosine monophosphate

NUDE in art
Marble and nudity. W. H. Gerdts. il Art in Am 59:60-7 My '71
NUDE in photography. See Human figure in photography
NUDIBRANCHS. See Sea slugs
NUDISM
Decline of nudism; Oakdale guest ranch. T. Tyler. il por Time 98:58-9 Jl 19 '71
NUDISM; story. See Pavese, C.
NUDIST colonies. See Nudism
NUDITY
Nakedness vs. nudity. A. West. il Vogue 157:116-19 My '71
Of cats and skinny-dipping; nude swimming. P. Leahy. il Time 98:42 Ag 2 '71
NUGENT, Luci Baines (Johnson)
LBJ's best friend: the love story of a man & his dog. il pors Ladies Home J 88:77-9+ Ap '71
NULF, Frank
Luigi Pirandello and the cinema. bibliog Film Q 24:40-8 Wint '70
NULTY, Leslie. See Nulty, T. jt. auth.
NULTY, Timothy, and Nulty, Leslie
Pakistan: the busy bee route to development. il Trans-Action 8:18-26+ F '71
NUMBER concept
Count-down on the 1-2-3's: counting and mathematical-concept books for the primary level. D. Thomas. bibliog il Library J 96:1083-90 Mr 15 '71
Did you know that . . ? a googol and other large numbers. F. L. Remington. Sci Digest 70:54 O '71
A million of anything is a lot. Nations Bsns 59:82 S '71
Who's afraid of modern math? N. W. Maertens. il Parents Mag 46:54+ Ag '71
#312-35-989 where did you go; story. See Jordan, E. H.
NUMBERS, Complex
How to use operator "j"; imaginary number used in electronic calculations. J. Collins. il Radio-Electr 42:49 F '71
Of imaginary numbers; Time essay. O. Friedrich. Time 98:37 Ag 2 '71
See also
Numbers, Real

NUMBERS, Imaginary. See Numbers, Complex
NUMBERS, Prime
$2^{19,937}-1$ is prime. Sci Am 224:56 Je '71
NUMBERS, Real
New models of the real-number line. L. A. Steen. il Sci Am 225:92-9 Ag '71
NUMBERS betting. See Gambling
NUMEIRY, Jaafar. See Nimieri, G. M.
NUMERATION
See also
Number concept
NUMERIC identification. See Identification
NUMERICAL indicator tubes. See Electron tubes
NUMISMATICS
Numismatics. C. F. French. See issues of Hobbies
Numismatics: at least you can't go broke. Bsns W p83-4 My 8 '71
See also
Coins
Medals
NUNLEY, Jay A.
Electronic combination lock. il Pop Electr 35:51-3+ Ag '71
NUNN, Annie Dyer
Venezuelan adventure. il Travel 137:54-7 Ja '72
NUNN, Richard
How to have power when there is none. il Pop Mech 136:156-8 D '71
NUNNERIES. See Convents and nunneries
NUNS
Asks priestly rights for nuns. Chr Cent 8:1160 O 6 '71
Sister Fuzz; nun as a Pontoon Beach juvenile officer. il pors Life 70:50-1 Mr 12 '71
Why I became a nun. A. M. Wolf. pors Ladies Home J 88:94+ My '71
See also
Convents and nunneries
Ex-nuns, priests, etc.
NUNS as teachers
Sisters desert racist institution; St Raymond's school, Detroit. America 124:194 F 27 '71
NUREEV, Rudolf
Ballet unlimited. H. Saal. il por Newsweek 77:48+ F 8 '71 *
NUREMBERG trials
Meaning of Calley. J. Goldstein. New Repub 164:13-14 My 8 '71
NURISTAN
Native races
Echoes of the Aryans. F. V. Grunfeld. il Horizon 13:102-4 Sum '71
NURNBERG stove; drama. See Howard, H. L.
NURSE midwives. See Midwives
NURSE sharks. See Sharks
NURSEMAIDS
Mary Poppins lives; nanny training school in England. M. Kupfer. il Newsweek 77:37-8 Mr 1 '71
NURSERIES (horticulture)
In Connecticut: a garden to visit; White flower farm, Litchfield, Conn. M. Perry. il Home Gard 58:38-9 Ap '71
San Diego's back country is the place for gardeners to see and shop subtropicals. il Sunset 146:82-3 Je '71
Your growing years. Y. Horn. il Har Yrs 11:16-19 Jl '71

Anecdotes, facetiae, satire, etc.
How to behave at a nursery. E. Harnett. House B 113:28-9 Je '71
NURSERIES, Day. See Day nurseries
NURSERY rhymes
Ecologic of nursery rhymes. J. Lear. il Sat R 54:73-6 N 6 '71
See also
Mother Goose
NURSERY schools
Nursery school on wheels; Appalachia educational laboratory. M. Cobb. il Parents Mag 46:60-1+ S '71
Nursery schools: a primer for parents. E. H. McCleary. il Ladies Home J 88:74+ N '71
Sense and nonsense about preschools. D. Elkind. il Parents Mag 46:51-3+ My '71
Should you force your child to go to nursery school? E. Peck. il Todays Health 49:58-62 Ag '71
See also
Day nurseries

NURSES and nursing
Introducing; the supernurse; nurse-practitioners as physicians assistants. L. Gross. McCalls 98:75+ Mr '71
Why are nurses shook-up over abortion? I. Fischl. Look 35:66 F 9 '71

Training
Mike the cop studies to be Mike the nurse. il pors Life 70:47-8+ My 14 '71
NURSING (infant feeding) See Breast feeding
NURSING homes
Caring for our aged poor. L. H. Henry. New Repub 164:17-22 My 22 '71
Eye on aged care. Sr Schol 98:16-17 Mr 8 '71
Flemming finds nation welcomes Nixon's concern over nursing homes. Aging 204:7 O '71
Nursing business. New Repub 165:8-9 N 27 '71
President urges nursing home reforms, hints action by U.S; excerpts from address, June 25, 1971. R. M. Nixon. Aging 201:5+ Jl '71
Story of a teen-age Nader raider. B. L. Collier. il pors N Y Times Mag p30-1+ Mr 14 '71; Discussion. p 102 Ap 4 '71

Fires and fire protection
Fire protection for nursing homes. Sci N 100:262 O 16 '71
NURSING schools
See also
Frontier nursing service
NUSSBAUM, Albert F.
Rehabilitation myth. Am Scholar 40:674-6 Aut '71
NUSSENZWEIG, Victor. See Bianco, C. jt. auth.
NUSSEY, Wilf, and Reuter, Henry
African round-up. il Sci Digest 69:42-8 Je '71
NUT trees
See also
Chestnut trees
NUTARAREAK, Tomasik
From the world of Tomasik Nutarareak. B. Skovbo. il Natur Hist 80:28-35 Ja '71
NUTCRACKER; ballet. See Ballets—Criticisms
NUTRIENT labeling of foods. See Food—Labeling
NUTRITION
Adelle Davis celebrates 25 years with Harcourt; interview, ed. by L. P. Freilicher. A. Davis. il por Pub W 199:56 Je 21 '71
Adelle Davis, earth mother to the foodists. J. Howard. il pors Life 71:67-8+ O 22 '71
Are we overfed but undernourished? S. M. Spencer. Read Digest 99:135-9 S '71
Does the way our food is grown affect our mental well-being? bibliog Org Gard & Farm 18:102-6+ My '71
Facts about nutrition. R. M. Leverton. Todays Ed 60:71-2 N '71
Gayelord Hauser: for my toast, I want butter. Vogue 157:24 Jl '71
Her believers eat right; A. Davis. B. Falconer. McCalls 98:45 Ag '71
Let's talk about food; questions and answers, ed. by P. L. White. See issues of Today's health
You are what you eat. il Sr Schol 98:2-7 F 8 '71
See also
Aged—Nutrition
Children—Nutrition
Diet
Food habits
Iron in diet
Starvation
Trace elements
Vitamins
Youth—Nutrition
NUTRITION and heart disease. See Heart—Diseases—Nutritional aspects
NUTRITION problems
See also
Food and agriculture organization of the United Nations

Guatemala
Guatemala: food for profit; Public law 480, food for peace. T. Bodenheimer. il Ramp Mag 10:23-5 O '71
Mayan nutrition, then and now. Chem 44:23-4 Jl '71

United States
Child is being beaten; the effects of hunger; address, March 21, 1971. B. Pasamanick. Vital Speeches 37:465-72 My 15 '71
Playing games with hunger. Nation 212:612 My 17 '71

Reality of American hunger. E. F. Hollings. Nation 212:518-21 Ap 26 '71
We are ignorant about nutrition; excerpts from comment to the press. J. Mayer. McCalls 98:78 F '71
NUTRITION workers
Careers in nutrition. R. P. Geyer. il por Chem 44:12-15 Ja '71
NUTRITIONISTS. See Nutrition workers
NUTS
See also
Cookery—Nuts
NUTS (machinery) See Bolts and nuts
NUTT, Charles S.
How to organize an outdoor art show. il Am Artist 35:24-9 Je '71
NUZUM, C. Thomas, and Snodgrass, P. J.
Urea cycle enzyme adaptation to dietary protein in primates. bibliog il Science 172:1042-3 Je 4 '71
NYAD, Diana
She takes a long swim off a short pier. D. Levin. por Sports Illus 35:38-40+ D 6 '71 *
NYDEN, Paul J.
Coal the killer. Nation 213:238-42 S 20 '71
Voting for their lives. Nation 212:206-10 F 15 '71
NYERERE, Julius Kambarage
Dead letter. por Newsweek 78:84+ S 20 '71 *
Profiles. W. E. Smith. por New Yorker 47:42-8+ O 16; 47-54+ O 23; 53-8+ O 30 '71 *
NYLON sails. See Sails
NYMPHAEA. See Water lilies
NYMPHS, Artificial. See Fishing lures, flies, etc.
NYQUIST, Ewald B.
All the isms are wasms; address, July 15, 1971. Vital Speeches 37:645-50 Ag 15 '71
Concept of open education. Ed Digest 37:9-12 N '71
NYQUIST, S. E. and others
Vitamin A: concentration in the rat liver Golgi apparatus. bibliog il Science 173:939-41 S 3 '71
NYREN, Dorothy
Voices of Brooklyn: report on a project funded by the National endowment for the humanities. il por Wilson Lib Bul 46:443-5 Ja '72

O

OAO (orbiting astronomical observatory) See Artificial satellites—Astronomical use
OAS. See Organization of American states
OBE. See United States—Business economics, Office of
OCR (optical character recognition) See Optical scanners
OECD. See Organization for economic cooperation and development
OEO. See United States—Economic opportunity, Office of
OEP. See United States—Emergency preparedness, Office of
OH radicals. See Hydroxyl
OIC. See Opportunities industrialization centers, inc.
OPA. See United States—Price administration, Office of
OPEC. See Organization of petroleum exporting countries
OPERA America. See Opera—United States
OPIC. See Overseas private investment corporation
OSO (orbiting solar observatory) See Artificial satellites
OTB. See Off-track betting corporation, New York
OTC trading. See Stocks—Marketing
OTDA. See United States—National aeronautics and space administration—Tracking and data acquisition, Office of
OAK ISLAND
Hidden treasure? il Newsweek 78:71-2 N 8 '71
OAKDALE guest ranch (nudist colony) See Nudism
OAKELEY, John D. A.
Booms; excerpts from Winning. il Yachting 130:82+ N '71
OAKES, John Bertram
Extra nickel's worth. il pors Time 97:36 Je 21 '71 *

OCCIDENTAL petroleum corporation
Occidental petroleum's unhappy ventures. il Bsns W p79-80+ D 18 '71
Overstaying his time? por Forbes 108:31-2 N 15 '71

OCCULT sciences
Occult. J. Ehrenwald. il Todays Ed 60:28-30 S '71
See also
Astrology
Magic
Mediums
Satanism
Spiritualism

OCCULTATIONS
Amateur scientist; groups are organized to observe the eclipse of stars by the moon. T. E. Bell. il Sci Am 226:108-11 Ja '72
Casting some (star) light on Jupiter's atmosphere. D. E. Thomsen. il Sci N 99: 267-8 Ap 17 '71
December grazing occultation of Iota Capricorni. H. R. Povenmire. il Sky & Tel 41:182-3 Mr '71
Grazing occultation observed with great accuracy. H. R. Povenmire and M. Dobbings. il Sky & Tel 41:393 Je '71
How to watch the moon hide a star. D. L. Heiserman. il Pop Sci 198:122+ F '71
Jupiter and Beta Scorpii. il Sky & Tel 41:328 My '71
Jupiter and Beta Scorpii. D. S. Evans and W. B. Hubbard. il por Sky & Tel 42:337-41 D '71
Jupiter and Io occult Beta Scorpii. il Sky & Tel 42:112-16 Ag '71
Mars occultation roundup. il Sky & Tel 42: 48-51 Jl '71
May occultation of Mars. D. W. Dunham. il Sky & Tel 41:326 My '71
Occultation highlights (cont) D. W. Dunham. il Sky & Tel 41:327; 42:184; 43:54-7 My, S '71, Ja '72
Occultation of Mars. T. D. Nicholson. il Natur Hist 80:78 My '71
Occultations during the lunar eclipse. E. M. Bram. il Sky & Tel 43:63 Ja '72
Pluto and a star. Sky & Tel 41:277 My '71
When you wish upon a Jupiter. Sci N 100: 261 O 16 '71

OCCUPATIONAL aptitude tests. See Aptitude tests

OCCUPATIONAL diseases. See Diseases, Industrial

OCCUPATIONAL education. See Vocational education

OCCUPATIONAL guidance. See Vocational guidance

OCCUPATIONAL mobility
Uses of adversity. il Newsweek 77:58+ Ja 18 '71
See also
Labor turnover

OCCUPATIONAL rehabilitation. See Vocational rehabilitation

OCCUPATIONAL retraining. See Retraining, Occupational

OCCUPATIONAL safety. See Industrial safety

OCCUPATIONAL surveys
New federal-state occupational employment statistics program: mail questionnaire survey of employment by occupation. H. Goldstein. Mo Labor R 94:12-17 O '71

OCCUPATIONS
Career choices. P. H. Abelson. Science 174: 1283 D 24 '71
Good careers that don't require college degrees. il Good H 172:179 Mr '71
Graduates and jobs: a grave new world. il Time 97:49-52+ My 24 '71
Job vacancies in 1970. R. Konstant. Mo Labor R 94:20-1 F '71
Jobs for tomorrow. il Time 97:70 F 15 '71
Jobs that can change your world. N. A. Comer. il Mlle 73:132-4+ S '71
Where the jobs will be in the '70s; excerpts from survey by U.S. Department of labor. il U S News 75:68-71 S 6 '71
See also
Negro women—Occupations
Occupational surveys
Professions
Woman—Occupations

OCCUPATIONS, Choice of. See Occupations

OCCUPATIONS for the blind. See Blind, Occupations for the

OCEAN
Health and beauty from the sea, by M. Castle. Review
House B 113:9 Jl '71. S. Lindsay
Oceans as alphabet soup: focus on DDT and PCB's. R. H. Gilluly. Sci N 101:30-1 Ja 8 '72

This watery plant; excerpt from Water and life. R. Platt. il Audubon 73:4-9 Mr '71
See also
Arctic Ocean
Coasts
Indian Ocean
Meteorology, Maritime
Oceanographic research
Oceanography
Pacific Ocean
Sea level changes
Sea water
Territorial waters
Waves

OCEAN-atmosphere interaction
Shifting world of Arctic sea ice. L. Purrett. il Sci N 100:80-1 Jl 31 '71

OCEAN bottom
Nonspreading crustal blocks at the mid-Atlantic ridge. E. Bonatti and J. Honnorez. bibliog il Science 174:1329-31 D 24 '71
Pacific's drift. Sci N 99:399 Je 12 '71
Submarine pingos in the Beaufort Sea. J. M. Shearer and others. bibliog il Science 174:816-18 N 19 '71
See also
Benthos
Faults (geology)
Marine sediments
Sounding and soundings
Submarine valleys

International aspects
Legal regulation of mineral exploitation in the deep seabed; address, April 19, 1971. J. R. Stevenson. Dept State Bul 65:48-55 Jl 12 '71
Search for equity on the seabeds; address, February 9, 1971. J. R. Stevenson. Dept State Bul 64:529-33 Ap 19 '71
See also
Seabed treaty
United Nations—Committee on the peaceful uses of the seabed and ocean floor

OCEAN currents
Antarctic bottom water: major change in velocity during the late Cenozoic between Australia and Antarctica. N. D. Watkins and J. P. Kennett. bibliog il Science 173: 813-18 Ag 27 '71
Southward flow under the Florida current. W. Düing and D. Johnson. bibliog il Science 173:428-30 Jl 30 '71
See also
Gulf Stream

OCEAN drilling and exploration company
Late tape. R. Brady. Duns 97:106 Mr '71

OCEAN fishing. See Salt water fishing

OCEAN floor. See Ocean bottom

OCEAN freight forwarders. See Forwarding companies

OCEAN in art
See also
Marine painting

OCEAN liners
Albatross queen; Queen Mary project. il Newsweek 77:80+ Mr 15 '71
Gathering: venture. New Yorker 47:31-4 Je 26 '71
Last voyage: no more American passenger ships to sail from an Atlantic Coast port. il Am Heritage 22:111 Ag '71
Logistics of glut; world cruise aboard the S.S. France. J. Wechsberg. il Esquire 76: 188-93+ D '71
Rather large vessel in Long Beach invites you to come aboard; Queen Mary. il Sunset 147:38-9 S '71
Sway of the grand saloon, by J. M. Brinnin. Review
Atlan 228:126-8+ D '71. L. Kronenberger
Whatever happened to the glamorous ocean Queens? il U S News 71:42 S 13 '71
See also
Ocean travel
Shipwrecks

OCEAN mining
Legal regulation of mineral exploitation in the deep seabed; address, April 19, 1971. J. R. Stevenson. Dept State Bul 65:48-55 Jl 12 '71

OCEAN pollution. See Marine pollution

OCEAN temperature
Depth habitats of growth stages of pelagic foraminifera. E. Emiliani. bibliog il Science 173:1122-4 S 17 '71
Gulf Stream and middle Atlantic bight: complex thermal structure as seen from an environmental satellite. P. K. Rao and others. il Science 173:529-30 Ag 6 '71

OCEAN travel
Afloat with freight. C. P. Weikel. il Har
  Yrs 11:19-23 O; 20-3 D '71
Once again: what to expect of freighter trav-
  el. F. G. Philcox. il Travel 135:55-7 F '71
Sway of the grand saloon, by J. M. Brinnin.
  Review
  Atlan 228:126-8+ D '71. L. Kronenberger
  New Yorker 47:181-2+ N 27 '71. L. E.
  Sissman
Sway of the grand saloon; excerpts. J. M.
  Brinnin. il Am Heritage 22:12-19+ O '71
  See also
  Cruising
  Ocean liners
  Voyages
  Voyages around the world
OCEAN trenches. See Submarine valleys
OCEAN waves
Patterns in ocean turbulence. il Chem 44:25
  Jl '71
OCEANIA
  See also
  Easter Island
  Fiji
  Islands of the Pacific
  Micronesia
  New Hebrides
  Norfolk Island
  Society Islands
  Tahiti

Antiquities
New hall: Peoples of the Pacific exhibition
  at the Museum of natural history. New
  Yorker 47:32-3 Ap 10 '71

Description and travel
Will Wally Hickel ever come home? with
  travel notes. R. Joseph. il por Esquire
  76:12, 91-7 Ag '71

Native races
Peoples of the Pacific; ed. by M. Mead and
  P. McClanahan. bibliog il pors Natur Hist
  80:33-70 My '71
OCEANIC basalt. See Basalt
OCEANOGRAPHIC research
Amateur scientist; experiments with salt
  fountains and related instabilities in water,
  ed. by C. L. Stong. il Sci Am 224:124-8 Je
  '71
  See also
  Underwater drilling
  Underwater exploration
  Underwater laboratories

Equipment
  See also
  Submarine research vehicles
OCEANOGRAPHY
  See also
  Challenger expedition, 1872-1876
  Marine microbiology
  Marine pollution
  Ocean
  Ocean-atmosphere interaction

Bibliography
Science of the sea in books. See issues of
  Sea frontiers

Study and teaching
Oceanographic odyssey; annual educational
  tour sponsored by the University of Wash-
  ington at Seattle. R. W. Sternberg and
  others. il Travel 137:50-3 Ja '72
  See also
  United States—Sea grant programs. Office
  of
OCEANOLOGY. See Oceanography
OCELLI. See Eye (insects)
OCHI, Norio
Changing trade policy in Japan. address, No-
  vember 1, 1971. Vital Speeches 38:102-5 D
  1 '71
OCHOA, Eduardo Martinez
Day the rebels attacked; ed. by O. Brooks.
  il pors Outdoor Life 147:44-7+ Ja '71
O'COLLINS, Gerald
Faith in focus. America 124:207-8, 237-8,
  264, 291-2, 320, 345, 410 F 27-Ap 3, 17 '71
O'CONNELL, Richard
Eight epigrams. Nat R 23:1109 O 8 '71
O'CONNELL, Timothy J.
Hope from Horizon house. il America 125:
  282-5 O 16 '71
Lettuce boycott reaches New York. America
  124:148-9 F 13 '71
O'CONNOR, Carroll
Meet Archie Bunker and the man who
  created All in the family; interview, ed.
  by P. Hudson. N. Lear. il pors Sr Schol
  99:6-7+ O 25 '71 *

O'CONNOR, Douglas F.
Renewal rangers. R. L. Shayon. Sat R 54:38
  Ag 21 '71 *
O'CONNOR, Flannery
Crop; story. Mlle 72:216-17 Ap '71
  about
Acts of grace. W. Clemons. por Newsweek
  78:115-17 N 8 '71 *
Even as the heathen rage. G. Davenport.
  Nat R 23:1473 D 31 '71 *
Flannery O'Connor and fundamental poverty;
  address, November 1970. C. Martin. Engl
  J 60:458-61 Ap '71 *
O'CONNOR, Frank
Call; story. Harper 242:90-3 Ap '71
O'CONNOR, J. F.
Fuller explanation; poem. Sat R 54:4 Ag
  14 '71
O'CONNOR, Jack
Getting the range. See issues of Outdoor
  life
How to choose an outfitter. il Outdoor Life
  148:49-51+ Ag '71
Nonresident license gouge. il Outdoor Life
  148:27-9+ D '71
Safari in the seventies. il Outdoor Life 147:
  55-7+ Mr '71
Sheep hunting is an art. il Outdoor Life 147:
  68-71+ F '71
Shooting. See issues of Outdoor life
Trophies to order. il Outdoor Life 147:40-1+
  Ja '71
O'CONNOR, U.
(tr) See Behan, B. Two poems; Jim Larkin;
  The versemaker's wish
OCTANDRE; ballet. See Ballets—Criticisms
OCTANE rating. See Gasoline—Anti-knock
  and anti-knock mixtures
OCTOPUS
Octopus trilogy. F. G. Wood; J. F. Gennaro,
  jr. il Natur Hist 80:14-16+ Mr '71
Shy monster, the octopus. G. L. Voss. il
  Nat Geog 140:776-99 D '71
OCTOPUSH. See Aquatic sports
ODD lot sales. See Stocks—Odd lots
ODD lot trading. See Stocks—Odd lots
O'DELL, Scott
Authors & editors; interview, ed. by P.
  Bragg. por Pub W 200:21-3 N 15 '71
ODETS, Clifford
Stormbird of the working class. S. Maloff.
  Commonweal 95:226-9 D 3 '71 *
O'DOHERTY, Brian
Hopper bequest at the Whitney. il Art in Am
  59:68-72 S '71
New conservatism in the seventies? Art in
  Am 59:23 Mr '71
What is post-modernism? Art in Am 59:19
  My '71
O'DONNELL, Richard W.
Sad, sad tale. Nat R 23:369 Ap 6 '71
O'DONNELL, William J.
New wrinkle in printmaking. il Am Artist
  35:52-3+ N '71
O'DONOVAN, Leo J.
Weekend of hope. America 125:319-21 O 23
  '71
ODORS
Home is where the nose is. J. Robbins. il
  Todays Health 49:48-9+ Ap '71
Left- and right-handed odors. Sci Am 225:
  46 Ag '71
Odor differences between enantiomeric isom-
  ers. G. F. Russell and J. I. Hills. bibliog
  il Science 172:1043-4 Je 4 '71
Odor incongruity and chirality. L. Fried-
  man and J. G. Miller. bibliog il Science
  172:1044-6 Je 4 '71
Present shock. D. M. Rorvik. Esquire 76:
  68+ O '71
S.M.E.L.L.S. v. smells; offensive odors from
  beet-processing plant in Hartford, Wis.
  Time 98:84 N 22 '71
  See also
  Deodorants
  Gardens, Fragrant
  Pheromones

Control
Low-cost odor control; Seattle. G. W. Isaac.
  il Am City 86:14 Je '71
Manure odor controls, how well do they
  work? B. Eftink. il Suc Farm 69:B2-3
  Ap '71
ODORS of animals
Mammalian scent marking. K. Ralls. bibliog
  il Science 171:443-9 F 5 '71
ODUM, Howard T.
Print-out of the future systems of man; ex-
  cerpt from Environment, power and society;
  with biographical sketch. il Natur Hist 80:6,
  24-9 bibliog(p 104) My; 10 O '71

O'DWYER, Paul
Lonely witness. Nation 213:549-50 N 29 '71 •
ODYA, Charles. See Itskovitz, H. D. jt. auth.
OEHLER, John H. and Schopf, J. W.
Artificial microfossils: experimental studies of
permineralization of blue-green algae in sil-
ica. bibliog il Science 174:1229-31 D 17 '71
OERKE, Andrew
Serengeti sunset; poem. New Repub 164:25
My 8 '71
Sun; poem. Poetry 119:22 O '71
OERTLE, V. Lee
Back-country camper. il Pop Mech 136:58 S
'71
On-the-go camping. See issues of Popular
mechanics to July 1971
Selecting the right outboard. il Yachting
129:66-7+ Ap '71
Smart ways to improve your recreational
vehicle. il Pop Mech 135:156+ My '71
OERWOOD braille trail, Pa. See Trails
OESPER, Ralph E.
(tr) See Schütz, W. Doebereiner and the
University of Jena
(tr) See Szabadvary, F. Great moments in
chemistry
OESTREICHER, Paul
Britain deports Rudi Dutschke. Chr Cent 88:
223-4 F 17 '71
O'FARRELL, S. See McNarry, L. R. jt. auth.
OFF-Broadway theater. See New York (city)—
Theater
OFF-road racing. See Motor vehicle racing
OFF-street parking. See Automobile parking
OFF-track betting. See Horse race betting
OFF-track betting corporation, New York
I got the horse right, where? OTB patrons.
P. Putnam. il Sports Illus 34:22-4+ Ap 19
'71
New game in town. il Time 97:66 My 31 '71
New York derby. il Newsweek 77:61 My 17
'71
Putting the case to Howie the horse; ed.
by W. Tower. E. B. Ryan. il por Sports
Illus 34:26-9 Je 28 '71
Two will get you, two? il Forbes 107:50 Ap
15 '71
OFFENBACH, Jacques
La Grande-duchesse de Gérolstein. Criticism
New Yorker 47:87 S 4 '71 •
Mozart of the boulevards. C. J. Luten. Opera
N 35:24-5 Ja 23 '71 •
Offenbach...and other Germans. J. Rock-
well. por Opera N 35:24-5 Ap 10 '71 •
La Perichole. Criticism
Opera N 35:24-5 Ja 23 '71 •
Opera N il 35:17-20 Ja 23 '71 •
Tales of Hoffman (Les contes d'Hoffmann)
Criticism
Hi Fi 20:MA14 D '70 •
Opera N il 35:17-20 Ap 10 '71 •
OFFENSES against the person
See also
Kidnapping
OFFERS, Jane M.
Books in brief. See issues of American West
OFFICE buildings
Office boom jolts the planners; RPA projec-
tions for New York. il Bsns W p59+ Ja 23
'71
Proposal to change the urban landscape by
redistributing a city's office space into 150-
story superframe towers. A. T. Swenson.
il Arch Forum 135:58-60 S '71
White elephant herd. il Newsweek 77:76+ F 8
'71
See also
Bank buildings
County buildings
Office layout
Skyscrapers
  also subhead Buildings under names of
cities, e.g. London—Buildings

Designs and plans
Building types study; low-rise office build-
ings. il Arch Rec 149:121-36 Je '71
Canadians build an office complex by Mies
van der Rohe in Toronto; with introd. by
M. F. Schmertz. il Arch Rec 149:105-14 Mr
'71
Common parts and legible spaces in Toron-
to's O.M.A. building. R. Jensen. il Arch
Rec 150:127-34 S '71
Elastic office building: GRT corporation.
Sunnyvale, Calif. R. Montgomery. il Arch
Forum 135:54-7 S '71
IBM in Boca Raton: Breuer builds on
Florida's flood plain. il Arch Rec 149:113-
18 F '71

Illinois Bell telephone company, Dorchester
building, Chicago. il Arch Rec 149:106 My
'71
Office buildings. il Arch Forum 134:28-57 Ja
'71
Fires and fire protection
See also
Skyscrapers—Fires and fire protection
Leasing and renting
See Offices—Leasing and renting
Location
See Location in business and industry
OFFICE, buildings, Remodeled
Renovated waterfront warehouse in San Fran-
cisco. il Arch Rec 150:102-4 Ag '71
OFFICE decoration
Record interiors of 1971. il Arch Rec 149:85-
104 Ja '71
OFFICE equipment and supplies
See also
Calculating machines, Electronic
Computers—Business use
Exhibitions
U.S. computers score; Western business ma-
chines at Leningrad's Systemotechnika-71.
Bsns W p60 O 23 '71
OFFICE equipment industry
See also
International business machines corporation
Great Britain
Profitable path to decimalization. Bsns W
p31+ Ja 23 '71
OFFICE for intellectual freedom. See American
library association—Office for intellectual
freedom
OFFICE furniture
See also
Alma desk company
OFFICE layout
Remodeled offices for an orthodontist. il
Arch Rec 149:150 Mr '71
OFFICE machines. See Office equipment and
supplies
OFFICE of business economics. See United
States—Business economics, Office of
OFFICE of communication of the United church
of Christ. See United church of Christ
OFFICE of economic opportunity. See United
States—Economic opportunity, Office of
OFFICE of education. See United States—
Education, Office of
OFFICE of emergency preparedness. See United
States—Emergency preparedness, Office of
OFFICE of foreign direct investments. See
United States—Foreign direct investments,
Office of
OFFICE of minority manpower. See Association
of American publishers—Office of minority
manpower
OFFICE of public safety. See United States—
Agency for international development—
Office of public safety
OFFICE of systems analysis. See United States
—Defense, Department of—Systems analy-
sis, Office of
OFFICE of tracking and data acquisition. See
United States—National aeronautics and
space administration—Tracking and data
acquisition, Office of
OFFICE signs. See Signs and signboards
OFFICE workers
Brighter demand for office help. Bsns W
p 15 Jl 3 '71
Office boom jolts the planners; RPA projec-
tions for New York. il Bsns W p59+ Ja 23
'71
Your clerical workers are ripe for unionism.
A. Vogel. il Harvard Bsns R 49:48-54 Mr
'71
See also
Secretaries
Salaries, allowances, etc.
Blue-collar/white-collar pay trends; sympo-
sium. bibliog il Mo Labor R 94:3-36 Je '71
Record increases in white-collar pay. il U S
News 72:65 Ja 3 '72
Regional pay differentials in white-collar oc-
cupations; with tables. H. F. Zeman. Mo
Labor R 94:53-6 Ja '71
White-collar salaries rise 6.2 percent. E. J.
Caramela. il Mo Labor R 94:57-9 Ja '71
Training
New skills for tomorrow's office worker. M.
W. Wood. Ed Digest 36:50-2 My '71
OFFICERS training corps. See United States—
Reserve officers training corps

OFFICES
Equip a good farm office for under $400. M. Hood. il Suc Farm 69:32-3 Ap '71
They share home office space. il Sunset 147:88 Jl '71
When the architect designs his own office. il Arch Rec 149:101-8 Ap '71

Leasing and renting
Office glut hits Los Angeles. il Bsns W p43 S 11 '71

OFFICIAL entertaining. See Government entertaining

OFFICIAL secrets
Reports and comment: Washington; use of secret information by government for self-serving purposes. R. H. Shackford. Atlan 228:18-20+ S '71
Roche paper. Newsweek 77:20 Ja 18 '71
Sloughs of secrecy; British official secrets acts. F. Feldkamp. il Harper 243:79-82 D '71
See also
Defense information, Classified
Executive privilege (government information)
Government and the press
Security classification (government documents)

OFFIT, Sidney
Pleasures and pitfalls of an int'l writers' congress. Pub W 200:32-4 Ag 16 '71

OFFSHORE boundaries. See Territorial waters

OFFSHORE oil fields. See Petroleum in submerged lands

OFFSHORE oil fires. See Oil fires

OFFSHORE platforms. See Artificial islands

O'FLAHERTY, Terrence
Cinderella network. il Am Ed 7:14-17 N '71; Same abr. with title PBS: the Cinderella network. Read Digest 99:43-8 N '71

OFSTHUN, Neil A.
Land acquisition: at no cost. Parks & Rec 6:40 Jl '71

OGALLALA, Neb.
One season in a quiet place. J. Shepherd. Look 35:48 Ja 12 '71

O'GARA, Robert J.
Designed into nature. il Design 73:10-11 Wint '71

OGBURN, Charlton, Jr
Modest proposal. il Harper 243:106-7 O '71

OGDEN, Anne
Limited editions for love and money. il House B 113:56+ N '71

OGDEN, Samuel R.
Vegetable that returns the most. il por Org Gard & Farm 18:38-40 D '71

OGDON, John
Unromantic romantic. por Time 97:78 F 22 '71

OGILVIE, Bruce Charles
We have a neurotic in the backfield, doctor. J. Jares. il pors Sports Illus 34:30-4 Ja 18 '71

OGILVY, David
Ogilvy pitch. R. Levy. por Duns 97:60+ F '71

OGILVY and Mather Inc.
Ogilvy pitch. R. Levy. por Duns 97:60+ F '71

OGLESBY, Arthur
Pheasant shooting in Britain. il Field & S 76:42-3+ D '71

OGLESBY, Carl
Contradictions. Ramp Mag 10:28-9+ O; 24+ N '71

OGLETREE, Earl J. and Rackauskas, J. A.
Creativity among west European pupils. bibliog Sch & Soc 99:377-8 O '71

OGNIBENE, Elaine R.
Black literature revisited: Sonny's blues. Engl J 60:36-7 Ja '71

OGNIBENE, Peter J.
ABCs of ABM. Commonweal 94:31-4 Mr 19 '71
Dodge to end the draft. il Nation 212:467-8 Ap 12 '71
Vietnam roulette. Commonweal 94:236-8 My 14 '71

O'GRADY, Joseph F.
You have to think service; interview, ed. by B. Foster. pors Am City 86:67-9 Je '71

OH, John K. C.
Premature aging of the Asian youth; address, October 29, 1971. Vital Speeches 38: 186-8 Ja 1 '72

O'HANLON, Michael J.
Alternate bookstore in St Louis, Missouri. Pub W 199:40 Je 14 '71
Bookselling at the center of the world. il Pub W 199:45 Mr 1 '71

O'HANLON, Thomas
Anarchy threatens the kingdom of coal. il por Fortune 83:78-82+ Ja '71

O'HARA, Frank
Sleeping on the wing; poem. New Repub 166: 28 Ja 1 '72
about
All the imagination can hold. K. Koch. New Repub 166:23-5 Ja 1 '72 *
New York pastoral. W. Clemons. por Newsweek 78:95-6 D 20 '71 *

O'HARA, Frederic James
Selected government publications. See issues of Wilson library bulletin

O'HARA, James Grant
Excerpt from debate, November 17, 1970. Cong Digest 50:86+ Mr '71

O'HIGGINS, Patrick
Christmas at the Ritz. il por Harp Baz 105:100-1 D '71
about
Authors & editors. L. P. Freilicher. il pors Pub W 200:23-4 Ag 16 '71 *
Madame; excerpt from Madame: an intimate biography of Helena Rubinstein. por McCalls 98:68-9+ Ag '71

OHIO
See also
Architecture, Domestic—Ohio
Booksellers and bookselling—Ohio
Canals—Ohio
Colleges and universities, State—Ohio
Education—Ohio
Fishing—Ohio
Great Miami River
Hunting—Ohio
Libraries—Ohio
Montgomery County
Paleobotany—Ohio
School libraries—Ohio

Social life and customs
Why Ohio? D. Hering. il Dance Mag 45:47-62 S '71

OHIO. Kent state university
Behind the headlines with a witness from Kent state; death of A. Krause. Seventeen 29:156+ Ag '70
Citizens battle for justice; Kent state shootings by Ohio national guard; with editorial comment. P. Davies. Nation 213: 547-8, 557-9 N 29 '71
Dismissals at Kent state. il Time 98:11 D 20 '71
James Michener speaks out; excerpts from remarks at press conference, April 27, 1971. J. A. Michener. por Pub W 199:17-18 My 10 '71
Kent remembers. il Newsweek 77:29 My 17 '71
Kent state. by J. Michener. Review Bsns W il p 12+ My 1 '71. J. R. Wilheim
   Nat R 23:707 Je 29 '71. D. Brudnoy
   Nation 213:54-6 Jl 19 '71. R. Walters
Kent state four; anniversary of the shootings. Nat R 23:514+ My 18 '71
Kent state in '72. Nation 213:612-13 D 13 '71
Kent state one year later: on the long road back. il U S News 70:17-20 Je 14 '71
Kent state revisited. W. Friedman. il Time 98:21 D 6 '71
Kent state: what happened and why; condensation. J. A. Michener. il Read Digest 98:57-63+ Mr; 217-20+ Ap '71
Loss of faith; no further action by the Department of justice. il Time 98:11 Ag 23 '71
New look at Kent state. Time 98:16+ Ag 2 '71
Parting shots: man who says he lost two daughters at Kent state. il por Life 71: 65 Ag 27 '71
Reporter at large; aftermath. P. Hamburger. New Yorker 47:106+ Je 5 '71

OHIO library association
Of note: seventy-sixth annual conference. R. H. Donahugh. Am Lib 2:1134 D '71

OHIO national guard. See United States—National guard

OHIO state library, Columbus
Dust from old photographs. il Am Lib 2:556-7 Je '71

OHIO university, Athens
$1 toy teaches photography. E. Truxell. il Pop Phot 68:116-17 Ja '71

OHLSSON, Garrick
Musician of the month. S. Fleming. por Hi Fi 21:MA8-9 Mr '71 *

OHMART, Robert D. and Lasiewski, R. C.
Roadrunners: energy conservation by hypothermia and absorption of sunlight. bibliog il Science 172:67-9 Ap 2 '71

OHNISHI, Eiji. See Sonobe, H. jt. auth.

O'HORGAN, Tom
Cerebral trip is over. por Time 98:68 O 25 '71 *
Do you mind critics calling you cheap, decadent, sensationalistic, gimmicky, vulgar, overinflated, megalomaniacal? J. Gruen. il por N Y Times Mag p 14-16+ Ja 2 '72 *
No one will leave feeling neutral. M. Paley. por Life 71:40 O 22 '71 *

OHTA, Tomoko, and Kimura, Motoo
Amino acid composition of proteins as a product of molecular evolution. bibliog il Science 174:150-3 O 8 '71

OIL, Tall. See Tall oil

OIL and gas leases
Raising the ante on North Sea oil. Bsns W p32-3 Ag 28 '71

OIL crayon. See Crayons

OIL field flooding
Ground rupture in the Baldwin Hills. D. H. Hamilton and R. L. Meehan. bibliog il Science 172:333-44 Ap 23 '71
Oil and earth movements; Baldwin Hills injections. il Sci N 99:300 My 1 '71

OIL filters
See also
Purolator, inc.

OIL fires
Holocaust on platform B; Shell oil company's drilling platform in Gulf of Mexico. J. P. Blank. il Read Digest 99:80-4 N '71

OIL imports. See Petroleum industry—Imports problem

OIL lands
Biggest buried treasure on earth; Piceance shale. R. Schiller. il Read Digest 99:157-60+ S '71

OIL pollution of lakes. See Oil pollution of rivers, harbors, etc.

OIL pollution of rivers, harbors, etc.
Barehanded battle to cleanse the Bay. P. T. White. il Nat Geog 139:866-81 Je '71
Biological and oceanographical survey of the Santa Barbara Channel oil spill 1969-1970. ed. by D. Straughan and R. L. Kolpack. Review
Environ il 13:48-52 S '71
Cordova fishermen; proposed Alaskan oil pipeline. Nation 213:580-1 D 6 '71
Disaster in the Bay. il Newsweek 77:48 F 1 '71
Effects of the Santa Barbara blowout. il U S News 70:54 F 8 '71
Horizon to horizon; brief review of worst oil spills November 1969 through January 1971. bibliog il Environ 13:13-21 Mr '71
More oil for our troubled waters; San Francisco and New Haven; with editorial comment. il Life 70:28, 36-43 F 5 '71
New Jersey of the Northwest; threat of expanding petroleum industry. H. Henkin. Nation 212:292-3 Mr 8 '71
Oil-eating lobsters. Sci Digest 70:25 D '71
Oil off two coasts: the promises, the problems il U S News 71:45-6 N 22 '71
Oil on troubled waters; oil spill in San Francisco Bay. il Time 97:61 F 1 '71
Oil pollution. M. Zeldin. il Audubon 73:99-119 My '71
Oil spills bring a call for action; San Francisco Bay and Long Island Sound. il Bsns W p20-1 Ja 30 '71
Oil's aftermath; report on 1969 spill in Santa Barbara Channel. il Time 97:37 Mr 1 '71
Pity the birds. Nation 212:165-6 F 8 '71
Small oil spill; impact of 1969 West Falmouth spill on the marine environment. M. Blumer and others. bibliog il Environ 13:2-12 Mr '71
Troubled oil on waters. J. Frye. il Sea Front 17:38-47 Ja '71

Control
Goo and more goo. New Repub 164:14 F 6 '71
Great ocean sweepstakes. M. Gruber. il Sea Front 17:146-59 My '71
Growing problem of oil spills: reasons and remedies. il U S News 70:52-4 F 8 '71
Slick-licker. S. Lindsay. il Sat R 54:95 D 4 '71
Slick-licker: the Oilevator, a Canadian invention. il Time 98:81 O 25 '71
Spread oil on the Sound's troubled waters and you'll be in hot water with the chief. S. Singer. il pors Todays Health 49:35-9+ O '71
Vacuum unit helps clean up local oil spill; Lake Wausau, Wis. il Am City 86:12 Jl '71
We're fighting oil pollution with bubbles, belts and beads. B. Ford. il Sci Digest 69:34-9 Mr '71

Laws and legislation
See Water pollution—Laws and legislation

Measurement
Earth resource technology used in pollution detection. B. M. Elson. il Aviation W 95:46-9 D 13 '71
Petroleum: tar quantities floating in the northwestern Atlantic taken with a new quantitative neuston net. B. F. Morris. bibliog il Science 173:430-2 Jl 30 '71

OIL refineries. See Petroleum refineries

OIL shale lands. See Oil lands

OIL shales
Elusive bonanza, by C. Welles. Review
New Repub 164:28-9 F 13 '71. P. Passell and L. Ross
Shale's elusive boom. il Newsweek 78:57 S 6 '71

OIL spills. See Oil pollution of rivers, harbors, etc.

OIL tankers. See Tank ships

OIL tanks
Tank on the bottom of the sea. M. Gruber. il Sea Front 17:26-9 Ja '71

OIL well drilling
Ghost at the feast. il Forbes 108:26 Jl 15 '71

OIL well drilling, Submarine
See also
Artificial islands
Petroleum in submerged lands

Safety devices and measures
Offshore fire singes oil's safety rules. Bsns W p48 O 23 '71

OILMAN; story. See Newman, M.

OILS and fats, Edible
FDA seems about to abandon its opposition to truthful labeling of factory-made foods; fat ingredients. il Consumer Bul 54:24-6 Ag '71
Questions and answers on fats and cholesterol. R. H. Smithies. il Good H 172:139-40 F '71
See also
Food—Fat content

OJAI, Calif.
Use air to sweep streets clean. il Am City 86:34 S '71

OJAI festival. See Music festivals—California

OJALA, William T.
Teacher behavior and English instruction. Clear House 45:435-8 Mr '71

OJHA, Ishwer C. and Tretiak, Daniel
Toward a new beginning. Cur 130:5-6 Je '71

OKA, Takashi
Emperor who meets the President today. il pors N Y Times Mag p44-5+ S 26 '71
Japan's self-defense force wins a skirmish with the past. il por N Y Times Mag p 12-13+ F 28 '71

OKAMOTO, Michiko, and others
Destruction of mammalian motor nerve terminals by black widow spider venom. bibliog il Science 172:733-6 My 14 '71

OKAMURA, Akihiko
Crossroads at Tchepone; photographs. il Life 70:29-31 Mr 26 '71
War in Laos; report and photographs. por Life 70:21-9 Mr 12 '71
—See Godfrey, M. jt. auth.

O'KANE, Joseph P.
As Arabs see it. il America 124:67-8 Ja 23 '71

OKEECHOBEE WATERWAY. See Waterways —United States

O'KEEFE, John A.
Tektite glass in Apollo 12 sample. bibliog il Science 168:1209-10; 170-200; 171:313-14 Je 5, O 9 '70, Ja 22 '71

O'KEEFE, Patrick A.
Movie's the message! Engl J 60:957-9 O '71

O'KEEFFE, Georgia
Georgia O'Keeffe at eighty-four. L. Janos. il por Atlan 228:114-17 D '71 *

O'KEEFFE, Vincent
Dear Bill Cosby. Clear House 46:56-8 S '71

OKINAWA
Agreement with Japan on reversion of Okinawa transmitted to the Senate. R. M. Nixon; W. P. Rogers. Dept State Bul 65:431-5 O 18 '71
End of a feud? il Newsweek 77:34 Je 21 '71
End of American rule on Okinawa; what it means. il U S News 70:42-3 Je 28 '71
Secretary Rogers urges early and favorable Senate action on agreement with Japan on reversion of Okinawa; statement, October 27, 1971. W. P. Rogers. Dept State Bul 65:565-8 N 15 '71

OKINAWA—*Continued*
Spear and the shield. il Time 97:37-8 Je 28 '71
U.S. and Japan sign agreement on reversion of Okinawa, statements, June 17, 1971; with Department announcement, text of the agreement, and texts of related documents. W. P. Rogers. Dept State Bul 65:33-9 Jl 12 '71

OKLAHOMA
Oklahoma, the adventurous one. R. P. Jordan. il Nat Geog 140:149-89 Ag '71
See also
Platt National Park
Wilderness areas—Oklahoma

State library commission
ALA asked to investigate Oklahoma County firing. pors Library J 96:3075+ O 1 '71
Oklahoma City-County library fires Betty Lou Townley. Library J 96:2417+ Ag '71

OKLAHOMA CITY
Theater
Mummers theater. P. Blake. il Arch Forum 134:30-7 Mr '71; Discussion. 134:15 My '71
Toward a new slang; Mummers theater: J. Johansen's design gay as a Tinker-toy. R. Hughes. il por Time 97:68-9 My 31 '71

OKLAHOMA CITY-COUNTY library
ALA asked to investigate Oklahoma County firing. pors Library J 96:3075+ O 1 '71
Oklahoma City-County library fires Betty Lou Townley. Library J 96:2417+ Ag '71
OKLAHOMA library commission. See Oklahoma—State library commission

OKONITE company
Rival offer stymies Ling's Okonite bid. Bsns W p30+ Mr 6 '71

OKPAKU, Joseph
Story behind the book: If they come in the morning, by A. Davis and other writers, published by Third press. R. H. Smith. por Pub W 200:52-3 N 15 '71 *
Why minority publishing? ed. by B. Chambers. il pors Pub W 199:42-4 Mr 15 '71 *

OKSENBERG, Michel
Strategies of Peking. For Affairs 50:15-29 O '71

OKTOBERFEST. See Festivals—Germany (Federal Republic)

OKUHARA, Tetsu
Gallery; photograph. Life 71:4-5 Jl 30 '71

OLATUNJI, Babatunde
Olatunji at the Manhattan school of music. il pors Hi Fi 21:MA10-11 Ag '71 *

OLAUS J. Murie-Harvey Broome memorial book awards. See Wilderness society

OLD, Anne
Campfire cooking with foil. Redbook 137:32 My '71

OLD age
Clue to senility. Newsweek 78:40 Ag 23 '71
Senility and how you can avoid it. W. A. Nolen. il McCalls 99:20 O '71
See also
Aged
Aging
Centenarians
Gerontology
Longevity

OLD age assistance
AoA grants $2.2 million for 9 new areawide model projects. Aging 201:12 Jl '71
AoA, SRS, and OEO grant $2.4 million for coordinated services for elderly. Aging 201:11+ Jl '71
Administration reverses itself; now asks more funds for administration on aging. T. Schuchat. Har Yrs 11:56 Je '71
Maryland begins statewide information, referral service. il Aging 195:10 Ja '71
Massachusetts creates new elder affairs executive office. il Aging 195:11 Ja '71
News of federal agencies. See issues of Aging
News of state agencies. See issues of Aging
Oregon Title III self-help program is community activity. il Aging 205:18 N '71
Senate committee urges fast action, starting now, on 23 proposals for elderly. il Aging 196:5-6+ F '71
Title II project assisting 874 in Oregon model city area; Portland's program. il Aging 196:8-9 F '71
See also
United States—Cabinet committee on aging
OLD age centers. See Senior centers

OLD age homes
Number of aged homes rises 14%, patients 40%, in 5 years. il Aging 200:16 Je '71
What can they teach us? J. R. Lange; H. C. Howes. il Har Yrs 11:35-8 My '71
See also
Nursing homes

OLD age market
Operation stretch your dollar; 10 per-cent discounts for the elderly. A. Z. Rose. il por Har Yrs 11:28-9 F '71
Over-65 set: a bonanza for business? il Nations Bsns 59:34-6 N '71
Power of the aging in the marketplace. il Bsns W p52-8 N 20 '71

OLD age pensions
See also
Pensions, Industrial
Retirement income

Europe, Western
Regulation of private pension plans in Europe. F. M. Kleiler. Mo Labor R 94:33-9 Ap '71

OLD bus; story. See Brautigan, R.
OLD DEERFIELD, Mass. See Deerfield, Mass.
OLD farmers almanac. See Almanacs
OLD Halvorson place; story. See Woiwode, L.
OLD maid (game) See Cards
OLD man minds his wife; drama. See Heshmati, L. B.
OLD Milwaukee days. See Festivals—Wisconsin
OLD people. See Aged
OLD SALEM, N.C. See Winston-Salem, N.C.
OLD SALEM village. See Winston-Salem, N.C.
OLD times; drama. See Pinter H.
OLD WESTBURY, N.Y.
18 months of nuisance-free operation. S. A. Bogen. il Am City 86:71-3 Je '71
OLD WESTBURY college. See New York (state). State university—College at Old Westbury
OLDENBOURG, Zoé
Authors & editors. H. R. Lottman. por Pub W 200:57-9 Jl 19 '71 *
OLDENBURG, Claes
Man and machine. il por Time 97:60-3 Je 28 '71 *
OLDENBURGER, Pyxie
Opera primer. Seventeen 31:32 Ja '72
OLDEST store museum. See St Augustine, Fla.
OLDS, Sally Wendkos
What we do, and don't know about miscarriage. il Todays Health 49:42-5 F '71
(ed) See Ostapowicz, F. Anesthesia and analgesia during childbirth
OLDSTONE, Michael B. A. and others
Activation of spontaneous murine leukemia virus-related antigen by lymphocytic choriomeningitis virus. bibliog il Science 174:843-5 N 19 '71
OLEFINS
Photochemically induced ionic reactions of cycloalkenes. J. A. Marshall; reply. C. E. Wulfman and S. Kumei. Science 172:1061 Je 4 '71
OLFACTORY bulb. See Brain
OLFACTORY nerves
Garfish olfactory nerve: easily accessible source of numerous long, homogeneous, nonmyelinated axons. D. M. Easton. bibliog il Science 172:952-5 My 28 '71
OLFSON, Lewy
Necklace; dramatization of story, by G. de Maupassant. Plays 30:51-7 My '71
Sail on! Sail on! drama. Plays 30:77-81 O '71
Three swine of most small stature; drama. Plays 30:91-5+ Mr '71
Try data-date! drama. Plays 30:77-80 My '71
OLIGOCENE period. See Paleontology—Oligocene
OLIN corporation
End of a company town; Saltville, Va; with editorial comment. J. Newcombe. il Life 70:3. 36-45 Mr 26 '71
OLIPHANT, Sir Mark
One culture. L. Morris. Chr Today 15:55-6 My 21 '71 *
OLIVAS, J. M.
Convertible room of loose platforms. il Pop Sci 199:100-1 S '71
OLIVE trees
If you like your olive trees minus their olives. il Sunset 146:281 My '71
OLIVER
Pop personality. por Seventeen 29:216 S '70
OLIVER, Daniel
Theater. Nat R 23:490-1 My 4 '71
OLIVER, Edith
Off Broadway. See issues of New Yorker
OLIVER, Jack, and Murphy, Leonard
WWNSS: seismology's global network of observing stations. bibliog il Science 174:254-61 O 15 '71

OLIVER, John W.
Jesus and nationalism. Chr Today 15:18-19 Ap 9 '71

OLIVER, Mary
Encounter; poem. New Repub 164:27 My 29 '71

OLIVERO, Magda
Music to my ears; first New York appearance. I. Kolodin. Sat R 54:75 N 20 '71 •

OLIVETTI
Why labor gives Olivetti peace in times of strife. il Bsns W p38 Je 26 '71

OLIVETTI corporation of America
More than just a volume; Pennsylvania Olivetti plant. J. M. Dixon. il Arch Forum 134:20-5 Ap '71
What happened to Underwood. il Fortune 83: 267 My '71

OLIVINE
Core binding energy difference between bridging and nonbridging oxygen atoms in a silicate chain. L. I. Yin and others. bibliog il Science 173:633-5 Ag 13 '71
Olivines: revelation of tracks of charged particles. S. Krishnaswami and others. bibliog il Science 174:287-91 O 15 '71

OLLY
From blossoms, birds, butterflies. A. Landau. il por Américas 22:36-7 N '70 •

OLMEC antiquities. See Mexico—Antiquities

OLMSTED, Frederick Law, 1822-1903
Civilizing American cities, ed. by S. B. Sutton. Review
Arch Forum 135:8+ O '71. H. H. Reed •

OLMSTED, George
Executive gap. il Nations Bsns 59:67-9 D '71

OLNEY, Richard
Open-fire cooking. il House & Gard 139:92-9 Je '71

OLOFSON, Shirley
Obituary
Wilson Lib Bul por 46:396 Ja '72

OLSEN, Edward, and Jarosewich, Eugene
Chondrules: first occurrence in an iron meteorite. bibliog il Science 174:583-5 N 5 '71

OLSEN, Jack
Oh brother! A pair to watch. il pors Sports Illus 34:36-8+ Mr 2 '71
Poisoning of the West. il Sports Illus 34: 80-4+ Mr 8; 36-40+ Mr 15; 34-6+ Mr 22 '71
Poisoning of the West; excerpt from Slaughter the animals, poison the earth. il Read Digest 99:69-74 Ag '71
Trade winds; interview. ed. by C. Amory. Sat R 54:20+ N 6 '71
(ed) See Alcindor, L. We've got to spread a little anarchy
(ed) See Blanda, G. Decade of revenge
(ed) See Blanda, G. I keep getting my kicks
(ed) See Blanda, G. That impossible season
(ed) See Dryden, K. Banned in Boston, knighted in Montreal

OLSEN, Leif Henry
Is the recession over? interview. Read Digest 99:123-6 Ag '71
Why consumers will spend. por Nations Bsns 59:66 S '71

OLSEN, Paul
Rock hound, and renaissance man. il Seventeen 31:8 Ja '72 •

OLSEN, Peter
Negro maritime worker and the sea. bibliog il Negro Hist Bull 34:38-41 F '71

OLSHANSKY, Simon
Vocational rehabilitation of the older handicapped worker. Ment Hy 55:507-10 O '71

OLSON, Allen Dale
America's most far-flung school system. il Am Ed 7:12-15 Ag '71; Same abr. Ed Digest 37:32-4 D '71

OLSON, Hank
QRP thing. il Pop Electr 34:39-44+ F '71

OLSON, Miles C.
School for the 70's: an immodest proposal. Clear House 45:488-92 Ap '71

OLSON, Russell F.
Adult education and the urban crisis. il Todays Ed 60:24-6 F '71

OLSON, Ted
Mending a sidewalk . . . making a poem. Sat R 54:33 N 27 '71

OLSON, Toby
Home; poem. Nation 212:670 My 24 '71

OLSON, William A.
Renew old sewers and then maintain them. il Am City 86:105-6 O '71

OLT, James R.
Double take. il pors Outdoor Life 148:72-5+ S '71

OLYMPIC athletes. See Athletes

OLYMPIC games
Brundage backs down. Newsweek 78:84 Ag 2 '71
See also
Pan American games

Economic aspects
Race for all that Olympic gold. Bsns W p58 S 11 '71

OLYMPIC games (winter)
As smooth as silk in Sapporo; Japanese rehearsal for 1972 Winter Olympic games. W. Johnson. il Sports Illus 34:16-19 F 22 '71
Go east, young Olympian; photographs by J. Cooke and others; with account by W. Johnson. Sports Illus 35:52-64 N 15 '71
Hard, cold facts of winter games. B. Ottum. Sports Illus 35:65-6 N 15 '71
Late try for the winter Olympics? hotel space in Sapporo, Japan. Sunset 147:24 D '71
Olympian snafu at Sniktau; Denver proposed Mt Sniktau. R. Rapoport. Sports Illus 34: 60-1 F 15 '71
Sapporo: city of the Olympics. il Newsweek 78:102-3 D 20 '71

OLYMPIC games, 1972
Emphasis Olympic! preparation for the 1972 games. E. Horan. il Yachting 129:71+ Je '71

OLYMPIC NATIONAL PARK
Olympic adventure: ridge of the wild goats. B. Horton. il Nat Parks & Con Mag 45: 30-4 My '71
Place to stretch your soul; Washington's Olympic beach. R. Kirk. il Nat Wildlife 9:42-7 Je '71

OMAHA, Neb.
Police
911 goes regional. Am City 86:37 Ap '71

Sanitary affairs
Natural gas engines cut energy costs. il Am City 86:44-5 Jl '71

O'MAHONY, T. P.
Ireland's rocky road to pluralism. il America 124:513-16 My 15 '71

O'MALLEY, Janet
Wedding is on Tuesday; story. Good H 172: 72-3 F '71

O'MALLEY, Walter F.
Few hundred words from the front office; interview. ed. by A. S. Young. il pors Ebony 26:44-6+ Ja '71

OMAN
Starting from scratch. il por Time 97:34-7 F 15 '71
See also
Guerrillas—Oman
Petroleum industry—Oman
United Nations—Oman

OMAR, Margaret K.
That magical moment when baby starts to talk. il Parents Mag 46:54-5+ S '71

O'MARA, Richard
Chile: a good neighbor. Nation 212:180-1 F 8 '71
Cuba: policy of malign neglect. Nation 213: 524-6 N 22 '71
Peron: the home sick dictator. Nation 213: 14-15 Jl 5 '71

OMBUDSMAN
Curbing an import. Nations Bsns 59:18 F '71
Educational ombudsman for New York city? S. P. Lachman and D. Bresnick. bibliog f Sch & Soc 99:168-70 Mr '71
Fastest scissors in the East? government's ombudsman for business. V. Louviere. por Nations Bsns 59:17 D '71
Now: a swing to ombudsmen by U.S. companies. il U S News 70:39 Ap 5 '71
Ombudsmen; corporate ombudsman. il Newsweek 78:57+ Jl 26 '71
Patient's friend. il Time 98:46 Ag 30 '71
Planning a children's advocacy system. Cur 125:3-4 Ja '71

OMBUDSMAN (education)
Ombudsman in the educational hierarchy. S. W. Brown and R. F. Dyer. bibliog il Clear House 46:234-8 D '71
Ombudsman: new BMOC. E. Kiester, jr. il Todays Health 49:34-7 Ap '71

OMDAHL, J. L. and DeLuca, H. F.
Strontium induced rickets: metabolic basis. bibliog il Science 174:949-51 N 26 '71

OMEGA-Alpha, inc.
Back at the old stand. il por Newsweek 78: 79-80 N 1 '71
Case study; how an MBA class might assess Omega-Alpha, inc. por Forbes 108:19-20 O 1 '71

OMEGA system. See Radio in aviation; Radio in navigation

OMELETS
Make an omelet: rolled, stuffed or flat. J. Pépin. il House B 113:167 O '71
Omelets for all occasions. il Ebony 26:128+ Mr '71
Perfect omelet every time. il McCalls 99: 76+ O '71
You cook omelets to order, right at the table. il Sunset 146:190 My '71

OMORI, Minoru
How we bombed Tokyo's press. A. Axelbank. Nation 213:205-6 S 13 '71 *

ON changing doctors; story. See Hochman, S.

ON the move; ballet. See Ballets—Criticisms

ON the Sound (periodical)
Sound idea. il Newsweek 77:60 Ja 25 '71

ON the town; musical comedy. See Musical comedies, revues, etc.—Criticisms, plots, etc.

ONA Indians. See Indians of South America

ONASSIS, Aristotle Socrates
Jackie and Ari and Tom and George and Spiro and... R. Fitch. il pors Ramp Mag 10:38-47+ Ja '72 *
Onassis servant tells all he knows, and then some. W. A. McWhirter. il por Life 71:85 N 12 '71 *

ONASSIS, Jacqueline Lee (Bouvier) Kennedy
Dream realized. por Ladies Home J 88:113+ S '71

about
Conversations with de Gaulle; excerpt from Fallen oaks. A. Malraux. il por Esquire 76:129-33+ D '71 *
Kennedy portraits; White House portraits by Aaron Shikler. pors U S News 70:88 F 15 '71 *
Marquesa decided to have a party, and look who came. il pors Life 71:98-100 D 10 '71 *
Meanwhile, on the island of Skorpios. il pors Life 71:88 D 31 '71 *
Occupation: Jackie-watcher. il pors Life 70: 32-7 F 12 '71 *

ONCOGENIC viruses. See Tumor viruses

ONE Bull (Sioux chief)
Echoes of the Little Bighorn. D. H. Miller. il pors Am Heritage 22:30-1 Je '71 *

ONE flew over the cuckoo's nest; drama. See Wasserman, D.

ONE in a million; drama. See Murray, J.

ONE of ours; story. See Walker, T.

ONE out of many; story. See Naipaul, V. S.

ONE reason why I married Henry; story. See Franco, M.

ONE-room schools. See Rural schools—One-teacher schools

ONE-teacher schools. See Rural schools—One-teacher schools

ONE ton cup competition. See Yacht racing

ONE touch of magic; story. See Cave, H.

ONE wish too many; drama. See Feather, J.

O'NEAL, Eddie S. See Mitchell, H. H. jt. auth.

O'NEAL, Ryan
How handsome the hero, how romantic his fate! interview, ed. by E. Miller. il pors Seventeen 29:111+ D '70

about
Love story's Ryan O'Neal. por Vogue 157:133 Mr 1 '71 *
Very brash young man. il pors Life 70:68-71 My 21 '71 *

O'NEIL, Dan, 4th
Ghetto kids, a dedicated teacher find adventure with photography. J. Deschin. il por Pop Phot 69:28+ S '71 *

O'NEIL, David
To Hobart by trimaran. Yachting 129:258-61 Ap '71

O'NEIL, Harold O.
Reddest of the red. il por Org Gard & Farm 18:46-7 Ap '71

O'NEIL, Isabel
Art of burnished gilding. il por House & Gard 140:124-5 O '71 *

O'NEIL, Paul
At play in the fields of the company. il Life 71:26-9+ S 3 '71
Black governor for Mississippi? il pors Life 70:59-60 My 14 '71
Prime time of Walter Cronkite. il pors Life 70:50-50B+ Mr 26 '71
Vitamin C mania. il por Life 71:55-6+ Jl 9 '71

O'NEIL, Wayne A.
Who says Thailand's next? New Repub 164: 23-7 Ja 2 '71

O'NEILL, Eugene Gladstone
Last will and testament of Silverdene Emblem O'Neill. il pors Look 35:39-40 Ap 20 '71; Same abr. Read Digest 99:193-4+ D '71
Long day's journey into night. Criticism
    Nation 212:605-6 My 10 '71 *
    New Repub 164:26+ Je 12 '71 *
    New Yorker 47:94+ My 1 '71 *
    Newsweek il 77:122 My 10 '71 *
    Time il 97:62 My 3 '71 *
Mourning becomes Electra. Criticism
    Sat R 54:33 Ag 7 '71 *

O'NEILL, Jennifer
Pretty Jenny. il pors Life 71:72-4 N 19 '71 *

O'NEILL, Joan
Saint David of the daffodils; story. Seventeen 30:132-3 Ap '71

O'NEILL, William D.
How we resolved a highway-park conflict. il Am City 86:65 Ag '71
We tried gunite to repair spalled curbs. il Am City 86:69 Ja '71

ONEONTA college. See New York (state). State university—College at Oneonta

ONIONS
Onion and I. L. W. Patterson. il Org Gard & Farm 18:55-7 Mr '71
Useful onion. K. Kraft and P. Kraft. il Horticulture 49:38-9+ F '71
    See also
Cookery—Vegetables
Shallots

ONLY human; story. See Cullinan, E.

ONO, Yoko
Lennon: the working-class hero turns red; interview, ed. by R. Blackburn and T. Ali. pors Ramp Mag 10:43-9 Jl '71

about
Art; exhibition of works at Everson museum, Syracuse. L. Alloway. Nation 213:477-8 N 8 '71 *
Leave it to the wind; exhibition at the Everson museum of art, Syracuse, N.Y. D. Davis. il por Newsweek 78:120-1 N 8 '71 *
Two women who broke up the Beatles. J. Goldman. pors McCalls 98:72-3+ Jl '71 *
Yoko Lennon's latest film has a cast of 200—flies. E. Washington. il por Life 71:61 Ag 6 '71 *

ONONDAGA COUNTY, N.Y.
Community thanks its policemen. V. Louviere. il Nations Bsns 59:18 Je '71

ONSALA space observatory. See Astronomical observatories—Sweden

ONTARIO
    See also
Algonquin Provincial Park
Paleontology—Ontario

Religious institutions and affairs
Worldaround. Chr Cent 88:779, 1304-5 Je 23, N 3 '71

ONTARIO, Calif.
Employee invents a speedy curb painter. G. H. Mim Mack. il Am City 86:90 Jl '71

ONTARIO, Calif. public library
We threw away our tennis shoes. M. A. Crush. il Am Lib 2:207 F '71

ONTARIO, LAKE
Runoff of deicing salt: effect on Irondequoit Bay, Rochester, New York. R. C. Bubeck and others. bibliog il Science 172:1128-32 Je 11 '71

ONTARIO 500. See Automobile racing

ONTARIO library association
Of note; annual meeting. Am Lib 2:922 O '71

ONTARIO motor speedway. See Speedways

OOCYTES. See Germ cells

OOKPIKJUAK. See Owls

OP amps. See Amplifiers

OP art. See Art, Modern

OPAL
Opal precipitation by marine gastropods (mollusca) H. A. Lowenstam. bibliog il Science 171:487-90 F 5 '71

OPALAK, John
Marixa. il Design 73:40-1 Fall '71
Yves Brayer. il Design 72:27-9 mid-Wint '71

OPALS
Australia: opals are a girl's best friend; black opals. N. Morgan. il Sat R 54:50-1+ O 23 '71

OPEL (automobile) See Automobiles, Foreign

OPEN admissions by colleges and universities. See Colleges and universities—Entrance requirements

OPEN-air museums
North of Victoria, forest museum. il Sunset 146:8 Je '71
See also
Villages, Restored

OPEN-air theater. See Theater, Open air

OPEN and closed shelves
Opening those closed shelves: advisory statement concerning restricted circulation of library materials. J. F. Krug and J. A. Harvey. Am Lib 2:755 Jl '71; Reply with rejoinder. E. J. Gaines. 2:923-4 O '71

OPEN-pit mining. See Strip mining

OPEN plan schools
Can British school reforms work here? Ed Digest 37:5-8 S '71
Concept of open education. E. B. Nyquist. Ed Digest 37:9-12 N '71
Division X: Catholic response to dull, drab classrooms. G. Elford. America 124:376-8 Ap 10 '71
Does school+joy=learning? il por Newsweek 77:60-2+ My 3 '71
Free school or chalk time; address, November 1970. M. R. Graham. Engl J 60:754-9 S '71
Inside the open classroom. M. P. Berson. il Am Ed 7:11-15 My '71
Integrated day workshop. A. Muskopf and J. Moss. Ed Digest 36:26-8 My '71
It's what's inside that counts. G. S. Zimbel. il Sat R 54:50-1 Jl 17 '71
Joy of learning in the open corridor. W. Schneir and M. Schneir. il por N Y Times Mag p30-1+ Ap 4 '71; Discussion. p95-6+ My 2 '71
Joyful classrooms; Great Britain. il Newsweek 77:86+ Ap 5 '71
Learning in the open classroom; with report by P. Trachtman. il Life 71:146-7+ D 17 '71
Lemonade stand education. W. D. Boutwell. PTA Mag 65:13-14 Je '71
Life-style education. W. Von Eckardt. il Sat R 54:64 Ap 3 '71
Open classroom. H. S. Resnik. il Todays Ed 60:16-17+ D '71
Open classroom: protect it from its friends. M. Hapgood. il Sat R 54:66-9+ S 18 '71
Open school: an experiment in learning through joy; New York city. S. G. Lanes. il Parents Mag 46:56-9 S '71
Open schools: the British and us. J. Featherstone. New Repub 165:20-5 S 11; 17-21 S 25 '71; Same abr. with title What role for open schools? Cur 134:41-51 N '71; Excerpt. Ed Digest 37:9-12 D '71
Open schools vs. traditional: which is right for your child? H. S. Resnik. Redbook 137: 60+ O '71
Sober chaos; informal education. il por Time 99:44 Ja 3 '72
Wide open for learning; Project SOLVE; schools without walls in New Hampshire. R. C. Wing and P. H. Mack. Ed Digest 36:19-21 F '71

OPEN sandwiches. See Sandwiches

OPEN space program. See Land utilization

OPEN university. See Adult education—Great Britain

OPENERS, Bottle. See Corkscrews

OPERA
Neapolitan intermezzo and its influence on the symphonic idiom. G. Lazarevich. bibliog il Mus Q 57:294-313 Ap '71
See also
Jewelry in opera
Libretto
Prompting

Appreciation
Applause. G. R. Marek. il Opera N 36:6-7 D 18 '71
Opera primer. P. Oldenburger. Seventeen 31: 32 Ja '72
Song of the lark; W. Cather. D. Beckman. por Opera N 35:6-7 F 27 '71

Chorus
Birth of an ensemble; Chicago's lyric opera. G. McElroy. il Opera N 36:16-18 O '71
We choristers. W. Zakariasen. il Opera N 35: 27-9 Ja 30 '71

Finance
Money man; Hadley the Met's director of finance. M. Mayer. por Opera N 35:28-9 Ap 3 '71

History and criticism
Aida's creator: Auguste Mariette. S. J. London. il por Hi Fi 21:52-6 Ag '71
Flame-spattered robe; changing the locale and characters of the Masked ball. O. Rachleff. Opera N 35:23 Ja 30 '71
Happy birthday, Aida! V. Sheean. Opera N 36:8-9 D 25 '71

How high was G? H. Pleasants. Opera N 35:24-5 F 20 '71
Johann Simon Mayr and his Ifigenia in Aulide. J. Freeman. bibliog f il Mus Q 57:187-210 Ap '71
King of the May; B. Britten's Albert Herring. il Opera N 36:16-17 S '71
Magic flute, Masonic opera, by J. Chailley. Review
Am Rec G por 37:636-8 My '71. R. W. Gutman
Making of Aida; Cairo opera house premiere, 1871. W. Weaver. il Sat R 54:45-7 D 25 '71
Mozart of the boulevards: J. Offenbach. C. J. Luten. Opera N 35:24-5 Ja 23 '71
Stravinsky and the natures of ballet and opera. G. Martin. Yale R 61:193-206 D '71
Why Luisa Miller? R. A. Tuggle. il Opera N 36:21-4 D 11 '71
Witches' cauldron: Strauss' Elektra. M. Carner. il Opera N 35:24-6 F 27 '71

Instruction and study
Opera Ruffino style. H. E. Phillips. il por Opera N 35:13-15 Ja 16 '71
Role in hand. S. Milnes. por Opera N 36: 12-14 O '71
School of hard knocks; Merola opera program. K. Monson. il Opera N 36:8-9 N '71
Yankees in Valhalla; American singers in Germany. W. Hutton. il Opera N 35:8-11 Mr 20 '71
See also
North Carolina school of the arts, Winston-Salem

Intermissions
Dear Texaco opera quiz . . . N. S. Ross. Opera N 36:16 D 11 '71
Time out; opera intermissions. R. Rushmore. Opera N 35:6-7 F 6 '71

Stage lighting
Let there be light. M. J. Matz. il pors Opera N 35:8-11 Ap 3 '71

Stage setting and scenery
Darling of San Francisco; designer of opera productions. S. Von Buchau. por Opera N 35:12-13 Mr 20 '71
Let there be light. M. J. Matz. il pors Opera N 35:8-11 Ap 3 '71
Meeting of minds: Resnik and Blatas, a new director-designer team. S. Jenkins. il pors Opera N 35:6-9 Ap 17 '71
Osie; interview, ed. by J. Ferris. O. Hawkins. il por Opera N 35:30-1 Ja 16 '71
Quaglio & son. F. Merkling. il Opera N 36:8-11 D 18 '71

Stories
See Libretto

Study and teaching
See Opera—Instruction and study

Australia
Sydney's operatic showcase and the show for the case; performances by the Australian opera company. I. Kolodin. Sat R 54: 22 Jl 17 '71

Brazil
Yerma reborn. J. W. Freeman. il por Opera N 35:6-7 Je 12 '71

Bulgaria
Letter from Paris; Bulgarian opera troupe from Sofia. Genêt. New Yorker 47:86 My 29 '71
See also
Canadian opera company

Canada

France
Letter from Paris; reopening of the Opéra and the comique. Genêt. New Yorker 47:70 Jl 10 '71

Germany (Democratic Republic)
Behind the opera curtain; productions of G. Friedrich. il Newsweek 78:82 D 6 '71

Germany (Federal Republic)
Opera house crisis. E. Helm. il Hi Fi 21: MA26+ S '71
Report:
Stanislaw Moniuszko's Haunted manor on joint opera stage of Krefeld and Mönchengladbach. H. Koegler. Opera N 35: 31 Mr 20 '71

Great Britain
Britten's Britons; the English opera group in San Francisco. J. W. Stedman and G. McElroy. il por Opera N 36:18-20 N '71

OPERA—*Continued*

Italy

In Stendhal's footsteps: an opera junket. M. R. Scott. il Opera N 35:10-11 Ap 17 '71
See also
Opera, Italian

Sweden

New man at the Met: Stockholm's Göran Gentele. W. Weaver. il por Sat R 54:33-5+ Je 26 '71

United States

Metropolitan opera spring tour. Opera N 35:35 Ap 10 '71
O.P.E.R.A. America; first annual meeting of O.P.E.R.A. America in the Philharmonic Hall. H. E. Phillips. Opera N 35:32 Mr 20 '71
Opera U.S.A.; new season. il Harp Baz 104:92-3 S '71
U.S. calendar. See issues of Opera news published during opera season
See also
American opera company
Central opera service
Clarion music society, inc.
New York city opera company
Radio broadcasting—Operas
Santa Fe opera company
Television broadcasting—Operas

OPERA, Amateur
Opera Ruffino style. H. E. Phillips. il por Opera N 35:13-15 Ja 16 '71

OPERA, French
Average sensual man; J. Massenet. M. Cooper. il por Opera N 35:6-11 Mr 27 '71
Despot of French opera; J. B. Lully. K. O. Hoover. il por Opera N 35:6-11 Mr 6 '71

OPERA, Italian
Merits of Mercadante; revivals reveal his quality. W. Weaver. Hi Fi 21:MA29-30 My '71
Shaw looks at Verdi; reprint from The Nation, July 7, 1917 issue. pors Opera N 35:24-5 Mr 13 '71

OPÉRA, Paris. See Opera houses

OPERA America. See Opera—United States

OPERA broadcasts. See Radio broadcasting—Operas

OPERA-comique, Paris. See Opera houses

OPERA company of Boston
Druids in Boston. H. Saal. il por Newsweek 77:95 Je 28 '71
Report:
Beverly Sills in Norma. J. W. Freeman. Opera N 36:24 S '71
Charpentier's Louise. H. Neville. Opera N 35:25 My 15 '71

OPERA conferences. See Music conferences

OPERA dancing. See Dancing

OPERA houses
Back to the Bijou; restoration of Penn theatre, Pittsburgh. A. Vells. il Opera N 36:12-14 S '71
Byways of Europe: Wiesbaden; Hessian state theater. E. Gerken. il Opera N 35:20-1 My 15 '71
Great opera houses:
Frankfurt. E. Davidson. il Opera N 35:12-15 Mr 27 '71
Letter from Paris; reopening of the Opéra and the comique. Genêt. New Yorker 47:70 Jl 10 '71
Making of Aida; Cairo opera house. W. Weaver. il Sat R 54:45-7 D 25 '71
Marble hall: Chicago's civic opera house. il Opera N 36:6-9 O '71
Miracle of Santa Fe; photographs by D. Brown. Opera N 35:8-11 Je 12 '71
Musical events; Santa Fe opera house. W. Sargeant. New Yorker 47:82+ S 4 '71
Sydney's sculpture in stone. I. Kolodin. Sat R 54:39 Je 26 '71
Temple of the opera; Colón theater, Buenos Aires. R. Caamano. il Américas 23:17-24 Ja '71
See also
Lincoln Center for the performing arts, New York—Opera house
London—Covent Garden

Fires and fire protection

Holocaust on the Golden Horn: Istanbul culture center. C. E. Adelsen. il Opera N 35:14-16 Ja 30 '71

OPERA intermissions. See Opera—Intermissions

OPERA orchestra of New York
Musical events; concert performance of Respighi's Belfagor. W. Sargeant. New Yorker 47:110 Ap 3 '71
Report:
Ottorino Respighi's Belfagor. J. W. Freeman. Opera N 35:23-4 My 15 '71

OPERA quiz. See Radio broadcasting—Operas

OPERA singers
Before their time; singers cut down in the prime of life. G. Jellinek. il Opera N 36:32-4 D 25 '71
How to say it: a pronunciation guide for the Metropolitan opera's 1971-72 broadcasts. Opera N 36:28-9 D 18 '71
I remember Emma. P. Wood. por Opera N 35:26-9 F 6 '71
In Stendhal's footsteps: an opera junket. M. R. Scott. il Opera N 35:10-11 Ap 17 '71
Recordings; sopranos. M. Mayer. Esquire 75:30 F '71
Stars eat out: singers' guide to New York restaurants. Q. Eaton. il Opera N 35:12-16 Mr 6 '71
See also
Negro opera singers
Singing
also names of opera singers, e.g. S. Milnes

OPERA society of Washington
Koanga, a corpse is resurrected, feebly. G. Gelles. Hi Fi 21:MA31 Ap '71
Report:
Alberto Ginaster's Beatrix Cenci. J. W. Freeman. Opera N 36:21 O '71
American premiere of Frederick Delius' opera, Koanga. K. F. Reuling. il Opera N 35:30 Ja 30 '71

OPERANT conditioning. See Conditioned responses

OPERAS
See also
Phonograph records—Operas
Television broadcasting—Operas

Analysis

Dream of love, in Tristan und Isolde. S. Jenkins. il Opera N 36:24-5 D 18 '71
Opera for grownups: Hansel and Gretel, ed. by D. Bamberger. il Opera N 36:15-18 D 25 '71

Criticisms, plots, etc.

See name of composer for full entry
Aida. G. Verdi
Albert Herring. B. Britten
Antony and Cleopatra. S. Barber
Ariodante. G. F. Händel
Arlecchino, F. Busoni
Un ballo in maschera. See Masked ball, below
Barber of Seville. G. Rossini
Il barbiere di Siviglia. See Barber of Seville, above
Beatrix Cenci A. Ginastera
La Bohème. G. Puccini
Boris Godunov. M. P. Musorgskii
Carmen. G. Bizet
Cavalleria rusticana. P. Mascagni
La clemenza di Tito. J. C. W. A. Mozart
Les contes d'Hoffmann. See Tales of Hoffmann, next page
Così fan tutte. J. C. W. A. Mozart
Crime and punishment. E. Petrovics
Don Carlo. G. Verdi
Don Giovanni. J. C. W. A. Mozart
Don Pasquale. G. Donizetti
Don Rodrigo. A. Ginastera
Elektra. R. Strauss
Ernani. G. Verdi
Faust. C. F. Gounod
Faust counter Faust. J. Gessner
Fidelio. L. van Beethoven
Der fliegende Holländer. See Flying Dutchman, below
Flying Dutchman. R. Wagner
Die frau ohne schatten. See Woman without a shadow, next page
Der freischütz. K. M. von Weber
La Grande-duchesse de Gérolstein. J. Offenbach
La guerra. R. Rossellini
Hansel and Gretel. E. Humperdinck
Huckleberry Finn. H. Overton
Knot garden. M. Tippett
Koanga. F. Delius
Losers. H. Farberman
Louise. G. Charpentier
Lovers. S. Barber
Lucia di Lammermoor. G. Donizetti
Luisa Miller. G. Verdi
Madame Butterfly. G. Puccini
Magic flute. J. C. W. A. Mozart
Makropoulos affair. L. Janáček
Maria Stuarda. G. Donizetti
Masked ball. G. Verdi
Mefistofele. A. Boito
Midsummer marriage. M. Tippett
Moses and Aaron. A. Schönberg
Most important man. G. C. Menotti
Mother of us all. V. Thomson
Norma. V. Bellini
Orfeo ed Euridice. C. W. Gluck

OPERAS—Criticisms, plots, etc.—*Continued*
Pagliacci. R. Leoncavallo
Parsifal. R. Wagner
La Perichole. J. Offenbach
Roberto Devereux. G. Donizetti
Samson and Delilah. C. Saint-Saëns
Semiramide. G. Rossini
Summer and smoke. L. Hoiby
Tales of Hoffmann. J. Offenbach
Tosca. G. Puccini
La Traviata. G. Verdi
Tristan und Isolde. R. Wagner
Il Trovatore. G. Verdi
Werther. J. Massenet
Woman without a shadow. R. Strauss
Yerma. H. Villa-Lobos
Die zauberflöte. See Magic flute, previous page
See also
Rock operas—Criticisms, plots, etc.
OPERATIC acting. See Acting
OPERATIC characters. See Characters in opera
OPERATIC composition. See Composition (music)
OPERATIC production and direction
La Carmencita; photographs of Carmen. Opera N 35:21-3 F 6 '71
From another world; photographs of Die frau ohne schatten. Opera N 35:21-3 Ja 16 '71
King's fortune; photographs of the Masked ball. Opera N 35:21-2 Ja 30 '71
Love story; photographs of Werther. Opera N 35:21-3 Mr 27 '71
Meeting of minds: Resnik and Blatas, a new director-designer team. S. Jenkins. il pors Opera N 35:6-9 Ap 17 '71
Night at the (Finnish) opera; production of Crime and punishment in Finnish. G. Loney. il Hi Fi 21:MA26-7 Ja '71
On the threshold: rehearsal of new production of Tristan and Isolde; interview. A. Everding. New Yorker 47:37-9 D 11 '71
Out of Prague; photographs of Don Giovanni. Opera N 35:21-3 Mr 20 '71
Regina Resnik's Carmen: pleases audiences but not critics. P. Moor. il Hi Fi 21:MA28-9 O '71
Revolution comes to opera: Minneapolis' center opera. C. L. Osborne. il Hi Fi 21:62-70 N '71
Rivals; photographs of Il Trovatore. Opera N 35:21-3 Mr 13 '71
S.R.O. in Atlanta; traveling Carmen. B. Thebom. il Opera N 36:27-9 D 25 '71
Sacred spear; photographs of Parsifal. Opera N 35:21-3 Ap 3 '71
Shadow play; photographs of Tristan. Opera N 36:21-3 D 18 '71
Singing lesson; photographs of The barber of Seville. Opera N 35:21-3 F 20 '71
Sorcerer's apprenticeship, ed. by F. Rizzo. F. Zeffirelli. il pors Opera N 35:6-10 F 13 '71
Spaced-out Tristan. R. T. Jones. il Time 98:63 N 29 '71
Speaking of Cav/Pag: discussion by eleven performers, ed. by A. M. Lingg. il Opera N 35:21-5 F 13 '71
Telling Tales; photographs of Tales of Hoffmann. Opera N 35:21-3 Ap 10 '71
Three kings and a shepherd's miracle; Amahl and the night visitors performed by Columbus boychoir. il Good H 173:62-3 D '71
Vengeance in the East; photographs of Electra at the State opera in East Berlin. Opera N 35:21-3 F 27 '71
Ways of love; photographs of La Perichole. il Opera N 35:21-3 Ja 23 '71
Wedding party; photographs of Madama Butterfly. Opera N 35:21 Ap 17 '71
See also
Opera—Chorus
OPERATIC rehearsals. See Operatic production and direction
OPERATIC societies
See also
National opera association
OPERATIC stage directors. See Operatic production and direction
OPERATION Breadbasket. See Southern Christian leadership conference
OPERATION Breakthrough. See United States—Housing and urban development, Department of
OPERATION SEEK. See New York (city). City university
OPERATION Springboard. See Naval maneuvers
OPERATIONAL amplifiers. See Amplifiers
OPERATIONS, Surgical. See Surgery
OPERATIONS research
ABM debate: learned society split by old grievance. N. Wade. Science 174:276-7 O 15 '71
See also
Critical path analysis

OPERATIONS research society of America
ABM debate: learned society split by old grievance. N. Wade. Science 174:276-7 O 15 '71
Judgment; ORSA ABM debate. Sci Am 225:48 N '71
OPERETTAS
Criticisms, plots, etc.
See name of composer for full entry
Candide. L. Bernstein
OPIATE antagonists. See Narcotic antagonists
OPIATES. See Narcotics
OPIE, Iona (Archibald)
—and Opie, Peter
Games (young) people play. il Horizon 13:16-19 Wint '71
about
Their work is child's play. R. Cowley. il pors Horizon 13:14-15 Wint '71 *
OPIE, Peter
—See Opie, I. A. jt. auth.
about
Their work is child's play. R. Cowley. il pors Horizon 13:14-15 Wint '71 *
OPINION, Public. See Public opinion
OPINION, Student. See Student opinion
OPINION, Teacher. See Teacher opinion
OPIPARE, Sue, and others
Breaking into jail. il pors Library J 96:2734-6 S 15 '71
OPIUM
Ultimate concession; Turkey abolishing poppy production. Time 98:29 Jl 12 '71
See also
Morphine
OPIUM smuggling. See Smuggling
OPIUM trade
International drug trade: poppy to pusher. il Sr Schol 98:11-13 My 17 '71

Asia, Southeastern

New opium war. F. Browning and B. Garrett. il Ramp Mag 9:32-9 My '71

Singapore

Gallery: government-run opium factory; photographed by C. Mydans. Life 70:4-6A Je 25 '71

Turkey

Anger anyone? A. R. Dolan. Nat R 23:1117 O 8 '71
Beating the habit; agreement with U.S. to ban poppy planting. Newsweek 78:38+ Jl 12 '71
Let's halt heroin at the source. W. Schulz. Read Digest 98:97-101 My '71
Opium: sweeping the sands. Nation 213:421 N 1 '71
United States hails Turkish decision to ban opium poppy production; statement and remarks of President Nixon, and news conference of Secretary Rogers and Ambassador Esenbel, June 30, 1971. R. M. Nixon; W. P. Rogers; M. Esenbel. Dept State Bul 65:74-7 Jl 19 '71
OPPEN, Mary
In my window; poem. Nation 212:606 My 10 '71
Occulting light; poem. Nation 212:507 Ap 19 '71
OPPENHEIMER, Joan
Birds in a summer garden; story. Seventeen 29:90-1 Jl '71
Gift of home; story. Seventeen 29:152-3 S '70
Images; story. il Seventeen 30:146-7 S '71
OPPERSDORFF, Mathias
Portrait of tinkers; photographs. Natur Hist 80:2, 25-35+ D '71
OPPORTUNITIES Industrialization centers, Inc.
Steps we must take: training, economic development and togetherness; address, July 6, 1971. L. H. Sullivan. Vital Speeches 37:676-9 S 1 '71
Unorthodox ministry of Leon H. Sullivan. P. Garland. il pors Ebony 26:112-14+ My '71
OPPORTUNITY cost. See Cost
OPPRESSION
Repressive violence. E. Currie. Trans-Action 8:12-14+ F '71; Same abr. with title Violent America: a new myth? Cur 128:29-33 Ap '71
OPTIC nerve
Receptive field organization of units in the first optic ganglion of diptera. D. W. Arnett. bibliog il Science 173:929-31 S 3 '71

OPTIC thalamus
Contours and contrast: responses of monkey lateral geniculate nucleus cells to luminance and color figures. R. L. De Valois and P. L. Pease. bibliog il Science 171:694-6 F 19 '71
Mutants with abnormal visual pathways: an explanation of anomalous geniculate laminae. R. W. Guillery and others. bibliog il Science 174:831-2 N 19 '71
Visual attention in the tree shrew: an ablation study of the striate and extrastriate visual cortex. H. Killackey and I. T. Diamond. bibliog il Science 171:696-9 F 19 '71
OPTICAL art. See Art, Modern
OPTICAL character recognition. See Optical scanners
OPTICAL communications systems. See Light communication systems
OPTICAL crystallography. See Crystal optics
OPTICAL data processing
See also
Optical pattern recognition
Optical scanners
OPTICAL fibers. See Fiber optics
OPTICAL illusions
Amateur scientists; generating visual illusions with two kinds of apparatus. C. L. Stong. il Sci Am 224:110-14 Mr '71
Fortification illusions of migraines. W. Richards. il Sci Am 224:88-94+ bibliog(p 132) My '71
Interocular apparent movement in depth: a motion preference effect. S. H. Ferris and N. Pastore. bibliog il Science 174:305-7 O 15 '71
Multistability in perception. F. Attneave. il Sci Am 225:62-71 D '71
Optical illusions, how one kind can cancel out another. R. Dreistadt. il Sci Digest 69:10-14 F '71
Visual illusions. M. Shaw. il Sch Arts 71:40 N '71
OPTICAL industry
See also
Bausch and Lomb, inc.
Photographic apparatus and supplies industry
Poly-Optics, inc
OPTICAL instruments
See also
Lenses
Schlieren apparatus
Spectrohelioscope
Telescopes
OPTICAL pattern recognition
Advances in pattern recognition. R. G. Casey and G. Nagy. il Sci Am 224:56-64 Ap '71
Extremely rapid visual search: the maximum rate of scanning letters for the presence of a numeral. G. Sperling and others. bibliog il Science 174:307-11 O 15 '71
See also
Optical scanners
OPTICAL pyrometers. See Pyrometers and pyrometry
OPTICAL reading machines. See Optical scanners
OPTICAL scanners
Automatic railroad-car identification; optical-electronic scanning system for freight cars. D. L. Heiserman. il Electr World 86:46-7 S '71
Optical character recognition. D. L. Heiserman. il Electr World 85:43-4+ Ap '71
Write it once and retain it; computer and optical character recognition. D. W. Brown. il por Am City 86:81-2 N '71
See also
Optical pattern recognition
OPTICAL spectrum analysis. See Spectrum analysis
OPTICAL tracking of space vehicles. See Space vehicles—Tracking
OPTICS
See also
Aberration (optics)
Electron optics
Electrooptics
Fiber optics
Magneto-optics
Nonlinear optics
Perspective
Photographic optics
Reflection (optics)
OPTICS, Physiological
Visual phenomena noted by human subjects on exposure to neutrons of energies less than 25 million electron volts. T. F. Budinger and others. bibliog il Science 172:868-70 My 21 '71
See also
Optical illusions
Sight

OPTIONS
See also
Put and call transactions
Stock purchase options
OPTOACOUSTIC spectroscopy. See Spectrum analysis
OPTOELECTRONICS. See Electron optics
OPUS Dei (secular institute)
Commune for conservatives; student residences. il Time 97:59 Mr 1 '71
In the twilight of the Franco era. S. G. Payne. For Affairs 49:342-54 Ja '71
O'QUIN, Sally
After the quake: the psychic tremors still shake people up. il Todays Health 49:20-2+ My '71
(ed) See Hayakawa, S. I. Most precious gift a father can give to his son
ORAL composition. See English language—Composition
ORAL contraceptives. See Contraceptives
ORAL history
Murrow's legatees; Columbia's oral scrapbook of the sixties. M. Kempton. il Hi Fi 21:63-4 My '71
Prestige of the spoken word; Africa. il UNESCO Courier 24:26-7 Ja '71
Tape documentaries start at home. J. Matcha. il Pop Phot 68:37-8 Je '71
ORANGE, N.J public library
Information exchange; Read and return collection of multiple copies of popular books. M. H. Scilken. il Wilson Lib Bul 46:104-5 S '71
ORANGE COUNTY, N.Y.
Architecture
See Architecture—New York (state)
ORANGE juice
See also
Tropicana products, inc.
ORANGEBURG, S.C.
Riots
Orangeburg massacare, by J. Nelson and J. Bass. Review
Cath World 214:39 O '71. R. E. Forbes
ORANGES
Organic oranges: California and Florida style. M. C. Goldman. il Org Gard & Farm 18:80+ N '71
See also
Cookery—Fruit
ORATORIOS
1803 version of Beethoven's Christus am Oelberge. A. Tyson. bibliog f il Mus Q 56: 551-84 O '70
See also
Phonograph records—Oratorios
ORATORY
Silence, gentlemen, please: prominent personages who have nothing to say. T. Beeson. Chr Cent 89:6-7 Ja 5 '72
ORBITAL motion of the earth. See Earth—Orbital motion
ORBITAL platforms. See Space stations
ORBITAL rendezvous (space flight)
Apollo 14's lunar ascent near perfect. il Aviation W 94:25 F 15 '71
Apollo-Salyut, Soyuz-Skylab dockings eyed. Z. Strickland. Aviation W 95:17-18 S 13 '71
Docking of Apollo-Soyuz proposed. Z. Strickland. Aviation W 94:16-17 Ap 12 '71
Docking the Apollo. il Space World H-5-89: 41-5 My '71
Post-Skylab plans focus on earth orbital missions. Z. Strickland. il Aviation W 95: 15-17 O 11 '71
Visibility problem in docking. Space World H-3-87:21 Mr '71
When Soyuz meets Skylab. Sci N 100:167 S 11 '71
ORBITING solar observatory. See Artificial satellites—Astronomical use
ORBITOLINA. See Foraminifera, Fossil
ORBITS
See also
Mechanics, Celestial
Space vehicles—Orbits
ORBITS of communications satellites. See Communications satellites—Orbits
ORCHARDS. See Fruit culture
ORCHESTRA shells
Technology; new acoustical spaces. il Arch Forum 134:64-7 Mr '71
ORCHESTRAL concerts. See Concerts
ORCHESTRAL music
See also
Phonograph records—Orchestral music
Symphonies

ORCHESTRAS
American festival orchestra goes to Italy. J. Strasser. il Hi Fi 21:MA10-11 F '71
Birth of an ensemble; Chicago's lyric opera. G. McElroy. il Opera N 36:16-18 O '71
Debuts & reappearances; New York concerts. See issues of High fidelity and Musical America
Orchestra coast to coast. il Newsweek 78:89 O 11 '71
    See also names of orchestras, e.g. Chicago symphony orchestra

ORCHIDS
Exquisite orchids. L. Marden. il Nat Geog 139:484-513 Ap '71
Inexpensive orchids; miniature cymbidium. il Sunset 147:197 D '71
Lisa Gordon's discovery; one orchid leads to another and another. il Sunset 146:230-1 Je '71
My love affair with orchids. R. Peterson. il Home Gard 58:46-7 Ap '71
Phalaenopsis, the moth orchids. H. R. Sweet. il Horticulture 49:24-5+ N '71

ORDINANCES, Municipal. See Municipal ordinances

ORDNANCE
    See also
Weapons systems

ORDÓÑEZ, Antonio
On offering the bull his body. J. McCormick. il pors Sports Illus 34:26-8+ Je 14 '71

ORDOVICIAN formation. See Geology, Stratigraphic—Ordovician

ORE deposits
    See also
Prospecting

OREGON
    See also
Columbia River
Fishing—Oregon
Forests and forestry—Oregon

Legislature
Deposit on litter; bill banning throwaway bottles and cans. Nation 213:6 Jl 5 '71

Politics and government
Oregon: gunning for Hatfield. R. Friedman. Nation 212:781-2 Je 21 '71

OREGON Shakespearean festival. See Shakespeare festivals

OREGONIAN (newspaper) See Portland, Ore.—Newspapers

O'REILLY, Anthony J. F.
Irish wunderkind joins U.S. Heinz. il por Bsns W p57-8 S 11 '71 *

O'REILLY, Don
(ed) See Passino, J. Racetrack is still Detroit's best test track!

O'REILLY, Jane
Colorado, the American family vacation state. il Holiday 49:42-9+ Mr '71
Kir. il Holiday 48:68-9 S '70

ORES
    See also
Chromium ores

ORFEO ed Euridice; opera. See Gluck, C. W.

ORFF, Carl
Theater of folk ritual. J. Rockwell. il por Opera N 35:8-12 Ja 16 '71 *

ORGAN, Troy
Cosmological Christology. Chr Cent 88:1293-5 N 3 '71

ORGAN, Electronic
Computer organ has virtually unlimited voicing. il Pop Electr 35:66-7 Ag '71
Electronic organs. il Consumer Bul 54:29-31 Mr '71

Equipment
Leslie effect simulator; all-electronic organ accessory. J. S. Simonton, jr. il Pop Electr 34:51-3+ Mr '71
Pipe speaker system. J. R. Smith. il Electr World 86:24-6 D '71

ORGAN music
In the mood for baseball; organ music between-innings at Shea Stadium. R. Cantwell. il Sports Illus 34:54-6+ Je 7 '71
    See also
Phonograph records—Organ music

ORGANELLES. See Cells

ORGANIC cosmetics. See Cosmetics

ORGANIC farm management. See Farm management

ORGANIC farmers. See Farmers

ORGANIC farms. See Farms, Organic

ORGANIC food. See Food, Organic

ORGANIC food stores. See Food stores

ORGANIC gardening
For farmers mainly. Org Gard & Farm 18:88-90 My '71
Garbage farming. M. Franz. il Org Gard & Farm 18:58-62 Ja '71
Garden calendar. See issues of Organic gardening and farming
Guru of the organic food cult. W. Greene. il pors N Y Times Mag p30-1+ Je 6 '71
High-altitude gardening, a success story. E. D. Johnson. il Org Gard & Farm 18:64-5 My '71
How to strengthen your organic family. R. Rodale. il Org Gard & Farm 18:32-7 D '71
Is organic gardening success easy? il Sunset 146:216-17 Mr '71
Know your organic farmer. M. C. Goldman. il Org Gard & Farm 18:69-72 Je '71
Life inside a hippie commune. L. Robinson. il Ebony 26:88-91+ N '70
Looking for the organic America; stickin' your neck out. F. Allen. il Org Gard & Farm 18:40-3 Je '71
My organic mother-in-law's lakeside garden. J. Vivian. il Org Gard & Farm 18:37-9 Ap '71
One-acre garden for $10.50. P. Wartiainen, jr. il Org Gard & Farm 18:86 My '71
Open letter from an apple grower. M. C. Loken. Org Gard & Farm 18:21-3 My '71
Organic farmer. il Org Gard & Farm 18:74-87+ O; 105-12+ N; 78-85+ D '71
Organic; magic word at the food counter, many doubts on the farm. G. Logsdon. il Farm J 95:20-1+ D '71
Our organic mobile home garden. E. M. Stevens. il Org Gard & Farm 18:53 D '71
Postscript to the California growers meeting. F. Allen. Org Gard & Farm 18:75-6 Je '71
Put it back! J. Olds. il Org Gard & Farm 18:48-50 Mr '71
Responsibility of being organic. R. Rodale. il Org Gard & Farm 18:34-8 Mr '71
Santa Barbara plan; organic community garden. F. Allen. il Org Gard & Farm 18:68-71 Ja '71
Shaping an organic America. J. H. Todd. il Org Gard & Farm 18:50-5 S; 78-85 O; 63-9 N; 57-61 D '71
Step-by-step to organic vegetable growing, by S. Ogden. Review
    Org Gard & Farm 18:79 Jl '71
Very personal garden of Harry Rogers; an easy-does-it organic garden. il House & Gard 140:64-7+ Jl '71
Young people, are they America's new peasantry? R. Rodale. il Org Gard & Farm 18:30-3 My '71
    See also
Compost
Food, Organic
Mulching
Vegetable gardening, Home

Study and teaching
Planting the organic seed. T. D. Fegely. il Org Gard & Farm 18:52-3 Mr '71

ORGANIC gardening and farming (periodical)
Catching up to Rodale press. il por Time 97:51 Mr 22 '71
Organic farmer section is reborn. J. Goldstein. il Org Gard & Farm 18:56-8 S '71
Why I started Organic gardening. J. I. Rodale. il por Org Gard & Farm 18:35-40 S '71

ORGANIC gardening clubs. See Garden clubs

ORGANIC phosphates. See Phosphates

ORGANIZATION, Social. See Social organization

ORGANIZATION for economic cooperation and development
Greening of technology. Sci Am 225:44 Ag '71
Tenth meeting of OECD ministerial council held at Paris; statements with text of communique, June 8, 1971. W. P. Rogers; N. Samuels; H. Stein. Dept State Bul 65:11-21 Jl 5 '71

ORGANIZATION of African unity
Address by president of Mauritania; summary of address, September 24, 1971. UN Mo Chron 8:66-7 O '71
Four wise men; African leaders on peace mission to Israel. il por Time 98:38 N 15 '71
Four wise men; mission to aid in the settlement of the Arab-Israeli dispute. Newsweek 78:42 N 15 '71

ORGANIZATION of American states
Hemisphere. See issues of Américas
Hemisphere foreign ministers meet in OAS General assembly; convention designed to curb terrorist crimes. Américas 23:44 Mr '71

ORGANIZATION of American states—*Cont.*
More balanced and reinvigorated partnership of the Americas; statement, April 15, 1971. W. P. Rogers. Dept State Bul 64:602-7 My 10 '71
OAS foreign ministers discuss coastal state fisheries question; statements, with text of resolution. J. J. Jova; J. N. Irwin. Dept State Bul 64:245-50 F 22 '71
OAS today; excerpt from address, October 18, 1970. G. Plaza. il por Américas 23:513-15 Ja '71
Review of the progress and problems of the Organization of American states; statement, July 26, 1971. J. J. Jova. bibliog f il Dept State Bul 65:284-93 S 13 '71
Third special session of the OAS general assembly adopts measures on kidnaping and terrorism; statements, with text of convention and resolution. W. P. Rogers. Dept State Bul 64:228-34 F 22 '71
What is the OAS doing? G. Plaza. il Américas 23:42 Ap '71
See also
Inter-American children's institute
Inter-American economic and social council

General assembly
Address by the Secretary-General to the Organization of American states; April 14, 1971. Thant. UN Mo Chron 8:42-9 My '71
First General assembly. G. Meek. il Américas 23:2-7 Je '71

ORGANIZATION of petroleum exporting countries
Big squeeze. il Newsweek 77:63 F 15 '71
Crisis in Teheran. Newsweek 77:72+ F 8 '71
Desert foxes. il Time 97:69-70 F 15 '71
Higher prices for oil: who will get hit. il U S News 70:52-4 Mr 1 '71
How the Arabs changed the oil business. G. Breckenfeld. il Fortune 84:112-16+ Ag '71
Is a cartel next for oilmen? il Bsns W p70-1 Ja 23 '71
Mideast oil pact: stability at a price. il Bsns W p23 F 20 '71
Oil countries grab a bigger share. il Bsns W p40 D 18 '71
Oil flows on. Sr Schol 98:15 Mr 15 '71
Oil giants brace for big changes. il Bsns W p 14-15 Ja 30 '71
Oil power. W. J. Levy. For Affairs 49:652-68 Jl '71
What is a fair price for oil? P. H. Abelson. Science 171:633 F 19 '71
What price oil for the lamps of the world? il Fortune 83:30 Mr '71
ORGANIZATIONAL change
Eclectic approach to organizational development. E. F. Huse and M. Beer. il Harvard Bsns R 49:103-12 S '71
ORGANIZATIONS. See Associations, institutions, etc.
ORGANIZED crime. See Crime and criminals—United States; Mafia
ORGANOMETALLIC compounds
Combination: method of joining noble metals with organic compounds. Newsweek 78: 101-2 D 20 '71
ORGANOTHERAPY. See Cellular therapy
ORGASM
Gospel of orgasm. il por Time 97:54-5 My 10 '71
ORGEL, L. E. See Lohrmann, R. jt. auth.
ORIENTAL American students
Yellow youth's psychological struggle; excerpts from essays. M. Maruyama. Ment Hy 55:382-90 Jl '71
ORIENTAL carpets. See Rugs and carpets, Oriental
ORIENTAL cookery. See Cookery, Oriental
ORIENTAL dolls. See Dolls
ORIENTAL house decoration. See House decoration, Oriental
ORIENTAL Jews. See Sephardim
ORIENTAL Lowestoft. See Pottery, Chinese
ORIENTAL poppies. See Poppies
ORIENTAL rites. See Catholic church—Oriental rites
ORIENTAL rugs. See Rugs and carpets, Oriental
ORIENTAL students in the United States. See Foreign students in the United States
ORIENTAL studies
See also
Chinese studies (Sinology)
ORIENTATION
Celestial navigation by migrating birds. Sky & Tel 41:80 F '71
Celestial rotation: its importance in the development of migratory orientation. S. T. Emlen; reply with rejoinder. E. G. F. Sauer. bibliog Science 173:459-61 Jl 30 '71

Color- and edge-sensitive channels in the human visual system: tuning for orientation. R. Held and S. R. Shattuck. bibliog il Science 174:314-16 O 15 '71
Flight orientation in locusts. J. M. Camhi. il Sci Am 225:74-81 bibliog(p 120) Ag '71
Homing in the harvester ant pogonomyrmex badius. B. Hölldobler. bibliog il Science 171: 1149-51 Mr 19 '71
Migratory bird navigation experiment. Space World H-11-95:43-4 N '71
See also
Echolocation (physiology)
ORIENTATION of teachers. See Teachers—Adjustment
ORIENTEERING (sport)
Correcting map declination. E. P. Doclar. jr. il Field & S 76:82 N '71
ORIGIN of life. See Life (biology)—Origin
ORIGIN of man. See Man—Origin and antiquity
ORIGIN of species. See Evolution
ORIGINALITY. See Creation (literary, artistic, etc)
ORIGO, Iris
Images and shadows, by I. Origo. Review Sat R 54:27-8 My 8 '71. G. Gersh •
Peripatetic reviewer. E. Weeks. Atlan 228: 101-2 Jl '71 •
Twentieth century renaissance woman. K. G. Chapin. New Repub 164:25-8 My 8 '71 •
ORINGER, Judy
(ed) See Nin, A. Anaïs Nin on women
ORIOLES (baseball) See Baseball clubs
ORISSA cyclone. See Cyclones
ORLANDO, Guido
Guido Orlando: cosa sua. D. Rader. il pors Esquire 75:134-7+ Ja '71 •
ORLANDO, Fla.

Music
Report:
Manon Lescaut. M. E. Peltz. Opera N 35:30 Ap 3 '71

Water supply
Unmanned satellite water plants. W. L. Birdyshaw. il Am City 86:97-9 Ag '71
ORLANDO press. See Publishers and publishing—Great Britain
ORLANS, Harold
Political uses of social research. Ann Am Acad 394:28-35 Mr '71
ORLÉANS, France
One right way to write and think? E. Morin's analysis of anti-Semitism. B. DeMott. Am Scholar 41:53-62 Wint '71
ORLEN, Steven
Sleeping on doors; Deserted husband; To a child courting death; poems. Poetry 119:71-3 N '71
ORLOW, Alexander
Art on the line. il Newsweek 77:80-3 Ap 12 '71 •
ORLY; story. See Monell, L.
ORMEN, Ian B.
Lasting piece of art. il Sch Arts 71:28-9 Ja '72
ORNAMENTAL cabbage. See Flowering cabbage
ORNAMENTAL cookery. See Cookery, Ornamental
ORNAMENTAL glass. See Glass, Ornamental
ORNAMENTAL grasses. See Grasses
ORNAMENTAL plants. See Plants, Ornamental
ORNAMENTS, Christmas tree. See Christmas decorations
ORNE, Jerrold
Renaissance of academic library building 1967-1971. il por Library J 96:3947-67 D 1 '71
ORNITHINE decarboxylase. See Decarboxylase
ORNITHOGALUMS
Pregnant onion will multiply. il Sunset 147: 263 N '71
ORNITHOPTERS
They wanted wings; birdmen in flying contest. il Time 98:25 Ag 23 '71
ORNITZ, Don
Nude as nature. J. Scully. il Mod Phot 34: 76-9 N '70 •
ORNSTEIN, Allan C.
Myths of liberalism and school integration. Sch & Soc 99:436-9 N '71
ORPHANS and orphan asylums
Bringing themselves up; the six orphaned Gregorys. M. Gross. il pors Good H 173: 42-4+ S '71
Nobody's children; orphans in Rome. il Time 97:27 Mr 8 '71
See also
Homes, institutional
ORPHEUS (operatic character) See Characters in opera

ORPHIREM, Hiram
Researching the parables. P. Steinfels. Commonweal 94:230 My 14 '71 *

ORR, Bobby
Hottest man on ice. B. Surface. il por Read Digest 98:219-20+ F '71 *
Orr effect. T. Dowling. il Atlan 227:62-8 Ap '71 *
Sporting scene. H. W. Wind. New Yorker 47:107-14 Mr 27 '71 *

ORR, Isabel
Granny Orr's great manure maneuver. M. Sweeney. Farm J 95:54 F '71 *

ORR, John D.
Put fun into camp dining room clean-up. il Camp Mag 43:50 Mr '71

ORRICK, Richard
Arts flash from Europe. Vogue 158:72-4 N 1 '71

ORSHEFSKY, Milton
Bulldozers carve out Israel's new frontiers. il Life 70:32-4 Mr 12 '71
Hildegard rides again. il pors Life 71:36-7 Jl 23 '71

ORSY, Ladislas M.
Priest: center of unity in the Christian community. America 125:205-8 S 25 '71
Theology, university and a brave new world. America 124:606-8 Je 12 '71

ORTEGO, Philip D.
Schools for Mexican-Americans: between two cultures. il Sat R 54:62-4+ Ap 17 '71

ORTH, Bob
To Brother Thomas Merton; poem. Cath World 213:40 Ap '71

ORTH, Charles D. 3d, and Jacobs, Frederic
Women in management: pattern for change. bibliog f Harvard Bsns R 49:139-47 Jl '71

ORTHODOX Eastern church
No private affair; renewal in the Greek church. Chr Today 15:23 Ag 27 '71; Reply. R. G. Stephanopoulos. 16:19 O 22 '71
Our far-flung correspondents; burial in Venice of l. F. Stravinsky. F. Steegmuller. New Yorker 47:99-103 My 1 '71
See also
Ethiopic church

ORTHODOX Eastern church, Russian
New patriarch in Moscow. America 124:642 Je 26 '71
New Russian patriarch: acceptable to both church and state. M. Bourdeaux. Chr Cent 88:932-3 Ag 4 '71
Pimen named patriarch of Russian church. Chr Cent 88:770 Je 23 '71
Russian orthodoxy in crucial council. M. Bourdeaux. Chr Cent 88:646-7 My 26 '71
Russia's new patriarch. por Newsweek 77:114 Je 14 '71

ORTHODOX Eastern church in the United States
American Orthodox Christians in search of mission. C. B. Ashanin. Chr Cent 88:465-6 Ap 14 '71

ORTHOPEDIA
Incomplete twin. il Time 97:57 Je 28 '71

ORTHOPYROXENES. See Pyroxenes

ORTIZ, Ralph
Culture and the people. Art in Am 59:27 My '71

ORVIS, Pat
Teen travel talk: where the Cochrans ski. il Seventeen 29:62 D '70

ORWELL, George, pseud.
George Orwell, by R. Williams. Review Nation 213:341-2 O 11 '71. G. Woodcock *

ORYXES. See Antelopes

OSAWATOMIE, Kan.

Lighting
Lighting adds glamor to downtown facelift. G. Schrader. il Am City 86:122+ Ap '71

OSBORN, Jeanne
Ghost of the hairy Javelin. il Am Lib 2:747-9 Jl '71

OSBORN, Lynn
Elegy for an old home. il Har Yrs 11:30-1+ O '71

OSBORN, Michelle
Crosstown is dead, long live the crosstown? il Arch Forum 135:39-41 O '71

OSBORN, Robert T.
Religion on the campus. il Chr Cent 88:1161-3 O 6 '71

OSBORNE, Conrad L.
Kubelik's Lohengrin. il Hi Fi 21:77-9 D '71
Pathé's complete Romeo et Juliette, 1912. il Hi Fi 21:78-9 Ap '71
Revolution comes to opera. il Hi Fi 21:62-70 N '71
Vocal reissues, Italian style. por Hi Fi 21:24+ Mr '71

OSBORNE, Grace S. and Hurlburt, A. S.
Credibility gap in supervision. bibliog Sch & Soc 99:415-17 N '71

OSBORNE, Grant R. See Pinnock, C. H. jt. auth.

OSBORNE, John, 1907-
Nixon watch. See issues of New republic

about
Watch on the Potomac. il por Time 97:72+ My 10 '71 *

OSBORNE, John P.
Growing alpines under glass. il Horticulture 49:34-5 F '71

OSBORNE, Karl
Rock riot at Nags Head. il pors Outdoor Life 148:56-7+ N '71

OSBORNE, T. Z. and Shaw, R. E.
Multipurpose water program. il Am City 86:95+ Ap '71

OSCARS (prizes) See Academy awards (moving pictures)

OSCILLATIONS
Overtones of free oscillations and the structure of the earth's interior. A. M. Dziewonski. bibliog il Science 172:1336-8 Je 25 '71
See also
Damping (mechanics)

OSCILLATORS
Build the fil-oscillator; sharp audio filter & versatile waveform generator. R. Melen and H. Garland. il Pop Electr 34:58-62 My '71
Designing a phase-shift oscillator. J. L. Turino. il Electr World 86:34-5 Jl '71
One IC audio generator. R. D. Crawford. il Radio-Electr 42:37-8 F '71
Relaxation oscillators, old and new. R. D. Clement and R. L. Starliper. il Electr World 85:36-7 My '71
See also
Multivibrators

OSCILLATORS, Crystal
Low-power crystal-controlled oscillator. J. H. Wujek. il Electr World 86:69 D '71

OSCILLOGRAPHS
Add triggered sweep to your scope. H. Garland and R. Melen. il Pop Electr 35:61-6 Jl '71
Build a scope camera for $45. J. Darr. il Radio-Electr 42:43-5 N '71
Kikusui alignment scope model 5121. il Radio-Electr 42:58 Jl '71
Leader LBO-54B oscilloscope. il Radio-Electr 42:14 Ag '71
Lectrotech TO-50 triggered-sweep scope. J. Fitzgibbon. Radio-Electr 42:22 Mr '71
Oscilloscopes for servicing; with tables. S. R. Prentiss. il Electr World 86:27-31+ N '71
Product gallery; Leader instruments LBO-501 oscilloscope. il Pop Electr 34:78-80 F '71
Transistor and FET curve tracer; scope adapter. D. Metzger. il Electr World 86:52-4 Ag '71
Why triggered sweep oscilloscopes? S. Prentiss. il Pop Electr 1:68+ Ja '72

OSCILLOSCOPE calibrators. See Calibrators

OSCILLOSCOPES. See Oscillographs

OSCO drug, inc.
Prescription prices lose their mystery. Bsns W p21-2 D 18 '71

OSIPOV, A.
New theory on excitations between spheres of the globe. Space World H-12-96:46 D '71

OSMOSIS
Amateur scientist; an osmotic pump, an unusual timer and how to enhance contrast in astronomical photographs. O. Levenspiel. il Sci Am 225:100 D '71
Invisible wall that purifies water; reverse osmosis filtration system. D. X. Manners. il Sci Digest 69:70-3 Je '71
Reversible osmotic opening of the blood-brain barrier. S. I. Rapoport and others. bibliog il Science 173:1026-8 S 10 '71
State of water in red cells. A. K. Solomon. il Sci Am 224:88-96 F '71
See also
Biological transport

OSORIO, Carlos Manuel Arana. See Arana Osorio, C. M.

OSPREYS
Last hope for the ospreys of Long Island Sound. D. R. Zimmerman. il por N Y Times Mag p38-40+ D 12 '71; Discussion. p28 Ja 9 '72

OSSA, Nena
Chile's Che Guevara? Nat R 23:307-8 Mr 23 '71

OSTAPOWICZ, Frank
Anesthesia and analgesia during childbirth; ed. by S. Olds. Redbook 136:12+ Ap '71

OSTEOGENESIS imperfecta
Progress report. G. Geisman. por Redbook 138:184 D '71
OSTEOGENIC sarcoma. See Sarcoma
OSTERMANN, Robert
Speechless page after page. New Repub 164:28-31 My 1 '71
OSTRANDER, Sheila, and Schroeder, Lynn
Birth control by astrology; excerpt from Psychic discoveries behind the Iron curtain. Harp Baz 104:104-5 F '71
OSTRIKER, Jeremiah P.
Nature of pulsars; with biographical sketch. il Sci Am 224:12, 48-60 Ja '71
OSTROVE, Geraldine
Harford theater is a group effort. il Hi Fi 21:MA20-2 N '71
OSTROVSKII, Aleksandr Nikolaevich
Diary of a scoundrel. Criticism
Newsweek il 78:86 N 22 '71
OSWALD, Lee Harvey
Oswald and the U-2. il por Newsweek 77:31 Mr 1 '71
OSWALD, Russell G.
Bloody Attica: furies unleashed. il pors Newsweek 78:22-6+ S 27 '71 *
War at Attica: was there no other way? il por Time 98:18-26 S 27 '71 *
OTEPKA, Otto F.
Amplification; editorial reply. N Y Time Mag p42-3 Je 27 '71 *
OTHELLO; drama. See Shakespeare, W.—Plays
OTIS, Amos
Noble mobile from Mobile. L. Keith. por Sports Illus 34:52 Je 21 '71 *
OTIS, Elisha Graves
World's fair stunt that lifted skylines. R. A. Weller. il pors Nations Bsns 59:82-3 Ja '71 *
OTIS elevator company
World's fair stunt that lifted skylines. R. A. Weller. il pors Nations Bsns 59:82-3 Ja '71
OTOLITHS. See Labyrinth (ear)
O'TOOLE, William
Spiro and the Buchwald blues. Commonweal 93:465 F 12 '71
OTTAWA
Ottawa is the capital of Canada, but what else is it? M. Richler. il Holiday 48:58-9+ N '70
OTTERBINE jet propulsion unit. See Motor boat engines
OTTERS
Confessions of an otter addict. M. Sprague. il Nat Wildlife 9:13-16 Ag '71
See also
Sea otters
OTTINA, John R.
Highlights of OE's 1972 budget. il Am Ed 7:36-7 Ag '71
OTTO, Dave
Up the down lakers. il por Outdoor Life 148:56-7+ Jl '71
OTTO, Frei
Architecture. F. Gutheim. Nation 213:190 S 6 '71 *
OTTO, Herbert A.
Communes: the alternative life-style. il Sat R 54:16-21 Ap 24 '71; Same abr. Cur 130:15-22 Je '71
OTTUM, Bob
Boog! The big baseball musical. il Sports Illus 35:50-4+ Jl 19 '71
OTVÖS, Gabor
What a conductor is for; interview, ed. by S. L. Fobel. por Opera N 36:30 D 25 '71
OUABAIN
Cooperative control of potassium accumulation by ouabain in vascular smooth muscle. J. Gulati and A. W. Jones. bibliog il Science 172:1348-50 Je 25 '71
OUACHITA RIVER
Float note; canoeing. Travel 137:27 Ja '72
One man's fight. E. E. Guess. il pors Outdoor Life 147:4+ F '71
OUBRE, Hayward
Art of wire sculpture. il Design 72:4-5 midWint '71 *
OUDES, Bruce J.
Sweet bonus for apartheid. Nation 212:719-21 Je 7 '71
OUGHTON, Diana
Diana: the making of a terrorist, by T. Powers. Review
Sat R 54:35 My 1 '71. F. J. Cook *
OUCLOGUEM, Yambo
Yambo Ouologuem on violence, truth and black history; interview, ed. by L. Kuehl. por Commonweal 94:311-14 Je 11 '71

about

Africa's past: another version. C. R. Larson. Nation 212:697-9 My 31 '71 *
Books. J. Updike. New Yorker 47:187-8+ N 13 '71 *

OUR little girl is lost; story. See Ernst, P.
OUR things fell off the mountain; story. See Cain, E.
OUT of class examinations. See Examinations
OUT of the blue; story. See Robinson, B.
OUTBOARD motor boat racing. See Motor boat racing
OUTBOARD motor boats
Aquarod. H. Kelly. il Mech Illus 67:66-70+ Mr '71
Lots of class for bass; fish-n-ski boat. G. Reiger. il Pop Mech 135:102 My '71
Seaworthy Seamaster. G. W. Reiger. il Pop Mech 136:96-9 Jl '71
Shark: the boat they're all out to beat. J. Roe. il Pop Sci 199:34+ O '71
Small fishing boats. il Consumer Rep 36:423-9 Jl '71
"Yachting" eyes a boat:
Outboard Wellcraft airslot 24. R. Marston. il Yachting 129:72-3+ Mr '71
OUTBOARD motors
Consumer's guide to outboard motors. Mech Illus 67:82 Mr '71
Electric trolling motors. il Consumer Rep 36:160-9 Mr '71
Gasoline outboards under 9 hp. il Consumer Rep 36:354-62 Je '71
I added power tilt to my outboard. V. G. Shaw. il Pop Sci 198:93 Je '71
1971 motor facts and figures; table. Outdoor Life 147:71 Ja '71
1972 outboards. M. Crook. il Yachting 130:64-5+ O '71
Outboard power for 1972. F. M. Paulson. il Field & S 76:90-5 D '71
Outboards for '71: the engine story. J. Roe. il Pop Sci 198:84-5+ F '71
Outboards '72: all-purpose power. C. Miller. il Motor B & S 128:60-1+ O '71
Preview of the 1972 outboards. B. McKeown. il Mech Illus 67:80-1+ O '71
Recycling outboards: recirculating fuel system. M. Crook. il Yachting 130:53 S '71
Selecting the right outboard. V. L. Oertle. il Yachting 129:66-7+ Ap '71
65 hp from a 3-cylinder lightweight; Mercury 650, with table. J. Roe. il Pop Sci 199:76-7+ D '71

Maintenance and repair

Outboard maintenance in a can. M. Schultz. il Mech Illus 67:138+ N '71
Outboard motor. C. Miller. il Motor B & S 127:96-7 Ap '71
What I learned at outboard motor school can help you. E. H. Arctander. il Pop Sci 198:98-9 My '71
Why outboards fail. il Mech Illus 67:34+ Je '71
OUTDOOR art shows. See Art—Exhibitions
OUTDOOR bowling. See Bowling
OUTDOOR carpets, Cleaning of. See Rugs and carpets, Outdoor—Care
OUTDOOR Christmas decorations. See Christmas decorations, Outdoor
OUTDOOR concerts. See Concerts
OUTDOOR cookery. See Cookery, Outdoor
OUTDOOR education
Hawkeye outdoorsmen of Wilson junior high. H. Bradshaw and V. Bradshaw. il Field & S 76:78-9+ My '71
See also
Camping—Educational aspects
Conservation of resources—Study and teaching
Nature study
Outward bound schools
OUTDOOR games. See Games
OUTDOOR life
Endless weekend; special issue on Americans at play; symposium. il Life 71:8-24+ S 3 '71
Next time around. R. Starnes. Field & S 76:12+ O '71
Out trail. E. A. Shead. Nat Parks & Con Mag 45:11 Ja '71
Outdoors with Wynn Davis. W. Davis. See issues of Mechanix illustrated
Time for living. C. S. Murdock. il Liv Wildn 35:13-16 Spr '71
See also
Camping
Camps
Country life
Hunting
Mountaineering
Outdoor meals
Picnics
Survival after airplane accidents, shipwrecks, etc.
Walking
Wilderness survival
Winter sports

OWENS VALLEY, Calif.
North of Bishop, where to look for petroglyphs and pupfish. il Sunset 147:46+ O '71

OWENSBORO, Ky.
Local governments share a computer. M. N. Rhoads. il Am City 86:52 F '71

OWL monkeys. See Monkeys

OWLS
How owls spot their prey. il Sci Digest 70:81-2 Jl '71
Mystery of the snowy owl. J. George. il Read Digest 99:219-20+ N '71
Ookpikjuak comes to Long Island; snowy owl. R. Caras. il Nat Wildlife 9:10-11 F '71

OWO excavations. See Nigeria—Antiquities

OWSLEY, David T.
London silver in Pittsburgh. il Antiques 101:177-84 Ja '72

OXALATES
See also
Hyperoxaluria

OXALIS. See Wood sorrel

OXFORD English dictionary. See English language—Dictionaries

OXFORD. University
Seven Yanks at Oxford; basketball club. il Newsweek 79:46 Ja 10 '72

OXFORD university press
Candet in medio litterarum mundo prelum universitatis oxoniensis. C. Booker. il Esquire 76:100-3+ Jl '71

OXIDASES
Detoxication enzymes in the guts of caterpillars: an evolutionary answer to plant defenses? R. I. Krieger and others. bibliog il Science 172:579-81 My 7 '71
Induction of microsomal oxidase in F_1 hybrids of a high and a low oxidase housefly strain. L. C. Terriere and others. bibliog il Science 171:581-3 F 12 '71
Iron- and riboflavin-dependent metabolism of a monoamine in the rat in vivo. A. L. Symes and others. bibliog il Science 174:153-5 O 8 '71

OXIDATION
History and stability of atmospheric oxygen. L. Van Valen. bibliog Science 171:439-43 F 5 '71; Reply with rejoinder. B. Gregor. 174:316-17 O 15 '71
Kinetics of single-layer graphite oxidation: evaluation by electron microscopy. E. L. Evans and others. bibliog il Science 171:174-5 Ja 15 '71
Riboflavin photosensitized oxidation of 2,4-dichlorophenol: assessment of possible chlorinated dioxin formation. J. R. Plimmer and U. I. Klingebiel. bibliog il Science 174:407-8 O 22 '71
This plastic will self-destruct. Sci N 100:92 Ag 7 '71
See also
Antioxidants

OXIDATION, Physiological
See also
Cytochromes

OXIDATION ditches. See Sewage lagoons

OXIDES
See also
Nitrogen oxides

OXTOBY, Willard G.
Middle East: from polemic to accommodation. bibliog il por Chr Cent 88:1192-7 O 13 '71

OXYGEN
Facts of life. E. Gibbons. Org Gard & Farm 18:117-21 S '71
History and stability of atmospheric oxygen. L. Van Valen. bibliog Science 171:439-43 F 5 '71; Reply with rejoinder. B. Gregor. 174:316-17 O 15 '71
Oxygen-carrying iridium complexes: kinetics, mechanism, and thermodynamics. L. Vaska and others. bibliog il Science 174:587-9 N 5 '71
See also
Ozone
Space vehicles—Cabin atmospheres

OXYGEN in the body
See also
Asphyxia

OXYGEN therapy
See also
Spirometers

OXYTOCIN
Leucylglycinamide released from oxytocin by human uterine enzyme. R. Walter and others. bibliog il Science 173:827-9 Ag 27 '71

OYEVAAR, Jan J.
Technological change and the future of shipping in developing countries. bibliog f il Int Concil 582:44-65 Mr '71

OYSTERS
Mammalian blood, new food for oysters. S. V. Jones. il Sci Digest 70:69 O '71
See also
Cookery—Shellfish

OZ, Amos
Crusade; story. Commentary 52:42-60 Ag '71
about
Israel postscript: two writers. D. N. Mount. Pub W 199:31 Je 7 '71 *

OZARK MOUNTAINS
Land of the fifth season. E. Waldron. Il Holiday 49:72-4+ Ap '71

OZMON, Howard
Bertrand Russell: Socrates of our age. Ed Digest 36:34-6 F '71

OZONE
Reduction of stratospheric ozone by nitrogen oxide catalysts from supersonic transport exhaust. H. Johnston. bibliog il Science 173:517-22 Ag 6 '71

OZTEMEL, Ara
Horse trader at the highest level. por Bsns W p89-90 Je 19 '71 *

P

PAET (planetary atmosphere experiments test)
See Space probes

PAHO. See Pan American health organization

PAS (passing aid system) See Electronics in traffic control

PAYE (pay as you earn) See Student loans

PCB (polychlorinated biphenyls) See Diphenyl compounds

PEN club
50 years of P.E.N. T. Fleming. Pub W 200:pt2 184-6 S 27 '71
P.E.N. elects Fleming, gives translation award. il Pub W 199:31 Je 14 '71
Pleasures and pitfalls of an int'l writers' congress. S. Offit. Pub W 200:32-4 Ag 16 '71

PEP (Pollution and environmental problems)
See Environmental associations, committees, etc.

PGA tournament. See Golf—Tournaments

Ph.D. degrees. See Degrees, Academic

POW. See Prisoners of war

PPB. See Program budgeting

PSA. See Photographic society of America

PTA. See National congress of parents and teachers; Parents and teachers associations

PUSH. See People united to save humanity (organization)

PX. See United States—Armed forces—Post exchanges

PAARLBERG, Don
Phase 2: what will it mean to you? interview, ed. by F. Bailey, jr. il Suc Farm 69:9+ N '71
Washington report; interview, ed. by F. Bailey, jr. il Suc Farm 69:7+ O '71

PACE, Judy
Judy Pace: the thinking man's star. L. Robinson. il pors Ebony 26:112-14+ Mr '71 *

PACEMAKER, Artificial (heart)
Cardiac pacemakers. H. J. Sanders. il Chem 44:14-17 Jl '71
Change of pace; pacemaker malfunction from electrical interference. Sci Am 224:59 Je '71

PACHECO, Gene
Root work is fun to him. il por Mech Illus 67:72 Ap '71 *

PACHELBEL, Johann
Reviews of records. L. Noss. Mus Q 57:166-9 Ja '71 *

PACIFIC basin economic council
Japan's executives turn to diplomacy. il Bsns W p36-7 My 22 '71

PACIFIC coast
See also
Marine pollution—Pacific coast

Evacuation
See World war, 1939-1945—Evacuation of civilians

PACIFIC countries
See also
Anzus council

PACIFIC CREST TRAIL
Mexico to Canada on the Pacific Crest trail.
M. W. Edwards. il pors Nat Geog 139:741-
79 Je '71
Trails: so who needs them? D. B. Huyck.
il Am For 77:22-4+ O '71
Twenty-five hundred miles on horseback. B.
Murray. il pors Life 71:60-6+ S 3 '71
PACIFIC Islands. See Islands of the Pacific
PACIFIC ISLANDS, TRUST TERRITORY OF.
See Trust Territory of the Pacific Islands
PACIFIC NORTHWEST. See Northwest
PACIFIC NORTHWEST library association
Of note; sixty-first annual conference. C. Sy-
mon. Am Lib 2:1032 N '71
PACIFIC OCEAN
North Pacific circumnavigation. H. Roth. il
Yachting 130:52-4+ Jl; 52-3+ Ag; 54-5+ S;
58-9+ O '71 (to be cont)
See also
Coral Sea
Micronesia
Oceania
PACIFIC regional ballet festival. See Dance
festivals
PACIFIC salmon. See Salmon
PACIFIC Southwest airlines
PSA canceling L-1011 orders. Aviation W
96:21 Ja 3 '72
PACIFIC telephone and telegraph company
Cutting down Ma Bell. New Repub 165:10-
11 Jl 17 '71
PACIFIC TRUST TERRITORY. See Trust Ter-
ritory of the Pacific Islands
PACIFICA stations. See Radio stations
PACIFICATION programs in Vietnam. See
Vietnamese war, 1957- —Pacification pro-
grams
PACIFISM
Reporter at large; American Friends service
committee Peace education division. G.
Jonas. New Yorker 47:99-104+ Mr 20 '71
See also
Conscientious objectors
Vietnamese war, 1957- —Protests, demonstra-
tions, etc, against
PACIFISTS. See Pacifism
PACK, Arthur Newton
AFA annual meeting awards. il pors Am
For 77:6-7 D '71 *
Museum joins the forest service. F. A. Tink-
er. il por Am For 77:32-5 My '71 *
PACKAGE tours. See Travel
PACKAGED foods
Upsetting facts about our diet; sugar added
to processed foods. B. T. Hunter. il Con-
sumer Bul 54:4+ Jl '71
PACKAGED mixes. See Food mixes
PACKAGERS, Book. See Publishers and pub-
lishing
PACKAGES, Wrapping of. See Wrapping of
packages
PACKAGING
Return to cave and candle? W. F. May. il
Nations Bsns 59:81-3 N '71
Silent servant; packaging industry and the
problems of pollution; address, October 4,
1971. J. H. Alexander. Vital Speeches 38:
112-15 D 1 '71
Throw-away syndrome. E. Keller. Chem 44:2
My '71
See also
Gianninoto, Frank, and associates, inc.
Pressure packaging
PACKARD, David
Packard opposes broad loan plan. Aviation W
95:16 Jl 26 '71 *
Packard plan adopted by DOD to fund ad-
vances in technology. C. Brownlow. Avia-
tion W 95:15-16 Ag 2 '71 *
Packard resigns. Time 98:8 D 20 '71 *
Project bosses get more power. il por Bsns
W p96+ Mr 20 '71 *
Resignation's wider ripple. por Bsns W p68
D 18 '71 *
PACKARD, William
I remember as a child; poem. Nation 212:380
Mr 22 '71
PACKER, Dorothy S.
François Rabelais, vaudevilliste. bibliog f il
Mus Q 57:107-28 Ja '71
PACKER, Herbert L.
Pornography caper. bibliog f Commentary 51:
72-7 F; 52:36 Jl '71
PACKER, James S.
It don't hurt much, ma'am. il Am Heritage
22:66-9 F '71
PACKER, Rod E.
Science's eye on the universe. il Sci Digest
69:67-72 F '71

PACKING of luggage
How to pack a suitcase. il Mech Illus 67:59
Mr '71
Travelingest photographer of them all shares
some most cherished secrets. S. Nathan.
il Pop Phot 69:56+ S '71
PADDEN, R. C.
Reflections of a gilded cage. Harper 242:88-91
F '71
PADDLE steamers. See Steamships and steam-
boats
PADDLE tennis
Paddle is no longer piddling. G. S. Brown. il
Sports Illus 34:81-2 Ap 19 '71
Paddle, the new executive sport. R. Levy.
il Duns 98:49-51 O '71
PADDOCK, Polly. See Arthur, W. jr, jt. auth.
PADILLA, Alberto Ibáñez. See Ibáñez Padilla,
A.
PADILLA, Heberto
Trouble in Cuba. Nation 212:708 Je 7 '71 *
When friends fall out. por Time 97:30+ My
24 '71 *
PADLOCKS. See Locks and keys
PADOVANO, Anthony T.
Authority and conscience. il Cath World 213:
79-82 My '71
PADS, Rug. See Rug pads
PADWE, Sandy
Move over Mayor Daley: here comes Frank
Rizzo. por Ramp Mag 10:27-9 Ag '71
PAESTUM
Spoils of Paestum. M. Gendel. il Art N 70:
27-31+ Sum '71
PAETRO, Madeline E.
Getting a head start. il Library J 96:2846-7
S 15 '71
PAGAN, Alfred R.
New and old storm drains team up. il Am
City 86:112 Ap '71
PAGAN, Burma
Pagan, on the road to Mandalay. W. E. Gar-
rett. il Nat Geog 139:340-65 Mr '71
PAGANINI, Niccolò
Luciferian legacy. por Time 98:63 N 29 '71 *
PAGANISM
Homage to Iemanjá; pagan practices in
Brazil. il Time 99:44-5 Ja 10 '72
New paganism; Jesus the superstar. G. Mei-
laender, jr. il Chr Today 15:4-6 S 24 '71
PAGE, Irvine
Institute of medicine. Science 172:635 My 14
'71
PAGE, Joseph A.
Little priest who stands up to Brazil's gen-
erals. il por N Y Times Mag p26-7+ My 23
'71
Will the FDA get the lead out? Commonweal
95:246-7 D 10 '71
PAGE, Warren
Land of the blue wolf. il Field & S 76:54-5+
Ag '71
Sheep that is a goat. il Field & S 76:76-7+ Je
'71
(ed) Shooting. See issues of Field & stream
about
Editorial. C. Conley. Field & S 76:8 Ag '71 *
PAGEANTS
Bear Mountain's Christmas festival. S.
Traiman. il Parks & Rec 6:24-6 F '71
Come to the fair. J. Beatty, jr. il Redbook
137:87-90 Jl '71
PAGES, Congressional. See United States—Con-
gress—Pages
PAGET'S disease
Why Beethoven became deaf. Sci Digest 70:
26-7 D '71
PAGLIACCI; opera. See Leoncavallo, R.
PAHLAVI university. See Colleges and univer-
sities—Iran
PAHLEVI, Mohammed Reza, shah of Iran.
See Mohammed Reza Pahlevi
PAHLS, Martin L.
Golden oldies revisited. il Hi Fi 21:55-60 F
'71
PAID holidays. See Vacations, Employee
PAIGE, LeRoy. See Paige, S.
PAIGE, Satchel
Hollow ring to fame. por Ebony 26:124-5 Ap
'71 *
Parting shots: everybody wants Satchel Paige,
except the majors. por Life 71:65 Ag 27
'71 *
PAIK, Woon Ki, and Kim, Sangduk
Protein methylation. bibliog il Science 174:
114-19 O 8 '71
PAILS. See Buckets (pails)

PAIN
Controlling pain at the gate; dorsal column stimulation and saline injection. Sci N 100:7 Jl 3 '71
How much pain can you stand? A. J. Snider. il Sci Digest 69:55 Je '71
Jamming the pain waves. Newsweek 77:97 Ap 5 '71
Now: an electronic pain killer; dorsal column stimulator. A. S. Freese. il Pop Mech 136:68-71+ Jl '71
Shock-elicited pain and its reduction by concurrent tactile stimulation. J. D. Higgins and others. bibliog il Science 172:866-7 My 21 '71
Somatosensory responses of bulboreticular units in awake cat: relation to escape-producing stimuli. K. L. Casey. bibliog il Science 173:77-80 Jl 2 '71
Why leg pains? K. Anderson. il Har Yrs 11:46-8 Ag '71
See also
Analgesia
Suffering

PAIN killing drugs. See Analgesics
PAINESVILLE, Ohio

Municipal Improvement
It took a spud. G. Russell. il Am City 86:77 Ap '71

PAINT
Interior latex paints. il Consumer Rep 36:176-9 Mr '71
Marine paints for every purpose. J. L. Duffett. Motor B & S 127:92-3 Ap '71
New paints & varnishes. J. Hand. Mech Illus 67:87 Ag '71
Paint chemistry. J. L. Duffett. Motor B & S 127:92-3 Ap '71
Topside boat paints. il Consumer Rep 36:284-7 My '71
Will the FDA get the lead out? J. A. Page. Commonweal 95:246-7 D 10 '71

Testing
X-ray fluorescence: detection of lead in wall paint. G. R. Laurer and others. bibliog il Science 172:466-8 Ap 30 '71

PAINT, Protective
Barnacles and grasses are a pain on the bottom. E. A. Zadig. Motor B & S 127:90-1+ Je '71

PAINT industry
See also
Sherwin-Williams company

PAINTED pottery. See Pottery—Decoration
PAINTER, Charlotte
Confession from the Malaga madhouse, by C. Painter. Review
Sat R 54:45-6 N 6 '71. F. Lamport •

PAINTING
Art: decline of easel painting. L. Alloway. Nation 213:60-1 Jl 19 '71
See also
Color
Cubism
Finger painting
Genre painting
Impressionism (art)
Landscape painting
Marine painting
Mural painting and decoration
Portrait painting
Realism in art
Still life painting

Competitions
See Art—Competitions

Exhibitions
See Art—Exhibitions

Study and teaching
Hollywood community adult school. E. Blangsted. il Sch Arts 70:36-7 F '71
Painting with a brayer. J. Macey. il Sch Arts 71:8 D '71
Poetry and paint. R. Moore. il Sch Arts 70:16-17 Je '71

Technique
Acrylics: the opaque technique; excerpt from Complete guide to acrylic painting. W. Blake. il Am Artist 36:52-9+ Ja '72
Arthur Seller by design; interview, ed. by R. Kolbe. A. Seller. il por Am Artist 35:42-7+ S '71
Human touch: Gerard Knipscher. J. Vanderwall. il por Am Artist 35:38-43+ D '71
Virtuoso technique of Richard Schmid. A. R. Bloeme. il por Am Artist 35:20-7+ Ag '71
See also
Chiaroscuro
Palettes (colors)
Water color painting

PAINTING, Abstract. See Art, Abstract
PAINTING, Amateur. See Art, Amateur
PAINTING, American
Art out of the attic. C. Davidson. il Am Heritage 23:66-71 D '71
Canvases brimming with color. il Life 71:74-9 S 24 '71
Give my regards to Eighth street. M. Feldman. il por Art in am 59:96-9 Mr '71
Grand opera and the small still voice. B. Novak. il Art in Am 59:64-73 Mr '71
Picnics long ago; with paintings by artists of the Hudson River school. Am Heritage 22:42-7 Je '71
Things are thoughts in America. L. Campbell. il Art N 69:34-7+ F '71
Young America; collection of genre paintings for exhibition at Corcoran gallery of art in Washington, D.C. H. W. Williams, jr. il Am Heritage 22:16-32 F '71
See also
Albers, J.
Artists, American
Barker, J. J.
Baziotes, W. A.
Brooks, J.
Brown, H. J.
Budd, D.
Carter, C. H.
Chumley, J. W.
Clark, D.
Collins, P.
Davis, R.
Demuth, C.
Eakins, T.
Earl, R. E. W.
Evans, J.
Frankenthaler, H.
Freilicher, J.
Handell, A.
Harnett, W. M.
Hofmann, H.
Hopper, E.
Jenkins, G.
Johns, J.
Johnson, L.
Katz, A.
Kelly, E.
Knipscher, G.
Kraus, O.
Kulicke, R.
Lack, R. F.
Leffel, D. A.
Levine, D.
Libhart, J. J.
Lichtenstein, R.
Lucioni, L.
Marin, J.
Midgette, W. F.
Miller, A. J.
Nast, T.
Neel, A.
Newman, B.
Noland, K.
Peale, C. W.
Pearlstein, S.
Portrait painting
Portraits, American
Reid, C.
Remenick, S.
Ridenhour, W.
Rivers, L.
Rockwell, N.
Rothko, M.
Schmid, R.
Shikler, A.
Silverman, B.
Sloan, J.
Stella, F.
Trumbull, J.
Warhol, A.
Whistler, J. A. M.
Whitney museum of American art, New York
Whittaker, J. B.
Wiley, W. T.
Williams, W. T.
Wyeth, N. C.
Youngerman, J.

PAINTING, Austrian
See also
Kubin, A.

PAINTING, Baroque
Pseudo-Caravaggisti; exhibition at the Cleveland museum. R. E. Spear. il Art N 70:38-41+ N '71

PAINTING, British
Hidden art scene. J. Russell. il Art in Am 59:120-2 Mr '71
See also
Bacon, F.
Freud, L.
Hogarth, W.
Lewis, W.
Rossetti, D. G.
Rudge, J.
Salmon, R.
Sharples, J, family

PAINTING, Canadian
See also
Bush, J. H.
Kane, P.
PAINTING, Childrens. See Childrens art
PAINTING, Dutch
London; Dutch pictures from the Royal collection. J. Russell. il Art N 70:38+ Sum '71
See also
Gogh, V. van
Mondriaan, P. C.
PAINTING, Ecuadorian
See also
Kingman, E.
PAINTING, English. See Painting, British
PAINTING, European
Opening it up; Metropolitan's reinstallation; interview. E. Fahy. New Yorker 47:45-7 N 13 '71
PAINTING, Flemish
See also
Rubens, P. P.
Weyden, R. van der
PAINTING, French
See also
Braque, G.
Brayer, Y.
Buren, D.
Cézanne, P.
Courbet, G.
Couture, T.
Degas, E.
Dubuffet, J.
Duchamp, M.
Gauguin, P.
Géricault, T.
Hélion, J
Ingres, J. A. D.
Léger, F.
Michaux, H.
Monet, C.
Redon, O.
Seurat, G.
Vuillard, E.
PAINTING, German
See also
Dürer, A.
Ernst, M.
PAINTING, Gothic
Late Gothic and renaissance painting in northern Europe. il Design 72:6-10 mid-Wint '71
PAINTING, Industrial and practical
5 ways to shape a room with paint. il House & Gard 140:118-21 S '71
Here's help on painting problems. Sunset 147:82 Jl '71
How to save money when you paint. T. Philbin. il Mech Illus 67:94-6+ N '71
See also
Automobiles—Painting
Boats—Painting
House painting
Paint
Varnish and varnishing
PAINTING, Irish
See also
Dixon, S.
PAINTING, Italian
Orphan celebrated; 18th century Italian painting. R. Hughes. il Time 97:50-3 Mr 8 '71
Pseudo-Caravaggisti; exhibition at the Cleveland museum. R. E. Spear. il Art N 70:38-41+ N '71
See also
Botticelli, S.
De Luigi, L
Giorgione da Castelfranco
Mantegna, A.
Morandi, G.
Salviati, F.
PAINTING, Japanese
Japanese screens. R. Davidson. il Antiques 99:132-9; 100:190-1 Ja, Ag '71
Screens against the wind; byōbu. R. Hughes. il Time 97:69-71 Mr 15 '71
See also
Arakawa, S.
PAINTING, Manuscript. See Illumination of books and manuscripts
PAINTING, Mexican
See also
Covarrubias, M.
PAINTING, Modern. See Art, Modern
PAINTING, Peruvian
Inca baroque; Cuzco paintings at the Brooklyn museum. S. C. Faunce. il Art N 70:24-5 D '71
PAINTING, Puerto Rican
San Juan muralists. J. Gómez-Sicre. il Américas 23:2-9 Ag '71

PAINTING, Renaissance
Humanists. V. Cronin. il Horizon 13:80-103 Wint '71
Late Gothic and renaissance painting in northern Europe. il Design 72:6-10 mid-Wint '71
PAINTING, Russian
When the renaissance came to Russia; 20th century Russian art. A. Hilton. bibliog il Art N 70:34-9+ D '71
See also
Rodchenko, A.
Titov, ITu.
PAINTING, Spanish
See also
Goya y Lucientes, F. J. de
Picasso, P.
Velázquez, D. R. de S. y
PAINTING, Swedish
See also
Fahlström, Ö.
PAINTING, Uruguayan
See also
Torres-García, J.
PAINTING and photography. See Art and photography
PAINTING of Easter eggs. See Easter eggs
PAINTING on book edges. See Book ornamentation
PAINTING on glass. See Glass painting and staining
PAINTING on stone
Rock painting for fun and profit. J. Windle. il pors Design 72:20-1 mid-Wint '71
PAINTING on textiles. See Textile painting
PAINTINGS
Expensive nineteenth century. G. Keen. Art in Am 59:29 S '71
Greening of Pittsburgh. H. A. La Farge. il Art N 70:39-43+ My '71
Thirty hours plus thirty years. G. C. Moore. Am Artist 35:5 O '71
See also
Pictures

Appreciation
See Art—Appreciation

Prices
See Art—Prices

Technique
Conversation with Philip Pearlstein; ed. by E. Schwartz. P. Pearlstein. il Art in Am 59:50-7 S '71
PAINTINGS, Photography of. See Photography of works of art
PAINTINGS, Theft of. See Art thefts
PAINTINGS in factories. See Art in factories
PAISLEY, Ernest H.
Non-hazardous cockroach control. il Am City 86:60-1 Ja '71
PAK, Chung Hi. See Park, C. H.
PAK, William L. See Alawi, A. A. jt. auth.
PAKE, George E.
Whither United States universities? Science 172:908-16; 174:9 My 28, O 1 '71
PAKISTAN
Eyewitness in East Pakistan: an occupied, conquered territory. il U S News 71:44 Ag 23 '71
Lament for Pakistan; failure of the impossible dream. J. A. Michener. il N Y Times Mag p 11-13+ Ja 9 '72
Pakistan: what never gets said. P. Deutschman. Nation 213:457-60 N 8 '71
Staggered Pakistanis seek new start. il U S News 72:16 Ja 3 '72
Terrible wave; Ganges Delta disaster. J. P. Blank. il Read Digest 98:90-4 My '71
See also
Airlines—Pakistan
Bangladesh
Dacca
Economic assistance in Pakistan
Elections—Pakistan
Guerrillas—Pakistan
Kashmir
Military assistance, American—Pakistan
Trials—Pakistan
Wealth—Pakistan

Air force
Indian air power isolates Pakistani forces in east. il Aviation W 95:15-16 D 13 '71

Armed forces
My classmate the enemy; top officers. il Newsweek 78:38 D 20 '71

Army
Atrocities
Terrible blood bath of Tikka Khan. T. Clifton. il Newsweek 77:43-4 Je 28 '71

PAKISTAN—*Continued*

Civil war, 1971

Atop the volcano. Newsweek 77:38 Mr 29 '71

Bangla-desh. New Repub 164:9-10 Ap 17 '71 •

Battle of Kushtia; report on the civil war. il Time 97:20-1 Ap 19 '71

Bengal: the murder of a people; with reports by L. Jenkins and T. Clifton. il Newsweek 78:26-30 Ag 2 '71

Bloody surgery of Pakistan. A. Ahmad. Nation 212:815-19 Je 28 '71

Case against Pakistan. America 124:645-6 Je 26 '71

Civil war ravages Bangla Desh. il Sr Schol 98:14 My 3 '71

Coming apart; East-West split. il Newsweek 77:54+ Mr 15 '71

Dacca, city of the dead. D. Coggin. il Time 97:28 My 3 '71

Death of an ideal; civil war; with report by L. Jenkins. il Newsweek 77:50+ Ap 12 '71

East Pakistan crisis poses grave questions for other nations. C. B. Firth. Chr Cent 88:806-7 Je 30 '71

East Pakistan: joy Bangla; joy Jesu. P. Parshall. Chr Today 15:34 Ap 23 '71

Genocide in East Pakistan. N. Cousins. Sat R 54:20-1 My 22 '71

Growing war threat. Time 98:30 Ag 16 '71

Humiliation or war. il Time 97:33-4 My 10 '71

Huq's rebellion. M. J. Kubic. il por Newsweek 77:50 My 10 '71

Jinnah's fading dream. il por Time 97:31 Mr 15 '71

Mujib's secret trial. il Time 98:16+ Ag 23 '71

Nehru's plan for peace. S. S. Harrison. New Repub 164:17-22 Je 19 '71

Notes and comment. New Yorker 47:17 Jl 3 '71

Pakistan: at the point of no return? il Newsweek 77:35-6 Mr 22 '71

Pakistan plunges into civil war; with report by L. Jenkins. il Newsweek 77:31-2+ Ap 5 '71

Pakistan: round 1 to the West. il Time 97:23-4 Ap 12 '71

Pakistan: the ravaging of golden Bengal. il Time 98:24-9 Ag 2 '71

Pakistan: toppling over the brink; civil war in East Pakistan. il Time 97:18-19 Ap 5 '71

Pakistan: vultures and wild dogs. il Newsweek 77:35-6 Ap 26 '71

Pakistan's agony. W. J. Barnds. il America 124:508-9+ My 15 '71

Polishing a tarnished image. il Time 97:33 My 24 '71

Political tidal wave that struck East Pakistan. P. Durdin. il por N Y Times Mag p24-5+ My 2 '71

Protracted war. il Newsweek 78:43-4 Jl 12 '71

Push toward the borders. il Time 97:39 Ap 26 '71

Rebellion in Pakistan: prelude to the Indian revolution? T. Ali. il Ramp Mag 9:16+ Je '71

Reign of terror. il Newsweek 77:52+ Ap 19 '71

Reports and comment. P. R. Kann and L. Lescaze. Atlan 228:26+ D '71

Second thoughts. M. J. Kubic. Newsweek 77:47-8 My 17 '71

Unwinnable war. A. De Borchgrave. Newsweek 78:50+ N 15 '71

Why Pakistan exploded: story behind a civil war. il U S News 70:31-2 Ap 12 '71

Why the East chose revolution. J. W. Milner. Nat R 23:530-1 My 18 '71

Will guerrilla war come to East Pakistan? Cur 129:61-3 My '71

Will of the people in Pakistan: is Eastern independence the answer? L. Howell. Chr Cent 88:595-9 My 12 '71

Defenses

Equal hatred, unequal odds. il Newsweek 78:40 D 13 '71

Economic conditions

Pakistan: the busy bee route to development. T. Nulty and L. Nulty. il Trans-Action 8: 18-26+ F '71

Economic policy

Pakistan: the transfer of power: address, June 28, 1971. A. M. Yahya Khan. Vital Speeches 37:650-4 Ag 15 '71

Foreign relations

Pakistan divided. S. H. Schanberg. For Affairs 50:125-35 O '71

France

See France—Foreign relations—Pakistan

India

See India—Foreign relations—Pakistan

United States

See United States—Foreign relations —Pakistan

Industries

Social information and government-sponsored development: a case study from West Pakistan; Pakistan industrial development corporation. Z. Shariff. bibliog f il Ann Am Acad 393:92-108 Ja '71

Politics and government

Agony of East Pakistan. D. Reed and J. E. Frazer. il Read Digest 99:66-71 N '71

Ali Bhutto begins to pick up the pieces. il por Time 99:32+ Ja 3 '72

America responds to Pakistan. H. A. Jack. Chr Cent 88:1137-8 S 29 '71

Avoiding disaster in South Asia. W. P. Bundy. Newsweek 78:62 O 25 '71

Church leaders prick Europeans' consciences over Pakistan tragedy. A. Woodrow. Chr Cent 88:912 Jl 28 '71

Dateline: Pakistan, East and West. J. C. Haughey. il America 125:365-7 N 6 '71

East Pakistan: even the skies weep. il Time 98:37-8 O 25 '71

Pakistan divided. S. H. Schanberg. For Affairs 50:125-35 O '71

Pakistan: the transfer of power; address, June 28, 1971. A. M. Yahya Khan. Vital Speeches 37:650-4 Ag 15 '71

Pakistan's new order. il Newsweek 79:21-2 Ja 3 '72

Peking's double game. J. M. Van Der Kroef. Nat R 23:928-9 Ag 24 '71

President on a tightrope. il por Newsweek 79:25-7 Ja 10 '72

Relief to East Pakistan: a political dilemma. L. Howell. il Chr Cent 88:1135-7 S 29 '71

Toward a revolution. il por Time 99:25 Ja 17 '72

What Pakistan wants. New Repub 165:9 O 16 '71

See also

Elections—Pakistan

Relief work

Church leaders prick Europeans' consciences over Pakistan tragedy. A. Woodrow. Chr Cent 88:912 Jl 28 '71

Major U.S. organizations for Pakistani relief. America 125:415 N 20 '71

Pakistani relief: compound of hope and tragedy. J. C. Haughey. il America 125:420-3 N 20 '71

President names advisory panel on south Asian relief assistance. Dept State Bul 65: 278 S 13 '71

President requests additional funds for south Asian relief; statement, October 1, 1971. R. M. Nixon. Dept State Bul 65:444 O 25 '71

Relief to East Pakistan: a political dilemma. L. Howell. il Chr Cent 88:1135-7 S 29 '71

U.S. announces measures for East Pakistan relief; Department announcements. Dept State Bul 64:823-4 Je 28 '71

U.S. continues disaster relief to Pakistan; statement, January 4, 1971. R. M. Nixon. Dept State Bul 64:138 F 1 '71

U.S. support for relief efforts in south Asia; statement, October 4, 1971. M. J. Williams. Dept State Bul 65:500-2 N 1 '71

U.S. supports U.N. program for East Pakistan relief. Dept State Bul 64:794 Je 21 '71

PAKISTAN-India war, 1971. See India-Pakistan war, 1971

PAKISTAN industrial development corporation. See Pakistan—Industries

PAKISTAN international airlines. See Airlines—Pakistan

PAKISTAN refugees. See Refugees, Pakistan

PAL, Nandita. See Goldstein, D. B. jt. auth.

PALACES

City of palaces: Mexico City. C. F. Marini. il Américas 23:2-9 S '71

Palace of Pavlovsk, near Leningrad. M. Chamot. il Antiques 99:725-31 My '71

See also

Castles

Versailles, Palace of

PALATABILITY. See Flavor

PALATNIK, Reizia

Demonstration at IFLA for Reizia Palatnik. il por Wilson Lib Bul 46:391 Ja '72 •

PALEN, Cole

Bad baron flies again. il Life 70:62-5 Ja 29 '71 •

PALEOANTHROPOLOGY. See Man, Prehistoric

PALEOBIOLOGY
See also
Paleoecology

PALEOBOTANY
See also
Petrified forests

Silurian

Early Silurian spore tetrads from New York: earliest New World evidence for vascular plants? J. Gray and A. J. Boucot. bibliog il Science 173:918-21 S 3 '71

Florida

Petrified forest of Key Biscayne. il Sci Digest 69:32-3 F '71

Montana

Digging in Montana's evolutionary past. H. F. Becker. il Am For 77:44-7+ Ap '71

New York (state)

Early Silurian spore tetrads from New York: earliest New World evidence for vascular plants? J. Gray and A. J. Boucot. bibliog il Science 173:918-21 S 3 '71

Ohio

Maize from an Adena mound in Athens County, Ohio. J. L. Murphy. bibliog il Science 171:897-8 My 5 '71

PALEOCLIMATOLOGY
Climate cycles. C. Emiliani. il Sea Front 17: 108-20 Mr '71
Last interglacial: paleotemperatures and chronology. C. Emiliani. bibliog il Science 171:571-3 F 12 '71
Late pleistocene paleotemperatures at Tongue of the ocean, Bahamas. G. W. Lynts and J. B. Judd. bibliog il Science 171: 1143-4 Mr 19 '71
Ocean-floor record links dinosaurs, plankton, climate; leg 19 of the Deep sea drilling project. Sci N 100:279 O 23 '71
Paleomagnetic chronology of pliocene-early pleistocene climates and the plio-pleistocene boundary in New Zealand. J. P. Kennett and others. bibliog il Science 171:276-9 Ja 22 '71
Paleotemperature variations across the plio-pleistocene boundary. C. Emiliani. bibliog il Science 171:60-2 Ja 8 '71
Pleistocene changes in the fauna and flora of South America. B. S. Vuilleumier. bibliog il Science 173:771-80 Ag 27 '71
Solar-climate relationships in the post-pleistocene. J. R. Bray. bibliog Science 171: 1242-3 Mr 26 '71
Tropics weren't so stable after all. L. Purrett. il Sci N 100:177 S 11 '71

PALEOECOLOGY
Recent brachiopod-coralline sponge communities and their paleoecological significance. J. B. C. Jackson and others. bibliog il Science 173:623-5 Ag 13 '71

PALEO-INDIANS
Early man in the Andes. R. S. MacNeish. il Sci Am 224:36-46 Ap '71
First American. by C. W. Ceram. Review
  Time 98:114+ N 22 '71. L. I. Barrett

PALEOLIMNOLOGY. See Paleontology

PALEOMAGNETISM. See Magnetism, Terrestrial

PALEONTOLOGY
Record in the rocks; find of archaeopteryx; with photographs by B. Ratcliffe. R. Moore. Audubon 73:13-29 Ja '71
See also
Man, Prehistoric
Mastodons

Methodology

Examining fossils by X-ray. il Chem 44:21 Je '71

Cenozoic

Arctic paleo-oceanography in late cenozoic time. Y. Herman; reply with rejoinder. K. Hunkins and others. bibliog Science 174: 962-3 N 26 '71
Paleotemperature variations across the plio-pleistocene boundary. C. Emiliani. bibliog il Science 171:60-2 Ja 8 '71
See also
Paleontology—Pliocene

Cretaceous

Orbitolina, a cretaceous larger foraminifer from Flemish cap: paleoceanographic implications. B. K. Sen Gupta and A. C. Grant. bibliog il Science 173:934-6 S 3 '71

Mesozoic

Ocean-floor record links dinosaurs, plankton, climate; leg 19 of the Deep sea drilling project. Sci N 100:279 O 23 '71

Miocene

Gorilla-sized ape from the miocene of India; Dryopithecus indicus. E. L. Simons and D. Pilbeam. bibliog il Science 173:23-7 Jl 2 '71

Oligocene

Reporter at large; final approval of Florissant Fossil Beds National Monument. B. Rouché. New Yorker 47:141-2+ N 13 '71

Pleistocene

Archeological traces of early hominid activities, east of Lake Rudolf, Kenya. G. L. Isaac and others. bibliog il Science 173: 1129-34 S 17 '71
Late pleistocene paleotemperatures at Tongue of the Ocean, Bahamas. G. W. Lynts and J. B. Judd. bibliog il Science 171: 1143-4 Mr 19 '71
Pleistocene changes in the fauna and flora of South America. B. S. Vuilleumier. bibliog il Science 173:771-80 Ag 27 '71

Pliocene

Fossil penguin from the late cenozoic of South Africa. G. G. Simpson. il Science 171: 1144-5 Mr 19 '71

Pre-Cambrian

Ancient algae; possible index to the Precambrian. Sci N 100:204 S 25 '71
Oldest fossils. E. S. Barghoorn. il Sci Am 224:30-42 bibliog(p 132) My '71
Precambrian columnar stromatolite diversity: reflection of metazoan appearance. S. M. Awramik. bibliog il Science 174:825-7 N 19 '71

Quaternary

Oxygen-18 studies of recent planktonic foraminifera: comparisons of phenotypes and of test parts. A. D. Hecht and S. M. Savin; reply with rejoinder. A. W. H. Bé and J. Van Donk. bibliog il Science 173: 167-9 Jl 9 '71
Paleolimnology of late quaternary deposits: Seibold site, North Dakota. A. M. Cvancara and others. bibliog il Science 171:172-4 Ja 15 '71

Africa

Humans before man; Australopithecus africanus. Sci Am 224:46-7 Mr '71

Antarctic Regions

Antarctic bottom water: major change in velocity during the late Cenozoic between Australia and Antarctica. N. D. Watkins and J. P. Kennett. bibliog il Science 173: 813-18 Ag 27 '71

Arctic Regions

Arctic paleo-oceanography in late cenozoic time. Y. Herman; reply with rejoinder. K. Hunkins and others. bibliog Science 174:962-3 N 26 '71

Bahama Islands

Late pleistocene paleotemperatures at Tongue of the Ocean, Bahamas. G. W. Lynts and J. B. Judd. bibliog il Science 171: 1143-4 Mr 19 '71

Canada

See also
Paleontology—Ontario

Colorado

Reporter at large; final approval of Florissant Fossil Beds National Monument. B. Rouché. New Yorker 47:141-2+ N 13 '71

India

Gorilla-sized ape from the miocene of India; Dryopithecus indicus. E. L. Simons and D. Pilbeam. bibliog il Science 173:23-7 Jl 2 '71

Kenya

More complete view of man's ancestors; Australopithecus. il Sci N 99:141 F 27 '71

Montana

Digging in Montana's evolutionary past. H. F. Becker. il Am For 77:44-7+ Ap '71

North Dakota

Paleolimnology of late quaternary deposits: Seibold site, North Dakota. A. M. Cvancara and others. bibliog il Science 171:172-4 Ja 15 '71

Ontario

Oldest fossils. E. S. Barghoorn. il Sci Am 224:30-42 bibliog(p 132) My '71

PALEONTOLOGY—*Continued*

Peru

Early man in the Andes. R. S. MacNeish. il Sci Am 224:36-46 Ap '71

South Africa

Fossil penguin from the late cenozoic of South Africa. G. G. Simpson. il Science 171: 1144-5 Mr 19 '71

Oldest fossils. E. S. Barghoorn. il Sci Am 224:30-42 bibliog(p 132) My '71

South America

Pleistocene changes in the fauna and flora of South America. B. S. Vuilleumier. bibliog il Science 173:771-80 Ag 27 '71

Utah

Where ancestors of the lobster left their marks in the shale; Antelope spring area. il Sunset 146:38+ My '71

Western states

Professor Cope vs. Professor Marsh; feud among the bones. J. Penick. il pors Am Heritage 22:4-13+ Ag '71

PALEOPATHOLOGY

Neanderthals had rickets. il Sci Digest 69:35-6 F '71

PALEOTEMPERATURE. See Paleoclimatology

PALÉS MATOS, Luis

Black poetry of Luis Palés Matos and its sources, by L. Torres. Review
  Américas il 23:40-1 Ap '71. M. R. Hoff •

PALESTINE
  See also
Zionism

Jewish-Arab problem

See Jewish-Arab relations

PALESTINIAN Arabs

Middle East: from polemic to accommodation. W. G. Oxtoby. bibliog il por Chr Cent 88: 1192-7 O 13 '71

Second-class citizens; Eisenstadt-Peres report. il Newsweek 77:40 F 8 '71

Terrorism & preventive detention: the case of Israel. A. M. Dershowitz; discussion. Commentary 51:33-4+ Je '71

Third way; Hebron's mayor Ja'bari. il por Time 98:33 S 13 '71

PALETTE, Pilar

John Wayne: his wife explains the man behind the legend; ed. by V. Scott. il pors Ladies Home J 88:72+ N '71

PALETTES (colors)

Palettes of the old masters. F. Birren. il Am Artist 35:38-43+ F '71

PALEVSKY, Max

Shoestring cinema of Max Palevsky; interview, ed. by T. Murray. por Duns 97:35 F '71

PALEY, Grace

Two stories. Atlan 227:66-7 My '71

PALEY, William

Trivets had it hot. il Hobbies 76:48-9 S '71

PALISADES nuclear power plant. See Atomic power plants

PALISADES park. See Amusement parks

PALKA, John. See Edwards, J. S. jt. auth.

PALLADIAN architecture. See Architecture, Italian

PALLATZ, Harold

Build a sonic cleaner. il Radio-Electr 42:46 D '71

Underground survey meter and metal locator. il Pop Electr 35:63-5 Ag '71

PALM BEACH, Fla.

Social life and customs

Palm Beach is the big stadium. . . . T. Buckley. il N Y Times Mag p26-9+ Mr 21 '71

PALM COAST, Fla. See New cities and towns

PALM SPRINGS, Calif.

Chic of Araby. D. Butwin. Sat R 54:59-60+ Mr 27 '71

Palm Springs. P. Benchley. il Holiday 49: 54-9+ D '70

Palm Springs back country. il Sunset 147: 74-9 N '71

PALMA, R. J. and Sund, E. H.

Spectrophotometric determinations of pKa's for substituted 2-nitrophenols. bibliog il pors Chem 44:26-8 My '71

PALMA, Ricardo

Ricardo Palma's tradiciones. L. A. Fox. il por Américas 23:31-6 Je '71 •

PALMBY, Clarence Donald

Washington report; interview, ed. by F. Bailey, jr. il por Suc Farm 69:7+ O '71

PALMER, Alison

Tally's triumph. por Time 98:20 S 6 '71 •

PALMER, Arnold

And for their next number. M. Cope. il pors Sports Illus 35:44+ Ag 9 '71 •

Arnie and Sam. por Newsweek 78:75 Ag 9 '71 •

Arnie re-arms while Lee flees. C. Kirkpatrick. il pors Sports Illus 35:20-1 Ag 2 '71 •

Arnie's desert campaign. Time 97:62 Mr 1 '71 •

Two for money, one for show. G. S. Brown. il pors Sports Illus 35:28-9 N 8 '71 •

PALMER, Charlene

O Lord, let us not seek false comforts anymore; poem. Chr Cent 38:1230 O 20 '71

PALMER, D. F. and Henyey, T. L.

San Fernando earthquake of 9 February 1971: pattern of faulting. il Science 172:712-15 My 14 '71

PALMER, Gail, and Jensen, Orville

Freedom to learn at Wilson campus school. Todays Ed 60:47-8 N '71

PALMER, Jeff

Brant! il Field & S 76:58-9+ N '71

Can you really see deer? il Field & S 76:31+ S '71

Timetable for bowhunters. il Field & S 76 46-7+ Jl '71

PALMER, John D.

Rhythm of the flowers; with biographical sketch. il Natur Hist 80:5, 64-73 Ag '71

PALMER, Norman D.

China's relations with India and Pakistan. bibliog f Cur Hist 61:148-53 S '71

PALMER, Paul F.

Christian breakthrough in Women's lib. America 124:634-7 Je 19 '71

Communal penance: what are the options? America 124:64-6, 411 Ja 23, Ap 17 '71

PALMER, Robert Roswell

American historical association in 1970; adaptation of address, December 28, 1970. Am Hist R 76:1-15 F '71

PALMER, Tally. See Palmer, A.

PALMERSTON, Henry John Temple, 3d viscount

Beloved bounder. A. Cooper. por Newsweek 77:82+ My 31 '71 •

Lord Palmerston, by J. Ridley. Review
  New Repub 164:30-2 Je 26 '71. J. Walt
  Sat R 54:22-3 Ag 28 '71. C. Miller •

PALMISTRY

Is the way to his heart through his hand? K. Parker. il Seventeen 29:100-1+ Jl '70

PALMS
  See also
Coconut

PALO ALTO, Calif

Education

Learning is an all-black thing; Nairobi day schools. J. Slater. il Ebony 26:88-90+ S '71

Finance

Computerized total-cost bidding. J. W. Wear. il Am City 86:60-1 F '71

Poor

Meet the need; East Palo Alto's program for needy food stamp purchasers. New Repub 164:11 Mr 6 '71

Veterans administration hospital

See United States—Veterans administration hospitals

PALOVIC, Clara Lora

Overdue. Wilson Lib Bul 46:268-9 N '71

PALYTOXIN. See Toxins and antitoxins

PAMPHLETS

Best in booklets. See issues of House & garden incorporating Living for young homemakers

Booklet bonanza; before you build, buy or decorate (title varies) (cont) House B 113: 80-2+ O '71

Booklets worth writing for. il Good H 172: 202 Ap '71

Hints for shoppers from trade associations. il Changing T 25:29-30 Jl '71

Publications worth writing for. C. Bilski. See issues of Popular mechanics

Teacher's survival guide to environmental education resources; booklets, etc. Schol Teach Jr/Sr High p40+ O '71

Things to write for. See every other issue of Changing times

Writer with a camera. R. Arnold. Writers Digest 51:14-16 F '71
  See also
Advertising mediums—Pamphlets

PAMTGG; ballet. See Ballets—Criticisms

PAN, M. L. and Wyatt, G. R.
Juvenile hormone induces vitellogenin synthesis in the monarch butterfly. bibliog il Science 174:503-5 O 29 '71

PAN-AFRICA-U.S.A. international track meet.
See Track athletics

PAN-AFRICANISM
Pan-Africanism and the black church; a search for solidarity. C. Rogers. il Chr Cent 88:1345-7 N 17 '71

PAN AM (airline) See Pan American world airways

PANAMA
See also
Coclé
Fishing—Panama
Mulatas Islands
Panama Canal
Portobelo
Public health—Panama
Yachts and yachting—Panama

PANAMA, ISTHMUS OF
How the Isthmus of Panama got there. il Sci N 99:279 Ap 24 '71

PANAMA CANAL
Celebrating the canal's completion. V. L. George. il Hobbies 76:148-9 Je '71
A man, a plan, a canal, Panama! J. F. Stevens. D. G. McCullough. il pors Am Heritage 22:64-71+ Je '71
Panama Canal on cards. V. L. George. il Hobbies 76:148-9 My '71
Whatever happened to the plans for a second Panama Canal? il U S News 71:94 O 25 '71

PAN AMERICAN conferences. See Inter-American conferences

PAN AMERICAN day and week
April 14, 1971; Pan American day. Américas 23:1 Ap '71
Pan American day and Pan American week, 1971, proclamation. R. M. Nixon. Dept State Bul 64:568 My 3 '71

PAN AMERICAN games
Carl Van Duyne on the Pan Am games. C. Van Duyne. il Yachting 130:31 O '71
Good things come in large packages; 205-pound prizefighter and a 304-pound weight lifter gold medals winners. P. Putnam. il pors Sports Illus 35:16-18+ Ag 23 '71
Having at a ball in new Havana. J. Kirshenbaum. il Sports Illus 35:18-21 Ag 30 '71
Marathon si, basketball no! Pan-Am games, Cali Colombia. P. Putnam. il Sports Illus 35:18-19 Ag 16 '71
No fun games. il Newsweek 78:53 Ag 23 '71
Pain-Am games. il Time 98:46 Ag 16 '71
Pan American games; a Brazilian sweep; sailing races. C. Van Duyne. Yachting 130:48+ O '71

PAN AMERICAN health organization
Canada asks admission to PAHO. Américas 23:44 Ag '71
Hemisphere health. il Américas 22:39 N '70

PAN AMERICAN highway
Bridging the Darien gap. il Américas 23:44 Je '71
Finally: last link for the Pan-American highway. il U S News 70:80 Mr 8 '71
U.S. Panama, and Colombia to build link to Pan American highway; statement, May 6, 1971. R. M. Nixon. Dept State Bul 64:673 My 24 '71

PAN AMERICAN union
Hemisphere art. See issues of Américas
Music. See issues of Américas

PAN AMERICAN world airways
And now Pan Am is in a nose dive. il Bsns W p63-4+ Je 26 '71
Board probing 747 takeoff accident. il Aviation W 95:26-7 Ag 9 '71
Executive jet CAB filing seeks to stop Pan Am Falcon charters. C. E. Schneider. Aviation W 95:17 Ag 30 '71
Information lack revealed in 747 probe. Aviation W 95:21-4 Ag 30 '71
Moscow makes the going tough. il Bsns W p20-1 My 8 '71
NTSB broadens 747 investigation. il Aviation W 95:29-30 Ag 16 '71
New blood at Pan Am. Newsweek 78:94+ N 15 '71
Pan Am laying off 1,750 workers. Aviation W 95:25 O 25 '71
Pan Am management realigned. Aviation W 94:30 Je 14 '71
Pan Am, Pakistan airlines hurt by war. J. P. Woolsey. Aviation W 96:24 Ja 3 '72
Pan Am picks a copilot. il por Time 98:80+ N 29 '71
Pan Am seeks lower North Atlantic fares. Aviation W 94:28 My 24 '71
Pan Am submerges Trippe regime. L. Doty. Aviation W 94:24-5 Je 21 '71

Pan Am takes a one-two-three punch. il Bsns W p80-1 O 2 '71
Pan American, carrier in crisis. por Time 98:84 O 25 '71
Pan American cuts Caribbean frequencies to 200/week. Aviation W 94:30 My 10 '71
Pan American plans stock sale. Aviation W 94:26 Mr 22 '71
Pan American seeks to localize advertising, marketing efforts. Aviation W 94:34 Ap 19 '71
Pan American sees merger with Eastern as main domestic hope. Aviation W 94:36 F 15 '71
Pan American upgrading entire 747 fleet. il Aviation W 94:26-7 Ja 18 '71
Two airlines ponder their losing runs. Bsns W p26 Ja 16 '71
U.S. Irish clash on Dublin rights. L. Doty. Aviation W 95:25-6 D 20 '71
Why Pan Am doesn't have a new president. pors Bsns W p 120-2 N 13 '71

PAN AMERICAN world airways-Trans World airlines merger (proposed) See Airlines—Consolidations and mergers

PAN AMERICANISM. See Inter-American relations

PANARABISM
Oil-rich country with an uncertain future; Libya. il US News 70:86-8 Je 7 '71
See also
Arab Republics, Federation of

PANCAKES. See Griddle cakes

PANCHAL, Mansaram
Color linocuts. il Sch Arts 71:12-13 D '71
Patterned objects. il Sch Arts 71:30 Ja '72

PANCHO, Juan. See Cabalquinto, L. jt. auth.

PANCREAS
See also
Insulin

PANDAS
How about a panda or two? possibility of acquiring pandas from China. Nation 213:100 Ag 16 '71

PANDION haliaetus. See Ospreys

PANEL discussion. See Discussion

PANELING
Facts on prefinished paneling. F. K. Coffee. il Mech Illus 67:87-9+ Ja '71
How to put up wall paneling without leftovers. G. Daniels. il Pop Sci 198:124 My '71
Panel a child's room with color. il Parents Mag 46:26 F '71
When and how to use furring strips. il Bet Hom & Gard 49:16+ My '71

PANETTA, Leon E.
Panetta's White House. J. Osborne. New Repub 164:7-9 My 8 '71 *

PANIC, Milan
Serbian boy builds his dream castle in the drug business. P. Siekman. il por Fortune 83:94-7+ Ja '71 *

PANISH, Morton B. and Hayashi, Izuo
New class of diode lasers; with biographical sketches. il Sci Am 225:14, 32-40 bibliog (p 122) Jl '71

PANISLAMISM
Pan-Islam and communism. America 125:526 D 18 '71

PANKEY, Kay
Expatriate chess on the other side of the wall. E. Shorris. il pors N Y Times Mag p36 My 23 '71 *

PANNELLA, Giorgio
Fish otoliths; daily growth layers and periodical patterns. bibliog il Science 173:1124-7 S 17 '71

PANOFSKY, Wolfgang K. H.
Roots of the strategic arms race: ambiguity and ignorance. Bul Atom Sci 27:15-20 Je '71
—See Kendall, H. W. jt. auth.

PANORAMA exhibition. See Exhibitions, Traveling

PANTALEONI, Helenka
UNICEF's 25th anniversary promise: a future for every child. por Parents Mag 46:32 D '71

PANTER, Carol
Man in the museum; story. Redbook 136:72-3 F '71

PANTER-DOWNES, Mollie
Letter from London (cont) New Yorker 47:101-3 F 27; 113-15 Ap 17; 64-6 Jl 3; 68-70 Ag 7; 138+ O 30; 177-80 N 13 '71
Profiles. New Yorker 46:40-4+ Ja 23; 31-43 Ja 30: 40-6+ F 6 '71
Profiles; the Pines, Putney, home of A. C. Swinburne and T. Watts-Dunton. New Yorker 46:40-4+ Ja 23; 31-43 Ja 30 '71

PANTHERS
See also
Pumas

PANTLEO, Paul M. See Crowther, B. jt. auth.

PANTOMIME
Silent tour of Buenos Aires. G. Nogués. il Américas 23:24-31 O '71
See also
American mime theatre
Mime
PANTY hose. See Hosiery
PANTYHOSE industry. See Hosiery industry
PAO, Y. K.
Y.K. who? por Time 98:65 Jl 5 '71 *
PAO-AN, China. See Villages—China (People's Republic)
PAOLINO, Ronald M. and Levy, H. M.
Amnesia produced by spreading depression and ECS: evidence for time-dependent memory trace localization. bibliog il Science 172:746-9 My 14 '71
PAOLOZZI, Eduardo
Machined mosaics. R. Hughes. il Time 98:86-7 O 11 '71 *
PAPAGALLO fishing
Baja roosterfish. J. Hardie. il Field & S 76:74-5+ Je '71
PAPAL encyclicals. See Encyclicals
PAPAL infallibility. See Popes—Infallibility
PAPANDREOU, Andreas
Jackie and Ari and Tom and George and Spiro and . . . R. Fitch. il pors Ramp Mag 10:38-47+ Ja '72 *
PAPANICOLAOU, Christos
Wait-listed for the pantheon. A. Verschoth. il pors Sports Illus 34:46+ F 1 '71 *
PAPAWS
Curious pawpaw. J. Sansregret. il Am For 77:37 Ap '71
PAPAYAS
See also
Cookery—Fruit
PAPER
Selecting the right watercolor paper. R. Fabri. il Am Artist 35:28-32+ Ag '71
See also
Feeding and feeding stuffs—Paper
Photographic paper
PAPER, Handmade. See Paper making
PAPER, Recycled. See Refuse. Utilization of
PAPER bag players. See Theater, Childrens
PAPER books. See Paperback books
PAPER container industry. See Container industry
PAPER cutting. See Paper work
PAPER folding. See Paper work
PAPER furniture. See Furniture, Paperboard
PAPER gold. See Special drawing rights
PAPER-hanging
Easy way to remove wallpaper. J. Savage. il Mech Illus 67:116-17+ F '71
Should you try wallpapering? Sunset 146:136 Je '71

Anecdotes, facetiae, satire, etc.
Spring hangup; excerpt from The complete book of pitfalls. D. Williamson. Sat R 54:6+ My 15 '71
PAPER houses. See Paperboard houses
PAPER industry
Wastepaper bag. il Newsweek 77:73+ Jl 12 '71
See also
Hammermill paper company
International paper company
Kimberly-Clark corporation
St Regis paper company
Saxon industries, inc.
Scott paper company
Strikes—United States—Paper industry
Union camp corporation
United States plywood-Champion papers, inc.
Weyerhaeuser company

Pollution
Paper's pollution problems. H. V. L. Bloomfield. il Am For 77:10-13+ N '71
Water lords, by J. M. Fallows. Review
Chr Cent 88:1420 D 1 '71. T. W. Rogers

Great Britain
See also
Bowater paper corporation. ltd.

Japan
Paper world of Mino. M. C. Dorst. il Craft Horiz 31:50-1 Je '71
PAPER making
Paper world of Mino. M. C. Dorst. il Craft Horiz 31:50-1 Je '71

History
Paper making history from the ancient Chinese to Ben Franklin and modern times; a Library of Congress traveling exhibit. K. V. Hostick. Hobbies 75:140 F '71

PAPER mills
Pollution
Hammermill urges you. Nation 212:485 Ap 19 '71
PAPER mobiles. See Mobiles
PAPER work
Combinatorial richness of folding a piece of paper. M. Gardner. il Sci Am 224:110-12+ My; 122-3 Je '71
Polish paper cutting. E. Mitsch. il Am Artist 35:58-9 Ap '71
See also
Papier-mâché
PAPERBACK book covers. See Book covers
PAPERBACK book fairs. See Book fairs
PAPERBACK books
Always an open door for the paperback category novel. D. R. Koontz. il Writers Digest 52:24-6+ Ja '72
Everybody into the pool; new wave in childrens paperbacks. J. Higgins. il por Library J 96:2842-5 S 15 '71
1970: some surprises in paperback best sellers. il Pub W 199:38-41 F 8 '71
Paperback revolution. jr. M. J. Bandler. Commonweal 95:182-5 N 19 '71
See also
Advertising mediums—Paperback books
Booksellers and bookselling—Paperback books
Libraries—Paperback books
Publishers and publishing—Paperback books

Bibliography
Books to come; childrens and adult; comp. by S. T. Halbreich; I. E. Stokvis. Library J 96:297-324 Ja 15 '71
Books to come; childrens and adult; comp. by A. Yazejian; I. E. Stokvis and C. Horwitz. Library J 96:1837-65, 2863-6+ My 15, S 15 '71
Current and choice in paperbacks. America 125:536-41+ D 18 '71
Mini reference library: 21 paperbacks; high school material. J. Higgins and A. Stellwag. il pors Library J 96:245-7 Ja 15 '71
Notable books in paperback, 1968-69. Am Lib 2:108 Ja '71
PW forecasts. See issues of Publishers' weekly
Paperback bag. J. E. Illig. Seventeen 29:66+ N '70
Paperback bookshelf. See every other issue of Changing times
Pick of the paperbacks. R. W. Saal. See issues of Saturday review
Teacher's survival guide to environmental education resources. Schol Teach Jr/Sr High p34+ O '71
PAPERBOARD
Designing cardboard play equipment. L. Whitesel. il Sch Arts 70:24-5 Mr '71
PAPERBOARD houses
Paper houses go on sale. il Bsns W p 100 Ag 14 '71
PAPERWEIGHTS
White rose. T. Capote. il por Ladies Home J 88:96-7+ Jl '71
PAPICH, Robert
Real camp program in a city park day camp. il Camp Mag 43:20-1 F '71
PAPIER-MACHÉ
Animal parade. M. Heinrich. il Sch Arts 71:22-3 O '71
Comic characters. G. Short. il Sch Arts 70:8-9 Je '71
Extra fine papier-mâché mix. M. B. Green, jr. il Sch Arts 71:26-7 N '71
Mini-armature. S. Hastings. il Sch Arts 70:12-13 Je '71
Molding history; good old days with paper. R. J. Lynch. il por Har Yrs 11:41-3 Ag '71
Sunbursts and papier-mâché. D. De La Rosa and D. D. Ebert. il Sch Arts 70:6-7 Je '71
PAPP, Joseph
Beyond coteries. il por Time 98:71 N 15 '71 *
Not to be missed. G. Trotta. il por Harp Baz 104:86-7 Je '71 *
Pitchman for free (and freewheeling) theater. R. Bongartz. il pors N Y Times Mag p 12-13+ Ag 15 '71; Reply. J Papp. p40 Ag 29 '71 *
Public affairs. J. Kroll. Newsweek 78:109-10 N 29 '71 *
Public fights for life. il por Newsweek 77:113-14 Mr 22 '71 *
Public theater. L. Lerman. il por Mlle 73:133-7 Je '71 *
PAPP, William J.
Allergies: not to be sneezed at! il Har Yrs 11:30-3+ Ap '71
More from your doctor. il Har Yrs 11:36-9 Je '71

PAPPALARDI, Felix
Mountain climbing. S. K. Oberbeck. il por Newsweek 77:88 My 3 '71 •
PAPPAS, Lou Seibert
Complete ice cream cookbook. il House & Gard 140:127-8+ S '71
PAPPAS, Thomas Anthony
Jackie and Ari and Tom and George and Spiro and . . . R. Fitch. il pors Ramp Mag 10:38-47+ Ja '72 •
PAPPENHEIM, Bertha
Glückel von Hameln: Bertha Pappenheim's idealized ancestor. G. H. Pollock. bibliog Am Imago 28:216-27 Fall '71 •
PAPPER, Emanuel Martin
New techniques to help save life for accident victims. Vogue 158:268-9+ S 1 '71
PAPUANS
19th century champion of anti-racism in New Guinea; excerpts from diaries, correspondence and other papers, ed. by N. A. Butinov. N. N. Miklukha-Maklaĭ. il por UNESCO Courier 24:24-7 N '71
PAPYROS (firm). See Publishers and publishing—Greece, Modern
PARABLES
See also
Jesus Christ—Parables
PARACELSUS
Cantankerous Paracelsus. il Chem 44:5 N '71 •
Iatrochemistry; tr. by R. E. Oesper. F. Szabadvary. il por Chem 44:18-20 Je '71 •
PARACHUTES
Parachute that glides like a plane; Paraplane. D. Garr. il Pop Sci 199:76-7+ Ag '71
PARACHUTING
Snow 'chuting. il Mech Illus 67:58 Ja '71
PARADES
See also subhead Parades under names of cities. e.g. Washington, D.C.—Parades
PARADISE park. See Honolulu—Parks and playgrounds
PARADZINSKI, Eugene
Blacktails for beginners. il Field & S 76:52-3+ O '71
PARAGUAY
See also
Paraná River

Politics and government
Paraguay's popular dictator: A. Stroessner. S. Rodman. il Nat R 23:759-60+ Jl 13 '71
PARALLAX
Parallaxes of faint stars. Sky & Tel 42:212 O '71
PARALYSIS
See also
Parkinson's disease
Poliomyelitis
PARALYTICS
Eye control. il Time 98:40 Jl 5 '71
PARAMEDICS. See Medical workers
PARAMOUNT, Calif.

Education
Design for learning. S. Lovelady. il Todays Ed 60:54-6 F '71
PARANA RIVER
Parks of the upper Paraná. L. C. Merriam, jr. Nat Parks & Con Mag 45:27 Ag '71
PARANOIA

Anecdotes, facetiae, satire, etc.
United States of bananas. il Esquire 75:97-103 Ap '71
PARAPLEGICS. See Paralytics
PARAPSYCHOLOGY
See also
Dreams
Extrasensory perception
Mediums
PARASITES
See also
Lice
Plasmodium (parasite)
Symbiosis

Insects
Host-seeking stimulant for parasite of corn earworm: isolation, identification, and synthesis. R. L. Jones and others. bibliog il Science 173:842-3 Ag 27 '71
PARASITIC diseases
See also
Measles in cattle
Toxoplasmosis
PARASITIC plants
Are there any plants that can attack other plants? Sci Digest 70:83-4 Ag '71
See also
Air plants

PARATHYROID hormones. See Hormones
PARCEL post rates. See Postal rates—United States
PARCHER, Emily Seaber
Right plants turn a shaded area into an asset. il Home Gard 58:24-7+ Ag '71
Wild flowers for the cultivated garden. il Horticulture 49:32-5 Mr '71
PARCHMAN penal farms. See Prisons—Mississippi
PARCHMENT
Scrap of parchment; second century A.D. Plato text. il Chem 44:3 My '71
PARDO, Richard
New assertion of rights. il por Am For 77:16-19+ My '71
Washington lookout. Am For 77:14-15 My; 10-11 Jl; 10-11 Ag; 8-9 S; 6+ O; 7+ N '71
PARDON
See also
Probation
PARDUE, Leonard G.
Hurricane season of 1970. bibliog il Weatherwise 24:24-33+ F '71
PARENT and child (law)
See also
Support (domestic relations)
PARENT and child centers. See Day nurseries
PARENT-child relationship
Between father and son. il Good H 172:54+ Ap '71
Boy's best teacher. H. G. Green. Read Digest 98:187-8 Je '71
Briefing for parents: how to get your child to listen to you and how to listen to your child. D. E. Hamachek. bibliog il Todays Ed 60:33-48 Ap '71
Children must leave home. T. I. Rubin. Ladies Home J 88:40 S '71
Daddy tells a story. S. A. Stutz. Parents Mag 46:48+ Je '71
Day Bobby learned about love. C. Alvarado. il por Redbook 136:10+ F '71
Dearest Meg. M. S. Hudnall. Good H 174:12 Ja '72
Don't shoot—we are your children! by J. A. Lukas. Review
Sat R il 54:34 My 1 '71. R. Cassidy
Few kind words for parents. I. Mothner. Look 35:50 Ja 26 '71
How many raindrops in the world? S. Streshinsky. il Redbook 136:53+ Ja '71
How not to embarrass your children; with study discussion program, by E. Harris and D. Harris. D. Graves. bibliog il PTA Mag 66:28-30, 34-5 S '71
How to talk to your parents about sex; ed. by M. Brenton. O. Rabinowitz. Seventeen 30:152-3+ Mr '71
Kids and drugs; address, May 1971. A. Linkletter. il PTA Mag 66:2-5 S; 2-5 O '71
Limits of parenthood; reprint. S. J. Harris. PTA Mag 65:33 Ap '71
Love is not enough. S. Chisholm. il por Parents Mag 46:52+ D '71
Most precious gift a father can give to his son; ed. by S. O'Quin. S. I. Hayakawa. il por Todays Health 49:21-3 Je '71
Mothers & daughters. M. Brenton. il Seventeen 30:92-3+ D '71
My parents drink too much; questions and answers. A. Wood. Seventeen 30:168+ Ap '71
Play it straight with your children. M. Angell. il Parents Mag 46:49-51+ O '71
Psychiatrists helping young mommas understand baby; new read-together books for parents and children, interview, ed. by P. A. Farrell. R. Switzer; J. C. Hirschberg. il pors Pub W 199:38-9 Je 28 '71
Teenagers: how to drive parents sane. H. Ginott. il Todays Health 49:20-3 N '71
U.S. journal: Manhattan and Atchison, Kan; the Maes family. C. Trillin. New Yorker 47:90-5 Je 12 '71
What to tell your daughter about Women's lib; questions and answers, ed. by T. Langleben. A. Landers. il pors Todays Health 49:52-5+ O '71
See also
Children—Management and training
Children of divorced parents
Family life
Fathers
Generation gap
Love, Maternal
Mothers

Anecdotes, facetiae, satire, etc.
Revenge of Erma Bombeck; excerpt from Just wait till you have children of your own. E. Bombeck and B. Keane. McCalls 98:24+ Ag '71

PARENT education
Evaluation of parent drug education. P. Thomas and others. bibliog Ment Hy 55: 456-60 O '71
For parent effectiveness: on-the-job training. R. Kramer. il N Y Times Mag p 102-3+ Mr 28 '71
PARENT effectiveness training. See Parent education
PARENT participation in school management. See School management and organization—Parent participation
PARENT-teacher associations. See Parents and teachers associations
PARENT-teacher cooperation. See School and the home
PARENTAL overprotection. See Parent-child relationship
PARENTAL responsibility ordinances. See Municipal ordinances
PARENTE, W. J.
Scissors superstar! il Sr Schol 99:42+ S 27 '71
PARENTEAU, Shirley
Welcome aboard, Cherie. il pors Motor B & S 127:54-5 My '71
PARENTERAL feeding. See Intravenous feeding
PARENTS
See also
Children
Family
Home life
School and the home
Stepparents
PARENTS and teachers associations
Editorial. B. B. Price. See issues of PTA magazine
How to's for leaders and members (cont) M. M. Conant. PTA Mag 65:36 F; 36 Mr; 34 My; 33 Je '71
Membership proclamation. E. Mallory. PTA Mag 66:9 O '71
PTA of the future. E. Mallory and others. il PTA Mag 65:14-16 F '71
PTA where the action is. See issues of PTA magazine
Solution-seekers in the seventies. P. B. Price. PTA Mag 65:2-3 F '71
What is a PTA member? por PTA Mag 66:24-5 O '71
See also
National congress of parents and teachers
PARENTS and teachers conferences. See School and the home
PARENTS liability. See Liability (law)
PARENTS' magazine
100 million American children: a rededication on our forty-fifth anniversary. G. J. Hecht. por Parents Mag 46:44 O '71
See also
Youth group achievement awards
PARENTS of the handicapped
Help for the exceptional parent. J. Cass. Sat R 54:39 Ag 21 '71
PARENTS responsibility (law) See Liability (law)
PARETTI, Andrew
Family business is wrecked by the poison. J. Howard. il pors Life 71:28-9 S 10 '71 *
PARETTI, Maria
Family business is wrecked by the poison. J. Howard. il pors Life 71:28-9 S 10 '71 *
PARIAN dolls. See Dolls
PARIS

Airports
Paris Nord concept keyed to expansion. D. E. Fink. il Aviation W 95:69-70+ N 15 '71

Art
Paris. M. Conil-Lacoste. See issues of Art news
Paris. M. Gibson. il Art in Am 59:128-9 Mr '71

Cemeteries
Necropolis: Père Lachaise cemetery. J. Bryan, 3d. il Nat R 23:821-2 Jl 27 '71

Commune
See Paris—History

Description
Changing face of Paris. il U S News 71: 56 Ag 9 '71
Even with traffic, Paris is still Paris. L. Barry. il Pop Phot 69:34+ Ag '71
Paris on parade. S. Turner. il Schol Teach Jr/Sr High p 18-19 Mr 8 '71
Travel notes; walking in the city. R. Joseph. Esquire 76:50+ S '71

Galleries and museums
Paris; unveiling of the Michel Monet bequest at Musée Marmottan. M. Conil-La-coste. il Art N 70:9 S '71
Prophet of light; musée Marmottan and the Monet bequest. R. Hughes. il Time 98:54-5 Jl 19 '71
See also
Louvre

History
Those costly barricades; centenary of the Paris commune of 1871. T. Beeson. Chr Cent 88:612 My 19 '71

Hotels, restaurants, etc.
Bazaar's bazar. M. Capron and G. Mazer. il Harp Baz 104:164-5 Mr '71
Christmas at the Ritz. P. O'Higgins. il por Harp Baz 105:100-1 D '71
What's new on the Paris hotel and restaurant scene? W. Root. il Holiday 48:76-9+ S '70
See also
Night clubs—France

Libraries
Paris plans for major public library. H. R. Lottman. Pub W 200:234 Ag 50 '71

Markets
Folding the parasols of Paris: Les Halles. il Time 98:28+ Jl 12 '71
Where have all the eggplants gone? English sculptor's account of his own monument to les Halles. R. Mason. il Art N 70:72-4+ N '71

Monuments, statues, etc.
Courbet and the column. C. R. Baldwin. il Art N 70:36-8 My '71
Paris must; Memorial to the martyrs of deportation. R. Goetz. Chr Cent 88:646 My 26 '71

Music
Opera buffa; new administrator for the Paris opéra. Newsweek 78:73-4 Ag 9 '71
Questions and answers; eight days of modern music. R. McMullen. il Hi Fi 21:MA28+ My '71
Report:
Die Walküre and Rossini's Pietra del paragone. D. Stevens. Opera N 36:30-1 D 11 '71

Newspapers
Pinch in Paris. il Time 98:53 D 27 '71

Police
Letter from Paris; street corner talks between police and students. Genêt. New Yorker 47: 95 Mr 27 '71

Stores
Turning on in Paris. H. Gault and C. Millau. il Holiday 48:72-5 S '70

Subways
Metro: the Paris subway adds a stylish line. il Life 70:84-9 My 7 '71

Theater
From Paris. S. Kauffmann. New Repub 165: 26+ Ag 7 '71
In Paris, the play "1789." M. Gottfried. il Vogue 158:58 Ag 15 '71
Letter from Paris; production of L'Amante Anglaise. Genêt. New Yorker 47:91-2 F 27 '71
Theatre; performances by Le Tréteau de Paris of L'Amante Anglaise, by M. Duras. B. Gill. New Yorker 47:93 Ap 24 '71
PARIS fashion shows. See Fashion shows
PARIS in art
Where have all the eggplants gone? English sculptor's account of his own monument to les Halles. R. Mason. il Art N 70:72-4+ N '71
PARIS international air show. See Aviation—Exhibitions
PARIS Nord airport. See Paris—Airports
PARIS Opéra. See Opera houses
PARIS peace talks. See Vietnamese war, 1957- —Peace mediation—Negotiation meetings, May 1968-
PARISH, Mrs Henry
Living in luxury with Sister Parish. C. Kriebel. il por Harp Baz 105:134 D '71 *
PARISHES
Holy secularity in a rural parish. L. R. Ward. il Cath World 212:259-63 F '71
School crisis, or parish crisis? with editorial comment. G. Elford. Commonweal 93:411-12, 418-20 Ja 29 '71

Caricatures and cartoons
Meanwhile, back at the polarized parish. J. Noonan. Cath World 213:93-4 My '71

PARISI, Mario, and others
Conductance changes produced by acetylcholine in lipidic membranes containing a proteolipid from electrophorus. bibliog il Science 172:56-7 Ap 2 '71

PARK, Brad
Loitering in this Park is forbidden. M. Mulvoy. il por Sports Illus 35:26-7 N 8 '71 *

PARK, C. H. and others
Ascorbic acid: a culture requirement for colony formation by mouse plasmacytoma cells. bibliog il Science 174:720-2 N 12 '71

PARK, Charles
Profiles. J. McPhee. por New Yorker 47:42-8+ Mr 20 '71 *

PARK, Chung Hee
Choosing the familiar. Newsweek 77:50 My 10 '71 *
Landslide for Stone Face. il por Time 97:27 My 10 '71 *

PARK, Ed
How to buy and use maps to improve your hunting. il Field & S 76:68-9+ O '71
Record trout lake you can drive to. il Field & S 76:38-9+ Jl '71
Trout fishing where history happened. il Field & S 76:53-5+ Je '71

PARK, Karen
Karen Park's ceramic wall reliefs. M. Blanchard. il por Ceram Mo 19:24-6 O '71 *

PARK, W. B.
Liberation of Melba Gast. il Look 35:46-7 O 5 '71

PARK and recreation departments
Labor relations. L. B. Eichhold and J. D. Redmond. il Parks & Rec 6:20-2+ N '71

Equipment
Make crews visible. il Am City 86:40 N '71

PARK buildings
Maintenance made easy. il Parks & Rec 6:31+ My '71

PARK crimes. See Crimes and criminals—United States

PARK employees
Labor relations. L. B. Eichhold and J. D. Redmond. il Parks & Rec 6:20-2+ N '71

PARK lane hotel. See New York (city)—Hotels, restaurants, etc.

PARK rangers. See Forest rangers

PARK service personnel. See National park personnel

PARK signs. See Signs and signboards

PARKE-Bernet galleries, inc.
Bull market. il Newsweek 77:113 My 17 '71
Ever upward. il Time 97:83 My 17 '71
Parke-Bernet opens a new west wing. il Bsns W p39 F 27 '71
Photographica at auction. J. Deschin and K. Poli. il Pop Phot 68:58+ Ap '71

PARKE, Davis and company
Health market gets a new giant. il por Bsns W p38-9+ F 20 '71
Special dispensation; overseas sales of chloromycetin. S. Sesser. New Repub 164:16-17 Mr 6 '71

PARKER, Don H.
Revolution or anarchy in our schools? Ed Digest 36:5-8 F '71

PARKER, Elaine
Don't let this go to waste. M. K. Murphy and C. E. Kozoll. il Am Ed 7:6-9 Mr '71 *

PARKER, Franklin
Creation of the Peabody education fund; excerpt from George Peabody: a biography. bibliog por Sch & Soc 99:497-500 D '71
1971 as a centennial year in the history of education. Sch & Soc 99:94-6 F '71

PARKER, Garland G.
Enrollment survey to appear in February issue. Sch & Soc 99:19 Ja '71
Statistics of attendance in American universities and colleges, 1970-71. bibliog f il Sch & Soc 99:105-26 F '71

PARKER, George G. C. and Segura, E. L.
How to get a better forecast. bibliog f il Harvard Bsns R 49:99-109 Mr '71

PARKER, Kallie
Is the way to his heart through his hand? il Seventeen 29:100-1+ Jl '70

PARKER, Maynard
Asia: how stand the dominoes? il Newsweek 78:47+ S 27 '71

PARKER, Paul
Escrow college: high school students study at community colleges. bibliog il Clear House 45:439-43 Mr '71

PARKER, Rod
And whose little boy are you? Criticism New Yorker 47:104-5 My 15 '71 *

PARKER, Sanford S. and others
Business roundup. See issues of Fortune

PARKER, W. R. See Wester, R. E. jt. auth.

PARKER brothers, inc.
Marvin's garden plays Monopoly. il Bsns W p42 N 13 '71

PARKIN, Curtis W. See Dyal, P. jt. auth.

PARKING, Automobile. See Automobile parking

PARKING garages. See Garages; Garages, Municipal

PARKING lots. See Automobile parking

PARKING meters
Home parking meters. il Time 98:102 O 11 '71
Square tubing looks better; Plymouth, Mich. il Am City 86:126 Ap '71

PARKINSON, C. Northcote
Making of college presidents. Cur 125:25-9 Ja '71
Trade winds; interview, ed. by C. Amory. Sat R 54:13 Jl 24 '71

about
Untold secrets. J. Yardley. New Repub 165:27 Jl 10 '71 *

PARKINSON, Norman
Forthright young princess comes of age; photographs. pors Life 71:30-3 Ag 20 '71
H.R.H. the Princess Anne; photographs. Vogue 158:54-7 Ag 15 '71

PARKINSON, Wenda
Place to raise rainbows. il Vogue 157:106-11 Ja 15 '71

PARKINSON'S disease
Melatonin and abnormal movements induced by L-dopa in mice. G. C. Cotzias and others. bibliog il Science 173:450-2 Jl 30 '71

PARKMAN, George
Disappearance of Dr Parkman, by R. Sullivan. Review
    New Repub 165:30 O 9 '71 *

PARKS, Carl
Pacific Northwest: revival in the underground. E. E. Plowman. Chr Today 15:34-5 Ja 29 '71 *

PARKS, Gordon, 1912-
Old master back in the ring; photographs. Life 71:74-9 N 5 '71
Trade winds; interview, ed. by C. Amory. Sat R 54:8 Jl 17 '71

PARKS, John R.
Deep dive for black coral. il Field & S 76:114-16+ D '71

PARKS, Rosa
Whatever happened to Mrs Rosa Parks? il pors Ebony 26:180-1 Ag '71 *

PARKS
See also
Amusement parks
Landscape architecture
Playgrounds
Recreation

Concessions
See Concessions (food, etc)

Equipment
Maintenance made easy. il Parks & Rec 6:31+ My '71

Finance
Broad new funding program, legacy of parks. D. F. Rettie. il Parks & Rec 6:35-8 Ap '71
Sound planning stretches capital funds; questions and answers. R. K. Brown. Parks & Rec 6:37-8+ Jl '71

Maintenance
Maintenance made easy. il Parks & Rec 6:31+ My '71
Maintenance team is born; District of Columbia. E. B. Willard. il Parks & Rec 6:53-4+ My '71
Put more green in the park maintenance budget; Medford, Ore. M. A. Starr. il Am City 86:81+ My '71
Sound planning stretches capital funds; questions and answers. R. K. Brown. Parks & Rec 6:37-8+ Jl '71

Management
Security, safety: two sides of the coin. R. Hall. bibliog il Parks & Rec 6:22+ D '71
See also
Park employees

Canada
See also
British Columbia—Parks and reserves

South America
Parks of the upper Paraná. L. C. Merriam, jr. Nat Parks & Con Mag 45:27 Ag '71

United States
Broad new funding program, legacy of parks. D. F. Rettie. il Parks & Rec 6:35-8 Ap '71
Local parks and recreation; charts and tables. Parks & Rec 6:17-31 Ag '71

PARKS—United States—*Continued*
1970: urban recreation and park... data bench mark year. D. R. Dunn. il por Parks & Rec 6:32-7+ F '71
Parks and recreation. See issues of American city
People's art. R. Sommer. il Natur Hist 80:40-5 F '71
Placing a dollar sign on urban parks; highway location. D. G. Brauer; reply. J. C. Whittaker. Parks & Rec 6:4 Ja '71
Sound planning stretches capital funds; questions and answers. R. K. Brown. Parks & Rec 6:37-8+ Jl '71
Time for appraisal: the legacy of parks; status of HUD's Legacy of the parks program. Parks & Rec 6:9 D '71
We will be ready, Mr President... Parks & Rec 6:20 Mr '71
See also
National parks and reserves—United States
State parks and reserves
also subhead Parks and reserves under names of states, e.g. New York (state)
—Parks and reserves; *also* subhead Parks and playgrounds under names of cities, e.g. Rye, N.Y.—Parks and playgrounds
PARKWAY program. See Philadelphia—Education
PARLIAMENTARY practice
Presidents, politics, and prime ministers; U.S, British, French systems. R. L. Tobin. Sat R 54:20 Ja 16 '71
PARLIAMENTARY union, Inter-. See Interparliamentary union
PARLOR cars. See Railroads—Cars
PARLOR games. See Games
PARMET, Robert D.
Schools for the freedmen. bibliog il Negro Hist Bul 34:128-32 O '71
PARNAS, I. and others
Synaptic transmission in the crayfish: increased release of transmitter substance by bacterial endotoxin. bibliog il Science 171:1153-5 Mr 19 '71
PARNASSUS, George
Out of this I am getting not a nyickl. R. Blount. il por Sports Illus 34:62-4+ My 31 '71 *
PARNELL, Dale
State superintendent teaches first grade. il por Todays Ed 60:29-30 O '71
PAROCHIAL schools. See Church schools
PAROCHIAL schools, Catholic. See Catholic schools
PAROCHIAL schools, Jewish. See Jews—Education
PAROLA, René
Harry Carmean: teacher of classical figure drawing. il por Am Artist 35:58-65+ Mr '71
PAROLE
No exit. W. Gaylin. il Harper 243:86-9+ N '71
One judge, one prisoner; Judge P. Shearin taking custody of T. Eisentrager. Time 98:42 Ag 2 '71
Reforming the prisons. Commonweal 94:467-8 S 17 '71
See also
Probation
PAROLE, Board of. See United States—Parole, Board of
PARRENT, Allan M.
Prayer amendment revisited. Chr Cent 88: 1220-1 O 20 '71
PARRILLA-BONILLA, Antulio, bp
Independence for Puerto Rico. America 125: 37-9 Jl 24 '71
PARRY, H. B. See Bignami, A. jt. auth.
PARRY, Jack
Bunnies by barometer. il Field & S 76:34-5+ S '71
How to match your truck and camper. il Pop Mech 135:166D+ My '71
PARSEGIAN, V. L.
New goals for atomic energy. por Bul Atom Sci 27:2-7 O '71
PARSIFAL; opera. See Wagner, R.
PARSLEY
Vegetable that returns the most. S. R. Ogden. il por Org Gard & Farm 18:38-40 D '71
PARSONS, Donald Holcombe
More tremors jolt a shaky empire. por Bsns W p24-5 F 20 '71 *
PARSONS, Ellen
What's cooking? Org Gard & Farm 18:94-5 Je '71
PARSONS, Melinda
For Steppenwolf; poem. Seventeen 30:80 Ja '71
PARSONS, Richard
Barge your way through France. il Holiday 49:56-60 My '71

PARSONS tables. See Tables
PART time employment
Back to work? Go on your own terms: shorter week or job sharing for women. M. Meade. McCalls 98:46 Jl '71
How to make money in your spare time. J. Kuh. See occasional issues of Ladies' home journal
PARTCH, Harry
Partch for all. L. Stempel. por Sat R 54:72-3 N 27 '71 *
PARTHENOCARPY
Morphactin-induced parthenocarpy in the cucumber. R. W. Robinson and others. bibliog il Science 171:1251 Mr 26 '71
PARTHENOGENESIS
Parthenogenesis: does it occur spontaneously in mice? W. K. Whitten. bibliog Science 171:406-7 Ja 29 '71
PARTHENOGENESIS (plants)
See also
Parthenocarpy
PARTICIPATORY art. See Art, Modern
PARTICLE accelerators. See Accelerators (electrons, etc)
PARTICLE board
New from the woods. J. Hand. Mech Illus 67:50 S '71
PARTICLES
See also
Dust
PARTICLES (nuclear physics)
Do second-class currents exist in beta decay? G. B. Lubkin. bibliog il Phys Today 24:18-20 N '71
Exotic atoms: elementary particles go into orbit. G. L. Wick. Science 172:46 Ap 2 '71
Gold in a silver mine; intermediate boson. Sci Am 225:42+ O '71
New subatomic particle appears; intermediate boson, or W particle. il Sci Digest 70:67-8 N '71
Parton: it works even if you don't believe in it. G. B. Lubkin. Phys Today 24:17+ F '71
Partons: new fundamental particles in the nucleons? A. L. Hammond. Science 173:1223-4 S 24 '71
Quark search gets help from Millikan. G. B. Lubkin. il Phys Today 24:17-18 My '71
Science's hunt for the missing links of nature; use of the periodic system. V. I. Gol'danskii. il UNESCO Courier 24:28-31 Je '71
Theory of early universe explains particle production. G. B. Lubkin. Phys Today 24:19 D '71
Twelve subnucleons. Sci N 99:144 F 27 '71
W particle may have been found. il Sci N 100:121-2 Ag 21 '71
Weak interaction: puzzle of the fourth force. D. E. Thomsen. il por Sci N 100:252-3 O 9 '71
See also
Hyperons
Mesons
Neutrinos
Neutrons
Protons
Scattering (physics)

Acceleration

Energetic protons. Sci Am 225:75 S '71
ISR experiment shows scaling behavior. G. B. Lubkin. bibliog il Phys Today 24:17-18 S '71
Photons as hadrons. F. V. Murphy and D. E. Yount. il Sci Am 225:94-104 bibliog (p 122) Jl '71
Physical sciences; report of 1971 particle accelerator conference. Sci N 99:183 Mr 13 '71
Proton-proton collisions. Sci N 100:55-6 Jl 24 '71
Superheavy nuclei from Orsay's Alice. Sci N 100:373 D 4 '71
What's in a proton? D. E. Thomsen. il Sci N 100:346-7 N 20 '71
PARTICLES, Virus-like. See Virus-like particles
PARTIES. See Balls (parties); Entertaining
PARTIN, Edward Grady
Hoffa and the witness; Hoffa-Partin affair. T. Bethell. Nation 212:678-9 My 31 '71 *
PARTITIONS
Dividing. N. Seney and J. Pinkham. il Bet Hom & Gard 49:44-5 My '71
Leading off with wood. il Bet Hom & Gard 49:133 D '71
Vertical stripes to hide and to divide. il Sunset 146:112 Mr '71
With partial walls, a better entry. il Sunset 147:143 N '71

PARTITIONS, Movable
Ingenious ways to turn one room into two;
sculptured plywood forms. il House & Gard
140:152-3 O '71
PARTNERSHIP
See also
Joint adventures
Limited partnership
PARTNERSHIP for the arts (organization)
First in war, first in space, and last in
support for the arts? D Preiss. il Am
Artist 35:5 Ap '71
PARTONS. See Particles (nuclear physics)
PARTRIDGE, David
Artist with nails. R. Fox. il pors Design 72:
16-17 mid-Wint '71 •
PARTRIDGE, Rondal
It's about too late for Tahoe; photographs.
Audubon 73:46-62+ My '71
PARTS of speech
Character parts in the drama of English
grammar. B. Berman. Clear House 45:380-2
F '71
PARTURIER, Françoise
One woman, one vote. por Time 97:33 Ja 25
'71 •
PARTY affiliation

Anecdotes, facetiae, satire, etc.
Scion. G. Ace. Sat R 54:6 O 30 '71
PARTY funds. See Campaign funds
PARTY games. See Games
PARVIN, Betty
Comment. P. Schjeldahl. Poetry 117:274-5 Ja
'71 •
PARVIN, Stuart A.
Miniaturia. See issues of Hobbies
PARVIN-Dohrmann company. See Recrion cor-
poration
PASADENA, Calif.
Rosy lighting for the Rose bowl. il Am City
86:124 Ap '71
Education
Concern for children; Pasadena public li-
brary, Calif; letter to the editor. B. L.
Ryder. Library J 96:1059+ Mr 15 '71
Parades
U.S. journal: waiting for the roses. C. Tril-
lin. New Yorker 46:85-9 Ja 16 '71
PASADENA, Calif, public library
Concern for children; letter to editor. B. L.
Ryder. Library J 96:1059+ Mr 15 '71
PASAMANICK, Benjamin
Child is being beaten; address, March 21,
1971. Vital Speeches 37:465-72 My 15 '71
PASCAL, Donald D.
Specialized profits. A. A. Butkus. por Duns
98:48-9 D '71 •
PASCHAL, Justin
Gift of Christmas; poem. America 125:558
D 25 '71
Grace; poem. Chr Cent 88:338 Mr 17 '71
PASEO houses. See Architecture, Domestic
—California
PASEWARK, Richard A. and Rardin, M. W.
Theoretical models in community mental
health. bibliog Ment Hy 55:358-64 Jl '71
PASKO, Donald G.
Saving a fish for tomorrow. il Cons 26:48-9+
Ag '71
PASOCHOA and Cotopaxi; story. See Pomeroy,
M. B.
PASQUALINI, François
How to sell articles to British magazines.
il Writers Digest 51:25-7 O '71
PASS-throughs
Pass-through for garbage cans. il Sunset
146:175 Ap '71
PASSAIC RIVER
? pollution of the water supply of—;
1887 lawsuit against industries polluting
the Passaic River. il Chem 44:19-20 Ap '71
PASSENGER fares. See Airlines—Fares
PASSENGER loading systems. See Airports
—Equipment
PASSENGER pigeons
Audubon. J. Shepherd. il Look 35:26-8 O 19
'71
PASSENGER service on airlines. See Airlines
—Passenger service
PASSENGER trains. See Railroads—Trains
PASSIFLORA. See Passion flowers
PASSING; story. See Morgan B.
PASSINO, Jacque
Racetrack is still Detroit's best test track!
interview, ed. by D. O'Reilly. il pors Pop
Mech 136:76-9 Ag '71

PASSION flowers
Butterfly-plant coevolution: has passiflora
adenopoda won the selectional race with
heliconiine butterflies? L. E. Gilbert. bib-
liog il Science 172:585-6 My 7 '71
PASSION music
See also
Phonograph records—Passion music
PASSION of Christ. See Jesus Christ—Passion
PASSION plays
Mesa del Nayar's strange Holy week; Cora
Indians celebration. G. Aldana E. il por
Nat Geog 139:780-95 Je '71
PASSIONS of the mind; story. See Stone, I.
PASSIVE resistance to government
See also
Tax evasion
PASSOVER
Is Passover Christian? il Time 97:70 Ap 12 '71
Passover telecast. W. G. Pippert. Chr Today
15:40 Mr 26 '71
PASSPORT restrictions. See Travel regulations
PASSPORTS
Additional post offices to accept passport
applications. Dept State Bul 64:765 Je 14
'71
International travel: consular operations; ad-
dress, February 16, 1971. B. M. Watson. Vi-
tal Speeches 37:463-5 My 15 '71
My visit to the United States; refusal of visa;
with editorial comment. E. Schumacher.
Nation 212:666-8 My 24 '71
Post offices throughout U.S. to accept pass-
port applications. Dept State Bul 65:109
Jl 26 '71
PAST, The
Nostalgia: sentimental craze for the past;
symposium. il Life 70:39-56+ F 19 '71
PASTA. See Cookery, Italian; Macaroni
PASTAN, Linda
Swimming last summer; poem. Esquire 75:
177 Ap '71
PASTEGA, Louie Leroy, family
It's all in this family, too. M. Frady. il Life
71:61-2+ N 19 '71
PASTEL drawing
See also
Crayon drawing
PASTON, Herbert S.
Oil crayon. il Design 72:11 mid-Wint '71
PASTORAL counseling
Minister's workshop. See issues of Chris-
tianity today
Pastoral counseling; with NAMH position
statement. R. B. Sloane and D. F. Horvitz.
bibliog Ment Hy 55:538-43 O '71
PASTORAL drama
Agazzari's Eumelio, a dramma pastorale. M.
F. Johnson. bibliog f il Mus Q 57:491-505
Jl '71
PASTORAL letters
Appeal for activism; apostolic letter ad-
dressed to Maurice Cardinal Roy of Quebec.
il por Time 97:46 My 24 '71
Variations on a theme; abortion pastoral.
Commonweal 94:229 My 14 '71
PASTORAL psychology. See Pastoral counseling
PASTORAL theology
Burying the Gospel. D. G. Bloesch. Chr To-
day 15:8-11 S 24; 16:12-14 O 8 '71
Counseling confab explores counterculture,
women's liberation and homosexuality. C. J.
Edson. Chr Cent 88:1473-4 D 15 '71
Urban training, English style; Urban minis-
try project. R. H. Luecke. Chr Cent 88:
1348-51 N 17 '71
PASTORE, Arthur R. Jr
Having wonderful time, wish you were there.
Writer 84:17-19+ O '71
PASTORE, Nicholas. See Ferris, S. H. jt.
auth.
PASTRY
Cruller that looks like a butterfly; Chinese
rosettes. il Sunset 146:151-2 Je '71
Gallic wedding treat; croquembouche, cream
puffs. R. A. Sokolov. il N Y Times Mag
p45 Ag 8 '71
Great Danes; with recipes. M. Happel. il
Ladies Home J 88:138-9 Mr '71
See also
Pie
Tarts
PASTURES
Here's a workable year-round pasture plan.
Suc Farm 69:no3 H6 F '71
928 pounds of beef an acre; irrigating dry-
land pasture. C. Peterson, jr. il Suc Farm
69:B4 Ag '71
Nitrogen can be applied safely on grassland.
C. E. Sommers. Suc Farm 69:40 N '71
See also
Grazing
Stock ranges

PATCHWORK
Patchwork: as American as blue jeans. il
House & Gard 139:68-9 F '71
Patchwork fashions; custom patching of
jeans. il Time 97:46-7 Jl 12 '71
Patchwork heritage, Appalachia's indigenous
quilting crafts. T. W. Moore. il Chr Cent
88:233-4 F 17 '71
PATCHWORK quilts. See Quilts
PATEL, C. K. N. See Kreuzer, L. B. jt. auth.
PATENT cooperation treaty. See Patents—
International aspects
PATENT laws and legislation
See also
Patents—Licensing
Patents and government-developed inventions
PATENT medicine. See Medicines, Patent, pro-
prietary, etc.
PATENT office (United States) See United
States—Patent office
PATENTS
Do patents pay? F. M. Butrick. il Pop Mech
135:68-9+ Je '71
Patent talk; how to get a patent. A. S.
Cookfair. Radio-Electr 42:53+ F '71
See also
Inventions
Pollution—Control—Patents
History
Patents reflect trends: lawn mowers. il Parks
& Rec 6:28-9 My '71
Staying afloat in the patent office. M. Sher-
wood. il Am West 8:16-17 My '71
International aspects
Patent cooperation treaty signed by 35 coun-
tries. Dept State Bul 64:218 F 15 '71
See also
World intellectual property organization
Licensing
Little colossus of holography. il Bsns W
p 122-3 S 11 '71
Patent system needs overhauling. il Bsns W
p65+ D 4 '71
Treasure chests of technology unlocked; GE
program. V. Louviere. Nations Bsns 59:15 F
'71
See also
International license agreements
PATENTS and government-developed inven-
tions
Gatorade and patent policy. Sci N 100:143
Ag 28 '71
White House adjusts patent policy. C. Holden.
Science 173:1007 S 10 '71
PATER, Walter Horatio
Walter Pater: humanist, by R. Crinkley. Re-
view
Nat R 23:265-6 Mr 6 '71. G. Davenport
PATERA, Ken
Good things come in large packages. P. Put-
nam. il pors Sports Illus 35:16-18+ Ag 23
'71 *
PATERNO, Joe
Trade winds; interview, ed. by C. Amory.
Sat R 55:6 Ja 1 '72
about
Saved by the itch to switch. P. Putnam. il
Sports Illus 35:24-5 O 25 '71 *
PATERSON, N.J.
Music
Report:
Anna Bolena. R. D. Daniels. il Opera N
36:37-8 D 25 '71
PATÉS. See Cookery—Meat
PATHMARK. See Supermarkets general cor-
poration
PATHOLOGISTS
Crime doctors; forensic pathologists. il News-
week 78:67-8 O 11 '71
PATHOLOGY
See also
Inflammation
Paleopathology
PATHS. See Garden walks; Trails
PATIENTS and physicians. See Physicians and
patients
PATIL, Shivanand R. and others
Identification of each human chromosome
with a modified Giemsa stain. bibliog il
Science 173:821-2 Ag 27 '71
PATIO furniture. See Furniture, Outdoor
PATIOS. See Outdoor rooms
PATMAN, Wright
Battle over $300-billion in bank trusts. il
por Bsns W p64-7 Jl 24 '71 *
Minor national monument. R. Sherrill. Na-
tion 212:137-41, F 1 '71; Reply. J. F.
Doherty. 212:418+ Ap 5 '71 *

Multiple warhead aimed at the banks. por
Bsns W p 19 Ap 24 '71 *
Patman's new threat to the bankers. por
Bsns W p20 Ap 3 '71 *
Profit motive and the public interest:
Wright Patman vs. the bankers. W. Sha-
piro. il Ramp Mag 9:16-20 My '71 *
PATON, Alan
Alan Paton: revisions. Nat R 23:852 Ag 10
'71 *
PATRIARCA, Raymond
Death of a mob family. T. Renner. Read Di-
gest 98:175-6+ My '71 *
PATRIOTISM
We need a new kind of patriotism. R. Nader.
por Life 71:4 Jl 9 '71
See also
Americanism
PATROL boats, Police. See Police boats
PATRONAGE, Art. See Art patronage
PATRONAGE, Political
Such good friends; investigation over choice
of underwriters for postal bonds. News-
week 78:82+ O 11 '71
Taking the politics out of the paycheck. Bsns
W p22 My 22 '71
To the victor, by M. Tolchin and S. Tol-
chin. Review
Commonweal 94:432-4 Ag 20 '71. R.
Whitehead, jr.
See also
Nepotism
PATRUSKY, Ben
Healthy mind? il Look 35:62 Je 1 '71
PATTEN, Donald L.
Portable sound systems for performers. il
Electr World 86:27-9+ Ag; 38-40 S '71
PATTEN, Irene M.
Civil war as romance of noble warriors and
maidens chaste. il Am Heritage 22:48-53+
Ap '71
PATTERN glass. See Glassware
PATTERN perception
Scanpaths in eye movements during pattern
perception. D. Noton and L. Stark. bibliog
il Science 171:308-11 Ja 22 '71; Reply with
rejoinder. H. H. Spitz. 173:753 Ag 20 '71
See also
Optical pattern recognition
PATTERNS (dress)
How to transfer a Sunset pattern. Sunset
146:131 Mr '71
PATTERSON, Claire
Coin of the realm. il Time 98:66 O 4 '71 *
PATTERSON, Doris
Our community sends its boys and girls to
college. il Parents Mag 46:52-3+ Ap '71
PATTERSON, Franklin
College presidents and students; interview.
Mlle 73:247+ Ag '71
PATTERSON, Herbert Parsons
Cutting down on lost causes. il pors Nations
Bsns 59:60-3 F '71
PATTERSON, Jack
Wall of zoning. Commonweal 94:283-5 My 28
'71
PATTERSON, Lois W.
Bibb lettuce, a very big return on a small
investment. il Org Gard & Farm 18:102+
O '71
Gain an extra growing season with artificial
lighting. il Org Gard & Farm 18:41-3 D
'71
Good deal, cottonseed meal. Org Gard &
Farm 18:102-3 S '71
Onion and I. il Org Gard & Farm 18:55-7 Mr
'71
PATTERSON, Monica
Women of Belfast. E. McCallion. il America
125:453-6 N 27 '71 *
PATTERSON, Wade N.
In-service micro-college. Todays Ed 60:53 F
'71
PATTON, Edward L.
Patience for a pipeline. A. A. Butkus. por
Duns 97:76 My '71 *
PATTON, George Smith, 1885-1945
My confrontation with General Patton; ex-
cerpt from The brass ring. B. Mauldin. il
pors Life 71:50-2+ Ag 6 '71 *
PATTON, Mary Lou
Open curriculum. il Schol Teach Jr/Sr High
p20-3 S '71
PATTON, Thomas F.
How a new steel emerged from a wreck. il
por Nations Bsns 59:84-5 Ja '71
PATUXENT wildlife research center
New hope at Patuxent. D. Farney. il Nat
Wildlife 9:44-7 O '71
PAUKEN, Thomas W.
Look inside Russia. il por U S News 71:64-7
Ag 2 '71

PAUL, Saint
Teachings
St Paul and the liberated woman. C. Miller. Chr Today 15:13-14 Ag 6 '71
PAUL VI, pope
Will to peace; excerpts from message, January 1, 1971. il UNESCO Courier 24:22-3 F '71
about
Appeal for activism. il por Time 97:46 My 24 '71 *
Can Christians aid violence? P. J. Riga. il Cath World 212:232-6 F '71 *
New "encyclical" on social justice. P. P. McDermott. por Chr Cent 88:748-51 Je 16 '71 *
Papal exhortation to religious. J. C. Haughey. America 125:34 Jl 24 '71 *
Paul VI: Octogesima adveniens. Nat R 23:628 Je 15 '71 *
Pope faces east. T. Beeson. Chr Cent 88:549 My 5 '71 *
Pope Paul's letter. Commonweal 94:299-300 Je 11 '71 *
Power and the glory are passing. J. Roddy. il Look 35:21-5 O 19 '71 *
Priesthood and papal anguish. America 124: 425 Ap 24 '71 *
Protestants and the Pope. L. Morris. Chr Today 15:53-4 F 26 '71 *
Rocking the Pope. il Time 97:41 Ap 26 '71 *
Traveling with humanity; the papal letter. America 124:554 My 29 '71 *
Visit to Asia and Pacific Region
Pope's visit Down Under: stress on unity. R. Mathias. Chr Cent 88:198 F 10 '71
Visit to Poland (proposed)
Papal visit to Poland? America 124:331-2 Ap 3 '71
PAUL, Claudine, and others
Structure of the hinge region of the mu heavy chain of human IgM immunoglobulins. bibliog il Science 172:69-72 Ap 2 '71
PAUL, Leslie
Theological college, or Mayfields novelty. Chr Cent 88:107-8+ Ja 27 '71
PAUL, Michael I, and others
Urinary adenosine 3',5'-monophosphate in the switch process from depression to mania. bibliog il Science 171:300-3 Ja 22 '71
PAUL, Roland A.
Laos: anatomy of an American involvement. il For Affairs 49:533-47 Ap '71
PAUL, Steven
Steven Paul; interview. New Yorker 46:28-31 F 13 '71
PAUL Taylor dance company
American dance season. W. Terry. il Sat R 54:79 Mr 13 '71
Paul Taylor dance company, ANTA theatre, NYC. L. Pastore. Dance Mag 45:96+ Ap '71
PAULING, Linus
Doctor Linus Pauling talks about vitamin C and, . ; interview, ed. by L. Kent. il por Vogue 157:130-1+ Ap 1 '71
about
Can vitamin C really prevent and cure colds? il Good H 172:173-5 Mr '71 *
Linus Pauling and the vitamin controversy. N. Cousins. Sat R 54:37-40+ My 15 '71 *
Pauling pickets. D. Shapley. il por Science 174:482 O 29 '71 *
Vitamin C, Linus Pauling and the common cold. Consumer Rep 36:113-14 F '71 *
Vitamin C mania. P. O'Neil. il por Life 71:55-6+ Jl 9 '71 *
PAULSON, F. M.
(ed) Boating. See issues of Field & stream
PAULSTON, Rolland G.
Education, revolution, and nationalism in Peru. bibliog Sch & Soc 99:361-4 O '71
Revolutionizing educational policy in Cuba. bibliog Sch & Soc 99:452-3 N '71
PAULY, Rose
Chased by the notes; interview, ed. by J. H. Sutcliffe. por Opera N 35:12-13 F 27 '71
PAVAROTTI, Luciano
Music to my ears; performance in La Bohème. I. Kolodin. Sat R 54:16+ Mr 27 '71 *
PAVEMENT markings. See Traffic markings
PAVEMENTS
See also
Curbs
Maintenance and repair
Concrete utility-cut repairs work best; San Diego, Calif. il Am City 86:28 Mr '71
Street cut repairs can be better than the original surface; Southampton, Pa. il Am City 86:35 D '71
See also
Pavements—Surface treatment
Streets—Maintenance and repair

Surface treatment
Grooving tried to prevent wet-weather accidents. il Am City 86:30 O '71
Ground tires reduce pavement cracking; College Station, Tex. L. L. James. il Am City 87:64-5+ F '71
Renew that deteriorated pavement; Cypress, Calif. A. W. Schatzeder. il Am City 86:109-10 Je '71
Seal coats are not enough; Portland, Me. il Am City 86:30 Ap '71
Traffic lines
See Traffic markings
PAVEMENTS, Asphalt
Cost-benefit factors of natural rubber in asphalt pavements. Am City 86:30 O '71
Full-depth asphalt to the rescue; stabilized bases in Ames, Ia. A. O. Chantland. il Am City 86:68+ D '71
See also
Pavements, Rubber asphalt
PAVEMENTS, Concrete
How to provide scale-resistant concrete. Am City 86:26 Ag '71
PAVEMENTS, Glasphalt
Glasphalt paves downtown city block; Omaha, Neb. il Am City 86:19 N '71
PAVEMENTS, Rubber asphalt
Ground tires reduce pavement cracking; College Station. Tex. L. L. James. il Am City 86:64-5+ F '71
PAVESE, Cesare
Nudism; story. Vogue 158:95-6 Jl '71
PAVILIONS
Water wonderland; Ontario place, Toronto. J. M. Dixon. il Arch Forum 135:30-7 Jl '71
See also
Music pavilions
PAVLOVSK palace. See Palaces
PAVÓN (fish) See Cichlids
PAWLOWSKI, Robert S.
Oedipus at Thule; poem. Commonweal 93:549 Mr 5 '71
PAWPAWS. See Papaws
PAX world fund, Inc. See Investment trusts
PAXTON, Harold William
Paxton to head new NSF division of materials research. G. B. Lubkin. il por Phys Today 24:61-2 S '71 *
PAXTON, Worthen
100 years of the Salmagundi club. il Am Artist 35:31+ D '71
PAY-as-you-see television. See Television broadcasting, Subscription
PAY board (United States) See United States —Pay board
PAY differentials. See Wage differentials
PAY television. See Television broadcasting, Subscription programs
PAYMENT
See also
Banks and banking—Bill payment service
Debtor and creditor
PAYMENTS, Balance of. See Balance of payments
PAYNE, Daniel Alexander, bp
Wilberforce university. C. Killian. bibliog il por Negro Hist Bul 34:83-7 Ap '71 *
PAYNE, Donald
How justice works: the people vs. Donald Payne. P. Goldman and D. Holt. il por Newsweek 77:22-4+ Mr 8 '71 *
PAYNE, Ernest
Payne pamphlet. T. Beeson. Chr Cent 88: 793 Je 30 '71
PAYNE, Leslie
Saguaro. il Nat Parks & Con Mag 45:29-31 Ap '71
PAYNE, Melvin M.
Mississippi odyssey begins 1971-72 series of special publications. il Nat Geog 139:882-6 Je '71
PAYNE, Mildred
Great Dismal Swamp. il Nat Parks & Con Mag 45:9-13 F '71
PAYNE, Roger S. and McVay, Scott
Songs of humpback whales. bibliog il Science 173:585-97 Ag 13 '71
PAYNE, Stanley G.
In the twilight of the Franco era. For Affairs 49:342-54 Ja '71
PAYNTER, John Henry
Lincoln graduate writes of Lincoln university, the old and the new; excerpts from Fifty years after. Negro Hist Bul 34:82 Ap '71

PAYTON, Leland
Last chance for the tall grass prairie. il Nat Wildlife 9:25-7 Ag '71

PAZ, Octavio
Configurations. A. Balakian. Sat R 54:28+ Jl 17 '71 *

PEABODY, George
Creation of the Peabody education fund; excerpt from George Peabody: a biography. F. Parker. bibliog por Sch & Soc 99:497-500 D '71 *

PEABODY, Judith
Books. Vogue 157:130+ Ap 15; 158:80 N 1 '71
On target: Judith Peabody. S. Harrington. por Vogue 157:98+ Je '71 *

PEABODY coal company
Bad day at Black Mesa. P. Barnes. New Repub 165:23-4 Jl 17 '71
Big dig at Black Mesa. J. Bishop, jr. il Newsweek 77:75-6 F 8 '71
How Kennecott got hooked with Catch-22. R. Loving, jr. il Fortune 84:98-101+ S '71
Murder of the Southwest. A. M. Josephy, jr. il Audubon 73:52-67 Jl '71
Trinkets for the Navajos. P. Barnes New Repub 165:15-16 Jl 3 '71

PEABODY education fund
Creation of the Peabody education fund; excerpt from George Peabody: a biography. F. Parker. bibliog por Sch & Soc 99:497-500 D '71

PEACE
American strength: the keystone of peace; address, May 29, 1971. R. M. Nixon. Dept State Bul 64:813-15 Je 28 '71
Catholics and peace. Commonweal 95:315-16 Ja 7 '72
Community of science and the search for peace; adaptation of address, April 26, 1971. P. Doty. Science 173:998-1002 S 10 '71
Foreign policy and the United Nations; address, October 4, 1971. W. P. Rogers. Vital Speeches 38:34-8 N 1 '71; Same with title Legacy of peace: our responsibility to future generations. Dept State Bul 65:437-44 O 25 '71
Hesse on peace; excerpt from If the war goes on, tr. by R. Mannheim. H. Hesse. Mlle 72:76-7 Ja '71
Is anybody ready for peace? F. K. Kelly. Sat R 54:16+ Ag 7 '71
It could be heaven; reprint from October 23, 1953 issue. D. Lawrence. U S News 71:112 N 15 '71
Overdue first word on peace and war; program of the Richmond, Va. diocese. E. Glynn. il America 125:396-7 N 13 '71
Peace: and the everlasting arms. Chr Today 15:36-7 S 24 '71
Peace: gift & task; pastoral letter. C. T. Dozier. Commonweal 95:289+ D 24 '71
Purpose of America's power; address, March 12, 1971. R. M. Nixon. Dept State Bul 64:487-9 Ap 5 '71
Will to peace; excerpts from message, January 1, 1971. Paul VI. il UNESCO Courier 24:22-3 F '71
World trend is toward peace, not war. D. Lawrence. U S News 71:116 O 18 '71
See also
Hague peace conferences
International organization
International relations
International security
Pacifism
Stockholm international peace research institute
United Nations—Special committee on peacekeeping operations
Vietnamese war, 1957- —Peace and mediation
War
 Study and teaching
Irenics: the study of peace. America 125:336 O 30 '71

PEACE (theology)
Toward a theology of peace. J. J. Fahey. il Cath World 213:64-8 My '71

PEACE and education. See War and education

PEACE conferences
Another evaluation of the CPC. P. Verghese. Chr Cent 88:1319 N 10 '71
Fun and games in the CPC. Chr Cent 88:1244 O 20 '71
Internal problems vitiate Christian peace conference. Chr Today 15:46 S 24 '71
Onward as to war? a report from Prague; Christian peace conference. M. Mayer. Chr Cent 88:1316-19 N 10 '71

PEACE corps. See United States—Peace corps

PEACE lobby. See Lobbying

PEACE of mind
Peace of mind; views of prominent Americans. il Look 35:20-4+ Jl 27 '71; Same abr. with title Prescriptions for peace of mind. Read Digest 99:61-5 N '71

PEACE posters. See Posters

PEACEFUL uses of atomic power. See Atomic power—Economic aspects

PEACHES
Hard times hit the peach growers. F. Allen. il Org Gard & Farm 18:58-63 My '71
 See also
Cookery—Fruit

PEACOCK pavón (fish) See Cichlids

PEALE, Charles Willson
Charles Willson Peale's portrait of Robert and Gouverneur Morris. C. C. Sellers. il pors Antiques 99:404-6 Mr '71 *

PEALE, Norman Vincent
Eight steps to a new life. Read Digest 99:121-4 N '71
Peace of mind. por Look 35:29 Jl 27 '71
We need their faith! Read Digest 99:138-41 D '71

PEALE, Ruth (Stafford)
Tested ways of saving your marriage; excerpt from The adventure of being a wife. Read Digest 99:72-5 Jl '71

PEANUT brittle. See Candy

PEANUTS (comic strip) See Comics (books, strips, etc)

PEARCE, J. B. and others
Mariner 6 and Mariner 7 ultraviolet spectrometer: in-flight measurements of simulated Jupiter atmosphere. bibliog il Science 172:941-3 My 28 '71

PEARL fisheries
Pearl hunting in Scotland. il Sci Digest 69:21-3 Ap '71

PEARL HARBOR, Attack on, 1941
Pearl Harbor survivors; reminiscences. il Newsweek 78:16-17 D 13 '71

PEARL Lang dance company
Pearl Lang and dance company, ANTA theatre, NYC. M. Marks. Dance Mag 45:96 Ap '71

PEARLE, Philip
Quantum theory fails the single system. por Phys Today 24:38 Ap '71

PEARLS
If oysters screamed. . . G. M. Semmes. il Holiday 49:41+ Jl '71

PEARLSTEIN, Philip
Conversation with Philip Pearlstein; ed. by E. Schwartz. il Art in Am 59:50-7 S '71

PEARLSTEIN, Seymour
Seymour Pearlstein. D. Hines. il por Am Artist 35:62-7+ F '71 *

PEARS
 Diseases and pests
Perfect fruit, it's in the bag; protecting Bartlett pears. C. Sauerland. Org Gard & Farm 18:93 S '71

PEARS, Pickled. See Pickles and relishes

PEARSON, Allen D. and Miller, J. A.
Tornado season of 1970. il Weatherwise 24:12-17 F '71

PEARSON, David
You aren't playing the course, you're playing the designer. il Esquire 75:130-5 Ap '71

PEARSON, John F.
Science worldwide. See issues of Popular mechanics

PEARSON, Keith L.
Watch out, you might assimilate; with biographical sketch. il Natur Hist 80:4, 24-33 Je '71

PEARSON, Lester Bowles
Experienced anti-American. L. Tiger. New Repub 164:30 F 13 '71 *

PEARSON, S. and son, ltd.
Clever person can always make money. il Forbes 108:24-5 Ag 15 '71

PEARSON, Sigfrid
Centralize your fleet for economy's sake. il por Am City 86:88+ Je '71

PEAS
Put sugar peas on your list; edible-podded peas. D. W. Weinsheimer. il Horticulture 49:45 Je '71
There are no peas like snow peas! A. G. Hodge. il Org Gard & Farm 18:62-4 D '71
Your peas can sprawl or they can climb. il Sunset 147:248 O '71
 See also
Cookery—Vegetables

PEAS, Edible-podded. See Peas
PEASANTRY
See also
Land tenure

Vietnam (Republic)
See also
Vietnamese war, 1957- —Pacification pro-
grams
PEASE, Deborah
Trade winds; interview, ed. by C. Amory.
Sat R 54:12 Je 12 '71
PEASE, Paul L. See De Valois, R. L. jt. auth.
PEBBLE pictures. See Pictures
PECCEI, Aurelio
Fade out for private cars? Cur 134:52-5 N
'71
PECHTER, William S.
Movies (title varies) (cont) Commentary 51:
76-8 Mr; 79-81 Ap; 87-9 Je; 52:84-6 Ag;
24+ S '71; 53:78-80 Ja '72
PECK, Ellen
Should you force your child to go to nur-
sery school? il Todays Health 49:58-62 Ag
'71
PECK, Jim. See Engelhardt, T. jt. auth.
PECK, John
Afterward; poem. New Yorker 47:128 N 13
'71
Hunger-trace; poem. New Yorker 47:36 Ag 14
'71
PECK, Ralph H.
Instant India. il Travel 136:28-35+ S '71
PECK, Richard
Can students evaluate their education? il
PTA Mag 65:4-7 bibliog(p36) F '71; Same
abr. Ed Digest 36:29-31 My '71
Street trio; poem. Sat R 54:6 S 4 '71
We can save our schools. il Parents Mag
46:51-3+ S '71
PECK, Royal L.
For Catholics, another 95-point crisis. Chr
Today 15:34 Ag 27 '71
PECKHAM, Kenneth L.
Teaching foreign languages: need for ac-
cord. Clear House 45:523 My '71
PECKINPAH, Sam
Peckinpah: primitive horror. il por Time 98:
85+ D 20 '71 *
Peckinpah's progress. D. Yergin. il pors
N Y Times Mag p 16-17+ O 31 '71 *
PECKVILLE, Pa.
No joy in Peckville; problems of theater
owner Nick Angeli, jr. J. Morgenstern.
Newsweek 77:17 Je 7 '71
PEDAGOGY. See Teaching
PEDDLERS and peddling
See also
Street trades
PEDERSEN, John D.
Mr Pedersen's secret weapon. C. Worman. il
Hobbies 75:150-1 F '71 *
PEDERSEN, Nelda. See Bolarsky, C. jt. auth.
PEDERSEN, Paul
Possibilities for violence in Malaysia. bibliog
f Cur Hist 61:339-44+ D '71
PEDERSEN, Richard F.
New trends in U.S. foreign policy; address,
February 17, 1971. Dept State Bul 64:322-7
Mr 15 '71
Youth, change, and foreign policy; address,
November 12. 1970. Dept State Bul 63:718-22
D 14 '70
PEDRAM, Manouchehr
Unique approach to inner-city teacher educa-
tion. Clear House 45:297-9 Ja '71
PEEKE, Harman V. S. and Herz, M. J.
Caudate nucleus stimulation retroactively
impairs complex maze learning in the rat.
bibliog il Science 173:80-2 Jl 2 '71
PEELE, David
Cataloging on the wall. Wilson Lib Bul 45:
772-4 Ap '71
PEEPHOLE in the gate; story. See Singer, I. B.
PEERCE, Jan
Musician of the month. J. Hiemenz. il por
Hi Fi 21:MA4-5 D '71 *
PEERMAN, Dean
Church-hopping in Havana. Chr Cent 88:
1435-8 D 8 '71
PEET, Creighton
Ultima Thule. il Am For 77:12-15+ Je '71
Your career in architecture. il Sci Digest 69:
60-4 Je '71
PEET, John
Expatriate chess on the other side of the
wall. E. Shorris. il pors N Y Times Mag
p32+ My 23 '71 *
PEIRCE, Jon
My brother's cooking. S. Peirce. por Seven-
teen 30:162 Mr '71 *

PEIRCE, Susan
My brother's cooking. por Seventeen 30:162
Mr '71
PEKING man. See Man, Prehistoric
PEKKANEN, John
If they get out of line, he'll bust their
heads. il Life 71:34 O 29 '71
PELAGIC foraminifera. See Foraminifera
PELAMIS platurus. See Sea snakes
PELICANS
Will the brown pelican survive? H. H. Har-
rison. il Nat Wildlife 9:25-7 Je '71
PELIKAN, Jaroslav Jan
Scholar's scholar. il por Newsweek 78:62 S
6 '71 *
PELL, Claiborne
U.N. adopts principles governing seabed ex-
ploitation and decides to convene compre-
hensive law-of-the-sea conference in 1973;
statement, November 26, 1970. Dept State
Bul 64:150-4 F 1 '71
U.N. General assembly urges humane treat-
ment of prisoners of war; statement, No-
vember 6, 1970. Dept State Bul 64:8-11 Ja 4
'71
United Nations adopts resolution on human
environment conference; statement, Decem-
ber 7, 1970. Dept State Bul 64:67-9 Ja 11 '71
Work of U.N. high commissioner for ref-
ugees commended by U.S; statement,
November 17. 1970. Dept State Bul 64:96-8
Ja '71
PELL, Roger, pseud.
Agonizing decision of Joanne and Roger
Pell. Good H 174:76-7+ Ja '72
PELLEGRINO, Edmund Daniel
Egeberg's successor. Time 97:42 Mr 29 '71 *
PELLETED feed. See Feeding and feeding
stuffs—Pelleted feed
PELOPONNESIAN war, 431-404 B.C. See
Greece, Ancient—History—Peloponnesian
war, 431-404 B.C.
PELTIER, Gary L. See Bartl, C. P. jt. auth.
PELTON, Gerald W.
Cooperation, mountain style. il Parks & Rec
6:34-5 N '71
PELTS. See Hides and skins
PELZER, David
Back into the future. il Cons 26:32-3 D '71
PEMBROKE, Trevor
Darkness in the North. il Nat R 23:868-70+
Ag 10 '71
PEN club. See PEN club
PENAL law. See Criminal law
PENAL reform. See Prisons
PENCILS
Don't chew your pencil. Sci Digest 70:29 N
'71
Lead in pencils, but not in the lead. Con-
sumer Rep 36:646-8 N '71
Lead poisoning: risks for pencil chewers?
J. Pichirallo. Science 173:509-10 Ag 6 '71
Pencil chewers beware. Chem 44:5 N '71
PENDERECKI, Krzysztof
Tragedy of Father Urbain. D. Hamilton.
il Hi Fi 21:69-70 Je '71 *
PENDLETON, Clarence M. jr
Crash funding won't do it! il por Parks &
Rec 6:39-41+ Ap '71
Penny's pavilion. il Parks & Rec 6:42+ My
'71
PENDULUM
See also
Gravity
PENGELLEY, Eric T. and Asmundson, S. J.
Annual biological cloak; with biographical
sketches. il Sci Am 24:14, 72-9 Ap '71
PENGUINS
Fairy penguins of Australia. il Sci Digest 69:
21 Je '71
PENGUINS, Fossil
Fossil penguin from the late cenozoic of
South Africa. G. G. Simpson. il Science 171:
1144-5 Mr 19 '71
PENICILLIN
Penicillin as an epileptogenic agent: effect on
an isolated synapse. G. F. Ayala and others.
bibliog il Science 171:915-17 Mr 5 '71
PENICILLIN allergy. See Drug allergy
PENICK, James
Professor Cope vs. Professor Marsh. il pors
Am Heritage 22:4-13+ Ag '71
PENITENCE. See Repentance
PENKNIVES. See Knives
PENMAN, Sheldon. See Zylber, E. A. jt. auth.
PENMANSHIP
Decade of research in handwriting. E. Askov,
and others. Ed Digest 36:43-6 Mr '71
PENMARRIC; novel. See Howatch, S.

PENN, Arthur
On directors and technicians. il Harp Baz 104:65 Jl '71
about
Difficulties of Little big man. L. Braudy. il Film Q 25:30-3 Fall '71 •
Pennmanship. C. L. Westerbeck, jr. il Commonweal 93:397-8 Ja 22 '71 •
PENN, Elizabeth E.
Elementary art education in Osaka, Japan. il Sch Arts 70:46-8 Ap '71
PENN, Irving
Love flowers; the rose; photographs. Vogue 158:151+ D '71
Veiled Morocco; photographs. Vogue 158:116-23 D '71
PENN Central company
Boxcar caper. Newsweek 77:86+ Mr 29 '71
Faint chance for the Penn Central. il Bsns W p70-2 My 29 '71
Foiling the wolf. Forbes 107:20 Mr 15 '71
Gravy train. Time 97:86 F 22 '71
Has Penn Central been nationalized? il Bsns W p 19 Ja 23 '71
House report puts Penphil under fire. il Bsns W p22 F 20 '71
How Penn Central lost in Liechtenstein. Bsns W p41 Mr 13 '71
Penn Central: a year later. il Bsns W p92+ Je 19 '71
Penn Central makes some mileage. Bsns W p24-5 Mr 6 '71
Penn Central: now the family jewels; forthcoming sale of real-estate. il Newsweek 77:79 Je 14 '71
Penn Central sells off. Time 97:82 Je 14 '71
Penn Central's blues. il Newsweek 78:79 N 1 '71
Right to know; trading of Penn Central stock before bankruptcy. Newsweek 77:85-6 Ap 12 '71
We're broke, he told the workers. We need your help. M. Smith. il pors Life 71:69-70+ S 24 '71
Who took the boxcars when PC wasn't looking? il Bsns W p34 Mr 27 '71
PENN Dixie cement corporation
Jerry Castle's ordeal. por Forbes 108:20-1 Jl 15 '71
PENNELL, Robert M. See Vandell, R. F. jt. auth.
PENNEY, Alexandra
Party maximus. House & Gard 140:32+ N '71
PENNEY, James Cash
Golden rule merchant. por Time 97:89 F 22 '71 •
Obituary
Chr Today 15:39 Mr 12 '71
Newsweek por 77:73 F 22 '71
PENNEY, J. C, company
Batten of J. C. Penney. il por Forbes 107:66 My 15 '71
Penney steps out. il Forbes 107:19 F 15 '71
PENNINGTON, Anne
(tr) See Popa, V. Give me back my rags
PENNINGTON, Malcolm W.
How to make the least of planning. il Nations Bsns 59:78-9 Je '71
PENNSAUKEN, N.J.
New and old storm drains team up. A. R. Pagan. il Am City 86:112 Ap '71
PENNSYLVANIA
See also
Allegheny County
Booksellers and bookselling—Pennsylvania
Camps—Pennsylvania
Education—Pennsylvania
Express highways—Pennsylvania
Finance—Pennsylvania
Fishing—Pennsylvania
Hunting—Pennsylvania
Justice. Administration of—Pennsylvania
Landscape protection—Pennsylvania
Lebanon County
Music festivals—Pennsylvania
Prisons—Pennsylvania
Reclamation of land—Pennsylvania
School libraries—Pennsylvania
Skis and skiing—Pennsylvania
Taxation—Pennsylvania
PENNSYLVANIA Amish. See Pennsylvania Germans
PENNSYLVANIA ballet
Pennsylvania ballet, Academy of music, Philadelphia. S. Smoliar. Dance Mag 45:71 F '71
PENNSYLVANIA Dutch. See Pennsylvania Germans
PENNSYLVANIA German pottery. See Pottery, American
PENNSYLVANIA Germans
Amish are wexelin. R. Gehman. il Holiday 49:60-3+ Ap '71

PENNSYLVANIA library association
Pennsylvania LA conference: elegant & upbeat. W. R. Eshelman. Wilson Lib Bul 46:312 D '71
PENNSYLVANIA New York Central transportation company. See Penn Central company
PENNSYLVANIA railroad station, New York. See New York (city)—Stations
PENNSYLVANIA state university
Mau-mauing at Penn state. H. Caton. Nat R 23:428 Ap 20 '71
PENNSYLVANIA. University, Philadelphia
Experimental colleges and communes. R. Kirk. Nat R 23:147 F 9 '71

Hospital
Hospital of the University of Pennsylvania in Philadelphia. il Antiques 99:520 Ap '71
PENPHIL (firm) See Investment trusts
PENROSE annual
Penrose annual, 1971; ed. by H. Spencer. Review
Pub W il 200:54-5 Ag 2 '71. C. B. Grannis
PENSACOLA, Fla.

Education
Place where learning happens; Escarosa humanities center. S. K. DeMarko. il Am Ed 7:21-3 My '71
PENSION benefits. See Pensions
PENSION funds and funding. See Pensions—Finance
PENSION trusts
Pensions: pitfalls in the fine print. il Time 98:48-9 Ag 23 '71
PENSIONS
Changes ahead in pension plans; interview. F. L. Griffin, jr. por U S News 70:88-92 Ap 5 '71
Early retirement time bomb. il Nations Bsns 59:20-4 F '71
Growth benefits in a cohort of pension plans. H. E. Davis. bibliog il Mo Labor R 94:46-50 My '71
Incidence of private retirement plans; with tables. E. Beier. Mo Labor R 94:37-40 Jl '71
More help for private pensions, the Nixon blueprint. il U S News 71:49-51 D 20 '71
Pension formula summarization: an emerging research technique; with tables. A. Strasser. bibliog f Mo Labor R 94:49-56 Ap '71
Pensions elite. J. H. Schultz. New Repub 164:9-10 My 15 '71
Pensions: pitfalls in the fine print. il Time 98:48-9 Ag 23 '71
Retirement age dilemma; address, November 9, 1970. E. S. Willis. Vital Speeches 37:204-6 Ja 15 '71
Searching look at pension plans. Bsns W p40 Ap 10 '71
See also
Municipal employees—Pensions
Old age pensions
State employees—Pensions
United mine workers of America—Welfare and retirement fund

Finance
Big steel's little switch; change in pension fund accounting. Forbes 108:50 D 1 '71
Danger ahead for pension funds. C. D. Ellis. il Harvard Bsns R 49:50-6 My '71
Navigation guide for pension funds. W. W. Wolbach. Nations Bsns 59:78A-78D Ap '71
Pension plan reforms. I. Ross. Har Yrs 11:19-21+ Ap '71; Same abr. with title What you should know about your pension. Read Digest 98:31-2+ Ap '71
Pressure on pension funds to perform; with editorial comment. il Bsns W p88-9+, 138 S 11 '71
That ever expanding pension balloon. G. Burck. il Fortune 84:100-3+ O '71
See also
Pension trusts

Laws and regulations
Great pension controversy. G. Rosen and A. Hershman. il Duns 97:33-5+ My '71
New pressures to safeguard pensions. il U S News 71:40-2 O 11 '71
Pension protection. New Repub 165:7-8 N 27 '71
Pensions gamble. New Repub 175:11-12 Ag 21 '71
Pressure on pension funds to perform; with editorial comment. il Bsns W p88-9+. 138 S 11 '71
Private pension legislative issues. Nations Bsns 59:21 F '71

PENSIONS—Laws and regulations—*Continued*
Proposed pension legislation; the administration's view; address, December 8, 1970. L. H. Silberman. Vital Speeches 37:197-200 Ja 15 '71
Reform on the way? Newsweek 78:76 D 20 '71
Urged: tighter rules on pension funds. U S News 70:46 Ap 12 '71
PENSIONS for teachers. See Teachers—Pensions
PENSKE, Roger
Slide-rule boys at Indy. R. F. Jones. il pors Sports Illus 34:32-4+ My 31 '71 *
PENTAGASTRIN
Thyrocalcitonin: stimulation of secretion by pentagastrin. C. W. Cooper and others. bibliog il Science 172:1238-40 Je 18 '71
PENTAGON papers. See Defense information, Classified; Vietnamese war, 1957- —History
PENTATHLON
Sixteen flags over Texas: Modern pentathlon world championship. A. Higgins. Sports Illus 35:80 O 25 '71
PENTECOSTAL churches
Black origins of the Pentecostal movement. J. S. Tinney. Chr Today 16:4-6 O 8 '71; Discussion. 16:31+ N 19 '71
Pentecostal evangelism: but will it work? J. S. Tinney. Chr Today 16:44 D 3 '71
Theology of joy. S. Darst. Nation 213:440+ N 1 '71
PENTECOSTAL churches in Canada
Deep in the heart of Quebec; Catholic Pentecostal movement. L. K. Tarr. Chr Today 16:44+ N 19 '71
PENTECOSTAL churches in Chile
Street seminaries of Chile. C. P. Wagner. il Chr Today 15:5-8 Ag 6 '71
PENTECOSTAL movement. See Pentecostal churches
PENTHOUSE (periodical)
Prodigal son makes it big. il por Forbes 107:19 Mr 1 '71
PEONIES
Graceful Japanese peonies. G. Wister. il Horticulture 49:20-2 O '71
Time now to plant peonies. M. Price. il Home Gard 58:18-19+ O '71
PEOPLE are living there; drama. See Fugard, A.
PEOPLE-to-people program
Citizen diplomacy; a challenge to Americans; address, March 25, 1971. A. A. Reich. Dept State Bul 64:706-8 My 31 '71
Mr Fraim elected board chairman of People-to-people program. J. P. Fraim. Dept State Bul 63:752 D 21 '70
PEOPLE united to save humanity (organization)
Jackson pushes on. il por Time 99:30 Ja 3 '72
PEOPLES, Clara
Plan for giving. il pors Ebony 27:96-8+ D '71 *
PEOPLES art. See Art, Amateur
PEOPLE'S coalition for peace and justice
Order of battle. il por Time 97:13-15 My 10 '71
PEOPLE'S liberation army. See China (People's Republic)—Armed forces
PEOPLES of the Pacific Hall. See American museum of natural history, New York
PEOPLES parks. See Parks
PEOPLE'S peace treaty
People's peace treaty. Ramp Mag 9:14-17 Ap '71
People's peace treaty. F. Greer and P. Katz. Mlle 73:234 My '71
Students sign a peace treaty. T. H. Ingram. Nation 211:646-8 D 21 '70
PEORIA, Ill.
Renew old sewers and then maintain them. W. A. Olson. il Am City 86:105-6 O '71
Water supply
Observation deck added to water tower. il Am City 86:34 Je '71
PEP (organization) See Environmental associations, committees, etc.
PEPE, Comandante. See Liendo, G. J.
PEPER, Erik. See Luce, G. G. jt. auth.
PEPIN, Arthur C.
IQ test: education's bugaboo. bibliog Clear House 45:278-80 Ja '71
PÉPIN, Jacques
House beautiful chef. See issues of House beautiful

PEPPER, Choral
Great American cookout. il Travel 136:56-61 O '71
Pareu parade. il Travel 135:48-52+ Ap '71
Vancouver vacation. il Travel 135:62-3 Je '71
West coast wanderings. See issues of Travel
PEPPER, Curtis Bill
(ed) See Grace Patricia, consort of Rainier III, prince of Monaco. H.S.H. Princess Grace of Monaco
(ed) See Hepburn, A. Audrey Hepburn Dotti and her family
PEPPERDINE university, Los Angeles
School of business
Where the boss gets an MBA on the job. il Bsns W p86-7 My 8 '71
PEPPERMINT tree. See Agonis
PEPPERS
Really red peppers and how they grow. L. Riotte. il Org Gard & Farm 18:44-5 My '71
See also
Cookery—Vegetables
PEPSICO, inc.
Pepsi's whiz kid. por Bsns W p80 F 6 '71
PEPTIC ulcers
Children with peptic ulcers. A. J. Snider. Sci Digest 69:71-2 My '71
Have a happy ulcer; peptic ulcer. A. J. Snider. il Sci Digest 69:57 Mr '71
How to prevent that ulcer from flaring up. Bsns W p65 Jl 31 '71
Rat race; cause of ulcers. il por Newsweek 78:74-5 S 27 '71
PEPTIDASES
See also
Carboxypeptidases
PEPTIDE biosynthesis. See Biosynthesis
PEPTIDES
Biological activity and synthesis of an encephalitogenic determinant. R. Shapira and others. bibliog il Science 173:736-8 Ag 20 '71
Collagen polypeptides: normal release from polysomes in the absence of proline hydroxylation. E. Lazarides and L. N. Lukens. bibliog il Science 173:723-5 Ag 20 '71
Glycopeptides from the surface of control and virus-transformed cells. C. A. Buck and others. bibliog il Science 172:169-71 Ap 9 '71
Gonadotropin-releasing hormone: one polypeptide regulates secretion of luteinizing and follicle-stimulating hormones. A. V. Schally and others. bibliog il Science 173:1036-8 S 10 '71
Intestinal secretion: stimulation by peptides. G. O. Barbezat and M. I. Grossman. bibliog il Science 174:422-4 O 22 '71
See also
Angiotensin
Glutathione
Pentagastrin
PEPYS, Samuel
Organizer of the ordinary day. V. Miller. Nat R 23:150-1 F 9 '71 *
World of Samuel Pepys, esqre. J. Kenyon. il Horizon 13:57-71 Sum '71 *
PERCEPTION
Cartography of the ecstatic and meditative states. R. Fischer. bibliog il Science 174:897-904 N 26 '71
Eye movements and visual perception. D. Noton and L. Stark. il Sci Am 224:34-43 bibliog(p 136) Je '71
In search of the mind's eye. R. Gore. il Life 71:56+ O 22 '71
Object in the world of the infant. T. G. R. Bower. il Sci Am 225:30-8 bibliog (p 120) O '71
Way of seeing. J. H. Kay. Writer 84:24-6 My '71
See also
Cognition
Extrasensory perception
Figural aftereffects
Human information processing
Motion perception
Pattern perception
Signal detection (psychology)
Sound perception
Space perception
Time perception
Visual discrimination
PERCEPTION, Disorders of
Hidden threats to your child's learning ability. M. Pines. Read Digest 98:29-30+ F '71
See also
Hallucinations and illusions
PERCEPTRONS
See also
Optical pattern recognition

PERCH fishing
Gassed up worms for walleyes. P. Shea. il Field & S 76:86 My '71
How to catch big walleyes. D. Walsh, Jr. il pors Outdoor Life 148:66-7+ N '71
Summer dog days walleye. R. A. Bartnett. il Field & S 76:82-3+ Je '71
Walleye wonderlake. B. Milek. il Field & S 75:76-7+ Ap '71
PERCHED soil. See Slopes (soil mechanics)
PERCIVAL, John
Mad Jack and the missionaries. L. McKee. il pors Am Heritage 22:30-7+ Ap '71 *
PERCIVAL, Lloyd
Testing for athletic talent. D. Newlands. il Look 35:67 Je 1 '71 *
PERCOLATORS, Coffee. See Coffee pots, percolators, etc.
PERCUSSION instruments, Electronic. See Musical instruments, Electronic
PERCUSSION music
See also
Phonograph records—Percussion music
PERCY, Charles Harting
Separation of powers. il Todays Ed 60:36-8 My '71
PERCY, Walker
Authors that bloom in the spring; excerpts from press conference. il por Pub W 199: 23-4 Mr 22 '71
about
Lapsometer legend. M. Duffy. por Time 97: 94 My 17 '71 *
Pilgrimage of Walker Percy. A. Kazin. Harper 242:81-6 Je '71 *
PEREGRINE falcons. See Falcons
PERELMAN, Michael
Second thoughts on the green revolution. New Repub 165:21-2 Jl 17 '71
PERELMAN, Sidney Joseph
Around the bend in eighty days. New Yorker 47:22-4 Ja 1 '72
Machismo mystique. il McCalls 98:88-9+ F '71
Mad about the girl. il Holiday 48:80-1 S '70
about
Verne hero lives. il por Sr Schol 98:6 F 1 '71 *
PERENCHIO, Andrew Gerald
In this corner Jerry Perenchio; interview, ed. by L. Gross. il pors Look 35:92-3+ Je 1 '71
PERENCHIO, Jerry
Ali vs. Frazier: a show-biz approach. por Bsns W p27 F 13 '71 *
Fight of the century has few losers. il Bsns W p44 Mr 13 '71 *
Purse snatchers. il pors Time 97:65-6 Ja 25 '71 *
Sport's $5 million payday. J. Kirshenbaum. il por Sports Illus 34:20-3 Ja 25 '71 *
Take the money and run. il por Newsweek 77:94-5 Mr 8 '71 *
PERENNIALS
Perennials for early bloom. E. S. Henderson. il Horticulture 49:38-41 N '71
Walk with perennials. W. B. Harris. House & Gard 140:76+ O; 64+ N '71
See also
Chrysanthemums
PERERA, Victor
Firewalkers of Udappawa. Harper 242:18+ My '71
Guatemala: always *la violencia.* il N Y Times Mag p 12-13+ Je 13 '71
PÉREZ, Galo René
Ariel today. il por Américas 23:23-4 Ap '71
PEREZ, Paul
It's a good, simple life in Mexico. N. Rothschild. il Pop Phot 68:16+ F '71 *
PEREZ, Rudy
Rudy Perez, in whose hands. M. Last. il pors Dance Mag 45:28-31+ Je '71 *
Stillness of Rudy Perez. D. Jowitt. il Art in Am 59:102-3 My '71 *
PÉREZ DE AYALA, Ramón
Ruera street; story; excerpt from Belarmino and Apolonio; tr. by M. Baumgarten and G. Berns. Yale R 60:383-9 Mr '71
PÉREZ-ESCLARÍN, Antonio
Theology of revolution for the third world. il Cath World 213:277-82 S '71
PEREZ-MORENA, Bianca Teresa
Pagan event. pors Newsweek 77:36 My 24 '71 *
PERFECTION (philosophy)
Perfectibility of man, by J. Passmore. Review Nation 213:185-6 S 6 '71 C. Bedient
PERFECTLY wonderful girl; story. See Soman, F. J.
PERFORMANCE appraisal. See Employees—Rating

PERFORMANCE contracts (education)
Banneker at bay. il Newsweek 77:93+ Mr 15 '71
Education experiment that could affect your children. il Good H 172:158-9 F '71
Gary's novel school, score after a year; contract education. il U S News 71:61 O 25 '71
Learning C.O.D: can the schools buy success? J. A. Mecklenburger and J. A. Wilson. il Sat R 54:62-5+ S 18 '71; Same abr. Ed Digest 37:1-4 N '71
Money-back schools: unclear balance sheet; Gary, Ind. il Time 98:78 O 11 '71
Performance contracting is a hoax! G. D. Hottleman. Ed Digest 37:1-4 S '71
Performance contracting: making it legal. R. Martin. Ed Digest 36:1-4 Ap '71
Performance contracting: proceed with caution. J. D. Reynolds. il Engl J 60:102-6+ Ja '71; Same abr. with title Performance contracting: adapted. Ed Digest 36:5-7 Ap '71
Performance contracting: some questions and answers. J. Schiller. il Am Ed 7:3-5 My '71
Question of survival for grand tour of planets. Sci N 100:246 O 9 '71
Success in Gary. Newsweek 78:66 O 11 '71
We'll educate your kids, or your money back. J. Star. il Look 35:56+ Je 15 '71
Will this boy's curriculum manager deserve an apple this year? Gary, Ind. Banneker school. B. Kaufman. il Todays Health 49: 20-3 S '71
PERFORMERS. See Actors and actresses
PERFORMING arts
Arts: a view from the wings; interviews. il Forbes 107:20-1 Ja 15 '71
Celebrity spotlight. E. N. Mintz. See issues of Travel
Multimedia. See last issue of each month of Saturday review. January 30, 1971–
Scenic world of Joseph Svoboda. J. M. Burian. il por Sat R 54:35-7+ Ag 28 '71
See also
Sex in the performing arts
Finance
Can the transistor save the arts? il Forbes 107:18-22 Ja 15 '71
PERFORMING arts, School of. See New York (city)—Education
PERFUMES
Gentleman's guide to giving the swell smells. R. Warfield. House & Gard 140:24+ D '71
Old masters. il Harp Baz 104:20 Je '71
Perfume is for wearing. Vogue 157:113 Je '71
Perfume people and the power of colorfulness. R. Warfield. House & Gard 140:41-2+ S '71
Scent perception. il Seventeen 30:104-7 D '71
Scents, and sense. Mlle 74:138-41 D '71
PERFUMES for men
Smelling Trouble; a new cologne for men. il Time 98:82 N 15 '71
PERGAMON press, ltd.
British study finds Maxwell reckless at Pergamon. Pub W 200:30 Ag 9 '71
Peace at Pergamon; Robert Maxwell returns to board. Pub W 199:38-9 My 17 '71
La **PERICHOLE**; opera. See Offenbach, J.
PERIDOTITE
Oxygen isotope ratios in eclogites from kimberlites. G. D. Garlick and others. bibliog il Science 172:1025-7 Je 4 '71
PERILYMPH. See Lymph
PERINETTI, André
French taste. S. Kauffmann. New Repub 165: 26+ Ag 7 '71 *
PERING, Katherine L. and Ponnamperuma, Cyril
Aromatic hydrocarbons in the Murchison meteorite. bibliog il Science 173:237-9 Jl 16 '71
PERINT, Gladys
At home in Paris with Madame Herve Alphand. por Harp Baz 104:179 F '71
At home in Paris with Susan Hampshire. Harp Baz 104:70 My '71
Countess of Cromer. Harp Baz 104:58 Mr '71
Memo from London. Harp Baz 104:40 Ap '71
PERIODIC law
Science's hunt for the missing links of nature; use of the periodic system. V. I. Gol'danskii. il UNESCO Courier 24:28-31 Je '71
That chart on the laboratory wall. G. Teterin and C. Terlon. il pors UNESCO Courier 24:24-7+ Je '71
PERIODIC tables. See Chemical elements
PERIODICAL advertising. See Advertising, Magazine

PERIODICAL articles
Are you that special person who can write inspirational articles? R. Peterman. Writers Digest 51:31-2+ D '71
Article writing today. W. B. Hartley. Writer 84:14-16+ S '71
Freelance market report: Harcourt Brace and Jovanovich trade journals. M. W. Fedo. il Writers Digest 51:28-30 N '71
Full-time freelancing in rural route U.S.A. C. Stowers. il Writers Digest 51:35-6+ Ap '71
Having wonderful time, wish you were there; travel writing. A. R. Pastore, jr. Writer 84:17-19+ O '71
Helen Gurley Brown tells what Cosmopolitan wants; reprint. H. G. Brown. Writer 84:47-8 Jl '71
How to sell articles to British magazines. F. Pasqualini. il Writers Digest 51:25-7 O '71
How to write for specialized magazines. M. H. Endres. Writer 84:24-5 S '71
Idea a day (cont) F. A. Dickson. por Writers Digest 51:12-13 F; 12+ Mr; 18-20 Je; 16-17+ Ag '71
Interviewing for trade journal articles. M. Tyson. il Writers Digest 51:25-7 Jl '71
Local history: a beginner's gold mine. A. Lynch. Writer 84:26 F '71
1971 articles contest. N. Kephart. Writers Digest 51:32 O '71
Writing article queries that sell. J. Fisher. Writer 84:18-20+ Je '71
Writing for the science and mechanics magazines. R. M. Benrey. Writer 84:26-7 N '71

Reprints
Dun's all over; re-publication of Dun's articles. Duns 97:3 My '71

PERIODICAL articles, Titles of. See Titles of books, stories, etc.
PERIODICAL columns. See Periodicals—Sections, columns, etc.
PERIODICAL literature
New York market letter. H. B. Jacobs. See issues of Writer's digest
Southern California market letter. D. Hellyer. Writers Digest 51:28-30+ My '71
Where to sell manuscripts. See issues of Writer
Writer's market; late news! See issues of Writer's digest
See also
Periodical articles
Trade journals
PERIODICAL postal rates

United States
See Postal rates—United States
PERIODICALS
See also
Employees magazines, handbooks, etc.
Freedom of the press
Illustration of books and periodicals
Journalism
Libraries—Periodical collections
Trade journals
also subhead Periodicals under various subjects, e.g. Poetry—Periodicals

Bibliography
Anima rising: little magazines in the sixties. L. Fulton. il Am Lib 2:25-47 Ja '71; Discussion. 2:345 Ap '71; Library J 96:1949 Je 1 '71
Another list, oh God! But a list as good as anyone else's list; with additional lists by C. Karpel and M. Mayer. Esquire 75:120-2+ My '71
Free & inexpensive magazines for schools; ed. by B. Katz. A. M. Smith. Library J 96:2065-6 Je 15 '71
Magazines; ed. by B. Katz. See issues of Library journal

Letters to the editor
Columnists mail: mixed bag; letters to LJ and the author. K. F. Kister. Library J 96:3735 N 15 '71
Letters you write to the editor. R. L. Tobin. Sat R 54:43-4 Ag 14 '71

Prices
Fa la la la la (why Century rates are rising) Chr Cent 88:1439 D 8 '71
Price indexes for 1971: U.S. periodicals. H. W. Tuttle. il Library J 96:2271-4 Jl '71

Sections, columns, etc.
Columnists mail: mixed bag; letters to LJ and the author. K. F. Kister. Library J 96:3735 N 15 '71

Argentina
Sur: 40 years. D. Lagmanovich. il pors Américas 23:10-14 S '71

Canada
See also
Books in Canada (periodical)

Europe, Western
New windows on the world; reading newspapers and journals from abroad. T. H. Barton. Harvard Bsns R 49:136-8+ S '71

France
Perils of JJSS; control of L'Express. por Newsweek 77:61+ Je 14 '71

Great Britain
Chilblains and strong tea on dark afternoons; microfilming British 18th and 19th century periodicals. D. Fader. il Library J 96:1330-2 Ap 15 '71
English little mags; ed. by B. Katz. Library J 96:1588-90 My 1 '71
How to sell articles to British magazines. F. Pasqualini. il Writers Digest 51:25-7 O '71
See also
Penrose annual
Punch (periodical)

Hong Kong
Chinese science: what the China watchers watch; China news analysis. D. Shapley. bibliog f Science 173:615-17 Ag 13 '71

Mozambique
Berman too much! concerning review of periodical Mozambique revolution. Library J 96:1305-6 Ap 15 '71; Discussion. 96:2022-3, 2562+ Je 15, S 1 '71

United States
New journalism. J. Ridgeway. bibliog il Am Lib 2:585-92 Je '71
Our shrinking magazines: time to change your page size. J. Tebbel. il Sat R 54:68-70 O 9 '71
That special treatment; sampling of newcomers. il Time 97:56 Ap 26 '71
Trimming down. Newsweek 77:54-5 Ja 18 '71
See also
Environmental news
Periodicals for women
also names of periodicals, e.g. Harper's magazine

PERIODICALS, Comic. See Comics (books, strips, etc)
PERIODICALS, Immoral. See Immoral literature and pictures
PERIODICALS, Publishing of. See Publishers and publishing—Periodicals
PERIODICALS, Trade. See Trade journals
PERIODICALS for men
See also
Penthouse (periodical)
Playboy (periodical)
PERIODICALS for women
Cashing in on fear & fantasy. K. Fisher. Nation 213:334-7 O 11 '71
Liberating magazines. il Newsweek 77:101 F 8 '71
Ms and the journalism of Women's lib. P. Howard. il Sat R 55:43-5+ Ja 8 '72
Women's lit; the feminist press. il Newsweek 77:65 Ap 26 '71
See also
Good housekeeping (periodical)
Ladies' home journal
Ms (periodical)
Woman's day magazine
PERIODICALS on microfilm
Chilblains and strong tea on dark afternoons; British 18th and 19th century periodicals. D. Fader. il Library J 96:1330-2 Ap 15 '71
PERIODICITY
See also
Biology—Periodicity
Botany—Periodicity
PERIODONTIA
Alternative to false teeth? marrow grafts. il Time 98:57 O 4 '71
PERIOPHTHALMUS. See Gobies
PERIWINKLES
It will grow and bloom in the hottest weather; vinca rosea. il Sunset 146:88-9 Je '71
PERJURY
See also
Trials (perjury)
PERKASIE, Pa.
Small size is no excuse. D. K. Price. il por Am City 86:60-2 My '71

PERSIAN literature
Romance of Varghe and Golshah. A. S. Melikian-Chirvani. il UNESCO Courier 24:26-9 O '71
See also
Authors, Persian

PERSIAN poetry
Epic of the kings: Persia's national saga the Shah-nama. J. Santa-Croce. il UNESCO Courier 24:32-3+ O '71

PERSIAN sculpture. See Sculpture, Persian

PERSIMMONS
Persimmons. J. C. McDaniel. il Horticulture 49:32-3+ S '71

PERSONAL beauty. See Beauty, Personal

PERSONAL confidences. See Confidential communications

PERSONAL criticism. See Self-evaluation

PERSONAL finance. See Finance, Personal

PERSONAL liberty. See Liberty

PERSONAL loans. See Loans, Personal

PERSONAL names. See Names, Personal

PERSONAL property. See Property

PERSONAL rapid transit. See Local transit

PERSONAL responsibility. See Reponsibility

PERSONAL rights. See Civil rights

PERSONAL selection. See Recruiting of employees

PERSONAL space
Etiquette of the new intimacy. il Esquire 76:59-64 Jl '71
Overcrowding and mental illness. A. J. Snider. Sci Digest 69:57-8 Ap '71

PERSONALITY
Does everybody want to be somebody? W. Cooper. il Harp Baz 104:134-5 My '71
Sleep stage and personality characteristics of natural long and short sleepers. W. B. Webb and J. Friel. bibliog il Science 171:587-8 F 12 '71
Tip-offs on personality traits; with study-discussion program, by M. M. Conant. L. Morgan. bibliog il PTA Mag 66:22-4+, 34 S '71
See also
Human relations
Identity (psychology)
Individuality
Leadership
Self
Typology (psychology)

PERSONALITY, Disorders of
See also
Schizophrenia

PERSONALITY tests
Battle royal over inkblot tests; are they useless? J. Benedict. il Sci Digest 70:43-8+ O '71
Changing identities; Rorschach test responses. il Newsweek 78:44-5 S 6 '71
Unisex in the laboratory; Rorschach inkblot test. il Time 98:48-9 S 6 '71

PERSONNEL management
Behavioral theory vs. reality. J. A. Lee. bibliog f Harvard Bsns R 49:20-2+ Mr '71
Behavioral theory vs. reality. J. A. Lee. bibliog f Harvard Bsns R 49:20-2+ Mr '71; Discussion. 49:31-2 S '71
Executives in ferment. G. J. Berkwitt; reply. R. S. Travis. Duns 97:11 Ap '71
Getting along with the boss. il Changing T 25:37-8 O '71
How companies deal with cutback jitters. Bsns W p88 Ap 24 '71
It's hell in personnel. T. J. Murray. il Duns 97:40-3 Mr '71
Public employee relations; address, March 19, 1971. J. R. Van De Water. Vital Speeches 37:556-63 Jl 1 '71
See also
Communication in management
Employees—Dismissal
Employees—Rating
Employees—Relocation
Employees magazines, handbooks, etc.
Factory management
Grievance procedures
Incentives in industry
Job satisfaction
Labor turnover
Layoff systems
Library administration
Profit sharing
Suggestion systems
Wage payment plans
Work rules

PERSONNEL service in education
Beware of false gods; utilizing technology in guidance. E. P. Dworkin. Ed Digest 36:27-9 Ja '71
See also
School psychologists
Student counselors

PERSONS, Wallace R.
Persons of Emerson electric. il por Forbes 107:52 My 15 '71 *

PERSPECTIVE
Feininger. A. Feininger. il Mod Phot 35:126+ Ag '71
Feininger; perspective, rectilinear or curvilinear. A. Feininger. Mod Phot 35:120-1 S '71
Perspective: know it, use it. E. Meyers. il Pop Phot 68:20+ Ap '71
What is a painting? the Pozzo phenomenon. M. Polanyi; discussion. Am Scholar 40:326-9 Spr '71

PERSPIRATION
By the sweat of their brow; polywater poohpoohed. il Sci N 99:62-3 Ja 23 '71
Polywater and sweat: similarities between the infrared spectra. D. L. Rousseau. bibliog il Science 171:170-2 Ja 15 '71

PERSUASION. See Rhetoric

PERSUASION (propaganda) See Propaganda

PERU
Eternal Peru. G. de Zéndegui. il Américas 23:S1-24 My '71
See also
Agricultural administration—Peru
Earthquakes—Peru
Forests and forestry—Peru
Huaylas, Callejón de
Incas
Investments, Foreign (in Peru)
Paleontology—Peru
Poor—Peru
Titicaca, Lake

Description and travel
Peru. I. Stanger. Harp Baz 104:72+ F '71

Economic policy
Peru: soldier in the saddle. il Time 98:33 Jl 26 '71
Peru's military populism. G. W. Grayson, jr. bibliog f Cur Hist 60:71-7+ F '71
Revolutionary nationalism in Peru. M. Niedergang. For Affairs 49:454-63 Ap '71

Native races
See also
Indians of South America—Peru

Politics and government
Peru's military populism. G. W. Grayson, jr. bibliog f Cur Hist 60:71-7+ F '71
Revolution in Lima. W. F. Buckley, jr. Nat R 23:217 F 23 '71
Speed of reforms slowed. E. Watlington. Chr Cent 88:500-1 Ap 21 '71

Reconstruction
From disaster to development; Callejón de Huaylas. P. L. Doughty. il Américas 23:25-35 My '71

Social conditions
Education, revolution, and nationalism in Peru. R. G. Paulston. bibliog Sch & Soc 99:361-4 O '71
See also
Poor—Peru

PERUTZ, Kathrin
Hair today, gone tomorrow. Seventeen 30:160+ Mr '71

PERUVIAN Indians. See Indians of South America—Peru

PERUVIAN painting. See Painting, Peruvian

PESCHEL, Harry
Richmond, Va. coliseum blends with the city. il Am City 86:58-9 D '71

PESQUEIRA, Ignacio
Henry A. Crabb, filibuster or colonizer? J. A. Stout. il pors Am West 8:4-9 My '71 *

PESSAGNO, Emile A. jr. See Mattson, P. H. jt. auth.

PESSEN, Edward
Egalitarian myth and the American social reality: wealth, mobility, and equality in the era of the common man. bibliog f il Am Hist R 76:989-1034 O '71

PESSIMISM
See also
Cynicism

PEST control
Agricultural pest control and the environment. G. W. Irving, jr; discussion. Science 171:16+ Ja 8 '71
Pest control is a year-round job. C. F. Sommers. Suc Farm 69:no 4 C12 Mr '71
Sensible ways to get rid of bugs and weeds. Changing T 25:31-3 Ag '71
See also
Slugs—Control

PEST control operators
When you need an exterminator. Good H 174: 139 Ja '72

PESTICIDE metabolism in insects. See Insects—Metabolism

PESTICIDE metabolism in soils. See Soil metabolism

PESTICIDE pollution. See Pesticides and the environment

PESTICIDES
Chemical control of pests. L. Lykken. bibliog il por Chem 44:18-21 Jl '71
Editorial; responsible use of pesticides. C. B. Lees. Horticulture 49:16 Ag '71
Just how safe are garden pesticides? Bet Hom & Gard 49:41+ F '71
Least hazardous pesticides for home use. Good H 172:177 Je '71
1971 look at pesticides and their use. il Home Gard 58:44-5 My '71
Pesticides: heroes or villains? C. E. Sommers. Suc Farm 69:no3 39 F '71
Pesticides: useful friends or deadly enemies? il Bet Hom & Gard 49:28+ Je '71
Plague descends on pesticides. il Bsns W p22 Jl 31 '71
Solve pesticide mixing problems. Suc Farm 69:no3 W28 F '71
See also
Fungicides
Herbicides
Insecticides
Spraying and dusting

Disposal
What to do with unused pesticides. Suc Farm 69:no3 W16 F '71

Injurious effects
Fright mongers. il Farm J 95:42 Jl '71
Lament for some companions of my youth. D. Moser. il Life 70:46-8+ Ja 22 '71
Nader on food. il Time 98:46-7 Ag 2 '71
Please pass the poison. R. Stout. il Org Gard & Farm 18:36-9 Je '71

Laws and legislation
New pesticide bill calls for farmers to be licensed. R. D. Wennblom. Farm J 95:29 N '71
New pesticide bill: how tough will it be? L. Palmer. Farm J 95:31 My '71
New problems: pesticide regulations. C. E. Sommers. Suc Farm 69:23 Ap '71
Pesticides bill that industry can live with. Bsns W p44-5 N 13 '71
See what's coming in pesticide regulation; interview, ed. by F. Bailey. R. E. Johnson. Suc Farm 69:7 Ap '71
Surprise! Nearly everyone backs new pesticide bill. L. Palmer. Farm J 95:34 Ap '71
Washington, spare that pesticide! M. Allen. New Repub 164:14-15 Je 12 '71
See also
United States—Agricultural research service—Pesticides regulation division

Testing
Group charges pesticides were tested on people. G. Reynolds. Farm J 95:38 Ap '71

PESTICIDES and the environment
Great caterpillar war and the ecopolitics of pesticides. P. Montague and K. Montague. il Audubon 73:50-8 Ja '71
Lament for some companions of my youth. D. Moser. il Life 70:46-8+ Ja 22 '71
Pesticides. il Sr Schol 97:15-17 Ja 11 '71
Soviet pesticides. P. R. Pryde. bibliog il Environ 13:16-24 N '71
Without pesticides, the world population will starve; excerpts from address, October 7, 1971. N. E. Borlaug. il por U S News 71:93 N 1 '71

PESTICIDES and wildlife
DDE residues and eggshell changes in Alaskan falcons and hawks. T. J. Cade and others bibliog il Science 172:955-7 My 28 '71
Last hope for the ospreys of Long Island Sound. D. R. Zimmerman. il por N Y Times Mag p38-40+ D 12 '71; Discussion. p28 Ja 9 '72
Will the brown pelican survive? H. H. Harrison. il Nat Wildlife 9:25-7 Je '71

PESTICIDES regulation division. See United States—Agricultural research service—Pesticides regulation division

PET food
See also
Cats—Food and feeding
Dogs—Food and feeding

PETCOFF, Darrell G. and others
Marihuana: identification of cannabinoids by centrifugal chromatography. bibliog il Science 173:824-6 Ag 27 '71

PETER, Emmett, Jr
Not quite black or white. New Repub 165: 13 D 25 '71

PETER, John
Mass urban transit. il Look 35:20-7 Ap 20 '71
Sand castles for keeps. il Look 35:84-6 Je 1 '71

PETER, Robert
Cassocks and communism. Nat R 23:1468-9 D 31 '71

PETER Abelard; drama. See Millar, R.

PETER and the wolf; drama. See Chermak, S.

PETERFI, William O.
United States-Vatican relations in the 1970's. il America 125:89-93 Ag 21 '71

PETERMAN, Edward
Transfer of orientation techniques to school libraries. Wilson Lib Bul 46:63 S '71

PETERMAN, Ruth
Are you that special person who can write inspirational articles? Writers Digest 51: 31-2+ D '71

PETERS, Art
Criminal law with a Johnson touch. il pors Ebony 26:93-4+ F '71

PETERS, C. Brooks
Gaelic sports. Sports Illus 34:88+ Ap 12 '71

PETERS, Charles
Low-keyed muckrakers. il Time 97:51 Mr 29 '71 *

PETERS, Dustin A.
Lincoln university in the nineteenth century. bibliog Negro Hist Bul 34:80-2 Ap '71

PETERS, Jean
Liberation of Mrs Howard Hughes. D. L. Lyons. il pors Ladies Home J 88:112+ Mr '71 *

PETERS, Joe
Best-of-all boat. il Outdoor Life 147:72+ Ja '71

PETERS, Roderic
Tom Edison's sales techniques. il pors Nations Bsns 59:52-6 Mr '71

PETERS, Ruth Marie
Color summer with annuals. il Home Gard 58:26-34 Ap '71

PETERS, Thomas R.
Experiment for the White House; address, February 23, 1971. Vital Speeches 37:379-82 Ap 1 '71

PETERS, William
Brown eyes, blue eyes; excerpt from A class divided. Read Digest 98:61-5 Ap '71

PETERSBURG, Ill.
Spoon River revisited. E. Laning. il por Am Heritage 22:14-17+ Je '71

PETERSEN, David
E is for empty. Flying 90:60-1 Ja '72

PETERSEN, Alan W. and Kieffaber, L. M.
Twilight flash of sodium. il Sky & Tel 41:344-5 Je '71

PETERSON, Arthur G.
Button panel, starred loop, and diamond ridge. il Hobbies 75:72-3 Ja '71

PETERSON, Dale. See Johnson, D. M. jt. auth.

PETERSON, Dennis
Viable approach to school assemblies. il Clear House 45:551-5 My '71

PETERSON, Esther
How you can make big business care about the little man; ed by J. C. G. Conniff. por Todays Health 49:19 D '71

PETERSON, Eugene H.
Discipleship; poem. Chr Today 15:10 S 10 '71

PETERSON, Everett H.
Commercial prunes don't taste like mine. Org Gard & Farm 18:125 S '71

PETERSON, Harold
Because it's nowhere. il pors Sports Illus 34:76-8+ My 3 '71
Golf. Sports Illus 35:48+ Ag 23 '71
Hollerin'. il Sports Illus 35:44-5 Jl 12 '71
Snowballing through the Rockies. il Sports Illus 35:68-70+ D 20 '71
Week; college basketball. Sports Illus 34:57-8 Ja 18; 42-3 Ja 25; 44 F 1; 45-6 F 8; 48-9 F 15; 35:66+ D 13 '71
Week; college football (cont) Sports Illus 35: 66+ O 11 '71

PETERSON, Harold L.
Dress parade; excerpts from America's fighting men. il Am Heritage 22:4-11 O '71

PETERSON, Lucky
Little Boy Blue. por Newsweek 77:73 Je 14 '71 *
On stage with Little Lucky. il pors Ebony 26:94-6+ O '71 *

PETERSON, Mike
Greatest athlete in Yates Center, Kansas. W. Johnson. il pors Sports Illus 35:26-31 Ag 9 '71 *

PETERSON, Norman. See Friedman, I. jt. auth.

PETERSON, Patti. See Altbach, P. G. jt. auth.

PETERSON, Peter G.
America: still the top producer, but . . interview. por U S News 71:34-7 Jl 12 '71
President Nixon establishes Council on international economic policy; excerpts from news conference, Janurary 19, 1971. Dept State Bul 64:169-72 F 8 '71

about

Mr Peterson's assignment. Fortune 83:63-4 Mr '71 •

PETERSON, Richard
My love affair with orchids. il Home Gard 58:46-7 Ap '71

PETERSON, Richard S. and Le Boeuf, B. J.
Fur seals are coming back to California. il Sci Digest 69:74-9 Ap '71

PETERSON, Robert
Josh Gibson was the equal of Babe Ruth, but. . il N Y Times Mag p 12-13+ Ap 11 '71

PETERSON, Robert (poet)
Resolutions; poem. Nation 213:56 Jl 19 '71

PETERSON, Russell Wilbur
He slammed the door in industry's face; interview. il por Nat Wildlife 10:50-1 D '71

PETERSON, S. W. and others
Antiprismatic coordination about xenon: the structure of nitrosonium octafluoroxenate (VI) bibliog il Science 173:1238-9 S 24 '71

PETERSON, Susan
California design XI. il Craft Horiz 31:52-3+ Je '71

PETERSON, Virgil W.
Development of local and state law enforcement. bibliog f Cur Hist 60:327-34 Je '71

PETITT, Dorothy
(ed) Professional publications. See issues of English journal

PETRAKIS, Nicholas L.
Cerumen genetics and human breast cancer. bibliog il Science 173:347-9 Jl 23 '71

PETRICCIANI, John C. and others
Subhuman primate diploid cells: possible substrates for production of virus vaccines. bibliog il Science 174:1025-7 D 3 '71

PETRICK, Helmutt
Tube that sees through the Wall; interview, ed. by R. Hemming. por Sr Schol 98:8+ Mr 8 '71

PETRIE, Graham
(tr) See Rohmer, E. Eric Rohmer: an interview

PETRIE, Paul
Scattered craft. J. Galassi. Poetry 118:291 Ag '71 •

PETRIFACTION. See Paleontology

PETRIFIED forests
Gingko, a petrified forest. H. D. Brown. il Hobbies 76:144+ Ag '71
Petrified forest of Key Biscayne. il Sci Digest 69:32-3 F '71

PETROGLYPHS
Brimhall saga: some remarkable discoveries in the cliffs of Utah. F. Brodie. il por Am West 8:4-9+, 18-23+ Jl, S '71
Riddle of America's elephant slabs. N. J. Harris. il Sci Digest 69:74-7 Mr '71
Semites first in America? B. Ford. il Sci Digest 71:43-8+ Ja '72
See also
Cave drawings and paintings

PETROLEUM
See also
Oil lands
Oil shales

Conservation
See also
Petroleum—Proration

International aspects
Is a cartel next for oilmen? il Bsns W p70-1 Ja 23 '71
Oil giants brace for big changes. il Bsns W p 14-15 Ja 30 '71
Politics behind the new oil hunt. il Bsns W p 104-6 Mr 6 '71
Showdown with oil nations: the stakes in prices, markets. il U S News 70:43-4 F 1 '71
What's good for oil and no one else. B. D. Nossiter. New Repub 164:17-18 F 6 '71
See also
Organization of petroleum exporting countries

Pipe lines
Alaska pipeline reports hit economics, safety. Nat Parks & Con Mag 45:31 Jl '71
Alaskan oil. A. W. Smith. Nat Parks & Con Mag 45:2+ Mr '71
Alaska's frustrating freeze in oil; report. P. Delaney. il Time 98:58 Jl 26 '71

Alaska's governor covets the pipeline. por Bsns W p44 N 13 '71
America must have the Alaskan oil. S. G. Slappey. il Nations Bsns 59:40-3 S '71
Archaeology along the pipeline; trans-Alaska pipeline. R. J. Trotter. il Sci N 100:396-7 D 11 '71
Are we about to plunder Alaska? R. Pollak. Cur 129:39-46 My '71
Blow to the pipeline; hearings in Alaska. Newsweek 77:81 Mr 1 '71
Cordova fishermen; proposed Alaskan oil pipeline. Nation 213:580-1 D 6 '71
Dealing with a northern sheik. il Time 98: 78 N 29 '71
Great pipeline flap; Alaskan route or a trans-Canadian route down the Mackenzie Valley. D. Coxe. Nat R 23:703+ Je 29 '71
Lawyers seek pipeline facts; Trans-Alaska oil pipeline. Liv Wildn 34:64-5 Wint '70
Morton questions pipeline project; with editorial comment. Liv Wildn 35:2, 45 Spr '71
New freeze on Alaskan oil; proposed Mackenzie Valley pipeline. il Time 97:48 Mr 29 '71
North slope boom is in a deep freeze. il Bsns W p 152-3+ My 15 '71
Oil across Alaska. Sci N 99:64 Ja 23 '71
Paris helps the Arabs build; unique Franco-Arab bank. il Bsns W p38 My 1 '71
Patience for a pipeline. A. A. Butkus. il por Duns 97:76 My '71
Pipeline; Alaska. New Repub 164:9 Ja 30 '71
Pipeline reports suppressed; proposed trans-Alaska pipeline. L. Aspin. por Nat Parks & Con Mag 45:25-8 Ap '71
Productivity in the petroleum pipelines industry. C. S. Fehd. il Mo Labor R 94:46-8 Ap '71
Search for alternatives; Alaska pipeline. Sci N 99:143 F 27 '71
Showdown nears for Alaska pipeline. il U S News 71:80-2 S 13 '71
State teetering between hope and despair. N. J. Margolin. il U S News 70:53-4 Mr 15 '71
Trans-Alaska pipeline: impact study receives bad reviews. R. Gillette. il Science 171:1130-2 Mr 19 '71
Trio of doubters; Alaska pipeline. Sci N 99:196 Mr 20 '71
Vote for the pipeline; Alaska. il Newsweek 77:71+ Ja 25 '71
Will oil and tundra mix? W. S. Ellis. il Nat Geog 140:484-517 O '71

Prices
Big squeeze. il Newsweek 77:63 F 15 '71
Higher prices for oil: who will get hit. il U S News 70:52-4 Mr 1 '71
How Libya set a stiffer price. il Bsns W p87 Ap 10 '71
Mideast oil pact: stability at a price. il Bsns W p23 F 20 '71
Power to the producers. Time 97:74+ Mr 1 '71
Tears in Teheran. Newsweek 77:76 Mr 1 '71
What is a fair price for oil? P. H. Abelson. Science 171:633 F 19 '71
What's good for oil and no one else. B. D. Nossiter. New Repub 164:17-18 F 6 '71

Production methods
See Petroleum engineering

Proration
Another shot fired at the oil producers; proposed suspension of Connally act. Bsns W p30 F 13 '71

Prospecting
Mr Prescott's class goes wildcatting. Ed Digest 37:32-4 O '71
Oiling the escalator: an economic incentive for winning the war? G. Kolko. New Repub 164:18-20 Mr 13 '71
Politics behind the new oil hunt. il Bsns W p 104-6 Mr 6 '71

Secondary recovery processes
See Petroleum engineering

Storage
See also
Oil tanks

Transportation
See also
Petroleum—Pipe lines
Tank ships

Alaska
Alaska pipeline reports hit economics, safety. Nat Parks & Con Mag 45:31 Jl '71
Alaska's frustrating freeze in oil; report. P. Delaney. il Time 98:58 Jl 26 '71
Are we about to plunder Alaska? R. Pollak. Cur 129:39-46 My '71

PETROLEUM—Alaska—*Continued*
Klondike '70, by D. J. Chasan. Review
  Newsweek il 77:73-4+ Ja 18 '71. R. A.
  Sokolov
Pipeline reports suppressed; proposed trans-
  Alaska pipeline. L. Aspin. por Nat Parks
  & Con Mag 45:25-8 Ap '71
Piper's tune. il Sr Schol 98:15-16 F 8 '71

Arctic Regions
See also
Petroleum—Alaska
Petroleum—Canada

Asia, Southeastern
Asian enigma. il Newsweek 78:92 N 29 '71
Little error that grew. L. Howell. Cur 131:63-4
  Jl '71
Offshore oil boom. B. Weisberg. il Nation 212:
  294-5 Mr 8 '71; Same with title Will an oil
  boom change U.S. policies? Cur 129:47-51
  My '71
Oil: hidden factor in the Vietnam equation? il
  Forbes 107:19-20 Mr 15 '71
Those mysterious oil leases. Nation 212:421 Ap
  5 '71

Canada
Legacy of the Manhattan. M. A. Galway.
  il Sea Front 17:292-7 S '71

Colorado
Biggest buried treasure on earth; Piceance
  shale. R. Schiller. il Read Digest 99:157-60+
  S '71

Florida
Newest trouble on Everglades waters. il Bsns
  W p44+ Je 5 '71

Indonesia
General and the gusher. A. A. Butkus. por
  Duns 98:34-5+ O '71

Kuwait
Curse of too much. il Forbes 107:33 Ap 1 '71

Latin America
Boom in the Andes. il Newsweek 78:104+
  O 18 '71

Mediterranean Region
Oil men scramble for their share; Spanish
  Mediterranean. il Bsns W p35 S 18 '71

Middle East
Challenge of change: petroleum and planning
  in the Middle East. J. A. Bill. bibliog il Fo-
  cus 22:1-5 S '71
Middle East: the makings of a boom. il Bsns
  W p86-7 Ap 10 '71

North Sea Region
Gusher in North Sea oil. J. Ross-Skinner. il
  Duns 98:50-2+ S '71
Oil fever strikes the Norwegians. Bsns W
  p40 Je 26 '71
Raising the ante on North Sea oil. Bsns W
  p32-3 Ag 28 '71

Russia
Now red bloc struggles with a fuel shortage.
  il U S News 71:84-5 O 25 '71

Vietnam (Republic)
Offshore oil activities in the Viet-Nam area;
  text of letters. D. M. Abshire. Dept State
  Bul 64:491-4 Ap 5 '71
Offshore oil. New Repub 164:8-9 Ap 3 '71
Offshore oil sweepstakes; with editorial
  comment. M. Tanzer. Nation 212:804, 814
  Je 28 '71
Oil in Vietnam. A. Bennion. il Ramp Mag
  9:8+ My '71
Oil on the waters. J. Deedy. Commonweal
  94:274 My 28 '71
Oiling the escalator: an economic incentive
  for winning the war? G. Kolko. New Re-
  pub 164:18-20 Mr 13 '71
Saigon affair. Newsweek 77:88+ Mr 22 '71

PETROLEUM engineering
Getting more oil from an oil field; Mara-
  flood recovery process. il Bsns W p 108
  Mr 6 '71
  See also
Oil field flooding

PETROLEUM equipment industry
  See also
Ocean drilling and exploration company

PETROLEUM exporting countries, Organization of. See Organization of petroleum exporting countries

PETROLEUM in submerged lands
Offshore oil boom; Southeast Asia. B. Weisberg. il Nation 212:294-5 Mr 8 '71; Same
  with title Will an oil boom change U.S.
  policies? Cur 129:47-51 My '71
Offshore oil; coastal oil in southeast Asia.
  New Repub 164:8-9 Ap 3 '71

Oil fever strikes the Norwegians; North Sea
  yield. Bsns W p40 Je 26 '71
On off two coasts: the promises, the prob-
  lems. il U S News 71:45-6 N 22 '71
  See also
Petroleum—Mediterranean Region
Petroleum—North Sea Region

PETROLEUM industry

Consolidations and mergers
Encouraging prospects. G. J. Henry. Forbes
  107:68 Ap 1 '71
Ties that may keep two oil giants apart; proposed merger of Continental oil co. with
  Britain's Burmah oil co. Bsns W p30 Mr 6
  '71

Finance
Energy; with yardsticks of management performance. il Forbes 109:138-9 Ja 1 '72
Five, four, three, two; full cost accounting.
  il Forbes 108:69 D 1 '71

Imports problem
Oil import control program modified by
  President Nixon; proclamation. R. M. Nix-
  on. Dept State Bul 64:147-9 F 1 '71
Protectionism, quotas and free enterprise,
  Texas-style. Consumer Rep 36:120-1 F '71

International aspects
See Petroleum—International aspects

Securities
Hurricane, blow! il Forbes 108:21 O 1 '71

Taxation
TRB from Washington; depletion allowance.
  New Repub 165:4 N 13 '71

Alaska
North slope boom is in a deep freeze. il Bsns
  W p 152-3+ My 15 '71

Algeria
Foreign legion routs the French. Bsns W
  p35 My 8 '71

Arab states
See Petroleum industry—Middle East

Australia
Encouraging prospects; Delhi-Santos interests.
  G. J. Henry. Forbes 107:68 Ap 1 '71

Canada
Canada continued. G. J. Henry. il Forbes
  108:57-8 Ag 1 '71

France
France's Total invades the U.S. il Bsns W
  p34-5 Ap 24 '71

Great Britain
See also
British petroleum company

Libya
Libya pours more trouble on oil; takeover
  of British petroleum-Nelson Bunker Hunt
  interests. Bsns W p79 D 11 '71

Maine
Hard test for Maine; building of oil-desulfur-
  ization plant at Penobscot Bay. Time 97:45-
  6 Ap 12 '71
Letter from Maine; oil and water. J. N. Cole.
  il Harper 243:42+ N '71
Oil and the environment: the view from
  Maine. J. McDonald. il Fortune 83:84-9+
  Ap '71

Middle East
Crisis in Teheran. Newsweek 77:72+ F 8 '71
How the Arabs changed the oil business. G.
  Breckenfeld. il Fortune 84:112-16+ Ag '71
Looking for a fair sheik. il Time 97:74-5 F 1
  '71

Oman
Maverick oilman battles the majors. il por
  Bsns W p78+ O 16 '71
Phillips of Arabia drops from favor. por Bsns
  W p41 S 25 '71

Singapore
Letter from Singapore; American investments. B. Weisberg. Nation 214:51-2 Ja 10
  '72

United States
Battle of the Atlantic. il Time 99:62 Ja 3 '72
Criticism, policy and reality: a national
  energy policy; address, May 28, 1971. F. N.
  Ikard. Vital Speeches 37:625-8 Ag 1 '71
Oil everywhere. P. Barnes. New Repub 165:
  21-3 N 6 '71

PETROLEUM industry—United States—*Cont.*
Oil: no need to scrape the bottom of the barrel. il Nations Bsns 59:28-31 Jl '71
Wide reach of oil. R. W. Dietsch. New Repub 164:16-17 Je 26 '71
    See also
General crude oil (firm)
Gulf oil corporation

Venezuela
Squeezing the oil concessions. il Time 98:59 S 6 '71

PETROLEUM laws and legislation
    See also
Oil and gas leases
Petroleum—Proration

PETROLEUM pipe lines. See Petroleum—Pipe lines

PETROLEUM pollution of waters. See Oil pollution of rivers, harbors, etc.

PETROLEUM products
Additives
    See also
Lubrizol corporation

PETROLEUM refineries
New Jersey of the Northwest; oil refining complex in Whatcom County, Wash. H. Henkin. Nation 212:292-3 Mr 8 '71
Oil and the environment: the view from Maine. J. McDonald. il Fortune 83:84-9+ Ap '71
    See also
Northeast petroleum industries

Location
Opinion: saving a town for the future: Tiverton, R.I. and the Northeast petroleum refining corporation. L. Durfee. Mlle 74:66+ D '71
Tempting of a small town; Tiverton and the oil refinery. R. Vaughan. il Life 71:50-1+ Jl 30 '71; Same abr. Read Digest 99:207-8+ O '71

PETROLOGY
Petrologic implications of plate tectonics; report of meeting. H. S. Yoder, jr. Science 170:464-6 Jl 30 '71

History
Beginnings of experimental petrology; excerpts from address, January 1971. H. P. Eugster. bibliog il Science 173:481-9 Ag 6 '71

PETRONE, Rocco A.
Apollo; an assessment; interview. il por Space World H-8-92:4-7 Ag '71
Is another moon trip necessary? interview. por U S News 71:21-2 Ag 2 '71

PETRONIO, Adriano
Prompter. E. Burns. il pors Opera N 35:27-9 Mr 27 '71

PETROSIAN, Tigran Vartanovich
Bobby makes his move. il pors Time 98:68+ N 8 '71 •
Peacock vs. the wren. il pors Newsweek 78:87-8+ O 18 '71 •

PETROV, Boris
Case for space automation. Space World H-3-87:36-7 Mr '71
Intercosmos: space program of socialist countries. Space World H-4-88:36-7 Ap '71

PETROVICS, Emil
Crime and punishment. Criticism
Hi Fi 21:MA26-7 Ja '71 •

PETRY, Ann
Witness; story. Redbook 136:80-1 F '71

PETS
Pet journal. il Ladies Home J 88:46 S; 68 O; 76 D '71; 89:130 Ja '72
Pet news. See issues of Ladies home journal to July 1971
Smooth the way for a second pet. Bet Hom & Gard 49:146 Ap '71
Snake: household's newest pet. Mech Illus 67:134-6 S '71
Some animals should't be pets. il Life 70:24-33 Ap 9 '71
Tips to keep a guest pet happy. Good H 173:192 O '71
What is a pet? excerpts. L. P. McGrath and J. Scobey. Good H 173:90-1 Jl '71
    See also
Travel with pets
    also names of animal pets, e.g. Cats

Care
Keep your pet healthy when it's hot. D. M. Lidster. Bet Hom & Gard 49:112+ Je '71
Pampered pets of France; pet vacation club. Time 98:37 Ag 30 '71
What makes your pet itch? D. M. Lidster. Bet Hom & Gard 49:93+ Ag '71

PETS and children. See Children and animals

PETTENGILL, Daniel W.
Writing the prescription for health care. Harvard Bsns R 49:37-43 N '71

PETTENGILL, G. H. and others
Martian craters and a scarp as seen by radar. bibliog il Science 174:1321-4 D 24 '71

PETTINELLI, Vincent D.
Coordinating a volunteer program. Ment Hy 55:516-18 O '71

PETTINGELL, Phoebe
Graven images; Labyrinths; poems. Poetry 119:23-4 O '71

PETTINGILL, Amos, pseud. See Harris, W. B.

PETTIS, Jerry Lyle
Technology gap in health: it has to be closed; address, June 1971. Vital Speeches 37:693-6 S 1 '71

PETTY, Richard
Earthly delights of stock-car racing. W. McIlwain. Harper 243:22+ S '71 •
Million-dollar Sunday driver. R. Blount. il por Sports Illus 35:16-17 Ag 9 '71 •
No recession for Mr Petty. R. F. Jones. Sports Illus 34:56 F 22 '71 •
Will Richard Petty retire? il pors Motor T 23:110 D '71 •

PETTY, Roy
(ed) See White, P. L. Which diets work, which don't

PETUNIAS
Perfect potted partners. T. Cruso. il McCalls 98:28+ Jl '71

PEUGEOT (automobile) See Automobiles, Foreign

PEW, John Howard
J. Howard Pew, 1882-1971. Chr Today 16:22-3 D 17 '71 •
Obituary
Chr Today 16:24 D 17 '71. L. N. Bell

PEW, Joseph Newton, 1886-1963
Left-wing Joe Pewism. S. Alsop. il Newsweek 78:128 O 25 '71 •

PEW, Thomas W. Jr
Greek editor sums up. Nation 213:654-6 D 20 '71
Peddling the great West. il Sat R 54:48-51 S 4 '71

PEWTER
European guild pewter: forms and functions. R. M. Vetter. il Antiques 101:201-8 Ja '72
Table guards and cake plates of pewter. R. M. Vetter. il Antiques 99:712-17 My '71

PEWTER casting. See Foundry practice

PEWTER tableware. See Tableware, Pewter

PFAFF, Donald W. and others
Telemetered recording of hormone effects on hippocampal neurons. bibliog il Science 172:394-5 Ap 23 '71

PFAFF, William
Reflections. New Yorker 47:32-8 Jl 3 '71

PFALTZGRAFF, Robert L. Jr
Should the United States retain a military presence in Europe and Asia? bibliog f Ann Am Acad 397:1-10 S '71

PFEFFER, Leo
Parochiaid decision. Todays Ed 60:63-4+ S '71

PFEIFER, Carl J.
Getting it together: the International catechetical congress. America 125:287-9 O 16 '71

PFEIFER, C. Boyd
Conowingo, Maryland's neglected bass lake. il Field & S 76:162-4+ My '71
Potomac: smallmouth paradise. il Field & S 76:52-3+ Jl '71

PFEIFER, E. W.
Land war. il pors Environ 13:3-8 N '71

PFEIFFER, John Edward
Man, the hunter. il Horizon 13:28-33 Spr '71

PFEIL, Mary Pat
Second vocabulary for Johnny. il Am Ed 7:16-20 My '71

PFIZER, Beryl
Poor woman's almanac. See issues of Ladies' home journal

PFOUTZ, Daniel R.
(comp) Sci-tech books '70. il por Library J 96:781-92 Mr 1 '71

PHAGOCYTES and phagocytosis
Melanin pigmentation: an in vivo model for studies of melanosome kinetics within keratinocytes. M. Wolff and K. Konrad. il Science 174:1034-5 D 3 '71
    See also
Macrophages
Pinocytosis

PHALAENOPSIS. See Orchids

PHALANGIDS. See Harvestmen

PHARMACEUTICAL industry. See Drug industry

PHARMACEUTICAL laboratories
　See also
Lederle laboratories
PHARMACEUTICAL research
　Ever-expanding armamentarium of drugs. G.
　　Gregory. il UNESCO Courier 24:12-14 Je
　　'71
PHARMACOGENETICS
　How genes control drugs. J. L. Arehart. il
　　Sci N 99:438-9 Je 26 '71
PHARMACOLOGY
　See also
Psychopharmacology
PHARMACOPOEIAS
　Western alchemy symbols in a Japanese med-
　　ical work; translation of 17th century
　　Dutch pharmacopoeia. T. Benfey. bibliog
　　il Chem 44:14-18 S '71
PHARMACY
　See also
American pharmaceutical association
PHASE rule and equilibrium
　See also
Critical point
PHEASANT shooting
　Changing pheasant. E. A. Bauer. il Outdoor
　　Life 148:60-3+ N '71
　Pheasant shooting in Britain. A. Oglesby. il
　　Field & S 76:42-3+ D '71
　Veterans' pheasant hunt. B. Gillette. il Out-
　　door Life 147:64-7+ Je '71
PHEASANTS
　See also
Cookery—Game
PHELAN, J. D.
　Steel industry and pollution. il Parks & Rec
　　6:20-2+ S '71
PHELPS, Flora L.
　Architecture, sculpture, environment. il
　　Américas 23:S12-15 Je '71
PHELPS, Robert
　Jupiter's brain: notes on sexual compati-
　　bility and astrology. il Mlle 73:130-1+ S
　　'71
　Music. Vogue 157:156 My '71
　Picasso and Braque, their cubist years. Vogue
　　157:125+ Ap 1 '71
PHENOBARBITAL
　Genetic aspects of increase in rat liver
　　aldehyde dehydrogenase induced by pheno-
　　barbital. R. A. Deitrich. bibliog il Science
　　173:334-6 Jl 23 '71
　Induction of liver acetaldehyde dehydro-
　　genase: possible role in ethanol tolerance
　　after exposure to barbiturates. G. Redmond
　　and G. Cohen. bibliog il Science 171:387-9
　　Ja 29 '71
PHENOLOGY
　See also
Plants, Flowering of
PHENOLS
　Spectrophotometric determination of pKa's
　　for substituted 2-nitrophenols. R. J. Palma
　　and E. H. Sund. bibliog il pors Chem 44:26-
　　8 My '71
　See also
Dichlorophenol
PHENOTHIAZINE
　Phenothiazine effects on auditory signal de-
　　tection in paranoid and nonparanoid
　　schizophrenics. M. Rappaport and others.
　　bibliog il Science 174:723-5 N 12 '71
PHENOTYPE. See Genotype and phenotype
PHENYLALANINE
　p-Chlorophenylalanine methyl ester; an
　　aphrodisiac? R. E. Whalen and W. C. Lut-
　　tge; reply. G. L. Gessa and others. Science
　　171:706 F 19 '71
　See also
Dopa
PHENYLMERCURIC acetate
　Phenylmercuric acetate: metabolic conversion
　　by microorganisms. F. Matsumura and
　　others. bibliog il Science 173:49-51 Jl 2 '71
PHEROMONES
　Attack by pheromone. Sci Am 225:45 Jl '71
　Chemical communication and propaganda
　　in slave-maker ants. F. E. Regnier and E.
　　O. Wilson. bibliog il Science 172:267-9 Ap
　　16 '71
　Chemical ecology. J. G. MacConnell and R.
　　M. Silverstein. il pors Chem 44:6-9 Jl '71
　Chemical languages of fishes. J. H. Todd.
　　il Sci Am 224:98-106+ My '71
　Knowing noses. Sci Am 225:76+ S '71
　1-Pentadecene production in tribolium confu-
　　sum. D. W. Von Endt and J. W. Wheeler.
　　bibliog Science 172:60 Ap 2 '71
　Pheromones isolation of male sex attractants
　　from a female primate. R. P. Michael and
　　others. bibliog il Science 172:964-6 My 28 '71
　Present shock. D. M. Rorvik. Esquire 76:
　　68+ O '71
　See also
Insect sex attractants

PHI epsilon pi. See College fraternities
PHIBBS, Brendan Pearse
　Wyoming's war on deadly strep. M.
　　Michaelson. il Todays Health 49:40-3+ Mr
　　'71 *
PHILADELPHIA
　　Architecture
　Philadelphia; United fund building. J. M.
　　Dixon. il Arch Forum 134:40-5 Ja '71
　　Banks
　Philadelphia's banks. R. Nathan and R. Lear.
　　New Repub 164:10+ Je 5 '71
　　City planning
　Dispirited '76 for Philadelphia. il Bsns W
　　p 108+ Ja 16 '71
　Dispirited '76. il Newsweek 78:55-6 Ag 2 '71
　Happy ending to Philadelphia's downtown
　　story; Franklin town. Bsns W p37 Ag 28
　　'71
　Old city's new town; Franklin town. il Time
　　97:62 Je 14 '71
　Price planners pay for secrecy; Franklin town
　　project. il Bsns W p28 Je 26 '71
　　Courts
　Court goes to court; seeking financial help.
　　Time 97:54 Mr 22 '71
　　Description
　Champ's town. D. Butwin. il Sat R 54:47-8+
　　Ap 3 '71
　Philadelphia, a triumph over time. J. Keats.
　　il Holiday 49:42-7+ Ap '71
　　Education
　American children with reading problems can
　　easily learn to read English represented
　　by Chinese characters. P. Rozin and others.
　　bibliog il Science 171:1264-7 Mr 26 '71
　First things first; financial pinch and high
　　school football. J. Cass. Sat R 54:75 O 16
　　'71
　High school without walls; school system's
　　experimental Parkway school. il Bsns W
　　p88 My 29 '71
　I get a very different feeling in that class;
　　affective education. K. Branan. il Schol
　　Teach Jr/Sr High p8-10 My 3 '71; Same
　　abr. Ed Digest 37:9-11 S '71
　Ousting a reformer; Philadelphia school
　　superintendent M. Shedd. il por Time
　　98:58 D 20 '71
　Philadelphia, football, & the economy. G.
　　Nikolaieff. il Sr Schol 99:12-14 N 15 '71
　Santa's workshop for teachers; Learning cen-
　　ters project and the Teacher center at Dur-
　　ham elementary school. A. Silberman. il
　　Am Ed 7:3-8 D '71
　Schoolgirl's album; Ogontz school for young
　　ladies, with photographs. Am Heritage 23:
　　72-9 D '71
　We expect them to storm the gates; no
　　varsity sports. R. Fimrite. il Sports Illus
　　35:20-2+ S 6 '71
　　Elections
　When law and order was voting issue. il por
　　U S News 70:54-5 My 31 '71
　　Finance
　Philadelphia, football, & the economy. G.
　　Nikolaieff. il Sr Schol 99:12-14 N 15 '71
　We expect them to storm the gates: no
　　varsity sports. R. Fimrite. il Sports Illus
　　35:20-2+ S 6 '71
　　Galleries and museums
　See also
Philadelphia museum of art
　　Historic houses, sites, etc.
　See also
Independence National Historical Park
　　History
　Centennial city. E. P. Richardson. il por Am
　　Heritage 23:17-32 D '71
　　Hospitals
　Getting something for the money: Penn-
　　sylvania's Blue cross. R. DeWolf. Nation
　　213:435-6 N 1 '71
　See also
Pennsylvania, University, Philadelphia—Hos-
　pital
　　Housing
　Court breaks new social ground in housing
　　policy. J. R. Hacala and J. M. Kakalec.
　　America 124:228-30 Mr 6 '71; Reply with re-
　　joinder. G. Cavanaugh. 124:589-91 Je 5 '71
　Happy ending to Philadelphia's downtown
　　story. Bsns W p37 Ag 28 '71
　Philadelphia story: the Tasker homes. G.
　　Bruce. il America 124:652-4 Je 26 '71

PHILADELPHIA—*Continued*

Libraries

Philadelphia project: decrease in students' use of public and school libraries between 4th and 12th grades. J. Q. Benford. il por Library J 96:2041-7 Je 15 '71
See also
Philadelphia free library

Music

Current chronicle; Philadelphia musical academy centennial anniversary celebration. D. Chittum. il Mus Q 57:129-41 Ja '71
See also
Academy of music, Philadelphia
Philadelphia lyric opera company
Philadelphia orchestra

Parks and playgrounds

Walk-to swimming pools. R. W. Crawford. il Am City 86:51-2 Ja '71
See also
Independence National Historical Park

Politics and government

City hall; Rizzo campaign. R. Mulligan, jr. New Repub 164:10-11 My 15 '71
Conservative's dilemma: F. Rizzo. G. Bruce. Nat R 23:1224 N 5 '71
Copping it; former police chief F. L. Rizzo as candidate for mayor. il por Newsweek 77:20+ My 31 '71
If they get out of line, he'll bust their heads; Rizzo running for mayor. J. Pekkanen. il Life 71:34 O 29 '71
Move over Mayor Daley: here comes Frank Rizzo. S. Padwe. por Ramp Mag 10:27-9 Ag '71
Night-stick candidate. G. Gilmore. il Nation 213:397-8 O 25 '71
Supercop; mayoral candidate. F. Rizzo. por Newsweek 77:32+ Mr 15 '71
Tough cop for mayor. il por Time 97:13 My 31 '71
Toughest cop in America campaigns for mayor of Philadelphia. L. E. Berson. il pors N Y Times Mag p30-1+ My 16 '71; Reply. F. L. Rizzo. p20 Je 13 '71

Race question

Philadelphia story: the Tasker homes. G. Bruce. il America 124:652-4 Je 26 '71

Rapid transit

See Philadelphia—Transit systems

Sanitary affairs

Bag your trash week brings lasting benefits. il Am City 86:16 Ap '71
Tests microstraining and ozone on stormwater overflow. il Am City 86:28 Ja '71

Schools

See Philadelphia—Education

Street traffic

Crosstown is dead, long live the crosstown. M. Osborn; D. S. Brown; M. Verman. il Arch Forum 135:38-45 O '71

Traffic problem

See Philadelphia—Street traffic

Transit systems

Little railroad that could; Lindenwold line. C. G. Burck. il Fortune 84:74-7 Jl '71

Water supply

Water resource leaders. W. S. Foster. il pors Am City 86:67-8 Mr '71
PHILADELPHIA centennial. See Centennials
PHILADELPHIA crosstown expressway. See Express highways—Pennsylvania
PHILADELPHIA Eagles (football club) See Football clubs
PHILADELPHIA free library
Ideological balance in the Free library of Philadelphia book collections; ed. by J. F. Krug and J. A. Harvey. G. Wilson. Am Lib 2:156-7 F '71
Jerry Rubin's Do it! still in. il Am Lib 2:137 F '71
Last minute reprieve in Philadelphia. Library J 96:431 F 1 '71
Model cities community information center. R. J. Luce. Am Lib 2:206-7 F '71
Philadelphia free wheeler on-the street service. il Library J 96:4138-9 D 15 '71
PHILADELPHIA furniture. See Furniture, American

PHILADELPHIA gas works
Balancing act; WFLN, WPEN and the T. Grant controversy. R. L. Shayon. Sat R 54:43 Je 5 '71; Reply with rejoinder. L. M. C. Smith. 54:19 Jl 10 '71
PHILADELPHIA grand opera company
Report:
Carmen, Lucia, and Meistersinger. M. De Schauensee. Opera N 35:32-3 Ja 16 '71
Mascagni's Amico Fritz. M. De Schauensee. Opera N 35:32 Mr 20 '71
PHILADELPHIA in art
Centennial city. E. P. Richardson. il por Am Heritage 23:17-32 D '71
PHILADELPHIA lyric opera company
Report:
Carmen. M. De Schauensee. Opera N 35:32 Mr 20 '71
Il Trovatore and Otello. M. De Schauensee. Opera N 35:33 F 20 '71
PHILADELPHIA museum of art
Museum samplers. M. Evans and D. L. Brightbill. il Am Home 74:96-7+ S '71
Reaching out to the city. D. Davis. Newsweek 77:93-4 Je 28 '71
PHILADELPHIA musical academy. See Academy of music, Philadelphia
PHILADELPHIA orchestra
Generations of Shostakovich; performance of Fourteenth symphony. I. Kolodon. Sat R 54:79 Ja 23 '71
Musical events; concerts in Philharmonic Hall (cont) W. Sargeant. New Yorker 47:168+ O 16 '71
Musical events; Shostakovich's Fourteenth symphony in Philharmonic Hall. W. Sargeant. New Yorker 46:93 Ja 16 '71
Music's handmaiden; performance of Shostakovich's Fourteenth symphony. H. Saal. por Newsweek 77:50 Ja 18 '71
PHILADELPHIA Phillies (baseball) See Baseball clubs
PHILADELPHIA public library. See Philadelphia free library
PHILADELPHIA symphony orchestra. See Philadelphia orchestra
PHILAE, Temples of. See Temples—Egypt
PHILANTHROPIC foundations. See Foundations, Charitable and educational
PHILANTHROPIST; drama. See Hampton, C.
PHILANTHROPY. See Giving
PHILATELY. See Postage stamps
PHILBIN, Tom
How to save money when you paint. il Mech Illus 67:94-6+ N '71
PHILBRICK, Charles
House call; evening; poem. Sat R 54:20 Mr 13 '71
PHILCOX, Frederick G.
Once again: what to expect of freighter travel. il Travel 135:55-7 F '71
PHILHARMONIC-symphony orchestra of New York. See New York philharmonic-symphony orchestra
PHILIDOR, François André Danican, 1726-1795
Life of Philidor, by G. Allen. Review
Am Rec G por 37:602-4 My '71. H. C. Schonberg *
PHILIP and Anna; story. See Warner, S. T.
PHILIPPINE cookery. See Cookery, Philippine
PHILIPPINE priests, inc. See Priests—Associations, institutions, etc.
PHILIPPINES
See also
Agriculture—Philippines
Church and social problems—Philippines
Communism—Philippines
Elections—Philippines
Luzon
Natural resources—Philippines
Research—Philippines
Terrorism—Philippines

Economic conditions

Philippines. A. Cutshall. bibliog il Focus 21:1-9 Mr '71

History

Insurrection, 1899-1901

Mylai was not the first time. D. B. Schirmer. New Repub 164:18-21 Ap 24 '71

Industries

See also
Philippines—Economic conditions

Native races

First glimpse of a stone age tribe; Tasaday tribe of Mindanao. il Nat Geog 140:880-2 D '71
Help for Philippine tribes in trouble; work of Panamin among Mindanao tribesmen. K. MacLeish. il pors Nat Geog 140:220-55 Ag '71

PHILIPPINES—Native races—*Continued*
Lost tribe of the Tasaday; Stone age people.
il Time 98:58+ O 18 '71
Travels with Charlie. E. Needham. il por
Esquire 75:90-1+ Mr '71

Politics and government
Binding up the wounds. Time 98:44 N 22 '71
Engulfed in strife: Philippines' Marcos. il
por U S News 70:56 Mr 29 '71
See also
Elections—Philippines

Race question
Help for Philippine tribes in trouble; work of
Panamin among Mindanao tribesmen. K.
MacLeish. il pors Nat Geog 140:220-55 Ag '71

Religious institutions and affairs
Worldaround. Chr Cent 88:606, 1054+, 1428
My 12, S 8, D 1 '71

PHILIPS' gloeilampen fabrieken. See Electric
industries—Netherlands
PHILLIES (baseball) See Baseball clubs
PHILLIPS, Cabell
Footbridge into the quagmire. New Repub
165:13-15 Jl 24 '71
Why not another WPA? New Repub 164:19
20 F 6 '71
PHILLIPS, Christopher H.
Twenty-fifth General assembly rejects move
to change representation of China in the
U.N; statement. November 12, 1970. Dept
State Bul 63:733-5 D 14 '70
U.N. force in Cyprus extended through June
1971; statement, December 10, 1970. Dept
State Bul 64:70-1 Ja 11 '71
United States calls for restraint in southern
Africa; statement, October 12, 1971. Dept
State Bul 65:608 N 22 '71
PHILLIPS, David L.
Revised refuse procedure cuts budget more
than 25%. il por Am City 86:66-9 Ap '71
PHILLIPS, Douglas
Old medium, new messages. il pors Ebony
27:33-6+ D '71 *
PHILLIPS, Gene D.
Personal vision of John Schlesinger. America
125:290-2 O 16 '71
PHILLIPS, Harvey E.
Friend of the working girl. por Opera N 35:
28-30 Mr 6 '71
Opera Ruffino style. il por Opera N 35:13-15
Ja 16 '71
(ed) See Baldani, R. Ruza
PHILLIPS, Howard
Build a $5 vehicle alarm system. il Radio-
Electr 42:35-6 N '71
PHILLIPS, James Charles
Chemical bond and solid-state physics; adap-
tation of address. March 1969. bibliog il por
Phys Today 23:23-30 F '70; 24:13+ F '71
PHILLIPS, Kevin P.
Will Agnew dump himself? il pors N Y
Times Mag p36-7+ N 14 '71
PHILLIPS, Louis
Woman is made of water & man of clay:
poem. Mlle 73:114 S '71
PHILLIPS, Richard A.
Run machines on profit-or-loss basis. il Am
City 86:84+ N '71
PHILLIPS, Wendell
Maverick oilman battles the majors. il pors
Bsns W p78+ O 16 '71 *
Phillips of Arabia drops from favor. por Bsns
W p41 S 25 '71 *
PHILLIPS, William
Cops on the take. il por Newsweek 78:48+
N 1 '71 *
Guarding the guardians. il por Time 98:22+
N 1 '71 *
PHILLIPS collection. See Art—Private collec-
tions
PHILLIPS curve. See Statistical methods
PHILLIPS Exeter academy, Exeter, N.H. See
Private schools
PHILOLOGY
See also
Language and languages
PHILOSOPHERS
Philosophical thought in America; sym-
posium. il Américas 23:S1-24 Ag '71
See also names of philosophers, e.g. M.
Buber
PHILOSOPHY
See also
Analysis (philosophy)
Atheism
Civilization
Consciousness
Evolution
Gnosticism
Humanism
Knowledge, Theory of

Life
Mind and body
Naturalism (philosophy)
Nihilism (philosophy)
Perfection (philosophy)
Political philosophy
Psychology
Reality
Space and time
Utilitarianism
also subhead Philosophy under vari-
ous subjects, e.g. Science—Philosophy
PHILOSOPHY, Analytical. See Analysis (phi-
losophy)
PHILOSOPHY, Brazilian
Philosophical thought in Brazil. L. W. Vita.
Américas 23:S18-23 Ag '71
PHILOSOPHY, Chinese
See also
Lao-tzu
PHILOSOPHY, English
See also
Bacon, R.
Bentham, J.
Russell, B. R.
PHILOSOPHY, French
Influence of French thought. J. L. Marti. il
Américas 23:S9-12 Ag '71
PHILOSOPHY, German
See also
Hegel, G. W. F.
Kant, I.
Nietzsche, F. W.
PHILOSOPHY, Greek
See also
Diogenes
PHILOSOPHY, Jewish
I'd rather dance with the Jews. R. E. Wentz.
Chr Cent 88:830-2 Jl 7 '71
Star of redemption, by F. Rosenzweig. Review
America 125:19 Jl 10 '71. J. Riemer
Time 98:50-1 Ag 9 '71
PHILOSOPHY, Latin American
Foundations of philosophy. J. C. Torchia-
Estrada. Américas 23:38 Ap '71
Philosophical thought in America; sym-
posium. il Américas 23:S1-24 Ag '71
PHILOSOPHY, Moral. See Ethics
PHILOSOPHY, Spanish
Ideology of the conquest. A. Salgado. il
Américas 23:S3-5 Ag '71
PHILOSOPHY and religion
Varieties of religious experience, by W.
James. Review
New Repub 165:28-31 O 2 '71. R. Coles
PHILOSOPHY and science
Chance and necessity, by J. Monod. Review
Atlan 228:125-30 N '71. G. Stent
Nation 213:568+ N 29 '71. J. H. Bryant
PHILOSOPHY of education. See Education—
Philosophy
PHILP, Richard
Béjart: the lingering impact. il Dance Mag
45:26-8 Ap '71
PHINIZY, Coles
In the wake of the capsize kid. il por Sports
Illus 35:28-30+ Jl 12 '71
Rediscovery of New York city. il Sports Illus
35:98-101+ N 22 '71
True love at first contusion. il por Sports
Illus 34:52-4 Mr 22 '71
You never know when you might need a mul-
let. il pors Sports Illus 34:54-6+ Ap 5 '71
PHIPPS, Welland W.
World of Weldy Phipps. S. Wilkinson. il Fly-
ing 88:54-63 Mr '71 *
PHIPPS, William E.
D. H. Lawrence's appraisal of Jesus. Chr
Cent 88:521-4 Ap 28 '71
PHLOGISTON theory
Great moments in chemistry; tr. by R. E.
Oesper. F. Szabadvary. il pors Chem 44:
14-17 D '71
PHOBIAS
Do you know what you're afraid of? quiz.
J. C. Stacey. Sci Digest 69:33 Ap '71
See also
School phobia
PHOBOS (satellite) See Satellites
PHOENICIAN civilization. See Civilization,
Phoenician
PHOENICIANS
See also
Carthaginians
PHOENIX, Ariz.
Leisurely cities. H. T. Blake. Harp Baz 104:
52-3 My '71

Art
Art in Arizona. Travel 135:15+ Ap '71

Description
Step by step through Phoenix. R. Deardorff.
il Travel 136:58-63 N '71

PHOENIX, Ariz.—*Continued*

Lighting

Lighting makes a city a showplace. J. J. Protis. il Am City 86:116 O '71

Parks and playgrounds

Learning at the zoo; Phoenix zoo's children's natural history and art program. F. J. Turkowski. il Parks & Rec 6:25-6 N '71

Religious institutions and affairs

North Phoenix's corporate ministry: a question mark. D. M. Lynch. Chr Cent 88:562-3+ My 5 '71

Sanitary affairs

BIRP proves practical and economically feasible in Phoenix, Ariz; Beverage industry recycling program. S. Carter. il Am City 86:28 D '71

PHOENIX (newspaper)

War of the weeklies. il Time 98:74+ N 15 '71

PHONOGRAPH

Cheerful earfuls. il Seventeen 29:136-9 S '70
Pioneer PL-12A record player. il Pop Electr 1:78-80 Ja '72

Control

Phono motor control. il Radio-Electr 42:54 My '71

History

Wonder of the age. G. Movshon. il Hi Fi 21:84-5 S '71

Maintenance and repair

Get better sound from your record player. P. Sutheim. il Radio-Electr 42:32-4 N '71

Pickup

Photoelectric phono pickups. F. Shunaman. il Radio-Electr 42:43 Mr '71
What's the difference between a $20 cartridge and an $80 cartridge? N. Eisenberg. Hi Fi 21:54 F '71
See also
Phonograph—Stereophonic pickup

Record changers

Buyer's guide to today's record-playing equipment. Hi Fi 21:52-3 My '71
Equipment report; Pioneer PL-A25 automatic turntable. Radio-Electr 42:84-5 O '71
Garrard Zero 100 automatic turntable. il Pop Electr 35:82-4 Ag '71
Hirsch-Houck lab tests automatic turntables. J. D. Hirsch. il Electr World 85:27-30+ Je '71
How important is stylus overhang? D. Gravereaux. il Hi Fi 21:52-3 F '71
Turntables and changers up to date. L. Zide. il Hi Fi 21:44-9 My '71

Stereophonic pickup

15 things we do know about phono cartridges. J. G. Holt. il Pop Electr 34:25-30 Je '71
Hi-fi product report; Pickering V-15 phase IV stereo cartridge. il Electr World 86:10 S '71
Stereo phono cartridges. il Consumer Rep 36:68-73 F '71
What makes a good stereo cartridge? L. Feldman. Hi Fi 21:45-51 F '71

Tone arm

How important is stylus overhang? D. Gravereaux. il Hi Fi 21:52-3 F '71
3 new zero-tracking-error turntables. C. P. Gilmore. il Pop Sci 199:94-5 N '71
Two tone arms: superior, but—. il Consumer Rep 36:192-3 Ap '71

Turntables

Buyer's guide to today's record-playing equipment. Hi Fi 21:52-3 My '71
Hi-Fi product report:
Rabco model ST-4 turntable/arm. il Electr World 85:14-15 Je '71
How good need a turntable be? J. G. Holt. il Pop Electr 1:7-10 Ja '72
Those new turntables. R. F. Scott. il Radio-Electr 42:61-3 Je '71
Turntables and changers up to date. L. Zide. il Hi Fi 21:44-9 My '71
What is a professional turntable? N. Eisenberg. Hi Fi 21:50-1 My '71
See also
Phonograph—Record changers

PHONOGRAPH, Portable

Portable stereo phonographs. il Consumer Rep 36:252-5 Ap '71

PHONOGRAPH record industry
See also
Atlantic recording corporation
Capitol records, inc.
Columbia records, inc.
Phonograph records—Recording

Germany (Federal Republic)

Component maker meets record company: the AR/DGG contemporary music project. D. Henahan. Hi Fi 21:96-7 F '71

Great Britain
See also
Electric and musical industries, ltd.

PHONOGRAPH records

Assisting artists in Edison cylinders. J. Walsh. il por Hobbies 76:37-8 Ap; 37-8+ My '71
Beethoven by the bushel from DGG. P. G. Davis. Hi Fi 20:116 D '70
Best records of the year. il Hi Fi 20:44-6 D '70; 21:24-5 D '71
Books and records to give for Christmas. J. Herbert. House & Gard 140:102+ D '71
Boston symphony chamber players; Schubert-Milhaud-Hindemith miscellany. A. Cohn. il Am Rec G 37:424-5 Mr '71
Building your own record library; interviews, ed. by R. Hemming. B. Haitink; H. W. Henze; H. Somer. il Sr Schol 97:21 Ja 11 '71
Checklist for a musical Christmas. il Seventeen 29:144-5 D '70
Close-up (cont of) Spotlight! E. Miller. See issues of Seventeen, April 1971-
Component maker meets record company: the AR/DGG contemporary music project. D. Henahan. Hi Fi 21:96-7 F '71
DGG in Boston. D. Hamilton. il Hi Fi 20:85-6 D '70
Delian delight; Appalachia and Brigg fair, Sir John Barbirolli's final recording. D. Henahan. por Hi Fi 21:77 Ap '71
DISCussions. R. Hemming; D. Finkle; B. Scoppa. See issues of Senior scholastic
Double-barreled Donizetti; Souliotis as Anna Bolena and Caballé in a collection of rarities. G. Movshon. por Hi Fi 20:90+ D '70
Favorite pioneer recording artists. J. Walsh. See issues of Hobbies
French sampler; income from recordings. P. Entremont. il Hi Fi 21:32+ N '71
Great recordings of the decade:
The classics. il Hi Fi 21:62-4+ Ap '71
Grotesqueries by Alkan and Lewenthal. H. Goldsmith. Hi Fi 21:86 O '71
His own man, the music of Elliott Carter. A. Cohn. il por Am Rec G 37:756-9 Jl '71
Historical records. A. Favia-Artsay. See issues of Hobbies
Hodeir on Finnegans wake; Anna Livia Plurabelle. I. Kolodin. Sat R 54:53 Ja 30 '71
In brief. See issues of High fidelity and Musical America
Lighter side. M. Ames and others. See issues of High fidelity and Musical America
Limited edition: twenty discsful of Toscaniniana. C. J. Luten. il Am Rec G 37:744-5+ Jl '71
Masterwork by Boulez; Pli selon pli. R. P. Morgan. por Hi Fi 21:70-1 Ag '71
Music in the round. Discus. See issues of Harper's magazine
New records in review. B. H. Haggin. See issues of Yale review
1971's best LPs. Time 99:55 Ja 3 '72
On the record; critic's choice. H. Saal. il Newsweek 78:38-9 D 27 '71
On the record: Music. See issues of Library journal
Other reviews. See issues of American record guide
Philips' import conversion, the first 28 releases. P. G. Davis. Hi Fi 21:100 S '71
Phonograph records. W. F. Grueninger. See issues of Consumer bulletin
Producer stars in DGG's first Boston Pops recording: Fabulous Broadway. R. D. Darrell. il por Hi Fi 20:86-7 D '70
Recordings. R. Jacobson. Sat R 54:58 F 27; 58 Ap 24; 51 Je 26; 50 Ag 28; 77 S 25; 80 N 27 '71
Recordings. M. Mayer. See issues of Esquire
Recordings in review. I. Kolodin. See issues of Saturday review
Recordings reports: miscellaneous LPs. I. Kolodin. See issues of Saturday review
Records:
Bizet-Corigliano-Hess: The naked Carmen. Opera N 35:35 F 13 '71
Spoleto festival album. Opera N 35:30 My 15 '71
Records (cont) D. Hamilton. Nation 211: 670; 212:381-2, 573, 701-2; 213:633-4 D 21 '70, Mr 22, My 3, 31, D 13 '71

PHONOGRAPH records—*Continued*
Records (title varies) (cont) W. F. Rickenbacker. Nat R 23:772 Jl 13 '71
Records I don't want to live without. A. Rich. Redbook 137:95+ S '71
Records: summer's choice. il Time 98:53 Ag 30 '71
Reviews of records. See issues of Musical quarterly
Reviews of records; works by H. Isaac. R. Cross. Mus Q 57:524-7 Jl '71
Season's best in low-priced records. il Changing T 25:17-18 D '71
Singer's choice. C. Ludwig. Hi Fi 21:27 Jl '71
Speaking of records. See issues of High fidelity and Musical America
Thin record; RCA's Dynaflex. Newsweek 77:80-1 Ja 25 '71
Two very different sides of Ned Rorem. P. L. Miller. Am Rec G 37:730-1 Je '71
What's become of the great recordings of 1951-61? Hi Fi 21:65 Ap '71
What's happening. G. Shalit. See issues of Ladies' home journal
Word thing from the kid with the Bic pen. R. Thompson. Harper 243:46-7 O '71
Year's best recordings; comp. by R. Freed. Sat R 54:84-5 N 27 '71
    See also
Copyright—Phonograph records
Libraries—Phonograph and phonograph records

Animal sounds
Songs of the humpback whale. A. Goldman. il Life 70:16 Ap 9 '71
Whale songs. J. Morgenstern. Newsweek 77:16-17 F 15 '71

Arias
About baseball giants, and the great Leontyne Price: Prima donna/volume three. W. Botsford. por(p273) Am Rec G 37:296-7+ Ja '71
Canadian releases. A. Favia-Artsay. il Hobbies 76:35-6+ D '71
Carole Bogard: a revelation. S. Lincoln. Am Rec G 37:722-3 Je '71
Even rarer Donizettiana from RCA. P. L. Miller. Am Rec G 37:279 Ja '71
Manuel Salazar. A. Favia-Artsay. pors Hobbies 75:35-6 Ja '71
Records:
    Amelita Galli-Curci, Louise Homer, Enrico Caruso. Opera N 35:34 Ja 30 '71
    Caballé/Martí duets. Opera N 36:33 D 11 '71
    Grace Bumbry; James King. Opera N 35:34 Ap 10 '71
    Joan Sutherland: French arias. Opera N 35:34 Mr 6 '71
    Kirsten Flagstad. Opera N 35:35 F 6 '71
    Luciano Pavarotti. Opera N 36:32 O '71
    Montserrat Caballé. Opera N 35:34 Ap 17 '71
    Montserrat Caballé in Donizetti rarities. Opera N 35:34 F 20 '71
    Mozart/Strauss: arias, songs. Opera N 35:34 F 27 '71
    Theo Adam; James King; Ruza Baldani; Mirella Freni. Opera N 35:35 Ja 23 '71
Solid bass; A. Kipnis: Song recital. D. Hamilton. por Hi Fi 21:64-5 My '71

Ballet music
Giselle and Coppélia for ears and feet. W. Terry. Sat R 54:88 N 27 '71

Baseball
Songs and music
Baseball recordings. J. Walsh. il Hobbies 76:37-8+ D '71

Benefit performances
Rock for Bangladesh; recording of George Harrison's benefit concert at New York's Madison Square Garden. il Newsweek 79:61 Ja 10 '72

Blues (songs, etc)
Bessie's blues. H. Saal. por Newsweek 77:44-5 F 1 '71
Complete Bessie Smith. L. Gerber. pors Am Rec G 37:340-2 F '71
Records; recordings of M. Waters. D. Lupoff. il Ramp Mag 10:67-8 N '71

Cantatas
Meanwhile in nearby Brattleboro. .; Bach festivals. P. L. Miller. Am Rec G 37:290 Ja 71
Prokofiev blockbuster; Cantata for the twentieth anniversary of the October revolution. R. S. Brown. Hi Fi 21:88+ Ja '71

Records:
    Bach: Cantatas. Opera N 35:32 Mr 13 '71
    Prokofiev: Cantata for the 20th anniversary of the revolution, and Shostakovich: The sun shines over our motherland. Opera N 35:32 Ap 3 '71

Cello music
Pablo Casals: a tribute. D. W. Moore. por Am Rec G 37:280-1 Ja '71

Chamber music
Fantasy world of Pierrot lunaire. D. Hamilton. il Hi Fi 21:70-1 Jl '71

Childrens records
On and off the avenue (cont) New Yorker 47:128-30 D 11 '71
Recommended recordings (cont) N. Langstaff. Horn Bk 47:322 Je '71
Recordings. J. L. Limbacher. See occasional issues of Library journal
Recordings: the oral tradition revived; with discography. A. Sperber. il por Library J 96:3813-15 N 15 '71
What records should you give to children? E. Kulleseid. il Hi Fi 20:79-83 D '70

Choral music
Out of the mouths of babes; Children's plea for peace. R. J. Watson. Chr Cent 88:1423-4 D 1 '71
Records:
    Vaughan Williams: Sea symphony and Sancta Civitas/Benedicite. Opera N 35:34 Mr 6 '71
    Verdi: Quattro pezzi sacri. Opera N 35:30 My 15 '71

Christmas music
Delightful music for all seasons, a Praetorius program from Nonesuch. J. W. Barker. il Am Rec G 37:209 D '70

Church music
Bad day for Blackwoods; Gospel music association's Dove awards. C. A. Forbes. Chr Today 16:44 N 19 '71
Cantiones sacrae 1575; English church music. J. W. Barker. pors Am Rec G 37:344-5+ F '71

Collectors and collecting
About collectors items. A. Favia-Artsay. il Hobbies 76:35-6+ Ap; 35-6+ My '71
Archive explosion. P. L. Miller. Opera N 35:28-9 Ja 23 '71
Pianist's choice. A. Foldes. il Hi Fi 21:24 Ja '71
Self-analysis of a music addict. A. Chipman. por Hi Fi 21:20 F '71
Tale of a record collector. I. Rotman. il Hobbies 76:35-6+ Ag '71

Concertos
Beethoven violin concerto for piano. H. Goldsmith. Hi Fi 21:92 N '71
Blazing virtuosity and intellect of William Kapell. M. N. Kanny. por Am Rec G 37:303+ Ja '71
Brahms by Arrau: two of his finest recorded performances. M. N. Kanny. Am Rec G 37:714 Je '71
Carter's Concerto for orchestra, a gripping musical experience. D. Hamilton. Hi Fi 21:82 Mr '71
Fox meets the rabbit; Rubinstein and Arrau play the two Brahms piano concertos. H. Goldsmith. il pors Hi Fi 21:61-2 My '71
In a class by itself: Bishop's Emperor. M. N. Kanny. il Am Rec G 37:240 D '70
Intriguing, and also extremely pleasant; real baroque Christmas. D. W. Moore. il Am Rec G 37:211 D '70
Jakob Gimpel: there is no mistaking the mastery. M. N. Kanny. Am Rec G 37:712 Je '71
Luciferian legacy: N. Paganini's third concerto. por Time 98:63 N 29 '71
Menuhin plays Walton, a brilliant show. S. Fleming. Hi Fi 21:80 My '71
Moszkowski's splashy piano concerto. R. W. Schaaf. Hi Fi 21:86+ Ja '71
Steal for the modest price asked; Mozart's Sinfonia concertante from Musical heritage society. Am Rec G 37:378 F '71
Three North American keyboard virtuosos give Bach a young look: Glenn Gould, Anthony Newman and I. Kipnis. R. P. Morgan; C. F. Gilmore. il Hi Fi 21:86-7 S '71

Dance music
Records for teachers. E. Le Mone. Dance Mag 45:94-5 Ap; 98+ O '71; 46:90 Ja '72
    See also
Phonograph records—Ballet music

PHONOGRAPH records—*Continued*

Documentary records
Facts about the only recording of Mr Edison's voice. J. Walsh. il Hobbies 76:37-8+ Ja '72
My last words concerning the controversial McKinley record. J. Walsh. il pors Hobbies 76:37-8+ O; 37-8+ N '71
Prey to charisma; The Groupies. C. E. Fager. Chr Cent 88:356 Mr 17 '71

Electronic music
Partch for all. L. Stempel. por Sat R 54:72-3 N 27 '71

Folk music
Folk music. L. Gerber. Am Rec G 37:330-1, 784-5 Ja, Jl '71

Gospel music
See Phonograph records—Church music

Harpsichord music
See also
Phonograph records—Concertos

History
Fabulous phonograph, in words and music; Wonder of the age: Mr Edison's new talking phonograph. R. Gelatt. il Sat R 54:78 S 25 '71
Four-channel discs, 1904. L. Marcus. il Hi Fi 21:65 Jl '71
Those were the days. Hi Fi 21:36 O '71
Victor record sales, from 1901 to 1942. J. Walsh. il Hobbies 76:37-8+ Je '71

Humorous records
Scorn along with Archie; All in the family album. il Time 99:47 Ja 17 '72

Incidental music
Delicately molded sensuality, bordering on the pornographic: Chansons de Bilitis and Satie's Socrate. J. Ringo. il Am Rec G 37:310-12 Ja '71

Italian music
Reviews of records; Musik aus der zeit von Boccaccios decamerone. A. Blachly. Mus Q 57:330-41 Ap '71

Jazz music
Jazz. J. S. Wilson. See issues of High fidelity and Musical America
Jazz records; B. Smith reissue project. W. Balliett. New Yorker 47:160-6+ N 6 '71
Musical events; L. Armstrong. W. Balliett. New Yorker 47:75-7 Ag 28 '71
Recordings reports: jazz LPs. S. Dance. See issues of Saturday review

Moving picture music
Potpourri for Beatrix Potter; Ballet film soundtrack. R. D. Darrell. il Hi Fi 21:98 O '71

Music, Popular (songs, etc)
Dance, saith the Lord; The Motown story. C. E. Fager. Chr Cent 88:1094 S 15 '71
Great recordings of the decade:
Pops. G. Lees. il Hi Fi 21:69-71 Ap '71
Music. D. Lupoff. Ramp Mag 10:61 S '71
Paul Siebel: homegrown weed. E. Sander. por Sat R 54:55 Ja 30 '71
Pilgrim's progress; K. Kristofferson's country or popular music. P. Axthelm. por Newsweek 77:105-6 My 24 '71
Songwriter & the record business today. A. Shaw. il Writers Digest 51:24-7+ N '71
Today's unwritten pop music. B. Mathieu. Writers Digest 51:25 N '71
Yowltide season; canine rendition of Jingle bells. Newsweek 79:46-7 Ja 3 '72
See also
Phonograph records—Rock music (songs, etc)

Musical comedies, revues, etc.
Gershwin's two Astaires; re-creations of Lady be good and Funny face. I. Kolodin. il Sat R 54:70 O 30 '71
Gilbert without Sullivan; recording of F. Clay's Ages ago. R. Jacobson. Sat R 54:58 F 27 '71

Negro music
In Desto albums, music by a dozen black composers. L. Gerber. il Am Rec G 476-9 Ap '71
In justice to George Washington Johnson; favorite records of The whistling coon and The laughing song. J. Walsh. il pors Hobbies 75:37-9+ Ja '71
Soul kaleidoscope: Aretha at the Fillmore. M. Lydon. il pors Ramp Mag 10:30-9 O '71
Sounds. P. Garland. See issues of Ebony

Operas
Ariadne auf Naxos. A. Sperber. il Am Rec G 37:350-2 F '71
At last, les Huguenots. G. L. Mayer. il por Am Rec G 37:484-7 Ap '71
Boulez Parsifal. R. Lawrence. Sat R 54:83 O 30 '71
Britten's Prodigal. R. Jacobson. Sat R 54:57 My 29 '71
Britten's The rape of Lucretia. D. Harris. il Hi Fi 21:80-1 O '71
Bumper crop of Wagner operas: Solti's Tannhäuser, Kubelik's Lohengrin and Karajan's Meistersinger. P. G. Davis; C. L. Osborne; D. Hamilton. il por Hi Fi 21:75-81 D '71
Caballé and early Bellini; Il pirata. H. Weinstock. Sat R 54:55 Ap 24 '71
Colin Davis on Figaro. G. L. Mayer. Sat R 54:79 N 27 '71
Double-barreled Donizetti: Souliotis as Anna Bolena and Caballé in a collection of rarities. G. Movshon. por Hi Fi 20:90+ D '70
Finally a Tippett opera. H. Weinstock. Sat R 54:52 Ag 28 '71
Fisher vs. Lang; Tamerlano controversy. C. P. Fisher; P. H. Lang. pors Hi Fi 21:18-19 Jl '71
Fresh view of Pelleas; Pierre Boulez' interpretation. D. Hamilton. por Hi Fi 21:63-4 F '71
Handel at half mast; Orlando. R. Jacobson. Sat R 54:51 Je 26 '71
History brought to life; Giulini conducts Don Carlo. G. Movshon. il Hi Fi 21:77-8 O '71
Kubelik-Nilsson Oberon. I. Kolodin. Sat R 54:74 N 27 '71
London's Anna Bolena. P. L. Miller. il Am Rec G 37:276-9 Ja '71
Magnificent baroque opera; Fischer-Dieskau and Troyanos as Hadel's Caesar and Cleopatra. P. H. Lang. Hi Fi 21:65-7 F '71
Manon à la Sills. R. Jacobson. Sat R 54:58 Ap 24 '71
Medea à la Mayr. R. Lawrence. Sat R 54:57 Ja 30 '71
Meyerbeer's bloody machine; Sutherland in Huguenots. P. G. Davis. Hi Fi 21:73-4 Ja '71
Midsummer marriage. E. Greenfield. il pors Am Rec G 37:696-8+ Je '71
Milestone Aida; Leontyne Price on RCA. G. Movshon. por Hi Fi 21:57-8 Ag '71
Mining the musical underground. B. Collins. il Hi Fi 21:74-6 N '71
Multilayered vision; Michael Tippett's Midsummer marriage. P. G. Davis. il por Hi Fi 21:68-70 Ag '71
My favorite recordings, and other related sources of controversy. G. London. Hi Fi 21:22+ My '71
Obviously produced with loving care: from London: die zauberflöte. R. W. Gutman. il Am Rec G 37:472-4 Ap '71
Original-cast Amahl. P. L. Miller. Am Rec G 37:208 D '70
Parsifal at Bayreuth: Boulez conducts. D. Hamilton. il Hi Fi 21:85-6 N '71
Pathe's complete Romeo et Juliette, 1912. C. L. Osborne. il Hi Fi 21:78-9 Ap '71
Pelléas et Mélisande. N. Rorem. il Am Rec G 37:405-7 Mr '71
Rebirth of Venus; Wagner's Paris Tannhäuser. R. T. Jones. Time 99:64 Ja 10 '72
Records:
Bellini: Il Pirata. Opera N 35:30 My 15 '71
Bizet: Carmen and Carmen (highlights) Opera N 35:35 F 13 '71
Blitzstein: The cradle will rock. Opera N 35:34 F 20 '71
Borodin: Prince Igor. Opera N 36:32 O '71
Britten: Noye's fludde. Opera N 35:34 Mr 27 '71
Debussy: Pelléas et Mélisande. Opera N 35:32 Mr 13 '71
Donizetti: Anna Bolena. Opera N 35:35 F 6 '71
Donizetti: Lucia di Lammermoor. il Opera N 35:34 Ja 16 '71
Giannini: Taming of the shrew. Opera N 36:42 D 25 '71
Gluck: Orfeo ed Euridice. il Opera N 35:35 Ja 23 '71
Gounod: Mireille. Opera N 35:34 Ap '17 '71
Handel: Giulio Cesare. Opera N 35:34 F 20 '71
Handel: Orlando and Ariodante. Opera N 36:32 O '71
Handel: Tamerlano. Opera N 35:34 Mr 27 '71
Hanson: Herry Mount (excerpts) Opera N 35:34 F 27 '71
Krenek: Jonny spielt auf. Opera N 35:32 Ap 3 '71
Lortzing: Der wildschütz. Opera N 36:30 S '71

PHONOGRAPH records—Operas—*Continued*
Records:—*Continued*
Massenet: Manon. Opera N 35:30 Je 12 '71
Mayr: Medea in Corinto. Opera N 35:34 F 27 '71
Menotti: The medium. Opera N 35:34 Ap 10 '71
Menotti: The old maid and the thief. Opera N 35:34 Mr 6 '71
The Met's first Butterfly. Opera N 36: 36 D 18 '71
Mozart: Die zauberflöte. Opera N 35:34 Mr 20 '71*
Owen: A fisherman called Peter. Opera N 35:34 Ap 10 '71
Penderecki: Devils of Loudun. Opera N 35:30 Je 12 '71
Rossini: Guillaume Tell (excerpts) Opera N 36:33 D 11 '71
Tchaikovsky: Maid of Orleans. Opera N 36:42 D 25 '71
Tippett: The midsummer marriage. il Opera N 36:30 S '71
Verdi: Aida. Opera N 36:30 S '71
Verdi: Don Carlo. il Opera N 36:32 N '71
Verdi: Un ballo in maschera. il Opera N 36:33 D 11 '71
Wagner: Parsifal. Opera N 36:36 D 18 '71
Webber/Rice: Jesus Christ superstar. Opera N 35:34 Ja 30 '71
Records. D. Hamilton. Nation 213:510; 214: 62 N 15 '71, Ja 10 '72
Records: Bizet's Carmen, Massenet's Manon. D. Hamilton. Nation 212:701-2 My 31 '71
Records: Gounod's Roméo et Juliette. D. Hamilton. Nation 212:381-2 Mr 22 '71
Sad days for Salome. R. Jacobson. Sat R 54:77 S 25 '71
Sills and Gedda star in an ideal Manon. G. Movshon. il Hi Fi 21:72-3 Je '71
Sills as Lucia. P. G. Davis. il Hi Fi 21:69-70 Mr '71
Souped-up savovards. H.M.S. Pinafore. R. Jacobson. Sat R 54:80 N 27 '71
Tamerlane and Julius Caesar. H. Weinstock. Sat R 54:79 Mr 27 '71
Tchaikovsky's Joan of Arc; excerpts. P. G. Davis. Hi Fi 21:96 Ag '71
Tragedy of Father Urbain; Devils of Loudun. D. Hamilton. il Hi Fi 21:69-70 Je '71
Weber's English opera in German: Oberon. D. Hamilton. Hi Fi 21:108 O '71
See also
Phonograph records—Rock operas
Tape recordings—Operas

Operettas

See Phonograph records—Musical comedies, revues, etc.

Oratorios

From the best Weihnachtsoratorium, the best: highlights. P. L. Miller. il Am Rec G 37:210 D '70
Music for the season: Handel's Messiah. J. Diether. il Am Rec G 37:204-8 D '70
Old warhorse rides again: Mendelssohn's Elijah. T. W. Moore. Chr Cent 88:390 Mr 24 '71
Records:
Cavalieri: Rappresentazione di anima e di corpo. Opera N 35:32 Ap 3 '71
Handel: Messiah. Opera N 35:34 Ap 17 '71
Mendelssohn: Elijah. Opera N 35:35 F 6 '71
Vaughan Williams: Sea symphony and Sancta Civitas/Benedicite. Opera N 35: 34 Mr 6 '71

Orchestral music

Herrmann's Holst: warmly recommended; The planets. J. Diether. Am Rec G 37:372 F '71
Strong, assertive voice: the music of Arthur Cohn. D. W. Moore. por Am Rec G 37:554 My '71
Thrilling live recording: Colin Davis conducting The last night of the proms. R. D. Darrell. il Hi Fi 21:79 O '71

Organ music

How slow is fast? Bach. W. F. Rickenbacker. Nat R 23:772 Jl 13 '71
Reviews of records; Bach family: organ works. L. Noss. Mus Q 57:163-6 Ja '71
Reviews of records; Böhm and Pachelbel: organ compositions. L. Noss. Mus Q 57:166-9 Ja '71
Reviews of records: Spanish and Portuguese organ music. L. Noss. Mus Q 57:169-72 Ja '71

Overtures

Ormandy declares war (on himself) Tchaikovsky: 1812 Overture. R. D. Darrell. Hi Fi 21:77 Je '71

Passion music

Recordings; Bach's St Matthew passion. M. Mayer. Esquire 76:26+ S '71
Saint Matthew sweepstakes, by Philadelphia, Stuttgart, Pro Arte. J. Hiemenz. Hi Fi 21:MA25 Jl '71
Total victory in the Bach revolution; St Matthew passion. C. F. Gilmore. il Hi Fi 21:67-8 Jl '71

Percussion music

Rather delightfully wild, the music of William Kraft. D. W. Moore. Am Rec G 37: 570 My '71

Piano music

Beethoven on records. H. Goldsmith. Hi Fi 21: 61-2 Ja '71
Forgotten romantics. Discus. Harper 243: 145-6 N '71
From the Musical heritage society, the complete works of Chopin. L. Richmond. il pors Am Rec G 37:488-93+ Ap '71
Memorable IPL release: Moszkowski. L. Gerber. il Am Rec G 37:282-4 Ja '71
Multum in parvo, Marlboro Mozart. M. N. Kanny. il Am Rec G 37:287-8 Ja '71
New tales of Josef Hofmann. R. Jacobson. il por Sat R 54:50 Ag 28 '71
Old masters remastered: recordings by Rachmaninoff, Lhevinne, Hofmann, and Schnabel. H. Goldsmith. il Hi Fi 21:71-3 Mr '71
Pianistic culminations. R. P. Morgan. por Hi Fi 21:20 Je '71
Piano rags by Scott Joplin. por Am Rec G 37: 354-5 F '71
Rachmaninoff eruption. H. Goldsmith. il Hi Fi 21:69-70 Jl '71
Sergei Rachmaninoff. L. Gerber. il Am Rec G 37:438-9 Mr '71
Super great recordings of the century: Backhaus. R. Kammerer. por Am Rec G 37:430-1 Mr '71
Three decades of Ellington: a fascinating Decca release. D. W. Moore. por Am Rec G 37:370 F '71
Truly extraordinary Brahms; with Stephen Bishop. M. N. Kanny. Am Rec G 37:364 F '71
Very first release, from RCA Victrola, of 1935-1938 recordings by Josef Hofmann. R. Kammerer. il por Am Rec G 37:480-1 Ap '71
Weissenberg: close to the very ultimate. L. Gerber. Am Rec G 37:448 Mr '71
With a brain in each of her fingers, Alicia de Larrocha. por Am Rec G 37:420-1 Mr '71
See also
Phonograph records—Concertos
Phonograph records—Sonatas

Recording

Baker/Boult/Brahms project. E. Greenfield. il Hi Fi 21:16+ My '71
Bernstein's Broadway Mass. P. G. Davis. Hi Fi 21:22 D '71
Britten's television opera; Owen Wingrave. E. Greenfield. il Hi Fi 21:19-20 Mr '71
La Calisto, Diana, and the oldest nymph in the business. E. Greenfield. il Hi Fi 21:26+ N '71
Chicago symphony in Vienna; recording Mahler's Eighth symphony. R. Dettmer. il Hi Fi 21:20-1 D '71
Classical recording techniques. F. Catero. il por Electr World 85:43+ My '71
Colin Davis' second marriage; Sir Michael Tippett's The Midsummer marriage. R. Wimbush. il por Hi Fi 21:17-18 Ag '71
Comic Klemperer: Mozart's four popular operas. E. Greenfield. por Hi Fi 21:10-12 Je '71
Concertgebouw in Amsterdam; recording Mahler's Eighth symphony. E. Greenfield. Hi Fi 21:21-2 D '71
High infidelity; swing bands of the '30s and '40s recreated by studio musicians. J. Morgenstern. Newsweek 78:9 Jl 19 '71
Karajan invades East Germany. P. Moor. il pors Hi Fi 21:20+ Ap '71
New quadraphonic disc system. il Radio-Electr 42:2+ S '71
Operatic cliffhangers with Sills and Souliotis. E. Greenfield. il Hi Fi 21:19-20+ Ja '71
Playing the hits like the heavies; rock music. L. Hutchinson. il Sr Schol 98:24+ Ap 26 '71
Previn meets Shankar. E. Greenfield. il Hi Fi 21:13+ S '71
Der Rosenkavalier; a Bernstein/Culshaw production. S. Gould. il Hi Fi 21:16-17 Ag '71
Sutherland's 1971 Lucia; Decca decennial Lucia. E. Greenfield. il Hi Fi 21:20+ O '71

PHONOGRAPH records—Recording—*Cont.*
Varèse sonic spectacular: Decca/London recording sessions with Zubin Mehta. K. Monson. Hi Fi 21:22 S '71
Where the music sounds best. J. G. Holt. il Pop Electr 34:86-9 My '71

Unauthorized recording

Mining the musical underground. B. Collins. il Hi Fi 21:74-6 N '71
Revolutionary war; bootlegging of records by black-market operators. il Time 97:72-3 Je 28 '71

Reissues

Classic recordings for a song; discography. J. R. Douglas. il por Library J 96:597-607 F 15 '71
Golden oldies revisited. M. L. Pahls. il Hi Fi 21:55-60 F '71
Historic master series: a last chance; with editorial comment. D. Shawe-Taylor. Am Rec G 37:468-71 Ap '71
Old gold; new releases of classical recordings. W. Bender. Time 97:73 Mr 15 '71
Old masters remastered: recordings by Rachmaninoff, Lhevinne, Hofmann, and Schnabel. H. Goldsmith. il Hi Fi 21:71-3 Mr '71
Repeat performance. P. G. Davis. See issues of High fidelity and Musical America to June 1971
Spirit of 78. Time 97:69 Ap 12 '71
Vocal reissues, Italian style; operatic recitals. C. L. Osborne. Hi Fi 21:24+ Mr '71

Religious records

Sweet and sour. T. W. Moore. il Chr Cent 88:785-6 Je 23 '71

Requiems

Flashes of greatness from the 25-year-old Bruckner: a moving, masterly Requiem. J. Diether. por Am Rec G 37:428-9+ Mr '71
Verdi requiem; from Angel and Columbia. P. L. Miller. Am Rec G 37:384-5 F '71

Rock music (songs, etc)

After all; Woodstock record album. C. E. Fager. Chr Cent 88:302 Mr 3 '71
Aretha, the Turners, and King Curtis. B. Korall. Sat R 54:59 D 25 '71
Beatles to remember, beatles to forget. B. Scoppa. Sr Schol 98:29+ Mr 29 '71
Cat Mother; new albums by Cat Mother and the All-Night Newsboys, and commander Cody and his Lost Planet Airmen. D. Lupoff. il Ramp Mag 10:64-6 Ja '72
Child is father to the rock and roll music. E. Sander. il Sat R 54:55 F 27; 75+ Mr 27 '71
Dylan's New morning. R. D. Campbell. por Chr Cent 88:1009 Ag 25 '71
George and John; LP's by G. Harrison and J. Lennon. E. Willis. New Yorker 47:95-7 F 27 '71
Grateful dead and the Life and times of Country Joe & the Fish from Haight-Ashbury to Woodstock. D. Lupoff. Ramp Mag 10:63-5 D '71
Heaviest Beatles of them all: solo albums by George Harrison and John Lennon. J. Gabree. il Hi Fi 21:70-1 Mr '71
Inside all-time rock 'n' roll poll; discography. il Sr Schol 99:22-3 D 13 '71
Jimmy Webb. B. Korall. Sat R 54:76 S 25 '71
Judy Collins: diary of a heart. E. Sander. Sat R 54:80 N 27 '71
Pink Floyd, Relics; and Maggot brain. Funkadelic. D. Lupoff. il Ramp Mag 10:65-6 O '71
Pop. E. Sander. Sat R 54:55 F 27; 75+ Mr 27: 57 Ap 24; 49 Je 26; 47 Ag 28 '71
Return of Satan's Jesters; Rolling Stones new record Sticky fingers. il Time 97:60 My 17 '71
Rock, etc; J. Joplin. E. Willis. New Yorker 47:81-2 Ag 14 '71
Rock for Bangladesh; recording of George Harrison's benefit concert at New York's Madison Square Garden. il Newsweek 79:61 Ja 10 '72
Rock music. J. Voigt. Wilson Lib Bul 46: 130-1 O '71
Songwriter & the record business today. A. Shaw. il Writers Digest 51:24-7+ N '71
Ten neglected rock classics. T. R. Bingham. il Hi Fi 21:28+ O '71

Rock operas

Here comes SuperJudas! Jesus Christ: superstar. S. M. Smith. Nat R 23:715 Je 29 '71
Jesus Christ superstar. N. Rorem. Harper 242:22-4 Je '71

New paganism; Jesus the superstar. G. Meilaender, jr. il Chr Today 15:4-6 S 24 '71
Rock gets religion: Jesus Christ superstar; interview, ed. by E. Miller. T. Rice; A. L. Webber. pors Seventeen 30:156-7+ Mr '71
Super profits from Superstar: Jesus Christ superstar. il Bsns W p46-7 S 11 '71

Sonatas

Eclecticism is always satisfying: Lowndes Maury. A. Cohn. Am Rec G 37:585 My '71
Eighteen minutes of glorious Schubert from Lili Kraus; sonato in A minor. L. Gerber. il Am Rec G 37:512-13 Ap '71
Great master of sonata form: the real Muzio Clementi. S. Lincoln. il pors Am Rec G 37:228-34 D '70
One of the great Mozart piano records: Sonata in A minor. L. Gerber. Am Rec G 37: 320 Ja '71
Schubert, transcendental amateur; W. Kempff reflectively explores the "complete" piano sonatas. D. Henahan. il por Hi Fi 21:71-2 Je '71
Serkin and Beethoven's Hammerklavier. H. Goldsmith. Hi Fi 21:86 D '71
Temperament and accuracy: violin sonata. D. W. Moore. Am Rec G 37:367 F '71

Songs

Composer's showcase: Robert Starer. D. W. Moore. Am Rec G 37:383 F '71
Elusive Jenny Lind record; discovery of wax cylinder. H. Birdoff. il por Hobbies 75:35-6+ F '71
Gunther Schuller, a very right man to interpret Ives. P. L. Miller. Am Rec G 37:353 F '71
House of many mansions: the songs of Charles Ives and the American experience. P. L. Miller. Am Rec G 37:563+ My '71
In justice to George Washington Johnson; favorite records of The whistling coon and The laughing song. J. Walsh. il pors Hobbies 75:37-9+ Ja; 37+ F '71
Louisville orchestra 100th golden edition 1954-1970. P. M. Miller. il Am Rec G 37: 422-3 Mr '71
Over 400 Schubert songs: Fischer-Dieskau and Gerald Moore. D. Hamilton. il Hi Fi 21:74-5 Ja '71
Puppet, pirate, poet, pawn, and king: a Sinatra retrospective. A. Shaw. il pors Hi Fi 21:65-8 Ag '71
Records:
    Alexander Kipnis. Opera N 35:31 Je 12 '71
    Stravinsky: songs. Opera N 35:34 Mr 20 '71
    Victoria de los Angeles: Spanish folk songs. Opera N 36:42 D 25 '71
Solid bass; A. Kipnis: Song recital. D. Hamilton. por Hi Fi 21:64-5 My '71
Touching and toe-tingling: a salute to Percy Grainger. R. Kennedy. Am Rec G 37:295 Ja '71
Toy pianos, musical saws and a great vocal tour de force; G. Crumb's Ancient voices of children. D. Hamilton. Hi Fi 21:78 Ag '71
See also
Phonograph records—Arias

Soul music

See Phonograph records—Negro music

Sounds

There's a tweeter in my tweeter; with selective list of sound-effects records. E. Endres. Hi Fi 21:61-5 Je '71
See also
Phonograph records—Animal sounds

Spoken records

European literary scene; recordings produced by Deutsche grammophon gesellschaft. R. J. Clements. Sat R 54:27 F 13 '71
Facts about the only recording of Mr Edison's voice. J. Walsh. il Hobbies 76:37-8+ Ja '72
Murrow's legatees; Columbia's oral scrapbook of the sixties. M. Kempton. il Hi Fi 21:63-4 My '71
On the record: Words. J. L. Limbacher. See issues of Library journal
Recommended recordings (cont) N. Langstaff. Horn Bk 47:322 Je '71
Recordings. J. L. Limbacher. See occasional issues of Library journal
Recordings: the oral tradition revived; with discography. A. Sperber. il por Library J 96:3813-15 N 15 '71
Silhouettes in courage; documentary history of black history. B. Teague. Hi Fi 21:102 Ap '71

PHONOGRAPH records—Spoken records—*Cont.*
Voice of Harriet Beecher Stowe; wax cylinder recording. H. Birdoff. il por Hobbies 76:35-6+ Jl '71
Wonder of the age. G. Movshon. il Hi Fi 21:84-5 S '71
Words only. S. Potter. See issues of American record guide
See also
Talking books

Stereophonic records
4-channel stereo records. il Radio-Electr 42:38 Mr '71
Other reviews. See issues of American record guide
Uncover extra stereo channels. M. Kahn. il Hi Fi 21:43-6 Je '71

String quartet music
Avant-garde music for conservatives. A. Frankenstein. Hi Fi 21:68 My '71
Eighteen chamber masterpieces, gloriously performed: string quartets from Hungary. H. Goldsmith. il Hi Fi 21:83-4 S '71
Four decades of the Budapest quartet: a discography, 1926-1966. S. Smolian. il Am Rec G 37:220-4+ D '70

String sextet music
Very rich, thoroughly convincing Brahms. M. N. Kanny. Am Rec G 37:288+ Ja '71

Symphonic poems
Souvenir of Sibelius centennial, the first American recording of Luonnotar. J. Diether. por Am Rec G 37:494-5+ Ap '71

Symphonies
Beethoven on records. P. H. Lang. Hi Fi 20:49-50+ D '70
Georg Solti's first Chicago recordings; Mahler symphonies i.o. 5 and no. 6. J. Diether. il Am Rec G 37:346-9 F '71
Grandiose transcendentalism: Horenstein and Abravanel in the Mahler Third symphony. G. S. Fox. Am Rec G 37:577+ My '71
Greatest orchestra in the world; Haydn symphonies: George Szell conducting. R. C. Marsh. Hi Fi 21:82 Je '71
Gustav Mahler: Das klagende lied. G. S. Fox. por Am Rec G 37:214-16+ D '70
In tender memory, what the *lobgesang* means to me; Mendelssohn's Second symphony. S. Lincoln. il por Am Rec G 37:412-16 Mr '71
Karajan's Mozart. P. H. Lang. il Hi Fi 21:82 O '71
Mahler's symphonies, the best complete set: Kubelik and DGG's engineers. R. C. Marsh. Hi Fi 21:83-4 N '71
Music from Marlboro. M. Kanny. il por Am Rec G 37:282-7 Ja '71
New era in Chicago (courtesy of England) H. Goldsmith. il por Hi Fi 21:71-2 Ja '71
On London: Solti the Hungarian; Mahler Fifth. R. C. Marsh. Hi Fi 21:72-3 Ja '71
One of the great ones, Haitnik's Brahms Third. M. N. Kanny. Am Rec G 37:503-4 Ap '71
Other Haydn. H. C. R. Landon. Hi Fi 21:100 D '71
Records
Shostakovich: Symphony no. 14. Opera N 35:35 Ja 23 '71
Shostakovich's Fourteenth, a new protest? R. S. Brown. por Hi Fi 21:64-5 F '71
Sibelius' forgotten masterpiece: Kullervo symphony. H. Goldsmith. por Hi Fi 21:87 N '71
That potent Koussevitzky-Sibelius magic. G. S. Fox. Am Rec G 37:382-3 F '71
Truly great Beethoven by Schmidt-Isserstedt. M. N. Kanny. Am Rec G 37:762-3 Jl '71
Unique pleasures of Haydn's 107 symphonies. R. C. Marsh. il Hi Fi 21:75-6 Ap '71
Winter dreams, the newest and best. M. Kanny. Am Rec G 37:592+ My '71

Tone poems
See Phonograph records—Symphonic poems

Viola music
Berio's anguished trinity. D. Henahan. Hi Fi 21:78 Mr '71

Violin music
Heifetz on television. S. Fleming. Hi Fi 21:92 Jl '71
Passion and elegance, Kyung-Wha Chung's disc debut: Sibelius: Concerto for violin and orchestra; Tchaikovsky: Concerto for violin and orchestra. S. Fleming. Hi Fi 21:104 Ap '71
See also
Phonograph records—Concertos

PHOSPHATES
From bone manure to superphosphate. V. Schatz and A. Schatz. il Org Gard & Farm 18:140-7+ Mr '71
See also
Diphosphoglycerate
Phosphorylation
PHOSPHATES in detergents. See Detergents
PHOSPHATIDES
Phosphatidylserine: selective enhancer of histamine release. A. Goth and others. bibliog il Science 173:1034-5 S 10 '71
Phospholipid-calcium phosphate complex: enhanced calcium migration in the presence of phosphate. J. M. Cotmore and others. bibliog il Science 172:1339-41 Je 25 '71
See also
Lecithin
PHOSPHATIDYLSERINE. See Phosphatides
PHOSPHODIESTERASE. See Esterases
PHOSPHOLIPIDS. See Phosphatides
PHOSPHORESCENCE
See also
Bioluminescence
PHOSPHORYLATION
Interchangeability of phosphorylation coupling factors in photosynthetic and respiratory energy conversion. B. A. Melandri and others. bibliog il Science 174:514-16 O 29 '71
Periplasmic galactose binding protein of escherichia coli. H. M. Kalckar. bibliog il Science 174:557-65 N 5 '71
Urea-inorganic phosphate mixtures as prebiotic phosphorylating agents. R. Lohrmann and L. E. Orgel. bibliog il Science 171:490-4 F 5 '71
PHOTO expo 71. See Photography—Exhibitions
PHOTO finishing. See Photographic finishing, Commercial
PHOTOCHEMISTRY
Carbon monoxide: its role in photochemical smog formation. K. Westberg and others. bibliog il Science 171:1013-15 Mr 12 '71
Normal atmosphere: large radical and formaldehyde concentrations predicted. H. Levy, 2d. bibliog il Science 173:141-3 Jl 9 '71
Particle formation during water-vapor photolysis. I. D. Clark and J. F. Noxon. bibliog Science 174:941-4 N 26 '71
Photochemical transformation of 5-alkyluracils and their nucleosides. E. Krajewska and D. Shugar. bibliog il Science 173:435-7 Jl 30 '71
Photochemically induced ionic reactions of cycloalkenes. J. A. Marshall; reply. C. E. Wulfman and S. Kumei. Science 172:1061 Je 4 '71
See also
Photosynthesis
PHOTOCOMPOSITION. See Phototypesetting
PHOTOCOPYING. See Copying processes
PHOTODECOMPOSITION. See Decomposition (chemistry)
PHOTOELECTRIC cells

Control use
Remote control for audio. il Radio-Electr 42:79 Je '71
PHOTOELECTRIC multipliers
Channel electron multipliers: new semiconductor radiation detectors. F. W. Holder. il Electr World 86:30-1+ D '71
PHOTOELECTRIC phonograph pickups. See Phonograph—Pickup
PHOTOELECTRON spectroscopy. See Spectrum analysis
PHOTO-essay books. See Picture books
PHOTOFABRICATION. See Photomechanical processes
PHOTOFRAGMENT spectroscopy. See Spectrum analysis
PHOTOGRAPHERS
Money, money, money! amateur vs. professional. S. Nathan. il Pop Phot 68:50+ Je '71
To become a photographer, interview, ed. by J. Foldes. A. Kertész. il por Pop Phot 68:72-5+ Mr '71
See also names of photographers, e.g. H. Cartier-Bresson
PHOTOGRAPHERS, French
New French photographers. J. Greenberg. il Mod Phot 36:76-85 Ja '72
PHOTOGRAPHIC apparatus and supplies industry
Looking for nuts and bolts? with directory. N. Goldberg. il Pop Phot 68:48+ Je '71
See also
Bell and Howell company
Eastman Kodak company
Polaroid corporation

PHOTOGRAPHIC apparatus and supplies industry—*Continued*

Australia

Camera maker aims at the U.S; Hanimex, ltd. il por Bsns W p66 My 15 '71

Germany (Federal Republic)

Keppler on the SLR:
How Zeiss wound up out of the camera business. H. Keppler. il Mod Phot 35: 30+ D '71

Japan

From those wonderful folks who brought you Pearl Harbor; Fuji photo. il Forbes 107: 35-6 Ja 15 '71

Mexico

Photography in a developing nation; Eastman Kodak plant in Guadalajara. N. Rothschild. il Pop Phot 68:22+ My '71

PHOTOGRAPHIC chemistry
See also
Photography—Processing

PHOTOGRAPHIC conferences
Need for images will increase in future, say parley members; Wilson Hicks international conference on communication arts. N. Rothschild. il Pop Phot 69:14+ S '71

PHOTOGRAPHIC enlargers. See Photography—Enlargers and enlarging

PHOTOGRAPHIC equipment. See Photography—Apparatus and supplies

PHOTOGRAPHIC exhibitions. See Photography—Exhibitions

PHOTOGRAPHIC films. See Photography—Films

PHOTOGRAPHIC filters. See Light filters

PHOTOGRAPHIC finishing, Commercial
Ed Scully on color; offbeat bargain bulk films. E. Scully Mod Phot 35:56 O '71
Photofinishing by mail. Consumer Bul 54:32 Ap '71
See also
Technicolor, inc.

PHOTOGRAPHIC humor. See Humor, Pictorial

PHOTOGRAPHIC illustration. See Illustration of books and periodicals

PHOTOGRAPHIC lenses. See Lenses, Photographic

PHOTOGRAPHIC literature
Seeing pictures; photographic annuals. J. Scully. Mod Phot 34:48+ N '70
Seeing pictures; trends in photo books. J. Scully. il Mod Phot 35:10+ S '71
See also
Booksellers and bookselling—Photographic literature
Photography—Bibliography
Publishers and publishing—Photographic literature

PHOTOGRAPHIC meters
Photographer's test meter. M. Lincoln. il Radio Electr 42:59-61 O '71
See also
Densitometers
Exposure meters

PHOTOGRAPHIC museums. See Photography—Galleries and museums

PHOTOGRAPHIC optics
Importance of the little item called the blur disk. N. Goldberg. il Pop Phot 69:54+ Ag '71
See also
Lenses, Photographic
Perspective

Terminology

Lens test glossary. N. Goldberg. il Pop Phot 68:112-13+ My '71

PHOTOGRAPHIC paper
At long last, painless glossy printing paper has arrived! C. W. Kennedy. il Pop Phot 69:20+ S '71
Grade 6 paper can save a rainy day. C. W. Kennedy. il Pop Phot 68:22+ Ap '71
Look what a difference the paper can make. S. M. Gallager. il Pop Mech 136:113 Ag '71
Wolfman on printing; make your own variable contrast paper. A. Wolfman. Mod Phot 35:124+ N '71
Wolfman on printing; special color based papers. A. Wolfman. Mod Phot 35:52+ O '71

PHOTOGRAPHIC posters. See Posters

PHOTOGRAPHIC processing. See Photography—Processing

PHOTOGRAPHIC research
Techniques tomorrow; Polaroid 20,000 speed negative material. B. Sherman. Mod Phot 35:36+ Jl '71

PHOTOGRAPHIC silk screen printing. See Silk screen printing

PHOTOGRAPHIC slides. See Transparencies

PHOTOGRAPHIC societies. See Photography—Societies

PHOTOGRAPHIC society of America
Service, fun, and fellowship are found in PSA membership. N. Rothschild. il Pop Phot 69:44+ Jl '71

PHOTOGRAPHIC supplies industry. See Photographic apparatus and supplies industry

PHOTOGRAPHS
Bold eye from India; photographs by R. Rai. Mod Phot 34:84-7 N '70
Gallery:
Ancient French town of Le Puy, photographed by Carlo Bavagnoli. Life 70: 6-7 Ap 2 '71
Bill Binzen's Trinidad Mardi gras. Life 70:8-9 F 19 '71
Burk Uzzle captures the bleak beauty of sand dunes. Life 70:6-7 Mr 12 '71
Chicago stockyards by H. Kluetmeier. il Life 70:4-5 F 26 '71
David Cavagnaro photograph of a spider and a glacial lake. Life 71:8-9 Jl 16 '71
David Douglas Duncan's photographic essays. Life 71:8-11 S 17 '71
David Plowden photographs our daily architecture. Life 70:6-7 Ja 22 '71
Don Worth photographs trees and rocks in San Francisco. Life 70:6-7 My 7 '71
E. J. Bellocq's portraits of New Orleans prostitutes. Life 70:6-9 Mr 26 '71
Early morning sculler on the Arno River by Tony Ruta. Life 70:8-9 Ap 16 '71
Edward Weston's graceful images of nature. Life 71:6-7 S 24 '71
Ernest Braun in Yosemite National Park. Life 70:8-9 Ap 9 '71
George Silk photographs royal terns in Texas. Life 78:6-7 Mr 19 '71
Government-run opium factory; photographed by C. Mydans. Life 70:4-6A Je 25 '71
Jan Weborg in Morocco. Life 70:4-5 F 12 '71
John Loengard in California. Life 70:4-7 F 5 '71
Lennart Nilsson explores the crystalline world of hormones. Life 70:6-9 Ap 23 '71
Lonely beauty of the Canyonlands. J. Loengard. Life 71:6-9 Ag 6 '71
Margaret Bourke-White has a retrospective. Life 70:6-9 Ja 29 '71
New York cemetery by Arthur Tress. Life 70:7 Je 18 '71
New York faces photographed by S. McCartney. Life 70:6-9 Je 4 '71
112-frame portrait by Tetsu Okuhara. Life 71:4-5 Jl 30 '71
Painter and his self-portrait; photographed by Alfred Eisenstaedt. Life 70: 8-9 My 21 '71
Reflections in rippled metal by L. Bassman. Life 71:8-9 Ag 20 '71
Stan Wayman photographs a sea otter's leisurely lunch. Life 70:8-9 My 14 '71
Still lifes by Dorothea Kehaya. Life 71: 8-9 O 8 '71
Stunt driver Jim Rusing jumps speedboats; photographed by G. Warren. Life 70:8-9 Ap 30 '71
Timeless glimpse of China, by F. Fischbeck. Life 70:6-7 My 28 '71
Tropical moths, by K. Sandved. Life 70: 8-9 Je 11 '71
Turn of the century scenes by Clarence H White. Life 71:8-9 S 10 '71
William Mundell's field of grazing horses. Life 70:8-9 Mr 5 '71
Wind-sculptured dunes of southwestern Utah. J. Schwarz Life 71:8-9 O 22 '71
Young Marilyn Monroe before the wave; photographs by William Burnside. Life 71:6-7 Jl 23 '71
Just plane flat; photographs by J. Mathews. J. Dreyfus. Mod Phot 34:80-1 N '70
Reflections by young poets and photographers. Seventeen 30:80-1 Ja '71
When reality becomes the unreal. il Pop Phot 68:80-5 Mr '71
Winners of the Life 1971 contest. il Life 71: 35-52+ Jl 9 '71
See also
Libraries—Picture collections
also subhead Photographs under various subjects, e.g. Current events—Photographs

Collections

Collector's item; excerpts from address, ed. by M. R. Weiss. il Sat R 54:36-7 Ag 7 '71
On and off the avenue; works of the masters. J. Malcolm. New Yorker 47:118+ My 1 '71

Exhibitions

See Photography—Exhibitions

PHOTOGRAPHS—*Continued*

Marketing

How to make your portfolio pay. A. Goldsmith. il Pop Phot 68:110-11 Je '71
Where's the action? J. Dreyfuss. Mod Phot 35:114+ Ap '71
Writer with a camera (cont) R. Arnold. por Writers Digest 51:16-18 Jl; 14+ S: 34-5+ N '71

Mounting

See Photographs—Trimming, mounting, etc.

Trimming, mounting, etc.

Home gallery of photographs without frames. il Sunset 146:118 Je '71
Make a dry-mount photo press. J. R. Eyton. il Pop Sci 198:112 Mr '71
Trout mount; photographic cutout. D. Shiner. il Design 72:12-13 mid-Sum '71
Wolfman on printing; keeping mounted prints down. A. Wolfman. il Mod Phot 35:56+ My '71

PHOTOGRAPHS, Composite. See Photomontage
PHOTOGRAPHS, Hanging of. See Pictures, Hanging of
PHOTOGRAPHS, Judging of. See Photography—Criticism, interpretation, etc.
PHOTOGRAPHS and prints division of the Library of Congress. See United States—Library of Congress—Prints and photographs division
PHOTOGRAPHS in books and periodicals. See Illustration of books and periodicals
PHOTOGRAPHS in education. See Pictures in education

PHOTOGRAPHY

Feininger. A. Feininger. See issues of Modern photography
Has success spoiled 35? with photographs. B. Schwalberg. Pop Phot 69:65-75+ S '71
Looking at both sides of a problem; art and technique. N. Rothschild. Pop Phot 68:12+ Ja '71
Now we can laugh at some classic goofs that were near-tragedies at the time. N. Rothschild. il Pop Phot 69:22+ O '71
35 look? What's that? with photographs. H. Birnbaum. Pop Phot 69:80-5+ S '71
Tool & techniques. C. W. Kennedy. See issues of Popular photography
Vagabond camera. F. Rohr. See issues of Travel
See also
Astronomical photography
Color photography
Creative photography
Electronics in photography
Lasers—Photographic use
Moving picture photography
Nature photography
Photomicrography
Radiography
Telephotography
Vietnamese war. 1957- —Photography

Anecdotes, facetiae, satire, etc.

Pro's secrets. A. Gescheidt. il Pop Phot 68:102-5+ F '71

Apparatus and supplies

And now, here's the windup! Photo expo in Chicago. il Mod Phot 35:64-5 Ag '71
Behind the scenes. See occasional issues of Modern photography
First look. See issues of Popular photography
Handy gadgets for 35. M. Frank. il Pop Phot 69:86-7 S '71
Have you a vested interest? photo vest. H. Keppler. il Mod Phot 35:116 Je '71
It's in the bag! H. Keppler. il Mod Phot 35:76-9 Jl '71
Little items that can make a big difference. C. W. Kennedy. il Pop Phot 69:42+ Ag '71
Once over lightly. il Mod Phot 35:130-1 Ja; 136 Mr; 32 Ap; 144 Je '71
Photokina 70. il Pop Phot 68:81-96 Ja '71
6 quick tips for photographers. il Pop Sci 198:122 Ap '71
Tele-converters: are they good or bad? N. Rothschild. il Pop Phot 68:82-5 Je '71
There's a tape for almost any task. A. Francekevich. il Pop Phot 68:18+ F '71
Tools & techniques. C. W. Kennedy. See issues of Popular photography
Try add-on optics for picture power. H. V. Fondiller. il Pop Phot 68:78-81+ Je '71
Umbrella is key to compact home studio; umbrella reflector. N. Goldberg. il Pop Phot 68:52+ My '71
Well, we found something! Photo expo in Chicago. il Mod Phot 35:46-9 Jl '71

What Westphalen is doing; Multifocal adapters. H. Keppler. il Mod Phot 35:76-7+ O '71
What's new? Look! il Mod Phot 35:63-78 Ja '71
Writer with a camera. R. Arnold. por Writers Digest 51:18-20 Ap '71; Discussion. 51:13-15 Jl '71
See also
Camera cases
Camera shutters
Camera tripods
Cameras
Exposure meters
Lenses, Photographic
Light filters
Moving picture photography—Apparatus and supplies
Photography—Electronic equipment
Photography—Enlargers and enlarging
Photography—Processing—Apparatus and supplies

Exhibitions

See Photography—Exhibitions

Storage

Wolfman on printing; storing paper. A. Wolfman. Mod Phot 35:88 S '71

Testing

Modern tests. See issues of Modern photography

Bibliography

Book review in brief. See issues of Popular photography
Books in review. See issues of Modern photography
Dry rot in photo books. il Mod Phot 35:100-1+ N '71
More photo books for less. V. D. Coke. il Mod Phot 35:176-9 D '71

Competitions

Bicentennial photography contest. Life 71:20D-21 Jl 9 '71
Capture the moment; winners in Kodak's annual international newspaper snapshot awards. il Parents Mag 46:126 O '71
Enter Home garden's color photo contest. il Home Gard 58:40-1 Ag '71
Home garden's winners of 1971 Color photo contest. Home Gard 58:59 D '71
Monthly contest. See issues of Modern photography
1971 Photo awards. Sr Schol 98:4-5 My 17 '71
Photo contests (cont) Pop Phot 68:76 Ja; 58 F '71
Pollution in all its incredible ugliness; winning photographs in the 1970 contest. Nat Wildlife 9:26-8 F '71
Seeing pictures; comments of Life photo contest judges. J. Scully. il Mod Phot 35:14+ Mr '71
We're looking for a picture that speaks to us; contest for amateurs only. R. Graves. il Life 70:3 Ap 2 '71
Winners of the Life 1971 contest. il Life 71:35-52+ Jl 9 '71
World travel photo contest. il Sat R 55:50-4 Ja 1 '72

Composition

See Composition (photography)

Copying

See also
University microfilms, inc.

Criticism, interpretation, etc.

Enigmatic image. R. Hattersley. il Pop Phot 68:116-19+ My '71
Opinionated group of experts. il Mod Phot 35:74-83 Je '71
Seeing pictures. J. Scully. See issues of Modern photography

Darkroom technique

See Photography—Processing

Darkrooms

See Photography—Studios and darkrooms

Developing and developers

1970 film developer roundup. A. Kramer. il Mod Phot 35:64-7+ F '71
View from Kramer; new way to get big sharp negatives. A. Kramer. il Mod Phot 35:20+ S '71

Drying (films and prints)

Print drying for cheapskates. D. W. Kennedy. il Pop Phot 68:26+ Ja '71

Educational use

See Photography in education

PHOTOGRAPHY—*Continued*

Electronic equipment

Auto flash is here! W. F. Wilson. il Pop Phot 68:82-5 My '71

Flashy change in Polaroid 400's. D. L. Miller. il Mod Phot 35:20+ My '71

Get out of the dark with modeling lights; electronic flash units with built-in modeling lights. N. Rothschild. il Pop Phot 68:86-7+ My '71

Low-light flash; Braun Hoodwinker. B. Schwalberg. il Pop Phot 69:92-3 Ag '71

Photo expo 71: flash. H. Birnbaum. il Pop Phot 69:85+ Ag '71

Phototronics. E. Farber. See issues of Modern photography

Rapid-flash; lightweight electronic flash unit. W. W. Schopp. il Electr World 85:68-9 Ap '71

They like impossible jobs; EG&G strobe systems. N. Carlisle. il Pop Mech 135:76-9+ F '71

3 fancy new flashguns. il Pop Mech 135:172-4+ My '71

21 auto-flash units compared. H. Keppler and D. L. Miller. il Mod Phot 35:86-7+ My '71

Wrap a ring light around your lens. B. Murphy. il Pop Mech 135:84-7+ F '71

Your photographic electronics and optics: keeping them in shape. N. Goldberg. il Pop Phot 68:70-1+ Mr '71

See also
Camera shutters—Control

Enlargers and enlarging

View from Kramer; Pavelle 402 color head for the Durst 138S enlarger. A. Kramer. il Mod Phot 36:36+ Ja '72

Exhibitions

Ansel Adams revisited: something old, something new; show at the Focus gallery, San Francisco. M. Mann. il Pop Phot 68:49+ My '71

At the Smithsonian, photography is treated with sophistication; Stephen Whealton's and Janine Niépce's shows. R. Bruns. il Pop Phot 68:52+ Ja '71

Cartier-Bresson's France. M. R. Weiss. il Sat R 54:46-8 F 13 '71

Double documentary; W. Evans and W. E. Smith retrospectives. M. R. Weiss. il Sat R 54:34-5 Mr 13 '71

Ed Scully on color; Interkamera '71 in Prague. E. Scully. Mod Phot 35:26+ S '71

Exhibit looks at process or pure trends in photography; Humboldt state college. M. Mann. il Pop Phot 69:48+ Ag '71

Gallery snooping. See issues of Modern photography

How the McLuhan generation speaks: Student view 1970 sponsored by Assn. for education in journalism. R. Bruns. il Pop Phot 68:-106-9 Ja '71

Invitation to have your photographs exhibited; Discovery galleries in New York. J. Deschin. il Pop Phot 69:18+ Jl '71

Look through a peephole and discover a landscape; show at the San Francisco museum of art. M. Mann. il Pop Phot 69:22+ S '71

Paul Strand: close-up on the long view. M. R. Weiss. il Sat R 54:20-1 D 18 '71

Photo education; Chicago Expo 71. E. Scully. Mod Phot 35:130-1 Ag '71

Photo expo 71; symposium. il Pop Phot 69:79-87+ Ag '71

Photography as media; exhibition at the Museum of contemporary crafts, N.Y. D. Hare. il Craft Horiz 31:14-17+ D '71

Photography has equal status in art competition; exhibit at the San Francisco art institute. M. Mann. il Pop Phot 69:106+ Jl '71

Photokina 70. il Pop Phot 68:81-96 Ja '71

Pre-surrealism photography: a trip into the subconscious; show at the Pasadena art museum. M. Mann. il Pop Phot 68:33+ Ap '71

Right moment; P. Strand retrospective. D. Davis. il Newsweek 78:106 D 6 '71

Seeing pictures; Photo Expo 71. J. Scully. il Mod Phot 35:16+ Ag '71

Seeing pictures: Photo media. J. Scully. Mod Phot 36:11+ Ja '72

Seeing pictures: Photokina. J. Scully. il Mod Phot 35:14+ Ja '71

Shooting it right; works of W. E. Smith at New York's Jewish museum. S. K. Oberbeck. il Newsweek 77:56 F 8 '71

Shows to see. See issues of Popular photography

Shows we've seen. See issues of Popular photography

Stephen Shore; exhibition at the Metropolitan museum of art. New Yorker 47:29-30 Mr 6 '71

Walker Evans retrospective; exhibition at the Museum of modern art. W. McQuade. il Life 70:12 Mr 5 '71

Exposure

Camera collector; actinometers and other ingenious devices. J. Schneider. il Mod Phot 36:14+ Ja '72

Can you follow the meter needle? H. Keppler and E. Scully. il Mod Phot 35:80-1 Jl '71

How to beat the numbers racket; film speed rating. E. Meyers. il Pop Phot 68:26+ Mr '71

Keppler on the SLR; automatic exposure. H. Keppler. Mod Phot 35:9+ My '71

Keppler on the SLR; Novoflex solution of the close-up exposure problem. H. Keppler. il Mod Phot 34:36-8 N '70

Lighting and exposure; symposium. il Pop Phot 68:81-101+ My '71

More than exposure. J. Scully. il Mod Phot 35:64-73 Jl '71

View from Kramer; bellows extension factors. A. Kramer. Mod Phot 35:28+ F '71

See also
Exposure meters

Films

Agfa contour film wins Interkamera medal. M. Edelson. il Pop Phot 69:60+ O '71

Color print film for daylight or blue flash. il Consumer Bul 55:13-14 Ja '72

Cost-cuttingest color film you can buy? it may be Anscochrome type 5470. N. Rothschild. il Pop Phot 68:100-1 Ja '71

Ed Scully on color; differences in color films. E. Scully. Mod Phot 35:46+ Mr '71

Ed Scully on color; offbeat bargain bulk films. E. Scully. Mod Phot 35:56 O '71

Ed Scully on color; total optical color. E. Scully. Mod Phot 35:42+ F '71

For better outdoor pictures. T. Trueblood. il Field & S 76:20+ Ag '71

Only in 35. N. Rothschild. il Pop Phot 69:76-9+ S '71

Roll film, sheet film round-up. N. Rothschild. il Pop Phot 68:68-71 Ap '71

Static marks on film: a mystery that still jolts the experts. N. Goldberg. il Pop Phot 68:84-5+ Ap '71

Variations on a b&w theme. N. Rothschild. il Pop Phot 69:86-9+ O '71

View from Kramer; three sheet films. A. Kramer. Mod Phot 35:56+ Mr '71

What film for lousy weather? H. Keppler. il Mod Phot 35:76-7 My '71

What's your film? J. Scully. il Mod Phot 35:68-73 Ap '71

Which film for your color slides? il Consumer Bul 54:14-16 My '71

X-rays can ruin your outing! screening of luggage. J. Samson. il Field & S 75:16 Ap '71

See also
Moving picture films

Storage

Hold what you've got! W. Hanson. il Pop Phot 69:83-5 O '71

Focusing

Coming: a camera that can focus itself! S. M. Gallager. il Pop Mech 135:82-3 Mr '71

Don't be felled by faulty focusing. C. W. Kennedy. il Pop Phot 68:32+ Je '71

Ed Scully on color; soft focus. E. Scully. il Mod Phot 35:16+ Je '71

How to make pictures appear sharp when they aren't. E. Meyers. il Pop Phot 69:40+ S '71

Minolta junks depth-of-field laws. H. Keppler. il Mod Phot 35:42 N '71

Polaroid's latest: a handy distance finder plus focused flash. il Pop Mech 136:42-3 S '71

Poor focus? Don't just blame the lens. N. Goldberg. il Pop Phot 68:28+ Ap '71

Pupillary problems; more about depth of field and depth of focus. B. Schwalberg. il Pop Phot 69:24+ S '71

Techniques tomorrow; automatic focusing. B. Sherman. Mod Phot 34:74+ D '70; 35:24+ F '71

Things you should know about depth of field & depth of focus. B. Schwalberg. il Pop Phot 69:26+ Ag '71

Think you get sharper pictures by stopping down, eh? Well, you don't! L. A. Mannheim. il Mod Phot 35:84-7+ N '71

PHOTOGRAPHY—Focusing—*Continued*

View from Kramer; view camera back and film holder alignment. A. Kramer. il Mod Phot 34:56+ N '70
See also
Diffusion technique (photography)
Lenses, Photographic
Moving picture photography—Focusing

Galleries and museums

Despite predictions of doom, this photo gallery survives; Focus gallery, San Francisco. M. Mann. il Pop Phot 68:30+ Ja '71
On and off the avenue: works of the masters. J. Malcolm. New Yorker 47:118+ My 1 '71
Photo education; George Eastman house. E. Scully. il Mod Phot 35:46+ O '71
Talk with Van Deren Coke, new man at the George Eastman house. J. Deschin. por Pop Phot 69:24+ Ag '71

Grain

Feininger; how to use film grain creatively. A. Feininger. Mod Phot 35:62+ Ja '71

History

Feininger; brief review of the past 50 years. A. Feininger. Mod Phot 35:48+ Je '71
History of photography from the camera obscura to the beginning of the modern era, by H. Gernsheim and A. Gernsheim. Review
Mod Phot 35:122 Ap '71

Landscapes

Landscapes: interpretation is in the eye of the beholder. C. Steinberg. il Pop Phot 69:96-101 O '71
Presenting Dean Brown. D. Brown. il Art in Am 59:82-5 Ja '71
Straight talk about scenics. J. Scully. il Mod Phot 35:64-71 Mr '71

Light

Available light: a modern primer. B. Pierce. il Pop Phot 99-101+ My '71
Camera flare: the real enemy? B. Bodenstein and H. Keppler. il Mod Phot 36:86-9 Ja '72
Feininger. A. Feininger. Mod Phot 35:34+ My '71
How to make the most out of available light. F Rohr. il Travel 135:74-6 Mr '71
Light and white on white. R. Hattersley. il Pop Phot 69:64-7 Ag '71
See also
Photography—Exposure

Lighting

Lighting and exposure; symposium. il Pop Phot 68:81-101+ My '71
Lighting problems and solutions; excerpts from Photographing your product. N. Nelson. il Ceram Mo 19:22-3 O '71
Shoot portraits with a single light. E. Hittig. il Pop Mech 135:130-1 Ap '71
Simple as 1,2,3; number of lights needed for portraits. E. Scully. il Mod Phot 35:76-7+ Ap '71
See also
Moving picture photography—Lighting

Marines

Look down and rediscover the ever-changing seascape. R. McCullough. il Pop Phot 68:92-5 Mr '71

Negatives

Scratching: a how-to-undo it guide. N. Goldberg. il Pop Phot 68:42+ Ja '71
Techniques tomorrow; Polaroid 20,000 speed negative material. B. Sherman. Mod Phot 35:36+ Jl '71

Periodicals

See also
Modern photography (periodical)

Philosophy

Family photography as a sacrament. R. Hattersley. il Pop Phot 68:106-9 Je '71

Portraits

August Sander: portraitist of a nation in transition. J. Scully and E. Scully. il Mod Phot 35:88-93 Ag '71
Camera eye of Thomas Eakins. il Life 71:54-9 Jl 23 '71
Ed Scully on color. E. Scully. Mod Phot 35:36+ N '71
Ed Scully on color; color portraits outdoors. E. Scully. Mod Phot 35:16+ My '71
Family photography as a sacrament. R. Hattersley. il Pop Phot 68:106-9 Je '71
Five portraits; excerpt from Faces of our time. Y. Karsh. il Sat R 54:13-15 Ag 28 '71

Gallery: Indian portraits by J. K. Dixon. Life 71:10-11 Jl 2 '71
Gallery: New York faces photographed by S. McCartney. Life 70:6-9 Je 4 '71
Gallery: painter and his self-portrait; photographed by Alfred Eisenstaedt. Life 70: 8-9 My 21 '71
Glamor by Gowland. P. Gowland. il Pop Phot 68:24 Ja '71
Ham on wry; humor by S. Klein. R. Hattersley. il Pop Phot 68:110-13 Ja '71
Picnics are great for people pix. F. Rohr. il Travel 136:24-6 Ag '71
Poets as people. M. R. Weiss. il Sat R 54: 52-3 My 15 '71
Schneider's sneaky setup. J. Schneider. il Mod Phot 35:84-5 Je '71
Shoot portraits with a single light. E. Hittig. il Pop Mech 135:130-1 Ap '71
Simple as 1,2,3; number of lights needed for portraits. E. Scully. il Mod Phot 35:76-7+ Ap '71
Studio at your doorstep; F. M. Gill. J. Scully. il Mod Phot 35:76-9 Mr '71
Three classic beauties, a photographic study by Richard Avedon. Vogue 158:64-9 Ag 1 '71
Tip for making really good family pictures: be prepared! E. Meyers. il Pop Phot 69: 38+ Ag '71
See also
Photography of women

Printing processes

Basic. color analysis. A. Kramer. il Mod Phot 35:74-5+ Ap '71
Bold color from b&w. H. Shaman. il Pop Phot 69:92-5 Jl '71
Ed Scully on color; Aeroprint's spray color process. Mod Phot 35:28+ Ag '71
Ed Scully on color; color printing at home. E. Scully. Mod Phot 36:48+ Ja '72
Filter your color negatives before you shoot. E. Meyers. il Pop Phot 69:30+ Jl '71
Great color print breakthrough? Aeroprint color process. E. Scully. il Mod Phot 36:90-1+ Ja '72
Greater than the sum of the parts. E. Meyers. il Pop Phot 68:34+ F '71
Simple way to analyze your color prints. A. Kramer. il Mod Phot 35:86-7+ Je '71
Special edition of platinum prints made available by N.Y. dealer. J. Deschin. il por Pop Phot 69:36+ O '71
Test matrix zeros in on true color. A. Francekevich. il Pop Phot 68:12+ My '71
Top pro prints them his way; J Loengard. J. Scully. il Mod Phot 35:68-77 F '71
What's new? Old techniques! J. Scully. il Mod Phot 35:78-85 My '71
Wolfman on printing. A. Wolfman. See issues of Modern photography
Wolfman on printing; bas-relief prints. il Mod Phot 35:56+ Ap '71

Processing

Color processing: anywhere, anytime. W. Hanson. il Pop Phot 69:90-1+ Jl '71
How you can salvage unsharp pictures. C. W. Kennedy. il Pop Phot 69:32+ Jl '71
Some more tips to make darkroom work easier. C. W. Kennedy. il Pop Phot 69:62+ O '71
See also
Photographic finishing, Commercial

Apparatus and supplies

Between the dark and the daylight; equipment for developing film without a darkroom. W. Hanson. il Pop Phot 68:86-8+ Je '71
Build an electronic darkroom temperature monitor. J. A. Gupton, jr. il Radio-Electr 42:40-2 F '71
Can a machine like this really replace tray processing? stabilization processors. E. Scully. il Mod Phot 34:82-3+ N '70
Color printing for any budget. A. Kramer. il Mod Phot 35:80-3+ Mr '71
Ed Scully on color; Agnekolor processor. E. Scully. il Mod Phot 34:66+ N '70
Ed Scully on color; darkroom equipment. E. Scully. Mod Phot 35:24+ D '71
New color processor handles up to 16x20's; Agnekolor. N. Rothschild. il Pop Phot 68:48+ Ja '71
Nuts and bolts of roll film processing. A. Kramer. il Mod Phot 34:96-7+ N '70
Photo expo 71: darkroom. E. Meyers. il Pop Phot 69:84+ Ag '71
Photo print dryer you can build for peanuts. J. A. Joyner. il Pop Mech 135:120-1 F '71
Processing film, no muss, no fuss: Merrick model 35-36 professor. D. Molner. il Schol Teach Jr/Sr High p28-9 Mr 8 '71

PHOTOGRAPHY—Processing—Apparatus and supplies—*Continued*
Solid-state darkroom timer. R. A. Walton. il Electr World 85:66-7 Je '71
Texture screens: back again. L. Drukker. il Pop Phot 68:86-7+ Ap '71
View from A. Kramer; Lowell softlight unit; print washers. A. Kramer. il Mod Phot 35:44+ Je '71
View from Kramer; Pavelle 400 colorhead. A. Kramer. il Mod Phot 34:46+ D '70
Wolfman on printing; Richard wash indicator and dust removal aids. A. Wolfman. il Mod Phot 35:30+ Je '71
Wolfman on printing; texture screens. A. Wolfman. il Mod Phot 34:66+ D '70; 35:18+ Ja '71
Wolfman on printing; texture screens. Amber fireball safelite. A. Wolfman. Mod Phot 35:22 Mr '71
See also
Exposure meters

Scientific use
Techniques tomorrow; Cornell aeronautical laboratories. B. Sherman. il Mod Phot 35:60+ Je '71
See also
Photomicrography

Social aspects
Polaroid: the ice breaker; how residents view their own community. J. Greenberg. il Mod Phot 35:82-3 Jl '71

Societies
Photo education; tutorial seminars and periodic conferences. Mod Phot 35:128-9 Jl '71
See also
Photographic society of America
Professional photographers of America, inc.

Still life
Lighting problems and solutions; excerpts from Photographing your product. N. Nelson. il Ceram Mo 19:22-3 O '71

Studios and darkrooms
Instant darkroom. R. M. Benrey. il Pop Sci 199:114 O '71
View from Kramer; electro static air scrubber for filtering darkroom air. A. Kramer. Mod Phot 35:18+ Ap '71

Study and teaching
Center of the eye; summer program; with student photographs. P. Caulfield. il Pop Phot 69:82-9+ Jl '71
Ghetto kids, a dedicated teacher find adventure with photography. J. Deschin. il por Pop Phot 69:28+ S '71
Hattersley class. R. Hattersley. See issues of Popular photography
Is Life the best teacher? excerpts from Life library of photography. il Mod Phot 35:58-75 S '71
$1 toy teaches photography; Ohio university course. E. Truxell. il Pop Phot 68:116-17 Ja '71
Photo education. E. Scully. See issues of Modern photography. October 1970-
Photo education; impressions of Aspen's Center of the eye. J. Scully. il Mod Phot 36:64+ Ja '72
Pinhole camera; photography in the elementary art program. T. Junger. il Sch Arts 71:14-15 D '71
Summer workshop '71. Mod Phot 35:116+ Jl '71
See also
Famous photographers school

Themes
Hand held! photographs by T. Yoshida. J. Greenberg. il Mod Phot 35:90-1 Je '71
On the right track: picture stories or sequences. R. Hattersley. Pop Phot 69:66-9 Jl '71
See also
Absurd, The

Japan
Japan has cameras galore, but where are the photographers? M. Mann. il Pop Phot 68:26+ F '71

PHOTOGRAPHY, Aerial
Corn blight watch experiment. il Space World H-9-93:46 S '71
How they'll spot corn blight from 11 miles up. B. Coffman. il Farm J 95:33 F '71
NASA to use U-2s. Aviation W 94:25 Ap 12 '71
NASA U-2s photograph earth in four spectrums. il Aviation W 95:22-3 N 1 '71

NASA using U-2s as ERTS simulators. il Aviation W 95:16 O 25 '71
There's money in the air. K. Chellis. il Pop Phot 68:80-1+ F '71
See also
Aerial reconnaissance
Mapping, Aerial

PHOTOGRAPHY, Artistic
Art and the photographic image. N. Rothschild. il Pop Phot 68:18+ Je '71
Come out from behind your viewfinder and see; with photographs by K. Biggs. M. Edelson. Pop Phot 68:97-9 Ja '71
Image variations; with photographs. E. Scully and J. Scully. Mod Phot 35:66-73 O '71
It's art, but is it photography? imagery of G. Obremski. C. Steinberg. il Pop Phot 68:76-9 Mr '71
Photography as media; exhibition at the Museum of contemporary crafts, N.Y. D. Hare. il Craft Horiz 31:14-17+ D '71
Yukio Shimizu: color as a strong but gentle medium; with photographs. R. Bruns. Pop Phot 69:74-8 Ag '71

PHOTOGRAPHY, Astronomical. See Astronomical photography

PHOTOGRAPHY, Close-up
Face to face with fanciful folk at the flea market. N. Rothschild. il Pop Phot 68:88-91 F '71
Getting close to Mother Nature. F. Rohr. Travel 135:74-6 Ap '71
Keppler on the SLR; Novoflex solution of the close-up exposure problem. H. Keppler. il Mod Phot 34:36-8 N '70
Pupillary problems: more date for close-up photography. B. Schwalberg. il Pop Phot 69:28+ O '71
What you've always wanted to know about close-ups. N. Rothschild. il Pop Phot 68:76-9+ F '71

PHOTOGRAPHY, Commercial
See also
Photography, Fashion
Photography, Journalistic
Photography as a profession

PHOTOGRAPHY, Composite. See Photomontage

PHOTOGRAPHY, Documentary
David Plowden: The hand of man on America; with photographs. R. Bruns. Pop Phot 68:98-103+ Je '71
Diary of a century, by J. H. Lartigue. Review
Mod Phot il 35:14+ Ap '71. J. Scully
Modern challenge: pictures that persuade and convince. M. Mann. il Pop Phot 68:52+ Mr '71
Seeing pictures. J. Scully. il Mod Phot 35:24+ My; 6+ Je '71

PHOTOGRAPHY, Electronic
Day the silver runs out... W. Hanson. il Pop Phot 68:61-3+ Mr '71

PHOTOGRAPHY, Fashion
On and off the avenue. K. Fraser. New Yorker 47:107-11 My 8 '71

PHOTOGRAPHY, Flashlight
Flash pictures: little tricks that make the big difference. S. M. Gallager and B. Murphy. il Pop Mech 136:114-18 D '71
Tele flash? You bet! It's simple. E. Scully. il Mod Phot 35:78-9 Ag '71

Apparatus and supplies
Simple rig for close-up flash. E. Borgeson. il Pop Mech 136:112 Ag '71

Electronic equipment
See Photography—Electronic equipment

PHOTOGRAPHY, Infrared
New light in electronic imagery; thermography. G. J. Berkwitt. il Duns 98:83-4+ N '71
Sharper eyes seek the world's resources. il Bsns W p54-5 N 27 '71
They can take your temperature with a camera. S. M. Gallager. il Pop Mech 136:88-9 Jl '71

PHOTOGRAPHY, Journalistic
Freelance market: TV news and features. B. Koenig. il Writers Digest 51:28-30 Je '71
Here's how the professionals do it. J. Deschin. il Pop Phot 68:20+ Ja '71
Is 35-mm less sharp? less dull! S. Nathan. il Pop Phot 68:40+ My '71
Need for images will increase in future, say parley members; Wilson Hicks international conference on communication arts. N. Rothschild. il Pop Phot 69:14+ S '71
New photojournalism market. R. Arnold. il Writers Digest 52:34-5 Ja '72
Rewards of photo-journalism; with market list. J. Tallon. Writer 84:25-8 Ap '71
Shooting your own pictures! E. R. Fenn. il Writers Digest 51:28-9+ F '71

PHOTOGRAPHY, Journalistic—*Continued*
There is more to pictures than meets the film. R. Graves. il Life 70:1 F 12 '71
W. Eugene Smith: let truth be the prejudice. R. Benedict. il por Pop Phot 68:88-93 Ap '71
Writer with a camera. R. Arnold **Writers** Digest 51:14-16 F; 16-18 Jl; 14+ S; 34-5+ N '71
PHOTOGRAPHY, Laser. See Lasers—Photographic use
PHOTOGRAPHY, Medical
See also
Brain—Photographs
PHOTOGRAPHY, Military
See also
Aerial reconnaissance
PHOTOGRAPHY, Nature. See Nature photography
PHOTOGRAPHY, Night
Shot in the dark. B. Murphy. il Pop Mech 136:108-11 Jl '71
PHOTOGRAPHY, Pinhole
Pinhole camera; photography in the elementary art program. T. Junger. il Sch Arts 71:14-15 D '71
PHOTOGRAPHY, Submarine
Filming in depth. R. Pinney. il Pop Phot 68:74-6 Ja '71
It's easy to take pictures underwater. F. Schulke. il Motor B & S 128:28-9+ Jl '71
Mzima, Kenya's spring of life. J. Root and A. Root. il pors Nat Geog 140:350-73 S '71

Apparatus and supplies
Underwater automatic. C. Conley. il Field & S 76:150 O '71
PHOTOGRAPHY, Time-lapse
From bud to blossom in seconds. R. Pinney. il Pop Phot 68:104-5 Ap '71
PHOTOGRAPHY, Travel. See Travel photography
PHOTOGRAPHY, Trick
Goof may prove to be the better idea; multiple exposures. S. Nathan. il Pop Phot 69: 70+ O '71
See also
Moving picture photography, Trick
PHOTOGRAPHY, Ultraviolet
Technique detects nitric oxide emissions. R. S. Kahn. il Aviation W 96:44-5 Ja 3 '72
PHOTOGRAPHY, Wide-angle
Wide-angle syndrome. H. Keppler. il Mod Phot 35:72-5 My '71
PHOTOGRAPHY and art. See Art and photography
PHOTOGRAPHY annuals. See Photographic literature
PHOTOGRAPHY as a profession
Photo education; career opportunities and pay. E. Scully. Mod Phot 35:112+ Ap '71
Seeing pictures; professional photographers who live where and how they want. J. Scully. Mod Phot 35:10+ S '71
PHOTOGRAPHY by children. See Children as photographers
PHOTOGRAPHY in criminal investigation, espionage, etc.
New super 8s catch thieves at work. V. Omelczenko. il Pop Sci 199:135 N '71
PHOTOGRAPHY in education
Using photography to amplify self-esteem in the primary grades. R. T. Tamashiro. Ed Digest 37:38-40 N '71
PHOTOGRAPHY models. See Models (persons)
PHOTOGRAPHY of animals
About face! M. Burnham. il Outdoor Life 147:90-3 Ap '71
For shutterbugs. T. Trueblood. il Field & S 76:26+ Jl '71
North country red. J. S. Crawford. il Outdoor Life 148:38-41+ Jl; 68-71+ Ag '71
Tips and tricks for your zoo pics. R. H. Rufa. il Travel 137:72+ Ja '72
See also
Animals—Photographs
Photography of reptiles
PHOTOGRAPHY of birds
Camera for the birds; excerpt from Portraits of tropical birds. J. S. Dunning. il Américas 23:14-17 O '71
For shutterbugs. T. Trueblood. il Field & S 76:26+ Jl '71
How we photograph birds. E. M. Woodford. il Horticulture 49:30-1 S '71
Photo safari by boat. F. M. Paulson. il Field & S 75:42-5+ Ja '71
There's a picture window in my muskrat house. F. A. Heidelbauer. il por Nat Wildlife 9:44-6 Ag '71
You can get killed shooting birds' eggs. H. H. Harrison. il Nat Wildlife 9:10-15 Ap '71

PHOTOGRAPHY of children
How to take better photographs of children. Good H 173:169 D '71
Keep a camera in your kitchen. M. Cobb. il Farm J 95:43 Ap '71
Photographing your baby: a mother's guide. S. Thaler. il Redbook 138:79+ D '71
See also
Children—Photographs
PHOTOGRAPHY of dancing
Barbara Morgan: one of America's great photographers reflects a decade of dance, 1935-1945. D. Hering. il por Dance Mag 45: 43-56 Jl '71
PHOTOGRAPHY of fishes
Shoot fish in a barrel; use of shallow aquarium. H. Grier. il Pop Phot 68:72-3+ Ap '71
PHOTOGRAPHY of flowers, plants, trees, etc.
In and out of this world; seed photography. il Design 73:18-21 Fall '71
Plotting prize winning garden photographs. D. Fell. il Home Gard 58:24-5 Ap '71
PHOTOGRAPHY of infants. See Photography of children
PHOTOGRAPHY of insects
Gallery: tropical moths. K. Sandved. Life 70: 8-9 Je 11 '71
PHOTOGRAPHY of light
Capture those Roman candles and batons. F. Rohr. il Travel 136:24-6 Jl '71
Lights, camera, action. D. Corry. il Mod Phot 35:82-3 F '71
PHOTOGRAPHY of mammals
Talk of a whale of an assignment! E. Meyers. il Pop Phot 68:42+ Je '71
PHOTOGRAPHY of moving objects
Add action. J. Scully. il Mod Phot 35:88-93 Ja '71
Capture those Roman candles and batons. F. Rohr. il Travel 136:24-6 Jl '71
Figure in motion. W. G. Larson. il Mod Phot 35:78-81 Ap '71
PHOTOGRAPHY of nature. See Nature photography
PHOTOGRAPHY of paintings. See Photography of works of art
PHOTOGRAPHY of reptiles
Snakes I met that day. H. Ellis. il Nat Wildlife 9:12-15 O '71
So you want to be a snake photographer... K. Severin. il pors Sci Digest 69:55-7 My '71
PHOTOGRAPHY of sports
Good water sport photos are a breeze. F. Rohr. il Travel 135:74-6 Je '71
See also
Baseball—Photographs
Football—Photographs
Sports—Photographs
PHOTOGRAPHY of the human figure. See Human figure in photography
PHOTOGRAPHY of weddings
How to get wedding pictures you'll love, honor & cherish. A. E. Woolley. il Today's Health 49:38-43 Je '71
I carried my camera to a wedding and shot between soup & dessert. E. Meyers. il Pop Phot 69:46+ O '71
PHOTOGRAPHY of women
Ikko: tradition meets a modern eye. R. Bruns. il Pop Phot 68:80-5 Ap '71
PHOTOGRAPHY of works of art
How Geoffrey Clements photographs fine art; interview, ed. by S. E. Meyer. G. Clements. il Am Artist 35:24-6 My '71
How to photograph your art. H. Keppler. il Am Artist 35:20-3+ My '71
PHOTOGRAPHY schools. See Photography—Study and teaching
PHOTOJOURNALISM. See Photography, Journalistic
PHOTOKINA. See Photography—Exhibitions
PHOTOLYSIS (chemistry) See Photochemistry
PHOTOMECHANICAL processes
Workshop: photofabrication. E. Moty. bibliog f il Craft Horiz 31:12-17 Je '71
PHOTOMETERS
See also
Transmissometers
PHOTOMETRY
See also
Spectrophotometry
PHOTOMETRY, Astronomical
Magnetoglow: a new geophysical resource. C. Y. Johnson and others. bibliog il Science 171:379-81 Ja 29 '71
See also
Stars—Scintillation
PHOTOMICROGRAPHY
Wilson Bentley, the snowflake man. D. C. Blanchard. bibliog il pors Weatherwise 23:260-9 D '70

PHOTOMONTAGE
Coming and going, now you see David, now his sister. il Sunset 147:154 N '71

PHOTOMULTIPLIER tubes. See Photoelectric multipliers

PHOTONS
Particles without mass: the enigma of the photon. D. E. Thomsen. il Sci N 100:46-7 Jl 17 '71
Photons as hadrons. F. V. Murphy and D. E. Yount. il Sci Am 225:94-104 bibliog (p 122) Jl '71
Simple technique produces photon echoes and optical nutation. G. B. Lubkin. Phys Today 24:17+ D '71

PHOTOOXIDATION. See Oxidation

PHOTOPERIODISM
Ethanol preference in the rat as a function of photoperiod. I. Geller. bibliog il Science 173:456-9 Jl 30 '71
Photoperiod evidence in the introduction of xanthium (cocklebur) to Australia. C. McMillan. bibliog il Science 171:1029-31 Mr 12 '71
Photoperiodically significant photoreception in sparrows: is the retina involved? H. Underwood and M. Menaker; discussion. Science 169:892-3; 172:293 Ag 28 '70, Ap 16 '71
Rhythm of the flowers. J. D. Palmer. il Natur Hist 80:64-73 Ag '71
Temporal synergism of corticosterone and prolactin controlling gonadal growth in sparrows. A. H. Meier and others. bibliog il Science 173:1240-2 S 24 '71

PHOTORECEPTORS. See Receptors, Neural

PHOTOSYNTHESIS
Control of photosynthetic carbon metabolism. J. A. Bassham. bibliog il Science 172:526-34 My 7 '71
Editorial. C. B. Lees. Horticulture 49:16 Jl '71
Flow of energy in the biosphere. D. M. Gates. il Sci Am 225:88-92+ bibliog(p244) S '71
History and stability of atmospheric oxygen. L. Van Valen. bibliog il Science 171:439-43 F 5 '71; Reply with rejoinder. B. Gregor. 174:316-17 O 15 '71
Let the sun shine in. R. J. Trotter. il Sci N 99:372-4 My 29 '71
Photosynthesis and photorespiration; report of meeting. R. O. Slatyer and N. E. Tolbert. Science 173:1162+ S 17 '71
Recycling: an old idea with new significance. R. Andrus and S. P. Mathur. il Cons 25:28-31 Je '71

PHOTOSYNTHETIC bacteria. See Bacteria, Photosynthetic

PHOTOTYPESETTING
Electronic typesetting. D. L. Heiserman. il Electr World 86:35-7+ Ag '71
Fairchild expands Electro set machine lines. il Pub W 200:41-2 Jl 5 '71

PHREATOPHYTES
See also
Streamside vegetation

PHTHALATE plasticizers. See Plasticizers

PHYFE, Duncan
Antiques. A. Winchester. il Antiques 99:96-7 Ja '71 *

PHYSALIA. See Portuguese man-of-war

PHYSARUM. See Slime molds

PHYSICAL education and training
See also
Exercise

PHYSICAL education and training of women
See also
Women as athletes

PHYSICAL examinations
How to help your doctor help you. D. Schultz. Ladies Home J 88:36+ Ag '71
Is an annual physical examination necessary for good health? Good H 173:185-7 O '71
Vital hour: your physical exam. V. Cohn. Ladies Home J 88:74 Ap '71

PHYSICAL exercise. See Exercise

PHYSICAL fitness
See also
Exercise
Health

PHYSICAL geography
See also
Climate
Islands
Lakes
Ocean

PHYSICAL metallurgy
Solid-state physicists and metallurgy; adaptation of address, March 1970. R. W. Schmitt. bibliog il Phys Today 24:44-8 Ja '71

PHYSICAL review
Sociology of refereeing. H. Zuckerman and R. K. Merton. bibliog il Phys Today 24:28-33 Jl '71

PHYSICAL theory. See Physics—Philosophy

PHYSICAL therapy
See also
Recreational therapy

PHYSICALLY handicapped. See Handicapped

PHYSICALLY handicapped teachers. See Teachers

PHYSICIANS
Doctor who practices what he preaches; work in a roadhouse clinic. S. Streshinsky. il por Redbook 138:78+ N '71
Interactional problems between mental health professionals and non-psychiatric physicians. M. R. Green and others. bibliog Ment Hy 55:206-13 Ap '71
Physician, what ails thee? study findings of G. E. Vaillant. Newsweek 78:84 O 18 '71
Prescribed environment; excerpt from Medicines for man. H. F. Dowling. Sat R 54:58-60 Ap 3 '71
$ profile of U.S. physicians. Sci Digest 70:60 D '71
They take vacations for humanity. C. W. Hall. il Read Digest 98:45-6+ Ap '71
See also
Chiropractors
Malpractice
Medical education
Medical service
Medicine—Practice
Surgeons
Women as physicians

Anecdotes, facetiae, satire, etc.
Patient. G. Ace. Sat R 54:8 S 25 '71

Fees
See Medical service, Cost of

Names
Anecdotes, facetiae, satire, etc.
Is Dr Doctor in? R. Armour. Read Digest 99:114-15 Jl '71

Recruiting
Doctor shortage, what's being done; armed forces medical school. il U S News 71:67 N 22 '71

Supply and demand
Doctor deficit. il Time 98:59 S 20 '71
Doctor for Vinton County; plight of a country doctor. il Time 98:82 N 1 '71
Doctor shortage, what's being done; armed forces medical school. il U S News 71:67 N 22 '71
Doctors for the poor. Commonweal 93:484 F 19 '71
Peace, health, and the doctor. J. Lear. Sat R 54:33-5+ Ap 17 '71
Where have our doctors gone? J. Star. il Look 35:15-17 Je 29 '71

PHYSICIANS and patients
How to work with your doctor. Bet Hom & Gard 49:32 D '71
I never dreamed medicine would be like this! first day in the emergency room. il pors Todays Health 49:40-5 O '71
More from your doctor. W. J. Papp. il Har Yrs 11:36-9 Je '71
Profiles: E. L. Schmidt, the only doctor in Jal, N.Mex. B. Roueché. por New Yorker 47:30-40 Ja 1 '72
Three who cared; with photographs by W. E. Smith. B. Roueché. Todays Health 49:52-7 S '71
When you and your doctor disagree; medical grievance committees. Bet Hom & Gard 49:128 Ap '71
Why we must see our doctors in a new light. W. Nolen. il Todays Health 49:70-1 D '71

PHYSICIANS as air pilots
Digging for the truth. R. B. Parke. Flying 89:40 Jl '71

PHYSICIANS assistants. See Medical workers

PHYSICISTS
See also
American physical society
Einstein, A.
Fermi, E.
Gamow, G.
Rutherford, E. R.
Women as scientists

PHYSICISTS—*Continued*
Supply and demand
Job shortage hit older physicists hardest. G.
B. Lubkin. il Phys Today 24:61-3 My '71
Job situation, more views; letters. il Phys
Today 24:9+ Je '71
On physics and employment of physicists in
1970. H. W. Koch. bibliog il Phys Today
24:23-7 Je '71
PHYSICISTS, Professional ethics for. See Scientists, Professional ethics for

PHYSICS
Chemists, please note; on the future of physics. Chem 44:4-5 Ja '71
Frontiers of physics today (cont) il Phys
Today 24:31-6+ Ja; 19-26 Jl '71
Future of physics; adaptation of address,
March 1970. F. J. Dyson; reply. R. M.
Pearlstein. Phys Today 24:15+ Ja '71
Physics and social change; adaptation of address, June 1971. G. E. Brown, jr. il pors
Phys Today 24:23-7 O '71
See also
American institute of physics
American physical society
Astrophysics
Atomic theory
Biological physics
Entropy
Field theory (physics)
Force and energy
Gravitation
Light
Magnetism
Nuclear physics
Physical metallurgy
Quantum theory
Relativity (physics)
Units
Bibliography
Books. See issues of Physics today
History
Jean Perrin: a pioneer of modern physics. P.
Auger. UNESCO Courier 23:45 D '70
Measurement of the man-day. E. S. Ferguson.
il Sci Am 225:96-103 O '71
See also
Electricity—History

Information services
See Science—Information services
Philosophy
Paul Ehrenfest, by M. Klein. Review
New Yorker 46:95-8 F 6 '71. J. Bernstein
Research
Lasers; applications in physics research. J. A.
Armstrong. bibliog il Phys Today 24:34-9
Mr '71
Physicist's research notes as historical documents. J. N. Warnow. Phys Today 24:9
O '71
Search & discovery. See issues of Physics
today
What next for programs dropped by AEC?
G. B. Lubkin. il Phys Today 24:57+ Jl '71
See also
Cambridge. University—Cavendish laboratory

Study and teaching
Teaching and the environmental challenge;
excerpts from address, June 1971. R. H.
Socolow. bibliog il Phys Today 24:32-4+ D
'71
Teaching physics in the corridors. H. L.
Davis. Phys Today 24:88 My '71
See also
Colleges and universities—Departments of
physics
International centre for theoretical physics,
Trieste, Italy

China (People's Republic)
C. N. Yang discusses physics in People's
Republic of China. G. B. Lubkin. por Phys
Today 24:61-3 N '71

Great Britain
Nuclear physics: does competition breed a
monstrous game? N. Wade. Science 174:932
N 26 '71
Japan
Physics in Japan: budgets still meager despite economic boom. H. L. Davis. il Phys
Today 24:69-71 Ag '71
PHYSICS and state. See Science and state
PHYSICS teachers
See also
American association of physics teachers

PHYSIOGNOMY
Does your face give you away? il Mlle 73:
194-6 My '71
PHYSIOLOGICAL apparatus
In vitro techniques for avoiding edge damage
in studies of frog skin. S. I. Helman and
D. A. Miller. bibliog il Science 173:146-8 Jl
9 '71
See also
Spirometers
PHYSIOLOGICAL effects of noise. See Noise
—Physiological effects
PHYSIOLOGICAL optics. See Optics, Physiological
PHYSIOLOGICAL psychology. See Psychology,
Physiological
PHYSIOLOGY
See also
Anatomy
Corpulence
Old age
Psychology, Physiological
Reproduction
Respiration
Starvation
Stress (physiology)
Weight (physiology)
also names of organs of the body, e.g.
Stomach
PIAGET, Jean
Early childhood education: a Piagetian perspective. D. Elkind. Ed Digest 37:28-31 D
'71 *
Measuring young minds. D. Elkind. por Horizon 13:32-7 Wint '71 *
Piaget undermined? pors Newsweek 78:61-2
S 13 '71 *
PIANISTS
See also
Bar-Illan, D.
Blake, E.
Ellington, D.
Watts, A.
Williams, M. L.
PIANKO, Irving. See Flinker, I. jt. auth.
PIANO
See also
Piano music
PIANO music
Beethoven and the London pianoforte
school. A. L. Ringer. bibliog f il Mus Q
56:742-58 O '70
Musical events; Alice Tully Hall sampler. W.
Sargeant. New Yorker 47:84 Je 19 '71
See also
Concertos
Phonograph records—Piano music
PIASECKI, Frank Nicholas
Where are they now? il por Newsweek 77:16
Mr 15 '71 *
PICA (pathology)
Lead poisoning. J. J. Chisolm, jr. il Sci Am
224:15-23 bibliog(p 130) F '71
PICARD, Gilbert Charles-. See Charles-Picard,
G.
PICASSO, Pablo
Anatomy of a minotaur. R. Hughes. il pors
Time 98:68-78 N 1 '71 *
Art; exhibition, homage to Picasso for his
90th birthday. Nation 213:285-6 S 27 '71 *
Master at 90, Picasso's great age seems only
to stir up the demons within. Brassaï. il
pors N Y Times Mag p30-1+ O 24 '71 *
Pablo Picasso at 90. D. Davis. il pors Newsweek 78:102-7 O 25 '71 *
Picasso and Braque, their cubist years. R.
Phelps. Vogue 157:125+ Ap 1 '71 *
Picasso at 90. il Art N 70:29+ O '71 *
Picasso at 90. H. Miller. il pors Life 71:52-4
O 29 '71 *
Picasso's iconoclasm. G. Vahanian. il Chr
Cent 88:1523-5 D 29 '71 *
Skulls of Picasso. L. Steinberg. bibliog il
por Art N 70:26-8+ O '71 *
PICCARD, Jacques
Dying oceans, poisoned seas; views presented
at United Nations symposium on the environment. Time 98:74+ N 8 '71
PICKERELL, James H.
It's not cloud 9, it's superbed! il Pop Mech
135:80-1 My '71
New garage where you pocket the labor costs.
il Pop Mech 135:88-9 Je '71
PICKET boats. See Boats and boating
PICKFORD, Mary
Doug Fairbanks: superstar of the silents. R.
Schickel. il pors Am Heritage 23:4-12+
D '71 *
PICKLES and relishes
Bazaar foods. il Bet Hom & Gard 49:74-5+
S '71
Little pears, rich and buttery. il Sunset 147:
151 D '71

PICKLES and relishes—*Continued*
September is the month to make relishes. il Sunset 147:132 S '71
Tart and tangy relishes. E. W. Manning. il Farm J 95:35-6 S '71
Vegetables in a pickled mix. il Sunset 147:200 O '71

PICKUP, Phonograph. See Phonograph—Pickup

PICKUP campers. See Campers and coaches, Truck

PICKUP trucks. See Motor trucks

PICNIC cookery. See Cookery, Outdoor

PICNIC tables. See Tables

PICNICS
Great getaways; with recipes. il Seventeen 30:138-41+ O '71
November is the month for spur-of-the-moment picnics. il Sunset 147:102-3 N '71
Party picnic: everyone brings something. il House & Gard 140:32-3 Jl '71
Party swim; with recipes. il Seventeen 29: 104-11+ Jl '70
Picnics are great for people pix. F. Rohr. il Travel 136:24-6 Ag '71
Picnics long ago; with paintings by artists of the Hudson River school. Am Heritage 22:42-7 Je '71
What's good about family reunions? Fabulous food! with recipes. E. W. Manning. il Farm J 95:42-3+ Je '71

PICÓ, Fernando
Time to go home. America 126:20-1 Ja 8 '72

PICO, Juan Vega
Exploring Spanish caves for cave-man art; tr. by K. Young. il Sci Digest 70:6-11 Jl '71

PICTON, Terence W. and others
Human auditory attention: a central or peripheral process? bibliog il Science 173: 351-3 Jl 23 '71

PICTORIAL embroidery. See Embroidery

PICTORIAL humor. See Humor, Pictorial

PICTURE books
New gift and art books; with portfolio. A. H. Johnston. Pub W 200:43-62 Ag 23 '71
Splurge of photo books. A. Caruba. il Pub W 199:24-34 My 3 '71
See also
Illustrated books

PICTURE books for children
Overdue; the golden age of the picture book. S. Wilbricht. por Wilson Lib Bul 46:186-7 O '71
Within the margins of a picture book. U. Shulevitz. il Horn Bk 47:309-12 Je '71
See also
Caldecott medal

PICTURE cards. See Advertising cards

PICTURE clocks. See Clocks

PICTURE collections
See also
Libraries—Picture collections

PICTURE frames
Classic picture frame. il Pop Sci 199:84 D '71
Plastic frames for your pictures. P. Stoddart. il Design 73:11 Fall '71

PICTURE post cards. See Post cards

PICTURE posters. See Posters

PICTURE signs. See Signs and signboards

PICTURE tubes, Color. See Television receivers, Color—Picture tubes

PICTURE writing, Maya. See Mayas—Writing

PICTUREPHONE. See Telephone—Television combination

PICTURES
Painting with beads; works of M. Galleher. R. Wrenn. il por Design 72:8-11 Sum '71
Painting with fingerprints; G. Jenkins. N. Hawkins. il por Design 72:20-1 Sum '71
Painting with pebbles. il Design 72:12-13 mid-Wint '71
Painting with petals. M. B. Hall. il Design 72:36 Spr '71
Shell painting. L. J. Miller il Design 72:40 Spr '71
See also
Illustration of books and periodicals
Libraries—Picture collections
Paintings
Still life painting
Framing
See Picture frames
Prices
See Art—Prices

PICTURES, Framing of. See Picture frames

PICTURES, Hanging of
Blow-ups; very large photographic prints on walls, on doors, on cabinets. il Sunset 146:100-1 Ap '71
Decorating with pictures. M. Kraft. il Good H 172:152 F '71
How to enjoy your family photographs. W. Baldwin. House & Gard 139:10+ Ap '71
How to really hang a picture. J. E. Kollas. il Design 72:40-1 mid-Wint '71

PICTURES, Immoral. See Immoral literature and pictures

PICTURES, Photography of. See Photography of works of art

PICTURES in education
Family of man in an English class. P. F. Skinner. Engl J 60:220-2 F '71
See also
Moving pictures in education

PICTURES in the hallway (dramatic reading)
See Dramatic readings

PIDGIN English
At peace with pidgin; special language of Hawaiian children. M. Altiery. il Am Ed 7:32-6 O '71

PIE
ABC's of chiffon pie. il Am Home 74:116 Ap '71
Bake a pie to beat the heat; frozen lime pie. R. A. Sokolov. il N Y Times Mag p24 Jl 11 '71
Fruit tarts & pies. H. McCully. il House B 113:86-7+ Je '71
How to make perfect piecrust. S. Whittier. il Good H 172:134 My '71
Party full of pies. il Ladies Home J 88:100-1+ O '71
Perfect apple pie. il McCalls 98:100+ S '71
Pick a fresh fruit pie; with recipes. il Good H 173:107-9+ Jl '71
Pies to please everyone in your family. R. Molter. il Parents Mag 46:80-3+ F '71
Three spectacular holiday pies. il Sunset 147:165 N '71
Under the lattice, sweet and tart; strawberry-rhubarb pie. il Sunset 146:218 My '71

PIECRUST mixes. See Food mixes

PIEDRACELISTAS. See Poets, Colombian

PIER glass. See Mirrors

PIER 1 imports, inc.
Pier 1: a retailer for cottage industries. il Bsns W p58-9 O 2 '71

PIERCE, Bill
Available light: a modern primer. il Pop Phot 68:99-101+ My '71
How to control diffusion. il Pop Phot 68: 120-1+ Ja '71

PIERCE, Charles
Charles Pierce: female impersonator as culture hero(ine) J. Stewart. il pors Ramp Mag 10:60-3 O '71 *

PIERCE, Edith Lovejoy
Fable; poem. Chr Cent 88:969 Ag 18 '71
Father of the prodigal; poem. Chr Cent 88: 460 Ap 14 '71
Park bench; poem. Chr Cent 88:1470 D 15 '71

PIERCE, Edward
Exploding supertankers. Time 97:43 Ja 25 '71 *

PIERCE, John Robinson
Time to take stock. Science 172:115 Ap 9 '71

PIERCE, Ruth
Opinion: on when a single girl becomes pregnant. Mlle 72:36+ Mr '71

PIERCE, S. S, company
Proxy fight shakes S.S. Pierce's teapot. Bsns W p26 Je 26 '71

PIERCE, Walter. See Getz, H. G. jt. auth.

PIERCE, Wilbur W.
Black capitalism: a study of struggle. il por Bsns W p96-8+ Ja 16 '71 *

PIERCY, Marge
Comment. S. Dobyns. Poetry 117:395 Mr '71 *

PIERONEK, Mitch
How to make a major addition to your home. il Mech Illus 67:103-7 Ap '71

PIERRE, Andrew J.
Nuclear diplomacy: Britain, France and America. For Affairs 49:283-301 Ja '71

PIERS, Bridge. See Bridges—Foundations and piers

PIERSON, George, and Hampf, F. E.
Salvaging New York harbor debris. il Cons 26:2-3 Ag '71

PIERSON, Jean
Now-and-forever diet. Vogue 157:98-9 F 15 '71

PIES. See Pie

PIES, Meat. See Cookery—Meat

PIFER, Alan
Call for higher education reform; excerpts from address, June 1971. por Sch & Soc 99:327-8 O '71
Jeopardy of private institutions. Ed Digest 36:34-7 My '71
Situation has worsened for women in colleges; excerpts from address, November 29, 1971. por U S News 71:82 D 13 '71

PIGANIOL, Pierre
Pondering the imponderable. il UNESCO Courier 24:28-32 Ap '71

PIGEON population
Control
See Bird populations—Control

PIGEON post
French pigeon post. H. Herst, jr. Hobbies 76:131+ Mr '71

PIGEON shooting
How to bag bandtails. W. Curtis. il Field & S 76:54-5+ S '71

PIGEONS
Classical conditioning of a complex skeletal response. E. Gamzu and D. R. Williams. bibliog il Science 171:923-5 Mr 5 '71; Reply with rejoinder. B. F. Skinner. 173:752-3 Ag 20 '71
Maternally derived transferrin in pigeon squabs. J. A. Frelinger. bibliog il Science 171:1260-1 Mr 26 '71
Melatonin: effect on punished and nonpunished operant behavior of the pigeon. R. I. Schoenfeld. bibliog il Science 171:1258-60 Mr 26 '71
See also
Passenger pigeons

PIGGY banks. See Banks, Coin

PIGMENTATION (biology) See Color of man

PIGMENTS
See also
Carbon black

PIGMENTS (biology)
See also
Carotenoids
Cytochromes
Hemes
Melanin
Melanophores

PIGNATELLI, Luciana, princess. See Avedon, L.

PIGS. See Swine

PIGS in literature. See Animals in literature

PIGWEED. See Purslane

PIKE, Albert V.
Lupins. il Horticulture 49:39+ My '71
Propagation by leaf cuttings. il Horticulture 49:36-7+ D '71

PIKE, John E.
Prostaglandins; with biographical sketch. il Sci Am 225:12, 84-92 bibliog(p 136+) N '71

PIKE
Too easy to catch. P. Bauer. il Nat Wildlife 9:10-11 Je '71

PIKE fishing
Art of pike fishing. A. J. McClane. il Field & S 75:104-5+ Ap '71
Bad winds and big pike of Kesagami. D. Richey. il Outdoor Life 147:56-9+ Je '71
How to lure lazy pike. J. R. Sundra. il Field & S 75:80-1+ Mr '71
Jumping jacks. E. A. Bauer. il Outdoor Life 147:82-5+ Ap '71
Landlocked monsters of Ireland. D. Knight. il Field & S 75:78-9+ F '71
Tourists, take your tackle. M. H. Garrell. il por Outdoor Life 147:78-9+ My '71

PIKE PLACE market. See Seattle—Markets

PILBEAM, David. See Simons, E. L. jt. auth.

PILCHER, J. R. and others
Land clearance in the Irish neolithic: new evidence and interpretation. bibliog il Science 172:560-2 My 7 '71

PILEGGI, Nicholas
From D.A. to dope lawyer. il pors N Y Times Mag p34-5+ My 16 '71
Making of The godfather: sort of a home movie. il N Y Times Mag p7+ Ag 15 '71

PILFERING. See Stealing

PILGRIM rebel; drama. See Hall, M.

PILGRIMAGES to Mecca
Israel's pilgrims to Mecca. America 125:498 D 11 '71
On the holy road to Mecca. E. Hughes. il Read Digest 99:27-8+ O '71

PILKINGTON, Betty
Mainland China at the UN door. Commonweal 94:420-1 Ag 20 '71
Whatever became of quiet diplomacy? Commonweal 94:53-4 Mr 26 '71

PILL (birth control) See Contraceptives

PILLA, Richard L.
Converge. Parks & Rec 6:29+ O '71

PILLAGE
Submarine thieves; objects looted from ancient shipwrecks. Sci Am 224:53 Ap '71

PILLET, Roger A.
Foreign languages: how pertinent? Ed Digest 37:54-6 O '71

PILLOW cases
Sheets & pillowcases: where to find the best buys. il Changing T 26:46 Ja '72

PILOCARPINE
Cholinergic sensitivity: normal variability as a function of stimulus background. L. Z Bito and others. bibliog il Science 172:583-5 My 7 '71

PILOT guides
Captain Spry's boat; picket boats used in tunnel construction. New Yorker 47:29-30 My 15 '71

PILOT training. See Air pilots—Training

PILPEL, Harriet F. and Norwick, K. P.
But can you do that? See issues of Publishers' weekly to March 29, 1971
—and Schwartz, A. U.
You can do that. Pub W 200:37 Ag 2 '71; 201:30-2 Ja 3 '72

PILSON, Michael E. Q. See Fanning, K. A. jt. auth.

PIMEN, patriarch
New patriarch in Moscow. America 124:642 Je 26 '71 *
New Russian patriarch: acceptable to both church and state. M. Bourdeaux. Chr Cent 88:932-3 Ag 4 '71 *
Pimen named patriarch of Russian church. Chr Cent 88:770 Je 23 '71 *
Russia's new patriarch. por Newsweek 77:114 Je 14 '71 *
Taking a troubled throne. il por Time 97:59 Je 14 '71 *

PIMLOTT, Douglas H.
Way of life of the timber wolf. il Liv Wildn 34:20-8 Aut '70

PIÑATAS
Blindfolded batsman and Mexico's piñata. il Sunset 147:74-5 D '71
Santa piñata party; excerpts from Piñatas; ed. by K. Surin. V. Brock. il Good H 173:178+ D '71

PINCAY, Laffit
He has them over a barrel. W. Tower. por Sports Illus 35:76+ D 6 '71 *

PINCHOT, Gifford
Conservation, for whom? J. A. Zivnuska. il por Am For 77:8-9+ Jl '71 *
Mike Frome; excerpts from The forest service. M. Frome. Am For 77:5+ Je '71 *

PINCOCK, Richard E. and others
Probability distribution of enantiomorphous forms in spontaneous generation of optically active substances. bibliog il Science 174:1018-20 D 3 '71

PINCUS, Walter
Campaign funding. New Repub 165:17-19 D 11 '71
Honesty in politics. New Repub 165:9-10+ D 4 '71

PINE
Beautiful, not big, and it takes it easy; mugho pine. il Sunset 147:169 S '71
Genetic improvement of southern pines. B. J. Zobel. il Sci Am 225:94-103 bibliog(p138) N '71
Pines of Ravenna. N. T. Mirov. il Natur Hist 80:24-6 Ja '71
See also
Tall oil

PINE BARRENS
Planning in the Pine Barrens. P. M. Tilden. il Nat Parks & Con Mag 45:22-6 Ag '71

PINE BLUFF laboratory. See Laboratories, Government

PINEAL body
Pineal function in sparrows: circadian rhythms and body temperature. S. Binkley and others. bibliog il Science 174:311-14 O 15 '71

PINEAPPLE family. See Bromeliads

PINEAPPLES
See also
Cookery—Fruit

PINES, Maya
Child's mind is shaped before age 2. il Life 71:63+ D 17 '71
Hidden threats to your child's learning ability. Read Digest 98:29-30+ F '71

PING pong. See Table tennis

PING pong tables. See Tables

PINGOS. Submarine. See Ocean bottom

PINGUSSON, Georges Henri
Pingusson's legacy. N. Pressman. il Arch Forum 134:52-5 Je '71 *

PINHOLE photography. See Photography, Pinhole

PINK Floyd (rock group) See Rock groups

PINK roses; story. See Stephens, R.

PINKHAM, Lydia (Estes)
Sweet extract of hokum. G. Carson. il pors Am Heritage 22:21-7+ Je '71 *

PINKVILLE; drama. See Tabori, G.

PINNACLES NATIONAL MONUMENT
Spring's the best time to dip into the rugged Pinnacles. il Sunset 146:46-8+ Ap '71

PINNER, Frank A.
Students a marginal elite in politics. bibliog f Ann Am Acad 395:127-38 My '71

PINNEY, Roy
Dream super 8 outfit. il por Pop Phot 68:114+ F '71
Filming in depth. il Pop Phot 68:74-6 Ja '71
From bud to blossom in seconds. il Pop Phot 68:104-5 Ap '71
Make a movie from your family album. il Pop Phot 68:112-13 Je '71

PINNOCK, Clark H. and Osborne, G. R.
Truce proposal for the tongues controversy. Chr Today 16:6-9 O 8 '71

PINOCYTOSIS
Pinocytosis and membrane dilation in uranyl-treated plant roots. H. Wheeler and P. Hanchey. bibliog il Science 171:68-71 Ja 8 '71

PINS
Diaper-pin derby, clip division. il Consumer Rep 37:6 Ja '72
Two winners in the diaper-pin derby. il Consumer Rep 36:269-70 My '71

PINSKY, Robert
Catatonic; View from the road; Destruction of Long Branch, N.J; Classic moment; poems. Poetry 118:316-20 S '71

PINSON, Penelope
(comp) Books for parents. See issues of Parents' magazine & better family living

PINTER, Harold
All of that; poem. Vogue 158:98 Jl '71
Conversation (pause) with Harold Pinter; interview, ed. by M. Gussow. il por N Y Times Mag p42-3+ D 5 '71

about

Birthday party. Criticism
New Yorker 46:78 F 13 '71 *
Time 97:52 F 22 '71 *
Homecoming. Criticism
America 125:70-1 Ag 7 '71
Nation 212:732-3 Je 7 '71 *
New Yorker 47:55 My 29 '71
Newsweek il 77:42 My 31 '71 *
Old times. Criticism
America 125:485 D 4 '71 *
Commonweal 95:278-9 D 17 '71 *
Life 71:16 S 17 '71 *
Nation 212:829-30 Je 28 '71 *
Nation 213:603-4 D 6 '71 *
New Repub 165:20+ D 18 '71 *
New Yorker 47:64-5 Jl 3 '71 *
New Yorker 47:89 N 27 '71 *
Newsweek il 77:70 Je 14 '71
Newsweek il 78:110-11 N 29 '71 *
Sat R 54:20 D 4 '71 *
Time 98:70-1 N 29 '71 *
Time il 97:76 Je 14 '71 *
Vogue 158:71 Ag 1 '71 *
Peopled wound, by M. Esslin. Review
Cath World 213:48-9 Ap '71. C. Hughes *

PIONEER life. See Frontier and pioneer life

PIONEER messenger service. See Vera institute of justice

PIONEER museum. See Tillamook, Ore.—Galleries and museums

PIOUS, Richard M.
Phony war on poverty in the Great society. bibliog f il Cur Hist 61:266-72 N '71
Pretrial and nontrial in the lower criminal courts. bibliog f Cur Hist 61:20-6+ Jl '71

PIPE bending
See also
Tube bending

PIPE laying
Highlining helps customers and contractors; San Diego, Calif. F. M. Conger. il Am City 86:30 Ja '71
New and old storm drains team up; Pennsauken, N.J. A. R. Pagan. il Am City 86:112 Ap '71
Plastic water main for hot soil; Denver. C. Carlson. il Am City 86:70 Je '71
1700-foot outfall laid in one day; Greenwood, S.C. C. A. Bell. il Am City 86:66-7 S '71

PIPE lines
See also
Gas, Natural—Pipe lines
Petroleum—Pipe lines
Williams companies

PIPE safes. See Safes

PIPER, John S.
Fours and fives; poem. Chr Cent 88:1466 D 15 '71

PIPER, Klaus
Piper's personal publishing; L'Express wades into books. H. Lottman. por Pub W 200:49-50 Jl 12 '71 *

PIPER, Leonora E.
The medium had the message: Mrs Piper and the professors; excerpts from Here, Mr Splitfoot. R. Somerlott. il pors Am Heritage 22:33-7+ F '71 *

PIPER aircraft corporation
Piper, Swearingen study link; latter developing business jet. E. J. Bulban. Aviation W 95:19 Jl 26 '71

PIPER verlag. See Publishers and publishing —Germany (Federal Republic)

PIPER'S hill hotel for children. See Stamford, Conn.—Hotels, restaurants, etc.

PIPES
See also
Sewer pipes
Tobacco pipes
Water pipes

PIPES, Plastic
1700-foot outfall laid in one day; Greenwood, S.C. C. A. Bell. il Am City 86:66-7 S '71
See also
Water pipes, Plastic

PIQUET, Howard S.
Free trade truths, and myths. il Nations Bsns 59:37-8+ F '71

PIRANDELLO, Luigi
Luigi Pirandello and the cinema. F. Nulf. bibliog Film Q 24:40-8 Wint '70 *

PIRATE radio stations. See Radio stations, Illegal

PIRATES (baseball) See Baseball clubs

PIRNIE, Jane
Jane Pirnie's puzzler. Wilson Lib Bul 45:778-9 Ap '71
Solution to Pirnie's April puzzler. il Wilson Lib Bul 45:831+ My '71

PISANI, Joseph
Christian nonviolent workshop. Cath World 214:31-4 O '71
Conscientious objection: no longer un-Catholic. Chr Cent 88:876-8 Jl 21 '71

PISCATAWAY, N.J.
Cloud comes to Quibbletown. D. Jackson. il Life 71:72-4+ D 10 '71

PISENGA, David
Good morning; poem. Seventeen 29:146 Jl '70

PISTOL; story. See Carpenter, D.

PISTOLS
Major Pitcairn's pistols; Scotch sidearms. C. Worman. il Hobbies 76:154-5 N '71
Pistols for two. C. Worman. il Hobbies 76:154-5 Ja '72
U.S. model 1836 pistol; flintlock pistol. C. Worman. il Hobbies 76:154-5 Je '71
Williamson deringer. C. Worman. il Hobbies 76:154-5 Ag '71
See also
Revolvers

Laws and regulations
See Firearms—Laws and regulations

PISZEK, Edward J.
One-man crusade against the Polish joke. M. Durham. il por Life 72:70-1 Ja 14 '72 *

PITCAIRN, John
Major Pitcairn's pistols. C. Worman. il Hobbies 76:154-5 N '71 *

PITCH, Musical. See Musical pitch

PITCHER, Joan A.
Interlude in the tropics. il Am For 77:28-30 D '71

PITCHERS, Baseball. See Baseball players

PITCHING (baseball)
How to throw the ultimate fast ball; V. Blue. W. Twombly. il pors N Y Times Mag p22-4+ Jl 25 '71
Pitching secrets. il Sports Illus 34:70-3 Ap 12 '71
Protecting boys' pitching arms. A. J. Snider. Sci Digest 70:56 N '71

PITCHMEN. See Salesmen and salesmanship

PITHA, Josef, and Pitha, P. M.
Antiviral resistance by the polyinosinic acid—poly(1-vinylcytosine) complex. bibliog il Science 172:1146-8 Je 11 '71

PITHA, Paula M. See Pitha, J. jt. auth.

PITMAN, Dorothy
I can't call you my sister yet; interview, ed. by M. Cantwell. por Mlle 73:182-3+ My '71

PITTENGER, Norman
E. M. Forster, homosexuality and Christian morality. Chr Cent 88:1468-71 D 15 '71
Quest at Cambridge. Chr Cent 88:150 F 3 '71

PITTOSPORUM
Indoor evergreen you'll love. D. Reay. il Org Gard & Farm 18:129+ F '71

PITTSBURGH
Back to the Bijou; restoration of Penn theatre. A. Velis. il Opera N 36:12-14 S '71

Air pollution
Pittsburgh: from smoky city to smog-less skies. E. L. Stockton. il UNESCO Courier 24:14-17 Jl '71
Pittsburgh goes after the big polluters. il Bsns W p 124+ Mr 13 '71

City planning
Big action belongs downtown. E. Faltermayer. il Life 71:20B O 29 '71

Courts
Pittsburgh's program for efficient courts. M. T. Bloom. Read Digest 98:215-16+ Je '71

Description
Making the best of a visit to Pittsburgh. Bsns W p 102 Mr 13 '71

Galleries and museums
See also
Carnegie institute

Libraries
Breaking into jail; Allegheny County jail. S. Opipare and others. il pors Library J 96: 2734-6 S 15 '71
See also
Carnegie library of Pittsburgh

Music
See also
Heinz Hall for the performing arts
Pittsburgh opera company

Politics and government
Mayor is nobody's boy. R. Z. Hallow. il Nation 212:492-6 Ap 19 '71

Public health
Pittsburgh narcotics addicts find hope in the methadone method. il Ebony 26:48-50+ N '70

Transit systems
Pittsburgh splits over Skybus. il Bsns W p25 Ag 7 '71

PITTSBURG, Kan.
Slurry seal for maintenance, remix for reconstruction. R. O. Yaeger. il Am City 86: 54-5 Jl '71

PITTSBURGH opera company
Report:
Aida. R. Croan. Opera N 36:27 D 11 '71

PITTSBURGH Pirates (baseball)   See Baseball clubs

PITTSBURGH Steelers (football club) See Football clubs

PITTSBURGH. University
Election recess fails trial. Sch & Soc 99:399 N '71
Should Pittsburgh save Forbes field? J. D. Morgan. il Arch Rec 150:119-22 Jl '71

PITTSBURGH World series victory celebration. See Celebrations

PITTSFIELD, Mass.
One town's hot & cold views of the freeze. G. Nikolaieff. il Sr Schol 99:11-13 O 11 '71
Utility conduit doubles as sidewalk. C. J. McMahon. il Am City 86:132-3 S '71

PITTSTON company
Open-door policy. il Forbes 107:66 Ap 15 '71

PITUITARY hormones
Diligence and luck pay off; synthesis of human growth hormone. il por Sci N 99:41-2 Ja 16 '71
Growth hormone and fetal nutrition. Sci N 100:373-4 D 4 '71
Human growth hormone. il por Newsweek 77:38+ Ja 18 '71
Prenatal cerebral development: effect of restricted diet, reversal by growth hormone. S. Zamenhof and others. bibliog il Science 174:954-5 N 26 '71
Revising the sequence; human growth hormone. por Sci N 99:230 Ap 3 '71
Synthesis of human growth hormone. Chem 44:20-1 Ap '71
See also
Gonadotropins
Melanotropin
Oxytocin

PITZ, Henry C.
Seymour Remenick: a quiet voice. il por Am Artist 35:44-9+ Ag '71

PITZER, Kenneth S.
Science and society: some policy changes are needed; adaptation of address, January 20, 1971. Science 172:223-6 Ap 16 '71

PIUS XI, pope
Pope Pius XI on rebuilding the social order. B. L. Masse. America 124:559 My 29 '71 *

PIZZA. See Cookery, Italian

PIZZA parlors. See Restaurants

PLACE, John Bassett Moore
Anaconda turns to a money man. por Bsns W p24-5 My 22 '71 *
Banking on an outsider. E. J. Tracy and others. por Fortune 83:33 Je '71 *

PLACE between; story. See Agudllo, T.

PLACE in the family; drama. See Thane, A.

PLACE names. See Names, Geographical

PLACEBO; story. See Masello, R.

PLACEMENT bureaus. See Employment agencies

PLACEMENT of teachers. See Teachers— Selection and appointment

PLACEMENT service in aging. See Institute of gerontology

PLACENTA
Mimicking the placenta with computer models. il Sci N 100:205 S 25 '71

PLACES of retirement. See Retirement, Places of

PLAGEMANN, Bentz
New life; story. Good H 172:92-3 Ap '71

PLAGIARISM by students. See Cheating in schoolwork

PLAGUE
Annals of medicine; case of bubonic plague from handling squirrel infected with sylvatic plague. B. Roueché. New Yorker 47: 70+ Ap 10 '71
Bubonic plague: it's still around but under control. A. Hamilton. il Sci Digest 69:9-13 My '71

PLAINCLOTHES men. See Detectives

PLAINCLOTHES women. See Detectives

PLAINS
See also
Great Plains

PLAISTED, Julian A.
Training teachers of teachers. il Am Ed 7: 33-5 Ja '71

PLANERS. See Planing machines

PLANETARIUMS
Armand N. Spitz, planetarium inventor. C. A. Federer. il pors Sky & Tel 41:354-5 Je '71
Czechoslovakian planetarium and public observatory. O. Oburka. il Sky & Tel 41:292-4 My '71

PLANETARY albedo. See Earth—Radiation

PLANETARY atmosphere experiments test. See Space probes

PLANETARY masses. See Planets—Mass

PLANETARY spectroscopy. See Astronomical spectroscopy

PLANETS
Astronomy. J. Stokley. See fourth issue of each month of Science news
Planets in December. il Sky & Tel 41:186-7 Mr '71
Sun, moon, and planets this month. R. C. Victor. See issues of Sky and telescope
Tenth planet? Chem 44:23-4 D '71
See also
Life on other planets
Mechanics, Celestial
Occultations
Satellites
also names of planets, e.g. Pluto (planet)

Mass
System of planetary masses. M. E. Ash and others. bibliog il Science 174:551-6 N 5 '71

Observations
See also
Mars (planet)—Observations

Spectra
Microwaves from the planets. D. E. Thomsen il Sci N 99:424-5 Je 19 '71

PLANING machines
All-purpose planer. R. J. De Cristoforo. il Mech Illus 67:92-3+ Ap '71
See also
Jointers (woodworking machinery)
Shapers

PLANKTON
Harvest of plankton; excerpt from The sea against hunger. C. P. Idyll. il Sea Front 17:258-67 S '71
What do you know about plankton? quiz. J. Daugherty and M. Daugherty. il Sci Digest 71:82-3+ Ja '72
See also
Diatoms
Water bloom
PLANNED parenthood. See Birth control
PLANNED parenthood federation of America. See Planned parenthood-world population (organization)
PLANNED parenthood-world population (organization)
Mrs Lieberman of Baltimore; Planned parenthood of Maryland. J. Corry. por Harper 242:92-5 F '71
PLANNING, Business. See Business planning
PLANNING, Educational. See Educational planning
PLANNING, Regional. See Regional planning
PLANNING, Social. See Social policy
PLANNING of cities. See City planning
PLANNING-programming-budgeting. See Program budgeting
PLANT, Gloria. See Eckley, M. jt. auth.
PLANT breeding
Blossoms for a brave new world. T. Cruso. il McCalls 98:34+ S '71
Induced mutations in plants. B. Sigurbjörnsson. il Sci Am 224:86-95 Ja '71
Where the new blooms start; nurseries and plant breeders of California. E. McDonald. il House B 113:70-2+ Mr '71
See also
Corn—Hybrids
Tree breeding
PLANT cells and tissues
See also
Chloroplasts
Chromosomes (botany)
Pinocytosis
Plants—Chemical analysis
Plastids
PLANT conservation
Our wildflowers. A. Holweg. il Cons 26:14-16 Ag '71
PLANT cuttings. See Plant propagation
PLANT dyes. See Dyes and dyeing
PLANT equipment. See Factories—Equipment
PLANT evolution. See Evolution
PLANT genetics
Correlation between gametophytic and sporophytic characteristics in zea mays L. D. L. Mulcahy. bibliog il Science 171:1155-6 Mr 19 '71
Multiple genotypes in individuals of Claytonia virginica. W. H. Lewis and others. bibliog il Science 172:564-5 My 7 '71; Discussion. 174:1044-5 D 3 '71
See also
Chromosomes (botany)
PLANT hairs. See Trichomes
PLANT houses. See Sheds
PLANT introduction
Breadfruit tree. H. M. Berry. il Horticulture 49:19+ Mr '71
Photoperiod evidence in the introduction of xanthium (cocklebur) to Australia. C. McMillan. bibliog il Science 171:1029-31 Mr 12 '71
PLANT location. See Location in business and industry
PLANT mitochondria. See Mitochondria
PLANT propagation
Bonsai from seed. C. E. Derderian. il Horticulture 49:42-3+ Ap '71
Coffee-can magic. L. Anthony. il Org Gard & Farm 18:118-19 Ap '71
Epiphyllums from seed. R. James. il Horticulture 49:18-19+ Je '71
Growing herbaceous plants from seed. P. Swindells. il Horticulture 49:40-1+ My '71
Multiplying your houseplants. K. S. Taylor. il Horticulture 49:30-3 F '71
New plants from old. D. A. Brown. il Home Gard 58:26-31 Je '71
Propagating your favorites by sand-rooting. B. Wahlfeldt. il Org Gard & Farm 18:54-5 F '71
Propagation by leaf cuttings. A. V. Pike. il Horticulture 49:36-7+ D '71
Time now to plant peonies. M. Price. il Home Gard 58:18-19+ O '71
See also
Seedlings
Seeds
PLANT relocation. See Location in business and industry

PLANT research. See Botanical research
PLANT roots. See Roots
PLANT succession
Stability and diversity at three trophic levels in terrestrial successional ecosystems. L. E. Hurd and others. bibliog il Science 173:1134-6 S 17 '71
PLANT supports. See Garden stakes and staking
PLANT tissue tests. See Plants—Chemical analysis
PLANT viruses. See Viruses, Plant
PLANTAR warts. See Warts
PLANTERS (farm machines)
Electronic monitors check your planter. P. B. Jones. il Suc Farm 69:24-5 Ap '71
High-speed planters "pit-stop" refills to beat the blight. il Farm J 95:30-3 Ap '71
Planning a toolbar planter system. G. L. Earle. Suc Farm 69:26-7 Ap '71
PLANTERS (flower boxes) See Flower boxes, planters, etc.
PLANTING. See Landscape gardening; Plants, Space arrangement of; Seeding; Transplanting
PLANTING, Roadside. See Roadside improvement
PLANTING machinery. See Planters (farm machines)
PLANTING of corn. See Corn—Seeding
PLANTS
Best plants. Home Gard 58:24-5 F; 62+ Ap '71
[Month] in your garden. See issues of Sunset
More new plants for 1971. il Horticulture 49:22-3+ F '71
Plant collector's corner:
Better name for sea oats is bamboo grass. il Sunset 146:127 Ja '71
From tubers, sticks, and twigs come the wonders of the neighborhood. il Sunset 146:213-15 Mr '71
Trees and plants section; symposium. il Am For 77:33-47+ Ap '71
See also
Alpine flora
Annuals (plants)
Berry bearing plants
Bulbs
Dormancy (plants)
Forcing (plants)
Hallucination and illusion producing plants
Herbs
Marsh plants
Parasitic plants
Perennials
Poisonous plants
Pollen
Roots
Transplanting
also names of plants, e.g. Hibiscus

Absorption of water

Water movement in plants. P. C. Bibb. il Horticulture 49:22-3+ Mr '71
Weatherman looks at the redwood tree; California's fog drinker. R. E. Burton. il Weatherwise 24:120-4 Je '71

All America selections

Our pick of the colorful new flowers. H. Mason. il Bet Hom & Gard 49:54-5 Mr '71
Roses for 1972: Apollo and Portrait. il Horticulture 49:20-1 Jl '71
Two new all-America roses with great fragrance. il Home Gard 58:22-3 Ag '71

Breeding

See Plant breeding

Chemical analysis

Tissue tests to your plants' rescue. R. Steffen. Org Gard & Farm 18:100+ D '71

Cold resistance

See Plants—Frost resistance

Disease and pest resistance

Cucumber beetle resistance and mite susceptibility controlled by the bitter gene in cucumis sativus L. C. P. Da Costa and C. M. Jones. bibliog il Science 172:1145-6 Je 11 '71

Dormancy

See Dormancy (plants)

Drought resistance

Desiccation-tolerant flowering plants in southern Africa. D. F. Gaff. bibliog il Science 174:1033-4 D 3 '71

PLANTS—*Continued*

Electrophysiology
See Electrophysiology of plants

Fertilization
See Fertilization of plants

Fire resistance
Brush fire and forest fire dangers in California are very real. What can you do? Sunset 146:272+ Ap '71

Frost resistance
Cold-resistant corn coming? Suc Farm 69: no5 M8 Mr '71

Hardiness
See also
Plants—Drought resistance
Plants—Frost resistance

Irritability and movements
Potassium flux: a common feature of albizzia leaflet movement controlled by phytochrome or endogenous rhythm. R. L. Satter and A. W. Galston. bibliog il Science 174:518-20 O 29 '71

Metabolism
Boron: possible role in plant metabolism. J. A. Rajaratnam and others. bibliog il Science 172:1142 Je 11 '71
Control of photosynthetic carbon metabolism. J. A. Bassham. bibliog il Science 172: 526-34 My 7 '71
How does a plant synthesize a molecule? P. Andermatt. il Chem 45:23-4 Ja '72

Movements
See Plants—Irritability and movements

Nutrition
See also
Eutrophication
Photosynthesis
Soil fertility

Reproduction
See also
Parthenocarpy

Resistance to insects
See Plants—Disease and pest resistance

Translocation
See Plants, Motion of fluids in

Water absorption
See Plants—Absorption of water

PLANTS, Aquatic. See Aquatic plants
PLANTS, Climbing. See Climbing plants
PLANTS, Cover. See Cover plants

PLANTS, Edible
Are wild foods dangerous? E. Gibbons. bibliog Org Gard & Farm 18:98-101 Je '71
Lights, camera and action in Canada. E. Gibbons. Org Gard & Farm 18:116-21 F '71
On the trail of the three sisters; food plants of the original Americans. E. Gibbons. Natur Hist 80:14-16+ F '71
Outdoor pantry. P. Foret. Horticulture 49: 27+ Ap '71
What's cooking?
English department epicure. J. Schwartz. il por Org Gard & Farm 18:126-9 Ja '71
Wild food with a college education. E. Gibbons. Org Gard & Farm 18:118+ Ja '71
Wild survival challenge in Arizona. E. Gibbons. Org Gard & Farm 18:121-2+ Mr '71
See also
Food. Wild
Greens, Edible

PLANTS, Effect of air pollution on
Air pollution and chrysanthemums. R. C. Bonham il Horticulture 49:30-1 O '71
Air pollution can injure your crops. C. E. Sommers. Suc Farm 69:H12 S '71
Lichens and air pollution. I. M. Brodo. il Cons 26:22-6 Ag '71
See also
Plants, Effect of smog on

PLANTS, Effect of boron on
Boron: possible role in plant metabolism. J. A. Rajaratnam and others. bibliog il Science 172:1142 Je 11 '71

PLANTS, Effect of carbon dioxide on
Plant response to carbon dioxide enrichment under field conditions: a simulation. L. H. Allen, jr. and others. bibliog il Science 173:256-8 Jl 16 '71

PLANTS, Effect of climate on
See also
Meteorology, Agricultural

PLANTS, Effect of cold on. See Plants, Effect of temperature on

PLANTS, Effect of drought on. See Plants—Drought resistance
PLANTS, Effect of humidity on
Humidify for healthier house plants. B. Thompson. Home Gard 58:74-5 Ap '71
PLANTS, Effect of lead on
On the trail of heavy metals in ecosystems. il Sci N 100:165-6 S 11 '71
PLANTS, Effect of light on
See also
Artificial light gardening
PLANTS, Effect of potassium on
Potassium flux: a common feature of albizzia leaflet movement controlled by phytochrome or endogenous rhythm. R. L. Satter and A. W. Galston. bibliog il Science 174:518-20 O 29 '71
PLANTS, Effect of radio waves on
Ultrahigh-frequency electromagnetic fields for weed control phytotoxicity and selectivity. F. S. Davis and others. bibliog il Science 173:535-7 Ag 6 '71
PLANTS, Effect of salt on
Select trees and shrubs that can tolerate de-icing salts. il Am City 86:21 S '71
PLANTS, Effect of smog on
Smog: the tree killer. E. Hay. il Am For 77:8-10+ O '71
PLANTS, Effect of solar radiation on
Why organic growers love the sun. R. Rodale. il Org Gard & Farm 18:30-4 O '71
PLANTS, Effect of temperature on
Temperature and forsythia buds. A. J. Fordham. il Horticulture 49:16-17 My '71
Why do some plants live through cold while others die? Sci Digest 69:70 Ap '71
See also
Plants—Frost resistance

PLANTS, Electroculture of. See Electrohorticulture

PLANTS, Flowering of
How lilacs and other plants time their blooming. J. M. Caprio. Horticulture 49:26-7+ S '71
Rhythm of the flowers. J. D. Palmer. il Natur Hist 80:64-73 Ag '71
Temperature and forsythia buds. A. J. Fordham. il Horticulture 49:16-17 My '71

PLANTS, Food. See Plants, Edible
PLANTS, Growth of. See Growth (plants)
PLANTS, Hallucinogenic. See Hallucination and illusion producing plants
PLANTS, Irritability and movements of. See Plants—Irritability and movements

PLANTS, Motion of fluids in
Mycorrhizal enhancement of water transport in soybean. G. R. Safir and others. bibliog il Science 172:581-3 My 7 '71
Water movement in plants. P. C. Bibb. il Horticulture 49:22-3+ Mr '71

PLANTS, Ornamental
Planting; plants in front of the Metropolitan museum of art. New Yorker 47:25-6 Ag 14 '71
See also
Anthuriums
Aspidistra
Coleus
Medinilla

PLANTS, Poisonous. See Poisonous plants

PLANTS, Potted
Big container plants add interest to indoor spaces, soften outdoor house lines. il Sunset 146:162-3 F '71
Extraordinary plants, but easy. H. Mason il Bet Hom & Gard 49:68-71 F '71
Grouping pot plants in roomy wood containers. il Sunset 147:134 N '71
Perfect potted partners; petunias and ivy. T. Cruso. il McCalls 98:28+ Jl '71
Pot gardener gone wild. il Sunset 147:92-3 O '71
Potfuls of vegetables. B. F. George. Horticulture 49:40 Jl '71
See also
Flower boxes, planters, etc.
Hanging baskets
House plants
Watering of plants

PLANTS, Protection of
Pollution protection for plants, ozone protection by benomyl. il Sci Digest 69:77 Je '71
Winter protection for roses. il Home Gard 58:42 D '71
See also
Frost protection
Mulching

PLANTS, Rock garden
Gentians for the rock garden. R. Murfitt. il Horticulture 49:26-7+ O '71
See also
Alpine flora

PLANTS, Sex in
See also
Algae, Sex in
PLANTS, Shade
Here are plants that make it in heavy shade. il Sunset 146:261 Ap '71
Right plants turn a shaded area into an asset. E. S. Parcher. il Home Gard 58:24-7+ Ag '71
Shade plants; two are standbys: two are special. il Sunset 147:152-3 Jl '71
See also
Clivias
PLANTS, Space arrangement of
Narrow row machinery experience. Suc Farm 69:no2 27 F '71
Timetable for narrow rows. W. Messerly. il Suc Farm 69:no4 48 Mr '71
PLANTS, Training of
Art of espaliering. E. McDonald. il House B 113:58-7 Jl '71
Camellia with flower garlands; camellia lutchuensis. il Sunset 147:213 D '71
Decorate with espaliered pyracantha. il Sunset 147:189 D '71
Training herbs. C. Stewart. il Horticulture 49:28+ Mr '71
See also
Trees, Training of
PLANTS, Watering of. See Watering of plants
PLANTS and sound. See Vegetation and sound
PLANTS as gifts
Natural gifts; Christmas plants. il Bet Hom & Gard 49:72-3 D '71
Small wonders with a fruitful gift. E. McDonald. il House B 113:44-6 D '71
PLANTS for shady places. See Plants, Shade
PLANTS in art
See also
Flowers in art
PLANTS in house decoration
Details that make the difference. W. Baldwin. House & Gard 139:10+ My '71
Real garden that is inside the house. il Sunset 146:108-11 My '71
PLANTS in soil erosion control. See Erosion prevention and control
PLANZ, Charles A.
It can work: busing inner city pupils to suburban schools. il Clear House 46:158-62 N '71
PLASMA (ionized gases)
Controlled nuclear fusion: status and outlook. D. J. Rose. bibliog il Science 172:797-808 My 21 '71
Looking for the harmony; theories of tokamaks. Sci N 99:434 Je 26 '71
Magnetic resonances and waves in simple metals. W. M. Walsh, jr. bibliog il Science 171:36-42 Ja 8 '71
Mirror, mirror on the wall, which is the fairest plasma of them all? D. E. Thomsen. il Sci N 101:28-9 Ja 8 '72
Physical sciences; 4th International conference on plasma physics and controlled nuclear fusion research. Sci N 100:10 Jl 3 '71
Plasma physics applied to cosmology. H. Alfvén. bibliog il Phys Today 24:28-31+ F '71
Plasma physics, space research, and the origin of the solar system; Nobel lecture, December 11, 1970. H. Alfvén. il Science 172:991-4 Je 4 '71
Prospects of fusion power. W. C. Gough and B. J. Eastlund. il Sci Am 224:50-64 F '71
Scyllac in operation at Los Alamos. Sci N 99:178 Mr 13 '71
See also
Solar wind
PLASMACYTOMA cells. See Tumor cells
PLASMALEMMA. See Membranes (biology)
PLASMINOGEN
Kidney: primary source of plasminogen after acute depletion in the cat. R. F. Highsmith and D. L. Kline. bibliog il Science 174:141-2 O 8 '71
PLASMODIUM (parasite)
Malaria resistance: artificial induction with a partially purified plasmodial fraction. L. E. D'Antonio and others; reply with rejoinder, R. T. Cook and M. Aikawa. bibliog Science 171:1175-6 Mr 19 '71
Plasmodium berghei: enhanced protective immunity after vaccination of white rats born of immune mothers. R. S. Desowitz. bibliog il Science 172:1151-2 Je 11 '71
Sporozoite-induced infections of plasmodium berghei administered by the oral route. M. Yoeli and H. Most. bibliog il Science 173:1031-2 S 10 '71
PLASMODIUM infection. See Malaria
PLASTER modeling. See Modeling

PLASTER work (craft)
Projects from plaster. L. J. Miller. il Design 72:34-5 mid-Sum '71
Young sculptors at the beach; sandcasting. il Sunset 146:86-7 Mr '71
PLASTIC adhesives. See Adhesives
PLASTIC airplanes. See Airplanes—Materials; Airplanes, Light—Materials
PLASTIC boats. See Boats—Materials
PLASTIC flooring. See Flooring, Plastic
PLASTIC foams
There's no place like foam: polyurethane foam. P. Knight. il Sports Illus 35:66-7 N 8 '71
PLASTIC furniture. See Furniture, Plastic
PLASTIC greenhouses. See Greenhouses
PLASTIC houses
House that grows; Diaz-Infante's modular house of plastic polyester. J. Sanger. il por Américas 23:16-24 Mr '71
Inflatable, portable house; Pneudome. il Vogue 158:116-17 Ag 1 '71
New foam homes. il Am Home 74:75-87 Ap '71
PLASTIC mulch. See Mulching
PLASTIC pipes. See Pipes, Plastic
PLASTIC sculpture
Experiment in sculpture; use of epoxy material. G. E. Toles. il Design 73:32-3 Wint '71
PLASTIC surgery. See Surgery, Plastic
PLASTIC water pipes. See Water pipes, Plastic
PLASTIC worms. See Fishing lures, flies, etc.
PLASTICIZERS
New-car smell; dangers of phthalate plasticizers. K. P. Shea. bibliog il Environ 13:2-9 O '71
Plasticizer found in heart muscle. il Chem 45:25 Ja '72
Plasticizers: new entry on list of suspected contaminants. Sci N 100:324 N 13 '71
Warning on plasticizers. Chem 44:24 Jl '71
PLASTICS
Glass that won't break; Texan. il Mech Illus 67:93 Ja '71
10,000 metamorphoses of plastics and synthetic fibres. G. Gregory. il UNESCO Courier 24:15-23 Je '71
See also
Epoxy resins
Flooring, Plastic
Plasticizers
Polyethylene
Polymers

Deterioration
Disappearing plastics start to appear. il Bsns W p 148 N 13 '71
This plastic will self-destruct. Sci N 100:92 Ag 7 '71
PLASTICS, Chromium plating of. See Chromium plating
PLASTICS in building
Foam: the new miracle building material. S. Schuler. Am Home 74:36+ Ap '71
Urethane foam becomes practical for housing; Heritage Village, Southbury, Conn. il Am City 86:75 F '71
PLASTICS industry
Plastics return the ecologists' fire. il Bsns W p25 Jl 10 '71
PLASTICS work
How to make see-through accessories. A. Lees. il Pop Sci 199:108 S '71
How to work with Corian; new man-made marble. R. J. DeCristoforo. il Pop Sci 198:105-7+ Mr '71
Plexiglas trio. il Mech Illus 67:114-15 F '71
Tools the pros use on plastic laminates. H. Wicks. il Pop Mech 136:170-2+ N '71
See also
Turning

Projects
Buffet wedge in plastic: simple and elegant. A. J. Hand. il Pop Sci 198:82 Ja '71
How to work with today's materials: acrylic plastic. il Bet Hom & Gard 49:51 Jl '71
Light, lustrous look of glass, and you can make them; Plexiglas projects. W. C. Leckey. il Pop Mech 135:148-51+ Mr '71
PLASTIDS
Glycogen plastids in Müllerian body cells of cecropia peltata, a higher green plant. F. R. Rickson. bibliog il Science 173:344-7 Jl 23 '71
PLASTOW, David
Rap 'n' pinion. por Motor T 23:14 Jl '71
about
Rebirth of Rolls? il por Forbes 108:77 O 15 '71 *

PLATE tectonics. See Geology, Structural

PLATED silverware. See Silverware

PLATELETS (blood) See Blood—Corpuscles and platelets

PLATES (dishes) See Pottery

PLATFORM tennis. See Paddle tennis

PLATFORMS
Climb up to better hunting; tree stand. il Field & S 76:6+ O '71
Treated wood structures; observation platforms at Ohiopyle state park. il Parks & Rec 6:32 My '71

PLATH, Sylvia
Six poems: Babysitters; Pheasant; Courage of shutting up; Apprehensions; For a fatherless son; By candlelight. New Yorker 47:36-7 Mr 6 '71
What I found out about Buddy Willard; story; excerpt from The bell jar. McCalls 98:86-7 Ap '71

about

Sylvia Plath: a partial disagreement. I. Howe. Harper 244:88-91 Ja '72 *
Sylvia Plath cult. A. Birstein. por Vogue 158:176 O 1 '71 *
Sylvia Plath: three poems and a remembrance. E. A. Stoianoff. por Mlle 73:160-1 S '71 *
Triumph of a tormented poet. M. Duffy. il pors Life 71:38A-38B N 12 '71 *
Waiting for the voice to crack. S. Maloff. New Repub 164:33-5 My 8 '71 *

PLATING
See also
Chromium plating
Gilding

PLATINUM compounds
New heat in a chilly argument; one-dimensional conductor, potassium tetracyano platinate. il Sci N 99:194 Mr 20 '71

PLATINUM printing. See Photography—Printing processes

PLATO
Plato parchment; earliest known Plato text in codex. il Sci Digest 70:62-3 Ag '71 *
Scrap of parchment; second century A.D. text. il Chem 44:3 My '71 *

PLATT, Robert Holmes
Wider spectrum at Magnavox. por Bsns W p 112 Mr 13 '71 *

PLATT, Rutherford
This water planet; excerpt from Water and life. il Audubon 73:4-9 Mr '71

PLATT NATIONAL PARK
It's a good ol' place: Uncle Sam's mini-park. J. Madson. il Audubon 73:30-5 Ja '71

PLATTEN, Donald C.
New monetary system for the 1980's, address, December 3, 1971. Vital Speeches 38:179-82 Ja 1 '72

PLAVEC, Miroslav. See Batten. A. H. jt. auth.

PLAY
Baby's play group is great, for mummy. S. Ramos. il N Y Times Mag p67-8+ Ap 25 '71; Reply. N. Mueller and J. M. Kennedy. p 16 My 23 '71; Rejoinder. p43 Jl 18 '71
Come out & play; with letter by Patricia Nixon. il Ladies Home J 88:8, 48+ Jl '71
Happy head start at home. M. A. Schatz. il Parents Mag 46:29-31+ Jl '71
Play and its theories re-examined. M. J. Ellis. Parks & Rec 6:51-5+ Ag '71
Play-in, teach-in for parents; with study-discussion program. M. M. Conant. bibliog il PTA Mag 65:14-17, 34 Mr '71
Play; symposium. il Natur Hist 80:44-77 D '71
What happens when a child plays? B. Bettelheim. Ladies Home J 88:34+ N '71
See also
Childrens amusements
Games
Recreation

PLAY apparatus. See Playgrounds—Equipment

PLAY houses. See Playhouses

PLAY production. See Theatrical production and direction

PLAY schools
See also
Nursery schools

PLAY Strindberg; drama. See Dürrenmatt. F.

PLAY writing. See Drama—Technique

PLAYBOY (periodical)
Continental Playboys. il Newsweek 78:51 S 13 '71
Gathering at Bunnymede; Playboy international writers' convocation. R. Todd. Atlan 229:86-8 Ja '72

PLAYBOY enterprises, inc.
Campus conquistador. por Time 97:71 Mr 8 '71
Can you bare it? with interview by H. Hefner. il pors Forbes 107:17-21 Mr 1 '71
Playboy forms book club; firm will go public soon. Pub W 199:45-6 Je 21 '71
Playboy goes public. il Time 98:88 S 27 '71

PLAYBOY of the western world; drama. See Synge, J. M.

PLAYBOY writers convocation. See Authors conferences

PLAYER, Gary
Flailings of a zealot. H. McIlvanney. il por Sports Illus 35:81-3 O 18 '71 *

PLAYGROUND apparatus. See Playgrounds—Equipment

PLAYGROUND sculpture. See Sculpture

PLAYGROUNDS
Adventure playgrounds; Milpitas thinks they can work in America. R. F. McGuire. il Parks & Rec 6:30-2 N '71
Miniparks: diminishing returns. N. Clay. il Parks & Rec 6:22-6 Ja '71
Parks and recreation. See issues of American city
See also
Athletic fields
Parks
also subhead Parks and playgrounds under names of cities, e.g. Oakland, Calif.—Parks and playgrounds

Equipment
Designing cardboard play equipment. L. Whitesel. il Sch Arts 70:24-5 Mr '71
Every playground has a theme; Abilene, Tex. il Am City 86:32 Ja '71
Play spacenet. il Arch Forum 135:70 Jl '71
Play's the thing. il Newsweek 78:30+ D 27 '71
Sculpture parks: can they work? Hong Kong. P. Selinger. il Parks & Rec 6:38-9+ F '71
Try poles for playgrounds; San Francisco. il Am City 86:28 S '71
Value of playground sculpture. S. Gendusa. il Parks & Rec 6:39+ Jl '71
Water sculpture. il Design 73:15-16 Wint '71
See also
Swings

PLAYGROUNDS, Home
Place to play. N. Skurka. il N Y Times Mag p54 S 19 '71

Equipment
Lawn boat bounces, rolls, jumps, wiggles. It's a stressed sheet of plywood. il Sunset 147:76 Ag '71
Swings, slide, playhouse, racetrack, sandbox, fountain. il Sunset 146:101-2 Mr '71
See also
Playhouses

PLAYHOUSES
Child's house. il Sunset 147:66-8 Jl '71
Super space for play and storage. E. McDonald. il House B 113:78-9 Ja '71
Team of fathers built this windowed shoe for $300. il Sunset 147:139-40 N '71
What is a house? children's play turns to house building. il Good H 173:94+ N '71

PLAYING cards. See Cards

PLAYLAND amusement park, Rye, N.Y. See Amusement parks

PLAYMATES
First steps to friendship. S. G. Streshinsky. il Parents Mag 46:66-9 F '71
What can a parent do about a neighborhood bully? B. Bettelheim. Ladies Home J 89:30+ Ja '72

PLAYROOMS
Up the pole to their play loft. il Sunset 146:126 Mr '71

PLAYS. See Childrens plays; Drama

PLAYS by children. See Children as authors

PLAYWRIGHTS. See Dramatists

PLAYWRIGHTS conferences. See Authors conferences

PLAYWRITING. See Drama—Technique; Moving picture authorship

PLAZA, Galo
Beyond the Alliance; excerpt from address, April 14, 1971. il Américas 23:2-4 My '71
Latin America today and tomorrow; excerpts. il Américas 23:41-3 Je '71
New decade of inter-American cooperation; statement, August 17, 1971. il Américas 23:44 S '71
New inter-American effort; excerpt from address, February 8, 1971. Américas 23:1 Mr '71

PLAZA, Galo—*Continued*
Next development decade; excerpts from address. Américas 23:42 Ja '71
OAS today; excerpt from address, October 18, 1970. il por Américas 23:S13-15 Ja '71
What is the OAS doing? Américas 23:42 Ap '71

PLAZAS
Plazas for people; San Luis Potosi, Mexico. P. D. Eimon. il Am City 86:88+ F '71

PLEA; story. See Cohea, B.

PLEAS (criminal procedure)
I have nothing to do with justice; M. Erdmann; the guilty always win, with editorial comment. J. Mills. il pors Life 70:2A, 56-8+ Mr 12 '71

PLEASANTS, Henry
How high was G? Opera N 35:24-5 F 20 '71

PLEASANTS, Mary Ellen
Historic recipes from Mammy Pleasant. il por Ebony 26:108+ F '71 *

PLEASE, Stanley
Social impact of the green revolution; comment. bibliog f il pors Int Concil 581:55-61 Ja '71

PLEASURE
Physiological role of pleasure. M. Cabanac. bibliog il Science 173:1103-7 S 17 '71

PLEDGE of allegiance. See Loyalty, Oaths of

PLEISTOCENE period. See Paleontology—Pleistocene

PLENTY Coups (Indian chief)
Crow chief's tribute to the unknown soldier. J. C. Ewers. il pors Am West 8:30-5 N '71 *

PLIGHT of Farmer Jones; drama. See Tennen, S.

PLIMMER, Jack R. and Klingebiel, U. I.
Riboflavin photosensitized oxidation of 2,4-dichlorophenol: assessment of possible chlorinated dioxin formation. bibliog il Science 174:407-8 O 22 '71

PLIMPTON, Calvin Hastings
Healer for Downstate. por Time 98:40-1 D 13 '71 *

PLIMPTON, Francis T. P.
When China gets into the U.N. il N Y Times Mag p29-30+ S 19 '71
about
Profiles. G. T. Hellman. por New Yorker 47:61-2+ D 4 '71 *

PLIMPTON, George
Alex Karras golf classic. Harper 242:60-5 My '71
And the curious facts about another 'the game'. il Sports Illus 35:40-2+ N 22 '71
In the mind's eye. Sports Illus 35:50-2+ Jl 5 '71
No requiem for a heavyweight. il por Sports Illus 34:84-6+ Ap 5 '71
Rajahs' game falls on hard times. il Sports Illus 35:20-2+ Jl 19 '71

PLIOCENE period. See Paleontology—Pliocene

PLIO-PLEISTOCENE boundary. See Geology, Stratigraphic—Cenozoic; Paleontology—Cenozoic

PLOTNICK, Harvey M.
What the eye sees, the heart already knows; poem. Chr Cent 88:974 Ag 18 '71

PLOTNIK, Arthur
Library life in Middle America. il Wilson Lib Bul 46:412-25 Ja '72
Spring, National library week, and an observer come to small-town library, U.S.A. (W.Va) ; or, Seed money, grass-roots, and the greening of the American library dream. il Wilson Lib Bul 45:932-40 Je '71

PLOTS (drama, novel, etc)
Turning novel cuts into short stories. R. E. Hayes. il Writers Digest 51:28-9+ Jl '71
Your story's too episodic. S. Smythe. Writers Digest 51:36-7+ Mr '71

PLOTT hounds. See Hounds

PLOWDEN, David
Gallery; photographs. Life 70:6-7 Ja 22 '71
The island that is. il Audubon 73:61-8 Mr '71
about
David Plowden: The hand of man on America; with photographs. R. Bruns. Pop Phot 68:98-103+ Je '71 *

PLOWING. See Tillage

PLUM puddings. See Puddings

PLUM trees
Commercial prunes don't taste like mine. E. H. Peterson. Org Gard & Farm 18:125 S '71

PLUMADORE, Paul
Paul Plumadore and company, the Cubiculo, NYC. T. Borek. Dance Mag 45:78-9 S '71 *
Paul Plumadore and company, the Cubiculo, NYC. D. Hering. Dance Mag 45:95 Ap '71 *

PLUMB, Barbara
Plumb line. See issues of American home

PLUMB, J. H.
The Edwardians. il Horizon 13:18-29+ Aut '71
Great change in children. il Horizon 13:4-13 Wint '71
Odd couples. il Horizon 13:60-1 Spr '71
Up from slavery. il Horizon 13:80-1 Sum '71

PLUMB bobs
Plumb bob reels out right length of line. A. Lees. il Pop Sci 199:114 Ag '71

PLUMBING
See also
Boats—Sanitation

Maintenance and repair
Fixing faucets and drains. il Bet Hom & Gard 49:148 Ap '71
How to fix a dripping faucet. il Sunset 147:98-9 Jl '71
How to make simple plumbing repairs. il Good H 173:144 Ag '71
No more leaky faucets. il McCalls 98:28 Ag '71
Right way to fix a leaking faucet. il Good H 172:157 F '71
7 plumbing repairs anyone can do. D. Demske. il Mech Illus 67:84-6+ Ja '71
Toilet tank fix-its. il McCalls 98:48 Ap '71

PLUMBING; story. See Updike, J.

PLUMBING supplies industry
Price-fixers get the plumbing bill. Bsns W p26 O 2 '71

PLUMLEY, H. Ladd
Discouraging a do-gooder. il Time 98:80 N 15 '71 *

PLUMLY, Stanley
Giraffe; poem. New Yorker 47:185 N 20 '71

PLUMMER, Mark A.
Taiwan's Chinese nationalist government. bibliog f Cur Hist 61:171-6 S '71

PLUNKETT, E. R.
Eye cups. bibliog il Hobbies 76:118-19 Mr '71

PLUNKETT, Eugenia
Sky-view drive-in: memory of psychotherapy; poem. Poetry 117:241 Ja '71

PLUTO (planet)
Shrinking mass of Pluto. D. E. Thomsen. il Sci N 100:154-5 Ag 28 '71
System of planetary masses. M. E. Ash and others. bibliog il Science 174:551-6 N 5 '71

PLUTONIUM
Another SST? questioning the development and proliferation of the so-called Liquid-metal-cooled fast breeder reactor. Environ 13:18-19 Jl '71
Black-market A-bombs? il Newsweek 77:59 Ap 26 '71
Plutonium and the energy decision. D. P. Geesaman. por Bul Atom Sci 27:33-6 S '71
Plutonium: reactor proliferation threatens a nuclear black market. D. Shapley. bibliog f Science 172:143-6 Ap 9 '71
See also
Dow chemical company—Rocky Flats division

Isotopes
Experimental cosmology. Sci Am 224:54-6 Je '71
Heaviest element in nature; plutonium-244. Chem 44:22 D '71
Plutonium-244: confirmation as an extinct radioactivity. E. C. Alexander, jr. and others. bibliog il Science 172:837-40 My 21 '71

PLUTONIUM workers. See Radiation workers

PLYMOUTH, Mass.
Sanitary affairs
Our plant must be a good neighbor. D. Smith. il Am City 86:89+ Ap '71

PLYMOUTH, Mich.
Square tubing looks better. il Am City 86:126 Ap '71

PLYMOUTH trouble shooting contest. See Automobile mechanics (persons)

PLYWOOD
How to work with today's materials. il Bet Hom & Gard 49:48-51 Jl '71
New from the woods. J. Hand. Mech Illus 67:50 S '71

PNEUMATIC street cleaners. See Street cleaning apparatus

PNEUMATIC tools
Air tools come to home shops. B. Bond and others. il Pop Sci 199:92-3+ Ag '71

PNEUMOCONIOSIS. See Lungs—Dust diseases

PNEUMONIA
What you should know about pneumonia. G. M. Knox. il Bet Hom & Gard 49:16+ F '71

PNEUMONIA, 1945; story. See Woiwode, L.

POACHING
Good guys, bad guys and the bighorn. E. Zern. il por Sports Illus 34:20-2+ Je 28 '71
That desert-sheep case; Swanson charged and sentenced. il Outdoor Life 148:8 N '71

POAGE, Roy
How to beat common confinement problems. il Farm J 95:H14-15 N '71

POBEREZNY, Paul H.
Another look at the BD-4. il Flying 89:71-3 Jl '71

POCKER, Y. and others
Carbonic anhydrase interaction with DDT, DDE, and dieldrin. bibliog il Science 174: 1336-9 D 24 '71

POCKET billiards. See Billiards
POCKET knives. See Knives
POCKETBOOKS. See Purses
POCONO raceway. See Speedways

PODESTA, Robert Angelo
Domestic aid for rural U.S. G. R. Rosen. por Duns 97:62-3 Je '71 •

PODGORNYI, Nikolai Viktorovich
Middle East: anxious visitors. il por Time 97:17-18 Je 7 '71 •
Russia's new coup in Egypt. il por Newsweek 77:43 Je 7 '71 •

PODHORETZ, Norman
Certain anxiety; address. Commentary 52: 4+ Ag '71
Issues. See issues of Commentary

about
Cooling of the intellectuals. P. Steinfels. Commonweal 94:255-61 My 21 '71 •

PODOCARPUS
Podocarpus were obliging. il Sunset 146:124 Ja '71

POE, Edgar Allan
Philosophy of furniture; excerpts. Antiques 99:64+ Ja '71

POEM for Geoff; story. See Gobel, W. jr

POEM forgotten; ballet. See Ballets—Criticisms

POEME de l'extase; ballet. See Ballets—Criticisms

POETICS
Function of stanzaic form. M. A. Kaplan. bibliog f Engl J 60:47-53 Ja '71
Haku mele: a poetry workshop program. P. Thompson. Engl J 60:215-19 F '71
On leaving the bench. J. Ciardi. Sat R 54: 23 Mr 13 '71
Poetry: how and why. J. Jerome. See issues of Writer's digest
Poet's workshop. F. Trefethen. See every other issue of Writer
Writing poems. D. Hall. Writer 84:19-21 F '71
See also
Poetry—Authorship
Rime

POETRY
Light, serious or in-between. J. D. Engle, jr. Writers Digest 51:26-7 F '71
Modern poets: an American-British anthology, ed. by J. M. Brinnin and B. Read. Review
Poetry 119:169-71 D '71. J. Atlas
Poetry place. See issues of Mademoiselle
Poets are remembering it well. J. F. Cotter. America 125:514-16 D 11 '71
Unconsenting spirit: poetry and politics. M. L. Rosenthal. Nation 212:149-50 F 1 '71
Untranslatable language. L. Perrine. bibliog f Engl J 60:54-61 Ja '71
See also
Childrens poems (by children)
Childrens poems (for children)
Christmas poetry
College verse
Computers—Literary use
Free verse
Nature in poetry
Negro poetry
Nursery rhymes
Poets
Political poetry
Religious poetry
Rime
Symbolism in literature
also subhead Poetry under various subjects, e.g. Time—Poetry; *also* American poetry; English poetry; etc.

Appreciation
Poetry and paint. R. Moore. il Sch Arts 70: 16-17 Je '71
Western wind and the complexity of poetry. R. W. French. Engl J 60:212-14 F '71

Authorship
Poetry: how and why. J. Jerome. See issues of Writer's digest

Bibliography
Around the corner. P. Schjeldahl. Poetry 117: 261-75 Ja '71
Books of poetry. Writers Digest 51:21 My '71
Poetry quarterly (cont) Sat R 54:31-3+ Ap 3; 39+ O 2; 37-41+ D 18 '71

Competitions
How to win poetry contests. N. W. Walter. Writers Digest 51:25-7 S '71
1971 poetry contest. J. Chimsky. Writers Digest 51:32-3+ O '71
1971 writing awards. Sr Schol 98:8 My 17 '71

History and criticism
Ringers in the tower, by H. Bloom. Review
Nation 213:278-80 S 27 '71. M. Lebowitz
Truth of poetry, by M. Hamburger. Review
Nation 213:280-1 S 27 '71. G. Schulman

Periodicals
Magazines; ed. by B. Katz. Library J 96: 3583-4 N 1 '71

Study and teaching
Baseball, film, and poetry. R. W. Reising. Clear House 45:317-18 Ja '71
Building blocks of poetry. N. Nathan and A. Berger. Engl J 60:42-6 Ja '71
Dylan Thomas: the experience, the picture, and the message. R. H. Meyer. bibliog f Engl J 60:199-204 F '71
Electrified term papers; multi-media poetry interpretations. D. McCoy. Engl J 60:107-10 Ja '71
Emily Dickinson: a poet for the now generation. T. D. McFadden. Engl J 60:462-4 Ap '71
Filming poetry; Max Cameron high school, British Columbia. T. Barker. il School Teach Jr/Sr High p 10-11 Ap 5 '71
Hart Crane and the contemporary search. P. J. Sheehan. Engl J 60:1209-13 D '71
Marshall McLuhan and Sir Patrick Spens. R. J. Goba. Engl J 60:62-4 Ja '71
Student poet power. D. J. Hannan. Engl J 60:913-20 O '71
See also
Poetry—Appreciation

Anecdotes, facetiae, satire, etc.
Poet and poem: an approach to genuis. B. N. S. Gooch and T. Westermark. Engl J 60:465-8 Ap '71

Technique
See Poetics

Themes
See Literature—Themes

Translations and translating
Onward and upward with the arts; a study of English and American poetry translated into German and French, with examples. V. Proetz. New Yorker 47:82+ My 22 '71

POETRY (periodical)
Announcement of prize awards for 1971. Poetry 119:112-13 N '71

POETRY, Influence of. See Literature, Influence of

POETRY and morals. See Literature and morals

POETRY and society. See Literature and society

POETRY contests. See Poetry—Competitions

POETRY magazines. See Poetry—Periodicals

POETS
Poets as people. M. R. Weiss. il Sat R 54:52-3 My 15 '71
Poet's workshop; the poet's perceptions and thought associations. F. Trefethen. Writer 85:18-21 Ja '72
See also
Children as poets

POETS, American
Contemporary American poets, ed. by M. Strand. Review
Poetry 119:109-11 N '71. D. Allen
Fresh airs; two collections of New York poetry. Poetry 119:39-44 O '71
Good omen? J. Naiden. Poetry 118:46-7 Ap '71
New England tradition. H. Carruth. bibliog il Am Lib 2:938-48 O '71

POETS, American—*Continued*
Young American poets, ed. by P. Carroll. Review
   Poetry 117:277-80 Ja '71
   See also
Aiken, C.
American poetry
Beatniks
Berge, C.
Berry, W.
Boyle, K.
Ciardi, J.
Crane, H.
Davison, P.
Dickey, J.
Dickinson, E.
Eberhart, R.
Elliott, G. P.
Farley, J.
Feldman, I.
Finkel, D.
Francis, R.
Frumkin, G.
Giovanni, N.
Glück, L.
Goodman, P.
Guthrie, R.
Hazel, R.
Hoffman, D.
Humphries, R.
Ignatow, D.
Kelly, R.
Koch, K.
Levertov, D.
Logan, J.
McGrath, T.
McKuen, R.
Meredith, W.
Merrill, J.
Mezey, R.
Moore, M.
Mundell, W. D.
Nash, O.
Niedecker, L.
Plath, S.
Pound, E.
Ransom, J. C.
Ray, D.
Sandburg, H.
Schevill, J. E.
Simic, C.
Smith, W. J.
Snyder, G.
Stein, G.
Stevens, W.
Tate, J.
Whalen, P. G.
Williams, J.
Wright, J.
POETS, Australian
   See also
Hope, A. D.
POETS, Brazilian
   See also
Brazilian poetry
POETS, British. See Poets, English
POETS, Canadian
   See also
Atwood, M.
Strand, M.
Swenson, M.
Waddington, M.
POETS, Chilean
   See also
Mistral, G.
Neruda, P.
POETS, Chinese
   See also
Mao, T. T.
POETS, Colombian
Poets of rock and sky; the Piedracelistas. M.
   De Semprún Donahue. il Américas 22:19-24
   N '70
POETS, Cuban
   See also
Padilla, H.
POETS, English
   See also
Auden, W. H.
Blake, W.
Bold, A.
Bunting, B.
Chaucer, G
Crozier, A.
Eliot, T. S.
English poetry
Graves, R.
Hamburger, M.
Herbert, G.
Holloway, J.
Hughes, T.
Parvin, D.
Read, H. E.
Rossetti, D. G.
Swinburne, A. C.

POETS, Finnish
   See also
Hollo, A.
POETS, French
   See also
Breton, A.
POETS, Greek
   See also
Cavafy, C. P.
Seferiades, G. S.
POETS, Hungarian
   See also
Csokonai Vitéz, M.
Juhász, F.
POETS, Irish
   See also
Liddy, J.
Yeats, W. B.
POETS, Italian
   See also
Dante Alighieri
POETS, Japanese
   See also
Sakutarō, H.
POETS. Mexican
   See also
Nervo, A.
POETS, Puerto Rican
   See also
Palés Matos, L.
POETS, Roman
   See also
Virgil
POETS, Russian
   See also
Blok, A. A.
Maiakovskii, V. V.
Mandel'shtam, O. E.
Pushkin, A. S.
POETS, Spanish
   See also
Bécquer, G. A.
POETS, Welsh
   See also
Early, T.
Thomas, D.
POETS, playwrights, editors, essayists, novelists club. See PEN club
POFF, Richard H.
Nixon's jinxed southern seat. por Newsweek
   78:22 O 11 '71 *
Poff, the Court and filibusters. America 125:
   276 O 16 '71 *
Tergiversation of Poff. Nat R 23:1156+ O 22
   '71 *
Wise decision. Nation 213:355-6 O 18 '71 *
POGONOMYRMEX badius. See Ants
POGREBIN, Letty Cottin
Working woman. See issues of Ladies' home
   journal
POINDEXTER, David R. jr
Verdict on Poindexter. por Newsweek 77:31
   Ap 26 '71 *
POINSETT, Alex
Black takeover of U.S. cities? il Ebony 26:
   76-9+ N '70
Dilemma of the black policeman. il Ebony 26:
   122-4+ My '71
Dixie schools charade. il Ebony 26:144-8 Ag
   '71
Metamorphosis of Howard university. il
   Ebony 27:110-12+ D '71
Newark a year later. il pors Ebony 27:124-
   6+ N '71
Watchdog for U.S. labor. il pors Ebony 26:
   95-100+ Ap '71
POINSETTIAS
Color it red and call it Christmas. M. Byrne.
   il Nat Wildlife 10:24-5 D '71
POINT, Critical. See Critical point
POINT BARROW, Alaska
Top of the world. D. Butwin. il Sat R 54:35-6
   Jl 31 '71
POINT REYES NATIONAL SEASHORE
Miracle of Point Reyes. W. Duddleson. il
   Liv Wildn 35:15-24 Sum '71
POINTERS (dogs)
Prescription for pointers. J. Falk. il Field &
   S 75:182+ F '71
POINTILLISM. See Impressionism (art)
POINTS, Ignition. See Automobile engines—
   Ignition
POIRET, Paul
Poiret: inspiration for artists, designers, and
   women. J. J. Sweeney. il por Vogue 158:
   186+ S 1 '71 *
POIRIER, Richard
How to be a culture hero. R. Berman. Nat
   R 23:658 Je 15 '71 *
Rap! Rap! Who's there! J. Seelye. New Republic 164:25-6 My 1 '71 *

POISON baits
Eagles are not for killing; illegal use of poison bait in Wyoming. R. Stebbins. il Am For 77:12-14+ O '71

POISON ivy
Poison ivy: its purpose has yet to be established. B. Roueché. il Todays Health 49:38-41+ My '71
That itchy ivy league. P. Kalman. il Field & S 76:54-5+ Jl '71

POISONING. See Poisons

POISONING, Blood. See Blood poisoning

POISONOUS gases. See Gases, Asphyxiating and poisonous

POISONOUS plants
Editorial. C. B. Lees. Horticulture 49:16 N '71
Tips for your home and family; veiled killers. Todays Health 49:69 Ag '71
What do you know about poisonous plants? quiz. J. Daugherty and M. Daugherty. il Sci Digest 70:90-1+ S '71
See also
Poison ivy

POISONOUS snakes. See Snakes

POISONS
Checklist of baby poisons. A. J. Snider. il Sci Digest 70:54-5 N '71
Poisoning of the West; excerpt from Slaughter the animals, poison the earth. J. Olsen. il Read Digest 99:69-74 Ag '71
Poisoning of the West; predator control programs. J. Olsen. il Sports Illus 34:80-4+ Mr 8; 36-40+ Mr 15; 34-6+ Mr 22 '71
See also
Botulism
Carbon monoxide
Lead poisoning
Mercury pollution of rivers, lakes, etc.
Poison baits
Strychnine
Venom

POISONS, Industrial
See also
Cadmium poisoning
Carbon tetrachloride
Mercury poisoning

POITIER, Sidney
Sidney Poitier on Carter G. Woodson. por Negro Hist Bul 33:158 N '70

about
Durango: Poitier meets Belafonte. G. Goodman. il pors Look 35:56-60+ Ag 24 '71 *
Expanding world of Sidney Poitier. L. Robinson. il pors Ebony 27:100-1+ N '71 *

POKER
Sawyer takes the pot anytime; poker heists in Huntsville, Ala. A. D. Livingston. il Sports Illus 35:41-2+ N 15 '71

POKER game robberies. See Robberies and assaults

POKER players
See also
Moss, J. H.

POLAND
See also
Arts and crafts—Poland
Communist party (Poland)
Jews in Poland
Labor and laboring classes—Poland
Land—Poland
Poles

Description and travel
American revisits Poland. J. F. Diggs. il U S News 70:35-6 Je 28 '71

Economic conditions
Exit Gomulka. T. Deutscher. il por Ramp Mag 9:12+ Mr '71
Making ends meet. P. Ben. New Repub 164:14 Ja 30 '71
See also
Labor and laboring classes—Poland

Economic policy
Patching it up. il por Newsweek 77:34 F 1 '71

Foreign relations
Beyond the Gomulka era. A. Bromke. For Affairs 49:480-92 Ap '71

Industries
See also
Construction industry—Poland

Politics and government
Beyond the Gomulka era. A. Bromke. For Affairs 49:480-92 Ap '71
Blue-collar revolution? J. Burnham. Nat R 23:261 Mr 9 '71
Exit Gomulka. T. Deutscher. il por Ramp Mag 9:12+ Mr '71

Iron triangle wobbles. J. K. Anderson. Nat R 23:137-9+ F 9 '71
Meeting with old mates. Time 97:31 F 8 '71
New course in Communist-ruled Poland? R. F. Staar. bibliog f il Cur Hist 60:269-75 My '71
Plan for man's needs. por Time 98:29 Jl 5 '71
Repairing a shaken regime. il por Time 97:30-1 Ja 25 '71
Will it fly? il por Newsweek 78:42+ D 20 '71
See also
Communist party (Poland)

Riots
Prices rise, Gomulka falls. il Sr Schol 97:6+ Ja 18 '71

POLANSKI, Roman
If you don't show violence the way it is . . . B. Weinraub. il pors N Y Times Mag p36-7+ D 12 '71 *
Macbeth by daylight. il por Time 97:45 Ja 25 '71 *
Polish imposition. K. Tynan. pors Esquire 76:122-5+ S '71 *

POLAR bear tagging. See Animal tagging

POLAR bears. See Bears

POLAR deserts. See Deserts

POLAR REGIONS
See also
Ice—Polar Regions
South Pole

POLAR research
See also
Antarctic research

POLARIZATION (light)
Astronomers' new tool; circular polarization. il Sci N 100:75 Jl 31 '71
Clouds of Venus: evidence for their nature. J. E. Hansen and A. Arking. bibliog il Science 171:669-72 F 19 '71
See also
Magneto-optics

POLAROID corporation
Polaroid apartheid: pull tab, wait 60 seconds. D. Schechter. il Ramp Mag 9:47-8+ Mr; 60 Ap '71
Polaroid approach to South Africa. G. M. Houser. Chr Cent 88:249-52 F 24 '71
Polaroid picture; South African issue. il Newsweek 77:66 Ja 25 '71
Polaroid stays put. il Newsweek 79:50+ Ja 10 '72
Reply to accusations against Polaroid: letter. S. A. Benton and others. Phys Today 24:9+ Ap '71

POLAROID Land cameras
Build a scope camera for $45. J. Darr. il Radio-Electr 42:43-5 N '71
Coming: a camera that can focus itself! S. M. Gallager. il Pop Mech 135:82-3 Mr '71
Ed Scully on color; Polaroid Big Shot. il Mod Phot 35:28 Ag '71
Flashy change in Polaroid 400's. D. L. Miller. il Mod Phot 35:20+ My '71
From Polaroid: a $20 one-purpose camera. E. H. Ortner. il Pop Sci 198:32 My '71
From Polaroid: cameras that focus the flash. E. H. Ortner. il Pop Sci 198:68 Ap '71
Is Polaroid turning square? D. L. Miller. il Mod Phot 35:18+ S '71
New Polaroid cameras on the way. Consumer Rep 36:195 Ap '71
Polaroid Big Shot does its thing only. il Consumer Rep 36:586-7 O '71
Polaroid cameras. il Consumer Rep 36:730-3 N '71
Polaroid: the ice breaker; how residents view their own community. J. Greenberg. il Mod Phot 35:82-3 Jl '71
Polaroids Big Shot for color portraits only. il Consumer Bul 54:27-8 S '71
Polaroid's horn of plenty does it again; the Square shooter. il Consumer Bul 54:24-5 O '71
Polaroid's latest: a handy distance finder plus focused flash. il Pop Mech 136:42-3 S '71
Polaroid's model changeover. il Consumer Bul 54:10-12 Ag '71
Techniques tomorrow; Polaroid scanning camera. B. Sherman. Mod Phot 35:44+ Ag '71
What's new about the Polaroid Colorpax III? Consumer Rep 36:337-8 Je '71

POLAROID negative material. See Photography—Negatives

POLE vaulting. See Vaulting (sport)

POLES
Passel of Poles to be proud of. il Life 72:71 Ja 14 '72

POLES, Wood. See Wood poles

POLICE
See also
Agents provocateurs
Computers—Police use
Detectives
Negro police
Strikes—United States—Police

Community relations
See Police—Public relations

Electronic equipment
See Electronics in criminal investigation, espionage, etc.

Equipment and supplies
Computerized police systems in the U.S? L. Webb. Cur 132:14-20 S '71
Weapons that don't kill. il Newsweek 78:81 O 18 '71

Health and hygiene
Training police sergeants in early warning signs of emotional upset. R. J. Sokol and M. Reiser. bibliog Ment Hy 55:303-7 Jl '71

Psychological aspects
See Police psychology

Public relations
Cop named Joe; community relations project, Asbury Park, N.J. F. Knebel. il Look 35:15-19 Jl 27 '71
Editor's choice; to be professional: police officer in William Steig's Sylvester and the magic pebble. J. G. Burke. il Am Lib 2:159 F '71
Gain mutiny; Oakland, Calif. por Newsweek 78:35 D 27 '71
Overdue; Sambo and Sylvester. D. MacCann. Wilson Lib Bul 45:880-1 My '71; Discussion. 46:43 S '71
Ox of a different color: Sylvester and the magic pebble; Little Black Sambo. J. F. Krug and J. A. Harvey. Am Lib 2:532-4 My '71
Police: ally or enemy of the comprehensive community mental health center? H. G. Whittington. bibliog Ment Hy 55:55-9 Ja '71
Poor old Sylvester and the magic pebble. Am Lib 2:226 Mr '71
Threat to freedom: Sylvester and the magic pebble in Toledo. R. V. Fitzgerald. il por Library J 96:1429-30 Ap 15 '71

Training
Pros & cons on joining the police. M. Spiegel. il Mech Illus 67:41-3+ Jl '71
Role of police forces in a changing world; address, August 13, 1971. U. A. Johnson. Dept State Bul 65:280-3 S 13 '71

Brazil
Brazilian death squads. America 125:80-1 Ag 21 '71
Rio's death squad. Newsweek 78:60 Ag 9 '71

California
See also
Santa Barbara County, Calif.—Police

France
See also
Paris—Police

Great Britain
British crime prevention. H. R. Horwitz. Am Scholar 40:677-85 Aut '71
Farewell to Bill Sikes. il Time 98:29-30 S 6 '71
See also
London—Police
Police power

Guatemala
Good neighbor; training and advising of Guatemalan military and police. New Repub 164:9 Ap 24 '71

Japan
Japan's way with protest. A. Axelbank. Nation 212:684 My 31 '71

Russia
See also
Secret service—Russia

Sweden
Copology; interview. P. Wahlöö; M. Sjöwall. New Yorker 47:28 My 22 '71

United States
Case of the Panther 28. Sr Schol 98:8-9 Ap 19 '71
Copology; interview. P. Wahlöö; M. Sjöwall. New Yorker 47:28 My 22 '71

Disarmament at home. Nation 211:643-4 D 21 '70
How to solve the police crisis; interviews, ed. by G. M. Chamberlain, C. M. Kelley; J. V. Wilson; J. P. Howard. pors Am City 86:94-5+ S; 88+ O; 106-8 N '71
How we handcuff our police. J. F. Ahern and V. H Bernstein. Redbook 136:79+ Ap '71
Police; P. V. Murphy and Q. Tamm excluded from White House meetings. New Repub 164:6 Je 19 '71
Politics of problems; New York's Commissioner of police not invited to conference in Washington. Nation 212:770 Je 21 '71
Reporter at large; C. R. Garry's list of Panthers allegedly killed by police, with case histories. E. J. Epstein. New Yorker 46:45-6+ F 13 '71; Reply with rejoinder. E. Kosner. 47:125 My 8 '71
White House and station house. il Newsweek 77:26-7 Je 14 '71
Who would want to be a cop? H. Whitman. Read Digest 99:168-9 S '71
See also
Police—Public relations
Police power
United States—Justice, Department of—Law enforcement assistance administration
also subhead Police under names of cities, e.g. New York (city)—Police

POLICE, State
Training
Pros & cons on joining the police. M. Spiegel. il Mech Illus 67:41-3+ Jl '71

POLICE automobiles. See Automobiles, Police

POLICE boats
Fire-police boat in one package, San Diego, Calif. il Am City 86:37 Ap '71
Police patrol boats cut crime, save lives; Miami Beach, Fla. il Am City 86:33 Jl '71
Pollution and policing; Lake George patrol. M. Crook. il Yachting 129:70+ Je '71

POLICE communication systems
911 goes regional; Omaha, Neb. Am City 86:37 Ap '71

POLICE corruption
Cops on the take; Knapp commission hearings. il por Newsweek 78:48+ N 1 '71
Crusader; F. Serpico's testimony on corruption. por Newsweek 77:24 My 31 '71
Guarding the guardians; hearings by Knapp commission. il por Time 98:22+ N 1 '71
Murphy among the meat-eaters. T. Buckley. il pors N Y Times Mag p 10-11+ D 19 '71
New York's rotten apples; report of the Knapp commission. Newsweek 78:78-9 Jl 12 '71
Of many things; Murphy and command responsibility. T. M. Gannon. America 125: inside cover S 18 '71
Plan to keep our police honest. A. Reiss, jr. il Todays Health 49:70-1 N '71
Policing the police; New York city. Newsweek 78:41 S 6 '71
Taking dirty money; New York city. il por Time 98:20 S 13 '71
Three ingredients of graft. W. J. Byron. il America 125:532-3 D 18 '71

POLICE ethics
Observing police misconduct. Sci N 99:367-8 My 29 '71

POLICE-fire boats. See Police boats

POLICE helicopters. See Helicopters in police work

POLICE in literature. See Literature—Themes

POLICE murders. See Murder

POLICE power
Judicial attempts to control the police. L. P. Tiffany. bibliog f Cur Hist 61:13-19+ Jl '71
Justice British style; lessons U.S. lawyers see. il U S News 71:36-7 Ag 2 '71
Public safety and police powers. America 124: 530 My 22 '71

POLICE psychology
Policeman complains; interview, ed. by R. Coles; excerpt from Middle Americans. il N Y Times Mag p 11+ Je 13 '71; Reply. F. C. Hughes. p2+ Jl 11 '71
When the cops pick up a black kid. Trans-Action 8:6+ N '70

POLICE records
Ever been arrested? DC court of appeals decision on arrest records. R. Cassidy. New Repub 165:14-16 D 4 '71
Presumption of guilt; maintenance and distribution of mistaken arrest records. T. R. Reid, 3d. New Repub 164:15-16 Ja 16 '71

POLICE records on microfilm
Microfilm system to aid law enforcement;
Essex County, N. J. il Am City 86:24 My
'71
Turn police files into information centers;
Baton Rouge, La. E. O. Bauer, jr. and E. B.
Morel. il Am City 86:105 My '71

POLICE-school cooperation
Most special ombudsman: a police-community
ambassador in Niagara Falls, N.Y. W. Vanderlip. Clear House 46:109 O '71

POLICE state. See Totalitarianism

POLICEMENS wives
Lonely fear of a policeman's wife; life of
Mary Ellen Streske. G. Sheehy. il McCalls
98:96-9+ Mr '71

POLICIES, Insurance. See Insurance—Policies

POLIOMYELITIS
How poliomyelitis was brought under control. P. Morrison. Sci Am 224:125-9 Ap '71

POLISH, David
Religious meanings in Jewish secularism. il
Chr Cent 88:649-55 My 26 '71

POLISH AMERICANS
One-man crusade against the Polish joke.
M. Durham. il por Life 72:70-1 Ja 14 '72

POLISH literature
Introduction to modern Polish literature. J.
M. Seamon. bibliog Engl J 60:38-41 Ja '71

POLISHERS, Electric
See also
Floor machines

POLISHES. See Furniture polishes; Polishing
materials

POLISHING machines
How to make a scalloped polishing wheel.
W. G. Waggoner. il Pop Sci 198:124 Ap '71

POLISHING materials
Fork clean is a special product necessary?
il Consumer Bul 54:39 My '71
See also
Furniture polishes

POLITBURO. See Communist party (Russia)—
Political bureau

POLITICAL affiliation. See Party affiliation

POLITICAL attitudes
Plausible and the wacky; conspiracy. L. P.
Ribuffo. Nation 213:251-4 S 20 '71
See also
Public opinion
Youth—Political attitudes

POLITICAL bureau of the Communist party.
See Communist party (Russia)—Political
bureau

POLITICAL campaigns
Battle for Congress: early look at '72 cam-
paign. il U S News 72:56-9 Ja 3 '72
Columbia conservatives for Buckley. J. Col-
lins. Mlle 72:138 Ja '71
How to run & win. J. Higgins; P. J. Mc-
Caffrey. Nation 211:648-53 D 21 '70
See also
Campaign funds
Campaign issues
Candidates, Political
Television in politics
also subhead Politics and government un-
der names of countries, states, cities, e.g.
New York (city)—Politics and government

India
Mrs Gandhi makes her bid. il por Newsweek
77:36-7 Mr 1 '71
Mrs Gandhi's goal: beating old guard. J. N.
Wallace. il por U S News 70:87 Mr 8 '71
Of sacred cows and squint-eyed uncles. il
Time 97:27 Mr 1 '71

Indonesia
Indonesia: things look up. T. Clifton and
J. Williams. il Newsweek 78:41-2 Jl 12 '71

Vietnam (Republic)
And then there were two. Time 98:29 Ag
16 '71
Mudslingers. il por Newsweek 78:38 Ag 2 '71
Trials of Ngo Cong Duc. il por Time 98:24-
5 S 6 '71

POLITICAL candidates. See Candidates, Political

POLITICAL cartoons. See Caricatures and
cartoons

POLITICAL clubs and associations
See also
Common cause (political organization)

France
Monsieur Charly; Service d'action civique. il
Newsweek 79:29 Ja 10 '72

POLITICAL contributors. See Campaign funds

POLITICAL conventions
See also
National conventions (political)
National conventions, Democratic
National conventions, Republican

POLITICAL corruption. See Politics, Corruption in

POLITICAL crimes and offenses
See also
Insurgency
Terrorism

Greece, Modern
See also
Political prisoners—Greece, Modern

India
Every day St Valentine's day; bitter feuding
between Marxist Communist party and
Naxalites in Calcutta. Time 97:31-2 Mr 15
'71

POLITICAL defectors. See Defectors, Political

POLITICAL education. See Political science—
Study and teaching

POLITICAL ethics
Pentagon papers; games presidents and oth-
er people play. E. J. McCarthy. New Re-
pub 165:14-17 Jl 10 '71
Pentagon papers; implications of deceit by
government. N. Cousins. Sat R 54:16 Jl 3;
18 Jl 10 '71
Radical man, by C. Hampden-Turner. Review
Nation 212:472-4 Ap 12 '71. W. Anderson
Three saints in politics. P. H. Douglas. Am
Scholar 40:223-32 Spr '71
See also
Government, Resistance to
Politics, Corruption in

POLITICAL films. See Moving pictures—Political films

POLITICAL forecasting
Battle for Congress: early look at '72 cam-
paign. il U S News 72:56-9 Ja 3 '72
Battle for the youth vote. R. T. Gray. il
Nations Bsns 59:60-2+ O '71
Four-year itch. H. Sidey. Life 71:4 N 26 '71
Governors size up the '72 election. il U S
News 71:26-8 S 27 '71
How will youth vote? il Newsweek 78:28-30+
O 25 '71
Is 1972 here already? D. Lawrence. U S
News 71:92 Ag 16 '71
Nixon's chances in '72, as top Republicans
see them. il U S News 71:37-9 Ag 9 '71
Nixon's chances in 1972. il por U S News 71:
16-18 Jl 5 '71
Outlook, '72: Nixon vs. the field: strategies
take shape. il U S News 72:50-3 Ja 10 '72
Six scenarios for 1980. W. Laqueur. il N Y
Times Mag p8-9+ D 19 '71
TRB from Washington: Nixon will lose. New
Repub 166:6 Ja 1 '72
Twenty-one theses; a radical perspective on
the '70s. A. I. Waskow. Commonweal 93:
463-5 F 12 '71
Why the '72 election is baffling the forecas-
ters. il U S News 70:40-2+ Je 7 '71

POLITICAL fundamentalism. See Conservatism

POLITICAL games. See Games

POLITICAL informers. See Informers (law)

POLITICAL kidnapping. See Kidnapping

POLITICAL leadership. See Leadership

POLITICAL liberty. See Liberty

POLITICAL literature
Literary criticism and literary radicals. I.
Howe. Am Scholar 41:113-20 Wint '71

POLITICAL parties

Membership
See Party affiliation

Canada
See also
Social credit party

Chile
Change in Chile; Christian democrats. J.
Deedy. Commonweal 93:506 F 26 '71
Chile's Che Guevara? Miristas' Commandante
or G. J. Liendo. N. Ossa. Nat R 23:307-8
Mr 23 '71

France
Radical alternative, by J. J. Servan-Schreiber
and M. Albert. Review
America 125:131-2 S 4 '71. F. K. Kelly
See also
Communist party (France)

POLITICAL parties—*Continued*

Germany (Federal Republic)

Adolf on the skids; defeat of West Germany's National democrats. il Time 97:35 My 10 '71

Challenger with two hats; new chairman of Christian democratic union. por Time 98: 45-6 O 18 '71

Choice not an echo; new leader of the Christian democratic union. il por Newsweek 78: 41 D 20 '71

Great Britain

See also
Labor party (Great Britain)

India

Every day St Valentine's day; bitter feuding between Marxist Communist party and Naxalites in Calcutta. Time 97:31-2 Mr 15 '71

India: a clear mandate for Mrs Gandhi. il por Time 97:22-3 Mr 22 '71

Indonesia

Indonesia's Suharto seeks vote of confidence in July 3 parliamentary election. B. Howell. Chr Cent 88:802-3 Je 30 '71

Italy

Almirante is no M-s---i-- yet. M. S. Davis. il por N Y Times Mag p27+ Je 6 '71

Il Duce's shadow; Italian social movement. il Newsweek 77:44-5 Je 28 '71

Sounding the alarm; neo-Fascist Italian social movement. il Time 97:40 Je 14 '71

Voters' *corrivo*; neo-Fascist party, Movimento sociale italiano gains. il Time 97:33 Je 28 '71

Japan

Conservative dominance in Japanese politics. G. L. Curtis. Cur Hist 60:207-12+ Ap '71

Russia

See also
Communist party (Russia)

United States

Candidates answer Senior's queries; third party presidential candidates: any chance of success or significant influence on the major parties? il Sr Schol 99:8-9 N 1 '71

Dr Spock for president; assembly meets in Dallas to launch fourth party. W. Murchison, jr. Nat R 23:1470 D 31 '71

Starting a fourth party. P. Barnes. New Repub 165:19-21 Jl 24 '71

Three, four, many parties? Nat R 23:357 Ap 6 '71

Trouble on the two-party line. H. Sidey. il Life 70:4 Je 4 '71

See also
Communist party (United States)
Democratic party
National conventions (political)
Populist party
Republican party

POLITICAL patronage. See Patronage, Political

POLITICAL philosophy

Between nothingness and paradise, by G. Niemeyer. Review
Nat R 23:875-6 Ag 10 '71. E. Sandoz

Hannibal for president. G. W. Johnson. Am Scholar 41:29-39 Wint '71

Notes and comment; views of L. Powell. New Yorker 47:43 N 13 '71

Nuclear tyranny and the divine right of kings. G. E. Christianson. il Bul Atom Sci 27:44-6 Ja '71

See also
Communism and democracy
Conservatism
Democracy
Liberalism
Political thought
Racism

POLITICAL poetry

Return of political poetry. T. Gitlin. Commonweal 94:375-80 Jl 23 '71

POLITICAL pressure. See Pressure groups

POLITICAL prisoners

Man's inhumanity to man; letter. M. M. Solomon. N Y Times Mag p6 Ag 22 '71

Who (and what) is a political prisoner? Time essay. L. Morrow. il Time 98:18-19 S 6 '71

See also
Ransom

Brazil

Daughter's lament; case of Rubens Beyrodt Paiva and family. Newsweek 77:42 F 15 '71

Price goes up; exchange rate on kidnapped ambassadors. Newsweek 77:44 Ja 25 '71

This is theater; Living theater troupe of New York. por Newsweek 78:40 Ag 16 '71

To the president of Brazil; open letter from a group of American churchmen. Chr Cent 88:1462-3 D 15 '71

China (People's Republic)

Hostage in Peking; condensation. A. Grey. il Read Digest 98:181-8+ Ja '71

Present from Chou; release of Richard Fecteau and Mary Ann Harbert. il Newsweek 78:25-6 D 27 '71

Two-fifths thaw; P. Fecteau and M. A. Harbert released from Chinese prison. pors Time 98:8 D 27 '71

Greece, Modern

Conspiracy of conscience; A. Fleming. il por Time 98:53 O 11 '71

I accept it; Lady Fleming, others. por Newsweek 78:38 O 11 '71

Letter in a bottle. G. Mangakis. il Atlan 228:53-9 O '71

Silenced lady; A. Fleming and others. por Newsweek 78:36+ S 13 '71

There's the Greece of Greeks and there's the tourists' Greece. A. Sotiris. il N Y Times Mag p 12-14+ Jl 25 '71

Two Greeces. M. Goldbloom. il Commonweal 93:441-4 F 5 '71

Israel

Terrorism & preventive detention: the case of Israel. A. M. Dershowitz; discussion. Commentary 51:33-4+ Je '71

Northern Ireland

Everyone but the terrorists. S. Cronin. Commonweal 94:470-1 S 17 '71

Russia

Government of Doctor Caligari: Soviet mental hospitals; address, December 3, 1971. B. D. Wolfe. Nat R 23:1461-2 D 31 '71

Psychoadaptation; or, How to handle dissenters. por Time 98:44-5 S 27 '71

Question of madness; excerpt. Z. A. Medvedev and R. A. Medvedev. il pors N Y Times Mag p34-5+ N 7 '71

Vietnam (Republic)

Vietnamese student; letter. D. Truong. New Repub 165:31 Jl 3 '71

POLITICAL psychology

Shafting of Mr Average. S. Alsop. Newsweek 77:132 Ap 19 '71

See also
Political attitudes
Propaganda
Public opinion

POLITICAL publicity. See Propaganda; Television in politics

POLITICAL responsibility. See Responsibility

POLITICAL rhetoric. See Rhetoric

POLITICAL science

See also
Authority
Civil rights
Decision making (political science)
Democracy
Divine right of kings
Fascism
Liberalism
Liberty
Majorities
Municipal government
Nationalism
Nations
Political philosophy
Political thought
Power (social sciences)
Radicalism
Totalitarianism
Utopias

Bibliography

Resources for preparing new voters; growing up political. Schol Teach Jr/Sr High p 10-11+ Ja '72

History

Politics and the stages of growth, by W. W. Rostow. Review
Nat R 23:1059+ S 24 '71. A. W. Green

Politics of authenticity, by M. Berman. Review
Commonweal 94:362-4 Jl 9 '71. L. Kriegel

Study and teaching

Fellows: program to train college students in city government in New York. New Yorker 46:28-30 Ja 16 '71

Preparing the new voters. C. H. Harrison. il Schol Teach Jr/Sr High p6-9 Ja '72

POLITICAL science—Study and teaching—
Continued
Telecture: an adventure in learning; social studies teachers at Dover high school, N.J. R. Schwartz and R. McNeely. Clear House 46:215-17 D '71
What schools are doing to train young voters. il U S News 71:92-5 O 18 '71
See also
Citizenship, Education for
Robert A. Taft institute of government

Aids and devices
Resources for preparing new voters: growing up political. Schol Teach Jr/Sr High p 10-11+ Ja '72
POLITICAL theory. See Political philosophy
POLITICAL thought
Roots of political thought. A. Lejeune. Nat R 23:88-9 Ja 26 '71
POLITICS
See also
Conservatism
Liberalism
Music and politics
Political campaigns
Political ethics
Political science
Television in politics
Women and politics
Women in politics
also subhead Politics and government under names of countries, states, etc. e.g. India—Politics and government

Anecdotes, facetiae, satire, etc.
Cruise director on the Titanic; A. Buchwald's column. T. Meehan. il pors N Y Times Mag p 10-11+ Ja 2 '72
See also
Presidents—United States—Anecdotes, facetiae, satire, etc.

Terminology
Words in the news (cont) Sr Schol 99:20 O 4 '71
POLITICS, Corruption in
Congressman convicted; case of J. Dowdy. por Time 99:13-14 Ja 10 '72
See also
Campaign funds

Illinois
Off to the races. il Newsweek 78:27-8 O 11 '71

Italy
Unsinkable Mafia; parliamentary report. il Newsweek 78:35+ Jl 26 '71

New Jersey
Weeding the Garden State. il por Time 98:12-13 Jl 19 '71

New York (state)
Percentage of the take, by W. Goodman. Review
Bsns W p8 F 20 '71. J. Patterson
Commentary 51:95-6 My '71. R. Starr
Life 70:10 F 26 '71. F. J. Cook

Texas
Promoter and the crime buster; relations between F. W. Sharp and W. R. Wilson, jr. D. Jackson. il pors Life 71:59-60+ S 24 '71

Vietnam (Republic)
Democracy in reverse? Newsweek 78:45 Ag 30 '71
Letter from Saigon. R. Shaplen. New Yorker 47:96+ S 11 '71
Making of a loser. il Time 98:24+ S 13 '71
Politics vs. democracy. Newsweek 78:25 S 6 '71
Saigon shambles. Nation 213:165 S 6 '71
South Viet Nam's fifth no. il Time 98:23-4 S 6 '71
Still a Thieu-way race in South Viet Nam. il por Time 98:23-4 Ag 30 '71
Viet Nam: a cancerous affliction. il Time 97: 22-3 Je 7 '71
POLITICS and business. See Business—
Political aspects
POLITICS and Christianity. See Church and politics
POLITICS and education
Politics and learned societies. D. S. Seckinger. bibliog Sch & Soc 99:345-6 O '71
What educational decisions by whom? J. I. Goodlad. Ed Digest 37:4-8 O '71
See also
College students—Political activities
Colleges and universities—Political control
High school students—Political activities
Teachers—Political activities

POLITICS and literature. See Literature and politics
POLITICS and music. See Music and politics
POLITICS and Negroes. See Negroes and politics
POLITICS and newspapers. See Newspapers and politics
POLITICS and religion
Conciliarism in America: what difference does it make? Chr Cent 88:1125 S 29 '71
See also
Church and politics
POLITICS and science. See Science and state
POLITICS and war
Dissent in three American wars, by S. E. Morison and others. Review
Trans-Action 8:100-2 N '70. S. Tax
POLITOFF, Alberto L. See Socolar, S. J. jt. auth.
POLK, Judd
International competition and production; address, January 14, 1971. Vital Speeches 37: 286-8 F 15 '71
POLK COUNTY, Fla.
Zoning by referendum. il Am City 86:98+ D '71
POLL lists. See Voters, Registration of
POLLACK, Harriet. See Smith, A. B. jt. auth.
POLLACK, Herman
Objectives of international cooperation in science and technology; statement, February 15, 1971. Dept State Bul 64:837-41 Je 28 '71
POLLACK, Irving Meyer
Sleuth of Wall Street. G. R. Rosen. por Duns 97:71-2 Mr '71 *
POLLAK, Richard
Are we about to plunder Alaska? Cur 129:39-46 My '71
POLLARD, Doug
Lumberjacks, miners, tourists keep a unique bookstore busy and solvent. J. R. Hunt. il por Pub W 199:57-8 Mr 8 '71 *
POLLARD, Frederick
Rose bowl star, 56 years ago. J. Barry. il pors Ebony 27:100-2+ Ja '72 *
POLLARD, Fritz. See Pollard, Frederick
POLLARD, Richard
Man who really relishes photo contests. R. Graves. por Life 71:3 Jl 9 '71 *
POLLEN, Daniel A. and others
How does the striate cortex begin the reconstruction of the visual world? bibliog il Science 173:74-7 Jl 2 '71
POLLEN
Correlation between gametophytic and sporophytic characteristics in zea mays L. D. L. Mulcahy. bibliog il Science 171:1155-6 Mr 19 '71
Pollen, a key to the history of the earth. R. J. N. Muller. bibliog il Sci Digest 70:19-23 Jl '71
Unique type of angiosperm pollen from the family annonaceae. J. W. Walker. bibliog il Science 172:565-7 My 7 '71
POLLETT, Jeanne
Legal rights for writers. Writer 84:22-4 Ap '71
POLLINATION. See Fertilization of plants
POLLOCK, George H.
Glückel von Hameln: Bertha Pappenheim's idealized ancestor. bibliog Am Imago 28: 216-27 Fall '71
POLLS, Public opinion. See Public opinion polls
POLLUTION
Case against the disaster lobby; address, January 28, 1971. T. R. Shepard, jr. il Liv Wildn 35:25-30 Sum '71
Causes of pollution. B. Commoner and others. bibliog il Environ 13:2-19 Ap '71
Closing circle, by B. Commoner. Review
Bsns W p 13 O 23 '71. S. B. Shepard
Earth watch. S. Lindsay. See issues of Saturday review
Ecological problem. R. Hotz. Aviation W 94:11 Ap 12 '71
Environment (cont of) Environmental sciences. See issues of Science news
Environment yes: hysteria no. il Bet Hom & Gard 49:30 Ap; 20+ My; 28+ Je; 4+ Jl; 12+ Ag; 34+ S; 14+ O; 18+ N '71
Environmental dilemma. P. E. Waggoner. il Horticulture 49:30-3+ My '71
Exaggeration: the other pollution peril; interview. P. Handler. pors Nation Bsns 59:30-3 Ap '71
Haste makes waste: pollution and entropy. H. A. Bent. bibliog il por Chem 44:6-15 O '71
The island that is. D. Plowden. il Audubon 73: 61-8 Mr '71

POLLUTION—*Continued*
Last days of mankind, by S. Mines. Review
  Am For 77:36+ **Ag** '71. M. Bush
Metallic menaces in the environment. G. By-
  linsky. il Fortune 83:110-13+ Ja '71
Pollution in all its incredible ugliness; win-
  ning photographs in the 1970 contest. Nat
  Wildlife 9:26-8 F '71
Pollution: talking not doing. il Chem 44:23-4
  N '71
Price of progress; conclusions of B. Com-
  moner. Time 98:79 N 1 '71
Reporter at large. B. Commoner. New York-
  er 47:44-8+ O 2 '71
S.O.S. environment; symposium. il UNESCO
  Courier 24:4-32 Jl '71
Silent servant; packaging industry and the
  problems of pollution; address, October 4,
  1971. J. H. Alexander. Vital Speeches 38:
  112-15 D 1 '71
Urban pollution: many long years ago. J. A.
  Tarr. il Am Heritage 22:65-9+ O '71
Why we are losing the battle against pollu-
  tion. F. Graham, jr. il Todays Health 49:14-
  15 S '71
Your environment and what you can do
  about it, by R. Saltonstall, jr. Review
  Consumer Bul 54:13+ O '71
  See also
Air pollution
Cruisers (pleasure boats)—Pollution
Paper industry—Pollution
Pesticides and the environment
Power plants—Pollution
Radioactive pollution
Steel works—Pollution
United States — Congress — Senate — Public
  works, Committee on—Environmental pol-
  lution, Subcommittee on
Water pollution

Anecdotes, facetiae, satire, etc.
Parting shots: the diary of a polluter. J.
  Howard. Life 70:71-2 Ap 23 '71

Bibliography
Children, books, and pollution. J. Verts.
  Am For 77:54-6 **Ag** '71

Control
Business and society; address, January 27,
  1971. R. W. Sarnoff. Vital Speeches 37:273-
  5 F 15 '71
Camp environment checklist. W. H. Wads-
  worth. Camp Mag 43:11-12 Je '71
Clean machine; U.S. steel Texas works. il
  Time 97:46 My 17 '71
Earth week. J. Shepherd; A. Rothenberg; M.
  M. McGlynn. il Look 35:19-30 My 4 '71
Environment boom; excerpts from Oppor-
  tunities in environmental careers. O. Fan-
  ning. il Sat R 54:60 My 1 '71
Has the environment a future? M. I. Gold-
  man. Nation 213:358-61 O 18 '71
How private industry combats pollution. il
  U S News 70:44-6+ F 15 '71
How REAP helps you pay for pollution con-
  trols. G. Reynolds. Farm J 95:38 Mr '71
Industry clean-up. B. Ford. il Sci Digest 70:
  80-5 D '71
1971 student burgesses at colonial Williams-
  burg; zeroing in on pollution. il Sr Schol
  98:19-20 Mr 29 '71
On urbanization: a worldwide process; excerpts from address, November 1970. B.
  Ward. por Sr Schol Teach ed 97:3 Ja 11
  '71
Pollution cure must not be worse than
  disease; reprint. F. R. Shumway. Yachting 130:29 O '71
Pollution fighters' newsletter. See issues of
  Popular mechanics
Pollution snoop troops; monitoring and surveillance program in St Petersburg, Fla. il
  Am City 86:102 O '71
Putting PEP into fighting pollution; Pollu-
  tion and environmental problems. A. Fer-
  rara. il Org Gard & Farm 18:144-18 Mr '71
Reducing pollution involves a trade-off! Con-
  sumer Bul 54:13-14 S '71
Responsibility of being organic. R. Rodale.
  il Org Gard & Farm 18:34-8 Mr '71
To catch a polluter. M. Palmer. il McCalls
  99:52 O '71
We must stop population growth. W. H.
  Davis. Field & S 76:20+ Je '71
What you can do now to fight pollution.
  A. Lake. il Redbook 137:56-7+ Jl '71
Who'll call the tune on pollution control?
  interview, ed. by B. Coffman. S. Aldrich.
  por Farm J 95:G1 Ap '71

You can get federal funds to control feedlot
  runoff; REAP funds. B. Eftink. il Suc Farm
  69:23 O '71
  See also
Aerospace industries—Pollution control ac-
  tivities
Electronics in pollution control
Environmental movement
Industry and the environmental movement
United States—Environmental protection
  agency
United States—National industrial pollution
  control council

Conferences
Pollution teleconference. Sat R 54:44-5 Jl
  3 '71
Second United States-Japan meeting on pollution held at Washington; joint communique, June 2, 1971. Dept State Bul 64:
  831-2 Je 28 '71
  See also
United Nations conference on the human
  environment

Economic aspects
Cleanup collides with the GNP; Netherlands.
  il Bsns W p35 Jl 10 '71
Cost of cleanliness. Sci Am 225:42 O '71
Dirty deal? smog control and jobs at Union
  carbide. Sr Schol 98:15-16 Mr 8 '71
Dow cleans up pollution at no net cost. il
  Bsns W p32-5 Ja 1 '72
Drive to find jobs for victims of pollution
  war. U S News 71:68-9 D 6 '71
Economic growth and ecology: an econo-
  mist's view. W. W. Heller. bibliog Mo La-
  bor R 94:14-21 N '71
Economics of pollution; who pays for the
  cleanup? il Sr Schol 98:11-12 Mr 8 '71
Economist's approach to pollution and its
  control; adaptation of address, December
  1970. R. M. Solow. bibliog Science 173:498-
  503 Ag 6 '71
Environment vs. poverty. H. C. Wallich.
  Newsweek 77:87 Je 7 '71
Environmental control and economic systems. H. Brabyn. il UNESCO Courier 24:
  24-7 Jl '71
Environmental economics, by T. D. Crock-
  er and A. J. Rogers. Review
  Nation 213:314-16 O 4 '71. S. D. Antler
From big polluters come small profits. Bsns
  W p25-6 Ag 7 '71
Measuring the real costs. Sci N 100:75-6 Jl
  31 '71
Mounting bill for pollution control. G. By-
  linsky. il Fortune 84:87-9+ Jl '71
Next big industry: environmental improve-
  ment. J. B. Quinn. il Harvard Bsns R 49:
  120-4+ S '71
No more golden eggs? il Nations Bsns 59:
  72-6 O '71
Official report on the cost of a cleaner en-
  vironment; excerpts from report of the
  Council on environmental quality. U S
  News 71:51 Ag 23 '71
Polluters raise the cleanup ante. il Bsns W
  p46 My 15 '71
Pollution and industry: pros, cons of growing
  fight. il U S News 71:60-2 N 22 '71
Price of cleaning up. il Newsweek 78:68-9
  Ag 16 '71
Saving the crusade. P. F. Drucker. il Harper
  244:66-71 Ja '72
Taxing U.S. polluters; excerpt from testi-
  mony before the Joint economic committee
  of Congress. L. I. Moss. Sat R 54:51 Ag
  7 '71
Wait a minute: address. July 15, 1971. M. H.
  Stans. Vital Speeches 37:690-3 S 1 '71
Way to finance environmental protection;
  proposed 10 per cent surtax on personal
  and corporate-income tax liabilities. A. K.
  Browne. Am City 86:6 Ja '71
What the pollution fight will cost business. il
  Time 97:82 My 31 '71
Where pollution control is slowing indus-
  trial growth. il U S News 71:47-50 Ag 23
  '71
  See also
Air pollution—Control—Economic aspects

History
Pollution: precedent and prospect. C. C.
  Humpstone. For Affairs 50:325-38 Ja '72

International aspects
Pollution: precedent and prospect. C. C.
  Humpstone. For Affairs 50:325-38 Ja '72

Patents
Trends: patent applications; priority processing to aid in curbing of environmental
  abuses. il Bul Atom Sci 27:33 Ja '71

POLLUTION—*Continued*

Economic aspects

Don't broadcast this, but pollution can get you fired! reprint. C. Gillespie. il Audubon 73:103-5 Ja '71

Dynamite in pollution; Jacksonville, Fla. TV station WJXT reports on local polluters. C. Gillespie; discussion. Nation 211:674; 212:258+ D 28 '70. Mr 1 '71

Economic growth and ecology: a biologist's view; with tables. B. Commoner. bibliog Mo Labor R 94:3-13 N '71

Laws and legislation

Ecologist; Richard Nixon's proposals. il Newsweek 77:23 F 22 '71

Great billboard battle. C. G. Rogers. il McCalls 99:36 N '71

Lip service vs. action. L. Edgerton and J. Edgerton. il Nat Wildlife 9:28-31 Je '71

Nixon offers large, mixed bag on environment. C. Holden. Science 171:659 F 19 '71

Nixon tries to follow Muskie's cleanup act. Bsns W p21-2 F 6 '71

Paying for pollution by the pound; effluent fees. il Bsns W p78 S 4 '71

Peace and pollution. J. B. Craig. Am For 77:12 Ag '71

Senator Muskie's foreign pollution policy; address to UN symposium, May 21, 1971. J. Lear. Sat R 54:20+ Je 12 '71

What the pollution fight will cost business. il Time 97:82 My 31 '71

See also
Air pollution—Laws and legislation
Water pollution—Laws and legislation

Measurement

Earth resource technology used in pollution detection. B. M. Elson. il Aviation W 95:46-9 D 13 '71

See also
Air pollution—Measurement
Oil pollution of rivers, harbors, etc.—Measurement

Physiological effects

See also
Environmental health

Protests, demonstrations, etc, against

See Environmental movement—Marches, rallies, etc.

Research

Pollution. J. MacQuarrie. il Horticulture 49:28-9+ Je '71

See also
Air pollution—Research

Asia

Pollution of Asia; report of the Conference on Asian environments. M. T. Farvar and others. bibliog il por Environ 13:10-17 O '71

Europe, Eastern

Smog Marxes on. Sr Schol 98:12-14 Mr 15 '71

Hawaii

Goodbye to you, blue Hawaii. il Life 71:58-64 N 26 '71

Pollution in paradise. il Newsweek 77:84 Mr 1 '71

Italy

Dark days in sunny Italy. il Time 97:44 Mr 15 '71

Japan

Kogai: environmental disruption in Japan. S. Tsuru. il UNESCO Courier 24:6-13 Jl '71

Russia

Soviet pesticides. P. R. Pryde. bibliog il Environ 13:16-24 N '71

POLLUTION control devices (airplanes) See Airplanes—Pollution control devices

POLLUTION control devices (motor vehicles) See Motor vehicles—Pollution control devices

POLLUTION control industries
See also
Johnson service company
Research-Cottrell, inc.

POLLUTION-industrial complex. See Industry and the environmental movement

POLLUTION of lakes. See Water pollution

POLLUTION policy. See Environmental policy

POLLUTION research. See Pollution—Research

POLNER, Murray
Sense of isolation. Nation 213:230-4 S 20 '71

POLO, Marco
Traveler nobody would believe. L. Thomas. il Read Digest 99:129-33 Jl '71 *

Drama

Travels of Marco Polo. A. Thane. Plays 30:81-92 My '71

POLO
Revival of an old rock festival; Britain and the U.S. H. McIlvanney. il Sports Illus 35:18-19 Ag 9 '71
See also
Bicycle polo

POLOS, Nicholas C.
Adventures in the multi-disciplinary world of the arts and humanities. il Sch Arts 71:34-5 S '71

POLS, Edward
Consciousness-makers and the autonomy of consciousness. Yale R 60:514-31 Je '71

POLSTER, Sandor M.
Insubordinate rank and file. Nation 212:782-5 Je 21 '71

POLUNIN, Ivan
Who says fish can't climb trees? il Nat Geog 141:84-91 Ja '72

POLY I:C
Antiviral activity of polyribocytidylic acid in cells primed with polyriboinosinic acid. E. de Clercq and P. de Somer. bibliog il Science 173:260-2 Jl 16 '71

Antiviral resistance by the polyinosinic acid—poly (1-vinylcytosine) complex. J. Pitha and P. M. Pitha. bibliog il Science 172:1146-8 Je 11 '71

Induction of interferon. M. R. Hilleman and A. A. Tytell. il Sci Am 225:26-31 Jl '71

POLYACRYLAMIDE gel electrophoresis. See Electrophoresis

POLYADENYLIC acid
Polyadenylic acid sequences: role in conversion of nuclear RNA into messenger RNA. J. E. Darnell and others. bibliog il Science 174:507-10 O 29 '71

POLYCHOLORINATED biphenyls. See Diphenyl compounds

POLYCYSTIC renal disease. See Kidneys—Diseases

POLYESTER fibers. See Textile fibers, Synthetic

POLYETHYLENE
Preparation of high-crystallinity polyethylene at low pressures. K. Hara and H. Schonhorn. bibliog il Science 172:562-4 My 7 '71

POLYGAMY
Whispered faith; Utah's Mormon polygamists. il Time 98:25 O 11 '71

POLYGLOTTISM. See Multilingualism

POLYGONUM. See Knotweeds

POLYGRAPH
Startling new research from the man who talks to plants. J. Robbins and C. Robbins. il pors Nat Wildlife 9:21-4 O '71

POLYHEDRONS
Plaiting of Plato's polyhedrons and the asymmetrical yin-yang-lee. M. Gardner. il Sci Am 225:204-6+ S '71

Quadratic elongation: a quantitative measure of distortion in coordination polyhedra. K. Robinson and others. bibliog il Science 172:567-70 My 7 '71

POLYINOSINIC-polycytidylic acid. See Poly I:C

POLYMERASE
DNA polymerase required for rapid repair of X-ray-induced DNA strand breaks in vivo. C. D. Town and others. bibliog il Science 172:851-4 My 21 '71

Interferon action: inhibition of vesicular stomatitis virus RNA synthesis induced by virion-bound polymerase. P. I. Marcus and others. bibliog il Science 174:593-8 N 5 '71

Viral RNA polymerases: electron microscopy of reovirus reaction cores. S. Gillies and others. bibliog il Science 174:694-6 N 12 '71

POLYMERS
Polyester fiber: from its invention to its present position. A. E. Brown and K. A. Reinhart. bibliog il Science 173:287-93 Jl 23 '71

Polymer whiskers grown from methyl 2-cyanoacrylate vapor. R. I. Smith-Johannsen. bibliog il Science 171:1246-7 Mr 26 '71

Polymers can relieve surcharged sewers. J. I. Cahalan and others. il Am City 86:87-8+ S '71

See also
Plastics
Polyethylene

POLYMORPHISM (biology)
Genetic polymorphisms in varied environments. J. R. Powell. bibliog il Science 174:1035-6 D 3 '71
Hemoglobin polymorphism. M. H. Crawford. Science 171:706 F 19 '71
Polymorphism of human constitutive heterochromatin. A. P. Craig-Holmes and M. W. Shaw. bibliog il Science 174:702-4 N 12 '71
Polymorphism of soluble glutamic-pyruvic transaminase: a new genetic marker in man. S. H. Chen and E. R. Giblett. bibliog il Science 173:148-9 Jl 9 '71
POLYNESIA
  See also
Easter Island
POLYNESIANS
Peoples of the Pacific; ed. by M. Mead and P. McClanahan. bibliog il pors Natur Hist 80:41-2 My '71
POLY-OPTICS, inc.
Genie in Poly-Optic's fiber lamps. il Bsns W p52 F 13 '71
POLYPEPTIDES. See Peptides
POLYRIBONUCLEOTIDES. See Nucleotides
POLYSACCHARIDES
Molecular structure of starch-type polysaccharides from hericium ramosum and hericium coralloides. D. A. McCracken and J. L. Dodd. bibliog Science 174:419 O 22 '71
  See also
Glycogen
POLYUNSATURATED fats. See Oils and fats, Edible
POLYURETHANE foam. See Plastic foams
POLYWATER. See Water
POMANDERS
Herbal gifts you can make or buy. House & Gard 140:103-4 D '71
POMARE, Eleo, dance company.   See Dance companies
POMERANCE, Jo. See Wadsworth, J. J. jt. auth.
POMERANZ, Virginia E. and Schultz, Dodi
How to keep your home safe for your children. il Todays Health 49:32-4 O '71
POMEROY, Kenneth B.
Roadblock or detour? por Am For 77:5 Jl '71
Time for action. il Am For 77:32-4+ F '71
World forest research congress. il Am For 77:32-6 Ag '71
POMEROY, Mary Barnas
Pasochoa and Cotopaxi; story. Américas 23:20-2 Ap '71
POMEROY, Ralph
Comment. L. Mueller. Poetry 117:330 F '71 •
POMONTI, Jean Claude
Other South Vietnam: toward the breaking point. For Affairs 50:253-69 Ja '72
POMPANO fishing
Fish you can't forget; permit fishing. J. Brooks. il Outdoor Life 147:90-2+ My '71
Grail still swims in the Yu Yum lagoon; permit fishing. C. Gammon. il Sports Illus 35:104-10+ D 6 '71
Quest for permit. G. Drake. il Field & S 75:64-5+ Ap '71
POMPEII
Dream city. R. Winter. il Sci Digest 69:52-5 Ap '71
POMPIDOU, Georges
Common market: good morning! pors Newsweek 77:29-30 My 31 '71 •
Europe: the British are coming? il pors Time 97:26+ My 31 '71 •
French tie that binds. il Time 97:37 F 15 '71 •
Honeymoon ends for France's Pompidou. il por U S News 70:70 Ap 12 '71 •
New European man runs France. K. Botsford. por N Y Times Mag p9+ Ag 29 '71 •
Pompidou gives Concorde support. D. E. Fink. il pors Aviation W 94:23-4 My 17 '71 •
Pompidou trip boosts Concorde's outlook. il Aviation W 95:15 D 20 '71 •
Pompidou's anthology. Time 97:37 F 8 '71 •
PONCE, John
At the desk; poem. Seventeen 30:132 Jl '71
POND, Alonzo W.
What's your survival quotient? true or false quiz. Field & S 75:72-3+ Mr '71
POND, Elizabeth
Tran-ngoc-Chau affair. Atlan 227:19-20+ My '71
POND life. See Fresh water biology
POND snails. See Snails
PONDS
  See also
Water gardens
PONNAMPERUMA, Cyril. See Pering, K. L. jt. auth.
PONS, William F.
His subject is a world-famous museum. J. Deschin. il por Pop Phot 68:32+ My '71 •

PONTIAC, Mich.
Education
Block those buses. D. Zwerdling. New Repub 165:14-17 O 23 '71
Pontiac survives its trial by fire. Bsns W p71 O 2 '71
Trouble in Pontiac. il Newsweek 78:33-4 S 20 '71
PONTIFICAL commission on justice and peace
  See also
Joint committee for society, development and peace
PONY express
Pony express. H. Herst, jr. Hobbies 76:131+ Je '71
PONZO, Marie
Opera by the book. il Wilson Lib Bul 46:335-7 D '71
POOL (game) See Billiards
POOL rooms
Clutch of odd birds. P. Jordan. il Sports Illus 35:56-60+ Ag 30 '71
POOLE, Peter A.
Ethnic minority groups: source of regional instability. il Focus 21:9-12 F '71
POOLHOUSES. See Bathhouses
POOLS. See Garden pools; Swimming pools
POOR, Henry Varnum
Obituary
Craft Horiz por 31:4 Ap '71
POOR
  See also
Tramps
Psychology
Environment and the poor: toward more realistic welfare policies. L. Goodwin. bibliog f il Cur Hist 61:290-6+ N '71
Why Uncle Sam is pulling back his dollars from healthful housing programs for the poor. R. Sherrill. il Todays Health 49:16-19+ Jl '71
Brazil
To hell and gone; Recife shantytowns. G. H. Dunne. il America 125:224-7 O 2 '71
India
India's endless troubles, and why they worry U.S. il U S News 71:86-9 N 8 '71
Israel
Black Panthers of Israel. A. Elon. il N Y Times Mag p33+ S 12 '71; Discussion. p8 O 17 '71
Poverty problem. il Newsweek 77:59-60 Ap 19 '71
Peru
To be poor in Peru. E. Watlington. Chr Cent 88:200+ F 10 '71
Puerto Rico
Poor in Puerto Rico. S. Steiner. New Repub 165:8-9 D 11 '71
United States
Any end to poverty? America's big problem. il U S News 71:52-7 Jl 12 '71
Bishops and poverty; Campaign for human development. J. Deedy. Commonweal 95:218 D 3 '71
Black humor of housing. R. Sherrill. Nation 212:397-402 Mr 29 '71
Flannery O'Connor and fundamental poverty; address, November 1970. C. Martin. Engl J 60:458-61 Ap '71
Future of poverty. A. T. Kapusinski. il America 125:346-9 O 30 '71
Home ownership for the poor? B. Friedan and J. Newman. il Trans-Action 7:47-53 O '70
How poverty area residents look for work. H. J. Hilaski. il Mo Labor R 94:41-5 Mr '71
Is poverty illegal? I. Silver. Commonweal 93:488-92 F 19 '71
Job training programs in urban poverty areas. R. V. McKay. il Mo Labor R 94:36-40 Ag '71
Let's break the hellish circle; USCC campaign. America 125:389 N 13 '71
On the road in Mississippi. A. V. Krebs, jr. Cath World 212:297-300 Mr '71
One woman's war against poverty; Interfaith task force for community services. C. Remsberg and B. Remsberg. il por Good H 173:91+ O '71
Other America, by M. Harrington. Review Fortune 83:130-1 Ap '71. D. Seligman
Poverty may be good for you. il Time 97:64 Je 21 '71
Scope of the poverty problem. J. F. Bauman. bibliog f Cur Hist 61:284-9+ N '71
Social cost of curbing inflation. B. L. Masse. America 124:644 Je 26 '71

POOR—United States—*Continued*
Supreme court and the rights of poor. America 124:477 My 8 '71
25 million poor in U.S: really? il U S News 70:40 My 24 '71
Unutilized manpower in poverty areas of 6 U.S. cities; with tables. H. J. Hilaski. bibliog Mo Labor R 94:45-52 D '71
White paper; race and poverty. il Newsweek 77:18-19 My 31 '71
Winking at poverty. Nation 212:642-4 My 24 '71
See also
Church and social problems
National welfare rights organization
Negroes—Social conditions
Public welfare—United States
also subhead Poor under names of cities, e.g. Portland, Ore.—Poor

POOR laws
United States
See also
Public welfare—United States
POOR relief. See Public welfare
POP lyrics. See Music, Popular (songs, etc)
POP mom moon; story. See Updike, J.
POP music. See Music, Popular (songs, etc)
POPA, Vasko
Give me back my rags; poem. tr. by A. Pennington. Atlan 228:118-20 D '71
POPAYAN, Colombia
Popayán revisited. R. E. Crist. il Américas 23:25-32 Ap '71
POPE, Saxton
Last stone age American; excerpt from The first American. C. W. Ceram. il pors Am Heritage 22:98-9 Ag '71 *
POPEIL brothers, inc.
Masters of the TV hard sell. il Bsns W p40-1 Ag 7 '71
POPES
Election
Who will be the next pope? A. Brady. il (p 112) Cath World 213:75-8 My '71
Infallibility
Infallibility fight. pors Newsweek 77:57 Ja 25 '71
Infallible? an inquiry, by H. Kung. Review New Repub 164:27-8 My 15 '71. E. H. Brill
Power and the glory are passing. J. Roddy. il Look 35:21-5 O 19 '71
Primacy
Breakfast by the lake; the bestowal of primacy upon Simon Peter. V. P. McCorry. America 124:440-1 Ap 24 '71
POPKIN, Henry
New stars, the new films. por Harp Baz 105: 71 D '71
POPKIN, Samuel Lewis
Strictly academic. il por Newsweek 78:47 N 8 '71 *
POPOLIZIO, Vincent J.
For the elementary teacher: holiday stereotypes. il Sch Arts 71:8-9 S '71
POPPIES
Oriental poppies. E. S. Henderson. il Horticulture 49:22-3 Jl '71
See also
Opium trade
POPPINO, Rollie E.
Brazil's third government of the revolution. Cur Hist 60:102-7+ F '71
POPPY, John
Loveable woman. Look 35:45-6 Ja 12 '71
Radical family. il Look 35:81-2+ Ja 26 '71
—and Cowan, Richard
Don't trust anyone over thirty. il McCalls 99:38+ O '71
POPPY; ballet. See Ballet—Criticisms
POPPY designs. See Design, Decorative—Plant forms
POPULAR culture
Mass media and mass culture. F. McDermott. il UNESCO Courier 24:15-17 Ja '71
See also
United States—Popular culture
POPULAR electronics (periodicals)
Merger! W. A. Stocklin. por Electr World 86:6 D '71
Popular electronics, including Electronics world. M. S. Snitzer. Pop Electr 1:16 Ja '72
POPULAR front of the liberation of Palestine. See Fedayeen
POPULAR music. See Music, Popular (songs, etc)
POPULAR songs. See Music, Popular (songs, etc)

POPULARITY
How to be popular. B. Spock. Seventeen 29: 156-7 S '70
POPULATION
See also
Birth control
Birth rate
also subhead Population under names of countries, states, cities, e.g. United States —Population
Overpopulation
After the population explosion. H. Brown. il Sat R 54:11-13+ Je 26 '71
Another approach to population control? N. De Nevers. Bul Atom Sci 27:34 Mr '71
Census sense; views of C. F. Taeuber and P. Ehrlich. Newsweek 77:78 Ja 25 '71
Nobody ever dies of overpopulation. G. Hardin. Science 171:527 F 12 '71
Peril of overpopulation: our greatest threat. G. M. Landau. por Parents Mag 46:56 N '71
Population explosion: is man really doomed? Time essay. O. Friedrich. il Time 98:58-9 S 13 '71
We must stop population growth. W. H. Davis. Field & S 76:20+ Je '71
See also
Malthusianism
Population, Increase of
POPULATION, Distribution of
Rural exodus: new census report. il U S News 70:37 F 22 '71
Where blacks are moving, and moving up. il U S News 70:24-6 Mr 1 '71
POPULATION, Increase of
Case against having children, by Anna Silverman and Arnold Silverman. Review Cath World 214:136-8 D '71. F. Julien
Development of institutions to meet the world population crisis; address, March 12, 1971. P. P. Claxton, jr. Dept State Bul 65: 165-72 Ag 16 '71
Impact of population growth. P. R. Ehrlich. and J. P. Holdren. bibliog il Science 171: 1212-17 Mr 26 '71; Discussion. 173:278+ Jl 23 '71
Optimism and population: NAS report. Sci Am 225:40 O '71
People in the machinery; views of Barry Commoner. P. R. Ehrlich and J. P. Holdren. Sat R 55:71 Ja 1 '72
Population; EQ index. il Nat Wildlife 9:38-9 O '71
Population growth and national development; address, June 14, 1971. D. L. Gamon. Dept State Bul 65:172-8 Ag 16 '71
Zero population growth, do we need it now? T. J. Jermann. America 124:538-40 My 22 '71
See also
Population—Overpopulation
POPULATION genetics
Cerumen genetics and human breast cancer. N. L. Petrakis. bibliog il Science 173:347-9 Jl 23 '71
Kinetic path of genes undergoing selection. H. N. Kirkman. bibliog il Science 174:68-70 O 1 '71
Population genetics and human origins. R. B. Eckhardt. il Sci Am 226:94-103 Ja '72
Sex and population differences in the incidence of a plasma cholinesterase variant. A. H. Lubin and others. bibliog il Science 173:161-4 Jl 9 '71
POPULATION growth. See Population, Increase of
POPULATION limitation. See Birth control
POPULISM
Now is the time, by F. R. Harris. Review New Repub 165:30-1 Ag 7 '71. W. F. Claire
POPULIST party
Populist dreams and Negro rights: east Texas as a case study: Grimes County, Tex. L. C. Goodwyn. bibliog f il Am Hist R 76: 1435-56 D '71
PORCELAIN. See Pottery
PORCELAIN, Chinese. See Pottery, Chinese
PORCHES
Play up a porch. P. Rumely. il Bet Hom & Gard 49:50-3 Je '71
PORK
See also
Cookery—Meat
Ham
Advertising
See Meat industry—Advertising
PORK grading. See Meat—Grading and standardization
PORK industry. See Meat industry

PORNOGRAPHY. See Immoral literature and pictures; Obscenity (law); Sex in moving pictures

PORPHYRIA
Chemically induced porphyria: increased microsomal heme turnover after treatment with allylisopropylacetamide. U. A. Meyer and H. S. Marver. bibliog il Science 171: 64-6 Ja 8 '71
George III and the mad business. by I. Macalpine and R. Hunter. Review
New Yorker 47:89-92 Je 26 '71. R. Coles
Uroporphyrinogen III cosynthetase activity in the fox squirrel (sciurus niger) E. Y. Levin and V. Flyger. bibliog il Science 174:59-60 O 1 '71

PORPHYRINS
Stereochemistry of hemes and other metalloporphyrins. J. L. Hoard. bibliog il Science 174:1295-302 D 24 '71

PORPOISES. See Dolphins (mammals)

PORT authority of New York. See Port of New York authority

PORT CHARLOTTE, Fla.
Working at a life of leisure: R. Walton in Fla. J. Kirshenbaum. il Sports Illus 34:52-6+ F 1 '71

PORT of New York authority
Academy panel kicks over traces; study of consequences of new runways in Jamaica Bay. C. Holden. Science 171:781 F 26 '71
Other agency turns to transit. Bsns W p91 F 20 '71
Port authority battles its critics. il Bsns W p48-51 Ap 3 '71
See also
World trade institute

PORT WASHINGTON, N.Y.
Balkanization of suburbia. S. Kaplan. il Harper 243:72-4 O '71

Education
Demise of the reluctant reader: television reading program. S. Fleming. il Schol Teach Jr/Sr High p 12-13+ Ja 11 '71

PORTABLE electric typewriters. See Typewriters. Electric

PORTABLE phonograph. See Phonograph, Portable

PORTABLE radar apparatus. See Radar— Antenna and scanning mechanisms

PORTABLE radio receivers. See Radio receivers. Portable

PORTABLE radio telephone. See Radio telephone. Portable

PORTABLE television receivers. See Television receivers, Portable

PORTER, Cole
Classic Cole Porter. L. Smit. il por Sat R 54:48-9+ D 25 '71 *
Cole; ed. by R. Kimball. Review
New Repub 165:23-4 D 11 '71. R. Whittemore
Sat R il por 54:50-1 D 25 '71 *
Cole Porter: the new nostalgia; excerpt. ed. by R. Kimball. il pors Harp Baz 105:116-17 N '71 *
Profiles. B. Gill. por New Yorker 47:48-50+ S 18 '71 *
Treasury of his unpublished songs. Cole Porter wasn't perfect, only incomparable. R. Severo. il por N Y Times Mag p 18-19+ O 10 '71; Discussion. p 114 N 14 '71 *

PORTER, Eliot
Eliot Porter: conservationist with a camera. M. R. Weiss. il Sat R 54:58-9 O 2 '71 *

PORTER, Joyce
Games writers play. Writer 84:9-10+ D '71

PORTER, Katherine Anne
And to the living. joy. McCalls 99:76-7 D '71
Spivvleton mystery; story. Ladies Home J 88:74-5 Ag '71

PORTER, Myra T. and others
Correction of abnormal cerebroside sulfate metabolism in cultured metachromatic leukodystrophy fibroblasts. bibliog il Science 172:1263-5 Je 18 '71

PORTER, Phil. See Ball. C. E. jt. auth.

PORTER, Russell Williams
Stellafane holds Porter centennial. D. Milon. il por Sky & Tel 42:208-11 O '71 *

PORTER, Stephen C.
Holocene eruptions of Mauna Kea volcano. Hawaii. bibliog il Science 172:375-7 Ap 23 '71

PORTER, Sylvia
Spending your money: questions and answers. See issues of Ladies' home journal

PORTER, Willard H.
American rodeo. il Am West 8:40-7+ Jl '71

PORTER, William E.
Radicalism and the young journalist. il Sat R 54:65-6 D 11 '71

PORTER, William J.
[Plenary sessions] on Vietnam held at Paris. See issues of Department of state bulletin September 9, 1971-

about
Ambassador Porter named to head U.S. delegation to Paris talks. Dept State Bul 65:181 Ag 16 '71 *
New man in Paris. por Time 98:20-1 Ag 9 '71 *
Talking tough in Paris. por Time 99:26 Ja 17 '72 *

PORTER, William W.
Matter of opinion: reclamation. Am West 8: 48 Ja '71

PORTES, Alejandro
Guatemala's right-wing terror. il Nation 214:47-8 Ja 10 '72

PORTLAND, Me.
Streets
Seal coats are not enough. il Am City 86:30 Ap '71

PORTLAND, Ore.
See also
Western forestry center

Fountains
See Fountains

Housing
East Burnside apartments. il Arch Rec 149: 84-5 mid-My '71

Newspapers
From token to the top; Oregonian's Negro city editor. il por Time 97:65 My 17 '71

Poor
Plan for giving; Community care self-help program. il pors Ebony 27:96-8+ D '71

PORTLAND cement concrete. See Concrete

PORTLAND rose festival. See Festivals—Oregon

PORTNOY, Sandra B. See Mogul, P. H. jt. auth.

PORTOBELO, Panama
Restoring Portobelo. Américas 23:45 My '71

PORTRAIT drawing
Will the real Jimmy please stand up? L. De Wyngaert. il Sch Arts 70:24-5 F '71

PORTRAIT painting
Camera eye of Thomas Eakins. il Life 71:54-9 Jl 23 '71
Children in pastel. I. E. Weidenaar. il Design 72:32-3 mid-Wint '71
Goya's portrait of Gen Nicolas Guye. P. Muller. il Art N 70:29+ D '71
Most talked-about painter of 1971: Aaron Shikler. J. Singer. il por Am Artist 35: 30-7+ S '71
Seymour Pearlstein. D. Hines. il por Am Artist 35:62-7+ F '71
Using reference materials to paint portraits; excerpts from Painting portraits. E. R. Kinstler. il por Am Artist 35:30-8 My '71

PORTRAIT sculpture
American in Paris. J. W. Freeman. il por Opera N 35:24-7 Mr 6 '71
Beesley and his bronze children. D. Cochrane. il por Am Artist 35:54-9+ S '71
Finial busts on eighteenth-century Philadelphia furniture. R. C. Smith. il Antiques 100:900-5 D '71

PORTRAITS
See also
Photography—Portraits
Portrait painting

PORTRAITS, American
Charles Willson Peale's portrait of Robert and Gouverneur Morris. C. C. Sellers. il pors Antiques 99:404-6 Mr '71
Three Tennessee painters. B. H. Bishop. il Antiques 100:432-7 S '71

PORTRAITS of children. See Children in art

PORTS
Another SST? artificial deep-water port. il Forbes 107:21-2 Ap 15 '71

PORTSMOUTH, Derek John Harford Worlock, bp of. See Worlock, D. J. H.

PORTUGAL
See also
Algarve
Church and state in Portugal
Nazaré
United Nations—Portugal

Colonies
Territories in southern Africa; consideration in Fourth committee. UN Mo Chron 8:77-80 N '71
See also
Macao

PORTUGAL—*Continued*

Description and travel

Instant Portugal: Lisbon, Algarve, Nazaré. il Holiday 49:47-55 F '71

Foreign relations
United States

See United States—Foreign relations—Portugal

Politics and government

Bread-and-butter politics. por Newsweek 77: 46 Je 28 '71

Religious institutions and affairs

See also
Catholic church in Portugal

PORTUGUESE
Gallery: N. Slavin's portraits of the Portuguese. Life 71:6-9 O 29 '71
PORTUGUESE EAST AFRICA. See Mozambique
PORTUGUESE GUINEA
Propaganda war? P. Webb. il Newsweek 78: 28-9 D 27 '71
PORTUGUESE man-of-war
Purple wind. W. Zeiller and G. Compton. il Sea Front 17:372-7 N '71
POSELL, George
Prompter. E. Burns. il pors Opera N 85:27-9 Mr 27 '71 *
POSEY, Sam
Now, when I am world champion. K. Chapin. il Sports Illus 35:32-4+ N 1 '71 *
POSITION of the planets; story. See Gilliatt, P.
POSITIONS, Applications for. See Applications for positions
POSNER, Richard
Love triangle; story. Ladies Home J 88:108 Mr '71
POSNER, Richard A.
Nader on antitrust. New Repub 164:11-14 Je 26 '71
POSNER, Victor
Prime target for the SEC. por Bsns W p56 Je 19 '71 *
POSPISIL, Alan
Oliver. Sat R 54:84 N 13 '71
POSSESSIONS. See Property
POST, Richard F.
Fusion power: the uncertain certainty; adaptation of address, April 26, 1971. il por Bul Atom Sci 27:42-8 O '71
POST, Troy Victor
Troy Post cashes in some big chips. il por Bsns W p20-1 Ja 23 '71 *
POST, Washington. See Washington post
POST cards
Celebrating the canal's completion. V. L. George. il Hobbies 76:148-9 Je '71
Missouri's 150th birthday. V. L. George. il Hobbies 76:152-3 S '71
Most unusual post card shrine. V. L. George. il Hobbies 76:158-9 O '71
Picture post card. See issues of Hobbies
Saving an American tradition: little country churches. V. L. George. il Hobbies 76:158-9 N '71
POST company. See Washington post company
POST exchanges. See United States—Armed forces—Post exchanges
POST libraries. See United States—Army—Libraries
POST office buildings
Post office as a pacesetter; Columbus, Ind. il Arch Forum 133:46-9 D '70
POSTAGE stamps
Apollo 15 brings post office to the moon. A. Hauck. il Sci Digest 71:89 Ja '72
Ascension Island space commemoratives. A. Hauck. il Sci Digest 70:84 S '71
Canada honors discoverers of insulin. A. Hauck. il Sci Digest 70:88 O '71
Nativity and a pear tree; motif on Christmas stamp. G. Everett. il Chr Today 16: 42 O 22 '71
Southern stamp strategy. C. Norwood. Commonweal 94:455-6 S 3 '71
Stamps. H. Herst, jr. See issues of Hobbies
Stamps against racism. il UNESCO Courier 24:23 N '71
Stamps honor ecological expedition; New Hebrides. A. Hauck. il Sci Digest 70:79 D '71
Stamps honor math formulas; Nicaragua. A. Hauck. il Sci Digest 70:78-9 N '71
Steins and other drinking vessels pictured on stamps. J. G. Lowenstein. il Hobbies 76:89-92 Jl '71
WHCOA stamped envelopes, 40 million, issued to honor conference. il Aging 205:8 N '71

Anecdotes, facetiae, satire, etc.

Parting shots: proposing some memorable commemoratives. il Life 70:66A-68 F 26 '71

Collectors and collecting

Absolutely stuck on stamps; philately. R. H. Boyle. il por Sports Illus 35:32-7 Ag 23 '71
Philately for fun, only! J. B. Raskin. il Mech Illus 67:64+ O '71
Stamp collecting: rich man's hobby lures investors. Bsns W p83 N 20 '71
Stampede for rare stamps. il U S News 71:57 D 13 '71
POSTAL censorship
Let's put the smut merchants out of business. W. M. Blount. il Nations Bsns 59:34-6+ S '71
Renewed effort at post office censorship. R. H. Smith. Pub W 200:32 S 20 '71
POSTAL rates

United States

AAP asks rollback of postal rate increases. S. Wagner. Pub W 199:44 Je 21 '71
AAP spokesman testifies on postal rate increase; excerpts ed. by L. Huston. R. W. Frase. Pub W 200:233 Ag 30 '71
Businessmen fight the new mail rates. il Bsns W p23 My 22 '71
Century goes up. J. Deedy. Commonweal 95: 314 Ja 7 '72
Death of Look. N. Cousins. Sat R 54:26-7 O 2 '71; Same with title What killed Look? U S News 71:104+ O 11 '71
Direct-mail ads will get more direct. il Bsns W p84+ N 27 '71
End of Look. R. H. Smith. Pub W 200:46 S 27 '71
Good ways to save on postage. il Good H 173:206 S '71
How to get the most from the mails. P. Cartwright. il Mech Illus 67:30+ My '71
Magazines in jeopardy. Time 99:43 Ja 10 '72
Mail robbery. Nation 212:581-2 My 10 '71
Paying for diversity; periodicals. New Repub 165:7 Jl 10 '71
Postage rate increases proposed. Pub W 199: 54 F 15 '71
Postal forum debates rates and service. S. Wagner. Pub W 200:30 O 4 '71
Postal increases up for review. S. Wagner. Pub W 199:47-8 My 24 '71
Price of first-class. Time 97:16 My 24 '71
Print media's plight; 2nd class mail increases. J. Deedy. Commonweal 94:322 Je 25 '71
Serious threat to magazines. Life 71:4 Ag 20 '71; Same. Forbes 108:19-20 S 15 '71
Up, up and away. Newsweek 77:60+ F 15 '71
What it costs you to mail letters now. il U S News 71:43 Jl 12 '71
Where rise in postal rates will hit hardest; mailing of magazines and newspapers. il U S News 70:56-7 F 22 '71
POSTAL scales. See Scales (weighing instruments)
POSTAL service
See also
Electronics in postal service
Pigeon post

Unordered merchandise

Obituary peddler; unsolicited merchandise received through the mail. Consumer Rep 36:404 Jl '71
Reader's digest agrees to NYC consumer ruling. Pub W 199:36-7 Ja 18 '71

Europe, Western

Europe is on the move in mail. il Nations Bsns 59:72-3 My '71

France

Mail must go through, but 100 years late? il Sci Digest 69:76-7 My '71

Great Britain

Pigeons and pirates. il Time 97:31-2 F 1 '71

United States

Big changes in mail service. il U S News 70:43 Ap 26 '71
Boom in private mail service: why it's catching on. il U S News 71:24-5 N 1 '71
Competition for the post office. Nation 212: 325-6 Mr 15 '71
Once again, the purple finger. D. Williamson. il Sat R 54:6+ S 4 '71
Postal reform faces heavy weather. il Bsns W p81-2 F 13 '71
Postal service gets down to business. il Bsns W p78-80 Je 26 '71
Rebellion at the mailbox. J. Snyder. McCalls 99:34 N '71

POSTAL service—United States—*Continued*
Season's greetings. Newsweek 78:44 D 27 '71
What new mail service means to you; interview. W. M. Blount. il por U S News 71:46-51 Jl 5 '71
Your stake in the new postal setup. il Nations Bsns 59:70-4 My '71
See also
Air mail service
Independent postal system of America
Postal rates—United States

History
See also
Pony express
POSTAL strike, Great Britain. See Strikes—Great Britain
POSTAL system of America, Independent. See Independent postal system of America
POSTCARDS. See Post cards
POSTEL, George
Postel's law. Newsweek 78:51 N 29 '71 *
POSTELLE, Yvonne
Mother, may I go out to swim? il Parents Mag 46:48-9+ Ag '71
New way to manage family finances. il Mech Illus 67:65-7+ S '71
Progress report on classroom integration. il Parents Mag 46:48-51 D '71
POSTERS
NLW poster protest: letters to the editor. il Library J 96:760, 1548 Mr 1, My 1 '71
Poster art and low-cost photographic reproductions. M. Mann. il Pop Phot 69:30+ O '71
Psychedelic posters. M. F. Bolger. il Sch Arts 71:40 S '71
Sunflower that grew and grew. D. Silverton. por McCalls 98:44 My '71
POSTS, Military. See Military posts
POSTURE
Magic of good posture. W. R. Young. Read Digest 99:151-2+ N '71
See also
Stature
POSVAR, Wesley W.
Reshaping our foreign policy; address, April 1971. bibliog f Ann Am Acad 396:105-14 Jl '71
POT. See Marijuana
POT roasting. See Cookery—Meat
POTASSIUM
See also
Plants, Effect of potassium on
POTASSIUM in the body
Cooperative control of potassium accumulation by ouabain in vascular smooth muscle. J. Gulati and A. W. Jones. bibliog il Science 172:1348-50 Je 25 '71
Sodium and potassium activities in normal and sodium-rich frog skeletal muscle. W. M. Armstrong and C. O. Lee. bibliog il Science 171:413-15 Ja 29 '71
POTATO spindle tuber virus. See Viruses, Plant
POTATOES
Bushels of late potatoes. B. Brinhart. il Org Gard & Farm 18:39-41 My '71
Raising potatoes under straw. J. Stuwe. Org Gard & Farm 18:51 Jl '71
See also
Cookery—Vegetables
Feeding and feeding stuffs—Potatoes
Sweet potatoes
History
Potato. D. Ugent; discussion. Science 171:955-6 Mr 12 '71
POTATOES, Dried
Instant potatoes. il Consumer Rep 36:435-7 Jl '71
POTATOES, Frozen. See Vegetables, Frozen
POTENTILLAS. See Cinquefoil
POTHOLM, Christian P.
Future of Africa South. bibliog f Cur Hist 60:146-50+ Mr '71
POTLATCH forests, Inc.
Potlatch's oil man. por Bsns W p79 Ap 17 '71
POTOMAC, Md.
Iron curtain; suburban opposition to low-income housing. New Repub 164:7-8 Ap 24 '71
POTOMAC RIVER
Little sturm und drang at Hunting creek. J. Sax. il Esquire 75:84-8+ F '71
Mike Frome; proposed landfill and high rise apartment construction at Hunting Creek. M. Frome. Am For 77:5+ Ag '71
Bridges
Is pressure legal? building of Three sisters bridge halted by court decision. il Time 98:69 N 22 '71

POTS and pans. See Kitchen utensils
POTTED plants. See Plants, Potted
POTTER, Beatrix
Linder collection of the works and drawings of Beatrix Potter. K. Clark. il Horn Bk 47:554-5 O '71 *
Some personal recollections of Beatrix Potter. W. Boultbee. il Horn Bk 47:586-8 D '71 *
POTTER, Charles H.
Grow cut flowers in your greenhouse. il Horticulture 49:18-19+ N '71
POTTER, Conrad H.
Cultivating student teachers in the Yakima Valley. il Am Ed 7:27-31 My '71
POTTER, Dale R.
Outdoor classroom. il Am For 77:44-6 O '71
POTTER, David Morris
Obituary
Am Hist R 76:1273-5 O '71. C. N. Degler
POTTER, Ray
New super oils for your car. il Pop Sci 198:45-7 Je '71
POTTER, Stephen
Words only. See issues of American record guide
POTTER, Van R. See Barbiroli, B. jt. auth.
POTTER instrument company
Potter problem. A. A. Butkus. il Duns 98:58 Jl '71
POTTERS
Ceramactivities; people, places and things. See issues of Ceramics monthly
See also
Brown, P. C.
Kriwanek, F.
Larson, J.
Martin, I.
Martin, K.
Natzler, O.
Novy, J.
Park, K.
Reitz, D.
Rippon, R.
Sanders, H.
Sterckx, A.
POTTERY
China chicanery. E. D. Craster. il Bet Hom & Gard 4978-81 Ap '71
Dangerous pottery removed from market; danger of lead poisoning. Consumer Rep 36:302 My '71
Lead in pottery. il Chem 44:23-4 S '71
Most costly dinner service; the Flora Danica. H. C. Howes. il Design 72:14-15 mid-Wint '71
Screening for lead in pottery. Chem 44:24 S '71
Stick-spatter ware. E. F. Robacker. il Antiques 99:245-51 F '71
Stoneware made by the White family in Utica, New York. B. Franco. il Antiques 99:872-6 Je '71
See also
Ceramic sculpture
Cloisonné
Cups
Glazes and glazing
Jugs
Majolica
Molds (for ceramic products)
Bibliography
New books. See occasional issues of Ceramics monthly
Decoration
Design sources of early China trade porcelain; Chinese Lowestoft. C. Le Corbeiller. il Antiques 101:161-8 Ja '72
Majolica technique for stoneware. A. C. Garzio. il Ceram Mo 20:19-22 Ja '72
Exhibitions
Ceramic statement 1971: San Francisco, Youngstown, Greencastle, Evanston. il Ceram Mo 19:30-1 Je '71
Cranbrook alumni gallery tour: Oakbrook invitational craft exhibition; South Carolina state art collection; Burke ceramics at Chicago public library. il Ceram Mo 19:17-18 D '71
Crock art; show at New York's Museum of contemporary crafts. D. Davis. il Newsweek 78:78 Jl 5 '71
Itinerary. See issues of Ceramics monthly
Laugh-in in clay; Clayworks: 20 Americans, exhibition at the Museum of contemporary crafts. R. Slivka. il Craft Horiz 31:39-47 O '71
Mid-South ceramic exhibition. il Ceram Mo 19:26-7 My '71
Natzler retrospective exhibition; M. H. de Young memorial museum, San Francisco. il Ceram Mo 19:14-15 O '71

POTTERY—Exhibitions—*Continued*
On and off the avenue; exhibition at the Museum of contemporary crafts: Clayworks: 20 Americans. J. Malcolm. New Yorker 47: 59-60 S 4 '71
To market, to market! R. Wolverton and M. Wolverton. il Ceram Mo 19:21+ My; 27+ Je '71
Toledo area artists annual exhibition; the Ceramic league of Miami. il Ceram Mo 19:21 O '71
Twelve Dutch potters. il Ceram Mo 19:31 N '71

Firing
Fluoride glazes for cones 06, 4 and 6. R. Behrens. il Ceram Mo 19:33 S '71
Low temperature frit porcelain. R. Behrens. il Ceram Mo 19:33 N '71
Raku unit for high school potters. A. C. Spray. il Ceram Mo 19:17-18 Ap '71

History
Artistic greatness of China. W. H. LeMaire. il Design 72:14-15 mid-Sum '71

Study and teaching
Potter's trip. K. Morton. Ceram Mo 19:32 S '71
Pottery workshop for children. il Design 73: 28-30 Fall '71
Primitive pottery at Red Dog. F. Ball. il Ceram Mo 19:29-32 My '71
Raku unit for high school potters. A. C. Spray. il Ceram Mo 19:17-18 Ap '71
Rome: milieu for ceramics; Centro internazionale di ceramica. il Craft Horiz 31:35 Ap '71
Room design and curriculum planning. C. Rash. il Ceram Mo 19:30-1 S '71
Summer workshops 1971. il Ceram Mo 19:19-26 Ap '71
See also
Haystack Mountain school of crafts, Deer Isle, Me.

Technique
Balloon forms from buttered clay. F. Staryos. il Ceram Mo 19:31 Mr '71
Bird feeders. N. Baldwin. il Ceram Mo 19: 16-20 O '71
Canteen forms adapted from stones. D. M. Johnson and D. Peterson. il Ceram Mo 19. 30-2 Ap '71
Ceramic forms from layered slabs. R. F. Eilenberger. il Ceram Mo 19:16-18 Je '71
Clay cooking pot. R. F. Eilenberger. il Ceram Mo 19:20-3 F '71
Conversation with Don Reitz and Bruce Breckenridge; ed. by C. Brawer. B. Breckenridge; D. Reitz. il pors Ceram Mo 19: 17-19 Mr '71
Decorating with a slip cup. R. F. Eilenberger. il Ceram Mo 19:26-8 Ja '71
Don Reitz; a Ceramics monthly portfolio. C. C. Brawer. pors Ceram Mo 19:19-26 D '71
John Novy demonstrates: centering with a leather strap. D. H. Sweetman. il Ceram Mo 19:14-16 Mr '71
Making double-spouted pots on the wheel. B. Lee and D. Lewis. il Ceram Mo 20:23-5 Ja '72
Pennsylvania German pottery, tools and processes. E. Powell. il Ceram Mo 19:18-22 N '71
Pot clusters. il Ceram Mo 19:28-9 Je '71
Raku beads. S. Hyman. il Ceram Mo 19:28-30 O '71
Raku unit for high school potters. A. C. Spray. il Ceram Mo 19:17-18 Ap '71
Relocating a plate rim; slab technique. R. F. Eilenberger. il Ceram Mo 19:23-5 N '71
Terra sigillata. R. Behrens. Ceram Mo 19:31 Ja '71
Three slip trailing techniques; excerpts from Ceramic creations. R. Fournier. il Ceram Mo 19:21-3 S '71
Throwing the covered pot. L. Helmuth. il Ceram Mo 19:26-9 N '71
Throwing the large plate. S. H. Lee. il por Ceram Mo 19:18-20 S '71
Tyrone and Julie Larson. T. Shafer. il pors Ceram Mo 19:14-16 Ap '71
See also
Glazes and glazing
Modeling

POTTERY, American
Grueby art pottery. R. W. Blasberg. il Antiques 100:246-9 Ag '71
Pennsylvania German pottery, tools and processes. E. Powell. il Ceram Mo 19:18-22 N '71

Reuben Kadish: in clay, where all details begin. D. Shapiro. il Craft Horiz 31:26-9 F '71
Sadie Irvine letters: a further note on the production of Newcomb pottery; excerpts from letters, ed. by R. W. Blasberg. S. Irvine. il Antiques 100:250-1 Ag '71

Exhibitions
See Pottery—Exhibitions

POTTERY, Chinese
Artistic greatness of China. W. H. LeMaire. il Design 72:14-15 mid-Sum '71
Design sources of early China trade porcelain; Chinese Lowestoft. C. Le Corbeiller. il Antiques 101:161-8 Ja '72
Tz'u-chou stoneware. il Ceram Mo 19:24-5 S '71

POTTERY, Danish
Most costly dinner service; the Flora Danica. H. C. Howes. il Design 72:14-15 mid-Wint '71

POTTERY, Dutch
Twelve Dutch potters; exhibition. il Ceram Mo 19:31 N '71

POTTERY, English
Cottages and castles in English ceramics: the collection of Mrs Lawrence K. Miller. il Antiques 99:122-6 Ja '71
Doulton stoneware. A. Beardsley. il Hobbies 76:120-1+ Je '71
English yellow-glazed earthenware from the Eleanor and Jack L. Leon collection. J. J. Miller, 2d. il Antiques 100:93-8, 236-40 Jl-Ag '71
Marianne de Trey: Shinners Bridge pottery. E. Lewenstein. il pors Ceram Mo 19:14-17 S '71
Spode, by L. Whiter. Review
Antiques 99:366 Mr '71. E. Collard
Three pottery workshops in England. R. A. Goettsch. il Ceram Mo 19:13-19 F '71

POTTERY, European
Museum accessions; ceramics. R. Davidson. il Antiques 99:816-17+ Je '71

POTTERY, French
French pottery and porcelain. S. B. Sherrill. il Antiques 99:622+ My '71

POTTERY, Iranian
Persian bestiary. il UNESCO Courier 24:10-11 O '71
Persian ceramics after Islam. il Ceram Mo 19:20-1 Ja '71

POTTERY, Italian
See also
Majolica

POTTERY, Japanese
Raku murals of Paul Rayar. P. Rothenberg. il Ceram Mo 19:14-15 Je '71

POTTERY, Persian. See Pottery, Iranian

POTTERY, Roman
Terra sigillata. R. Behrens. Ceram Mo 19:31 Ja '71

POTTERY, Spanish
Pottery in Manises; Moorish-influenced majolica of southern Spain. T. Shafer and Y. Shafer. il Ceram Mo 20:14-18 Ja '72

POTTERY, Welsh
Collection of Swansea and Nantgarw porcelain. A. N. Morgan. il Antiques 100: 596-601 O '71

POTTERY industry
Grueby art pottery. R. W. Blasberg. il Antiques 100:246-9 Ag '71

POTTERY kilns. See Kilns

POTTING (electronics) See Electronic circuits— Plastic embedment

POTTING sheds. See Sheds

POUGH, F. Harvey
Leech-repellent property of eastern red-spotted newts. notophthalmus viridescens bibliog il Science 174:1144-6 D 10 '71

POULENC, Francis
Musical events. W. Sargeant. New Yorker 47: 181-3 N 13 '71 *
Report. R. D. Daniels. il Opera N 36:30-1 D 18 '71 *

POULLAIN, Ludwig
Virtuoso German banker moves center stage. pors Bsns W p56-7 Mr 27 '71 *

POULTRY
Chickens before eggs. N. Bubel. il Org Gard & Farm 18:44-7 D '71
Galactose toxicity in the chick: hyperosmolality. J. I. Malone and others. bibliog il Science 174:952-4 N 26 '71
How to buy and store chicken. il Bet Hom & Gard 49:85 My '71
Intersexes and sex determination in chickens. F. Abdel-Hameed and R. N. Shoffner. bibliog il Science 172:962-4 My 28 '71
See also
Carving (meat, etc)
Cookery—Poultry
Jungle fowls
Turkeys

POULTRY—*Continued*

Anecdotes, facetiae, satire, etc.

Chickens used to be like people! J. Campbell. Farm J 95:58 Ap '71

Breeding

See Poultry breeding

Prices

Buying chicken? Compare prices and save. il Changing T 25:37 S '71

POULTRY, Dressing of

How to cut up a chicken. il Bet Hom & Gard 49:81 My '71

How to cut up chicken. il Am Home 74:78 S '71

Simple tricks to boning meat. M. Happel. il Ladies Home J 88:132-3 S '71

POULTRY, Freezing of. See Freezing of food

POULTRY breeding

Chicken little. Sci Am 224:59 Je '71

Anecdotes, facetiae, satire, etc.

It's a breed, it's a strain, it's superchicken! D. M. Dunne. il Farm J 95:19 N '71

POULTRY stuffing. See Cookery—Poultry

POUND, Ezra

Discretions, by M. de Rachewiltz. Review
  Nat R 23:933+ Ag 24 '71. H. Kenner
  Nation 214:23-4 Ja 3 '72. C. D. Heymann *
  New Repub 165:26-7 Jl 3 '71. R. Whittemore *

Ezra Pound's voice of silence. A. Levy. il pors N Y Times Mag p 14-15+ Ja 9 '72 *

Knee-high to Ezra Pound. B. Darrach. il por Time 98:66 Ag 2 '71 *

POUND cake. See Cake

POUND ritual of Negro soldiers. See Salutations

POUSSAINT, Alvin F.

Blacks and the sexual revolution. il por Ebony 26:112-14+ O '71

—and Comer, J. P.

Question every black parent asks: what shall I tell my child? il Redbook 136:64-5+ Ja '71

POVE, Xavora

Cosmic conditioning of hair. See issues of Harper's bazaar

Eye on the sky. See issues of Harper's bazaar

POVERTY

Catch 22 of world poverty. P. Steinfels. Commonweal 94:302 Je 11 '71

See also

Poor

United States

See Poor—United States

POVERTY POINT excavations. See Louisiana—Antiquities

POWDER propellants. See Rockets—Fuel

POWDER puff derby. See Airplane racing

POWELL, Adam Clayton, 1908-

Adam Clayton Powell resigns church pastorate. Chr Cent 88:520 Ap 28 '71 *

End of the politics of pleasure. R. M. Levine. por Harper 242:45-8+ Ap '71 *

Old order changeth . . . pors Ebony 26:116-17 Ja '71 *

POWELL, Anthony Dymoke

Discords in the music of time. H. Howarth. Commentary 53:70-5 Ja '72 *

POWELL, Bernard, family

Lifestyle. il pors Am Home 74:14+ O '71

POWELL, Boog

Boog! The big baseball musical; with editorial comment. B. Ottum. il Sports Illus 35:4,50-4+ Jl 19 '71 *

POWELL, David S.

Right out of the roaring twenties. il Pop Mech 136:76H N '71

POWELL, E. R.

West View's water plant is different. il Am City 86:103-4+ Je '71

POWELL, Elizabeth

Pennsylvania German pottery, tools and processes. il Ceram Mo 19:18-22 N '71

POWELL, Evan

How ice makers work, what to do if they don't. il Pop Sci 198:87-9+ Je '71

How to prevent appliance breakdowns. il Pop Sci 199:86-7+ Jl '71

POWELL, Jeffrey R.

Genetic polymorphisms in varied environments. bibliog il Science 174:1035-6 D 3 '71

POWELL, Lawrence Clark

Who is Lawrence Clark Powell? Am Lib 2:682 Jl '71

POWELL, Lewis Franklin, 1907-

What Nixon's court nominees have said about key issues; excerpts from speeches and writings. por U S News 71:40-2 N 8 '71

about

Check and double-check. il pors Newsweek 78:38 N 8 '71 *

Facts about wiretapping. N. Lewin. New Repub 165:16-17 N 20 '71 *

Hansel and Gretel. por Time 98:27 N 22 '71 *

Lonely witness. Nation 213:549-50 N 29 '71 *

Notes and comment. New Yorker 47:43 N 13 '71 *

Powell: a Virginia gentleman. il por Newsweek 78:18-19 N 1 '71 *

Powell, Rehnquist and the Court. America 125:387-8 N 13 '71 *

Powell speaks. Nat R 23:1396 D 17 '71 *

President's two nominees. il pors Time 98:18-19 N 1 '71 *

Remaking the Supreme court. Nixon sets a pattern. il pors U S News 71:15-17 N 1 '71 *

POWELL, Renee

Lady pros seek golf glory. il pors Ebony 26:106-8+ Jl '71 *

POWELL, Sue

Painting with wax. il Design 73:39 Wint '71

POWELL, William

Doing it. por Newsweek 77:98 Ap 12 '71 *

POWELL, LAKE

Cathedral in the canyon. F. C. Clark, jr. il Motor B & S 127:94-7+ Mr '71

POWELSON, D. Harvey

Drug scene, has it changed? il PTA Mag 66:3-4 bibliog(p35) D '71

POWER, Edward J.

Changing student in the Catholic college; excerpt from Catholic higher education in America: a history. bibliog f Sch & Soc 99:493-6 D '71

POWER, Jonathan

Whither the black power movement? Cur 134:21-4 N '71

POWER, Lawrence V.

Avant gardener. il Am Home 74:28+ Je; 24+ Jl; 58+ S; 56+ O '71

Containers for easy patio gardening. il Am Home 74:88-91+ Ap '71

How to grow houseplants 15 stories high. il Am Home 74:46-7+ F '71

Petaled perfection. il Am Home 74:36 Mr '71

—See McDonald, E. jt. auth.

POWER (mechanics)

See also

Force and energy

Horsepower (mechanics)

POWER (social sciences)

After the revolution, by R. A. Dahl. Review
  Nation 213:117-21 Ag 16 '71. T. Gitlin

Game of nations. R. Barnet. il Harper 243:53-9 N '71

More power to everybody. M. Ways. Read Digest 98:199+ Je '71

Technical power and people. A. W. Benn. Bul Atom Sci 27:23-6 D '71

POWER, Muscular. See Muscular power

POWER amplifiers. See Amplifiers

POWER boat racing. See Motor boat racing

POWER boats. See Motor boats

POWER brakes. See Brakes, Automobile

POWER conversion. See Force and energy

POWER cruisers. See Cruisers (pleasure boats)

POWER failures. See Electric power failures

POWER garden tools. See Garden tools, equipment, and supplies

POWER industry. See Fuel industry

POWER lawn mowers. See Lawn mowers

POWER line poles. See Electric lines—Poles

POWER lines. See Electric lines

POWER plants

See also

Atomic power plants

Electric plants

Hydroelectric plants

Steam power plants

Location

Rocky Mountain coal fever. J. Ridgeway. il Ramp Mag 10:4+ O '71

Trinkets for the Navajos. P. Barnes. New Repub 165:15-16 Jl 3 '71

Pollution

Energy crisis; views of an environmentalist; address, June 15, 1971. M. McCloskey. Vital Speeches 37:621-5 Ag 1 '71

Less power to the people? il Sr Schol 98:16-17 F 15 '71

POWER plants—Pollution—*Continued*
Power generation and the environment. R. Eliassen. il por Bul Atom Sci 27:37-42 S '71
Power pollution: are we living better electrically or worse? il Bet Hom & Gard 49:12+ Ag '71
Rocky Mountain coal fever. J. Ridgeway. il Ramp Mag 10:4+ O '71
Utilities and the environment. Sci N 99:163-4 Mr 6 '71

POWER pools. See Electric plants—Interconnection

POWER production, Electric. See Electric power production

POWER resources
America's energy needs; address, January 12, 1971. H. M. Dole. Vital Speeches 37:322-7 Mr 15 '71
Are we running out of fuel? I. Bengelsdorf. il Nat Wildlife 9:4-9 F '71
Atomic power: what are our alternatives? R. Gannon. il Sci Digest 70:18-23 D '71
Burning up our resources. R. E. Lapp; R. W. Dietsch. New Repub 164:14-17 Je 26 '71
Cleaning of America (don't hold your breath) J. Ridgeway. Ramp Mag 9:17-18 Mr '71
Continuing increase in use of energy. P. H. Abelson. Science 172:795 My 21 '71
Criticism, policy and reality; a national energy policy; address, May 28, 1971. F. N. Ikard. Vital Speeches 37:625-8 Ag 1 '71
Energy crisis. P. R. Ehrlich and J. P. Holden. Sat R 54:50-1 Ag 7 '71
Energy crisis; address, December 10, 1970. F. R. Shumway. Vital Speeches 37:209-12 Ja 15 '71
Energy crisis; symposium. il Bul Atom Sci 27:2-53 S; 2-56 O; 38-56 N '71
Energy crisis; views of an environmentalist; address, June 15, 1971. M. McCloskey. Vital Speeches 37:621-5 Ag 1 '71
Energy; President asks $3 billion for breeder reactor, fuel studies. R. Gillette. Science 172:1114-16 Je 11 '71
Energy resources of the earth. M. K. Hubbert. il Sci Am 225:60-70 bibliog(p244) S '71
Energy, technology and future options. il Sci N 100:53-4 Jl 24 '71
Flow of energy in an industrial society. E. Cook. il Sci Am 225:134-42+ bibliog(p244) S '71
Getting more power to the people. il Time 97:72-4 Ap 19 '71
Heading off an energy crisis. il Nations Bsns 59:26-36 Jl '71
Less power to the people? il Sr Schol 98:16-17 F 15 '71
No energy to waste. J. Lear. Sat R 54:37-9 Jl 3 '71
Power crisis: electricity, oil, coal; interview. T. F. Bradshaw. il por U S News 70:84-6+ My 10 '71
Print-out of the future systems of man; excerpt from Environment, power and society. H. T. Odum. il Natur Hist 80:24-9 bibliog(p 104) My '71; Discussion. 80:10 O '71
Recycling: an old idea with new significance. R. Andrus and S. P. Mathur. il Cons 25:28-31 Je '71
Solutions to the power problem. Chem 44:22 O '71
US to spend more on new energy programs. G. B. Lubkin. Phys Today 24:69-70 Ag '71
Why we have a fuel and power shortage. R. K. Bennett. Read Digest 98:74-8 Ja '71
Year of the firefly. J. Lear. Sat R 55:59 Ja 1 '72
You can't make a power plant look like a tree; or, Waste not, want not. W. F. Wagner, jr. Arch Rec 150:9-10 N '71
See also
Fuel
Fuel supply
Solar energy

Economic aspects
Economic geography of energy. D. B. Luten. il Sci Am 225:164-71+ S '71

POWER sprayers. See Spraying apparatus
POWER steering. See Automobiles—Steering gear
POWER supplies for electronic apparatus. See Electronic apparatus and appliances—Power supply
POWER supply. See Power resources
POWER supply, Electric. See Electric power
POWER tools. See Electric tools

POWER transmission
Transmission they said wouldn't work; kinetic energy control. E. F. Lindsley. il Pop Sci 198:112-13 Ap '71
See also
Belting

POWERS, John James, 1912-
Government structure; address, June 21, 1971. Vital Speeches 37:628-31 Ag 1 '71

POWERS, Thomas
Autopsy on Old Westbury. il Harper 243:52-3+ S '71
Learning to die. il Harper 242:72-4+ Je '71

POWERS, Separation of. See Separation of powers

POWILLS, Dorothy
Playing cards. See issues of Hobbies

POWLEDGE, Fred
H. Ross Perot pays his dues. il pors N Y Times Mag p 16-17+ F 28 '71

POZZO phenomenon (perspective) See Perspective

PRACTICE teaching. See Student teaching

PRAETORIUS, Michael
Delightful music for all seasons, a Praetorius program from Nonesuch. J. W. Barker. il Am Rec G 37:209 D '70 *

PRAGER, Arthur
Edward Stratemeyer and his book machine. il por Sat R 54:15-17+ Jl 10 '71

PRAGMATISM
See also
Utilitarianism

PRAGUE

Description
Interloper in Wechsberg country. H. Sutton. il Sat R 54:16+ Je 26 '71

Music
Report:
Le Malade imaginaire, by J. Pauer. P. Eckstein. il Opera N 35:31 Ja 23 '71

PRAIRIE dogs
Habituation of electrically induced readiness to gnaw. R. E. Cain and others. bibliog il Science 173:262-4 Jl 16 '71

PRAIRIE ecology
Grassland biome network: results of first year. J. L. Arehart. il Sci N 100:282-3 O 23 '71
Lasater ranch: applied range ecology. F. T. Colbert. il Nat Parks & Con Mag 45:18-20 Mr '71
Last chance for the tall grass prairie. L. Payton. il Nat Wildlife 9:25-7 Ag '71
Tallgrass prairie park. A. Bohling. il Nat Parks & Con Mag 45:6-10 Mr '71

PRAIRIE NATIONAL PARK (proposed) See National parks and reserves—United States

PRAIRIES
Grasslands; symposium. il Nat Parks & Con Mag 45:4-28 Mr '71
Last chance for the tall grass prairie. L. Payton. il Nat Wildlife 9:25-7 Ag '71
Tallgrass Prairie National Park. E. R. Hall. il Am For 77:16-21 D '71
Window on yesterday. R. Gogerty. il Farm J 95:42-3 Ja '71

PRALINE soufflé. See Soufflés

PRALL, Ivan E.
Buy a jet for your jon. il Pop Mech 136:10 S '71

PRAMER, David
Soil transforms. il Environ 13:42-6 My '71

PRANG prints. See Lithographs

PRATT, George W. 3d
Face to face with a boy who took his own case to court. por Seventeen 30:139 Jl '71

PRATT, Wallace E.
Striking it big, the unorthodox way. T. D. Barrow. il pors Nations Bsns 59:68-9 Ja '71 *

PRATT and Whitney aircraft division. See United aircraft corporation—Pratt and Whitney aircraft division

PRATTE, Richard
New sensorium: the new student. Sch & Soc 99:160-3 Mr '71

PRAYER
At night in prayer. N. Ayo. il Chr Cent 88:1494-7 D 22 '71
Getting things from God. Chr Today 15:23 Ja 29 '71
Misunderstanding of prayer. D. G. Bloesch. Chr Cent 88:1492-4 D 22 '71

PRAYER in the schools. See Public schools and religion

PRAYER meetings
One mayor's breakfast; Mayor's youth prayer breakfast in Modesto, Calif. L. Roddy. Chr Today 15:42 F 26 '71

PRAYERS
Ask, receive. V. P. McCorry. America 125: inside back cover O 9 '71
New Year's prayer; excerpt from issue of January 2, 1942. D. Lawrence U S News 72:80+ Ja 10 '72
Prayer. A. Solzhenitsyn. il Vogue 158:87 D '71
Prayer for Americans. B. Strohm. il Nat Wildlife 10:3-12 D '71
PRAYING mantis
Meet the mighty mantis. S. Seegers. il Read Digest 99:33-41+ Jl '71
Using yesterday's ways to stop today's bugs! M. C. Goldman. il Org Gard & Farm 18:52-7 Jl '71
PREACHING
Crisis in preaching. E. P. Echlin. il Commonweal 94:423-6 Ag 20 '71; Discussion. 95:70-1 O 15 '71
Future shape of preaching, by T. Hall. Review
Chr Cent 88:1476-7 D 15 '71. D. J. Randolph
Hearts that burn. L. N. Bell. Chr Today 15:27-8 Jl 16 '71
Preaching is social action. W. S. Reid. Chr Today 15:10-11 Je 4 '71
See also
Sermons
PREAKNESS horse race. See Horse racing
PREAMPLIFIERS. See Amplifiers
PREBIOTIC synthesis. See Biosynthesis
PRE-CAMBRIAN period. See Geology, Stratigraphic — Pre-Cambrian; Paleontology—Pre-Cambrian
PRECAST concrete. See Concrete, Precast
PRECESSION
Rotation of the earth. D. E. Smylie and L. Mansinha. il Sci Am 225:80-8 bibliog(p 120) D '71
PRECIOUS metals
Combination; method of joining noble metals with organic compounds. Newsweek 78: 101-2 D 20 '71
PRECIOUS stones
Gemland U.S.A; gem-hunting in South Dakota. il Travel 135:6 Ap '71
Gems and minerals. H. D. Brown. See issues of Hobbies
See also
Gems
Lapidary work
Opals
Pearls
PRECIOUS stones, Artificial
See also
Diamonds, Artificial
PRECIPITATION (meteorology)
See also
Hail
Rain and rainfall
Snow
Measurement
Record snowstorms and problems of snow measurement on Mount Washington. J. E. Howe. il Weatherwise 23:280-2 D '70
PRECISION flying. See Aviation—Formation flying
PRECOGNITION. See Extrasensory perception
PRE-COLUMBIAN art. See Art, Pre-Columbian
PRECONDITIONING of cattle. See Cattle, Beef—Preconditioning
PRECOOKED food, Frozen. See Food, Frozen
PREDATION (zoology)
Nest predation affecting the breeding season of the clay-colored robin, a tropical song bird. E. S. Morton. bibliog il Science 171: 920-1 Mr 5 '71
See also
Insects, Predatory
PREDATOR and rodent control. See United States—Fish and wildlife service
PREDATOR control. See Animals, Predatory—Control
PREDATORY animals. See Animals, Predatory
PREDATORY birds. See Birds of prey
PREDATORY insects. See Insects, Predatory
PREDICTED log competitions. See Navigation—Competitions
PREDICTION. See Forecasting
PREDICTION of scholastic success
Self-fulfilling prophecy. T. L. Good and J. E. Brophy. il Todays Ed 60:52-3 Ap '71
PRE-ENGINEERED buildings. See Buildings, Prefabricated
PREFABRICATED bathrooms. See Bathrooms
PREFABRICATED buildings. See Buildings, Prefabricated
PREFABRICATED fireplaces. See Fireplaces
PREFABRICATED furniture. See Furniture, Prefabricated

PREFABRICATED houses. See Houses, Prefabricated
PREFABRICATED school building. See School buildings, Prefabricated
PREFABRICATION
See also
Houses, Prefabricated
PREFERRED stocks. See Stocks
PREGNANCY
Do's and don'ts of pregnancy. il Good H 173: 205 S '71
Expectant mother:
Emotional changes during pregnancy. N. A. Newton. Redbook 138:10+ D '71
High blood pressure during pregnancy; ed. by E. Jacobs. C. I. Bryans, jr. Redbook 136:20+ F '71
Modern obstetric care. E. B. Connell. Redbook 137:16+ Je '71
Skin changes during pregnancy. E. B. Connell. por Redbook 137:50+ O '71
Giving more of our infants the lives they deserve. T. Berland. il Todays Health 49: 16-19+ Ag '71
Help for girls in trouble; special high schools in New York city. B. Shanas. Parents Mag 46:42-3+ Je '71
Help for high school mothers; Citrus high, Azusa, Calif. program. R. Woodbury. il Life 70:34-41 Ap 2 '71
Little girl who shared my pregnancy. P. Dobson. il por Redbook 137:23-4 Jl '71
Pregnancy: no time to diet. D. Calloway. il McCalls 98:54+ My '71
Pregnancy: the three phases; psychological effects. il Time 98:64+ D 20 '71
Problems of pregnancy; National research council report on nutrition in pregnancy. R. W. Gause. il PTA Mag 65:24-6 Ja '71
School-age mothers go to classes. J. W. Martin. Ed Digest 36:44-5 Ja '71
Weight gains in pregnancy; care with diet still required. Sci N 100:262 O 16 '71
See also
Abortion
Amniotic liquid
Birthright centers
Childbirth
Fetus
Prenatal influences

Signs and diagnosis
New improved pregnancy tests. Good H 172: 165 F '71
Pregnant? Find out early. Newsweek 78:68 N 29 '71
PREGNANCY, Complications of
See also
Abortion
PREGNANCY diet. See Diet
PREGNANCY in animals
Prenatal cerebral development: effect of restricted diet, reversal by growth hormone. S. Zamenhof and others. bibliog il Science 174:954-6 N 26 '71
PREGNANCY tests. See Pregnancy—Signs and diagnosis
PREHISTORIC agriculture. See Agriculture, Prehistoric
PREHISTORIC man. See Man, Prehistoric
PREISS, David
First in war, first in space, and last in support for the arts? il Am Artist 35:5 Ap '71
Seymour Chwast: a Coney Island of the head. il por Am Artist 35:40-5+ O '71
PREJUDICE
How tolerant are we? il Sr Schol 99:2-5 O 25 '71
Language of prejudice. S. Steinberg. il Todays Ed 60:14-17 F '71
Prejudice. A. Whitman. Seventeen 29:118-19+ D '70
Prejudice: a hair across your cheek; Senior youthview. il Sr Schol 99:8-9 O 25 '71
See also
Race prejudice
PREMACK, David
Language in chimpanzee? bibliog il Science 172:808-22 My 21 '71
PREMATURE infants. See Infants, Premature
PREMINGER, Otto
My Laura and Otto's. V. Caspary. il Sat R 54:36-7 Je 26 '71 *
PREMIUM pay. See Overtime
PREMIUMS
Advertising premiums to beguile the mind; classics by Sam Loyd, master puzzle-poser. M. Gardner. il Sci Am 225:114-16+ N '71
Big boxtop bargains. il Mech Illus 67:76-7+ D '71
Cadillacs for free? First state bank of Chicago. il Time 97:89 F 22 '71

PRENATAL care. See Pregnancy
PRENATAL diagnosis. See Fetus—Diseases—Diagnosis
PRENATAL influences
Chemical-cue preferences of newborn snakes: influence of prenatal maternal experience. G. M. Burghardt. bibliog il Science 171:921-3 Mr 5 '71
DNA (cell number) in neonatal brain: second generation (F₂) alteration by maternal (F₀) dietary protein restriction. S. Zamenhof and others. bibliog il Science 172:850-1 My 21 '71
PRENSKY, Sol D.
Do you know these electronic abbreviations? il Electr World 86:57 O '71
PRENTISS, Karl
Body beautiful. il Holiday 48:84-7 S '70
PRENTISS, S. Gilbert
Library leadership and the state library agency. il Am Lib 2:186-91 F '71
PRENTISS, Stanton R.
Oscilloscopes for servicing. il Electr World 86:27-31+ N '71
Test equipment scene. il Pop Electr 1:68+ Ja '72
Zenith goes plug-in. il Radio-Electr 42:62-3+ O '71
PREPAREDNESS, Military
See also
United States—Defenses

Egypt
See also
Egypt—Defenses

Russia
Our four-star military mess; with editorial comment. G. P. Hunt. il Life 70:3, 50-2+ Je 18 '71
See also
Russia—Defenses
PREROGATIVE, Royal
No more whales' tails for Her Majesty; loss of royal rights. il Time 97:37 F 8 '71
PRESBYTERIAN church in Canada
Canadian Presbyterians: down in the middle of the road. L. K. Tarr. Chr Today 15:33 Jl 2 '71
PRESBYTERIAN church in the U.S.A.
Massanetta mandates. R. Chandler. Chr Today 15:32 Jl 16 '71
PRESBYTERIAN church in the United States (general)
Presbyterian revolution of love; celebration of evangelism. J. Adams. Chr Today 16:41 O 22 '71
See also
United Presbyterian church in the U.S.A.
PRESBYTERIAN church in the United States (South)
Conservative fallout. R. Chandler. Chr Today 15:42-3 S 24 '71
Death knell for southern Presbyterians? R. Chandler. Chr Today 15:31 Jl 2 '71
Dixieterian secession. Chr Cent 88:1017 S 1 '71
Plea for a sympathizing tear. Chr Today 15:21 Jl 16 '71
Protestant schism. Newsweek 78:62-3 S 6 '71
Southern Presbyterians continue Liberal-Conservative debate at 111th General Assembly. T. M. McMillan, jr. Chr Cent 88:959-61 Ag 11 '71
PRESBYTERIAN journal
Founder of Presbyterian journal resigns over withdrawal plan. Chr Cent 88:1043 S 8 '71
PRESCHOOL children
See also
Child study

Education
Discovery center hustle. A. Cook and H. Mack. Ed Digest 36:50-3 Mr '71
Early childhood education: a Piagetian perspective. D. Elkind. Ed Digest 37:28-31 D '71
Headstart plus; Mondale child development bill. New Repub 165:10 S 11 '71
Parent education and cultural inheritance. D. Tanner and L. N. Tanner. bibliog Sch & Soc 99:21-4 Ja '71
Pre-schoolers are in school. R. H. Smith. Pub W 200:23 N 1 '71
Reform of preschool education in West Germany. Sch & Soc 99:288-9 Sum '71
Should you force your child to go to nursery school? E. Peck. il Todays Health 49:58-62 Ag '71
Sources of early-childhood curriculum; why are current theories not appropriate? B. Spodek. Ed Digest 36:49-52 Ja '71

Which way for pre-K: wishes or reality? L. T. DiLorenzo. il Am Ed 7:28-32 Ja '71
Young explorers start out; Hofstra university's child development center. il Parents Mag 46:38-9 Je '71
See also
Kindergarten
Nursery schools
Reading
See Childrens reading
Russia
Who raises Russia's children? S. Jacoby. il Sat R 54:40-3+ Ag 21 '71
PRESCHOOL education. See Preschool children—Education
PRESCHOOL literature. See Childrens literature
PRESCOTT, Peter S.
Looking at books. See issues of Look
PRESCOTT, Robert William
Prescott of Flying tiger. por Forbes 107:206-7 My 15 '71 *
PRESCRIPTIONS
Anecdotes, facetiae, satire, etc.
Defiling the prescription; plans for new labeling of prescription drugs. G. Ace. Sat R 54:4 My 8 '71
PRESERVATION hall concerts. See New Orleans—Music
PRESERVATION of architecture. See Architecture—Conservation and restoration
PRESERVATION of landmarks, scenery, etc. See Landscape protection
PRESERVATIVES for feed. See Feed preservation and preservatives
PRESERVES. See Jelly, jam, etc.
PRESERVING. See Canning and preserving
PRESIDENTIAL advisers
Nixon's inner circle of businessmen. il por Bsns W p52-3+ Jl 31 '71
PRESIDENTIAL assistants. See Public officers
PRESIDENTIAL campaigns
See also
Campaign funds
Campaign management
National conventions (political)
National conventions, Democratic
Presidential candidates
Presidents—United States—Election
1972
As Republicans prepare for '72 campaign. il U S News 70:14-16 F 1 '71
Best way to run for president. il por Newsweek 78:26-7 N 22 '71
Campaign costs: floor, not ceiling; Time essay. Time 97:18-19 My 17 '71
Elections '72. Sr Schol 99:1-15 N 1 '71
1972 campaign. Nat R 23:626 Je 15 '71
Nixon in '72: views of party governors. il U S News 70:21 My 3 '71
Nixon: opening moves. Nat R 23:1337 D 3 '71
Nixon's secret strategy. R. Reeves. Harper 243:96-8 D '71
Obstacle course; presidential primary calendar '72. il Newsweek 77:20-1 My 24 '71
Politics: the G.O.P. gears for '72. il Time 98:18-19 N 22 '71
'Tis the season to be nasty. H. Sidey. il Life 71:4 D 3 '71
PRESIDENTIAL candidates
See also
Presidential campaigns
1972
Any number can play scenario. R. Reeves. il N Y Times Mag p7-9+ Ap 11 '71
As Democrats look to '72. il U S News 71:24-6 Ag 2 '71
Battle lines drawn for '72 election; union, White House showdown. il por U S News 71:11-13 D 6 '71
Birch Bayh's bid. por Newsweek 77:43 Ap 19 '71
Brain-trust race for '72; advisers to potential Democratic contenders. C. Roberts. il Newsweek 77:30+ Mr 15 '71
Brooke scenario. il por Time 98:13 D 13 '71
Countdown to '72. Cato. Nat R 23:74 Ja 26 '71
Democratic roller-coaster. Cato. Nat R 23:468 My 4 '71
Democrats. pors Time 98:22 N 22 '71
Democrats: on the threshold of adventure. H. Sidey. il Time 97:16-18 My 17 '71
Ed Muskie asks you to trust him; with editorial comment. B. Brower. il pors Life 71:3, 58-60+ N 5 '71
Enter Jackson. Cato. Nat R 23:522 My 18 '71
Facing up to the indecisiveness issue. por Time 97:15 My 3 '71

PRESS releases
 See also
 Government and the press
PRESS subpoenas. See Subpoenas
PRESSMAN, Norman
 Pingusson's legacy. il Arch Forum 134:52-5 Je
 '71
PRESSON, Gene M.
 Reliable electronic intrusion alarm. il Electr
 World 86:31 S '71
PRESSURE
 Ball stands still in the air; demonstrating
 radiation pressure with laser beams. il Sci
 N 100:309-10 N 6 '71
 See also
 High pressure (science)
PRESSURE, Atmospheric. See Atmospheric
 pressure
PRESSURE, Political. See Pressure groups
PRESSURE groups
 Can we bust the Highway trust? Highway
 action coalition. D. Hayes. il por Sat R
 54:48-53 Je 5 '71; Discussion. 54:58 S 4 '71
 Fight quickens over city highways. M.
 Smith. McCalls 99:43 D '71
 Highway lobby in ambush; public opinion
 survey of Highway users federation for
 safety and mobility. B. Kelley. Nation 213:
 496-500 N 15 '71
 New voice for children; California children's
 lobby. D. Silverton. McCalls 99:50 D '71
 Public policy making; why the churches strike
 out. V. C. Blum. America 124:224-8 Mr 6 '71;
 Discussion. 124:348-9 Ap 3 '71
 See also
 Common cause (political organization)
 Lobbying
 Protests, demonstrations, etc.
PRESSURE packaging
 Aerosol containers. Good H 174:6 Ja '72
 Deactivator of metal aerosol cans. il Consum-
 er Rep 36:64-5 F '71
 Mix with care; interaction between PB and
 Freon in aerosol dispensers. J. McCaull.
 bibliog il Environ 13:39-42 Ja '71
 Q & A on sprays. il Electr World 85:41 My
 '71
 Safe disposal of aerosol cans! il Consumer
 Bul 54:25-6 F '71
PRESTA, Julius F.
 Colonial weaving. il Sch Arts 70:22-3 Mr '71
PRESTAGE, Robin
 Englishman in apple-pie land. Sat R 55:38+
 Ja 1 '72
PRESTON, Betty Braxton
 Quiz for the teacher-buyer. Todays Ed 60:
 36-7 Ja '71
PRESTON, Richard K. and Roth, E. B.
 Loving, learning, and little ones. il Am Ed
 7:9-11 Je '71
PRETRIAL detention. See Preventive detention
PRE-TRIAL procedure
 Pretrial and nontrial in the lower criminal
 courts. R. M. Pious. bibliog f Cur Hist 61:
 20-6+ Jl '71
PRETTYMAN, Alfred
 Why minority publishing? ed. by B. Cham-
 bers. il pors Pub W 199:36-7 Mr 15 '71 *
PREUS, Jacob A. O.
 Sent to reconcile; excerpt from report to
 Missouri synod. Chr Today 15:16-18+ S 10
 '71
 about
 Lutherans to the right. il por Newsweek
 78:64-5 Jl 12 '71 *
 Missouri waltz; whose tunes? with editorial
 comment. R. Chandler. Chr Today 15:24,
 31-2 Ag 6 '71 *
 POW crusade. Chr Today 15:31 F 26 '71 *
 Preus on Concordia; no progress reports. R.
 Chandler. Chr Today 15:48 F 26 '71 *
PREVENTION (periodical)
 Catching up to Rodale press. il por Time 97:51
 Mr 22 '71
PREVENTION of accidents. See Accidents—
 Prevention
PREVENTION of crime. See Crime prevention
PREVENTION of cruelty to animals. See Ani-
 mals—Treatment
PREVENTION of suicide. See Suicide—Preven-
 tion
PREVENTIVE detention
 Annals of justice; G. Russier case in Mar-
 seille. M. Gallant. New Yorker 47:47-52+ Je
 26 '71
 Pretrial and nontrial in the lower criminal
 courts. R. M. Pious. bibliog f Cur Hist 61:
 20-6+ Jl '71
 Terrorism & preventive detention: the case
 of Israel. A. M. Dershowitz; discussion.
 Commentary 51:33-4+ Je '71
PREVENTIVE psychiatry. See Mental hygiene

PREVIN, André
 Mamma mia, that'sa some musical meatball!
 H. Lawrenson. il Esquire 76:94-7+ Jl '71 *
PREVIN, Dory
 Songs to live by. por Time 98:84+ D 6 '71 *
PREVISIONS
 See also
 Dreams
PRÉVOST, Antoine François
 Perfide Manon and abbé Prévost. M. Bishop.
 il por Horizon 13:76-7 Aut '71 *
PRICE, Charles
 Golf and country. Holiday 49:84-5 Mr '71
PRICE, Donald K.
 Small size is no excuse. il por Am City 86:
 60-2 My '71
PRICE, Gerald B. and others
 Age-associated changes in the DNA of mouse
 tissue. bibliog il Science 171:917-20 Mr 5 '71
PRICE, John
 Notes from the cavern. J. Osborne. New
 Repub 165:13-14 D 4 '71 *
PRICE, Leontyne
 About baseball giants, and the great Leontyne
 Price. W. Botsford. por(p273) Am Rec G
 37:296-7+ Ja '71 *
 Milestone Aida. G. Movshon. por Hi Fi 21:
 57-8 Ag '71 *
PRICE, Molly
 Pick of the iris. il Home Gard 58:24-5+ Je
 '71
 Time now to plant peonies. il Home Gard
 58:18-19+ O '71
PRICE, P. Buford. See Cowsik, R. jt. auth.
PRICE, Pearl B.
 Editorial. See issues of PTA magazine
PRICE, Vincent
 Last of the ghouls. J. Kroll. por Newsweek
 77:105+ Je 14 '71 *
PRICE administration, Office of. See United
 States—Price administration, Office of
PRICE commission (United States) See United
 States—Price commission
PRICE control. See Price regulation by gov-
 ernment
PRICE cutting
 See also
 Discount houses (retail trade)
 Dumping (commercial policy)
PRICE earnings ratio. See Stocks—Price earn-
 ings ratios
PRICE fixing, Retail. See Price maintenance
 by industry
PRICE indexes
 Anatomy of price change:
 First quarter, 1971. J. G. Thomas. il Mo
 Labor R 94:73-5 Je '71
 Second quarter, 1971. T. Nakayama. il
 Mo Labor R 94:55-8 O '71
 Third quarter, 1971. T. Nakayama. il
 Mo Labor R 94:62-5 D '71
 Anatomy of price change in 1970. W. J.
 Layng and T. Nakayama. il Mo Labor R 94:
 38-41 F '71
 At last, good news on living costs. il U S
 News 70:62 Je 7 '71
 Consumer price index; how it measures in-
 flation; questions and answers. il U S
 News 71:36-7 O 4 '71
 Determining the effects of quality change
 on the CPI. J. E. Triplett. bibliog il Mo
 Labor R 94:27-32 My '71
 Here's what's been happening to your living
 costs. il Changing T 25:7-14 Ap '71
 Prices; tables. See issues of Monthly labor
 review
 Silent majority's market basket; consumer
 price index. il Forbes 108:38 O 1 '71
 Toward comprehensive measurement of
 prices. A. D. Searle. bibliog f il Mo Labor R
 94:9-22 Mr '71
 What does the consumer price index mean
 to you? M. Daly. Bet Hom & Gard 49:26+ O
 '71
 What freeze did to the cost of living. il U S
 News 71:20 D 6 '71
 Where the index of prices begins; price data
 collectors. il Bsns W p23 O 9 '71
 Yardstick has to measure up; consumer price
 index. W. D. Arant. por Nations Bsns 59:
 75 My '71
PRICE maintenance by industry
 Price-fixers get the plumbing bill. Bsns W
 p26 O 2 '71
PRICE marks
 Retailers search for the right price tag;
 machine readable systems. il Bsns W p52-3
 Ja 23 '71
 They'd rather switch; tag-switching. il News-
 week 78:76-7 Jl 12 '71
 See also
 Unit pricing

PRICE regulation by government
Who will control the price-controllers? il
 Consumer Rep 36:612-14 O '71
    See also
Wage-price policy

Canada

    See also
Wage-price policy—Canada

United States

BMI: 39th annual meeting. il Pub W 200:20-5
 D 13 '71
Complex formula for prices. il Time 98:30 N
 22 '71
Fight for price controls. W. F. Buckley, jr.
 Nat R 23:102 Ja 26 '71
New plea for price control exemption. S.
 Wagner. Pub W 200:51 N 15 '71
Royalties, copyrights freed from price con-
 trols. S. Wagner. Pub W 200:19 N 22 '71
Silver lining? M. Friedman. Newsweek 77:56
 F 1 '71
Wage-price exemption fails in Congress. S.
 Wagner. Pub W 200:30 D 20 '71
    See also
United States—Price administration, Office of
United States—Price commission

PRICE supports, Agricultural. See Agricultural
 administration—United States
PRICE tags. See Price marks
PRICE-wage policy. See Wage-price policy
PRICES
    See also
Inflation (finance)
Profiteering
Value (economic theory)
    also subhead Prices under various sub-
 jects, e.g. Gasoline—Prices; *also* headings
beginning Price

Economic aspects

Economic growth and ecology; an economist's
 view. W. W. Heller. bibliog Mo Labor R
 94:14-21 N '71
    See also
Wage-price policy

Regulation

See Price regulation by government

United States

After four months of controls, price rises
 spreading, and still more to come. il U S
 News 71:15-17 D 20 '71
Anatomy of inflation: 1953-1975. W. H. Fish-
 er. il Sci Am 225:15-21 N '71
As some prices turn down. il U S News
 70:15-16 Ja 25 '71
Cracks in the freeze. il Time 98:23-4 N 15
 '71
How shoppers and merchants size up the
 price freeze. il U S News 71:30-3 N 15 '71
How to shop aggressively and save. il Mech
 Illus 67:44-6+ Ja '71
Inflation crunch: why President acted. il U S
 News 70:18-19 Mr 8 '71
Inflation looks stubborn to business; with
 editorial comment. il Bsns W p26-7, 104
 My 1 '71
Parting shots: some old nickel bargains still
 linger on. il Life 71:62-4 Ag 6 '71
Prices (cont of) Consumer prices; tables and
 Wholesale prices; tables. See issues of
 Monthly labor review
Ready to spend, but still wary. il Bsns W
 p 19-20 F 20 '71
What's good for profits can be bad for prices.
 il Fortune 84:18 Ag '71
    See also
Cost of living—United States
Price indexes
Price regulation by government—United
 States
    also subhead Prices under various sub-
 jects, e.g. Steel—Prices

PRICES of books. See Books—Prices
PRICKLY pears
Prickly pear: desperado of the range? W.
 Rominger. il Org Gard & Farm 18:90 Je
 '71
PRIDE, Charley
Charley Pride and the chicken ladies. M.
 Shestack. por Esquire 75:102-5+ Mr '71

    about
This pitcher won't make it. il pors Ebony
 26:45-6+ My '71 •
PRIDE and vanity
Pride goes before avarice: social change and
 the vices in Latin Christendom. L. K.
 Little. bibliog f il Am Hist R 76:16-49 F
 '71

PRIDEAUX, Tom
Four patron saints in one great act: the
 Steins. il por Life 70:56-60+ Ap 23 '71
Is there a magician in the house? il Life 71:
 114-16+ D 17 '71
PRIESTHOOD. See Priests
PRIESTMAN, Brian
Englishman comes to Denver. A. Young. por
 Hi Fi 21:MA30-1 Je '71 •
PRIESTS
Aftermath of Detroit; Roman document on
 the priesthood. America 124:501-2 My 15 '71
Anonymous priesthood. J. W. Glaser; discus-
 sion. Commonweal 93:407, 483+ Ja 22, F 19
 '71
Backlash and the bishops. W. Wallace. Com-
 monweal 94:253-4 My 21 '71
Canon law: justice by variety. M. J. Mc-
 Manus. America 125:257-9 O 9 '71
Catholic priest in the United States, ed. by
 J. T. Ellis. Review
 America 125:406 N 13 '71. J. Hennesey
Clergy drain. J. Deedy. Commonweal 94:26
 Mr 19 '71
Communities of freedom; Pope's Apostolic
 exhortation on the renewal of the religious
 life. T. Beeson. Chr Cent 88:968-9 Ag 18
 '71
Cutbacks in priesthood. America 124:137-8 F
 13 '71
Episcopal survey reveals priestly role prob-
 lems. Chr Cent 88:95 Ja 27 '71
Exodus of priests: growing worry for Catho-
 lics il U S News 71:78-9 Ag 23 '71
Freedom, not celibacy, major issue, says
 Catholic report. Chr Cent 88:551 My 5 '71
Marriage for priests? What surveys show.
 U S News 70:83 Ap 26 '71
Might the synod surprise? H. ten Kortenaar.
 Commonweal 95:4-5 O 1 '71
New norms for laicization. America 124:365
 Ap 10 '71
1971 synod: a summons to service; with edi-
 torial comment. A. O. Sigur. America 125:
 inside cover, 223 O 2 '71
Nonclerical priests: Vatican's new instruc-
 tions on dispensation from priestly vows.
 T. Beeson. Chr Cent 88:484-5 Ap 21 '71
Papal exhortation to religious. J. C. Haughey.
 America 125:34 Jl 24 '71
Priest-bishop relations: American perspective.
 J. C. Haughey. America 124:518-20 My 15 '71
Priest: center of unity in the Christian com-
 munity. L. Orsy. America 125:205-8 S 25 '71
Priest power in Baltimore. J. J. Egan. Com-
 monweal 94:101-2 Ap 9 '71
Priesthood and papal anguish. America 124:
 425 Ap 24 '71
Priestly problems. R. Chandler. Chr Today
 15:44-5 My 21 '71
Priests vs. bishops. Newsweek 77:97 Ap 26 '71
Question of freedom. Time 97:73 Ap 26 '71
Red and the black: two Italian priests. L.
 Cunningham. Commonweal 94:502-4 S 24 '71
Synod and the study: NORC study of the
 American priesthood. Commonweal 94:
 205-6 My 7 '71
Vatican study reveals sharp increase in
 clergy dropouts. Chr Cent 88:994 Ag 25 '71
Why I am staying in the church. H. Küng.
 il America 124:281-3 Mr 20 '71; Discussion.
 124:358 Ap 10 '71
Why older priests need the Synod. J. B.
 Healey. America 125:210-13 S 25 '71
    See also
Celibacy
Chaplains, Military
Clergy
Ex-nuns, priests, etc.
Marriage of priests

Associations, institutions, etc.

Clerical confusion in Geneva; European as-
 sembly of priest delegates. A. Woodrow.
 Commonweal 94:277-8 My 28 '71
European priests' Geneva conference: div-
 ision and consensus. A. Woodrow. Chr
 Cent 88:805-6 Je 30 '71
Philippine priests organization grows in
 strength and influence. Chr Cent 88:771 Je
 23 '71
To bring the people of God together. T. J.
 Durkin. Chr Cent 88:927-30 Ag 4 '71
    See also
National federation of priests councils

Caricatures and cartoons

Anybody for the priesthood? J. Noonan. Cath
 World 214:35-6 O '71

PRIESTS—*Continued*

Salaries, allowances, etc.

Of celibacy and stipends. E. C. Bianchi. Cath World 213:35-8 Ap '71

Of salary and celibacy. D. Kucharsky. Chr Today 15:52 S 10 '71

PRIGOZY, Ruth
Matter of measurement. Commonweal 95:103-6+ O 29 '71

PRIMACK, Phil
Second rape of Appalachia. Nation 213:530-2 N 22 '71

PRIMACY of the Pope. See Popes—Primacy

PRIMARIES
Fitting up for the primaries. il Time 98:10-11 Jl 19 '71

In re New Hampshire: question of John Ashbrook's candidacy in presidential primary. Nat R 23:1449 D 31 '71

Letter from Washington. Cato, pseud. Nat R 23:1451 D 31 '71

Little Lord; District of Columbia's Democratic primary. New Repub 166:12 Ja 1 '72

Looking ahead; McCloskey. Nat R 23:792 Jl 27 '71

Obstacle course; presidential primary calendar '72. il Newsweek 77:20-1 My 24 '71

Primary nonsense. R. Reeves. il Harper 244:41-4 Ja '72

States race for the gold in primaries. il Bsns W p66+ Je 12 '71

Timetable of Democrats' '72 primaries for president. il US News 71:13 D 6 '71

PRIMARY education. See Education, Elementary

PRIMARY elections. See Primaries

PRIMATES
At play in the fields. P. Dolhinow. il Natur Hist 80:66-71 D '71

Primate populations and biomedical research. C. H. Southwick and others; reply. G. Bermant and S. Chandrasekhar. Science 171:628-9 F 19 '71

Reporter at large. E. Hahn. New Yorker 47:46-8+ Ap 17; 46-50+ Ap 24 '71

Watchers in a green world. P. Rodman and C. Rodman. il pors Life 72:56-63 Ja 14 '72

What do you know about the primates? quiz. J. Daugherty and M. Daugherty. il Sci Digest 70:90-1+ O '71
See also
Apes
Chimpanzees
Emory university, Atlanta, Ga.—Yerkes primate research center
Monkeys

PRIME ministers conferences
Commonwealth: crash course. Time 97:32+ Ja 25 '71

Commonwealth on collision course; meeting in Singapore. il Newsweek 77:35 Ja 25 '71

Delaying a showdown. Time 97:32 F 1 '71

Great imponderable; Commonwealth conference. il Newsweek 77:35 F 1 '71

PRIME numbers. See Numbers, Prime

PRIME rates. See Interest

PRIMEAU, Ernest
Primeau on pulpits. Commonweal 95:74 O 22 '71

PRIMERS
See also
Hornbooks

PRIMITIVE society. See Society, Primitive

PRIMROSES
Walk the primrose path. K. A. Sullivan. il Org Gard & Farm 18:44-6 Jl '71

PRINCE, Alain Wood
Hunting beneath the reef. il Field & S 75:68-9+ F '71

People's choice. il por Outdoor Life 148:84+ Ag '71

PRINCE, Hal
How to play at Hal Prince. H. Saal. il por Newsweek 78:68-70 Jl 26 '71 *

Prince & his follies. L. Botto. il pors Look 35:34-8 My 18 '71 *

PRINCE, Harold S. See Prince, H.

PRINCE EDWARD ISLAND
Uptight little island. D. Levin. il Sports Illus 35:38-40+ O 4 '71

PRINCE GEORGES COUNTY

Education
See Education—Maryland

PRINCETON, III.
Liquid coagulant eases operating problems. E. Finn. il Am City 86:24 D '71

PRINCETON, N.J.
Town tries to block study of its affluence. Pub W 200:235+ Ag 30 '71

PRINCETON particle accelerator. See Accelerators (electrons, etc)

PRINCETON university
Fiscal Houdini for Princeton. il por Bsns W p78+ D 4 '71

From Goheen to "Boheen". por Time 98:42 D 13 '71

Goheen goes. Time 97:45 Ap 5 '71

Lady in a tiger. D. Leff. il Seventeen 29:124-5+ O '70

Princeton chose me. J. Robinson. il por Redbook 136:68-9+ F '71

PRINCETON university press
Companionable design for definitive Thoreau. C. B. Grannis. il por Pub W 200:44+ O 4 '71

PRINCIGALLI, Ada
Our woman in Peking. por Newsweek 78:71 S 20 '71 *

PRINCIPALS, School. See School superintendents and principals

PRINGLE, Laurence
Upper Hudson: whitewater or washwater? il Audubon 73:88+ Mr '71

PRINGLE'S pride; story. See Brody, S.

PRINT collections. See Prints—Collectors and collecting

PRINT council of America
Collector's item; excerpts from address, ed. by M. R. Weiss. il Sat R 54:36-7 Ag 7 '71

PRINTED circuits
Adhesive stencil technique for PC boards. T. Anderson. il Pop Electr 35:71+ D '71

Break through radio pollution: use etched coils in FM preamp. R. B. Cooper, jr. il Radio-Electr 42:33-7 Je '71

Look at the PC market. A. W. Burawa. il Pop Electr 1:46-50 Ja '72

Making the PC board. il Pop Sci 198:96-7+ Mr '71

PRINTED textiles. See Textile fabrics

PRINTERS
See also
International typographical union

PRINTERS (computers) See Computers—Print-out equipment

PRINTING
Penrose '71: can printers keep up with new developments? C. B. Grannis. il Pub W 200:54-5 Ag 2 '71
See also
Embossing (typography)
Lithography

History
Book that never was, by J. R. Dunlap. Review
Pub W il 200:45-6 D 6 '71. C. B. Grannis

Private presses
See Private presses

PRINTING (photography) See Photography—Printing processes

PRINTING, Linoleum block. See Linoleum block printing

PRINTING industry
Future isn't what it used to be; adaptation of address, 1970. A. E. Gardner. Pub W 199:42-5 Ja 11 '71

Hurry-up job of printing prospectuses. R. Levy. il Duns 97:62-5 Ap '71
See also
Colish, A. inc.

PRINTING paper (photography) See Photographic paper

PRINTMAKING. See Prints—Technique

PRINTS
Colonial life in the West Indies as depicted in prints. N. Connell. il Antiques 99:732-7 My '71

Graphics: fair game for the treasure-seekers. A. Ogden. House B 113:22+ D '71

Making the gallery scene; Japanese prints at the Brooklyn museum. B. Wasserman. il Sch Arts 71:28-31 N '71

New wrinkle in printmaking; a wrinkle print. W. J. O'Donnell. il Am Artist 35:52-3+ N '71

Young printmakers in Latin America. E. L. Johnson. il Art in Am 59:116-17 Ja '71
See also
Lithographs

Collectors and collecting
Print collection at Winterthur. N. E. Richards. il Antiques 100:586-90 O '71 (to be cont)

Some pre-Revolutionary prints and broadsides; Middendorf collection of American historical prints. W. J. Shadwell. il Antiques 99:262-7 F '71
See also
Libraries—Print collections
New York public library—Print collection

PRINTS—*Continued*

Exhibitions

Art; L'estampe originale, exhibition at the New York cultural center. L. Alloway. Nation 212:189-90 F 8 '71

Technique

Carry a big stick and print with it. S. Gruenberg. il Sch Arts 70:22-3 F '71

Just ink and print with fruit or vegetable. il Sunset 147:152 N '71

Luigi Rist: printmaker in the Japanese tradition. B. Whipple. il por *Am Artist* 35: 38-43+ Ag '71

Making a cardboard print. E. Palmatier. il Todays Ed 60:66 N '71

No bones about it; bone printing. S. Deutchman. il Sch Arts 71:42-3 D '71

Roll a multi-colored print. N. Finley. il Sch Arts 71:10-11 D '71
See also
Linoleum block printing

PRINTS, Drying of. See Photography—Drying (films and prints)

PRINTS, Finger. See Fingerprints

PRINTS and photographs division of the Library of Congress. See United States—Library of Congress—Prints and photographs division

PRISON architecture. See Prisons—Architecture

PRISON bands
Song of freedom; Sonny Brown and his bands and choirs. por Newsweek 77:115 My 17 '71

PRISON camps

Russia

24 years in the life of Lyuba Bershadskaya. T. Vocse. il por N Y Times Mag p27-9+ Mr 14 '71

PRISON drama. See Prison recreation

PRISON escapes. See Escapes

PRISON guards. See Prisons—Officials and employees

PRISON industries
See also
Federal prison industries, inc.

PRISON labor. See Convict labor

PRISON libraries
Breaking into jail; Allegheny County jail, Pittsburgh. S. Opipare and others. il pors Library J 96:2734-6 S 15 '71

Dorothy Carter, prison librarian, emeritus; King County jail, Seattle, Wash. il pors Wilson Lib Bul 46:408-10 Ja '72

Good news in prison library reform. Wilson Lib Bul 46:222+ N '71

Library service for prisons aim of new organizations. Library J 97:20 Ja 1 '72

Roundelay for Attica and other prison libraries based on an old song. D. E. Stadius. il por Wilson Lib Bul 46:246-7 N '71
See also
Libraries—Services to prisons

PRISON recreation
Playwrights in residence; Later, Jason, written by inmate of Virginia state penitentiary presented on TV. il por Time 98:43 Jl 26 '71

PRISON reform. See Prisons

PRISON riots
Attica. Chr Cent 88:1123 S 29 '71
Attica prison riot: what happened? Why? What now? il Sr Schol 99:14-15 O 18 '71
Attica prison's bloody Monday; with editorial comment, reports and interview with N. Morris, ed. by J. Pekkanen. il Life 71:3, 26-36 S 24 '71
Attica rebellion. il Newsweek 78:21 S 20 '71
Attica: the hostages' story. W. H. Hanson. il N Y Times Mag p 18-19+ O 31 '71; Same abr. with title Attica revisited. Nat R 23: 1274 N 19 '71; Reply with rejoinder. A. O. Eve. N Y Times Mag p 18 N 28 '71
Attica: Vietnam at home. J. Leo; P. Steinfels. Commonweal 95:6-8 O 1 '71
Attican rights. W. F. Buckley, jr. Nat R 23: 1137 O 8 '71
Attica's legacy. il Newsweek 78:23 O 4 '71
Bloody Attica; furies unleashed. il pors Newsweek 78:22-6+ S 27 '71
Dead end at Attica. New Repub 165:9-10 S 25 '71; Reply. T. K. Dalglish. 165:31 O 23 '71
Exploiting Attica. il Nat R 23:1101-2 O 8 '71
Learning lessons from Attica. America 125: 251 O 9 '71
Of life and death; blacks can learn from Attica. il Ebony 27:168-9 N '71
Order and Attica. New Repub 165:7-8 O 23 '71

Religious reaction to Attica. Chr Cent 88: 1159 O 6 '71
Remember Attica; Rahway insurrection. il Newsweek 78:26+ D 6 '71
Riot in the penitentiary; Raiford state penitentiary, Florida. J. Blake. Am Scholar 40:672-3 Aut '71
Slaughter at Attica. Nation 213:258 S 27 '71
Storm over Attica. il Life 71:26-9 O 1 '71
Tragedy averted; uprising at Rahway, N.J. il Time 98:19 D 6 '71
Uprising in Attica. il Time 98:12-14 S 20 '71
War at Attica: was there no other way? il por Time 98:18-26 S 27 '71
We're reaping a harvest of permissiveness; interview. F. T. Wilkinson. il por U S News 71:22 S 27 '71
Why U.S. prisons are exploding; Attica, N.Y. il U S News 71:19-21 S 27 '71
William Kunstler for the defense, of himself; performance at Attica. T. Moore. por Life 71:77 O 1 '71

PRISON visits. See Prisons—Visits with inmates

PRISONER of Second avenue; drama. See Simon, N.

PRISONERS
George Jackson radicalizes the brothers in Soledad and San Quentin. T. Szulc. il pors N Y Times Mag p 10-11+ Ag 1 '71
Prisoner power: a radical turn. il Newsweek 78:38 S 27 '71
What prisoners are reading. Am Scholar 40: 701-7 Aut '71
Where waiting is like dying. il Newsweek 77: 30-1 My 17 '71
See also
Escapes
Melville, S.
Parole
Political prisoners
Prisons
Prisons—Visits with inmates

Employment
See Convict labor

Legal status, laws, etc.
Burger court & the penal system. S. Rubin. Nation 212:785-8 Je 21 '71
Due process behind prison walls. M. O. Tobriner. Nation 213:367-9 O 18 '71

Recreation
See Prison recreation

Rehabilitation
From jailhouse to journalism; Sidney Cassese, a trainee on Richmond's Times-Dispatch. Time 98:62+ N 22 '71
Heroin and the black community. V. E. Taylor. Am Scholar 40:691-4 Aut '71
Inside the prison-industrial complex. J. Castelli. Commonweal 95:124-5 N 5 '71
Is the prison becoming obsolete? R. W. England, jr. bibliog f il Cur Hist 61:35-9+ Jl '71
Jaycees in prison. il Time 98:60+ S 20 '71
Pre-posthumous conversation with myself. E. Smith. pors Esquire 75:112-15+ Je '71
Prisons: the way to reform. il Time 98:26+ S 27 '71
Reforming prison reform. D. G. Shockley. Commonweal 94:497-8 S 24 '71
Rehabilitation myth. A. F. Nussbaum. Am Scholar 40:674-6 Aut '71
There's more to crime control than the get tough approach. D. L. Skoler. bibliog f Ann Am Acad 397:28-39 S '71

Treatment
Attica graduate tells his story. W. R. Coons. il por N Y Times Mag p20-1+ O 10 '71; Reply. p30+ N 7 '71
Attica: part of an overall pattern. R. Arens. Commonweal 95:52-3 O 15 '71
Attica's eloquence. Chr Today 16:31 O 8 '71
Case for skepticism: San Quentin shoot-out. A. H. Sigman. Nation 213:424-9 N 1 '71
From revenge to resocialization; changing perspectives in combating crime. D. Glaser. Am Scholar 40:654-61 Aut '71
Gorilla cowed his keepers; Kayo Konigsberg at the United States medical center for federal prisoners, Springfield, Mo. with editorial comment. D. Walsh. il pors Life 70 3, 42-8+ Je 25 '71
. . . I am not free. A. I. Waskow. Sat R 55: 20-1 Ja 8 '72
Life behind bars. Commonweal 93:508 F 26 '71
My cure for prison riots: end prison racism. W. E. Moore. il pors Ebony 27:84-6+ D '71
Prison: the new academy. B. Jackson. il Nation 213:584-9 D 6 '71

PRISONERS—Treatment—*Continued*
Prisoner and the union: efforts to aid prisoners and ex-convicts in Calif. D. Seidman. Nation 213:6-7 Jl 5 '71
Scandal in Virginia; ruling by U.S. District court. il Newsweek 78:39 N 15 '71
Square's night behind bars; Nevada graduate course for judges. P. E. Wilson. por Nation 212:200-6 F 15 '71
Unusual experiment at Stanford dramatizes the brutality of prison life. N. Faber. il Life 71:82-3 O 15 '71

PRISONERS, Discharged
Bargain for freedom; E. H. Smith. Newsweek 78:30 D 20 '71
Hoffa home free. por Time 99:29 Ja 3 '72
Neither truth nor victory; freeing of Edgar Smith. il por Time 98:51 D 20 '71
Return of Edgar Smith. W. F. Buckley, jr. Nat R 23:1455 D 31 '71
See also
Parole

PRISONERS, Political. See Political prisoners

PRISONERS, Women
Teacher who chose to go to jail. D. Gallagher. il por Redbook 136:58-9+ Ja '71
Women in prison. K. Burkhart. il Ramp Mag 9:20-9 Je '71

PRISONERS as artists
Artists in prison. R. Weiner. Am Artist 36:8 Ja '72

PRISONERS as authors
Long wait; new trial for death house author. E. Smith por Time 97:22+ My 24 '71
Playwrights in residence; Later, Jason, written by inmate of Virginia state penitentiary presented on TV. il por Time 98:43 Jl 26 '71

PRISONERS as dramatists. See Prisoners as authors

PRISONERS of war
See also
Geneva conventions
Vietnamese war, 1957- —Prisoners and prisons

Families
See Service mens families

Wives
See Service mens wives

PRISONERS of war, Returned
One for one; release of J. C. Sexton. il por Newsweek 78:68 O 25 '71

PRISONERS of war in Korea
See also
Korean war, 1950-1953—Prisoners and prisons

PRISONERS of war in Vietnam. See Vietnamese war, 1957- —Prisoners and prisons

PRISONS
See also
Indeterminate sentence
Prison riots
Probation

Architecture
Building types study. il Arch Rec 150:109-24 Ag '71

Officials and employees
Waiting for a riot; guard in the tombs fights problems no one can solve. J. Mills. il Life 71:30-5 O 1 '71

Visits with inmates
Opening the gates to new prison reform; conjugal visits for convicts. il Life 71:24-9 Ag 13 '71

Arkansas
New chapter in horror; Cummins prison farm. N. C. Chriss. il Nation 214:49-50 Ja 10 '72

California
Case for skepticism: San Quentin shoot-out. A. H. Sigman. Nation 213:424-9 N 1 '71
Closing Q: San Quentin. Time 99:10 Ja 17 '72
Crime wave; San Quentin penitentiary. Newsweek 77:33 Ap 26 '71
Death in San Quentin: G. Jackson. il por Time 98:17-18 S 6 '71
George Jackson radicalizes the brothers in Soledad and San Quentin. T. Szulc. il pors N Y Times Mag p 10-11+ Ag 1 '71
Instant clothes checking in a jail; Orange County jail. il Am City 86:36 O '71
Jackson's legacy. il Newsweek 78:17-18 S 13 '71
Kind and usual punishment in California. J. Mitford. il Atlan 227:45-52 Mr '71; Discussion. 227:34+ My '71
Pistol in the Afro wig; escape attempt by G. Jackson from San Quentin. Nat R 23:970+ S 10 '71
San Quentin massacre. il por Newsweek 78:29 Ag 30 '71

San Quentin story: the prisons are getting a tougher class of convicts. K. Lamott. il por N Y Times Mag p28-9+ My 2 '71
Setback for prison reform? killings at San Quentin. il U S News 71:49 S 6 '71
Sifting the facts about George Jackson. il por Sr Schol 99:15-16 O 18 '71
Way to lick the jail habit; RODEO program. L. Velie. Read Digest 98:142-6 F '71
What about the other five? slaughter at San Quentin. G. Kirk. Nat R 23:1058 S 24 '71
What happened at San Quentin. il Newsweek 78:18-20 S 6 '71

Connecticut
Danbury strikes. Commonweal 94:442 S 8 '71

Florida
Riot in the penitentiary; Raiford state penitentiary. J. Blake. Am Scholar 40:672-8 Aut '71

Great Britain
Dose of medicine. Newsweek 78:30 S 6 '71

Indiana
Violence to reform to apathy. M. King. Nation 213:325-7 O 11 '71

Mississippi
Delta prison. J. T. Fargason, jr. Am Scholar 40:667-71 Aut '71

Nevada
Square's night behind bars. P. E. Wilson. por Nation 212:200-6 F 15 '71

New Jersey
Remember Attica; Rahway insurrection. il Newsweek 78:26+ D 6 '71
Tragedy averted; uprising at Rahway. il Time 98:19 D 6 '71

New York (state)
Attica. Chr Cent 88:1123 S 29 '71
Attica. il Life 71:28-9 D 31 '71
Attica aftermath. il Time 98:24 O 11 '71
Attica prison riot: what happened? Why? What now? il Sr Schol 99:14-15 O 18 '71
Attica prison's bloody Monday; with editorial comment, reports and interview with N. Morris, ed. by J. Pekkanen. il Life 71:3, 26-36 S 24 '71
Attica rebellion. il Newsweek 78:21 S 20 '71
Attica: the hostages' story. W. H. Hanson. il N Y Times Mag p 18-19+ O 31 '71; Same abr. with title Attica revisited. Nat R 23:1274 N 19 '71; Reply with rejoinder. A. O. Eve. N Y Times Mag p 18 N 28 '71
Attica: Vietnam at home. J. Leo; P. Steinfels. Commonweal 95:6-8 O 1 '71
Attican rights. W. F. Buckley, jr. Nat R 23:1137 O 8 '71
Attica's legacy. il Newsweek 78:23 O 4 '71
Bloody Attica; furies unleashed. il pors Newsweek 78:22-6+ S 27 '71
Dead end at Attica. New Repub 165:9-10 S 25 '71; Reply. T. K. Dalglish. 165:31 O 23 '71
Exploiting Attica. il Nat R 23:1101-2 O 8 '71
Letters from Attica and elsewhere; with introduction. S. Melville. il por Ramp Mag 10:45-50 D '71
Order and Attica. New Repub 165:7-8 O 23 '71
Religious reaction to Attica. Chr Cent 88:1159 O 6 '71
Slaughter at Attica. Nation 213:258 S 27 '71
Storm over Attica. il Life 71:26-9 O 1 '71
Uprising in Attica. il Time 98:12-14 S 20 '71
War at Attica: was there no other way? il por Time 98:18-26 S 27 '71
Why U.S. prisons are exploding; Attica, N.Y. il U S News 71:19-21 S 27 '71

Pennsylvania
Reflections from the pig farm; Lewisburg federal penitentiary. T. Lewis. Commonweal 94:499-500 S 24 '71

See also
Prison camps—Russia

Russia

United States
Black liberation and the prisons. C. Rogers. Chr Cent 88:1462 D 15 '71
Drive to halt prison violence. il U S News 71:37-9 D 27 '71
Gorilla cowed his keepers; Kayo Konigsberg at the United States medical center for federal prisoners, Springfield, Mo; with editorial comment. D. Walsh. il pors Life 70:3, 42-8+ Je 25 '71
. . I am not free. A. I. Waskow. Sat R 55:20-1 Ja 8 '72

PRIX de l'Arc de triomphe. See Horse racing
—France
PRIZE fighters. See Boxers
PRIZES. See Rewards, prizes, etc.
PRO football. See Football clubs
PRO musica (organization) See New York pro
musica antiqua (organization)
PROBABILITIES
See also
Distribution (probability theory)
Stochastic processes
PROBATE law and practice
See also
Executors and administrators
PROBATION
Better than prison. Time 97:39 Je 7 '71
PROBES, Testing. See Testing instruments
PROBLEM children
Teachers look at classroom behavior problems,
a survey. R. H. Burns and A. McCullen.
Ment Hy 55:504-6 O '71
See also
Juvenile delinquency
Runaway boys and girls
School children—Adjustment

Education
Relieving anxiety through art activity in an
inner city school. E. Scott. bibliog il Sch
Arts 70:44-6 Mr '71
See also
Mentally handicapped children—Education
Special classes and special schools
PROBLEM drinking. See Alcoholism
PROBLEM solving
Don't solve problems, prevent them. J. J.
Cribbin. il Nations Bsns 59:57-8 O '71
PROBST, Gerald G.
Coming of age at Univac. por Bsns W p 116+
S 11 '71 •
PROCEDURE (law)
Pittsburgh's program for efficient courts.
M. T. Bloom. Read Digest 98:215-16+ Je
'71
See also
Appellate procedure
Conduct of court proceedings
Courts martial and courts of inquiry
Criminal procedure
PROCESS theology
Process philosophy: a post-conciliar op-
tion? R. Lauder. Cath World 213:13-16 Ap
'71
PROCRASTINATION
Helping the procrastinating child. B. Spock.
il Redbook 136:20+ Ja '71
PROCTER and Gamble company
See also
Clorox company
PROCTOR, Alexander Phimister
Mustangs; excerpts from Alexander Phimister
Proctor, sculptor in buckskin. il pors Design
73:4-7 Fall '71 •
PROCTOR, Mac
Addiction, the counter-culture. Nation 212:
623-7 My 17 '71
PROCTOR, Samuel D.
Revolution in a technological society; address,
October 22, 1970. por Negro Hist Bul 34:6-9
Ja '71
PROCUREMENT, Government. See Purchas-
ing, Government
PRODIGIES, Musical. See Children as musi-
cians
PRODUCE trade
See also
Farm produce—Marketing
Geest industries, ltd.
PRODUCTION
Capital goods may get a growing share; re-
lationships between capital and output.
L. A. Mayer. il Fortune 83:96-9+ Je '71
See also
Gross national product
Input-output analysis
Inventories
Labor productivity
PRODUCTION, Agricultural
Social impact of the green revolution; with
discussion. L. R. Brown. bibliog f il pors
Int Concil 581:5-61 Ja '71
Where green revolution is ending food crises.
il U S News 71:91-3 N 1 '71
See also
Crop yields
Surplus products, Agricultural
PRODUCTION control
See also
Critical path analysis
PRODUCTIVITY, Labor. See Labor produc-
tivity
PRODUCTS, Certification of. See Commercial
products, Certification of

PRODUCTS, Commercial. See Commercial
products
PRODUCTS, New
Exciting new products. C. Bilski. See issues
of Popular mechanics
Good news. D. L. Gregg and D. M. Lidster.
See issues of Better homes and gardens
New products. See fourth issue of each month
of Science news
New products. See issues of Popular elec-
tronics
New products. See issues of Radio-electron-
ics
New products & literature. See issues of
Electronics world
New products and processes. See issues of
American city
Product gallery. See issues of Popular elec-
tronics
Some of the 500's new products. il Fortune
83:152-7 My '71
12 convenience items worth buying. F. Casey.
il Mech Illus 67:74-5 Jl '71
What's new. See issues of Hot rod
PRODUCTS, Quality of. See Quality of prod-
ucts
PROETZ, Victor
Onward and upward with the arts. New
Yorker 47:82+ My 22 '71
PROFESSIONAL basketball. See Basketball
teams
PROFESSIONAL basketball players. See Bas-
ketball players
PROFESSIONAL education
See also
Library schools and education
PROFESSIONAL ethics
See also
Business ethics
Librarians, Professional ethics for
Medical ethics
Scientists, Professional ethics for
PROFESSIONAL football clubs. See Football
clubs
PROFESSIONAL football players. See Football
players
PROFESSIONAL golfers' association of Ameri-
ca
What every well-bred rookie should know;
qualifying school of the PGA's tournament
players division. B. Gilbert. il Sports Illus
34:42-3 Ja 11 '71
PROFESSIONAL golfers' association tourna-
ment. See Golf—Tournaments
PROFESSIONAL photographers of America,
inc.
Photo education. E. Scully. Mod Phot 35:133+
Ja '71
PROFESSIONAL secrets. See Confidential com-
munications
PROFESSIONAL sports. See Sports
PROFESSIONAL tennis. See Tennis
PROFESSIONAL women. See Business and
professional women
PROFESSIONALISM (sports) See Amateurism
(sports)
PROFESSIONS
Choosing careers: the big shift. il U S News
70:22-4 My 31 '71
See also
Negro women—Occupations
Occupations
Self employed
also Librarianship as a profession;
Teaching as a profession; etc.
PROFESSORS. See College professors and in-
structors
PROFFITT, Nicholas C.
A day in the dwindling war. il Newsweek
78:40-1 S 13 '71
PROFIT
Effect on profits. C. Morgello. il Newsweek
78:98 N 22 '71
Profits and Phase two. M. L. Weidenbaum.
Duns 98:11 N '71
Putting a lid on profits: who gets squeezed.
il U S News 71:55-7 N 29 '71
Trend of profits now. il U S News 71:34-6
N 1 '71
See also
Corporations—Finance
PROFIT sharing
Profit-sharing plans: other needs, other
goals. Harvard Bsns R 49:52 My '71
See also
Bonus system
PROFITEERING
Profit puzzle in procurement; GAO study. il
Bsns W p44+ Mr 6 '71
See also
War profits
PROFITS tax, Excess. See Excess profits tax

PROGRAM budgeting
ABC's of PPB; planning-programming-budgeting at Lancaster County library. H. R. Jenkins. bibliog il por Library J 96:3089-93 O 1 '71
Change in budgetary thinking: PPBS; address, June 1971. W. Summers. bibliog il Am Lib 2:1174-80 D '71
From analysis to evaluation. A. Schick. bibliog f Ann Am Acad 394:57-71 Mr '71
McNamara, media and you; PPBS (program planning and budgeting system) and school libraries. J. Meyers and R. Barber. bibliog il Library J 96:1079-81, 1743+ Mr 15, My 15 '71
Program budgeting works in nonprofit institutions. R. K. Macleod. il Harvard Bsns R 49:46-56 S '71
Toward PPBS in the public library; planning-programming-budgeting system at Vigo County public library. E. N. Howard. bibliog il Am Lib 2:386-93 Ap '71
PROGRAM evaluation and support, Committee on. See American library association—Program evaluation and support, Committee on
PROGRAMMABLE calculators. See Calculating machines, Electronic
PROGRAMMED instruction
See also
Computers—Educational use
PROGRAMMING (computers) See Computer programming
PROGRAMMING languages (computers) See Computer languages
PROGRESS
Dodo didn't make it; survival and betterment. K. E. Boulding. Bul Atom Sci 27:19-22 My '71
What's happened to the brain business? P. Schrag. il Sat R 54:12-15+ Ag 7 '71
See also
Change
Social progress
PROGRESS, Technical. See Technological change
PROGRESSIVE education
Education in depth; overcoming failure of life adjustment education. M. Rafferty. Ed Digest 36:9-11 Mr '71
See also
Open plan schools
PROHIBITION
India
Return of the toddy tappers. Time 98:26 S 13 '71
PROJECT management. See Business management and organization
PROJECT Rover. See Rockets, Atomic powered
PROJECT Sanguine. See Radio communication, Naval
PROJECT SOAR (Save our American resources project) See Conservation of resources—Study and teaching
PROJECT SPOKE. See Norton, Mass.—Education
PROJECT Stratoscope. See Balloons—Research use
PROJECT teaching
See also
Art—Study and teaching—Projects
PROJECT UNIQUE. See Rochester, N.Y.—Education
PROJECT Wingspread. See Chicago—Education
PROJECTION, Television. See Television projection
PROJECTION of transparencies. See Transparencies—Projection
PROJECTORS
How to choose a projector like an expert. L. Drukker. il Pop Phot 68:104-5+ Ja '71
Last look at Photokina '70. W. F. Wilson. il Pop Phot 68:110+ F '71
New from Kodak: the quiet ones; slide projectors. il Consumer Bul 54:21 D '71
Photo expo 71. N. Rothschild. il Pop Phot 69:85+ Ag '71
Portable battery-operated slide projector. il Consumer Bul 54:28 Mr '71
Slide projectors. il Consumer Bul 54:7-11+ Je '71
See also
Moving picture projectors
Television projection
PROKOF'EV, Sergei Sergeevich
Prokofiev blockbuster. R. S. Brown. Hi Fi 21:88+ Ja '71 *
PROMENADE concerts, London. See London—Music
PROMETHIUM
Promethium in S stars. Sky & Tel 42:279 N '71
Promethium in the star HR 465. M. F. Aller. il Sky & Tel 41:220-2 Ap '71

PROMISCUITY. See Sexual ethics
PROMOTERS and promoting
Ali vs. Frazier: a show-biz approach. por Bsns W p27 F 13 '71
But it looked like a great new racket; pro tennis, ed. by F. Deford. B. Briner. il Sports Illus 34:56-8+ Ap 19 '71
Fight of century has few losers; Ali-Frazier match. il Bsns W p44 Mr 13 '71
Greed creed: will it pay off? closed circuit TV in sports. Newsweek 77:75D-76 Mr 22 '71
In this corner Jerry Perenchio; interview, ed. by L. Gross. A. G. Perenchio. il pors Look 35:92-3+ Je 1 '71
New enemy; Ali-Frazier fight and business profits. S. J. Adamo. America 124:321 Mr 27 '71
Take the money and run; Muhammad Ali-Joe Frazier fight promoters. il pors Newsweek 77:94-5 Mr 8 '71
Trade winds; efforts to block closed-circuit bullfight in Madison Square Garden. C. Amory. Sat R 54:10-11 Jl 3 '71
See also
Impresarios
Parnassus, G.
Perenchio, J.
PROMPTING
Prompter. E. Burns. il pors Opera N 35:27-9 Mr 27 '71
PRONZINI, Bill
Uses and abuses of dialogue. Writer 84:12-14+ My '71
PROOF (law) See Evidence (law)
PROPAGANDA
Dilemma of cultural propaganda: let it be; American propaganda. A. Goodfriend. Ann Am Acad 398:104-12 N '71
Promotion of chaos: the three major catalysts; address, July 17, 1971. R. E. L. Eaton. Vital Speeches 37:687-90 S 1 '71
Propaganda: morally questionable and morally unquestionable techniques. R. K. White. bibliog f Ann Am Acad 398:26-35 N '71
Selling Uncle Sam in the seventies. K. R. Sparks. bibliog f Ann Am Acad 398:113-23 N '71
Six 'big lies' about America. A. Belchman. il N Y Times Mag p32-3+ Je 6 '71
See also
Moving pictures—Propaganda films
Propaganda, International
Vietnamese war. 1957- —Propaganda
PROPAGANDA, American. See Propaganda
PROPAGANDA, Anti-American. See Propaganda
PROPAGANDA, British
Changing role of British international propaganda. H. Beeley. Ann Am Acad 398:124-9 N '71
PROPAGANDA, Chilean
Red red riding hood; government's comic books. il Newsweek 78:38 O 11 '71
PROPAGANDA, Communist
See also
Propaganda, Russian
PROPAGANDA, International
Propaganda in international affairs; symposium, ed. by L. J. Martin. bibliog f il Ann Am Acad 398:1-139 N '71
PROPAGANDA, Russian
Soviet international propaganda: its role, effectiveness, and future. Z. Nagorski, jr. bibliog f Ann Am Acad 398:130-9 N '71
PROPAGATION of plants. See Plant propagation
PROPANE
See also
Automobile engines—Fuel
Liquefied petroleum gas
PROPANE torches. See Torches
PROPANIL
Soil transforms; metabolism of aniline-based pesticides to TCAB and other azo compounds. D. Pramer. il Environ 13:42-6 My '71
PROPELLANTS, Rocket. See Rockets—Fuel
PROPER motion of the stars. See Stars—Motion
PROPERTY
Searching mind of men and property. T. L. Shaffer. il Todays Ed 60:25-7 N '71
See also
Church property
Heirlooms
Vested rights
Wills
PROPERTY, Intellectual
See also
Copyright
World intellectual property organization
PROPERTY insurance. See Insurance, Property

PROPERTY tax
Ahead, a shift away from property taxes. il U S News 71:93-4 D 6 '71
California doctrine. A. E. Wise. il Sat R 54: 78-9+ N 20 '71
California scraps its school tax system. Bsns W p59-60 S 4 '71
Dividing the cake; California Supreme court decision on property tax school finance. il Time 98:47 S 13 '71
Exit the property tax? California Supreme court decision. Newsweek 78:61 S 13 '71
Fresh blow against financing schools with property taxes. U S News 72:66 Ja 10 '72
Nationwide shake-up in property taxes. G. Lorang. il Farm J 95:22-3 N '71
Paying for public education; California Supreme court decision. Nation 213:226 S 20 '71
Property tax spiral: what can you do to stop it? M. Daly. Bet Hom & Gard 49:16+ Ag '71
Revolt in a grab bag; inequities in California. il Newsweek 78:93 D 6 '71
Rising taxes on homes, and the search for a way out. il U S News 71:71-3 Jl 12 '71
School-tax ruling that could overturn financing in most states. U S News 71:90 S 13 '71
School taxes; decision by the California Supreme court. New Repub 165:9-10 O 2 '71
Trouble with property taxes. R. Cassidy. New Repub 164:15-16 My 15 '71; Reply. A. L. Grey, jr. 165:33 Jl 3 '71
Trying to change an unfair tax. il Time 97: 81-2 My 3 '71
Welcome blow at the school tax; California decision. Fortune 84:68 O '71

PROPHECIES
Prophecy: fluke, fraud or psychological syndrome? J. Ehrenwald. bibliog Am Imago 28:79-83 Spr '71
　　See also
Astrology
Bible—Prophecies
Forecasting
Prophets

PROPHETS
Who are today's true prophets? E. H. Merrill. Chr Today 15:8-10+ Mr 12 '71

PROPOSITION; musical comedy. See Musical comedies, revues, etc.—Criticisms, plots, etc.

PROPRIETARY medicines. See Medicines, Patent, proprietary, etc.

PROSHANSKY, Harold M.
Finding elbowroom in a crowded world. il por Bsns W p60 N 27 '71 *

PROSPECT school, North Bennington, Vt. See Schools, Experimental

PROSPECTING
Termites reveal hidden gold treasure. il Sci Digest 70:78-81 O '71
　　See also
Petroleum—Prospecting

PROSPECTUSES. See Securities—Prospectuses

PROSPERITY
　　See also
Business conditions

PROSTAGLANDINS
Aspirin inhibits prostaglandins. Sci Am 225: 45 Ag '71
Aspirin: new perspective on everyman's medicine. A. L. Hammond. Science 174:48 O 1 '71
For the 1970s: a new group of wonder drugs? Good H 173:161 Jl '71
How aspirin works. il Sci N 100:38 Jl 17 '71
Mysteries of aspirin. Time 98:36 Jl 19 '71
New mystery, maybe miracle drug. L. Galton. il N Y Times Mag p46-7+ D 5 '71
Once-a-month birth-control pill. D. Moreau. Vogue 158:95 Ag 1 '71
Prostaglandins. J. E. Pike. il Sci Am 225:84-92 bibliog(p 136+) N '71
Prostaglandins: a new wonder drug? E. B. Connell. Redbook 138:11-12+ Ja '72
Prostaglandins; report of third international conference. G. G. Anderson and L. Speroff. il Science 171:502-4 F 5 '71
Radioimmunoassay for prostaglandins. B. M. Jaffe and others. bibliog il Science 171:494-6 F 5 '71
Rapid research advances. Sci N 99:230 Ap 3 '71
Two more possibilities; arthritis treatment. Sci N 99:44+ Ja 16 '71

PROSTATE gland
I am Joe's prostate. J. D. Ratcliff. il Read Digest 99:99-102 D '71

PROSTITUTION
Carnal knowledge: a portrait of four hookers. K. Coleman. il Ramp Mag 10:16-28 D '71
Legal prostitution spreads in Nevada. G. Astor. il Look 35:34-6 Je 29 '71
Prostitutes: the new breed. il Newsweek 78: 78 Jl 12 '71

Reflections on the sad profession; Time essay. O. Friedrich. il Time 98:34-5 Ag 23 '71
Scattering the pigeons; crackdown on New York's prostitutes. il Time 98:21 Jl 26 '71
Should prostitution be legalized? M. Mead. Redbook 136:50+ Ap '71
Sodom on the Hudson. il Newsweek 78:77 Jl 26 '71
Story behind the book: The lively Commerce. L. P. Freilicher. Pub W 199:53 My 24 '71
　　See also
Illegitimacy

PROSTRATION, Heat. See Heatstroke

PROTEASES
　　See also
Renin

PROTECTION (tariff) See Free trade and protection

PROTECTION against burglary. See Burglary protection

PROTECTION from frost. See Frost protection

PROTECTION of animals. See Animals—Protection

PROTECTION of cities and towns. See Cities and towns—Protection

PROTECTION of plants. See Plants, Protection of

PROTECTION of the president. See Presidents—United States—Protection

PROTECTIVE coatings
　　See also
Metal coating

PROTECTIVE mechanisms (biology) See Defense mechanisms (biology)

PROTECTIVE paint. See Paint, Protective

PROTEIN biosynthesis. See Biosynthesis

PROTEIN feed supplements. See Feeding and feeding stuffs—Protein supplements

PROTEIN metabolism
　　See also
Amyloidosis

PROTEINASES
Alkyl isocyanates as active site-specific inhibitors of chymotrypsin and elastase. W. E. Brown and F. Wold. bibliog il Science 174:608-10 N 5 '71

PROTEINS
Amyloid fibril proteins: proof of homology with immunoglobulin light chains by sequence analyses. G. G. Glenner and others. bibliog il Science 172:1150-1 Je 11 '71
Chemoreception in nassarius obsoletus: the role of specific stimulatory proteins. S. Gurin and W. E. Carr. bibliog il Science 174:293-5 O 15 '71
Creation of "amyloid" fibrils from Bence Jones proteins in vitro. G. G. Glenner and others. bibliog il Science 174:712-14 N 12 '71
Juvenile hormone induces vitellogenin synthesis in the monarch butterfly. M. L. Pan and G. R. Wyatt. bibliog il Science 174:503-5 O 29 '71
Now the villain is protein; hardening of the arteries. il Sci N 100:123-4 Ag 21 '71
Protein methylation. W. K. Paik and S. Kim. bibliog il Science 174:114-19 O 8 '71
Questions and answers on meat and other high protein foods: with recipes. R. H. Smithies. il Good H 173:167-68+ S '71
Urea cycle enzyme adaptation to dietary protein in primates. C. T. Nuzum and P. J. Snodgrass. bibliog il Science 172:1042-3 Je 4 '71
　　See also
Amino acids
Bacterial proteins
Collagen
Elastin
Fish protein concentrate
Food substitutes
Gelatin
Glycoproteins
Grain—Protein content
Insulin
Interferon
Lipoproteins
Nucleoproteins
Proteolysis
Tryptophan

PROTEOLIPIDS. See Lipids

PROTEOLYSIS
Creation of "amyloid" fibrils from Bence Jones proteins in vitro. G. G. Glenner and others. bibliog il Science 174:712-14 N 12 '71
Taking proteins apart; intracellular protein degradation. D. E. Thomsen. il por Sci N 101:14-15 Ja 1 '72

PROTESTANT churches
See also
Catholic church—Relations—Protestant churches
Christian holiness association
Ecumenical movement
Women and the church

Clergy
See Clergy

Missions
See Missions

England
See also
British council of churches

Germany (Democratic Republic)
East German churches support controversial WCC program. F. Lüpsen. Chr Cent 88:258 F 24 '71

Japan
See also
United church of Christ in Japan

Latin America
High theology in the Andes; Fraternity of Latin American theologians. C. P. Wagner; reply. C. R. Padilla. Chr Today 15: 31 My 7 '71
Latin American theology, by C. P. Wagner. Review
Chr Cent 88:698-700 Je 2 '71. M. Arias

New Zealand
See also
Church union—New Zealand

United States
See also
National council of churches

History
Christian America, by R. T. Handy. Review
America 125:493 D 4 '71. F. X. Curran
PROTESTANT churches and race problems. See Church and race problems
PROTESTANT churches and social problems. See Church and social problems
PROTESTANT churches in Ireland
Irish Protestants weigh withdrawal from WCC over African grants. J. Horgan. Chr Cent 88:959 Ag 11 '71
PROTESTANT Episcopal church
Cannibalism in the Episcopal church; 1971 New York Episcopal convention. D. K. Mano. Nat R 23:867+ Ag 10 '71
Curious anniversary; Thirty-nine articles. G. W. Bromiley. Chr Today 16:5-6 O 22 '71
What ever happened to God? Nat R 23:746 Jl 13 '71

Bishops
Plowshares into swords; Bishop Hobgood's consecration. T. W. Moore. il Chr Cent 88:294+ Mr 3 '71

Clergy
Uncorinthian Philadelphians; Suzanne Radley Hiatt ordained. T. W. Moore. por Chr Cent 88:930-1 Ag 4 '71
See also
Protestant Episcopal church—Bishops
PROTESTANT missions. See Missions
PROTESTANTISM
Cultural strain and Protestant liberalism; liberal movement in American theology from 1875 to World war I. W. R. Hutchinson. bibliog f il Am Hist R 76:386-411 Ap '71; Reply with rejoinder. D. E. Bigham. 76: 1631-3 D '71
PROTESTANTS in the United States
Righteous empire, by M. E. Marty. Review
Cath World 213:41-2 Ap '71. J. M. King
Sat R 54:32-3 F 6 '71. W. Arnold
PROTESTANTUS, Theophilus, pseud.
Authority. Cath World 213:146-7 Je '71
Place to stand. Cath World 213:296 S '71
Resist your funeral. Cath World 212:312 Mr '71
Three crosses. Cath World 213:243 Ag '71
Watch your umbrella. Cath World 213:87 My '71
We're still shooting our own troops. Cath World 213:39 Ap '71
PROTESTS, demonstrations, etc.
Jane Fonda, nonstop activist; with account by J. Frook. il por Life 70:50-1+ Ap 23 '71
Mass intimidation. F. S. Meyer. Nat R 23: 594 Je 1 '71
Of politics and prophecy; student activism today. R. C. Johansen. il Chr Cent 88:219-23 F 17 '71
Public safety and police powers. America 124:530 My 22 '71

See also
Lexington, Mass.—Protests, demonstrations, etc.
New York (city)—Protests, demonstrations, etc.
Student demonstrations
Washington, D.C.—Protests, demonstrations, etc.
Womens liberation movement

Chile
Empty pots and Yankee plots. il Time 98: 26 D 13 '71
March of the empty pots; demonstration against the Allende government. il Newsweek 78:53-4 D 13 '71

Israel
Middle East: Israel's other war; Panther demonstration. il Time 97:30+ Je 21 '71

Japan
Japan's way with protest. A. Axelbank. Nation 212:684 My 31 '71

Turkey
Welcome that wore thin. il Time 97:22 Mr 1 '71
PROTESTS against Vietnamese war. See Vietnamese war, 1957- —Protests, demonstrations, etc, against
PROTHRO, James Thompson, 1920-
Big names in the biggest game. il por Time 98:60+ O 4 '71 *
It's how you played the game. T. Maule. il por Sports Illus 35:24-5 Ag 16 '71 *
PROTHRO, Tommy. See Prothro, J. T. jr
PROTOCOL, Office of. See United States— State, Department of
PROTON accelerators. See Accelerators (electrons, etc)
PROTON magnetic resonance. See Magnetic resonance
PROTONS
Another level of structure. Sci N 99:315 My 8 '71
How many quarks in a proton? I. Asimov. Sci Digest 70:82-3 O '71
ISR experiment shows scaling behavior. G. B. Lubkin. bibliog il Phys Today 24:17-18 S '71
Proton-proton collisions. Sci N 100:55-6 Jl 24 '71
Structure of the proton and the neutron. H. W. Kendall and W. H. Panofsky. il Sci Am 224:60-6+ Je '71
What's in a proton? D. E. Thomsen. il Sci N 100:346-7 N 20 '71
PROTOPLASM
See also
Golgi apparatus
Melanophores
PROTOZOA
See also
Amebas
Euglena
Foraminifera
Plasmodium (parasite)
Sporozoites
PROULX, Cynthia, and Keown, Ian
France for loving couples; nests along the Loire. il Sat R 54:58-9+ Mr 13 '71
PROULX, E. A.
Baroque marble; story. Seventeen 29:162-3 S '70
PROUST, Marcel
Lunch; excerpt from On reading; tr. by W. S. Burford. Vogue 158:118-19+ N 1 '71
Proust's prefaces to Ruskin; excerpts, ed. by J. Autret and W. Burford. Nation 212: 565-9 My 3 '71
about
A la recherche de Marcel Proust. il por Time 98:30+ Jl 5 '71 *
Eat. M. Cantwell. Mlle 74:94+ N '71 *
Letter from Paris. Genêt. New Yorker 47:53 Jl 3 '71 *
Marcel Proust: a centennial volume, ed. by P. Quennell. Review
Time il por 98:106 O 11 '71. M. Maddocks *
One hundred years of Proust. H. Moss. New Yorker 47:124+ D 18 '71 *
Proust: a prophet remembered. M. Maddocks. Atlan 228:92-5 Jl '71 *
Unfinished cathedrals. P. Schneider. il Vogue 158:96-101+ D '71 *
Woman in Proust's life. S. de Gramont. por Harp Baz 104:54-5 Je '71 *
PROUTY, Winston Lewis
Excerpt from debate, September 17, 1970. Cong Digest 50:83+ Mr '71

PROVENCE

Description and travel

Christmas traveler: Provence. M. R. Henry. Mlle 74:144-5+ D '71

PROVIDENT hospital. See Chicago—Hospitals

PROVINCETOWN, Mass, fisheries. See Fisheries—United States

PROVING grounds

See also

Bombing and gunnery ranges

PROVOCATEURS, Agents. See Agents provocateurs

PROWSE, Juliet

South Africa's diamond. M. Veljkovic. il pors Dance Mag 45:24-5 O '71 *

PROXIES

Ambush of generation gap; proxy fights. pors Time 97:84 My 3 '71

Milstein around the neck; proxy fight. il Forbes 107:21 Mr 15 '71

New proxy warfare. il Nations Bsns 59:58-63 Ag '71

New turmoil in proxies. J. Perham. il Duns 97:54-6 My '71

Philadelphia's banks. R. Nathan and R. Lear. New Repub 164:10+ Je 5 '71

Proxy activists turn on the SEC. Bsns W p39 Ap 17 '71

Proxy wars flare up anew. Bsns W p50 My 15 '71

Return engagement. Newsweek 77:86 My 10 '71

20th century-Fox presents: proxy war. il Bsns W p68-70 My 8 '71

War of the noses; proxy fights. Time 97:90+ Ap 26 '71

PROXIMITY warning indicators

Army plans test of improved PWI. P. J. Klass. il Aviation W 94:46-8 F 15 '71

Beacon proximity warning unit outlined. il Aviation W 95:74+ S 20 '71

Testing

FAA plans tests of low-cost radar proximity warning unit. il Aviation W 95:82-3 S 20 '71

PROXMIRE, William

No one is in charge. Newsweek 77:16-17 Ja 18 '71 *

What makes Proxmire run. por Bsns W p84-5 Mr 27 '71 *

What makes Proxmire run. J. Herbers. il pors N Y Times Mag p28-9+ Ap 4 '71; Reply. B. K. Taylor. p98 My 2 '71 *

William Proxmire, the giant killer. por Time 97:13 Mr 29 '71 *

PRPIC, George J.

Yugoslavia at the crossroads. il America 125:147-50 S 11 '71

PRUITT-Igoe housing development. See St Louis—Housing

PRUNES

Commercial prunes don't taste like mine. E. H. Peterson. Org Gard & Farm 18:125 S '71

PRUNING

Overgrown boxwood calls for radical pruning. il Sunset 146:267 Ap '71

There's a time and a way to prune. E. V. Alfrey. il Org Gard & Farm 18:94-9 Ja '71

PRUNING apparatus and equipment

Some shears for the snipper. il Consumer Bul 54:35-7 Jl '71

Tools you need for pruning. il Home Gard 58:36-7 My '71

PRUNTY, Dorothy

Happiness is...making a puppet. il Sch Arts 70:34-5 Je '71

PRYBYLA, Jan S.

Foreign aid: the Chinese are coming. bibliog f il Cur Hist 61:142-7+ S '71

Soviet man in the ninth plan. bibliog f Cur Hist 61:227-34+ O '71

PRYDE, Philip R.

Soviet pesticides. bibliog il Environ 13:16-24 N '71

PRYOR, Helen B. and Martin, M. C.

Baby step out. il Parents Mag 46:40-1+ D '71

PRYTZ, John M.

Applied exobiology. Space World H-11-95:34-5 N '71

PSALMS. See Bible—Old Testament—Psalms

PSENCIK, Leroy F.

Social studies: specialists in state education departments. Clear House 45:341-5 F '71

PSEUDOHEMOPHILIA. See Von Willebrand's disease

PSEUDOMONAS

Psuedomonas aeruginosa: growth in distilled water from hospitals. M. S. Favero and others. bibliog il Science 173:836-8 Ag 27 '71

PSORIASIS

Psoriasis: a perilous cure. il Newsweek 78:68 O 11 '71

Skin disease victims protest. Sci Digest 69:60 Mr '71

PSYCHEDELIC drugs. See Hallucinogenic drugs

PSYCHEDELIC light-show systems. See Light shows—Apparatus

PSYCHIATRIC clinics

See also

Hospitals, Psychiatric—Outpatient service

PSYCHIATRIC consultants

Coordinated patient care: a consultant's view. M. King. Ment Hy 55:461-6 O '71

PSYCHIATRIC consultation

See also

Television in psychiatry

PSYCHIATRIC hospital aides. See Hospitals, Psychiatric—Staff

PSYCHIATRIC hospitals. See Hospitals, Psychiatric

PSYCHIATRIC insurance. See Insurance, Mental health

PSYCHIATRIC patients. See Mentally ill

PSYCHIATRIC personnel

See also

Hospitals, Psychiatric—Staff

PSYCHIATRIC research

Evaluation research: the consequences of program evaluation. D. Harper and H. Babigian. bibliog Ment Hy 55:151-6 Ap '71

PSYCHIATRIC social work

On call for crises; psychiatric counseling by nurses in Rutland, Vt. D. Robinson. il por Good H 172:92-3+ Mr '71

PSYCHIATRIC social workers. See Social workers

PSYCHIATRISTS

Interactional problems between mental health professionals and non-psychiatric physicians. M. R. Green and others. bibliog Ment Hy 55:206-13 Ap '71

Psychiatrist in a superior court setting. E. J. Balcanoff. bibliog Ment Hy 55:45-50 Ja '71

See also

Hospitals, Psychiatric—Staff

Psychiatric consultants

PSYCHIATRY

Carpeting the ward: an exploratory study in environmental psychiatry. F. E. Cheek and others. bibliog Ment Hy 55:109-18 Ja '71

See also

American psychiatric association

Child psychiatry

Forensic psychiatry

Group psychotherapy

Mental illness

Psychiatric social work

Social psychiatry

Television in psychiatry

Bibliography

Book reviews. See issues of Mental hygiene

Study and teaching

Writer's insight; premedical students learn from drama. il Time 98:60 N 29 '71

Sweden

Swedish psychiatry today; adaptation of address; July 1969. H. G. Leche. Ment Hy 55:404-6 Jl '71

PSYCHIATRY, Military

Lest their minds become casualties of the war; excerpt from 365 days. R. J. Glasser. il Todays Health 49:50-5+ N '71

PSYCHIATRY and religion

Denominational membership, expression of religious sentiments and status upon admission to a psychiatric hospital. G. Siskind. Ment Hy 55:246-7 Ap '71

PSYCHIATRY and society

Psychiatric reappraisal; excerpts from The politics of therapy. S. Halleck. Cur 131:43-50 Jl '71

Psychiatry and the survival of man. J. Marmor. Sat R 54:18-19+ My 22 '71

PSYCHOACTIVE drugs. See Psychopharmacology

PSYCHOANALYSIS

Freud and the Americans, by N. G. Hale, jr. Review

America 125:520-2 D 11 '71. J. F. Lee

Géza Róheim: psychoanalytic anthropologist or radical Freudian? R. C. Calogeras. bibliog Am Imago 28:146-57 Sum '71

Psycho-cultural shifts in ego defenses. F. X. Schupper and R. C. Calogeras. bibliog Am Imago 28:53-70 Spr '71

PSYCHOANALYSIS—*Continued*
Some implications of sexual activity for mental illness. G. H. Rozan and others. bibliog Ment Hy 55:318-23 Jl '71
See also
Complexes (psychology)
Dreams
International psycho-analytical association
Symbolism (psychology)

Bibliography
Reviews of current books. Am Imago 28:91-104 Spr '71

PSYCHOANALYSIS and literature
Lorca's two farces: Don Perlimplin and Don Cristóbal. C. Feal-Deibe. bibliog Am Imago 27:358-78 Wint '70
Mythopoesis and psychoanalysis. J. E. Gedo. bibliog Am Imago 27:329-37 Wint '70
Shakespeare; symposium. bibliog Am Imago 27:197-297 Fall '70

PSYCHOANALYSIS in literature
Freud's literary style: some observations. W. G. Niederland. bibliog f Am Imago 28:17-23 Spr '71

PSYCHOANALYSTS
See also
Freud, S.

PSYCHOLOGICAL apparatus
Animal guidance systems; use of Skinner box for training. L. G. Lawrence. il Electr World 86:27-9+ D '71

PSYCHOLOGICAL counseling. See Counseling

PSYCHOLOGICAL games. See Games

PSYCHOLOGICAL research
They throw money away on purpose; experiments in the social psychology of pro-social behavior. S. Bacon. il Sci Digest 69:39-44 F '71

PSYCHOLOGICAL societies
See also
American psychological association
Association for humanistic psychology

PSYCHOLOGICAL stress. See Stress (physiology)

PSYCHOLOGICAL tests
See also
Intelligence tests
Personality tests

PSYCHOLOGICAL types. See Typology (psychology)

PSYCHOLOGICAL warfare
See also
Terrorism

PSYCHOLOGISTS
Psychologist and minimal brain dysfunction: ten steps to maximum incompetence. L. J. Aronson. Ment Hy 55:523-5 O '71
See also
Adler, A.
Freud, S.
Hospitals, Psychiatric—Staff
Piaget, J.
School psychologists

PSYCHOLOGY
Farther reaches of human nature, by A. H. Maslow. Review
Sat R 54:56 N 6 '71. R. Muska
Pollution of the psychological environment. C. H. H. Branch. bibliog Ment Hy 55:519-22 O '71
See also
Aggressiveness (psychology)
American psychological association
Art—Psychology
Association (psychology)
Attention
Attitudes
Behavior (psychology)
Behaviorism
Change (psychology)
Child study
Cognition
Complexes (psychology)
Drawing—Psychological applications
Environmental psychology
Ethnopsychology
Genius
Habits
Hostility (psychology)
Human relations
Hypnotism
Imagination
Memory
Motivation (psychology)
Political psychology
Psychology, Religious
Recognition (psychology)
Self
Self love
Sex (psychology)
Social psychology

Stage fright
Symbolism (psychology)
Television broadcasting—Psychological aspects
Typology (psychology)
Violence
also subhead Psychology under various subjects, e.g. Middle age—Psychology

Industrial applications
See Psychology, Industrial

Periodicals
See also
Psychology today (periodical)

Study and teaching
Integrity group seminars; graduate study at University of Illinois. il Sch & Soc 99:333 O '71

PSYCHOLOGY, Applied
See also
Negotiation
Peace of mind
Psychology, Industrial

PSYCHOLOGY, Comparative
See also
Animals—Habits and behavior

PSYCHOLOGY, Educational
Early childhood education: a Piagetian perspective. D. Elkind. Ed Digest 37:28-31 D '71
Roles, goals, and failure. W. Glasser. il Todays Ed 60:20-1+ O '71; Same abr. Ed Digest 37:25-7 D '71
Self-image; Project IMPACT for humanizing the classroom. R. J. Trotter. il Sci N 100:130-1 Ag 21 '71
See also
Abstraction
Intelligence levels
School psychologists

PSYCHOLOGY, Forensic
See also
Forensic psychiatry

PSYCHOLOGY, Industrial
Therapy by dummies; self-control room used by Japanese workers. il Time 98:60-1 O 18 '71
See also
Employee morale
Job satisfaction

PSYCHOLOGY, Pathological
Herodotus: observer of sexual psychopathology. C. P. Rosenbaum and R. Rossi. bibliog Am Imago 28:71-8 Spr '71
Psychopathology of racism. J. Daniels; reply. V. R. Mollenkott. Chr Today 15:6-8 Mr 26 '71
See also
Hallucinations and illusions
Hypochondria
Psychotherapy

PSYCHOLOGY, Physiological
Biology of behavior. R. J. Williams. Sat R 54:17-19+ Ja 30 '71
Mind over body, mind over mind. G. Luce and E. Peper. il N Y Times Mag p34-5+ S 12 '71
Neural events and the psychophysical law. S. S. Stevens; reply with rejoinder. M. Buchsbaum. Science 172:502 Ap 30 '71
See also
Avoidance (psychology)
Body image
Brain—Localization of functions
Color sense
Conditioned responses
Figural aftereffects
Left- and right-handedness
Memory
Mind and body
Motor responses
Optical illusions
Pain
Reinforcement (psychology)
Senses and sensation
Sex psychology
Signal detection (psychology)
Sleep
Space perception
Time perception

PSYCHOLOGY, Police. See Police psychology

PSYCHOLOGY, Religious
Varieties of religious experience, by W. James. Review
New Repub 165:28-31 O 2 '71. R. Coles

PSYCHOLOGY, Sex. See Sex (psychology)

PSYCHOLOGY of learning. See Learning, Psychology of

PSYCHOLOGY today (periodical)
Applied psychology. il Newsweek 77:59 My 24 '71

PSYCHOPATHOLOGY. See Psychology, Pathological

PSYCHOPHARMACOLOGY
Drug advertising and perception of mental illness; with reply by G. Usdin. R. Seidenberg. bibliog Ment Hy 55:21-34 Ja '71

PSYCHOPHYSICS. See Psychology, Physiological

PSYCHOSES
Chemistry of madness. R. Campbell. il Life 71:66-8+ N 26 '71
Urinary adenosine 3',5'-monophosphate in the switch process from depression to mania. M. I. Paul and others. bibliog il Science 171:300-3 Ja 22 '71
See also
Depression, Mental

PSYCHOSURGERY. See Brain—Surgery

PSYCHOTHERAPISTS
Analyzing the psychotherapist. D. I. Templer. Ment Hy 55:234-6 Ap '71
Effects of the psychotherapeutic experience on emerging psychotherapists. H. B. Roback and others. Ment Hy 55:228-9 Ap '71

PSYCHOTHERAPY
Can primal therapy shortcut the return to happiness? A. Goldman. il por Vogue 158:270-1 S 1 '71
Definition of psychotherapy. J. M. Reisman. bibliog Ment Hy 55:413-17 Jl '71
Effects of the psychotherapeutic experience on emerging psychotherapists. H. B. Roback and others. Ment Hy 55:228-9 Ap '71
Final-exam jitters. il Newsweek 77:49 My 24 '71
New look at the meaning of reality. R. H. Gilluly. il por Sci N 99:335-7 My 15 '71
Primal screamer. il por Newsweek 77:97 Ap 12 '71
Psychotherapy in a public mental hospital. W. B. Simon and J. E. Wood, jr. bibliog Ment Hy 55:221-4 Ap '71
Sense in humor; excerpt from Laughter and liberation. H. Mindess. Sat R 54:10-12 Ag 21 '71
Sensuous therapist. il por Newsweek 78:66 S 20 '71
Therapy failure: pride and/or predjudice of the therapist? S. V. Didato. bibliog Ment Hy 55:219-20 Ap '71
Tyranny of the male therapist; interview, ed. by C. Bigwood. P. Chesler. Harp Baz 104:52-3 Jl '71
Where to turn for help. J. Brothers. Good H 172:48+ My '71
See also
Behavior therapy
Child psychotherapy
Family psychotherapy
Group psychotherapy
Psychiatry and religion

PSYCHOTROPIC drugs. See Psychopharmacology

PTARMIGAN shooting
Ptarmigan. B. Brister. il Field & S 76:36-7+ S '71
Pterrible ptemperature ptarmigan. N. Karas. il Field & S 75:64-5+ Mr '71

PUBERTY
Height and weight at menarche and a hypothesis of critical body weights and adolescent events. R. E. Frisch and R. Revelle; discussion. bibliog Science 174:1148-9 D 10 '71

PUBLIC address amplifiers. See Amplifiers

PUBLIC address systems. See Loud speaking apparatus

PUBLIC administration
Public policymaking reexamined. by Y. Dror. Review
Trans-Action 7:55-7 O '70. M. J. Shapiro
See also
Bureaucracy
Executive advisory bodies
Municipal government
also subhead Politics and government under names of countries, states, etc. e.g.
France—Politics and government

PUBLIC broadcasting service
All in the network. R. L. Shayon. Sat R 54:16+ O 30 '71
Cinderella network. T. O'Flaherty. il Am Ed 7:14-17 N '71; Same abr. with title PBS: the Cinderella network. Read Digest 99:43-8 N '71
Great scissors debate. R. L. Shayon. Sat R 54:68 D 4 '71
PBS, NET and the FBI. il Newsweek 78:127 O 18 '71

PUBLIC buildings
GSA advocates new financing techniques for public buildings. A. F. Sampson. Arch Rec 150:65-6 S '71

Public buildings, portfolio of facilities for assembly, exhibition, and information. il Arch Forum 135:36-57 N '71
See also
County buildings
Courthouses
Library architecture
Municipal buildings
Post office buildings
also subhead Public buildings under names of cities, e.g. Washington, D.C.—Public buildings

Location
Housing black workers; implications of relocating federal facilities. R. Cassidy. New Repub 165:16-17 Jl 17 '71

PUBLIC equity corporation
Anti-corporation. Newsweek 78:93-4 N 29 '71

PUBLIC health
See also
Camp sanitation
Cleaning of cities, towns, etc.
Environmental health
Epidemics
Health facilities
Infant mortality
Insects as carriers of infection
Malaria
Meat inspection
Sewage disposal
Smoke prevention
Venereal diseases

Appalachian Region
Appalachia gets a program it trusts; ALCOR, inc. il Bsns W p54-5 O 16 '71

California
U.S. journal: Imperial County; doctors' views on the Clinica de salubridad de campesinos. C. Trilling. New Yorker 46:83-9 F 13 '71
Where the doctors police the doctors; peer review system. il Bsns W p58-9 S 4 '71
See also
Los Angeles—Public health

China (People's Republic)
China; medical reform program. H. Yu. Chr Cent 88:1010 Ag 25 '71
Population care and control. E. Snow. New Repub 164:22-3 My 1 '71
Prescriptions of Chairman Mao; symposium. il Time 99:60-1 Ja 10 '72

Kentucky
Health care: what the poor people didn't get from Kentucky project; Floyd County project. R. J. Bazell. il Science 172:458-60 Ap 30 '71; Discussion. 173:191-2 Jl 16 '71
OEO hedges on Kentucky program. R. J. Bazell. Science 174:45 O 1 '71

Missouri
See also
St Louis—Public health

New York (state)
See also
New York (city)—Public health
New York (state)—Mental hygiene, Department of

North Carolina
Army snow job; D. Middleton's story on the army's Nation-building program. W. L. Robb. New Repub 165:15-17 D 11 '71
Nation-mending at home. il por Time 97:20 Je 21 '71

Panama
Panama Canal: a medical history. H. H. Ziperman. il Américas 23:8-18 Je '71

United States
Health programs: slum children suffer because of low funding. R. J. Bazell. il Science 172:921-5 My 28 '71
See also
Nutrition problems—United States
also subhead Public health under names of cities, e.g. Seattle—Public health

Washington (state)
See also
Seattle—Public health

West Virginia
Biological tyranny; OEO's family planning projects. W. Hern. New Repub 164:15-17 F 27 '71

Wyoming
Wyoming's war on deadly strep. M. Michaelson. il Todays Health 49:40-3+ Mr '71

PUBLIC health clinics. See Health facilities
PUBLIC holidays. See Holidays
PUBLIC houses (Great Britain) See Bars and barrooms
PUBLIC housing projects. See Housing projects, Government
PUBLIC information act. See Information, Freedom of
PUBLIC land law review commission. See United States—Public land law review commission
PUBLIC lands
    See also
Wilderness areas

Alaska

Unfreezing Alaska. P. Barnes. New Repub 165:15-17 S 11 '71

United States

Big lockout. M. Frome. Field & S 76:66-7+ O '71
Cloud in the big sky; locked gates bar hunters and fishermen from public lands. W. A. Fairhurst and B. East. il Outdoor Life 148: 31-3+ Jl '71
For Cal from Uncle Sam, with well; leasing of Camp Pendleton and San Onofre beachfront to the state of California. R. W. Johnston. Sports Illus 35:86+ S 13 '71
Let's put the public back in the public lands. M. Frome. Field & S 76:42+ O '71
New homestead; OEO Oklahoma program. il Time 99:10 Ja 17 '72
Reviewing our public land use policies. D. Jackson. Cur 127:24-8 Mr '71
    See also
National forests
National parks and reserves—United States
United States—Land management, Bureau of
United States—Public land law review commission

History

Great American land grab. P. Barnes. New Repub 164:19-23 Je 5 '71
PUBLIC libraries. See Libraries
PUBLIC officers
Doubt about Newsweek tribute; Catholics in public office. B. L. Masse. America 125:361 N 6 '71
Man who is in; White House staffer. C. Colson. por Newsweek 78:16 S 6 '71
Nixon's Haldeman: power is proximity. C. S. Wren. il pors Look 35 :15-19 Ag 24 '71
Wages of truth. il por Time 98:34 O 11 '71
Watch Peter Flanigan. G. R. Rosen. il pors Duns 98:28-31+ Jl '71
What do special assistants specialize in? W. Sparks. Atlan 227:64-6+ F '71
White House padre; J. J. McLaughlin. por Newsweek 78:27 Jl 26 '71
    See also
Cabinet officers
Conflict of interests (public office)
Governors
Negro public officers
Political ethics
Presidential advisers
United States—Executive office of the president
United States—President's commission on personnel interchange
Women as public officers

Anecdotes, facetiae, satire, etc.

Profiles in Courrèges. C. Trillin. il Atlan 228: 121-3 N '71

Recreation

License plates of Burning Tree; Washington, D.C. New Yorker 46:20-2 Ja 30 '71

Recruiting

Administration talent search: alternatives to the buddy system. N. Wade. por Science 173:1216-18 S 24 '71
PUBLIC officers, Resignation of
Logic of defection: ex-Kissinger aides. Nat R 23:301 Mr 23 '71
PUBLIC opinion
    See also
Attitudes
Knowledge, Sociology of
National opinion research center
Propaganda
Rumor
Student opinion
Teacher opinion
Vietnamese war, 1957- —Public opinion
    also subhead Foreign opinion under names of countries, e.g. United States—Foreign opinion

Arab states
    See also
United States—Foreign opinion—Arab

Australia

What's wrong with Australia? M. Parker. il por Newsweek 79:24-6 Ja 3 '72

Canada

Public and modern art; Unesco-backed inquiry; with report by D. F. Cameron. il UNESCO Courier 24:4-34 Mr '71

China (People's Republic)
    See also
China (People's Republic)—Foreign opinion
United States—Foreign relations—China (People's Republic)

Europe, Western
    See also
United States—Foreign opinion—European

France
    See also
Vietnamese war, 1957- —Public opinion

Germany (Federal Republic)
    See also
Vietnamese war, 1957- —Public opinion

Great Britain

British economists talk down the EEC. il Bsns W p85-6+ Ap 3 '71
    See also
United States—Foreign opinion—British
Vietnamese war, 1957- —Public opinion

Ireland

Dublin conversation: do you support the I.R.A.? W. Sheed. il N Y Times Mag p32-3+ O 24 '71

Israel

Israelis and Jews, by S. N. Herman. Review Commentary 53:84-6 Ja '72. M. Sklare
    See also
Israeli-Arab war, 1967- —Public opinion

New Zealand
    See also
Vietnamese war, 1957- —Public opinion

Russia
    See also
United States—Foreign opinion—Russian

Sweden
    See also
United States—Foreign opinion—Swedish

Turkey
    See also
United States—Foreign opinion—Turkish

United States

Analyzing the crisis of confidence. D. C. Anderson. Cur 132:7-11 S '71
Are you personally afraid of crime? Readers speak out. il Life 72:28-31 Ja 14 '72
Average man might fool you. R. Coles. por Life 70:4 My 7 '71
Bad news from the pollsters. H. Sidey. il Life 70:2B Mr 19 '71
Demands of Consciousness II. H. J. Gans. Nation 212:275-7 Mr 1 '71
Dissent in three American wars, by S. E. Morison and others. Review
    Trans-Action 8:100-2 N '70. S. Tax
Guarded optimism at the top; new Fortune 500-Yankelovich survey. R. Loving, jr. il Fortune 83:168-9+ My '71
How shoppers and merchants size up the price freeze. il U S News 71:30-3 N 15 '71
Inflated view of company profits. il Bsns W p26 D 18 '71
Keynesian Nixon gets passing marks. il Bsns W p 15-16 F 6 '71
Listening to America, by B. Moyers. Review
    Newsweek 77:114 Mr 15 '71. P. S. Prescott
Mood of America: wait-and-see optimism. il U S News 71:50-5 S 13 '71
Per Angela ad astra: reactions to cases of Angela Davis and Simonas Kudirka. Nat R 23:67-8 Ja 26 '71
Poll reveals tolerance tempered by doubts; black/white dating. il Life 70:66-7 My 28 '71
Real issues in today's America: Congress nears from home. il U S News 70:9-11 My 3 '71
Season of our discontent? America 126:1-2 Ja 8 '72
Taxi chorus; sampling after Lindsay's conversion. il Time 98:8 Ag 23 '71
Violent Americans; attitudes toward civil violence. R. J. Trotter. il Sci N 100:14-15 Jl 3 '71
Vote for Nixonomics; how Americans feel now about the freeze. il Newsweek 78:75 O 11 '71

PUBLIC opinion—United States—*Continued*
What moonwalk? What moon? P. Steinfels.
Commonweal 93:487 F 19 '71
What the people think. B. W. Roper and J.
Heinig. il Cur 132:5-7 S '71
What the people think of today's America.
il U S News 70:32-6 Mr 29 '71
See also
China (People's Republic)—Foreign opinion—
American
Vietnamese war, 1957- —Public opinion

PUBLIC opinion polls
How schools can listen to the community.
N. Stark. il Am Ed 7:8-11 Jl '71
Later George, not now, nonrecognition of
candidates. New Repub 164:5-6 My 8 '71
Latest poll. Nixon leads four top Democrats.
U S News 71:64 D 20 '71
See also
Scholastic research center

PUBLIC purchasing. See Purchasing, Government

PUBLIC records
See also
Archives
United States—Transportation, Department of
—Public records

PUBLIC relations
Public relations. L. L. L. Golden. See issues
of Saturday review
Tour, talk, tell and build: North Mankato,
Minn. il Am City 86:116+ Mr '71
See also
Corporate image
Customer relations
Investor relations programs
Presidents—United States—Public relations
School and the community
also subhead Public relations under vari-
ous subjects, e.g. Libraries—Public rela-
tions

Bibliography
Books in communications. S. W. Little. See
issues of Saturday review

PUBLIC relations consultants
See also
Orlando, G.

PUBLIC relations directors
See also
Women as public relations directors

PUBLIC relations society of America
Making of a profession? L. L. L. Golden. Sat.
R 54:74 O 9 '71

PUBLIC schools
See also
Education and state
Negro schools
School management and organization
Special classes and special schools
also headings beginning School

Appraisal
See Education—Evaluation

Desegregation
American tragedy. Nation 213:196-7 S 13 '71
Attack on de facto; federal court ruling in
Detroit. Time 98:23-4 O 11 '71
Battle for the South: phase two. C. Ful-
wood. il Ramp Mag 10:36-9 Jl '71
Call it desegregation. J. Osborne. New Repub
164:12-13 Ja 30 '71
Discrimination and professional ethics; NEA
task force findings. Todays Ed 60:34-5 Mr
'71
Dixie schools charade. A. Poinsett. il Ebony
26:144-8 Ag '71
Feasibility of public school desegregation. R.
A. Ellis. bibliog Sch & Soc 99:433-6 N '71
How much progress is enough? J. Cass. Sat
R 54:41 Jl 17 '71
Loneliness of being black; senior year at
an integrated school. L. Williams. il Sev-
enteen 30:118-19+ Jl '71
Looking back: Little Rock Nine; interview.
E. Green. New Yorker 47:30-2 My 8 '71
More desegregation. J. Osborne. New Repub
164:15-16 Je 12 '71
Myths of liberalism and school integration.
A. C. Ornstein. Sch & Soc 99:436-9 N '71
New Orleans schools ten years later. F.
Guillory. America 125:93-5 Ag 21 '71
Now Supreme court sets rules for busing
students. il U S News 70:12-14 My 3 '71
Numbers game southern-style. Sat R 54:70
Ap 17 '71
Progress report on classroom integration. Y.
Postelle. il Parents Mag 46:48-51 D '71
Public school desegregation: legal perspec-
tives. N. C. Amaker. Negro Hist Bul 33:
174-7 N '70
Public schools and desegregation. America
124:447-8 My 1 '71

Race and education; summary of reports. M.
Perry. bibliog il Am Lib 2:1051-4 N '71
Residential segregation: its effects on edu-
cation. A. Downs. Ed Digest 36:12-15 Ap '71
School daze, policy maze. Chr Cent 88:1071-2
S 15 '71
Small victories in Americus. M. Frady. il Life
70:46B-46D+ F 12 '71
South moving ahead in mixed schools. U S
News 70:44 Ja 25 '71
Spreading the blame; court ruling against
segregation in Detroit. Newsweek 78:28 O
11 '71
To end school segregation: a city-suburb
linkup? il U S News 71:36 O 18 '71
Where school desegregation isn't happening.
D. E. Wagoner. il Ed Digest 37:21-4 D '71
Yazoo, by W. Morris. Review
Sat R 54:31-3 Je 5 '71. W. F. Holmes
You've got to get them involved. Alice Deal
junior high, Washington, D.C. S. McBee.
il por McCalls 98:28+ My '71
See also
School children—Transportation for integra-
tion

Finance
See School finance

Health service
Mental health consultation to schools. R. G.
Hirschowitz. Ment Hy 55:237-41 Ap '71

History
Father of American public education. P. W.
Schmidtchen. il Hobbies 76:135-6+ N '71

Mental health service
See Public schools—Health service

Public relations
See also
School and the community

Statistics
See Education—Statistics

United States
Crisis in the classroom, by C. E. Silberman.
Review
Schol Teach Jr/Sr High p24 Mr 8 '71
Giving public education a run for its money.
R. Goetz. Chr Cent 88:516-17 Ap 28 '71;
Discussion. 88:722-4, 889-90 Je 9, Jl 21 '71
How to survive in your native land, by J.
Herndon. Review
Life il por 70:14 Ap 23 '71. R. Gross
Literature in the ghetto school. S. Bachner.
Clear House 46:147-50 N '71
New ideas for better schools; interview. S.
P. Marland, jr. il por U S News 71:80-5
N 1 '71
Schools for failure; ghetto schools. L. Velie.
il Read Digest 99:147-51 Jl '71
What's going on in schools & colleges. See
every other issue of Changing times
See also
Education—United States
Equalization, Educational
High schools
Junior colleges
Rural schools
Rural schools—One-teacher schools
School districts
School year
Voucher plan in education

Political control
See Politics and education

PUBLIC schools and religion
American education as metaphysics: the re-
ligious consequence. F. K. Davis. Yale R
61:57-68 O '71
Another push to allow prayer in the schools.
il U S News 71:102 O 4 '71
Evangelical responsibility in public educa-
tion. B. Menkus. Chr Today 15:10-12 F 12
'71
High school scene: what prayer amendment?
E. E. Plowman. Chr Today 16:40 D 3 '71
House defeats prayer amendment. America
125:416 N 20 '71
Making no amends for prayer. Chr Today
16:31 D 3 '71
Not a prayer. il Newsweek 78:89 N 22 '71
Perfect love casteth out fear. M. McGrory.
America 125:444 N 27 '71
Prayer amendment. Commonweal 95:124 N
5 '71
Prayer amendment. W. F. Buckley, jr. Nat R
23:1375 D 3 '71
Prayer amendment coercive says Father
Drinan. Chr Cent 88:899 Jl 28 '71
Prayer amendment defeated by religious lead-
ers. Chr Cent 88:1375 N 24 '71

PUBLIC schools and religion—*Continued*
Prayer amendment; misconceived move.
America 125:307 O 23 '71
Prayer amendment revisited. A. M. Parrent.
Chr Cent 88:1120-1 O 20 '71
Prayer amendment; second wind. Chr Today
15:37 Ag 27 '71
Prayer bill hasn't one. R. Chandler. il Chr
Today 16:39-40 D 3 '71
Prayer in the public schools, by W. K. Muir.
Review
Trans-Action 8:53-4 Ja '71. J. G. Deutsch
Religion in the public schools; with study-
discussion program, by C. Harris and D.
Harris. J. S. Ackerman. bibliog il PTA Mag
65:2-5, 32-3 My '71
Who teaches? Catholic and Amish parents
vs. schools over compulsory attendance. Sr
Schol 98:10-11 Mr 29 '71
PUBLIC schools and the community See
School and the community
PUBLIC service advertising. See Advertising,
Public service
PUBLIC service advertising awards. See Ad-
vertising awards
PUBLIC services. See Municipal services
PUBLIC speaking
For top rating on the speaker's platform.
Bsns W p93 Ja 16 '71
Fringe benefits for freelancers. N. Davis.
Writers Digest 51:24 Jl '71
Giving a speech? Start 'em laughing! il
Changing T 25:39-40 D '71
How to line up a speaker for your program.
Bsns W p81 Ap 3 '71
See also
Lectures and lecturing
Oratory
Rhetoric
Television public speaking
PUBLIC television. See Television broadcast-
ing, Noncommercial
PUBLIC transportation. See Local transit
PUBLIC utilities
See also
Electric utilities
Government investigations—Public utilities
Waterworks
Finance
Ouch! with table. Forbes 107:41 Ap 1 '71
Utilities; with yardsticks of management
performance. il Forbes 109:169-70+ Ja 1 '72
Rates
See also
Water rates
Regulation
See also
Electric utilities—Regulation
Securities
Clearance sale? il Forbes 108:47 Jl 15 '71
Statistics
50 largest utilities; with directory. Fortune
83:200-1 My '71
Taxation
Utilities get in on the write-off bill. Bsns W
p41 F 27 '71
PUBLIC welfare
Law
Day-care jungle; legislation, federal pro-
grams, and new proposals. S. Boyer. il Sat
R 54:50-1 F 20 '71
California
Governor Reagan's private war; California
rural legal assistance. L. T. King. Com-
monweal 94:358-9 Jl 9 '71
Poor betrayed; refunding the California rural
legal assistance program. J. Osborne. New
Repub 164:13-15 F 13 '71
Reagan the revolutionary. Nat R 23:1075 S
24 '71
Reagan versus the poverty lawyers. P.
Barnes. New Repub 164:15-17 Ja 23 '71;
Reply. L. C. Battle. 164:33 F 13 '71
Reagan's welfare deal. J. Osborne. New Re-
pub 164:11-12+ My 15 '71
Saving the states from bankruptcy. R.
Reagan. il por Nations Bsns 59:56-60 My
'71
War on the poor? OEO grant for the Califor-
nia rural legal assistance program vetoed
by state. il Newsweek 77:18-19 Ja 18 '71
Welfare costs: new drive by 2 top governors.
il U S News 70:52-3 Mr 22 '71
Connecticut
What one state is doing about the burden
of relief; interview. H. C. White. il por
U S News 71:65-8 O 25 '71

Massachusetts
See also
Boston—Public welfare

New York (state)
Welfare costs: new drive by 2 top governors.
il U S News 70:52-3 Mr 22 '71
See also
New York (city)—Public welfare

Switzerland
Social welfare in Calvin's Geneva; adaptation
of address, December 30, 1968. R. M. Kingdon. bibliog f Am Hist R 76:50-69 F '71

United States
Any end to poverty? America's big problem.
il U S News 71:52-7 Jl 12 '71
Big package of welfare reform. America 124:
557 My 29 '71; Reply. R. P. Kennedy. 124:
656-7 Je 26 '71
Case for federal welfare. A. L. Schorr. Na-
tion 212:555-7 My 3 '71
Case for the President's plan; Family assistance plan, ed. by G. Wierzynski. D. P.
Moynihan. por Time 97:23 F 8 '71
Church agencies, civic groups press for welfare reform. Chr Cent 88:551 My 5 '71
Coming revolution in welfare. il U S News 70:
30-2+ Je 14 '71
Crackdown on welfare payments. il U S News
71:13-16 Ag 9 '71
Dump FAP; alteration to Family assistance
plan. Nat R 23:624-6 Je 15 '71
Ending poverty; HR 1 proposals. New Repub 165:8-9 Ag 7 '71
Family assistance; proposed Family assis-
tance plan. L. M. Salamon. New Repub 164:
17-18 F 20 '71
House approves 5% social security rise, new
welfare program; Nixon hails bill. Aging
201:3-4 Jl '71
How the states are attacking the welfare
mess. il Nations Bsns 59:58-9+ Jl '71
Is poverty illegal? L. Silver. Commonweal 93:
488-92 F 19 '71
More than welfare reform; the President's
Family assistance plan. America 125:4 Jl
10 '71
Nixon and Mills bill; family assistance plan.
il por Time 98:22 Jl 5 '71
Notes from the road. J. Burnham. Nat R 23:
191 F 23 '71
Overhauling welfare, social security; the
latest plan. il U S News 70:49-50 My 24 '71
Plan to guarantee income: chances now. il
U S News 71:52 Jl 5 '71
Policy options for welfare reform. G. Y.
Steiner. bibliog f Mo Labor R 94:23-31 Mr
'71
Progress of welfare reform. America 124:
499 My 15 '71
Punishing the poor. Commonweal 94:491-2
S 24 '71
Putting off the poor. New Repub 165:10 S 18
'71
Relief from the welfare mess; the House bill.
Life 70:36+ Je 25 '71
Runaway rise in welfare spending. il U S
News 72:43 Ja 3 '72
Small step, big symbol; welfare backlash. il
Time 98:10-11 D 27 '71
Stamp of disapproval; should strikers receive
welfare aid? Nations Bsns 59:28+ Ap '71
Stemming the welfare tide; results of latest
survey; with interview with H. C. White.
il U S News 71:62-8 O 25 '71
TRB; out of joint. New Repub 164:6 My 1 '71
Three ways to solve the welfare problem.
H. J. Gans. il N Y Times Mag p26-7+ Mr
7 '71; Discussion. p6+ Mr 28 '71
Waaaait a minute! Nat R 23:300-1 Mr 23 '71
Waiting for welfare; the Ribicoff bill. M. J.
Ulmer. New Repub 165:10-11 N 13 '71
Welfare: America's no. 1 problem; interview.
R. Reagan. il por U S News 70:36-40 Mr 1
'71
Welfare and the new federalism; sympo-
sium. bibliog f il Cur Hist 61:257-96+ N
'71
Welfare costs: sky-high or down to earth?
interview. R. B. Long. il por Nations
Bsns 59:50-2+ My '71
Welfare crackdown. Newsweek 78:20-1 S 20
'71
Welfare employables. J. Deedy. Common-
weal 95:26 O 8 '71; Reply with rejoinder.
W. D. Duggan. 95:99+ O 29 '71
Welfare front. Nat R 23:1044 S 24 '71
Welfare-industrial complex. M. Gruber. Na-
tion 212:808-11 Je 28 '71
Welfare myths vs. facts; HEW's own re-
port. il U S News 71:54-5 D 20 '71

PUBLIC welfare—United States—*Continued*
Welfare out of control: story of financial crisis cities face. il U S News 70:30-4 F 8 '71
Welfare reform; address, September 3, 1971. A. K. Davis. Vital Speeches 37:765-8 O 1 '71
Welfare: the best of intentions, the worst of results; theories of Frances Fox Piven and Richard A. Cloward. I. Kristol. Atlan 228:45-7 Ag '71
Welfare, the shame of a nation; present system and the proposed Family assistance plan; with interview with D. P. Moynihan. il Newsweek 77:22-6+ F 8 '71
Welfare: trying to end the nightmare. il Time 97:14-18+ F 8 '71
Welfare vs. jobs: President sees a threat to America; excerpts from address, April 19, 1971. R. M. Nixon. U S News 70:67 My 3 '71
What it's like: four cases. il Time 97:16-17 F 8 '71
Why enforced work won't work in welfare. A. L. Schorr. Sat R 54:17-19+ Je 19 '71
Work and welfare; Mills bill. M. J. Ulmer. il New Repub 165:12-14 Jl 3 '71; Reply. S. Nathanson. 165:31-2 Jl 17 '71
See also
Child welfare—United States
Food relief—United States
National welfare rights organization
PUBLIC welfare workers. See Social workers
PUBLIC works
New federal program in professional contracts. E. Mickel. Arch Rec 149:57-8 F '71
See also
Dams

Canada
He'll develop Quebec's TVA; James Bay project. por Bsns W p56 N 27 '71

Quebec
See Public works—Canada

United States
See Public works
PUBLIC works equipment. See Municipal equipment
PUBLICATIONS, Library. See Library publications
PUBLICITY
See also
Advertising
Television in politics
PUBLIK (periodical) See Catholic press
PUBLISHERS and authors. See Authors and publishers
PUBLISHERS and libraries. See Libraries and publishers
PUBLISHERS and publishing
Book business; book packagers. A. Green. Sat R 54:48-9 O 30 '71
Universal Xerox life compiler machine. W. Jovanovich. Am Scholar 40:249-55 Spr '71
See also
Authors and publishers
Best sellers
Books—Advertising
Books—Marketing
Books—Prices
Booksellers and bookselling
Computers—Publishing use
Copyright
Literary agents
Negro publishers and publishing
Royalties
also names of publishers, e.g. Doubleday and company

Anecdotes, facetiae, satire, etc.
How did Amanda get into this? D. Horne. Pub W 199:41 Ja 11 '71

Art literature
Book business; interview, ed. by A. Green. H. N. Abrams. Sat R 54:43+ N 27 '71
Wide open approach to the wide open spaces; publication of The art of the Old West, by David C. Hunt and Paul A. Rossi. A. DeMirjian, jr. il Pub W 200:30-3 N 1 '71

Biographies
Atlantic brief lives: an ambitious undertaking. B. A. Bannon. il Pub W 199:38-9 My 17 '71

Childrens literature
Art vs. adventitious circumstances. W. Chappell. il Horn Bk 47:456-61 O '71

Dictionaries
I and the camera; Oxford English dictionary compact edition. A. De Mirjian, jr. il Pub W 200:42-3 O 4 '71

Educational literature
Is educational reform conceivable? conference of Open court publishing company. R. Kirk. Nat R 23:872 Ag 10 '71
New look at educational publishing; interview. R. C. Hagel. Pub W 200:27-8 D 13 '71
Why minority publishing? educational publishers; ed. by B. Chambers. il pors Pub W 199:48-50 Mr 15 '71

Erotic literature
Erotica for women; Orlando press. Newsweek 78:63 D 27 '71

Facsimiles
See Book rarities—Facsimiles

Finance
AAP spokesman testifies on postal rate increase; excerpts ed. by L. Huston. R. W. Frase. Pub W 200:233 Ag 30 '71
BMI: 39th annual meeting. il Pub W 200:20-5 D 13 '71
Book industry, financial trends reviewed. Pub W 200:22-3 N 22 '71
New plea for price control exemption. S. Wagner. Pub W 200:51 N 15 '71
No Fahrenheit 451 yet. R. E. Bye. Library J 96:3577 N 1 '71
Wage-price exemption fails in Congress. S. Wagner. Pub W 200:30 D 20 '71
Where's the money: hard cover or paperback? S. Marlowe. il Writers Digest 51:28-30+ S '71

International aspects
Buying around: in search of solutions; problem between American and British publishers. R. H. Smith. Pub W 200:57 N 15 '71
Espionage career of General Gehlen; a publishing controversy. B. A. Bannon. por Pub W 201:33-4 Ja 3 '72
See also
Association for the promotion of the international circulation of the press
International publishers association

Maps
See also
Hammond, inc.

Microforms
AAUP: microforms, reprints, computers and creativity. C. B. Grannis. il Pub W 199:42+ Je 14 '71
GPO receives first micropublishing recommendations. S. Wagner. Pub W 200:28 O 4 '71
Publishing the pre-shrunk; books in microfiche at Toronto university press; reprint. I. Montagnes. il Pub W 200:13-15 N 22 '71

Negro literature
Advocacy. E. Geller. Library J 96:675 F 15 '71
Story behind the book: if they come in the morning, by A. Davis and other writers, published by Third press. R. H. Smith. por Pub W 200:52-3 N 15 '71

Paperback books
Bantam introduces new series of all-color paperbacks. Pub W 200:35 S 20 '71
Returns. E. Lottman. Pub W 200:16-17 D 20 '71

Periodicals
Magazines in jeopardy. Time 99:43 Ja 10 '72
See also
Harper's magazine press

Photographic literature
Low-cost print collecting gets a new boost; famous photographers portfolios by Doubleday. N. Rosenheck. il Pop Phot 69:104+ S '71

Religious literature
Hip religions spark contemporary publishing. M. R. Kraner. il Pub W 199:50-5 My 17 '71
New world language? a chance to mediate the Christian message. A. Deeken. il America 126:11-14 Ja 8 '72
Religious publishers confident they can keep pace with the 70s. C. B. Grannis. Pub W 199:33-4+ Mr 8 '71
Religious publishing: a decline but not a demise. M. E. Marty. il Chr Cent 88:524-8 Ap 28 '71
Seven religious books analyzed at AAP meeting. Pub W 199:33-4 Je 7 '71
Whatever happened to theology? R. P. McBrien. Commonweal 94:129-33 Ap 16 '71
See also
Herder and Herder, inc.
Methodist publishing house
Revell, Fleming H, company

PUBLISHERS and publishing—*Continued*

Scientific literature

New firm to publish in history of science. Pub W 200:24 D 6 '71

Sci-tech publishers wary about proposed UNESCO information network: world science information system, UNISIST. Pub W 200:28 N 8 '71

See also
Publishers and publishing—Technical literature
Science service, inc.

Securities

Book industry stock reports. See occasional issues of Publishers' weekly

Consider the textbook stocks. C. Rolo. il Forbes 108:58-9 S 1 '71

Statistics

1970: a big boost in book titles, as recorded in PW. il Pub W 199:32-3 F 8 '71

1970 in review. il Pub W 199:50-3 F 8 '71

No Fahrenheit 451 yet. R. E. Bye. Library J 96:3577 N 1 '71

Rise of women in publishing, plus some other useful statistics for the manager planning ahead. Pub W 199:66+ F 15 '71

Title output; tables (cont) Pub W 199:60 Ap 12; 200:31 Jl 26; 21 N 1 '71

Technical literature

Sci-tech-business publishers bullish in face of higher costs, greater specialization. C. B. Grannis. Pub W 199:23-5 Ap 12 '71

Sci-tech publishers wary about proposed UNESCO information network: World science information system, UNISIST. Pub W 200:28 N 8 '71

Textbooks

Educational publishing. California. D. N. Mount. Pub W 200:22 D 6 '71

Is educational reform conceivable? conference of Open court publishing company. R. Kirk. Nat R 23:872 Ag 10 '71

1970 in review. Pub W 199:46 F 8 '71

Publishers and prisoners; letter to the editor. O. W. Walter. Library J 96:1306-7 Ap 15 '71

Textbooks are progressive. R. N. Saveland. Pub W 200:17-18 D 6 '71

What is college publishing all about? E. D. Gustafson. Pub W 200:63-4 N 15 '71

Austria

Letter from Vienna. T. Weyr. Pub W 200: pt2 178-80 S 27 '71

California

West coast publishing: San Francisco. D. N. Mount. Pub W 200:14-17 D 13 '71

West coast publishing scene: Los Angeles. D. N. Mount. Pub W 200:19-22 D 6 '71

Canada

Canadian government bailing out publishers. Pub W 199:29-30 Mr 22 '71

Canadian publishing takes a searching look at itself. Pub W 199:29-30 Ap 5 '71

Commission established to study Canadian publishing. Pub W 199:47 Ja 11 '71

McClelland and Stewart next Canadian publisher to sell? Pub W 199:49 Mr 8 '71

Ontario cracks the whip on foreign distributors. Pub W 200:35-6 Ag 16 '71

Where is publishing heading? P. A. Farrell il Pub W 200:40-2 S 13; 22-5 S 20 '71

See also
British Columbia university press
Toronto university press

Europe, Western

European scene. H. R. Lottman. See issues of Publishers' weekly

France

Calmann-Lévy: back into French publishing's mainstream. H. R. Lottman. il Pub W 199:24-5 Ap 19 '71

French publishing takes a hard look at itself. H. R. Lottman. Pub W 200:39 Ag 2 '71

Hachette: reception at the Plaza for the Marquis I. de Roquemaurel. New Yorker 47:35-6 O 23 '71

Hachette sees firm future in Africa. H. R. Lottman. Pub W 200:21 S 20 '71

Jean-Jacques slips behind the scenes; le Groupe express. il por Bsns W p33 Ja 23 '71

Opera Mundi: the many facets of a versatile firm. H. R. Lottman. il Pub W 199:33-5 Je 28 '71

Piper's personal publishing; L'Express wades into books. H. Lottman. por Pub W 200:50 Jl 12 '71

Sibling rivalry; clash over management of Le Groupe express. pors Newsweek 77:54 Ja 18 '71

Germany (Federal Republic)

Letter from West Germany (cont) D. Lattmann. Pub W 199:23 My 3 '71

Piper's personal publishing; L'Express wades into books. H. Lottman. por Pub W 200:49-50 Jl 12 '71

West Germany's largest book publisher: Bertelsmann company. D. Lattmann. il Pub W 200:24-6 O 25 '71

Great Britain

Authors & editors: Sir G. Weidenfeld cofounder of Weidenfeld & Nicolson's. B. A. Bannon. por Pub W 199:17-19 Je 21 '71

Erotica for women; Orlando press. Newsweek 78:63 D 27 '71

From Denmark, with love; English publication of The little red schoolbook. H. R. Mayes. Sat R 54:8-9 Jl 3 '71

London notebook (cont) B. Kolins. Pub W 199:34 Mr 1; 25-6 My 17; 50-1 Je 28; 200: pt2 163-5 S 27 '71

London's most remarkable publishing firm; Allison and Busby. il pors Ebony 26:43-6+ Mr '71

See also
International publishing corporation
Nonesuch press
Oxford university press
Pergamon press, ltd.

Greece, Modern

History without tears; new illustrated historical monthly produced by Papyros. P. S. Nathan. Pub W 199:63 F 1 '71

Israel

Graphic design in Israel. E. Reichl. il Pub W 199:48-9 Je 7 '71

Israeli publishing and printing industry eager to export. D. N. Mount. il Pub W 199:29-30+ Je 7 '71

Italy

Obituary: A. Mondadori, founder of Arnoldo Mondadori editore. Pub W 199:43 Je 28 '71

Rise of Signora Broggi. H. Lottman. Pub W 199:30 Je 14 '71

Japan

Japan: the world's third largest publishing conglomeration. L. E. Kern, jr. il por Pub W 200:pt2 172-4 S 27 '71

Japanese royalties: two points of view. T. Mori; L. E. Kern, jr. Pub W 199:17-18 My 3 '71

Massachusetts

Boston book scene. B. A. Bannon. il Pub W 199:22-4 My 10 '71

Russia

Russian book publishing: inexorably wedded to censorship. S. Jacoby. il Pub W 200:pt2 169-71 S 27 '71

Spain

Spain: the death of a publishing house; Editorial Estela. H. R. Lottman. Pub W 200: 23 S 6 '71

United States

ABA is the working liaison: retail stores and publishers; letter to the editor. R. Brigham. Pub W 199:20 Je 21 '71

Book business. A. Green. See last issue of each month of Saturday review

Buying around: in search of solutions; problem between American and British publishers. R. H. Smith. Pub W 200:57 N 15 '71

If you have hidden talent and like to eat, have we got an expense account for you! D. Mount. Esquire 76:214-15+ D '71

Modern technology and modern publishing; excerpts from Books for the millions. F. Comparato. Pub W 200:34+ N 1 '71

Multi-media: who's afraid? C. B. Grannis. Pub W 199:62 Ap 12 '71

1970 in review. il Pub W 199:42-53 F 8 '71

Publisher-bookseller issues: bookselling problems; highlights of panel discussion, June 1, 1971. il Pub W 199:34-5+ Je 21 '71

Vanity by any other name. L. Conger. Writer 84:7-8 F '71

See also
Associations of American publishers
Cope program
Publishers and publishing—California
Publishers and publishing—Massachusetts
also names of publishers, e.g. Princeton university press

PUBLISHERS catalogs. See Catalogs, Publishers

PUBLISHERS' weekly
International title output figures: are they really comparable? F. Fico. Pub W 200:pt2 187 S 27 '71
Some innovations at PW. A. W. Ehrlich. Pub W 200:63 Ag 23 '71

PUBLISHING. See Publishers and publishing

PUBS (Great Britain) See Bars and barrooms

PUCCINI, Giacomo
La Bohème. Criticism
Hi Fi 21:MA13 Je '71 •
Opera N il 35:17-20 Mr 6 '71 •
Sat R 54:16+ Mr 27 '71 •
Kirsten on Puccini; interview, ed. by J. Rockwell. D. Kirsten. il por Opera N 35:21-3 Mr 6 '71 •
Madame Butterfly. Criticism
Hi Fi 20:MA15 D '70 •
Hi Fi il 20:MA16+ D '70 •
Opera N il 35:17-20 Ap 17 '71 •
Tosca. Criticism
Nation 213:572 N 29 '71 •

PUCINSKI, Roman C.
High noon for Pucinski. Nat R 23:577-8 Je 1 '71 •

PUDDINGS
Christmas treat; plum pudding. Redbook 138:60 D '71
Hasty puddings. M. Happel. il Ladies Home J 88:86-7+ Ja '71
Pears or apples in this pudding. il Sunset 146:96 Ja '71
Pumpkin pudding. il Bet Hom & Gard 49:92 D '71
Rice pudding again? with recipes. il Sunset 147:176 D '71

PUDDINGS, Canned. See Canned food

PUEBLO; drama. See Greenberg, S. R.

PUEBLO Indians
U.S. Journal Tesuque, N.M. C. Trillin. New Yorker 47:93-7 D 18 '71
Watch out, you might assimilate. K. L. Pearson. il Natur Hist 80:24-33 Je '71
See also
Taos Indians

PUEBLO ovens. See Ovens

PUERTO RICAN painting. See Painting, Puerto Rican

PUERTO RICAN students in the United States
See also
Spanish speaking students

PUERTO RICANS in New York city. See Puerto Ricans in the United States

PUERTO RICANS in the United States
Culture and the people; Museo del bario. R. Ortiz. Art in Am 59:27 My '71
Puerto Rican migration: right place, wrong time? N. Glazer. America 125:339-41 O 30 '71
Time to go home. F. Picó. America 126:20-1 Ja 8 '72

PUERTO RICO
See also
Church and social problems—Puerto Rico
Culebra Island
Hotels, taverns, etc.—Puerto Rico
Music festivals—Puerto Rico
Poor—Puerto Rico
San Juan
Tourist trade—Puerto Rico
United Nations—Puerto Rico

Description and travel
Puerto Rico: the alternatives. R. S. Kane. il Harp Baz 104:72+ O '71
Puerto Rico: where the past grows young. G. Bradshaw. il Vogue 157:88-9+ Ja 15 '71

Economic conditions
Clouds over Puerto Rico. il Time 97:84 My 24 '71
Puerto Rico: a surging economy; address, July 27, 1971. L. A. Ferre. Vital Speeches 37:741-3 O 1 '71
Two bright spots in the troubled Caribbean. C. Migdail. il U S News 70:55-6 Mr 15 '71

Nationalism
Independence for Puerto Rico. A. Parrilla-Bonilla. America 125:37-9 Jl 24 '71

Social conditions
See also
Poor—Puerto Rico

PUERTO RICO and the United States
Independence for Puerto Rico. A. Parrilla-Bonilla. America 125:37-9 Jl 24 '71

PUERTO VALLARTA, Mex.
Mexico's new stars. N. Lynn. il Travel 137:28-33+ Ja '72

PUESCHEL, Rudolf F. See Ellis, H. T. jt. auth.

PUGET SOUND
See also
San Juan Islands

PUGH, Grace Huntley
Watercolor page; with biographical sketch. il por Am Artist 35:62-5+ My '71

PUGH, Marshall
Le camping: the cheapest way to go. il Holiday 49:70-1+ F '71

PUGLIESE, Gilbert
Conscience of a steel worker. B. Ehrenreich and J. Ehrenreich. il Nation 213:268-71 S 27 '71 •

PUGLIESE, Joe
Ron Nagle: the potter. il Craft Horiz 31:35-7 Je '71

PUGWASH conferences on science and world affairs
Community of science and the search for peace; adaptation of address, April 26, 1971. P. Doty. Science 173:998-1002 S 10 '71
Disarmament and arms limitation: Pugwash assessment. Bul Atom Sci 27:20-3 Mr '71
SALT and international security; excerpt from statement. Bul Atom Sci 27:17-19 D '71
Student's view of Pugwash. A. H. Cahn. Bul Atom Sci 27:36-7 Ap '71
21st Pugwash conference on science and world affairs. B. T. Feld. Science 174:1150+ D 10 '71

PULLING teeth. See Teeth—Extraction

PULLMAN, Inc.
Big switch at Pullman. A. A. Butkus. il por Duns 98:30-3 D '71
Sale in Macy's basement? il Forbes 108:63 O 15 '71
See also
Swindell-Dressler company

PULMONARY diseases. See Lungs—Diseases

PULMONARY embolism. See Embolism

PULSARS
Nature of pulsars. J. P. Ostriker. il Sci Am 224:48-60 Ja '71
Neutron stars vs. black holes. D. E. Thomsen. il Sci N 99:151-2 F 27 '71
Pulsars for coded communication. S. V. Jones. il Sci Digest 69:71 Ap '71
Pulsating X-ray source might be neutron star or black hole. il Phys Today 24:17+ Je '71
Starquakes: have they been observed? L. C. Green. il Sky & Tel 41:76-9 F '71

PULSE generators. See Signal generators

PULSE techniques (electronics)
Signal averaging techniques. S. L. Silver. il Electr World 85:45-8 My '71
Understanding complex waveforms. L. S. Nickel. il Electr World 86:68-9 Jl '71

PUMA (sports car) See Sports cars

PUMA hunting
Cat in Pace Canyon. M. R. James. il Outdoor Life 147:56-7+ Ja '71
Cougar does attack. D. D. Ellis. il Outdoor Life 148:64-7+ S '71
Encounter with a cougar. S. Udall. il Field & S 76:64-5+ N '71
Lion of a lifetime. L. Bamford. il Field & S 76:64-5+ Ag '71

PUMARA, Hazel L. Diaz. See Diaz Pumara, H. L.

PUMAS
Hailing the elusory mountain lion. E. Hoagland. New Yorker 47:26-33 Ag 7 '71
Living with lions. W. H. Carr. il Am For 77:4-5+ F '71

PUMPED-storage hydroelectric plants. See Hydroelectric plants

PUMPING machinery
Cranes go round and round; St Louis. il Am City 86:34 Ag '71

PUMPKIN faces. See Halloween

PUMPKIN pudding. See Puddings

PUMPKIN seeds
In Latin America they're pepitas. il Sunset 147:159 S '71

PUMPKINS
See also
Cookery—Vegetables

PUNCH (beverage)
Convivial punch bowl; with recipes. F. M. Crawford. il Am Home 74:76 N '71
Drink. A. Fraser. Mlle 74:50 D '71
Wine punch with a fruit flavor. il Sunset 146:215 My '71
Wine to welcome the New Year. il Bet Hom & Gard 49:70+ Ja '71

PUNCH (periodical)
Big bunny. il Newsweek 78:79 N 22 '71

PUNCTUALITY
    See also
    Tardiness
PUNIC wars
    Eight centuries of Carthaginian civilization.
        G. C. Picard. il UNESCO Courier 23:17-21+
        D '70
    Grandeur and decline of the Punic city-state;
        rise of Carthage. H. Slim. il UNESCO Cour-
        ier 23:9-16 D '70
PUNISHMENT
    Crime and punishment. Sci Am 224:50-1 My
        '71
        See also
    Capital punishment
    Hell
    Indeterminate sentence
    Prisons
    Probation
PUNITIVE expedition to Mexico, 1916. See
    United States—History—Punitive expedition
    to Mexico, 1916
PUNKE, Harold H.
    Simple tools and complex learning.   Sch
        & Soc 99:513-14 D '71
    —and Hall, J. F.
    Functional community philosophy of educa-
        tion. Ed Digest 36:26-8 Mr '71
PUNNETT, Thomas
    Environmental control of photosynthetic
        enhancement. bibliog il Science 171:284-6
        Ja 22 '71
PUNS and punning
    Cesium properties of puns. W. R. Charlton. il
        Chem 44:25 Ap '71
    Puns in the sports world. L. Kahn. Chem 44:
        31 Je '71
PUNTA CAÑA club. See Seaside resorts—
    Dominican Republic
PUPFISH. See Killifishes
PUPPETS and puppet plays
    Happiness is. . .making a puppet. D. Prunty.
        il Sch Arts 70:34-5 Je '71
    It's Howdy Doody time, again. il pors Life
        70:90-2 My 7 '71
    Magic mushrooms. D. C. Jones. Plays 30:63-5
        Ap '71
    Marionette project. M. M. Kissel. il Sch Arts
        70:14-15 Je '71
    Puppets. P. A. Fraschetti. il Sch Arts 70:36-
        8 Je '71
    Puppets: The little players. J. B. Myers. il
        Craft Horiz 31:27-9+ D '71
PURCELL, Gary R.
    Reference books of 1970. il por Library J 96:
        1325-9 Ap 15 '71
PURCELL, Theodore V.
    Case of the borderline black. il Harvard Bsns
        R 49:128-30+ N '71
PURCHASE, Mary E.
    Detergents. House & Gard 140:44+ Jl '71
PURCHASING
    See also
    Consumers
    Consumption (economics)
    Quality of products
    Shopping and shoppers
        also subhead Purchasing under various
        subjects, e.g. Automobiles—Purchasing
PURCHASING, Cooperative
    Buy with a group and save? il Changing T
        25:40-2 Jl '71
    Families that buy together save together;
        buying clubs. McCalls 98:39 Je '71
    Food conspiracy; buying groups. Ramp Mag
        9:8 Ap '71
    How to set up an organic food co-op. J.
        Cox. Org Gard & Farm 18:64-8 O '71
    We started our own co-op. E. M. Hasse. il
        Har Yrs 11:14-15 Ap '71
    You can shave costs 5-10 per cent. R.
        Krumme and J. Davis. il Suc Farm 69:no3
        32-3 F '71
        See also
    Purchasing, Municipal
PURCHASING, Government
    Contract guidelines change asked. Avia-
        tion W 96:61 Ja 10 '72
    Federal buyers will flex Phase II muscle.
        Bsns W p24 Ja 1 '72
    Government book purchasing: a fed-
        eral commission takes a look. S. Wagner.
        Pub W 199:40-2 Je 28 '71
    Gov't book purchasing: procedural changes
        sought. S. Wagner. Pub W 200:30+ Jl 5 '71
    Government book purchasing: the dictionary
        controversy. S. Wagner. Pub W 199:36-8 My
        17 '71
    Salad days at the Pentagon. J. Drake and
        G. Gersmehl. Commonweal 93:485-6 F 19 '71
    Standardization. R. P. Raskowitz. Electr
        World 86:66-7 S '71

Washington cracks down on computer costs.
    il Bsns W p73-4 O 23 '71
    See also
Contracts, Government
United States—Air force—Procurement
United States—Commission on government
    procurement
United States—General services administra-
    tion
United States—National aeronautics and
    space administration—Procurement
PURCHASING, Household
    Make food orders clear, specific and in writ-
        ing. Camp Mag 43:26 F '71
    Pitfalls in purchasing. D. E. Doherty. il To-
        days Ed 60:60-1 Mr '71
    You & your diet: 55 food-buying facts. R. H.
        Smithies. il Good H 172:233-6 Ap '71
        See also
    Consumer education
    Food—Prices
    New York (city)—Consumer affairs, Depart-
        ment of
    Quality of products
PURCHASING, Military
    U.S. look at a French missile. il Bsns W p78
        Ja 23 '71
        See also
    United States—Air force—Procurement
    United States—Defense, Department of—Pro-
        curement

Israel

    Agreement may open parts line to Israel.
        D. E. Fink. Aviation W 95:15-16 N 22 '71

Latin America

    New muscle in arms; sales to Latin Amer-
        ica. il Time 98:57-8 Jl 12 '71

Pakistan

    See also
    Military assistance, American—Pakistan

South Africa

    When silence is not golden; English Roman
        Catholic hierarchy. T. Beeson. Chr Cent
        88:645 My 26 '71
PURCHASING, Municipal
    Tips on purchasing from the British. R. G.
        Wessells. il Am City 86:90+ Mr '71
    You have to think service; interview, ed. by
        B. Foster. J. F. O'Grady. pors Am City
        86:67-9 Je '71
        See also
    Municipal contracts
PURCHASING power
    Two measures of purchasing power con-
        trasted. P. M. Schwab. bibliog f il Mo
        Labor R 94:3-14 Ap '71

Russia

    Purchasing power of workers in the Soviet
        Union. E. Nash. bibliog il Mo Labor R
        94:39-45 My '71
PURCHASING power bonds. See Bonds, Gov-
    ernment
PURDUE airlines
    Financial squeeze sparks Purdue cutback. H.
        D. Watkins. Aviation W 95:28-9 Ag 30 '71
PURDY, Barbara A. and Brooks, H. K.
    Thermal alteration of silica minerals: an
        archeological approach. bibliog il Science
        173:322-5 Jl 23 '71
PURDY, James
    I am Elijah Thrush; story. il Esquire 76:
        194-201 D '71
PURDY, Susan
    Four fanciful dolls. il Ladies Home J 88:182
        S '71
PURIFICATION of water. See Water purifica-
    tion
PURINE nucleotides. See Nucleotides
PURITANISM
    Puritan ethic today. R. L. Tobin. Sat R 55:
        16 Ja 1 '72
        See also
    Puritans
PURITANS
    Mathers, by R. Middlekauff. Review
        Sat R 54:30 Jl 10 '71. N. Pettit
    Our Puritan heritage. R. A. Hasler. Chr
        Today 15:23-4 F 26 '71
PURKINJE cells. See Nerve cells
PURKO, Joe
    Los Angeles builds separate helicopter fa-
        cility. il Am City 86:97 Je '71
PUROLATOR, Inc.
    Oil filters to clinics. R. Levy. Duns 98:60 N
        '71
PURPLE martins. See Martins
PURSES
    Just two bangles and a bandanna. il Sunset
        147:107 D '71

PURSLANE
Purslane a weed? The French and the Mexicans use it in salads; with recipes. il Sunset 147:97 Ag '71

PURSUITS; story. See Goldschmidt, J.

PUSHCARTS. See Street trades

PUSHKIN, Aleksandr Sergeevich
Pushkin, by H. Troyat. Review
Nation 213:246-7 S 20 '71. D. Fanger •

PUSHRODS, Automobile. See Automobile engines

PUT and call transactions
Wall Street's new options il Fortune 84: 211-13 N '71

PUTMAN, Clay
Some grass roots of peace in Pacific Heights South; story. Atlan 228:114-15 O '71

PUTNAM, George
Stocks in '72; steady gains; interview. il por U S News 72:58-60 Ja 10 '72

about

It's Put-put time in California. Cyclops. por Life 70:18 Je 25 '71 •

PUTNAM, John J.
Ganges, river of faith. il Nat Geog 140:445-83 O '71

PUTNAM, Patrick F.
Back in the running. il pors Sports Illus 34: 10-13 F 1 '71
Backer of a bearback ride. il por Sports Illus 34:36-8+ Je 28 '71
Boxing. il Sports Illus 34:54-5 F 22 '71
But Alabama poses another threat. il Sports Illus 35:25-1 D 6 '71
College football (cont) Sports Illus 35:61-2 S 27; 54+ O 4; 56-7 N 1; 67+ N 22 '71
Dream comes true. il pors Sports Illus 34:18-21 My 24 '71
Good things come in large packages. il pors Sports Illus 35:16-18+ Ag 23 '71
He takes off, he takes it in. il pors Sports Illus 34:26-8+ My 17 '71
I got the horse right, where? il Sports Illus 34:22-4+ Ap 19 '71
Marathon si, basketball no! il Sports Illus 35:18-19 Ag 16 '71
Nature. il Sports Illus 35:44-6 Ag 30 '71
No practice makes almost perfect. il por Sports Illus 34:18-19 F 8 '71
Phooey on the fortune cookie. il por Sports Illus 34:22-3 Mr 1 '71
Pride in the red jersey. il Sports Illus 35: 18-21 O 11 '71
Saved by the itch to switch. il Sports Illus 35:24-5 O 25 '71
Track & field (title varies) (cont) Sports Illus 34:64+ Mr 22; 54-6 Je 28 '71
—and Myslenski, Skip
Firstest, fastest and mostest. il Sports Illus 35:18-21 Jl 5 '71

PUTNEY, London. See London

PUTTERMAN, Seth J. and Rudnick, Isadore
Quantum nature of superfluid helium. bibliog il Phys Today 24:39-43+ Ag '71

PUTTING (golf)
Putting is a family affair. M. Mulvoy. il por Sports Illus 34:86-7 Ap 12 '71

PUY, LE, France
Gallery; ancient French town. C. Bavagnoli. il Life 70:6-7 Ap 2 '71

PUZO, Mario
My mother, right or wrong. McCalls 98:111 My '71

PUZZLES
Advertising premiums to beguile the mind; classics by Sam Lloyd, master puzzle-poser. M. Gardner. il Sci Am 225:114-16+ N '71
New puzzles from the game of Halma, the noble ancestor of Chinese checkers. M. Gardner. il Sci Am 225:104-7 O '71
Princeps puzzle; first all-electronic puzzle. J. W. Cuccia. il Pop Electr 34:26-32 My '71
Up the cerebral cortex. I. Morris. il Esquire 75:92-5 Ja '71

PYES, Craig
Rip Torn: the case of the Hollywood 1. il pors Ramp Mag 9:40-6 Mr '71

PYLE, Christopher
How the U.S. army spies on citizens. il por Life 70:20-7 Mr 26 '71 •

PYLE, Howard
Brandywine school. D. Davis. il Newsweek 77:93 Je 28 '71 •

PYLE, Robert Michael
Is there wilderness in western Europe? il Liv Wildn 34:44-8 Wint '70

PYLONS (aeronautics) See Jet airplane engines—Mounting

PYRACANTHA. See Firethorns

PYRAMID-style investment plans. See Investments

PYRAMIDS
Secrets of the great pyramid; excerpts. P. Tompkins. il Horizon 13:38-49 Wint '71
What do you know about pyramids? quiz. J. Daugherty and M. Daugherty. il Sci Digest 70:80-1+ N '71

Construction

Make-work on the Nile. il Time 97:40 My 10 '71

PYRETHRINS
Mix with care. J. McCaull. bibliog il Environ 13:39-42 Ja '71

PYRIMIDINES
See also
Thymine
Uracil

PYROGRAPHY
Pyrography and plywood. L. J. Miller. il Design 73:27 Fall '71

PYROMETERS and pyrometry
How accurately can temperature be measured? use of optical pyrometers. W. T. Gray and D. I. Finch. il Phys Today 24:39-40 S '71

PYROXENES
Cation disorder in shocked orthopyroxene. R. W. Dundon and S. S. Hafner. bibliog il Science 174:581-3 N 5 '71
Core binding energy difference between bridging and nonbridging oxygen atoms in a silicate chain. L. I. Yin and others. bibliog il Science 173:633-5 Ag 13 '71

PYRUVATES
Hyperoxaluria in L-glyceric aciduria: possible pathogenic mechanism; effect of hydroxypyruvate. H. E. Williams and L. H. Smith, jr. bibliog il Science 171:390-1 Ja 29 '71

Q

QABUS bin Said, sultan of Muscat and Oman
Starting from scratch. il por Time 97:34-5 F 15 '71 •

al-QADDAFI, Muammar
Gaddafi to the rescue. por Time 99:27-8 Ja 17 '72 •
Libya: the enfant terrible. il por Time 98: 22 Ag 2 '71 •
Libya's Qaddafi: candidate for Arab world's strong man. por U S News 71:77 Ag 23 '71 •
Rich young rebel. por Newsweek 78:38-9 Ag 30 '71 •

QANTAS airways. See Airlines—Australia

QATAR
See also
United Nations—Qatar

QUACKS and quackery
You're not Mrs Hatfield. . . B. Lindeman. pors Todays Health 49:25-7+ F '71
See also
Medicines, Patent, proprietary, etc.

QUADE, Roy G.
Making an 8-inch refractor objective. il Sky & Tel 41:243-6 Ap '71

QUADRAGESIMO anno. See Encyclicals

QUADRIPHONIC sound. See Sound—Stereophonic recording and reproducing

QUADRIPLEGICS. See Paralytics

QUAIL shooting
Best way to bag bobwhite. W. Davis. il Mech Illus 68:58+ Ja '72
Bobwhite is no gentleman anymore! B. Brister. il Field & S 75:34-5+ Ja '71
Bobwhite leftovers. C. Elliott. il Outdoor Life 148:40-1+ D '71
Breadbasket bobwhites. J. M. Vance. il Field & S 76:72-3+ N '71
Mr Bob is full of beans. B. H. Brady. il Outdoor Life 147:72-3+ F '71

QUAILS
Eggshell thinning in Japanese quail fed mercuric chloride. G. S. Stoewsand and others. bibliog il Science 173:1030-1 S 10 '71

QUAINTANCE, Charles W.
Race, evolution and Mormonism. Chr Cent 88:586-9 My 12 '71

QUAKER relief work. See American Friends service committee

QUAKERS. See Friends, Society of

QUALIFICATIONS of librarians. See Librarians—Qualifications

QUALITY of products
America, inc, by M. Mintz and J. S. Cohen.
Review
Time 97:71 Je 28 '71
Determining the effects of quality change
on the CPI. J. E. Triplett. bibliog il Mo
Labor R 94:27-32 My '71
Institute reports on:
Aerosol containers. Good H 174:6 Ja '72
Baby food: a good-sense guide. il Good
H 172:6 Mr '71
Carpet padding: basic facts & buying
advice. il Good H 172:6 F '71
Differences in drain cleaners. Good H
173:6 Jl '71
Fashions in GH. il Good H 172:6 Je '71
How GH evaluates toys. il Good H 173:
6 N '71
No-phosphate detergents. il Good H
173:6 O '71
Resilient flooring. il Good H 173:6 S '71
Stamping out static electricity in fabrics
and carpets. Good H 173:6 Ag '71
Those colorful cookware finishes. il Good
H 172:6 Ap '71
Reliability physics: a response to consum-
erism's crisis of confidence; address. April
1, 1971. J. Hillier. Vital Speeches 37:474-7
My 15 '71
Speaker for the house. C. Montgomery. See
issues of Good housekeeping
Sweet inflation. il Time 97:79 F 8 '71
See also
Commercial products. Certification of
Food industry—Quality control
United States—National commission on prod-
uct safety
QUANDT, Richard E. See Malkiel, B. G. jt.
auth.
QUANTITY cookery. See Cookery, Quantity
QUANTUM mechanics. See Quantum theory
QUANTUM theory
Einstein's rejection of quantum theory: a
personal motive. H. M. Schey. bibliog f
il Am Imago 28:186-90 Sum '71
Quantum mechanics and reality: dilemma
of indeterminism. B. S. DeWitt; discus-
sion. bibliog il Phys Today 24:36-44 Ap;
11+ O '71
Scientific establishment and the transmission
of quantum mechanics to the United States.
1919-32. S. Coben. bibliog f Am Hist R 76:
442-66 Ap '71
See also
Energy band theory of solids
Relativity (physics)
QUARANTINE
See also
United States—Manned spacecraft center—
Lunar receiving laboratory
QUARKS. See Particles (nuclear physics)
QUARRELS
Is your marriage a fighting affair? il Chang-
ing T 25:25-7 F '71
QUARTERBACKS. See Football players
QUARTERMAIN, David, and others
Suppression of food intake with intragastric
loading: relation to natural feeding cycle.
bibliog il Science 173:941-3 S 3 '71
QUARTZ
Quartz: synthesis at earth-surface condi-
tions. F. T. MacKenzie and R. Gees. bib-
liog il Science 173:533-5 Ag 6 '71
See also
Agates
QUASARS
Antiquity of quasars. Sci Am 224:47 Ja '71
Brighter than 10 trillion suns; Seyfert galax-
ies. il Sci N 99:209 Mr 27 '71
Does annihilation power quasars? J. T. Scott.
il Phys Today 24:32 F '71
Evidence for internal structure in quasars.
Sci N 99:245 Ap 10 '71
Evolution of quasars. M. Schmidt and F.
Bello. il Sci Am 224:54-62+ bibliog (p 132)
My '71; Discussion. 225:6 Ag '71
Illusion of plus-C velocity. Sci N 99:278-9 Ap
24 '71
Observational paradoxes in extragalactic
astronomy. H. Arp. bibliog il Science 174:
1189-200 D 17 '71
Pinning down the quasars. J. P. Wiley, jr.
Natur Hist 80:79 My '71
Quasars are relatively local. Except those
that are not. J. T. Scott. il Phys Today 24:
13+ Jl '71
Quasars, galaxies and superlight velocities.
Sci N 100:405-6 D 18 '71
Quasars: millisecond-of-arc structure revealed
by very-long-baseline interferometry. C. A.
Knight and others. bibliog il Science 172:
52-4 Ap 2 '71

Quasars revisited: rapid time variations
observed via very-long-baseline interferometry. A. R. Whitney and others. bibliog il Science 173:225-30 Jl 16 '71
Rapidly changing radio images. A. Cavaliere
and others. bibliog il Science 173:525-8 Ag
6 '71
Statistics of quasars. il Sky & Tel 42:335
D '71
Spectra
Attacking the redshift. Sci N 99:367 My 29
'71
Quasars: new evidence for cosmological dis-
tances. Sci N 99:193 Mr 20 '71
QUASTEL, David M. J. and others
Calcium: is it required for transmitter se-
cretion? bibliog il Science 172:1034-6 Je 4
'71
QUATERNARY period. See Geology, Strati-
graphic—Quaternary; Paleontology—Qua-
ternary
QUAYLE, Eric
Juvenile incunabula. il por Wilson Lib Bul
46:326-34 D '71
QUEBEC (city)
Quebec: French city in an Anglo-Saxon
world. K. MacLeish. il Nat Geog 139:416-
42 Mr '71
QUEBEC (province)
See also
Architecture, Domestic—Quebec (province)
French Canadians
Gaspé Peninsula
Description and travel
Flaming fall foliage. N. D. Ford. il por Har
Yrs 11:6-16 Ag '71
Nationalism
Oh! Canada! The eruption of a revolution.
R. Salutin. Harper 243:26-31 Jl '71: Dis-
cussion. 243:9-10 S '71
Smoldering resentment in French Canada.
R. F. Hafter. Cur 132:46-50 S '71
See also
Front for the liberation of Quebec
Politics and government
Aftermath of Quebec crisis: a new mood
emerges. C. De Mestral. Chr Cent 88:666+
My 26 '71
Sequel to a crisis. C. de Mestral. Chr Cent
88:501-2 Ap 21 '71
Religious institutions and
affairs
World around us (cont) Chr Cent 88:501-2
Ap 21 '71
QUEBEC liberation front. See Front for the
liberation of Quebec
QUEEN Anne beds. See Beds
QUEEN Elizabeth (ship). See Ocean liners
QUEEN Mary (ship) See Ocean liners
QUEENS, N.Y.
Housing
Fear in Forest Hills. il Time 98:25-6 N 29
'71
Rage in Forest Hills. il Newsweek 78:82
N 29 '71
Romney on Forest Hills. Time 98:20-1 D
6 '71
Turmoil in Forest Hills. America 125:472 D
4 '71
When the melting pot doesn't melt. N.
Glazer. il N Y Times Mag p 12-13+ Ja 2 '72
QUEENS borough public library
Black librarians' caucus formed in Queens,
N.Y. Library J 96:3555-6 N 1 '71
QUEENSTOWN, New Zealand
New Zealand's resort king. T. R. Talamini.
il Travel 135:46-51 Mr '71
QUEENY, Edgar Monsanto
Dealing with a disaster. C. H. Sommer. il
pors Nations Bsns 59:78-9 Ja '71 *
QUELER, Eve
Musician of the month. C. Contos. por Hi
Fi 21:MA6 My '71 *
QUENNELL, Peter
Kenneth Clark: a man for all media. il por
Sat R 54:10-12+ Ag 28 '71
QUENUM, Olympe Bhely-. See Bhely-Quenum,
O.
QUESADILLAS. See Cookery, Mexican
QUESTER, George H.
Missiles in Cuba, 1970. For Affairs 49:493-
506 Ap '71
QUESTION of time; story. See Salinger, P.
QUESTIONING
Questions teachers ask: by-passes or thru-
ways? C. R. Duke. Clear House 45:468-7
Ap '71

QUESTOR corporation
From steady profits to swinging losses. il
Bsns W p 106+ Ag 14 '71
QUESTOR Grand prix. See Automobile racing
QUETICO-Superior committee. See United
States—President's Quetico-Superior com-
mittee
QUETICO-SUPERIOR country. See Wilderness
areas—Minnesota
QUICHE. See Cookery, French
QUIETUDE. See Silence
QUIGLEY, Carroll
Youths heroes have no haloes. Todays Ed
60:28-9 F 71, Same abr. Ed Digest 36:46-8
Ap 71
QUILTS
American quilts. D. Shapiro. il Craft Horiz
31:42-5+ D '71
Joy of quilting. il Newsweek 79:42 Ja 10 '72
On and off the avenue; exhibition at the
Whitney: Abstract design in American
quilts. J. Malcolm. New Yorker 47:60-2 S 4
'71
Quilts as art; exhibition at the Whitney
museum. S. B. Sherrill. il Antiques 100:
162+ Ag '71
West Virginia women find cash in quilts with
aid of VISTA man. Aging 198:14 Ap '71
See also
Patchwork
QUINLIVAN, Francis John
Christian apathy. il Cath World 213:187-8 Jl
'71
QUINN, Sister Bernetta
Comment. Poetry 118:97-8 My '71
Symbolic landscapes. Poetry 118:288-9 Ag '71
QUINN, George
Beginner's luck; story. Todays Ed 60:34-5 Ja
'71
QUINN, James
Reaganism in Connecticut. New Repub 164:
17 My 29 '71
QUINN, James Brian
Next big industry: environmental improve-
ment. il Harvard Bsns R 49:120-4+ S '71
QUINN, John Robert
Anatomy of faith; poem. Chr Cent 88:1085 S
15 '71
QUINN, Robert P. See Herrick, N. Q. jt. auth.
QUINN, Tom
Baseball. il Sports Illus 34:77-8 Ap 19 '71
QUINTUPLETS
Keeping up with the quints. A. Lake. il
Good H 173:96-9+ S '71
Quints go into action; the Kienast babies.
A. Lake. il pors Good H 172:72-7+ Mr '71
QUIST, George
Dirty dozen outfit cleans up in Itel deal. por
Bsns W p21 Ja 23 '71 *
QUIZ kids. See Children, Gifted
QUIZ shows. See Television programs—Quiz
shows
QUIZZES. See Information tests
QUMRAN Covenanters (sect) See Jewish sects
QUMRAN scrolls. See Dead Sea scrolls
QUOIREZ, Françoise. See Sagan, F. pseud.
QUOTATIONS
Quotable quotes. See issues of Reader's di-
gest
See also
Children—Sayings
QUTUB, Musa Y.
Mars is nearing earth. bibliog il Space
World H-7-91:4-10 Jl '71

R

R Cancri. See Stars, Variable
RANN (research applied to national needs)
program. See United States—National sci-
ence foundation
RCA corporation
$500-million write-off at RCA. il Fortune 84:34
N '71
Peddler. il por Time 97:66 Je 28 '71
RCA bows out. Newsweek 78:87+ S 27 '71
RCA digs in. il Forbes 107:23-4 Ja 15 '71
RCA switches on its videovoice. il Bsns W
p 120+ Je 19 '71
RCA takes off on a building spree; new
European plants. il Bsns W p30 Jl 3 '71
RCA's diversity yields a president. Bsns W
p43 Je 5 '71
Thin record. Newsweek 77:80-1 Ja 25 '71
$250-million disaster that hit RCA; sale of
computer division. il Bsns W p34-6 S 25 '71

RCA Victor division
Victor record sales, from 1901 to 1942. J.
Walsh. il Hobbies 76:37-8+ Je '71
REA express, inc.
Executive jungle? il por Forbes 107:60 F 15
'71
REACT (radio emergency associated citizens
teams) See React (organization)
REAP (Rural environmental assistance pro-
gram) See United States—Agricultural
stabilization and conservation service
REIT. See Real estate investment trusts
RETRO (Regional environmental training and
research organization project) See Re-
training, Occupational
RFC. See Reconstruction finance corporation
R. H. Macy and company. See Macy, R. H.
and company
R. J. Reynolds industries See Reynolds, R. J.
industries, inc.
RNA
Actinomycin D: renewed RNA synthesis after
removal from mammalian cells. A. Schluederberg and others. bibliog il Science 172:
577-9 My 7 '71
Adenosine   3',5'-monophosphate   increases
capacity for RNA synthesis in rat liver
nuclei. L. A. Dokas and L. J. Kleinsmith.
bibliog il Science 172:1237-8 Je 18 '71
Cross-linked transfer RNA functions in all
steps of the translation process. L. Chaffin
and others. bibliog il Science 172:854-5 My
21 '71
Enzymatic modification of transfer RNA. D.
Söll. bibliog il Science 173:293-9 Jl 23 '71
Expression of allelic immunoglobulin in homozygous rabbits injected with RNA extract.
C. Bell and S. Dray. bibliog il Science 171:
199-201 Ja 15 '71
Interferon action: inhibition of vesicular stomatitis virus RNA synthesis induced by virion-bound polymerase. P. I. Marcus and
others. bibliog il Science 174:593-8 N 5 '71
Molecular conformation of dihydrouridine:
puckered base nucleoside of transfer RNA.
M. Sundaralingam and others. bibliog il
Science 172:725-7 My 14 '71
Nucleotide sequence of the denaturable leucine transfer RNA from yeast. S. Kowalski
and others. bibliog il Science 172:385-7 Ap
23 '71
Polyadenylic acid sequences: role in conversion of nuclear RNA into messenger RNA.
J. E. Darnell and others. bibliog il Sci-
ence 174:507-10 O 29 '71
Preparation of highly labeled [32P]nucleic
acids from yeast; isolation of denaturable
leucine acceptor transfer RNA. S. Kowalski
and J. R. Fresco. bibliog il Science 172:384-
5 Ap 23 '71
RNA-directed DNA synthesis. H. M. Temin.
il Sci Am 226:24-33 bibliog(p 122) Ja '72
Rabbit blood from a frog. Sci Am 225:40
D '71
Raman spectrum of a transfer RNA. M.
Tsuboi and others. bibliog il Science 174:
1142-4 D 10 '71
Reverse transcription: one year later. B. J.
Culliton. Science 172:926-8 My 28 '71
Ribosomal RNA synthesis and the multiple,
atypical nucleoli in cleaving embryos. C. P.
Emerson, jr. and T. Humphreys. bibliog il
Science 171:898-901 Mr 5 '71
Ribosome-catalyzed polyester formation. S.
Fahnestock and A. Rich. bibliog il Science
173:340-3 Jl 23 '71
Rule of amino acids in ribosomal RNA syn-
thesis. Sci N 100:374 D 4 '71
Simultaneous detection of reverse transcrip-
tase and high molecular weight RNA unique
to oncogenic RNA viruses. J. Schlom and
S. Spiegelman. bibliog il Science 174:840-3
N 19 '71
Specialization of rabbit reticulocyte transfer
RNA content for hemoglobin synthesis. D.
W. E. Smith and A. L. McNamara. bib-
liog il Science 171:577-9 F 12 '71; Correc-
tion. 171:1040 Mr 12 '71
Synthesis of 5S and 4S RNA in metaphase-
arrested HeLa cells. E. A. Zylber and S.
Penman. bibliog il Science 172:947-9 My 28
'71
Viral RNA polymerases: electron microscopy
of reovirus reaction cores. S. Gillies and
others. bibliog il Science 174:694-6 N 12 '71
X-ray diffraction patterns of transfer RNA
consistent with the presence of short
parallel helices in the molecule. T. Sakurai
and others. bibliog il Science 172:1234-7
Je 18 '71
See also
Poly I:C
RNA tumor forming viruses. See Tumor viruses

ROI (return on investment) See Corporations
—Finance
ROTC. See United States—Reserve officers
training corps
RTE corporation
Marriage, Swedish-American style; RTE-
ASEA. il Forbes 107:50 F 15 '71
RA expeditions
Ra expeditions. by T. Heyerdahl. Review
Sat R il 54:63 S 4 '71. S. A. Jacobson
Time il 98:54 Ag 30 '71. M. Maddocks
Sight I shall never forget: The Ra expeditions
by Thor Heyerdahl. A. H. Johnston. il Pub
W 199:28-9 Je 14 '71
Voyage of Ra II. T. Heyerdahl. il pors Nat
Geog 139:44-71 Ja '71
Voyages of Ra; condensed from The Ra
expeditions. T. Heyerdahl. il por Read Di-
gest 99:187-90+ Ag '71
RAAB, Earl
Deadly innocences of American Jews. Com-
mentary 50:31-9 D '70; 18 Ap '71
Quotas by any other name. Commentary 53:
41-5 Ja '72
RAAB, Lawrence
Eight landscapes from the tarot deck; poem.
Poetry 117:300-3 F '71
Magritte: the song of the glass keys and
the cape of storms; poem. Am Scholar
41:111-12 Wint '71
RABB, Charles
Mr Buckley goes to Washington. Common-
weal 94:181-2 Ap 30 '71
Roman collar in the House. Commonweal 94:
276 My 28 '71
Sniffing out the super-snoopers. Commonweal
94:126-7 Ap 16 '71
RABBIS
Two rabbis rock the boat. pors Time 97:
65-6 Mr 15 '71
See also
Central conference of American rabbis
Riskin, S.
RABBIT hunting
Bunnies by barometer. J. Parry. il Field & S
76:34-5+ S '71
Bunny bagging, America's favorite sport!
W. Davis. il Mech Illus 67:83+ N '71
Cottontail hunting, eastern style. C. Nansen.
il Field & S 76:54-5+ O '71
[Future farmers of America rabbit drive in
Idaho] P. Henault. il Ramp Mag 9:12 Ap '71
Guzzler cottontails. J. R. Higley. il por Out-
door Life 148:62-3+ Jl '71
How the English hunt rabbits. F. Taylor.
il pors Field & S 75:84-5+ Mr '71
Madcap of the swamps; snowshoe rabbit. D.
Knight. il Field & S 76:46-7+ N '71
New ways to hunt rabbits. P. Curtis. il Field
& S 75:36-7+ Ja '71
Snowshoes in the wind. R. L. Tucker. il pors
Outdoor Life 148:58-9+ N '71
RABBITS
Estrogen receptor in the rabbit corpus lu-
teum. C. Lee and others. bibliog il Science
173:1032-3 S 10 '71
Expression of allelic immunoglobulin in homo-
zygous rabbits injected with RNA extract.
C. Bell and S. Dray. bibliog il Science 171:
199-201 Ja 15 '71
Raising rabbits right. J. D. Belanger. il Org
Gard & Farm 18:120-1 Ap '71
We call our place Rabbit run. L. Block. il
Org Gard & Farm 18:104-10 F '71
See also
Cookery—Game
RABBITS, Dressing of. See Game, Dressing of
RABBIT'S evening out; story. See Updike. J.
RABBIT'S foot; drama. See Miller, H. L.
RABBITT, Thomas
Exodus; poem Nation 213:379 O 18 '71
Farm rental; poem. Nation 213:61 Jl 19 '71
Letter from a dog with mange; poem. Nation
213:279 S 27 '71
RABE, David
Rabe; interview. New Yorker 47:48-9 N 20
'71
about
Basic training of Pavlo Hummel. Criticism
Nation 212:733 Je 7 '71
New Yorker 47:55 My 29 '71 •
Newsweek il 77:70 Je 14 '71 •
Sat R 54:36 Jl 10 '71
Experience thing. por Newsweek 78:58+ D
20 '71 •
Sticks and bones. Criticism
Nation 213:539 N 22 '71 •
New Repub 165:22+ D 4 '71 •
New Yorker 47:114+ N 20 '71 •
Newsweek 78:110 N 29 '71 •
Sat R il 54:70-1 N 27 '71 •
Time il 98:93 N 22 '71 •
RABELAIS, Francois
Francois Rabelais, vaudevilliste. D. S. Pack-
er. bibliog f il Mus Q 57:107-28 Ja '71 •

RABIES
Boy who didn't die. R. Rhodes. il Redbook
137:58-60+ Ag '71; Same abr. Read Digest
99:227-8+ D '71
RABINOVE, Samuel
Between order and violence: the middle
ground. America 125:311-12 O 23 '71
RABINOWITCH, Eugene
Mounting tide of unreason. por Bul Atom
Sci 27:4-9 My '71
Role of scientists: thoughts for 1971; adapta-
tion of address, September 9, 1970. por Bul
Atom Sci 27:2-4 Ja '71
RABINOWITZ, Dorothy
Advocate. Commentary 51:69-71 Mr '71
RABINOWITZ, Joseph L. and Hercker, E. S.
Thyroxine: conversion to triiodothyronine by
isolated perfused rat heart. bibliog Science
173:1242-3 S 24 '71
RABINOWITZ, Oscar
How to talk to your parents about sex; ed.
by M. Brenton. Seventeen 30:152-3+ Mr
'71
RACCOON hunting
Where raccoons come tough. H. Bradshaw.
il Field & S 75:56-7+ Ja '71
RACCOONS
I've learned to love raccoons. L. L. Rue, 3d.
il Nat Wildlife 9:36-8 Ap '71
RACE attitudes
Attitudes toward racial integration. A. M.
Greeley and P. B. Sheatsley. il Sci Am 225:
13-19 bibliog(p 120) D '71
RACE cooperation. See Interracial cooperation
RACE differences. See Racial differences
RACE discrimination
Brown eyes, blue eyes; excerpt from A class
divided. W. Peters. Read Digest 98:61-5 Ap
'71
Elimination of racial discrimination; Third
committee begins consideration. UN Mo
Chron 8:106 N '71
New attacks on discrimination; Hawkins v.
town of Shaw. il Time 97:59 F 22 '71
Rap on race; excerpts. M. Mead; J. Baldwin.
pors McCalls 98:84-5+ Je '71
Rogue Elk; Negro membership controversy.
il por Newsweek 78:70 D 13 '71
Some progress, more myth: the new, new
South. R. W. Dietsch. Nation 212:615-18
My 17 '71
U.S. discusses actions to combat racism and
discrimination; statements, October 26 and
November 3, 1971. A. A. Fletcher. Dept
State Bul 65:628-39 N 29 '71
Washington scores Moose for snub of black
librarian; S. Finley from Timberland
regional library. il por Library J 97:11 Ja
1 '72
Will revenue-sharing mean power-sharing? D.
Lawrence. U S News 70:100 F 15 '71
See also
Discrimination in education
Discrimination in employment
Discrimination in housing
International day for the elimination of racial
discrimination
International year for action to combat racism
and racial discrimination, 1971
Race prejudice
RACE equality. See Equality
RACE horse auctions. See Auctions
RACE horse training. See Horse training
RACE horses
¡Arriba! Canonero does it again: at the
Preakness. W. Tower. il Sports Illus 34:22-
5 My 24 '71
Bold Ruler's legend. Newsweek 78:80 Jl 26 '71
Experiment in drugs at Santa Anita; legal-
izing Butazolidin for thoroughbreds. W.
Leggett. il Sports Illus 34:18-19 Ja 25 '71
Half-mast; Hoist The Flag. il Newsweek 77:
74 Ap 12 '71
It may be adios to Canonero; Preakness at
Pimlico. W. Tower. il Sports Illus 34:80+
My 17 '71
Last year's crop of misses is starting to hit;
thoroughbred colts. W. Tower. il Sports Illus
34:50-1 F 15 '71
Missing data unavailable; Venezuela's Can-
onero II. W. Tower. il Sports Illus 34:18-21
My 10 '71
Mostest hoss: Man o' War. P. Chew. il Am
Heritage 22:24-9+ Ap '71
On the fence about winning; His Majesty.
W. Tower. il Sports Illus 34:54 Mr 1 '71
One more blur in a confusion Derby: no fa-
vorite for Kentucky Derby. W. Tower. il
Sports Illus 34:20-1 Ap 26 '71
People's horse; Canonero II. il Newsweek 77:
74 Je 14 '71

RACE horses—*Continued*
Pretenders to the crown; Hoist The Flag's likely successors. W. Tower. il Sports Illus 34:26-9 Ap 12 '71
Race track. A. Minor. See issues of New Yorker
Saratoga auction: the very elegant crap game; report. C. Winfrey. il Time 98:12 Ag 23 '71
Son of the Axe chops 'em; Executioner winner of Flamingo stakes. W. Tower. il Sports Illus 34:22-3 Mr 15 '71
They're all running after The Flag; Hoist The Flag. W. Tower. il Sports Illus 34:28-31 Ap 5 '71
Unconscious, List and Twist; Kentucky Derby. W. Tower. il Sports Illus 34:32-3 My 3 '71
What a fiesta we will have! trio of Venezuelans; owner, trainer and jockey of Canonero. W. F. Reed. il pors Sports Illus 34:26-8+ My 31 '71

Caricatures and cartoons
What hath Roth got? drawings of harness horses. A. Roth. Sports Illus 35:30-5 Jl 26 '71

Doping
See Doping in sports

Training
See Horse training
RACE horses, Doping of. See Doping in sports
RACE improvement. See Eugenics
RACE prejudice
Pride of color; excerpt from issue of August 23, 1957. D. Lawrence. U S News 71:104 O 4 '71
Rap on race; excerpts. M. Mead; J. Baldwin. pors McCalls 98:84-5+ Je '71
See also
Anti-Semitism
Racism
RACE problems
See also
Business and race problems
Church and race problems
Ethnopsychology
Intermarriage of races
Interracial cooperation
Minorities
Race relations
United States—Race question
also subhead Race question under names of continents, countries, cities, etc. e.g. Newark, N.J.—Race question
RACE psychology. See Ethnopsychology
RACE relations
Bad day in Memphis; the only major southern city to have a major racial incident this year. N. C. Chriss. Nation 213:653-4 D 20 '71
Ballet of umbrellas. il UNESCO Courier 24:18-19 N '71
Been down home so long it looks like up to me. J. B. Cumming, jr. il Esquire 76:84-90+ Ag '71
Black/white dating; with result of national poll. J. Downs. il Life 70:56-67 My 28 '71
Integration and acceptance; excerpt from The forum for residential therapy. M. Brackeen. por Camp Mag 43:12-14 F '71
Interview of the week; ed. by R. Hemming. N. Wilson. por Sr Schol 98:22 F 1 '71
Jacksonville: so different you can hardly believe it. J. Fischer. Harper 243:20-2+ Jl '71
Journey through black America; condensation of Odyssey: journey through black America; with editorial comment. E. Selby and M. Selby. Read Digest 99:11-13, 223-8+ S '71
Learning the three T's in school: tolerance, toil, and teamwork. A. A. Mazrui. il UNESCO Courier 24:28-30+ N '71
Liberal mayor's advice to blacks: think white; excerpts from address, October 6, 1971. S. Massell. por U S News 71:94-5 N 1 '71
Myths of liberalism and school integration. A. C. Ornstein. Sch & Soc 99:436-9 N '71
Paradox without promise: a dream deferred; address; April 21, 1971. F. A. Rodgers. Vital Speeches 37:521-5 Je 15 '71
Powder keg in cities. il U S News 71:45 Jl 5 '71
Profiles: J. U. Monro, white director of freshman studies. E. J. Kahn, jr. New Yorker 47:43-8+ Ap 10 '71
Rap on race, by M. Mead and J. Baldwin. Review
Newsweek 77:100+ My 24 '71

Rap on race: how James Baldwin and I talked a book. M. Mead. il por Redbook 137:70-2+ S '71
Some of my best friends; letter to the editor. V. M. Puryear. Am Lib 2:233 Mr '71
Stepin Fetchit talks back; interview, ed. by J. McBride. S. Fetchit. pors Film Q 24:20-6 Sum '71
Violence flares: just a start? U S News 70:29 Je 7 '71
When the melting pot doesn't melt; the fight over a public housing project in Forest Hills, N.Y.C. N. Glazer. il N Y Times Mag p 12-13+ Ja 2 '72
White hopes and other coalitions; adaptation of address at convention of the National urban league. L. Bennett, jr. il Ebony 26:33-4+ O '71
White man's strategy for black victory. J. C. Van Leuven. Yale R 61:183-92 D '71
Wingspread: where people are people; black-white student exchanges in Chicago. M. Cleary. il Am Ed 7:21-4 Ap '71
See also
Black power
Interracial cooperation

Anecdotes, facetiae, satire, etc.
Brother's keeper. J. C. Bledsoe. Esquire 76:81-2+ N '71
Some of my kid's best friends are black. M. Elkoff. Esquire 76:10+ D '71

Periodicals
Magazines; ed. by B. Katz. Library J 96:4077-8 D 15 '71
RACE tracks
Chairman: New York racing association; interview. A. G. Vanderbilt. New Yorker 47:33-5 Ap 17 '71
Thoroughbred can of worms; 1¼-mile race for 3-year-olds at Saratoga. W. Tower. Sports Illus 35:53-4 Ag 30 '71
See also
Speedways
RACEMIZATION
Marine sediments: dating by the racemization of amino acids. J. L. Bada and others; reply with rejoinder. M. C. McKenna. Science 172:503 Ap 30 '71
Racemization of amino acids in marine sediments. J. Wehmiller and P. E. Hare. bibliog il Science 173:907-11 S 3 '71
RACHEWILTZ, Mary de
Impassioned reticence. H. Kenner. Nat R 23:933+ Ag 24 '71 *
RACHLEFF, Owen S.
Flame-spattered robe. Opera N 35:23 Ja 30 '71

about
Conversation with a witch-debunker. K. Bryn. Sci Digest 69:27 Je '71 *
RACHMANINOFF, Sergei
Rachmaninoff eruption. H. Goldsmith. il Hi Fi 21:69-70 Jl '71 *
Weissenberg: close to the very ultimate. L. Gerber. Am Rec G 37:448 Mr '71 *
RACIAL attitudes. See Race attitudes
RACIAL differences
Intelligence and race. W. F. Bodmer and L. L. Cavalli-Sforza; discussion. Sci Am 224:6-8 Ja '71
Race and I.Q. excerpts from Race and psychology. O. Klineberg. il UNESCO Courier 24:4-9+ N '71
Race, social class, and IQ. S. Scarr-Salapatek. bibliog il Science 174:1285-95 D 24 '71
See also
Ethnopsychology
RACIAL discrimination. See Race discrimination
RACIAL doctrine. See Racism
RACIAL equality. See Equality
RACIAL zoning. See Zoning
RACINE, Jean Baptiste

Bibliography
Psychological bibliography of Jean Racine; comp. by E. P. Chanover. Am Imago 28:84-90 Spr '71
RACING. See Airplane racing; Motorcycle racing; Snowmobile racing; and similar headings
RACING car models. See Automobile models
RACING car tires. See Tires, Automobile
RACING cars. See Automobiles, Racing
RACING tires. See Tires, Automobile

RACISM
Answers to racism; symposium. il UNESCO Courier 24:4-33 N '71
Aryan myth. M. D. Biddiss. il por Horizon 13:96-101 Sum '71
Confessions of a white racist, by L. L. King. Review
  Life 70:16 Je 11 '71. M. Frady
Defining racism. R. Caselli. Clear House 46:98-101 O '71
Dilemma of the black policeman. A. Poinsett. il Ebony 26:122-4+ My '71
Psychopathology of racism. J. Daniels; reply. V. R. Mollenkott. Chr Today 15:6-8 Mr 26 '71
  See also
Race prejudice
RACKAUSKAS, John A. See Ogletree, E. J. jt. auth.
RACKETEERING
Second business at our airports: theft. D. Walsh. il Life 70:16-23 F 12 '71
RACKS. See Shelves
RACKS, Gun. See Gun racks
RACKS, Magazine. See Magazine stands, racks, etc.
RACKS, Spice. See Spice racks
RACKS, Wine. See Wine racks
RADAR
  See also
Motor vehicles—Radar equipment

Antenna and scanning mechanisms
Giant billboard antennas for space-age radars. E. A. Lacy. il Pop Electr 35:44-7+ D '71
New airborne test antenna. il Pop Electr 1:62 Ja '72
Portable radar becomes a reality. R. Humphrey. il Pop Electr 35:67-8+ Jl '71

Military use
Are modern military radars infallible? A. E. Judd. il Pop Electr 35:45-51 S '71
HF radar detects Soviet ICBMs. P. J. Klass. il Aviation W 95:38-40 D 6 '71
New radars, fire control aids displayed. P. J. Klass. il Aviation W 94:39-41+ Je 7 '71
Soviet radar expertise expands. B. Miller. il Aviation W 94:14-16 F 15 '71
Soviet radars disclose clues to doctrine. B. Miller. il Aviation W 94:42-3+ F 22 '71
Soviets closing gap in avionics, computer science military development. C. Brownlow and B. Miller. il Aviation W 95:40-3+ O 25 '71
  See also
Airplanes, Military—Radar equipment
RADAR astronomy. See Radar in astronomy
RADAR beacons. See Radar in aviation
RADAR defense networks
  See also
Ballistic missile early warning system
RADAR in astronomy
Mapping the topography of Mars with radar. Sci N 100:277 O 23 '71
Mars radar observations, a preliminary report. G. S. Downs and others. bibliog il Science 174:1324-7 D 24 '71
Martian craters and a scarp as seen by radar. G. H. Pettengill and others. bibliog il Science 174:1321-4 D 24 '71
RADAR in aviation
ARTS-3 readied for FAA service; automated radar terminal system. P. J. Klass. il Aviation W 94:44-7+ Ja 25 '71
Discrete address beacon plan set. P. J. Klass. il Aviation W 95:45-6 O 18 '71
Everything you always wanted to know about radar. W. Berkley. il Flying 88:44-6 F '71
FAA to seek bids on new automated radar. Aviation W 94:20 My 10 '71
New ASR-7 radar installed near Dallas. il Aviation W 94:61 Je 14 '71
Radar and the VFR pilot. W. Berkley. Flying 88:57-8 My '71
  See also
Airplanes, Military—Radar equipment
Helicopters—Radar equipment
Proximity warning indicators
RADAR in surveying
Sharper eyes seek the world's resources. il Bsns W p54-5 N 27 '71
Side-looking radar maps terrain details. il Aviation W 94:44-5 Ap 19 '71
RADBURN, N. J.
Radburn revisited. H. N. Wright. bibliog il Arch Forum 135:52-7 Jl '71
RADEBAUGH, Byron F. and Johnson, J. A.
Excellent teachers: what makes them outstanding? Phase II. il Clear House 45:410-18 Mr '71

RADEKE, Duane L.
CATV story in St Cloud. il Todays Ed 60:58-9 N '71
RADER, Dotson
Feminization of the American male. por Harp Baz 105:106-7+ N '71
Guido Orlando: cosa sua. il pors Esquire 75:134-7+ Ja '71
RADERSTORF, Jerry
Land acquisition: a country's responsibility. Parks & Rec 6:41+ Jl '71
RADFORD, Jeff
Chile's reasonable revolution: Allende after a year. Nation 213:422-4, 642 N 1, D 20 '71
RADIAL drill press. See Drilling and boring machinery
RADIAL saws. See Saws
RADIAL tires. See Tires, Automobile
RADIATION
  See also
Cosmic rays
Gamma rays
Mössbauer effect
Radioactivity
Radiology
Stars—Radiation
Television receivers, Color—Radiation hazards
Ultraviolet rays

Effect on metals
See Metals, Effect of radiation on

Laws and regulations
Precautions are being taken by those who know: an inquiry into the power and responsibilities of the AEC. P. Jacobs. Atlan 227:45-56 F '71; Discussion. 227:30+ Ap; 36 My; 36 Je '71
State radiation law loses in court. C. Holden. Science 171:45 Ja 8 '71

Measurement
Channel electron multipliers: new semiconductor radiation detectors. F. W. Holder. il Electr World 86:30-1+ D '71
  See also
Remote sensing systems

Physiological effects
Fallout from the peaceful atom. P. Winslow. Nation 212:557-61 My 3 '71. Reply with rejoinder. J. A. Harris. 212:738 Je 14 '71
Precautions are being taken by those who know: an inquiry into the power and responsibilities of the AEC. P. Jacobs. Atlan 227:45-56 F '71 Discussion. 227:30+ Ap; 36 My; 36 Je '71
  See also
Atomic medicine
Aviation—Radiation hazards
Microwaves—Physiological effects

Safety devices and measures
Another round on radiation. Sci N 99:78 Ja 30 '71
Ionizing-radiation standards for population exposure; adaptation of address. July 1971. J. A. Lieberman. il Phys Today 24:32-8 N '71
Never do harm. K. Z. Morgan. bibliog il Environ 13:28-38 Ja '71
New emission guidelines. B. I. Spinrad. Bul Atom Sci 27:7 S '71
Nuclear plant controversy; AEC's standards. R. E. Lapp. New Repub 164:17-21 F 27 '71
Nuclear power and the public, ed. by H. Foreman. Review
  Science 171:790-3 F 26 '71. L. Loevinger
Radiation standards: are the right people making decisions? P. M. Boffey. Science 171:780-3 F 26 '71; Reply. F. Forscher. 172:632-3 My 14 '71
Reactor emissions: AEC guidelines move toward critics' position. R. Gillette. Science 172:1215-16 Je 18 '71; Discussion. 174:1280-1 D 24 '71
Reviving the radiation scare. Bsns W p83 My 29 '71
RADIATION, Atomic. See Radioactivity
RADIATION, Terrestrial. See Earth—Radiation
RADIATION biology. See Radiobiology
RADIATION chemistry. See Radiochemistry
RADIATION detectors. See Radiation—Measurement
RADIATION pressure. See Pressure
RADIATION standards. See Radiation—Safety devices and measures
RADIATION workers
Plutonium cancer shadow hangs over Rocky Flats, AEC. D. Shapley. Science 174:570 N 5 '71

RADIATOR coolant additives. See Automobile engines—Cooling

RADIATORS
What an ugly radiator can do for a room. il Pop Mech 135:138-41+ F '71

RADICAL left (politics) See Radicalism

RADICAL party. See Political parties—France

RADICAL theology. See Theology

RADICALISM
Bobby Seale's birthday cake. J. A. Lukas. il por N Y Times Mag p42+ O 31 '71
Catholic left. J. Deedy. Commonweal 94:466 S 17 '71
Catholic radicals. J. Deedy. Commonweal 94: 50 Mr 26 '71
Grand jury network; how the Nixon administration has secretly perverted a traditional safeguard of individual rights. F. J. Donner and E. Cerruti. il Nation 214:5-15+ Ja 3 '72
Inside the revolutionary left. T. E. Mosher. Read Digest 99:53-7 S '71
Lennon: the working-class hero turns red; interview, ed. by R. Blackburn and T. Ali. Y. Ono; J. Lennon. pors Ramp Mag 10: 43-9 Jl '71
Of politics and prophecy: student activism today. R. C. Johansen. il Chr Cent 88:219-23 F 17 '71
Radical chic is out. P. Douglas. Chr Today 15:12 Mr 26 '71
Radical man, by C. Hampden-Turner. Review
Nation 212:472-4 Ap 12 '71. W. Anderson
Radicals in America: who, what, where, and why? Sr Schol 98:4-14 Ap 19 '71
Radicals: time out to retrench. J. Birnbaum. il Time 97:11-12 F 22 '71
Rules for radicals, by S. D. Alinsky. Review
Nation 213:373-7 O 18 '71. T. Gitlin. Reply. S. D. Alinsky. 213:500 N 15 '71
Short course in the three types of radical professors. J. Hitchcock. il N Y Times Mag p30-1+ F 21 '71; Discussion. p80 Mr 21 '71
Six 'big lies' about America. A. Beichman. il N Y Times Mag p32-3+ Je 6 '71
You are the target; address, December 3, 1970. T. E. Bishop. Vital Speeches 37:238-41 F 1 '71
See also
New university conference

RADICALS (chemistry)
Free radical inhibitory effect of some anticancer compounds. K. K. Georgieff. bibliog il Science 173:537-9 Ag 6 '71
Free radicals in the liquid phase: structure and reactivity; report of meeting. G. A. Russell. Science 173:1042+ S 10 '71
See also
Hydroxyl

RADICALS, Student. See Student militants

RADICALS, Young. See Young militants

RADICALS and radicalism. See Radicalism

RADIN, Doris
In my hands I hold an ancient drinking vessel; poem. Nation 213:606 D 6 '71

RADIO advertising
But first a message; U.S. Court of appeals on paid public-issue announcements. Newsweek 78:72-3 Ag 16 '71
See also
Cigarettes—Advertising

RADIO alarms. See Fire alarms

RADIO amateurs. See Radio operators, Amateur

RADIO amplifiers. See Amplifiers

RADIO antennas
Case of a custom job too well done. J. T. Bailey. il Radio-Electr 42:54 N '71
Equipment report; Simpson model A 2-meter FM transceiver with Hy-Gain MMG-150 mobile whip and Mosely Diplomat-2 2-meter ground-plane. il Radio-Electr 42:22+ N '71
Giant antennas for use in deep space probes. il Space World H-12-96:37-8 D '71
See also
Communications satellites—Ground stations
Radio telescopes

RADIO apparatus
Build FM stereo adapter. L. D'Airo. il Radio-Electr 42:68-70 Mr '71
New products. See issues of Popular electronics

RADIO apparatus on ships, boats, etc.
Show me the way to go home. C. Miller. il Motor B & S 128:66-7+ Ag '71
See also
Radio telephone on ships, boats, etc.

RADIO apparatus on space vehicles. See Space vehicles—Radio equipment

RADIO astronomy
Antares as a radio source. Sky & Tel 41:212-13 Ap '71
Cyclops: eye on the universe. Sci N 99:435 Je 26 '71
Ingredients for life in outer space. R. Amidei. bibliog il Sci Digest 70:24-9 S '71
Microwaves from the planets. D. E. Thomsen. il Sci N 99:424-5 Je 19 '71
Radio emission from Antares B. Sky & Tel 43:10 Ja '72
Radio emission from X-ray sources. Sky & Tel 42:335 D '71
Radio photography of the sky. il Sky & Tel 42:205-6 O '71
Radio stars. R. M. Hjellming and C. M. Wade. bibliog il Science 173:1087-92 S 17 '71
Rapidly changing radio images. A. Cavaliere and others. bibliog il Science 173:525-8 Ag 6 '71
See also
Interstellar communication
Quasars
Radio telescopes

RADIO beacons
FAA will issue crash locator beacon specification. Aviation W 94:43 Ja 25 '71

RADIO broadcasting
See also
Radio stations

Automobile racing
See Radio broadcasting—Sports

Censorship
Balancing act; WFLN, WPEN and the T. Grant controversy. R. L. Shayon. Sat R 54:43 Je 5 '71; Reply with rejoinder. L. M. C. Smith. 54:19 Jl 10 '71

Comedy
See Radio broadcasting—Humor

Conversation programs
How to promote your book on radio and TV interviews. R. Hull. il Writers Digest 51: 28-30+ Ag '71

Horse racing
See Radio broadcasting—Sports

Humor
Amos and Andy at ease. il Newsweek 78:23 N 15 '71
Illegal use
See also
Radio stations, Illegal

International aspects
Future of international broadcasting. F. S. Ronalds, jr. bibliog f Ann Am Acad 398:71-80 N '71
See also
World administrative radio conference

Licenses
See Radio laws and regulations

Multiplex system
Build FM stereo adapter. L. D'Airo. il Radio-Electr 42:68-70 Mr '71
Unique stereo decoder. S. Reich. il Pop Electr 35:53-5+ O '71

Music
How New York's pioneer classical station has fallen upon sorry Times: WQXR. C. Briefer. il pors Hi Fi 21:74-9 S '71
See also
Disc jockeys
Radio broadcasting—Operas

Negro programs
Black-oriented; study findings of Stanford university's Institute for communications research. R. L. Shayon. Sat R 54:18 S 25 '71

News
Unusual typecasting for radio newscasters; corporate executives on Cleveland's station WERE. V. Louviere. il Nations Bsns 59:21 N '71

Operas
Dear Texaco opera quiz... N. S. Ross. Opera N 36:16 D 11 '71
Forty seasons of Metropolitan opera broadcasts, 1931-71. il Opera N 35:24-5 Ap 17 '71
Musical events; broadcast of Werner Egk's The betrothal in Santo Domingo. New Yorker 47:118-19 S 25 '71
Texaco-Metropolitan opera radio network (cont) Opera N 36:14-15 D 11 '71

RADIO broadcasting—*Continued*

Propaganda
Who needs it? New Repub 164:7 Je 5 '71
See also
Radio free Europe

Religious programs
Radio priest; Father Coughlin's Golden hour. pors Newsweek 78:15 O 4 '71
Religious broadcasting marks fiftieth year; the KDKA program. R. Chandler. Chr Today 15:48-9 F 12 '71
Spanish radio: The friendly voice. D. Foster. Chr Today 16:45 Ja 7 '72

Social aspects
Hey, radio, help me make it through the night. P. Fornatale. il por Sr Schol 99:32-4 O 25 '71
TV-radio; Upper midwestern conference on broadcasting and the people. R. L. Shayon. Sat R 54:54 My 15 '71
See also
MINERVA system

Sports
And here, to bring you the play by play: baseball announcers. J. Kirshenbaum. il Sports Illus 35:32-5+ S 13 '71
How Mel Allen started a lifelong love affair. J. A. Lukas. il N Y Times Mag p38-9+ S 12 '71; Discussion. p 18+ O 17 '71
Man who blew a Derby: C. McCarthy. B. Greenspan. il por Sports Illus 34:40-2+ My 17 '71
Sid Collins; Indianapolis motor speedway radio network announcer. R. Guldahl, jr. il pors Hot Rod 24:44-6 My '71

Stereophonic transmission
Instant quadriphony. R. Long. il Hi Fi 21:42-3 S '71
Surrounding the listener with hi-fi. il Bsns W p89 O 2 '71

Weather forecasts
How's the weather? J. West. il Yachting 130:68-9+ D '71
Transcribed weather broadcast service. il Weatherwise 24:236 O '71
See also
United States—National weather service

Australia
See also
Australian broadcasting commission

Mexico
Radio broadcasting agreements with Mexico enter into force. Dept State Bul 63:736 D 14 '70

United States
Night the martians didn't land; dramatization of H. G. Wells novel, October 30, 1938. il Life 70:56B F 19 '71
Radio broadcasting agreements enter into force. Dept State Bul 63:736 D 14 '70

RADIO broadcasting, **Short wave**
Shortwave broadcasts of solar and geophysical information. il Sky & Tel 42:120-1 Ag '71

RADIO broadcasting, **Stereophonic.** See Radio broadcasting—Stereophonic transmission

RADIO broadcasting stations. See Radio stations

RADIO circuits
Introduction to direct-conversion radio receivers; with glossary. R. F. Scott. bibliog il Radio-Electr 42:62-3+ N '71
New squelch for CB receiver; solid-state circuit. G. Neal. il Radio-Electr 42:37 N '71

RADIO City music hall. See New York (city) —Radio City music hall

RADIO commentators. See Radio broadcasting —News

RADIO communication
See also
Communications satellites
Space flight—Communication systems

Emergency use
CB and the coast guard. R. Humphrey. il Pop Electr 35:42-4 S '71
See also
React (organization)

Interference
See Radio interference

International aspects
See also
Radio broadcasting—International aspects

RADIO communication, **Municipal.** See Radio in municipal government

RADIO communication, **Naval**
Talking to ourselves; Sanguine communications system. M. McClintock and others. bibliog f il Environ 13:16-19+ S '71

RADIO communication, **Short wave**
Who rules the microwaves? il Newsweek 77:56 Mr 22 '71
See also
Citizens radio service
Microwave communications, inc.

RADIO communication in aviation. See Radio in aviation

RADIO converters
VHF frequency converter. L. E. Greenlee. il Pop Electr 35:52-3+ D '71

RADIO corporation of America. See RCA corporation

RADIO fire alarms. See Fire alarms

RADIO free Europe
Don't ask; CIA funding. New Repub 164:13-14 F 6 '71
Radio free Europe. il Newsweek 77:102 F 8 '71

RADIO frequency
Changes in design, higher costs expected with new allocations; communications satellite bands. il Aviation W 95:89-92 Ag 23 '71

Allocation
See Radio frequency allocation

RADIO frequency allocation
Report on the World administrative radio conference. R. G. Gould. Pop Electr 35:69-70+ D '71
Satellite radio spectrum expanded. P. J. Klass. Aviation W 95:14-15 Ag 2 '71

RADIO frequency signal generators. See Signal generators

RADIO generators. See Signal generators

RADIO in aviation
Landing aid for army progresses; A-Scan landing guidance units. K. J. Stein. il Aviation W 95:42-4 O 4 '71
Omega navaid aviation use studied. P. J. Klass. il Aviation W 95:38-42 N 29 '71
Pro's nest; phraseology. T. H. Block. Flying 89:70 Jl '71
See also
Airplanes, Military—Radio equipment
Helicopters—Radio equipment
United States—Federal aviation administration—Flight service stations

RADIO in defense
See also
Radio communication, Naval

RADIO in education
Educational broadcasting facilities program; grants for educational television and radio. il Am Ed 7:24 N '71
Everyman's alma mater; Britain's Open university. il Newsweek 77:52+ Ja 25 '71

RADIO in meteorology
Detecting tornadoes by radio. L. Purrett. il Sci N 100:12-13 Jl 3 '71
Modifying the ionosphere with intense radio waves. W. F. Utlaut and R. Cohen. bibliog il Science 174:245-54 O 15 '71

RADIO in municipal government
Go total communications; Upper Arlington, Ohio. A. C. Neer. il Am City 86:117-18 Ap '71
Street cleaning that pays its way; two-way radio, Akron, Ohio. il Am City 86:42 N '71

RADIO in navigation
New navigator that never sleeps; Minidec. E. A. Zadig. il Motor B & S 127:128+ Mr '71
Soviets using Omega-like navaid system. P. J. Klass. Aviation W 95:22 N 22 '71
See also
Radio apparatus on ships, boats, etc.

RADIO in surveying
News from the world of space exploration; satellite-Doppler survey receivers. Space World H-9-93:49 S '71

RADIO instruments
See also
Calibrators

RADIO interference
Radio interference: causes & cures. J. T. Frye. Pop Electr 1:94-6 Ja '72

RADIO interferometry. See Interferometry

RADIO laws and regulations
Should the FCC reward stations that do a good job? granting of licenses. M. Cohn. il Sat R 54:45-7 Ag 14 '71
Staying on the air; Pastore bill and license renewals. New Repub 164:9 Je 26 '71
Very cold turkey; banning of lyrics referring to illegal drugs. R. L. Shayon. Sat R 54:22 My 1 '71
See also
Radio frequency allocation

RADIO licenses. See Radio laws and regulations

RADIO operators. Amateur
Incentive licensing for hams: progress or discrimination? R. Humphrey. Pop Electr 1: 52-3 Ja '72
See also
React (organization)

RADIO plays
Huckleberry Finn; dramatization of a story by Mark Twain. G. DuBois. Plays 30:71-80 Ap '71
Juggler of Our Lady; dramatization of story by A. France. W. Hackett. Plays 31:89-94 D '71
Necklace; dramatization of story, by G. de Maupassant. L. Olfson. Plays 30:51-7 My '71

RADIO receivers
All about scanning monitor receivers. R. F. Scott. il Radio-Electr 42:58-9+ D '71
Cheerful earfuls. il Seventeen 29:136-9 S '70
Introduction to direct-conversion radio receivers; with glossary. R. F. Scott. bibliog il Radio-Electr 42:62-3+ N '71
Small radios for general purpose listening in the home. il Consumer Bul 54:27-30 D '71
Table-model radios. il Consumer Bul 54:7-12 Mr '71
Ten-Tec model RX-10 amateur radio receiver. il Pop Electr 34:78-82 My '71
See also
Clock radios

Design
Technical topics; relationship of receiver selectivity to the i.f. R. F. Scott. il Radio-Electr 42:51-3 Mr '71

Frequency modulation receivers
Unique stereo decoder. S. Reich. il Pop Electr 35:53-5+ O '71

Maintenance and repair
Sweep alignment speeds troubleshooting. J. Darr. il Radio-Electr 42:62-3+ S '71

Single sideband receivers
Single sideband for CB is now! H. Friedman. il Pop Electr 35:25-9 Ag '71

RADIO receivers, Portable
Lafayette Guardian-6000 portable 6-band receiver. il Pop Electr 35:81-2 O '71

RADIO receivers, Short wave
Worldwide adventures on the airwaves. L. Buckwalter. il Pop Sci 198:60+ Ap '71

RADIO receivers, Stereophonic
Hi-Fi product report:
Marantz model 19 stereo-FM receiver. il Electr World 86:11-12+ N '71
Sansui model 2000A AM/stereo-FM receiver. il Electr World 85:12+ Je '71
Scott 387 Am/stereo-FM receiver. il Electr World 86:7-8 Jl '71
Sony ST-5100 AM/stereo-FM tuner. il Electr World 86:7-8 Jl '71
Pioneer SX-2500 stereo receiver. il Pop Electr 35:83-5 D '71
R-E builds Heath AR-1500 stereo receiver. C. H. Lawrence. il Radio-Electr 42:36-8 D '71

RADIO relay systems
See also
Communications satellites

RADIO stars. See Radio astronomy

RADIO stations
Balancing act; WFLN WPEN and the T. Grant controversy. R. L. Shayon. Sat R 54:43 Je 5 '71; Reply with rejoinder. L. M. C. Smith. 54:19 Jl 10 '71
Black-oriented; study findings of Stanford university's Institute for communication research. R. L. Shayon. Sat R 54:18 S 25 '71
Bombs to the right of them; Houston Pacifica. N. C. Chriss. Nation 212:243-4 F 22 '71
Radio stunt man; D. Whittington on KGIL. il por Newsweek 77:64 My 17 '71
Riding shotgun on justice; question of funds for Pacifica foundation's station in Houston. R. L. Shayon. Sat R 54:50-1 Ja 23 '71
Should the FCC reward stations that do a good job? granting of licenses. M. Cohn. il Sat R 54:45-7 Ag 14 '71
Texaco-Metropolitan opera radio network (cont) Opera N 36:14-15 D 11 '71

History
How New York's pioneer classical station has fallen upon sorry Times: WQXR. C. Briefer. il pors Hi Fi 21:74-9 S '71

RADIO stations. Amateur
See also
Citizens radio service

Equipment
See also
Radio transmitters

RADIO stations, Illegal
Warring pirates; Radio Northsea and competing pirate radio ship, Veronica. il Time 97:39+ My 31 '71

RADIO telephone

Maintenance and repair
Troubleshooting CB transceivers. A. J. Mueller. il Radio-Electr 42:47-50 Je '71

RADIO telephone, Portable
Equipment report; Simpson model A 2-meter FM transceiver. il Radio-Electr 42:22+ N '71
SBE Catalina 23-channel CB transceiver. il Pop Electr 1:82-4 Ja '72

RADIO telephone on aircraft
Number pleeyuz... Flying 89:15-16+ S '71
Product news; Flite Fone. il Flying 90:102 Ja '72

RADIO telephone on ships, boats, etc.
They've changed the rules for marine radio; with tables. F. H. Belt. il Pop Sci 199:65-7+ D '71
What'll you do in seventy-two? C. Miller. il Motor B & S 128:73+ Jl '71
Why? When? What? about DSB, SSB and VHF radiotelephones? J. West. il Yachting 130:63+ Jl '71

RADIO telecopes
Arecibo resurfacing. Sci N 100:377 D 4 '71
Illinois 120-foot radio telescope. A. H. Schriefer. jr and others. il Sky & Tel 41:132-8 Mr '71
Improvements at Arecibo. Sky & Tel 41:352 Je '71
Indian radio telescope. Sky & Tel 41:339 Je '71
Mars tracking station. il Space World H-8-92:21-3 Ag '71
New ear to the heavens; West Germany's Effelsberg telescope. il Time 97:55 Je 7 '71
Stanford's high-resolution radio interferometer. R. N. Bracewell and others. il pors Sky & Tel 42:4-9 Jl '71

RADIO transmission
Moon as transmitter. Newsweek 78:83-4 N 22 '71

RADIO transmitters
Transmitter for the neglected band; 1750 meter band. J. White. il Pop Electr 1:58-61 Ja '72

Transistor transmitters
QRP thing; battery-operated 40-meter transmitter. H. Olson. il Pop Electr 34:39-44+ F '71

RADIO waves
Whistling in the culvert; exploring analogies between sound waves and electromagnetic waves traveling in a channel. Sci Am 225:84 S '71
See also
Microwaves
Pulse techniques (electronics)
Radio frequency

Physiological effects
See also
Plants, Effect of radio waves on

RADIOACTIVE dating
Acadian orogeny: an abrupt and brief event. R. S. Naylor. bibliog il Science 172:558-60 My 7 '71
Dating of moon samples: pitfalls and paradoxes. E. Driscoll. Sci N 101:12-14 Ja 1 '72
Resetting the carbon clock. il por Time 98:64 N 29 '71
Uranium distributions in archeologic ceramics; dating of radioactive inclusions; fission-track mapping. D. W. Zimmerman. bibliog il Science 174:818-19 N 19 '71
See also
Radiocarbon dating

RADIOACTIVE fallout
End to fallout? Newsweek 78:84 N 22 '71
See also
Radioactive pollution

Physiological effects
See Radioactivity—Physiological effects

RADIOACTIVE halos. See Halos (mineralogy)

RADIOACTIVE iodine. See Iodine—Isotopes

RADIOACTIVE pollution
Nuclear sword of Damocles. L. Marshall. Liv
  Wildn 35:17-19 Spr '71
Radiation pollution of the environment. P.
  J. Lindop and J. Rotblat. il por Bul Atom
  Sci 27:17-24 S '71
Seventeen million years; half-life of iodine-
  129. S. Novick. bibliog il Environ 13:42-7
  N '71
  See also
Atomic power plants—Pollution
RADIOACTIVE substances
  See also
Promethium
Thorium

Transportation
Radioactive cargoes: record good but the
  problems will multiply. D. Shapley. bib-
  liog f il Science 172:1318-22 Je 25 '71
RADIOACTIVE waste disposal
AEC has something for Kansas. R. Brown.
  Nation 212:712-16 Je 7 '71
AEC has trouble salting away waste. Bsns
  W p30 O 16 '71
Dear Sir: your house is built on radioactive
  uranium waste; Grand Junction, Colo. H.
  P. Metzger. il N Y Times Mag p 14-15+
  O 31 '71
EPA and AEC. Sci N 99:416 Je 19 '71
Hanford revisited. S. Novick. il Environ 13:
  48-9 My '71
Hot sands; Grand Junction, Colo. Newsweek
  78:46 O 18 '71
Hot town; Grand Junction, Colo. Time 98:56
  D 20 '71
Kansas geologists and the AEC; plan to bury
  cannisters of nuclear wastes. il Sci N 99:161
  Mr 6 '71
Nuclear graveyard. il Newsweek 77:60 Mr 29
  '71
Nuclear sword of Damocles. L. Marshall. Liv
  Wildn 35:17-19 Spr '71
Nuclear waste: Kansans riled by AEC plans
  for atom dump. C. Holden. il Science 172:
  249-50 Ap 16 '71
Radioactive salt mine; with comments and
  summary. R. S. Lewis. il Bul Atom Sci
  27:27-31+ Je '71
Radioactive tailings; Colorado uranium pollu-
  tion. Nation 213:389 O 25 '71
Residential radioactivity; sharing of respon-
  sibility; houses in western Colorado. Sci
  N 100:390 D 11 '71
RADIOACTIVITY
  See also
Plutonium

Accidents and injuries
Radioactive cargoes: record good but the
  problems will multiply. D. Shapley. bibliog f il Science 172:1318-22 Je 25 '71

Physiological effects
Great nuclear debate: are our newborn babies'
  lives in danger? M. Hope and J. Young.
  Redbook 138:16+ Ja '72
Health effects from radiation; address. July
  14, 1971. E. J. Sternglass. bibliog Vital
  Speeches 37:699-703 S 1 '71
Hiroshima time bomb; research by the
  Atomic bomb casualty commission. il Time
  97:73 Je 14 '71
Nuclear plant controversy. R. E. Lapp. New
  Repub 164:17-21 F 27 '71
Radiation and leukemia rates; letter. E. L.
  Saenger and others. bibliog Science 171:
  1096+ Mr 19 '71; Reply. E. B. Lewis. 174:454
  O 29 '71
Radiation controversy; a challenge to health
  physicists; address. July 15, 1971. P. Turner.
  Vital Speeches 37:696-9 S 1 '71
Radiation pollution of the environment. P.
  J. Lindop and J. Rotblat. il por Bul Atom
  Sci 27:17-24 S '71
  See also
Atomic bomb casualty commission
Radiobiology

Safety devices and measures
  See also
Nuclear reactors—Safety devices and mea-
  sures
RADIOBIOLOGY
Squaring an infinite circle: radio-biology and
  the value of life. J. Lederberg. Bul Atom
  Sci 27:43-5 S '71
RADIOCARBON dating
Carbon 14 and the prehistory of Europe. C.
  Renfrew. il Sci Am 225:63-70+ bibliog (p
  120) O '71
Land clearance in the Irish neolithic: new
  evidence and interpretation. J. R. Pilcher
  and others. bibliog il Science 172:560-2 My
  7 '71

RADIOCHEMISTRY

Conferences
Radiation chemistry; report of meeting of
  the Hungarian chemical society. J. G. Burr.
  Science 174:616 N 5 '71
RADIOGRAPHY
Early warning system; using xeroradio-
  graphy in breast cancer detection. il Time
  98:41 D 27 '71
Neutron radiography for nondestructive
  testing. H. Berger. il Electr World 86:40-1+
  Ag '71
Now N rays show what X rays can't. H.
  Berger. il por Pop Sci 198:57-9+ Je '71
Xerox machine that prints X-rays. il Bsns
  W p60 My 29 '71
RADIOHALOS. See Halos (mineralogy)
RADIOIMMUNOASSAY. See Biological assay
RADIOISOTOPES
  See also subhead Isotopes under names
  of chemical elements, e.g. Lead—Isotopes

Decay
  See also
Isotopic power generators
RADIOLOGICAL physics. See Radiology
RADIOLOGY
Radiological physics characteristics of the
  extracted heavy ion beams of the beva-
  tron. C. A. Tobias and others. bibliog il
  Science 174:1131-4 D 10 '71
RADIOLOGY, Medical
Never do harm. K. Z. Morgan. bibliog il En-
  viron 13:28-38 Ja '71
Signal detectability and medical decision-
  making. L. B. Lusted. bibliog il Science
  171:1217-19 Mr 26 '71
  See also
Diagnosis, Radioscopic
RADIOMETERS
Radiometer ILS monitor studied; airbone
  microwave radiometer. il Aviation W 94:42-
  3+ My 17 '71
RADIOTHERAPY
  See also
Cancer—Therapy
RADISHES
  See also
Cookery—Vegetables
RADMER, Richard, and Kok, Bessel
Unified procedure for the detection of life
  on Mars. bibliog il Science 174:233-9 O 15
  '71
RADVÁNYI, Netty (Reiling) See Seghers, A.
  pseud.
RADZIWILL, Lee (Bouvier) princess
Country house in flower; Radziwill's Tur-
  ville Grange. P. Devlin. il pors Vogue 158:
  100-7+ Jl '71 •
RAFAELA 300 Indy. See Automobile racing—
  Argentina
RAFFERTY, Max
Education in depth. Ed Digest 36:9-11 Mr
  '71
RAFFETTO, Francis
Dining in big D. il por Library J 96:1923-6 Je
  1 '71
RAFTING of boats. See Anchorage
RAGWEED
Romance of roadside ragweed. F. E. Egler.
  Cons 26:27 Ag '71
RAHE, Jurgen, and Donn, Bertram
Visual observation of comets. il Sky & Tel
  41:214-16 Ap '71
RAHM, Neal M.
Regional forester bites the bullet. il por Am
  For 77:38-9+ F '71
RAHMAN, Mujibur. See Mujibur Rahman
RAHMEIER, Paul W.
Abortion and the reverence for life. Chr Cent
  88:556-60 My 5 '71
RAHNER, Karl
Follow-up on the Küng-Rahner feud. Chr
  Cent 88:997-1000 Ag 26 '71 •
Infallibility fight. pors Newsweek 77:57 Ja 25
  '71 •
Küng and Rahner: dueling over infallibility.
  B. Van Voorst. por Chr Cent 88:617-22
  My 19 '71 •
Küng-Rahner debate. G. C. Berkouwer. Chr
  Today 15:45-6 My 7 '71 •
RAHWAY prison, N.J. See Prisons—New Jer-
  sey
RAI, Raghu
Bold eye from India; photographs. Mod Phot
  34:84-7 N '70
RAILINGS. See Hand railings
RAILPAX. See National railroad passenger
  corporation
RAILROAD accidents. See Railroads—Accidents
RAILROAD cars. See Railroads—Cars

RAILROAD crossings. See Railroads—Crossings
RAILROAD excursions. See Excursions
RAILROAD law
Fight shaping up on rail labor law. il Bsns W p45 Ja 23 '71
New plea to curb transport strikes. U S News 70:79-80 F 15 '71
Rail peace may stymie legislation. il Bsns W p21 My 22 '71
RAILROAD management. See Railroads—Management
RAILROAD passengers. See Railroad travel
RAILROAD rates. See Railroads—Rates
RAILROAD signal men's strike. See Strikes—United States—Railroads
RAILROAD stations. See Railroads—Stations
RAILROAD stations, Remodeled. See Buildings, Remodeled
RAILROAD strikes. See Strikes—United States—Railroads
RAILROAD supplies industry
    See also
Pullman. inc
RAILROAD trains. See Railroads—Trains
RAILROAD travel
Do yuh hear that whistle down the line? ballplayers leisurely train travel. M. Kram. il Sports Illus 35:106-10+ N 29 '71
Give the trains a chance Life 71:42 D 3 '71
Is 1971 your year to discover or rediscover the railroad adventure? il Sunset 146:100-5 My '71
    See also
National railroad passenger corporation
RAILROAD whistles. See Locomotives—Whistles
RAILROAD work rules. See Railroads—Work rules
RAILROADS
    See also
Train ferries

Accidents

Nightmare in Laurel. J. H. Winchester. il Read Digest 99:82-6 Jl '71

Automobile parking lots

See Automobile parking

Cars

Automatic railroad-car identification; optical-electronic scanning system for freight cars. D. L. Heiserman. il Electr World 86:46-7 S '71
Miracle of rare device; Santa Fe's Super chief. K. R. Zimmermann. Nat R 23:655+ Je 15 '71
Tough route from jets to rail cars; new designs for rapid transit cars. il Bsns W p96-7+ My 1 '71
Vegas on end; Vert-a-pac railroad car. il Mech Illus 67:46 Je '71
    See also
Pullman. inc.

Commuter service

Little railroad that could; Lindenwold line. C. G. Burck. il Fortune 84:74-7 Jl '71

Crossings

Rubber RR crossing an unqualified success; Charleroi, Pa. D. S. Bosson. il Am City 86:20 Jl '71

Employees

No-day week; Burlington northern railroad. il Newsweek 77:85 My 10 '71
    See also
Strikes—United States—Railroads
United transportation union

Finance

Fight to save the railroads. il U S News 70:10-12 My 31 '71
Numbers game. Newsweek 77:77-8 Ap 26 '71
Rich get richer. il Forbes 108:24 S 1 '71

Freight cars

See Railroads—Cars

Freight rates

See Railroads—Rates

Freight service

Portland freight run. E. Hoagland. Atlan 227:26+ F '71

Freight trains

Fast freight: across the U.S. on Super C. K. Johnson. il Time 98:14 Jl 19 '71

Government ownership

See Railroads and state

History

    See also
Railroads—United States—History

Law

See Railroad law

Management

We're broke, he told the workers. We need your help; B. Moore of Penn Central. M. Smith. il pors Life 71:69-70+ S 24 '71

Operation

See Railroads—Management

Parlor cars

See Railroads—Cars

Passenger service

Fight over cuts in rail service. il U S News 70:47 F 1 '71
On the track: the trains in Spain, etc (cont) D. Butwin. il Sat R 54:36-9 Ja 16; 80-1 Ja 23 '71
    See also
Auto-train corporation
National railroad passenger corporation
Railroad travel
Railroads—Commuter service

Passenger traffic

    See also
Commuters

Photographs

On the right track. J. de Elorza. Pop Phot 69:66-9 Jl '71

Rates

Freight rate hikes hit a roadblock. Bsns W p22 Ja 1 '72
Modules look for a cheaper ride. il Bsns W p22-3 My 22 '71

Real estate operations

Penn Central: now the family jewels; forthcoming sale. il Newsweek 77:79 Je 14 '71
Penn Central sells off. Time 97:82 Je 14 '71

Safety devices and measures

See also
Locomotives—Whistles

Stations

How do railroad stations retire? V. A. Schlich. il Har Yrs 11:14-16 D '71
Railroad stations: an endangered species. il Arch Rec 150:120-3 D '71
    See also
New York (city)—Stations
Subway stations

Strikes

See Strikes—United States—Railroads

Trains

Amtrak's one-way ticket to the dole. il Newsweek 78:69 D 20 '71
Auto-train miracle. il Newsweek 79:38 Ja 3 '72
Miracle of rare device; Santa Fe's Super chief. K. R. Zimmermann. Nat R 23:655+ Je 15 '71
Overland cruise to Florida; auto-bearing passenger train from Alexandria, Va, to Sanford, Fla. il Time 98:91 N 8 '71
This is a railroad? Amtrak. il Time 98:75 D 20 '71
Train that takes your auto along; combination passenger and auto-ferry service to Florida. il Bsns W p26-7 O 30 '71
    See also
Railroads—Freight trains

Wages and hours

    See also
Collective bargaining—Railroads

Work rules

New drive to cut railroad featherbedding. il U S News 71:49-50 Jl 19 '71
Railroads break a union's work rules. il Bsns W p 14 Jl 24 '71

Africa, East

Tortoise and the hare; Chinese-built Tanzania-Zambia project. il Newsweek 78:56 O 25 '71

Canada

How Canada's railroads handle freedom. il Bsns W p54+ Jl 10 '71
National dream, by P. Berton. Review Nation 212:696-7 My 31 '71. R. Ginger
    See also
Canadian national railways

RAILROADS—*Continued*

Europe, Western
Sea going trains. il Travel 135:53-5 Ap '71

Germany (Federal Republic)
Debt rides a German state-run railroad; Deutsche Bundesbahn. il Bsns W p34-5 Ja 23 '71

Great Britain
See also
Railroads and state—Great Britain

Iran
New rail link completed between Iran and Turkey. Dept State Bul 65:418 O 18 '71

Japan
Japan's troubled railroads. il Bsns W p38+ Ap 24 '71

Russia
See also
Trans-Siberian railway

Turkey
New rail link completed between Iran and Turkey. Dept State Bul 65:418 O 18 '71

United States
Five keys to railroad productivity and service; address, November 8, 1971. B. F. Biaggini. Vital Speeches 38:130-4 D 15 '71
Future of passenger trains; interview. B. F. Biaggini. il por U S News 72:44-8 Ja 3 '72
I got those disappearing railroad blues. K. R. Zimmermann. il Sr Schol 99:30-1 D 13 '71
Numbers game. Newsweek 77:77-8 Ap 26 '71
On the track; faded velvet, tinny tunes. D. Butwin. il Sat R 54:36-9 Ja 16 '71
See also
Collective bargaining—Railroads
Railroads—Management
Railroads, Short line
Railroads and state—United States
also names of railroads, e.g. Burlington Northern, inc.

History
Lincoln's other dream. T. Fleming. il Read Digest 98:134-9 Je '71
Man who met the longhorns with a railroad. J. S. Reed. il por Nations Bsns 59:50-1 Ja '71

Zambia
How the railroads export knowhow. il Bsns W p35 F 6 '71

RAILROADS, Air cushion. See Air cushion vehicles

RAILROADS, Logging
Don't run over the train; Michigan's Pinconning & Blind River railroad. F. Nofziger. il Travel 135:70-3 Je '71

RAILROADS, Magnetic. See Air cushion vehicles

RAILROADS, Narrow gage
See also
Railroads, Logging

RAILROADS, Short line
Letter from the editor; Valley railroad ride from Essex to Deep River, Conn. O. Jensen. il Am Heritage 23:2 D '71
Scenic railway; Cass scenic railroad, Cass, W.Va. B. Thomas. il Travel 136:35-7 Jl '71
Wonderful day; reopening of the Valley railroad company run from Essex to Deep River, Conn. New Yorker 47:24-5 S 4 '71

RAILROADS, Single rail
New rapid transit system tested; prototype computer-controlled system. M. L. Yaffee. il Aviation W 95:44-6+ N 8 '71
300 MPH monorail started with a broomstick; tri-mono-trans system. M. Lamm. il Pop Mech 136:81-3+ N '71

RAILROADS, Small size
See also
Railroads, Logging

RAILROADS and state

Germany (Federal Republic)
Debt rides a German state-run railroad. il Bsns W p34-5 Ja 23 '71

Great Britain
British railways: or, How to lose money at a profit. Forbes 107:23 Ap 1 '71

United States
Fight to save the railroads. il U S News 70:10-12 My 31 '71
Has Penn Central been nationalized? il Bsns W p 19 Ja 23 '71

Hunting a rail-strike cure; growing pressures for action. U S News 70:45-6 My 31 '71
Is anyone listening? address, May 20, 1971. J. S. Reed. Vital Speeches 37:569-72 Jl 1 '71
Last chance for Railpax. America 124:63 Ja 23 '71
Meany for nationalization. il Time 97:73 F 1 '71
Railroad industry: is nationalization the answer? address, December 14, 1970. B. F. Biaggini. Vital Speeches 37:212-16 Ja 15 '71
Will big brother ride the rails? il Forbes 107:22-3 Ap 1 '71
See also
National railroad passenger corporation

RAILSBACKS, Thomas F.
Excerpt from debate, September 15, 1971. Cong Digest 50:276+ N '71

RAILWAY accidents. See Railroads—Accidents

RAILWAY labor acts. See Railroad law

RAIN and rainfall
Carbon monoxide in rainwater. J. W. Swinnerton and others. bibliog il Science 172:943-5 My 28 '71
La Porte precipitation fallacy; letter. B. G. Holzman. Science 171:847 Mr 5 '71; Discussion. bibliog 172:987 Je 4 '71
Some precipitation aspects of Florida showers and thunderstorms. W. L. Woodley and others. bibliog il Weatherwise 24:106-13+ Je '71
See also
Droughts
Floods
Storms

RAIN making
As rainmakers try to end drought. il U S News 70:63-4 My 31 '71
Cloud seeding experiments; possible bias. S. M. Stigler. bibliog Science 173:850 Ag 27 '71
Doubling rainfall during Florida's drought. Sci N 100:389 D 11 '71
NOAA to try rescue rainmaking. A. L. Hammond. Science 172:40 Ap 2 '71
Rain made to order. R. Gannon. il Pop Sci 199:49-51+ S '71
Rainmaker cometh; cloud-seeding experiment in Florida. il Sat R 54:44 Jl 3 '71
Rainmaking comes of age. B. Funk. il Read Digest 98:145-9 Je '71
Rainmaking in Florida. il Sci N 99:246 Ap 10 '71
Seeding cumulus in Florida; new 1970 results. J. Simpson and W. L. Woodley. bibliog il Science 172:117-26 Ag 9 '71
Weather modification; a technology coming of age. A. L. Hammond. Science 172:548-9 My 7 '71

RAIN of fishes, insects, etc. See Fishes, insects, etc, Rain of

RAINBOW
Infrared rainbow. R. G. Greenler. bibliog il Science 173:1231 S 24 '71

RAINBOW trout. See Trout

RAINBOW trout fishing. See Trout fishing

RAINEY Glenn W.
Where they live; address, November 1970. Engl J 60:787-91 S '71

RAINEY, Sarita R.
Expressions in three-dimensional design. il Sch Arts 71:6-7 Ja '72

RAINIER III, prince of Monaco
Prince as MBA; an interview with Rainier of Monaco; ed. by A. Jones. il por Forbes 108:64+ S 15 '71

RAINIER, MOUNT
Mt Rainier: now you see it, now you don't. G. S. Zeigler and others. bibliog il Weatherwise 24:114-19 Je '71
Summit firn caves, Mount Rainier, Washington. E. P. Kiver and M. D. Mumma. bibliog il Science 173:320-2 Jl 23 '71
See also
Mount Rainier National Park

RAINMAN, Eva Schindler-. See Schindler-Rainman, E.

RAINSTORMS. See Storms

RAINWATER, Dorothy T. and Hackler, R. E. A.
Silver from Iolani palace, Honolulu. il Antiques 99:272-7 F '71

RAINWATER. See Rain and rainfall

RAISES, Pay. See Wages

RAISINS
See also
Cookery—Fruit

RAISMAN, Geoffrey, and Field, P. M.
Sexual dimorphism in the preoptic area of the rat. bibliog il Science 173:731-3 Ag 20 '71

RAJARATNAM, J. A. and others
Boron: possible role in plant metabolism.
bibliog il Science 172:1142 Je 11 '71
RAJWAR, L. M. S.
Trade and shipping needs of developing
countries. bibliog f il Int Concil 582:7-26
Mr '71
RAKSTIS, Ted J.
New help for nonsleepers. il Todays Health
49:16-19+ S '71
Secret of full-time freelancing: get a re-
tainer. il Writers Digest 51:28-30 D '71
Which summer camp is right for your child.
il Todays Health 49:35-7+ My '71
RAKU beads. See Beads
RAKU ware. See Pottery, Japanese
RALLIES, Automobile. See Automobile driv-
ing—Competitions
RALLS, Katherine
Mammalian scent marking. bibliog il Science
171:443-9 F 5 '71
RALLYE des champions, France. See Competi-
tions
RAMADAN
Ramadan: month of fast in Tangier. A.
Waugh. Nat R 23:87 Ja 26 '71
RAMAN, Sir Chandrasekhara Venkata
Obituary
Phys Today por 24:79 Mr '71. S. Chand-
rasekhar
RAMAN effect
Raman spectrum of a transfer RNA. M.
Tsuboi and others. bibliog il Science 174:
1142-4 D 10 '71
RAMAPO-Catskill library system
Divorce: N.Y. style. K. Nyren. il Library J
96:2257-62 Jl '71
Spring Valley, N.Y. library secedes from
system. Library J 96:909-10 Mr 15 '71
What price cooperation? W. R. Eshelman.
Wilson Lib Bul 45:733 Ap '71
RAMER, Earl M. See Cox, R. L. jt. auth.
RAMEY, Estelle
Why women are tougher. Read Digest 98:73-5
Ap '71
RAMM, Bernard
Double and Romans 7. Chr Today 15:14+ Ap
9 '71
RAMO, Simon
Coming social-industrial complex; address,
October 21, 1971. Vital Speeches 38:80-6 N
15 '71
RAMOS, Suzanne
Parent and child. N Y Times Mag p67-8+ Ap
25; 43 Jl 18; 83-4+ N 14 '71
RAMPS
Down goes tonnage, easily, safely. il Sun-
set 147:128-9 Ag '71
Safe ramps for car work. R. K. McLemore. il
Pop Sci 199:133 O '71
RAMS (football club) See Football clubs
RAMSAY, John M.
Appalachian folk school. il Nat Parks & Con
Mag 45:22-4 Jl '71
RAMSEY, Arthur Michael, abp
Rebutting Dr Ramsey. T. Beeson. Chr Cent
88:364-5 Mr 24 '71 *
Showing who's boss. J. D. Douglas. Chr To-
day 15:40-1 Mr 26 '71 *
RANA clamitans. See Frogs
RANCH life
Vacation getaways; dude or working ranches
in Wyoming. F. Shemanski. il Schol Teach
Jr/Sr High p21 My 3 '71
RANCHES
Back at the ranch: profits, pride, and a
tax shelter. Bsns W p77 Ag 21 '71
Lasater ranch: applied range ecology. F. T.
Colbert. il Nat Parks & Con Mag 45:18-20
Mr '71
Range war in Florida. il Time 97:71 F 15 '71
See also
Ranch life
RAND, Abby
10 rugged western slopes for the skier in
quest of the ultimate run. il Holiday 48:30-
1 N '70
10 swinging alpine resorts for the very best
in European skiing. il Holiday 48:34-5 N
'70
RAND corporation
Anguish at Rand. il Bsns W p70-2+ Jl 17 '71
Guard you hire may be dangerous; Rand
study. Bsns W p25-6 D 4 '71
New security rules for Rand. J. Walsh.
Science 173:411 Jl 30 '71
Pentagon papers: repercussions for Rand
and other think tanks? J. Walsh. Science
173:311+ Jl 23 '71
Plugging leaks in a think tank. il Newsweek
78:28-9 Jl 12 '71
RANDALL, Belle
Attention please; Afterward; poems. Poetry
119:67-8 N '71

RANDALL, Charles Edgar
Big Scrub makes the grade. il Am For 77:28-
31+ N '71
Hiawatha national forest by the big-sea-
water. il Am For 77:32-5+ Mr '71
Superior forest. il Am For 77:26-9+ S '71
RANDALL, Dudley
Why minority publishing? ed. by B. Cham-
bers. il pors Pub W 199:44-5 Mr 15 '71; Re-
ply. C. D. Kinsman and M. A. Tennenhouse.
199:19-20 Je 21 '71 *
RANDALL, Florence Engel
How a book grows. Writer 85:11-13+ Ja '72
RANDALL, George
Safe on the streets. il PTA Mag 65:5-7 bib-
liog(p35) Ap '71
RANDALL, John E.
Progress in marine parks; with biographical
sketch. il Sea Front 17:2-16, 63 Ja '71
RANDALL, Julia
Comment. D. Aldan. Poetry 118:35-7 Ap '71 *
RANDEL, Don M.
Emerging triadic tonality in the fifteenth
century. bibliog f il Mus Q 57:73-86 Ja '71
RANDER, Andrea
POW wife. il pors Ebony 26:110-11+ Je '71 *
RANDER, Donald
POW wife. il pors Ebony 26:110-11+ Je '71 *
RANDOLPH, A. Philip, Institute. See A. Philip
Randolph institute
RANDOLPH, Asa Philip
Vote mobilization for the 1970s. il por Ebony
26:84-6 Jl '71 *
RANDOLPH, Benjamin
Benjamin Randolph, cabinetmaker. M. K. Al-
bers. il Design 72:8-9 Spr '71 *
Finial busts on eighteenth-century Philadel-
phia furniture. R. C. Smith. il Antiques
100:900-5 D '71 *
RANDOLPH, Jennings
Senator looks at forestry. il por Am For 77:
12-15+ Ja '71
RANDOLPH, Michael M.
They didn't believe it would work. il Am
City 86:91 Ag '71
RANDOM processes. See Stochastic processes
RANDORF, Gary A.
Haiku: ancient poetry for today's ecology;
with biographical sketch. il Cons 26:8-13,
40 D '71
Kauai, nature's paradise. il Liv Wildn 35:20-3
Spr '71
Walk, look and learn. il Cons 26:6-8 Ap '71
RANDSIGHT. See Blind. Apparatus for the
RANDT, Clark T. and others
Norepinephrine biosynthesis inhibition: ef-
fects on memory in mice. bibliog il Science
172:498-9 Ap 30 '71
RANEY, Ona
We grow the biggest mustard. Org Gard &
Farm 18:74 S '71
RANGEFINDER cameras. See Cameras
RANGERS, Rogers'. See United States—His-
tory—French and Indian war, 1755-1763
RANGERS, Park. See Forest rangers
RANGES. See Stock ranges
RANGES, Kitchen. See Electric stoves; Stoves
RANGO, Albert
Waterwise. il Weatherwise 24:68-73 Ap '71
RANGOON
Reports & comment. P. Theroux. Atlan 228:
37+ N '71
RANK, D. M. and others
Interstellar molecules and dense clouds. bib-
liog il Science 174:1083-101 D 10 '71
RANK-Xerox, ltd.
Xerox: shortcut. il Forbes 109:26-7 Ja 1 '72
RANKIN, Allen
Gorilla is a paper tiger. il Read Digest 98:
210-14+ Ap '71
RANLY, Ernest W.
What are people for? il por Commonweal
94:207-11 My 7 '71
RANSOM, Jay Ellis
Big Horn medicine wheel, an American Stone-
henge? il Am West 8:16-17+ Mr; 64 S 71
RANSOM, John Crowe
Ransom's new selected poems. J. Mazzaro.
Poetry 117:275-6 Ja '71 *
RANSOM
Price goes up; exchange rate on kidnapped
ambassadors in Brazil. Newsweek 77:44 Ja
25 '71
Ransoms for revolution; plots in Turkey, in
Venezuela, in Uruguay. Time 97:39 Mr 15
'71
RANSTEAD, Donald D.
Chile con Allende. Commonweal 95:253-6 D
10 '71
RANUNCULUS. See Anemones

RAO, P. K. and others
Gulf Stream and middle Atlantic bight: complex thermal structure as seen from an environmental satellite. il Science 173:529-30 Ag 6 '71

RAO, Y. V. Lakshmana
Propaganda through the printed media in the developing countries. bibliog f Ann Am Acad 398:93-103 N '71

RAPE
Couple-speak: rape, true and false. S. de Gramont; N. R. de Gramont. pors Vogue 157:108-9+ Je '71
Rape: the all-American crime. S. Griffin. il Ramp Mag 10:26-35 S '71
Rape: the unmentionable crime. A. Lake. Good H 173:104-5+ N '71
Violence is a part of the times; interview. M. A. Lipton. por U S News 70:73-4 Ja 25 '71

RAPE trials, Military. See Courts martial and courts of inquiry

RAPER, John R. See Hoffman, R. M. jt. auth.

RAPHAEL Minichiello airplane hijacking trial. See Trials—Italy

RAPID-American corporation
Meshulam Riklis: the power, the profit and the glory. il Forbes 107:24-6+ Mr '71

RAPID transit. See Local transit

RAPID transit cars. See Railroads—Cars

RAPOPORT, Debra
Tapisserie vivant. il Craft Horiz 31:24-5+ O '71

RAPOPORT, Roger
Conservation. Sports Illus 35:68-9 N 1 '71
Disney's war against the wilderness. il Ramp Mag 10:27-33 N '71
Skiing. il Sports Illus 34:60-1 F 15; 72+ My 3 '71

RAPOPORT, Sheva
Toothpaste. il Consumer Bul 54:7-9 Ag '71

RAPOPORT, Stanley I. and others
Reversible osmotic opening of the blood-brain barrier. bibliog il Science 173:1026-8 S 10 '71

RAPPAPORT, M. and others
Phenothiazine effects on auditory signal detection in paranoid and nonparanoid schizophrenics. bibliog il Science 174:723-5 N 12 '71

RAPPAPORT, Roy A.
Flow of energy in an agricultural society; with biographical sketch. il Sci Am 225:25+, 116-22+ bibliog(p244) S '71

RAPTORIAL birds. See Birds of prey

RARDIN, Max. See Pasewark, R. A. jt. auth.

RARE animals
All animals are happy. il Esquire 76:128-9 O '71
Does the whale's magnitude diminish?—Will he perish? growing list of endangered species. S. McVay. il Bul Atom Sci 27:38-41 F '71
Easy chair; species being saved by transplantation to the American Southwest. J. Fischer. Harper 243:16+ O '71
Endangered species. il Nat Parks & Con Mag 45:32-3+ Ap; 9-13 My; 18-21 Ag '71
See also
Ferrets
Pandas
Sea otters

RARE book dealers. See Booksellers and bookselling—Book rarities

RARE books. See Book rarities

RARICK, John R.
Excerpt from debate, November 17, 1970. Cong Digest 50:89+ Mr '71
Excerpt from report, March 3, 1971. Cong Digest 50:121+ Ap '71

RASCOE, Judith
Small sounds and tilting shadows; story. Atlan 228:53-5 Jl '71

RASH, Charles D.
Room design and curriculum planning. il Ceram Mo 19:30-1 S '71

RASKIN, A. H.
What the 'Little Fellow' says to the teamsters is what counts. il pors N Y Times Mag p 12-13+ My 30 '71; Correction. p20 Je 13 '71

RASKIN, Eugene
Are our cities dying? Read Digest 99:167-8+ Ag '71

RASKIN, J. B.
Philately for fun, only! il Mech Illus 67:64+ O '71

RASKOWITZ, Robert P.
Standardization. Electr World 86:66-7 S '71

RASKY, Harry
Television. Nation 212:218-19+ F 15 '71

RASMUSSEN, Boyd
Editorial. C. Conley. Field & S 76:8 Ag '71 •

RASMUSSEN, Frederick A. and Holobinko, Paul
New idea for merit pay, teachers rate themselves. bibliog Clear House 46:207-11 D '71

RASMUSSEN, Howard. See Allen, J. E. jt. auth.

RASMUSSEN, Victor
Towards a freer school. Ed Digest 36:22-5 My '71

RASOF, Elvin
Detroit combines students' worlds. Am Ed 7:25-7 Je '71

RASOOL, S. I. and Schneider, S. H.
Atmospheric carbon dioxide and aerosols: effects of large increases on global climate. bibliog il Science 173:138-41 Jl 9 '71

RASPBERRIES
Reddest of the red. H. O. O'Neil. il por Org Gard & Farm 18:46-7 Ap '71
See also
Cookery—Fruit

RASPS. See Files and rasps

RAT control
Control of rats. A. Squire. il Cons 26:26 O '71
Rats and how your students can fight them R. E. Novick. il Todays Ed 60:26-8 O '71
Super-rats are coming. il Time 98:49 N 29 '71

RAT liver. See Liver

RATCLIFF, Carter
Anne Arnold. il por Craft Horiz 31:18-21+ Je '71
Robert Ryman's double positive. il Art N 70:54-6+ Mr '71

RATCLIFF, John Drury
How to handle the summer sun. Read Digest 99:106-8 Jl '71
I am Joe's adrenal gland. il Read Digest 98:127-30 My '71
I am Joe's ear. il Read Digest 99:131-4 O '71
I am Joe's intestine. il Read Digest 99:75-8 Ag '71
I am Joe's prostate. il Read Digest 99:99-102 D '71
I am Joe's spine. il Read Digest 98:87-90 Mr '71
Versailles reborn. il Read Digest 99:166-71 O '71
(ed) See Whipple, G. H. Disease that always killed

RATCLIFFE, Bill
Canyonlands; photographs. Audubon 73:33-48 Jl '71
Record in the rocks; photographs. Audubon 73:17-28 Ja '71

RATE, Hank
Are you tough enough to hunt big game? il Field & S 76:50-3+ Ag '71
Guide was a dude. il Field & S 76:32-3+ S '71

RATES. See Telephone—Rates; Water rates

RATES, Money. See Interest

RATHBONE, Richard
Politics and factionalism in Ghana. bibliog f Cur Hist 60:164-7+ Mr '71

RATHJENS, George W.
ABCs of ABMs. Bul Atom Sci 30:14-16 Mr '71
Breakthrough in arms control? il Bul Atom Sci 27:4-5 Je '71

RATHS, James D.
Teaching without specific objectives. Ed Digest 37:9-12 O '71

RATING of baseball players. See Baseball players—Rating

RATING of employees. See Employees—Rating

RATING of executives. See Executives—Rating

RATING of station wagons. See Station wagons—Rating

RATING of teachers. See College professors and instructors—Rating; Teachers—Rating

RATING services. See Credit—Rating

RATIONALISM
On the ethics of principle. D. Little. por Chr Cent 88:1441-4 D 8 '71
See also
Enlightenment

RATIOS, Financial. See Financial ratios

RATLIFF, Frank E.
Accountability: at what cost? address, November 1970. Engl J 60:485-90 Ap '71

RATLIFF, Mike
Big name for the small colleges. W. F. Reed. il por Sports Illus 35:77-9 N 29 '71 •

RATNER, Albert. See Adamo, N. J. jt. auth.

RATNER, Rochelle
Hands; poem. Nation 212:502 Ap 19 '71

RATNER, Victor M. See Mandelbaum, B. jt. auth.

RATS
Acetoacetyl-coenzyme A thiolase in brain, liver, and kidney during maturation of the rat. C. Dierks-Ventling and A. L. Cone. bibliog il Science 172:380-2 Ap 23 '71
Amnesia produced by spreading depression and ECS: evidence for time-dependent memory trace localization. R. M. Paolino and H. M. Levy. bibliog il Science 172:746-9 My 14 '71
Cardiac rate regulated by nutritional factor in young rats. M. A. Hofer. bibliog il Science 172:1039-41 Je 4 '71
Cerebellar hypoplasia in neonatal rats caused by lymphocytic choriomeningitis virus. A. A. Monjan and others. bibliog il Science 171:194-6 Ja 15 '71
Ceroid pigment formation and irreversible sterility in vitamin E deficiency. C. Raychaudhuri and I. D. Desai. bibliog il Science 173:1028-9 S 10 '71
Copulatory behavior can inhibit pregnancy in female rats. N. T. Adler and S. R. Zoloth; reply with rejoinder. P. Dziuk. bibliog Science 171:311-12 Ja 22 '71
DDT administered to neonatal rats induces persistent estrus syndrome. W. L. Heinrichs and others. bibliog il Science 173: 642-3 Ag 13 '71
DNA synthesis and interaction between controlled feeding schedules and partial hepatectomy in rats. B. Barbiroli and V. R. Potter. bibliog il Science 172:738-41 My 14 '71
Ethanol preference in the rat as a function of photoperiod. I. Geller. bibliog il Science 173:456-9 Jl 30 '71
Monosodium glutamate: lack of effects on brain and reproductive function in rats. N. J. Adamo and A. Ratner; reply with rejoinder. J. W. Olney. bibliog Science 172: 294 Ap 16 '71
Nuclear localization of histamine in neonatal rat brain. A. B. Young and others. bibliog il Science 173:247-9 Jl 16 '71
Of pot and rats. Time 98:71 S 27 '71
Rat! Friend, foe and unwanted companion. E. M. Reilly, jr. il Cons 26:22-5 O '71
Recuperation from illness: flavor enhancement for rats. K. F. Green and J. Garcia. bibliog il Science 173:749-51 Ag 20 '71
Suppression of food intake with intragastric loading: relation to natural feeding cycle. D. Quartermain and others. bibliog il Science 173:941-3 S 3 '71
Taste stimuli: quality coding time. B. P. Halpern and D. N. Tapper. bibliog il Science 171:1256-8 Mr 26 '71
Transplanted precursors of nerve cells: their fate in the cerebellums of young rats. G. D. Das and J. Altman. bibliog il Science 173:637-8 Ag 13 '71
RATTAZZI, Susanna (Agnelli) contessa. See Agnelli, S.
RATTI, John
Comment. H. Witt. Poetry 118:41-2 Ap '71 *
RATTIGAN, Terence
Bequest to the nation. Criticism
Cath World 212:313 Mr '71 *
RATZ, Margaret
Keys to success in learning. il Parents Mag 46:56-7+ O '71
RAUBINGER, Fred M.
Long-term contracts for superintendents? Ed Digest 37:12-13 S '71
RAUCH, Jerome S.
Medical library association, the movement, and the world outside. Wilson Lib Bul 46:38-9 S '71
RAUCH, John
Shuffle off in Buffalo. por Newsweek 78:83 Ag 2 '71 *
RAUCH, Rudolph S. 3d
Ounce of prevention for the banks and the bogs. il Sports Illus 35:48-51 N 22 '71
RAUH, Joseph Louis, 1911-
Left-wing Joe Pewism. S. Alsop. il Newsweek 78:128 O 25 '71 *
RAUP, Henry A.
Cairngorm wildlands of Scotland. il Liv Wildn 35:24-9 Spr '71
RAVEN, Peter H. and others
Origins of taxonomy. bibliog Science 174: 1210-13 D 17 '71
RAVENAL, Earl C.
Approaching China, defending Taiwan. For Affairs 50:44-58 O '71
Nixon doctrine and our Asian commitments. For Affairs 49:201-17 Ja '71
RAVENNA, Italy
Pines of Ravenna. N. T. Mirov. il Natur Hist 80:24-6 Ja '71
RAVENTOS, Bill
Speakers for PA. il Radio-Electr 42:52-4 My '71

RAW food. See Food, Raw
RAW materials
Raw materials. il Forbes 108:20-5 Ag 1 '71
Prices
Is the party over? il Forbes 108:22-3 Ag 1 '71
RAWLS, Joseph
East of the Andes. il Américas 23:15-24 Ag '71
RAWSON, Eleanor
Market for book manuscripts. Writer 84:18-19 Jl '71
RAWSON, Guillermo
Guillermo Rawson's idealistic vision of the United States. J. Villaverde. il pors Américas 23:25-35 Ag '71 *
RAY, Cyril
Classic fruit brandies. il Holiday 49:76-8 Mr '71
Dutch food. il Holiday 48:60-1+ N '70
Roasted goose in the Tower of London. il Holiday 48:12-13 N '70
RAY, David
Comment. A. Williamson. Poetry 118:171-2 Je '71 *
RAY, James Earl
Frame-up, by H. Weisberg. Review
Sat R 54:23-4 Ap 10 '71. F. J. Cook *
RAYAR, Paul
Raku murals of Paul Rayar. P. Rothenberg. il Ceram Mo 19:14-15 Je '71 *
RAYCHAUDHURI, C. and Desai, I. D.
Ceroid pigment formation and irreversible sterility in vitamin E deficiency. bibliog il Science 173:1028-9 S 10 '71
RAYMOND, Lowell W.
Chiselers and social security. Cath World 214: 117-19 D '71
RAYMOND'S run; story. See Bambara, T. C.
RAYS (fishes)
Manta pup. R. Fabbri. il Sea Front 17:332-4 N '71
RAYTHEON company
Raytheon ATC computer contract terms changed. Aviation W 94:28 Mr 22 '71
RAZA movement. See Mexican Americans
RAZOR, Jack E.
Hosts for athletic contests. Clear House 45: 305-8 Ja '71
RAZOR blades
Razor blades. il Consumer Bul 54:4 Ap '71
Shaving on Mad. ave; Schick super chromium razor blades. Consumer Rep 36:585-6 O '71
See also
Gillette company
RAZORS
See also
Gillette company
REACT (organization)
CB and the snowmobile: how REACT can save your life. W. J. Hawkins. il Pop Sci 199:78-9+ S '71
REACTIONARIES. See Conservatism
REACTIONS, Chemical. See Chemical reactions
REACTORS, Nuclear. See Nuclear reactors
READ, David Haxton Carswell
Right to convert. Chr Today 15:9-12 Ag 27 '71
READ, Sir Herbert Edward
Life as a mandala. G. Woodcock. Nation 213: 181-3 S 6 '71 *
READABILITY (literary style)
Readability, what it is and isn't. A. M. Blair. Ed Digest 37:50-1 O '71
READERS (books)
New readings on reading. il Time 97:59-60 Mr 29 '71
READERS and libraries. See Libraries and readers
READER'S digest
How I learned to stop worrying and to enjoy life on the far right. M. E. Marty. Chr Cent 88:1279 O 27 '71
In-Digest-ible charges. Chr Cent 88:1219 O 20 '71; Discussion. 88:1342, 1504-5 N 17, D 22 '71
Of many things; Reader's digest views of regrettable views of WCC actions. D. R. Campion. America 125:inside cover N 6 '71
READERS digest association, inc.
Biggest sweepstakes; FTC files complaint. il Newsweek 77:61 Ja 18 '71
Reader's digest agrees to NYC consumer ruling. Pub W 199:36-7 Ja 18 '71
READER'S digest sweepstakes. See Lotteries
READERS of Catholic newspapers. See Newspapers—Readers
READINESS for school
See also
Reading readiness

READING

Lunch; excerpt from On reading; tr. by W. S. Burford. M. Proust. Vogue 158:118-19+ N 1 '71

Significant unsolved problems in reading. H. M. Robinson. Ed Digest 36:42-5 F '71

Special feature on reading; symposium. bibliog il Todays Ed 60:44-54 O '71

See also

Right to read program

Aids and devices

DOVACK's machines help children read. M. Wills. il por Am Ed 7:3-8 Je '71

See also

Reading laboratories

Readiness

See Reading readiness

Remedial teaching

Demise of the reluctant reader; Port Washington, N.Y. television reading program. S. Fleming. il Schol Teach Jr/Sr High p 12-13+ Ja 11 '71

Do drag racers need to know how to read? Yuba County reading-learning center. H. Bottel. il Am Ed 7:3-7 O '71

Performance contracting: proceed with caution. J. D. Reynolds. il Engl J 60:102-6+ Ja '71; Same abr. with title Performance contracting: adapted. Ed Digest 36:5-7 Ap '71

Practical reading courses for the slow learner in high school. B. Ashton. il Engl J 60:97-101 Ja '71

Programed tutor: Programed tutorial reading project in Indianapolis public schools. J. White. il Am Ed 7:18-21 D '71

Remedial reading via TV; Electric company. M. E. Ricketts. Todays Ed 60:51-2 O '71

Study and teaching

Evaluation and decision making. R. Farr and V. L. Brown. Ed Digest 36:40-3 Ap '71

Letter-name vs. letter-sound knowledge in learning to read. S. J. Samuels. Ed Digest 37:49-51 S '71

Middle school tries contractual reading. L. L. Smith and J. Riebock. Clear House 45: 404-6 Mr '71

New readings on reading. il Time 97:59-60 Mr 29 '71

Oust ABC's, teach reading by color; Gattegno method. C. Meyer. il McCalls 98:41-2 F '71

Project RISE for elementary schools and high schools. PTA Mag 65:26-8+ My; 23-6 Je '71

Reading, the fundamental R: what parents can do to upgrade school programs. J. E. Allen, jr. por Parents Mag 46:32 My '71

Why they teach your child to read that way. il Changing T 25:48-51 D '71

See also

Reading clinics

Reading readiness

Right to read program

Aids and devices

Communication skills through self-recording. L. Smith and others. il Todays Ed 60:18-20 Ja '71

READING air show. See Aviation—Exhibitions

READING aloud. See Books and reading—Reading aloud

READING and television. See Television and reading

READING by children. See Childrens reading

READING clinics

Do drag racers need to know how to read? Yuba County reading-learning center. H. Bottel. il Am Ed 7:3-7 O '71

Hilo reads with aloha spirit; Hilo reading clinic, Hawaii. T. Kaser. il Am Ed 7:16-20 Ap '71

Our high school reading center. E. Elmore. Todays Ed 60:40 Ja '71

READING comprehension

Reading and writing exposition and argument: the skills and their relationships. M. Finder. Engl J 60:615-20 My '71

READING disability

American children with reading problems can easily learn to read English represented by Chinese characters. P. Rozin and others. bibliog il Science 171:1264-7 Mr 26 '71; Discussion. 173:190-1 Jl 16 '71

Dyslexic child. R. M. N. Crosby. Todays Ed 60:46-8 O '71

Is there such a thing as a learning disabled child? N. E. Silberberg and M. C. Silberberg. Ed Digest 37:14-17 S '71

Learned ape; experiments to study dyslexia. il Newsweek 78:78 O 25 '71

Reading disability, tendency toward delinquency? W. H. Miller and E. Windhauser. bibliog Clear House 46:183-7 N '71

READING laboratories

Recipe for reading. W. B. Ziegenfuss. il Todays Ed 60:44-5 O '71

READING lists

See also

Books and reading—Best books

READING of maps. See Map reading

READING readiness

Putting parents into the reading picture; with study-discussion program, by M. M. Conant. W. D. Boutwell. bibliog il PTA Mag 66:6-8+, 35 O '71

READING research

Research in the teaching of English. D. V Gunderson. bibliog Engl J 60:547-53 Ap '71

READING to children. See Books and reading—Reading aloud

READINGS, Dramatic. See Dramatic readings

READY, William

Llyfrgell Genedlaethol Cymru: the National library of Wales. bibliog il Wilson Lib Bul 45:962-5 Je '71

READY-to-cook food. See Food—Ready-to-cook food

REAGAN, Robert H.

Easiest trout fishing going. il Field & S 75: 56-7+ Ap '71

REAGAN, Ronald

Saving the states from bankruptcy. il por Nations Bsns 59:56-60 My '71

Welfare: America's no. 1 problem; interview. il por U S News 70:36-40 Mr 1 '71

about

Crisis facing key states: what Reagan, Rockefeller are doing. pors U S News 70:41-2 My 17 '71 *

Governor Reagan's private war. L. T. King. Commonweal 94:358-9 Jl 9 '71 *

Poor betrayed. J. Osborne. New Repub 164: 13-15 F 13 '71 *

Reagan and taxes. W. F. Buckley, jr. Nat R 23:609 Je 1 '71 *

Reagan model; veto of California rural legal assistance. M. E. Leary. Nation 212:134-5 F 1 '71 *

Reagan the revolutionary. Nat R 23:1075 S 24 '71 *

Reagan versus the poverty lawyers. P. Barnes. New Repub 164:15-17 Ja 23 '71; Reply. L. C. Battle. 164:33 F 13 '71 *

Reagan's privacy; his finances. Nation 212:646 My 24 '71 *

Ronald Reagan's slow fade. K. Fleming. il por Newsweek 78:28-9 D 20 '71 *

Showdown with Reagan. J. Osborne. New Repub 165:9-11 Jl 10 '71 *

Taxing Reagan. Newsweek 77:32 My 17 '71 *

REAL estate advertising. See Real property—Advertising

REAL estate agents

How to make an (almost) trouble-free transfer. J. Ingersoll. House B 113:24-5 Ja '71

REAL estate auctions. See Auctions

REAL estate business

California's coast: the developers win. il Bsns W p1-2 N 27 '71

Job for patient money: J. Cowan of Phipps land company. por Forbes 107:45+ F 15 '71

Trammell Crow: Big. Bigger. Biggest? por Forbes 107:53-4+ Ap 15 '71

See also

Aerospace industries—Real estate operations

Corporations—Real estate operations

Offices—Leasing and renting

Railroads—Real estate operations

Finance

Land sales: a lower key. il Bsns W p84+ Ja 23 '71

REAL estate investment

Apartment house goes public. A. Hershman. il Duns 98:36-8 N '71

Betting on death; British sale of reversions. Newsweek 77:66+ Ja 25 '71

Big land rush: no slowdown in sight; land sales are booming. il U S News 71:32-4 D 13 '71

Florida: boom! boom! boom? symposium. il Look 35:17-28+ Ap 6 '71

Land speculators play Disney's money machine. il Bsns W p80+ S 11 '71

New boom: Disneyland East. il Newsweek 77:103-4 Ap 19 '71

Nice piece of desert: Cochiti Lake, a fraud in the recreational city business. R. A. Jones. il Nation 213:616-26 D 13 '71

REAL estate investment—*Continued*
US as slumlord. K. Hartnett. New Repub 165:11-13 D 11 '71
Wall Street's new fashions. il Forbes 108:22-6 Jl 15 '71
Who owns New York? il Forbes 107:24-6+ Je 1 '71

REAL estate investment trusts
Are real estate trusts a good investment? M. Daly. Bet Hom & Gard 49:26 O '71
Investing in real estate, without buying property. il U S News 70:47-8 My 17 '71
Real estate trusts are a money magnet. il Bsns W p 112+ O 23 '71
Retreat of the REIT. Newsweek 78:87-8 D 6 '71

REAL estate titles. See Land titles

REAL numbers. See Numbers, Real

REAL property
See also
Land titles
Mortgages
Real estate business

Advertising
Land development sales gimmicks. Consumer Bul 54:21-2 Ap '71
Marvin's garden plays Monopoly. il Bsns W p42 N 13 '71

Valuation
How an expert appraises land. M. Hood. il Suc Farm 69:G24 S '71

REALE, Nicholas
Watercolor page; with biographical sketch. il por Am Artist 35:56-7+ Mr '71

REALISM in art
Art; exhibition of works at the Wadsworth atheneum, Hartford. L. Alloway. Nation 213:605-6 D 6 '71
Portrait of the artist as a portrait of the artist; work of W. Midgette. D. Rosand. il por Art N 70:32-5+ Mr '71
Who was Théodore Géricault? L. Eitner. il Art N 70:30-5+ O '71
See also
Genre painting

REALISM in literature
New realism. R. Burch. bibliog f il Horn Bk 47:257-64 Je '71
Realism, truth, and honesty; address, July 1970. M. Q. Steele. Horn Bk 47:17-27 F '71

REALISM in moving pictures
Two types of film theory. B. Henderson. Film Q 24:33-42 Spr '71

REALITY
Collision with reality; Institute for advanced Christian studies conference. C. F. H. Henry. Chr Today 16:37-8 D 3 '71

REALS, Lucile Farnsworth
Antique silver spoon. il Hobbies 76:128 Je '71
Let's enjoy Emile Galle's glass. il Hobbies 76:91 My '71

REALTORS. See Real estate agents

REAPPORTIONMENT. See Apportionment (election law)

REARDEN, Jim
They're threatening Alaska's big game hunting. il Nat Wildlife 9:21-3 F '71

REASON
See also
Rationalism

REASONER, Harry, family
Boyhood joys of Christmas. J. Egan. il pors Good H 173:44+ D '71

REAVELL, George
Nation-mending at home. il por Time 97:20 Je 21 '71 *

REAVEY, Edward P. Jr
Critical consumer need; address, May 17, 1971. Vital Speeches 38:25-7 O 15 '71

REAY, Devon
Indoor evergreen you'll love. Org Gard & Farm 18:129+ F '71

REBAY, Luciano
(tr) See Montale, E. After a flight

REBELLIONS. See Revolutions

REBINDING. See Bookbinding

REBOZO, Charles Gregory
Portrait of Bebe Rebozo, Nixon family's closest friend. il pors U S News 71:68-9 O 11 '71 *

REBUILT automobiles. See Automobiles, Remodeled

RECALL (psychology)
Free recall and abstractness of stimuli. W. Bevan and J. A. Steger. bibliog il Science 172:597-9 My 7 '71

RECAPPING of tires. See Tires, Rubber—Retreading and recapping

RECEPTIONS
See also
Government entertaining

RECEPTORS, Neural
Cyclic adenosine monophosphate: function in photoreceptors. W. H. Miller and others. bibliog il Science 174:295-7 O 15 '71
Insect photoreceptor: an internal ocellus is present in sphinx moths. J. L. Eaton. bibliog il Science 173:822-3 Ag 27 '71
Molecular biology of synaptic receptors. E. de Robertis. bibliog il Science 171:963-71 Mr 12 '71
Morphological basis for a mechanical linkage in otolithic receptor transduction in the frog. D. E. Hillman and E. R. Lewis. bibliog il Science 174:416-19 O 22 '71
Photoreceptors in primitive chordates: fine structure, hyperpolarizing receptor potentials, and evolution. A. L. F. Gorman and others. bibliog il Science 172:1052-4 Je 4 '71
Potassium ion release and enzyme secretion: adrenergic regulation by α- and β-receptors. S. Batzri and others. bibliog il Science 174:10291-31 D 3 '71
Receptors: localization and specificity of binding of serotonin in the central nervous system. S. G. A. Alivisatos and others. bibliog il Science 171:809-12 F 26 '71

RECEPTORS, Visual. See Rod and cone cells

RECESSION, Business. See Business depression

RECHNITZ, G. A. and Mohan, M. S.
Potassium-adenosine triphosphate complex: formation contant measured with ion-selective electrodes. bibliog il Science 168:1460; 171:1268 Je 19 '70, Mr 26 '71

RECIFE, Brazil
To hell and gone; Recife shantytowns. G. H. Dunne. il America 125:224-7 O 2 '71

RECIPES. See Cookery

RECIPROCATING engines (aircraft) See Airplane engines

RECK, Tom S.
Exile of pirates & princes. Commonweal 95:155-8 N 12 '71

RECK-MALLECZEWEN, Friedrich Percyval
Books. R. Coles. New Yorker 46:92-5 Ja 30 '71 *

RECLAMATION of land
Peeling back the land for coal; with report by G. Mendes. il Newsweek 77:69-72+ Je 28 '71
Sharp conflict on strip-mine reclamation. il Sci N 99:297-8 My 1 '71
See also
Irrigation

Mexico
See also
Chinampas

Pennsylvania
Taming the strip-mine monster. E. Faltermayer. il Life 71:21 O 1 '71

West Virginia
Jay and the strippers. R. Starnes. Field & S 76:8+ Je '71

RECLAMATION of waste water. See Water reuse

RECLUSES
See also
Hermits

RECOGNITION (psychology)
Chimp with a self concept? il Sci Digest 70:46-50 Jl '71

RECONCILIATION
Reconciliation. V. P. McCorry. America 124:300-inside back cover Mr 20 '71

RECONNAISSANCE, Aerial. See Aerial reconnaissance

RECONNAISSANCE satellites. See Artificial satellites—Military use

RECONSTRUCTION (Civil war)
See also
Freedmen

RECONSTRUCTION finance corporation
Professional SOB. por Forbes 108:16 Ag 1 '71

RECONSTRUCTIONIST Judaism
Reconstructionism in American Jewish life, by C. S. Liebman. Review
Commentary 51:74-6 Mr '71. M. A. Meyer; Discussion. 52:28+ Ag '71

RECONSTRUCTIVE surgery. See Surgery, Plastic

RECORD, Jeffrey
Viet Cong: image and flesh. il Trans-Action 8:46-52 Ja '71

RECORD changers. See Phonograph—Record changers

RECORD players. See Phonograph

RECORDING instruments
See also
Oscillographs

RECORDS
See also
Aviation records
Business records
Farm records
Household records
Medical records
Police records
Weather records

Preservation
See Archives
RECORDS, Phonograph. See Phonograph records
RECORDS, School. See School reports and records
RECORDS, World. See World records
RECOVERY, inc.
Recovery, inc: aid in the transition from hospital to community. D. T. Lee. bibliog Ment Hy 55:194-8 Ap '71
RECREATION
Trends; with editorial comment. il Parks & Rec 6:26-57+ My '71
See also
Forest recreation
Industrial recreation
Leisure
Outdoor life
Parks
Play
Playgrounds
Prison recreation
Recreational therapy
United States—Armed forces—Recreation

Accidents and injuries
Matter of life or death. J. L. Hecht. Parks & Rec 6:39-40+ Mr '71
Security, safety: two sides of the coin. R. Hall. bibliog il Parks & Rec 6:22+ D '71
Youth camp safety act. A. Ribicoff. por Parks & Rec 6:23+ S '71

Activities
Do's and don'ts of citizen involvement in good park and recreation programs. J. J. Bannon. Am City 86:20 F '71
Park programs on a bare-bones budget; Boston, Mass. J. E. Curtis. il por Am City 86:51-3 D '71
See also
Boats and boating
Camping—Activities
Childrens plays
Picnics
Recreation for the handicapped
Singing

Administration
Citizen leadership; coordination councils. R. M. Artz. Parks & Rec 6:109-10+ Ja '71
Establishing a harmonious relationship between recreation departments and organized youth leagues. W. D. Martin. il Parks & Rec 6:42-3+ Jl '71
Now if the Frederickson revolt would only spread; reprint. Parks & Rec 6:17 Ja '71

Economic aspects
Economics of leisure today. R. Kraus. bibliog Parks & Rec 6:62-6+ Ag '71

Equipment and supplies
Product news. See issues of Parks & recreation

Finance
Investing in companies that profit from pleasure. il Changing T 25:35-40 Je '71

Safety devices and measures
Matter of life or death. J. L. Hecht. Parks & Rec 6:39-40+ Mr '71
Youth camp safety act. A. Ribicoff. por Parks & Rec 6:23+ S '71

Study and teaching
Outdoor classroom. D. R. Potter. il Am For 77:44-6 O '71
Recreation and park education; charts. il Parks & Rec 6:35-43 Ag '71
See also
Recreation workers—Training

United States
Do's and don'ts of citizen involvement in good park and recreation programs. J. J. Bannon. Am City 86:20 F '71
Endless weekend: special issue on Americans at play; symposium. il Life 71:8-24+ S 3 '71
Outdoor America. B. Thomas. il Travel 136: 28-39+ Jl '71

Parks & recreation essay. W. W. Brown. Parks & Rec 6:38-9 Je '71
Stretching outdoor recreation. R. Moses. il por Cons 26:28-9 D '71
Unfinished business. Parks & Rec 6:13 Ap '71
See also
National recreation and park association
also subhead Recreation under names of cities, e.g. Greensboro, N.C.—Recreation
RECREATION, industrial. See Industrial recreation
RECREATION areas
Corporate move to leisure towns. E. Carruth. il Fortune 83:72-9 Ap '71
Lessons from the land; ventures in leisure-time communities. il Time 97:86 Ap 12 '71
We will be ready, Mr President. . . Parks & Rec 6:20 Mr '71
See also
Parks

Arizona
Watershed recreation without water; J. David Lee Dam, Thatcher, Ariz. J. L. Knisley, jr. il Parks & Rec 6:27 Ja '71

California
Between Gilroy and Los Banos there's a new recreation area. il Sunset 146:76 Ap '71
Disney's war against the wilderness; Mineral King controversy. R. Rapoport. il Ramp Mag 10:27-33 N '71

Indiana
Indiana's new lakes. B. Thomas. il Travel 135:45-51+ F '71

Wyoming
Flaming Gorge. B. Thomas. il Travel 135: 42-6 My '71
RECREATION buildings
Building for recreation. il Arch Forum 135: 29-51 Jl '71
RECREATION centers
Ellis memorial & Eldredge house, inc, Boston. il Antiques 100:526 O '71
Hard lesson; Eugene, Ore. drop-in youth centers. N. Murray. il Parks & Rec 6:28-31+ F '71
See also
School buildings as social centers
RECREATION conferences
Coming events. See issues of Parks & recreation
See also
Congress for recreation and parks
RECREATION departments. See Park and recreation departments
RECREATION education. See Recreation—Study and teaching
RECREATION for the aged
High school remembers the senior citizen. D. L. Berne. Clear House 45:545-6 My '71
Seniors, Girl scouts cooperate for community service in N.Y. town; Friendship club of senior citizens, Clarence, Erie County. il Aging 203:6 S '71
See also
Senior centers
RECREATION for the blind
Sailing blind. C. E. Leonard. il Yachting 130:62-3+ Ag '71
RECREATION for the handicapped
Camping with a coronary. W. L. Trotter. il Har Yrs 11:37-8 Mr '71
Give youth a volunteering chance: Saturday morning recreation program for handicapped children, Madison, Wis. C. M. Anderson. il Parks & Rec 6:44-5 O '71
There's a wheelchair in the woods; Forest service trails. E. H. Stone. il Parks & Rec 6:18-21+ D '71
See also
Recreation for the blind
Recreational therapy
RECREATION research
1970: urban recreation and park. . .data bench mark year. D. R. Dunn. il por Parks & Rec 6:32-7+ F '71
RECREATION rooms
Instant family-room theater; convertible basement recreation room. H. Wicks. il Pop Mech 136:148-51 N '71
RECREATION vehicle show. See Recreational vehicles—Exhibitions
RECREATION workers
Labor relations. L. B. Eichhold and J. D. Redmond. il Parks & Rec 6:20-2+ N '71
Parks & recreation essay. W. W. Brown. Parks & Rec 6:38-9 Je '71
People. See issues of Parks & recreation

RECREATION workers—*Continued*

Certification
Certification; Georgia. H. D. Leavitt. Parks & Rec 6:123+ Ja '71

Supply and demand
Role of civil service. F. A. Cosgrove and R. Kraus. il Parks & Rec 6:27-9+ Je '71

Training
Careers in recreation; Evanston, Ill. S. Sarkisian. il Parks & Rec 6:40-1+ F '71
Case for graduate school education in recreation. A. A. Shuster and S. K. Shuster. Parks & Rec 6:116-17+ Ja '71

RECREATION workers, Volunteer
Volunteers in parks program inaugurated. il Parks & Rec 6:5-6 F '71

RECREATIONAL therapy
Therapeutic recreation; charts. il Parks & Rec 6:57-61 Ag '71

RECREATIONAL vehicles
Camping out in comfort. A. F. Rush. il McCalls 98:104-5+ Je '71
Colorful world of RVs. il Mech Illus 67:92 O '71
Editorial; responsible use of recreational vehicles. C. B. Lees. Horticulture 49:20 S '71
Facts on financing an RV. F. C. Kilburn. il Mech Illus 67:58-9+ Ag '71
LPG in your RV; butane, propane, or bottled gas. B. Behme. il Field & S 76:142-4 Ag '71
New RVs. Mech Illus 67:108 Mr '71
New wheels for the wild country, which one is for you? H. Shuldiner. il Pop Sci 198:86-9+ Mr '71
Recreation roundup. H. Shuldiner. See issues of Popular science monthly
Recreation vehicles for 1971; what's new in campers, trailers and motor homes. B. Behme. il Field & S 75:66-9+ Ap '71
See also
Automobile trailers
Campers and coaches, Truck
Motor vehicles, Amphibious
Snowmobiles and snowmobiling

Exhibitions
Bigger and better rec-vees; National recreation vehicle exposition. C. B. Colby. il Outdoor Life 147:96-8+ Mr '71
Trucks for fun roll into high. il Bsns W p43 N 13 '71

Leasing and renting
Great way to go; fly-and-rent. B. Behme. il Field & S 76:54-6 Je '71

Maintenance and repair
Cold-weather tips for RV owners. V. L. Oertle. il Pop Mech 136:151-3+ O '71

Storage
Storage lots for trailers, campers, Sunset 146:140 Mr '71

Testing
Great RV binge; Chevrolet Blazer, Ford Bronco and AMC Jeepster. C. Koch. il Motor T 23:62-4+ Je '71
Great RV binge; Jeep CJ-5, Toyota Land Cruiser, International Scout II and the Suzuki Brute IV. C. Koch. il Motor T 23:42-7 Ag '71

RECRION corporation
Las Vegas operator deals a new hand; Nevada gambling enterprise. Bsns W p21 Ag 7 '71

RECRUITING agencies. See Employment agencies

RECRUITING and enlistment. See United States—Armed forces—Recruiting and enlistment; United States—Army—Recruiting and enlistment

RECRUITING for librarianship. See Librarians—Recruiting

RECRUITING of athletes. See Athletes—Recruiting

RECRUITING of employees
Company recruiters still shun the campus. Bsns W p36-7 D 11 '71
Farm help: how to find it. R. Sanders. il Suc Farm 69:no3 26-7 F '71
See also
College professors and instructors—Recruiting
Computers—Employment use
Discrimination in employment
Executives—Recruiting
Public officers—Recruiting

RECRUITING of physicians. See Physicians—Recruiting

RECRUITING of students. See Colleges and universities—Student recruiting

RECRUITING of teachers. See Teachers—Recruiting

RECTIFIERS. See Electric current rectifiers

RECUPERATION. See Convalescence

RECYCLED paper. See Refuse, Utilization of

RECYCLED water. See Water reuse

RECYCLING of waste. See Refuse, Utilization of

RED blood cells. See Erythrocytes

RED cedar. See Juniper

RED cedar, Western. See Arborvitae

RED cestrum. See Cestrums

RED cross
United States
President pays tribute to international relief efforts of American Red cross; remarks, May 19, 1971. R. M. Nixon. Dept State Bul 64:800-3 Je 21 '71
Red cross national aquatic and small-craft schools (cont) Camp Mag 43:30-1 Ap '71

RED foxes. See Foxes

RED guard. See Youth movement—China (People's Republic)

RED peppers. See Peppers

RED RIVER
One-inch journey; excerpt from The unforeseen wilderness. W. Berry. il Audubon 73:4-11 My '71

RED SEA
Hot spots in the Red Sea. L. Purrett. il Sci N 99:388-9 Je 5 '71
See also
Suez Canal

RED shift. See Quasars—Spectra

RED Sox (baseball) See Baseball clubs

RED tape. See Bureaucracy

RED tide
Parting shots: a tide of death that pollution didn't cause. il Life 71:64 Ag 13 '71

RED wines. See Wine

RED Wings (hockey team) See Hockey teams

RED yucca. See Yucca

REDDICK, Thomas L.
New educational games for social studies classes. Clear House 46:127-8 O '71

REDDING, Anita
Unusual catch. il Yachting 130:54-5 N '71

REDDY, John
Are dirty movies on the way out? PTA Mag 66:2-5 N '71; Same abr. Read Digest 99:110-13 N '71
Bill Buckley: blithe spirit of the right. por Read Digest 99:112-16 S '71
Comeuppance for Newark's unholy alliance. il Read Digest 98:113-17 Ja '71
Get up with Hugh Downs. por Read Digest 98:45-6+ F '71
School that love built. por Read Digest 99:149-50+ '71
Washington: a state for all seasons. il Read Digest 99:142-8 D '71

REDEMPTION. See Salvation

REDEMPTION of bonds. See Bonds—Redemption

REDFORD, Robert
Skiing the American West. por Harp Baz 105:38+ D '71
about
Robert Redford: husband, father and sex symbol. S. Davidson. por Redbook 137:81+ My '71 •

REDFORD, Robert, family
Lifestyle. il pors Am Home 74:12+ O '71

REDGRAVE, Vanessa
People are talking... por Vogue 158:120-1 N 1 '71 •

REDISTRICTING. See Apportionment (election law)

REDLICH, Don
Don Redlich dance company, ANTA theatre, NYC. M. Marks. Dance Mag 45:89 My '71 •

REDMOND, D. E. Jr, and others
Social behavior of monkeys selectively depleted of monoamines. bibliog il Science 174:428-31 O 22 '71

REDMOND, Geoffrey, and Cohen, Gerald
Induction of liver acetaldehyde dehydrogenase: possible role in ethanol tolerance after exposure to barbiturates. bibliog il Science 171:387-9 Ja 29 '71

REDMOND, Jeffrey D. See Eichhold, L. B. jt. auth.

REDMOND, Wash.

Education

High school newsreels. J. A. Newman. il Schol
Teach Jr/Sr High p22-3 Mr 8 '71

REDON, Odilon

Eternal garden of Monsieur Redon. W. A. H.
Birnie. il Read Digest 99:122-8 S '71 •

REDUCING. See Corpulence

REDUCING diet. See Diet

REDUCING exercises. See Exercise

REDWOOD

Redwoods: a population model. C. A. Bosch.
bibliog il Science 172:345-9 Ap 23 '71; Discussion. 174:435-6 O 22 '71

Redwoods: saved or sorry? A. W. Smith. il
Nat Parks & Con Mag 45:12-20 Ja '71

Weatherman looks at the redwood tree:
California's fog drinker. R. E. Burton. il
Weatherwise 24:120-4 Je '71

REDWOOD burls

How to raise a redwood burl. il Sunset 147:
124-5 Ag '71

REDWOOD NATIONAL PARK

Men and events behind Redwood National
Park. E. C. Crafts. il Am For 77:20-8+
My '71; Reply. R. D. Butcher. 77:2-3 Ag
'71

Oversight. J. Morgenstern. Newsweek 77:9
My 24 '71

Redwoods: saved or sorry? A. W. Smith. il
Nat Parks & Con Mag 45:12-20 Ja '71

REDWOOD planters. See Flower boxes, planters, etc.

REDWOOD shores project. See Housing projects

REDWOOD sorrel. See Wood sorrel

REECE, Bonnie B. See Greyser, S. A. jt. auth.

REECE, Norval D.

Politics for rich & poor. New Repub 164:
8-9 Ja 16 '71

REED, Beverley

Amy Jacques Garvey: black, beautiful & free.
B. Reed. il pors Ebony 26:45-6+ Je '71

REED, Cerid

Erie Canal state park. il Parks & Rec 6:24-
6+ S '71

REED, David

Comeback in the Congo. por Read Digest
98:134-8 Ap '71

Golda Meir: Israel's tough grandmother-
prime minister. por Read Digest 99:109-13
Jl '71

—and Frazer, J. E.

Agony of East Pakistan. il Read Digest 99:
66-71 N '71

REED, Eugenia

Iris caper. Har Yrs 11:18 Ap '71

REED, G. W. and others

Surface-related mercury in lunar samples.
bibliog il Science 172:258-61 Ap 16 '71

REED, Herbert O.

Law & order; address, August 4, 1971. Vital
Speeches 37:730-6 S 15 '71

REED, John R.

Gallery of spiders; poem. Poetry 118:192-4
Jl '71

REED, John Shedd

Is anyone listening? address, May 20, 1971.
Vital Speeches 37:569-72 Jl 1 '71

Man who met the longhorns with a railroad. il por Nations Bsns 59:50-1 Ja '71

REED, Judith

Following through in Macon County. il Am
Ed 7:7-12 N '71

REED, Nathaniel

Eloquent ecologist. M. Von Matthiessen. por
Harp Baz 104:96 Jl '71 •

REED, Peter J.

Self-sparing usages of English; or, Why my
cat got sick in Atlanta. Engl J 60:1123-6
N '71

REED, Raymond S.

F. A. O. Schwarz: tougher selling in toyland.
il Bsns W p46-9 D 18 '71 •

REED, Rex

(ed) See Williams, T. Tennessee Williams
turns sixty

REED, T. M.

Analytic philosophy in the 20th century. bibliog Am Lib 2:1161-8 D '71

REED, William F. Jr

All business for the Big Bird. il Sports Illus
35:14-15 Ag 23 '71

Baseball. il Sports Illus 34:69+ Je 7 '71

Big name for the small colleges. il por Sports
Illus 35:77-9 N 29 '71

College football (cont) Sports Illus 35:71-2
N 15 '71

Fastest man afloat. il por Sports Illus 34:16-
19 Mr 1 '71

Good times come to Cajun country. il por
Sports Illus 35:20-1 D 20 '71

Harness racing (cont) il Sports Illus 35:92-5
S 13; 66-7 O 4; 83-4 D 13 '71

He who laughs last. il por Sports Illus 35:
26-8 S 6 '71

Ho, ho, ho went the jolly white giant. il por
Sports Illus 34:20-1 Je 21 '71

Ineligible married man. il por Sports Illus
34:42-4+ Ap 12 '71

Irish stew for LSU. il Sports Illus 35:26-7
N 29 '71

It's the Hoosier title wave. il Sports Illus
34:28-30+ Mr 22 '71

Queen of the divers is King. il por Sports
Illus 35:31-3 Ag 16 '71

Roaring grand lights 100 candles. il Sports
Illus 34:28-30+ Je 21 '71

Swimming (cont) Sports Illus 34:77-9 Ap 5;
35:46-7+ S 6 '71

Swing shift, sweet chariot. il Sports Illus
35:22-3 Ag 30 '71

Week; baseball. Sports Illus 34:52 Je 28 '71

Week; college football (cont) Sports Illus 35:
70+ N 22 '71

What a fiesta we will have! il pors Sports
Illus 34:26-8+ My 31 '71

—See Ress, P. jt. auth.

REED, Willis

Solitary hunter stands in the way. W. Artis,
jr. il por Look 35:70-1 Ap 6 '71 •

Sports. R. Kahn. Esquire 75:34+ Mr '71 •

REEDER, Norm, and Machan, Cathy

Can dairymen control production? Farm J 95:
D6+ D '71

REEF coral. See Corals

REEFS

See also

Coral reefs and islands

REELS

Reels for hoses keep them stored but handy.
il Suc Farm 69:D12 O '71

RE-ENLISTMENT in the armed forces. See
United States—Armed forces—Recruiting
and enlistment

REES, Albert

Statistical needs for setting policy. Mo
Labor R 94:43-5 S '71

REEVE, F. D.

Faces at the bottom. Poetry 118:234-8 Jl
'71

Fresh airs. Poetry 119:39-44 O '71

Last game for the new life; poem. Poetry
118:218 Jl '71

Through the fire screen. Poetry 117:388-91
Mr '71

REEVE, Michael R.

Deadly arrow worm; with biographical sketch.
il por Sea Front 17:175-83,191 My '71

REEVES, Richard

Any number can play scenario. il N Y Times
Mag p7-9+ Ap 11 '71

Are our cities dying? Read Digest 99:172+
Ag '71

Feud. Life 70:54-6 Je 25 '71

Nixon's secret strategy. Harper 243:96-8 D
'71

Norman Rockwell is exactly like a Norman
Rockwell. il pors N Y Times Mag p 14-15+
F 28 '71

Primary nonsense. il Harper 244:41-4 Ja '72

Statehood for cities: the impossible dream.
Sat R 54:18-21 S 4 '71

REFEREEING of scientific literature. See Scientific literature

REFERENCE books

See also

Biographical dictionaries

Booksellers and bookselling—Reference books

Dictionaries

Encyclopedias

Bibliography

Current reference books. F. N. Cheney. See
issues of Wilson library bulletin

Mini reference library: 21 paperbacks; high
school material. J. Higgins and A. Stellwag. il pors Library J 96:245-7 Ja 15 '71

Reference books of 1970: recommendations of
a committee of the Reference services division of ALA. G. R. Purcell. il por Library J 96:1325-9 Ap 15 '71

SR's semiannual reference book roundup
(cont) D. M. Glixon. Sat R 54:39-43+ Ap
17: 44+ D 4 '71

REFERENCE services division. See American
library association—Reference services division

REFERENCE work. See Libraries—Reference
work

REFERENDUM

Cleanup battle jolts California. Bsns W p35
D 25 '71

Initiatives. New Repub 165:10 N 6 '71

REFF, Theodore

Butterfly and the old ox. il pors Art N 70:26-
31+ Mr '71

REFINERIES
    See also
    Petroleum refineries
REFINISHING furniture.   See   Furniture—
    Finishing
REFLECTING telescope. See Telescopes
REFLECTION (optics)
    Reflectors in fishes. E. Denton. il Sci Am
    224:64-72 Ja '71
REFLECTION nebulae. See Nebulae
REFLECTION spectra. See Spectrum—Reflec-
    tion spectra
REFLECTIONS; ballet. See Ballets—Criticisms
REFLECTIONS; story. See Canzoneri, R.
REFLECTORS   (photography)   See   Photog-
    raphy—Apparatus and supplies
REFLEXES
    See also
    Conditioned responses
    Tremor
REFORESTATION
    Total support for total reforestation. E. W.
    Allen jr. il por Am For 77:30-1 Ag '71
    See also
    Forest planting
    Forests and forestry
REFORMATION
    Women of the reformation in Germany and
    Italy, by R. H. Bainton. Review
    Chr Cent 88:1008 Ag 25 '71. M. Fousek
REFORMATORIES
    Residential treatment unit for delinquent
    youths; Hawthorne, N.Y. il Arch Rec 149:
    146-7 Mr '71
    Toward moral maturity; teaching ethics in
    the reformatory. il por Time 97:48 Je 28
    '71
    See also
    Wiltwyck school for boys, Yorktown Heights,
    N.Y.
REFORMED church in America
    Reformed church: growing old alone. Chr
    Today 15:33 Jl 2 '71
REFORMED church in Canada
    Radical departure; Canadian Christian re-
    formed church. L. K. Tarr. Chr Today
    16:46 Ja 7 '72
REFORMED churches
    Christian reformed synod: mirror, mirror
    J. Daane. Chr Today 15:35 Jl 16 '71
REFRACTING telescope. See Telescopes
REFRESHMENT   stands.   See   Concessions
    (food, etc)
REFRIGERATION and refrigerating machinery
    See also
    Ice—Manufacture
REFRIGERATION on boats
    Anatomy of a powerboat; refrigeration sys-
    tems. J. West. il Yachting 129:70-1+ Mr '71
    Ice—making and keeping it. J. Hart. il Yacht-
    ing 129:70+ Ap '71
REFRIGERATORS, Electric
    Compact refrigerators. il Consumer Rep 37:
    20-6 Ja '72
    Compact refrigerators and a freezer. il Con-
    sumer Bul 54:18-23 N '71
    No-frost, top-freezer refrigerators. il Consu-
    mer Rep 36:562-71 S '71
REFUELING of airplanes. See Airplanes—Re-
    fueling
REFUGEES
    Dispossessed. H. Bowser. Sat R 54:14 Ap 10
    '71
    See also
    International rescue committee
    United Nations—High commissioner for refu-
    gees
    United Nations relief and works agency for
    Palestine refugees in the Near East

    Resettlement
    Government and private agency partnership in
    refugee assistance programs; address, March
    14, 1971. F. L. Kellogg. Dept State Bul 64:
    576-8 My 3 '71
REFUGEES, Arab
    See also
    United Nations relief and works agency for
    Palestine refugees in the Near East
REFUGEES, Cambodian
    Indochina: a generation of refugees. il Time
    97:24-6 My 10 '71
    Refugee problems in Laos and Cambodia;
    statement, April 22, 1971. W. H. Sullivan.
    Dept State Bul 64:648-54 My 17 '71
REFUGEES, Cuban
    End of the freedom flights. Time 98:34 S 13
    '71
    Flight from Cuba: Castro's loss is U.S. gain.
    il U S News 70:74-7 My 31 '71
    Miami: the Cuban flavor. A. Burt. il Nation
    212:299-302 Mr 8 '71; Reply with rejoinder.
    J. D. Garst. 212:450 Ap 12 '71
    Why Castro is halting the airlift. il U S News
    71:91 S 13 '71

REFUGEES, Egyptian
    Suez exodus. il Newsweek 77:38 F 15 '71
REFUGEES, European
    Refugees: two kinds of exodus. il Time 97:
    31+ F 8 '71
    See also
    Intergovernmental committee for European
    migration
REFUGEES, German
    One of the comrades is missing; K. Bley's es-
    cape from East German ship; ed. by K.
    Schaefer. K. Agnew. il Read Digest 98:78-
    82 Ap '71
    Vanguard from the east; Germans from
    Poland. il Time 97:31+ F 8 '71
REFUGEES, Jewish
    Few who got out. il Time 97:35 F 8 '71
REFUGEES, Laotian
    Indochina: a generation of refugees. il Time
    97:24-6 My 10 '71
    Indochina: a slaughter of innocents. E. M.
    Kennedy. Nation 212:806-8 Je 28 '71
    Indochina war casualties. Ramp Mag 9:14
    My '71
    One-third of a nation uprooted; with editorial
    comment. G. M. Kahin. New Repub 165:10,
    19-21 Ag 7 '71
    Refugee problems in Laos and Cambodia;
    statement, April 22, 1971. W. H. Sullivan.
    Dept State Bul 64:648-54 My 17 '71
    Reports & comment. H. D. S. Greenway.
    Atlan 228:6+ Jl '71
REFUGEES, Pakistan
    Bengal: the murder of a people; with re-
    ports by L. Jenkins and T. Clifton. il
    Newsweek 78:26-30 Ag 2 '71
    Bengal: tragedy beyond belief. Chr Today
    15:32-3 Ag 27 '71
    Bengali refugees: a surfeit of woe. il Time 97:
    25-6 Je 21 '71
    Better place to live. il Newsweek 77:36+ Je
    21 '71
    Dubious haven. T. Clifton. il Newsweek 77:
    53-4 Je 14 '71
    East Pakistan crisis poses grave questions
    for other nations. C. B. Firth. Chr Cent
    88:806-7 Je 30 '71
    East Pakistan: even the skies weep. il Time
    98:37-8 O 25 '71
    Faces emptied of all hope. J. Saar. il Life
    70:22-9 Je 18 '71
    Gifts and questions; Gulf-Western industries
    gift. America 125:499 D 11 '71
    Kennedy's searing trip through Pakistani
    grief. il por Life 71:26-9 Ag 27 '71
    Letter from West Bengal. V. Mehta. New
    Yorker 47:166+ D 11 '71
    Millions of refugees, calamity for India. J.
    Wallace. il U S News 70:41 Je 21 '71
    No place worse than home. il Newsweek 78:
    31 D 6 '71
    Our brothers and sisters in Bengal. Ameri-
    ca 125:413-14 N 20 '71
    Pakistan refugee; how many will die? ad-
    dress, August 26, 1971. E. M. Kennedy.
    Vital Speeches 37:738-41 O 1 '71
    Pakistan: the ravaging of golden Bengal. il
    Time 98:24-9 Ag 2 '71
    Pakistani relief: compound of hope and
    tragedy. J. C. Haughey. il America 125:
    420-3 N 20 '71
    Refugee-related assistance to India outlined
    by Department. Dept State Bul 65:109-10
    Jl 26 '71
    Saga of shame; East Bengal and the plight
    of the refugees. Commonweal 95:75 O 22
    '71
    U.S. responds to U.N. appeal for blankets
    for refugees in India. Dept State Bul 65:
    620 N 29 '71
    U.S. to assist India in meeting burden of
    East Pakistan refugees. Dept State Bul
    65:82 Jl 19 '71
    U.S. urges international community to con-
    tinue relief to south Asia; statement,
    November 19, 1971. W. T. Bennett, jr.
    Dept State Bul 65:717-19 D 20 '71
    U.S. welcomes U.N. appeal for East Pakistan
    refugees. Dept State Bul 64:764 Je 14 '71
    Unbelievable happens in Bengal. J. K. Gal-
    braith. il por N Y Times Mag p 13+ O 31
    '71
    Why they fled Pakistan, and won't go back.
    K. Singh. il N Y Times Mag p 12-15 Ag
    1 '71
REFUGEES, Political
    See also
    Emigrés
    Refugees, European
    Refugees, Jewish
REFUGEES, Tibetan
    Lama in exile: prospects for an expatriate
    tradition. M. Jeschke. por Chr Cent 88:443-
    6 Ap 7 '71

REFUGEES, Vietnamese
Indochina: a generation of refugees. il Time 97:24-6 My 10 '71
Indochina: a slaughter of innocents. E. M. Kennedy. Nation 212:806-8 Je 28 '71; Reply. R. Boyd. 213:130 Ag 30 '71

REFUSE, Utilization of
Aluminum peddles its own recycle. il Bsns W p21 Ja 30 '71
BIRP proves practical and economically feasible in Phoenix, Ariz; Beverage industry recycling program. S. Carter. il Am City 86:28 D '71
Back in circulation; trash-collection project of Ecology action of Florida, inc. J. G. Meyer. il Environ 13:30-3 S '71
City turns trash into money; recycling plant; Franklin, Ohio. Bsns W p 120 Je 19 '71
Clean new gas; methane from feedlot wastes. H. L. Bohn. bibliog il Environ 13:4-9 D '71
Closing the circle; use of totally recycled paper in Environment. il Environ 13:34-7 S '71
Computer improves recycling process. Am City 86:36 S '71
Earth; the recycling picture. P. Swatek. Mlle 73:56-7 Je '71
Empty cans give scientists double-edged dome; geodesic dome material for bubble chamber. P. Wahl. il Pop Sci 199:82 O '71
End product; bricks from manure. il Newsweek 78:62 Jl 26 '71
From rice hulls to carbon black. il Bsns W p 18 Jl 3 '71
Garbage into gold. R. Hill. il Pop Sci 199: 40 N '71
Garbage pollution: what you can do to help. il Bet Hom & Gard 49:14+ O '71
Gold in garbage. Time 97:61 F 1 '71
Good ideas on land; using New York's garbage. Time 98:50 D 6 '71
Homemade storage devices for recycling rubbish. J. Hand. il Pop Sci 198:94-5+ Je '71
How science will help us get rid of our mountain of junk. C. P. Gilmore. il Pop Sci 198:70-3+ Ap '71
Industrial alcohol from waste paper. Chem 44:23 N '71
Ingenuity and determination for our ailing environment. il Chem 44:4-5 N '71
Let's speak up on solid wastes, truthfully. W. A. Xanten. il Am City 86:100-1 Je '71
Market unfolds for ecology paper. il Bsns W p86 Jl 17 '71
New drive to get rid of trash. il U S News 70:65-8 Je '71
New low-cost manure disposal system; Barriered landscape water renovation system. Suc Farm 69:H2 N '71
No energy to waste. J. Lear. Sat R 54:37-9 Jl 3 '71
No trees destroyed; Recycled paper products co. of Chicago. McCalls 99:46-7 D '71
Option for survival. R. S. Berry. Bul Atom Sci 27:22-7 My '71
Put it back! R. Adams; T. Brown; J. Olds. il Org Gard & Farm 18:50-5 Je '71
Reclaimed fibers for quality printing; excerpts from address, December 7, 1971, ed. by C. B. Grannis. W. R. Thompson. Pub W 201:48-9 Ja 3 '72
Recycling: an old idea with new significance. R. Andrus and S. P. Mathur. il Cons 25: 28-31 Je; 26:10-11 Ag '71
Recycling wastes. il Nat Wildlife 9:37 O '71
Return to cave and candle? W. F. May. il Nations Bsns 59:81-3 N '71
Rise of rejasing; re-using junk as something else. il Time 97:55 Ap 19 '71
Salvaging New York harbor debris. G. Pierson and F. E. Hampf. il Cons 26:2-3 Ag '71
Stamford mines a garbage lode. Bsns W p 142 S 25 '71
Tires, new and old. il Chem 44:3-4 Jl '71
Trash: how to put it to good use. M. Roche. House & Gard 140:47+ Jl '71
Trashing. il Newsweek 77:74 F 22 '71
Wastepaper bag. il Newsweek 78:73+ Jl 12 '71
What has business done? A. Rothenberg. Look 35:23 My 4 '71
Wisconsin develops intermediate composting. J. Olds. il Org Gard & Farm 18:65-7 Ja '71
See also
Filling (earthwork)
National conference on composting and waste recycling
Refuse as fertilizer

REFUSE and refuse disposal
Art of garbage analysis; with photographs of garbage of four celebrities. A. J. Weberman. il Esquire 76:113-17 N '71
Bears, dumps and people. G. T. Chase. il Cons 26:5 Ag '71
Campers vs. litter: practical ecology in camp. A. H. Seed, jr. il Camp Mag 43:13+ Je '71
Contractor refuse collection wouldn't do; Town of Union, N.Y. R. R. Blessing. il Am City 86:46+ Jl '71
Grinding refuse is no experiment; Madison, Wis. E. J. Duszynski. il Am City 86:61-3 S '71
How MTM can improve refuse collection. R. Stone. il Am City 86:74+ O '71
How much refuse in your city? study in six Texas cities. il Am City 86:64-6 Mr '71
Let's speak up on solid wastes, truthfully. W. A. Xanten. il Am City 86:100-1 Je '71
Manage solid wastes as a utility; Tacoma, Wash. R. M. Clark and others. il Am City 86:45-7 F '71
Mass transfer and urban problems. E. S. Savas. Science 174:365 O 22 '71
Paper and beer cans win; roadside litter count survey; Dallas County. Tex. J. C. Makens. il Am City 86:53 Ja '71
Plastics return the ecologists' fire. il Bsns W p25 Jl 10 '71
Refuse collection & disposal. See issues of American city
Solid waste demonstration programs. E. F. Spitzer. il Am City 86:58-60+ Jl '71
Third pollution, by W. E. Small. Review Commonweal 95:208-10 N 26 '71. J. Kretchmer
What's happening in solid wastes. Am City 86:96 Jl '71
Whisking the garbage; Sweden's vacuum system. B. B. Johansson. il Sat R 54:40-3 Jl 3 '71
See also
Cleaning of cities, towns, etc.
Radioactive waste disposal
Refuse collection trucks
Refuse containers
Refuse incinerators
Sewage disposal
Street cleaning
Timber disposal
Trade waste disposal
Waste disposal in the ocean
Water pollution
also subhead Sanitary affairs under names of cities, e.g. New York (city)—Sanitary affairs

Apparatus
Ecological can crusher. il Mech Illus 67:56 D '71
Garbage compactors end air-pollution problem; West New York, N.J. il Am City 86:28 Je '71
Kitchen machines to squash your trash. il Changing T 25:11-12 S '71
Will test home trash smashing; experiment in Atlanta. il Am City 86:34 Mr '71

Conferences
American city holds solid waste seminar; Pittsfield, Mass. il Am City 86:14 Jl '71

REFUSE as fertilizer
Garbage farming. M. Franz. il Org Gard & Farm 18:58-62 Ja '71
His process digests trash. por Bsns W p58 F 13 '71
See also
Compost

REFUSE bags. See Refuse containers

REFUSE collection trucks
Ideal refuse truck. Am City 86:8 Jl '71
Monsters on the prowl; Scottsdale, Ariz. C. O. Port. McCalls 98:40 Ap '71

REFUSE compactors. See Refuse and refuse disposal—Apparatus

REFUSE containers
Bag your trash week brings lasting benefits; Philadelphia. il Am City 86:16 Ap '71
Let's organize about plastic bags. J. Olds. Org Gard & Farm 18:72 F '71
Paper sacks prove profitable; Pasadena, Tex. C. Doyal. il por Am City 86:68-9 N '71
Penguin litter receptacle; Clearwater, Fla. il Am City 86:32 Ja '71
Plastic trash carts to the rescue; Bella Villa, Mo. G. J. Appel. il Am City 86:77-8 Jl '71
Polyethylene scrap bags. il Consumer Bul 54: 33 Ap '71
Revised refuse procedure cuts budget more than 25%; Lynn. Mass. D. L. Phillips. il por Am City 86:66-9 Ap '71

REFUSE containers—*Continued*
Sticker condemns that old garbage can; Atlanta, Ga. il Am City 86:32 S '71
33 cubic yards per trailer load; city ordinance requiring plastic bags in Arlington, Tex. il Am City 86:29 O '71
Trash-box demise improves environment; West Allis, Wis. il Am City 86:8 Ja '71
Two systems for sorting out waste. il Sunset 146:133 Je '71
Wheeled refuse containers please everyone; Atlanta, Ga. R. Hulsey. il Am City 86:113 S '71

REFUSE grinders
Grinding refuse is no experiment; Madison, Wis. E. J. Duszynski. il Am City 86:61-3 S '71
You can install a waste disposer. W. C. Leckey. il Pop Mech 136:168-70+ O '71

REFUSE incinerators
High-performance incinerator; New Orleans. J. Cassreino, and others. il Am City 86:54-7 Ja '71
How to give incinerators half a chance. W. S. Foster. bibliog il Am City 86:41-3 Jl; 76+ Ag '71
Small town incinerator; Durham, N.H. H. Le Clair. il Am City 86:63-4 My '71
What about incinerators, Professor? interview, ed. by B. Foster. E. R. Kaiser. pors Am City 86:70+ D '71
Zero-residue incinerator? Am City 86:8 Ap '71

REFUSE receptacles. See Refuse containers

REGAN, Gerald A.
Future of American investment; address October 8, 1971. Vital Speeches 38:92-6 N 15 '71

REGAN, James D. and others
Xeroderma pigmentosum: a rapid sensitive method for prenatal diagnosis. bibliog il Science 174:147-50 O 8 '71

REGAN (literary character) See Shakespeare, W.—Characters

REGATTAS
Emphasis Olympic! preparation for the 1972 games. E. Horan. il Yachting 129:71+ Je '71
Forty years of madness; frostbiting. J. Sutphen. il Motor B & S 127:56-7 F '71
Gold-plated regatta; Block Island week. il Life 71:38-43 Jl 23 '71
Islands & race weeks; Block Island; Antigua. B. Robinson. il Yachting 130:48-51+ Ag '71
Month in yachting. See issues of Yachting
Offshore in Idaho; racing on Lake Coeur d'Alene. R. S. Larrigan. il Yachting 129:58+ My '71
Regatta results. See occasional issues of Yachting
Taking stock. N. Freeman. il Yachting 130:66-7+ Jl '71

REGENCY furniture. See Furniture, English

REGENERATION (biology)
DNA synthesis and interaction between controlled feeding schedules and partial hepatectomy in rats. B. Barbiroli and V. R. Potter. bibliog il Science 172:738-41 My 14 '71
Killer whale has a nose bob. W. Hartley and E. Hartley. il Sci Digest 70:12-13 Jl '71
Limb regeneration in mammals. il por Sci N 100:322-3 N 13 '71
Neural regeneration: delayed formation of central contacts by insect sensory cells. J. S. Edwards and J. Palka. bibliog il Science 172:591-4 My 7 '71
Portal blood factor as the humoral agent in liver regeneration. B. Fisher and others. bibliog il Science 171:575-7 F 12 '71

REGENSTEIN, Joseph, library. See Chicago. University—Libraries

REGIONAL airlines. See Local service airlines

REGIONAL libraries. See Libraries, Regional

REGIONAL library associations. See Library associations

REGIONAL organizations. See International organizations, Regional

REGIONAL plan association, New York
Office boom jolts the planners. il Bsns W p59+ Ja 23 '71

REGIONAL planning
Air resource management and regional planning. E. J. Croke and J. J. Roberts. il Bul Atom Sci 27:8-12 F '71
Culture of cities, by L. Mumford. Review
New Repub 165:29-30 O 23 '71. H. J. Muller
Rural poverty and the urban crisis, by N. M. Hansen, and French regional planning, by N. M. Hansen. Reviews
New Repub 164:27-9 My 29 '71. G. Gappert
See also
Parks
Rural planning
Shopping centers

New Jersey
Planning in the Pine Barrens. P. M. Tilden. il Nat Parks & Con Mag 45:22-6 Ag '71

New York (state)
Mid-Hudson. A. E. Weintraub and D. J. Knorr. il Cons 25:6-9 F '71
See also
Regional plan association, New York

REGISTER of copyrights (United States) See United States—Copyright office

REGISTER of scientific and technical personnel. See National register of scientific and technical personnel

REGISTRATION of architects. See Architects—Licenses and registration

REGISTRATION of voters. See Voters, Registration of

REGNERY, Henry, company
Regnery, Chicago firm, buys Cowles book company. Pub W 199:49 Mr 8 '71

REGNIER, F. E. and Wilson, E. O.
Chemical communication and propagation in slave-maker ants. bibliog il Science 172:267-9 Ap 16 '71

REGRESSION analysis
Clearer crystal ball? R. Levy. il Duns 98:50-1+ Jl '71
How to get a better forecast. G. G. C. Parker and E. L. Segura. bibliog f il Harvard Bsns R 49:99-109 Mr '71

REGULATORS, Voltage. See Voltage regulators

REGULATORY commissions. See Independent regulatory commissions

REHABILITATION
Miracle worker on campus; bringing hope to handicapped students. P. Bailey. il pors Ebony 26:80-1+ S '71
See also
Vocational rehabilitation

REHABILITATION centers
Center for child development and rehabilitation; University of Oregon. il Arch Rec 149:143-5 Mr '71
Horizon house, a place for readjusting to community living; Philadelphia. il Arch Rec 149:148-9 Mr '71
See also
Hospitals, Psychiatric—Rehabilitation centers
Narcotic addicts—Rehabilitation

REHABILITATION of juvenile delinquents
Way to lick the jail habit; RODEO program. L. Velie. Read Digest 98:142-6 F '71
When children collide with the law. G. Samuels. il N Y Times Mag p44-5+ D 5 '71
See also
Reformatories

REHABILITATION of prisoners. See Prisoners—Rehabilitation

REHBERGER, Gustav
Art of Rock; exhibition. D. Davis. il por Newsweek 77:64+ F 22 '71 *

REHEARSALS, Ballet. See Dance production

REHEARSALS, Operatic. See Operatic production and direction

REHNQUIST, William Hubbs
Excerpt from testimony before the Subcommittee on constitutional rights, March 9, 1971. Cong Digest 50:244+ O '71
What Nixon's court nominees have said about key issues; excerpts from speeches and writings. por U S News 71 42-4 N 8 '71

about
Check and double-check. il pors Newsweek 78:38 N 8 '71 *
Hansel and Gretel. por Time 98:27 N 22 '71 *
How Congress packs it in. il por Newsweek 78:20-1 D 20 '71 *
Is Rehnquist a counterrevolutionary? Nat R 23:1283 N 19 '71 *
Memo from Rehnquist. por Newsweek 78:32+ D 13 '71 *
Myth and William Rehnquist. S. Alsop. Newsweek 78:124 D 6 '71 *
Now that there's a Nixon court. U S News 71:18 D 20 '71 *
Powell, Rehnquist and the Court. America 125:387-8 N 13 '71 *
President's two nominees. il pors Time 98:18-19 N 1 '71 *
Rehnquist: a lawyer's lawyer. il por Newsweek 78:18-19 N 1 '71 *
Rehnquist fight. Nat R 23:1338-9 D 3 '71 *
Rehnquist file. il por Newsweek 78:31-2 N 15 '71 *
Remaking the Supreme court. Nixon sets a pattern. il pors U S News 71:15-17 N 1 '71 *
TRB from Washington. New Repub 165:6 N 6 '71 *
Up-to-date conservative. P. Steinfels. Commonweal 95:174 N 19 '71 *

REIBSTEIN, Janet
Pioneer in Peru. il pors Dance Mag 45:68-9 F '71

REICE, Sylvie
Reel winner. il Am Home 74:58+ N '71

REICH, Alan A.
Citizen diplomacy; a challenge to Americans; address, March 25, 1971. Dept State Bul 64: 706-8 My 31 '71

REICH, Bernard
Israel's quest for security. bibliog f Cur Hist 62:1-5+ Ja '72

REICH, Charles A.
Reflections. New Yorker 47:52-7 Je 19 '71
—and Carroll, Douglas, 3d
After the gold rush. Nat Parks & Con Mag 45:4-5 Ap '71

about

I-less in Gaza; the Greening of Charles A. Reich. L. E. Sissman. Atlan 227:26+ Je '71 *
Yale is no. 1 with the promoter & the idol. P. Wilkes. il pors Look 35:60-2 Ap 6 '71 *

REICH, David L.
Independent study project at Dallas. il por Wilson Lib Bul 46:441-2 Ja '72

REICH, Kenneth
Postscript to the Medina trial. Nation 213: 433-5 N 1 '71

REICH, Seymour
Unique stereo decoder. il Pop Electr 35: 53-5+ O '71

REICH, Wilhelm
Gospel of orgasm. il por Time 97:54-5 My 10 '71 *
Wilhelm Reich: the psychoanalyst as revolutionary. D. Elkind. il pors N Y Times Mag p25-7+ Ap 18 '71; Discussion. p36+ My 16 '71 *
Wilhelm Reich's theory: ethical implications. M. B. Zweig. Am Imago 28:268-86 Fall '71 *

REICHERT, Philip
Engineers & doctors, a new partnership. Radio-Electr 42:39 F '71

REICHL, Ernst
Graphic design in Israel. il Pub W 199:48-9 Je 7 '71

REICHLEY, A. James
Muskie's problem is how to keep being himself. il por Fortune 83:76-9+ Je '71
Our critical shortage of leadership. il Fortune 84:88-93+ S '71
That elusive political majority. il por Fortune 83:68-73+ Mr '71

REICHLIN, Seymour. See Mitnick, M. jt. auth.

REID, Alastair
Flying time; poem. New Yorker 47:64 Ag 7 '71
Tidings; poem. New Yorker 46:30 F 6 '71

REID, Charles
Charles Reid: the direct approach. C. M. Daugherty. il por Am Artist 35:44-9+ D '71 *

REID, Kenneth H.
Periodical cicada: mechanism of sound production. bibliog il Science 172:949-51 My 28 '71

REID, Morgan
U.S. corporation in Canada. por Nations Bsns 59:87 Ap '71

REID, P. Nelson
Financing higher education in Ohio. New Repub 164:13-14 Je 12 '71

REID, Stephen
Desdemona's guilt. bibliog Am Imago 27: 245-62 Fall '70
In defense of Goneril and Regan. bibliog Am Imago 27:226-44 Fall '70
Winter's tale. bibliog Am Imago 27:263-78 Fall '70

REID, Thomas R. 3d
Presumption of guilt. New Repub 164:15-16 Ja 16 '71

REID, Virginia M.
NCTE councilletter. Engl J 60:390-1 Mr '71

REID, W. Stanford
Preaching is social action. Chr Today 15:10-11 Je 4 '71

REIDEL, Carl H.
Christianity and the environmental crisis; interview. Chr Today 15:4-8 Ap 23 '71

REIF, Rita
Home (cont) il N Y Times Mag p54-5 Ja 24; 54-5 F 28; 82-3 Mr 28; 78-9 My 2; 86-7 Je 6 '71
Up and down house. il N Y Times Mag p90-1 N 14 '71

REIGER, George W.
Honeymoon on a houseboat. il Pop Mech 135: 102-5+ F '71

REILLY, Edgar M. jr
Rat! Friend, foe and unwanted companion. il Cons 26:22-5 O '71

REILLY, John H.
Drama. Chr Cent 88:603-4 My 12 '71

REIMER, Everett
Does the shoe fit? il America 124:69-70 Ja 23 '71

REIMER, Milton K.
Areas of concern for comprehensive community colleges. bibliog f Sch & Soc 99: 47-9 Ja '71
Critique of sensitivity training. bibliog Sch & Soc 99:356-7 O '71

REIN, Bert W.
Current policy problems in international aviation; address. November 17, 1970. Dept State Bul 64:15-18 Ja 4 '71

REINBOLD, James S.
Family portrait; story. Esquire 75:96-7 Mr '71
Mr Staal; story. Esquire 76:118-19 N '71

REINDEER
Reaction of reindeer to obstructions and disturbances. D. R. Klein. bibliog il Science 173:393-8 Jl 30 '71
See also
Cookery—Game
REINDEER on the roof; drama. See Hark, M. and McQueen, N.

REINEMER, Vic. See Metcalf, L. jt. auth.

REINERT, Jeanne
What your sense of time tells about you. il Sci Digest 69:8-12 Je '71

REINFELDER, Al
Menhaden system. il Field & S 75:194-7+ Ap '71

REINFORCEMENT (psychology)
Signaled reinforcing brain stimulation facilitates operant behavior under schedules of intermittent reinforcement. M. B. Cantor. bibliog il Science 174:610-13 N 5 '71
See also
Reward (psychology)

REINHARDT, Richard
Nice piece of real estate. il Am Heritage 23:42-7+ D '71

REINHART, Kenneth A. See Brown, A. E. jt. auth.

REINSTATEMENT of employees. See Employees—Reinstatement

REIS, Herbert
U.N. General assembly calls for study to further the work of the International court of justice; statement. November 18, 1970. Dept State Bul 64:121 Ja 25 '71

REIS, Lois
1971 short story contest. Writers Digest 51:31-2 O '71

REISCHAUER, Edwin Oldfather
Don't take Japan for granted; interview. ed. by E. Klein. il Newsweek 78:36 O 4 '71
Fateful triangle: the United States, Japan and China. il N Y Times Mag p 12-13+ S 19 '71
Yes to China must not be no to Japan. por Life 71:4 S 10 '71

REISE, Barbara
Presenting Gilbert & George, the living sculptures. il pors Art N 70:62-5+ N '71

REISER, Martin. See Sokol, R. J. jt. auth.

REISFIELD, R. A. and others
Salt extraction of soluble HL-A antigens. bibliog il Science 172:1134-6 Je 11 '71

REISING, R. W.
Baseball, film, and poetry. Clear House 45: 317-18 Ja '71

REISMAN, John M.
Definition of psychotherapy. bibliog Ment Hy 55:413-17 Jl '71

REISS, Albert, jr
Plan to keep our police honest. il Todays Health 49:70-1 N '71

REISS, James
¿Habla usted espanol? poem. Sat R 54:26 O 2 '71
Remember me? poem. Sat R Ap 3 '71

REISSUES of phonograph records. See Phonograph records—Reissues

REITZ, Donald
Conversation with Don Reitz and Bruce Breckenridge; ed. by C. Brawer. il pors Ceram Mo 19:17-19 Mr '71

about

Don Reitz. C. C. Brawer. pors Ceram Mo 19:19-26 D '71 *

REJNIS, Ruth
Hot tips on heating your home. Read Digest 99:21-2 N '71

REJUVENATION
Youth pill. P. M. McGrady, jr. il Ladies Home J 88:72-4+ Jl '71

RELATIVISM. See Relativity

RELATIVITY
Relativism in organizations. G. F. F. Lombard. bibliog f Harvard Bsns R 49:55-65 Mr '71

RELATIVITY (physics)
Arguments concerning relativity and cosmology. O. Klein. bibliog il Science 171:339-45 Ja 29 '71
Einstein theory appears valid. Chem 44:24-5 My '71
Einstein theory upheld. Space World H-4-88:24 Ap '71
Question of time; round-the-world flight to test Albert Einstein's controversial clock paradox. il pors Time 98:63 O 18 '71
Relativity wins again. Sci Digest 71:23-4 Ja '72
Resolution of the clock paradox. M. Sachs. bibliog il Phys Today 24:23-9 S '71
See also
Field theory (physics)
Gravity waves
Quantum theory

Anecdotes, facetiae, satire, etc.
Troubled romance of little Mary Mass and speedy Edward Energy. F. S. Levine. il Chem 44:32 My '71

RELAXATION
How to relax without pills. L. A. Knight, jr. Read Digest 98:139-41 F '71
How to unwind; symposium. il House & Gard 139:116-17+ Ap '71
See also
Hydrotherapy

RELAXATION oscillators. See Oscillators

RELIABILITY (engineering)
See also
Computers—Reliability

RELIABILITY of products. See Quality of products

RELIANCE electric company
Good gambles can also lose. il Forbes 108:32-3 N 15 '71

RELICS and reliquaries
See also
Holy Shroud

RELIEF (sculpture)
Cardboard relief. J. Fasciott. il Sch Arts 70:46 Je '71
Panels of clay applique. M. Rothenberg. il Design 72:26-8 mid-Sum '71

RELIEF work
See also
Food relief
International rescue committee
Medical relief work
Vietnamese war, 1957- —Relief work

RELIGION
Second chance for the neo-orthodox. J. P. Crossley, jr. Chr Cent 88:1048-51 S 8 '71
Wayside adjustments. E. M. Blaiklock. Chr Today 15:9 Je 4 '71
See also
Atheism
Children—Religion
Christianity
Faith
God
Humanism
Modernism
Mysticism
Paganism
Prayer
Psychiatry and religion
Public schools and religion
Religious education
Revivals
Satanism
Sects
Secularism
Sin
Spirituality
Television programs—Religious programs
Women and religion
Worship
Youth—Religion
also subhead Religious institutions and affairs under names of countries, states, cities, etc. e.g. United States—Religious institutions and affairs

Bibliography
Books in review. See issues of Christianity today
Books to come (cont) Library J 96:2677+; 97:91+ S 1 '71. Ja 1 '72
Essential(?) religious books. Chr Cent 88:543 Ap 28 '71
Review of books. Chr Cent 88:1386-8+ N 24 '71

Spring religious books: surprising variety and riches. L. M. Scribner. Chr Cent 88:529-31 Ap 28 '71
Spring religious highspots; March through August. il Pub W 199:37-48 Mr 8 '71
See also
Catholic literature—Bibliography

Periodicals
See Religious newspapers and periodicals

Philosophy
See also
Philosophy and religion

Study and teaching
Boom in religion studies; graduate programs. por Time 98:83-4 O 18 '71

RELIGION, Comparative. See Religions
RELIGION and art. See Art and religion
RELIGION and communism. See Communism and religion

RELIGION and ecology
Christianity and the environmental crisis; interview; with editorial comment. C. H. Reidel. Chr Today 15:4-8, 26-7 Ap 23 '71
Ecological challenge to Christian ethics. J. C. Livingston. il Chr Cent 88:1409-12 D 1 '71
Ecology, an American heresy? J. V. Schall. America 124:308-11 Mr 27 '71
Ecology and apocalypse. W. L. Bullock. Chr Today 15:20-1+ Ap 23 '71
Is ecology heresy? il Time 98:29-30 Ag 23 '71
Saving the earth: a challenge to our religious traditions. E. B. Fiske. il Redbook 137:78+ Je '71

RELIGION and education. See Public schools and religion
RELIGION and labor. See Church and labor
RELIGION and language
Overcoming Babel. G. M. Cowan. Chr Today 15:8-10 Jl 16 '71
Some comments on linguistics; or, How to overcome the world with a few trick phrases. D. F. Cox. Chr Cent 88:1498-9 D 22 '71

RELIGION and law
Christianity and criminality. J. B. Shepherd. il Chr Cent 88:796-8 Je 30 '71
RELIGION and magic. See Christianity and magic
RELIGION and medicine. See Medicine and religion
RELIGION and music
Glide to glory; Glide memorial united Methodist church. L. Robinson. il por Ebony 26:44-6+ Jl '71
RELIGION and philosophy. See Philosophy and religion
RELIGION and science
More on Teilhard's spirituality. D. A. Drennen. America 124:413-14 Ap 17 '71
New scientific thought: data and dogma as compatible. L. J. Crabb, jr. Chr Today 15:7-8 Mr 12 '71
Sir Alister Hardy: science and religious experiences. D. Cohen. il por Sci Digest 70:18-23 S '71
Spirit: who will make the choices of life and death? il Time 97:48+ Ap 19 '71
See also
Evolution
Religion and technology
RELIGION and sex. See Sex and religion
RELIGION and social problems. See Church and social problems
RELIGION and technology
It takes two for dialogue; Interpretation and dialogue between the science-technology community and the church. E. M. Hawk. Chr Cent 88:1418-20 D 1 '71
Primitivism or technocracy: must we choose? D. J. Elwood. il Chr Cent 88:1413-18 D 1 '71
RELIGION and war. See War and religion
RELIGION editors. See Editors and editing
RELIGION in fiction. See Religion in literature
RELIGION in literature
Mr Sammler and the God of Our fathers. J. W. Sire. Chr Today 15:6-9 Je 4 '71
See also
Mysticism
RELIGION in public schools. See Public schools and religion
RELIGIONS
Historical notes on the (in)comparable Christ. E. M. Yamauchi. il Chr Today 16:7-11 O 22 '71

RELIGIONS—*Continued*
New religions, by J. Needleman. Review
    Commonweal 94:386-7 Jl 23 '71. M. Zeik
See also
Bahaism
Buddha and Buddhism
Christianity and other religions
Confucius and Confucianism
Cults
Gnosticism
Indians of North America—Religion and mythology
RELIGIOUS advertising
Packaging Jesus; TV campaign. R. L. Shayon.
    Sat R 54:78 Mr 13 '71

Anecdotes, facetiae, satire, etc.
Killed with the Holy Ghost. Chr Cent 88: 939 Ag 4 '71
RELIGIOUS architecture. See Church architecture
RELIGIOUS art. See Christian art and symbolism
RELIGIOUS art objects See Religious articles
RELIGIOUS articles
Treasure on earth; Heenan on sale of valuable ornaments. T. Beeson. Chr Cent 88: 1405-6 D 1 '71
RELIGIOUS books. See Religious literature
RELIGIOUS ceremonies. See Rites and ceremonies
RELIGIOUS conferences
Beyond sexual politics; conference of religious feminists at Graymoor, N.Y. D. Grumbach.
    Commonweal 95:292-3 D 24 '71
CICOP: 1971. America 124:84-5 Ja 30 '71
Can evangelicals reform Methodism? Convocation of United Methodists for evangelical Christianity. J. L. Adams. Chr Today 15:35-6 Ag 6 '71
Catholics get the spirit; International conference on the charismatic renewal in the Catholic church. E. E. Plowman. il Chr Today 15:31-2 Jl 16 '71
Change of mood at CICOP. J. McLellan. Commonweal 93:508-10 F 26 '71
Collision with reality; Institute for advanced Christian studies conference. C. F. H. Henry. Chr Today 16:37-8 D 3 '71
Future theology: hope or suffering? Hope and the future of man conference. D. J. Turner. Chr Today 16:42+ N 5 '71
Jesus is right on: Billy Graham crusade school of evangelism. Chr Today 15:31 Ag 27 '71
Shattering stereotypes; United Methodist congress on evangelism. R. Chandler. Chr Today 15:32 Ja 29 '71
Weekend of hope; Hope and the future of man. L. J. O'Donovan. America 125:319-21 O 23 '71
Writing on the wall: Colonnese go home; Catholic inter-American cooperation program; with editorial comment. G. Maceoin. Commonweal 94:492-3 S 24 '71
See also
Conference of major superiors of men
Methodist world conference
World conference of religion for peace
World council of churches

Australia
Australian evangelicals up from Down Under; National evangelical congress of Australia. L. Morris. Chr Today 16:52+ O 8 '71

Europe
CEC builds bridges of understanding. F. Murphy. Chr Cent 88:758 Je 16 '71

Europe, Western
European conference on evangelism listens to youth delegates. T. Cosmades. Chr Cent 88:1241-2+ O 20 '71
European congress: getting to know you; with editorial comment. J. J. Van Capelleveen. il Chr Today 15:39, 40-1 S 24 '71

Germany (Federal Republic)
Christian television festival: making ultimate concern visual. M. Furlong. Chr Cent 88: 779-80 Je 23 '71

Great Britain
Missionary mandate at home and abroad; Assembly of evangelicals in London. J. D. Douglas. Chr Today 15:32+ Je 4 '71
Taming of the evangelicals; National assembly of evangelicals. T. Beeson. Chr Cent 88:680-1 Je 2 '71

Israel
Bible prophecy in the prophets' city. D. L. Baker. Chr Today 15:29-30 Jl 16 '71
Lamp of prophecy; the Jerusalem conference on Biblical prophecy. C. F. H. Henry. Chr Today 15:34-5 Ap 9 '71
Prophetic hope; Jerusalem conference on biblical prophecy. C. F. H. Henry. Chr Today 15:40-1 S 10 '71
Prophets in Jerusalem; conference on biblical prophecy. il Newsweek 77:62 Je 28 '71

Italy
Catechetical congress cites problems. Chr Cent 88:1223 O 20 '71
Getting it together: the International catechetical congress. C. J. Pfeifer. America 125:287-9 O 16 '71

Kenya
See also
Anglican consultative council

Latin America
Latin America's own work corps: 180,000 religious; Confederation of Latin American religious. J. F. Talbot. il America 124:343-4 Ap 3 '71
RELIGIOUS contemplation. See Meditation
RELIGIOUS cooperation
Jewish Lent; rabbis leading Christians in observing Lent. Chr Cent 88:331 Mr 17 '71
Key 73: a continental call. D. Kucharsky. il Chr Today 16:38 N 19 '71
Key 73: on the bridge together. E. E. Plowman. Chr Today 15:32 Je 18 '71
Women of Belfast; women together movement. E. McCallion. il America 125:453-6 N 27 '71
RELIGIOUS denominations. See Sects
RELIGIOUS discrimination in employment. See Discrimination in employment
RELIGIOUS education
Christian educationists parley in Peru: World council of Christian education. S. Bliss. Chr Cent 88:968 Ag 18 '71
Curriculum scandal. I. V. Cully. Chr Cent 88:879-82 Jl 21 '71; Discussion. 88:1146-7, 1300-2 S 29, N 3 '71
Design for religion: toward ecumenical education, by G. Moran. Review
    America 125:43 Jl 24 '71. B. S. Gresh
    Commonweal 94:146-9 Ap 16 '71. G. S. Sloyan
Religious education-community. G. Moran. America 124:86-9 Ja 30 '71
See also
Catechetics
Catholic church—Education
Church colleges
Moral education
Theological education
RELIGIOUS experience. See Experience (religion)
RELIGIOUS faith. See Faith
RELIGIOUS history. See Church history
RELIGIOUS institutions and affairs
Worldaround. See issues of Christian century continuing New Christian
    See also subhead Religious institutions and affairs under names of countries, states, etc. e.g. Canada—Religious institutions and affairs
RELIGIOUS intermarriages. See Marriages, Mixed
RELIGIOUS Journalism. See Journalism, Religious
RELIGIOUS life. See Christian life
RELIGIOUS literature
Boring heresy. T. Beeson. Chr Cent 88:738 Je 16 '71
Literary style in religious writing. C. D. Linton. Chr Today 15:5-6+ Je 18; 8-12 Jl 2 '71
Religion and the scriptures, today. A. W. Swarthout. bibliog il por Wilson Lib Bul 45: 664-73 Mr '71
Religious literature of the West, ed. by J. R. Whitney and W. Howe. Review
    Chr Cent 88:1093 S 15 '71. M. E. Marty
    See also
Booksellers and bookselling—Religious literature
Jewish literature
Publishers and publishing—Religious literature
Religion—Bibliography
RELIGIOUS music. See Church music
RELIGIOUS news
Top '71 religious news: world revival. R. Chandler. Chr Today 16:40-1 Ja 7 '72
    See also
Church and the press

RELIGIOUS newspapers and periodicals
Target/Lengo: open window on East Africa.
K. Strong. Chr Cent 88:1451-2 D 8 '71
See also
Christian century (periodical)
Journalism, Religious
Worldview (periodical)
RELIGIOUS orders
Friars' new creation. Chr Cent 88:1157 O 6
'71
Renewal in the church: two mentalities in
conflict; pressure from the Congregation
for religious. T. E. Clarke. America 124:
234-7 Mr 6 '71; Discussion. 124:459-61 My 1
'71
Vanishing religious order and the new hu-
man community. R. Ruether. Chr Cent 88:
425-9 Ap 7 '71
What are religious: avant-garde or civil
servants? T. E. Clarke. America 125:232-3
O 2 '71
See also
Carmelites
Conference of major superiors of men
Jesuits
Sisterhoods
RELIGIOUS poetry
Holy Mr Herbert. E. E. Ericson, jr. Chr To-
day 15:7-8+ S 10 '71
RELIGIOUS psychology. See Psychology,
Religious
RELIGIOUS radio programs. See Radio broad-
casting—Religious programs
RELIGIOUS records. See Phonograph records—
Religious records
RELIGIOUS revivals. See Revivals
RELIGIOUS rites and ceremonies. See Rites
and ceremonies
RELIGIOUS schools. See Catholic schools;
Church schools
RELIGIOUS services. See Church services
RELIGIOUS systems data center
Researching the parables. P. Steinfels. Com-
monweal 94:230 My 14 '71
RELIGIOUS thought
See also
Puritanism
RELIGIOUS vocation. See Vocation in reli-
gion
RELISHES. See Pickles and relishes
RELOCATION of Japanese Americans. See
World war, 1939-1945—Evacuation of ci-
vilians
RELOCATION of tenants. See Housing proj-
ects—Relocation of tenants
REMAK, Joachim
Law and order, said Hitler, or, did he? por
Commonweal 94:429-32 Ag 20 '71
REMARRIAGE
American way of marriage: remarriage. B.
Rollin. Look 35:62+ S 21 '71
Here comes the bride: again. S. Nirenberg.
House B 113:114-15 O '71
Second marriages. E. Havemann. il Ladies
Home J 88:106+ My '71
Seven on a honeymoon. G. U. Stark. il Par-
ents Mag 46:445+ My '71
Why get married? H. Alpert. Har Yrs 11:6-
10+ Ap '71
REMBAR, Charles
Paper victory: the United States v. the New
York times and the Washington post. Atlan
228:61-6 N; 46+ D '71

about

Threats to intellectual freedom; address, June
1971. E. T. Moore. il por Library J 96:3563-
7 N 1 '71; Same abr. with title Rise of a
new censorship? Cur 135:3-8 D '71 *
REMEDIAL reading. See Reading—Remedial
teaching
REMEDIAL teaching
See also
English language—Remedial teaching
Reading—Remedial teaching
REMEMBRANCE of things future; story. See
Cousins, M.
REMENICK, Seymour
Seymour Remenick: a quiet voice. H. C.
Pitz. il por Am Artist 35:44-9+ Ag '71 *
REMINGTON, Frank J.
Role of the Supreme court. bibliog f Cur
Hist 60:353-6+ Je '71
REMINGTON rifles. See Rifles
REMINISCENCE
Growing up in Newport; excerpts from Al-
pha omega. W. T. Scott. il Am Heritage
22:54-7+ Ag '71
I won't look back. A. S. Zuffa. Har Yrs 11:
42-3 S '71

Little Johnny slept here. C. M. Williams.
Read Digest 98:82-5 F '71
Presenting the past. A. Vivante. Writer 84:
9-11 My '71
Summer's magical music. A. Sherman. Read
Digest 99:58-60 Jl '71
REMODELED automobile engines. See Auto-
mobile engines
REMODELED automobiles. See Automobiles,
Remodeled
REMODELED buildings. See Buildings, Re-
modeled
REMODELED houses. See Houses, Remodeled
REMODELED motor trucks. See Motor trucks,
Remodeled
REMODELING (architecture)
See also
Apartments, Remodeled
Houses, Remodeled
Office buildings, Remodeled
REMOTE control
Low-voltage remote power control; two-way
switching system. N. Johnson. il Pop
Electr 35:69-70+ Jl '71
See also
High fidelity sound systems—Control
Photoelectric cells—Control use
Television receivers—Control
REMOTE sensing systems
Advanced sensors used to survey Algeria. il
Aviation W 94:42 Mr 15 '71
Archeological methodology and remote sens-
ing. G. J. Gumerman and T. R. Lyons.
bibliog il Science 172:126-32 Ap 9 '71
CARETS: remote sensing for environmental
studies. il Sci N 99:413-14 Je 19 '71
Conference of remote sensing of the Chesa-
peake Bay. Space World H-6-90:49-50 Je '71
How we're reading nature's secrets from the
sky. J. R. Berry. il Pop Mech 136:68-72 S
'71
Multispectral scanner promising. K. J. Stein.
il Aviation W 94:39-41 My 24 '71
Scanner to tell if mother earth is sick or
well. il Space World H-10-94:47-8 O '71
Science's eye on the universe; head-coupled
television systems. R. E. Packer. il Sci
Digest 69:67-72 F '71
Scientific spy eyes for NASA. il Sci N 99:248
Ap 10 '71
Sharper eyes seek the world's resources. il
Bsns W p54-5 N 27 '71
War toys for adults. R. Barkan. New Repub
165:7-8 D 11 '71
See also
Infrared rays—Measurement use
REMOTE switches. See Electric switches
REMSBERG, Bonnie. See Remsberg, C. jt. auth.
REMSBERG, Charles, and Remsberg, Bonnie
5 who fight pollution. pors Seventeen 30:128-
9+ Ap '71
One woman's war against poverty. il por
Good H 173:91+ O '71
Stormy aftermath of abortion reform. Good H
172:86-7+ F '71
RENAISSANCE
See also
Humanism
RENAISSANCE pleasure faire. See Festivals—
California
RENAISSANCE spa, Nassau. See Health
resorts, watering places, etc.
RENAL diseases. See Kidneys—Diseases
RENAL hypertension. See Hypertension
RENAUD, Madeleine
Letter from Paris. Genêt. New Yorker 47:91-2
F 27 '71 *
RENAULT, Pierre F. and others
Marihuana: standardized smoke administra-
tion and dose effect curves on heart rate
in humans. bibliog il Science 174:589-91 N 5
'71
RENAULT (automobile) See Automobiles, For-
eign
RENAULT automobile company. See Automo-
bile industry—France
RENDEZVOUS (space) See Orbital rendezvous
(space flight)
RENÉ, Denise
Denise undaunted. D. Davis. il por Newsweek
78:81-2 Jl 19 '71 *
RENEGOTIATION of government contracts.
See Contracts, Government—Renegotiation
RENEWAL of copyright. See Copyright—
Duration
RENEWAL of the church. See Church renewal
RENFREW, Colin
Carbon 14 and the prehistory of Europe;
with biographical sketch. il Sci Am 225:12,
63-70+ bibliog(p 120) O '71

about

Pyramids from France? il Newsweek 77:50
Ap 5 '71 *
Resetting the carbon clock. il por Time 98:64
N 29 '71 *

RENIN
Renin secretion: an anatomical basis for tubular control; juxtaglomerular apparatus. L. Barajas. bibliog il Science 172:485-7 Ap 30 '71

RENNER, Bruce
Mending; poem. Esquire 76:32 Jl '71

RENNER, Frederic G.
Schoolboy's sketchbook. il por Am Heritage 22:70-1 O '71

RENNER, Tom
Death of a mob family. Read Digest 98:175-6+ My '71

RENNIE, Drummond
Doctorcito, don't let them abandon us. il por Todays Health 49:23-4+ My '71

RENO, Nev.
Description
Finding the real Reno. P. Zauner. il Travel 136:56-9+ D '71

Recreation
Dream came true; junior ski program. G. A. Broten and G. R. Twardokens. il Parks & Rec 6:111+ Ja '71

RENO national championship air races. See Airplane racing

RENOUARD, Yves
Yves Renouard and the economic history of the middle ages. D. Herlihy. Am Hist R 76:127-31 F '71 •

RENSBERGER, Boyce
When Americans are a swallow away from death; 1971. il Todays Health 49:40-3+ S '71

RENSHAW, C. Jr
(ed) See Buck, P. S. Visit with Pearl Buck

RENT
Rent boosts, the word on how much. U S News 72:30 Ja 3 '72
Why rents will rise still higher. il Changing T 25:29-30 F '71
See also
Landlord and tenant
Leases

RENT laws
New York: eviction notice; abolition of rent control. Newsweek 77:117 Je 7 '71

RENTED clothes. See Clothing and dress—Renting

RENTING of automobiles. See Automobiles—Leasing and renting

RENTING of motor trucks. See Motor trucks—Leasing and renting

RENTING of moving pictures. See Moving pictures—Renting

RENTMEESTER, Co
Southwest bakes in a ruinous drought; photographs. Life 70:26-31 Je 4 '71

REORGANIZATION, Congressional. See United States—Congress—Reorganization

REPAIR men. See Repairmen

REPAIR shops
See also
Automobile service stations

REPAIRING
Rising anger over costly and slipshod services. il U S News 70:37-9 Ap 5 '71
See also subheads Repairing, and Maintenance and repair under various subjects, e.g. Roofs—Maintenance and repair

REPAIRMEN
Something this country needs: lots of good repairmen. il Changing T 25:21-3 Ap '71

REPARATION
Public pay for crime victims: an idea that is spreading. il U S News 70:40-2 Ap 5 '71
When crime victims are paid for losses. Good H 172:160 F '71
See also
Negroes—Reparations

REPEATING rifles. See Rifles

REPELLENTS, Insect. See Insect baits and repellents

REPENTANCE
Repentance as a church priority. V. Havner. Chr Today 15:12+ Mr 12 '71

REPETITION (rhetoric)
Importance of being repetitious. H. R. Struck. Engl J 60:474-8+ Ap '71

REPLANSKY, Naomi
Weeping sea-beast; poem. Nation 212:668 My 24 '71

REPORTERS and reporting
Bread and roses too, by J. Newfield. Review Commonweal 95:110-13 O 29 '71. R. Whitehead, jr
Covering the Court; Supreme court's press corps. Newsweek 78:127-8 O 18 '71
Freedoms to write and read and be informed; E. Caldwell case. R. H. Smith. Pub W 200: 29 D 13 '71
Insight's latest headlines; a select team on London's Sunday times. il Time 98:87 N 1 '71

Motor monk; R. W. Irvin. il por Newsweek 78:54 D 27 '71
Operate your own wire service for a dime. J. McLendon. Writers Digest 51:35 N '71
Ouster at the U.N; Taiwan reporters excluded. Time 99:50 Ja 3 '72
Pirates win; then jubilant celebration or mass brawl? il Sr Schol 99:15-16 N 15 '71
What it's like to be a newspaper reporter. il Changing T 26:19-21 Ja '72
What riot? contrasting news reports of Pittsburgh's post-World series victory celebration. il Newsweek 78:82 N 1 '71
See also
Confidential communications—Press
Crime and the press
Environmental news
Foreign correspondents
Government and the press
Journalists
National press club
Negro journalists
News
Newspaper court reporting
Radio broadcasting—Sports
Science news
Television broadcasting—News
Vietnamese war, 1957- —Censorship
War correspondents
Women as foreign correspondents
Women as journalists
Women as reporters

REPORTS
See also
Corporation reports
Library reports

Anecdotes, facetiae, satire, etc.
Annual report, Horace C. Smith family, inc. il Changing T 26:24 Ja 72

REPOTTING of plants. See Plants, Potted

REPRESENTATIVE government and representation
See also
Democracy
Referendum

REPRINTS. See Books—Reprints

REPRODUCTION
How the fetus develops. E. B. Connell. por Redbook 137:10+ Ag '71
Nest predation affecting the breeding season of the clay-colored robin, a tropical song bird. E. S. Morton. bibliog il Science 171:920-1 Mr 5 '71
See also
Fertility, Human
Fetus
Ovulation
Parthenogenesis
Sex determination and control
Spontaneous generation

Research
Regulation of mammalian reproduction; report of meeting. R. Crozier. Science 174: 1157-9 D 10 '71

REPRODUCTION, Asexual
See also
Clones (biology)

REPRODUCTIONS of works of art
See also
Multiple art

REPTILES
See also
Alligators
Lizards
Nervous system—Reptiles
Snakes
Turtles

REPTILES, Fossil
See also
Dinosaurs

REPUBLIC corporation
New president to repair Republic. pors Bsns W p40+ F 13 '71

REPUBLIC steel corporation
How a new steel emerged from a wreck. T. F. Patton. il por Nations Bsns 59:84-5 Ja '71

REPUBLICAN party
Around city hall. A. Logan. New Yorker 47:64-70 Ag 21 '71
As Republicans prepare for '72 campaign. il U S News 70:14-16 F 1 '71
Conversion of John Lindsay. il pors Time 98:7-9 Ag 23 '71
Disenchanted; Republicans denounce R. Nixon. il Newsweek 78:35+ N 8 '71
End of liberalism; New York state. P. Hoffman. Nation 212:457-61 Ap 12 '71
Enduring Republican minority. V. Fingerhut. New Repub 165:18-20 S 11 '71
Exit Lindsay. W. F. Buckley, jr. Nat R 23: 1010-11 S 10 '71

REPUBLICAN party—*Continued*
Forging a majority, by M. F. Holt. Review
  Trans-Action 8:104-6 N '70. C. O. Jones
G.O.P.'s strange appeal to business. R. D. Corwin and L. Gray. il Fortune 84:127-8 Jl '71
Happiness at Ripon. Nat R 23:1011 S 10 '71
Lindsay: a switch in time? il pors Newsweek 78:15-16+ Ag 23 '71
Looking ahead: McCloskey. Nat R 23:792 Jl 27 '71
McCloskey's rebellion. Nation 212:484-5 Ap 19 '71
Monday master; National committee's weekly. por Time 98:48 S 13 '71
1964 and 1972. W. F. Buckley, jr. Nat R 23:1374-5 D 3 '71
Politics: the G.O.P. gears for '72. il Time 98:18-19 N 22 '71
President dumping. P. R. Wieck. New Repub 164:11-14 Ap 24 '71
Rebel Republican; McCloskey in motion. R. Kuttner. Commonweal 94:380-2 Jl 23 '71
Right wing v. Nixon. il Time 98:12-13 Ag 16 '71
Southern strategy, by R. Murphy and H. Gulliver. Review
  Bsns W p7+ Ag 7 '71. R. Smith
Two parties and two prospects. M. McGrory. America 125:549 D 25 '71
  See also
National conventions, Republican
REPURCHASE of stocks. See Stocks—Repurchase
REQUIEMS
  See also
Phonograph records—Requiems
RESCUE apparatus. See Life saving equipment
RESCUE at sea. See Survival after airplane accidents, shipwrecks, etc.
RESCUE beacons. See Radio beacons
RESCUE work
Ordeal on Mt Kenya. L. Elliott. il Read Digest 99:92-7 S '71
Reporter at large; Alpine accidents and rescues. J. Bernstein. New Yorker 47:118-32+ O 30 '71
  See also
Artificial satellites—Use in rescue work
Space rescue work
Survival after airplane accidents, shipwrecks, etc.
Underwater rescue work
RESEARCH
Brave new world (title varies) D. M. Rorvik. Esquire 75:66 Ap; 76:26 Ag '71
Dictation to science by laymen; excerpt from 1946 Carnegie institution of Washington year book. V. Bush. Science 174:11 O 1 '71
Student attitudes on science; summary of interviews. il Bul Atom Sci 27:31-5 My '71
TV tapes as research materials; with text of bill. H. H. Baker. Am Lib 2:951-2 O '71
  See also
Artificial satellites—Use in research
Communication in science
Experimental design
Libraries and research
National research council
  also Atmospheric research; Cancer research; and similar headings

Anecdotes, facetiae, satire, etc.
Great race: virus find awakens hope for sufferers; Wagonband theory of nobelogenesis. N. Wade. Science 174:1112 D 10 '71

Federal aid
Brains on the shelf. il Nations Bsns 59:66-9 My '71
Grant K6-MH-21775; B. F. Skinner's project. Nation 214:37 Ja 10 '72
Matter of perspective. H. Newell. Science 172:331 Ap 23 '71
Science in America: we're still in first place, but—; interview. P. Handler. il pors U S News 70:30-4 Ja 18 '71
Scientific starvation today; a second-rate nation tomorrow; address, April 14, 1971. R. Anderson. Vital Speeches 37:502-5 Je 1 '71; Excerpts. Aviation W 94:9 My 17 '71
To be first in everything. il Sci N 99:93-4 F 6 '71

China (People's Republic)
Revolution in China's laboratories. il Bsns W p88-9 Ag 21 '71

Japan
Flaw in Japan's boom. il Bsns W p42-3 Jl 10 '71

Philippines
Brain drain in the Philippines; a case study. A. Muriel; reply. M. J. Moravcsik. Bul Atom Sci 27:36 F '71

Russia
Russian press reports on Soviet science. I. Agnew. See issues of Science digest
  See also
Atomic research—Russia

United States
Another voice raised. C. A. Anderson. Aviation W 95:7 O 18 '71
Science in America: we're still in first place, but—; interview. P. Handler. il pors U S News 70:30-4 Ja 18 '71
Senseless war on science. L. Lessing. il Fortune 83:88-91+ Mr '71
U.S. agencies seek concepts to spur R&D. W. H. Gregory. il Aviation W 95:14-16 Ag 30 '71
Unrealistic demands on science and medicine. P. H. Abelson. Science 172:989 Je 4 '71
  See also
Colleges and universities—Research
Government research
Research institutions
United States—National science foundation
RESEARCH, Freedom of. See Science, Freedom of
RESEARCH and development contracts
  See also
Patents and government-developed inventions
RESEARCH and industry. See Industrial research
RESEARCH applied to national needs program. See United States—National science foundation
RESEARCH-Cottrell, inc.
Can pollution pay off? il Bsns W p46-7 Ja 16 '71
RESEARCH in colleges. See Colleges and universities—Research
RESEARCH institutions
Of Rand Mitre, Bellcom, et al; federal contract research centers. Trans-Action 7:4+ O '70
Think tanks, by P. Dickson. Review
  Bsns W p 11+ O 30 '71. R. E. Lapp
Thumbs down on think tanks. N. Walsh. Science 174:1008 D 3 '71
Troubled think tanks. Newsweek 77:73+ Ja 25 '71
  See also
Rand corporation
System development corporation
RESEARCH laboratories
Industrial laboratories: wither basic research? D. Shapley. Science 174:1214-15 D 17 '71
  See also
Bell telephone laboratories
Cambridge. University—Cavendish laboratory
General motors technical center
RESEARCH libraries
Along the academic way; with editorial comment. E. Mason. il por Library J 96:1657, 1671-6 My 15 '71; Discussion. 96:2408-9 Ag '71
Instant classification: improving reference service. D. A. Diefenbach. por Library J 96:801-2 Mr 1 '71; Discussion. 96:1547 My 1 '71
RESEARCH natural areas. See Wilderness areas
RESEARCH ships. See Ships, Research
RESEARCH submarines. See Submarine research vehicles
RESEGREGATION of schools. See Segregation in education
RESERPINE
Effects of long-term reserpine treatment on brain tyrosine hydroxylase and behavioral activity. D. S. Segal and others. bibliog il Science 173:847-9 Ag 27 '71
RESERVATIONS, Airline. See Airlines—Reservation systems
RESERVATIONS, Hotel. See Hotels, taverns, etc.—Reservation systems
RESERVATIONS, Indian. See Indians of North America—Reservations
RESERVE forces (United States) See United States—Armed forces—Reserves
RESERVE officers training corps. See United States—Reserve officers training corps
RESERVOIRS
Exchange water keeps Denver's taps flowing; Williams Fork reservoir. R. E. Wiedemann. il por Am City 86:79-80+ Je '71
Great Lakes of the Missouri. C. L. Cadieux. il Yachting 129:58-9+ Je '71

RESERVOIRS—*Continued*
Keep that stored water fresh; West Chester, Pa. J. R. McCullough. il por Am City 86: 63-5 Ap '71
Lunkers at large; public fishing at Tomhannock reservoir. A. Woldt. il Cons 25:2-3 Je '71
Multipurpose water program; Greensboro, N.C. T. Z. Osborne and R. E. Shaw. il Am City 86:95+ Ap '71
Reservoir designed not to be seen; Boulder, Colo. R. G. Westdyke. il Am City 86:19 S '71
Reservoir loading and earthquakes. il Sci N 99:368 My 29 '71
You have to make reservoirs look good; Spokane, Wash. R. E. Saty. il Am City 86:58-9 Ag '71
RESETTLEMENT of refugees. See Refugees—Resettlement
RESIDENCE halls. See Dormitories
RESIDENTIAL zoning. See Zoning
RESIGNATION of public officers. See Public officers, Resignation of
RESILIENT flooring. See Flooring, Plastic
RESINOUS products
See also
Epoxy resins
Plasticizers
RESINS. See Gums and resins
RESISTANCE to disease. See Immunity
RESISTANCE to government. See Government, Resistance to
RESISTANCE to insecticides. See Insects, Injurious and beneficial—Resistance to control
RESISTANCE to insects in plants. See Plants—Disease and pest resistance
RESISTORS, Electric. See Electric resistors
RESNICK, Milton
Fathomless field. H. Rosenstein. il por Art N 70:69-71+ N '71 *
RESNIK, H. L. P. and Wittlin, B. J.
Abortion and suicidal behaviors: observations on the concept of endangering the mental health of the mother. bibliog Ment Hy 55: 10-20 Ja '71
—See Winickoff, S. A. jt. auth.
RESNIK, Henry S.
Open classroom. il Todays Ed 60:16-17+ D '71
Open schools vs. traditional: which is right for your child? Redbook 137:60+ O '71
Promise of change in North Dakota. il Sat R 54:67-9+ Ap 17 '71
Rock pile. il Sat R 54:48-50 Ja 30 '71
Television (cont) Vogue 157:157 Mr 1; 158:62 Ag 15 '71
Yin, yang, macrobiotics, and me. il Redbook 137:58-9+ Jl '71
RESNIK, Muriel
Movies. il Vogue 158:60-1 Ag 15; 178-9 O 1 '71
RESNIK, Regina
Meeting of minds. S. Jenkins. il pors Opera N 35:6-9 Ap 17 '71 *
Regina Resnik's Carmen. P. Moor. il Hi Fi 21:MA28-9 O '71 *
RESNIK, Solomon, and Kaplan, Barbara
Report card on open admissions: remedial work recommended. il N Y Times Mag p26-8+ My 9; 21+ Je 6 '71
RESOLUTIONS
See also
New Years resolutions
RESONANCE, Magnetic. See Magnetic resonance
RESORPTION (physiology) See Absorption (physiology)
RESORT hotels. See Hotels, taverns, etc.
RESORTS. See Health resorts, watering places, etc; Seaside resorts; Winter resorts
RESOURCES, Conservation of. See Conservation of resources
RESOURCES, Natural. See Natural resources
RESPIGHI, Ottorino
Report:
Ottorino Respighi's Belfagor. J. W. Freeman. Opera N 35:23-4 My 15 '71 *
RESPIRATION
Liquid breathing in humans fact or fiction? C. Dickson. il Sea Front 17:268-71 S '71
See also
Asphyxia
Spirometers
RESPIRATORY apparatus
See also
Life support systems (submarine environment)
RESPIRATORY intensive care units. See Hospital care

RESPIRATORY organs
See also
Gills
Lungs

Birds
How birds breathe. K. Schmidt-Nielsen. il Sci Am 225:72-9 bibliog(p 120) D '71

Diseases
See also
Air pollution—Physiological effects
Hyaline membrane disease
Influenza
Lungs—Diseases
Pneumonia
RESPONSE, Motor. See Motor responses
RESPONSIBILITY
Drugs, morals and family responsibilities. E. J. Faux. Ment Hy 55:260-3 Ap '71
Nader and the scientists: a call for responsibility. P. M. Boffey. Science 171: 549-51 F 12 '71
Personal accountability; address, June 9, 1971. E. R. Zumwalt, Jr. Vital Speeches 37: 605-8 Jl 15 '71
Reflections: the limits of duty; with case histories. C. A. Reich. New Yorker 47:52-7 Je 19 '71
See also
Assistance in emergencies

Anecdotes, facetiae, satire, etc.
On breathing and other ills. R. W. Murphy. Harper 242:22+ My '71
RESS, Paul
(ed) See McCarthy, M. Underpinning of birds of America
—and Reed, W. F. jr
Skating for gold on thin ice. il Sports Illus 34:18-19 F 15 '71
REST
See also
Relaxation
REST homes. See Nursing homes
RESTAURANT menus. See Menus
RESTAURANT workers. See Restaurants—Employees
RESTAURANTS
International chef. M. Woodward. See issues of Travel
See also subhead Hotels, restaurants, etc. under names of cities, e.g. London—Hotels, restaurants, etc.

Employees
Où est la cuisine d'antan? desperate help situation. N. Hazelton. Nat R 23:1366 D 3 '71
See also
Walters and waitresses

Franchise system
Danner feasts on food franchising. il por Bsns W p 120 O 23 '71
Fast-food stands sprout on the Ginza. il Bsns W p41 O 16 '71

Europe, Western
Europe's finest restaurants 1971. S. Spitzer and H. Spitzer. Holiday 49:95-102 F '71
Fortune from fowl fare; Wienerwald restaurants. por Time 98:80+ N 15 '71

France
See also
Paris—Hotels, restaurants, etc.

Great Britain
Hamburger goes abroad. E. Herzberg. il Duns 97:83-4+ My '71
See also
Lyons, J, and company, ltd.

Hong Kong
How to eat in Chinese. P. Brooks. Sat R 54:81-2 O 23 '71

Japan
See also
Tokyo—Hotels, restaurants, etc.

Netherlands
Dutch food. C. Ray. il Holiday 48:60-1+ N '70

United States
Back roads to the best food in America; backcountry restaurants. G. Logsdon. il Farm J 95:18-19+ Ag '71
Holiday's choice of North American restaurants. S. Spitzer and H. Spitzer. Holiday 49:17-20+ Jl '71
In-most places. P. D. Dibble. Ladies Home J 88:66 My '71

RESTAURANTS—United States—*Continued*
Palate revolution; pizza parlors. il Forbes 107:35+ F 15 '71
They made it big in the restaurant biz: students' restaurant at Harvey's Lake, Pa. il Seventeen 30:158-9 Mr '71
See also
Benihana of Tokyo, inc.

RESTON, James Barrett, 1909-
State of Uncle Sam. Read Digest 98:167-8 Ap '71
View from China. Read Digest 99:117-22 D '71

about
Appendicitis papers. G. Ace. Sat R 54:12 S 4 '71 *
Mr Reston's revolution. W. F. Buckley, jr. Nat R 23:1136-7 O 8 '71 *
Please don't eat the lotus leaves; concerning interview with Chou En-lai. il por Time 98:32 Ag 23 '71 *
Reston and Chou. Nat R 23:912 Ag 24 '71 *

RESTON, James Barrett, 1941-
Vietnam amnesty: a proposal to the President. New Repub 165:21-2 O 9 '71

RESTON, Sally
Dinner with Chou En-lai. Vogue 158:89 N 15 '71

RESTORATION of books. See Books—Conservation and restoration

RESTORATION of buildings. See Architecture—Conservation and restoration

RESTORATION of works of art. See Art—Conservation and restoration

RESTORED airplanes. See Airplanes, Restored

RESTORED automobiles. See Automobiles, Restored

RESTORED villages. See Villages, Restored

RESTRAINT of trade
See also
Boycott
Patents—Licensing
Price maintenance by industry

RESTRICTED stock options. See Stock purchase options

RESTRICTION on travel. See Travel regulations

RESURFACING of roads. See Roads—Surface treatment

RESURRECTION
See also
Immortality
Jesus Christ—Resurrection and ascension

RESUSCITATION
Bringing back the dead. I. Agnew. Sci Digest 69:30-2 Ap '71

RETAIL trade
If you wear it, it's selling well. il Bsns W p21 Jl 10 '71
Over-the-counter views of 1971. il Bsns W p27 Ja 16 '71
Parents provide the fall sales action. il Bsns W p40-1 S 11 '71
Retail trade moves up. il U S News 70:11-13 My 10 '71
Spring budding of optimism; Easter business. il Bsns W p31 Ap 17 '71
Still no rush to buy: Story of the cautious consumer. il U S News 70:20-1 Mr 22 '71
Things look brighter to retailers: a survey. il U S News 71:26-7 S 20 '71
Why shoppers are back in the stores. il U S News 70:345 My 31 '71
See also
Business hours
Canvassing
Chain stores
Charge accounts (retail trade)
Christmas business
Department stores
Discount houses (retail trade)
Gift shops
Mail order business
Penney, J C, company
Pier 1 imports, inc.
Premiums
Price marks
Sales
Salesmen and salesmanship
Sears, Roebuck and company
Shopping centers
Specialty stores
Supermarkets
Supermarkets general corporation

Finance
Distribution; with yardsticks of management performance. il Forbes 109:190-3 Ja 1 '72
Ratios of retailing; with table (cont) Duns 98:76-7 S '71

Statistics
50 largest retailing companies; with directory. Fortune 83:196-7 My '71

RETAINING walls
Easily built retaining wall takes care of a change in grade. il Sunset 146:100 F '71
See also
Bulkheads

RETARDED children. See Mentally handicapped children

RETENTION communications systems, inc.
Late tape. R. Brady. Duns 97:9-10 Je '71

RETI, Ladislao
Leonardo on bearings and gears; with biographical sketch. il Sci Am 224:12, 100-7+ F '71

RETINA
Irreversible effects of visible light on the retina: role of vitamin A. W. K. Noell and R. Albrecht. bibliog il Science 172:76-80 Ap 2 '71
Vitamin A deficiency effect on retina: dependence on light. W. K. Noell and others. bibliog il Science 172:72-6 Ap 2 '71
See also
Electroretinography
Rod and cone cells

RETIRED military personnel

Employment
Roll-call of colonels that industry hires. il Bsns W p20 N 27 '71

RETIRED senior volunteer program. See Volunteer service

RETIREES as guides. See Guides

RETIREMENT
Adventures in retirement; North Carolina. W. M. Baker. il pors Am For 77:28-31+ Je; 38-9+ Ag; 36-9+ S '71
Don't let your brain go down the drain. R. Little. il pors Fortune 84:164-8+ N '71
Early retirement time bomb. Nations Bsns 59:20-4 F '71
First of the '30 and outs'. il Bsns W p60 My 22 '71
Inquiring about retiring; questions and answers. T. Collins. See issues of Harvest years
Look ahead to a place to retire. il Changing T 25:43-5 F '71
Men who still hang on to the reins. pors Bsns W p40+ O 2 '71
More managers fade away early. Bsns W p41-2 S 11 '71
News desk; retirement information. T. Schuchat. See issues of Harvest years
Old bosses bequeath new problems; incoming chief executives. il Bsns W p50-1 Ja 1 '72
Retired and want to work? Changing T 25:44 Je '71
Thirty-and-outers opt for late retirement. il Bsns W p82-3 O 9 '71
Time to retire. Nations Bsns 59:20 Je '71
Working at a life of leisure; R. Walton in Fla. J. Kirshenbaum. il Sports Illus 34:52-6+ F 1 '71
See also
Farmers—Retirement

RETIREMENT, Places of
Florida: still good for retirement? N. D. Ford. il Har Yrs 11:16-20+ Je '71
Florida: the impact of an aging population. il Bsns W p57 N 20 '71
See also
Port Charlotte, Fla.

RETIREMENT boats. See Cruisers (pleasure boats)

RETIREMENT income
Pension formula summarization: an emerging research technique; with tables. A. Strasser. bibliog f Mo Labor R 94:49-56 Ap '71
Senate considers House changes in retirement income tax credit. Har Yrs 11:4 Ag '71
Tax reforms bring advantages and credits in retirees' 1970 package. Har Yrs 11:4-5 Ja '71
See also
Pensions
Teachers—Pensions

RETRAINING, Occupational
Engineers are redesigning their own profession. J. Gooding. il Fortune 83:72-5+ Je '71
Federal aid program offers few jobs. Aviation W 94:64 Je 7 '71
More engineer retraining studied. Aviation W 95:14-15 S 6 '71
Re-entry from space; project RETRO. Newsweek 77:88-9 Je 7 '71
Switch to urban problems; aerospace retraining. Sci N 99:180 Mr 13 '71
U.S. rescues trade casualties. il Bsns W p66 Jl 3 '71
Urban engineers. il Newsweek 78:126+ N 15 '71

RETREAD tires. See Tires, Automobile

RETREADING of tires. See Tires, Rubber—Retreading and recapping

RETREATS, Spiritual
And now, the Yoga retreat. G. A. Maloney. America 124:591-3 Je 5 '71

RETRIEVER trials. See Field trials (dogs)

RETRIEVERS
Duck dog in the uplands. J. Falk. il Field & S 76:156+ S '71
Fetching comparisons. D. M. Duffey. il Outdoor Life 147:204+ Ap '71

Training
See Dogs—Training

RETROACTIVE pay. See Wages—United States

RETROGRADE amnesia. See Amnesia

RETTENMUND, Merv
Well, he's that kind of guy. R. Fimrite. por Sports Illus 35:28-30+ O 4 '71 *

RETTIE, Dwight F.
Broad new funding program, legacy of parks. il Parks & Rec 6:35-8 Ap '71
Will NRPA survive? remarks before the 1971 Congress for recreation and parks. Parks & Rec 6:23-4+ D '71

about
Dwight F. Rettie to head NRPA. por Parks & Rec 6:13 S '71 *

RETURNABLE containers. See Containers

RETURNED prisoners of war. See Prisoners of war, Returned

REUBEN, David R.
Doctor David Reuben answers your questions See issues of McCall's
Questions everyone asks about sex. Read Digest 98:66-8 F '71
Sexual problems of women alone. por McCalls 98:62+ F '71

REUCASSEL, Dick
Impala's struggle for life; photographs. Life 70:70-4 Je 4 '71

REUNION; story. See Gilmore, J. L.

REUNIONS, Family. See Family reunions

REUSS, Henry Schoellkopf
Needed: an about-face for the corps of engineers. Read Digest 99:129-32 N '71
Reuss: harbinger in the House. por Bsns W p 18-19 S 18 '71 *

REUSSWIG, F. W. See Anderson, R. H. jt. auth.

REUTER, Henry
Modern Masai. il pors Ebony 26:87-91 Ap '71
—See Nussey, W. jt. auth.

REUTERS news service
Reuters hits Dow with Lightfoot Leo. il Bsns W p40 F 27 '71

REUTHER, Ronald T.
New zoo view. il Parks & Rec 6:17-19+ S '71

REVANS, Reginald William
Executive-swapping in Europe. J. Ross-Skinner. il Duns 97:77-8+ Mr '71 *

REVEL, Jean François
Foreign vision of the coming American revolution; excerpts from The new American revolution. Time 97:18-19 F 22 '71
Without Marx or Jesus; excerpts, tr. by J. Bernard. il Sat R 54:14-31 Jl 24 '71

REVELL, Fleming H, company
Story behind the book: Revell's Bible quiz book. B. A. Bannon. il Pub W 200:36 S 20 '71

REVELLE, Keith
Collection for la raza. il por Library J 96:3719-26 N 15 '71

REVELS, Hiram Rhoades
Hundred years of history. G. A. Sewell. bibliog il pors Negro Hist Bul 34:78-9 Ap '71 *

REVENUE, Municipal. See Municipal finance

REVENUE sharing. See Intergovernmental tax relations

REVERE, Jonathan
Gull skeleton; poem. Poetry 118:22 Ap '71

REVERE, Paul
Boston massacre and Crispus Attucks. il Negro Hist Bul 34:52-4 Mr '71 *

REVERSE osmosis. See Osmosis

REVERSION (law)
Betting on death; British sale of reversions. Newsweek 77:66+ Ja 25 '71

REVIEWS of books. See Book reviews

REVIEWS of moving pictures. See Moving picture plays—Criticisms, plots, etc.

REVIEWS of plays. See Dramas—Criticisms, plots. etc.

REVITALIZATION corps. See Interracial cooperation

REVIVALS
Asbury revisited. J. F. Nelson. Chr Today 15:51+ F 12 '71
Billy and Aimee. F. Russell. Nat R 23:716 Je 29 '71
California capitol: revolution on the steps. A. Eggebroten. Chr Today 15:50+ Mr 12 '71
Coming world revival? with editorial comment. R. E. Coleman. Chr Today 15:10-12, 20-1 Jl 16 '71
Fire on the prairie; spiritual renewal Saskatoon. Chr Today 16:33 D 3 '71
Greening of revival: the Jesus revolution and other signs. E. Jorstad. il Cath World 213:265-8 S '71
Jesus and the star system. D. Donnelly. America 125:350-2 O 30 '71
Jesus movement is upon us; California. B. Vachon. il Look 35:15-21 F 9 '71
Jesus movement: now it's in the hamlets. E. E. Plowman. Chr Today 15:35-6 Je 18 '71
Jesus revolution. America 124:646 Je 26 '71
Marks of the Jesus movement; excerpt from address to the European congress on evangelism. B. Graham. Chr Today 16:4-5 N 5 '71
New rebel cry: Jesus is coming! il Time 97:56-63 Je 21 '71; Same abr. with title Jesus revolution. Read Digest 99:135-8 D '71
1971: religion on the rebound. Chr Today 16:23 D 17 '71
Pacific Northwest: revival in the underground; street Christians in Spokane, Wash. E. E. Plowman. Chr Today 15:34-5 Ja 29 '71
Recalling revival. D. Kucharsky. Chr Today 15:42-3 My 21 '71
Repentance as a church priority. V. Havner. Chr Today 15:12+ Mr 12 '71
Revival in Canada. R. Greenslade and E. E. Plowman. il Chr Today 16:31-2 D 17 '71
Shape of the coming renewal. R. Lovelace. il Chr Cent 88:1164-7 O 6 '71
Taking stock of Jesus rock; Jesus people's festival of Christian music. E. E. Plowman. Chr Today 15:32-3 F 26 '71
That old-time religion. il Sr Schol 99:15 D 13 '71
We need their faith! N. V. Peale. Read Digest 99:138-41 D '71
Youth lead more revivals. Chr Today 15:50 Mr 12 '71

REVOIR, Dan
I never want a bigger moose. il Outdoor Life 147:60-1+ Je '71

REVOLTS, Student. See Student demonstrations

REVOLUTION, Social. See Social revolution

REVOLUTIONARIES. See Revolutionists

REVOLUTIONARY war (United States) See United States—History—Revolution

REVOLUTIONISTS
Are we ready for an American Lenin? B. Mazlish. il Horizon 13:48-55 Aut '71
Arrogant cult of youth. M. Geltman. Nat R 23:140-1 F 9 '71
Free who? views of underground newspaper. Free you. New Repub 165:5-6 Ja 16 '71
In with the outs; haven for exiled revolutionaries in Santiago. il por Time 97:36 Ja 25 '71
See also
Student militants

REVOLUTIONS
On the meaning of revolution. R. F. Gibbs. Nat R 23:699-700 Je 29 '71
Prescription for revolution; excerpts from Lenin's letter, ed. by P. Harvey. V. I. Lenin. Read Digest 98:93-4 Ja '71
Theology of revolution for the third world. A. Pérez-Esclarin. il Cath World 213:277-82 S '71
See also
Government, Resistance to
Insurgency
Revolutionists

REVOLVERS
Something really new in revolvers; Wesson W-12. G. C. Nonte, jr. il Pop Mech 136:107 Ag '71
Springfield .45-70 trapdoor. C. Worman. il Hobbies 75:150-1 Ja '71

REVSON, Peter
Peter, Peter, Donohue beater. R. F. Jones. il por Sports Illus 34:34-6+ My 24 '71 *
Peter Revson. K. Given. il pors Motor T 23:74-6+ D '71 *

REWALD, John
Vincent van Gogh, 1880-1971. il pors Art N 69:53-5+ F '71

REWARD (psychology)
Altruism is rewarding. R. F Weiss and others. bibliog il Science 171:1262-3 Mr 26 '71
Hyperactive engineering. V. Krauch. il Am Ed 7:12-13+ Je '71

REWARD (theology)
Paradox of doing good; excerpts from address, June 6, 1971. M. Friedman. Read Digest 99:189-90 O '71

REWARDS, prizes, etc.
Senior achievement awards. il Har Yrs 11:26-9 My '71
Spring awards in the media. P. C. Rule. America 124:461-2 My 1 '71
See also names of organizations, societies, etc. granting awards, e.g. American forestry association; *also* names of awards, e.g. Nobel prizes; *also* Advertising awards, Television awards, and similar headings

Anecdotes, facetiae, satire, etc.
Achievement. R. Angell. New Yorker 47:24-8 Ag 21 '71
LJ's annual awards. J. Berry, 3d. and others. Library J 96:4043 D 15 '71

REX, Michelle B.
They'll never see you cry. il Good H 172:42+ Ap '71

REX, Robert W.
Geothermal energy, the neglected energy option. il por Bul Atom Sci 27:52-6 O '71

REYBURN, Jerry H.
Wilderness program for one-week campers. il Camp Mag 43:14 Je '71

REYER, W. B.
Start a rebellion; build a calico camper. il Pop Sci 199:76-7+ Jl '71

REYES, Jorge Muñoz. See Muñoz Reyes, J.

REYES BASUALTO, Neftali Ricardo. See Neruda, P.

REYKJAVIK, Iceland
Place to cool it. D. Butwin. il Sat R 54:30+ Ag 21 '71

REYNAL, Jeanne
Jeanne Reynal. B. Guest. il Craft Horiz 31:40-3 Je '71 *

REYNARD, Carolyn C.
I can't draw. il Sch Arts 71:48-9 N '71

REYNOLDS, Alan
Case against wage and price control. il Nat R 23:1051-5 S 24 '71
Unions: scapegoat for inflation. Nat R 23:1463-4+ D 31 '71

REYNOLDS, Hudson G.
Austrians call it: *landwirtschaftlichebetreid*. il Am For 77:14-17+ S '71

REYNOLDS, Jerry D.
Performance contracting: proceed with caution. il Engl J 60:102-6+ Ja '71; Same abr. with title Performance contracting: adapted. Ed Digest 36:5-7 Ap '71

REYNOLDS, Judith
Buying a used camera. il Consumer Bul 54:28-32 N '71

REYNOLDS, Marc
Plant a little spring indoors this fall. il Horticulture 49:28-31 N '71
Tulips. il Horticulture 49:18-19+ O '71

REYNOLDS, Margaret
England restricts freedom to publish. Pub W 200:27-8 Jl 26 '71

REYNOLDS, Paul Revere
Literary agent's notebook. Writer 84:15-17+ D '71
Man in the middle: excerpts from The middle man. por Pub W 200:21-3 O 18 '71

REYNOLDS, R. J., industries, inc.
Voyages into the unknown. il Forbes 108:30-2+ D 1 '71

REYNOLDS, R. Neil
Toward relevancy, curriculum, and the social order. Sch & Soc 99:29-30 Ja '71

REYNOLDS, Richard Joshua
Reynolds saga: the sweet with the bitter. il por Forbes 108:32-3 D 1 '71 *

REYNOLDS, Richard Samuel, 1881-1955
Alarmist whose thinking was sound. R. S. Reynolds, jr. il por Nations Bsns 59:86-7 Ja '71 *

REYNOLDS, Richard Samuel, 1908-
Alarmist whose thinking was sound. il por Nations Bsns 59:86-7 Ja '71

REYNOLDS, W. Ann, and others
Monosodium glutamate: absence of hypothalamic lesions after ingestion by newborn primates. bibliog il Science 172:1342-4 Je 25 '71

REYNOLDS, William J.
To describe it all, growl softly. Engl J 60:267-9 F '71

REYNOLDS and company
Real Reynolds story. Forbes 107:41 Mr 1 '71

REYNOLDS metals company
Alarmist whose thinking was sound. R. S. Reynolds, jr. il por Nations Bsns 59:86-7 Ja '71
Two more Reynolds creations. Forbes 108:36 D 1 '71

REZNIKOFF, Marvin, and Domino, George
What do you want for Christmas? Ladies Home J 88:62+ D '71

RHEAULT, Robert B.
Books & ideas. il Fortune 83:163-4 Je '71

RHENIUM
Ida Noddack, 75 & element 75. F. Habashi. bibliog il por Chem 44:14-15 F '71

RHESUS monkeys. See Monkeys

RHETORIC
Foolish American ism: utopianism. I. Kristol. il N Y Times Mag p31+ N 14 '71; Reply. A. F. Reel. p32+ D 5 '71
Language of statesmen. L. J. Halle. il Sat R 54:30-1 O 16 '71
You'd better believe it's loaded; adaptation of address, November 1970. L. B. Salomon. Engl J 60:353-8 Mr '71
See also
English language—Composition
Oratory
Repetition (rhetoric)

RHEUMATIC fever
Wyoming's war on deadly strep. M. Michaelson. il Todays Health 49:40-3+ Mr '71

RHEUMATIC heart disease. See Heart—Diseases

RHEUMATISM
See also
Arthritis

RHEUMATOID arthritis. See Arthritis

RHEUMATOID factor. See Immunoglobulins

RHINELANDER, John B.
International conference on air law approves convention on aircraft hijacking; statement, December 16, 1970. Dept State Bul 64:51-2 Ja 11 '71

RHINOCEROS
They're out to save the black rhino. G. Frame. il Sci Digest 70:33-8 N '71

Anecdotes, facetiae, satire, etc.
Rhinoceros: an appreciation. C. Tomkins. New Yorker 47:59-61 N 20 '71

RHINOPLASTY. See Surgery, Plastic

RHIZOPUS. See Fungi

RHOADS, Geraldine
How to sell a magazine one issue at a time. il por Sat R 54:61-3 S 11 '71

RHOADS, Max N.
Local governments share a computer. il Am City 86:52 F '71

RHODE, Eric
(ed) See Updike, J. Grabbing dilemmas

RHODE ISLAND
See also
Architecture, Domestic—Rhode Island
Banks and banking—Rhode Island
Block Island
Camps—Rhode Island
Conservation of resources—Rhode Island
Fishing—Rhode Island
Libraries—Rhode Island
Music festivals—Rhode Island

RHODE ISLAND furniture. See Furniture, American

RHODE ISLAND historical society
Painting collection of the Rhode Island historical society. F. H. Goodyear, jr. il Antiques 100:749-57 N '71

RHODE ISLAND library association
Rhode Island librarians meet censorship fan: Reverend Mr Ennio Cugini. Library J 96:2249 Jl '71

RHODES, Lynwood Mark
Why cholera is the disease nations try to hide. il Todays Health 49:51-3 Je '71

RHODES, Maribelle
Community of crafts: Peters Valley. il Craft Horiz 31:38+ Ap '71

RHODES, Philip L.
Great yacht designers. B. Robinson. il por Yachting 129:66-7+ Je '71 *

RHODES, Richard
Boy who didn't die. il Redbook 137:58-60+ Ag '71; Same abr. Read Digest 99:227-8+ D '71
Credences of summer. il Harper 243:57-60 Ag '71
Of dogs. il Harper 242:94-7 Ap '71
Packaged sentiment. il Harper 243:61-6 D '71

RHODESIA
Far from ideal. Newsweek 78:44+ D 6 '71
Having another go. il por Newsweek 78:37 N 29 '71
In civilized hands. il por Time 98:37 D 6 '71
Reports and comment. J. Grimond. Atlan 228:24+ O '71

RHODESIA—*Continued*
Rhodesia through the eye of faith. T. Beeson. Chr Cent 88:1460-1 D 15 '71
Why the sudden concern over Rhodesia; with interview with I. Smith. il U S News 71:40-1 N 29 '71
  See also
Catholic church in Rhodesia
Church and state in Rhodesia
Collective farms—Rhodesia
Great Britain—Foreign relations—Rhodesia
United Nations—Rhodesia
Zimbabwe

Commerce
Why the U.S. ban on chrome was lifted. il Bsns W p23 N 27 '71
  See also
United States—Commerce—Rhodesia

Economic relations
  See also
Great Britain—Economic relations—Rhodesia

Foreign relations
United States
  See United States—Foreign relations—Rhodesia

Native races
  See also
Rhodesia—Race question

Politics and government
Rhodesia: a crucial issue for the Christian conscience. R. E. Kendall. Chr Cent 88:1086-8 S 15 '71
Something new has been added; compromise agreement between Great Britain and Ian Smith. Nat R 23:1396+ D 17 '71

Race question
Rhodesia: a crucial issue for the Christian conscience. R. E. Kendall. Chr Cent 88:1086-8 S 15 '71
  See also
Church and race problems in Rhodesia
RHÔNE-Poulenc, s.a. See Chemical industries —France
RHUBARB
Three vegetables that come back. il Sunset 146:158+ F '71
  See also
Cookery—Rhubarb
RHYME. See Rime
RHYNE, Charles S.
Mr Rhyne heads U.S. delegation to UNHCR executive committee. Dept State Bul 65:470 O 25 '71 *
RIAD, Mahmoud
Middle East: a case of jitters. il por Time 98:36-7 D 6 '71 *
RIBAKOVE, Barbara
(ed) See Susann, J. Jacqueline Susann's bedtime stories
RIBAKOVE, Sy
(ed) See Susann, J. Jacqueline Susann's bedtime stories
RIBES, Jacqueline, vicomtesse de
Spanish sunaways: fresh places to go; interview. il pors Vogue 157:136-47+ Ap 15 '71
RIBICOFF, Abraham A.
Youth camp safety act. por Parks & Rec 6:23+ S '71
  about
Crusader. por Newsweek 77:27 My 3 '71 *
Ecopolitics. Forbes 108:52 Jl 15 '71 *
RIBMAN, Ronald
Fingernails blue as flowers. Criticism
Nation 214:29 Ja 3 '72 *
Time 99:57 Ja 3 '72 *
RIBOFLAVIN. See Vitamins—Vitamin B₂
RIBONUCLEIC acid. See RNA
RIBOSOMES. See Nucleoproteins
RIBOUD, Marc
China: a sense of initiative. il Newsweek 78:28-35 S 13 '71
China: three photographic insights. Vogue 158:156-61 D '71
China's amazing art discoveries, jade and gold body suits; photographs. Vogue 158:94-7 O 15 '71
RICCARDO, John J.
American businessman; address, March 12, 1971. Vital Speeches 37:434-6 My 1 '71
RICCIARDI, Mirella
African elegance; photographs from Vanishing Africa. Life 71:56-64 O 8 '71
  about
African adventures of an elegant farm girl. R. Graves. il por Life 71:3 O 8 '71 *

RICCIUTI, Florence, and Ruddle, F. H.
Biochemical and cytological evidence for triple hybrid cell line formed from fusion of three different cells. bibliog il Science 172:470-2 Ap 30 '71
RICE, Berkeley
B-1 bomber. il Sat R 54:20-2+ D 11 '71
C-5A+L-1011=Lockheed's financial crisis: what price Lockheed? il N Y Times Mag p24-5+ My 9 '71
C-5A: postmortem on a mess. Look 35:80-1 My 18 '71
Cold-war college. Nation 213:304-8 O 4 '71
RICE, Charles Owen
Wild Rice. S. J. Adamo. America 124:238-9 Mr 6 '71 *
RICE, Tim
Hosanna! a year of Superstar. il Mlle 74:104-5 D '71
Rock gets religion; interview, ed. by E. Miller. pors Seventeen 30:156-7+ Mr '71
RICE
Looking for the organic America: raising rice the right way. F. Allen. Org Gard & Farm 18:66-8+ Jl '71
Talc-treated rice and Japanese stomach cancer. R. R. Merliss. bibliog il Science 173:1141-2 S 17 '71
  See also
Cookery—Rice
International rice research institute
RICE pudding. See Pudding
RICH, Alan
High fidelity moves into its second generation. il Hi Fi 21:57+ Ap '71
On the off-beat (cont) Hi Fi 21:MA9+ F '71
Records I don't want to live without. Redbook 137:95+ S '71
RICH, Alexander. See Fahnestock, S. jt. auth.
RICH, Frank
Q: do the claims of conscience outweigh the duties of citizenship? il por Esquire 76:154-5+ D '71
RICH, Leslie
Newark's parent-powered school. il Am Ed 7:35-9 D '71
Teaching for the real world. il Am Ed 7:3-6 Ag '71
RICH, The
Radical chic & mau-mauing the flak catchers, by T. Wolfe. Review
Harper 242:104-9 F '71. I. Howe
RICH people are happier than poor; healthy, happier than sick; young, happier than old; story. See Mountzoures, H. L.
RICHARD III, king of England
We speak no treason, by R. H. Jarman and Killing of Richard III, by R. Farrington. Reviews
Time il 99:68 Ja 3 '72. B. Darrach *
RICHARD, J. F.
Let George do it? Commonweal 94:11-15 Mr 12 '71
Remaking of Muskie. por Nation 212:235-40 F 22 '71
RICHARD II; drama. See Shakespeare, W.—Plays
RICHARD III; drama. See Shakespeare, W.—Plays
RICHARDS, Arlene
What do students really want? il Todays Ed 60:57-8 Ap '71
RICHARDS, D. Boyd
Back to basics. il Flying 88:57-8 F '71
RICHARDS, Lindsay. See Kanegis, A. jt. auth.
RICHARDS, Nancy E.
Print collection at Winterthur. il Antiques 100:586-90, 734-9 O-N '71
RICHARDS, Reuben F.
Money for sale. por Forbes 107:49-50 Ap 1 '71 *
RICHARDS, Whitman
Fortification illusions of migraines; with biographical sketch. il Sci Am 224:12, 88-94+ bibliog(p 132) My '71
RICHARDSON, Bernard E.
Manly art. il Library J 96:446-9 F 1 '71
Quo jure? il Am Lib 2:304-5 Mr '71
RICHARDSON, Brenda
(ed) See Nelson, G. Women, wives, filmmakers
(ed) See Wiley, D. Women, wives, filmmakers
RICHARDSON, Edgar P.
Centennial city. il por Am Heritage 23:17-32 D '71
RICHARDSON, Elliot Lee
Next big effort. il Am Ed 7:11-12 Ja '71
Nixon behind the scenes. por Newsweek 77:16-17 F 1 '71
  about
Boston Brahmin in Heartbreak house. J. Cameron. il pors Fortune 84:88-91+ O '71 *
Call it desegregation. J. Osborne. New Repub 164:12-13 Ja 30 '71 *

RICHARDSON, Elliot Lee—about—*Continued*
Clark Kent at HEW. por Time 98:19 Ag 9
'71 •
HEW struggles to deliver the American
dream. il por Bsns W p62-6 My 1 '71 •
Secretary Richardson. J. Osborne. New Repub
164:11-12 Ja 23 '71 •
RICHARDSON, Jack
Ali on Peachtree. il Harper 242:46-9+ Ja '71
Requiem for Feldman. Harper 243:116-18 O '71
Theater. Commentary 51:78-80 F; 76-8 Ap;
52:77-80 Jl '71
RICHARDSON, John, 1921-
Impact of American business on world af-
fairs; address, April 7, 1971. Dept State Bul
64:608-12 My 10 '71
RICHARDSON, Larry
Larry Richardson & dance company, Gener-
oso Pope theatre, Fordham university,
NYC. L. Pastore. Dance Mag 45:82 Ag '71 •
RICHARDSON, Paul R.
Nevergreen in Groton: special news analy-
sis. S. C. Scott. il pors Wilson Lib Bul 45:
818-20+ My '71 •
RICHARDSON, Sir Ralph
Sir Ralph Richardson; interview, ed. by J.
Gruen. por Vogue 158:87-8+ N 15 '71
RICHARDSON, Ron
Even in Siberia it's the age of ecology. il
por Am For 77:24-7+ Mr '71
RICHARDSON, W. L.
Rev Richardson's football farm. L. J. Banks.
il pors Ebony 27:104-9 D '71 •
RICHARDSON, William J.
President Nixon's China trip. il America 125:
84-7 Ag 21 '71
RICHEY, David
Bad winds and big pike of Kesagami. il Out-
door Life 147:56-9+ Je '71
RICHLER, Mordecai
Authors & editors; interview. por Pub W
199:29-31 Je 28 '71
Canada: an immensely boring country, un-
til now. il Life 70:54-54B+ Ap 9 '71
Ottawa is the capital of Canada, but what
else is it? il Holiday 48:58-9+ N '70
RICHMOND, Lee J.
Symbol and theme in Eudora Welty's Petrified
man. Engl J 60:1201-3 D '71
RICHMOND, LeRoy
From the Musical heritage society, the com-
plete works of Chopin. il pors Am Rec G
37:488-93+ Ap '71
RICHMOND, Tom
Change color pix tubes faster. il Radio-Electr
42:33-5 My '71
RICHMOND, Va.
Answer the ecologists; pollution abatement
program. P. D. Eimon. il Am City 86:118+
O '71
    Churches
First Unitarian church of Richmond, Vir-
ginia. il Arch Rec 150:108-9 Jl '71
    Coliseum
Richmond, Va. coliseum blends with the
city. H. Peschel. il Am City 86:58-9 D '71
    Education
For racial balance: city-to-county busing?
U S News 71:32 Ag 30 '71
Governor's dilemma; integration. il por
Newsweek 77:69 F 15 '71
Year of the bus. R. G. Holland. Nat R 23:
475+ My 4 '71
    Newspapers
See also
Times-Dispatch
    Parks and playgrounds
No caged birds. il Am City 86:28 Ap '71
    Recreation
See also
Richmond, Va.—Parks and playgrounds
    Religious institutions and affairs
Overdue first word on peace and war. E.
Glynn. il America 125:396-7 N 13 '71
RICHSTONE, May
Good manners? poem. Good H 172:44 F '71
RICHTER, Charles F.
Expert assesses the danger; interview. il
por U S News 70:35-6 F 22 '71
RICK, Cary
Cary Rick, Athenaeum theater, Chicago. A.
Barzel. Dance Mag 45:80 Jl '71 •
RICKENBACKER, William F.
Land of the free. Nat R 23:1181, 1355 O 22,
D 3 '71
Records (title varies) (cont) Nat R 23:209-10,
772 F 23, Jl 13 '71
    about
Irrepressible and irresistible. J. Chamberlain.
Nat R 23:373 Ap 6 '71 •

RICKERBY, Arthur
Wedge meets the headhunters; photographs.
Life 71:32-9 D 3 '71
RICKETS
Rickets. W. F. Loomis; reply with rejoinder.
T. H. Jukes. il Sci Am 224:6 F '71
Serum parathyroid hormone in X-linked
hypophosphatemia. C. Arnaud and others.
bibliog il Science 173:845-7 Ag 27 '71
Strontium induced rickets; metabolic basis.
J. L. Omdahl and H. F. DeLuca. bibliog il
Science 174:949-51 N 26 '71
RICKETTS, Mary E.
Remedial reading via TV. Todays Ed 60:51-2
O '71
RICKSON, Fred R.
Glycogen plastids in Müllerian body cells
of cecropia peltata, a higher green plant.
bibliog il Science 173:344-7 Jl 23 '71
RIDDLE; story. See Midwood, B.
RIDE a black horse; drama. See Scott, J.
RIDENHOUR, William
652 Broadway. D. Shapiro. il por Art N 70:
50-2+ Ap '71 •
RIDGES, Ocean. See Ocean bottom
RIDGEWAY, James
Cleaning of America (don't hold your
breath) Ramp Mag 9:17-18 Mr '71
Hard times. See issues of Ramparts
Mum's the word. New Repub 165:17-19 Ag 21
'71
New journalism. bibliog il Am Lib 2:585-92
Je '71
There's a Toyota in their future! il Ramp
Mag 10:40-1 N '71
—See Kopkind, A. jt. auth.
RIDGWAY, Matthew B.
Indochina: disengaging. For Affairs 49:583-92
Jl '71
RIDICULOUS theatrical company. See New
York (city)—Theater
RIDING. See Horseback trips
RIDLAND, John
Density; poem. Nation 213:184 S 6 '71
RIEBOCK, James. See Smith, L. L. jt. auth.
RIECHERT, Susan
Spying on spiders. il Chem 44:18 O '71 •
RIECKEN, Henry W.
Federal government and social science pol-
icy. Ann Am Acad 394:100-13 Mr '71
RIEDER, Werner
Circuit breakers; with biographical sketch. il
Sci Am 224:12, 76-84 Ja '71
RIEGE, Walter H.
Never too late. Sci Am 225:84 S '71 •
—and Cherkin, Arthur
One-trial learning and biphasic time course
of performance in the goldfish. bibliog il
Science 172:966-8 My 28 '71
RIEGLE, Donald Wayne, 1938-
Dump Nixon campaign. Look 35:79-80 Je 1
'71
    about
Happy, humble drive to dump Nixon. il pors
Time 97:10-11 Je 7 '71 •
RIELLY, John E.
Global poverty and underdevelopment; ad-
dress, March 15, 1971. Vital Speeches 37:
496-502 Je 1 '71
RIENDEAU, Albert J.
Charge, sir knight! il Parks & Rec 6:31-4+
Ap '71
RIENOW, Leona Train
Salt in our lives. Audubon 73:100-3 Jl '71
RIESE chain of restaurants. See New York
(city)—Hotels, restaurants, etc.
RIESER, Leonard M.
Governance of the association. Science 171:
755 F 26 '71
RIESSEN, Marty
Marty just might be the man. F. Deford. il
por Sports Illus 35:47-8 Ag 30 '71 •
RIESSMAN, Frank, and Gartner, Alan
Employer of first resort. Nation 212:434-5
Ap 5 '71
RIFLE, Colo.
Curtain time. il por Newsweek 78:37-8 O 18
'71
RIFLE sights. See Firearms—Sights
RIFLES
All-around rifle for big game. W. Davis. il
Mech Illus 67:74+ Ja '71
All outdoors; commemorative firearms. G.
Reiger. il Pop Mech 136:28 O '71
Confederate sharps carbine. C. Worman. il
Hobbies 76:154-5 Jl '71
Is there really an all-around rifle? G. C.
Nonte. il Pop Mech 136:106-8+ S '71
Lever country; new Browning lever action
rifle. W. Page. il Field & S 75:150-2+ Mr
'71
Mr Pedersen's secret weapon; rifle with
semi-automatic action. C. Worman. il Hob-
bies 75:150-1 F '71

RIFLES—*Continued*
New CO$_2$ fun gun fires like a six-shooter.
P. Wahl. il Pop Sci 199:57 D '71
New Sharps rifle. J. O'Connor. il Outdoor
Life 148:102+ Ag '71
Notes on the sheep rifle. J. O'Connor. il Out-
door Life 148:64+ D '71
On changing point of impact. J. O'Connor. il
Outdoor Life 147:164+ Ap '71
7mm. Remington magnum. J. O'Connor. il
Outdoor Life 147:166+ Mr '71
Spencer's horizontal shot tower. C. Worman.
il Hobbies 76:154-5 D '71
Springfield .45-70 trapdoor.　C. Worman. il
Hobbies 75:150-1 Ja '71
Taste of nostalgia; the Stevens Favorite. J.
O'Connor. il por Outdoor Life 147:122+ Je
'71
.22 rimfire: still the fun gun. L. J. Bashline.
il Field & S 76:100-1+ O '71

RIFT zones (geology) See Faults (geology)
RIGA, Peter J.
Can Christians aid violence? il Cath World
212:232-6 F '71
Catholic theologian today. Cath World 214:
128-31 D '71
International war crimes. il Cath World 213:
130-3 Je '71
Plight of the ethnics. il Cath World 212:
289-91 Mr '71
Time to draft the clergy. America 125:456-7
N 27 '71
RIGALI, Norbert J.
Catholics and liberalized abortion laws. il
Cath World 213:283-5 S '71
RIGGALL, Dan J.
Evangelical college students: an opinion
sampler; excerpts from college newspapers.
Chr Today 15:11-14 My 21 '71
RIGGING. See Masts and rigging
RIGGS, Bobby
Chips, chops, drops and lobs. G. S. Brown.
il por Sports Illus 34:60+ Ja 18 '71 *
RIGHT and left (political science)
Behind the political debate. P. Steinfels.
Commonweal 95:126 N 5 '71
Campus characteristics and campus unrest. K.
Keniston and M. Lerner. bibliog f il Ann
Am Acad 395:39-53 My '71
Changing sources of power, by F. G. Dutton.
Review
Bsns W il p 13 Je 26 '71. B. A. Agnew
Deradicalized intellectuals. E. Goodheart.
Nation 212:177-80 F 8 '71
Development of the new left; excerpts from
The development of a new left in the United
States, 1960-1965. J. P. O'Brien. bibliog f
Ann Am Acad 395:15-25 My '71
Leonard Boudin: the left's lawyer's lawyer.
P. Wilkes. il por N Y Times Mag p38-40+
N 14 '71
Liberal draws the line. S. McCracken. il Nat
R 23:1402-6 D 17 '71
Libertarianism: a new right credo? S. Lehr
and L. Rossetto, jr. Cur 127:29-38 Mr '71
Meaning of left and right. T. Szamuely.
il Nat R 23:923-7+ Ag 24 '71
My Jewish problem, and ours; Israel, the
left, and the Jewish establishment.　S.
Stern. il Ramp Mag 10:30-40 Ag '71
New-left economics. P. A. Samuelson. News-
week 78:94 D 6 '71
New left: why violence? J. Ciardi. Sat R
54:12+ Ja 23 '71
New right credo: libertarianism. S. Lehr
and L. Rossetto, jr; discussion. N Y
Times Mag p32 F 14 '71
Notes on the election of '72. M. S. Evans.
Nat R 23:205 F 23 '71; Reply. S. M. Lipset.
23:552 My 18 '71
On being deradicalized. N. Glazer; discussion.
Commentary 50:30-1 O '70; 51:20-3 Ja; 22+
Ap '71
Organizing the new politics; a proposal. S.
Lynd. Ramp Mag 10:14-15+ D '71
Orwellians left and right. P. Steinfels. Com-
monweal 94:6 Mr 12 '71
Radical chic is dead. S. Alsop. Read Digest
98:103-4 F '71
Right-radicals. W. F. Buckley, jr. Nat R
23:162 F 9 '71
Same old new left. Nat R 23:1394+ D 17 '71
Snobberies of the left; abusive articles about
Blackpool. P. Worsthorne. Nat R 23:76 Ja
26 '71
Socialism of fools: the new left calls it anti-
Zionism. S. M. Lipset; discussion. N Y
Times Mag p39 Ja 31; 16+ Mr 14 '71
Tin star state. G. Cartwright. il Esquire
75:95-9+ F '71
Twenty-one theses; a radical perspective on
the '70s. A. I. Waskow. Commonweal 93:
463-5 F 12 '71

Violence: left and middle; use as a political
tactic. M. C. Segers. il Cath World 212:307-
8+ Mr '71
What's left? attitudes in the 1930's.　R.
Starr. Commentary 52:35-41 Ag '71
Will Mr William Kunstler please step down?
a dissenting opinion on the practice of
new left law. J. W. Bishop, jr. il pors
Esquire 75:115-17+ Ap '71
Willis Carto. C. H. Simonds. il por Nat R
23:978-89 S 10 '71
See also
Conservatism
Liberalism
Radicalism
RIGHT- and left-handedness. See Left- and
right-handedness
RIGHT and wrong. See Ethics
RIGHT of asylum. See Asylum, Right of
RIGHT of dissent. See Free speech
RIGHT of privacy. See Privacy, Right of
RIGHT of way
Clouds in the big sky; locked gates bar
hunters and fishermen from public lands.
W. A. Fairhurst and B. East. il Outdoor
Life 148:31-3+ Jl '71
RIGHT On (nightclub) See Night clubs
RIGHT to read program
Rallying to the reading challenge; with
study-discussion program, by E. Harris
and D. Harris. L. Fay and W. Blanton.
bibliog il PTA Mag 65:9-12, 32-3 Ja '71
Right to read. D. Dempsey. Sat R 54:22-3
Ap '71
Right to read program goes into operation.
Pub W 200:29-30 N 8 '71
Right to read: the national scene. il PTA
Mag 65:31 Mr '71
RIGHT wing (politics) See Right and left
(political science)
RIGHTS, Bill of. See United States—Constitu-
tion—Bill of rights
RIGHTS, Vested. See Vested rights
RIGHTS of artists. See Artists rights
RIGHTS of authors. See Authors rights
RIGHTS of employees. See Employees—Civil
rights
RIGHTS of way. See Right of way
RIHM, Kurt
Some deep-sky photographs. il Sky & Tel
43:22-4 Ja '72
RIKLIS, Meshulam
Meshulam Riklis: the power, the profit and
the glory. il Forbes 107:24-6+ Mr 15 '71 *
RIKLIS, Pinhas
Fathers & sons. il por Forbes 107:39 Mr 15
'71 *
RILES, Wilson C.
Man who beat Max Rafferty; with inter-
view, ed. by J. Fried. il pors Life 70:30-1
F 26 '71
about
California's new education boss. L. Robin-
son. il pors Ebony 26:54-6+ My '71 *
Getting smarter sooner. il por Time 98:38 Jl
26 '71 *
RILEY, Frank
Australia: a quiet place to fossick. il Sat
R 54:52-3+ O 23 '71
RILEY, Nord
Paddy's grouse. il Outdoor Life 148:80-3+
Ag '71
Uproar is the name of the game. il Outdoor
Life 147:76-9+ Mr '71
RILEY, Robert Q.
Build the yellow jacket for $400. il Pop
Mech 135:126-9+ Mr '71
RILLING, Helmuth
Music to my ears. I. Kolodin. Sat R 54:18 My
1 '71 *
RIME
Poet's workshop; relationship of rhyme to
poetry. F. Trefethen. Writer 84:16-18+ N
'71
RINEHART, George
Ability grouping: out or in? . . . Ed Digest
36:49-51 F '71
RINEHART, William D.
Excerpt from statement, November 1971. Cong
Digest 50:303+ D '71
RINFRET, Pierre André
Is a tax cut coming? interview, ed. by G.
R. Rosen. por Duns 97:14-16+ Ap '71
RING, Betty
Memorial embroideries by American school-
girls. il Antiques 100:570-5 O '71
RING compounds. See Cyclic compounds
RINGEL, Robert L.
Say rabbit, not wabbit. il Newsweek 77:98
Mr 22 '71 *

RINGER, Alexander L.
Beethoven and the London pianoforte school. bibliog f il Mus Q 56:742-58 O '70

RINGER, Barbara A.
International copyright turns another corner. Pub W 200:22-5 N 8' 71

about

Barbara Ringer endorsed by former copyright chief. S. Wagner. Pub W 200:30 O 18 '71 *

Barbara Ringer wins round one in Copyright office fight. S. Wagner. Pub W 200:42 S 27 '71 *

Cary appointed register: action contested by Ringer. Library J 97:12+ Ja 1 '72 *

Cary renamed register of copyrights. S. Wagner. Pub W 200:29 N 8 '71 *

Race & sex bias are issues as Ringer takes LC to court. pors Library J 96:3262-3 O 15 '71 *

RINGLE, William M.
They've never lost a decision. il Nations Bsns 59:62-4 Je '71

RINGLING brothers, Barnum and Bailey circus. See Circus

RINGO, James
Delicately molded sensuality, bordering on the pornographic. il Am Rec G 37:310-12 Ja '71

RINGS
Banding together; bright wedding things. il Mlle 72:118 Ja '71

RINKS, Skating. See Skating rinks

RINPOCHE, Chime. See Chime Rinpoche

RIO DE JANEIRO
See also
Stock exchange—Rio de Janeiro

Cemeteries

Raising the dead; skyscraper cemetery. il Time 98:72 N 29 '71

RIOS, Angelyn. See Simmons, R. L. jt. auth.

RIOT control
Self-control for riot controllers. il Bsns W p50-1 Jl 3 '71
See also
Police—Equipment and supplies

RIOTS
See also
Prison riots
also subhead Riots *under names of continents, countries, cities, etc, e.g. Mexico (city)—Riots*

RIOTTE, Louise
Grapes grow great in Oklahoma. il Org Gard & Farm 18:105-6+ Ja '71

Really red peppers and how they grow. il Org Gard & Farm 18:44-5 My '71

Wanted: brussels sprouts in Oklahoma. il Org Gard & Farm 18:56-7 Ag '71

What's cooking? Org Gard & Farm 18:140+ Ap '71

RIPARIAN vegetation. See Streamside vegetation

RIPP, Judith
(ed) Family movie guide. See issues of Parents' magazine & better family living

RIPPED off; story. See Adams, A.

RIPPER, José E. See D'Asaro, L. A. jt. auth.

RIPPIN, Sarah
Birth. il por Redbook 137:48+ S '71

RIPPLE, Gail G.
Lookout Mountain. il Travel 135:47-9 My '71

Sequoyah country. il Travel 136:26-7 D '71

RIPPON, Ruth
Ruth Rippon retrospective exhibition. il Ceram Mo 19:20-1 Mr '71 *

RISEBROUGH, Robert W. See Hays, H. jt. auth.

RISK
See also
Hedging

RISK (insurance)
Avoid losses through risk management. F. X. McCahill, jr. Harvard Bsns R 49:57-65 My '71

RISKIN, Steven
Sound of the shofar. il por Time 98:69 O 4 '71 *

RIST, Luigi
Luigi Rist: printmaker in the Japanese tradition. B. Whipple. il por Am Artist 35:38-43+ Ag '71 *

RISTORI, Allen J.
Montauk, small-boat paradise. il por Field & S 75:172-5+ Mr '71

RITALIN. See Methylphenidate

RITE aid corporation
Rite aid network. A. Hershman. Duns 98:69-70 S '71

RITES and ceremonies
Baptism by theater. il Time 99:49 Ja 3 '72
Have Americans gone mad. M. Maddocks. Cur 125:5-9 Ja '71
See also
Circumcision
Festivals
Fire walking
Marriage customs and rites
Passover

India

Bizarre rites of the cobra shrine; Indian god Tajaji credited with saving snake bite victims. K. Severin. il Sci Digest 69:52-5 Mr '71

New Hebrides

Social climbing in the New Hebrides *nimangi* ceremoney. K. Muller. il Natur Hist 80:66-75 O '71

Surinam

Under the power of the Gran Gadu; Bush Negro witchcraft. L. C. Whiton. il Natur Hist 80:14-16+ Ag '71

RITTENHOUSE, Jack D.
Santa Fe profile. il Am West 8:42-7 S '71

RITTER, Lawrence S.
Battling the balance sheet. il Sat R 54:22-5 O 9 '71

RITUAL. See Catholic church—Liturgy and ritual; Liturgies; Rites and ceremonies

RITUAL acrobats of Persia. See Acrobats and acrobatism

RITZ in Paris. See Paris—Hotels, restaurants, etc.

RIVALRY
See also
Competition (psychology)

RIVER; ballet. See Ballets—Criticisms

RIVER boats. See Barges; Steamships and steamboats

RIVER ecology. See Fresh water ecology

RIVER EDGE, N.J.

Monuments, statues, etc.

Fine arts; The soldier in Veterans' memorial park. C. J. McNaspy. America 124:263 Mr 13 '71

RIVER pearl fisheries. See Pearl fisheries

RIVER towboats. See Tugboats

RIVER trips
Another world, another time; a trip on the Delta Queen. B. Atkinson. il Audubon 73:66-71 Ja '71

Back-yard float trip. G. Haman. il Pop Mech 136:92-4+ Jl '71

Death ran with the river; rapids on Middle Fork of Salmon. A. E. Couture. il pors Outdoor Life 147:53-7+ My '71

Mighty Columbia. L. Barber. il Yachting 129:60-1+ My '71

Rafting down a jungle river in Jamaica. il Sunset 147:75 O '71

Rip-roaring river, the rumbling Colorado. M. Litton. il Holiday 49:50-3 My '71

River runs in the West in 1971, here are some of your 600 choices. Sunset 146:42+ My '71

Sea chanties & marlinspikes; life aboard the ecology-inspired Clearwater. D. Kasanof. il Motor B & S 127:88-9+ Mr '71

Shannon cruise. G. Fitzsimons. il Travel 136:40-3+ Jl '71

Steamin' up the River; from Memphis to New Orleans on the Delta Queen. D. Butwin. il Sat R 54:36-8 My 29; 44-6+ Je 5; 36+ Je 12 '71

There's thunder in the Canyon; Grand Canyon safari. N. A. Winter, jr. il Nat Wildlife 10:17-20 D '71

Wild rivers; wilderness waterways. E. Welke. il Bet Hom & Gard 49:119-24 Mr '71
See also
Canoe trips

RIVERA, Diego
Blowup. D. Davis. il por Newsweek 78:77 Jl 5 '71 *

RIVERA, Luis
Luis Rivera Spanish dance company, 92nd street Y, NYC. L. Pastore. Dance Mag 45:85 My '71 *

RIVERBANK vegetation. See Streamside vegetation

RIVERDALE, Robert Arthur Balfour, 2d baron
After 50,000 miles. il Yachting 129:68-9+ Je '71

RIVERDALE, Calif.
Low-budget sports lighting. il Am City 86:72 Ja '71

RIVERS, Caryl
Growing up Catholic in mid-century America. il pors N Y Times Mag p 16-17+ O 10 '71

RIVERS, Joan
I'm glad I'm a middle-aged sex object. por McCalls 99:78+ O '71

RIVERS, Jonny
Backer of a bearback ride. P. Putnam. il por Sports Illus 34:36-8+ Je 28 '71 •

RIVERS, Larry
Bronx is beautiful. R. Hughes. il pors Time 97:68-9 F 8 '71 •
Sanguinary saga; Some American history exhibition. T. W. Moore. il Chr Cent 88: 864-5 Jl 14 '71 •

RIVERS, Mark E.
West Pointer for Watts mfg. por Bsns W p29 O 2 '71 •

RIVERS
Wild rivers; wilderness waterways. E. Welke. il Bet Hom & Gard 49:119-24 Mr '71
See also
Erosion
Water pollution
Watersheds
Waterways
also names of rivers, e.g. Green River

Regulation
How to tame a wild river; reformation of the Floyd River in Sioux City, Ia. J. H. Brouwer. il Am City 86:84+ D '71
Needed: a bill of rights for our rivers. J. N. Miller. Read Digest 99:161-2+ Jl '71
See also
Colorado River

Temperature
Now: total fishing:
Blueprint for success. S. Lievense. il por Outdoor Life 147:58-9+ My '71
Neglected tool, thermometer. S. Lievense. il Outdoor Life 147:75-7+ Ap '71
State's thermal profile; temperature of New York's waters. D. H. Shafer. il Cons 25: 31-2 F '71

RIVERS, lakes, etc.

Clearing
See Clearing of lakes, rivers, etc.

RIVERSIDE, Calif.
Make tree-well covers attractive. il Am City 86:40 D '71

Hotels, restaurants, etc.
Farewell to the Glenwood mission inn. M. C. Muchmore. il Hobbies 76:156+ Ja '72

RIVERSIDE park. See New York (city)—Parks and playgrounds

RIVERSIDE university, Riverside, Calif.
On the up side of down. il Time 97:60 Mr 29 '71

RIVETS and riveting
Custom rivets from memory plastic. J. Hand. il Pop Sci 198:63 F '71

RIVIERA
Battle of the beaches. il por Time 98:26 Ag 30 '71
French Riviera. M. Gough. House B 113:62+ O; 27-8+ N '71
In the land of the voluptuaries. H. Sutton. il Sat R 54:34-5 Ag 7; 37-8 Ag 14 '71

RIZER, Murle
Live-aboard trailering. il Motor B & S 127: 89+ My '71

RIZZO, Francis
Diary of two deadlines. Opera N 35:26-8 Mr 13 '71
Rossini's tragic mask. il Opera N 36:10-11 O '71
(ed) See F. Zeffirelli. Sorcerer's apprenticeship

RIZZO, Frank L.
City hall. R. Mulligan, jr. New Repub 164: 10-11 My 15 '71 •
Conservative's dilemma. G. Bruce. Nat R 23: 1224 N 5 '71 •
Copping it. il por Newsweek 77:20+ My 31 '71 •
Move over Mayor Daley: here comes Frank Rizzo. S. Padwe. por Ramp Mag 10:27-9 Ag '71 •
Night-stick candidate. G. Gilmore. il Nation 213:397-8 O 25 '71 •
Only in America. New Repub 165:10 N 13 '71 •
Running back into the past; with reports by J. Pekkanen and B. Brigham. il pors Life 71:32-4+ O 29 '71 •
Supercop. por Newsweek 77:32+ Mr 15 '71 •
Tough cop for mayor. il por Time 97:13 My 31 '71 •

Toughest cop in America campaigns for mayor of Philadelphia. L. E. Berson. il pors N Y Times Mag p30-1+ My 16 '71; Reply. F. L. Rizzo. p20 Je 13 '71 •
When law and order was voting issue. il por U S News 70:54-5 My 31 '71 •

ROACH, Mary
Leaf plug sparks tree growth. Org Gard & Farm 18:43 O '71
Wool-gathering produces two-pound tomatoes. il Org Gard & Farm 18:70-2 Mr '71

ROACH, William N.
Bulls of Barriere. il pors Outdoor Life 148: 84-7+ O; 80-3+ N; 54-7+ D '71
I wanted it wild. il pors Outdoor Life 148:84-7+ O '71 (to be cont)

ROAD guards. See Roads—Safety guards

ROAD runners (birds)
Roadrunners: energy conservation by hypothermia and absorption of sunlight. R. D. Ohmart and R. C. Lasiewski. bibliog il Science 172:67-9 Ap 2 '71

ROAD signs
Louvered signs lessen highway hazards. Am City 86:112 O '71
Make signs simple; freeway signs. Am City 86:122 S '71

ROAD traffic
On the road; highway flag girl. T. Mocabee. il Seventeen 30:70 Jl '71
See also
Electronics in traffic control

Automatic control
See also
Computers—Traffic control use

ROADRUNNERS. See Road runners (birds)

ROADS
Lifelines for the developing world; new highway systems across continents. W. H. Owens. il UNESCO Courier 24:17+ F '71
Road. G. Brinkman. il Liv Wildn 34:18-22 Wint '70
See also
Snow and ice removal
Trails
Tunnels and tunneling
Wilderness areas—Roads

Federal aid
See Express highways—Federal aid

Interchanges and intersections
Controlling an over-the-hill blind intersection; DeKalb County, Ga. R. W. Roseveare. il Am City 86:116+ N '71
How we resolved a highway-park conflict; Manchester, Conn. W. D. O'Neill. il Am City 86:65 Ag '71
Overlooked cloverleaf; Manchester compromise to keep recreational facilities. il Time 98:30 Ag 23 '71

Lighting
Road-level lighting provides a carpet of light; San Francisco. il Am City 86:84 Jl '71

Location
Parting shots: some Texas folks suggest where a hated superhighway can go. il Life 71:66-7 Ag 27 '71
Reporter at large; house and highway. W. Balliett. New Yorker 47:40-5 D 25 '71
Showdown in the park; conservationists' action over building U.S. highway through Overton park, Memphis. Time 97:44 Mr 15 '71

Maintenance and repair
See also
Roads—Surface treatment

Resurfacing
See Roads—Surface treatment

Safety devices and measures
See also
Roads—Safety guards

Safety guards
New steel median barrier introduced; Washington, D.C. il Am City 86:112 Mr '71

Surface treatment
1.9 miles resurfaced per day; New Mexico. il Am City 86:64-5 S '71

Brazil
Taming the green hell; Transamazon highway. il Life 71:26-31 N 12 '71
Transamazonia: the last frontier. il Time 98:36+ S 13 '71

ROADS—*Continued*

California

How to irrigate median strips; Palm Springs and Santa Rosa, Calif. il Am City 86:14 Mr '71

Colombia

See also
Pan American highway

Latin America

See also
Pan American highway

Panama

See also
Pan American highway

Tanzania

Tortoise and the hare; U.S.-built road. il Newsweek 78:56 O 25 '71

Texas

See also
Express highways—Texas

United States

See also
Express highways
Pan American highway

Wyoming

Who needs the Clark's Fork Canyon road? V. Huser. il Am For 77:24-7 D '71

ROADS, International

U.S. to assist Botswana and Zambia in developing regional road link; Department announcement. Dept State Bul 63:723 D 14 '70

ROADSIDE diners. See Lunchrooms, Roadside

ROADSIDE improvement

How to irrigate median strips; Palm Springs and Santa Rosa, Calif. il Am City 86:14 Mr '71

Ideas for street-side planting. J. Fanning. il House & Gard 139:31+ Je '71

M.I.T. professor challenges garden clubs. J. Clarkson. Horticulture 49:32-5 Je '71

90 serious people armed with shovels plant at almost 500 trees-per-hour. il Sunset 146: 138-9 Mr '71

Whatever happened to the drive to beautify highways? il U S News 71:93 S 20 '71

See also
Billboards

ROADSIDE marketing

Popular garden stand features organic produce. G. Shearer. il Org Gard & Farm 18: 110-13 Ja '71

ROADSIDE planting. See Roadside improvement

ROADSIDE stands. See Roadside marketing

ROALMAN, A. R.

How to tow a trailer. il Pop Mech 135:141-2+ My '71

ROASTING. See Cookery—Meat; Cookery—Poultry

ROASTING utensils. See Kitchen utensils

ROBACK, Howard B. and others

Effects of the psychotherapeutic experience on emerging psychotherapists. Ment Hy 55:228-9 Ap '71

ROBACKER, Earl F.

Stick-spatter ware. il Antiques 99:245-50 F '71

ROBB, Frances Woolley

Where are they now? il pors Newsweek 77:18 Je 14 '71 *

ROBB, Lynda Bird (Johnson)

Once upon a time. il Ladies Home J 88:62+ N '71

(ed) See Nixon, T. Tricia Nixon: my wedding

ROBB, William L.

Army snow job. New Repub 165:15-17 D 11 '71

ROBBERIES and assaults

Behind the upsurge in bank robberies. il U S News 71:30-2 Jl 5 '71

My friend *flic*; bank robberies in France. il Time 97:40 Mr 29 '71

Sawyer takes the pot anytime; poker heists in Huntsville, Ala. A. D. Livingston. il Sports Illus 35:41-2+ N 15 '71

See also
Brigands and robbers

ROBBERS. See Brigands and robbers

ROBBERSON, Elbert

Distress signals. il Yachting 129:70-2+ My '71

ROBBERSON, Winifred

Boating business. See issues of Yachting

ROBBERY insurance. See Insurance, Burglary

ROBBINS, Anne Jerene

Lady in the shower? P. Jordan. por Sports Illus 34:50 Mr 1 '71 *

ROBBINS, Anthony

Physician's role in hospital management. Mo Labor R 94:60-2 Ap '71

—See White, W. D. jt. auth.

ROBBINS, Jane

AALS at Berkeley. por Library J 96:932-3 Mr 15 '71

ROBBINS, Jerome

Robbins; interview. New Yorker 47:21-3 Je 19 '71

about

Classic achieved. J. T. Elson. il por Time 97: 69 Je 21 '71 *

Dance laughter. W. Terry. il Sat R 55:8 Ja 1 '72 *

Genius of Robbins. W. Terry. il Sat R 54:32 Jl 3 '71 *

Going for baroque. H. Saal. il Newsweek 77: 72 Je 7 '71 *

ROBBINS, Jhan

Home is where the nose is. il Todays Health 49:48-9+ Ap '71

ROBBINS, Leonard R. and Kacen, N. M.

Human being inside the child. Todays Ed 60:28-35 My '71

ROBBINS, Norman, and Yonezawa, Takeshi

Developing neuromuscular junctions: first signs of chemical transmission during formation in tissue culture. bibliog il Science 172:395-8 Ap 23 '71

ROBBINS, Warren M.

Totem and taboo. il Newsweek 77:85-6 Je 21 '71 *

ROBERSON, Sam

Stump merchants. Field & S 75:16+ Mr '71

ROBERT A. Taft institute of government

Teaching the teacher. P. S. Coyne. Nat R 23:1302+ N 19 '71

ROBERT college, Istanbul, Turkey. See Colleges and universities—Turkey

ROBERT Fleming and company. See London —Banks

ROBERT Joffrey ballet. See City center Joffrey ballet

ROBERT Lehman collection. See Art— Private collections

ROBERT Wood Johnson foundation

New focus on role of foundations. il U S News 71:52 D 20 '71

ROBERTIS, Eduardo de

Molecular biology of synaptic receptors. bibliog il Science 171:963-71 Mr 12 '71

ROBERTO Devereux; opera. See Donizetti, G.

ROBERTS, A. Hood. See Malkoc, A. M. jt. auth.

ROBERTS, Arthur D. and Dyril, O. E.

Environmental education. Clear House 45: 451-5 Ap '71

ROBERTS, Benjamin C.

Social cost of bargaining: a European perspective. Mo Labor R 94:56-9 Ag '71

ROBERTS, Catherine

Debate: animal experimentation and evolution. Am Scholar 40:497-502 Sum '71

ROBERTS, Cokie, and Roberts, S. V.

Venereal disease pandemic. il N Y Times Mag p62+ N 7 '71

ROBERTS, Doris G.

Sweet memories: glass toy containers. il Hobbies 76:98 Jl '71

ROBERTS, Elsa. See Fraser, B. jt. auth.

ROBERTS, Gary L.

West's gunmen. il Am West 8:10-15+ Ja; 18-23+ Mr '71

ROBERTS, J. J. See Croke, E. J. jt. auth.

ROBERTS, Mark

Work your science interest into your holiday. il Sci Digest 71:60-4 Ja '72

ROBERTS, Millard George

Making college pay. il por Newsweek 78:56 D 20 '71 *

ROBERTS, Myron, and Haynes, Lincoln

TV: Archie's hang-ups. Nation 213:509-10 N 15 '71

ROBERTS, Nancy

Discovering the excitement of science. il Am Ed 7:24-7 Jl '71

Teaching the mentally retarded. il Sat R 54: 70-1+ S 18 '71

ROBERTS, Steven V.

Halfway between dropping out and dropping in. il N Y Times Mag p44-6+ S 12 '71

—See Roberts, C. jt. auth.

ROBERTS, William E.

Calculated risk. por Forbes 107:193 My 15 '71 *

ROBERTSON, Abel Lazzarini, Jr, and Khairallah, P. A.

Angiotensin II: rapid localization in nuclei of smooth and cardiac muscle. bibliog il Science 172:1138-9 Je 11 '71

ROBERTSON, Al
Monumental brass rubbings. il Design 73:36-8 Wint '71
ROBERTSON, Bryan
Museum and the democratic fallacy. il Art in Am 59:58-65 Jl '71
ROBERTSON, Gary J. and Mitchell, B. C.
School grade-age relationship, 1918-69. bibliog Sch & Soc 99:447-51 N '71
ROBERTSON, Ian, and Fishkin, Jim
Ghettoizing culture in South Africa. Commonweal 94:156-7 Ap 23 '71
ROBERTSON, James D.
Forum. Duns 98:73 Ag '71
ROBERTSON, James Louis
Poison of disrespect for law is spreading; excerpts from address, April 29, 1971. il pors U S News 70:66+ My 24 '71
ROBERTSON, Josephine
Sons and daughters of the Soddies. il Har Yrs 11:20 Jl '71
ROBERTSON, Oscar
With Oscar and Lew, Milwaukee is basketball's best, but . . . P. Wilkes. pors Look 35:68-70 Ap 6 '71 •
ROBERTSON, Reuben, 3d
Fasten your seat belts. New Repub 164:17-18 Ja 2 '71
ROBERTSON, Wyndham, and others
Personal investing. See issues of Fortune
ROBESON, Kenneth, pseud. See Dent, L.
ROBIE house, Chicago. See Chicago—Historic houses, etc.
ROBIN, Stanley S.
Observations in a mental hospital: a sociological perspective. bibliog Ment Hy 55:253-9 Ap '71
ROBIN, Steve
Travels with Banovitch. pors Dance Mag 45: 36-7 Je '71
ROBIN Hood and the Gentle knight; drama. See Morley, O.
ROBINS
Nest predation affecting the breeding season of the clay-colored robin, a tropical song bird. E. S. Morton. bibliog il Science 171: 920-1 Mr 5 '71
Rare escape from DDT. E. V. Johnson. il Cons 25:2-3 F '71
ROBINSON, Barbara
Out of the blue; story. Good H 173:118-19 O '71
Summer after; story. Redbook 137:79 Ag '71
ROBINSON, Betty
Checkpoint for travelers. See issues of House beautiful
ROBINSON, Bill
Cruising yachtsman. See issues of Yachting
Editor's page. See issues of Yachting
Height of luxury; excerpts from Legendary yachts. il Yachting 130:66-7+ N '71
Toms River challenge cup is the sport's oldest continuous competition. il Yachting 130: 60-1+ Jl '71
Two thirds to windward. il Yachting 129: 44-7+ Ap '71
ROBINSON, C. E.
Golf courses. il Parks & Rec 6:50-1+ O '71
ROBINSON, Cervin
Late cast iron. il Arch Forum 135:46-9 S '71
ROBINSON, Donald
America's seventy-five most important women. pors Ladies Home J 88:71-3 Ja '71
On call for crises. il por Good H 172:92-3+ Mr '71
ROBINSON, Donald W.
Nobel prizes. il Todays Ed 60:16-19 Ap '71
ROBINSON, Duane, and Clayton, Donald
Ecological man and leisure man. Parks & Rec 6:81-2 Ag '71
ROBINSON, Edwin Arlington
New England tradition. H. Carruth. bibliog il Am Lib 2:940-8 O '71 •
ROBINSON, Francis
Lady without whom we would not be here today; excerpt from intermission talk on the Texaco-Metropolitan opera broadcast, March 13, 1971. Opera N 35:6-7 My 15 '71
ROBINSON, Frank, 1935-
Champagne and aspirin. pors Newsweek 78: 75 O 25 '71 •
ROBINSON, Frankie Isaac
Whatever happened to "Sugar Chile" Robinson? il pors Ebony 26:178 Je '71 •
ROBINSON, Gail
Pops' girl Gail makes it at the Met. il pors Life 70:57-61 Ap 2 '71 •
ROBINSON, Gerold Tanquary
Obituary
Am Hist R 76:1642-3 D '71. H. L. Roberts

ROBINSON, Helen M.
Significant unsolved problems in reading. Ed Digest 36:42-5 F '71
ROBINSON, Jackie, 1946-1971
Sports. R. Kahn. Esquire 76:24+ N '71 •
ROBINSON, James M.
Early Christian manuscripts from the sands of the Nile. il UNESCO Courier 24:4-8+ My '71
ROBINSON, Jan
Princeton chose me. il por Redbook 136:68-9+ F '71
ROBINSON, Jerome B.
Ducks from a red canoe. il Outdoor Life 148: 64-5+ O '71
Float trip for crows. il pors Outdoor Life 147: 66-7+ My '71
Lakers along the shore. il por Outdoor Life 147:62-3+ Je '71
—and Carroll, Hanson
Mountaintop trout. il Field & S 75:58-9+ Ja '71
ROBINSON, Jimmie C. See Kirby, T. B. jt. auth.
ROBINSON, John Arthur Thomas
God without God? Chr Cent 88:1379-82 N 24 '71
ROBINSON, John P. Jr
Tyrian purple; with biographical sketch. il por Sea Front 17:76-82, 126 Mr '71
ROBINSON, Keith, and others
Quadratic elongation: a quantitative measure of distortion in coordination polyhedra. bibliog il Science 172:567-70 My 7 '71
ROBINSON, Kenneth
PTA people of the month. pors PTA Mag 66: 16-17 D '71 •
ROBINSON, Louie
Ann of Mount Angel abbey. il pors Ebony 26: 29-30+ F '71
California's new education boss. il pors Ebony 26:54-6+ My '71
Expanding world of Sidney Poitier. il pors Ebony 27:100-1+ N '71
Glide to glory. il por Ebony 26:44-6+ Jl '71
Judy Pace: the thinking man's star. il pors Ebony 26:112-14+ Mr '71
Life inside a hippie commune. il Ebony 26: 88-91+ N '70
Man and boy. il pors Ebony 26:42-4+ Ap '71
Mexico: a haven for disabled vets. il Ebony 27:31-4+ Ja '72
Return of a native. il pors Ebony 26:120-5 Ag '71
ROBINSON, R. W. and others
Morphactin-induced parthenocarpy in the cucumber. bibliog il Science 171:1251 Mr 26 '71
ROBINSON, Richard M.
Buckwheat does it all. il Org Gard & Farm 18: 33-5 Je '71
ROBINSON, Smokey
Miracle of the Miracles. L. J. Banks. il pors Ebony 26:164-6+ O '71 •
ROBINSON, Victoria
Late bloomer; story. Redbook 136:95 Ap '71
ROBINSON, W. R.
Are the glaciers coming back? il Sci Digest 70:52-7 D '71
ROBISCH, Dave
Rave for Dave. H. L. Masin. por Sr Schol 97:19 Ja 11 '71 •
ROBISON, Howard Winfield
Excerpt from address, February 22, 1971. Cong Digest 50:114+ Ap '71
ROBOTS. See Automatons
ROBSON, William Wallace
Comment. H. Witt. Poetry 118:42-3 Ap '71 •
ROCHE, Eamonn Kevin
You can't see the foyer for the trees. W. Von Eckardt. il pors Horizon 13:40-7 Sum '71 •
ROCHE, James Michael
Competitive system; address, March 25, 1971. il por Vital Speeches 37:445-8 My 1 '71; Same abr. with title Let's stop blaming business! Read Digest 99:123-5 Jl '71; Excerpts. U S News 70:91-3 Ap 12 '71
James M. Roche of General motors; interview. il pors Nations Bsns 59:50-4+ O '71

about

Exit Jim Roche. por Newsweek 78:88 D 6 '71 •
For Roche of G.M. happiness is a 10% surcharge. W. Serrin. il pors N Y Times Mag p36-7+ S 12 '71 •
How GM reacts to the pressure. il por Newsweek 77:76-7 My 24 '71 •
Roche of General motors. il por Forbes 107: 48 My 15 '71 •

ROCHE, John P.
Jigsaw puzzle of history; adaptation of address. il por N Y Times Mag p 14-15+ Ja 24; 4 F 14; 62 F 21 '71

about

Roche paper. Newsweek 77:20 Ja 18 '71 •

ROCHE, Kevin. See Roche, E. K.

ROCHE, Mary
Ecology for your own backyard. il House & Gard 139:56-7+ Je '71

ROCHE, Paul
Pompeii revisited; poem. New Yorker 47:52 O 23 '71

ROCHE institute of molecular biology
Molecular biology: corporate citizenship and potential profit. R. J. Bazell. Science 174: 275-6 O 15 '71

ROCHESTER, Minn.
Stainless steel poles add charm to suburbia. il Am City 86:122 Ap '71

ROCHESTER, N.Y.

Education

It can be work: busing inner city pupils to suburban schools; Project UNIQUE. C. A. Planz. il Clear House 46:158-62 N '71

ROCHESTER, N.Y. University
University of Rochester psychology building, Rochester, New York. il Arch Rec 149:100-1 My '71

Eastman school of music

Eastman. R. Zachary. il Opera N 35:26-30 F 20 '71
Report:
Richard Strauss' Silent woman. J. Echaniz. il Opera N 35:30-1 Ja 30 '71

ROCHESTER Institute of technology, Rochester, N.Y.
College arts complex shaped by a strong master plan. il Arch Rec 149:93-100 Ap '71

ROCK, J. S.
New math: the day they bombed Wisconsin. Ramp Mag 9:32-4 F '71

ROCK apes. See Monkeys

ROCK ballet. See Ballet

ROCK bands. See Rock groups

ROCK bass fishing. See Bass fishing

ROCK carvings. See Petroglyphs

ROCK climbing. See Mountaineering

ROCK concerts. See Concerts

ROCK crystal. See Quartz

ROCK drills
Tunnel technology and the hot-hole digger. il Sci N 101:23-4 Ja 8 '72

ROCK fertilizers. See Fertilizers and manures

ROCK festivals. See Music festivals

ROCK fishing. See Fishing

ROCK garden plants. See Plants, Rock garden

ROCK groups
Also *sprach* Grand Funk Railroad. R. Goldstein. Harper 243:32+ O '71
Buffalo Springfield: this time around. J.-C. Costa. il Sr Schol 98:24-5 My 17 '71
Chicago and the great dream machine. A. Goldman. Life 70:14 My 28 '71
Esquire's heavy 89. il Esquire 76:148-51 O '71
Family reunion; Mamas and the Papas. il Newsweek 78:77+ N 15 '71
Female rock. il Time 97:68-9 Ap 12 '71
From the Cockettes with love and squalor. J. Stewart. il Ramp Mag 10:52-6 D '71
Gideon's bible; Gideon and Power. il por Newsweek 78:73 Ag 9 '71
Grand Funk Railroad: pro, con. D. Goldberg; P. Baird. il Sr Schol 99:21-4 S 27 '71
Grateful dead and the Life and times of Country Joe & the Fish from Haight-Ashbury to Woodstock. D. Lupoff. Ramp Mag 10:63-5 D '71
Jackson Five. il Life 71:50-1 S 24 '71
Jackson Five at home. T. Tyler. il Time 97: 64+ Je 14 '71
Mick Jagger shoots birds; Rolling Stones' tour of Europe, 1970. S. Davidson. Atlan 227:96-8+ My '71
Miracle of the Miracles. L. J. Banks. il pors Ebony 26:164-6+ O '71
Mountain climbing. S. K. Oberbeck. il por Newsweek 77:88 My 3 '71
New heights for the Jackson Five. il Ebony 26:126-8+ S '71
Out of the sandbox; Beach Boys. il Time 98: 45 S 6 '71
Pink Floyd. Relics; and Maggot brain. Funkadelic. D. Lupoff. il Ramp Mag 10:65-6 O '71
Poco's comin' up fast. P. Baird. il Sr Schol 98:26 My 17 '71

Purple lights; Grateful Dead dance marathon at the Manhattan center. New Yorker 47: 35 Ap 17 '71
Return of Satan's Jesters; Rolling Stones new record Sticky fingers. il Time 97:60 My 17 '71
Rock & roll is here to stay; Creedence Clearwater Revival. il Pub W 199:250-2 Ja 25 '71
Rock, etc. concert at Monticello raceway. E. Willis. New Yorker 47:120+ S 25 '71
Rock, etc; the Who at the Performing arts center in Saratoga Springs. E. Willis. New Yorker 47:78+ Ag 28 '71
Rock stars at home with their parents. il Life 71:46-55 S 24 '71
Roots and crafts; the British are coming. E. Sander. Sat R 54:57 Ap 24 '71
Sunday's Child. il Ebony 26:57-8+ Ap '71
The Temptations: a group in tune with the times. C. Higgins. il Ebony 26:64-8+ Ap '71
See also
Beatles

ROCK hunting. See Rocks—Collectors and collecting

ROCK ISLAND corporation
Acquisition drive aimed at losers. por Bsns W p27 Je 26 '71

ROCK jasmines
Androsaces in the garden. M. Helleiner. il Horticulture 49:32 Jl '71

ROCK lyrics. See Rock music (songs, etc)

ROCK mulch. See Mulching

ROCK music (songs, etc)
Fading of a fantasy. il Time 98:8 Jl 19 '71
Fillmore: final night of the Fillmore East. New Yorker 47:23 Jl 10 '71
Good-by to the Fillmores. H. Saal. il por Newsweek 78:89 Jl 12 '71
In my opinion; hard rock is dead! D. Strongin. por Seventeen 30:208 Ap '71
James Taylor: one man's family of rock. il pors Time 97:45-50+ Mr 1 '71
Memorable song for our times; American pie. P. F. Kluge. il pors Life 72:44A-44B+ Ja 14 '72
New folk musical: do the answers ring true? New vibrations. C. A. Forbes. Chr Today 15:38 Mr 26 '71
Playing the hits like the heavies; recording session. L. Hutchinson. il Sr Schol 98:24+ Ap 26 '71
Pop. E. Sander. Sat R 54:55 F 27; 75+ Mr 27; 57 Ap 24; 56 My 29; 47+ Jl 31; 47 Ag 28 '71
Report:
Survival of St Joan, a medieval rock opera by Hank and Gary Ruffin. S. Jenkins. il Opera N 35:31 Mr 27 '71
Revolt into style. by G. Melly. Review Sat R il 54:31-3 N 20 '71. E. Dowling
Rock and its new role. il Sr Schol 98:5-10 My 3 '71
Rock and rebellion, from modern jazz to hard rock, a sociological view. I. L. Horowitz. il Commonweal 93:466-9 F 12 '71
Rock and the Jesus movement. il Sr Schol 99:6-12 D 18 '71
Rock, etc. concert at the Fillmore East a week before closing, with B. B. King and Moby Grape band. E. Willis. New Yorker 47:58 Jl 10 '71
Rock pile; movies. H. S. Resnik. il Sat R 54:48-50 Ja 30 '71
Study: post-rock trend towards jazz; interview. H. Hancock. New Yorker 47:29 Je 12 '71
Through the eyes of sister Kate; interview, ed. by E. Miller. K. Taylor. il pors Seventeen 30:226-7+ Ag '71
Women in rock. J. Marks. Vogue 157:112 Mr 1 '71
See also
Phonograph records—Rock music (songs, etc)
Religion and music
Rock groups
Rock singers

Bibliography

Rock music. J. Voight. Wilson Lib Bul 46: 130-1 O '71; Discussion. 46:318 D '71

ROCK music and society. See Music and society

ROCK music literature. See Music literature

ROCK 'n' roll music (songs, etc) See Rock music (songs, etc)

ROCK operas

Criticisms, plots, etc.

See name of composer for full entry
Jesus Christ superstar. A. L. Webber

ROCK paintings. See Cave drawings and paintings

ROCK phosphates. See Phosphates

ROCK singers
King as queen? il Time 98:52 Jl 12 '71
Melanie is love. M. English. Look 35:37-8 Ja 12 '71
Music: Joplin and Hendrix: a note on the rhetoric of death. M. Josephson. il pors Art in Am 59:96-7 S '71
New minstrels. pors Harp Baz 104:56-9 Je '71
Rock, etc; women's movement in rock. E. Willis. New Yorker 47:168-70+ O 23 '71
That lonely feeling; the Taylors. S. K. Oberbeck. il por Newsweek 77:48 F 8 '71
Women is losers. A. M. Micklo. il Sr Schol 98:22-3+ Ap 26 '71
See also
Narcotics and musicians
also names of rock singers, e.g. J. Taylor
ROCK songs. See Rock music (songs, etc)
ROCKEFELLER, David
David Rockefeller of Chase Manhattan bank; interview. pors Nations Bsns 59:34-8 D '71
New towns, urban rehabilitation; address, February 16, 1971. Vital Speeches 37:354-7 Ap 1 '71
What it will take to bring cities back to life; interview. il por U S News 70:50-2+ Je 7 '71
ROCKEFELLER, John Davison, 1874-1960
I believe. il Am For 77:4-5 Ap '71

about
Ludlow massacre revisited. F. Lang. il Ramp Mag 10:20-2 Ja '72 *
ROCKEFELLER, John Davison, 1906-
Reconciling youth and the Establishment; excerpt from address, December, 1970. Sat R 54:27-9+ Ja 23 '71
ROCKEFELLER, John Davison, 1937-
Break for West Virginia. W. E. Chilton, 3d. Nation 213:390-2 O 25 '71 *
Jay and the strippers. R. Starnes. Field & S 76:8+ Je '71 *
ROCKEFELLER, Martha (Baird)
Obituary
Opera N por 35:28-9 Ap 10 '71. F. Merkling
ROCKEFELLER, Nelson Aldrich, 1908-
Bloody Attica: furies unleashed. il pors Newsweek 78:22-6+ S 27 '71 *
Crisis facing key states: what Reagan, Rockefeller are doing. pors U S News 70:41-2 My 17 '71 *
Rockefeller and Lindsay feud. R. Reeves. pors Life 70:54-6 Je 25 '71 *
Rocky's road. J. L. Sax. il Am Heritage 22:78-83+ F '71 *
Timetable of a bloodbath. J. Leo. Commonweal 95:6-7 O 1 '71 *
What price glory on the Albany Mall? E. Carruth. il por Fortune 83:92-5+ Je '71 *
ROCKEFELLER, Rodman C.
Turn public problems to private account. Harvard Bsns R 49:131-8 Ja '71
ROCKEFELLER, Sharon Lee (Percy)
When I was 17; interview. ed. by B. Kevles. pors Seventeen 30:131+ O '71
ROCKEFELLER public service awards
Talk of the town. New Yorker 47:25-7 D 25 '71
ROCKERS. See Chairs
ROCKET cars. See Automobiles, Racing
ROCKET engines
See also
Guided missiles—Propulsion systems
Space vehicles—Propulsion systems

Design
Solid-propellant technology gains spurred. M. L. Yaffee. il Aviation W 95:48-9+ Ag 16 '71
Specifications
U.S. rocket motors; tables (cont) Aviation W 94:90-1+ Mr 8 '71
Thrust control
Controlling the thrust of rocket engines. N. A. Zarin. il por Space World H-5-89:30-4 My '71
ROCKET fuel. See Rockets—Fuel
ROCKET models
Model rockets useful teaching aids. il Space World H-4-88:41-2 Ap '71
ROCKET propellants. See Rockets—Fuel
ROCKET propulsion
See also
Rockets, Atomic powered
ROCKET ships. See Rockets, Interplanetary
ROCKETDYNE division. See North American Rockwell corporation

ROCKETS
See also
Guided missiles
Fuel
Lox/propane fuel studied for shuttle booster. Aviation W 95:12 O 25 '71
Powder-fueled rocket motor static fired. il Aviation W 95:64-5 D 20 '71
Meteorological use
Two rocket launches scheduled. Aviation W 94:20 Ap 19 '71
Specifications
Leading U.S. international research rockets; tables (cont) Aviation W 94:74-5 Mr 8 '71
Use in research
Vertical 2. A. Gorokhov. Space World H-12-96:45 D '71
ROCKETS, Atomic powered
Congress probes Rover fund cuts. K. Johnsen. Aviation W 94:14-15 Mr 1 '71
Rover reoriented as shuttle complement. K. Johnsen. Aviation W 94:55 F 22 '71
Use of Nerva reactor heat to make electricity studied. R. G. O'Lone. il Aviation W 95:36-7 Jl 26 '71
ROCKETS, Interplanetary
Rocket ships: from Kibalchich to Korolev. Y. Biryukov. Space World H-6-90:4-6 Je '71
ROCKEY, Linda
Dark days for the white collar. il Todays Health 49:16-19 Mr '71
ROCKFORD, Ill.

Parks and playgrounds
Real camp program in a city park day camp. R. Papich. il Camp Mag 43:20-1 F '71; Reply. D. M. Lonheim. 43:30 Je '71
ROCKFORD college, Rockford, Ill.
Adair plaques adorn new Rockford library. il Ceram Mo 20:26-7 Ja '72
ROCKHOUNDS. See Rocks—Collectors and collecting
ROCKING chairs. See Chairs
ROCKS
See also
Geodes
Petrology
Collectors and collecting
Pocketful of treasure: agate supplies of Iowa and the shores of Lake Superior. L. Seamer. por Hobbies 75:144 F '71
Rockhound at Moody air force base. H. D. Brown. il Hobbies 76:148-9 Ja '72
Thickinich Lake; agate prospecting at Mount Rainier. H. D. Brown. il Hobbies 76:150+ D '71
Deformation
Cation disorder in shocked orthopyroxene. R. W. Dundon and S. S. Hafner. bibliog il Science 174:581-3 N 5 '71
Weathering
What is rock weathering? Sci Digest 71:80 Ja '72
ROCKS, Crystalline and metamorphic
See also
Quartz
ROCKS, Igneous
Evolving subduction zones in the western United States, as interpreted from igneous rocks. P. W. Lipman and others. bibliog il Science 174:821-5 N 19 '71
See also
Anorthosite
Basalt
Peridotite
Volcanic ash, tuff, etc.
ROCKVILLE, Md.

Parks and playgrounds
Land acquisition: at no cost. N. A. Ofsthun. Parks & Rec 6:40 Jl '71
ROCKWELL, John
Offenbach. . .and other Germans. por Opera N 35:24-5 Ap 10 '71
Theater of folk ritual. il por Opera N 35:8-12 Ja 16 '71
(ed) See Kirsten, D. Kirsten on Puccini
ROCKWELL, Norman
Audubon observing the passenger pigeon; painting. Look 35:26-7 O 19 '71

about
Homage to Norman Rockwell; with photographs by R. Borowski. Esquire 75:84-5 Ap '71 *
Norman Rockwell album. W. A. H. Birnie. il pors Read Digest 98:145-54 Ap '71 *

ROCKWELL, Norman—about—*Continued*
Norman Rockwell is exactly like a Norman
Rockwell. R. Reeves. il pors N Y Times
Mag p 14-15+ F 28 '71 *
Norman Rockwell's 78th spring. A. Hurlburt.
il pors Look 35:26-30 Je 1 '71 *
Recommended reading. il Am Artist 35:64+
N '71 *
Thanksgiving with Norman Rockwell. il por
Ladies Home J 88:113-21+ N '71 *
ROCKWELL, Pete
Sea and the sky. il Motor B & S 128:44-5
bibliog(p58) Jl '71
ROCKWELL, Willard Frederick, 1888-
Colonel takes command at Rockwell. por
Bsns W p22 My 29 '71 *
Hats worn by a company head. V. Louviere.
Nations Bsns 59:24 S '71 *
ROCKWELL manufacturing company
Colonel takes command at Rockwell. por
Bsns W p22 My 29 '71
ROCKY FLATS division. See Dow chemical
company—Rocky Flats division
ROCKY MOUNTAIN goat hunting
Don't shoot the bearded lady. D. Grave-
stock. il Outdoor Life 147:60-3+ Ja '71
Guide was a dude. H. Rate. il Field & S 76:
32-3+ S '71
ROCKY MOUNTAIN goats
Olympic adventure: ridge of the wild goats.
B. Horton. il Nat Parks & Con Mag 45:30-4
My '71
ROCKY MOUNTAIN laboratory. See United
States—National institutes of health—Rocky
Mountain laboratory
ROCKY MOUNTAIN NATIONAL PARK
Rocky Mountain National Park. V. Huser. il
Nat Parks & Con Mag 45:4-9 Ag '71
ROCKY MOUNTAIN sheep hunting. See Moun-
tain sheep hunting
ROCKY MOUNTAIN spotted fever
Rising fever. Sci Am 225:44 Jl '71
Rocky Mountain laboratory: a monument to
the tick. B. Nelson. il Science 173:1009-10
S 10 '71
ROCKY MOUNTAINS
Springtime in the Rockies. M. Sprague. il
Nat Wildlife 9:26-8, 29-31 Ap '71

Canadian Rockies
For American profit and Japanese steel,
they're tearing down the Canadian Rock-
ies. G. Laycock. il Audubon 73:77-84 Ja '71 *
See also
Banff, Alberta
ROCKY RIVER, Ohio
You don't necessarily need aerobes. il Am
City 86:61-2 Ap '71
ROD and cone cells
Light adaptation in the rat retina: evidence
for two receptor mechanisms. D. G. Green.
bibliog il Science 174:598-600 N 5 '71
Red-green cone interactions in the incre-
ment-threshold spectral sensitivity of pri-
mates. H. G. Sperling and R. S. Harwerth.
bibliog il Science 172:180-4 Ap 9 '71
ROD and custom magazine. See Hot rod (per-
iodical)
RODAHL, Kaare
Be fit for life! condensation. il Read Digest
98:140-8 My '71
RODALE, Jerome Irving
From the writings of J. I. Rodale. Org Gard
& Farm 18:41-5 S '71
Miscellany. il Org Gard & Farm 18:26 F;
26-8+ Ap '71
Organic miscellany. Org Gard & Farm 18:26+
Mr; 66-8 My; 77-80 Je; 86-9 Jl; 67-70 Ag '71
Why I strated Organic gardening. il por Org
Gard & Farm 18:35-40 S '71

about

Catching up to Rodale press. il por Time 97:
51 Mr 22 '71 *
Death of a salesman. Newsweek 77:69 Je 21
'71 *
Guru of the organic food cult. W. Greene. il
pors N Y Times Mag p30-1+ Je 6 '71; Reply.
M. Feher. p4+ Je 27 '71 *
In memoriam; J. I. Rodale. R. Rodale. il por
Org Gard & Farm 18:36-41 Ag '71 *
J. I. Rodale's greatest contribution. R.
Rodale. il pors Org Gard & Farm 18:28-34
S '71 *

Obituary
Pub W 199:52 Je 21 '71
Organic gospel according to J. I. Rodale. P.
A. Farrell. il por Pub W 200:49-50 N 15
'71 *
Shaping an organic America. J. H. Todd.
Org Gard & Farm 18:50-5 S '71 *

Eulogies
Letters in tribute to J. I. Rodale. Org Gard &
Farm 18:46-9 S '71

RODALE, Robert
In memoriam; J. I. Rodale. il por Org Gard
& Farm 18:36-41 Ag '71
Organic gospel according to J. I. Rodale. P.
A. Farrell. il por Pub W 200:49-50 N 15
'71 *
RODALE press, inc.
Organic gospel according to J. I. Rodale. P.
A. Farrell. il por Pub W 200:49-50 N 15
'71
RODBARD, D. See Chrambach, A. jt. auth.
RODCHENKO, Aleksandr
Rodchenko, practicing constructivist. J. Licht.
bibliog il por Art N 70:60-3+ Ap '71 *
RODDY, Joseph
Hippie saint. il pors Look 35:31-7 Ap 20 '71
Igor Stravinsky (1882-1971) Look 35:58 Je 1
'71
Julius Rudel: Washington's music man. por
Look 35:38 S 21 '71
New 'in' group is the Guarneri. il N Y Times
Mag p30-1+ Mr 7 '71
Notes on a cellist in trouble. Look 35:32 F
23 '71
Power and the glory are passing. il Look 35:
21-5 O 19 '71
RODENTS
See also names of rodents, e.g. Ground
squirrels
RODENTS as carriers of infection
See also
Plague
RODEO tailors, inc. See Tailors
RODEOS
American rodeo: sport and spectacle. W. H.
Porter. il Am West 8:40-7+ Jl '71
And they laid it on the Lyne at the O. C.
corral: National finals at Oklahoma fair-
grounds arena. J. Kirshenbaum. il por
Sports Illus 35:85+ D 20 '71
Best damn cowboy in the world; L. Mahan.
J. Stewart-Gordon. il Read Digest 99:215-
16+ S '71
Ride 'em cowboy, gently. il Newsweek 77:
83 Je 27 '71
RODGERS, Dorothy, and Rodgers, Mary
Of two minds. See issues of McCalls
RODGERS, Frederick A.
Paradox without promise: address; April 21,
1971. Vital Speeches 37:521-5 Je 15 '71
RODGERS, Lionel M.
Too many political traffic signals. il Am City
86:69 F '71
RODGERS, Mary. See Rodgers, D. jt. auth.
RODGERS, Mary Augusta
Christmas sun. il Good H 173:58+ D '71
Indoor ecology: cleaning up from basement
to attic to closets. Good H 172:33-4+ Je '71
When children break the law. Good H 173:
67+ Jl '71
RODGERS, R. Bruce, and Ernst, R. C.
Wind Cave National Park. il Nat Parks &
Con Mag 45:15-17 Je '71
RODGERS, Rod A.
Rod Rodgers dance company, Clark center for
the performing arts, NYC. P. G. Rich-
mond. Dance Mag 45:76 F '71 *
RODGERS, Samuel A. See Elton, C. F. jt.
auth.
RODIA, Sam. See Rodilla, S.
RODILLA, Simon
U.S. journal: Watts, the towers. C. Trillin.
New Yorker 47:136+ D 4 '71 *
RODIN, Auguste
Auguste Rodin affair: exhibition at the
National gallery. K. Kuh. il Sat R 54:22-3
D 25 '71 *
Rodin drawings, true and false. J. K. T.
Varnedoe. il Art N 70:30-3+ D '71 *
RODMAN, Carol. See Rodman, P. jt. auth.
RODMAN, Carole Cleaver
San Blas: untrammeled islands off Panama.
Harp Baz 104:60+ Ap '71
RODMAN, Peter, and Rodman, Carol
Watchers in a green world. il pors Life 72:
56-63 Ja 14 '72
RODMAN, Selden
Don't underestimate Brazil. il Nat R 23:860-3
Ag 10 '71
Mas'. Nat R 23:371 Ap 6 '71
Paraguay's popular dictator. il Nat R 23:
759-60+ Jl 13 '71
What drives Latin Americans left? il Nat R
23:1348-50+ D 3 '71
RODÓ, José Enrique
Ariel today. G. R. Pérez. il por Américas
23:23-4 Ap '71 *
RODRIGUEZ, Henry S.
Feeding the children. il Parks & Rec 6:55+
My '71

RODRIGUEZ, Pedro
¡Ay chihuahua! What a race. R. F. Jones. il
por Sports Illus 34:20-1 F 8 '71 *
RODRIGUEZ, Zhandra
Brief biography. S. Goodman. pors Dance
Mag 46:70-1 Ja '72 *
RODS, Fishing. See Fishing tackle
ROE, Jim
Cruising Lake Michigan. il por Yachting 130:
58-9+ Jl '71
ROELOFS, Wendell L. and Cardé, R. T.
Hydrocarbon sex pheromone in tiger moths
(arctiidae) bibliog il Science 171:684-6 F 19
'71
—and others
Sex attractant of the codling moth: char-
acterization with electroantennogram tech-
nique. bibliog il Science 174:297-9 O 15 '71
ROESCH, Roberta
Should you have another baby? Read Digest
98:111-13 My '71
ROESCH, William R.
Waiting for tenure at Jones & Laughlin. por
Bsns W p20 Ja 23 '71 *
ROESELER, Wolfgang Guenther
How to plan regionally for a regional air-
port. il Am City 86:70+ Mr '71
ROESSLER, David
Easy reading in Redcar. il Arch Forum 135:
48-51 N '71
ROGEN, B. R.
Build R-E's $15 color convergence generator.
il Radio-Electr 43:50-2 Ja '72
ROGERS, Bennett M.
Mighty Mooney Mite. il Flying 88:60-4 Je '71
ROGERS, Carl
Forget you are a teacher. Ed Digest 37:17-19
N '71
ROGERS, Cornish
Pan-Africanism and the black church: a
search for solidarity. il Chr Cent 88:1345-7
N 17 '71
Peace breaks out at ABC convention. Chr
Cent 88:682 Je 2 '71
Soul and sense. Chr Cent 88:148, 276-7, 550,
769; 921-2, 1286, 1340, 1462, F 3, Mr 3, My
5, Je 23, Ag 4, N 3, 17, D 15 '71
UCC synod narrows behavior-belief gap. Chr
Cent 88:850 Jl 14 '71
ROGERS, Del Marie
Forest; poem. Nation 213:87 Ag 2 '71
ROGERS, Franklyn C.
Underground nuclear power plants. il por Bul
Atom Sci 27:38-41+ O '71
ROGERS, Michael
Great feeling; story. Esquire 75:94-6 Ap '71
ROGERS, Paul G.
Cancer legislation: pro-NIH bill advances in
House. N. Wade. por Science 174:389 O 22
'71 *
ROGERS, Robert
Americans as guerrilla fighters: Robert Rog-
ers and his rangers. J. T. Hubbard. il por
Am Heritage 22:81-6 Ag '71 *
ROGERS, Robert L.
Chicago ecumenism: changes in style and
agenda. il Chr Cent 88:626-31 My 19 '71
Environmental workbook on church space. il
Chr Cent 88:948-51 Ag 11 '71
ROGERS, Steffen H. and Bueding, Ernest
Hycanthone resistance: development in schi-
stosoma mansoni. bibliog il Science 172:
1057-8 Je 4 '71
ROGERS, Warren
Kennedy's comeback: will he or won't he? il
pors Look 35:13-20+ Ag 10 '71
ROGERS, Will
Little human happiness; excerpt from The
lion. A. P Hout. por Read Digest 99:121-
2 O '71 *
ROGERS, William Pierce
Agreement with Japan on reversion of
Okinawa transmitted to the Senate; report,
September 5, 1971. Dept State Bul 65:433-5
O 18 '71
China, Mideast, Berlin: Rogers states U.S.
policy; excerpts from address, October 5,
1971. il por US News 71:104-6 O 18 '71
Congress, the president, and the war pow-
ers; statement, May 14, 1971. bibliog f Dept
State Bul 64:721-33 Je 7 '71
Death of President Tubman of Liberia; remarks, July 28, 1971. Dept State Bul 65:
180-1 Ag 16 '71
Department reviews the doctrine of executive privilege; statement, August 4, 1971.
bibliog Dept State Bul 65:246-8 Ag 30 '71
Department urges Senate approval of Geneva
protocol on poisonous gases and biological
warfare; statement, March 5, 1971. Dept
State Bul 64:455-9 Mr 29 '71
Fiscal 1972 budget request for development
assistance and security assistance; statement, September 8, 1971. Dept State Bul
65:336-9 S 27 '71

Foreign assistance and the U.S. national interest; statement, with transcript of news
conference, October 30 and November 2,
1971. Dept State Bul 65:577, 583-6 N 22 '71
Foreign policy and the United Nations; address, October 4, 1971. Vital Speeches 38:
34-8 N 1 '71; Same with title Legacy of
peace: our responsibility to future generations. Dept State Bul 65:437-44 O 25 '71;
Excerpts. Cur Hist 62:44+ Ja '72
Growing ties between science and foreign
policy; address, May 21, 1971. Dept State
Bul 64:766-8 Je 14 '71
IJC completes report on pollution of the
lower Great Lakes; statement, January 14,
1971. Dept State Bul 64:203 F 15 '71
Joint Japan-U.S. committee on trade and
economic affairs holds eighth meeting at
Washington; opening remarks, September
9, 1971. Dept State Bul 65:346-50 O 4 '71
More balanced and reinvigorated partnership
of the Americas; statement, April 15, 1971.
Dept State Bul 64:602-7 My 10 '71
New foreign service and the job of modern
diplomacy; remarks, November 16, 1971.
Dept State Bul 65:675-6 D 13 '71
North Atlantic council ministerial meeting
held at Brussels; arrival statement, De-
cember 2, 1970. Dept State Bul 64:1 Ja 4
'71
Our permanent interests in Europe; address,
December 1, 1971; with questions and
answers. Dept State Bul 65:693-702 D 20 '71
Peace and stability in the Middle East and
Asia; statement, December 8, 1970. Dept
State Bul 64:61-7 Ja 11 '71
Principles and pragmatism in American
foreign policy; address, August 31, 1971.
Dept State Bul 65:297-302 S 20 '71
Quadripartite agreement on Berlin signed
at Berlin concluding first phase of negotia-
tions; statement, September 3, 1971. Dept
State Bul 65:317 S 27 '71
Relating our national idealism to interna-
tional realities; address, May 30, 1971.
Dept State Bul 64:795-9 Je 21 '71
Restoring our common purpose in world af-
fairs; statement concerning report on
United States foreign policy 1969-1970. Dept
State Bul 64:507 Ap 12 '71
Rogers: dealing with realities of the world
today; text of statement, August 2, 1971. il
por U S News 71:20-1 Ag 16 '71
Secretary gratified at decision of Senate on
NATO forces; statement, May 15, 1971.
Dept State Bul 64:740-1 Je 7 '71
Secretary Rogers accepts task force reports
on Department of state management reform; statement and text of letter, December 4, 1970. Dept State Bul 63:794 D 28
'70
Secretary Rogers announces U.S. policy on
Chinese representation in the U.N; statement, August 2, 1971. Dept State Bul 65:
193-6 Ag 23 '71
Secretary Rogers attends SEATO and
CENTO meetings and visits four Arab
states, Israel and Rome; statements and
transcripts of interviews, April 26-May 9,
1971. Dept State Bul 64:681-701 My 31 '71
Secretary Rogers discusses Middle East and
southeast Asia in interview on CBS Morning news; January 15, 1971. Dept State Bul
64:133-6 F 1 '71
Secretary Rogers discusses new Cabinet
committee on international narcotics control; news conference, September 7, 1971.
Dept State Bul 65:357-9 O 4 '71
Secretary Rogers discusses United Nations
decision on Chinese representation; transcript of news conference, October 26, 1971.
Dept State Bul 65:541-7 N 15 '71
Secretary Rogers interviewed for Yugoslav
television; transcript of interview, Octo-
ber 22, 1971. Dept State Bul 65:596-8 N 22
'71
Secretary Rogers interviewed on Face the
Nation; transcript of program, October 10,
1971. Dept State Bul 65:479-86 N 1 '71
Secretary Rogers interviewed on Meet the
press; program, May 16, 1971. Dept State
Bul 64:734-40 Je 7 '71
Secretary Rogers' news conference:
December 23, 1970. Dept State Bul 64:37-
48 Ja 11 '71
January 29, 1971. Dept State Bul 64:189-
97 F 15 '71
March 16, 1971. Dept State Bul 64:478-86
Ap 5 '71
April 23, 1971. Dept State Bul 64:593-600
My 10 '71
June 15, 1971. Dept State Bul 65:1-9 Jl
5 '71
July 1, 1971. Dept State Bul 67:78-82
Jl 19 '71
September 3, 1971. Dept State Bul 65:
326-33 S 27 '71

ROGERS, William Pierce—*Continued*
Secretary Rogers pays tribute to the NATO
alliance; excerpt from remarks, December
10, 1970. Dept State Bul 64:6-7 Ja 4 '71
Secretary Rogers reviews U.S. objectives in
the world; remarks, with questions and
answers, November 12, 1971. Dept State Bul
65:647-58 D 6 '71
Secretary Rogers urges early and favorable
Senate action on agreement with Japan on
reversion of Okinawa; statement, October
27, 1971. Dep State Bul 65:565-8 N 15 '71
Self-help and the search for peace; statement, November 25, 1970. Dept State Bul
63:713-17 D 14 '70
Seventeenth anniversary of SEATO, statement, September 8, 1971. Dept State Bul
65:356 O 4 '71
Supplemental assistance and basic U.S. poli-
cies in the Middle East and East Asia.
Dept State Bul 64:19-26 Ja 4 '71
Tenth meeting of OECD ministerial council
held at Paris; statement, June 7, 1971.
Dept State Bul 65:11-13 Jl 5 '71
Third special session of the OAS general as-
sembly adopts measures on kidnaping and
terrorism; statements, January 27 and
February 2, 1971. Dept State Bul 64:228-31
F 22 '71
Thirty minutes with William P. Rogers; in-
terview on PBS program, March 9, 1971.
Dept State Bul 64:440-8 Mr 29 '71
U.S. and Japan sign agreement on reversion
of Okinawa, statements, June 17, 1971. Dept
State Bul 65:33-4 Jl 12 '71
U.S. and Thailand sign memorandum of
understanding of international narcotics
control; remarks, September 28, 1971. Dept
State Bul 65:411-12 O 18 '71
U.S. and U.S.S.R. sign agreements to reduce
risk of nuclear war; remarks, September 30,
1971. Dept State Bul 65:399-400 O 18 '71
U.S.-Canadian economic committee meets at
Ottawa; statement, November 25, 1970.
Dept State Bul 63:730 D 14 '70
U.S. foreign policy in a technologcal age;
address, January 26, 1971. Dept State Bul 64:
198-202 F 15 '71
U.S. responds to Chilean decision on compensation for expropriation; statement, Oc-
tober 13, 1971. Dept State Bul 65:478 N 1
'71
U.S. sets a new course; interview. por U S
News 71:30-4 N 22 '71
United States and Japan: common interests
and common problems; address, June 30,
1971. Dept State Bul 65:69-73 Jl 19 '71
United States foreign policy 1969-1970; a report of the Secretary of state; letter of
transmittal and introductory comment.
Dept State Bul 64:465-77 Ap 5 '71
United States hails Turkish decision to ban
opium poppy production, news conference,
June 30, 1971. Dept State Bul 65:75-7 Jl
19 '71
Vienna convention on the law of treaties
transmitted to the Senate; report. Dept
State Bul 65:684-9 D 13 '71

about
Flashing the signal. Newsweek 78:61+
O 18 '71 *
Israel: does geography matter? por News-
week 77:37-8 Mr 29 '71 *
Kissinger and Rogers. J. Osborne. New Re-
pub 164:13-15 Mr 27 '71 *
Mideast: the Phantom 'No'. il por Newsweek
78:31-2 N 29 '71 *
President defends a policy and a man; tele-
vised press conference, March 4, 1971. il
pors Time 97:13 Mr 15 '71 *
Secretary of state marches on. W. F. Buck-
ley, jr. Nat R 23:498 Ag 24 '71 *
Who's secretary of state? il pors Newsweek
77:26-7 Mr 15 '71 *

Visit to the Middle East, 1971
Big gamble in the Middle East. il por News-
week 77:41+ My 10 '71
Mission to the Middle East. il por Time 97:
23-4 My 3 '71
On the road in search of peace. il pors
Newsweek 77:35-6 My 17 '71
Rogers on the road. il por Time 97:34 My 10
'71
Rogers trip, how successful? il pors U S
News 70:26 My 17 '71
Secretary Rogers attends SEATO and
CENTO meetings and visits four Arab
states, Israel and Rome; statements, trans-
cripts of interviews, and texts of commu-
niques, April 26-May 9, 1971. W. P. Rog-
ers. Dept State Bul 64:681-702 My 31 '71

ROGERS' rangers. See United States—History
—French and Indian war, 1755-1763
ROGET, Peter Mark
Peter Mark Roget, by D. L. Emblen. Review
Writer 84:7-8 Mr '71. L. Conger *
ROGIN, Gilbert
Address to the orgiasts; story. New Yorker
47:39-45 Je 5 '71
La-dah-dah-dah-dum; story. New Yorker
47:32-4 D 18 '71
Spanish house; story. New Yorker 47:32-4 My
15 '71
about
Socks washed in tears. J. Skow. por Time
98:87+ N 29 '71 *
ROGIN, Richard
East New York: this place makes Bedford-
Stuyvesant look beautiful. il N Y Times
Mag p30-1+ Mr 28 '71
ROHDE, William L.
Horses and riders: a galloping growth. il
Cons 25:13+ Ap '71
RÓHEIM, Géza
Géza Róheim: psychoanalytic anthropologist
or radical Freudian? R. C. Calogeras. bib-
liog Am Imago 28:146-57 Sum '71 *
ROHLF, John A.
Your beef business. See issues of Farm
journal
ROHLFS, Mrs Marcus
Year of the woman for Baptists, Presby-
terians. E. E. Plowman. por Chr Today 15:
27 Je 4 '71 *
ROHM and Haas company
Rohm & Haas: new pathway. il Forbes 109:
29 Ja 1 '72
ROHMER, Eric
Eric Rohmer: an interview; tr. by G. Petrie.
il Film Q 24:34-41 Sum '71

about
Current cinema. P. Kael. New Yorker 47:
136+ Mr 20 '71 *
Films. R. Hatch. Nation 212:574 My 3 '71 *
Mystifier. P. D. Zimmerman. il por News-
week 77:100-1 My 3 '71 *
Reputation of Eric Rohmer. W. S. Pechter.
Commentary 52:84-6 Ag '71 *
Rohmer's formula: boy talks with girl, boy
argues with girl, boy says. M. S. Davis. il
pors N Y Times Mag p38-9+ N 21 '71 *
ROHNERT PARK, Calif.
Master-planned for progress. T. West. il
Parks & Rec 6:36+ Mr '71
ROHR, Frank, jr
Vagabond camera. See issues of Travel
ROHR corporation
Tough route from jets to rail cars. il Bsns
W p96-7+ My 1 '71
ROIPHE, Anne Richardson
Family is out of fashion. il por N Y Times
Mag p 10-11+ Ag 15 '71 *
Mad diary of a Manhattan ecologist. il N Y
Times Mag p6+ O 17: 98 N 7 '71
Up the sandbox! story, excerpt from novel.
Redbook 136:167-89 F '71
ROIZMAN, Bernard, and Spear, P. G.
Herpesvirus antigens on cell membranes de-
tected by centrifugation of membrane-
antibody complexes. bibliog il Science 171:
298-300 Ja 22 '71
ROJAS, Billy
Textbook of the future. Sch & Soc 99:315-
17 Sum '71
ROLAND, Mitchell
Doesn't anybody need a Ph.D. chemist? il
por Life 71:84 N 5 '71 *
ROLE playing
Brown eyes, blue eyes; excerpt from A class
divided. W. Peters. Read Digest 98:61-5
Ap '71
I became a bum to understand their prob-
lems. S. Bacon. il pors Sci Digest 69:40-7
My '71
Improvisational techniques: American Shake-
speare festival's Center for theatre tech-
niques in education, or CTTE, and other
workshops. T. Mofford and J. Mofford. bib-
liog il Schol Teach Jr/Sr High p 14-16 Ja
'72
Parting shots; a professor dresses up zool-
ogy; R. Eakin of Berkeley campus. il pors
Life 71:62-3 Jl 23 '71
Roar, lion, roar! theater where children take
over. il Life 71:155-6 D 17 '71
ROLFS, Mary Jane
Sisterhood; story. Redbook 137:197-219 O '71
ROLL-on, roll-off freighters. See Freighters
ROLLER skating
Roller derby. il Life 71:56-9 Ag 13 '71
ROLLERS, Appliance. See Casters, glides, etc
(hardware)

ROLLIN, Betty
   American way of marriage: remarriage. Look
      35:62+ S 21 '71
   Backlash against Women's lib! il Look 35:
      15-19 Mr 9 '71
   George C. Scott: nothing ever really helps.
      il pors Look 35:78-80+ Ap 20 '71
   What's women's lib doing to the family?
      Plenty! Look 35:40 Ja 26 '71
ROLLING (metal work)
   One-trip sheetmaking goes on stream; tan-
      dem casting-rolling mill. il Bsns W p55
      O 9 '71
   Sheet metal with fewer wrinkles. il Bsns W
      p60 Jl 17 '71
ROLLS. See Bread
ROLLS-Royce, ltd.
   Carriers, banks queried in L-1011 accord. J.
      P. Woolsey. Aviation W 94:22-3 Ap 5 '71
   Collapse of Rolls-Royce adds to Lockheed's
      woes. il U S News 70:95 F 15 '71
   Conway leaves position at Rolls after head-
      quarters restructuring. Aviation W 95:18 S
      27 '71
   Highfliers. Nation 212:260-1 Mr 1 '71
   How the U.S. (and Britain and Germany...)
      got involved in Lockheed. R. Fitch. il
      Ramp Mag 10:44-6+ S '71
   In Burbank and Derby, they wait. il News-
      week 78:52 Ag 9 '71
   Legend may go under the hammer. il Bsns
      W p67 F 13 '71
   Lockheed, British reopen talks on future of
      RB.211 for TriStar. Aviation W 94:185 Mr
      8 '71
   Lockheed's rough ride with Rolls-Royce. il
      Time 97:68-9 F 15 '71
   Lockheed's search for survival. il Bsns W
      p64-8 F 13 '71
   Meetings to weigh RB.211 future. Aviation
      W 94:25-6 F 22 '71
   New RB.211 contract hinges on U.S. guar-
      antees. Aviation W 94:15 My 17 '71
   Offer of costly salvation; Lockheed engine
      contract for TriStar jet. Time 97:78 Mr 15
      '71
   On the skids. il Sr Schol 98:14-15 Mr 8 '71
   RB.211 deadline extended for negotiation. H.
      J. Coleman. Aviation W 94:23-4 Mr 1 '71
   RB.211 problem spurs Rolls layoff study.
      Aviation W 94:24 Mr 15 '71
   Rolls fiber interests readied for sale. H. J.
      Coleman. Aviation W 95:17 O 25 '71
   Rolls nationalization clouds RB.211 future.
      H. J. Coleman. Aviation W 94:26-7 F 8 '71
   Rolls on the rocks. il Newsweek 77:65 F 15
      '71
   Rolls receiver reassures debenture holders.
      Aviation W 94:25 Ap 26 '71
   Rolls-Royce: the trap of technological pride.
      il Time 97:84+ F 22 '71
   Rolls seeks new RB.211 contract. Aviation W
      94:32-4 F 15 '71
   Salvage of the Lockheed 1011. H. B. Meyers.
      il por Fortune 83:66-71+ Je '71
   TriStar engine may be U.S.-made; with
      commentary. il por Bsns W p42-3 Mr 13 '71
   TriStar: the cost of buying American. Bsns
      W p29 Mr 20 '71
   U.K. government officials join Lockheed-
      Rolls talks in U.S. J. E. Woolsey. Avia-
      tion W 94:26 Mr 29 '71
ROLLS-Royce motors, ltd.
   Auto aristocrat is going public. il Bsns W
      p39 O 2 '71
   Rap 'n 'pinion. D. Plastow. por Motor T
      23:14 Jl '71
   Rebirth of Rolls? il por Forbes 108:77 O 15
      '71
ROLO, Charles J.
   Stock buying: what to look for in industries.
      Bet Hom & Gard 49:24+ O '71
   Stock trends (cont) por Forbes 107:63 Mr 1;
      66-7 Ap 1; 50 My 1; 54-5 Ag 1; 108:58-9 S 1;
      98-9 D 1 '71
   Wall street view (cont) por Forbes 107:58-
      9 F 1 '71
ROM, Patricia
   Anachronisms of another day. W. R. Eshel-
      man. Wilson Lib Bul 45:719 Ap '71 •
ROMAINE, Howard
   Why a black man should run. Nation 213:
      264-8 S 27 '71
ROMAN Catholic church. See Catholic church
ROMAN Catholics. See Catholics
ROMAN empire. See Rome
ROMAN imperialism. See Imperialism
ROMAN pottery. See Pottery, Roman
ROMANCE: ballet. See Ballets—Criticisms
ROMANCE of Varghe and Golshah. See Per-
   sian literature
ROMANIES. See Gypsies

ROMANO, Salvatore
   It floats. C. R. Baldwin. il Art N 70:36-7+ N
      '71 •
ROMANOFF, Valentin
   That's show biz. Newsweek 78:74 D 13 '71 •
ROMANTIC love. See Love
ROMANTIC poets. See Romanticism
ROMANTICISM
   Beards, buildings and romantics. R. Lynes.
      Art in Am 59:19 Ja '71
   Decline of flower power. P. C. Rule. America
      124:141-5 F 13 '71
   New (?) romanticism. J. Jerome. Writers
      Digest 51:14-17 N '71
   On the road to Manderley. M. Duffy. il
      Time 97:95+ Ap 12 '71
   Ricardo Palma's tradiciones. L. A. Fox. il
      por Américas 23:31-6 Je '71
   Ringers in the tower, by H. Bloom. Review
      Nation 213:278-80 S 27 '71. M. Lebowitz
ROMANTICISM in music
   Beethoven and romantic irony. R. M. Long-
      year. bibliog f il Mus Q 56:647-64 O '70
   Classical nature of Schubert's lieder. W. Gray.
      bibliog f Mus Q 57:62-72 Ja '71
ROME
   Coin of the realm. il Time 98:66 O 4 '71

      Anecdotes, facetiae, satire, etc.
   Night they auctioned off the Roman empire.
      E. Segal. il Horizon 13:36-9 Sum '71

      History
   Carthage through the eyes of Greece and
      Rome. M. Fantar. il UNESCO Courier 23:
      29-33 D '70
         Historiography
   Zosimus, the first historian of Rome's fall.
      W. Goffart. bibliog f Am Hist R 76:412-41
      Ap '71
         Republic, 265-30 B.C.
   M. Licinius Crassus, loser; excerpt from
      From the jaws of victory. C. Fair. il Hori-
      zon 13:112-17 Spr '71
   On war and greed in the second century
      B.C; economic motives of Roman imperi-
      alism. W. V. Harris. bibliog f Am Hist
      R 76:1371-85 D '71
ROME (city)

      Anecdotes, facetiae, satire, etc.
   Man in the ruins: from a Roman journal.
      C. Strout. Yale R 61:151-60 O '71

      Art
   Rome. M. Gendel. Art N 70:43 Ap '71

      Churches
      See also
   Rome (city)—St Peter's cathedral

      Description
   Travel notes: walking in the city. R. Joseph.
      Esquire 76:50+ S '71
      See also
   Rome (city)—Gardens

      Gardens
   Rome's glorious garden; Villa Borghese. A.
      Menen. il Holiday 49:34-9+ My '71

      Music
   Report:
      Cosi fan tutte. E. Rizzo. Opera N 35:
         33 F 13 '71
      La favorita and Khovanshchina. E.
         Rizzo. il Opera N 35:31 Mr 13 '71

      St Peter's cathedral
   St Peter's. A. Menen. il Nat Geog 140:864-
      79 D '71
ROME (city) in art
   Ingres in Rome. P. Hattis. il Art N 70:26-9+
      My '71
ROMEO and Juliet; ballet. See Ballets—Criti-
   cisms
ROMER, Karen T. and Secor, Cynthia
   Time is here for Women's liberation. Ann
      Am Acad 397:129-39 S '71
ROMERO, Fernando
   Sailing by Caravel. il Américas 23:S7-10 O '71
ROMERO, Francisco
   Course of Latin American philosophy. il
      Américas 23:S13-17 Ag '71
ROMINGER, Wray
   Prickly pear: desperado of the range? il Org
      Gard & Farm 18:90 Je '71
ROMNES, Haakon Ingolf
   H. I. Romnes of AT&T; interview. por Na-
      tions Bsns 59:56-60+ Ap '71
         about
   Romnes of AT&T. il por Forbes 107:54 My
      15 '71 •

ROMNEY, George, 1907-
Reply to Life's editorial on Nixon. por Life
70:62A F 5 '71
ROMNEY, Lenore (LaFount)
Men, women, and politics. Look 35:11 Ap
'71
RON, Harold. See Lurie, A. jt. auth.
RON, Rahamim
Brief biography. S. Goodman. il pors Dance
Mag 45:66-7 F '71 *
RONALDS, Francis S. Jr
Future of international broadcasting. bibliog
f Ann Am Acad 398:71-80 N '71
RONAN, Margaret
Films. See issues of Senior scholastic
RONAN, William John
New York transit boss rides out the storm.
il por Bsns W p90-2 F 20 '71 *
RONDEAU, Noah John
Noah John Rondeau: Adirondack hermit,
by M. C. DeSormo. Review
Liv Wildn por 35:42-4 Spr '71. W. K.
Verner *
RONNING, Chester A.
China: a traveler's diary. P. Stursberg. il
Newsweek 77:48+ My 17 '71 *
ROOBOL, Norman R.
Chromium plating on plastics. il por Chem
44:10-13 N '71
ROOD, Ronald
Trade winds; interview, ed. by C. Amory.
Sat R 54:10-11 Ag 7 '71
ROOF decks. See Outdoor rooms
ROOF gardens
Garden in the clouds; with editorial com-
ment. S. N. Shurcliff. il Horticulture 49:
20, 22-5 My '71
ROOF heliports. See Heliports
ROOFS
Ingenuity simplifies construction of a com-
plex concrete roof. il Arch Rec 150:125-6
Ag '71
Use this easy method to tie-in the roof. R.
F. Dempewolff. il Pop Mech 135:128-30 Je
'71
    See also
Boats—Roofs
Domes
        Maintenance and repair
Don't forget to check your roof. il Chang-
ing T 25:43-5 Jl '71
How to patch a shingled roof. il Bet Hom
& Gard 49:26 Ap '71
Repair system for copper roof. Am City 86:48
O '71
ROOM air conditioners. See Air conditioning
equipment
ROOM deodorizers. See Deodorants
ROOM dividers. See Partitions
ROOM for a King; drama. See DuBois, G.
ROOM furnishings. See Household furnishings
ROOM models. See Rooms, Miniature
ROOM painting. See Painting, Industrial and
practical
ROOMS
Case of the disappearing bed. N. Mandel-
baum. il Ladies Home J 88:126-9 S '71
Convertible room of loose platforms. J. M.
Olivas. il Pop Sci 199:100-1 S '71
Create your own winter hospitality room. il
House B 113:162-3+ O '71
Everything in one enormous room. il House
& Gard 140:102-11 O '71
15 great rooms and what makes them worth
studying. il House B 113:74-83 Ap '71
First step to a beautiful room: the floor plan.
W. Baldwin. il House & Gard 140:6+ N
'71
How to bring your rooms up to date. W.
Baldwin. House & Gard 140:6+ Jl '71
Immediate style: 5 rooms for today. L.
Grundy. il House B 113:139-45 O '71
New room: no furniture, cubes and plat-
forms to replace furniture. il Time 97:60+
Ap 26 '71
    See also
Attics
Bathrooms
Bedrooms
Childrens rooms
Dens (rooms)
Dining rooms
Furniture, Arrangement of
Guest rooms
House decoration
Kitchens
Music rooms and equipment
Outdoor rooms
Playrooms
Recreation rooms
Sewing rooms
Studies (rooms)
Studios

ROOMS, Miniature
On and off the avenue; model rooms on dis-
play at Bloomingdale's. J. Malcolm. New
Yorker 47:172-3 N 13 '71
ROOMS, Remodeled. See Houses, Remodeled
ROOSA, Robert Vincent
Strategy for winding down inflation. il
Fortune 84:70-3+ S '71
ROOSA, Stuart A.
    See also
Space flight to the moon—Manned flights—
Apollo 14 flight
ROOSEVELT, Eleanor (Roosevelt)
Eleanor and Franklin. by J. P. Lash. Review
Atlan 228:136-9 N '71. M. Mannes *
Bsns W por p8+ O 16 '71. G. Hicks *
Life il pors 71:10 O 15 '71. J. M. Burns *
Nat R il 23:1357-8 D 3 '71. J. Chamber-
lain *
New Repub 165:19-23 O 16 '71. D.
Meyer *
New Yorker 47:177-81 O 16 '71. B. Gill *
Newsweek il por 78:116+ O 18 '71. W.
Clemons *
Sat R il pors 54:44-7 O 16 '71. G.
Culligan *
Time il pors 98:86+ N 29 '71. M. Duffy *
Vogue 158:68 D '71. J. Stafford *
Eleanor; excerpt from Eleanor and Franklin.
J. P. Lash. il pors McCalls 99:92-3+ O '71 *
Miss Eleanor Roosevelt; excerpts. K. S.
Davis. il pors Am Heritage 22:48-59 O '71 *
ROOSEVELT, Franklin Delano, 1882-1945
Before the colors fade: The true-blue Demo-
crat; interview, ed. by V. V. Hamilton. J.
A. Farley. il pors Am Heritage 22:38-43+
Ag '71 *
Eleanor and Franklin, by J. P. Lash. Re-
view
Life il pors 71:10 O 15 '71. J. M. Burns *
Nat R il 23:1357-8 D 3 '71. J. Chamber-
lain *
New Repub 165:19-23 O 16 '71. D. Meyer *
New Yorker 47:177-81 O 16 '71 B. Gill *
Sat R il pors 54:44-7 O 16 '71 G. Culligan *
Time il pors 98:86+ N 29 '71. M. Duffy. *
Vogue 158:68 D '71. J. Stafford *
Franklin Roosevelt as world leader. R.
Dallek. bibliog f Am Hist R 76:1503-13
D '71 *
Miss Eleanor Roosevelt; excerpts. K. S.
Davis. il pors Am Heritage 22:48-59 O '71 *
Prince, American style. A. Kazin. il Vogue
157:132-3+ F 1 '71 *
Roosevelt: the soldier of freedom, by J. M.
Burns. Review
Commentary 51:83-4+ Ap '71. R. H. S.
Crossman
New Yorker 46:81-2+ Ja 9 '71. N.
Bliven *
        Memorials
Where are they now? proposed official monu-
ment. il Newsweek 78:13 S 20 '71
ROOSEVELT, Franklin D. library, Hyde Park,
N.Y. See Franklin D. Roosevelt library,
Hyde Park, N.Y.
ROOSEVELT, Theodore
T.R. on the writing of history. il Am Her-
itage 22:112 Ap '71

            about
A man, a plan, a canal, Panama! J. F.
Stevens. D. G. McCullough. il pors Am
Heritage 22:64-71+ Je '71 *
T.R. and the nature fakers. G. Carson. il por
Am Heritage 22:60-5+ F '71 *
ROOSTERFISH fishing. See Papagallo fishing
ROOT, Alan. See Root, J. jt. auth.
ROOT, Joan, and Root, Alan
Mzima, Kenya's spring of life. il pors Nat
Geog 140:350-73 S '71
ROOT, Lin
Italian idyll: Elba. il Travel 136:28-35+
N '71
ROOT, Samuel L. pseud.
I sold my company (a horror story) il Duns
97:48-50 F '71
ROOT, Waverley
What's new on the Paris hotel and restau-
rant scene? il Holiday 48:76-9+ S '70
—and Eckley, Mary
Secret of great women chefs. il McCalls 98:
70-7+ Ag '71
ROOT carving. See Carving (art industries)
ROOT cellars. See Basements and cellars
ROOTS, John McCook
(ed) See Ben Gurion, D. Peace is more im-
portant than real estate

ROOTS
Look at your plant roots. V. Schatz and A. Schatz. Org Gard & Farm 18:96-7 Je '71
Pinocytosis and membrane dilation in uranyl-treated plant roots. H. Wheeler and P. Hanchey. bibliog il Science 171:68-71 Ja 8 '71
Plant roots and productive growth. C. M. Wilson. Org Gard & Farm 18:114-16 Ja '71

ROOTWORMS, Corn. See Corn rootworms

ROPE
See also
Knots and splices

ROPER, Burns W. and Heinig, Jean
What the people think. il Cur 132:5-7 S '71

ROPER, Elmo
Obituary
Sat R por 54:21 My 22 '71. N. Cousins and W. D. Patterson

ROPER, James E.
Legacy of David Scull. por Read Digest 99: 33-6 Ag '71
Man behind the ban on cigarette commercials. por Read Digest 98:213-14+ Mr '71
Why our fishing fleet is sinking. il Read Digest 99:182-6+ O '71

ROQUEMAUREL, Ithier, marquis de
Hachette: reception at the Plaza. New Yorker 47:35-6 O 23 '71

ROREM, Ned
Pelléas et Mélisande. il Am Rec G 37:405-7 Mr '71
Performing arts. Harper 242:22-4 Je '71
Some notes on Debussy. por Am Rec G 37: 404+ Mr '71
about
Musical events; Symphony no. 3 was played by the Utah symphony in Carnegie Hall. W. Sargeant. New Yorker 47:88 Je 12 '71 •
Two very different sides of Ned Rorem. P. L. Miller. Am Rec G 37:730-1 Je '71 •

RORSCHACH test. See Personality tests

RORVIK, David M.
Beyond the pill. Look 35:17-19 Je 15 '71
Present shock (cont of) Brave new world. Esquire 75:24 F; 66 Ap; 76:26 Ag; 68+ O; 48+ D '71
Test-tube baby is coming. il Look 35:83-6+ My 18 '71
You can stop worrying about menopause. McCalls 99:102-3+ O '71

ROSALEE Pritchett; drama. See Molette, C. and Molette, B.

ROSAND, David
Portrait of the artist as a portrait of the artist. il por Art N 70:32-5+ Mr '71

ROSAPEPE, James C.
Statement in black and white. Commonweal 94:421-2 Ag 20 '71

ROSE, Ann Zias
Operation stretch your dollar. il por Har Yrs 11:28-9 F '71

ROSE, Barbara
Art. il Vogue 157:156 Mr 1; 74 Mr 15; 161 Ap 1; 128 Ap 15; 158:88 Jl; 70 Ag 1; 284-5 S 1; 177-8 O 1; 169 D '71
Books. Vogue 157:156+ My '71
Jack Youngerman. por Vogue 157:143 F 1 '71
Movies. il Vogue 158:70 N 1 '71

ROSE, Ben
Day the lion ate franks and beans. J. Deschin. il por Pop Phot 68:10+ Je '71 •

ROSE, Carl
Obituary
New Yorker 47:68 Jl 3 '71

ROSE, David J.
Controlled nuclear fusion: status and outlook. bibliog il Science 172:797-808 My 21 '71

ROSE, Dick
Racing clinic. See issues of Yachting

ROSE, Dixie E.
Trailing the wild iris. il Horticulture 49:48-9 My '71

ROSE, Don
New voices of newsmen: local journalism reviews. il Nation 214:43-6 Ja 10 '72

ROSE, Leonard
Talk with Leonard Rose. D. J. Soria. por Hi Fi 21:MA6-8 Ap '71 •

ROSE, Noel R. See Vladutiu, A. O. jt. auth.

ROSE, P. I.
Protein-metal ion binding site: determination with proton magnetic resonance spectroscopy. bibliog il Science 171:573-4 F 12 '71

ROSE, Sanford
Capital is something that doesn't love a wall. il Fortune 83:100-3+ F '71
Our strange new hard line on trade. il Fortune 84:136-9+ N '71
U.S. foreign trade: there's no need to panic. il Fortune 84:109-11+ Ag '71

ROSE, Stephen C.
Drama. Chr Cent 88:1333-4 N 10 '71
UPUSA and social revivalism. Chr Cent 88: 712-13 Je 9 '71
(ed) See Alinsky, S. D. Discerning power realities
about
Announcement. Chr Cent 88:713 Je 9 '71 •

ROSE, Stephen T.
Peephole into the world of work. K. E. Aylor. il Am Ed 7:29-30 Mr '71 •

ROSE and the ring; drama. See Thane, A.

ROSE festival, Portland. See Festivals—Oregon

ROSE for Miss Emily; ballet. See Ballets— Criticisms

ROSE gardens
I promised myself a rose garden. O. Friedrich. il McCalls 98:90-1+ Je '71

ROSE petals; story. See Jhabvala, R. P.

ROSÉ wines. See Wine

ROSEBLOOM; drama. See Perr, H.

ROSEBUD; story. See Allen, E.

ROSEN, Charles
Should music be played wrong? il Hi Fi 21: 54-8 My '71
about
Musical mandarin. por Newsweek 77:88+ My 3 '71 •

ROSEN, Gerald R.
International business. Duns 98:81-2+ S '71
Washington desk. See issues of Dun's

ROSEN, Jeffrey, and others
Recovery of function after serial ablation of prefrontal cortex in the rhesus monkey. bibliog il Science 173:353-6 Jl 23 '71

ROSEN, Louis
Relevance of particle accelerators to national goals; adaptation of address, March 1971. bibliog il Science 173:490-7 Ag 6 '71

ROSEN, Roslyn
We tried to live the EQ way. il pors Nat Wildlife 9:8-9 Ap '71

ROSENBAUM, C. Peter
Supportive outpatient treatment. bibliog Ment Hy 55:225-7 Ap '71
—and Rossi, Romolo
Herodotus: observer of sexual psychopathology. bibliog Am Imago 28:71-8 Spr '71

ROSENBAUM, Mary
Two faiths and one love. il por Redbook 138: 33-4+ D '71

ROSENBAUM, Ron
Run, Tommy, run! il Esquire 76:51-8+ Jl '71
Secrets of the little blue box. il Esquire 76: 116-25+ O '71

ROSENBERG, Alex
From J&B to Dali. por Duns 98:59-60 Jl '71 •

ROSENBERG, Harold
Art world (cont) New Yorker 46:71-5 Ja 30; 47:73-7 Mr 6; 117-20 Mr 27; 102-5 My 8; 101-5 Je 12; 62-5 Jl 24; 147-53 O 16; 201-4+ N 20 '71; 43-6 Ja 1 '72
Books. Vogue 158:72 Ag 1 '71
On the de-definition of art. Art N 70:23 D '71
about
Act and the actor: making the self. by H. Rosenberg. Review
Vogue 157:158 My '71. A. Kazin •

ROSENBERG, Laura
Embers glow; story. Har Yrs 11:14-15 Je '71

ROSENBERG, Max
Educators' quiz. See issues of Education digest

ROSENBERG, Roger N. and others
Kinetics of acetylcholine synthesis and hydrolysis in myasthenia gravis. bibliog il Science 173:644-5 Ag 13 '71

ROSENBERG, Sharon, and Wiener, Joan
Recycling old clothes. il pors Seventeen 30: 244-5 Ag '71

ROSENBERGER, David S. See Beck, W. R. jt. auth.

ROSENBERRY, Terrone L. See Bartels, E. jt. auth.

ROSENBLATT, Joan R. and Filliben, J. J.
Randomization and the draft lottery. bibliog Science 171:306-8 Ja 22 '71

ROSENBLATT, Joe
Poem for a dying bumblebee; poem. Nation 213:58 Jl 19 '71

ROSENBLOOM, Morris Victor
From limousines to casaba melons. Nations Bsns 59:41 Ag '71

ROSENBLOOM, Shelley. See Aronson, E. jt. auth.

ROSENFELD, Albert
What is the right number of children? il Life 71:97+ D 17 '71

ROSENFELD, Isaac
Midtown and the Village. A. Kazin. il
Harper 242:82-9 Ja '71 *
ROSENHECK, Natalie
Low-cost print collecting gets a new boost.
il Pop Phot 69:104+ S '71
ROSENSTEIN, Harris
Beyond control. il Art N 69:48-9+ F '71
Fathomless field. il por Art N 70:69-71+ N '71
Lipton's code. il Art N 70:46-7+ Mr '71
ROSENSTIEL, Lewis S.
Schenley chapter. H. Messick. il Nation 212:
428-31 Ap 5 '71 *
ROSENSTIEL, Susan
Schenley chapter. H. Messick. il Nation 212:
428-31 Ap 5 '71 *
ROSENTHAL, Alan
Today's health news. Todays Health 49:7-8
S '71
—and Rosenthal, Beverly
So you're taking the kids this summer? il
Todays Health 49:44-7+ Ap '71
ROSENTHAL, Benjamin Stanley
Excerpt from testimony, September 16, 1969.
Cong Digest 50:46-7+ F '71
Role of the lawyer; address, February 8, 1971.
Vital Speeches 37:407-10 Ap 15 '71
**ROSENTHAL, Beverly. See Rosenthal, A. jt.
auth.**
ROSENTHAL, David
Alba, for a strange land; poem. Nation 212:
313 Mr 8 '71
Warpoem to my classmates. Nation 212:438
Ap 5 '71
Winter in the imperial city; poem. Nation
214:56 Ja 10 '72
ROSENTHAL, Jack
Tale of one city. il N Y Times Mag p4-5+
D 26 '71
ROSENTHAL, M. L.
Plastic possibilities. Poetry 119:99-104 N '71
Two parables. Nation 212:506-7 Ap 19 '71
Unconsenting spirit: poetry and politics. Na-
tion 212:149-50 F 1 '71
ROSENTHAL, Marilynn
Where rumor raged. il Trans-Action 8:34-43
F '71
ROSENTHAL, Raymond
(tr) See Landolfi, T. Fable
ROSENTHAL, Richard
Winners in WD's first annual cartoon &
gag writing contest. Writers Digest 51:
32-3 My '71
ROSENZWEIG, Franz
God, man; world. M. A. Meyer. Commentary
52:83-7 Jl '71 *
Path to utter freedom. il por Time 98:50-1 Ag
9 '71 *
Star of redemption, by F. Rosenzweig. Re-
view
America 125:19 Jl 10 '71. J. Riemer *
Chr Cent 88:662 My 26 '71. J. Riemer *
ROSENZWEIG, Michael L.
Paradox of enrichment: destabilization of ex-
ploitation ecosystems in ecological time.
bibliog il Science 171:385-7 Ja 29 '71
ROSENZWEIG, Rafael, and Tamarin, Georges
Israel's power elite. il Trans-Action 7:26-33+
Jl '70; 8:4 Ja '71
ROSES
Fabulous floribunda roses. G. Ohlaus. il Home
Gard 58:36-7 F '71
Guide to planting roses. il Good H 172:199
Ap '71
Love flowers; with photographs by I. Penn.
A. West. Vogue 158:150-5+ D '71
New roses. E. McDonald. il House B 113:90-1
F '71
Peace: proud parent of a great rose family.
U. Toomey. il Home Gard 58:34 Je '71
Rose with many uses; fairy, or pink cushion
rose. il Home Gard 58:72 Ap '71
Roses as shrubs. K. P. Jones. il Horticulture
49:38-40 O '71
Roses in the landscape, yes or no? il Sunset
146:122-3 Ja '71
Winter protection for roses. il Home Gard
58:42 D '71
Your new choice in roses for 1971. il Sunset
146:116+ Ja '71
See also
Plants—All America selections
Rose gardens
ROSEWALL, Ken
Winner takes $50,000 loser, $1 million. J.
Jares. il por Sports Illus 35:28-9 D 6 '71
about
Cliffhanger at Longwood. B. Collins. il Sports
Illus 35:65-7 Ag 16 '71 *
ROSIN, Mark
Woody Allen: the power of an imperfec-
tionist. il por Harp Baz 105:62-3 D '71

ROSIN. See Gums and resins
ROSKO, Milt
Fishing tropical waters. il Travel 136:44-9 Ag
'71
**ROSMARIN, Trude Weiss-. See Weiss-Rosma-
rin. T.**
ROSOW, Jerome M.
Human resources: retooling our manpower.
il Sat R 54:40-1+ Ja 23 '71
Productivity; address, February 9, 1971. Vital
Speeches 37:488-91 Je 1 '71
ROSS, Bob
Dropouts heavy in Sydney-Hobart. il Yacht-
ing 129:49+ Mr '71
ROSS, David F.
Fishy business. New Repub 166:19-21 Ja 1 '72
Progress is not just around the corner. New
Repub 164:20-1 Ja 2 '71
ROSS, Diana
Ross rage. pors Harp Baz 104:84-9 Ap '71
ROSS, Dick, and associates (firm)
Film firm faces financial failure. E. E. Plow-
man. Chr Today 16:44 Ja 7 '72
ROSS, Frank E.
Escape from mediocrity: making English de-
partments work. Engl J 60:896-901 O '71
ROSS, Helen
Of books and love. il PTA Mag 65:24-5 Ap
'71
ROSS, Irwin
Magic lady; story. Har Yrs 11:24-5 N '71
ROSS, Irwin, 1919-
Case for revenue sharing. Read Digest 98:77-
81 Je '71
Credit card's painful coming-of-age. il For-
tune 84:108-11+ O '71
Do-it-yourself man from Parkersburg, West
Virginia. il pors Fortune 84:98-102+ Jl '71
George Shultz: strong right arm of the pre-
sidency. por Read Digest 98:143-7 Mr '71
Legalized gambling: is it a good bet? Read
Digest 99:94-8 N '71
Most powerful man in Congress. por Read
Digest 98:101-5 Ja '71
Pension plan reforms. Har Yrs 11:19-21+ Ap
'71; Same abr. with title What you should
know about your pension. Read Digest
98:31-2+ Ap '71
President's bold plan to streamline govern-
ment. Read Digest 99:61-5 Jl '71
ROSS, Jeanette H.
Paint-in. il Sch Arts 70:49 My '71
ROSS, Madeline D.
I remember the bears. il Har Yrs 11:46-7 F
'71
ROSS, Marianne
Wife and mother; story. Good H 172:84-5 My
'71
ROSS, Mike
Typist's plea; poem. Good H 173:188 Jl '71
ROSS, Nancy S.
Dear Texaco opera quiz. . .   Opera N 36:16
D 11 '71
ROSS, Philip
NLRB's regulation of union job control. Mo
Labor R 94:59-62 Mr '71
ROSS, Richard S.
ABC's of busing furor; interview. il U S
News 71:82-5 N 15 '71
ROSS, Russell, and Bornstein, Paul
Elastic fibers in the body; with biographical
sketches. il Sci Am 224:16, 44-52 bib-
liog(p 136) Je '71
ROSS, Walter Sanford
Vitamin C: does it really help? Read Digest
98:129-32 Je '71
ROSS-SKINNER, Jean
International business (cont) il Duns 97:77-
8+ Mr; 79-80+ Je; 98:61-2+ D '71
Wall Street beat. Duns 97:85-6 Ap '71
ROSSBACH, Ed
Mats of Nabeul. il Craft Horiz 31:33-4+ Ap
'71
Thoughts on Jack Lenor Larsen and the
textile horizon. il por Craft Horiz 31:12-13
Ap '71
ROSSELLINI, Renzo
La guerra. Criticism
New Yorker 47:93 Mr 27 '71 *
ROSSETTI, Dante Gabriel
Rossetti and the fair lady, by D. Sonstroem.
Review
Poetry 118:343-4 S '71. V. Burnett *
ROSSETTO, Louis, jr. See Lehr, S. jt. auth.
ROSSI, Anthony T.
What makes Rossi run? por Forbes 108:50-1
N 15 '71 *
ROSSI, Romolo. See Rosenbaum, C. P. jt. auth.

ROSSINI, Gioacchino
Barber of Seville (Il barbiere di Siviglia)
Criticism
Hi Fi 21:MA15-16 My '71 *
Opera N 35:24-5 F 20 '71 *
Opera N il 35:17-20 F 20 '71 *
Sat R 54:44 F 13 '71 *
Life of Rossini, by Stendhal. Review
New Repub 164:27-9 F 27 '71. R. Evett *
Rossini's tragic mask: Semiramide. F. Rizzo.
il Opera N 36:10-11 O '71 *
Semiramide. Criticism
Opera N 36:10-11 O '71 *

ROSSITER, Charles M. Jr
How we can listen faster with compressed
speech. il Sci Digest 70:66-8 D '71

ROSSITER, Elizabeth
Between love and longing; story; excerpt
from A marriage of convenience. Good H
174:60-1 Ja '72 (to be cont)

ROSSOVICH, Tim
He's burning to be a success. J. Underwood.
il pors Sports Illus 35:90-3+ S 20 '71 *

ROSTAND, Edmond
Cyrano de Bergerac. Criticism
Sat R 54:18 Ag 21 '71 *

ROSTOW, Eugene Victor
L.B.J. reconsidered. por Esquire 75:118-19+
Ap '71

ROSTOW, Walt Whitman
Dangers that remain in the Vietnam war;
interview. il pors U S News 71:80-4 N 8 '71
Vietnam was it worth it? Look 35:68+ S 21
'71

about

Mr Rostow and what went wrong. Nat R 23:
791 Jl 27 '71 *

ROSTROPOVICH, Mstislav
Music to my ears; Bach by Rostropovich.
I. Kolodin. Sat R 54:60 D 25 '71 *
Musical events; recital in Philharmonic Hall.
W. Sargeant. New Yorker 47:116-17 D 18
'71 *
Notes on a cellist in trouble. J. Roddy. Look
35:32 F 23 '71 *

ROSY-cheeked ghost; drama.   See Blaine,
B. G.

ROTARY heat exchangers. See Heat exchangers

ROTARY lawn mowers. See Lawn mowers

ROTARY piston engines. See Automobile engines

ROTARY rasps. See Files and rasps

ROTATING combustion engines. See Gas and
oil engines

ROTATION of stars. See Stars—Rotation

ROTATION of the earth. See Earth—Rotation

ROTBLAT, Joseph. See Lindop, P. J. jt. auth.

ROTH, Arnold
What hath Roth got? Sports Illus 35:30-5
Jl 26 '71

ROTH, Chester Haskell
Roth ponders a bid. por Bsns W p67 Ja 23
'71 *

ROTH, Edith B. See Preston, R. K. jt. auth.

ROTH, Eugene F. Jr, and Kochen, Joseph
Acridine orange potentiation of actinomycin
D uptake and activity. bibliog il Science
174:696-8 N 12 '71

ROTH, Hal
North Pacific circumnavigation. il Yachting
130:52-4+ Jl; 52-3+ Ag; 54-5+ S; 58-9+
O '71 (to be cont)

ROTH, Helga
Volunteering: the happening of the 1970s. il
Parks & Rec 6:70-3+ Ag '71

ROTH, Herbert, 1928-
Defense contractor goes civilian. il pors Bsns
W p74-5 Mr 6 '71 *

ROTH, Philip
Courting disaster (or, Serious in the fifties)
story. Esquire 75:93-101 My '71
On satirizing presidents; interview. ed. by
A. Lelchuk. il Atlan 228:81-8 D '71
Unlikely heroes; dramatization. See Arrick, L.

about

After Portnoy, what? Roth's work-in-prog-
ress. R. H. Smith. Pub W 199:57 Ap 12 '71 *
Joking in the square. por Newsweek 78:110+
N 8 '71 *
Philip Roth emerges from the men's room.
J. Greenway. Nat R 23:1389 D 17 '71 *

ROTH, Robert, 1901-
Rapid change of sentiment. Ann Am Acad
397:83-7 S '71

ROTH, William Victor, 1921-
That big government haystack. il por Nations
Bsns 59:64-6 F '71

ROTHENBERG, Al
Big hassle: your car vs. clean air. Look 35:51-
2+ Mr 23 '71
Name of the game is change; Look's sixteenth
annual new car preview. il Look 35:44-53+
S 21 '71
Stealing your car. il pors Look 35:74-6 Je
29 '71

ROTHENBERG, Marian S.
APS-AAPT meet in New York. il Phys Today
24:25+ Ja '71

ROTHENBERG, Maurice
Panels of clay applique. il Design 72:26-8 mid-
Sum '71

ROTHENBERG, Polly
Electroformed enamels. il Ceram Mo 19:22-5
Mr '71
Footed cloisonne bowl. il Ceram Mo 19:25-7
F '71
Raku murals of Paul Rayar. il Ceram Mo 19:
14-15 Je '71
Slab-built cylinders from improvised molds.
il Ceram Mo 19:34-5 My '71

ROTHENBERG, Germany
Down and out in Dinkelsbühl. R. Atcheson.
il Sat R 54:42+ Mr 13 '71

ROTHKO, Mark
Art; paintings in chapel at Texas medical
center, Houston. L. Alloway. Nation 212:
349-50 Mr 15 '71 *
Mark Rothko, American genius; with four
paintings. por Vogue 157:110-11 Mr 1 '71 *
Maximum of poignancy. K. Kuh. por Sat R
54:52+ Ap 17 '71 *
Rothko's black paintings. R. Goldwater. il
Art in Am 59:58-63 Mr '71 *

ROTHKO chapel. See Houston, Tex.—Chapels

ROTHNEY, John W. M.
Who gets counseled and for what? Ed Digest
37:41-4 N '71

ROTHSCHILD, Norman
Offbeat. See issues of Popular photography
What you've always wanted to know about
close-ups. il Pop Phot 68:76-9+ F '71

ROTHSCHILD, Pauline, baronne de
Two literary travellers: a dialogue. pors
Vogue 157:122-3 Ap 15 '71

ROTHSCHILDS; musical comedy. See Musical
comedies, revues, etc.—Criticisms, plots,
etc.

ROTHSTEIN Herbert M.
Humanistic approach to behavioral objectives. Engl J 60:760-2 S '71

ROTMAN, Charles B. and Clayman, C. S.
Human relations training for camp staff
members. il Camp Mag 43:10+ Ap '71

ROTMAN, Irving
Tale of record collector. il Hobbies 76:35-6+
Ag '71

ROTMIL, Charles
Apocalypse is a nice place to visit, but . . . Sat
R 54:4+ N 27 '71

ROTORS (helicopters) See Helicopters—Rotors

ROTTENBERG, Dan
How about a game of Mob strategy or Adultery? il Todays Health 49:46-9 Ag '71

ROTUNDO, Barbara
Literary lights were always bright at 148
Charles street. il pors Am Heritage 22:10-15
F '71

ROUECHÉ, Berton
Annals of medicine (cont) New Yorker 47:
70+ Ap 10; 72-81+ Ag 21; 66-72+ S 4 '71
Poison ivy: its purpose has yet to be estab-
lished. il Todays Health 49:38-41+ My '71
Profiles: E. L. Schmidt. por New Yorker 47:
30-40 Ja 1 '72
Reporter at large. New Yorker 47:141-2+ N
13 '71
Three who cared; with photographs by W. E.
Smith. Todays Health 49:52-7 S '71
When Americans are a swallow away from
death; 1949; reprint. il Todays Health 49:
40-3+ S '71

ROUGH ROCK demonstration school. See Indians of North America—Education

ROUND table on the social responsibilities
of libraries. See American library association—Social responsibilities of libraries
round table

ROUNDHILL, Kenneth S.
Speaking and hearing the truth in love. Chr
Today 16:7-9 Ja 7 '72

ROUNDTREE, Richard
From model to movie star. il pors Ebony
26:128+ Je '71 *

ROUP, Walter
People find the street he lives on. R. Bednar.
Org Gard & Farm 18:50 D '71 *

ROURA, Octavio González. See González Roura,
O.

ROUSEY, Clyde L. See Filippi, R. jt. auth.

ROUSSEAU, D. L.
Polywater and sweat: similarities between the infrared spectra. bibliog il Science 171: 170-2 Ja 15 '71
ROUSSEAU, Jean Jacques
Rousseau, Beaumarchais, and Figaro. A. Livermore. bibliog f il Mus Q 57:466-90 Jl '71 •
ROUSSEAU, Theodore
Historic duty. Hobbies 76:100+ Jl '71
ROUSSELIERE, Guy Mary-. See Mary-Rousselière, G.
ROVER nuclear rocket program. See Rockets, Atomic powered
ROVERE, Richard Halworth
Eisenhower revisited: a political genius? A brilliant man? il pors N Y Times Mag p 14-15+ F 7 '71
Letter from Washington. See occasional issues of New Yorker
ROW, W. Harold
Obituary
Chr Cent 88:898 Jl 28 '71
ROW houses
Australia's terrace houses. K. Woolley. il Arch Forum 134:46-51 My '71
Islandia, Alameda, Calif. il Arch Rec 149:90-1 mid-My '71
Tidesfall townhouses, Columbia, Md. il Arch Rec 149:92-3 mid-My '71
Warren gardens inc, Roxbury, Mass. il Arch Rec 149:86-7 mid-My '71
Well-built house; Richmond, Va. J. H. Ingersoll. il House B 113:46 My '71
We're the third white house from the corner; Daly City, San Francisco. il Life 71:78-9 O 1 '71
ROW spacing of plants. See Plants, Space arrangement of
ROWAN, Carl Thomas
Nigeria's spectacular rebound. Read Digest 98:156-8+ Je '71
South Africa: a nation at war with its conscience. Read Digest 99:140-4 S '71
'South of freedom' 1971. il pors Ebony 26:134-9 Ag '71
—and Mazie, D. M.
Let's fight the bad-driver menace. Read Digest 99:123-6 O '71
ROWE, James D.
Navigation contest. il Motor B & S 127:78+ Mr '71
ROWE, Mass, nuclear power station. See Atomic power plants
ROWEN, James
Bombing forests. New Repub 164:12 Mr 6 '71
ROWES, Barbara Gail
Toronto dance theatre. il Dance Mag 45:70-3 Ap '71
ROWING
Anchors aweigh for the IRA; U.S. naval academy crew on Lake Onondaga, Syracuse, N.Y. H. D. Whall. Sports Illus 34:57 Je 21 '71
Cornell fishes out a big one at last, IRA champions. H. D. Whall. il Sports Illus 34:59-60 Je 28 '71
Lurch, wobble and gobble 'em up; crew of the University of Washington. H. D. Whall. il Sports Illus 34:24-5 My 31 '71
Rowing: a similarity analysis. T. A. McMahon. bibliog il Science 173:349-51 Jl 23 '71
ROWITZ, Louis, and Levy, Leo
State mental hospital in transition: an approach to the study of mental hospital decentralization. bibliog Ment Hy 55:68-76 Ja '71
ROXON, Lillian
Intelligent woman's guide to sex manuals. il Mlle 73:118-19+ Jl '71
ROYAL, Darrell
Oklahoma wins the Wishbone war. D. Jenkins. il Sports Illus 35:24-7 O 18 '71 •
ROYAL astronomical society of New Zealand
Astronomy in New Zealand. G. A. Eiby. il Sky & Tel 42:18-20 Jl '71
ROYAL collection, Great Britain. See Art—Private collections
ROYAL Copenhagen porcelain. See Pottery, Danish
ROYAL Dutch airlines. See Airlines—Netherlands
ROYAL family of Great Britain. See Great Britain—Royal family
ROYAL family of Monaco. See Monaco—Royal family
ROYAL military college, Sandhurst. See Sandhurst, Royal military college
ROYAL Netherlands aircraft factories Fokker. See Airplane industry—Netherlands

ROYAL opera, Great Britain
Ordinary bloke; work of artistic director C. Davis. por Time 99:54-5 Ja 3 '72
Report:
Beverly Sills in Donizetti's Lucia. F. G. Barker. Opera N 35:30 F 13 '71
Eugene Onegin at Covent Garden. F. G. Barker. il Opera N 35:32-3 Ap 10 '71
Sir Michael Tippett's Knot garden. F. G. Barker. il Opera N 35:33 F 6 '71
Tristan and Isolde and Ballo in maschera. F. G. Barker. il Opera N 36:25 S '71
ROYAL opera house, London. See London—Covent Garden
ROYAL rights. See Prerogative, Royal
ROYAL Swedish ballet. See Ballet—Sweden
ROYAL Winnipeg ballet
Idea: Arnold Spohr and the Royal Winnipeg ballet. O. Maynard. il por Dance Mag 45: 38-45 Ap '71
Royal Winnipeg ballet, Royce Hall, Los Angeles, Calif. V. H. Swisher. Dance Mag 45:87 D '71
Royal Winnipeg ballet, Symphony Hall, Newark. J. Gale. Dance Mag 45:90 My '71
ROYALTIES
French sampler: income from recordings. P. Entremont. il Hi Fi 21:32+ N '71
Japanese royalties: two points of view. T. Mori; L. E. Kern, jr. Pub W 199:17-18 My 3 '71
Royalties, copyrights freed from price controls. S. Wagner. Pub W 200:19 N 22 '71
ROYALTY. See Kings and rulers
ROYAN festival. See Music festivals—France
ROYCROFT shop, East Aurora, N.Y.
Commune in East Aurora. R. L. Beisner. il pors Am Heritage 22:72-7+ F '71
ROZAN, Gerald H. and others
Some implications of sexual activity for mental illness. bibliog Ment Hy 55:318-23 Jl '71
ROZELL, Bruce
Turnips in your cover crop? Org Gard & Farm 18:98-9 S '71
ROZIN, Paul, and others
American children with reading problems can easily learn to read English represented by Chinese characters. bibliog il Science 171: 1264-7 Mr 26 '71
RUBBER bands
Amateur scientist; some delightful engines driven by the heating of rubber bands. P. B. Archibald. il Sci Am 224:118-22 Ap '71
RUBBER gloves. See Gloves, Rubber
RUBBERMAID, Inc.
Plum that couldn't be picked. il Forbes 107:13-14 Ja 15 '71
RUBBINGS
Can rubbings be creative? M. J. Acosta. il Design 72:30-1 mid-Wint '71
Gravestone rubbings in New England. J. H. Mofford. il Travel 135:52-5 Mr '71
Instant souvenirs. N. Levy. il Har Yrs 11:45 9 S '71
Monumental brass rubbings. A. Robertson. il Design 73:36-8 Wint '71
RUBBISH disposal. See Refuse and refuse disposal
RUBELLA
Vaccines
Rubella: will vaccination prevent birth defects? M. M. Eichhorn. bibliog Science 173: 710-11 Ag 20 '71
Second look at the German measles vaccine. B. Goodheart. il Todays Health 49:46-7+ Mr '71
RUBENS, Sir Peter Paul
Rubens' Ceres in Leningrad. L. Steinberg. bibliog f il Art N 70:42-3 D '71 •
RUBENSTEIN, Joshua
Refreezing the thaw. il por Art N 70:40-1+
RUBIDIUM in the body
Rubidium and lithium: opposite effects on amine-mediated excitement. B. J. Carroll and P. T. Sharp. bibliog il Science 172: 1355-7 Je 25 '71
RUBIN, Bernard
International film and television propaganda: campaigns of assistance. bibliog f il Ann Am Acad 398:81-92 N '71
RUBIN, Emanuel, and Lieber, C. S.
Alcoholism, alcohol, and drugs. bibliog il Science 172:1097-102 Je 11 '71
RUBIN, J. and others
Crystal structure of a naturally occurring dinucleoside monophosphate: uridylyl (3',5') adenosine hemihydrate. bibliog il Science 174:1020-2 D 3 '71
RUBIN, Sol
Burger court & the penal system. Nation 212:785-8 Je 21 '71

RUBIN, Theodore Isaac
Dr Rubin. See issues of Ladies' home journal
Statistics show that women usually outlive
men. Ladies Home J 88:34 Ja '71; Same
abr. with title What wives can do to help.
Read Digest 98:76-7 Ap '71

RUBINSTEIN, Alvin Z.
Egypt since Nasser. Cur Hist 62:6-13 Ja '72

RUBINSTEIN, Amnon
Plan for the Sinai: something less than peace
in return for something less than total
withdrawal. il N Y Times Mag p 12-13+
Ja 17 '71
Why the Israelis are being difficult. il N Y
Times Mag p32-3+ Ap 18 '71

RUBINSTEIN, Artur
Rubinstein; interview. ed. by G. Gould. il
pors Look 35:52-8 Mr 9 '71

about

Fox meets the rabbit. H. Goldsmith. il pors
Hi Fi 21:61-2 My '71 *
Music to my ears; Chopin program in Phil-
harmonic Hall. I. Kolodin. Sat R 54:79
Ja 23 '71 *

RUBINSTEIN, G. See Delcoigne, G. C. jt. auth.

RUBINSTEIN, Helena
Authors & editors. L. P. Freilicher. il pors
Pub W 200:23-4 Ag 16 '71 *
Madame, by P. O'Higgins. Review
Bsns W por p 11 Jl 31 '71. D. Anderson *
Time il por 98:66-7+ Ag 9 '71. G. Clarke
Madame; excerpt from Madame: an intimate
biography of Helena Rubinstein. P. O'Hig-
gins. por McCalls 98:68-9+ Ag '71 *

RUCKELSHAUS, Jill
Lifestyle. il por Am Home 74:14 My '71 *

RUCKELSHAUS, William Doyle
Beginning of the new American revolution;
address, April 1971, with questions and
answers. Ann Am Acad 396:13-24 Jl '71
Coming government moves in war against
pollution: interview. il por U S News 70:
70-5 Mr 29 '71
Man in the eye of the storm: interview,
ed. by J. Edgerton. il por Nat Wildlife
9:28-31 Ag '71
Mr Clean; excerpts from address, January
12, 1971. por Am For 77:7+ Jl '71
Ruckelshaus on accountability; excerpts from
address, September 13, 1971. Science 174:43
O 1 '71

about

Exhaustive test for Detroit. por Time 98:51
Jl 12 '71 *
Introducing William Ruckelshaus, who? J.
Shepherd. il pors Look 35:20-2 My 4 '71 *
Lifestyle. il por Am Home 74:14 My '71 *
Nixon's pollution fighter faces a backlash. il
pors Bsns W p54-5+ Ag 21 '71 *
Ruckelshaus' first year. il por Time 99:53-4
Ja 3 '72 *

RUDAHL, Kurt T.
Integrated circuit audio generator. il Electr
World 86:60-1 S '71

RUDDER, Cynthia
How do I get them to go home? Ed Digest
36:32-4 Mr '71

RUDDERS. See Boats—Steering gear

RUDDLE, Frank H. See Ricciuti, F. jt. auth.

RUDEL, Julius
Celebration of the spirit. H. Saal. il por
Newsweek 78:33 S 20 '71
Julius Rudel: Washington's music man. J.
Roddy. por Look 35:38 S 21 '71 *
Julius the cool. pors Time 98:80-1 N 1 '71 *
Not to be missed. G. Trotta. pors Harp Baz
104:118-19 Ap '71 *

RUDEL, Reinhardt, and Taylor, S. R.
Striated muscle fibers: facilitation of contrac-
tion at short lengths by caffeine. bibliog il
Science 172:387-8 Ap 23 '71

RUDERMAN, Malvin A.
Solid stars; with biographical sketch. il
Sci Am 224:12, 24-31 F '71

RUDGE, John
Death of an artist. A. Nebolsine. Commonweal 94:167-8 Ap 23 '71 *

RUDNICK, Isadore. See Putterman, S. J. jt.
auth.

RUDNIK, Sister Mary Chrysantha
What every librarian should know about li-
brary technical assistants. bibliog il por
Wilson Lib Bul 46:67-72 S '71

RUDOFF, Alvin, and Lucken, Dorothy
Engineer and his work: a sociological perspective. bibliog Science 172:1103-8 Je 11 '71

RUDOFSKY, Bernard
Fashionable body; excerpt from The unfash-
ionable human body. il Horizon 13:56-65
Aut '71

God has given you one face, and you make
yourselves another. il Horizon 13:72-9 Sum
'71
Shelter for a dark age. il Horizon 13:62-73
Spr '71

RUDOLPH, Paul Marvin
Sibyl Moholy-Nagy. Arch Forum 134:29 Je
'71

about

County government center by Paul Rudolph.
il Arch Rec 150:83-92 Ag '71 *

RUDOLPH, Susanne Hoeber
From Madras: a view of the southern film.
Yale R 60:468-80 Mr '71

RUE, Leonard Lee, 3d
I've learned to love raccoons. il Nat Wild-
life 9:36-8 Ap '71
Visit to a walrus island. il Audubon 73:36-7
My '71

RUERA street; story. See Pérez De Ayala, R.

RUETHER, Rosemary
Black theology of James Cone. por Cath
World 214:18-20 O '71
Vanishing religious order and the new hu-
man community. Chr Cent 88:425-9 Ap 7 '71

RUFA, Robert H.
How not to waste a weekend. il Travel 136:
68-71 Ag '71
Tips and tricks for your zoo pics. il Travel
137:72+ Ja '72

RUFALO, Betty
Teacher who chose to go to jail. D. Gallagher. il por Redbook 136:58-9+ Ja '71 *

RUFFINI, Eugene
Police, the press & the legend; call it Mafia.
il Nation 213:520-4 N 22 '71

RUFFINI, Remo
Gravity waves may come from black holes.
D. E. Thomsen. il por Sci N 98:480-1 D
26 '70 *
—and Wheeler, J. A.
Introducing the black hole; excerpt from
The significance of space research for
fundamental physics. bibliog il Phys Today
24:30-6+ Ja '71

RUFFINO, Marguerite
Opera Ruffino style. H. E. Phillips. il por
Opera N 35:13-15 Ja 16 '71 *

RUG cleaning. See Rugs and carpets—Care

RUG making. See Rugs and carpets

RUG pads
Carpet padding: basic facts & buying advice.
il Good H 172:6 F '71

RUGBY football
Whiffenpoofs and Wallabies; Australian na-
tional rugby team vs U.S. All-Stars from
Eastern rugby union. D. Levin. il Sports
Illus 35:73-4 D 13 '71

RUGEN, Karen
More than a house of books. il Am Lib 2:876-
81 S '71

RUGOFF, Donald S.
Right on with Rugoff. H. Alpert. il por Sat
R 54:61-3+ S 25 '71 *

RUGS and carpets
Kitchen carpets; are they really stain resis-
tant? il Consumer Bul 54:30-3 O '71
Mats of Nabeul; Tunisia. E. Rossbach. il
Craft Horiz 31:33-4+ Ap '71
New carpets: showy shags to no-fuss flats.
V. D. Hahn. Am Home 74:18 Ap '71
Q&A on easy, inexpensive do-it-yourself car-
peting. A. A. Latour. il Good H 173:208 S
'71
Soft touch beneath your feet. A. Ogden.
il House B 113:169-80 O '71
Your own rug under foot. il Sunset 147:81-2+
S '71

Care

Carpet cushions lengthen carpet life. il Con-
sumer Bul 54:38-9 My '71
First aid for carpet stains. House B 113:
275 O '71
How to care for your carpet. Bet Hom &
Gard 49:118-19 O '71
New vacuums and groomers make strides in
shag-carpeting care. J. M. Bauer. Am
Home 74:68 S '71
Vacuum is a rug's best friend. House B 113:
28 Mr '71

Purchasing

Carpeting and rugs: how to choose what's
best for your home. R. Rumely. il Bet Hom
& Gard 49:56-63 S '71
Your first big investment in carpets and
rugs. J. R. Cary. il Parents Mag 46:102-5
Mr '71

RUGS and carpets, Oriental
Kazak rugs. S. B. Sherrill. il Antiques 100:
820 D '71
Seven hundred years of oriental carpets. M.
S. Dimand. Antique 99:484+ Ap '71

RUGS and carpets, Outdoor

Care

Care and cleaning of indoor-outdoor carpets.
E. Taylor. il Good H 173:130 Ag '71

RUHEN, Olaf
Involvement: action and reaction. Writer 84:
16-18 F '71

RUIDOSO, N.Mex.
After a mountain of money; quarter-horse
racing. B. Gilbert. il Sports Illus 35:28-9
S 20 '71

RUINED cities. See Cities and towns, Ruined,
extinct, etc.

RUKEYSER, William Simon
Books & ideas. Fortune 83:235-6 My '71
Walter Kidde's stormy voyage with U.S. lines.
il Fortune 84:82-5+ Jl '71

RULE, Philip C.
Communications. America 124:461-2, 541-2,
570-2; 125:71-2, 404 My 1, 22-9, Ag 7, N 13
'71
Decline of flower power. America 124:141-5
F 13 '71
Middle Catholic's anguish. il America 125:
96-9 Ag 21 '71
Reflections on the publication of a Sex book.
America 125:128 S 4 '71

RULE of law
Poison of disrespect for law is spreading;
excerpts from address, April 29, 1971. J. L.
Robertson. il pors U S News 70:56+ My
24 '71

RULERS. See Kings and rulers

RULES of war. See War, Laws of

RULING class; drama. See Barnes, P.

RUM
Rum without the garbage. il Esquire 76:104-
5 Jl '71

RUM cake. See Cake

RUMANIA
See also
Clothing industry—Rumania
Investments, Foreign (in Rumania)
Jews in Rumania
Transylvania

Cultural relations
See also
Exchange of persons programs

Description and travel
Roumania: angels among the roses; painted
churches of Moldavia. M. Sulzberger.
Vogue 157:194 My '71

Foreign relations
Russia
See Russia—Foreign relations—Rumania

Industries
See also
Airplane industry—Rumania

Politics and government
Turn of the screw. il por Newsweek 78:36+
Ag 9 '71

*Religious institutions
and affairs*
International Byzantine congress: East-West
communication. C. S. Calian. Chr Cent 88:
1472-3 D 15 '71

Social conditions
Keeping Rumania pure. America 125:445 N 27
'71

RUMINANTS
See also
Camels

RUMOR
Where rumor raged; Detroit in the winter of
1967-68. M. Rosenthal. il Trans-Action 8:34-
43 F '71

RUMPELSTILTSKIN revisited; drama. See
Dewey, P. B.

RUMSEY, Marian
Sails across Florida. il Motor B & S 127:
66-7+ F '71

RUMSFELD, Donald
How controls will be enforced; interview. il
pors U S News 71:42-6 D 13 '71

RUNAWAY boys and girls
Runaways. L. Ambrosino. il Todays Ed 60:26-
8 D '71

RUNNING
Back in the running; J. Ryun. P. Putnam. il
pors Sports Illus 34:10-13 F 1 '71
Boston's marvelous marathon. B. Surface.
il Read Digest 98:122-6 Ap '71
Champion of the armchair athletes; D.
Meriwether. R. H. Boyle. il pors Sports
Illus 34:20-2+ F 22 '71

Doctor Meriwether saga. pors Time 98:40 Jl
12 '71
Dream comes true; M. Liquori vs. J. Ryun.
P. Putnam. il pors Sports Illus 34:18-21
My 24 '71
Happy runners; race at the Martin Luther
King games in Philadelphia. il pors News-
week 77:36 My 31 '71
Hey, I can beat those guys; D. Meriwether.
S. Treadwell. il por Sports Illus 34:14-15
Ja 18 '71
Long and the shorter of it: cross-country
race. G. S. Brown. il por Sports Illus 35:
94-5 D 6 '71
Match-up for Munich; Dr Martin Luther
King jr. International freedom games in
Philadelphia. il pors Time 97:66-7 My 31
'71
Phooey on the fortune cookie; K. O'Brien
world indoor two-mile record. P. Putnam.
il por Sports Illus 34:22-3 Mr 1 '71
Run around the houses; Brazil's São
Sylvestre marathon. F. Dickenson. il
Américas 23:36-40 Ag '71
Secrets of speed; ed. by G. S. Brown. B.
Bowerman. il Sports Illus 35:22-9 Ag 2 '71
They take the scenic route: cross-country
marathon; photographs, with account by
K. Moore. Sports Illus 35:44-53 N 1 '71
What makes Ryun run again? P. Berger. il
pors Look 35:56-8+ Jl 27 '71
Whoosh goes the Wasco whiz. G. Curry. il
por Sports Illus 34:66+ My 3 '71
See also
Hurdle racing
Jogging

RUNOFF
Newest findings on fertilizer runoff. B.
Coffman. Farm J 95:20-2 Ag '71
Runoff of deicing salt; effect on Irondequoit
Bay, Rochester, New York. R. C. Bubeck
and others. bibliog il Science 172:1128-32 Je
11 '71
Sea level as affected by river runoff, eastern
United States. R. H. Meade and K. O.
Emery. bibliog il Science 173:425-8 Jl 30 '71

RUNSICK, Arlita J.
Treasures of the Ozarks. il por Travel 136:
50-4 Ag '71

RUPTURE. See Hernia

RURAL churches. See Country churches

RURAL development programs. See Rural planning

RURAL education. See Rural schools

RURAL environmental assistance program. See
United States—Agricultural stabilization
and conservation service

RURAL hospitals. See Hospitals, Rural

RURAL housing. See Housing, Rural

RURAL industries
Helping hand for smaller towns. il U S
News 71:95 N 22 '71

RURAL life. See Farm life

RURAL medical service. See Medical service,
Rural

RURAL parishes, Catholic. See Parishes

RURAL planning
How will you spend the money? il Farm J
95:58 My '71
Rural & urban growth. New Repub 165:12-13
S 25 '71
Will we get city's problems. D. Hanson. Suc
Farm 69:A5 My '71; Reply. D. R. Fessler.
69:A2 S '71

RURAL poverty
United States
See Poor—United States

RURAL schools
Small school can be a good school. F. L.
Heesacker. Ed Digest 36:12-15 Ja '71

One-teacher schools
Daring educational experiment: the one-room
schoolhouse. W. Griffith. il N Y Times Mag
p 14-16+ My 30 '71

United States
See also
School districts

RURAL-urban conflict. See City and country

RURAL water supply. See Water supply,
Rural

RURAL zoning. See Zoning

RUSCH, Harold P. See LeStourgeon, W. M.
jt. auth.

RUSH, Anna Fisher
Appliances: try thinking small. il McCalls
99:94-7 O '71
Camping out in comfort. il McCalls 98:104-5+
Je '71
Fisherman's luck. il McCalls 98:58+ S '71
Taking the terror out of moving. il McCalls
98:102-3+ Mr '71

RUSH, Kenneth
Berlin agreement: an assessment; address, September 22, 1971. Dept State Bul 65:489-97 N 1 '71
Protectionism or free trade: a decision for our time; address, May 3, 1971. Dept State Bul 64:749-53 Je 7 '71
Quadripartite agreement on Berlin signed at Berlin concluding first phase of negotiations; statement, September 3, 1971. Dept State Bul 65:318 S 27 '71
Rush job. il por Newsweek 78:29 S 6 '71 *

RUSHING, William A.
Occupation, income and mental hospitalization. bibliog il Ment Hy 55:248-52 Ap '71

RUSHMORE, Robert
Time out. Opera N 35:6-7 F 6 '71

RUSK, Dean
Pentagon study; the other side; television interview, July 2, 1971. il pors U S News 71:68-76 Jl 19 '71
about
Meet Dean Rusk, early dove. por Time 98: 10 Jl 5 '71 *
New respect for the old Dino. H. Sidey. il Life 71:4 Jl 23 '71 *

RUSK (bread) See Toast

RUSKAY, Joseph A.
Loopholes still with us. Nation 212:368-71 Mr 22 '71

RUSKIN, Arnold M.
Financing environmental improvements. il Am City 86:70+ N '71

RUSKIN, John
Proust's prefaces to Ruskin; excerpts, ed, by J. Autret and W. Burford. M. Proust. Nation 212:565-9 My 3 '71*

RUSKIN college. See Adult education—Great Britain

RUSS, Lavinia
Viking and Atheneum authors are 1970 Newbery and Caldecott winners. il pors Pub W 199:116-18 F 22 '71

RUSSELL, Bertrand Russell, 3d earl
Bertrand Russell: Socrates of our age. H. Ozmon. Ed Digest 36:34-6 F '71 *

RUSSELL, Beverly
Financing a restoration. House & Gard 140: 10+ Ag '71
How to unwind. il House & Gard 139:116-17+ Ap '71
Tradition: why some live with it and others can't. il House & Gard 140:52+ Ag '71
What is the American talent for living? House & Gard 139:46-7+ F '71

RUSSELL, Charles Marion
Schoolboy's sketchbook; with drawings. F. G. Renner. por Am Heritage 22:70-3 O '71 *

RUSSELL, Clifford S. and Landsberg, H. H.
International environmental problems: a taxonomy. bibliog Science 172:1307-14 Je 25 '71

RUSSELL, Francis
Billy and Aimee. Nat R 23:716 Je 29 '71
Morning greetings to Old Glory; reminiscence by our regular contributor. Am Heritage 22:74 Je '71
Movies. Nat R 23:1479-80 D 31 '71
Mummy of Red Square. Nat R 23:865-6 Ag 10 '71

RUSSELL, Franklin
Legend of a lake. il Am Heritage 22:14-23+ Ap '71

RUSSELL, G. F. and Hills, J. I.
Odor differences between enantiomeric isomers. bibliog il Science 172:1043-4 Je 4 '71

RUSSELL, Greg
It took a spud. il Am City 86:77 Ap '71

RUSSELL, Helen Ross
Nature's plastic surgeon. il Cons 25:17 Je '71

RUSSELL, Jane
Parting shots: The outlaw girl, Broadway's newest star. T. Thompson. il por Life 71: 68 Jl 2 '71 *

RUSSELL, John, 1919-
Francis Bacon: a retrospective and a preview. por Horizon 13:78-87 Aut '71
London. See issues of Art news
London. il Art in Am 59:120-2 Mr; 106-9 S '71
Lucian Freud: clairvoyeur. il Art in Am 59: 104-6 Ja '71
Vuillard: melancholy mastered. il por Art N 70:48-50 S '71

RUSSELL, John J.
Is advertising education relevant? Sat R 54: 95+ Mr 13 '71

RUSSELL, Ken
Case of the sacred monster; interview, ed. by Leo Lerman. pors Mlle 74:136-7+ N '71
about
Current cinema (cont) P. Kael. New Yorker 46:76-9 Ja 30 '71 *
Director in a caftan. il por Time 98:53 S 13 '71 *
Great lives on TV. R. Schickel. Harper 242: 28+ Ja '71 *
Russell: spoofing the spoof. il por Time 98: 87-8 D 20 '71 *

RUSSELL, Louis Byron, jr
World's leading heart transplant sets super pace. L. J. Banks. il pors Ebony 26:106-8+ Ap '71 *

RUSSELL, Richard Brevard
Death comes for the bandleader. por Time 97:19 F 1 '71 *
Obituary
Nat R 23:129 F 9 '71. D. Brudnoy
New Repub 164:10 F 6 '71
Newsweek por 77:22+ F 1 '71

RUSSELL, Robert
World will never be so small again; a Thanksgiving story from a blind reader. il Wilson Lib Bul 46:238-45 N '71

RUSSELL, Robert S.
Using volumetric measurements for glazes. il Sch Arts 71:26-7 Ja '72

RUSSELL lupines. See Lupines

RUSSELL Sage foundation conference. See Educational conferences

RUSSETT, Bruce Martin
Licensing: for cars and babies. Bul Atom Sci 26:15-19 N '70; 27:3+ My '71

RUSSIA
Soviet Union, 1971; symposium. bibliog f il Cur Hist 61:193-239+ O '71
See also
Aeronautics, Commercial—Russia
Agriculture—Russia
Airlines—Russia
Airplanes, Military—Russia
Airports—Russia
Atomic power—Russia
Atomic research—Russia
Automobile industry—Russia
Baikal, Lake
Ballet—Russia
Business management and organization—Russia
Caspian Sea
Censorship—Russia
Childrens literature—Russia
City planning—Russia
Civil rights—Russia
Conservation of resources—Russia
Disarmament—Russia
Education—Russia
Hunting—Russia
Immigration and emigration—Russia
Investments, Foreign (in Russia)
Jews in Russia
Leningrad
Marriage customs and rites—Russia
Military research—Russia
Petroleum—Russia
Political prisoners—Russia
Pollution—Russia
Prison camps—Russia
Research—Russia
Secret service—Russia
Space research—Russia
Technology—Russia
Trials—Russia
United Nations—Russia
United States—Commerce—Russia
United States—Trade missions—Russia
Visitors, Foreign—Russia
Wages—Russia
Water pollution—Russia
Wilderness areas—Russia
World war, 1939-1945—Russia

Air force
Playing chicken over the Mediterranean. W. H. Honan. il Read Digest 98:77-81 Mr '71

Antiquities
Tracking the Scythians. il Time 99:36 Ja 17 '72

Armed forces
See also
Russia—Navy

Civilization
Reflections: A. de Custine's account of visit in 1839. G. F. Kennan. New Yorker 47:48-50+ My 1 '71

Commerce
Looking to open new trade doors. Bsns W p34-5 S 18 '71
Russians look west for computers. Bsns W p34-5 F 6 '71
See also
Russia—Industries

RUSSIA—Commerce—*Continued*

United States
See United States—Commerce—Russia

Cultural relations
Soviet chattel. catalan duo; embargo on concert tours to Britain. I. Kolodin. Sat R 54:82 N 27 '71

Defenses
Adequate defense posture; Soviet superiority; address, December 4, 1970. B. M. Goldwater. Vital Speeches 37:230-2 F 1 '71
Arms race hasn't stopped. H. Sidey. il Life 71:4 O 15 '71
Good news at last. S. Alsop. Newsweek 77:116 Je 14 '71
Our turn to blink? missile program. S. Alsop. Newsweek 78:100 N 1 '71
Selling of the Soviet Pentagon. M. M. Drach-kovitch. bibliog f il Nat R 23:694-6 Je 29 '7
What's going in the holes? Newsweek 77:124 My 10 '71
Who watches the watchman? J. Burnham. Nat R 23:1105 O 8 '71
See also
Guided missiles
Radar—Military use
Russia—Armed forces
Russia—Navy

Description and travel
From Alaska to Russia by the back door. il Sunset 146:68+ Ap '71

Economic conditions
Rising expectations. E. Klein. il Newsweek 77:35-6 Je 21 '71
Soviet Union: the risks of reform. il Time 97:27-30+ Mr 29 '71
Why Russia can't catch up without western know-how. il U S News 70:52-7 Ja 25 '71
See also
Agriculture—Russia
Russia—Industries
Wages—Russia

Economic policy
And then there was one; 24th Soviet party congress on the ninth five-year plan. il Time 97:26+ Ap 19 '71
Coddling the consumer; new five-year plan. il Time 97:23 Mr 1 '71
More heat in the Soviet hothouse. M. I. Gold-man. bibliog f il Harvard Bsns R 49:4-6+ Jl '71
Promises, promises; new five-year plan. News-week 77:40+ Mr 1 '71
Russia's new 5-year plan: crucial test for red system. il U S News 70:20-2 Ap 5 '71
Soviet man in the ninth plan. J. S. Prybyla. bibliog f Cur Hist 61:227-34+ O '71
See also
Wage-price policy—Russia

Foreign relations
American images of Soviet foreign policy, by W. Welch. Review
Nation 212:603-4 My 10 '71. D. F. Fleming
Feathers and foie grass. il pors Newsweek 78:54 N 8 '71
Great squeeze. Z. Brzezinski. Newsweek 78:44 O 11 '71
Hopeful talks with the Soviet leaders. W. A. Harriman. il por Life 70:30-1 F 5 '71
Image and reality in Indochina. H. E. Salis-bury. For Affairs 49:381-94 Ap '71
Kremlin's grand design. A. De Borchgrave. il Newsweek 78:55 O 18 '71
More power for Brezhnev: what it means to U.S. por U S News 70:18 Ap 26 '71
Moscow globetrotters. il Time 98:43-4 S 27 '71
Moscow globetrotters; forthcoming state visits. il Newsweek 78:43-5 S 20 '71
Moscow globe-trotters: what they are after. il U S News 71:63 O 4 '71
Nikita Khrushchev 1894-1971. il pors Sr Schol 99:16-17 O 11 '71
Our foreign policy: peaceful coexistence; address, April 6, 1971. A. A. Gromyko. Vital Speeches 37:427-30 My 1 '71
Russia drives east of Suez. il Newsweek 77:27+ Ja 18 '71
Russia's game plan: has it really changed? U S News 71:18-21 Jl 26 '71
Soother in Havana; visit of A. Kosygin. il pors Time 98:40+ N 8 '71
Soviet Union, 1971; symposium. bibliog f il Cur Hist 61:193-239+ O '71
Soviet victories. E. v. Kuehnelt-Leddihn. Nat R 23:1415 D 17 '71

Super B and the new Soviet surge. il pors Newsweek 78:29-30+ N 1 '71
United States, our NATO allies, and the Soviet Union in an era of changing foreign relations; address, February 19, 1971. U. A. Johnson. Dept State Bul 64:315-21 Mr 15 '71
See also
Berlin question, 1945-
Communist strategy
Cuban crisis, 1962
Military assistance, Russian

Arab states
As Arabs see it; with editorial comment. J. P. O'Kane. il America 124:62-3, 67-8 Ja 23 '71
Communism and the Arab world. America 125:83 Ag 21 '71

Asia
Red giants battle over Asia. J. N. Wallace. il U S News 71:42-5 S 20 '71

Asia, Southeastern
Russia in southeast Asia. il Newsweek 77:49-50 Ap 12 '71

Asia, Southern
Super powers and southern Asia. Cur 130:11-14 Je '71

Canada
Canada switches targets. D. Coxe. Nat R 23:1177 O 22 '71
Is Kosygin damaging U.S.-Canada ties? il U S News 71:44-5 N 1 '71
My friend Trudeau. il por Time 98:51 N 1 '71
Suitor next door. il por Newsweek 78:33 N 1 '71

China (People's Republic)
Authors & editors; concerning Nations in darkness by J. Stoessinger. D. N. Mount. por Pub W 200:15-17 S 20 '71
Coming war between Russia and China, by H. Salisbury. Review
Bul Atom Sci 27:54-6 S '71. E. Rabino-witch
Communist giants poise for possible conflict. il U S News 71:70 S 13 '71
Russia and China: controlled conflict. R. Lowenthal. For Affairs 49:507-18 Ap '71
Sino-Soviet relations in the Brezhnev era. H. C. Hinton. bibliog f Cur Hist 61:135-41+ S '71
Sino-Soviet relations: the view from Moscow. J. R. Thomas. Cur Hist 61:210-14+ O '71

Cuba
Kosygin in Cuba: a visit with a high-priced ally. il por U S News 71:60 N 8 '71
Stronger voice now for Russia in Cuba. il U S News 70:26 Ja 18 '71

Czechoslovakia
See also
Czechoslovakia—Occupation, 1968-

Egypt
Gasoline by an open fire. il Time 98:29-30 O 25 '71
See also
Russia—Treaties—Egypt

Europe, Eastern
Imperial dilemmas. Z. Brzezinski. Newsweek 78:62 N 22 '71
Russia in eastern Europe: hegemony with-out security. R. F. Byrnes. For Affairs 49:682-97 Jl '71
Self-determination of peoples? D. Lawrence. U S News 70:92 Mr 29 '71
Soviet tutelage in east Europe. C. Gati. bib-liog f Cur Hist 61:206-9+ O '71

Europe, Western
Europe between the superpowers. A. Hartley. For Affairs 49:271-82 Ja '71
Soviet policies in west Europe. T. Gilberg. bibliog f Cur Hist 61:198-205 O '71

France
Charmer in Paris: visit of Brezhnev. il pors Time 98:38+ N 8 '71

Germany (Federal Republic)
German policy toward east Europe. R. G. Wesson. Cur Hist 60:295-301+ My '71
Opening to the East. P. Wohl. il Nation 212:142-5 F 1 '71
See also
Berlin question, 1945-

Great Britain
See Great Britain—Foreign relations—Russia

RUSSIA—Foreign relations—*Continued*

India

America and Russia in India. C. Bowles. For Affairs 49:636-51 Jl '71

New worries for U.S. in Asia, aftermath of Indian-Pakistani war. il U S News 72:14-17 Ja 3 '72

Israel

Moscow makes a move. Time 98:24+ Jl 5 '71

Soft on Russia? il Newsweek 78:50 N 22 '71

Tale of two travelers; visit of V. Louis. il pors Newsweek 78:37-8 Jl 12 '71

Mexico

Plot the Russians muffed. C. Foley. Nat R 23:479-80 My 4 '71

Soviet plot to destroy Mexico; excerpt from KGB. J. Barron. il Read Digest 99:227-32+ N '71

Middle East

See also
Israeli-Arab war, 1967- —Russian participation

Rumania

Crimean summit. por Time 98:25-6 Ag 16 '71

Open window to the West chills Russia. il Bsns W p57 S 11 '71

Turn of the screw. il por Newsweek 78:36+ Ag 9 '71

Sudan

Black eye for Moscow. il por Newsweek 78:30+ Ag 9 '71

United States

See United States—Foreign relations—Russia

Yugoslavia

Battle Stalin lost, by V. Dedijer. Review Nat R 23:318-19+ Mr 23 '71, M. Padev Sat R il por 54:26-7 Ja 30 '71. S. K. Padover

Man from Moscow; L. Brezhnev. il por Newsweek 78:44+ O 4 '71

No illusions. D. Tinnin. il Time 98:44+ O 4 '71

History

See also
Nicholas II, emperor of Russia
Russian-Japanese war, 1904-1905

19th century

Reflections: A. de Custine's account of visit in 1839. G. F. Kennan. New Yorker 47:48-50+ My 1 '71

Industries

Why Russia can't catch up without western know-how. il U S News 70:52-7 Ja 25 '71

See also
Aerospace industries—Russia
Automobile industry—Russia
Machine tool industry

Intellectual life

Despair in Russia. G. Heath. Read Digest 98:125-8 Je '71

Dissent in Russia: the thin wedge. il por Newsweek 77:29-34 F 1 '71

Letter from Moscow. J. Kraft. New Yorker 47:64+ My 29 '71

Medvedev papers, by Z. A. Medvedev. and A question of madness, by Z. A. Medvedev and R. A. Medvedev. Reviews
    Sat R pors 54:35-7 N 20 '71. S. Jacoby

New quest for the old Russia. G. A. Geyer. il Sat R 54:14-17 D 25 '71

Question of madness, by Z. Medvedev and R. Medvedev. Review
    Time il 98:84 D 13 '71. R. Z. Sheppard

Labor policy

Soviet labor policies. Mo Labor R 94:61 N '71

Military policy

Growing threat. C. Brownlow and B. Miller. il Aviation W 95:12-15 O 4; 36-40 O 11; 34-7 O 18; 40-3+ O 25; 38-43 N 8 '71; Discussion 95:7 O 4; 96 N 1 '71

Growing threat; with editorial comment. C. Brownlow and B. Miller. il Aviation W 95:7, 12-15 O 4 '71

Letter to a Soviet friend. C. Yost. por Life 71:4 S 24 '71

Moscow and the missile race. B. S. Lambeth. bibliog f Cur Hist 61:215-21+ O '71

Soviet first strike? H. Scoville, jr. New Repub 165:17-19 O 2 '71; Reply with rejoinder. J. R. Rumbaugh. 165:32-3 D 25 '71

Strategic transition; views of J. Erickson. il Newsweek 78:36 S 13 '71

Will success sober Moscow? il Newsweek 78:30-1 N 1 '71

See also
Preparedness, Military—Russia
Russia—Defenses

Navy

America as island? Nat R 23:1452 D 31 '71

Look at U.S.-Soviet rivalry in the Mediterranean; interview. I. C. Kidd, jr. il por U S News 71:110-11 N 15 '71

Mediterranean tide runs for the Russians. A. De Borchgrave. il Newsweek 78:34-5 Jl 19 '71

Red star over the Indian Ocean. A. Harrigan. Nat R 23:421-3 Ap 20 '71

Russia drives east of Suez. il Newsweek 77:27+ Ja 18 '71

Soviet moves highlight Guantanamo role. C. Brownlow. il Aviation W 94:16-17 Ja 25 '71

Soviet threat to NATO's northern flank. il Time 98:39 O 18 '71

Soviet thrust in the Mediterranean; Black Sea fleet and Sixth fleet. il Time 97:27-8 Je 28 '71

Where Russian threat keeps growing; interview. E. R. Zumwalt, jr. il por U S News 71:72-7 S 13 '71

Submarine service

Soviet submarines: new challenge from Cuba. K. O. Gilmore. il Read Digest 98:63-7 My '71

Photographs

Gallery. M. Bourke-White. Life 70:6-9 Ja 29 '71

Politics and government

Collective or personal rule in the U.S.S.R? D. T. Cattell. Cur Hist 61:235-9 O '71

Computerizing Soviet society. V. Zorza. Cur 132:23-30 S '71

Khrushchev remembers, by N. S. Khrushchev. Review
    Commentary 51:96+ Je '71. T. Frankel

Kremlin scoop? Khrushchev memoirs. Sr Schol 97:7-8 Ja 18 '71

Nikita Khrushchev 1894-1971. il pors Sr Schol 99:16-17 O 11 '71

Sakharov: a man for our times. W. C. Clemens, jr. il Bul Atom Sci 27:4-6+ D '71

Soviet vulnerability. Z. Brzezinski. Newsweek 78:45 N 1 '71

Trade and ideology. Z. Brzezinski. Newsweek 78:56 D 13 '71

See also
Communism—Russia
Communist party (Russia)

Relations (diplomatic)

Catholic church

See Catholic church—Relations (diplomatic)—Russia

Religious institutions and affairs

Flame of faith is not out in the U.S.S.R. P. Verghese. Chr Cent 88:580-1 My 12 '71

Moscow's methods. Chr Today 16:18 D 17 '71

Pravda on unbelief: counterevangelization. America 125:443 N 27 '71

See also
Christians in Russia
Orthodox Eastern church, Russian

Social conditions

Look inside Russia. T. W. Pauken. il por U S News 71:64-7 Ag 2 '71; Discussion 71:64 S 20 '71

See also
Jews in Russia

Social history

See also
Education—Russia—History

Treaties

Canada

Behind Trudeau's pact with Soviets. il por U S News 70:46 Je 7 '71

Egypt

Middle East: anxious visitors; Russia signing a 15-year friendship treaty with Egypt. il por Time 97:17-18 Je 7 '71

One-man show; treaty of friendship and cooperation. Newsweek 77:44 Je 14 '71

Russia's new coup in Egypt; treaty of friendship and cooperation. il por Newsweek 77:43 Je 7 '71

Germany (Federal Republic)

Changing East-West relations in Europe: the Bonn-Moscow treaty of August 1970; address, December 18, 1970. D. L. Bark. Vital Speeches 37:216-18 Ja 15 '71

RUSSIA—Treaties—*Continued*

India

Moscow: success in India, fear of China. il Time 98:14+ Ag 23 '71
Very best of friends. il Newsweek 78:27-8 Ag 23 '71

RUSSIA and the United States
See also
United States—Foreign opinion—Russian
RUSSIA and the West. See World politics, 1945-
RUSSIA-United States airline service. See Airlines—International services
RUSSIAN academy of sciences. See Academy of sciences of the USSR
RUSSIAN art. See Art, Russian
RUSSIAN artificial satellites. See Artificial satellites, Russian
RUSSIAN astronauts. See Astronauts
RUSSIAN authors. See Authors, Russian
RUSSIAN basketball players. See Basketball players
RUSSIAN blockade of Berlin. See Berlin—History—Russian blockade
RUSSIAN bonds. See Bonds, Government—Russia
RUSSIAN chess players. See Chess players
RUSSIAN communications satellites. See Communications satellites, Russian
RUSSIAN Communist party. See Communist party (Russia)
RUSSIAN composers. See Composers, Russian
RUSSIAN culture. See Russia—Intellectual life
RUSSIAN economic assistance. See Economic assistance, Russian
RUSSIAN guided missiles. See Guided missiles
RUSSIAN intellectuals. See Intellectuals
RUSSIAN-Japanese war, 1904-1905
Blow struck for the revolution; tr. by S. Wincelberg. J. Marateck. Commentary 53: 62-6 Ja '72
RUSSIAN Jews. See Jews in Russia
RUSSIAN literature
See also
Underground literature
RUSSIAN military assistance. See Military assistance, Russian
RUSSIAN Orthodox church. See Orthodox Eastern church, Russian
RUSSIAN painting. See Painting, Russian
RUSSIAN poetry

Translations into English

Confessions of an old story-teller; tr. by L. G. Leighton (cont) K. I. Chukovskii. il por Horn Bk 47:28-39 F '71
Elm log: Storm in the mountains; poems tr. by M. Glenny. A. I. Solzhenitsyn. Mlle 73:74 Je '71
Tribute to Satchmo. E. A. Evtushenko. Harp Baz 104:214-15 S '71
RUSSIAN propaganda. See Propaganda, Russian
RUSSIAN scientists. See Scientists, Russian
RUSSIAN space vehicles. See Space vehicles, Russian
RUSSIAN spies. See Spies
RUSSIAN strategy. See Strategy
RUSSIAN technical assistance. See Technical assistance, Russian
RUSSIAN track team. See Track athletics
RUSSIAN underground literature. See Underground literature
RUSSIANS in Cuba
Soviet submarines: new challenge from Cuba. K. O. Gilmore. il Read Digest 98:63-7 My '71
RUSSIANS in Mexico
Soviet plot to destroy Mexico; excerpt from KGB. J. Barron. il Read Digest 99:227-32+ N '71
RUSSIANS in southeastern Asia
Russia in southeast Asia. il Newsweek 77: 49-50 Ap 12 '71
RUSSIANS in the Sudan
Soviet Viet Nam. il Time 97:30+ Mr 1 '71
RUSSIER, Gabrielle
Affair of Gabrielle Russier. J. Peabody. Vogue 158:80 N 1 '71 *
Annals of justice. M. Gallant. New Yorker 47:47-52+ Je 26 '71 *
RUSSO-German war, 1941-1945. See World war, 1939-1945—Campaigns and battles—Russia
RUST. See Corrosion and anticorrosives
RUSTIN, Bayard
Blacks and the unions. il Harper 242:73-6+ My '71

RUSTLERS, Cattle. See Cattle thieves
RUSTOW, Dankwart A.
Relevance in social science, or the proper study of mankind. Am Scholar 40:487-96 Sum '71
RUSTS (botany)
Identification of the germination self-inhibitor from wheat stem rust uredospores. V. Macko and others. bibliog Science 173:835-6 Ag 27 '71
RUTA, Tony
Gallery; photographs. Life 70:8-9 Ap 16 '71
RUTH, Leo
The scene. Engl J 60:656-63, 1243-51+ My, D '71
RUTHERFOORD, Jim
Death hovers over Santeeland. Field & S 76:124+ Je '71
RUTHERFORD, Alta
So sweet to eat! il Org Gard & Farm 18:128-31 Ap '71
RUTHERFORD, Ernest Rutherford, 1st baron
Importance of being Ernest Rutherford. L. Badash. Science 173:873 S 3 '71 *
Recollections of Rutherford and the Cavendish; adaptation of address, August 1971. S. Devons. il pors Phys Today 24:38-45 D '71 *
RUTLEDGE, Archibald
My most memorable deer hunt. il Outdoor Life 148:44-5+ Jl '71
Not wholly; poem. Good H 172:193 F '71
RUTSALA, Vern
By the Willamette; poem. New Yorker 47:82 Ag 14 '71
Nursing home; poem. Esquire 76:56 N '71
Other lives; poem. New Repub 164:25 Mr 13 '71
RUWENZORI MOUNTAINS
This is a vacation? climbing the Mountains of the Moon. N. Ellena. il por Todays Health 49:34-6+ F '71
RYAN, Allen J.
Origin of playing cards. il Hobbies 76:142-4 My; 142-3+ Je '71
Origin of the suits. il Hobbies 76:156-7+ S '71
RYAN, E. Barry
Putting the case to Howie the horse; ed. by W. Tower. il por Sports Illus 34:26-9 Je 28 '71
RYAN, Henry B.
Stone age or twentieth century. il Américas 23:19-24 S '71
RYAN, John Fergus
American Christmas; story. Atlan 228:92-4 D '71
RYAN, John T.
Pursuit of souls: betrayal of soul. Cath World 212:245-8 F '71
RYAN, Joseph L. See Kritzeck, J. jt. auth.
RYAN, Margaret-Rose
Oklahoma summer; poem. Mlle 73:307 Ag '71
RYAN, Mary
Art classrooms without walls in the Toledo, Ohio public schools. il Sch Arts 70:40 Je '71
RYAN, Nancy
Poem: Heat rises from our bodies. Mlle 73:114 S '71
Vagabond (after bosch); poem. Mlle 74:88 D '71
RYAN, Patricia
Grim run to fiscal daylight. il Sports Illus 34:18-20+ F 1 '71
Motor sports. Sports Illus 34:48+ F 8 '71
Nature. Sports Illus 34:44 Ja 11 '71
Sporting look. Sports Illus 34:73-5 Mr 8 '71
RYAN, W. E.
Of switches and buttons; poem. America 124: 150 F 13 '71
RYBAK, Rose Kacherian
Day the Marsmen landed; drama. Plays 30: 37-42 Ap '71
RYBAR, Valerian
Valerian Rybar travels; interview. por Vogue 157:65+ Ap 15 '71
RYBURN, Beverly H.
Trilliums. il Horticulture 49:24-5+ O '71
RYDEN, Hope
Good-by to the wild horse? excerpt from America's last wild horses. il Read Digest 98:227-30+ My '71
On the track of the West's wild horses. il Nat Geog 139:94-109 Ja '71
RYDER, Robert
Opinion: on marriage. Mlle 72:17+ Ja '71
RYDER cup matches. See Golf—Tournaments
RYDER system, Inc.
Leave the driving to them. il Time 97:79 Mr 15 '71
RYDER truck lines, Inc.
Making small shipments pay their way. por Bsns W p82-4 Jl 17 '71

RYE, N.Y.

Gardens
Garden in the grand manner. E. McDonald il House B 113:110-13 Ap '71

Parks and playgrounds
Family playground; Playland amusement park. F. A. Seitz. il Parks & Rec 6:42-3+ Ap '71

Religious institutions and affairs
Groovy Christians of Rye, N.Y. J. Howard. il Life 70:78-82+ My 14 '71

RYE
How to handle three-foot winter rye. R. J. Lemp. il Org Gard & Farm 18:110-11 Je '71
See also
Feeding and feeding stuffs—Rye
RYE bread. See Bread
RYMAN, Robert
Robert Ryman's double positive. C. Ratcliff. il Art N 70:54-6+ Mr '71 *
RYSANEK, Leonie
Rysanek on Strauss; ed. by S. Jenkins. por Opera N 35:24-7 Ja 16 '71
RYTHER, John H. and Dunstan, W. M.
Nitrogen, phosphorus, and eutrophication in the coastal marine environment. bibliog il Science 171:1008-13 Mr 12 '71
RYUKYU ISLANDS
President issues executive order pertaining to Ryukyuan elections; White House announcement and text of executive order. R. M. Nixon. Dept State Bul 65:384 O 11 '71
Volatile issues mark Ryukyuan-American relations. E. E. Bollinger. Chr Cent 88:162 F 3 '71
RYUN, Jim
Back in the running. P. Putnam. il pors Sports Illus 34:10-13 F 1 '71 *
Dream comes true. P. Putnam. il pors Sports Illus 34:18-21 My 24 '71 *
Happy runners. il pors Newsweek 77:86 My 31 '71 *
Match-up for Munich. il pors Time 97:66-7 My 31 '71 *
What makes Ryun run again? P. Berger. il pors Look 35:56-8+ Jl 27 '71 *

S

S-3A (airplane) See Airplanes, Military—United States
S&H green stamps. See Sperry and Hutchinson company
SAB. See School of American ballet, inc.
SAC. See United States—Air force—Strategic air command
SACB. See United States—Subversive activities control board
SAG. See Screen actors' guild
SALT. See Strategic arms limitation talks
SAP (stockholders action program) See Stockholders
SAS. See Scandinavian airlines system, inc.
SBA. See United States—Small business administration
SBIC. See Small business investment companies
SCLC. See Southern Christian leadership conference
SCM corporation
One-armed paperhangers. il Forbes 108:44-5 Ag 1 '71
SCOPE. See International council of scientific unions—Special committee on problems of the environment
SCR (silicon controlled rectifier) See Electric current rectifiers
SDC. See System development corporation
SDR. See Special drawing rights
SDS. See Students for a democratic society (organization)
SEATO. See Southeast Asia treaty organization
SEC. See United States—Securities and exchange commission
SEED (special elementary education for the disadvantaged) See Socially handicapped children—Education
SEEK (search for education, elevation and knowledge) See New York (city). City university

SEMA. See Specialty equipment manufacturers association
SERVE (serve and enrich retirement by volunteer experience) See Community service
SES (surface effect ships) See Air cushion vehicles
SESPA. See Scientists and engineers for social and political action (organization)
SEWS (Satellite early warning system) See Ballistic missile early warning system
SIPI. See Scientists' institute for public information
SIPRI. See Stockholm international peace research institute
SKF industries, inc.
Did SKF sell out to the enemy? il Bsns W p22-3 Jl 10 '71
Still on top. il Forbes 108:18-19 Ag 1 '71
SLA See Special libraries association
SLAC (Stanford linear accelerator) See Accelerators (electrons, etc)
SLR cameras. See Single-lens reflex cameras
SMIC (study of man's impact on climate) See Man—Influence on nature
SOAR (Save our American resources) project. See Conservation of resources—Study and teaching
SOBS. See Sons of bosses international
SORC (Southern ocean racing conference) See Yacht racing
SOS. See Signals and signaling
SPAM (soil-plant-atmosphere model) See Computers—Agricultural use
SRAM (short range attack missile) See Guided missiles—Launching from airplanes
SRO (Southern regional opera) See Atlanta—Music
S. S. Pierce company. See Pierce, S. S, company
SST. See Airplanes, Supersonic
SSU (semiconductor storage unit) See Memory devices (computers)
STOL airplanes. See Airplanes, Short take-off and landing
STP (scientifically treated petroleum) See Lubrication and lubricants—Additives
STP corporation
Mouse-milk man. il por Newsweek 77:72+ Ap 5 '71
Racer's sludge. il por Time 98:106 N 1 '71
SWLA. See Southwestern library association
SAAB-Scania (firm) See Aerospace industries—Sweden
SAAL, Hubert
Who ever heard of a German ballet company? il por N Y Times Mag p 10-12 +Jl 18 '71
SAAL, Rollene W.
Pick of the paperbacks. See issues of Saturday review
SAAR, John
Faces emptied of all hope. il Life 70:22-9 Je 18 '71
Frantic night on the edge of Laos. Life 70:26-31 F 19 '71
Hunting for Mukti Bahini behind the lines. il Life 71:32-4 D 10 '71
Ignominious and disorderly retreat. il Life 30:24-8 Ap 2 '71
Visit to a friendly neighborhood sorcerer. il Life 71:34-5 Ag 13 '71
Whole country being worked very hard. il por Life 70:32-4 Ap 30 '71
SAARINEN, Eero
General motors revisited. C. Eames. il Arch Forum 134:21-8 Je '71 *
You can't see the foyer for the trees. W. Von Eckardt. il pors Horizon 13:40-7 Sum '71 *
SABBATICAL leaves. See Employees—Leaves of absence
SABELLARIID worms. See Annelids
SABER, Mourad (literary character) See Characters in literature
SABICH, Vladimir
Spider who finally came in from the cold. G. S. Brown. il por Sports Illus 35:92+ D 20 '71 *
SABIN, Francene
Willing your child. Ladies Home J 88:194 My '71
SABIN, Louis
Pledge of love. il Todays Health 49:24-5+ Jl '71
SABLE, Arnold P.
What has to be said: a personal statement. il Wilson Lib Bul 46:338-47 D '71
SABLE antelope. See Antelopes
SABOL, Blair, and Truscott, L. K. 4th
Politics of the costume. il Esquire 75:123-34 My '71

SABOTAGE
Warring pirates; Radio Northsea and competing pirate radio ship, Veronica. il Time 97:39+ My 31 '71
SABRY, Aly
Odd man out. il por Newsweek 77:36 My 17 '71 *
SACCHARIDES
Two decades of research on the biosynthesis of saccharides; Nobel lecture, December 11, 1970. L. F. Leloir. bibliog il Science 172: 1299-303 Je 25 '71
See also
Polysaccharides
SACCO-Vanzetti case
Sacco and Vanzetti: reflections in the radical mirror. bibliog il Sr Schol 98:2-3 Ap 19'71
SACHAROFF, Mark
(comp) Bibliography of recent and forthcoming books on US war crimes in Indochina. New Repub 164:29+ Ja 2 '71
Which edition of the Pentagon papers do you buy? Wilson Lib Bul 46:313-14+ D '71
SACHET. See Toilet preparations
SACHS, Ignacy
Industrialization without pollution: a challenge to the developing world. il UNESCO Courier 24:30-2 Jl '71
SACHS, Marvin L. See Clibbon, S. jt. auth.
SACHS, Mendel
Alternative to quantum mechanics. por Phys Today 24:39-41 Ap '71
Resolution of the clock paradox. bibliog il Phys Today 24:23-9 S '71
SACK, John
Authors that bloom in the spring; excerpts from press conference. il por Pub W 199: 24-6 Mr 22 '71
(ed) See Calley, W. L. jr. Confessions of Lieutenant Calley

about
Third installment. il por Newsweek 77:44 F 1 '71 *
SACRAMENTO, Calif.

Education
Survival training: bonus for life; sixth-graders at Orange Grove school. K. Hoff. bibliog il Schol Teach Jr/Sr High p 18-19+ O '71

Religious institutions and affairs
California capitol: revolution on the steps. A. Eggebroten. Chr Today 15:50+ Mr 12 '71
SACRAMENTO, COUNTY, Calif.
Herbicide clears sewer roots. Am City 86:16-17 S '71
SACRAMENTO foods (firm)
National tomato juice goes organic. il Org Gard & Farm 18:42-5 N '71
SACRAMENTS
See also
Confirmation
Lords Supper
SACRED choruses. See Choruses, Sacred
SACRED congregation for religious. See Vatican—Sacred congregation for religious and secular institutes
SACRED congregation for the doctrine of the faith. See Congregation for the doctrine of the faith
SACRED Heart, Devotion to
Eloquent image; devotion to the Sacred Heart. V. P. McCorry. America 124:640-1 Je 19 '71
SACRED music. See Church music
SACRED places. See Jerusalem—Holy places
SACRIFICE, Human
Dance drama: Mayan sacrifice. L. Mattlage. il Dance Mag 45:20-2 My '71
SADAT, Anwar
Arab Socialist union; address, June 10, 1971. Vital Speeches 37:580-3 Jl 15 '71
Sadat: we are now back to square one; interview. ed. by A. de Borchgrave. il pors Newsweek 78:43-4+ D 13 '71
Talk with Sadat on peace terms; interview. ed. by A. de Borchgrave. pors Newsweek 77:40-1 F 22 '71

about
Egypt: alone at the top. Newsweek 77:30+ My 31 '71 *
Egypt moves west. F. Halliday. por Ramp Mag 10:41-4 Ag '71 *
Egypt: Sadat in the saddle. il por Time 97: 34+ My 31 '71 *
Egypt's Sadat: cooling the hawks. il por U S News 70:36 My 31 '71 *
Just ask the sheik. il por Time 97:41-2 Je 14 '71 *

Letter from Cairo. J. Kraft. il New Yorker 47:76+ S 18 '71 *
Middle East: a case of jitters. il por Time 98:36-7 D 6 '71 *
Middle East: the underrated heir. il pors Time 97:23-6+ My 17 '71 *
Mideast: back from the brink. il por Newsweek 77:37-8 F 15 '71 *
Mideast war? Sadat holds key. il U S News 71:83 O 25 '71 *
Power of positive thinking. Newsweek 77: 33-4 Mr 1 '71 *
Preemptive purge in Cairo. il Time 97:28+ My 24 '71 *
Real Sadat and the demythologized Nasser. E. R. F. Sheehan. il pors N Y Times Mag p6-7+ Jl 18 '71 *
Religion and politics in Anwar el Sadat. J. C. Haughey. America 124:605 Je 12 '71 *
Reports & comment. G. G. Stevens. Atlan 229: 12-16 Ja '72 *
Sadat rattles his saber. por Newsweek 78: 40+ D 6 '71 *
Sadat's shake-up. il por Newsweek 77:35-6 My 24 '71 *
SADDLEBAGS for bicycles. See Bicycles—Equipment
SADLER'S Wells opera
Report:
Lohengrin. F. G. Barker. Opera N 36: 28 N '71
SADLER'S Wells theatre. See London—Theater
SAENGER, Eugene L, and others
Radiation and leukemia rates; letter. bibliog Science 171:1096+ Mr 19 '71
SAFARI. See Hunting—Africa; Hunting—Africa, East; Hunting—Chad
SAFDIE, Moshe
Beyond habitat, by M. Safdie. Review
Arch Forum 135:10 Jl '71. R. Banham *
SAFE deposit boxes
How safe is your safe deposit box? Bet Hom & Gard 49:4 My '71
SAFEGUARD anti-ballistic missile system. See Guided missiles—Defenses
SAFES
Hideaway safe for your valuables. il Mech Illus 67:109+ N '71
SAFETY, Industrial. See Industrial safety
SAFETY at sea
See also
Navigation
SAFETY belts
See also
Automobiles—Safety belts
SAFETY devices and measures
Home unsafe home. R. Nader. Ladies Home J 89:70+ Ja '72
In cold weather, safety-first counts. Good H 174:140-1 Ja '72
Safe & sane in the summertime. il Changing T 25:16-17 Jl '71
See also
Accidents—Prevention
also subhead Safety devices and measures under various subjects, e.g. Boats and boating—Safety devices and measures
SAFETY education
See also
Accidents—Prevention
Automobile driving—Study and teaching
Camping—Safety devices and measures
SAFETY engineering
See also
Underwriters' laboratories, inc.
SAFETY eyeglasses. See Eyeglasses
SAFETY guards. See Roads—Safety guards
SAFETY helmets. See Helmets
SAFETY Inspection of automobiles. See Automobiles—Inspection
SAFETY laws and legislation
See also
Industrial safety—Laws and regulations
SAFETY movement
See also
National safety council
SAFETY pins. See Pins
SAFETY-razor blades. See Razor blades
SAFETY seats. See Automobiles—Safety devices and measures
SAFEWAY stores, inc.
Last lap? il Forbes 107:21 Ap 1 '71
SAFIR, G. R. and others
Mycorrhizal enhancement of water transport in soybean. bibliog il Science 172:581-3 My 7 '71
SAFIRE, William
It's time for a change of political slogans. il N Y Times Mag p8-9 D 26 '71
SAFRAN, Nadav
Fleeting opportunity. il Nation 212:425-8 Ap 5 '71

SAGAN, Carl
—and Khare, B. N.
Long-wavelength ultraviolet photoproduction
of amino acids on the primitive earth. bibliog il Science 173:417-20 Jl 30 '71

about

Super hurricanes on Mars? Space World
H-11-95:37 N '71 •
SAGAN, Françoise, pseud.
Few hours of sunlight; story. Ladies Home J
88:189-96 Mr; 131-8 Ap '71
SAGER, Donald J.
Working with foundations: how to start a
local arts council. bibliog il Wilson Lib Bul
45:744-9 Ap '71
SAGITTA. See Arrowworms
SAGUARO. See Cactus
SAGUARO NATIONAL MONUMENT
Saguaro. L. Payne. il Nat Parks & Con
Mag 45:29-31 Ap '71
SAGUENAY RIVER
Where the white whales play. E. G. Beckett.
il Yachting 129:65+ F '71
SAHARA DESERT
See also
Geology—Sahara Desert

Description and travel

Sahara safari. R. Harrington. il Travel 136:
48-55 O '71
SAHLBERG, George
Trouble off Bergen Point! T. Gallagher. il
Read Digest 99:58-62 Ag '71 •
SAIGON

Economic conditions

Quail sales fail. Sr Schol 98:7 Ap 5 '71
SAIL on! Sail on! drama. See Olfson, L.
SAILBOAT masts. See Masts and rigging
SAILBOAT racing
Forty years of madness; frostbiting. J. Sut-
phen. il Motor B & S 127:56-7 F '71
Half ton, all race; no handicaps, no adjusted
finishes, fastest boat wins. H. D. Whall. il
Sports Illus 35:14-17 Ag 16 '71
It's harder than it looks! the 1971 Sunfish
world championships. P. Smyth. il Motor B
& S 127:27-9+ My '71
Post time for college sailing. G. M. Hall. il
Yachting 129:66-7+ Mr '71
Toms River challenge cup is the sport's old-
est continuous competition; catboat racing.
B. Robinson. il Yachting 130:60-1+ Jl '71
Winning is the only thing; International 14
class team racing series. J. Lawson. il
Yachting 130:64-5+ Ag '71
With the racing classes. E. Horan. See is-
sues of Yachting
See also
Catamaran racing
Regattas
Yacht racing

Canada

YOTS: Canada pans for gold; Youth Olympic
training seminar. D. Rose. Yachting 130:
36+ N '71
SAILBOATS
Build PM's top-performance sailboat: the
Glen L 10. H. Wicks. il Pop Mech 135:142-6
F '71
Hoist sails and away: on water, land, or
ice; Water beetle. B. Kocivar. il Pop Sci
199:60 Ag '71
It's harder than it looks! the 1971 Sunfish
world championships. P. Smyth. il Motor B
& S 127:27-9+ My '71
No fuel, no noise: just the wind and you. B.
Smith. il Pop Sci 198:90-2+ F '71
Taking stock. N. Freeman. il Yachting 130:
66-7+ Jl '71
Two new easy-breezy Snarks. D. D. Vigren.
il Pop Sci 199:46+ N '71
Yachting's preview of 1972 sailboats and
sailboat shows. il Yachting 130:63-71+ S
'71
See also
Catamarans
Masts and rigging
Trimarans
Yachts and yachting

Design

Designs; ed. by B. D. Barker, 3d. See issues
of Yachting
Drop the keel, pop the top; cruising sailboats. H. D. Whall. il Sports Illus 34:
70+ Ap 19 '71

Gary Mull's cold-molded Improbable. il
Motor B & S 128:62-3 Ag '71
New cruising sailboats: suddenly every-
body's in the act. M. Johnson. il Motor
B & S 128:48-51+ O '71

Equipment

Clever gadgets for '72. D. Rose. il Yachting
130:34+ D '71
Self-tacking trapeze. G. Hall. il Yachting
130:33+ Ag '71
Yachting's boat show (cont) il Yachting 129:
206-11 F '71

Exhibitions

See Boats—Exhibitions

Photographs

Sun, snow and sails. Yachting 129:59 My
'71

Steering gear

See Boats—Steering gear
SAILFISH fishing
Acres of action; Panama's Pacific coast. M.
J. Sosin. il pors Outdoor Life 147:68-71+
Mr '71
Big sails and marlin too. B. Warner. il Field
& S 75:78-9+ Mr '71
SAILING
Motor boating & sailing USA. See issues
of Motor boating & sailing to June 1971
Purring along with the cats: Hobie Cat
14 National championships. D. Levin. il
Sports Illus 35:88+ D 6 '71
Sailing blind. C. E. Leonard. il Yachting 130:
62-3+ Ag '71
Sailing through summer. D. Siegel. il Par-
ents Mag 46:36-7+ Jl '71
Trim to win. S. Allan. il Motor B & S 127:
78-9 F '71
See also
Boats and boating
Cruising
Navigation
Regattas
Sailboat racing
Yachts and yachting

Accidents

See Boats and boating—Accidents

Study and teaching

Instant sailing: two days before, behind,
above and below the mast. C. Born. il
Motor B & S 128:62-3+ O '71
Post time for college sailing. G. M. Hall. il
Yachting 129:66-7+ Mr '71
Sailing without water; automatic sailing
simulator. N. Hemingway. il Motor B & S
127:40+ Je '71
School for sailors. N. Levy. il Har Yrs 11,
30-4 Jl '71
YOTS: Canada pans for gold; Youth Olympic
training seminar. D. Rose. Yachting 130:
36+ N '71
SAILING cruisers. See Cruisers (pleasure
boats)
SAILING schools. See Sailing—Study and teach-
ing
SAILING ships. See Sailing vessels
SAILING vessels
After 50,000 miles; appraisal of ketch, Blue-
bird of Thorne. Lord Riverdale. il Yacht-
ing 129:68-9+ Je '71
Cape Horn; voyage of the sailing ship, British
Isles. E. Bunster. il Américas 23:2-11 Mr
'71
Cruise aboard this space-age sailing ship;
Dynaship. P. Wahl. il Pop Sci 198:48-9 Je '71
See also
Junks
SAILING yachts. See Yachts and yachting
SAILORS. See Seamen
SAILORS songs
Sea chanties & marlinspikes; life aboard the
ecology-inspired Clearwater. D. Kasanof.
il Motor B & S 127:88-9+ Mr '71
SAILORS uniforms. See Uniforms, Naval
SAILPLANES. See Gliders (aeronautics)
SAILS
De-wrapping the spinnaker. C. L. Moore. il
Yachting 129:65+ Je '71
Light weight spinnaker cloth; nylon cloth. D.
Rose. Yachting 130:32+ Ag '71
Non-mysteries of tuning. P. Smyth. il
Motor B & S 127:116+ Ap '71
Sails and rigging. J. Duffett. Motor B & S
127:101 Ap '71
Sails, spars & rigging. See issues of Motor
boating & sailing to June 1971

SAILS—*Continued*
Trim to win. S. Allan. il Motor B & S 127: 78-9 F '71
Your genoa: to cut or not to cut. J. Sutphen. il Yachting 129:58-9+ Ap '71
Your mainsail, to cut or not to cut. J. Sutphen. il Yachting 129:60-2+ Mr '71
SAINOVIC, Radenko
Helping to decide in Yugoslavia. il por Newsweek 77:39-40 Ap 5 '71 •
ST AUGUSTINE, Fla.

Galleries and museums
Museum world; Oldest store museum. J. L. Stoughtenburgh. il Hobbies 76:138-9 Ap '71
ST BERNARD'S school, Gladstone, N.J. See Private schools
ST CHARLES COUNTY, Mo, library, St Charles
Library wins tax referendum. il Am Lib 2: 559 Je '71
ST CLAIR, F. B.
(ed) See Hebert, B. Two for the desert
ST CLOUD, Minn.

Education
CATV story in St Cloud. D. L. Radeke. il Todays Ed 60:58-9 N '71
SAINT DAVID of the daffodils; story. See O'Neill, J.
ST DAVIDS, Elisabeth
In the lee of Angel Island. il Motor B & S 127:56-7+ Je '71
ST ELMO'S fire
St Elmo's fire. il Chem 44:3 Je '71
SAINT EXUPÉRY, Antoine de
Antoine de Saint-Exupéry, by C. Gate. Review
New Yorker 47:133-4 Mr 13 '71. N. Bliven •
ST HELENA (island)
Edmond Halley at St Helena. J. Ashbrook; reply. W. G. Tatham. Sky & Tel 41:280 My '71
ST HILL, Thomas Nast
Life and death of Thomas Nast; excerpts from Thomas Nast's Christmas drawings for the human race. il pors Am Heritage 22:81-96 O '71
SAINT-JEAN-VIANNEY, Quebec, landslide. See Landslides
ST JOAN of the stockyards; drama. See Brecht, B.
ST JOE paper company
Why strikers fear Ed Ball. por Bsns W p 102 O 16 '71
ST JOHN, Francis R.
Obituary
Pub W 200:31 Ag 9 '71
ST JOHN the Divine, Cathedral of. See New York (city)—St John the Divine, Cathedral of
ST JOHN'S wort
It flowers yellow in spring, it isn't very demanding, and it covers the ground; hypericum coris. il Sunset 147:229 N '71
ST LAURENT, H.
Build a moisture sensor. il Pop Electr 34: 67-9 Mr '71
ST LAURENT, Yves Mathieu
Au revoir, haute couture. il por Newsweek 78:49 Ag 23 '71 •
Oasis in Paris. il por Vogue 158:158-63 N 1 '71 •
Yves St debacle. il Time 97:62 F 15 '71 •
Yves Saint Laurent. J. Brady. por Harp Baz 104:102-3 O '71 •
Yves St Laurent, new king of off-the-rack fashion. N. Liber. por Life 71:93 O 8 '71 •
ST LAWRENCE SEAWAY
Strike-harried ships jam the Seaway. Bsns W p46 N 13 '71
ST LOUIS
City owned and operated TV stations. G. M. Chamberlain. il Am City 86:103-4+ Ap '71

Air pollution
Episode 104. V. Brodine. bibliog il Environ 13:2-24+ Ja '71

Airports
Air-force type fire fighter for airports; Lambert field. il Am City 86:12 F '71

Architecture
St Louis; Ralston purina headquarters. il Arch Forum 134:50-3 Ja '71

Description
Step by step through St Louis. R. Deardorff. il Travel 135:56-61 Je '71

Education
St Louis' educational supermarket; Junior college district. N. P. Salus. il Am Ed 7: 24-8 Mr '71
St Louis public school named for Crispus Attucks. J. Davis. Negro Hist Bul 34:57 Mr '71
To "stay" with tax-supported love; dropout project in St Louis. K. Marshall. il Am Ed 7:6-10 Ap '71

Housing
Tragedy of Pruitt-Igoe. il Time 98:38 D 27 '71

Lighting
$12 million for new street lights. il Am City 86:124 Je '71

Monuments, statues, etc.
Giant arch enhances the waterfront. L. Barry. il Pop Phot 68:32+ Ja '71

Public health
Half step forward; concern with lead poisoning. D. T. Magidson. il Environ 13:10-13 Je '71

Sanitary affairs
Cranes go round and round. il Am City 86: 34 Ag '71
Money down the drain. C. F. Buettner. il Am City 86:60-2 Ag '71
ST LOUIS civic ballet. See Ballet companies
ST LOUIS university, St Louis, Mo.
Private higher education; St Louis university self-scrutiny. America 125:500 D 11 '71
ST MARTIN (island)
Under a double standard. D. Butwin. il Sat R 54:32+ Ap 10 '71
ST MARY'S cathedral, San Francisco. See San Francisco—Churches
ST PATRICK'S day
Old Muldoon. New Yorker 47:34 Mr 27 '71

Drama
Finnegan at the fair. F. B. Watts. Plays 30: 39-44, 78 Mr '71
ST PAUL

Banks
Sinologist at St Paul; travel unit of First national bank of St Paul. R. Levy. Duns 98:61 O '71

Description
Minneapolis/St Paul: living and working in the Twin Cities. A. M. Cunningham. Mlle 73: 152+ S '71

Education
Museum for fun and learning; public schools volunteer services program and the Minnesota museum of art. M. A. Grossmann. il Am Ed 7:24-5 My '71

Music
See also
St Paul opera association

Politics and government
Mayor for all seasons. il por Newsweek 77:59 F 8 '71
ST PAUL civic opera association. See St Paul opera association
ST PAUL opera association
Hoiby's Summer and smoke hits home; opera based on Tennessee Williams' play. J. Gerstel. il Hi Fi 21:MA20-1 S '71
Report:
Lee Hoiby's Summer and smoke. P. Gainsley. Opera N 36:22 S '71
St Paul's summer; world premiere of L. Hoiby's Summer and smoke. M. A. Feldman. il por Opera N 36:18-20 S '71
ST PAUL'S cathedral, London. See London—St Paul's cathedral
ST PAUL'S school, Concord, N.H. See Private schools
ST PETER'S cathedral, Rome. See Rome (city) —St Peter's cathedral
ST PETERSBURG, Fla.
Artificial turf turns median strip into beauty spots. il Am City 86:24+ Je '71
Pollution snoop troops. il Am City 86:102 O '71

Education
Battle for the South: phase two. C. Fulwood. il Ramp Mag 10:36-9 Jl '71
ST REGIS paper company
Seeing the forest for the trees; advertising campaign for The secret life of the forest. L. L. L. Golden. Sat R 54:50 Ap 10 '71; Same. Am For 77:45 S '71
Stairway to heaven. il Forbes 107:43 My 1 '71

SAINT-SAËNS, Camille
Samson and Delilah. Criticism
  Sat R 54:60 D 25 '71 *

ST VINCENT (island)
  See also
Bequia (island)

SAINTE-MARIE, Buffy
Singular woman. M. Smith. por McCalls 98:
  45 Mr '71 *

SAJER, Guy
Everything was permitted. J. Walt. New Repub 164:28-9 F 20 '71 *

SAKAS, Joseph
William Torrey Harris: pioneer in comparative education. bibliog por Sch & Soc 99:
  230-2 Ap '71

SAKATA, Harold
Odd job gets a new job. P. Hudson. por Sr
  Schol 99:44-5 S 27 '71 *

SAKHAROV, Andreï Dmitrievich
—and others
Sakharov on human rights. Sat R 54:24 Ja
  16 '71
           about
Sakharov: a man for our times. W. C.
  Clemens, jr. il Bul Atom Sci 27:4-6+ D '71 *

SAKURAI, T. and others
X-ray diffraction patterns of transfer RNA
  consistent with the presence of short parallel helices in the molecule. bibliog il Science 172:1234-7 Je 18 '71

SAKUTARō, Hagiwara
Comment. F. D. Reeve. Poetry 118:234-5 Jl
  '71 *

SALAD dressings
ABC'S of salad dressing. il Am Home 74:
  130 N '71
Crazy mixed-up salad dressings. il Bet Hom
  & Gard 49:131 D '71
Good match, shallot dressing and crisp vege-
  tables. il Sunset 147:139 S '71

SALAD greens. See Greens, Edible

SALADS
Chicken salad is really a meal. il Sunset 146:
  174 Je '71
Cold roast and shredded lettuce. il Sunset
  146:180 Mr '71
Easy salads: with meat from the icebox or
  delicatessen. il Sunset 147:135 Jl '71
Fast and fancy cranberry salads. il Bet Hom
  & Gard 49:103-4 N '71
Fast and fancy vegetable salads. il Bet Hom
  & Gard 49:77-8 My '71
For cool eating on hot days count on sal-
  ads. R. Molter. il Parents Mag 46:52-5+
  Je '71
Fresh bean sprouts with seafood. Sunset
  146:186 Mr '71
Good-buy salads. F. M. Crawford. Am Home
  74:46 Mr '71
Help-yourself salad plate. il Sunset 146:148
  Mr '71
Help yourself to summer. F. M. Crawford.
  il Am Home 74:62-3+ Je '71
Holiday salad platters with marinated vege-
  tables. il Sunset 147:134 D '71
Instead of celery, asparagus victor. il Sun-
  set 146:232 Ap '71
Lively salads from the Near East. il Sun-
  set 146:88 Ja '71
Main dish salads made in a mold. Sunset
  147:180 N '71
Make-ahead meat and salad trays. il Sunset
  146:166 Je '71
Midwinter green salads, each with a surprise.
  il Sunset 146:104 Ja '71
Putting fruit and seafood together. il Sunset
  146:178+ Je '71
Salad days. il Redbook 137:102-6+ Je '71
Salads from the sea with squid. il Sunset
  147:183 N '71
Spectacular salad entrée; shrimp and rice;
  with menu and recipe. H. McCully. il House
  B 113:70-1 Jl '71
Strawberries, special in salads. il Bet Hom &
  Gard 49:69+ My '71
12-year-old chef makes Caesar salad at the
  table while everybody watches. il Sunset
  146:110-11 F '71
24 salads all dressed up. M. Happel. il Ladies
  Home J 88:78-81+ Je '71
What's for salad? Dandelion greens. il Sunset
  146:196 My '71

SALAMANDERS
  See also
Newts

SALAMENSKY, Carl
I can't take any more. il por Newsweek
  78:51-2 Jl 26 '71 *
Kidney in time. il por Newsweek 78:45 Ag
  2 '71 *

SALAMI; story. See Wohlstattar, T.

SALAMON, Lester M.
Family assistance. New Repub 164:17-18 F 20
  '71

SALAMY, Joseph G. See Morrell, L. K. jt.
  auth.

SALAPATEK, Sandra Scarr-. See Scarr-Sa-
  lapatek, S.

SALARIES
Blue-collar/white-collar pay trends: a com-
  ment on the findings. P. Henle. Mo Labor
  R 94:35-6 Je '71
Trimmed paychecks put back lost weight.
  Bsns W p35 Jl 17 '71
  See also
Bonus system
Minimum wage
Non-wage payments
    also subhead Salaries, allowances, etc.
  under various subjects, e.g. College pro-
  fessors and instructors—Salaries, allow-
  ances, etc.

SALAS, Floyd
Notes on a second novel. Writer 84:12-15 F
  '71

SALAZAR, Filoteo Samaniego. See Samaniego
  Salazar, F.

SALAZAR, Manuel
Manuel Salazar. A. Favla-Artsay. pors Hobbies 75:35-6 Ja '71 *

SALEH, Dennis
Meadow; Sexuality; Trout; For light; White
  apple; Snake; poems. Poetry 118:327-32 S '71

SALEM, Mass.
                Antiquities
They're digging up witch lore in Salem. S. S.
  McKern. il Sci Digest 69:27-8+ My '71

SALEM, N.C. See Winston-Salem, N.C.

SALEM witchcraft. See Witchcraft

SALES, Bob
She's just one of the guys. il pors Todays
  Health 49:19-22+ Ap '71

SALES
How to turn your unwanted possessions into
  money: attic sales, barn sales, etc. J. W.
  Johnson. il Mech Illus 67:57-8+ D '71

SALES conventions
Why sales meetings? G. J. Berkwitt. il Duns
  97:37-9 F '71

SALES forecasting
As government sees it: sales outlook for 66
  major industries. U S News 70:19 Ap 5 '71
How to choose the right forecasting technique. J. C. Chambers and others. bibliog
  f il Harvard Bsns R 49:45-74 Jl '71

SALES promotion
  See also
Entertaining in sales promotion
Premiums
Samples (merchandising)

SALES tax
  See also
Motor fuels—Taxation
Value added tax

SALESMANSHIP. See Salesmen and salesman-
  ship

SALESMEN and salesmanship
Fast-buck gospel; enterprises of G. W. Tur-
  ner. il por Time 98:76+ N 29 '71
Last of the supersalesmen; pitchmen on At-
  lantic City's boardwalk. il Bsns W p50+
  S 18 '71
  See also
Automobile salesmen
Booksellers and bookselling
Canvassing
Sales conventions

                Audio visual aids
Suit yourself, with mirrors; Synoptic mirror system. P. Wahl. il Pop Sci 198:57 F
  '71

SALGADO, Antonio
Ideology of the conquest. il Américas 23:S3-
  5 Ag '71

SALICYLATES
Glycoproteins: isolation from cell membranes
  with lithium diiodosalicylate. V. T. Marchesi and E. P. Andrews. bibliog il Science
  174:1247-8 D 17 '71
Salicylate: effect on membrane permeability
  of molluscan neurons. J. L. Barker and H.
  Levitan. bibliog il Science 172:1245-7 Je 18
  '71

SALINA, Kan.
Trim the border for an attractive street. il
  Am City 86:38 Ap '71

SALINE water
Amateur scientist; experiments with salt
  fountains and related instabilities in water,
  ed. by C. L. Stong. il Sci Am 224:124-8 Je
  '71

SALINGER, Pierre
Question of time; story; excerpt from On
instructions of my government. Good H
172:77-9 My; 88-9 Je '71
SALISBURY, Charlotte Y.
Enlightened travelers. pors Vogue 158:134-
5+ O 15 '71
SALISBURY, Harrison E.
Enlightened travelers. pors Vogue 158:134-
5+ O 15 '71
Image and reality in Indochina. For Affairs
49:381-94 Ap '71
about
Extra nickel's worth. il por Time 97:36 Je
21 '71 •
SALM, Walter G.
CATV and the wired city. il Radio-Electr
42:36-8 My '71
Cassette or cartridge: which tape machine
for you? il Pop Mech 135:72-5+ F '71
Clock timers: easy way to automate your
home. il Pop Mech 136:112-15+ S '71
Home video recording, or is it? il Radio-
Electr 42:13-15+ Jl '71
Look what they've done with the lowly cas-
sette! il Pop Mech 136:100-5+ D '71
SALMAGUNDI club, New York
100 years of the Salmagundi club. W. Pax-
ton. il Am Artist 35:31+ D '71
SALMON, Larry
Jack Lenor Larsen in Boston. il **Craft Horiz**
31:14-23 Ap '71
SALMON, Paul D.
Schoolman of the hour. por **Newsweek 77:**
80 My 31 '71 •
SALMON, Robert W.
Robert Salmon: painter of ship and shore.
J. Wilmerding. il Antiques 99:257-61 F '71 •
SALMON, Sydney, and others
Lymphocyte stimulation: selective destruc-
tion of cells during blastogenic response
to transplantation antigens. bibliog il Sci-
ence 172:490-2 Ap 30 '71
SALMON
Little salmon: planted kokanee in eastern
lakes. L. J. Bashline. il Field & S 76:38 Je
'71
Vicissitudes of the Pacific salmon. A. Netboy.
il Sea Front 17:83-93 Mr '71
Wild hope from some tame Atlantic salmon;
Norwegian fish farms. C. Gammon. il
Sports Illus 35:94+ N 29 '71
See also
Cookery—Fish
SALMON fisheries. See Fisheries
SALMON fishing
Fall salmon snagging. R. F. Eggert. il Field
& S 76:114+ Ag '71
Follow that fish. D. Stair. il **Field & S 75:**
74-5+ Ap '71
Go light for kings. D. H. Smith. il Field & S
75:60-1+ Mr '71
Kings of the spring. W. Curtis. il Outdoor
Life 147:64-5+ Mr '71
Kings on the rocks. E. Demeter. il Field &
S 75:80-1+ F '71
Labrador discovery. N. Karas. il **Field & S**
76:58-9+ Jl '71
Maine thing. J. Brooks. il Outdoor Life 147:
116-19+ F '71
Miramichi goes public. J. **Fisk.** il por Out-
door Life 147:64-5+ My '71
Salmon fishing in America: the Indians vs.
the state of Washington. P. Collier. il Ramp
Mag 9:29-31+ Ap '71
Salmon fishing . .; pure and simple. A. J.
McClane. il Field & S 76:84-7 Jl '71
Sebago comeback. T. Janes. il Outdoor Life
147:88-9+ Ap '71
Steelhead or Atlantic salmon? J. Brooks.
il Outdoor Life 148:68-9+ S '71
Witch salmon. H. Hyman. il por **Field & S**
76:110-13+ Jl '71
SALMON RIVER
Death ran with the river; rapids on Middle
Fork of Salmon. A. E. Couture. il pors Out-
door Life 147:53-7+ My '71
SALMONELLA. See Bacteria, Pathogenic
SALMONELLOSIS
Annuals of medicine outbreak of salmonella
cubana at Massachusetts general hospital
caused by contaminated carmine dye. B.
Roueché. New Yorker 47:66-72+ S 4 '71
Pet turtles and salmonella poisoning. il Con-
sumer Rep 36:405-6 Jl '71
SALOMON, Louis B.
You'd better believe it's loaded; adaptation
of address, November 1970. Engl J 60:353-
8 Mr '71

SALONE, Ivory, Jr
Window wishing for 1971; poem. Negro Hist
Bul 34:20 Ja '71
SALT
Salt. R. C. Murray. il Natur Hist 80:46-53
O '71
Salt in our lives. L. T. Rienow. Audubon
73:100-3 Jl '71
Salt in snack foods. D. M. Strietelmeier.
il Chem 44:20-2 D '71
SALT glands. See Glands
SALT LAKE CITY
Urban shadows fall on sunny Salt Lake City.
H. Waters. il Newsweek 77:102+ Mr 15 '71
See also
Stock exchange—Salt Lake City

Banks
Theft from Ute Indians; the First security
bank, transfer agent. Ramp Mag 10:7 Ag '71
SALT marsh ecology. See Marsh ecology
SALT marsh plants. See Marsh plants
SALT marshes. See Marshes, Tide
SALT mines and mining

United States
Radioactive salt mine; with comments and
summary. R. S. Lewis. il Bul Atom Sci
27:27-31+ Je '71
SALT talks. See Strategic arms limitation
talks
SALT tolerance of plants. See Plants, Effect
of salt on
SALT water. See Saline water
SALT water fishing
Inshore seamanship; surf fishing. J. A. Em-
mett. il Outdoor Life 148:20+ Jl '71
Lure of the surf. N. Bryant. Atlan 227:108+
My '71
Salt water. G. Heinold. **See issues of Out-
door life**
Surf fishing with a 4-wheel drive. G. W.
Linnane. il Pop Mech 135:106-7+ F '71
Surfman's savvy. G. Heinhold. il Outdoor
Life 148:38+ N '71
With the sport fishermen. F. T. Moss. See
issues of Yachting
You never know when you might need a mul-
let. C. Phinizy. il pors Sprts Illus 34:54-6+
Ap 5 '71
See also
Barracuda fishing
Bass fishing
Bluefish fishing
Bonefish fishing
Dolphin fishing
Marlin fishing
Pompano fishing
Sailfish fishing
Shark fishing
Snook fishing
Tarpon fishing
Tuna fishing
SALTON, Gerard
Computers & libraries. bibliog il por Li-
brary J 96:3277-82 O 15 '71
SALTS
Polywater: evidence from electron spec-
troscopy for chemical analysis (ESCA) of
a complex salt mixture. R. E. Davis and
others. bibliog il Science 171:167-70 Ja 15
'71
SALTS in snow and ice removal. See Snow and
ice removal
SALTVILLE, Va. See Company towns
SALUS, Naomi P.
St Louis' educational supermarket. il Am
Ed 7:24-8 Mr '71
SALUTATIONS
"Pound", a new unity sign; ritual greeting
of black soldiers in Vietnam. F. C.
Anthony. America 124:147-8 F 13 '71
SALUTIN, Rick
Oh! Canada! The eruption of a revolution.
Harper 243:26-31 Jl '71
SALVADOR
See also
Earthquakes—Salvador
Fishing—Salvador
SALVADOR, Brazil
Bahia: papaya every morning, voodoo every
night. C. Tressilian. il Holiday 48:62-5+
S '70
SALVAGE (ships)
Men against the sea. D. Barney. il Pop Mech
136:92-7+ D '71
SALVAGE (waste)
See also
Automobiles—Wrecking
Refuse, Utilization of

SALVATION
Cosmological Christology. T. Organ. Chr Cent
88:1293-5 N 3 '71
Elusive trail from is to ought. Chr Today
15:20-1 Ag 27 '71
Star of redemption, by F. Rosenzweig. Review
Commentary 52:83-7 Jl '71. M. A. Meyer
SALVATION army
Biting the hand that feeds you; reply. E.
Fritz. Trans-Action 7:60+ O '70
Mercenaries for Christ. il Newsweek 78:50
D 27 '71
SALVI, Giancarlo
Roughneck from Bologna. por Bsns W p43
Je 5 '71
SALVIATI, Francesco
Salviati's beheading of St John the Baptist.
L. Steinberg. il Art N 70:46-7 S '71 *
SALYUT. See Space stations
**SALZBURG Easter festival. See Music festivals
—Austria**
SALZBURG festival
Festival retains its glamor. G. Movshon. Hi
Fi 21:MA28-9 N '71
Report:
Mozart's Mitridate, rè di ponto, Donizetti's Don Pasquale, Berg's Wozzeck,
and Monteverdi's Orfeo. D. Norris. il
Opera N 36:24-5 O '71
SALZKAMMERGUT, Austria
Salzburg connection. J. T. Starr. il Am For
77:28-31+ F '71
SALZMAN, Herbert
Man from OPIC. G. R. Rosen. por Duns 97:
70+ Ap '71 *
SAMANIEGO SALAZAR, Filoteo
Venus of Valdivia. il Américas 23:25-31 Mr
'71
SAMFORD, Clarence D.
Social studies: then and now. il Clear House
45:337-40 F '71
SAMMARTINO, Bruno
Little agony, a little ecstasy. L. A. Gutkind.
il por Sports Illus 35:36-8+ S 27 '71 *
SAMPLERS
Museum samplers. M. Evans and D. L.
Brightbill. il Am Home 74:96-7+ S '71
SAMPLES (merchandising)
Selective samplers find the customers. il
Bsns W p34-5 Jl 3 '71
SAMPLING
See also
Grain sampling
SAMPSELL, Paul H.
Anniversary meditation; poem. Chr Cent
88:992 Ag 25 '71
SAMPSON, Arthur F.
GSA advocates new financing techniques for
public buildings. Arch Rec 150:65-6 S '71
SAMS, Jonathan
Angling theologically. il Field & S 76:40-1+
D '71
SAMSON, Jack
Game for gourmets. il Field & S 75:69-70+ F
'71
**SAMSON and Delilah; opera. See Saint-Saëns,
C.**
SAMSONITE corporation
Paternalism dies at Samsonite. il por Bsns W
p58 D 25 '71
SAMUELS, Charles Thomas
Antonioni: two decades of film. il Art in Am
59:72-7 Ja '71
Bresson's gentleness. Am Scholar 40:309-15
Spr '71
Cinema in the sixties; with filmography. il
Am Lib 2:461-73 My '71
Sightings (cont) Am Scholar 40:482-6, 695-
700; 41:134-8 Sum-Wint '71
SAMUELS, Gertrude
Thank God it's Thursday! Coming soon? The
four-day week. il N Y Times Mag p32-3+
My 16 '71
When children collide with the law. il N Y
Times Mag p44-5+ D 5 '71
SAMUELS, H. J.
Hunter cooks. il Outdoor Life 147:84+ F '71
SAMUELS, Howard Joseph
New York derby. il Newsweek 77:61 My 17
'71 *
SAMUELS, Nathaniel
Aims of President Nixon's economic program
presented to the GATT council; statement,
August 24, 1971. Dept State Bul 65:305-8
S 20 '71
Inter-American economic and social council
meets at Panama City; statement, September 13, 1971. Dept State Bul 65:379-82
O 11 '71
International economic policy scene; address,
November 15, 1971. Dept State Bul 65:669-74
D 13 '71

International trade issues for the seventies;
statement, May 20, 1971. Dept State Bul 64:
807-12 Je 21 '71
Tenth meeting of OECD ministerial council
held at Paris; statements, June 7 and 8,
1971. Dept State Bul 65:13-19 Jl 5 '71
U.S. foreign economic policy: problems and
prospects; excerpts from address, February
25, 1971. Dept State Bul 64:327-8 Mr 15 '71
SAMUELS, S. Jay
Letter-name vs. letter-sound knowledge in
learning to read. Ed Digest 37:49-51 S '71
SAMUELSON, Paul Anthony
[Column on economic questions] See issues
of Newsweek
Maximum principles in analytical economics;
Nobel lecture, December 11, 1970. bibliog
il Science 173:991-7 S 10 '71
Where has all the money gone? interview,
ed. by O. Coombs. por Redbook 137:48+ Jl
'71
Who's fooling with it? il Look 35:59-61 Ap
20 '71
SAN ANDREAS fault. See Faults (geology)
**SAN ANTONIO grand opera festival. See Music
festivals—Texas**
**SANASARDO, Paul, dance company. See
Dance companies**
SANASESSION. See Exercise
SAN BLAS, Mexico
San Blas for slow-paced vacations. il Sunset
147:54+ N '71
**SAN BLAS ISLANDS, Panama. See Mulatas
Islands**
SANCHEZ, Luis Alberto
Role of the colonial university. il Américas
23:S6-8 Ag '71
SANCHEZ, Manuel
President's man. il pors Time 97:14 Mr 1 '71 *
SANCHEZ, Phillip V.
Old-fashioned U.S. success story. il pors U S
News 71:80 O 4 '71 *
SANCHEZ, Ricardo
Why minority publishing? ed. by B. Chambers. il pors Pub W 199:38-40 Mr 15 '71
SANCTIONS (international law)
Department reviews U.S. position on Southern Rhodesia; statement. J. D. D.
Newsom. Dept State Bul 65:111-15 Jl 26 '71
SANCTUARY (law) See Asylum, Right of
SAND, George X.
Alaska's valley of death. il Sci Digest 69:
24-9 Ap '71
Hunting and fishing Alaska by train. il
Field & S 76:156-8+ O '71
New fishing chart opens flooded Everglades
wilderness. il Field & S 76:172-4+ Je '71
SAND blast
Product of the month; A.L.C. model C sandy
jet abrasive blaster. B. Bryan. il Hot Rod
24:120-1 Jl '71
SAND casting. See Plaster work (craft)
SAND crabs. See Crabs
SAND dunes
See also
White Sands National Monument
**SAND LAKE national wildlife refuge. See
Wildlife sanctuaries—South Dakota**
SAND skis and skiing
Without snow or sand still they ski; Monte
Kaolino at Hirschau, Western Germany.
H. Zenker. il Travel 135:66-9 My '71
SAND storms. See Dust storms
SANDA, Dominique
Dominique Sanda, the mad and the beautiful. H. Ehrlich. il pors Look 35:66-72+ O 5
'71 *
SANDBACH, Walker
Other Ralph Nader. R. Levy. por Duns 98:
42-3 D '71 *
**SANDBERG-DIMENT, Erik. See Langer, R.
W. pseud.**
SANDBURG, Helga
Comment. N. Sullivan. Poetry 119:109 N '71 *
SANDEEN, Ernest
Cricket sound; poem. Sat R 54:21 F 13 '71
Little folding of the hands to sleep; poem.
Sat R 54:55 Ja 30 '71
SANDER, August
August Sander: portraitist of a nation in
transition. J. Scully and E. Scully. il Mod
Phot 35:88-93 Ag '71 *
SANDER, Ellen
Pop. Sat R 54:55 F 27; 75+ Mr 27; 57 Ap 24;
56 My 29; 49 Je 26; 47+ Jl 31; 47 Ag 28;
80 N 27 '71
SANDER, Ernest
Paul Siebel: homegrown weed. por Sat R
54:55 Ja 30 '71
SANDERS, C. J.
Sex pheromone specificity and taxonomy of
budworm moths (choristoneura) bibliog il
Science 171:911-13 Mr 5 '71

SANDERS, Charles L.
Aretha. il pors Ebony 27:124-6+ D '71
Radicalization of Angela Davis. pors Ebony 26:114+ Jl '71
(ed) See King, C. S. Finally I've begun to live again

SANDERS, Ed
Charlie and the devil; excerpt from The Family. il por Esquire 76:105-12+ N '71

SANDERS, Gladys
Bitten by the water bug. il House B 113:66-7+ Jl '71

SANDERS, Herbert
Herbert Sanders. F. Ball. il por Ceram Mo 19:14-17 N '71 •

SANDERS, Howard J.
Cardiac pacemakers. il Chem 44:14-17 Jl '71

SANDERS, Ralph
Beef management. See issues of Successful farming
(ed) Successful beef managemnt. Suc Farm 69: Bl O; Bl O '71

SANDERS, Thomas G.
Family planning in Latin America: image and reality. il America 124:203-7 F 27 '71
SANDERS. See Sanding machines

SANDERS associates, inc.
Sanders fights to break its financial bind. il Bsns W p42+ S 18 '71
Settlement cuts Sanders' equity. Aviation W 95:17 Jl 26 '71

SANDERSON, Derek
Ice hockey's best-hated villain; with report by B. Bruns. il pors Life 70:46-51 Ap 9 '71 •
Sports. R. Kahn. Esquire 75:50+ Ja '71 •

SANDERSON, R. T.
How should periodic groups be numbered? il por Chem 44:17-18 N '71

SANDERSON, Robert
Robert Sanderson in England. Mrs G. E. P. How. il Antiques 99:718-19 My '71 •

SANDHURST, Royal military college
Updating Sandhurst. A. Deming. il Newsweek 77:40+ F 8 '71

SAN DIEGO, Calif.
Commuter's convention site. il Newsweek 78: 18 Ag 2 '71
Playground divided; difficulty supporting professional sports. R. W. Johnston. il por Sports Illus 35:78-81+ N 8 '71
San Diego backs into a smoke-filled room; bid for 1972 Republican convention. il Bsns W p23 Jl 10 '71
Sewage reservoir solves overflow problem. F. M. Conger. il Am City 86:103 N '71

Community centers
San Diego's Cardijan center. America 125: 136-7 S 11 '71

Description
San Diego watered down. D. Butwin. il Sat R 54:32-3 Jl 10 '71

Education
Improving school-community relations; O'Farrell junior high school. G. T. Frey. il Todays Ed 60:14-17 Ja '71

Harbor
Fire-police boat in one package. il Am City 86:37 Ap '71

Stores
Yab Yum, a sensory experience in 4000 sq. ft. M. Clark. il Pub W 199:43-5 My 3 '71

Streets
Concrete utility-cut repairs work best. il Am City 86:28 Mr '71

Water supply
Highlining helps customers and contractors. F. M. Conger. il Am City 86:30 Ja '71
Pure water from sewage. R. E. Dodson. il por Am City 86:43-4 F '71

SAN DIEGO COUNTY, Calif.
Need better news coverage? il Am City 86: 80 S '71

SANDIMANIE, Ellen A.
Liberian lady wears three hats. E. B. Thompson. il pors Ebony 27:54-6+ Ja '72 •

SANDING machines
Finishing sanders. il Consumer Rep 36:554-9 S '71
Lathe-powered band sander. A. E. Hartman. il Pop Sci 198:110 Je '71
Salvaged motor makes a handy shop sander. R. S. Hedin. il Pop Mech 136:172+ D '71
Turning a sander into a sander-grinder. W. Waggoner. il Mech Illus 67:114-15+ N '71

SANDOVAL, Orlando
Revolution? Not here, not yet. America 124: 94-6 Ja 30 '71

SANDS, Barbara
Mercury monitoring highlights Long Island swordfish tournament. il por Cons 26:27-31 O '71

SANDS measurement corporation
How to weigh a moving train. il Bsns W p 102 Je 26 '71

SANDVED, Kjell
Gallery; photographs. Life 70:8-9 Je 11 '71

SANDWICH glass. See Glassware

SANDWICHES
Beer on a bun. il Bet Hom & Gard 49:24 Ap '71
Italy and the sandwich. J. Ferris. Sat R 54:6 Jl 24 '71
Man-sized sandwiches. il Bet Hom & Gard 49:86 Jl '71
Open-faced sandwiches using vegetables, seeds, eggs, cheese. il Sunset 147:182 O '71
Tortilla roll-ups for a picnic. il Sunset 146: 216 My '71

SANDY, Stephen
Joshua's poem. Yale R 60:390 Mr '71
November larches; poem. Harper 242:60 Ja '71

SAN FERNANDO VALLEY quake. See Los Angeles—Earthquake, 1971

SANFORD, David
Last and leased. New Repub 165:17-20 S 4 '71
What can you do in a canoe? New Repub 164:17-18 My 29 '71

SANFORD, Steven
Doughnuts to dollars. il por Time 95:58-9 Ag 9 '71 •

SAN FRANCISCO
Monster mast; television antenna to rise above city. il Time 99:54 Ja 3 '72

Airports
Bay area seeks greater airport capacity. R. G. O'Lone. il Aviation W 95:98-100 N 15 '71
See also
Skyscrapers

Architecture

Banks
Make your MBO pragmatic; Wells Fargo bank program. J. B. Lasagna. il Harvard Bsns R 49:64-9 N '71

Churches
Glide to glory; Glide memorial united Methodist church. L. Robinson. il por Ebony 26:44-6+ Jl '71
On building cathedrals and tearing them down; St Mary's cathedral, San Francisco. J. V. Schall. il Cath World 212:301-6 Mr '71
Saint Mary's cathedral, San Francisco. E. K. Thompson. il Arch Rec 150:113-20 S '71

City planning
Design becomes part of a master plan. il Bsns W p64 S 4 '71
Skylines v. skyscrapers. il Time 97:35 Mr 8 '71
Who needs skyscrapers? conservationists petition for height limitation. New Repub 164:10 Ja 30 '71

Crime
Beware the *wah ching!* il Newsweek 78:63-4 Ag 30 '71

Description
San Francisco: its cool charm is summerproof. Bsns W p79-80 Jl 17 '71
San Francisco scene. B. Bryant. il Mlle 72: 180+ F '71

Earthquake and fire, 1906
San Francisco earthquake, by G. Thomas and M. M. Witts. Review
Atlan 228:114-15 S '71. E. Weeks
Bsns W il p 13 Ag 21 '71. R. Lamb

Education
Boycotting the buses. il Newsweek 78:43 S 27 '71
New breed principal brings peace to Pelton; T. Carroll of San Francisco's Pelton junior high school. il pors Ebony 27:144-6+ N '71
Quotas by any other name; deselection of administrators. E. Raab. Commentary 53: 41-5 Ja '72

Fountains
See Fountains

Galleries and museums
Despite predictions of doom, this photo gallery survives: Focus gallery. M. Mann. il Pop Phot 68:30+ Ja '71

Gardens
Strybing arboretum and botanical garden. R. L. Hudson. il Horticulture 49:36-7+ Je '71

SAN FRANCISCO—*Continued*

Historic houses, etc.
Fort under Golden Gate bridge. il Sunset 147:26 N '71

History
Nice piece of real estate: J. Y. Limantour's claim. R. Reinhardt. il Am Heritage 23:42-7+ D '71

Hospitals
Models for financially healthy hospitals; Saint Francis memorial hospital. G. C. Forsyth and D. G. Thomas. il Harvard Bsns R 49:106-17 Jl '71

Housing
We're the third white house from the corner; Daly City. il Life 71:78-9 O 1 '71

Lighting
Road-level lighting provides a carpet of light. il Am City 86:84 Jl '71

Moral conditions
San Francisco: Sodom revisited; Examiner editorial. Chr Today 15:23 Ja 29 '71
Ungluing of San Francisco. D. Brudnoy. il Nat R 23:592 Je 1 '71

Music
Britten's Britons; the English opera group in San Francisco. J. W. Stedman and G. McElroy. il por Opera N 36:18-20 N '71
Opera, ballet, jazz, or symphony in a San Francisco forest; Sigmund Stern grove. il Sunset 146:84-5 Je '71
See also
San Francisco opera company

Newspapers
See also
San Francisco examiner

Parks and playgrounds
Opera, ballet, jazz, or symphony in a San Francisco forest; Sigmund Stern grove. il Sunset 146:84-5 Je '71
Plan for action. J. Caverly. il Parks & Rec 6:18-19+ N '71
Try poles for playgrounds. il Am City 86:28 S '71

Police department
Keystone cops; report of Committee on crime. Newsweek 77:67 Je 28 '71
New-breed cop; program of new sheriff. R. Hongisto. New Repub 165:7 D 4 '71

Politics and government
Odds on Alioto. il por Newsweek 78:26-7 O 11 '71
Sheriff of San Francisco. Nation 213:518 N 22 '71

Publishers and publishing
See Publishers and publishing—California

Recreation
See also
San Francisco—Parks and playgrounds

Social problems
Churches and the homosexual; San Francisco's gay community; with editorial comment. J. A. Coleman. America 124:inside cover. 113-17 F 6 '71

Streets
San Francisco's Union street. il Sunset 146:112-15 My '71

Strikes
See also
Strikes—United States—Teachers

Transit systems
All aboard BART, the commuter's dream. M. Walker. il Read Digest 99:97-100 Jl '71
BART: the way to go for the '70s. M. Walker. il Pop Sci 198:50-3+ My '71
Martini commuters; ferry from Sausalito to San Francisco. il Time 98:46 Jl 12 '71
Rapid transit: a real alternative to the auto for the Bay area? R. J. Bazell. il Science 171:1125-8 Mr 19 '71
San Franciscans fight for that cable-car charm. il Bsns W p62-4 S 4 '71

Water supply
See also
Hetch Hetchy water supply project

SAN FRANCISCO art institute
Photography has equal status in art competition. M. Mann. il Pop Phot 69:106+ Jl '71

SAN FRANCISCO BAY
Imminent death of San Francisco Bay. L. Green. il Field & S 75:10+ Ap '71

SAN FRANCISCO BAY bridges
High lighting for an upper level. il Am City 86:70 Ja '71

SAN FRANCISCO BAY oil slicks. See Oil pollution of rivers, harbors, etc.

SAN FRANCISCO examiner
San Francisco; Sodom revisited. Chr Today 15:23 Ja 29 '71

SAN FRANCISCO 49ers (football club) See Football clubs

SAN FRANCISCO Giants (baseball) See Baseball clubs

SAN FRANCISCO International airport. See San Francisco—Airports

SAN FRANCISCO museum of art
Look through a peephole and discover a landscape. M. Mann. il Pop Phot 69:22+ S '71

SAN FRANCISCO-OAKLAND BAY bridge. See San Francisco-Bay bridges

SAN FRANCISCO opera company
Hapless queen of Scots; Donizetti's Mary Stuart in San Francisco. R. D. Daniels. il pors Opera N 36:10-15 N '71
Paskalis, McCracken cheered in San Francisco Otello. A. Frankenstein. Hi Fi 21:MA22 F '71
Report:
    American premiere of Benjamin Britten's Midsummer night's dream. J. Rockwell. Opera N 36:27 D 11 '71
    Bohème, Cinderella, Gianni Schicchi and The medium. J. Rockwell. Opera N 35:23 Je 12 '71
    Donizetti's Maria Stuarda. J. Rockwell. il Opera N 36:36 D 25 '71
    Rosenkavalier, Manon and Meistersinger. S. Jenkins. il Opera N 36:24-5 N '71
    Il Trovatore and Un ballo in maschera. J. Rockwell. il Opera N 36:31-2 D 18 '71
    School of hard knocks; Merola opera program. K. Monson. il Opera N 36:8-9 N '71
    Spring opera goes theatrical. A. Frankenstein. il Hi Fi 21:MA26-7 Ag '71
    Thomas triumphs as Siegfried. A. Frankenstein. il Hi Fi 20:MA26+ D '70

SAN FRANCISCO public library
BARC and the consumer: Bay Area reference center. G. McNamee. bibliog il Library J 96:3292-4 O 15 '71

SANGER, Elliott M.
How New York's pioneer classical station has fallen upon sorry Times. C. Briefer. il pors Hi Fi 21:74-9 S '71 *

SANGER, Jonathan
Bogotá builds. il Américas 23:25-30 Je '71
House that grows. il por Américas 23:16-24 Mr '71

SANGLEY, POINT. See Navy yards and naval stations

SANGUINE communication system. See Radio communication. Naval

SANITARY affairs. See subhead Sanitary affairs under names of countries, states, cities, e.g. Stamford, Conn.—Sanitary affairs

SANITARY engineering
See also
Drainage
Pipe laying
Refuse and refuse disposal
Sewer cleaning
Snow and ice removal

SANITARY fills. See Filling (earthwork)

SANITARY napkins, tampons, etc.
Female hygiene and the TV code. Bsns W p 100 S 11 '71

SANITATION
See also
Camp sanitation
Privies
Sewage disposal
Smoke prevention

SANITATION workers
Garbageman, ed. by K. Lasson. R. Murdock. il Atlan 228:78-82 O '71

SANJEK, Betty
Motion picture previews (cont) il PTA Mag 65:38-40 Ja '71

SAN JOSE, Calif.

Politics and government
When you negotiate with municipal labor unions. R. R. James. Am City 86:140-2 Je '71

SAN JUAN, Puerto Rico
Four hundred fiftieth anniversary of San Juan. Américas 23:1 Ag '71

Architecture
Vivienda '70 in Puerto Rico: Shelley system's first project is nearly complete. il Arch Rec 149:116-19 Ap '71

SAN JUAN CAPISTRANO, Calif.
Poking around in the mission village of San Juan Capistrano. il Sunset 146:46-8 Je '71
SAN JUAN ISLANDS
Exploring the border islands. il Sunset 147: 44-51 Jl '71
Music to the gourmet's ears. Puget Sound. J. Low. il Holiday 49:70-1+ Ap '71
San Juan: pride of the Northwest. E. Crimmin. il Motor B & S 127:55+ Je '71
SAN LORENZO branch library. See Alameda County, Calif. library, Hayward—Branches
SAN LUIS POTOSI, Mexico
Plazas for people. P. D. Eimon. il Am City 86:88+ F '71
SAN MARCO satellites. See Artificial satellites, Italian
SAN MATEO COUNTY, Calif. free library, Belmont
East Palo Alto federal library project. M. Keller. il Am Lib 2:631-5 Je '71
SAN MIGUEL DE ALLENDE, Mexico
Easter week processions at San Miguel de Allende. il Sunset 146:32 Mr '71
SAN ONOFRE bluffs state beach park. See California—Parks and reserves
SAN QUENTIN prison. See Prisons—California
SAN SIMEON (estate) See California—Parks and reserves
SANSREGRET, Jane
Curious pawpaw. il Am For 77:37 Ap '71
SANTA ANA, Calif.

Churches
Gulf spanned at Calvary. Chr Today 15:21 Ja 29 '71
SANTA BARBARA, Calif.

Airports
Protests spark Cessna facility location shift. E. J. Bulban. Aviation W 95:20-1 O 4 '71
SANTA BARBARA COUNTY, Calif.

Police
Dr Strange cop. por Newsweek 78:28 N 29 '71
SANTA BARBARA oil slicks. See Oil pollution of rivers, harbors, etc.
SANTA CATALINA ISLAND
Development of Santa Catalina Island. M. J. Renton. il Forbes 107:11 Ap 1 '71
SANTA CLAUS
Should parents encourage their children to believe in Santa Claus? B. Bettelheim. Ladies Home J 88:14+ D '71
Two Christmas stories. S. A. Mateer. il Chr Today 16:5-7 D 3 '71
Your child can get a letter from Santa. Good H 173:170 D '71
SANTA-CROCE, Joseph
Epic of the kings. il UNESCO Courier 24: 32-3+ O '71
SANTA CRUZ campus. See California. University—Santa Cruz campus
SANTA FE, N. Mex.

City planning
Santa Fe capitalizes on its atmosphere. il Bsns W p 112+ Ap 10 '71

Description
Santa Fe offers charm and culture. Bsns W p98 Ap 10 '71

History
Post card album; 300 years of history on cards. V. L. George. il Hobbies 75:158-9 Ja '71
Santa Fe profile. J. D. Rittenhouse. il Am West 8:42-7 S '71

Music
Musical events; Santa Fe opera. W. Sargeant. New Yorker 47:82+ S 4 '71
See also
Santa Fe opera company

Social life and customs
New trail to Santa Fe. D. Butwin. il Sat R 54:35-6 Jl 3 '71
SANTA FE opera company
Mixed medea; performance of Yerma. Newsweek 78:74 Ag 23 '71
Report:
Flying Dutchman. premiere of Villa-Lobos' Yerma, Offenbach's La Grande Duchesse and Mozart's Magic flute. S. Jenkins. Opera N 36:21-2 O '71
Santa Fe opera 1957-71: a chronicle of artists and repertory. Opera N 35:16-17 Je 12 '71
Villa-Lobos' Yerma bogs down; but Offenbach's Grande duchesse proves delightful. M. Bernheimer. Hi Fi 21:MA16-17 N '71

SANTA FE opera house. See Opera houses
SANTA FE railway. See Atchison, Topeka and Santa Fe railway
SANTAMARIA, Carlos Sanz de. See Sanz de Santamaría, C.
SANTA MONICA, Calif.

Education
Hyperactive engineering. V. Krauch. il Am Ed 7:12-13+ Je '71
SANTA MONICA MOUNTAINS
Giant mountain park for Los Angeles? il Sunset 146:60-3 F '71
SANTANA, Mary Carmen
Mary Carmen Santana, school librarian. il pors Wilson Lib Bul 45:646-7 Mr '71 *
SANTEE LAKES, Calif. See Lakes, Artificial
SANTEE swamp, S.C. See Marshes
SANTIAGO, Luciano P. R.
Ulysses complex. bibliog il Am Imago 28: 158-86 Sum '71
SANTIAGO, Spain
Pilgrim's trail. P. Brooks. Nat R 23:1003-4 S 10 '71
SANTIAGO de Compostela, Spain. See Santiago, Spain
SANTO, Ron
These major-leaguers succeeded in spite of . . . E. Kiester. il pors Todays Health 49: 46-8 O '71 *
SANTO DOMINGO (Republic) See Dominican Republic
SANYO electric company. See Electric industries —Japan
SANZ DE SANTAMARIA, Carlos
Journalistic ideal; excerpts from statement. May 1971. Américas 23:1 Je '71
SAO PAULO (city)

Brazil
Plight of São Paulo. il Newsweek 79:44-5 Ja 10 '72
SÃO SYLVESTRE marathon, Brazil. See Running
SAPPINGTON, Margo
Now a Swan lake swan. N. M. Stoop. il por Dance Mag 46:36-9+ Ja '72 *
SAPPORO, Japan
Go east, young Olympians; photographs by J. Cooke and others; with account by W. Johnson. Sports Illus 35:52-64 N 15 '71
Sapporo: city of the Olympics. il Newsweek 78:102-3 D 20 '71
SARACENI, Remo
Discoveries. il House & Gard 139:108-9 My '71
SARACEVIC, Tefko
Bellies and ASIS. il Library J 96:167-8 Ja 15 '71
SARACH, Marian
Marian Sarach and dance company. Isidor Straus theater, NYC. T. Borek. Dance Mag 45:76+ F '71 *
Marian Sarach and dance company, Judson memorial church, NYC. M. Marks. Dance Mag 45:77-8 Je '71 *
SARAH O'Loughlin Foley award. See Literary prizes
SARASOTA, Fla.

Ringling center
Theater; productions of Asolo, the State theater company. H. Hewes. Sat R 54:17 My 15 '71

Van Wezel performing arts hall
West Coast symphony, in purple; new home for West Coast symphony orchestra. R. B. Baumel. il Hi Fi 20:24-5 D '70
SARASY, Phyllis (Powell)
From Manhattan brownstone. . . to San Francisco Bay. H. Brown; N. C. Gray. il pors Am Home 74:98-101+ My '71 *
SARATOGA race track. See Race tracks
SARCOMA
Love that lights the last days of a brave young mother; osteogenic sarcoma. M. Michaelson. il pors Todays Health 49:48-53+ D '71
SARCOPLASMIC reticulum. See Muscle
SAREPTA excavations. See Lebanon—Antiquities
SARGASSUM
Gulf weed communities of south Florida. T. W. Thompson. il Sea Front 17:95-101 Mr '71
SARGEANT, Winthrop
Musical events. See issues of New Yorker
Parasitic profession; interview, ed. by R. T. Jones; with introduction. por Time 99:64 Ja 10 '72
Profiles; B. Sills. por New Yorker 47:42-6+ Mr 6 '71

SARIS, Anthony
Anthony Saris: variations on an angel's theme. N. Meglin. il Am Artist 35:22-5 D '71 *

SARKISIAN, Sevan
Careers in recreation. il Parks & Rec 6:40-1+ F '71

SARNOFF, David
Fellow on the bridge. il pors Time 98:57 D 27 '71 *
Obituary
Newsweek il pors 78:47 D 27 '71

SARNOFF, Robert W.
Business and society: address, January 27, 1971. Vital Speeches 37:273-5 F 15 '71

SAROYAN, William
Apple pie and crazy people. Nation 213:629-30 D 13 '71
Lord Chugger of Cheer; story. il McCalls 99:98-9 D '71
Najari Levon's old country advice to the young Americans on how to live with a snake; story. Atlan 228:71-2 Ag '71

SARRA, Barbara
Alfred I. DuPont education association. Todays Ed 60:56 Ap '71

SARREL, Lorna J. See Sarrel, P. M. jt. auth.

SARREL, Philip M. and Sarrel, L. J.
Abortion: what you should know. Vogue 158: 93-4 Ag 1 '71
Are you killing love with sex problems you create? Vogue 158:269-70 S 1 '71

SARRIS, Andrew
Aesthete at the movies. Commentary 51:81-4 F '71
Couple-speak: happy marriage. pors Vogue 157:106+ Je '71
Movies. il Vogue 158:287 S 1 '71

SARRIS, Molly (Haskell)
Couple-speak: happy marriage. pors Vogue 157:107+ Je '71

SARSON, Evelyn
She ACTs against television. M. Meade. il McCalls 99:46 D '71 *

SARTON, May
Gardens are a demanding joy. Vogue 158:52-3+ Ag 15 '71
Invocation of Kali; poem. Poetry 117:314-321 F '71
Man from another time; excerpt from Plant dreaming deep. il Read Digest 98:61-4 Je '71

SARTORI, Franco. See Merlino, S. jt. auth.

SARTRE, Jean Paul
Sartre accuses the intellectuals of bad faith; interview, ed. by J. Gerassi. il pors N Y Times Mag p38-9+ O 17 '71

about
Europe's first feminist has changed the second sex. C. Cate. il pors N Y Times Mag p38-44 Jl 11 '71 *
Letter from Paris; new book on G. Flaubert. Genêt. New Yorker 47:106+ Je 12 '71 *

SARVISTREE. See Serviceberries (tree)

SARZETAKIS, Christos
Epilogue to Z, an Athenian tragedy. R. McDonald. New Repub 164:25 Je 12 '71 *

SASKATCHEWAN
See also
Saskatoon

SASKATOON, Saskatchewan
Fire on the prairie; spiritual renewal Saskatoon. Chr Today 16:33 D 3 '71

SASSOON, Vidal
Voila Vidal! Flowers with a Sassoon flair. E. McDonald. il por House B 113:102-4 N '71 *

SATAN. See Devil

SATANISM
Evil, anyone? il Newsweek 78:56-7 Ag 16 '71
Rosemary's babies; case of Patrick Michael Newell. il Newsweek 78:22 Jl 19 '71
Sex and the supernatural. J. R. Moore. Chr Today 15:7-8+ My 7 '71

SATCHIDANANDA (Indian yogi)
And now, the Yoga retreat. G. A. Maloney. America 124:591-3 Je 5 '71 *

SATELLITE early warning system. See Ballistic missile early warning system

SATELLITE viruses. See Viruses

SATELLITES
Christopher Scheiner's observations of an object near Jupiter. J. Ashbrook. bibliog il Sky & Tel 42:344-5 D '71
Disk photography of a Jovian satellite; Io. il Sky & Tel 42:10-11 Jl '71
Infrared measures of Ganymede. Sky & Tel 42:205 O '71
Jupiter: its captured satellites. J. M. Bailey. bibliog il Science 173:812-13 Ag 27 '71

Jupiter's atmosphere and an eclipse of Ganymede. il Sky & Tel 41:151-2 Mr '71
Lumpy miniworlds of Phobos and Deimos. il Sci N 100:372 D 4 '71
Observing the satellites of Saturn. il Sky & Tel 42:122-3 Ag '71
Satellites of the outer planets: thermal models. J. S. Lewis. bibliog il Science 172: 1127-8 Je 11 '71
Timings of inferior geocentric conjunctions. E. J. Reese. il Sky & Tel 41:318-19 My '71
See also
Artificial satellites
Moon

SATIE, Erik
Delicately molded sensuality, bordering on the pornographic. J. Ringo. il Am Rec G 37:310-12 Ja '71 *
Erik Satie, 1866-1925. R. Phelps. Vogue 157: 156 My '71 *

SATISFACTION
Self-conceptions of mental health among the aged. J. F. Gubrium. bibliog Ment Hy 55: 398-403 Jl '71

SATISFACTION in work. See Job satisfaction

SATO, Eisaku
Slow and steady: a talk with Eisaku Sato; excerpts from interview, ed. by B. Krisher. il por Newsweek 78:38 S 20 '71

about
Bad dream come true. il Time 98:29-30 Ag 9 '71 *
Facing facts. il Newsweek 78:32-3 S 6 '71 *
Japan: on Nixon's China bandwagon. il por Newsweek 78:29 Ag 9 '71 *
Trying to make up with Japan. il por Time 99:11 Ja 17 '72 *

SATRA corporation
Horse trader at the highest level. por Bsns W p89-90 Je 19 '71

SATTER, Ruth L. and Galston, A. W.
Potassium flux: a common feature of albizzia leaflet movement controlled by phytochrome or endogenous rhythm. bibliog il Science 174:518-20 O 29 '71

SATTERTHWAITE, P. J.
Old records and new technology find a water supply. il Am City 86:68+ S '71

SATTERWHITE, R. B.
New winter trails: North Carolina. il Travel 136:28-33+ D '71

SATTINGER, Irvin J.
Satellites to monitor earth resources. il Parks & Rec 6:10-13+ D '71

SATTLEY, Helen H.
Run twice as fast: service to children. bibliog il Am Lib 2:843-9 S '71

SATURDAY evening post
Good old ways. il Newsweek 78:74 D 13 '71
Return of the Post. il por Time 97:70 Je 14 '71

SATURDAY review
Bargaining for a baby. por Time 98:30 Jl 19 '71
Consummate professional. por Time 98:74+ D 6 '71
Cousins quits. Time 98:58 N 29 '71
End of an era. il Newsweek 78:51 N 29 '71
Facts vs. conclusions. N. Cousins. Sat R 54: 28 S 11 '71
Final report to the readers. N. Cousins. Sat R 54:32-3 N 27 '71
Letters you write to the editor. R. L. Tobin. Sat R 54:43-4 Ag 14 '71
New man at the Review. il Newsweek 78: 70 D 6 '71
New owners for SR, McCall book division. Pub W 200:95 Jl 19 '71
New tycoons. pors Newsweek 78:64 Jl 26 '71
Report to the readers. N. H. Charney. por Sat R 54:26-7 D 11; 26-7 D 18; 20-1 D 25 '71
Report to the readers. J. J. Veronis. Sat R 54:32-3 D 4 '71
Report to the readers; history of ownership. N. Cousins. Sat R 54:16-17 Jl 31 '71
Revamping the Review. il pors Time 98:62 N 22 '71
SR television awards/1971. Sat R 54:55-6 My 8 '71
SR's nineteenth annual advertising awards. R. L. Tobin. Sat R 54:51-5 Ap 10 '71
See also
Anisfield-Wolf awards

SATURDAY review press
McCall name change due; SR announces book club. Pub W 200:20 N 1 '71

SATURN (boosters) See Space vehicles—Propulsion systems

SATURN (planet)
Saturn's rings. J. Stokley. il Sci N 100:284 O 23 '71

Satellites
See Satellites

SATY, Richard E.
You have to make reservoirs look good. il Am City 86:58-9 Ag '71

SATZ, Arthur
Boulez and new breezes. por Hi Fi 21:MA12+ Ag '71

SAUCERS, Flying. See Flying saucers

SAUCES
Almost anything tastes good in this wonderful sauce: garlic butter. il Sunset 147:213 N '71
Good gravy! il Bet Hom & Gard 49:104 D '71
King of desserts: ice cream and sauces. H. McCully. il House B 113:66-7+ Ag '71
Know your sauces. Bet Hom & Gard 49:84 My '71
Nut butters: great on vegetables. il Sunset 147:118 Jl '71
Sauces for spaghetti lovers. il Redbook 136: 104-5+ F '71
Story behind: Lea & Perrins Worcestershire sauce. il Changing T 25:24 Jl '71
Things mother never taught you about holiday sauces. il Ladies Home J 88:144 N '71
Work wonders with barbecue sauce. il Ladies Home J 88:104+ Jl '71

SAUDAN, Sylvain
He conquers high mountains from the top down. A. Verschoth. il por Sports Illus 34: 62 Mr 15 '71 *

SAUDI ARABIA
Saudi Arabia: the hole in the map. Q. Crewe. il Holiday 49:64-7+ Mr '71
See also
Red Sea

Foreign relations

United States
See United States—Foreign relations— Saudi Arabia

SAUER, George, Jr
Sports: disillusioned professional football players. J. Scott. Ramp Mag 10:68-70 N; 65-8 D '71

SAUERBRATEN. See Cookery—Meat

SAUERLAND, Caroline
Perfect fruit, it's in the bag. Org Gard & Farm 18:93 S '71
Preserving the wild in your garden. il Org Gard & Farm 18:44-6 Je '71
Space-savers for the small garden. il Org Gard & Farm 18:91-3 Ja '71

SAUL, Ralph Southey
Saul details his First Boston job. por Bsns W p86 O 23 '71 *
Saul steps down. por Newsweek 77:83 Mr 29 '71 *
Saul's broad role at First Boston. por Bsns W p32 Mr 20 '71 *
Time for a switch. por Time 97:78 Mr 29 '71 *

SAULNIER, Raymond J.
Doubts about an iffy budget. por Nations Bsns 59:37 Jl '71
Will controls work? por Nations Bsns 59: 64-6 D '71

SAUNA
Bathtub sauna. A. Lees. il Pop Sci 199:200 S '71
Sauna experience: discover how life can be beautiful at 200°F. D. McCluggage. Am Home 74:40+ F '71

SAUNDERS, David M.
Those dangerous encounters. Yachting 130: 44+ N '71

SAUNDERS, Sara Bradford
Doors of the past. Hobbies 76:147 Ja '72
Treasured diaries. Hobbies 76:141 O '71

SAUNDERS-Stiver and company
Swinger who struck out. il por Bsns W p78+ Mr 13 '71

SAUROPODS. See Dinosaurs

SAUSAGE
See also
Cookery—Meat

SAVAGE, Duke. See Schollander, D. jt. auth.

SAVAGE, Gail. See Savage, N. jt. auth.

SAVAGE, John
Easy way to remove wallpaper. il Mech Illus 67:116-17+ F '71
Make your own miniature golf course. il Mech Illus 67:80-2 My '71

SAVAGE, Norbert, and Savage, Gail
J. Evans, painter. il Antiques 100:782-7 N '71

SAVAGE, Wilbert Nathan
Covered bridges: historic reminders. il Am For 77:40-3+ Je '71

SAVANNAH, Ga.
Leisurely cities. H. T. Blake. Harp Baz 104: 52-3 My '71
Mrs Wilkes's boarding house: dining in Old Savannah. R. A. De Groot. il Esquire 76: 150-1+ N '71
Saving Savannah. il Life 70:48-55+ My 7 '71
Write your own computer specs. il Am City 86:84+ My '71

SAVANNAH (ship) See Ships, Atomic powered

SAVAS, Emanuel S.
Mass transfer and urban problems. Science 174:365 O 22 '71
Municipal monopoly. il Harper 243:55-60 D '71

SAVE our American resources project. See Conservation of resources—Study and teaching

SAVE the children federation
Authors & editors: A. Cornelisen as social worker in Lucania, Italy. B. A. Bannon. por Pub W 200:9-11 N 1 '71

SAVED; drama. See Bond, E.

SAVELAND, Robert N.
Textbooks are progressive. Pub W 200:17-18 D 6 '71

SAVILLE, Anthony
Conflict: new emphasis in leadership. Clear House 46:52-5 S '71

SAVIN, Samuel M. See Hecht, A. D. jt. auth.

SAVING and savings
Big payoffs for savers coming to an end. il U S News 70:72-3 Ap 5 '71
Buy, brother, buy. il Forbes 107:36 Mr 1 '71
Should you be building an emergency fund? il Changing T 25:33-5 Ap '71
Why the savings rate is still so high. il Bsns W p96+ D 4 '71
See also
Bonds
Finance, Personal
Investment clubs
Investments

SAVINGS and loan associations
California's S&Ls are regaining their heft. il Bsns W p56-7 Jl 3 '71
Pair of S&Ls bedevils the Fed. Bsns W p38 S 18 '71
Ralph Nader, where are you? Nat R 23:356 Ap 6 '71
S&Ls break out of the boom-bust mold. il Bsns W p38 O 9 '71

Securities
If savings and loan associations issue stock. il U S News 70:35-6 My 10 '71

SAVINGS banks
See also
Savings and loan associations

SAVINGS bonds. See Bonds, Government

SAVINGS deposits

Interest
Maybe we need truth in savings, too. il Changing T 25:7-10 F '71
Ralph Nader, where are you? Nat R 23:356 Ap 6 '71
Savings accounts: different types pay different interest. Good H 172:180 Je '71

SAW guards. See Machinery—Safety devices and measures

el SAWI, Abdel Moneim
Nubia: victory of international solidarity. il UNESCO Courier 24:60-2 Ag '71

SAWICKI, Dorothea L. and others
Immunochemical detection of minor bases in nucleic acids. bibliog il Science 174:70-2 O 1 '71

SAWING
Cutting party knockdowns from single plywood sheets. R. Capotosto. il Pop Sci 198:108-10 Ap '71
See also
Miter boxes, gages, etc.

SAWMILL workers. See Lumber workers

SAWS
Build these power hacksaws. il Suc Farm 69: no2 B8 F '71
Guide to hacksaw blades. E. Dussault. il Mech Illus 67:88-9 Ag '71
Hole saw, makes the intricate easy. D. A. Ashe. il Bet Hom & Gard 49:62-3 F '71
Kindest cut of all comes from a cared-for chain saw. H. Wicks. il Pop Mech 136:174-6+ N '71
Lightweight chain saw that purrs. E. F. Lindsley. il Pop Sci 199:108 O '71
Little tool with a big bite: jeweler's saw. W. E. Burton. il Pop Mech 135:168-70 Ap '71
PM tests Skil's 10-in. electric chain saw. W. C. Leckey. il Pop Mech 136:188 O '71

SAWS—*Continued*
Sears' best radial: you get what you pay for. H. Wicks. il Pop Mech 136:120-2+ Ag '71
Which blades for a circular saw? il Sunset 147:140+ O '71
See also
Jigsaws
SAWTOOTH wilderness area. See Wilderness areas—Idaho
SAWYER, Peter Roland
Profiles. J. Bainbridge. por New Yorker 47: 40-50+ Ag 14 '71 •
SAX, Joseph L.
Environment and the bureaucracy. New Repub 164:9-10 Je 19 '71
Little sturm und drang at Hunting creek. il Esquire 75:84-8+ F '71
Pollution fight before the U.S. courts. il UNESCO Courier 24:20-3 Jl '71
Rocky's road. il Am Heritage 22:78-83+ F '71
SAXE, Ralph
Un-easy rider. il Sr Schol 99:32+ N 29 '71
SAXITOXIN. See Toxins and antitoxins
SAXON, Davidyne
Anyone here want to buy a Rubens? Esquire 75:58+ Ja '71
SAXON industries, inc.
Saxon industries thrives on buying trouble. Bsns W p62+ N 27 '71
SAYERS, Wilson B.
King is dead, long live the king. il Am For 77:20-3+ N; 22-3+ D '71
SAYINGS. See Aphorisms and apothegms
SAYLE, Murray
Defeat on Everest. il por Life 71:22-9 Jl 2 '71
SAYLOR, Charles Proffer
Case of the flowing roof. il Chem 44:19-20 D '71
SAYLOR, Leslie E.
Bellevue education association. Todays Ed 60:66 Mr '71
SAYRE, Nora
Politics (cont) Esquire 75:36+ Ja '71
(ed) See Gilliatt, P. Penelope Gilliatt talks about Sunday bloody Sunday
SAYRE, Roxanna
Econotes. Audubon 73:100-2 Ja; 125-6 Mr; 95-8 My; 96-7 Jl '71
SCADUTO, Anthony
Won't you listen to the lambs. Bob Dylan. il pors N Y Times Mag p34-6+ N 28 '71
SCALES (weighing instruments)
Danish, but not pastry a Danish postal scale. il Consumer Bul 54:15-16 O '71
How to weigh a moving train. il Bsns W p 102 Je 26 '71
Make a magnetic postal scale. P. E. Fiechter. il Pop Sci 198:108 F '71
Your best weapon against overweight. C. Mitchell. Read Digest 99:94-6 Jl '71
SCALI, John Alfred
Nixon's new voice. por Newsweek 77:95 Ap 19 '71 •
Recruiting the opposition. por Time 97:65 Ap 19 '71 •
SCALLOPS
See also
Cookery—Shellfish
SCALP
Beauty: how to stop killing your hair; and your scalp. il Mlle 74:122-5 Ja '72
SCAMMON, Richard Montgomery
Memo from Richard Scammon. il por Newsweek 79:12 Ja 10 '72
Tough facts of life for black politicians. il por Newsweek 77:33 Je 7 '71
SCAN-Data corporation
Scanning for sales. A. Hershman. por Duns 98:48 D '71
SCANDINAVIA
See also
Booksellers and bookselling—Scandinavia
Cruising—Scandinavia
Description and travel
Northland memory (cont) C. Mitchell. il Yachting 129:60-1+ F '71
Scandinavian spectacular. F. Lemkowitz. il Schol Teach Jr/Sr High p68 Mr 8 '71
Economic policy
Reports & comment; question of EEC membership. D. Cook. Atlan 229:6+ Ja '72
SCANDINAVIAN airlines system, inc.
SAS inaugurates transsiberian service. D. E. Fink. il Aviation W 94:25-7 Ap 19 '71
SCANLAN, Alfred L.
Maryland's scholarship plan. America 124:563-4 My 29 '71

SCANLAN'S monthly
Scanlan's bomb; issue on Guerrilla war in the U.S.A. A. Wolff. il Newsweek 77:61 Ja 25 '71
SCANNING devices, Optical. See Optical scanners
SCANNING electron microscope. See Electron microscope and microscopy
SCANNING monitor receivers. See Radio receivers
SCARBROUGH, Bryan
Talent unlimited. D. Herbert. il por Design 72:26-8 Sum '71 •
SCARF, Maggie
Man who gave us inferiority complex, compensation, overcompensation, aggressive drive and style of life. il pors N Y Times Mag p 10-11+ F 28 '71
Normality is a square circle or a four-sided triangle. il pors N Y Times Mag p 16-17+ O 3 '61
SCARFF, Edward L.
Acquisition drive aimed at losers. por Bsns W p27 Je 26 '71 •
SCARICH, Kathryn, and Trumpeter, Margo
Dope that users can't find. pors Wilson Lib Bul 46:256-9 N '71
SCARPETTA, Olga
Fight for baby Lenore. E. L. Hughes. il pors Ladies Home J 88:58+ S '71 •
Mothers talk about the anguish of their fight. pors Life 70:36 Je 11 '71
SCARR-SALAPATEK, Sandra
Race, social class, and IQ. bibliog il Science 174:1285-95 D 24 '71
Unknowns in the IQ equation. bibliog Science 174:1223-8 D 17 '71
SCATTERGUNS. See Shotguns
SCATTERING (physics)
Muon-pair experiment: no new particles. G. B. Lubkin. il Phys Today 24:17-18 Mr '71
Structure of the proton and the neutron. H. W. Kendall and W. K. H. Panofsky. il Sci Am 224:60-6+ Je '71
Surprising proton-proton data from CERN; results from elastic proton-proton scattering. G. B. Lubkin. bibliog il Phys Today 24:17-18 Ag '71
SCENARIO; story. See Jurkowski, J.
SCENE designers. See Designers
SCENE designing. See Theater—Stage setting and scenery
SCENERY, Preservation of. See Landscape protection
SCENERY, Stage. See Theater—Stage setting and scenery
SCENES from American life; drama. See Gurney, A. R. jr
SCENES from the almost revolution; story. See Jones, J.
SCENT. See Perfumes
SCENTED geraniums. See Geraniums
SCHAAF, Robert W.
Moszkowski's splashy piano concerto. Hi Fi 21:86+ Ja '71
SCHACHNER, Erwin
Erwin Schachner makes a linocut. il por Am Artist 35:40-5 N '71
SCHACHTER, Oscar, and Serwer, Daniel
Marine pollution, potential for catastrophe. UN Mo Chron 8:28-49 Mr '71
SCHAEFER, Hermann J.
Radiation exposure in air travel. bibliog il Science 173:780-3 Ag 27 '71
SCHAEFER, Kenneth
(ed) See Agnew, K. One of the comrades is missing
SCHAEFER, Marilyn
Illustrator in the courtroom: Hal Ashmead. il por Am Artist 36:30-5+ Ja '72
SCHAEFER, Paul
To Hanging Spear Falls with Zahnie. il Liv Wildn 34:23-7 Wint '70
SCHAEFER, Vincent Joseph
Threat of the unseen. il Sat R 54:55-7 F 6 '71
SCHAEFER, Wil A.
Theology for swingers. Chr Cent 88:447 Ap 7 '71 •
SCHAEFFER, Janet
Earth week 1971. il Nat Parks & Con Mag 45:17-19 Ap '71
SCHAEFFLER, Willy
I've never taught a boy how to lose. il pors Life 70:46-9 Mr 12 '71 •
SCHAFER, Ann
Genealogy: the mystery hobby. il Har Yrs 11:24-5+ Ag '71
SCHAFER, Edward H.
Playing grownup. il Horizon 13:20-3 Wint '71

SCHAFER, Walter E. and others
Programmed for social class: tracking in high school. il Trans-Action 7:39-46+ O '70
SCHAFFER, Noel
Superclinic, science-fiction structure takes the pain out of medical treatment. il Arch Forum 135:30-5 N '71 •
SCHALL, James V.
Conditions of freedom revisited. Commonweal 95:9-13 O 1 '71
Does a bell toll for the nation-state? America 125:59-63 Ag 7 '71
Ecology, an American heresy? America 124: 308-11 Mr 27 '71
End of sadness and history. il Cath World 213:222-6 Ag '71
On building cathedrals and tearing them down. il Cath World 212:301-6 Mr '71

about

Is ecology heresy? il Time 98:29-30 Ag 23 '71 •
SCHALLER, George B.
Imperiled phantom of Asian peaks. il Nat Geog 140:702-7 N '71
SCHALLY, Andrew V.
—and others
Gonadotropin-releasing hormone: one poly-peptide regulates secretion of luteinizing and follicle-stimulating hormones. bibliog il Science 173:1036-8 S 10 '71

about

Toward birth control by peptides. por Sci N 100:37 Jl 17 '71 •
SCHANBERG, Sydney H.
Pakistan divided. For Affairs 50:125-35 O '71
SCHANCHE, Don A.
Toxoplasmosis. McCalls 99:56+ N '71
SCHANZER, Beverly
Accidents that don't have to happen: what parents should know. il Redbook 137:60-1+ Jl '71
SCHARBAUER, Clarence
After a mountain of money. B. Gilbert. il Sports Illus 35:28-9 S 20 '71 •
SCHARDT, Arlie
Crack in Hoover's fortress; conference at Woodrow Wilson school of Princeton university. Nation 213:526-30 N 22 '71
SCHARFFENBERGER, George T.
Chameleon. il Forbes 107:20-1 Je 1 '71 •
SCHARY, Dore
Artist life. D. J. Soria. por Hi Fi 20:MA4-6+ D '70 •
SCHATZ, Albert. See Schatz, V. jt. auth.
SCHATZ, Mary Ann
Happy head start at home. il Parents Mag 46:29-31+ Jl '71
SCHATZ, Vivian, and Schatz, Albert
From bone manure to superphosphate. il Org Gard & Farm 18:140-7+ Mr '71
Look at your plant roots. Org Gard & Farm 18:96-7 Je '71
SCHATZEDER, A. W.
Renew that deteriorated pavement. il Am City 86:109-10 Je '71
SCHAWN, Norman
Build a cartop camper. il Mech Illus 67:69-71 Je '71
SCHECHNER, Richard
Commune. Criticism
America 124:265 Mr 13 '71 •
Vogue il 157:142 F 1 '71 •
Communing with Commune. C. R. Hughes. America 124:265 Mr 13 '71 •
Grotowski and Schechner: the servitudes of freedom. T. Hoffman. il Art in Am 59:74-81 Mr '71 •
SCHECHTER, Daniel
Polaroid apartheid: pull tab, wait 60 seconds. il Ramp Mag 9:47-8+ Mr; 60 Ap '71
SCHECHTER, Philip E.
Two rabbis rock the boat. pors Time 97:65-6 Mr 15 '71 •
SCHEDULES, School
Flexible scheduling: facts, fantasies and fads; address, November 1970. J. J. Backen. Engl J 60:363-8+ Mr '71
Mod mod world of flexible modular scheduling. D. J. Dieterich. bibliog Engl J 60:1264-71 D '71
Variable scheduling. E. T. Kelly and J. P. Turano. il Clear House 45:365-8 F '71
SCHEDULES of reinforcement. See Reinforcement (psychology)
SCHEEL, Walter
One more whirl. Newsweek 78:29 Jl 19 '71 •
SCHEFFER, Victor B.
Go now and look for beauty; excerpts from The seeing eye. il Nat Wildlife 9:8-12 Ag '71

SCHEFRIN, Rita A.
Barriers to and barriers of library security. bibliog il por Wilson Lib Bul 45:870-8 My '71
SCHEIN, Muriel
Only on Sundays; with biographical sketch. il Natur Hist 80:10, 52-61 Ap '71
SCHEINER, Christoph
Christopher Scheiner's observations of an object near Jupiter. J. Ashbrook. bibliog il Sky & Tel 42:344-5 D '71 •
SCHELL, Orville, jr
Silent Vietnam: how we invented ecocide and killed a country. il Look 35:55+ Ap 6 '71
SCHELLING, Thomas C.
Defense: the savings of accommodation. Sat R 54:38 Ja 23 '71
What is the business of organized crime? bibliog f Am Scholar 40:643-53 Aut '71
SCHELSKE, Claire L. and Stoermer, E. F.
Eutrophication, silica depletion, and predicted changes in algal quality in Lake Michigan. bibliog il Science 173:423-4 Jl 30 '71
SCHEMMER, Benjamin F.
What happened to Howard Hughes. il por Look 35:21-5 Je 1 '71
SCHENKEL, Chris
TV talk. F. Deford. Sports Illus 34:16 My 24 '71 •
SCHERER, Silvester N.
Grandparent insurance. il Har Yrs 11:46-7 D '71
SCHERLE, William J.
Excerpt from debate, November 17, 1970. Cong Digest 50:91+ Mr '71
Frustrations of a rural Republican; interview, ed. by J. Cook. il por Time 98:21 N 22 '71
SCHERMAN, Katharine
Island in the sea. il Audubon 73:4-7 Jl '71
SCHERP, Henry W.
Dental caries: prospects for prevention. bibliog il Science 173:1199-205 S 24 '71
SCHERY, Robert W.
Fescues, the hard-working grasses for home lawns. il Home Gard 58:24-5+ Mr '71
Lawn renovation the modern way. il Home Gard 58:38-9+ My '71
Top turfgrasses. il Horticulture 49:22-3+ Ap '71
SCHEUER, Paul J. See Moore, R. E. jt. auth.
SCHEVILL, James Erwin
Comment. J. Jacobsen. Poetry 118:166 Je '71 •
Comment. P. Schjeldahl. Poetry 117:272 Ja '71 •
SCHEY, H. M.
Einstein's rejection of quantum theory: a personal motive. bibliog f il Am Imago 28:187-90 Sum '71
SCHIAPARELLI, Elsa
Where are they now? il pors Newsweek 77:16 Mr 29 '71 •
SCHICK, Allen
From analysis to evaluation. bibliog f Ann Am Acad 394:57-71 Mr '71
SCHICK, Edgar B.
University as paradox. Sch & Soc 99:84-6 F '71
SCHICK, Frank L.
Library statistics: a century plus. Am Lib 2:727-31 Jl '71
SCHICK, Tom
New NCCL faces prompt challenge. il America 125:483-4 D 4 '71
SCHICKEL, Richard
Books. Harper 242:104-8 Ap; 243:10 Jl '71
Doug Fairbanks: superstar of the silents. il pors Am Heritage 23:4-12+ D '71
Lecture notes. il Harper 243:30+ D '71
Life movie review. See issues of Life
Performing arts (cont) Harper 242:28+ Ja; 24+ Mr; 14-15 Ap; 243:18+ Ag '71
Silents weren't just voiceless talkies. il N Y Times Mag p32-3+ N 28 '71
Stars and celebrities. Commentary 52:61-5 Ag '71
SCHIESSLER, Robert Walter
Excerpt from letter, February 1971. Cong Digest 50:306+ D '71
SCHIFF, Frank W.
Control of inflation and recession; address, April 1971, with questions and answers. Ann Am Acad 396:90-104 Jl '71
SCHIFF, Leonard Isaac
Obituary
Phys Today por 24:54-5 Jl '71. F. Bloch and J. D. Walecka
SCHIFFMAN, Frank
Apollo: mecca of black show business; excerpts from Uptown; the story of Harlem's Apollo theatre. J. Schiffman. il por Ebony 26:114-16+ Ap '71 •

SCHMIDT, John R. and Whalen, W. E.
Put the lid on. New Repub 164:16-17 Je **5** '71
SCHMIDT, Maarten, and Bello, Francis
Evolution of quasars; with biographical
sketches. il Sci Am 224:12, 54-62+ bibliog
(p 132) My '71
SCHMIDT, Michael
Well at Balankanche; Alone, and in a lonely
place; Underwater; poems. Poetry 118:147-
50 Je '71
SCHMIDT, Michael J. and others
Cyclic adenosine monophosphate in brain
areas: microwave irradiation as a means of
tissue fixation. bibliog il Science 173:1142-3
S 17 '71
SCHMIDT-NIELSEN, Knut
How birds breathe; with biographical sketch.
il Sci Am 225:10, 72-9 bibliog (p 120) D '71
SCHMIDTCHEN, Paul W.
History in books. See issues of Hobbies
SCHMIEDESKAMP, Jay
Slow consumer comeback in 1972; interview.
por Bsns W p40-1 Ja 1 '72

about

Mouthpiece for the consumer's mood. por
Bsns W p82 Ag 14 '71 *
SCHMITT, Harrison
Scientist gets the nod for the final moon
flight. il por Sci N 100:137 Ag 28 '71 *
SCHMITT, Roland W.
Solid-state physicists and metallurgy; adap-
tation of address, March 1970. bibliog il
Phys Today 24:44-8 Ja '71
SCHMITT, Roman A. See Wakita, H. jt. auth.
SCHMITZ, Dennis
Comment. A. Williamson. Poetry 118:173-4 Je
'71 *
SCHNEIDER, Allen M. See Kapp, B. S. jt.
auth.
SCHNEIDER, Jason
Camera collector. See issues of Modern pho-
tography
—and Bodenstein, Bennett
How shaky is your camera? il Mod Phot 35:
90-3 My '71
SCHNEIDER, John H.
Selective dissemination and indexing of sci-
entific information. bibliog il Science 173:
300-8 Jl 23 '71
SCHNEIDER, Kenneth R.
Architecture of urban space. Arch Forum
134:48-51+ Je '71
SCHNEIDER, Lorraine
Sunflower that grew and grew. D. Silverton.
por McCalls 98:44 My '71 *
SCHNEIDER, Nicholas
Grandeur that was Penn station; drawings.
Arch Forum 133:60-2 D '70
SCHNEIDER, Nina
He saith among the trumpets, ha, ha; and
he smelleth the battle afar off; poem.
Mlle 74:88 D '71
SCHNEIDER, Pierre
Unfinished cathedrals. il Vogue 158:96-101+
D '71
SCHNEIDER, Romy
Parting shots; well-kept-secret weapon in
the sexual revolution. W. A. McWhirter.
il por Life 71:69 Jl 9 '71 *
SCHNEIDER, S. H. See Rasool, S. I. jt. auth.
SCHNEIDER-SIEMSSEN, Günther
Günther and Eva; interview, ed. by Q.
Eaton. il por Opera N 36:26-7 D 18 '71
SCHNEIR, Miriam. See Schneir, W. jt. auth.
SCHNEIR, Walter, and Schneir, Miriam
Joy of learning in the open corridor. il por
N Y Times Mag p30-1+ Ap 4; 95-6 My 2
'71
SCHNITTKER, John A. See Allen, M. jt. auth.
SCHNITZER, Bertram, and others
Erythrocytes: pits and vacuoles as seen with
transmission and scanning electron micro-
scopy. bibliog il Science 173:251-2 Jl 16 '71
SCHNOEBELEN, Sister Anne
Cazzati vs. Bologna: 1657-1671. bibliog f il
Mus Q 57:26-39 Ja '71
SCHOENBERG, Arnold. See Schönberg, A.
SCHOENFELD, Lawrence S. and others
We like us. Ment Hy 55:171-3 Ap '71
SCHOENFELD, R. I.
Melatonin: effect on punished and non-
punished operant behavior of the pigeon.
bibliog il Science 171:1258-60 Mr 26 '71
SCHOENHUT, Anton Wilhelm
Hang on to your Schoenhuts. C. H. Fawcett.
il Hobbies 76:40+ Je '71 *
SCHOENHUT all wood dolls. See Dolls

SCHOENSTEIN, Ralph
Day that revolution became one of the three
R's. il Todays Health 49:48-9 N '71
Don't let anyone catch you using your naked
eye. il Todays Health 49:28-31 Je '71
Plowshares, anyone? New Yorker 47:52-3 D
11 '71
What even your best friend, the dog, won't
tell you. il Todays Health 49:50-3 Jl '71
SCHOLARS
China scholars. il Time 98:44+ Ag 9 '71
See also
College professors and instructors
Negro college professors and instructors
SCHOLARS, Russian. See Russia—Intellectu-
al life
**SCHOLARSHIP, education and defense fund
for racial equality**
Black power enclave. D. S. Glick. New Re-
pub 164:12 Ja 16 '71
SCHOLARSHIPS and fellowships
Our community sends its boys and girls to
college. D. Patterson. il Parents Mag 46:
52-3+ Ap '71
Scholarship shrinkage. Time 97:60 Mr 29 '71
Unesco fellowships for study abroad. R.
Greenough. Sch & Soc 99:442-3 N '71
White House fellow. il pors Ebony 26:98-
100+ My '71
See also
Ford foundation
Loucye Gordy Wakefield scholarship
Student aid
SCHOLASTIC achievements. See Student
achievements
SCHOLASTIC aptitude test. See College en-
trance examination board—Scholastic apti-
tude test
SCHOLASTIC aptitude tests. See Aptitude
tests
SCHOLASTIC institute of student opinion. See
Scholastic research center
SCHOLASTIC magazines, inc.
Presenting the 1971 Scholastic awards. Sr
Schol 98:2-10+ My 17 '71
SCHOLASTIC research center
Make marijuana laws easier? Most young
people say no: Scholastic's National Insti-
tute of student opinion. Sr Schol 99:7 N
29 '71
NISO poll results: students' views of na-
tional issues. Sr Schol 99:12 D 6 '71
SCHOLASTIC success, Prediction of. See Pre-
diction of scholastic success
SCHOLL, Phoebe K.
Oh, say, can you see? il Sch Arts 70:12-13
Ap '71
Structure needn't stifle. il Sch Arts 71:12-13
S '71
To feel y'self gettin' better. il Sch Arts 71:
30-1 D '71
SCHOLLANDER, Don, and Savage, Duke
Not the triumph but the struggle; conden-
sation from Deep water. il pors Read Di-
gest 98:221-4+ Je '71
SCHÖNBERG, Arnold
Fantasy world of Pierrot lunaire. D. Hamil-
ton. il Hi Fi 21:70-1 Jl '71 *
Moses and Aaron. Criticism
Nation 213:670 D 20 '71 *
SCHONBERG, Harold C.
Music (cont) Harper 242:11-12 F; 110+ Ap;
113-14 My; 243:96-7 Jl; 103-4 S; 130+ D '71
Strange malady called Fischer fear. il pors
N Y Times Mag p32-3+ N 14 '71

about

Harold and the wolf. il Time 97:56 Ap 26
'71 *
SCHÖNEFELD airport. See Berlin (East Ber-
lin)—Airports
SCHONHORN, H. See Hara, K. jt. auth.
SCHOOL administration. See School manage-
ment and organization
SCHOOL administrators
See also
Heads of departments
School superintendents and principals
SCHOOL age
School grade-age relationship, 1918-69; with
tables. G. J. Robertson and B. C. Mitchell.
bibliog Sch & Soc 99:447-51 N '71
SCHOOL and social and economic problems
High school fights for its life. . .and a prin-
cipal, for his; George Washington high
school, Denver. L. Gross. il pors Look 35:
20-5+ Mr 9 '71
See also
Children of migrant laborers—Education
Socially handicapped children—Education

SCHOOL children—Adjustment—*Continued*
Panel sanctions amphetamines for hyperkinetic children. R. J. Bazell. Science 171: 1223 Mr 26 '71
Pills for classroom peace? E. T. Ladd. Ed Digest 36:1-4 F '71
To "stay" with tax-supported love; social adjustment classes. K. Marshall. il Am Ed 7:6-10 Ap '71
    See also
Problem children

Food
See School lunches

Grading and promotion
See Grading and marking (students)

Migration
See Children of migrant laborers

Nutrition
See Children—Nutrition

Reading
See Childrens reading

Transportation
Bus stop. il Life 71:143-5 D 17 '71

Transportation for integration
ABC's of busing furor; interview. R. S. Ross. il U S News 71:82-5 N 15 '71
Acquiring wisdom and virtue by bus. R. Kirk. Nat R 23:1306 N 19 '71
Agony of busing moves north. il Time 98:57-60+ N 15 '71
Austin story. J. Osborne. New Repub 165: 13-15 Ag 21 '71
Back to busing. New Repub 165:5-6 D 18 '71
Betrayal in the House; adoption of anti-bussing amendment. Nation 213:515-17 N 22 '71
Big, ugly sleeper. S. Alsop. Newsweek 78: 130 O 18 '71
Block those buses; white militance in Michigan. D. Zwerdling. New Repub 165:14-17 O 23 '71
Boycotting the buses; San Francisco. il Newsweek 78:43 S 27 '71
Br'er George; busing policy. Newsweek 78:21 Ag 23 '71
Bus or not? Latest in uproar. U S News 71: 37 S 6 '71
Bus stop. il Time 98:10-11 Ag 16 '71
Bus stop at the House. il New Repub 165:1+ N 20 '71; Discussion. 165:26-7 D 18 '71
Buses are running. il Time 98:42+ S 13 '71
Business about bussing; Supreme court decision. Nation 212:647-8 My 3 '71
Busing. il Time 98:14 S 20 '71
Busing and politics. J. Osborne. New Repub 164:19-20 My 29 '71
Busing crisis hits a peak. il U S News 71:30-2 Ag 30 '71
Busing judge. por Time 97:40 My 3 '71
Busing: stop and go; the President's turn-around on busing in the South. il Newsweek 78:47 Ag 16 '71
Busing; Supreme court decision on southern schools. New Repub 164:11-12 My 1 '71
Busing: the court rules. il Newsweek 77:26-7 My 3 '71
Busing: the North reports; findings of the Center for urban education. Sat R 54:52 Je 19 '71
Busing the South; Supreme court decision. Sr Schol 98:16 My 17 '71
Busing: U.S. civil rights commission. 1970. il Negro Hist Bul 34:68 Mr '71
Confusing retreat on bussing. il Life 71: 4 Ag 27 '71
Dixie takes the bus. il Newsweek 78:14-15 S 13 '71
Fall madness over school busing. il Bsns W p70-1 O 2 '71
Far-reaching school decision, in the Court's own words; excerpts. U S News 70:40-2 My 3 '71
Green light for busing. il Sat R 54:68 My 22 '71
It can work: busing inner city pupils to suburban schools; Rochester's Project UNIQUE. C. A. Planz. il Clear House 46: 158-62 N '71
Latest in the furor over school busing. il U S News 71:72 N 8 '71
Let 'em eat cake; private schools for children of United States liberals. Nat R 23: 1398-9 D 17 '71
On the overturning of two school buses in Lamar, S.C.   W. F. McIlwain. il Esquire 75: 98-103+ Ja '71
Outflanking the President; busing policy. Time 98:10-11 Ag 23 '71

Progress in Jackson. E. Clift. il Newsweek 78:34 S 20 '71
Raging again: battle over school busing. U S News 71:38 Ag 16 '71
School busing and forced integration: a dissenting opinion; address. September 8, 1971. R. C. Byrd. Vital Speeches 38:7-11 O 15 '71
School-busing battle spreads to North and West; with excerpts from remarks by W. E. Burger. il U S News 71:22-3 S 13 '71
School busing: confusing ends and means; concerning President's statement. America 125:82 Ag 21 '71
Southern editors size up busing decision. U S News 70:49-50 My 10 '71
Supreme court yes to busing. il Time 97:13-14 My 3 '71
To bus or not to bus. Newsweek 78:16-17 S 6 '71
Trouble in Pontiac. il Newsweek 78:33-4 S 20 '71
Truth and busing. J. Osborne. New Repub 165:11-12 S 11 '71
Votes against the poor; busing to integrate schools. il Time 97:16-17 My 10 '71
What happens after busing starts. J. N. Miller. Read Digest 99:86-90 O '71
Year of the bus; Richmond, Va. R. G. Holland. Nat R 23:475+ My 4 '71
SCHOOL children, Free food for. See School lunches
SCHOOL counselors. See Student counselors
SCHOOL discipline
Vice principal: more than a disciplinarian. S. Winston. Clear House 46:78-81 O '71
    See also
Classroom management
Corporal punishment
SCHOOL districts
Educational cooperatives. C. C. Todd, jr. Clear House 45:383-4 F '71
SCHOOL drama. See College and school drama
SCHOOL employees
    See also
School personnel management
SCHOOL enrollment. See School attendance
SCHOOL excursions
Schools where education comes alive. G. W. Weinstein. il Parents Mag 46:33-5+ Je '71
SCHOOL exhibits
    See also
Childrens art—Exhibitions
SCHOOL finance
Ahead for big-city schools: penny-pinching and turmoil. il U S News 71:24-6+ S 13 '71
Bad way to pay for schools. Life 71:42 D 10 '71
California doctrine. A. E. Wise. il Sat R 54: 78-9+ N 20 '71
California scraps its school tax system. Bsns W p59-60 S 4 '71
Can we afford to educate our children? G. M. Knox. il Bet Hom & Gard 49:56+ N '71
Comparative expenditures on education. Sch & Soc 99:396 N '71
Crisis in school costs: what can be done? G. M. Knox. Bet Hom & Gard 49:6+ O '71 (to be cont)
Crisis in school finance. J. S. Berke. Ed Digest 37:5-8 N '71
Dayton's school situation. America 125:446 N 27 '71
Dividing the cake; California Supreme court decision. il Time 98:47 S 13 '71
Education's rigged lottery; address, October 12, 1971. S. P. Marland, jr. Vital Speeches 38:122-5 D 1 '71
Exit the property tax? California Supreme court decision. Newsweek 78:61 S 13 '71
Financial crisis for public schools. il U S News 71:48-50 N 8 '71
Financing education in the 70's. H. Calkins. Todays Ed 60:30-2 F '71
Fresh blow against financing schools with property taxes. U S News 72:66 Ja 10 '72
Lessons from the schools of other nations; two pilot programs of the Office of education's Institute of international studies. D. Sweeney. il Am Ed 7:11-12 O '71
Nationwide shake-up in property taxes. G. Lorang. il Farm J 95:22-3 N '71
New financing for schools. America 125:363 N 6 '71
Paying for good schools. New Repub 165: 5-6 D 11 '71
Paying for public education; California Supreme court decision. Nation 213:226 S 20 '71
Political techniques in school bond and millage elections. J. W. Maguire. bibliog Sch & Soc 99:514-15 D '71
Private wealth and public education, by J. E. Coons and others. Review
    Sat R 54:76-7+ Ap 17 '71. A. E. Wise

SCHOOL finance—*Continued*
Recasting of public education; address. July 5, 1971. J. E. Allen, jr. Vital Speeches 37: 654-8 Ag 15 '71
Runaway school taxes: can we corral them? G. W. Wormley. il Farm J 95:26-7+ My '71
School-tax ruling that could overturn financing in most states. US News 71:90 S 13 '71
School taxes; decision by the California Supreme court. New Repub 165:9-10 O 2 '71
Schools go begging. il Newsweek 77:98+ Je 7 '71
Squeezing the schools. il Time 98:72+ O 4 '71
Summer budget troubles. il Sat R 54:52 Jl 17 '71
Toward equity in school finance; National educational finance project. R. L. Johns. Am Ed 7:3-6 N '71
Yes was a big word at Reavis; Don Depa and the school tax referendum for high school in Burbank, Ill. Sr Schol 99:3 O 11 '71
    See also
Education—Economic aspects
Education—Federal aid
Education and state

Statistics
Facts on school enrollments and finance. Sch & Soc 99:74 F '71
SCHOOL for wives; drama. See Molière, J. B. P.
SCHOOL gardens
    See also
Childrens gardens
SCHOOL girls. See Girls
SCHOOL gymnasiums. See Gymnasiums
SCHOOL hygiene
    See also
Public schools—Health service
SCHOOL journalism. See College and school journalism
SCHOOL laws and legislation
How to live with due process. G. Triezenberg. Ed Digest 36:18-21 My '71
    See also
Teachers—Tenure

California
Dividing the cake; California Supreme court decision on property tax school finance. il Time 98:47 S 13 '71
Exit the property tax? California Supreme court decision. Newsweek 78:61 S 13 '71
Paying for public education; Supreme court decision. Nation 213:226 S 20 '71
School-tax ruling that could overturn financing in most states. US News 71:90 S 13 '71
School taxes; decision by the California Supreme court. New Repub 165:9-10 O 2 '71
Welcome blow at the school tax. Fortune 84: 68 O '71

Michigan
Public: court of last resort; reversing the polls on rejected parochiaid. C. M. Whelan. America 124:568-70 My 29 '71

United States
Civil rights of public school students; recent judicial decisions. R. M. Blankenburg. Cur 131:35-42 Jl '71
Education as a source of power. J. M. Shaman. Sch & Soc 99:166-8 Mr '71
Law and punishment status of state statutes. J. G. Brown. Clear House 46:106-9 O '71
NEA's concerns in the new Congress. Todays Ed 60:33 Ja '71
Performance contracting: making it legal. R. Martin. Ed Digest 36:1-4 Ap '71
Religion and education: cooperation or conflict? G. A. Kizer. bibliog Sch & Soc 99: 152-6 Mr '71
Student rights find a friend in court (s) L. W. Knowles. Ed Digest 36:15-17 My '71
With education in Washington. T. Schuchat. See issues of Education digest
    See also
Compulsory education
SCHOOL librarians
Disenfranchised: school librarians at NYLA. Library J 96:3797-8 N 15 '71
Librarians & AECT. E. Geller. il Library J 96:1749, 1771-4+ My 15 '71; Discussion. 96: 2805 S 15 '71
School librarians: are we for real? excerpts. C. Leopold. il por Library J 96:1424-8 Ap 15 '71
    See also
American association of school librarians

Education
Experimental models for school library media education. R. N. Case. bibliog il por Library J 96:4151-6 D 15 '71

Qualifications
Who should do what in the media center. R. N. Case. por Wilson Lib Bul 45:852-5 My '71

Supply and demand
School library manpower project: a report on phase 1. R. N. Case and A. M. Lowrey. il Am Lib 2:98-101 Ja '71
SCHOOL librarians institutes. See Library institutes and workshops
SCHOOL libraries
Library as a teaching asset. J. F. McAteer. Clear House 45:510-12 Ap '71
SLJ news roundup. P. Schuman. il Library J 96:4145-50 D 15 '71
To answer the taxpayer; duplication of library service for children by public and school libraries. J. Berry. Library J 96: 2027 Je 15 '71
    See also
School librarians

Administration
    See School libraries—Supervisors and supervision

Audio-visual materials
    See School libraries and audio-visual materials

Book selection
School children and book selection; use of elementary student reviewers for Learning resource centers in Canton, Ohio. W. Measel and L. L. Crawford. il pors Am Lib 2:955-7 O '71

Censorship
Book business. A. Green. Sat R 54:21-2 Je 26 '71
Down these mean streets: book banning in Teaneck, N.J. W. R. Eshelman. Wilson Lib Bul 46:123 O '71
Library media committee; statement, May 5, 1971. S. Mendlow and I. Morris. Am Lib 2: 789-90 S '71
School censors hit N.Y, Ohio, Maryland and California. il Library J 96:228-30 Ja 15 '71

Federal aid
ESEA report notes growth of unified media concept. Library J 96:230-1 Ja 15 '71
Editor's choice; USOE commissioner's conference. Am Lib 2:357 Ap '71
Education revenue sharing. Wilson Lib Bul 45:1005-6 Je '71
Federal sell-out. E. Geller. Library J 96:1407 Ap 15 '71
Libraries look to the state agency. M. F. K. Johnson. bibliog il Am Lib 2:736-9 Jl '71
Revenue sharing plan unveiled by OE ESEA, NDEA to be consolidated. Library J 96: 1411-12 Ap 15 '71

Finance
Better look at budgets; cooperation to improve media programs. L. Howard. il Library J 96:1081-2 Mr 15 '71
McNamara, media and you; PPBS (program, planning and budgeting system) and school libraries. J. Meyers and R. Barber. bibliog il Library J 96:1079-81, 1743+ Mr 15, My 15 '71

Instruction in use
School librarians: are we for real? excerpts. C. Leopold. il por Library J 96:1424-8 Ap 15 '71
Transfer of orientation techniques to school libraries. E. Peterman. Wilson Lib Bul 46: 63 S '71

Map collections
Acquisition of maps for school and other small libraries. C. E. Current. bibliog il por Wilson Lib Bul 45:578-83 F '71

Periodical collections
Free & inexpensive magazines for schools; ed. by B. Katz. A. M. Smith. Library J 96: 2065-6 Je 15 '71

Supervisors and supervision
Getting a head start; how to organize for the school year. M. E. Paetro. il Library J 96:2846-7 S 15 '71
What price professionalism? High school of performing arts, New York city. R. Feinberg. il por Library J 96:691-4 F 15 '71

California
Concern for children; Pasadena public library, Calif; letter to the editor. B. L. Ryder. Library J 96:1059+ Mr 15 '71

SCHOOL libraries—California—*Continued*
Edna Hill Banks, exemplary elementary school librarian; George Washington elementary school, Compton. il pors Wilson Lib Bul 45:946-7 Je '71
Mary Carmen Santana, school librarian; East Los Angeles high school. il pors Wilson Lib Bul 45:646-7 Mr '71

Great Britain

Stirrings in a new school library movement. F. L. Carroll and M. Friday. Wilson Lib Bul 45:983-6 Je '71

Maryland

Professionalism; letter to the editor. M. W. Stoer. Library J 96:1062-3 Mr 15 '71

Mississippi

Education in Mississippi; Leflore County. L. Hogue. il Am Lib 2:985-6 O '71

New Jersey

Down these mean streets; book banning in Teaneck, N.J. W. R. Eshelman. Wilson Lib Bul 46:123 O '71

New York (state)

Disenfranchised: school librarians at NYLA. Library J 96:3797-8 N 15 '71
Educationists and librarians; NYLA conference. J. Berry. Library J 96:153 Ja 15 '71
Future of children's service discussed in Finger Lakes. Library J 96:1068 Mr 15 '71
Is CCLD all that bad? patterns of children's library service. M. R. Sive. il por Library J 96:3442-5 O 15 '71
NYLA 77th annual conference, November 1970. il Am Lib 2:5-6 Ja '71
Pilot program on alternatives in children's service to test school library recommendation in CCLD report. il Library J 96:223-5+ Ja 15 '71
Where will all the children go? J. G. Burke. bibliog il Am Lib 2:56-61 Ja '71; Discussion. 2:448-9, 601-4, 783-4, My-Je, S '71
Will Shakespeare knew that all along; actress F. Foster's visit to library of George Westinghouse vocational and technical high school, Brooklyn. S. C. Aksel. il por Wilson Lib Bul 45:754-7 Ap '71

Ohio

School children and book selection; use of elementary student reviewers for Learning resource centers in Canton. W. Measel and L. L. Crawford. il pors Am Lib 2:955-7 O '71

Pennsylvania

Philadelphia project: decrease in students' use of public and school libraries between 4th and 12th grades. J. Q. Benford. il por Library J 96:2041-7 Je 15 '71
Sacred cows: the CCLD report; New York findings and Philadelphia schools. C. Field. il por Library J 96:3445-7 O 15 '71

Southern states

Coddling segregation; the case for ALA action. E. J. Josey. por Library J 96:1778-9 My 15 '71
Southern integration: writing off the black librarian. P. Schuman. il Library J 96:1775-7 My 15 '71

Virginia

Va. school & library join to form community library; Aurora Hills library, Arlington. Library J 96:3061 O 1 '71

SCHOOL libraries and audio-visual materials
Accountability: notes toward a definition; address, 1971. R. L. Darling. il por Library J 96:3805-8 N 15 '71
Better look at budgets; cooperation to improve media programs. L. Howard. il Library J 96:1081-2 Mr 15 '71
Experimental models for school library media education. R. N. Case. bibliog il por Library J 96:4151-6 D 15 '71
McNamara, media and you; PPBS (program planning and budgeting system) and school libraries. J. Meyers and R. Barber. bibliog il Library J 96:1079-81, 1743+ Mr 15, My 15 '71
Overdue; librarian and the AV specialist: less talk of either/or, more of both. C. K. Silver. por Wilson Lib Bul 46:461+ Ja '72
Systems for individual study. E. Fleischer. il por Library J 96:695-8 F 15 '71
SCHOOL libraries and drama. See Libraries and drama

SCHOOL libraries and Negroes
Coddling segregation; the case for ALA action. E. J. Josey. por Library J 96:1778-9 My 15 '71
Southern integration: writing off the black librarian. P. Schuman. il Library J 96:1775-7 My 15 '71
SCHOOL libraries and social and economic problems
What price professionalism? High school of performing arts, New York city. R. Feinberg. il por Library J 96:691-4 F 15 '71
Will Shakespeare knew that all along; actress F. Foster's visit to library of George Westinghouse vocational and technical high school, Brooklyn. S. C. Aksel. il por Wilson Lib Bul 45:754-7 Ap '71
SCHOOL library instruction. See School libraries—Instruction in use
SCHOOL library journal
Lillian N. Gerhardt appointed SLJ editor-in-chief. por Library J 96:3423 O 15 '71
SCHOOL library orientation. See School libraries—Instruction in use
SCHOOL library supervisors. See School libraries—Supervisors and supervision
SCHOOL lockers. See Lockers
SCHOOL lunches
Feeding needy children. America 125:335 O 30 '71
Feeding the children; National school lunch program. H. S. Rodriguez. il Parks & Rec 6:55+ My '71
Next: free lunches to all schoolchildren? il U S News 71:51-2 N 8 '71
SCHOOL management and organization
Benefits of regional education authorities. J. Elkind. Clear House 45:328 F '71
Community control of schools, ed. by H. M. Levin. Review
  America 124:576 My 29 '71. F. Griffith
Desirable characteristics of decentralized school systems. S. M. Brownell. Ed Digest 36:8-11 Ap '71
Imperatives in urban education; address, July 16, 1971. H. B. Scribner. Vital Speeches 37:669-72 Ag 15 '71
Managing the unmanageable; address, July 13, 1971. F. A. J. Ianni. Vital Speeches 37:683-7 S 1 '71
New York's mini-schools. D. Divoky. Sat R 54:60-1+ D 18 '71
Pressures on students. F. M. Raubinger. Todays Ed 60:46 D '71
Reorganization of education in metropolitan areas. R. J. Havighurst. Ed Digest 36:5-8 My '71
School system: a look into the future. R. T. Grant. Clear House 45:535-7 Mv '71
Theory and practice: why nothing seems to work. D. A. Erlandson and E. R. House. Ed Digest 37:34-7 S '71
  See also
Ability grouping in education
Colleges and universities—Administration
Corporal punishment
Schedules, School
School districts
School finance
School personnel management
School superintendents and principals
School year
Teacher-administrator relationships
Teachers—Tenure
Teaching

Parent participation

All the isms are wasms; New York state's Project Redesign; address, July 15, 1971. E. Nyquist. Vital Speeches 37:645-50 Ag 15 '71
Newark's parent-powered school; Springfield avenue community school. L. Rich. il Am Ed 7:35-9 D '71
Parent participation. W. D. Boutwell. PTA Mag 65:30 My '71
Parental control of schools urged by Catholic group. Chr Cent 88:1103 S 22 '71

Student participation

Bored of education? No, sir! teenage Larry Hamm of Newark, N.J. Sr Schol 99:3 S 20 '71
Story behind the book: The little red schoolbook. L. P. Freilicher. pors Pub W 200:32-3 D 13 '71
Student power: want to start a school? il Seventeen 29:132-3+ N '70
Students lay it on the line. C. H. Harrison. il Schol Teach Jr/Sr High p6-8+ Ap 5 '71

Teacher participation

Helping spend school dollars wisely; teachers councils on curriculum development. D. J. Stangel. Todays Ed 60:38-9 Ja '71
Teachers as change agents. C. H. Hill. bibliog Clear House 45:424-8 Mr '71

SCHOOL music
See also
Music educators national conference
SCHOOL newspapers. See College and school journalism
SCHOOL of American ballet, Inc.
Time of the crocus. O. Maynard. il Dance Mag 45:60-3 Je '71
SCHOOL of performing arts. See New York (city)—Education
SCHOOL organization. See School management and organization
SCHOOL personnel management
Differentiation : a means for improving staff utilization. R. G. Telfer. Clear House 46: 112-15 O '71
SCHOOL phobia
Reinforcement approach to the elimination of a child's school phobia. C. V. Edlund. bibliog Ment Hy 55:433-6 O '71
Why some kids hate school. Newsweek 78:57-8 O 4 '71

Anecdotes, facetiae, satire, etc.
Scholastis adolescum: a disease every kid has the cure for; excerpts from Sons of the great society. A. Buchwald. il Todays Health 49:44-5 S '71
SCHOOL plays. See College and school drama
SCHOOL-police cooperation. See Police-school cooperation
SCHOOL prayer. See Public schools and religion
SCHOOL prayer decision. See United States —Supreme court—Decisions
SCHOOL principals. See School superintendents and principals
SCHOOL psychologists
How school psychologists can be important to your child. il Good H 172:200 Ap '71
SCHOOL public relations. See School and the community
SCHOOL refusal. See School phobia
SCHOOL reports and records
Appeal for public school archives. P. A. Kalisch. Clear House 45:562 My '71
Guidelines on pupil records; report of Russell Sage foundation conference. Sch & Soc 99: 283-5 Sum '71
School records can be an invasion of privacy; Russell Sage foundation conference guidelines. V. S. Teitelbaum. Todays Ed 60:43-5 My '71
SCHOOL schedules. See Schedules, School
SCHOOL sessions. See School year
SCHOOL sickness. See School phobia
SCHOOL statistics. See Education—Statistics
SCHOOL superintendents and principals
Accountable leadership. R. T. McGee. Clear House 46:170-2 N '71
Administrative leadership and curriculum change. R. L. Swihart. Clear House 46: 146 N '71
Administrator: target for today. E. J. Cereghino. Clear House 45:528-31 My '71
Assistant principal: a job in limbo. R. Kindsvatter and D. J. Tosi. bibliog Clear House 45:456-64 Ap '71
Current problems of the school superintendent. M. S. Norton. il Clear House 46:15-19 S '71
Elementary school principalship, 1980. W. D. Southworth. Clear House 46:136-40 N '71
Games principals shouldn't play with teachers. B. Demsch and D. Muller. Clear House 45:473-5 Ap '71
Is anybody in charge here? G. E. Flower. Ed Digest 37:1-4 D '71
Long-term contracts for superintendents? F. M. Raubinger. Ed Digest 37:12-13 S '71
Man we call superintendent. R. T. Gregg and S. J. Knezevich. Ed Digest 37:21-3 O '71
Managing the unmanageable; address, July 13, 1971. F. A. J. Ianni. Vital Speeches 37: 683-7 S 1 '71
Matter of principals; with study-discussion program by E. Harris and D. Harris. S. P. Wiggins. bibliog il PTA Mag 65:2-5, 32 Je '71
New breed principal brings peace to Pelton; T. Carroll of San Francisco's Pelton junior high school. il pors Ebony 27:144-6+ N '71
New kind of principal. W. W. Wayson. Ed Digest 36:1-4 My '71
Ousting a reformer; Philadelphia school superintendent M. Shedd. il por Time 98: 58 D 20 '71
Principal as a change agent. L. E. Annese. bibliog Clear House 45:273-7 Ja '71
Vice principal; more than a disciplinarian. S. Winston. Clear House 46:78-81 O '71

Anecdotes, facetiae, satire, etc.
Glossary of administrative birds. H. E. Marchie. Clear House 46:226 D '71

Education in service
AASA's nonacademic academy. L. L. Gray. Am Ed 7:21-4 O '71

Training
New path to educational leadership; the National program for educational leadership. B. Gifford. Am Ed 7:9-12 D '71
SCHOOL supervision and supervisors
Credibility gap in supervision. G. S. Osborne and A. S. Hurlburt. bibliog Sch & Soc 99:415-17 N '71
See also
Supervisors of student teaching
SCHOOL tax system. See School finance
SCHOOL teaching. See Teaching
SCHOOL terms. See School year
SCHOOL volunteer programs. See Volunteer workers in education
SCHOOL year
Autumn vacation; staggered schedules at Valley View school district outside Chicago. Time 98:66 N 1 '71
Developing flexible all-year schools. J. McLain. Ed Digest 36:12-14 My '71
Diary of the year-round school. M. K. Murphy. il Schol Teach Jr/Sr High p 16-19 N '71
How to think about the extended school year; with comment by E. F. Schmidt. il Camp Mag 43:4, 8-12 S '71
New trend: year-round schools. il U S News 71:35-7 Jl 26 '71
School around the calendar; Valley View elementary district, Lockport, Ill. T. F. Driscoll. il Am Ed 7:21-3 Mr '71
Valley View's 45-15 year-round school. S. C. Thomas. Todays Ed 60:42-3 N '71
SCHOOLROOMS. See Classrooms
SCHOOLS
See also
Catholic schools
Correspondence schools and courses
Education
Forestry schools and education
Library schools and education
Military post schools, American
Negro schools
Private schools
Private schools, Negro
Public schools
School buildings
Schools, Experimental
Summer schools
Sunday schools

Statistics
See Education—Statistics

England
England comprehensive; London secondary school. il Arch Forum 134:52-5 My '71

France
Trouble at Normale. il Newsweek 77:110 Ap 19 '71

United States
See also
Education—United States
John C. Campbell folk school, Brasstown, N.C.
Public schools—United States
SCHOOLS, Community control of. See School management and organization
SCHOOLS, Elementary. See Education, Elementary; Public schools
SCHOOLS, Experimental
Case for permissipline; informal teaching at Wilde Lake middle school; Columbia, Md. il Time 97:54 Je 21 '71
Chaos and learning: the free schools; report on Exploring family school, El Cajon, Calif. B. Hillenbrand. il Time 97:81-2 Ap 26 '71
English in experimental schools. B. Leondar. Engl J 60:748-53 S '71
School of your children's dreams; Prospect school, North Bennington, Vt. A. Silberman. il Good H 172:69+ Mr '71
See also
Open plan schools
Vineland, N.J.—Education
SCHOOLS, Traveling
Nursery school on wheels; Appalachia educational laboratory. M. Cobb. il Parents Mag 46:60-1+ S '71
SCHOOLS, Ungraded. See Ungraded classes
SCHOOLS and libraries. See Libraries and schools

SCHOOLS and museums. See Museums and schools

SCHOOLS and politics. See Politics and education; Teachers—Political activities

SCHOOLS and social and economic problems. See School and social and economic problems

SCHOOLS for the blind. See Blind—Education

SCHOOLS of education
Programmed unhappiness: when will schools of education make teaching a relevant act? R. V. Iannone. bibliog Clear House 46:102-5 O '71

SCHOONER racing. See Yacht racing

SCHOPF, J. William. See Oehler, J. H. jt. auth.

SCHOPP, Walter W.
Rapid-flash. il Electr World 85:68-9 Ap '71

SCHORR, Alvin L.
Case for federal welfare. Nation 212:555-7 My 3 '71

SCHORR, Daniel Louis
Bad check. por Newsweek 78:79-80 N 22 '71 *
Case of Daniel Schorr. America 125:445-6 N 27 '71 *
Dan Schorr affair. J. Osborne. New Repub 165:11-13 N 27 '71 *

SCHOTT, B. sons. See Music publishing

SCHOTT, Francis H.
Interest rate outlook. por Nations Bsns 59:73 D '71

SCHRADER, Hans Joachim
Fecal pellets: role in sedimentation of pelagic diatoms. bibliog il Science 174:55-7 O 1 '71

SCHRAG, Peter
Age of Willie Mays. il pors Sat R 54:15-17+ My 8 '71
Dossier dictatorship. Sat R 54:24-5 Ap 17 '71
Ellsberg affair. por Sat R 54:34-9 N 13 '71
McGovern in South Dakota. Atlan 228:6+ O '71
New beat in the heart of Dixie. il por Sat R 54:42-5+ Mr 20 '71
What's happened to the brain business? il Sat R 54:12-15+ Ag 7 '71

SCHRAMM, Richard
Return; poem. Poetry 118:206-7 Jl '71
Silt shallows; poem. New Yorker 47:69 My 22 '71
Snow line; poem. New Yorker 46:65 Ja 9 '71

SCHREIBER, Jean Jacques Servan-. See Servan-Schreiber, J. J.

SCHREIBER, Jean Louis Servan-. See Servan-Schreiber, J. L.

SCHREIBER, Norman B.
Going up! por Forbes 108:79 S 15 '71

SCHRIEFER, Arno H. Jr, and others
Illinois 120-foot radio telescope. il Sky & Tel 41:132-8 Mr '71

SCHRODER, Naess and Thomas (firm)
Game gets more dangerous; interview. R. Wilson. pors Forbes 108:39-42 Ag 1 '71
(ed) See MacMurray, J. H. Magic of a good marriage
(ed) See Young, R. Robert Young: TV's Dr Welby; his frank and personal replies to fans

SCHROEDER, Dolores M. See Ebbesson, S. O. E. jt. auth.

SCHROEDER, Henry A.
Metals in the air. bibliog il por Environ 13:18-24+ O '71

SCHROEDER, Leslie
Bees. il Horticulture 49:24-5+ F '71
Hummingbirds. il Horticulture 49:28-9+ S '71

SCHROEDER, Lynn. See Ostrander. S. jt. auth.

SCHROEDER, M. S.
Handy light control for your darkroom. il Pop Mech 136:116-18 S '71

SCHROEDER, Theodore Albert
Comstock's nemesis. D. Brudnoy. Nat R 23:1064+ S 24 '71 *

SCHUBERT, Franz Peter
Classical nature of Schubert's lieder. W. Gray. bibliog f Mus Q 57:62-72 Ja '71 *
Eighteen minutes of glorious Schubert from Lili Kraus. L. Gerber. il Am Rec G 37:512-13 Ap '71 *
Over 400 Schubert songs: Fischer-Dieskau and Gerald Moore. D. Hamilton. il Hi Fi 21:74-5 Ja '71 *
Schubert: discoveries of the last decade. M. J. E. Brown. bibliog f il por Mus Q 57:351-78 Jl '71 *
Schubert, transcendental amateur. D. Henahan. il por Hi Fi 21:71-2 Je '71 *
Schubert's Beethoven. E. T. Cone. bibliog f il Mus Q 56:779-93 O '70 *

SCHUBERTH, Christopher J.
Long Island's ocean beaches; with biographical sketch. il Sea Front 17:350-62, 383 N '71

SCHUCHAT, Theodor
News desk. See issues of Harvest years
With education in Washington. See issues of Education digest

SCHUCK, Linda. See Hirst, E. jt. auth.

SCHULER, Stanley
Foam: the new miracle building material. Am Home 74:36+ Ap '71
Livin' is easy. il Nations Busns 59:86-90 O '71
20 steps to a more fire-safe home. Am Home 74:90 N '71

SCHULITZ, Helmut C.
Structure for change and growth. il Arch Forum 134:60-3 Mr '71

SCHULKE, Flip
It's easy to take pictures underwater. il Motor B & S 128:28-9+ Jl '71

SCHULLER, Robert H.
Spiritual shopping center. il por Newsweek 78:51 Jl 5 '71 *

SCHULMAN, Grace
Border; Abbess of Whitby; In the police state; poems. Nation 213:663 D 20 '71

SCHULMAN, Samuel
Instant millionaires from the basketball war; with account by D. Fisher. il por Life 70:32-4 Ap 23 '71 *

SCHULTE and Dieckhoff GmbH. See Hosiery industry

SCHULTZ, A. Jay, and Thompson, W. P.
New era in environmental education. il Am For 77:28-31+ Ap '71

SCHULTZ, Dodi
Family doctors' health guide. Ladies Home J 88:34+ Ag '71
Safety starts at home. Ladies Home J 88:170 S '71
—See Chambers, C. D.; Pomeranz, V. E. jt. auths.

SCHULTZ, Michael John, Jr
After all. Todays Ed 60:80 N '71

SCHULTZ, Morton J.
Automobile clinic; questions and answers. See issues of Popular mechanics
Coming: a computerized collision-avoidance system. il Pop Mech 135:90-3+ F '71
How the airlines hope to stop bombs and bomb scares. il Pop Mech 135:94-7+ Mr '71
How to buy a used mini bike. il Mech Illus 67:76-7 Jl '71
How to repair a fiberglass boat. il Pop Mech 135:116-19+ Mr '71
How to service small engines. il Pop Mech 135:130-5 Mr; 134-9 Ap '71
It's your business. il Pop Mech 136:82-5+ S '71
Outboard maintenance in a can. il Mech Illus 67:138+ N '71
Saturday mechanic. See issues of Popular mechanics
Those new gasolines: how to pick the right one for your car. il Pop Mech 135:122-5 F '71
What's wrong with the 747? il Mech Illus 67:60-1+ Je '71
Your pollution-free car of 1975. il Sci Digest 69:48-54 My '71

SCHULTZ, Myron Gilbert
Doctor Jekyll and Mr Cocaine. Sci N 99:264 Ap 17 '71 *

SCHULTZ, Paul
Windshield wiper pause control. il Radio-Electr 42:52-3 D '71

SCHULZ, Ann T.
Leadership role for Iran in the Persian Gulf? bibliog f il Cur Hist 62:25-30+ Ja '72

SCHULZ, Charles Monroe
What Peanuts means to Schulz. il Newsweek 78:42 D 27 '71

about

Good grief, $150 million! il pors Newsweek 78:40-4 D 27 '71 *

SCHULZ, James H.
Pension elite. New Repub 164:9-10 My 15 '71

SCHULZ, John W.
Technician's perspective. See issues of Forbes

SCHULZ, Mark
Boy in search of a man. il pors Life 71:65-6+ S 24 '71 *

SCHULZ, William
Let's halt heroin at the source. Read Digest 98:97-101 My '71
Mob's grip on New Jersey. Read Digest 98:111-15 F '71

SCHULZE, Franz
Art news in Chicago. il Art N 70:45-55 N '71

SCHUMACHER, E. F.
Small is beautiful: toward a theology of enough; address. Chr Cent 88:900-2 Jl 28 '71

SCHUMACHER, Ernst
My visit to the United States. Nation 212:666-8 My 24 '71

SCHUMAN, Patricia
SLJ news roundup. il Library J 96:4145-50
D 15 '71
—and Detlefsen, E. G.
Sisterhood is serious: an annotated bibliography. il pors Library J 96:2587-94 S 1 '71
SCHUMANN, Maurice
Foreign policy and the United Nations. Vital
Speeches 38:45-9 N 1 '71
SCHUPPER, Fabian X. and Calogeras, R. C.
Psycho-cultural shifts in ego defenses. bibliog Am Imago 28:53-70 Spr '71
SCHUSTER, F. L. See Dunnebacke, T. H. jt.
auth.
SCHUSTER, Marjorie
Lowering the dropout rate. Clear House 45:
329-32 F '71
SCHÜTZ, Klaus
Peace as a process. Nation 213:195 S 13 '71 •
SCHÜTZ, Wilhelm
Doebereiner and the University of Jena; tr.
by R. E. Oesper. il pors Chem 45:10-11 Ja
'72
SCHUYLER, George W. and Zschock, D. K.
Venezuelan progress reconsidered. bibliog f
Cur Hist 60:95-101+ F '71
SCHUYLER, James
Evening wind; poem. New Yorker 47:127 O 9
'71
Light from Canada: poem. New Yorker 47:
57 Jl 31 '71
SCHUYLER, Keith C.
Indians were only first. il Field & S 76:52-
3+ S '71
SCHUYLER, Peter
Four Indian kings in London. M. Bishop. il
Am Heritage 23:62-5 D '71 •
SCHWAB, Judith
Man at the counter, poem. Chr Cent 88:
522 Ap 28 '71
SCHWAGER, Myron
Beethoven's septet, Opus 20: an arrangement for military band. bibliog f il Mus Q
56:727-41 O '70
SCHWALBERG, Bob
Handling the Canon F-1. il Pop Phot 68:120-
1+ My '71
Photography's electronic future. il Pop Phot
68:64-9+ Mr '71
Schwalberg at large. por Pop Phot 69:20+ Jl;
26+ Ag; 24+ S '71
SCHWALBERG, Carol
How to read a menu. il Travel 135:63-5 F '71
SCHWARTZ, Alan U. See Pilpel, H. F. jt.
auth.
SCHWARTZ, Barbara
Carl and Heidi Bucher need your body. il
Craft Horiz 31:27-9+ Je '71
Self in city space and in clothed space. il
por Craft Horiz 31:30-5 Ag '71
SCHWARTZ, Barry
Museums: art for who's sake? il Ramp Mag
9:38-49 Je '71
SCHWARTZ, Daniel
Daniel Schwartz the realist's view. P. A.
Dreyfus. il por Am Artist 35:40-8+ My '71 •
SCHWARTZ, Donald M.
Arms control and supra-nationalism: Bul
Atom Sci 27:38-41 Ap '71
SCHWARTZ, Elizabeth
Ecology, conservation, etc; ed. by B. Katz.
Library J 96:3304-6 O 15 '71
SCHWARTZ, Ellen
(ed) See Pearlstein, P. Conversation with
Philip Pearlstein
SCHWARTZ, Gary E. and Higgins, J. D.
Cardiac activity preparatory to overt and
covert behavior. bibliog il Science 173:1144-
6 S 17 '71
SCHWARTZ, Harry
Health care in America: a heretical diagnosis. il Sat R 54:14-17+ Ag 14 '71
SCHWARTZ, Jane
What's cooking? il por Org Gard & Farm
18:126-9 Ja '71
SCHWARTZ, Jonathan Matthew
Letter home; poem. Nation 213:477 N 8 '71
SCHWARTZ, Joseph A.
Positives outweigh negatives for camps using
convenience foods. il Camp Mag 43:20-2 My
'71
SCHWARTZ, Raymond, and McNeely, Richard
Telecture. Clear House 46:215-17 D '71
SCHWARTZ, Robert L.
Great change in living values. pors House &
Gard 140:100-1+ O '71
SCHWARTZ, Sheila
Science fiction: bridge between the two cultures. bibliog f Engl J 60:1043-51 N '71
SCHWARTZ, Stan
Why farmers "forget" their farm organization dues; ed. by B. Coffman. Farm J 95:
22C Jl '71

SCHWARZ, Boris
Little-known Beethoven sketch in Moscow.
bibliog f il Mus Q 56:539-50 O '70
SCHWARZ, Dietrich W. F. and Fredrickson,
J. M.
Rhesus monkey vestibular cortex: a bimodal
primary projection field. bibliog il Science
172:280-1 Ap 16 '71
SCHWARZ, F. A. O. (firm)
F. A. O. Schwarz: tougher selling in toyland. il Bsns W p46-9 D 18 '71
SCHWARZ, Helmut Julius
Optical modulation of electron beam. G. B.
Lubkin. il Phys Today 24:17-19 Je '71 •
SCHWARZ, John C.
Celibacy: the foundations have shifted. Cath
World 212:254-8 F '71
SCHWARZ, Jon
Gallery; photographs. Life 71:8-9 O 22 '71
SCHWARZ, Klaus, and Milne, D. B.
Growth effects of vanadium in the rat. bibliog il Science 174:426-8 O 22 '71
SCHWEID, Barry
Short tempers on the high bench. Nation
213:15-17 Jl 5 '71
SCHWEIKER, William
Does video violence make Johnny hit back?
Sci Digest 71:57 Ja '72 •
SCHWEITZER, Albert
Schweitzer: prophet of radical theology, by
J. L. Ice. Review Commonweal 95:258-60 D 10 '71. R. P.
McBrien •
SCHWETZINGEN festival. See Music festivals
—Germany (Federal Republic)
SCHWITTERS, Kurt
Out of the midden heap, retrospective in
Düsseldorf, Germany. R. Hughes. il por
Time 97:64-6 Mr 1 '71 •
SCIENCE
Evaluation of basic science. D. Stetten, Jr.
Science 174:105 O 8 '71
Isaac Asimov explains: questions and answers. I. Asimov. See issues of Science
digest
On the use and misuse of science. A. W. Galston. Yale R 60:458-63 Spr '71; Same with
title Education of a scientific innocent. Natur Hist 80:16-18 Je '71
Physical sciences. See occasional issues of
Science news
Science: endless horizons or golden age? address. December 28, 1970. B. Glass. bibliog
Science 171:23-9 Ja 8 '71; Discussion. 172:
111-12; 173:103-4 Ap 9, Jl 9 '71
Science in review. A. W. Galston. See issues
of Yale review
Student attitudes on science; summary of
interviews. il Bul Atom Sci 27:31-5 My
'71
See also
British association for the advancement of
of science
Communication in science
Environmental sciences
Religion and science
Research
Scientific societies
Underdeveloped areas—Science
also headings beginning Scientific

Authorship
See Technical writing

Awards, prizes, etc.
See also
Kalinga prize

Bibliography
Book reviews. See issues of Science
Book reviews. See issues of Space world
Books. See issues of Physics today
Books. See issues of Science digest
Books of the week. See issues of Science
news
Books to come (cont) Library J 96:867-8+,
2383-5+, 3647+ Mr 1, Jl, N 1 '71
Emphasis is on here and now: April through
September science and technology books. il
Pub W 199:31-47 Ap 12 '71
Library at large. See issues of Chemistry
Reviews. See issues of Environment
Science & technology; a selection of books
planned for publication November, 1971
through May, 1972. il Pub W 200:29-42 N 15
'71
Sci-tech books '70; one hundred outstanding
titles for general library collections; comp.
by D. R. Pfoutz. il por Library J 96:781-92
Mr 1 '71

Experiments
See also
Experimental design

SCIENCE—*Continued*

Federal aid
See Research—Federal aid

Fiction
See Science fiction

History
See also
Biology—History
Electricity—History
Physics—History

Information services
Current physics information. H. W. Koch. bibliog il Science 174:918-22 N 26 '71
Keeping up with what's going on in physics; AIP's Current physics information program; with editorial comment. A. Herschman. bibliog il Phys Today 24:23-9. 80 N '71

International aspects
Consortium of academies: a new way to found international scholarly institutions. W. M. Todd and J. Voss. Bul Atom Sci 27:29-32 F '71
Crisis in science and UNESCO. W. N. Ellis. Bul Atom Sci 27:33-5 F '71
Growing ties between science and foreign policy; address, May 21, 1971. W. P. Rogers. Dept State Bul 64:766-8 Je 14 '71
Inquisitive mind; Unesco's work. W. McEwing. il UNESCO Courier 24:30-2+ Ag '71
International cooperation in science. C. MacLeod and H. A. Minners. Science 173:1085 S 17 '71
National science policy, prelude to global cooperation; statement to House committee on science and astronautics at meeting with Panel on science and technology, Jan. 26-28, 1971. E. Q. Daddario. por Bul Atom Sci 27:21-4 Je '71
Objectives of international cooperation in science and technology; statement, February 15, 1971. H. Pollack. Dept State Bul 64:837-41 Je 28 '71
Research and development: international cooperation; address, January 27, 1971. E. E. David, jr. Vital Speeches 37:311-13 Mr 1 '71
U.S.-Japan scientific committee meets at Tokyo; Department announcement with text of joint communique. Dept State Bul 65:197-8 Ag 23 '71
See also
International centre for theoretical physics, Trieste, Italy
United Nations—Advisory committee on the application of science and technology to development

Juvenile literature
See Scientific literature for children

Methodology
Access to data; letter. T. D. Sterling. Science 173:676-7 Ag 20 '71
Myth of teaching for critical thinking. B. Skinner. bibliog f Clear House 45:372-6 F '71
Sensuous-intellectual complementarity in science. T. R. Blackburn. bibliog Science 172:1003-7 Je 4 '71; Discussion. 173:1191-2+ S 24 '71
See also
Experimental design
Research

Moral aspects
See Science and ethics

Periodicals
U.K. science press: New scientist absorbs sibling Science journal. M. Butler. Science 171:157-60 Ja 15 '71
See also
Environment (periodical)
Science (periodical)

Philosophy
Books. G. Steiner. New Yorker 47:98+ Mr 6 '71
Sensuous-intellectual complementarity in science. T. R. Blackburn. bibliog Science 172:1003-7 Je 4 '71; Discussion. 173:1191-2+ S 24 '71
See also
Physics—Philosophy

Popularization
See Science news

Religious aspects
See Religion and science

Social aspects
Accelerating protons and social reform; National accelerator laboratory. C.-G. McDaniel. Chr Cent 88:1032-4 S 1 '71
General scientific association: a bridge to society at large; adaptation of address, March 22, 1971. W. Bevan. Science 172:349-52 Ap 23 '71
How scientists can really help; adaptation of address, October 26, 1970. M. Gell-Mann. il Phys Today 24:23-5 My '71
In defense of science. Time 97:56 Mr 8 '71
Mounting tide of unreason. E. Rabinowitch. por Bul Atom Sci 27:4-9 My '71
National science policy, prelude to global cooperation; statement to House committee on science and astronautics at meeting with Panel on science and technology, Ja. 26-28 ,1971. E. Q. Daddario. por Bul Atom Sci 27:21-4 Je '71
New frontiers of the mind; address, December 30, 1970. G. T. Seaborg. Vital Speeches 37:282-6 F 15 '71
New goal for science; excerpt from address. M. Tishler. il Sat R 54:56-8 Je 5 '71
On the social deployment of science. A. G. Mencher. il Bul Atom Sci 27:34-8 D '71
Public interest: new group seeks redefinition of scientists' role. C. Holden. il Science 173:131-2 Jl 9 '71
Science and our understanding of ourselves. L. L. Whyte. Bul Atom Sci 27:32-3 Mr '71
Social control of science and technology. M. S. Baram. bibliog il Science 172:535-9 My 7 '71
Social responsibility of the scientist, ed. by M. Brown. Review
Bul Atom Sci 27:36-7 Je '71. L. F. Gorr
What's happened to the brain business? P. Schrag. il Sat R 54:12-15+ Ag 7 '71
See also
British society for social responsibility

Study and teaching
Application of science principles to teaching. K. T. Henson. bibliog Clear House 46:143-6 N '71
Discovering the excitement of science. N. Roberts. il Am Ed 7:24-7 Jl '71
Inquisitive mind; Unesco's work. W. McEwing. il UNESCO Courier 24:30-7 Ag '71
See also
Nature study
Science teachers
Scientific education
also subhead Study and teaching under names of sciences, e.g. Physics—Study and teaching

Africa
Scientific safari to Africa. G. T. Seaborg; discussion. Science 172:987 Je 4 '71

China (People's Republic)
Chinese science: what the China watchers watch; China news analysis. D. Shapley. bibliog f Science 173:615-17 Ag 13 '71
From ping pong to science: cautious hope. Sci N 99:313 My 8 '71
Year of the dove? possible scientific exchange. D. Shapley. Science 172:457 Ap 30 '71

Great Britain
Letter from London:
Changing the guard. Aurum. Bul Atom Sci 27:42-3 F '71
Development and the Kalinga prize. Aurum. Bul Atom Sci 27:24+ Mr '71
Technology and democratic performance. Aurum. Bul Atom Sci 27:41-2 My; 25-6 Je '71

India
Science education in India. H. L. Strauss. Bul Atom Sci 27:10-13 Mr '71

Iran
Scientific legacy of Iran. D. Stewart. il UNESCO Courier 24:12-15 O '71

Russia
See also
Research—Russia

Underdeveloped areas
See Underdeveloped areas—Science

Vietnam (Democratic Republic)
Education and science in North Vietnam. A. W. Galston and E. Signer. bibliog Science 174:379-85 O 22 '71

SCIENCE (periodical)
AAAS: what it is and what it tries to do. P.
M. Boffey. Science 172:544-6 My 7 '71
Editing of Science. P. H. Abelson. Science
171:1101 Mr 19 '71
Instructions for contributors (cont) Science
171:xv-xvi Mr 26; Same. 172:xv-xvi Je 25;
173:xv-xvi S 24; 174:xv-xvi D 24 '71
Science censored. D. Shapley. Science 174:
273 O 15 '71
SCIENCE, Freedom of
Protecting the scientist. Sci N 100:61 Jl 24
'71
SCIENCE, Social. See Social sciences
SCIENCE and children. See Children and science
SCIENCE and civilization
Bus line in the sky and other expensive indignities. L. E. Sissman. Atlan 228:34-5 S
'71
Can science survive in the modern age? C. P.
Snow lecture, January 19, 1971. H. Brooks.
bibliog Science 174:21-30 O 1 '71
Good use of scientists; adaptation of address. J. Coulomb. Bul Atom Sci 27:39-41+
Ja '71
In defense of science; address, May 26, 1971.
P. Handler. Vital Speeches 37:715-20 S 15
'71
In defense of science; excerpts from address,
May 26, 1971. P. Handler. Science 172:1320
Je 25 '71
Mounting tide of unreason. E. Rabinowitch.
por Bul Atom Sci 27:4-9 My '71
Science alone is not enough. D. P. Young. il
por Chem 44:14-16 N '71
Science and society: some policy changes are
needed; adaptation of address, January 20,
1971. K. S. Pitzer. Science 172:223-6 Ap 16
'71
Science and technology: a positive outlook;
excerpts from address, May 27, 1971. W.
Von Braun. Space World H-11-95:24-5 N '71
Scientist as prophet. L. Eiseley. il Harper
243:96-8 N '71
Scientists as politicians. D. S. Greenberg. Cur
128:19-24 Ap '71
Those good new days; excerpt from address.
G. T. Seaborg. Sat R 54:52-3 Mr 6 '71
What's happened to the brain business? P.
Schrag. il Science 173:12-15+ Ag 7 '71
See also
Technology and civilization
SCIENCE and ethics
Science and human values. J. E. Wise. bibliog Sch & Soc 99:90-2 F '71
SCIENCE and industry. See Industrial research
SCIENCE and literature. See Literature and
science
SCIENCE and philosophy. See Philosophy and
science
SCIENCE and religion. See Religion and science
SCIENCE and society. See Science and civilization
SCIENCE and state
After the Pentagon papers: talk with Kistiakowsky, Wiesner; interviews, ed. by E.
Langer. J. Wiesner; G. Kistiakowsky. pors
Science 174:923-8 N 26 '71
Can democracy cope with man's predicament? E. Q. Daddario. Cur 133:9-16 O '71
David on neutrality of NAS, PSAC; excerpts
from interview. E. E. David. Science 174:
1109 D 10 '71
Era of big science; adaptation of address,
December 1970. E. Teller. il Bul Atom Sci
27:34-6 Ap '71
Federal government and the scientific community; address, December 26, 1970. P.
Handler. bibliog Science 171:144-51 Ja 15 '71;
Discussion. 172:425-7, 896+ Ap 30, My 28 '71
Good use of scientists; adaptation of address. J. Coulomb. Bul Atom Sci 27:39-41
Ja '71
Knowledge, power, and Democratic theory.
S. A. Lakoff. bibliog f Ann Am Acad 394:
4-12 Mr '71
Letter from London:
Technology and democratic performance.
Aurum. Bul Atom Sci 27:41-2 My; 25-6
Je '71
Letter from Washington:
Ministry of science, U.S. style. H. R.
Vohra. il Bul Atom Sci 27:29-32 Ja '71
Preventive technology: rival proposals
in Congress. H. R. Vohra. Bul Atom
Sci 27:25-6 Mr '71
Science in Congress. H. R. Vohra. Bul
Atom Sci 27:44-6 F '71
More favor for applied science. Sci N 99:44
Ja 16 '71
On the control of science; symposium. il
Bul Atom Sci 27:23-38 D '71

Prospects for physics support continue to
deteriorate. M. S. Rothenberg. il por Phys
Today 24:91-2 Ja '71
Research and development: international cooperation; address, January 27, 1971. E. E.
David, jr. Vital Speeches 37:311-13 Mr 1 '71
Science and policy for a new decade. C. P.
Haskins. bibliog f For Affairs 49:237-70 Ja
'71
Science policy. Sci N 99:50 Ja 16 '71
Science policy: an insider's view of LBJ,
DuBridge, and the budget. P. M. Boffey.
Science 171:874-6 Mr 5 '71
Scientist and public. chapter and verse from
David. D. Shapley. Science 172:1010 Je 4
'71
Senseless war on science. L. Lessing. il Fortune 83:88-91+ Mr '71
Steps toward a national policy for academic
science. C. M. York. bibliog il Science 172:
643-8 My 14 '71
See also
Social sciences and state
Technology and state
United States—National science foundation

Chile
Chile: planning for science faces obstacles
old and new. N. Hawkes. Science 174:1217-19
D 17 '71
Great Britain
British science policy: a crisis of confidence.
J. Walsh. Science 174:572-4 N 5 '71
Notes on science policy in Britain. Bul Atom
Sci 27:21-2 D '71
Russia
Medvedev papers, by Z. A. Medvedev. Review
Science 174:937 N 26 '71. R. Pipes
Singapore
Science and government in Singapore. R. S.
Bhathal. Bul Atom Sci 27:20-1+ Ja '71
SCIENCE and the humanities
English in a sea of science; address, November 1970. W. D. Boutwell. Engl J 60:326-32
Mr '71
Future literacy. G. Steiner. il Atlan 228:40-4
Ag '71
See also
Literature and science
SCIENCE as a profession
What are scientists like? M. Goodstein. bibliog il por Chem 44:11-13 S '71
See also
Chemistry as a profession
SCIENCE cities
See also
Akademgorodok, Siberia
SCIENCE education. See Scientific education
SCIENCE fiction
Books about it. T. Sturgeon. il Nat R 23:
1245-6 N 5 '71
Changing role of science fiction in children's
literature. S. L. Engdahl. il Horn Bk 47:
449-55 O '71
Father of science fiction. P. W. Schmidtchen.
il por Hobbies 76:135-6+ D '71
Future grok. R. Z. Sheppard. il Time 97:86+
Mr 29 '71
Science fiction and how it got that way. R.
Zelazny. Writer 84:15-17 My '71
Science fiction as education for change. L.
Ruth. Engl J 60:1243-51+ D '71
Science fiction: bridge between the two cultures. S. Schwartz. bibliog f Engl J 60:
1043-51 N '71
Science fiction: emerging from its exile in
limbo. J. Williamson. il Pub W 200:16-20
Jl 5 '71
What are people for? man, fate and Kurt Vonnegut. E. W. Ranly. il por Commonweal 94:
207-11 My 7 '71
See also
Moving pictures—Science fiction films

Drama
Day the Marsmen landed. R. K. Rybak.
Plays 30:37-42 Ap '71
My cousin from Tycho. C. Boiko. Plays 31:
37-46 N '71
Star fever. C. Boiko. Plays 30:15-24 Mr '71

Technique
Building four-dimensional people in science
fiction. J. Brunner. Writer 84:21-4 D '71

Themes
How, instead of being educated in college, I
was graduated from libraries; or, Thoughts
from a chap who landed on the moon in
1932; address, with questions and answers.
R. Bradbury. il por Wilson Lib Bul 45:842-
51 My '71

SCIENCE fiction writers of America
Nebula awards, 1971. il Am Lib 2:441 My '71
SCIENCE herbicide assessment commission. See
American association for the advancement
of science
SCIENCE in literature
See also
Science fiction
SCIENCE information. See Communication in
science
SCIENCE museums
San Francisco museum stresses involvement.
G. L. Matloff. il Phys Today 24:62 Je '71
SCIENCE news
Russian press reports on Soviet science. I.
Agnew. See issues of Science digest
Science and the popular press. J. J. Fortman
and others. Chem 44:20-1 O '71
Science month. See issues of Science digest
Science newsfront. A. Fisher. See issues of
Popular science monthly
Science worldwide. J. F. Pearson. See is-
sues of Popular mechanics
Search & discovery. See issues of Physics to-
day
See also
Medical news
SCIENCE service, inc.
NSF to the rescue. R. Gillette. Science 173:
218 Jl 16 '71
SCIENCE students
See also
Science talent search—1971 (30th)
SCIENCE talent search

1971 (30th)
Creative and skeptical. il Sci N 99:164 Mr 6
'71
Forty winners. Sci N 99:81 Ja 30 '71
SCIENCE teachers
Science teachers: ignored in a crisis; letter.
J. H. Woodburn. Science 171:127-8 Ja 15
'71
SCIENCE teaching. See Science—Study and
teaching
SCIENCE writing. See Technical writing
SCIENCES, Social. See Social sciences
SCIENTIFIC apparatus and instruments
New products. See fourth issue of each month
of Science news
Role of scientific instrumentation. P. H. Abel-
son. Science 174:1081 D 10 '71
Science junk: funding cuts make used equip-
ment pile up. D. Shapley. Science 171:879-
82 Mr 5 '71
See also
Physiological apparatus
Psychological apparatus
also names of scientific apparatus and
instruments, e.g. Microscope and micro-
scopy
SCIENTIFIC conferences
Aerospace calendar. See issues of Aviation
week & space technology
Calendar. See issues of Physics today
Forthcoming events. See occasional issues of
Science
Meetings. See issues of Science
See also
Astronomical conferences
Biological conferences
Gordon research conferences
Pugwash conferences on science and world
affairs
also subhead Conferences under names of
sciences, e.g. Molecular biology—Conferen-
ces
SCIENTIFIC education
Do-it-yourself science: Man-made world
project. il Newsweek 77:102 Ap 12 '71
One objective for science teaching; excerpts
from address, March 27, 1971. E. E. David,
jr. Science 172:901 My 28 '71
Science education in India. H. L. Strauss.
Bul Atom Sci 27:10-13 Mr '71
Science education, process or content? ex-
cerpt from The timely and the timeless. B.
Glass. Science 171:851 Mr 5 '71
What people know. R. J. Trotter. Sci N 99:306
My 1 '71
See also
Science—Study and teaching
SCIENTIFIC exchanges. See Exchange of per-
sons programs
SCIENTIFIC expeditions
Hovercraft to the heart of Africa; Trans-
african hovercraft expedition. il Sci Digest
70:38-45+ D '71
Hovercraft to the wilderness; Amazonas
hovercraft expedition. D. Smithers. il por
Sci Digest 70:8-17+ N '71
See also
Archeological expeditions
Challenger expedition, 1872-1876

SCIENTIFIC freedom. See Science, Freedom of
SCIENTIFIC illustration
See also
Medical illustration
SCIENTIFIC information. See Communication
in science
SCIENTIFIC information services. See Science
—Information services
SCIENTIFIC instruments. See Scientific ap-
paratus and instruments
SCIENTIFIC libraries
See also
New York public library—Science and tech-
nology division
SCIENTIFIC literature
Sociology of refereeing. H. Zuckerman and
R. K. Merton. bibliog il Phys Today 24:28-
33 Jl '71
See also
Information storage and retrieval systems—
Science
Publishers and publishing—Scientific litera-
ture
Science—Bibliography
SCIENTIFIC literature for children
Views on science books. H. C. Stubbs. See
issues of Horn book magazine

Bibliography
Books about science for the younger reader:
an annual Christmas survey. P. Morrison
and P. Morrison. Sci Am 225:106-15 D '71
SCIENTIFIC method. See Science—Methodol-
ogy
SCIENTIFIC names. See subhead Nomencla-
ture under various subjects, e.g. Zoology—
Nomenclature
SCIENTIFIC news. See Science news
SCIENTIFIC research. See Research
SCIENTIFIC societies
Consortium of academies: a new way to
found international scholarly institutions.
W. M. Todd and J. Voss. Bul Atom Sci 27:
29-32 F '71
Reflections on the decline of science in Amer-
ica and on some of its causes; adaptation
of address, March 22, 1971. A. Thackray.
bibliog Science 173:27-31 Jl 2 '71
See also
American association for the advancement
of science
British association for the advancement of
science
SCIENTIFIC writing. See Technical writing
SCIENTIST-astronauts. See Astronauts
SCIENTISTS
Good use of scientists; adaptation of ad-
dress. J. Coulomb. Bul Atom Sci 27:39-41 Ja
'71
On trying to understand scientific genius.
G. Holton. bibliog Am Scholar 41:95-110
Wint '71
Role of scientists: thoughts for 1971; adap-
tation of address, September 9, 1970. E.
Rabinowitch. por Bul Atom Sci 27:2-4 Ja
'71
Scientists and citizens: when are they differ-
ent? Sci N 101:21-2 Ja 8 '72
Should you marry a scientist? M. Goran. por
Chem 44:16 Ap '71
Social responsibility of the scientist, ed. by
M. Brown. Review
Bul Atom Sci 27:36-7 Je '71. L. F. Gorr
See also
Chemists
Engineers
Physicists
Science as a profession
Women as scientists

Poetry
Curriculum vitae: a man of his times. J.
Walsh. Science 172:1218 Je 18 '71

Political activities
After the Pentagon papers: talk with Kis-
tiakowsky, Wiesner; interviews, ed. by E.
Langer. J. Wiesner; G. Kistiakowsky. pors
Science 174:923-8 N 26 '71
Politics and scholarship; reprint. Science 174:
1187. D 17 '71
Sakharov: a man for our times. W. C.
Clemens, jr. il Bul Atom Sci 27:4-6+ D
'71
Science is too important to stay out of
politics; letter. L. D. Longo and G. G.
Power. Science 171:334 Ja 29 '71
See also
British society for social responsibility
Federation of American scientists
Scientists and engineers for social and polit-
ical action (organization)

SCIENTISTS—*Continued*

Supply and demand

Hard times for scientists. Time 97:48 Ap 12 '71

Job prospects: science graduates face worst year in two decades. D. Shapley. Science 172:823-4 My 21 '71

Manpower in science and engineering, based on a saturation model; adaptation of address, November 23, 1970. W. R. Brode. bibliog il Science 173:206-13 Jl 16 '71

Quaint minority group. Newsweek 77:60-1 Ap 5 '71

Scientific manpower for 1970-1985; adaptation of address. December 27, 1970. A. M. Carter. bibliog il Science 172:132-40 Ap 9 '71; Discussion. 173:6-7; 174:771-2 Jl 2, N 19 '71

Statement of Senator Edward M. Kennedy on re-employing defense scientists and engineers. E. M. Kennedy. por Bul Atom Sci 27:41-3 Mr '71

Story of a science depression. il U S News 70:24-6 Ja 25 '71

Supply of scientific and engineering manpower: surplus or shortage? F. E. Terman. bibliog il Science 173:399-405 Jl 30 '71

Training scientists for new jobs. P. H. Abelson. Science 174:651 N 12 '71

Underemployment of scientists and engineers. P. H. Abelson. Science 172:221 Ap 16 '71

Unemployment: what Nixon is/isn't doing to help jobless scientists. P. M. Boffey. Science 171:985-7 Mr 12 '71

When the brains can't get work. il Bsns W p90-2+ F 13 '71

See also
Brain drain
Chemists—Supply and demand
Physicists—Supply and demand

SCIENTISTS, Amateur

Amateur scientist; ed. by C. L. Stong. See issues of Scientific American

SCIENTISTS, American

See also
Federation of American scientists
National register of scientific and technical personnel

SCIENTISTS, Exchange of. See Exchange of persons programs

SCIENTISTS, German

Project Paperclip. by C. G. Lasby. Review Sat R 54:39-40 D 11 '71. S. Schultz

SCIENTISTS, Professional ethics for

Nader and the scientists: a call for responsibility. P. M. Boffey. Science 171:549-51 F 12 '71

Nuclear physics: does competition breed a monstrous game? N. Wade. Science 174:932 N 26 '71

Time to take stock. J. R. Pierce. Science 172:115 Ap 9 '71

SCIENTISTS, Russian

Dissent in Russia: the thin wedge. il por Newsweek 77:29-34 F 1 '71

Science in Siberia. W. R. Shelton. il Bul Atom Sci 27:23-8 F '71

See also
Russia—Intellectual life
Sakharov, A. D.

SCIENTISTS and engineers for social and political action (organization)

Visitors ask M.I.T. faculty to renounce military research. T. P. Southwick. Science 171:156 Ja 15 '71; Reply. L. Grodzins. 172:214+ Ap 16 '71

SCIENTISTS as astronauts. See Astronauts

SCIENTISTS in government

Administration talent search: alternatives to the buddy system. N. Wade. por Science 173:1216-18 S 24 '71

SCIENTISTS' Institute for public information

Another SST? complaint filed against Atomic energy comission. Environ 13:18-19 Jl '71

SCIENTOLOGY

FDA versus scientology. Chr Today 15:21 Je 4 '71

Setback for scientology; loss of libel action in Britain. J. D. Douglas. Chr Today 15:33 Ja 29 '71

SCILKEN, Marvin H.

Information exchange. il Wilson Lib Bul 46:104-5 S '71

SCINTILLATION of stars. See Stars—Scintillation

SCISSORS and shears

Electric scissors; battery-operated. il Consumer Bul 54:27 Mr '71

Kitchen cutups. il Bet Hom & Gard 49:102 O '71

SCLERODERMA

Scleroderma and the subcutaneous tissue. R. Fleischmajer and others. bibliog il Science 171:1019-21 Mr 12 '71

SCLEROSIS, Multiple

Farm practices influencing the incidence of multiple sclerosis. J. A. Shield. bibliog il Org Gard & Farm 18:102-6+ Ap '71

Picking up the pieces. M. Shonbrun. il Good H 172:10+ F '71

SCOBEY, Joan. See McGrath, L. P. jt. auth.

SCOBIE, W. I.

Mau-mauing Dr Teller. Nat R 23:697-8 Je 29 '71

Theater (cont) Nat R 23:714-15 Je 29 '71

SCOFIELD, John

Lower Keys, Florida's out islands. il Nat Geog 139:72-93 Ja '71

SCOPES. See Oscillographs

SCOPPA, Bud, and others

DISCussions. See issues of Senior scholastic

SCOTCH whiskey. See Whiskey

SCOTLAND

See also
Cairngorm Mountains
Hebrides
Highlands of Scotland
Hunting—Scotland

Description and travel

With Scott in the land of Brigadoon. V. Waite. il Sat R 54:37-9+ Mr 13 '71

SCOTLAND, Church of. See Church of Scotland

SCOTT, Byron

Give a damn heals. il Todays Health 49:38-40 Ap '71

SCOTT, Carole B.

Hi mom, what's for lunch? il Parents Mag 46:26 Jl; 35 S; 98 O; 105 N; 18 D '71

SCOTT, Charlie

Charlie is their darling. P. Carry. il por Sports Illus 34:69+ Mr 22 '71 *

SCOTT, David C.

Allis: the turnaround got stuck. il por Bsns W p96-7 Mr 13 '71 *

SCOTT, David R.

Apollo 15: three views of the moon. il Read Digest 99:72-4 N '71

about

High-flying crew for Apollo. por Time 98:39 Ag 2 '71 *

Mission into the moon's past. E. Driscoll. il pors Sci N 100:28-30 Jl 10 '71 *

See also
Space flight to the moon—Manned flights—Apollo 15 flight

SCOTT, Dorothea

Persistence of Indonesian libraries. bibliog il Wilson Lib Bul 45:976-82 Je '71

SCOTT, Elizabeth

Breathtaking; poem. Liv Wildn 34:62 Aut '70

SCOTT, Emily

Relieving anxiety through art activity in an inner city school. bibliog il Sch Arts 70:44-6 Mr '71

SCOTT, George C.

Reluctant Oscars; interview, ed. by C. Irving. pors McCalls 98:12+ Jl '71

Scott on some aspects of acting. Time 97:66 Mr 22 '71

about

George C. Scott: nothing ever really helps. B. Rollin. il pors Look 35:78-80+ Ap 20 '71 *

George C. Scott: tempering a terrible fire. il pors Time 97:63-6+ Mr 22 '71 *

In search of evil. H. Alpert. Sat R 54:40 My 8 '71 *

Meat parade. por Time 97:40 Mr 8 '71 *

SCOTT, Harold B.

As I see it; interview. il por Forbes 108:43-4+ O 1 '71

SCOTT, Hazel

Hazel weaves a new black magic. T. Thompson por Life 70:14 Je 18 '71 *

SCOTT, Jack

It's not how you play the game, but what pill you take. il N Y Times Mag p40-1+ O 17 '71

Sports. Ramp Mag 10:67-8 O; 68-70 N; 65-8 D '71; 64 Ja '72

about

Jack Scott draws blood from sportsmanship. P. Axthelm. Vogue 157:163 Ap 1 '71 *

Jeremiah of Jock liberation. il por Time 97:88-9+ My 24 '71 *

SCOTT, Jack Denton

Even muskrats believe in life insurance. il Nat Wildlife 9:58-61 O '71

No one badgers the badger. il Nat Wildlife 9:18-20 F '71

Snow free. il Nat Wildlife 10:41-3 D '71

Steer clear of the grizzly. il Nat Wildlife 9:12-15 Je '71

SCOTT, John
Electronic data processing in urban government. il Am City 86:69-72 My '71
—See Laird, C. W. jt. auth.
SCOTT, John (playwright)
Ride a black horse. Criticism
New Yorker 47:100 Je 5 '71 •
SCOTT, June Gyneth
Whoa! Where are you heading? Har Yrs 11:
33 My '71
SCOTT, Linton
Flight unlimited. il pors Ebony 26:123-4+
O '71 •
SCOTT, Michael R.
In Stendhal's footsteps: an opera junket.
il Opera N 35:10-11 Ap 17 '71
SCOTT, Ralph L.
$1,000 misunderstanding: UM's index to its
Dissertation abstracts international. Wilson
Lib Bul 46:73-6 S '71
SCOTT, Robert E.
Proceedings and findings pertaining to a
request for action submitted by Robert E.
Scott, under the Program of action in
support of the Library bill of rights. Am Lib
2:316-17 Mr '71 •
SCOTT, Robert F.
All about scanning monitor receivers. il Ra-
dio-Electr 42:58-9+ D '71
New color circuits for '72. il Radio-Electr
43:42-5 Ja '72
Technical topics (cont) il Radio-Electr 42:
51-3 Mr; 62-3+ My; 62-3+ N '71
Those new turntables. il Radio-Electr 42:61-3
Je '71
SCOTT, Stephen C.
Nevergreen in Groton: special news analysis.
il pors Wilson Lib Bul 45:818-20+ My '71
SCOTT, Vernon
Gunsmoke's mysterious... il pors Ladies
Home J 88:90+ My '71
(ed) See Palette, P. John Wayne: his wife ex-
plains the man behind the legend
SCOTT, Sir Walter, bart
Sir Walter Scott, by E. Johnson. Review
New Yorker 47:117-23 F 20 '71. W. H.
Auden •
With Scott in the land of Brigadoon. V.
Waite. il Sat R 54:37-9+ Mr 13 '71 •
SCOTT, Winfield Townley
Growing up in Newport; excerpts from Alpha
omega. il Am Heritage 22:54-7+ Ag '71
SCOTT family
Scott coat-of-arms. H. K. Eilers. il Hobbies
76:138-9 S '71
SCOTT paper company
Dunning of Scott paper. por Forbes 107:192
My 15 '71
His job: to turn Scott around. por Bsns W
p46 Ag 21 '71
SCOTTISH HIGHLANDS. See Highlands of
Scotland
SCOTTISH pistols. See Pistols
SCOTTSBORO, Ala.
Alabama's magic Monday. J. Goodrum. il
Travel 135:34-9+ Mr '71
SCOTTSDALE, Ariz.
Scottsdale's new civic center. il Arch Rec
149:119-24 Mr '71
SCOURING pads
Scouring pads and powders. il Consumer Rep
36:489-91 Ag '71
SCOURING powders. See Cleaning composi-
tions
SCOURS in swine. See Swine—Diseases and
pests
SCOUTING, Baseball. See Baseball scouting
SCOUTING, Football. See Football scouting
SCOUTS and scouting
    See also
Boy scouts
SCOVIL, H. E. D. See Bobeck, A. H. jt. auth.
SCOVILL, Janet
Understanding myself and others. por Sr
Schol 98:14 F 15 '71
SCOVILLE, Herbert, Jr
Latest red scare. New Repub 164:16-19 My
15 '71
Limitation of offensive weapons; with
biographical sketch. il Sci Am 224:12, 15-
25 bibliog(p 122) Ja '71
Missile myths. New Repub 165:17-19 O 2;
19-20 O 9; 33 D 25 '71
SCOVILLE, John
Kitchens. M. Davidson. il pors Ladies Home
J 88:26 Je '71 •
SCRAGG, Alan H. and others
Cell-free protein synthesizing system from
yeast mitochondria. bibliog il Science 171:
908-10 Mr 5 '71
SCRAPIE (disease) See Sheep—Diseases and
pests

SCRATCH; drama. See MacLeish, A.
SCREEN actors' guild
Screen hopefuls battle the stars. Bsns W p95-
6 N 20 '71
SCREEN doors. See Screens (doors, windows,
etc)
SCREEN painting, Japanese. See Painting, Ja-
panese
SCREEN printing. See Silk screen printing
SCREEN writing. See Moving picture author-
ship
SCREENPLAYS. See Moving picture scripts
SCREENS; drama. See Genet, J.
SCREENS (doors, windows, etc)
Sliding screens get it all together. il House B
113:70 N '71
SCREENS (fences) See Fences
SCREENS (furniture)
Movable feasts; Japanese screens. A. Soper.
il Art N 69:40-3+ F '71
SCREENS (photography) See Photography—
Processing—Apparatus and supplies
SCREW (periodical)
No place to go but up. il pors Time 97:65
Ap 19 '71
SCREW threads
Racer's threads, do-it-yourself sparkplug-port
repair kit. il Pop Mech 135:180 F '71
SCRIABIN, Alexander Nicholaevich. See Skria-
bin, A. N.
SCRIBNER, Charles, 1921-
Some thoughts on a 125th anniversary; in-
terview. il por Pub W 200:24-5 S 6 '71
SCRIBNER, Harvey Bertram
Imperatives in urban education; address.
July 16, 1971. Vital Speeches 37:669-72 Ag
15 '71
    about
Chancellor Harvey Scribner: the most power-
ful man in the school system, on paper.
J. Lelyveld. il pors N Y Times Mag p30-1+
Mr 21 '71 •
SCRIBNER'S, Charles, sons
Some thoughts on a 125th anniversary; inter-
view. C. Scribner, jr. il por Pub W 200:
24-5 S 6 '71
SCRIMSHAW, Nevin S. See Young, V. R. jt.
auth.
SCRIPPS submarine canyon. See Submarine
valleys
SCRIPT writing, Audio-visual. See Audio-
visual script authorship
SCRIPT writing, Television. See Television
authorship
SCRIPTS, Moving pictures. See Moving picture
scripts
SCRIPTURES. See Bible
SCRIVEN, Eldon G. and Harrison, A. Jr
Student dress codes. Ed Digest 36:40-1 F '71
SCROLLS from the Dead Sea. See Dead Sea
scrolls
SCRUBBERS (chemical technology)
Sulfur is the major problem. il Bsns W p56+
F 6 '71
SCUBA diving. See Skin diving
SCULL, David
Legacy of David Scull. J. E. Roper. por Read
Digest 99:33-6 Ag '71 •
SCULLY, Ed
Ed Scully on color. See issues of Modern
photography
Photo education. See issues of Modern pho-
tography. October 1970-
SCULLY, Julia
Photo education. il Mod Phot 36:64+ Ja
'72
Seeing pictures. See issues of Modern pho-
tography
SCULPTORS
    See also
Sculpture
SCULPTORS materials. See Artists materials
SCULPTURE
Value of playground sculpture. S. Gendusa.
il Parks & Rec 6:39+ Jl '71
    See also
Animal sculpture
Bronzes
Carving (art industries)
Ceramic sculpture
Garden ornaments
Horses in art
Human figure in art
Metal sculpture
Modeling
Monuments
Plastic sculpture
Portrait sculpture
Relief (sculpture)
Wire sculpture
Wood sculpture

SCULPTURE—*Continued*

Competitions
See Art—Competitions

Private collections
See Art—Private collections

Study and teaching
Children's sculpture. J. W. Burgner. il Sch Arts 71:42-4 O '71

Figures of clay and plaster. C. Heiple. il Sch Arts 71:28-9 O '71

Functional sculpture. T. K. Stevens. il Sch Arts 71:26-7 O '71

Non-objective sculpture. E. G. Zang. il Sch Arts 71:26-7 S '71

See also
Modeling

Materials
Art from dry plant stems. F. Walker. il Sch Arts 70:17-21 F '71

Beach stone sculpture. P. A. Sladek. il Sch Arts 70:29 F '71

Found object sculpture. J. Comins. il Sch Arts 70:14-15 F '71

Making it in 3-D. E. Stein. il Sch Arts 71:10-13 O '71

See also
Papier-mâché

Technique
Tony Smith: talk about sculpture; interview, ed. by L. R. Lippard. T. Smith. il Art N 70:48-9+ Ap '71

See also
Modeling

SCULPTURE, African
African sculpture at Notre Dame. il Design 72:41 Sum '71

Collector collects; Gaston de Havenon collection. L. Hess. il Harp Baz 104:186 S '71

Dance of the Chi Wara; Gaston de Havenon collection. B. Forgery. il Art N 70:46-9+ Sum '71

Makonde sculpture. J. L. Block. il Craft Horiz 31:31-2+ Ap '71

SCULPTURE, American
Don Judd's less is more art. B. Rose. il Vogue 158:88 Jl '71

George Quix, or Don Quixote? il Design 73:31-3 Fall '71

Marble and nudity. W. H. Gerdts. il Art in Am 59:60-7 My '71

See also
Andre, C.
Arnold, A.
Beesley, J. C.
Bufano, B. B.
Davidson, J.
Di Suvero, M.
Fogel, J.
Frank, M.
Greenough, H.
Jonas, L. P.
Judd, D.
Liberman, A.
Lipton, S.
Nevelson, L.
Newman, B.
Reynal, J.
Serra, R.

SCULPTURE, Ancient
Cincinnati's new look. K. Kuh. il Sat R 54:34-5 F 27 '71

Sacred source of the Seine; Celtic sculpture as offerings to goddess. S. A. Deyts. il Sci Am 225:65-73 Jl '71

SCULPTURE, Architectural. See Decoration and ornament, Architectural

SCULPTURE, British
See also
Newman, R.
Paolozzi, E.

SCULPTURE, Canadian
See also
Vaillancourt, A.

SCULPTURE, Celtic. See Sculpture, Ancient

SCULPTURE, Childrens. See Childrens art

SCULPTURE, Chilean
See also
Dominguez, L.

SCULPTURE, Egyptian
Split king; broken statue of Ny-user-ra in Cairo fits Rochester fragment. il Time 97:53 Je 21 '71

SCULPTURE, English. See Sculpture, British

SCULPTURE, European
Three artists in three dimensions: Louis Pons, Jean Amado, and Aeppli. M. Gibson. il Art in Am 59:112-13 Ja '71

SCULPTURE, French
See also
Aslan
Dubuffet, J.
Lipchitz, J.

SCULPTURE, German
See also
Marcks, G.

SCULPTURE, Greek
Archeological find named Iris Love; Praxiteles's Aphrodite of Knidos. E. Stevens. il pors N Y Times Mag p32-4+ Mr 7 '71; Discussion. p 16+ Ap 4 '71

When Love came to Cnidus. Cyclops. il Life 70:18 Je 11 '71

SCULPTURE, Italian
See also
Lucchesi, B.

SCULPTURE, Metal. See Metal sculpture

SCULPTURE, Mobile. See Mobiles

SCULPTURE, Persian
Sassanian royal hunt. il UNESCO Courier 24:34-8 O '71

SCULPTURE, Photography of. See Photography of works of art

SCULPTURE, Pre-Columbian
Before Cortés. E. P. Benson. il Américas 23:5̄2-11 Je '71

Making the gallery scene; ancient art of the New World. B. Wasserman. il Sch Arts 71:30-3 O '71

SCULPTURE, Snow. See Snow modeling

SCULPTURE of children. See Children in art

SCURVY
Once a limey, never a squirt. Sr Schol 98:8 F 8 '71

SCYLLAC devices. See Plasma (ionized gases)

SCYTHIANS
Tracking the Scythians. il Time 99:36 Ja 17 '72

SEA. See Ocean

SEA-air interaction. See Ocean-atmosphere interaction

SEA anemones
Anemone's strange attachment. D. P. de Sylva. il Sea Front 17:213 Jl '71

Biphasic feeding response in a sea anemone: control by asparagine and glutathione. K. J. Lindstedt. bibliog il Science 173:333-4 Jl 23 '71

SEA bathing. See Swimming

SEA beaches. See Beaches

SEA birds
Shore theater; drama by dawn's early light. M. Mayer. il Holiday 49:36-7 Jl '71

Accidents and hazards
See Birds—Accidents and hazards

SEA burials. See Burial at sea

SEA coasts. See Coasts

SEA crows. See Skimmers (birds)

SEA floor. See Ocean bottom

SEA-floor spreading. See Ocean bottom

SEA food
See also
Cookery—Sea food
Shellfish

SEA food salads. See Salads

SEA grant programs, Office of. See United States—Sea grant programs, Office of

SEA ice. See Ice—Polar Regions

SEA ISLANDS
Sea Islands. J. Cerruti. il Nat Geog 139:366-93 Mr '71

See also
Cumberland Island

SEA-level canal. See Canals—Central America

SEA level changes
Sea level as affected by river runoff, eastern United States. R. H. Meade and K. O. Emery. bibliog il Science 173:425-8 Jl 30 '71

What would happen if the ice-caps melted? I. Asimov. Sci Digest 71:79-80 Ja '72

SEA life. See Seafaring life

SEA lions. See Seals (animals)

SEA oats. See Grasses

SEA OF CORTEZ. See California, Gulf of

SEA otters
Otter life. M. Shearly. Nat Parks & Con Mag 45:35 Ap '71

Return of the sea otter. K. W. Kenyon. il Nat Geog 140:520-39 O '71

Sea otters ambushed. il Nat Parks & Con Mag 45:32-4+ Ap '71

SEA PINES plantation, S.C. See Housing projects
SEA planes. See Seaplanes
SEA power
Erosion of surface naval power. P. Cohen. For Affairs 49:330-41 Ja '71
Look at U.S.-Soviet rivalry in the Mediterranean; interview. I. C. Kidd, jr. il por U S News 71:110-11 N 15 '71
Mediterranean tide runs for the Russians. A. De Borchgrave. il Newsweek 78:34-5 Jl 19 '71
SEA serpents
Sea serpents: what they really are; rotting carcass of basking shark. D. Cohen. il Sci Digest 69:27-8 Mr '71
  See also
Loch Ness monster
SEA slugs
Giant brain cells in mollusks. A. O. D. Willows. il Sci Am 224:68-75 F '71
Naked gills and recycled stings. W. Zeiller. il Natur Hist 80:36-41 D '71
SEA snakes
Consequences of a sea-level canal. R. H. Gilluly. il Sci N 99:52-3 Ja 16 '71
Panama Canal warning: possibility of yellow-bellied sea snake and crown-of-thorns starfish in Atlantic with sea-level canal. Sr Schol 98:9 Mr 29 '71
Sea snakes: an unusual salt gland under the tongue. W. A. Dunson and others. bibliog il Science 173:437-41 Jl 30 '71
Sea snakes are coming. W. A. Dunson. il Natur Hist 80:52-61 N '71
SEA songs
  See also
Sailors songs
SEA stars. See Starfishes
SEA travel. See Ocean travel
SEA urchins
Pink urchin of the deep sea. J. W. Hoyt. il Sea Front 17:140-5 My '71
Sea urchin embryos are permeable to actinomycin. G. A. Greenhouse and others. bibliog il Science 171:686-9 F 19 '71
Underwater battle; southern California's Pacific coastline. G. T. Bowden. il Parks & Rec 6:22-4 Jl '71
SEA venture (ship) See Ocean liners
SEA water
Hot spots in the Red Sea. L. Purrett. il Sci N 99:388-9 Je 5 '71
Magnesium-iron replacement in clay minerals in anoxic marine sediments. J. I. Drever. bibliog il Science 172:1334-6 Je 25 '71
Seawater can be a-wham-peaceful retriever of health. il Harp Baz 104:84-5 My '71
  Desalting
Arid land agriculture: Shaikh up in Arizona research. R. J. Bazell. il Science 171:989-90 Mr 12 '71
How is desalination used to make sea water drinkable? Sci Digest 70:45 Jl '71
  Pollution
  See Marine pollution
SEA waves. See Waves
SEABED. See Ocean bottom
SEABED treaty
Exempting the seas; 63 nations sign. il Newsweek 77:45 F 22 '71
Law for the seas. W. Smith. Nat Parks & Con Mag 45:2+ Je '71
No deep secrets. Sr Schol 98:13-14 Mr 8 '71
Seabed arms control treaty transmitted to the Senate; President Nixon's message, Secretary Rogers' report. R. Nixon and W. Rogers. Dept State Bul 65:185-7 Ag 16 '71
To guard the sea. E. Young. For Affairs 50:136-47 O '71
Treaty banning emplacement of nuclear weapons on the seabed signed by 62 nations at Washington; remarks by Secretary Rogers, British Ambassador Lord Cromer, Soviet Ambassador Anatoliy F. Dobrynin, and President Nixon at the signing ceremony. Dept State Bul 64:288-90 Mr 8 '71
SEABOARD coast line railroad company
Overland cruise to Florida; auto-bearing passenger train from Alexandria, Va. to Sanford, Fla. il Time 98:91 N 8 '71
SEABORG, Glenn T.
General conference of the International atomic energy agency holds 15th session at Vienna; statement, September 22, 1971. Dept State Bul 65:419-24 O 18 '71
New frontiers of the mind; address, December 30, 1970. Vital Speeches 37:282-6 F 15 '71
Nuclear power plants, boon or blight? il por Nat Wildlife 9:21-3 Ap '71

Scientific safari to Africa. il Science 169:554-61; 172:987 Ag 7 '70, Je 4 '71
Those good new days; excerpt from address. Sat R 54:52-3 Mr 6 '71
  about
Change at the AEC. pors Time 98:47 Ag 2 '71 *
Glenn T. Seaborg, president-elect 1971. G. F. Tape. por Science 171:707-9 F 19 '71 *
On misunderstanding the atom; adaptation of address, March 22, 1971. il por Bul Atom Sci 27:46-53 S '71
Seaborg will leave AEC. C. Holden. il por Science 173:407 Jl 30 '71 *
SEABURY, Paul
Berkeley: a tale of one city. Commentary 52:66-72 Ag '71
SEAFARING life
  History
Mad Jack and the missionaries. L. McKee. il pors Am Heritage 22:30-7+ Ap '71
SEAFOOD
  See also
Fish as food
SEAGER, Laura
All the pretty little horses; story. Mlle 73:197 My '71
SEAGRAM, Joseph E, and sons
Seagram's hears the suburbs calling. il Bsns W p48 S 11 '71
SEAGULL, Louis M.
Youth vote and change in American politics. bibliog f il Ann Am Acad 397:88-96 S '71
SEAL hunting
Slaughter of the seals. il Sci N 100:188 S 18 '71
SEALANTS. See Sealing compounds
SEALE, Bobby G.
Black Panther thrust in American revolution. R. Chrisman. il Sat R 54:35-8 Jl 24 '71 *
Bobby and Ericka: free at last, until next time. A. Goldberg. Ramp Mag 10:45-8 Ag '71 *
Bobby Seale's birthday cake. J. A. Lukas. il por N Y Times Mag p42+ O 31 '71 *
Freed in New Haven. pors Time 97:12-13 Je 7 '71 *
Trials of the system. il por Newsweek 77:27-8 Je 7 '71 *
SEALE, William
History in houses. il Antiques 100:241-5 Ag '71
SEALING (technology)
Dam the water; cure for leaks. T. Tappett. il Mech Illus 67:98-100+ Mr '71
SEALING compounds
Product of the month; Loctite, the liquid safety wire. B. Bryan. il Hot Rod 24:114-15 Ag '71
Sealants & bedding compounds. J. Duffett. Motor B & S 127:94 Ap '71
  See also
Caulking compounds
SEALS (animals)
Aggression of the breeding bulls; elephant seals. B. J. Le Boeuf. il Natur Hist 80:82-94 F '71
Fur seals are coming back to California. R. S. Peterson and B. J. Le Boeuf. il Sci Digest 69:74-9 Ap '71
Leptospirosis epizootic among California sea lions. N. A. Vedros and others. bibliog il Science 172:1250-1 Je 18 '71
New York seal data sheet. bibliog il Cons 26:32-3 Ag '71
Tropical seals; Hawaiian monk seals. G. C. Whittow. il Sea Front 17:285-7 S '71
SEALS of approval. See Commercial products, Certification of
SEAMAN, Elizabeth (Cochrane) See Cochrane, E.
SEAMANSHIP
Racing clinic. D. Rose; G. Hall. See issues of Yachting
Seasoned skipper. il Motor B & S 128:62-3+ Jl; 14+ Ag; 8+ S; 26+ O '71
  See also
Knots and splices
Navigation
SEAMEN
Jobs at sea. il Changing T 25:45-7 My '71
Seamen and modernization of merchant shipping: 55th International (maritime) labor conference, Geneva, Switzerland. J. P. Goldberg. Mo Labor R 94:49-54 F '71
  See also
Negro seamen
Seafaring life
  History
Sailing by Caravel; age of discovery. F. Romero. il Américas 23:S7-10 O '71

SEAMER, Lorraine
Pocketful of treasure. por Hobbies 75:144 F '71
SEAMON, James M.
Introduction to modern Polish literature. bibliog Engl J 60:38-41 Ja '71
SEAMOUNTS. See Ocean bottom
SEAMS
Gluing a fine seam. Chem 44:3 My '71
SEANCES. See Spiritualism
SEAPLANE bases
New York city studies hydroport usage. R. S. Kahn. il Aviation W 95:29-30 S 20 '71
SEAPLANES
STOL flying boat makes a splash. P. Wahl. il Pop Sci 198:54 My '71
   See also
Airplanes, Amphibious
SEARCH and rescue operations
   See also
Missing persons—Search and rescue operations
SEARCH warrants. See Warrants (law)
SEARCHES and seizures
Ballew raid. J. Mann. New Repub 165:12-13 S 11 '71
From Burger: a call for action to stop freeing the guilty. por U S News 71:33 Jl 5 '71
Judicial attempts to control the police. L. P. Tiffany. bibliog f Cur Hist 61:13-19+ Jl '71
Mapp v. Ohio, 1961. Cur Hist 61:43-5 Jl '71
SEARCY, Charles M.
I remember Vietnam; address, May 4, 1971. il Chr Cent 88:828-30 Jl 7 '71
SEARLE, G. D, and company
Tax man smiles. Forbes 107:41 Mr 15 '71
SEARLE, Ronald
Dissertation on the beaver; cartoons; with biographical sketch. il Natur Hist 80:4, 8+ Je '71
SEARLES, John R.
(comp) More sources of free and inexpensive material. Engl J 60:797-804 S '71
—and Blount, N. S.
(eds) Teaching materials. See Issues of English journal
SEARS, Jerry A.
Unintentional discoveries. bibliog il por Chem 44:16-18 Ja '71
SEARS, Stephen W.
Hell's highway to Arnhem. il Am Heritage 22:60-3+ Je '71
SEARS, Roebuck and company
Everything's rosy in Sears, Roebuck country. il Fortune 84:34 O '71
Sears allies itself with Latin progress. V. Louviere. il Nations Bsns 59:17 Je '71
Sears strikes again. il Forbes 108:19 D 15 '71
Sears way. A. A. Butkus. Duns 97:54-6 Mr '71
   See also
Allstate insurance company
SEARS women's world classic. See Golf—Tournaments
SEASCAPE photography. See Photography—Marines
SEASHORE
   See also
Beaches
Coasts
SEASHORE houses. See Beach architecture
SEASICKNESS
Sway of the grand saloon; excerpts. J. M. Brinnin. il Am Heritage 22:16-19+ O '71
SEASIDE resorts
Southern California beaches. L. Burton. il Travel 135:28-35+ Ap '71
        History
Once more on to the beach; with paintings. G. Carson. il Am Heritage 22:58-80+ Ag '71
        Bahama Islands
Fly-in resorts; table. Flying 89:51 N '71
        Dominican Republic
Place in the sun; Punta Caña club. il Forbes 108:21 O 15 '71
        England
   See also
Blackpool, England
        France
France's new Riviera; Languedoc-Roussillon coast. T. Mackay. il Travel 135:28-33 Je '71
        Israel
Four seas of Israel. S. Goodstone. il Holiday 48:54-7+ N '70
        Spain
Golden ruler. il Newsweek 79:54-5 Ja 10 '72

SEASONAL industries
   See also
Construction industry
SEASONAL labor
   See also
Migrant labor
SEASONINGS
   See also
Garlic
Herbs
Salt
SEASONS
   See also
Autumn
Spring
Summer
Winter
SEAT belts, Automobile. See Automobiles—Safety belts
SEATRAIN lines, inc.
Drawing to an inside straight. il Forbes 107:26 F 1 '71
Order at the docks; terminal at Weehauken, N.J. il Arch Forum 134:32-5 Ap '71
SEATS
   See also
Airplanes—Seats
Motorcycles—Seats
SEATTLE
        Air pollution
Mt Rainier: now you see it, now you don't. G. S. Zeigler and others. bibliog il Weatherwise 24:114-19 Je '71
        Airports
Airport ends the long walk; Seattle-Tacoma international airport. S. Lindsay. Sat R 54:62-3 Ap 3 '71
New baggage system planned by airport; Seattle-Tacoma international airport. R. S. Kahn. il Aviation W 94:34-5 Ja 18 '71
        City planning
Battle in Seattle; movement to preserve Pike Place market area. Newsweek 77:94 My 17 '71
        Economic conditions
Good neighbor policy; sister city, Kobe, Japan donates food to hungry people of Seattle. Nation 214:4 Ja 3 '72
        Education
Seattle's concentration on careers. V. Hedrich. il Am Ed 7:12-15 Jl '71; Same. Ed Digest 37:34-7 N '71
        History
Mercer girls. S. C. Shulsinger. il por Am West 8:28-9 Jl '71
        Housing
Oistad apartment building. il Arch Rec 149:82-3 mid-My '71
        Markets
Battle in Seattle; movement to preserve Pike Place market area. Newsweek 77:94 My 17 '71
Seattle's Pike place market. il Sunset 147:70-3 S '71
        Music
Report:
La Bohème. F. J. Warnke. Opera N 36:27 N '71
   See also
Seattle opera assocation
        Parks and playgrounds
City camping calls for coordination; day camps. D. M. Lonheim. Camp Mag 43:20-1 Ap '71
        Police
Staked out for slaughter; case of L. E. Ward. J. R. Waltz. Nation 213:19-20 Jl 5 '71
        Politics and government
End to tolerance; corruption indictments. Newsweek 78:25-6 Ag 9 '71
        Public health
Dark days for the white collar. L. Rockey. il Todays Health 49:16-19 Mr '71
Seattle helps its Neighbors in need. R. Ruppert. Chr Cent 88:1508-10 D 22 '71
        Sanitary affairs
How Seattle cleaned up. E. W. Kenworthy. il Audubon 73:105-6 Ja '71
Low-cost odor control. G. W. Isaac. il Am City 86:14 Je '71
        Streets
What do you do with street triangles? L. W. Johnson. il Am City 86:26 S '71

SEATTLE opera association
Report:
Don Carlo. F. J. Warnke. Opera N 35:25
My 15 '71
Le nozze di Figaro. F. J. Warnke. Opera
N 35:32 Mr 20 '71
Who's Tommy. J. Rockwell. il Opera N 35:
22-3 Je 12 '71
SEATTLE seven trial. See Trials (conspiracy)
SEAWEED
Harvest of seaweed; excerpt from The sea
against hunger. C. P. Idyll. il Sea Front
17:342-8 N '71
See also
Agar
Kelp
Sargassum
SEAWELL, William Thomas
Pan Am picks a copilot. il por Time 98:80+
N 29 '71 *
Why Pan Am doesn't have a new president.
pors Bsns W p 120-2 N 13 '71 *
SEAY, James
Comment. J. Jacobsen. Poetry 118:167 Je
'71 *
SEBRING races. See Automobile racing
SECHZER, Jeri A. and others
Developmental behaviors: delayed appearance
in monkeys asphyxiated at birth. bibliog
il Science 171-1173-5 Mr 19 '71
SECKINGER, Donald S.
Politics and learned societies. bibliog Sch &
Soc 99:345-6 O '71
SECOND advent
God and the future. Chr Today 15:20 Je 4 '71
Past and future coming. V. P. McCorry.
America 125:440 N 20 '71
SECOND chance; story. See McKimmey, J.
SECOND thoughts on the subject of mother;
story. See Ballard, H.
SECONDARY education. See Education, Sec-
ondary
SECONDHAND boats. See Boats, Used
SECONDHAND cameras. See Cameras, Used
SECOR, Cynthia. See Romer, K. T. jt. auth.
SECRECY (law)
See also
Confidential communications
SECRET agents. See Spies
SECRET defense information. See Defense in-
formation, Classified
SECRET languages. See Languages, Secret
SECRET police, Russian. See Secret service
—Russia
SECRET service
See also
Intelligence service
World war, 1939-1945—Secret service

Russia
Beyond endurance; complaint by A. Solz-
henitsyn. Time 98:26-7 Ag 30 '71
How Russia spies: a new game; KGB net-
work. il por Newsweek 78:31-2+ O 11 '71
Poor Wilfred Burchett. W. F. Buckley, jr.
Nat R 23:668 Je 15 '71
Solzhenitsyn complains of secret police harass-
ment Pub W 200:38 Ag 23 '71
Soviet plot to destroy Mexico; excerpt from
KGB. J. Barron. il Read Digest 99:227-32+
N '71
Spies: foot soldiers in an endless war. il
Time 98:41-2+ O 11 '71

United States
By invitation only; tactics used during Day-
ton, Ohio, visit of R. M. Nixon. New
Repub 165:9 S 18 '71
See also
Presidents—United States—Protection
United States—Central intelligence agency
SECRET societies
See also
Elks, Benevolent and protective order of
Freemasons
Ku Klux klan
Moose, Loyal order of
SECRET treasure; story. See Cave, H.
SECRETAN, Luc
Simple yoke mounting for a 12-inch reflector.
il Sky & Tel 41:114-16 F '71
SECRETARIAT of the United Nations. See
United Nations—Secretariat
SECRETARIES
Working woman. L. C. Pogrebin. por Ladies
Home J 88:46+ N '71
See also
Corporation secretaries

SECRETARIES of defense (United States)
See also
Laird, M.
McNamara, R. S.
SECRETARIES of labor (United States)
See also
Shultz, G. P.
SECRETARIES of state (United States)
Eclipse of the State department. D. Acheson.
For Affairs 49:593-606 Jl '71
Pungent memories from Mr Acheson; ex-
cerpts from interview, ed. by K. Harris. D.
G. Acheson. il pors Life 71:51-2+ Jl 23 '71
See also
Rogers, W. P.
Snyder, J. W.
SECRETARIES of the treasury (United States)
See also
Connally, J.
SECRETARY General of the United Nations.
See United Nations—Secretary General
SECRETION, Intestinal. See Intestines
SECRETIONS
See also
Pheromones
SECRETS, Official. See Official secrets
SECRETS, Personal. See Confidential commu-
nications
SECRETS, Professional. See Confidential com-
munications
SECTIONS, Microscopic. See Microscopic sec-
tions
SECTS
On separation. L. N. Bell. Chr Today 16:26-7
O 8 '71
See also
Children of God (movement)
Christian holiness association
Church of God
Hutterite Brethren
Jewish sects
Mennonites
Mormons and Mormonism
Seventh day Adventists
Worldwide church of God
SECULARISM
Ecumenism: who cares? K. McDonnell. Com-
monweal 95:55-9 O 15 '71; Reply. L. D.
Jordahl. 96:147+ N 12 '71
World come full circle. H. A. Snyder. Chr
Today 16:9-13 Ja 7 '72
SECURITIES
What's behind the tombstones; announce-
ments of major underwritings. Bsns W p67
Mr 6 '71
See also
Bonds
Dividends
Investment banking
Investments
Stock exchange
Stocks
also subhead Securities under various
subjects, e.g. Banks and banking—Securi-
ties

Laws and regulations
New look at role of big investors. il U S
News 70:44 Mr 22 '71

Marketing
Charon's toll; securities auctions. por Forbes
107:25-6 My 1 '71
Looking to the public. C. Morgello. il News-
week 78:91 D 13 '71
Quiet turnaround in private placements. A.
Hershman. il Duns 98:53-5 S '71
Restructuring the securities industry; the
two market system; address, May 17, 1971
J. J. Needham. Vital Speeches 37:549-52 Jl
1 '71
Specialist speaks; interview. J. C. Kellogg,
3d. pors Forbes 107:49-50 Mr 15 '71
Specialists lose their old-time grip. il Bsns W
p72-5 D 4 '71
Unreconstructed specialists. il Fortune 84:183-
5 Ag '71
Wall Street's favorite bureaucrat, now. por
Time 98:99 N 22 '71

Private placement
See Securities—Marketing

Prospectuses
Hurry-up job of printing prospectuses. R.
Levy il Duns 97:62-5 Ap '71

Theft
See Securities, Theft of

Australia
Dateline Australia. G. J. Henry. Forbes 108:
97 D 1 '71

SECURITIES—*Continued*

Germany (Federal Republic)

Whose grass is greener? interview. N. K. Siegel. por Forbes 108:54+ N 15 '71

SECURITIES, Privately placed. See Securities —Marketing

SECURITIES, Tax exempt
See also
Municipal bonds

SECURITIES, Theft of
Crime on the Street; McClellan permanent subcommittee on investigations hearings. Newsweek 77:79-80 Je 21 '71
Stealing on Wall Street: growing threat. U S News 70:85 Je 21 '71
Stolen stocks and bonds for sale. Changing T 25:28 F '71
Toll mounts on stock theft. il Bsns W p82 Je 26 '71

Prevention
See Brokers—Security measures

SECURITIES and exchange commission. See United States—Securities and exchange commission

SECURITIES dealers, National association of. See National association of securities dealers, inc.

SECURITY, Internal. See National security

SECURITY analysts. See Investment advisers

SECURITY classification (government documents)
Anderson's brass ring. il por Time 99:34 Ja 17 '72
Bureaucratic odyssey of a space mapping camera; with editorial comment. E. Driscoll. Sci N 100:354, 362-3 N 27 '71
GENDIS: burn before reading. il Newsweek 78:21-2 Jl 5 '71
Kissinger tilt; deliberations of Washington special action group. Time 99:15 Ja 17 '72
Oswald and the U-2; declassified papers from the Warren report. il por Newsweek 77:31 Mr 1 '71
Top secret: who decides. il U S News 71:20-1 Jl 5 '71
U.S. mania for classification. Time 98:14-15 Jl 5 '71
Underworld of government; government operations subcommittee hearings. New Repub 165:5-7 Jl 10 '71
See also
Defense information, Classified
Official secrets

Great Britain
Secrecy: the British way; D-notice system. Time 97:39 Jl 5 '71

SECURITY council of the United Nations. See United Nations—Security council

SECURITY measures in industry. See Industry—Security measures

SECURITY service. See Secret service

SEDATIVES
See also
Barbiturates

SEDER. See Passover

SEDIMENTATION and deposition
Fossil fuel combustion and the major sedimentary cycle. K. K. Bertine and E. D. Goldberg. bibliog il Science 173:233-5 Jl 16 '71
See also
Marine sediments

SEDITION
See also
Freedom of the press

SEDITIOUS libel
See also
Trials (seditious libel)

SEDLMAYR, Julius H.
Bonds in '72: higher yields; interview. por U S News 72:60-1 Ja 10 '72

SEDULUS, pseud.
Television. See issues of New republic

SEDUMS
Stonecrop, a decorative and rugged container plant. P. Gunn. il Home Gard 58:68 Ap '71
To-be-looked-at sedum and Australia's super lily. il Sunset 146:262-3 My '71

SEE, Carolyn
Veterinarian. il Atlan 228:95-8+ O '71

SEEBURG corporation
Spinoff to break a fall. il Bsns W p38-9 S 25 '71

SEED, Allen H. Jr
Campers vs. litter: practical ecology in camp. il Camp Mag 43:13+ Je '71

SEED germination. See Germination

SEED photography. See Photography of flowers, plants, trees, etc.

SEED tapes
Novel way to sow seeds. il Home Gard 58:33 Je '71

SEEDING
Sowing now in open ground. Sunset 147:263 O '71
See also
Corn—Seeding
Seed tapes

SEEDLINGS
Start your corn indoors. A. A. Hardiman. il Org Gard & Farm 18:83 My '71

SEEDS, Nicholas W. and Gilman, A. G.
Norepinephrine stimulated increase of cyclic AMP levels in developing mouse brain cell cultures. bibliog il Science 174:292 O 15 '71

SEEDS
Do you save seeds? Watch it! R. Stout. il Org Gard & Farm 18:50-3 Ja '71
Every gardener his own seedman? C. B. Wilson. Horticulture 49:46-8 D '71
Native and rare plants from seed. il Sunset 147:272 O '71
Seed: what would it cost to. . . C. E. Sommers. il Suc Farm 69:24-5 N '71
See also
Corn—Seed
Dormancy (plants)
Germination
Pumpkin seeds
Soybeans—Seed
Sunflowers—Seed

Germination
See Germination

SEEDS; story. See Levin, R.

SEEGER, Murray
Washington desk. Duns 98:5-6 Ag '71
Washington: Wilbur D. Mills of Arkansas. Atlan 228:6+ Ag '71

SEEGER, Pete
My dirty stream. Audubon 73:85-6 Mr '71
about
A man, a boat, a river, a dream. J. Hope. il por Audubon 73:80-7 Mr '71 *

SEEGERS, Kathleen Walker. See Seegers, S. jt. auth.

SEEGERS, Scott
Meet the mighty mantis. il Read Digest 99:33-4+ Jl '71
—and Seegers, K. W.
Father of the green revolution. por Read Digest 98:134-8 Mr '71

SEELEY, John Ronald
Stances and substances. Ann Am Acad 395:95-104 My '71

SEELY, Janet E. and others
Cigarette smoking: objective evidence for lung damage in teen-agers. bibliog il Science 172:741-3 My 14 '71

SEELYE, John
Inquest; poem. New Repub 165:34 Jl 17 '71

SEFERIADES, Giorgos Stylianou
Death of a poet. H. J. Cargas. Commonweal 95:112 O 29 '71 *

SEFERIS, George. See Seferiades, G. S.

SEFRIOUI, Ahmed
Veiled Morocco; with photographs by I. Penn. Vogue 158:116-23+ D '71

SEGAL, David S. and others
Cycloheximide: its effects on activity are dissociable from its effects on memory. bibliog il Science 172:82-4 Ap 2 '71
Effects of long-term reserpine treatment on brain tyrosine hydroxylase and behavioral activity. bibliog il Science 173:847-9 Ag 27 '71

SEGAL, Erich Wolf
Erich Segal's identity crisis; interview, ed. by P. Goldberger; reprint. il pors N Y Times Mag p 16-17+ Je 13 '71
Erich Segal's last last interview; ed. by J. Y. Mercier. il por Vogue 158:89+ Ag 1 '71
Is the family obsolete; interview, ed. by J. Kronenberger. Look 35:35-6 Ja 26 '71
Night they auctioned off the Roman empire. il Horizon 13:36-9 Sum '71
about
Love story; runaway hit: why? M. Cousins. il Vogue 157:130-2+ Mr 1 '71 *
Mush. N. Ephron. il pors Esquire 75:89-92+ Je '71 *
Parting shots; plight of Mr Love Story. B. Darrach. il por Life 70:77 Je 4 '71 *
Segal the scholar. por Time 97:52+ Mr 15 '71 *
Yale is no. 1 with the promoter & the idol. P. Wilkes. il pors Look 35:60-2 Ap 6 '71 *
Yellow submarine passenger list; letter. L. Minoff. N Y Times Mag p3 Jl 4 '71 *

SEGAL, Julius
How much sleep do you need? interview.
Read Digest 98:185-6+ My '71
SEGALL, Joel E.
Pollution tax is boomeranging. por Bsns W
p40-1 Ap 10 '71 *
SEGEL, Joseph Myron
Franklin mint. il por Nations Bsns 59:74-5+
D '71 *
SEGERS, Mary C.
Violence: left and middle. il Cath World
212:307-8+ Mr '71
SEGHERS, Anna, pseud.
Quest for Christa T, by C. Wolf. Review
Sat R 54:31-2 My 8 '71. P. Moscoso-Gón-
gora *
SEGRAVE, Edmond
Obituary
Pub W 199:60 Ap 12 '71
SEGREGATION, Social
See also
Discrimination in housing
SEGREGATION in education
Blot for Boston; charge of maintaining seg-
regated schools. il Newsweek 78:62 D 13 '71
Coddling segregation; the case for ALA ac-
tion. E. J. Josey. por Library J 96:1778-9
My 15 '71
Rebel yell academies. E. Tornquist. il Ramp
Mag 10:12+ S '71
Segregated classrooms? Newsweek 77:86 Ap
5 '71
White academies in the South, booming de-
spite obstacles. il U S News 70:75-6 Ap
19 '71
See also
Negroes—Education
SEGREGATION in sports
Before you could say Jackie Robinson; black
players. J. Holway. il Look 35:46-50 Jl 13
'71
Parting shots: Sharon Poole, girl star, gets
the little league thumb. il Life 71:64 Jl 23
'71
SEGREGATION of libraries. See Libraries and
Negroes
SEGURA, Edilberto L. See Parker, G. G. C. jt.
auth.
SEICK, John D.
How publishers can benefit from the new
minicomputers. il Pub W 200:24-6 Ag 9 '71
SEIDENBERG, Robert
Drug advertising and perception of mental
illness. bibliog Ment Hy 55:21-31 Ja '71
SEIDMAN, Aaron
Barriers to technical innovation. il Bul Atom
Sci 27:29-31 Mr '71
SEIDMAN, David
Prisoner and the union. Nation 213:6-7 Jl 5
'71
SEIDMAN, Hugh
Comment. F. MacShane. Poetry 118:296-7 Ag
'71 *
SEIDMAN, Jerry
Academy graduates; letter. New Repub 164:31
Ap 10 '71
SEISMOGRAPH stations. See Seismological sta-
tions
SEISMOLOGICAL research. See Earthquakes—
Research
SEISMOLOGICAL stations
WWNSS: seismology's global network of ob-
serving stations. J. Oliver and L. Murphy.
bibliog il Science 174:254-61 O 15 '71
SEISMOLOGY
Apollo seismic net finds quakes occur as
deep in moon as earth. Aviation W 95:20
S 6 '71
Ascent stage impact aids seismic tests.
Aviation W 95:21 Ag 9 '71
Astronaut to set off explosions in search for
water on the moon: Apollo 14 ALSEP ex-
periments. Space World H-4-88:43 Ap '71
Composition and evolution of the mantle and
Core, D. L. Anderson and others. bibliog
il Science 171:1103-12 Mr 19 '71
Moonquakes. G. Latham and others. bibliog
il Science 174:687-92 N 12 '71
Moonquakes show volcanic symptoms. Avia-
tion W 94:60 My 3 '71
Seismology meets politics; nuclear detec-
tion. il Sci N 100:22-3 Jl 10 '71
See also
Earth movements
SEITZ, Frank A.
Family playground. il Parks & Rec 6:42-3+
Ap '71
SEIZURE of vessels and cargoes
What goes on down there? Cubans seize
Bahamas lines freighter. Nation 214:3-4 Ja
3 '72
SEIZURES. See Searches and seizures
SEKBER Golkar (political party) See Polit-
ical parties—Indonesia

SEKULA, Sonia
Who was Sonia Sekula? with excerpts from
her journals and comments. N. Foote. il
Art in Am 59:73-80 S '71 *
SELAGINELLA
Butterfly feeding on lycopsid. M. C. Singer
and others. bibliog il Science 172:1341-2 Je
25 '71
SELBY, Earl, and Selby, Miriam
Journey through black America; condensa-
tion of Odyssey: journey through black
America. Read Digest 99:223-8+ S '71
Mojave Desert; a treasure in trouble. il Nat
Wildlife 9:52-7 O '71; Same abr. with title
Trouble in the Mojave. Read Digest 99:45-
8+ O '71
SELBY, Miriam. See Selby, E. jt. auth.
SELECTION, Natural. See Natural selection
SELECTION of bishops. See Bishops—Selec-
tion
SELECTION of librarians. See Librarians—
Selection and appointment
SELECTION of students. See Student selection
SELECTION of teachers. See Teachers—Selec-
tion and appointment
SELECTIVE objectors. See Conscientious ob-
jectors
SELECTIVE service, Military. See Military
service, Compulsory
SELENOLOGY. See Lunar geology
SELF, Charles R. Jr
How to choose a crash helmet. il Mech Illus
67:59-61+ S '71
Motorcycle mania: new magazine market re-
port. il Writers Digest 51:24-6+ Mr '71
SELF, Maurine
Our need for perspective. bibliog f Engl J 60:
603-6 My '71
SELF
Addiction as a necessity and opportunity;
address, April 20, 1970. E. H. Land. Sci-
ence 171:151-3 Ja 15 '71
Psycho-cultural shifts in ego defenses. F. X.
Schupper and R. C. Calogeras. bibliog Am
Imago 28:53-70 Spr '71
See also
Consciousness
Identity (psychology)
Satisfaction
SELF-accusation; drama. See Handke, P.
SELF concept. See Self perception
SELF confidence. See Self reliance
SELF control
Steps toward self control; with study-dis-
cussion program, by M. M. Conant. J. W.
Kessler. bibliog il PTA Mag 65:14-16, 32
Ja '71
SELF defense
Bad night at no-name cove. R. Starnes.
Field & S 76:8+ D '71
SELF-destructing plastics. See Plastics—De-
terioration
SELF discipline. See Self control
SELF disclosure
Fear that cheats us of love. S. M. Jourard
and A. Whitman. Redbook 137:82-3+ O '71
SELF employed
Earn money at home, a handful of ideas. il
Changing T 26:30 Ja '72
It's your business. M. Schultz. il Pop Mech
136:82-5+ S '71
On the job: how to succeed in business by
really trying. Mlle 74:146 Ja '72
31 enterprising ways to work/live. il Mlle 74:
69-71+ Ja '72
Whole sell catalogue. N. A. Comer. Mlle
72:188-90 Mr '71
SELF esteem. See Self love
SELF evaluation
How not to embarrass your children; with
study discussion program, by E. Harris
and D. Harris. D. Graves. bibliog il PTA
Mag 66:28-30, 34-5 S '71
Judgment. E. Glynn. America 124:96-7 Ja
30 '71
Not like the rest. V. P. McCorry. America
125:inside back cover O 16 '71
Speaking and hearing the truth in love. K.
S. Roundhill. Chr Today 16:7-9 Ja 7 '72
There is no real you. M. Tumin. Mlle 72:
140-1+ F '71
See also
Self perception
SELF government. See Democracy
SELF government in education
Can students evaluate their education? with
study-discussion program. C. Smallen-
burg and H. Smallenburg. R. Peck. bibliog
il PTA Mag 65:4-7, 35-6 F '71; Same abr. Ed
Digest 36:29-31 My '71

SELF government in education—*Continued*
Student council: useful or useless? M. O.
Miklos and L. D. Miklos. Ed Digest 36:
47-9 Mr '71
Too idealistic? student dominated classroom.
J. J. Roy. Clear House 45:376 F '71
What do students really want? A. Richards.
il Todays Ed 60:57-8 Ap '71
SELF-hypnosis diet. See Hypnotism—Ther-
apeutic use
SELF image. See Self perception
SELF love
Raising student self-esteem for a change. W.
P. Ferris. Engl J 60:379-81 Mr '71
Self-image; Project IMPACT for human-
izing the classroom. R. J. Trotter. il Sci
N 100:130-1 Ag 21 '71
Topography of love; excerpt from The
death of the family. D. Cooper. Vogue 157:
104-5+ Ja 15 '71
Using photography to amplify self-esteem in
the primary grades. R. T. Tamashiro. Ed
Digest 37:38-40 N '71
SELF perception
Self image: a theory of the dynamics of be-
havior, updated. C. M. Anderson. Ment Hy
55:365-8 Jl '71
See also
Body image
SELF preservation
Self image: a theory of the dynamics of be-
havior, updated. C. M. Anderson. Ment Hy
55:365-8 Jl '71
SELF rating of baseball players. See Baseball
players—Rating
SELF realization
See also
Satisfaction
SELF recognition. See Recognition (psychol-
ogy)
SELF reliance
Confident beauty. Harp Baz 104:108 F '71
Dare to be great! super-huckster. G. W.
Turner. T. Thompson. il pors Life 70:68-
68B My 28 '71
SELF revelation. See Self disclosure
SELIGMAN, Daniel
Bad new era for common stocks. il Fortune
84:73-5+ O '71
Books & ideas (cont) Fortune 83:130-1 Ap '71
SELIGSON, Marcia
Tricia got her rose garden. il pors Life 70:
32-5 Je 25 '71
SELINGER, Paul
Sculpture parks: can they work? il Parks &
Rec 6:38-9+ F '71
SELISKAR, Carl J. and Brand, Ludwig
Solvent dependence of the luminescence of
N-arylaminonaphthalenesulfonates. bibliog
il Science 171:799-800 F 26 '71
SELLER, Arthur
Arthur Seller by design; interview. ed. by
R. Kolbe. il por Am Artist 35:42-7+ S '71
SELLERS, Charles Coleman
Charles Willson Peale's portrait of Robert
and Governeur Morris. il pors Antiques 99:
404-6 Mr '71
SELLERS, Jerry. See Folkes, G. C. jt. auth.
SELLERS, Patricia
Freelance job idea, writing paperback cover
copy. il Writers Digest 52:26 Ja '72
SELLERS, Robert C.
Excerpt from testimony, June 9, 1971. Cong
Digest 50:308+ D '71
SELLERSVILLE, Pa.
Sellers of Sellersville. D. Coll. il Am City 86:
64 Jl '71
SELLING. See Salesmen and salesmanship
SELLING of the president; musical comedy.
See Musical comedies, revues, etc.—Criti-
cisms, plots, etc.
SELTZER, R. W.
Public education: is its demise near? Clear
House 46:6-9 S '71
SELZER, Michael
Normalizing the Jews. H. Halkin; reply with
rejoinder. M. Selzer. Commentary 51:22+
My '71 *
SEMANTICS
Some comments on linguistics; or, How to
overcome the world with a few trick
phrases. D. F. Cox. Chr Cent 88:1498-9
D 22 '71
SEMBENE, Ousmane
Ousmane Sembene; interview. New Yorker
47:37-9 S 25 '71
SEMEN
Frozen assets; sperm banks. il Time 99:52 Ja
3 '72
Frozen human sperm banks successful. A.
J. Snider. Sci Digest 70:54 N '71

Now it's ice-cube babies; artificial insemina-
tion with frozen sperm. il por Newsweek
78:81 Jl 12 '71
Sperm on deposit. il Newsweek 78:58 Ag 30
'71
SEMI-AUTOMATIC rifles. See Rifles
SEMICONDUCTOR industry. See Electronic in-
dustries
SEMICONDUCTOR memories. See Memory
devices (computers)
SEMICONDUCTORS
Junction lasers. L. A. D'Asaro and J. E.
Ripper. bibliog il Phys Today 24:42-8 Mr
'71
Model for amorphous semiconductors pre-
dicts energy band gaps. M. S. Rothenberg.
bibliog il Phys Today 24:17+ N '71
New semiconductors. il Radio-Electr 42:72
Jl; 80 Ag '71
New tubes and semiconductors (cont) Radio-
Electr 42:95 Mr '71
Semiconductor market growth predicted. il
Aviation W 95:15 D 27 '71
Solid state. L. Garner. See issues of Popular
electronics
Solid state; charge-coupled image device. L.
Garner. il Pop Electr 35:79-81+ Jl '71
Theory of amorphous semiconductors; adap-
tation of address, February 1971. M. H.
Cohen. bibliog il Phys Today 24:26-32 My
'71
See also
Diodes
Electric current rectifiers
Electroluminescence
Transistors
SEMINARIANS
Church needs Christian lovers, not oedipal
boys; ordination sermon. G. A. Benson.
Chr Cent 88:101-4 Ja 27 '71
Pearly gates amendment and congressional
images of church and ministry; question of
draft exemption for ministerial students.
P. Deats. jr. Chr Cent 88:486-7 Ap 21 '71
SEMINARIES. See Theological seminaries
SEMINARS
Seminars try to cut the Phase II fog. Bsns W
p46 O 23 '71
SEMIRAMIDE: opera. See Rossini, G.
SEMIVAN, John
Observations; poem. New Repub 164:32 My 22
'71
SEMMES, Granville M.
Gourmet in New Orleans. Holiday 49:20 Mr
'71
If oysters screamed... il Holiday 49:41+ Jl
'71
SENATE investigations. See Government in-
vestigations
SENATE voting. See United States—Congress
—Senate—Voting
SENATORS
Is America going isolationist? Size-up by
key senators; interviews. pors U S News
70:24-31 Je 28 '71
Parting shots; in the Senate, it's all in the
family. il Life 70:74A-76 Mr 12 '71
Some tax fiction to the home folk; Senate
tax bill amendments. Bsns W p 24 N 20
'71
Who's new in the Congress. il Time 97:15
F 1 '71
Salaries, allowances, etc.
Senatorial fringe benefit; fees for speeches
and articles. il U S News 70:35 Je 7 '71
SENATORS (baseball) See Baseball clubs
SENDAI virus. See Viruses
SENDAK, Maurice
Introduction to pictures by Maurice Sendak.
il Pub W 200:40 D 6 '71
Sendak sampler; interview. ed. by A. De-
Mirjian. jr. il Pub W 200:37-9 D 6 '71
SENDAK, Theodore Lorraine
Criminal violence; address, May 12, 1971.
Vital Speeches 37:574-6 Jl 1 '71
SENDLER, David
(ed) See Brown, H. G. What it will be like
when we elect a woman president
SENEGAL
Ousmane Sembene; interview. O. Sembene.
New Yorker 47:37-9 S 25 '71
See also
United Nations—Senegal
SENEGALESE dancing. See Dancing, African
SENEGALESE national dance company. See
Dancing, African
SENGHOR, Léopold Sédar
Four wise men. il por Time 98:38 N 15 '71 *
SEN GUPTA, Barun K. and Grant, A. C.
Orbitolina, a cretaceous larger foraminifer,
from Flemish cap: paleoceanographic im-
plications. bibliog il Science 173:934-6 S 3 '71

SENILITY. See Old age
SENIOR centers
Arkansas senior center still going strong more than year after title III grants stop. il Aging 199:7 My '71
Brunswick, Me, senior club is Evergreen year round, sometimes seven days a week. il Aging 196:14-15 F '71
Center brings education they want to the elderly; South County senior center, inc, Edmonds, Wash. il Aging 203:8-9 S '71
Connecticut Title III center, less than year old, booming. il Aging 201:14 Jl '71
GAB, used toys, civic support build Wisconsin senior center; Appleton, Wis. il Aging 198:9 Ap '71
Tennessee model city starts senior center as part of improvement. il Aging 199:11 My '71
    See also
National institute of senior centers
Recreation for the aged
SENIOR citizen achievement awards. See Rewards, prizes, etc.
SENIOR citizens clubs. See Recreation for the aged
SENIOR citizens month
1971 Senior citizens month keyed to November's White House conference. il Aging 198:4 Ap '71
SENKEVITCH, Anatole, Jr
Nineteenth-century public buildings in Nashville. il Antiques 100:222-7 Ag '71
SENNETT, Tomas
Room for one more; with photographs. J. Scully. Mod Phot 35:78-83 N '71 *
SENSE of humor. See Humor
SENSES and sensation
Development of polysensory responses in association cortex of kitten. K. S. Mayers and others. bibliog il Science 171:1038-40 Mr 12 '71
Physiological role of pleasure. M. Cabanac. bibliog il Science 173:1103-7 S 17 '71
    See also
After images
Brain
Chemoreceptivity
Hearing
Pain
Perception
Sight
Smell
Taste
Time perception
SENSING systems, Remote.   See Remote sensing systems
SENSITIVITY training. See Group relations training
SENSORS. See Detectors
SENSUALITY
How sensuous are you? test. J, pseud. il Ladies Home J 88:74+ F '71
SENTENCE, Indeterminate. See Indeterminate sentence
SENTENCES, Imposing of. See Justice, Administration of
SENYK, George, and others
Immunogenicity of glucagon: determinants responsible for antibody binding and lymphocyte stimulation. bibliog il Science 171:407-8 Ja 29 '71
SEPARATION (chemistry)
    See also
Chromatographic analysis
SEPARATION (law)
Bonds of acrimony, by R. DeWolf. Review Newsweek 77:109-109A+ Mr 15 '71
SEPARATION (technology)
    See also
Adsorption
SEPARATION anxiety. See Maternal deprivation
SEPARATION of Isotopes. See Isotope separation
SEPARATION of powers
Secrecy in a free society; executive privilege. S. J. Ervin, jr. il Nation 213:451-7 N 8 '71
Separation of powers. C. H. Percy. il Todays Ed 60:36-8 My '71
    See also
Executive privilege (government information)
SEPHARDIM
Black Panthers of Israel. A. Elon. il N Y Times Mag p33+ S 12 '71
Grandees, by S. Birmingham. Review
Nat R 23:768-9 Jl 13 '71. E. Roditi
Sat R 54:32 Mr 20 '71. A. Churchill
SEPHERIADES, Giorgos Stylianou. See Seferiades, G. S.
SEPPUKU. See Harakiri

SEPULCHRAL monuments
Say it in stone; gravestones in Highgate cemetery, London. H. R. Mayes. Sat R 54:14-15 S 4 '71
Stones with the raised hands; funerary art of the Bogomils. M. Krleza. il UNESCO Courier 24:17-22 My '71
    See also
Pyramids
SEPÚLVEDA WHITTLE, Tomás
Jaime Zudánez, illustrious unknown. il Américas 23:9-13 O '71
SEQUESTERING agents
Methyl mercury and inorganic mercury collection by a selective chelating resin. S. L. Law. bibliog il Science 174:285-7 O 15 '71
    See also
Ethylenediamine tetraacetic acid
SEQUOIA, Giant
Some problems relating to the giant trees; reprint from 1866 article. C. B. Bradley. il por Am For 77:29-31+ My '71
SEQUOIA sempervirens. See Redwood
SERAGLIO. See Harem
SERBO-CROATIAN poetry

Translations into English
Give me back my rags; tr. by A. Pennington. Atlan 228:118-20 D '71
SEREBNICK, Judith, and others
(ed) Book review. See issues of Library journal
SEREBRIER, José
Adventures of an itinerant conductor. por Hi Fi 21:MA25+ S '71
SERIAL publications
Price indexes for 1971: Serials services. W. H. Huff and N. B. Brown. il Library J 96:2274-5 Jl '71
SERIALS (moving pictures) See Moving pictures—Serial films
SERIES, Book
Edward Stratemeyer and his book machine. A. Prager. il por Sat R 54:15-17+ Jl 10 '71
Story behind the books: Lucia is alive and well. E. Erdosi. Pub W 200:49 Ag 9 '71
Woman behind great thinkers: unique publisher on universal themes. H. Rosenberg. por Vogue 158:72 Ag 1 '71
SERMONS
Hell discovered! news on the sermon front. Chr Cent 88:143 Ja 27 '71
Let's update Bible and sermon. P. R. Gastonguay. il Cath World 213:232-5 Ag '71
Some notes on liturgy. J. Nilssen. il Chr Cent 88:924-7 Ag 4 '71
    See also
Preaching
SEROTONIN
Brain serotonin content: increase following ingestion of carbohydrate diet. J. D. Fernstrom and R. J. Wurtman. bibliog il Science 174:1023-5 D 3 '71
Brain serotonin content: physiological dependence on plasma tryptophan levels. J. D. Fernstrom and R. J. Wurtman. bibliog il Science 173:149-52 Jl 9 '71
Narcotic tolerance and dependence: lack of relationship with serotonin turnover in the brain. D. L. Cheney and others. bibliog il Science 171:1169-70 Mr 19 '71
Persistent increase in brain serotonin turnover after chronic administration of LSD in the rat. J.-L. Diaz and M. O. Huttunen. bibliog il Science 174:62-4 O 1 '71
Receptors: localization and specificity of binding of serotonin in the central nervous system. S. G. A. Alivisatos and others. bibliog il Science 171:809-12 F 26 '71
Serotonin: two different inhibitory actions on snail neurons. H. M. Gerschenfeld. bibliog il Science 171:1252-4 Mr 26 '71
SERPICO, Frank
Crusader. por Newsweek 77:24 My 31 '71 *
Up against the cops. il por Time 97:52+ My 31 '71 *
SERRA, Richard
Serra's visit and after. M. Amaya. il Art in Am 59:122-3 My '71 *
SERRIN, William
Assembly line. il Atlan 228:62-8+ O '71
For Roche of G.M. happiness is a 10% surcharge. il pors N Y Times Mag p36-7+ S 12 '71
Ford's Iacocca: apotheosis of a used car salesman. il pors N Y Times Mag p8-9+ Jl 18 '71
SERSIC, J. L.
First century of Cordoba observatory. il Sky & Tel 42:347-50 D '71
SERUM
    See also
Antilymphocytic serum

SERUM hepatitis. See Hepatitis
SERUM hepatitis virus. See Hepatitis viruses
SERVAAS, Beurt
Good old ways. il Newsweek 78:74 D 13 '71 *
Return of the Post. il por Time 97:70 Je 14 '71 *
SERVAAS, Sandra
For want of a teeshot. il Holiday 49:38-40+ Jl '71
SERVAN-SCHREIBER, Jean Jacques
Jean-Jacques slips behind the scenes. il por Bsns W p33 Ja 23 '71 *
Perils of JJSS. por Newsweek 77:61+ Je 14 '71 *
Reports & comment. J. K. Glassman. Atlan 227:6+ F '71 *
Sibling rivalry. pors Newsweek 77:54 Ja 18 '71 *
SERVAN-SCHREIBER, Jean Louis
Sibling rivalry. pors Newsweek 77:54 Ja 18 '71 *
SERVANTS. See Household employees
SERVERS (cabinets) See Cabinets (furniture)
SERVETUS, Michael
Heretical map verso. P. W. Schmidtchen. il por Hobbies 75:134-6 F '71 *
SERVICE, John Stewart
Old China hands. pors Time 98:14-15 Ag 2 '71 *
SERVICE, William
Feeling one's way across the chasm. il Sports Illus 35:62-4+ Jl 26 '71
Letter from the publisher. J. R. Munro. il por Sports Illus 35:4 Jl 26 '71 *
SERVICE, Community. See Community service
SERVICE, Compulsory non-military
Alternative service locates in Appalachia. J. DeMuth. il America 125:374-5 N 6 '71
National service: worse than the draft; report on idea of Universal national service. J. Castelli. Chr Cent 88:315-16 Mr 10 '71
Replacing the draft: a limited national service system. J. B. Bingham. New Repub 164: 17-21 Ja 16 '71; Reply with rejoinder. B. A. Sheridan 164:33-4 F 13 '71
SERVICE, Volunteer. See Volunteer service
SERVICE clubs. See Clubs
SERVICE d'action civique. See Political clubs and associations—France
SERVICE industries
Address book. E. Kinard. See issues of House beautiful
Booming business service business. il Changing T 25:39-43 S '71
Headed for stagnation? M. R. Gainsbrugh. por Nations Bsns 59:91 O '71
It's your business. M. Schultz. il Pop Mech 136:82-5+ S '71
Next, the hospitality conglomerate. Bsns W p61 Je 12 '71
Please tell me . . . House & Gard 139:70 My; 140:66+ S '71
Productivity: industry isn't the only place where it's a problem; interview. P. E. Haggerty. il por Forbes 107:43-5 F 1 '71
Services grow while the quality shrinks. il Bsns W p50-1+ O 30 '71
Shift to the production of services. P. E. Haggerty. Science 173:679 Ag 20 '71
They board up the windows; Board-up services. il Bsns W p90 My 1 '71
See also
Homeowners emergency services, inc.
Moving and storage companies
Repairing

Advertising

Advertising a service business. J. Frye. Electr World 86:52-3 Jl '71
SERVICE men
See also
Military life
Narcotics and service men

Pay, allowances, etc.

See United States—Armed forces—Pay, allowances, etc.
SERVICE men, Discharged. See Veterans
SERVICE men and narcotics. See Narcotics and service men
SERVICE mens benefits. See Veterans—Benefits
SERVICE mens clubs. See Clubs
SERVICE mens early educational counseling. See Veterans—Education
SERVICE mens entertainments. See United States—Armed forces—Recreation
SERVICE mens families
Billions for defense but. . ; need for welfare aid. New Repub 164:8 Mr 27 '71

Dear Mr President, the P.O.W. families. J. Lelyveld. il N Y Times Mag p 14-15+ O 3 '71
Speaking out; meeting of National league of families of American prisoners and missing in southeast Asia. il Time 98:21 O 11 '71
They also serve; activist groups lobby government. Newsweek 78:17-18 D 27 '71
SERVICE mens graves
See also
Unknown soldiers
SERVICE mens publications
See also
Stars and stripes (newspapers)
SERVICE mens wives
Aid for war wives; legal assistance through Young lawyers section of the American bar association. il Time 98:98 N 1 '71
POW wife. il pors Ebony 26:110-11+ Je '71
SERVICE stations, Airplane. See Airplane service stations
SERVICEBERRIES (tree)
Small tree for all seasons; the sarvistree. J. Flory. il Home Gard 58:30 Mr '71
SERVING carts
Bucket-grill barbecue cart. B. Fifer. il Pop Sci 199:82-4 Ag '71
Rollaway party wall. il Pop Mech 136:140-1 Ag '71
SERVING equipment. See Tableware
SERVING of food. See Food
SERWER, Daniel. See Schachter, O. jt. auth.
SESSER, Stanford N.
Special dispensation. New Repub 164:16-17 Mr 6 '71
SET design. See Theater—Stage setting and scenery
SETO, Dexter S. Y. See Carver, D. H. jt. auth.
SETON, Anya
Katherine by Anya Seton for high school seniors. R. P. Hildebrand. Engl J 60: 746-7+ S '71 *
SETTERS
Black and tan setters; Gordon setters. D M. Duffey. il Outdoor Life 147:162+ My '71
Irish luck improved; Irish setters. L. Mueller. il Field & S 76:168-70+ O '71
Pride of the setters; 1970 National field trial championship. L. Mueller. il Field & S 76: 192+ Je '71
SETTLES, Gary S.
Amateur scientist. il Sci Am 224:118-22+ My '71
SEURAT, Georges
Sunday afternoon on the Island of La Grande Jatte. R. McMullen. il por Horizon 13:82-95 Sum '71 *
SEVAREID, Eric
Dissent within a lawful society; address, December 4, 1970. Vital Speeches 37:251-3 F 1 '71
SEVENTH army. See United States—Army—Forces in Europe
SEVENTH-day Adventists
Day of the Adventists. il Newsweek 77:65-6 Je 7 '71
Growing quarrel among Seventh-day Adventists. S. G. Sturges. Chr Today 15:12-13 Je 18 '71
Revival reaches out; SDA students carry it on. E. E. Plowman. Chr Today 15:35-6 Mr 26 '71
SEVENTH day Baptists
At 300, still alive. A. Eggebroten. Chr Today 15:46 S 10 '71
SEVENTH fleet. See United States—Navy
70, girls, 70; musical comedy. See Musical comedies, revues, etc.—Criticisms, plots, etc.
SEVERIN, Kurt
Bizarre rites of the cobra shrine. il Sci Digest 69:52-5 Mr '71
Medicine dolls and primitive peoples. il Sci Digest 69:65-9 Je '71
Rescuing the golden marmosets. il Sci Digest 70:46-8 D '71
So you want to be a snake photographer . . . il pors Sci Digest 69:55-7 My '71
SEVERINSEN, Carl. See Severinsen, D.
SEVERINSEN, Doc
Hip hokum. pors Time 99:71-2 Ja 3 '72 *
SEVERO, Richard
Treasury of his unpublished songs, Cole Porter wasn't perfect, only incomparable. il por N Y Times Mag p 18-19+ O 10 '71
SEVERS, Helen G.
Return; poem. Todays Ed 60:36-7 F '71
SEVERTSON, Susan, and Banks, George
Toward the library-bookstore. bibliog il pors Library J 96:163-6 Ja 15 '71

SEVILLE, Spain
¡Sevilla! where Carmen lived and died; photographs. T. Eigeland. Opera N 35:8-13 F 6 '71
SEVIN. See Insecticides
SEWAGE as fertilizer
It's not sludge, it's fertilizer; Winston-Salem, N.C. F. Styers. il Am City 86:48-50 F '71
New directions in water pollution abatement. R. H. Gilluly. il Sci N 99:286-7 Ap 24 '71
Value of sludge; projects in Chicago. il Time 98:93+ S 27 '71
SEWAGE disposal
Challenge for the President; proposed bill of Senator Muskie's subcommittee. J. Lear. Sat R 54:47 S 4 '71
Sewer shortage halts the builders. il Bsns W p54+ O 2 '71
Wastewater collection and treatment. See issues of American city
    See also
Privies
Sewage as fertilizer
Sewage lagoons
Trade waste disposal
Waste disposal in the ocean
Water pollution
    Rates
Try units to finance sewerage construction; Bath, N.Y. L. E. Bower. Am City 86:10 My '71
SEWAGE disposal plants
Camouflaged sewage plant; Freehold, N.J. S. Lindsay. il Sat R 54:56 S 4 '71
Cheaper way to burn sewage; demonstration plant in Freehold, N.J. Bsns W p38-9 Ag 7 '71
Cranes go round and round; St Louis. il Am City 86:34 Ag '71
Our plant must be a good neighbor; Plymouth, Mass. D. Smith. il Am City 86:89+ Ap '71
Pilot tests show promise of big savings; Unox wastewater-treatment; Sayreville, N.J. il Am City 86:13 Ap '71
Portable plant meets tertiary requirements; Colorado Springs. il Am City 86:63 Mr '71
Treat septic-tank wastes separately; Babylon, N.Y. R. MacCallum. il Am City 86:48-9 Ja '71
You don't necessarily need aerobes; Rocky River, Ohio. il Am City 86:61-2 Ap '71
    Automatic control
Natural gas engines cut energy costs; Omaha, Neb. il Am City 86:44-5 Jl '71
    Design
What about turnkey and wastewater projects? Am City 86:6 N '71
    Equipment
How to make digesters work faster; Bergen County, N.J. Am City 86:26 D '71
SEWAGE flow
Polymers can relieve surcharged sewers. J. I. Cahalan and others. il Am City 86:87-8+ S '71
Sewage reservoir solves overflow problem; San Diego, Calif. F. M. Conger. il Am City 86:103 N '71
SEWAGE lagoons
Oxidation ditch: best way yet to handle waste? W. Kester. il Farm J 95:B8-10 Ap '71
Oxidation ditches: their progress and problems. B. Eftink. il Suc Farm 69:28-9 Ag '71
Oxidation wheel that works. R. Wilmore. il Farm J 95:14-15 S '71
Propellor whips air into manure slurry. il Farm J 95:H9-10 N '71
SEWAGE pumps
Natural gas engines cut energy costs; Omaha, Neb. il Am City 86:44-5 Jl '71
SEWAGE purification
Breakthrough in water pollution; tertiary system at Lake Tahoe. L. A. Stevens. il Read Digest 98:167-8+ Je '71
Instant pH readings serve twofold purpose. A. Monaco. il Am City 86:42 O '71
New directions in water pollution abatement. R. H. Gilluly. il Sci N 99:286-7 Ap 24 '71
Phosphates and nitrates in surf waters. K. E. Glines. Chem 44:25-6 Mr '71
Tests microstraining and ozone on stormwater overflow; Philadelphia. il Am City 86:28 Ja '71
Treat septic-tank wastes separately; Babylon, N.Y. R. MacCallum. il Am City 86:48-9 Ja '71
Wastewater collection and treatment. See issues of American city
    See also
Sewage disposal plants
Water reuse

    Activated sludge method
Let's reunderstand activated sludge. B. L. Goodman. bibliog il Am City 86:63-7 O '71
Odor-prevention insurance; installing neutralizer at waste water purification plant, Clearwater, Fla. L. A. McDowell. il Am City 86:54+ F '71
Pilot tests show promise of big savings; Unox wastewater-treatment; Sayreville, N.J. il Am City 86:13 Ap '71
    Aeration
18 months of nuisance-free operation; Old Westbury, N.Y. S. A. Bogen. il Am City 86:71-3 Je '71
You don't necessarily need aerobes; Rocky River, Ohio. il Am City 86:61-2 Ap '71
    See also
Sewage lagoons
    Radioactive treatment
Recycled water: pure enough to drink because of cobalt-60. E. Hartley. il Sci Digest 70:82-6 N '71
SEWAGE treatment plants. See Sewage disposal plants
SEWELL, George A.
Hundred years of history. bibliog il pors Negro Hist Bul 34:78-9 Ap '71
SEWELL, Richard
Ledge pond; poem. New Yorker 46:36 F 13 '71
SEWER cleaning
Herbicide clears sewer roots; County of Sacramento, Calif. Am City 86:16-17 S '71
Jet-vacuum sewer cleaning; South Bend, Ind. il Am City 86:83 Jl '71
SEWER pipe laying. See Pipe laying
SEWER pipes
    See also
Sewer cleaning
    Leakage
Money down the drain; locating and stopping infiltration into the sanitary sewers; St Louis. C. F. Buettner. il Am City 86:60-2 Ag '71
    Maintenance and repair
Liner saves sewer replacement; Houston, Tex. il Am City 86:33 N '71
Money down the drain; locating and stopping infiltration into the sanitary sewers; St Louis. C. F. Buettner. il Am City 86:60-2 Ag '71
SEWER service charges. See Sewage disposal—Rates
SEWERAGE
Renew old sewers and then maintain them; Peoria, Ill. W. A. Olson. il Am City 86:105-6 O '71
    See also
Drainage
Pipe laying
Sewage disposal
Storm sewers
SEWERS. See Sewerage
SEWERS, Storm. See Storm sewers
SEWING
How home sewing can be profitable. Good H 173:196 O '71
Recycling old clothes. S. Rosenberg and J. Weiner. il pors Seventeen 30:244-5 Ag '71
7 easy ways to sew your own slipcover, tablecloths, curtains, pillows, tableskirt. il House & Gard 139:102-3 Ap '71
Sew your own decorator flourishes. il House B 113:69-78 bibliog(p 127) Ag '71
    See also
Curtains and draperies
Dressmaking
Needlework
    Study and teaching
How to teach your little girl to sew. il Good H 172:194 Mr '71
SEWING baskets. See Baskets
SEWING by men
Man that needle! with editorial comment. il Life 70:3, 80-3 My 28 '71
SEWING centers. See Sewing rooms
SEWING equipment
Sewing new knit and stretch fabrics. il Sunset 146:156 Ap '71
SEWING machines
Which sewing machine is best for you? J. L. Heckroth. il Bet Hom & Gard 49:160 N '71
SEWING patterns. See Patterns (dress)
SEWING rooms
Creativity thrives in an organized sewing center. il House B 113:76-8 Ag '71

SEWING rooms—*Continued*
Everything wall; laundry-sewing center. M. K. Spencer. il Am Home 74:76-8 F '71
Family-size sewing center. il Bet Hom & Gard 49:153 O '71
Sewing center that goes into hiding. il Sunset 146:153 Ap '71

SEX
Questions everyone asks about sex. D. Reuben. Read Digest 98:66-8 F '71
See also
Orgasm

Anecdotes, facetiae, satire, etc.
Sex tips. G. Keillor. New Yorker 47:31 Ag 14 '71

Research
See Sex research

SEX (biology)
Intersexes and sex determination in chickens. F. Abdel-Hameed and R. N. Shoffner. bibliog il Science 172:962-4 My 28 '71
See also
Estrus

SEX (psychology)
Feminization of the American male. D. Rader. por Harp Baz 105:106-7+ N '71
Herodotus: observer of sexual psychopathology. C. P. Rossenbaum and R. Rossi. bibliog Am Imago 28:71-8 Spr '71
My husband was afraid of sex. il Good H 174:34+ Ja '72
Opinion: a lesbian and a homosexual on female sexuality. J. Johnston; L. Skir. Mlle 74:76+ N '71
Sex: up with the stock market. B. Wysor. Vogue 157:87-8+ F 15 '71
See also
Sex role

SEX, Change of. See Change of sex

SEX and law
Sex & the law. H. Colton. Harp Baz 104:108-9+ Ag '71
See also
Prostitution

SEX and religion
Pious pornography. N. M. Tischler. Chr Today 15:14-15 Ap 23 '71
Sex and the supernatural. J. R. Moore. Chr Today 15:7-8+ My 7 '71
Sexual revolution, would you believe? Graymoor conference. D. Grumbach. Commonweal 94:180-1 Ap 30 '71

SEX attractants (insects) See Insect sex attractants

SEX behavior. See Sexual behavior

SEX control. See Sex determination and control

SEX crimes
What sex offenders say about poronography. G. D. Shultz. Read Digest 99:53-7 Jl '71
See also
Child molesters
Rape
Sex and law

SEX determination and control
Intersexes and sex determination in chickens. F. Abdel-Hameed and R. N. Shoffner. bibliog il Science 172:962-4 My 28 '71
Present shock. D. M. Rorvik. Esquire 76:26 Ag '71

SEX differences
Biological superiority: female or male? R. Winter; K. Anderson. il Sci Digest 70:44-7+ Ag '71
Case against Unisex. H. Perlman. Ed Digest 36:32-3 F '71
FemLib case against Sigmund Freud. R. Gilman. il pors N Y Times Mag p 10-11+ Ja 31 '71; Discussion. p6+ Mr 7 '71
Male chauvinist Spock recants, well almost. B. Spock. N Y Times Mag p98+ S 12 '71
Sex difference in the number of sympathetic neurons in the spinal cord of the cat. F. R. Calaresu and J. L. Henry. bibliog il Science 173:343-4 Jl 23 '71
Sex differences in I.Q. pattern of children with congenital heart defects. M. P. Honzik and others. bibliog il Science 174:1042-4 D 3 '71
There are sex differences in the mind, too. T. Alexander. il Fortune 83:76-9+ F '71

SEX education. See Sex instruction

SEX hormones. See Hormones, Sex

SEX in algae. See Algae, Sex in

SEX in literature
Everything you always wanted to know about censorship (but were afraid to ask) explained. E. M. Oboler. bibliog il Am Lib 2:194-8 F '71
Pious pornography. N. M. Tischler. Chr Today 15:14-15 Ap 23 '71
Sex and the single child; symposium. bibliog il Wilson Lib Bul 46:144-76 O '71

SEX in moving pictures
Are dirty movies on the way out? J. Reddy. PTA Mag 66:2-5 N '71; Same abr. Read Digest 99:110-13 N '71
Eroticism and the art of film; address, 1970. G. W. Jones. il Library J 96:3809-10 N 15 '71
From hot panting to hotpants. D. Newman and R. Benton. il Mlle 73:82-3+ Jl '71
No more sex? S. Kauffmann. New Repub 164:24+ My 22 '71
Pornography and politics: effects of sex in movies and plays on our standards of personal privacy and political freedom. R. Ward. Nat R 23:1178-9+ O 22 '71
See also
Moving pictures in sex instruction

Anecdotes, facetiae, satire, etc.
Oh, that Danish blue! F. Shakespeare. Nat R 23:192+ F 23 '71

SEX in the performing arts
Pornography and politics; effects of sex in movies and plays on our standards of personal privacy and political freedom. R. Ward. Nat R 23:1178-9+ O 22 '71
See also
Sex in moving pictures

SEX instruction
Born knowing. il Good H 173:76+ S '71
Finally: a serious, humane book about sex. D. N. Mount. il Pub W 199:122-5 My 31 '71
How to talk to your parents about sex; ed. by M. Brenton. O. Rabinowitz. Seventeen 30:152-3+ Mr '71
Pornography, ho-hum. C. H. Simonds. Nat R 23:705 Je 29 '71
Reflections on the publication of a Sex book. P. C. Rule. America 125:128 S 4 '71
Sex at Sunday school. il Newsweek 78:50-1 D 27 '71
Sex book, by M. Goldstein and others. Review
America 125:129-30 S 4 '71. M. S. Calderone
Sex book. il Newsweek 77:56 My 17 '71
Sex dictionary. il Time 97:72 My 17 '71
Sex education for the whole society. M. S. Calderone. Ed Digest 37:43-5 O '71
Sex education in America. E. Berne. Harp Baz 104:140-1 Mr '71
Sex education in the secondary curriculum: problems and pseudo-problems. P. M. Collins. Sch & Soc 99:357-9 O '71
Sex education: time for appraisal. G. H. Gumm. Clear House 46:110-11 O '71
Sex goes to college. A. H. Malcolm. il Todays Health 49:26-9 Ap '71
Sex on the phone; Community sex information and education service Inc. Time 98:33 Jl 19 '71
Special sex education survey. M. Hunt. il Seventeen 29:94-7+ Jl '70
Teacher opinion poll. il Todays Ed 60:60 Ja '71
What schoolgirls want to know about sex. J. L. Block. il Good H 173:64-5+ Ag '71
Who teaches? Catholic parents vs. schools over compulsory sex education. Sr Schol 98:10-11 Mr 29 '71
See also
Moving pictures in sex instruction

Bibliography
More than moral indignation. A. Eggebroten. Chr Today 16:15-18+ N 19 '71
Sex is not a four-letter word. E. T. White and R. Friedman. bibliog il pors Wilson Lib Bul 46:153-62 O '71
Views on science books. H. C. Stubbs. Horn Bk 47:69-71 F '71

SEX manuals. See Marriage—Handbooks, manuals, etc.

SEX pheromones (insects) See Insect sex attractants

SEX ratio
Parthenogenesis: does it occur spontaneously in mice? W. K. Whitten. bibliog Science 171:406-7 Ja 29 '71

SEX relations
Advice to married couples. W. H. Masters and V. E. Johnson. il Redbook 137:92-3+ S '71
Advice to young women; questions and answers. W. H. Masters and V. E. Johnson. il Redbook 138:78-9+ Ja '72
Are you killing love with sex problems you create? P. M. Sarrel and L. J. Sarrel. Vogue 158:269-70 S 1 '71
Doctor William H. Masters and Virginia E. Johnson: advice on married love. W. H. Masters and V. E. Johnson. Redbook 137:75+ My '71; Same abr. with title Real role of love in marriage. Read Digest 99:129-32 Ag '71

SEX relations—*Continued*
Female sexuality: what it is and isn't; symposium. il Mlle 73:108-17 Jl '71
Fighting words: American women are lousy lovers. S. Rattazzi. Vogue 158:91+ Jl '71
Jupiter's brain: notes on sexual compatibility and astrology. R. Phelps. il Mlle 73:130-1+ S '71
Opinion: on man and woman. J. M. Ganguli. por Mlle 73:38+ My '71
Premarital sex. D. Reuben. McCalls 98:50+ Mr '71
Report on a consciousness-raising group. il Mlle 73:80-1+ Jl '71
Sex questions people don't ask and should; interview, ed. by L. Kent. V. E. Johnson; W. A. Masters il pors Vogue 158:88-91 Ag 15 '71
Sexually sensible woman H. La Barre. Ladies Home J 88:50+ Ag '71
Will liberalized sex kill romantic love? J. Brothers. il Good H 172:62+ Je '71

SEX research
Sex questions people don't ask and should; interview, ed. by L. Kent. V. E. Johnson; W. A. Masters. il pors Vogue 158:88-91 Ag 15 '71

SEX role
Challenge to every marriage. A. Shulman. Redbook 137:57+ Ag '71
Changing identities; Rorschach test responses. il Newsweek 78:44-5 S 6 '71
Courage to see; religious implications of the new sisterhood. M. Daly. Chr Cent 88:1108-11 S 22 '71
Does your child want to grow up to be just like mommy or daddy? B. Bettelheim. Ladies Home J 88:30+ Jl '71
Feminist manifesto; excerpt from address. L. Komisar. Read Digest 99:105-8 Ag '71
50/50 marriage: is this what women want? S. North. il Look 35:57-61 O 5 '71
Gloria Steinem, writer and social critic, talks about sex, politics and marriage; interview, ed. by L. Smith. G. Steinem. il Redbook 138:68-76 Ja '72
How ideology shapes women's lives. J. Lipman-Blumen. il Sci Am 226:34-42 Ja '72
How to make tapioca pudding; Karen Jensen; photographs. Esquire 76:68-71 Jl '71
Ibsen's Nora and ours; meeting of the Theatre for ideas J. Richardson. Commentary 52:77-80 Jl '71
Liberated woman. M. Decter; discussion. Commentary 51:12+ F '71
Male chauvinist Spock recants, well, almost. B. Spock. N Y Times Mag p98+ S 12 '71
Men who envy women. Newsweek 77:58 Mr 29 '71
Mother Portnoy's complaints. P. Bart. il Trans-Action 8:69-74 N '70
Must marriage cheat today's young women? P. E. Slater. il Redbook 136:66-7+ F '71
My Mailer problem. G. Greer. por Esquire 76:90-3+ S '71
Myths that keep women down. C. Bird. Ladies Home J 88:68+ N '71
Opinion: on the subtle chauvinism of Princeton males. K. Boals. por Mlle 72:56+ Ap '71
Prisoner of sex. N. Mailer. bibliog f il por(p4) Harper 242:41-6+ Mr '71; Discussion. 242: 6+ Je; 243:16+ Jl '71
Rape: the all-American crime. S. Griffin. il Ramp Mag 10:26-35 S '71
Role of male and female in children's books, dispelling all doubt. M. R. Key. bibliog il por Wilson Lib Bul 46:167-76 O '71
Sexism in the head. A. Croce. bibliog f Commentary 51:63-8 Mr '71
Sexual stereotypes start early; excerpt from address. F. Howe. il Sat R 54:76-7+ O 16 '71
Status is the name of the game. Trans-Action 8:6+ F '71
Unisex in the laboratory; Rorschach ink-blot test. il Time 98:48-9 S 6 '71
Why children's films are not rated R. H. Miller. il Wilson Lib Bul 46:183-4 O '71
Woman problem; with account by R. Gilman. il Life 71:40-8+ Ag 13; 46-51 Ag 27 '71
Women: the new image; address, June 3, 1971. A. S. Fraser. Vital Speeches 37:599-605 Jl 15 '71
Women's liberation: humanizing rather than polarizing. J. D. Mandle. bibliog f Ann Am Acad 397:118-28 S '71
Women's liberation: or, Exploding the fairy princess myth. A. G. West. bibliog f Schol Teach Jr/Sr High p6-11 N '71
You've come a long way, Buddy. B. Farrell. il Life 71:52+ Ag 27 '71

SEX role in literature
Sexism (Sic) in children's books; report of panel discussion. il Pub W 199:20-2 Mr 22 '71

SEXTANTS
How it works: the marine sextant. C. Miller. il Motor B & S 127:118+ Ap '71

SEXTON, Anne
Boat; poem. New Yorker 47:30 Ag 7 '71
Three poems: For Mr death who stands with his door open; Doctor of the heart; Ambition bird. il Sat R 54:18-19 Ag 14 '71
Wedlock; poem. New Repub 165:23 D 11 '71

about

Transformations, by A. Sexton. Review
New Repub 165:29-30 O 16 '71. L. Coxe •

SEXTON, John C. Jr
One for one. il por Newsweek 76:68 O 25 '71 •

SEXUAL behavior
Blacks and the sexual revolution. A. F. Poussaint. il por Ebony 26:112-14+ O '71
Facts versus fears: why should we worry about pornography? W. C. Wilson. bibliog f Ann Am Acad 397:105-17 S '71
Group sex. il Newsweek 77:98-9 Je 21 '71
I don't regard sex as fun; interview. N. Shainess. Mlle 73:78-9+ Jl '71
Is virginity outmoded? D. A. Sugarman and R. Hochstein. il Seventeen 30:120-1+ O '71
Man talk: rated X; the nature of female sexuality. D. Newman and R. Benton. Mlle 72:54 F '71
Sex before sport? il Time 97:54 Mr 15 '71
Sexual problems of women alone. D. Reuben. por McCalls 98:62+ F '71
Social control of pornography and sexual behavior. B. L. Bonniwell. bibliog f Ann Am Acad 397:97-104 S '71
Too much sex too little joy? excerpt from Love and will. R. May. Read Digest 98:68-70 My '71
What's happening to American morals; symposium. U S News 70:68-74 Ja 25 '71
See also
Aged—Sexual behavior
College students—Sexual behavior
Middle age—Sexual behavior

Bibliography
New sexistentialism. B. DeMott. Sat R 54: 21-5+ Jl 10 '71
Birds
See also
Courtship of birds

Crustaceans
Metachronal limb movements by artemia salina: synchrony of male and female during coupling. C. M. Lent. bibliog il Science 173:1247-8 S 24 '71

SEXUAL behavior in animals
p-Chlorophenylalanine methyl ester; an aphrodisiac? R. E. Whalen and W. C. Luttge; reply. G. L. Gessa and others. Science 171:706 F 19 '71
Copulatory behavior can inhibit pregnancy in female rats. N. T. Adler and S. R. Zoloth; reply with rejoinder. P. Dziuk. bibliog Science 171:311-12 Ja 22 '71

SEXUAL crimes. See Sex crimes
SEXUAL dimorphism. See Dimorphism (biology)
SEXUAL diseases. See Venereal diseases
SEXUAL ethics
American way of swinging. il Time 97:51 F 8 '71
Fair way to end prostitution? L. Kanowitz. McCalls 99:38 N '71
Invasion of compulsory sex-morality, by W. Reich. Review
New Repub 165:27 O 30 '71. J. Wilton •
Plea for privacy. M. Holmes. il PTA Mag 65:10-12 Mr '71
Radical family. J. Poppy. il Look 35:81-2+ Ja 26 '71
Sell-out; notions of morality. D. Newman and R. Benton. Mlle 74:92 N '71
7 snares that lead men to affairs; extramarital relationships. W. M. Fine. Harp Baz 104:98-9 Ap '71
Sexual revolution, would you believe? Graymoor conference. D. Grumbach. Commonweal 94:180-1 Ap 30 '71
See also
Sex instruction
Sex relations
Virginity

SEXUAL maturity. See Puberty
SEXUAL perversion
See also
Homosexuality
SEXUAL sterilization. See Sterilization, Sexual

SEYCHELLES (islands)
Promiscuous isles. P. Webb. il Newsweek 78:
55 D 6 '71
See also
Aldabra Island
Zoology—Seychelles (islands)
SEYFERT galaxies. See Galaxies
SEYMOUR, Dorothy Z.
Black children, black speech. Commonweal
95:175-8 N 19 '71
SHACKFORD, R. H.
Reports and comment: Washington. Atlan
228:18-20+ S '71
SHAD fishing
Shad, the spring fish. J. Brooks. il Outdoor
Life 147:114+ Ap '71
SHADBLOWS. See Serviceberries (tree)
SHADBUSHES. See Serviceberries (tree)
SHADE
See also
Sunlight
SHADE plants. See Plants, Shade
SHADRACK ole Sainepu (Masai tribesman)
Modern Masai. H. Reuter. il pors Ebony 26:
87-91 Ap '71 •
SHADWELL, Wendy J.
Some pre-Revolutionary prints and broad-
sides. il Antiques 99:262-7 F '71
SHAFER, Donald H.
State's thermal profile. il Cons 25:31-2 F '71
SHAFER, Tom
Tyrone and Julie Larson. il pors Ceram Mo
19:14-16 Ap '71
—and Shafer, Yvonne
Pottery in Manises. il Ceram Mo 20:14-18
Ja '72
SHAFER, Yvonne. See Shafer, T. jt. auth.
SHAFFER, Anthony
Sleuth. Criticism
Nat R 23:324 Mr 23 '71 •
SHAFFER, Elaine
Ladies' week in the world of music. I. Kolo-
din. Sat R 54:44 F 13 '71 •
SHAFFER, Ellen
Hornbook, an invitation to learning. il Horn
Bk 47:85-91 F '71
SHAFFER, Kenneth R.
Decision making; excerpts. il por Library J
96:1677-80 My 15 '71
Library systems: tough times ahead? il por
Library J 96:2263-5 Jl '71
SHAFFER, Raymond F.
With several ways to go, he chose up. il
pors Nations Bsns 59:60-1 Ja '71
SHAFFER, Thomas L.
Searching mind of men and property. il To-
days Ed 60:25-7 N '71
SHAH, Dinesh O. and Hamlin, R. M. Jr
Structure of water in microemulsions: elec-
trical, birefringence, and nuclear magnetic
resonance studies. bibliog il Science 171:
483-5 F 5 '71
SHAHEEN, John M.
Daily will try where others failed. por Bsns
W p27-8 O 16 '71 •
SHAHN, Ben
Education of an artist; excerpt from The
shape of content. Am Artist 35:5 My '71
SHAINESS, Natalie
I don't regard sex as fun; interview. Mlle
73:78-9+ Jl '71
Mental health movement meets women's lib;
interview. Ment Hy 55:1-9 Ja '71
SHAKESPEARE, Francis
Oh, that Danish blue! Nat R 23:192+ F 23 '71
SHAKESPEARE, William
Shakespeare, with an eye to ophthalmology.
il Todays Health 49:71 Mr '71 •

Characters
Desdemona: an innocent victim? R. Dickes.
bibliog Am Imago 27:279-97 Fall '70
Desdemona's guilt. S. Reid. bibliog Am Imago
27:245-62 Fall '70
Falstaff behind the arras. M. D. Faber. bibliog Am Imago 27:197-225 Fall '70
In defense of Goneril and Regan. S. Reid.
bibliog Am Imago 27:226-44 Fall '70

Criticism and interpretation
Breath of clowns and kings, by T. Weiss.
Review
Nation 213:122-3 Ag 16 '71. T. H. Jame-
son
Othello: the justice of it pleases. M. D.
Faber. bibliog Am Imago 26:228-46 Fall
'71
Shakespeare's sexual comedy: a mirror for
lovers, by H. M. Richmond. Review
America 126:27-8 Ja 8 '72. T. H. Stahel

Moving pictures
Shakespeare on screen. H. L. Hennedy.
Commonweal 95:134-5 N 5 '71

Plays
Cymbeline
Full stretch; New York Shakespeare festival.
J. Kroll. il Newsweek 78:82 Ag 30 '71
King Lear
In defense of Goneril and Regan. S. Reid.
bibliog Am Imago 27:226-44 Fall '70
Macbeth
Off Broadway; production directed by Dino
DeFilippi at the Mercer-O'Casey. E. Oliver.
New Yorker 46:75 Ja 16 '71
Merry wives of Windsor
0 for 2. T. E. Kalem. il Time 98:57 Jl 5 '71
Midsummer night's dream
Bottom's song: Shakespeare in junior high.
E. Eidenier. Engl J 60:208-11 F '71
Broadway and the British; Brook's dream.
C. Hughes. il Cath World 212:315 Mr '71
Circus in the Forest of Arden; Peter Brook's
production. T. Prideaux. Life 70:12 F 26
'71
Dream for mortals; Peter Brook's new Royal
Shakespeare company production. H. Hewes.
Sat R 54:48+ F 6 '71
Dream of love; production by P. Brook.
J. Kroll. il Newsweek 77:73 F 1 '71
Frolicking with the bard. T. E. Kalem. Time
97:76 F 1 '71
Midsummer's night re-dreamed; Peter
Brook's production. M. Warner. il Vogue
157:56-7 Ja 15 '71
Shakespeare and Beckett; Peter Brook's pro-
duction. J. Richardson. Commentary 51:76-
7 Ap '71
Swinging Shakespeare. il Life 70:64-7+ Ap 9
'71
Theatre; P. Brook's production. H. Clurman.
Nation 212:188-9 F 8 '71
Theater; Peter Brook's production. S. Kauff-
mann. New Repub 164:24+ F 20 '71
Theatre; Royal Shakespeare company pro-
duction directed by Peter Brook. B. Gill.
New Yorker 46:54 Ja 30 '71
Othello
Desdemona: an innocent victim? R. Dickes.
bibliog Am Imago 27:279-97 Fall '70
Desdemona's guilt. S. Reid. bibliog Am Imago
27:245-62 Fall '70
Othello: the justice of it pleases. M. D.
Faber. bibliog Am Imago 26:228-46 Fall
'71 •
Wounded animal; revival at Los Angeles'
Mark Taper forum. T. E. Kalem. por Time
97:75 Ap 26 '71
Richard II
New Barrymore. T. E. Kalem. por Time 97:
74 Ap 26 '71
Richard III
Richard III. Shakespeare, and history. S.
E. Leas. bibliog Engl J 60:1214-16+ D '71
Tempest
0 for 2. T. E. Kalem. il Time 98:57 Jl 5 '71
Winter's tale
Winter's tale. S. Reid. bibliog Am Imago
27:263-78 Fall '70

Psychology
Shakespeare: symposium. bibliog Am Imago
27:197-297 Fall '70

Staging and acting of plays
Peter Brook's Midsummer night's dream. il
Life 70:64-7+ Ap 9 '71

Study and teaching
Shakespeare: why ignore the comedies and
the histories? M. O. Fisher. Engl J 60:587-90
My '71
SHAKESPEARE festival public theater. See
New York Shakespeare festival
SHAKESPEARE festivals
Ashland in 1971: more and earlier. Sunset
146:67 Mr '71
See also
American Shakespeare festival theatre and
academy, Stratford, Conn.
New York Shakespeare festival
SHALES, Oil See Oil shales
SHALIT, Gene
Look at the movies. See occasional issues of
Look to October 19, 1971
What's happening. See issues of Ladies' home
journal
SHALLOTS
Arkansas shallots stay versatile. M. Bobbitt.
il Org Gard & Farm 18:82-3 My '71

SHAMAN, Harvey
  Bold color from b&w. il Pop Phot 69:92-5 Jl
  '71
SHAMAN, Jeffrey M.
  Education as a source of power. Sch & Soc
  99:166-8 Mr '71
SHAMAN. See Medicine men
SHAMPOOS
  Great color wash-in. il Harp Baz 104:18 Je
  '71
SHANAS, Bert
  Help for girls in trouble. Parents Mag 46:42-
  3+ Je '71
SHANE, Harold G. and Nelson, O. N.
  What will the schools become? Ed Digest 37:
  1-3 O '71
SHANE, Rita
  Lulu; interview, ed. by G. Loney. por Opera
  N 35:26 Ap 17 '71
SHANIDAR cave excavation. See Iraq—An-
  tiquities
SHANKAR, Ravi
  Colossal event. J.-C. Costa. il pors Sr Schol
  99:32-4 S 27 '71 *
  Concert. New Yorker 47:28-30 Ag 14 '71 *
SHANNON, Claude Elwood
  Energy and information. M. Tribus and E. C.
  McIrvine.   il Sci Am 225:179-84+ bib-
  liog(p244+) S '71 *
SHANNON, Joseph
  All the birds and the beasts were there. J.
  Ashbery. il por Art N 70:36-7+ Mr '71 *
SHANNON, William V.
  Death of time; reprint. Am Heritage 23:107
  D '71
SHANNON RIVER
  Shannon cruise. G. Fitzsimons. il Travel 136:
  40-3+ Jl '71
  Soothing lethargy. M. Badham. il Yachting
  129:64+ F '71
SHANTIES (songs) See Sailors songs
SHAPELL industries, inc.
  Shapell's own housing boom. il Duns 98:58-9
  Jl '71
SHAPERS
  Meet the molders. R. J. De Cristoforo. il Mech
  Illus 67:117-19 My '71
SHAPIRA, R. and others
  Biological activity and synthesis of an en-
  cephalitogenic determinant. bibliog il Sci-
  ence 173:736-8 Ag 20 '71
SHAPIRO, David, 1947-
  American quilts. il Craft Horiz 31:42-5+ D
  '71
  Homage to Albers. il por Art N 70:30-3+ N
  '71
  Imago mundi. il pors Art N 70:40-1+ O '71
  Reuben Kadish. il Craft Horiz 31:26-9 F '71
  652 Broadway. il por Art N 70:50-2+ Ap '71
SHAPIRO, Harry L.
  Strange, unfinished saga of Peking man; with
  biographical sketch. il Natur Hist 80:2,
  8-10+ N '71
SHAPIRO, Lucille, and others
  Bacterial differentiation. bibliog il Science
  173:884-92 S 3 '71
SHAPIRO, Paula Melnetz
  Innovator for tomorrow. il pors Dance Mag
  45:62-5 F '71
SHAPIRO, Peter. See Connolly, S. jt. auth.
SHAPIRO, Theodore
  Symbolic process: a colloquium. bibliog Am
  Imago 28:195-215 Fall '71
SHAPIRO, Walter
  Profit motive and the public interest: Wright
  Patman vs. the bankers. il Ramp Mag 9:16-
  20 My '71
SHAPLEN, Robert
  Letter from Hong Kong. New Yorker 47:58-
  60+ Jl 31 '71
  Letter from Indo-China (cont) New Yorker
  47:78+ Mr 6; 104-12+ Ap 24 '71
  Letter from Saigon (cont) New Yorker 47:
  96+ S 11 '71
  Letter from Vietnam. New Yorker 47:77-8+
  N 13 '71
SHAPLEY, Harlow
  Harlow Shapley, cosmographer; man of the
  world. B. J. Bok; K. F. Mather. Am Scholar
  40:470-81 Sum '71
SHAPP, Milton J.
  Educational process; address. September 23,
  1971. Vital Speeches 38:49-51 N 1 '71
  Need for increased public investment. Ann
  Am Acad 397:40-7 S '71

  about

  Battle over bankruptcy. il Time 98:11-12 Jl
  19 '71 *
SHARBAUGH, H. Robert
  Unleash the people; address. March 1, 1971.
  Vital Speeches 37:413-16 Ap 15 '71

SHARE-cropping
  Unchanged South. J. E. White, jr. il Ebony
  26:126-8+ Ag '71
SHARE-the-work plan. See Part time employ-
  ment
SHARECROPPERS. See Share-cropping
SHAREHOLDERS. See Stockholders
SHAREHOLDERS meetings. See Stockholders
  meetings
SHARIFF, Zahid
  Social information and government-sponsored
  development: a case study from West
  Pakistan. bibliog f il Ann Am Acad 393:
  92-108 Ja '71
SHARK fishing
  Thing in Hatchet Bay. R. D. Legg. il pors
  Outdoor Life 148:80-1 S '71
SHARKNAS, Jenevie
  After all. Todays Ed 60:64 D '71
SHARKS
  Blue meridian, by P. Matthiessen. Review
    Natur Hist il 80:94-6+ My '71. W. F.
    Herrnkind
  Connections on the nurse shark's telencepha-
    lon. S. O. E. Ebbesson and D. M. Schroe-
    der bibliog il Science 173:254-6 Jl 16 '71
  Great white shark. il Life 70:58-63 Mr 26 '71
  In the blue mist; excerpts from Blue merid-
    ian. P. Matthiessen. il Audubon 73:4-12
    Ja '71
  Invasion of sharks. E. S. Hodgson. il Natur
    Hist 80:92-101 D '71
  Killer shark may save your life. G. Young.
    il Pop Mech 135:70-4+ Je '71
  Sea serpents: what they really are; rotting
    carcass of basking shark. D. Cohen. il Sci
    Digest 69:27-8 Mr '71
  Shark! A. J. McClane. il Field & S 75:38 Mr
    8 '71
  Shark; excerpt from The shark: splendid
    savage of the sea. J. Y. Cousteau and P.
    Cousteau. il Read Digest 99:103-8 S '71
  Shark vs porpoise. R. F. Burgess. bibliog il
    Sci Digest 69:36-40 Je '71
  Ultimate predator; great white shark. J.
    Lipscomb. il Sports Illus 35:22-6+ Ag 23
    '71
SHARM EL SHEIKH, Egypt
  Policing the peace. New Repub 164:8 Ap 10 '71
  Sharm el Sheikh: a nice place to live. M.
    Levin. il Time 97:24 My 3 '71
SHARMAN, Bill
  Why L.A. loves the Lakers. il por Newsweek
    78:73 D 13 '71 *
SHARNIK, Morton
  Buckeyes' don't have it. il Sports Illus 35:
    30-2+ Jl 5 '71
  Super bowl. il por Sports Illus 34:19-20+ Ja
    18 '71
  (ed) See Frazier, J. I got a surprise for Clay
  —See Maule, T. jt. auth.
SHARON steel corporation
  Prime target for the SEC. por Bsns W p56
    Je 19 '71
SHARP, Frank W.
  Big names in a Texas stock scheme. por
    Bsns W p77 Ja 23 '71 *
  Enforcer steps down. Time 98:16+ O 25 '71 *
  Founder. il por Time 97:18+ F 15 '71
  High wind in Texas.Newsweek 77:61 F 1
    '71 *
  I.O.U.'s of Texas are upon us. America 124:
    139 F 13 '71 *
  Promoter and the crime buster. D. Jackson.
    il pors Life 71:59-60+ S 24 '71 *
  Taint in the Justice department. por Time
    98:12-13 S 13 '71 *
  Texas does it big. Nation 213:324 O 11 '71 *
  Widening impact of a Texas scandal. Bsns W
    p22 Ja 30 '71 *
  Will Wilson's loans. il pors Newsweek 78:
    16-17 S 13 '71 *
SHARP, Kenneth J.
  Abortion's psychological price. Chr Today 15:
    4-6 Je 4 '71
SHARP, Michael Bruce
  Will somebody please welcome this hero
    home? B. Lindeman. il pors Todays Health
    49:54-6+ Je '71 *
SHARP, Peter T. See Carroll, B. J. jt. auth.
SHARPENERS
  Now, sharpen your drills like a pencil; Black
    & Decker electric sharpener. E. F. Linds-
    ley. il Pop Sci 199:128 O '71
  Super-sharp sharpener. C. Conley. il Field &
    S 75:185 Ap '71
SHARPENING
    See also
  Grinding machines
SHARPLES, James, family
  Sharples family of painters. A. Wilson. il
    Antiques 100:740-3 N '71
SHARPLESS, D. R.
  To be of special services. il Parks & Rec 6:45-
    52 My '71

SHARPS rifles. See Rifles
SHARPSTOWN state bank. See Houston, Tex.
—Banks
SHARR, F. A.
Proper study of librarianship; address, February 1971. il por Library J 96:3727-30 N 15 '71
SHASTA LAKE
Off-season cruising in a Shasta Lake houseboat. il Sunset 147:34+ N '71
SHATTERLY, Daniel. See Verden, P. jt. auth.
SHATTUCK, Stefanie R. See Held, R. jt. auth.
SHAUB, Benjamin M.
Woody flowering natives. il Horticulture 49:36-7+ Mr '71
SHAVER, Samuel M.
Three Tennessee painters. B. H. Bishop. il Antiques 100:432-7 S '71 •
SHAVING
See also
Razor blades
SHAW, Arnold
Puppet, pirate, poet, pawn, and king. il pors Hi Fi 21:65-8 Ag '71
Songwriter & the record business today. il Writers Digest 51:24-7+ N '71
SHAW, Bernard. See Shaw, G. B.
SHAW, F. Alden
Essentialist challenge to American education. bibliog Sch & Soc 99:210-14 Ap '71
SHAW, George Bernard
Our lost honesty. il Harper 243:96-9 O '71
about
George Bernard Shaw's vegetarian recipes. R. J. Minney. il por Harp Baz 104:151-3 O '71 •
Shaw looks at Verdi; reprint from The Nation, July 7, 1917 issue. pors Opera N 35:24-5 Mr 13 '71 •
SHAW, Jane
One long fight that preservationists lost. il Arch Rec 150:10 D '71
SHAW, John F.
Heresy of John F. Shaw: a purloined letter. Nation 212:173-7 F 8 '71
about
Atrocious judgment. Nation 212:131-2 F 1 '71 •
SHAW, Margery W. See Craig-Holmes, A. P. jt. auth.
SHAW, Martha E.
Art education and the public taste. Am Artist 35:5 Ag '71
SHAW, Mildred
Visual illusions. il Sch Arts 71:40 N '71
SHAW, Peter
On Ford Madox Ford. Commentary 52:79-82 S '71
SHAW, Ray E. See Osborne, T. Z. jt. auth.
SHAW, Robert B.
As he is. Poetry 118:349-51 S '71
Janus; Not answering letters; There; poems. Poetry 117:227-30 Ja '71
Poets in midstream. Poetry 118:228-33 Jl '71
SHAW, Ruth Mepham
Women as forest workers. il Liv Wildn 35:30-1 Spr '71
SHAW, Tommy
Aloha for a bright young blond. D. Jenkins. il por Sports Illus 34:20-1 F 15 '71 •
SHAW, Vincent G.
I added power tilt to my outboard. il Pop Sci 198:93 Je '71
SHAW, Wally
Dream super 8 outfit. il por Pop Phot 68:115-16 F '71
SHAW, Miss.
New attacks on discrimination; Hawkins v. town of Shaw. il Time 97:59 F 22 '71 •
SHAWE-TAYLOR, Desmond
Historic master series: a last chance. Am Rec G 37:468-71 Ap '71
SHAWN, Ted
Anniversaries of Ted Shawn. W. Terry. il pors Dance Mag 45:26-9+ N '71 •
Ted Shawn: a father at eighty. W. Terry. il pors Sat R 54:22+ O 23 '71 •
SHAWNEE, Kan.
Education
NEA of Shawnee Mission. N. K. Nichols. Todays Ed 60:54 My '71
SHAYON, Robert Lewis
TV-radio. See issues of Saturday review
Television. New Repub 165:22+ D 11 '71
SHE stoops to conquer; drama. See Goldsmith, O.
SHEA, Gordon F.
Treasure; drama. Plays 30:76-8 Mr '71

SHEA, Kevin P.
Infectious cure. il Environ 13:43-5 Ja '71
New-car smell. bibliog il Environ 13:2-9 O '71
Old weapons are best. bibliog il Environ 13:40-9 Je '71
SHEAD, Edward A.
Out trail. Nat Parks & Con Mag 45:11 Ja '71
SHEAHEN, Al
Guaranteed annual income: a hope and question mark. America 125:503-7 D 11 '71
SHEARER, Derek
Evening with Henry. il Nation 212:296-9 Mr 8 '71
Reader's guide to the warfare state. bibliog Ramp Mag 9:55-9 Je '71
Reorganizing the lines of power. Nation 212:618-23 My 17 '71
SHEARER, Goldie
Popular garden stand features organic produce. il Org Gard & Farm 18:110-13 Ja '71
SHEARER, J. M. and others
Submarine pingos in the Beaufort Sea. bibliog il Science 174:816-18 N 19 '71
SHEARER, Sybil
Sybil Shearer and co, Chicago. A. Barzel. Dance Mag 45:87 My '71 •
SHEARLY, Mary
Otter life. Nat Parks & Con Mag 45:35 Ap '71
SHEARS. See Scissors and shears
SHEARSON, Hammill and company
See also
First Harlem securities corporation
SHEATSLEY, Paul B. See Greeley, A. M. jt. auth
SHECTER, Leonard
Fall and rise of Muhammad Ali. il pors Look 35:62-6 Mr 9 '71
Making of Fat city: craft beats art by a T.K.O. il Look 35:88-90 O 19 '71
What if they had a world series and nobody came? Look 35:22+ O 5 '71
You're gonna pay, baby. il Look 35:42-5 S 7 '71
(ed) See Bouton, J. I'm glad you didn't take it personally
SHEDD, Margaret Cochran
Authors & editors. B. A. Bannon. por Pub W 199:21-3 Mr 1 '71 •
SHEDD, Mark R.
Ousting a reformer. il por Time 98:58 D 20 '71 •
SHEDENHELM, W. R. C.
Back from Baja. il Motor T 23:50-1 F '71
SHEDLIN, Michael
(ed) See Hall, C. Conrad Hall: an interview
SHEDS
Anybody can build a backyard toolshed. il Changing T 25:45-6 Je '71
Her plant house beside the deck is a winter growing place for seedlings, a summer buffet for entertaining. il Sunset 146:46-7 Ja '71
See also
Agricultural machinery—Storage
Garden houses, shelters, etc.
SHEEAN, Vincent
Happy birthday, Aida! Opera N 36:8-9 D 25 '71
SHEED, Wilfrid
Dublin conversation: do you support the I.R.A? il N Y Times Mag p32-3+ O 24 '71
Thurber carnival. il Horizon 13:16-17 Aut '71
about
Critic, review thyself. V. Mercier. Nation 213:662-4 D 20 '71 •
SHEEHAN, B. Choyce
Coo-hoo. Har Yrs 11:34 Ap '71
SHEEHAN, Bobby
Bobby Boston doesn't own. M. Mulvoy. il por Sports Illus 35:60+ N 1 '71 •
SHEEHAN, Edward R. F.
Real Sadat and the demythologized Nasser. il pors N Y Times Mag p6-7+ Jl 18 '71
Second most important man in Egypt, and possibly the world's most powerful journalist. il pors N Y Times Mag p 12-13+ Ag 22 '71
SHEEHAN, Ethna
Children's books at Christmastime. il America 125:486-91 D 4 '71
SHEEHAN, John Eugene
Fed gets a businessman. por Bsns W p31 Ja 1 '72 •
SHEEHAN, Neil
Changing Times. por Newsweek 77:59 Ap 5 '71 •
Leaker, leakee. il por Newsweek 78:26 Jl 26 '71 •
SHEEHAN, Peter J.
Hart Crane and the contemporary search. Engl J 60:1209-13 D '71

SHEEHAN, Susan
Battling Buckley women. il McCalls 99:82-3+ O '71
SHEEHY, Gail
Lonely fear of a policeman's wife. il McCalls 98:96-9+ Mr '71
SHEEP

Diseases and pests

Aggregations of 35-nanometer particles associated with neuronal cytopathic changes in natural scrapie. A. Bignami and H. B. Parry. bibliog il Science 171:389-90 Ja 29 '71
Susceptibility of mink to sheep scrapie. R. P. Hanson and others. bibliog il Science 172:859-61 My 21 '71
SHEEP farms
Housewife at the end of the world: Tierra del Fuego. R. N. P. Goodall. il pors Nat Geog 139:130-50 Ja '71
SHEERAN, Michael J.
Home scene. America 125:438-9 N 20 '71
SHEERIN, John B.
Editorial. See issues of Catholic world
Synod: hope deferred; last editorial. Cath World 214:99-100 D '71

about

Father Sheerin retires as editor. K. A. Lynch. Cath World 214:100 D '71 *
SHEETS
How you can create a romantic bedroom, sheet mix-up. il House & Gard 139:42-9 Ja '71
Sheets & pillowcases: where to find the best buys. il Changing T 26:46 Ja '72
SHEEHAN, Lawrence Joseph, cardinal
Harrisburg conspiracy. Nation 212:133 F 1 '71 *
SHEIBE, W. G.
Fenceless pool in congress city. il Parks & Rec 6:32 Mr '71
SHEIKDOMS. See Arab states
SHEIN, Bob, and Tallon, Robert
Hands: inky fun with your fingers. il Life 71:156-60 D 17 '71
SHELANSKI, Michael L. and others
Isolation of filaments from brain. bibliog il Science 174:1242-5 D 17 '71
SHELBY, Shelby, fierce and free; story. See Trott, S.
SHELDON, Charles
Time for living. C. S. Murdock. il Liv Wildn 35:13-16 Spr '71 *
SHELL jewelry. See Jewelry
SHELL oil company
Moving time. L. L. L. Golden. Sat R 54:63 Je 12 '71
Shell: American, British or Dutch? il Forbes 109:28-9 Ja 1 '72
SHELL pictures. See Pictures
SHELLENBERGER, Donald
Plea for keeping camping both relevant and sane. il Camp Mag 43:11-12 Mr '71
SHELLEY, Percy Bysshe
Lovers; excerpt from The nympho and other maniacs. I. Wallace. pors Ladies Home J 88:127-33 F '71 *
SHELLFISH
Poison in shellfish. Newsweek 79:39 Ja 10 '72
See also
Cookery—Shellfish
Lobsters
SHELLFISH, Frozen
Frozen breaded shrimp. il Consumer Rep 37: 27-32 Ja '72
SHELLFISH culture
Raising crayfish in the farm pond. W. O. McLarney. Org Gard & Farm 18:84-5+ D '71
SHELLFISH fisheries
Ama, sea nymphs of Japan. L. Marden. il Nat Geog 140:122-35 Jl '71
Crab that shakes hands. C. P. Idyll. il Nat Geog 139:254-71 F '71
Fishery; New England fishery for deep-sea lobsters; letter. J. R. Uzmann. Harper 242: 18 F '71
See also
Pearl fisheries

International aspects

Lobster stew; Russia-U.S. discuss incidents. il Newsweek 77:23 My 31 '71
SHELLS (conchology)
Beach-combing. M. E. Slate. il Motor B & S 128:50-1 bibliog (p158) Jl '71
Natural history. A. G. Melvin. See issues of Hobbies

Shell provinces. A. G. Melvin. il Hobbies 76:148-9 O; 148 N; 148-9 D '71
See also
Nautilus
SHELLS, Orchestra. See Orchestra shells
SHELTER ROCK public library, Albertson, N.Y.
Albertson, N.Y: luxurious in Long Island. il Library J 96:3981 D 1 '71
SHELTERS
Build this low-cost winter home for your boat. D. G. Fenwick. il Pop Mech 136:119 N '71
No-cost vacation shelters let you recycle trash. A. Lees. il Pop Sci 199:72-5 Ag '71
See also
Garden houses, shelters, etc.
SHELTON, Richard
Requiem for sonora; poem. New Yorker 47: 30 S 4 '71
Totem; poem. New Yorker 47:154 O 23 '71
Winter; poem. New Yorker 46:102 F 13 '71
SHELTON, William R.
Science in Siberia. il Bul Atom Sci 27:23-8 F '71
SHELTON college, Cape May, N.J.
Degree decree. Chr Today 15:45 F 12 '71
Forecast for Shelton: a few degrees warmer? R. Chandler. Chr Today 15:42 Mr 26 '71
SHELVES
Shelves that move with you. R. W. Weed. il Pop Sci 198:150 My '71
Tall, slim and showy; open hi-fi rack. J. Hand. il Pop Mech 136:142-3 N '71
Wall-hung storage. cost about $36. il Sunset 146:146 My '71
SHEMANSKI, Frances
Europe on a budget. il Schol Teach Jr/Sr High p 16-17 Mr 8 '71
(comp) 1972 world travel calendar. Sat R 55: 43-7 Ja 1 '72
Travelguide. Schol Teach Jr/Sr High p34-5 S '71
Vacation getaways. il Schol Teach Jr/Sr High p20-2 My 3 '71
SHEMELLA, Betty
Birding by boat. il Motor B & S 128:52-3 bibliog (p58) Jl '71
SHEN, James C. H.
What now for Nationalist China; interview. il por U S News 71:42-5 Ag 2 '71
SHENKER, Israel
Borges, a blind writer with insight; reprint. il por Pub W 199:20-1 My 10 '71
Chomsky is difficult to please. . . il por Horizon 13:104-9 Spr '71
SHENOUDA III, Coptic patriarch
True Jews. il Newsweek 78:48 N 29 '71 *
SHEPARD, Alan Bartlett, 1923-
Once a fighter pilot. . . ; interview. il pors Space World H-4-88:20-3 Ap '71

about

From Mercury to Apollo 14. il pors Newsweek 77:62-3 F 1 '71*
Grand old man of space. por Time 97:46 F 1 '71 *
Old pro gets his shot at the moon. L. Wainwright. por Read Digest 98:88-92 Ja '71 *
Old pro goes all the way. il pors Life 70:32-5 F 19 '71 *
See also
Space flight to the moon—Manned flights—Apollo 14 flight
SHEPARD, Martin
Sensuous therapist. il por Newsweek 78:66 S 20 '71 *
SHEPARD, Roger N. and Metzler, Jacqueline
Mental rotation of three-dimensional objects. il Science 171:701-3 F 19 '71
SHEPARD, Sam
Mad dog blues. Criticism
America 124:408 Ap 17 '71 *
SHEPARD, Thomas R. Jr
Case against the disaster lobby; address, January 28, 1971. il Liv Wildn 35:25-30 Sum '71
We're going too far on consumerism! excerpts from address. Read Digest 98:147-50 F '71
SHEPHERD, Cybill
New stars, the new films. B. L. Feitler. por Harp Baz 105:70 D '71 *
SHEPHERD, J. Barrie
Christianity and criminality. il Chr Cent 88: 796-8 Je 30 '71
Shall these bones live? America 126:15-17 Ja 8 '72
SHEPHERD, Jack
America, you're beautiful. Look 35:33 Ja 12 '71
Introducing William Ruckelshaus, who? il pors Look 35:20-2 My 4 '71
One season in a quiet place. Look 35:48 Ja 12 '71

SHEPHERD, Jack—*Continued*
Polis '76. Look 35:43-4 Ja 12 '71
Trade winds; interview, ed. by C. Amory.
Sat R 54:8+ Mr 27 '71
SHEPHERD dogs
See also
German shepherd dogs
SHEPPARD, Carl F.
Specifying a custom sportfisherman. il
Motor B & S 127:35+ Je '71
SHEPPARD, Eugenia
Dashing young men. il Harp Baz 104:132 Mr
'71
Eligibles. Harp Baz 104:218-19 S '71
Eternal triangle. Harp Baz 104:88-9 Jl '71
Is marriage going out of style? il Harp Baz
104:168-9 O '71
Purposeful people. Harp Baz 104:134-5 F '71
Sleeping around. Harp Baz 105:138-9 N '71
SHEPPARD, Harold L.
Discontented blue-collar workers; a case
study. il Mo Labor R 94:25-32 Ap '71
SHEPPARD, John R. and others
Cell-surface changes after infection with on-
cogenic viruses: requirement for synthesis
of host DNA. bibliog il Science 172:1345-
6 Je 25 '71
SHEPPARD, Sam
Sheppard v. Maxwell, 1966. Cur Hist 61:106-
10+ Ag '71 *
SHEPPARD, Samuel H.
F. Lee Bailey's The defense never rests; ex-
cerpt from The defense never rests; ed. by
A. Aronson. F. L. Bailey. il pors Ladies
Home J 88:93-5+ O '71 *
SHERBET. See Ice cream, ices, etc.
SHERIDAN, Barbara
5 who fight pollution. C. Remsberg and B.
Remsberg. pors Seventeen 30:129+ Ap '71 *
SHERIDAN, David
At Cape Kennedy, a case of middle aged sag.
por Life 70:2A F 26 '71
SHERIDAN, James
Abacus, American style. il pors Nations
Bsns 59:76-7 Ja '71
SHERIDAN, Judson D. See Johnson, R. G. jt.
auth.
SHERIFFS
See also
Hongisto, R.
SHERIN, Ray
Youth art show. il Sch Arts 70:32-3 F '71
SHERLOCK, Holmes and the second stain;
drama. See Holmes, O. J.
SHERLOCK Holmes stories. See Doyle, A. C.
SHERMAN, Allan
Question of honor. il Read Digest 98:77-80 My
'71
Summer's magical music. Read Digest 99:58-
60 Jl '71
SHERMAN, Bennett
Techniques tomorrow. See issues of Modern
photography
SHERMAN, Edward F.
Bureaucracy adrift. Nation 212:265-75 Mr 1
'71
SHERMAN, Gordon B.
Ambush of generation gap. pors Time 97:
84 My 3 '71 *
SHERMAN, Howard, and others
Getting on talk shows. Writers Digest 51:30
Ag '71
SHERMAN, J. K.
Immortality and the freezing of human
bodies; with biographical sketch. Natur
Hist 80:2, 16-18+ D '71
SHERMAN, Joan R.
Poet with a purpose. bibliog Negro Hist Bul
34:163-4 N '71
SHERMAN, Nate H.
Ambush of generation gap. pors Time 97:84
My 3 '71 *
SHERMAN, R. G. and Atwood, H. L.
Synaptic facilitation: long-term neuromuscu-
lar facilitation in crustaceans. bibliog il Sci-
ence 171:1248-50 Mr 26 '71
SHERR, Lynn
Why astrology stays sky-high! il Seventeen
29:126-7+ N '70
SHERRILL, Robert G.
Before you believe those exercise and diet
ads read the following report. il Todays
Health 49:34-6+ Ag '71
Black humor of housing. Nation 212:397-402
Mr 29 '71
Education of a conservative. Nation 213:
105-10 Ag 16 '71
Embodiment of poor white power. il pors N Y
Times Mag p9+ F 28 '71
Eulogies and evasions. Nation 212:197-200
F 15 '71
Happy ending (maybe) of The selling of the
Pentagon. il N Y Times Mag p25-7+ My
16; 4+ Jl 18 '71

Invisible senator. por Nation 212:584-9 My 10
'71
Minor national monument. Nation 212:137-
41, 435 F 1, Ap 5 '71
Naked power of monopoly. Nation 213:589-92
D 6 '71
Saturday night special and other hardware.
il N Y Times Mag p 15+ O 10 '71
Why Uncle Sam is pulling back his dollars
from healthful housing programs for the
poor. il Todays Health 49:16-19+ Jl '71
SHERRILL, Sarah B.
Current and coming. See issues of Antiques
SHERTZER, Karen
Children in the morning; story. Seventeen 30:
86-7 Ja '71
SHERWIN, Judith Johnson
Grasses; poem. Poetry 118:20-1 Ap '71
SHERWIN-Williams company
Turning an art into science. E. C. Baldwin.
il por Nations Bsns 59:88-9 Ja '71
SHERWOOD, E. Stephen-. See Stephen-Sher-
wood, E.
SHERWOOD, Glen
Carnage at Sand Lake. il Audubon 72:66-73
N '70; 73:105-6 Mr '71
SHERWOOD, Morgan
Staying afloat in the patent office. il Am
West 8:16-17 My '71
SHESTACK, Melvin
Charley Pride and the chicken ladies. por
Esquire 75:102-5+ Mr '71
SHETTLES, Landrum B.
Test-tube baby is coming. D. M. Rorvik. il
pors Look 35:83-6+ My 18 '71 *
SHETTY, Taranath
Photic responses in hyperkinesis of child-
hood. bibliog Science 174:1356-7 D 24 '71
SHEWMON, P. G.
Radiation-induced swelling of stainless steel.
bibliog il Science 173:987-91 S 10 '71
SHIDELER, Mary McDermott
Amicable divorce. il Chr Cent 88:553-5 My 5
'71
SHIEH, C. Y. See Collins, F. jt. auth.
SHIEK, Harriet
Better to know you; story. Good H 172:116-17
Ap '71
SHIELD, James Asa
Does the way our food is grown affect our
mental well-being? bibliog Org Gard &
Farm 18:102-6+ My '71
Farm practices influencing the incidence of
multiple sclerosis. bibliog il Org Gard &
Farm 18:102-6+ Ap '71
SHIELDING (heat)
See also
Space vehicles—Shielding (heat)
SHIELDS, Jody
Grand tour. Seventeen 30:148 Ap '71
SHIELDS, John Potter
Build a liquid-crystal wattmeter. il Radio-
Electr 42:43-4 D '71
SHIELDS, Rodney
High cost of shareholder democracy. Duns
98:112 S '71 *
SHIERS, George
Induction coil; with biographical sketch. il
Sci Am 224:12, 80-7 My '71
SHIFFRIN, Richard M.
Forgetting: trace erosion or retrieval failure?
bibliog il Science 168:1601-3; 173:1040-1 Je
26 '70, S 10 '71
—See Atkinson, R. C. jt. auth.
SHIFTERS for automobiles. See Automobiles
—Transmission
SHIFTING cultivation
Flow of energy in an agricultural society.
R. A. Rappaport. il Sci Am 225:116-22+
bibliog(p244) S '71
SHIKLER, Aaron
Painting of a legend. il pors McCalls 98:76-
81+ Mr '71
about
Most talked-about painter of 1971: Aaron
Shikler. J. Singer. il por Am Artist 35:30-
7+ S '71 *
Traditional revolutionists. il por Newsweek
77:84 My 3 '71 *
SHIMAHARA, Nobuo. See Wheeler, J. jt. auth.
SHIMBORI, Michiya
Student radicals in Japan. bibliog f il Ann
Am Acad 395:150-8 My '71
SHIMIZU, Akira, and others
Variation and homology in the mu and gam-
ma heavy chains of human immunoglob-
ulins. bibliog il Science 173:629-33 Ag 13
'71
SHIMIZU, Yukio
Yukio Shimizu: color as a strong but gentle
medium; with photographs. R. Bruns. Pop
Phot 67:74-8 Ag '71 *
SHINE on, Pecos Bill; drama. See Winther, B.

SHINER, Don
Bell ringing project. il Design 72:30-1 Spr '71
Build this cabana now, use it all year. il Pop
Mech 135:154-7 Ap '71
Tell-time table. il Design 72:34-5 Spr '71
Trout mount. il Design 72:12-13 mid-Sum '71
SHINKER, Laura Latham
Why only Orson? poem. Chr Cent 88:528 Ap
28 '71
SHINNECOCK swordfish tournament. See
Fishing—Competitions
SHIP and boat models
Mini Tahiti. il Mech Illus 67:86 N '71
Tankers in the Alps: a school for skippers. R.
Dyment. il Sea Front 17:72-5 Mr '71
SHIP building. See Shipbuilding
SHIP canals. See Canals
SHIP hijacking
Attack in the Caribbean; piratical act of
Cuban patrol boat. Time 98:33 D 27 '71
Hijacked! a peaceful cruise interrupted at
gunpoint. L. Barber. il Yachting 129:59+
Mr '71
Piracy in the Pacific! B. Benson. il Motor
B & S 128:46-7+ O '71
SHIP museums. See Naval museums
SHIP owners. See Shipowners
SHIP signals. See Signals and signaling
SHIPBUILDING
U.S. merchant fleet: it's still hard aground.
il U S News 71:82-3 S 6 '71
What a way to build a ship! W. R. Kreh.
il Sci Digest 70:92 N '71
See also
Levingston shipbuilding company
Litton industries, inc.
Shipyards
Tank ships
SHIPLER, David K.
Two John Lindsays. New Repub 164:16-20
My 1; 34 Je 26 '71
SHIPMENT of books. See Books—Transporta-
tion
SHIPMENT of goods
How to ship that yuletide package. Bet Hom
& Gard 49:174-5 N '71
Notes for the corporate nomad: shipping
things home. Fortune 84:48 S '71
See also
Forwarding companies
SHIPOWNERS
Poker faces; tanker owners. il Forbes 107:22
Ap 15 '71
SHIPPEE, William R.
Amplifier quiz. Electr World 86:51 D '71
Logic terms quiz. Electr World 86:8+ N '71
SHIPPING
See also
Barge lines
Freighters
Panama Canal
Tank ships
Underdeveloped areas—Shipping

International aspects
Seamen and modernization of merchant shipping: 55th International (maritime) labor
conference. Geneva, Switzerland. J. P.
Goldberg. Mo Labor R 94:49-54 F '71

Rates
Fast drop in rates keeps tankers in port.
il Bsns W p35 Jl 31 '71
Freight rates foundering. il Time 98:59 Ag 9
'71

Arctic Regions
Legacy of the Manhattan. M. A. Galway.
il Sea Front 17:292-7 S '71

Great Lakes
See Inland water transportation

Israel
Maritime fruit's twisting course. Bsns W p32
My 29 '71

Italy
Italy casts off; nearly all intercontinental
passenger service eliminated. il Newsweek
78:68+ Ag 30 '71

Japan
Y.K. who? por Time 98:65 Jl 5 '71

Norway
Tanker shortage brings joy to Oslo. Bsns W
p31 Ja 30 '71

Underdeveloped areas
See Underdeveloped areas—Shipping

United States
See also
Inland water transportation
Merchant marine—United States

SHIPPING companies
See also
Seatrain lines, inc.
United States lines, inc.
SHIPPING containers. See Containers for
shipping
SHIPPING terminal buildings. See Terminal
buildings
SHIPROCK, N.Mex, housing project. See
Housing projects
SHIPS
See also
Freighters
Hospital ships
Ice breaking vessels
Missing ships
Ocean liners
Sailing vessels
Salvage (ships)
Shipwrecks
Sloops
Steamships and steamboats
Tank ships
Tugboats
Warships

Crews
See Seamen

Fires and fire protection
Saga of the Antilles. P. W. Adams. il Yachting 129:62-3+ My '71

Fouling
See Marine fouling

Manufacture
See Shipbuilding

SHIPS, Atomic powered
Whatever happened to America's atom-
powered merchant ship? il U S News 71:49
Ag 16 '71
SHIPS, Hospital. See Hospital ships
SHIPS, Model. See Ship and boat models
SHIPS, Research
Deep-water archeology; use of Alcoa Sea-
probe. W. Bascom. bibliog il Science 174:
261-9 O 15 '71
Glomar Challenger drills deep-sea peephole
into earth's past. A. Hamilton. il Pop Sci
198:58-60+ My '71
Salvaging ancient ships; Alcoa Seaprobe. il
Newsweek 78:84 N 22 '71
SHIPS in art
See also
Marine painting
SHIPWRECKS
Byzantine trading venture. G. F. Bass. il Sci
Am 225:22-33 bibliog (p 120) Ag '71
15,000 wrecks in the Great Lakes await ad-
venture and treasure hunters. F. F.
Hollister. Motor B & S 127:202 Mr '71
Landlocked sailors; USS Wateree cast ashore
by tidal wave in 1868. R. Clancy. il Sea
Front 17:241-2 Jl '71
Last temptation of Delilah; 26 days aboard a
sinking schooner. J. Tompkins. Motor B &
S 127:72-3+ Ap '71
Saga of the Antilles; French cruise ship on
fire in the Grenadines. P. W. Adams. il
Yachting 129:62-3+ My '71
See also
Salvage (ships)
Survival after airplane accidents, shipwrecks,
etc.
SHIPYARDS
Red Clyde; workers seize control of John
Brown yard. il Newsweek 78:37+ Ag 16 '71
Sailor Ted's sinking shipyards; or, All's not
bonny on Clyde. il por Time 98:31 Ag 16 '71
SHIRLEY, George
Black performer. il Opera N 35:6-13 Ja 30 '71
about
Recordings. M. Mayer. Esquire 76:72 D
'71 *
SHIRTS
Back to the button-down. Time 99:74 Ja 10
'72
Men's shirts. il Consumer Bul 54:23-6 Ap
'71
Peacock revolution. il Forbes 108:61-2 N 15
'71
SHISEIDO company. See Cosmetics industry—
Japan
SHIVERING
Shivering, one of nature's danger signals. D.
L. Dudley. il Field & S 76:42+ My '71
SHLAER, Robert
Shift in binocular disparity causes compen-
satory change in the cortical structure of
kittens. bibliog il Science 173:638-41 Ag
13 '71

SHNAYERSON, Robert
Signs of life. Harper 243:12+ S '71

about

About this issue. por Harper 243:4 S '71 •
Filling the Morris chair. Newsweek 77:61 Je
28 '71 •
New head at Harper's. por Time 97:46 Je
28 '71 •
SHOCK
Shock treatment; MSS for shock lung. il
Newsweek 77:68 Je 14 '71
See also
Electric shock
Traumatism
SHOCK absorbers
Apollo shock absorbers could be adapted to
cars. S. V. Jones. il Sci Digest 70:49 D '71
See also
Automobiles—Shock absorbers
SHOCK deformation of rocks. See Rocks—
Deformation
SHOCK of recognition; story. See Du Maurier,
D.
SHOCK waves
Sound from Apollo rockets in space. D. Cot-
ten and W. L. Donn. bibliog il Science 171:
565-7 F 12 '71
See also
Atomic weapons—Testing. Underground
Sonic boom
SHOCKLEY, Donald G.
Reforming prison reform. Commonweal 94:
497-8 S 24 '71
SHOCKLEY, William Bradford
Is intelligence racial? H. Simmons. il por
Newsweek 77:69-70 My 10 '71 •
SHOE industry
Bally who? Melville joint venture. Forbes
108:32-3 N 15 '71
Cuban shoe-in; Suave shoe corp. Time 97:
76 Je 7 '71
New boom bubbles up in the boot business;
foam ski boots. F. Lee. il Sports Illus 34:
50-1 Ja 25 '71
$100-million object lesson: Corfam problems.
il Fortune 83:109 Ja '71
See also
Beck industries, inc.
Interco, inc.
Nettleton, A. E. company

Imports problem

Learning to play by the new rules. il Bsns
W D20 Ag 28 '71
SHOEMAKER, William J. and Wurtman, R. J.
Perinatal undernutrition: accumulation of
catecholamines in rat brain. bibliog il
Science 171:1017-19 Mr 12 '71
SHOEMAKER, Willie
World's winningest jockey. B. Surface. il
por Read Digest 98:123-6 My '71 •
SHOES
Baby steps out. H. B. Pryor and M. C.
Martin. il Parents Mag 46:40-1+ D '71
Favor your feet. T. P. Garigan. il Field & S
76:14+ S '71
Freaky feet. il Newsweek 78:94 N 15 '71
Shooing out myths about footwear. J. Nel-
son. il Todays Health 49:32-4 My '71
These heels were made for gawking; high
heels for men. il Life 71:54-6 N 5 '71
See also
Slippers

Trade and manufacture
See Shoe industry
SHOFFNER, R. N. See Abdel-Hameed, F. jt.
auth.
SHOMON, Joseph James
More greenspace for urban America; with
biographical sketch. il Cons 26:14-17, 40
D '71
SHONBRUN, Margaret
Picking up the pieces. il Good H 172:10+
F '71
SHOOTING
Case for the lung shot. B. Milek. il Field & S
76:44-5+ Ag '71
Indoor wingshooting is here. P. Wahl. il Pop
Sci 198:65 F '71
Late season bird hunting. W. Davis. il Mech
Illus 67:44+ D '71
Right-eyed or left-eyed? J. Samson. il Field
& S 76:22+ Jl '71
Shooting. J. O'Connor. See issues of Outdoor
life
Shooting; ed. by W. Page. See issues of Field
& stream
Shooting; ed. by S. Williams. See issues of
Field & stream November 1971-

Two new shooting editors for a growing
sport; S. Williams and B. Brister. M. J.
O'Neill and C. Conley. pors Field & S
76:8-9 O '71
See also
Archery
Game birds
Geese, Wild
Hunting
Rifles
also Duck shooting and similar headings
Competitions
Shooting against the world; International
shooting union. W. Page. il Field & S 75:
74-7 Mr '71

Study and teaching
Of boys and guns. T. Trueblood. il Field & S
76:12+ D '71
SHOP management. See Factory management
SHOPLIFTING
Diary of a shoplifter. il Seventeen 29:134-5+
N '70
Is there a shoplifter in your family? I. Bar-
mash. Harp Baz 104:127 O '71
They'd rather switch; tag-switching. il News-
week 78:76-7 Jl 12 '71
Youth in trouble; shoplifters. R. S. Davis.
il Todays Ed 60:31-2+ S '71
SHOPPERS guides. See Consumer education
SHOPPING and shoppers
Hints for shoppers from trade associations.
il Changing T 25:29-30 Jl '71
In-most places. P. D. Dibble. Ladies Home J
88:66 My '71
Mrs Conservative loses out; car buying. C.
Dawson. McCalls 99:37 N '71
Parting shots; some old nickel bargains still
linger on. il Life 71:62-4 Ag 6 '71
Save money when you buy. F. K. Coffee. il
Mech Illus 67:70-1+ Ap '71
Six steps to smarter shopping. W. Wirsig.
Read Digest 99:29-30+ D '71
Special on meat; how to buy ham. L. Wing.
il Good H 173:160 D '71
Sunday shopping spree; for physically handi-
capped. L. Hoffman. il Har Yrs 11:44-5 F '71
Where the buys are in your food market. E.
Alston. il Look 35:64-5 Ap 20 '71
See also
Consumers

Europe, Western
Europe's flea markets. N. Beare. il Travel
135:36-41 Ap '71
France
Bazaar's bazar. M. Capron and G. Mazer. il
Harp Baz 104:164-5 Mr '71

Great Britain
Memo from London. G. Perint. Harp Baz
104:40 Ap '71
SHOPPING centers
Bazaar bookshop in an empty nest com-
munity; Village Green shopping center in
Heritage Village, Southbury, Conn. il Pub
W 199:246-8 Ja 25 '71
Heritage Village bazaar. il Arch Rec 149:107-10
My '71
Shopping centers, boon or bust? H. D.
Greene. 3d. Pub W 199:54-5 F 1: 70-1 F 8 '71
Shopping centers grow into shopping cities.
il Bsns W p34-8 S 4 '71
Updated bazaar; Heritage Village, Southbury,
Conn. il Arch Forum 134:58-60 Ap '71
SHOPPING malls
It took a spud; salvaging downtown Paines-
ville, Ohio. G. Russell. il Am City 86:77 Ap
'71
SHORE, Dinah
Someone's in the kitchen with Dinah; ex-
cerpts. il por Ladies Home J 89:100+ Ja '72
SHORE, Maxine
Catastrophe Clarence; drama. Plays 31:37-
46, 72 O '71
SHORE, Stephen
Stephen Shore; exhibition at the Metropol-
itan museum of art. New Yorker 47:29-30
Mr 6 '71 •
SHORE birds
See also
Sea birds
Water birds
SHORE lines
See also
Coast changes
SHORE protection
See also
Beach erosion
Coasts
SHORES, Louis
Library-university. Sch & Soc 99:163-6 Mr
'71

SHORING and underpinning
Popsicle pipe, freezing the ground so you
can build on it. il Sci Digest 69:94-5 F '71
SHORR, Mimi
Self in chambered space. il Craft Horiz 31:
26-9+ Ag '71
SHORRIS, Earl
Expatriate chess on the other side of the
wall. il pors N Y Times Mag p30-2+ My 23
'71
How 114 washing machines came to the
Crow reservation; excerpt from The death
of the Great Spirit. Atlan 227:73-7 F '71
SHORT, Alison. See Short. L. jt. auth.
SHORT, Bobby
I remember Ivie; excerpt from Black and
white keys. por Sat R 54:50-1+ F 27 '71
SHORT, Georgianna
Comic characters. il Sch Arts 70:8-9 Je '71
SHORT, Lester
Woodpeckers without woods; with biographi-
cal sketch. il Natur Hist 80:8, 66-74 Mr
'71
—and Short, Alison
How to protect your camp from electrical
fires. Camp Mag 43:18-19+ F '71
SHORT, Robert E.
Bad case of the Short shorts. R. Fimrite. il
Sports Illus 35:20-2+ Ag 9 '71 *
Baseball's odd couple meets the wild bunch.
J. Mann. il pors Look 35:71-2+ My 4 '71 *
Short cuts to Texas. il por Newsweek 78:47
O 4 '71 *
Short end? por Newsweek 78:57-8 Ag 30 '71 *
SHORT line railroads. See Railroads, Short
line
SHORT men. See Stature
SHORT stories
See also
Childrens stories
SHORT story
Big secret. R. McInerny. Writer 84:9-11 F '71
Fiction from fact. V. M. Gillette. Writer 84:
11-13 Ap '71
5 writing problems in the short story. J.
Chimsky. il Writers Digest 51:24-7+ My '71
How to turn fact into fiction; newspapers as
story sources. G. Antonich. il Writers Di-
gest 51:37-9+ Ap '71
Let nothing your readers dismay; writing
a Christmas story. L. Conger. Writer 84:
7-8 D '71
Short stories: bridges to vision. P. D. Boles.
Writer 84:9-11 Mr '71
Short story checklist. H. J. Chadwick.
Writers Digest 51:33 N '71; 52:27 Ja '72
Turning novel cuts into short stories. R. E.
Hayes. il Writers Digest 51:28-9+ Jl '71
Writing the male confession. J. D. Harsh.
Writer 84:18-19 My '71
See also
Detective and mystery stories

Study and teaching
Alienation and isolation in Nelson Algren's
A bottle of milk for mother. D. R. Sil-
kowski. Eng J 60:724-7 S '71
Critical menagerie in The short happy life
of Francis Macomber. T. L. Gaillard, jr.
Engl J 60:31-5 Ja '71
Jackson's The witch; a satanic gem. R. L.
Kelly. Engl J 60:1204-8 D '71
Symbol and theme in Eudora Welty's Pet-
rified man. L. J. Richmond. Engl J 60:
1201-3 D '71
SHORT story contests. See Fiction—Competi-
tions
SHORT subject films. See Moving pictures—
Short subject films
SHORT wave radio receivers. See Radio re-
ceivers, Short wave
SHORTBREAD. See Cookies
SHORTER, Frank
Long and the Shorter of it. G. S. Brown.
il por Sports Illus 35:94-5 D 6 '71 *
SHORTS. See Clothing and dress
SHORTWAVE radio. See Radio broadcasting,
Short wave
SHOSHONE national forest. See National for-
ests
SHOSTACK, Kenneth, and Eddy, Charles
Management by computer graphics. il Har-
vard Bsns R 49:52-63 N '71
SHOSTAKOVICH, Dmitrii Dmitrievich
Generations of Shostakovich; performance of
Fourteenth symphony by the Philadelphia
orchestra. I. Kolodin. Sat R 54:79 Ja 23 '71 *
Musical events; Fourteenth symphony per-
formed by Philadelphia orchestra in Phil-
harmonic Hall. W. Sargeant. New Yorker
46:93 Ja 16 '71 *
Music's handmaiden; performance of Fourteenth symphony by the Philadelphia orchestra. H. Saal. por Newsweek 77:50 Ja
18 '71 *

Shostakovich's Fourteenth, a new protest? R.
S. Brown. por Hi Fi 21:64-5 F '71 *
Shostakovich's the Nose sparkles in Munich.
R. S. Brown. Hi Fi 21:MA25 Je '71 *
SHOSTROM, Everett L. and Kavanaugh,
James
Did you marry the right man? quiz; excerpt
from Between man and woman. Ladies
Home J 88:100+ Mr '71
SHOT putting
No practice makes almost perfect; Matson,
the Olympic champion. P. Putnam. il por
Sports Illus 34:18-19 F 8 '71 *
SHOTGUN shells. See Cartridges
SHOTGUNS
Airweight battery. W. Page. il Field & S
75:86-9 Ja '71
Gun that grows with your son. C. F. Rees.
il Field & S 76:108-9 S '71
How experts finish gun stocks. J. O'Con-
nor. il Outdoor Life 148:86+ S '71
Of boys and guns. T. Trueblood. il Field & S
76:12+ D '71
Open choke. J. O'Connor. il por Outdoor Life
148:92+ N '71
Shotgun fits. T. Trueblood. il Field & S
76:84-6+ S '71
Star quality: Model 12 Winchester scatter-
guns. W. Page. il Field & S 76:164-6 Je
'71
What's new in the shooting world. S. Wil-
liams. il Field & S 76:76-8 D '71
SHOUP, Carl Sumner
Story behind the book: Revell's Bible quiz
book. B. A. Bannon. il Pub W 200:36
S 20 '71 *
SHOUP, David Monroe
Where are they now? il pors Newsweek 78:11
N 29 '71 *
SHOUSE, Catherine (Filene)
Wolf Trap, a gala opening. B. Belt. por
Hi Fi 21:MA20+ O '71 *
SHOW dogs. See Dogs
SHOW me; musical comedy. See Musical come-
dies, revues, etc.—Criticisms, plots, etc.
SHOW Stoppers (group) See Entertainers
SHOW windows
Santa and the summer rotisserie. M. B.
Green, jr. il Design 73:24-7 Wint '71
SHOWER curtains. See Curtains and draperies
SHOWERS. See Rain and rainfall
SHOWLER, Janice
Growing up absurd in a mad, mad, mad,
mad world. Engl J 60:223-5 F '71
SHRAKE, Edwin
Bundini: Svengali in Ali's corner. pors Sports
Illus 34:32-6 F 15 '71
Name of the game is O.J. por Sports Illus
35:18-19 S 6 '71
What are they doing with the sacred game
of pro football? pors Sports Illus 35:96-9+
O 25 '71
World's best poker player. il por Sports
Illus 34:56-8 Ja 25 '71
SHREDDERS, Compost. See Compost grinders
and grinding
SHREVEPORT, La.
Music
Report:
Tosca and Mourning becomes Electra. il
O. Chism. Opera N 35:32 Ja 30 '71
SHREWS
Visual attention in the tree shrew: an abla-
tion study of the striate and extrastriate
visual cortex. H. Killackey and I. T.
Diamond. bibliog il Science 171:696-9 F 19
'71
SHRIMPS
Bidding up shrimp. il Time 99:63 Ja 3 '72
Metachronal limb movements by artemia
salina: synchrony of male and female dur-
ing coupling. C. M. Lent. bibliog il Science
173:1247-8 S 24 '71
See also
Cookery—Shellfish
SHRIMPS, Frozen. See Shellfish, Frozen
SHRINES
See also
Lourdes, France
SHRINES, War. See War memorials
SHROUD, Holy. See Holy Shroud
SHRUBS
Flowers in abundance from trees and shrubs.
G. Taloumis. il Home Gard 58:22-3+ Mr
'71
Woody flowering natives. B. M. Shaub. il
Horticulture 49:36-7+ Mr '71
See also
Berry bearing plants
also names of shrubs, e.g. Firethorns
SHUB, Anatole
Supermarket or superpower? il Harper 244:
57-63 Ja '72

SHUB, Elizabeth
Adventure in translation. Horn Bk 47:265-7 Je '71
SHUGART, Diana
Whole earth view of bookselling; excerpts from The whole earth catalog. por Pub W 200:20-1 S 6 '71
SHULDINER, Herbert
Recreation roundup. See issues of Popular science monthly
SHULEVITZ, Uri
Within the margins of a picture book. il Horn Bk 47:309-12 Je '71
SHULMAN, Alix
Challenge to every marriage. Redbook 137:57+ Ag '71
SHULMAN, Marshall D.
What does security mean today? For Affairs 49:607-18 Jl '71
SHULSINGER, Stephanie Cooper
Mercer girls. il por Am West 8:28-9 Jl '71
SHULTZ, George Pratt
Economic policy on course, says top Nixon aide; excerpts from address, April 22, 1971 por U S News 70:55-7 My 10 '71
It could be verse. Science 172:829 My 21 '71
Looking beyond wage-price freeze; interview. il pors U S News 71:32-6 S 6 '71
President Nixon establishes Council on international economic policy; excerpts from news conference, January 19, 1971. Dept State Bul 64:169-72 F 8 '71

about

Architect of Nixon's new economics. il pors Bsns W p72-5 Mr 20 '71 *
George Shultz: general manager of the United States? il pors Nations Bsns 59:34-8 Mr '71 *
George Shultz: strong right arm of the presidency. I. Ross. por Read Digest 98:143-7 Mr '71 *
Nixon: check it with George. por Newsweek 78:86 N 15 '71 *
Nixon's man for all seasons. por U S News 70:29 Mr 29 '71 *
Shultz learns that Packard means it. Bsns W p96 Mr 20 '71 *
SHULTZ, Gladys Denny
What sex offenders say about pornography. Read Digest 99:53-7 Jl '71
SHUMAN, A. B.
Marking time. E. Dahlquist. por Motor T 23:6 O '71 *
SHUMAN, James B.
Anti-drug program that works. Read Digest 98:139-42 Mr '71
SHUMWAY, F. Ritter
Energy crisis; address, December 10, 1970. Vital Speeches 37:209-12 Ja 15 '71
SHUNAMAN, Fred
Photoelectric phono pickups. il Radio-Electr 42:43 Mr '71
SHURCLIFF, Sidney N.
Garden in the clouds. il Horticulture 49:22-5 My '71
SHURR, G. G. and Martens, C. R.
Caulk your way to a better paint job. il Pop Mech 136:120-1 S '71
SHUSTER, Alvin
What happened at Tchepone? reprint. Ramp Mag 9:12 Je '71
SHUSTER, Arnold A. and Shuster, S. K.
Case for graduate school education in recreation. Parks & Rec 6:116-17+ Ja '71
SHUSTER, Harry
King of the jungle. T. J. Murray. il por Duns 98:59-60 N '71 *
SHUSTER, Susan K. See Shuster, A. A. jt. auth.
SHUTTERS, Camera. See Camera shutters
SHUTTLE service, Airline. See Airlines—Shuttle service
SHUTTLESWORTH, Fred L.
Birmingham revisited. il pors Ebony 26:114-18 Ag '71
SHYER, Marlene Fanta
Helpmate; story. Good H 173:114-15 O '71
You want to go to Pittsburgh; story. Redbook 137:86-7 Je '71
SHYNESS. See Bashfulness
SIAM. See Thailand
SIAMESE cats. See Cats
SIAMESE twins
Joined at birth, separated they thrive; Bunton twins. W. Cole. il Good H 173:60+ O '71
SIBELIUS, Jean Julius Christian
Sibelius and his world, by R. Layton. Review
Am Rec G 37:735 Je '71. L. Richmond
Sibelius' forgotten masterpiece. H. Goldsmith. por Hi Fi 21:87 N '71 *

Souvenir of Sibelius centennial, the first American recording of Luonnotar. J. Diether. por Am Rec G 37:494-5+ Ap '71 *
That potent Koussevitzky-Sibelius magic. G. S. Fox. Am Rec G 37:382-3 F '71 *
SIBERIA
Last frontier. J. Axelbank. il Newsweek 79:31-2 Ja 10 '72
See also
Akademgorodok
Ecology—Siberia
SIBERIAN tigers. See Tigers
SIBLEY, Antoinette
Carousel; photo essay. Dance Mag 45:38-9 Je '71 *
SIBLINGS
My brother's keeper, my brother's friend. J. D. Miller. il por Redbook 137:42+ Je '71
Oh jealous love. S. G. Streshinsky. il Parents Mag 46:39-41+ Ag '71
They never stop fighting. R. A. Gardner. il N Y Times Mag p69+ N 28 '71
SIBSON, Robert E.
Executive pay: the long term is where the action is; excerpt from Seventh annual study of management compensation. il Nations Bsns 59:29-32+ N '71
SICILY
See also
Art—Sicily

History

Kingdom in the sun, 1130-1194, by J. Norwich. Review
Sat R 54:38-9 Mr 6 '71. G. Gersh
SICK, The
Caring for the ill at home. Good H 172:174 Je '71
Some lessons on dying; reactions of terminal patient and staff. B. Hale. il por Chr Cent 88:1076-9 S 15 '71
See also
Incurables
Sick children
Physicians and patients
SICK children
Human being inside the child. L. R. Robbins and N. M. Kacen. Todays Ed 60:28-35 My '71
Little girl who shared my pregnancy. P. Dobson. il por Redbook 137:23-4 Jl '71
Noel Charron's courage alone makes him the toughest kid on the block; living with rheumatoid arthritis. B. Lindeman. il Todays Health 49:46-51 S '71
See also
Mentally ill children
SICKLE cell anemia. See Anemia
SICKLER, Richard C.
Dutch hutch. il Mech Illus 67:64-6 Ag '71
Fine-furniture filing cabinets. il Mech Illus 67:110+ Ap '71
SICKNESS
See also
Convalescence
SICRE, José Gómez-. See Gómez-Sicre, J.
SIDE effects of drugs. See Drugs—Physiological effects
SIDEMAN, Andrew
In my opinion. por Seventeen 29:390 Ag '70
SIDEREAL time. See Time measurement
SIDEWALKS, Elevated
Walk in the sky. Newsweek 77:73-4 F 15 '71
SIDEY, Hugh
Don't they know we're getting out? il por Life 70:2 F 12 '71; Same abr. Read Digest 98:131-2 My '71
Down home in the happy kingdom of L.B.J. il pors Life 70:44-52 My 21 '71
John Connally. il pors Life 70:38-41 My 7 '71
Nixon's economic bombshell. il por Life 71:20-1 Ag 27 '71
Presidency. See issues of Life
SIDNEY, Margaret, pseud. See Lothrop, H. M. S.
SIEBEL, Paul
Paul Siebel: homegrown weed. E. Sander. por Sat R 54:55 Ja 30 '71 *
SIEBERT, Muriel
Money game: playing to win. A. M. Watkins. McCalls 99:38 My '71 *
SIEGEL, Dorothy
Sailing through summer. il Parents Mag 46:36-7+ Jl '71
SIEGEL, Eric
Alternate video. H. S. Resnik. Vogue 158:62 Ag 15 '71 *
SIEGEL, Jeanne
(ed) Around Barnett Newman. il pors Art N 70:42-7+ O '71
SIEGEL, Martin
Two rabbis rock the boat. pors Time 97:65-6 Mr 15 '71 *

SIEGEL, Norbert K.
Whose grass is greener? interview. por
Forbes 108:54+ N 15 '71
SIEGEL, Robert
Bear; poem. Poetry 117:371 Mr '71
Late shopper; poem. Chr Cent 88:1491 D 22
'71
Mr Fiddler; poem. Atlan 227:77 F '71
Rock; poem; reprint. America 124:594 Je 5 '71
SIEGMAN, Henry
Peace of Jerusalem. il Chr Cent 88:1203-5 O
13 '71
SIEGMEISTER, Elie
Beyond the avant garde. il Hi Fi 21:MA13-
14+ D '71
SIEHL, George H.
Literature subsequent to the environmental
nova. il por Library J 96:2266-70 Jl '71
SIEKMAN, Philip
Plane that could teach an industry to fly. il
Fortune 83:96-9+ Ap '71
Serbian boy builds his dream castle in the
drug business. il por Fortune 83:94-7+ Ja
'71
SIEMENS ag. See Electric industries—Ger-
many (Federal Republic)
SIEMSSEN, Günther Schneider-. See Schneid-
er-Siemssen, G.
SIENA, Italy
Music
On a hill in Tuscany; Accademia musicale
Chigiana. B. Fischer-Williams. il Opera N
35:16-18 My 15 '71
Student makes music in Siena. K. Wilson. il
Hi Fi 21:MA10-11 Ap '71
SIERRA, Sali
Drug abuse: where to find the facts. il
Todays Health 49:57-8 Mr '71
SIERRA club
Adopt an island; Lovell's island in Boston
harbor. L. D. Harris. il Am For 77:4-5 My
'71
Warning: the chain saw cometh; Tongass
national forest. P. Brooks. il Atlan 228:
95-9 D '71
SIERRA LEONE
Back to Africa: a history of Sierra Leone and
Liberia, by R. West, and Liberia: black Af-
rica in microcosm, by C. M. Wilson. Re-
views
Sat R 54:41-2 My 15 '71. C. Miller
Politics and government
Sierre Leone: political liberty deteriorates.
J. Power. Chr Cent 88:162+ F 3 '71
SIERRA LEONE national dance company. See
Dancing, African
SIERRA NEVADA MOUNTAINS
High country in season; excerpt from The
mighty Sierra: portrait of a mountain
world. P. Webster. il Am West 8:20-9 N
'71
SIEVERS, Harry J.
History. America 124:546-7 My 22 '71
SIEVING, Molecular. See Adsorption
SIFNEOS, Peter
Patients' views on relocation. Ment Hy 55:
495-8 O '71
SIGBAND, Norman B.
How to meet with success. il Nations Bsns
59:76-8 Mr '71
SIGGINS, G. R. and others
Cyclic adenosine monophosphate and nore-
pinephrine: effects on transmembrane prop-
erties of cerebellar Purkinje cells. bibliog
il Science 171:192-4 Ja 15 '71; Reply with
rejoinder. 174:1257-9 D '71
SIGHT
Extremely rapid visual search: the maxi-
mum rate of scanning letters for the pres-
ence of a numeral. G. Sperling and oth-
ers. bibliog il Science 174:307-11 O 15 '71
Eyes have it; improve your night sight. E.
Slepian. Motor B & S 127:80+ My '71
How does the striate cortex begin the recon-
struction of the visual world? D. A. Pollen
and others. bibliog il Science 173:74-7 Jl 2
'71
How well does your baby see? R. Mlynarczyk.
il Parents Mag 46:58-60+ O '71
Right-eyed or left-eyed? J. Samson. il Field
& S 76:22+ Jl '71
When the eyes don't have it. W. A. Nolen.
McCalls 99:27 N '71
See also
After images
Color blindness
Color sense
Contact lenses
Eye
Eyeglasses
Figural aftereffects

Motion perception
Optic thalamus
Optical illusions
Optics, Physiological
Space perception
Visual discrimination
SIGHT (animals)
Anomalous retinal pathways in the Siamese
cat: an inadequate substrate for normal
binocular vision. R. E. Kalil and others.
bibliog il Science 174:302-5 O 15 '71
Eye marks in vertebrates: aids to vision.
R. W. Ficken and others. bibliog il Science
173:936-9 S 3 '71
Illness-induced aversions in rat and quail:
relative salience of visual and gustatory
cues. H. C. Wilcoxon and others. bibliog il
Science 171:826-8 F 26 '71
Shift in binocular disparity causes compen-
satory change in the cortical structure of
kittens. R. Shlaer. bibliog il Science 173:
638-41 Ag 13 '71
SIGHT and shooting. See Shooting
SIGHT reduction tables. See Navigation—
Tables
SIGHT testing
How well does your baby see? early testing
prevents minor visual problems. R.
Mlynarczyk. il Parents Mag 46:58-60+ O '71
SIGHTS for firearms. See Firearms—Sights
SIGMAN, Alfred H.
Case for skepticism: San Quentin shoot-out.
Nation 213:424-9 N 1 '71
SIGMAN, Carl T.
Little firehouse for the backyard. il Pop Sci
198:106-7+ Ap '71
SIGMUND Stern grove. See San Francisco—
Music
SIGN language
No thanks, said the ape. il Newsweek 78:101
D 20 '71
When they talk with their hands, what are
they saying? industrial signals. N. Sklare-
witz. il Pop Mech 135:72-3 My '71
SIGNAL companies
Signal helps itself and bails out Mecom. il
Bsns W p20 D 25 '71
SIGNAL detection (psychology)
Brain as a parallel coherent detector. A.
Trehub. bibliog il Science 174:722-3 N 12
'71
Phenothiazine effects on auditory signal de-
tection in paranoid and nonparanoid
schizophrenics. M. Rappaport and others.
bibliog il Science 174:723-5 N 12 '71
Signal detectability and medical decision-
making. L. B. Lusted. bibliog il Science
171:1217-19 Mr 26 '71
SIGNAL generators
Accurate d.c.-less clock-pulse generator. F.
H. Tooker. il Electr World 86:69 Ag '71
Build a pocket pipper; fast risetime pulse
generator. T. Annes. il Radio-Electr 42:46-
8 F '71
Build the fil-oscillator; sharp audio filter &
versatile waveform generator. R. Melen
and H. Garland. il Pop Electr 34:58-62 My
'71
14 ways to use R-E's tone-burst generator.
T. Annes. il Radio-Electr 42:32-5+ Ag '71
Hi-fi product report; Sound technology 1000A
FM alignment generator. il Electr World
85:14+ Ap '71
Integrated circuit audio generators. K. T.
Rudahl. il Radio World 86:60-1 S '71
Low-cost 10.7-MHz signal generator. R. F.
Lewis. il Pop Electr 34:61-3+ Mr '71
Precision square-wave audio generator. R.
A. Walton. il Electr World 85:54-5 My '71
RC time constants in UJT circuits. R. M.
Cartoscelli. il Electr World 86:23 D '71
RCA WR-514A Sweep Chanalyst. Radio-Electr
42:28+ Ap '71
R-E's dual-function generator; pulse and
square-wave generator. P. Harms. il Ra-
dio-Electr 42:36-40 S '71
Sencore SM-168 speed aligner. Radio-Electr
42:24+ Ap '71
Tune up your stereo; build a tone-burst
generator. T. Annes. il Radio-Electr 42:22-7
Jl '71
What's a frequency synthesizer? L. Allen. il
Radio-Electr 42:50-2 F '71
See also
Oscillators
SIGNALS; ballet. See Ballets—Criticisms
SIGNALS, Electric. See Electric signals
SIGNALS, Traffic. See Traffic signals
SIGNALS and signaling
Distress signals; safety equipment for boats.
E. Robberson. il Yachting 129:70-2+ My '71
See also
Drum language
Traffic signals

SIGNER, Ethan. See Galston, A. W. jt. auth.

SIGNS and signboards
Can you read outdoor sign language? new picture signs in national parks and forests. il Pop Sci 199:89 Ag '71
Don't blink; you'll miss the message; office signs. A. F. Gonzalez, jr. Nations Bsns 59:53 Jl '71
Images for a new California City. R. Jensen. il Arch Rec 149:117-20 Je '71
New park signs, Yosemite is first. il Sunset 147:24 N '71
Signs of our time. R. Almquist. il Design 72:38-9 Sum '71
See also
Billboards
Road signs
Street signs

SIGOLOFF, Sanford Charles
New president to repair Republic. pors Bsns W p40+ F 13 '71 *

SIGUR, Alexander O.
Detroit's Cardinal Dearden: a cautious progressive. Chr Cent 88:671-3 My 26 '71
1971 synod: a summons to service. America 125:223 O 2 '71

SIGURBJÖRNSSON, Björn
Induced mutations in plants; with biographical sketch. il Sci Am 224:13, 86-95 bibliog(p 122) Ja '71

SIHANOUK, Norodom. See Norodom Sihanouk

SIHLER, William W.
Framework for financial decisions. bibliog f il Harvard Bsns R 49:123-35 Mr '71

SIKKIM
Enlightened travelers. H. E. Salisbury; C. Y. Salisbury. pors Vogue 158:134-5+ O 15 '71

SIKORSKY aircraft division. See United aircraft corporation—Sikorsky aircraft division

SILAGE
Hay chopping hints. il Suc Farm 69:38 Je '71

Moisture content
These feeders are sold on high-moisture grain; corn and milo. il Suc Farm 69:24-5 S '71

SILAGE handling
Tagalong silage truck. il Suc Farm 69:no2 B5 F '71

SILBER, John Robert
Quest for a silver unicorn. E. Kern. il pors Life 70:61-2+ Je 4 '71 *

SILBER, Robert L.
Where do we begin? Chem 44:2 D '71

SILBERBERG, Margaret C. See Silberberg, N. E. jt. auth.

SILBERBERG, Norman E. and Silberberg, M. C.
Is there such a thing as a learning disabled child? Ed Digest 37:14-17 S '71

SILBERBERG, Sophie C.
Turning on parent power. Sat R 54:58-9 N 13 '71

SILBERMAN, Arlene
How to rate your child's school. Ladies Home J 88:39-40+ F '71; Same abr. with title How good is your child's school? Read Digest 98:70-4 Mr '71
No wheelchair for Steven. il Good H 173:99+ N '71
Santa's workshop for teachers. il Am Ed 7:3-8 D '71
School of your children's dreams. il Good H 172:69+ Mr '71

SILBERMAN, Charles E.
Even student teaching is dismal; excerpt from Crisis in the classroom. il Todays Ed 60:22-5+ Ja '71
Identity crisis in the consumer markets. il Fortune 83:92-5+ Mr '71
U.S. economy in an age of uncertainty. il Fortune 83:72-7+ Ja '71; Same abr. with title Era of new uncertainties. Cur 127:3-14 Mr '71
about
Does school+joy=learning? il por Newsweek 77:60-2+ My 3 '71 *

SILBERMAN, Eve
In my opinion. por Seventeen 30:186 N '71

SILBERMAN, Laurence H.
Proposed pension legislation; the administration's view; address, December 8, 1970. Vital Speeches 37:197-200 Ja 15 '71

SILENCE
Quiet, please! Please. J. Howard. il Life 71:75-6+ D 3 '71

SILENT films. See Moving pictures—Silent films

SILICA
Eutrophication, silica depletion, and predicted changes in algal quality in Lake Michigan. C. L. Schelske and E. F. Stoermer. bibliog il Science 173:423-4 Jl 30 '71
See also
Chert
Opal

SILICATES
See also
Aluminum silicates
Barium silicates
Kaolinite
Mica
Peridotite
Pyroxenes
Zoisite

SILICON controlled rectifiers. See Electric current rectifiers

SILICONE rubber implantation. See Surgery. Plastic

SILK, George
Gallery; photograph of royal terns in Texas. Life 70:6-7 Mr 19 '71
Gold-plated regatta; photographs. Life 71:38-43 Jl 23 '71
More oil for our troubled waters. il Life 70:40-1 F 5 '71

SILK screen printing
Silkscreening. il Sunset 147:98-101 N '71

SILK trees
Potassium flux: a common feature of albizzia leaflet movement controlled by phytochrome or endogenous rhythm. R. L. Satter and A. W. Galston. bibliog il Science 174:518-20 O 29 '71

SILKOWSKI, Daniel R.
Alienation and isolation in Nelson Algren's A bottle of milk for mother. Engl J 60:724-7 S '71

SILKWORMS
Silkworm bombyx mori L: nature of diapause factor. H. Sonobe and E. Ohnishi. bibliog il Science 174:835-8 N 19 '71

SILKY acacias. See Silk trees

SILL, William
Headboard for night owls. il Pop Sci 198:102-3 Mr '71

SILLITOE, Alan
Night Enoch slept downstairs by the fire; story. Redbook 137:106-7 My '71

SILLS, Beverly
Beverly Sills: the fastest voice alive. il pors Time 98:74-6+ N 22 '71 *
Manon à la Sills. R. Jacobson. Sat R 54:58 Ap 24 '71
Operatic cliffhangers with Sills and Souliotis. E. Greenfield. il Hi Fi 21:19-20+ Ja '71 *
Profiles. W. Sargeant. por New Yorker 47:42-6+ Mr 6 '71 *

SILLS, Paul
Fairy tales redone; Story theater. R. Crinkley. Nat R 23:155-6 F 9 '71 *
Saving the evening. il pors Time 97:60 Mr 1 '71 *
Story theatre. Criticism
America 124:637 Je 19 '71 *

SILLS of Cambridge. See Tailors

SILO, Inc.
Appliance dealer with a real clout. il por Bsns W p76+ N 6 '71

SILOS
Sealed storage: will it fit your livestock system. J. R. Borcherding and R. Lutz. il Suc Farm 69:B1-5 Je '71

SILURIAN period. See Paleobotany—Silurian

SILVA, Father
Orphan-boys circus. M. Del Castillo. il por Vogue 158:104-7+ D '71 *

SILVER, Alice Moolten
Candlelight; poem. Ladies Home J 88:76 O '71

SILVER, Carole K.
Overdue. por Wilson Lib Bul 46:461+ Ja '72

SILVER, George A.
Money won't solve everything. il Nation 213:110-14 Ag 16 '71

SILVER, Isidore
Is poverty illegal? Commonweal 93:488-92 F 19 '71
Last picture show: a concurring opinion. Commonweal 95:348-50 Ja 14 '72
Secrets and security. Commonweal 94:399-402 Ag 6 '71

SILVER, Sidney L.
Electronics fights noise pollution. il Pop Electr 35:61-6 O '71
Electronics helps fight air pollution. il Electr World 86:41-4+ S '71
Signal averaging techniques. il Electr World 85:45-8+ My '71

SILVER
Day the silver runs out . . . W. Hanson. il Pop Phot 68:61-3+ Mr '71
See also
Silverware

SILVER—*Continued*

Prices
No shine in silver. il Time 98:94+ D 6 '71

SILVER as money
Coin Harvey: the free silver movement's frustrated promoter. O. Stephens. il por Am West 8:4-9 S '71
Coin of the realm; fall of the Roman empire. il Time 96:66 O 4 '71

SILVER coins. See Coins

SILVER dollars. See Coins

SILVER iodide
Ice nucleation by coprecipitated silver iodide and silver bromide. B. Vonnegut and H. Chessin. bibliog il Science 174:945-6 N 26 '71

SILVER marks. See Hall marks

SILVER mines and mining

United States
Golden dreams and silver realities; excerpts from Gold and silver in the West. T. H. Watkins. il Am West 8:34-43 My '71
Silver boom that fizzled; Hughes rush to buy Nevada mines. il Bsns W p42 O 16 '71

SILVER polishes. See Polishing materials

SILVER question. See Silver as money

SILVERA, Doug
Up on the props and out ahead. H. D. Whall. il por Sports Illus 34:24-5 Je 14 '71 •

SILVERMAN, Burton
Burton Silverman captures the moment. E. Case. il por Am Artist 35:36-43+ Je '71 •

SILVERMAN, Fred
How a network boss picks shows. T. Thompson. il pors Life 71:46-50+ S 10 '71 •

SILVERMAN, Martin
Professionalizing your staff development. il Camp Mag 43:13-14 Mr '71

SILVERSMITHING
Early silversmiths and the silver trade in Georgia; with check list of Georgia marks. K. G. Farnham and C. H. Efird. il Antiques 99:380-5 Mr '71
See also
Silverware

SILVERSMITHS
Early silversmiths and the silver trade in Georgia; with check list of Georgia marks. K. G. Farnham and C. H. Efird. il Antiques 99:380-5 Mr '71
Mobile silversmiths and jewelers 1820-1867; with check list of Mobile silversmiths. S. A. Smith. il Antiques 99:407-11 Mr '71
Tennessee silversmiths. B. H. Caldwell, jr. il Antiques 100:382-5 S '71
Tennessee silversmiths prior to 1860: a check list. B. H. Caldwell, jr. il Antiques 100:906-13 D '71

SILVERSTEIN, Robert M. See MacConnell, J. G. jt. auth.

SILVERSTEIN, Zona
In the Housatonic Valley; poem. Nation 213:311 O 4 '71
Rachel; poem. Nation 213:661 D 20 '71

SILVERWARE
American silver: the seventeenth century; excerpt from American silver; a history of style, 1650-1900. G. Hood. il Antiques 100:576-9 O '71
Bermuda's antique furniture & silver, by B. B. Hyde. Review
Antiques il 100:502-3 O '71. M. G. Fales and D. A. Fales, jr
Gold, silver and stainless flatware. il Changing T 25:39-41 '71
Nineteenth-century silver in Natchez. H. P. Bacot and B. B. Lambdin. il Antiques 99:412-17 Mr '71
Remember, it's the silver anniversary. S. Lindsay and S. Nirenberg. il House B 113:22+ My '71
Rundell, Bridge and Rundell, aurifices regis. J. F. Hayward. il Antiques 99:860-5; 100:110-15 Je-Jl '71
Sallie Morris' silver. L. C. Belden. il Antiques 100:214-16 Ag '71
Silver celebration. il Mlle 72:100-1 Ja '71
Silver from Iolani palace, Honolulu. D. T. Rainwater and R. E. A. Hackler. il Antiques 99:271-7 F '71
Southern silver. D. B. Warren. il Antiques 99:374-9 Mr '71
Sterling in the '70s; Sterling silver design competition at New York's Lever house. D. Smith. Craft Horiz 31:12-17 O '71
Tennessee silversmiths. B. H. Caldwell, jr. il Antiques 100:382-5 S '71
See also
Silversmithing
Spoons

Care
See also
Polishing materials

Collectors and collecting
London silver in Pittsburgh; the Ailsa Mellon Bruce collection at the Carnegie institute. D. T. Owsley. il Antiques 101:177-84 Ja '72

SIM, Thomas
Lightning and the plastic airplane. Flying 89:6-7 Jl '71

SIMIAN viruses
Simian tumor virus isolate: demonstration of cytopathic effects in vitro. D. L. Fine and others. bibliog il Science 174:420-1 O 22 '71

SIMIC, Charles
Body; Grass; Pillow; Flies; Suffering; poems. Poetry 118:187-91 Jl '71
Rooster; poem. Esquire 75:52 Mr '71
Sunflowers; poem. New Yorker 47:127 Je 5 '71

about
Comment. D. Wakoski. Poetry 118:357 S '71 •

SIMMON, Kay
Manhattan safari. il Natur Hist 80:72-7 My '71

SIMMONS, Gene
On the moon with Apollo 15. il Space World H-10-94:4-37 O '71

SIMMONS, James A.
Echolocation in bats: signal processing of echoes for target range. bibliog il Science 171:925-8 Mr 5 '71
—and others
Periodical cicada: sound production and hearing. il Science 171:212-13 Ja 15 '71

SIMMONS, Richard L. and Rios, Angelyn
Immunotherapy of cancer: immunospecific rejection of tumors in recipients of neuraminidase-treated tumor cells plus BCG. bibliog il Science 174:591-3 N 5 '71

SIMMONS, Robert
Sending a boy to do a job you wouldn't even wish on a man; photographs. Todays Health 49:44-9 Jl '71

SIMON. See Nathan, Simon

SIMON, Arthur
Operation Breadbasket campaigns against A&P at the national level. Chr Cent 88:349-50 Mr 17 '71
Stroke of the pen. Commonweal 93:391-5 Ja 22 '71

SIMON, Hilda
Splendor of iridescence. il Pub W 199:35-8 Mr 22 '71 •

SIMON, Joanna
Ladies' week in the world of music. I. Kolodin. Sat R 54:44 F 13 '71 •

SIMON, John
Movie studies: read all about it. R. Schickel. Harper 242:24+ My '71; Reply with rejoinder. J. Simon. 242:10+ My '71 •

SIMON, Neil
Gingerbread lady. Criticism
New Repub 164:22+ Ja 16 '71 •
Last of the red-hot writers. S. Kauffmann. New Repub 164:22+ Ja 16 '71 •
Prisoner of Second avenue. Criticism
Nation 213:573 N 29 '71 •
New Yorker 47:111 N 20 '71 •
Newsweek il 78:86+ N 22 '71 •
Sat R 54:20+ D 4 '71 •
Time il 98:93 N 22 '71 •
When the funniest writer in America tried to be serious. R. Meryman. pors Life 70:60B-60D+ My 7 '71 •

SIMON, Norton, inc.
Moving in; interview. D. Mahoney. New Yorker 47:28-9 My 29 '71
Norton Simon to sell McCall book to CRM. Pub W 200:51 Jl 12 '71
Report to the readers; history of ownership of Saturday review. N. Cousins. Sat R 54:16-17 Jl 31 '71

SIMON, Samuel A.
Catch in amnesty. Nation 213:308-9 O 4 '71

SIMON, Walter B. and Wood, J. E. jr
Psychotherapy in a public mental hospital. bibliog Ment Hy 55:221-4 Ap '71

SIMON, William
Back-to-the-wall effect? il Science 174:774-5 N 19 '71

SIMONDS, C. H.
For now (cont) por Nat R 23:145, 370, 532, 705, 931, 1118, 1305, 1471 F 9, Ap 6, My 18, Je 29, Ag 24, O 8, N 19, D 31 '71
Willis Carto. il por Nat R 23:978-89 S 10 '71

SIMONIS, Adrianus Johannes, bp
Episcopacy and power politics. Chr Cent 88:94 Ja 27 '71 •
Papal politics. Newsweek 77:52 Ja 18 '71 •

SIMONS, Elwyn L. and Pilbeam, David
Gorilla-sized ape from the miocene of India. bibliog il Science 173:23-7 Jl 2 '71

SIMONS, Marlise
From Martinique to Malmaison. il por Sat R
54:49-50+ Mr 13 '71
SIMONS, Myron
Stock trends. See second issue of each month
of Forbes
SIMONT, Marc
In Spain they say ski, ski; drawings. Sports
Illus 34:46-51 Mr 15 '71
SIMONTON, John S. Jr
Drummer boy. il Pop Electr 35:25-35+ Jl '71
In-out annunciator. il Pop Electr 34:48-52+
Ap '71
Leslie effect simulator. il Pop Electr 34:51-
3+ Mr '71
Solid-state bird. il Pop Electr 35:58-60 S '71
SIMPLIFICATION in industry
See also
Standardization
SIMPLIFIED spelling. See Spelling
SIMPSON, Cedric Keith
Sherlock Holmes lives again. J. Stewart-
Gordon. Read Digest 98:203-6+ F '71 •
SIMPSON, Dwight James
Turkey: a time of troubles. Cur Hist 62:38-
43+ Ja '72
SIMPSON, Eileen Berryman
Woman took up the myth that this talent
was uniquely hers. Vogue 158:60+ S 15
'71
SIMPSON, George Gaylord
Fossil penguin from the late cenozoic of
South Africa. il Science 171:1144-5 Mr 19 '71
SIMPSON, Joanne, and Woodley, W. L.
Seeding cumulus in Florida: new 1970 re-
sults. bibliog il Science 172:117-26 Ap 9
'71
SIMPSON, Kitty M.
Hodges gardens. il Horticulture 49:48-9 Mr
'71
SIMPSON, O. J.
Name of the game is O.J. E. Shrake. por
Sports Illus 35:18-19 S 6 '71 •
SIMPSON, Robert
Understanding insurance; questions and
answers. Har Yrs 11:40-1 Ap: 34-5 S '71
SIMPSON, Robert H. See Wise, C. W. jt.
auth.
SIMPSON timber company
25 years later: the circle that works; Shel-
ton working circle. C. Collins. il Am For
77:15-20+ O '71
SIMROSS, Lynn
College football. il Sports Illus 35:82+ N 29
'71
Harness racing (cont) il Sports Illus 34:74+
My 24; 35:48-9 Jl 19; 84 O 18 '71
SIMS, Harold R.
Whitney Young's open society; address, April
1971, with questions and answers. Ann Am
Acad 396:70-8 Jl '71
SIMS, Mary Inglis
Safeguard your baby's sense of hearing. il
Parents Mag 46:62-3+ N '71
SIMS, Nicholas A.
Douglas-Home's oceanic policy. por(p481)
Chr Cent 88:490-3 Ap 21 '71
SIMS, Virginia
Youth conference in Colorado. il Sr Schol
98:14-15 My 17 '71
SIMULATION in education
Student involvement in social studies through
simulation. G. Kachaturoff. Clear House 45:
541-4 My '71
SIMULATION methods
See also
Economic models
Mathematical models
SIMULATORS
Driving a go-cart on the moon. R. Gannon.
il pors Pop Sci 198:70-2+ Ja '71
Live training in nuclear power. V. Louviere.
il Nations Bsns 59:18 D '71
Simulating the ocean; pressure chamber com-
plex. il Sci Digest 69:82 F '71
Study in depth; Pennsylvania experiment in
deep diving chamber. Newsweek 78:60-1
S 6 '71
This train goes nowhere; locomotive sim-
ulator. B. Goldrath. il Mech Illus 67:34 My
'71
See also
Space flight simulators
SIN
One way. L. N. Bell. Chr Today 16:20-1 Ja 7
'72
See also
Atonement
Confession
SINAI (peninsula)
Plan for the Sinai: something less than
peace in return for something less than
total withdrawal. A. Rubinstein. il N Y
Times Mag p 12-13+ Ja 17 '71
See also
Sharm el Sheikh

SINANTHROPUS. See Man, Prehistoric
SINATRA, Frank
Ali-Frazier fight; photographs. il pors Life
70:cover. 20-1 Mr 19 '71
about
As Bess weighs in Frank says so long. il pors
Life 71:56-7 D 31 '71 •
Chairman emeritus. il pors Time 97:58 Ap 5
'71 •
For now. C. H. Simonds. Nat R 23:532 My 18
'71 •
How Frank Sinatra taught me friendship;
ed. by J. Bacon. S. Davis, Jr. il pors To-
days Health 49:30-3 N '71 •
Mafia is not an equal opportunity employer,
by N. Gage. Review
Sat R il 54:49 O 9 '71. F. J. Cook •
Parting shots: Frank Sinatra's swan song. T.
Thompson. il pors Life 70:70A-74 Je 25 '71 •
Puppet, pirate, poet, pawn, and king. A.
Shaw. il pors Hi Fi 21:65-8 Ag '71 •
Sinatra, that certain style. G. Lees. por Sat
R 54:45+ Ag 28 '71 •
SINCERITY
Anecdotes, facetiae, satire, etc.
Humbug for beginners. A. Lunn. Nat R 23:
1292 N 19 '71
SINCLAIR, Carolyn
Miracle baby of Carolyn Sinclair. J. L. Block
and J. Stein. il por Good H 172:86-7+ Je
'71 •
SINCLAIR, John
P.E.N. protests writer's conviction on pot
charges. Pub W 199:51-2 Mr 15 '71 •
SINDLINGER, Albert
Direct line to consumers. por Bsns W p46
Ap 24 '71 •
SING the songs of Thanksgiving; drama. See
Fisher, A.
SINGAPORE
Modest insurance premium; departure of
British forces. Time 98:31-2 N 15 '71
See also
Investments, Foreign (in Singapore)
Natural resources—Singapore
Newspapers—Singapore
Opium trade—Singapore
Science and state—Singapore
History
Singapore. Y. M. Yeung. bibliog il Focus 21:
1-8 Ap '71
Politics and government
Lee cracks down. por Newsweek 77:49 Je 7
'71
Press lord without portfolio. Time 97:71 My
31 '71
Sanitary affairs
Asia's Mr Clean. il Time 97:44 Ja 25 '71
SINGER, Alma
(tr) See Singer, I. B. Cabalist of East
Broadway
SINGER, David
Rebirth of Jewish mysticism. il Commonweal
93:492-5 F 19 '71
SINGER, Isaac Bashevis
Cabalist of East Broadway; tr. by A. Singer
and H. Lottman. New Yorker 47:32-4 Mr 6
'71
Day in Coney Island; tr. by the author and
L. Colwin. New Yorker 47:33-7 Jl 31 '71
Egotist; story, tr. by the author and D.
Straus. New Yorker 46:32-6 Ja 16 '71
Magazine; tr. by the author and L. Colwin.
New Yorker 47:33-7 My 22 '71
Peephole in the gate; story, tr. by the author
and R. S. Finkel. Esquire 75:124-7 Ap '71
Third one; story, tr. by the author and L
Colwin. New Yorker 47:30-5 Jl 17 '71
SINGER, James W. and Dolan, T. J.
Panther raid coverup. New Repub 165:21-3 Jl
24 '71
SINGER, Joe
Most talked-about painter of 1971: Aaron
Shikler. il por Am Artist 35:30-7+ S '71
SINGER, Laura J. and Buskin, Judith
Sex education on film; with list of film and
filmstrip references. il pors Wilson Lib Bul
46:177-82 O '71
SINGER, Lynn Teper
Yoga proves valuable camp program addi-
tion. il Camp Mag 43:13 N '71
SINGER, Michael C. and others
Butterfly feeding on lycopsid. bibliog il Sci-
ence 172:1341-2 Je 25 '71
SINGER, Richard G.
Home is where the vote is. Nation 213:202-5
S 13 '71

SINGER, Siegfried Fred
How did Venus lose its angular momentum? bibliog Science 170:1196-8; 173:170 D 11 '70, Jl 9 '71
SINGER, Stephen
Shall we rule these TV egos guilty of unnecessary roughness? il Todays Health 49: 40-3 D '71
Spread oil on the Sound's troubled waters and you'll be in hot water with the chief. il pors Todays Health 49:35-9+ O '71
SINGER company
Whatever happened to Singer? il por Forbes 108:31-3 Ag 1 '71
SINGERS
America is still singing; a catalogue of modern minstrels. T. Glover. il Sr Schol 98: 36-7+ Mr 29 '71
Debuts & reappearances; New York concerts. See issues of High fidelity and Musical America
Men of the high C's: countertenors. il por Newsweek 79:60-1 Ja 10 '72
Musical whirl; photographs. See issues of High fidelity and Musical America
Superstars, poets, pickers, prophets; country singers. W. Hedgepeth. il Look 35:28-30+ Jl 13 '71
Young artists, 1971; photographs. Hi Fi 21: MA10-14 Jl '71
   See also
Opera singers
Rock singers
   also names of singers, e.g. K. Kristofferson
SINGH, Arjan
Tiger. il Nat Parks & Con Mag 45:18-21 Ag '71
SINGH, Khushwant
Why they fled Pakistan, and won't go back. il N Y Times Mag p 12-15 Ag 1 '71
SINGH, Swaran
Foreign Minister of India visits Washington; statement, June 17, 1971. Dept State Bul 65: 41 Jl 12 '71 *
SINGING
Bird on Nellie's hat; singing yesteryear's songs in costume. G. Klewans. il Har Yrs 11:14-15 Ja '71
How high was G? H. Pleasants. Opera N 35:24-5 F 20 '71
Marilyn Horne becomes a prima donna. M. Mayer. il pors N Y Times Mag p 14-15+ Ja 17 '71
Processo alla Callas: bel canto style; interview. M. Callas. New Yorker 47:31-2 Ap 24 '71
Riding a wild horse; singing Tristan. J. Thomas. por Opera N 36:12-13 D 18 '71
Strauss and the low voice. J. Madeira. por Opera N 35:27 F 27 '71
   See also
Singers

Diction
When everybody wins. D. Uris. Opera N 36: 6-7 D 25 '71
SINGING teachers
Some of my best friends are phonies. W. Alderson; discussion. Opera N 35:35 F 20 '71
SINGLE-lens reflex cameras
And now there are four automatic 35mm focal plane shutter through lens meter single lens reflexes. H. Keppler. il Mod Phot 35:82-3 Ap '71
Annual guide to 47 top cameras. il Mod Phot 35:75-122 D '71
Canon SLR goes after the Nikon; F-1 system. E. Scully. il Mod Phot 34:40+ D '70
China's one-eyed seagull. F. L. Lee. il Pop Phot 69:40 O '71
Everything's new on the Nikon F2. E. H. Ortner. il Pop Sci 199:16 O '71
Handling the Canon F-1. B. Schwalberg. il Pop Phot 68:120-1+ My '71
It's a (gulp!) 4x5 SLR: Arca-Swiss reflex. N. Rothschild. il Pop Phot 68:102-3 Ja '71
Keppler on the SLR. H. Keppler. See issues of Modern photography
Lab report:
Argus/Cosina STL. N. Goldberg; R. Bruns. il Pop Phot 68:118-19+ Ja '71
Exa IIa. N. Goldberg and M. Frank. il Pop Phot 68:102-3+ Ap '71
Fujica ST 701. N. Goldberg. il Pop Phot 69:96-7+ Jl '71
Kowa SETR 2. N. Goldberg; M. Snyder. Pop Phot 69:94-5+ O '71
Mamiya RB67. N. Perry; N. Goldberg. il Pop Phot 68:102-3+ Mr '71
Norita 66. N. Goldberg; R. Kinne. il Pop Phot 68:104-5+ Je '71
Pentax 6x7. N. Goldberg; B. Pierce. il Pop Phot 69:88-9+ Ag '71
Zeiss Contarex super electronic. N. Rothschild; N. Goldberg. il Pop Phot 68:106-7+ F '71

Modern photography's annual guide to 45 top cameras. il Mod Phot 34:85-130 D '70
Modern tests:
Canon F-1. il Mod Phot 35:94-6+ My '71
Canon FTb. il Mod Phot 35:96-7 Ag '71
Chinese SLR, Seagull DF. M. Tsuji. Mod Phot 35:20+ O '71
Olympic FTL 35mm SLR. il Mod Phot 35:78-9 O '71
Perfect? No! Ideal? Almost! Pentax 6x7. S. Nathan. il Pop Phot 68:50+ Ap '71
Photo expo 71. N. Rothschild. il Pop Phot 69:80+ Ag '71
Readers' report:
Canon FT. il Mod Phot 35:95+ Ap '71
Exaktas. il Mod Phot 35:99+ Ag '71
Hasselblad 500C. M. Solon. il Mod Phot 35:91 Mr '71
Mamiya 500, 1000 TL's & DTL's. M. Solon. il Mod Phot 36:112-13 Ja '72
Minolta SR-T 101. il Mod Phot 35:97+ My '71
Miranda. il Mod Phot 35:78-9+ F '71
Nikon SLR cameras. il Mod Phot 35:90-1 Jl '71
Rollei goes after the Pentax; SL 35. L. A. Mannheim. il Mod Phot 34:51+ D '70
35mm focal-plane SLR's compared. D. L. Miller. il Mod Phot 35:80-7 Ag '71
35mm leaf shutter and 120 SLR's compared. D. L. Miller. il Mod Phot 35:76-8 S '71
SINGLE men
Bachelor executives: the bold new minority. G. Berkwitt. il Duns 98:44-6 D '71
Ebony's 1971 bachelors. il Ebony 26:136-40+ Je '71
Eligibles. E. Sheppard. Harp Baz 104:218-19 S '71
SINGLE parent adoption. See Adoption
SINGLE people
   See also
Cohabitation
SINGLE sideband receivers. See Radio receivers—Single sideband receivers
SINGLE women
Eligible single girls of 1971. il Ebony 26:149-52+ Ap '71
How I escaped a time clock. B. Bobrowski. por Redbook 136:38+ Ap '71
Sexual problems of women alone. D. Reuben. por McCalls 98:62+ F '71
Single wasn't so swell. J. Viorst. Redbook 137:81+ O '71
Young woman's story (cont) Redbook 136: 10+ Ja '71
   See also
Mothers, Unmarried
SINGLETON, Joe
Surfers invade sailing. il Motor B & S 127: 37+ F '71
SINIAVSKII, Andrei Donat'evich
Man whose alter ego is Abram Tertz. T. Solotaroff. Sat R 54:23-4+ F 27 '71 *
SINISTRALS. See Left- and right-handedness
SINO-Indian border dispute, 1957-
India's China war, by N. Maxwell. Review Life il 70:10 My 28 '71. C. Elliott
Lesson in astigmatism; disputed Aksai Chin. il Time 97:43 Je 14 '71
SINOLOGY. See Chinese studies (Sinology)
SIODMAK, Alex
Dream super 8 outfit. il Pop Phot 68:115-16 F '71
SIOUX CITY, Ia.
How to tame a wild river. J. H. Brouwer. il Am City 86:84+ D '71

Parks and playgrounds
Normal vs. emergency chipping. il Am City 86:37 Ag '71

Sanitary affairs
They didn't believe it would work. M. M. Randolph. il Am City 86:91 Ag '71
SIOUX FALLS college, Sioux Falls, S.D.
TV-radio; Upper midwestern conference on broadcasting and the people. R. L. Shayon. Sat R 54:54 My 15 '71
SIPAY, Edward R. See Vellutino, F. R. jt. auth.
SIPHONOPHORA
Purple wind. W. Zeiller and G. Compton. il Sea Front 17:372-7 N '71
SIPHONS
Dielectric siphons. T. B. Jones and others. bibliog il Science 174:1232-3 D 17 '71
SIPLE, Molly
Volunteer lawyers for the arts. Art in Am 59:31 S '71
SIPPLE, James B.
D. H. Lawrence and Man's ontological solitude. Chr Cent 88:1365-6 N 17 '71

SIRE, James W.
  Mr Sammler and the God of Our fathers. Chr
    Today 15:6-9 Je 4 '71
SIRIK MATAK, Sisowath
  Man behind the symbol. por Time 97:39 My
    17 '71 *
SIRIO satellite. See Communications satellites,
    Italian
SIROTA, David, and Greenwood, J. M.
  Understand your overseas work force; with
    folded charts. il Harvard Bsns R 49:53-60
    Ja '71
SISAL hemp
  Great sisal scheme. D. R. Gross. il Natur
    Hist 80:48-55 Mr '71
SISCO, Joseph John
  Assistant Secretary Sisco interviewed on
    Face the Nation program, February 14, 1971.
    Dept State Bul 64:291-6 Mr 8 '71
  Fluid and evolving situation in the Middle
    East; address, November 6, 1970. Dept
    State Bul 63:748-51 D 21 '70
            about
  Dialogue of the deaf. Newsweek 78:32 Ag 9
    '71 *
  Say it with flowers. il por Newsweek 78:34+
    Ag 16 '71 *
SISK, J. Kelly
  Mass media; address, February 11, 1971. Vital
    Speeches 37:404-7 Ap 15 '71
SISKIND, George
  Denominational membership, expression of
    religious sentiments and status upon ad-
    mission to a psychiatric hospital. Ment Hy
    55:246-7 Ap '71
SISSMAN, Louis Edward
  Big rock-candy mountain; poem. New Yorker
    46:28-9 Ja 9 '71
  Convenient to Victoria; poem. New Yorker
    47:40 Mr 20 '71
  Innocent bystander (cont) Atlan 227:40-1 F;
    34+ Mr; 26+ Ap; 30+ My; 26+ Je; 228:20+
    Jl '71
  Mouth-organ tunes: the American lost and
    found; poem. New Yorker 47:43 F 27 '71
  Temporary measures; a book of hours;
    poem. New Yorker 47:42-3 Je 26 '71
SISTER cities. See Intercommunity coopera-
    tion
SISTERHOOD; story. See Rolfs, M. J.
SISTERHOODS
  Renewal in the church: two mentalities in
    conflict; pressure from the Congregation
    for religious. T. E. Clarke. America 124:
    234-7 Mr 6 '71; Discussion. 124:459-61 My 1
    '71
  Sisters unite separately. America 124:276 Mr
    20 '71
      See also
  Carmelites
  Convents and nunneries
  Nuns
SITE planning. See Building sites; Housing
    projects—Site planning
SITES, Building. See Building sites
SITES, Historic. See Historic houses, sites,
    etc.
SITES, Industrial. See Location in business
    and industry
SITKA spruce. See Spruce
SITTEL, Edward
  Movies. il Vogue 158:170 N 1 '71
SITUATION ethics
  Situation ethics in a changing situation.
    J. Fletcher. por Chr Cent 88:1444-6 D 8 '71
SIURU, William D. Jr, and Holder, W. G.
  Aerospace museums. il Travel 136:58-65 Jl
    '71
SIVE, Mary Robinson
  Is CCLD all that bad? il por Library J 96:
    3442-5 O 15 '71
SIVERNS, L. E.
  Walkathon; poem. Chr Cent 88:801 Je 30 '71
SIX, Robert Forman
  Bob Six show rolls on. T. J. Murray. il por
    Duns 97:34-7+ Je '71 *
SIX; musical comedy. See Musical comedies,
    revues, etc.—Criticisms, plots, etc.
SIX flags over mid-America (amusement park)
    See Amusement parks
6:27 p.m; story. See Oates, J. C.
SIX year term for president. See Presidents
    —United States—Term
SIXKILLER, Sonny
  Magic number is Sixkiller. R. Blount, jr. il
    pors Sports Illus 35:34-7 O 4 '71 *
SIXTH committee of the General assembly.
    See United Nations—Legal committee
SIXTH fleet. See United States—Navy
SIXTY nine cents shops
  How 69¢ stores ring the bell. il Bsns W p 138
    My 15 '71

SIZE of man. See Body size
SJÖWALL, Maj
  Copology; interview. New Yorker 47:28 My
    22 '71
            about
  Authors & editors. B. A. Bannon. il por
    Pub W 200:13-15 S 6 '71 *
SKALNY, Jan. See Daugherty, K. E. jt. auth.
SKATES
  Sleds & skates for fun in the cold. il Chang-
    ing T 25:15-16 D '71
SKATING
      See also
  Roller skating
          Competitions
  Skating for gold on thin ice: American teen-
    agers in Finland. P. Ress and W. F. Reed.
    il Sports Illus 34:18-19 F 15 '71
SKATING rinks
  From tennis courts to skating rinks, fast;
    Vail, Colo. il Am City 86:23 My '71
  Sure you can ice skate in warm weather;
    Wyandotte, Mich. B. F. Yack. il Am City
    86:54 Ap '71
SKEIN; story. See Walker, T.
SKELETONS, Plastic. See Anatomical models
SKELL, Philip S.
  Combination. Newsweek 78:101-2 D 20 '71 *
  Free atoms: a whole new basic chemistry.
    il por Sci N 100:390 D 11 '71 *
SKELTON, Red
  So long, clown. M. Williams. Nat R 23:823-4
    Jl 27 '71 *
SKETCH boards. See Drawing boards, tables,
    etc.
SKI bindings. See Skis and skiing—Equipment
SKI coaches. See Coaches (athletics)
SKI houses. See Vacation houses
SKI resorts. See Winter resorts
SKI tours. See Skis and skiing
SKIDDING of automobiles. See Automobiles—
    Skidding
SKIDMORE, James Albert, 1932-
  Recruiter's recruit. por Bsns W p84-5 Mr 6
    '71 *
SKIERS
      See also
  Women as skiers
SKIING. See Skis and skiing
SKILLET cookery. See Cookery
SKILLETS
  Most indispensable utensil. J. Pépin. il
    House B 113:140 My '71
SKIMMERS (birds)
  Cutwater. F. K. Truslow. il Audubon 73:8-11
    Jl '71
SKIN
  In vitro techniques for avoiding edge damage
    in studies of frog skin. S. I. Helman and D.
    A. Miller. bibliog il Science 173:146-8 Jl 9 '71
  Skin: keeping in touch. Vogue 157:109 Ap 1
    '71
  Skin shows emotional problems. A. J. Snider.
    il Sci Digest 69:59-60 Ap '71
      See also
  Sunburn
          Care and hygiene
  Don't be another pebble on the beach. Harp
    Baz 104:82 Je '71
  Good-earth way to glow; Klinger salon. il
    pors Mlle 72:170-3 Mr '71
  Skin care appliances. Bet Hom & Gard 49:
    88 O '71
  Skin deep. T. H. Sternberg. McCalls 98:28
    F '71
  Skin sense. C. Valmy. il por Harp Baz 104:
    38 Mr '71
  Winter beauty. C. Bartel. il Am Home 74:24
    D '71
  Your skin & you. il Seventeen 29:126-7 O '70
          Diseases
  Xeroderma pigmentosum: a rapid sensitive
    method for prenatal diagnosis. J. D. Re-
    gan and others. bibliog il Science 174:
    147-50 O 8 '71
      See also
  Hives (urticaria)
  Psoriasis
  Scleroderma
  Warts
SKIN, Color of. See Color of man
SKIN cancer. See Cancer
SKIN color. See Color of man
SKIN diving
  Ama, sea nymphs of Japan. L. Marden. il
    Nat Geog 140:122-35 Jl '71
  Deep dive for black coral. J. R. Parks. il
    Field & S 76:114-16+ D '71

SKIN diving—*Continued*
It's another world, the underwater world. il
Sunset 146:90-5 Ap '71
Skin diving for boatmen. B. McKeown. il
Mech Illus 67:81+ S '71
You're not too old to scuba dive! G. Tinker.
il Motor B & S 127:30-1+ Ap '71
See also
Spear fishing

Equipment and supplies
Underwater equipment. G. Tinker. il Motor
B & S 127:32+ Ap '71
SKIN pigmentation. See Color of man
SKINNER, Ballou
Myth of teaching for critical thinking. bib-
liog f Clear House 45:372-6 F '71
SKINNER, Burrhus Frederic
Nice new world of B. F. Skinner; inter-
view, ed. by A. Gross. pors Mlle 74:90-3+
Ja '72
about
Beyond freedom and dignity, by B. F. Skin-
ner. Review
Atlan 228:122-5 O '71. G. Kateb •
Sat R 54:47-8+ O 9 '71. W. Arnold •
Brave new behaviorism. por Newsweek 78:
95 S 20 '71 •
Case of Dr Skinner, for & against; reactions
to Beyond freedom and dignity. Mlle 74:
90-3+ Ja '72 •
Freedom and funding; Skinner support
queried. por Sci N 100:420-1 D 25 '71 •
Grant K6-MH-21775. Nation 214:37 Ja 10 '72 •
He envisions a happier age. C. McCarry. il
McCalls 99:35 N '71 •
Misplaced zeal. New Repub 166:14 Ja 1 '72 •
Modifying man's behavior; three reviews of
Beyond freedom and dignity. Cur 135:9-18 D
'71 •
Skinner's utopia: panacea, or path to hell?
il pors Time 98:47-52+ S 20 '71 •
Ultimate conclusions of a mod behaviorist.
R. J. Trotter. por Sci N 100:96-7 Ag 7 '71;
Discussion. 100:134+ Ag 28 '71 •
SKINNER, Deborah
Skinnerian innovation: baby in a box. il pors
Time 98:51 S 20 '71 •
SKINNER, Gwen
Visit to the San Blas Indians takes you
backward in time. il Yachting 129:66-7+
F '71
SKINNER, Jean Ross-. See Ross-Skinner, J.
SKINNER, Patrick F.
Family of man in an English class. Engl J
60:220-2 F '71
SKINNER, Wickham
Anachronistic factory. bibliog f il Harvard
Bsns R 49:61-70 Ja '71
SKINNER, William Alfred
Is a mustache just peanuts? G. S. Brown.
il por Sports Illus 34:38-40+ Je 14 '71 •
SKINNER box. See Psychological apparatus
SKINNING of rabbits. See Game, Dressing of
SKINNING of squirrels. See Game, Dressing of
SKINS. See Hides and skins
SKIPPER, Howard E.
What's happening in cancer research? il Sat
R 54:16-19 Ja 16 '71
SKIR, Leo
Opinion: a lesbian and a homosexual on
female sexuality. Mlle 74:76+ N '71
SKIRTS, Length of. See Clothing and dress
SKIS and skiing
Cross-country craze; ski touring. il Life
72:64-6 Ja 14 '72
Executive schuss. R. Levy. il Duns 97:66-
8 Mr '71
Going things; snow story '71-'72 U.S.A.
and Canada. S. Cuneo and A. Donohue.
Mlle 74:100-2+ N '71
He conquers high mountains from the top
down; S. Saudan. A. Verschoth. il por
Sports Illus 34:62 Mr 15 '71
Jamais vu! il Time 97:60 F 22 '71
Ski-tour trails. R. Massow. il Seventeen 30:
141 D '71
Ski touring. S. Cuneo. Mlle 74:170-1+ N '71
Skiing, the easy way; ski touring. il Time
99:68 Ja 17 '72
Snow people. C. G. Rogers. il McCalls 99:47
D '71
Spider who finally came in from the cold;
ex-Olympian Sabich. G. S. Brown. il por
Sports Illus 35:92+ D 20 '71
Teen travel talk: where the Cochrans ski. P.
Orvis. il Seventeen 29:62 D '70
Total exercise: cross-country skiing. Vogue
158:149 N 1 '71

Winter sport: some new ways to go. G. G.
Greer. il Bet Hom & Gard 49:6+ D '71
See also
Sand skis and skiing
United States—Army—Ski troops
Water skis and skiing

Accidents and injuries
Breaks of the game. il Time 97:58+ F 8 '71
See also
National ski patrol system

Equipment
Skiers in a bind. Newsweek 78:62 N 29 '71
Technology of the ski. A. Greenberg. il Es-
quire 76:202-7 D '71

Study and teaching
Dream came true; junior ski program in
Reno, Nev. G. A. Broten and G. R. Twar-
dokens. il Parks & Rec 6:111+ Ja '71

Canada
Going things; snow story '71-'72 U.S.A. and
Canada. S. Cuneo and A. Donohue. Mlle 74:
100-2+ N '71
Skiing Canada's big back country; photographs by J. G. Zimmerman; with account
by A. Verschoth. Sports Illus 35:48-55 D
6 '71

Chile
Chile dilly: Mt Villarrica. Travel 136:27 N '71

Colorado
Aspen's new kind of ski bum. il Life 70:
62-7 Mr 5 '71
Those beautiful new ski bums. C. S. Wren.
il pors Look 35:35-8+ F 23 '71

Europe, Western
Ski in Europe and hit a slide in price. Bsns
W p81-2 Ja 23 '71
Summer ski tours for teens. il Travel 135:69
Mr '71
10 swinging alpine resorts for the very best
in European skiing. A. Rand. il Holiday
48:34-5 N '70

Maine
Win one and they give you the ax; World
cup and Tall timber classic. W. Johnson.
il Sports Illus 34:24-6+ Mr 1 '71

North Carolina
New winter trails: North Carolina. R. B.
Satterwhite. il Travel 136:28-33+ D '71

Northeastern states
Skiing anyone? il Ebony 26:100-5 Ja '71
Snowbirding the Northeast. M. Cohen. Red-
book 138:151 Ja '72

Pennsylvania
Skiing down a garbage pile: sanitary landfills. il Bsns W p90 N 6 '71

Spain
In Spain they say ski, ski; drawings by A.
Simont. Sports Illus 34:46-51 Mr 15 '71

Switzerland
New winter trails: Switzerland. R. Deardorff.
il Travel 136:34-9 D '71

United States
See Skis and skiing

Utah
Alta is for skiing. D. Thomas. il Holiday 48:
26-9 N '70

Vermont
Dreams of maple sugar plums. H. Sutton. il
Sat R 54:38-9+ Mr 20 '71

Western states
Pleasures of ski touring. il Sunset 146:54-9
F '71
Skiing the American West. R. Redford. por
Harp Baz 105:38+ D '71
10 rugged western slopes for the skier in
quest of the ultimate run. A. Rand. il Holi-
day 48:30-1 N '70
SKITTLES
Skittle bowl has automatic pin setter. il Pop
Mech 136:154-7 S '71
SKLAR, Anna
Library services well-suited to automation.
il Am City 86:79 D '71
SKLAR, Robert
Hollywood's new wave. il Ramp Mag 10:60-6
N '71
SKLAREWITZ, Norman
When they talk with their hands, what are
they saying? il Pop Mech 135:72-3 My '71

SKOKIE, III.
Parking problems in residential areas. J. Matzer, jr. il Am City 86:68 Jl '71
3 cities, innovative reporting. il Am City 86:132+ Je '71

SKOLER, Daniel L.
There's more to crime control than the get tough approach. bibliog f Ann Am Acad 397:28-39 S '71

SKOLIMOWSKI, Jerzy
Current cinema. P. Gilliatt. New Yorker 47:56-7 S 4 '71 •

SKOLNICK, Jerome H.
Neighborhood police. Nation 212:372-3 Mr 22 '71
Violence commission violence. il Trans-Action 7:32-8 O '70
—and Brick, S. A.
Fair trial for Angela Davis? por Nation 213: 46-50 Jl 19 '71

SKOVBO, Bob, pseud.
From the world of Tomasik Nutarareak; with biographical sketch. il Natur Hist 80:2, 28-35 Ja '71

SKRIABIN, Aleksandr Nikolaevich
Discussions. R. Hemming. por Sr Schol 99: 21 Ja 10 '72 •
Man with the astral body. R. Evett. Atlan 228:128-31 O '71 •

SKULL
Face of Tamerlane; M. Gerasimov's reconstructions based on skull studies. il por Newsweek 77:70 Mr 8 '71

SKURKA, Norma
Home. See issues of New York times magazine

SKURNIK, W. A. E.
United States role in Africa. Cur Hist 60: 129-35+ Mr '71

SKY
Star gazing the easy way. M. Lincoln. il Pop Sci 199:122+ O '71
Star-studded show. J. C. Miller. il Motor B & S 128:54-5 bibliog(p58) Jl '71
See also
Airglow

SKY, Color of
Sky color. G. Benford and D. Book. bibliog il Natur Hist 80:32-9+ F '71

SKY diving. See Parachuting

SKY marshals. See Airplane hijacking—Prevention

SKYBOLT (guided missile) See Guided missiles —Launching from airplanes

SKYBUS. See Pittsburgh—Transit systems

SKYJACKING. See Airplane hijacking

SKYLAB. See Space stations

SKYLIGHTS
How to install a skylight. D. Huff. il Pop Sci 198:130 Ap '71
Inside kitchen, flooded with sky light. il Sunset 147:64-5 Ag '71

SKYSCRAPERS
Skylines v. skyscrapers; San Francisco. il Time 97:35 Mr 8 '71
See also
New York (city)—Empire State building
Fires and fire protection
Are our office buildings firetraps? N. A. Martin. il Duns 98:50-2+ N '71
50-story firetraps. A. S. Freese. il Pop Mech 136:53-6+ Ag '71
Tougher fire safety code for skyscrapers. il Bsns W p46-7 Ag 7 '71

SLABINSKI, Victor J.
Optical tracking of spacecraft. il Sky & Tel 42:202-4 O '71

SLACK, Warner
Computer-based interviewing system dealing with nonverbal behavior as well as keyboard responses. bibliog il Science 171: 84-7 Ja 8 '71

SLADEK, John R. Jr
Differences in the distribution of catecholamine varicosities in cat and rat reticular formation. bibliog il Science 174:410-12 O 22 '71

SLADEK, Pat A.
Beach stone sculpture. il Sch Arts 70:29 F '71

SLAG; drama. See Hare, D.

SLAMECKA, Vladimir
Filling the computer gap. J. Poindexter. por Duns 97:77-8 My '71 •

SLANG
If you think it's groovy to rap, you're shucking. M. Jahn. il N Y Times Mag p28-9+ Je 6 '71; Discussion. p4 Je 20; 42 Je 27 '71

SLANTS, Ed
Rod Stewart. il por Sr Schol 99:30-1 N 29 '71

SLAPPEY, Sterling G.
America must have the Alaskan oil. il Nations Bsns 59:40-3 S '71
Going somewhere from the road to nowhere. il Nations Bsns 59:66-9 Je '71
Heading off an energy crisis. il Nations Bsns 59:26-9 Jl '71

SLASH-and-burn farming. See Shifting cultivation

SLATE, John H.
So you're going to build an ocean liner; reprint. il Motor B & S 127:55+ F '71

SLATE, Mary Ellen
Beach-combing. il Motor B & S 128:50-1 bibliog(p58) Jl '71
Cypress Gardens rides again. il Motor B & S 127:10-11 Mr '71

SLATE, Theodore
Ted Slate, special librarian. il pors Wilson Lib Bul 46:138-9 O '71 •

SLATER, Jack
Guard changes in Berkeley. il pors Ebony 26:74-6+ O '71
Learning is an all-black thing. il Ebony 26:88-90+ S '71

SLATER, Philip E.
Must marriage cheat today's young women? il Redbook 136:66-7+ F '71

SLATER, Robert Edward
Strike three? por Forbes 108:78 N 1 '71 •

SLATER, Walker securities, ltd.
British lion that beat the bear. por Bsns W p56 My 8 '71

SLATKIN, William
15 years of video recording. il Electr World 86:36-8+ N '71

SLATTED barn floors. See Barns and stables— Floors

SLAUGHTERING and slaughterhouses
See also
Meat inspection

SLAVE trade in art
Eyeview history of the Atlantic slave trade. M. Teague and Z. Cowan. il Art in Am 59:58-67 Ja '71

SLAVERY
United States
Best white friend black Americans ever had: Thaddeus Stevens. G. P. Morrill. il por Read Digest 99:169-70+ Jl '71
World of the slave. L. Bennett, jr. il Ebony 26:44-6+ F '71
Emancipation
Translation of Act of emancipation manuscript. J. Derham. il Negro Hist Bul 33: 165 N '70
Insurrections, etc.
See also
Southampton insurrection, 1831

SLAVES, Emancipation of. See Slavery— United States—Emancipation

SLAVIN, Neal
Gallery; photographs. Life 71:6-9 O 29 '71

SLAYMAKER, S. R. 2d
Deadly anytime anywhere. il Field & S 76: 30+ Je '71

SLAYTON, William L.
Don't oversell new towns. Am City 86:8 My '71

SLEDS
Sleds & skates for fun in the cold. il Changing T 25:15-16 D '71
Winter sport: some new ways to go. G. G. Greer. il Bet Hom & Gard 49:6+ D '71

SLEEP
Acetylcholine liberation from cerebral cortex during paradoxical (REM) sleep. H. H. Jasper and J. Tessier. bibliog il Science 172:601-2 My 7 '71
Anemia in sleep-deprived rats receiving anticoagulants. R. R. Drucker-Colin and others. bibliog il Science 174:505-7 O 29 '71
How much sleep do you need? interview. J. Segal. Read Digest 98:185-6+ My '71
News from the world of space exploration; NASA-developed sleep analyzer. Space World H-10-94:41-2+ O '71
Report on sleep research. Sci Digest 69:57-8 Je '71
Retrograde amnesia: electroconvulsive shock effects after termination of rapid eye movement sleep deprivation. W. Fishbein and others. bibliog il Science 172:80-2 Ap 2 '71
Single neuron activity in cat gigantocellular tegmental field: selectivity of discharge in desynchronized sleep. R. W. McCarley and J. A. Hobson. bibliog il Science 174:1250-2 D 17 '71
Sleep stage and personality characteristics of natural long and short sleepers. W. B. Webb and J. Friel. bibliog il Science 171: 587-8 F 12 '71

SLEEP—*Continued*
Stage 4 sleep: influence of time course variables. W. B. Webb and H. W. Agnew, jr. bibliog il Science 174:1354-6 D 24 '71
  See also
Dreams
Insomnia
Narcolepsy
SLEEP deprivation. See Sleep
SLEEP learning
Learn Russian and sleep. il Sci Digest 70:79 S '71
Present shock: experiments in learning. D. M. Rorvik. il Esquire 76:48+ D '71
SLEEP therapy
New help for nonsleepers. T. J. Rakstis. il Todays Health 49:16-19+ S '71
Sleep machine: electrosleep therapy. il Newsweek 77:70 My 17 '71
SLEEP walking. See Somnambulism
SLEEPING bags
Pads with a punch; Air cap. H. K. Cox. il Field & S 75:24 Ap '71
Sleeping bags. il Consumer Rep 36:350-3 Je '71
There's no place like foam; polyurethane foam. P. Knight. il Sports Illus 35:66-7 N 8 '71
SLEEPING garments. See Nightgowns, pajamas, etc.
SLEEPING mountains; drama. See Winther, B.
SLEEPING sickness, Equine. See Encephalomyelitis
SLEEPLESSNESS. See Insomnia
SLEEPWALKING. See Somnambulism
SLEEPWEAR. See Nightgowns, pajamas, etc.
SLEET, Moneta, Jr
In Montgomery; photographs. Ebony 26:42-8 Ag '71
SLEGERS-Forbes (firm) See Motorcycle industry
SLEIGHS and sleighing
Snowballing through the Rockies: sleigh racing. H. Peterson. il Sports Illus 35:68-70+ D 20 '71
SLEPIAN, Edward L.
Eyes have it. Motor B & S 127:80+ My '71
SLEPIAN, J. See Konishi, T. jt. auth.
SLESINGER, Tess
Small servings of pathos. G. Weales. Commonweal 94:360-2 Jl 9 '71 •
SLEUTH; drama. See Shaffer, A.
SLEUTHS. See Detectives
SLICK, Grace
God of Grace. il por Newsweek 77:95 Mr 15 '71 •
Rock family affair. il por Life 71:53 S 24 '71 •
SLIDE projectors. See Projectors
SLIDE rule
Slide rules you make yourself. M. Lincoln. il Pop Sci 198:136 My '71
SLIDES. See Transparencies
SLIM, Hedi
Grandeur and decline of the Punic city-state. il UNESCO Courier 23:9-16 D '70
SLIME eel. See Hagfish
SLIME molds
Adenosine 3',5'-monophosphate phosphodiesterase in the growth medium of physarum polycephalum. A. W. Murray and others. bibliog il Science 171:496-8 F 5 '71
Nuclear acidic protein changes during differentiation in physarum polycephalum. W. M. LeStourgeon and H. P. Rusch. bibliog il Science 174:1233-6 D 17 '71
SLINGSHOTS
    Anecdotes, facetiae, satire, etc.
For use on giants not turkeys. D. Mannix. il Sports Illus 34:44-6+ Je 14 '71
SLIP covers
How to make a slipcover like an expert. il House & Gard 140:150 O '71
Sew up some beautiful savings. M. B. Smith. il Bet Hom & Gard 49:64-7 Mr '71
SLIPPERS
Washable slippers, easy to make. il Sunset 146:133 Ap '71
SLIPYJ, Josyf, cardinal
Ukrainians on the march. G. A. Maloney. por Cath World 214:109-12 D '71 •
SLIVKA, Rose
Laugh-in in clay. il Craft Horiz 31:39-46 O '71
SLOAN, John
John Sloan as an illustrator. E. J. Bullard. il Am Artist 35:52+ O '71 •
SLOANE, Leonard
Madison avenue. Sat R 54:69 S 11; 76 O 9; 97 N 13 '71

SLOANE, R. Bruce, and Horvitz, D. F.
Marital counseling. bibliog Ment Hy 55:534-7 O '71
Pastoral counseling. bibliog Ment Hy 55:538-43 O '71
SLOCHOWER, Harry
Mythopoesis and psychoanalysis. J. E. Gedo. bibliog Am Imago 27:329-37 Wint '70 •
SLOGANS
It's time for a change of political slogans. W. Safire. il N Y Times Mag p8-9 D 26 '71
SLOOPS
Letter from Long Island Sound. M. Hunt. New Yorker 47:62+ Ag 28 '71
Sea chanties & marlinspikes; life aboard the ecology-inspired Clearwater. D. Kasanof. il Motor B & S 127:88-9+ Mr '71
Setting sail for yesterday; maiden voyage of Clearwater. B. Atkinson. il Audubon 73:73-9 Mr '71
SLOPES (soil mechanics)
Romance of perched soil. A. R. Croft. il Am For 77:38-9+ Mr '71
SLOT machines. See Gambling machines
SLOTNICK, D. L.
Fastest computer; with biographical sketch. il Sci Am 224:12, 76-87 F '71
SLOTNICK, Henry B.
Do thirteen year olds write as well as seventeen year olds? il Engl J 60:1109-15 N '71
—and Knapp, J. V.
Essay grading by computer: a laboratory phenomenon? bibliog f Engl J 60:75-80+ Ja '71
SLOTTEN, Ralph
Alleluia lamb; poem. Chr Cent 88:427 Ap 7 '71
Divine wit of miraculous conceptions; poem. Chr Cent 88:317 Mr 10 '71
Orthodoxy for April fools' day; poem. Chr Cent 88:397 Mr 31 '71
SLOVAKIA
  See also
Hotels, taverns, etc.—Slovakia

    Description and travel
High hopes in the Slovak uplands. H. Sutton. il Sat R 54:31-2 Je 19 '71
SLOW learning children

    Education
Kindergarten plus. N. Voldstad. il Parents Mag 46:72-3+ F '71
Moral dilemma, a teaching unit for slow learners. R. G. Brown. Engl J 60:924-6+ O '71
Our son was failing in school. il Good H 172:16+ My '71
Progress chart for slow learners. J. Marusek. Clear House 45:312-13 Ja '71
SLOYAN, Gerard S.
New servant class? Commonweal 94:56-60 Mr 26 '71
SLOYAN, Patrick J.
Full of air. New Repub 164:9 Mr 20 '71
SLUDGE as fertilizer. See Sewage as fertilizer
SLUGS
    Control
Will beer really get slugs, snails? Sunset 146:253 Ap '71
SLUGS, Sea. See Sea slugs
SLUM clearance. See Urban renewal
SLUMLORDS. See Landlord and tenant
SLUMS
Housing abandonment. Arch Forum 134:42-5 Ap '71
Let's keep the inner city black. il Ebony 27:108-9 Ja '72
Urban wilderness; excerpt from CEQ report. il Sat R 54:52-5 S 4 '71
SLUTZ, Merton H.
Tic-tac-toe you can play anywhere. il Pop Mech 135:153 Ap '71
SLUZKI, Carlos E. See Goldenberg, M. jt. auth.
SMALL, Dorothy May
Nature's jewels; photographs. Am For 77:44-5 F '71
SMALL, William J.
Melvin Laird and CBS. Sedulus. New Repub 165:29-30 Jl 10 '71 •
SMALL arms. See Firearms
SMALL business
  See also
Cottage industries
Self employed

    Federal aid
Lease guarantees help small firms obtain prime locations. Nations Bsns 59:20 D '71
Occupational safety and health loans: an advance look for small businessmen. Nations Bsns 59:20 O '71

SMALL business—*Continued*

Finance

How to go about buying a business. il
Changing T 25:17-20 F '71
What going into business costs. il Changing
T 25:25-9 Je '71
What's worrying small businessmen. il U S
News 70:13-14 My 31 '71
SMALL business administration. See United
States—Small business administration
SMALL business investment companies
Business fights the social ills: in a recession.
il Bsns W p60-2 Mr 6 '71
Let's write off MESBICs. R. S. Rosenbloom
and J. K. Shank; discussion. Harvard
Bsns R 48:170-1 N '70; 49:25 Ja '71
Venture capital vehicle is picking up momentum; Minority enterprise small business investment companies. Nations Bsns
59:16 N '71
See also
Narragansett capital corporation
SMALL claims courts
Buyer vs. seller in small claims court. il
Consumer Rep 36:624-31 O '71
SMALL colleges
Best colleges have the least effect; Project
on student development in small colleges.
A. W. Chickering. il Sat R 54:48-50+ Ja
16 '71
Out of sight, out of mind. Newsweek 78:
83 N 15 '71
Small colleges; football 1971. Sports Illus
35:79-80 S 13 '71

Finance

Any future for private colleges? interview.
J. A. Howard. il por U S News 71:43-6 S 6
'71
SMALL expectations; story. See Hearon, S.
SMALL sounds and tilting shadows; story. See
Rascoe, J.
SMALL town life. See City and town life;
Village life
SMALLENBURG, Carol, and Smallenburg,
Harry
School behavior: whose problem? il PTA
Mag 65:18-21 bibliog(p35) F '71
SMALLENBURG, Harry. See Smallenburg, C.
jt. auth.
SMALLMOUTH fishing. See Bass fishing
SMALLPOX
End of smallpox? il Newsweek 77:65 Mr 1
'71
See also
Vaccination
SMATHERS, George
Smathers machine. J. Ridgeway. por Ramp
Mag 10:26-8 Ja '72 *
SMELL
Chemical languages of fishes. J. H. Todd.
il Sci Am 224:98-106+ My '71
See also
Odors
SMETANA, Bedřich
Smetana. by B. Large. Review
Am Rec G il por 37:628-30 My '71. L.
Richmond *
SMILEY, Albert, family
Great homes away from home: Mohonk mountain house. J. Edgan. il Am Home 74:42+
O '71 *
SMILEY, Sam
5 ways to sell your play. il Writers Digest
51:22-5 D '71
SMIT, Leo
Classic Cole Porter. il por Sat R 54:48-9+ D
25 '71
SMITH, Adeline M.
Free & inexpensive magazines for schools;
ed. by B. Katz. Library J 96:2065-6 Je 15
'71
SMITH, Alexander B. and Pollack, Harriet
Crimes without victims. Sat R 54:27-9 D
4 '71
SMITH, Alexis
Alexis Smith & Craig Stevens: nostalgic? Not
on your life! A. G. Mazer. pors Harp Baz
105:107 D '71 *
SMITH, Alice Upham
Cool it with trees. il Horticulture 49:18-21
Ag '71
SMITH, Anthony
Story behind the book: Mato Grosso. A. H.
Johnston. il Pub W 200:26-7 N 8 '71 *
SMITH, Anthony Wayne
New forestry program; testimony. Nat Parks
& Con Mag 45:35-7 My '71
SMITH, Arnholt
Playground divided. R. W. Johnston. il por
Sports Illus 35:78-81+ N 8 '71 *

SMITH, Asa
Asa Smith leaves the war; ed. by B. Catton.
il Am Heritage 22:54-9+ F '71
SMITH, Bessie
Bessie's blues. H. Saal. por Newsweek 77:
44-5 F 1 '71 *
Complete Bessie Smith. L. Gerber. pors Am
Rec G 37:340-2 F '71 *
Jazz records. W. Balliett. New Yorker 47:
160-6+ N 6 '71 *
SMITH, Beverly Bush
More fun than play dough. il Todays Health
49:58-61 F '71
SMITH, Bob
No fuel, no noise: just the wind and you.
il Pop Sci 198:90-2+ F '71
SMITH, Bob, 1918?-
It's Howdy Doody time, again. il pors Life
70:90-2 My 7 '71 *
SMITH, Brian H.
Narrow path: Reinhold Niebuhr (1892-1971)
America 125:63-5 Ag 7 '71
SMITH, Brian Sutton-. See Sutton-Smith, B.
SMITH, Bruce L.
What price Tillich? Chr Today 16:16-18 D
17 '71 (to be cont)
SMITH, Bubba
Beasts of Baltimore. L. L. King. il por Atlan
229:70-7 Ja '72 *
SMITH, C. Arnholt
California goes after a transportation octopus. por Bsns W p54 S 25 '71 *
Mr San Diego. por Forbes 108:26 Ag 15 '71 *
SMITH, Charles Aaron. See Smith, Bubba
SMITH, Damion
Our plant must be a good neighbor. il Am
City 86:89+ Ap '71
SMITH, David H.
Go light for kings. il Field & S 75:60-1+ Mr
'71
SMITH, David Jeddie
Case in plot; poem. Nation 213:602 D 6 '71
SMITH, David W. E. and McNamara, A. L.
Specialization of rabbit reticulocyte transfer
RNA content for hemoglobin synthesis. bibliog il Science 171:577-9 F 12 '71
SMITH, Delbert D.
Educational satellite telecommunication: the
challenge of a new technology. il Bul Atom
Sci 27:14-18 Ap '71
SMITH, Dennis
. . . Or a firefighter? Read Digest 99:169-70
S '71
SMITH, Desmond
Hamtramck: waiting for Pilsudski. Nation
214:41-3 Ja 10 '72
SMITH, Dido
Sterling in the '70s. il Craft Horiz 31:12-17
O '71
SMITH, Donald F.
Micronesian culture vs. American education.
bibliog il Sch & Soc 99:279-82 Sum '71
SMITH, Douglas
Telling it on the mountain. I. Eldad. Chr
Cent 88:886 Jl 21 '71 *
SMITH, E. Harold
Catholic crisis. Commonweal 95:320-3 Ja 7 '72
SMITH, Edgar
Pre-posthumous conversation with myself.
pors Esquire 75:112-15+ Je '71
about
Bargain for freedom. Newsweek 78:30 D 20
'71 *
Edgar Smith case. W. F. Buckley, jr. Nat R
23:777 Jl 13 '71 *
Edgar Smith's big day. il Nat R 23:574 Je 1
'71 *
Long wait. por Time 97:22+ Mv 24 '71 *
Neither truth nor victory. il por Time 98:
51 D 20 '71 *
Return of Edgar Smith. W. F. Buckley, jr.
Nat R 23:1455 D 31 '71 *
SMITH, Edward C.
Coming of the black ghetto-state. Yale R
61:161-82 D '71
SMITH, Elinor Goulding
What! You're not going to Thorshavn? il
Travel 136:74-6 D '71
Woman who couldn't lie; story. Redbook
137:73-4 Ag '71
SMITH, Elmore
Elmore the Great. il por Newsweek 77:67
Mr 29 '71 *
SMITH, Emily Anne
Homes: new and remodeled. M. Kraft. il por
Good H 172:140-7+ Ap '71 *
SMITH, F. G. Walton
Real sea; excerpt from The seas in motion. il Sea Front 17:298-311 S '71
SMITH, Fred
America is a growing country; address, May
22, 1971. Vital Speeches 37:534-7 Je 15 '71

SMITH, G. Roysce
How many books make a bookstore? il Pub
W 200:18-20 D 20 '71
How to become a bookseller. Pub W 200:
25-7 N 29 '71
SMITH, Gail
Omit the general contractor; how to save
construction costs. il Am City 86:77 N '71
SMITH, Gene A. See Zima, J. P. jt. auth.
SMITH, Gerard Coad
U.S. and Soviet Union begin fifth phase of
SALT talks; statement, July 6, 1971. Dept
State Bul 65:98 Jl 26 '71
U.S. and Soviet Union begin sixth phase
of SALT talks; statement, November 13,
1971. Dept State Bul 65:659-60 D 6 '71
SMITH, Gordon S.
Trees of Cape Cod. il Am For 77:6-7 Je '71
SMITH, Grace Ferguson
Theme editor: English teacher's ally. Clear
House 46:116-18 O '71
SMITH, Grace Sands
Closing the gap. il Sch Arts 70:29 Mr '71
SMITH, H. Allen
Sampling of worries. Sat R 54:6+ F 13 '71
SMITH, Harrison
Obituary
Pub W 199:38 Ja 18 '71
Sat R por 54:30 Ja 23 '71
SMITH, Ian Douglas
Black-white war inevitable? interview, ed.
by R. Knight. por U S News 71:41 N 29
'71
about
Far from ideal. Newsweek 78:44+ D 6 '71 *
In civilized hands. il por Time 98:37 D 6 '71*
SMITH, J. Roy
Pipe speaker system. il Electr World 86:24-
6 D '71
SMITH, Jack
Gadgets and gilhickies. See issues of Yachting
Holiday in Holland. il Yachting 129:62-3+
F '71
SMITH, Jack E. Jr
From puritans to panthers. Clear House
46:125-6 O '71
180 days: observations of an elective year.
Engl J 60:229-30+ F '71
SMITH, James D.
West Pointer's wild preview of the volun-
teer army. C. S. Wren. il pors Look 35:
24-7 F 23 '71 *
SMITH, Jeffrey H.
Omaha De Porres club. bibliog Negro Hist
Bul 33:194-9 D '70
SMITH, Joan (Irvine)
Irvine ranch fights regulation. por Bsns W
p57-8 Jl 3 '71 *
SMITH, Joanmarie
Knowing isn't everything. America 124:286-8
Mr 20 '71
SMITH, John C.
Play ball! Nat R 23:481 My 4 '71
What's up underground. Nat R 23:1130 O 8
'71
SMITH, John K.
Federal mule administration. il Nations
Bsns 59:49 O '71
SMITH, Joseph B.
Project restoration: Ohio's scenic canal
routes. il Travel 135:58-62 F '71
(ed) See Bauer, E. A. Work while the fish
are biting
SMITH, K. Wayne
Notes from the cavern. J. Osborne. New Re-
pub 165:13-14 D 4 '71 *
SMITH, Ken
Winter poem. Nation 212:698 My 31 '71
SMITH, Larry
How are you? Don't tell me; story. Redbook
137:104-5 S '71
SMITH, Lawrence L. and Riebock, James
Middle school tries contractual reading.
Clear House 45:404-6 Mr '71
SMITH, Lewis, and others
Communication skills through self-recording.
il Todays Ed 60:18-20 Ja '71
SMITH, Liz
Coming of age in America. il por Vogue
157:90-2+ Je '71
(ed) See Steinem, G. Gloria Steinem, writer
and social critic, talks about sex, politics
and marriage
SMITH, Lloyd H. Jr. See Williams, H. E.
jt. auth.
SMITH, M. L. See Malina, J. F. jr, jt. auth.
SMITH, M. Rolfson
Forgotten Faeroes. il Travel 136:38-43+ Ag
'71
SMITH, Maggie
New Lunts? No, the original Stephenses;
with interview, ed. by D. Lurie. il pors
Life 71:62-6 Jl 16 '71 *

SMITH, Margaret (Chase)
Is America going isolationist? interview. por
U S News 70:27-8 Je 28 '71
SMITH, Margarita G.
Girl named Carson. il pors Redbook 137:90-
1+ O '71
(ed) See McCullers, C. S. Like that;
Breath from the sky; Instant of the hour
after
SMITH, Marshall
We're broke, he told the workers. We need
your help. il pors Life 71:69-70+ S 24 '71
SMITH, Mortimer
Education 1970: a short review. Ed Digest
36:29-31 Ap '71
SMITH, Ned
Wildlife sketchbook. See issues of National
wildlife
SMITH, Olcott D.
Crowbar governor was a man of many
parts. pors Nations Bsns 59:42-3 Ja '71
SMITH, Oliver
Oliver Smith talks about theatre; interview,
ed. by G. Trotta. il por Harp Baz 104:190-1
S '71
SMITH, Patrick J.
Book reviews. See issues of High fidelity and
Musical America
SMITH, R. C.
America's 10 best hospitals. il Todays Health
49:24-9+ N '71
Today's health news. Todays Health 49:7-8 D
'71
SMITH, R. Seymour
Your district does have a public relations
program. Ed Digest 37:20-2 N '71
SMITH, Richard J.
Reading, writing, and creativity. bibliog f
il Clear House 45:350-4 F '71
SMITH, Robert C.
Finial busts on eighteenth-century Philadel-
phia furniture. il Antiques 100:900-5 D '71
SMITH, Robert H.
Anonymous ally. il por Time 97:52 F 8 '71 *
SMITH, Robert L.
Obituary
Consumer Rep por 36:468 Ag '71
SMITH, Robert S.
Dilemma of foreign investment in South
Africa; remarks, April 30, 1971. Dept State
Bul 64:825-7 Je 28 '71
SMITH, Scottie (Fitzgerald)
Trade winds; interview, ed. by C. Amory.
Sat R 54:6+ Ja 16 '71
—See McLendon, W. jt. auth.
SMITH, Sheila
It's my turn to be lucky. P. Bosworth. il pors
Todays Health 49:24-7+ D '71 *
SMITH, Sheldon Moody
Dead-end dialogue. Nat R 23:367-8 Ap 6 '71
Here comes SuperJudas! Nat R 23:715 Je 29
'71
Three British Christians. Nat R 23:545+ My
18 '71
SMITH, Sidney Adair
Mobile silversmiths and jewelers 1820-1867. il
Antiques 99:407-11 Mr '71
SMITH, Stan
Closing up the longest Open. L. Keith. il
Sports Illus 35:73 S 27 '71 *
He was more like a regiment. G. Brown.
il por Sports Illus 35:28-9 O 18 '71 *
Man named Smith. il por Time 98:61 S 27
'71 *
SMITH, Stanford H. See Aron, W. I. jt. auth.
SMITH, Syd, and Bogen, R. W.
CATV story in Nashville. Todays Ed 60:57-8
N '71
SMITH, Tedd
New folk musical: do the answers ring
true? C. A. Forbes. Chr Today 15:38 Mr
26 '71 *
SMITH, Tony
Tony Smith: talk about sculpture; inter-
view, ed. by L. R. Lippard. il Art N 70:
48-9+ Ap '71
SMITH, Una and others
Endothelial projections as revealed by scan-
ning electron microscopy. bibliog il Science
173:925-7 S 3 '71
SMITH, Victor
Puget Sound's war within a war. I. Doig.
il Am West 8:22-7 My '71 *
SMITH, W. Eugene
Three who cared; photographs. Todays
Health 49:52-7 S '71
about
Double documentary. M. R. Weiss. il Sat R
54:84-5 Mr 13 '71 *
Shooting it right. S. K. Oberbeck. il News-
week 77:56 F 8 '71 *
W. Eugene Smith: let truth be the prejudice.
R. Benedict. il por Pop Phot 68:88-93 Ap
'71 *

SMITH, Walter L.
Walter L. Smith: blind librarian for the blind. il pors Wilson Lib Bul 45:838-9 My '71 •

SMITH, William Edgett
Profiles; J. K. Nyerere. por New Yorker 47:42-8+ O 16; 47-54+ O 23; 53-8+ O 30 '71

SMITH, William Jay
Comment. W. H. Pritchard. Poetry 119:163-4 D '71

SMITH, William L.
Ending the isolation of the handicapped. il Am Ed 7:29-33 N '71

SMITH-JOHANNSEN, R. I.
Polymer whiskers grown from methyl 2-cyanoacrylate vapor. bibliog il Science 171:1246-7 Mr 26 '71

SMITH-Corona-Marchant. See SCM corporation

SMITHERS, David
Hovercraft to the heart of Africa. il Sci Digest 70:38-45+ D '71
Hovercraft to the wilderness. il por Sci Digest 70:8-17+ N '71

SMITHIES, Oliver, and others
Deletions in immunoglobulin polypeptide chains as evidence for breakage and repair in DNA. bibliog il Science 172:674-7 My 7 '71

SMITHIES, Ronald H.
You & your diet. See issues of Good housekeeping

SMITH'S transfer corporation
Living, well, on leftovers. il Forbes 108:38 O 15 '71

SMITHSONIAN institution
Museums: art for who's sake? Anacostia neighborhood museum. B. Schwartz. il Ramp Mag 9:38-49 Je '71
125 years and going strong. il U S News 71:54-7 S 27 '71
Peace corps and Smithsonian: deploying environmental experts. D. P. Teter. Science 172:1317-18 Je 25 '71

Astrophysical observatory

See also
International satellite geodesy experiment

Center for short-lived phenomena

Compendium of curious events reported by the Center for short-lived phenomena. P. Morrison. Sci Am 225:116-19 Ag '71
Frog wars and blackbird explosions. S. Wymelenberg. il Life 71:16 O 15 '71

SMOG
Carbon monoxide: its role in photochemical smog formation. K. Westberg and others. bibliog il Science 171:1013-15 Mr 12 '71
Smog formation simplified. R. W. Medeiros. bibliog il por Chem 45:16-18 Ja '72
Smog threat: a bad summer on the way? U S News 70:77 My 3 '71
Space technology to aid smog research. Space World H-10-94:45+ O '71
See also
Los Angeles—Air pollution
Plants, Effect of smog on

SMOKE
Sulfur is the major problem. il Bsns W p56+ F 6 '71
See also
Smog

SMOKE ovens
How to buy & cook on the new smoke cookers. P. K. Snook. il Mech Illus 67:89-90+ Jl '71
Make your own smoke cooker. P. Snobk. il Mech Illus 67:108-10+ Ag '71

SMOKE prevention
Air resource management and regional planning. E. J. Croke and J. J. Roberts. Bul Atom Sci 27:8-12 F '71
Smoke rings may help air pollution problem. G. Williams. il Sci Digest 69:86-7 Mr '71
See also
Pittsburgh—Air pollution

SMOKED fish. See Fish, Smoked

SMOKING
Ban on public smoking? por Newsweek 77:90-1 Ja 25 '71
Beating the cigarette habit. A. De Saint Phalle. il Seventeen 30:108-9+ N '71
Breaking the habit; European congress on smoking and health. Newsweek 78:56-7 S 20 '71
Methods that have helped many people to stop smoking. il Good H 172:183 Mr '71
New warning on smoking. Time 97:58 F 8 '71
New wrinkles in smoking. il Newsweek 78:62 D 20 '71
Public nuisance? Sr Schol 98:6-7 F 15 '71

Still dying for a smoke? L. Elliott. Read Digest 99:49-52 Jl '71
What's burning? experiments with new smoking materials to break the smoking habit. Newsweek il 77:95-6+ My 3 '71
Why health hazards are rising for women smokers. Good H 173:195 O '71
See also
Cigars
Tobacco pipes

SMOKING and youth
Cigarette smoking: objective evidence for lung damage in teen-agers. J. E. Seely and others. bibliog il Science 172:741-3 My 14 '71
Young smokers, beware. Newsweek 77:40+ My 31 '71

SMOLIAN, Steven
Four decades of the Budapest quartet. il Am Rec G 37:220-4+ D '70

SMOOTH muscle. See Muscle

SMOTHERS brothers
TV screen. E. Miller. pors Seventeen 29:105+ Ag '70

SMUGGLING
Agro-frauders. Time 97:85 My 31 '71
America's battle against the white death; opium problem. il Newsweek 77:41-3 Mr 29 '71
Anger anyone? opium smuggling route from Turkey to Marseilles and the United States. A. R. Dolan. Nat R 23:1117 O 8 '71
French connection: heroin smuggling. il pors Newsweek 78:38 N 29 '71
French connection: spy turned heroin smuggler. il por Time 98:26 N 29 '71
Gains in the war against drug smugglers; interview. M. J. Ambrose. il por U S News 70:60-2+ Je 21 '71
Iron curtain bibles: smugglers too smug? P. Geiger. Chr Today 15:35 Jl 16 '71; Discussion. 15:15 Ag 27 '71
Jungle cocks, trout flies, and smugglers. E. N. Layne and S. Hartgen. il Audubon 73:38-43 My '71
Travelers warned of penalties for drug violations abroad; Department announcement. Dept State Bul 65:56-7 Jl 12 '71

SMYLIE, D. E. and Mansinha, L.
Rotation of the earth; with biographical sketches. il Sci Am 225:10, 80-8 bibliog (p 120) D '71

SMYRNA, Turkey
Smyrna affair, by M. Housepian. Review Nation 213:57-8 Jl 19 '71. P. Sourian

SMYTH, Paul
First altar; poem. Am Scholar 41:50-2 Wint '71
Thistles and thorns; lyrics of Abraham and Sarah; excerpt; poem. Poetry 118:249-54 Ag '71

SMYTH, Pete
Artifacts everywhere. Motor B & S 128:57-8 Jl '71
EPA drops the other shoe. Motor B & S 127:2+ Je '71
How to dig your own channel. il Motor B & S 127:66-9+ Je '71
Sign of things to come? il Motor B & S 128:64-7+ Jl '71

SMYTHE, Sandra
Your story's too episodic. Writers Digest 51:36-7+ Mr '71

SNACKS
Help-yourself mini-meal for drinks. J. Beard. il por House & Gard 140:50-1 Jl '71
High-flavor low-calorie snacks for dieters. il Parents Mag 46:68 Ag '71
Lots of friends, lots of food. il Bet Hom & Gard 49:68-9+ Ja '71
Man-sized football snacks. il Ebony 26:156+ N '70
9 midnight snacks you'll want to lose sleep over. S. Marston. il Todays Health 49:48-50 Je '71
Spin a deli-go-round; with recipes. il Seventeen 29:272-3+ Ag '70
What's new besides hamburgers? Great American snacks; with recipes. il Seventeen 30:144-7+ Ap '71

SNAG in the harp; story. See Ullian, R.

SNAILS
Chemoreception in nassarius obsoletus: the role of specific stimulatory proteins. S. Gurin and W. E. Carr. bibliog il Science 174:293-5 O 15 '71
Lancers of the reef; cone snails. M. Gruber. il Sea Front 17:30-7 Ja '71
Meet the good snails; they can benefit a garden pond. il Sunset 146:247-8 My '71
Snails: slow motion on a leaf trapeze. il Sci Digest 70:60-3 O '71
See also
Cookery—Snails

SNAKE bite. See Venom

SNAKE chief; drama. See Brown, B. S.

SNAKE RIVER
Fight to save the Snake. A. Tussing. Field & S 76:22+ O '71

SNAKE RIVER DAM. See Dams

SNAKE toxins. See Toxins and antitoxins

SNAKE venom. See Venom

SNAKES
Chemical-cue preferences of newborn snakes: influence of prenatal maternal experience. G. M. Burghardt. bibliog il Science 171: 921-3 Mr 5 '71
In praise of snakes. A. Carr. il Audubon 73:18-27 Jl '71
Mamba! G. Young and R. Dempewolff. il Sci Digest 70:58-64 Jl '71
Night of the cottonmouth. P. E. Allen. il por Outdoor Life 148:58-61+ Jl '71
See also
Copperheads
Sea snakes

SNAKES, Photography of. See Photography of reptiles

SNAKES as pets. See Pets

SNAPP, Thomas
Foundry; poem. New Yorker 47:50 N 13 '71
Night running; poem. New Yorker 47:36 Jl 31 '71

SNAPPERS
See also
Cookery—Fish

SNAPPING turtles. See Turtles

SNEAD, Carlyle
Putting is a family affair. M. Mulvoy. il por Sports Illus 34:86-7 Ap 12 '71 •

SNEAD, Sam
Arnie and Sam. por Newsweek 78:75 Ag 9 '71 •
Old pro teaches the teachers. G. S. Brown. por Sports Illus 35:85-6 O 25 '71 •

SNEIDER, Vern
Two-level story. Writer 84:21-2 Je '71

SNELL, Adelbert H.
Equipment adjusts to the storm. il Am City 86:103-4 S '71

SNELL, Bradford C.
Collusion of style. Nation 213:5 Jl 5 '71

SNELL, David
Family that raised the art of giving to its noblest form. il Todays Health 49:20-5+ O '71

SNIDER, Arthur J.
Medicine. See issues of Science digest

SNITZER, Milton S.
Direct & current. Pop Electr 35:7 Ag; 7 S; 7 O '71

SNODGRASS, Philip J. See Nuzum, C. T. jt. auth.

SNODGRASS, W. D.
Old apple trees; poem. New Yorker 47:41 My 1 '71

SNODGRESS, Carrie
American good looks. por Vogue 157:164-5 F 1 '71
about
Carrie Snodgress. G. Goodman. pors Look 35:50-3 Ap 6 '71 •

SNOGREN, Richard C.
All you need to know about adhesives; with tables. Pop Sci 199:92-7 D '71

SNOOK, Fred G.
Wall fish. il Outdoor Life 148:50-1+ D '71

SNOOK, Patrick K.
Getting your snowmobile ready. il Mech Illus 67:92-3+ N '71
Guide to snowmobile trails. il Mech Illus 67:63-4+ N '71
How to buy & cook on the new smoke cookers. il Mech Illus 67:89-90+ Jl '71
Make your own smoke cooker. il Mech Illus 67:108-10+ Ag '71

SNOOK fishing
Snook by the roadside. G. Heinold. il Outdoor Life 147:120+ F '71

SNOW, Charles Percy, baron Snow of Leicester. See Snow of Leicester, C. P. S.

SNOW, Edgar
Aftermath of the cultural revolution. New Repub 164:18-21 Ap 10 '71
Army and the party. New Repub 164:9-12 My 22 '71
China will talk from a position of strength. il pors Life 71:22-7 Jl 30 '71
China's 70,000 communes. New Repub 164: 19-23 Je 26 '71
Conversation with Mao Tse-tung. il por Life 70:46-8 Ap 30 '71
Open door. New Repub 164:20-3 Mr 27 '71

Population care and control. New Repub 164:20-3 My 1 '71
Why Nixon is relatively good. il por Time 98:13 Ag 2 '71
about
Dialogues with Chou. pors Newsweek 77:59 Ap 12 '71 •

SNOW, Gene
Snow storms. R. Guldahl, jr. il Hot Rod 24:48-50 Je '71 •

SNOW, John
Is it cricket? il por Newsweek 78:77 S 13 '71 •

SNOW, Lois Wheeler
All you need to know for a trip to China. il Sat R 54:36-9 O 23 '71
Caves of Pao-an. il Nation 212:690-2 My 31 '71
How Chinese women live and work. Vogue 158:157+ D '71

SNOW of Leicester, Charles Percy Snow, baron
Q: do the claims of conscience outweigh the duties of citizenship? por Esquire 76:159+ D '71
Two aspects of science's giant. Life 71:14 Ag 20 '71
about
Sage's summa. S. Weintraub. New Repub 165:23-5 N 27 '71 •

SNOW
Extremes of snowfall: United States and Canada; with editorial comment. Weatherwise 23:259, 286-94 D '70
Snow rollers in Minnesota. il Weatherwise 24:230-1 O '71
Snowfall season of 1969-1970. D. M. Ludlum. il Weatherwise 24:18-23+ F '71
Up went the ash, down came snow; man-induced snowfall. il Sci N 100:168 S 11 '71
See also
Snow crystals
Snow storms

SNOW and ice removal
Equipment adjusts to the storm; Stafford Township, N.Y. A. H. Snell. il Am City 86:103-4 S '71
Graders take on the big drifts; Buffalo, N.Y. il Am City 86:22 Ja '71
New ways to attack old snow-ice problems. J. P. Coombes. il por Am City 86:63-5 N '71
Of salts and safety; dangers of de-icing salts. Time 97:37 Mr 1 '71
Pollution from salt. il Newsweek 79:45 Ja 3 '72
Put speed and control in your snow fighting program; Indianapolis, Ind. il Am City 86:37 D '71
Runoff of deicing salt: effect on Irondequoit Bay, Rochester, New York. R. C. Bubeck and others. bibliog il Science 172:1128-32 Je 11 '71
Snow and ice control. See occasional issues of American city
Winter ice control, art or science? Dayton, Ohio. il Am City 86:24 Ag '71
You can't see your best snow fighting tool; public cooperation in Arlington, Mass. J. E. Bowler. il Am City 86:81-2 D '71

SNOW blowers, throwers, etc.
Mount the blower in the bucket, fast! equipment used in Kalamazoo, Mich. D. H. Swets. il Am City 86:40 O '71
Snowthrowers: winter fun machines. G. Kratsch. il Pop Mech 136:50+ N '71
Maintenance and repair
Snowthrowers: love 'em; don't leave 'em neglected. E. F. Lindsley. il Pop Sci 199: 70-2 N '71

SNOW camping. See Camping

SNOW crystals
Lifetime of snowflakes; with photographs by W. A. Bentley. H. Borland. Audubon 73: 59-65 Ja '71
Odds are with it; question of identical snowflakes. B. Targan. Sat R 54:20 F 6 '71
Six-sided snowflake. bibliog il Chem 44:19-21 S '71
Wilson Bentley, the snowflake man. D. C. Blanchard. bibliog il pors Weatherwise 23: 260-9 D '70

SNOW flakes. See Snow crystals

SNOW leopards. See Leopards

SNOW measurement. See Precipitation (meteorology)—Measurement

SNOW modeling
Snow sculpture. M. Turner. il Design 73: 28 Wint '71

SNOW peas. See Peas

SNOW removal equipment
Snow rake for the roof. C. A. Fenner. il Pop Sci 199:132 N '71

SNOW removal equipment, Municipal
Equipment adjusts to the storm; Stafford Township, N.Y. A. H. Snell. il Am City 86:103-4 S '71
Larger than usual, but not too big; Grand Rapids, Mich. G. Sweder. il Am City 86: 53 N '71
They didn't believe it would work; Sioux City, Ia. **M. M. Randolph. il Am City 86: 91 Ag '71**

SNOW sculpture. See Snow modeling

SNOW slides. See Avalanches

SNOW storms. See Snowstorms

SNOW throwers. See Snow blowers, throwers, etc.

SNOW tire studs. See Tires, Automobile

SNOW trails. See Animal tracks and trails

SNOW White and Rose Red; drama. See Creegan, G. R.

SNOWDON, Antony Charles Robert Armstrong-Jones, 1st earl of
Reigning family of Monaco; photographs. Vogue 158:109-15 D '71

SNOWFALLS. See Snow

SNOWFLAKES. See Snow crystals

SNOWMOBILE engines
Inside the new snowmobile engines. E. F. Lindsley. il Pop Sci 199:97-9+ O '71
See also
Spark plugs

SNOWMOBILE racing
Cool 125.87 mph. il Hot Rod 24:92 S '71

SNOWMOBILE trails. See Trails

SNOWMOBILES

Equipment
Bolt-on speed booster for snowmobiles. il Mech Illus 68:18 Ja '72

Laws and regulations
What the law makers may do. Field & S 76: S 20 O '71

Maintenance and repair
Getting your snowmobile ready. P. K. Snook. il Mech Illus 67:92-3+ N '71
How to get your snowmobile ready for snow. H. B. Notrom. il Pop Mech 136:122-5 N '71
How to keep your snowmobile going. il Suc Farm 69:G22 S '71

Specifications
Snowmobiles in '72. G. Reiger. il Pop Mech 136:154-7 O '71

SNOWMOBILES and snowmobiling
Cook, fast fun, and trouble, too. il Life 70: 20-5 F 26 '71
Dan Gurney on snowmobiles; interview. ed. by G. Reiger. D. Gurney. il pors Pop Mech 136:148-50+ O '71
Expanding world of snowmobiles. B. Behme. il Field & S 76:S1-4+ O '71
Extras for your snowmobile. G. L. Earle. il Suc Farm 69:G18 S '71
Fun cars, a boom that's running into trouble. il U S News 72:32-3 Ja 3 '72
New snowmobiles. il Mech Illus 67:82-5+ O '71
Sizzling snow. J. Maxam. il Har Yrs 11:32-3 F '71
Ski-doo or ski-don't? D. Butwin. il Sat R 54:40-2 Mr 6 '71
Snowmobile fever really turns you on. O. Sweet. il Pop Sci 198:80-1 Ja '71
Snowmobile sales hit the skids. il Bsns W p 134 Mr 13 '71
Snowmobiles; love 'em or hate 'em. L. Line; J. D. Perry. Nat Wildlife 10:21-3 D '71
Snowmobiling. il Consumer Bul 54:27-32 F '71
Snowmobiling in Yellowstone. B. Behme. il Field & S 76:38-9 D '71
They put snowmobiles to work. G. L. Earle. Suc Farm 69:D6 O '71
Utah's secret snow country. **G. Reiger. il Pop Mech 136:72-4 D '71**
See also
Arctic enterprises, inc.

Accidents and injuries
Ordeal on Beartooth Mountain. J. Klobuchar. il Pop Mech 136:84-9+ N '71
Snowmobiler's back. il Time 97:62 Mr 15 '71

Bibliography
Free booklets, films, maps, etc. for snowmobilers. H. Bradshaw and V. Bradshaw. il Field & S 75:38-9+ Ja '71

Laws and regulations
Let's harness those go-anywhere machines. Bet Hom & Gard 49:8-9 Ja '71

Safety devices and measures
CB and the snowmobile: how REACT can save your life. W. J. Hawkins. il Pop Sci 199:78-9+ S '71

SNOWPLOWS for automobiles. See Automobiles—Equipment

SNOWSHOE rabbit hunting. See Rabbit hunting

SNOWSHOEING
Snowshoe country. V. N. DeFelice. il Am For 77:20-3+ F '71
Snowshoeing: it's fun, inexpensive, and strenuous. il Sunset 147:38+ D '71

SNOWSLIDES. See Avalanches

SNOWSTORMS
Montreal's great snowstorm of '69. M. E. H. Trueman. il Weatherwise 23:270-3 D '70
Ordeal on Beartooth Mountain. J. Klobuchar. il Pop Mech 136:84-9+ N '71
Record snowstorms and problems of snow measurement on Mount Washington. J. E. Howe. il Weatherwise 23:280-2 D '70
Snow free. J. D. Scott. il Nat Wildlife 10:41-3 D '71

SNOWY owls. See Owls

SNUFF
Clean your mind with snuff. S. P. Friedman. Esquire 76:84+ D '71

SNUG HARBOR boat club. See Boat clubs

SNYDER, Beverly Stonebraker
More women in ag careers. il Farm J 95: 22-3+ O '71

SNYDER, Edward F.
Churches' role in Washington. Chr Cent 88: 69-71 Ja 20 '71

SNYDER, Gary
Prayer for the great family. il Look 35:54-9 Ja 26 '71
about
Comment. R. E. Teele. Poetry 118:174-6 Je '71 *

SNYDER, Howard A.
World come full circle. Chr Today 16:9-13 Ja 7 '72

SNYDER, Jean
How to use your head when your hair starts falling out. il Todays Health 49:32-4+ Jl '71
What you'd better know about the meat you are buying. il Todays Health 49:37-9+ D '71

SNYDER, Jimmy
Sports. R. Kahn. il **Esquire 76:14+ S '71 ***

SNYDER, John Wesley
Where are they now? il pors Newsweek 78: 8 Jl 12 '71 *

SNYDER, Solomon H.
What we have forgotten about pot. il N Y Times Mag p26-7+ D 13 '70; 6 Ja 17 '71
—See Taylor, K. M. jt. auth.

SOAP
Non-enzyme laundry detergents and soaps. il Consumer Bul 54:13-16 Mr '71
See also
Cleaning compositions

SOAP industry
As the soapers' world turns. il **Time 97:72 Mr 8 '71**

SOARING (aeronautics) See Gliding and soaring

SOBEL, Sheila
Sheila Sobel and ensemble, the Cubiculo NYC. T. Borek. Dance Mag 45:83-4 Ag '71 *

SOBELL, Henry M.
Now visible, in 3-D. il por Sci N 99:436 Je 26 '71 *

SOBHAN, Rehman
Bailing out Pakistan. New Repub 164:14-15 Je 5 '71
Genesis of resistance. Nation 213:686-9 D 27 '71

SOCCER
Are we finally starting to dig the world's game? H. McIlvanney. il Sports Illus 35: 64-5 O 4 '71
But the south shall rise again (and again!) H. McIlvanney. il Sports Illus 34:22-5 My 17 '71
Honor the Octopus; international all-stars v. Russian stars. il por Newsweek 77:75-6 Je 14 '71

SOCCER players
See also
Tashin, L. I.

SOCIAL action
Catholic social action: where do we go from here? E. A. Marciniak; discussion. America 123:517-19; 124:126-8 D 12 '70, F 6 '71
Preaching is social action. W. S. Reid. Chr Today 15:10-11 Je 4 '71
Social action in the P.I. America 125:359 N 6 '71

SOCIAL adjustment. See Adjustment, Social
SOCIAL agencies
 See also
Involvement corps
SOCIAL aspects of science. See Science—Social aspects
SOCIAL attitudes. See Attitudes
SOCIAL behavior of animals. See Animals—Habits and behavior
SOCIAL behavior of birds. See Birds—Habits and behavior
SOCIAL change
Affluence and the world tomorrow. L. S. Wehrle. For Affairs 49:419-28 Ap '71
Being and doing, by M. G. Raskin. Review Sat R 54:24-5 Jl 3 '71. R. A. Gross
Changing priorities: hard choices, new price tags. J. L. Miller. il Sat R 54:36-7+ Ja 23 '71
Crisis prediction. P. Wiles. Ann Am Acad 393:32-9 Ja '71
Demands of Consciousness II. H. J. Gans. Nation 212:275-7 Mr 1 '71
Despairing optimist. R. Dubos. Am Scholar 41:16-18+ Wint '71
Focus on the future: the small town; address, January 28, 1971. J. W. Joanis. Vital Speeches 37:275-9 F 15 '71
Foreign vision of the coming American revolution; excerpts from The new American revolution. J. F. Revel. Time 97:18-19 F 22 '71
Future shock, by A. Toffler. Review Nation 212:117-20 Ja 25 '71. R. Claiborne
Great change in living values. J. L. Larsen; R. L. Schwartz. pors House & Gard 140:100-1+ O '71
Life party. N. Johnson. New Repub 164:21-3 Ap 10 '71
One and a half cheers for progress. J. A. Michener. il N Y Times Mag p9+ S 5 '71; Discussion. p98 S 26 '71
Physics and social change; adaptation of address, June 1971. G. E. Brown, jr. il pors Phys Today 24:23-7 O '71
Rebirth: Americans moving on; symposium. Look 35:33-8+ Ja 12 '71
Schools and social change. C. Weinberg. Sch & Soc 99:487-9+ D '71
Sweet bird of youth. I. J. Hutchison, jr. il Parks & Rec 6:46-7+ O '71
Violence and social change. M. Mead. Redbook 137:60+ Je '71
Virgin again. J. Morgenstern. Newsweek 77:10-11 F 1 '71
 See also
Acculturation
Educational sociology
Social progress
Social revolution
Asia
Premature aging of the Asian youth; address, October 29, 1971. J. K. C. Oh. Vital Speeches 38:186-8 Ja 1 '72
SOCIAL classes
Race, social class, and IQ. S. Scarr-Salapatek. bibliog il Science 174:1285-95 D 24 '71
 See also
Elite (social sciences)
Middle classes
SOCIAL conditions
 See also
Civilization
Social problems
Social surveys
 also subhead Social conditions under names of countries, states, cities, e.g. Atlanta—Social conditions
SOCIAL conflict
Conflict: new emphasis in leadership. A. Saville. Clear House 46:52-5 S '71
Is it time to break the silence on violence? curriculums of American elementary schools. R. J. Munnelly. Ed Digest 36:16-18 Ap '71
Toward managing social conflict. H. Henderson. bibliog f Harvard Bsns R 49:82-90 My '71
 See also
Youth-adult relationship
SOCIAL cooperation, international. See International cooperation
SOCIAL credit party
Exit Social credit. D. Kucharsky. Chr Today 15:41 S 24 '71
SOCIAL crisis games. See Games
SOCIAL democracy. See Socialism
SOCIAL development. See Social progress
SOCIAL dimensions fund. See Investment trusts

SOCIAL diseases. See Venereal diseases
SOCIAL drinking. See Drinking customs
SOCIAL education
Down and out in Boston; students spending week as derelicts. il Time 98:34 S 6 '71
Education's role: dignity of the individual. R. D. Strom. bibliog Clear House 46:163-9 N '71
Getting high on high school; new alternatives. K. Branan. il Schol Teach Jr/Sr High p 12-14+ F 1 '71
Schools and population. S. Viederman. Ed Digest 37:26-8 N '71
 See also
Citizenship, Education for
Group relations training
Sex instruction
Social sciences—Study and teaching
SOCIAL ethics
Growth with social justice: India today; address, November 6, 1970. L. K. Jha. Vital Speeches 37:218-21 Ja 15 '71
 See also
Altruism
Business ethics
Christian ethics
Church and race problems
Crime and criminals
Political ethics
Sexual ethics
Social problems
SOCIAL evolution. See Social change; Social progress
SOCIAL exchange
Interpersonal and economic resources. U. G. Foa. bibliog il Science 171:345-51 Ja 29 '71
SOCIAL forecasting
Desperation of Calcutta; Latin American prospects. E. Flores. Nation 212:652-3 My 24 '71
Soviet scientist looks at futurology. I. V. Bestuzhev-Lada. il UNESCO Courier 24:22-7 Ap '71
SOCIAL games. See Games
SOCIAL gerontology. See Gerontology
SOCIAL gospel
Cultural strain and Protestant liberalism. W. R. Hutchison. bibliog f il Am Hist R 76:386-411 Ap '71; Reply with rejoinder. D. E. Bigham. 76:1631-3 D '71
SOCIAL history
 See also
Middle classes
Negroes—Social history
 also subhead Social history under names of countries, states and cities, e.g. Geneva, Switzerland—Social history
SOCIAL institutions
Government agencies are failing our people; address, June 29, 1971. D. F. Linowes. Vital Speeches 37:759-62 O 1 '71
SOCIAL interaction
 See also
Social exchange
SOCIAL isolation
Human circadian rhythms in continuous darkness: entrainment by social cues. J. Aschoff and others. bibliog il Science 171:213-15 Ja 15 '71
 See also
Alienation (social psychology)
Loneliness
SOCIAL isolation in literature
Hunting for America. R. W. Murphy. Harper 242:16-18+ Je '71
SOCIAL justice. See Social ethics
SOCIAL legislation
 See also
Pensions—Laws and regulations
Unemployment—Relief measures
United States
Working conditions survey as a source of social indicators. N. Q. Herrick and R. P. Quinn. il Mo Labor R 94:15-24 Ap '71
SOCIAL norm
Give us this day our daily surrealism. J. Ciardi. Sat R 54:48 Je 12 '71
SOCIAL organization
Uses of information: when social information becomes desired. Z. Bauman. bibliog f Ann Am Acad 393:20-31 Ja '71
SOCIAL perception
 See also
Group relations training
SOCIAL planning. See Social policy
SOCIAL policy
Education for survival. W. H. Boyer. Ed Digest 36:1-4 Mr '71
Future shock, by A. Toffler. Review Trans-Action 8:102-4 N '70. A. Etzioni

SOCIAL policy—*Continued*
Limits of social policy; excerpt from address, September 1970. N. Glazer. Commentary 52:51-8 S '71
See also subhead Social policy under names of countries, e.g. United States—Social policy

SOCIAL problems
Coming social-industrial complex; address, October 21, 1971. S. Ramo. Vital Speeches 38:80-6 N 15 '71
Crisis prediction. P. Wiles. Ann Am Acad 393:32-9 Ja '71
Social problem indicators: Israel. L. Guttman. bibliog f il Ann Am Acad 393:40-6 Ja '71
See also
Church and social problems
Crime and criminals
Family
Homosexuality
Illegitimacy
Juvenile delinquency
Libraries and social and economic problems
Marriage
Narcotic habit
Poor
Progress
Prostitution
Social action
Social surveys
Standard of living
Suicide
Technology and civilization
Woman—Social and moral questions
also subhead Social problems under names of cities, e.g. San Francisco—Social problems

SOCIAL problems and art. See Art and society

SOCIAL problems in education. See Educational sociology

SOCIAL progress
Analysis of socio-economic development through a system of indicators. D. V. McGranahan. bibliog f il Ann Am Acad 393:65-81 Ja '71
One and a half cheers for progress. J. A. Michener. il N Y Times Mag p9+ S 5 '71; Same abr. Read Digest 99:209+ D '71; Discussion. N Y Times Mag p98 S 26 '71
Practical significance of social information. J. Drewnowski. bibliog f Ann Am Acad 393:82-91 Ja '71
Puzzle for U.S: growth vs. social progress; address. D. P. Eastburn. il por U S News 71:64-6 Jl 12 '71
Social information for what? I. Galnoor. bibliog f Ann Am Acad 393:1-19 Ja '71
See also
Social change

SOCIAL psychiatry
Background of today's social psychiatry. C. E. Goshen. Ment Hy 55:526-32 O '71
Our unsure society: mental health and the Nation; address, October 16, 1970. L. Bellak. Vital Speeches 37:279-82 F 15 '71
Transcultural aspects of community psychiatry. J. Hartog. bibliog Ment Hy 55:35-44 Ja '71

SOCIAL psychology
One right way to write and think?; E. Morin's analysis of anti-Semitism in Orléans, France. B. DeMott. Am Scholar 41:53-62 Wint '71
Picking and choosing. C. H. Simonds. Nat R 23:370 Ap 6 '71
Psychology of social control. C. M. Lowe. bibliog Ment Hy 55:124-9 Ja '71
See also
Alienation (social psychology)
Anomy
Crowds
Ethnopsychology
Fads
Family
Groups (sociology)
Human relations
Leadership
Morale, National
Political attitudes
Political psychology
Public opinion
Social conflict
Social psychiatry
Violence

SOCIAL reform. See Social problems; Social revolution

SOCIAL research. See Social science research

SOCIAL responsibilities round table. See American library association—Social responsibilities round table

SOCIAL responsibility. See Responsibility

SOCIAL revolution
Changing ways of life and the struggle for cultural identity. F. McDermott. il UNESCO Courier 24:13-14 Ja '71
Financing social revolutions; address, October 28, 1971. J. T. Connor. Vital Speeches 38:105-9 D 1 '71
Liberal antecedents of the revolt; excerpt from Youth and dissent. K. Keniston. Cur 134:3-20 N '71
Without Marx or Jesus, by J. F. Revel. Review
Chr Today 16:60-1 O 8 '71. J. W. Montgomery
Life 71:12 S 17 '71. A. Schlesinger, jr
Nation 213:312-14 O 4 '71. G. G. Eckstein
New Repub 165:25-6+ S 25 '71. S. McCracken
Without Marx or Jesus: the new American revolution has begun; excerpt; tr. by J. Bernard. J. F. Revel. il Sat R 54:14-31 Jl 24 '71
See also
Counter culture

Anecdotes, facetiae, satire, etc.
Requiem for Feldman. J. Richardson. Harper 243:116-18 O '71

SOCIAL role
See also
Sex role

SOCIAL science. See Social sciences

SOCIAL science research
Government structure: inherent inability to change; address, June 21, 1971. J. J. Powers, jr. Vital Speeches 37:628-31 Ag 1 '71
Indians and sociologists: science or exploitation? J. Trotter. Sci N 100:234 O 2 '71
R&D processing of domestic programs. A. Etzioni. Science 171:1203 Mr 26 '71
See also
Computers—Social science use
Little, Arthur D. inc.
National institute of economic and social research, London
Social surveys

SOCIAL sciences
Conditions favoring major advances in social science. K. W. Deutsch and others. bibliog il Science 171:450-9 F 5 '71; Discussion. 172:1191-2 Je 18 '71
Social science impact. Time 97:47 Mr 29 '71
See also
Behavior (psychology)
Civilization
Economics
Power (social sciences)
Social scientists
Sociology

Philosophy
Relevance in social science, or the proper study of mankind. D. A. Rustow. Am Scholar 40:487-96 Sum '71

Research
See Social science research

Study and teaching
Are civic education courses worth keeping? R. E. Cleary. bibliog Sch & Soc 99:35-9 Ja '71
Change and resistance to the new social studies. I. J. Winn. bibliog Sch & Soc 99:182-4+ Mr '71
Educational objectives and the new social studies. R. A. Gerlach. bibliog Sch & Soc 99:180-2 Mr '71
Is it time to break the silence on violence? curriculums of American elementary schools. R. J. Munnelly. Ed Digest 36:16-18 Ap '71
Meaningful tests in social studies. J. Eulie. bibliog f Clear House 45:333-6 F '71
New educational games for social studies classes. T. L. Reddick. Clear House 46:127-8 O '71
Social education: is it Zing, Zang, or Zong? J. Hantula. bibliog Clear House 46:40-3 S '71
Social science in early education. Sch & Soc 99:465-6 D '71
Social studies: specialists in state education departments. L. F. Psencik. Clear House 45:341-5 F '71
Social studies: then and now. C. D. Samford. il Clear House 45:337-40 F '71
Student involvement in social studies through simulation. G. Kachaturoff. Clear House 45:541-4 My '71
See also
Citizenship. Education for
History—Study and teaching
National council for the social studies
Social education

SOCIAL sciences—*Continued*

Textbooks

Minorities in social studies textbooks. Negro Hist Bul 33:166-7 N '70

Minorities: what textbooks don't say; excerpt from Minorities in textbooks. M. B. Kane. Cur 129:13-16 My '71

SOCIAL sciences and state

Social science and the federal government; symposium, ed. by G. M. Lyons. bibliog f Ann Am Acad 394:1-128 Mr '71

SOCIAL scientists

Obligations of American social scientists. P. Green. bibliog f Ann Am Acad 394:13-27 Mr '71

See also
Gerontologists

SOCIAL security. See Insurance, Social

SOCIAL security administration. See United States—Social security administration

SOCIAL security benefits—United States. See Insurance, Social—United States

SOCIAL security taxes

Social-security tax: another boost. U S News 70:37 My 10 '71

Truth in advertising; booklet. Your social security. M. Friedman. Newsweek 77:88 Je 14 '71

SOCIAL status

Status inconsistency theory and flying saucer sightings (cont) D. I. Warren; discussion. Science 171:956-9 Mr 12 '71

Who sees flying saucers? il Sci Digest 69:34-5 F '71

SOCIAL structure. See Social organization

SOCIAL studies. See Social sciences

SOCIAL surveys

Social information for developing countries; symposium, ed. by I. Galnoor. bibliog f il Ann Am Acad 393:1-121 Ja '71

Working conditions survey as a source of social indicators. N. Q. Herrick and R. P. Quinn. il Mo Labor R 94:15-24 Ap '71

SOCIAL thought

Social theory of Herbert Marcuse. R. Goodwin. por Atlan 227:68-70+ Je '71

SOCIAL values

Literature and society's values; address, November 1970. D. T. Turner. bibliog f Engl J 60:577-86 My '71

Senile society: a theory. S. Goldberg. Yale R 61:1-25 O '71

Social values and the elderly. R. A. Kalish. Ment Hy 55:51-4 Ja '71

Toward a new reformation. I. H. Wilson. Cur 131:18-23 Jl '71

SOCIAL welfare

See also
Public welfare
United Nations—Commission for social development

SOCIAL work

See also subhead Social work under names of cities, e.g. Van Nuys, Calif.—Social work

SOCIAL work, Psychiatric. See Psychiatric social work

SOCIAL work conferences

See also
National conference on social welfare

SOCIAL workers

Charity; case worker in Chicago. S. Dybeck. Commonweal 95:248-52 D 10 '71

Welfare-industrial complex. M. Gruber. Nation 212:808-11 Je 28 '71

Education

Meeting social work's challenge in community mental health. P. P. Evans and N. F. Bracht. Ment Hy 55:295-7 Jl '71

SOCIALISM

Confronting reality with reason; P. Baran's views. P. Clecak. Nation 212:245-8+ F 22 '71

Development: a Soviet countermodel. R. Bosc. il America 124:504-8 My 15 '71

History and class consciousness, by G. Lukács. Review
Nat R 23:595-6 Je 1 '71. T. Szamuely

I am not a Marxist, I am Marx. M. Harrington. Nation 213:694-6 D 27 '71

Our lost honesty. G. B. Shaw. il Harper 243:96-9 O '71

Third world development, can east and west agree? R. Bosc. il America 124:532-4 My 22 '71

What's a Marxist? Sr Schol 98:10 F 1 '71

See also
Collective settlements
Collectivism
Communism
Government ownership
Industrial democracy
Utopias

History

Short history of socialism, by G. Lichtheim. Review
Commentary 52:72-7 Jl '71. N. Birnbaum

Africa

African gift. S. Mayo. Chr Cent 88:252-3 F 24 '71

Czechoslovakia

See also
Communism—Czechoslovakia

SOCIALIST International congress, Helsinki, 1971

International. il Newsweek 77:44+ Je 7 '71

SOCIALLY handicapped

Mending lives at a PCC, the West Virginia parent and child center. M. P. Berson. il Am Ed 7:22-7 D '71

Education

Predicting college success of the educationally disadvantaged; adaptation of address, June 1970. J. C. Stanley. bibliog Science 171:640-7 F 19 '71; Discussion. 173:1079 S 17 '71

Employment

Top drivers make the grade; Transportation opportunity program in Los Angeles. J. Jones. il Am Ed 7:34-40 N '71

See also
Cope program
Negroes—Employment
Opportunities industrialization centers, inc.

SOCIALLY handicapped and libraries. See Libraries—Services to socially handicapped

SOCIALLY handicapped children

Domain of sorts; excerpt from Children of crisis: migrants, sharecroppers and mountaineers. R. Coles. il Harper 243:116-18+ N '71

See also
Negro children

Education

Can slum children learn? University of Wisconsin infant education center project. S. P. Strickland. il Am Ed 7:3-7 Jl '71

Cargo of career education. W. Wood. il Am Ed 7:16-20 O '71

Colleges and minorities especially some colleges; no comfort from Washington. America 124:247-8 Mr 13 '71

Creating group cohesion in inner city classrooms. F. P. Bazeli. bibliog Clear House 45:547-50 My '71

Design for learning. S. Lovelady. il Todays Ed 60:54-6 F '71

Earlier head start. Sci N 100:24 Jl 10 '71

English literature for the disadvantaged; here's how, but why? W. W. West. Engl J 60:902-5 O '71

Give us this day our ABCs. L. Velie. Read Digest 99:126-30 D '71

Home visitation and parent involvement. V. K. Burney. Todays Ed 60:10-11 O '71

In the car shop; inside a boys technical high school. T. J. Cottle. il Sat R 54:49-51+ Je 19 '71

Intellectual development in early childhood education. H. H. Spicker. Ed Digest 37:35-8 O '71

Is there such a thing as a learning disabled child? N. E. Silberberg and M. C. Silberberg. Ed Digest 37:14-17 S '71

Lowering the dropout rate; transition classes. M. Schuster. Clear House 45:329-32 F '71

New York's mini-schools. D. Divoky. Sat R 54:60-1+ D 18 '71

Next big effort; increasing number of homes that encourage learning. E. L. Richardson. il Am Ed 7:11-12 Ja '71

Project SEED: mathematics in the ghetto. il Phys Today 24:71-2 Mr '71

Second-chance academy; Chicago school for drop-outs. il Ebony 26:39-42 Ja '71

Stop trying to make equal education. L. C. Solmon. Nat R 23:1106-9 O 8 '71

Tests that destroy. il Newsweek 78:97 S 20 '71

Three programs for needy students; Talent search, Upward bound, and Special services. il Am Ed 7:31-2 Mr '71

To be nobody-but-yourself. S. Fleming. il Schol Teach Jr/Sr High p 18-19 F 1 '71

To sing the street; using a community film program to teach composition. H. Foley. Engl J 60:1101-8 N '71

Which way for pre-K. wishes or reality? L. T. DiLorenzo. il Am Ed 7:28-32 Ja '71

See also
Children of migrant laborers—Education
Mexican Americans—Education
Performance contracts (education)
Voucher plan in education

SOCIALLY handicapped children—*Continued*

Recreation

Camping with inner-city kids; trip with teacher's family. R. Blume and D. E. Blume. il Todays Ed 60:32-3 Mr '71
Idea from below nowhere; P. Bellesen and his youth organization. E. Crimmin. il por Motor B & S 127:12+ My '71
Miniparks; diminishing returns. N. Clay. il Parks & Rec 6:22-6 Ja '71
See also
Camps for the socially handicapped

SOCIETIES
See also
Art clubs and societies
Associations, institutions, etc.
Negroes—Clubs, societies, etc.
Scientific societies
SOCIETIES, Insect. See Insect societies
SOCIETY, Primitive
Lost tribe of the Tasaday; Stone age people in the Philippines. il Time 98:58+ O 18 '71
See also
Indians of North America—Culture
Taboo

SOCIETY and art. See Art and society
SOCIETY and law. See Rule of law; Sociological jurisprudence
SOCIETY and literature. See Literature and society
SOCIETY and music; Society and war; etc. See Music and society; War and society; etc.
SOCIETY and the arts. See The Arts and society
SOCIETY and the church. See Church and the world
SOCIETY and the individual. See Individual and society
SOCIETY and youth. See Individual and society
SOCIETY columns. See Newspapers—Sections, columns, etc.
SOCIETY for religion in higher education
Religion in higher education. M. Novak. Commonweal 93:395-6 Ja 22 '71
SOCIETY ISLANDS
Pareu parade. C. Pepper. il Travel 135:48-52+ Ap '71
SOCIETY of American travel writers
Heritage; annual convention in Greece. Nation 213:550 N 29 '71
SOCIETY of British aerospace companies
SBAC says government support could help double U.K. sales. Aviation W 96:19 Ja 10 '72
SOCIETY of compassionate friends
Therapeutic friendship. il Time 97:45 My 3 '71
SOCIETY of Friends. See Friends. Society of
SOCIETY of priests for a free ministry. See Priests—Associations, institutions, etc.
SOCIO-ECONOMIC status of students. See Students—Social and economic status
SOCIOLOGICAL jurisprudence
Angry young lawyers. P. Vanderwicken. il Fortune 84:74-7+ S '71
Burger; don't look for courts to reshape society; excerpts from address, September 17, 1971. W. E. Burger. por U S News 71:19 O 4 '71
Law and justice. M. Cane. Am Scholar 40:583 Aut '71
Reflections of a jurist on civil disobedience. G. W. Crockett, jr. Am Scholar 40:584-91 Aut '71
SOCIOLOGICAL research. See Social science research
SOCIOLOGY
Coming crisis in western sociology, by A. W. Gouldner. Review
Commentary 50:95-7 D '70. S. Rothman; Reply with rejoinder. A. W. Gouldner. 51:20-1 Ap '71
See also
Culture
Economics
Family
Malthusianism
Power (social sciences)
Progress
Property
Social psychology
SOCIOLOGY, Christian
Contemplative life and the sociologist. M. Rowe; discussion. Chr Cent 88:20, 319 Ja 6, Mr 10 '71
Cult of Jacques Ellul. D. D. McFerran. America 124:122-4 F 6 '71
Our thing; some further reflections on space ship earth. R. G. Howes. Cath World 213:169-73 Jl '71
See also
Church and social problems
Social gospel

SOCIOLOGY, Educational. See Educational sociology
SOCIOLOGY, Urban
Are our cities dying? E. Raskin; S. Tenenbaum; R. Reeves. Read Digest 99:167-8+ Ag '71
Urban affairs, right on; social studies course in Dayton, Ohio high schools. W. L. Bombeck. il Todays Ed 60:38-9 O '71
See also
Cities and towns
Urban renewal
SOCIOLOGY of knowledge. See Knowledge, Sociology of
SOCKS. See Hosiery
SOCOLAR, Sidney J. and Politoff, A. L.
Uncoupling cell junctions in a glandular epithelium by depolarizing current. bibliog il Science 172:492-4 Ap 30 '71
SOCOLOW, Robert H.
Teaching and the environmental challenge; excerpts from address, June 1971. bibliog il Phys Today 24:32-4+ D '71
SOD
Sod creates instant park. J. E. Howland. il Parks & Rec 6:27+ N '71
SODA. See Sodium bicarbonate
SODEPAX. See Joint committee for society, development and peace
SÖDERSTRÖM, Elisabeth
Artist life. D. J. Soria. por Hi Fi 21:MA4+ O '71 *
Söderström honors Jenny Lind. F. Hedman. il por Hi Fi 21:MA16 Ja '71 *
SODIUM acetate
Polywater or sodium acetate? W. M. Madigosky. bibliog il Science 172:264-5 Ap 16 '71
SODIUM bicarbonate
Outdoors with soda. M. Mihelick. il Field & S 76:68-70 D '71
SODIUM carbonates

Manufacture

Solvay process. D. L. Morris. il Chem 44:15-17 Je '17
SODIUM chloride. See Salt
SODIUM in the body
Sodium and potassium activities in normal and sodium-rich frog skeletal muscle. W. M. Armstrong and C. O. Lee. bibliog il Science 171:413-15 Ja 29 '71
SODIUM nitrate
Nitrosamines; a universal cancer-causing chemical? B. T. Hunter. il Consumer Bul 54:25 Mr '71
SOEDERSTROEM, Elisabeth. See Söderström, E.
SOEHARTO. See Suharto
SOEIRO, Renato de Azevedo Duarte
Colonial architecture in Brazil. il Américas 23:S22-4 Ap '71
SOFAS
Comfort round the clock; mobile seating with style. il Am Home 74:66-8 F '71
Sofas; new and renewed. M. Kraft. il Good H 172:124-31 My '71
SOFAS, Built in. See Furniture. Built in
SOFAS, Convertible. See Furniture, Convertible
SOFFEN, Gerald A. and Martin. J. S. jr
How we'll search for life on Mars. il Pop Sci 198:51-3+ F '71
SOFFER, Gad
Education corps. il Focus 21:9-12 Ja '71
SOFT contact lenses. See Contact lenses
SOFT drink industry
Price of success; Coke and Pepsi in Japan. Newsweek 78:88+ D 6 '71
See also
Coca-Cola company
SOFT drinks. See Beverages
SOFTBALL
It's tough to beat this Queen of diamonds; R. Beaird of group called the Queen and her maids. D. Chapin. il pors Todays Health 49:35-9+ Jl '71
SOFTENING of water. See Water softening
SOHN, David A.
Taste and aftertaste; address, November 1970. Engl J 60:369-72 Mr '71
SOHO. See New York (city)—SoHo
SOIFER, David, and others
Insulin and microtubules in rat adipocytes. bibliog il Science 172:269-71 Ap 16 '71
SOIL absorption
Fate of air pollutants; removal of ethylene, sulfur dioxide, and nitrogen dioxide by soil. F. B. Abeles and others. bibliog il Science 173:914-16 S 3 '71

SOIL acidity
Nitrogen can make soils acid. C. E. Sommers. Suc Farm 69:C8 N '71

SOIL-atmosphere interaction
SPAM: a computer views a cornfield. il Sci N 100:292-3 O 30 '71
Sun's work in a cornfield. E. Lemon and others. bibliog il Science 174:371-8 O 22 '71

SOIL compaction
Reduce soil compaction for better yields. C. E. Sommers. il Suc Farm 69:32-3 O '71

SOIL conservation
Drought, land and ecology; Great Plains states. Sci N 99:316 My 8 '71
Whatever happened to soil conservation? W. E. Swegle. Suc Farm 69:37 My '71
  See also
Cover crops
Terraces (agriculture)

SOIL conservation service. See United States—
Soil conservation service

SOIL fertility
Does the way our food is grown affect our mental well-being? bibliog Org Gard & Farm 18:102-6+ My '71
Health and vigor depend on the soil. P. H. DeHart and R. M. DeHart. bibliog il Org Gard & Farm 18:102-7 Je '71
How my garden soil grew and grew. J. J. Meeker. il Org Gard & Farm 18:39-43 F '71
Organic soil keeps the insects away. R. Rodale. il Org Gard & Farm 18:28-32 Je '71
  See also
Humus
Soil productivity rating

SOIL fungi
  See also
Mycorhiza

SOIL mechanics
  See also
Slopes (soil mechanics)

SOIL metabolism
Soil transforms; metabolism of aniline-based pesticides to TCAB and other azo compounds. D. Pramer. il Environ 13:42-6 My '71

SOIL microbiology
Soil: a natural sink for carbon monoxide. R. E. Inman and others. bibliog il Science 172:1229-31 Je 18 '71
  See also
Soil metabolism

SOIL moisture
Sun's work in a cornfield. E. Lemon and others. bibliog il Science 174:371-8 O 22 '71
Your soil does affect irrigation. il Suc Farm 69:B16 My '71
  See also
Soil compaction

SOIL packing. See Soil compaction

SOIL percolation
  See also
Soil absorption

SOIL preparation in gardens. See Gardening—
Soil preparation

SOIL productivity rating
Soil; EQ index. il Nat Wildlife 9:32 O '71

SOIL temperature
Implications of soil temperatures in May. M. Franz. il Org Gard & Farm 18:74-80 My '71

SOIL testing. See Soils—Analysis

SOILS
Crop managment. C. E. Sommers. See issues of Successful farming
Our homestead in suburbia; transformation from hardpan to topsoil. C. F. D'Amico. il Org Gard & Farm 18:49-52 O '71
Topsoil depth, how important? il Suc Farm 69:no4 C28 Mr '71
  See also
Clay
Compost
Gardening—Soil preparation
Humus

Analysis
When to test your soils. Suc Farm 69:no3 B8 F '71

Carbon monoxide content
Carbon monoxide sink. Sci Am 225:47 Ag '71
Soil: a natural sink for carbon monoxide. R. E. Inman and others. bibliog il Science 172:1229-31 Je 18 '71

Composition
See Soil compaction; Soil fertility

Lead content
On the trail of heavy metals in ecosystems. il Sci N 100:165-6 S 11 '71

Mineral content
Health and vigor depend on the soil. P. H. DeHart and R. M. DeHart. bibliog il Org Gard & Farm 18:102-7 Je '71
Make sure your soil has trace minerals. J. Cox. Org Gard & Farm 18:58-61 Jl '71

Moisture
See Soil moisture

Nitrogen content
Nitrogen can make soils acid. C. E. Sommers. Suc Farm 69:C8 N '71

Temperature
See Soil temperature

Testing
See Soils—Analysis

Water content
See Soil moisture

SOILS, Freezing of. See Frozen ground

SOKOL, Robert J. and Reiser, Martin
Training police sergeants in early warning signs of emotional upset. bibliog Ment Hy 55:303-7 Jl '71

SOKOLOV, Raymond A.
Food. il N Y Times Mag p66 Je 13; 36 Je 20; 16 Jl 4; 24 Jl 11; 39 Jl 25; 34 Ag 1; 45 Ag 8; 57 S 19; 82 O 3; 89 O 24; 86 N 7; 83 N 28; 34 D 19; 22 D 26 '71; 29 Ja 2 '72
Food beat; interview. New Yorker 47:20-2 Ag 21 '71
  about
Critic in the kitchen. il por Newsweek 77: 65+ Ap 26 '71 •

SOLAR batteries
Huge solar array for space station. il Space World H-3-87:50 Mr '71
New glass means longer life for satellites. il Space World H-10-94:45 O '71
New look at the sun. P. E. Glaser. il Cons 25:22-7 Je '71
Solar array capabilities increase. B. M. Elson. il Aviation W 95:50-1+ S 13 '71
Solar arrays' particle resistance tested. Aviation W 94:66-7 Je 14 '71

SOLAR cells. See Solar batteries

SOLAR-climate relationships. See Sun and meteorology

SOLAR cookers
Solar cooker is an ecologist's delight. D. D. Vigren. il Pop Sci 199:55 Ag '71

SOLAR corona. See Sun—Corona

SOLAR eclipses. See Eclipses, Solar

SOLAR energy
Is it time for a new look at solar energy? A. B. Meinel and M. P. Meinel. il pors Bul Atom Sci 27:32-7 O '71
New look at the sun. P. E. Glaser. il Cons 25:22-7 Je '71
Solar energy: a feasible source of power? A. L. Hammond. Science 172:660 My 14 '71
Solar energy researchers try a new way. il Bsns W p72 Je 12 '71
Solar power. N. C. Ford and J. W. Kane. il pors Bul Atom Sci 27:27-31 O '71
Why organic growers love the sun. R. Rodale. il Org Gard & Farm 18:30-4 O '71
  See also
Solar batteries

SOLAR magnetic fields. See Magnetic fields (cosmic physics)

SOLAR neutrinos. See Neutrinos

SOLAR power. See Solar energy

SOLAR prominences. See Sun—Prominences

SOLAR radiation
Lockheed experiment will map sun's X-rays; X-ray heliometer experiment. Space World H-11-95:43 N '71
Mars 3 explores the sun: automatic interplanetary station studying radio-frequency radiation. Space World H-11-95:48 N '71
Shock waves of cosmic rays. G. Lyubimov. Space World H-12-96:46-7 D '71
  See also
Atmospheric turbidity
Birds, Effect of solar radiation on
Energy budget (geophysics)
Plants, Effect of solar radiation on
Soil-atmosphere interaction
Solar cookers
Solar energy
Solar wind

Measurement
Solar particle tracks in glass from the Surveyor 3 spacecraft. G. Crozaz and R. M. Walker. bibliog il Science 171:1237-9 Mr 26 '71

SOLAR system
  See also
  Planets
SOLAR water heaters. See Water heaters
SOLAR wind
  Novel solar-wind experiment. Sky & Tel 41:
    83 F '71
  Permanent lunar surface magnetism and its
    deflection of the solar wind. A. Barnes and
    others. bibliog il Science 172:716-18 My 14
    '71
  Storms from the sun. I. Asimov. Sci Digest
    70:87-8 S '71
  Whole body response of the moon to electro-
    magnetic induction by the solar wind. C. P.
    Sonett and others. bibliog il Science 172:
    256-8 Ap 16 '71
SOLDER and soldering
  Microelectronic soldering. E. H. Breslin. il
    por Electr World 86:53 N '71
  Solder and soldering tools. J. Frye. il Electr
    World 85:45-8+ Je '71
SOLDERING apparatus
  Would you believe a rechargeable soldering
    iron?. W. J. Hawkins. il Pop Sci 199:101
    Jl '71
SOLDIERS
  See also
  Military life
SOLDIERS, Negro. See United States—Army
  —Negroes
SOLDIERS, Unknown. See Unknown soldiers
SOLE (fish)
  See also
  Cookery—Fish
SOLEDAD prison. See Prisons—California
SOLERI, Paolo
  Architecture shaped by nature. il por House
    & Gard 139:50-5 Je '71 *
  Beyond civilization. P. Bohannan. il Natur
    Hist 80:50-67 F '71 *
  Portfolio: coming of age at Haystack. F. B.
    Merritt. il Ceram Mo 19:19-26 Je '71 *
  Soleri's arcology: a new design for the city?
    S. Kostof. il Art in Am 59:90-5 Mr '71 *
SOLHEIM, Wilhelm Gerhard, 1924-
  New light on a forgotten past. il Nat Geog
    139:330-9 Mr '71
SOLID propellant rockets. See Rocket engines
SOLID-state research. See Electronics research
SOLID wastes. See Refuse and refuse disposal
SOLIDS
  See also
  Energy band theory of solids
SOLIFLUCTION
  Solifluction: a model experiment. A. Higashi
    and A. E. Corte. il Science 171:480-2 F 5 '71
SOLIS-COHEN, Lita H.
  Living with antiques. il Antiques 99:386-90
    Mr '71
SOLITAIRE/double solitaire; drama. See An-
  derson, R. W.
SOLITUDE
  Involvement. P. B. Price. PTA Mag 65:13
    Ja '71
  Ultimate spring of solitude; excerpt from
    Alone at high noon. E. Cailliet. Chr Today
    15:12 Jl 16 '71
  See also
  Loneliness
SÖLL, Dieter
  Enzymatic modification of transfer RNA. bib-
    liog il Science 173:293-9 Jl 23 '71
SOLMON, Lewis C.
  Stop trying to make equal education. Nat R
    23:1106-9 O 8 '71
SOLNIT, Albert
  Wear and tear in the communes. il Nation
    212:524-7 Ap 26 '71; Same abr. Cur 130:22-6
    Je '71
SOLOMON, Arthur K.
  State of water in red cells; with biographical
    sketch. il Sci Am 224:12, 88-96 F '71
SOLOMON, Ezra
  What Solomon will bring to the CEA. por
    Bsns W p 17 My 29 '71 *
SOLOMON, Joe
  Last of the schlockmeisters. R. Ebert. il
    pors Esquire 76:152-5+ N '71 *
SOLOMON, Maynard
  Beethoven's birth year. bibliog f Mus Q 56:
    702-10 O '70
SOLOMON, Stephen
  Now computers guide you through traffic
    snarls. il Pop Sci 198:51-3+ Ja '71
SOLOMON R. Guggenheim museum, New York
  Art; T. M. Messer and the Haacke exhibi-
    tion. L. Alloway. Nation 213:93-4 Ag 2 '71
  Artists vs. museums; Haacke-Guggenheim
    affair. E. C. Baker. Art N 70:25+ My '71;
    Discussion. 70:21+ S '71
  Last International? D. Davis. il Newsweek
    77:64 F 22 '71

SOLOMONS, Gus, Jr
  Gus Solomons, jr. and company, Judson me-
    moral church, NYC. L. Pastore. Dance
    Mag 45:78 Jl '71 *
SOLON, John
  Dealing with administrators and analysts;
    excerpts from address, May 16, 1971. Pub
    W 199:23-4 Je 14 '71
SOLOTAROFF, Theodore
  Reality and socialist realism. Sat R 54:59-62
    Ja 23 '71
SOLOVIOFF, Nicholas
  New beat in the heart of Britain; repro-
    ductions of paintings. Fortune 83:98-105
    Ja '71
SOLOW, Robert M.
  Economist's approach to pollution and its
    control; adaptation of address, December
    1970. bibliog Science 173:498-503 Ag 6 '71
SOLTI, Georg
  Music to my ears; concert version of Wag-
    ner's Das Rheingold. I. Kolodin. Sat R 54:
    19 My 15 '71 *
  Musical events; concert in Carnegie Hall,
    performed by Chicago symphony orchestra.
    W. Sargeant. New Yorker 47:97 N 27 '71 *
  Solti is special. R. C. Marsh. por Hi Fi 21:
    MA26-7 Ap '71 *
SOLUNAR theory. See Fishing
SOLUTION (chemistry)
  Stress collisions and constants. D. L. Morris.
    il por Chem 44:10-12 Ap; 15-19 My; 15-17
    Je '71
SOLVANG, Calif.
  Detour 85 miles northwest of L.A. to see
    horses, flowers, history and Danes. il Sun-
    set 147:60-1 Ag '71
SOLVAY process. See Sodium carbonates—
  Manufacture
SOLVENTS
  See also
  Carbon tetrachloride
  Cleaning compositions
  Methylene chloride
  Plasticizers
SOLZHENITSYN, Aleksandr Isaevich
  Elm log; Storm in the mountains; poems, tr.
    by M. Glenny. Mlle 73:74 Je '71
  Prayer. il Vogue 158:87 D '71
  Soldier's death: from Solzhenitsyn's August
    1914. il Time 97:34 Je 28 '71
  Solzhenitsyn: three short stories; with bio-
    graphical sketch. Vogue 157:90-3 F 15 '71

  about
  Alexander Solzhenitsyn: religious writer. M.
    Bourdeaux. Chr Cent 88:202-3 F 10 '71 *
  Battle of August 1914. B. A. Bannon. Pub
    W 200:37 Ag 16 '71 *
  Beyond endurance. Time 98:26-7 Ag 30 '71 *
  Big prize; publishing rights to August 1914.
    il por Newsweek 78:55 Jl 19 '71 *
  Books. E. Wilson. New Yorker 47:83-7 Ag 14
    '71 *
  Dissent in Russia: the thin wedge. il por
    Newsweek 77:29-34 F 1 '71 *
  Embarrassing award. Time 98:30+ S 13 '71 *
  God is upper-case. il por Time 97:29 Je 21
    '71
  Life worth loving. P. S. Prescott. Newsweek
    78:73A+ Jl 26 '71 *
  Look at Solzhenitsyn. M. Mayne. Engl J 60:
    205-7 F '71 *
  New War and peace. Newsweek 77:45-6 Je
    28 '71 *
  Solzhenitsyn, by L. Labedz. Review
    New Repub 165:30 O 16 '71. P. Blake *
  Solzhenitsyn complains of secret police
    harassment. Pub W 200:38 Ag 23 '71 *
  Solzhenitsyn, ed. by L. Labedz; Aleksandr
    Solzhenitsyn, by A. Rothberg; Solzhenit-
    syn, by G. Lukács. Reviews
    Sat R 54:54+ D 4 '71. M. Friedberg *
  Solzhenitsyn's tributes. il por Newsweek 79.
    23 Ja 3 '72 *
SOMAN, Florence Jane
  Game of hearts; story. Good H 173:106-7 N '71
  Perfectly wonderful girl; story. Good H 172:
    72-3 Je '71
  Surprising stranger; story. Good H 173:70-1
    D '71
  Up above the world so high; story. il Good H
    173:66-7 Ag '71
SOME grass roots of peace in Pacific Heights
  South; story. See Putman, C.
SOMER, P. de. See Clercq, E. de, jt. auth.
SOMERLOTT, Robert
  The medium had the message: Mrs Piper
    and the professors; excerpts from Here,
    Mr Splitfoot. il pors Am Heritage 22:33-7+
    F '71
SOMERS, Florence
  New movies. See issues of Redbook

SOMERSON, Norman L. and others
Pulmonary compliance: alteration during infection. bibliog il Science 171:66-8 Ja 8 '71
SOMERVILLE, Rose M.
Women's studies. Todays Ed 60:35-7 N '71
SOMLYO, Andrew P. See Somlyo, A. V. jt. auth.
SOMLYO, Avril V. and Somlyo, A. P.
Strontium accumulation by sarcoplasmic reticulum and mitochondria in vascular smooth muscle. bibliog il Science 174:955-8 N 26 '71
SOMMARS, Julie
Can two TV beauties survive TV? interview, ed. by R. Meryman. il pors Life 70:54-6 Ja 22 '71
SOMMER, Charles H.
Dealing with a disaster. il pors Nations Bsns 59:78-9 Ja '71
SOMMER, Robert
People's art; with biographical sketch. il Natur Hist 80:10. 40-5 F '71
Time for every purpose; with biographical sketch. il Natur Hist 80:4. 24-5+ bibliog(p96) Ag '71
SOMMER, Susan Thiemann
New York: a week of Josquin. il Hi Fi 21: MA14-15 O '71
SOMMERS, Charles E.
Crop management. See issues of Successful farming
SOMNAMBULISM
Why children may sleepwalk. il Good H 172: 162 F '71
SONAR
See also
Echolocation (physiology)
SONATAS
See also
Phonograph records—Sonatas
SONDHEIM, Stephen
Sondheim on songwriting. por Time 97:72-3 My 3 '71 *
SONDHEIMER, E. and others
Asymmetry, its importance to the action and metabolism of abscisic acid. bibliog il Science 174:829-31 N 19 '71
SONETT, C. P. and others
Whole body response of the moon to electromagnetic induction by the solar wind. bibliog il Science 172:256-8 Ap 16 '71
SONFIST, Alan
Alchemist and the phenomenologist. C. Nemser. bibliog il Art in Am 59:100-3 Mr '71 *
SONG of Grendel; story. See Gardner, J.
SONG writers. See Composers
SONG writing. See Composition (music)
SONGMY massacre. See Vietnamese war, 1957- —Atrocities—My Lai massacre
SONGS
See also
Carols
Christmas carols
Folk songs
Hymns
Phonograph records—Songs
SONGS, American
See also
Campaign songs
Folk songs, American
Star spangled banner (song)
SONGS, Campaign. See Campaign songs
SONGS, Indian. See Indians of North America— Music
SONGS, Popular. See Music, Popular (songs, etc)
SONIC boom
Can science quiet the sonic boom? B. Kocivar. il Pop Sci 199:62-4+ Ag '71
SONIC cleaning. See Metal cleaning
SONIC holography See Holography
SONNICHSEN, C. L.
Instant millionaire. bibliog il pors Am West 8:4-9+ N '71
SONOBE, Haruyuki, and Ohnishi, Eiji
Silkworm bombyx mori L: nature of diapause factor. bibliog il Science 174:835-8 N 19 '71
SONORA (state), Mexico
By back roads to Sonora's one and only boojum forest. il Sunset 147:24+ O '71
SONS and daughters of the Soddies, inc.
Sons and daughters of the Soddies. J. Robertson. il Har Yrs 11:20 Jl '71
SONS and fathers. See Parent-child relationship
SONS of bosses international
Oedipus hex. il Time 97:71-2 Mr 22 '71
SONTAG, David
Project Adam and Eve. Harper 243:43 Ag '71
SONTAG, Frederick
Ill-tempered Christians. Chr Cent 88:316-17 Mr 10 '71

SONTAG, John
Presenting the next great western movie. L. E. Sissman. Atlan 228:40+ D '71 *
SONTAG, Susan
Susan Sontag speaks up; interview. ed. by L. Kent. por Vogue 158:88+ Ag 1 '71
SOON; musical comedy. See Musical comedies, revues, etc.—Criticisms, plots, etc.
SOPER, Alexander
Movable feasts. il Art N 69:40-3+ F '71
SOPER, Leonard G.
California cities form data center partnership. il Am City 86:113-14 My '71
SOPHOCLES
Antigone. Criticism
    Nation 212:700-1 My 31 '71 *
    New Repub 164:26 Je 12 '71 *
    New Yorker 47:56 My 22 '71 *
    Newsweek il 77:88 My 24 '71 *
    Sat R 54:55 My 29 '71 *
    Time il 97:48 My 24 '71 *
SOPORIFICS. See Hypnotics
SOPRANOS. See Opera singers
SORCERY. See Witchcraft
SOREL, Edward
Richard M. Nixon library. il Atlan 227:85-92 F '71
SOREL, Nancy (Caldwell)
Trade winds; interview. ed. by C. Amory. Sat R 54:6+ Mr 6 '71
SORGHUM
Keep weeds out of sorghum. Suc Farm 69: no5 D3 Mr '71
See also
Feeding and feeding stuffs—Sorghum
Milo
    Hybrids
How to make sorghum-sudan hybrids pay off. Suc Farm 69:B4 My '71
75 bu. sorghum; 40 bu. wheat same year. Suc Farm 69:38 N '71
SORIA, Dorle J.
Artist life. See issues of High fidelity and Musical America
SOROKA, Margery
Watercolor page; with biographical sketch. il por Am Artist 35:48-9+ F '71
SORREL
See also
Wood sorrel
SORRELLS, Helen
Amputation; poem. Esquire 75:20 Ja '71
SORROW
See also
Bereavement
Crying
SORROWFUL woman; story. See Godwin, G.
SOSIN, Mark J.
Acres of action. il pors Outdoor Life 147: 68-71+ Mr '71
SOSNOFF, Martin T.
Market trends (cont) por Forbes 107:74-5 F 15; 74-5 Je 1; 108:96-7 S 15 '71; 109: 202-3 Ja 1 '72
SOTH, Lauren
Obsolete dream machine. il Nation 212:687-90 My 31 '71
SOTHEBY and company
Victoria's return. il Newsweek 78:90+ N 8 '71
SOTIRIS, Angelos, pseud.
There's the Greece of Greeks and there's the tourists' Greece. il N Y Times Mag p 12- 14+ Jl 25 '71
SOTOGRANDE colony. See Seaside resorts— Spain
SOTSKOV, Boris
Automatic craft on space routes. Space World H-6-90:8-9 Je '71
SOUFFLÉS
Cold soufflé. S. Whittier. il Good H 173: 164 S '71
Food from afar: France. il Bet Hom & Gard 49:126 Ap '71
How to make an absolutely superb dessert. il Redbook 137:78-81+ Jl '71
McCall's cooking school: chocolate soufflé. il McCalls 98:124-5+ F '71
Some experiments with soufflés. Sunset 146: 145 F '71
Surefire soufflé. J. Jaffry. il Am Home 74: 102-4+ My '71
Virtuoso's legacy; Michael Field's praline souffle fifi, and sweet cream waffles. R. A. Sokolov. il N Y Times Mag p83 N 28 '71
SOUL
Psychical research society awarded funds to prove soul's existence. Chr Cent 88:947 Ag 11 '71
See also
Spirit
SOUL CITY, N.C.
Soul City. G. Gould. New Repub 165:9-11 Jl 3 '71

SOUL food. See Cookery, American
SOUL music. See Negro music
SOUL of Christmas; story. See King, H. H.
SOULIOTIS, Elena
Operatic cliffhangers with Sills and Souliotis. E. Greenfield. il Hi Fi 21:19-20+ Ja '71 •
SOUND
Breaking through the sound barrier; H. Jones' timesthetic projects. R. T. Coe. il Art N 70:44-5+ Sum '71
   See also
Acoustics, Architectural
Electroacoustics
Hearing
Noise
Sound waves

Apparatus
Distortionless audio compressor. C. Caringella. il Pop Electr 35:25-30 D '71
EW lab tested. See issues of Electronics world
Fidelity figures can confuse. L. Brown. il Pop Phot 69:55+ Ag '71
Focus on sound. R. Pinney. See issues of Popular photography
4-channel audio mixer. il Radio-Electr 42:75 Jl '71
Low-distortion hi-fi volume expander. R. Wilt. il Electr World 85:54-5 Je '71
Portable sound systems for performers; mixers. D. L. Patten. il Electr World 86:27-9+ Ag '71
Solid-state bird. J. S. Simonton, jr. il Pop Electr 35:58-60 S '71
   See also
Amplifiers
Headphones
Loud speaking apparatus
Magnetic recorders and recording
Microphones
Moving picture cameras—Sound equipment
Phonograph

Attenuation
   See also
Vegetation and sound

Recording and reproducing
Focus on sound. R. Pinney. See issues of Popular photography
   See also
High fidelity sound systems
Magnetic recorders and recording
Moving picture sound recording
Moving pictures, Amateur—Sound effects
Phonograph records—Recording
Sound—Stereophonic recording and reproducing

Stereophonic recording and reproducing
Build a four-channel stereo decoder. G. Meyerle. il Pop Phot 35:52-3+ Jl '71
Do we need 4-channel stereo? F. Krausser. il Electr World 86:42-4 Ag '71
Experiment with 4-channel stereo. H. E. Maynard. il Radio-Electr 42:33-8 Mr '71
Four-channel discs, 1971. R. Long. il Hi Fi 21:64 Jl '71
Four-channel stereo. il Hi Fi 21:48-54 Ja '71
4-channel stereo is here. A. W. Burawa. il Pop Electr 35:47-51 Jl '71
Four-channel stereo sound. D. M. Berk. il Consumer Bul 54:29-30 My '71
4-channel stereo: symposium with editorial comment. H. E. Maynard. il por Radio-Electr 42:4, 33-45+ O '71
4-channel stereo synthesizer. C. H. Lawrence. il Radio-Electr 42:71-3 Mr '71
Instant quadriphony. R. Long. il Hi Fi 21:42-3 S '71
Quadaphonic quandary. I. Berger. Sat R 54:84 O 30 '71
   See also
Magnetic recorders and recording—Stereophonic recorders
Stereophonic sound systems
SOUND control. See Noise control
SOUND effects. See subhead Sound effects under various subjects, e.g. Moving pictures, Amateur—Sound effects
SOUND in literature
Auditory experience in Joyce's Portrait. R. Tarbox. bibliog Am Imago 27:301-28 Wint '70
Sounds of fiction. M. Franco. Writer 84:11-13 O '71
SOUND of trumpets; story. See Huffstutler, S. A.

SOUND perception
Auditory evoked potentials during speech perception. C. C. Wood and others. bibliog il Science 173:1248-51 S 24 '71
Evoked potential correlates of auditory signal detection. S. A. Hillyard and others. bibliog il Science 172:1357-60 Je 25 '71
Speech perception in infants. P. D. Eimas and others. bibliog il Science 171:303-6 Ja 22 '71
Unilateral ablation of the auditory cortex in the cat impairs complex sound localization. J. Cranford and others. bibliog il Science 172:286-8 Ap 16 '71
SOUND production by animals
Can leviathan long endure so wide a chase? song of the humpback whale. S. McVay. il Natur Hist 80:36-41 Ja '71
   See also
Animal sounds
SOUND production by insects. See Insect sounds
SOUND waves
Acoustic surface-wave devices. J. R. Fisk. il Pop Electr 34:27-33 Mr '71
Sound from Apollo rockets in space. D. Cotten and W. L. Donn. bibliog il Science 171:565-7 F 12 '71
Whistling in the culvert; exploring analogies between sound waves and electromagnetic waves traveling in a channel. Sci Am 225:84 S '71
SOUNDING and soundings
Tales of sea floor soundings. B. G. Ledbetter. il Sea Front 17:274-84 S '71
   See also
Depth indicators
SOUNDPRINTING
   See also
Voiceprints
SOUNDS
   See also
Phonograph records—Sounds
SOUPHANOUVONG, prince of Laos, 1902-
Two brothers vying for control of Laos. pors U S News 70:71 F 22 '71 •
SOUPS
Basic bisque. C. Claiborne. il N Y Times Mag p70 F 21 '71
Bean soup bargains. il Bet Hom & Gard 49:92-3 Ap '71
Borscht: icy cold and colorful. Sunset 146:182 Je '71
Canned and dry-mix soups. Consumer Rep 36:536-40 S '71
Chopstick soups. il Sunset 146:106-7 My '71
Consommé: the consummate soup. J. Pépin. il House B 113:40-1 S '71
Eat: watercress soup. M. Cantwell. Mlle 73:80+ My '71
Fava beans make a great soup. il Sunset 147:191 O '71
Food from afar: Mexico; gazpacho. il Bet Hom & Gard 49:80 Je '71
Fresh vegetables and chicken broth; cold soups. Sunset 147:100 Ag '71
Green thoughts in a green shade; puree of artichoke, and puree of asparagus soups. R. A. Sokolov. il N Y Times Mag p36 Je 20 '71
Meal-in-itself, Bavarian soup. il Sunset 146:126 F '71
Out of the pumpkin, Aztec soup from Mexico. il Sunset 147:100-1 O '71
Soups and stews the world over; excerpts. L. Driggs. il Har Yrs 11:35-8 Ap '71
Soups with gusto. il Bet Hom & Gard 49:80-1+ S '71
Soups you serve cold! il Bet Hom & Gard 49:87 My '71
South of the border soup; corn soup. il N Y Times Mag p29 S 5 '71
Thoughts for the hostess. M. M. Hemingway. House & Gard 140:24+ N '71
Two broth-soups, easy, delicious. il Sunset 146:206 My '71
We can dream, can't we? cheap and non-fattening soups. N. Hazelton. Nat R 23:430 Ap 20 '71
Work wonders with dried soups. il Ladies Home J 89:98+ Ja '72
   See also
Campbell soup company
Chowder
SOUPS, Dry. See Food, Dried
SOUSA, John Philip
Pied Piper. A. M. Lingg. il pors Opera N 36:10-14 D 25 '71 •
SOUSTELLE, Jacques
Jacques is back. por Newsweek 77:42+ F 22 '71 •

SOUTH
Whistling Dixie. Life 70:36 F 19 '71
See also
Colleges and universities—Southern states
Education—Southern states
Forests and forestry—Southern states
Justice, Administration of—Southern states
Libraries—Southern states
Mountaineers (southern states)
Negroes—Southern states
School libraries—Southern states
Women—Southern states

Description and travel
South today. il Ebony 26:33+ Ag '71

Economic conditions
Black business is tops in South. S. Booker.
   il Ebony 26:56-8+ Ag '71
New environment of the South. G. Clay.
   Arch Forum 133:42-5 D '70
On the road in Mississippi. A. V. Krebs, jr.
   Cath World 212:297-300 Mr '71
Some progress, more myth. R. W. Dietsch.
   Nation 212:615-18 My 17 '71

History
See also
Ku Klux klan
Negroes—History
United States—History—Civil war

Industries
When industry goes south. A. A. Fletcher. il
   pors Ebony 26:168-71 Ag '71
See also
Cotton industry

Politics
Black politics in the new South. C. C. Doug-
   las. il Ebony 26:27-30+ Ja '71
Black politics in the South. H. Walton, jr.
   il Ebony 26:140-3 Ag '71
Democrats' comeback in South: a political key
   to '72. il U S News 70:22-4 Mr 29 '71
New breed? southern governors. Sr Schol 98:
   17 F 8 '71
Of many things. T. H. Clancy. America 124:
   inside cover My 15 '71
South today. il Ebony 26:64-5 Ag '71

Race question
Black voices of the South; symposium. il
   Ebony 26:50-4 Ag '71
White voices of the South; symposium. il
   Ebony 26:164-7 Ag '71

Social conditions
Been down home so long it looks like up to
   me. J. B. Cumming, jr. il Esquire 76:84-90+
   Ag '71
New day a'coming in the South. il por
   Time 97:14-20 My 31 '71
Notes from the road. J. Burnham. Nat R
   23:191 F 23 '71
Old illusions and new Souths; with editorial
   comment. L. Bennett, jr. il Ebony 26:33,
   35-8+ Ag '71
See also
Negroes—Social conditions

Statistics
South today. il Ebony 26:64-5 Ag '71

SOUTH AFRICA
See also
Astronomical observatories—South Africa
Botany—South Africa
Censorship—South Africa
Church and race problems in South Africa
Drag racing—South Africa
Geology—South Africa
Investments, Foreign (in South Africa)
Paleontology—South Africa
Purchasing, Military—South Africa
Television industry—South Africa
Trials—South Africa
United Nations—South Africa
Zambia

Foreign relations
Great Britain
   See Great Britain—Foreign relations—
   South Africa
Malawi
Red carpet for a black man; H. K. Banda
   visit. por Time 98:28 Ag 30 '71

History
See also
South African war, 1899-1902

Intellectual life
Ghettoizing culture in South Africa. I. Rob-
   ertson and J. Fishkin. Commonweal 94:156-7
   Ap 23 '71

Native races
Passage through Botswana. E. McCarthy.
   Commonweal 95:131-2 N 5 '71
See also
South Africa—Race question
Zulus

Politics and government
South Africa: the politics of fragmentation.
   N. Curtis. For Affairs 50:283-96 Ja '72

Race question
Alan Paton: revisions; attitude toward apartheid. Nat R 23:852 Ag 10 '71
Apartheid: cracks in the façade. il Time 98:
   50-1 N 1 '71
Arresting a bishop. J. Deedy. Commonweal
   94:154 Ap 23 '71
Australians divided on South Africans' rug-
   by, cricket tours. R. Mathias. Chr Cent 88:
   668-9 My 26 '71
CBS and South Africa. Nat R 23:415 Ap 20 '71
Case against dean flawed; trial of Dean Gon-
   ville Ffrench-Beytagh. J. Squire. Chr Cent
   88:1329-30 N 10 '71
Cricket controversy: sport and social protest. W. Clarnette; R. Mathias. Chr Cent
   88:1267-9 O 27 '71
Englishman tries to understand apartheid.
   T. Stacey. il Nat R 23:581-4 Je 1 '71
Father Desmond's mistake. America 125:22 Jl
   24 '71
Hazardous courses in southern Africa. G. F.
   Kennan. For Affairs 49:218-36 Ja '71; Same
   abr. with title What policies toward
   southern Africa? Cur 127:50-63 Mr '71
I won't come out alive; Dean Ffrench-Bey-
   tagh of Johannesburg's Anglican cathedral.
   por Time 98:43 N 15 '71
Inequality before the law in South Africa.
   il UNESCO Courier 24:14-17 N '71
Joint meeting on problems of southern Afri-
   ca. UN Mo Chron 8:21-37 Je '71
Over the bunkers; racially mixed South
   African professional golf association
   championship. il Newsweek 78:44 D 6 '71
Polaroid apartheid: pull tab, wait 60 seconds.
   D. Schechter. il Ramp Mag 9:47-8+ Mr;
   60 Ap '71
Polaroid approach to South Africa. G. M.
   Houser. Chr Cent 88:249-52 F 24 '71
Policies of apartheid of government of South
   Africa; consideration by Special political
   committee. UN Mo Chron 8:72-7 N '71
Reply to accusations against Polaroid; letter.
   S. A. Benton and others. Phys Today 24:9+
   Ap '71
South Africa: a nation at war with its con-
   science. C. T. Rowan. Read Digest 99:140-4
   S '71
South Africa: the politics of fragmentation.
   N. Curtis. il For Affairs 50:283-96 Ja '72
South African bishop attacks apartheid. Chr
   Cent 88:1287 N 3 '71
South African violence, black or white? M.
   Magee. Commonweal 93:388-9 Ja 22 '71
South African visit reveals black anger, white
   apathy; with editorial comment. D. M.
   Parker. Chr Cent 88:874, 882-3 Jl 21 '71
South Africa's black mood. P. R. Webb. il
   por Newsweek 77:47-8+ My 10 '71
U.S. business in South Africa. il Newsweek
   77:80+ Mr 29 '71
U.S. should cut loose. J. R. Hollingsworth.
   Nation 212:390-4 Mr 29 '71
United States options in southern Africa; ad-
   dress, December 8, 1970. D. D. Newsom.
   Dept State Bul 64:80-4 Ja 18 '71
Zulus: black nation in a land of apartheid.
   J. Judge. il Nat Geog 140:738-51 D '71
See also
Church and race problems in South Africa
Colored people (South Africa)
United Nations—Special committee on apar-
   theid

Religious institutions and affairs
See also
Christians in South Africa
Church and state in South Africa
Church of England in South Africa

SOUTH African war, 1899-1902
Scramble for Africa, by A. Nutting. Review
   Sat R il 54:29 Jl 17 '71. C. Miller

SOUTH AFRICAN Zionists. See Zulus—Religion

SOUTH AMERICA
See also
Horn, Cape
Latin America
Paleontology—South America
Parks—South America
Tierra del Fuego

SOUTH AMERICA—Continued

Commerce
See Latin America—Commerce

History
Jaime Zudánez, illustrious unknown. T.
Sepúlveda Whittle. il Américas 23:9-13 O
'71

Native races
See Indians of South America

Politics
See Latin America—Politics
SOUTH AMERICAN Indians. See Indians of
South America
SOUTH BEND, Ind.

Sanitary affairs
Jet-vacuum sewer cleaning. il Am City 76:83
Jl '71
SOUTH CAROLINA
See also
Architecture, Domestic—South Carolina
Chattooga River
Gardens—South Carolina
Hilton Head Island
Negroes—South Carolina
Sea Islands
Wildlife conservation—South Carolina

Economic conditions
Showdown at Hilton Head. il Bsns W p 102
Ap 17 '71

Historic houses, etc.
See also
Columbia, S.C.—Historic houses, etc.

Industries
Showdown at Hilton Head. il Bsns W p 102
Ap 17 '71

Politics and government
Education of a conservative; E. Hollings. R.
Sherrill. Nation 213:105-10 Ag 16 '71
Parting shots: a political charmer in Dixie
diapers; Nancy Moore Turmond. il por
Life 71:69 Jl 16 '71
SOUTH CAROLINA. University, Columbia
Big man on campus. il pors Ebony 26:106-8+
Ag '71

Graduate library school
S.C. library school to design curriculum. Li-
brary J 96:3935-6 D 1 '71
SOUTH COMMONS, Chicago. See Chicago—
City planning
SOUTH DAKOTA
Gemland U.S.A; gem-hunting. il Travel 135:6
Ap '71
See also
Hunting—South Dakota
Wildlife sanctuaries—South Dakota
Wind Cave National Park

State library commission
South Dakota state library under fire. Am Lib
2:1027 N '71
SOUTH DAKOTA library association
Governor proposes program; meeting. il por
Am Lib 2:1032-3 N '71
SOUTH DAKOTA library commission. See
South Dakota—State library commission
SOUTH in art
John Faulkner's vanishing South; with ex-
cerpts from works of Faulkner. R. S. Sugg,
jr. il pors Am Heritage 22:65-75 Ap '71
SOUTH in literature
Continuing trial of Jesse Hill Ford. M.
Frady. il pors Life 71:56-56B+ O 29 '71
John Faulkner's vanishing South; with ex-
cerpts from works of Faulkner. R. S. Sugg,
jr. il por Am Heritage 22:65-75 Ap '71
Romance vs. cruelty: the South, seen by two
famous women. E. Hardwick. Vogue 158:62
N 1 '71
SOUTH POLE
Sahara Desert ice cap. R. W. Fairbridge. il
Natur Hist 80:66-73 Je '71
Will our Simon Nathan really get back to
the South Pole? S. Nathan. il Pop Phot
69:56+ Ag '71
SOUTH POLE stations. See Antarctic re-
search
SOUTH SEA ISLANDS. See Oceania
SOUTHAMPTON, N.Y.

Stores
On and off the avenue; womens clothing
shops. K. Fraser. New Yorker 47:72-4 Ag
7 '71

SOUTHAMPTON, Pa.
Street cut repairs can be better than the
original surface. il Am City 86:35 D '71
SOUTHAMPTON, Pa, free library
Southampton Pa: Bucks County compact. il
Library J 96:3985 D 1 '71
SOUTHAMPTON insurrection, 1831
Nat Turner's rebellion. il Sr Schol 99:8-9 N 8
'71
SOUTHBURY, Conn.
Heritage Village bazaar. il Arch Rec 149:107-
10 My '71
Updated bazaar; Heritage Village. il Arch
Forum 134:58-60 Ap '71
Urethane foam becomes practical for hous-
ing; Heritage Village. il Am City 86:75 F
'71
SOUTHEAST ASIA. See Asia, Southeastern
SOUTHEAST ASIA treaty organization
Goldwater: Congress knew what it was doing
on Vietnam; address July 29, 1971. B. M.
Goldwater. il por U S News 71:88-91 Ag
16 '71
Questions for Senator Javits: SEATO and
US troop withdrawals. W. F. Buckley, jr.
Nat R 23:330 Mr 23 '71
Secretary Rogers attends SEATO and CENTO
meetings and visits four Arab states, Is-
rael and Rome; statements, transcripts of
interviews and texts of communiques, April
26-May 9, 1971. W. P. Rogers. Dept State
Bul 64:681-702 My 31 '71
Seventeenth anniversary of SEATO, state-
ment, September 8, 1971. W. P. Rogers.
Dept State Bul 65:356 O 4 '71
SOUTHEASTERN regional ballet festival. See
Dance festivals
SOUTHERN AFRICA. See Africa, Southern
SOUTHERN belles. See Women—Southern
states
SOUTHERN CALIFORNIA counseling center.
See Mental health centers
SOUTHERN CALIFORNIA university, Los An-
geles
Report:
Luigi Dallapiccola's Job and Carl Orff's
Trionfo di Afrodite. J. Rockwell.
Opera N 35:31 Ja 30 '71
Tale of two universities. E. Holsendolph. il
Fortune 83:104-8+ F '71
SOUTHERN Christian leadership conference
Abernathy woos Communists as U.S. backing
drops. Chr Today 16:43 O 22 '71
Jackson pushes on. il por Time 99:30 Ja 3
'72
Jesse Jackson quits SCLC after being sus-
pended. Chr Cent 88:1488 D 22 '71
Operation Breadbasket campaigns against
A&P at the national level. A. Simon. Chr
Cent 88:349-50 Mr 17 '71
SCLC: faithful to its function. C. Rogers.
Chr Cent 88:550 My 5 '71
SCLC to sponsor strategy meetings for blacks,
minorities, students. Chr Cent 88:95 Ja 27
'71
Sit-in at A&P was no tea party; Operation
Breadbasket. il Bsns W p21 F 6 '71
Split in SCLC. il por Newsweek 78:27-8 D
20 '71
SOUTHERN company
Loss of innocence? il Forbes 108:58 D 1 '71
SOUTHERN cookery. See Cookery, American
SOUTHERN forest experiment station. See
United States—Agriculture, Department of
SOUTHERN Methodist university, Dallas, Tex.
Celebration, not sensation: Advent service.
J. C. Evans. Chr Cent 89:4-6 Ja 5 '72

School of business administration
B-school students run a real company. il
Bsns W p 100+ My 1 '71
Bootstrap teaching: while undergraduates. il
Time 98:82 N 15 '71
SOUTHERN ocean racing conference. See
Yacht racing
SOUTHERN pine. See Pine
SOUTHERN Presbyterian church. See Presby-
terian church in the United States (South)
SOUTHERN railway company
Southern's system for using the computer.
V. Louviere. Nations Bsns 59:15 Jl '71
SOUTHERN regional opera. See Atlanta—
Music
SOUTHERN states. See South
SOUTHFIELD, Mich.
Super-roundhouse for public works. A. F.
Wilusz. il Am City 86:84+ Ag '71
SOUTHWEST
See also
Agriculture—Southwestern states
Air pollution—Southwestern states
Conservation of resources—Suothwestern
states
Law—Southwestern states
Water supply—Southwestern states

SOUTHWEST—*Continued*

Description and travel

Southwest. A. M. Cunningham. Mlle 72:272-3
Ap '71
Two wheels along the Mexican border. W. A.
Allard. il por Nat Geog 139:591-635 My '71

Economic conditions

Hello, energy: goodbye, big sky. J. Neary.
il Life 70:61-4+ Ap 16 '71

History

Frontier law and order, by P. D. Jordan.
Review
Am West 8:49 Ja '71. R. Trennert
Henry A. Crabb, filibuster or colonizer? Son-
ora expedition in 1857. J. A. Stout. il pors
Am West 8:4-9 My '71

Photographs

Presenting Dean Brown. D. Brown. il Art in
Am 59:82-5 Ja '71

SOUTHWEST AFRICA
See also
Namibia
United Nations—Southwest Africa

SOUTHWEST airlines company
Fare war in Texas. Newsweek 78:56+ Jl 5 '71
Love is ammunition for a Texas airline. il
Bsns W p24-5 Je 26 '71
New Texas airline plans start. Aviation W 94:
41 My 31 '71

SOUTHWEST forest industries, inc.
He won Riegel for Southwest. por Bsns W
p42 Je 19 '71

SOUTHWEST in literature
Frontier myth and southwestern literature. L.
Goodwyn. bibliog il Am Lib 2:161-7, 359-66
F, Ap '71; Reply. L. C. Powell. 2:682 Jl '71

SOUTHWESTERN library association
Of note; policy for projects of the South-
western library interstate collaborative ef-
fort council. known as SLICE. P. S. Grove.
Am Lib 2:1138 D '71
SWLA twenty-third biennial conference. P.
S. Grove. Am Lib 2:145-6 F '71

SOUTHWESTERN regional ballet festival. See
Dance festivals

SOUTHWORTH, William D.
Elementary school principalship. 1980. Clear
House 46:136-40 N '71

SOUVANNA Phouma, prince of Laos
Future of Laos; interview, ed. by G. M.
Kahin. New Repub 165:15-16 Jl 24 '71

about

Two brothers vying for control of Laos. pors
U S News 70:71 F 22 '71 *

SOVIET-AMERICAN arms control talks. See
Strategic arms limitation talks
SOVIET education. See Education—Russia
SOVIET government. See Russia—Politics and
government
SOVIET minorities. See Minorities
SOVIET UNION. See Russia
SOVIET writers. See Authors, Russian
SOW collars. See Swine—Confinement methods
SOWERS, David W. jr
Who's the smartest fellow around? il Am
For 77:8+ Mr '71
SOWING. See Seeding
SOWINSKI, Richard. See Levine, S. jt. auth.
SOWS. See Swine
SOYBEAN mosaic virus. See Viruses, Plant
SOYBEANS
Growers see higher acreage for '72 beans.
Suc Farm 69:36 N '71
Mycorrhizal enhancement of water transport
in soybean. G. R. Safir and others. bibliog
il Science 172:581-3 My 7 '71
Touring with the champs; annual Elanco
Treflan soybean champions' tour. D. Han-
son. Suc Farm 69:L4 Ag '71
You can get 10 more bushels from every
acre; ed. by R. Lutz. il Suc Farm 69:SB3-
5+ N '71
See also
American soybean association
Cookery—Vegetables
Feeding and feeding stuffs—Soybeans

Cultivation

How to boost soybean yields. T. McCartney.
il Suc Farm 69:no5 M24 Mr '71
New soybean growing tips. C. E. Sommers.
il Suc Farm 69:23-7 My '71
Piggyback sprays: new way to clean out
weeds in soybeans. D. Seim. il Farm J 95:
29 Ap '71
Weed control for soybeans. Suc Farm 69:no3
W4 F '71

What we learned about soybeans. N. Bubel.
il por Org Gard & Farm 18:60-3 Je '71
You can get 10 more bushels from every
acre; ed. by R. Lutz. il Suc Farm 69:SB3-5
N '71

Diseases and pests

Plant diseases, more problems ahead. C. E.
Sommers and E. W. Palm. il Suc Farm 69:
50-1 Ap '71

Harvesting

How fast can you harvest? P. B. Jones. il
Suc Farm 69:25 Je '71
Make an extra $10 per hour combining soy-
beans. P. B. Jones. il Suc Farm 69:C12 O
'71

Marketing

Does storing soybeans pay? il Suc Farm 69:
32 Je '71
Get a premium for soybeans. R. Krumme.
il Suc Farm 69:33 Je '71

Prices

Soybean outlook '72. R. Reiman. il Suc Farm
69:SB17 N '71

Seed

Here are recommended varieties. il Suc Farm
69:SB12 N '71
New test for carryover soybean seed. Suc
Farm 69:38 Ap '71

Yield
See Crop yields

SOYUZ (space vehicle) See Space vehicles. Rus-
sian
SOYUZ flights. See Space flight—Manned
flights—Soyuz flights
SPACE (architecture)
All-year vacation house: a surge of space.
A. Stagg. il House & Gard 139:114-21 Mr '71
Self in chambered space; A. Kasuba. M.
Shorr. il Craft Horiz 31:26-9+ Ag '71
6 interiors; A. Kasuba's New York apart-
ment. il Arch Rec 150:93-5 Ag '71
Space as live-in sculpture; G. El-Zoghby. il
House B 113:44-9 Jl '71
SPACE, Outer
Isaac Asimov explains; low temperature of
space. I. Asimov. Sci Digest 69:76-7 F '71

Exploration

Importance of space exploration. C. R. Kon-
kel. Space World H-4-88:44-5 Ap '71
SPACE, Personal. See Personal space
SPACE and time
Time for every purpose. R. Sommer. il Natur
Hist 80:24-5+ bibliog(p96) Ag '71
See also
Relativity (physics)
SPACE arrangement of plants. See Plants,
Space arrangement of
SPACE cameras. See Space vehicles—Equip-
ment
SPACE communication. See Interstellar com-
munication
SPACE cooperation. See Space research—Inter-
national aspects
SPACE docking. See Orbital rendezvous (space
flight)
SPACE exploration. See Space, Outer—Explor-
ation
SPACE flight
Close look at the outer planets. il Sci N
99:77-8 Ja 30 '71
How we'll explore the outermost planets.
W. Von Braun. il Pop Sci 198:77-9+ Ja '71
Sirens of Titan: grand-tour missions. Sci
Am 226:46 Ja '72
Soviet space flights in 1970. A. Dmitriev.
Space World H-6-90:34-5 Je '71
Space travel in the seventies; interview. W.
Von Braun. il por Holiday 49:8-10 Mr '71
See also
International astronautical federation
Navigation (space flight)
Orbital rendezvous (space flight)
United States—National aeronautics and
space administration

Accidents

Cause sought in Soyuz tragedy; with edi-
torial comment. il Aviation W 95:7, 12-15
Jl 5 '71
Depressurization of Soyuz confirmed by So-
viet commission. il Aviation W 95:15 Jl
19 '71
Ill-fated Soyuz 11. R. N. Watts, jr. il Sky &
Tel 42:138 S '71
Impact of Soviet space tragedy. il U S News
71:39 Jl 12 '71
Soyuz 11, death in space. il Newsweek 78:90-1
Jl 12 '71

SPACE flight—Accidents—*Continued*
Soyuz 11: what happened. Newsweek 78:46 Jl 26 '71
Soyuz seal failure. Sci N 100:38-9 Jl 17 '71
Tragedy in space. il Sci N 100:22 Jl 10 '71
Triumph and tragedy of Soyuz 11. il Time 98:38-9 Jl 12 '71
See also
Space vehicles—Fires and fire protection

Communication systems
Giant antennas for use in deep space probes. il Space World H-12-96:37-8 D '71
See also
Space vehicles—Radio equipment

Finance
Uncertain future for space explorers. il U S News 72:68-9 Ja 10 '72

Food problems
Cold food diet is becoming a thing of the past in oute: space. Y. Marinin. Space World H-12-96:44 D '71
Soviet space man's menu. V. Dupik. Space World H-12-96:42+ D '71
What Soviet spacemen eat. V. Yefimov and others. Space World H-3-87:40 Mr '71

International aspects
Apollo-Salyut. Soyuz-Skylab dockings eyed. Z. Strickland. Aviation W 95:17-18 S 13 '71
Diplomatic flurry over joint manned mission. Sci N 100:388 D 11 '71
Docking of Apollo-Soyuz proposed. Z. Strickland. Aviation W 94:16-17 Ap 12 '71
Plan to rescue stranded astronauts; Apollo-Salyut common docking module. Bsns W p 112 N 6 '71

Manned flights
Man in space or chip in space? R. Jastrow. il N Y Times Mag p 14-15+ Ja 31 '71
Manned space flight; description of programs. il Space World H-3-87:42-3 Mr '71
Soviets plan more manned flights. Aviation W 95:16 N 1 '71
Surplus Apollos may fill hiatus in manned flights. Z. Strickland. Aviation W 95:18 Ag 2 '71
10th anniversary of U.S. manned space flight. il Space World H-8-92:17-20 Ag '71
See also
Astronauts
Orbital rendezvous (space flight)
Space flight to Mars
Space flight to the moon—Manned flights

Accidents
See Space flight—Accidents

Extravehicular activity
Worden takes first deep space walks. Aviation W 95:22-3 Ag 9 '71
See also
Space flight to the moon—Manned flights—Extravehicular activity

Soyuz flights
Cause sought in Soyuz tragedy; with editorial comment. il Aviation W 95:7, 12-15 Jl 5 '71
First laboratory in space; Soyuz 11. R. N. Watts, jr. il Sky & Tel 42:83+ Ag '71
Ill-fated Soyuz 11. R. N. Watts, jr. il Sky & Tel 42:138 S '71
Impact of Soviet space tragedy. il U S News 71:39 Jl 12 '71
Salyut boosts self to higher orbit. il Aviation W 94:14-15 My 3 '71
Salyut flight stresses biomedical studies. il Aviation W 94:17-19 Je 21 '71
Salyut marks major space station step. il Aviation W 94:27-8 Je 14 '71
Salyut mission starts research on astrophysics. il Aviation W 94:22-3 Je 28 '71
Soviet Soyuz 10 links with an orbiting space station. R. N. Watts, jr. il Sky & Tel 41:350 Je '71
Soyuz 10 link a mystery. Sci N 99:298-9 My 1 '71
Soyuz 11: death in space. il Newsweek 78:90-1 Jl 12 '71
Soyuz 11: what happened. Newsweek 78:46 Jl 26 '71
Soyuz review leaves puzzles unresolved. Aviation W 94:19 My 10 '71
Tragedy in space. il Sci N 100:22 Jl 10 '71
Triumph and tragedy of Soyuz 11. il Time 98:38-9 Jl 12 '71

Military use
USAF studies shuttle missions. Aviation W 95:25 N 8 '71

Physiological aspects
After the final Apollo flight, says an astrophysicist, we should deploy machines, not men, in space. T. Gold. il N Y Times Mag p 16-17 Ag 22 '71
NASA reviews Apollo 16 crew workloads. E. J. Bulban. Aviation W 95:21-2 Ag 23 '71
Salyut flight stresses biomedical studies. il Aviation W 94:17-19 Je 21 '71
See also
Life support systems (space environment)
Space medicine

Religious aspects
See also
Space flight to the moon—Religious aspects

Safety devices and measures
See also
Space flight to the moon—Manned flights—Safety devices and measures
Space rescue work
SPACE flight accidents. See Space flight—Accidents
SPACE flight in art
Robert McCall, illustrator of aerospace exploration. P. A. Dreyfus. il por Am Artist 35:80-5+ Mr '71
SPACE flight simulators
NASA simulator shows Apollo 14 descent toward landing site in Fra Mauro Region; photographs. Aviation W 94:40-1 Ja 18 '71
News from the world of space exploration; flight of delta lifting body simulator. il Space World H-9-93:48 S '71
Simulations of shuttle aid NASA. W. S. Heironymus. Aviation W 95:45+ O 4 '71
SPACE flight to Jupiter
Journey to Jupiter. il Time 97:56+ Mr 15 '71
Pioneering way to Jupiter. E. Driscoll. il Sci N 100:330-1 N 13 '71
Pioneers to Jupiter. Sci Am 225:44 O '71
SPACE flight to Mars
Album: photo story of 1981 Mars mission. il Space World H-3-87:23-35 Mr '71
Appointment with Mars; Mariner 9. il Newsweek 78:83 N 22 '71
Destination Mars; Mariner 9. Sci N 99:383 Je 5 '71
Dust storm dims early data from Mariner. il Aviation W 95:24-6 N 22 '71
En route to Mars. M. Borisov. Space World H-12-96:41 D '71
Exploration of Mars. R. N. Watts, jr. Sky & Tel 42:15 Jl '71
First launch of Mariner orbiter set May 7, second for May 17. Z. Strickland. Aviation W 94:16 My 3 '71
Getting aboard Viking: no room on the Mars lander; alpha scattering instrument to analyse martian soil. S. Jacobsen. il Bul Atom Sci 27:49-56 D '71
How we'll search for life on Mars. C. A. Soffen and J. S. Martin, jr. il Pop Sci 198:51-3+ F '71
Mariner Mars 1971 launches. il Space World H-7-91:11-27 Jl '71
Mariner 9 approaches Mars. R. N. Watts, jr. il Sky & Tel 42:270 N '71
Mariner 9 to Mars. W. Von Braun. il Pop Sci 199:62-4+ N '71
Mariner 9 to orbit Mars. R. N. Watts, jr. il Sky & Tel 41:347-50 Je '71
Mars Mariner loss stalls second shot. Aviation W 94:20 My 17 '71
New orbit planned to permit Mariner 9 greater capability. Aviation W 94:57 Je 14 '71
No men on Mars, but a surprise anyway. il U S News 71:46 N 29 '71
On the way to Mars; Mars 2. Sci N 99:367 My 29 '71
Race to see if there's life on Mars. il U S News 70:72 Je 14 '71
Racing toward Mars. il Time 98:45-6 N 15 '71
Red flag on Mars. il Newsweek 78:67 D 13 '71
Rendezvous with Mars; U.S. Mariner 9. il Time 98:61 N 22 '71
Russians land hammer and sickle on Mars. Sci N 100:373 D 4 '71
Soviets glean broad Martian data. il Aviation W 96:12-15 Ja 3 '72
Soviets land TV on Mars; blame failure on wind, dust. Aviation W 95:20 D 13 '71
Tale of trouble with Mars lander. Sci N 100:422 D 25 '71
Then there was one; Mars orbiter. il Sci N 99:330-1 My 15 '71
Three spacecraft study the red planet. il Sky & Tel 43:14-17 Ja '72
Toward the red planet. Time 97:50 My 31 '71
U.S. USSR to share Martian data. Aviation W 95:15 O 25 '71

SPACE flight to Mars—*Continued*
Uncertain future for space explorers. il U S News 72:68-9 Ja 10 '72
Unmasking the Martian mysteries. il Sci Digest 70:71-5 Jl '71

SPACE flight to the moon
Apollo: an assessment; interview. R. A. Petrone. il por Space World H-8-92:4-7 Ag '71
See also
Orbital rendezvous (space flight)

Bibliography

Apollo books available. R. N. Watts, jr. Sky & Tel 43:17 Ja '72

Cost

Are U.S. moon shots worth the money? il U S News 70:24 F 8 '71

Luna flights

Luna 16's trophies; excerpts from address, October 28, 1970. M. Keldysh. Space World H-6-90:18-19 Je '71

Manned flights

Authors & editors; interview, ed. by B. A. Bannon. N. Mailer. por Pub W 199:177-9 Ja 25 '71
Decision to go to the moon, by J. M. Logsdon, and Of a fire on the moon, by N. Mailer. Reviews
Commonweal 94:216-18 My 7 '71. R. A. Schroth
Is another moon trip necessary? interview. R. A. Petrone. por U S News 71:21-2 Ag 2 '71
Moon, by S. A. Bedini and others. Review
Natur Hist il 80:76-8 Mr '71. I. Asimov
Moon men and moon robots. Nat R 23:184 F 23 '71
On the way to the moon shot. J. Dos Passos. Nat R 23:135-6 F 9 '71
See also
Astronauts—Training
Moon—Exploration

Apollo 11 flight

Of a fire on the moon, by N. Mailer. Review
Commentary 51:83-4 My '71. J. P. Sisk.
Esquire 75:52 Mr '71. B. Midwood
Nation 212:378-81 Mr 22 '71. H. Maurer
Sat R 54:25-7+ Ja 16 '71. B. DeMott

Apollo 14 flight

Apollo 14 aids lunar cartography. E. J. Bulban. Aviation W 94:52+ F 22 '71
Apollo 14 first EVA, equipment shown. il Aviation W 94:2-3 Mr 1 '71
Apollo 14: golf on the moon. il Newsweek 77:50-2 F 15 '71
Apollo 14: journey to the moon. il Newsweek 77:54-5 F 8 '71
Apollo 14 preliminary time line. Space World H-3-87:46-8 Mr '71
Apollo 14 stresses experiments, geology; photographs. Aviation W 94:18-19 Mr 1 '71
Apollo 14's moon mission. R. N. Watts, jr. il Sky & Tel 41:200-8 Ap '71
Apollo on the way. il Sci N 99:97 F 6 '71
Apollo: what U.S. hopes to learn. il U S News 70:22-4 F 8 '71
Astronaut to set off explosions in search for water on the moon. Space World H-4-88:43 Ap '71
Cause of Apollo 14 docking delay unclear. E. J. Bulban. il Aviation W 94:24-5 F 8 '71
Climb up Cone crater. A. J. Hall. il Nat Geog 140:136-48 Jl '71
Drama of Apollo 14 moon landing depicted; photographs. Space World H-7-91:28-9 Jl '71
Electrophoresis demonstration planned for Apollo 14. il Space World H-4-88:28-30 Ap '71
End of Apollo; end of an era. R. S. Lewis. il Bul Atom Sci 27:26-8 Ja '71
From Mercury to Apollo 14. il pors Newsweek 77:62-3 F 1 '71
Future of space program: a lot depends on Apollo 14 trio. il U S News 70:45-6 F 1 '71
Home from the hills of the moon. il Newsweek 77:82-83D F 22 '71
Letter from the space center: gathering moon samples. H. S. F. Cooper, jr. New Yorker 47:120+ Ap 17 '71
Letter from the space center: preparations. H. S. F. Cooper, jr. New Yorker 46:66-74 Ja 9 '71
Lunar terrain may confuse Apollo crews. Aviation W 94:184 Mr 8 '71
Man's return to the moon: second attempt at Fra Mauro Region. E. Driscoll. il Sci N 99:66-7 Ja 23 '71

Man's third lunar landing: more time for science. il Sci N 99:110-12 F 13 '71
Man's triumphant return. il Time 97:11-13 F 15 '71
Old pro goes all the way. il pors Life 70:32-5 F 19 '71
Probing the lunar badlands. il U S News 70:29-30 F 15 '71
Return of Kitty Hawk. il Time 97:44+ F 22 '71
Some optical observations of Apollo 14. il Sky & Tel 41:251-6 Ap '71
Special report: Apollo 14; symposium, with editorial comment. il Aviation W 94:9, 17-25 F 15 '71
Take-off for the moon; photographs. Space World H-5-89:23-9 My '71
Terrain hampers second Apollo 14 EVA. E. J. Bulban. il Aviation W 94:17-20 F 15 '71
To Fra Mauro and beyond. Time 97:46+ F 1 '71
Varied experiments planned for Apollo 14. il Aviation W 94:18-19 Ja 25 '71
What's left to gain from more moon walks. il U S News 70:21-2 F 22 '71
White tracks on the moon; experiments in geology and telepathy. il por Life 70:26-9 F 26 '71

Apollo 15 flight

Apollo 15: a giant step for science. il Time 98:19-20 Ag 16 '71
Apollo 15: boldest space mission yet. il U S News 71:18-20 Ag 2 '71
Apollo 15: drilling into the moon's surface. E. A. Zadig. il Pop Sci 199:58-9 D '71
Apollo 15 landing site. Space World H-2-86:45 F '71
Apollo 15 pictorial. J. A. Ashbrook. Sky & Tel 42:192-201 O '71
Apollo 15: the most daring mission yet. il Bsns W p 18 Jl 24 '71
Apollo 15: three views of the moon. D. R. Scott; J. B. Irwin; A. M. Worden. il Read Digest 99:72-7 N '71
Apollo 15 timeline. il Space World H-8-92:36 Ag '71
Apollo 15 to set length, scientific marks. Z. Strickland. il Aviation W 95:36-43 Jl 5 '71
Apollo 15's discoveries, the real meaning. il U S News 71:39-41 Ag 16 '71
Close-ups of the moon from cameras of Apollo 15. il U S News 71:32-3 Ag 23 '71
Dangerous assault on the Sea of Rains. il Time 98:38-9 Ag 2 '71
From the good earth to the Sea of Rains. il Time 98:10-15 Ag 9 '71
Great leap for the scientists. il Newsweek 78:24-7 Ag 16 '71
Letter from the space center; plans. H. S. F. Cooper, jr. New Yorker 47:40-2+ Jl 17 '71
Lunar reflections. P. L. Buckley. Nat R 23:909-10+ Ag 24 '71
Maturing Apollo program. R. Hotz. Aviation W 95:7 Jl 19 '71
Mission into the moon's past. E. Driscoll. il pors Sci N 100:28-30 Jl 10 '71
Mountains of the moon. il Newsweek 78:46 Jl 26 '71
News from the world of space exploration; electric drill to be used by Apollo 15 crew. il Space World H-6-90:48-9 Je '71
Off to the Apennines. il Sci N 100:74 Jl 31 '71
On the moon with Apollo 15. G. Simmons. il Space World H-10-94:4-37 O '71
Revised engine procedures permit Apollo 15 lunar flight to continue. Aviation W 95:19 Ag 2 '71
Roving through the mountains of the moon. il Life 71:26-9 Ag 20 '71
Search for moon secrets. il U S News 71:17 Ag 9 '71
Some plans for Apollo 15. C. A. Federer. il Sky & Tel 42:80-3 Ag '71
Special report: symposium, with editorial comment. il Aviation W 95:7, 13-23 Ag 9; 14-22+ Ag 16 '71
Weekend drive on the moon. il Newsweek 78:46-8 Ag 9 '71

Apollo 16 flight (proposed)

Apollo 16 site selection. Space World H-11-95:44+ N '71
NASA firms Apollo 16 schedule. il Aviation W 95:16 N 1 '71
NASA reviews Apollo 16 crew workloads. E. J. Bulban. Aviation W 95:21-2 Ag 23 '71

Apollo 17 flight (proposed)

Scientist gets the nod for the final moon flight. il por Sci N 100:137 Ag 28 '71

SPACE flight to the moon—Manned flights—
Continued

Extravehicular activity

Apollo 15: drilling into the moon's surface.
E. A. Zadig. il Pop Sci 199:58-9 D '71
Apollo 15's discoveries, the real meaning. il
U S News 71:39-41 Ag 16 '71
Close-ups of the moon from cameras of
Apollo 15. il U S News 71:32-3 Ag 23 '71
First manned rover on moon. Z. Strickland.
il Aviation W 95:13-17 Ag 9 '71
Great leap for the scientists. il Newsweek
78:24-7 Ag 16 '71
Paydirt at Hadley/Apennine. il Sci N 100:
89-90 Ag 7 '71
Roving through the mountains of the moon;
Apollo 15. il Life 71:26-9 Ag 20 '71
Stunning scenes from a desolate moonscape.
il Time 98:26-7 Ag 23 '71

Safety devices and measures

News from the world of space exploration;
playing it safe on the moon. il Space World
H-8-92:45 Ag '71

Philosophy

Lunar meditations. N. Cousins. Sat R 54:20
Ag 14 '71

Public opinion

Earth from far away, and close up; questions
and answers to student burgesses in Williamsburg, ed. by E. Sparn. il Sr Schol 98:
17 Mr 15 '71

Religious aspects

Spiritual implications of exploring the moon.
R. W. Johnson. Chr Today 16:4-6 Ja 7 '72

Anecdotes, facetiae, satire, etc.

Free-wheeler in space. Chr Cent 88:891 Jl 21
'71

Surveyor flights

Blowing of lunar soil by Apollo 12: Surveyor 3 evidence. L. D. Jaffe. bibliog il
Science 171:798-9 F 26 '71
Solar particle tracks in glass from the Surveyor 3 spacecraft. G. Crozaz and R. M.
Walker. bibliog il Science 171:1237-9 Mr 26
'71

SPACE flight to Venus
Exploration of Venus. il Sky & Tel 41:81-3
F '71
Onward from Venus: unmanned space probe
Venera 7. Time 97:66 F 8 '71
Soviets say Venus 7 transmitted 23 min.
data on planet's surface. il Aviation W
94:22 F 1 '71
SPACE foods. See Space flight—Food prob-
lems
SPACE law
Exploration of the moon: some aspects of
legal regulation. E. G. Vasilevskaia. Space
World H-11-95:27-31 N '71
Moon and international law: problems and
prospects G. Zhukov. Space World H-12-96:
45-6 D '71
SPACE medicine
NASA, press differ on release of Apollo
crew medical data. Aviation W 95:22 Ag
23 '71
SPACE navigation. See Navigation (space
flight)
SPACE perception
Mental rotation of three-dimensional objects.
R. N. Shepard and J. Metzler. il Science
171:701-3 F 19 '71
Space perception in early infancy: perception
within a common auditory-visual space.
E. Aronson and S. Rosenbloom. bibliog il
Science 172:1161-3 Je 11 '71
Stereoscopic depth movement: two eyes less
sensitive than one. C. W. Tyler. bibliog
il Science 174:958-61 N 26 '71
See also
Orientation
SPACE photography
Techniques tomorrow. B. Sherman. Mod
Phot 36:58+ Ja '72
See also
Earth—Photographs from space
Mars (planet)—Photographs from space
Moon—Photographs from space

Apparatus and supplies

Lunar photos reveal new details. W. H. Greg-
ory. il Aviation W 95:66-73 D 20 '71
SPACE platforms. See Space stations
SPACE probes
Mariner Mars 1971 launches. il Space World
H-7-91:11-27 Jl '71
Planetary atmosphere experiments test. il
Space World H-9-93:28-34 S '71
Test of NASA atmospheric probe slated. R.
G. O'Lone. il Aviation W 94:59 Je 14 '71
See also
Space flight to Mars

SPACE propulsion. See Space vehicles—Pro-
pulsion systems
SPACE rescue work
Plan to rescue stranded astronauts; Apollo-
Salyut common docking module. Bsns W
p 112 N 6 '71
Rescue plan devised for Skylab. Aviation W
94:23 Mr 22 '71
SPACE research
Aerospace. See occasional issues of Science
news
Case for space automation. B. Petrov. Space
World H-3-87:36-7 Mr '71
Plasma physics, space research, and the or-
igin of the solar system; Nobel lecture, De-
cember 11, 1970. H. Alfvén. il Science 172:
991-4 Je 4 '71
Space sciences. Sci N 100:212,249, 375, 423;
101:27 S 25, O 9, D 4, 25 '71, Ja 8 '72
See also
International astronautical federation
International council of scientific unions—
Committee on space research

Economic aspects

NEO space: the case for the space program. il
Space World H-12-96:27-30 D '71
Overlooked space program benefits; excerpts
from address. J. F. Clayton. Aviation W
94:11 Mr 15 '71

International aspects

Exchange set on biomedical data. Aviation
W 96:51 Ja 10 '72
German-U.S. barium-ion cloud experiment.
il Space World H-7-91:42-3 Jl '71
International programs. Space World H-3-87:
10-13 Mr '71
Optimism remains on post-Apollo pact despite
unsuccessful parley. Aviation W 94:20 F 22
'71
Space meteorology; cooperation between
NASA and the Russian academy of sciences.
Space World H-7-91:33-5 Jl '71
U S. and Soviets to share data on Mars
missions. Sci N 100:291-2 O 30 '71
U.S. and U.S.S.R. agree to increase coopera-
tion in space activities; joint communique.
Dept State Bul 64:202 F 15 '71
U.S.-Europe space system talks center on
shuttle, tug, station. Aviation W 95:21 N
15 '71
U.S.-Soviet agreement for cooperation
in space exploration. Space World H-7-91:
30-1 Jl '71
U.S. USSR to share Martian data. Aviation
W 95:15 O 25 '71
See also
International satellite geodesy experiment
Space flight—International aspects

Social aspects

Overlooked space program benefits; excerpts
from address. J. F. Clayton. Aviation W
94:11 Mr 15 '71

Europe, Western

Disunity impedes European space effort. D.
E. Fink. il Aviation W 94:46+ Mr 8 '71
See also
European space conference
European space research organization

France

French space technology. il Space World H-
9-93:23-7 S '71
See also
France—National center for space studies

Japan

Realigned national space program adopted
by Japanese. il Aviation W 95:64-6 N 1
'71

Russia

Progress of space exploration and research. A.
Blagonravov. il Space World H-9-93:12-21 S
'71
Reliability of automation versus manned
spaceflight. B. Evseev. Space World H-8-
92:31-3 Ag '71
Russians in space, by E. Riabchikov. Re-
view
Sat R il por 54:41-3+ O 30 '71. W. Shel-
ton
Soviet civil space shakeup seen. Aviation
W 95:14-15 O 11 '71
Soviet space program. E. Driscoll. il Sci N
99:303-5 My 1 '71
Soviets mark 10th anniversary of Yuri Gaga-
rin's spaceflight; symposium. Space World
H-6-90:4-13 Je '71

SPACE research—Russia—*Continued*
Soviets plan further Salyut tests; push unmanned systems. Aviation W 94:20 My 17
'71
Soviets prepare for manned moon landing.
D. C. Winston. il Aviation W 94:43+ Mr 8
'71

United States

After the final Apollo flight, says an astro-
physicist, we should deploy machines, not
men, in space. T. Gold. il N Y Times Mag
p 16-17+ Ag 22 '71; Reply. W. P. O'Neill.
p98 S 26 '71
After the moon missions: exploring earth
from space. il U S News 71:18-19 Ag 9 '71
Can we afford the loss of momentum in the
Nation's aerospace program? A. Bell. Space
World H-9-93:36-7 S '71
Case for the space shuttle: address. C. P.
Anderson. Aviation W 94:9 My 10 '71
Future space objectives. D. J. Fink. Avia-
tion W 94:9 Ja 25 '71
Is another moon trip necessary? interview.
R. A. Petrone. por U S News 71:21-2 Ag
2 '71
On revitalizing space. J. Karth. Space World
H-11-95:32 N '71
Post-Skylab plans focus on earth orbital
missions. Z. Strickland. il Aviation W
95:15-17 O 11 '71
Relevance of space; adaptation of address,
October, 1970. A. Kantrowitz. il Bul Atom
Sci 27:32-3 Ap '71; Discussion. 27:2-3 D '71
Sounder planning required. R. Hotz. Avia-
tion W 95:9 Ag 16 '71
Space program: pro and con; address, J. Clark.
Space World H-12-96:32-5 D '71
What next in space? J. P. Wiley, jr. il Natur
Hist 80:74-5 Ag '71
See also
Space flight to the moon
United States—National aeronautics and
space administration

History

Decision to go to the moon, by J. M. Logsdon. Review
Science 173:317-18 Jl 23 '71. L. V. Blank-
enship
SPACE sciences

Study and teaching

More than a space science center: space
science lab for elementary school complex
in Middletown, R.I. N. D. Field. il To-
days Ed 60:32-3 O '71
SPACE shuttle. See Space vehicles
SPACE stations
After the moon missions: exploring earth
from space. il U S News 71:18-19 Ag 9 '71
Apollo-Salyut, Soyuz-Skylab dockings eyed.
Z. Strickland. Aviation W 95:17-18 S 13
'71
Beyond Apollo: flying labs in space. il U S
News 70:22-4 F 22 '71
Concepts; Grumman study on living in a
space station. New Yorker 47:32-4 F 27 '71
First laboratory in space; Soyuz 11. R. N.
Watts, jr. Sky & Tel 42:83+ Ag '71
Freight car in the sky; Salyut. il Newsweek
77:97 Je 21 '71
Manning the orbital lab; Soyuz 11 cosmo-
nauts. Sci N 99:399 Je 12 '71
Mars 3 explores the sun: automatic inter-
planetary station studying radio-frequency
radiation. Space World H-11-95:48 N '71
Money called key to second Skylab flight. Z.
Strickland. Aviation W 95:19 D 20 '71
Moscow high, Houston low. Time 97:49 Je 28
'71
1977: homes in outer space. B. Kocivar. Mc-
Calls 98:43 Mr '71
Non-race in space; Salyut and Skylab. R. G.
Gillette. Science 172:654-5 My 14 '71
One giant space step for Russia; Salyut I.
il Bsns W p74-5 Ap 24 '71
Orbiting station to provide direct benefits
to earth. Space World H-3-87:20 Mr '71
Raised Salyut orbit may signal new visit. il
Aviation W 95:14-15 Jl 12 '71
Russian success. il Time 97:35 Je 21 '71
Russians operate their first space station.
I. Agnew. Sci Digest 69:41+ Je '71
Salute: man's first manned orbital station.
Space World H-9-93:4-8 S '71
Salyut and Soyuz 10. il Newsweek 77:92 My
3 '71
Salyut boosts self to higher orbit. il Aviation
W 94:14-15 My 3 '71
Salyut for Russia. il Time 97:68 My 3 '71
Salyut marks major space station step. il
Aviation W 94:27-8 Je 14 '71

Salyut may be space station test. Aviation
W 94:22 Ap 26 '71
Salyut reluctantly destroyed; films, tapes,
experiments lost. Aviation W 95:14 O 25 '71
Skylab, the 12-man orbiting space station. il
Space World H-3-87:4-6 Mr '71
Soviet space house: why? il U S News 70:29
Je 21 '71
Soviets push satellite station. Aviation W
94:22 Ap 19 '71
Soyuz 10 link a mystery. Sci N 99:298-9 My 1
'71
Space platforms: why they should be built.
A. A. Blagonravov. Space World H-8-92:
34-5 Ag '71
Space station: key to the future. il Space
World H-2-86:6-44 F '71
Spaced out? Newsweek 77:70+ My 10 '71
Station in space; Russian program. Sci N 99:
278 Ap 24 '71
They live in Skylab. B. Frisch. il Sci Digest
70:9-14 O '71
Troubled Salyut. Time 97:40 My 10 '71
SPACE technology
Bonanza from space. A. S. Freese. il Pop
Mech 136:58-61 Jl '71
European avionics firms focus on space ap-
plications projects. il Aviation W 94:186-9
My 31 '71
Expanding international cooperation in space
activities; address, May 3, 1971. G. Bush.
Dept State Bul 64:709-10 My 31 '71
Extraterrestrial imperative: excerpts from
address, February 1971. K. A. Ehricke. il
Bul Atom Sci 27:18-26 N '71
NEO space: the case for the space program.
il Space World H-12-96:27-30 D '71
New technology for civil uses evolving. il
Aviation W 95:79+ Ag 23 '71
Skylab will have first factory in space. S. V.
Jones. Sci Digest 69:73 F '71
Space station: key to the future. il Space
World H-2-86:6-44 F '71
U.S. reviews progress in sharing benefits of
space technology; statement. July 6. 1971.
A. W. Frutkin. Dept State Bul 65:217-19 Ag
23 '71
SPACE vehicles
Boost for NASA; proceeding with space
shuttle. il Time 99:36-7 Ja 17 '72
Europeans seek guarantees on space tug. E.
H. Kolcum. Aviation W 95:17-18 O 4 '71
Key space shuttle decisions near. Aviation
W 94:45-6 Mr 29 '71
Liftoff to economy: the space shuttle. H. W.
Cannon. il Space World H-11-95:11-15 N '71
Military to drop present boosters for NASA
space shuttle system. K. Johnsen. Aviation
W 94:19 Ap 5 '71
NASA plans concurrent booster, orbiter. Z.
Strickland. il Aviation W 95:12-13 O 25
'71
Orbiter selection due by mid-1972. Aviation
W 94:16 Je 28 '71
Shuttle decision hailed as NASA victory.
Aviation W 96:15-16 Ja 10 '72
Shuttle is weathering the storm. il Sci N 100:
56+ Jl 24 '71
Space science and applications, future pro-
gram. Space World H-4-88:38-40 Ap '71
Space shuttle: a giant step for NASA and
the military? R. Gillette. il Science 171:
991-3 Mr 12 '71
Under way: battle for billions to build U.S.
space shuttle. il U S News 70:69 My 10 '71
Who will win the shuttle port? J. Waugh.
Nation 212:679-80 My 31 '71
Will the space shuttle follow SST? il Bsns W
p36-7 Ap 10 '71
See also
Lunar vehicles
Rockets, Interplanetary
Space probes
Television cameras on space vehicles

Air locks

See Air locks

Atomic power plants

New modular space power system under
study; Isotope-Brayton modular power
system. il Space World H-7-91:36-7 Jl '71

Cabin atmospheres

Modified cryogenic oxygen tanks for Apollo
14. il Space World H-6-90:14-17 Je '71

Control systems

Automatic craft on space routes. B. Sotskov.
Space World H-6-90:8-9 Je '71
Reliability of automation versus manned
spaceflight. B. Evseev. Space World H-8-
92:31-3 Ag '71

SPACE vehicles—*Continued*

Cost
Space shuttle: studies open cost-benefit conflict. R. Gillette. il Science 172:1112 Je 11 '71; Reply. T. A. Heppenheimer. bibliog 174:646+ N 12 '71

Crews
See Astronauts

Design
Changing shuttle concepts studied. W. S. Hieronymus. il Aviation W 94:36-8 Ap 5 '71
NASA weights reports on shuttles. M. L. Yaffee. il Aviation W 94:55-61 Je 7 '71
Program changes boost Grumman shuttle. M. L. Yaffee. il Aviation W 95:36-9 Jl 12 '71
Shuttle orbiter concept, control panel shown. il Aviation W 94:83 My 10 '71
Shuttle performance gain planned. Aviation W 94:16 F 8 '71

Electronic equipment
Earth to spacecraft; integrated command and measuring complexes. A. Alexandrov. Space World H-6-90:6-7 Je '71
Shuttle avionics concepts studied. W. S. Hieronymus. il Aviation W 94:58-9 Je 28 '71

Equipment
Apollo optical bar panoramic camera il Space World H-11-95:16-23 N '71
Bureaucratic odyssey of a space mapping camera; with editorial comment. E. Driscoll. Sci N 100:354, 362-3 N 27 '71
Techniques tomorrow; Lunar Orbiter cameras. B. Sherman. Mod Phot 35:26+ N '71
See also
Life support systems (space environment)

Fires and fire protection
Capsule fire flares up again: a widow's lawsuit and an engineer's story about the Apollo disaster. il pors Life 71:24-9 S 17 '71

Fuel
See Rockets—Fuel

Landing
Landing made with only two parachutes; Apollo 15. il Aviation W 95:43 Ag 16 '71

Landing systems
X-24A lifting body to be reshaped. Space World H-11-95:50 N '71

Mars
Mars Viking systems take shape. Z. Strickland. il Aviation W 96:40-3 Ja 10 '72

Launching
Sound from Apollo rockets in space. D. Cotten and W. L. Donn. bibliog il Science 171:565-7 F 12 '71

Launching pads
ELDO pad attains operational goal. D. E. Fink. il Aviation W 96:48-50 Ja 3 '72
Launch pad damage from Saturn 5 cut. il Aviation W 95:38-9 S 6 '71

Materials
Non-metallics studied for shuttle. W. S. Hieronymus. il Aviation W 94:36-7+ Ja 18 '71
See also
Space vehicles—Shielding (heat)

Orbits
Salyut moved to higher orbit. Aviation W 95:20 S 6 '71

Piloting
See also
Navigation (space flight)
Orbital rendezvous (space flight)

Power supply
See also
Solar batteries
Space vehicles—Atomic power plants

Propulsion systems
British employ Black arrow to launch Prospero satellite. Aviation W 95:25 N 1 '71
Delta refined for bigger payloads. Z. Strickland. il Aviation W 95:12-13 Jl 19 '71
Expendable booster gains favor as NASA studies phased shuttle. Z. Strickland. Aviation W 94:19 Je 21 '71
Failure clouds European launcher future. D. E. Fink. il Aviation W 95:20-1 N 15 '71
Old Saturn V may loft Orbiter. il Bsns W p 130 S 25 '71

P&W shuttle engine based on XLR129. M. L. Yaffee. il Aviation W 94:51-2+ Je 14 '71
Rocketry's ageless wonders; Atlas and Thor. il Space World H-5-89:4-15 My '71
Shuttle engine awarded to Rocketdyne. Aviation W 95:12 Jl 19 '71
Shuttle engine proposals submitted. il Aviation W 94:21 Ap 26 '71
Shuttle engine still on schedule. Aviation W 95:21 S 13 '71
Space shuttle may change course. Bsns W p 17 Jl 3 '71
Space shuttle; phase B engine program completed. il Space World H-6-90:43-4 Je '71
Space vehicle propulsion systems; space shuttle technology conference. il Space World H-6-90:50 Je '71
Three shuttle booster concepts studies. W. S. Hieronymus. il Aviation W 96:46-8 Ja 10 '72
Titan 3L studied as expendable booster. Z. Strickland. il Aviation W 95:40-1 Ag 2 '71
Winged Saturn studied for shuttle. Z. Strickland. Aviation W 95:16-17 S 20 '71
See also
European launcher development organization
Space vehicles—Atomic power plants

Design
$1-billion shuttle engine program seen. W. S. Hieronymus. il Aviation W 94:60-3 Je 21 '71

Failure
Europa 2 loss laid to guidance system. Aviation W 95:19 N 22 '71
Gas leaks cited as Delta problem. Aviation W 96:17 Ja 3 '72
Mars Mariner loss stalls second shot. Aviation W 94:20 My 17 '71
Then there was one; Mars orbiter. il Sci N 99:330-1 My 15 '71

Specifications
U.S. launch vehicles; International launch vehicles; tables (cont) Aviation W 94:67-8 Mr 8 '71

Radio equipment
Changes in design, higher costs expected with new allocations; communications satellite bands. il Aviation W 95:89-92 Ag 23 '71

Safety devices and measures
See also
Space vehicles—Fires and fire protection

Shielding (heat)
Ablative use on shuttle studied. Aviation W 94:82 My 10 '71
High-temperature resistant carbon. il Space World H-10-94:50 O '71
Non-metallics studied for shuttle. W. S. Hieronymus. il Aviation W 94:36-7+ Ja 18 '71

Specifications
Leading U.S. & international spacecraft; tables. Aviation W 94:65-6 Mr 8 '71

Tracking
Mars tracking station. il Space World H-8-92:21-3 Ag '71
Optical tracking of spacecraft. V. J. Slabinski. il Sky & Tel 42:202-4 O '71
Some optical observations of Apollo 14. il Sky & Tel 41:251-6 Ap '71
See also
United States—National aeronautics and space administration—Tracking and data acquisition, Office of

SPACE vehicles, Russian
How the Vostok spaceship was developed. F. Morev. il Space World H-8-92:26-7 Ag '71
Soviet Soyuz erection sequence detailed. il Aviation W 95:14 Jl 19 '71
Soyuz 10 readied for launch; photographs. Aviation W 94:24-6 My 24 '71

SPACEMEN. See Astronauts
SPACESUITS. See Astronauts—Clothing
SPACEWALK. See Space flight—Manned flights —Extravehicular activity
SPACKS, Barry
Rising; To a computer writing verses; poems. Poetry 118:325-6 S '71
Woman; poem. Atlan 228:97 S '71
SPADY, James G.
Ancient Zimbabwe empire. il Negro Hist Bul 34:33-4 F '71
SPAGHETTI. See Macaroni
SPAGHETTI sauce. See Sauces
SPAGNOLI, John J.
What's happening to our salt water marshes? il Cons 25:22-3+ Ap '71

SPAIN, Jayne Baker
Woman could be president; address,
February 25, 1971. Vital Speeches 37:357-9
Ap 1 '71

SPAIN
See also
Automobile racing—Spain
Business consolidations and mergers—Spain
Church and state in Spain
Hunting—Spain
Manises
Montserrat
Music festivals—Spain
Publishers and publishing—Spain
Santiago
Seaside resorts—Spain
Skis and skiing—Spain
Taxation—Spain
Trials—Spain

Army
After Franco, who will reign in Spain? views
of army officer. M. Acoca. il Newsweek 77:
42-4 Ja 25 '71

Description and travel
Spanish sunaways: fresh places to go; inter-
view. J. de Ribes. il pors Vogue 157:136-47+
Ap 15 '71

Foreign relations
United States
See United States—Foreign relations—
Spain

History
Arab period, 711-1492
Christian-Islamic confrontation in the west:
the thirteenth-century dream of conversion.
R. I. Burns. bibliog f il Am Hist R 76:
1386-434 D '71

Ferdinand and Isabella,
1479-1516
That August third; Columbus departs Spain
in 1492. G. de Zéndegui. il Américas 23:S3-6
O '71

Civil war, 1936-1939—Memorials
See War memorials

Intellectual life
Ortega y Gasset: the partly faithful professor; excerpt from Man and his circumstances: Ortega as educator. R. McClintock. bibliog Sch & Soc 99:304-15 Sum '71

Politics and government
After Franco, who will reign in Spain? views
of army officer and a union man. M. Acoca.
il Newsweek 77:42-4 Ja 25 '71
Behind the visit of Spain's future king. il
por U S News 70:86 F 8 '71
Beyond Franco. il Time 98:38+ O 11 '71
In the twilight of the Franco era. S. G.
Payne. For Affairs 49:342-54 Ja '71
Spain: still totalitarian. T. Beeson. Chr Cent
88:183 F 10 '71

Religious institutions and affairs
Spanish radio: The friendly voice. D. Foster.
Chr Today 16:45 Ja 7 '72
Texan's crusade. il Time 98:92 N 8 '71
Worldaround. Chr Cent 88:290, 759, 1452 Mr 3,
Je 16, D 8 '71
See also
Evangelistic work—Spain

SPALDING, Alice Cooke, house. See Honolulu
academy of arts

SPANIELS
Brittany owner speaks up. D. M. Duffey. il
Outdoor Life 148:92-4+ D '71

SPANISH American art. See Art, Latin American

SPANISH AMERICAN fiction. See Latin American fiction

SPANISH AMERICANS in the United States.
See Latin Americans in the United States

SPANISH cookery. See Cookery, Spanish

SPANISH dancing. See Dancing, Spanish

SPANISH explorers. See Explorers, Spanish

SPANISH Grand prix. See Automobile racing—
Spain

SPANISH house; story. See Rogin, G.

SPANISH Jews. See Sephardim

SPANISH language

Textbooks
Spanish I goes relevant; text entitled Modern
Spanish. L. Polon and D. Bland. Nat R
23:185 F 23 '71

SPANISH missions in California. See California—Missions

SPANISH moss
Did you know that. .? Sci Digest 69:85 Je '71

SPANISH philosophy. See Philosophy, Spanish

SPANISH poetry
See also
Gallegan poetry

Translations into English
Israel 1969, tr. by N. T. Di Giovanni. J. L.
Borges. Nation 213:346 O 11 '71
Southside; Rose; tr. by N. T. Di Giovanni.
J. L. Borges. New Yorker 47:40 My 15 '71
To smile with the joyful sadness of the olive
tree; tr. by T. Baland. M. Hernandez. New
Repub 165:23 N 27 '71

SPANISH pottery. See Pottery, Spanish

SPANISH speaking students
Aqui estoy . . . here I am; storefront English
language center for Spanish speakers. A.
Gaber. il por Am Ed 7:18-22 Ja '71
See also
Mexican American students

SPANISH tragedy; drama. Kyd, T.

SPANISH wines. See Wine

SPARANO, Vin T.
(ed) Where to go. See issues of Outdoor
life

SPARE time. See Leisure

SPARERIBS. See Cookery—Meat

SPARGUR, Ronn
Passion of the women; poem. Chr Cent 88:
429-30 Ap 7 '71

SPARK plugs
Choosing the right plugs. W. Heyman. il
Motor B & S 127:97+ Ap '71
50 easy horses. J. Dianna. il Hot Rod 24:120-1
Ap '71
How to change points. il Motor T 23:82 O
'71
How to change spark plugs. il Motor T 23:71
Jl '71
Right plug for your snowmobile. M. Schultz.
il Pop Mech 136:106-8 D '71

SPARKLING wines. See Wine

SPARKS, Kathlene
Saucepan dreams; poem. Seventeen 30:180
Ap '71

SPARKS, Kenneth R.
Selling Uncle Sam in the seventies. bibliog f
Ann Am Acad 398:113-23 N '71

SPARKS, Richard K.
Are we ready for national certification of
professional educators? Ed Digest 36:16-18
Ja '71

SPARKS, Will
What do special assistants specialize in? Atlan 227:64-6+ F '71

SPARROWS
Elusive seringo. D. Zochert. il Natur Hist
80:8-10 D '71
Photoperiodically significant photoreception in
sparrows: is the retina involved? H. Underwood and M. Menaker; discussion. Science 169:892-3; 172:293 Ag 28 '70, Ap 16 '71
Pineal function in sparrows: circadian
rhythms and body temperature. S. Binkley
and others. bibliog il Science 174:311-14 O
15 '71
Temporal synergism of corticosterone and
prolactin controlling gonadal growth in
sparrows. A. H. Meier and others. bibliog
il Science 173:1249-2 S 24 '71

SPARS. See Masts and rigging

SPARTANS industries, inc. See Arlen realty
and development corporation

SPAS. See Health resorts, watering places, etc.

SPATER, George A.
What is needed to get the airlines out of
trouble; interview. il por U S News 71:
62-7 Ag 9 '71

SPATIAL conceptualization. See Space perception

SPATTER ware. See Pottery

SPEAKERS. See Loud speaking apparatus

SPEAKERS, Guest. See Public speaking

SPEAKING. See Lectures and lecturing; Public speaking

SPEAKING in tongues. See Gift of tongues

SPEAR, Patricia G. See Roizman, B. jt. auth.

SPEAR, Richard E.
Pseudo-Caravaggisti. il Art N 70:38-41+
N '71

SPEAR fishing
Game for gourmets; stalking lobsters. J.
Samson. il Field & S 75:69-70+ F '71
Hunting beneath the reef. A. W. Prince. il
Field & S 75:68-9+ F '71

SPEAR lilies
To-be-looked-at sedum and Australia's super lily. il Sunset 146:262-3 My '71

SPECIAL action office for drug abuse prevention. See United States—Drug abuse prevention, Special action office for (proposed)

SPECIAL classes and special schools
Drugs: a new way out? experiment at Savannah, Georgia high school. E. Clift. McCalls 99:46 O '71
Help for girls in trouble; special high schools in New York city. B. Shanas. Parents Mag 46:42-3+ Je '71
Lowering the dropout rate; transition classes. M. Schuster. Clear House 45:329-32 F '71
Scenes from a special classroom. J. Kaplan. Commentary 51:69-76 My '71
School that love built; human resources school. J. Reddy. por Read Digest 99:149-50+ S '71
    See also
Blind—Education
Slow learning children—Education

SPECIAL committee on problems of the environment. See International council of scientific unions—Special committee on problems of the environment

SPECIAL committee to investigate economic and financial concentration (proposed) See United States—Congress—Senate—Special committee to investigate economic and financial concentration (proposed)

SPECIAL committees of the United Nations. See name of the committee as subhead under United Nations, e.g. United Nations—Special committee on peacekeeping operations

SPECIAL day; story. See Ledecky, B.

SPECIAL days, weeks and months
Come out & play; with letter by Patricia Nixon. il Ladies Home J 88:8, 48+ Jl '71
Voluntary overseas aid week and human development month; proclamation. R. Nixon. Dept State Bul 64:754 Je 7 '71
World law day, 1971, proclamation. R. M. Nixon. Dept State Bul 65:110 Jl 26 '71
    See also names of special days, weeks, and months, e.g. Senior citizens month

SPECIAL drawing rights
Dollars or SDR? H. C. Wallich. Newsweek 78:81 O 11 '71

SPECIAL libraries. See Libraries, Special

SPECIAL libraries association
Fragmented personalities: the lessons of SLA; annual conference. A. Plotnik. il Wilson Lib Bul 46:30-4 S '71
SLA-ASIS merger friction aired by New Jersey SLA. Library J 96:1184 Ap 1 '71
SLA in SF: merger, no! Cooperation, yes! S. Havens. il Library J 96:2464-6 Ag '71

SPECIAL litigation section of the Department of Justice. See United States—Justice, Department of—Internal security division

SPECIAL services, Army. See United States—Army—Special services

SPECIAL virus cancer program. See United States—National cancer institute

SPECIALISTS, Stock. See Securities—Marketing

SPECIALTY equipment manufacturers association
SEMA scene. See issues of Hot rod

SPECIALTY stores
Boutique mystique: second National boutique show. New Yorker 46:25-7 F 6 '71
Making life easier for lefties. J. F. Pearson. il Pop Mech 135:66-7 Je '71
On and off the avenue; Narcissa, designer boutique. K. Fraser. New Yorker 47:122+ N 20 '71
Pants, slacks, jeans, bells, cords for everyone; Sid's pants chain. Fortune 83:73 F '71
    See also
Lane Bryant, inc

SPECIATION. See Species

SPECIES
Continental drift and the diversity of species. L. Purrett. il Sci N 100:394-5 D 11 '71
Immortality; excerpt from Mosquito safari. C. B. Worth. il Audubon 73:28-31 Jl '71
Pleistocene changes in the fauna and flora of South America. R. S. Vuilleumier. bibliog il Science 173:771-80 Ag 27 '71
Tropics weren't so stable after all. L. Purrett. il Sci N 100:177 S 11 '71
    See also
Natural selection

SPECIFIC gravity
    See also
Gravity

SPECIFIC heat
Determining specific heats by ice calorimetry. H. W. Edwards and L. G. Brouwer. bibliog il pors Chem 44:23-4 Ap '71

SPECIFICATIONS
    See also subhead Specifications under various subjects, e.g. Automobiles—Specifications

SPECTACLES. See Eyeglasses

SPECTOR, N. Herbert
Alcohol breath tests: gross errors in current methods of measuring alveolar gas concentrations. bibliog il Science 172:57-9; 174:772+ Ap 2, N 19 '71

SPECTOR, Robert M.
Changed role of the modern university president. bibliog Sch & Soc 99:276-9 Sum '71; Same abr. Ed Digest 37:46-9 O '71

SPECTOR, Sydney, and Flynn, E. J.
Barbiturates: radioimmunoassay. bibliog il Science 174:1036-8 D 3 '71

—and Vesell, E. S.
Disposition of morphine in man. bibliog il Science 174:421-2 O 22 '71

SPECTROHELIOSCOPE
Compact prizewinning spectrohelioscope. C. Horne. il Sky & Tel 42:238-40 O '71

SPECTROMETERS
Hyperfine Zeeman effect atomic absorption spectrometer for mercury. T. Hadeishi and R. D. McLaughlin. bibliog il Science 174:404-7 O 22 '71
New eye on the air; correlation spectrometer. A. Coble and others. bibliog il por Environ 13:34-41 My '71
    See also
Mass spectrometry

SPECTROPHOTOMETRY
Spectrophotometric determinations of pKa's for substituted 2-nitrophenols. R. J. Palma and E. H. Sund. bibliog il pors Chem 44:26-8 My '71

SPECTROSCOPY. See Spectrum analysis

SPECTRUM
    See also
Stars—Spectra

Reflection spectra
Alteration of lunar optical properties: age and composition effects. J. B. Adams and T. B. McCord. bibliog il Science 171:567-71 F 12 '71

SPECTRUM, Infrared
Polywater and sweat: similarities between the infrared spectra. D. L. Rousseau. bibliog il Science 171:170-2 Ja 15 '71

SPECTRUM, Ultraviolet
    See also
Photography, Ultraviolet

SPECTRUM analysis
By the sweat of their brow; polywater poohpoohed. il Sci N 99:62-3 Ja 23 '71
How we're reading nature's secrets from the sky; multispectral analysis. J. R. Berry. il Pop Mech 136:68-72 S '71
Nitric oxide air pollution: detection by optoacoustic spectroscopy. L. B. Kreuzer and C. K. N. Patel. bibliog il Science 173:45-7 Jl 2 '71
Nobel prize for chemistry; Herzberg and molecular spectroscopy. A. E. Douglas. por Science 174:672-3 N 12 '71
Optical system analyzes engines. B. M. Elson. il Aviation W 94:48-9+ Mr 1 '71
Photofragment spectroscopy looks at excited states. M. S. Rothenberg. bibliog il Phys Today 24:19-20 Ap '71
Polywater: evidence from electron spectroscopy for chemical analysis (ESCA) of a complex salt mixture. R. E. Davis and others. bibliog il Science 171:167-70 Ja 15 '71
Studying electron behavior; photoelectron spectroscopy. Sci N 100:187 S 18 '71
    See also
Astronomical spectroscopy
Mass spectrometry
Nuclear magnetic resonance
Raman effect

SPECULATION
    See also
Arbitrage
Commodity exchanges
Investments
Real estate investment

SPEECE, Donna
Composition; poem. Seventeen 30:81 Ja '71

SPEECH
Language production: electroencephalographic localization in the normal human brain. D. W. McAdam and H. A. Whitaker. bibliog il Science 172:499-502 Ap 30 '71; Reply with rejoinder. L. K. Morrell and D. A. Huntington. 174:1359-61 D 24 '71
    See also
Children—Language
Compressed speech
Silence

Study and teaching
See Speech education

SPEECH, Freedom of. See Free speech
SPEECH, Parts of. See Parts of speech
SPEECH correction. See Speech therapy
SPEECH education
 We're failing to teach effective talking. T.
  F. Nelson. Todays Ed 60:43 O '71
  See also
 Children—Language
SPEECH of animals. See Animal communication
SPEECH perception. See Sound perception
SPEECH therapy
 Say it right and they will too; David Push-
  aw's developmental language and speech
  center, Grand Rapids, Mich. M. Lloyd. il
  Am Ed 7:5-7 Ja '71
 Say rabbit, not wabbit. il Newsweek 77:98
  Mr 22 '71
SPEECHES, addresses, etc.
  See also
 Baccalaureate addresses
SPEED (drugs) See Amphetamines
SPEED boats. See Motor boats
SPEED indicators
  See also
 Computers—Traffic control use
 Logs (nautical instruments)
 Speedometers
 Tachometers
SPEED of birds. See Birds—Flight
SPEED records, Automobile. See Automobile
  speed records
SPEEDOMETERS
 How to troubleshoot your speedometer. M.
  Schultz. il Pop Mech 135:136-9 Mr '71
SPEEDWAYS
 Captain Marvel presents Captain Nice; Po-
  cono raceway. B. Yates. il por Sports Illus
  35:18-19 Jl 12 '71
 U.S. Grand prix. K. Ludvigsen. il Motor T
  23:46-9 D '71
    Equipment
 Computerized scoring and timing system for
  auto racing; Ontario motor speedway sys-
  tem. P. Harms. il Electr World 86:32-3
  N '71
 Pro-start system. J. Dianna. il Hot Rod 24:
  66 F '71
SPEEDY trial
 By the sea of confusion; problems over new
  deadlines. Time 98:80 N 8 '71
SPEER, Albert
 Books. G. Steiner. New Yorker 47:70-5 Jl
  24 '71 *
 How to succeed though innocent. V. H.
  Bernstein. Nation 212:376-8 Mr 22 '71 *
 In Hitler's service. L. S. Dawidowicz; discus-
  sion. Commentary 51:32+ Mr '71 *
SPELLING
 No more frater trafic; end of simplified spell-
  ing in Chicago tribune. Time 97:47 Ja 25 '71
SPENCER, Elizabeth
 Finder; story. New Yorker 46:30-9 Ja 23 '71
 Storytelling, old and new. Writer 85:9-10+
  Ja '72
SPENCER, John R.
 University museum: accidental past, pur-
  poseful future? il Art in Am 59:84-90 Jl '71
SPENCER, Jonathan
 It's the perfect days that get you. Flying 88:
  93 Je '71
SPENCER, Michael Jon
 Applause, applause. McCalls 98:46 Ag '71 *
SPENCER, Scott
 News; story. Redbook 137:82-3 My '71
SPENCER, Steven M.
 Are we overfed but undernourished? Read
  Digest 99:135-9 S '71
 New strides in the battle against birth de-
  fects. Read Digest 98:159-60+ My '71
SPENCER, Terence
 Gallery; photograph. Life 71:2-3 Ag 27 '71
 Tourists find the forgotten islands; photo-
  graphs. Life 71:44-51 O 29 '71
SPENCER-BOOTH, Yvette. See Hinde, R. A.
  jt. auth.
SPENCER rifle. See Rifles
SPENDER, Stephen
 Q: do the claims of conscience outweigh the
  duties of citizenship? por Esquire 76:158+
  D '71
SPENDING. See Consumption (economics)
SPERBER, Ann
 Ariadne auf Naxos. il Am Rec G 37:350-2 F
  '71
 Recordings: the oral tradition revived. il
  por Library J 96:3813-15 N 15 '71

SPERLING, George, and others
 Extremely rapid visual search: the maximum
  rate of scanning letters for the presence
  of a numeral. bibliog il Science 174:307-11
  O 15 '71
SPERLING, Godfrey, 1915-
 Breakfast with Budge. Newsweek 78:64-5 Jl
  26 '71 *
SPERLING, H. G. and Harwerth, R. S.
 Red-green cone interactions in the increment-
  threshold spectral sensitivity of primates.
  bibliog il Science 172:180-4 Ap 9 '71
 —See Harwerth, R. S. jt. auth.
SPERM banks. See Semen
SPERMATOZOA
  See also
 Semen
SPERRY and Hutchinson company
 Bucking the trend; S&H green stamps. il
  Forbes 107:18-19 F 1 '71
 Sticky time at Sperry & Hutchinson. il Bsns
  W p 102+ Mr 20 '71
SPERRY Rand corporation
    Univac division
 Coming of age at Univac. por Bsns W p
  116+ S 11 '71
 Tougher Univac? A. A. Butkus. por Duns
  97:58 F '71
 Univac picks up where RCA left off. Bsns W
  p25 N 27 '71
SPHERES, isolation. See Isolation chambers
SPHINX moths. See Moths
SPICE cabinets. See Kitchen cabinets
SPICE racks
 Nostalgia comes to the kitchen: jars and
  bottles with an old-time flavor. il House B
  113:54 N '71
SPICER, Edward H.
 Persistent cultural systems. bibliog Science
  174:795-800 N 19 '71
SPICES
 Botany of a fruitcake. M. A. Gamble. il Hor-
  ticulture 49:50-4 Mr '71
SPICKER, Howard H.
 Intellectual development in early childhood
  education. Ed Digest 37:35-8 O '71
SPIDER venom. See Venom
SPIDERS
 Hop skip, jump and a pounce. M. Byrne. il
  Nat Wildlife 9:40-1 Je '71
 Spying on spiders. il Chem 44:18 O '71
 Test your knowledge of spiders. J. Daugherty
  and M. Daugherty. il Sci Digest 69:74-5+
  F '71
 What's so special about spiders? P. A. Zahl.
  il Nat Geog 140:190-219 Ag '71
SPIEGEL, Marshall
 News on wheels (cont) il Sr Schol 97:26+ Ja
  18; 98:30-2 Ap 26; 33+ My 17; 99:40 S
  27; 26-7+ O 25 '71
 Old man of the brickyard tries again and
  again and again. il por Mech Illus 67:57-
  9+ My '71
 Pros & cons on joining the police. il Mech
  Illus 67:41-3+ Jl '71
SPIEGELMAN, S. See Schlom, J. jt. auth.
SPIEKER, Edmund M.
 Schöpf, Maclure, Werner, and the earliest
  work on American geology. bibliog Science
  172:1333-4 Je 25 '71
SPIER, Peter
 . . . And God saw that it was good. il Nat
  Wildlife 10:26-7 D '71
SPIERS, Al
 How to get hooked on tarpon. il Field & S
  75:54-5+ Mr '71
SPIERS, Ronald Ian
 U.S. national security policy and the In-
  dian Ocean area; statement, July 28, 1971.
  Dept State Bul 65:199-203 Ag 23 '71
SPIES
 Beyond Britain: what red spies are doing all
  over world. il U S News 71:25-6 O 11 '71
 Britain boots out 105 Soviets as spies. Sr
  Schol 99:15 O 25 '71
 Not-so-classy exit; departure of Russians
  named as spies, from Great Britain. il
  Time 98:45 O 18 '71
 Spies by the thousands: report from Ger-
  many. F. Ungeheuer. Harper 242:26-9 Je
  '71
 Spies who are out in the cold; British ex-
  pulsion of Soviet officials. il Time 98:49-50
  O 4 '71
 To Russia without love; mass ouster of spies
  from Britain. il Newsweek 78:43 O 4 '71
  See also
 Agents provocateurs
 Cohen, E.
 Espionage
 Secret service
 World war, 1939-1945—Secret service

SPIES—*Continued*

Anecdotes, facetiae, satire, etc.

Dossier on Leonardo Michelangelo. J. Beatty, jr. Esquire 75:184+ Je '71

SPILHAUS, Athelstan F.
AAAS meeting in Mexico City. Science 174:549 N 5 '71

SPINACH
Alternative to regular spinach; New Zealand spinach. il Sunset 146:248 Ap '71

SPINAL column. See Spine

SPINAL cord
Histochemical and functional correlations in anterior horn neurons of the cat spinal cord. J. F. Campa and W. K. Engel. bibliog il Science 171:198-9 Ja 15 '71

SPINAL fluid. See Cerebrospinal fluid

SPINALE, Angela
In my opinion. por Seventeen 30:346 Ag '71

SPINE
I am Joe's spine. J. D. Ratcliff. il Read Digest 98:87-90 Mr '71

Diseases

Lethal legacy; spinal cerebellar degeneration, a hereditary nerve disease. il Time 97:56+ Ja 25 '71

SPINNAKERS. See Sails

SPINNERS. See Fishing lures, flies, etc.

SPINNING
Hand spinning for the 'seventies. A. Fannin. il por Craft Horiz 31:20-5+ F '71

SPINNING wheels
Wheels are spinning; shop at Wind Lake, Wis. il pors Design 73:16-17 Fall '71

SPINOFF (technology) See Technology transfer

SPINOZA, Baruch. See Spinoza, Benedictus de

SPINOZA, Benedictus de
Freedom of the mind and other essays. by S. Hampshire. Review
New Repub 165:24-5+ O 23 '71. P. Caws *

SPINRAD, Bernard I.
America's energy crisis: reality or hysteria? por Bul Atom Sci 27:3-6 S '71
Implications of SALT. Bul Atom Sci 27:22-5 Ja '71

SPINRAD, Hyron
Worlds beyond the dust. il Newsweek 77:89 Ja 25 '71 *

SPINRAD, William
Fighting back. Nation 212:802 Je 28 '71

SPINSTERS. See Single women

SPIRIT
Healing Christ. L. N. Bell. Chr Today 16:34+ D 3 '71
Spirit: who will make the choices of life and death? il Time 97:48+ Ap 19 '71

SPIRIT, Holy. See Holy Spirit

SPIRIT communication. See Spiritualism

SPIRIT writings. See Spiritualism

SPIRITUAL life
Difference, yes; dichotomy, no. V. P. McCorry. America 125:inside back cover Jl 10 '71
Double and Romans 7. B. Ramm. Chr Today 15:14+ Ap 9 '71

SPIRITUAL retreats. See Retreats, Spiritual

SPIRITUALISM
Report from heaven. il por Newsweek 79:52 Ja 3 '72
Spirited sites; Camp Chesterfield, Ind. B. Thomas. il Travel 136:40-3 O '71
Supernatural symphonies; excerpt from Unfinished symphonies. R. Brown. il por Ladies Home J 88:92+ S '71
See also
Mediums

SPIRITUALITY
How are your eyes? L. N. Bell. Chr Today 15:20-1 Mr 26 '71

SPIRO, Howard Marget
Have a happy ulcer. A. J. Snider. il Sci Digest 69:57 Mr '71 *

SPIROMETERS
Yawn box for post-op; incentive spirometer. A. J. Snider. Sci Digest 69:57-8 F '71

SPITZ, Armand N.
Armand N. Spitz, planetarium inventor. C. A. Federer. il pors Sky & Tel 41:354-5 Je '71 *
Obituary
Weatherwise por 24:99+ Je '71

SPITZ, Mark
Still a big fish in a big (Olympic-size) pond. W. F. Reed. il por Sports Illus 35:46-7+ S 6 '71 *

SPITZER, Elroy F.
Solid waste demonstration programs. il Am City 86:58-60+ Jl '71

SPITZER, Helen. See Spitzer, S. jt. auth.

SPITZER, Hugh
Two who rejected the business world; interview. il pors Fortune 83:102-3 Mr '71

SPITZER, Paul
Last hope for the ospreys of Long Island Sound. D. R. Zimmerman. il por N Y Times Mag p38-40+ D 12 '71 *

SPITZER, Silas
Champagne & caviar. il Holiday 49:72-3+ D '70
—and Spitzer, Helen
Europe's finest restaurants 1971. Holiday 49:96-102 F '71
Holiday's choice of North American restaurants. Holiday 49:17-20+ Jl '71

SPIVACK, George. See Turner, C. O. jt. auth.

SPIVACK, Kathleen
Blurring; poem. Atlan 229:80 Ja '72
Lobotomy; poem. Atlan 227:62 Je '71
Rain; poem. Poetry 117:361-2 Mr '71

SPIVVLETON mystery; story. See Porter, K. A.

SPLICES. See Knots and splices

SPOCK, Benjamin
Don't blame me! Look 35:37-8 Ja 26 '71; Same abr. with title Doctor Spock speaks out. Cur 127:19-23 Mr '71
How to be popular. Seventeen 29:156-7 S '70
[Monthly column] See issues of Redbook
Parent and child. por N Y Times Mag p98+ S 12 '71

about

Dr Spock for president. W. Murchison, jr. Nat R 23:1470 D 31 '71 *

SPOCK, Michael
Lifestyle. il por Am Home 74:12 My '71 *

SPODE, Josiah, 1733-1797
Spode, by L. Whiter. Review
Antiques 99:366 Mr '71. E. Collard *

SPODE, Josiah, 1754-1827
Spode, by L. Whiter. Review
Antiques 99:366 Mr '71. E. Collard *

SPODE pottery. See Pottery, English

SPODEK, Bernard
Sources of early-childhood curriculum. Ed Digest 36:49-52 Ja '71

SPOFFORD, Walter R. and Chase, Greenleaf
Golden eagle rediscovered. il Cons 26:6-8 Ag '71

SPOHR, Arnold
Idea; Arnold Spohr and the Royal Winnipeg ballet. O. Maynard. il por Dance Mag 45:38-45 Ap '71 *

SPOILING of children. See Children—Management and training

SPOILS system. See Patronage, Political

SPOKANE, Wash.

Water supply

You have to make reservoirs look good. R. E. Saty. il Am City 86:58-9 Ag '71

SPOKEN English. See English language—Pronunciation

SPOKEN phonograph records. See Phonograph records—Spoken records

SPOLETINI, Pasquale M.
Roman question and Italian politics. il America 124:336-40 Ap 3 '71

SPOLETO festival. See Festivals—Italy

SPONGE cake. See Cake

SPONGES
Recent brachiopod-coralline sponge communities and their paleoecological significance. J. B. C. Jackson and others. bibliog il Science 173:623-5 Ag 13 '71

SPONSORS, Advertising. See Television advertising

SPONTANEOUS abortion. See Abortion

SPONTANEOUS generation
Probability distribution of enantiomorphous forms in spontaneous generation of optically active substances. R. E. Pincock and others. bibliog il Science 174:1018-20 D 3 '71

SPOONS
Antique silver spoon; caddy spoon. L. F. Reals. il Hobbies 76:128 Je '71

SPORES (botany)
Identification of the germination self-inhibitor from wheat stem rust uredospores. V. Macko and others. bibliog Science 173:835-6 Ag 27 '71

SPORES (botany), Fossil
Early Silurian spore tetrads from New York; earliest New World evidence for vascular plants? J. Gray and A. J. Boucot. bibliog il Science 173:918-21 S 3 '71

SPOROZOITES
Sporozoite-induced infections of plasmodium berghei administered by the oral route. M. Yoeli and H. Most. bibliog il Science 173:1031-2 S 10 '71

SPORT fisheries and wildlife, Bureau of. See
   United States—Fish and wildlife service
SPORT fishing boats. See Fishing boats
SPORT knives. See Bowie knives
SPORT trophies. See Trophies, Sport
SPORTFISHERMEN. See Fishermen
SPORTING goods
   What's new. See issues of Outdoor life
      See also
   Hunting outfits
SPORTING goods industry
      See also
   Herter's, inc.
SPORTS
   How healthy is your sport? G. M. Knox.
      Bet Hom & Gard 49:10+ My '71
   1972 world travel calendar: comp. by F.
      Shemanski. Sat R 55:43-7 Ja 1 '72
   Outdoors with Wynn Davis. W. Davis. See
      issues of Mechanix illustrated
   Sports world; 1971. il Life 71:50-1 D 31 '71
      See also
   Amateurism (sports)
   Aquatic sports
   Athletes
   Canoe trips
   College athletics
   Doping in sports
   Industrial recreation
   Mountaineering
   Pan American games
   Photography of sports
   Radio broadcasting—Sports
   Recreation
   School athletics
   Segregation in sports
   Sports for children
   Sportsmanship
   Television broadcasting—Sports
   Tournaments
      also names of sports, e.g. Track athletics

Accidents and injuries
Healthy body? C. Mangel. il Look 35:61-2 Je
   1 '71
      See also
   Football—Accidents and injuries
   Hockey—Accidents and injuries
   Skis and skiing—Accidents and injuries
   Snowmobiles and snowmobiling—Accidents
      and injuries

Anecdotes, facetiae, satire, etc.
One last impossible shot at fame. H. Groen-
   ing. il Sports Illus 35:56-8+ D 6 '71
Time for all good men . . . help defend
   American sports clichés. F. Deford. Sports
   Illus 35:54+ N 22 '71

Bibliography
Babe Ruth still in his heaven. J. Yardley.
   New Repub 165:21-3 D 18 '71

Caricatures and cartoons
Disappearing, inch by inch. il por Time 97:
   46 Ja 25 '71
Sporting scene. J. Markow. Writers Digest
   51:16-17+ D '71

Economic aspects
Pro sports: a business boom in trouble. il
   U S News 71:56-8 Jl 5 '71
Winning is a many splendored thing. il Na-
   tions Bsns 59:70-2 D '71

Ethical aspects
Mud flies all over the track: R. Wilson,
   owner of a thoroughbred racing stable and
   pro football's Buffalo Bills. R. H. Boyle.
   il por Sports Illus 35:30-1 N 1 '71

Laws and regulations
Woolf at the door. il por Time 98:69 N 29 '71

Medical aspects
See Sports medicine

Periodicals
      See also
   Sports illustrated (periodical)

Photographs
Oh, Jonah he lived on a whale. UNESCO
   Courier 24:18-19 Ja '71
Sport is a double exposure. M. Kauffman.
   Sports Illus 35:98-107 D 20 '71

Statistics
They do it by the numbers; NFL statistic-
   ians. J. Marshall. Sports Illus 35:100+ N
   29 '71

Afghanistan
Grab the goat and ride. Omar! sport known
   as buzkashi. R. H. Boyle. il Sports Illus
   34:58-61 My 17 '71

England
   See also
Cricket (game)
Soccer

France
Gymnastics and sports in fin-de-siècle France:
   opium of the classes? E. Weber. bibliog f
   il Am Hist R 76:70-98 F '71

Ireland
Consorting with the enemy; Gaelic athletic
   association rules. C. B. Peters. Sports Illus
   34:88+ Ap 12 '71

Japan
   See also
Baseball clubs—Japan

Mexico
Doctor tries a transplant; importing fron-
   tenis from Mexico. T. Thompson. il por
   Sports Illus 34:34-6 My 17 '71

Russia
   See also
Soccer

Spain
   See also
Bullfights

United States
Antitrusters take on professional sports. il
   Bsns W p60-1+ O 9 '71
For the record. See issues of Sports illus-
   trated
Jeremiah of Jock liberation. il por Time 97:
   88-9+ My 24 '71
Sports. H. L. Masin. See issues of Senior
   scholastic
      See also
Recreation—United States
Segregation in sports
SPORTS announcers. See Radio broadcasting
   —Sports; Television broadcasting—Sports
SPORTS car racing. See Automobile racing
SPORTS cars
   Brazilian Corvette; Puma GTE 1600. K. Lud-
      vigsen. il Motor T 23:54-6+ My '71
   Ford's new mid-engine sports car. G. Wilk-
      ins. il Mech Illus 67:48-9 Jl '71
   In retrospect:
      1957 fuel—injected Corvette W. Wyss.
         il Motor T 23:58-61 D '71
   Jaguar XKE V12 vs. Corvette LT-1V8. E.
      Dahlquist. il Motor T 23:36-8 Ap '71
   Motor trend investigative report: the great
      Corvette controversy. il Motor T 23:26-31
      D '71
   New visas for Europe's kings of the road.
      Bsns W p97 Ap 10 '71
   Sports cars for the man who has everything;
      Mercedes-Benz 350SL and Jaguar V12.
      J. P Norbye. il Pop Sci 199:52-4 Ag '71
   3 positions of Lotus: Europa, Elan S4 and
      Elan +2. J. Christy. il Motor T 23:30-5+
      Ag '71

Testing
Z; Datsun 240Z. C. Koch. il Motor T 23:
   64-6+ Mr '71
SPORTS clothes. See Clothing and dress—
   Sports clothes
SPORTS clubs
   Consorting with the enemy; Gaelic athletic
      association rules. C. B. Peters. Sports Illus
      34:88+ Ap 12 '71
   Metal buildings for sport: Wightman tennis
      center, Weston, Mass. il Arch Forum 135:
      50-1 Jl '71
   Unusual archery club; APG bowmen. G. H.
      Gillelan. il Outdoor Life 147:36+ Mr '71
SPORTS fans
   Hockey fanatics; fans of the New York
      Rangers. J. Greenfield. Harper 244:16-18+
      Ja '72
   Other side of paradise; Augusta national golf
      club. B. Gilbert. Sports Illus 34:40-8+ Ap 5
      '71
   Playground divided; difficulty supporting pro-
      fessional sports. R. W. Johnston. il por
      Sports Illus 35:78-81+ N 8 '71
      See also
   Football fans
SPORTS films. See Moving pictures—Sports
   films
SPORTS for children
   At age 9, they're bowl game veterans; Junior
      pee wee league. il Life 71:101-2 D 17 '71
   How good are organized sports for your
      child? symposium. il Look 35:61-2+ Je 1
      '71
   New awakening in Orr land; little league
      mania. M. Maddocks. il Sports Illus 35:32-7
      O 11 '71
   Rod Laver holds court. R. Laver. il pors
      Ladies Home J 88:88+ S '71

SQUASHES
Here's the surprise plant of the squash family; spaghetti squash. il Sunset 146:274-5 My '71
Waltham butternut squash. P. F. Frese. Horticulture 49:55 F '71

SQUAW VALLEY
For sale: one hunk of American history; location of 1960 Winter Olympics. R. Rapoport. il Sports Illus 34:72+ My 3 '71

SQUIDS
See also
Cookery—Shellfish

SQUINTING. See Strabismus

SQUIRE, Albert
Control of rats. il Cons 26:26 O '71

SQUIRES, James Robert
All those electronic chemicals. Electr World 85:44 My '71
Pick the right system for you. il Radio-Electr 42:23-7+ N '71

SQUIRREL hunting
Big red of the Ozarks. B. Gooch. il pors Outdoor Life 148:90-2+ O '71
Foggy float for squirrel. L. Kreh. il Field & S 75:32-3+ Ja '71
Greatest hunting dog you'd never guess. B. Dalrymple. il Field & S 76:48-9+ S '71

SQUIRRELS
Uroporphyrinogen III cosynthetase activity in the fox squirrel (sciurus niger) E. Y. Levin and V. Flyger. bibliog il Science 174:59-60 O 1 '71
See also
Ground squirrels

SQUIRRELS, Skinning of. See Game, Dressing of

SQUIRRELS as carriers of infection
See also
Plague

SRINIVASAN, B. and others
Iodine-129 in terrestrial ores. bibliog il Science 173:327-8 Jl 23 '71

STAAR, Richard F.
New course in Communist-ruled Poland? bibliog f il Cur Hist 60:269-75 My '71

STAATS, Elmer Boyd
Public private eye. por Forbes 108:76 N 1 '71 *

STABILITY of automobiles. See Automobiles—Stability and stabilizers

STABILIZATION, Economic. See Economic stabilization

STABILIZATION of wages. See Wages—Regulation

STABILIZATION processors. See Photography—Processing—Apparatus and supplies

STABLE flies. See Ecdysone

STACEY, Nicolas
Man of vision. T. Beeson. Chr Cent 87:825-6 Jl 7 '71 *

STACEY, Tom
Englishman tries to understand apartheid. il Nat R 23:581-4 Je 1 '71

STACK, Julia F.
She went through fire. il Hobbies 75:45 Ja '71

STACK, Robert
Thanks to the hunter! Nat Wildlife 9:17 O '71

STACKERS. Hay. See Hay stackers

STACKPOLE, Christopher W. and others
Cell surface antigens; serial sectioning of single cells as an approach to topographical analysis. bibliog il Science 172:472-4 Ap 30 '71

STADIUMS
Financial hero in New Orleans. il por Bsns W p80 S 18 '71
Innovative engineering leads to new stadium designs. H. Bandel. il Arch Rec 150:139-42 N '71
Let me make one thing clear; New Orleans $130 million pleasure dome. J. Kirshenbaum. il Sports Illus 34:34-6+ Je 7 '71
Should Pittsburgh save Forbes field? J. D. Morgan. il Arch Rec 150:119-22 Jl '71
Stadiums for small communities. A. Gobar. il Parks & Rec 6:31-4+ Je '71
Yankees, stay home! Newsweek 77:70 Mr 15 '71
Lighting
Lighting adds color to new stadium; Cincinnati. il Am City 86:82 F '71
Rosy lighting for the Rose bowl; Pasadena, Calif. il Am City 86:124 Ap '71

STADIUS, Donald E.
Roundelay for Attica and other prison libraries based on an old song. il por Wilson Lib Bul 46:246-7 N '71

STADTMAN, Thressa C.
Vitamin B₁₂. bibliog il Science 171:859-67 Mr 5 '71

STAFF committee on mediation, arbitration and inquiry. See American library association—Mediation, arbitration and inquiry, Staff committee on

STAFFORD, Jean
Books. il Vogue 158:282-3 S 1; 68 D '71; 159:122 Ja 1 '72
Children's books for Christmas. New Yorker 47:177-84+ D 4 '71
Intimations of hope. McCalls 99:77+ D '71
Suffering summering houseguests. Vogue 158:112 Ag 15 '71
Unexpected joys of a simple garden. il Redbook 137:79+ Je '71

STAFFORD, William
British Columbia; poem. Am Scholar 40:481 Sum '71
In a time of need; Oak; Stories to live in the world with; poems. Poetry 119:127-9 D '71
New letters from Thomas Jefferson; poem. Esquire 75:205 My '71
Our story; poem. New Repub 165:27 S 4 '71
Poem: Some days of its gift; Hide and go seek at the cemetery. Harper 243:58 O '71
Trying to remember a town; poem. New Yorker 47:116 O 2 '71
Two cold rivers; poem. Am Scholar 41:120 Wint '71
about
Symbolic landscapes. B. Quinn. Poetry 118:288-9 Ag '71 *

STAFFORD, N.Y.
Equipment adjusts to the storm. A. H. Snell. il Am City 86:103-4 S '71

STAGE coaches. See Coaches and coaching

STAGE fright
Stage fright. L. Hutchinson. il Sr Schol 98:29 F 15 '71

STAGE lighting
See also
Opera—Stage lighting

STAGE scenery. See Opera—Stage setting and scenery; Theater—Stage setting and scenery

STAGECOACHES. See Coaches and coaching

STAGG, Anne
All-year vacation house: a surge of space. il House & Gard 139:114-21 Mr '71
(ed) See Goldfinger, M. Architect speaks his mind

STAGGERED hours. See Hours of labor

STAGGERS, Harley Orrin
CBS versus Congress. W. F. Buckley, jr. Nat R 23:829 Jl 27 '71 *
Quiet man who cried foul. por Newsweek 78:25 Jl 26 '71 *
Selling of Congress. il por Newsweek 78:24-5 Jl 26 '71 *

STAHL, O. Glenn
Case against strikes. Read Digest 99:128-30 O '71

STAHL, Robert. See Dauterman, P. jt. auth.

STAHLKE, Otto F.
New syncretistic dialogue. Chr Today 16:8-9 D 3 '71

STAHR, Elvis J.
Camp: the ideal place for teaching environmental urgencies. il Camp Mag 43:20+ Mr '71

STAINED glass. See Glass painting and staining

STAINLESS steel. See Steel, Stainless

STAINLESS steel blades. See Razor blades

STAINS, Removal of. See Cleaning

STAINS and staining (microscopy)
Acridine orange potentiation of actinomycin D uptake and activity. E. F. Roth, jr. and J. Kochen. bibliog il Science 174:696-8 N 12 '71
Identification of each human chromosome with a modified Giemsa stain. S. R. Patil and others. bibliog il Science 173:821-2 Ag 27 '71
Pathways in the brain. L. Heimer. il Sci Am 225:48-57+ Jl '71
Sorting out chromosomes; use of Giemsa stain. il Sci N 100:200 S 25 '71

STAIR, Dan
Follow that fish. il Field & S 75:74-5+ Ap '71
To catch a steelhead. il Field & S 76:56-7+ Ag '71

STAIR, Lois H.
Madame moderator. por Newsweek 77:85 My 31 '71 *

STAIRCASES. See Stairways

STAIRWAYS
Child-safe stairway. il Bet Hom & Gard 49:102 D '71
See also
Garden steps

STALIN, Iosif
Battle Stalin lost, by V. Dedijer. Review
 Nat R 23:318-19+ Mr 23 '71. M. Padev *
 Sat R il por 54:26-7 Ja 30 '71. S. K.
 Padover *
Let history judge, by R. A. Medvedev. Review
 Newsweek il 79:55 Ja 3 '72. S. K. Oberbeck *
 Sat R il pors 55:25-8 Ja 8 '72. R. C.
 Tucker *
 Time il por 99:66+ Ja 17 '72. S. Talbott *
Nation killers; the Soviet deportation of nationalities, by R. Conquest. Review
 Nat R 23:483-4 My 4 '71. F. Russell *
New indictment of Stalin. Time 98:42 N 1
 '71 *
STALKING of game. See Tracking and trailing
STALL barns. See Barns and stables
STALLS, Airplane. See Airplanes—Stalling
STALLWORTHY, Jon
Comment. A. Williamson. Poetry 118:172-3
 Je '71 *
STAMFORD, Conn.

Education
Sensible new plan to fight drugs in our schools; excerpt from The nightmare route: the truth about drugs in suburbia. F. W. Chinnock. Ladies Home J 88:68-70+ Ap '71

Hotels, restaurants, etc.
Grand hotel; Piper's hill hotel for children.
 il Newsweek 77:107+ My 10 '71

Sanitary affairs
Stamford mines a garbage lode. Bsns W
 p 142 S 25 '71
STAMP collecting. See Postage stamps—Collectors and collecting
STAMPS, Food. See Food relief—United States
STAMPS, Postage. See Postage stamps
STANCHION barns. See Barns and stables
STANDARD brands, inc.
 See also
Fleischmann distilling corporation
STANDARD of living
Affluence and the world tomorrow. L. S.
 Wehrle. For Affairs 49:419-28 Ap '71
Analysis of socio-economic development through a system of indicators. D. V. McGranahan. bibliog f il Ann Am Acad 393: 65-81 Ja '71
Personal testimony on the standard of living. D. Lambert. il Nat Parks & Con Mag 45:23-6 Je '71
Practical significance of social information. J. Drewnowski. bibliog f Ann Am Acad 393: 82-91 Ja '71
 See also
Budget, Household
Income
STANDARD oil company (Indiana)
Why Indiana Standard grows so well. il por Bsns W p57+ D 4 '71
STANDARD oil company (New Jersey)
Harlem prep gets another boost. Nations Bsns 59:19 My '71
Jamieson and Brisco of Jersey standard.
 il Forbes 107:74 My 15 '71
 See also
International petroleum company
STANDARD oil company of California
Enforcer. il por Newsweek 78:101 O 18 '71
Relief, but no cure. il Forbes 108:44 Jl 1 '71
 See also
Chevron oil company
STANDARD pressed steel company
SPS: trouble at the top. A. A. Butkus. por
 Duns 97:72 Mr '71
STANDARDIZATION
Standardization. R. P. Raskowitz. Electr
 World 86:66-7 S '71
STANDARDS. See Commercial products, Certification of; also subhead Standards under various subjects, e.g. Lasers—Standards
STANDARDS, Engineering
When a standard doesn't measure up. Bsns
 W p54-5 Jl 24 '71
 See also
Building—Standards
STANDARDS, Library. See Libraries—Standards
STANDARDS, National bureau of. See United States—Standards, National bureau of
STANDS, Roadside. See Roadside marketing
STANFORD, Alfred
Pleasures of sailing. Motor B & S 127:76-7+
 Mr '71
STANFORD, Edward B.
British university library buildings. bibliog
 il por Library J 96:4067-71 D 15 '71

STANFORD, Frank
Belladonna; poem. Nation 213:314 O 4 '71
STANFORD, Gene
Word study that works. Engl J 60:111-15 Ja
 '71
STANFORD university, Palo Alto, Calif.
Bombing of SLAC: a question of why? Sci N
 100:406 D 18 '71
Inciting to violence; H. B. Franklin fired.
 il por Time 99:41 Ja 17 '72
Limits of academic freedom; case of radical professor H. B. Franklin. il por Time 97:51 Mr 15 '71
Tame spring, troubled Stanford. Time 97:62
 My 10 '71

Institute for communications research
Black-oriented; study findings. R. L. Shayon.
 Sat R 54:18 S 25 '71

School of medicine
Stanford school of medicine:
 Clinicians make an issue. J. Walsh. il
  Science 171:654-7 F 19 '71
 Problems over more than money. J.
  Walsh. il Science 171:551-3 F 12 '71
 Varieties of medical experience. J. Walsh.
  Science 171:785-7 F 26 '71
STANGEL, Donald J.
Helping spend school dollars wisely. Todays
 Ed 60:38-9 Ja '71
STANGER, Ila
Dance. Harp Baz 104:150 O '71
Television to turn on. il Harp Baz 105:74+ N;
 77 D '71
Travel bazaar. Harp Baz 104:72+ F; 84+ S;
 105:64+ N '71
STANKY, Eddie
Brat is a winner for old USA. R. Fimrite. il
 por Sports Illus 34:62-3 My 3 '71 *
STANLEY, Julian C.
Predicting college success of the educationally disadvantaged; adaptation of address, June 1970. bibliog Science 171:640-7. 173; 1079 F 19, S 17 '71
STANLEY-BROWN, Joseph
My friend Garfield; excerpt from memoir, with editorial comment. il pors Am Heritage 22: 49-53+ Ag '71
STANLEY steamer. See Automobiles, Steam
STANNARD, Una
Adam's rib; or, The woman within. il Trans-Action 8:24-32+ N '70
STANOLIND. See Standard oil company (Indiana)
STANS, Maurice Hubert
Doing business with Russia; interview. il
 pors U S News 71:56-60+ D 20 '71
Excerpt from letter, July 1971. Cong Digest
 50:298 D '71
Technology's vital role; excerpts from testimony before House subcommittee on science, research and development. Aviation W 95:7 Ag 30 '71
Wait a minute; address, July 15, 1971.
 Vital Speeches 37:690-3 S 1 '71
Where will we be 20 years from now? por
 Nations Bsns 59:26-8 F '71

about
Beyond protocol in Greece. por Time 97:16 My
 3 '71 *
Can the U.S. do business with the Russians?
 il por Newsweek 78:85 N 29 '71 *
Mission to Moscow. il por Time 98:26 D
 6 '71 *
Sounding the alarm. il Newsweek 78:57-8
 Ag 9 '71 *
Stans style. il por Time 98:58 Ag 2 '71 *
STANTON, Edward S.
Religion (cont) America 124:547-8, 125:437-8
 My 22, N 20 '71
STANTON, Frank
Selling of Congress. il por Newsweek 78:24-5
 Jl 26 '71
Stanton's no. por Time 98:68 Jl 5 '71 *
Unblinking eye of CBS. Time 98:19 Jl 26 '71 *
Who is big brother? por Newsweek 78:25 Jl
 5 '71 *
STANTON, Will
Dishwasher that brought out the worst in everybody; story. Redbook 137:108-9 My '71
Farewell Roxane; story. Ladies Home J 88:
 54 Jl '71
Friend of the family's; story. Redbook 137:
 80-1 Ag '71
Just call me cupid. il Read Digest 98:91-3
 F '71
There's no mayonnaise in Ireland. il Read
 Digest 98:153-4+ My '71
STAPLETON, Maureen
People are talking about. . . . A. Talmey.
 por Vogue 157:144-5 F 1 '71 *

STAPLETON, Peter T.
English for free; English for the hell of it; address, November 1970. Engl J 60:500-4 Ap '71

STAR, Jack
Cook County: hospital; the terrible place. il Look 35:24-30+ My 18 '71
Great purple martin controversy! il por Look 35:24-6 Ag 10 '71
Homosexual couple. il Look 35:69-71 Ja 26 '71
How Silastic transformed breast surgery. Look 35:12 Jl 27 '71
J.F.K. college won't die. Look 35:47 Ja 12 '71
Jam-up: crisis in our criminal courts. il Look 35:32-4+ Mr 23 '71
We'll educate your kids, or your money back. il Look 35:56+ Je 15 '71
Where have our doctors gone? il Look 35: 15-17 Je 29 '71

STAR clusters. See Stars—Clusters

STAR fever; drama. See Boiko, C.

STAR motions. See Stars—Motion

STAR spangled banner (song)
America's song of songs; The star spangled banner. W. F. Gavin. il Read Digest 99: 126-8 Jl '71

STARBUCK, George
Barraclough foofarough; poem. New Yorker 47:81 D 18 '71
Hush of rugs, the banter of the benign; poem. Sat R 54:92 Ja 23 '71

STARCH (for clothes)
Body and ease of ironing in a can; aerosol spray starches, sizings, and finishes. il Consumer Bul 54:33-6 Je '71

STARE, Fredrick J.
Diet that's killing our kids. il Ladies Home J 88:70+ O '71

STARER, Robert
Composer's showcase: Robert Starer. D. W. Moore. Am Rec G 37:383 F '71 *

STARFISHES
Coral-eating sea stars acanthaster planci in Hawaii. J. M. Branham and others. bibliog il Science 172:1155-7 Je 11 '71
Panama Canal warning: possibility of yellow-bellied sea snake and crown-of-thorns starfish in Atlantic with sea-level canal. Sr Schol 98:9 Mr 29 '71

STARGELL, Willie
Big man, big bat, big heart. L. J. Banks. il pors Ebony 26:132-4+ O '71 *
Sugar Bear, formerly Gentle Ben. il por Time 98:54-5 Ag 2 '71 *
Willie at the bat. Newsweek 77:91 My 3 '71 *

STARK, Gail U.
Seven on a honeymoon. il Parents Mag 46: 44-5 My '71

STARK, Harry F.
Economic indicators issued by states. il Mo Labor R 94:47-50 S '71

STARK, Lawrence. See Noton, D. jt. auth.

STARK, Nancy
How schools can listen to the community. il Am Ed 7:8-11 Jl '71

STARKE, John
Sad story of crazy Frenchie and me. por Sr Schol 98:15 F 15 '71

STARKEY, J. Albert
What is it? il Am For 77:44-5 Je '71

STARKMAN, Ernest Seymour
GM's pollution man. por Bsns W p80 F 6 '71 *

STARLIPER, R. L.
Programmable zener applications. il Electr World 85:60-1 Je '71
—See Clement, R. D. jt. auth.

STARNES, Richard
[Monthly article on outdoor life] See issues of Field & stream

STARR, Chauncey
Electric power crisis in America; interview. Look 35:37-40+ Ag 10 '71
Energy and power; with biographical sketch. il Sci Am 225:25, 36-49 bibliog(p244) S '71

STARR, John T.
Salzburg connection. il Am For 77:28-31+ F '71

STARR, Knight
Our geodesic greenhouse. il Org Gard & Farm 18:100-1 S '71

STARR, Michael A.
Put more green in the park maintenance budget. il Am City 86:81+ My '71

STARR, Nina Howell
Stay young with photography. R. Hattersley. il Pop Phot 69:90-3+ O '71 *

STARR, Roger
Decline and decline of New York. il N Y Times Mag p31+ N 21; 26 D 12 '71
What's left? Commentary 52:35-41 Ag '71

STARS
Astronomy. J. Stokley. See fourth issue of each month of Science news
Deep-sky wonders. W. S. Houston. See issues of Sky and telescope
Star gazing the easy way. M. Lincoln. il Pop Sci 199:122+ O '71
Star-studded show. J. C. Miller. il Motor B & S 128:54-5 bibliog(p 58) Jl '71
See also
Astrophysics
Galaxies
Neutron stars
Occultations
Parallax

Age
Time scales for lithium depletion and rotational braking in solar-type main-sequence stars; age determination for the Hyades. E. P. J. van den Heuvel and P. Conti. bibliog il Science 171:895-6 Mr 5 '71

Clusters
Dynamics of star clusters. I. R. King. il Sky & Tel 41:139-43 Mr '71
Nearest galaxy or richest globular? IRC-20 385. il Sky & Tel 42:273 N '71
Time scales for lithium depletion and rotational braking in solar-type main-sequence stars; age determination for the Hyades. E. P. J. van den Heuvel and P. Conti. bibliog il Science 171:895-6 Mr 5 '71

Density
Solid stars. M. A. Ruderman. il Sci Am 224: 24-31 F '71

Evolution
Nature of pulsars. J. P. Ostriker. il Sci Am 224:48-60 Ja '71
Stellar old age. A. L. Hammond. il Science 171:994-5, 1133-4, 1228 Mr 12-26 '71
Two new chapters in the story of U Cephei. A. H. Batten and M. Plavec. il Sky & Tel 42:213-15 O '71

Motion
Progress on the Lick survey. Sky & Tel 42: 191 O '71

Radiation
Cetus radio arc. il Sky & Tel 42:12 Jl '71
Radio observations of Scorpius X-1. il Sky & Tel 41:86 F '71

Rotation
Time scales for lithium depletion and rotational braking in solar-type main-sequence stars. E. P. J. van den Heuvel and P. Conti. bibliog il Science 171:895-6 Mr 5 '71

Scintillation
Seeing and scintillation. A. T. Young. bibliog il Sky & Tel 42:139-41+ S '71

Spectra
Mira stars with hydroxyl emission lines. Sky & Tel 41:352 Je '71
Promethium in the star HR 465. M. F. Alter. il Sky & Tel 41:220-2 Ap '71
Two new chapters in the story of U Cephei. A. H. Batten and M. Plavec. il Sky & Tel 42:147-50 S '71

STARS, Double
On the invisible trail of binary black holes. il Sci N 100:419-20 D 25 '71
696 visual binaries. Sky & Tel 41:154 Mr '71
Some bright visual binary stars (cont) J. Meeus. il Sky & Tel 41:88-92 F '71
Theta Coronae Borealis as a double star. Sky & Tel 42:206 O '71
See also
Stars, Eclipsing binary

STARS, Dwarf
New work on Sirius B. Sky & Tel 43:13 Ja '72
Polarized light from white-dwarf star. G. B. Lubkin. bibliog il Phys Today 24:19-20 Ja '71
Stellar old age: white dwarfs, neutron stars, and black holes. A. L. Hammond. il Science 171:994-5 Mr 12 '71

STARS, Eclipsing binary
CH Cygni: an eclipsing binary? Sky & Tel 42:334-5 D '71
Eclipsing binary LY Aurigae. il Sky & Tel 41: 212 Ap '71
Two new chapters in the story of U Cephei. A. H. Batten and M. Plavec. il Sky & Tel 42:147-50, 213-15 S-O '71

STARS, Giant
Antares as a radio source. Sky & Tel 41:212-13 Ap '71
Luminosities of red supergiants. Sky & Tel 41:152-3 Mr '71

STATIC electricity. See Electricity, Static

STATION wagon camping. See Camping

STATION wagons
PM owners report:
International Travelall. il Pop Mech 135:132-5+ My '71
Slick new Scout. M. Lamm. il Pop Mech 136:100-2 N '71
Spirit of '76; Chevrolet's new super Suburban. E. Dahlquist. Motor T 23:68-70 N '71
Station wagons. il Consumer Rep 36:217-18 Ap '71
Station wagons; Dodge Monaco, Ford Country Squire, Pontiac Safari, AMC Hornet Sportabout, Chevrolet Vega. il Consumer Rep 36:340-9 Je '71

Equipment
Chevy's Superblazer takes all jobs in stride. J. Davis. il Pop Sci 199:78-9 D '71

Four wheel drive
V8 power + four-wheel drive=terrific terrain goers. J. P. Norbye and J. Dunne. il Pop Sci 199:23-4+ Ag '71

Rating
Bus wagons: Chevrolet Sportvan; Dodge Sportsman; Ford Club wagon and VW bus wagon. il Consumer Rep 36:493-501 Ag '71

Testing
Movable feast; VW station wagon, Royal Sportsman 300, Beauville Sportvan and Chateau Club wagon. W. Wyss. il Motor T 23:82-6 Ap '71
Popular science car test:
'71 Matador, Coronet, and Montego. J. P. Norbye and J. Dunne. il Pop Sci 198:20+ Mr '71
Small buses. J. P. Norbye and J. Dunne. il Pop Sci 199:20+ Jl '71
Standard wagons. J. P. Norbye and J. Dunne. il Pop Sci 198:42+ Ap '71
Real American station wagon test. C. Koch. il Motor T 23:70-2+ S '71
Tom McCahill tests:
International Travelall station wagon. T. McCahill. il Mech Illus 67:50-2+ Ja '71
Wagons ho! Hornet Sportabout, Volkswagen, Toyota Mark II and Ford. J. Brokaw. il Motor T 23:82-6+ Jl '71

STATIONS, Seismological. See Seismological stations

STATIONS in space. See Space stations

STATISTICAL methods
Inflation versus unemployment: another view of the trade-off; shift in Phillips curve. S. S. Wallack. bibliog Mo Labor R 94:49-54 N '71
Living with a higher jobless rate; Phillips curve. il Bsns W p36-8 D 25 '71
See also
Experimental design
Regression analysis
Stochastic processes
United States—Labor statistics, Bureau of

STATISTICS
See also
Computers—Statistical use
Economic statistics
Gross national product
Statistical methods
also subhead Statistics under various subjects, e.g. Marriage—Statistics

Study and teaching
Statistics: a vital educational tool; adaptation of address. J. F. McNamara. Clear House 45:558-61 My '71

STATUE and the bust; story. See Hazzard, S.

STATUES
See also
Crazy Horse (Sioux Indian)—Statues, portraits, etc.
Monuments

STATURE
Height and antisocial behavior in XY and XYY boys. E. B. Hook and D. S. Kim. bibliog il Science 172:284-6 Ap 16 '71
Heightism; American bias against the short man. il Time 98:64 O 4 '71
No one roots for Goliath. F. Katz. il Todays Health 49:24-9 S '71

STAUB, William J. and Blase, M. G.
Genetic technology and agricultural development. bibliog il Science 173:119-23 Jl 9 '71

STAUBACH, Roger
Bullet Bob v. Roger the Dodger. il pors Time 99:42-5 Ja 17 '72 *

STAUFFER chemical company
Chemists produce a change in students. V. Louviere. il Nations Bsns 59:16 Jl '71

STAUTH, Lorraine
Have we forsaken our teen-agers. il Parents Mag 46:54-6+ My '71

STAVN, Diane (Gersoni) See Gersoni, D.

STEAD, Christina
About woman's insight, there is a sort of folklore we inherit. Vogue 158:61+ S 15 '71
Azhdanov tailors; story. Commentary 52:55-8 Jl '71

STEAK See Cookery—Meat

STEAK tartare. See Food, Raw

STEALING
New York crime and the religious sector; church burglaries. T. Early. Chr Cent 88:977-8 Ag 18 '71
One touch of larceny; employee thefts; study findings of L. R. Zeitlin. Newsweek 77:84+ Je 14 '71
Ripping off, the new life style. M. Drosnin. il N Y Times Mag p 12-13+ Ag 8 '71
Viet Nam: a cancerous affliction. il Time 97:22-3 Je 7 '71
Watch out for thieves that prey on travelers. il Changing T 25:40-2 My '71
Why employes steal; interview. N. Jaspan. il por U S News 70:78-82 My 3 '71; Same abr. Read Digest 99:83-6 S '71
See also
Airport thefts
Art thefts
Automobiles, Theft of
Burglary and burglars
Cattle thieves
Securities, Theft of
Shoplifting

STEAM, Natural
Fuel that truly is pollution-free; geothermal energy. E. Yenay. il Mech Illus 67:63-5+ Mr '71
Geothermal energy, the neglected energy option. R. W. Rex. il por Bul Atom Sci 27:52-6 O '71
Geothermal power. J. Barnea. il Sci Am 226:70-7 bibliog(p 122) Ja '72
Hot springs fuel Iceland's hopes; proposed chemical complex. il Bsns W p 124 Ap 10 '71
Power from the earth; geothermal energy. D. Fenner and J. Klarmann. bibliog il Environ 13:19-26+ D '71
Steam inside. il Newsweek 77:95+ Je 7 '71
Ultima Thule; report on Iceland's use of geothermal energy. C. Peet. il Am For 77:12-15+ Je '71

STEAM automobiles. See Automobiles, Steam

STEAM engines
Steam engine festivals. B. Thomas. il Travel 136:33-5 Jl '71
See also
Locomotives

STEAM engines, Automotive. See Automobile engines

STEAM irons, Electric. See Electric irons

STEAM motor buses. See Motor buses, Steam

STEAM power plants
Fuel that truly is pollution-free; geothermal energy. E. Yenay. il Mech Illus 67:63-5+ Mr '71
See also
Steam, Natural

STEAM ships. See Steamships and steamboats

STEAM-spray irons, Electric. See Electric irons

STEAM tractor models. See Tractor models

STEAM turbine generators. See Electric generators

STEAMBOATS. See Steamships and steamboats

STEAMERS (ships) See Steamships and steamboats

STEAMING (cookery)
Things mother never taught you about steaming. il Ladies Home J 88:144 Mr '71

STEAMSHIP lines
See also
Cunard steamship company
Hudson River day lines
Ocean liners

STEAMSHIPS and steamboats
All ashore; final trip for Alexander Hamilton, last of the Hudson River sidewheelers. il Am Heritage 23:109 D '71
Another world, another time; a trip on the Delta Queen. B. Atkinson. il Audubon 73:66-71 Ja '71
Fight for the Queen; or Two cheers for Congress. O. Jensen. il Am Heritage 22:4-7+ Ap '71

STEAMSHIPS and steamboats—*Continued*
Postcards from the Hudson; farewell to the Alexander Hamilton. A. Hiss. il New Yorker 47:54-65 N 13 '71
Steamin' up the River; from Memphis to New Orleans on the Delta Queen. D. Butwin. il Sat R 54:36-8 My 29; 44-6+ Je 5; 36+ Je 12 '71
See also
Ocean liners
Ocean travel

History
Sway of the grand saloon, by J. M. Brinnin. Review
  Time 99:68+ Ja 3 '72. J. Skow
STEBBINS, Doris E.
Glads go petite. il Horticulture 49:30-1+ Je '71
STEBBINS, J. R.
Equipment basics for the backpacker. il Field & S 76:72-3+ Je '71
STEBBINS, Ray
Eagles are not for killing. il Am For 77:12-14+ O '71
STECKLER, Larry
Microwave ovens. il Radio-Electr 42:68-70 F '71
STEDMAN, Jane W. and McElroy, George
Britten's Britons. il por Opera N 36:18-20 N '71
STEEGMULLER, Francis
Onward and upward with the arts. New Yorker 46:70-5 Ja 23 '71
Our far-flung correspondents. New Yorker 47:99-103 My 1 '71
Stravinsky at work. il Sat R 54:44-5 My 29 '71
STEEL, Ronald
  (ed) See Lippmann, W. World we're in
STEEL

Marketing
I sell Japanese steel. N. A. Martin. por Duns 77:49-50+ Je '71

Prices
Battle over steel prices; pattern for other industries. il U S News 70:33-4 F 1 '71
Bethlehem caper. Newsweek 78:66 Ag 23 '71
Cool climate for steel price hikes. il Bsns W p25 Ag 14 '71
Jawbone hits steel. Newsweek 77:63-4 Ja 25 '71
Silver lining? M. Friedman. Newsweek 77:56 F 1 '71
Slap for steel, a spur for machinery. il Time 97:64-5 Ja 25 '71
Users shrug off steel price hike. Bsns W p 16 Ja 23 '71

Stockpiling
See Stockpiling

Welding
He custom-builds light steel beams; Thermatool continuous-welding process. il Bsns W p92 Je 26 '71
STEEL, Stainless
Designs in steel; 1970-1 Design in steel award program. il Design 72:4-7 Sum '71
Radiation-induced swelling of stainless steel. P. G. Shewmon. bibliog il Science 173:987-91 S 10 '71
Steel for space hardware. il Space World H-10-94:48 O '71
STEEL alloys
How a new steel emerged from a wreck. T. F. Patton. il por Nations Bsns 59:84-5 Ja '71
STEEL company of Canada
North of the border. il Forbes 108:44+ O 15 '71
STEEL construction
See also
American institute of steel construction
Steel houses
STEEL houses
Quiet gamble on a steel house. il Bsns W p 108 F 27 '71
STEEL industry
See also
Steel workers
Steel works

Consolidations and mergers
Two steelmakers tempt antitrust; proposed National steel corp.-Granite city steel co. merger. Bsns W p21 Ap 24 '71

Finance
Bending big steel. Sr Schol 98:16-17 F 8 '71
Making money work; steel stocks. S. Meisenberg. Har Yrs 11:52-3 S '71
Metals; with yardsticks of management performance. il Forbes 109:101-2+ Ja 1 '72

Imports problem
Imports bite into specialty steel. il Bsns W p78 Jl 31 '71
Irony of quotas that protect imports. Bsns W p31 Ja 23 '71
Steel fabricators fight the foreigners. il Bsns W p26 N 20 '71
Steel imports: the economic effect; address, February 3. 1971. J. P. Molony. Vital Speeches 37:307-9 Mr 1 '71
Steel industry negotiates to survive. il Bsns W p92-5+ My 15 '71
Trouble ahead for steel, strike or no strike. il U S News 70:81-2 Je 7 '71
Will imports crimp new steel prices? Bsns W p29 Ja 16 '71

International aspects
See also
International iron and steel institute

Securities
Fundamental problems. C. Morgello. il Newsweek 77:60 F 1 '71

Wages and hours
Inflation alert: first step toward steel-pay showdown. U S News 70:91-2 Ap 26 '71
Steel industry negotiates to survive. il Bsns W p92-5+ My 15 '71
31% raise. Time 97:80 Je 14 '71
See also
Collective bargaining—Steel industry

Canada
See also
Steel company of Canada

Great Britain
See also
Guest, Keen and Nettlefolds, ltd.

Japan
Straw and steel; Daido steel co. il Chem 44:4 S '71

United States
Big industry in trouble. il U S News 71:26-7 Jl 26 '71
Rift in the ranks. Time 98:52 Ag 23 '71
Rough road ahead for an ailing industry. il U S News 71:66-9 O 4 '71
Slap for steel, a spur for machinery. il Time 97:64-5 Ja 25 '71
Steel hedge-buying is off to a late start. il Bsns W p39-40 Mr 13 '71
Steel; recasting an industry under stress. A. T. Demaree. il Fortune 83:74-7+ Mr '71
Steel's new year looks cheerier. il Bsns W p20 D 18 '71
Steel's past ills linger tenaciously. il Bsns W p20 My 29 '71
See also
Collective bargaining—Steel industry
United steelworkers of America
  also names of steel companies, e.g.
United States steel corporation
STEEL mills. See Steel works
STEEL sculpture. See Metal sculpture
STEEL service centers
See also
Marcrest-Pacific company
STEEL tire cord. See Tire fabrics
STEEL workers
Grim outlook for steelworkers. Bsns W p33 N 6 '71
New cloud over Gary. il Newsweek 78:59 S 13 '71
See also
United steelworkers of America
STEEL works
Where the mills went wrong. Bsns W p82-4 Je 5 '71
See also
Jones and Laughlin steel corporation

Pollution
Big steel union makes war on pollution; Local 1557's fight to clean up coke plant. il Bsns W p34-5 D 25 '71
Birmingham's grim lesson. il Bsns W p20-1 N 27 '71
Conscience of a steel worker. B. Ehrenreich and J. Ehrenreich. il Nation 213:268-71 S 27 '71
STEELE, John
Pick & choose among stereo headphones. il Pop Electr 34:44-7+ Ap '71
STEELE, Mary Q.
Realism, truth, and honesty; address, July 1970. Horn Bk 47:17-27 F '71
STEELE, Robert
Movie (title varies) Chr Cent 88:234-5 F 17 '71

STEELE, Robert Hampton
　Our most dangerous epidemic. il por Nations Bsns 59:46-8 Jl '71
　Dzu story. por Time 98:18+ Jl 19 '71 •
STEELERS (football club) See Football clubs
STEELHEAD trout fishing. See Trout fishing
STEELWORKERS union. See United Steelworkers of America
STEEN, Lynn Arthur
　New models of the real-number line; with biographical sketch. il Sci Am 225:13, 92-9 Ag '71
STEENBOCK, Harry
　Discovery of vitamin D. il Chem 44:19 O '71 •
STEEPLECHASE. See Hurdle racing
STEERING gear
　　See also
　Automobiles—Steering gear
　Boats—Steering gear
STEES, Arthur R.
　Fly El Elijah! Chr Cent 88:1471-2 D 15 '71
STEFFEN, Don Carl
　Multimedia classroom. il Am Ed 7:28-30 Ag '71
STEFFEN, Robert
　Agricultural research and the small farm. Org Gard & Farm 18:84-6 My '71
　Back to the land with Bob Steffen. See issues of Organic gardening and farming
　Establishing and managing alfalfa seedlings. Org Gard & Farm 18:114-17 N '71
　Tissue tests to your plants' rescue. Org Gard & Farm 18:100+ D '71
　Using rock fertilizers on the farm. il Org Gard & Farm 18:58-9 Mr '71
　Why we must grow good beef without hormones or high-energy rations. il Org Gard & Farm 18:61-3 Ap '71
STEFFENS, Lincoln
　Autobiography of Lincoln Steffens. Review
　　New Repub 165:29-31 N 6 '71. A. M. Greeley •
STEGER, Joseph A. See Bevan, W. jt. auth.
STEGNER, Wallace
　Angle of repose; story. McCalls 98:103-10 Ap '71
STEIGER, William Albert
　Excerpt from debate, November 17, 1970. Cong Digest 50:90+ Mr '71
　Excerpt from remarks, February 17, 1971. Cong Digest 50:152+ My '71
STEIN, Andrew
　Noise study takes legislator to U.K. Aviation W 94:58 Mr 1 '71 •
　Stein's sound barrier. il por Newsweek 77:78 Mr 1 '71 •
STEIN, Elizabeth
　Making it in 3-D. il Sch Arts 71:10-13 O '71
STEIN, Gerald
　America's #1 husband; story. Redbook 137:88-9 O '71
STEIN, Gertrude
　Rose is a rose is a rose; excerpt from The world is round. Harp Baz 104:126 Ag '71
　　　about
　Art world. H. Rosenberg. New Yorker 46:71-5 Ja 30 '71 •
　Continuous present. F. Stevenson. il por Opera N 35:8-13 Ap 10 '71 •
　Four patron saints in one great act: the Steins. T. Prideaux. il por Life 70:56-60+ Ap 23 '71 •
　G.M.P. J. Ashbery. il Art N 69:44-7+ F '71 •
　Gertrude Stein in pieces, by R. Bridgman. Review
　　Nat R 23:89-90 Ja 26 '71. H. Kenner •
　Gertrude Stein, master librettist. P. J. Smith; S. Fleming. il por Hi Fi 21:MA10-11 N '71 •
　Liberation of Gertrude Stein. F. Gervasi. il pors Sat R 54:13-14+ Ag 21 '71 •
　Seemingly wise. H. Kenner. New Repub 164:25-6+ Ja 16 '71 •
STEIN, Harry
　(ed) See Bowder, E. R. Marx's disenchanted salesman
STEIN, Herbert
　Tenth meeting of OECD ministerial council held at Paris; statement, June 7, 1971. Dept State Bul 65:13-14 Jl 5 '71
　What to watch for in prices, pay, profits, rents; interview. il pors U S News 71:28-32 N 8 '71
　　　about
　Herb Stein's comfortable purgatory. por Time 98:25 D 6 '71 •
　Herbert Stein: free marketer at the controls. por Bsns W p76 D 4 '71 •
　Moving up: the chief architect of Phase 2. il por U S News 71:62 D 6 '71 •

STEIN, Howard
　Lion's roar. Newsweek 77:76 Ja 25 '71 •
　Stein's salon. Newsweek 77:90+ Mr 22 '71 •
STEIN, Jane. See Block, J. L. jt. auth.
STEIN, Larry, and Wise, C. D.
　Possible etiology of schizophrenia: progressive damage to the noradrenergic reward system by 6-hydroxydopamine. bibliog il Science 171:1032-6 Mr 12 '71
STEIN, M. L.
　Black reporter and his problems. il Sat R 54:58-60 F 13 '71
　Everything changes even the newsroom. Sat R 54:45-6+ Jl 10 '71
　Journalism education, a matter of coexistence. Sat R 54:71-3 O 9 '71
　Missouri's freedom of information center. il Sat R 54:93-4+ Mr 13 '71
　News access isn't only a Washington problem. il Sat R 54:50-1+ Ag 14 '71
　Reporting from the ghettos. Sat R 54:95-6 N 13 '71
　West Germany's adversary press. Sat R 54:47-8 My 8 '71
STEIN, Ralph M.
　Excerpt from testimony before the Subcommittee on constitutional rights, February 24, 1971. Cong Digest 50:253+ O '71
STEIN, Sol
　Trade winds; interview. ed. by C. Amory. Sat R 54:12 My 1; 24 D 4 '71
STEIN, Stanley
　Unforgettable Stanley Stein. L. G. Blochman. il por Read Digest 98:88-92 Je '71 •
STEIN collection. See Art—Private collections
STEINBACH, Donald L.
　Digital instruments you can build (title varies) (cont) il Electr World 85:32-3+ Mr '71
STEINBACH, Josef
　Wheeling and dealing in Rumania. il por Newsweek 77:39 Ap 5 '71 •
STEINBERG, Alfred
　Mini-businesses of junior achievement. Read Digest 98:19-22+ My '71
　They know where it's at. il Read Digest 99:116-20 Jl '71
STEINBERG, Claire
　It's art, but is it photography? il Pop Phot 68:76-9 Mr '71
　Power of one-color color. il Pop Phot 69:72-7 Jl '71
STEINBERG, David
　Funny man for this season. S. Davidson. il pors N Y Times Mag p26-7+ Ap 25 '71 •
　Uncensored Steinberg; interview. ed. by M. B. Rosin. por Harp Baz 104:138-9+ F '71 •
STEINBERG, J. L.
　European astronomers decide to consolidate their journals. Science 172:451-2 Ap 30 '71
STEINBERG, Leo
　Mantegna's Judith in Washington. il Art N 70:42-3 N '71
　Rubens' Ceres in Leningrad. bibliog f il Art N 70:42-3 D '71
　Salviati's beheading of St John the Baptist. il Art N 70:46-7 S '71
　Skulls of Picasso. bibliog il por Art N 70:26-8+ O '71
　Water carrier of Velazquez. il Art N 70:54-5 Sum '71
STEINBERG, Michael
　Felsenstein thing. por Hi Fi 21:MA8-9 Ag '71
　New chamber music. Hi Fi 21:MA28+ Mr '71
STEINBERG, Philip
　He custom-builds light steel beams. il Bsns W p92 Je 26 '71 •
STEINBERG, Saul
　How's that again? por Forbes 107:14-15 Ja 15 '71 •
　Saul Steinberg and high school composition. L. Mueller. bibliog il Engl J 60:1095-100 N '71 •
STEINBERG, Stephen
　How Jewish quotas began. Commentary 52:67-76 S '71; 53:22+ Ja '72
　Language of prejudice. il Todays Ed 60:14-17 F '71
STEINEM, Gloria
　Gloria Steinem, writer and social critic, talks about sex, politics and marriage; interview. ed. by L. Smith. il Redbook 138:68-76 Ja '72
　　　about
　Coming of age in America. L. Smith. il por Vogue 157:90-2+ Je '71 •
　Feminist forum. Newsweek 78:104 N 8 '71 •
　Gloria Steinem. il pors Newsweek 78:51-4+ Ag 16 '71 •
　Miss Davis and Steinem. W. F. Buckley, jr. Nat R 23:1486 D 31 '71 •
　She. L. Levitt. il por Esquire 76:87-9+ O '71 •

STEINER, George
Future literacy. il Atlan 228:40-4 Ag '71
In Bluebeard's castle: some notes towards
the redefinition of culture, by G. Steiner.
Review
Nation 214:53-4 Ja 10 '72. R. S. Pic-
ciotto •
STEINER, Gilbert Y.
Policy options for welfare reform. bibliog f
Mo Labor R 94:23-31 Mr '71
STEINER, Henry J. and Trubek, D. M.
Brazil: all power to the generals. For Af-
fairs 49:464-79 Ap '71
STEINER, Paul
Chamisa road with Paul & Meredith. by P.
Steiner and M. Maran. Review
Sat R 54:27 Jl 31 '71. J. Luria •
STEINER, Rolf
Africa's Nuremberg trial. il por Newsweek
78:31 S 6 '71 •
Armed missionary. por Time 98:53 N 22 '71 •
Soldier of misfortune. D. Robison. il por
Newsweek 77:44+ My 10 '71 •
STEINER, Shari
(ed) See West, M. Exclusive interview with
Morris West
STEINER, Stan
Poor in Puerto Rico. New Repub 165:8-9 D
11 '71
STEINFELD, Jesse L.
Ban on public smoking? por Newsweek 77:
90-1 Ja 25 '71 •
STEINFELS, Peter
Choice of wars. Commonweal 95:319+ Ja 7
'72
Cooling of the intellectuals. Commonweal
94:255-61, 367 My 21, Jl 9 '71
How we perceive the enemy. Commonweal
95:7-8 O 1 '71
Why I went to jail. Commonweal 94:158 Ap
23 '71
STEINGASS, David
Comment. H. Witt. Poetry 118:41 Ap '71 •
STEINGESSER, M.
Life; poem. Nation 213:186 S 6 '71
STEINHACKER, Charles
Moody woman called Superior; excerpts from
Superior: portrait of a living lake; photo-
graphs. il Nat Wildlife 9:43-7 F '71
STEINHAUSER, Margaret N.
Experiments in self-expression. il Sch Arts
70:24-6 Ap '71
STEINMAN, Clay
In my opinion. por Seventeen 29:152 Jl '70
STEINMANN, Marion
Fighting the genetic odds. il pors Life 71:
18-25 Ag 6 '71
New discoveries about how immunity works.
il Life 70:54 My 28 '71
Washday question. il Life 70:35-7 My 21 '71
STEINMETZ, Charles Proteus
Wizards meet; excerpts from The 42nd paral-
lel. J. Dos Passos. il por Am Heritage 22:
96-7 Ap '71 •
STEINS. See Drinking vessels
STELCO. See Steel company of Canada
STELLA, Frank
Frank Stella, revival and relief. E. C. Baker.
il Art N 70:34-5+ N '71 •
STELLAFANE convention. See Astronomical
conferences
STELLAR evolution. See Stars—Evolution
STELLAR motion. See Stars—Motion
STELLAR parallax. See Parallax
STELLAR systems. See Stars—Clusters
STELLWAG, August. See Higgins, J. jt. auth.
STEMPEL, Larry
Parisian view of Varèse. Sat R 54:71 O 30 '71
Partch for all. por Sat R 54:72-3 N 27 '71
STENCIL work
Craft of mimeography; book publishing. C.
Moore. il por Craft Horiz 31:30-3 F '71
How to stencil from the floor up. il House
& Gard 139:98-101 Ap '71
Stencil a cover-up for the floor. il House B
113:72-3+ Ja '71
STENERUD, Jan
Jan Stenerud is no football player but he
wins football games. B. Surface. il por
N Y Times Mag p 10-11+ S 19 '71 •
Kick that failed. il por Newsweek 79:46 Ja
10 '72 •
STENNIS, John Cornelius
Is America going isolationist? interview. por
U S News 70:25 Je 28 '71
STENSLAND, Anna Lee
American Indian culture: promises, problems,
and possibilities. bibliog Engl J 60:1195-200
D '71
STENTON, Sir Frank Merry
Sir Frank Stenton (1880-1967) V. H. Gal-
braith. Am Hist R 76:1116-23 O '71 •

STENVIG, Charles S.
Life under Stenvig. C. Roberts. il por News-
week 77:37-8 Je 14 '71 •
Moderation in Minneapolis. E. J. Gaines.
il pors Library J 96:1681-3 My 15 '71 •
STEPHANOS, Robert C.
Citizens' corporations as true community
mental retardation and mental health cen-
ters. Ment Hy 55:410-12 Jl '71
STEPHEN-SHERWOOD, E. and others
Thymine: a possible prebiotic synthesis. bib-
liog il Science 173:446-7 Jl 30 '71
STEPHEN, Steve, Stevie; story. See Walker,
T.
STEPHEN T. Mather training center. See
United States—National park service
STEPHENS, Cleo
Where to find ideas. il Writers Digest 51:33-5
Mr '71
STEPHENS, Mark
Lady who stole trees; story. Redbook 137:
110-11 S '71
STEPHENS, Oren
Coin Harvey. il por Am West 8:4-9 S '71
STEPHENS, Robert
New Lunts? No, the original Stephenses;
with interview, ed. by D. Lurie. il pors
Life 71:62-6 Jl 16 '71 •
STEPHENS, Rosemary
Pink roses; story. il Seventeen 30:142-3 S '71
STEPHENSON, Marion
Blind people do not fear snakes; address,
May 25, 1971. Vital Speeches 37:583-6 Jl 15
'71
STEPMOTHERS. See Stepparents
STEPPARENTS
Confessions of a wicked stepmother. G. L.
Cox. il Ladies Home J 88:104+ Mr '71
STEPS, Garden. See Garden steps
STERBA, James P.
Report from the majority of the world. il
N Y Times Mag p 12-13+ S 5 '71
STERCKX, Anthony
Studio. R. Goettsch. il por Ceram Mo 19:
18-19 F '71 •
STEREO amplifiers. See Amplifiers
STEREO cartridges. See Phonograph—Stereo-
phonic pickup
STEREO headphones. See Headphones
STEREOCHEMISTRY
Hydrogen-bond stereochemistry and anom-
alous water. B. Kamb. bibliog il Science
172:231-42 Ap 16 '71; Discussion. 173:1252
S 24 '71
Stereochemistry of hemes and other metallo-
porphyrins. J. L. Hoard. bibliog il Science
174:1295-302 D 24 '71
See also
Isomers and isomerism
STEREOPHONIC phonograph records. See
Phonograph records—Stereophonic records
STEREOPHONIC pickup. See Phonograph—
Stereophonic pickup
STEREOPHONIC radio receivers. See Radio
receivers, Stereophonic
STEREOPHONIC recorders. See Magnetic re-
corders and recording—Stereophonic re-
corders
STEREOPHONIC sound. See Sound—Stereo-
phonic recording and reproducing
STEREOPHONIC sound systems
Compact stereo systems. il Consumer Rep
36:711-15 N '71
Four-channel sound: where will it all end?
H. Fantel. il Pop Sci 199:86-8+ N '71
4-channel stereo, here at last! H. Fantel. il
Pop Mech 136:66-70+ Ag '71
4-channel stereo; Iras multisonic system. il
Radio-Electr 42:22 D '71
From two channels to four, with a little bit
o' pluck. R. S. Lanier. il Hi Fi 21:78-81
N '71
Newest: 4-channel stereo. R. Angus. il Mech
Illus 67:118-20+ N '71
Peg board: meet jack field. G. Movshon. il
Hi Fi 20:70-4 D '70
Smile, you're on four channels now! S. M.
Gallager. il Pop Mech 136:130-5+ N '71
Sound dollar: best buys in stereo. H. Fantel.
il Opera N 36:8-11 D 11 '71
Sound of music; music, music, music. T. Zito.
il Esquire 76:162-4+ N '71
Status report on four-channel stereo. J. D.
Hirsch. il Electr World 86:13-14 Ag '71
Stereo scene. See issues of Popular electron-
ics
Equipment
Good stereo at a glance; easy-to-make bal-
ance meter. R. Bloch. il Pop Mech 135:126-8
Ap '71
Stereo stocking stuffers, for under $23. R.
Long. il Hi Fi 21:66-70 D '71

STEREOPHONIC sound systems—*Continued*

Volume control

Those redundant volume controls. J. G. Holt. il Pop Electr 34:81-3+ Je '71

What's behind the knob? layman's guide to audio controls. L. Feldman. il Hi Fi 21:56-63 Jl '71

STEREOSCOPIC cameras. See Cameras

STERILITY, Induced. See Sterilization, Sexual

STERILITY in animals

Ceroid pigment formation and irreversible sterility in vitamin E deficiency. C. Raychaudhuri and I. D. Desai. bibliog il Science 173:1028-9 S 10 '71

STERILITY in insects

Chemosterilant action of anthramycin: a proposed mechanism. S. B. Horwitz and others. bibliog il Science 174:159-61 O 8 '71

STERILIZATION (birth control) See Sterilization, Sexual

STERILIZATION, Sexual

Birth control for men; vasectomy. E. M. Wylie. Read Digest 98:53-6 Ja '71

For men only: foolproof birth control; vasectomy. E. Dunbar. Look 35:45-6+ Mr 9 '71

Let George do it; vasectomy revolution. A. Gross. Mlle 73:160-1+ O '71

New birth-control freedom for women. E. M. Wylie. Read Digest 99:153-6 Ag '71

Offer band-aid sterilization for women; laparoscopy. E. Clift. McCalls 98:39 Jl '71

Pledge of love: vasectomy. L. Sabin. il Todays Health 49:24-5+ Jl '71

Question of sterilization; ed. by E. Edelson. W. M. Wolfe. Redbook 136:22+ Mr '71

Questions parents ask about sterilization. H. Edey. Parents Mag 46:66-7+ Mr '71

Vasectomy. D. Reuben. McCalls 98:26+ Jl '71

Vasectomy that is reversible. il Bsns W p72 S 4 '71

Voluntary sterilization. Consumer Rep 36: 384-6 Je '71

STERK, Sam

How to give real meaning to CIT programs. il Camp Mag 43:15-16 Mr '71

STERLING, Claire

Aswan Dam looses a flood of problems. il Life 70:46-46A F 12 '71

Aswan disaster. il Nat Parks & Con Mag 45: 10-13 Ag '71

STERLING, Theodor D.

Difficulty of evaluating the toxicity and teratogenicity of 2,4,5-T from existing animal experiments. bibliog Science 174:1858-9 D 24 '71

STERLING airways. See Airlines—Denmark

STERLING ball. See Balls (parties)

STERLING drug, inc.

He wants to lengthen antitrust's reach; supply space concept. por Bsns W p38+ My 22 '71

STERLING silver. See Silverware

STERN, Adele H.

Dedalus speaks to Bobby Dylan; address, November 1970. Engl J 60:610-14 My '71

STERN, Lothar, and Carroll, I. R.

Optoelectronic revolution. il Electr World 86: 46-8+ Jl '71

STERN, Richard Martin

About creative writing. Writer 84:9-10 Jl '71

STERN, Sol

Berkeley city council will never be the same. il N Y Times Mag p 14-16+ Ag 29 '71

Campaign to free Angela Davis, and Ruchell Magee. il por N Y Times Mag p8-9+ Je 27 '71

My Jewish problem, and ours. il Ramp Mag 10:30-40 Ag '71

STERN college for women. See Yeshiva university, New York

STERNBERG, R. W. and others

Oceanographic odyssey. il Travel 137:50-3 Ja '72

STERNBERG, Thomas H.

Skin deep. McCalls 98:28 F '71

STERNGLASS, Ernest J.

Health effects from radiation; address, July 14, 1971. Vital Speeches 37:699-703 S 1 '71

about

Great nuclear debate: are our newborn babies' lives in danger? M. Hope and J. Young. Redbook 138:16+ Ja '72 •

STERNLIEB, George S.

Are big cities worth saving? interview. il por U S News 71:42-6+ Jl 26 '71

STERNWHEELERS. See Steamships and steamboats

STEROID hormones. See Hormones, Sex

STEROIDS

See also
Corticosteroids
Lipids
Methylprednisolone
Testosterone

STETLER, C. Joseph

Hospital pharmacy-industry cooperation; address, December 10, 1970. Vital Speeches 37: 232-5 F 1 '71

STETTEN, DeWitt, Jr

Evaluation of basic science. Science 174:105 O 8 '71

Projected changes in medical school curriculum. bibliog il Science 174:1308-6 D 24 '71

STEVENS, A. C.

Here comes the Electric company. il Am Ed 7:18-23 N '71

STEVENS, Craig

Alexis Smith & Craig Stevens: nostalgic? Not on your life! A. G. Maser. pors Harp Baz 105:107 D '71 •

STEVENS, David

(ed) See Mesplé, M. Flair for precision

STEVENS, Elisabeth

Archeological find named Iris Love. il pors N Y Times Mag p32-4+ Mr 7 '71

STEVENS, George, 1904-

Above and beyond capital punishment. il Sat R 54:28-9 S 25 '71

Book designers are a pain in the neck. Sat R 54:20 F 6 '71

Ogden Nash: a memoir. Sat R 54:19 Je 19 '71

STEVENS, Georgiana G.

Egypt. Atlan 229:12-16 Ja '72

Suez. Atlan 228:16-19 Jl '71

STEVENS, J. P, and company

Flaw in the fabric at J. P. Stevens. il Bsns W p64-6 N 13 '71

STEVENS, Jack G. and Cook, M. L.

Latent herpes simplex virus in spinal ganglia of mice. bibliog il Science 173:843-5 Ag 27 '71

STEVENS, James Frank

John F. Stevens: pathfinder for western railroads. E. Clark. bibliog il pors Am West 8:28-33+ My '71 •

STEVENS, John Frank

A man, a plan, a canal, Panama! D. G. McCullough. il pors Am Heritage 22:64-71+ Je '71 •

STEVENS, Joseph

Hazards of journalism. Nation 212:773 Je 21 '71 •

STEVENS, Leonard A.

Breakthrough in water pollution. il Read Digest 98:167-8+ Je '71

STEVENS, Leslie

Up from the underground. P. S. Nathan. Pub W 200:40 O 25 '71 •

STEVENS, Preston, Jr

What can you do about ethnic change? il Am City 86:99-100 N '71

STEVENS, Robert Warren

Military spending & dollars abroad. il Nation 213:554-7 N 29 '71

STEVENS, Roger L.

Book committee elects Stevens, honors E. B. White. il Pub W 200:34 D 20 '71 •

STEVENS, S. S.

Neural events and the psychophysical law. bibliog il Science 170:1043-50; 172:502 D 4 '70, Ap 30 '71

STEVENS, Shane

Rat packs of New York. il N Y Times Mag p28-9+ N 28 '71

Writer's real world. Writer 84:11-12+ Jl '71

STEVENS, Thaddeus

Best white friend black Americans ever had. G. P. Morrill. il por Read Digest 99:169-70+ Jl '71 •

STEVENS, Thelma K.

Functional sculpture. il Sch Arts 71:26-7 O '71

STEVENS, Wallace

Comment. D. Hine. Poetry 119:171-2 D '71 •

STEVENS, Weston A.

Alas for him who never sees; excerpt from address. Read Digest 99:103-4 O '71

STEVENS Favorite (rifle) See Rifles

STEVENS PASS

John F. Stevens: pathfinder for western railroads. E. Clark. bibliog il pors Am West 8:28-33+ My '71

STEVENSON, Anne

Comment. R. J. Mills, jr. Poetry 117:334 F '71 •

STEVENSON, Charles

Wage madness in the construction industry. Read Digest 98:47-51 Ja '71

STEVENSON, Florence

Continuous present. il por Opera N 35:8-13 Ap 10 '71

Shooting star. il Opera N 35:24-6 Mr 27 '71

Three operas by Janacek. il Hi Fi 20:MA28-9 D '70

STEVENSON, James
Billy's design. New Yorker 46:26-7 Ja 9 '71
Communicating with your head. il New York-
er 47:40-1 O 16 '71
Discovery. New Yorker 47:30-1 Jl 3 '71
Metropolitan comics. New Yorker 47:36-9 Jl
17 '71
Metropolitan New York points of interest. il
New Yorker 46:38 F 6 '71
Oberfest. New Yorker 47:43 My 8 '71
Our local correspondents. New Yorker 47:
116+ N 13 '71; 47-9 Ja 1 '72
Pastry in motion. il New Yorker 47:32-4 S
4 '71
What to do on a Saturday. il New Yorker
47:34-6 Ag 7 '71

STEVENSON, John R.
Department urges Senate advice and consent
to ratification of hijacking convention; state-
ment, June 7, 1971. Dept State Bul 65:84-8
Jl 19 '71
International conference on air law approves
convention on aircraft hijacking; statement,
December 2, 1970. Dept State Bul 64:50-1 Ja
11 '71
Legal regulation of mineral exploitation in
the deep seabed; address, April 19, 1971.
Dept State Bul 65:48-55 Jl 12 '71
Search for equity on the seabeds; address,
February 9, 1971. Dept State Bul 64:529-33
Ap 19 '71
U.N. adopts principles governing seabed ex-
ploitation and decides to convene comprehensive law-of-the-sea conference in 1973:;
statement, December 8, 1970. Dept State
Bul 64:154-5 F 1 '71.
U.S. draft articles on territorial sea, straits,
and fisheries submitted to U.N. seabeds
committee; statement, August 3, 1971. Dept
State Bul 65:261-8 S 6 '71
U.S. oral statement on continued presence
of South Africa in Namibia presented before
the International court of justice; statement, March 9, 1971. Dept State Bul 64:542-
9 Ap 26 '71
War powers legislation: practical and constitutional problems; statement, June 2,
1971. Dept State Bul 64:833-6 Je 28 '71

STEVENSON, Robert Louis
Doctor Jekyll and Mr Cocaine. Sci N 99:264
Ap 17 '71 •
Silverado museum recalls Robert Louis Stev-
enson. il Sunset 146:28 Ja '71 •

STEVENSON, W. Taylor
Here today, here tomorrow. Chr Cent 88:
856-7 Jl 14 '71

STEVER, H. Guyford
Nixon makes it official: Stever in for McElroy. por Sci N 100:341 N 20 '71 •

STEW
Accent is garlic; daube. il N Y Times Mag
p47 Je 27 '71
Irish way and two other ways. Sunset 146:
156-7 Mr '71
Rosemary stew. il N Y Times Mag p47 Ag
15 '71
Slow-cooking stews. D. Eby and J. McCloskey.
il Bet Hom & Gard 49:76-7+ S '71
Soups and stews the new way; excerpts. L.
Driggs. il por Har Yrs 11:35-8 Ap '71
Stew: heterogenius mix. L. Witt. il Todays
Health 49:48-51 Mr '71
Stew surprises from the Caribbean. Sunset
146:139 F '71

STEWARDESSES, Air. See Airlines—Hostesses

STEWART, Charlotte
Training herbs. il Horticulture 49:28+ Mr '71

STEWART, Clay C.
There's a bird in the frog house! il Org Gard
& Farm 18:70-1 D '71
Tricks with leaves. il Org Gard & Farm
18:46-8 O '71

STEWART, Desmond
Scientific legacy of Iran. il UNESCO Courier
24:12-15 O '71

STEWART, Don
Man from Miracle Valley. Chr Today 16:43
O 8 '71 •

STEWART, Horace
Kindling a hope in the disadvantaged: a
study of the Afro-American healer. bibliog Ment Hy 55:96-100 Ja '71

STEWART, Jackie
Can-do Scot in the Can-Am. R. F. Jones.
il por Sports Illus 35:22-3 Jl 5 '71 •
How to last eleven laps and be happy. H.
Whall. il por(cover) Sports Illus 35:43-5 S
6 '71 •
It's not how long you wear your hair
but... G. S. Brown. il por Sports Illus 34:
70-1 Ap 5 '71 •

STEWART, James
Jimmy Stewart's personal picture album.
il pors Good H 172:88-91 Ap '71

STEWART, James Thompson
USAF prototype plans; excerpts from address, November 1971. Aviation W 95:9 N 29
'71

STEWART, John
John Stewart. J. Hiemenz. por Hi Fi 21:
MA18-19 D '71 •

STEWART, John Young
Lift a pint to the king, luv. R. F. Jones.
il por Sports Illus 35:14-17 Jl 26 '71 •

STEWART, Jon
Jack Nicholson looks east. il pors Ramp
Mag 10:51-4 S '71

STEWART, Maxwell S.
Nixon's new federalism: is it the answer?
Cur Hist 61:279-83+ N '71

STEWART, Natacha
Grief; story. New Yorker 47:45-9 O 9 '71

STEWART, Potter
Three points of view from the Court. Time
98:10-11 Jl 12 '71

STEWART, Robert
Migrant quarters; poem. America 125:403 N
13 '71

STEWART, Rod
Rod Stewart. E. Slants. il por Sr Schol 99:30-
1 N 29 '71 •

STEWART-GORDON, James
Best damn cowboy in the world. il Read
Digest 99:215-16+ S '71
Bike is back and booming! il Read Digest
99:185-8+ D '71
Mysterious jinx of the Hope diamond. il
Read Digest 99:25-30 Ag '71
Secret witness: new weapon against crime. il
Read Digest 99:190-1+ N '71
Sherlock Holmes lives again. Read Digest
98:203-6+ F '71
Take a bow, Lew Alcindor. il por Read Di-
gest 98:118-22 Ja '71

STEWIG, John Warren
Library books for leftover class time. bib-
liog il por Wilson Lib Bul 45:681-4 Mr '71;
Correction. 45:836 My '71

STEWS. See Stew

STICKERS. See Labels

STICKS and bones; drama. See Rabe, D.

**STIEPER, Donald R. See McClellan, T. A. jt.
auth.**

STIGGERS, Lester
Way for Lester. por Time 98:53 Jl 12 '71 •

STIGLER, Stephen M.
Cloud seeding experiments: possible bias.
bibliog Science 173:850 Ag 27 '71

STIGNANI, Ebe
All about Ebe; interview, ed. by E. Davidson.
por Opera N 35:28-9 Mr 20 '71

about

Historical records. A. Favia-Artsay. por Hobbies 76:36 Ja '72 •

STIGWOOD, Robert
J.C. superstar enterprises, inc. M. Haskell.
il Sat R 54:65-7+ O 30 '71 •

STILBESTROLS
Court suit asks ban on stilbestrol. L. Palmer.
Farm J 95:25 D '71
Hormonal time bomb? treatment with di-
ethylstilbestrol, cause of vaginal cancer.
Time 98:52-3 Ag 2 '71
Morning-after pill; diethylstilbestrol. Sci N
100:293 O 30 '71
Morning-after pill: diethylstilbestrol. Time
98:67 N 8 '71
Morning-after pill; diethylstilbestrol. il News-
week 78:74 N 8 '71
Now it's beef and mutton; DES controversy.
il Newsweek 78:85 N 8 '71
Price of beef; diethylstilbestrol residues. D.
Cottrell. bibliog il Environ 13:44-7+ Jl '71
What you'd better know about the meat you
are buying. J. Snyder. il Todays Health
49:37-9+ D '71

STILES, F. Gary
Time, energy, and territoriality of the anna
hummingbird (calypte anna) bibliog il
Science 173:818-21 Ag 27 '71

STILL life painting
Bric-a-brac still life. W. H. Gerdts. il An-
tiques 100:744-8 N '71
See also
Trompe-l'oeil

**STILL-life photography. See Photography—Still
life**

STILL point; ballet. See Ballets—Criticisms

STILLMAN, Beatrice
(tr) See Baranskaîa, N. Alarm clock in the
cupboard

STILLMAN, Irwin Maxwell, and Baker, S. S.
Doctor's quick teen-age diet; excerpt. il Mc-
Calls 98:78-9+ Ap '71

STILLWELL, Marjorie
Shelling bench. il por Org Gard & Farm
18:66 Ag '71

STILWELL, Joseph Warren
Retreat from Burma; excerpts from Stilwell and the American experience in China, 1911-45. B. W. Tuchman. il pors Am Heritage 22:38-43+ F '71 •
Stilwell and the American experience in China, 1911-45, by B. W. Tuchman. Review
  Bsns W il por p6 F 13 '71. J. K. Fairbank •
  Nat R 23:432-3+ Ap 20 '71. D. Brudnoy •
  Nation 212:533+ Ap 26 '71. A. S. Whiting •
  New Repub 164:25-6 Mr 27 '71. J. K. Fairbank •
  New Yorker 47:141-2+ My 15 '71. N. Bliven
  Newsweek por 77:85-6 F 15 '71. P. S. Prescott •
  Sat R il por 54:25-7+ F 20 '71. O. E. Clubb •

STIMSON, Allen
Space-age workbench has color-coded storage. il Pop Sci 199:88-90+ S '71

STIMULANTS
  See also
Amphetamines
Coffee
Methylphenidate

STIMULATION (physiology)
Activity change as the cause of apparent aversiveness during prolonged hypothalamic stimulation. J. W. Hu; J. Mendelson. bibliog il Science 172:84-6 Ap 2 '71
Analgesia from electrical stimulation in the brainstem of the rat. D. J. Mayer and others. bibliog il Science 174:1351-4 D 24 '71
Caudate nucleus stimulation retroactively impairs complex maze learning in the rat. H. V. S. Peeke and M. J. Herz. bibliog il Science 173:80-2 Jl 2 '71
Habituation of electrically induced readiness to gnaw. R. E. Cain and others. bibliog il Science 173:262-4 Jl 16 '71
Pineal N-acetyltransferase activity: effect of sympathetic stimulation. P. H. Volkman and A. Heller. bibliog il Science 173:839-40 Ag 27 '71
  See also
Electronic behavior control

STIMULUS and response
Dissociation of impairment after lateral and medial prefrontal lesions in dogs. J. Dabrowska. bibliog il Science 171:1037-8 Mr 12 '71
Never too late; increase in brain weight in mature rats by environmental stimulation. Sci Am 225:84 S '71
Perception of changes in certain exteroceptive stimuli. J. M. Notterman and others. bibliog il Science 173:1206-11 S 24 '71
Visual and auditory inputs into the cuneate nucleus. S. J. Jabbur and others. bibliog il Science 174:1146-7 D 10 '71
  See also
Motor response

STINNETT, Caskie
How to get and keep the upper hand with a French menu. Holiday 49:8+ F '71
On Holiday. il por Newsweek 77:60 Ja 25 '71 •

STIRLING, Marion W.
Olmec: America's first civilization. il Américas 23:S23-31 Je '71

STIRLING engines. See Heat engines

STITCHES. See Needlework

STITES, D. P. and others
Factor VIII detection by hemagglutination inhibition: hemophilia A and von Willebrand's disease. bibliog il Science 171:196-7 Ja 15 '71

STITH, Richard
Secular case against abortion on demand. Commonweal 95:151-4 N 12 '71

STOBART, John
John Stobart marine artist. L. Chmelik. il por Am Artist 35:46-51+ N '71 •

STOCHASTIC processes
Randomization and social affairs: the 1970 draft lottery. S. E. Fienberg. bibliog il Science 171:255-61 Ja 22 '71; Reply with rejoinder. C. J. Scheirer. 172:630+ My 14 '71
Randomization and the draft lottery; with tables. J. R. Rosenblatt and J. J. Filliben. bibliog Science 171:306-8 Ja 22 '71

STOCK, Henry M.
Historymobile. Parks & Rec 6:25+ Jl '71

STOCK, Robert
One of the old ones; poem. Yale R 60:393 Mr '71

STOCK averages. See Stocks—Price indexes and averages

STOCK brokers. See Brokers

STOCK car drivers. See Automobile racing drivers

STOCK car racing. See Automobile racing

STOCK certificates. See Stocks—Certificates
STOCK control (bookstores) See Booksellers and bookselling—Stock
STOCK dividends. See Dividends
STOCK exchange
Another unbelievable year in the stock market. Brutus. il Atlan 229:81-5 Ja '72
Market comment. L. O. Hooper. See issues of Forbes
Market outlook. S. B. Lurie. See issues of Forbes
More protection for investors: latest moves; recommendation of the Martin report. il U S News 71:55-7 Ag 16 '71
Outlook for securities markets. W. L. Cary and W. Werner. Harvard Bsns R 49:16-18+ Jl '71
Stock analysis. H. H. Biel. See issues of Forbes
Stock trends. See second issue of each month of Forbes
Why stock market is jittery. il U S News 71:40-2 Jl 12 '71
  See also
Arbitrage
Brokers
Computers—Investment use
Government investigations—Stock exchange
Put and call transactions
Stocks—Marketing

Crisis, October 1929
Day the stock market crashed. D. Wharton. il Read Digest 99:57-9+ O '71

Records
Back-office crunch haunts the Street. il Bsns W p74 F 13 '71
Meeting the volume test. C. Morgello. il Newsweek 77:80 F 22 '71
Tighter rules for heavier trading. Bsns W p72+ F 27 '71
Watchdog moves in on the back office. Bsns W p39 Ap 17 '71

Regulation
Market structure: remodel or reform? proposals of P. Kolton. por Bsns W p47-8 O 23 '71
More protection for investors: latest moves; with interview with W. J. Casey. il U S News 71:50-7 Ag 16 '71
Rendering the rest of the bill. Forbes 107:17 My 1 '71
Tighter rules for heavier trading. Bsns W p72+ F 27 '71
Unbelievable last months of Hayden, Stone. C. J. Loomis. il Fortune 83:114-16+ Ja '71
Whistle-blowing on Wall Street; case of Loeb, Rhoades & co. D. McClintick. New Repub 165:20-5 S 4 '71
  See also
United States—Securities and exchange commission

Chicago
Midwest solution for back-office paper; Signet 80. Bsns W p36-7 Je 19 '71

New York (city)
Aftershocks; big board's suit against Orvis brothers & co. Newsweek 78:68+ Jl 12 '71
Back-office crunch haunts the Street. il Bsns W p74 F 13 '71
Big board bows to Perot. Bsns W p22 My 8 '71
Big board starts defogging; special trust fund payments to houses in liquidation. il Bsns W p80 Ja 16 '71
Big board study brings Martin back. por Bsns W p 16-17 Ja 30 '71
Big buyers start to bargain; block trading. il Bsns W p74 Ap 3 '71
Big step backward: proposed creation of a national stock exchange system; the W. M. Martin report. C. Mathews. il Nation 213:593-5 D 6 '71
Calling Bill Martin. Newsweek 77:52 F 1 '71
Coming wounds of Wall Street. L. H. Lapham. Harper 242:47-50+ My '71
Costs of change. C. Morgello. il Newsweek 77:82 F 8 '71
Double blow for the big board. il Time 97:75-6 Ap 19 '71
Fat in the fire; institutional memberships. Newsweek 77:80 F 8 '71
Fleecing the lambs, by C. Elias. Review Sat R 54:55+ O 16 '71. J. Brooks
Free trade comes to Wall Street. il Newsweek 77:97-8 Ap 19 '71
Haack steps down. Time 98:106 N 1 '71
How Martin would reform the markets. Bsns W p23-4 Ag 7 '71
Institutions get a foot on the floor. il Bsns W p 15-16 Ja 30 '71

STOCK exchange—New York (city)—*Cont.*
Jefferies case: cracking the exchange; anti-
trust suit. Bsns W p73 O 16 '71
Keeping the funds at arm's length; institu-
tional membership. Bsns W p44 F 27 '71
Leaving the big board; loss of block trades. il
Fortune 83:145-6 Ja '71
Martin is about to end the suspense. Bsns
W p25 Jl 31 '71
**Mr Nice Guy goes to Wall St. por Time 97:
85-6 My 3 '71**
**New scenario for the big board. il por Bsns
W p64 My 22 '71**
Power to the SEC? Newsweek 79:50 Ja 10
'72
Rating the new rates. C. Morgello. il News-
week 78:100 O 25 '71
Saul steps down. por Newsweek 77:83 Mr 29
'71
Second wind. Time 97:78 Mr 29 '71
Somewhere over the rainbow. it's 1972. il
Bsns W p38 Mr 13 '71
Tantrums among the giants. il Time 97:77-8
F 8 '71
Tempered enthusiasm; market moves into
new year. il Time 99:21 Ja 17 '72
To thine own self be true: reply with re-
joinder. L. J. Weil. Nat R 23:118+ F 9 '71
Unbelievable last months of Hayden, Stone.
C. J. Loomis. il Fortune 83:114-16+ Ja '71
Wall Street. C. Morgello. See issues of News-
week
Wall Street security risk by H. Baruch.
Review
Newsweek 78:90+ S 13 '71
Wall Street: the Martin report. il por News-
week 78:61-2 Ag 16 '71
Woes of Wall Street: interview. ed. by R.
Brady. F. Carr. il por Duns 98:8-9+ S '71
See also
Wall Street

Rio de Janeiro
Rio's stocks samba to a boomtime beat.
il Bsns W p43 Ja 16 '71

Salt Lake City
Penny saved... il Newsweek 77:88 Je 7 '71

Tokyo
Street's pipeline to Japanese stocks. il Bsns W
p66+ My 29 '71
STOCK exchange specialists. See Securities—
Marketing
STOCK fraud. See Fraud
STOCK market. See Stock exchange
STOCK market clubs. See Investment clubs
STOCK option contracts. See Put and call
transactions
STOCK ownership, Employee. See Employees as
stockholders
STOCK purchase options
Industry gropes for a better option plan.
il Bsns W p50+ Ag 21 '71
New executive perk: loans for options. J.
Perham. il Duns 97:39-41 Je '71
Riskless options? Duns 97:71 Je '71
Stock options: hope springs eternal. il Forbes
108:42-3 Ag 15 '71
Top men demand new kinds of pay. il Bsns
W p65-6 Ja 23 '71
STOCK ranges
Cloud in the big sky; locked gates bar hunt-
ers and fishermen from public lands. W. A.
Fairhurst and B. East. il Outdoor Life 148:
31-3+ Jl '71
Lasater ranch: applied range ecology. F. T.
Colbert. il Nat Parks & Con Mag 45:18-20
Mr '71
STOCK specialists. See Securities—Marketing
STOCK ticker machines
GM . . . X . . . DD . . . hic; nonbrokerage
house locations. il Time 98:72 S 20 '71
STOCK trailers. See Trailers
STOCKBROKERS. See Brokers
STOCKDALE, Frank E.
DNA synthesis in differentiating skeleta
muscle cells: initiation by ultraviolet light.
bibliog il Science 171:1145-7 Mr 19 '71
STOCKHAUSEN, Karlheinz
Cosmic anthems. H. Saal. por Newsweek 77:
93 Mr 8 '71 *
Music to my ears; performance of Hymnen
by New York philharmonic. I. Kolodin.
Sat R 54:24 Mr 13 '71 *
Musical events; Hymnen in Philharmonic
Hall. W. Sargeant. New Yorker 47:127 Mr
13 '71 *
New resonances from Stockhausen's Stim-
mung. I. Kolodin. Sat R 54:19 D 11 '71 *
STOCKHOLDERS
Are small investors souring on stocks? il
U S News 71:68-9 Ag 2 '71

Controlling shareholder servicing costs; re-
purchasing small shareholdings. A. Young
and W. Marshall. bibliog f il Harvard Bsns
R 49:71-8 Ja '71
Disenchantment of the odd-lotter. il Bsns W
p22-3 O 30 '71
Dying breed? por Forbes 108:17 Jl 15 '71
High cost of shareholder democracy. Duns
98:112 S '71
**Money game: playing to win. A. M. Watkins.
McCalls 98:38 My '71**
Moral power of shareholders. il Bsns W p76+
My 1 '71
SAP! Power to women. McCalls 99:47 O '71
See also
Employees as stockholders
Investor relations programs
Proxies
Women as investors

Anecdotes, facetiae, satire, etc.
Confessions of a stockbroker. Brutus. Atlan
228:46-52 Jl '71

Psychology
Sex: up with the stock market. B. Wysor.
Vogue 157:87-8+ F 15 '71
STOCKHOLDERS meetings
Annual meeting, 1971. J. Perham. Duns 97:
31-5+ Mr '71
New gadflies; Japanese stockholders' meet-
ings. il Newsweek 77:83 Je 14 '71
Social activists switch to proxy power. il
Bsns W p86-7 F 13 '71
With the volume lower, the issues are heard.
il Bsns W p21-2 My 1 '71

Anecdotes, facetiae, satire, etc.
Annual meeting of the corporation. W. Zins-
ser. il N Y Times Mag p9+ My 16 '71
STOCKHOLM

Description
Stockholm when the Swedes split. D. But-
win. il Sat R 54:50-2 O 9 '71
STOCKHOLM international peace research in-
stitute
Merchants of death; SIPRI study of the in-
ternational trade in arms. Sci Am 226:44-5
Ja '72
STOCKHOLM protocol. See Copyright
STOCKING of streams, lakes, etc. See Fish
culture
STOCKINGER, Joe, and Stockinger, N. F.
Who says you can't grow blueberries in
Kansas? il por Org Gard & Farm 18:50-3
F '71
STOCKINGER, Niles F. See Stockinger, J. jt.
auth.
STOCKINGS. See Hosiery
STOCKLIN, William A.
Be cool: cook with a microwave oven. il
Electr World 86:44-5 Jl '71
Merger! por Electr World 86:6 D '71
STOCKPILING
Steel hedge-buying is off to a late start.
il Bsns W p39-40 Mr 13 '71
STOCKS
Analysis bet on consumers; consumer-ori-
ented stock group. il Bsns W p94 Ap 10 '71
Bad new era for common stocks. D. Selig-
man. il Fortune 84:73-5+ O '71
Earnings are what really count. il Forbes
108:63 D 1 '71
Investing in companies that profit from plea-
sure. il Changing T 25:35-40 Je '71
Is preferred the right word? il Forbes 108:46
Jl 1 '71
Is this any time to be putting money into
stocks? il Changing T 26:7-11 Ja '72
Loaded laggards: 1971. il Forbes 108:31 Jl 1
'71
Making money work: should you buy con-
vertible stocks and bonds? S. Meisenberg.
Har Yrs 11:44-5 Ag '71
Market as contact (lens) sport. S. H. Brown.
il Life 71:8 Ag 13 '71
New new-issues boom? with table. Forbes
108:40 D 15 '71
Rebound candidates: they're down, but are
they out? table. Forbes 108:48 N 1 '71
6 per cent payers: bargains or leftovers?
table. Forbes 107:38 F 15 '71
Stockbuying: what to look for in industries.
C. J. Rolo. Bet Hom & Gard 49:24+ O '71
These are times of technical adjustment; ed.
by R. H. Boyle. Sports Illus 35:95-6+ O 18
'71
What they bought went up; what they sold
went up, too! tables. Forbes 108:65 Jl 15
'71
Where big investors are putting their money.
il U S News 70:18-20 Mr 29 '71

STOCKS—*Continued*
Who's where in growth; tables. Forbes 109: 51-2+ Ja 1 '72
See also
Bonds
Dividends
Stock exchange
Stock purchase options
also subhead Securities under various subjects, e.g. Banks and banking—Securities

Certificates
Closing in on the stock certificate. il Bsns W p 19 Jl 3 '71

Marketing
Action over-the-counter; views of security analysts, ed. by A. Hershman. il Duns 97: 29-33 Je '71
Happy mood in the market. Time 97:78 F 8 '71
Higher meaning of NASDAQ; market for over-the-counter stocks. il Fortune 83:141-2+ Ap '71
New issues rouse investors. Bsns W p74 S 18 '71
See also
National association of securities dealers
Stocks—Repurchase

Odd lots
Are small investors souring on stocks? il U S News 71:68-9 Ag 2 '71
Disenchantment of the odd-lotter. il Bsns W p22-3 O 30 '71
How odd of the public. C. Morgello. il Newsweek 78:68 Ag 2 '71
Look at the little guy; odd-lot sales. C. Morgello. il Newsweek 77:64 Ja 18 '71

Price earnings ratios
Melting multiple? C. Morgello. il Newsweek 78:102 N 8 '71

Price forecasting
Boom, we'll be at 1,000. C. Morgello. Newsweek 78:84 O 11 '71
Brokers' choice. C. Morgello. il Newsweek 77:92 Je 14 '71
Econometric stab at stock forecasting; Shilling and Keran models. il Bsns W p36+ My 26 '71
Going up. N. B. Schreiber. por Forbes 108:79 S 15 '71
Groups to watch. C. Morgello. il Newsweek 77:72 Ja 25 '71
How the pros see it now. C. Morgello. Newsweek 77:90 Mr 29 '71
Outlook for stocks as the analysts see it. il U S News 70:51-3 My 31 '71
Phase 2 and the stock market, a look ahead. il U S News 71:26+ O 18 '71
Stocks in '72: steady gains; interview. G. Putnam. il por U S News 72:58-60 Ja 10 '72
Where stocks are headed. il U S News 70:17-19 F 15 '71

Price indexes and averages
Bears march again in Wall Street. il Bsns W p24 Ag 7 '71
Boom in stocks: what it means. il U S News 70:17-19 My 3 '71
Breather after a skid. il Bsns W p21 Je 26 '71
Bulls return to Wall Street. il Bsns W p75-6 Ag 21 '71
Contrarian; views of J. Neff of the Windsor fund. R. Brady. por Duns 97:100A-100B Mr '71
Descent into limbo. il Time 98:22 N 8 '71
Does stock market indicate a trend? il U S News 71:30-1 D 13 '71
Freeze, float, surcharge: impact on investors abroad. il U S News 71:88-90 S 13 '71
Garden of wallflowers; table. Forbes 107:62 Ap 15 '71
Hopes go higher with the market. il Bsns W p 16 Ja 30 '71
Investors rally, in a cautious way. il Bsns W p 16 D 25 '71
Keeping on top of the market. C. Rolo. Bet Hom & Gard 49:18-19 Ja '71
Market rides on new confidence. il Bsns W p 19 Ag 28 '71
Nixon rally sets a record. il Newsweek 78:20-1 Ag 30 '71
Phase II scares the stock market. Bsns W p26+ N 27 '71
Quarterly survey of corporate performance; with tables. Bsns W p41-52+ My 8; 47-54+ Ag 14; 71-8+ N 13 '71
Runaway market stops for breath. Bsns W p28 My 22 '71
Share in the market. C. Morgello. il Newsweek 77:84 Ap 26 '71

Technician's perspective. J. W. Schulz. See issues of Forbes
Tiny bull walks on Wall Street. il Bsns W p34 N 6 '71
Uncertainty kills the Nixon bull market. il Bsns W p84 O 23 '71
Uneasy stock market: what experts think. il U S News 71:17-19 Ag 23 '71
Wall Street:
  Analyzing the rally. C. Morgello. il Newsweek 78:46 D 27 '71
  Bull's waning signs. C. Morgello. il por Newsweek 78:59 Ag 9 '71
  Devaluation values. C. Morgello. il Newsweek 79:40 Ja 3 '72
  Drip-drip and a bounce. C. Morgello. il Newsweek 78:99 D 6 '71
  Gauging the Nixon rally. C. Morgello. il Newsweek 78:96 S 13 '71
  Here we go again. C. Morgello. il Newsweek 77:66 F 15 '71
  How high is up? C. Morgello. il Newsweek 77:90 Mr 15 '71
  How sweet it was. C. Morgello. il Newsweek 77:82 Mr 1 '71
  Hunting for bargains. C. Morgello. il Newsweek 78:75 D 20 '71
  Marking time. C. Morgello. il Newsweek 78:68 N 1 '71
  Name of the game. C. Morgello. il Newsweek 77:90 My 17 '71
  Will the Dow top 1000? C. Morgello. Newsweek 77:74 My 3 '71
Wall Street ignores the money crisis. il Bsns W p 106+ My 15 '71
Wall Street's first reading; 50 best, and 50 worst performers. il Forbes 108:60-1 S 15 '71
What's happening in the stock market, and why. il U S News 71:26-7 N 15 '71
Where big investors are putting their money. il U S News 70:18-20 Mr 29 '71
Where stocks are headed. il U S News 70:17-19 F 15 '71
Where the action is; table. Forbes 107:33 My 1 '71
Why stock market is jittery. il U S News 71:40-2 Jl 12 '71
Why the tumble. C. Morgello. il Newsweek 77:70 My 31 '71

Anecdotes, facetiae, satire, etc.
Mr Sullivan discusses the stock market (with apologies to Mr Arbuthnot) H. Morgan. Sat R 54:4 Ja 23 '71

Repurchase
Controlling shareholder servicing costs. A. Young and W. Marshall. bibliog f il Harvard Bsns R 49:71-8 Ja '71

Valuation
See Corporations—Valuation
STOCKS, Repurchasing of. See Stocks—Repurchase
STOCKSTILL, Louis R.
Don't ever forget! Read Digest 98:117-20 My '71
Inside the prisons of Hanoi. Read Digest 98: 67-72 Ap '71
STOCKTON, Edward L.
Pittsburgh: from smoky city to smog-less skies. il UNESCO Courier 24:14-17 Jl '71
STOCKTON, Peter D. H. and Newman, Barbara
Another flight of fancy. Nation 212:653-6 My 24 '71
STODDART, Phil
Plastic frames for your pictures. il Design 73:11 Fall '71
STOERMER, Eugene F. See Schelske, C. L. jt. auth.
STOESSINGER, John G.
Authors & editors. D. N. Mount. por Pub W 200:15-17 S 20 '71 •
(comp) Recent books on international relations. See issues of Foreign affairs
STOEWSAND, Gilbert S. and others
Eggshell thinning in Japanese quail fed mercuric chloride. bibliog il Science 173:1030-1 S 10 '71
STOHLMAN, Martha Lou
Appellations. Sat R 54:4+ Ja 23 '71
STOKER, Bram
Dracula: Sabbat; dramatization. See Katz, L.
STOKES, Allen W. See Watts, C. R. jt. auth.
STOKES, Carl Burton
Carl Stokes drops out. il por Time 97:18-19 Ap 26 '71 •
STOKES, Donald Gresham, baron Stokes of Leyland. See Stokes of Leyland, D. G. S.
STOKES, Fanny Wister
House at Broad and Locust. il Opera N 35: 8-12 Ja 23 '71

STOKES, Terry
Getting the company to back our relationship; poem. Esquire 76:24 D '71
Natural disasters; poem. Esquire 75:123 Je '71
Spending your life killing yourself; poem. Nation 214:58 Ja 10 '72
Through the window; poem. Esquire 75:40 My '71
Winter light; poem. Nation 212:220 F 15 '71
STOKES of Leyland, Donald Gresham Stokes, baron
Motor trend interview. il pors Motor T 23: 86+ Ag '71
STOKINGER, H. E.
Sanity in research and evaluation of environmental health. bibliog Science 174:662-5 N 12 '71
STOKLEY, James
Astronomy. See fourth issue of each month of Science news
STOKVIS, Irene Ellen
(comp) Adult paperbacks. Library J 96: 299-324 Ja 15 '71
(ed) First novelists; spring-summer-fall, 1971. il Library J 96:505-11, 2118-21, 3164-8 F 1 Je 15, O 1 '71
—and Horwitz, Carey
(comps) Adult paperbacks. Library J 96:1839-65, 2866+ My 15, S 15 '71
STOLLEY, Richard B.
Family jest blossoms into the real thing. il Life 71:30-6 O 22 '71
STOLZ, Alan J.
Let's put an end to lost camper hazards on trips. Camp Mag 43:14 Mr '71
STOMACH
Why the stomach does not digest itself. H. W. Davenport. il Sci Am 226:86-93 bibliog(p 122) Ja '72
  See also
Peptic ulcers

Diseases
  See Foreign bodies (physiology)
STOMACH cancer. See Cancer
STOMACH ulcers. See Peptic ulcers
STONE, Charles Edward
Teacher retirement systems. Ed Digest 37:42-4 D '71
STONE, Edward H.
There's a wheelchair in the woods. il Parks & Rec 6:18-21+ D '71
STONE, Gene
In my opinion. por Seventeen 29:216 N '70
STONE, Gerald
Healthier and less perplexed. il por Time 97: 36-7 My 24 '71 *
STONE, Gregory P. See Mahigel, E. L. jt. auth.
STONE, Irving
Passions of the mind; story. McCalls 98:133-40 Mr '71
STONE, Irwin
Vitamin C mania. P. O'Neil. il por Life 71: 55-6+ Jl 9 '71 *
STONE, Isidor Feinstein
Armchair revolutionary. M. M. Uhlmann. Nat R 23:437-9 Ap 20 '71 *
End of the Stone age. por Time 98:52 D 20 '71 *
Investigator. G. Wolff. por Newsweek 77: 92 F 8 '71 *
Washington's venerable rebel. S. McBee. McCalls 98:43 S '71 *
STONE, Michael
Movie. Chr Cent 88:955 Ag 11 '71
STONE, Ralph
How MTM can improve refuse collection. il Am City 86:74+ O '71
STONE, Ronald
Arraignment in Harrisburg. Chr Cent 88:589-92 My 12 '71
Politics of the kingdom of God. Chr Cent 88:337-40 Mr 17 '71
STONE, Ruth
Inner world where poets wander. J. Kessler. Sat R 54:50 O 2 '71 *
STONE, William T.
Washington report. See issues of Yachting
STONE, Artificial
  See also
Marble, Artificial
STONE age
Sea shells from what seashore? Unusual pattern of Neolithic trade. Sci Am 224:47 F '71
Seashells and an ancient trade route. il Chem 44:22-3 F '71
  See also
Man, Prehistoric
Stone implements and weapons

Ireland
Land clearance in the Irish neolithic: new evidence and interpretation. J. R. Pilcher and others. bibliog il Science 172:560-2 My 7 '71

STONE Implements and weapons
Early man in the Andes. R. S. MacNeish. il Sci Am 224:36-46 Ap '71
Thermal alteration of silica minerals: an archeological approach. B. A. Purdy and H. K. Brooks. bibliog il Science 173:322-5 Jl 23 '71
  See also
Indians of North America—Implements
STONE painting. See Painting on stone
STONE pictures. See Pictures
STONE rubbings. See Rubbings
STONE sheep hunting. See Mountain sheep hunting
STONEBURNER, Tony
Metamorphoses of energy; poem. Chr Cent 88:188 F 10 '71
Photographer of fog; poem. Chr Cent 88:68 Ja 20 '71
STONECROPS. See Sedums
STONE'S, I. F. bi-weekly. See I. F. Stone's bi-weekly
STONESIFER, Howard
Grooving with film. il Har Yrs 11:6-8 S '71
STONEWARE. See Pottery
STONEWARE, American. See Pottery, American
STONG, C. L.
(ed) Amateur scientist. See issues of Scientific American
STONINGTON, Conn.
Profiles. A. Bailey. New Yorker 47:36-44+ Jl 24; 38-52+ Jl 31 '71
STONY BROOK campus, State university of New York. See New York (state). State university—Stony Brook campus
STONY BROOK school, N.Y. See Church schools
STOOP, Norma McLain
Not a Swan lake swan. il por Dance Mag 46:36-9+ Ja '72
Of time and Alvin Ailey. il por Dance Mag 45:28-33 D '71
Reviewing the tube. Dance Mag 45:102 N '71; 46:89-90 Ja '72
(tr) See Christout, M. F. Béjart's Nijinsky: Clown of God
STOPPERS, Bottle. See Bottle caps and seals
STORAGE
  See also
Garden houses, shelters, etc.
  also subhead Storage under various subjects, e.g. Farm produce—Storage
STORAGE batteries
Electric cars: the battery problem; adaptation of address, December, 1970. V. Wouk. il Bul Atom Sci 27:19-22 Ap '71
Everything you always wanted to know about all those little batteries. E. F. Lindsley. il Pop Sci 198:46-8+ Ja '71
Just add water, and this battery goes to work. il Pop Sci 198:126 Ap '71
New story on batteries: your car's battery. T. Tappett. il Mech Illus 67:108+ O '71
Racer's test; Juice box battery. J. Dianna. il Hot Rod 24:112-13 Je '71

Care
Follow these ABC's of good battery care. Suc Farm 69:G26 Ap '71
How to store your boat battery for the winter. M. Schultz. il Pop Mech 136:120-1+ N '71
Phototronics; ways to get more out of nickel-cadmium batteries. E. Farber. Mod Phot 35:128-9 Ja '71
Start with cold-weather battery care. P. B. Jones. il Suc Farm 69:C1 N '71
Tools and techniques for a battery service center. R. Day. il Pop Sci 199:114 S '71

Charging
Phototronics; recharging Vivitar flash units. E. Farber. Mod Phot 36:125 Ja '72
STORAGE battery chargers
Phototronics; cadmium-cadmium coulometer. E. Farber. Mod Phot 35:73-4 N '71
Phototronics; McCulloch rapid charger for Honeywell units. E. Farber. Mod Phot 35: 42+ O '71
Pick the best battery charger for your boat. C. Miller. il Motor B & S 127:78-9+ My '71
STORAGE cabinets. See Cabinets (furniture)
STORAGE cellars. See Basements and cellars
STORAGE in boats. See Boats—Equipment
STORAGE in the home
Build your own storage. il Bet Hom & Gard 49:140 D '71
Double-duty units expand a country condominium. H. Brown. il Am Home 74:59-62 F '71

STORAGE in the home—*Continued*
4 ways to solve storage problems. R. Adams.
il House B 113:88-9 Ap '71
Homes on a corner lot: a storage maze in
the front yard. il Pop Sci 198:76 Ja '71
How to find those hidden storage spaces.
J. Hand. il Mech Illus 67:95-6+ F '71
Order out of chaos. A. Lees. il Pop Sci 199:
92-4 S '71
Our new super kitchen; wide open storage.
il House & Gard 139:38-9 Ja '71
Search for space; bright ideas in the kitchen.
il House B 113:110-11+ S '71
Space-makers. M. Davidson. il Ladies Home
J 88:102 S '71
Spectacular new storage strategies. il House
& Gard 139:98-103 Mr '71
Storage cubes resemble grocery-store cartons.
il Consumer Rep 37:7 Ja '72
Storage ideas for a bigger, better house. N.
Seney. il Bet Hom & Gard 49:54-65 O '71
Storage ideas plus new equipment; new
kitchen life. il House & Gard 140:70-1 Jl '71
Storage units that swing. il Bet Hom & Gard
49:150 Ap '71
Where can I put it all? il Redbook 136:68-9+
Ja '71
See also
Closets
Kitchen cabinets
Storage walls
STORAGE of food. See Food—Storage
STORAGE rings. See Accelerators (electrons,
etc)
STORAGE tanks. See Water tanks
STORAGE walls
All systems go for space. V. D. Hahn. il Am
Home 74:63-5 F '71
Behind those handsome walls: storage galore.
H. Wicks. il Pop Mech 136:144-7 O '71
Everything wall; laundry-sewing center. M.
K. Spencer. il Am Home 74:76-8 F '71
Nifty hobby wall everybody will like. il
Farm J 95:47 Ja '71
Ringbound storage wall from a kit. H. Wicks.
il Pop Mech 136:94-6 S '71
Working walls. N. Seney and J. Pinkham. il
Bet Hom & Gard 49:56-7 My '71
STORANDT, Priscilla
Bread. New Yorker 47:30-2 Ap 3 '71 *
STORE hours
Back in ten minutes. J. Ferris. Sat R 55:6
Ja 8 '72
See also
Business hours
STORED grain. See Grain, Stored
STORES
Design for merchandising. il Arch Rec 149:89-
104 F '71
See also
Chain stores
Department stores
Food stores
Furniture stores
Retail trade
Salesmen and salesmanship
Shopping centers
Specialty stores
Supermarkets
also subhead Stores under names of
cities, e.g. New York (city)—Stores

Employees
See also
Booksellers and bookselling—Employees
STORES, Self service
See also
Supermarkets
STOREY, David
Contractor. Criticism
Newsweek il 78:114 D 13 '71 *
Time 98:55 D 27 '71 *
STORIES. See Childrens stories; Fairy tales
STORIES of operas. See Libretto
STORKS
Courtship of storks. M. P. Kahl. il Natur
Hist 80:36-45 O '71
Parting shots: Vienna's operation stork. il
Life 71:64-5 Jl 30 '71
STORLI, Tom J.
Riding a giant's coattails. Flying 89:82+
O '71
STORM, Frank, family
Fighting the genetic odds. M. Steinmann.
il pors Life 71:18-25 Ag 6 '71 *
STORM sewers
New and old storm drains team up: Penn-
sauken, N.J. A. R. Pagan. il Am City 86:
112 Ap '71
STORM water. See Storm sewers
STORM windows. See Windows
STORMS
Anatomy of a squall. J. McCollam. il Yacht-
ing 129:64-5+ Ap '71

Lessons from the squall. G. J. Hess. il Yacht-
ing 129:64+ Je '71
Our far-flung correspondents; big rain and
floods over Nelson County, Va. E. Kin-
kead. New Yorker 47:66+ Jl 31 '71
Record severe storms in a dense meteoro-
logical network. S. A. Changnon, jr. and J.
W. Wilson. bibliog il Weatherwise 24:152-63
Ag '71
Safety-first measures to take in major wind-
storms. Good H 172:189 My '71
See also
Dust storms
Hail
Hurricanes
Ice storms
Snowstorms
Thunderstorms
Tornadoes
Winds
STORR, Anthony
Genius: what is it? Who has it? Vogue 157:
108+ Mr 1 '71
STORY telling
Caldecott award acceptance; address, June
21, 1971. G. E. Haley. Horn Bk 47:363-8 Ag
'71
Daddy tells a story. S. A. Stutz. il Parents
Mag 46:48+ Je '71
Jacqueline Susann's bedtime stories; inter-
view, ed. by S. Ribakove and B. Ribakove.
il Todays Health 49:30-3+ S '71
STORY telling records. See Phonograph records
—Childrens records
STORY theatre; drama. See Sills, P.
STORYTELLING. See Story telling
STOTLER, Donald
Environmental education as liberation. Ed
Digest 36:38-41 My '71
STOUGHTENBURGH, John L.
Museum world. See issues of Hobbies
STOUT, Joe A.
Henry A. Crabb, filibuster or colonizer? il
pors Am West 8:4-9 My '71
STOUT, Rex
Do orchids have the right to privacy? il
Holiday 48:19-21 S '70
STOUT, Robert Joe
Norther coming in; poem. Chr Cent 88:776
Je 23 '71
STOUT, Ruth
Do you save seeds? Watch it! il Org Gard
& Farm 18:50-3 Ja '71
Please pass the poison. il Org Gard & Farm
18:36-9 Je '71
Visit with Ruth Stout at 87; interview, ed.
by M. C. Goldman. il por Org Gard & Farm
18:56-8 O '71
You can thumb your nose at fall frost! por
Org Gard & Farm 18:59-61 S '71
STOUT, Thomas M. See Dooley, A. R. jt. auth.
STOVALL, Robert
Wall Street view. por Forbes 107:60 Ja 15;
79 Mr 15; 84-5 Ap 15; 68 Je 15; 108:77
Jl 15; 86 Ag 15; 86-7 O 1; 95 O 15; 109-10
N 15; 96 D 1; 58-9 D 15 '71
STOVES
What you should know about today's ranges.
J. R. Cary. il Parents Mag 46:73-5 O '71
See also
Camp stoves
Electric stoves
Solar cookers
STOWE, Harriet Elizabeth (Beecher)
Voice of Harriet Beecher Stowe. H. Birdoff.
il por Hobbies 76:35-6+ Jl '71 *
STOWE, Leland
Hokkaido: Japan's frontier wonderland. il
Read Digest 99:138-44 N '71
STOWERS, Carlton
Full-time freelancing in rural route U.S.A. il
Writers Digest 51:35-6+ Ap '71
Pride of Lions in cattle country. il Sports
Illus 35:38-42 N 1 '71
STRABISMUS
Anomalous retinal pathways in the Siamese
cat; an inadequate substrate for normal
binocular vision. R. E. Kalil and others.
bibliog il Science 174:302-5 O 15 '71
STRACKBEIN, O. R.
Changing basis for protectionism; address,
February 24, 1971. Vital Speeches 37:401-4
Ap 15 '71
STRADLEY, William E.
Getting to the top of the staff totem pole.
Clear House 45:538-40 My '71
STRAGE, Mark
VD: the clock is ticking. il Todays Health
49:16-18+ Ap '71
STRAIGHT, Michael
Caravaggio. Criticism
Sat R 54:34 Jl 24 '71 *
STRAIGHT, Michael Whitney
Arts & society; address, November 15, 1970.
Vital Speeches 37:394-8 Ap 15 '71

STRAIN, E. William
Prison escape. il por Library J 96:169-70
Ja 15 '71
STRAINS and stresses
See also
Wind-pressure
STRAIT of Juan de Fuca. See Juan de Fuca
Strait
STRAITS of Florida. See Florida, Straits of
STRAN-steel corporation
How a library project got off the shelf;
Stran-steel employees involved in commu-
nity improvement. V. Louviere. Nations
Bsns 59:21 N '71
STRAND, Mark
Formulas for oblivion; poem. Harper 242:93
Je '71
about
Comment. J. Martin. Poetry 118:347-8 S '71 •
STRAND, Paul
Paul Strand: close-up on the long view. M.
R. Weiss. il Sat R 54:20-1 D 18 '71 •
Right moment. D. Davis. il Newsweek 78:
106 D 6 '71 •
STRANDBERG, Warren. See Perrone, V. jt.
auth.
STRANGE-dreaming Charlie, cow-eyed Charlie;
story. See Batki, J.
STRASSER, Jonathan
American festival orchestra goes to Italy.
il Hi Fi 21:MA10-11 F '71
STRATE, Grant
Dance with a liberal education. G. Thomson.
il por Dance Mag 45:66-7 Ap '71 •
STRATEGIC air command. See United States—
Air force—Strategic air command
STRATEGIC arms limitation talks
Agreeing to try to agree. il Newsweek 77:
15-16 My 31 '71
Arms and the men: seeking a cutback. il
Newsweek 77:26-7 My 31 '71
Best chance; ban on MIRV. Sci Am 224:44
Mr '71
Breakthrough in arms control? G. W. Rath-
jens. il Bul Atom Sci 27:4-5 Je '71
Bridging the gap. Newsweek 78:55 N 22 '71
China and the bomb. B. T. Feld. Bul Atom
Sci 27:inside cover, 31 S '71
Disarmament: SALT up to date. Time 97:38+
My 17 '71
Economics of an arms pact. il Bsns W p 18-
19 My 29 '71
Freeze on missile testing. J. Lederberg. Bul
Atom Sci 27:4-6+ Mr '71
Global morale booster. Newsweek 78:64 S 27
'71
Implications of SALT; B. I. Spinard. Bul
Atom Sci 27:22-5 Ja '71
Japan and the world of SALT. R. Imai. por
Bul Atom Sci 27:13-16 D '71
Limitation of offensive weapons. H. Scoville,
jr. il Sci Am 224:15-25 bibliog(p 122) Ja '71
Myth of arms control and disarmament. B. M.
Becker. Bul Atom Sci 27:5-8+ Ap '71
Patience of Mr Nixon. W. F. Buckley, jr.
Nat R 23:669 Je 15 '71
Perl, Drell, York differ on SALT future. H.
L. Davis. il pors Phys Today 24:57-9 Jl '71
President announces major step in SALT ne-
gotiations; statement, May 20, 1971. R. M.
Nixon. Dept State Bul 64:741-2 Je 7 '71
Ready to give on arms control. il Bsns W
p86 Mr 13 '71
Real issue in arms talks. J. Fromm. il U S
News 70:26 Mr 22 '71
Round 4 in Vienna. Newsweek 77:38+ Mr 22
'71
SALT and international security; excerpt
from statement. Bul Atom Sci 27:17-19 D
'71
SALT and its illusions. M. L. Perl. il Bul
Atom Sci 27:7-12 D '71
SALT seasoning. New Repub 164:11-12 My
29 '71
SALT: signs of a new savor. il Time 97:9-11
My 31 '71
SALT talks in Helsinki: out of the cellar?
H. A. Jack. Chr Cent 88:1053-4 S 8 '71
Significant development; address, May 20,
1971. R. M. Nixon. por U S News 70:19
My 3 '71
Souring on SALT? Time 97:26+ F 1 '71
State of SALT. Sci Am 224:48 Ap '71
Strategic balance; the future of freedom; ad-
dress, April 15, 1971. H. M. Jackson. Vital
Speeches 37:482-5 Je 1 '71
Sufficiency for war or peace? Z. Brzezinski.
Newsweek 77:45 Ap 26 '71
Sweet talk at SALT. Newsweek 78:30 Jl 19
'71
Troops, trade and diplomacy. R. E. Hunter.
il Nation 212:776-80 Je 21 '71

U.S. and Soviet Union begin fifth phase
of SALT talks; statement, July 6, 1971.
G. C. Smith. Dept State Bul 65:98 Jl 26
'71
U.S. and Soviet Union begin sixth phase of
SALT talks; statement, November 13, 1971.
G. C. Smith. Dept State Bul 65:659-60 D
6 '71
U.S. and U.S.S.R. conclude fifth phase of
strategic arms limitation talks; text of
joint communique, September 24, 1971. Dept
State Bul 65:403-4 O 18 '71
U.S. and U.S.S.R. conclude third phase of
strategic arms limitation talks; text of
communique, December 18, 1970. Dept State
Bul 64:55 Ja 11 '71
U.S. and U.S.S.R. sign agreements to reduce
risk of nuclear war; White House announcement; with remarks by Secretary Rogers
and Foreign Minister Gromyko, September
30, 1971 and texts of agreements. Dept State
Bul 65:399-403 O 18 '71
U.S.-Soviet breakthrough: who stands to gain
in arms pact. U S News 70:19 My 31 '71
STRATEGY
Deterrence through defense. C. Benson. il Nat
R 23:251-9 Mr 9 '71; Discussion. 23:240,
342+, 356-7 Mr 9, Ap 6 '71
Erosion of U.S. military strength: can there
be peace without power? address, July 14,
1971. J. L. Buckley. Vital Speeches 37:
642-4 Ag 15 '71
Roots of the strategic arms race: ambiguity
and ignorance. W. K. H. Panofsky. Bul
Atom Sci 27:15-20 Je '71
U.S. strategic superiority has ended. Read
Digest 99:89-93 Jl '71
See also
Communist strategy
Vietnamese war, 1957- —Strategy
World war, 1939-1945—Strategy
STRATEMEYER, Edward
Edward Stratemeyer and his book machine.
A. Prager. il por Sat R 54:15-17+ Jl 10 '71 •
STRATFORD, Conn. Shakespeare festival. See
American Shakespeare festival theater and
academy, Stratford, Conn.
STRATMAN, Hardin
Filing technical articles. il por Electr World
85:58 F '71
STRATOSCOPE project. See Balloons—Re-
search use
STRATOSPHERE. See Atmosphere
STRAUB, Peter
Desert motion; Bow; Using the bow;
Sleepers; On Hampstead Heath with wom-
en; poems. Poetry 117:243-7 Ja '71
Encantadas; poem. Poetry 119:91-3 N '71
STRAUS, Dorothea
(tr) See Singer, I. B. Egotist
about
People are talking about... J. Stafford. il por
Vogue 158:282-3 S 1 '71 •
STRAUS, Ellen Sulzberger
Propose new status for volunteers; interview.
McCalls 98:39 Mr '71
STRAUSS, Egon
TV scope. il Radio-Electr 42:44-5 D '71
STRAUSS, Herbert L.
Science education in India. Bul Atom Sci 27:
10-13 Mr '71
STRAUSS, Levi, and company
Blue jeans are the hot pants. il Bsns W p32-3
Ap 24 '71
Dynamic growth companies. il Nations Bsns
59:76-8 N '71
Levi's tries on a troika for size. il Bsns W
p50 S 4 '71
Rough beginning. Forbes 108:25 S 1 '71
STRAUSS, Richard
Ariadne auf Naxos. A. Sperber. il Am Rec G
37:350-2 F '71 •
Elektra. Criticism
Hi Fi 21:MA15 Ap '71 •
Opera N il 35:17-20 F 27 '71 •
Opera N il 35:24-6 F 27 '71 •
Gielen's chromatic, traumatic evening; per-
formance of Metamorphosen by the New
York philharmonic. I. Kolodin. Sat R 54:85
O 30 '71 •
Rysanek on Strauss; ed. by S. Jenkins. L.
Rysanek. por Opera N 35:24-7 Ja 16 '71 •
Sad days for Salome. R. Jacobson. Sat R 54:
77 S 25 '71 •
Strauss and the low voice. J. Madeira. por
Opera N 35:27 F 27 '71 •
Witches' cauldron. M. Carner. il Opera N 35:
24-6 F 27 '71 •
Woman without a shadow (Die frau ohne
schatten) Criticism
Hi Fi 21:MA15 My '71 •
Opera N il 35:17-20 Ja 16 '71 •
Sat R 54:14 Ja 30 '71 •
Sat R 54:44 F 13 '71 •

STRAVINSKY, Igor Fedorovich
Editorial. P. H. Lang. Mus Q 57:506-18 Jl
'71 *
Igor Fyodorovitch Stravinsky. J. McClure.
por Hi Fi 21:20 Jl '71 *
Igor Stravinsky (1882-1971) J. Roddy. Look
35:58 Je 1 '71 *
Last rite of spring. il pors Life 70:50-1 Ap 16
'71 *
Obituary
Dance Mag por 45:15 My '71
Newsweek pors 77:108-9 Ap 19 '71. H.
Saal
Opera N por 35:20 Je 12 '71. G. Fitzgerald
Sat R 54:24 Ap 24 '71. L. Kolodin
Sr Schol por 98:15 My 3 '71
Rightness of his wrongs. pors Time 97:68-9
Ap 19 '71 *
Rolls-Royce of composers. R. Evett. Atlan
228:96-8 Jl '71 *
Stravinsky and the century; symposium. il
por Sat R 54:39-41+ My 29 '71 *
Stravinsky and the natures of ballet and
opera. G. Martin. Yale R 61:193-206 D '71 *
Stravinsky remembered. Cyclops. il Life 71:13
N 19 '71
Stravinsky's sacred music. R. Thibodeau. il
Commonweal 94:384-5 Jl 23 '71 *

Funeral rites and ceremonies
Our far-flung correspondents. F. Steegmuller.
New Yorker 47:99-103 My 1 '71
STRAVINSKY, Soulima
Son of Stravinsky. por Newsweek 78:64
D 20 '71 *
STRAW hat theater. See Theater—United
States
STRAW mulch. See Mulching
STRAWBERRIES
From stream bed to strawberries. R. Hamp-
ton. il Org Gard & Farm 18:44-6 F '71
How we built a fresh strawberry factory,
to grow a midwinter crop. il Sunset 147:
180 S '71
New way to bigger, tastier strawberries. G.
L'Allemand. il Home Gard 58:60-1 Mr '71
Our permanent strawberry bed. R. Kreun.
il Org Gard & Farm 18:46-8 F '71
Strawberries show-me style. H. G. Lendle.
il Org Gard & Farm 18:48-50 My '71
Strawberry marvels. il Sunset 147:54-5 S '71
We grow our strawberries in huge straw-
berry boxes. L. M. Hardwick. il Org Gard
& Farm 18:48-9 F '71
See also
Cookery—Fruit
STRAY dogs. See Dogs
STREAMERS (fishing flies) See Fishing lures,
flies, etc.
STREAMSIDE vegetation
Wildlife versus irrigation; phreatophyte re-
moval in Arizona. R. H. Gilluly. il Sci N
99:194-5 Mr 13 '71
STREET Christians. See Hippies—Religion
STREET cleaning
Street cleaning. See issues of American city
Systems approach to street sweeping; Louis-
ville, Ky. E. D. Alston. il Am City 86:91-
2+ N '71
Trim the border for an attractive street;
Salina, Kan. il Am City 86:38 Ap '71
See also
Cleaning of cities, towns, etc.
Gutters—Cleaning
Snow and ice removal
STREET cleaning apparatus
How do you sweep sand? El Paso, Tex. il
Am City 86:38 D '71
How street sweepers perform today; 152
cities responding to sweeper survey. C. W.
Laird and J. Scott. il Am City 86:58-62 Mr
'71
Pneumatic street cleaning? New York city. il
Am City 86:26 F '71
Street cleaning. See issues of American city
Street cleaning that pays its way; two-way
radio, Akron, Ohio. il Am City 86:42 N '71
Use air to sweep streets clean; Ojai, Calif. il
Am City 86:34 S '71
STREET fairs. See Fairs
STREET lighting
Blinding the big eyes; glare of city lights, an
astronomical disaster. il Time 97:48 Ap 12
'71
Outdoor lighting. See issues of American city
See also
Street lighting fixtures
also subhead Lighting under names of
cities, e.g. Muncie, Ind.—Lighting
STREET lighting fixtures
Old lighting system with a new twist; right-
of-way line, Orlando, Fla. W. A. Dixon,
jr. il Am City 86:112 N '71

Stainless steel poles add charm to suburbia;
Rochester, Minn. il Am City 86:122 Ap '71
Street lighting, a growth service; Lansing,
Mich. il Am City 86:110 Mr '71

Maintenance and repair
Dirt and light don't mix. Am City 86:112+
N '71
Don't blame the lamp, blame the dirt. Am
City 86:116 My '71
STREET markets, Paris. See Paris—Markets
STREET markings. See Traffic markings
STREET musicians
Enclaves of harmony; San Francisco's corps
of street minstrels. il Time 97:57 Ap 5 '71
STREET name signs. See Street signs
STREET names
On the street where I live. L. Torok. Sat R
54:4 Ag 28 '71
STREET paving. See Pavements
STREET rod nationals. See Drag racing
STREET rod of the year award. See Hot rod
(periodical)
STREET rods. See Automobiles, Remodeled
STREET signs
Color-coded street name signs; Minneapolis.
il Am City 86:114 Mr '71
STREET sweepers. See Street cleaning ap-
paratus
STREET sweeping. See Street cleaning
STREET trades
Business is blooming; flower children to
sell carnations on the streets. il Time 97:
71 F 1 '71
Indian markets of South America. E. A.
Gerling. il Travel 135:42-7 F '71
On the street; leather belt peddler on Fifth
avenue. New Yorker 47:27-9 Je 12 '71
On the street; open-air market between Fif-
ty-ninth and Sixtieth streets on Fifth ave-
nue. New Yorker 47:29-30 S 11 '71
Street capitalism. il Newsweek 78:86+ N 29
'71
STREET traffic. See City traffic
STREET trees. See Trees in cities
STREET vendors. See Street trades
STREETS
See also
Gutters
Pavements
Street trades

Drainage
Ever try diagonal grate inlets? il Am City
86:35 D '71
Intersections
What do you do with street triangles? Se-
attle. L. W. Johnson. il Am City 86:26 S '71
Maintenance and repair
Computerized street maintenance; methods
used in Denver. B. Gilbert. il Am City 86:
70-2 O '71
Poor streets cost more than good ones;
Union City, Tenn. W. D. Frizzell. il por
Am City 86:98+ Mr '71
Slurry seal for maintenance, remix for recon-
struction; Pittsburg, Kan. R. O. Yeager. il
Am City 86:54-5 Jl '71
Street construction & maintenance. See is-
sues of American city
See also
Pavements—Maintenance and repair
Pavements—Surface treatment

Names
See Street names

Traffic lines
See Traffic markings
STREIFTHAU, Donna
Cincinnati cabinet- and chairmakers, 1819-
1830. il Antiques 99:896-905 Je '71
STREPTOCOCCAL infections
Wyoming's war on deadly strep. M. Michael-
son. il Todays Health 49:40-3+ Mr '71
STRESHINSKY, Shirley G.
Doctor who practices what he preaches. il por
Redbook 138:78+ N '71
First steps to friendship. il Parents Mag 46:
66-9 F '71
How many raindrops in the world? il Red-
book 136:53+ Ja '71
Oh jealous love. il Parents Mag 46:39-41+
Ag '71
STRESS (physiology)
Body time; excerpts (title varies) G. G. Luce.
Vogue 158:156-7+ N 1; 132-3+ N 15 '71
Mineral element correlation with adenohy-
pophyseal-adrenal cortex function and
stress. A. Flynn and others. bibliog il Sci-
ence 173:1035-6 S 10 '71

STRESS (physiology)—*Continued*
Rat race; cause of ulcers. il por Newsweek 78:74-5 S 27 '71
Stress and behavior. S. Levine. il Sci Am 224:26-31 bibliog(p 122) Ja '71
Tension: the everyday threat to American women, and what to do about it. A. A. Hutschnecker. Vogue 157:120-1+ Je '71
Where to turn for help. J. Brothers. Good H 172:48+ My '71
See also
Traumatism

STRETCH, Bonnie Barrett
White House conference on youth. il Sat R 54:66-7+ My 22 '71

STRICKLAND, Stephen P.
Can slum children learn? il Am Ed 7:3-7 Jl '71
Integration of medical research and health policies: adaptation of address, December 1970. bibliog Science 173:1093-103 S 17 '71

STRICKLER, John K.
Who says trees don't grow in Kansas? il Am For 77:28-9 Jl '71

STRIKES
See also
Trade agreements
Trade unions

Law
See Labor laws and legislation— United States

Canada
Lost strike goes on and on; ITU strike against Toronto's three daily newspapers. Bsns W p90+ F 6 '71

Europe, Western
Social cost of bargaining: a European perspective. B. C. Roberts. Mo Labor R 94: 56-9 Ag '71

France
Letter from Paris; coal miners, and others. Genêt. New Yorker 47:91 F 27 '71
Letter from Paris; train strike. Genêt. New Yorker 47:54+ Jl 3 '71
Locking up the boss. Newsweek 77:61+ Ja 18 '71
Western Europe: the luxury strikes. il Time 97:24+ Mr 8 '71

Germany (Federal Republic)
Strike nobody wants; IG metall employees. il Newsweek 78:80 D 13 '71

Great Britain
Can Heath hold the line? C. Brogan. Nat R 23:634+ Je 15 '71
Letter from London; postal workers strike. M. Panter-Downes. New Yorker 47:101-2 F 27 '71
Life without mail. il Newsweek 77:80 Mr 8 '71
Mail strike? Look at Britain. il U S News 70: 72 F 15 '71
New battle of Britain: government vs. strikers. il U S News 70:84-5 Ap 5 '71
Pigeon service; post-office workers. il Newsweek 77:35-6 F 1 '71
Pigeons and pirates. il Time 97:31-2 F 1 '71
Postal strike tests British mettle. Bsns W p22 Ja 23 '71
Postal strike tests policy of Tories. U S News 70:54 F 1 '71
Strikes in Britain: fewer but longer. U S News 71:50 Ag 2 '71
When a government cracks down on pay raises. il U S News 70:78 F 15 '71

Italy
Unwelcome mat. il Newsweek 77:46+ Je 7 '71

Sweden
Paradise lost. R. J. Korengold. il Newsweek 77:50 Mr 15 '71
Sweden: mass walkout, tough response; government employes. U S News 70:72 Mr 15 '71
Western Europe: the luxury strikes. il Time 97:24 Mr 8 '71

United States
Any cure for big strikes? interview. J. D. Hodgson. il pors U S News 71:68-72 N 29 '71
Case against strikes. O. G. Stahl. Read Digest 99:128-30 O '71
Chances of labor peace in year ahead. il U S News 72:47-8 Ja 10 '72
Ford weighing aid for strikers; opposition by GM official; excerpts from address, June 3, 1971. G. B. Morris. U S News 70: 88 Je 21 '71
Fresh wave of strikes in key industries. il U S News 71:28-9 Jl 26 '71
Labor: a plague of strikes. Time 98:20 O 11 '71

Labor-management disputes; tables. See issues of Monthly labor review
On reinstatement of strikers. Mo Labor R 94:62-4 bibliog(p66) N '71
Rash of big strikes and the outlook for more. il U S News 71:48-9 O 18 '71
Stamp of disapproval; should strikers receive welfare aid? Nations Bsns 59:28+ Ap '71
Strike outlook grows darker for last half of the year. il U S News 71:83-4 Jl 12 '71
Strikes of '71: costing a lot, and more to come. il U S News 71:77-8 Ag 9 '71
U.S. economy off the tracks. il Newsweek 78:15-16 Ag 9 '71
Why all the strikes? America 124:85 Ja 30 '71
See also
Arbitration, Industrial—United States

Authors
Be good to your authors; consequences of a strike. R. Armour. Pub W 200:23 Ag 9 '71

Cemetery workers
Bury the dead; Colna, San Francisco. il Newsweek 78:105-6 O 11 '71

Coal mines and mining
Big test of government power to end strikes. il U S News 71:87-8 N 15 '71
Coal walks out before it bargains. por Bsns W p37 Je 19 '71
Deadlock in soft-coal strike. U S News 71:78 N 1 '71
Ludlow massacre revisited; Colorado strike, 1913-14. F. Lang. il Ramp Mag 10:20-2 Ja '72
Steam goes out of the coal talks. Bsns W p98 O 30 '71
Two for the money. il Newsweek 78:75-6 O 11 '71

Construction industry
No-strike boards for construction? U S News 71:86-7 N 22 '71
Work stoppages. Mo Labor R 94:2 F '71

Government employees
See also
Strikes—United States—Municipal employees

Government intervention
Bigger hand for government in strike crises; steel and railroad settlements. U S News 71:69-70 Ag 16 '71
Dock strikers feel the Nixon jawbone. il Bsns W p28 O 2 '71
Government intervention in railroad disputes. M. Cimini. bibliog Mo Labor R 94:27-34 D '71
Threat of intervention angers longshoremen. il Bsns W p28-9 Ag 14 '71

Hospital employees
Recognition, negotiation, and work stoppages in hospitals. D. D. Pointer and H. Graham. bibliog il Mo Labor R 94:54-8 My '71
Revolt of the hospital workers; local 1199. il Ebony 26:53-6+ Mr '71

Maritime workers
All-coasts strike threatens the docks. il Bsns W p 14-15 Jl 24 '71
Big test of government power to end strikes. il U S News 71:87-8 N 15 '71
Decision on the docks. il Time 98:33 O 18 '71
Dock strike mess. il Time 98:75 N 29 '71
Dock strikers feel the Nixon jawbone. il Bsns W p28 O 2 '71
Dock truce, but not a peace treaty. il Bsns W p28+ O 9 '71
Dockers form a common front. il Bsns W p55 N 6 '71
Hopeful sign from the Pacific docks. il Bsns W p66-7 S 4 '71
How dock strike is hurting Hawaii. U S News 71:94-5 O 4 '71
Labor: dead days on the docks. il Time 98: 74-5 S 13 '71
Rising costs of the dock strike. U S News 71:70-1 Ag 16 '71
Silence on the docks. Newsweek 78:87 S 27 '71
Troubled respite in the dock strife. il Bsns W p29-30 D 4 '71
Two for the money. il Newsweek 78:75-6 O 11 '71
Walkout maroons a sea of books. il Bsns W p47 N 13 '71
Western dock strike: its impact. U S News 71: 96-7 S 20 '71
Why West coast dock strike hangs on. U S News 71:65 Ag 23 '71

Miners
See also
Coeur d'Alene strike, 1892

STRIKES—United States—*Continued*

Municipal employees

See also
New York (city)—Strikes

Museum workers

Walking out on MOMA. il Newsweek 78:53 Ag 30 '71

Paper industry

Why strikers fear Ed Ball. por Bsns W p 102 O 16 '71

Police

Cop-out in New York. il Newsweek 77:59 Ja 25 '71
New York: the cops return. il Newsweek 77:47-8 F 1 '71
Shortage of blue; New York police. Time 97:23-4 Ja 25 '71
When police walked out in New York. il U S News 70:42 F 1 '71

Railroads

Government intervention in railroad disputes. M. Cimini. bibliog Mo Labor R 94:27-34 D '71
Great train strike. il Newsweek 77:61+ My 31 '71
How many strikes to put us out? il Newsweek 78:55 Ji 26 '71
Hunting a rail-strike cure: growing pressures for action. U S News 70:45-6 My 31 '71
Line must be drawn. Nat R 23:572-3 Je 1 '71
Rail strikes begin to hurt everywhere. Bsns W p20 Jl 3 '71
Selective railroad strikes; railroad unions. Mo Labor R 94:62-3 S '71
Untracked again; strike by Brotherhood of railroad signalmen. il Time 97:82+ My 31 '71
Wave of labor unrest. il Newsweek 78:61 Ag 2 '71

Teachers

Daley's magic; agreement in Chicago. il Newsweek 77:52 Ja 25 '71
N.Y. teachers' strike. J. Deedy. Commonweal 95:266 D 17 '71
Parochial pickets; New York city and San Francisco. il Newsweek 78:62-3 D 13 '71
Plight of Newark. America 124:426 Ap 24 '71
Savage strike in Newark. il Time 97:66 Ap 19 '71
Strike one! Yer' out! A short count for the student teacher in a school strike? L. M. Chaffee and R. D. Alley. Clear House 45:503-6 Ap '71
Teacher opinion poll: should teachers strike? il Todays Ed 60:27 F '71
Teacher who chose to go to jail; Newark strike. D. Gallagher. il por Redbook 136:58-9+ Ja '71
When teachers strike; Los Angeles public schools. V. Bartel. il Parents Mag 46:68-70+ Mr '71

Telephone workers

Phone supervisors answer the call. il Bsns W p21-2 N 20 '71
Phone workers swell the picket population. il Bsns W p33 Jl 17 '71

Transportation workers

New try at curbing transportation strikes. Bsns W p 116 Je 19 '71

Truck drivers

Strange alliance; NAACP helping striking timber haulers. Newsweek 78:48 N 8 '71

STRING quartets
Musicians of the month. S. Fleming. il Hi Fi 21:MA8-9 Je '71
Musicians of the month: the Juilliard quartet. J. Hiemenz. il Hi Fi 21:MA8-9 O '71
New 'in' group is the Guarneri. J. Roddy. il N Y Times Mag p30-1+ Mr 7 '71; Discussion. p6 Mr 28 '71
See also
Phonograph records—String quartet music

STRING sextet music. See Phonograph records —String sextet music

STRINGED instruments
See also names of stringed instruments, e.g. Lute

STRINGFELLOW, Martha Marian
Teacher of the year, 1971. W. J. McKean. il pors Look 35:51-4 My 4 '71 *

STRINGFELLOW, William
Harboring of Daniel Berrigan. R. Wool. il Esquire 76:156-61+ N '71 *
Stringfellow-Towne indictment; with statement. J. R. Nelson. Chr Cent 88:60-1 Ja 20 '71 *

STRIP films. See Film strips

STRIP mine dumps, Reclamation of. See Reclamation of land

STRIP mining
Adversary classrooms vs. strip mines. J. Goldstein. il Org Gard & Farm 18:58-61 Ag '71
Appalachia, like the flayed back of a man. J. Branscome. il N Y Times Mag p30-1+ D 12 '71
Appalachian inferno. il Ramp Mag 9:10 Je '71
Big dig at Black Mesa. J. Bishop, jr. il Newsweek 77:75-6 F 8 '71
Coal companies rediscover the West. il Bsns W p92+ D 11 '71
For American profit and Japanese steel, they're tearing down the Canadian Rockies. G. Laycock. il Audubon 73:77-84 Ja '71
Jay and the strippers. R. Starnes. Field & S 76:8+ Je '71
Let's look toward an early end of strip mining. R. Starnes. il Field & S 76:12+ Ag '71
Mountaineers in the affluent society. H. M. Caudill. il Nat Parks & Con Mag 45:17-21 Jl '71
My land is dying, by H. M. Caudill. Review Sat R il 55:30 Ja 1 '72. R. Cassidy
Peeling back the land for coal; with report by G. Mendes. il Newsweek 77:69-72+ Je 28 '71
Price of strip mining; ravaged hills of Appalachia. il Time 97:47 Mr 22 '71
Sharp conflict on strip-mine reclamation. il Sci N 99:297-8 My 1 '71
Strip mining. J. Trawick. il Nat Parks & Con Mag 45:10-14 Jl '71; Same abr. with title Ravaging land by strip mining. Cur 132:31-5 S '71
Strip mining: coast to coast. H. M. Caudill. Nation 212:488-90 Ap 19 '71
Stripping for pleasure and profit. J. Branscome. Commonweal 95:229-31 D 3 '71
TVA ravages the land. K. Hechler. Nat Parks & Con Mag 45:15-16 Jl '71
Taming the strip-mine monster; Pennsylvania reclamation law. E. Faltermayer. il Life 71:21 O 1 '71
West Virginia turns against strip mining. il Bsns W p29 Mr 6 '71

STRIPED bass fishing. See Bass fishing

STRISIK, Paul
Watercolor page; with biographical sketch. il por Am Artist 35:50-1+ Ap '71

STROBOSCOPIC lighting
Dancing fluorescent strobes. C. L. Andrews. il Radio-Electr 42:46-7 Jl '71

STROESSNER, Alfredo
Paraguay's popular dictator. S. Rodman. il Nat R 23:759-60+ Jl 13 '71 *

STROETZEL, Donald, and Stroetzel, Dorothy
To tame the mighty Mekong. il Read Digest 98:192-4+ Je '71

STROETZEL, Dorothy. See Stroetzel, Donald, jt. auth.

STROH, Nicholas
End of a dream. por Newsweek 78:70-1 Ag 2 '71 *

STROH, Ruth K.
Art of needle painting. il Design 73:17 Wint '71

STROHM, Bob
Prayer for Americans; with biographical sketch. il Nat Wildlife 10:2-12 D '71

STROKE, George
DNA double helix: photo sends controversy spiraling. B. Nelson. il Science 173:800-1 Ag 27 '71 *

STROKE. See Cerebrovascular disease

STROLLERS (infants) See Baby carriages

STROM, Robert D.
Education's role: dignity of the individual. bibliog Clear House 46:163-9 N '71

STROMATOLITES. See Algae, Fossil

STRONER, Sandra
Media programming for children; address, 1970. il Library J 96:3811-13 N 15 '71

STRONG, Laurence E.
Metallic hydrogen. Chem 44:24 D '71

STRONG, Maurice Frederick
Cleanup man Maurice Strong. S. Lindsay. il por Sat R 54:43-7+ Ag 7 '71 *

STRONGIN, Dan
In my opinion; hard rock is dead! por Seventeen 30:208 Ap '71

STRONGIN, Lynn
Andromache; Dutch painting; poems. Poetry 119:142-3 D '71

STRONTIUM in the body
Strontium accumulation by sarcoplasmic reticulum and mitochondria in vascular smooth muscle. A. V. Somlyo and A. P. Somlyo. bibliog il Science 174:955-8 N 26 '71
Strontium induced rickets: metabolic basis. J. L. Omdahl and H. F. DeLuca. bibliog il Science 174:949-51 N 26 '71

STROTHER, Robert S.
Great airbag hassle. Nat R 23:812+ Jl 27 '71;
Same abr. Read Digest 99:53+ N '71
STROUT, Cushing
Man in the ruins: from a Roman journal.
Yale R 61:151-60 O '71
STRUCK, Herman R.
Importance of being repetitious. Engl J 60:
474-8+ Ap '71
STRUCTURAL carbon. See Carbon, Structural
STRUCTURAL geology. See Geology, Struc-
tural
STRUCTURE, Biological. See Anatomy
STRUCTURES, Moving of. See Moving of struc-
tures, etc.
STRUGGLE for existence
Competition between species: frequency de-
pendence. F. J. Ayala. bibliog il Science 171:
820-4 F 26 '71
STRUNG, Norman
Northerns are in. il Field & S 76:52-3+ N '71
Prospecting for mountain trout. il Field & S
75:52-3+ Mr '71
STRYBING arboretum and botanical garden.
See San Francisco—Gardens
STRYCHNINE
Warning. E. Keller. Chem 44:2 Je '71
STRYK, Lucien
Elegy for a long-haired student; poem. Na-
tion 212:378 Mr 22 '71
Hyde park Sunday; poem. Sat R 54:24 Je 19
'71
STUART, Dabney
Trial; poem. New Yorker 47:74 S 18 '71
STUART, Dee
Research at Uncle Sam's bookstore. Writer
84:24-5+ Jl '71
STUART, Lyle
Outrageous Lyle, B. Darrach. il pors Life 70:
61-4+ Je 11 '71 *
Sensuous publisher. il por Forbes 107:57 Je
15 '71 *
STUBBINS, Bert
Recreating the mediocre and the discard.
il Sch Arts 70:11 Mr '71
STUBBS, Harry C.
Views on science books. See issues of Horn
book magazine
STUCKER, Gilbert
Youth, rebellion & the environment. il Nat
Parks & Con Mag 45:6-9 Ap '71
STUD farms. See Horse breeding
STUDDED tires. See Tires, Automobile
STUDEBAKER-Worthington, inc.
Half the way home? il Forbes 108:66-7 N
15 '71
STUDENT achievements
Is there such a thing as a learning disabled
child? N. E. Silberberg and M. C. Silber-
berg. Ed Digest 37:14-17 S '71
See also
Accountability (education)
Performance contracts (education)
Prediction of scholastic success
Underachievers
STUDENT activism. See Student movement
STUDENT activists. See Student militants
STUDENT activities
Student activities in the schools of the
seventies. R. L. Buser. Ed Digest 37:48-50
N '71
See also
College and school journalism
College students—Political activities
Fund raising
High school students—Political activities
STUDENT aid
College funds for descendants of veterans.
Bet Hom & Gard 49:6+ Jl '71
Greening of education; House defeats pro-
posal to help more poor college students.
New Repub 165:8 N 13 '71
Helping the poor to college; the Pell bill.
America 125:51 Ag 7 '71
Higher education: funds rise while basic
changes are debated. D. P. Teter. il Sci-
ence 173:309-11 Jl 23 '71
Higher education: will federal aid favor stu-
dents or institutions? J. Walsh. Science 171:
1217-21 Mr 26 '71
More U.S. aid for college students? il U S
News 70:44 Mr 8 '71
See also
Medical students—Aid
Scholarships and fellowships
Student loans
STUDENT attitudes. See Students—Attitudes
STUDENT Christian movements
Asian to head IFES. Chr Today 15:46 S 24 '71
London's university of the streets; problems
of an urban community. C. Barker. Chr
Cent 88:378-9 Mr 24 '71
STUDENT clothing. See Clothing and dress—
Students

STUDENT counselors
High school counseling: how much help is it?
G. G. Greer. Bet Hom & Gard 49:16+ Ap
'71
Parent conferences: guidelines for the coun-
selor. W. R. Barda. Clear House 45:520-3
My '71
Pitfalls a guidance counselor should avoid.
F. Griffith. Clear House 46:105 O '71
Student counsel; hired professionals to de-
fend students' interests at the University
of Texas. il Time 97:57 F 1 '71
Who gets counseled and for what? J. W.
M. Rothney. Ed Digest 37:41-4 N '71
STUDENT demonstrations
James Michener speaks out; excerpts from
remarks at press conference, April 27, 1971.
J. A. Michener. por Pub W 199:17-18 My 10
'71
Students protest; symposium, ed. by P. G.
Altbach and R. S. Laufer. bibliog f il Ann
Am Acad 395:1-194 My '71
See also
Student movement

Bibliography
Selected references on student protest. K.
Keniston and M. Lerner. Ann Am Acad
395:184-94 My '71

History
Student protest and university response. J.
R. Gusfield. bibliog f Ann Am Acad 395:
26-38 My '71

Africa
Student protest in independent Black Africa.
W. J. Hanna. bibliog f il Ann Am Acad 395:
171-83 My '71

France
Letter from Paris; street-corner talks be-
tween police and students. Genêt. New
Yorker 47:95 Mr 27 '71
Sources of student protest in France. R.
Boudon. il Ann Am Acad 395:139-49 My '71

Japan
End to play-acting; Narita. il Time 98:46 S 27
'71

Korea (Republic)
Clampdown on the campus. il Time 98:43 O
25 '71

United States
Beginning: Berkeley, 1964, by M. Heirich. Re-
view
Nation 212:599-600 My 10 '71. B. Aptheker
Free speech movement; charges against par-
ticipants in the Sanders theater affair at
Harvard. il Newsweek 77:73 Ap 12 '71
High school as a focus of student unrest. E.
Z. Friedenberg. bibliog f Ann Am Acad
395:117-26 My '71
How to cure a major cause of unrest. D.
Lawrence. U S News 70:96 Je 21 '71
Hysteria on the campus; who is responsible?
address, March 2, 1971. L. Fertig. Vital
Speeches 37:454-9 My 15 '71
Kent state, by J. A. Michener. Review
Nat R 23:707 Je 29 '71. D. Brudnoy
Kent state: what happened and why; conden-
sation. J. A. Michener. il Read Digest 98:
57-63+ Mr; 217-20+ Ap '71
Menace of ignorance. D. Lawrence. U S
News 70:96 Je 7 '71
Of politics and prophecy: student activism
today. R. C. Johansen. il Chr Cent 88:219-23
F 17 '71
Storm warnings. il Newsweek 77:68+ Ap 12
'71
Students against campus violence; excerpt
from The riot makers. E. H. Methvin. Read
Digest 98:62-6 Ja '71
Were campuses really quiet? Time 98:74 O 4
'71

History
Student response to faculty power. L. G.
Geiger. Sch & Soc 99:424-6 N '71

Yugoslavia
Crisis in Croatia. il Time 98:32 D 27 '71
Yugoslavia's future; Tito as Diocletian; riot-
ing in the Croatian capital of Zagreb. M.
M. Mestrovic. Commonweal 95:317-18 Ja 7
'72
STUDENT employment
Dim outlook for summer jobs. il U S News
70:13-14+ My 24 '71
Employment of school-age youth; with tables
and chart. H. Hayghe. bibliog Mo Labor R
94:13-18 Ag '71
Here he is, ranger, and he's all yours; sum-
mer employment in the virgin forests. B.
Gilbert. il Sports Illus 34:48-50+ My 17 '71

STUDENT employment—*Continued*
Party corps; Hostess helper course of the Youth employment service, Montclair, N.J. McCalls 98:40 Ap '71
Students and summer jobs. V. C. Perrella. il Mo Labor R 94:55-62 F '71
Students join the idle poor. Bsns W p21 My 29 '71
Summer job for your kids; detasseling corn. Farm J 95:34 My '71
This summer, don't just sit there on a sight-seeing bus, do something. S. Cuneo. il Mlle 72:191-8 Mr '71
Working through college in the nude. D. DeVoss. il Time 98:16 D 13 '71
See also
United States—Youth conservation corps
STUDENT fees. See Colleges and universities—Finance
STUDENT forums. See Forums (discussion and debate)
STUDENT government. See Self government in education
STUDENT health. See College students—Health and hygiene
STUDENT life
See also
College students
STUDENT life insurance policies. See Insurance, Life—Policies
STUDENT loans
Academic rip-offs. Time 98:40 Ag 2 '71
College costs: easing the burden. il Duns 98: 51+ D '71
Education on the installment plan. Nat R 23:354+ Ap 6 '71
Financing higher education in Ohio. P. N. Reid. New Repub 164:13-14 Je 12 '71
Gilligan plan; Ohio plan. Newsweek 77:73 Ap 12 '71
Give power to the students; self-help on campus. F. R. Buckley. Nat R 23:424-5+ Ap 20 '71
Going to Yale on a 35-year loan. Bsns W p32 F 13 '71
Guaranteed loans for college students. Sch & Soc 99:275 Sum '71
Learn now, pay if you feel like it; United student aid fund (USAF) Nat R 23:1217-18 N 5 '71
Learn now, pay later; PAYE (pay as you earn) scheme. Time 97:57 F 1 '71
Learn now, pay later; Yale plan. New Repub 164:12-13 F 20 '71
Out of pocket in academe. Sat R 54:70-1 Ap 17 '71
Pay as you earn. Newsweek 77:69 F 15 '71
Yale plan: study now, pay for 35 years. U S News 70:28 F 22 '71
Yale's tuition postponement plan. Sch & Soc 99:273-5 Sum '71
Your bank can help meet the high cost of learning. Bsns W p61 Jl 24 '71
See also
Student aid
STUDENT lounges
Segregation comes to Columbia; granting of Malcolm X liberation center and other student groups' demand for lounges. F. K. Lowell. Nat R 23:1236 N 5 '71
STUDENT militants
Activist youth of the 1960's: summary and prognosis. J. L. Horn and P. D. Knott. bibliog il Science 171:977-85 Mr 12 '71
California's Isla Vista: From anathema to dialogue. N. Cousins. Sat R 54:22-4 Je 5 '71
Class of '68 revisited: a cooler anger. il Time 97:55-6 My 17 '71
Distinguishing fact from fiction in social crises. W. P. Moellenberg. bibliog Sch & Soc 99:420-4 N '71
Don't trust anyone over thirty; views of ex-campus radicals. J. Poppy and R. Cowan. il McCalls 99:38+ O '71
High school as a focus of student unrest. E. Z. Friedenberg. bibliog f Ann Am Acad 395:117-26 My '71
Mau-mauing Dr Teller. W. I. Scobie. Nat R 23:697-8 Je 29 '71
Policeman complains; interview, ed. by R. Coles; excerpt from Middle Americans. il N Y Times Mag p 11+ Je 13 '71
Psychoanalyst looks at student revolutionaries. R. Hendin. il N Y Times Mag p 16-17+ Ja '71; Discussion. p59 F 21 '71
Self-confrontation: rehearsal for renaissance. W. F. Amar. Clear House 45:294-6 Ja '71
Students protest; symposium, ed. by P. G. Altbach and R. S. Laufer. bibliog il Ann Am Acad 395:1-194 My '71

Time to get radical: radical students' lack of education. A. H. Leitch. Chr Today 15: 61-2 Mr 12 '71
See also
Negro student militants
Students for a democratic society (organization)

Anecdotes, facetiae, satire, etc.
Day that revolution became one of the three R's. R. Schoenstein. il Todays Health 49: 48-9 N '71

Bibliography
Selected references on student protest. K. Keniston and M. Lerner. Ann Am Acad 395:184-94 My '71

Japan
Student radicals in Japan. M. Shimbori. bibliog f il Ann Am Acad 395:150-8 My '71

Mexico
Student activism in Mexico. A. Liebman. bibliog f Ann Am Acad 395:159-70 My '71
STUDENT movement
Eva Jefferson: young voice of change; Associated student government of Northwestern university, Evanston, Ill. H. H. King. il pors Ebony 26:71-4+ Ja '71
Kent state again? S. Melvin. il Todays Health 49:30-3 Ap '71
Protests of young people should be considered seriously. H. Taylor. por Parents Mag 46:34+ F '71
Quiet campus? il Newsweek 77:45-6 Je 21 '71
Shall these bones live? J. B. Shepherd. America 126:15-17 Ja 8 '72
Student activism: a perspective and strategy. R. E. Jennings. Clear House 46:86-90 O '71
Student movement: where do you stand? B. McGhan. bibliog f Clear House 46:91-5 O '71
Toward radical reform: excerpt from How to change colleges. H. Taylor. Cur 130:27-35 Je '71
Union and campus: talking together. J. Higgins. Nation 213:171-4 S 6 '71
Working to change the system; Public interest research groups. Mlle 73:52 S '71
Youth and dissent. by K. Keniston. Review Newsweek il 78:62+ N 1 '71. J. K. Footlick
See also
College students—Political activities

History
Before Berkeley: historical perspectives on American student activism. P. G. Altbach and P. Peterson. bibliog f Ann Am Acad 395:1-14 My '71
Development of the new left; excerpts from The development of a new left in the United States, 1960-1965. J. P. O'Brien. bibliog f Ann Am Acad 395:15-25 My '71

United States
See Student movement
STUDENT newspapers. See College and school journalism
STUDENT opinion
Earth from far away, and close up; questions and answers to student burgesses in Williamsburg. ed. by E. Sparn. il Sr Schol 98: 17 Mr 15 '71
Evangelical college students: an opinion sampler; excerpts from college newspapers. D. J. Riggall. Chr Today 15:11-14 My 21 '71
Faculty-student views on colleges; Carnegie commission on higher education survey. Sch & Soc 99:262+ Sum '71
First-time voters: what they want in a candidate; Senior youthview. il Sr Schol 99: 14-15 N 1 '71
Guest editor journal: what we're doing, thinking, hoping; discussion. il Mlle 73:314-17+ Ag '71
Let's hear it from Hamtramck; St Ladislaus high school. il Sr Schol 98:18-19 Ap 19 '71
Nasty shock: results of polls in West Germany. E. von Kuehnelt-Leddihn. Nat R 23:758 Jl 13 '71
Opinion on the campus; analysis of, and commentary on questions and responses of National review poll. il Nat R 23:635-50 Je 15 '71
Polls and protests; Vietnam war; excerpt from They would rather be left, by S. M. Lipset and G. Schaflander. S. M. Lipset. For Affairs 49:548-55 Ap '71
Real opinion gap. Trans-Action 8:8+ N '70
Student leaders in high school: what they think. U S News 71:66 D 13 '71
Student leaders on selected current social issues. B. C. Wheatley and W. B. Cash. Sch & Soc 99:445-7 N '71

STUDENT opinion—*Continued*
Ten years in the wrong direction; National review's Opinion on the campus. A. H. Leitch. Chr Today 15:55-6 S 10 '71
Today and tomorrow. il Sr Schol 98:7-8 My 10 '71
Tuning in on tomorrow's voters; polls of high school students by the National institute of student opinion. W. D. Boutwell. PTA Mag 65:14 Je '71
U.S. campus mood, '71: a Newsweek poll. il Newsweek 77:61-3 F 22 '71
What do high school students think? high school student weltanschauung. Sch & Soc 99:74-5 F '71
What teenagers think about the 16 people and the dog on our cover; Senior youthview. il Sr Schol 99:16-18 S 20 '71
See also
Students—Attitudes
STUDENT participation in school administration. See School management and organization—Student participation
STUDENT plagiarism. See Cheating in schoolwork
STUDENT radicals. See Student militants
STUDENT records. See School reports and records
STUDENT recruiting. See Colleges and universities—Student recruiting
STUDENT residences. See College students—Housing; Dormitories
STUDENT rights. See Students—Civil rights
STUDENT selection
How Jewish quotas began. S. Steinberg. Commentary 52:67-76 S '71; Discussion. 53:16+ Ja '72
Minorities still underrepresented. Sat R 54:52-3 Je 19 '71
See also
Colleges and universities—Attendance
STUDENT teachers
Strike one! Yer' out! A short count for the student teacher in a school strike? L. M. Chaffee and R. D. Alley. Clear House 45:503-6 Ap '71
STUDENT teaching
Cultivating student teachers in the Yakima Valley. C. H. Potter. il Am Ed 7:27-31 My '71
Even student teaching is dismal; excerpt from Crisis in the classroom. C. E. Silberman. il Todays Ed 60:22-5+ Ja '71; Discussion. 60:22-3+ Ap '71
S.I.T.E: a suggested answer to the pollution in art teacher development A. W. Beck. il Sch Arts 71:36-7 S '71
Unique approach to inner-city teacher education; Cooperative Urban Teacher Education project. M. Pedram. Clear House 45:297-9 Ja '71
See also
Teachers—Education
STUDENT teaching, Supervisors of. See Supervisors of student teaching
STUDENT travel
America's vagabond ambassadors; interviews. ed. by D. Butwin. C. Wolkowitz; P. Wilk; A. Mullen. il por Sat R 54:59-62+ F 20 '71
As young Americans swarm over Europe. il U S News 71:32-5 Ag 16 '71
CAB to scrutinize European charters. L. Doty. Aviation W 95:26-7 S 6 '71
Going things. Mlle 73:100-2+ S '71
Ready, Europe? Here they come. il Life 71:28-31 Jl 9 '71
Rites of passage: the knapsack nomads. il Time 98:66-7 Jl 19 '71
Student travelers should. . . D. Kaye. il Sat R 54:63 F 20 '71
This summer, don't just sit there on a sightseeing bus, do something. S. Cuneo. il Mlle 72:191-8 Mr '71
See also
Travel study courses
STUDENT tutors. See Tutors and tutoring
STUDENT union buildings. See College architecture
STUDENT volunteer service. See Volunteer service
STUDENT withdrawals. See Dropouts
STUDENTS
Pressures on students. F. M. Raubinger. Todays Ed 60:46 D '71
See also
College students
Engineering students
Foreign students in the United States
French students
High school students
Jewish students
Law students
Medical students
Negro students
School management and organization—Student participation
Underachievers

Attitudes
Adolescent grievances at school; with study-discussion program, by C. Smallenburg and H. Smallenburg. D. Graves. bibliog il PTA Mag 66:26-8, 36 O '71
Changing mood of youth. N. Cousins. Sat R 54:22 F 20 '71
College youth attitudes today. R. A. Weil. Sch & Soc 99:246-7 Ap '71
Evolution or revolution? G. H. Darling. Clear House 46:26 S '71
How new ideas about sex are changing our lives. J. Cuber. Redbook 136:85+ Mr '71
More podunks than Harvards; views of S. M. Lipset. por Newsweek 77:62-3 F 22 '71
New tensions on campus. W. J. McGill. por Life 71:55 O 8 '71
Segregation comes to Columbia; granting of Malcolm X liberation center and other student groups' demand for lounges. F. K. Lowell. Nat R 23:1236 N 5 '71
Spring love and hate. il Chr Cent 88:613-14 My 19 '71
Student attitudes on science; summary of interviews. il Bul Atom Sci 27:31-5 My '71
Students reveal negative attitudes toward technology. L. R. McNarry and S. O'Farrell. Science 172:1060-1 Je 4 '71
Today's campus: the eerie calm. G. M. Sykes. Nation 212:490-1 Ap 19 '71
What are today's college-age counselors really like? excerpts from address. O. E. Jones. il por Camp Mag 43:11-12+ Ja '71
Witnessing; or, The myth of the global village. B. R. Tanner. Engl J 60:740-5 S '71
Youth and establishment collaboration? Yankelovich survey. Cur 127:15-19 Mr '71

Civil rights
Civil rights of public school students; recent judicial decisions. R. M. Blankenburg. Cur 131:35-42 Jl '71
How to live with due process. G. Triezenberg. Ed Digest 36:18-21 My '71
Locker searches and the law. H. C. Hudgins, jr. Todays Ed 60:30-2 N '71
Student rights find a friend in court (s) L. W. Knowles. Ed Digest 36:15-17 My '71
Students' rights and responsibilities: the New York city experience; with text of resolution; study-discussion program by C. Smallenburg and H. Smallenburg. S. P. Lachman. bibliog il PTA Mag 65:14-17, 33 My '71
Why students want their constitutional rights. N. Hentoff. il Sat R 54:60-3+ My 22 '71; Same abr. bibliog Ed Digest 37:39-42 O '71

Employment
See Student employment

Grading and promotion
See Grading and marking (students)

Political activities
Problem of student registration. Harper 243:38 S '71
Young lobbyists. Seventeen 29:164-5+ S '70
See also
People's peace treaty

Rating
Informative feedback: an educational controversy. W. Baller and E. Lower. bibliog Sch & Soc 99:417-19 N '71

Social and economic status
Changing social base of the American student movement. M. Mankoff and R. Flacks. bibliog f il Ann Am Acad 395:54-67 My '71
STUDENTS, Mentally superior. See High school students, Mentally superior
STUDENTS and environmental problems. See Environmental movement
STUDENTS and teachers. See Teachers and students
STUDENTS and war. See High school students and war
STUDENTS as guides. See Guides
STUDENTS contests. See Competitions
STUDENTS for a democratic society (organization)
Run, Tommy, run! R. Rosenbaum. il Esquire 76:51-8+ Jl '71
See also
Weathermen (organization)
STUDENTS socio-economic status. See Students—Social and economic status
STUDENTS verse. See College verse
STUDIES (rooms)
Home study center. H. Kelly. il Mech Illus 67:112-14 S '71
What makes a good study center? il Bet Hom & Gard 49:32+ N '71

STUDIOS
Add a studio/sitting room. E. McGough. il Mech Illus 67:118-20+ O '71
Working place; home studio. il Sunset 146: 64-9 F '71
See also
Artists studios
Moving picture studios
STUDS, Tire. See Tires, Automobile

STUDY
See also
Note taking
STUDY centers. See Studies (rooms)

STUDY halls
Junior high study hall: boredom v. discipline. J. A. Miller. Clear House 46:230 D '71
STUDY of man's impact on climate. See Man —Influence on nature
STUDY tours. See Travel study courses
STUDY-work plan. See Education, Cooperative
STUFFING. See Cookery—Meat

STULMAN, Julius
Creative systems in housing; address, December 28, 1970. Vital Speeches 37:241-5 F 1 '71

STUNT flying. See Aviation—Stunt flying

STUNT men
Charging full tilt into a bloody fray; jousting 1971 style. C. Gammon. il Sports Illus 35: 26-8+ S 13 '71
Gallery; stunt driver Jim Rusing jumps speedboats; photographs. Life 70:8-9 Ap 30 '71

STUNT motorcycling. See Motorcycling—Stunt cycling

STUNT women
Hollywood stunt girl; P. Jones. W. P. Burrell. il pors Ebony 27:147-8+ D '71

STUPAK, Ronald J.
Student as enemy of the student. Cur 125: 20-5 Ja '71

STURGES, Stanley G.
Growing quarrel among Seventh-day Adventist. Chr Today 15:12-13 Je 18 '71

STURGES, Tom
No chicken counting. il Yachting 129:68-9+ My '71

STURM, I. E. and Lipton, Herbert
Countering defeatism in psychiatric vocational placement. bibliog Ment Hy 55:230-3 Ap '71

STUTTGART, Germany

Music

Report:
Don Giovanni. D. Norris. Opera N 35:26 Je 12 '71
Lehár's Merry widow. D. Norris. Opera N 35:26 My 15 '71

STUTTGART ballet
Dance. N. Goldner. Nation 212:731-2 Je 7 '71
Dance; Poème de l'extase. J. Maskey. il Hi Fi 21:MA11 O '71
Germany's elegant troupe of storytellers. C. Barnes. il por Life 70:10 My 21 '71
Goyas and dolls. il Time 97:70 My 10 '71
Is an opera house a home? D. Hering. il Dance Mag 45:57-63 Jl '71
Love danced in; opening night program at the Metropolitan opera house. W. Terry. il Sat R 54:41 My 8 '71
Musical events:
Ballets presented at the Metropolitan opera house. W. Sargeant. New Yorker 47: 136+ My 15 '71
Carmen. W. Sargeant. New Yorker 47:91 My 8 '71
Eugene Onegin. W. Sargeant. New Yorker 47:110 My 1 '71
Mixed program; including The catalyst, Salade, Black Swan pas de deux, Jeu de cartes. W. Sargeant. New Yorker 47:58-9 My 29 '71
Romeo and Juliet. W. Sargeant. New Yorker 47:110 My 1 '71
On supering with the Stuttgart. S. McDermott. il Dance Mag 45:50-7 Je '71
Stuttgart ballet. R. Zachary. Opera N 35: 28 Je 12 '71
Stuttgart ballet. Poeme de l'extase, Metropolitan opera house, NYC. N. M. Stoop. Dance Mag 45:86 S '71
Team; New York season. W. Terry. il pors Sat R 54:42 Je 5 '71
Who ever heard of a German ballet company? H. Saal. il por N Y Times Mag p 10-12+ Jl 18 '71

STUTZ, Sara D.
Curtain going up! il Parents Mag 46:60-1+ Mr '71

STUTZ, Sidney A.
Daddy tells a story. il Parents Mag 46:48+ Je '71

STUWE, Jane
Raising potatoes under straw. Org Gard & Farm 18:51 Jl '71
STUYVESANT town housing project. See New York (city)—Housing
STY of the blind pig; drama. See Dean, P. H.

STYERS, Frank
It's not sludge, it's fertilizer. il Am City 86: 48-50 F '71

STYLE, Literary
Literary style in religious writing. C. D. Linton. Chr Today 15:5-6+ Je 18; 8-12 Jl 2 '71
See also
Readability (literary style)
Words
STYLE, Musical
Musical mannerism; effeteness or virility? excerpts from address. M. R. Maniates. bibliog f Mus Q 57:270-93 Ap '71
On Beethoven's thematic structure. D. Bartha. bibliog f il Mus Q 56:759-78 O '70
On Frescobaldi's chromaticism and its background. R. Jackson. bibliog f il Mus Q 57:255-69 Ap '71
See also
Classicism in music
Composition (music)
STYLE, Personal. See Individuality
STYLE in dress. See Fashion
STYLING, Automobile. See Automobiles—Design

STYRON, William
Marriott, the marine; story; excerpt from The way of the warrior. il Esquire 76: 100-4 S '71

SU, Che, and others
[3H] adenosine triphosphate: release during stimulation of enteric nerves. bibliog il Science 173:336-8 Jl 23 '71
SUÁREZ, Hugo Banzer. See Banzer Suárez, H.
SUAVE shoe corporation. See Shoe industry
SUBACUTE sclerosing panencephalitis. See Encephalitis
SUBARU (automobile) See Automobiles, Foreign
SUB-COMPACT cars. See Automobiles, Compact

SUBCONSCIOUSNESS
See also
Dreams
Hallucinations and illusions
Hypnotism

SUBCONTRACTING
See also
Contracts, Government—Subcontracting
SUBDIVISION of land. See Land—Subdivision

SUBJECT headings
Children, idiots, the underground, and others; excerpts from Prejudices and antipathies: a tract on the LC subject heads concerning people. S. Berman. bibliog f il por Library J 96:4162-7 D 15 '71
SUBJECT to fits; drama. See Montgomery. R.
SUBJECTS, Literary. See Literature—Themes
SUBLIMATING; story. See Updike, J.
SUBLIMNOS (underwater laboratory) See Underwater laboratories
SUBMARINE archeology. See Archeology, Submarine

SUBMARINE boats
Build this two-man sub for $400. W. K. Markham. il Pop Mech 135:94-7+ Je '71
Erosion of surface naval power. P. Cohen. For Affairs 49:330-41 Ja '71
Secret of sunken sub: U-166 off New Orleans during World war II. Sr Schol 98:15 Ap 26 '71
SUBMARINE boats, Research. See Submarine research vehicles
SUBMARINE boats, Russian. See Russia—Navy —Submarine service
SUBMARINE cables. See Cables, Submarine
SUBMARINE canyons. See Submarine valleys
SUBMARINE diving. See Diving, Submarine
SUBMARINE erosion. See Erosion
SUBMARINE exploration. See Underwater exploration

SUBMARINE geology
See also
Marine sediments
Ocean bottom
SUBMARINE laboratories. See Underwater laboratories
SUBMARINE photography. See Photography, Submarine
SUBMARINE pingos. See Ocean bottom

SUBMARINE research vehicles
Deepstar explores the ocean floor. R. Church. il por Nat Geog 139:110-29 Ja '71
See-all-around bubble sub; Johnson-Sea-Link. A. Fisher. il Pop Sci 199:80-4 S '71
Subs that see in the deep! il Mech Illus 67: 112-13 N '71

SUBMARINE topography. See Ocean bottom

SUBMARINE valleys
Submarine canyon erosion: contribution of marine rock burrowers; Scripps submarine canyon. J. E. Warme and others. bibliog il Science 173:1127-9 S 17 '71
Tectonic movement in the Chile trench. C. R. B. Lister. bibliog il Science 173:719-22 Ag 20 '71

SUBMARINE vehicles
Easy ride under the water; Sea scuta. R. Hill. il Pop Sci 199:55 Ag '71

SUBMARINE weapons. See Weapons systems

SUBMERSIBLES. See Submarine research vehicles

SUBPOENA; story. See Barthelme, D.

SUBPOENAS
Getting CBS. Newsweek 77:95 Ap 19 '71
Privilege in a time of violence; Caldwell ruling and press subpoenas. V. Blasi. Nation 211:653-6 D 21 '70
Third installment; J. Sack and the William L. Calley tapes. il por Newsweek 77:44 F 1 '71

SUBSCRIPTION television. See Television broadcasting, Subscription

SUBSIDIES
See also
Agricultural administration—United States
Federal aid
Tobacco subsidies

SUBSTITUTE products
See also
Food substitutes
Leather substitutes
Sugar substitutes

SUBSTITUTE teachers
Notes of a substitute teacher. P. Berlinrut. Commentary 51:53-62 Ap '71

SUBURBAN churches
Church alive and changing; southern California suburbs. J. C. Hough, jr. il Chr Cent 89:8-12 Ja 5 '72

SUBURBAN life
Suburbia: the new American plurality; with correspondents' reports of four different type suburbs. il Time 97:14-20 Mr 15 '71
Survival in the suburbs; the Thorndikes of West Granby, Conn. J. Egan. il Good H 172:74-5+ Je '71

SUBURBAN offices. See Location in business and industry

SUBURBS
Balkanization of suburbia. S. Kaplan. il Harper 243:72-4 O '71
Battle of the suburbs. il Newsweek 78:61-4+ N 15 '71
Burglars in the suburbs. Newsweek 78:102 O 4 '71
City and suburb: instead of shouting, how about talking? W. F. Wagner, jr. il Arch Rec 150:9-10 O '71
Government renews pressure for integrated suburbs. il U S News 70:47-8 Je 28 '71
Residential segregation: its effects on education. A. Downs. Ed Digest 36:12-15 Ap '71
Shift in policy on housing? low-cost housing in the suburbs. il U S News 70:63 Ap 5 '71
Suburbia: the new American plurality; with correspondents' reports of four different type suburbs. il Time 97:14-20 Mr 15 '71
Suburbs have to open their gates. L. Davidoff and others. il N Y Times Mag p40-4+ N 7 '71
Wall of zoning; suburban racial and economic front. J. Patterson. Commonweal 94:283-5 My 28 '71

Negroes
Will the suburbs beckon? il Ebony 26:112-13 Jl '71

SUBVERSIVE activities
SISS mischief; testimony against NSCM. Chr Cent 88:365-6 Mr 24 '71
You are the target; address, December 3, 1970. T. E. Bishop. Vital Speeches 37:238-41 F 1 '71
See also
Communism—United States
Espionage
Terrorism
United States—Subversive activities control board

Vietnam (Republic)
Quislings; the new meaning. Nation 212:804 Je 28 '71

SUBWAY stations
Low maintenance transit stations. il Am City 86:122 S '71

SUBWAYS
See also subhead Subways under names of cities. e.g. Mexico (city)—Subways

SUCCESS
Following their footsteps: teens on their way talk to five who have made it; symposium. il pors Seventeen 30:94-7+ Ja '71

Teaching children the habit of success. J. Brothers. il por Good H 173:72+ O '71
Winning and losing in life: a survey of opinions about causes. H. J. Wahler. bibliog Ment Hy 55:91-5 Ja '71
See also
Self reliance

SUCCESSION, Plant. See Plant succession

SUCCULENT plants
See also
Cactus
Sedums
Spear lilies
Spurges

SUCHODOLSKI, Bogdan
Aims and requirements of modern education. Sch & Soc 99:409-10 N '71

SUDAN
Soviet Viet Nam; civil war. il Time 97:30+ Mr 1 '71
Ten years of fratricide. S. Meisler. il Nation 213:582-4 D 6 '71
See also
Communist party (Sudan)
Russia—Foreign relations—Sudan
Russians in the Sudan
Trials—Sudan

Politics and government
Revolving-door coup. Time 98:21-3 Ag 2 '71
Showdown season in the Middle East. il por Newsweek 78:34-5 Ag 2 '71

SUDAN GRASS
Hybrids
See also
Sorghum—Hybrids

SUDILOVSKY, Oscar, and others
Cyclic adenosine 3′,5′-monophosphate during glucose repression in the rat liver. bibliog il Science 174:142-4 O 8 '71

SUELZLE, Marijean
Women in labor. il Trans-Action 8:50-8 N '70

SUENENS, Léon Joseph, cardinal
Does the church need a constitution? J. B. Sheerin. Cath World 214:3-4 O '71 *
Suenens proposal. J. Deedy. Commonweal 95:170 N 19 '71 *

SUEZ CANAL
Behind the pressure to reopen Suez Canal. il U S News 70:34-6 Ap 19 '71
If Suez were open. W. P. Bundy. Newsweek 77:40 Je 21 '71
Masada complex. S. Alsop. Newsweek 78:92 Jl 12 '71
New dangers in Mideast; key questions and answers. il U S News 71:40-2 D 6 '71
Reports and comment: Suez. G. G. Stevens. Atlan 228:16-19 Jl '71
Ship canals and aquatic ecosystems. W. I. Aron and S. H. Smith. bibliog il Science 174:17-19 O 1 '71
Suez Canal: beer and boredom. il Time 97:28 My 17 '71
Uncorking the Suez. G. Owens and S. A. Blumberg. Nation 211:656-7 D 21 '70

SUFFERING
Word to suffering saints. Chr Today 16:24 D 17 '71

SUFFOLK COUNTY, N.Y, library association
Major New York County LA critical of state plan. Library J 96:908 Mr 15 '71

SUFFRAGE
See also
Voters, Registration of

United States
All eyes on new young voters; with chart. il Sr Schol 99:2-3 S 20 '71
Battle for the youth vote. R. T. Gray. il Nations Bsns 59:60-2+ O '71
Candidates answer Senior's queries: most significant thing to tell a young person voting for the first time in 1972? il Sr Schol 99:12-13 N 1 '71
Countdown toward a lower voting age. il U S News 70:38 Je 14 '71
18-year-old vote. New Repub 164:7 My 8 '71
18-year-old vote: a 50-state survey. il U S News 70:58-60 Mr 8 '71
18-year-old vote could beat Nixon in '72. S. Lubell. il Look 35:64+ Jl 13 '71
Elections '72: Americans from age 17 to 23. il Sr Schol 99:6 N 29 '71
Electoral values old and new. R. L. Tobin. Sat R 54:16 My 29 '71
How will the young vote? il Time 98:9-10 Ag 23 '71
Lower voting age: one more hurdle to go. il U S News 70:64-5 Ap 5 '71
Now that the voting age is lower. il U S News 71:58 Jl 12 '71
Old hometown: question of student residency. D. Baskin. New Repub 165:11 N 6 '71

SUFFRAGE—United States—*Continued*
Open letter to the new voters. J. Ciardi. Sat
R 54:8+ S 11 '71
Rapid change of sentiment: lowering the
voting age. R. Roth. Ann Am Acad 397:
83-7 S '71
Sometime eighteen-year-old vote: bizarre de-
cision by the Court. N. Lewin. New Repub
164:21-2 Ja 2 '71
Upsets recorded by student voters, an omen
for candidates in 1972? il U S News 71:25
N 15 '71
Vote at 18. Sr Schol 98:14 Ap 26 '71
Vote for 18-year-olds: what justices said on
both sides. il U S News 70:88-9 Ja 25 '71
What will the 135 million do? R. L. Tobin.
Sat R 54:23 O 9 '71
Youth vote and change in American politics.
L. M. Seagull. bibliog f il Ann Am Acad
397:88-96 S '71
See also
Woman suffrage—United States

SUFISM
Ancient way to new freedom. D. Lessing.
Vogue 158:98+ Jl '71

SUGAR
Upsetting facts about our diet; sugar added
to processed foods. B. T. Hunter. il Con-
sumer Bul 54:4+ Jl '71
See also
Glucose

SUGAR cane technologists, International society
of. See International society of sugar cane
technologists

SUGAR CREEK, Tex. See New cities and towns

SUGAR in the body
See also
Blood sugar

SUGAR industry
Department discusses Sugar act extension
before Senate committee; statement, June
16, 1971. J. L. Katz. Dept State Bul 65:
89-91 Jl 19 '71
Department gives views on sugar legislation; address, May 6, 1971. J. L. Katz. Dept
State Bul 64:778-82 Je 14 '71

Imports problem
Sugar: the lobbyists' dream. Nation 212:773-
4 Je 21 '71
Sweet bonus for apartheid; sugar quota issue. B. F. Oudes. Nation 212:719-21 Je 7 '71

SUGAR peas. See Peas

SUGAR substitutes
On sweetness and sweeteners. il Chem 44:21-2
N '71

SUGARMAN, Daniel A. and Hochstein, Rollie
Is virginity outmoded? il Seventeen 30:120-1+
O '71
Many faces of love. il Seventeen 29:112-13+
D '70
Searching for a new faith. il Seventeen 29:
134-5+ S '70

SUGARS
See also
Saccharides

SUGG, Redding S. Jr
John Faulkner's vanishing South. il por Am
Heritage 22:65-75 Ap '71

SUGGESTION
See also
Hypnotism

SUGGESTION systems
Boom in bright ideas. R. Levy. Duns 97:67-8+
My '71

SUHARTO, 1925-
Electing God's government. il por Time 98:
25-6 Jl 12 '71 *
Indonesia: transition to stability? D. B.
H. Denoon. bibliog f il Cur Hist 61:332-8+
D '71 *

SUHOR, Charles
Pattern practices: we bombed in New Orleans. Engl J 60:1221-4 D '71

SUICA, J. Salom
Power development in Yugoslavia. il por Bul
Atom Sci 27:42-6 N '71

SUICIDE
Abortion and suicidal behaviors: observa-
tions on the concept of endangering the
mental health of the mother. H. L. P.
Resnik and B. J. Wittlin. bibliog Ment Hy
55:10-20 Ja '71
Adolescent suicide: results of study by P.
Cantor. Time 99:57 Ja 3 '72
Alternative to suicide. Time 97:48 Ap 26 '71
Attempt; excerpt from The savage God. A.
Alvarez. il Atlan 227:84-6+ Ap '71
Black suicide, by H. Hendin. Review
Atlan 227:108-10+ F '71. J. Updike
Extent and significance of suicide among
American Indians today. R. J. Havighurst.
bibliog il Ment Hy 55:174-7 Ap '71

Student suicide. S. A. Winickoff and H.
L. P. Resnik. bibliog Todays Ed 60:30-2+
Ap '71
Suicide in college. Trans-Action 8:10 F '71
Youthful suicides. Newsweek 77:70-1 F 15 '71
See also
Harakiri

Prevention
Evaluation and treatment of suicide-prone
youth. M. King. bibliog Ment Hy 55:344-50
Jl '71
Present suicide taboo in the United States.
C. J. Frederick. bibliog Ment Hy 55:178-83
Ap '71
Suicide prevention programs and mental
health associations. R. K. McGee. bibliog
Ment Hy 55:60-7 Ja '71

SUITCASES. See Luggage

SUITE no. 3; ballet. See Ballets—Criticisms

SUITS at law. See Actions and defenses

SUKHOMLINOV, Vladimir Aleksandrovich
Sukhomlinov effect. R. A. Beaumont and
B. J. James. il por Horizon 13:66-9 Wint
'71 *

SULFONATES
Solvent dependence of the luminescence of
N-arylaminonaphthalenesulfonates. C. J.
Seliskar and L. Brand. bibliog il Science
171:799-800 F 26 '71

SULFUR
Prices
Sulfur from gas is glutting the market. il
Bsns W p60 Jl 24 '71

SULFUR in the body
Add six years to your life; sulfur compounds
to combat free radicals. il Sci Digest 70:
76-7 D '71

SULICA, Andrei, and others
Stimulation in vitro with protein carrier of
antibodies against a hapten. bibliog il Science 171:1165-7 Mr 19 '71

SULLIVAN, Charles Loten
If not Charles Evers, who? interview ed. by
R. Branson. Chr Cent 88:906-8 Jl 28 '71

SULLIVAN, Ed
Winner is, the losers are. . . il pors Time 97:
50-1 Mr 29 '71 *

SULLIVAN, Frank, 1892-
Greetings, friend! poem. New Yorker 47:31
D 25 '71

SULLIVAN, George A. Jr
Judge George Sullivan: lawbreaker for peace;
interview, ed. by C. E. Fager. il Chr Cent
88:852-5 Jl 14 '71

about
Turnabout trials. il por Time 98:44-5 Jl 19
'71 *

SULLIVAN, Godfrey
Political activities of the teacher. bibliog f
Clear House 46:212-14 D '71

SULLIVAN, James
Paean (in the old style) poem. Commonweal
94:168 Ap 23 '71

SULLIVAN, K. A.
Walk the primrose path. il Org Gard & Farm
18:44-6 Jl '71

SULLIVAN, Leon Howard
Steps we must take: training, economic development and togetherness; address, July
6, 1971. Vital Speeches 37:676-9 S 1 '71

about
Black director pushes reforms at GM. il pors
Bsns W p 100-3 Ap 10 '71 *
Unorthodox ministry of Leon H. Sullivan.
P. Garland. il pors Ebony 26:112-14+ My
'71 *

SULLIVAN, Louis Henry
Down comes a masterpiece; Louis Sullivan's
old Stock exchange building. il Life 71:40-1
N 5 '71
One long fight that preservationists lost.
J. Shaw. il Arch Rec 150:10 D '71 *

SULLIVAN, Nancy
Beyond saying; poem. New Repub 165:28 D
11 '71
Iconodule and iconoclast. Poetry 119:107-9
N '71

SULLIVAN, Pat
Underneath that 7 is an S. P. Putnam. il
Sports Illus 35:67+ N 22 '71 *

SULLIVAN, Peggy
Gaping across the gap. bibliog il Library J
96:1767-70 My 15 '71

SULLIVAN, Robert
Other Illinois. il Travel 135:56-61 Ap '71

SULLIVAN, Robert J.
Reluctant rebels. il Parents Mag 46:56-7+ Ap
'71

SULLIVAN, Ronald
How two influential fathers turned family drug tragedies into a triumph for the public. il Todays Health 49:42-5 My '71
SULLIVAN, William Cornelius
File on J. Edgar Hoover. il pors Time 98: 14-16 O 25 '71 *
SULLIVAN, William H.
Refugee problems in Laos and Cambodia; statement, April 22, 1971. Dept State Bul 64:648-54 My 17 '71
SULLY, François
Frustration near the front. por Time 97:45-6 Mr 8 '71 *
Obituary
Newsweek il por 77:75 Mr 8 '71
SULZBERGER, Arthur Ochs
Its business is much more than the news. il por Bsns W p75-6 Je 28 '71 *
Project X. il por Time 97:45-6 Je 28 '71 *
SULZBERGER, Marina
Roumania: angels among the roses. Vogue 157:194 My '71
SUMBERG, M. S.
10 key specs for effective PA. il Radio Electr 42:45-7 My '71
SUMITOMO chemical company. See Chemical industries—Japan
SUMMER
Credences of summer; boys' home on a farm. R. Rhodes. il Harper 243:57-60 Ag '71
Summer glimpses. New Yorker 47:24-6 Jl 31 '71
SUMMER after; story. See Robinson, B.
SUMMER and smoke; opera. See Hoiby, L.
SUMMER camping. See Camping
SUMMER cookery. See Cookery
SUMMER entertaining. See Entertaining
SUMMER furniture. See Furniture, Summer
SUMMER homes
Cliffhanging retreat for a three-career man. W. McQuade. il Fortune 83:105-7 Mr '71
Veranda set; Lee Eastmans' cottage in East Hampton. R. Reif. il N Y Times Mag p86-7 Je 6 '71
SUMMER jobs for students. See Student employment
SUMMER meals. See Meals
SUMMER menus. See Menus
SUMMER resorts
See also
Deauville, France
Mount Desert Island
Seaside resorts
SUMMER safety devices and measures. See Safety devices and measures
SUMMER school of music of Yale university. See Music schools
SUMMER schools
School of the arts in Port Townsend. il Sunset 146:30+ Je '71
Summer school: a time for imagination. T. V. Muller. Clear House 45:422-3 Mr '71
Summer school outdoors. D. N. Haerer. il Todays Ed 60:18-19 F '71
See also
International summer school on disarmament and arms control
School year
SUMMER theater. See Theater—United States
SUMMER vacations. See Vacations
SUMMER workshops. See Educational workshops
SUMMERLIN, Edgar
Month's jazz. Am Rec G 37:394-5, 523 F; Ap '71
SUMMERS, Claude M.
Conversion of energy; with biographical sketch. il Sci Am 225:28, 148-60 S '71
SUMMERS, F. William
Change in budgetary thinking; address, June 1971. bibliog il Am Lib 2:1174-80 D '71
State library standards, revised: a critique. Library J 96:1191-2 Ap 1 '71
SUMMERS, Scott K. and Teton, A. P.
Paddle your own canoe. il por Parks & Rec 6:35-6 Jl '71
SUMMERS, William. See Summers, F. W.
SUMMERTON, Margaret
Sweetcrab; story. Redbook 136:125-47 Ja '71
SUMMIT conferences. See International conferences
SUMNER, Charles
Charles Sumner and the rights of man, by D. Donald. Review
New Repub 164:36-8 Ja 2 '71. H. N. Meyer *
Sat R 54:32-4 F 20 '71. T. H. Williams *
SUMNER, John Saxton
Obituary
Pub W 200:56 Jl 12 '71

SUN
Sun, moon, and planets this month. R. C. Victor. See issues of Sky and telescope
When the sun was young. Newsweek 79:45 Ja 3 '72
Your life depends on the sun. il Nat Wildlife 9:10-11 O '71
See also
Eclipses, Solar
Spectrohelioscope

Atmosphere
See also
Sun—Corona

Corona
Apollo photos aid sun energy flow study. il Aviation W 96:49 Ja 10 '72
Geometry of the coronal magnetic field. M. D. Altschuler. il Sky & Tel 41:146-50 Mr '71
See also
Solar wind

Prominences
Solar prominences and their magnetic fields. E. Tandberg-Hanssen. il Sky & Tel 42:72-5, 142-5 Ag-S '71
SUN and cancer. See Cancer—Causes
SUN and meteorology
Solar-climate relationships in the postpleistocene. J. R. Bray. bibliog Science 171:1242-3 Mr 26 '71
SUN burn. See Sunburn
SUN dials. See Sundials
SUN glasses
Focus on eyes: the newest eye wardrobes create a whole new point of view. il Harp Baz 104:12 Jl '71
Sunglasses. Mech Illus 67:73 Jl '71
Sunglasses. il Consumer Bul 54:32-4+ Jl '71
Tips on tinted glasses. P. Van Wagenen. il Parents Mag 46:30 Ap '71
SUN in literature
Our busy and versatile literary sun. R. Lipez. Sat R 54:18 Ag 7 '71
SUN light. See Sunlight
SUN oil company
Longest night. il Forbes 107:22-3 Je 1 '71
SUN tan. See Tan
SUN tan preparations. See Cosmetics
SUNBEAM corporation
Shadow on Sunbeam. il Forbes 108:55 Jl 15 '71
SUNBURN
Tan now, pay in 1986, danger of skin cancer. C. Carpentieri. il Mech Illus 67:62-3+ Jl '71
SUNBURN lotions. See Cosmetics
SUND, Eldon H. See Palma, R. J. jt. auth.
SUNDARALINGAM, M. and others
Molecular conformation of dihydrouridine: puckered base nucleoside of transfer RNA. bibliog il Science 172:725-7 My 14 '71
SUNDAY horse racing. See Horse racing
SUNDAY legislation
Blue laws: more confusion than conviction. Bsns W p98 O 16 '71
Editorial: no hunting allowed on Sunday. C. Conley. Field & S 75:6 F '71
See also
Business hours
SUNDAY opening of libraries. See Libraries—Hours of opening
SUNDAY opening of stores. See Business hours
SUNDAY schools
Sex at Sunday school. il Newsweek 78:50-1 D 27 '71
SUNDAY times, London
Insight's latest headlines. il Time 98:87 N 1 '71
London notebook. B. Kolins. Pub W 199:25-6 My 17 '71
SUNDAY's Child (rock group) See Rock groups
SUNDERLIN, Sylvia
Fashion show centennial. il Har Yrs 11: 49-51 Ag '71
SUNDEWS
Fly in the sundew. T. Ashley and J. F. Gennaro, jr. il Natur Hist 80:80-5+ D '71
SUNDIALS
On the trail of old sundials. O. Lindberg. il Sci Digest 70:69-72 S '71
Riverside sun-dial. O. R. Hagans. il Hobbies 76:126-8+ N '71
Sundials are fun: and they also tell you the time. il Sunset 147:158 Jl '71
Tell-time table. D. Shiner. il Design 72:34-5 Spr '71
SUNDRA, Jon R.
How to lure lazy pike. il Field & S 75:80-1+ Mr '71
SUNFISH (boats) See Sailboats

SUNFISH fishing
  Bluegills and blubbers. J. N. Mannix. il por
    Outdoor Life 147:86-8+ My '71
  Deer hair and bluegill. T. Nixon. il Field & S
    76:80-1+ My '71
  Don't forget the bluegills. B. W. Dalrymple.
    il Outdoor Life 147:74-5+ F '71
  People's choice; pint-size bluegills. A. W.
    Prince. il por Outdoor Life 148:84+ Ag '71
SUNFLOWERS
  Sunflowers! R. L. Higby; H. G. Lendle; M.
    Miller. il Org Gard & Farm 18:68-76 Ap '71

      Seed

  Will the Russians bury us in sunflower seeds?
    R. Rodale. il Org Gard & Farm 18:35-8 Ja
    '71
SUNGLASSES. See Sun glasses
SUNKEN treasure. See Treasure trove
SUNLIGHT
  Sun machine previews shadows. P. Wahl. il
    Pop Sci 199:121 Ag '71
      See also
  Photosynthesis
SUNRISE
  Dawn watch. J. Ciardi. Sat R 54:26 N 6 '71
SUNRISE services, Easter. See Easter
SUNSCREEN preparations. See Cosmetics
SUNSET (periodical)
      See also
  Western home awards
SUNSET CRATER NATIONAL MONUMENT
  Arizona prehistory, a loop north of Flag-
    staff. il Sunset 147:56-7 O '71
SUNSET garden contest. See Gardening—Com-
    petitions
SUNSET phenomena
  Twilight flash of sodium. A. W. Peterson and
    L. M. Kieffaber. il Sky & Tel 41:344-5 Je '71
  [Violet flash, observed] R. H. Wilson, jr.
    Sky & Tel 42:327+ D '71
      See also
  Sky, Color of
SUNSHINE. See Sunlight
SUNSPOTS
  USNO sunspot program. Sky & Tel 41:152
    Mr '71
SUNTAG, Murray
  Radio & television news. See issues of Elec-
    tronics world
SUNTAN. See Tan
SUOMI, Stephen J. and Harlow, H. F.
  Monkeys at play. il Natur Hist 80:72-7 D '71
SUPER, John H.
  New use for SK-5. il Sea Front 17:272-3 S
    '71
SUPER chief (train) See Railroads—Trains
SUPER 8 cameras. See Moving picture cam-
    eras
SUPER markets. See Supermarkets
SUPERCHARGERS
      See also
  Automobile engines—Superchargers
SUPERCONDUCTING magnets. See Magnets
SUPERCONDUCTIVITY
  Along two dimensions. Sci N 100:140 Ag 28
    '71
  Electronics with superconduction junctions;
    Josephson devices. J. Clarke. bibliog il
    Phys Today 24:30-7 Ag '71
  Search for high-temperature superconduc-
    tors. B. T. Matthias. bibliog il Phys Today
    24:23-8 Ag '71
  Superconductivity at high pressure. N. B.
    Brandt and N. I. Ginzburg. il Sci Am 224:
    83-8+ Ap '71
      See also
  Superfluidity
SUPERCONDUCTORS
  Electron microscopy and diffraction of lay-
    ered, superconducting intercalation com-
    plexes. H. Fernández-Morán and others.
    bibliog il Science 174:498-500 O 29 '71
  Intercalation complexes of Lewis bases and
    layered sulfides: a large class of new su-
    perconductors. F. R. Gamble and others.
    bibliog il Science 174:493-7 O 29 '71
  Magnetic structure of superconductors. U.
    Essmann and H. Träuble. il Sci Am 224:
    74-84 Mr '71
  New heat in a chilly argument; high-tem-
    perature superconductors. il Sci N 99:194
    Mr 20 '71
  New superconductors. T. H. Geballe. il Sci
    Am 225:22-33 N '71
  Superconducting glass. Sci Am 224:47 F '71
SUPERCOOLING
  Ice nucleation by coprecipitated silver iodide
    and silver bromide. B. Vonnegut and H.
    Chessin. bibliog il Science 174:945-6 N 26
    '71

SUPERFLUIDITY
  Quantum nature of superfluid helium. S. J.
    Putterman and I. Rudnick. bibliog il Phys
    Today 24:39-43+ Ag '71
      See also
  Superconductivity
SUPERGIANT stars. See Stars, Giant
SUPERHEATING
  Modified superheating of purified water. K.
    Hickman and I. White. bibliog il Science
    172:718-22 My 14 '71
SUPERINTENDENTS, School. See School
    superintendents and principals
SUPERIOR, LAKE
  Moody woman called Superior; excerpts from
    Superior: portrait of a living lake. A. Kar-
    len. il Nat Wildlife 9:43-7 F '71
  Superior cruising. G. E. Miller. il Motor B &
    S 127:62-5+ My '71
SUPERIOR colliculus. See Brain
SUPERIOR national forest, Minn. See Nation-
    al forests
SUPERMARKET unit pricing. See Unit pric-
    ing
SUPERMARKETS
  Blitzing the supermarket customer with
    books. P. A. Farrell. Pub W 200:71-2 Ag
    23 '71
  Chains woo consumers with open dating. il
    Bsns W p48+ Ja 16 '71
  Penney steps out. il Forbes 107:19 F 15 '71
  Supermarket trap, by J. Cross. Review
    Ramp Mag 9:59-60 Mr '71. H. Lippincott
      See also
  Colonial stores, inc.
  Great Atlantic and Pacific tea company
  Safeway stores, inc.
  Thriftimart, inc.

      Advertising

  Truth in advertising: supermarket specials.
    Consumer Rep 36:465-6 Ag '71

      Finance

  Late tape. R. Brady. Duns 97:9-10 My '71

      Public relations

  How Pathmark disarms the crusaders. il Bsns
    W p62+ My 8 '71

      Securities

  Making money work; investments in super-
    market chains. S. Meisenberg. Har Yrs 11:
    54-5 Je '71

      Japan

  Mao in the supermarket. il por Time 97:74 Je
    28 '71
SUPERMARKETS general corporation
  How Pathmark disarms the crusaders. il
    Bsns W p62+ My 8 '71
SUPERNATURAL
      See also
  Occult sciences
SUPERNATURAL in literature
  C. S. Lewis: apostle to the imagination.
    D. Downing. por Chr Today 16:10-12 O
    8 '71
  Figure of the dybbuk. H. Fisch. Commen-
    tary 51:70-5 Ap '71
SUPERNATURAL moving pictures. See Mov-
    ing pictures—Horror films
SUPERNOVA. See Stars, New
SUPERPHOSPHATES. See Phosphates
SUPERSONIC air travel. See Air travel
SUPERSONIC airplane engines. See Jet air-
    plane engines
SUPERSONIC airplanes. See Airplanes, Super-
    sonic
SUPERSTITION
  I'm not superstitious, but . . . J. H. Win-
    chester. il Read Digest 98:21-4 F '71
      See also
  Medicine men
  Occult sciences
  Taboo
  Witchcraft
SUPERTANKERS. See Tank ships
SUPERVISED study
      See also
  Study halls
SUPERVISION of schools. See School supervi-
    sion and supervisors
SUPERVISORS
  Where they make believe they're the boss;
    assessment technique. il Bsns W p34-5 Ag
    28 '71
SUPERVISORS, Library. See Library adminis-
    tration
SUPERVISORS, School. See School supervision
    and supervisors
SUPERVISORS of student teaching
  Criteria for selecting supervising teachers. S.
    A. Gregory. il Clear House 46:178-82 N '71

SUPERVISORS of student teaching—*Continued*
Dedicated sponsors for student teachers. E.
A. King. Clear House 46:206 D '71
Guide for the supervising teacher. B. E.
Long. Clear House 46:151-4 N '71
SUPPERS
Follow-up food. il Bet Hom & Gard 49:66-7+
Ja '71
Guess what's coming for dinner: covered
dish suppers. il McCalls 98:92-8+ My '71
Party supper: a main course all in one dish;
with recipes. il House & Gard 140:34-5+ Jl
'71
SUPPLEMENTAL airlines. See Airlines—Non-
scheduled operations; Local service air-
lines
SUPPLEMENTARY employment
Moonlight dims for professors. il Bsns W
p52-5 Jl 3 '71
Multiple jobholding in 1970 and 1971; with
tables. H. V. Hayghe and K. Michelotti.
il Mo Labor R 94:38-45 O '71
SUPPORT (domestic relations)
EDP keeps tabs on wife supporters; Dane
County, Wis. A. Larson. il Am City 86:82
My '71
SUPPORTS, Plant. See Garden stakes and
staking
SUPREME court judges. See United States—
Supreme court
SUPREME court of the United States. See
United States—Supreme court
SUPREME court press corps. See Reporters
and reporting
SUR (periodical) See Periodicals—Argentina
SURF fishing. See Salt water fishing
SURF riding
All aboard for the big flush; Collegiate in-
land surfing classic. A. Napier. il Sports
Illus 34:80+ Ap 5 '71
Brutal is the word; body-surfing area. New-
port Beach, Calif. il Life 71:72-5 O 1 '71
Closest thing to being born; body surfing. C.
Kirkpatrick. il Sports Illus 34:60-4+ F 22
'71
Surfers invade sailing. J. Singleton. il Motor
B & S 127:37+ F '71
Winter surfing in Rhode Island. M. P.
Manheim. il Travel 136:52-5 D '71
You can always surf on it; Smirnoff world
pro-am surfing championship at Sunset
Beach. R. W. Johnston. il Sports Illus 35:
102-3 D 6 '71
SURF sailing. See Surf riding
SURFACE, Bill
Boston's marvelous marathon. il Read Di-
gest 98:122-6 Ap '71
Hottest man on ice. il por Read Digest 98:
219-20+ F '71
Jan Stenerud is no football player but he
wins football games. il por N Y Times
Mag p 10-11+ S 19 '71
Pitcher; baseball's tormented magician. il
Read Digest 99:115-18 Ag '71
Pro football's one-man demolition squad.
il Read Digest 99:149-52 O '71
World's winningest jockey. il por Read Di-
gest 98:123-6 My '71
SURFACE effect ships. See Air cushion veh-
icles
SURFACE effect vehicles. See Air cushion vehi-
cles
SURFACE electrical properties experiment. See
Moon—Exploration—Equipment
SURFACE films. See Films
SURFACES
See also
Thin films
Measurement
Surface microtopography; adaptation of ad-
dress, March 1971. R. D. Young. bibliog il
Phys Today 24:42-9 N '71
SURFING. See Surf riding
SURGEONS
Mistakes surgeons make most often. W. A.
Nolen. Vogue 158:92-3 Ag 1 '71
SURGERY
Patients hear during surgery? A. J. Snider.
Sci Digest 69:57 F '71
They cut her open and then just sewed her
back up. R. Drake. Chr Cent 88:288-9 Mr
3 '71
Unkindest cut. il Newsweek 79:51 Ja 3 '72
White hurts surgeons' eyes. Sci Digest 69:57
Je '71
See also
Anesthesia
Chemosurgery
Orthopedia
Surgeons
Veterinary surgery
also subhead Surgery under names of
organs and regions of the body, e.g. Throat
—Surgery

History
See Medicine—History
SURGERY, Cosmetic. See Surgery, Plastic
SURGERY, Plastic
Breast sculpture. S. Morini. il Vogue 157:82-
5+ Ja 15 '71
Can a nose job change your life? B. Wagner.
pors Seventeen 30:136+ N '71
Face-lifts; excerpt from Body sculpture. S.
Morini. il Vogue 158:114-17+ S 15 '71
Happy specialty. il Newsweek 77:39-40 My 31
'71
How Silastic transformed breast surgery. J.
Star. Look 35:12 Jl 27 '71
My new face. A. Vanderbilt. pors Ladies
Home J 88:52+ Ap '71
New aid to plastic surgery: silicone. S.
Morini. il Vogue 157:84-7+ Mr 15 '71
Operation facelift. R. Barnette. Har Yrs 11:
22-3 F '71
Other face of plastic surgery: the disappoint-
ed patient. F. C. Macgregor and B. Ford.
Sci Digest 69:16-20 Ap '71
Plastic surgery: rhinoplasty. H. LaBarre. il
Ladies Home J 88:102+ My '71
So people won't stare; reconstructive surgery.
T. Irwin. il Todays Health 49:28-9 F '71
Take 15 years off your face. il McCalls 98:
68-71 Ap '71
SURINAM
See also
Rites and ceremonies—Surinam
SURO, Dario
Painter of hands. il Américas 23:37-40 Je '71
SURPLUS products
Boeing's surplus is on the block. il Bsns W
p35-6 Ap 17 '71
Science junk; funding cuts make used equip-
ment pile up. D. Shapley. Science 171:879-
82 Mr 5 '71
Surplus scene:
Today's surplus dealers. A. W. Burawa.
il Pop Electr 1:116 Ja '72
See also
B and F enterprises (firm)
SURPLUS products, Agricultural
Brighter outlook for farmers; interview. C
M. Hardin. il por U S News 70:58-62 Je 28
'71
Corn crop so big it's a real headache. il
U S News 71:42 N 29 '71
SURPRISE parties. See Entertaining
SURPRISING stranger; story. See Soman, F. J.
SURREALISM
André Breton: magus of surrealism, by A.
Balakian. Review
America 125:327-8 O 23 '71. J. D. Gauthier
Pre-surrealism photography: a trip into the
subconscious. M. Mann. il Pop Phot 68:
33+ Ap '71
Venice revisited. G. Highet. il Horizon 13:
54-7 Wint '71
SURSUM corda, Washington, D.C. See Hous-
ing projects. Government
SURTEES, Dennis
Search for speed. il Yachting 129:50-1+ Ap
'71
SURVEYING
See also
Radio in surveying
United States—National ocean survey
SURVEYING, Aerial
See also
Mapping, Aerial
Photography, Aerial
Radar in surveying
SURVEYOR flights. See Space flight to the
moon—Surveyor flights
SURVEYOR fund, Inc. See Investment trusts
SURVIVAL after airplane accidents, ship-
wrecks, etc.
Noble savage, 1971: suggestions for survival
reading. M. A. Crush. bibliog il por Wil-
son Lib Bul 45:864-9 My '71
Staying alive in a raft. G. Webb and J.
Webb. il Motor B & S 128:41+ Ag '71
When in trouble: lessons from three rescue
operations and a severe squall. S. Chasa-
low; R. Williams; G. J. Hess. il Yachting
129:60-4+ Je '71
See also
Survival and emergency equipment
Wilderness survival
SURVIVAL after death. See Immortality
SURVIVAL and emergency equipment
Using survival equipment? B. D. Barker, 3d.
il Yachting 130:68-9 Jl '71
SURVIVAL of man. See Man—Survival
SUSANN, Jacqueline
Jacqueline Susann's bedtime stories: inter-
view, ed. by S. Ribakove and B. Ribakove.
il Todays Health 49:30-3+ S '71
SUSPENSE novels. See Detective and mystery
stories

SUSPENSION, Automobile. See Automobiles—
   Springs and suspension
SUSSMAN, Marvin B.
   Family systems in the 1970's: analysis, poli-
   cies, and programs; address, April 1971,
   with questions and answers. bibliog f Ann
   Am Acad 396:40-56 Jl '71
SUSUE Jo; story. See Garrison, R. H.
SUTCLIFFE, James Helme
   (ed) See Dernesch, H. Recipe for Brünn-
     hilde
   (ed) See Kubelik, R. Kubelik speaks
   (ed) See Martin, J. No elbows
   (ed) See Pauly, R. Chased by the notes
SUTER, Carrie Rice
   I am black; poem. Negro Hist Bul 34:88 Ap
   '71
SUTFIN, Lloyd V. and others
   Microanalysis of individual mitochondrial
   granules with diameters less than 1000
   angstroms. bibliog il Science 174:947-9 N
   26 '71
SUTHEIM, Peter
   Experimenter's delight. Radio-Electr 42:41-5+
   Ag '71
   Get better sound from your record player.
   il Radio-Electr 42:32-4 N '71
SUTHERLAND, Don
   Good home movie is not necessarily well
   made. il Pop Phot 69:122-3+ O '71
   How to shoot from the hip. il Pop Phot 69:
   102-3+ S '71
   Rarely is the medium well done. il Pop Phot
   69:102-3+ Jl '71
SUTHERLAND, Earl Wilbur, 1915-
   1971 Nobel prize for physiology or medicine.
   I. H. Pastan. por Science 174:392-3 O 22
   '71 *
   1971 Nobel prizes in science. por Chem 45:23
   Ja '72 *
   Nobelist in Nashville. por Newsweek 78:109-
   10 O 25 '71 *
   Second messenger. por Time 98:63 O 25 '71 *
   Sutherland's cyclic AMP work brings him
   1971 Nobel prize. por Sci N 100:278 O 23
   '71 *
SUTHERLAND, Joan
   Sutherland: a separate greatness. por Time
   98:81 N 22 '71 *
SUTHERLAND, Zena
   Books for young people. See issues of Satur-
     day review
   Children's books for spring. il Sat R 54:45-8
   My 15 '71
SUTOR, D. June. See Lonsdale, K. jt. auth.
SUTPHEN, Jack
   Forty years of madness. il Motor B & S
   127:56-7 F '71
   Your genoa: to cut or not to cut. il Yacht-
   ing 129:58-9+ Ap '71
   Your mainsail, to cut or not to cut. il
   Yachting 129:60-2+ Mr '71
SUTRO, Adolph G.
   Lift-off from San Francisco Bay. il Read Di-
   gest 99:110-14 D '71
SUTTER, Janet Bascom
   Speaking of books. il Home Gard 58:52 Ag
   '71
SUTTLER, David
   Parents' guide to the new draft. il Ladies
   Home J 88:56+ D '71
SUTTON, Edwin C.
   Making tubes for NO_2—N_2O_4 equilibrium re-
   action. il por Chem 45:28 Ja '72
SUTTON, Horace
   Booked for travel (cont) il Sat R 54:34+
   Ap 24: 16+ Je 26; 34-5 Ag 7: 37-8 Ag 14:
   56-8 S 25; 63-4+ N 6 '71; 55:22-3 Ja 8 '72
   Does anyone want to visit the U.S.A? il Sat
   R 55:36-7+ Ja 1 '72
   Fanon. il por Sat R 54:16-19+ Jl 17 '71
   Guide to the beauty of the French West
   Indies. il McCalls 99:90-1+ N '71
   Palm tree revolt. il Sat R 54:15-19+ F 27 '71
   Prague, spring '71. il Sat R 54:19-21+ Je 5 '71
   Special travel correspondent (cont) il Holi-
   day 48:14-17 S; 8-11 N; 49:11+ D '70
SUTTON, Isaac
   Quiet family life of Muhammad Ali; photo-
   graphs. Ebony 26:118-22 Ja '71
SUTTON, Willie
   Medicare mob. il pors Esquire 76:99 Ag '71 *
SUTTON-SMITH, Brian
   Children at play. il Natur Hist 80:54-9 D '71
SUWANNEE RIVER wilderness preserve. See
   Wilderness areas—Florida
SUZMAN, Janet
   New stars, the new films. H. Popkin. por
   Harp Baz 105:71 D '71 *
SUZUKI, Kunihiko. See Suzuki, Y. jt. auth.
SUZUKI, Yoshiyuki, and Suzuki, Kunihiko
   Krabbe's globoid cell leukodystrophy: defi-
   ciency of galactocerebrosidase in serum,
   leukocytes, and fibroblasts. bibliog il Sci-
   ence 171:73-5 Ja 8 '71

SUZY, pseud. See Mehle, A.
SVEDIN, Lulli
   Dance in Sweden. il Dance Mag 45:50+ My
   '71
SVOBODA, Josef
   Scenic world of Joseph Svoboda. J. M. Burian.
   il por Sat R 54:35-7+ Ag 28 '71 *
SVOBODA, William S.
   Case for out-of-class exams. Clear House
   46:231-3 D '71
SWADOS, Harvey
   Joys and terrors of sending the kids to col-
   lege. il N Y Times Mag p 12-13+ F 14 '71
SWALLOW-tailed kites. See Kites (birds)
SWALLOWS
   See also
   Martins
SWAMP plants. See Marsh plants
SWAMP rabbit hunting. See Rabbit hunting
SWAMPS. See Marshes
SWAN, Jimmy
   If not Charles Evers, who? interview ed. by
   R. Biranson. Chr Cent 88:906-8 Jl 28 '71
            about
   Swan's song. Newsweek 78:20+ Ag 16 '71 *
SWAN, Jon
   Fall below zero in New England winter;
   poem. Atlan 227:95 F '71
   Idyll, with siren; poem. New Yorker 46:75
   F 6 '71
   Only fitting; poem. New Yorker 47:44 S 25 '71
SWAN, Margaret
   And now for the resurrection. R. Blount. il
   por Sports Illus 34:96-100+ Ap 12 '71 *
SWAN, Paul
   Tips on A.I. from a real pro. pors Suc Farm
   69:no3 D10 F '71
SWAN LAKE iris gardens. See Gardens—
   South Carolina
SWANN, Brian
   Naxos; poem. Commonweal 93:444 F 5 '71
SWANN, G. A. and others
   Geologic setting of the Apollo 14 samples.
   bibliog il Science 173:716-19 Ag 20 '71
SWANN, Robert
   Culebra: island besieged. Nation 212:262-5
   Mr 1 '71
SWANS
   Australia's black swan is a people bird. il
   Sci Digest 69:56 Mr '71
SWANSEA porcelain. See Pottery, Welsh
SWANSON, Dick
   Wild beast that devours the dry forests;
   photographs. il Life 71:28-33 Jl 23 '71
SWANSON, Gary
   Good guys, bad guys and the bighorn. E.
   Zern. il por Sports Illus 34:20-2+ Je 28 '71 *
   That desert-sheep case. il Outdoor Life 148:8
   N '71 *
SWANSON, Gloria
   Gloria Swanson is back, full of organic beans.
   M. Paley. por Life 71:77 S 17 '71 *
SWANSON, Stephen O.
   Foreign aid; poem. Chr Cent 88:1131 S 29 '71
SWAPPING. See Barter
SWARTHMORE college, Swarthmore, Pa.
   How G-men win their letter on campus. T.
   DeFrank. il Newsweek 77:24 Ap 26 '71
SWARTHOUT, Arthur W.
   Religion and the scriptures, today. bibliog il
   por Wilson Lib Bul 45:664-73 Mr '71
SWARTS, Helene
   Priorities; poem. Chr Cent 88:558 My 5 '71
SWARTZ, Roderick G.
   (ed) Humanities in the library: the role of
   the National endowment for the humani-
   ties. il por Wilson Lib Bul 46:426-45 Ja '72
   Pride in heritage: one library's approach. il
   Wilson Lib Bul 46:431-5 Ja '72
SWARTZBERG, Irvin
   Swartzberg's misfortune. G. R. Rosen. por
   Duns 98:74 S '71 *
SWASTIKA on our door; story. See Adams, A.
SWATEK, Paul
   Earth. Mlle 73:56-7 Je '71
SWAZILAND
   C'est si bon. por Newsweek 78:61-2 N 22 '71
   Most African country in Africa. J. Morris.
   il Holiday 49:50-3+ Mr '71
             Royal family
   Six royal Africans at an Indiana college. il
   Ebony 26:66-8+ F '71
SWEARER, Donald K.
   Appeal of Buddhism: a Christian perspective.
   il Chr Cent 88:1289-93 N 3 '71
SWEARINGEN, John Eldred, 1918-
   Why Indiana Standard grows so well. il por
   Bsns W p57+ D 4 '71 *

SWEARINGEN aircraft (firm)
Fairchild subsidiary to buy assets, resume Swearingen production. Aviation W 95:22 N 8 '71
Piper, Swearingen study link; latter developing business jet. E. J. Bulban. Aviation W 95:19 Jl 26 '71

SWEAT. See Perspiration

SWEATERS
Fashion is an honest sweater. il Time 98:66-70 N 15 '71

SWEDEN
See also
Airplanes, Military—Sweden
Astronomical observatories—Sweden
Automobile industry—Sweden
Ballet—Sweden
Banks and banking—Sweden
Business management and organization—Sweden
Environment policy—Sweden
Environmental movement—Sweden
Opera—Sweden
Police—Sweden
Psychiatry—Sweden
Strikes—Sweden

Armed forces
Parting shots; about face! Fix hairnets! Forward march! il Life 70:76 Je 18 '71

Description and travel
Skerry place. D. Butwin. il Sat R 54:52+ O 2 '71

Economic conditions
Good life. P. A. Samuelson. Newsweek 77:66 Ja 18 '71
Gunnar Myrdal talks about troubles in Utopia; interview, ed. by S. G. Slappey. G. Myrdal. il por Nations Bsns 59:44-5+ Ap '71
Model welfare state runs into trouble. il U S News 70:92-4 My 10 '71
Setback for the Swedes. America 124:252-3 Mr 13 '71
Stagflation of the economy. J. E. Wikstrom. Chr Cent 88:961-2 Ag 11 '71

Industries
See also
Aerospace industries—Sweden
Automobile industry—Sweden
Iron mines and mining—Sweden

Religious institutions and affairs
See also
Church and state in Sweden

Social conditions
See also
Women—Sweden

SWEDES in the United States
See also
Bishop Hill, Ill.

SWEENEY, Don
Lessons from the schools of other nations. il Am Ed 7:8-13 O '71

SWEENEY, James Johnson
Poiret: inspiration for artists, designers, and women. il por Vogue 158:186+ S 1 '71

SWEENEY, John A. H.
Paintings in the Winterthur collection. il Antiques 100:758-67 N '71

SWEENEY, Marian
Granny Orr's great manure maneuver. Farm J 95:54 F '71

SWEEP generators. See Signal generators

SWEEPERS, Street. See Street cleaning apparatus

SWEEPING, Street. See Street cleaning

SWEEPSTAKES. See Lotteries

SWEET, A. Porter S.
Whistle talk. il Am Heritage 22:108-9 Ag '71

SWEET, Herman R.
Phalaenopsis, the moth orchids. il Horticulture 49:24-5+ N '71

SWEET, James S.
Science sells. il Writers Digest 51:28-30+ O '71

SWEET, Ossian H.
Man's home, a man's castle, by K. G. Weinberg. Review
New Repub 165:26-7 O 30 '71. R. Margolis •

SWEET, Ozzie
Snowmobile fever really turns you on. il Pop Sci 198:80-1 Ja '71

SWEET peppers. See Peppers

SWEET potatoes
Sweet surprise. P. A. Boggs. il Org Gard & Farm 18:53 Ag '71
Toxic sweet potatoes. Chem 45:26-7 Ja '72
See also
Cookery—Vegetables

SWEETBREADS
See also
Cookery—Meat

SWEETCRAB; story. See Summerton, M.

SWEETENING agents. See Sugar substitutes

SWEETMAN, Donald H.
John Novy demonstrates: centering with a leather strap. il Ceram Mo 19:14-16 Mr '71
John Novy, third generation potter. il por Ceram Mo 19:13 Mr '71

SWEGLE, Wayne E.
Across the editor's desk. Suc Farm 69:no2 26 F; no5 L4 Mr; A2 Je; A4 O '71
It's time for some plain talk about trade. Suc Farm 69:no5 L8-9 Mr '71

SWENERTON, Helene, and Hurley, L. S.
Teratogenic effects of a chelating agent and their prevention by zinc. bibliog il Science 173:62-4; 174:102 Jl 2, O 8 '71

SWENSON, Alfred T.
Proposal to change the urban landscape by redistributing a city's office space into 150-story superframe towers. il Arch Forum 135:58-60 S '71

SWENSON, Gene
Art critic as social reformer, with a question mark. G. Battcock. il por Art in Am 59:26-7 S '71 •
Critic's conscience. D. Davis. por Newsweek 78:79-80 N 29 '71 •

SWENSON, May
Celebration; poem. Am Lib 2:1047 N '71
On the edge; poem. Sat R 54:23 Mr 6 '71
Red moonset; poem. Harper 242:97 Ja '71
Speed; poem. New Yorker 47:44 O 23 '71

about
Comment. N. Sullivan. Poetry 119:107-8 N '71 •
Two poets. R. Knudson. il pors Am Lib 2:1046 N '71 •

SWIDDEN farming. See Shifting cultivation

SWIFT, Joan
Line-up; poem. Yale R 60:391-2 Mr '71

SWIFT, Jonathan
Don't put it down! A teacher's session with Hair. Engl J 60:626-8 My '71

SWIFT, Lloyd W. and Swift, R. W.
Going west to West Virginia. il pors Am For 77:16-19 Mr '71

SWIFT, Rose W. See Swift, L. W. jt. auth.

SWIFT de la Plata (firm) See Meat industry—Argentina

SWIFTY; drama. See Willment, F.

SWIHART, Thelma
What is humanization? Engl J 60:1225-7 D '71

SWIMMING
Fastest man afloat; D. Edgar and his coach R. Bussard. W. F. Reed. il por Sports Illus 34:16-19 Mr 1 '71
Fastest splash in the West; S. Gould at Santa Clara. J. Kirshenbaum. il pors Sports Illus 35:18-19 Jl 19 '71
Girl has to suffer. J. Lebow. il Look 35:60-2+ Je 29 '71
It's the Hoosier title wave; Indiana swimming team at NCAA competitions. W. F. Reed. il Sports Illus 34:28-30+ Mr 22 '71
Not the triumph but the struggle; condensation from Deep water. D. Schollander and D. Savage. il pors Read Digest 98:221-4+ Je '71
Of cats and skinny-dipping; nude swimming. P. Leahy. il Time 98:42 Ag 2 '71
Once more on to the beach; with paintings. G. Carson. il Am Heritage 22:58-80+ Ag '71
She takes a long swim off a short pier. D. Levin. por Sports Illus 35:38-40+ D 6 '71
Still a big fish in a big (Olympicsize) pond; top U.S. swimmers: topmost being M. Spitz. W. F. Reed. il por Sports Illus 35:46-7+ S 6 '71
What the fans came to see is what they got; Hoosiers' fourth NCAA swimming and diving championship. W. F. Reed, jr. Sports Illus 34:77-9 Ap 5 '71
See also
Diving
Swimming, Synchronized

Safety devices and measures
Basic guide to safe swimming. Good H 173:157 Jl '71
Mother, may I go out to swim? Y. Postelle. il Parents Mag 46:48-9+ Ag '71
Survival swimming. il Field & S 75:86+ Ap '71
Swimtime; when a camp director needs a friend; Camp Birchwood, Minn. J. C. Bredemus. il Camp Mag 43:23+ Ap '71

Study and teaching
Master-planned for progress; city of Rohnert Park, Calif. T. West. il Parks & Rec 6:36+ Mr '71

SWIMMING—Study and teaching—*Continued*
Mother, may I go out to swim? Y. Postelle.
il Parents Mag 46:48-9+ Ag '71
Water babies. il Life 71:56-9 Ag 6 '71
Why isn't my child a deep-water swimmer?
a director answers. H. Zeitz and M. Domsky. il Camp Mag 43:17 Je '71

SWIMMING, Synchronized
And now for the resurrection: Mrs Swan
and her Cygnets. R. Blount. il por Sports
Illus 34:96-100+ Ap 12 '71

SWIMMING pool heaters. See Water heaters

SWIMMING pools
See also
Diving platforms, boards, etc.

SWIMMING pools, Home
The day the pool became a painting. il House
B 113:63 Ag '71
Easy backyard living. A. J. Maher. Am Home
74:32+ Je '71
Extend your swimming season with sun
power. E. McGough. il Mech Illus 67:98-9 S
'71
How to keep your pool crystal clear. il Pop
Mech 135:154-7 Je '71
Pool enclosures: from domes to greenhouses.
Bsns W p67 Ag 28 '71
Pools deck out for play. J. Levy. il Am
Home 74:56-9 Je '71
Swimming pool stacks away. R. Frederick. il
Pop Sci 198:104-5+ Ap '71
What you should know before buying a pool.
il Home Gard 58:38-9 Je '71

Lighting
Gas-lit torches around their pool. il Sunset
147:100 Jl '71

Maintenance and repair
What it really costs to maintain a swimming
pool. F. La Gregga. il Mech Illus 67:63 Ag
'71

SWIMMING pools, Municipal
Fishing, at the swimming pool; National city,
Calif. A. F. Maley. il Parks & Rec 6:112-15
Ja '71
Sellers of Sellersville. D. Coll. il Am City 86:
64 Jl '71
Swimming pool gets second life; Greensburg,
Pa. il Parks & Rec 6:40+ My '71
Swimming pools '71; symposium. il Parks &
Rec 6:29-36+ Mr '71
Walk-to swimming pools; Philadelphia. R. W.
Crawford. il Am City 86:51-2 Ja '71
Waves for family fun; Decatur, Ala. J
Brown. il Am City 86:101-2 O '71

SWIMSUITS. See Bathing suits

SWINBURNE, Algernon Charles
At the pines. by M. Panter-Downes. Review
Sat R il 54:23 Ag 21 '71. L. Untermeyer •
Profiles. M. Panter-Downes. il New Yorker
46:40-4+ Ja 23; 31-43 Ja 30; 40-6+ F 6 '71 •

SWINDELL-Dressler company
First contract for Kama River. Bsns W
p30 Ja 1 '72

SWINDELLS, Philip
Growing herbaceous plants from seed. il Horticulture 49:40-1+ My '71

SWINDLERS and swindling. See Fraud

SWINE
Checklist for buying better boars. il Suc
Farm 69:H16 O '71
Feet and leg problems to avoid. M. Fink and
R. J. Fee. il Suc Farm 69:H2-3 Ap '71
Hog extra. See issues of Farm journal
Hog management. R. J. Fee. See issues of
Successful farming
How I select replacement gilts. K. Baum-
gartner. il Suc Farm 69:H15 Ap '71
Nine tips on how to buy feeder pigs. Suc
Farm 69:no3 B12 F '71
Our far-flung correspondents; visit to pig
farm called Real farms, inc. in Tipton, Pa.
W. Whitworth. il New Yorker 46:64+ Ja 30
'71

Branding
Easy way to keep track of sows. il Suc Farm
69:no5 43 Mr '71

Care
Farrowing details that save you money. W.
R. Prafka. il Farm J 95:H17 Mr '71

Confinement methods
How to beat common confinement problems.
R. Poage. il Farm J 95:H14-15 N '71
Shakedown for gestation housing. J. Russell.
il Farm J 95:H11-13+ Ag '71
Sow collars, how they're working. R. J. Fee.
il Suc Farm 69:no5 H4-5 Mr '71
Wean pigs into cages. R. Wilmore. il Farm J
95:H5-7 N '71
See also
Swine farrowing crates and pens

Diseases and pests
Animal health: new test for atrophic rhinitis.
il Suc Farm 69:no4 H14 Mr '71
Animal health: what causes pre-farrowing
losses. B. Eftink. il Suc Farm 69:H20 Ap
'71
Bleeding pig disease. Suc Farm 69:H10 Ap '71
Eight-point plan to halt baby pig scours. R.
J. Fee. il Suc Farm 69:no3 24-5 F '71
How to handle milk scours. J. Russell. Farm
J 95:33 Ag '71
Swine arthritis, a long-range problem. Suc
Farm 69:H3 N '71
See also
Hog cholera
Leptospirosis
Lungworms
Worms, Intestinal and parasitic

Feeding
Feed additives on the firing line. J. Russell.
Farm J 95:H16 My '71
How these livestock men reduce feeding
costs il Suc Farm 69:J4 N '71
New way to feed lactating sows. R. Wil-
more. Farm J 95:24E Ag '71
Will processing grain for hogs pay? R. Wil-
more. Farm J 95:H12+ Mr '71
See also
Feeding and feeding stuffs—Corn
Swine self feeders

Grading and standardization
Sonoray hits the road. il Suc Farm 69:H16
Ap '71

Marketing
Coordination without contracts does work.
J. Russell. il Farm J 95:H10+ Mr '71

**Performance records and
registration**
Selection pointers from a pro. D. Huinker.
il Suc Farm 69:H2-3 O '71

Prices
Big corn crop: no boon for hogmen. R. Wil-
more. il Farm J 95:H24 O '71
Market analysis. See issues of Farm journal
Money management; interview. D. Vander-
fluct. il por Suc Farm 69:10 Ap '71
Nothing surprises him; T. Meyer. B. Coff-
man. il por Farm J 95:H18-19 S '71
Pig-pricing formula for feeders. il Suc Farm
69:H10 O '71
Price forecast. See issues of Farm journal
Producers tell USDA what they think of the
situation. R. Wilmore. il Farm J 95:H24
Mr '71
What affects hog prices. R. Krumme; R. J.
Fee. il Suc Farm 69:no2 54-5 F '71

SWINE breeding
Confinement breeding system that works. D.
K. O'Brien. il Farm J 95:H8-9 S '71
Fastest way to boost litter size: double mat-
ing. A. D. Leman. Farm J 95:H12 S '71
Hog breeding shake-up ahead. J. Russell.
Farm J 95:H12 Ap '71
How they're trying to build you a better
hog. J. Russell. il Farm J 95:26-7+ O '71
Pig production Texas style: 100,000 head/year.
il Suc Farm 69:H6 O '71
Replacement selection made easy. R. Wil-
more. Farm J 95:H7+ S '71

SWINE cholera. See Hog cholera

SWINE farm management
Fast way to sharpen management; com-
puters. J. Russell. il Farm J 95:H6-7+ Ap
'71
Father-son agreement for a growing hog
business. R. J. Fee. il Suc Farm 69:H6
S '71
Feeder pig production cooperative style. il
Suc Farm 69:H3 My '71
How much time do you waste? R. Wilmore.
Farm J 95:H18-19 Ap '71
No room for average hogman. Suc Farm 69:
H6-7 Ap '71
Old-fashioned, but profitable. W. Kester. il
Farm J 95:H12-13 N '71
Successful hog management (cont) il Suc
Farm 69:no4 H1-3+ Mr; H1 Ap; H1 Ag;
H1 O '71
U.S. know-how improves primitive hog pro-
duction; Ecuador experiment station. J.
Boyd. il Farm J 95:H13 Mr '71
Wanted: woman to run 200-sow hog farm.
R. Wilmore. il Farm J 95:H6-8 My '71
See also
Farm records

SWINE farms
100,000 hogs a year; Yugoslavia's largest hog
farm, with editorial comment. R. Wilmore.
il Farm J 95:H7-9, H20 Ag '71

SWINE farms—*Continued*
Our far-flung correspondents; visit to pig farm called Real farms, inc. in Tipton, Pa. W. Whitworth. il New Yorker 46:64+ Ja 30 '71

Equipment
See also
Swine—Confinement methods

SWINE farrowing crates and pens
Farrowing house remodeling, less than $350 per sow. il Suc Farm 69:no4 H16 Mr '71
Farrowing house with a new slant. il Suc Farm 69:H16 Ag '71
Free-stall farrowing with slats saves labor. W. Waltner and E. Waltner. il Suc Farm 69:H14 Ap '71
He switched to slats after two years. T. McCartney. il Suc Farm 69:no3 H4 F '71
Low-cost, low-labor farrowing; free stall farrowing pens. R. Wilmore. il Farm J 95: H17 O '71
More on hog housing: farrowing. il Suc Farm 69:H10 Ag '71
Three farms, three ways to farrow. R. J. Fee. il Suc Farm 69:30-1 My '71

SWINE feeders. See Swine self feeders

SWINE houses
Finishing house tips from the experts. B. Eftink. il Suc Farm 69:H2-3 Ag '71
Free-stall gestation house that eases sow handling. R. Wilmore. il Farm J 95:H11 Mr '71
Twice the pigs, half the labor. il Suc Farm 69:no4 H17 Mr '71
See also
Swine—Confinement methods

Equipment
See also
Swine farrowing crates and pens

Floors
Remodeling ideas for heated slats; heated concrete and carpet, too. il Suc Farm 69:no4 H2-3+ Mr '71
Slat floor finishing for less than $20 per pig. J. Fee. il Suc Farm 69:C15 N '71

Heating and ventilation
Finishing house with natural ventilation. W. Waltner and E. Waltner. il Suc Farm 69: H6 Ag '71
Viewpoint: another look at hog house heating. R. J. Fee. il Suc Farm 69:no4 H1 Mr '71

SWINE in literature. See Animals in literature

SWINE self feeders
More on hog housing: feeding. il Suc Farm 69:H11 Ag '71

SWINGING games. See Games
SWINGING-lens cameras. See Cameras

SWINGS
Backyard swing sets. il Consumer Rep 36:272-8 My '71
Build this old-time yard swing. W. C. Leckey. il Pop Mech 135:140-3+ Ap '71
Sling swing with room for three. il Sunset 146:137 Ap '71

SWINNERTON, J. W. and others
Carbon monoxide in rainwater. bibliog il Science 172:943-5 My 28 '71

SWISHER, Viola Hegyi
UCLA graduate dance center. il Dance Mag 45:76-9 D '71

SWISS chard. See Chard
SWISS cookery. See Cookery, Swiss
SWITCHES, Electric. See Electric switches
SWITCHING of price tags. See Shoplifting

SWITCHING systems
Solid-state band-switching circuits. W. G. Wheeler. il Electr World 85:34-5 Je '71
Stereo speaker headphone switching. J. A. Rome. il Radio-Electr 42:42 F '71
Switching logic quiz. R. P. Balin. il Pop Electr 34:50+ Mr '71
Switching regulator power supply. F. Heath. il Electr World 86:43-4+ O '71

SWITZER, George S.
Questing for gems. il Nat Georg 140:834-63 D '71

SWITZER, Robert
Psychiatrists helping young mommas understand baby; interview, ed. by P. A. Farrell. il pors Pub W 199:38-9 Je 28 '71

SWITZERLAND
Europe's Tibet: Switzerland, a military democracy. E. M. von Kuehnelt-Leddihn. il Cath World 214:120-3 D '71
See also
Airplanes, Military—Switzerland
Arts and crafts—Switzerland
Banks and banking—Switzerland
Bern (city)
Public welfare—Switzerland
Villages—Switzerland
Water pollution—Switzerland

Description and travel
Back-country Switzerland. B. Ellison. il Travel 135:50-3 My '71
New look in Heidiland. J. Harayda. Sat R 54:34 Ag 28 '71
Switzerland isn't all work by any means. Bsns W p 102 F 27 '71
Switzerland's perennial pleasures. il Holiday 49:58-63 Mr '71

Economic conditions
Switzerland: progress against the communes. B. R. Barber. il Trans-Action 8:27-31+ F '71

Foreign relations
See also
Switzerland—Neutrality

Industries
See also
Aerospace industries—Switzerland
Hoffman-La Roche, F, and company

Neutrality
Switzerland: absent host to the United Nations. W. B. Lloyd, jr. Bul Atom Sci 27:42-3 Ja '71

Religious institutions and affairs
See also
Catholic church in Switzerland

SWITZERLAND-United States air agreement. See Aviation—International aspects
SWOFFORD, James Oliver. See Oliver

SWOMLEY, John M. jr
Parochiaid and taxes. Chr Cent 88:1024-5 S 1 '71

SWORTZELL, Lowell
Why the peacock is proud; drama. Plays 31: 47-51 O '71

SYCAMORE, Ill.
Pumpkin fever. T. Bennett. il Travel 136:46-7 S '71

SYDENHAM hospital. See New York (city)—Hospitals

SYDNEY, Australia

Architecture
See also
Architecture, Domestic—Australia

Description
City under Capricorn. H. Sutton. il Sat R 55: 22-3 Ja 8 '72

SYDNEY-Hobart race. See Yacht racing—Australia
SYDNEY opera house. See Opera houses

SYKES, Gresham M.
New crimes for old. Am Scholar 40:592-8 Aut '71
Today's campus: the eerie calm. Nation 212: 490-1 Ap 19 '71

Les SYLPHIDES; ballet. See Ballets—Criticisms
SYLVATIC plague. See Plague

SYMBIOSIS
Communication between ants and their guests. B. Hölldobler. il Sci Am 224:86-93 Mr '71
Sensuous symbionts of the sea. L. Thomas. il Natur Hist 80:28-37+ bibliog(p96) Ag '71
Symbiosis and evolution; origin of organelles. L. Margulis. il Sci Am 225:48-57 bibliog(p 120) Ag '71

SYMBOLISM
Fragging the beast; dehumanizing the enemy. F. H. Borsch. Chr Cent 88:720-2 Je 9 '71

SYMBOLISM (psychology)
Symbolic process: a colloquium. T. Shapiro. bibliog Am Imago 28:195-215 Fall '71

SYMBOLISM in architecture. See Architecture—Philosophy

SYMBOLISM in art
Skulls of Picasso. L. Steinberg. bibliog il por Art N 70:26-8+ O '71

SYMBOLISM in literature
Furnace and the tower: a new look at the symbols in Native son. D. R. Merkle. Engl J 60:735-9 S '71
Poet's workshop. F. Trefethen. Writer 84:20-3 Jl '71

SYMBOLISM in medicine
Western alchemy symbols in a Japanese medical work; translation of 18th century Dutch pharmacopoeia. T. Benfey. bibliog il Chem 44:14-18 S '71
SYMBOLS
Mark of man; shrines. W. Hedgepeth. il Look 35:58-63 Ja 12 '71
Ugly and ordinary architecture; or, The decorated shed; excerpts from Learning from Las Vegas. R. Venturi and D. S. Brown. il Arch Forum 135:64-7 N '71
SYMES, Aston L. and others
Iron- and riboflavin-dependent metabolism of a monoamine in the rat in vivo. bibliog il Science 174:153-5 O 8 '71
SYMINGTON, Stuart
Is America going isolationist? interview. por U S News 70:28-9 Je 28 '71

about
Education of a senator. F. Lewis. por Atlan 228:55-64 D '71 *
Not-so-secret war. Newsweek 77:26+ Je 21 '71 *
Rites of spring. Nation 212:387-8 Mr 29 '71 *
SYMMETREL. See Amantadine hydrochloride
SYMMETRY (biology)
Bilateral symmetry in chick embryo determination by gravity. S. Kochav and H. Eyal-Giladi. bibliog il Science 171:1027-9 Mr 12 '71
On telling left from right. M. C. Corballis and I. L. Beale. il Sci Am 224:96-104 bibliog(p 124) Mr '71
SYMONDS, Martin, and Hellman, J. R.
How to cope with those middle-age blues. Read Digest 99:101-4 N '71
SYMPATHECTOMY. See Nervous system—Surgery
SYMPHONIE communications satellite. See Communications satellites, European
SYMPHONIES
Beethoven's new way and the Eroica. P. G. Downs. bibliog il Mus Q 56:585-604 O '70
Beethoven's Pastoral symphony as a Sinfonia caracteristica. F. E. Kirby. bibliog f il Mus Q 56:605-23 O '70
See also
Phonograph records—Symphonies
SYMULA, James F.
Censorship and teacher responsibility. Engl J 60:128-31 Ja '71
SYNAPSES
Cholinergic synapse and the site of memory. J. A. Deutsch. bibliog il Science 174:788-94 N 19 '71
Penicillin as an epileptogenic agent: effect on an isolated synapse. G. F. Ayala and others. bibliog il Science 171:915-17 Mr 5 '71
Sexual dimorphism in the preoptic area of the rat. G. Raisman and P. M. Field. bibliog il Science 173:731-3 Ag 20 '71
Synaptic adjustment after deafferentation of the superior colliculus of the rat. R. D. Lund and J. S. Lund. bibliog il Science 171:804-7 F 26 '71
SYNAPTIC receptors. See Receptors, Neural
SYNCHRONEX system. See Moving picture cameras—Sound equipment
SYNCHRONIZED swimming. See Swimming, Synchronized
SYNDICATE material, Newspaper. See Newspapers—Syndicate service
SYNERGISM
Synergy of ethanol and a natural soporific—gamma hydroxybutyrate. E. R. McCabe and others. bibliog il Science 171:404-6 Ja 29 '71
SYNERGISTS for insecticides. See Insecticides
SYNGE, John Millington
Playboy of the western world. Criticism
Nation 212:124-5 Ja 25 '71 *
New Repub 164:24+ Ja 30 '71 *
New Yorker 46:75 Ja 16 '71 *
Newsweek il 77:79 Ja 18 '71 *
Sat R 54:75-6 Ja 23 '71 *
That enquiring man, John Synge. D. H. Greene. Nation 213:150-2 Ag 30 '71 *
Writings of J. M. Synge. by R. Skelton, and J. M. Synge and his world, by R. Skelton. Reviews
Sat R 54:36 My 1 '71. S. Callery
SYNOD of bishops, 1971
After the synod. A. M. Greeley. America 125:424-6 N 20 '71
Bishops in Rome: no final solutions. Chr Today 16:37 O 22 '71
Bishops meet. il Newsweek 78:52 O 11 '71
Bishops, the CO's and amnesty. America 125:362-3 N 6 '71
Forbidden topic. Newsweek 78:127 O 25 '71
Go, and synod no more. H. ten Kortenaar. Commonweal 95:196-7 N 26 '71

Hope for the synod. Commonweal 95:3-4 O 1 '71
Hopes and expectations for the Synod; symposium, with editorial comment. America 125:inside cover, 189-208, 210-13 S 25 '71
How goes the 1971 Synod? America 124:305 Mr 27 '71
Might the synod surprise? H. ten Kortenaar. Commonweal 95:4-5 O 1 '71
New vs. old, the struggle among Catholics. il U S News 71:31-3 N 1 '71
1971 synod: a summons to service; with editorial comment. A. O. Sigur. America 125:inside cover, 223 O 2 '71
No revelation in Rome. il Time 98:84 N 15 '71
Parochial education. K. L. Woodward. Newsweek 78:105 N 15 '71
Press handcuffed. S. J. Admao. America 125:376-7 N 6 '71
Report on the Catholic synod. U S News 71:55 N 22 '71
Still in the woods. W. Willoughby. Chr Today 16:46-7 N 5 '71
Strengthening Paul's hand. il Time 98:83 O 18 '71
Synod begins il Time 98:63-4 O 11 '71
Synod: hope deferred; last editorial. J. B. Sheerin. Cath World 214:99-100 D '71
Synod notebook. D. R. Campion. America 125:253, 278, 308, 338, 364, 391, 418-19 O, 9-N 20 '71
Synod of bishops: failure of vision. W. Triggs. il Chr Cent 88:1484-7 D 22 '71
Synod of bishops: new era or disillusion? W. Triggs. Chr Cent 88:1188-9 O 13 '71
Synod of small expectations. H. ten Kortenaar. Commonweal 94:28-9 Mr 19 '71
Third roman synod. F. X. Murphy. America 124:454-6 My 1 '71
Time of anxiety for Pope and bishops. il U S News 71:28 O 11 '71
Toward a more fallible church; Time essay. M. Mohs. il Time 98:84-5 N 15 '71
Trying to undo the Council; the Fundamental law issue on bishops' agenda. H. T. Kortenaar. Commonweal 94:348-9 Jl 9 '71
SYNODINOS, Demetrious. See Snyder, J.
SYNSEPALUM dulcificum. See Miracle fruit
SYNTAX. See English language—Syntax
SYNTHESIS
Primitive earth synthesis of nicotinic acid derivatives. N. Friedmann and others. bibliog il Science 171:1026-7 Mr 12 '71
See also
Biosynthesis
SYNTHETASES
Uroporphyrinogen III cosynthetase activity in the fox squirrel (sciurus niger) E. Y. Levin and V. Flyger. bibliog il Science 174:59-60 O 1 '71
SYNTHETIC diamonds. See Diamonds, Artificial
SYNTHETIC fibers. See Fibers
SYNTHETIC fur. See Fur, Artificial
SYNTHETIC textile fibers. See Textile fibers, Synthetic
SYNTHETIC turf. See Turf, Artificial
SYRACUSE, N.Y.

Parks and playgrounds
Movie bus. P. S. Gallivan. il Parks & Rec 6:37+ S '71

Recreation
See also
Syracuse, N.Y.—Parks and playgrounds
SYRACUSE, N.Y. public library
Some hope in Syracuse. W. R. Eshelman. Wilson Lib Bul 46:7 S '71
Syracuse public library faces budget disaster. Library J 96:2029-30 Je 15 '71
SYRACUSE university, Syracuse, N.Y.
Grass and hash business at Syracuse university L Kramer. il Fortune 84:102-3 S '71
Young Ifshin objects. W. F. Buckley, jr. Nat R 23:496 My 4 '71
SYRIA
Syria: warming toward U.S. il por U S News 71:43 D 6 '71
See also
Arab Republics, Federation of
SYRINGES, Hypodermic. See Injections, Hypodermic
SYSTEM development corporation
Think-tank strives harder to be a business. Bsns W p91-2 N 27 '71
SYSTEMIC insecticides. See Insecticides
SYSTEMS analysis
How scientists can really help; adaptation of address, October 26, 1970. M. Gell-Mann. il Phys Today 24:23-5 My '71
See also
United States—Defense, Department of—Systems analysis, Office of

SYSTEMS analysis in education
ES '70s: the educational innovation of the 1970's? W. H. Drost. bibliog Sch & Soc 99:224-7 Ap '71
SYSTEMS building. See Buildings, Prefabricated
SYSTEMS management
See also
Computer systems management
SZABADVARY, Ferenc
Great moments in chemistry; tr. by R. E. Oesper (cont) il por Chem 44:18-20 Je; 14-17 D '71
SZABO, Daniel
U.S. trade policy and Latin America; statement, July 12, 1971. Dept State Bul 65: 239-46 Ag 30 '71
SZAMUELY, Tibor
Meaning of left and right. il Nat R 23:923-7+ Ag 24 '71
Pure essence of totalitarianism. il Nat R 23:595-6 Je 1 '71
Technological fraud. Nat R 23:201-3 F 23 '71
SZASZ, Tnomas S.
Normality is a square circle or a four-sided triangle. M. Scarf. il pors N Y Times Mag p 16-17+ O 3 '71; Discussion. p6+ N 14 '71 *
SZE, William C.
Social variables and their effect on psychiatric emergency situations among children. bibliog il Ment Hy 55:437-43 O '71
SZENT-GYORGYI, Albert
New theory on cancer. Chem 44:23 Jl '71 *
SZULC, Tad
George Jackson radicalizes the brothers in Soledad and San Quentin. il pors N Y Times Mag p 10-11+ Ag 1 '71
Letter from the Azores. New Yorker 47:54-8 Ja 1 '72
SZUPROWICZ, Bohdan
Steak, yes, martinis, no. il Duns 98:71-2+ O '71
SZYMANOWSKI, Karol
Music to my ears. l. Kolodin. Sat R 54:24 Ap 25 '71 *

T

T-groups. See Group relations training
TCAB (tetrachloroazobenzene) See Azo compounds
TCC. See Texas conference of churches
THC
Activity of Δ^8-and Δ^9-tetrahydrocannabinol and related compounds in the mouse. H. D. Christensen and others. bibliog il Science 172:165-7 Ap 9 '71
Delta-9-tetrahydrocannabinol: metabolism and disposition in long-term marihuana smokers. L. Lemberger and others. bibliog il Science 173:72-4 Jl 2 '71
Electroencephalographic and behavioral alterations produced by Δ^1-tetrahydrocannabinol. C. H. Hockman and others. bibliog il Science 172:968-70 My 28 '71
6β-Hydroxy-Δ^1-tetrahyocrocannabinol synthesis and biological activity. Z. Ben-Zvi and others. bibliog il Science 174:951-2 N 26 '71
Inhibition of normal growth by chronic administration of Δ-9-tetrahydrocannabinol. F. J. Manning and others. bibliog il Science 174:424-6 O 22 '71
Marihuana components: effects of smoking on Δ^9-tetrahydrocannabinol and cannabidiol. F. Mikes and P. G. Waser. bibliog il Science 172:1158-9 Je 11 '71
TIFS (total in-flight simulator) See Airplanes, Training
TRIBE (teaching and research in bicultural education) See Indians of North America —Education
TRW, Inc.
GE, TRW disclose aerospace financial results. il Aviation W 94:53 Mr 29 '71
Teamwork through conflict. il Bsns W p44-5+ Mr 20 '71
TUC. See Trades union congress
TVA. See Tennessee Valley authority
TWA. See Trans World airlines
TAAGEPERA, Rein
Revolt of the thinking class. Nation 212: 681-4 My 31 '71
TABAK, May Natalie
Tamarind lithography workshop (title varies) (cont) il Craft Horiz 31:34-7+ F '71

TABERNACLE
Tabernacle furnishings: recreating the divine design. D. Baker. il Chr Today 15:43 Mr 12 '71
TABLE, The. See Table setting
TABLE decoration
Double-duty centerpiece for your home. R. E. Donegan. il Pop Sci 199:83 D '71
Fruit color hangs high over the holiday table. il Sunset 147:52-3 D '71
Party whirl. il Seventeen 29:116-17+ D '71
Razzle-dazzle table settings. il McCalls 99: 106-7 D '71
Setting the mood. N. Skurka. il N Y Times Mag p27 D 26 '71
TABLE linen
From tablecloth to skirt. N. O'Leary. il Ladies Home J 88:72-3+ Je '71
Romance at table: a play of ribbon. il Ladies Home J 88:82+ S '71
TABLE manners. See Etiquette
TABLE mats, tiles, etc.
Coaster: an absorbing problem. House B 113: 36 N '71
TABLE setting
All set for the holidays: dozens of Christmas-table ideas. il Good H 173:124-9 D '71
Down-to-earth dining. il Bet Hom & Gard 49:142 O '71
Holiday table settings. H. Brown. Am Home 74:69 N '71
Many moods of a holiday table. A. Wiglama. il House B 113:122-9 N '71
Numbers game; how can you juggle eight plates and 16 guests? M. Wallace. il Am Home 74:56+ N '71
Party tables set like gardens. il House & Gard 139:120-6 My '71
Proper way to set a table. il Good H 173: 142-3 Ag '71
Summer table settings: alfresco the easy way. S. Lindsay. il House B 113:64-5 Ag '71
View from the table; the California way. M. Miller and S. Lindsay. il House B 113:90-3 Mr '71
Wake up to color and breakfast. il House & Gard 139:106-11 Mr '71
Where dinner is always a party: the Oscar de la Rentas' town house. il Vogue 158: 74-7 N 15 '71
Why is this table different? il Mlle 73:194-7 O '71
TABLE tennis
Backspin on the Chinese serve. Chr Cent 88: 483 Ap 21 '71
Exterminating a ping-pong pest. D. Miles. il Sports Illus 34:30-5 Je 28 '71
Fastest wrists in the East. il Time 97:60 Ap 19 '71
How the ball bounces. il por Newsweek 77: 71-2 My 3 '71
How to play ping-pong like a Chinese champ. L. M. Chui. il pors Esquire 76:122-7 N '71
How to play winning ping-pong. T. Boggan. il por Mech Illus 67:82-3+ S '71
MI at large: ping-pong pains. D. Barnett. il Mech Illus 67:23+ S '71
My China visit as a ping pong diplomat. G. Brathwaite. il pors Ebony 27:84-6+ N '71
Peek into Peking; ping-pong gambit. Sr Schol 98:15 Ap 26 '71
Peking puts no spin on table tennis sales. Bsns W p 17 Ap 24 '71
Ping heard round the world: American ping pong players in China. il Time 97:25-8+ Ap 26 '71
Ping pong anyone? Chinese invitation to the U.S. team. Nation 212:514 Ap 26 '71
Ping-pong diplomat. J. Bochenski. il por Seventeen 30:142+ O '71
Ping-pong parlor; Marty Reisman's establishment on Broadway. New Yorker 47:30 My 1 '71
Ping-pong star's get-rich plans. il por Bsns W p26 My 8 '71
They still swing a mean paddle; red China's athletes at the World table tennis championship. D. Miles. il Sports Illus 34:32-3 Ap 12 '71
TABLECLOTHS. See Table linen
TABLES
Anyone can build this coffee table for $35. W. C. Leckey. il Pop Mech 136:174-6 S '71
Apartment ping-pong table. B. Berger. il Mech Illus 67:102-3 D '71
Beside their pool, a roomy sun table. il Sunset 146:114 Je '71
Build this 'glass-top' wagon-wheel table. E. Waltner and W. Waltner. il Pop Mech 135: 182D-182G F '71
Child can do it; mosaic coffee table. K. J. Griffin. il Design 73:8-9 Wint '71

TABLES—*Continued*
Clean lines, generous size, and the chopping-block look. il Sunset 147:144+ N '71
Easy-to-build ping-pong table. il Mech Illus 67:84-5+ S '71
Fold-flat picnic table lets you put it away. P. Bell. il Pop Mech 136:130-1 Ag '71
$45 worth of beauty and convenience you can build for $21; wall-hung pier set. R. Capotosto. il Pop Mech 135:134-7 Je '71
Glass-topped coffee table: easy-to-make elegance. R. Benrey. il Pop Sci 199:95 Ag '71
How to build a contemporary pedestal table. J. Hand. il Pop Mech 135:162-4 Ap '71
How to build a table the Chinese way. D. Warren. il por Pop Sci 199:104-6+ N '71
How to make and keep a smart fish bowl under the table. J. Hand. il Pop Sci 199:78-9+ Jl '71
Indoor-outdoor rolling tables. il Sunset 146:144 My '71
Making baskets into play tables, patio tables, end tables. il Sunset 146:105-6 Mr '71
Martini table. J. Capotosto. il Mech Illus 67:90+ My '71
New face and a new life for yesterday's card table. il Sunset 147:146+ O '71
Portable, adjustable table for the beach, patio, inside the house. il Sunset 147:88 S '71
Portable picnic table. il Mech Illus 67:80-1 Je '71
Sides are cedar, the tops marble. il Sunset 146:122 Mr '71
Table that tops off a wall. il Pop Sci 198:80-1+ Je '71
Tiny turned tables; woodworking project. J. Capotosto. il Mech Illus 67:106-8 N '71
Top is 2 by 2's glued, the base is 1 by 2's around a paper drum. il Sunset 146:140 Ap '71
We assmbled this Parsons table in 30 minutes. Cost: about $7. il Sunset 147:75 Ag '71
Wood slabs make a patio table. il Sunset 146:116+ Ap '71
Work-space table for your outdoor grill. E. V. Bloom. il Pop Sci 199:103 Ag '71
TABLES, calculations, etc.
See also
Navigation—Tables
TABLEWARE
How to serve food at the table. il Redbook 136:86-90 F '71
Pleasant realities for the 1971 bride. il House B 113:18-20 Je '71
Shopping for your kitchen in Honolulu. il Sunset 146:86-7 Je '71
See also
Pottery
TABLEWARE, Pewter
Pewter. M. Evans. il Am Home 74:94-8+ Ap '71
TABOO
Can we live without taboos? M. Mead. Redbook 138:42+ D '71
Present suicide taboo in the United States. C. J. Frederick. bibliog Ment Hy 55:178-83 Ap '71
TABORI, George
Pinkville. Criticism
Newsweek il 77:109 Mr 29 '71 •
TABORI, Kristoffer
Kids want to see movies about people the way we are! il pors Seventeen 31:96+ Ja '72
TABS (boats)
Keep in trim. G. Byrnes. il Motor B & S 127:64-5+ Je '71
TABUN. See Gases, Asphyxiating and poisonous
TACHOMETERS
Dynamic dwell/tachometer. J. Colt. il Electr World 85:78-80 My '71
How to use the tach-dwell for perfect tune-ups. M. Schultz. il Pop Mech 135:126-9 F '71
TACKE, Gerd
Foreign minister. por Forbes 108:80 D 1 '71 •
TACOMA, Wash.

Sanitary affairs
Manage solid wastes as a utility. R. M. Clark and others. il Am City 86:45-7 F '71
TACTILE vision substitution system. See Blind, Apparatus for the
TACTUAL perception. See Touch
TAEUBER, Conrad
Federal government as a source of data. bibliog f Ann Am Acad 394:144-24 Mr '71
Too many Americans? A population expert's view; excerpts from address, January 13, 1971. il por U S News 70:62-4 F 15 '71

about
Census sense. Newsweek 77:78 Ja 25 '71 •

TAFFY. See Candy
TAFT, Robert, 1917-
Legal services; address, April 15. 1971. Vital Speeches 37:615-18 Ag 1 '71; Excerpt. Cong Digest 50:210+ Ag '71
TAFT, Robert A, institute of government. See Robert A. Taft institute of government
TAFT-Hartley law. See Labor laws and legislation—United States—Taft-Hartley law
TAFT institute of government. See Robert A. Taft institute of government
TAG-switching. See Shoplifting
TAGGART, Robert, 3d. See Levitan, S. A. jt. auth.
TAGGING of animals. See Animal tagging
TAHITI
Taking a cooler in Tahiti. D. Messinesi. Vogue 158:130 Ag 1 '71
Will Tahiti lose its virginity? il Forbes 108:34 Ag 15 '71
TAHOE, LAKE
Breakthrough in water pollution. L. A. Stevens. il Read Digest 98:167-8+ Je '71
It's about too late for Tahoe. W. Bronson. il Audubon 73:46-62+ Mv '71
This is no ordinary lake; Indian Creek reservoir, California. il Am City 86:34 O '71
TAI Chi (exercise) See Exercise
TAIGANIDES, E. Paul
There's no more away; excerpts from address. Suc Farm 69:20 Ap '71
TAILORS
Bespoke is for the carriage trade; Sills of Cambridge. Fortune 83:73 F '71
Nudie the tailor; Rodeo tailors, inc. il por Newsweek 78:90 S 13 '71
Tom Nutter. C. Kriebel. por Harp Baz 104:180 F '71
TAIPEI, Taiwan

Hotels, restaurants, etc.
How to eat in Chinese. P. Brooks. Sat R 54:82 O 23 '71
TAIRA, Koji
Japan's economic relations with Asia. bibliog f Cur Hist 60:225-30+ Ap '71
TAIWAN
Agenda in Peking. New Repub 165:5-7 Ag 7 '71
Peking's terms for closer ties with U.S. il U S News 71:22 Ag 9 '71
This country is a reality; interview. H. Y. Kao. por U S News 71:24 N 8 '71
U.N. plebiscite for Taiwan. L. C. Chen. Chr Cent 88:952-3 Ag 11 '71
Uneasy Taiwan awaits results of Nixon's Peking trip. G. F. Hall. Chr Cent 88:1149 S 29 '71
See also
Investments, Foreign (in Taiwan)
United Nations—Taiwan

Economic conditions
Taiwan, scorned by U.N. still has a lot going for it. il U S News 71:22-4 N 8 '71

Economic policy
Taiwan's strategy for survival. L. Kraar. il Fortune 84:124-31+ N '71

Foreign relations
Meanwhile, in Taiwan. il por Time 98:14 Ag 2 '71
Tense triangle: what to do about Taiwan. il Time 97:23-4 Je 7 '71
What now for Nationalist China; interview. J. C. H. Shen. il por U S News 71:42-5 Ag 2 '71

United States
See United States—Foreign relations—Taiwan

Politics and government
Chiang's last redoubt: future uncertain. il pors Time 98:32-3 N 8 '71
Notes and comment. New Yorker 47:41-3 N 6 '71
Other China: prospering, and worried. il U S News 70:32 Mv 24 '71
Repression in Taiwan. P. Ginsburg. New Repub 165:15 Jl '71
Taiwan: reality intrudes on a dogged dream. il Newsweek 78:24 N 8 '71
Taiwan's Chinese nationalist government. M. A. Plummer. bibliog f Cur Hist 61:171-6 S '71
TAKAHASHI, Kunitaro, and others
Development of excitability in embryonic muscle cell membranes in certain tunicates. bibliog il Science 171:415-18 Ja 29 '71
TAKE home examinations. See Examinations

TAKINS
Tell me that U Mishmi, Gracie; a pair of takins at the Bronx zoo. C. Trillin. il Life 71:18 N 5 '71

TAL, Wasfi
Black day in Cairo. il Newsweek 78:50 D 13 '71 •

TALAMINI, Thomas R.
New Zealand's resort king. il Travel 135:46-51 Mr '71

TALARICO, Ross
Beginning; poem. Nation 213:566 N 29 '71

TALBOT, John F.
Latin America's own work corps; 180,000 religious. il America 124:343-4 Ap 3 '71

TALBOT COUNTY, Md.
All the difference; Talbot County. W. W. Gormly. il Travel 135:38-41+ My '71

TALCOTT, James, inc.
Talcott lends aid and wins a factor; Mill factors corp. Bsns W p 19 My 29 '71

TALENT search programs (education)
Three programs for needy students. il Am Ed 7:31-2 Mr '71

TALENT testing. See Aptitude tests

TALES of Hoffmann; opera. See Offenbach, J.

TALESE, GAY
Honor thy father; excerpts. il pors Esquire 76:45-53+ Ag; 116-21+ S; 140-7+ O '71

about
Dying out. P. S. Nathan. il Pub W 200:53 Ag 2 '71 *

TALIAFERRO, Margaret
Why can't a woman... il Yachting 129:65+ My '71

TALIESIN WEST. See Frank Lloyd Wright school of architecture

TALKING books
World will never be so small again; a Thanksgiving story from a blind reader. R. Russell. il Wilson Lib Bul 46:238-45 N '71

TALKING drums. See Drum language

TALL men. See Stature

TALL oil
Tall oil, a valuable by-product. J. T. Geoghegan and W. E. Bambrick. bibliog il pors Chem 44:6-10 Ja '71

TALL tale tournament; drama. See Boiko, C.

TALL timber classic. See Skis and skiing—Maine

TALLGRASS PRAIRIE NATIONAL PARK (proposed) See National parks and reserves —United States

TALLIS, Thomas
Cantiones sacrae 1575. J. W. Barker. pors Am Rec G 37:344-5+ F '71 *

TALLMAN, Frank
Tallman speaking; interview, ed. by P. Garrison. il pors Flying 88:44-51 Ap '71

TALLON, James
Mexico's madcap fish market. il Outdoor Life 157:80-3+ F '71
Rewards of photo-journalism. Writer 84:25-6+ Ap '71
Wahweap jumpoff il Outdoor Life 148:56-9+ S '71

TALLON, Robert. See Shein, B. jt. auth.

TALMEY, Allene
Books. Vogue 158:286 S 1 '71
People are talking about...(cont) Vogue 157:52-3 Ja 15; 144-5 F 1 '71
(ed) See Kennedy, R. Family-power all the way

TALMON, Shemaryahu
New covenanters of Qumran; with biographical sketch. il Sci Am 225:12, 72-81 bibliog(p 136) N '71

TALOUMIS, George
Flowers in abundance from trees and shrubs. il Home Gard 58:22-3+ Mr '71

TAMARIN, Georges. See Rosenzweig, R. jt. auth.

TAMARIND lithography workshop, inc.
Tamarind lithography workshop (title varies) (cont) M. N. Tabak. il Craft Horiz 31:34-7+ F '71

TAMARIND seed; story. See Anthony, E.

TAMASHIRO, Roy T.
Using photography to amplify self-esteem in the primary grades. Ed Digest 37:38-40 N '71

TAMERLANE
Face of Tamerlane; facial reconstruction by M. Gerasimov. il por Newsweek 77:70 Mr 8 '71

TAMERS, Murry A.
Language gap: must we all speak English? Bul Atom Sci 27:38-40 Mr '71

TAMM, Igor' Evgen'evich, 1895-1971
Obituary
Phys Today por 24:71+ S '71. B. Bolotovsky

TAMM, Quinn
Police. New Repub 164:6 Je 19 '71 •

TAMMEN, Ronald L.
Letter from Washington. il Bul Atom Sci 27:42-4 My '71
Wolf at the Pentagon door. New Repub 164:13-14 Mr 20 '71

TAMOR, Phyllis
Countdown for summer slimness. il Todays Health 49:58-61 Ap '71
Football brunch. il Todays Health 49:40-3 N '71

TAMPA, Fla.
Kids play outside every day; life of the Ellis family. J. Kronenberger. il Look 35:38-41+ Ap 6 '71

Airports
Nation's newest airport complex; International airport. il Am City 86:76+ S '71
Tampa design keyed to shuttle system. Z. Strickland. il Aviation W 95:91+ N 15 '71
Transfer at Tampa; Florida airport terminal. il Arch Forum 135:34-7 O '71

City planning
Show and sell with slides and sound. il Am City 86:126+ S '71

Foreign population
Romeo & Julieta; growing up among Cuban relatives. J. Yglesias. New Yorker 47:107-8+ O 16 '71

Immigrants
See Tampa, Fla.—Foreign population

Lighting
Demonstration for better lighting. il Am City 86:116 My '71

Parks and playgrounds
Dining out in the park; Busch gardens, Tampa, Fla. T. Barrett. il Parks & Rec 6:19-22+ Ap '71

TAMPA international airport. See Tampa, Fla.—Airports

TAMPLIN, Arthur R.
Issues in the radiation controversy. por Bul Atom Sci 27:25-7 S '71

about
Fallout from the peaceful atom. P. Winslow. Nation 212:557-61 My 3 '71. Reply with rejoinder. J. A. Harris. 212:738 Je 14 '71 *

TAMPONS. See Sanitary napkins, tampons, etc.

TAN
Don't be another pebble on the beach. Harp Baz 104:82 Je '71
How to handle the summer sun; skin cancer and solar radiation. J. D. Ratcliff. Read Digest 99:106-8 Jl '71
Love affair with the sun. E. Sheppard. Harp Baz 104:94-5 Je '71
Or would you rather be a fish? Harp Baz 104:85 Je '71
Sun talk. il Mlle 73:210-11 My '71
Sun-worshiper's strategy. Ladies Home J 88:133 Jl '71
Suntan preparations. il Consumer Rep 36:408-11 Jl '71
Tan now, pay in 1986; danger of skin cancer. C. Carpentieri. il Mech Illus 67:62-3+ Jl '71
Travel and beauty care. J. Clark. Holiday 49:124+ D '70

TANAGER gallery. See New York (city)—Galleries and museums

TANAKA, Tomiko. See Zbar, B. jt. auth.

TANAKA, Yasumasa
Psychological factors in international persuasion. bibliog f Ann Am Acad 398:50-60 N '71

TAND, Oege M.
Sharing his hobbies has made thousands happy. S. A. Parvin. il Hobbies 76:140-1 My '71

TANDBERG-HANSSEN, E.
Solar prominences and their magnetic fields. il Sky & Tel 42:72-5, 142-5 Ag-S '71

TANGANYIKA
See also
Tanzania

TANGE, Kenzō
Kenzo Tange, 1946-1969, architecture and urban design, by U. Kultermann. Review Arch Forum 135:8 O '71. R. Boyd •

TANGIER, Morocco
Ramadan: month of fast. A. Waugh. Nat R 23:87 Ja 26 '71

TANIA (artist)
Canvas 33 stories high. D. Davis. Newsweek 78:65-6 Ag 9 '71 *

TANK ship models. See Ship and boat models
TANK ship owners. See Shipowners
TANK ships
Big doesn't mean efficient; case of the Torrey Canyon. R. E. Lapp. New Repub 165:26-7 N 20 '71
Exploding supertankers; oil tanker explosions; explanation of E. Pierce. Time 97:43 Ja 25 '71
Giant alternative to the Suez Canal. il Fortune 84:117 Ag '71
Oil bombs; mammoth tankers. Nation 212:229 F 22 '71
Racing to build supertankers. il Bsns W p45 Ag 7 '71
Tankerman's eerie world; aboard Europoort; report. W. Rademaekers. il Time 97:48-9 Mr 29 '71
There's a lot of gravy in hauling oil. il Bsns W p36-7 F 20 '71
Trouble off Bergen Point! tugboat Julia C. Moran, rescue operation. T. Gallagher. il Read Digest 99:58-62 Ag '71
Two-piece tanker cuts shipping costs; Tug-barge. P. Wahl. il Pop Sci 199:61 D '71
TANKERS. See Tank ships
TANKERSLEY, Anthony
Recantations of a reformed Berkeley bomber; ed. by G. Anderson. Time 97:12-13 F 22 '71
TANKS
See also
Oil tanks
Water tanks
TANKS, Military
Analysis of a dream tank; the XM803. W. Overend. Nation 212:755-6 Je 14 '71
TANNER, Bernard R.
Witnessing; or, The myth of the global village. Engl J 60:740-5 S '71
TANNER, Daniel, and Tanner, L. N.
Parent education and cultural inheritance. bibliog Sch & Soc 99:21-4 Ja '71
TANNER, Laurel N. See Tanner, D. jt. auth.
TANNER, William F.
Net kinetic energy in littoral transport. bibliog Science 172:1231 Je 18 '71
Our moving beaches. il Américas 23:2-8 O '71
TANNING
Tan a snakeskin. il Field & S 76:14 Jl '71
Tan deer hides. J. Palmer. il Field & S 76:14+ Ag '71
TANZANIA
Good show for the blimps; tenth anniversary of independence. il Time 98:42 D 20 '71
See also
Ecology—Tanzania
National parks and reserves—Tanzania
Roads—Tanzania

Foreign relations
Border incident; Uganda and Tanzania. Newsweek 78:30-1 S 6 '71

History
Profiles; J. K. Nyerere. W. E. Smith. por New Yorker 47:42-8+ O 16; 47-54+ O 23 '71

Politics and government
Profiles; J. K. Nyerere. W. E. Smith. por New Yorker 47:42-8+ O 16; 47-54+ O 23; 53-8+ O 30 '71

Religious institutions and affairs
Worldaround. Chr Cent 89:19-20 Ja 5 '72
TANZER, Michael
Offshore oil sweepstakes. Nation 212:814 J 28 '71
TAORMINA, Anthony S.
Art and science of composting. il Cons 26:48-9+ O '71
TAOS, N. Mex.
Taos remembered; with prologue and epilogue by T. H. Watkins. H. Fergusson. il pors Am West 8:38-41 S '71
TAOS COUNTY, N.Mex.
Commune way keeps spreading because: maybe it'll be different here. W. Hedgepeth. il Look 35:63-6+ Mr 23 '71
TAOS Indians
Battle for Blue Lake. D. O. Collins. il Am West 8:32-7 S '71
Taos Indians have a small generation gap. W. Griffith. il N Y Times Mag p26-7+ F 21 '71
Taos Indians train for the future. il Am For 77:34-5 S '71
TAP additives. See Gasoline—Additives
TAP dancing
Reveille for taps. il Time 98:44-5 Jl 5 '71
Tap, tapping and tappers. M. Horosko. il Dance Mag 45:32-7 O '71
TAP rooms. See Bars and barrooms

TAPE
See also
Adhesive tape
TAPE, Cassette. See Magnetic tape
TAPE, Magnetic. See Magnetic tape
TAPE decks. See Magnetic recorders and recording
TAPE players. See Magnetic tape players
TAPE recorders and recording. See Magnetic recorders and recording
TAPE recordings
Ampex and instant publishing. I. Berger. Sat R 54:47-8 Ag 28 '71
Electronic tourism for the '70s; Tours on tapes. G. Haber. il Pop Phot 68:42+ F '71
Great recordings of the decade; Tapes. R. D. Darrell. il Hi Fi 21:71-3 Ap '71
Measuring tapes; cassette recordings on many subjects. il Time 97:51 F 1 '71
Nine cassettes to show off and test your tape playback system. R. D. Darrell. Hi Fi 21:48-9 Ag '71
Playing it by ear; taped tours. H. Sutton. Holiday 49:11+ D '70
Sound of deceit: alibi tapes. Time 97:65 Ap 26 '71
Tape deck. R. D. Darrell. See issues of High fidelity and Musical America
Tapester's timer; pre-programmed tape recorder. R. Angus. il Pop Phot 68:47+ Ja '71
See also
Libraries—Tape recordings
Oral history

Anecdotes, facetiae, satire, etc.
More functional than Muzak. Chr Cent 88:639 My 19 '71

Operas
Case for cassettes: taped opera. H. Fantel. il Opera N 35:14-16 F 20 '71

Stereophonic recordings
Great 4-channel tape snarl. I. Berger. Sat R 54:91 N 27 '71
Quadraphonic quandary. I. Berger. Sat R 54:84 O 30 '71

Storage
Tapes & stripes forever. R. Pinney. il Pop Phot 69:27+ O '71

Unauthorized recording
See Magnetic recorders and recording—Unauthorized recording
TAPED seed. See Seed tapes
TAPESTRY
Calder tapestries. M. Welish. il Craft Horiz 31:40-1 D '71
Chinese silk tapestries. S. B. Sherrill. il Antiques 99:304+ Mr '71
Tapestries: a versatile approach; linoleum block printing and creative stitchery. B. Culley. il Sch Arts 71:10-11 Ja '72

Exhibitions
Two views of the fifth tapestry biennale. J. L. Larsen; D. Rapoport. il Craft Horiz 31:22-30+ O '71
TAPEWORMS
See also
Measles in cattle
TAPP, Robert B.
On the rise of demotheology. Chr Cent 88:153-6 F 3 '71
TAPPER, Daniel N. See Halpern. B. P. jt. auth.
TAPPETT, Tom
Car care. See issues of Mechanix illustrated
TAPPLY, Horace G.
Sportsman's notebook. See issues of Field & stream
TARBOX, Raymond
Auditory experience in Joyce's Portrait. bibliog Am Imago 27:301-28 Wint '70
TARDINESS
In slight praise of tardiness; Time essay. G. Clarke. il Time 97:50-1 Je 28 '71
TARGAN, Barry
Odds are with it. Sat R 54:20 F 6 '71
TARGET/Lengo (periodical) See Religious newspapers and periodicals
TARGET missiles. See Guided missiles
TARIFF
See also
Balance of trade
Free trade and protection
General agreement on tariff and trade
Smuggling

Europe, Western
Europeans urge retaliatory import duties. D. E. Fink. Aviation W 95:19-20 O 25 '71
See also
European economic community

TARIFF—*Continued*

United States

Advice to Connally: quit while you're ahead. D. Grove. il Time 98:24 O 4 '71

After the blow, Japan picks up the pieces. il Bsns W p60-1 Ag 28 '71

Aims of President Nixon's economic program presented to the GATT council; statement, August 24, 1971, with text of terms of reference. N. Samuels. Dept State Bul 65:305-8 S 20 '71

Barriers to trade. New Repub 165:7-8 O 2 '71

Dollar: a power play unfolds; surtax on imports. il Time 98:14+ Ag 30 '71

Dollar devaluation. il Newsweek 78:16-18 Ag 30 '71

Import surcharge jolts the retailers. il Bsns W p68 Ag 21 '71

Imposition of supplemental duty for balance of payments purposes; proclamation. R. Nixon. il Dept State Bul 65:256-7 S 6 '71

Lament for lost U.S. markets. il Bsns W p40 O 30 '71

Living with the Nixon measures. Fortune 84:49-51 O '71

More things change; effects of import surtax. J. Burnham. Nat R 23:977 S 10 '71

Multinationals take it in stride. il Bsns W p59 Ag 28 '71

Our strange new hard line on trade. S. Rose. il Fortune 84:136-9+ N '71

View of America: down and out or up and punching; a Time symposium. il Time 98: 24-5 O 25 '71

See also
Free trade and protection

TARIFF commission. See United States—Tariff commission

TARKENTON, Fran

Wages of greed. P. Axthelm. por Newsweek 78:53+ Ag 23 '71 •

TARLING, D. H.

Other extreme; Gondwana reconstructions. il Sci N 99:49 Ja 16 '71

TAROT

Tarot takeoff, a new game that strips off psychic layers. J. M. G. Norwood. Vogue 157:85+ F 15 '71

Tarot talk. D. Powills. il Hobbies 75:154-5 Ja '71

TARPON fishing

How to get hooked on tarpon. A. Spiers. il Field & S 75:54-5+ Mr '71

Sojourn in Santa Marta. G. Gresham. il Field & S 76:48-9+ Jl '71

Where tarpon fishing is color-coded. R. Marston. il Motor B & S 128:24+ Jl '71

TARR, Curtis W.

As draft is renewed; interview. il por U S News 71:30-2 O 4 '71

How Congress should change the draft; interview. il pors U S News 70:28-32 F 1 '71

Winds of change in the draft; interview. il pors Nations Bsns 59:48-50+ F '71

about

Greetings' man; with interview, ed. by M. Byers. il pors Life 70:57-8 Je 11 '71 •

TARR, Joel A.

Urban pollution: many long years ago. il Am Heritage 22:65-9+ O '71

TARSIS, Valerii

Where are they now? il por Newsweek 77:6 Je 28 '71 •

TARTOF, Kenneth D.

Increasing the multiplicity of ribosomal RNA genes in drosophila melanogaster. bibliog il Science 171:294-7 Ja 22 '71

TARTS

Canterbury tarts for dessert. il Sunset 147: 194 N '71

Fabulous flan. il Ladies Home J 88:82+ Je '71

Fruit tarts & pies. H. McCully. il House B 113:86-7+ Je '71

TASADAY tribe. See Philippines—Native races

TASCA, Henry J.

Our man in Athens. il por Newsweek 77: 48+ My 3 '71 •

TASMANIA

See also
De Witt's Island
Macquarie Island

TASMANIAN devils

Tasmanian devil, Australia's meat-eating marsupial. il Sci Digest 69:15 F '71

TASTE

Accounting for taste. F. Warshofsky. Read Digest 98:31-2+ Je '71

Blowflies: alteration of adult taste responses by chemicals present during development. V. G. Dethier and N. Goldrich. bibliog il Science 173:242-4 Jl 16 '71

Illness-induced aversions in rat and quail: relative salience of visual and gustatory cues. H. C. Wilcoxon and others. bibliog il Science 171:826-8 F 26 '71

Matter of taste; idiopathic hypogeusia. Newsweek 78:71 Ag 16 '71

On sweetness and sweeteners. il Chem 44:21-3 N '71

Taste of water in the cat; effects on sucrose preference. L. M. Bartoshuk and others. bibliog il Science 171:699-701 F 19 '71

Taste pathways in rat brainstem. R. Norgren and C. M. Leonard. bibliog il Science 173: 1136-9 S 17 '71

Taste stimuli: quality coding time. B. P. Halpern and D. N. Tapper. bibliog il Science 171:1256-8 Mr 26 '71

Tortured tastes; idiopathic hypogeusia. Time 98:45 Ag 16 '71

See also
Flavor

TASTE (aesthetics) See Aesthetics

TASTE, Musical. See Music—Philosophy and aesthetics

TATE, James

Comment. J. Atlas. Poetry 119:45-6 O '71 •

TATE, Judith

What an arrival that would be; poem. Commonweal 95:257 D 10 '71

TATE murder case. See Murder

TATI, Jacques

Current cinema. P. Gilliatt. New Yorker 47:58+ Ag 28 '71 •

TATTING

Art from a tatting shuttle. T. Messick. il Design 73:34-6 Fall '71

TATTOOING

Pins and needles; exhibition at the Museum of American folk art. New York. D. Davis. il Newsweek 78:113 D 13 '71

Zoo tattoos identify animals. J. Fix. il Sci Digest 69:61 Ap '71

TATUM, Goose. See Tatum, R.

TATUM, L. A.

Southern corn leaf blight epidemic. bibliog Science 171:1113-16 Mr 19 '71

TATUM, Reece

Basketball's black entrepreneur. A. S. Young. il pors Ebony 26:96-8+ Mr '71 •

TAUBER, Peter

See here, Private Tauber. A. Cooper. Newsweek 78:82 Ag 16 '71 •

TAUKE, M. S.

Bull Bailey, I love you; story. New Yorker 47:36-8 Je 5 '71

TAUTAVEL man. See Man. Prehistoric

TAVERNS. See Bars and barrooms

TAX auditing

How it feels to be audited by IRS. G. Reynolds. il Farm J 95:32 Je '71

How your tax return will be handled. il U S News 70:38-40 Ap 26 '71

If your tax return is questioned: case histories, what to expect; with interview with R. W. Thrower. il U S News 70:23-6 Je 14 '71

TAX collection

See also
Tax returns
United States—Internal revenue service

TAX courts

Court for small taxpayers; how it's working out. il U S News 71:112+ O 18 '71

See also
United States—Tax court

TAX deductions. See Income tax—Deductions

TAX evasion

Race-track scandal; case of O. Kerner. il por Time 98:15 D 13 '71

Withholding war taxes. P. Barnes. New Repub 164:15-17 Ap 10 '71

TAX exemption. See Taxation, Exemption from

TAX forms

Notes on a tax form. H. C. Wallich. Newsweek 77:82 Ap 26 '71

One form for all tax receipts; Litchfield, Minn. H. T. Curtis. Am City 86:62 Ja '71

TAX law. See Taxation—Law

TAX loopholes. See Taxation, Exemption from

TAX planning

Booby traps in executive taxes; interview, ed. by G. R. Rosen. B. Grund. por Duns 97:10-12+ F '71

Save on taxes with these year-end tips. il Changing T 25:11-12 N '71

Taxes: the crucial sixty days. L. Williams. il Duns 98:71-2 N '71

12 legal ways to reduce your income tax. il Suc Farm 69:12-13 N '71

Your portfolio: reminders on tax-selling. Bsns W p 131-2 N 13 '71

TAX reduction. See Taxation—United States

TAX relations, intergovernmental. See Intergovernmental tax relations

TAX returns
Facing the guns of April. W. B. Furlong. Todays Health 49:50-3 Ap '71
How to make the 1970 tax reform changes pay off. P. Lindberg. il Bet Hom & Gard 49:6+ F '71
How to make your taxes into a one-evening job. il Mech Illus 67:60-1+ Ap '71
Story that tax returns tell. U S News 71: 57-8 N 29 '71

Auditing
See Tax auditing

TAX selling. See Tax planning

TAX sharing. See Intergovernmental tax relations

TAX write-off program. See Amortization deductions

TAXATION
See also
Intergovernmental tax relations
Value added tax
  also subhead Taxation under various subjects, e.g. Church property—Taxation

Law
Booby traps in executive taxes; interview, ed. by G. R. Rosen. B. Grund. por Duns 97:10-12+ F '71
Package that Nixon will like. Bsns W p25 O 2 '71
Tax calendar for '71: dates you need to watch. U S News 70:73 Ja 18 '71
Tax reform act (cont) I. Fisher. Dance Mag 45:83 F; 108 Ap '71

California
California scraps its school tax system. Bsns W p59-60 S 4 '71
Revolt in a grab bag; inequities in California. il Newsweek 78:93 D 6 '71

Canada
Tax proposals don't hurt much after all. Bsns W p28-9 Je 26 '71

Great Britain
Tax cuts and easier credit. il U S News 71:33 Ag 2 '71
Tax-reform start in Britain. U S News 70: 43-4 Ap 12 '71

Pennsylvania
Pennsylvania tax decision. America 125:3 Jl 10 '71

Spain
Opening the tax books. Sr Schol 98:5-6 Ap 5 '71

United States
Back to business; measures before Congress. Newsweek 78:15-16 S 13 '71
Billions in tax cuts inch ahead. U S News 71:98 N 22 '71
Connally explains how new tax plan will help people; excerpts from testimony before House ways and means committee. J. Connally. il por U S News 71:83-5 S 20 '71
Have we been here before? R. Lekachman. Duns 97:13 Je '71
How big a tax cut ahead? il U S News 71: 17-18 S 27 '71
Is a tax cut coming? interview, ed. by G. R. Rosen, with editorial comment. P. A. Rinfret. por Duns 97:14-16+, 104 Ap '71
Measured portion of economic stimulus. il Bsns W p24-5 Ag 21 '71
Outlook for the President's tax plans; interviews with key men in Congress. W. D. Mills and others. pors U S News 71:19-20 S 6 '71
Outlook now for tax cuts. il U S News 70: 15-16 Mr 29 '71
Plan for tax changes. il U S News 71:33-5 Ag 30 '71
Progress on several fronts; tax-reduction bill. il Time 98:20 D 13 '71
Selling out the future. M. K. Udall. New Repub 165:12-13 N 20 '71
70,000 taxpayers speak out: tax questionnaire report. P. Lindberg. Bet Hom & Gard 49:58-9+ Mr '71
Slap for steel, a spur for machinery. il Time 97:64-5 Ja 25 '71
Some tax fiction for the home folk; Senate tax bill amendments. Bsns W p24 N 20 '71
TRB from Washington. New Repub 164:4 Ap 10 '71
TRB from Washington: brass tax. New Repub 165:4 D 11 '71

Tax cuts push the deficit higher. il Bsns W p32 D 11 '71
Taxes: still headed in the same direction. Nations Bsns 59:50-2 Ag '71
Way to finance environmental protection; proposed 10 per cent surtax on personal and corporate-income tax liabilities. A. K. Browne. Am City 86:6 Ja '71
Why you don't notice tax cuts. il U S News 70:22-3 Mr 1 '71
With the latest cut, tax changes you will get. il U S News 71:25-8 D 27 '71
See also
Excess profits tax
Income tax—United States
Libraries—Finance
Local taxation
Property tax
Social security taxes
Tariff—United States
Tax evasion
Taxation, State
United States—Internal revenue service

TAXATION, Double
Tax convention with Finland enters into force. Dept State Bul 64:124-5 Ja 25 '71
Tax convention with Trinidad and Tobago enters into force. Dept State Bul 64:187 F 8 '71
U.S.-Netherlands tax convention enters into force. Dept State Bul 64:251 F 22 '71
United States and Japan sign new income tax convention. Dept State Bul 64:461-2 Mr 29 '71

TAXATION, Exemption from
Artists and Irish taxes. Art in Am 59:23 My '71
Court ruling may limit religious publishers' tax-exempt status. Chr Cent 88:1489 D 22 '71
Loopholes still with us. J. A. Ruskay. Nation 212:368-71 Mr 22 '71
Tax issue; refusal of tax exempt status for organizations engaged in efforts to protect or restore the environment. Liv Wildn 34:3 Aut '70
Trying to change an unfair tax. il Time 97: 81-2 My 3 '71
Where 40 billion in tax subsidies go. il U S News 71:29 D 27 '71
See also
Church property—Taxation
Foundations, Charitable and educational— Taxation

Anecdotes, facetiae, satire, etc.
Re: how segregation ended in the early seventies. C. F. Eyre. Nat R 23:1303-4 N 19 '71

TAXATION, Municipal. See Local taxation

TAXATION, State
Gambling revenue tempting more states. U S News 70:80 Ja 25 '71
Grass-roots taxes: no cause for cheer. il U S News 71:58 O 18 '71
Parochiaid and taxes. J. M. Swomley, jr. Chr Cent 88:1024-5 S 1 '71
State, local tax loads: why no relief in sight. il U S News 70:59-61 Je 7 '71
State taxes, yours and others'; with tables. il Changing T 25:39-47 O '71
States reach for a bigger slice. il Bsns W p26+ F 20 '71
You've paid federal tax, but—. il U S News 70:20 My 3 '71
See also
Income tax, State

TAXATION for education. See School finance

TXATION for library service. See Libraries— Finance

TAXATION of corporations. See Corporations —Taxation

TAXATION of foreign investments. See Investments, Foreign—Taxation

TAXICABS
Fares
Survival of the fittest. il Time 97:62-3 Ap 12 '71
Taxis galore; New York. il Newsweek 77:53-4 Mr 22 '71

TAXONOMY. See Biology—Classification

TAY-Sachs disease. See Amaurotic family idiocy

TAYLOR, Bob L.
Teacher education: put it where the action is. Clear House 45:532-4 My '71

TAYLOR, Desmond Shawe-. See Shawe-Taylor, D.

TAYLOR, Dick
Simple test for telephone courtesy. il Am City 86:134+ My '71

TAYLOR, Edmond
Rise and fall and rise of Leon Trotsky. il pors Horizon 13:34-43 Spr '71
TAYLOR, Eleanor Ross
Skipped page; poem. Poetry 117:299 F '71
TAYLOR, Elizabeth, 1932-
Our marriage after 7 years; interview. ed. by R. Bain. por Ladies Home J 88:88+ Ap '71

about
Travelling with Elizabeth. R. Burton. il pors Vogue 157:68-71 Ap 15 '71 *
TAYLOR, Emily
Keeping house with Emily Taylor. See issues of Good housekeeping
TAYLOR, Fannie
Audiences, what's happened to them? Hi Fi 20:MA10-12+ D '70
Care and feeding of an arts administrator. Hi Fi 21:MA10-11 S '71
TAYLOR, Fred J.
How the English hunt rabbits. il pors Field & S 75:84-5+ Mr '71
TAYLOR, Frederick Winslow
Measurement of the man-day. E. S. Ferguson. il Sci Am 225:96-103 O '71 *
TAYLOR, Gary R.
Bell curve has an ominous ring. il Clear House 46:119-24 O '71
TAYLOR, George W.
Income policy and the price system. bibliog Mo Labor R 94:45-8 Ag '71
TAYLOR, Harold
Curriculum for peace. Sat R 54:22-3 S 4 '71
Protests of young people should be considered seriously. por Parents Mag 46:34+ F '71
Toward radical reform; excerpt from How to change colleges. Cur 130:27-35 Je '71
TAYLOR, Harriet (Hardy) See Mill, H. H.
TAYLOR, James
In rock, it's a bad, mad world. A. Goldman. pors Life 70:12 Mr 12 '71 *
James Taylor, a new troubadour. S. Braudy. il pors N Y Times Mag p28-9+ F 21 '71 *
James Taylor: one man's family of rock. il pors Time 97:45-50+ Mr 1 '71 *
New minstrels. pors Harp Baz 104:58 Je '71 *
Sweet appeal of James Taylor. E. Dunbar. il Redbook 137:75+ Je '71 *
That lonely feeling. S. K. Oberbeck. il por Newsweek 77:48 F 8 '71
TAYLOR, Kate
Through the eyes of sister Kate; interview. ed. by E. Miller. il pors Seventeen 30:226-7+ Ag '71
TAYLOR, Kathryn S.
Multiplying your houseplants. il Horticulture 49:30-3 F '71
TAYLOR, Kenneth M. and Snyder, S. H.
Brain histamine: rapid apparent turnover altered by restraint and cold stress. bibliog il Science 172:1037-9 Je 4 '71
TAYLOR, Kenneth Nathaniel
Updating the Bible. il por Newsweek 78:102 S 27 '71 *
TAYLOR, Lauriston Sale
Another round on radiation. Sci N 99:78 Ja 30 '71 *
TAYLOR, Livingston
In rock, it's a bad, mad world. A. Goldman. pors Life 70:12 Mr 12 '71 *
TAYLOR, Marcy
Flag girl. Nation 212:710 Je 7 '71 *
TAYLOR, Milton W. and others
New class of purine mutants of Chinese hamster ovary cells. bibliog il Science 172:162-3 Ap 9 '71
TAYLOR, Otis
Call it catch-as-catch-can. R. H. Boyle. il por Sports Illus 35:84+ N 15 '71 *
TAYLOR, Paul, dance company. See Paul Taylor dance company
TAYLOR, Paul S.
Matter of opinion: reclamation. Am West 8:48+ Jl '71
TAYLOR, Roger
Teachers and the drug scene. il Schol Teach Jr/Sr High p23 F 1 '71
TAYLOR, Ronald B.
Reagan's legal aid. Nation 212:645 My 24 '71
Why Chavez spurns the Labor act. il Nation 212:454-6 Ap 12 '71
TAYLOR, Stuart R. See Rüdel, R. jt. auth.
TAYLOR, Suzanne
Young and hungry; excerpts. il Ladies Home J 88:146-7+ My '71
TAYLOR, Telford
Judging Calley is not enough. il Life 70:20-3 Ap 9 '71
Who is responsible? excerpt from Nuremberg and Vietnam. Cur 126:52-64 F '71

about
Guilt by comparison. R. L. Shayon. Sat R 54:34 Jl 3 '71 *

TAYLOR, Tucker
Airplane as a teaching tool. Flying 89:54-6 D '71
TAYLOR, Victor E.
Heroin and the black community. Am Scholar 40:691-4 Aut '71
TAYLOR, Zack
Can you and should you build your own boat? Motor B & S 127:52-5 F '71
TCHAIKOVSKY, Peter Ilyltch
Ormandy declares war (on himself) R. D. Darrell. Hi Fi 21:77 Je '71 *
Tchaikovsky at home. C. Jolly. il por Opera N 35:10-15 My 15 '71 *
Tchaikovsky's Joan of Arc; excerpts. P. G. Davis. Hi Fi 21:96 Ag '71 *
Winter dreams, the newest and best. M. Kanny. Am Rec G 37:592+ My '71 *
TCHAIKOVSKY international competition. See Music—Competitions
TCHIDIMBO, Raymond Marie, abp
La bizarrérie in Guinea. America 124:107 F 6 '71 *

TEA
Glossary of popular teas and how to brew them. Good H 173:190 O '71
Tea as a medicine. Sci Digest 69:53-4 Je '71
What's cooking?
Teapot in my garden; herb teas. N. C. Tucker. Org Gard & Farm 18:127-8+ S '71

TEA caddy spoons. See Spoons
TEA industry
See also
Brooke Bond Liebig, ltd.
TEA tax (American colonies)
See also
Boston tea party, 1773
TEACHER-administrator relationships
Teacher-administrator relations: a continuing hiatus. Y. Chussil. bibliog f Clear House 45:387-91 Mr '71
TEACHER education. See Teachers—Education
TEACHER evaluation. See Teachers—Rating
TEACHER librarian training. See School librarians—Education
TEACHER morale. See Morale
TEACHER opinion
Faculty-student views on colleges; Carnegie commission on higher education survey. Sch & Soc 99:262+ Sum '71
Here's what junior-college faculties think. Todays Ed 60:67-8 Mr '71
Teacher opinion poll. See issues of Today's education
What will the schools become? H. G. Shane and O. N. Nelson. Ed Digest 37:1-3 O '71
TEACHER participation in school administration. See School management and organization—Teacher participation
TEACHER-pupil relations. See Teachers and students
TEACHER rating. See Teachers—Rating
TEACHER shortage. See Teachers—Supply and demand
TEACHERS
Dear Bill Cosby. V. O'Keeffe. Clear House 46:56-8 S '71
Games principals shouldn't play with teachers. B. Demsch and D. Muller. Clear House 45:473-5 Ap '71; Same abr. with title Games that principals shouldn't play. Ed Digest 37:18-19 S '71
Man's touch; male kindergarten teachers. il Newsweek 77:76-7 Mr 8 '71
Middle school, specially trained teachers are vital to its success. S. Clarke. bibliog f Clear House 46:218-22 D '71
Person teacher; self-concept of a teacher. J. M. Beniskos. Ed Digest 36:34-6 Ap '71
She fought to teach; J. Heumann first physically handicapped teacher E. Blaustein. il pors Good H 173:56+ S '71
Teacher of the year 1971; M. M. Stringfellow. W. J. McKean. il pors Look 35:51-4 My 4 '71
Urban teachers for urban youth. E. Kruszynski. bibliog Sch & Soc 99:511-13 D '71
What happened to a teacher who touched kids; male teacher of fourth grade incorrectly charged with child molesting. R. B. Kaiser. il Look 35:64-8 Ag 10 '71
See also
American teachers in Canada
Collective bargaining—Teachers
Dance teachers
English teachers
Future teachers of America
National education association
Nuns as teachers
School and the home

TEACHERS—See also—*Continued*
School management and organization—Teacher participation
Science teachers
Substitute teachers
Teaching
Women as teachers

Adjustment

Beginning teacher; symposium. il por Todays Ed 60:54-9 S '71
My first year of teaching; excerpt from Don't smile until Christmas, ed. by K. Ryan. W. Crawford. Todays Ed 60:46-7 F '71

Anecdotes, facetiae, satire, etc.

Game of one downsmanship or one upsmanship down. R. Burns and R. L. Harrell. Clear House 46:96-7 O '71
Light touch. See issues of Today's education

Appointment

See Teachers—Selection and appointment

Certification

Are we ready for national certification of professional educators? R. K. Sparks. Ed Digest 36:16-18 Ja '71
Certification: an educational necessity. B. King. il Dance Mag 45:71-3 Je '71
Teaching high school in Texas; letter. R. B. Clark. Phys Today 24:9 My '71; Reply with rejoinder. R. D. McConnell. 24:9+ N '71

Civil rights

Discriminating against the pregnant teacher. il Todays Ed 60:33-5 D '71

Contracts

See also
College professors and instructors—Tenure
Teachers—Tenure

Dismissal

Due process: rights of the non-tenured teacher. H. C. De Bruin. Clear House 45:369-71 F '71
Union retires a teacher; case of Margaret Maki. Nations Bsns 59:69 Jl '71

Duties

Teacher evaluates teacher for pay differentials. R. A. Engel. Clear House 45:407-9 Mr '71

Education

AMIGOS: a friendly title for a new teacher education program. E. L. McCullough. Clear House 45:476-9 Ap '71
COP's cause for celebration; Career opportunities program; with list of project sites and funds. W. Anderson. il Am Ed 7:28-35 Jl '71
Class room control should be a vital part of teacher education. D. A. Wesley. bibliog Clear House 45:346-9 F '71
Experiment in teacher education; Rutgers univ. J. Wheeler and others. Sch & Soc 99:220-3 Ap '71
Improving courses in methods of teaching. K. T. Henson. bibliog Sch & Soc 99:413-15 N '71
New role for foundations courses in teacher education. J. W. Wagener. Ed Digest 36: 29-31 Mr '71
New school; North Dakota's teacher preparation program. V. Perrone and W. Strandberg. Ed Digest 37:13-16 O '71
Statistics: a vital educational tool; adaptation of address. J. F. McNamara. Clear House 45:558-61 My '71
Teacher education: put it where the action is. B. L. Taylor. Clear House 45:532-4 My '71
Training teachers for excellence. A. A. Glatthorn. il Parents Mag 46:68-70+ S '71
Training teachers of teachers: an agent of change; Office of education program at Clark university. J. A. Plaisted. il Am Ed 7:33-5 Ja '71
Wide-open classroom to teach the teachers; New school for behavioral studies, Grand Forks, N.D. il Life 71:60+ O 1 '71
See also
Educational workshops
Mathematics teachers—Education
National commission on teacher education and professional standards
Schools of education
Student teachers
Student teaching

Education in service

Antidote: when teaching sours; National leadership methods labs. M. Manley. Ed Digest 36:46-8 Ja '71

Ending the isolation of the handicapped; teacher training programs under the Education professions development act. W. L. Smith. il Am Ed 7:29-33 N '71
In-service micro-college. W. N. Patterson. Todays Ed 60:53 F '71
Proposal for helping the beginning teacher. P. Marashio. Clear House 45:419-21 Mr '71
Santa's workshop for teachers; Learning centers project and the Teacher center at Durham elementary school, Philadelphia. A. Silberman. il Am Ed 7:3-8 D '71
State superintendent teaches first grade. D. Parnell. il por Todays Ed 60:29-30 O '71
This mini seems here to stay; Minicourse: television taping of a teacher's performance improves teaching skills. W. Wood. il Am Ed 7:14-17 D '71
Videotape recorder: aids self-improvement. J. L. Klingstedt. Clear House 45:360 F '71
See also
Robert A. Taft institute of government

Health and hygiene

Troubled teachers whose behavior disturbs our kids. M. Brenton. il Todays Health 49:16-19+ N '71

Legal status, laws, etc.

Due process: rights of the non-tenured teacher. H. C. De Bruin. Clear House 45: 369-71 F '71
Governance is integral to accountability. L. Williams. Todays Ed 60:59-60 Ap '71
Tenure and the teacher. J. G. Brown. Clear House 45:355-60 F '71

Migration

Work satisfaction and teacher mobility. R. G. Davison. bibliog Clear House 45:265-8 Ja '71

Morale

See Morale

Pensions

Teacher retirement. Todays Ed 60:46-7 My '71
Teacher retirement systems. C. E. Stone. Ed Digest 37:42-4 D '71

Placement

See Teachers—Selection and appointment

Political activities

Organizing for political action. Todays Ed 60:51 N '71
Political activities of the teacher. G. Sullivan. bibliog f Clear House 46:212-14 D '71
See also
College professors and instructors—Political activities

Promotion

Getting to the top of the staff totem pole. W. E. Stradley. Clear House 45:538-40 My '71; Reply. P. J. Viel. 46:200-2 D '71

Qualifications

Excellent teachers: what makes them outstanding? Phase II. B. F. Radebaugh and J. A. Johnson. il Clear House 45:410-18 Mr '71
We're trapped by degrees. Todays Ed 60:31 Mr '71
See also
Teachers—Certification

Rating

Grading the educators. America 124:195 F 27 '71
New idea for merit pay, teachers rate themselves. F. A. Rasmussen and P. Holobinko. bibliog Clear House 46:207-11 D '71
Outstanding teachers: who are they? M. Zax. Clear House 45:285-9 Ja '71
Process for improvement (title varies) T. J. Watman. Clear House 46:190-2, 254-6 N-D '71
Professional evaluation. T. P. Kromer. Clear House 46:14 S '71
Testing teachers. C. H. Harrison. il Schol Teach Jr/Sr High p 14-17 S '71

Rating by students

See also
College professors and instructors—Rating by students

Recruiting

For mavericks only; Teacher dropout center. il Newsweek 78:74 Ag 30 '71
Operating in the school job market. T. L. McGreal and C. Hughes. Clear House 45: 397-403 Mr '71
Teacher recruitment. C. W. Caress. Clear House 45:392-6 Mr '71

TEACHERS—*Continued*
Salaries, allowances, etc.
New idea for merit pay, teachers rate themselves. F. A. Rasmussen and P. Holobinko. bibliog Clear House 46:207-11 D '71
Rewarding teacher competence; merit pay. W. D. Boutwell. PTA Mag 66:10 S '71
Teacher evaluates teacher for pay differentials. R. A. Engel. Clear House 45:407-9 Mr '71
Teacher opinion poll: differentiated pay and overtime pay. Todays Ed 60:10 Mr '71
Thaw in the freeze: pay hikes for thousands of teachers. il U S News 71:23 S 6 '71
We're trapped by degrees. Todays Ed 60:31 Mr '71
See also
Strikes—United States—Teachers

Selection and appointment
Criteria for selecting supervising teachers. S. A. Gregory. il Clear House 46:178-82 N '71
Interview: guidelines for making it a more effective hiring device. J. L. Morris. il Clear House 46:35-9 S '71
Operating in the school job market; suggestions for job candidates. T. L. McGreal and C. Hughes. Clear House 45:397-403 Mr '71

Social status
See also
College professors and instructors—Social status

Supply and demand
As the surplus of teachers grows—. il U S News 71:44 O 25 '71
Teacher exodus; Germany takes U.S. surplus. il Newsweek 78:76 Ag 9 '71
Teacher numbers game. D. Davies. Ed Digest 36:1-4 Ja '71
Teacher surplus: fact or fancy? Sch & Soc 99:393-5 N '71
Transplanting teachers; Germany imports U.S. surplus. il Time 98:45 Ag 9 '71
See also
Teachers—Recruiting

Tenure
How teachers feel about tenure. G. Nikolaieff. Schol Teach Jr/Sr High p2 D '71
Tenure and the teacher. J. G. Brown. Clear House 45:355-60 F '71
Testing teachers. C. H. Harrison. il Schol Teach Jr/Sr High p 14-17 S '71
See also
College professors and instructors—Tenure
Teachers—Dismissal

Training
See Teachers—Education
TEACHERS, New. See Teachers—Adjustment
TEACHERS, Women. See Women as teachers
TEACHERS aides
COP's cause for celebration; Career opportunities program, with list of project sites and funds. W. Anderson. il Am Ed 7:28-35 Jl '71
Children who had to be found; high school aides helping handicapped preschoolers; interview. ed. by W. E. Densham. A. Davis. il Am Ed 7:11-14 Mr '71
Living lab for high school students; Nursery teacher aide training program at Berkeley, Calif. high school. M. P. Larson. il Todays Ed 60:22-4 Mr '71
Newark's parent-powered school; Springfield avenue community school. L. Rich. il Am Ed 7:35-9 D '71
Paraprofessionals. il Newsweek 78:47 Jl 26 '71
Theme editor: English teacher's ally. G. F. Smith. Clear House 46:116-18 O '71
TEACHERS and students
After all. J. Sharknas. Todays Ed 60:64 D '71
Annals of justice; G. Russier case in Marseille. M. Gallant. New Yorker 47:47-52+ Je 26 '71
Are you listening to or talking at? C. F. Greiner. Todays Ed 60:38-9 N '71
Black literature and the non-black teacher of black students. R. Bizot. Engl J 60:889-95 O '71
Classroom incident. See Issues of Today's education
Forget you are a teacher. C. Rogers. Ed Digest 37:17-19 N '71
Generation gap. J. Ciardi. Sat R 55:24 Ja 8 '72
How not to teach English in high school. E. Luis. Ed Digest 36:32-3 Ja '71
How to kill individuality: two viewpoints. M. Greer; M. Langenbach and T. W. Wiggins. il Todays Ed 60:42-3 D '71

Human being inside the child; the teacher and the chronically ill pupil. L. R. Robbins and N. M. Kacen. Todays Ed 60:28-35 My '71
Interaction briefs. Todays Ed 60:73 S; 60 O '71
Notes. R. C. Longe. Todays Ed 60:40 Mr '71
Perceptive youth and sound curricula. R. C. Dobbs. Clear House 46:43 S '71
Process for improvement (title varies) T. J. Watman. Clear House 46:254-6 D '71
Responsible freedom for the secondary school press: a cooperative effort. E. M. Deal. Engl J 60:960-2 O '71
School which lives. J. O'Brien. Clear House 46:59-61 S '71
Teachers look at classroom behavior problems, a survey. R. H. Burns and A. McCullen. Ment Hy 55:504-6 O '71
Things ain't the way they used to be in the English classroom. J. Yatvin. Engl J 60:1080-5 N '71
Verbal patterns of teachers in the classroom; interactional analysis of verbal behavior. J. Bondi. Ed Digest 37:44-5 S '71
Wanted. H. M. Krahulik. Todays Ed 60:20-1 Ap '71
What can I do about racism? K. Branan. Schol Teach Jr/Sr High p26+ S '71
What happened to a teacher who touched kids; male teacher of fourth grade incorrectly charged with child molesting. R. B. Kaiser. il Look 35:64-8 Ag 10 '71
What my students taught me; ed. by J. C. G. Conniff. H. H. Humphrey. il por Todays Health 49:20-3+ Ag '71
Youth speaks out about teachers; Future teachers of America survey. C. Boiarsky and N. Pedersen. il Todays Ed 60:44-6 N '71
See also
Contract plan (education)
TEACHERS assistants. See Teachers aides
TEACHERS associations. See Educational associations
TEACHERS colleges
See also
Schools of education
Teachers—Education
TEACHERS councils. See School management and organization—Teacher participation
TEACHERS meetings
Strangers in the hallways. E. J. Weber. Clear House 46:141-2 N '71
TEACHERS pensions. See Teachers—Pensions
TEACHERS salaries. See Teachers—Salaries, allowances, etc.
TEACHERS strikes. See Strikes—United States—Teachers
TEACHERS unions
Professors, unite! M. Lieberman. Harper 243:61-4+ O '71; Same abr. Cur 135:27-25 D '71; Discussion. Harper 243:9+ D '71
Talking union; college professors. il Newsweek 77:76-7 Je 14 '71
Unionizing college faculties. il Sat R 54:52 Je 19 '71
Unions woo the college faculties. il Bsns W p69-70+ My 1 '71
TEACHERS workshops. See Educational workshops
TEACHING
Case against behavioral objectives. J. B. MacDonald and B. J. Wolfson. Ed Digest 36:22-5 F '71
How to survive in your native land, by J. Herndon. Review
    Sat R 54:72 S 18 '71. B. DeMott
Humanities-science: a natural for team teaching. G. T. Capps. Clear House 45:361-4 F '71
Moving toward a new direction; multi-discipline approach to education. P. Marashio. Clear House 46:252-3 D '71
Opening up the classroom; inquiry teaching. S. J. Immitt. Engl J 60:505-7 Ap '71
Teaching: an educational adventure. K. E. Myers. bibliog Clear House 46:131-5 N '71
We can't be objective about current issues. J. Tinsman. Todays Ed 60:60 N '71
What do I do Monday? by J. Holt. Review
    Sat R 54:50 Ag 21 '71. L. Weber
See also
Classroom management
Colleges and universities—Teaching
Contract plan (education)
Discussion method (education)
Education, Experimental
Future teachers of America
Individual instruction
Lecture method in teaching
Motivation (education)

TEACHING—See also—*Continued*
Psychology, Educational
Questioning
Special classes and special schools
Teachers—Education
Teachers—Rating
Team teaching
    also subhead Study and teaching under various subjects, e.g. English language—Study and teaching

Aids and devices

Educational materials in the third world; meeting of the German foundation for developing countries. H. Lottman. il Pub W 200:16-18 N 22 '71
Learning directory 1970-71. Review
    Library J 96:248-9 Ja 15 '71. J. Eubanks. Reply with rejoinder. R. K. Randall. 96:1741 My 15 '71
Mediaguide. Schol Teach Jr/Sr High p30-1+ S; 24 N; 12 D '71; 21-2 Ja '72
New educational materials (cont) Schol Teach Jr/Sr High p20-1 Ja 11; 28-9+ F 1; 25-7+ Mr 8; 17+ Ap 5; 30-4 My 3 '71
Quiz for the teacher-buyer. B. B. Preston. Todays Ed 60:36-7 Ja '71
Teacher in a multi-mediated setting. I. W. Dible. Ed Digest 36:26-8 F '71
Teaching tips; suggestions sent in by teachers (cont) Schol Teach Jr/Sr High p35 F 1; 36 Mr 8; 22 Ap 5; 32 S; 66 O '71; 23 Ja '72
    See also
Audio-visual aids
Bulletin boards
Computers—Educational use
Education market
English language—Study and teaching—Aids and devices
Environmental education—Aids and devices
Film strips
Instructional materials centers
Magnetic recorders and recording—Educational use
Moving pictures in education
Photography in education
Political science—Study and teaching—Aids and devices
Radio in education
Telephone in education
Television in education

Anecdotes, facetiae, satire, etc.

Light touch. See issues of Today's education

Bibliography

Teacher's bookshelf (cont) Schol Teach Jr/Sr High p 15 Ja 11; 24 Mr 8; 26+ My 3; 49+ O '71

TEACHING, Freedom of. See Academic freedom
TEACHING as a profession
Dedicated teacher is the teaching profession's greatest enemy. E. Edwards. Ed Digest 36: 22-3 Ja '71
Special feature on governance of the profession. il Todays Ed 60:18-25 D '71
TEACHING efficiency. See Teachers—Rating
TEACHING machines
    See also
Computers—Educational use
TEACHING plans. See Lesson plans
TEACHINGS of Saint Paul. See Paul, Saint —Teachings
TEAGUE, Bob
Silhouettes in courage. Hi Fi 21:102 Ap '71
TEAGUE, Michael, and Cowan, Zélide
Eyeview history of the Atlantic slave trade. il Art in Am 59:58-67 Ja '71
TEAGUE, W. Dorwin
Amateur yacht research society. il Motor B & S 127:90-1+ Mr '71
Reefing through the Leewards. il Yachting 130:52-3+ N '71
TEAKETTLES. See Kettles
TEAL, Alice
Turf; poem. Seventeen 30:132 Jl '71
TEALE, Edwin Way
Big Thicket: crossroads of nature. il Audubon 73:12-32 My '71
TEAM teaching
Humanities-science: a natural for team teaching. G. T. Capps. Clear House 45:361-4 F '71
Toward greater success in team teaching. F. T. Arone. Clear House 45:501-2 Ap '71
TEAMS, Baseball. See Baseball clubs
TEAMSTERS union. See International brotherhood of teamsters, chauffeurs, warehousemen and helpers of America
TEAR gas
Tear gas in Vietnam and the return of poison gas; testimony before the Defense subcommittee of the Senate appropriations committee, May 1970. M. Meselson. Bul Atom Sci 27:17-19 Mr '71

TEARS
    See also
Crying
TEASDALE, Sara
Appraisal; poem. Good H 172:174 My '71
TEATRO Colón, Buenos Aires. See Opera houses
TEAYS VALLEY (preglacial valley)
New River: one of the oldest. R. E. Janssen. il Nat Parks & Con Mag 45:16-17 Ag '71
TEBBEL, John
Changing American newsboy. il Sat R 54:56-8 F 13 '71
Eyes and ears of the world. il Sat R 54:60-2 Je 12 '71
Inside Soviet television. Sat R 55:48-9 Ja 8 '72
Micrographics: a growing industry. Sat R 54:48-50 Jl 10 '71
Miniaturization of the book. Cur 126:46-51 F '71
Old new journalism. Sat R 54:96-7 Mr 13 '71
Our shrinking magazines: time to change your page size. il Sat R 54:68-70 O 9 '71
What tomorrow's front page will look like. il Sat R 54:50-2 My 8 '71
What's happening to the underground press? Sat R 54:89-90 N 13 '71
World press and the teaching of journalism. il Sat R 54:64-5+ S 11 '71
TECHNICAL assistance
    See also
Agricultural assistance
Underdeveloped areas
United Nations—Development program
TECHNICAL assistance, American
U.S. to assist Botswana and Zambia in developing regional road link; Department announcement. Dept State Bul 63:723 D 14 '70
    See also
United States—Peace corps
TECHNICAL assistance, Israeli
Israel's stake in black Africa. il Time 97:38+ My 31 '71
TECHNICAL assistance, Russian

Cuba

Russia tightens grip on Castro. il U S News 71:34-5 Ag 23 '71
TECHNICAL assistance in Africa
Israel's stake in black Africa. il Time 97:38+ My 31 '71
Scientific safari to Africa. G. T. Seaborg; discussion. Science 172:987 Je 4 '71
TECHNICAL chemistry. See Chemistry, Technical
TECHNICAL conferences
Engineering foundation conferences. S. S. Cole. Science 172:603-4 My 7 '71
    See also
Urban technology conference
TECHNICAL education
    See also
Industrial arts
John C. Campbell folk school, Brasstown, N.C.
TECHNICAL high schools. See Trade schools
TECHNICAL literature
    See also
Publishers and publishing—Technical literature
Technology—Bibliography
TECHNICAL processes in libraries. See Libraries—Technical processes
TECHNICAL writing
Credo of a tech writer. J. Frye. Electr World 85:50-1 Je '71
Full-time freelancing in technical writing. P. Franklin; reply. G. Adcock. Writers Digest 51:8 Mr '71
Science sells. J. S. Sweet. il Writers Digest 51:28-30+ O '71
TECHNICIANS in industry
Technicians in Britain. E. A. Bromfield. Electr World 86:36 Jl '71
    See also
Comprehensive designers, inc.
TECHNICOLOR, inc.
Brighter palette for Technicolor. Bsns W p22 N 20 '71
Technicolor: red to black. T. J. Murray. por Duns 98:70+ S '71
TECHNICON corporation
Man in a fish bowl. il por Forbes 107:19-20 Je 15 '71
TECHNIQUE (art) See Art—Technique; Painting—Technique
TECHNOLOGICAL aids in education. See Teaching—Aids and devices
TECHNOLOGICAL change
Barriers to technical innovation. A. Seidman. il Bul Atom Sci 27:29-31 Mr '71
Future shock, by A. Toffler. Review
    Trans-Action 8:102-4 N '70. A. Etzioni

TECHNOLOGICAL change—*Continued*
Luddites were not all wrong. W. Greene and S. Golden. il por N Y Times Mag p40-2+ N 21 '71
Man and meaning; excerpts from address, November 1970. G. Wald. por Sr Schol Teach ed 97:4 Ja 11 '71
Mounting tide of unreason. E. Rabinowitch por Bul Atom Sci 27:4-9 My '71
One and a half cheers for progress. J. A. Michener. il N Y Times Mag p9+ S 5 '71; Same abr. Read Digest 99:209+ D '71; Discussion. N Y Times Mag p98 S 26 '71
Revolution in a technological society; address, October 22, 1970. S. D. Proctor. por Negro Hist Bul 34:6-9 Ja '71
Technological change; address, October 20, 1971. C. L. Hogan. Vital Speeches 38:139-42 D 15 '71
Technological change and the future of shipping in developing countries. J. J. Oyevaar. bibliog f il Int Concil 582:44-65 Mr '71
Technology and manpower in nonelectrical machinery. L. T. O'Carroll. bibliog il Mo Labor R 94:56-62 Je '71
Unbound Prometheus, by D. S. Landes. Review
　Am Hist R 76:467-74 Ap '71. R. M. Hartwell and R. Higgs; Reply. D. S. Landes. 76:1633-7 D '71
　See also
Technology assessment
Technology transfer

TECHNOLOGICAL forecasting
Make TF serve corporate planning. P. H. Thurston. Harvard Bsns R 49:98-102 S '71
Naysayers never die; excerpt from Down the centuries with the prophets. C. Leinbach and W. E. Jackman. Aviation W 94:9 Mr 22 '71
　See also
Technology assessment

TECHNOLOGICAL innovations. See Technological change

TECHNOLOGICAL obsolescence. See Obsolescence

TECHNOLOGICAL research. See Industrial research

TECHNOLOGY
Enemy within. L. Mumford. por Forbes 108: 46 N 15 '71
Magruder in White House: SST man plans new technology take-off. D. Shapley. por Science 174:386-8 O 22 '71
New initiatives in technology. P. H. Abelson. Science 174:895 N 26 '71
Technology's vital role; excerpts from testimony before House subcommittee on science, research and development. M. H. Stans. Aviation W 95:7 Ag 30 '71
U.S. technology: looking for a better mousetrap; interviews, ed by R. Nash. E. Q. Daddario; E. E. David, jr; S. Melman. il pors Forbes 108:36-8+ N 15 '71
　See also
Space technology
Underdeveloped areas—Technology

Bibliography
Books to come (cont) Library J 96:867-8+, 2383-5+, 2647+ Mr 1, Jl, N 1 '71
Emphasis is on here and now; April through September science and technology books. il Pub W 199:31-47 Ap 12 '71
Sci-tech books '70; one hundred outstanding titles for general library collections; comp. by D. R. Pfoutz. il por Library J 96:781-92 Mr 1 '71
Science & technology; a selection of books planned for publication November, 1971 through May, 1972. il Pub W 200:29-42 N 15 '71

History
Leonardo on bearings and gears. L. Reti. il Sci Am 224:100-7+ F '71

International aspects
Growing ties between science and foreign policy; address, May 21, 1971. W. P. Rogers. Dept State Bul 64:766-8 Je 14 '71
Objectives of international cooperation in science and technology; statement; February 15, 1971. H. Pollack. Dept State Bul 64:837-41 Je 28 '71
Technology and world trade: is there cause for alarm? P. M. Boffey. il Science 172:37-41 Ap 2 '71
U.S. foreign policy in a technological age; address, January 26, 1971. W. P. Rogers. Dept State Bul 64:198-202 F 15 '71

Chile
Chile: trying to cultivate small base of technical excellence. N. Hawkes. Science 174: 1311-13 D 24 '71

Great Britain
Britain stages a technological retreat. il Bsns W p 114-15 Mr 13 '71

Russia
Russia sells its knowhow; wrapped in red tape. il Bsns W p59-60 My 8 '71
Scientists' lament: we live in another epoch. il Newsweek 77:32 F 1 '71

Underdeveloped areas
See Underdeveloped areas—Technology

United States
See Technology

TECHNOLOGY and art. See Art and technology

TECHNOLOGY and civilization
Aerospace and the common good; excerpts from address, January 1971. C. M. Kearns. jr. Aviation W 94:9 Ja 18 '71
Building the city of man, by W. W. Wagar. Review
　Sat R 54:57-8 N 6 '71. R. J. Barnet
Closing circle, by B. Commoner. Review
　Bsns W p 13 O 23 '71. S. B. Shepard
Coping with future shock; excerpt from Future shock. A. Toffler. Read Digest 99:81-6 Ag '71
Culture of machine living. M. Lerner. il UNESCO Courier 24:23-7 My '71
Design, technology, and the pursuit of ugliness; excerpt from The synthetic garden. G. Nelson. il Sat R 54:22-5+ O 2 '71
Despairing optimist. R. Dubos. Am Scholar 40:389-90+ Sum '71
Doubts about technology: are they valid? il Space World H-8-92:14-16 Ag '71
Engineer and his work: a sociological perspective. A Rudoff and D. Lucken. bibliog Science 172:1103-8 Je 11 '71; Discussion. 174:645 N 12 '71
Future shock, by A. Toffler. Review
　Ramp Mag 9:57-8 Mr '71. A. Sklar
Greening of America, by C. A Reich. Review
　Bul Atom Sci 27:33-7 N '71. E. Rabinowitch
Impossibility of dropping out. A. Hartley. il Horizon 13:104-5 Aut '71
Is man over adapting to his environment? R. Dubos. Cur 128:34-9 Ap '71
Need for technological assessment. J. Lederberg. Cur 128:24-8 Ap '71
$1-billion monthly cost foreseen to apply technology to social ills. Aviation W 95:46 N 29 '71
Our thing: some further reflections on space ship earth. R. G. Howes. Cath World 213: 169-73 Jl '71
People in the machinery; views of Barry Commoner. P. R. Ehrlich and J. P. Holdren. Sat R 55:71 Ja 1 '72
Revolt of the thinking class. R. Taagepera. Nation 212:681-4 My 31 '71
SST, end product of Consciousness II. P. P. McDermott. America 124:171-4 F 20 '71
Saving the crusade. P. F. Drucker. il Harper 244:66-71 Ja '72
Science and technology; an age of anxiety; address, April 30, 1971. A. H. Aymond. Vital Speeches 37:492-4 Je 1 '71
Small is beautiful: toward a theology of enough; address. E. F. Schumacher. Chr Cent 88:900-2 Jl 28 '71
Taming technology; address, December 27, 1970. L. M. Branscomb. bibliog Science 171:972-7 Mr 12 '71
Technology and society: a challenge to private enterprise; address, April 1971. I. K. MacGregor. Vital Speeches 37:525-9 Je 15 '71
Technology and society: the real issues. M. Tribus. il Bul Atom Sci 27:27-30 D '71
Technology for the poor. P. R. Ehrlich and J. P. Holdren. Sat R 54:46-7 Jl 3 '71
Two cheers for technology. S. Chase. Sat R 54:20-1+ F 20 '71
Ungodly city; a theological response to Jacques Ellul. H. Cox. il Commonweal 94: 351-7 Jl 9 '71
View from the year 2000. B. Farrell. il pors Life 70:46-8+ F 26 '71
War in man, by F. D. Wilhelmsen and J. Bret. Review
　Nat R 23:208-9 F 23 '71. F. S. Meyer
Youth and the future: how to avoid future shock. il por Sr Schol 98:3-6 My 10 '71
　See also
Social problems
Technological change
Technology assessment

TECHNOLOGY and education. See Education and technology

TECHNOLOGY and society. See Technology and civilization
TECHNOLOGY and state
Quest for national technological goals. Sci N 101:21 Ja 8 '72
Technical power and people. A. W. Benn. Bul Atom Sci 27:23-6 D '71
TECHNOLOGY assessment
On the social deployment of science. A. G. Mencher. il Bul Atom Sci 27:37-8 D '71
Participatory technology. J. D. Carroll. bibliog Science 171:647-53 F 19 '71
Technology and the law; technology assessment by private tort action. Sci Am 224: 45-6 F '71
TECHNOLOGY transfer
Aerospace giant tries earthwork; Boeing's new directions. il Time 98:79 N 15 '71
Benefits from space. Space World H-9-93: 39-40 S '71
Bonanza from space. A. S. Freese. il Pop Mech 136:58-61 Jl '71
Medical spin-offs from the space program. W. Von Braun. il Pop Sci 198:62-4 Mr '71
Organize for technology transfer. R. N. Foster. bibliog il Harvard Bsns R 49:110-20 N '71
School control, statistical aids devised from space technology. Aviation W 94:19 My 24 '71
TECTONICS. See Geology, Structural
TEDESCO, Thomas A. and Mellman, W. J.
Galactosemia: evidence for a structural gene mutation. bibliog il Science 172:727-8 My 14 '71
TEELE, Roy E.
Two poets and Japan. Poetry 118:174-7 Je '71
TEEN-age automobile drivers. See Automobile drivers
TEEN-age employment. See Youth—Employment
TEEN-age literature. See Young adults literature
TEEN-age marriage
Married students vs. married dropouts. J. Huber. Ed Digest 36:42-3 Ja '71
Ups and downs of young marriage. E. M. Wylie. il Seventeen 30:236-7+ Ag '71
TEEN-age pregnancy. See Pregnancy
TEEN-age suicide. See Suicide
TEEN-agers. See Adolescence; Youth
TEENAGERS and smoking. See Smoking and youth
TEETH
See also
Dentistry
Care and hygiene
Agriculture and teeth; reprint. E. B. Carpenter. Org Gard & Farm 18:88-91 Ag '71
Toothpaste. S. Rapoport. il Consumer Bul 54: 7-9 Ag '71
What do you really know about dental health? G. M. Knox. Bet Hom & Gard 49: 30+ Mr '71
See also
Dental caries—Prevention
Dentifrices
Toothpicks, Electric
Diseases
See also
Dental caries
Extraction
What to do after a tooth is pulled. Changing T 25:18 S '71
TEETH, Artificial
Care and hygiene
Denture cleaners. il Consumer Rep 36:432-4 Jl '71
TEFLON
Spray-on nonstick coating. il Mech Illus 67:46 S '71
TEHAN, William H.
Can you top this? por Forbes 108:62 D 1 '71 *
TEHERAN university. See Colleges and universities—Iran
TEILHARD DE CHARDIN, Pierre
More on Teilhard's spirituality. D. A. Drennen. America 124:413-14 Ap 17 '71 *
Promise of Teilhard, by P. Hefner. Review Chr Cent por 88:633-4 My 19 '71. E. Wing *
TEITELBAUM, Vivien Stewart
School records can be an invasion of privacy. Todays Ed 60:43-5 My '71
TE KANAWA, Kiri
Maori Mozart. il por Newsweek 79:47 Ja 3 '72 *
TEKTITE (underwater laboratory) See Underwater laboratories

TEKTITES
Export of lunar glass. Sci Am 225:50 N '71
New family of tektites? Australites. il Sci Digest 70:55-7 O '71
Tektite glass in Apollo 12 sample. J. A. O'Keefe; discussion. Science 170:199-200; bibliog 171:312-14 O 9 '70, Ja 22 '71
TEL AVIV museum
Israel's newest museum; with introd. by H. L. Smith, jr. il Arch Rec 150:119-22 O '71
TELDEC videodisc system. See Video playback systems
TELECOMMUNICATION
International telecommunications organizations and how they affect you. R. G. Gould. il Electr World 85:38-40+ F '71
See also
Communications satellites
Data transmission systems
Facsimile transmission
Multiplex system
Multiple access techniques add flexibility. il Aviation W 95:84-8 Ag 23 '71
TELE-CONVERTERS. See Photography—Apparatus and supplies
TELECTURES. See Telephone in education
TELEFACTORS. See Man amplifiers
TELEFUNKEN computer GMBH. See Computer industry—Germany (Federal Republic)
TELEGRAPH companies
See also
Western union telegraph company
TELELECTURES. See Telephone in education
TELEMETER
See also
Aerospace telemetry
Remote sensing systems
TELEMETRY, Biological. See Biotelemetry
TELEPATHY
See also
Extrasensory perception
TELEPHONE
See also
Bell telephone laboratories
Facsimile transmission
Radio telephones on ships, boats, etc.
Air pollution reports
Forum; telephone recording of daily air pollution report. P. Blake. il Arch Forum 134: 19 My '71
Anecdotes, facetiae, satire, etc.
Secrets of the little blue box. R. Rosenbaum. il Esquire 76:116-25+ O '71
Apparatus and supplies
Attachments to your telephone. W. H. Bushsbaum. il Electr World 86:27-9+ Jl '71
Interconnect. C. J. Rolo. por Forbes 108: 54-5 Ag 1 '71
Revolution in the phone business. il Bsns W p66-9+ N 6 '71
Emergency use
See also
Police communication systems
Telephone in counseling
International aspects
Hello, Shanghai, will you answer? il Bsns W p26 Ag 7 '71
Rates
Cutting down Ma Bell. New Repub 165:10-11 Jl 17 '71
How to make more phone calls for less money. Bsns W p93 Mr 6 '71
Why Bell system wants higher rates. il Bsns W p36-7 F 27 '71
Why your phone bill is going to go up. il U S News 71:78-9 N 22 '71
Religious use
Ringing in the sheaves. J. R. Greisch. Chr Today 16:24-5 N 19 '71
Television combination
RCA switches on its videovoice. il Bsns W p120+ Je 19 '71
See-while-you-talk telephone service. J. R. Free. il Pop Sci 198:65+ Mr '71
Wire tapping
See Wire tapping
TELEPHONE centers, nooks, etc.
Keep the directory near your kitchen phone. A. Lees. il Pop Sci 198:101 F '71
Plan a telephone center. il Good H 172:188 Mr '71

TELEPHONE companies
Revolution in the phone business. il Bsns W p66-9+ N 6 '71
See also
American telephone and telegraph company
Collective bargaining—Telephone companies
Florida telephone corporation
New York telephone company
Pacific telephone and telegraph company

Employees
See also
Strike—United States—Telephone workers
Telephone operators

TELEPHONE etiquette
Simple test for telephone courtesy; Inglewood, Calif. D. Taylor. il Am City 86:134+ My '71
Teaching telephone techniques. B. Earls. Todays Ed 60:41 F '71

TELEPHONE in business
New fed-beef Tel-O-auctions. J. D. Boyd. il Farm J 95:32 S '71

TELEPHONE in counseling
At the Talk center, they talk of drugs; drug help line, White Plains, N.Y. L. Greenhouse. il N Y Times Mag p67-9+ F 21 '71
On the hot line. M. Hodgkinson. il Har Yrs 11:48-50 N '71
Take your troubles to the Hotline. J. N. Bell. il Seventeen 29:242-3+ Ag '70

TELEPHONE in education
Telecture: an adventure in learning; social studies teachers at Dover high school, N.J. R. Schwartz and R. McNeely. Clear House 46:215-17 D '71
Wisconsin uses phone network in training title III staff workers. il Aging 203:12 S '71

TELEPHONE in government
Need better news coverage? San Diego County, Calif. il Am City 86:80 S '71

TELEPHONE in municipal government. See Telephone in government

TELEPHONE lines
See also
Electric conduits

TELEPHONE numbers
911 covers all emergencies; Springfield, Mass. Am City 86:12+ N '71
911 goes regional; Omaha, Neb. Am City 86:37 Ap '71

TELEPHONE on aircraft. See Radio telephone on aircraft

TELEPHONE operators
Telephone operator, ed. by K. Lasson. D. P. Neal. il Atlan 228:74-8 O '71
See also
Telephone in business

TELEPHOTO lenses. See Lenses, Photographic

TELEPHOTOGRAPHY
Pros tell why teles. J. Scully. il Mod Phot 35:68-77 Ag '71
Tele—flash? You bet? It's simple. E. Scully. il Mod Phot 35:78-9 Ag '71

TELEPROMPTER corporation
His voice is still loud above the static. por Bsns W p46+ Je 26 '71
Scandal clouds the CATV picture. il Bsns W p88 N 6 '71

TELESCOPE lenses. See Lenses

TELESCOPE mirrors. See Mirrors for telescopes

TELESCOPE models
Working model of a 70-inch telescope. M. Kaufman. il por Sky & Tel 42:170-3 S '71

TELESCOPE mountings
Simple yoke mounting for a 12-inch reflector. L. Secretan. il Sky & Tel 41:114-16 F '71

TELESCOPES
Australian 12½-inch Buchroeder relay telescope. A. E. Coombs. il Sky & Tel 42:302-8 N '71
Carnegie plans telescope in Chile. C. Holden. Science 171:557 F 12 '71
Collapsible lightweight Cassegrain telescope. V. G. Nikolashin. il Sky & Tel 41:382-3 Je '71
Fixed-eyepiece refractor with heated observatory. W. Fellows. il Sky & Tel 41:310-13 My '71
4½-inch unobstructed Maksutov telescope. A. E. Crowe, jr. il Sky & Tel 43:47-52 Ja '72
German amateur's 12-inch Newtonian reflector. M. Lammerer. il Sky & Tel 41:379-81 Je '71
Gleanings for ATM's; ed. by R. E. Cox. See issues of Sky and telescope
New Michigan 52-inch reflector. P. A. Wehinger and O. C. Mohler. il Sky & Tel 41:72-5 F '71
Southern hemisphere 100-inch telescope; instrument in Chile. Sky & Tel 41:131+ Mr '71
See also
Mirrors for telescopes
Radio telescopes

Control
Amateur-built chain drive for a 12¼ inch reflector. C. Nash. il Sky & Tel 42:378-80 D '71

Equipment
Simple knife-edge focusing attachment. R. C. Dickinson. il Sky & Tel 42:235-7 O '71

History
First Newtonian. R. A. Wells. bibliog il por Sky & Tel 42:342-4 D '71

TELESESSION company
Cooks, travelers, everybody can learn by telephone. McCalls 98:42 Ap '71

TELETHON (firm)
Pap art; Telethon's Television environment shown at art museums. il pors Time 98:90 N 1 '71

TELEVIDEO productions (firm)
Commercial; observing production of TV ads for McGregor sportswear. il New Yorker 47:21-3 Ag 7 '71

TELEVISION
Radio & television news. M. Suntag. See issues of Electronics world
Television scene. F. H. Belt. Pop Electr 1:112-15 Ja '72

Color
See Television, Color

Police use
See Television in criminal investigation

Social aspects
See Television broadcasting—Social aspects

United States
Television; special section. il Life 71:35-44+ S 10 '71

TELEVISION, Closed circuit
Fight: Ali-Frazier battle. New Yorker 47:32-5 Mr 20 '71
Greed creed: will it pay off? closed circuit TV in sports. Newsweek 77:75D-76 Mr 22 '71
TV talk:
Closed-circuit, TV. F. Deford. Sports Illus 34:14+ Mr 8 '71
Television guards a power plant: Seal Beach, Los Angeles. R. K. Morten. il Am City 86:42+ S '71
See also
Television in business

TELEVISION, Color
Color TV from black and white film. S. V. Jones. il Sci Digest 70:53 N '71
Crumbling resistance to color TV. J. Frye. Electr World 85:50+ Ap '71

TELEVISION, Experimental
Alternate video; E. Siegel. H. S. Resnik. Vogue 158:62 My 15 '71
Video underground. C. Aaron. il Art in Am 59:74-9+ My '71

TELEVISION actors and actresses. See Television broadcasting—Performers

TELEVISION advertising
Advertising the army. New Repub 165:10 O 2 '71
Are TV commercials insulting to women? GH poll. il Good H 172:68+ My '71
But first a message; U.S. Court of appeals on paid public-issue announcements. Newsweek 78:72-3 Ag 16 '71
Children's hour. J. Morgenstern. Newsweek 78:9 Ag 16 '71
Children's TV: slow learner; international survey. Sat R 54:48 Ag 21 '71
El Exigente meets the Pepsi generation; commercials in the curriculum. R. Maynard. il Schol Teach Jr/Sr High p 12-14 My 3 '71
Environment. Sedulus. New Repub 164:27-8 Mr 20 '71
Female hygiene and the TV code. Bsns W p 100 S 11 '71
How will television feel after it gives up smoking? M. Mayer. il Fortune 83:86-9+ Ja '71
Is television messing with your mind? N. Johnson. Vogue 158:92 Jl '71
Lion, lion, burning bright; new rulings on Fairness doctrine and paid controversial announcements. R. L. Shayon. Sat R 54:18+ S 11 '71
Masters of the TV hard sell. il Bsns W p40-1 Ag 7 '71
Name of the game. Sedulus. New Repub 164:31-2 F 20 '71
Quieting the children's hour. il Time 97:75 Ap 19 '71
Short commercial. G. Ace. Sat R 54:12 N 27 '71

TELEVISION advertising—*Continued*
TV ads: shorter pitches at better prospects.
il Bsns W p88-9 Ja 23 '71
TV time sells out at premium prices. il Bsns
W p43 My 15 '71
Tanks but no tanks; fairness doctrine and
Chevron's claims. T. Asher. New Repub 164
17-19 Je 26 '71
That's entertainment! il Look 35:22-3 S 7
'71
Think small; extending the cigarette doc-
trine to automobile advertising. Newsweek
78:63 Ag 30 '71
Uncommon cold; deceptive commercials. G.
Ace. Sat R 54:6 F 20 '71
Unselling the war. il Newsweek 77:69 Je 21 '71
Why producers give TV programs away. il
Bsns W p41 Ap 10 '71
See also
Books—Advertising
Television productions (firm)

Cigarettes
See Cigarettes—Advertising

TELEVISION advertising, Religious. See Re-
ligious advertising
TELEVISION amplifiers. See Amplifiers
TELEVISION and children. See Television
broadcasting and children
TELEVISION and copyright. See Copyright—
Broadcasting rights
TELEVISION and libraries. See Libraries and
television
TELEVISION and moving pictures. See Mov-
ing pictures and television
TELEVISION and reading
Remedial reading via TV; Electric company.
M. E. Ricketts. Todays Ed 60:51-2 O '71
TELEVISION antennas
Build a mini-pyramidal UHF TV antenna.
G. J. Monser. il Pop Electr 35:40-3 D '71
Costly TV antenna that offers little. il Con-
sumer Rep 36:645-6 N '71
How to beat those football blackouts. R. M.
Benrey. il Pop Sci 199:57-9+ S '71
How to select a TV antenna. F. H. Belt. il
Electr World 85:32-5+ My '71
Little antenna with a big reception; Sensar
SR-20. W. Hawkins. il Pop Sci 198:61 Mr
'71
Multi-set TV-FM systems for the home.
T. R. Haskett. il Electr World 85:32-5+
Ap '71
See also
CATV system
Equipment
TV antenna accessories. R. G. Middleton.
il Radio-Electr 42:33-5+ S '71
TELEVISION antennas lead-in line. See Tele-
vision cables
TELEVISION apparatus
Add-on converter turns your B&W TV into
a color set. R. M. Benrey. il Pop Sci 199:
45-7 D '71
Science's eye on the universe; head-coupled
television systems. R. E. Packer. il Sci
Digest 69:67-72 F '71
See also
Television receivers—Control
Video playback systems
Video recorders and recording
TELEVISION apparatus industry
Color TV sales look brilliant. Bsns W p25
D 4 '71
Japan
Boycott tunes down Japan's TV makers. il
Bsns W p41 Mr 6 '71
TELEVISION apparatus on aircraft
TV in helicopter aids New York police. K.
J. Stein. il Aviation W 95:42-5 Ag 2 '71
TELEVISION audiences
But do we like what we watch? Life 71:40-4
S 10 '71
Who watches what, why? H. Resnik. Vogue
157:157 Mr 1 '71
TELEVISION authorship
Pilot for a new TV show; Funny face. N.
Vogel. il Writers Digest 51:31-4 Ag '71
Selling the comedy bit. G. Q. Lewis. il
Writers Digest 51:31 S '71
Should the new TV writer go to Hollywood?
ed. by N. Vogel. H. Meinert and D. Marsh.
por Writers Digest 51:32-5+ Je '71
TELEVISION awards
Irony of a succès de'Emmy. Cyclops. Life
70:11 Je 18 '71
SR television awards/1971. Sat R 54:55-6 My
8 '71

TELEVISION broadcasting
TV is civilisation. K. M. C. Clark. pors
Look 35:50 S 7 '71
See also
Communications satellites
Television public speaking
Television stations
Video recorders and recording

Advertising
See Television advertising

Anecdotes, facetiae, satire, etc.
Open letters. M. Williams Nat R 23:1315
N 19 '71

Animated cartoons
Cartoonist Q's; magazine cartooning on TV.
J. Markow. Writers Digest 51:38-9 Je '71

Baseball
See Television broadcasting—Sports

Basketball
See Television broadcasting—Sports

Boxing
See Television broadcasting—Sports

Bullfights
See Television broadcasting—Sports

Censorship
Most unkindest cut of all; comedy writers
and censors. G. Ace. Sat R 54:4 Je 26 '71
Passover passed over; with editorial com-
ment. W. G. Pippert. Chr Today 15:28, 33
Ap 23 '71
Very cold turkey; banning of lyrics referring
to illegal drugs. R. L. Shayon. Sat R 54:22
My 1 '71

Children, Effect on
See Television broadcasting and children

Childrens programs
See also
Action for children's television (organiza-
tion)

Conversation programs
How to promote your book on radio and TV
interviews. R. Hull. il Writers Digest 51:28-
30+ Ag '71

Criticism
See Television criticism

Documentary programs
See Television programs, Documentary

Drama
Medium is the motivation; movies, TV and
paperbacks. K. Cremonini. il Schol Teach
Jr/Sr High p 12-14 Ap 5 '71
Stuart history a la PBS; The first Churchills.
T. H. Clancy. America 124:262-3 Mr 13 '71

Football
See Television broadcasting—Sports

Frequency standards
See Frequency standards

Government use
Image blues; President Nixon's TV appear-
ances. Nation 212:453 Ap 12 '71

History
Member of the first TV generation looks
back. J. Greenfield. il N Y Times Mag p8-
11 Jl 4 '71
Our first TV star; Felix the cat. il Life
71:68 S 10 '71
This was our life. G. Shalit. il Look 35:24-6
S 7 '71

Interference
See Television interference

International aspects
World boom in television and book transla-
tion. Unesco yearbook reports. UNESCO
Courier 24:14-15 F '71
See also
World administrative radio conference

Laws and regulations
See Television laws and regulations

Licenses
See Television laws and regulations

Merchandising tie-in
Toy maker builds on a TV name; Romper
room kiddie show. il por Bsns W p 116+
Mr 13 '71

TELEVISION broadcasting—*Continued*

Moral aspects

Does video violence make Johnny hit back?
Sci Digest 71:57 Ja '72
Murder on televison and the fourteen-year-old. R. L. Tobin. Sat R 55:39-40 Ja 8 '72
Pest control: the TV problem; with study-discussion program, by M. M. Conant. M. Harris. bibliog il PTA Mag 65:6-8+, 32 My '71
Television violence; revised code on Independent television authority. T. Beeson. Chr Cent 88:1438-9 D 8 '71

Moral aspects

This program may be harmful to your child; federal study on TV and violence. R. L. Tobin. il Sat R 54:63-4 O 9 '71

Moving pictures

Every night at the movies. H. Ehrlich. il Look 35:62-3 S 7 '71
Movies make it, even on T.V. P. Hudson. il Sr Schol 98:34+ Mr 29 '71
See also
Moving pictures and television

Music

Recordings. M. Mayer. Esquire 76:50+ N '71
Young people's concert; how not to win friends. Hi Fi 21:MA24 My '71

News

ABC advances; Nielsen ratings. Newsweek 77:93+ Ap 12 '71
Art of cut and paste. il Time 97:56+ Ap 12 '71
Authors & editors; interview, ed. by A. Johnston. W. Cronkite. por Pub W 199:15-17 My 3 '71
Broadcasting and the first amendment; address, November 11, 1971. R. Frank. Vital Speeches 38:125-7 D 1 '71
CBS, the White House and the myth of objectivity. P. C. Rule. America 124:541-2 My 22 '71
Chancellor on his own. il por Newsweek 78:71 Ag 2 '71
Day in the life of Walter Cronkite. P. Hudson. il pors Sr Schol 99:10-11+ O 18 '71
Edith Efron's murderous adding machine; TV bias. J. Chamberlain. Nat R 23:1225-6+ N 5 '71
Fighting film fakery. Time 98:86 S 20 '71
Growing up with the media. P. C. Rule. il America 125:71-2 Ag 7 '71
Happy ending (maybe) of The selling of the Pentagon. R. Sherrill. il N Y Times Mag p25-7+ My 16 '71; Reply with rejoinder. E. Sonderling. p4+ Jl 18 '71
Happy news. il Time 97:65 F 8 '71
Is the truth incredible? quotations, ed. by F. Trippett. Look 35:46+ S 7 '71
It's Put-put time in California; G. Putnam. Cyclops. por Life 70:18 Je 25 '71
Melvin Laird and CBS; question of editing. Sedulus. New Repub 165:29-30 Jl 10 '71; Reply. K. D. Tiven. 165:33 Jl 24 '71
Networks and Congress; charges of deceptive editing. America 125:51-2 Ag 7 '71
New breed; female reporters. il Newsweek 78:62 Ag 30 '71
News twisters. by E. Efron. Review Fortune il 84:183+ N '71
News twisters; E. Efron's study of broadcasts. Nat R 23:1159 O 22 '71
Newscasting, 1971. J. Leonard. Life 70:12-13 F 5 '71
Nixon vs. the media. il Newsweek 77:54+ Ap 5 '71
No news was bad news: continuous information about Los Angeles earthquake from KNBC only. P. Hudson. Sr Schol 98:22 Mr 15 '71
Pressure on the media. Nation 212:420-1 Ap 5 '71
Sander Vanocur. a very confused man. B. L. Freund. por Harp Baz 105:108 D '71
TV: delusions of infallibility: address, March 30, 1971. A. Capp. Vital Speeches 37:477-8 My 15 '71
TV tapes as research materials; with text of bill. H. H. Baker. Am Lib 2:951-2 O '71
Television and the First amendment. F. W. Friendly. Sat R 55:46-7+ Ja 8 '72
Television newsmens' opinions on the air? interview, ed. by P. Hudson. F. McGee. pors Sr Schol 99:19 Ja 10 '72
Upsurge in TV news girls. il Ebony 26:168-70+ Je '71
What it's like to broadcast news; excerpt from address. W. Cronkite; discussion. Sat R 54:46+ Ja 9; 52-3+ F 13 '71

Operas

Abduction from the Seraglio (NET opera theater) P. J. Smith. Hi Fi 21:MA12 Ja '71
Cockerel and nightingale: Le coq d'or and Le rossignol. S. Jenkins. Opera N 36:35 D 18 '71
Musical events; NET opera theatre production, Monteverdi's Orfeo. W. Sargeant. New Yorker 46:90 Ja 30 '71
Musical events; Tchaikovsky's Queen of spades. W. Sargeant. New Yorker 47:94 F 27 '71
NET opera: Hansel and Gretel. S. Jenkins. Opera N 35:33 Ja 30 '71
Orpheus: two versions; NET opera theater. J. W. Freeman. il Opera N 35:33 Mr 20 '71
Queen of spades; NET opera. S. Jenkins. il Opera N 35:33 Mr 20 '71
Tourel as the countess in a TV Queen of spades. I. Kolodin. Sat R 54:6+ Mr 20 '71
See also
Television operas

Performers

Becoming Susan Dey. B. Vachon. il pors Look 35:64-6+ Jl 27 '71
Exciting new TV star goes into orbit; Sandy Duncan of Funny face. M. Davidson. il pors Good H 173:102-3+ N '71
Invasion of the Hollywoodites. M. Williams. Nat R 23:1192 O 22 '71
Now you see 'em, now you don't; nine deposed stars; interviews, ed. by L. Botto. il Look 35:70-3 S 7 '71
Through the years with the blacklist. O. Bean. il Nat R 23:193-5+ F 23 '71
Would you let your daughter do it? views of TV actresses, ed. by J. Hamilton. il Look 35:32-4+ S 7 '71
See also
Nelson, Ozzie, family

Political programs

See Television in politics

Program production

New Van Dyke family blooms in the desert. il pors Life 71:38-9+ S 17 '71
Pilot for a new TV show; Funny face. N. Vogel. il Writers Digest 51:31-4 Ag '71

Program recording

See also
Video recorders and recording

Programming

ABC makes it a three-way race. il Bsns W p28 N 20 '71
Blackmail is beautiful. G. Ace. Sat R 54:4 Ja 16 '71
Hello and goodbye season. G. Ace. Sat R 55:4 Ja 8 '72
How a network boss picks shows. T. Thompson. il pors Life 71:46-50+ S 10 '71
Hunger pangs: 1971-72 season. R. L. Shayon. Sat R 54:22+ S 18 '71
I found a five-and-ten-cent movie in a million-dollar TV set. G. Ace. Sat R 54:8 My 1 '71
Local stations try filling prime time. il Bsns W p 100 S 11 '71
Prime mistake? Newsweek 78:99-100 O 4 '71
Same old tunnel; minority programming. R. L. Shayon. Sat R 54:46 S 4 '71

Programs

See Television programs

Propaganda

International film and television propaganda: campaigns of assistance. B. Rubin. bibliog f il Ann Am Acad 398:81-92 N '71

Psychological aspects

Seeing isn't believing. Sedulus. New Repub 164:30-2 Mr 13 '71
TV's impact on society. D. J. Boorstin. il Life 71:36-9 S 10 '71

Social aspects

Archie Bunker: is bigotry a laughing matter? symposium. il Seventeen 31:108+ Ja '72
Dr Rubin: watching television. T. I. Rubin. il Ladies Home J 89:40 Ja '72
Ecumenical group reflects on woman's image in the media. F. S. Smith. Chr Cent 88:1002+ Ag 25 '71
Looking for a different approach to sadism. C. Horman. il Commonweal 95:281-3 D 17 '71
My phony neighbors and yours. Sedulus. New Repub 164:36-7 Ap 17 '71
Speak up, man. Sedulus. New Repub 164:34-6 Mr 27 '71

TELEVISION broadcasting—Social aspects—
Continued
TV-radio; Upper midwestern conference on broadcasting and the people. R. L. Shayon. Sat R 54:54 My 15 '71
TV; speaking about the unspeakable; reactions to All in the family, with reports by A. R. Martin and J. Morgenstern. il Newsweek 78:52-4+ N 29 '71
TV; the challenge of the 70s; quantity plus quality; excerpts. M. Esslin. il UNESCO Courier 24:4-7+ F '71
Test pattern for living. N. Johnson. il por Sat R 54:12-15+ My 29 '71
Two immodest proposals. Sedulus. New Repub 164:32-3 F 13 '71
See also
MINERVA system
Television broadcasting—Psychological aspects
Television broadcasting and Negroes
Television broadcasting and the deaf

Sound effects
Last laugh; use of laugh tracks. J. Morgenstern. Newsweek 77:12 Ap 12 '71

Sports
And here, to bring you the play by play; baseball announcers. J. Kirshenbaum. il Sports Illus 35:32-5+ S 13 '71
Basketball is black. Cyclops. il Life 70:8 My 28 '71
Fight: Ali-Frazier battle. New Yorker 47:32-5 Mr 20 '71
New champ? closed circuit vs network television. R. L. Shayon. Sat R 54:31 Ap 10 '71
Shall we rule these TV egos guilty of unnecessary roughness? ABC pro football broadcast. S. Singer. il Todays Health 49:40-3 D '71
Super spectator and the electric Lilliputians, by W. O. Johnson, jr. Review
Bsns W il p6+ Mr 6 '71. P. Osborne
TV talk:
Announcers in the bullpen. F. Deford. Sports Illus 34:10 Je 28 '71
Closed-circuit, TV. F. Deford. Sports Illus 34:14+ Mr 8 '71
College football on television. J. Craig. Sports Illus 35:11 N 8 '71
NBA championships on ABC. F. Deford. Sports Illus 34:16 My 24 '71
Sports announcing. F. Deford. Sports Illus 34:14 Mr 29 '71
Super bowl. F. Deford. Sports Illus 34:12 F 8 '71
Tennis is increasing in popularity. F. Deford. Sports Illus 35:10 S 13 '71
Wide world of sports. F. Deford. Sports Illus 34:77 Ap 26 '71
They hardly ever knock the products. Cyclops. por Life 71:12 Ag 13 '71
Time of the television football freak. il por Time 99:45 Ja 17 '72
Trade winds; efforts to block closed-circuit bullfight in Madison Square Garden. C. Amory. Sat R 54:10-11 Jl 3 '71
What are they doing with the sacred game of pro football? E. Shrake. pors Sports Illus 35:96-9+ O 25 '71
Wide world of sports. Cyclops. il Life 71:8 Jl 9 '71
You're gonna pay, baby. L. Schecter. il Look 35:42-5 S 7 '71

Study and teaching
Demise of the reluctant reader; Port Washington, N.Y. television reading program. S. Fleming. il Schol Teach Jr/Sr High p 12-13+ Ja 11 '71

Tennis
See Television broadcasting—Sports

Time signals
See Time signals

Canada
End of momma. Sedulus. New Repub 164:29-30 Ja 23 '71

Germany (Federal Republic)
Tube that sees through the Wall: Radio free Berlin; interview, ed. by R. Hemming. H. Petrick. por Sr Schol 98:8+ Mr 8 '71

Great Britain
English channels. G. K. Hodenfield. PTA Mag 65:32-3 F '71
Television violence; revised code on Independent television authority. T. Beeson. Chr Cent 88:1438-9 D 8 '71

Italy
Art of selling; advertising interlude, Carosello. Newsweek 78:85 D 20 '71

Russia
Inside Soviet television. J. Tebbel. Sat R 55:48-9 Ja 8 '72

United States
Stay tuned for the future. Sr Schol 98:21 My 10 '71
TV-radio. R. L. Shayon. See issues of Saturday review
TV: turn-on or turn-off? symposium. il Look 35:14-15+ S 7 '71
What's ahead for television. il Newsweek 77:72-9 My 31 '71
See also
American broadcasting companies
Columbia broadcasting system, inc.
Metromedia, inc.
Television industry—United States

TELEVISION broadcasting, Noncommercial
And now the fourth network. il Newsweek 77:110-11 Mr 29 '71
Carrot for the brute; financing PTV. N. Mark. New Repub 165:24+ D 25 '71
Lid comes off the box. B. Dunn. il Life 70:42-6+ Ap 2 '71
Public vs. private TV. Cyclops. Life 71:12 Jl 23 '71
What's different about public TV? G. Astor. il Look 35:14-15 S 7 '71

TELEVISION broadcasting, Subscription
Up-to-date report on pay TV. il Good H 172:196 My '71

TELEVISION broadcasting and children
Does video violence make Johnny hit back? Sci Digest 71:57 Ja '72
Pest control: the TV problem; with study-discussion program, by M. M. Conant. M. Harris. bibliog il PTA Mag 65:6-8+, 32 My '71
Quieting the children's hour. il Time 97:75 Ap 19 '71
Rx children's television. N. Johnson. PTA Mag 66:21-4 D '71
Sight & sound: a few sensible words about children's TV. M. J. Arlen. McCalls 98:34+ F '71
See also
Television programs—Childrens programs
TELEVISION broadcasting and Negroes
Black-and-white TV. E. Dunbar. il Look 35:31 S 7 '71
TELEVISION broadcasting and the deaf
Hearing and listening. R. L. Shayon. Sat R 54:47 F 6 '71
TELEVISION broadcasting for children. See Television programs—Childrens programs
TELEVISION broadcasting from space
Apollo 15 television from the moon. il Sky & Tel 42:136-8 S '71
TELEVISION broadcasting stations. See Television stations
TELEVISION cables
Antenna lead-ins for TV. F. H. Belt. il Electr World 86:32-4 Ag '71
TELEVISION cameras on space vehicles
TV camera helps diagnose Apollo 14 in-flight problems. Aviation W 94:54 F 22 '71
TELEVISION censorship. See Television broadcasting—Censorship
TELEVISION channels. See Television stations
TELEVISION circuits
All about new no-switch, no-button TV tuning, more on selectivity. R. F. Scott. il Radio-Electr 42:62-3+ My '71
Automatic tint correction in color TV. F. H. Belt. il Electr World 86:45-8 Ag '71
Color TV for 1971. F. H. Belt. il Electr World 85:43-4+ Mr '71
New color circuits for '72. R. F. Scott. il Radio-Electr 43:42-5 Ja '72
Red drive control update. il Radio-Electr 42:95 S '71
Vertical output circuits (title varies) J. Darr. il Radio-Electr 42:77-8 My; 70-2 Je; 65-6 Jl; 64+ Ag '71
TELEVISION commentators. See Television broadcasting—News
TELEVISION commercials. See Television advertising
TELEVISION converters. See Television apparatus
TELEVISION criticism
Notes on a viewer's album. J. Barthel. il Life 71:60-7 S 10 '71
What the viewers say, and do. il Newsweek 77:74 My 31 '71
TELEVISION couplings. See Couplings, Electric
TELEVISION drama. See Television broadcasting—Drama
TELEVISION editing. See Television broadcasting—News
TELEVISION editorials. See Editorials

TELEVISION In aviation
Time/frequency CAS data may be sent via
TV. Aviation W 95:63 S 27 '71
  See also
Television apparatus on aircraft
TELEVISION in business
TV replaces stacks of paperwork. il Bsns W
p48+ Ja 30 '71
TELEVISION in criminal investigation
TV in helicopter aids New York police. K. J.
Stein. il Aviation W 95:42-5 Ag 2 '71
TV patrol; electronic surveillance system,
Mount Vernon, N.Y. Time 97:46 My 10 '71
TELEVISION in education
Big Bird, meet Dick and Jane; a critique of
Sesame street. J. Holt. Atlan 227:72-4+ My
'71
Big sister on Sesame street. il Seventeen 29:
112+ Jl '70
CATV story in Nashvile. S. Smith and R.
W. Bogen. Todays Ed 60:57-8 N '71
CATV story in St Cloud. D. L. Radeke.
il Todays Ed 60:58-9 N '71
Everyman's alma mater; Britain's Open uni-
versity. il Newsweek 77:52+ Ja 25 '71
El Exigente meets the Pepsi generation; com-
mercials in the curriculum. R. Maynard. il
Schol Teach Jr/Sr High p 12-14 My 3 '71
Growing up with the media. P. C. Rule. il
America 125:71-2 Ag 7 '71
Here comes the Electric company. A. C.
Stevens. il Am Ed 7:18-23 N '71
Is Sesame authoritarian? Newsweek 78:68+
S 20 '71
Jewish studies course via TV; City university
of New York. Sch & Soc 99:402 N '71
Sesame under attack. il pors Newsweek 77:
52 My 24 '71
Some things you've wanted to know about
Sesame street. G. A. Bogatz and S. Ball.
il Am Ed 7:11-15 Ap '71; Same. Ed Digest
37:23-6 S '71
Special feature on cable television. il Todays
Ed 60:52-6 N '71
TV education role gains world interest. il
Aviation W 95:70-2+ Ag 23 '71
What's happened to educational TV? F. H.
Belt. il Pop Electr 35:31-5 D '71
  See also
Television broadcasting—Study and teaching
Television stations, Educational
TELEVISION in meteorology
Here's latest on detecting tornadoes by TV.
R. Lutz. il Suc Farm 69:34 My '71
TELEVISION in navigation
Under way with the USPS. R. A. Green.
il Motor B & S 127:26+ Ap '71
TELEVISION in politics
Elections and image building. R. E. Cleary.
il Todays Ed 60:30-2+ D '71
Politics for rich & poor. N. D. Reece. New
Repub 164:8-9 Ja 16 '71; Reply. M. Gravel.
164:32-3 F 20 '71
Reports & comment: Washington. E. B.
Drew. Atlan 227:18+ Mr '71
Time to talk back; Fairness doctrine for
political communication. R. L. Shayon. Sat
R 54:13 D 25 '71
TELEVISION in psychiatry
Consultation by television aids psychiatric
treatment. Todays Health 49:60 My '71
TELEVISION in traffic control
TV monitors a bridge; Verrazano-Narrows
bridge. il Am City 86:76-7 Ja '71
TELEVISION industry
  See also
Confidential communications—Television

Finance
How will television feel after it gives up
smoking? M. Mayer. il Fortune 83:86-9+
Ja '71
Pruning old friends. Time 97:76 F 15 '71

Great Britain
Top grade; L. Grade. por Time 98:80 O 4 '71

South Africa
Apartheid television. Time 97:27 My 10 '71

United States
Black Friday; employee cutbacks. Newsweek
77:55-6 F 22 '71
[Dollar signs] S. Kanfer. il por Time 98:90+
N 1 '71
Future schlock; network retrenchment. Time
97:64 F 1 '71
Madison avenue; TV announcements to woo
young men to the proposed all-volunteer
army. H. Maneloveg. Sat R 54:49+ My 8 '71
TV networks shrug off new competition;
cassettes, cable-TV, and government. il
Bsns W p90-4+ Mr 27 '71
Trade winds; interview. ed. by C. Amory. L.
Brown. Sat R 54:14+ N 13 '71
  See also
Metromedia, inc.

TELEVISION Interference
Battle over a TV antenna; World trade center interference controversy. il Bsns W
p27 N 20 '71
TELEVISION journalism. See Television
broadcasting—News
TELEVISION laws and regulations
Blacks challenge the airwaves; FCC license
contests. P. Garland. il Ebony 26:35-8+
N '70
Captive medium; TV & the First amend-
ment; address, November 23, 1970. B.
Monroe. Vital Speeches 37:267-70 F 15 '71
Chickens and foxes; cases involving secrecy
of program records of broadcasters whose
license renewals are challenged by citizen
groups. R. L. Shayon. Sat R 54:73 O 16
'71
Controversial time; challenge to new rulings.
R. L. Shayon. Sat R 54:12 N 20 '71
Lion, lion, burning bright; new rulings on
Fairness doctrine and paid controversial
announcements. R. L. Shayon. Sat R
54:18+ S 11 '71
Should the FCC reward stations that do a
good job? granting of licenses. M. Cohn. il
Sat R 54:45-7 Ag 14 '71
Staying on the air; Pastore bill and license
renewals. New Repub 164:9 Je 26 '71
Tanks but no tanks; fairness doctorine. T.
Asher. New Repub 164:17-19 Je 26 '71
Television and the First amendment. F. W.
Friendly. Sat R 55:46-7+ Ja 8 '72
Think small; extending the cigarette doc-
trine to automobile advertising. Newsweek
78:63 Ag 30 '71
Time to talk back; Fairness doctrine for
political communication. R. L. Shayon. Sat
R 54:13 D 25 '71
Very cold turkey; banning of lyrics referring
to illegal drugs. R. L. Shayon. Sat R 54:22
My 1 '71
Who will make TV's new rules? il Newsweek
77:76-7 My 31 '71
  See also
Television broadcasting—Censorship
TELEVISION licenses. See Television laws
and regulations
TELEVISION news. See Television broadcast-
ing—News
TELEVISION operas
New Tv opera by Britten; Owen Wingrave.
I. Kolodin. Sat R 54:52 My 22 '71
Opera *mundi*; B. Britten's Owen Wingrave.
W. Bender. il Time 97:74 My 24 '71
Owen Wingrave; Benjamin Britten's televis-
ion opera. S. Jenkins. Opera N 35:27 Je
12 '71
Taping Le rossignol for television. J. Hie-
menz. il Hi Fi 21:71-3 N '71
Tippett's Knot garden. Britten's Owen Win-
grave. E. Greenfield. il Hi Fi 21:MA30-1
Ag '71
TELEVISION performers. See Television
broadcasting—Performers
TELEVISION production. See Television broad-
casting—Program production
TELEVISION programming. See Television
broadcasting—Programming
TELEVISION programs
But where's the Eurasian lady consumer pro-
tectionist? D. Brudnoy. il Nat R 23:269-70
Mr 9 '71
Close-up (cont of) Spotlight! E. Miller. See
issues of Seventeen
Crime in the screens; fall season. G. Ace.
Sat R 54:6 O 23 '71
Hunger pangs; 1971-72 season. R. L. Shayon.
Sat R 54:22+ S 18 '71
Life TV review. Cyclops. See issues of Life
Medium where even the grass won't grow
up. Cyclops. Life 71:16 D 31 '71
New? Season. il Look 35:20-1 S 7 '71
New season. R. Burgheim. il Time 98:58-9 S
27:70-1 O 4 '70
New TV shows. N. Vogel. il Writers Digest
51:32-3+ Jl '71
1971's ten most. Time 99:72 Ja 3 '72
Public season; fall lineup of Public broad-
casting service. R. Burgheim. il Time 98:
78+ O 18 '71
Recycled waste; reruns and replacements. R.
Burgheim. il Time 97:64+ F 1 '71
Rich half hour of everything; programs of
community interest over Boston's UHF
channel. Cyclops. il Life 71:14 N 12 '71
Sight & sound. C. Irving. See issues of Mc-
Call's
Sorry season. il Newsweek 78:78+ S 27 '71
TV year of social critique; 1970-71 television
season. R. L. Shayon. Sat R 54:54 My 8 '71
Teleguide. A. D. Beck. il Sr Schol Teach ed
99:5 N 15 '71
Teleguide. A. Berle. il Schol Teach Jr/Sr
High p31 Ja '72

TELEVISION programs—*Continued*
Teleguide. K. Bobrowsky. il Schol Teach Jr/Sr High p28 Ja '72
Teleguide. K. C. Cremonini. Schol Teach Jr/Sr High p48 S '71
Teleguide. L. Gardner. il Schol Teach Jr/Sr High p31 N '71
Teleguide. F. S. Gross. il Schol Teach Jr/Sr High p 15 D '71
Teleguide. S. Jantzen. Sr Schol Teach ed 99:4 Ja 10 '72
Teleguide. L. A. Markham. il Sr Schol Teach ed 99:7 N 15 '71
Teleguide. T. Willis. il Schol Teach Jr/Sr High p35 My 3 '71
Television. P. Hudson. See issues of Senior scholastic
Television. Sedulus. See issues of New republic
Television to turn on. I. Stanger. il Harp Baz 105:74+ N: 77 D '71
Time out for TV. See issues of PTA magazine
Viewer. G. Ace. Sat R 54:4 S 11 '71
What to do with TV? Nat R 23:1005 S 10 '71
What's ahead for television. il Newsweek 77: 72-9 My 31 '71
What's happening. G. Shalit. See issues of Ladies' home journal
Why producers give TV programs away. il Bsns W p41 Ap 10 '71
Winner is, the losers are . . . il pors Time 97: 50-1 Mr 29 '71
  See also
Environmental news
Television broadcasting—Drama
Television broadcasting, Noncommercial
Television criticism

Ballet
See Television programs—Dance programs

Biographical programs
Great lives on TV. R. Schickel. Harper 242: 28+ Ja '71

Childrens programs
Children's hour. J. Morgenstern. Newsweek 78:9 Ag 16 '71
Children's TV: slow learner: international survey. Sat R 54:48 Ag 21 '71
Child's guide to television. P. Pierce. il McCalls 98:48 S '71
Junior season opens. K. Kelly. il Time 98: 82+ S 20 '71
New TV shows for children. C. Terry. il Good H 173:88 O '71
This program may be harmful to your child; federal study on TV and violence. R. L. Tobin. il Sat R 54:63-4 O 9 '71
Time out for TV. See issues of PTA magazine
Wrong way down Sesame street. il Life 71: 18 O 15 '71
  See also
Television in education

Conversation programs
Atlanta's charmer on channel 5; weekly black talk show. il pors Ebony 26:134-6+ N '70
Back here: doing talk shows in London; interview. D. Cavett. New Yorker 47:34-5 Je 5 '71
Chicago's Underground news. Cyclops. Life 71:14 Jl 2 '71
Profiles; J. Franklin. W. Whitworth. por New Yorker 47:44-6+ My 22 '71
Soliology of dumb: one evening too many with Carson, Griffin, and Cavett. C. Wells. il Esquire 75:102-8+ My '71
Today; a TV institution. T. Thompson. il Life 71:67-8 D 10 '71

Anecdotes, facetiae, satire, etc.
Doing what comes fatuously. G. Ace. Sat R 54:6 My 22 '71

Cookery programs
Critic in the kitchen. il por Newsweek 77: 65+ Ap 26 '71

Crime programs
Private eye. Cyclops. Life 71:12 Ag 27 '71
Private eyes and heavy lids. Cyclops. il Life 71:18 O 22 '71

Dance programs
Bert Bacharach special. M. Harriton. Dance Mag 45:95 My '71
Dames at sea goes dancing. R. Zachary. il Dance Mag 45:28-31 O '71
Fanfare: Alicia Alonso, NET (channel 13) N. M. Stoop. Dance Mag 45:81 Jl '71

Fanfare: ambassadors of dance, NET (channel 13) N. M. Stoop. Dance Mag 45:98 Ag '71
Fanfare: Cullberg, NET (channel 13) N. M. Stoop. Dance Mag 45·81 Jl '71
L'oiseau de feu, French television service. M. Marks. Dance Mag 45:81 Jl '71
Nijinsky by Bejart, parts I & II, Camera three. N. M. Stoop. Dance Mag 46:89-90 Ja '72
Poppy series: Soul. N. M. Stoop. Dance Mag 45:102 N '71

Dancing
Dance as filler: TV's use and abuse. V. H. Swisher. il Dance Mag 45:78-80 O '71

Documentary programs
See Television programs, Documentary

Dramas
Can two TV beauties survive TV? interview, ed. by R. Meryman. P. Lipton; J. Sommars. il pors Life 70:54-6 Ja 22 '71
Phasing out Ivan the Terrible. R. L. Shayon. Sat R 54:22 N 27 '71
That family sure has its share of problems; daytime serials. L. Botto. il por Look 35:64-5 S 7 '71

Foreign language programs
End of momma. Sedulus. New Repub 164: 29-30 Ja 23 '71

Garden programs
Lady who talks to plants; interview, ed. by M. Mercer. T. Cruso. il pors McCalls 98:80-1+ Ap '71

Humorous programs
Archie Bunker: is bigotry a laughing matter? symposium. il Seventeen 31:108+ Ja '72
Blackmail is beautiful. G. Ace. Sat R 54:4 Ja 16 '71
Meet Archie Bunker and the man who created All in the family: interview. ed. by P. Hudson. N. Lear. il pors Sr Schol 99:6-7+ O 25 '71

Negro programs
Atlanta's charmer on channel 5: weekly black talk show. il pors Ebony 26:134-6+ N '70
Blacks challenge the airwaves; FCC license contests. P. Garland. il Ebony 26:35-8+ N '70

Operas
Musical events; NET opera theatre broadcast of Offenbach's Tales of Hoffmann. W. Sargeant. New Yorker 47:158+ D 11 '71

Program rating
But do we like what we watch? Life 71:40-4 S 10 '71

Quiz shows
Air. R. Adler. New Yorker 47:46-9 D 25 '71

Religious programs
Christian television festival: making ultimate concern visual. M. Furlong. Chr Cent 88: 779-80 Je 23 '71
Electronic evangelist. il por Time 97:70+ My 17 '71

Reviews, etc.
All in the family
  Life il 70:10 Mr 19 '71
  Life il 71:61-2+ N 19 '71
  Nation 213:509-10 N 15 '71
  Newsweek 77:55 Ja 18 '71
  Newsweek il 77:64+ Mr 15 '71
  Newsweek il 78:52-4+ N 29 '71
  Sat R 54:20 Mr 27 '71
  Sat R 55:8 Ja 8 '72
  Sr Schol il 99:20-1 S 20 '71
  Sr Schol il 99:6-7+ O 25 '71
All the way home
  Sr Schol il 99:20-1 N 15 '71
  Sr Schol Teach ed il 99:7 N 15 '71
Bold ones
  Life 70:11 Je 18 '71
Cade's county
  Writers Digest 52:51-2 Ja '72
Carol Burnett show
  Life il 70:10 Ap 2 '71
Catch 44
  Life il 71:14 N 12 '71
Caught in the middle
  Sat R 54:46 S 4 '71
Decisions! Decisions!
  Sat R 54:18 O 9 '71
Dick Cavett show
  Life por 71:12 D 10 '71
  Sat R 55:7 Ja 1 '72

TELEVISION programs—Reviews, etc.—*Cont.*
Eagle and the hawk
    Sr Schol Teach ed il 99:5 N 15 '71
Electric company
    Am Ed il 7:18-23 N '71
    Newsweek il 78:66-7 Jl 5 '71
    Newsweek il 78:82+ N 1 '71
    Time il 98:46 O 25 '71
Firing line
    Life 71:11 Jl 16 '71
First Churchills
    America 124:262-3 Mr 13 '71
    Life il 70:18 Mr 5 '71
    Time il 97:66 F 8 '71
    Vogue 157:158 Ap 1 '71
Funny face
    Life il 71:8 N 26 '71
Great American dream machine
    Bsns W p23 F 6 '71
    Life 70:16 F 19 '71
    McCalls il 98:14+ My '71
    New Repub 164:33 Ja 30 '71
    Newsweek il 77:55 Ja 18 '71
    Time 97:65-6 F 8 '71
    Vogue 157:116 Mr 15 '71
Idea of North
    Sat R 54:43 F 13 '71
It couldn't be done
    Sr Schol 98:20-1 F 8 '71
Jane Eyre
    Sr Schol il 98:22-3 Mr 15 '71
Joyce and Barbara: for adults only
    Newsweek il 77:93 Ap 12 '71
Jude the obscure
    Life il 71:13 N 5 '71
    Schol Teach Jr/Sr High p48 S '71
Lassie
    Life il 71:11 O 29 '71
Marcus Welby, M.D.
    Life il por 70:18 My 14 '71
    Look il 35:56-9 Mr 23 '71
NET playhouse
    Time 97:66 F 8 '71
New Dick Van Dyke show
    Chr Cent 88:1530-1 D 29 '71
New performers
    Sr Schol 98:22 Ap 5 '71
Odd couple
    Writers Digest 52:47-8+ Ja '72
Penelope's Hellenic hour
    New Repub 164:29-30 Ja 23 '71
Peyton Place
    Esquire il 76:160-8+ D '71
Plot to murder Hitler
    Sr Schol 99:19 D 6 '71
Possessed
    Life il 70:10 Je 4 '71
Red Skelton show
    Nat R 23:823-4 Jl 27 '71
Sesame street
    Am Ed 7:11-15 Ap '71
    Atlan 227:72-4+ My '71
    Life il 71:18 O 15 '71
    Newsweek il 77:52 My 24 '71
    UNESCO Courier il 24:8-9 F '71
Shirley's world
    Sat R 54:26 O 23 '71
    Sr Schol il 99:18 O 11 '71
Sit down, shut up or get out
    Sat R 54:23 Jl 17 '71
Six wives of Henry VIII
    Life 71:14 Ag 6 '71
    Sat R 54:18 Ag 28 '71
    Time il 98:51 Ag 9 '71
    Vogue 158:74 Ag 1 '71
Snow goose
    Schol Teach Jr/Sr High p31 N '71
    Sr Schol il 99:18-19 N 8 '71
Song of summer
    Harper 242:28+ Ja '71
Sonny and Cher
    Life il 71:18 S 17 '71
Story theatre
    Life il 71:6 D 3 '71
To be young, gifted and black
    Life il 72:14 Ja 14 '72
Today
    Life il 71:67-8 D 10 '71
Turned on crisis
    Sr Schol il 98:20-1 F 1 '71
Vanished
    Sr Schol il 98:22 Mr 8 '71
You are there
    Life il 71:20 O 8 '71
TELEVISION programs, Documentary
Television. H. Rasky. Nation 212:218-19+ F 15 '71
    See also
Television programs—Biographical programs

Reviews, etc.
Advocates
    Life il 71:10 Jl 30 '71
American revolution: 1770-1783
    Time il 97:46+ Ap 5 '71

Archaeology on CBS
    Life il 70:18 Je 11 '71
Basic training
    Life 71:10 O 1 '71
    Newsweek 78:99 O 4 '71
Behind the lines
    Sat R 54:16+ O 30 '71
Black view of South Africa
    Nat R 23:415 Ap 20 '71
Boating with the power squadron
    Motor B & S 127:26+ Ap '71
But what if the dream comes true?
    Time il 98:64 D 13 '71
Death of Diem
    Schol Teach Jr/Sr High il p 15 D '71
Heifetz
    Sat R il pors 54:45-7 Ap 24 '71
    Sr Schol 98:20 Ap 19 '71
Hello, Philadelphia, the world is watching
    Sat R 54:50 Jl 24 '71
Last tribes of Mindanao
    Schol Teach Jr/Sr High il p31 Ja '72
Mysterious spring: Africa's Mzima
    Schol Teach Jr/Sr High il p28 Ja '72
Nader report
    New Repub 164:40-2 Ja 2 '71
Nuremberg and Vietnam: who is guilty?
    Sat R 54:34 Jl 3 '71
Part of the family
    Sat R 54:53 Je 12 '71
Passover
    Chr Today 15:40 Mr 26 '71
    Chr Today 15:33 Ap 23 '71
Red China
    Life il 71:12 S 10 '71
Say good-bye
    Field & S 75:6 Ap '71
    Field & S 76:4 My '71
Selling of the Pentagon
    America 124:541-2 My 22 '71
    Harper 242:30-3+ Je '71
    Harper 243:40+ D '71
    N Y Times Mag il p25-7+ My 16 '71
    Nat R 23:855-7+ Ag 10 '71
    Nation 212:581 My 10 '71
    Newsweek il 77:74 Mr 8 '71
    Sat R 54:40 Mr 20 '71
    Time 97:68 Jl 5 '71
    Time il 97:46 Ap 5 '71
    Time il 97:56+ Ap 12 '71
Stravinsky remembered
    Life il 71:13 N 19 '71
Suffer the little children
    Sr Schol Teach ed 99:4 Ja 10 '72
Thirty minutes
    Newsweek il por 78:74-5 D 13 '71
This child is rated X
    Sat R 54:51 My 22 '71
Under surveillance
    Time il 99:72 Ja 3 '72
Venice be damned
    Schol Teach Jr/Sr High il p35 My 3 '71
Youth speaks
    Sr Schol 98:22 Ap 5 '71
TELEVISION projection
Thin-film mirror simplifies projection TV. J. R. Free. il Pop Sci 198:16 Mr '71
TELEVISION public speaking
Setting a TV image for businessmen. Bsns W p77 Ja 30 '71
TELEVISION receivers
Black-and-white TV sets. il Consumer Rep 36:363-7 Je '71
Cheerful earfuls. il Seventeen 29:136-9 S '70
1972 TV sets are more automated. il Consumer Bul 54:7-12 D '71

Color receivers
  See Television receivers, Color

Control
Remote U.H.F.-TV signal-seeking system. P. LeFevre. il Electr World 86:66-7 Jl '71

Maintenance and repair
Eliminating hum bars. il Radio-Electr 43:70 Ja '72
How to repair your own TV. il Mech Illus 67:106-8 S '71
In the shop, with Jack. J. Darr. See issues of Radio-electronics to April 1971
Kwik-fix picture and waveform charts. See issues of Radio-electronics
Switching diodes for TV front ends. J. Darr. il Radio-Electr 43:72+ Ja '72
TV scope; making a TV set trace its own i.f. response curve. E. Strauss. il Radio-Electr 42:44-5 D '71
Testing IC's in TV receivers. F. H. Belt. il Electr World 86:49-52+ N '71
    See also
Television service shops

Picture tubes
  See also
Television receivers, Color—Picture tubes

TELEVISION receivers—*Continued*

Safety devices and measures

TV service and safety. R. E. Herzog. il Electr World 85:30-1 F '71

TELEVISION receivers, Color

Bigger, better Sony color-TV set. il Consumer Rep 36:524 S '71

Color TV consoles. il Consumer Rep 37:8-14 Ja '72

Color TV for 1971. F. H. Belt. il Electr World 85:23-6+ F; 43-4+ Mr '71

Color TV 1972; symposium. il Radio-Electr 43:33-45+ Ja '72

For hobbyists: a good color TV kit, but; Heathkit GR270 color TV kit. il Consumer Rep 36:466-8 Ag '71

For '72, color TV goes modular and solid state. J. R. Free. il pors Pop Sci 199:82-5 N '71

Heathkit GR-169 solid-state portable color television kit. il Radio-Electr 42:74 Jl '71

Kit-builder's dream job; Heathkit. S. M. Gallager. il Pop Mech 136:118-19 Ag '71

Zenith goes plug-in. S. Prentiss. il Radio-Electr 42:62-3+ O '71

Design

Color TV goes modular for '72. L. Allen. il Radio-Electr 43:33-7+ Ja '72

Maintenance and repair

Change color pix tubes faster. T. Richmond. il Radio-Electr 42:33-5 My '71

Color I.F. alignment techniques. R. L. Goodman. il Radio-Electr 42:38-42 N '71

Color-killer adjustments. il Radio-Electr 42:72 Ap '71

Color TV; frequency-of-repair records. il Consumer Rep 37:15-17 Ja '72

Lightning and color TV sets. E. Cunningham. il Radio-Electr 42:48 Jl '71

Symptom: no color. A. Margolis. il Radio-Electr 42:23-5 D '71

TV repair woes: light at the end of the tube? il Consumer Rep 36:438-41 Jl '71

Picture tubes

Trinitron versus shadowmask. F. H. Belt. il Radio-Electr 43:38-41 Ja '72

Radiation hazards

Measuring color-TV generated X-rays. J. G. Ello. il Electr World 86:37-9+ Jl '71

Safety devices and measures

X-ray monitor for TV; of limited use. Consumer Rep 36:136 Mr '71

Tuning

Automatic tint controls for everyone. H. O. Maxwell. il Radio-Electr 43:53-6+ Ja '72

TELEVISION receivers, Portable

Portable TVs you can play at a picnic, on a patio, by a pool. L. Buckwalter. il Pop Mech 136:104-7 Jl '71

TELEVISION receivers industry. See Television apparatus industry

TELEVISION relay systems
    See also
Communications satellites

TELEVISION reporters. See Television broadcasting—News

TELEVISION script writing. See Television authorship

TELEVISION scripts. See Television authorship

TELEVISION service shops

Licenses

TV repair woes: light at the end of the tube? il Consumer Rep 36:438-41 Jl '71

TELEVISION stations

Channel crossing; Boston's WHDH-TV. Newsweek 78:48+ S 13 '71

Chickens and foxes; cases involving secrecy of program records of broadcasters whose license renewals are challenged by citizen groups. R. L. Shayon. Sat R 54:73 O 16 '71

Don't broadcast this, but pollution can get you fired! reprint. C. Gillespie. il Audubon 73:103-5 Ja '71

Dynamite in pollution; Jacksonville, Fla. TV station WJXT reports on local polluters. C. Gillespie; discussion. Nation 211:674; 212:258+ D 28 '70, Mr 1 '71

Should the FCC reward stations that do a good job? granting of licenses. M. Cohn. il Sat R 54:45-7 Ag 14 '71
    See also
American broadcasting companies
Metromedia, inc.

TELEVISION stations, Educational

Cinderella network. T. O'Flaherty. il Am Ed 7:14-17 N '71; Same abr. with title PBS: the Cinderella network. Read Digest 99:43-8 N '71

Educational broadcasting facilities program; grants for educational television and radio. il Am Ed 7:24 N '71

Living library; Texas tech university station. KTXT-TV. J. D. Mertes and others. il pors Parks & Rec 6:34-5+ O '71

TELEVISION stations, Municipal

City-owned and operated TV stations; Denver and St. Louis. G. M. Chamberlain. il Am City 86:103-4+ Ap '71

TELEVISION studio bands. See Bands (music)

TELEVISION technicians. See Television workers

TELEVISION telephone combination. See Telephone—Television combination

TELEVISION test apparatus. See Testing instruments

TELEVISION time signals. See Time signals

TELEVISION towers

Monster mast; television antenna to rise above city. il Time 99:54 Ja 3 '72

TELEVISION transmission

Interference

See Television interference

TELEVISION workers

Vocation profile: the TV product-service technician. R. E. Herzog. il por Electr World 85:40-1 Je '71

TELEVISION writing. See Television authorship

TELFER, Richard G.

Differentiation: a means for improving staff utilization. Clear House 46:112-15 O '71

TELLEEN, Robert

Informal dramatics can provide the means. il Camp Mag 43:12-13 My '71

TELLER, Aaron Joseph

Specialist in pollution control. il por Bsns W p59 Mr 6 '71 *

TELLER, Edward

Era of big science; adaptation of address, December 1970. il Bul Atom Sci 27:34-6 Ap '71
    about

Mau-mauing Dr Teller. W. I. Scobie. Nat R 23:697-8 Je 29 '71 *

TELTSCHER, Herry O.

How to analyze your child's handwriting; excerpt from Handwriting. Ladies Home J 88:92+ Mr '71

TEMIN, Howard Martin

RNA-directed DNA synthesis; with biographical sketch. il Sci Am 226:10, 24-33 bibliog(p 122) Ja '72
    about

Reverse transcription: one year later. B. J. Culliton. Science 172:926-8 My 28 '71 *

Teminism and cancer. J. L. Arehart. Sci N 100:317 N 6 '71 *

War on cancer: progress report. il Newsweek 77:84-6+ F 22 '71 *

TEMPER
    See also
Anger

TEMPERAMENT

Difficult baby is born that way. B. W. Wyden. il N Y Times Mag p67+ Mr 21 '71; Discussion. p60-1 Ap 11 '71
    See also
Typology (psychology)

TEMPERANCE societies
    See also
Woman's Christian temperance union

TEMPERATURE
    See also
Atmospheric temperature
Climate
Lakes—Temperature
Ocean temperature
Plants, Effect of temperature on
Rivers—Temperature
Soil temperature

Measurement

How accurately can temperature be measured? W. T. Gray and D. I. Finch. il Phys Today 24:32-40 S '71
    See also
Thermocouples
Thermometers and thermometry

Physiological effects

Hippocrates, thermal stress, and stroke mortality, 1966. L. A. Helfand and C. Bridger. il Weatherwise 24:100-4 Je '71

TEMPERATURE—Physiological effects—*Cont.*
Sugar transport: effect of temperature on concentrative uptake of α-methylglucoside by kidney cortex slices. P. McNamara and others. bibliog il Science 172:1033-4 Je 4 '71
  See also
Fishes, Effect of temperature on

TEMPERATURE, Animal and human
On cooling hot dogs. Chem 44:5 My '71
Pineal function in sparrows: circadian rhythms and body temperature. S. Binkley and others. bibliog il Science 174:311-14 O 15 '71
Thermosensitivity of neurons in the sensorimotor cortex of the cat. J. L. Barker and D. O. Carpenter; reply with rejoinder. J. S. Eisenman and H. M. Edinger. bibliog Science 172:1360-2 Je 25 '71
  See also
Hypothermia

TEMPERATURE changes, Global. See Global temperature changes

TEMPERATURE inversions
Episode 104. V. Brodine. bibliog il Environ 13:2-24+ Ja '71

TEMPERATURES, Low. See Low temperatures

TEMPEST; drama. See Shakespeare, W.— Plays

TEMPLE, Henry John, 3d viscount Palmerston. See Palmerston. H. J. T.

TEMPLE, Shirley
U.S. discusses priorities for the 1972 U.N. conference on the human environment; statement, September 20, 1971. Dept State Bul 65:531-4 N 8 '71
When I was 17; interview, ed. by B. Kevles. pors Seventeen 30:131+ O '71

TEMPLE music institute. See Temple university, Philadelphia

TEMPLE university, Philadelphia
Temple festival gets a roof over its head. J. Felton. Hi Fi 21:MA19+ N '71

TEMPLE university music festival. See Music festivals—Pennsylvania

TEMPLER, Donald I.
Analyzing the psychotherapist. Ment Hy 55: 234-6 Ap '71

TEMPLES

Egypt
5 million dollars needed to save Philae monuments. il UNESCO Courier 24:62-3 Ag '71
To save the Pearl of Egypt; temples of Philae. il Sat R 54:73 O 2 '71
  See also
Abu Simbel, Temples of

Hawaii
Restored temple in Makaha Valley. il Sunset 147:22 D '71

TEMPLIN, Phillip S.
Washington front (cont) America 124:83, 110, 193 Ja 30-F 6, 27 '71

TEMPO (music)
  See also
Metronomes

TEMPTATION
Grace to say no! L. N. Bell. Chr Today 15:36-7 Mr 12 '71
One way. L. N. Bell. Chr Today 16:20-1 Ja 7 '72

TEMPTATIONS (rock group) See Rock groups

TENANT farming. See Farm tenancy

TENANTS. See Landlord and tenant

TENCIN, Claudine Alexandrine Guérin de
Liberation of Mme de Tencin. M. Bishop. por Horizon 13:54-6 Sum '71 •

TENENBAUM, Samuel
Are our cities dying? Read Digest 99:170-2 Ag '71

TENER, Morton
Training your staff to handle ecological programs. Camp Mag 43:11 F '71

TENNECO, Inc.
Fun vs. games. il Forbes 108:35-6 Jl 1 '71

TENNEN, Steven
Plight of Farmer Jones; drama. Plays 31: 66-8 N '71

TENNESSEE
  See also
Architecture, Domestic—Tennessee
Great Smoky Mountains National Park
Hunting—Tennessee
Lookout Mountain

Antiquities
Did Jews reach America first? il Sci Digest 70:39-40 Ag '71

Historic houses, etc.
Hermitage, home of Andrew Jackson. S. F. Horn. il Antiques 100:413-17 S '71
Historic sites in Tennessee. R. M. McBride. il Antiques 100:394-401 S '71

History
Antiques; in Tennessee; symposium. il Antiques 100:376-441 S '71

Maps
Tennessee, historical introduction. W. T. Alderson. il Antiques 100:378-81 S '71

Politics and government
Annals of politics: senatorial campaign: A. Gore vs. W. E. Brock. R. E. Harris. New Yorker 47:34-54 Jl 10 '71
End of a populist; A. Gore. D. Halberstam. il por Harper 242:35-45 Ja '71

TENNESSEE cabinetmakers. See Cabinetmakers

TENNESSEE furniture. See Furniture, American

TENNESSEE-Tombigbee waterway project. See Waterways—United States

TENNESSEE. University, Knoxville
Is a mustache just peanuts? G. S. Brown. il por Sports Illus 34:38-40+ Je 14 '71

TENNESSEE VALLEY authority
Let's look toward an early end of strip mining. R. Starnes. il Field & S 76:12+ Ag '71
Striking the balance; TVA use of 2,4-D to control Eurasian watermilfoil. E. Hirst and H. Bank. bibliog il Environ 13:34-41 N '71
TVA ravages the land. K. Hechler. Nat Parks & Con Mag 45:15-16 Jl '71; Same Cur 132:35-9 S '71

TENNEY committee. See California—Legislature—Joint fact-finding committee on un-American activities

TENNIS
Big reach for a net profit: R. Laver in Tennis champions classic at Madison Square Garden. A. Wright. il por Sports Illus 34: 56-7 Mr 29 '71
But it looked like a great new racket; pro tennis, ed. by F. Deford. B. Briner. il Sports Illus 34:56-8+ Ap 19 '71
Chips, chops, drops and lobs: B. Riggs. G. S. Brown. il por Sports Illus 34:60+ Ja 18 '71
Chrissie; United States Open championships. por Newsweek 78:58 S 20 '71
Cliffhanger at Longwood; U.S. professional tennis championship. B. Collins. il Sports Illus 35:65-7 Ag 16 '71
Closing up the longest Open. L. Keith. il Sports Illus 35:73 S 27 '71
Happiness is six hours a day with your eye on the ball; C. Evert. L. Keith. il por Sports Illus 45:58-61 Jl 26 '71
He was more like a regiment. G. Brown. il por Sports Illus 35:28-9 O 18 '71
Hollywood tennis does socko biz. D. Haber. il Sports Illus 34:42-4+ Mr 8 '71
Little red machine misses a beat; Philadelphia International. W. Bingham. Sports Illus 34:59 F 22 '71
Man named Smith; U.S. Open. il por Time 98:61 S 27 '71
Marty just might be the man; best bet for U.S. victory at Forest Hills. F. Deford. il por Sports Illus 35:47-8 Ag 30 '71
More Joan of Arc than Shirley Temple: C. Evert. R. Blount. il pors Sports Illus 35: 30-1 S 20 '71
Respectable rocket; R. Laver. por Time 98: 43 Jl 5 '71
Rocket heard round the world. J. Underwood. il pors Sports Illus 34:80-4+ My 31 '71
She's just one of the guys. B. Sales. il por Todays Health 49:19-22+ Ap '71
Singalong with Goolagong; winner of Wimbledon tournament. il pors Life 71:32-3 Jl 16 '71
Sporting scene; troubles. H. W. Wind. New Yorker 47:98-108+ O 2 '71
Tennis: the smash sport of the '70s. R. Daley. il Vogue 157:126-9+ My '71
Waltz at Wimbledon. W. Bingham. il pors Sports Illus 35:14-17 Jl 12 '71
Winner takes $50,000 loser, $1 million; Rosewall beat Laver to win World championship tennis. J. Jares. il por Sports Illus 35:28-9 D 6 '71
Women lobbers; ladies' pro tennis tour. il pors Newsweek 77:90-1 My 3 '71
  See also
International lawn tennis federation
Paddle tennis

TENNIS—*Continued*

Anecdotes, facetiae, satire, etc.

In the mind's eye; competing at Wimbledon. G. Plimpton. Sports Illus 35:50-2+ Jl 5 '71
Serving up a new game of life. S. Dryer. il Sports Illus 34:46-8+ Ap 26 '71

Equipment and supplies

Tennis for one, anyone? il Consumer Rep 36: 644 N '71

History

Sphairistiké, anyone? E. M. Halliday. il Am Heritage 22:48-59 Je '71

Study and teaching

Rod Laver holds court; teach the game to your children. R. Laver. il pors Ladies Home J 88:88+ S '71

TENNIS, Table. See Table tennis

TENNIS balls
Tennis balls. il Consumer Rep 36:412-14 Jl '71

TENNIS clubs. See Sports clubs

TENNIS courts
Have you tried platform tennis? Maplewood, N.J. W. D. Carew. il Am City 86:22 Jl '71
Making the most of tennis courts. il Parks & Rec 6:37 My '71

Lighting

Tennis court lighting for pros and amateurs; Brookline, Mass. il Am City 86:114 N '71

TENNIS elbow. See Epicondylitis

TENNIS players
Billie Jean King goes for the net profits. R. Woodbury. il por Life 71:77 N 19 '71
Sporting scene; troubles. H. W. Wind. New Yorker 47:98-108+ O 2 '71
See also
International lawn tennis federation
United States lawn tennis association
also names of tennis players, e.g. R. G. Laver

TENNY, Ralph
Operational amplifier. il Pop Electr 35:30-5+ Ag; 61-6 S '71

TENONING machines
Build a tenoning attachment for your table saw. R. K. Wallace. il Pop Mech 136:146-7 Jl '71

TENORS. See Singers

TENSION (psychology) See Stress (physiology)

TENT trailers. See Automobile trailers

TENTS
And now the RV tent. C. B. Colby. il Outdoor Life 148:12+ Ag '71
Giving camping a second chance. C. B. Colby. il Outdoor Life 148:12+ S '71
How to choose a tent. T. Trueblood. il Field & S 75:22+ Mr '71
New sheik; tent by Angelo Donghia. il Vogue 157:104-5 Mr 15 '71
Tents. il Consumer Rep 36:296-301 My '71
Tot's play tent you can make in one day. C. Houck. il Parents Mag 46:56 Jl '71

TENURE, Academic. See College professors and instructors—Tenure

TENURE, Teacher. See Teachers—Tenure

TENURE of union officers. See Trade unions —Officials—Tenure

TEPE YAHYA excavations. See Iran—Antiquities

TERATOLOGY. See Abnormalities (animals)

TERESA, Mother
Mother Teresa of Calcutta. America 125:335 O 30 '71 *
No substitutes. R. Haughton. il Cath World 213:167-8 Jl '71 *
Something beautiful for God, by M. Muggeridge. Review
America 125:380-2 N 6 '71. Q. Lauer *
Commonweal 95:163-4 N 12 '71. M. Ward *
New Repub 165:35-6 O 16 '71. P. O'Donovan *

TERESA, Vincent
Pay the Piranha. por Time 98:22 Ag 9 '71
Rogue's gallery. por Newsweek 783:23 Ag 9 '71 *

TERLON, Claire. See Teterin, G. jt. auth.

TERM insurance. See Insurance, Life—Policies

TERM papers. See English language—Composition

TERMAN, Frederick E.
Supply of scientific and engineering manpower: surplus or shortage? bibliog il Science 173:399-405 Jl 30 '71

TERMINAL buildings
Order at the docks; Seatrain terminal at Weehauken, N.J. il Arch Forum 134:32-5 Ap '71

TERMINAL buildings, Airport. See Airport buildings

TERMINAL disease. See Diseases

TERMINALS (transportation)
See also
Chicago—Stations

TERMINOLOGY. See subhead Terminology under various subjects, e.g. Investments— Terminology

TERMITES
Termite Mary; Formosan termites. Newsweek 78:111-12 N 15 '71
Termites reveal hidden gold treasure. il Sci Digest 70:78-81 O '71

TERNS
Early warning of the terns. H. Hays and R. W. Riseborough. il Natur Hist 80:38-47 N '71
What a place to lay an egg! T. R. Howell. il Nat Geog 140:414-19 S '71

TERRA sigillata (pottery) See Pottery, Roman

TERRACES (agriculture)
Terrace gardens are easy with a tiller. J. R. Coggins. il Org Gard & Farm 18:58-9 Je '71
They work together to solve erosion problems. C. E. Sommers. il Suc Farm 69:24-5 Ag '71

TERRACES (outdoor living areas) See Outdoor rooms

TERRARIUMS
Bottle garden, the easy way. J. Capotosto. il Mech Illus 67:73 My '71
First you get yourself a very big bottle. il Sunset 147:250 O '71
Garden under glass. il Bet Hom & Gard 49: 132 Mr '71
See-through gardens. L. V. Power. il Am Home 74:58+ S '71
See also
Gardens, Miniature

TERRE HAUTE, Ind.

Libraries
See also
Vigo County, Ind. public library

TERRESTRIAL magnetism. See Magnetism, Terrestrial

TERRIERE, L. C. and others
Induction of microsomal oxidase in F₁ hybrids of a high and a low oxidase housefly strain. bibliog il Science 171:581-3 F 12 '71

TERRILL, Ross
800,000,000: the real China; excerpts. il Atlan 228:90-6+ N '71; 229:39-54+ Ja '72
Japan: the land of the re-rising sun. il Atlan 227:78-82+ Mr '71
about
Closeup on China. por Time 98:72+ N 15 '71 *

TERRITORIAL waters
Fishy business; who owns the oceans? D. F. Ross. New Repub 166:19-21 Ja 1 '72
Great tuna war. Newsweek 78:28 D 27 '71
Great tuna war; Ecuador vs. United States. Time 97:24 F 8 '71
Lobster stew; Russia-U.S. discuss New England incidents. il Newsweek 77:23 My 31 '71
OAS foreign ministers discuss coastal state fisheries question; statements, with text of resolution. J. J. Jova; J. N. Irwin. Dept State Bul 64:245-50 F 22 '71
Shrinking the oceans; 200-mile limit claimed by Latin America. il Time 98:61 Ag 16 '71
See also
Fishery laws and legislation

TERRORISM
Anarchist cookbook, by W. Powell. Review
Commonweal 94:16-19 Mr 12 '71. E. Capouya
Nat R 23:819-20 Jl 27 '71. M. Geltman
As bombings in U.S. soar; who's to blame, the motives. il U S News 70:95 My 17 '71
Bomb in the Senate. il Time 97:25 Mr 15 '71
Bombing of SLAC: a question of why? Sci N 100:406 D 18 '71
Bombing the banks. il Time 99:18 Ja 17 '72
Bombs to the right of them; Houston Pacifica. N. C. Chriss. Nation 212:243-4 F 22 '71
Convention on terrorism transmitted to the Senate; message, May 11, 1971. R. M. Nixon. Dept State Bul 65:28 Jl 5 '71
Drive to halt terror bombings. il U S News 70:17-19 Mr 15 '71
Hemisphere foreign ministers meet in OAS General assembly. Américas 23:44 Mr '71
Houston: the terrorists. il Newsweek 77:54+ My 3 '71
How do you keep bombs away? blast in Capitol. il Sr Schol 98:13-14 Mr 22 '71
Inside the revolutionary left. T. E. Mosher. Read Digest 99:53-7 S '71

TERRORISM—*Continued*

Madness past midnight. S. Alsop. Newsweek 77:116 Mr 15 '71

Material witness; L. Bacon held as witness in Capitol bombing case. il por Newsweek 77:26-27B My 10 '71

No more tribute for terror. Time 97:31 Mr 22 '71

On the bombing of a linear accelerator. D. E. Thomsen. Sci N 100:418 D 25 '71

Price; bombing of the Capitol. Nation 212: 322 Mr 15 '71

Ransoms for revolution; plots in Turkey, in Venezuela, in Uruguay. Time 97:39 Mr 15 '71

Terrorist acts against United Nations missions. UN Mo Chron 8:61-70 N '71

Terrorists among us: an intelligence report. R. K. Bennett. il Read Digest 99:115-20 O '71

Third special session of the OAS general assembly adopts measures on kidnaping and terrorism; statements, with text of convention and resolution. W. P. Rogers. Dept State Bul 64:228-34 F 22 '71

Trashing the Capitol. il Newsweek 77:28-9 Mr 15 '71

U.S. condemns shooting incident at Soviet mission to the U.N; statement, October 21, 1971. G. Bush. Dept State Bul 65:598 N 22 '71

Violence: left and middle; use as a political tactic. M. C. Segers. il Cath World 212:307-8+ Mr '71

See also
Bomb scares
Kidnapping
Sabotage
Vietnamese war, 1957- —Atrocities

Bangladesh

Vengeance in victory; Bengali retaliation against Pakistani soldiers. il Time 99:33-4 Ja 3 '72

Brazil

Brazil: what terror is like. M. M. Alves. Nation 212:337-41 Mr 15 '71

Great Britain

New way of life; R. Carr's home bombed. il por Newsweek 77:44 Ja 25 '71

Shades of Guy Fawkes. Time 98:40 N 15 '71

Guatemala

Guatemala: always *la violencia*. V. Perera. N Y Times Mag p 12-13+ Je 13 '71

Guatemala: terror in silence. J. C. Goulden. Nation 212:365-8 Mr 22 '71

Inside a state of siege: legalized murder in Guatemala. S. Bodenheimer. il Ramp Mag 9:50-2 Je '71

Northern Ireland

Acceptable violence? il Time 98:32+ D 27 '71

Everyone but the terrorists. S. Cronin. Commonweal 94:470-1 S 17 '71

Fierce women of Ulster; with report by J. Bonfante. il Life 71:24B-30 D 3 '71

Fury grows in Ulster. il Life 71:35-7 N 12 '71

In the shadow of the gunmen. il Time 99: 30-4+ Ja 10 '72

Last gasp for Irish terrorists? il U S News 72:39 Ja 3 '72

Murder of Santa Claus. il Time 98:40 D 20 '71

Northern Ireland: Britain's Vietnam? il U S News 71:52 S 20 '71

Ulster: bloody Dodge City. Time 98:46+ N 22 '71

War of attrition. il Time 99:42 Ja 3 '72

Philippines

Death in the Plaza Miranda. Time 98:27 Ag 30 '71

Turkey

Getting tough; kidnaping of 4 U.S. airmen. il Newsweek 77:53-4 Mr 15 '71

Tempting target; Israeli diplomat E. Elrom. Time 97:37 My 31 '71

Vietnam (Republic)

Mood turns violent; Saigon. il Time 98:46+ S 27 '71

TERRY, Bob. See Sheehan, B.

TERRY, Carroll
Movie report. See issues of Good housekeeping
TV report. il Good H 173:88 O '71

TERRY, Mark
Hello Ents, good-bye Aristotle; excerpts from Teaching for survival; with biographical sketch. Natur Hist 80:2, 6-8+ bibliog(p84) Ja '71

TERRY, Walter
Anniversaries of Ted Shawn. il pors Dance Mag 45:26-9+ N '71

Black ballet can be beautiful. il por Sat R 54:48-9 F 27 '71

Dancer's composer. il Sat R 54:42-3+ My 29 '71

Markova on mime. il por Sat R 54:40-1 Ag 28 '71

Miriam Winslow: dancer-sculptress. il pors Dance Mag 45:25-7 D '71

World of dance. See issues of Saturday review

TERTZ, Abram, pseud. See Siniavskii, A. D.

TESICH, Steven
Carpenters. Criticism
New Yorker 46:75-6 Ja 16 '71 •
Lake of the woods. Criticism
Nation 214:29 Ja 3 '72 •
Time il 99:57 Ja 3 '72 •

TESLA, Nikola
Nikola Tesla's bold adventure. H. L. Goldman. il por Am West 8:4-9 Mr '71 *

TESLA coils
Nikola Tesla's bold adventure. H. L. Goldman. il por Am West 8:4-9 Mr '71

TESSENDORF, K. C.
Old man of the western sea. il Américas 23: 25-32 S '71

TESSIE, the tea bag maker; drama. See Huff, B. T.

TESSIER, Jacques. See Jasper, H. H. jt. auth.

TEST anxiety. See Anxiety

TEST probes. See Testing instruments

TEST tube babies. See Fertilization (in vitro)

TESTES. See Testicles

TESTICLES
Follicle-stimulating hormone and the regulation of testosterone secretion in rabbit testes. B. H. Johnson and L. L. Ewing. bibliog il Science 173:635-7 Ag 13 '71

TESTIMONY. See Witnesses

TESTIMONY and demeanor; story. See Casey, J.

TESTING
See also subhead Testing under various subjects, e.g. Automobiles—Testing

TESTING, Educational. See Educational tests and measurements

TESTING instruments
Analyzer in automatic home appliances. J. Darr. Radio-Electr 42:16 S '71

Appliance tester you can build. R. M. Benrey. il Pop Sci 199:124+ S '71

B&K model 162 transistor FET tester. A. Cunningham. Radio-Electr 42:92 Mr '71

B&K 747 Dyna-jet tube tester. il Radio-Electr 43:26 Ja '72

Build a digi-viewer; automatic in-operation testing of digital IC's. D. Lancaster. il Pop Electr 34:41-6 Mr '71

Build R-E's $15 color convergence generator. B. R. Rogen. il Radio-Electr 43:50-2 Ja '72

Color-bar generators for servicing. F. H. Belt. il Electr World 86:34-7+ S '71

Make this appliance test block. W. H. McClay. il Pop Mech 135:153 F '71

Non-destructive transistor tester. J. L. Keith. il Pop Electr 34:47-9 Mr '71; Correction. 34:10+ My '71

Test capacitors fast. H. Linton. il Radio-Electr 42:60-1 D '71

Test equipment product report. See issues of Electronics world

Test equipment scene. S. Prentiss. il Pop Electr 1:68+ Ja '72

Test instrument tricks. J. Darr. il Radio-Electr 42:69-70 N '71

Transistor testers for servicing. F. H. Belt. il Electr World 86:40-3 Jl '71

Triplett 990 industrial maintenance analyzer. il Radio-Electr 42:91 S '71

2 dream workbenches. J. Darr; P. Sutheim. il Radio-Electr 42:36-45+ Ag '71

Using an impedance tester. H. A. Ankermann. il Radio-Electr 42:82-3+ Je '71

Using the right probes. R. G. Middleton. il Radio-Electr 42:23-5+ Ag '71

See also
Calibrators
Dynamometers
Electric meters
Signal generators
Wheatstone bridges

TESTING laboratories
See also
Aeronautic laboratories
Cornell aeronautical laboratory, inc.
Underwriters' laboratories, inc.
United States—Manned spacecraft center— Lunar receiving laboratory

TESTOSTERONE
Follicle-stimulating hormone and the regulation of testosterone secretion in rabbit testes. B. H. Johnson and L. L. Ewing. bibliog il Science 173:635-7 Ag 13 '71

TESTS, Information. See Information tests

TESTS and scales. See Educational tests and measurements

TESUQUE Indians. See Pueblo Indians

TETANUS

Vaccination
Tetanus still kills, needlessly. il Changing T 25:23-4 Je '71

TETERIN, Ghenrikh, and Terlon, Claire
That chart on the laboratory wall. il pors UNESCO Courier 24:24-7+ Je '71

TETLEY, Glen
Dutch mutations; interview. ed. by G. Loney. il Dance Mag 45:55-9 F '71

TETON, Andrew P. See Summers, S. K. jt. auth.

TETRA pak international (firm) See Container industry

TETRACYCLINES
New antibiotic finally gets born; Minocin. il Bsns W p56+ O 16 '71

TETRADRACHMA. See Coins, Ancient

TETRAHYDROCANNABINOL. See THC

TEXACO, Inc.
Texaco's long steps aside again. Bsns W p36 D 11 '71

TEXACO opera quiz. See Radio broadcasting—Operas

TEXAS
Dust bowl 1971. il Newsweek 77:32-3 Ap 26 '71
Tin star state. G. Cartwright. il Esquire 75:95-9+ F '71
See also
Architecture, Domestic—Texas
Automobile touring—Texas
Banks and banking—Texas
Big Bend National Park
Big Thicket
Chisos Mountains
Dallas County
Express highways—Texas
Fishing—Texas
Hunting—Texas
Irrigation—Texas
Music festivals—Texas
Politics, Corruption in—Texas
Wildlife management—Texas

Aeronautics commission
Turmoil in Texas. Flying 88:92-3 My '71

Description and travel
Highland lakes of Texas; a series of impoundments of the Colorado River. C. L. Cadieux. il Yachting 130:54-5+ O '71
Shunpiking through Texas. N. D. Ford. il Har Yrs 11:6-13+ F '71

Politics and government
Big Ben. il por Newsweek 77:36+ Je 28 '71
John Connally: Nixon's new quarterback. R. Dugger. Atlan 228:82-6+ Jl '71; Reply with rejoinder. D. I. Shapiro. 228:40+ O '71

TEXAS conference of churches
Chicano workers, Rio Grande farmers agree to meet. N. D. Phillips. Chr Cent 88:84-6 Ja 20 '71
Ecumenism, Texas style. M. Moss. Chr Today 15:47-8 Ap 9 '71

TEXAS Gulf sulphur company
Playing for big stakes. il Forbes 107:16-17 F 1 '71

TEXAS instruments, inc.
At play in the fields of the company. P. O'Neil. il Life 71:26-9+ S 3 '71
Texas instruments wins MRCA role. Aviation W 95:21 O 25 '71

TEXAS international airlines
Control of Texas international gained by Jet capital group. J. P. Woolsey. Aviation W 95:27 D 20 '71

TEXAS library association
TLA annual conference. R. Bohachevsky. Am Lib 2:563-4 Je 12 '71

TEXAS refinery corporation
Social-security swingers. il Newsweek 79:37 Ja 3 '72

TEXAS state fair. See Agricultural exhibitions

TEXAS tech television station. See Television stations, Educational

TEXAS tech university station, KTXT-TV. See Television stations, Educational

TEXAS, University
Hooking horns at UT; denunciation by William Arrowsmith. il por Newsweek 77:46 F 1 '71
LBJification of U.T. F. Lang. Ramp Mag 10: 8+ D '71

College of education
Degrees in bilingual education. Sch & Soc 99:332 O '71

TEXTBOOKS
Campus best sellers. Newsweek 77:46 F 1 '71
New guidelines against racism in textbooks. R. H. Smith; reply. R. F. Hogan. Pub W 199:32-3 F 1 '71
Textbook of the future. B. Rojas. Sch & Soc 99:315-17 Sum '71
Textbooks, propaganda, and librarians. A. J. Dyson. bibliog il por Wilson Lib Bul 46: 260-7 N '71
Untested textbooks. il Time 97:33 Je 7 '71
See also
Booksellers and bookselling—Textbooks
Hornbooks
Publishers and publishing—Textbooks
Readers (books)
Social sciences—Textbooks
Spanish language—Textbooks
United States—History—Textbooks
World history—Textbooks

TEXTILE design
Art power at work; Bedford Stuyvesant's Design works. N. Schram. il House B 113: 113-15 N '71
Current translations; American Indian designs of Billy McCarty. il House B 113:60-1 Je '71
Taste for the East. il Look 35;30-4+ S 21 '71
Thoughts on Jack Lenor Larsen and the textile horizon. E. Rossbach. il por Craft Horiz 31:12-13 Ap '71
Workshop: adire eleko. L. Brooks. il Craft Horiz 31:12-15 Ag '71
See also
Batik
Weaving

TEXTILE exhibits. See Textile fabrics—Exhibitions

TEXTILE fabrics
Decorating with fabrics; excerpt from David Hicks on decoration—with fabrics. D. Hicks. il McCalls 98:80-7 S '71
Golden twist for textiles; success of double knits. il Time 98:100 N 8 '71
Outdoor decorating: brief guide to rain-or-shine fabrics. V. Griffin. Good H 172:158 Je '71
Printed textiles, English and American cottons and linens, 1700-1850, by F. M. Montgomery. Review
Antiques 99:230+ F '71. R. Davidson
Tennessee textiles. R. H. Hulan. il Antiques 100:386-9 S '71
See also
Spinning
Weaving

Dyeing
See Dyes and dyeing

Exhibitions
Jack Lenor Larsen in Boston; Museum of fine arts. L. Salmon. il Craft Horiz 31:14-23 Ap '71

TEXTILE fabrics, Fire resisting
Glass fabric with cotton's feel; laminate called Fibercoat. il Bsns W p62+ Mr 27 '71
How to beat the heat and stay alive; Nomex nylon. il Sci Digest 71:18-19 Ja '72
You can stay cool in hot pants; Nomex fabrics. J. F. Pearson. il Pop Mech 136: 86-7 D '71

TEXTILE fabrics, Flammable
Burned children. R. Nader. New Repub 165: 19-21 Jl 3 '71

TEXTILE fabrics, Knitted. See Knit goods

TEXTILE fabrics, Synthetic
Gluing a fine seam. Chem 44:3 My '71
Quick guide to man-made fibers. J. Van Leeuwen. Good H 173:186 N '71

TEXTILE fabrics, Wrinkle resistant
How to iron less and enjoy it more; questions and answers. Redbook 136:57+ Mr '71
Questions and answers on today's no-iron fabrics and finishes. A. A. Latour. il Good H 172:164 My '71

TEXTILE fibers, Synthetic
Polyester fiber: from its invention to its present position. A. E. Brown and K. A. Reinhart. bibliog il Science 173:387-93 Jl 23 '71

TEXTILE industry
See also
Wool industry

Imports problem
Costly trade victory over Japan. il Time 98:23 O 25 '71
Deal from Japan. Newsweek 77:80 Mr 8 '71
Double whammy. por Forbes 108:26 Jl 1 '71

TEXTILE industry—Imports problem—*Cont.*
Japanese plan eases trade row. Bsns W p26 Mr 6 '71
Japanese textile curbs may get a trial. il Bsns W p26 Mr 20 '71
President Nixon continues to seek solution to textile problem; statement, March 11, 1971. R. M. Nixon. Dept State Bul 64:490 Ap 5 '71
Story behind the textile war with Japan. il U S News 71:47-50 O 11 '71
Textiles still cry for help. Bsns W p22 Ag 28 '71
Trading with the enemy; U.S. vs. Tokyo, Hong Kong, Taiwan and South Korea. Newsweek 78:101+ O 18 '71
U.S.-Japanese textile squabble: is it economics? Is it politics? or did our industry goof? interview. A. W. Gutenberg. por Forbes 108:22-3 O 15 '71

Wages and hours

Wages in synthetic fibers manufacturing; with table. D. Ridzon. Mo Labor R 94:55 N '71

France

Boussac tries to save his empire. por Bsns W p31 Jl 3 '71

Japan

Textile exporters may fight quotas. il Bsns W p41 O 30 '71

Morocco

Sheila Hicks at Rabat. B. Werther. il por Craft Horiz 31:30-3 Je '71

United States

Golden twist for textiles; success of double knits. il Time 98:100 N 8 '71
Tennessee textiles. R. H. Hulan. il Antiques 100:386-9 S '71
Textiles: more demand but fiercer competition. il Bsns W p48-9 D 25 '71
See also
Burlington industries, inc.
Duplan corporation
Stevens, J. P. and company

TEXTILE painting
Creativity with textile paint. F. O. Howling. il Sch Arts 70:18-19 Mr '71
Day my whole class dyed. W. McAllister. il Sch Arts 70:18-19 Je '71

TEXTILE workers
See also
Cotton mills—Employees
Textile industry—Wages and hours

TEXTILES. See Textile fabrics

TEXTRON, inc.
Textron goes its own way. il Forbes 108:58 S 15 '71
Textron's big gulp; proposed merger with Kendall. Fortune 84:33 O '71

TEXTURE (photography) See Photography—Grain

TEXTURE screens in photography. See Photography—Processing—Apparatus and supplies

TEXTURED walls. See Wall coverings

THACKERAY, William Makepeace
Rose and the ring; dramatization. See Thane, A.

about
Bout of Thackeray. R. Hatch. Nation 212:309-11 Mr 8 '71 *

THACKRAY, Arnold
Reflections on the decline of science in America and on some of its causes; adaptation of address, March 22, 1971. bibliog Science 173:27-31 Jl 2 '71

THAILAND
See also
Anti-Communist movements—Thailand
Communism—Thailand
United States—Foreign relations—Thailand

Antiquities

Early center of bovine husbandry in southeast Asia; Non Nok Tha. C. F. W. Higham and B. F. Leach. bibliog il Science 172:54-6 Ap 2 '71

Economic conditions

Paradise lost. il Time 98:60 Ag 2 '71

Foreign relations

Thailand and multipolarity. K. T. Young. bibliog f Cur Hist 61:327-31+ D '71

Politics and government

Coup that wasn't. Newsweek 78:38+ N 29 '71
Same old crowd. il por Time 98:39 N 29 '71
Thai coup. New Repub 165:9 D 4 '71
Who says Thailand's next? W. A. O'Neil. New Repub 164:23-7 Ja 2 '71

THALAMUS. See Optic thalamus

THALASSEMIA. See Anemia

THALER, Susan
Photographing your baby: a mother's guide. il Redbook 138:79+ D '71

THAMES RIVER
Charming charter on the Thames. C. Howland. il Motor B & S 128:60-1+ Jl '71

THANAT Khoman
U.S. and Thailand sign memorandum of understanding on international narcotics control; remarks, September 28, 1971. Dept State Bul 65:412 O 18 '71

THANATOLOGY. See Death

THANE, Adele
Big Paul Bunyan; drama. Plays 30:29-36 Ap '71
Conspiracy; dramatization of excerpt from The old curiosity shop, by C. Dickens. Plays 30:85-96 F '71
Hare, the hippo, and the elephant; dramatization of An African folk tale. Plays 30:58, 59-65 My '71
Place in the family; drama. Plays 30:51-6 Ap '71
Rose and the ring; dramatization of a story by W. M. Thackeray. Plays 30:79-90 Mr '71
Travels of Marco Polo; drama. Plays 30:81-92 My '71

THANKS. See Thanksgiving

THANKSGIVING
Every day is Thanksgiving day; reprint from December 5, 1958 issue. D. Lawrence. U S News 71:96 D 6 '71
Today; let's give thanks. K. Hillyard. il Har Yrs 11:42-3 N '71
See also
Gratitude

THANKSGIVING day
Thanksgiving with a Lebanese flavor. A. Eisenberg and H. Eisenberg. il por Good H 173:84+ N '71

Drama

Pilgrim rebel. M. Hall. Plays 31:13-24 N '71
Sing the songs of Thanksgiving; reprint from November 1958 issue. A. Fisher. Plays 31:69-78 N '71
Thanksgiving postscript; reprint from November 1958 issue. M. Hark and N. McQueen. Plays 31:47-56 N '71

THANKSGIVING dinners
Little birds, big feast: rock cornish hens. il Ebony 27:188+ N '71
Thanksgiving with Norman Rockwell; with recipes. il por Ladies Home J 88:113-21+ N '71
This year, try something different; menus with recipes. il McCalls 99:104-10+ N '71

THANKSGIVING postscript; drama. See Hark, M. and McQueen, N.

THANT, 1909-
Address by the Secretary-General to the Organization of American states; April 14, 1971. UN Mo Chron 8:42-9 My '71
Governments, systems, ideologies, and institutions come and go, but humanity remains; excerpts from address, September 1971. Sat R 54:19 O 23 '71
Human rights day, 10 December 1970, message. UN Mo Chron 7:i D '70
International year for action to combat racism and racial discrimination 1971; message, March 21, 1971. UN Mo Chron 8:i-ii Mr '71
Introduction to the report of the Secretary-General on the work of the organization. UN Mo Chron 8:92-166 O '71
Pakistan; Middle East; statement and interview. UN Mo Chron 8:24-6 My '71
Pakistan; statement. UN Mo Chron 8:49-50 Je '71
People are asking why? address, May 5, 1971. UN Mo Chron 8:82-7 Je '71
Role of the Secretary-General; address, September 16, 1971. UN Mo Chron 8:178-87 O '71
Secretary-General's press conference; January 18, 1971. UN Mo Chron 8:24-34 F '71
Secretary-General's press conference; May 27, 1971. UN Mo Chron 8:75-81 Je '71
Secretary-General's press conference; September 14, 1971. UN Mo Chron 8:167-77 O '71
Toward world literacy; excerpts from address, September 8, 1970. por Sch & Soc 99:282-3 Sum '71
United Nations and some problems of public understanding; address, December 3, 1970. UN Mo Chron 8:98-105 Ja '71
United Nations day 24 October 1971; message. UN Mo Chron 8:i-ii O '71

about
Secretary-General; activities during November. UN Mo Chron 7:80 D '70 *
Secretary-General; activities during December. UN Mo Chron 8:66-7 Ja '71 *

THANT, 1909- —about—*Continued*
Secretary-General; activities during February, April. UN Mo Chron 8:12-14 Mr; 24 My '71 *
Secretary-General; activities during September, October UN Mo Chron 8:85-6 O; 95-8 N '71

THAT time of year; drama. See Cable, H.

THAWLEY, John
Drive ya buggy. See issues of Hot rod

THEATER
See also
Actors and actresses
Drama
Dramatic criticism
Masks (plays)
Mime
Pantomime
Puppets and puppet plays
Theater, Experimental

Stage setting and scenery
Oliver Smith talks about theatre; interview, ed. by G. Trotta. O. Smith. il por Harp Baz 104:190-1 S '71
Scenic world of Joseph Svoboda. J. M. Burian. il por Sat R 54:35-7+ Ag 28 '71

Czechoslovakia
Black light theatre of Prague. New York city center, NYC. D. Hering. Dance Mag 45:91 N '71

France
See also
Paris—Theater

Germany (Federal Republic)
All or nothing; production of P. Weiss's Hölderlin. Newsweek 78:92 O 11 '71
From Germany. S. Kauffmann. New Repub 165:24+ Jl 10; 26+ Jl 24 '71

Great Britain
See also
London—Theater

Japan
National theatres of Japan. Carnegie Hall, NYC. M. Marks. Dance Mag 45:22-3 Je '71
See also
Kabuki

United States
Every weekend this summer in California's Mother Lode; melodramas, musicals, straw hats and stovepipes. il Sunset 146:98-101 Je '71
It's showtime in the park. il Life 71:30-3 Ag 27 '71
Jean Dalrymple's theater notes. il Holiday 49:18-20 My '71
When the stars fell on California. M. Gottfried. Vogue 158:87 Jl '71
See also
Theater, Negro
also subhead Theater under names of cities, e.g. Los Angeles—Theater

THEATER, Childrens
Paper bag players in Hot Feet, Hunter college playhouse, NYC. N. Mason. Dance Mag 45:78 F '71
Saving the evening; Story theater. il por Time 97:60 Mr 1 '71
See also
Childrens plays

THEATER, Experimental
Dance of death; hierophantic theater: The grey lady cantata performed by the Bread and puppet theater. T. E. Kalem. il Time 97:47-8 Mr 8 '71
Grotowski and Schechner: the servitudes of freedom. T. Hoffman. il Art in Am 59:74-81 Mr '71
Kiss in the dark; the James Joyce memorial liquid theatre. il Newsweek 78:86 N 1 '71
New theatre, now. H. Clurman. Harper 242:28-34 '71; Reply with rejoinder. R. Hornby. 242:15-16 My '71
Non-verbal; Deafman glance. New Yorker 47:29-30 Mr 27 '71
Off Broadway; the James Joyce memorial liquid theatre performed at the Guggenheim museum by the Company theatre of Los Angeles. E. Oliver. New Yorker 47:101-2 O 16 '71
Roar, lion, roar! theater where children take over. il Life 71:155-6 D 17 '71
Singing in the sun; Lincoln Center street theater festival. J. Kroll. il Newsweek 78:73 S 6 '71
Theatre & films; James Joyce memorial liquid theatre. H. Clurman. Nation 213:444-6 N 1 '71

THEATER, Negro
Apollo: mecca of black show business; excerpts from Uptown; the story of Harlem's Apollo theatre. J. Schiffman. il por Ebony 26:114-16+ Ap '71

Of Harlem and Verona. C. Hughes. America 125:534-5 D 18 '71
See also
Negro drama

THEATER, Open-air
It's showtime in the park. il Life 71:30-3 Ag 27 '71

THEATER, Traveling
See also
Moving picture theaters, Traveling

THEATER and libraries. See Libraries and drama

THEATER architecture. See Theater buildings

THEATER audiences. See Audiences

THEATER buildings
Guidelines for good seeing. R. H. Wadsworth. il Arch Rec 149:137-44 Je '71
Theater buildings. il Arch Forum 134:29-51 Mr '71
See also
Dressing rooms, Theater
Opera houses
Sarasota, Fla.—Van Wezel performing arts hall

THEATER festivals. See Drama festivals

THEATER tickets
See Broadway shows at half price; twofers. il Changing T 25:6 F '71
Two on the isle; New York and London prices. H. R. Mayes. Sat R 54:6-7 Je 5 '71

THEATERS. See Theater buildings

THEATRICAL audiences. See Audiences

THEATRICAL direction. See Theatrical production and direction

THEATRICAL directors
See also names of theatrical directors, e.g. H. Prince

THEATRICAL glass. See Glassware

THEATRICAL music. See Music, Incidental

THEATRICAL production and direction
Do you mind critics calling you cheap, decadent, sensationalistic, gimmicky, vulgar, overinflated, megalomaniacal? production of Jesus Christ superstar. J. Gruen. il por N Y Times Mag p 14-16+ Ja 2 '72
How to play at Hal Prince. H. Saal. il por Newsweek 78:68-70 Jl 26 '71
Prince & his follies. L. Botto. il pors Look 35:34-8 My 18 '71
Superstar becomes a circus; with report by M. Paley. il Life 71:38-40 O 22 '71
When the funniest writer in America tried to be serious; with comments by N. Simon and others. R. Meryman. pors Life 70:60B-60D+ My 7 '71
Writing for the theatre today; practical advice on getting a play produced. Writer 85:22-7 Ja '72
See also
College and school drama
Moving picture production and direction
Operatic production and direction
Shakespeare, W.—Staging and acting of plays

THEBERGE, John B.
Wolf music; with biographical sketch. il Natur Hist 80:10, 36-43 bibliog(p84) Ap '71

THEBOM, Blanche
S.R.O. in Atlanta. il Opera N 36:27-9 D 25 '71

THEFT. See Shoplifting; Stealing

THEFT insurance. See Insurance. Burglary

THEME editors. See Teachers aides

THEME writing. See English language—Composition

THEODORACOPULOS, Taki
Détente in the Mideast. Nat R 23:312+ Mr 23 '71
Mr Agnew goes home again. Nat R 23:1412+ D 17 '71

THEOHARIS, Athan G.
Thirty years of wire tapping. Nation 212:744-50 Je 14 '71

THEOLOGIANS
Rome unbends a bit; dealing with theologians. Chr Cent 88:309 Mr 10 '71
Watching our language. G. O'Collins. America 124:207-8 F 27 '71
See also
Barth, K.
Cone, J.
Ellul, J.
Küng, H.
Moltmann, J.
Niebuhr, R.
Tillich, P.
Women as theologians

THEOLOGICAL education
Theological education 1971; symposium. Chr Cent 88:91-3+ Ja 27 '71
See also
Theological seminaries

THEOLOGICAL seminaries
Ailing seminaries: unfit to be tied? United Presbyterian schools. Chr Today 15:39-40 Mr 12 '71
Black theological education; successes and failures. C. Rogers. Chr Cent 88:129-31 Ja 27 '71
Drought hits the halls of divinity. Chr Cent 88:91-3 Ja 27 '71
Fact book reveals no substantial change in seminary enrollment. Chr Cent 88:740 Je 16 '71
Lineaments of seminary renewal. B. Barr. Chr Cent 88:97-101 Ja 27 '71; Discussion. 88:291-2 Mr 3 '71
See also
Central Baptist theological seminary, Kansas City, Kan.
Concordia theological seminary, St Louis

Finance
Financing theological education. J. I. McCord and others. Chr Cent 88:106-7 Ja 27 '71
Squeeze at the seminaries. Newsweek 77:85 My 31 '71

Great Britain
Seminaries and skulduggery: Church of England report. T. Beeson. Chr Cent 88:333 Mr 17 '71
Theological college, or Mayfields novelty. L. Paul. Chr Cent 88:107-8+ Ja 27 '71

THEOLOGICAL seminaries, Catholic
Renewing the ministry, prescription for reforming seminary training. Commonweal 94:125-6 Ap 16 '71
Theology, university and a brave new world. L. M. Orsy. America 124:606-8 Je 12 '71

THEOLOGY
Catholic theologian today; legacy of Vatican II. P. J Riga. Cath World 214:128-31 D '71
Christianity and evolution, by P. T. de Chardin. Review
  America 125:563 D 25 '71. C. F. Mooney
Dialogue on black theology. J. Cone and W. Hordern. Chr Cent 88:1079-80+ S 15 '71
Does theology come in colors? H. B. Kuhn. Chr Today 15:43-4 Ap 23 '71
Hans Küng replies to Gregory Baum. H. Küng. Commonweal 94:326-30 Je 25 '71
Here today, here tomorrow. W. T. Stevenson. Chr Cent 88:856-7 Jl 14 '71
I'd rather dance with the Jews. R. E. Wentz. Chr Cent 88:830-2 Jl 7 '71
Introduction to theology. C. F. H. Henry. Chr Today 15:25-6 Je 4 '71
It's back to work they go. G. C. Berkouwer. Chr Today 15:42 Ag 6 '71
Latin American theology, by C. P. Wagner. Review
  Chr Cent 88:698-700 Je 2 '71. M. Arias
Moral theology: hope for revival? E. Colborn. America 124:312-15 Mr 27 '71
Poor of God and the black Christian in America. R. A. Jeffers. il Cath World 213:126-9 Je '71
Rome's new approach; unorthodox theological opinion. Commonweal 93:484-5 F 19 '71
Schweitzer: prophet of radical theology, by J. L. Ice. Review
  Commonweal 95:258-60 D 10 '71. R. P. McBrien
Survey of Catholic theology, by T. M. Schoof. Review
  Cath World 213:97-8 My '71. G. MacEoin
Symposium on Hans Küng's Infallible? an inquiry. A. Dulles; M. A. Fahey; G. A. Lindbeck. America 124:427-33 Ap 24 '71
Theology en masse; World council of churches faith and order commission. T. Beeson. Chr Cent 88:1016-17 S 1 '71; Reply. G. G. Beazley, jr. 88:1305 N 3 '71
Theology, university and a brave new world. L. M. Orsy. America 124:606-8 Je 12 '71
Truth in theology. R. Hazelton. il Chr Cent 88:772-4 Je 23 '71
What price Tillich? B. L. Smith. Chr Today 16:16-18 D 17 '71; 13-15 Ja 7 '72
Whatever happened to theology? R. P. McBrien. Commonweal 94:129-33 Ap 16 '71
See also
Catechetics
Christian life
Christianity
Devil
Freedom (theology)
Good and evil
Grace (theology)
Hell
Jesus Christ
Love (theology)
Man (theology)
Modernism

Pastoral theology
Peace (theology)
Religion
Salvation
Secularism
Truth

Bibliography
Books on church history and theology, 1970. G. W. Bromiley. Chr Today 15:4-6 F 26 '71

Study and teaching
New Society is born; study of black religion. Chr Cent 88:1342 N 17 '71
Within and without the circle of faith; end of Illinois plan. D. B. Larson. il Chr Cent 88:1172-4 O 6 '71; Reply. R. B. Garrison. 88:1430 D 1 '71
See also
Theological education
Theological seminaries
Theological seminaries, Catholic

THEOLOGY, Doctrinal
See also
Process theology

THEOPHILUS Protestantus, pseud. See Protestantus, T. pseud.

THERA (island)
New thought on lost Atlantis. il Chem 44:5 Ja '71

THERAPEUTIC communities. See Hospitals, Psychiatric

THERAPEUTICS
See also
Acupuncture
Cellular therapy
Electrotherapy
Psychotherapy
Recreational therapy

THERE'S one in every marriage; drama. See Feydeau, G.

THERESE Dolores McFadden, Sister. See McFadden, T. D.

THERMAL-knit underwear. See Underwear

THERMAL inversions. See Temperature inversions

THERMAL pollution. See Air pollution; Pollution; Water pollution

THERMATOOL process. See Steel—Welding

THERMIONIC converters
Soviets report successful thermionic unit. Sci N 99:231 Ap 3 '71

THERMOCHARGER compressed-air boost system. See Automobile engines—Superchargers

THERMOCOUPLES
How accurately can temperature be measured? W. T. Gray and D. I. Finch. il Phys Today 24:37-9 S '71
How to replace a thermocouple. il Sunset 147:85 Jl '71

THERMODYNAMICS
Option for survival. R. S. Berry. Bul Atom Sci 27:22-7 My '71
See also
Entropy

THERMOGRAPHY, infrared. See Photography, Infared

THERMOLUMINESCENCE
What new methods are being developed for dating the past? Sci Digest 70:88-9 S '71

THERMOMETERS, Cooking
Meat thermometers. il Consumer Bul 54:38-40 F '71

THERMOMETERS and thermometry
Build an electronic darkroom temperature monitor. J. A. Gupton, jr. il Radio-Electr 42:40-2 F '71
Digital thermometer module for the digital measurements lab. D. Meyer. il Pop Electr 34:69-71+ Je '71
Low-temperature thermometers discussed at symposium. G. B. Lubkin. bibliog il Phys Today 24:17-18 O '71
New electronic temperature taker. C. Conley. il Field & S 76:107 D '71
Solid-state probe thermometer; use of silicon diodes. G. Gregg. il Electr World 85:70-1 Mr '71
Three-range electronic thermometer. R. M. Benrey. il Pop Sci 198:102-3 F '71
See also
Thermocouples

THERMOS containers
Picnic tableware and coolers. il Bet Hom & Gard 49:78-9 Je '71
Thermal jugs. il Consumer Bul 54:12-15 Je '71

THEROUX, Paul
Burma. Atlan 228:37+ N '71
Killing of Hastings Banda. Esquire 76:22+ D '71

THETA Coronae Borealis. See Stars, Double

THEUS, Robert
Dropouts: prevention and cure. Clear House 46:95 O '71

THIBODEAU, Ralph
Media is the mass. Commonweal 95:17-18 O 1 '71
Stravinsky's sacred music. il Commonweal 94:384-5 Jl 23 '71
THICKET, BIG. See Big Thicket
THICKNESS measurement
See also
Micrometers
THIESENHUSEN, William C.
Latin America's employment problem. bibliog il Science 171:868-74 Mr 5 '71
THIEU, Nguyen-van-. See Nguyen-van-Thieu
THIEVES
Thieves are after your gear. J. Weiss. il Field & S 76:48+ My '71
See also
Burglary and burglars
Cattle thieves
Shoplifting
Stealing
THIGH exercises. See Exercise
THIN films
Evaporation retardation by monolayers: another mechanism. J. Wu. bibliog il Science 174:283-5 O 15 '71
THINK tanks. See Research institutions
THINKING. See Thought and thinking
THINKING machines. See Artificial intelligence
THIOKOL chemical corporation
Thiokol chosen as second source SRAM rocket motor supplier. Aviation W 95:19 N 29 '71
Thiokol grapples with diversification. W. H. Gregory. il Aviation W 94:47-50 Mr 29 '71
THIOLASE. See Enzymes
THIOPHENECARBOXYLIC acid. See Carboxylic acids
THIRD life of Grange Copeland; story. See Walker, A.
THIRD one; story. See Singer, I. B.
THIRD party movement. See Political parties—United States
THIRKELL, Angela (Mackail)
Angela Thirkell is back! E. Lottman. Pub W 200:33 D 6 '71 •
THIRTEEN; drama. See Martens, A. C.
35mm cameras. See Cameras
THIRTY-nine articles. See Church of England—Articles of religion
THOM, Rose Anne
My whole life has been a matching grant. il Dance Mag 45:20-1+ S '71
THOMAN, Roy E.
Iraq under Baathist rule. bibliog f Cur Hist 62:31-7+ Ja '72
THOMAS Aquinas, Saint
Homosexuality, Aquinas, and the church. J. A. McCaffrey. Cath World 213:183-6 Jl '71 •
THOMAS More, Saint. See More, T.
THOMAS, Bill
Alabama's Tennessee playground. il Travel 135:46-7 Je '71
Biking through history. il Parents Mag 46: 46-9+ My '71
Flaming Gorge. il Travel 135:42-6 My '71
Indiana's new lakes. il Travel 135:48-51+ F '71
Maryland's idle gold. il Travel 136:36-9 N '71
Outdoor America. il Travel 136:28-39+ Jl '71
Spirited sites. il Travel 136:40-3 O '71
Talking the classroom outdoors. il Parents Mag 46:48-9+ Ap '71
THOMAS, Carol Sue
Those beautiful new ski bums. C. S. Wren. il pors Look 35:35-8+ F 23 '71 •
THOMAS, Charles William
Relevance of black power in Haiti. New Repub 164:11-13 Je 19 '71
Undiplomatic reforms. il por Time 98:20 N 15 '71 •
THOMAS, D. Glyn. See Forsyth, G. C. jt. auth.
THOMAS, Danny
Thanksgiving with a Lebanese flavor. A. Eisenberg and H. Eisenberg. il por Good H 173:84+ N '71 •
THOMAS, Della
Count-down on the 1-2-3's. bibliog il Library J 96:1083-90 Mr 15 '71
THOMAS, Donald
Five clues to a good school. Ed Digest 36:29-31 F '71
THOMAS, Duane
Troubles of Thomas. por Newsweek 78:57 Ag 30 '71 •
THOMAS, Dylan
Dylan Thomas: the experience, the picture, and the message. R. H. Meyer. bibliog f Engl J 60:199-204 F '71 •
Dylan's boathouse. B. Brower. il Esquire 75: 96-7+ Ja '71 •

THOMAS, Jess
Riding a wild horse. por Opera N 36:12-13 D 18 '71
THOMAS, Joe
This Joe had better be good. J. Underwood. il pors Sports Illus 35:42-4+ D 13 '71 •
THOMAS, John R.
Sino-Soviet relations: the view from Moscow. Cur Hist 61:210-14+ O '71
THOMAS, Joseph
Precious blood of Joe Thomas. il pors Ebony 26:72-4+ My '71 •
THOMAS, Lewis
On insect; poem. New Yorker 47:27 Jl 10 '71
THOMAS, Lewis, 1913-
Sensuous symbionts of the sea; with biographical sketch. il Natur Hist 80:4, 28-37+ bibliog(p96) Ag '71
THOMAS, Lowell, 1892-
Traveler nobody would believe. il Read Digest 99:129-33 Jl '71
THOMAS, Michael Tilson
Following their footsteps. M. Makarski. il pors Seventeen 30:96-7+ Ja '71 •
He reminds me of me at that age, says Leonard Bernstein. D. Henahan. il pors N Y Times Mag p36-8+ O 24 '71 •
Music to my ears; at the Philharmonic. I. Kolodin. Sat R 54:75 N 20 '71 •
Musical events. W. Sargeant. New Yorker 47:183-4 N 13; 188 N 20 '71 •
On the upbeat. il por Newsweek 77:67 Mr 1 '71 •
THOMAS, Norman C. See Cronin, T. E. jt. auth
THOMAS, Orlando Pendleton
Top man leaps from oil to tires. por Bsns W p22-3 S 18 '71 •
THOMAS, Paul M.
Every tomato is a beauty! il Org Gard & Farm 18:60-2 Mr '71
THOMAS, Peter, and others
Evaluation of parent drug education. bibliog Ment Hy 55:456-60 O '71
THOMAS, Roger J. and Maran, S. P.
What two sun-observing satellites tell us. il pors Sky & Tel 41:268-72 My '71
THOMAS, Steven C.
Valley View's 45-15 year-round school. Todays Ed 60:42-3 N '71
THOMAS, Veronica
Arans, Ireland's invincible isles. il Nat Geog 139:544-73 Ap '71
THOMAS, Walter L.
Showdown at generation gap. il Farm J 95: 32-3+ Mr '71
THOMAS, William F. 1924-
Chandler's change of heart. Time 97:46 Je 28 '71 •
THOMAS and Betts corporation
Late tape. R. Brady. Duns 97:10 My '71
THOMAS Cook & son. See Cook, Thomas, and son
THOMASON, Ronald
Watercolor page; with biographical sketch. il por Am Artist 35:30-3+ N '71
THOMPSON, Betty
After China, can Cuba be far behind? Chr Cent 88:944-5 Ag 11 '71
THOMPSON, Bill
Sons of the bitter mango. Nation 213:551-4 N 29 '71
THOMPSON, Bob
Humidify for healthier house plants. Home Gard 58:74-5 Ap '71
THOMPSON, C. Lamar
Themes in A separate peace. Clear House 46: 188-9 N '71
THOMPSON, Carl
Animal trainer who's big on love. il pors Ebony 26:120-2+ S '71 •
THOMPSON, Charley
Don't broadcast this, but pollution can get you fired! reprint. G. Gillespie. il Audubon 73:103-5 Ja '71 •
Dynamite in pollution. C. Gillespie; discussion. Nation 211:674; 212:258+ D 28 '70, Mr 1 '71 •
THOMPSON, Claude
Social reform: an evangelical imperative. Chr Today 15:8-12 Mr 26 '71
THOMPSON, Dorothy Barclay
Happy marriage, is it real? Vogue 158:117+ N 1 '71
THOMPSON, Era Bell
I was a cancer coward. il por Ebony 26: 64-8+ S '71
Liberian lady wears three hats. il pors Ebony 27:54-6+ Ja '72
Paradise returned. il Ebony 26:84-8+ F '71
THOMPSON, Henry O.
Interracial marriage and the Bible. bibliog il Negro Hist Bul 34:103-6 My '71
THOMPSON, J. Walter, company
Jewel from the crown; Pinto-Maverick-Mustang advertising accounts. Newsweek 78:67 Jl 19 '71

THOMPSON, John
 Books (cont) Harper 242:90-2 Ja; 99-101 Mr;
  94-8 Je; 243:89-91 Ag; 120-5 O '71
THOMPSON, Marilyn
 Dawn; poem. Nation 213:252 S 20 '71
 Klimt's justice; One woman; Two women;
  poems. Nation 213:632 D 13 '71
 Outpost; poem. Nation 212:638 My 17 '71
THOMPSON, Paul H. See Dalton, G. W. jt.
  auth.
THOMPSON, Phyllis
 Haku mele: a poetry workshop program. Engl
  J 60:215-19 F '71
THOMPSON, Robert
 Record album notes. Harper 243:46-7 O '71
THOMPSON, Sir Robert Grainger Ker
 If U.S. pulls out of Vietnam too fast; inter-
  view. il por U S News 70:36-8 Ap 12 '71
 Is ground war over for U.S. in Vietnam? in-
  terview. il por U S News 71:64-5 N 1 '71
THOMPSON, Sada
 Four faces of Sada. pors Newsweek 78:109
  N 29 '71 •
 From the coloring book. T. E Kalem. por
  Time 98:70 N 29 '71 •
THOMPSON, Thomas
 Battle of the undefeated giants. il pors Life
  70:40-9 Mr 5 '71
 Dare to be great! il pors Life 70:68-68B+
  My 28 '71
 Doctor tries a transplant. il por Sports Illus
  34:34-6 My 17 '71
 Film ratings flunk out. il Life 71:50B+ Ag
  20 '71
 How a network boss picks shows. il pors Life
  71:46-50+ S 10 '71
 Nixon's price freeze heats up Atlanta's lots.
  il Life 71:34-7 O 8 '71
 Parting shots. il por Life 71:68 Jl 2 '71
 Parting shots: Frank Sinatra's swan song.
  il pors Life 70:70A-74 Je 25 '71
 Today. il Life 71:67-8 D 10 '71
 Year they changed hearts; excerpt from
  Hearts. il Life 71:56-56B+ S 17 '71
THOMPSON, Thomas W.
 Gulf weed communities of south Florida;
  with biographical sketch. il por Sea Front
  17:95-101, 126 Mr '71
THOMPSON, William Irwin
 Planetary vistas. bibliog il Harper 243:71-8 D
  '71
   about
 Bear and the hummingbird. J. Seelye. New
  Repub 164:28-31 Je 19 '71 •
THOMPSON, William P. See Schultz, A. J. jt.
  auth.
THOMPSON, William R.
 Reclaimed fibers for quality printing; ex-
  cerpts from address, December 7, 1971, ed.
  by C. B. Grannis. Pub W 201:48-9 Ja 3 '72
THOMPSON Ramo Woolridge, inc. See TRW,
  inc.
THOMS, Wayne
 MI flies McCulloch's new hoppercopter! il
  Mech Illus 67:60-1+ My '71
THOMSON, Greg
 Dance with a liberal education. il por Dance
  Mag 45:66-7 Ap '71
THOMSON, James C. jr
 Recollections of a cultural imperialist (j.g.)
  Atlan 228:35-9 Ag '71
THOMSON, John
 John Thomson of Barclays bank ltd; inter-
  view. il pors Nations Bsns 59:44-8 Ag '71
THOMSON, Thyra
 Some second thoughts on Women's lib. Read
  Digest 98:95-7 Je '71
THOMSON, Virgil
 Homage. New Yorker 47:39 D 25 '71 •
 Mother of us all. Criticism
  Hi Fi il 21:MA10-11 N '71 •
 Musical events; birthday concert performed
  by Clarion music society in Alice Tully Hall.
  W. Sargeant. New Yorker 47:97-8 N 27 '71 •
 Musician of the month. P. J. Smith. por
  Hi Fi 21:MA8-9 N '71 •
 Virgilian knack. por Time 98:84 D 6 '71 •
THOMSON-CSF (firm) See Avionics industry
  —France
THORARINSSON, Sigurdur
 Hellfire; with biographical sketch. il Natur
  Hist 80:5, 58-63 Ag '71
THOREAU, Henry David
 Right on, Henry David! excerpts from Tho-
  reau's world, ed. by C. R. Anderson. Natur
  Hist 80:22-4+ F '71
   about
 Companionable design for definitive Thoreau.
  C. B. Grannis. il por Pub W 200:44+ O 4
  '71 •
 Elusive seringo. D. Zochert. il Natur Hist 80:
  8-10 D '71 •
 Thoreau and the endless beach. E. Kinkead.
  il Sat R 54:40+ Mr 13 '71 •

THORIUM
 Alpha-recoil thorium-234: dissolution into
  water and the uranium-234/uranium-238
  disequilibrium in nature. K. Kigoshi. bib-
  liog il Science 173:47-8 Jl 2 '71
THORNBERRY, Homer
 Where are they now? il por Newsweek 78:
  10 N 1 '71
THORNBERRY, William Homer. See Thorn-
  berry, H.
THORNDIKE, Dean, family
 Survival in the suburbs. J. Egan. il Good H
  172:74-5+ Je '71
THORNTON, Douglas N.
 Grinding-wheel dresser assures square edge.
  il Pop Mech 135:165 Ap '71
THORNTON, P. K.
 Room arrangements in the mid-eighteenth
  century. il Antiques 99:556-61 Ap '71
THOROUGHBRED horses. See Race horses
THORP, Roderick, and Blake, Robert
 Wives; excerpts from Wives: an investiga-
  tion. il Ladies Home J 88:186-91 S '71
THORSEN, Karen
 Our real security is in each other. Life 71:
  32-3 N 19 '71
THORSON, Gunnar Axel Wright
 Obituary
  Sea Front 17:127 Mr '71
THOUGHT and thinking
 Creativity: an implicit goal in education.
  S. Cohen. bibliog Sch & Soc 99:174-6 Mr
  '71
 Critical thinking in the English classroom.
  J. P. Madison. bibliog Engl J 60:1133-40+
  N '71
 Does anyone have time to think? reprint
  from March 26, 1955, issue. N. Cousins.
  Sat R 54:32 S 18 '71
 Myth of teaching for critical thinking. B.
  Skinner. bibliog f Clear House 45:372-6 F
  '71
   See also
 Abstraction
 Association (psychology)
 Cognition
 Intuition
 Self
THOUSAND and one nights. See Arabian nights
  entertainments
THREE little kittens' Christmas; drama. See
  Christmas, J. S.
3M company. See Minnesota mining and manu-
  facturing company
THREE-mile limit. See Territorial waters
THREE swine of most small stature; drama.
  See Olfson, L.
THREE wheel automobiles. See Automobiles,
  Three wheel
THREE wise men. See Magi
THREE'S a family; story. See Cave, H.
THRESHING
 Old-style threshing bees this month and next.
  il Sunset 147:62-3 Ag '71
THRIFT
   See also
 Domestic finance
THRIFTIMART, inc.
 How Thriftimart shelved a challenge. il Bsns
  W p26 Ag 14 '71
THROAT
   Diseases
   See also
 Goiter
   Surgery
 Should those tonsils really come out? il
  Changing T 25:31-3 O '71
THROMBOPHLEBITIS
 Boots and blood clots. il Newsweek 78:64 D 13
  '71
THROWER, Randolph William
 We need more manpower; excerpts from testi-
  mony before the House subcommittee on
  treasury, post office and general appropria-
  tions. U S News 70:25-6 Je 14 '71
THROWERS, Snow. See Snow blowers, throw-
  ers, etc.
THRUST reversers. See Jet airplane engines—
  Thrust reversers
THUJA. See Arborvitae
THUNDERHEAD (mountain) See Crazy Horse
  (Sioux Indian)—Statues, portraits etc.
THUNDERHEADS. See Clouds
THUNDERSTORMS
 Some precipitation aspects of Florida showers
  and thunderstorms. W. L. Woodley and
  others. bibliog il Weatherwise 24:106-13+
  Je '71
 Thunderstorms: effects on ionosphere. il Sci
  N 100:142 Ag 28 '71

THUNDERSTORMS—*Continued*
Water vapor: stratospheric injection by thunderstorms. P. M. Kuhn and others. bibliog il Science 174:1319-21 D 24 '71
See also
Lightning

THURBER, James
Thurber carnival. W. Sheed. il Horizon 13: 16-17 Aut '71 *

THURMOND, Strom
How Strom Thurmond does it. C. Roberts. il pors Newsweek 78:19-20 S 13 '71 *
Parting shots: a political charmer in Dixie diapers: Nancy Moore Thurmond. il por Life 71:69 Jl 16 '71 *

THURSTON, Philip H.
Make TF serve corporate planning. Harvard Bsns R 49:98-102 S '71

THYMINE
Thymine: a possible prebiotic synthesis. E. Stephen-Sherwood and others. bibliog il Science 173:446-7 Jl 30 '71

THYMOCYTES
Immunocompetent cells among mouse thymocytes: a minor population. E. Leckband and E. A. Boyse. bibliog il Science 172:1258-60 Je 18 '71 *

THYMUS gland
See also
Thymocytes

THYROCALCITONIN. See Calcitonin

THYROID gland
See also
Thyroxine

Diseases
See also
Goiter

THYROID hormones
See also
Calcitonin

THYROTROPIN
Thyrotropin-releasing hormone: biosynthesis by rat hypothalamic fragments in vitro. M. Mitnick and S. Reichlin. bibliog il Science 172:1241-3 Je 18 '71

THYROXINE
Thyroxine: conversion of triiodothyronine by isolated perfused rat heart. J. L. Rabinowitz and E. S. Hercker. bibliog Science 173: 1242-3 S 24 '71

TIBERIUS, emperor of Rome
Shadow of a man. P. W. Schmidtchen. il pors Hobbies 76:135-7+ Ag '71

TIBET
Lama in exile: prospects for an expatriate tradition. M. Jeschke. por Chr Cent 88:443-6 Ap 7 '71

TIBETAN refugees. See Refugees, Tibetan

TICE, George A.
Special edition of platinum prints made available by N.Y. dealer. J. Deschin. il por Pop Phot 69:36+ O '71 *

TICK-tack-toe. See Games

TICK-tack-toe, Electronic. See Electronic games

TICKER machines, Stock. See Stock ticker machines

TICKETS
See also
Theater tickets

TICKLING
Ticklish question. Sci Am 225:45 Jl '71

TICKS as carriers of infection
Rocky Mountain laboratory: a monument to the tick. B. Nelson. il Science 173:1009-10 S 10 '71

TICKSEED
Sunny color spring to fall; coreopsis. il Sunset 146:276 Ap '71

TIC-TAC-TOE. See Games

TIC-tac-toe. See Games

TIDAL marshes. See Marshes, Tide

TIDAL waves
Krakatoa, the killer wave. J. D. Truby. il Sea Front 17:130-9 My '71
Landlocked sailors; USS Wateree cast ashore by tidal wave in 1868. R. Clancy. il Sea Front 17:241-2 Jl '71
Warning: tsunamis! T. Harvey. il Pop Sci 199:62-4+ D '71

TIDES
Sea and the sky. P. Rockwell. il Motor B & S 128:44-5 bibliog(p 58) Jl '71

TIDYMAN, Ernest
What's happening to Ernest Tidyman's Shaft on the way to the screen. B. A. Bannon. il Pub W 199:22-3 Ap 19 '71 *

TIE-dyeing. See Dyes and dyeing

TIE-in merchandise. See Merchandising

TIED and dyed work. See Dyes and dyeing

TIERNEY, Charles G.
Unidentified stationary objects. Sat R 54:30 D 18 '71

TIERNEY, J. D.
It's a wise child. Nat R 23:704 Je 29 '71

TIERRA DEL FUEGO
Housewife at the end of the world. R. N. P. Goodall. il pors Nat Geog 139:130-50 Ja '71
Lola: last surviving Ona Indian. A. M. Chapman. il Natur Hist 80:32-41 Mr '71

TIES (neckwear) See Neckties

TIETJEN, Mary Louise
Hunt; poem. Cath World 212:300 Mr '71

TIETJENS, Therese
Tietjens the beloved. R. D. Daniels. por Opera N 35:24-6 Ja 30 '71 *

TIFFANY, Lawrence P.
Judicial attempts to control the police. bibliog f Cur Hist 61:13-19+ Jl '71

TIFFIN, Gerald C.
Education: the good old days that never were. Chr Today 15:4-6 F 12 '71

TIGER moths. See Moths

TIGERS
Tiger. A. Singh. il Nat Parks & Con Mag 45:18-21 Ag '71
Way to extinction: the Siberian tiger; with painting by G. Coheleach. Audubon 73:36-7 Ja '71

TIGERS (baseball) See Baseball clubs

TIGHE-FORD, David
Barnacles and hormones; with biographical sketch. il Sea Front 17:243-50, 255 Jl '71

TILDEN, Paul M.
New hope for the American chestnut. il Nat Parks & Con Mag 45:25-8 Jl '71
Ocean of grass. il Nat Parks & Con Mag 45:4-5 Mr '71
Planning in the Pine Barrens. il Nat Parks & Con Mag 45:22-6 Ag '71

TILE laying
How to lay vinyl floor tiles. Good H 172:201 Ap '71
Tiling is now easier than ever. W. C. Leckey. il Pop Mech 136:142-5 S '71

TILE printing. See Block printing

TILES
How to make decorative concrete tiles. il Bet Hom & Gard 49:52+ Ap '71
Printing with tiles; use of clay tiles for blocks. I. Kettner. il Ceram Mo 19:30-1 D '71
Tiling is now easier than ever; adhesive-backed tile. W. C. Leckey. il Pop Mech 136:142-5 S '71

TILLAGE
Better crops with the chisel plow. S. Durin. il Org Gard & Farm 18:86-7+ O '71
Double digging improves soil twice as deep. il Sunset 146:206 Mr '71
Minimum tillage helps him farm bigger. il Suc Farm 69:B14 Je '71
Plow at 8 mph to cut costs? G. W. Wormley. il Farm J 95:28B N '71
Reduced tillage, what's it worth? R. Sanders. il Suc Farm 69:no3 28-31 F '71
Tips on good soil tillage. Suc Farm 69: A7 S '71
See also
Terraces (agriculture)

TILLAMOOK, Ore.

Galleries and museums
Birds on display in Tillamook; Pioneer museum. Sunset 146:26 F '71

TILLERS. See Cultivators

TILLERS, Marine. See Boats—Steering gear

TILLICH, Paul
Paul Tillich's dialectical humanism, by L. F. Wheat. Review
Chr Cent 88:1062+ S 8 '71. R. Kysar *
What price Tillich? B. L. Smith. Chr Today 16:16-18 D 17 '71; 13-15 Ja 7 '72 *

TILLINGHAST, Jack
Thing of use and beauty; poem. Am For 77: 50 Ag '71

TILLMAN, Rollie
Rise of the conglomerchant. il Harvard Bsns R 49:44-51 N '71

TILLOTSON, Brooks
Musical events; recital in Alice Tully Hall. W. Sargeant. New York 47:120-1 Je 5 '71 *

TILT, Albert, Jr
East Side house settlement. il Antiques 99: 66 Ja '71

TIM, Tiny. See Tiny Tim

TIMBER
Timber; EQ index. il Nat Wildlife 9:35 O '71
See also
Lumber industry

TIMBER cutting. See Lumbering

TIMBER disposal
Non-polluting tree disposal; using the Chiparvestor in Wayne County, Mich. il Am City 86:34 N '71

TIMBER wolves. See Wolves

TIMBERDOODLE shooting. See Woodcock shooting

TIMBERLAND regional library, Olympia, Wash.
Washington scores Moose for snub of black librarian. il por Library J 97:11 Ja 1 '72

TIME
Now, the leap second. Time 98:54 D 27 '71
See also
Past, The
Space and time

Poetry

Poet's workshop. F. Trefethen. Writer 84:19-22 Mr '71

TIME (periodical)
Harry Luce and the Russian century. J. Chamberlain. Nat R 23:524-5+ My 18 '71
Letter from the publisher; reporter-researchers. H. Luce. il Time 97:8-9 Ja 25 '71
Man of the year. il Time 99:10-13+ Ja 3 '72

TIME, Inc.
Old soldier. pors Forbes 107:56 F 15 '71
Time inc. stalks some new markets. Bsns W p32 Je 12 '71

TIME, Cognition of. See Time perception

TIME, Use of
Death of time; reprint. W. V. Shannon. Am Heritage 23:107 D '71
Getting the most out of odd moments. J. Bradford. Read Digest 98:82-4 Je '71
How to get on top of your job. C. R. Murrah. il Nations Bsns 59:68-9 S '71
What's your time worth in the pool hall? R. Sanders. il Suc Farm 69:no2 H4 F '71

TIME compressed speech. See Compressed speech

TIME-lapse photography. See Photography, Time-lapse

TIME measurement
Finding sidereal time R. H. Hardie and M. E. Krebs. il Sky & Tel 41:288-9 My '71; Discussion. 42:204 O '71
What is the smallest possible unit of time? I. Asimov. Sci Digest 70:74-5 D '71
See also
Sundials
Timing devices

TIME perception
Time for every purpose. R. Sommer. il Natur Hist 80:24-5+ bibliog(p96) Ag '71
What your sense of time tells about you. J. Reinert. il Sci Digest 69:8-12 Je '71

TIME sharing computers. See Computers—Time sharing systems

TIME signals
Piggybacking on TV waves. Bsns W p 123 S 11 '71

TIME was village museum, Mendota, Ill. See Museums

TIMERS. See Timing devices

TIMES (London)
Correspondence course; letters to the editor. H. R. Mayers. Sat R 54:10+ D 4 '71

TIMES, Los Angeles. See Los Angeles times

TIMES, New York. See New York times

TIMES, Sunday. See Sunday times, London

TIMES-Dispatch, Richmond, Va.
From jailhouse to journalism. Time 98:62+ N 22 '71

TIMIDITY
See also
Bashfulness

TIMING devices
Amateur scientist; an osmotic pump, an unusual timer and how to enhance contrast in astronomical photographs. R. A. Wolf. il Sci Am 225:100-3 D '71
Clock timers; easy way to automate your home. W. G. Salm. il Pop Mech 136:112-15+ S '71
Kitchen timers. il Consumer Bul 54:10-11 N '71
Tapester's timer; pre-programmed tape recorder. R. Angus. il Pop Phot 68:47+ Ja '71
Timing tower under the dash. S. Kelly. il Hot Rod 24:108-9 My '71
See also
Electric lighting—Control

TIMM, Eric
Psychology of auto accidents. il Sci Digest 70:38-42 O '71

TIMMONS, Jeffry A.
Black is beautiful: it it bountiful? bibliog f il Harvard Bsns R 49:81-94 N '71

TIMMONS, Virginia G.
Clipboard. See issues of School arts
Organizing for art. il Sch Arts 70:12-13 F '71
Resource materials. See issues of School arts

TIN can sculpture. See Metal sculpture

TINKER, Frank A.
I flew it. il Pop Mech 136:88-91+ Ag '71
Museum joins the forest service. il por Am For 77:32-5 My '71
New Mexico nuggets. il Travel 136:36-9+ S '71
Unsafe trucks can kill you! il Pop Mech 135:63-7+ My '71

TINKER, Gene
Underwater equipment. il Motor B & S 127:32+ Ap '71
You're not too old to scuba dive! il Motor B & S 127:30-1+ Ap '71

TINKER, Hugh
Can urban guerrilla warfare succeed? Cur 129:52-7 My '71

TINKERS. See Gypsies in Ireland

TINNEY, James S.
Assemblies' line. Chr Today 15:45-6 S 10 '71
Black origins of the Pentecostal movement. Chr Today 16:4-6 O 8 '71

TINSLEY, I. J. and others
Binding of DDT to lecithin. bibliog il Science 174:145-7 O 8 '71

TINSLEY, Russell
Try station wagon camping. il Nat Wildlife 9:20-3 Ag '71

TINSMAN, Jay
We can't be objective about current issues. Todays Ed 60:60 N '71

TINTING of fabrics. See Dyes and dyeing

TINY Tim
My mother, right or wrong. McCalls 98:110 My '71

TIPPETT, Sir Michael
Finally a Tippett opera. H. Weinstock. Sat R 54:52 Ag 28 '71 •
Knot garden. Criticism
Hi Fi il 21:MA30-1 Ag '71 •
Midsummer marriage. Criticism
Esquire 76:72+ D '71 •
Midsummer marriage. E. Greenfield. il pors Am Rec G 37:696-8+ Je '71 •
Multilayered vision. P. G. Davis. il por Hi Fi 21:68-70 Ag '71 •
Tippett's Knot garden, Britten's Owen Wingrave. E. Greenfield. il Hi Fi 21:MA30-1 Ag '71 •

TIPPING
Notes for the corporate nomad: how much to tip. il Fortune 83:94 My '71
Wages and tips in restaurants and hotels; with tables and a chart. C. M. O'Connor. Mo Labor R 94:47-51 Jl '71
When should you tip? A. Vanderbilt. Ladies Home J 88:48 Ag '71

TIPTON, James
Evening in October; poem. Nation 212:156 F 1 '71

TIPTON, Stuart Guy
Perspective on consumerism; excerpts from address. Aviation W 95:9 Jl 12 '71

TIRE cord. See Tire fabrics

TIRE fabrics
Bigger stakes in tire belting. Bsns W p34 Ap 24 '71
In the eye of the storm; production of radial-type wire. il Forbes 108:64 D 1 '71

TIRE industry
Radial tire gives Akron a turn. il Bsns W p27 My 22 '71
See also
General tire and rubber company
Goodrich, B. F, company
Goodyear tire and rubber company

Consolidations and mergers

Tiremakers in a tug-of-war; battle for N. V. Rubberfabriek Vredestein. Bsns W p32 Ap 24 '71

Finance

Learning to play by the new rules. il Bsns W p20-1 Ag 28 '71

France

Michelin steps up its radial attack on Akron. il Bsns W p40 Ag 14 '71

TIRE wire. See Tire fabrics

TIRES, Automobile
Battle of the belts. il Time 97:92 Ap 26 '71
Drag racing tires. J. Dianna. il Hot Rod 24:38-40 Ag '71
Facts on glass tires. P. Weissler. il Mech Illus 67:65-7 Ja '71
Hot line report; all-season tires. B. Irvin. Mech Illus 67:73 N '71
New story on retreads. T. Tappett. il Mech Illus 67:94-6+ D '71
Radial tire gives Akron a turn. il Bsns W p27 My 22 '71
Removing the mystery from tire buying. D. Gregg. il Bet Hom & Gard 49:32-3+ My '71
Snow tires with studs, for safer driving on icy roads. il Consumer Bul 54:7-9 N '71

TIRES, Automobile—*Continued*
Street/racing tire. il Hot Rod 24:132-3 Jl '71
This year your studded snow tires may be illegal! M. Schultz. il Pop Mech 136:36 N '71
Tires. il Consumer Rep 36:472-7 Ag '71
Tires for your car. J. P. Norbye. il Pop Sci 198:65-7+ Ap '71
Tires, new and old. il Chem 44:3-4 Jl '71
See also
Goodrich, B. F. and company
Tire fabrics

Care
Doing it: tire care. il Motor T 23:78 D '71
How to double the life of your tires. M. Schultz. il Pop Mech 136:158-61+ O '71
Small-tire care. D. L. Gregg. Bet Hom & Gard 49:6+ Je '71
Steps to delay deterioration of tires and rubber goods. Consumer Bul 54:23 Ag '71

Testing
Tire safety gets a heavier tread. il Bsns W p 124+ My 15 '71
TIRES, Rubber
Moon tires are flat tires on earth. il Space World H-9-93:9-11 S '71

Retreading and recapping
Bandag gets a bounce out of retreads. il Bsns W p44+ My 22 '71
TIRES, Tractor
Questions and answers about tractor tires. P. B. Jones. il Suc Farm 69:no5 28-9 Mr '71
TIRRELL, Ruth
Beets are good from top to bottom. Org Gard & Farm 18:68-9 D '71
What's cooking?
So who needs perfect apples? Org Gard & Farm 18:130+ O '71
Which vegetables for the new garden? Org Gard & Farm 18:74-6 Jl '71
TISCH, Laurence Alan
How the Tisches run their little store. C. G. Burck. il por Fortune 83:158-61+ My '71 •
TISCHLER, Nancy M.
Pious pornography. Chr Today 15:14-15 Ap 23 '71
TISHLER, Max
New goal for science; excerpt from address. il Sat R 54:56-8 Je 5 '71
TISSUE banks
Vaccine makers set up cell banks. il Bsns W p72-3 S 4 '71
TISSUE fixation. See Tissues—Preservation
TISSUES
See also
Elastic tissues
Melanophores
Muscle

Culture
Ascorbic acid: a culture requirement for colony formation by mouse plasmacytoma cells. C. H. Park and others. bibliog il Science 174:720-2 N 12 '71
Developing neuromuscular junctions: first signs of chemical transmission during formation in tissue culture. N. Robbins and T. Yonezawa. bibliog il Science 172:395-8 Ap 23 '71
Functional sequences modulated by morphological transitions in human lymphoid cells grown in vitro. B. Drewinko and others. bibliog il Science 171:185-6 Ja 15 '71
Glucocorticoid receptors in lymphoma cells in culture: relationship to glucocorticoid killing activity. J. D. Baxter and others. bibliog il Science 171:189-91 Ja 15 '71
Histidase activity in cultivated human amniotic fluid cells. S. B. Melancon and others. bibliog il Science 173:627-8 Ag 13 '71
Human leukemic cells: in vitro growth of colonies containing the Philadelphia (Ph¹) chromosome. P. A. Chervenick and others. bibliog il Science 174:1134-6 D 10 '71
Hybrid cell line from a cloned immunoglobulin-producing mouse myeloma and a non-producing mouse lymphoma. B. Mohit and K. Fan . bibliog il Science 171:75-7 Ja 8 '71
Immunoglobulin production by human lymphocytoid lines and clones: absence of genic exclusion. A. D. Bloom and others. bibliog il Science 172:382-3 Ap 23 '71
Induction of murine C-type viruses from clonal lines of virus-free BALB/3T3 cells. S. A. Aaronson and others. bibliog il Science 174:157-9 O 8 '71
Junctions between cancer cells in culture: ultrastructure and permeability. R. G. Johnson and J. D. Sheridan. bibliog il Science 174:717-19 N 12 '71

Nerve trophic function: in vitro assay of effects of nerve tissue on muscle cholinesterase activity. T. L. Lentz. bibliog il Science 171:187-9 Ja 15 '71
Production of hemadsorption-negative areas by serums containing Australia antigen. D. H. Carver and D. S. Y. Seto. bibliog il Science 172:1265-7 Je 18 '71
Subhuman primate diploid cells: possible substrates for production of virus vaccines. J. C. Petricciani and others. bibliog il Science 174:1025-7 D 3 '71
Trout leukocytes: growth in oxygenated cultures. J. R. Heckman and others. bibliog Science 173:246 Jl 16 '71
Vaccine makers set up cell banks. il Bsns W p72-3 S 4 '71
See also
Culture media

Preservation
Cyclic adenosine monophosphate in brain areas: microwave irradiation as a means of tissue fixation. M. J. Schmidt and others. bibliog il Science 173:1142-3 S 17 '71
Dr Hsu's frozen zoo; preserving cells of animals doomed to extinction. Time 95:57 D 6 '71
TITAN (boosters) See Space vehicles—Propulsion systems
TITANIUM
Titanium follows aerospace nosedive. il Bsns W p20-1 S 4 '71
TITANIUM castings. See Metal castings
TITANIUM ores
See also
Ilmenite
TITICACA, LAKE
Biography of a lake. J. M. Reyes. il Américas 23:11-16 Ja '71
Titicaca, abode of the sun. L. Marden. il Nat Geog 139:272-94 F '71
TITLE pages
ANSI approves format for title leaves of a book. Pub W 199:33 Je 14 '71
Greatest invention since the title-page? auto-bibliography from incipit to cataloging-in-publication. V. W. Clapp. bibliog il Wilson Lib Bul 46:348-59 D '71
TITLE searching. See Land titles
TITLES (land) See Land titles
TITLES of books, stories, etc.
Much ado about titles. A. Gingrich. Esquire 76:6+ N '71

Anecdotes, facetiae, satire, etc.
Winners! results of contest in matching the titles of familiar books to familiar persons. N. Hazelton. Nat R 23:314+ Mr 23 '71
TITMUSS, Richard
Gift of blood; excerpt from The gift relationship. il Trans-Action 8:18-26+ Ja '71
TITO
President Tito of Yugoslavia visits the United States; exchange of greetings, toasts, October 28, 1971 Dept State Bul 65:590-1, 592-4 N 22 '71
about
Balkanization in Titoland. M. M. Mestrovic. Commonweal 94:252-3 My 21 '71 •
Battle Stalin lost by V. Dedijer. Review Nat R 23:318-19+ Mr 23 '71. M. Padev •
Closing the triangle. il por Time 98:42 N 1 '71 •
Dictatorships and gerontocracy. G. W. Ball. Newsweek 78:60 N 8 '71 •
Maverick red gets red carpet welcome. il por U S News 71:92 N 8 '71 •
Nonaligner in Washington. il por Time 98: 46+ N 8 '71 •
Tito's way. por Newsweek 77:42 My 17 '71 •
VIP from Belgrade. il por Newsweek 78:57+ N 8 '71 •
Working against time. por Time 97:37 My 17 '71 •
Yugoslavia: Tito's daring experiment. il Time 98:24+ Ag 9 '71 •
Yugoslavia's future: Tito as Diocletian. M. M. Mestrovic. Commonweal 95:317-18 Ja 7 '72
TITOV, Iurii
Yuri Titov: profile of a Soviet artist. M. Bourdeaux. Chr Cent 88:1264-6 O 27 '71 •
TIVERTON, R.I.
Opinion: saving a town for the future; Tiverton, R.I. and the Northeast petroleum refining corporation. L. Durfee. Mlle 74:66+ D '71
TJAARDA, Tom
Sinthesis 2000. W. Wyss. il pors Motor T 23:75 Je '71 •

TO live another summer, to pass another winter; musical comedy. See Musical comedies, revues, etc.—Criticisms, plots, etc.

TOAST
Croutons & other toasty tricks. il Ladies Home J 88:140 S '71
Delicious with cheese and jelly? rusks. il Sunset 147:188 O '71

TOASTERS, Electric. See Electric toasters

TOBACCO
See also
Cigarettes
Cigars

History
Tobacco among the Karuks. C. Miles. il Hobbies 76:146-7+ N '71

TOBACCO industry
Filtering out theft and tax increases. il Bsns W p22 Ap 3 '71
Uses of adversity. Newsweek 78:64+ Jl 19 '71
See also
American brands, inc.

Advertising
See also
Cigarettes—Advertising

Canada
Will the ad ban spread north? il Bsns W p24-5 My 1 '71

TOBACCO pipes
Lure and lore of pipes. Mech Illus 67:32 Ja '71
Tobacco among the Karuks. C. Miles. il Hobbies 76:146-7+ N '71

TOBACCO subsidies
America's quiet crimes against people. C. Rogers. Chr Cent 88:769 Je 23 '71

TOBACH, Ethel
Mental health movement meets women's lib; interview. Ment Hy 55:1-9 Ja '71

TOBAGO (island)
See also
Architecture, Domestic—Tobago (island)

TOBIAS, Andrew
Funny money game, by A. Tobias. Review Bsns W p8 D 25 '71. J. Madrick •

TOBIAS, C. A. and others
Radiological physics characteristics of the extracted heavy ion beams of the bevatron. bibliog il Science 174:1131-4 D 10 '71

TOBIAS, Tobi
And if you're a good girl, I'll take you to a Makarova rehearsal. il pors Dance Mag 45:38 My '71
Nikolais and Louis: a new space. il pors Dance Mag 45:46-54 F '71

TOBIN, Richard L.
(ed) Communications. See Communications issues of Saturday review
Jungle, desert, icebergs, and hunger. il Sat R 54:20 O 23 '71
Puritan ethic today. Sat R 55:16 Ja 1 '72

TOBIN, Ronald W.
Man in the middle: the college professor. il America 125:176-8 S 18 '71

TOBOGGANS and tobogganning
See also
Sleds

TOBRINER, Mathew O.
Due process behind prison walls. Nation 213: 367-9 O 18 '71

TOCQUEVILLE, Alexis de
Time, work and leisure today. G. J. Dahl. Chr Cent 88:185-9 F 10 '71 •

TODD, Charles C. jr
Educational cooperatives. Clear House 45: 383-4 F '71

TODD, John H.
Chemical languages of fishes; with biographical sketch. il Sci Am 224:12, 98-106+ My '71
Shaping an organic America. il Org Gard & Farm 18:50-5 S; 78-85 O; 63-9 N; 57-61 D '71

TODD, Michael
Around the bend in eighty days. S. J. Perelman. New Yorker 47:22-4 Ja 1 '72 •

TODD, Paul, and others
Spatial distribution of biological effect in a 3.9-Gev nitrogen ion beam. bibliog il Science 174:1127-8 D 10 '71

TODD, Richard
Gathering at Bunnymede. Atlan 229:86-8 Ja '72
Masks of Kurt Vonnegut, jr. il pors N Y Times Mag p 16-17+ Ja 24 '71
Notes on corporate man. il Atlan 228:83-8+ O '71

TODD, W. M. and Voss, John
Consortium of academies: a new way to found international scholarly institutions. Bul Atom Sci 27:29-32 F '71

TODTENBIER, Ed
Field & stream interviews: the Nation's best topwater bass fisherman? interview. il por Field & S 76:36-7+ D '71

TOFFEE. See Candy

TOFFLER, Alvin
Coping with future shock; condensation. Read Digest 99:81-6 Ag '71
How to cope with Future shock; interview. il Seventeen 30:146-7+ Mr '71
Is the family obsolete; interview, ed. by J. Kronenberger. Look 35:35 Ja 26 '71
about
Youth and the future: how to avoid future shock. il por Sr Schol 98:3-6 My 10 '71 •

TOILET
See also
Beauty, Personal

TOILET articles
Father's day specials. P. Van Wagenen. il Parents Mag 46:18 Je '71

TOILET preparations
Beauty & the bath. S. Lindsay. See issues of House beautiful
Natural beauty. il Redbook 137:46, 70-1 Jl '71
Sweet smell of sachet. il Ladies Home J 88:74 D '71
See also
Bath preparations
Cosmetics
Deodorants
Shampoos

TOILET training. See Infants—Care and hygiene

TOILETS
Finally, an end to toilet-tank trickle. il Pop Mech 136:176 D '71
Goodbye to the flush toilet. R. Rodale. Org Gard & Farm 18:28-32 N '71
Modernizing an old W.C. il Mech Illus 67:116+ Ap '71

TOILETS for boats. See Boats—Toilet facilities

TOKAMAK devices. See Plasma (ionized gases)

TOKAY geckos. See Lizards

TOKSÖZ, M. Nafi, and Kehrer, H. H.
Underground nuclear explosions: tectonic utility and dangers. bibliog il Science 173: 230-3 Jl 16 '71

TOKYO
Tokyo: the problem city after the shock. il Bsns W p66-9 O 9 '71
See also
Stock exchange—Tokyo

Air pollution
Blue sky for Tokyo. il Time 97:40 Ap 12 '71
Kogai: environmental disruption in Japan. S. Tsuru. il UNESCO Courier 24:6-13 Jl '71

Airports
Tokyo's new airport delayed by land acquisition disputes. C. Brownlow. il Aviation W 95:110-12 N 15 '71

Architecture
Night in the capsule. il Newsweek 77:117 Je 7 '71
Tokyo; New sky building. il Arch Forum 134:54-7 Ja '71

City planning
Blue sky for Tokyo. il Time 97:40 Ap 12 '71

Crime
World's safest city. il Newsweek 78:76 D 6 '71

Description
No cumshaw, no rickshaw. N. Algren. il Holiday 49:32-5+ Jl '71 (to be cont)
Tokyo, directed by Fellini. il Nation 212: 114-16 Ja 25 '71
Tokyo entertains visitors western style. Bsns W p75-6 O 9 '71
Tokyo in bloom. D. Butwin. Sat R 54:45-6+ My 1 '71

Hotels, restaurants, etc.
Fast-food stands sprout on the Ginza. il Bsns W p41 O 16 '71

Music
Report:
Fledermaus. S. P. Chizeck. Opera N 35: 33 Ap 10 '71

TOLAND, John
Trade winds; interview, ed. by C. Amory. Sat R 54:22 Ja 23 '71

TOLAND, Toshiko
Trade winds; interview, ed. by C. Amory. Sat R 54:22 Ja 23 '71

TOLEDO, Ohio

Education, Board of
Threat to freedom: Sylvester and the magic pebble. R. V. Fitzgerald. il por Library J 96:1429-30 Ap 15 '71

School board
See Toledo, Ohio—Education, Board of
TOLEDO, Ohio, public library. See Toledo-Lucas County, Ohio, public library
TOLEDO, Ore
No outside help wanted. C. R. Meek. il Am City 86:79 Mr '71
TOLEDO-LUCAS COUNTY, Ohio, public library
Threat to freedom: Sylvester and the magic pebble. R. V. Fitzgerald. il por Library J 96:1429-30 Ap 15 '71
TOLERANCE. See Toleration
TOLERANCE of pain. See Pain
TOLERATION
Born free, of bigotry; with study-discussion program, by M. M. Conant. B. W. Overstreet. bibliog il PTA Mag 65:8-10, 34 F '71
How tolerant are we? il Sr Schol 99:2-5 O 25 '71
See also
Prejudice
TOLES, George E.
Ancient art of batik making. il Design 72:8-10 mid-Sum '71
Experiment in sculpture. il Design 73:32-3 Wint '71
TOLL bridges
See also
Chesapeake Bay bridge-tunnel
TOLLETT, Kenneth S.
Southern justice for blacks. il por Ebony 26:58-60+ O '71
TOLSON, Melvin B.
The new Negro; poem. Negro Hist Bul 34:88 Ap '71
TOLSTOI, Lev Nikolaevich, graf
Last year of Leo Tolstoy, by V. Bulgakov. Review
Nation 213:276-7 S 27 '71. H. McLean •
Newsweek por 77:92 Mr 8 '71
Tolstoy, my father, by I. Tolstoy. Review
Sat R 54:47-9 N 20 '71. M. Friedberg •
TOLSTOY, Leo. See Tolstoi, L. N.
TOM, Theodore Benton
Rap 'n 'pinion. por Motor T 23:12 F '71
TOM Castro, the implausible impostor; story. See Borges, J. L.
TOMA, David
Cop for all seasons. il por Newsweek 78:40 Jl 19 '71 •
TOMALES BAY
Hour and half north of San Francisco is Tomales Bay. il Sunset 146:60-1+ My '71
TOMASINI, René
Agnew à la mode. Time 97:24 Mr 1 '71 •
Tomasini vs. judges. il Newsweek 77:40 Mr 1 '71 •
TOMASSI, Jacquelyn
La mama exposée; poem. Am Scholar 40:322 Spr '71
TOMASSO, Enrico
Young man with a horn. por Time 98:64 S 13 '71 •
TOMATO juice
See also
Sacramento foods (firm)
TOMATOES
Cherry tomatoes halved, stuffed. il Sunset 147:148 S '71
Snow job for tomatoes; whitewashing. F. L. Elam. il Farm J 95:24 Jl '71
Tomatoes! symposium. il Org Gard & Farm 18:60-77 Mr '71
Two-by-four tomatoes, P. Medway. Org Gard & Farm 18:28-9 My '71
When tomatoes don't set fruit. Sunset 147:144 Jl '71
See also
Cookery—Vegetables

Hybrids
Three outstanding tomato varieties. Org Gard & Farm 18:64-5 Mr '71
TOMB of the unknown soldier. See Unknown soldiers
TOMBS
Raising the dead; skyscraper cemetery. il Time 98:72 N 29 '71
See also
Lenin, V. I.—Tomb
TOMBS (prison) See New York (city)—Prisons and reformatories
TOMBSTONES. See Sepulchral monuments
TOMHANNOCK reservoir, N.Y. See Reservoirs

TOMKIEVICZ, Shirley
Flaubert's Madame Bovary. il pors Horizon 13:114-19 Wint '71
TOMKINS, Calvin
How now? New Yorker 46:28 Ja 23 '71
Profiles: H. Geldzahler. por New Yorker 47:58-60+ N 6 '71
Rhinoceros: an appreciation. New Yorker 47:59-61 N 20 '71
TOMKINS, George S.
Canada. bibliog il Focus 21:1-8 Je '71
TOMLIN, Lily
Lily Tomlin at the circus; interview. New Yorker 47:33-4 Ap 10 '71
Most wanted '71: funny Lily Tomlin; interview, ed. by L. Kent. pors Vogue 157:102-3+ Je '71
TOMLINSON, Kenneth Y.
Our VA hospitals are in trouble. Read Digest 98:163-4+ Mr '71
Watch on the Potomac. Read Digest 98:117-18 Je '71
—and Denison, George
Watch on the Potomac. Read Digest 98:205-6 Ap; 99:25-7+ Jl '71
TOMMY; ballet. See Ballets—Criticisms
TOMORROW is too late; story. See Morrow, S.
TOMPKINS, Jan
Last temptation of Delilah. Motor B & S 127:72-3+ Ag '71
TOMPKINS, Peter
Secrets of the great pyramid; excerpts. il Horizon 13:38-49 Wint '71
TOMPKINS, Warwick, Jr
Outfitting for offshore. il Motor B & S 128:46-7+ Ag '71
TOMS RIVER, N.J. yacht club. See Yacht clubs
TOMS RIVER challenge cup race. See Sailboat racing
TONALITY
Emerging triadic tonality in the fifteenth century. D. M. Randel. bibliog f il Mus Q 57:73-86 Ja '71
Musical events; atonality: New York Philharmonic concert in Philharmonic Hall. W. Sargeant. New Yorker 47:164 O 23 '71
TONE arm, Phonograph. See Phonograph—Tone arm
TONE-burst generators. See Signal generators
TONGASS national forest, Alaska. See National forests
TONGUE
See also
Taste
TONGUES, Gift of. See Gift of tongues
TONGYAI, Thomas
Run, Tommy, run! R. Rosenbaum. il Esquire 76:51-8+ Jl '71 •
TONKIN GULF incident, 1964
From Roots of involvement; excerpt. M. Kalb and E. Abel. Sat R 54:33 Mr 27 '71
Tonkin Gulf, by E. G. Windchy. Review
New Repub 165:26+ S 18 '71. C. Marcy
Tonkin repeal. Sr Schol 98:2 F 1 '71
TONKS, Lewi
Obituary
Phys Today 24:75 N '71. K. H. Kingdon
TONOPAH, Nev.
Silver boom that fizzled; Hughes rush to buy Nevada mines. il Bsns W p42 O 16 '71
TONSILLECTOMY. See Throat—Surgery
TOOKER, Frank H.
Accurate d.c.-less clock-pulse generator. il Electr World 86:69 Ag '71
Digital frequency dividers for any ratio. il Electr World 86:60-2 Ag '71
Don't bypass the hobby shop. il Pop Electr 35:50-2+ O '71
Equivalency in RTL circuits. il Pop Electr 34:49-53+ F; 39-46 Je '71
Make your own integrated-circuit modules. il Electr World 85:62-3 Mr '71
Novel counter, decoder, readout. il Electr World 86:40-2 D '71
Power-supply improvement. il Electr World 86:73 S '71
Unusual, but useful, digital circuits. il Electr World 85:36-7+ Ap '71
TOOL and die industry
Faster way to turn out dies. il Bsns W p86 Ja 30 '71
TOOL research and engineering corporation
Thriving company in a slow industry. il Bsns W p22-3 D 18 '71
TOOL sheds. See Sheds
TOOLS
All those electronic chemicals. J. R. Squires. Electr World 85:44 My '71
Chemicals for electronics. L. Cantor. il Pop Electr 34:25-8+ Ap; 63-6 My '71

TOOLS—*Continued*

Don't bypass the hobby shop; hard-to-find tools and materials. F. H. Tooker. il Pop Electr 35:50-2+ O '71

Hand tools for the technician. J. Frye. il Electr World 86:48-50+ S '71

Handy tool kits for a lady when husband's not in reach. il Sunset 146:145-6 Ap '71

Little-known tools you'll want to add to your toolbox. H. Wicks. il Pop Mech 136:162-4 D '71

McCall's handywoman: 12 tools to begin with. il McCalls 98:182 F '71

New tools for improving your home. H. Wicks. il Pop Mech 135:38-9 My '71

Special tools for your equipment, tinkers only. N. Goldberg. il Pop Phot 69:56+ Jl '71

Spray chemicals for servicing. J. Frye. il Electr World 85:39-42+ My '71

13 tools every man should own. R. J. De-Cristoforo. il Mech Illus 67:112-14+ Ja '71

Tools for tuning and sprucing up. J. Duffett. Motor B & S 127:90-1 Ap '71

Tools the pros use on plastic laminates. H. Wicks. il Pop Mech 136:170-2+ N '71

Woodworker's discovery, Japanese tools. il Sunset 147:56-9 S '71

See also

Electric tools
Hydraulic tools
Pneumatic tools
Stone implements and weapons
  also names of tools, e.g. Augers

Anecdotes, facetiae, satire, etc.

So you want the right tool for the job? excerpt from The complete book of pitfalls. D. Williamson. il Read Digest 98:148-50 Mr '71

Storage

See also
Sheds

TOOLS, Rescue. See Life saving equipment

TOOLSHED; story. See Kean, G.

TOOMEY, Bill

—and Toomey, Mary
  Exercises for the two of you; interview, ed. by S. Obre. il pors Ladies Home J 88:90-1 Ap '71
  Ineligible married man. W. F. Reed. il por Sports Illus 34:42-4+ Ap 12 '71 *

TOOMEY, Mary. See Toomey, B. jt. auth.

TOOMEY, Ursula
  Peace: proud parent of a great rose family. il Home Gard 58:34 Je '71

TOOTH decay. See Dental caries

TOOTH powders and pastes. See Dentifrices

TOOTHBRUSHES
  Appliances that keep you smiling. Bet Hom & Gard 49:136 N '71
  Toothbrushes. il Changing T 25:13-14 My '71

TOOTHPICKS, Electric
  Appliances that keep you smiling. Bet Hom & Gard 49:136 N '71
  Dental irrigators. il Consumer Rep 36:387-92 Je '71

TOPKAPI Sarayi museum. See Istanbul—Galleries and museums

TOPOGRAPHIC maps
  Maps for going afield. T. Fegely. il Field & S 76:150 Je '71

TOPOL, Chaim
  Topol: fiddler on the screen; with report by J. Bonfante. il pors Life 71:87-90 D 3 '71 *

TOPPER corporation
  Dawn: plastic doll at sixty-eighth annual American toy fair. New Yorker 47:31-2 Mr 20 '71

TOPPING, Audrey
  Acupuncture: myth cure? il Vogue 159:94-5+ Ja 1 '72
  Return to changing China. il por Nat Geog 140:800-33 D '71
    about
  Topping the Times. il por Newsweek 77:60 My 24 '71 *

TOPS, Bottle. See Bottle caps and seals

TOPSOIL. See Soils

TORCHES
  Pinpoint propane torch. J. R. Walker. il Mech Illus 67:92 Ja '71
    See also
  Electric torches
  Gas torches

TORELL, Bruce N.
  He's bullish on jet engines. por Bsns W p70 Jl 10 '71 *

TORN, Rip
  Rip Torn: the case of the Hollywood 1. C. Pyes. il pors Ramp Mag 9:40-6 Mr '71 *

TORNABENE, Lyn
  How America lives. il Ladies Home J 88:82-3+ Ja '71
  Liberation of Betty Friedan. il McCalls 98:84-5+ My '71
  Where the rich grow young. il Ladies Home J 89:86-7+ Ja '72

TORNADO detection. See Tornadoes

TORNADOES
  Detecting tornadoes by radio. L. Purrett. il Sci N 100:12-13 Jl 3 '71
  Devastation in the Delta. R. Rein. il Time 97:17 Mr 8 '71
  Here's latest on detecting tornadoes by TV. R. Lutz. il Suc Farm 69:34 My '71
  Tornado season of 1970. A. D. Pearson and A. J. Miller. il Weatherwise 24:12-17 F '71

TORNERO, Sergio Gonzales. See Gonzales Tornero, S.

TORNHEIM, Keith. See Lowenstein, J. jt. auth.

TORNQUIST, Elizabeth
  Rebel yell academies. il Ramp Mag 10:12+ S '71

TORO (asteroid) See Asteroids

TOROK, Lou
  How you help the burglar. il por Pop Mech 136:86-7 S '71
  On the street where I live. Sat R 54:4 Ag 28 '71

TORONTO

Architecture

Canadians build an office complex by Mies van der Rohe in Toronto; with introd. by M. F. Schmertz. il Arch Rec 149:105-14 Mr '71

Common parts and legible spaces in Toronto's O.M.A. building. R. Jensen. il Arch Rec 150:127-34 S '71

Water wonderland; Ontario place. J. M. Dixon. il Arch Forum 135:30-7 Jl '71

Art

Toronto. M. Amaya. il Art in Am 59:122-3 My; 102:5 S '71

Newspapers

Lost strike goes on and on; ITU strike against Toronto's three daily newspapers. Bsns W p90+ F 6 '71

Stores

Corporate Rip Van Winkle; Eaton's. il Forbes 107:37 Je 15 '71

TORONTO dance theatre. See Dance companies

TORONTO public library
  Toronto's new library stalled by disagreement. Library J 96:1316 Ap 15 '71

TORONTO university press
  Publishing the pre-shrunk; reprint. I. Montagnes. il Pub W 200:13-15 N 22 '71

TORPEDOES
  Westinghouse gets torpedoed; Mark 48 guided torpedo. Bsns W p 19 Jl 10 '71

TORQUE wrenches
  What you should know about torque wrenches. E. F. Lindsley. il Pop Sci 198:87-9 Ja '71

TORRE, Joe
  Aesop is the official scorer. M .Mulvoy. il por Sports Illus 35:18-19 Jl 26 '71 *

TORRES, Camilo
  Catholic revolutionaries: part of the solution or part of the problem? J. Finn. Commonweal 94:456-8 S 3 '71 *
  Postscript on Torres. J. Deedy. Commonweal 94:26 Mr 19 '71 *

TORRES, Juan José
  One more time. il Time 98:27 Ag 30 '71 *
  Push from the right. Newsweek 78:39-40 Ag 30 '71 *

TORRES-GARCIA, Joaquín
  Joaquín Torres-García. B. Duncan. il pors Américas 22:11-18 N '70 *

TORRES STRAIT
  Rugged run to New Guinea. P. Fitzgerald. il por Motor B & S 127:58-9+ F '71

TORREY, E. Fuller
  Of babalawos and shamans. M. Pines. McCalls 98:43 Ag '71 *

TORRIENTE, José de la
  Cuba is there. Nation 213:517-18 N 22 '71 *

TORTA. See Cookery, Italian

TORTA rustica. See Cookery, Italian

TORTE. See Cake

TORTILLAS. See Cookery, Mexican

TORTOISE; story. See Hernández, A. D.

TORTOISES
  Slow and serene; interview. P. Wohl. New Yorker 47:30-2 My 1 '71

TORTOLA (island)
  Tortola. B. Bell. il Travel 136:60-3 D '71

TORTS
Technology and the law; technology by private tort action. Sci Am 224:45-6 F '71

TOSCA; opera. See Puccini, G.

TOSCANINI, Arturo
Limited edition; twenty discsful of Toscaniniana. C. J. Luten. il Am Rec G 37:744-5+ Jl '71 *

TOSI, Donald J. See Kindsvatter, R. jt. auth.

TOTAL in-flight simulator. See Airplanes, Training

TOTALITARIANISM
Meaning of left and right. T. Szamuely. il Nat R 23:923-7+ Ag 24 '71
Notes and comment; effect of My Lai on American democracy and totalitarianism. New Yorker 47:29-32 Ap 10 '71
See also
Fascism

TOTEM poles
Trees of the totem culture; excerpts from Edge of a continent. D. G. Kelley. il Am West 8:18-21+ My '71

TOUCH
Touch sparks love. il Good H 173:14+ Ag '71

TOUCH of nature; story. See Hayden, J.

TOURÉ, Halima
People who discovered the beauty of black. il Redbook 136:91+ Mr '71
(ed) See McElin, T. W. Hysterectomy

TOURÉ, Sékou
Blood rites. Newsweek 77:36 F 8 '71 *

TOURISM. See Tourist trade

TOURIST blight. See Landscape protection

TOURIST tapes. See Tape recordings

TOURIST trade
Paradox. il Forbes 108:57 S 15 '71
Tourism tries to shake a bad trip. il Bsns W p 18 Ap 24 '71
Travel: the going things. S. Cuneo. il Mlle 74:78-80+ D '71; 40-2 Ja '72
Winter season starts off warm. il Bsns W p30 D 4 '71
See also
Travel—Economic aspects
Travel agencies and agents

Africa, East
East Africa's tourist boom begins. il Fortune 83:84-91 Je '71
Safari may answer your vacation dilemma. Bsns W p 113 S 25 '71

Australia
Going things. il Mlle 73:120-2+ O '71

China (People's Republic)
Slow boat to China. Newsweek 78:64+ Ag 2 '71
Traveling in China: tips for the tourist. Newsweek 77:20-1 Ap 26 '71
What the tourists are finding in mainland China. Bsns W p85 O 30 '71

Dominican Republic
It's one for fun in tomorrow's sun. W. Johnson. il Sports Illus 34:39-41 F 1 '71

Europe
Travel Europe, with an eye on economy; symposium. il Holiday 49:45-71+ F '71

Europe, Eastern
New boom in travel through the iron curtain. W. MacDougall. il U S News 70:33-5 Je 28 '71

Europe, Western
Booked for travel; prospects of summer travel abroad. D. Butwin. Sat R 54:50+ My 15; 54-7 My 22 '71
Bright ideas for this year's Europe-bound. J. Harayda. il Mlle 72:106-7+ Mr '71
Europe on a budget. F. Shemanski. il Schol Teach Jr/Sr High p 16-17 Mr 8 '71

Florida
Airlines, space center weighing impact of Disney on Florida tourism. W. H. Gregory. il Aviation W 95:34-5+ Ag 16 '71

France
Paris on parade. S. Turner. il Schol Teach Jr/Sr High p 18-19 Mr 8 '71

Greece, Modern
Going things: getting to Greece. S. Cuneo. il por Mlle 73:58-60 Jl '71

Hawaii
Dreams come true in Buru Hawaii. C. Black. il Sat R 54:62-4 O 23 '71
Hawaii pursues the Japanese yen. il Bsns W p26 My 22 '71

Hawaii's impossible choice; jobs and progress vs. Beauty and ecology. il Forbes 108: 31-4 Ag 15 '71

Israel
Fly El Elijah! A. R. Stees. Chr Cent 88:1471-2 D 15 '71

Italy
Unwelcome mat; tourists and strikes. il Newsweek 77:46+ Je 7 '71

Japan
Hard, cold facts of winter games. B. Ottum. Sports Illus 35:65-6 N 15 '71

Puerto Rico
Clouds over Puerto Rico. il Time 97:84 My 24 '71

Swaziland
C'est si bon. por Newsweek 78:61-2 N 22 '71

United States
Does anyone want to visit the U.S.A? with views of D. K. Inouye. H. Sutton. il Sat R 55:36-7+ Ja 1 '72
President signs bill to promote travel to the United States. Dept State Bul 63:729 D 14 '70

Venezuela
Venezuela talk. D. Messinesi. il Vogue 158: 16 O 15 '71

West Indies
West Indies vacation. il Ebony 26:148-50+ Je '71

TOURISTS. See Travelers

TOURISTS, Church work with. See Church work with tourists, travelers, etc.

TOURISTS and customs administration. See Customs service and tourists

TOURNAMENT of champions. See Golf—Tournaments

TOURNAMENT of roses. See Pasadena, Calif. —Parades

TOURNAMENTS
Charge, sir knight! National jousting championship. A. J. Riendeau. il Parks & Rec 6: 31-4+ Ap '71
Charging full tilt into a bloody fray; jousting 1971 style. C. Gammon. il Sports Illus 35:26-8+ S 13 '71

TOURNIER, Michel
Letter from Paris. Genêt. New Yorker 47: 116 Mr 13 '71 *

TOURS, Package. See Air travel; Travel

TOVATT, Anthony, and DeVries, Ted
This world of English. See issues of English journal

TOWBOATS. See Tugboats

TOWE, Kenneth M. See Gibson, T. G. jt. auth.

TOWELL, William Earnest
Great Alaskan inconsistency. Am For 77:46-7 S '71
Soaring with the scouts. il Am For 77:38-9+ Je '71

TOWELS
Sensational sun towels. il Redbook 137:96-7+ Je '71

TOWER, John Goodwin
Labor law reform: essential to fight inflation. por Nations Bsns 59:42-5 D '71

TOWER, Whitney
¡Arriba! Canonero does it again. il Sports Illus 34:22-5 My 24 '71
Happy story ends. il Sports Illus 34:18-21 Je 14 '71
Missing data unavailable; Venezuela's Canonero II. il Sports Illus 34:18-21 My 10 '71
One more blur in a confusion Derby. il Sports Illus 34:20-1 Ap 26 '71
Pretenders to the crown. il Sports Illus 34: 26-9 Ap 12 '71
Son of the Axe chops 'em. il Sports Illus 34:22-3 Mr 15 '71
They're all running after the Flag. il Sports Illus 34:28-31 Ap 5 '71
Unconscious, List and Twist. il Sports Illus 34:32-3 My 3 '71
You can't blame a girl for trying. il Sports Illus 35:30-1 N 22 '71
(ed) See Ryan, E. B. Putting the case to Howie the horse

TOWERS
Elgin clock tower (title varies) O. R. Hagans. il Hobbies 76:125-7 Ag; 126-8 S; 126-7 O '71
See also
Television towers
Water towers

Anecdotes, facetiae, satire, etc.
Re the tower project. G. Keillor. New Yorker 47:25 Ag 28 '71

TOWING
How to tow a trailer. A. R. Roalman. il Pop Mech 135:141-2+ My '71
Trailering, it helps to practice. Sunset 146:70+ Je '71
What science can tell you about trailer towing. J. Dunne. il Pop Sci 199:94-5 Jl '71
See also
Boats—Towing

TOWN, Christopher D. and others
DNA polymerase required for rapid repair of X-ray-induced DNA strand breaks in vivo. bibliog il Science 172:851-4 My 21 '71

TOWN houses. See City houses

TOWN life. See City and town life

TOWN ordinances. See Municipal ordinances

TOWNE, Anthony
Harboring of Daniel Berrigan. R. Wool. il Esquire 76:156-61+ N '71 •
Stringfellow-Towne indictment; with statement. J. R. Nelson. Chr Cent 88:60-1 Ja 20 '71 •

TOWNHOUSES. See City houses

TOWNLEY, Betty Lou
ALA asked to investigate Oklahoma County firing. pors Library J 96:3075+ O 1 '71 •
Oklahoma City-County library fires Betty Lou Townley. Library J 96:2417+ Ag '71 •

TOWNS, Elmer L.
Big churches? Yes! Chr Today 16:6+ N 5 '71

TOWNS, Abandoned. See Abandoned towns

TOWNS, New. See New cities and towns

TOWNS, Restored. See Villages, Restored

TOWNSEND, Charles L.
Osmotic pump, an unusual timer and how to enhance contrast in astronomical photographs. il Sci Am 225:103-4 D '71

TOWNSEND, Claire
Story of a teen-age Nader raider. B. L. Collier. il pors N Y Times Mag p30-1+ Mr 14 '71; Discussion. p 102 Ap 4 '71

TOWNSEND, John Rowe
Children's books in Britain: aiming hard for a new golden age. il Pub W 200:67-9 Jl 19 '71
In literary terms; excerpt from A sense of story. bibliog Horn Bk 47:347-53 Ag '71

TOWY RIVER
Return to the river of yesterday. C. Gammon. il Sports Illus 34:78-80+ My 24 '71

TOXINS and antitoxins
Aflatoxin P₁: a new aflatoxin metabolite in monkeys. J. Dalezios and others. bibliog il Science 171:584-5 F 12 '71
Batrachotoxin: chemistry and pharmacology. E. X. Albuquerque and others. bibliog il Science 172:995-1002 Je 4 '71
Palytoxin: a new marine toxin from a coelenterate. R. E. Moore and P. J. Scheuer. bibliog il Science 172:495-8 Ap 30 '71
Poison in shellfish. Newsweek 79:39 Ja 10 '72
Snake neurotoxins: effect of disulfide reduction on interaction with electroplax. E. Bartels and T. L. Rosenberry. bibliog il Science 174:1236-7 D 17 '71
Synaptic transmission in the crayfish: increased release of transmitter substance by bacterial endotoxin. I. Parnas and others. bibliog il Science 171:1153-5 Mr 19 '71
Toxic sweet potatoes. Chem 45:26-7 Ja '72
See also
Red tide

TOXOPLASMOSIS
Mother, put the cat out. il Newsweek 78:67-8 N 29 '71
Toxoplasmosis. D. A. Schanche. McCalls 99:56+ N '71

TOY houses. See Doll houses

TOY industry
Look who's playing with toys! il Forbes 108:22-4+ D 15 '71
Safe and lovable toys; Vermont wooden toy company. B. Baer. il por Am Home 74:94-5+ S '71
Toy battle is no game. il Bsns W p38 F 27 '71
See also
Hasbro industries
Mattel, inc.
Topper corporation

Great Britain
See also
Lesney products, ltd.

TOYLI, Matthew, and Gerhardt, John
Educational film program of the American meteorological society; with list of films. Weatherwise 24:228-9+ O '71

TOYNBEE, Arnold Joseph
Our English cousin. Am Heritage 22:109 O '71 •

TOYOTA (automobile) See Automobiles, Foreign

TOYS
Are toys passé? with study-discussion program, by M. M. Conant. P. Levenstein. il PTA Mag 66:16-18 N '71
Children's furniture & just-for-fun things. M. Kraft. il Good H 172:116-21 Mr '71
Clackers: a fun toy, but how safe? Good H 173:204 S '71
Educational toys no help. il Sci Digest 69:59 Mr '71
Great toy tangle. M. Sutphen. il House B 113:64-5+ D '71
How Good housekeeping institute evaluates toys. il Good H 173:6 N '71
New surge in toys that teach. il Ebony 26:114-16+ N '70
On and off the avenue (cont) New Yorker 47:109-10+ D 11 '71
Remember these? Old-timey toys to make. D. Ashe. il Bet Hom & Gard 49:52-3+ D '71
Safe and lovable toys; Vermont wooden toy company. B. Baer. il por Am Home 74:94-5+ S '71
Toys for the handicapped. il Time 97:48 Ap 26 '71
Toys that bring joy and challenge. M. Michaelson. il Todays Health 49:34-6+ D '71
Trouble in Toyland. il Time 98:76 D 13 '71
Water toys for the tides of summer. S. H. Schraub. il House B 113:77 Jl '71
Yo-yo power! A. Hoffman. il por Esquire 76:106-7+ O '71
See also
Christmas gifts for children
Creative playthings, inc.
Dolls
Hoops
Playgrounds, Home—Equipment
Schwarz, F. A. O (firm)
Toy industry

History
George Brown toy sketchbook, ed. and intro. by E. F. Barenholtz. Review
Antiques 100:354+ S '71. K. D. Barron

Safety devices and measures
Uncle Sam moves on unsafe toys, slowly. Consumer Rep 36:143-4 Mr '71

TOYS, Hazardous
Balls of fire: inflammable plastic-foam balls. il Consumer Rep 37:4-5 Ja '72
Cap pistol standards not good enough. Consumer Rep 36:527 S '71
Caution: toys ahead. il Good H 173:112-13+ N '71
Dangerous toys. il Life 71:79-82 N 12 '71
This ball is a ball of fire; Nerf ball. il Consumer Rep 36:132 Mr '71
Toys that don't care. by E. Swartz. Review Nation 212:763-4 Je 14 '71. J. Cross
Two toys, two hazards. Terry toy; Magnetic train set. il Consumer Rep 36:339 Je '71
Will the Toy safety act achieve its intended purpose? il Consumer Bul 54:2+ D '71

TRACE elements
Dietary trace elements and antioxidants. il Chem 44:23-4 Ja '71
Trace elements: no longer good vs. bad. J. L. Arehart. il Sci N 100:112-13 Ag 14 '71

TRACHTMAN, Paul
Parent endorses classroom chaos. Life 71:149-52 D 17 '71

TRACING cloth drawing. See Drawing

TRACK athletics
Africa, U.S. begin track series; Pan Africa-USA international track meet, Durham, N. C. il por Ebony 26:143-6+ O '71
Africa was right on in Dixie; Pan-Africa-U.S.A. international track meet, Durham, N.C. P. Carry. il Sports Illus 35:20-3 Jl 26 '71
Firstest, fastest and mostest; AAU track and field championships in Eugene, Ore. P. Putnam and S. Myslenski. il Sports Illus 35:18-21 Jl 5 '71
He takes off, he takes it in; UCLA freshman. J. McAlister. P. Putnam. il pors Sports Illus 34:26-8+ My 17 '71
Still something of a summit meeting; U.S.-Russian track meet. G. S. Brown. il Sports Illus 35:20-1 Jl 12 '71
This one was for James; NCAA track and field championships in Seattle. P. F. Putnam. il Sports Illus 34:54-6 Je 28 '71
See also
Decathlon
Jumping
Pan American games
Pentathlon
Running
Vaulting (sport)

TRACKING (education) See Ability grouping
in education
TRACKING and trailing
Fundamentals of deer stalking. D. Harbour.
il Field & S 76:42-3+ Ag '71
Looping for whitetail. A. Mitchell. il Field
& S 76:50-1+ O '71
TRACTOR driving
Can you pass the tractor driver's test? Suc
Farm 69:23 Ag '71
TRACTOR engines
They convert to V-8 tractor engines. G. L.
Earle. il Suc Farm 69 no3:B10 F '71
TRACTOR industry
  See also
Brown, David, corporation
Caterpillar tractor company
TRACTOR models
You can make this model steam tractor. R.
Kouhoupt. il Pop Mech 135:94-7+ F '71
TRACTOR pulling contests. See Competitions
TRACTOR tires. See Tires, Tractor
TRACTORS
All-electric tractors. M. Franz. il Org Gard &
Farm 18:51-5 N '71
More muscle for little tractors. J. M. Liston.
il Pop Mech 135:112-15+ Ap '71
Two workhorse tractors for tough jobs. E. F.
Lindsley. il Pop Sci 198:116-17+ Ap '71

Anecdotes, facetiae, satire, etc.
Country's toughest tractor? J. Carlson. Farm
J 95:55 Mr '71
Equipment
8-row tool bar that floats. C. E. Ball. il Farm
J 95:18-19 Mr '71
Maintenance and repair
Easy ways to keep hydraulic systems going.
P. B. Jones. il Suc Farm 69:26-7 Ag '71
Safety devices and measures
Pinned beneath a tractor. M. Etten. Farm J
95:22K S '71
TRACTORS, Municipal
Can you trim trees with a tractor? Winder-
mere, Fla. il Am City 86:12 My '71
TRACTORS, Used
Hints on buying a used tractor. il Suc Farm
69:no2 21 F '71
TRACY, Philip
Watch out, Uncle Sam is angry. Common-
weal 94:472 S 17 '71
TRACY, Spencer
He-she chemistry of Katherine Hepburn and
Spencer Tracy; excerpts from Tracy and
Hepburn. G. Kanin. il pors Vogue 158:
142-3+ N 1 '71 •
Tracy and Hepburn, by G. Kanin. Review
Sat R pors 55:29+ Ja 8 '72. R. Hector •
TRADE. See Commerce
TRADE, Balance of. See Balance of trade
TRADE agreements
Bigger hand for government in strike crises;
steel and railroad settlements. U S News
71:69-70 Ag 16 '71
Break in Florida's nine-year strike. por Bsns
W p 18 D 25 '71
Calendar of wage increases and negotiations
for 1971; with tables. L. Bornstein and L.
W. Bolton. Mo Labor R 94:31-44 Ja '71
Developments in industrial relations. See is-
sues of Monthly labor review
Emerging wage pattern: 30 per cent raise
over 3 years. U S News 71:48-9 Ag 2 '71
Labor agreements breach the guidelines. il
Bsns W p20-1 N 20 '71
Layoff and recall provisions in major agree-
ments. W. L. Tillery. il Mo Labor R 94:41-
6 Jl '71
Major collective bargaining agreements ex-
piring in [month] tables (title varies) See
issues of Monthly labor review
Sudden thaw at the bargaining tables. Bsns
W p 13-14 Jl 24 '71
USW pattern holds some hope for 1972. il
Bsns W p38-9 Je 5 '71
Union power and the new inflation. G. Burck.
il Fortune 83:65-9+ F '71; Same abr. with
title High cost of wage inflation. Read Di-
gest 98:139-43 Ap '71
  See also
Collective bargaining
TRADE catalogs. See Catalogs, Trade
TRADE fairs. See Exhibitions
TRADE journals
Blandness, bias, mar many trade journals.
Am City 86:8 Mr '71
Freelance market report: Harcourt Brace and
Jovanovich trade journals. M. W. Fedo. il
Writers Digest 51:28-30 N '71

Interviewing for trade journal articles. M.
Tyson. il Writers Digest 51:25-7 Jl '71
Interviewing for trade journals. O. Henry.
Writer 84:22-5 F '71
Trade magazines: the largest market. C. Mc-
Intosh. Writer 84:22-4 Ag '71
  See also
Publishers' weekly
TRADE marks and trade names
Farewell to Esso? new brand name, Exxon.
Time 98:86+ O 25 '71
Making of a trademark. J. S. Lorr. il Design
72:34-5 Sum '71
Story behind:
Changing times weather vane. il Chang-
ing T 26:42 Ja '72
Greyhound. il Changing T 25:30 My '71
Lea & Perrins Worcestershire sauce. il
Changing T 25:24 Jl '71
Oscar. il Changing T 25:30 Mr '71
Pepsi-Cola. il Changing T 25:30 S '71
Pocket books' Gertrude. il Changing
T 25:44 N '71
TRADE missions
  See also
United States—Trade missions
TRADE names. See Trade marks and trade
names
TRADE regulation
  See also
Export controls
Foreign trade regulation
TRADE routes
Taking to the sea, 9,000 years ago; evidence
for sea trade between Melos and mainland
Greece. il Sci N 100:225 O 2 '71
TRADE schools
In the car shop; inside a boys technical
high school. T. J. Cottle. il Sat R 54:49-
51+ Je 19 '71
Those computer schools you can't count on.
il Good H 172:163 F '71
TRADE shows. See Exhibitions
TRADE union leaders. See Trade unions—Of-
ficials
TRADE union mergers. See Trade unions—
Consolidations and mergers
TRADE unions
Foreign labor briefs. See issues of Monthly
labor review
  See also
Collective bargaining
Computers—Trade union use
Industrial relations
Trade agreements

Anecdotes, facetiae, satire, etc.
Forum. R. W. Dana. Duns 97:113 My '71
Consolidations and mergers
Strength through merger. il Bsns W p76 O 2
'71
Union merger pace quickens; with tables. L.
M. Dewey. Mo Labor R 94:63-70 Je '71
Dues, fees, etc.
No compulsion wanted; political use of com-
pulsory union dues. Nations Bsns 59:22-3
D '71
Employees
But they can't do that to us! organizing
union employees. W. M. Ringle. il Nations
Bsns 59:24-7 Ag '71
Ethical aspects
  See Labor ethics
Finance
Union wealth; growing despite hard times. il
U S News 71:73-5 Jl 5 '71
International aspects
Unions move against the multinationals.
Bsns W p48-9+ Jl 24 '71
  See also
International labor organization
Law
  See Labor laws and legislation—United
States
Membership
Challenge to labor; discrimination in union
membership. America 125 :111 S 4 '71
Dated study of union membership. America
124:446 My 1 '71
Insubordinate rank and file. S. M. Polster.
Nation 212:782-5 Je 21 '71
Labor relations. L. B. Eichhold and J. D.
Redmond. il Parks & Rec 6:20-2+ N '71
Unions slip from past gains. il Bsns W p77 O
2 '71
Women in labor unions. L. M. Dewey. bibliog
il Mo Labor R 94:42-8 F '71
  See also
Trade unions—Negro membership

TRAFFIC accidents—*Continued*
Town fights past its grief; Gunnison, Colo. varsity football bus accident. L. Wainwright. il Life 71:40-1 O 8 '71
See also
Automobile driving
Automobiles—Skidding
Drinking and traffic accidents
Insurance, Automobile
Life saving equipment

Prevention
See Traffic safety

Statistics
Death by the mile. Sci Am 224:46 F '71
Safety in numbers. Sci Am 224:52 Ap '71
TRAFFIC control, Airway. See Air traffic control
TRAFFIC detectors. See Detectors
TRAFFIC engineering
New patterns for a metropolis; midtown Manhattan. S. Van Ginkel and B. Van Ginkel. il Arch Forum 135:28-33 O '71
TRAFFIC in arms. See Munitions
TRAFFIC lights. See Traffic signals
TRAFFIC markings
Employee invents a speedy curb painter; Ontario, Calif. G. H. Mim Mack. il Am City 86:90 Jl '71
TRAFFIC regulations
See also
Computers—Traffic control use
Traffic signals
Traffic violations
TRAFFIC safety
Rap 'n 'pinion. J. A. Volpe. por Motor T 23:10 Ag '71
See also
Automobile driving
TRAFFIC signals
Too many political traffic signals; Norwalk, Conn. L. M. Rodgers. il Am City 86:69 F '71
Traffic signal receives technical award. il Am City 86:84 F '71
Traffic signals come of age; use of vandal-resistant polycarbonate resin. G. M. Chamberlain. il Am City 86:93-4+ Ag '71

Control
Electronics in Moscow's streets. il Am City 86:106 Ag '71
Mickey Mouse traffic-signal interconnect; Anaheim, Calif. E. F. Granzow. il Am City 86:55-7 Ag '71
TRAFFIC signs
Caution: new signs. il Time 99:52-3 Ja 3 '72
TRAFFIC violations
Bumper stickers and the cops; effect or Black Panther stickers. F. K. Heussenstamm. il Trans-Action 8:32-3 F '71
TRAGER, Frank N.
China question, once again. Nat R 23:585-6+ Je 1 '71
TRAGER, Ruth
Moratorium history committee. il Am Lib 2:1157-60 D '71
TRAGER, William F. See Breck, G. D. jt. auth.
TRAIL bikes. See Motorcycles
TRAIL cookery. See Cookery, Outdoor
TRAIL riders of the wilderness
Going west to West Virginia. L. W. Swift and R. W. Swift. il pors Am For 77:16-19 Mr '71
New leader for trail riders. il por Am For 77:36 Mr '71
TRAIL rides. See Horseback trips
TRAILER towing. See Towing
TRAILERABLE houseboats. See Houseboats—Automobile trailer combination
TRAILERING. See Towing
TRAILERS
Build this hydraulic hog trailer. il Suc Farm 69:H2 Je '71
See also
Automobile trailers
TRAILS
American trails, rediscovered. G. D. Hofe, jr. il Parks & Rec 6:41-8 Mr '71
Backpacking: offers a freedom found in no other type of travel. F. D. Nofziger. il Travel 136:62-7+ S '71
Guide to snowmobile trails. P. K. Snook. il Mech Illus 67:63-4+ N '71
Horses and riders: a galloping growth; increasing use of horse trails. W. L. Rohde. il Cons 25:13+ Ap '71
Mormon trails in the Midwest. S. Murdock. il Travel 137:58-63+ Ja '72
Pathways for the blind; Oerwood braille trail, Pa. J. J. Brett. il Cons 25:13-16 Je '71

There's a wheelchair in the woods; Forest service trails for the handicapped. E. H. Stone. il Parks & Rec 6:18-21+ D '71
Walk, look and learn. G. Randorf. il Cons 26:6-8 Ap '71
See also
Appalachian Trail
California Trail
National parks and reserves—Trails
Pacific Crest trail
TRAIMAN, Stephen
Bear Mountain's Christmas festival. il Parks & Rec 6:24-6 F '71
TRAIN, Russell E.
Without troubling of a star; interview; excerpts from Deena Clark's Moment with show. Am For 77:42-3+ My '71
about
Mr Train named to NATO committee on the challenges of modern society. Dept State Bul 64:197 F 15 '71 *
TRAIN ferries
Sea going trains; western Europe. il Travel 135:53-5 Ap '71
TRAIN travel. See Railroad travel
TRAIN whistles. See Locomotives—Whistles
TRAINED dogs. See Dogs—Training
TRAINING airplanes. See Airplanes, Training
TRAINING devices. See Simulators
TRAINING of animals. See Animals—Training
TRAINING of children. See Children—Management and training
TRAINING of dogs. See Dogs—Training
TRAINING of plants. See Plants, Training of
TRAINING schools for teachers. See Teachers—Education
TRAINING ships
Pioneer: big city schooner. T. Walton. il Motor B & S 128:22 Ag '71
TRAINS. See Railroads—Trains
TRAMMELL, Archie
FAR sight. il Flying 89:104 S; 38+ O; 17 N '71; 90:101 Ja '72
TRAMPS
I became a bum to understand their problems. S. Bacon. il pors Sci Digest 69:40-7 My '71
See also
Vagrancy
TRAN-ngoc-Chau
Tran-ngoc Chau affair. E. Pond. Atlan 227:19-20+ My '71 *
TRANQUILIZING drugs
Schizoid therapy. il Newsweek 77:77 Je 7 '71
See also
Haloperidol
Phenobarbital
Reserpine
TRANSAFRICAN hovercraft expedition. See Scientific expeditions
TRANS-ALASKA pipeline system. See Petroleum—Pipe lines
TRANS-AMAZON highway. See Roads—Brazil
TRANS-AMERICAN league. See Football clubs
TRANS-AMERICAN racing. See Automobile racing
TRANSATLANTIC airline service. See Airlines—International services—Transatlantic
TRANSATLANTIC airline traffic. See Airlines—Traffic
TRANSATLANTIC flights. See Aviation—Transatlantic flights
TRANS AUSTRALIA airlines. See Airlines—Australia
TRANSCEIVERS. See Radio telephone
TRANSCEIVERS, Portable. See Radio telephone, Portable
TRANSCENDENCE of God
God without God? The way of transcendence, by A. Kee. Review
Chr Cent 88:1379-82 N 24 '71. J. A. T. Robinson
TRANSCENDENTAL meditation. See Meditation
TRANSFER of technology. See Technology transfer
TRANSFERASES
Pineal N-acetyltransferase activity: effect of sympathetic stimulation. P. H. Volkman and A. Heller. bibliog il Science 173:839-40 Ag 27 '71 *
Polymorphism of soluble glutamic-pyruvic transaminase: a new genetic marker in man. S. H. Chen and E. R. Giblett. bibliog il Science 173:148-9 Jl 9 '71
TRANSFERRIN
Maternally derived transferrin in pigeon squabs. J. A. Frelinger. bibliog il Science 171:1260-1 Mr 26 '71
TRANSFORMERS, Electric. See Electric transfomers

TRANSFUSION of blood. See Blood—Transfusion

TRANSISTOR circuits
Design for stereo; bias circuits for bipolar circuits. M. Horowitz. il Radio-Electr 42:58-61+ My '71
9 experiments with multipurpose semiconductors. P. Franson. il Radio-Electr 42:48-51 Ap '71
Programmable zener applications. R. L. Starliper. il Electr World 85:60-1 Je '71
RC time constants in UJT circuits. R. M. Cartoscelli. Electr World 86:23 D '71
6 easy projects for beginners. M. Mandl. il Radio-Electr 42:60-2 Ap '71
  See also
Radio circuits
Switching systems
Television circuits

Design
Design for stereo; biasing the bipolar transistor. M. Horowitz. il Radio-Electr 42:22-5+ Mr '71
Equivalency in RTL circuits. F. H. Tooker. il Pop Electr 34:49-53+ F; 39-46 Je '71

TRANSISTOR testers. See Testing instruments

TRANSISTORS
Design for stereo; transistor types and characteristics. M. Horowitz. il Radio-Electr 42:64+ F '71
Don't throw good power diodes away. J. Colt. il Radio-Electr 42:37 Jl '71
Hot spots and heat sinks. J. Darr. il Radio-Electr 42:69-70 O '71
New solid-state device could improve amplifier performance; gallium arsenide field effect transistors il Aviation W 95:42 N 29 '71
Nomogram for power in switching transistors. J. E. McAlister. il Electr World 86:44-5 N '71
Replacement transistors. J. Darr. il Radio-Electr 42:33-6 F; 57-60+ Mr '71
Solid state; evolution of the transistor. L. Garner. il Pop Electr 34:71+ My '71

TRANSITRON electronics corporation
Dream deferred. il Forbes 107:16-17 Ja 15 '71

TRANSLATIONS and translating
World boom in television and book translation, Unesco yearbook reports. UNESCO Courier 24:14-15 F '71
  See also
Childrens literature—Translations and translating
Machine translating
Poetry—Translations and translating

TRANSLATORS
Way with language. Ladies Home J 88:175 Mr '71

TRANSLOCATION in plants. See Plants, Motion of fluids in

TRANSMEDITERRANEAN airways. See Air freight service—Lebanon

TRANSMISSION Automobile. See Automobiles—Transmission

TRANSMISSION of power. See Power transmission

TRANSMISSOMETERS
Automatic visual range reporting tested. K. J. Stein. il Aviation W 94:48-50 Ap 12 '71

TRANSMITTERS, Radio. See Radio transmitters

TRANSMUTATION (chemistry)
  See also
Alchemy

TRANSPAC race. See Yacht racing

TRANSPACIFIC airline service. See Airlines—International services—Transpacific

TRANS-PACIFIC yacht race. See Yacht racing

TRANSPARENCIES
Positive use for negatives; art slides composed of formerly unwanted film. J. Cassidy. il Design 73:12-14 Wint '71

Projection
Ed Scully on color; slide show preparation. E. Scully. Mod Phot 34:42+ D '70
Slide presentations; excerpt from Architectural delineation's, a photographic approach to presentation. E. Burden. il Arch Rec 150:55-8 Jl '71
Suit yourself, with mirrors; Synoptic mirror system. P. Wahl. il Pop Sci 198:57 F '71

Storage
Ed Scully on color; conservation of color slides. E. Scully. Mod Phot 35:22+ Ap '71

TRANSPLANTATION of organs, tissues, etc.
Alternative to suicide. Time 97:48 Ap 26 '71
Cancer and transplants; study of tumor-destroying lymphocytes. il pors Newsweek 77:98 My 10 '71
  See also
Eye—Transplantation
Eye donors
Hair—Transplantation
Heart—Transplantation
Immunological tolerance
Kidneys—Transplantation
Lungs—Transplantation
Marrow—Transplantation
Nerves—Transplantation

Moral and religious aspects
Transplant trepidation. R. Chandler. Chr Today 15:32 Ag 6 '71

Psychological aspects
Transplants and identity crises. A. J. Snider. Sci Digest 69:57 Ap '71

TRANSPLANTING
Spring journey for daylilies. il Org Gard & Farm 18:108-9 Je '71

TRANSPLANTING of trees. See Tree planting

TRANSPO-72. See Transportation—Exhibitions

TRANSPORT, Biological. See Biological transport

TRANSPORT theory
  See also
Energy budget (geophysics)

TRANSPORTATION
  See also
Carriers
Motor bus lines
Roads
Urban transportation
Vehicles
Waterways
  also subhead Transportation under various subjects, e.g. Animals—Transportation

Exhibitions
Aerospace role diminishes at Transpo-72. Aviation W 95:26 Ag 23 '71
Construction pace, theme cloud Transpo. D. A. Brown. Aviation W 95:20-1 N 1 '71
Soviet SST, delegation expected at U.S. transportation exhibit. Aviation W 96:19 Ja 3 '72
Transpo seeks buyers as key to success. D. A. Brown. Aviation W 95:17 D 13 '71
Transpo seeks traffic solution; highway access to Dulles international airport. D. A. Brown. Aviation W 95:22 N 29 '71

Federal aid
Nixon transportation trust fund idea hit. D. C. Winston. Aviation W 94:27 Mr 29 '71
Priorities or trust funds? B. Kelley and R. Hebert. Nation 212:497-500 Ap 19 '71
Transport turns to Congress for help. il Bsns W p39-40 Jl 17 '71
Where money's really needed; intercity transportation. Life 70:40 Mr 19 '71
  See also
Local transit—Federal aid

History
Stanley get the steam up, we're going for a ride. il Sr Schol 99:15 S 20 '71

Laws and regulations
Deregulation is off to a halting start. Bsns W p46 N 13 '71
It's time to unload the regulators. D. Cordtz. il Fortune 84:64-7+ Jl '71
Rules carriers want to live with. Bsns W p24 Je 26 '71
Transport turns to Congress for help. il Bsns W p39-40 Jl 17 '71

Research
See Transportation research

Speed
  See also
Transportation, High speed

Statistics
50 largest transportation companies; with directory. Fortune 83:198-9 My '71

California
California goes after a transportation octopus. por Bsns W p54 S 25 '71
San Franciscans fight for that cable-car charm. il Bsns W p62-4 S 4 '71

France
  See also
Canals—France

TRANSPORTATION—*Continued*

Japan
See also
Railroads—Japan

New Jersey
Showcase for integrated transport: Newark-Elizabeth complex. il Bsns W p42-4 N 27 '71

New York (state)
Rebellion against concrete: bond issue. Nation 213:514 N 22 '71

United States
Can Northeast avert a transport crisis? Boston to Washington. il U S News 71:53 S 27 '71
Free market in transportation? Duns 97:120 Mr '71
Great American motion sickness, by J. Burby. Review
  Bsns W p7 Ag 7 '71. B. Welling, jr
Our transportation system that gets us nowhere. V. H. Bernstein. Redbook 136:89+ Mr '71
Strike-legislation showdown expected. U S News 70:58 Ja 18 '71
Traffic and transportation. See issues of American city
U.S. transportation system and how to make it run; symposium; with editorial comment. il Fortune 84:51, 58-85+ Jl '71
Where money's really needed; intercity transportation. Life 70:40 Mr 19 '71
See also
Citizens' committee on public transportation
Railroads—United States
United States—Transportation, Department of
Waterways—United States

History
Legendary Concords. S. B. Duncan. il por Am West 8:16-17+ Ja '71
See also
Pony express

TRANSPORTATION, High speed
High-speed ground transit at a profit. il Am City 86:74+ Ja '71
High-speed rail transport for the Northeast corridor. Sci N 100:204 S 25 '71
Magnetic force studied for intercity travel. il Aviation W 94:50-1 Mr 22 '71

TRANSPORTATION, Military
See also
United States—Military airlift command

TRANSPORTATION, Municipal. See Local transit; Urban transportation

TRANSPORTATION industry. See Transportation

TRANSPORTATION of camp children. See Camp children—Transportation

TRANSPORTATION of school children. See School children—Transportation

TRANSPORTATION research
Rap 'n 'pinion. J. A. Volpe. por Motor T 23:10 Ag '71
See also
National research council—Highway research board
United States—Transportation, Department of—Transportation systems center

TRANSPORTATION systems center. See United States—Transportation, Department of—Transportation systems center

TRANSPORTATION workers
See also
Strikes—United States—Transportation workers

TRANSPOSITION of the great vessels. See Heart—Abnormities and deformities

TRANSRACIAL adoption. See Adoption

TRANSSEXUALISM. See Change of sex

TRANSSIBERIAN airline service. See Airlines —International services—European-Asiatic

TRANS-SIBERIAN railway
8:00 p.m. from Moscow to Peking is dead on time. C. Mullin. il por N Y Times Mag p40-1+ D 5 '71

TRANSUBSTANTIATION
See also
Catholic church—Eucharist

TRANSURANIUM elements
Ida Noddack, 75 & element 75. F. Habashi. bibliog il por Chem 44:14-15 F '71
Transastronomy at the Dubna conference; International conference on heavy ion physics. B. Kuchowicz. Sky & Tel 41:358 Je '71

TRANSVAAL
See also
South African war, 1899-1902

TRANS WORLD airlines
American, TWA ponder stock offerings as market declines. W. H. Gregory. Aviation W 94:29 Je 28 '71
TWA proposing lower North Atlantic fares. Aviation W 94:28-9 Je 7 '71
TWA says operating revenues, passenger traffic fell in August. Aviation W 95:31 S 27 '71
TWA stock sale nets $35:5 million. Aviation W 95:22 Jl 26 '71
Turnaround from disaster at TWA. il Bsns W p60-1+ O 30 '71
U.S, Irish clash on Dublin rights. L. Doty. Aviation W 95:25-6 Jl 20 '71
Why TWA is the Sears of the air. il Bsns W p68 Ap 17 '71

TRANS WORLD airlines-Pan American world airways merger (proposed) See Airlines—Consolidations and mergers

TRANSWORLD art, Inc.
From J&B to Dali. por Duns 97:59-60 Jl '71

TRANSYLVANIA
Dracula the man. il Newsweek 78:56 D 6 '71

TRAN-tuan-Nham
Two men who didn't make it; with editorial comment. il pors Life 71:24-5, 32 S 10 '71 •

TRAP shooting
Grand American; trapshooting tournament. B. A. Foxworthy. il Holiday 49:52-6 Jl '71

TRAPPING
Boy's introduction to a trapline. D. J. Anderson. il Field & S 76:50-1+ D '71
See also
Lobster trapping

TRAPS
See also
Mousetraps

TRAPS, Insect. See Insect traps

TRAPSHOOTING. See Trap shooting

TRASH carts. See Refuse containers

TRASH mashers. See Refuse and refuse disposal—Apparatus

TRASTEVERE; story. See Lavin, M.

TRÄUBLE, Hermann. See Essmann, U. jt. auth.

TRAUFFER, Art
Hi-fi amplifier module. il Pop Electr 35:59-60 D '71

TRAUMATISM
After the quake: the psychic tremors still shake people up. S. O'Quin. il Todays Health 49:20-2+ My '71
Aftershock; children emotionally traumatized by California's earthquake. il Newsweek 77:76 Mr 8 '71
Earthquake jitters; children's reactions to Los Angeles aftershocks. il Time 97:59 Mr 8 '71
New techniques to help save life for accident victims. E. M. Papper. Vogue 158:268-9+ S 1 '71
Trauma treatment; the Illinois plan. il Newsweek 78:80-1 N 1 '71

TRAVEL
Ask Holiday. Holiday 49:114-18 D '70
Ask Holiday; questions and answers. Holiday 49:80 F '71
Booked for travel. D. Butwin. See issues of Saturday review
Checkpoint for travelers. B. Robinson. See issues of House beautiful
Family travel. See issues of Better homes and gardens
Go Vogue; where, how, why to go. il Vogue 157:74-89 Ap 15 '71
Great Christmas presents. D. Messinesi. Vogue 158:44+ N 15 '71
Holiday travel forecast: 1971. Holiday 48:52-3+ N '70
How people really travel. il Vogue 157:116-21 Ap 15 '71
Over in Dulgence; trial run of the Renaissance tour for the overprivileged. H. Sutton. il Sat R 54:63-4+ N 6 '71
Roaming the globe. See issues of Travel
Spring and the traveler: in search of a romantic world; symposium. il Sat R 54:37-42+ Mr 13 '71
Temple bells and blue atolls; symposium. il Sat R 54:35-42+ O 23 '71
Time for adventure. P. A. Dickinson. il Har Yrs 11:45-53 Jl '71
Tips for tourists. Todays Ed 60:74-5 Mr '71
Travel. M. Gough. See issues of House beautiful
Travel bazaar. See issues of Harper's bazaar
Travel digest. See issues of Travel
Travel guidelines. E. M. Mills. il Consumer Bul 54:38-40 Jl '71
Travel tips (cont) Schol Teach Jr/Sr High p33 Mr 8; 24-6 My 3 '71
Traveler's camera. L. Barry. See issues of Popular photography

TRAVEL—*Continued*
Travelguide. F. Shemanski. Schol Teach Jr/Sr High p34-5 S '71
Two literary travellers: a dialogue. P. de Rothschild and E. Bruce. pors Vogue 157: 122-3 Ap 15 '71
Weekend traveler: there's a small hotel. il Mlle 73:184-7 S '71
  See also
Air travel
Business travel
Cruising
Customs service and tourists
Guidebooks
Motor bus travel
Ocean travel
Packing of luggage
Railroad travel
Student travel
Tourist trade
Vacations
  also subhead Description and travel under names of countries, states. etc. e.g. Japan—Description and travel

Anecdotes, facetiae, satire, etc.
Don't let anyone catch you using your naked eye. R. Schoenstein. il Todays Health 49: 28-31 Je '71
What! You're not going to Thorshavn? E. G. Smith. il Travel 136:74-6 D '71

Caricatures and cartoons
Innocents abroad. il Read Digest 99:146-7 Ag '71

Economic aspects
How to save money when you travel. L. David. Read Digest 98:53-4+ Je '71
How to spend your travel dollars wisely. F. K. Coffee. il Mech Illus 67:56-7+ Je '71
Travel bargains around the world. il U S News 70:30-3 Ap 5 '71
  See also
Airlines—Fares
Tourist trade

Anecdotes, facetiae, satire, etc.
Undivided attention. New Yorker 47:20-3 Jl 10 '71

Health aspects
Doctor packs his black bag for travellers. Vogue 157:154 Ap 15 '71

Social aspects
Sex on the go. P. S. Catling. il Vogue 157: 100+ Ap 15 '71
TRAVEL (periodical)
  See also
Mr Travel award
TRAVEL, Space. See Space flight
TRAVEL agencies and agents
Curse of Russia is Intourist; letter. A. S. Romer. Science 172:326 Ap 23 '71; Discussion. 172:1294 Je 25 '71
Four oarsmen of the epochal trips. R. Joseph. il Esquire 75:82-3+ F '71
Services a travel agent can provide. Good H 172:192-3 My '71
Waiting for that visa to China; World youth visit exchange association USA. R. Dudman. New Repub 165:17-19 Jl 3 '71; Discussion. 165:32 Jl 24 '71
  See also
Banks and banking—Travel departments
Cook, Thomas, and son
TRAVEL and education. See Student travel
TRAVEL books. See Travel literature
TRAVEL guides. See Guidebooks
TRAVEL literature
Tripping with books; travel writing, spring-summer, 1971. il Pub W 199:47-53 F 15 '71
  See also
Guidebooks
TRAVEL news. Newspapers—Travel news
TRAVEL photography
How to make your travel movies better. F. Rohr. il Travel 135:72-4 F '71
TRAVEL regulations
Passports, visas and customs inspections. E. Welke. Bet Hom & Gard 49:10+ Ja '71
U.S. passports remain invalid for travel to certain areas. Dept State Bul 64:510-11 Ap 12 '71
TRAVEL restrictions. See Travel regulations
TRAVEL study courses
Africa: frontier for summer study. J. Mandelstam. il Schol Teach Jr/Sr High p 17-19 Ja 11 '71
Teen travel talk; foreign study tour great experience or grim letdown. il Seventeen 29:199 N '70
  See also
Foreign study

TRAVEL tapes. See Tape recordings
TRAVEL with children
Children welcome! L. Fine. il Ladies Home J 88:56 My '71
Daddy's travels with a diaper bag. D. Cooper. il Good H 172:69-70+ Ap '71
Have baby, will travel. M. Martin. Parents Mag 46:40-1+ My '71
So you're taking the kids this summer? A. Rosenthal and B. Rosenthal. il Todays Health 49:44-7+ Ap '71
TRAVEL with pets
Notes for the corporate nomad: taking pets overseas. Fortune 84:50 O '71
Pet news. il Ladies Home J 88:64 My '71
TRAVELERS
Cosmopolitan-san. il Time 98:39 S 6 '71
Great romantic travellers. A. West. il Vogue 157:90-3+ Ap 15 '71
How to cope with European culture (without really trying) S. Mead. il Travel 135: 64-9 Je '71
Travelers warned of penalties for drug violations abroad; Department announcement. Dept State Bul 65:56-7 Jl 12 '71
Traveling on your own in Europe. G. Bush. il Bet Hom & Gard 49:95-101 F '71
Travelling with Elizabeth. R. Burton. il pors Vogue 157:68-71 Ap 15 '71
Valerian Rybar travels; interview. V. Rybar. por Vogue 157:65+ Ap 15 '71
Watch out for thieves that prey on travelers. il Changing T 25:40-2 My '71
  See also
Church work with tourists, travelers, etc.
Women as travelers

Caricatures and cartoons
American tourist, as others see us. Holiday 49:88-9 F '71
TRAVELERS checks
  See also
American express company
TRAVELING bags. See Luggage
TRAVELING moving picture theaters. See Moving picture theaters, Traveling
TRAVELING schools. See Schools, Traveling
TRAVELING wave tubes
New allocations spur device development. B. M. Elson. il Aviation W 95:46-7+ Ag 30 '71
TRAVELS
  See also
Horseback trips
Travel
Travelers
Voyages
TRAVELS of Marco Polo; drama. See Thane, A.
TRAVERS, Pamela Lyndon
Authors & editors; interview, ed. by P. Bragg. por Pub W 200:7-9 D 13 '71
La TRAVIATA; opera. See Verdi, G.
TRAWICK, Jack
Strip mining. il Nat Parks & Con Mag 45: 10-14 Jl '71; Same abr. with title Ravaging land by strip mining. Cur 132:31-5 S '71
TRAWLERS (boats) See Fishing boats
TRAXLER, Patricia
Our finest hour; poem. Nation 212:665 My 24 '71
TRAY meals. See Meals
TRAYLOR, Everett
Making an ocarina by the slip-cast method. il Ceram Mo 19:28-9 F '71
TRAYS
Chain-border tray; three versions. E. Gaines. il Antiques 100:256-7 Ag '71
Day of the tray. N. Mandelbaum. il Ladies Home J 88:130-3 My '71
Trays by ten artists. M. Amaya. il Art in Am 59:48-57 Ja '71
TREADWELL, Sandy
College basketball. Sports Illus 34:42 Ja 25; 58+ Mr 22 '71
Hey, I can beat those guys. il por Sports Illus 34:14-15 Ja 18 '71
Week; baseball. Sports Illus 34:70+ My 31 '71
Week; college basketball. Sports Illus 34:47-8 F 22; 50-1 Mr 1; 66+ Mr 8 '71
TREADWELL, Sherwood A.
Ecology of Easter; poem. Chr Cent 88:397 Mr 31 '71
TREASER, Richard
Watercolor page; with biographical sketch. il por Am Artist 36:36-9+ Ja '72
TREASURE; drama. See Shea, G. F.
TREASURE finders. See Metal detectors
TREASURE trove
Buried treasure, hot new hobby for RVers F. Coffee. il Mech Illus 67:100-2+ S '71

TREASURE trove—*Continued*
15,000 wrecks in the Great Lakes await adventure and treasure hunters. F. F. Hollister. Motor B & S 127:202 Mr '71
Hidden treasure? Oak Island. il Newsweek 78:71-2 N 8 '71

TREASURY department (United States) See United States—Treasury, Department of the

TREATIES
See also
Geneva conventions
United Nations conference on the law of treaties
also subhead Treaties under names of countries, e.g. Germany (Federal Republic) —Treaties

TREATMENT of prisoners. See Prisoners— Treatment

TREBILCOCK, Dorothy
Dunes at sunset. Nat Parks & Con Mag 45: 20 Ap '71
Reflection; poem. il Nat Parks & Con Mag 45:21 Ja '71

TRECKER, Janice Law
Woman's place is in the curriculum. il Sat R 54:83-6+ O 16 '71

TREE breeding
Breeding pollution resistant trees for cities. il Sci Digest 70:80-1 Ag '71
Genetic improvement of southern pines. B. J. Zobel. il Sci Am 225:94-103 bibliog(p 138) N '71
Now scientists are breeding super trees. M. Margolin. il Sci Digest 69:40-4 Mr '71

TREE disposal. See Timber disposal

TREE felling
How to remove a troublesome tree. il Home Gard 58:44 O '71

TREE planting
Editorial. C. B. Lees. Horticulture 49:16 O '71
How the highway planters plant. Sunset 147: 244 O '71
To jump three thousand years; Brooks Range wilderness, Alaska. S. Wright. il por Am West 8:24-7 Mr '71
With chicken wire and hay hook; moving a tree. il Sunset 147:240-1 O '71
See also
Forest planting
Reforestation

TREE rings
Carbon 14 and the prehistory of Europe. C. Renfrew. il Sci Am 225:63-70+ bibliog (p 120) O '71

TREE shrews. See Shrews

TREE trimmers. See Pruning apparatus and equipment

TREES
AFA's Social register of big trees. il Am For 77:24-31 Ja '71
Man's best friend: the tree, excerpts. il Am For 77:8-9 Ap '71
Support your local tree; photographs UNESCO Courier 24:18-19 Jl '71
Tall pine or mighty oak from seed. il Sunset 147:260-1 O '71
Trees and plants section: symposium. il Am For 77:33-47+ Ap '71
Trees of Cape Cod. G. S. Smith. il Am For 77:6-7 Je '71
See also
Annonaceae
Catkins
Christmas trees
Flowering trees
Forest conservation
Forests and forestry
Landscape gardening
Leaves
Roadside improvement
Tree breeding
Tree felling
Tree planting
Tree rings
also names of trees, e.g. Chestnut trees

Diseases and pests

See also
Gypsy moths
also subhead Diseases and pests under names of trees, e.g. Elm—Diseases and pests

Growth

See Growth (plants)

Identification

On not knowing the trees by their leaves. E. A. Menninger. il Am For 77:12-15 D '71

Planting

See Tree planting

Poetry

Tree planter. E. D. Merry. Am For 77:48 Ja '71

TREES, Dwarf
Bonsai from seed. C. E. Derderian. il Horticulture 49:42-3+ Ap '71
Prized art of bonsai. A. Lee. bibliog il Har Yrs 11:18-21 F '71
See also
Fruit trees, Dwarf

TREES, Effect of salt on. See Plants, Effect of salt on

TREES, Fossil
See also
Petrified forests

TREES, Moving of. See Tree planting

TREES, Training of
Upholding vines and trees. il Sunset 146:96-9 Ap '71

TREES in cities
Make tree-well covers attractive; Riverside, Calif. il Am City 86:40 D '71

TREFETHEN, Florence
Poet's workshop. See every other issue of Writer

TREHUB, Arnold
Brain as a parallel coherent detector. bibliog il Science 174:722-3 N 12 '71

TRELLISES
Upholding vines and trees. il Sunset 146:96-9 Ap '71

TREMATODES
See also
Schistosomes

TREMOR
Physiological tremor. O. Lippold. il Sci Am 224:65-73 Mr '71

TREMULIS, Alex Sarantos
Tucker: a modern American tragedy. A. B. Shuman. il pors Motor T 23:69-70 My '71 *

TRENCHES, Ocean. See Submarine valleys

TRENT, Council of, 1545-1563
Ecumenical "if"; D. Lainez's letter. C. J. McNaspy. il America 124:655-6 Je 26 '71

TREPHINING
Aboriginal trephination: case from southern New England? B. W. Powell; reply with rejoinder. H. H. Gass. Science 171:1268 Mr 26 '71

TRESS, Arthur
Gallery; photograph. Life 70:6-7 Je 18 '71

TRESSILIAN, Charles
Bahia: papaya every morning, voodoo every night. il Holiday 48:62-5+ S '70

TRETIAK, Daniel. See Ojha, I. C. jt. auth.

TREVINO, Lee
Arnie re-arms while Lee flees. C. Kirkpatrick. il pors Sports Illus 35:20-1 Ag 2 '71 *
Golf's biggest money winner. il pors Newsweek 78:57-61 Jl 19 '71 *
Lee Trevino: Cantinflas of the country clubs. il pors Time 98:47-51 Jl 19 '71; Same abr. with title Clown prince of golf. Read Digest 99:105-9 N '71 *
Mad golfer. B. Bruns. il pors Life 71:34-5 Jl 2 '71 *
Now for the Mexican Open. D. Jenkins. il por Sports Illus 35:12-15 Jl 19 '71 *
Remember the battle of Merion. D. Jenkins. il pors Sports Illus 34:12-15 Je 28 '71
Sportsman of the year. C. Kirkpatrick. il pors Sports Illus 35:34-9 D 20 '71 *
Triumph of Supermex. il por Newsweek 78: 64-5 Jl 5 '71 *
Two for money, one for show. G. S. Brown. il pors Sports Illus 35:28-9 N 8 '71 *

TREVOR, William
Access to the children; story. Redbook 136: 80-1 Ap '71

TREZISE, Philip H.
Assistant Secretary Green and Assistant Secretary Trezise interviewed for Japanese national television; February 26, 1971. Dept State Bul 64:449-54 Mr 29 '71
Department gives views on Eximbank legislation; statement, March 9, 1971. Dept State Bul 64:459-60 Mr 29 '71
Department gives views on export finance legislation; statement, May 26, 1971. Dept State Bul 65:27-8 Jl 5 '71
Multinational corporation; address, May 3, 1971. Vital Speeches 37:494-6 Je 1 '71; Same with title Some policy implications of the multinational corporation. Dept State Bul 64:669-72 My 24 '71
Western business in eastern Europe; address, December 29, 1970. Dept State Bul 64:85-8 Ja 18 '71; Same with title East-West trade. Vital Speeches 37:313-15 Mr 1 '71

TRI, Do-cao-. See Do-cao-Tri

TRIAL by Jury. See Jury

TRIAL of Christ. See Jesus Christ—Trial

TRIAL of the Catonsville nine; drama. See Berrigan, D.

TRIAL practice. See Procedure (law)
TRIAL reporting. See Newspaper court reporting
TRIALS
Second jury; courtroom buffs. L. Levitt. il Time 97:42-3 Mr 15 '71
  See also
Actions and defenses
Jury
Mock trial
Newspaper court reporting
Video recorders and recording—Court use

Cameroon Republic
Africa's dangerous precedent: sentencing Catholic bishops. O. Okite. Chr Today 15: 45-6 F 26 '71
Bishop in the dock; trial of Bishop Ndongmo. America 124:60 Ja 23 '71

France
Tiercé king. il por Newsweek 78:48-50 D 27 '71

Greece, Modern
I accept it; Lady Fleming, others. por Newsweek 78:38 O 11 '71

Italy
Lex romana. Time 97:34 My 3 '71

New Jersey
  See also
Trials (extortion)

Pakistan
Mujib on trial. il por Newsweek 78:28 Ag 23 '71

Russia
Jewish outcry; protests against Leningrad trial. il Newsweek 77:51-2 Ja 18 '71
Leningrad nine. il Time 97:39 My 31 '71
Protests on Jews; Soviet hijack trial. Sr Schol 98:4 F 1 '71

South Africa
Case against dean flawed; trial of Dean Gonville Ffrench-Beytagh. J. Squire. Chr Cent 88:1329-30 N 10 '71
Cut it out; trial of G. A. Ffrench-Beytagh. por Newsweek 78:40+ Ag 16 '71
South African cleric found guilty. Chr Cent 88:1343 N 17 '71
South African show trial: Dean Ffrench-Beytagh. America 125:417 N 20 '71

Spain
No firing squads in Spain: Burgos trial. E. von Kuehnelt-Leddihn. Nat R 23:134 F 9 '71
Trial for Spain; appeals save Basques charged at Burgos. Sr Schol 98:5 F 1 '71

Sudan
Africa's Nuremberg trial. il por Newsweek 78:31 S 6 '71
Armed missionary; case of Rolf Steiner. por Time 98:53 N 22 '71
Black eye for Moscow; trial of A. K. Mahgoub. il por Newsweek 78:30+ Ag 9 '71
Revenge in the Sudan; Communists, army officers executed. il por Time 98:26-7 Ag 9 '71

United States
How fair a trial can you get today? viewpoints. Sr Schol 99:6-7 N 8 '71
TRIALS (assault and battery)
Socking it to a rough union; E. Lassitter sues Fort Lauderdale operating engineers. il Time 98:42-3 D 27 '71
TRIALS (civil rights)
Catching up with Natchez. N. C. Chriss. Nation 213:592-3 D 6 '71
TRIALS (conspiracy)
Conspiracy trial; this worn-out piece of tyranny. J. R. Waltz. Nation 212:589-92 My 10 '71
Great conspiracy trial, by J. Epstein, and Trial, by T. Hayden. Reviews
  Esquire 75:16+ F '71. M. Muggeridge
Judging the Chicago trial. A. M. Bickel; discussion. Commentary 51:10+ My '71
Justice for the Panthers. Nation 212:674-5 My 31 '71
Not guilty of what? Black Panthers in New York city. E. Kennebeck. il Nation 213:296-304 O 4 '71
Orderly perversion of justice; Seattle conspiracy trial. B. Weiner. Nation 212:145-8 F 1 '71
TRIALS (extortion)
Wedding the Garden State. il por Time 98: 12-13 Jl 19 '71

TRIALS (libel)
  See also
Trials (seditious libel)
TRIALS (murder)
Bobby and Ericka: free at last, until next time. A. Goldberg. Ramp Mag 10:45-8 Ag '71
Continuing trial of Jesse Hill Ford. M. Frady. il pors Life 71:56-56B+ O 29 '71
Death for the family; Charles Manson and others. il Newsweek 77:40 Ap 12 '71
Death sentence for Manson clan, but—. il U S News 70:26 Ap 12 '71
Disappearance of Dr Parkman, by R. Sullivan. Review
  Newsweek 78:77-8+ Ag 23 '71. A. Cooper
Environmentalist. por Time 98:14 D 13 '71
F. Lee Bailey's strangest murder case; Coppolino case; excerpt from The Defense never rests, ed. by H. Aronson. F. L. Bailey. il por Ladies Home J 88:122-3+ N '71
F. Lee Bailey's The defense never rests; Sheppard case: excerpt from The defense never rests, ed. by A. Aronson. F. L. Bailey. il pors Ladies Home J 88:93-5+ O '71
Finally, a jury; New Haven kidnap-murder trial of Black Panther B. Seale and E. Huggins. Time 97:52+ Mr 22 '71
Freed in New Haven; B. G. Seale and E. Huggins of Black Panther party. pors Time 97:12-13 Je 7 '71
Hell in the factory; verdict in J. Johnson case, Detroit. il por Time 97:39 Je 7 '71
Hung jury for Huey. por Time 98:11 Ag 23 '71
Identity crisis; Gilbert twins. il Newsweek 77:30 Mr 29 '71
Life among the Manson jurors. il Time 97: 42+ Ap 12 '71
Life with father. il Time 97:23 F 15 '71
Los siete de la raza. M. Heins. il Ramp Mag 9:19-26 Mr; 10:50 Jl '71
Magical mystery tour; Charles Manson murder trial. Time 97:22-3 F 22 '71
Manson convicted. Nat R 23:128-9 F 9 '71
Manson jury; end of the long ordeal. H. Farrell. il por Life 70:44-8 Ap 16 '71
Murderers as heroes; case of Lieut. Tom Massie; letter. W. Reich. Nation 212:674 My 31 '71
Panthers acquitted. il Time 97:22 My 24 '71
There'll be no jail for Jesse Ford, except the prison of his mind. L. L. King. il pors Todays Health 49:28-33+ D '71
To whom it may concern; the Harlem six. Nation 213:101 Ag 16 '71
Trials of the system: charges dropped against B. G. Seale and E. Huggins. il por Newsweek 77:27-8 Je 7 '71
Verdict on Manson. il Newsweek 77:31 F 8 '71
Verdict on the Panthers. il Newsweek 77:24 My 24 '71
  See also
Sacco-Vanzetti case
TRIALS (perjury)
Alger Hiss case revisited. A. Weinstein. Am Scholar 41:121-32 Wint '71
TRIALS (seditious libel)
Case of John Peter Zenger. L. Barnett. il pors Am Heritage 23:33-41+ D '71
TRIALS, Dog. See Field trials (dogs)
TRIALS, Military. See Courts martial and courts of inquiry
TRIARYL phosphate additives. See Gasoline —Additives
TRIBES and tribal systems
  See also
Society, Primitive
TRIBOLIUM. See Flour beetles
TRIBUS, Myron
Applying science to industry: why America falls behind; excerpts from address, December 2, 1970. por U S News 70:35-6 Ja 18 '71
Engineering education; address. February 2, 1971. Vital Speeches 37:410-13 Ap 15 '71
Technology and society: the real issues. il Bul Atom Sci 27:27-30 D '71
—and McIrvine, E. C.
Energy and information; with biographical sketches. il Sci Am 225:32, 179-84+ bibliog (p244+) S '71
TRICHOMES
Butterfly-plant coevolution: has passiflora adenopoda won the selective race with heliconiine butterflies? L. E. Gilbert. bibliog il Science 172:585-6 My 7 '71
TRI-CITIES opera (Binghamton, Endicott and Johnson City, N.Y.)
Report:
  Binghamton's Masonic temple. H. E. Phillips. Opera N 35:28 Ap 17 '71
TRICK or treat for UNICEF; drama. See Boiko, C.

TRICK photography. See Photography, Trick

TRICKS
See also
Conjuring

TRIEZENBERG, George
How to live with due process. Ed Digest 36:
18-21 My '71

TRIGGS, William
Synod of bishops: failure of vision. il Chr
Cent 88:1484-7 D 22 '71
View from Rome. Chr Cent 88:484, 582-3,
824-5, 896-7, 1188-9 Ap 21, My 12, Jl 7,
28, O 13 '71

TRIGLYCERIDES. See Glycerides

TRIJET. See Airplanes, Jet

TRILLIN, Calvin
Gourmet of the golden browns. il Life 71:
14 Ag 27 '71
Profiles in Courrèges. il Atlan 228:121-3 N '71
Tell me that U Mishmi, Gracie. il Life 71:18
N 5 '71
U.S. journal (cont) New Yorker 46:85-9 Ja 16;
83-9 F 13; 47:100-2+ F 20; 86+ Mr 27; 102+
Ap 17; 104+ My 1; 60+ My 22; 90-5 Je 12;
57-8+ Jl 3; 103-4+ S 18; 108+ S 25; 120+ O
9; 173-4+ N 6; 136+ D 4; 93-7 D 18 '71
What enormous problems a man can cause
himself by answering his mail! il N Y
Times Mag p30-1+ My 2 '71
(ed) See Cavett, D. Dick Cavett talks
about

TRILLING, Lionel
Authenticity and the modern unconscious.
Commentary 52:39-50 S '71

TRILLIUMS
Trilliums. B. H. Ryburn. il Horticulture 49:
24-5+ O '71

TRILOBITES
Where ancestors of the lobster left their
marks in the shale; Antelope spring area. il
Sunset 146:38+ My '71

TRIM tabs. See Tabs (boats)

TRIMARANS
Are trimarans seaworthy? excerpts from
Racing and cruising trimarans. R. B. Har-
ris. il Motor B & S 127:60-1+ F '71
Building a cartop trimaran. M. F. Daniels. il
Mech Illus 67:72-4+ Mr '71
Slick new tri-hull. G. Reiger. il Pop Mech
136:84-6 Ag '71
To Hobart by trimaran; Sydney-Hobart race.
D. O'Neil. Yachting 129:258-61 Ap '71

TRINIDAD (island)
Carnival in Trinidad. H. La Fay. il Nat
Geog 140:690-701 N '71

TRINIDAD, Calif.
Once a year two dollars buys all the crab
you can eat. il Sunset 146:55 Ap '71

TRINIDAD and Tobago
Politics and government
See also
Elections—Trinidad and Tobago

TRINITY
Divine community. V. P. McCorry. America
124:601 Je 5 '71
Man as an image of the Trinity. A. Deeken. il
Cath World 214:9-13 O '71

TRINITY; ballet. See Ballets—Criticisms

TRIOLO, Tony
Cold cold heart of hockey. il Sports Illus 34:
24-31 Ja 25 '71

TRIPE
See also
Cookery—Meat

TRIPLE crown. See Horse racing

TRIPLETT, Jack E.
Determining the effects of quality change
on the CPI. bibliog il Mo Labor R 94:27-
32 My '71

TRIPODS, Camera. See Camera tripods

TRIPP, Carroll D.
We made mistakes, but we did not connive.
Chr Cent 88:379+ Mr 24 '71

TRIPP, Vollie
Getting seeds to germinate. Org Gard & Farm
18:114-15 Ap '71

TRIPPETT, Frank
He won in a walk. Look 35:46-7 Ja 12 '71
Key West, to have and have not. Look 35:
44-5 Ap 6 '71
Lindsay, Aurelio & co. hit the road. il pors
N Y Times Mag p36-7+ N 21 '71
Spiro. il Look 35:28-9 S 7 '71

TRIPS, Student. See School excursions

TRISTAN, Flora
Eternal pariah. B. Roszak. Nation 213:598-9
D 6 '71 *

TRISTAN und Isolde; opera. See Wagner, R.

TRITONIA. See Sea slugs

TRIUMPH (automobile) See Automobiles, Foreign

TRIVETS
Making a tile into a trivet. il Sunset 146:
78 Ja '71
Trivets had it hot; horseshoe trivets. W.
Paley. il Hobbies 76:48-9 S '71

TROMPE-l'oeil
Eye on the object; W. Harnett's freshly discovered painting, Ease. il por Newsweek
78:98 S 27 '71

TRONICK, Edward. See Ball, W. jt. auth.

TROPHIES, Sport
Second-guessing the Heisman. J. Newcombe.
Life 71:12 N 26 '71
See also
Hunting trophies

TROPICAL forests. See Forests and forestry
—Tropics

TROPICAL plants
See also
Bromeliads
Medinilla

TROPICANA products, Inc.
What makes Rossi run? por Forbes 108:50-1
N 15 '71

TROPICS
See also
Forests and forestry—Tropics

Climate
Global meteorology:
Experiments in the tropics; BOMEX,
GARP and GATE. A. L. Hammond. il
Science 174:2788-9 O 15 '71
Tropics weren't so stable after all. L. Pur-
rett. il Sci N 100:177 S 11 '71

TROTSKY, Leon
Rise and fall and rise of Leon Trotsky. E.
Taylor. il pors Horizon 13:34-43 Spr '71 *

TROTT, Susan
Bones of contention; story. Redbook 137:
86-8 My '71
Shelby, Shelby, fierce and free; story. Redbook 136:84-5 Ap '71

TROTTA, Geri
Not to be missed. See issues of Harper's
bazaar
Travel bazaar (cont) Harp Baz 104:34-5 Ag
'71
(ed) See Smith, O. Oliver Smith talks about
theatre

TROTTER, F. Thomas
End to professional self-pity. Chr Cent 88:
1040 S 8 '71

TROTTER, W. L.
Camping with a coronary. il Har Yrs 11:
37-8 Mr '71

TROTTERS. See Race horses

TROTTING races. See Harness racing

TROUBADOURS; story. See Boles, P. D.

TROUT
New trout for old waters. W. A. Flick. il Cons
25:18-21 Je '71
Residues of total mercury and methylmer-
curic salts in lake trout as a function of
age. C. A. Bache and others. bibliog il Sci-
ence 172:951-2 My 28 '71
Trout leukocytes: growth in oxygenated cul-
tures. J. R. Heckman and others. bibliog
Science 173:246 Jl 16 '71
Trout trilogy:
Brown trout. A. J. McClane. il Field &
S 76:96-9 D '71
The rainbow. A. J. McClane. il Field &
S 76:142-4+ N '71

TROUT fishing
Affair with the South Fork. V. L. Hoss.
il pors Outdoor Life 148:64-7+ Ag '71
Angling and some acts of God; rainbows
in British Columbia. T. McGuane. il Sports
Illus 35:32-7 Ag 9 '71
Battle of the lakers. J. Brooks. il pors Out-
door Life 148:78-9+ N '71
Boating winter steelhead. E. Bradner. il
Field & S 76:70-1+ N '71
But big for its size. J. C. Ericson. il por
Outdoor Life 148:78-9+ Ag '71
Can we save Rock Creek? T. Wendelburg.
il Outdoor Life 147:64-7+ F '71
Early trout. T. Trueblood. il Field & S 76:22+
My '71
Easiest trout fishing going. R. H. Reagan. il
Field & S 75:56-7+ Ap '71
Fishing at the swimming pool; National city,
Calif. A. F. Maley. il Parks & Rec 6:112-15
Ja '71
Hatch on a hot lake. M. W. Fong. il pors Out-
door Life 147:68-71+ My '71
Hooking big brookies. W. Davis. il Mech
Illus 67:26+ Je '71
How to fish low water. H. Wixom. il Field
& S 76:64-5+ Je '71
How to fool big brown trout. H. Wixom. il
Field & S 76:56-7+ My '71

TROUT fishing—*Continued*
Iowa eye-opener. F. Wensel. il Outdoor Life 147:96-7+ Ap '71
Jamison Loop. B. Nauheim. il por Outdoor Life 147:80-3+ Je '71
Klamath steelhead. B. Grant. il Field & S 76:48-9+ D '71
Lakers along the shore; Allagash Lake. J. B. Robinson. il por Outdoor Life 147:62-3+ Je '71
Lunkers of Slave Lake. J. Brooks. il Outdoor Life 147:104-6+ Mr '71
Lunkers on the surface. N. Smith. il Field & S 76:10 Jl '71
Minnows a different way. J. J. Hudock. il Field & S 76:10+ D '71
Mountaintop trout. J. B. Robinson and H. Carroll. il Field & S 75:58-9+ Ja '71
My greatest trout float. P. Curtis. il Field & S 75:50-1+ Ap '71
New York's ice trout bonanza. A. Glowka. il Outdoor Life 148:38-9+ D '71
No. 1 brown in U.S. il Outdoor Life 148:8 Ag '71
North Platte float trip. C. J. Farmer. il Outdoor Life 148:52-5+ Ag '71
North Umpqua story. J. Hemingway. il Field & S 75:52-3+ F '71
Prospecting for mountain trout. N. Strung. il Field & S 75:52-3+ Mr '71
Purist; 12-year-old preparing for opening day. P. McManus. il Field & S 75:54-5+ F '71
Rainbows run up to 2 pounds. il Sunset 147:22 N '71
Record trout lake you can drive to. E. Park. il Field & S 76:38-9+ Jl '71
Return to the Roaring Kill; Catskill Mountains. P. Barrett. il Field & S 76:62-3+ My '71
River named Smith. G. Laycock. il Field & S 75:50-1+ Ja '71
Sagebrush rainbows. E. Bradner. il Field & S 75:62-3+ F '71
Saving a fish for tomorrow. D. G. Pasko. il Cons 26:48-9+ Ag '71
Steelhead or Atlantic salmon? J. Brooks. il Outdoor Life 148:68-9+ S '71
Those brainy browns. J. G. McCue, jr. il Field & S 75:52-3+ Ap '71
Three flies for trout. A. J. McClane. il Field & S 75:98-100+ Ja '71
Timber vs. trout; Rock Creek, Mont. D. A. Burk. Field & S 75:12+ Ja '71
To catch a steelhead. D. Stair. il Field & S 76:56-7+ Ag '71
Tops in the Rockies. J. Brooks. il Outdoor Life 148:34-7+ Jl '71
Triple take at Double Lake; in Shoshone national forest. N. D. Weis. il Outdoor Life 148:66-9+ O '71
Trout agitator. E. P. Haddon. il Field & S 75:68-9+ Mr '71
Trout fishing where history happened; Missouri River. E. Park. il Field & S 76:53-5+ Je '71
Up the down lakers. D. Otto. il por Outdoor Life 148:56-7+ Jl '71
Wall fish. F. G. Snook. il Outdoor Life 148:50-1+ D '71
Will we let the pink and silver warrior die? steelhead fishing. J. Hemingway. il pors Nat Wildlife 9:34-7 Ag '71
Winter is the time for steelhead. L. J. Bashline. il Field & S 75:40-1+ Ja '71
Year of the giant steelhead. H. Williams. il Field & S 76:58-9+ O '71
See also
Grayling fishing

Il TROVATORE; opera. See Verdi, G.

TRUBEK, David M. See Steiner, H. J. jt. auth.

TRUBY, J. David
Krakatoa, the killer wave; with biographical sketch. il por Sea Front 17:130-9, 191 My '71

TRUCK campers. See Campers and coaches, Truck

TRUCK drivers. See Motor truck drivers

TRUCK drivers strikes. See Strikes—United States—Truck drivers

TRUCK rental. See Motor trucks—Leasing and renting

TRUCKING
Making small shipments pay their way. por Bsns W p82-4 Jl 17 '71
See also
Associated truck lines
Motor trucks—Laws and regulations

Rates
Freight rate hikes hit a roadblock. Bsns W p22 Ja 1 '72

TRUCKS
See also
Motor trucks

TRUDEAU, Margaret (Sinclair)
Pictures of a secret wedding. il pors Life 70:42-3 Mr 19 '71 *
Secret ceremony. il pors Time 97:37 Mr 15 '71 *
Trudeau takes his bride to Moscow. il pors Life 70:32-4 Je 4 '71 *

TRUDEAU, Pierre Elliott
Behind Trudeau's pact with Soviets. il por US News 70:46 Je 7 '71 *
Canada switches targets. D. Coxe. Nat R 23:1177 O 22 '71 *
My friend Trudeau. il por Time 98:51 N 1 '71 *
Pictures of a secret wedding. il pors Life 70:42-3 Mr 19 '71 *
Secret ceremony. il pors Time 97:37 Mr 15 '71 *
TRB from Washington. New Repub 165:4 D 18 '71 *
Trudeau in power, by W. Stewart. Review Sat R por 55:30-1 Ja 8 '72. C. Cocking *
Trudeau takes his bride to Moscow. il pors Life 70:32-4 Je 4 '71 *

TRUEBLOOD, David Elton
Gospel for the affluent; the playboy cult. Chr Today 15:14 Jl 2 '71

TRUEBLOOD, Ted, pseud.
[Monthly article on outdoor life] See issues of Field & stream
Shooting. Field & S 76:84-6+ S '71

TRUEMAN, Mark E. H.
Montreal's great snowstorm of '69. il Weatherwise 23:270-3 D '70

TRUFFAUT, François
Talking with Truffaut; interview, ed. by C. T. Samuels; excerpt from Encountering directors. Am Scholar 40:482-6 Sum '71

about
Current cinema. P. Kael. New Yorker 46:89-92 F 6 '71 *
Movies. W. S. Pechter. Commentary 51:88-9 Je '71 *

TRUFFLES
No truffling matter. il Time 97:42 My 31 '71 *

TRUMAN, Harry S.
Harry Truman chuckles dryly. R. A. Aurthur. il Esquire 76:136-9+ F '71 *
Wit and sass of Harry S. Truman. R. A. Arthur. il pors Esquire 76.62-7+ Ag '71 *

TRUMBO, Dalton
Story behind the book; Johnny got his gun. D. N. Mount. Pub W 200:39 Ag 23 '71 *

TRUMBULL, John
Thomas Jefferson and Maria Cosway. C. B. Van Pelt. il pors Am Heritage 22:22-5+ Ag '71 *

TRUMBULL, Robert
Bed and board at Aggie Grey's. il Sat R 54:60-1+ O 23 '71

TRUMBULL, Van
Washington lookout. See issues of American forests to April 1971

TRUMPETER, Margo. See Scarich, K. jt. auth.

TRUONG, David
Vietnamese student; letter. New Repub 165:31 Jl 3 '71

TRUSCOTT, Alan
Bridge. See issues of New York times magazine

TRUSCOTT, Lucian K. 4th
Good soldiers. Nation 213:517 N 22 '71
—See Sabol, B. jt. auth.

TRUSLOW, Frederick Kent
Cutwater. il Audubon 73:8-11 Jl '71

TRUST departments of banks. See Banks and banking—Trust departments

TRUST houses Forte, ltd. See Hotels, taverns, etc.—Great Britain

TRUST in God
Hang loose. L. N. Bell. Chr Today 15:18-19 Ag 27 '71
What about tomorrow. V. P. McCorry. America 125:inside back cover Jl 24 '71

TRUST TERRITORY OF THE PACIFIC IS-LANDS
Seniors active in island groups 6,000 miles from West coast. il Aging 204:16-17 O '71
Staging area imperialism. S. Connolly and P. Shapiro. Nation 213:330-4 O 11 '71
Trust territory of the Pacific Islands; statement, May 26, 1971. E. E. Johnston. Dept State Bul 65:209-17 Ag 23 '71
See also
Micronesia

TRUSTEES, Library. See Libraries—Trustees, boards, committees, etc.

TRUSTEES of colleges. See College trustees

TRUSTEESHIP council. See United Nations—Trusteeship council

TRUSTS, Industrial
See also
Business consolidations and mergers
Competition

International trusts
Antitrusters nip a steel cartel bid. Bsns W
p42 Mr 6 '71
Concan challenge. J. Ross-Skinner. il Duns
98:61-2+ D '71

Law
Antitrust & the $. Forbes 107:21 Je 15 '71
Antitrust: storm signals. il Forbes 108:23
N 1 '71
Antitrusters take on professional sports. il
Bsns W p60-1+ O 9 '71
How Kennecott got hooked with Catch-22. R.
Loving. ir. il Fortune 84:98-101+ S '71
How to succeed in business without being
tried; address, May 4, 1971. L. Loevinger.
Vital Speeches 37:529-34 Je 15 '71
Nader on antitrust. R. A. Posner. New Re-
pub 164:11-14 Je 26 '71; Reply. M. Green.
165:31-2 Jl 10 '71
See also
United States—Justice, Department of—Anti-
trust division

United States
Antitrust: new life in an old issue. il Time
97:70-2 Je 28 '71
Naked power of monopoly; El Paso natural
gas corp. R. Sherrill. Nation 213:589-92 D 6
'71
See also
United States—Justice, Department of—Antitrust division

TRUSTS, Pension. See Pension trusts

TRUSTS and trustees
See also
Art—Galleries and museums—Trustees,
boards, committees, etc.

TRUTH
Experiments with truth. P. W. Schmidtchen.
il pors Hobbies 76:134-7 Je '71
It makes sense; God's revealed truth. L. N.
Bell. Chr Today 15:22-3 My 7 '71
Truth in theology. R. Hazelton. il Chr Cent
88:772-4 Je 23 '71
See also
Sincerity

**TRUTH about Croesus; drama. See Nightin-
gale, E. M.**

**TRUTH in lending legislation. See Consumer
credit—Laws and legislation**

TRUXELL, Elizabeth
$1 toy teaches photography. il Pop Phot
68:116 Ja '71

TRY data-date! drama. See Olfson, L.

TRYON, Dwight William
Art of Dwight W. Tryon. S. B. Sherrill. il
Antiques 99:458+ Ap '71 *

TRYON, Thomas
Soon ripe, soon rotten. L. Anderson. Sat R
54:24 F 20 '71 *

TRYPTOPHAN
Brain serotonin content: physiological dependence on plasma tryptophan levels. J.
D. Fernstrom and R. J. Wurtman. bibliog
il Science 173:149-52 Jl 9 '71
L-Dopa: disaggregation of brain polysomes
and elevation of brain tryptophan. B. F.
Weiss and others. bibliog il Science 173:
833-5 Ag 27 '71
Histochemical fluorescence of raphe neurons: selective enhancement by tryptophan. G. K. Aghajanian and I. M. Asher.
bibliog il Science 172:1159-61 Je 11 '71

TRYTHALL, Gilbert
Current chronicle. R. L. Weaver. il Mus Q
57:317-22 Ap '71 *

TSANG, Tung. See Ghose, S. jt. auth.

**TSARIST bonds. See Bonds, Government—
Russia**

**TSEMBAGA tribe. See New Guinea—Native
races**

TSIOLKOVSKII, Konstantin Eduardovich
Russians in space, by E. Riabchikov. Review
Sat R il por 54:41-3+ O 30 '71. W. Shelton *

TSUBOI, Masamichi, and others
Raman spectrum of a transfer RNA. bibliog
il Science 174:1142-4 D 10 '71

TSUDA, Margaret
Hard questions; poem. Liv Wildn 34:50 Aut
'70

TSUJI, Frederick I. See Haneda, Y. jt. auth.

TSUKOMOTO, Marie
Untitled poem. Wilson Lib Bul 45:751 Ap '71

TSUNAMIS. See Tidal waves

TSUR, Muki
Trade winds; interview, ed. by C. Amory.
Sat R 54:12-13 Ap 3 '71

TSURU, Shigeto
Kogai: environmental disruption in Japan. il
UNESCO Courier 24:6-13 Jl '71

TSURUMI, Yoshi
Myths that mislead U.S. managers in Japan.
Harvard Bsns R 49:118-27 Jl '71

TUBE bending
How to make perfect bends in tubing. R.
Kouhoupt. il Pop Mech 135:169 Mr '71

TUBE testers. See Testing instruments

TUBERCULOSIS

Diagnosis
Mobile TB X-ray units: an obsolete technology lingers. B. Nelson. Science 174:1114-
15 D 10 '71

Therapy
New drug for tuberculosis. il Chem 44:19-20
O '71

TUBMAN, William Vacanarat Shadrach
Death of President Tubman of Liberia;
statement, remarks. R. M. Nixon; W. P.
Rogers. Dept State Bul 65:180-1 Ag 16 '71 *
Liberia: end of the Tubman era. H. J. Mas-
saquoi. il por Ebony 26:46-8+ O '71 *
Obituary
Negro Hist Bul por 34:139 O '71
Passing of Uncle Shad. por Newsweek 78:33
Ag 2 '71 *
Patriarch yields the reins. il por Time 98:30-1
Ag 2 '71 *

TUCCI, Robert
New politics for Christians; address. America 125:112-16 S 4 '71

TUCHMAN, Barbara W.
Retreat from Burma; excerpts from Stilwell
and the American experience in China,
1911-45. il pors Am Heritage 22:38-43+ F
'71

TUCK, James A.
Iroquois confederacy; with biographical
sketch. il Sci Am 224:12, 32-42 F '71

TUCKER, N. C.
What's cooking? Org Gard & Farm 18:127-
8+ S '71

TUCKER, Preston Thomas
Tucker: a modern American tragedy. A. B.
Shuman. il pors Motor T 23:68-70+ My
'71 *

TUCKER, Robert L.
Snowshoes in the wind. il por Outdoor Life
148:58-9+ N '71

TUCKER, Wallace H.
Soft X-rays from the Cygnus loop; interpretation. bibliog il Science 172:372-4 Ap 23
'71
—See Gorenstein, P. jt. auth.

TUCKERMAN, Anne
China vote. Nation 213:452 N 8 '71
Our man at the U.N. Nation 212:389 Mr 29
'71
U.N. patterns for 1971. Nation 213:322-3 O 11
'71

TUCSON, Ariz.

Lighting
Star bright, street light, which will they see
tonight? R. J. Bazell. il Science 171:461 F
5 '71

TUCSON, Ariz, public library
Emergency employment act: Tucson library
proposals. Library J 96:2721 S 15 '71

TUDOR, Antony
Living by the star system. R. T. Jones. il
Time 98:51 Ag 2 '71 *

TUDOR, Dean
Canadian forecast: overcast, with possible
secessions. por Library J 96:2462-3, 3531+
Ag, N 1 '71

TUDOR, Nancy
Rehashing and beefing up: Canadian LA conference. Wilson Lib Bul 46:40-1 S '71

TUFFTRIDING. See Case hardening

TUG-barge systems. See Freighters

TUGBOATS
Life on the Mississippi: 1971 style. il U S
News 71:68 S 20 '71
Trouble off Bergen Point! tugboat Julia C.
Moran, rescue operation. T. Gallagher. il
Read Digest 99:58-62 Ag '71

TUGGLE, Robert A.
Why Luisa Miller? il Opera N 36:21-4 D 11 '71

TUITION. See College education—Cost

**TUITION fees. See Colleges and universities
—Finance**

TULANE university, New Orleans
On campus. N. A. Comer. il por Mlle 73:202+
My '71

TULANE university, New Orleans—*Continued*
Newcomb college
Sadie Irvine letters: a further note on the production of Newcomb pottery; excerpts from letters, ed. by R. W. Blasberg. S. Irvine. il Antiques 100:250-1 Ag '71

TULIP time festival. See Holland, Mich.—Tulip time festival

TULIPS
Growing daffodils and tulips in kitchen pots and pans. il Sunset 147:237-8 N '71
Tulips. M. Reynolds. il Horticulture 49:18-19+ O '71

TULLIBEE fishing. See Cisco fishing

TULSA, Okla.
Housing
Tulsa, Okla: Center plaza. il Arch Forum 134:28-31 My '71

TULSA, Okla, city-county library system
Decision in Tulsa: an issue of censorship. A. B. Martin. il Am Lib 2:370-4 Ap '71
Pride in heritage: one library's approach; use of National endowment for the humanities funds. R. G. Swartz. il Wilson Lib Bul 46:431-5 Ja '72
Pride in heritage, or resentment? A sociologist analyzes library staff reaction. N. G. Feldman. il Wilson Lib Bul 46:436-40 Ja '72

TUMA, Harold J.
Don't lower beef quality! Farm J 95:B10 Mr '71

TUMANOV, Aleksandr
Soviet space research chronicle. Space World H-6-90:11-13 Je '71

TUMIN, Melvin
How to survive life: the cynic's guide. Mlle 73:290-1+ Ag '71
There is no real you. Mlle 72:140-1+ F '71

TUMOR cells
Ascorbic acid: a culture requirement for cology formation by mouse plasmacytoma cells. C. H. Park and others. bibliog il Science 174:720-2 N 12 '71
Functional sequences modulated by morphological transitions in human lymphoid cells grown in vitro. B. Drewinko and others. bibliog il Science 171:185-6 Ja 15 '71
Glucocorticoid receptors in lymphoma cells in culture: relationship to glucocorticoid killing activity. J. D. Baxter and others. bibliog il Science 171:189-91 Ja 15 '71
Herpesvirus type 2 isolated from cervical tumor cells grown in tissue culture. L. Aurelian and others. bibliog il Science 174:704-7 N 12 '71
Hybrid cell line from a cloned immunoglobulin-producing mouse myeloma and a nonproducing mouse lymphoma. B. Mohit and K. Fan. bibliog il Science 171:75-7 Ja 8 '71
Microwave absorption by normal and tumor cells. S. J. Webb and A. D. Booth. bibliog il Science 174:72-4 O 1 '71
Selective stimulation of allelic expression: effect of antibodies to allotypic markers on lymphoid cells. A. Frensdorff and others. bibliog il Science 171:391-4 Ja 29 '71

TUMOR viruses
Cancer and viruses: need for caution. il Sci N 100:185-6 S 18 '71
Cancer: quest for a virus. il Newsweek 78:64 D 13 '71
Cell-surface changes after infection with oncogenic viruses: requirement for synthesis of host DNA. J. R. Sheppard and others. bibliog il Science 172:1345-6 Je 25 '71
Isolation and culture of a virus from human cancer tissue. il Sci N 100:21 Jl 10 '71
More candidates for a human cancer virus. il Sci N 100:388-9 D 11 '71
Progress on breast cancer. il por Newsweek 77:129 Ap 19 '71
Progress on cancer. il Time 98:40 D 13 '71
RNA-directed DNA synthesis. H. M. Temin. il Sci Am 226:24-33 bibliog(p 122) Ja '72
Reverse transcription: one year later. B. J. culliton. Science 172:926-8 My 28 '71
Simian tumor virus isolate: demonstration of cytopathic effects in vitro. D. L. Fine and others. bibliog il Science 174:420-1 O 22 '71
Simultaneous detection of reverse transcriptase and high molecular weight RNA unique to oncogenic RNA viruses. J. Schlom and S. Spiegelman. bibliog il Science 174:840-3 N 19 '71
Teminism and cancer; connection between RNA viruses and cancer genesis. J. L. Arehart. Sci N 100:317 N 6 '71
See also
Leukemia viruses

TUMORS
DNA constancy in heteroploidy and the stem line theory of tumors. P. M. Kraemer and others. bibliog il Science 174:714-17 N 12 '71
Epithelial origin of polyoma salivary tumors in mice: evidence based on chromosome-marked cells. C. J. Dawe and others. bibliog il Science 171:394-7 Ja 29 '71
Suppression of urethan-induced lung adenomas in mice treated with trehalose-6,6-dimycolate (cord factor) and living bacillus Calmette Guérin. A. Bekierkunst and others. bibliog il Science 174:1240-2 D 17 '71
Tumor immunity: tumor suppression in vivo initiated by soluble products of specifically stimulated lymphocytes. I. D. Bernstein and others. bibliog il Science 172:729-31 My 14 '71
See also
Mesothelioma
Sarcoma

TUMORS, Blood. See Leukemia

TUNA fish
Tuna on toast, please. Newsweek 77:70 F 15 '71

TUNA fisheries. See Fisheries

TUNA fishing
New world record tuna. G. Gibson. il por Outdoor Life 148:49-51+ S '71
Pity the poor porpoise. il Newsweek 78:60 S 6 '71
Uptight little island: Prince Edward Island. D. Levin. il Sports Illus 35:38-40+ O 4 '71

TUNDER, Bertha
We did it. il House B 113:38 Mr '71

TUNE ups, Automobile. See Automobile engines—Maintenance and repair

TUNICATES
Development of excitability in embryonic muscle cell membranes in certain tunicates. K. Takahashi and others. bibliog il Science 171:415-18 Ja 29 '71
Photoreceptors in primitive chordates: fine structure, hyperpolarizing receptor potentials, and evolution. A. L. F. Gorman and others. bibliog il Science 172:1052-4 Je 4 '71

TUNING
See also
Musical pitch

TUNIS
Antiquities
Carthage must not be destroyed. J. el Kafi. il UNESCO Courier 23:4-8 D '70
Tunis: a jewel of Islam. G. Fradier. il UNESCO Courier 23:34-41 D '70

TUNISIA
See also
Americans in Tunisia
Arts and crafts—Tunisia
Antiquities
See also
Tunis—Antiquities

TUNLEY, Roul
He brings them back to life. il por Read Digest 98:193-4+ Ap '71
Smooth path at Rough Rock. il Am Ed 7:15-20 Mr '71

TUNNELS and tunneling
Digging the world's first freeze-dried tunnel. E. A. Zadig. il Pop Sci 198:56-7 Mr '71
Low-cost tunnel renovation; West rock tunnel in New Haven, Conn. il Am City 86:14 F '71
Steel tunnels: Southern California's Hollywood park. il Parks & Rec 6:36 My '71
See also
Rock drills

TUNNELS and tunneling, Underwater
See also
Chesapeake Bay bridge-tunnel

TUNNEY, John Varick
Bandwagon gambit. pors Newsweek 78:22+ D 20 '71 •
John Tunney, Kennedy's friend in Muskie s corner. J. Leslie. il pors N Y Times Mag p4-5+ D 26 '71 •
Lifestyle. il pors Am Home 74:8+ Jl '71 •

TUPAMAROS. See Guerrillas—Uruguay

TURANO, John P. See Kelly, E. T. jt. auth.

TURBIDITY, Atmospheric. See Atmospheric turbidity

TURBINES
See also
Gas turbines
Gas turbines, Marine

TURBOCHARGERS. See Airplane engines—Superchargers; Automobile engines—Superchargers

TURBOFAN airplane engines. See Jet airplane engines

TURBOJETS. See Jet airplane engines

TURBOPROP airplane engines. See Jet airplane engines

TURBULENCE
See also
Atmospheric turbulence

TURCO, Lewis
Cell; poem. Poetry 117:356 Mr '71
Children of Rome; Song; poems. Poetry 118:262-3 Ag '71
In the garden; poem. Commonweal 95:109 O 29 '71
Tick; poem. Sat R 54:54 Jl 31 '71

TURF. See Lawns

TURF, Artificial
Artificial turf turns median strip into beauty spots; St Petersburg, Fla. il Am City 86:24+ Je '71
Disputed turf. il Newsweek 78:92 N 22 '71
New slant on the mod sod; AstroTurf, Tartan Turf and Poly-Turf. J. Underwood. il Sports Illus 35:32-4+ N 15 '71
Very rough season for synthetic turf. il Bsns W p35 N 6 '71

Anecdotes, facetiae, satire, etc.
Warring of the green. R. D. Buechner. il Parks & Rec 6:57+ My '71

TURFGRASS. See Grasses

TURING machine theory. See Machine theory

TURINO, Jon L.
Designing a phase-shift oscillator. il Electr World 86:34-5 Jl '71

TURK, Midge
Up and over. D. Grumbach. New Repub 164:32-3 Je 12 '71 *

TURKEVICH, Anthony
Getting aboard Viking: no room on the Mars lander. S. Jacobsen. il Bul Atom Sci 27:49-56 D '71 *

TURKEY
See also
Agriculture—Turkey
Ani
Colleges and universities—Turkey
Cruising—Turkey
Folklore—Turkey
Guerrillas—Turkey
Istanbul
Opium trade—Turkey
Protests, demonstrations, etc.—Turkey
Railroads—Turkey
Smyrna
Terrorism—Turkey

Air force
Turkish air fleet causes NATO concern. E. H. Kolcum. il Aviation W 96:56-7 Ja 3 '72

Antiquities
Ancient man: farmer or villager first? Cayönü excavations. il Sci Digest 69:76-7 Je '71
Archeological find named Iris Love. E. Stevens. il pors N Y Times Mag p32-4+ Mr 7 '71
Prehistoric domestication of animals: effects on bone structure. I. M. Drew and others. bibliog il Science 171:280-2 Ja 22 '71
When Love came to Cnidus. Cyclops. il Life 70:18 Je 11 '71
See also
Art, Turkish

Army
Turkey: a time of troubles. D. J. Simpson. Cur Hist 62:38-43+ Ja '72

Foreign relations
See also
Cyprus
United States
See United States—Foreign relations—Turkey

Intellectual life
Turkish culture; Minister of culture, T. S. Halman. New Yorker 47:46-7 N 20 '71

Politics and government
Pride of authorship; new military government. il por Time 97:26+ Mr 22 '71
Tagmac memorandum. Newsweek 77:42+ Mr 22 '71
Turkey: a time of troubles. D. J. Simpson. Cur Hist 62:38-43+ Ja '72
Turkey in turmoil. L. Hansen. Chr Cent 88:840-2 Jl 7 '71
We won't give up. il por Newsweek 77:36 Ja 18 '71

Social life and customs
See also
Harem
TURKEY as food. See Cookery—Poultry

TURKEY calling. See Bird calling

TURKEY carving. See Carving (meat, etc)

TURKEY hunting
How to call spring gobblers. J. M. Vance. il Field & S 75:64-5+ F '71
Putt, putt, and gone. B. Warner. il por Field & S 75:82-3+ Mr '71
Team turkey. C. Elliott. il por Outdoor Life 147:66-7+ Mr '71
Turkeys talk in Texas. B. W. Dalrymple. il Outdoor Life 147:98-101+ Ap '71

TURKEYS
Unexpected nuclear spin-off; Atlas of the domestic turkey. D. E. Abrahamson. Science 173:1191 S 24 '71

TURKEYS, Wild
Old gobblers and old trees. B. Towell. Am For 77:40 Ja '71
Social order of turkeys. C. R. Watts and A. W. Stokes. il Sci Am 224:112-18 Je '71
See also
Turkey hunting

TURKISH Armenia. See Armenia

TURKISH art. See Art, Turkish

TURKOWSKI, Frank J.
Learning at the zoo. il Parks & Rec 6:25-6 N '71

TURNABOUT; drama. See Edwards, M. B.

TURNBULL, Gael
Comment. R. J. Mills, jr. Poetry 117:333 F '71 *

TURNCOATS
See also
Defectors, Political

TURNER, Camille Orso, and Spivack, George
Staff-patient interaction, race and patient behavior on a psychiatric ward. bibliog Ment Hy 55:499-503 O '71

TURNER, Darwin T.
Literature and society's values; address, November 1970. bibliog f Engl 60:577-86 My '71

TURNER, Ewart E.
Anti-Nazi resisters: a few remain. Chr Cent 88:1266-7 O 27 '71

TURNER, Glenn Wesley
Dare to be great! T. Thompson. il pors Life 70:68-68B+ My 28 '71 *
Fast-buck gospel. il por Time 98:76+ N 29 '71 *

TURNER, Ike
Ike & Tina Turner. il pors Ebony 26:88-90+ My '71 *

TURNER, Mary
Snow sculpture. il Design 73:28 Wint '71

TURNER, Nat
Nat Turner's rebellion. il Sr Schol 99:8-9 N 8 '71 *

TURNER, Paul
Radiation controversy; a challenge to health physicists; address, July 15, 1971. Vital Speeches 37:696-9 S 1 '71

TURNER, Robert Edward
In the wake of the capsize kid. C. Phinizy. il por Sports Illus 35:28-30+ Jl 12 '71 *

TURNER, Sheila
Paris on parade. il Schol Teach Jr/Sr High p 18-19 Mr 8 '71
Tales of a Levantine guru. il por Sat R 54:54-5+ Mr 13 '71

TURNER, Ted
Will Ted do it? il pors Yachting 130:65+ D '71 *

TURNER, Tina
Ike & Tina Turner. il pors Ebony 26:88-90+ My '71 *

TURNER, W. P.
Grid-dip meter extension. il Radio-Electr 42:61 S '71

TURNER, Wallace
All the Hughes that's fit to print. Esquire 76:65-7+ Jl '71

TURNER'S Negro insurrection, 1831. See Southampton insurrection, 1831

TURNING
7 smart tricks for a wood lathe. R. J. De Cristoforo. il Pop Sci 199:108 D '71
Tiny turned tables; woodworking project. J. Capotosto. il Mech Illus 67:106-8 N '71
Tired of turning metals? Try rigid plastic. W. E. Burton. il Pop Mech 135:160-4 Je '71
See also
Lathes

TURNIPS
Turnips, encore vegetables for double harvests. W. Masson. il Org Gard & Farm 18:112-13 Mr '71
Turnips in your cover crop? B. Rozell. Org Gard & Farm 18:98-9 S '71

TURNOVER of labor. See Labor turnover

TURNTABLE Junction. See Flemington, N.J.

TURNTABLES. See Phonograph—Turntables

TURNTABLES, Automatic. See Phonograph—
  Record changers

TURTLES
  Durable snapping turtle. D. A. Hammer. il
    Natur Hist 80:58-65 Je '71
  Pet turtles and salmonella poisoning. il Con-
    sumer Rep 36:405-6 Jl '71
  Slow and serene; interview. P. Wohl. New
    Yorker 47:30-2 My 1 '71
  What do you know about turtles? quiz. J.
    Daugherty and M. Daugherty. il Sci Digest
    70:56-7+ Jl '71

TUSCALOOSA Bryce hospital. See Hospitals,
  Psychiatric

TUSSING, Annette
  Fight to save the Snake. Field & S 76:22+
    O '71
  Women in the wilderness. il Liv Wildn 34:
    44-9 Aut '70

TUTEUR, Mary
  Grace for my twenty-fifth year; poem. Na-
    tion 213:573 N 29 '71

TUTHILL, Jack
  Pro who runs the tour. W. Bingham. il pors
    Sports Illus 34:52-5 Mr 15 '71 *

TUTHILL, Sue
  Today's health news. Todays Health 49:7-8
    O: 7-8 N '71

TUTKO, Thomas
  We have a neurotic in the backfield, doctor.
    J. Jares. il pors Sports Illus 34:30-4 Ja
    18 '71 *

TUTORS and tutoring
  Learning by tutoring others; sixth graders
    tutor younger children. M. M. Harris. To-
    days Ed 60:48-9 F '71
  Teaching writing to the non-academic stu-
    dent; student tutors. R. Lebda. Clear House
    46:39 S '71
  Tutoring for credit. L. Goodman. il Am Ed
    7:26-7 Ap '71

TUTTLE, Anthony
  8 items or less; story. Redbook 136:78-9 F '71

TUTTLE, Helen Welch
  Price indexes for 1971: U.S. periodicals. il
    Library J 96:2271-4 Jl '71
  Women in academic libraries. Library J 96:
    2594-6 S 1 '71

TUTTLE, Hugh
  300 years on the same piece of land. il pors
    Life 71:44-53 S 17 '71 *

TUTUOLA, Amos
  Amos Tutuola: emerging African literature.
    P. Neumarkt. bibliog Am Imago 28:129-45
    Sum '71 *

TUYET-mai-Ky. See Nguyen-cao-Ky, Mme

TVARDOVSKII, Aleksandr Trifonovich
  Solzhenitsyn's tributes. il por Newsweek 79:
    23 Ja 3 '72 *

TWAIN, Mark, pseud. See Clemens, S. L.

TWARDOKENS, G. R. See Broten, G. A. jt.
  auth.

TWEETER speakers. See Loud speaking apparatus

TWELFTH night. See Epiphany

TWELFTH night parties. See Entertaining

TWELVE days of Christmas; drama. See
  Wright, D. G.

TWELVE-mile limit. See Territorial waters

TWELVE-tone system
  Music of George Perle. L. Kraft. bibliog f il
    Mus Q 57:444-65 Jl '71
  Webern's twelve-tone sketches. G. Perle. bib-
    liog f il Mus Q 57:1-25 Ja '71

TWENTIETH century-Fox film corporation
  Backstage power who replaces Zanuck. por
    Bsns W p41 Je 19 '71
  Cliff-hanger for Fox shareholders. il Bsns
    W p24 My 22 '71
  SEC wants a close-up of Fox. il Bsns W
    p31 Je 12 '71
  20th century-Fox presents: proxy war. il Bsns
    W p68-70 My 8 '71

TWICE-told tales. See Borges, J. L.

TWIGGY (model)
  Tea with Twiggy; interview. New Yorker
    47:30-1 D 18 '71
  Twiggy model into movie star. il pors Mlle 74:
    138-41 N '71
    about
  Now blooming Twiggy. H. Ehrlich. il pors
    Look 35:58-63 My 4 '71 *
  Now it's Twiggy's turn. il pors Harp Baz
    105:112-13 D '71 *

TWIGS; drama. See Furth, G.

TWILIGHT flash. See Sunset phenomena

TWIN-lens cameras
  Camera collector (cont) J. Schneider. il
    Mod Phot 34:16+ N; 22-3+ D '70

Lab report; Field check; Instrument readouts:
    Meopta Flexaret Automat VII. H. Mar-
      tin; N. Goldberg. il Pop Phot 68:108-9+
      F '71
  Readers' report:
    Yashica TLR's. il Mod Phot 35:79+ S '71

TWINS
  Quiet family life of Muhammad Ali; photo-
    graphs by J. Sutton. Ebony 26:118-22 Ja
    '71
    See also
  Siamese twins

TWO by two; musical comedy. See Musical
  comedies, revues, etc.—Criticisms, plots,
  etc.

2,4-D. See Herbicides

2,4,5-T. See Herbicides

TWO gentlemen of Verona; musical comedy.
  See Musical comedies, revues, etc.—Criticisms, plots, etc.

TWO lane blacktop; screenplay. See Wurlitzer,
  R. and Corry, W.

TWO more under the Indian sun; story See
  Jhabvala, R. P.

TWO party system. See Political parties—
  United States

200-mile limit. See Territorial waters

TWOMBLY, Wells
  How to throw the ultimate fast ball. il pors
    N Y Times Mag p22-4+ Jl 25 '71

TWORKOV, Jack
  Quartered and drawn. D. Crimp. il Art N 70:
    48-9+ Mr '71 *

TWYMAN, Jack
  Baseball where the players are. il Parks &
    Rec 6:27+ S '71

TYLER, Anne
  With all flags flying; story. Redbook 137:
    88-9 Je '71

TYLER, C. William
  Stereoscopic depth movement: two eyes less
    sensitive than one. bibliog il Science 174:
    958-61 N 26 '71

TYLER, Edward T.
  Now it's ice-cube babies. il por Newsweek
    78:81 Jl 12 '71 *

TYLER, John D.
  Cast-iron cooking vessels. il Antiques 100:
    217-21 Ag '71

TYLER, Parker
  Aesthete at the movies. A. Sarris. Commen-
    tary 51:81-4 F '71 *

TYLER, Ralph W.
  Testing for accountability. Ed Digest 36:12-
    14 Mr '71

TYNAN, Kathleen
  Vain servile bores are we. por Vogue 157:131
    Ap 15 '71
  (ed) See Greer, G. Germaine Greer

TYNAN, Kenneth
  Polish imposition. pors Esquire 76:122-5+ S
    '71

TYPES, Psychological. See Typology (psychology)

TYPEWRITERS
  Q W E R T U I O P ? * ! ? Dvorak simpli-
    fied keyboard. W. T. Boyd. il Writers Di-
    gest 51:37+ F '71
    See also
  Olivetti corporation of America

TYPEWRITERS, Automatic
  See also
  Wang laboratories. inc.

TYPEWRITERS, Electric
  Portable electric typewriters. il Consumer
    Bul 54:33-40 S '71

TYPEWRITING
  See also
  Art typing

TYPOLOGY (psychology)
  What your sense of time tells about you.
    J. Reinert. il Sci Digest 69:8-12 Je '71

TYRIAN purple. See Dyes and dyeing

TYRONE Guthrie theatre. See Minneapolis—
  Theater

TYROSINE hydroxylase. See Hydroxylases

TYSON, Alan
  1803 version of Beethoven's Christus am Oel-
    berge. bibliog f il Mus Q 56:551-84 O '70

TYSON, Brady
  Dom Helder Camara as a symbolic man.
    Cath World 213:178-82, 235-9 Jl-Ag '71

TYSON, Mildred
  Interviewing for trade journal articles. il
    Writers Digest 51:25-7 Jl '71

TYTELL, Alfred A. See Hilleman, M. R. jt.
  auth.

TYTELL, John
  Coming of consciousness III. Cath World 212:
    265-6 F '71

U

U Cephei. See Stars, Eclipsing binary
U-2 (airplane) See Airplanes, Military—United
   States
U-2 incident, 1960
   Oswald and the U-2; declassified papers from
   the Warren report. il por Newsweek 77:31
   Mr 1 '71
UAW. See United automobile, aerospace and
   agricultural implement workers of America
UCC. See United church of Christ
UCLA. See California. University—Los An-
   geles campus
UCLA graduate dance center. See California.
   University—Los Angeles campus
UDC. See New York (state)—Urban develop-
   ment corporation
UFO (unidentified flying objects) See Flying
   saucers
UFWOC. See American federation of labor and
   Congress of industrial organizations—
   United farm workers organizing committee
UMTA. See United States—Urban mass
   transportation administration
UMW. See United mine workers of America
UN. See United Nations
UNCITRAL. See United Nations—Commission
   on international trade law
UNCTAD. See United Nations conference on
   trade and development
UNDP. See United Nations—Development pro-
   gram
UNEPRO. See United Nations East Pakistan
   relief operation
UNESCO. See Unesco
UNHCR. See United Nations—High commis-
   sioner for refugees
UNICEF. See United Nations children's fund
UNRWA. See United Nations relief and works
   agency for Palestine refugees in the Near
   East
UNV. See United Nations volunteer corps
UNW. See University of the New World
USCC. See United States Catholic conference
USDA. See United States—Agriculture, Depart-
   ment of
USDESEA (United States dependents schools,
   European area) See Military post schools,
   American
USM corporation
   Some British snap for a fastener maker. por
   Bsns W p42 Mr 20 '71
USO. See United service organizations
USOE. See United States—Education, Office of
USPS. See United States power squadrons, inc.
USSR (Union of Soviet Socialist Republics)
   See Russia
USVBA. See United States volleyball associa-
   tion
USWA. See United steelworkers of America
UUA. See Unitarian universalist association
UBELL, Shirley
   Why am I driven? K. S. Cunningham. il por
   Dance Mag 46:56-61 Ja '72 *
UBLEIS, Adolf
   He gave 'em the Vienna waltz. L. Simross.
   il por Sports Illus 34:74+ My 24 '71 *
UDALL, Morris King
   Selling out the future. New Repub 165:12-13
   N 20 '71

about

Road to power in Congress. L. L. King.
   Harper 242:39-42+ Je '71 *
Spoils of politics? Newsweek 78:53-4 Ag 9
   '71 *
Such good friends. Newsweek 78:82+ O 11 '71 *
UDALL, Scott
   Encounter with a cougar. il Field & S 76:
   64-5+ N '71
UDALL, Stewart Lee
   Homage to windmills. il Read Digest 98:95-6
   My '71
   Ivory tower is under siege; adaptation of ad-
   dress, December 1970. Audubon 73:118-19
   Mr '71
   Simple joys of roughing it. il McCalls 98:
   106 Je '71
UDENFRIEND, Sidney. See Dairman, W. jt.
   auth.
UDOFF, Yale
   Gun play. Criticism
   Sat R 54:16+ F 20 '71*
UEMURA, Kogoro
   Japan and the U.S. a call for harmony. por
   Nations Bsns 59:28-31 Ag '71

UGANDA
Uganda: Africa's uneasy heartland. H. La
   Fay. il Nat Geog 140:708-35 N '71
   See also
   Ruwenzori Mountains

Foreign relations

Border incident; Uganda and Tanzania.
   Newsweek 78:30-1 S 6 '71

Native races

Naked repression; Karamojong tribe. il por
   Time 98:31 Ag 2 '71

Politics and government

Big daddy takes charge. il pors Time 97:38
   F 8 '71
Gold-dust twins; coup. il por Newsweek 77:
   35 F 8 '71
Naked repression; Karamojong tribe. il por
   Time 98:31 Ag 2 '71
UHL, Edward G.
   Breaking with tradition; excerpts from ad-
   dress. Aviation W 95:9 Ag 2 '71
UHL, Joseph N.
   Consumer education; everybody needs it. il
   Am Ed 7:13-17 Ja '71
UHLER, Lowell D.
   Blue frogs. il Cons 26:4 Ag '71
UHNAK, Dorothy
   Madame Sleuth confesses. M. Meade. Mc-
   Calls 98:43 Jl '71 *
UKRAINE
   See also
   Conservation of resources—Ukraine
UKRAINIAN Catholics in the United States.
   See Catholics, Ukrainian in the United
   States
UKRAINIAN rite. See Catholic church—By-
   zantine rite (Ukrainian)
ULAM, Adam B.
   Twenty-fourth Soviet party congress. Cur
   Hist 61:222-6+ O '71
ULBRICHT, Walter
   Disciple departs. por Time 97:32+ My 17 '71 *
   Don't go, comrade Ulbricht. Time 98:38 D
   6 '71 *
   East Germany changes bosses. il por News-
   week 77:36-7+ My 17 '71 *
   Merit of Ulbricht. P. Wohl. Nation 212:613
   My 17 '71 *
   Toward a triumvirate. il por Time 97:36 Je 28
   '71 *
ULCERS
   See also
   Peptic ulcers
UL'IANOVA, Nadezhda Konstantinovna. See
   Krupskaia, N. K.
ULLIAN, Robert
   Celebration; story. Mlle 72:86-7 Ja '71
   Snag in the harp; story. il Esquire 75:78-81
   F '71
ULLMAN, Albert Conrad
   Al Ullman smiles an I told you so. por Bsns
   W p 15-16 S 4 '71 *
ULLMAN, Leslie
   Opinion; on living in the country. por Mlle
   72:20+ F '71
ULMAN, Lloyd
   Inflation policies and collective bargaining.
   Mo Labor R 94:48-52 Ag '71
ULMANN, Doris
   Gallery; photographs. Life 71:8-9 O 1 '71
ULMER, Melville J.
   Applied Nixonomics. New Repub 164:15-18 Ap
   24 '71
   Better than revenue sharing. New Repub 164:
   16-19 F 13 '71; Same abr. with title Alter-
   native 1: tax credits. Cur 128:46-50 Ap '71
   Limitations of revenue sharing. bibliog f Ann
   Am Acad 397:48-59 S '71
   Non-answer to Nixonomics. New Repub 165:
   19-21 D 11; 31 D 25 '71; 166:31 Ja 1 '72
   Who's making it in Mexico? New Repub 165:
   21-3 S 25 '71
ULTRAMINIATURE cameras. See Cameras
ULTRASONIC alarms. See Alarms
ULTRASONIC burglar alarms. See Burglar
   alarms
ULTRASONIC waves

Medical use

Sounding out the womb. J. L. Arehart. il
   Sci N 100:424-5 D 25 '71
   See also
   Eye—Surgery
ULTRAVIOLET photography. See Photography,
   Ultraviolet
ULTRAVIOLET rays
   Long-wavelength ultraviolet photoproduction
   of amino acids on the primitive earth. C.
   Sagan and B. N. Khare. bibliog il Science
   173:417-20 Jl 30 '71

ULTRAVIOLET rays—_Continued_

Physiological effects

Chromatid breakage: cytosine arabinoside-induced lesions inhibited by ultraviolet irradiation. W. F. Benedict and M. Karon. bibliog il Science 171:680-2 F 19 '71

DNA synthesis in differentiating skeletal muscle cells: initiation by ultraviolet light. F. E. Stockdale. bibliog il Science 171:1145-7 Mr 19 '71

Eye lens color: formation and function. S. Zigman. bibliog il Science 171:807-9 F 26 '71; Reply with rejoinder. D. Kennedy and R. Milkman. 173:654-5 Ag 13 '71

Ultraviolet light: a new stimulus for the induction of platelet aggregation. R. C. Dickson and others. bibliog il Science 172:1140-2 Je 11 '71

ULYSSES complex. See Complexes (psychology)

UMAN, Martin A.

Lightning and you; excerpts from Understanding lightning. il Sci Digest 70:45-8+ S; 21-5+ O '71

When lightning strikes, are you safe in a plane? excerpt from Understanding lightning. il Sci Digest 70:69-72 D '71

UMANS, Shelley

Computers in the classroom. il Parents Mag 46:62-3+ Mr '71

UN-AMERICAN activities committee. See United States—Congress—House—Internal security. Committee on

UN-AMERICAN activities committee of the California legislature. See California—Legislature—Joint fact-finding committee on un-American activities

UNAMUNO Y JUGO, Miguel de

In Bluebeard's castle: some notes towards the redefinition of culture. by G. Steiner. Review

Nation 214:53-4 Ja 10 '72. R. S. Picciotto *

UNARCO industries, Inc.

Fabricating growth. Fortune 83:138 Je '71

UNAUTHORIZED phonograph records. See Phonograph records—Recording—Unauthorized recording

UNAUTHORIZED reprints. See Copyright—Unauthorized reprints

UNAUTHORIZED tape recording. See Magnetic recorders and recording—Unauthorized recording

UNCLE Vanya; drama. See Chekhov. A. P.

UNCOMPROMISING girl; story. See Franco, M.

UNDERACHIEVERS

Academic underachiever in an industrialized world. C. P. Bartl and G. L. Peltier. bibliog Sch & Soc 99:24-7 Ja '71

UNDERDEVELOPED areas

Are the developing countries really developing? adaptation of address, August 23, 1970. G. Myrdal. Bul Atom Sci 27:5-8 Ja '71

Basic problems of development: the World bank; address, September 27, 1971. R. S. McNamara. Vital Speeches 38:17-21 O 15 '71

Development: a Soviet countermodel. R. Bosc. il America 124:504-8 My 15 '71 (to be cont)

Dollar crises and the developing countries. C. Elliott. Chr Cent 88:1520-2 D 29 '71

Global poverty and underdevelopment; address, March 15, 1971. J. E. Rielly. Vital Speeches 37:496-502 Je 1 '71

Industrialization without pollution: a challenge to the developing world. I. Sachs. il UNESCO Courier 24:30-2 Jl '71

Institutional problems in the developing countries; address, February 15, 1971. J. A. Hannah. Dept State Bul 64:297-301 Mr 8 '71

New educational methods and developing nations. Sch & Soc 99:399-400+ N '71

No muscle is the message; meeting of underdeveloped nations of Africa, Asia and Latin America. A. Bono. Commonweal 95:316-17 Ja 7 '72

Poor lands spawn big squalid cities. B. L. Masse. America 124:166 F 20 '71

Social information for developing countries; symposium, ed. by I. Galnoor. bibliog f il Ann Am Acad 393:1-121 Ja '71

Third world development, can east and west agree? R. Bosc. il America 124:532-4 My 22 '71

See also

Economic assistance in underdeveloped areas

International basic economy corporation

Investments, Foreign (in underdeveloped areas)

United States—Foreign relations—Underdeveloped areas

Agriculture

Genetic technology and agricultural development. W. J. Staub and M. G. Blase. bibliog il Science 173:119-23 Jl 9 '71

Green revolution: for bread and peace; address, December 1971. N. E. Borlaug. por Bul Atom Sci 27:6-9+ Je '71

Second thoughts on the green revolution. M. Perelman. New Repub 165:21-2 Jl 17 '71; Reply. R. J. Muscat. 165:33-5 Ag 21 '71

When North and West try to help. R. L. Tobin. Sat R 54:26 My 1 '71

Who's for DDT, views of N. E. Borlaug. por Time 98:84 N 22 '71

Will the green revolution ruin our export markets? W. Swegle. il Suc Farm 69:no3 B4-5 F '71

Commerce

Have-nots and the export dilemma. R. L. Tobin. Sat R 54:16 Ag 21 '71

See also

Underdeveloped areas—Shipping

Defenses

Merchants of death; SIPRI study of the international trade in arms. Sci Am 226:44-5 Ja '72

Education

Adult education and economic planning as weapons against unemployment. T. Kristensen. Sch & Soc 99:232-4 Ap '71

Center for concern; study of world peace, justice and development. America 124:531 My 22 '71

Correspondence courses for in-service training of primary teachers in developing countries. Sch & Soc 99:386 O '71

Educational materials in the third world; meeting of the German foundation for developing countries. H. Lottman. il Pub W 200:16-18 N 22 '71

Propaganda through the printed media in the developing countries. Y. V. L. Rao. bibliog f Ann Am Acad 398:93-103 N '71

Publishers participate in Third world meeting; UNESCO participation. H. Lottman. Pub W 199:45 Je 21 '71

Forests and forestry

World's wasteful woodsmen. G. Dorsey. il Am For 77:20-3+ Jl '71

Hospitals

Thriving market in turn-key hospitals. il Bsns W p37 O 9 '71

Public health

Progress in health: what index of what progress? W. Malenbaum. bibliog f il Ann Am Acad 393:109-21 Ja '71

Science

Science and policy for a new decade. C. P. Haskins. bibliog f For Affairs 49:237-70 Ja '71

Science, technology and the developing countries; statement to House committee on science and astronautics at meeting with Panel on science and technology, Jan. 26-28, 1971. H. Brown. por Bul Atom Sci 27:10-14 Je '71

Shipping

Shipping and developing countries; symposium. bibliog f il Int Concil 582:7-79 Mr '71

Technology

Science, technology and the developing countries; statement to House committee on science and astronautics at meeting with Panel on science and technology, Jan. 26-28, 1971. H. Brown. por Bul Atom Sci 27:10-14 Je '71

Unemployment

First and third world unemployment. T. Beeson. Chr Cent 88:872 Jl 21 '71

Marginal men: the global unemployment crisis. J. P. Grant. For Affairs 50:112-24 O '71

Plight of many in the third world. B. L. Masse. America 125:305 O 23 '71

Youth

Too many young? poor chances of getting either a job or an education. Sr Schol 98:8 Mr 29 '71

UNDERDRIVE transmission. See Automobiles—Transmission

UNDERGROUND; story. See Aguallo, T.

UNDERGROUND atomic power plants. See Atomic power plants

UNDERGROUND atomic testing. See Atomic bombs—Testing, Underground

UNDERGROUND employee press. See Employees magazines, handbooks, etc.
UNDERGROUND literature
Alien porn; new Russian books. il Newsweek 78:50+ N 22 '71
See also
Underground press
UNDERGROUND newspapers. See Underground press—United States
UNDERGROUND nuclear explosions. See Atomic weapons—Testing, Underground
UNDERGROUND nuclear explosions, Detection of. See Atomic weapons—Testing, Detection of
UNDERGROUND press

United States

Jesus presses are rolling. H. E. Flowman. Chr Today 15:38 Ap 9 '71
What's happening to the underground press? J. Tebbel. Sat R 54:89-90 N 13 '71
What's up underground. J. C. Smith. Nat R 23:1130 O 8 '71
See also
Newspapers—United States
UNDERGROUND press, Student. See College and school journalism
UNDERGROUND river; story. See Kittredge, W.
UNDERGROUND television. See Television, Experimental
UNDERGROUND water. See Water, Underground
UNDERSEA research vehicles. See Submarine research vehicles
UNDERSTANDING. See Comprehension
UNDERSTUDIES. See Actors and actresses
UNDERWATER archeology. See Archeology, Submarine
UNDERWATER cameras. See Cameras
UNDERWATER drilling
Birth of the Caribbean; leg 15 of the Deep sea drilling project. L. Purrett. il Sci N 99:169-70 Mr 6 '71
Deep sea drilling: age and composition of an Atlantic basaltic intrusion. D. Macdougall. bibliog il Science 171:1244-5 Mr 26 '71
Extension through 1975; Deep-sea drilling project. il Sci N 99:399 Je 12 '71
Glomar Challenger drills deep-sea peephole into earth's past. A. Hamilton. il Pop Sci 198:58-60+ My '71
How the Isthmus of Panama got there; leg 16 of Deep sea drilling project. il Sci N 99:279 Ap 24 '71
Leg 4 of the Deep sea drilling project; western Atlantic and Caribbean basins. bibliog il Science 172:1197-205 Je 18 '71
Ocean-floor record links dinosaurs, plankton, climate; leg 19 of the Deep sea drilling project. Sci N 100:279 O 23 '71
Undersea reentry. Sci N 99:43 Ja 16 '71
When the Pacific crustal plate reversed itself; leg 20 of the Deep sea drilling project. il Sci N 100:405 D 18 '71
Where plate meets plate; leg 18 of the Deep sea drilling project. il Sci N 100:90 Ag 7 '71
UNDERWATER exercises. See Exercise
UNDERWATER exploration
See also
Skin diving

History

Tales of sea floor soundings. B. G. Ledbetter. il Sea Front 17:274-84 S '71
UNDERWATER laboratories
Bargain basement habitat; Sublimnos. D. L. Hicks. il Pop Mech 135:194-7+ Ap '71
Helgoland underwater laboratory. R. Burton. il Sea Front 17:335-41 N '71
My two weeks under the sea. S. A. Earle and J. Devaney. il por Redbook 136:75-7+ Ad '71
New lab beneath the Bahamian Sea. J. S. Bunt. il Sea Front 17:171-4 My '71
Tektite II:
Science's window on the sea. J. G. Vanderwalker; S. A. Earle. il por Nat Geog 140:256-96 Ag '71
Tektite unlocks secrets from the ocean's floor. C. B. Jackson. il Nat Wildlife 9:50-5 Ap '71
UNDERWATER photography. See Photography, Submarine
UNDERWATER rescue work
We cannot let him die! R. Schiller. il Read Digest 99:105-9 O '71
UNDERWATER sports. See Aquatic sports
UNDERWATER structures
See also
Garages, Underwater
UNDERWATER treasure. See Treasure trove

UNDERWATER vehicles. See Submarine vehicles
UNDERWATER weapons. See Weapons systems
UNDERWEAR
Thermal underwear: best way to keep out the cold. il Good H 173:176 D '71
UNDERWOOD, Bob
Best bass bait in the world. il Outdoor Life 147:74-5+ Mr '71
Florida's lunker bass king. il Field & S 75:56-7+ F '71
UNDERWOOD, Herbert, and Menaker, Michael
Photoperiodically significant photoreception in sparrows: is the retina involved? bibliog il Science 167:298-301; 169:893; 172:293 Ja 16, Ag 28 '70; Ap 16 '71
UNDERWOOD, John
And this man is at the top. il por Sports Illus 35:52-7 S 13 '71
He's burning to be a success. il pors Sports Illus 35:90-3+ S 20 '71
New slant on the mod sod. il Sports Illus 35:32-4+ N 15 '71
No bird, no plane, just Superjack. il pors Sports Illus 34:32-5+ My 10 '71
Poms, butcher-birds and bogeymen. il Sports Illus 35:70-3+ N 1 '71
Pro football. il Sports Illus 35:71+ O 25 '71
Purple people eaters eaten. il Sports Illus 35:26-7 O 4 '71
Rocket heard round the world. il pors Sports Illus 34:80-4+ My 31 '71
They're ho-hummers no more. il por Sports Illus 34:26-8+ Mr 15 '71
This Joe had better be good. il pors Sports Illus 35:42-4+ D 13 '71
(ed) See Agnew, S. T. Not infected with the conceit of infallibility
(ed) See Chandler, A. B. Gunned down by the heavies
(ed) See Chandler, A. B. How I jumped from clean politics into dirty baseball
UNDERWOOD corporation. See Olivetti corporation of America
UNDERWRITERS' laboratories, inc.
Behind the UL label. G. J. Burnett. il Electr World 85:25-7+ Ap '71
UNDERWRITING. See Securities
UNEMPLOYED. See Unemployment
UNEMPLOYMENT
Foreign labor briefs. See issues of Monthly labor review
See also
Employment
Tramps

Relief measures

Aid for jobless scientists. C. Holden. Science 172:142 Ap 9 '71
And the jobless; veto of public service employment bill. Nation 212:228 F 22 '71
Employer of first resort. F. Riessman and A. Gartner. Nation 212:434-5 Ap 5 '71
First aid for the recession's casualties. il Bsns W p24-5 Mr 27 '71
Human resources reserve? U S News 71:66 Ag 23 '71
Job program gets into gear. il Bsns W p22+ S 4 '71
Jobless funds for 14 cities; unemployed engineers. Sci N 99:264 Ap 17 '71
Money for jobless: a growing worry. il U S News 71:93-4 O 4 '71
Money to test the jobs program; public service employment program. Bsns W p28 O 16 '71
Nixon's new tonics for the jobless. Bsns W p34-5 Ap 17 '71
President signs emergency employment act. G. Krettek and E. D. Cooke. Wilson Lib Bul 46:97-9 S '71
Public employment. New Repub 165:12 S 25 '71
Public service jobs; Emergency employment act of 1971. New Repub 165:11 O 2 '71
Public-service jobs for the unemployed: a new WPA? il U S News 71:22 Ag 23 '71
Scramble starts for new public jobs; public service employment bill. Bsns W p 16 Jl 24 '71
This month's feature: Congress & public service employment. Cong Digest 50:69-79+ Mr '71
See also
Loans, Personal
Retraining, Occupational
United States—Work projects administration

Statistics

Matter of jobs. Nation 213:579 D 6 '71
Unemployment: official & real; change in counting procedures. Nation 212:100 Ja 25 '71
Unemployment statistics and what they mean; with tables. J E Bregger bibliog Mo Labor R 94:22-9 N '71

UNEMPLOYMENT—*Continued*

California

Southern California: a pickup in jobs. Bsns W p47 N 13 '71

West coast jobless try activism. B. M. Elson. il Aviation W 94:36-7 My 17 '71

Canada

Number of jobless grows in Canada. U S News 70:81-2 F 8 '71

Colombia

ILO plan for solving the job crisis in Colombia. R. E. Ginnold. bibliog f il Mo Labor R 94:32-40 Mr '71

Connecticut

When the paychecks stopped; Tim Reilly. R. Hochstein. il Good H 173:108-9+ S '71

Great Britain

Britain's jobless: a rapid rise. U S News 70: 84-5 My 24 '71

Indiana

New cloud over Gary. il Newsweek 78:59 S 13 '71

Latin America

See also
Unemployment—Colombia

Massachusetts

Jobless scientists bus to Washington; testimonies before the House subcommittee on science, research, and development. il Bsns W p22 Je 26 '71

Route 128: jobless in a dilemma about politics, their professions. D. Shapley. Science 172:1116-18 Je 11 '71

Underdeveloped areas

See Underdeveloped areas—Unemployment

United States

Applied Nixonomics; inflation/unemployment seesaw. M. J. Ulmer. New Repub 164:15-18 Ap 24 '71

Brains on the shelf. il Nations Bsns 59:66-9 My '71

Changes in employment and unemployment in 1970; with tables and charts. P. O. Flaim and P. M. Schwab. Mo Labor R 94:12-23 F '71

Drive to find jobs for victims of pollution war. U S News 71:68-9 D 6 '71

Fall-off in jobs. il Fortune 83:272 My '71

For the jobless, old skills are not enough. il Bsns W p38-9 D 25 '71

Graduates and jobs: a grave new world. il Time 97:49-52+ My 24 '71

Grim outlook for steelworkers. Bsns W p33 N 6 '71

How to cope with being out of work. L. David. il Mech Illus 67:53-5+ Mr '71

Inflation versus unemployment: another view of the trade-off. S. S. Wallack. bibliog Mo Labor R 94:49-54 N '71

Inflation versus unemployment: the worsening trade-off; excerpt from Changing labor markets and inflation. G. L. Perry. il Mo Labor R 94:68-71 F '71

Job squeeze: a look ahead. U S News 70:22-4 Ap 19 '71

Jobless rate could lag behind more than usual. Bsns W p31 Ap 10 '71

Joblessness hits a decade's high. il Newsweek 77:57 Ja 18 '71

Jobs for all: any time soon? il U S News 71: 30-2 Ag 2 '71

Labor market twist, 1964-69; with charts. D. F. Johnston. bibliog f Mo Labor R 94:26-36 Jl '71

Living with a higher jobless rate. il Bsns W p36-8 D 25 '71

Manpower approach to the unemployment-inflation dilemma. C. C. Holt and others. Mo Labor R 94:51-4 My '71

Nixon's new chief spokesman sizes up the economy; excerpts from news conference, June 29, 1971. J. B. Connally. por U S News 71:76-8 Jl 12 '71

Over 40 . . . and fired. E. H. Graham. il por Mech Illus 67:69-71+ My '71

Puzzling aspects of unemployment. il Fortune 83:22 F '71

Statement of Senator Edward M. Kennedy on re-employing defense scientists and engineers. E. M. Kennedy. por Bul Atom Sci 27:41-3 Mr '71

Unemployment. il Sr Schol 97:9-14+ Ja 11 '71

Unemployment as a way of life. il Bsns W p24-5 Je 12 '71

Unemployment: what Nixon is/isn't doing to help jobless scientists. P. M. Boffey. Science 171:985-7 Mr 12 '71

Victims of a good, glamorous cause. il Time 97:78-9 Ap 5 '71

When the brains can't get work. il Bsns W p90-2+ F 13 '71

Why America's unemployment stays so high. il U S News 71:53 D 20 '71

Why unemployment will be so stubborn. il Bsns W p90+ Ap 17 '71

See also
Labor supply—United States
Unemployment—Relief measures

UNEMPLOYMENT, Technological
See also
Unemployment—United States

UNEMPLOYMENT compensation. See Insurance, Unemployment

UNEMPLOYMENT insurance. See Insurance, Unemployment

UNESCO

Crisis in science and UNESCO. W. N. Ellis. Bul Atom Sci 27:33-5 F '71

Cultural policy: a modern dilemma; intergovernmental conference on administrative, institutional and financial aspects of cultural policies; symposium. il UNESCO Courier 24:4-32 Ja '71

In the minds of men; excerpts. UNESCO Courier 24:43+ Ag '71

International title output figures: are they really comparable? F. Fico. Pub W 200:pt2 187 S 27 '71

New int'l body forecast for educational materials. Pub W 199:58-9 F 8 '71

New UNESCO committee. il Américas 23:45 My '71

Publishers participate in Third world meeting. H. Lottman. Pub W 199:45 Je 21 '71

Sci-tech publishers wary about proposed UNESCO information network: World science information system. UNISIST. Pub W 200:28 N 8 '71

Seasons of the mind. W. McEwing. il por UNESCO Courier 24:9-58 Ag '71

Some facts and figures about Unesco. UNESCO Courier 24:64 Ag '71

25 years of Unesco viewed by a student of 25. E. Naraghi. il UNESCO Courier 24:6-7 Ag '71

Unesco activities in 1970. Sch & Soc 99:287-8 Sum '71

UNESCO reports on developing nations. Pub W 199:31-2 Je 14 '71

Youth of the world, youth of Unesco. R. Maheu. UNESCO Courier 24:4-5 Ag '71

See also
International book year, 1972
International centre for theoretical physics, Trieste, Italy
Kalinga prize

History

UNESCO: record of success. R. L. Tobin. Sat R 54:34 N 6 '71

International copyright information center

UNESCO's copyright information center. Pub W 200:28-9 Jl 5 '71

Publications

25 years of Unesco publications on art. UNESCO Courier 24:35-6 Mr '71

World boom in television and book translation, Unesco yearbook reports. UNESCO Courier 24:14-15 F '71

UNESCO fellowships. See Scholarships and fellowships

UNFAIR labor practices. See Industrial relations

UNGAR, Sanford J.
Fingerprints. New Repub 164:20-1 Je 12 '71
To the boondocks. New Repub 165:11-12 O 2 '71

UNGARO, Emanuel
Ungaro's triumph. il por Newsweek 78:45 Ag 9 '71 *

UNGEHEUER, Friedel
Foreign report. Harper 242:26-9 Je '71

UNGRADED classes
Daring educational experiment: the one-room schoolhouse. W. Griffith. il N Y Times Mag p 14-16+ My 30 '71

UNICELLULAR organisms
See also
Amebas

UNIDENTIFIED flying objects. See Flying saucers

UNIFORM nutrient labeling. See Food—Labeling

UNIFORMITY. See Standardization

UNIFORMS
Uniformity pays off for career clothes. il Bsns W p38-9 Jl 24 '71

UNIFORMS, Military
Dress parade; excerpts from America's fighting men; with paintings by P. Copeland. H. L. Peterson. Am Heritage 22:4-11 O '71
Sukhomlinov effect. R. A. Beaumont and B. J. James. il por Horizon 13:66-9 Wint '71
See also
Great Britain—Army—Brigade of guards—Uniforms

UNIFORMS, Naval
Dress parade; excerpts from America's fighting men; with paintings by P. Copeland. H. L. Peterson. Am Heritage 22:4-11 O '71

UNIFORMS, Sports
Curtain up on a mod new act: thoroughly modern Phillies. R. Blount, jr. il Sports Illus 34:30-3 Ap 19 '71

UNION asbestos and rubber company. See Unarco industries, inc.

UNION camp corporation
Water lords, by J. M. Fallows. Review Chr Cent 88:1420 D 1 '71. T. W. Rogers

UNION carbide corporation
Corporate polluter learns the hard way; with editorial comment. il Bsns W p52-6, 94 F 6 '71
Dirty deal? smog control and jobs. Sr Schol 98:15-16 Mr 8 '71
Story of Lloyd M. Cooke. S. P. Massie. il Chem 44:11 My '71
Thorny task at Union carbide. il Fortune 83:29 Mr '71
Union carbide: the whole truth? environmental claim under SEC scrutiny. Bsns W p27 Mr 20 '71

UNION CENTER, N.Y.
Contractor refuse collection wouldn't do; Town of Union, N.Y. R. R. Blessing. il Am City 86:46+ Jl '71

UNION CITY, Tenn.
Poor streets cost more than good ones. W. D. Frizzell. il por Am City 86:98+ Mr '71

UNION dues. See Trade unions—Dues, fees, etc.

UNION for experimenting colleges and universities. See Colleges and universities, Experimental

UNION leader (Manchester) See Manchester union leader

UNION membership. See Trade unions—Membership

UNION of Soviet Socialist Republics. See Russia

UNION work rules. See Work rules

UNIONIDAE. See Mussels, Fresh water

UNIONS, Teachers. See Teachers unions

UNIONS, Trade. See Trade unions

UNIT construction. See Buildings, Prefabricated

UNIT pricing
Progress report on unit pricing. il Consumer Rep 36:84-5 F '71
Supermarket unit pricing: do people use it? Changing T 25:14 O '71
Unit pricing in markets: what it means to shoppers. il Good H 172:204 Ap '71

UNITARIAN universalist association
Sex at Sunday school. il Newsweek 78:50-1 D 27 '71
UUA assembly: black power, red ink. H. A. Jack. Chr Cent 88:859-60 Jl 14 '71

UNITAS, John
Keeping it short and sweet. T. Maule. il por Sports Illus 35:14-19 D 20 '71 *
To kill a memory that still hurts. R. F. Jones. il por Sports Illus 34:18-21 Ja 11 '71 *

UNITED air lines
Can a hotelman run an airline? il Fortune 83:31-2 F '71
Carlson moves to decentralize United. H. D. Watkins. Aviation W 94:28-9 My 17 '71
DC-10 demonstrates scheduling versatility; with tables. H. D. Watkins. il Aviation W 96:26-30 Ja 4 '72
DC-10 meeting operational goals. H. D. Watkins. il Aviation W 95:23-6 D 13 '71
DC-10s delivered to United, American. il Aviation W 95:26 Ag 2 '71
Decentralization of United extended into operations. H. D. Watkins. Aviation W 95: 27-8 O 11 '71
Is this any way to run an airline? por Time 98:101 N 8 '71
Modification of United JT8Ds on schedule. R. G. O'Lone. il Aviation W 94:27-8 Ap 26 '71
More 747, DC-10 commuter use planned. Aviation W 95:30 D 6 '71
New test equipment saves time. B. M. Elson. il Aviation W 94:41-3 Ap 19 '71

Two airlines ponder their losing runs. Bsns W p26 Ja 16 '71
United drive seeks larger share of California commuter market. Aviation W 96:26 Ja 10 '72
United jockeys for first DC-10 service. Aviation W 95:24 Jl 26 '71
United R-Hav flights use inertial navaid. Aviation W 95:38 Jl 19 '71
United to use 747s on commuter route. Aviation W 95:28 Ag 16 '71

UNITED aircraft corporation
Another Litton manager wants to run his own show. il por Fortune 84:33 N '71
Engine delay dims UAC outlook. Aviation W 95:23 N 15 '71
New engine man; H. J. Gray. por Time 98:98 O 11 '71
United aircraft goes outside for new president. Aviation W 95:21 O 4 '71
United aircraft picks a savvy outsider. por Bsns W p29-30 O 2 '71
United carrying overdue receivables at interest. il Aviation W 94:14 Mr 1 '71

Pratt and Whitney aircraft division
Fight delays NASA shuttle. Bsns W p78 Ag 28 '71
He's bullish on jet engines. por Bsns W p70 Jl 10 '71
Shuttle engine protest detailed. Aviation W 95:23 Ag 23 '71

Sikorsky aircraft division
Sikorsky uncertain about army's UTTAS. Aviation W 95:47 S 27 '71

UNITED auto brokers, inc.
How to buy your next new car for $125 over dealer cost. il Motor T 23:41-2 Je '71

UNITED automobile, aerospace and agricultural implement workers of America
Aircraft unions hold their fire. il Bsns W p 118 My 15 '71
Another challenge for Pay board. U S News 71:90 D 20 '71
Auto workers still in debt. U S News 71: 61 N 29 '71
Check it with Leonard. por Bsns W p63-4 My 29 '71
Close look at Leonard Woodcock; interview. L. Woodcock. il pors Nations Bsns 59:27-8+ Mr '71
First of the '30 and outs'. il Bsns W p60 My 22 '71
Needed, world-wide environment solutions; United auto workers and the United Nations explore pollution problems. S. Margold. il Am City 86:74+ Mr '71
Thirty-and-outers opt for late retirement. il Bsns W p82-3 O 9 '71
UAW agrees to settle for less. Bsns W p34 Ap 17 '71
UAW plan for wages and prices. B. L. Masse. America 124:221 Mr 6 '71
UAW struggles to pay its debts. il Bsns W p40-1 N 13 '71
UAW will ask government aid for 4-day week. Aviation W 94:22 Mr 29 '71
See also
Alliance for labor action

UNITED church of Canada
New Canadian hymnal brings Anglican-UCC union a step closer. G. Lane. Chr Cent 89: 18-19 Ja 5 '72

UNITED church of Christ
Rejuvenating the UCC? E. E. Plowman. Chr Today 15:36 Jl 16 '71
Renewal rangers; Office of communication. R. L. Shayon. Sat R 54:38 Ag 21 '71
UCC synod narrows behavior-belief gap. C. Rogers. Chr Cent 88:850 Jl 14 '71

UNITED church of Christ in Japan
Kyodan reports decrease in membership. Chr Cent 88:1519-D 29 '71

UNITED farm workers organizing committee. See American federation of labor and Congress of industrial organizations—United farm workers organizing committee

UNITED HIAS service, inc.
Government and private agency partnership in refugee assistance programs; address, March 14, 1971. F. L. Kellogg. Dept State Bul 64:576-8 My 3 '71

UNITED industrial corporation
Short by $22,000. Fortune 83:149 Je '71

UNITED KINGDOM atomic energy authority. See Great Britain—Atomic energy authority

UNITED Methodist church
Black Methodists celebrate soul. C. R. Rogers. il Chr Cent 88:377-8 Mr 24 '71
Can evangelicals reform Methodism? Convocation of United Methodists for evangelical Christianity. J. L. Adams. Chr Today 15:35-6 Ag 6 '71

UNITED Methodist church—*Continued*
Homosexual minister? por Newsweek 77:114+ Je 14 '71
James Cone and the Methodists. C. Rogers. Chr Cent 88:1340 N 17 '71
Key 73: bridge over troubled waters. Chr Today 15:21 Ja 29 '71
Pax fund invests in peace. Bsns W p56 S 4 '71
UNITED Methodist congress on evangelism. See Religious conferences
UNITED mine workers of America
Anarchy threatens the kingdom of coal. T. O'Hanlon. il por Fortune 83:78-82+ Ja '71
Bombshell from the Yablonski trial. Bsns W p30 Je 26 '71
Boyle's law. New Repub 164:7-8 Mr 27 '71
Coal: new fuel for inflation? il Time 98:78 O 4 '71
Coal walks out before it bargains. por Bsns W p37 Je 19 '71
Death and the mines; by B. Hume. Review Nation 214:56-8 Ja 10 '72. T. N. Bethell
Newsweek il 79:57 Ja 3 '72. P. S. Prescott
Ghost of John L. por Newsweek 77:86+ My 10 '71
Heirs of John L. Lewis. Nation 212:196 F 15 '71
Indictment for Boyle. il por Newsweek 77:78+ Mr 15 '71
More trouble for Tony. il por Time 97:26 Mr 15 '71
Voting for their lives. P. J. Nyden. Nation 212:206-10 F 15 '71
Years of trial for the UMW. il Bsns W p88+ F 6 '71

District 50
District 50: a feud threatens its merger. Bsns W p23 Ap 24 '71

Welfare and retirement fund
Boyle's law. New Repub 164:9 My 15 '71
Drop in miners' welfare fund. U S News 71:101 O 11 '71
UNITED NATIONS
Address by president of Mexico; summary of address, October 5, 1971. UN Mo Chron 8:71-2 N '71
Dialogue for understanding; panel discussion, October 30, 1970. J. L. Borges; M. Albornoz; E. Z. de T. Duggan. por Américas 23:12-15 Mr '71
Foreign policy and the United Nations. W. P. Rogers; A. A. Gromyko; M. Schumann. Vital Speeches 38:34-49 N 1 '71
Future of the United Nations; address, April 3, 1971. S. DePalma. Dept State Bul 64:517-21 Ap 19 '71
Governments, systems, ideologies, and institutions come and go, but humanity remains; excerpts from address, September 1971. Thant. Sat R 54:19 O 23 '71
Human environment, new challenge for the United Nations. UN Mo Chron 8:35-48 F '71
Humanitarian and social concerns of the United Nations; address, June 28, 1971. G. Bush. Dept State Bul 65:99-102 Jl 26 '71
Improving the effectiveness of the United Nations; statement, October 13, 1971. S. DePalma. Dept State Bul 65:569-755 N 15 '71
Injection of truth. Nation 214:2 Ja 3 '72
Introduction to the report of the Secretary-General on the work of the organization; major issues confronting the organization. Thant. UN Mo Chron 8:92-166 O '71
Notes of the month. See issues of UN monthly chronicle
People are asking why? address, May 5, 1971. Thant. UN Mo Chron 8:32-7 Je '71
Switzerland: absent host to the United Nations. W. B. Lloyd, jr. Bul Atom Sci 27:42-3 Ja '71
That elusive internationalism; UNA-USA study. America 125:222 O 2 '71
UN lost in an ideological cloud. America 125:501-2 D 11 '71
U.N's disastrous situation. Chr Cent 88:1373 N 24 '71
United Nations and some problems of public understanding; address, December 3, 1970. Thant. UN Mo Chron 8:98-105 Ja '71
United Nations faces the next twenty-five years. T. P. Melady. il Cath World 213:189-93 Jl '71
United Nations in a disorderly world; excerpt from address. E. Warren. il Sat R 54:16-18 O 23 '71
See also
Food and agriculture organization of the United Nations
International court of justice. The Hague
International day for the elimination of racial discrimination
International year for action to combat racism and racial discrimination, 1971

United States—President's commission for the observance of the twenty-fifth anniversary of the United Nations

Administrative and budgetary committee
Budget estimates 1971. UN Mo Chron 8:83-95 Ja '71
Fifth committee action; budget estimates. UN Mo Chron 8:107-12 N '71

Advisory committee on the application of science and technology to development
Advisory committee holds fourteenth session. UN Mo Chron 8:16-17 Mr '71

Anecdotes, facetiae, satire, etc.
Plowshares, anyone? R. Schoenstein. New Yorker 47:52-3 D 11 '71

Armed forces
Forces in Cyprus
Peace watch on Cyprus; Canadian soldiers on the Green line. J. C. Fleck. America 124:587-9 Je 5 '71
Security council extends stationing of peacekeeping force; with text of resolution. UN Mo Chron 8:19-27 Ja; 3-21 Je '71
U.N. force in Cyprus extended through June 1971; statement, December 10, 1970. C. H. Phillips. Dept State Bul 64:70-1 Ja 11 '71
U.N. force in Cyprus extended through December 1971; statement, May 26, 1971. G. Bush. Dept State Bul 64:842-3 Je 28 '71

Budget
See United Nations—Finance

Charter
Declaration on the strengthening of international security. L. N. Kutakov. UN Mo Chron 8:88-101 Je '71
Good news about the U.N; question of review. Sat R 54:16+ F 6 '71
Strengthening of international security: Assembly adopts declaration. UN Mo Chron 8:33-5 Ja '71

Commission for social development
Hold twenty-second session. UN Mo Chron 8:27-9 Ap '71

Commission on human rights
Concludes twenty-seventh session. UN Mo Chron 8:32-42 Ap '71
Twenty-seventh session begins. UN Mo Chron 8:21-2 Mr '71

Commission on international trade law
Commission opens fourth session. UN Mo Chron 8:43-4 Ap '71
Fourth session concluded. UN Mo Chron 8:35-40 My '71
International trade law; working group concludes session. UN Mo Chron 8:90 O '71
Sixth committee recommendation. UN Mo Chron 8:112 N '71

Commission on narcotic drugs
Conference adopts convention on psychotropic substances. UN Mo Chron 8:14-15 Mr '71
U.S. urges stronger multilateral commitments to narcotics control; statement, October 1, 1971. J. E. Ingersoll. Dept State Bul 65:523-9 N 8 '71

Committee for development planning
Opens seventh session. UN Mo Chron 8:30-1 Ap '71

Committee for programme and coordination
Opens eighth session. UN Mo Chron 8:30 Ap '71

Committee of twenty-four
See United Nations—Special committee on the situation with regard to the implementation of the declaration on the granting of independence to Colonial countries and peoples

Committee on disarmament
Assembly adopts 11 resolutions. UN Mo Chron 8:29-33 Ja '71
Bottling the Satan bug; Soviet proposal for controls on chemical and biological weapons. il Newsweek 77:48 Ap 12 '71
Geneva disarmament conference agrees on draft text of bacteriological weapons convention; statement with text of draft convention, September 28, 1971. J. F. Leonard. Dept State Bul 65:504-10 N 1 '71

UNITED NATIONS—Commitee on disarmament—*Continued*
Sound limitations on armaments urged by President Nixon; message, February 23, 1971. Dept State Bul 64:310-11 Mr 15 '71
U.S. and U.S.S.R. table draft biological weapons convention at Geneva disarmament conference; statement, August 5, 1971; with text of draft convention. J. F. Leonard. Dept State Bul 65:221-6 Ag 30 '71
U.S. states views on conventional arms restraints; statement, August 26, 1971. J. F. Leonard. Dept State Bul 65:309-15 S 20 '71
United States reviews major disarmament issues facing the U.N. General assembly; statement, with text of resolution. C. W. Yost. Dept State Bul 63:803-7 D 28 '70

Committee on natural resources
Concludes first session. UN Mo Chron 8:29 Ap '71

Committee on the elimination of racial discrimination
U.S. discusses actions to combat racism and discrimination; statements, October 26 and November 3, 1971. A. A. Fletcher. Dept State Bul 65:628-39 N 29 '71

Committee on the peaceful uses of outer space
Assembly adopts four resolutions. UN Mo Chron 8:35-7 Ja '71
Peaceful uses of outer space; committee adopts report. UN Mo Chron 8:82-3 O '71

Committee on the peaceful uses of the seabed and the ocean floor
Committee holds session. UN Mo Chron 8:21-6 Ap '71
Peaceful uses of sea-bed; committee begins consideration. UN Mo Chron 7:46 D '70
Peaceful uses of the sea-bed. UN Mo Chron 8:37-42 Ja '71
U.N. adopts principles governing seabed exploitation and decides to convene comprehensive law-of-the-sea conference in 1973; U.S. statements, with texts of resolutions. C. Pell; J. R. Stevenson. Dept State Bul 64:150-9 F 1 '71
U.S. draft articles on territorial sea, straits, and fisheries submitted to U.N. seabeds committee; statement with texts of articles. J. R. Stevenson. Dept State Bul 65:261-3 S 6 '71

Committee on trust and non-self-governing territories
See United Nations—Trusteeship committee

Conference of the committee on disarmament
See United Nations—Committee on disarmament

Credentials committee
Credentials of representatives; Assembly adopts resolution. UN Mo Chron 7:25-6 D '70

Delegates
Madison avenue Maoists; arrival of ten man delegation from China. il por Time 98:36+ N 22 '71
New face from China. il pors Life 71:38-9 N 19 '71
Peking in New York. il Newsweek 78:44-5 N 22 '71
Top team; Chinese delegates. il Newsweek 78:54+ N 15 '71
United Nations: Mao's men in Manhattan. il Time 98:26+ N 15 '71

Development program
Hoffman's decade of aid. por Time 99:31 Ja 17 '72
Needed, world-wide environment solutions; United auto workers and the United Nations explore pollution problems. S. Margold. il Am City 86:74+ Mr '71
UNDP governing council; pre-investment projects. UN Mo Chron 8:13-22 F '71

Economic and financial committee
Economic questions, consideration in Second committee. UN Mo Chron 8:98-101 N '71
Second committee; programme of work approved. UN Mo Chron 8:86 O '71
Second committee; recommendations approved. UN Mo Chron 7:82-7 D '70

Economic and social council
Challenges facing the economic and social council; statement, July 7, 1971. G. Bush. Dept State Bul 65:122-6 Ag 2 '71
Housing building and planning committee holds session; adopts report. UN Mo Chron 8:102-3 N '71
United States discusses report of economic and social council; statement, October 11, 1971. B. Zagorin. Dept State Bul 65:605-7 N 22 '71
See also
United Nations—Commission for social development
United Nations—Committee on natural resources

Meetings, 1970
Continues resumed forty-ninth session. UN Mo Chron 7:87-8 D '70

Meetings, 1971
Economic and social council adopts resolutions on human rights. UN Mo Chron 8:59-68 Je '71
Economic and social council, resumes fifty-first session. UN Mo Chron 8:101-2 N '71 Je '71
Fiftieth session ends. UN Mo Chron 8:51-7 Je '71
Fiftieth session opens. UN Mo Chron 8:12-13 F '71
Fiftieth session resumed. UN Mo Chron 8:26-7 My '71

Economic commission for Africa
Holds first conference of ministers. UN Mo Chron 8:18-20 Mr '71

Economic commission for Asia and the Far East
Holds twenty-seventh session. UN Mo Chron 8:29-30 My '71
To tame the mighty Mekong. D. Stroetzel and D. Stroetzel. il Read Digest 98:192-4+ Je '71

Economic commission for Europe
Meeting in Prague; symposium on the problems of the environment. D. N. Leff. il Environ 13:29-33 N '71
Twenty-sixth session. UN Mo Chron 8:27-9 My '71

Economic commission for Latin America
Concludes session. UN Mo Chron 8:57-8 Je '71
Fourteenth session in Santiago. UN Mo Chron 8:30-1 My '71

Employees
See also
United Nations—Secretariat

Fifth committee
See United Nations—Administrative and budgetary committee

Finance
Budget estimates 1971. UN Mo Chron 8:83-95 Ja '71
Fifth committee action; budget estimates. UN Mo Chron 7:94-7 D '70
Problem of UN finances. America 125:470-1 D 4 '71
U.S. reviews financial plight of the United Nations; statement, October 15, 1971. G. Bush. Dent State Bul 65:556-8 N 15 '71
Why majority in U.N. turned on U.S. il U S News 71:17-19 N 8 '71

First committee
See United Nations—Political and security committee

Fourth committee
See United Nations—Trusteeship committee

General assembly
Assembly decisions on economic questions. UN Mo Chron 7:81-2 D '70
Youth and human rights; Assembly adopts resolution. UN Mo Chron 7:92-3 D '70

Sessions (25th)
Assembly decisions on economic questions. UN Mo Chron 8:67-70 Ja '71
Assembly decisions on social questions. UN Mo Chron 8:71-83 Ja '71
Closing of the twenty-fifth session. UN Mo Chron 8:27-66 Ja '71
Twenty-fifth General assembly rejects move to change representation of China in the U.N; statement, November 12, 1970. C. H. Phillips. Dept State Bul 63:733-5 D 14 '70
25th session of the United Nations General assembly; summary of developments during the session from U.S. point of view. Dept State Bul 64:173-86 F 8 '71
U.N. General assembly establishes committee on procedures; statement, with text of resolution, November 9, 1970. S. M. Finger. Dept State Bul 63:762-4 D 21 '70

UNITED NATIONS—General assembly—*Cont.*

Sessions (26th)

Agenda of the 26th regular session of the U.N. General assembly. Dept State Bul 65: 536-9 N 8 '71

China: Assembly decides to restore its rights to People's Republic of China. UN Mo Chron 8:34-61 N '71

Close call; sniper attack on the building housing the Soviet mission. Newsweek 78: 40+ N 1 '71

General debate; summary of statements. UN Mo Chron 8:188-233 O; 122-202 N '71

Gentle reminder. Newsweek 78:40+ N 29 '71

Issues before the 26th General assembly; ed. by V. Kallab and N. Aggarwala. bibliog f il Int Concil 584:1-222 S '71

Opening of twenty-sixth session. UN Mo Chron 8:51-66 O '71

Peking's wordy debut. il Time 98:37 N 29 '71

Planetary spirit. Time 98:40 O 11 '71

Take that! And that!! Chinese-Soviet debate. Time 98:46 D 6 '71

U.N. patterns for 1971. A. Tuckerman. Nation 213:322-3 O 11 '71

U.N: will it run, or punt? il Newsweek 78: 44+ S 27 '71

Win some, lose some. il Newsweek 78:44 O 4 '71

Headquarters

Should the U.N. switch? Time 97:41 Je 14 '71

High commissioner for refugees

Assembly adopts resolution. UN Mo Chron 7:88-9 D '70

Work of U.N. high commissioner for refugees commended by U.S; statement, November 17, 1970. C. Pell. Dept State Bul 64:96-8 Ja 18 '71

Legal committee

Assembly acts on legal items. UN Mo Chron 8:95-6 Ja '71

Assembly acts on legal items; recommendations of Sixth committee. UN Mo Chron 7:97-9 D '70

International watercourses; Sixth committee recommendations. UN Mo Chron 7:100 D '70

Sixth committee recommendation. UN Mo Chron 8:112 N '71

Membership

Chinese representation items inscribed on U.N. General assembly agenda; statements, with texts of U.S. draft resolutions. G. Bush. Dept State Bul 65:425-7 O 18 '71

Facing up to the realities; two Chinas. il Newsweek 78:31-2 Ag 16 '71

General assembly admits Oman. UN Mo Chron 8:70 N '71

Go-betweens; question of China's membership in the United Nations. il Newsweek 77:43 My 10 '71

Paving the way for Peking's entry. il Time 98:22+ Ag 16 '71

Representation of China; Assembly decision. UN Mo Chron 7:27-40 D '70

Sacrificing principle for expediency. D. Lawrence. U S News 71:108 N 8 '71

Security council agrees to recommend Bhutan for United Nations membership. UN Mo Chron 8:3 Mr '71

Twenty-fifth General assembly rejects move to change representation of China in the U.N; statement, November 12, 1970. C. H. Phillips. Dept State Bul 63:733-5 D 14 '70

Two Chinas in the U.N, the U.S. states its case; excerpts from statement, October 18, 1971. G. Bush. il por U S News 71:74-5 N 1 '71

UN charter says no; two-China solution. America 125:252 O 9 '71

U.N. plebiscite for Taiwan. L. C. Chen. Chr Cent 88:952-3 Ag 11 '71

U.S. supports admission of Bahrain to the United Nations; statement, August 18, 1971. G. Bush. Dept State Bul 65:294-5 S 13 '71

U.S. supports admission of Qatar to the United Nations; statement, September 15, 1971. G. Bush. Dept State Bul 65:468 O 25 '71

Ultima Thule, and them some. P. L. Buckley. Nat R 23:1340+ D 3 '71

United Nations admits Oman to membership, statement, October 7, 1971. G. Bush. Dept State Bul 65:607 N 22 '71

United Nations member states; including 42 black African members. Negro Hist Bul 34: 32 F '71

Non-governmental organizations

Phased withdrawal; report on church efforts at the United Nations. P. Dietterich. Chr Cent 88:1326-9 N 10 '71

Political and security committee

Disarmament: discussion in First committee. UN Mo Chron 7:47-52 D '70

Peaceful uses of sea-bed: committee begins consideration. UN Mo Chron 7:46 D '70

Question of Korea: consideration in First committee. UN Mo Chron 7:43-5 D '70

Strengthening of international security. First committee holds general debate. UN Mo Chron 8:94 N '71

Publications

See also
UNESCO—Publications

Bibliography

Documents; selected list. See issues of UN monthly chronicle

Publications, official records. See issues of UN monthly chronicle

United Nations documents: a selected bibliography. See issues of Department of state bulletin

Secretariat

What's wrong at the United Nations. H. L. Keenleyside. Sat R 54:11-13+ Je 19 '71

Secretary General

Job opening? il Time 97:26 F 1 '71

New S-G. por Newsweek 79:24 Ja 3 '72

New S-G: front runners and long shots. il Newsweek 78:45 S 27 '71

Role of the Secretary-General; address, September 16, 1971. Thant. UN Mo Chron 8:178-87 O '71

U.N. a man who casts no shadow. il Time 98:32+ N 29 '71

U.N: madness or heroism? accession of K. Waldheim. Chr Cent 89:3 Ja 5 '72

United Nations: Mao on the threshold; candidates. il Time 98:38+ S 27 '71

Viennese compromise: K. Waldheim succeeds U Thant. il por Time 99:39-40 Ja 3 '72

What's wrong at the United Nations. H. L. Keenleyside. Sat R 54:11-13+ Je 19 '71

Security council

Berlin blockade and the use of the United Nations. P. C. Jessup. bibliog f For Affairs 50:163-73 O '71

Meetings, 1970

Record of the month:
Complaint by Guinea. UN Mo Chron 7:11-16 D '70

Complaint by Guinea. UN Mo Chron 8:3-19 Ja '71

Cyprus. UN Mo Chron 8:19-27 Ja '71

Southern Rhodesia. UN Mo Chron 7:3-10 D '70

Meetings, 1971

Late show at the U.N: discussion in the Security council on the Pakistani-Indian war. Nation 213:642 D 20 '71

Record of the month:
Complaint by Zambia. UN Mo Chron 8: 3-13 N '71

Complaints by Senegal and Guinea. UN Mo Chron 8:46-51 O '71

Cyprus. UN Mo Chron 8:3-21 Je '71

Namibia. UN Mo Chron 8:31-46 O '71

Situation in Namibia; with text of resolution. UN Mo Chron 8:13-34 N '71

Situation in the Middle East. UN Mo Chron 8:3-9 F '71

Situation in the Middle East. UN Mo Chron 8:3-5 Ap '71

Situation in the Middle East. UN Mo Chron 8:3-30 O '71

Record of the month. UN Mo Chron 8:3-4 Mr; 3-19 My '71

Sixth committee

See United Nations—Legal committee

Social, humanitarian and cultural committee

Elimination of racial discrimination: report of the Third committee. UN Mo Chron 7: 89-92 D '70

Elimination of racial discrimination: Third committee begins consideration. UN Mo Chron 8:106 N '71

Human rights in armed conflicts: Assembly adopts five resolutions. UN Mo Chron 8:80-3 Ja '71

Social questions. UN Mo Chron 8:87 O '71

World social situation, Third committee approves two resolutions. UN Mo Chron 8:103-5 N '71

Special committee on apartheid

Apartheid in South Africa: Assembly adopts six resolutions. UN Mo Chron 8:42-5 Ja '71

UNITED NATIONS—Special committee on apartheid—*Continued*

Apartheid in South Africa: committee approves six resolutions. UN Mo Chron 7:55-8 D '70

Apartheid in South Africa: Special committee considers work programme for 1971. UN Mo Chron 8:9-10 F '71

Apartheid in South Africa; special committee discusses report of mission to Europe and Africa. UN Mo Chron 8:80-2 O '71

International year for action to combat racism and racial discrimination; commemoration by Special committee on apartheid. UN Mo Chron 8:5-12 Ap '71

Special committee considers dialogue with South Africa. UN Mo Chron 8:37-45 Je '71

Special committee plans session to combat racism. UN Mo Chron 8:4-7 Mr '71

Special committee sends letter to United States. UN Mo Chron 8:19-22 My '71

Special committee on peace-keeping operations

Special committee begins 1971 work. UN Mo Chron 8:22-4 My '71

U.S. calls for agreed guidelines for U.N. peacekeeping; statement, April 1, 1971. G. Bush. Dept State Bul 64:626 My 10 '71

United States calls for concrete actions to strengthen U.N. peacekeeping; statement, with text of resolution. C. W. Yost. Dept State Bul 64:89-92 Ja 18 '71

Working group asked to continue efforts. UN Mo Chron 8:46-9 Je '71

Special committee on the question of defining aggression

Committee concludes session. UN Mo Chron 8:44-6 Ap '71

Committee holds fourth session. UN Mo Chron 8:24-7 Mr '71

Special committee on the situation with regard to the implementation of the declaration on the granting of independence to colonial countries and peoples

Assembly adopts resolution. UN Mo Chron 8:60-5 Ja '71

Opening of 1971 session; summary of statements. UN Mo Chron 8:7-11 Mr '71

Special committee of twenty-four ends work for 1970. UN Mo Chron 8:65-6 Ja '71

Special committee of twenty-four; report on military activities in colonial territories. UN Mo Chron 7:77-80 D '70

Special committee on decolonization. UN Mo Chron 8:12-21 Ap; 3-19 My '71

Special committee on decolonization; adopts resolutions. UN Mo Chron 8:80-93 N '71

Special committee on decolonization; adopts three resolutions. UN Mo Chron 8:68-80 O '71

U.S. informs U.N. of withdrawal from decolonization committee; text of letter, January 11, 1971. C. W. Yost. Dept State Bul 64:186 F 8 '71

Special committee to investigate Israeli practices affecting the human rights of the population of the occupied territories

Report of Special committee to investigate Israeli practices: Assembly adopts resolution. UN Mo Chron 8:78-80 Ja '71

Report of the Special committee to investigate Israeli practices affecting the human rights of the population of the occupied territories. UN Mo Chron 8:50-87 My '71

Second report of the Special committee to investigate Israeli practices affecting the human rights of the occupied territories; the texts of the letter of transmittal, the findings of the committee and its recommendations. UN Mo Chron 8:114-21 N '71

Special political committee

Apartheid in South Africa: committee approves six resolutions. UN Mo Chron 7:55-8 D '70

Peace-keeping operations: Special political committee adopts draft resolution. UN Mo Chron 7:52-5 D '70

Policies of apartheid of government of South Africa; consideration by Special political committee. UN Mo Chron 8:72-7 N '71

Technical assistance program
See also
United Nations—Development programme

Trusteeship committee

Assembly action. UN Mo Chron 8:54-60 Ja '71

Territories in southern Africa; consideration in Fourth committee. UN Mo Chron 8:77-80 N '71

Territories in southern Africa: recommendations of Fourth committee. UN Mo Chron 7:64-77 D '70

Trusteeship council

Begins annual review. UN Mo Chron 8:68-73 Je '71

Voting

Blackmail on Turtle Bay. America 125:360 N 6 '71

China: a stinging victory. il Time 98:26-8+ N 8 '71

China vote. Chr Today 16:27 N 19 '71

China vote. A. Tuckerman. Nation 213:452 N 8 '71

China vote: choler on the right. il Time 98:16-17 N 8 '71

Chinese are coming. il Newsweek 78:22-8 N 8 '71

Glee club; China vote. G. Ace. Sat R 54:4 N 20 '71

There goes Taipei; with report by P. Young and editorial comment. il pors Life 71:28-36 N 5 '71

Afghanistan

Assistance in cases of natural disaster. Assembly calls for assistance to Afghanistan. UN Mo Chron 8:103 N '71

Africa

Address by president of Mauritania; summary of address, September 24, 1971. UN Mo Chron 8:66-7 O '71

African issues at the U.N.: the United States position; address, September 21, 1971. D. D. Newsom. Vital Speeches 38:14-17 O 15 '71

Africa, Southern

Apartheid in South Africa; special committee discusses report of mission to Europe and Africa. UN Mo Chron 8:80-2 O '71

Look at African issues at the United Nations; address, September 21, 1971. D. D. Newsom. Dept State Bul 65:373-8 O 11 '71

Problems of southern Africa; joint meeting adopts consensus. UN Mo Chron 8:67-8 O '71

Territories in southern Africa; consideration in Fourth committee. UN Mo Chron 8:77-80 N '71

United States calls for restraint in southern Africa; statement, with text of resolution, October 12, 1971. C. H. Phillips. Dept State Bul 65:608 N 22 '71

Bahrein

U.S. supports admission of Bahrain to the United Nations; statement, August 18, 1971. G. Bush. Dept State Bul 65:294-5 S 13 '71

Bhutan

Security council agrees to recommend Bhutan for United Nations membership. UN Mo Chron 8:3 Mr '71

China (People's Republic)

Ambassador; interview. G. H. W. Bush. New Yorker 47:33-4 O 16 '71

Anticlimax on China. Chr Cent 88:967 Ag 18 '71

Barriers to a deal between U.S. and red China; interview. R. MacFarquhar. il por U S News 70:30-2 My 3 '71

Blackmail on Turtle Bay. America 125:360 N 6 '71

Burden of George Bush. W. F. Buckley, jr. Nat R 23:1198-9 O 22 '71

China: a stinging victory. il Time 98:26-8+ N 8 '71

China and the UN. R. H. Wilbur. New Repub 165:10-12 S 18 '71

China & the U.S: the twain shall meet. A. H. Grossman. il Harper 243:86-8+ O '71

China: Assembly decides to restore its rights to People's Republic of China. UN Mo Chron 8:34-61 N '71

China debate finally begins; Dilemma for the U.S. il Time 98:26+ O 25 '71

China policy: time for a thaw. il Newsweek 77:33-4 F 8 '71

China vote: choler on the right. il Time 98:16-17 N 8 '71

China's UN debut. Nat R 23:1336 D 3 '71

Chinese are coming. il Newsweek 78:22-8 N 8 '71

Chinese representation items inscribed on U.N. General assembly agenda; statements, with texts of U.S. draft resolutions. G. Bush. Dept State Bul 65:425-7 O 18 '71

UNITED NATIONS—Namibia—*Continued*
U.S. supports Security council resolution on Namibia; statement, October 20, 1971. W. T. Bennett, jr. Dept State Bul 65:609-12 N 22 '71

Oman

General assembly admits Oman. UN Mo Chron 8:70 N '71
United Nations admits Oman to membership, statement, October 7, 1971. G. Bush. Dept State Bul 65:607 N 22 '71

Pakistan

Assistance to Pakistan; appeal by Assembly president and Secretary-General. UN Mo Chron 7:27 D '70

Portugal

Security council condemns Portugal and demands compensation; with text of resolution. UN Mo Chron 8:3-19 Ja '71

Puerto Rico

Proposal to discuss Puerto Rico rejected by U.N. General assembly; statements, September 23 and 24, 1971. G. Bush. Dept State Bul 65:427-9 O 18 '71

Qatar

U.S. supports admission of Qatar to the United Nations; statement, September 15, 1971. G. Bush. Dept State Bul 65:468 O 25 '71

Rhodesia

Security council adopts resolution; with text of resolution. UN Mo Chron 7:3-10 D '70
Southern Rhodesia; Assembly action. UN Mo Chron 8:52 Ja '71
Toying with Rhodesia. Nation 213:354-5 O 18 '71
U.S. gives views on U.N. resolution on Rhodesian chrome imports; statement by W. E. Schaufele, jr, November 11, 1971; with text of resolution. Dept State Bul 65:690-1 D 13 '71

Russia

Foreign policy and the United Nations; address, October 4, 1971. A. A. Gromyko. Vital Speeches 38:38-45 N 1 '71
U.S. condemns shooting incident at Soviet mission to the U.N; statement, October 21, 1971. G. Bush. Dept State Bul 65:598 N 22 '71

Senegal

Security council considers reports of special missions to Senegal and Guinea. UN Mo Chron 8:46-51 O '71

South Africa

Joint meeting on problems of southern Africa. UN Mo Chron 8:21-37 Je '71
Security council calls on South Africa to respect sovereignty of Zambia; with text. UN Mo Chron 8:3-13 N '71
Security council considers South Africa's presence in Namibia. UN Mo Chron 8:13-34 N '71
See also
United Nations—Africa, Southern

Southwest Africa

Hazardous courses in southern Africa. G. F. Kennan. For Affairs 49:218-36 Ja '71; Same abr. with title What policies toward southern Africa? Cur 127:50-63 Mr '71
See also
United Nations—Namibia

Taiwan

Ambassador; interview. G. H. W. Bush. New Yorker 47:33-4 O 16 '71
Burden of George Bush. W. F. Buckley, jr. Nat R 23:1198-9 O 22 '71
China and the U.N. R. H. Wilbur. New Repub 165:10-12 S 18 '71
China: Assembly decides to restore its rights to People's Republic of China. UN Mo Chron 8:34-61 N '71
China vote: choler on the right. il Time 98:16-17 N 8 '71
Chinese are coming. il Newsweek 78:22-8 N 8 '71
Crisis that is bringing U.N. to life; with interview with G. Bush. il U S News 71:46-8 S 20 '71
Facing up to the realities. il Newsweek 78:31-2 Ag 16 '71
How to solve the China problem. J. Burnham. Nat R 23:693 Je 29 '71
Let Taiwan decide. L. C. Chen. New Repub 164:16 My 29 '71
Mr Nixon twists and turns admission of China to the United Nations. Nation 213:482-3 N 15 '71

One vote: Malta on the Peking-versus-Taiwan issue. New Yorker 47:43-4 N 6 '71
Ouster at the U.N; Taiwan reporters excluded. Time 99:50 Ja 3 '72
Paving the way for Peking's entry. il Time 98:22+ Ag 16 '71
Republic of China; address, October 25, 1971. S. K. Chow. Vital Speeches 38:101-2 D 1 '71
Sacrificing principle for expediency. D. Lawrence. U S News 71:108 N 8 '71
Sort of all-out effort. il Newsweek 78:55-6 O 25 '71
Taiwan: the crunch. Nat R 23:1216-17 N 5 '71
Taiwan: Washington's dilemma. A. S. Whiting. Nation 211:644 D 21 '70
Tense triangle: what to do about Taiwan. il Time 97:23-4 Je 7 '71
Test of strength; U.S. resolutions. il Time 98:29 O 4 '71
Trail of the dragon. Nat R 23:1282 N 19 '71
Two Chinas in the U.N, the U.S. states its case; excerpts from statement, October 18, 1971. G. Bush. il por U S News 71:74-5 N 1 '71
U.N. admits red China; U.S. reaction divided. il Sr Schol 99:17-18+ N 29 '71
United Nations votes to seat People's Republic of China and expel representatives of Republic of China; statements, October 18 and 25, 1971; with text of resolution. G. Bush. Dept State Bul 65:548-56 N 15 '71

United States

Adventure in shrinkage. N. Cousins. Sat R 54:36 O 30 '71
End of the United Nations? address, October 29, 1971. W. F. Buckley, jr. il Nat R 23:1300-1+ N 19 '71
Foreign policy and the United Nations; address, October 4, 1971. W. P. Rogers. Vital Speeches 38:34-8 N 1 '71; Same with title Legacy of peace: our responsibility to future generations. Dept State Bul 65:437-44 O 25 '71
Our man at the U.N. A. Tuckerman. Nation 212:389 Mr 29 '71
Policy on two Chinas; advantages of U.N; interview. G. Bush. il por U S News 71:47-8 S 20 '71
U.N. admits red China; U.S. reaction divided. il Sr Schol 99:17-18+ N 29 '71
U.S. participation in the U.N. during 1970; text of letter from President Nixon transmitting to Congress, September 20, 1971. R. M. Nixon. Dept State Bul 65:502-3 N 1 '71
Why majority in U.N. turned on U.S. il U S News 71:17-19 N 8 '71

Zambia

Security council calls on South Africa to respect sovereignty of Zambia; with text. UN Mo Chron 8:3-13 N '71

UNITED NATIONS bank for reconstruction and development. See International bank for reconstruction and development

UNITED NATIONS childrens fund
Executive board meets. UN Mo Chron 8:32-5 My '71
For the world's children, UNICEF at 25. H. R. Labouisse. il UN Mo Chron 8:48-60 Ap '71
UNICEF at 25. Chr Cent 88:1253 O 27 '71
UNICEF greeting cards. il UNESCO Courier 24:33 N '71
UNICEF's 25th anniversary promise: a future for every child. Mrs G. Pantaleoni, jr. por Parents Mag 46:32 D '71

UNITED NATIONS commission for the unification and rehabilitation of Korea
Question of Korea: Assembly adopts resolution. UN Mo Chron 8:28-9 Ja '71

UNITED NATIONS conference on the human environment
Global pollution. J. Lear; S. Lindsay; R. N. Gardner. il Sat R 54:41-50 Ag 7 '71
Human environment conference: citizen advisers muddle through. R. Gillette. Science 174:479-81 O 29 '71
Human environment conference: slow start toward Stockholm. R. Gillette. Science 172:1011-13 Je 4 '71
Human environment conference: the rush for influence. R. J. Bazell. Science 174:390-1 O 22 '71
Human environment, new challenge for the United Nations. UN Mo Chron 8:35-48 F '71
1972 conference on the human environment; Preparatory committee concludes second session. UN Mo Chron 8:15-16 Mr '71
Official emblem for conference on human environment. il Sch & Soc 99:332-3 O '71
Preparatory committee adopts report. UN Mo Chron 8:88-9 O '71

UNITED NATIONS conference on the human environment—_Continued_
Secretary Rogers names committee on the human environment. Dept State Bul 64:755 Je 7 '71
Senator Baker to head committee on U.N. environment conference. H. Baker. Dept State Bul 64:333 Mr 15 '71
U.N. as policeman. R. N. Gardner. Sat R 54: 47-50 Ag 7 '71; Same with title Can the UN be a policeman? Cur 133:34-40 O '71
UN conference in Stockholm; letter. J. R. Goldsmith. Science 172:216+ Ap 16 '71
U.S. discusses priorities for the 1972 U.N. conference on the human environment; statements, September 16, 20 and 24, 1971. C. A. Herter, jr; S. Temple. Dept State Bul 65:530-6 N 8 '71
U.S. government develops topics for U.N. environment conference. Dept State Bul 65: 390 O 11 '71
U.S. initiatives for the 1972 U.N. conference on the human environment; statement, February 9, 1971. C. A. Herter, jr. Dept State Bul 64:334-9 Mr 15 '71
United Nations adopts resolution on human environment conference; statement, with text of resolution. C. Pell. Dept State Bul 64:67-70 Ja 11 '71
UNITED NATIONS conference on the law of the sea, 1973
Law for the seas. A. W. Smith. Nat Parks & Con Mag 45:2+ Je '71
UNITED NATIONS conference on the law of treaties
Vienna convention on the law of treaties transmitted to the Senate; President's message, November 22, 1971; with Secretary Roger's report. R. M. Nixon; W. P. Rogers. Dept State Bul 65:684-9 D 13 '71
UNITED NATIONS conference on the problems of human environment. See United Nations conference on the human environment
UNITED NATIONS conference on trade and development
New international wheat agreement. UN Mo Chron 8:20 Mr '71
Trade and development board; concludes eleventh session. UN Mo Chron 8:87-8 O '71
UNITED NATIONS council for Namibia
Decides on itinerary for visit to Africa. UN Mo Chron 8:45 Je '71
UNITED NATIONS day
United Nations day, 1971, proclamation. R. M. Nixon. Dept State Bul 65:126 Ag 2 '71
United Nations day 24 October 1971; messages. A. Malik; Thant. UN Mo Chron 8:1-11 O '71
UNITED NATIONS development decade, 2d
Secretary-General's press conference; May 27, 1971. Thant. UN Mo Chron 8:75-81 Je '71
Unesco in the second development decade. H. Brabyn. il UNESCO Courier 24:12-16 F '71
UNITED NATIONS East Pakistan relief operation
U.S. urges international community to continue relief to south Asia; statement, November 19, 1971. W. T. Bennett, jr. Dept State Bul 65:717-19 D 20 '71
UNITED NATIONS educational, scientific and cultural organization. See UNESCO
UNITED NATIONS environment conference. See United Nations conference on the human environment
UNITED NATIONS food and agriculture organization. See Food and agriculture organization of the United Nations
UNITED NATIONS fund for drug abuse control
U.S. pledges $2 million to U.N. fund for drug abuse control. Dept State Bul 64:290 Mr 8 '71
United States presents $1 million to U.N. drug abuse control fund; statement, and remarks, April 1, 1971. G. Bush; J. E. Ingersoll. Dept State Bul 64:574-5 My 3 '71
UNITED NATIONS fund for population activities. See United Nations trust fund for population activities
UNITED NATIONS high commissioner for refugees
Mr Rhyne heads U.S. delegation to UNHCR executive committee. Dept State Bul 65:470 O 25 '71
U.S. urges international community to continue relief to south Asia; statement, November 19, 1971. W. T. Bennett, jr. Dept State Bul 65:717-19 D 20 '71
United States discusses report of UNHCR; statement, November 17, 1971. D. P. Moynihan. Dept State Bul 65:716-17 D 20 '71
UNITED NATIONS human rights day and week. See Human rights day and week
UNITED NATIONS international atomic energy agency. See International atomic energy agency

UNITED NATIONS international conference on the peaceful uses of atomic energy. See International conference on the peaceful uses of atomic energy, 4th Geneva, 1971
UNITED NATIONS monetary and financial conference
Deadlock over the dollar; with editorial comment. il Bsns W p82-6+, 144 S 25 '71
New monetary system for the 1980's, the spirit of Bretton Woods; address, December 3, 1971. D. C. Platten. Vital Speeches 38:179-82 Ja 1 '72
UNITED NATIONS relief and works agency for Palestine refugees in the Near East
Assembly adopts six resolutions. UN Mo Chron 8:45-52 Ja '71
Educational aid for the Palestine refugees. R. Maheu. UNESCO Courier 24:38-9 Mr '71
Palestine refugees. UN Mo Chron 7:58-64 D '70
Secretary-General: Palestine refugees. UN Mo Chron 8:11 F '71
U.S. urges support for UNRWA's efforts to provide essential services to Palestine refugees; statement, with text of resolution. R. H. Gimer. Dept State Bul 64:93-6 Ja 18 '71
UNITED NATIONS trust fund for population activities
U.S. pledges $12.5 million to U.N. population fund. Dept State Bul 64:259 Mr 1 '71
UNITED NATIONS volunteer corps
U.S. presents initial contribution to U.N. volunteers fund; statements, with text of letter, June 17, 1971. G. Bush; J. H. Blatchford. Dept State Bul 65:138-9 Ag 2 '71
UNITED NATIONS wheat conference. See United Nations conference on trade and development
UNITED Negro college fund
Friend at Burlington. por Bsns W p92 Mr 20 '71
UNITED Presbyterian church in the U.S.A.
Ailing seminaries: unfit to be tied? Chr Today 15:39-40 Mr 12 '71
Angela and the Presbyterians. Chr Cent 88: 823 Jl 7 '71; Discussion. 88:979-80 Ag 18 '71
Confronting church lobbyists. Chr Today 16: 32 N 5 '71
Ecclesiastical McCarthyism; William Thompson critical of lay committee. Chr Today 15: 21 Je 18 '71
Gulf oil kneels to church wishes. Bsns W p39 F 27 '71
It takes two for dialogue. E. M. Hawk. Chr Cent 88:1418-20 D 1 '71
Madame moderator; L. H. Stair elected. por Newsweek 77:85 My 31 '71
Packaging Jesus. R. L. Shayon. Sat R 54:78 Mr 13 '71
Presbyterians weigh pacts. J. M. Boice. Chr Today 15:29 Je 18 '71
Protestant schism. Newsweek 78:62-3 S 6 '71
UPUSA and social revivalism. S. C. Rose. Chr Cent 88:712-13 Je 9 '71
United Presbyterians: Jesus saves; Mrs L. H. Stair, named moderator. J. M. Boice. Chr Today 15:28 Je 4 '71
Up the down roller coaster: Presbyterians protest Angela. R. Chandler. Chr Today 15:35-6 Jl 2 '71
UNITED Presbyterian general assembly. See United Presbyterian church in the U.S.A.
UNITED REPUBLIC of Tanganyika and Zanzibar. See Tanzania
UNITED service organizations
U.S.O. New Yorker 47:30-2 S 11 '71
UNITED shoe machinery corporation. See USM corporation
UNITED STATES
America we love; excerpts. L. Day. il Ladies Home J 88:64+ Jl '71
America: where are we headed? il Sr Schol 99:6-12 S 27 '71
American future: what kind of a society do we want? H. H. Humphrey. il America 125:476-9 D 4 '71
America's most challenging objectives; symposium, ed. by R. D. Lambert. bibliog f Ann Am Acad 396:1-114 Jl '71
Case for optimism. N. Cousins. Sat R 54: 28-9 N 20 '71
Cooling of America; symposium. il Time 97: 10-19 F 22 '71
I love America. J. Atkins. Read Digest 98: 187-8 Mr '71
Listening to America, by B. Moyers; and U.S. journal, by C. Trillin. Reviews
    Sat R 54:26-7 My 8 '71. J. K. Hutchens
New directions at home and abroad. il U S News 71:19 N 15 '71
Real issues in today's America: Congress hears from home. il U S News 70:9-11 My 3 '71

UNITED STATES—*Continued*

Seven polarizing issues in America today; symposium, ed. by M. K. Whiteleather. bibliog f il Ann Am Acad 397:1-139 S '71
State of Uncle Sam. J. Reston. Read Digest 98:167-8 Ap '71
This country isn't kid stuff anymore. R. Graves. Life 70:3 My 21 '71
Transformation. Look 35:65 Ja 12 '71
25 amazing years; changes in the U.S. since World war II. il U S News 71:40-3 N 15 '71
Without Marx or Jesus, by J. F. Revel. Review
    Life 71:12 S 17 '71. A. Schlesinger. jr
    New Repub 165:25-6+ S 25 '71. S. Mc-Cracken
Without Marx or Jesus: the new American revolution has begun; excerpt; tr. by J. Bernard. F. Revel. il Sat R 54:14-31 Jl 24 '71
    See also
Americans
Indians of North America
States (United States)
    also names of sections. states. e.g. New England; *also* subhead United States under various subjects, e.g. Aerospace industries—United States

Action corps

All set: the super peace corps. il U S News 70:57 Je 28 '71
Getting it all together in the name of Action; merger of the Peace corps, VISTA and smaller government volunteer groups. il por Time 97:11-12 Je 7 '71
    See also
Volunteers in service to America

Administration on aging

AoA makes $329,990 training grants to six black colleges. Aging 203:4 S '71

Advanced research projects agency

    See United States—Defense, Department of—Advanced research projects agency

Advisory commission on international, educational and cultural affairs

Four new members join Commission on educational and cultural affairs. Dept State Bul 65:676 D 13 '71

Advisory council on executive organization

    See United States—President's advisory council on executive organization

Agency for international development

AID, voluntary agencies celebrate 25 years of cooperation overseas. Dept State Bul 64:753-4 Je 7 '71
Environment and development committee established by AID. Dept State Bul 65:155-6 Ag 9 '71
New educational methods and developing nations. Sch & Soc 99:399-400+ N '71
Supporting assistance bureau established by AID. Dept State Bul 65:198 Ag 23 '71

Office of public safety

Good neighbor; training and advising of Guatemalan military and police. New Repub 164:9 Ap 24 '71

Aging, Administration on

AoA budget request increased: FY '72 to be more than 20%. Aging 199:5+ My '71
Aging agency at White House level urged by Senate group. Aging 205:16-17 N '71
Martin appointed coordinator on HEW aging priority. Aging 204:4 O '71

Agricultural research service

Pesticides regulation division

Eradicate them one more time; fire ant eradication program. G. Laycock. Field & S 76:46-7+ D '71

Agricultural stabilization and conservation service

How REAP helps you pay for pollution controls. G. Reynolds. Farm J 95:38 Mr '71
You can get federal funds to control feedlot runoff; REAP funds. B. Eftink. il Suc Farm 69:23 O '71

Agriculture, Department of

Abolish the Department of agriculture! Farm J 95:78 Mr '71
Down on the farm. il por Newsweek 78:22 D 6 '71

Jobs in the southern forests. B. E. Griessman and K. A. Argow. il Am For 77:42-3+ Ja '71
Mirex and the fire ant: decline in fortunes of perfect pesticide. D. Shapley. il Science 172:358-60 Ap 23 '71
Moths 65, USDA 0. N. Wade. Science 174:41 O 1 '71
Nader on food. il Time 98:46-7 Ag 2 '71
Nader's newest raid for tougher meat inspection; with editorial comment. J. Carlson. Farm J 95:13+. 42 S '71
New help in getting carcass information; USDA ear tag pilot project. W. Kester. Farm J 95:B7 Ap '71
Washington report; reasons for reorganizing. W. E. Swegle. il Suc Farm 69:7 My '71
What will you lose if you lose USDA? F. Bailey. Suc Farm 69:no5-7 Mr '71
    See also
United States—Agricultural stabilization and conservation service
United States—Soil conservation service

Air force

Peacetime air force of the seventies; less money, fewer people, more technology; address, September 29, 1971. J. C. Meyer. Vital Speeches 38:56-8 N 1 '71
    See also
Airplanes, Military—United States
United States air force academy, Colorado Springs

Aero propulsion laboratory

Air force laboratory studies jet engine pollution control. M. L. Yaffee. Aviation W 94:58-9 F 1 '71
USAF propulsion interests detailed. M. L. Yaffee. Aviation W 94:54-7 Mr 1 '71

Arnold engineering development center

    See United States—Arnold engineering development center

Procurement

Project bosses get more power; B-1 management. il por Bsns W p96+ Mr 20 '71
USAF development policies; excerpts from address. G. S. Brown. Aviation W 95:9 S 6 '71
USAF prototype plans; excerpts from address, November 1971. J. T. Stewart. Aviation W 95:9 N 29 '71
USAF tightens B-1 management. C. Brownlow. il Aviation W 94:56-9 F 22 '71

Strategic air command

Survival as a free country depends on modern weapons; interview. B. K. Holloway. il por U S News 71:52-5 D 27 '71

Systems command

USAF unit seeks integrator role; Aeronautical systems division. M. L. Yaffee. Aviation W 94:14-15 My 10 '71
    See also
United States—Arnold engineering development center

Anti-Communist measures

    See United States—Foreign relations—Anti-Communist measures

Antiquities

    See also
Indians of North America—Antiquities

Appropriations and expenditures

Dollars and logic of reordered priorities. L. S. Ritter; S. Melman. il Sat R 54:22-7+ O 9 '71
New domestic spending bills: destructive trends; address, April 6, 1971. C. T. Curtis. Vital Speeches 37:486-8 Je 1 '71
Nixon's nest egg. il Newsweek 77:98 Ap 19 '71
Tax cuts, social security, welfare reform; interview. W. Mills. il pors U S News 70:42-4+ Mr 15 '71
Watch on the Potomac. K. Y. Tomlinson. Read Digest 98:117-18 Je '71
Why Nixon refuses to spend billions voted by Congress. il U S News 70:42-3 Ap 19 '71
    See also
Budget—United States
Federal aid
Government spending policy
United States—Defense, Department of—Appropriations and expenditures
United States—Economic policy
    also subhead Appropriations and expenditures under names of government departments, e.g. United States—Armed forces—Appropriations and expenditures

UNITED STATES—*Continued*

Armed forces

Bureaucracy adrift. E. F. Sherman. Nation 212:265-75 Mr 1 '71

Our four-star military mess; with editorial comment. G. P. Hunt. il Life 70:3. 50-2+ Je 18 '71

Our gravest military problem is manpower. J. Cameron. il Fortune 83:60-3+ Ap '71

See also

Courts martial and courts of inquiry

Discipline, Military

United States—Defense, Department of

United States—Marine corps

United States—Navy

United States—Reserve officers training corps

Appropriations and expenditures

Bad week for the doves. Time 98:21 O 11 '71

Budget aspects and national security; address. December 10, 1970. T. H. Moorer. Vital Speeches 37:194-7 Ja 15 '71

Congress can do it. New Repub 164:9-10 F 27 '71

Double-talk bookkeeping; military budget. R. F. Kaufman. Nation 213:429-32 N 1 '71

Erosion of U.S. military strength: can there be peace without power? address July 14, 1971. J. L. Buckley. Vital Speeches 37: 642-4 Ag 15 '71

First signs of an upturn in defense spending. il U S News 71:62-3 O 11 '71

Foreign-policy war; bill. Newsweek 78:22 N 29 '71

Major advanced weapon systems funded; with tables. Aviation W 94:16-17 F 1 '71

Military spending & dollars abroad. R. W. Stevens. il Nation 213:554-7 N 29 '71

Navy nets more of the budget. il Bsns W p62+ F 6 '71

Nixon's blueprint for defense. il U S News 70:29 F 8 '71

Real problem: how to cut defense billions. il U S News 70:30-2+ Je 21 '71

Roots of the strategic arms race: ambiguity and ignorance. W. K. H. Panofsky. Bul Atom Sci 27:15-20 Je '71

Second time around. Newsweek 78:22 O 11 '71

Toward a military welfare state? N. Cousins. Sat R 54:26-7 Mr 27 '71

Viability of the United States; address, September 17, 1971. G. S. Brown. Vital Speeches 38:53-6 N 1 '71

See also

Military-industrial complex

United States—Defense, Department of—Appropriations and expenditures

Bibliography

Military references. J. M. Hillard. Wilson Lib Bul 46:405 Ja '72

Clothing

See also

Uniforms, Military

Desertions

AWOL in Japan. R. Sklar. il Ramp Mag 10: 26-7 O '71

America's sad young exiles; draft evaders and deserters in Canada. K. Fleming. il Newsweek 77:28-30 F 15 '71

Anti-Americanism in Sweden: some of the bad blood is gone. il U S News 70:93 My 10 '71

Education

See also

United States—Armed forces staff college

Equipment and supplies

Military as litterbug. il Time 98:78+ O 25 '71

See also

Vietnamese war, 1957- —Equipment and supplies

Forces in Asia

Should the United States retain a military presence in Europe and Asia? R. L. Pfaltzgraff, jr. bibliog f Ann Am Acad 397:1-10 S '71

See also

United States—Armed forces—Forces in the Far East

Forces in Europe

Bring the boys home? Nat R 23:572 Je 1 '71

First line of defense. A. de Borchgrave. Newsweek 77:43 Je 14 '71

Foreign policy: Mansfield's rebellion. il por Newsweek 77:18-19 My 24 '71

Give and take at the summit, the stakes for America. il U S News 71:38-9 D 20 '71

Great trip-wire delusion. A. Cranston. Sat R 54:14 Je 19 '71

Mansfield ruckus. Nation 212:675-6 My 31 '71

Nato today; the Russian threat; address. September 2, 1971. A. J. Goodpaster. Vital Speeches 37:743-9 O 1 '71

NATO troops; Senate rejection of Mansfield resolution. New Repub 164:11 My 29 '71

President Nixon urges Senate to reject European forces reduction measures; text of letter to J. C. Stennis, November 22, 1971. R. M. Nixon. Dept State Bul 65:702-3 D 20 '71

Pros and cons of NATO troop withdrawal. il Time 97:18 My 24 '71

Purpose and policy; question of withdrawal. Z. Brzezinski. Newsweek 77:47 F 22 '71

Should the United States retain a military presence in Europe and Asia? R. L. Pfaltzgraff, jr. bibliog f Ann Am Acad 397:1-10 S '71

Sledgehammer; lobby to reduce America's troop commitments to NATO. il Newsweek 77:16-17 My 31 '71

Troops, trade and diplomacy. R. E. Hunter. il Nation 212:776-80 Je 21 '71

Voices of spring; question of withdrawal. G. W. Ball. por Newsweek 77:43 Mr 1 '71

Why U.S. forces will stay in Europe. il U S News 70:20 My 31 '71

Why U.S. must stay in Europe; interview, ed. by R. Haeger. W. Brandt. il pors U S News 70:39-42+ Je 14 '71

Forces in foreign countries

U.S. forces abroad, biggest drop in 16 years. il U S News 72:18-20 Ja 3 '72

Forces in Japan

AWOL in Japan. R. Sklar. il Ramp Mag 10: 26-7 O '71

U.S. and Japan adjust realignment of U.S. forces and facilities; text of joint U.S.-Japan statement. Dept State Bul 64:528 Ap 19 '71

U.S. and Japan discuss realignment of U.S. forces and facilities; text of joint statement. Dept State Bul 64:77-9 Ja 18 '71

Forces in Korea

All over Asia, GI's are leaving. il U S News 70:18 Ap 19 '71

U.S. and Korea agree on U.S. troop reduction and Korean modernization. Dept State Bul 64:263 Mr 1 '71

Forces in Laos

Not-so-secret war; secret session of the Senate. Newsweek 77:26+ Je 21 '71

United States gives position on foreign forces in Laos; Department statement. Dept State Bul 65:227-8 Ag 30 '71

Forces in the Far East

Why U.S. must stay in Asia; interview. H. Kahn. il pors U S News 70:60-4 F 8 '71

Forces in Vietnam

Amer-Asian children in Vietnam. D. Luce. Chr Cent 88:996-7 Ag 25 '71; Discussion. 88:1181-2 O 6 '71

Death of a soldier; fragging. Nation 212:612 My 17 '71

GI's other enemy: heroin. il Newsweek 77: 26+ My 24 '71

In defense of the military. G. W. Ball. Newsweek 78:48 Jl 5 '71; Same abr. with title Let's get off our soldiers' backs! Read Digest 99:155-6 O '71

Where U.S. will make its last stand in Vietnam. il U S News 71:41 S 20 '71

See also

Narcotics and service men

United States—Army—Forces in Vietnam

Vietnamese war, 1957- —American participation

Vietnamese war, 1957- —American troop withdrawals

Forces in Vietnam—Recreation

See United States—Armed forces—Recreation

History

Dress parade; excerpts from America's fighting men; with paintings by P. Copeland. H. L. Peterson. Am Heritage 22:4-11 O '71

Libraries

See also

United States—Army—Libraries

Medical and sanitary affairs

See also

Vietnamese war, 1957- —Medical and sanitary affairs

See also

World war, 1939-1945—Medical and sanitary affairs

UNITED STATES—Armed forces—*Continued*

Morale

Death of a soldier; fragging. Nation 212:612 My 17 '71

Incident on Route 9. D. Greenway. il Time 97:25 Ap 5 '71

Negroes

Armed forces: black powerlessness; Race rumblings at McClellan. il Time 98:24 N 29 '71

See also
United States—Army—Negroes

Officers, Retired

See Retired military personnel

Pay, allowances, etc.

Draft uncompromise. M. Friedman. il Newsweek 78:59 S 6 '71

Record pay increase. il U S News 71:32 O 4 '71

See also
United States—Army—Pay, allowances, etc.

Political activities

Conscience and command, ed. by J. Finn. Review
Commonweal 94:289-90 My 28 '71. W. C. McWilliams

Post exchange

Military exchanges think black; Westover air force base. il Ebony 26:54-6+ Jl '71

Procurement

Defense operation, procurement, RDT&E and construction; tables. Aviation W 94:14-15 F 1 '71

Public relations

I didn't raise my boy to be an eyebrow; Mole's living monument photographs. il Life 71:82-3 S 24 '71

See also
United States—Armed forces—Relations with civilians

Publications

See also
Stars and stripes (newspaper)

Recreation

Armed forces recreation; with tables. Parks & Rec 6:67-9 Ag '71

Typhoon Jane. il por Time 99:71 Ja 3 '72

See also
United service organization

Recruiting and enlistment

Beards, beer, no reveille: new lures for recruits. il U S News 70:38-40 Ja 18 '71

Whatever happened to military service for youths below 1-A? il U S News 71:56 S 6 '71

See also
Military service, Voluntary

Regulations

Beards, beer, no reveille: new lures for recruits. il U S News 70:38-40 Ja 18 '71

Military goes mod. Read Digest 98:100-4 Mr '71

Relations with civilians

Military and American society. R. G. Gard, jr. For Affairs 49:698-710 Jl '71

My Lai and the state of the army. D. A. Zoll. Nat R 23:1112-14 O 8 '71

Reserves

Sunshine soldiers, by P. Tauber. Review
Bsns W p22+ My 15 '71. E. R. Ray

Training

See Military training

Armed forces staff college

Black coed at Armed forces college. il pors Ebony 26:108-10+ N '70

Arms control and disarmament agency

Tenth annual report of ACDA transmitted to the Congress; President Nixon's letter of transmittal; with introduction of the report. R. M. Nixon. Dept State Bul 64:534-6 Ap 19 '71

Army

American strength: the keystone of peace; address, May 29, 1971. R. M. Nixon. Dept State Bul 64:813-15 Je 28 '71

Colonel Herbert v. the army. il por Time 98:24+ N 22 '71

Good soldiers. L. K. Truscott, 4th. Nation 213:517 N 22 '71

How the U.S. army spies on citizens. il por Life 70:20-7 Mr 26 '71

Invisible intruders; army's justification for collection of domestic political information. P. Schrag. Sat R 54:20-1 Ja 30 '71

Maverick; resignation of Lt Col A. Herbert. por Newsweek 78:40 N 22 '71

On being monitored; J. M. O'Brien charges army with political snooping. J. R. Waitz. Nation 212:113-14 Ja 25 '71

Surveillance surveyed; hearings by the Senate subcommittee on constitutional rights. Newsweek 77:54+ Mr 8 '71

West Pointer's wild preview of the volunteer army. C. S. Wren. il pors Look 35:24-7 F 23 '71

See also
Courts martial and courts of inquiry
Discipline, Military
Military posts

Clothing

See also
Uniforms, Military

Corps of engineers

Environment repair; the U.S. army engineers' new assignment. J. Lear. il Sat R 54:47-52 My 1 '71

Little sturm und drang at Hunting creek. J. Sax. il Esquire 75:84-8+ F '71

Needed: an about-face for the Corps of engineers. H. S. Reuss. Read Digest 99:129-32 N '71

Education

See also
United States—Armed forces staff college
United States military academy, West Point

Equipment and supplies

See also
Tanks, Military

Forces in Europe

Forgotten Seventh army. il Time 98:18-10 O 4 '71

Neglected and troubled Seventh army. B. van Voorst and R. Koch. il Newsweek 77:28-9 My 31 '71

Forces in Vietnam

Americal goes home. il Time 98:18-19 N 8 '71

Army at sea; comments on D. Kirk's article. Nation 213:291-2 O 4 '71

As fighting slows in Vietnam; breakdown in GI discipline. il U S News 70:16-17 Je 7 '71

A day in the dwindling war; Bravo company, fourth battalion, 31st infantry. N. Proffitt. il Newsweek 78:40-1 S 13 '71

Demoralization of an army: fragging and other withdrawal symptoms. E. Linden. il Sat R 55:12-17+ Ja 8 '72

Disorder in the ranks. Time 98:21 Ag 9 '71

Eyewitness report on drugs, race problems and boredom. W. S. Merick. il U S News 70:30-3 Ja 25 '71

Hell at Mary Ann; 23rd Americal division in Quang Tin province. N. C. Proffitt. il Newsweek 77:45 Ap 12 '71

Incident on Route 1; U.S. army tractor trailer accident. Time 98:38+ O 25 '71

Money king of Viet Nam; Senate permanent subcommittee on investigations study of army corruption. il por Time 97:19 Mr 8 '71

Shootout at Quang Tri; GI shoots officers. Newsweek 77:49 Ja 25 '71

War within the war; drugs, insubordination and racial tension in Viet Nam. Time 97:34-5 Ja 25 '71

Who has been fighting in Vietnam. il U S News 70:34 Mr 1 '71

Who wants to be the last American killed in Vietnam? D. Kirk. il N Y Times Mag p9+ S 19 '71

Withdrawal pains; C. Abrams broadside on carelessness. il Newsweek 77:41 Je 7 '71

Libraries

Army libraries profiled: a big, busy organization. Library J 96:1920 Je 1 '71

Military libraries: a defense; letter to the editor. B. E. Stevens. Library J 96:4041 D 15 '71

Materiel command

New facility to reduce R&D costs; army missile command's advanced simulation facility. M. L. Yaffee. il Aviation W 95:44-6 Jl 19 '71

Medical corps

Simpler creed; excerpt from 365 days. R. J. Glasser. il Harper 243:86-7 Jl '71

Military posts

See Military posts

Missile command

See United States—Army—Materiel command

UNITED STATES—Army—*Continued*

Morale

Demoralization of an army: fragging and other withdrawal symptoms. E. Linden. il Sat R 55:12-17+ Ja 8 '72

Eyewitness report on drugs, race problems and boredom. W. S. Merick. il U S News 70:30-3 Ja 25 '71

My Lai and the state of the army. D. A. Zoll. Nat R 23:1112-14 O 8 '71

Negroes

Black cadet at West Point; J. C. Whittaker case. J. F. Marszalek, jr. il pors Am Heritage 22:30-7+ Ag '71; Reply. T. J. Fleming. 22:111 O '71

See also
Brownsville, Tex.—Riot, 1906
Vietnamese war, 1957- —Negroes

Officers

Troubled army brass. K. Fleming. il Newsweek 77:21-3 My 24 '71

West Pointer's wild preview of the volunteer army. C. S. Wren. il pors Look 35:24-7 F 23 '71

See also
Generals

Pay, allowances, etc.

Money talks. Newsweek 77:23 Je 21 '71

Prisons

Military prisons: about face. il Time 97:63 My 17 '71

Public relations

Army ad blitz. Nation 212:357 Mr 22 '71

Big account. Nation 212:580-1 My 10 '71

Madison avenue; TV announcements to woo young men to the proposed all-volunteer army. H. Maneloveg. Sat R 54:49+ My 8 '71

Recreation

See also
United service organizations
United States—Army—Special services

Recruiting, enlistment, etc.

Advertising the army. New Repub 165:10 O 2 '71

Enlistment blues. Newsweek 77:29 Je 14 '71

Of cameras and screens. J. Morgenstern. Newsweek 77:9 Ap 26 '71

See also
Military service, Voluntary

Regulations

Getting nowhere through channels; distributing dissenting materials in the army. J. V. H. Dippel. New Repub 164:13-17 My 22 '71

How soldiers like life in the new army. il U S News 70:29-30 Ap 19 '71

Memories of an old soldier. W. Zinsser. Sat R 54:6-7 Jl 3 '71

Relations with civilians

See United States—Armed forces—Relations with civilians

Ski troops

Phantoms of the snow: 10th mountain division. W. Johnson. il Sports Illus 34:54-6+ F 8 '71

Special forces

Army snow job; D. Middleton's story on the army's Nation-building program in North Carolina. W. L. Robb. New Repub 165:15-17 D 11 '71

Nation-mending at home; Green Beret civic action teams. il por Time 97:20 Je 21 '71

Special services

To be of special services. D. R. Sharpless. il Parks & Rec 6:45-52 My '71

Army library service

See United States—Army—Libraries

Arnold engineering development center

AEDC facilities busy, despite cuts. M. L. Yaffee. il Aviation W 94:36-7+ Ap 26 '71

Art

See Art, American

Atomic energy commission

AEC asks billions for breeder reactors. Bsns W p82-4 My 29 '71

AEC considers environmental impact of power reactors. S. M. Hein. Phys Today 24:62 N '71

AEC has something for Kansas. R. Brown. Nation 212:712-16 Je 7 '71

AEC to nuclear industry: we're no longer your protector. Sci N 100:290 O 30 '71

AEC to referee, not promote, industry; excerpts from address, October 1971. J. R. Schlesinger. Science 174:478 O 29 '71

AEC transmutation. A. L. Hammond. Science 174:930 N 26 '71

AEC's new environmental rules for nuclear plants may open new debate, extend delays, raise plant costs. R. Gillette. Science 173:1112-13 S 17 '71

Another failure in communication. H. L. Davis. Phys Today 24:88 D '71

Atomic shield 1947/1952, by R. G. Hewlett and F. Duncan. Review
    Bul Atom Sci 27:48-50 Ja '71. H. P. Green

Atoms and dollars. il Forbes 108:24-6+ O 1 '71

Big shift at the AEC. G. R. Rosen. por Duns 98:34-5+ N '71

Breeding power. il Newsweek 77:67 Je 14 '71

Change at the AEC. pors Time 98:47 Ag 2 '71

Confusion on Amchitka. Nation 213:229 S 20 '71

Cooling threat to nuclear power. Bsns W p46 Je 5 '71

Court decision jolts AEC; dawdling in implementation of the National environmental policy act. C. Holden. Science 173:799 Ag 27 '71

Dear Sir: your house is built on radioactive uranium waste; Grand Junction, Colo. H. P. Metzger. il N Y Times Mag p 14-15+ O 31 '71

Economist for a chemist. il Sci N 100:76 Jl 31 '71

Fallout from the peaceful atom. P. Winslow. Nation 212:557-61 My 3 '71. Reply with rejoinder. J. A. Harris. 212:738 Je 14 '71

Great nuclear debate: are our newborn babies' lives in danger? M. Hope and J. Young. Redbook 138:16+ Ja '72

Harnessing the A.E.C. J. Deedy. Commonweal 95:146 N 12 '71

Hell in a very small place; Amchitka blast. W. K. Wyant, jr. Nation 213:132 Ag 30 '71

Kansas geologists and the AEC; plan to bury cannisters of nuclear wastes. il Sci N 99:161 Mr 6 '71

New man at the AEC. por Newsweek 78:49 Ag 2 '71

Notes and comment: test at Amchitka. New Yorker 47:45-6 N 20 '71

Nuclear graveyard. il Newsweek 77:60 Mr 29 '71

Nuclear plant controversy. R. E. Lapp. New Repub 164:18-21 Ja 23; 20-3 F 6; 17-21 F 27 '71; Same abr. with title Nuclear power for electricity. Cur 127:42-9 Mr '71

Nuclear power and the public, ed. by H. Foreman. Review
    Science 171:790-3 F 26 '71. L. Loevinger

Nuclear power loses a battle in court. Bsns W p24 Jl 31 '71

Nuclear reactor safety: a new dilemma for the AEC. R. Gillette. il Science 173:126-30 Jl 9 '71

Nuclear tests: big Amchitka shot target of mounting opposition. R. J. Bazell. il Science 172:1219-21 Je 18 '71

Nuclear waste: Kansans riled by AEC plans for atom dump. C. Holden. il Science 172:249-50 Ap 16 '71

Plutonium: reactor proliferation threatens a nuclear black market. D. Shapley. bibliog f Science 172:143-6 Ap 9 '71; Reply. R. L. Stetson. 173:7 Jl 2 '71

Precautions are being taken by those who know: an inquiry into the power and responsibilities of the AEC. P. Jacobs. Atlan 227:45-56 F '71. Discussion. 227:30+ Ap; 36 My; 36 Je '71

Radioactive salt mine; with comments and summary. R. S. Lewis. il Bul Atom Sci 27:27-31+ Je '71

Reactor emissions: AEC guidelines move toward critics' position. R. Gillette. Science 172:1215-16 Je 18 '71; Discussion. 174:1280-1 D 24 '71

Role of the AEC. Sci Am 225:40 D '71

Round 2 at Amchitka; environmentalists suit against the AEC. Time 98:41 Jl 19 '71

Schlesinger's bomb. por Newsweek 78:76+ N 1 '71

Seaborg will leave AEC. C. Holden. il por Science 173:407 Jl 30 '71

Tough manager takes over at AEC. Bsns W p20 Jl 24 '71

Unexpected nuclear spin-off; Atlas of the domestic turkey. D. E. Abrahamson. Science 173:1191 S 24 '71

What next for programs dropped by AEC? G. B. Lubkin. il Phys Today 24:57+ Jl '71

See also
Argonne national laboratory
Hanford works, Richland, Wash.

UNITED STATES—Atomic energy commission—*Continued*

Appropriations and expenditures
Politics and the AEC budget. il Sci N 99: 349-50 My 22 '71
Selective cuts. Sci N 99:96 F 6 '71

Attorney General
See United States—Justice, Department of

Boundaries
U.S.-Mexico boundary treaty transmitted to the Senate; President's letter of transmittal with Secretary Rogers' report of March 22, 1971. R. M. Nixon. il Dept State Bul 64: 674-8 My 24 '71
United States and Mexico sign boundary treaty; Department announcement. November 23, 1970. Dept State Bul 63:765-6 D 21 '70

Bureau of Indian affairs
See United States—Indian affairs, Bureau of

Business economics, Office of
New profit figures shock the experts. il Bsns W p57 Jl 31 '71

Cabinet
Tough road to reorganization; with editorial comment. il Bsns W p70, 88 Ja 30 '71
Who's who at White House now: shifts in the Nixon team. il U S News 70:16-18 Je 28 '71
See also
Secretaries of state (United States)

Anecdotes, facetiae, satire, etc.
Parting shots: a cabinet for all reasons. il Life 70:67-8 Ja 29 '71

Cabinet committee on aging
Nixon appoints Cabinet committee to coordinate policies on aging. T. Schuchat. Har Yrs 11:4 D '71
Nixon establishes domestic council cabinet-level committee on aging. Aging 205:6 N '71

Cabinet committee on international narcotics control
Secretary Rogers discusses new Cabinet committee on international narcotics control; news conference, with text of memorandum from President Nixon. W. P. Rogers. Dept State Bul 65:357-9 O 4 '71

Capitol
Bomb in the Senate. il Time 97:25 Mr 15 '71
Drive to halt terror bombings. il U S News 70:17-19 Mr 15 '71
Hideaways. il Newsweek 77:29 Mr 15 '71
How do you keep bombs away? il Sr Schol 98:13-14 Mr 22 '71
Price; bombing. Nation 212:322 Mr 15 '71
Trashing the Capitol. il Newsweek 77:28-9 Mr 15 '71

Census
America's new look, as the census sees it. il Changing T 25:13-14 Ag '71
Census of 1970. P. M. Hauser. il Sci Am 225: 17-25 bibliog(p 122) Jl '71
Census surprises. Newsweek 77:80 F 15 '71
How many of us are there? P. S. Templin. America 124:110 F 6 '71
1970 census shows 20 million 65+, more women than men. Aging 198:6 Ap '71

Centennial celebrations, etc.
American bicentennial, 1776-1976. D. Powills. il Hobbies 76:156-7 Jl '71
Bicentennial photography contest. Life 71: 20D-21 Jl 9 '71
Centennial city: Philadelphia. E. P. Richardson. il por Am Heritage 23:17-32 D '71
Dispirited '76. il Newsweek 78:55-6 Ag 2 '71
Dispirited '76 for Philadelphia. il Bsns W p 108+ Ja 16 '71
Philadelphia wedding; KYW-TV program. R. L. Shayon. Sat R 54:50 Jl 24 '71
Polis '76. J. Shepherd. Look 35:43-4 Ja 12 '71
200th anniversary of our independence. C. French. Hobbies 76:132 Ja '72

Central intelligence agency
CIA: an attack and a reply. V. Marchetti; L. B. Kirkpatrick, jr. il pors U S News 71:78-82+ O 11 '71
CIA and decision-making. C. L. Cooper. For Affairs 50:223-36 Ja '72
CIA as cop. J. Ridgeway. Ramp Mag 10:16 Ja '72
CIA on CIA. New Repub 164:10 My 1 '71

Congress and the CIA. Nation 213:548-9 N 29 '71
Don't ask; CIA funding. New Repub 164: 13-14 F 6 '71
Global intelligence: the Democratic society; address, April 14, 1971. R. Helms. Vital Speeches 37:450-4 My 15 '71; Excerpts. il por U S News 70:84-6 Ap 26 '71
H-L-S of the C.I.A. B. Welles. il pors N Y Times Mag p34-5+ Ap 18 '71
It won't wash. Nation 212:546-7 My 3 '71
Lansdale's secret war; the Saigon military mission. il por Newsweek 78:16 Jl 19 '71
Laos secrets. New Repub 165:9 Ag 21 '71
Letter from Washington. R. H. Rovere. New Yorker 47:125-7 Je 5 '71
New espionage American style. il Newsweek 78:28-32+ N 22 '71
Place to begin. Nation 212:163-4 F 8 '71
Radio free Europe. il Newsweek 77:102 F 8 '71
Spying and a free society: CIA chief speaks out; excerpts from address, April 14, 1971. R. Helms. il por U S News 70:84-6 Ap 26 '71
Why not? dissemination of CIA-gathered intelligence to Congress. Nation 213:68 Ag 2 '71

Chamber of commerce
See Chamber of commerce of the United States of America

Civil aeronautics board
American-Western merger opposed. L. Doty. Aviation W 96:20 Ja 3 '72
CAB allows more flexibility in discounts. H. D. Watkins. Aviation W 95:27-8 S 20 '71
CAB authorizes capacity talks in 13 markets; others denied. Aviation W 94:30 My 24 '71
CAB control of scheduling feared. L. Doty. il Aviation W 95:19-20 Ag 30 '71
CAB denies added cargo rights. Aviation W 95:18 N 22 '71
CAB financial advisors disbanded. L. Doty. Aviation W 94:28 Je 7 '71
CAB issues fare ruling deluge; major new bids hang on case. H. D. Watkins. Aviation W 94:21-2 Ja 18 '71
CAB non-affinity proposal adds fuel to charter feud. R. S. Kahn. Aviation W 95:25-6 Ag 30 '71
CAB orders fare reasonableness action, affirms merger position. Aviation W 94:187 Mr 8 '71
CAB pushes for international fares power. L. Doty. Aviation W 95:24 O 25 '71
CAB reopens tentative seating decisions. Aviation W 95:25 Jl 5 '71
CAB studies increased payments to local carriers despite budget. H. D. Watkins. il Aviation W 94:23 F 8 '71
CAB to scrutinize European charters. L. Doty. Aviation W 95:26-7 S 6 '71
CAB unit urges new air taxi standards. H. D. Watkins. Aviation W 94:29-30 Ap 26 '71
Case for grounding the CAB. il Fortune 84: 66+ Jl '71
Consumer pressure spurs CAB scrutiny. Aviation W 94:32-4 Mr 29 '71
Crying the blues; Senate hearings. Newsweek 77:64-5 F 15 '71
Dismal outlook spurs capacity cut drive. L. Doty. Aviation W 94:29 Ap 12 '71
Fare level spurs sharp divergence. H. D. Watkins. Aviation W 94:24 F 1 '71
Fasten your seat belts. R. Robertson, 3d. New Repub 164:17-18 Ja 2 '71; Discussion. 164: 34-5 F 13 '71
Giving the CAB transatlantic power. il Bsns W p26-7 O 16 '71
Just one more time. il Newsweek 77:78+ Ap 26 '71
Merger opinion may alter labor clauses. H. D. Watkins. Aviation W 95:28 N 8 '71
Nonskeds soar with CAB ruling. il Bsns W p 18-19 F 6 '71
North Atlantic fare increases approved. Aviation W 94:29 Mr 29 '71
Potential market seen in eased taxi rules. H. D. Watkins. Aviation W 95:26 O 4 '71
Rulings add incentive for capacity cuts. H. D. Watkins. il Aviation W 94:28-9 Ap 19 '71
Stormy weather for CAB's Secor Browne. il pors Nations Bsns 59:73-5 Mr '71

Civil rights commission
See United States—Commission on civil rights

Civilization
Abuse of myth. J. Castelli. il Cath World 213:88-92 My '71
After the revolution. by R. A. Dahl. Review Harper 242:12+ Mr '71. J. Fischer

UNITED STATES—Civilization—*Continued*
America may be in its last phase of adolescence. J. Lukacs. il N Y Times Mag p48+ D 5 '71
American institutions and ecological ideals; adaptation of address, December 29, 1969. L. Marx; discussion. Science 171:1095-6 Mr 19 '71
American manifesto, by R. J. Barnet and M. G. Raskin. Review
    New Repub 164:29 Ja 2 '71
Best of times, the worst of times. J. B. Sheerin. Cath World 212:227-8 F '71
Dissent within a lawful society; address, December 4, 1970. E. Sevareid. Vital Speeches 37:251-3 F 1 '71
Government structure: inherent inability to change; address, June 21, 1971. J. J. Powers, jr. Vital Speeches 37:628-31 Ag 1 '71
Greening of America, by C. Reich. Review
    Cath World 212:265-6 F '71. J. Tytell
    Cur 125:9-11 Ja '71. H. Marcuse
    Cur 125:11-14 Ja '71. P. Marin
    Harper 242:12+ Mr '71. J. Fischer
    Ramp Mag 9:51-2 Mr '71. A. Kopkind
Long night's journey into day; reprint. C. Julien. Nation 212:431-4 Ap 5 '71
Notes on being at home and abroad. A. Lewis. il Atlan 227:58-62 Je '71
Our unsure society: mental health and the Nation; address, October 16, 1970. L. Bellak. Vital Speeches 37:279-82 F 15 '71
Pride in America; address, October 30, 1971. L. Bushnell. Vital Speeches 38:142-5 D 15 '71
Roots of lawlessness. H. S. Commager. por Sat R 54:17-19+ F 13 '71
Searching mind of men and property. T. L. Shaffer. il Todays Ed 60:25-7 N '71
Tools of our tools; dehumanization of American life; address. August 14, 1971. J. H. Adamson. Vital Speeches 37:720-3 S 15 '71
Toward a new reformation. I. H. Wilson. Cur 131:18-23 Jl '71
Unhappy Americans: who they are, what they want. il U S News 70:90-4+ Ap 19 '71
Without Marx or Jesus, by J. F. Revel. Review
    Commonweal 95:303-4 D 24 '71. V. C. Ferkiss
    Time 98:89 S 20 '71. M. Maddocks
World and U.S. problems; address, July 6, 1971. R. M. Nixon. Vital Speeches 37:611-15 Ag 1 '71; Excerpts. U S News 71:46-7 Ag 2 '71; Dept State Bul 65:93-7 Jl 26 '71
    See also
United States—Intellectual life
United States—Popular culture
United States—Social conditions

Anecdotes, facetiae, satire, etc.
United States of bananas. il Esquire 75:97-103 Ap '71

Climate
Abnormal weather pattern, portent for the winter? il U S News 71:80 N 22 '71
    See also subhead Climate under names of states, sections, etc. e.g. Florida—Climate

Coast guard
CB and the coast guard. R. Humphrey. il Pop Electr 35:42-4 S '71
Futile leap; would-be defector, Simas Kudirka. Sr Schol 97:5 Ja 11 '71

Boats
New use for SK-5. J. H. Super. il Sea Front 17:272-3 S '71

Coast guard auxiliary
Under the blue ensign. B. Woodward. See issues of Motor boating & sailing

Commerce
As I see it; interview. H. B. Scott. il por Forbes 108:43-4+ O 1 '71
Connally's blunt talk on trade and the dollar; excerpts from address, November 16, 1971. J. B. Connally, jr. por U S News 71:88-9 N 29 '71
Crisis in U.S. trade policy. C. F. Bergsten. bibliog f For Affairs 49:619-35 Jl '71
Economic warfare. New Repub 165:7 D 4 '71
Impact of American business on world affairs; address, April 7, 1971. J. Richardson, jr. Dept State Bul 64:608-12 My 10 '71
In a more competitive world, U.S. takes a tougher line; interview with P. G. Peterson. il U S News 71:31-7 Jl 12 '71
New American imperialism?
    Does the U.S. economy require it? S. M. Miller and others. Cur 125:42-50 Ja '71
    Logic of imperialism. H. Magdoff. Cur 125:51-63 Ja '71

Nixonomics spreads gloom among traders. il Bsns W p78-9+ N 20 '71
Our foreign economic crisis; address, February 22, 1971. W. C. Armstrong. Vital Speeches 37:327-31 Mr 15 '71
Our strange new hard line on trade. S. Rose. il Fortune 84:136-9+ N '71
President reaffirms proposals for trade legislation; text of letter. R. M. Nixon. Dept State Bul 64:29 Ja 4 '71
Protectionism in America; address, October 30, 1970. J. A. Greenwald. Dept State Bul 63:724-9 D 14 '70
Protectionism or free trade: a decision for our time; address, May 3, 1971. K. Rush. Dept State Bul 64:749-53 Je 7 '71
Rekindling the spirit of '76. H. Sidey. il por Life 71:4 Ag 13 '71
Report on trade agreements program transmitted to the Congress; message, December 30, 1970. R. M. Nixon. Dept State Bul 64:114-15 Ja 25 '71
Report on trade agreements program transmitted to the Congress; message, December 1, 1971. R. M. Nixon. Dept State Bul 65:714-15 D 20 '71
Trade battle is far from over. il Bsns W p44 O 23 '71
U.S. foreign trade: there's no need to panic; with editorial comment. S. Rose. il Fortune 84:105-6, 109-11+ Ag '71
U.S. searches for a realistic trade policy. il Bsns W p64-7+ Jl 3 '71
    See also
Export trade
Imports
Merchant marine—United States
Tariff—United States
United States—Industries
World trade week

Canada
Future of American investment; address, October 8, 1971. G. A. Regan. Vital Speeches 38:92-6 N 15 '71

China (People's Republic)
Air conditioners to zinc dust. il Newsweek 77:33 Je 21 '71
Doing business with China; address, November 1, 1971. L. C. McQuade. Vital Speeches 38:151-5 D 15 '71
Farm exports to China? L. Palmer. Farm J 95:28F O '71
First on the spot: AMA meeting on doing business with red China. New Yorker 47:47-8 N 13 '71
First trickle of Chinese wares. Bsns W p42-3 O 23 '71
For Peking; fertilizer, yes: jets, no. il U S News 70:14 Je 21'71
Little red order book. il Time 97:88+ Ap 26 '71
New regulations announced on trade with the People's Republic of China; Department announcement; with announcements by the departments of Treasury, Commerce, and Transportation. Dept State Bul 64:702-4 My 31 '71
President Nixon reduces controls on trade with mainland China; text of announcement, June 10, 1971; with General license list. Dept State Bul 64:815-17 Je 28 '71; Excerpts. Cur Hist 61:182 S '71
There's a certain sense of mystery; interview. A. Eckstein. il por U S News 70:19-20 My 10 '71
Trader as diplomat, prospects for U.S.-China relations; address, October 20, 1971. N. E. Halaby. Vital Speeches 38:145-8 D 15 '71
U.S. companies visit by proxy; Canton trade fair. Bsns W p44 D 4 '71
U.S. faces a reluctant dragon; with editorial comment. il Bsns W p 16-17, 94 Ap 24 '71
What U.S. industry hopes China will buy. il Bsns W p26-7 My 22 '71
Wings for China? il Forbes 108:25-6 S 15 '71
    See also
Imports

Communist countries
What can you do in a canoe? law against sales to citizens of Communist countries. D. Sanford. New Repub 164:17-18 My 29 '71
    See also
United States—Commerce—Europe, Eastern

Europe, Eastern
Ecopolitics. Forbes 108:52 Jl 15 '71
Western business in eastern Europe; address, December 29, 1970. P. H. Trezise. Dept State Bul 64:85-8 Ja 18 '71; Same with title East-west trade: U.S. self interest. Vital Speeches 37:313-15 Mr 1 '71

UNITED STATES—Commerce—*Continued*

Japan

As U.S. and Japan pull apart, can the breach be healed? il U S News 71:42-4 N 22 '71

Changing trade policy in Japan; address, November 1, 1971. N. Ochi. Vital Speeches 38: 102-5 D 1 '71

Costly trade victory over Japan. il Time 98:23 O 25 '71

Deal with Japan. il por Newsweek 78:101 N 22 '71

Doing business in Japan; address, October 19, 1971. D. L. Williams. Vital Speeches 38:76-80 N 15 '71

End of an economic era. America 125:139 S 11 '71

Into round three. Sr Schol 98:11 Mr 29 '71

Japan corners Alabama's coal. il Bsns W p45 My 15 '71

Japanese textile curbs may get a trial. il Bsns W p26 Mr 20 '71

Nixon v. Mills; showdown on trade policy. por Time 97:70-1 Mr 22 '71

Nixon's rebuff to Japan. Newsweek 77:79 Mr 22 '71

Now that U.S. has ended the honeymoon with Japan. il U S News 71:36-8 Ag 30 '71

One-way street. il Forbes 107:15-16 My 1 '71

Relentless breeze; stopover in Japan. il por Time 98:33 N 22 '71

Story behind the textile war with Japan. il U S News 71:47-50 O 11 '71

Turn of the screw. Newsweek 77:84+ Mr 29 '71

See also

Japan-California association

Joint United States-Japan committee on trade and economic affairs

Latin America

CIAP protests protectionism. Américas 23:44 Ja '71

U.S. to consult Latin Americans on effects of new economic policy, Department announcement, August 19, 1971, with text of letter to chairman of CIAP, C. A. Meyer. Dept State Bul 65:278 S 13 '71

U.S. trade policy and Latin America; statement, July 12, 1971. D. Szabo. Dept State Bul 65:239-46 Ag 30 '71

Rhodesia

Chrome-plated blunder. New Repub 165:7 N 27 '71

Russia

Big breakthrough in East-West trade; with editorial comment. il Bsns W p34-8, 126 Je 19 '71

Big deal in Russia. Newsweek 78:91 D 13 '71

Break for the bulldog. il Newsweek 78:68-9 Ag 23 '71

Bulldog and the bear; Mack deal. Newsweek 77:80 Je 28 '71

Can the U.S. do business with the Russians? il por Newsweek 78:85 N 29 '71

Cooking big deals with Russia. il Bsns W p28-9 D 4 '71

Cracks in the ice. Time 98:78 D 13 '71

Doing business with Russia; interview. M. H. Stans. il pors U S News 71:56-60+ D 20 '71

Kama truck project gets rolling; export license issued to Swindell-Dressler co. il Bsns W p32 Ag 14 '71

Mission to Moscow; visit of M. Stans. il por Time 98:26 D 6 '71

Picking up where Mack left off. il Bsns W p42-3 S 25 '71

Rules ease on trade with Russia. il Bsns W p94-6 Je 12 '71

Thaw in U.S.-Soviet trade? il U S News 71: 39 N 15 '71

Trade, corn and politics. Nation 213:550 N 29 '71

Trade talks aim at an open port policy. il Bsns W p50+ D 11 '71

Trade with the U.S. gains new vigor. il Bsns W p58+ N 13 '71

South Africa

Sweet bonus for apartheid; sugar quota issue. B. J. Oudes. Nation 212:719-21 Je 7 '71

Commerce, Department of

See also

United States—Business economics, Office of

United States—Economic development administration

United States—Foreign direct investments, Office of

United States—International commerce, Bureau of

United States—National industrial pollution control council

Commercial policy

See United States—Economic policy

Commercial treaties and agreements

Cotton textile agreement with Japan extended. Dept State Bul 64:125 Ja 25 '71

U.S. and Japan exchange notes on cotton textile arrangement. il Dept State Bul 65:119 Jl 26 '71

U.S. and U.S.S.R. sign agreements on Northeastern Pacific fisheries. Dept State Bul 64:460-1 Mr 29 '71

U.S. and Yugoslavia conclude cotton textile agreement. Dept State Bul 64:159 F 1 '71

United States and China extend cotton textile agreement. Dept State Bul 65:340 S 27 '71

United States and China sign cotton textile agreement. Dept State Bul 64:103 Ja 18 '71

United States and Colombia sign new cotton textile agreement. Dept State Bul 65:163 Ag 9 '71

United States and Czechoslovakia extend cotton textile agreement. Dept State Bul 64:679 My 24 '71

United States and Greece sign new cotton textile agreement. Dept State Bul 65:143 Ag 2 '71

United States and Hong Kong sign cotton textile agreement. Dept State Bul 64:72 Ja 11 '71

United States and Italy sign cotton textile agreement. Dept State Bul 64:125 Ja 25 '71

United States and Korea extend cotton textile agreement. Dept State Bul 64:219 F 15, 372 O 4 '71

United States and Malta extend cotton textile agreement. Dept State Bul 64:187 F 8 '71

United States and Romania sign cotton textile agreement. Dept State Bul 64:186 F 8 '71

United States and Singapore sign cotton textile agreement. Dept State Bul 64:218 F 15 '71

United States and Spain sign cotton textile agreement. Dept State Bul 64:71 Ja 11 '71

Commission on civil rights

Civil rights ombudsman. Nation 212:805 Je 28 '71

Civil rights report. J. Osborne. New Repub 164:8-9 My 22 '71

Report on the beast. Time 97:21-2 My 24 '71

Commission on financial structure and regulation

Another call to revamp the financial system. il Bsns W p40 D 25 '71

Bank, thrift unit overhaul urged; summary of report. U S News 72:52-3 Ja 3 '72

Commission on government procurement

Congress expected to extend life for commission on procurement. K. Johnsen. Aviation W 94:17 My 3 '71

Government book purchasing: a federal commission takes a look. S. Wagner. Pub W 199:40-2 Je 28 '71

Gov't book purchasing: procedural changes sought. S. Wagner. Pub W 200:30+ Jl 5 '71

Commission on obscenity and pornography

Coalition asks fair debate on national porno report; with editorial comment. Pub W 199:45, 48 F 1 '71

NCOP report. Queens case, debated at NYLA. il Library J 96:3796-7 N 15 '71

No evidence pornography causes crime; interview. W. C. Wilson. por U S News 70:74 Ja 25 '71; Reply. M. A. Hill. por U S News 70:78 F 22 '71

Pornography caper. H. L. Packer. bibliog f Commentary 51:72-7 F '71; Discussion. 52:30+ Jl '71

Report that shocked the Nation. C. H. Keating, Jr. Read Digest 98:37-41 Ja '71

Comptroller of currency, Office of

Banks and consumers. New Repub 165:12 Jl 17 '71

Congress

Bearding the beast; R. Nader to investigate the Congress. New Repub 165:9 N 27 '71

Congress today: what U.S. gets for $396,000,000. il U S News 70:17-19 Mr 22 '71

Congressional information processes for national policy. N. Beckman. bibliog f Ann Am Acad 394:84-99 Mr '71

Goldwater: Congress knew what it was doing on Vietnam; address, July 29, 1971. B. M. Goldwater. il por U S News 71:88-91 Ag 16 '71

UNITED STATES—Congress—*Continued*
Inefficient Congress? rebuttal from Capitol hill; interview. H. Boggs. por U S News 70: 80-1 Mr 22 '71
Is Congress up to it? G. W. Ball. Newsweek 77:43 My 24 '71
Oiling the machinery of Congress; interview, ed. by J. Mandelstam. por Sr Schol 98:12 Mr 1 '71
Size-up of President Nixon; interview. M. J. Mansfield. il pors U S News 71:56-61 D 6 '71
TRB from Washington; need for reform. New Repub 164:4 Ja 16 '71
10 most frequently asked questions about Congress. Sr Schol 98:2-3 Mr 1 '71
See also
Congressmen
Congresswomen
Legislation—United States
Lobbying
Negro congressmen
Presidents—United States—Relations with Congress

Committees
Congressional chairmen. il Todays Ed 60: 40-2 My '71
Congressional hearings: a trap for businessmen? A. Maier. il Duns 97:44-6+ Mr '71
Stirrings of major reform; seniority system. il Newsweek 77:19 Ja 25 '71
Third branch; conference committees. il Newsweek 78:21 D 20 '71

Joint committee on atomic energy
High energy physics: in-group talks funds, possible closeouts. D. Shapley. Science 173: 897-9 S 3 '71

Joint committee on the environment (proposed)
Joint irresolution. R. Gillette. Science 174: 930-1 N 26 '71
Responsibility of Congress. J. Lear. Sat R 54:49 F 6 '71

Joint committee to investigate the origins of the Vietnamese war (proposed)
Inquiry. New Repub 165:9 Jl 17 '71

Joint economic committee
Nixon men defend their optimisim. il Bsns W p22-3 F 13 '71

Pages
Face to face with a female Senate page; ed. by M. E. Kinsley. E. McConnell. por Seventeen 30:52 N '71
Girl turns page in Senate history; P. M. Desell. por Sr Schol 98:16 Mr 1 '71

Powers and duties
Rise of Congress in foreign policy-making. J. F. Manley. bibliog f il Ann Am Acad 397:60-70 S '71
Sharing responsibility for war. A. M. Bickel. New Repub 165:15-17 S 25 '71
War power. New Repub 164:9-10 Je 12 '71

Reorganization
Making Congress work; redistributing power on Capitol hill R. Nader. New Repub 165: 19-21 Ag 21 '71; Same. Cur 133:17-21 O '71
Reform in the 92nd Congress. il Sr Schol 98: 13 Mr 1 '71

Rules and practice
Stirrings of major reform. il Newsweek 77:19 Ja 25 '71
TRB from Washington; need for reform. New Repub 164:4 Ja 16 '71

Salaries
See Congressmen—Salaries, allowances, etc.

Voting
Congressional test flight; defeat of supersonic transport support. Nation 212:418-20 Ap 5 '71
How Congress voted on SST funding. il Aviation W 94:32-4 Ap 5 '71
No-shows; Margaret Chase Smith's amendment. Newsweek 79:13 Ja 3 '72
See also
United States—Congress—House—Voting
United States—Congress—Senate—Voting

91st Congress
Laws you may have missed. U S News 70: 77 Ja 18 '71
TRB from Washington. New Repub 164:10 Ja 2 '71

92d Congress
92d Congress at work. il Sr Schol 98:2-13 Mr 1 '71
Profile of the new Congress. il U S News 70:42-3 Ja 25 '71
See also
Nixon, R. M.—Relations with Congress

92d Congress—1st session
Albert has dashed the reformers' hopes. por Bsns W p32-3 D 11 '71
Child care veto; day-care plan. il Time 98: 8-9 D 20 '71
Coming battle between President and Congress. il pors Time 97:12-14+ F 1 '71
Congress. il Newsweek 77:21 F 8; 27-8 F 15; 23-4 Mr 1; 54+ Mr 8; 27 Je 7; 28-9 Je 14; 31-2 Je 28; 78:25 Jl 5; 35 Jl 12; 21 Jl 19; 16-17 Ag 2; 23 Ag 9; 16-17 Ag 16; 15-16 S 13; 40+ S 27; 22 O 11; 22 N 29; 15-16 D 27 '71; 79:13 Ja 3 '72
Congress. il Time 97:12 Ap 5 '71
Congress: a fight to the finish. il Time 98: 8-9 D 20 '71
Congress bones up on Nixon economics. il Bsns W p 14-15 S 4 '71
Congress is nicer than Nixon expected. Bsns W p 15-16 Jl 24 '71
Eyeball to eyeball, Congress blinked. il Time 98:11-12 D 13 '71
How Congress packs it in. il por Newsweek 78:20-1 D 20 '71
Month in Congress. Cong Digest 50:65-8, 97-8, 129, 161+ Mr-Je '71
Nixon and Congress, score card on '71 session. il U S News 71:16-18 D 27 '71
Slow pace in Congress: the reasons. il U S News 71:20-2 Ag 23 '71
Small step, big symbol; welfare backlash. il Time 98:10-11 D 27 '71
Sporting life. il Newsweek 78:21 D 6 '71

92d Congress—2d session
Big issues Congress faces in '72. il Nations Bsns 59:24-5 D '71
Outlook, '72; showdown in Congress. il U S News 72:24-5 Ja 10 '72

House
Eulogies and evasions; the Mississippi challenge. R. Sherrill. Nation 212:197-200 F 15 '71
Mississippi challenge. New Repub 164:7-8 Ja 16 '71
Road to power in Congress; campaign for majority leader. L. L. King. Harper 242: 39-42 +Je '71
Udall and O'Hara; candidates for majority leader. New Repub 164:7 Ja 16 '71
See also
Apportionment (election law)
Congressmen

House—Aging, Committee on (Proposed)
House names committee to study aging needs. T. Schuchat. Har Yrs 11:4 N '71

House—Appropriations, Committee on
Critical hearings on SST opened. Aviation W 94:182-3 Mr 8 '71
Critical voting nears for SST funding. D. C. Winston. Aviation W 94:26-8 Mr 15 '71

House—Banking and currency, Committee on
How Penn Central lost in Liechtenstein. Bsns W p41 Mr 13 '71

House—Committees
Close call; seniority system vote. por Newsweek 77:27-8 F 15 '71
Getting rid of the seniority system. N. C. Miller. Cur 126:26-8 F '71

House—Interior and insular affairs, Committee on
House at the crossroads. M. Frome. Field S 76:46+ My '71

House—Internal security, Committee on
How much longer? Nation 212:676-7 My 31 '71
Open letter to the Honorable Richard Ichord. J. Ciardi. Sat R 54:14-15+ My 15 '71
TRB from Washington. New Repub 165:4 N 13 '71
Thirty years of treason: excerpts from hearings before the House committee on un-American activities, 1938-1968, by E. Bentley. Review
    Atlan 228:122-6 D '71. J. Mitford
    Newsweek il 78:114+ D 6 '71. W. Clemons

UNITED STATES—*Continued*

Continental Congress

Business of the highest magnitude; or, Don't put off until tomorrow what you can ram through today. R. C. Alberts. il Am Heritage 22:48-53+ F '71

Copyright office

Barbara Ringer endorsed by former copyright chief. S. Wagner. Pub W 200:30 O 18 '71

Barbara Ringer wins round one in Copyright office fight. S. Wagner. Pub W 200:42 S 27 '71

Cary appointed register: action contested by Ringer. Library J 97:12+ Ja 1 '72

Carey is new copyright head; Ringer sues, charging bias. Pub W 200:29 S 6 '71

Cary renamed register of copyrights. S. Wagner. Pub W 200:29 N 8 '71

New Register of copyrights expected this year. S. Wagner. Pub W 199:35 Ja 18 '71

Race & sex bias are issues as Ringer takes LC to court. pors Library J 96:3262-3 O 15 '71

Cost of living council

CLC warms up to its job. Bsns W p 18 Ag 28 '71

Dividend raisers feel the chill. Bsns W p42-3 S 11 '71

Down to the details on Phase II plans. Bsns W p36 S 25 '71

How controls will be enforced; interview. D. Rumsfeld. il pors U S News 71:42-6 D 13 '71

New pay-price rules; how Phase 2 will work. il U S News 71:21-3 N 22 '71

Out of phase. J. Osborne. New Repub 165:11-13 O 23 '71

Phase 2 controls; with text of Nixon's address, October 7, 1971. il U S News 71:21-6+ O 18 '71

President makes a costly bargain. Bsns W p104 O 16 '71; Reply. P. M. Flanigan. p5 O 23 '71

Putting on the freeze; Cost of living council. il Time 98:7 Ag 30 '71

We don't want to be heavy-handed. il Newsweek 78:73-4 S 20 '71

Who the watchdogs will be watching. Bsns W p51 N 13 '71

Who's in charge of wage-price curbs; Cost of living council. U S News 71:18 Ag 30 '71

See also
United States—Health services industry. Committee on the
United States—Interest and dividends. Committee on
United States—Pay board
United States—Price commission

Council of economic advisers

CEA's foundation: faith and hope. Bsns W p 15 Ja 23 '71

Foggy forecast from the CEA. il Bsns W p 16-17 F 6 '71

Herb Stein's comfortable purgatory. por Time 98:25 D 6 '71

Herbert Stein: free marketer at the controls. por Bsns W p76 D 4 '71

Inflation alert: first step toward steel-pay showdown. U S News 70:91-2 Ap 26 '71

Inflation alert with a louder ring; with editorial comment. Bsns W p33. 124 Ap 17 '71

McCracken bows out. il por Newsweek 78:96 D 6 '71

Macro-economics for macro-policy. E. S. Flash, jr. bibliog f Ann Am Acad 394:46-56 Mr '71

Mixed signals from the coaches. Bsns W p20-1 My 22 '71

Moving up: the chief architect of Phase 2. il por U S News 71:62 D 6 '71

Nixon men defend their optimism. il Bsns W p22-3 F 13 '71

Unions spurn the inflation alert. il Bsns W p72-3 Ap 24 '71

United States in the international economy; excerpts from annual report. il Dept State Bul 64:264-78 Mr 1 '71

What Solomon will bring to the CEA. por Bsns W p 17 My 29 '71

Will the predictions pan out? R. Lekachman. Duns 97:9 Mr '71

Council on environmental quality

Cost of cleanliness. Sci Am 225:42 O '71

Official report on the cost of a cleaner environment; excerpts from report. U S News 71:51 Ag 23 '71

Price of cleaning up; annual report. il Newsweek 78:68-9 Ag 16 '71

State of the ecology. il Time 98:35 Ag 16 '71

Tax issue: refusal of tax exempt status for organizations engaged in efforts to protect or restore the environment. Liv Wildn 34:3 Aut '70

Uncle Sam's environment troika: CEQ, EPA and NOAA. G. Fishbein. il Nation Bsns 59:34-6 Ap '71

Urban wilderness; excerpt from report. il Sat R 54:52-5 S 4 '71

Vital step on land use. Time 97:54 F 8 '71

Without troubling of a star; interview; excerpts from Deena Clark's Moment with show. R. Train. Am For 77:42-3+ My '71

Council on international economic policy

Mr Peterson's assignment. Fortune 83:63-4 Mr '71

President Nixon establishes council on international economic policy; White House announcement, remarks, excerpts from news conference and text of President Nixon's memorandum. R. M. Nixon; G. Shultz; P. G. Peterson. Dept State Bul 64:167-72 F 8 '71

Courts

See Courts—United States

Cultural relations

Dilemma of cultural propaganda: let it be. A. Goodfriend. Ann Am Acad 398:104-12 N '71

U.S.A: countdown for IBY. S. Wagner. il Pub W 200:pt2 150-1 S 27 '71

See also
People-to-people program

Culture, Popular

See United States—Popular culture

Declaration of independence

Business of the highest magnitude; or, Don't put off until tomorrow what you can ram through today. R. C. Alberts. il Am Heritage 22:48-53+ F '71

Centennial celebrations, etc.
See United States—Centennial celebrations, etc.

Defense, Department of

Aftermath of Lockheed's defeat. Bsns W p22-3 F 6 '71

C-5A: postmortem on a mess. B. Rice. Look 35:80-1 My 18 '71

DOD to coordinate laser-weapon efforts. P. J. Klass. Aviation W 95:24 N 8 '71

Laird plans Pentagon management changes. Aviation W 94:17 Mr 15 '71

McNamara and the Pentagon: limits of the management view. J. Walsh. Science 172: 1008-9+ Je 4 '71

Packard resigns; Deputy Secretary of defense. Time 98:8 D 20 '71

Pentagon propaganda machine, by J. W. Fulbright. Review
Bul Atom Sci 27:43-8 Ap '71. H. I. Schiller

Political pro who runs Defense: M. R. Laird. J. Duscha. il pors N Y Times Mag p 18-19+ Je 13 '71

Project bosses get more power. il por Bsns W p96+ Mr 20 '71

Tighter bridle on defense R&D. Bsns W p58+ O 16 '71

Toward a military welfare state? N. Cousins. Sat R 54:26-7 Mr 27 '71

U.S. strategic superiority has ended. Read Digest 99:89-93 Jl '71

You can't run wars with a computer. il Bsns W p 122 Je 5 '71

Advanced research projects agency
Counterinsurgency's proving ground; Project AGILE in Thailand. M. T. Klare. il Nation 212:527-31 Ap 26 '71

NSF may pick up ARPA's interdisciplinary laboratories. G. B. Lubkin. il Phys Today 24:61-2 F '71

Appropriations and expenditures
Conferees clear $21.3-billion defense bill. D. C. Winston. Aviation W 95:22 N 15 '71

Congress nears accord on DOD funding. D. C. Winston. Aviation W 95:17 N 1 '71

Congress votes conferees' figure of $70.52 billion for defense. D. C. Winston. Aviation W 95:18 D 20 '71

DOD funding bill clears House; Senate to act after Thanksgiving. Aviation W 95:16 N 22 '71

DOD funding bill faces conferees. D. C. Winston. Aviation W 95:14 N 29 '71

UNITED STATES—Defense, Department of—
Appropriations and expenditures—*Continued*
Defense cut bid threatens B-1 bomber. D.
C. Winston. Aviation W 94:16-17 My 10 '71
Defense debate. R. Hotz. Aviation W 94:9
My 3 '71
Defense dept. makes a timely purchase. il
Bsns W p27 Ag 14 '71
Draft bill shows DOD funding in Senate.
Aviation W 95:21 S 20 '71
Employment effects of reduced defense spend-
ing; with tables. R. P. Oliver. bibliog Mo
Labor R 94:3-11 D '71
Extraneous proposals may slow defense pro-
curement conference. D. C. Winston. Avia-
tion W 95:20 O 11 '71
Mansfield aide discusses amendment impact;
interview. by G. B. Lubkin. C. Ferris.
il por Phys Today 24:61-2 S '71
Military-industrial complexities. C. Wolf, jr.
Bul Atom Sci 27:19-22 F '71
Military maneuvers; reply. E. B. Staats. New
Repub 164:35 F 6 '71
Mission-oriented R&D. R. W. Nichols. bib-
liog Science 172:29-37 Ap 2 '71
New strategy, new threats, the fiscal 1972
military budget; with glossary. R. L. Tam-
men. il Bul Atom Sci 27:42-4 My '71
No one is in charge; Joint economic sub-
committee hearings on foreign aid funds.
Newsweek 77:16-17 Ja 18 '71
Occupational impact of defense expenditures;
with tables. R. Dempsey and D. Schmude.
Mo Labor R 94:12-15 D '71
Pentagon power. New Repub 164:7-8 F 6
'71
Pentagon will drop to second place by 1974;
comparison with Department of health, ed-
ucation and welfare. il U S News 70:36 My
17 '71
Reader's guide to the warfare state. D.
Shearer. bibliog Ramp Mag 9:55-9 Je '71
Reports & comment: Washington. E. B.
Drew. Atlan 227:8+ Ap '71
Senate committee restores F-14 funding.
Aviation W 95:22 Ag 9 '71
Senate unit hits soaring costs in reporting
DOD authorization. D. C. Winston. Avia-
tion W 95:22-3 S 13 '71
$3-billion cut expected in Defense requests.
D. C. Winston. Aviation W 94:16-17 Ap 19
'71
U.S. strategy beyond Vietnam; interview. M.
R. Laird. il por U S News 70:27-30+ My 17
'71
Upturn in defense buying seen by FY '73.
Aviation W 95:10 D 27 '71
See also
United States—Armed forces—Appropriations
and expenditures

Procurement

Cleaning up the marketplace. R. Hotz. Avia-
tion W 95:9 O 11 '71
DOD asks $67.5 million to fund prototype
effort; with editorial comment. C. Brown-
low. Aviation W 95:11, 17-18 S 27 '71
DOD urged to find cost overrun causes. K.
Johnsen. il Aviation W 94:21-2 Mr 29 '71
How much is enough? by A. C. Enthoven and
K. W. Smith. Review
Bsns W il p6-7 Ja 30 '71. H. Chesire
New Repub 164:26-8 F 20 '71. P. Passell
and L. Ross
Packard acts to bolster defense industry.
C. Brownlow. Aviation W 95:18-19 O 11
'71
Packard plan adopted by DOD to fund ad-
vances in technology. C. Brownlow. Avia-
tion W 95:15-16 Ag 2 '71
Profit puzzle in procurement; GAO study. il
Bsns W p44+ Mr 6 '71
Tighter rein on financing. il Bsns W p78-9
Ja 23 '71
Using the trick that built U-2s; crash team
R&D approach. Bsns W p 130 My 15 '71
Why prototyping is making a comeback. il
Bsns W p 102-3 Ag 14 '71

Public affairs, Office of

Pentagon propaganda machine. by J. W. Fulbright. Review
New Repub 164:28-9 Ja 23 '71. T. Hoopes

Public relations

Congressional pandora; Rep Staggers' in-
vestigation of The selling of the Penta-
gon. Nation 212:581 My 10 '71
Happy ending (maybe) of The selling of the
Pentagon. R. Sherrill. il N Y Times Mag
p25-7+ My 16 '71
Selling of the Selling of the Pentagon. R. J.
Irvine. Nat R 23:855-7+ Ag 10 '71
Unselling of The selling of the Pentagon.
F. W. Friendly. Harper 242:30-3+ Je '71

Systems analysis, Office of

How much is enough, by A. C. Enthoven
and K. W. Smith. Review
Nation 212:629-30 My 17 '71. R. F. Kaufman

Defense intelligence agency

Church and Defense; Catholic personnel of
DIA graduate school. Nation 213:261 S 27 '71

Defenses

Adequate defense posture; Soviet superiority;
address, December 4, 1970. B. M. Gold-
water. Vital Speeches 37:230-2 F 1 '71
Arms race hasn't stopped. H. Sidey. il Life
71:4 O 15 '71
Defense crisis. F. S. Meyer. Nat R 23:372 Ap
6 '71
For the defense: Melvin R. Laird. C. J. V.
Murphy. por Read Digest 99:49-53 Ag '71
Meaning of latest shift in U.S. defense. il U S
News 70:23-5 Mr 22 '71
Our four-star military mess; with editorial
comment. G. P. Hunt. il Life 70:3, 50-2+ Je
18 '71
Realistic deterrence; address, April 12, 1971.
G. S. Brown. Vital Speeches 37:514-16 Je
15 '71
State of flux marks U.S. defense posture. C.
Brownlow. il Aviation W 94:21-6 Mr 8 '71
Things old, things new. Time 97:14 Mr 22 '71
Toward a new definition of national security.
I. J. Winn. Bul Atom Sci 27:35-7 Mr '71
U.S. national security policy and the Indian
Ocean area; statement, July 28, 1971. R. I.
Spiers. Dept State Bul 65:199-203 Ag 23 '71
U.S. superiority has ended; summary of
statement by Citizens' panel on defense.
il U S News 70:49-50+ Ap 5 '71
What next in Indo-China; interview. T.
H. Moorer. il por U S News 70:44-8 Ap 5
'71
Who watches the watchman? J. Burnham.
Nat R 23:1105 O 8 '71
Wolf at the Pentagon door. R. L. Tammen.
New Repub 164:13-14 Mr 20 '71
See also
Atomic warfare—Defenses
Guided missiles
Guided missiles—Defenses
North American air defense command
United States—Air force
United States—Armed forces
United States—Army
United States—Defense, Department of
United States—Navy

Description and travel

Best short vacations in mid-America. G.
Greer. il Bet Hom & Gard 49:99-103 Je '71
Discover America (cont) il Pop Sci 198:70-5+
My '71
Englishman in apple-pie land. R. Prestage.
Sat R 55:38+ Ja 1 '72
Excursions; here are family-tailored ideas
for vacation side trips. E. Welke. il Bet
Hom & Gard 49:138-41 Ap '71
Finding the good green earth, fresh air, and
adventure in America. S. Cuneo; D. Wag-
oner; A. M. Cunningham. il Mlle 72:244-6+
Ap '71
Go! To the happening places: travel U.S.A.
Harp Baz 104:57-60 My '71
How to see America and never leave home.
G. Helgeland. il Nat Wildlife 9:46-9 Ap '71
Make it a vacation in Indian crafts country.
M. Gough. House B 113:30-2 Je '71
Redbook guide to American Heritage trails
(cont) W. Hartley and E. Hartley. il Red-
book 136:87-94 Ap '71
Travel U.S.A; symposium. il Holiday 49:41-
55+ Ap '71

Diplomatic and consular service

Death in the code room; Equatorial Guinea.
por Newsweek 78:38-9 S 13 '71
Easy chair; a welcome to Vienna. J Fischer.
il Harper 243:14 O '71
International travel: consular operations;
address, February 16, 1971. B. M. Watson.
Vital Speeches 37:463-5 My 15 '71
Rush job. il por Newsweek 78:29 S 6 '71
Tally's triumph; T. Palmer wins sex dis-
crimination case. por Time 98:20 S 6 '71
U.S. protests Soviet violation of embassy
premises at Moscow; text of note. Dept
State Bul 64:509 Ap 12 '71
See also
Ambassadors
United States—State, Department of

Discovery and exploration
See America—Discovery and exploration

UNITED STATES—*Continued*

Draft resisters

See Military service, Compulsory—Draft resisters

Drug abuse prevention, Special action office for (proposed)

Drug abuse control: policy turns toward rehabilitation. J. Walsh. Science 173:32-4 Jl 2 '71

Trying to treat the white plague. il Sci N 99:433 Je 26 '71

War on drugs. il pors Newsweek 77:32+ Je 28 '71

Economic conditions

Balancing the books; national myth of progress. Commonweal 93:539-40 Mr 5 '71

Basis for progress: free & open markets; address, November 30, 1971. P. W. McCracken. Vital Speeches 38:137-9 D 15 '71

Bitchy society will be an inflationary society, and other responses to a questionnaire. E. L. Dale, jr. il N Y Times Mag p 18-19+ S 26 '71

Burns on business; recovery, but new dangers of inflation; excerpts from testimony, February 19, 1971. A. Burns. por U S News 70:55-7 Mr 1 '71

Cautious consumers, wary executives. il Time 97:76-7 Mr 15 '71

Cities where business is best; with tables. il U S News 71:76-9 S 27 '71

Cooling off inflation. Time 97:82 My 3 '71

Dollar under attack abroad; impact on U.S. il U S News 70:9-10 My 24 '71

Economic blues. il Time 98:9-10 Ag 16 '71

Economic game plan, thoughts from labor; address, October 4, 1971. L. Woodcock. Vital Speeches 38:73-6 N 15 '71

Economic growth and ecology: a biologist's view; with tables. B. Commoner. bibliog Mo Labor R 94:3-13 N '71

Economic growth and ecology: an economist's view. W. W. Heller. bibliog Mo Labor R 94:14-21 N '71

Economics annual 1971. il Sr Schol 98:9-21 Ap 5 '71

Economics in the news (cont) Sr Schol 97:9-14+ Ja 11; 18-19 Ja 18; 98:18 F 1; 16 Mr 22; 99:7-9 S 20; 11-13 O 11 '71

Economy. See issues of Dun's

Economy. See issues of Newsweek

Economy at midyear: a size-up by Arthur Burns; statement before the Joint economic committee, July 23, 1971. A. F. Burns. por U S News 71:49-52 Ag 9 '71

Economy: fair and warmer, so far. il Newsweek 77:71-2 Ap 26 '71

Economy: 1065 and all that. il Newsweek 77: 77 Mr 15 '71

Expert views the freeze and the future; interview, ed. by W. A. McWhirter. O. Eckstein. por Life 71:22-6 Ag 27 '71

First readings on the new game plan. M. Friedman. Newsweek 78:100 N 8 '71

Freeze: planning for thin ice. il Newsweek 78:83-4 S 13 '71

Hey, big spender. Newsweek 77:83-4 Mr 29 '71

House divided: self discipline & economic freedom; address, October 14, 1971. R. H. Larry. Vital Speeches 38:58-61 N 1 '71

How to buck up the U.S. economy. il Newsweek 79:35-6 Ja 3 '72

Inflation scores on the game plan. il Newsweek 78:59-60 Ag 16 '71

Labor and the economy in 1970. R. W. Fisher. bibliog il Mo Labor R 94:3-13 Ja '71

Labor month in review. See issues of Monthly labor review

Last readings on the old game plans. M. Friedman. il Newsweek 78:95 S 27 '71

Nowadays, all that glitters is the gold. il Life 71:6-7 D 31 '71

Phase II: the nagging uncertainty. Time 98:30 N 1 '71

Recovery starts with a low profile. il Bsns W p22-3 Mr 6 '71

Rekindling the spirit of '76. H. Sidey. il por Life 71:4 Ag 13 '71

Sizing up 1970. il Sr Schol 98:10-11 Ap 5 '71

Stirrings of spring in the economy. Fortune 83:33 My '71

Technician's perspective. J. W. Schulz. See issues of Forbes

That elusive spark of confidence. Fortune 84:17-18 Ag '71

U.S. economy in an age of uncertainty. il Fortune 83:72-7+ Ja; 80-5+ F; 92-5+ Mr; 68-71+ Ap; 162-7+ My; 96-9+ Je; 84:87-9+ Jl; 136-9+ Ag '71; Same abr. with title Era of new uncertainties. Cur 127:3-14 Mr '71

U.S. economy off the tracks. il Newsweek 78:15-16 Ag 9 '71

Uses of economic adversity; role of recession in calming of America. P. Vanderwicken. il Time 97:17 F 22 '71

Welfare reform; address, September 3, 1971. A. K. Davis. Vital Speeches 37:765-8 O 1 '71

Working conditions survey as a source of social indicators. N. Q. Herrick and R. P. Quinn. il Mo Labor R 94:15-24 Ap '71

See also

Business conditions

Conservation of resources

Consumption (economics)

Cost of living—United States

Labor and laboring classes—United States

Negroes—Economic conditions

Prices—United States

Unemployment—United States

United States—Business economics, Office of

United States—Industries

Wages—United States

Economic development administration

Domestic aid for rural U.S. G. R. Rosen. por Duns 97:62-3 Je '71

Economic history

Can anybody manage a free economy? il U S News 71:26-8 Ag 30 '71

Putting it into perspective: progress report of the U.S. economy, 1850-present; table. Sr Schol 98:12 Ap 5 '71

Unfree nonenterprisers; the permanent war to save free enterprise. F. Getlein. Chr Cent 88:461-5 Ap 14 '71

See also

Stock exchange—Crisis, October 1929

Economic opportunity, Office of

Angry young lawyers of OEO; Legal services program. L. Velie. Read Digest 98:193-4+ My '71

Biological tyranny; family planning projects in West Virginia. W. Hern. New Repub 164 15-17 F 27 '71

Governors and mayors view the poverty program. D. H. Haider. bibliog f Cur Hist 61:273-8+ N '71

Health care: what the poor people didn't get from Kentucky project; Floyd County project. R. J. Bazell. il Science 172:458-60 Ap 30 '71; Discussion. 173:191-2 Jl 16 '71

New exploitation: California rural legal assistance (CRLA) Nat R 23:68 Ja 26 '71

New homestead. il Time 99:10 Ja 17 '72

OEO hedges on Kentucky program. R. J. Bazell. Science 174:45 O 1 '71

Old-fashioned U.S. success story; P. V. Sanchez. il pors U S News 71:80 O 4 '71

Phony war on poverty in the Great society. R. M. Pious. bibliog f il Cur Hist 61:266-72 N '71

Public corporation for poverty lawyers; Legal services program. il Bsns W p52 My 15 '71

Showdown with Reagan; funding California rural legal assistance, inc. J. Osborne. New Repub 165:9-11 Jl 10 '71

Taking over the OEO; Governor Williams's attempt to take control of OEO programs. J. R. Hood. Nation 213:646-9 D 20 '71

See also

Voucher plan in education

Economic policy

Administration blockbuster; 90-day freeze, with editorial comment. Bsns W p21-30+, 96 Ag 21 '71

Administration takes on the Fed; with editorial comment. pors Bsns W p 18-19, 80 Jl 31 '71

After the disappointing rebound. il Fortune 83:17 Ap '71

After the freeze: what comes next. il U S News 71:15-16 S 27 '71

Alternative to Nixon's game plan; Democratic critics in Congress. U S News 70:66 Ap 12 '71

America is a growing country; address, May 22, 1971. F. Smith. Vital Speeches 37:534-7 Je 15 '71

Are the elephant and the donkey twins? Nat R 23:303 Mr 23 '71

As Nixon looks beyond the freeze; remarks, September 23, 1971. R. M. Nixon. il por U S News 71:77-9 O 4 '71

Assessing the new Nixonomics; press reactions. il Time 98:34 Ag 30 '71

Boost for growth, a slap at prices. il Bsns W p22-3 Ja 16 '71

Bottom line in a controlled economy. Fortune 84:17 N '71

Bright new outlook, some new questions. Fortune 84:17-18 S '71

UNITED STATES—Economic policy—*Cont.*

Business under the freeze: a top executive's appraisal; interview. T. V. Learson. il por U S News 71:36-9 S 13 '71

Can we afford tomorrow? J. R. Meyer; J. V. Lindsay. il Sat R 54:44-8 Ja 23 '71

Congress bones up on Nixon economics. il Bsns W p 14-15 S 4 '71

Connally's hard sell against inflation. il pors Bsns W p62-6 Jl 10 '71

Control of inflation and recession; address, April 1971, with questions and answers. F. W. Schiff. Ann Am Acad 396:90-104 Jl '71

Deceptive package. R. Nader. New Repub 165:15-17 S 4 '71

Dollar crisis and the developing countries. C. Elliott. Chr Cent 88:1520-2 D 29 '71

Down the primrose path. F. S. Meyer. Nat R 23:994 S 10 '71

Down to the details on Phase II plans. Bsns W p36 S 25 '71

Drastic plan to save the dollar. il Bsns W p21-2 Ag 21 '71

Economic game plan, thoughts from labor; address, October 4, 1971. L. Woodcock. Vital Speeches 38:73-6 N 15 '71

Economic policy on course, says top Nixon aide; excerpts from address, April 22, 1971. G. P. Shultz. por U S News 70:55-7 My 10 '71

Economist. G. Ace. Sat R 54:10 S 18 '71

Economy. See issues of Dun's

Economy at midyear; a size-up by Arthur Burns; statement before the Joint economic committee, July 23, 1971. A. F. Burns. por U S News 71:49-52 Ag 9 '71

Fresh strategy to win world markets. il Bsns W p 19-20 My 22 '71

From the freeze to Phase 2. Life 71:32 S 10 '71

Galbraith gives Nixon an A-minus; interview. J. K. Galbraith. pors Bsns W p74-6 O 16 '71

Game plan: will it work? il Newsweek 78:19 Ag 9 '71

Great debate begins; Phase 2. Time 98:23 S 20 '71

How Nixon sizes up his prosperity plan now; excerpts from news conference, September 16, 1971. R. M. Nixon. por U S News 71:80-1 S 27 '71

How Nixon spells out his postfreeze program; address, October 7, 1971. R. M. Nixon. U S News 71:82-3 O 18 '71; Same with title Economic plan; Phase II. Vital Speeches 38: 2-4 O 15 '71; Same abr. with title Fighting inflation is everybody's business. Read Digest 99:77-80 D '71

I am now a Keynesian; President Nixon. Nation 212:99-100 Ja 25 '71

Incomes policy by any other name. Bsns W p 14-15 Ja 23 '71

Inflation policies and collective bargaining. L. Ulman. Mo Labor R 94:48-52 Ag '71

Jawbone hits steel. Newsweek 77:63-4 Ja 25 '71

Jobs, inflation: what Nixon's top economist expects; excerpts from statement before the Joint economic committee. July 8, 1971. P. W. McCracken. il por U S News 71:57-9 Jl 26 '71

Letter from Washington; Nixon administration. R. H. Rovere. New Yorker 46:85-90 Ja 23 '71

Letter from Washington; Nixon's new policy. R. H. Rovere. New Yorker 47:157-8 O 23 '71

Living with the Nixon measures. Fortune 84: 49-51 O '71

Matter of models. Nation 213:99 Ag 16 '71

Meeting our responsibilities abroad; excerpt from remarks, November 9, 1971. R. M. Nixon. Dept State Bul 65:613-14 N 29 '71

Mills: cut taxes, curb wages, prices; excerpts from address, July 16, 1971. W. D. Mills. por U S News 71:73 Jl 26 '71

Mr Nixon's new economic policy. America 125:109-10 S 4 '71

Mixing politics and economics. C. H. Madden. por Nations Bsns 59:40+ Mr '71

Money explodes. M. Friedman. Newsweek 77:81 My 3 '71

Moral rules and economic quarterbacks. B. L. Masse. America 125:475 D 4 '71

NEP of a different color. Nat R 23:1043 S 24 '71

Need for increased public investment. M. J. Shapp. Ann Am Acad 397:40-7 S '71

New assault on U.S. problems. U S News 70: 13 F 1 '71

New economic policy. Fortune 84:65-6 S '71

New economic program; western Europe; address, September 14, 1971. M. Mansfield. Vital Speeches 38:4-7 O 15 '71

New Nixonomics. New Repub 165:7-8 S 4 '71

New prosperity: hard sell begins. il por U S News 71:21 S 20 '71

New U.S. campaign. por Newsweek 77:63 My 31 '71

Newest Nixon looks Galbraithian. il por Bsns W p37 S 25 '71

1971: the year of the consumer? with reports by M. Friedman; P. A. Samuelson; H. C. Wallich. il Newsweek 77:55-6+ F 15 '71

1971 will be a good year; TV interview, January 4, 1971. R. M. Nixon. il por U S News 70:62-9 Ja 18 '71; Same abr. with title Conversation with the President, January 1971. Dept State Bul 64:105-10 Ja 25 '71

Nixon economics. P. A. Samuelson. Newsweek 78:70 Ag 2 '71

Nixon in the pulpit: economic evangelism; summary of address, September 6, 1971. R. M. Nixon. il por Time 98:11-12 S 20 '71

Nixon sets a new course. il U S News 70: 11-12 Ja 18 '71

Nixon steps up the pace. U S News 70:15 Mr 8 '71

Nixon tries the treatment. il pors Newsweek 78:18-19 S 20 '71

Nixonomics. D. Dowd. il Ramp Mag 10:13-16 N '71

Nixonomics: how the game plan went wrong. R. Evans, jr. and R. D. Novak. Atlan 228:66-76+ Jl '71

Nixon's dilemma': a boxed-in economy. il Time 98:62 Jl 5 '71

Nixon's economic bombshell; with editorial comment and interview with O. Eckstein. H. Sidey. il por Life 71:4, 20-5 Ag 27 '71

Nixon's four-point do-nothing plan. il pors Newsweek 78:67 Jl 12 '71

Nixon's frozen, floating dollar. il Newsweek 78:10-21 Ag 30 '71

Nixon's game plan. Sr Schol 97:18-19 Ja 18 '71

Nixon's grand design for recovery. il por Time 98:4-14+ Ag 30 '71

Nixon's N.E.P. Chr Cent 88:992 Ag 25 '71

Nixon's N.E.P. & the Constitution. A. S. Miller. il Nation 213:293-6 O 4 '71

Nixon's new chief spokesman sizes up the economy; excerpts from news conference, June 29, 1971. J. B. Connally. por U S News 71:76-8 Jl 12 '71

Nixon's new economic policy: hints of a resurgence for R&D. N. Wade. Science 173:794-6 Ag 27 '71

Nixon's new economic policy; with interview with P. W. McCracken. il U S News 71:15-24+ Ag 30 '71

Nixon's new keep-them-guessing policy. Time 97:70 F 1 '71

Nixon's power play. R. B. Du Boff. Commonweal 95:86-7 O 22 '71

Nixon's quadriad gets back in step. il Bsns W p88+ My 8 '71

Nixon's stunning turnabout; televised address, August 15, 1971. por Newsweek 78: 14-15 Ag 23 '71

Nixon's target: inflation, not unemployment. il Bsns W p 14-15 Jl 3 '71

Non-answer to Nixonomics. M. J. Ulmer. New Repub 165:19-21 D 11 '71; Discussion. 165:31 D 25 '71; 166:30-1 Ja 1 '72

Out in the freeze. Commonweal 94:443-4 S 3 '71

Overriding issue. Time 98:18-19 Jl 26 '71

Phase II. Time 98:24+ O 4 '71

Phase two. H. C. Wallich. Newsweek 78:69 N 1 '71

Phase 2 controls; with text of Nixon's address, October 7, 1971. il U S News 71:21-6+ O 18 '71

Phase II looks like a long, long freeze. il Bsns W p20 O 9 '71

Pitfalls ahead for Phase 2. il U S News 71: 23-6 O 25 '71

Policy of self-fulfilling prophecy. il Time 97: 76-7 F 8 '71

Policy without a plan. Fortune 84:68 O '71

President Nixon briefs editors and publishers from 12 southern states; excerpts from remarks, May 25, 1971. R. M. Nixon. Dept State Bul 64:757-63 Je 14 '71

President's economic policy in his own words; address, August 15, 1971. R. M. Nixon. por U S News 71:62-5 Ag 30 '71; Same with title Challenge of peace. Dept State Bul 65:253-6 S 6 '71; Same with title New economic policy. Vital Speeches 37:674-6 S 1 '71

Pressure forces a policy shift. Bsns W p19-20 Ag 7 '71

Price stability and full employment too? G. L. Bach. il Harvard Bsns R 49:68-78 S '71

Puzzle for U.S.: growth vs. social progress; address. D. P. Eastburn. il por U S News 71:64-6 Jl 12 '71

UNITED STATES—Economic policy—*Cont.*
Questions and answers. P. A. Samuelson.
 Newsweek 78:72 O 4 '71
Recovery, controls, taxes, trade war; inter-
 view. J. Connally. il pors U S News 70:52-7
 Ap 12 '71
Richard Nixon's NEP. Nat R 23:969 S 10 '71
Scorecard on the freeze. Time 98:13 S 13 '71
Shooting at the bluebirds of happiness. il
 pors Time 98:17-18 Ag 9 '71
Showdown fight over inflation. il Time 98:
 64-70 Ag 16 '71
State of the Union; address, January 22, 1971.
 R. M. Nixon. il pors U S News 70:66-70
 F 1 '71; Same. Vital Speeches 37:226-30 F 1
 '71; Excerpts. Cur Hist 60:171-4 Mr '71
Steady as you go. M. Friedman. Newsweek
 78:62 Jl 26 '71
Storm clouds do not change the course;
 with editorial comment. il Bsns W p23-4,
 98 Je 12 '71
Strong economy and a strong national de-
 fense; address, August 19, 1971. R. M.
 Nixon. Dept State Bul 65:273-6 S 13 '71
Struggle to stay competitive. Time 97:79-80
 My 31 '71
TRB from Washington: a policy of passiv-
 ity. New Repub 165:4 Jl 10 '71
TRB from Washington; a primer from
 Washington. New Repub 165:6 S 4 '71
TRB from Washington: leave it to papa. New
 Repub 165:6 O 30 '71
Technology stimulation plan seen. W. H.
 Gregory. Aviation W 95:16-18 Ag 23 '71
Teeth in Phase two. il por Newsweek 78:
 84+ S 27 '71
Thunderclap politics. Nation 213:164 S 6 '71
Tough, risky U.S. trade offensive. il News-
 week 77:81 Je 7 '71
Training a pleasant demon. R. Lekachman. il
 Sat R 54:15-18 Mr 6 '71
Turnabout. J. Osborne. New Repub 165:11-13
 S 4 '71
Two years of Nixonomics. New Repub 164:
 11-12 Ja 2 '71
U.S. agencies seek concepts to spur R&D.
 W. H. Gregory. il Aviation W 95:14-16 Ag
 30 '71
Uncertainties of Phase two. America 125:
 306-7 O 23 '71
United States in the international economy;
 excerpts from annual report of the Coun-
 cil of economic advisors. il Dept State Bul
 64:264-78 Mr 1 '71
Vehement policy of no change. il Time 98:
 54-5 Jl 12 '71
Verdict of Newsweek's three economists. M.
 Friedman; P. A. Samuelson; H. C. Wallich.
 Newsweek 78:22-3 Ag 30 '71
Waning game plan. R. Lekachman. Duns 98:
 13 Ag '71
Washington report; export and trade impli-
 cations; interviews, ed. by F. Bailey, jr.
 C. Palmby; D. Paarlberg. il por Suc Farm
 69:7+ O '71
Watch out: prosperity is just around the
 corner (again) D. Dowd. il Ramp Mag 9:34-
 9 Mr '71
Watershed of the American economy. D.
 Deitch. Nation 213:198-202 S 13 '71; Reply
 with rejoinder. J. Yuccas. 213:386+ O 25
 '71
What ails the dollar. G. Freeman. il For-
 tune 83:47-8+ Je '71
What follows the freeze. il Bsns W p 16-17
 S 4 '71
What to do about the economy. E. J. Mc-
 Carthy. New Repub 165:16-18 Ag 7 '71
What U.S. needs to do now: the President's
 size-up; message to Congress, September
 9, 1971. R. M. Nixon. il por U S News 71:
 31-4 S 20 '71; Same with title President
 Nixon asks congressional support for new
 economic program. Dept State Bul 65:362-6
 O 4 '71; Same with title Wage price freeze.
 Vital Speeches 37:706-9 S 15 '71
World and U.S. problems; address, July 6,
 1971. R. M. Nixon. Vital Speeches 37:
 611-15 Ag 1 '71; Excerpts. U S News 71:
 46-7 Ag 2 '71; Dept State Bul 65:93-7 Jl
 26 '71

See also
Budget—United States
Campaign issues
Government spending policy
Price regulation by government—United
 States
Tariff—United States
Taxation—United States
United States—Appropriations and ex-
 penditures
United States—Council of economic advisers
United States—Council on international eco-
 nomic policy
United States—Fiscal policy
Wage-price policy

Anecdotes, facetiae, satire, etc.
Willmoore Wheeler rides again. W. F. Rickenbacker. Nat R 23:1181 O 22 '71

Economic relations
Behind Nixon's 5 meetings with allies. il
 U S News 71:19-21 D 13 '71
International economic policy scene; address,
 November 15, 1971. N. Samuels. Dept State
 Bul 65:669-74 D 13 '71
International trade issues for the seventies;
 statement, May 20, 1971. N. Samuels. Dept
 State Bul 64:807-12 Je 21 '71
Internationalism or isolationism. il Time 98:
 18 Ag 30 '71
Lest we forget friends. America 126:3-4 Ja
 8 '72
New economics and U.S. foreign policy. C. F.
 Bergsten. For Affairs 50:199-222 Ja '72
Nixon's NEP and the developing world. P. J.
 Henriot. il America 125:448-50 N 27 '71
President affirms U.S. cooperation in world
 economic affairs; remarks, September 29,
 1971. R. M. Nixon. Dept State Bul 65:450-
 2 O 25 '71
U.S. foreign economic policy: problems and
 prospects; excerpts from address, February
 25, 1971. N. Samuels. Dept State Bul 64:327-
 8 Mr 15 '71
U.S. taking a hard line on dollar, trade. il
 U S News 71:70-1 S 27 '71
See also
Economic assistance, American
United States—Commerce

Algeria
Algeria's drive to be top Arab power. F.
 C. Painton. il U S News 71:46-8 Jl 12 '71

Canada
Canada: coping with a twitchy elephant.
 Time 98:26 O 18 '71
Exporting political trouble. W. P. Bundy.
 Newsweek 78:39 S 13 '71
Is Canada turning away from U.S? il U S
 News 71:66-7 Jl 19 '71
New strains between Canada and U.S. il
 U S News 71:58-60 O 25 '71
See also
Joint United States-Canadian committee on
 trade and economic affairs

Chile
Chile is not Cuba, or is it? R. Kuttner.
 Commonweal 94:405-7 Ag 6 '71

Egypt
U.S. and Egypt agree in principle on debt
 payment, October 2, 1971. Dept State Bul
 65:405 O 18 '71

Europe, Western
New economic program: western Europe
 address, September 14, 1971. M. Mansfield.
 Vital Speeches 38:4-7 O 15 '71
Striking out the wage gap. il Time 98:77-
 D 13 '71

Far East
Challenge of constructive cooperation in east
 Asia; address, October 4, 1971. M. Green.
 Dept State Bul 65:459-62 O 25 '71

Japan
Japan and the U.S., a call for harmony.
 K. Uemura. por Nations Bsns 59:28-31
 Ag '71
Japan woos the U.S. il Newsweek 78:25-6
 Jl 19 '71
Japanese speak their mind; views of five top
 Japanese businessmen. il Bsns W p61+
 Ag 28 '71
Japan's foothold in Alaska. il U S News 71:
 36 S 27 '71
Pearl Harbor in reverse. F. Gibney. il Harper
 244:49-51+ Ja '72
Trends in United States-Japan relations; ad-
 dress, October 18, 1971. U. A. Johnson. Dept
 State Bul 65:513-17 N 8 '71
U.S. and Japan on collision course; meeting
 in Washington; with interview with E.
 Sato. il Newsweek 78:37-9 S 20 '71
United States and Japan: common interests
 and common problems; address, June 30,
 1971. W. P. Rogers. Dept State Bul 65:69-
 73 Jl 19 '71
We have our protectionists too. por Forbes
 108:78 O 15 '71
See also
Joint United States-Japan committee on
 trade and economic affairs
United States—Commerce—Japan

Latin America
Colonialism lives in South America. E. K.
 Culhane. il America 125:67-9 Ag 7 '71; Re-
 ply. A. Shea. 125:301 O 23 '71

UNITED STATES—Economic relations—Latin
America—*Continued*
Cutting off aid to expropriators. R. M. Hall.
jr. New Repub 165:15-17 O 2 '71
Latin America slams the door. P. Lernoux.
Nation 213:271-5 S 27 '71
Marxist label pasted on wrong bottle; study
of inter-American development efforts by
Organization of American states. B. L.
Masse. America 125:137 S 11 '71
Neocolonialism in Latin America; excerpt
from Revolution next door. G. MacEoin.
bibliog Chr Cent 88:685-97 Je 2 '71
New economic policy hurts Latin America.
Américas 23:45 O '71
Son of dollar diplomacy. J. Barnes. il News-
week 77:44-5 My 3 '71
U.S. calls for joint solutions to western
hemisphere problems; statement, April 29,
1971. J. J. Jova. Dept State Bul 64:783-6
Je 14 '71
U.S. policy toward a changing Latin Amer-
ica; adaptation of address, January 29,
1971. S. Weintraub. Dept State Bul 64:550-4
Ap 26 '71
U.S. policy toward Latin America; where
we stand today; address, October 25, 1971.
C. A. Meyer. Dept State Bul 65:559-64 N 15
'71. Save Vital Speeches 38:109-12 D 1 '72
What drives Latin Americans left? S. Rod-
man. il Nat R 23:1348-50+ D 3 '71
See also
Inter-American economic and social council

Yugoslavia
U.S. and Yugoslavia conclude economic dis-
cussions; text of joint communique. Dept
State Bul 64:601 My 10 '71

Education, Department of
(proposed)
Nation needs a secretary of education; symposium. il Todays Ed 60:12-15 Ap '71

Education, Office of
Career education. S. P. Marland, jr. il To-
days Ed 60:22-5 O '71
Editor's choice; USOE commissioner's con-
ference. Am Lib 2:357 Ap '71
Education special revenue sharing proposal;
Commissioner's conferences held by USOE.
G. Krettek and E. D. Cooke. Am Lib 2:
380-1 Ap '71
Environmental education cannot win; with
editorial comment. S. P. Marland, jr. il
Am Ed 7:inside cover. 6-10 My '71
Guide to OE-administered programs, fiscal
year 1972. il Am Ed 7:38-44 Ag '71
Loving, learning, and little ones; OE model
day care center. R. K. Preston and E. B.
Roth. il Am Ed 7:9-11 Je '71
Marland on career education; questions and
answers. S. P Marland. jr. pors Am Ed
7:25-8 N '71
New U.S. commissioner of education. por
Sch & Soc 99:205 Ap '71
See also
United States—National institute of educa-
tion (proposed)

Appropriations and expenditures
Congress approves final USOE funds. S.
Wagner. Pub W 200:52-3+ Jl 12 '71
Education forces prepare for Senate fight to
increase USOE appropriations. S. Wagner.
Pub W 199:30-1 Ap 19 '71
Good and bad news for publishing in Nixon
budget. S. Wagner. Pub W 199:58 F 8 '71
Highlights of OE's 1972 budget. J. R. Ot-
tina. il Am Ed 7:36-7 Ag '71
Senate vote on USOE monies delayed. S.
Wagner. Pub W 199:36 Je 7 '71

*Libraries and educational
technology, Bureau of*
Toward a federal strategy in library training; address, January 15, 1971. B. E. Lamkin. pors Am Lib 2:496-9 My '71

*Libraries and educational technology,
Bureau of—Library programs,
Division of*
OE library agency aide heads resurgent union.
Library J 96:578 F 15 '71

Library programs, Division of
See United States—Education, Office of
—Libraries and educational technology,
Bureau of—Library programs, Division of

Emergency preparedness, Office of
OEP: disaster is its specialty. Newsweek 78:
14-15 Ag 30 '71
OEP puts the chill on. il Newsweek 78:47
S 6 '71
Taking out the chill. il Time 98:8-9 Ag
30 '71

Environmental policy
See Environmental policy

Environmental protection agency
Air resource management and regional planning. E. J. Croke and J. J. Roberts. il Bul
Atom Sci 27:8-12 F '71
Autos, emission reports and the public. Sci N
99:280 Ap 24 '71
Beginning of the new American revolution;
address, April 1971, with questions and
answers. W. D. Ruckelshaus. Ann Am Acad
396:13-24 Jl '71
Decision on 2,4,5-T: leaked reports compel
regulatory responsibility. N. Wade. Science
173:610-12+ Ag 13 '71; Discussion. 174:545-7
N 5 '71
EPA drops the other shoe: federal water
quality standards. P. Smyth. Motor B & S
127:2+ Je '71
EPA moves on refuse act. C. Holden. Science
173:901 S 3 '71
Environment repair: the U.S. army engineers' new assignment. J. Lear. il Sat R 54:
47-52 My 1 '71
Environmental protection agency: chaos or
creative tension? R. Gillette. Science 173:
703-7 Ag 20 '71
Introducing William Ruckelshaus, who? J.
Shepherd. il pors Look 35:20-2 My 4 '71
Ionizing-radiation standards for population
exposure; adaptation of address, July 1971.
J. A. Lieberman. il Phys Today 24:32-8 N
'71
Lead in the air: industry weight on Academy
panel challenged. R. Gillette. Science 174:
800-2 N 19 '71
Letter from Washington:
Environmental protection agency: teeth-
ing troubles. H. R. Vohra. Bul Atom
Sci 27:30-1 Ap '71
Man in the eye of the storm; interview, ed.
by J. Edgerton. W. D. Ruckelshaus. il por
Nat Wildlife 9:28-31 Ag '71
Meaningful boost. Sci N 99:96 F 6 '71
Mr Clean; excerpts from address, January 12,
1971. W. D. Ruckelshaus. por Am For 77:7+
Jl '71
New target in the antipollution drive; sewage
treatment, with editorial comment. il Bsns
W p 104-5+. 112 Ja 16 '71
Nixon's pollution fighter faces a backlash.
il pors Bsns W p54-5+ Ag 21 '71
Nixon's second round. Time 97:67 F 22 '71
Official exhaust sniffer; Ann Arbor, Mich,
laboratory to test emissions of motor ve-
hicles and engines. S. Lindsay. Sat R 54:
94-5 D 4 '71
Probing advisory committees: EPA shows
independence. Sci N 100:260 O 16 '71
Puckelshaus' first year. il por Time 99:53-4
Ja 3 '72
Uncle Sam's environment troika: CEQ, EPA
and NOAA. G. Fishbein. il Nations Bsns
59:34-6 Ap '71
Washington report. P. A. Douglas. Yachting
129:90 Mr '71
What about it. water-pollution engineers?
Am City 86:8 O '71
What future for the auto? il Sci N 99:329-30
My 15 '71

Water quality office
Clear prose, strained tone. Sci N 99:262 Ap
17 '71; Discussion. 99:364 My 29 '71
Nader group sees water wasteland. C. Holden. Science 172:455 Ap 30 '71

Environmental science services
administration
See United States—National oceanic and
atmospheric administration

Equal employment opportunity
commission
Bias in jobs: tighter rules in sight. il U S
News 71:90-1 S 27 '71
Equal opportunities. New Repub 165:10 O 30
'71
Let's be fair about equal employment. P. H.
Dominick. por Nations Bsns 59:40-2 O '71
This month's feature: Congress & EEOC
enforcement power. Cong Digest 50:257-88
N '71
Utilities land on the hiring carpet. il Bsns W
p23 N 20 '71

Executive advisory bodies
See Executive advisory bodies

Executive departments
Government agencies are failing our people;
address, June 29, 1971. D. F. Linowes. Vital
Speeches 37:759-62 O 1 '71

UNITED STATES—Executive department—
Continued
President and his experts. G. M. Lyons. bibliog f Ann Am Acad 394:36-45 Mr '71
President's bold plan to streamline government. I. Ross. Read Digest 99:61-5 Jl '71
U.S. agencies seek concepts to spur R&D. W. H. Gregory. il Aviation W 95:14-16 Ag 30 '71
Who's who in the White House. il Sr Schol 99:12 O 4 '71
Why the federal government needs restructuring. R. Ash. Fortune 83:64+ Mr '71
See also
United States—President's advisory council on executive organization

Anecdotes, facetiae, satire, etc.
Federal mule administration. J. K. Murray. il Nations Bsns 59:49 O '71

Public relations
Publishing on the Potomac: the selling of the government. S. Wagner. Pub W 200:28-9 Ag 9 '71

Executive office of the president
Courage and hesitation, by A. Drury and F. Maroon. Review
  Bsns W il p 10+ N 27 '71. B. Agnew
Inside the White House 1971; excerpts from Courage and hesitation. A. Drury. il pors Look 35:42+ O 19 '71
Nixon tightrope. J. M. Burns. il pors Life 70:48B-48D+ Ap 2 '71
Notes and comment; anti-democratic trends in the government. New Yorker 47:21-2 Jl 24 '71
Who's in charge here H. Sidey. il Life 71:4 D 10 '71
Who's who at White House now: shifts in the Nixon team. il U S News 70:16-18 Je 28 '71

Expenditures
See United States—Appropriations and expenditures

Farm labor and rural manpower service
Skunk is a skunk. Nation 212:740 Je 14 '71

Farmers home administration
Scandal of rural housing. C. L. Cochran. Arch Forum 134:52-5 Mr '71

Federal aviation administration
Airport, airways funding status remains clouded. J. P. Woolsey. Aviation W 94:135-7+ Mr 8 '71
FAA plans to lower positive control base. Aviation W 95:19 Jl 19 '71
FAA readies inspection program, standards of safety for airports. Aviation W 94:24 Ja 25 '71
FAA to seek bids on new automated radar. Aviation W 94:20 My 10 '71
FAA will issue crash locator beacon specification. Aviation W 94:43 Ja 25 '71
FAA would broaden use of flight plans. Aviation W 95:24 N 1 '71
FAR sight. A. Trammell. il Flying 89:104 S; 38+ O; 17 N '71; 90:101 Ja '72
New pilot qualifications proposed. Aviation W 94:46 Ap 5 '71
Operators, FAA seek jet noise solution. J. P. Woolsey. il Aviation W 95:50-1+ S 20 '71
Rules, economics hold keys to future growth. C. E. Schneider. il Aviation W 95:39+ S 20 '71
Shift of ATC design from FAA urged. P. J. Klass. Aviation W 94:20-1 Mr 15 '71
Transcribed weather broadcast service. il Weatherwise 24:236 O '71
Was the Wichita state crash avoidable? C. S. Wren. il Look 35:73-6 Mr 9 '71

Appropriations and expenditures
FAA operations get user fees. Aviation W 94:17 F 1 '71
FAA spurs R&D to curtail costs. P. J. Klass. il Aviation W 94:72-4 My 10 '71

Flight service stations
How to put more service in flight service stations. R. L. Collins. il Flying 88:S1-8 Ap '71

Federal bureau of investigation
After Hoover, who? a deluge of prospects. il Newsweek 77:31 My 10 '71
Atrocious judgment. Nation 212:131-2 F 1 '71
Boggs file. Newsweek 77:29 My 3 '71
Bugging Hoover. Time 97:17-18 Ap 26 '71
Bugging J. Edgar Hoover. por Time 97:15-16 Ap 19 '71

Crack in Hoover's fortress; conference at Woodrow Wilson school of Princeton university. A. Schardt. Nation 213:526-30 N 22 '71
Enemy within: the FBI's forgotten past. J. Ridgeway. Ramp Mag 10:4-7 Jl '71
FBI and its critics. America 125:388 N 13 '71
FBI inspection; proposal for investigation by a select Senate committee. New Repub 164:9-11 My 29 '71
FBI story; removal of documents from Pennsylvania offices by Citizens' commission to investigate the FBI. New Repub 164:5-7 Ap 10; 9-10 My 1 '71
FBI talk. W. F. Buckley, jr. Nat R 23:556 My 18 '71
FBI today:
  Case for effective control. H. H. Wilson. Nation 212:169-72 F 8 '71; Same. Cur 128:53-8 Ap '71
  Heresy of John F. Shaw: a purloined letter; with editorial comment. J. F. Shaw. Nation 212:172-7 F 8 '71
FBI's Hoover: what fight is all about. il por U S News 70:89 Ap 19 '71
File on J. Edgar Hoover. il pors Time 98:14-16 O 25 '71
Fingerprints; case of Dale B. Menard and distribution of files by the Identification division. S. J. Ungar. New Repub 164:20-1 Je 12 '71
G-man under fire; with report by T. Wicker. il pors Life 70:39-45 Ap 9 '71
Heat on Hoover? Sr Schol 98:17 My 10 '71
Hoover's FBI: time for a change? il pors Newsweek 77:28-32+ My 10 '71
Hoover's woes. por Newsweek 77:39 Ap 12 '71
Internal security of the U.S. depends upon the F.B.I. D. Lawrence. U S News 70:112 Ap 19 '71
No more fingerprints; ruling by G. A. Gesell. New Repub 165:8 Jl 3 '71
Notes and comment. New Yorker 47:29-30 My 8 '71
Of Hoover and Clark. por Time 97:16-17 My 3 '71
PBS, NET and the FBI. il Newsweek 78:127 O 18 '71
Presumption of guilt; maintenance and distribution of mistaken arrest records. T. R. Reid, 3d. New Repub 164:15-16 Ja 16 '71
Public justice v. J. Edgar Hoover. W. F. Buckley, jr. Nat R 23:1322 N '19 '71
Purloined letters. Newsweek 77:21-2 Ap 5 '71
Real conspiracy; use of informers by the FBI in political cases. Nation 212:101 Ja 25 '71
Ripping off the FBI; theft of documents dealing with surveillance of radical black student groups. por Time 97:15 Ap 5 '71
Sovereign FBI. Nation 212:514-15 Ap 26 '71
Spotlight on the FBI. Nation 213:386-7 O 25 '71
Watch out, Uncle Sam is angry; arrest of the Camden 28. P. Tracy. Commonweal 94:472 S 17 '71
What's bugging Boggs; electronic tabs on Capitol hill. por Newsweek 77:35 Ap 19 '71
Who dug for dirt on Earth day? FBI spying at last year's Earth day celebration. il Newsweek 77:23-4+ Ap 26 '71
Who's retiring? il por Newsweek 79:19 Ja 10 '72

Federal communications commission
Battle shapes up; question of ownership and operation of a domestic communications satellite system network. Sci N 99:195-6 Mr 20 '71
Bird watching; proceedings regarding establishment of domestic satellite services. R. L. Shavon. Sat R 54:57 Ap 17 '71
Cable revisions. R. L. Shayon. Sat R 54:14 D 11 '71
Cable vs. satellite in an FCC showdown. Bsns W p29-30 Je 12 '71
Captive medium: TV & the First amendment; address. November 23, 1970. B. Monroe. Vital Speeches 37:267-70 F 15 '71
Chickens and foxes; cases involving secrecy of program records of broadcasters whose license renewals are challenged by citizen groups. R. L. Shayon. Sat R 54:73 O 16 '71
Collision course; U.S. court of appeals reverses 1970 policy statement. R. L. Shayon. Sat R 54:38 Ag 7 '71
Controversial time; challenge to new rulings. R. L. Shayon. Sat R 54:12 N 20 '71
Great Scissors debate. R. L. Shayon. Sat R 54:68 D 4 '71
Local stations try filling prime time. il Bsns W p 100 S 11 '71
Pact that cuts little ice for CATV. Bsns W p78-9 N 27 '71

UNITED STATES—Federal communications commission—*Continued*
Phone company papers: a peek at the books. J. C. Goulden. il Nation 214:37-41 Ja 10 '72
Ruling the rule-makers; CATV issue. R. L. Shayon. Sat R 54:16 Je 19 '71
Should the FCC reward stations that do a good job? granting of licenses. M. Cohn. il Sat R 54:45-7 Ag 14 '71
Tanks but no tanks; fairness doctrine and Chevron's claims. T. Asher. New Repub 164:17-19 Je 26 '71
Two bites of the apple. R. L. Shayon. New Repub 165:22+ D 11 '71
Very cold turkey; banning of lyrics referring to illegal drugs. R. L. Shayon. Sat R 54:22 My 1 '71
What boundaries for federal censorship? banning pro-drug lyrics. R. H. Smith. Pub W 199:39 My 3 '71
White House office recommends approving all U.S. sat com bids Aviation W 95:20 N 8 '71
Who rules the microwaves? il Newsweek 77:56 Mr 22 '71
Who will make TV's new rules? il Newsweek 77:76-7 My 31 '71
Word from our censor; lyrics that advocate the use of drugs. New Repub 164:9-10 Mr 27 '71
See also
Television laws and regulations

Federal convention, 1787
See United States—Constitutional convention, 1787

Federal deposit insurance corporation
See Federal deposit insurance corporation

Federal housing administration
FHA housing used to fleece poor; 235-program suspended. P. S. Templin. America 124:83 Ja 30 '71
Fight on fraud in FHA programs. Bsns W p39 S 25 '71
Let George Romney play King Canute: FHA-VA mortgages. Nat R 23:848+ Ag 10 '71
Mr Secretary: please reconsider; letter to George Romney. T. M. Hesburgh. America 124:238-9 Mr 6 '71
Sometimes Uncle Sam helps pay the mortgage. Changing T 25:44 S '71

Federal insurance administration
Crime coverage, federal style. Bsns W p28 Ja 16 '71

Federal mediation and conciliation service
FMCS and arbitration: problems and prospects. W. J. Kilberg. il Mo Labor R 94: 40-5 Ap '71

Federal power commission
FPC chief faces a grilling on gas. Bsns W p40+ Jl 17 '71
Gas price rule hits a maverick. Bsns W p20 Ap 3 '71
Trying to spark a rush for gas. il Bsns W p60 My 1 '71

Federal reserve board
Administration takes on the Fed; with editorial comment. pors Bsns W p 18-19, 80 Jl 31 '71
Arthur the independent. il por Time 97:70 Mr 1 '71
Big money question. C. Morgello. il Newsweek 77:80 Je 28 '71
Changes at Federal reserve under Arthur Burns. il por U S News 71:60-3 Ag 23 '71
Checks that come back fast; Fed's check-clearing system. il Bsns W p72+ N 27 '71
Fear of inflation rules the markets. il Bsns W p37-8 Jl 17 '71
Fed acts cautiously on one-bank issue. Bsns W p20 Ja 30 '71
Fed gets a businessman. por Bsns W p31 Ja 1 '72
Fed says it can't do more; with editorial comment. Bsns W p23-4, 112 Mr 6 '71
Fed widens its portfolio. Bsns W p40 S 25 '71
Growing fight over easy money. il U S News 70:35-6 Mr 15 '71
Growth rate bedevils the Fed. il Bsns W p25 Je 12 '71
High marks for the Fed's freshman boss. il por Bsns W p38-9 Ja 30 '71
How far will the Fed go? Duns 93:116 Je '69
Inflation, threat of another round. il U S News 70:13-15 Je 28 '71
Irresponsible monetary policy. M. Friedman. il Newsweek 79:57 Ja 10 '72

Long and short of the Fed's problem. il Bsns W p26-7 Mr 20 '71
Nixon's recovery plan: will it work? il U S News 70:20-1 F 15 '71
Now the Fed can work more freely. il Bsns W p51 Ag 28 '71
Practical politician at the Fed. L. Malkin. il por Fortune 83:148-51+ My '71
Prime dilemma for the bankers; with editorial comment. il Bsns W p34, 126 Je 19 '71
Surprising turns in Operation Twist. Bsns W p32 My 1 '71
U.S. move to keep dollars safe at home. il Bsns W p25 Ja 16 '71

Federal trade commission
Admen burn over baker's bow to FTC. Bsns W p25-6 Jl 10 '71
Advertising claims to get closer scrutiny. U S News 70:53 Je 21 '71
Ally for admen against the FTC. Bsns W p39 Je 19 '71
Another consumer drive: taming the bill collector. il U S News 70:88-90 Mr 8 '71
Biggest sweepstakes; complaint against the Digest. il Newsweek 77:61 Ja 18 '71
Burden of proof. Newsweek 77:72+ Je 21 '71
Closer and cleaner? Newsweek 78:58 S 6 '71
Consumer credit and shoddy goods. U S News 71:59 O 4 '71
Door-to-door sales: industry proposal better. R. W. Frase. Pub W 199:18-19 My 3 '71
Drive to protect the buyer. il U S News 70:20-1 Ja 18 '71
FTC gets tougher on misleading ads. Bsns W p35 D 11 '71
FTC is staring at fuel companies. Bsns W p25 My 22 '71
FTC means business; recent actions. L. Sloane. Sat R 64:69 S 11 '71
FTC postpones hearing on door-to-door sales. Pub W 199:46 F 1 '71
FTC says book ads have free speech guarantees. S. Wagner. Pub W 200:29-30 Jl 26 '71
FTC takes new tack on door-to-door book sales. S. Wagner. Pub W 200.29 Jl 26 '71
FTC zooms in on better buys. il Bsns W p20-1 F 20 '71
He wants to lengthen antitrust's reach; supply space concept. por Bsns W p38+ My 22 '71
How Kennecott got hooked with Catch-22. R. Loving, jr il Fortune 84:98-101+ S '71
Justice dusts off a sharp weapon; criminal contempt actions. Bsns W p30 O 9 '71
More consumer action by the FTC; interview. M. W. Kirkpatrick. pors Nations Bsns 59: 38-40 Ja '71
Promoting self-policing; actions to root out deceptive ads. Time 97:81-2 Je 14 '71
Reform at the FTC. J. Osborne. New Repub 165:13-15 O 2; 10-11 O 16 '71
Shutting the gates on area franchises. Bsns W p22 Ja 23 '71
Tell it like it is; automakers ordered to produce documentation for advertising claims. Newsweek 78:63 Jl 26 '71

Fiscal policy
Applied Nixonomics. M. J. Ulmer. New Repub 164:15-18 Ap 24 '71
It's wait and see on fiscal stimulus. Bsns W p30 Mr 27 '71
What Mr Burns really said; testimony before Joint congressional economic committee. America 124:223 Mr 6 '71
See also
United States—Monetary policy

Fish and wildlife service
Can all the king's men put fish and wildlife together again? Audubon 73:114 Mr '71
Little sturm und drang at Hunting creek. J. Sax. il Esquire 75:84-8+ F '71
Poisoning of the West; predator control programs. J. Olsen. il Sports Illus 34:80-4+ Mr 8; 36-40+ Mr 15; 34-6+ Mr 22 '71

Food and drug administration
Chemicals we eat, by M. A. Benarde. Review
Consumer Bul 54:4+ S '71. B. T. Hunter
Drug efficacy study: FDA yields on fixed combinations. R. J. Bazell. Science 172: 1013-15 Je 4 '71; Discussion. 174:227-9 O 15 '71
FDA as activist. Time 99:67 Ja 17 '72
FDA: guidelines chiseled in stone; letter. R. L. Dean; reply. J. Freud and L. W. Preston. bibliog Science 171:334-5 Ja 29 '71
FDA science activities get mixed review. Sci N 99:383 Je 5 '71

UNITED STATES—Food and drug administration—*Continued*

FDA seems about to abandon its opposition to truthful labeling of factory-made foods; fat ingredients. il Consumer Bul 54:24-6 Ag '71

FDA versus scientology. Chr Today 15:21 Je 4 '71

FDA wants to widen its watchdogging. il Bsns W p 19 Jl 24 '71

Food and drug administration: is protecting lives the priority? R. J. Bazell. Science 172: 41-3 Ap 2 '71; Reply with rejoinder. C. C. Edwards. 173:379 Jl 30 '71

Hexachlorophene: FDA temporizes on brain-damaging chemical. N. Wade. Science 174: 805-7 N 19 '71

Hospital pharmacy-industry cooperation; case for closer ties; address, December 10, 1970. C. J. Stetler. Vital Speeches 37:232-5 F 1 '71

How safe is the food you buy? Good H 173: 155-7 Jl '71

More drugs to think twice about. Consumer Rep 36:180-1 Mr '71

Some medicines you may want to avoid. Consumer Rep 36:114-17 F '71

Technology gap in health: it has to be closed; address, June, 1971. J. L. Pettis. Vital Speeches 37:693-6 S 1 '71

Ugly truths about today's beauty aids. E. Kiester, jr. il Todays Health 49:16-20+ Je '71; Reply. J. B. Jerome. 49:70-1 S '71

Washington's diet for food companies; nutritional labeling. il Bsns W p28 Mr 20 '71

What are the facts about food additives? A. Q. Maisel. Read Digest 98:81-5 My '71

Will the FDA get the lead out? J. A. Page. Commonweal 95:246-7 D 10 '71

You and the big vitamin battle. J. M. Flagler. il Look 35:34-6+ Je 1 '71

Veterinary medicine, Bureau of

What you must do to keep your feed additives; interview, ed. by J. A. Rohlf. C. D. Van Houweling. il por Farm J 95:22-3+ Je '71

Foreign claims and settlement commission

They've never lost a decision. W. M. Ringle. il Nations Bsns 59:62-4 Je '71

Foreign direct investments, Office of

Capital is something that doesn't love a wall. S. Rose. il Fortune 83:100-3+ F '71

Foreign economic policy

See United States—Economic relations

Foreign opinion

As others see us; comp. by N. G. Balint. See issues of Saturday review

Of many things; how other peoples react to the U.S.A? D. R. Campion. America 124: inside cover F 13 '71

Outlook, '72: how world sees U.S. now. il U S News 72:16-18 Ja 10 '72

What is the American talent for living? Seven candid opinions. B. Russell. House & Gard 139:46-7+ F '71

Arab

As Arabs see it; with editorial comment. J. P. O'Kane. il America 124:62-3, 67-8 Ja 23 '71

British

Letter from Europe. A. Burgess. Am Scholar 40:514+ Sun '71

European

Are U.S. and Europe nearing a showdown? J. Fromm. il U S News 70:68-72 My 3 '71

Vietnam and western Europe; official positions of Great Britain, France and West Germany. S. Hoffmann. New Repub 164:18-23 Ja 30 '71

Viewed from abroad. H. H. Biel. il Forbes 108:94-5 N 1; 101-2 N 15 '71

Russian

Know thy enemy. Z. Brzezinski. Newsweek 78:40 Ag 30 '71

Per Angela ad astra: reactions to cases of Angela Davis and Simonas Kudirka. Nat R 23:67-8 Ja 26 '71

Swedish

Anti-Americanism in Sweden: some of the bad blood is gone. il U S News 70:93 My 10 '71

Turkish

Welcome that wore thin. il Time 97:22 Mr 1 '71

Vietnamese

U.S. as scapegoat. il Time 98:22-3 Jl 12 '71

Foreign population

See also
Cubans in the United States
Immigration and emigration—United States
Japanese in the United States

Foreign relations

After neo-isolationism, what? L. P. Bloomfield. Bul Atom Sci 27:9-13 Ap '71

Alliance politics. by R. E. Neustadt. Review New Yorker 47:85-7 Je 19 '71. J. Kraft

Assistant Secretary Green and Assistant Secretary Trezise interviewed for Japanese national television; February 26, 1971. M. Green; P. H. Trezise. Dept State Bul 64: 449-54 Mr 29 '71

Candidates answer Senior's queries: most important issue facing U.S. today? il Sr Schol 99:10-11 N 1 '71

Changing U.S. role in the world; address February 25, 1971. R. M. Nixon. il U S News 70:49-52 Mr 8 '71; Same with title Redefinition of the United States role in the world. Dept State Bul 64:305-10 Mr 15 '71; Excerpt. Cur Hist 61:357-8+ D '71

Chauvinism in the marketplace. G. W. Ball. Newsweek 78:45 N 29 '71

China, Mideast, Berlin: Rogers states U.S. policy; excerpts from address, October 5, 1971. W. P. Rogers. il por U S News 71: 104-6 O 18 '71

Community of the developed nations. Z. Brzezinski. Newsweek 77:40 F 1 '71

Dean Acheson, RIP. Nat R 23:1219-20 N 5 '71

Death of doctrine. W. P. Bundy. por Newsweek 77:44 F 15 '71

Diplomatic notes. L. H. Gelb and M. H. Halperin. il Harper 243:28-30+ N '71

Down the primrose path. F. S. Meyer. Nat R 23:994 S 10 '71

Dozens of Vietnams. J. Burnham. Nat R 23: 1050 S 24 '71

Enemy, by F. Greene. Review New Repub 164:35 My 29 '71. J. Gilbert

For a new policy balance. J. V. Lindsay. For Affairs 50:1-14 O '71

Foreign policy. Mansfield's rebellion. il por Newsweek 77:18-19 My 24 '71

From LBJ: some warnings about today's America; address, November 15, 1971. L. B. Johnson. il por U S News 71:92-3 N 29 '71

Game of nations. R. Barnet. il Harper 243: 53-9 N '71

Getting along with our friends too. il Life 71:42 D 10 '71

How not to look backward. G. W. Ball. por Newsweek 77:45 Mr 22 '71

How politicians in Congress weaken American foreign policy. D. Lawrence. U S News 71:96 N 1 '71

How real is neo-isolationism? Time essay. J. L. Steele. Time 97:24-5 My 31 '71

In search of Kissinger. J Kraft. por Harper 242:54-61 Ja '71

In the name of security; letter. L. G. Wolf. Nation 213:162+ S 6 '71

India-Pakistan war. A. J. Goldberg. New Repub 165:7-9 D 18 '71

International outlook. See issues of Business week

International roundup. Commonweal 94:275-6 My 28 '71

Is America going isolationist? Size-up by key senators; interviews. pors U S News 70:24-31 Je 28 '71

Is it safe to trust Washington? Newsweek 78:25 S 13 '71

Isolationism? F. S. Meyer. Nat R 23:1356 D 3 '71

Joys and sorrows of empire. J. Burnham. Nat R 23:749 Jl 13 '71

L.B.J. reconsidered E. V. Rostow. por Esquire 75:118-19+ Ap '71

Letter from Washington (cont) R. H. Rovere. New Yorker 47:155-7 O 23; 157-61 N 13; 82+ D 18 '71

Looking forward to the harvest; Nixon's future. H. Sidey. Life 70:8 Je 25 '71

Meet the President. Nation 212:386 Mr 29 '71

Meeting our responsibilities abroad; excerpt from remarks, November 9, 1971. R. M. Nixon. Dept State Bul 65:613-14 N 29 '71

Myth of neo-isolationism. Commonweal 94: 51-2 Mr 26 '71

New economics and U.S. foreign policy. C. F. Bergsten. For Affairs 50:199-222 Ja '72

UNITED STATES—Foreign relations—*Cont.*

Bibliography
Congressional documents relating to foreign policy. See issues of Department of state bulletin

History
Franklin Roosevelt as world leader. R. Dallek. bibliog f Am Hist R 76:1503-13 D '71
History as she is re-writ. G. W. Ball. Newsweek 78:64 O 18 '71
Misuse of power. H. S. Commager. New Repub 164:17-21 Ap 17 '71
Pungent memories from Mr Acheson; excerpts from interview, ed. by K. Harris. D. G. Acheson. il pors Life 71:51-2+ Jl 23 '71
Vantage point, by L. B. Johnson. Review
Sat R il pors 54:37-8+ N 6 '71. J. K. Galbraith

Africa
African issues at the U.N: the United States position; address, September 21, 1971. D. D. Newsom. Vital Speeches 38:14-17 O 15 '71
United States role in Africa. W. A. E. Skurnik. Cur Hist 60:129-35+ Mr '71

Africa, North
North Africa: lessons from the past and future directions; address, November 18, 1971. D. D. Newsom. Dept State Bul 65:677-83 D 13 '71
U.S. and North Africa: lessons from the past and future directions; address, November 18, 1971. D. D. Newsom. Vital Speeches 38:162-6 Ja 1 '72

Africa, Southern
Africa and America: the seventies; address, March, 1971 S. Khama. Vital Speeches 37:679-83 S 1 '71
Assistant Secretary Newsom reports to Congress on his visit to southern Africa; statement, December 3, 1970. D. D. Newsom. Dept State Bul 64:27-9 Ja 4 '71
Look at African issues at the United Nations; address, September 21, 1971. D. D. Newsom. Dept State Bul 65:373-8 O 11 '71
United States options in southern Africa; address, December 8, 1970. D. D. Newsom. Dept State Bul 64:80-4 Ja 18 '71
United States role in Africa. W. A. E. Skurnik. Cur Hist 60:129-35+ Mr '71

Arab states
As Arabs see it; with editorial comment. J. P. O'Kane. il America 124:62-3, 67-8 Ja 23 '71
Quiet revolution. Time 97:23 Mr 8 '71

Asia
Anticlimax on China. Chr Cent 88:967 Ag 18 '71
Asia feels the Nixon shock. H. Sidey. Life 71:4 S 17 '71
Asian triangle. W. P. Bundy. Newsweek 78:49 D 6 '71
Contradictions. C. Oglesby. Ramp Mag 10:28-9+ O; 24+ N '71
Despite Red China thaw, crucial tests for Nixon. il por U S News 71:15-17 Jl 26 '71
Eyes turned east. America 126:2-3 Ja 8 '72
Five major blunders by the U.S. in Asia. C. Bowles. il por Sat R 54:28-31 N 6 '71
Korea-U.S. relations: dilemmas and opportunities in the future of northeast Asia. C. H. Germany. Chr Cent 88:285-7 Mr 3 '71
See also
United States—Foreign relations—Asia, Southeastern

Asia, Southeastern
Collective security in Asia; address, August 31, 1971. J. S. McCain, jr Vital Speeches 37:749-57 O 1 '71
From Roots of involvement; excerpt. M. Kalb and E. Abel. Sat R 54:33 Mr 27 '71
Image and reality in Indochina. H. E. Salisbury. For Affairs 49:381-94 Ap '71
New tides in Southeast Asia. W. P. Bundy. For Affairs 49:187-200 Ja '71
Nixon doctrine in southeast Asia. R. Butwell. bibliog f Cur Hist 61:321-6+ D '71
President is the problem. T. Hoopes. New Repub 164:23-7 Mr 6 '71
President Nixon interviewed at newspaper editors meeting; excerpts, April 16, 1971. R. M. Nixon. Dept State Bul 64:561-7 My 3 '71
Quieter China in a calmer Asia. il Time 97:19-20 Ap 19 '71
Security assistance programs in east Asia; statement, May 4, 1971. M. Green. Dept State Bul 64:714-19 My 31 '71

Vietnam was it worth it? W. W. Rostow. Look 35:68+ S 21 '71
Who dies for what. N. Cousins. Sat R 54:20+ Ap 3 '71

Australia
Just a passing glance. il Time 98:34 N 15 '71
Prime Minister McMahon of Australia meets with President Nixon; remarks, November 2, 1971. R. M. Nixon. Dept State Bul 65:646 D 6 '71

Cambodia
Remember Cambodia? Nation 213:418-19 N 1 '71
See also
Military assistance, American—Cambodia

Canada
Canada switches targets. D. Coxe. Nat R 23:1177 O 22 '71
Foreign policy of the new Canada. I. L. Head. For Affairs 50:237-52 Ja '72
Is Kosygin damaging U.S.-Canada ties? il U S News 71:44-5 N 1 '71
See also
International joint commission (United States and Canada)

Chile
Chile going Marxist? What it means to the U.S. il por Sr Schol 98:8-15 F 1 '71
China and Chile. Nation 212:516 Ap 26 '71
Department comments on policy toward Chile; statement, October 15, 1971. C. A. Meyer. Dept State Bul 65:498-500 N 1 '71

China
Stilwell and the American experience in China, 1911-45, by B. W. Tuchman. Review
Nat R 23:432-3+ Ap 20 '71. D. Brudnoy
Nation 212:533+ Ap 26 '71. A. S. Whiting
New Repub 164:25-6 Mr 27 '71. J. K. Fairbank
New Yorker 47:141-2+ My 15 '71. N. Bliven
Sat R il por 54:25-7+ F 20 '71. O. E. Clubb

China (People's Republic)
After-dinner speech. il Newsweek 78:47-8 Jl 5 '71
After twenty years; recognition proposed by G. McGovern. Nation 212:164-5 F 8 '71
Authors & editors; concerning Nations in darkness by J. Stoessinger. D. N. Mount. por Pub W 200:15-17 S 20 '71
Barriers to a deal between U.S. and red China; interview. R. MacFarquhar. il por U S News 70:30-2 My 3 '71
Beckoning a new generation. R. Berger. Nation 213:361-7 O 18 '71
Changing great power alignments. J. C. Harsch. Cur 132:56-7 S '71
China and America. M. Oksenberg; J. A. Cohen; E. C. Ravenal. For Affairs 50:15-58 O '71
China and the bomb. B. T. Feld. Bul Atom Sci 27:inside cover, 31 S '71
China and the United States: beyond ping-pong. O. E. Clubb. bibliog f Cur Hist 61:129-34+ S '71
China gamble. J. Osborne. New Repub 165:11-12 Ag 7 '71
China policy: the balance sheet; reprint. Nat R 23:517-18 My 18 '71
China policy: time for a thaw. il Newsweek 77:33-4 F 8 '71
China question, once again. F. N. Trager. Nat R 23:585-6+ Je 1 '71
China's plans: an informed guess. O. E. Clubb. Nation 212:613-15 My 17 '71
Chou's shopping list. il por Newsweek 78:31 Ag 23 '71
Dealing with China; symposium. Cur 130:3-11 Je '71
Department lists steps taken on contacts with mainland China; announcement. Dept State Bul 64:510 Ap 12 '71
Drumfire on China. New Repub 165:11 S 25 '71
Go-betweens; question of China's membership in the United Nations. il Newsweek 77:43 My 10 '71
How Nixon signaled his China policy four years ago. R. M. Nixon. U S News 71:23 Ag 16 '71
How to live with both Peking and Taiwan. A. D. Barnett. por Life 71:17 Ag 13 '71
Leaf from Metternich. F. W. Neal. Nation 213:162-4 S 6 '71
Let a hundred flowers bloom. F. S. Meyer. Nat R 23:482 My 4 '71
Letter from Washington. R. H. Rovere. New Yorker 47:116-17 My 1 '71
Make way for the new China hands. J. Hohenberg. Sat R 55:41-2 Ja 8 '72

UNITED STATES—Foreign relations—China (People's Republic)—*Continued*
Needed: an Asian policy. G. W. Ball. Newsweek 78:45 Ag 16 '71
Negotiating with China. A. S. Whiting. New Repub 165:17-19 Jl 10 '71
Newthink. Nat R 23:741-2 Jl 13 '71
Nixon confuses Chou. Nation 212:771 Je 21 '71
Nixon: I will go to China. il pors Newsweek 78:16-21 Jl 26 '71
Old China hands. pors Time 98:14-15 Ag 2 '71
One China. New Repub 164:5-6 Ap 24 '71
Parrying a policy. por Time 97:23-4 Mr 29 '71
Parting of the bamboo curtain. America 124:447 My 1 '71
Path to Peking; with editorial comment. W. C. McWilliams. Commonweal 94:395, 397-8 Ag 6 '71
Peking's terms for closer ties with U.S. il U S News 71:22 Ag 9 '71
President Nixon eases restrictions on mainland China trade and travel; statement, April 14, 1971. R. M. Nixon. Dept State Bul 64:567 My 3 '71; Same with title Easing trade and travel restrictions in China. Cur Hist 61:178-9+ S '71
President Nixon interviewed at newspaper editors meeting; excerpts, April 16, 1971. R. M. Nixon. Dept State Bul 64:565-6 My 3 '71
President Nixon's China trip. W. J. Richardson. il America 125:84-7 Ag 21 '71
Question of timing. J. Burnham. Nat R 23:1401 D 17 '71
Red China, friend or foe? D. Lawrence. U S News 71:96 N 29 '71
Reopening the door to China. Life 70:52 Ap 30 '71
Shopping list for Peking. Time 97:26-7 Je 21 '71
Signals to Mao. J. Osborne. New Repub 164:15-16 My 1 '71
Sorry about that: resurrection of China experts. Nation 213:98-9 Ag 16 '71
Thirsting to get into China. H. Sidey. Life 70:4 Ap 30 '71
To and beyond the summits. New Repub 165:5-6 O 23 '71
Top challenge now: ending the missile race; excerpts from message to Congress, February 25, 1971. R. M. Nixon. il U S News 70:53-4 Mr 8 '71
Two-China policy? views of S. T. Agnew. Newsweek 77:28-9 My 3 '71
U.S. and China: new pages. Sr Schol 98:15-17 My 10 '71
U.S. and China: the thaw starts, how far will it go? il U S News 70:15-17 Ap 26 '71
We need a new Asia policy. il Life 70:44 Mr 12 '71
Welcome on the Great Wall, and another in the United Nations. il Life 71:42-4 D 31 '71
We've broken the ice with Communist China; excerpts from news conference, April 29, 1971. R. M. Nixon. por U S News 70:27 My 10 '71
Whose serve? J. Burnham. Nat R 23:469 My 4 '71
Why Nixon is relatively good. E. Snow. il por Time 98:13 Ag 2 '71
Why Washington is warming up to Communist China. U S News 70:13-14 Je 21 '71
World and U.S. problems; address, July 6, 1971. R. M. Nixon. Vital Speeches 37:611-15 Ag 1 '71; Excerpts. U S News 71:46-7 Ag 2 '71; Dept State Bul 65:93-7 Jl 26 '71
Yes to China must not be no to Japan. E. O. Reischauer. por Life 71:4 S 10 '71
See also
Kissinger, H. A.—Visits to China (People's Republic) 1971
Nixon, R. M.—Visit to China (People's Republic) 1972 (proposed)

China (People's Republic)—History
Making of America's China policy. D. Horowitz. il Ramp Mag 10:40-7 O '71

Colombia
Rhetoric or policy? W. F. Buckley, jr. Nat R 23:216 F 23 '71

Communist countries
See also
United States—Commerce—Communist countries

Cuba
Another Kennedy on Cuba. Chr Cent 88:1254 O 27 '71
Cuba: policy of malign neglect. R. O'Mara. Nation 213:524-6 N 22 '71
United States policy toward Cuba; statement, September 16, 1971. R. A. Hurwitch. Dept State Bul 65:391-5 O 11 '71

What goes on down there? Cubans seize Bahamas lines freighter. Nation 214:3-4 Ja 3 '72
Why not Cuba? Nation 213:98 Ag 16 '71

Ecuador
Great tuna war; Ecuador vs. United States. Time 97:24 F 8 '71
On the hook; fishing limit war. Newsweek 77:45 F 8 '71
Tuna war: much ado about what? il U S News 70:40 F 15 '71

Europe
Europe's answer to Connally. R. Beardwood. Time 98:19 D 13 '71
Our permanent interests in Europe; address, December 1, 1971; with questions and answers. W. P. Rogers. Dept State Bul 65:693-702 D 20 '71
United States, our NATO allies, and the Soviet Union in an era of changing foreign relations; address, February 19, 1971. U. A. Johnson. Dept State Bul 64:315-21 Mr 15 '71
Western European unity and inter-European reconciliation; address, July 19, 1971. J. N. Irwin. Dept State Bul 65:145-50 Ag 9 '71
See also
United States—State, Department of—Advisory council on European affairs

Europe, Eastern
President Nixon on European détente; excerpts from message to Congress, February 25, 1971. R. M. Nixon. Cur Hist 60:302 My '71
United States and east Europe. R. S. Whitcomb. bibliog f Cur Hist 60:263-8+ My '71

Europe, Western
Critical tasks facing western Europe and the United States in a period of change and transition; address, May 13, 1971. M. J. Hillenbrand. Dept State Bul 64:743-8 Je 7 '71
Europe between the superpowers. A. Hartley. For Affairs 49:271-82 Ja '71
New European defense community. F. Duchêne. For Affairs 50:69-82 O '71
Troops, trade and diplomacy. R. E. Hunter. il Nation 212:776-80 Je 21 '71

Far East
Letter from Washington; Nixon doctrine. R. H. Rovere. New Yorker 46:85-90 Ja 23 '71
Nixon doctrine: a progress report; address, January 19, 1971. M. Green. Dept State Bul 64:161-5 F 8 '71
Nixon doctrine; address, March 29, 1971. M. Mansfield. Vital Speeches 37:418-21 My 1 '71
Nixon doctrine and our Asian commitments. E. C. Ravenal. For Affairs 49:201-17 Ja '71
Packing the trunks for China. G. W. Ball. il Newsweek 78:53+ S 27 '71
Shanghai crisis of 1932; the basis of British policy. C. Thorne; reply. G. B. Ostrower. Am Hist R 76:1265-7 O '71

Germany (Federal Republic)
As Willy Brandt looks east: worries for U.S. and Germany. il por U S News 70:55-6 F 8 '71
Hectoring Herr Brandt. New Repub 164:7-8 Ja 23 '71
Opening to the East. P. Wohl. il Nation 212:142-5 F 1 '71

Ghana
Prime Minister Busia of Ghana meets with U.S. officials; statement, November 4, 1971. Dept State Bul 65:589 N 22 '71

Great Britain
Britain picks Europe, impact on America. il U S News 71:85 N 8 '71
Prime Minister Heath of the United Kingdom visits Washington; exchange of greetings, toasts, December 17, 1970. R. M. Nixon; E. Heath. Dept State Bul 64:56-60 Ja 11 '71
Where is Britain heading? interview, ed. by J. Fromm. E. Heath. por Read Digest 98:115-18 Mr '71

Greece, Modern
Air and conscience. Time 98:14 Ag 16 '71
Jackie and Ari and Tom and George and Spiro and . . . R. Fitch. il pors Ramp Mag 10:38-47+ Ja '72
Our man in Athens. il por Newsweek 77:48+ My 3 '71
Permanency of colonels. Nation 212:549 My 3 '71

UNITED STATES—Foreign relations—Greece, Modern—*Continued*
Rebellion in the House; House foreign affairs committee voting to cut off aid to Greece and Pakistan. Time 98:19 Jl 26 '71
Two U.S. allies drifting away. J. N. Wallace. il U S News 70:54-6 Mr 22 '71
United States policy toward Greece; statement, July 12, 1971. R. P. Davies. Dept State Bul 65:161-3 Ag 9 '71

Honduras
Swans, spooks and boobies; agreement to cede Great Swan and Little Swan islands to Honduras. il Time 98:43 D 6 '71

India
America and Russia in India. C. Bowles. For Affairs 49:636-51 Jl '71
Choosing sides in the subcontinent. il Newsweek 78:18-19 D 20 '71
Foreign Minister of India visits Washington; statement, June 17, 1971. Dept State Bul 65:41 Jl 12 '71
Involve ourselves in India? W. F. Buckley, jr. Nat R 23:1487 D 31 '71
Kissinger tilt; deliberations of Washington special action group. Time 99:15 Ja 17 '72
Losing battle; visit of I. Gandhi. il Newsweek 78:50 N 15 '71
Prime Minister Gandhi of India visits the United States; exchange of greetings, toasts; November 4, 1971. R. M. Nixon; I. N. Gandhi. Dept State Bul 65:615-20 N 29 '71
Tragic birth of Bangla Desh. Chr Cent 88:1517 D 29 '71
Trying to cap a hot volcano; I. Gandhi's Washington visit. il por Time 98:32+ N 15 '71
U.S.: a policy in shambles; India and Pakistan. il Time 98:28 D 20 '71
View from Washington, self-inflicted wound. il Time 98:15 Ag 23 '71
War in Asia, failure of U.S. diplomacy? a senator's criticism; with White House answer. il U S News 71:68-70 D 20 '71
War in Asia, why India spurned U.S. peace efforts. il U S News 71:11-14 D 20 '71
Who makes foreign policy? America 125:547 D 25 '71

Indochina
U.S. and Indochina. F. Lewis. Atlan 227:6+ Mr '71
See also
Cambodian-Vietnamese conflict—American participation

Ireland
Prime Minister of Ireland visits Washington; exchange of greetings. R. M. Nixon; J. Lynch. Dept State Bul 64:508-9 Ap 12 '71

Israel
American pressures on Israel. J. B. Sheerin. Cath World 213:59-60 My '71
Dialogue of the deaf; visit of J. Sisco. Newsweek 78:32 Ag 9 '71
Fleeting opportunity; mutual defense treaty. N. Safran. il Nation 212:425-8 Ap 5 '71
Israel quagmire; thoughts for the U.S. citizen; address, December 3, 1970. A. M. Lilienthal. Vital Speeches 37:206-9 Ja 15 '71
Israel: the 51st state? D. G. Nes. Cur 131:16-17 Jl '71
Mrs Meir: a phantom smile? il por Newsweek 78:42 D 13 '71
Phantoms and bargains. Time 99:27 Ja 17 '72
Say it with flowers; visit of J. Sisco. il por Newsweek 78:34+ Ag 16 '71
Strain between friends. il Time 97:24 Mr 29 '71
Tale of two travelers; visit of Helms. il pors Newsweek 78:37-8 Jl 12 '71

Italy
Prime Minister Colombo of Italy visits the United States; exchange of greetings, toasts, February 18, 1971. R. M. Nixon; E. Colombo. Dept State Bul 64:329-33 Mr 15 '71

Japan
As Nixon and Hirohito meet, can allies heal a split? pors U S News 71:35-6 S 27 '71
Assistant Secretary Green and Assistant Secretary Trezise interviewed for Japanese national television; February 26, 1971. M. Green; P. H. Trezise. Dept State Bul 64:449-54 Mr 29 '71
Don't take Japan for granted; interview, ed. by E. Klein. E. O. Reischauer. il Newsweek 78:36 O 4 '71
Fateful triangle: the United States, Japan and China. E. O. Reischauer. il N Y Times Mag p 12-13+ S 19 '71
Japan: adjusting to the Nixon *shokku.* il Time 98:34+ O 4 '71

Japan's global engagement. Z. Brzezinski. For Affairs 50:270-82 Ja '72
Needed: an Asian policy. G. W. Ball. Newsweek 78:45 Ag 16 '71
Of mills, textiles and Okinawa. Time 97:14+ Mr 29 '71
Playing with the fire of the Rising Sun. G. W. Ball. Newsweek 77:65 Ap 12 '71
President issues executive order pertaining to Ryukyuan elections; White House announcement and text of executive order. R. M. Nixon. Dept State Bul 65:384 O 11 '71
President Nixon and Emperor Hirohito of Japan meet in Alaska; statement and exchange of greetings, September 26, 1971. R. M. Nixon; Emperor Hirohito. Dept State Bul 65:397-8 O 18 '71
Putting pressure on Tokyo. il Newsweek 78:31+ Ag 30 '71
Secretary Rogers urges early and favorable Senate action on agreement with Japan on reversion of Okinawa; statement, October 27, 1971. W. P. Rogers. Dept State Bul 65:565-8 N 15 '71
Some airport diplomacy for the Emperor of Japan. S. Chang. il por Life 71:77 S 17 '71
Time to make up with Japan. Life 71:42 O 8 '71
Trying to make up with Japan; meeting between Nixon and Sato. il por Time 99:11 Ja 17 '72
U.S. and Japan: broadening bonds of understanding; address, October 27, 1971. M. Green. Dept State Bul 65:623-4 N 29 '71
U.S. and Japan sign agreement on reversion of Okinawa statements, June 17, 1971; with Department announcement, text of the agreement, and texts of related documents. W. P. Rogers; K. Aichi. Dept State Bul 65:33-41 Jl 12 '71
United States and Japan: common interests and common problems; address, June 30, 1971. W. P. Rogers. Dept State Bul 65:69-73 Jl 19 '71
View from Japan. F. Gibney. For Affairs 50:97-111 O '71
Volatile issues mark Ryukyuan-American relations. E. E. Bollinger. Chr Cent 88:162 F 3 '71
Yes to China must not be no to Japan. E. O. Reischauer. por Life 71:4 S 10 '71
See also
United States—Commerce—Japan
United States—Treaties—Japan

Korea (Republic)
Korea-U.S. relations; dilemmas and opportunities in the future of northeast Asia. C. H. Germany. Chr Cent 88:285-7 Mr 3 '71
See also
Korean war, 1950-1953—American participation

Laos
Laos: anatomy of an American involvement. R. A. Paul. il For Affairs 49:533-47 Ap '71

Latin America
Crumbling hemisphere. D. Lawrence. U S News 70:88 F 22 '71
Imperial dilemmas. Z. Brzezinski. Newsweek 78:62 N 22 '71
Latin America, no longer a U.S. sphere of influence: interview. E. F. Montalva. il por U S News 71:77-80 D 20 '71
Mismanagement of Latin American affairs; address, November 6, 1970. R. F. Delaney. Vital Speeches 37:235-8 F 1 '71
New direction for our Latin American policy. M. C. Needler. Yale R 60:333-41 Mr '71
Our nonpolicy toward Latin America. S. Linowitz. por Life 70:4 Je 18 '71
Price of misdeeds. Time 98:32 S 6 '71
Progress is not just around the corner. D. F. Ross. New Repub 164:20-1 Ja 2 '71
Rhetoric or policy? W. F. Buckley, jr. Nat R 23:216 F 23 '71
Schism between action and doctrine. I. L. Horowitz. Cur 135:43-52 D '71
Trend that failed. J. Barnes. il por Newsweek 78:44+ D 20 '71
U.S. policy toward Latin America: where we stand today; address, October 25, 1971. C. A. Meyer. Dept State Bul 65:559-64 N 15 '71
Writing on the wall: Colonnese go home; Catholic inter-American cooperation program; with editorial comment. G. Maceoin. Commonweal 94:492-3 S 24 '71

Madagascar
Big frame-up; expulsion of the U.S. ambassador. il por Newsweek 78:44+ Jl 5 '71

UNITED STATES—Foreign relations—*Cont.*

Mexico

See also
United States—History—Punitive expedition to Mexico, 1916
United States—Treaties—Mexico

Middle East

American policy toward the Middle East; address, January 10, 1971. P. T. Hart. Vital Speeches 37:370-4 Ap 1 '71
Rogers trip; how successful? il pors U S News 70:26 My 17 '71
Stalemate or settlement. Z. Brzezinski. Newsweek 77:50 My 17 '71
Those Arabists in the State department. J. Kraft. il N Y Times Mag p38-9+ N 7 '71; Reply. D. G. Nes. p 16+ N 28 '71

Pakistan

Aid and conscience. Time 98:14 Ag 16 '71
America responds to Pakistan. H. A. Jack. Chr Cent 88:1137-8 S 29 '71
Bailing out Pakistan. R. Sobhan. New Repub 164:14-15 Je 5 '71
Choosing sides in the subcontinent. il Newsweek 78:18-19 D 20 '71
Kissinger tilt; deliberations of Washington special action group. Time 99:15 Ja 17 '72
Mounting tragedy of East Bengal. E. M. Kennedy. Cur 135:53-62 D '71
Pakistan. F. Lang. Ramp Mag 10:17+ S '71
Pakistan refugee; how many will die? address, August 26, 1971. E. M. Kennedy. Vital Speeches 37:738-41 O 1 '71
Politics of relief. il Newsweek 78:28 Ag 2 '71
Rebellion in the House; House foreign affairs committee voting to cut off aid to Greece and Pakistan. Time 98:19 Jl 26 '71
U.S.: a policy in shambles; India and Pakistan. il Time 98:28 D 20 '71
War in Asia, failure of U.S. diplomacy? a senator's criticism; with White House answer. il U S News 71:68-70 D 20 '71

Portugal

Foreign minister of Portugal meets with U.S. officials; U.S.-Portuguese joint statement. Dept State Bul 63:722-3 D 14 '70

Rhodesia

Department reviews U.S. position on Southern Rhodesia; statement, July 7, 1971. D. D. Newsom. Dept State Bul 65:11-15 Jl 26 '71
Toying with Rhodesia. Nation 213:354-5 O 18 '71

Russia

America and Russia in a changing world. by W. A. Harriman. Review
Life 70:10 Ja 22 '71. J. K. Galbraith
Changes and chances in American-Soviet relations. H. J. Morgenthau. For Affairs 49:429-41 Ap '71
Era of negotiations with Russia? interview. ed. by J. Fromm. Read Digest 98:57-61 Ja '71
Exit the cold warrior? G. W. Ball. por Newsweek 77:45 F 8 '71
From trust to terror: the onset of the cold war, 1945-1950. by H. Feis. Review
Nat R 23:152-3 F 9 '71. J. Lukacs
Hopeful talks with the Soviet leaders. W. A. Harriman. il por Life 70:30-1 F 5 '71
How not to negotiate with the Russians. H. M. Jackson. por Nations Bsns 59:52+ Ap '71
Improbable triumvirate: Khrushchev. Kennedy, and Pope John. N. Cousins. pors Sat R 54:24-35 O 30 '71
In his own words: why Nixon is going to Moscow; news conference. October 12. 1971. R. M. Nixon. il por U S News 71:102-3 O 25 '71
Leaf from Metternich. F. W. Neal. Nation 213:162-4 S 6 '71
Learning to live with Russia; excerpts. R. M. Nixon. Time 97:14 Mr 8 '71
Let a hundred flowers bloom. F. S. Meyer. Nat R 23:482 My 4 '71
New nuclear ideas. Z. Brzezinski. por Newsweek 77:55 Je 7 '71
New tension between Russia and U.S: anti-Russian violence. il U S News 70:20-1 Ja 25 '71
New understanding: Soviet base on Cuba. Newsweek 77:33-4 Ja 18 '71
Rivals. by A. B. Ulam. Review
Sat R 54:38-40 N 20 '71. H. Schwartz
Soviet-American relations. J. C. Campbell. bibliog f Cur Hist 61:193-7+ O '71
Top challenge now: ending the missile race; excerpts from message to Congress. February 25. 1971. R. M. Nixon. il U S News 70:53-4 Mr 8 '71

U.S.-Russian thaw: prospects, and problems. il U S News 70:11-12+ Je 7 '71
Why not invite Brezhnev to visit the United States? D. Lawrence. U S News 71:80 Ag 23 '71
See also
Cuban crisis, 1962
Nixon, R. M.—Visit to Russia, 1972 (proposed)
Strategic arms limitation talks

Saudi Arabia

King Faisal of Saudi Arabia visits the United States; exchange of greetings, May 27, 1971. R. M. Nixon; King Faisal. Dept State Bul 64:763-4 Je 14 '71

South Africa

U.S. should cut loose. J. R. Hollingsworth. Nation 212:390-4 Mr 29 '71

Spain

Prince Juan Carlos of Spain visits the United States; exchange of greetings and toasts. R. M. Nixon; Prince Juan Carlos. Dept State Bul 64:236-9 F 22 '71

Taiwan

End of the United Nations? address, October 29. 1971. W. F. Buckley, jr. il Nat R 23:1300-1+ N 19 '71
Fat and unhappy. il Newsweek 77:43-4 Mr 29 '71
How to live with both Peking and Taiwan. A. D. Barnett. por Life 71:17 Ag 13 '71
Parrying a policy. por Time 97:23-4 Mr 29 '71
Recognizing China. J. A. Cohen. For Affairs 50:30-43 O '71
What about Taiwan? R. W. Barnett. Cur 130:7-11 Je '71
What now for Nationalist China; interview. J. C. H. Shen. il por U S News 71:42-5 Ag 2 '71
See also
United States—Treaties—Taiwan

Thailand

U.S. and Thailand sign memorandum of understanding on international narcotics control; remarks, with text of memorandum, September 28, 1971. W. P. Rogers; Thanat Khoman. Dept State Bul 65:411-13 O 18 '71
Who says Thailand's next? W. A. O'Neil. New Repub 164:23-7 Ja 2 '71

Turkey

Drug abuse: a challenge to U.S.-Turkish cooperation in the seventies; address, December 14, 1970. H. R. Wellman. Dept State Bul 64:140-6 F 1 '71
Two U.S. allies drifting away. J. N. Wallace. il U S News 70:54-6 Mr 22 '71

Underdeveloped areas

Sources of United States policy in the world. T. J. Farer. Yale R 60:321-32 Mr '71

Vietnam (Democratic Republic)

See also
Vietnamese war, 1957- —American participation

Vietnam (Republic)

After Saigon, Peking ahead. il por Time 98:31-2 O 18 '71
Spotlight turns to the Kennedy years; Pentagon papers. il Newsweek 78:19-21 Jl 5 '71
See also
Vietnamese war, 1957-

Yugoslavia

Closing the triangle. il por Time 98:42 N 1 '71
Nonaligner in Washington; Tito's visit. il por Time 98:46+ N 8 '71
President Tito of Yugoslavia visits the United States; exchange of greetings, toasts; with text of joint statement, October 28 and 30, 1971. R. M. Nixon; Tito. Dept State Bul 65:590-6 N 22 '71
Secretary Rogers interviewed for Yugoslav television; transcript of interview, October 22. 1971. W. P. Rogers. Dept State Bul 65:596-8 N 22 '71
VIP from Belgrade. il por Newsweek 78:57+ N 8 '71

Foreign service

Department announces new emphasis in Foreign service recruitment, September 16, 1971. Dept State Bul 65:360-1 O 4 '71
New foreign service and the job of modern diplomacy; remarks, November 16, 1971. W. P. Rogers. Dept State Bul 65:675-6 D 13 '71

UNITED STATES—Foreign service—*Continued*
Undiplomatic reforms; tragic case of C. W. Thomas. il por Time 98:20 N 15 '71
See also
United States—Diplomatic and consular service
United States—State, Department of
Women as foreign service employees

Forest service

Crisis of our national forests. J. N. Miller. il Read Digest 99:91-6 D '71
Disney's war against the wilderness; Mineral King controversy. R. Rapoport. il Ramp Mag 10:27-33 N '71
Forest service in the seventies. E. P. Cliff. por Am For 77:11 Ja '71
Here he is, ranger, and he's all yours; summer employment in the virgin forests. B. Gilbert. il Sports Illus 34:48-50+ My 17 '71
In the service: a Christmas story. A. W. Greeley. il por Am For 77:10-11+ D '71
Mike Frome. M. Frome. Am For 77:7+ Mr '71
Mike Frome; Bolle report on timber cutting in Bitterroot national forest. M. Frome. Am For 77:5+ Ja '71
Mike Frome; excerpts from The forest service. M. Frome. Am For 77:5+ Je '71
Mining the national forests; findings of the Bolle committee on the Bitterroot national forest. D. A. Burk. il Nation 212:110-13 Ja 25 '71
Montana's select committee; studying management practices on the Bitterroot national forest. J. B. Craig. il por Am For 77:35-7+ F '71
Museum joins the forest service; Ghost ranch museum, Abiquiu, N.Mex. F. A. Tinker. il por Am For 77:32-5 My '71
Regional forester bites the bullet; land management practices in the Bitterroot national forest. N. M. Rahm. il por Am For 77:38-9+ F '71
Stump merchants; timbering Alaska's national forests. S. Roberson. Field & S 75:16+ Mr '71
Timber mining: accusation or prospect? R. W. Behan. il Am For 77:4-6+ N '71
Tumult over timbering; endorsing clear cutting. Time 97:55-6 Ap 19 '71
Warning: the chain saw cometh; Tongass national forest. P. Brooks. il Atlan 228:95-9 D '71
Wreckreation in our national forests. R. B. Ditton. il Parks & Rec 6:22-6+ Je '71

Appropriations and expenditures
Areas of agreement; with editorial comment. Am For 77:10-11+ Je '71

General accounting office

Biggest racket; GAO report on defense contract profits. Nation 212:452-3 Ap 12 '71
Congress urged to base profits on investments. K. Johnsen. Aviation W 94:15 My 10 '71
DOD urged to find cost overrun causes. K. Johnsen. il Aviation W 94:21-2 Mr 29 '71
GAO report cites low defense profits. Aviation W 94:18 Mr 22 '71
Military maneuvers; reply. E. B. Staats. New Repub 164:35 F 6 '71
New battle over defense profits. il Time 97:70-1 My 8 '71
New design for the bottom line; change in Pentagon's system for negotiating profits on defense contracts. Bsns W p66+ Mr 27 '71
Pentagon power. New Repub 164:7-8 F 6 '71
Profit puzzle in procurement; GAO study. il Bsns W p44+ Mr 6 '71
Public private eye. Forbes 108:76 N 1 '71

General services administration

GSA's shopping list. Newsweek 78:92+ N 8 '71
See also
Consumer product information index

National archives and records service
Paper trust. B. A. Weisberger. il Am Heritage 22:38-41+ Ap '71

Geological survey

Pick up the phone and learn the earth's secrets. C. V. Glines. il Nations Bsns 59:48-51 D '71
Volcano watchers. il Newsweek 78:123 S 27 '71

Government

See United States—Politics and government

Government printing office

GPO receives first micropublishing recommendations. S. Wagner. Pub W 200:28 O 4 '71

Publishing on the Potomac: competition with the private sector. S. Wagner. Pub W 200:40-1 Ag 23 '71
Publishing on the Potomac: full steam ahead at the Government printing office. S. Wagner. il Pub W 200:36-9 Ag 16 '71
Research at Uncle Sam's bookstore. D. Stuart. Writer 84:24-5+ Jl '71

Government publications

See Government publications

Health, education and welfare, Department of

Assistant secretary for health: this time the job is on trial. J. Walsh. Science 172:1111+ Je 11 '71
Boston Brahmin in Heartbreak house. J. Cameron. il pors Fortune 84:88-91+ O '71
Clark Kent at HEW. por Time 98:19 Ag 9 '71
Columbia's lion gets a bearding. Bsns W p48 N 13 '71
DuVal for Egeberg. por Sci N 99:348 My 22 '71
Egeberg's successor. Time 97:42 Mr 29 '71
Federal advisory processes: advice and discontent; educational policy advisers. T. E. Cronin and N. C. Thomas. bibliog il Science 171:771-9 F 26 '71
HEW struggles to deliver the American dream. il por Bsns W p62-6 My 1 '71
Inside HEW: women protest sex discrimination. J. Chase. Science 174:270-4 O 15 '71
Is Mr Nixon in command of his own shop? HEW peace activities. Nat R 23:513 My 18 '71
More desegregation. J. Osborne. New Repub 164:15-16 Je 12 '71
Nursing business. New Repub 165:8-9 N 27 '71
Panetta's White House. J. Osborne. New Repub 164:7-9 My 8 '71
Secretary Richardson. J. Osborne. New Repub 164:11-12 Ja 23 '71
Welfare myths vs. facts; HEW's own report. il U S News 71:54-5 D 20 '71
See also
United States—Aging, Administration on
United States—Education, Office of
United States—National institutes of health

Appropriations and expenditures
Health programs: slum children suffer because of low funding. R. J. Bazell. il Science 172:921-5 My 28 '71
Pentagon will drop to second place by 1974; comparison with Department of health, education and welfare. il U S News 70:36 My 17 '71
Significant changes. Sci N 99:95 F 6 '71

Health services industry, Committee on the

Lid is clamped on health costs. Bsns W p 112+ N 13 '71

Historic houses, sites, etc.

Artifacts everywhere. P. Smyth. Motor B & S 128:57-8 Jl '71
Reporter at large; house and highway. W. Balliett. New Yorker 47:40-5 D 25 '71
Vitality of American tradition; with editorial comment. il House & Gard 140:33, 34-6+ Ag '71
See also
National trust for historic preservation

History

Letter from the editor. O. Jensen. il Am Heritage 22:2 O '71
See also
Education—United States—History
Frontier and pioneer life—United States
United States—Continental Congress
United States—Declaration of independence
United States—Economic history
United States—Foreign relations—History
United States—History, Military

Bibliography
Portrait of a nation. il Schol Teach Jr/Sr High p30-1 Mr 8 '71

Discovery and exploration
See America—Discovery and exploration

Historiography
Consciousness and ideology in American history: the burden of Daniel J. Boorstin. J. P. Diggins. bibliog f Am Hist R 76:99-118 F '71; Reply with rejoinder. O. Berland. 76:1245-54 O '71

UNITED STATES—History—*Continued*

Periodicals

See also
American heritage (periodical)

Study and teaching

American history: innovating or enervating.
H. G. Miller. il Clear House 45:483-7 Ap
'71
Use of new interpretations in American
history. T. J. Kerr. 4th. Ed Digest 37:46-8
S '71
See also
Negroes—History—Study and teaching

Textbooks

NAACP unit issues new multi-racial history
syllabus. Negro Hist Bul 33:167 N '70
Struggle for the inclusion of Negro history
in our text-books: a California experience; address, October 24, 1970. M. M.
Dymally. Negro Hist Bul 33:188-91 D
'70

Colonial period

See also
Jamestown, Va.
New England—History—Colonial period
Puritans

18th century

Meet Dr Franklin; excerpts. R. B. Morris.
il por Am Heritage 23:80-91 D '71

French and Indian war, 1755-1763

Americans as guerrilla fighters: Robert
Rogers and his rangers. J. T. Hubbard. il
por Am Heritage 22:81-6 Ag '71

Revolution

Emerging nations and the American revolu-
tion, by R. B. Morris. Review
Nation 213:24-5+ Jl 5 '71. R. Powers
England's Vietnam: the American revolution.
R. M. Ketchum. bibliog il Am Heritage 22:
6-11+ Je '71
Men of the Revolution. R. M. Ketchum. por
Am Heritage 22:20-1 Ag; 20-1 O; 23:48-9
D '71
Vietnam and the American revolution. D.
V. J. Bell and A. E. Goodman. Yale R
61:26-34 O '71
See also
Boston massacre, 1770
Boston tea party, 1773
Yorktown, Va.—Siege, 1781

Revolution—American forces

North Carolina continentals, by H. F. Rankin.
Review
Sat R 54:40 My 22 '71. J. Shy

Revolution—Campaigns and battles

Crossing, by H. Fast. Review
Atlan 227:125-6 F '71. E. Weeks
See also
Concord, Battle of, 1775
Lexington, Battle of, 1775

Revolution—Causes

On the meaning of revolution. R. F. Gibbs.
Nat R 23:699-700 Je 29 '71

Revolution—Drama

Molly meets the general. M. Hall. Plays 30:47-
54, 64 F '71

Revolution—Personal narratives

Voices of Lexington and Concord; eyewitness
accounts; excerpts from Voices of 1776,
comp. by R. Wheeler. il Am Heritage 22:8-
13+ Ap '71

*Revolution—Personal narratives—
British*

Voices of Lexington and Concord; eyewitness
accounts; excerpts from Voices of 1776,
comp. by R. Wheeler. il Am Heritage 22:8-
13+ Ap '71
See also
Indians of North America—Wars

1815-1861

Birth of modern America, 1820-1850, by D.
T. Miller. Review
Nation 213:310-12 O 4 '71. R. Powers

War with Mexico, 1845-1848

Land grants and land grabs. il Sr Schol
99:10-11 Ja 10 '72

Civil war

Puget Sound's war within a war. I. Doig.
il Am West 8:22-7 My '71

War for the Union, by A. Nevins. Review
Sat R 54:59-62 N 20 '71. G. G. Van
Deusen
See also
Confederate States of America—Army

Civil war—Campaigns and battles

See also
New Market, Battle of, 1864

Civil war—Damage to property

See United States—History—Civil war—
Destruction and pillage

Civil war—Destruction and pillage

New York is worth twenty Richmonds. N.
Brandt. il Am Heritage 22:74-80+ O '71

Civil war—Fiction

Civil war as romance of noble warriors and
maidens chaste. I. M. Patten. il Am Heritage 22:48-53+ Ap '71

Civil war—Personal narratives

Asa Smith leaves the war; ed. by B. Catton.
A. Smith. il Am Heritage 22:54-9+ F '71

1865

Age of energy, by H. M. Jones. Review
Nation 213:567-8 N 29 '71. A. R. Bentley
Sat R 54:39-41+ D 4 '71. D. E. Fortuna

1865-1898

See also
Indians of North America—Wars
Little Big Horn, Battle of the, 1876

Philippine insurrection, 1899-1901

See Philippines—History—Insurrection,
1899-1901

European war, 1914-1918

See European war, 1914-1918—United
States

Punitive expedition to Mexico, 1916

Great pursuit, by H. M. Mason, jr. Review
Am West 8:49 Mr '71. F. Egan

World war, 1939-1945

See World war, 1939-1945—United States

Korean war, 1950-1953

See Korean war, 1950-1953—American participation

History, Military

Speaking of unnecessary wars . . . R. L. Tobin. Sat R 54:20 Jl 17; Discussion. 54:17 Ag
28; 28 O 2 '71

Housing and urban development,
Department of

Big move to new towns. E. Carruth. il For-
tune 84:94-7+ S '71
Can we build enough homes for everybody?
Operation Breakthrough. A. M. Watkins.
Redbook 136:75+ Ap '71
Court breaks new social ground in housing
policy; Philadelphia court decision. J. R.
Hacala and J. M. Kakalec. America 124:228-
30 Mr 6 '71
HUD's other shoe drops on Cleveland. Bsns
W p22+ Ja 30 '71
Homecoming for Sam Jackson; HUD assis-
tant secretary. il pors Ebony 26:60-1+ Jl
'71
Meet Ginnie Mae. A. Hershman. il Duns 97:
72+ Mr '71
Pressure to build outside the ghettos. il Bsns
W p24 O 9 '71
Race is on for new towns. Bsns W p 130+
Mr 13 '71
Technology; Operation Breakthrough. M. Vil-
lecco. il Arch Forum 134:58-62 My '71
Time for appraisal: the legacy of parks;
status of HUD's Legacy of the parks pro-
gram. Parks & Rec 6:9 D '71
US as slumlord. K. Hartnett. New Repub
165:11-13 D 11 '71
Why so many mortages are being foreclosed.
il U S News 72:25-6 Ja 3 '72
See also
United States—Federal insurance administra-
tion

Indian affairs, Bureau of

Forked tongue. Nation 213:260 S 27 '71
See also
Indians of North America—Government re-
lations

Industries

Ability to compete, costs & benefits; address, November 4, 1971. R. F. Barker. Vital
Speeches 38:157-60 D 15 '71
Chemicals: a turnabout in profits and productivity. il Bsns W p44 D 25 '71

UNITED STATES—Industries—*Continued*
New industrial state, by J. K. Galbraith. Review
  Sat R 54:40+ O 2 '71. R. Eisner
Panorama of the nation's business. See issues of Nation's business
Who's where within the industry groups; with yardsticks of management performance. Forbes 109:91 Ja 1 '72
  See also
Rural industries
United States—Commerce
United States—Economic conditions
  also names of industries, e.g. Glass industry
  also subhead industries under names of sections, states, cities, etc. e.g. Delaware—Industries

Intellectual life
On being deradicalized. N. Glazer; discussion. Commentary 50:30-1 O '70; 51:20-3 Ja; 22+ Ap '71
Rediscovering American labor. P. Kemble. Commentary 51:45-52 Ap '71; Reply with rejoinder. H. A. Gray. 52:22 Ag '71
Role of the intellectuals; excerpt from address. N. Glazer. Commentary 51:55-61 F '71
School gap or age gap? Sr Schol 98:14 Mr 1 '71
  See also
Books and reading
Colleges and universities—United States
Miami, Fla.—Intellectual life
United States—Popular culture

Interest and dividends, Committee on
How planners set the first guideline. Bsns W p43 N 6 '71
Monetary monitors without much muscle. il Bsns W p24-5 O 16 '71

Interior, Department of
Exit Secretary Hickel, enter Secretary Morton. Audubon 73:94 Ja '71
Mike Frome; proposed landfill and high rise apartment construction at Hunting Creek. M. Frome. Am For 77:5+ Ag '71
  See also
United States—Fish and wildlife service
United States—National park service

Internal revenue service
Charge IRS intimidate church bodies. Chr Cent 88:1518 D 29 '71
Enforcing the freeze: an inside look; interview. A. Weber. por U S News 71:63-6 S 27 '71
How to cope with unreasonable compensation claims. R. S. Holzman. bibliog f Harvard Bsns R 49:79-81 S '71
If your tax return is questioned: case histories, what to expect; with interview with R. W. Thrower. il U S News 70:23-6 Je 14 '71
Library record snooping: more thumbs down. Library J 96:1182 Ap 1 '71
Official tax calendar (title varies) Nations Bsns 59:98 Ja; 67-9 F; 79-83 Mr '71
What happens if you complain, investigation of price-violation complaints. il U S News 71:33 N 15 '71

International commerce, Bureau of
You, too, can sell abroad; projects for increasing exports. il Nations Bsns 59:84-6 S '71

Interstate commerce commission
Entrenched ICC fights off the reformers. il Bsns W p48-9 O 9 '71
Free market in transportation? Duns 97:120 Mr '71
Freight rate hikes hit a roadblock. Bsns W p22 Ja 1 '72
It's time to unload the regulators. D. Cordtz. il Fortune 84:64-7+ Jl '71
Numbers game. Newsweek 77:77-8 Ap 26 '71

John F. Kennedy center for the performing arts
  See John F. Kennedy center for the performing arts, Washington, D.C.

John F. Kennedy space center
Airlines, space center weighing impact of Disney on Florida tourism. W. H. Gregory. il Aviation W 95:34-5+ Ag 16 '71
At Cape Kennedy, a case of middle aged sag. D. Sheridan. por Life 70:2A F 26 '71

Justice, Department of
Clash of absolutes; Pentagon's Vietnam studies. New Repub 165:5-7 Jl 3 '71

In the courts: the government vs. the press; Pentagon papers. il Newsweek 77:27+ Je 28 '71
Justice dept. slows AT&T system case. il Aviation W 95:38-40 Ag 23 '71
Kennedy justice, by V. S. Navasky. Review Commentary 53:82-4 Ja '72. J. Q. Wilson Nat R 23:1312-13 N 19 '71. G. F. Will New Repub 165:26+ O 9 '71. J. J. Fried No. 1 in Cabinet, and in controversy; J. N. Mitchell. il pors U S News 71:58-9 Ag 2 '71
Split of Comsat, terrestrial carriers urged. K. Johnsen. Aviation W 94:18 Ja 18 '71
  See also
United States—Federal bureau of investigation

Antitrust division
Antitrust: change at the top, but no change in policy. il por U S News 71:29-30 D 20 '71
Crime in the suites; report by Center for the study of responsive law. Newsweek 77:86 Je 14 '71
Fallout from McLaren's fast exit. por Bsns W p31 D 11 '71
How to succeed in business without being tried; address, May 4, 1971. L. Loevinger. Vital Speeches 37:529-34 Je 15 '71
McLaren out. Time 98:75 D 20 '71
McLaren's march to the sea; interview. R. W. McLaren. pors Forbes 109:129+ Ja 1 '72
Nader on antitrust. R. A. Posner. New Repub 164:11-14 Je 26 '71; Reply. M. Green. 165:31-2 Jl 10 '71
Views on bigness are contradictory. il Bsns W p58-63 Ag 7 '71

Civil rights division
Bias suits ask for back pay. U S News 71:96 O 4 '71
More desegregation. J. Osborne. New Repub 164:15-16 Je 12 '71

Internal security division
Internal security makes a comeback. F. Lang. il Ramp Mag 10:10+ Ja '72
Red squad; Special litigation section. il por Newsweek 77:17-18 My 31 '71
Tough new man at Justice. por Time 97:53 F 1 '71

Law enforcement assistance administration
Drive to halt prison violence. il U S News 71:37-9 D 27 '71
U.S. aid for lawmen comes under fire; with interview with Jerris Leonard. U S News 71:34-8 O 11 '71

Special litigation section
  See United States—Justice, Department of—Internal security division

Labor, Department of
Jobs-for-veterans drive is launched. U S News 70:70 Je 28 '71
Unemployment: official & real; change in counting procedures. Nation 212:100 Ja 25 '71
Watchdog for U.S. labor. A. Poinsett. il pors Ebony 26:95-100+ Ap '71
  See also
United States—Farm labor and rural manpower service
United States—Labor statistics, Bureau of

Labor policy
Any cure for big strikes? interview. J. D. Hodgson. il pors U S News 71:68-72 N 29 '71
At last, a national manpower policy. il Bsns W p48-9 Ag 7 '71
Dual labor market and manpower policy. R. E. Klitgaard. bibliog Mo Labor R 94:45-8 N '71
Human resources: retooling our manpower. J. M. Rosow. il Sat R 54:40-1+ Ja 23 '71
Jobs for all: any time soon? il U S News 71:30-2 Ag 2 '71
Nixon aides warn labor of crackdown. U S News 70:88-9 Mr 22 '71
Who cares about the public interest? compulsory arbitration; reprint. D. Lawrence. U S News 70:84 My 31 '71
  See also
Labor laws and legislation—United States
United States—National labor relations board

Labor statistics, Bureau of
In search of doughnuts. il Newsweek 78:82 O 11 '71
Numbers game shakes the BLS. Bsns W p22 O 9 '71
  See also
North American conference on labor statistics

UNITED STATES—*Continued*

Land management, Bureau of

Big lockout. M. Frome. Field & S 76:66-7+ O '71

Vehicle and environmental responsibility. B. Behme. il Field & S 75:142-4+ Ap '71

When a law fights a law: Mining law of 1872 vs Environmental act. B. Gilbert. il Sports Illus 34:30-2+ Ap 26 '71

Library of Congress

Barred from LC, ALA team interviews underground; investigating racism charges. Wilson Lib Bul 46:389 Ja '72

Black bias charges pressed at Library of Congress. Library J 96:2032 Je 15 '71

Black caucus charges Mumford evades ALA probe of LC. il Library J 97:14+ Ja 1 '72

Fauntroy to introduce bill on discrimination at LC. Library J 96:3262 O 15 '71

Library of Congress launches cataloging in publication program. S. Wagner. Pub W 200:51-2 Ag 2 '71

Preservation through documentation; exhibition of graphic and photographic records from the Nation's archive of historic architecture. K. V. Hostick. Hobbies 76:159 Ap '71

Protests end at LC: Congress may probe changes. Library J 96:3061-4+ O 1 '71

Thirteen fired by library of Congress: protesting black staff members. Library J 96:2415-16 Ag '71

See also

United States—Copyright office

Documents expediting project

Doc ex. J. W. Brewster; discussion. bibliog Wilson Lib Bul 45:513-15 Ja; 46:136 O '71

Prints and photographs division

Seeing pictures; photographic gold mine in Washington, D.C. J. Scully. Mod Phot 35:12+ O '71

Literary landmarks

See Literary landmarks

Management and budget, Office of

George Shultz: general manager of the United States? il pors Nations Bsns 59:34-8 Mr '71

Nixon's man for all seasons; G. Shultz. por U S News 70:29 Mr 29 '71

Shrewd diplomat. G. R. Rosen. por Duns 98:59 Jl '71

Manned spacecraft center

NASA's Captain Video. il por Time 98:12 Ag 9 '71

Lunar receiving laboratory

Letter from the space center; gathering moon samples on Apollo 14 flight. H. S. F. Cooper, jr. New Yorker 47:120+ Ap 17 '71

Letter from the space center; plans for the Apollo 15 project. H. S. F. Cooper, jr. New Yorker 47:40-2+ Jl 17 '71

Letter from the space center; preparations for the Apollo 14 mission. H. S. F. Cooper. jr. New Yorker 46:66-74 Ja 9 '71

Maps

Popular science 1971 travel map of the United States; with guide. il Pop Sci 198:68-73 My '71

Marine corps

Commandant Cushman. por Newsweek 78:37 D 13 '71

Harrier program seeks broad VTOL data. D. A. Brown. il Aviation W 95:47-8+ O 25 '71

Marines fit Harrier to own tactics. D. A. Brown. il Aviation W 95:38-44 O 18 '71

Marines' new chief: a man Nixon never forgot. por U S News 71:39 D 13 '71

New top leatherneck: R. E. Cushman. por Time 98:13-14 D 13 '71

Parting shots: a marine who could handle the tank. por Life 71:69 Jl 16 '71

President Nixon honors first marine division; remarks. R. M. Nixon. Dept State Bul 64:665-6 My 24 '71

U.S. marines: well in hand. il Newsweek 78:20-2 N 29 '71

Washington: the monks at Eighth and I. il Time 98:23 Ag 9 '71

Prisons

Military prisons: about face. il Time 97:63 My 17 '71

Military airlift command

Bill spurs MAC use of airlines. Aviation W 95:29 N 8 '71

Fuel tax dispute may affect results of Overseas national. W. H. Gregory. Aviation W 95:28 N 29 '71

Military policy

America as island? Nat R 23:1452 D 31 '71

Big bad bear. New Repub 164:9 Mr 27 '71

Kind word for the military. E. McCarthy. por Life 70:38 Mr 5 '71

Letter to a Soviet friend. C. Yost. por Life 71:4 S 24 '71

Military establishment: its impacts on American society, by A. Yarmolinsky. Review Nat R 23:267 Mr 9 '71. W. D. Jacobs

Nixon doctrine and our Asian commitments. E. C. Ravenal. For Affairs 49:201-17 Ja '71

President and the military. M. H. Halperin. For Affairs 50:310-24 Ja '72

Strategy for tomorrow, by H. W. Baldwin. Review Fortune por 83:163-4 Je '71. R. B. Rheault

U.S. strategy beyond Vietnam; interview. M. R. Laird. il por U S News 70:27-30+ My 17 '71

What would you do? S. Alsop. Newsweek 77:92 F 15 '71

Words of peace, works of war. Chr Cent 88:211 F 7 '71

See also

Military assistance, American

United States—Defenses

Vietnamese war, 1957- —American participation

Mines, Bureau of

Mine safety slips through a loophole. Bsns W p19 Ja 30 '71

Minority business enterprise, Office of

Let's write off MESBICs. R. S. Rosenbloom and J. K. Shank; discussion. Harvard Bsns R 48:170-1 N '70; 49:25 Ja '71

Monetary policy

Burns on business: recovery, but new dangers of inflation; excerpts from testimony, February 19, 1971. A. Burns. por U S News 70:55-7 Mr 1 '71

Fiscal or monetary? H. C. Wallich. Newsweek 77:88 Mr 15 '71

Irresponsible monetary policy. M. Friedman. il Newsweek 79:57 Ja 10 '72

Money, tight or easy? M. Friedman. il Newsweek 77:80 Mr 1 '71

Mutual responsibility for maintaining a stable monetary system; address, May 28, 1971. J. B. Connally. Dept State Bul 65:42-6 Jl 12 '71; Excerpts with title Tough talk to U.S. allies on trade, defense. U S News 70:51-3 Je 14 '71

Nixon's expansion policy irks Europeans. il Bsns W p88-9 Mr 13 '71

Tough talk to U.S. allies on trade, defense; excerpts from address, May 28, 1971. J. B. Connally. il por U S News 70:51-3 Je 14 '71

See also

Credit

United States—Federal reserve board

Moral conditions

American way of swinging. il Time 97:51 F 8 '71

Are we a nation of adulterers? H. Colton. Harp Baz 104:124-6 O '71

Cases of conscience; reactions to Calley verdict. J. Ciardi. Sat R 54:4+ My 1 '71

Child is being beaten; the effects of hunger; address, March 21, 1971. B. Pasamanick. Vital Speeches 37:465-72 My 15 '71

Cottonwoods astir. A. MacLeish. Sat R 54:40-1 N 13 '71

Cry, our beloved country. W. Barthelmes. Commonweal 94:186-7 Ap 30 '71

Death of the American ethic. O. S. Kramer. Yale R 61:69-75 O '71

Easter and the American conscience. America 124:364, 421 Ap 10, 24 '71

Ecology, an American heresy? J. V. Schall. America 124:308-11 Mr 27 '71

Ellsberg and the new heroism. T. Gitlin. Commonweal 94:447-51 S 3 '71

From hot panting to hotpants. D. Newman and R. Benton. il Mlle 73:82-3+ Jl '71

International war crimes; conduct of the war in Vietnam. P. J. Riga. il Cath World 213:130-3 Je '71

New consciousness. C. F. H. Henry. Chr Today 16:28-9 O 8 '71

Of many things; moral dilemmas. D. R. Campion. America 124:inside cover My 1 '71

UNITED STATES—Moral conditions—*Cont.*
Prudery and passion, by M. Rugoff. Review
Sat R 54:30+ Jl 10 '71. P. MacManus
See everything, do everything, feel nothing.
N. Cousins. Sat R 54:31 Ja 23 '71
What's happening to American morals; symposium. U S News 70:68-74 Ja 25 '71
See also
Crime and criminals—United States
Prostitution
Violence

National academy of sciences
See National academy of sciences

National advisory commission on civil disorders
Social scientists and the riot commission. M. Lipsky. bibliog f Ann Am Acad 394:72-83 Mr '71

National aeronautics and space administration
Advanced technology transport delayed. D. A. Brown. Aviation W 94:22 Mr 22 '71
Apollo: where is its poetry? il Time 98:14 Ag 9 '71
Boost for NASA; proceeding with space shuttle. il Time 99:36-7 Ja 17 '72
Can NASA keep its program aloft? Bsns W p23 F 13 '71
Fletcher to head NASA. Sci N 99:162 Mr 6 '71
Industry talks will seek policy on STOL proposal. Aviation W 94:25 Mr 29 '71
Infrared exploration, new light on the environment. J. Lear. il Sat R 54:53-7 Ap 3 '71
International programs. Space World H-3-87: 10-13 Mr '71
NASA building STOL transports. M. L. Yaffee. il Aviation W 95:44-7 S 13 '71
NASA, city group set target priorities. Aviation W 94:66 Je 7 '71
NASA takes a shot at general aviation. T. H. Block. Flying 89:S1-5 Ag '71
NASA to aid study of corn leaf blight. Aviation W 94:19 Ap 19 '71
NASA to use U-2s. Aviation W 94:25 Ap 12 '71
NASA using U-2s as ERTS simulators. il Aviation W 95:16 O 25 '71
NASA's new chief. por Newsweek 77:73 Mr 15 '71
1970: NASA records results. Space World H-5-89:46-7 My '71
Proposal for joint STOL opposed. D. A. Brown. Aviation W 94:27 Ap 5 '71
Science-mission reliability. Sci N 99:416 Je 19 '71
Shuttle decision hailed as NASA victory. Aviation W 96:15-16 Ja 10 '72
Some treats, some headaches; NAS recommendations for space science in the 1970's. Sci N 99:179-80 Mr 13 '71
Space meteorology; cooperation between NASA and the Russian academy of sciences. Space World H-7-91:33-5 Jl '71
Space science and applications, future program. Space World H-4-88:38-40 Ap '71
Tasks pile up for new NASA chief. por Bsns W p90 Mr 6 '71
Two Apollos, Mariners highlight 1971 NASA space launch plans. Aviation W 94:39 Ja 18 '71
See also
United States—John F. Kennedy space center
United States—Manned spacecraft center

Appropriations and expenditures
Fat-free diet for the space program. Bsns W p73+ Ja 16 '71
Grand tour, shuttle threatened. Sci N 100: 187 S 18 '71
House unit cuts NASA funding to $29 million below request. Aviation W 94:17 Je 28 '71
More cuts, but less drastic. Sci N 99:95 F 6 '71
NASA asks post-Skylab planning funds. Z. Strickland. Aviation W 95:15-16 N 29 '71
NASA funding trend levels; with tables. Aviation W 94:18-19 F 1 '71
NASA keys manned flight to shuttlecraft. Z. Strickland. il Aviation W 94:39-41 Mr 8 '71
Question of survival for grand tour of planets. Sci N 100:246 O 9 '71
Senate committee boosts funds for Rover nuclear rocket project. K. Johnsen. Aviation W 94:18 My 24 '71
Tight budgets continue to restrain NASA. il Aviation W 95:16 D 27 '71
Viking Mars, space shuttle, Nerva delayed by NASA budget slashes. D. C. Winston. Aviation W 94:17 F 8 '71

Communications network
NASA ponders relay satellites. il Aviation W 95:66+ Ag 23 '71
NASA's manned space flight network. il Space World H-4-88:31-3 Ap '71

Electronics research center
See also
United States—Transportation. Department of—Transportation systems center

Procurement
Study spurs tighter NASA procurement. Z. Strickland. Aviation W 95:18-19 Jl 12 '71

Tracking and data acquisition, Office of
How satellites are tracked and data acquired. il Space World H-8-92:10-13 Ag '71

National archives
New research source: archives branches. B. C. Harding. bibliog il Am Lib 2:306-7 Mr '71

National bureau of standards
See United States—Standards, National bureau of

National cancer institute
Best way to attack cancer. il Bsns W p62 Ap 3 '71
Cancer compromise: NCI looks to future. Sci N 100:404-5 D 18 '71
Cancer politics: NIH backers mount late defense in House. N. Wade. Science 174:127-31 O 8 '71
Cancer research goes political. Sci N 99:347-8 My 22 '71
Special virus cancer program: travails of a biological moonshot. N. Wade. il Science 174:1306-11 D 24 '71

National commission on libraries and information science
Library commission begins study. S. Wagner. Pub W 200:24 D 6 '71
National commission appointments. Am Lib 2:666 Jl '71

National commission on product safety
Ten deadliest household products. L. David. il Mech Illus 67:64-6+ F '71
Whatever happened to Product safety? M. Lemov. New Repub 164:12-13 Ap 3 '71

National commission on productivity
Productivity group gains some muscle. Bsns W p23 Ja 16 '71

National commission on reform of federal criminal laws
Death penalty on the way out? proposed new federal criminal code. il U S News 70:55 Ja 18 '71

National commission on the causes and prevention of violence
Thomas Jefferson, won't you please come home? address, April 1971, with questions and answers. L. N. Cutler. bibliog f Ann Am Acad 396:25-39 Jl '71
Violence commission violence. J. H. Skolnick. il Trans-Action 7:32-8 O '70

National forest service
See United States—Forest service

National foundation for higher education (proposed)
National foundation for higher education. G. Krettek and E. D. Cooke. Am Lib 2: 379-80 Ap '71

National foundation on the arts and the humanities
Arts and humanities in the library: a guide for federal aid to libraries. C. M. Hall. il Am Lib 2:201-2 F '71
Development of federal assistance to the humanities; address, April 1971, with questions and answers. W. B. Edgerton. Ann Am Acad 396:1-12 Jl '71
Humanities in the library: the role of the National endowment for the humanities; symposium, ed. by R. G. Swartz. il por Wilson Lib Bul 46:426-45 Ja '72
In support of freedom; National endowment for the arts: adaptation of address. February 17, 1971. N. Hanks. il Parks & Rec 6:44-5+ Ag '71
Making faces across the gulf: National endowment for the arts. N. Hanks. Science 173:479 Ag 6 '71

UNITED STATES—National foundation on the arts and the humanities—*Continued*
NEH supports definitive editions of American authors. S. Wagner. Pub W 199:47-8 Ja 11 '71
Not only red tape, but millions for a lot of claptrap; excerpts. H. R. Gross. il por U S News 71:30-1 Jl 19 '71
Willingly to school. N. Hanks. il PTA Mag 65:18-21 Ap '71

National guard
Behind the headlines with a witness from Kent state; death of A. Krause. Seventeen 29:156+ Ag '70
Citizens battle for justice; Kent state shootings by Ohio national guard; with editorial comment. P. Davies. Nation 213:547-8, 557-9 N 29 '71
From those wonderful people who gave you Kent state. J. Berendt. Esquire 75:38+ Ap '71
Self-control for riot controllers. il Bsns W p50-1 Jl 3 '71
Without a draft, can national guard survive? with interview. il U S News 71:61-3 N 8 '71

Caricatures and cartoons
Call out the guard! J. Noonan. Cath World 212:264 F '71

National highway traffic safety administration
Safety: the argument over air bags. Consumer Rep 36:221-2 Ap '71

National industrial pollution control council
Closed-door policy. New Repub 164:7 Ap 24 '71
Industry leaders hunt: practical answers to pollution. il Nations Bsns 59:18-20+ Ja '71

National institute of education (proposed)
Toward parental support of a national institute of education. S. P. Marland, jr. por Parents Mag 46:42 S '71

National institute of mental health
Freedom and funding: Skinner support queried. por Sci N 100:420-1 D 25 '71
Mental health industry: this way lies madness. A. Kopkind and J. Ridgeway. il Ramp Mag 9:38-44 F '71
Misplaced zeal; inquiry into grant to B. F. Skinner. New Repub 166:14 Ja 1 '72
Pop report: still inconclusive. Time 97:46 F 15 '71

National institute of neurological diseases and stroke
Two cultures note: criticism of NINDS director for travel on government time and money. J. Walsh. Science 174:128-9 O 8 '71

National institutes of health
Cancer legislation: pro-NIH bill advances in House. N. Wade. Science 174:388-9 O 22 '71
Male bias of NIH. F. Moog. Science 171:236 Ja 22 '71
Money won't solve everything. G. A. Silver. il Nation 213:110-14 Ag 16 '71
See also
United States—National cancer institute
United States—National institute of neurological diseases and stroke

Appropriations and expenditures
Graduate support: NIH grants threatened by Nixon priorities. R. J. Bazell. Science 171:554-6 F 12 '71
Research grants: new awards bore brunt of NIH cutbacks. R. Gillette. Science 172:43-5 Ap 2 '71

Rocky Mountain laboratory
Rocky Mountain laboratory: a monument to the tick. B. Nelson. il Science 173:1009-10 S 10 '71

National labor relations board
High-court rulings: labor wins 1 of 3. U S News 71:90-1 D 20 '71
Labor board rejects engineers bid for collective bargaining right. Aviation W 95:24 N 15 '71
NLRB petitions that are dismissed or withdrawn. J. Krislov. il Mo Labor R 94:71-2 Je '71
NLRB remedies for unfair labor practices. J. H. Fanning. bibliog f Mo Labor R 94:53-7 Mr '71
NLRB's regulation of union job control; purpose of labor management relations. P. Ross. Mo Labor R 94:59-62 Mr '71

Nixon looks warily for a new NLRB czar. Bsns W p43 My 15 '71
Significant decisions in labor cases. See issues of Monthly labor review

National ocean survey
They know where it's at. A. Steinberg. il Read Digest 99:116-20 Jl '71

National oceanic and atmospheric administration
Climate change study by NOAA. il Weatherwise 24:63 Ap '71
ESSA assumes control of SPAN solar network. Space World H-2-86:47 F '71
NOAA and oceanographic research: wet NASA idea dries up. J. Chase. Science 173:216-17+ Jl 16 '71
NOAA charts a course. Sci N 99:212 Mr 27 '71
Uncle Sam's environment troika; CEQ, EPA and NOAA. G. Fishbein. il Nations Bsns 59:34-6 Ap '71
See also
United States—National weather service

National park service
Harpers Ferry: arsenal of awareness; Stephen T. Mather training center. R. B. Kasparek. il Nat Parks & Con Mag 45:22-6 Ja '71
People parks. R. Starnes. Field & S 76:8+ S '71
Postscript to tragedy: a father's crusade. M. Cohen. il Redbook 137:76-7+ Je '71
Profiles; G. Hartzog. J. McPhee. por New Yorker 47:45-8+ S 11 '71
Volunteers in parks program inaugurated. il Parks & Rec 6:5-6 F '71
See also
Forest rangers
National park personnel

National parks and reserves
See National parks and reserves—United States

National reading council
Aid for the one in four who can't read well. V. Louviere. Nations Bsns 59:16 Jl '71
Reading, the fundamental R: what parents can do to upgrade school programs. J. E. Allen, jr. por Parents Mag 46:32 My '71
Right to read. D. Dempsey. Sat R 54:22-3 Ap 17 '71

National science board
Breaking down the boundaries. Sci N 100:40 Jl 17 '71
NSB promotes environmental science; excerpt from annual report. Science 173:313 Jl 23 '71

National science foundation
Jaundiced eye; refusal of grant to Environment. Environ 13:53 O '71
Kennedy and McElroy differ. C. Holden. Science 174:573 N 5 '71
McElroy leaving NSF. por Sci N 100:54-5 Jl 24 '71
NSF: is applied research at the take off point? R. J. Bazell. Science 172:1315-17 Je 25 '71
NSF may pick up ARPA's interdisciplinary laboratories. G. B. Lubkin. il Phys Today 24:61-2 F '71
NSF official resigns protesting science education cuts. N. Wade. por Science 173:1109 S 17 '71
NSF prods scientists to coordinate Bay research, but academic rivalries snag badly needed studies. A. L. Hammond. Science 172:827-30 My 21 '71
Nixon makes it official: Stever in for McElroy. por Sci N 100:341 N 20 '71
No part-time agency for basic research! H. L. Davis. Phys Today 24:80 My '71; Reply. W. D. McElroy. 24:9 Ag '71
Paxton to head new NSF division of materials research. G. B. Lubkin. il por Phys Today 24:61-2 S '71
Statement of Senator Edward M. Kennedy on re-employing defense scientists and engineers. E. M. Kennedy. por Bul Atom Sci 27:41-3 Mr '71
See also
National register of scientific and technical personnel
United States—Sea grant programs, Office of

Appropriations and expenditures
Budget outlook bright or dim, depending on your viewpoint. G. B. Lubkin. il Phys Today 24:65+ Ap '71
Exhilarating new role. il Sci N 99:94 F 6 '71

UNITED STATES—National science foundation
—Appropriations and expenditures—*Cont.*
Fellowship panel protests cutbacks. P. M.
Boffey. Science 171:1127 Mr 19 '71
Handler dissents on NSF budget. C. Holden.
Science 172:247 Ap 16 '71; Reply. P. Handler.
172:792 My 21 '71
NSF aide resigns over budget. **Sci N** 100:
186 S 18 '71
NSF asks for 23% budget increase as agency
research support drops. G. B. Lubkin. Phys
Today 24:61 Je '71
NSF makes headway. J. Walsh. Science 172:
828-9 My 21 '71
NSF to the rescue; grant to Science service,
inc. R. Gillette. Science 173:218 Jl 16 '71
RANN gets rundown. Sci N 99:331 My 15 '71

National security council

CIA and decision-making. C. L. Cooper.
For Affairs 50:223-36 Ja '72
Instruments of American foreign policy. C.
W. Yost. For Affairs 50:63-8 O '71
Kissinger and Rogers. J. Osborne. New
Repub 164:13-15 Mr 27 '71

National tourism resources review commission

President Nixon appoints members of tourism resources commission. Dept State Bul
64:303 Mr 8 '71

National transportation safety board

NTSB recommends descent warning aid.
Aviation W 95:55 D 6 '71

National weather service

NOAA VHF weather radio broadcasts. il
Weatherwise 24:237 O '71
Tropical analysis program of the National
hurricane center. C. W. Wise and R. H.
Simpson. bibliog il Weatherwise 24:164-73
Ag '71

Navy

Look at U.S.-Soviet rivalry in the Mediter-
ranean; interview. I. C. Kidd, jr. il por U S
News 71:110-11 N 15 '71
Mediterranean tide runs for the Russians. A.
De Borchgrave. il Newsweek 78:34-5 Jl 19
'71
Naval rivalry; Seventh fleet in the Indian
Ocean. il Time 99:26 Ja 17 '72
Personal accountability; address, June 9,
1971. E. R. Zumwalt, jr. Vital Speeches 37:
605-8 Jl 15 '71
Playing chicken over the Mediterranean. W.
H. Honan. il Read Digest 98:77-81 Mr '71
Soviet thrust in the Mediterranean; Black
Sea fleet and Sixth fleet. il Time 97:27-8
Je 28 '71
Where Russian threat keeps growing; in-
terview. E. R. Zumwalt, jr. il por U S
News 71:72-7 S 13 '71
See also
Naval maneuvers
Navy yards and naval stations

Boats
See also
Warships—United States

Clothing
See also
Uniforms, Naval

Communication systems
Indian Ocean naval communications facil-
ity planned by U.S. and U.K. joint an-
nouncement, December 15, 1970. Dept State
Bul 64:14 Ja 4 '71
See also
Radio communication, Naval

Office of emergency preparedness
See United States—Emergency preparedness, Office of

Parole, Board of
No exit. W. Gaylin. il Harper 243:86-9+ N
'71

Patent office
Patent system needs overhauling. il Bsns W
p65+ D 4 '71

Pay board
Aerospace pact tests the Pay board. Bsns
W p34 D 11 '71
Another challenge for Pay board; aerospace
wage contract. U S News 71:90 D 20 '71
As construction industry sets own pay pat-
tern. il U S News 71:78 D 6 '71
Bonuses as usual, but not for all; executive
compensation regulations. Bsns W p 19 Ja
1 '72
Breaks in the wage-price spiral. il por Time
99:20 Ja 17 '72

Catching 22. il Time 98:30+ N 1 '71
Chance for a Phase II deal with labor.
il Time 98:21 N 8 '71
Chances of labor peace in year ahead. il
U S News 72:47-8 Ja 10 '72
Coal miners, others to get bigger pay. U S
News 71:62 N 29 '71
Confusion at Pay board as Congress moves in.
U S News 71:47 D 27 '71
Congress wants Nixon to win this one. Bsns
W p51 N 13 '71
Decisions, decisions. il Newsweek 78:45-6 D
27 '71
Drive to beat inflation and Democrats; Blur-
ry banner for Phase II; program presented
by President Nixon, October 7, 1971. il por
Time 98:10-12+ O 18 '71
Getting set to start new controls. il U S News
71:26-7+ N 8 '71
Headaches piling up for the Pay board. il
U S News 71:104-6 D 13 '71
How big the big bump? Newsweek 78:86 D
6 '71
How Nixon spells out his postfreeze pro-
gram; address, October 7, 1971. R. M.
Nixon. U S News 71:82-3 O 18 '71; Same
with title Economic plan: Phase II. Vital
Speeches 38:2-4 O 15 '71; Same abr. with
title Fighting inflation is everybody's busi-
ness. il Read Digest 99:77-80 D '71
Is a pattern already set for Pay board's wage
controls? il U S News 71:76-8 N 1 '71
Labor's disturbing challenge; President
Nixon and G. Meany as speakers at AFL-
CIO convention. pors Time 98:29 N 29 '71
Living with the Pay board, strategy of big
unions. il U S News 71:59-60 N 29 '71
Look at a Pay-board day. U S News 71:48 D
27 '71
Mr Nixon knows what he can do. il pors
Newsweek 78:16-18 N 29 '71
New controllers, and new doubts. il pors
Newsweek 78:67-9 N 1 '71
Nixon's plan for more controls. il U S News
71:18-19 N 1 '71
Now the Pay board trips over aerospace.
Bsns W p31 D 18 '71
Pay board: dispute over '72 raises. U S
News 72:66 Ja 3 '72
Pay board irks aerospace unions. Aviation
W 96:21 Ja 10 '72
Pay board meets, and disputes begin. il U S
News 71:37-9 N 8 '71
Pay-board poker; labor holds the ace. News-
week 78:85-6+ N 15 '71
Pay board postpones action on aerospace
wages. Aviation W 96:16 Ja 3 '72
Pay board puts off the aerospace issue. Bsns
W p 19 D 25 '71
Pay board takes the middle road. il Bsns W
p 108-11 N 13 '71
Pay board's toughest dilemma: deferred wage
increases. il Bsns W p43 N 6 '71
Pay-price gap. il Newsweek 78:78-80 D 13
'71
Pay rules: official guidelines; statement by
the Board, November 8, 1971. U S News 71:
88 N 22 '71
Phase 2 controls; with text of Nixon's ad-
dress, October 7, 1971. il U S News 71:21-
6+ O 18 '71
Phase II: how it will work. il Bsns W p21-3
O 16 '71
Phase two: living with controls. il pors News-
week 78:26-32 O 18 '71
Phase II team sets up shop. il Bsns W p23-4
O 30 '71
Pitfalls ahead for Phase 2. il U S News 71:23-
6 O 25 '71
Raises running too high? A debate that is
heating up. il U S News 71:88-9 D 20 '71
Swallowing hard. il Newsweek 78:69-70 D 20
'71
Union threats that haunt the Pay board;
with editorial comment. il Bsns W p78+, 128
O 23 '71
Unions approach showdown: what to do about
Pay board; looking ahead to the AFL-
CIO convention. il U S News 71:85-6 N 22
'71
Wage and contract problems the unions see
coming. il U S News 71:48-50 O 25 '71
What the soft-coal decision means. Bsns W
p37 D 4 '71
What to watch for in prices, pay, profits,
rents; interview. H. Stein. il pors U S News
71:28-32 N 8 '71
Wobbly line on nonunion pay. Bsns W p31
N 27 '71

Forms, blanks, etc.
Pay board forms harass all sides. Bsns W
p24 Ja 1 '72

Peace corps
Age is an asset, says Peace corps, now seek-
ing more senior volunteers. il Aging 204:9
O '71

UNITED STATES—Peace corps—*Continued*
Agents of the new empire. M. Windmiller.
    Nation 212:592-6 My 10 '71
Killing of Hastings Banda; spying for the
    free world in the peace corps. P. Theroux.
    Esquire 76:22+ D '71
Peace corps and Smithsonian: deploying en-
    vironmental experts. D. P. Teter. Science
    172:1317-18 Je 25 '71
Peace corps forestry. S. Ellis. il Am For 77:
    36-8 My '71
Super Peace corps at home and abroad? il
    U S News 70:63-5 F 1 '71
This man wants you, to help them; with
    editorial comment. W. E. Swegle. il Suc
    Farm 69:no2 7, 26 F '71
What ever happened to the Peace corps?
    with firsthand views of J. Scovill and
    J. Starke. il Sr Schol 98:9-15 F 15 '71

Politics and government

Bring us together: Nixon as President and
    partisan. il pors Sr Schol 97:16-17 Ja 18 '71
Can we afford tomorrow? symposium, with
    introd. by W. C. Stolk. il Sat R 54:35-8+
    Ja 23 '71
Candidates answer Senior's queries: most im-
    portant issue facing U.S. today? il Sr Schol
    99:10-11 N 1 '71
Changing sources of power, by F. G. Dutton.
    Review
    Bsns W il p 13 Je 26 '71. B. A. Agnew
    New Repub 164:24-5 Je 5 '71. A. Schles-
    inger, jr
    Sat R 54:27 Jl 10 '71. L. L. Golden
Clear your mind of cant. S. Alsop. News-
    week 77:96 Mr 8 '71; Reply. Chr Cent 88:
    415 Mr 31 '71
Crime & the liberal audience. J. Q. Wilson;
    discussion. Commentary 51:26+ My '71
Demands of Consciousness II. H. J. Gans.
    Nation 212:275-7 Mr 1 '71
Dump Nixon campaign. D. W. Riegle, jr; A.
    K. Lowenstein. Look 35:79-80 Je 1 '71
Education of Pat Moynihan. Nat R 23:742+
    Jl 13 '71
Enduring Republican minority. V. Finger-
    hut. New Repub 165:18-20 S 11 '71
For a new policy balance. J. V. Lindsay.
    For Affairs 50:1-14 O '71
Freeze on politics. D. Lawrence. U S News
    71:108 D 13 '71
From the Democrats: a reply to Nixon;
    excerpts from interview. M. J. Mansfield.
    por U S News 70:37 F 8 '71
Future of the United States government, ed.
    by H. S. Perloff. Review
    Harper 243:89-91 Ag '71. J Thompson
Is bureaucracy out of control? il U S News
    70:61-4 My 17 '71
Issues to watch in the 92nd Congress. Sr
    Schol 98:7-8 Mr 1 '71
JFK, bitter memories of a cold day. G.
    Clarke. New Repub 164:13-15 Ja 16 '71
Jigsaw puzzle of history; adaptation of
    address. J. P. Roche. il por N Y Times
    Mag p 14-15+ Ja 24 '71; Discussion. p4
    F 14; 59+ F 21; 12 Mr 14 '71
Kennedy years: what endures. K. Auchin-
    closs. il pors Newsweek 77:20-2 F 1 '71
Letter from Washington. R. H. Rovere. See
    occasional issues of New Yorker
Letter from Washington (cont) Cato. Nat R
    23:74, 132, 190, 243, 302, 354, 410, 468, 522,
    625, 688, 740, 794, 910, 1045, 1096, 1160, 1213,
    1278, 1342, 1394 Ja 26-My 18, Je 15-Jl 27,
    Ag 24, S 24-D 17 '71
Life party. N. Johnson. New Repub 164:21-
    3 Ap 10 '71
Middle America is not back where it started.
    H. Sidey. il Time 97:18-19 F 22 '71
Moynihan report: after six months of benign
    neglect; interview. ed. by H. Brandon. D.
    P. Moynihan. il por N Y Times Mag p 10-
    11+ Je 27 '71; Reply. A. Hacker. p20 Jl 25
    '71
National affairs. See issues of Newsweek
New assault on U.S. problems. U S News
    70:13 F 1 '71
New nation gropes for better government.
    M. Ways. il Fortune 84:136-9+ Ag '71
Nixon in the White House, by R. Evans,
    jr. and R. D. Novak. Review
    Nat R 23:1307+ N 19 '71. W. A. Rusher
Nixon questions. Nat R 23:1042-3 S 24 '71
Nixon tightrope. J. M. Burns. il pors Life
    70:48B-48D+ Ap 2 '71
Nixon watch. J. Osborne. See issues of New
    republic
Nixon year III: the year of the presidential
    hat. Life 70:30-1 Ja 22 '71; Reply. G.
    Romney. 70:62A F 5 '71
Nixonology. Nat R 23:180+ F 23 '71

Off course: from Truman to Nixon, by R. G.
    Tugwell. Review
    Nat R 23:487-8 My 4 '71. G. F. Will
Pentagon papers; games presidents and other
    people play. E. J. McCarthy. New Repub
    165:14-17 Jl 10 '71
Pentagon papers; implications of deceit b''
    government. N. Cousins. Sat R 54:16 Jl 3
    '71
Perverted priorities of American politics, by
    D. Lockard. Review
    Nation 212:503-5 Ap 19 '71. H. S. Kariel
Points of rebellion, by W. O. Douglas. Review
    Nat R 23:526-8 My 18 '71. E. Van Den
    Haag
Polemics and prophecies 1967-1970, by I. F.
    Stone. Review
    Sat R 54:61 F 13 '71. S. W. Little
Politics, 1971. A. Schlesinger, jr Vogue 157:
    138-9 F 1 '71
Politics of the sixties: from the new fron-
    tier to the new revolution. E. J. Hughes.
    il N Y Times Mag p24-5+ Ap 4 '71; Reply
    with rejoinder. S. Alsop. p4+ Ap 25 '71
Presidency. H. Sidey. See issues of Life
Reports & comment: Washington (cont of
    Reports: Washington) See issues of Atlan-
    tic
Roots of lawlessness. H. S. Commager. por
    Sat R 54:17-19+ F 13 '71
Rush of events. il U S News 71:15 Jl 12 '71
Same old gang turns up in Washington.
    S. Brown. por Life 70:2 Ja 29 '71
Scenario for an American renaissance; ex-
    cerpt from address. H. Brown. Sat R 54:
    18-19 D 25 '71
Settling of America. Commonweal 93:387-8
    Ja 22 '71
State of the Union; address, January 22,
    1971. R. M. Nixon. il pors U S News 70:
    66-70 F 1 '71; Same. Vital Speeches 37:
    226-30 F '71; Excerpts. Cur Hist 60:171-4
    Mr '71
State of the Union, state of the President.
    il pors Time 97:10-11 Ja 25 '71
TRB from Washington:
    Back to normal. New Repub 164:6 My 15
    '71
    Might-have-beens. New Repub 164:6 Ja
    23 '71
That elusive political majority. A. J. Reiech-
    ley. il por Fortune 83:68-73+ Mr '71
Two years more of political irresponsibility? the
    need for one party responsibility for the
    presidency and Congress. D. Lawrence.
    U S News 70:80 F 1 '71
U.S. meets new tests at home and abroad.
    il U S News 70:9 My 31 '71
U.S. tempo speeds up. il U S News 71:15
    S 13 '71
Uneasy doubts about Nixon. F. S. Meyer.
    Nat R 23:706 Je 29 '71
Unfinished business of America; views of
    prominent Americans. il Look 35:56-7+ Jl
    13 '71
Vantage point, by L. B. Johnson. Review
    Newsweek il pors 78:22+ N 1 '71. C. Rob-
    erts
Vote of confidence; role of the Senate. E.
    J. McCarthy. Nation 212:423-5 Ap 5 '71
Voter or the politician? F. S. Meyer. Nat
    R 23:1120 O 8 '71
Washington outlook. See issues of Business
    week
Washington report. See issues of Successful
    farming
White House: the President in motion. il
    pors Time 98:18-19 O 11 '71
World we're in; excerpts from interview, ed.
    by R. Steel. W. Lippmann. New Repub 165:
    18-23 N 13 '71
    See also
Business—Political aspects
Campaign issues
Candidates, Political
Conservatism
Democratic party
Elections—United States
Fascism—United States
Federal government
Legislation—United States
Lobbying
Northwest—Politics
Political parties—United States
Populism
Presidential candidates
Presidents—United States
Presidents—United States—Relations with
    Congress
Primaries
Republican party
Right and left (political science)
South—Politics
State governments
Suffrage—United States

UNITED STATES—Politics and government—
    See also—*Continued*
Trade unions—Political activities
United States—Congress
United States—Constitution
United States—Executive departments
    also subhead Politics and government un-
    der names of states, cities, e.g. New York
    (city)— Politics and governnment

Anecdotes, facetiae, satire, etc.
On breathing and other ills. R. W. Murphy.
    Harper 242:22+ My '71
    See also
Presidents—United States—Anecdotes, face-
    tiae. satire, etc.

Popular culture
American thing: a view of southern Califor-
    nia. C. Holland. Mlle 72:207+ Ap '71
Audience as artist. A. Goldman. Vogue 157:
    135-6 F 1 '71
Identity crisis in the consumer markets.
    C. E. Silberman. il Fortune 83:92-5+ Mr
    '71
If an artist wants to be serious and respected
    and rich, famous and popular, he is suffer-
    ing from cultural schizophrenia. R. Brus-
    tein. il N Y Times Mag p 12-13+ S 26 '71;
    Discussion. p 16 O 24 '71
Look at the '50s. R. Goldstein. il Mlle 74:
    134-5+ N '71
Nostalgia: who says it's only for over-30's?
    D. Carlinsky. il Seventeen 30:114-15+ Jl '71

Population
Ahead for America: biggest baby boom. il
    U S News 70:37 Je 14 '71
How U.S. is growing. race by race. il U S
    News 71:91 N 8 '71
Middle America; center of population. il
    Newsweek 77:37 My 10 '71
New profile of U.S: latest from census. il
    U S News 70:24-5 Mr 15 '71
New questions about the U.S. population.
    L. A. Mayer. il Fortune 83:80-5+ F '71
Patterns of change in the United States; ad-
    dress, January 25, 1971. G. H. Brown.
    Vital Speeches 37:261-3 F 15 '71; Excerpts.
    por U S News 70:25 F 8 '71
Population; EQ index. il Nat Wildlife 9:38-9
    O '71
Population growth and public policy. J. T.
    McHugh. il America 125:368-9+ N 6 '71
Too many Americans? A population expert's
    view; excerpts from address, January 13,
    1971. C. Taeuber. il por U S News 70:
    62-4 F 15 '71
Who makes the babies? P. R. Ehrlich and
    J. P. Holdren. il Sat R 54:60 F 6 '71
Zero population growth, do we need it now?
    T. J. Jermann. America 124:538-40 My 22
    '71
    See also
Birth rate—United States
Migration, Internal
Negroes
United States—Census

Post office department
    See also
Postal service—United States

Postal service
    See Postal service—United States

President's advisory council on executive organization
New plan for regulating industry. il U S
    News 70:44-5 F 22 '71
Regulating the regulators; Ash commission.
    New Repub 164:10-11 F 20 '71

President's aviation advisory committee
Snowbound. R. B. Parke. Flying 89:30 Ag '71

President's commission for the observance of the twenty-fifth anniversary of the United Nations
Commission on the 25th anniversary of the
    United Nations submits final report to
    President Nixon; text of letter from Presi-
    dent Nixon to Ambassador Lodge. R. M.
    Nixon. Dept State Bul 65:127-36 Ag 2 '71

President's commission on campus unrest
Campus unrest; excerpts from report, with
    reactions to the report. Todays Ed 60:41-
    8+ Ja '71
Epistle to the Americans; Scranton report.
    R. A. Nisbet; discussion. Commentary 51:
    26+ Ap '71

President Nixon's comments on the Scranton
    report; excerpts. R. Nixon. Todays Ed
    60:59 F '71
Report of the President's commission on
    campus unrest. Review
    Nat R 23:207 F 23 '71. P. C. Roberts

President's commission on civil disorders
    See United States—National advisory
commission on civil disorders

President's commission on personnel interchange
Middle managers swap jobs; Executive inter-
    change program. il Bsns W p68 O 16 '71

President's commission on the assassination of President Kennedy
Oswald and the U-2; declassified papers from
    the Warren report. il por Newsweek 77:31
    Mr 1 '71

President's committee on employment of the handicapped
Hope and jobs for America's handicapped.
    B. L. Masse. America 125:529 D 18 '71

President's council on environmental quality
    See United States—Council on environ-
mental quality

President's foreign intelligence advisory board
Governor Connally named member. Foreign
    intelligence advisory board. Dept State Bul
    64:84 Ja 18 '71

President's Quetico-Superior committee
President's Quetico-Superior committee. Liv
    Wildn 34:54-8 Wint '70

Price administration, Office of
Have controls ever worked? il Newsweek
    78:84+ S 13 '71
Nixon of the O.P.A. M. Viorst. pors N Y
    Times Mag p70+ O 3 '71

Price commission
Catching 22. il Time 98:30+ N 1 '71
Chance for a Phase II deal with labor. il Time
    98:21 N 8 '71
Drive to beat inflation, and Democrats; Blur-
    ry banner for Phase II; program presented
    by President Nixon, October 7, 1971. il por
    Time 98:10-12+ O 18 '71
Getting set to start new controls. il U S
    News 71:26-7+ N 8 '71
Grayson sees no letup soon. il por Bsns W
    p22 D 25 '71
Hanging tough. il Newsweek 78:70-1 D 20 '71
How Nixon spells out his postfreeze pro-
    gram; address, October 7, 1971. R. M.
    Nixon. U S News 71:82-3 O 18 '71; Same
    with title Economic plan: Phase II. Vital
    Speeches 38:2-4 O 15 '71; Same abr. with
    title Fighting inflation is everybody's busi-
    ness. il Read Digest 99:77-80 D '71
How to deliver your price request. Bsns W
    p41 D 11 '71
Learning to live with Phase II. il Time 98:
    31 N 29 '71
New controllers, and new doubts. il pors
    Newsweek 78:67-9 N 1 '71
New tack on price hikes. Bsns W p41 D 11 '71
Nixon's plan for more controls. il U S News
    71:18-19 N 1 '71
Phase 2 controls; with text of Nixon's ad-
    dress, October 7, 1971. il U S News 71:21-
    6+ O 18 '71
Phase two: living with controls. il pors News-
    week 78:26-32 O 18 '71
Phase II team sets up shop. il Bsns W p23-4
    O 30 '71
Pitfalls ahead for Phase 2. il U S News 71:23-
    6 O 25 '71
Price controllers are reaching out. Bsns W
    p31 D 18 '71
Price controls get tougher. U S News 71:40
    D 13 '71
Price rules: official guidelines; statement is-
    sued by the Commission, November 11,
    1971. U S News 71:88-9 N 22 '71
Price rulings gather speed. il Bsns W p31
    N 27 '71
Proving the case for a price hike. il Bsns W
    p34+ D 4 '71
Rent boosts, the word on how much. U S
    News 72:30 Ja 3 '72
Take charge price czar; C. Jackson Gray-
    son. jr. por Time 98:19 D 20 '71
What controls mean to medical care. Bsns
    W p38-9 Ja 1 '72

UNITED STATES—Price commission—*Cont.*
What to watch for in prices, pay, profits, rents; interview. H. Stein. il pors U S News 71:28-32 N 8 '71
Zigs and zags of setting prices. Bsns W p32 N 20 '71

Public buildings
See Public buildings

Public health service
Ban on public smoking? por Newsweek 77: 90-1 Ja 25 '71

Public land law review commission
Reviewing our public land use policies. D. Jackson. Cur 127:24-8 Mr '71
Seven gut issues on public lands. W. E. Towell. Am For 77:7 Ja '71

Public opinion
See Public opinion—United States

Public works
See Public works

Quetico-Superior committee
See United States—President's Quetico-Superior committee

Race question
Attitudes toward racial integration. A. M. Greeley and P. B. Sheatsley. il Sci Am 225:13-19 bibliog(p 120) D '71
Jesus bag, by W. H. Grier and P. M. Cobbs. Review
  Nation 213:281 S 27 '71. P. Roazen
Why summer was mostly cool. il Time 98:16 S 20 '71
See also
Church and race problems
Negroes
  also subhead Race question under names of cities, e.g. Philadelphia—Race question

Reconstruction finance corporation
See Reconstruction finance corporation

Relations (diplomatic)
Catholic church
See Catholic church—Relations (diplomatic)—United States

Religious institutions and affairs
Religion in the age of Aquarius. D. Gelpi. il America 125:392-5 N 13 '71
Religion of the Republic, ed. by E. A. Smith. Review
  Commonweal 94:412-13 Ag 6 '71. G. H. Frein
See also
American council of Christian churches
Catholic church in the United States
Church and state
Churches—United States
Lutheran church in the United States
Lutherans in the United States
Mennonites
Presbyterian church in the U.S.A.
Presbyterian church in the United States (South)
Protestant churches—United States
Protestant Episcopal church
Protestants in the United States
Puritans
Reformed church in America
United church of Christ
  also subhead Religious institutions and affairs under names of states, cities, e.g. Chicago—Religious institutions and affairs

Reserve officers training corps
Another worry for services: sharp drop in ROTC students. il U S News 70:40 Ja 18 '71
ROTC: education groups' reforms stress flexibility, fuller funding. D. P. Teter. il Science 172:1216-19 Je 18 '71
ROTC stages a comeback. il U S News 71:31-2 O 11 '71
Science of war? L. G. Callahan, jr. Nat R 23:313 Mr 23 '71
Yes ma'am, colonel. Newsweek 77:98 Je 7 '71

Revenue
See also
Taxation—United States

Riots
Ghetto worries about the heat. il Bsns W p24 Jl 10 '71
See also
Riot control

Sea grant programs, Office of
Sea grant: four years later. L. Purrett. il Sci N 100:348-9 N 20 '71

Secretary of state
See Secretaries of state (United States)

Securities and exchange commission
Annual reports bare long-hidden facts. il Bsns W p65-6 Ap 3 '71
Big names in a Texas stock scheme. por Bsns W p77 Ja 23 '71
Big step backward: proposed creation of a national stock exchange system; the W. M. Martin report. C. Mathews. il Nation 213:593-5 D 6 '71
Casey: an SEC chairman Wall Street loves; with editorial comment. il por Bsns W p70-3, 104 O 16 '71
Casey at the bat. por Newsweek 77:64 F 15 '71
Casey at the bat. por Time 97:74 Mr 22 '71
Casey safe on first. por Newsweek 77:90 Mr 22 '71
Casey the reformer? Newsweek 77:64-5 My 31 '71
Companies tell more, mostly to the SEC. Bsns W p26 O 30 '71
Cracking down on pyramid plans. il Bsns W p 104+ D 11 '71
High wind in Texas; stock-fraud suit. Newsweek 77:56+ F 1 '71
I.O.U.'s of Texas are upon us; involvement of the Houston Jesuits. America 124:139 F 13 '71
Less room to play with customer cash. Bsns W p41 N 13 '71
Making it official. por Forbes 108:68 O 1 '71
More protection for investors: latest moves; with interview with W. J. Casey. il U S News 71:50-7 Ag 16 '71
New look at role of big investors. il U S News 70:44 Mr 22 '71
New man to guide the troubled SEC. por Bsns W p 18 F 6 '71
Past haunts an SEC nominee. Bsns W p35 F 27 '71
Power to the SEC? Newsweek 79:50 Ja 10 '72
Proxy activists turn on the SEC. Bsns W p39 Ap 17 '71
SEC puts a bite on funds of funds. il Bsns W p70+ F 27 '71
SEC study ducks some hard questions. Bsns W p39 Mr 13 '71
SEC wants a close-up of Fox. il Bsns W p31 Je 12 '71
SEC wants more disclosure. Bsns W p21-2 My 8 '71
SEC's own money problems. Bsns W p 19 Ap 3 '71
Sizing up the clout; study of institutional investors. C. Morgello. il Newsweek 77:94 Mr 22 '71
Sleuth of Wall Street; I. Pollack of the Division of trading and markets. G. R. Rosen. por Duns 97:71-2 Mr '71
Tighter rein on securities industry? U S News 72:75 Ja 10 '72
Tough task for new SEC chief. por U S News 70:77 F 15 '71
Wall Street's favorite bureaucrat, now. por Time 98:99 N 22 '71
Watchdog moves in on the back office. Bsns W p39 Ap 17 '71
Why the SEC wants more policing power. Bsns W p 16 Ja 1 '72
Widening impact of Texas scandal; closing of Sharpstown state bank. Bsns W p22 Ja 30 '71

Small business administration
Bigger help to small business? interview. T. S. Kleppe. il por Nations Bsns 59:26-30 My '71
New day at the SBA. G. R. Rosen. il Duns 97:42-4 Je '71
SBA report. Nations Bsns 59:20 O; 16 N; 20 D '71

Social conditions
Are the rules changing? R. Barta. America 125:341-5 O 30 '71
Are we really coming apart? M. Lerner. Cur 132:3-5 S '71
Bus line in the sky and other expensive indignities. L. E. Sissman. Atlan 228:34-5 S '71
Family portraits U.S.A. A. Gagnebin. il Look 35:22-9 Ja 26 '71
Hitching a ride across America. R. Brook. il pors Time 71:36-41 Ag 27 '71
Is America falling apart? A. Burgess. il N Y Times Mag p99-104 N 7 '71
Listening to America. B. Moyers; discussion. Harper 242:6+ F '71
Looking back on the seventies: notes toward a cultural history. B. DeMott. Atlan 227:59-64 Mr '71

UNITED STATES—Social conditions—*Cont.*
Moynihan at the UN; treatment of the United States in his analysis of 1970 report on the world social situation D. P. Moynihan. Nat R 23:1322-3 N 19 '71
Need for internal reform; excerpts from address, June 1971. K. G. Myrdal. por Sch & Soc 99:325 O '71
Now for the next 25 years. Nations Bsns 59:18 Ag '71
Repressive violence. E. Currie. Trans-Action 8:12-14+ F '71; Same abr. with title Violent America: a new myth? Cur 128:29-33 Ap '71
TRB from Washington; brutal problems facing the Nation. New Repub 164:6 My 29 '71
Today's campus: the eerie calm. G. M. Sykes. Nation 212:490-1 Ap 19 '71
White majority, ed. by L. K. Howe. Review America 125:242-4 O 2 '71. T. M. Gannon
Without Marx or Jesus, by J. F. Revel. Review
Chr Today 16:60-1 O 8 '71. J. W. Montgomery
Life 71:12 S 17 '71. A. Schlesinger, jr
Nation 213:312-14 O 4 '71. G. G. Eckstein
New Repub 165:25-6+ S 25 '71. S. McCracken
Without Marx or Jesus: the new American revolution has begun; excerpt; tr. by J. Bernard. J. F. Revel. il Sat R 54:14-31 Jl 24 '71
See also
Child labor—United States
Children—United States
Cities and towns—United States
Crime and criminals—United States
Divorce—United States
Labor and laboring classes—United States
Negroes
Poor—United States
Recreation—United States
Violence
Women—United States
Youth—United States
also subhead Social conditions under names of cities, e.g. Detroit—Social conditions

Bibliography
Home scene. M. J. Sheeran. America 125:438-9 N 20 '71

History
See United States—Social history

Social history
Egalitarian myth and the American social reality: wealth, mobility, and equality in the era of the common man. E. Pessen. bibliog f il Am Hist R 76:989-1034 O '71
See also
Education—United States—History
Labor and laboring classes—United States—History
Negroes—History
West—Social history

Social life and customs
Have Americans gone mad? M. Maddocks. Cur 125:5-9 Ja '71
See also
Balls (parties)
Christmas—United States
Family reunions
Suburban life
Thanksgiving day

Social policy
America is a growing country; address, May 22, 1971. F. Smith. Vital Speeches 37:534-7 Je 15 '71
Beginning the debate on a national planning policy. J. Barnett. Arch Rec 149:117-18 My '71
Benign neglect in the United States. R. L. Heilbroner. il Trans-Action 7:15-22 O '70
Changing priorities: hard choices, new price tags. J. I. Miller. il Sat R 54:36-7+ Ja 23 '71
Costs mount in war to end poverty. U S News 71:56-7 Jl 12 '71
From analysis to evaluation. A. Schick. bibliog f Ann Am Acad 394:57-71 Mr '71
Government agencies are failing our people; address, June 29, 1971. D. F. Linowes. Vital Speeches 37:759-62 O 1 '71
Government structure: inherent inability to change; address, June 21, 1971. J. J. Powers, jr. Vital Speeches 37:628-31 Ag 1 '71
Nixon's domestic program. F. S. Meyer. Nat R 23:262 Mr 9 '71
Phony war on poverty in the Great society. R. M. Pious. bibliog f il Cur Hist 61:266-72 N '71
Puzzle for U.S. growth vs. social progress; address. D. P. Eastburn. il por U S News 71:64-6 Jl 12 '71
See also
Public welfare—United States

Social security administration
For social security, it works like a dream. il Bsns W p 110+ Je 5 '71
Subverting the black lung law. J. DeMuth. America 125:530-2 D 18 '71

Soil conservation service
Soil conservation service, treasure chest of knowledge. R. Steffen. Org Gard & Farm 18:92-3 Je '71

Special action office for drug abuse prevention (proposed)
See United States—Drug abuse prevention, Special action office for (proposed)

Standards, National bureau of
Information on textiles, tires, and glue from the federal government. Consumer Bul 54:17-18 My '71
NBS urges 10-year metric conversion plan. C. Holden. Science 173:613 Ag 13 '71
Nation's standard setter gets a congressional review. Sci N 100:225-6 O 2 '71
Piggybacking on TV waves. Bsns W p 123 S 11 '71

State, Department of
Conference on economic nationalism sponsored by Department. Dept State Bul 65:660 D 6 '71
Diplomacy for the seventies: a program of management reform for the Department of state. Dept State Bul 63:775-802 D 28 '70
Eclipse of the State department. D. Acheson. For Affairs 49:593-606 Jl '71
Foreign affairs fudge factory, by J. F. Campbell. Review
Sat R 54:26-7 Jl 3 '71. N. King
Instruments of American foreign policy. C. W. Yost. For Affairs 50:59-68 O '71
Interagency group to coordinate federal foreign affairs research; Department announcement. Dept State Bul 64:612-13 My 10 '71
Last to know: President's personal monopoly on information and power. Nation 213:610-11 D 13 '71
Publications. See issues of Department of state bulletin
Savvy skipper of protocol. N. F. Busch. por Read Digest 99:161-5 O '71
Secretary Rogers announces management reforms; text of announcement, with text of Mr Macomber's report. Dept State Bul 65:103-9 Jl 26 '72
Secretary Rogers names committee on the human environment. Dept State Bul 64:755 Je 7 '71
Secretary Rogers receives 90-day report on progress of management reform; text of letter, March 15, 1971; with text of enclosure. W. B. Macomber, jr. Dept State Bul 64:579-81 My 3 '71
Those Arabists in the State department. J. Kraft. il N Y Times Mag p38-9+ N 7 '71
Reply. D. G. Nes. p 16+ N 28 '71
Youth, change, and foreign policy; address, November 12, 1970. R. F. Pedersen. Dept State Bul 63:718-22 D 14 '70
See also
United States—Foreign relations
United States—Foreign service

Advisory council on European affairs
Department names Advisory council on European affairs, September 2, 1971. Dept State Bul 65:359-60 O 4 '71

Advisory panel on international law
Department names advisory panel on international law. Dept State Bul 64:18 Ja 4 '71

Educational and cultural affairs, Bureau of
New private cooperation office to assist voluntary groups. Dept State Bul 64:708 My 31 '71

Subversive activities control board
...And no place to go. Newsweek 78:17 Ag 2 '71
Fear of freedom. Nation 213:484-5 N 15 '71
New mandate for inquisitors. Chr Cent 88:1041 S 8 '71
Subversives wanted. Newsweek 78:31 Jl 26 '71

Supreme court
Awful truth: Nixon-Mitchell nominees. Nation 213:450-1 N 8 '71
Changing Supreme court: new faces, new philosophy. il U S News 71:18-19 O 4 '71

UNITED STATES—Supreme court—*Continued*
Check and double-check; hearings on nominees. il pors Newsweek 78:38 N 8 '71
Chief justice looks at crime and the courts; interview. W. E. Burger. por Read Digest 98:113-16 Ap '71
Chosen two. J. Osborne. New Repub 165:12-13 N 6 '71
Court appointments. New Repub 165:7-8 N 6 '71
Court is supreme, after all. il Newsweek 78:16-21 N 1 '71
Crippling the Supreme court. America 125:249-50 O 9 '71
Hope in the law? America 126:4 Ja 8 '72
How Congress packs it in. il por Newsweek 78:20-1 D 20 '71
Lonely witness; testimony against appointment of L. F. Powell. Nation 213:549-50 N 29 71
Memo from Rehnquist. por Newsweek 78:32+ D 13 '71
Mr Justice Black. por Newsweek 78:40 S 27 '71
Myth and William Rehnquist. S. Alsop. Newsweek 78:124 D 6 '71
Nixon court. il Newsweek 78:18-22 O 4 '71
Nixon poker: six of a kind. il Newsweek 78:22+ O 25 '71
Nixon's court. Nation 213:290-1 O 4 '71
Nixon's court: its making and its meaning; President's two nominees. il pors Time 98:14-20 N 1 '71
Nixon's jinxed southern seat. por Newsweek 78:22 O 11 '71
Nixon's not so Supreme court. il Time 98:12-13 O 25 '71
Nixon's odd view of the Court. Life 71:36 N 5 '71
Now that there's a Nixon court. U S News 71:18 D 20 '71
Now, the Nixon court and what it means. il pors Time 98:15-16 O 4 '71
Now there are seven. Newsweek 78:35 O 18 '71
On choosing justices; Time essay. il Time 98:70 O 18 '71
Our creaking courts; interview. W. E. Burger. por Read Digest 98:217-19+ My '71
Poff, the Court and filibusters. America 125:276 O 16 '71
Powell, Rehnquist and the Court. America 125:387-8 N 13 '71
Powell speaks. Nat R 23:1396 D 17 '71
President and the Court. Nation 213:388 O 25 '71
Pro-antitrust, but within limits. Bsns W p27 O 2 '71
Rehnquist fight. Nat R 23:1338-9 D 3 '71
Rehnquist file. il por Newsweek 78:31-2 N 15 '71
Remaking the Supreme court, Nixon sets a pattern. il pors U S News 71:15-17 N 1 '71
Role of the Supreme court. F. J. Remington. bibliog f Cur Hist 60:353-6+ Je '71
Role of the Supreme court; Nixon gives his criteria; address, October 21, 1971. R. M. Nixon. por U S News 71:62-3 N 1 '71
Self-inflicted wound, by F. P. Graham. Review
  Nat R 23:153-4 F 9 '71. J. McClellan
Senate and the Court. Commonweal 95:27-8 O 8 '71
Senate's job. Nation 213:451-2 N 8 '71
Short tempers on the high bench. B. Schweid. Nation 213:15-17 Jl 5 '71
Should a woman be on the Supreme court? Certainly. D. Lawrence. U S News 71:104 O 25 '71
Supreme court and self-interest; justices and business litigation. America 125:138 S 11 '71
Supreme court and the idea of progress, by A. Bickel. Review
  Trans-Action 8:56+ Ja '71. L. H. Carter
Supreme court considers basic obscenity statutes. Pub W 199:45-6 F 1 '71
Supreme court: end of an era. il Time 97:41-2+ Je 21 '71
TRB from Washington: nine oracles. New Repub 165:6 N 20 '71
TRB from Washington: race against time. New Repub 165:8 S 25 '71
TRB from Washington: vending-machine justice. New Repub 165:6 N 6 '71
Toward the legal showdown; Pentagon papers case. il Time 98:13 Jl 5 '71
2 named to fill Supreme court vacancies. il Sr Schol 99:16-17 N 15 '71
Two whats for the Supreme court? W. F. Buckley, jr. Nat R 23:1258-9 N 5 '71
Up-to-date conservative; nomination of W. H. Rehnquist. Commonweal 95:174 N 19 '71
Vacancies on the Court. New Repub 165:8-9 O 2 '71

Who's who in the Supreme court. il Sr Schol 99:14 O 4 '71
  See also
Women as judges

Decisions
All or nothing for C.O.s. il Time 97:52 Mr 22 '71
Ballots, loyalty, obscenity: latest Supreme court rulings. U S News 70:68 Je 21 '71
Blow to the smut trade. Chr Today 15:22 Je 4 '71
Burger court & the penal system. S. Rubin. Nation 212:785-8 Je 21 '71
Busing. New Repub 164:11-12 My 1 '71
Busing judge. por Time 97:40 My 3 '71
Busing: the court rules. il Newsweek 77:26-7 My 3 '71
Busing the South. Sr Schol 98:16 My 17 '71
Business about bussing; Supreme court decision. Nation 212:547-8 My 3 '71
Conscientious objection. New Repub 164:7 Mr 27 '71
Counter to the current; four actions promoting liberal causes. il Time 98:80 N 8 '71
Court allows publication of Pentagon study; Bantam to publish N.Y. times version. il Pub W 200:51 Jl 12 '71
Court ruling on secrets: where it will lead. il U S News 71:22-4 Jl 12 '71
Court starts work; highlights of decisions. il Time 98:52 O 25 '71
Court's new rule on job testing. U S News 70:82-3 Ap 12 '71
Decision for Allah; draft and Muhammad Ali. por Newsweek 78:61+ Jl 12 '71
Don't call me champ; ruling on Muhammad Ali's draft. Nation 213:37 Jl 19 '71
Everybody out of the pool; ruling for Jackson, Miss. Newsweek 77:36 Je 28 '71
Far-reaching school decision, in the Court's own words; excerpts. U S News 70:40-2 My 3 '71
Fatal decision; Supreme court on death penalty. il Time 97:64 My 17 '71
First no to sex bias; victory for Mrs Sally Reed of Boise, Idaho. Time 98:71 D 6 '71
From Burger: a call for action to stop freeing the guilty. por U S News 71:33 Jl 5 '71
Gauntlet for the poor; decision on public housing. Nation 212:611 My 17 '71
Great disappointment; the Negré-Gillette decision. Chr Cent 88:363 Mr 24 '71
Green light for busing. il Sat R 54:68 My 22 '71
High court: where now? J. J. Kilpatrick. il Nat R 23:1287-91 N 19 '71
Higher wall around suburbia. Bsns W p24 My 1 '71
How High court ruled on three disputed issues; welfare, abortion, obscenity. U S News 70:58 Ja 25 '71
Is this strict construction? two decisons, expanding constitutional rights of the poor. Time 97:42 Mr 15 '71
Just one cheer; publication of the Pentagon papers. Nation 213:35-6 Jl 19 '71
Ladies' day; victory for Mrs Sally Reed in sex bias case. Newsweek 78:23-4 D 6 '71
Lessons from the school aid decisions. C. M. Whelan. America 125:32-3 Jl 24 '71
McGautha v. California, May, 1971. Cur Hist 61:40-2+ Jl '71
Mapp v. Ohio, 1961. Cur Hist 61:43-5 Jl '71
More of the same? ruling on use of intelligence tests by employers. Nat R 23:352 Ap 6 '71
Need for reasons. Time 97:47+ Je 21 '71
Neighborhood veto: a ruling on housing. il U S News 70:38 My 10 '71
New confusion on church-state school issue. R. H. Smith. Pub W 200:33 Jl 5 '71
No censorship by government; newspaper publication of Vietnam papers. R. H. Smith. Pub W 200:57 Jl 12 '71
Notes and comment. New Yorker 47:39 O 30 '71
Notes and comment; excerpt from letter to the editor of the Times approving nominations of L. F. Powell, jr. and W. H. Rehnquist. J. L. McClellan. New Yorker 47:39-40 N 27 '71
Now Supreme court sets rules for busing students. il U S News 70:12-14 My 3 '71
Onward and upward. Nat R 23:302-3 Mr 23 '71
Paper victory: the United States v. the New York times and the Washingon post. C. Rembar. Atlan 228:61-6 N '71; Reply with rejoinder. A. M. Rosenthal. 228:46+ D '71
Parochiald decision. L. Pfeffer. Todays Ed 60:63-4+ S '71
Parochial opinion; ruling on state aid. il Newsweek 78:55 Jl 12 '71

UNITED STATES—Supreme court—Decisions
—*Continued*
Parochial school aid. New Repub 165:7 Jl
10 '71
Parochial school tangle. il Sat R 54:48 Ag 21
'71
Parting shots: faces that go with the
decisions. il Life 70:62-3 F 5 '71
Pivotal parking lot. D. Kucharsky. il Chr
Today 16:42 Ja 7 '72
Prayer amendment. W. F. Buckley, jr. Nat R
23:1375 D 3 '71
Press wins and presses roll. il Time 98:10-12
Jl 12 '71
Privacy and the third-party bug; case of
James White. N. Lewin. New Repub 164:
12-17 Ap 17 '71
Psalm 151? Chr Cent 88:847 Jl 14 '71
Question of life or death. il Newsweek 77:30-2
My 17 '71
Racial balance in every school is not re-
quired; excerpts from remarks; August 31,
1971. W. E. Burger. por U S News 71:23
S 13 '71
Right to publish. N. Lewin. New Repub 165:
11-13 Jl 10 '71
Right to turn down advertising. R. L. Tobin.
Sat R 54:55-6 Je 12 '71
Right turn; Burger court on Miranda warn-
ings. il Time 97:38 Mr 8 '71
School aid decisions. C. M. Whelan. Amer-
ica 125:8-11 Jl 10 '71
Secrets and security; postscript to the Penta-
gon papers. I. Silver. Commonweal 94:399-
402 Ag 6 '71
Selective conscientious objectors decision.
America 124:278 Mr 20 '71
Self-inflicted wound, by F. P. Graham.
Review
America 124:296-7 Mr 20 '71. T. H.
Clancy
Sheppard v. Maxwell, 1966. Cur Hist 61:106-
10+ Ag '71
Significant decisions in labor cases. See
issues of Monthly labor review
Sometime eighteen-year-old vote. N. Lewin.
New Repub 164:21-2 Ja 2 '71
Southern editors size up busing decision.
U S News 70:49-50 My 10 '71
Splintering in the Supreme court. N. Lewin.
New Repub 164:13-15 F 27 '71
Strange case of libel; suits against newspa-
pers and magazines. S. G. Blackman. Sat
R 54:48-9+ Ap 10 '71
Stricter standards for personnel tests.
Bsns W p34 Mr 20 '71
Supreme court and abortion. America 124:
443 My 1 '71
Supreme court and the flag; question of
desecrating the flag through art. F. Gra-
ham. Art in Am 59:27 Mr '71
Supreme court and the rights of poor. Amer-
ica 124:477 My 8 '71
Supreme court: signs of a thaw. America
124:252 Mr 13 '71
Supreme court: yes and no. America 125:335
O 30 '71
Supreme court yes to busing. il Time 97:
13-14 My 3 '71
Swimming pools: black and white; Jackson,
Miss. closure. America 124:645 Je 26 '71
U.S. Supreme court as prophet; Pennsylvania
and Rhode Island laws furnishing aid to
church-related schools declared unconstitutional. W. W. Brickman. Sch & Soc 99:330-1
O '71
Ultimate question; death penalty. Nation
212:610 My 17 '71
Victory for the press; Supreme court ruling
on publication of the secret Pentagon his-
tory of the Vietnam war; with excerpts
from opinions of 5 justices. il Newsweek
78:16-19 Jl 12 '71
Viet objectors overruled. Sr Schol 98:12 Mr
22 '71
Vote for 18-year-olds: what justices said on
both sides. il U S News 70:88-9 Ja 25 '71
Votes against the poor; busing to integrate
schools. il Time 97:16-17 My 10 '71
Win one, lose one: the Supreme court;
Catholic schools and colleges. W. C. Mc-
Innes. America 125:170-3 S 18 '71
You can do that; Pentagon papers, obscenity and libel decisions. H. F. Pilpel
and A. U. Schwartz. Pub W 200:37-8 Ag 2
'71

History
Story behind the book; Holmes Devise fund's
history of U.S. Supreme court. R. H.
Smith. il Pub W 200:20 N 1 '71
Twelve great justices of all time. il Life 71:
52-4+ O 15 '71

Tariff commission
Lifelines for import victims. il Nations Bsns
59:28+ Je '71

Tax court
Now: a break for the small taxpayer;
Small tax case division. il U S News 70:
46-9 F 22 '71

Territories and possessions
See also
Guam
Micronesia
Trust Territory of the Pacific Islands
Virgin Islands

Trade missions

Japan
They took the American look to Tokyo. il
Bsns W p82+ O 16 '71

Russia
Toolmakers' mission to Moscow. il Bsns W
p24-5 Mr 20 '71
Trading with Russia gets down to hardware.
il Bsns W p95 Je 12 '71

Trade policy
See United States—Commerce

Transportation, Department of
DOT seen impeding landing aid program. C.
E. Schneider. il Aviation W 95:53-4 N 15
'71
DOT using mathematical models to study
SST climate effects. Aviation W 94:42 Ja
25 '71
Deregulation is off to a halting start. Bsns
W p46 N 13 '71
Foggy guidelines for airline mergers. il
Bsns W p22 S 4 '71
SST termination process begins; with ed-
itorial comment. Aviation W 94:9, 14-16
Mr 29 '71
Shame on you, DOT. R. L. Collins. Flying
90:14-15 Ja '72
Weak national plan chugs in behind schedule.
il Bsns W p76 S 18 '71
See also
United States—National highway traffic
safety administration
United States—Urban mass transportation ad-
ministration

Appropriations and expenditures
Administration yields on trust fund use. D.
C. Winston. Aviation W 94:20-1 Je 28 '71
Senate would halt trust fund loss. D. C.
Winston. Aviation W 95:14-15 Jl 26 '71

Public records
Cut that tape. il Time 98:94 D 6 '71

Transportation systems center
R&D conversion; former NASA lab now
working on transportation. D. Shapley.
Science 171:286-9 Ja 22 '71

Travel service
See also
United States—National tourism resources
review commission

Treasury, Department of the
As Connally sees his Cabinet job; excerpts
from testimony before the Senate finance
committee. J. B. Connally. por U S News
70:36 F 15 '71
John Connally: Mr Nixon's no. 2 man? il
pors Newsweek 78:16-20 Ag 9 '71
Nixon-Connally arrangement. R. J. Whalen.
por Harper 243:29-33+ Ag '71
Rough road to the Treasury. por Bsns W
p 17 F 6 '71
TRB from Washington; R. Nader and others file suit to block fast depreciation allowances. New Repub 165:6 Jl 17 '71
See also
United States—Comptroller of currency, Office of

Treaties
Honor among nations. J. Deedy. Common-
weal 95:146 N 12 '71
Treaty information. See issues of Depart-
ment of state bulletin
Vindication of John Bricker; Vienna protocol
treaty giving U.N. authority over control of
psychotropic drugs in U.S. J. Kaplan. Nat
R 23:1413-14 D 17 '71
See also
United States—Commercial treaties and
agreements

Honduras
United States and Honduras sign Swan Islands treaty. Dept State Bul 65:691 D 13 '71

UNITED STATES—Treaties—*Continued*

Japan

Agreement with Japan on reversion of Okinawa transmitted to the Senate. R. M. Nixon; W. P. Rogers. Dept State Bul 65: 431-5 O 18 '71

End of a feud? il Newsweek 77:34 Je 21 '71

End of American rule on Okinawa: what it means. il U S News 70:42-3 Je 28 '71

Spear and the shield; restoring Okinawa to Japanese control. il Time 97:37-8 Je 28 '71

United States-Japanese treaty on Okinawa; text. Cur Hist 61:359-60+ D '71

Mexico

Land grants and land grabs: Treaty of Guadalupe Hidalgo. il Sr Schol 99:10-11 Ja 10 '72

United States and Mexico sign boundary treaty; Department announcement. November 23, 1970. Dept State Bul 63:765-6 D 21 '70

Taiwan

Approaching China, defending Taiwan: Mutual defense treaty of 1954. E. C. Ravenal. For Affairs 50:44-58 O '71

Urban mass transportation administration

Can $30 billion buy a better ride? il Newsweek 77:48 Ja 18 '71

Mass transit's optimist. G. R. Rosen. por Duns 98:58-9 N '71

Veterans administration

Hearing aids; with Veterans administration ratings. il Consumer Rep 36:310-20 My '71

Let George Romney play King Canute: FHA-VA mortgages. Nat R 23:848+ Ag 10 '71

1971 hearing aid selections by the Veterans administration. il Consumer Bul 54:31-2 My '71

Veterans administration hospitals

Hospital holiday; army's Valley Forge general hospital; excerpt from How to say yes to life. C. L. Miller. il Good H 173:68-9+ D '71

Little help for the wounded; veterans' hospital care. Life 70:4 My 28 '71

Ordeal of the wounded veteran. A. Cranston. Redbook 136:78+ Ap '71

Our VA hospitals are in trouble. K. Y. Tomlinson. Read Digest 98:163-4+ Mr '71

Wounded wait in line. J. Castelli. Nation 213:178-80 S 6 '71; Reply with rejoinder. D. E. Johnson. 213:322+ O 11 '71

Drug treatment centers

Growing worry over drug-hooked GI's. il U S News 70:30 Ap 12 '71

Trying to help the GI addicts; Palo Alto VA hospital program; with editorial comment. il Life 71:3, 20-7 Jl 23 '71

VA given task of developing programs for GI addicts. J. Walsh. Science 173:33 Jl 2 '71

Violence commission

See United States—National commission on the causes and prevention of violence

Vital statistics

See also
Mortality
United States—Census
United States—Population

Weather bureau

See United States—National weather service

Work projects administration

WPA art: rescue of a U.S. treasure. il U S News 70:75-8 Je 21 '71

Why not another WPA? C. Phillips. New Repub 164:19-20 F 6 '71

Works progress administration

See United States—Work projects administration

Youth conservation corps

It's a natural. Sr Schol 98:12 Mr 15 '71

UNITED STATES air force academy, Colorado Springs

Captivating Air force academy. Chr Today 16:32 D 3 '71

UNITED STATES amateur championship. See Golf—Tournaments

UNITED STATES amateur publinx championship. See Golf—Tournaments

UNITED STATES and Canada; United States and Cuba; etc. See Canada and the United States; Cuba and the United States; etc.

UNITED STATES-Canadian committee on trade and economic affairs. See Joint United States-Canadian committee on trade and economic affairs

UNITED STATES Catholic bishops conference. See National conference of Catholic bishops

UNITED STATES Catholic conference

Dumping the draft; USCC testimony. Commonweal 94:52 Mr 26 '71

Let's break the hellish circle. America 125: 389 N 13 '71

Preserving a U.N. presence; possible closing of USCC's Office for United Nations affairs. Commonweal 95:123-4 N 5 '71

Scandal of silence. G. C. Zahn. Commonweal 95:79-85 O 22 '71

Unwarranted dismissal; L. M. Colonnese. Chr Cent 88:1102 S 22 '71

UNITED STATES chamber of commerce. See Chamber of commerce of the United States of America

UNITED STATES conference of mayors

Mayor's complaint. Newsweek 77:53 F 22 '71

Mayors' revolt; voyage to Washington to press support for President Nixon's revenue-sharing plan. il Newsweek 77:94 My 24 '71

UNITED STATES dependents schools, European area. See Military post schools, American

UNITED STATES-Dominican Republic air agreement. See Aviation—International aspects

UNITED STATES flag. See Flags—United States

UNITED STATES foreign service. See United States—Foreign service

UNITED STATES fuel and gas championship race. See Drag racing

UNITED STATES girls' junior championship. See Golf—Tournaments

UNITED STATES Grand prix. See Automobile racing

UNITED STATES in art

See also
New York city in art
Philadelphia in art
South in art
West in art

UNITED STATES in literature

Benjamin, Edgar, Humbert, and Jay, M. Banta. Yale R 60:532-49 Je '71

See also
New England in literature
South in literature
Southwest in literature

UNITED STATES-Japan conference on natural resources. See Natural resources—Conferences

UNITED STATES-Japan cooperative medical science committee. See Medical research—International cooperation

UNITED STATES-Japan ministerial conference on environmental pollution. See Pollution—Control—Conferences

UNITED STATES Jaycees (organization)

Jaycees in prison. il Time 98:60+ S 20 '71

UNITED STATES-Korea (Republic) air agreement. See Aviation—International aspects

UNITED STATES lawn tennis association

Keep it clean, chaps. il Newsweek 77:79-80 F 15 '71

UNITED STATES lines, inc.

Hot potato, maritime division. il Forbes 108:27-8 D 1 '71

Walter Kidde's stormy voyage with U.S. lines. W. S. Rukeyser. il Fortune 84:82-5+ Jl '71

UNITED STATES marine hospital, Carville, La. See Leprosy and lepers

UNITED STATES military academy, West Point

Black cadet at West Point; J. C. Whittaker case. J. F. Marszalek, jr. il pors Am Heritage 22:30-7+ Ag '71; Reply. T. J. Fleming. 22:111 O '71

Getting it together at the Point. P. Bailey. il Ebony 27:136+ D '71

UNITED STATES Open golf tournament. See Golf—Tournaments

UNITED STATES plywood-Champion papers, inc.

Alaska's Tongass suit: the exercise at Juneau. M. Miller. il Am For 77:28-31+ Mr '71

Dealer network for U.S. plywood. Bsns W p59 O 2 '71

Fight for the trees in the Tongass. M. Miller. il Am For 77:16-19 Jl '71

Warning: the chain saw cometh; Tongass national forest. P. Brooks. il Atlan 228:95-9 D '71

UNITED STATES postal service. See Postal service—United States
UNITED STATES power squadrons, inc.
57 years of service to the boating public. R. A. Green. Motor B & S 127:151 Je '71
Under way with the USPS. R. A. Green. See issues of Motor boating & sailing
UNITED STATES professional tennis championship. See Tennis
UNITED STATES-Russia airline service. See Airlines—International services
UNITED STATES sailboat show. See Boats—Exhibitions
UNITED STATES steel corporation
Big steel union makes war on pollution; Local 1557's fight to clean up coke plant. il Bsns W p34-5 D 25 '71
Big steel's little switch; change in pension fund accounting. Forbes 108:50 D 1 '71
Liberation of Gary, Indiana. E. Greer. il por Trans-Action 8:30-9+ Ja '71
Roof heliport keyed to 21st century; facility atop new U.S. steel headquarters in Pittsburgh. il Aviation W 95:50-1 O 18 '71
Water polluters tangle with the law, and lose. il Bsns W p64-5 O 9 '71
UNITED STATES-Switzerland air agreement. See Aviation—International aspects
UNITED STATES volleyball association
First stop for the U.S. on the road to Havana. J. Jares. il Sports Illus 34:72+ My 17 '71
UNITED steelworkers of America
Big steel union makes war on pollution; Local 1557's fight to clean up coke plant. il Bsns W p34-5 D 25 '71
Decent guys a little too long; interview, ed. by T. Joyce and J. Lowell. I. W. Abel. por Newsweek 77:51 F 1 '71
Rumblings of a steel strike get louder. il Bsns W p69 F 27 '71
Steel: labor's showdown of the year. il Newsweek 77:77 Ap 12 '71
Steelworkers conservation program. I. W. Abel. il por Nat Parks & Con Mag 45:25-8 F '71
Steelworkers' militant mood deepens. il Bsns W p76+ Ap 3 '71
Steelworkers set out to rescue steel. il Bsns W p58-9 D 11 '71
Steelworkers set the price for peace. Bsns W p31-2 Mr 20 '71
31% raise. Time 97:80 Je 14 '71
Trying to avoid an unwanted strike. il pors Time 97:77-8 My 24 '71
USW whets its c-o-l clause; unlimited cost-of-living. Bsns W p82 F 20 '71
UNITED transportation union
Railroad pact breaks new ground. Bsns W p56-7 Ag 7 '71
Railroads break a union's work rules. il Bsns W p 14 Jl 24 '71
Wave of labor unrest. il Newsweek 78:61 Ag 2 '71
UNITS
Mathematician's version of the fine-structure constant. G. B. Lubkin. bibliog il por Phys Today 24:17-19 Ag '71; Discussion. 24:9 N '71
UNIVAC division. See Sperry Rand corporation—Univac division
UNIVERSAL copyright convention. See Copyright
UNIVERSAL declaration of human rights
Secretary-General's press conference; January 18, 1971. Thant. UN Mo Chron 8:24-34 F '71
UNIVERSAL Negro improvement association
Amy Jacques Garvey: black, beautiful & free. B. Reed. il pors Ebony 26:45-6+ Je '71
UNIVERSAL symbols. See Symbols
UNIVERSE
Energy in the universe. F. J. Dyson. il Sci Am 225:50-9 S '71
Lunokhod 1 on the expansion of the universe. S Mandelshtam Space World H-4-88:46 Ap '71
Support for the theory of a hyperbolic universe. Sci N 100:291 O 30 '71
Theory of early universe explains particle production. G. B. Lubkin. Phys Today 24:19 D '71
What is beyond the universe? I. Asimov. Sci Digest 69:69-70 Ap '71
See also
Cosmology
Creation
UNIVERSITIES. See Colleges and universities
UNIVERSITY administration. See Colleges and universities—Administration
UNIVERSITY art galleries and museums. See College art galleries and museums
UNIVERSITY bands. See Bands (music)

UNIVERSITY CITY, Mo.
Try a city-school park program. C. I. Linhart. il Am City 86:82-3 Mr '71
UNIVERSITY computing company
Heady dreams at University computing. il por Bsns W p54-5+ My 1 '71
Wyly's Texas-style dream; Datran. A. A. Butkus. por Duns 98:54 Ag '71
UNIVERSITY extension
Another approach to higher education; proposal for a video university. A. M. Mood. Ed Digest 37:13-16 D '71
Big move to non-campus colleges. E. L. Boyer and G. C. Keller. il Sat R 54:46-9+ Jl 17 '71
College without a campus; SUNY programs. Time 97:56+ Mr 1 '71
Different type of college; it comes to the student. il U S News 71:40-2 O 4 '71
Internationalized university without walls. Sch & Soc 99:397-8 N '71
Open university is born; University without walls. C. Holden. Science 171:881 Mr 5 '71
Opening the ivory tower; external degree programs. il Sat R 54:49 Mr 20 '71
Universities without walls. Sch & Soc 99:201-2 Ap '71
University extension and accreditation. E. J. Durnall. Sch & Soc 99:87-8 F '71
When college is open to all: the experiment in Britain; Open university. il U S News 70:63-4 Mr 1 '71
UNIVERSITY government. See Colleges and universities—Administration
UNIVERSITY investments. See Colleges and universities—Investments
UNIVERSITY librarians. See College librarians
UNIVERSITY libraries. See College libraries
UNIVERSITY microfilms, inc.
$1,000 misunderstanding; UM's index to its Dissertation abstracts international; with reply by R. F. Asleson. R. L. Scott. Wilson Lib Bul 46:73-7 S '71
UNIVERSITY of Pennsylvania

Hospital

See Pennsylvania. University, Philadelphia—Hospital
UNIVERSITY of Rochester. See Rochester, N.Y. University
UNIVERSITY of southern California. See Southern California university, Los Angeles
UNIVERSITY of Texas. See Texas. University
UNIVERSITY of the air. See Adult education—Great Britain
UNIVERSITY of the New World
Brand new: a university to save the world? Mlle 72:282 Ap '71
UNIVERSITY police force. See Colleges and universities—Security measures
UNIVERSITY presidents. See College presidents
UNIVERSITY presses
1970 in review. Pub W 199:46 F 8 '71
Professors are too sophisticated. A. Kazin. Sat R 54:23-4+ My 22 '71
Scholarly publishing and the university library; address, May 1971. R. E. Ellsworth. il por Library J 96:3568-72 N 1 '71
See also
Association of American university presses
British Columbia university press
Oxford university press
Princeton university press
Toronto university press
UNIVERSITY professors. See College professors and instructors
UNIVERSITY research. See Colleges and universities—Research
UNIVERSITY students. See College students
UNIVERSITY trustees. See College trustees
UNIVERSITY without walls. See University extension
UNKNOWN soldiers
Crow chief's tribute to the unknown soldier. J. C. Ewers. il pors Am West 8:30-5 N '71
UNLEADED gasoline. See Gasoline—Additives
UNLIKELY heroes; drama. See Arrick, L.
UNMARRIED couples. See Cohabitation
UNMARRIED fathers. See Fathers, Unmarried
UNMARRIED mothers. See Mothers, Unmarried
UNMARRIED women. See Single women
UNORDERED merchandise. See Postal service—Unordered merchandise
UNOX process. See Sewage purification—Activated sludge method
UNRAU, Ruth
Reading before writing. Writer 84:25 D '71

UNRUH, Jesse Marvin
Jess Unruh and his moment of truth. J.
Larner. pors Harper 242:62-8 Ap '71 •
UNSER, Al
Motor trend interview. il pors Motor T
23-72+ Mr '71

about

Johnny Lightning drives through the wreck-
age. R. F. Jones. il por Sports Illus 34:26-9
Je 7 '71 •
UNSER, Bobby
Motor trend interview. il pors Motor T 23:
72+ Mr '71
UNTERECKER, John
Hero: poem. Poetry 119:26-7 O '71
UNTERMEYER, Louis
Law of order, the promise of poetry. Sat R
54:18-20+ Mr 20 '71
UNWORTHY friend; story. See Borges, J. L.
UP above the world so high: story. See Soman,
F. J.
UP the sandbox; story. See Roiphe, A. R.
UPDIKE, John
Baluchitherium; story. New Yorker 47:39 Ag
14 '71
First lunar invitational. New Yorker 47:35-6 F
27 '71
Grabbing dilemmas; interview. ed. by E.
Rhode. por Vogue 157:140-1+ F 1 '71
Jesus on Honshu; story. New Yorker 47:
29-30 D 25 '71
Love: first lessons; story. New Yorker 47:
46-7 N 6 '71
Marching through a novel; poem. Sat R 54:
24 Jl 3 '71
Plumbing; story. New Yorker 47:34-7 F 20 '71
Pop mom moon; story. Atlan 228:48-51 Ag '71
Rabbit's evening out; story; excerpt from
Rabbit Redux. il Esquire 76:109-12 S '71
Sublimating; story. Harper 243:82-5 S '71
Sunday rain; poem. Sat R 54:59 Ap 17 '71

about

Holding the fort on Audubon Terrace. M.
Cowley. il Sat R 54:17+ Ap 3 '71 •
Updike on the present. C. T. Samuels. New
Repub 165:29-30 N 20 '71 •
UPDIKE, Linda Grace (Hoyer) See Hoyer,
L. G.
UPHOLSTERY
See also
Automobiles—Upholstery
UPPER ARLINGTON, Ohio
Go total communications. A. C. Neer. il Am
City 86:117-18+ Ap '71
UPPER atmosphere. See Atmosphere, Upper
UPWARD bound (program)   See Socially
handicapped children—Education
URACIL
Photochemical transformation of 5-alkyl-
uracils and their nucleosides. E. Krajewska
and D. Shugar. bibliog il Science 173:435-7
Jl 30 '71
URANIUM
Isotopes
Alpha-recoil thorium-234: dissolution into
water and the uranium-234/uranium-238
disequilibrium in nature. K. Kigoshi. bib-
liog il Science 173:47-8 Jl 2 '71
URANIUM compounds
See also
Uranyl compounds
URANYL compounds
Pinocytosis and membrane dilation in uranyl-
treated plant roots. H. Wheeler and P.
Hanchey. bibliog il Science 171:68-71 Ja
8 '71
URBAN, Elizabeth Hope
Erin a la cart. il Travel 135:52-4 F '71
URBAN administration. See Municipal govern-
ment
URBAN center, Columbia university. See Col-
umbia university—Urban center
URBAN coalition (organization)
Life in the inner city: even worse since
1968. il Sci N 100:226 O 2 '71
Of budgets & media. P. Steinfels. Common-
weal 94:30 My 19 '71
URBAN constitutional convention (proposed)
See Constitutional conventions
URBAN design. See City planning
URBAN development. See Urban renewal
URBAN development corporation. See New
York (state)—Urban development corpora-
tion
URBAN education. See Education, Urban
URBAN growth. See Cities and towns—Growth
URBAN housing. See Housing
URBAN law institute
Disowned. New Repub 164:8-9 Ap 10 '71

URBAN league, National. See National urban
league
URBAN life. See City and town life
URBAN poverty. See Poor—United States
URBAN renewal
Building types study; with introd. by J. D.
Morgan. il Arch Rec 150:123-38 O '71
Developing the whole city. R. S. Danforth.
Cur 127:39-41 My '71
New town in town. il Newsweek 78:40+ Jl
19 '71
Public housing and urban renewal; Singa-
pore. Y. M. Yeung. bibliog il Focus 21:9-
12 Ap '71
What it will take to bring cities back to life;
interview. D. Rockefeller. il por U S News
70:50-2+ Je 7 '71
What really is relevant? Am City 86:8 S '71
See also
City planning
Urban coalition (organization)
also subhead City planning under cities,
e.g. Philadelphia—City planning

New York (state)

See also
New York (state)—Urban development corporation

Pennsylvania

See also
Philadelphia—City planning
URBAN-rural conflict. See City and country
URBAN services. See Municipal services
URBAN studies. See Sociology, Urban—Study
and teaching
URBAN teachers. See Teachers
URBAN technology conference
Aerospace's urban role debated. W. H. Greg-
ory. Aviation W 94:62-4+ Je 7 '71
URBAN transportation
Agony of the commuter. il Newsweek 77:
44-7+ Ja 18 '71
Environment, autos and the public. il Sci N
100:371-2 D 4 '71
Environment; summaries of papers at the
5th international conference on urban
transportation. Sci N 100:189 S 18 '71
Mass urban transit. J. Peter. il Look 35:20-7
Ap 20 '71
More woes for mass transit, and no end in
sight. il U S News 71:100-1 O 25 '71
Transportation in the cities: pessimism over
solutions. R. H. Gilluly. Sci N 100:250 O
9 '71
See also
Local transit
United States—Urban mass transportation
administration
URBAN water supply. See Water supply
URBANA, Ill.

Education

Students profit from classroom drilling;
course at Norris L. Brookens junior high
school. V. Louvière. il Nations Bsns 59:17
O '71
URBANISM. See Cities and towns
URBANIZATION
On urbanization: a worldwide process; ex-
cerpts from address, November 1970. B.
Ward. por Sr Schol Teach ed 97:3 Ja 11 '71
URBANIZED areas. See Metropolitan areas
URCH, George E.
Language and the schools in Kenya. bibliog
Sch & Soc 99:373-7 O '71
URCHINS, Sea. See Sea urchins
URDANG, Constance
Dusk to dawn; poem. New Repub 164:27 Je
12 '71
Images; Street thief; Day the houses sank;
poems. Poetry 118:141-2 Je '71
URDU poetry
Department of amplification. V. Mehta. New
Yorker 47:121-4 Mr 13 '71

Translations into English

Ghazal XXXIV, translations by Aijaz Ah-
mad, Adrienne Rich and William Stafford.
Ghālib. Mlle 74:50 Ja '72
UREDOPORES. See Spores (botany)
URETHANE foam. See Plastic foams
URETHANES
DEP, cancer and beverages. Sci N 100:422 D
25 '71
Diethyl pyrocarbonate: formation of urethan
in treated beverages. G. Löfroth and T.
Gejvall. bibliog il Science 174:1248-50 D 17
'71
UREY, Harold Clayton
Was the moon originally cold? bibliog Sci-
ence 172:403-5 Ap 23 '71

URIC acid
Uric acid dihydrate in bird urine. K. Lonsdale and D. J. Sutor. bibliog il Science 172: 958-9 My 28 '71
See also
Lesch-Nyhan syndrome
URIDINE
See also
Bromodeoxyuridine
Isododeoxyuridine
URINE
Analysis
Uric acid dihydrate in bird urine. K. Lonsdale and D. J. Sutor. bibliog il Science 172:958-9 My 28 '71
URIS, Dorothy
When everybody wins. Opera N 36:6-7 D 25 '71
UROPORPHYRINOGEN III cosynthetase. See Synthetases
URTICARIA. See Hives (urticaria)
URUGUAY
See also
Elections—Uruguay
Guerrillas—Uruguay
Investments, Foreign (in Uruguay)
Economic conditions
Yankees do business under fire. il Bsns W p42 D 4 '71
Politics and government
Chaos itself. Newsweek 78:37 O 11 '71
Test for the frente. Time 98:41-2 N 29 '71
USDIN, Gene L.
Coin needn't smell: a response to the Seidenberg thesis. Ment Hy 55:32-4 Ja '71
USE of time. See Time, Use of
USED automobiles. See Automobiles, Used
USED boats. See Boats, Used
USED cameras. See Cameras, Used
USED car industry. See Automobile industry—Used cars
USED car trade. See Automobile industry—Used cars
USED planes. See Airplanes, Used
USED tractors. See Tractors, Used
USERY, Willie J. 1923-
Labor's troubleshooter. por Newsweek 78: 60-1 Ag 16 '71 *
President's negotiator. por Duns 97:76-7 My '71 *
Rails flag a new contract negotiator. Bsns W p30 O 30 '71 *
USHERWOOD, Bob
British library world, 1971. il por Wilson Lib Bul 45:952-61 Je '71
USHIBA, Nobuhiko
Japan looks to the 1970's; address, September 16, 1971. Vital Speeches 38:11-13 O 15 '71
Pacific trade challenge; address, March 15, 1971. Vital Speeches 37:390-2 Ap 15 '71
about
We have our protectionists too. por Forbes 108:78 O 15 '71 *
USTINOV, Peter
Authors & editors; interview, ed. by D. N. Mount. por Pub W 200:15-17 O 25 '71
UTAH
See also
Arches National Monument
Canyonlands National Park
Fishing—Utah
Geology—Utah
Hunting—Utah
Mormons and Mormonism
Paleontology—Utah
Skis and skiing—Utah
Antiquities
Brimhall saga. F. Brodie. il por Am West 8:4-9+, 18-23+ Jl, S '71
Description and travel
Utah's secret snow country. G. Reiger. il Pop Mech 136:72-4 D '71
UTAH symphony orchestra
Musical events; concert in Carnegie Hall. W. Sargeant. New Yorker 47:88 Je 12 '71
UTE Indian museum. See Indians of North America—Museums
UTE Indians
Theft from Ute Indians. Ramp Mag 10:7 Ag '71
UTERUS
Leucylglycinamide released from oxytocin by human uterine enzyme. R. Walter and others. bibliog il Science 173:827-9 Ag 27 '71
See also
Placenta

Surgery
Hysterectomy; ed. by. H. Touré. T. W. McElin. Redbook 137:48+ My '71
UTERUS, Artificial
Obsolescent mother. E. Grossman. il Atlan 227:39-50 My '71
UTICA, N.Y.
Utica's hearty handshake. il Am City 86: 126+ My '71
Housing
Urban development corporation housing for Utica, New York. il Arch Rec 150:110-11 Jl '71
UTILITARIANISM
Mummy's curse; J. Bentham's philosophy. J. W. Burrow. il por Horizon 13:42-7 Aut '71
UTILITY poles, Wood. See Wood poles
UTLAUT, William F. and Cohen, Robert
Modifying the ionosphere with intense radio waves. bibliog il Science 174:245-54 O 15 '71
UTLEY, Robert M.
Epilogue. il Am Heritage 22:40-1 Je '71
UTOPIAS
Foolish American ism: utopianism. I. Kristol. il N Y Times Mag p31+ N 14 '71; Reply. A. F. Reel. p32+ D 5 '71
More's Utopia: confessional modes. D. Bleich. bibliog f Am Imago 28:24-52 Spr '71
UZMANN, Joseph R. See Cooper, R. A. jt. auth.
UZZELL, Thomas, and Corbin, K. W.
Fitting discrete probability distributions to evolutionary events. bibliog il Science 172: 1089-96 Je 11 '71
UZZLE, Burk
Gallery; photographs. Life 70:6-7 Mr 12 '71

V

V-belts. See Belting
VA. See United States—Veterans administration
VA hospitals. See United States—Veterans administration hospitals
VASCAR (visual average speed computer and recorder) See Computers—Traffic control use
VAT. See Value added tax
VD. See Venereal diseases
VEE (Venezuelan equine encephalomyelitis) See Encephalomyelitis
VISTA. See Volunteers in service to America
VOM. See Voltohmmeters
V/STOL (vertical or short take-off and landing) airplanes. See Airplanes, Vertical take-off and landing
VTOL airplanes. See Airplanes, Vertical take-off and landing
VTR (video tape recorders) See Video recorders and recording
VTVM (vacuum tube voltmeter) See Voltmeters
VACATION cabins. See Cabins
VACATION camps. See Camps
VACATION clothing. See Clothing and dress
VACATION houses
All-year vacation house: a surge of space. A. Stagg. il House & Gard 139:114-21 Mr '71
Block Island sanctuary. B. Plumb. il Am Home 74:86-9 S '71
Buy a vacation place all your own? il Changing T 25:24-8 Ag '71
Dome on the range, on the beach and in the bay. il Esquire 75:76-7 F '71
Four vacation houses. il Arch Rec 150:121-8 N '71
House by the side of the trail. N. Skurka. il N Y Times Mag p70-1 Mr 14 '71
How do you try out a vacation place idea? Here's a case history. il Sunset 147:74-6 S '71
How to make money while relaxing in the country. S. Burns. Vogue 159:12 Ja 1 '72
Season it Caribbean. J. Peter. il Look 35: 70-1 O 19 '71
Secluded weekend house for city dwellers. il Arch Rec 149:120-1 My '71
Second homes that can become first! il Pop Mech 135:144-52 Ap '71
Second-house dilemma: where do you really live? M. S. Welch. House B 113:71+ Je '71

VACATION houses—*Continued*
Ski-country casual. N. Skurka. il N Y Times
Mag p52-3 Ja 9 '72
Sky-lit room for dull days, a window seat
for storms. il Sunset 146:122 Je '71
Snow place; Richard Hodgsons' retreat,
Snowmass, Colo. R. Reif. il N Y Times
Mag p54-5 Ja 24 '71
Treehouse deep in the woods. il House B 113:
45-9 Ja '71
Variety in modules. N. Skurka. il N Y Times
Mag p60-1 My 9 '71
Weekend house that looks after itself. il
House & Gard 139:56+ Ja '71
Well-built house: a redwood and glass se-
cond home in Alpine Meadows, Calif. J.
H. Ingersoll. il House B 113:6 Mr '71
Windmill house rebuilt for family weekends.
il House & Gard 140:72-5 Ag '71
See also
Beach architecture
Summer homes

Leasing and renting
If you want to rent a villa here's how to
do it. H. Sutton. il Holiday 48:8-11 N '70
VACATION schools. See School year; Summer
schools
VACATION shelters. See Shelters
VACATION villages
Club Mediterranée. il Newsweek 77:68+ Ap 5
'71
Is the Club Méditerranée really that great?
You bet! L. Barry. il Pop Phot 69:48+ S
'71
Simple form of affluence; Club Méditer-
ranée. il Forbes 108:34 Ag 1 '71
VACATIONS
How not to waste a weekend; family ex-
cursions. R. H. Rufa. il Travel 136:68-71
Ag '71
Six of the healthiest vacation spots in the
U.S.A. R. Joseph. il Todays Health 49:24-
7+ Je '71
Swap your pad for a villa. L. Carpenter. il
McCalls 98:41 Je '71
Taking the kids and surviving it: a case for
togetherness. B. Brower. il Life 71:20-1 S 3
'71
This year, take a different vacation. il Chang-
ing T 25:30-1 Je '71
Try station wagon camping. R. Tinsley. il
Nat Wildlife 9:20-3 Ag '71
Where to get help in planning vacations. il
Good H 172:192-3 My '71
Where to go; ed. by V. T. Sparano. See is-
sues of Outdoor life
See also
Travel

Anecdotes, facetiae, satire, etc.
How to make a million dollars on your vaca-
tion; rain free insurance. L. S. Bernstein.
Holiday 49:26-7 Jl '71
Last resort; vacation at home. H. Chad-
wick. il Todays Health 49:50-2 My '71
Two weeks in another town. J. Viorst. Red-
book 137:62-3+ Ag '71
VACATIONS, Employee
Deprived Americans. il Time 98:58 S 6 '71
VACCINATION
End of smallpox? il Newsweek 78:58-9+ O
4 '71
Immunization: an ounce (or less) of preven-
tion. D. Schultz. Ladies Home J 88:34+ Ag
'71
See also
Immunity
Tetanus—Vaccination
VACCINES
Subhuman primate diploid cells: possible
substrates for production of virus vaccines.
J. C. Petricciani and others. bibliog il
Science 174:1025-7 D 3 '71
Vaccine makers set up cell banks. il Bsns W
p72-3 S 4 '71
Vaccines. F. Lang. Ramp Mag 10:28 Ja '72
See also subhead Vaccines under names
of diseases, e.g. Influenza—Vaccines
VACHON, Brian
Becoming Susan Dey. il pors Look 35:64-6+
Jl 27 '71
Jesus movement is upon us. il Look 35:15-21
F 9 '71
Witches are rising. il pors Look 35:40-4 Ag
24 '71
VACUUM bottles. See Thermos containers
VACUUM cleaners
Vacuum cleaners. il Consumer Rep 36:241-9
Ap '71
Vacuum is a rug's best friend. House B 113:
28 Mr '71

Repairing
Curing your sick vacuum cleaner. il McCalls
98:52 Jl '71
VACUUM collection and disposal system. See
Refuse and refuse disposal
VACUUM tubes
See also
Electron tubes
Traveling wave tubes
VAGABONDS
See also
Tramps
Vagrancy
VAGINAL cancer. See Cancer
VAGRANCY
Down and out in Boston; students spending
week as derelicts. il Time 98:34 S 6 '71
See also
Tramps
VAHANIAN, Gabriel
Picasso's iconoclasm. il Chr Cent 88:1523-5
D 29 '71
VAIL, Colo. See Winter resorts
VAILLANCOURT, Armand
War whoop for freedom. il por Time 97:64
My 3 '71 *
VAILLANT, George E.
Physician, what ails thee? Newsweek 78:84
O 18 '71 *
Writer's insight. il Time 98:60 N 29 '71 *
Les VAINQUEURS; ballet. See Ballets—Criti-
cisms
VALENCIA, Calif.
Paseo houses. S. Mead. il Bet Hom & Gard
49:40-1 Ag '71
VALENTE, Murillo Gurgel
Participation of developing countries in
shipping. bibliog f il Int Concil 582:27-43
Mr '71
VALENTI, Jack
In defense of the voluntary film rating pro-
gram. il Harp Baz 104:68-9 Jl '71
about
Pains of love. por Newsweek 77:74 F 1 '71 *
VALENTINE, Richard J.
Laboratory IC power supply. il Pop Electr
34:31-5 Je '71
VALENTINE; ballet. See Ballets—Criticisms
VALENTINES
Valentines. V. Duncan. il Hobbies 75:48-9+
F '71

Anecdotes, facetiae, satire, etc.
Just call me cupid. W. Stanton. il Read
Digest 98:91-3 F '71
VALENTINES day

Drama
Cupid on the loose; reprint from February
1955 issue. H. L. Miller. Plays 30:31-8
F '71
King's valentine tarts. F. B. Watts. Plays
30:39-46 F '71
VALENTINO
Valentino. J. Brady. por Harp Baz 105:53 D
'71 *
VALERO, Senja
Stalking Euell Gibbons. Org Gard & Farm
18:106 Jl '71
VALLE, José Cecilio del
Precursors of the inter-American system.
por Américas 23:S6-7 Ja '71 *
VALLEE, Rudy
Presentation: record album called MacAr-
thur's legacy presented to Mrs MacArthur.
New Yorker 47:24-5 Jl 17 '71 *
VALLEY FORGE general hospital. See United
States—Veterans administration hospitals
VALLEY of ten thousand smokes. See Katmai,
Mount
VALLEY of the fallen. See War memorials
VALLEYS
See also
Erosion
Submarine valleys
VALLIÈRES, Pierre
Revolt in the North. V. Dedijer. Nation
212:726-7 Je 7 '71 *
White niggers of America: the precocious
autobiography of a Quebec terrorist, by
P. Vallières. Review
Sat R por 54:29 My 8 '71. L. L. L. Gol-
den *
VALMY, Christine
Skin sense. il por Harp Baz 104:38 Mr '71
VALUATION
See also
Real property—Valuation
VALUATION (psychology) See Value (psy-
chology)

VALUE
    See also
  Cost
VALUE (economic theory)
  Evaluation of basic science. D. Stetten. Jr.
    Science 174:105 O 8 '71
VALUE (philosophy) See Worth
VALUE (psychology)
  Model for teaching valuing. T. F. Adams.
    bibliog il Clear House 45:507-9 Ap '71
VALUE added tax
  Another sales tax. New Repub 166:13-14 Ja
    1 '72
  Brewing interest in VAT. H. C. Wallich. il
    Fortune 83:94-5+ Ap '71
  New tax under study: here's how it would
    work. il U S News 70:27-8 Je 21 '71
  One for the money. il Newsweek 78:71-2 D 20
    '71
  Trouble with the value-added tax. il Bsns
    W p 100 Ap 17 '71
  Value-added tax: the case against. S. S.
    Surrey; discussion. Harvard Bsns R 49:
    31-2 Mr '71
  Value-added tax: the case for. D. T. Smith;
    discussion. Harvard Bsns R 49:31-2 Mr '71
VALUE analysis
    See also
  Cost effectiveness
VALUE of college education. See College educa-
    tion, Value of
VALUES, Social. See Social values
VAN, George E.
  Charisma repeats Bayview-Mackinac win.
    Yachting 130:43+ S '71
VAN BUSKIRK, Pat
  Loser wins out. il Read Digest 98:41-2+ Mr
    '71
VAN campers. See Campers and coaches, Truck
VANADIUM
  Growth effects of vanadium in the rat. K.
    Schwarz and D. B. Milne. bibliog il Science
    174:426-8 O 22 '71
VANCE, Barry T.
  Counselors' post-camp Canadian canoe trip
    brings staff back again next year. il Camp
    Mag 43:16-17 Je '71
VANCE, Joel M.
  Breadbasket bobwhites. il Field & S 76:72-3+
    N '71
  How to call spring gobblers. il Field & S 75:
    64-5+ F '71
  Marijuana is for the birds. il Outdoor Life
    147:53-5+ Je '71
VANCE, Paul C.
  PTA people of the month. pors PTA Mag
    66:16-17 D '71 *
VAN COEVERING, Jack
  Truth about mercury. Field & S 76:14+ My
    '71
VANCOUVER, British Columbia

    Description
  Vancouver vacation. C. Pepper. il Travel 135:
    62-3 Je '71
VANCOUVER ISLAND
    See also
  Juan Fuca Strait
VANCOUVER opera association
  Report:
    Madama Butterfly. F. B. St Clair. Opera
      N 35:33 Mr 27 '71
VANDALIA, Ohio
  Grand American; trapshooting tournament.
    B. A. Foxworthy. il Holiday 49:52-6 Jl '71
VANDALISM
  JFK rip-off. il Newsweek 78:37 D 13 '71
  People are pigs. D. L. Gilbert. Cons 25:33 Ap
    '71
  They board up the windows. il Bsns W p90
    My 1 '71
  Young defacers; parental neglect. Life 70:34
    Ap 9 '71
VAN DE GRAAFF accelerators. See Accelera-
    tors (electrons, etc)
VANDELL, Robert F. and Pennell, R. M.
  Tight-money financing. il Harvard Bsns R
    49:82-97 S '71
VANDENBERGH, C. W.
  Easy way out; poem. Chr Cent 88:150 F
    3 '71
VAN DEN BOSCH, Robert
  Melancholy addiction of Ol'King Cotton; with
    biographical sketch. il Natur Hist 80:4. 86-
    91 bibliog(p 120) D '71
VAN DEN HAAG, Ernest
  Art and the mass audience. il Art in Am 59:
    52-7 Jl '71
  Justice Douglas' book. Nat R 23:526-8 My
    18 '71
  There is more sex and less love; inter-
    view. por U S News 70:71-3 Ja 25 '71
  To southeast Asia, with reservations. il
    Nat R 23:1068-9 S 24 '71

  U.S. crimes in Vietnam; excerpts. il Nat R
    23:1171-6 O 22 '71
  When is a crime a war crime? excerpts. il
    Nat R 23:1227-32 N 5 '71
VANDERBILT, Alfred Gwynne
  Chairman; interview. New Yorker 47:33-5 Ap
    17 '71
VANDERBILT, Amy
  [Monthly column] See issues of Ladies' home
    journal
  My new face. pors Ladies Home J 88:52+
    Ap '71
VANDERBILT, Gloria
  Gingham checks in; excerpt from Gloria
    Vanderbilt book of collage. il por Ladies
    Home J 88:80-1 Ap '71

    about
  Decorate-it-yourself inspiration. il House &
    Gard 139:86-93 Ap '71 *
VANDERBILT university, Nashville, Tenn.
  New sound in Nashville; battle over Vander-
    bilt university's plans for expansion. il
    Newsweek 78:105 O 11 '71
VANDERFLUGT, Daryl
  Money management; interview. il por Suc
    Farm 69:10 Ap '71
VANDERGRIFF, Tommy
  Carnival in Texas. Newsweek 78:98 D 13 '71 *
VANDERHOEF, Ray W.
  College textbooks crisis of the 1970's. Pub
    W 200:24-5 O 4 '71
VANDER JAGT, Guy
  One day in the life of Guy Vander Jagt
    (R.-Mich.) J. Corry. por Harper 242:70-9
    Ap '71 *
VANDERKOOI, Garret
  Evolution as a scientific theory. Chr Today
    16:13-14 My 7 '71
VAN DER KROEF, Justus M.
  Peking's double game. Nat R 23:928-9 Ag 24
    '71
VANDERLIP, William
  Most special ombudsman. Clear House 46:
    109 O '71
VAN DER POST, Laurens Jan
  Nepal: a violent crescendo of mountains. il
    Holiday 48:56-7+ S '70

    about
  Noble prisoner. P. S. Prescott. Newsweek
    77:69A-69B+ F 1 '71 *
VANDERWALKER, John G.
  Tektite II. il por Nat Geog 140:256-89 Ag '71
VANDERWALL, Judith
  Human touch: Gerard Knipscher. il por Am
    Artist 35:38-43+ D '71
VANDERWICKEN, Peter
  Angry young lawyers. il Fortune 84:74-7+ S
    '71
  Toward the socialization of injury. il For-
    tune 84:160-3+ N '71
VAN DE WATER, John R.
  Public employee relations; address, March
    19, 1971. Vital Speeches 37:556-63 Jl 1 '71
VAN DINE, Alan
  Rhymes and ditties for middle-size cities:
    Seattle; poem. Sat R 54:10 N 27 '71
VAN DUYN, Mona
  Talker; poem. New Repub 164:25 F 20 '71

    about
  Comment. J. Jacobsen. Poetry 118:168-9 Je
    '71 *
VAN DYKE, Dick
  Faith, hope and hilarity; excerpts. Read
    Digest 98:231-2 F '71

    about
  Dick Van Dyke: having it his way. J.
    Wilkie. il pors Good H 173:92-3+ S '71 *
  New Van Dyke family blooms in the desert.
    il pors Life 71:38-9+ S 17 '71 *
VANETTES, William
  Instant communication. il Am City 86:130+
    My '71
VAN GELDER, Lindsy
  Aesthetics of childbirth. Ramp Mag 9:48-51
    My '71
  Bernardine Dohrn is weighed in the balance
    and found heavy. il pors Esquire 75:164+
    Ap '71
VAN GERBIG, Victoria
  House boat anchors life for Mr and Mrs
    Barend Van Gerbig, 2d. il pors Vogue 157:
    112-15 Ap 15 '71 *
VAN GINKEL, Blanche. See Van Ginkel, S.
    jt. auth.
VAN GINKEL, Sandy, and Van Ginkel, Blanche
  New patterns for a metropolis; midtown
    Manhattan. il Arch Forum 135:28-33 O '71

VAN HOUWELING, C. D.
What you must do to keep your feed additives; interview, ed. by J. A. Rohlf. il por Farm J 95:22-3+ Je '71
VANISHING animals. See Rare animals
VANITY publishing. See Publishers and publishing—United States
VANKE, Arlen
Akron Arlen Vanke. J. Dianna. il pors Hot Rod 24:62-4 Ap '71 *
VAN KLEY, Edwin J.
Europe's "discovery" of China and the writing of world history. bibliog f Am Hist R 76:358-85 Ap '71
VAN LEUVEN, Jon C.
White man's strategy for black victory. Yale R 61:183-92 D '71
VAN MATRE, Steve
Your camp ecology program. il Camp Mag 43:8-10 Je '71
VAN MESDAG, Rob
They really dig canals. il Motor B & S 128: 59+ Jl '71
VANN, John Paul
Where peace is returning in Vietnam; interview. il por U S News 70:29-31 My 31 '71
VAN NESS, Glenn B.
Ecology of anthrax. bibliog Science 172:1303-7 Je 25 '71
VAN NUYS, Calif.

Social work
Mrs Cox's double life; caseworker for the Los Angeles County public social services department. M. Kasindorf. il por Newsweek 77:101 My 10 '71
VAN NUYS municipal airport. See Los Angeles —Airports
VANOCUR, Sander
Constructive hostility? por Newsweek 78:70 D 6 '71 *
Sander Vanocur, a very confused man. B. L. Freund. por Harp Baz 105:108 D '71 *
VAN PEEBLES, Melvin
Parting shots; sweet Melvin's very hot. very cool black movie. B. Darrach. il por Life 71:61 Ag 13 '71 *
Power to the Peebles. por Time 98:47 Ag 16 '71 *
Sweet song of success. il por Newsweek 77: 89 Je 21 '71 *
Sweetback in wonderland. L. Bennett, jr. il por Ebony 26:106-8+ S '71 *
VAN PELT, Charles B.
Thomas Jefferson and Maria Cosway. il pors Am Heritage 22:22-5+ Ag '71
VAN PELT, W. F. and others
Laser (cont) il Radio-Electr 42:43-5 F; 61-3 Mr; 69-70 My '71 (to be cont)
VAN VALEN, Leigh
History and stability of atmospheric oxygen. bibliog Science 171:439-43; 174:317 F 5, O 15 '71
VAN VOORST, Bruce
Küng and Rahner: dueling over infallibility. por Chr Cent 88:617-22 My 19 '71
Placid Holland boils over. il Newsweek 77: 53+ My 10 '71
VAN WAGENEN, Pamela
Stay young and beautiful (title varies) See issues of Parents' magazine & better family living
VAN WEZEL performing arts hall. See Sarasota, Fla.—Van Wezel performing arts hall
VAN WICKLEN, Ellie
Some slants on asparagus. Org Gard & Farm 18:111-13 O '71
Sow and save. il Org Gard & Farm 18:116 S '71
VANZETTI, Bartolomeo
See also
Sacco-Vanzetti case
VAPORS
See also
Evaporation
Water vapor
VAQUEROS. See Cowboys
VARACTOR diodes. See Diodes
VARÈSE, Edgard
Parisian view of Varèse. L. Stempel. Sat R 54:71 O 30 '71 *
VARGHE and Golshah, Romance of. See Persian literature
VARIABLE-rate mortgages. See Mortgages
VARIABLE stars. See Stars, Variable
VARIATION (biology)
See also
Mutation (biology)
VARICOSE veins
Varicose veins: why put up with them? W. A. Nolen. McCalls 98:30 Ag '71
VARIETY stores
See also
Sixty nine cents shops

VARMECKY, John A.
Relating art to the secondary student's environment. il Sch Arts 71:38-9 S '71
VARN, Wilfred
Eye-opener for Will. por Newsweek 78:19-20 D 27 '71 *
VARNEDOE, J. Kirk T.
Rodin drawings, true and false. il Art N 70:30-3+ D '71
VARNISH and varnishing
New paints & varnishes. J. Hand. Mech Illus 67:87 Ag '71
Now, urethane varnish in rainbow colors. J. Hand. il Pop Sci 198:101+ Ap '71
See also
Furniture—Finishing
Lacquer and lacquering
VARRO, Stephen, Jr
His process digests trash. por Bsns W p58 F 13 '71 *
VARSI, Diane
Where are they now? il pors Newsweek 77: 10 My 31 '71 *
VASATURO, Mike
Company for dinner? Engine 310, Ladder 174, Brooklyn, that is. K. V. Brown. il pors Todays Health 49:46-9+ My '71 *
VASCULAR muscle. See Muscle
VAS DIAS, Robert
Spider; poem. Nation 213:474 N 8 '71
VASECTOMY. See Sterilization, Sexual
VASILEVSKAΙΑ, E. G.
Exploration of the moon: some aspects of legal regulation. Space World H-11-95:27-31 N '71
VASKA, L. and others
Oxygen-carrying iridium complexes: kinetics, mechanism, and thermodynamics. bibliog il Science 174:587-9 N 5 '71
VASQUEZ, Edward
Getting used to the system. Nat R 23:587-8+ Je 1 '71
VATICAN
Lateran leverage: forty-second anniversary of pact with Italy. R. L. Peck. Chr Today 15:55-6 Mr 12 '71
See also
Catholic church—Relations (diplomatic)

Finance
Diversification at the Vatican. il Time 97: 67-8 Ja 25 '71

Sacred congregation for religious and secular institutes
Renewal in the church: two mentalities in conflict. T. E. Clarke. America 124:234-7 My 6 '71; Discussion. 124:459-61 My 1 '71
VATICAN and the press
Press handcuffed. S. J. Adamo. America 125: 376-7 N 6 '71
VATICAN council, 2d
Catholic crisis. E. H. Smith. Commonweal 95:320-3 Ja 7 '72
Catholic theologian today; legacy of Vatican II. P. J. Riga. Cath World 214:128-31 D '71
See also
Popes—Infallibility
VAUGHAN, Maury S.
Change in education: the new and the not so new. bibliog Sch & Soc 99:341-5 O '71
VAUGHAN, Roger
Tempting of a small town. il Life 71:50-1+ Jl 30 '71; Same abr. Read Digest 99:207-8+ O '71
VAUGHN, Susan
Monster movies? il Library J 96:3439-41 O 15 '71
VAULTING (sport)
Wait-listed for the pantheon; C. Papanicolaou. A. Verschoth. il pors Sports Illus 34:46+ F 1 '71
VAUPEL, Louis
Louis Vaupel, master glass engraver. C. U. Fauster. il por Antiques 99:696-701 My '71 *
VAZQUEZ DE CORONADO, Francisco
Trial of Coronado. W. J. Buchanan. il Americas 23:28-38 Ja '71 *
VEAL
See also
Cookery—Meat
VEALEY, Claude E.
Man named Tony. il por Newsweek 78:56 Jl 5 '71 *
VECTOR analysis
Vectored-thrust maneuverability explored. D. A. Brown. il Aviation W 95:36-9 D 13 '71
VECTORS (biology) See Insects as carriers of infection
VEDROS, Neylan A. and others
Leptospirosis epizootic among California sea lions. bibliog il Science 172:1250-1 Je 18 '71

VEECK, Bill
Bad boy of baseball. il por Newsweek 77:12 My 17 '71 •

VEGETABLE diet. See Vegetarianism

VEGETABLE gardening
See also
Beans
Carrots
Companion crops

VEGETABLE gardening, Home
Eating garden-fresh all winter long. M. Franz. Org Gard & Farm 18:92+ F '71
Home garden's experts design a mini-vegetable garden for $10. il Home Gard 58:26-34 F '71
It's for zinnias, corn, radishes, Swiss chard, zucchini, and two little girls. il Sunset 146: 232-3 My '71
Outdoor pantry. P. Foret. Horticulture 49: 27+ Ap '71
Part-time farming is easy if everybody pitches in. il Sunset 146:264-5 My '71
Plant now for a vegetable harvest right in the dead of winter. il Sunset 147:178-9 S '71
Potfuls of vegetables. B. F. George. Horticulture 49:40 Jl '71
Put the world in your garden. J. Meeker. Org Gard & Farm 18:33-7 N '71
Sow and save. E. Van Wicklen. il Org Gard & Farm 18:116 S '71
Space-savers for the small garden. C. Sauerland. Org Gard & Farm 18:91-3 Ja '71
Succeeding with succession crops. N. W. Bubel. il Org Gard & Farm 18:44-9 Ja '71
Try earlier planting. J. R. Coggins. il Org Gard & Farm 18:46-7 Mr '71
What's the big idea? M. C. Goldman. il Org Gard & Farm 18:34-8 My '71
Which vegetables for the new garden? R. Tirrell. Org Gard & Farm 18:74-6 Jl '71
Why don't you grow your own vegetables? W. B. Harris. House & Gard 139:32+ Ap '71
You can thumb your nose at fall frost! R. Stout. por Org Gard & Farm 18:59-61 S '71
See also
Cold frames

VEGETABLE protein foods. See Food substitutes

VEGETABLE salads. See Salads

VEGETABLE stands. See Roadside marketing

VEGETABLES
Which vegetables for the new garden? R. Tirrell. Org Gard & Farm 18:74-6 Jl '71
See also
Canning and preserving
Cookery—Vegetables
Greens, Edible
Vegetable gardening, Home
Vegetarianism
also names of vegetables, e.g. Onions

Harvesting
Home harvester's art: when to pick, which ones to pick. il Sunset 147:54-5 Ag '71
How to tell when vegetables are ready. Sunset 147:126-7 Ag '71

Marketing
Buy your food direct-from-the-grower. J. Olds. Org Gard & Farm 18:91 My '71

VEGETABLES, Freezing of. See Freezing of food

VEGETABLES, Frozen
Frozen french fries. il Consumer Rep 36: 632-4 O '71

VEGETABLES, Pickled. See Pickles and relishes

VEGETARIANISM
Nature's table. il Seventeen 30:166+ S '71

VEGETATION
See also
Streamside vegetation

VEGETATION and sound
Plant to reduce noise pollution. il Home Gard 58:36-7+ Ap '71
Plants filter noises. D. E. Aylor. Horticulture 49:28+ F '71

VEHICLES
Personal rapid transit. P. Wahl. il Pop Sci 199:73-7+ N '71
See also
Bicycles
Coaches and coaching
Motor vehicles
Wheels

Anecdotes, facetiae, satire, etc.
Weekender's companion. O. Jensen. il Horizon 13:105-12 Sum '71

VEIL nebula. See Nebulae

VEILS
Veils: the net returns. il Life 70:46-8 Mr 26 '71

VEINS
See also
Thrombophlebitis
Varicose veins

Transplantation
See Blood vessels—Transplantation

VEINS (botany)
Disjunct foliar veins in Hawaiian euphorbias. D. Herbst. bibliog il Science 171:1247-8 Mr 26 '71

VELASCO ALVARADO, Juan
No love for the Yanqui dollar. por Bsns W p62 My 15 '71 •

VELASQUEZ, Conchita
Historical records. A. Favia-Artsay. por Hobbies 76:36 Ja '72 •

VELAZQUEZ, Diego Rodriguez de Silva y
Historic duty; acquisition of Juan de Pareja by Metropolitan museum. Hobbies 76:100+ Jl '71 •
Notes and comment; acquisition of portrait of Juan de Pareja by Metropolitan museum. New Yorker 47:31 Je 5 '71 •
Secret choice. il Time 97:68 My 24 '71 •
Water carrier of Velazquez. L. Steinberg. il Art N 70:54-5 Sum '71 •

VELIE, Lester
Angry young lawyers of OEO. Read Digest 98:193-4+ My '71
Give us this day our ABCs. Read Digest 99:126-30 D '71
Schools for failure. Read Digest 99:147-51 Jl '71
Way to lick the jail habit. Read Digest 98:142-6 F '71
Why insurance is so hard to get. Read Digest 98:83-8 Ap '71

VELIKOVSKY, Immanuel
Velikovsky controversy. Chem 44:17 O '71 •

VELIS, Andrea
Back to the Bijou. il Opera N 36:12-14 S '71

VÉLIZ, Claudio
Chilean experiment. For Affairs 49:442-53 Ap '71

VELJKOVIC, Morag
South Africa's diamond. il pors Dance Mag 45:24-5 O '71

VELLUM. See Parchment

VELLUTINO, Frank R. and Sipay, E. R.
Learning disabilities. Ed Digest 36:35-8 Mr '71

VENABLE, Clinton A.
Low-cost computer halves driving time. il Am City 86:105-6 Mr '71

VENATION (botany) See Veins (botany)

VENDING machines
Creeping technology. Time 97:63 Ap 5 '71
Smoke gets in your ears; commercial from cigarette vending machines. il Time 97:88 My 3 '71

VENDÔME column. See Paris—Monuments, statues, etc.

VENDORS, Street. See Street trades

VENEERS and veneering
Gardner & company of New York. K. Ames. il Antiques 100:252-5 Ag '71
New art of veneering. R. J. De Cristoforo. il Pop Sci 198:104-6 F '71

VENERA flight. See Space flight to Venus

VENEREAL diseases
VD. A. Blanzaco. Todays Ed 60:41 D '71
VD: the clock is ticking. M. Strage. il Todays Health 49:16-18+ Ap '71
Venereal disease. D. Rubin. McCalls 98:64+ Je '71
Venereal disease pandemic. C. Roberts and S. V. Roberts. il N Y Times Mag p62+ N 7 '71; Reply. H. I. Fienberg. p4+ Ja 2 '72
See also
Gonorrhea

VENEZUELA
See also
Fishing—Venezuela
Petroleum industry—Venezuela
Tourist trade—Venezuela

Description and travel
Travel plot: real life journal. S. Feigen. il pors Vogue 158:136-43+ O 15 '71
Venezuelan adventure. A. D. Nunn. il Travel 137:54-7 Ja '72

Economic conditions
Venezuelan progress reconsidered. G. W. Schuyler and D. K. Zschock. bibliog f Cur Hist 60:95-101+ F '71

Expropriation policy
Squeezing the oil concessions. il Time 98:59 S 6 '71

VENEZUELAN equine encephalitis. See Encephalitis

VENEZUELAN equine encephalomyelitis. See Encephalomyelitis

VENICE
Venetian notes: experiencing the city. D. Handlin. Am Scholar 41:65-78 Wint '71
Venetian recollection. H. Sutton. il Sat R 54:59-60+ O 30 '71

Churches
Our far-flung correspondents; funeral service for I. F. Stravinsky in Santi Giovanni e Paolo. F. Steegmuller. New Yorker 47:99-103 My 1 '71

Music
Report:
Abduction from the Seraglio and Tristan und Isolde. P. Elvins. Opera N 35:27 Je 12 '71

VENICE biennale. See Music festivals—Italy

VENICE in art
Venice revisited. G. Highet. il Horizon 13:54-7 Wint '71

VENISON
To venison with love. C. J. Anderson. il Field & S 76:62-3+ O '71
See also
Cookery—Game

VENOM
Bizarre rites of the cobra shrine; Indian god Tajaji credited with saving snake bite victims. K. Severin. il Sci Digest 69:52-5 Mr '71
Chemistry: turning an insect into a possible lifesaver; fire ant venom to fight fungi infections. il Bsns W p43 Ja 1 '72
Destruction of mammalian motor nerve terminals by black widow spider venom. M. Okamoto and others. bibliog il Science 172:733-6 My 14 '71
Some facts about snakebite. K. N. Anderson. Sci Digest 70:83 Jl '71

VENTILATION
See also
Air conditioning

VENTLING, Christa Dierks-. See Dierks-Ventling, C.

VENTRICULAR muscle. See Heart—Muscle

VENTURA manufacturing company
Lockheed sale of Ventura aimed at small business work. Aviation W 94:84 My 10 '71

VENTURE capital. See Capital, Venture

VENTURES, Joint. See Joint adventures

VENTURI, Denise (Lakofski) Scott Brown
Less is more: Mies van der Rohe; less is a bore: Robert Venturi. P. Goldberger. il N Y Times Mag p34-7+ O 17 '71 *

VENTURI, Robert
—and Brown, D. S.
Ugly and ordinary architecture or the decorated shed; excerpts from Learning from Las Vegas. il Arch Forum 135:64-7 N '71

about
Images for a new California City. R. Jensen. il Arch Rec 149:117-20 Je '71 *
Less is more: Mies van der Rohe; less is a bore: Robert Venturi. P. Goldberger. il N Y Times Mag p34-7+ O 17 '71 *

VENUS (planet)
Venera on Venus. Sci Am 225:44 Jl '71
Venus: what we know about this planet. M. Marov. Space World H-6-90:33-4 Je '71
See also
Space flight to Venus

Atmosphere
Clouds of Venus: evidence for their nature. J. E. Hansen and A. Arking. bibliog il Science 171:669-72 F 19 '71

Rotation
How did Venus lose its angular momentum? S. F. Singer; reply with rejoinder. B. M. French. bibliog Science 173:169-70 Jl 9 '71

VENUS probes. See Space flight to Venus

VERA institute of Justice
Vera: cleaning of Bethesda fountain, in Central park and other rehabilitation projects of the Pioneer messenger service. New Yorker 47:39-41 D 11 '71

VERDEN, Paul, and Shatterly, Daniel
Alcoholism research and resistance to understanding the compulsive drinker. bibliog Ment Hy 55:331-6 Jl '71

VERDI, Giuseppe
Addenda to Don Carlos, new episodes reveal new pleasures; episodes presented at Carnegie recital hall. M. Mayer. Hi Fi 21:MA22 Je '71 *

Aida. Criticism
New Yorker 47:88 Je 12 '71 *
Opera N 36:8-9 D 25 '71 *
Sat R il 54:45-7 D 25 '71 *
Don Carlo. Criticism
Hi Fi il 21:MA15+ D '71 *
Nation 213:443-4 N 1 '71 *
New Yorker 47:119 O 2 '71 *
Sat R 54:20 O 9 '71 *
Ernani. Criticism
Hi Fi il 20:MA13-14 D '70 *
History brought to life. G. Movshon. il Hi Fi 21:77-8 O '71 *
Luisa Miller. Criticism
Nation 213:572 N 29 '71 *
Opera N il 36:17-20 D 11 '71 *
Masked ball (Un ballo in maschera) Criticism
Hi Fi 21:MA16-17 D '71 *
New Yorker 47:110 Ap 3 '71 *
Opera N il 35:17-20 Ja 30 '71 *
Milestone Aida. G. Movshon. por Hi Fi 21:57-8 Ag '71 *
Report:
Don Carlos as lecture-concert at Carnegie recital hall. H. E. Phillips. Opera N 35:23 My 15 '71 *
Shaw looks at Verdi; reprint from The Nation, July 7, 1917 issue. pors Opera N 35:24-5 Mr 13 '71 *
La Traviata. Criticism
Hi Fi 20:MA14-15 D '70 *
New Yorker 47:119-20 S 25 '71 *
Il Trovatore. Criticism
Hi Fi 21:MA13 Je '71
New Yorker 47:127-8 Mr 13 '71 *
New Yorker 47:88-9 Je 12 '71 *
Opera N il 35:18-20 Mr 13 '71 *
Verdi requiem. P. L. Miller. Am Rec G 37:384-5 F '71 *
Why Luisa Miller? R. A. Tuggle. il Opera N 36:21-4 D 11 '71 *

VEREINIGTE flugtechnische werke. See Airplane industry—Germany (Federal Republic)

VERGHESE, Paul
Another evaluation of the CPC. Chr Cent 88:1319 N 10 '71
Flame of faith is not out in the U.S.S.R. Chr Cent 88:580-1 My 12 '71
Forward with brakes on! Chr Cent 88:848 Jl 14 '71

VERLAINE, Paul Marie
Verlaine, by J. Richardson. Review
Sat R 54:49-50 S 25 '71. A. Balakian *

VERMAN, Marvin
Crosstown is dead, long live the crosstown? il Arch Forum 135:44-5 O '71

VERMEULE, Emily
Golden links to the bronze age. il Horizon 13:50-3 Wint '71

VERMEULEN, Monette
Mudra: Maurice Béjart's gesture. N. M. Stoop. il pors Dance Mag 45:30-7 N '71 *

VERMONT
See also
Architecture, Domestic—Vermont
Art—Vermont
Booksellers and bookselling—Vermont
Education—Vermont
Environmental policy—Vermont
Geology—Vermont
Hunting—Vermont
Landscape protection—Vermont
Music festivals—Vermont
Skis and skiing—Vermont

Economic conditions
Who owns Vermont? excerpt from Colonialism and underdevelopment in Vermont. L. Webb. Ramp Mag 10:13 D 11 '71

VERNA, Tony
Time of the television football freak. il por Time 99:45 Ja 17 '72 *

VERNE, Jules
Father of science fiction. P. W. Schmidtchen. il por Hobbies 76:135-6+ D '71 *

VERNER, William K.
Art and the Adirondacks. il Antiques 100:84-92 Jl '71

VERNIER calipers. See Calipers

VERNON, Raymond
Multinational enterprise: power versus sovereignty; excerpts from Sovereignty at bay. For Affairs 49:736-51 Jl '71

VERNON, Calif.
Pipeline rehabilitation proved better, cheaper. R. H. King. il por Am City 86:80+ O '71

VERONA, Italy
Music
Report:
Aida, Nabucco and Macbeth. S. Gould. il Opera N 36:25 O '71

VERONIS, John J.
Report to the readers. Sat R 54:32-3 D 4 '71
about
New owners for SR. McCall book division.
Pub W 200:95 Jl 19 '71 *
New tycoons. pors Newsweek 78:64 Jl 26
'71 *
Report to the readers. N. Cousins. Sat R 54:
16-17 Jl 31 '71 *
Revamping the Review. il pors Time 98:62
N 22 '71 *
VERRAZANO-NARROWS bridge. See New
York (city)—Bridges
VERRETT, Shirley
On target: Shirley Verrett. por Vogue 157:
98-9 Je '71 *
VERSAILLES, Palaces of
Versailles reborn. J. D. Ratcliff. il Read Di-
gest 99:166-71 O '71
VERSCHOTH, Anita
He's at it again, as high as a kite. il por
Sports Illus 35:60-2+ O 18 '71
Skiing (cont) Sports Illus 34:62 Mr 15; 35:
86-7 N 22 '71
Track & field (title varies) (cont) il Sports
Illus 34:46+ F 1; 52-3 F 22; 84-5 Je 7 '71
VERSE. See Poetry
VERSIFICATION
See also
Rime
VERVOORT, John P.
Minneapolis money machine; interview, ed.
by R. J. Flaherty. il por Forbes 108:43-4+
S 15 '71
VERY small shipwreck; story. See Jerrard, M.
VESCO, Robert L.
Cornfeld's colonels try an IOS revolt. il Bsns
W p25-6 Je 26 '71 *
VESELL, Elliott S. See Spector, S. jt. auth.
VESELY, David L. and Hadley, M. E.
Calcium requirement for melanophore-stimu-
lating hormone action on melanophores.
bibliog il Science 173:923-5 S 3 '71
VESEY, Denmark
Trial record of Denmark Vesey. T. D. Perry.
Negro Hist Bul 34:45 F '71 *
VESSELS, Seizure of. See Seizure of vessels
and cargoes
VESTA (asteroid) See Asteroids
VESTED rights
Vesting: a key issue in the debate. Bsns W
p96 S 11 '71
VESTIBULAR cortex. See Cerebral cortex
VESTS
Have you a vested interest? photo vest. H.
Keppler. il Mod Phot 35:116 Je '71
VESTVILLE, Ga. See Villages, Restored
VETCH
Turnips in your cover crop? B. Rozell. Org
Gard & Farm 18:98-9 S '71
VETERANS
Homecoming of Chris Mead. K. Fleming. il
pors Newsweek 77:28-9 Mr 29 '71
No victory parades: the return of the Viet-
nam veteran, by M. Polner. Review
Commonweal 95:165-7 N 12 '71. J. Cas-
telli
Nation 213:344-5 O 11 '71. J. Finn
Sat R 54:28-9 Jl 31 '71. W. Beauchamp
Peace demonstrations, 1971. Nation 212:578-
9 My 10 '71
Reporter at large; Vietnam veteran. D. Lang.
New Yorker 47:35-40+ S 4 '71
Sense of isolation. M. Polner. Nation 213:230-
4 S 20 '71
Society and the Vietnam veteran. J. Castelli;
discussion. Cath World 213:213-14 Ag '71
TRB from Washington; April march on
Washington. New Repub 164:4 My 8 '71
Ten vets who went back. A. Maupin, jr. Nat
R 23:1465-7 D 31 '71
Veterans' pheasant hunt. B. Gillette. il Out-
door Life 147:64-7+ Je '71
Vietnam vet: no one gives a damn. il News-
week 77:27-8+ Mr 29 '71
Where are the leaders of our country? ex-
cerpts from testimony before the Senate
committee on foreign relations. J. F. Ker-
ry. New Repub 164:15-18 My 8 '71
Why Vietnam veterans feel like forgotten
men. il U S News 70:42-4 Mr 29 '71
Will somebody please welcome this hero
home? B. Lindeman. il pors Todays Health
49:54-6+ Je '71
See also
Negro veterans
United States—Veterans administration hos-
pitals
Associations, institutions, etc.
See also
American legion
Vietnam veterans against the war (organi-
zation)

Benefits
As Johnny comes marching home; inad-
equate benefits for Viet Nam veterans. il
Time 97:26-7 Mr 15 '71
Benefits available to veterans. Ebony 27:
42-3 N '71
Bigger benefits for veterans but no rush
of takers. il U S News 70:48-9 F 1 '71
College funds for descendants of veterans.
Bet Hom & Gard 49:6+ Jl '71
What a vet should do with his group life
insurance. Changing T 25:12 O '71
See also
Veterans—Education

Education
Educational counseling; counseling service-
men and women in southeast Asia, the
Far East, and Europe on educational op-
portunities. Sch & Soc 99:469+ D '71
Educational enrollments. Sch & Soc 99:469 D
'71
Long way from Vietnam; veterans on the
GI bill. il Newsweek 78:50+ O 4 '71

Employment
Employment situation of Vietnam era vet-
erans. E. Waldman and K. R. Gover. il
Mo Labor R 94:3-11 S '71
Home from the war; unemployment rate.
New Repub 164:11 Ja 30 '71
Hunt-Wesson's business; pledge to hire
draft resisters and anti-war veterans. New
Repub 164:8 Ap 24 '71
Job placement lags for Vietnam vets. U S
News 71:102 O 11 '71
Jobs-for-veterans drive is launched. U S News
70:70 Je 28 '71
Plight of Viet Nam era vets. Time 98:57 D
27 '71
Returning heroes get the cold shoulder. il
Bsns W p46-8 Jl 31 '71
This store has much to offer; Goodyear's
participation in Project Transition pro-
gram. Nations Bsns 59:20 My '71
Veteran comes home, to limbo. C. Leinster.
il pors Life 70:28-38 Ap 16 '71
Viet Nam veterans are counting on business-
men. il Nations Bsns 59:44+ S '71
Vital service for ex-servicemen: Jobs for
veterans program. V. Louviere. il Nations
Bsns 59:15 F '71

Loans
VA home loans now include mobile homes.
Har Yrs 11:5 Ja '71
VETERANS, Disabled
Mexico: a haven for disabled vets. L. Robin-
son. il Ebony 27:31-4+ Ja '72

Rehabilitation
Society and the Vietnam veteran. J. Castelli;
discussion. Cath World 213:213-14 Ag '71
VETERANS administration. See United States
—Veterans administration
VETERINARIANS
Veterinarian. C. See. il Atlan 228:95-8+ O
'71
VETERINARY medicine
Animal health: a practical plan for your herd.
A. Leman. Suc Farm 69:H14-15 O '71
Animal health: plan a veterinary treatment
center. R. Lutz. il Suc Farm 69:no4 D4 Mr
'71
Animal health: they contract veterinary care.
R. Lutz. il Suc Farm 69:no5 B8 Mr '71
Feedlot health. J. G. Clark. See issues of
Farm journal
Making treatment easier. A. Wesely. il Suc
Farm 69:no3 D24 F '71
See also
Veterinarians

Study and teaching
See also
Cornell university, Ithaca, N.Y.—School of
veterinary medicine
VETERINARY medicine, Bureau of. See
United States—Food and drug administra-
tion—Veterinary medicine, Bureau of
VETERINARY research
See also
Cornell university, Ithaca, N.Y.—School of
veterinary medicine
VETERINARY surgery
Challenge of horse surgery. K. Bryn. il Sci
Digest 70:72-5 Ag '71
VETRA, Vija
Vija Vetra, the Cubiculo, NYC. T. Borek.
Dance Mag 45:78 Jl '71 *
VETTER, Robert M.
European guild pewter: forms and functions.
il Antiques 101:201-8 Ja '72
Table guards and cake plates of pewter. il
Antiques 99:712-17 My '71

VIBRATION
 See also
Damping (mechanics)
Oscillations
VIBRATION-suppressing alloys. See Alloys
VICE
 See also
Immoral literature and pictures
VICE-PRESIDENTIAL candidates
1972
For a black vice president in 1972. A. M.
 Greeley. il N Y Times Mag p28+ S 19 '71;
 Discussion. p8+ O 17 '71
Is Spiro Agnew necessary? Time 98:11-12 Ag
 16 '71
VICE-PRESIDENTS
United States
 See also
Agnew, S. T.
VICTIMOLOGY. See Victims of crime
VICTIMS of crime
Criminal violence; how about the victim?
 address, May 12, 1971. T. L. Sendak. Vital
 Speeches 37:574-6 Jl 1 '71
Is the victim guilty? victimology investiga-
 tions. il Time 98:42 Jl 5 '71
 See also
Reparation
VICTOR, Florence
People in Europe were starving; poem.
 Poetry 119:77-8 N '71
VICTOR, Robert C.
Sun, moon, and planets this month. See issues
 of Sky and telescope
VICTOR talking machine company. See RCA
 corporation—RCA Victor division
VICTORIA
Australia's pacesetter state, Victoria. A. C.
 Fisher, jr. il Nat Geog 139:218-53 F '71
VICTORIA, British Columbia
Victoria's hanging baskets. R. Baird. il Hor-
 ticulture 49:24 Jl '71
VICTORIAN art objects. See Art objects, Vic-
 torian
VICTORIAN furniture, English. See Furniture,
 English
VICTORIAN jewelry. See Jewelry
VICTORIAN period (English literature) See
 English literature
VIDAL, Gore
Best man, '72. Esquire 75:102-5 Je '71
VIDEO disc players. See Video playback sys-
 tems
VIDEO discs. See Video records
VIDEO phone. See Telephone—Television com-
 bination
VIDEO playback systems
A is for abacus; EVR recordings. I. Kolodin.
 il Sat R 54:66-7 Mr 27 '71
Amazing video disc plays through your TV;
 Teldec video disc. A. Fisher. il Pop Sci
 198:60-1 Ja '71
Buy now, play later boom. S. H. Brown. il
 Life 71:8 D 3 '71
Canned video. J. P. Dessauer. il Pub W 199:
 32-4 Ja 18 '71
Cartridge TV; a new kind of entertainment.
 Good H 172:176 Je '71
Cassette-TV. H. Alpert; I. Berger. il Sat R
 54:42-7+ Ja 30 '71
Cassettes. il Newsweek 77:78 My 31 '71
Coming: color movies from black-and-white
 film! camera for use with electronic video
 recording process. S. M. Gallager. il Pop
 Mech 135:76-8 My '71
Coming: your super-8 movies on your own
 TV. A. Fisher. il Pop Sci 199:60 D '71
Photography's electronic future. B. Schwal-
 berg. il Pop Phot 68:64-9+ Mr '71
Report from Cannes; First international
 cartridge TV. videocassette and video disc
 conference. H. R. Lottman. Pub W 199:
 27-31 My 17 '71
Stand by for the cartridge TV explosion. L.
 Lessing. il Fortune 83:80-3+ Je '71
Teldec television disc. A. Harris. il Electr
 World 85:36-7+ F '71
 See also
Computer television, inc.
VIDEO recorders and recording
Cassette deck features mixing; Ampex micro
 52. il Hi Fi 21:42 Ja '71
Cassette-TV. il Sat R 54:42-7+ Ja 30; 51 F 27;
 66-7 Mr 27 '71
15 years of video recording. W. Slatkin. il
 Electr World 86:36-8+ N '71
Home video recording, or is it? W. G. Salm.
 il Radio-Electr 42:13-15+ Jl '71
Instant replay; TV's electronic magic. R.
 Dunlop. il Pop Mech 136:108-12 +N '71

Lights... action... tape; using videotape
 to make movies. il Newsweek 78:111 D 6
 '71
Looking ahead. D. Lachenbruch. Radio-Electr
 42:4+ Ag '71
Photography's electronic future. B. Schwal-
 berg. il Pop Phot 68:64-9+ Mr '71
Selecting a video tape recorder A. Harris. il
 Electr World 85:32-5+ F '71
TV tapes as research materials; with text
 of bill. H. H. Baker. Am Lib 2:951-2 O '71
Video underground. C. Aaron. il Art in Am
 59:74-9 My '71
Videomagnifier: Stephen Stills rock concert
 at Madison Square Garden; interview. J.
 White. New Yorker 47:19-20 Ag 28 '71
 See also
Video playback systems
Business use
Videotape brings the résumé alive. il Bsns
 W p36+ Jl 10 '71
Court use
TV goes to court. il Time 98:42 D 27 '71
Educational use
Theatre on film and tape; project of New
 York public library at Lincoln Center. B.
 Harte. il Am Lib 2:1065-8 N '71
This mini seems here to stay; Minicourse:
 television taping of a teacher's perform-
 ance improves teaching skills. W. Wood.
 il Am Ed 7:14-17 D '71
Videotape recorder: aids self-improvement.
 J. L. Klingstedt. Clear House 45:360 F '71
Videotapes in public schools. A. R. Davis.
 Ed Digest 37:52-3 S '71
VIDEO records
Amazing video disc plays through your TV;
 Teldec video disc. A. Fisher. il Pop Sci
 198:60-1 Ja '71
Color TV from a video disc. P. Moor. Sat
 R 54:73 S 25 '71
Is next year the year for video records?
 H. R. Lottman. il Pub W 200:pt2 153-62
 S 27 '71
LP's for TV's. D. Molner. il Schol Teach
 Jr/Sr High p22 F 1 '71
 See also
Copyright—Video records and tapes
VIDEO tape recorders and recording. See
 Video recorders and recording
VIDEO tape recordings
Film. D. Hare. Craft Horiz 31:10+ D '71
Video cassettes: problem or solution? R.
 Gilkey. Clear House 45:319-20 Ja '71
 See also
Copyright—Video records and tapes
Educational use
Another approach to higher education; pro-
 posal for a video university. A. M. Mood.
 Ed Digest 37:13-16 D '71
VIDILI, Claude
Womb with a view. il Time 98:44 Jl 5 '71 *
VIEDERMAN, Stephen
Schools and population. Ed Digest 37:26-8 N
 '71
VIEL, Paul J.
Up the hierarchy. Clear House 46:200-2 D
 '71
VIENNA
Description
Vienna: it's still an operetta. J. Wechsberg.
 il Holiday 49:74-7+ D '70
Music
Behind the scenes. R. Dettmer. il Hi Fi 21:
 20-1 D '71
Behind the scenes. S. Gould. il Hi Fi 21:16-17
 Ag '71
Report:
 Die Aegyptische Helena, by R. Strauss.
 J. Wechsberg. Opera N 35:33 Ja 23 '71
 Gottfried von Einem's Der besuch der
 alten dame. J. Wechsberg. Opera N
 36:25-6 S '71
 Mozart's Idomeneo. J. Wechsberg. Op-
 era N 35:26 My 15 '71
Vienna opera intrigues and vocal discoveries.
 Hi Fi 20:134 D '70
VIENNA, S.D.
Quiet falls across the plains. D. Wittner. il
 Life 70:22-31 Je 25 '71
VIENNA convention on the law of treaties.
 See United Nations conference on the law
 of treaties
VIENNA opera ballet. See Ballet—Austria
VIENNA talks. See Strategic arms limitations
 talks
VIENNESE cookery. See Cookery, Austrian
VIERBUCHEN, R. C. See Doehring, D. O. jt.
 auth.

VIERTEL, Gösta
Dirigible (cont) il **Harp Baz** 104:**124-5** F; 156-7 Mr; 140-1 Ap; 144-5 My '71

VIET CONG
Viet Cong comeback: a rising danger. il U S News 71:23-4 Ag 23 '71
Viet Cong: image and flesh. J. Record. il Trans-Action 8:46-52 Ja '71

VIETNAM
See also
Ecology—Vietnam
Land—Vietnam
Mekong River Delta

Economic history

Strange economics of the Vietnam war. B. Garrett. il Ramp Mag 10:34-9 N '71

Native races

See also
Montagnards

VIETNAM (Democratic Republic)
Vietnam. il Focus 22:1-8 D '71
See also
Catholics in Vietnam
Electronics—Vietnam (Democratic Republic)
Floods—Vietnam (Democratic Republic)
Morale, National—Vietnam (Democratic Republic)
Science—Vietnam (Democratic Republic)

Economic conditions

Answers to a mystery: why North Vietnam fights on. il U S News 71:40-1 Ag 9 '71

Foreign relations

Image and reality in Indochina. H. E. Salisbury. For Affairs 49:381-94 Ap '71

Politics and government

Impact in Hanoi; strategy of Le Duan. R. Critchfield. Nation 213:102-5 Ag 16 '71
See also
Elections—Vietnam (Democratic Republic)

VIETNAM (Republic)
Vietnam. il Focus 22:1-8 D '71
See also
Agriculture—Vietnam (Republic)
American property in Vietnam (Republic)
Archives—Vietnam (Republic)
Catholics in Vietnam
Children—Vietnam (Republic)
Election laws—Vietnam (Republic)
Elections—Vietnam (Republic)
Investments, Foreign (in Vietnam [Republic]
Military assistance, American—Vietnam (Republic)
Petroleum—Vietnam (Republic)
Political campaigns—Vietnam (Republic)
Political prisoners—Vietnam (Republic)
Politics, Corruption in—Vietnam (Republic)
Subversive activities—Vietnam (Republic)
Terrorism—Vietnam (Republic)
United States—Armed forces—Forces in Vietnam
United States—Foreign relations—Vietnam (Republic)
Vietnamese war, 1957- —Protests, demonstrations, etc, against—Vietnam (Republic)

Air force

Can choppers be Vietnamized? il Newsweek 77:41 Mr 15 '71
Saigon's choppers: a crash waiting to happen; problem of maintenance. E. Behr. il Newsweek 77:35 Mr 29 '71

Armed forces

Is ground war over for U.S. in Vietnam? interview. R. Thompson. il por U S News 71:64-5 N 1 '71
South Vietnam's chances of making it alone. il U S News 71:30-3 S 13 '71

Army

Assessing the Laos invasion; with report by B. Smith. il Newsweek 77:25-6+ Ap 5 '71
Can the South Vietnamese win their own war? il U S News 70:19-20 Mr 1 '71
Vietnamization: the reality and the myth. il Newsweek 78:38-9 Ag 2 '71
What it means for Vietnamization. Time 97:25-6 Ap 5 '71

Commerce

Japanese boom. il Newsweek 77:63-4 F 15 '71

Economic conditions

Phase Thieu. Time 98:39 N 29 '71
Review of progress and problems in Viet-Nam; address, January 21, 1971. E. Bunker. Dept State Bul 64:206-11 F 15 '71

South Vietnam's chances of making it alone. il U S News 71:30-3 S 13 '71
See also
Saigon—Economic conditions

Foreign opinion

Departing words. Newsweek 77:37 My 3 '71

Foreign relations

United States
See United States—Foreign relations—Vietnam (Republic)

History

United States in Vietnam: a study in futility. D. G. Marr. Ann Am Acad 397:11-18 S '71

Industries

There's a Toyota in their future? J. Ridgeway. il Ramp Mag 10:40-1 N '71

Politics and government

Aftermath of a victory. il por Newsweek 77:42+ Ap 12 '71
Diem document. il por Time 98:29 Ag 2 '71
For Thieu, biggest test still ahead. il por U S News 71:20 O 4 '71
Generals. New Repub 165:8-9 **S 4** '71
Is this written in the stars? See it through with Nguyen van Thieu. T. Buckley. il pors N Y Times Mag p 14-15+ S 26 '71
Let politics live in Vietnam; D. Luce's testimony. Chr Cent 88:711 Je 9 '71
Letter from Indo-China (cont) R. Shaplen. New Yorker 47:89-91 Mr 6; 112+ Ap 24 '71
Letter from Vietnam. R. Shaplen. New Yorker 47:77-8+ N 13 '71
No Ky and a big win? por Newsweek 78:30 Ag 16 '71
Other South Vietnam: toward the breaking point. J. C. Pomonti. For Affairs 50:253-69 Ja '72
Plot against Diem, as told by Pentagon papers; with interview with F. E. Nolting, jr. por U S News 71:66-70 Jl 26 '71
Prelude to a fiery campaign. il Time 97:38 Je 28 '71
Puppet pulls the strings. K. Buckley. il Newsweek 78:25 O 4 '71
South Viet Nam: two against Thieu. il pors Time 98:22+ Jl 26 '71
South Vietnams' chances of making it alone. il U S News 71:30-3 S 13 '71
Tran-ngoc-Chau affair. E. Pond. Atlan 227:19-20+ My '71
Two men who didn't make it. South Vietnam; with editorial comment. il pors Life 71:24-5, 32 S 10 '71
Vietnam: how Nixon plans to win the war; the Huntington-Kissinger strategy. B. Garrett. il por Ramp Mag 9:26-31 F '71
See also
Elections—Vietnam (Republic)
Political campaigns—Vietnam (Republic)

Relief work

Whatever happened to Vietnam's other war? R. Engel. il Chr Cent 88:350-3 Mr 17 '71
See also
Vietnamese war, 1957- —Relief work

Religious institutions and affairs

See also
Buddhists
Catholic church in Vietnam (Republic)

VIETNAM disengagement act. See Vietnamese war, 1957- —American troop withdrawals

VIETNAM veterans against the war (organization)
Farewell to arms. por Newsweek 77:25 My 3 '71
Hearts with one purpose alone. M. McGrory. America 124:476 My 8 '71
John Kerry's speech. W. F. Buckley, jr. Nat R 23:722-3 Je 29 '71
Liberty liberated. il Time 99:10 Ja 10 '72
Portrait of a protester: J. B. Crumb. H. Mitgang. New Repub 164:14-15 My 8 '71
Statue of Liberty play. il Newsweek 79:20 Ja 10 '72
Veterans' march to Boston. D. King. il New Repub 164:11-13 Je 12 '71
Vietnam vets: the anti-war army. A. Goldberg. il Ramp Mag 10:10-17 Jl '71
Warriors oppose the war. T. M. Gannon. il America 124:516-18 My 15 '71
Who is Al Hubbard? W. Overend. Nat R 23:589+ Je 1 '71

VIETNAM victory rally. See Washington, D.C.—Parades

VIETNAMESE
Quiet heroes of South Vietnam. A. Abrams. Read Digest 99:142-6 O '71
See also
Montagnards

VIETNAMESE war, 1957—American participation *—Continued*

United States in Vietnam: a study in futility. D. G. Marr. Ann Am Acad 397:11-18 S '71

Viet-Nam: ending U.S. involvement in the war; statement, May 3, 1971: J. N. Irwin, 2d. Dept State Bul 64:711-14 My 31 '71

Vietnam: the facts and the falsehoods. H. W. Baldwin. il Read Digest 99:211-12+ N '71

Vietnam veteran speaks out against continuing the war. R. M. Herhold. Chr Cent 88: 833-5 Jl 7 '71

Vietnam was it worth it? W. W. Rostow. Look 35:68+ S 21 '71

War according to the Pentagon papers. il Newsweek 77:17-21 Je 28 '71

We can't wait until 1973. New Repub 164:7-8 Mr 13 '71

What chance is reasonable in Vietnam? L. H. Gelb and M. H. Halperin. pors Life 71: 4 Jl 16 '71

What liberals don't understand about Vietnam. J. B. Burnham. Nat R 23:77-80 Ja 26 '71

What Nixon didn't say. New Repub 164:7-8 Ap 17 '71

What price victory? three important aspects of our involvement. H. J. Morgenthau. New Repub 164:21-3 F 20 '71; Same abr. with title Will we use our nuclear option? Cur 128:4-8 Ap '71

Where are the leaders of our country? excerpts from testimony. J. F. Kerry. New Repub 164:15-18 My 8 '71

Where U.S. will make its last stand in Vietnam. il U S News 71:41 S 20 '71

See also

Conscientious objectors

United States—Armed forces—Forces in Vietnam

Vietnamese war, 1957- —American troop withdrawals

Vietnamese war, 1957- —History

Vietnamese war, 1957- —Pacification programs

Anecdotes, facetiae, satire, etc.

Vietnam vocabulary; terms suitable for various groups. Chr Cent 88:87 Ja 20 '71

American troop withdrawals

Are the POW's the real issue? il Newsweek 77:18-19 Je 21 '71

As Nixon speeds Vietnam pullout. il U S News 70:15-17 Ap 19 '71

As Vietnam gets set for faster pullout. il U S News 71:45-6 N 15 '71

Best way home from the war in Vietnam. il Life 70:30-1 Ap 2 '71

Blockbuster three? S. Alsop. Newsweek 78:112 S 13 '71

Border recessional: the return of Con Thien. Time 98:23 Jl 19 '71

Cambodia: key to U.S. plan for Vietnam pullout. il U S News 71:36-7 N 29 '71

Can South Vietnam survive without U.S? interview, ed. by W. S. Merick. E. Bunker. il por U S News 71:24-6 Jl 5 '71

Don't they know we're getting out? H. Sidey. il por Life 70:2 F 12 '71; Same abr. Read Digest 98:131-2 My '71

Follow the leader. New Repub 164:7-8 Ap 3 '71

Hatfield-McGovern; Vietnam disengagement act. New Repub 164:10 Je 26 '71

How to set a date for getting out of Vietnam. T. Hoopes. il N Y Times Mag p20-1+ My 9 '71

Hunkered down for the last act. H. Sidey. il Life 70:4 Ap 16 '71

If U.S. pulls out of Vietnam too fast; interview. R. Thompson. il por U S News 70: 36-8 Ap 12 '71

Indochina: disengaging. M. B. Ridgway. For Affairs 49:583-92 Jl '71

Indochina: Nixon's strategy of withdrawal. il Time 97:19 Mr 1 '71

Indo-China story today as U.S. changes its role. J. N. Wallace. il U S News 70:19-22 Je 21 '71

It is important how we end this war; address, April 7, 1971. R. M. Nixon. il por U S News 70:79-81 Ap 19 '71; Same abr. with title Indochina progress report: an assessment of Vietnamization. Dept State Bul 64:537-40 Ap 26 '71

Letter from Hong Kong. R. Shaplen. New Yorker 47:58-60+ Jl 31 '71

Letter from Vietnam. R. Shaplen. New Yorker 47:77-8+ N 13 '71

Letter from Washington. R. H. Rovere. New Yorker 47:70+ Jl 17 '71

McGovern: the meaning; total withdrawal. Nat R 23:124+ F 9 '71

Movable war. New Repub 64:9-10 F 13 '71

Muskie on withdrawal. New Repub 164:14 F 20 '71

New pressures to end it. il Time 97:17 Je 21 '71

New stall. Nation 213:419-20 N 1 '71

Next problem in Vietnam: getting out safely; with interview with J. M. Gavin. il U S News 70:23-5 Ap 26 '71

Next question? Hugh Scott and the opinion research poll. New Repub 164:10-11 Je 12 '71

Nixon on Vietnam: more of the same; television address, April 7, 1971. il por Newsweek 77:26-7 Ap 19 '71

Nixon's latest Vietnam pullout. il U S News 71:28 N 22 '71

No decent exit from Viet Nam for the U.S. il Time 98:11 S 13 '71

100,000 homeward bound; Nixon's Viet plan. il Sr Schol 98:13-14 Ap 26 '71

President Nixon announces increased troop withdrawal from Viet-Nam; excerpts from news conference, November 12, 1971. R. M. Nixon. Dept State Bul 65:641-6 D 6 '71

President Nixon reiterates policy on withdrawal from Indochina; statement, November 17, 1971. R. M. Nixon. Dept State Bul 65:658 D 6 '71

President Nixon's news conference of April 29, 1971. R. M. Nixon. Dept State Bul 64: 629-33 My 17 '71

Promise Nixon didn't make. Life 70:40 Ap 16 '71

Questions for Senator Javits: SEATO and US troop withdrawals. W. F. Buckley, jr. Nat R 23:330 Mr 23 '71

Setback for the doves; votes on McGovern-Hatfield, Chiles amendments. il Newsweek 77:31-2 Je 28 '71

Thirty minutes with William P. Rogers; interview on PBS program, March 9, 1971. W. P. Rogers. Dept State Bul 64:440-8 Mr 29 '71

Time to furl flags and head for home. il Life 71:46-7 D 31 '71

Turn off the faucet; resolution by House Democrats. New Repub 164:10 Ap 10 '71

U.S. pulls out of Vietnam. il Life 71:34-8+ N 26 '71

Vietnam: booby trap? S. Alsop. Newsweek 77:112 My 3 '71

Viet-Nam: ending U.S. involvement in the war; statement, May 3, 1971. J. N. Irwin, 2d. Dept State Bul 64:711-14 My 31 '71

Vietnam: Nixon's way out. il Newsweek 78: 27-8 N 22 '71

Viet Nam: one more step; President Nixon's announcement. il Time 98:23-4 N 22 '71

Vietnam pullout: Nixon's new problems. il U S News 71:18-19 Jl 19 '71

Vietnam: the case for immediate withdrawal; with editorial comment. N. Glazer. Commentary 51:6+, 33-7 My '71

Vietnamization: the reality and the myth. il Newsweek 78:38-9 Ag 2 '71

Wanted: the first president brave enough to lose a war. R. Shnayerson. Harper 243: 12+ S '71

War policy: historic vote; Mansfield end-the-war amendment. U S News 71:29 Jl 5 '71

We hear you, Abe Rosenthal. Nat R 23:126-7 F 9 '71; Reply. B. W. Wolff. 23:248 Mr 9 '71

You don't see any hawks around here; Republican senators discussion with Melvin Laird. il Newsweek 77:27-9 Ap 19 '71

Art

Marine combat artist. il por Ebony 26:104-6+ My '71

Atrocities

And now a general. il por Newsweek 77:29 Je 14 '71

Bird of prey: Operation Phoenix, a program of terror and assassination. Commonweal 94:396 Ag 6 '71

Bringing the war home; Vietnam veterans against the war winter soldier investigation into American war crimes. P. Michelson. il New Repub 164:21-5 F 27 '71

Charge of a general. por Time 97:21 Je 14 '71

Colonel Herbert tried to go by the book in Vietnam: how a supersoldier was fired from his command. J. T. Wooten. il pors N Y Times Mag p 10-11+ S 5 '71; Discussion. p97 S 26 '71

Compounding the tragedy; Colonel Herbert reporting atrocities. Time 97:16 Mr 22 '71

Confessions of the winter soldiers. D. Jackson. il Life 71:22-7 Jl 9 '71

Day America could have used a psychiatrist. B. Asbell. il por Todays Health 49:24-9+ Ag '71

VIETNAMESE war, 1957—Atrocities—*Cont.*

Hard times; testimonies of Vietnam veterans given before the National committee for a citizens' commission of inquiry on US war crimes in Vietnam; ed. by F. Lang. il Ramp Mag 9:12+ F '71

In the uproar over Calley's conviction; other cases. il U S News 70:20 Ap 19 '71

International war crimes. P. J. Riga. il Cath World 213:130-3 Je '71

Is this justice? the case of A. B. Herbert. M McGrory. America 125:337 O 30 '71

Lieutenant Calley's army. R. A. Gross. il Esquire 76:154-8+ O '71

More atrocities? por Newsweek 77:26 Mr 22 '71

Mylai mentality; excerpt from War crimes and the American conscience, ed. by E. Knoll and J. N. McFadden. D. Ellsberg. New Repub 165:19-20 Jl 17 '71

Notes and comment; news coverage of firing of Lieut. Col. A. B. Herbert. New Yorker 47:35 O 23 '71

Reporter at large; America division's Rules of engagement, and the Ky Chanh incident. S. M. Hersh. New Yorker 47:101-2+ O 9 '71

U.S. crimes in Vietnam; excerpts. E. Van Den Haag. il Nat R 23:1171-6 O 22 '71

War crimes in high places. J. B. Sheerin. Cath World 213:163-4 Jl '71

War crimes: made in U.S.A. M. Sacharoff. Nation 212:120-1 Ja 25 '71; Reply. R. Schoenman. 212:354 Mr 22 '71

What's to be done? P. Barnes. New Repub 164:26-30 Ap 24 '71

Whose war crimes? views of Telford Taylor. il Newsweek 77:29 F 22 '71

Winter soldier confab reveals more My Lais. J. Best. Chr Cent 88:289-90 Mr 3 '71

Winter soldier; Vietnam veterans against the war investigation; reprint. L. Winfrey Nation 212:229 F 22 '71

Winter soldiering in Detroit. J. Mahoney. Commonweal 93:540-1 Mr 5 '71

Worst massacre of all; men and boys from the Roman Catholic Vietnamese community. D. Warner. il Look 35:67-8+ Je 15 '71

My Lai massacre

Calley and the public conscience. P. Steinfels. Commonweal 94:128 Ap 16 '71

Calley case re-examined. S. Lesher. il pors N Y Times Mag p6-7+ Jl 11 '71

Calley takes the stand; with excerpts from testimony. il pors Life 70:22-8 Mr 5 '71

Calley's defense: anger, hate, fear, orders. por Newsweek 77:51-2 Mr 8 '71

Captain who commanded Lieutenant Calley. T. Buckley. il por N Y Times Mag p8-9+ Je 20 '71

Confessions of Lieutenant Calley, interview, ed. by J. Sack. W. L. Calley. jr. Esquire 76:85-9+ S '71

Men accused in My Lai massacre. il U S News 70:29 Mr 8 '71

My Lai: a question of orders. il pors Time 97:24 Ja 25 '71

MyLai and the national conscience. M. Novak; W. Barthelmes. Commonweal 94:183-7 Ap 30 '71

My Lai and the state of the army. D. A. Zoll. Nat R 23:1112-14 O 8 '71

My Lai killings: 12 out of 13 accused are free. il U S News 71:101 O 4 '71

Notes and comment; effect on American democracy and totalitarianism. New Yorker 47:29-32 Ap 10 '71

What has happened to the men charged with Mylai. Life 70:27 Mr 5 '71

Who is responsible? excerpts from Nuremberg and Vietnam. T. Taylor. Cur 126:52-64 F '71

Who is responsible for My Lai? por Time 97:18-19 Mr 8 '71

Wound reopened. il Time 97:12-13 Ap 12 '71

Wounded knee and My Lai. Chr Cent 88:59 Ja 20 '71

Bibliography

Bibliography of recent and forthcoming books on US war crimes in Indochina; comp. by M. Sacharoff. New Repub 164:29+ Ja 2 '71

Three faces of war. J. B. Breslin. America 125:314-16 O 23 '71

Campaigns and battles

Fall back. Newsweek 78:45 Ag 30 '71

Hanoi's rainy-season surge. il Time 97:28-9 Je 21 '71

Hell at Mary Ann; 23rd American division in Quang Tin province. N. C. Proffitt. il Newsweek 77:45 Ap 12 '71

Massacre at fire base Mary Ann. J. Larsen. il Time 97:26 Ap 12 '71

Operation Steel Tiger. Newsweek 77:25 Ja 18 '71

Tet! by D. Oberdorfer. Review

New Repub 165:36-7 O 16 '71. R. Dudman

Time il 98:108+ N 8 '71. J. L. Schecter

See also

Laotian campaign

Casualties

Air war in Indochina: some responses. R. R. Fernandez. il Chr Cent 88:1404-5 D 1 '71

America's second most costly war. il U S News 71:17 Jl 26 '71

Death of a fighting general; Do cao Tri. il por Time 97:21 Mr 8 '71

Expendable Americans; death rate of Belen, N.Mex. citizens. J. Rowen. Ramp Mag 10:8-9 N '71

Frustration near the front. por Time 97:45-6 Mr 8 '71

In praise of wounded men. J. B. Gerald. il Harper 242:98-100+ Ap '71

Indochina: a slaughter of innocents. E. M. Kennedy. Nation 212:806-8 Je 28 '71

Larry Burrow's Vietnam. Life 70:34-45 F 26 '71

'To each his turn, today yours, tomorrow mine'; death of F. Sully, dean of the Saigon press corps. il por Newsweek 77:75 Mr 8 '71

War within the war; nonhostile fatalities. Time 97:34-5 Ja 25 '71

See also

Committee of responsibility to save war-burned and war-injured Vietnamese children

Censorship

Case of the leaky embargo; news blackout on Operation Dewey Canyon II. Newsweek 77:22 F 15 '71

Deeper and deeper. Commonweal 94:3-4 Mr 12 '71

How we bombed Tokyo's press. A. Axelbank. Nation 213:205-6 S 13 '71

Information freeze. Newsweek 77:46 Mr 1 '71

Right to know; Laos campaign. R. L. Tobin. Sat R 54:41-2 Ap 10 '71

Chemical warfare

Chemical war; National liberation front film. S. N. Novick. il Environ 13:44-7 Mr '71

Tear gas in Vietnam and the return of poison gas; testimony before the Defense subcommittee of the Senate appropriations committee, May 1970. M. Meselson. Bul Atom Sci 27:17-19 Mr '71

Children

Mascots of war; case of Le Van Cau. J. Marti. il Ramp Mag 10:52-3 Ja '72

Cost

Cost of the war after it's over. il Time 97:12 Ap 19 '71

Damage to property

See Vietnamese war, 1957- —Destruction and pillage

Destruction and pillage

Land war. E. W. Pfeiffer; A. H. Westing. il pors Environ 13:2-15 N '71

Silent Vietnam: how we invented ecocide and killed a country. O. Schell, jr. il Look 35:55+ Ap 6 '71

Starvation as a policy; report of the Science-herbicide assessment commission. P. R. Ehrlich and J. P. Holdren. Sat R 54:91 D 4 '71

War crimes: made in U.S.A. M. Sacharoff. Nation 212:120-1 Ja 25 '71; Reply. R. Schoenman. 212:354 Mr 22 '71

Economic aspects

Getting Thieu through '72. New Repub 165:5-6 N 27 '71

Millions for defense but . . ; unpopularity of war among businessmen. J. Clotfelter. il Nation 212:108-10 Ja 25 '71

Political economy of war. D. F. Dowd. Nation 212:811-15 Je 28 '71

Strange economics of the Vietnam war. B. Garrett. il Ramp Mag 10:34-9 N '71

Equipment and supplies

No abandoned arsenals this time. il U S News 71:19-20 Jl 19 '71

Quartermaster to the VC. il Newsweek 79:23 Ja 10 '72

Technology vs. guerrillas. E. Hymoff. il Bul Atom Sci 27:27-30 N '71

Foreign participation

Allies join the parade home. il U S News 71:21 Jl 19 '71

Viet-Nam troop contributors hold conference at Washington; communique, April 23, 1971. Dept State Bul 64:635-8 My 17 '71

VIETNAMESE war, 1957—*Continued*

History

Big lead; report published in New York times. Nation 212:802-3 Je 28 '71

Case of the Pentagon papers. America 125: 6-7 Jl 10 '71

Ellsberg affair. P. Schrag. por Sat R 54:34-9 N 13 '71

For whose eyes only? Pentagon papers. Nation 213:2 Jl 5 '71

Goldwater: Congress knew what it was doing on Vietnam; address, July 29, 1971. B. M. Goldwater. il por U S News 71:88-91 Ag 16 '71

Government vs. the press; Pentagon study. il por Newsweek 78:17-19 Jl 5 '71

High drama in foggy bottom; three editions of The Pentagon papers. J. Mirsky. il Sat R 55:23-6+ Ja 1 '72

Lansdale's secret war; the Saigon military mission. il por Newsweek 78:16 Jl 19 '71

Let it all come out. W. P. Bundy. Newsweek 78:49 Jl 12 '71

New respect for the old Dino. H. Sidey. por Life 71:4 Jl 23 '71

Notes and comment; keeping secret the Pentagon study of the war's origins and development. New Yorker 47:17-19 Jl 3 '71

Notes and comment; Pentagon's secret study on the conduct of the war. New Yorker 47:29-30 Je 26 '71; Same with title Leadership or suspended government? Cur 131:3-5 Jl '71

Notes on the Pentagon papers. P. Steinfels. Commonweal 94:350 Jl 9 '71

Of betrayal and loyalty. Chr Cent 88:792-Je 30 '71

On reading the Pentagon papers. E. G. Windchy. New Repub 165:21-5 Ag 7 '71

Particular tragedy of Robert McNamara. por Time 98:21 Jl 5 '71

Pentagon papers. Life 71:6 Jl 2 '71

Pentagon papers: did the public win or lose? questions and answers. Sr Schol 99:4-5 S 20 '71

Pentagon papers; games presidents and other people play. E. J. McCarthy. New Repub 165:14-17 Jl 10 '71

Pentagon papers: the secret war. il Time 97: 11-14 Je 28 '71

Pentagon study: the other side; television interview, July 2, 1971; with questions by B. Walters and E. Newman. D. Rusk. il pors U S News 71:68-76 Jl 19 '71

Round two: what the new documents show. il por Time 98:15-16 Jl 5 '71

Round 3: more Pentagon disclosures; excerpts from documents. il Time 98:12-13 Jl 12 '71

Secret decisions that altered the Vietnam war; storm over leaked documents. il U S News 70:21-3 Je 28 '71

Secret history of the war. il Newsweek 78: 21-2+ Jl 12 '71

Secret history of Vietnam; Pentagon study, commissioned by R. McNamara. il pors Newsweek 77:12-22+ Je 28 '71

Sources of insurgency. T. Buckley. N Y Times Mag p91 S 26 '71

Spotlight turns to the Kennedy years; Pentagon papers. il Newsweek 78:19-21 Jl 5 '71

TRB from Washington; Pentagon papers. New Repub 164:6 Je 26 '71

Today's lessons from the Pentagon papers. L. H. Gelb. por Life 71:34-6 S 17 '71

Tragedy of the Pentagon study. D. Lawrence. U S News 71:80 Ag 9 '71

Vantage point, by L. B. Johnson. Review Newsweek il pors 78:22+ N 1 '71. C. Roberts

Vietnam build-up: the story the "leaks" don't tell. il U S News 71:22-3 Jl 5 '71

Was Lyndon Johnson a liar? S. Alsop. Newsweek 78:80 Jl 5 '71

Which are the true papers? J. Burnham. Nat R 23:864 Ag 10 '71

Anecdotes, facetiae, satire, etc.

National review papers. W. F. Buckley, jr. Nat R 23:850 Ag 10 '71

Secret papers they didn't publish: documents leaked to National review. Nat R 23:798-811 Jl 27 '71; Discussion. 23:904, 915-18, 975-6 Ag 24-S 10 '71

Korean participation

Money for men. New Repub 165:1+ O 9 '71

Legal aspects

Reporter at large; America! division's Rules of engagement, and the Ky Chanh incident. S. M. Hersh. New Yorker 47:101-2+ O 9 '71

Wanted: an inquiry into the war. New Repub 164:56 My 22 '71

Why impeachment; case against Mr Nixon. R. A. Falk. New Repub 164:13-14 My 1 '71

Medical and sanitary affairs

Lest their minds become casualties of the war; excerpt from 365 days. R. J. Glasser. il Todays Health 49:50-5+ N '71

Our finest achievement. D. Weller. Chr Cent 88:1263-4 O 27 '71

Please read this; excerpt from 365 days. R. J. Glasser. Redbook 137:64+ Ag '71

Simpler creed; excerpt from 365 days. R. J. Glasser. il Harper 243:86-7 Jl '71

See also

Committee of responsibility to save war-burned and war-injured Vietnamese children

Moral and religious aspects

After Vietnam, another witchhunt? L. J. Halle. il N Y Times Mag p36-8+ Je 6 '71

American bishop blasts hierarchy on Vietnam silence, quits post. Chr Cent 88:794 Je 30 '71

Appeal to the bishops; a call for condemnation of war in Indochina. Commonweal 94:155-6 Ap 23 '71

Bishops and just war. M. Bordelon. America 126:17-19 Ja 8 '72

Bishops and the war. W. F. Buckley, jr. Nat R 23:1434 D 17 '71

Bishops speak on Vietnam; pastoral letter from bishops of the ecclesiastical province of Boston. America 124:623-4 Je 19 '71

Bishop's study: war no more. R. Chandler. Chr Today 16:35-6 D 17 '71

Call to action; four religious journals publish joint editorial. il Newsweek 77:101 Ap 12 '71

Call to penitence and action. Chr Cent 88: 419-20 Ap 7 '71; Same. Commonweal 94:99-100 Ap 9 '71; Discussion. Chr Cent 88:636-8 My 19 '71

Captivating Air force academy. Chr Today 16:32 D 3 '71

Judging Calley is not enough. T. Taylor. il Life 70:20-3 Ap 9 '71

Necessary amorality of foreign affairs. A. Schlesinger, jr. Harper 243:72-7 Ag '71; Discussion. 243:6+ O '71

Spring love and hate. il Chr Cent 88:613-14 My 19 '71

Unconditional withdrawal; strategy for peace? D. Kucharsky. Chr Today 15:37-8 Ap 23 '71

Vietnam: what is left of conscience? B. Moyers. Sat R 54:20-1 F 13 '71

Who else is guilty? K. Auchincloss. il Newsweek 77:30-2 Ap 12 '71

Wisdom of doves. Chr Cent 88:607 My 12 '71

Negotiations

See Vietnamese war, 1957- —Peace and mediation

Negroes

"Pound", a new unity sign; ritual greeting of black soldiers in Vietnam. F. C. Anthony. America 124:147-8 F 13 '71

Pacification programs

Civilian forced labor in Ba Chuc minefields. A. Shimkin. Chr Cent 88:297-8 Mr 3 '71

Letter from Indo-China; new standards for Hamlet evaluation system. R. Shaplen. New Yorker 47:111-12 Ap 24 '71

Notes and comment. New Yorker 47:27-8 My 29 '71

Notes and comment; project to deport people from the northernmost provinces of South Vietnam to southern provinces. New Yorker 46:23-4 Ja 23 '71

Peace and mediation

Chance to bargain on Vietnam. Life 71:34 Jl 23 '71

Changing U.S. role in the world: address February 25, 1971. R. M. Nixon. il U S News 70:49-52 Mr 8 '71; Same with title Redefinition of the United States role in the world. Dept State Bul 64:305-10 Mr 15 '71; Excerpt. Cur Hist 61:357-8+ D '71

Clark Clifford sounds the alarm. P. Anderson. il pors N Y Times Mag p8-9+ Ag 8 '71

Gathering climate of negotiation. il Time 98: 9-10 Jl 19 '71

How not to end a war. N. Cousins. Sat R 54:24 S 4 '71

How to set a date for getting out of Vietnam. T. Hoopes. il N Y Times Mag p20-1+ My 9 '71

Last chance to make peace? il Newsweek 78:14-15 Jl 19 '71

VIETNAMES war, 1957—Peace and mediation—*Continued*
Moment for restraint. Z. Brzezinski. Newsweek 78:37 Jl 19 '71
Negotiations: the view from Hanoi; proposals offered by the NLF's Provisional revolutionary government at Paris. July 1971. G. M. Kahin. New Repub 165:13-16 N 6 '71
Nixon's chance to end the war; Vietcong proposal of July 1. New Repub 165:7-8 Jl 17 '71
Opposing peace plans: still miles apart. il U S News 71:16 Jl 26 '71
Round II: peace movement vs. Vietnamization. P. P. McDermott. il Cath World 213: 6-12 Ap '71
To the people of North Vietnam. D. Lawrence. U S News 70:104 Ap 5 '71
U.S. and Indochina. F. Lewis. Atlan 227:6+ Mr '71
When the war might have ended; excerpt from The labour government, 1964-70. H. Wilson. il pors Life 70:54B-56+ My 21 '71
See also
People's peace treaty

Negotiation meetings, May 1968-
Ambassador Bruce resigns as head of U.S. delegation to Paris talks; with exchange of letters. July 28, 1971. R. M. Nixon; D. E. Bruce. Dept State Bul 65:179-80 Ag 16 '71
Ambassador Porter named to head U.S. delegation to Paris talks. Dept State Bul 65: 181 Ag 16 '71
Going nowhere in Paris. G. M. Kahin; reply. C. Dabezies. New Repub 164:32 Ja 23 '71
Hanoi: bearing gifts. Nat R 23:789-90 Jl 27 '71
Leapfrogging the Paris talks. il Newsweek 78:22 Jl 26 '71
Letter from Hong Kong. R. Shaplen. New Yorker 47:58-60+ Jl 31 '71
New man in Paris. por Time 98:20-1 Ag 9 '71
Nixon's objective in Paris. R. L. Leggett. Nation 213:610 D 13 '71
[Plenary sessions] D. K. E. Bruce. See issues of Department of state bulletin
Talking tough in Paris; work of Ambassador Porter. por Time 99:26 Ja 17 '72
War: stirrings at the peace table. il Time 98:8-9 Jl 12 '71
Way to end the war? Communist offer. il Newsweek 78:15 Jl 12 '71

Personal narratives
Confessions of Lieutenant Calley; interview, ed. by J. Sack. W. L. Calley, jr. Esquire 75:55-9+ F: 76:85-9+ S '71
Confessions of the winter soldiers. D. Jackson. il Life 71:22-7 Jl 9 '71
Conversation at Chu Lai hospital; excerpt from letter of Quaker worker. R. Marshall. Chr Cent 88:237-8 F 17 '71
A day in the dwindling war. N. Proffitt. il Newsweek 78:40-1 S 13 '71
Election time comes to Saigon. R. J. Willis. il America 125:400-2 N 13 '71
Forty days with the enemy, by R. Dudman. Review
New Repub 164:34-5 Je 5 '71. D. Halberstam
GI's Vietnam photo book; excerpt from The Vietnam photo book. M. Jury. il Look 35: 22-6+ S 21 '71
Gloria Emerson's Vietnam diary. G. Emerson. il pors Vogue 159:74-7+ Ja 1 '72
Hey, lady, what are you doing here? G. Emerson. il por McCalls 98:61+ Ag '71
I remember Vietnam; address. May 4, 1971. C. M. Searcy. il Chr Cent 88:828-30 Jl 7 '71
Let's get out, summary of interview. ed. by K. Buckley and N. Proffitt. por Newsweek 78:34 Jl 5 '71
Letter from Vietnam. Negro Hist Bul 34: 98 My '71
Lieutenant Calley's army. R. A. Gross. il Esquire 76:154-8+ O '71
Mylai mentality; excerpt from War crimes and the American conscience, ed. by E. Knoll and J. N. McFadden. D. Ellsberg. New Repub 165:19-20 Jl 17 '71
No victory parades, by M. Polner. Review
Sat R 54:28-9 Jl 31 '71. W. Beauchamp
Pete McCloskey. il pors Life 70:28B-29 My 7 '71
Satan one-five. R. Starnes. Field & S 75: 22-3 Ja '71
365 days, by R. J. Glasser. Review
Atlan 228:125-8 O '71. J. Bunting
Time il 98:113+ N 1 '71. L. Morrow
War of the innocents, by G. B. Flood. Review
Sat R 54:29 F 27 '71. J. Reed

Photographs and photography
Faces of war. N. Rosenheck. Pop Phot 68: 106+ Ap '71
GI's Vietnam photo book; excerpt from The Vietnam photo book. M. Jury. il Look 35: 22-6+ S 21 '71
Larry Burrow's Vietnam. Life 70:34-45 F 26 '71

Press reports
Vietnam: how the press went along; excerpt from Communication in international politics, ed. by R. L. Merritt. S. Welch. Nation 213:327-30 O 11 '71; Discussion. 213: 418, 450 N 1-8 '71
See also
Vietnamese war, 1957- —Censorship

Prisoners and prisons
Ambassador Bruce discusses problem of U.S. prisoners of war in southeast Asia; text of news conference, December 1, 1970. D. K. E. Bruce. il Dept State Bul 63:737-45 D 21 '70
Are the POW's the real issue? il Newsweek 77:18-19 Je 21 '71
Brouhaha over POWs advertising campaign. L. Sloane. Sat R 54:97 N 13 '71
Continuing U.S. efforts on behalf of prisoners of war and missing in southeast Asia; remarks, September 28, 1971. R. M. Nixon; M. R. Laird. Dept State Bul 65:447-50 O 25 '71
Cruelty of North Vietnam. D. Lawrence. U S News 70:92 Mr 8 '71
Day-trippers; Communist POW's torpedo repatriation. il Newsweek 77:40 Je 14 '71
Despite red China thaw, crucial tests for Nixon. il por U S News 71:15-17 Jl 26 '71
Don't ever forget! L. R. Stockstill. Read Digest 98:117-20 My '71
Families are frantic. il Time 98:17-18 Jl 26 '71
Forty days with the enemy, by R. Dudman. Review
New Repub 164:34-5 Je 5 '71. R. Halberstam
Sat R 54:26-7 Je 26 '71. J. Barry
H. Ross Perot pays his dues. F. Powledge. il pors N Y Times Mag p 16-17+ F 28 '71
Hanoi: bearing gifts. Nat R 23:789-90 Jl 27 '71
How to bring them all home. R. L. Leggett. Nation 212:394-7 Mr 29 '71
Inside the prisons of Hanoi. L. R. Stockstill. Read Digest 98:67-72 Ap '71
More on the prisoners. Nation 211:646 D 21 '70
Notes and comment: North Vietnamese prisoners refusal of repatriation offer. New Yorker 47:19 Je 19 '71
POW crusade. Chr Today 15:31 F 26 '71
POW wife. il pors Ebony 26:110-11+ Je '71
POWs and the professor; R. Falk. W. F. Buckley. jr. Nat R 23:828 Jl 27 '71
PR for POWs. New Repub 164:7 Je 19 '71
Power of a woman; Ladies home journal delegation at Paris. il Ladies Home J 88: 46+ Jl '71
Power of a woman; open letter to Communist leaders in Vietnam and Laos. Ladies Home J 88:50 Ap '71
President Nixon pledges continued efforts on behalf of U.S. prisoners of war; text of letter, December 26, 1970. R. M. Nixon. Dept State Bul 64:73-4 Ja 18 '71
President pays tribute to captives and missing in southeast Asia; statement, March 13, 1971. R. M. Nixon. Dept State Bul 64: 489 Ap 5 '71
President welcomes South Viet-Nam's initiative on prisoners of war, statement, April 14, 1971. R. M. Nixon. Dept State Bul 64:568 My 3 '71
Prisoners: a ray of hope. il Newsweek 77:41 Je 7 '71
Prisoners and policy. W. P. Bundy. Newsweek 77:34 My 31 '71
Proportional repatriation. Nation 212:324 Mr 15 '71
Red cross contribution; Write Hanoi campaign. New Repub 164:10 Ap 3 '71
Rules of the game: Geneva conventions of 1949. il Sr Schol 99:13-14 N 29 '71
Signals in the fog. il Time 97:19 My 24 '71
These men had dropped from sight. il Life 70:26-9 F 12 '71
They also serve; activist groups lobby government. Newsweek 78:17-18 D 27 '71
U.N. General assembly urges humane treatment of prisoners of war; statements with text of resolution. C. Pell; C. W. Yost. Dept State Bul 64:8-13 Ja 4 '71
United States concern for prisoners of war; address. May 17, 1971. S. T. Agnew. Dept State Bul 64:803-6 Je 21 '71; Excerpts. U S News 70:73 My 31 '71

VIETNAMESE war, 1957- —Prisoners and prisons—*Continued*

Week of concern for Americans captured and missing in action; proclamation. R. M. Nixon. Dept State Bul 64:506 Ap 12 '71

We've not given up on POW's; excerpts from address, May 17, 1971. S. Agnew. U S News 70:73 My 31 '71

What's a POW-MIA, and what are high school students doing about it? il Sr Schol 99:8-12 N 29 '71

See also
Prisoners of war. Returned

Photographs

Our missing men: silent faces, somber facts. Read Digest 98:114-16 My '71

Propaganda

But who hath measured the ground? unreliable and falsified figures and information. il Time 97:30 Mr 15 '71

Protests, demonstrations, etc, against

Academy graduates; letter. J. Seidman. New Repub 164:31 Ap 10 '71

After the rhetoric; pledge to vote only for anti-war candidates. Nation 212:579 My 10 '71

Ambush at the courthouse; antiwar raid on federal offices in Camden, N.J. il por Time 98:16 S 6 '71

Another plea for peace and a reservation. America 124:474 My 8 '71

Barbarians at the gates. J. Burnham. Nat R 23:523 My 18 '71

Biggest bust. il Newsweek 77:24-8+ My 17 '71

Bob Brown: reluctant radical; interview, ed. by R. M. Herhold. R. M. Brown. il por Chr Cent 88:745-7 Je 16 '71

Bureaucracy adrift; anti-war dissent within the U.S. military. E. F. Sherman. Nation 212:265-75 Mr 1 '71

Chess of ending a war. il Time 97:12-13 My 10 '71

Clergy and laymen: broadening the concern. R. S. Lecky. Commonweal 94:468 S 17 '71

Connie stay home; San Diego, Calif. il Newsweek 78:23-4 O 4 '71

Cornell vs. Wichita; Catholic peace fellowship. J. Deedy. Commonweal 94:346 Jl 9 '71

Countdown on the home front. Nat R 23:298+ Mr 23 '71

Demo time again. il Time 97:16 Ap 26 '71

Exercise in disruption and despair; Washington. il Life 71:36-7 D 31 '71

Getting nowhere through channels; distributing dissenting materials in the army. J. V. H. Dippel. New Repub 164:13-17 My 22 '71

Holy Week, Easter marked by antiwar activities. Chr Cent 88:519-20 Ap 28 '71

Informer; raids on draft-board offices in Camden, N.J. and Buffalo, N.Y. il Newsweek 78:23 S 6 '71

Invasion; traffic-blocking demonstrators in Washington, D.C. Sedulus. New Repub 164:36 My 15 '71

Is Mr Nixon in command of his own shop? HEW peace activities. Nat R 23:513 My 18 '71

Liberty liberated; Viet Nam veterans against the war occupy Statue of Liberty. il Time 99:10 Ja 10 '72

New peace movement; proposals. P. Steinfels. Commonweal 93:462 F 12 '71; Reply. R. Ruether. 94:22 Mr 12 '71

New wave of war protests, with a difference. il U S News 70:21-2 My 10 '71

Notes and comment. New Yorker 47:39 N 27 '71

Once again, witless violence. H. Sidey. Life 70:4 My 14 '71

Once more a time for protest; Washington; San Francisco; House and Senate hearings. il Newsweek 77:24-5 My 3 '71

One woman's walk for peace. A. Lake. il pors Good H 173:70-1+ Jl '71

Peace movement is using the wrong strategy. M. Harrington. il N Y Times Mag p 10-11+ My 30 '71

Protest: a week against the war. il Time 97:10-13 My 3 '71

Protests; San Francisco, April 28. W. F. Buckley, jr. Nat R 23:556-7 My 18 '71

Publishers for peace mass in N.Y.C. protest. Pub W 199:41 Ap 26 '71

Son of Mayday; Washington, D.C. il Newsweek 78:45+ N 8 '71

Spring offensive. Nation 212:259-60 Mr 1 '71

Spring offensive; plans for April 24. Newsweek 77:29-30 Ap 26 '71

Statue of Liberty play; seizure by members of Vietnam veterans against the war. il Newsweek 79:20 Ja 10 '72

Status of the movement: the energy levels are low. J. Lelyveld. il pors N Y Times Mag p36-7+ N 7 '71; Reply with rejoinder. R. A. Falk. p 14+ N 28 '71

Street protests: a decline in the tumult and shouting. il U S News 71:43 N 29 '71

Suing to stop the war; National emergency civil liberties committee suits. Nation 213:228 S 20 '71

TRB from Washington; Quaker vigil outside the White House. New Repub 165:4 O 23 '71

Telling it on the mountain; D. Smith on Mount Shasta. I. Eldad. Chr Cent 88:886 Jl 21 '71

Town and gown for peace; Eugene, Ore. anti-war resolution vote. Nation 212:741 Je 14 '71

Two days in May; Zinn at Boston. D. Brudnoy. Nat R 23:573 Je 1 '71

U.S. journal: Kansas. C. Trillin. New Yorker 47:60+ My 22 '71

Unselling of the Vietnam war. P. D. Maines. il Nat R 23:858-9 Ag 10 '71

Variations on a theme; abortion pastoral. Commonweal 94:229 My 14 '71

Watch out, Uncle Sam is angry; arrest of the Camden 28. P. Tracy. Commonweal 94:472 S 17 '71

Wave of other protests in U.S. il U S News 70:18 My 17 '71

Who is prolonging the war? reprint from issue of November 17, 1969. D. Lawrence. U S News 71:80 Jl 5 '71

Why I went to jail; the Holy week witness. P. Steinfels. Commonweal 94:158 Ap 23 '71

Winter soldier confab reveals more My Lais. J. Best. Chr Cent 88:289-90 Mr 3 '71

Withholding war taxes. P. Barnes. New Repub 164:15-17 Ap 10 '71

You don't see any hawks around here. il Newsweek 77:27-9 Ap 19 '71

See also
Boston—Protests, demonstrations, etc.
Lexington, Mass.—Protests, demonstrations, etc.
Military service. Compulsory—Draft resisters
People's coalition for peace and justice
People's peace treaty
Student demonstrations
Vietnam veterans against the war (organization)
Washington, D.C.—Protests, demonstrations, etc.

Caricatures and cartoons

Peace march. J. Noonan. Cath World 213:287 S '71

Vietnam (Republic)

Viet Catholics for peace; the Committee for the formation of a Catholic movement working for peace. J. Deedy. Commonweal 94:124 Ap 16 '71

Psychological aspects

Day America could have used a psychiatrist. B. Asbell. il por Todays Health 49:24-9+ Ag '71

Public opinion

Greatest tragedy of all; excerpts from letter to President Nixon. A. Daniel, 3d. il Time 97:13 Ap 19 '71

Hopes and fears; findings of Potomac associates, inc. New Repub 165:8 Jl 3 '71

Millions for defense but . . ; unpopularity of war among businessmen. J. Clotfelter. il Nation 212:108-10 Ja 25 '71

MyLai and the national conscience. M. Novak; W. Barthelmes. Commonweal 94:183-7 Ap 30 '71

New Zealand; antiwar sentiment grows. R. M. O'Grady. Chr Cent 88:469-70 Ap 14 '71

Power of a woman; open letter to Communist leaders in Vietnam and Laos. Ladies Home J 88:50 Ap '71

Power to the people; survey findings of the American institute of public opinion. Nation 212:261 Mr 1 '71

Question. Nation 212:258-9 Mr 1 '71

U.S. journal: Kansas. C. Trillin. New Yorker 47:60+ My 22 '71

Vietnam and western Europe; official positions of Great Britain, France and West Germany. S. Hoffmann. New Repub 164:18-23 Ja 30 '71

What liberals don't understand about Vietnam. J. B. Burnham. Nat R 23:77-80 Ja 26 '71

See also
Student opinion

Relief work

Ten vets who went back. A. Maupin, jr. Nat R 23:1465-7 D 31 '71

Social aspects

Agony of going home; settlements in Quang Nam province. J. Larsen. il Time 97:26 My 10 '71

VIETNAMESE war, 1957- —*Continued*
Statistics
Notes and comment; pacification programs.
New Yorker 47:27-8 My 29 '71

Strategy
About Vietnamization. P. M. Lake. Nat R
23:761 Jl 13 '71
Another route to peace. Nation 213:546-7 N
29 '71
Changing the ground rules? il Sr Schol 98:
5-6 F 15 '71
Dark night. Commonweal 93:459-60 F 12 '71
Generals of the new army; W. DePuy. il por
Ramp Mag 10:16-17 S '71
How the invasion was planned. il Newsweek
77:32 F 22 '71
If Giap were a U.S. general. W. C. Moore.
por U S News 70:35 My 3 '71
Impact in Hanoi; strategy of Le Duan. R.
Critchfield. Nation 213:102-5 Ag 16 '71
Indispensable lifeline; Ho Chi Minh trail.
il Time 97:28 F 15 '71
Military art of people's war: selected writings
of General Vo Nguyen Giap, ed. by Stetler.
Review
    Nation 212:764-5 Je 14 '71. L. P. Liggio
New respect for the old Dino. H. Sidey. por
Life 71:4 Jl 23 '71
Nixon doctrine; address, March 29, 1971. M.
Mansfield. Vital Speeches 37:418-21 My 1
'71
Nixon tightrope. J. M. Burns. il pors Life
70:48B-48D+ Ap 2 '71
Nuclear weapons, next? Commonweal 93:507
F 26 '71
Particular tragedy of Robert McNamara.
por Time 98:21 Jl 5 '71
President digs in on Viet Nam. il Time 97:11
Ap 19 '71
President on Indo-China; excerpts from
news conference, February 17, 1971. R. M.
Nixon. por U S News 70:21 Mr 1 '71; Ex-
cerpts. Dept State Bul 64:281-6 Mr 8 '71
President's double finesse. S. Alsop. News-
week 77:98 Mr 1 '71
Round II: peace movement vs. Vietnamiza-
tion. P. P. McDermott. il Cath World 213:
6-12 Ap '71
Theory and fallacies of counterinsurgency.
E. Ahmad. il Nation 213:70-85 Ag 2 '71
Today's lessons from the Pentagon papers.
L. H. Gelb. por Life 71:34-6 S 17 '71
U.S. strategy beyond Vietnam; interview. M.
R. Laird. il por U S News 70:27-30+ My 17
'71
Untold story of the Ho Chi Minh trail. il
U S News 70:23-4 F 15 '71
Vietnam: as war winds down new worries
spring up. il U S News 72:19-20 Ja 10 '72
Vietnam: how Nixon plans to win the war;
the Huntington-Kissinger strategy. B. Gar-
rett. il por Ramp Mag 9:26-31 F '71
Vietnam: the case for immediate withdrawal;
with editorial comment. N. Glazer. Com-
mentary 51:6+, 33-7 My '71
Vietnam: the next round. Nation 212:738 Je
14 '71
War according to the Pentagon papers. il
Newsweek 77:17-21 Je 28 '71
War of continuing illusions. D. Halberstam.
Cur 128:3-4 Ap '71
What chance is reasonable in Vietnam? L.
H. Gelb and M. H. Halperin. pors Life 71:
4 Jl 16 '71
White House conversation: the President and
Howard K. Smith; excerpts from TV inter-
view, March 22, 1971. R. M. Nixon. Dept
State Bul 64:497-506 Ap 12 '71
Who is prolonging the war? reprint from
issue of November 17, 1969. D. Lawrence.
U S News 71:80 Jl 5 '71
Widening the war to wind it down? il
Newsweek 77:18-19 F 8 '71
Will red China now risk war? il U S News
70:17 Mr 8 '71
Would U.S. support an invasion of North
Vietnam? President's news conference,
March 4, 1971. R. M. Nixon. il por U S
News 70:41 Mr 15 '71; Same. Dept State
Bul 64:433-9 Mr 29 '71
See also
Laotian campaign

Anecdotes, facetiae, satire, etc.
TRB from Washington: swift solution: use of
small, tactical, nuclear weapons in Laos.
New Repub 164:4 Mr 20 '71

Student opinion
See Student opinion

Veterans
See Veterans

War aims
Trap of rationality. G. W. Ball. Newsweek
78:43 Jl 26 '71

War correspondents and photographers
And now there are nine. Time 97:27 My 10 '71
And now there are ten; no word from C.
Webb. por Time 97:33 My 3 '71
As seen by gloomy Gloria. G. Kirk. Nat R
23:426 Ap 20 '71
Edge of the sword; four photographers pre-
sumed dead. il por Newsweek 77:55 F 22
'71
Frustration near the front. por Time 97:45-6
Mr 8 '71
Gloria Emerson's Vietnam diary. G. Emer-
son. il pors Vogue 159:74-7+ Ja 1 '72
Hey, lady, what are you doing here? G.
Emerson. il por McCalls 98:61+ Ag '71
Kate Webb's story. il por Newsweek 77:59-60
My 24 '71
This strange war fascinates me. il por Time
97:70 F 22 '71
'To each his turn, today yours, tomorrow
mine'; death of F. Sully. il por Newsweek
77:75 Mr 8 '71
VIETNAMESE war and college students. See
College students and war
VIETNAMESE war and high school students.
See High school students and war
VIEUX CARRE. See New Orleans
VIEW cameras. See Cameras
VIGILANCE (psychology)
See also
Signal detection (psychology)
VIGILANCE committees

Illinois
Chicago's black vigilantes; anti-drug Afro-
American group attack team. il Newsweek
78:75+ S 27 '71

New Jersey
It would not be fun. S. Alsop. Newsweek 77:
116 My 17 '71
VIGO COUNTY, Ind, public library, Terre
Haute
Budget cut contested by Vigo library board.
Library J 96:3548 N 1 '71
Toward PPBS in the public library; plan-
ning-programming-budgeting system. E. N.
Howard. bibliog il Am Lib 2:386-93 Ap '71
VIGREN, David D.
Experts advise you: how to pick a safe
boat. il Pop Sci 198:58-9+ Ja '71
VIGUERS, Ruth Hill
Obituary
Horn Bk por 47:255 Je '71. E. C. Hau-
gaard
Well done, old squirrel! F. C. Sayers. Horn
Bk 47:127 Ap '71 *
VIKING press, inc.
Gurus on parade; Modern masters series. A.
Cooper. Newsweek 77:93-4 Je 21 '71
Viking, Esquire, dropped from Calley law
suit. Pub W 199:37 Ja 18 '71
Viking press explains position on publica-
tion of Lieutenant Calley. A. J. Johnston.
il por Pub W 199:42 Ap 26 '71; Reply. W.
Greenhaw. 199:14 My 17 '71
VIKING program. See Space vehicles—Land-
ing systems—Mars
VIKINGS (football club) See Football clubs
VILAR, Esther
Who's exploiting whom? por Newsweek 78:
41-2 D 20 '71 *
VILLA BORGHESE gardens. See Rome (city)
—Gardens
VILLA-LOBOS, Heitor
Yerma. Criticism
Hi Fi il 21:MA16-17 N '71 *
New Yorker 47:85 S 4 '71 *
Newsweek 78:74 Ag 23 '71 *
Time il 98:36 Ag 23 '71 *
Yerma reborn. J. W. Freeman. il por Opera
N 35:6-7 Je 12 '71 *
VILLAGE life
Back to podunk! C. H. Simonds. Nat R
23:931 Ag 24 '71
Livin' is easy; small town life. S. Schuler.
il Nations Bsns 59:86-90 O '71
Profiles: Stonington, Conn. A. Bailey. New
Yorker 47:36-44+ Jl 24; 38-52+ Jl 31 '71
VILLAGE voice (newspaper)
Responsibilities of Carter Burden. Nat R 23:
557 My 18 '71
VILLAGES
See also
Village life

VILLAGES—*Continued*

China (People's Republic)

Caves of Pao-an; visit to Mao's past. L. W. Snow. il Nation 212:690-2 My 31 '71
Life inside a Chinese commune; interview, ed. by K. M. Chrysler. M. Wakabayashi. il por U S News 70:70-1 F 15 '71

Greece, Modern

To understand Greece, go to Lia. N. Gage. il por N Y Times Mag p 16-17+ Ja 31 '71; Reply with rejoinder. S. Bartzokis. p92 Mr 7 '71

Indonesia

Report from the majority of the world. J. P. Sterba. il N Y Times Mag p 12-13+ S 5 '71

Switzerland

Switzerland: progress against the communes. B. R. Barber. il Trans-Action 8:27-31+ F '71
VILLAGES, Restored
Holland's 17th century village for modern people; De Zaanse Schans. L. Barry. il Pop Phot 69:54+ Jl '71
Where it's always 1850; Westville, Ga. W. Wood. il Am Ed 7:17-23 Je '71
See also
Deerfield, Mass.
VILLARREAL, Carlos Castaneda
Mass transit's optimist. G. R. Rosen. por Duns 98:58-9 N '71 *
VILLAS BOAS, Orlando
Stone age of twentieth century. H. B. Ryan. il Américas 23:19-24 S '71 *
VILLAVERDE, Carmen, marquesa de
Marquesa decided to have a party, and look who came. il pors Life 71:98-100 D 10 '71 *
VILLAVERDE, Juan
Guillermo Rawson's idealistic vision of the United States. il pors Américas 23:25-35 Ag '71
Latin America's antinomy. il Américas 22:2-10 N '70
VILLECCO, Marguerite
Technology. il Arch Forum 135:68-70 N '71
VILLELLA, Edward
Movement. il pors Harp Baz 104:76-7 Ap '71
about
Encounter with an athlete. M. Kram. il pors Sports Illus 35:92-4+ S 27 71 *
VILLIERS, Alan
Man who mapped the Pacific. il por Nat Geog 140:297-349 S '71
VINCA rosea. See Periwinkles
VINCENNES university, Vincennes, Ind.
Six royal Africans at an Indiana college. il Ebony 26:66-8+ F '71
VINCENT, J. Austin
Time for recognition. P. A. Dickinson. il pors Har Yrs 11:36-40 Ja '71 *
VINCENT, John J.
Christology as secular dynamic. Chr Cent 88: 375-7 Mr 24 '71
VINCENT, Richard
Lenox arts center. Hi Fi 21:MA18 N '71
VINCENT, Wesley A.
Diode quiz. il Electr World 86:8 S '71
VINCI, Leonardo da. See Leonardo da Vinci
VINEGAR
Don't forget the vinegar! H. G. Tapply. il Field & S 75:82 F '71
Many uses of vinegar. Good H 174:140 Ja '72
VINELAND, N.J.

Education

Teaching for the real world; Micro-social learning center. L. Rich. il Am Ed 7:3-6 Ag '71
VINES. See Climbing plants
VINNEDGE, Harlan H.
Airs above the ground. New Repub 165:15-17 Ag 21 '71
Drugs for children. New Repub 164:13-15 Mr 13; 29 Ap 10 '71
VINOGRADOV, Aleksandr Pavlovich
Chemism of lunar rock; excerpts from address, October 28, 1970. Space World H-6-90: 19-20 Je '71
VINOPAL, Robert T. See Bayliss, F. T. jt. auth.
VINSON, Carlos
Dove shooter's fever. il Outdoor Life 148:52-3+ D '71
VINSON, Joe A.
Testing suntan preparations. il por Chem 44: 27 Je '71
VINYL floor tile laying. See Tile laying
VINZ, Mark
Detour: North Dakota, heading east; poem. Nation 214:23 Ja 3 '72

VIOLENCE
Biology of violence: focus on the brain. il Sci N 100:403-4 D 18 '71
Can Christians aid violence? P. J. Riga. il Cath World 212:232-6 F '71
Cry, our beloved country. W. Barthelmes. Commonweal 94:186-7 Ap 30 '71
Despairing optimist. R. Dubos. Am Scholar 40:565-6+ Aut '71
Fear in the streets. J. Wideman. Am Scholar 40:611-22 Aut '71
In a blood-stained mirror. J. Forest. Cath World 213:151-2 Je '71
Longing for Armageddon. L. H. Lapham. il Harper 243:10+ Ag '71
Notes and comment; interpretation of D. Berrigan's statement. New Yorker 47:29 Mr 27 '71
Notes and comment; recent American tragedies. New Yorker 47:29-30 O 2 '71
Positive carriers of violence among children: detection by speech deviations; with replies by B. Fraser and E. Roberts. R. Filippi and C. L. Rousey. bibliog Ment Hy 55:157-64 Ap '71
Powder keg in cities. il U S News 71:45 Jl 5 '71
Redefining violence. il Time 97:49 Je 14 '71
Repressive violence. E. Currie. Trans-Action 8:12-14+ F '71; Same abr. with title Violent America: a new myth? Cur 128:29-33 Ap '71
13 ways to deal with violence; excerpt from Violence against society. il U S News 70: 75 Je 28 '71
Violence and social change. M. Mead. Redbook 137:60+ Je '71
Violence and the brain, by V. H. Mark and F. R. Ervin. Review
  Nation 212:664-6 My 24 '71. J. Gliedman
Violence as a negation of freedom. C. Bay. Am Scholar 40:634-41 Aut '71
Violence flares; just a start? racial disturbances. U S News 70:29 Je 7 '71
Violence: left and middle; use as a political tactic. M. C. Segers. il Cath World 212: 307-8+ Mr '71
Violence or brotherhood? A religious dilemma. S. A. Fineberg. il Cath World 213:17-20 Ap '71
Violent Americans; attitudes toward civil violence. R. J. Trotter. il Sci N 100:14-15 Jl 3 '71
War on violence. R. Drinnon; reply. J. Jamieson. Wilson Lib Bul 45:236 N '70; rejoinder. 45:545 F '71
See also
Assault and battery
Terrorism
United States—National commission on the causes and prevention of violence
VIOLENCE in moving pictures. See Moving pictures—Moral aspects
VIOLENCE in television programs. See Television broadcasting—Moral aspects
VIOLIN music
See also
Phonograph records—Violin music
VIORST, Judith
Me I'm going to be. il Redbook 138:66-7+ Ja '72
Single wasn't so swell. Redbook 137:81+ O '71
Those eight-pound blues: a dieter's lament. il Redbook 136:90-1+ Mr '71
Two weeks in another town. Redbook 137: 62-3+ Ag '71
VIORST, Milton
Nixon of the O.P.A. pors N Y Times Mag p70+ O 3 '71
VIRAL hepatitis. See Hepatitis
VIRGIL
Dante and Virgil. R. Montano. Yale R 60: 550-61 Je '71
VIRGIN Mary. See Mary, Virgin
VIRGIN ISLANDS
See also
Architecture, Domestic—Virgin Islands
Buck Island Reef National Monument
Camps—Virgin Islands

Description and travel

Look at the U.S. Virgin Islands. S. Cuneo. Mlle 73:215+ My '71

Economic conditions

Two bright spots in the troubled Caribbean. C. Migdail. il U S News 70:55-6 Mr 15 '71

Politics and government

Governor of paradise; M. H. Evans inaugurated. il pors Ebony 26:105-6+ Mr '71

Race question

Plaint of the Virgin Islands: we have been encroached on, invaded, engulfed. J. A. Lukas. il N Y Times Mag p30-1+ Ap 18 '71

VIRGIN ISLANDS, BRITISH. See British Virgin Islands
VIRGINIA Heines, Sister. See Heines, V.
VIRGINIA
See also
Architecture, Domestic—Virginia
Camping—Virginia
Camps—Virginia
Chesapeake Bay
Dismal swamp
Fairfax County
Festivals—Virginia
Fishing—Virginia
Gardens—Virginia
Henrico County
James River
Landscape protection—Virginia
New River
Prisons—Virginia
School libraries—Virginia
Wildlife sanctuaries—Virginia
Wolf Trap Farm Park for the performing arts

Description and travel
Other side of the James. J. Bowen. il Travel
135:42-7 Ap '71

Historic houses, etc.
Colonial Gunston Hall. Home Gard 58:15 Mr '71
Mansion that got away from the Russians; Soviet bid for Wellington estate. il U S News 71:46 N 1 '71
Other side of the James. J. Bowen. il Travel 135:42-7 Ap '71
See also
Monticello (historic house)
Mount Vernon (historic house)

Parks and reserves
Chippokes plantation. B. H. Bolen. il Parks & Rec 6:33 N '71
VIRGINIA floods. See Floods—United States
VIRGINIA Kirkus bulletin (periodical) See Kirkus bulletin (periodical)
VIRGINITY
Is virginity outmoded? D. A. Sugarman and R. Hochstein. il Seventeen 30:120-1+ O '71
Virginity was my problem. M. Cahill. por Redbook 137:38+ Ag '71
VIROID. See Virus-like particles
VIRTUE
Good and, or virtuous life. P. W. Schmidt-chen. il Hobbies 76:134-6 My '71
VIRUS and cancer. See Cancer—Causes
VIRUS diseases
See also names of Virus diseases, e.g. Herpes simplex
VIRUS diseases in plants
See also
Mosaic diseases
Viruses, Plant
VIRUS-like particles
Infectious agent from a free-living soil amoeba, naegleria gruberi. T. H. Dunnebacke and F. L. Schuster. bibliog il Science 174:516-18 O 29 '71
New virus-like particle; viroid. Chem 44:18 O '71
VIRUS vaccines. See Vaccines
VIRUSES
Activation of spontaneous murine leukemia virus-related antigen by lymphocytic choriomeningitis virus. M. B. A. Oldstone and others. bibliog il Science 174:843-5 N 19 '71
Cerebellar hypoplasia in neonatal rats caused by lymphocytic choriomeningitis virus. A. A. Monlan and others. bibliog il Science 171:194-6 Ja 15 '71
Fertilization of rabbit ova in vitro by sperm with absorbed sendai virus. R. J. Ericsson and others. bibliog il Science 173:54-5 Jl 2 '71
Isolation of mycoplasmatales viruses and characterization of MVL1, MVL52, and MVG51. A. Liss and J. Maniloff. bibliog il Science 173:725-7 Ag 20 '71
It's a virus. S. Blakeslee. House & Gard 139:74-5 Ja '71
Nonencapsidated infectious DNA of adeno-satellite virus in cells coinfected with herpesvirus. D. W. Boucher and others. bibliog il Science 173:1243-5 S 24 '71
See also
Bacteriophage
Hepatitis viruses
Herpes simplex virus
Herpesvirus
Leukemia viruses
Measles virus
Simian viruses
Tumor viruses
Virus-like particles

Inactivation
Antiviral activity of polyribocytidylic acid in cells primed with polyriboinosinic acid. E. de Clercq and P. de Somer. bibliog il Science 173:260-2 Jl 16 '71
Antiviral resistance by the polyinosinic acid—poly(1-vinylcytosine) complex. J. Pitha and P. M. Pitha. bibliog il Science 172:1146-8 Je 11 '71
Virus killer. Time 97:68 Ap 26 '71
See also
Interferon
VIRUSES, Insect
Infectious cure. K. P. Shea. il Environ 13:43-5 Ja '71
VIRUSES, Oncogenic. See Tumor viruses
VIRUSES, Plant
Enter the viroid; potato spindle tuber virus. il Newsweek 78:58+ Ag 30 '71
Watch for other corn plant diseases: maize dwarf mosaic and soybean mosaic virus. Suc Farm 69:no4 B1 Mr '71
VISAS. See Passports
VISCARDI, Henry, 1912-
School that love built. J. Reddy. por Read Digest 99:149-50+ S '71 •
VISES
How to know a nice vise when you see one. R. J. DeCristoforo. il Mech Illus 67:112-13+ F '71
Little vise with the big bite. A. J. Hand. il Pop Sci 198:60 Je '71
New jaws for an old vise. W. E. Burton. il Pop Sci 198:136 Mr '71
Woodworking vises. il Consumer Rep 36.484-8 Ag '71
VISION. See Sight
VISION (animals) See Sight (animals)
VISION tests. See Sight testing
VISIT home; story. See Ledecky, B.
VISITING, Hospital. See Hospitals, Visitors
VISITING cards
Composer calls. S. Jenkins. il Opera N 35:6-7 F 20 '71
VISITORS, Foreign

Africa
Look into blackness; 20-year-old Afro-American's summer trip. H. V. Lino, jr. por Sr Schol 98:10-11+ Mr 22 '71
Once and future diplomat; A. Ashe government-sponsored tour of Africa. F. Deford. il por Sports Illus 34:62-6+ Mr 1 '71

Africa, West
Identity crisis in black Americans visiting West Africa. A. A. Messer. bibliog Ment Hy 55:375-81 Jl '71

Asia, Southeastern
To southeast Asia, with reservations. E. Van Den Haag. il Nat R 23:1068-9 S 24 '71

Australia
Home on the range. A. Conrad. il Seventeen 30:108+ Ja '71

China (People's Republic)
Americans in China. B. P. Clark; E. G. Dimond. il Sat R 54:14-19+ D 18 '71
China: a traveler's diary. P. Stursberg. il Newsweek 77:48+ My 17 '71
China; Chinese invitation to the U.S. table tennis team. H. Yu. Chr Cent 88:674 My 26 '71
China; Committee of concerned Asian scholars tour. H. Yu. Chr Cent 88:1150 S 29 '71
China; more signals. il Time 97:26 My 3 '71
Closeup on China. por Time 98:72+ N 15 '71
Half-Baedeker for China tourists. il Time 98:47 Ag 2 '71
Inside China; eyewitness report by J. Saar, photographs by F. Fischbeck; with editorial comments and E. Snow's talk with Mao. Life 70:3-4, 22-34+ Ap 30 '71
No green light yet from red China. il Bsns W p 17-18 Jl 3 '71
Parting the bamboo curtain; U.S. newsmen to accompany the table tennis team. il Time 97:54 Ap 26 '71
Please don't eat the lotus leaves; J. Reston-Chou En-lai interview. il por Time 98:32 Ag 23 '71
Two eyewitnesses behind the bamboo curtain. J. Saar and F. Fischbeck. il Time 97:27 Ap 26 '71
Uses of charm and chill; students from the Committee of concerned Asian scholars. il por Time 98:29 Ag 9 '71
View from China. J. Reston. Read Digest 99:117-22 D '71

VISITORS, Foreign—China (People's Republic)
—*Continued*
What the tourists are finding in mainland China. Bsns W p85 O 30 '71
You have opened a new page. il Newsweek 77:16-18+ Ap 26 '71

Cuba
Church-hopping in Havana. D. Peerman. Chr Cent 88:1435-8 D 8 '71
Having at a ball in new Havana; North-Central American and Caribbean zonal Olympic qualification tournament. J. Kirshenbaum. il Sports Illus 35:18-21 Ag 30 '71

Denmark
On the backpack trail: the siege of Copenhagen. D. Butwin. il Sat R 54:40-2 S 4 '71

Europe, Western
As young Americans swarm over Europe. il U S News 71:32-5 Ag 16 '71
Grand tour. J. Shields. Seventeen 30:148 Ap '71

Far East
East is West? K. Nott. Commentary 52:65-71 Jl '71

France
Bonjour, Paris! Here's Mona Grant in her beauty whirl. il pors Seventeen 29:112-15+ N '70

Hawaii
Dreams come true in Buru Hawaii. C. Black. il Sat R 54:62-4 O 23 '71

Iran
Confessions of a religious junketeer. H. A. Jack. Chr Cent 88:1448-9 D 8 '71

Ireland
Ireland revisited. F. Howe. Atlan 227:113-16 F '71

Japan
Table tennis, anyone? Peking's ping pong team in Japan. S. Liu. il Newsweek 77:57+ Ap 12 '71

Latin America
South America preparing for the new climate. Bsns W p83-4 F 6 '71

Morocco
Happenings in Morocco. D. J. Soria. por Hi Fi 21:MA4-5+ Ag '71

Nepal
Himalayan trek or treat. J. Bruce. il Sports Illus 34:86-8+ Je 7 '71

Netherlands
On the backpack trail: Freedom city; Amsterdam's youthful visitors. D. Butwin. il Sat R 54:48+ S 11 '71

Russia
Curse of Russia is Intourist; letter. A. S. Romer. Science 172:326 Ap 23 '71; Discussion. 172:1294 Je 25 '71
Detained in Russia: an American Jewish family's ordeal. M. H. Walling. Chr Cent 88:1114 S 22 '71
Flame of faith is not out in the U.S.S.R. P. Verghese. Chr Cent 88:580-1 My 12 '71
Geophysicists in Moscow: signs of easier relations. P. H. Abelson. Science 173:797-800 Ag 27 '71
In Russia, a problem of rubles. L. Barry. il Pop Phot 68:36+ My '71
Look inside Russia. T. W. Pauken. il por U S News 71:64-7 Ag 2 '71; Discussion 71:64 S 20 '71
Love and marriage, Russian-style. L. Barry. il Pop Phot 68:26+ Je '71
Soviet Jews. J. Kaplan. New Repub 165:18-21 D 25 '71
Trudeau takes his bride to Moscow. il pors Life 70:32-4 Je 4 '71

United States
Englishman in apple-pie land. R. Prestage. Sat R 55:38+ Ja 1 '72
Summer diplomat U.S.A: guide for G. Yogtiba of Ghana and S. Nganoubara of Burundi. A. Adams. por Seventeen 29:270-1+ Ag '70

Vietnam (Democratic Republic)
Education and science in North Vietnam. A. W. Galston and E. Signer. bibliog Science 174:379-85 O 22 '71

Zambia
Black Africa: the white man's future. C. W. Casewit. il America 125:15-17 Jl 10 '71

VISITORS, Hospital. See Hospitals—Visitors

VISITS with prison inmates. See Prisons—Visits with inmates

VISSCHER, Maurice B.
Animal welfare act of 1970. Science 172:916-17 My 28 '71

VISTA. See Volunteers in service to America

VISTA-dome cars. See Railroads—Cars

VISUAL acuity. See Sight

VISUAL aids in selling. See Salesmen and salesmanship—Audio visual aids

VISUAL average speed computer and recorder. See Computers—Traffic control use

VISUAL cells. See Rod and cone cells

VISUAL discrimination
Contours and contrast: responses of monkey lateral geniculate nucleus cells to luminance and color figures. R. L. De Valois and P. L. Pease. bibliog il Science 171:694-6 F 19 '71
See also
Optical pattern recognition

VISUAL illusions. See Optical illusions

VISUAL perception. See Perception

VISUAL pigments
See also
Rod and cone cells

VITA, Luis Washington
Philosophical thought in Brazil. il Américas 23:S18-23 Ag '71

VITAL statistics
See also
Birth rate
Infant mortality
Suicide

VITAMINS
How to feel better all over. Harp Baz 104:81 My '71
How to guarantee yourself the vitamins you need. D. Calloway. il McCalls 98:68 Je '71
Relation of organic fertilizers to vitamins. Org Gard & Farm 18:96-8 Jl '71
Vitamins you really need. Good H 173:137-9 Ag '71
You and the big vitamin battle. J. M. Flagler. il Look 35:34-6+ Je 1 '71

Vitamin A
Irreversible effects of visible light on the retina: role of vitamin A. W. K. Noell and R. Albrecht. bibliog il Science 172:76-80 Ap 2 '71
Vitamin A: concentration in the rat liver Golgi apparatus. S. E. Nyquist and others. bibliog il Science 173:939-41 S 3 '71
Vitamin A deficiency effect on retina: dependence on light. W. K. Noell and others. bibliog il Science 172:72-6 Ap 2 '71

Vitamin B complex
See also
Choline
Nicotinic acid

Vitamin B2
Iron- and riboflavin-dependent metabolism of a monamine in the rat in vivo. A. L. Symes and others. bibliog il Science 174:153-5 O 8 '71
Riboflavin photosensitized oxidation of 2,4-dichlorophenol: assessment of possible chlorinated dioxin formation. J. R. Plimmer and U. I. Klingebiel. bibliog il Science 174:407-8 O 22 '71

Vitamin B12
Chemical methylation of inorganic mercury with methlocobalamin, a vitamin B12 analog. N. Imura and others. bibliog il Science 172:1248-9 Je 18 '71
Vitamin B12. T. C. Stadtman. bibliog il Science 171:859-67 Mr 5 '71

Vitamin C
Ascorbate sulfate: a urinary metabolite of ascorbic acid in man. E. M. Baker, 3d. and others. bibliog il Science 173:826-7 Ag 27 '71
Ascorbic acid: a culture requirement for colony formation by mouse plasmacytoma cells. C. H. Park and others. bibliog il Science 174:720-2 N 12 '71
C is for controversy. Newsweek 78:102+ D 6 '71
Can vitamin C really prevent and cure colds? il Good H 172:173-5 Mr '71
Doctor Linus Pauling talks about vitamin C and. . ; interview, ed. by L. Kent. L. Pauling. il por Vogue 157:130-1+ Ap 1 '71
Linus Pauling and the vitamin controversy. N. Cousins. Sat R 54:37-40+ My 15 '71
On vitamin C, cholesterol, and heart attack. il Chem 44:24-5 Je '71

VITAMINS—Vitamin C—*Continued*
Streamlines: vitamin C. Seventeen 30:126 Jl
'71
Vitamin C, a preventive of the common
cold? Consumer Bul 54:23-5 S '71
Vitamin C and the common cold, by L.
Pauling. Review
Nation 212:440-2 Ap 5 '71. D. Planz
Vitamin C: does it really help? W. S. Ross.
Read Digest 98:129-32 Je '71
Vitamin C, Linus Pauling and the common
cold. Consumer Rep 36:113-14 F '71
Vitamin C mania. P. O'Neil. il por Life 71:
55-6+ Jl 9 '71
Vitamin C on the cold front: cure or craze?
Sr Schol 98:8 F 8 '71
Warning on vitamin C. Newsweek 77:90 Ja
25 '71
Warning: you can take too much vitamin C.
C. G. King. McCalls 98:65 Mr '71

Vitamin D
Discovery of vitamin D. il Chem 44:19 O '71
1,25-dihydroxycholecalciferol: identification
of the proposed active form of vitamin D_3
in the intestine. A. W. Norman and others.
bibliog il Science 173:51-4 Jl 2 '71
Rickets. W. F. Loomis; reply with rejoinder.
T. H. Jukes. il Sci Am 224:6 F '71
Vitamin D: a cholecalciferol metabolite highly
active in promoting intestinal calcium transport. J. F. Myrtle and A. W. Norman. bibliog il Science 171:79-82 Ja 8 '71
Vitamin D metabolism: the role of kidney
tissue. R. Gray and others. bibliog il Science 172:1232-4 Je 18 '71
Vitamin D_3: induction of calcium-binding
protein in embryonic chick intestine in
vitro. R. A. Corradino and R. H. Wasserman. bibliog il Science 172:731-3 My 14 '71

Vitamin E
Ceroid pigment formation and irreversible
sterility in vitamin E deficiency. C. Ray-
chaudhuri and I. D. Desai. bibliog il Sci-
ence 173:1028-9 S 10 '71
VITELLOGENIN. See Proteins
VITÉZ, Mihály Csokonai. See Csokonai Vi-
téz, M.
VITICULTURE
Tradition and technology blend nicely in the
Napa Valley. il Fortune 84:83-7 S '71
See also
Wine making
VITREOUS humor
Sight saver. il Time 97:40 My 24 '71
VITTERT, Mark
Campus conquistador. por Time 97:71 Mr 8
'71 *
VIVALDI, Antonio
Antonio Vivaldi, by W. Kolneder. Review
Am Rec G por 37:620-1 My '71. J. W.
Barker *
VIVANTE, Arturo
Presenting the past. Writer 84:9-11 My '71
VIVATI Vivat Regina; drama. See Bolt, R.
VIVIAN, John
Doctoring old apple trees. il por Org Gard &
Farm 18:65-7 D '71
My organic mother-in-law's lakeside garden.
il Org Gard & Farm 18:37-9 Ap '71
VIVIAN Beaumont theater. See Lincoln Cen-
ter for the performing arts. New York—
Vivian Beaumont theater
VIVISECTION
Antivivisection: the reluctant Hydra. R. J.
White. Am Scholar 40:503-512 Sum '71
See also
Animals—Treatment
VLAD II, Dracul, prince of Wallachia
Dracula the man. il Newsweek 78:56 D 6 '71 *
VLAD II, Tepes. See Vlad II, Dracul, prince of
Wallachia
VLADIMIROFF, Pierre
Pierre Vladimiroff: a memoir, ed. by M.
Horosko. F. Doubrovska. il pors Dance
Mag 45:43-5 F '71 *
VLADUTIU, Adrian O. and Rose, N. R.
Autoimmune murine thyroiditis relation to
histocompatibility (H-2) type. bibliog il
Science 174:1137-9 D 10 '71
VOCABULARY
Word study that works. G. Stanford. Engl J
60:111-15 Ja '71
See also
Words
VOCABULARY tests
It pays to increase your word power. P.
Funk. See issues of Reader's digest
Sporting words. R. Maltby, jr. Harp Baz 104:
146 My '71
VOCAL music. See Singing
VOCATION in religion
Call and response. V. P. McCorry. America
124:132-inside back cover F 6 '71

Careers with Christian impact. D. Kuchar-
sky. Chr Today 15:11-14+ S 24 '71
End to professional self-pity. F. T. Trot-
ter. Chr Cent 88:1040 S 8 '71
Hearkening to the call; south London's aux-
iliary ministers. T. Beeson. Chr Cent 88:
945-6 Ag 11 '71
No substitutes. R. Haughton. Cath World
213:167-8 Jl '71
See also
Clergy—Appointment, call and election
VOCATIONAL aptitude tests. See Aptitude
tests
VOCATIONAL education
Blue-collar training gets a white-collar look.
il Bsns W p76-7 Jl 31 '71
Career education. S. P. Marland, jr. il To-
days Ed 60:22-5 O '71
Career education: a new job for the schools;
interviews, ed. by M. K. Murphy; S. P.
Marland, jr. il por Schol Teach Jr/Sr High
p4-7 D '71
Career education now; address, January 23,
1971. S. P. Marland, jr. Vital Speeches 37:
334-7 Mr 15 '71; Same abr. Ed Digest 36:9-11
My '71
Cargo of career education. W. Wood. il Am
Ed 7:16-20 O '71
Increase in vocational-technical education
programs. Sch & Soc 99:467-8 D '71
Job training programs in urban poverty
areas. R. V. McKay. il Mo Labor R 94:
36-40 Ag '71
Learning to earn. il Newsweek 78:74-5 Ag
30 '71
Marland on career education; questions and
answers. S. P. Marland, jr. pors Am Ed 7:
25-8 N '71
Models in career education, S. P. Marland's
views. W. D. Boutwell. PTA Mag 66:9
S '71
New priorities and old prejudices. E. D.
Koontz. Todays Ed 60:25-6 Mr '71
Position paper on occupational education;
program described by New York state
board of regents. Sch & Soc 99:329 O '71
Schools for failure; ghetto schools. L. Velie.
il Read Digest 99:147-51 Jl '71
Seattle's concentration on careers. V. Hed-
rich. il Am Ed 7:12-15 Jl '71; Same. Ed
Digest 37:34-7 N '71
Vocational (career) education; with editorial
comment. W. G. Loomis. il Am Ed 7:inside
cover. 3-5 Mr '71
See also
Education. Cooperative
VOCATIONAL guidance
How to cure a major cause of unrest. D.
Lawrence. U S News 70:96 Je 21 '71
Peephole into the world of work; Cleveland's
Kennard junior high school. K. E. Aylor.
il Am Ed 7:29-30 Mr '71
See also
Vocational education
VOCATIONAL rehabilitation
Relationship therapy in vocational rehabilita-
tion. M. Durie and others. Ment Hy 55:242-
5 Ap '71
Vocational rehabilitation of the older hand-
icapped worker. S. Olshansky. Ment Hy
55:507-10 O '71
See also
Abilities, inc.
United States—President's committee on em-
ployment of the handicapped
VOCATIONAL schools. See Vocational educa-
tion
VOCATIONAL stories. See Childrens literature
VOCSE, Trudie, pseud.
24 years in the life of Lyuba Bershadskaya. il
por N Y Times Mag p27-9+ Mr 14 '71
VODKA
Riding high on a Moscow mule. J. G. Martin.
il pors Nations Bsns 59:66-7 Ja '71
VOGAN, James O.
Sheepmen vs. eagles: slaughter in the sky.
C. Leinster. il Life 71:36-8 Ag 20 '71 *
Slaughter of the eagles. il Newsweek 78.23 Ag
16 '71 *
Sluicing the eagles. il Time 98:36 Ag 16 '71 *
VOGEL, Alfred
Your clerical workers are ripe for unionism.
il Harvard Bsns R 49:48-54 Mr '71
VOGEL, Herb
Give me a brr, bmm, bmm, brr, bmm, bmm.
H. Weiskopf. il por Sports Illus 34:33-5 Mr
29 '71 *
VOGEL, Nancy
New TV shows. il Writers Digest 51:32-3+
Jl '71
Pilot for a new TV show. il Writers Digest
51:31-4 Ag '71

VOGEL, Nancy—*Continued*
Television and film writing (cont) por Writers Digest 52:47-8+ Ja '72
(ed) See Meinert, H. Should the new TV writer go to Hollywood?

VOGEL, William, and others
EEG responses in regularly menstruating women and in amenorrheic women treated with ovarian hormones. bibliog il Science 172:388-91 Ap 23 '71

VOGLER, Stephen H.
Grading themes: a new approach; a new dimension. Engl J 60:70-4+ Ja '71

VOGUE (periodical)
Vogue for the new. pors Newsweek 77:54-5 My 31 '71

VOHRA, Hans R.
Letter from Washington. il Bul Atom Sci 27:29-32 Ja; 44-6 F; 25-6 Mr; 30-1 Ap '71

VOICE
See also
Humming
Singing

VOICE culture
See also
Singing

VOICE prints. See Voiceprints

VOICE spectrograms. See Voiceprints

VOICEPRINTS
Speak, voiceprint. il Time 99:59 Ja 10 '72

VOIGT, John
Rock music. Wilson Lib Bul 46:130-1 O '71

VOLCANIC ash, tuff, etc.
Caribbean eocene volcanism and the extent of horizon A. P. H. Mattson and E. A. Pessagno jr. bibliog il Science 174:138-9 O 8 '71
Hellfire. S. Thorarinsson. il Natur Hist 80:58-63 Ag '71

VOLCANIC glass. See Obsidian

VOLCANIC rocks. See Rocks, Igneous

VOLCANOES
Fire rivers and fire falls in Hawaii. il Sunset 147:50-3 S '71
Obsidian hydration dating applied to dating of basaltic volcanic activity. I. Friedman and N. Peterson. bibliog il Science 172:1028 Je 4 '71
Recent volcanism and the stratosphere. J. F. Cronin. bibliog il Science 172:847-9 My 21 '71
Volcano. J. Mossman. il Travel 136:46-7+ N '71

See also
Etna, Mount
Hekla, Mount
Katmai, Mount
Krakatoa (island)
Mauna Kea
Mauna Loa
Rainier, Mount
Thera (island)
Volcanic ash, tuff, etc.

VOLCKER, Paul A.
World inflation and the international payments system; address, January 14, 1971. Dept State Bul 64:212-18 F 15 '71

about
New activist in central banking. Bsns W p 120 S 11 '71 •

VOLDSTAD, Natalie
Kindergarten plus. il Parents Mag 46:72-3+ F '71

VOLKMAN, Paul H. and Heller, Alfred
Pineal N-acetyltransferase activity: effect of sympathetic stimulation. bibliog il Science 173:839-40 Ag 27 '71

VOLKSWAGEN. See Automobiles, Foreign

VOLKSWAGEN engines. See Automobile engines

VOLKSWAGENWERKE, gmbh. See Automobile industry—Germany (Federal Republic)

VOLLERS, Lud
Top executive hunts for a job. M. Durham. il pors Life 70:44-50C Mr 19 '71 •

VOLLEYBALL
See also
United States volleyball association

VOLOWSEK, F. Drago
How to develop multinational executives. il pors Bsns W p88+ Je 12 '71 •

VOLPE, John Anthony
Excerpt from statement, March 18, 1971. Cong Digest 50:172+ Je '71
Excerpt from testimony before the Subcommittee on constitutional rights. March 11, 1971. Cong Digest 50:232+ O '71

Rap 'n 'pinion. por Motor T 23:10 Ag '71
Volpe pledges aviation tax fund integrity. C. E. Schneider. Aviation W 94:23-4 My 3 '71

about
Cut that tape. il Time 98:94 D 6 '71 •
Timid step toward reform. il por Time 97:82+ Mr 29 '71 •

VOLTAGE
What dimouts do to your electrical equipment. J. R. Free. il Pop Sci 198:58-9+ F '71

VOLTAGE-regulating diodes. See Diodes

VOLTAGE regulators
New in power supplies: hybrid IC regulator. W. Roy. il Radio-Electr 42:57 My '71
Power supplies using the uA723. W. G. Jung. il Radio-Electr 42:49-50 Jl '71
VR12 voltage regulator. C. R. Ball, jr. il Pop Electr 34:65-70+ Ap '71
Zener diodes & voltage-regulator design. K. Butler. il Electr World 86:32-4+ D '71

VOLTMETERS
Calibrating digital voltmeters. D. L. Kierstead. il Electr World 85:36+ Je '71
Forgotten gauges. il Hot Rod 24:46-8 N '71
High-impedance voltmeter. C. R. Lewart. il Radio-Electr 42:25 D '71
Understanding digital voltmeters. J. Frye. Electr World 86:43-4 D '71
V.T.V.M. battery eliminator. W. G. Heller. il Electr World 85:72 Ap '71

VOLTOHMMETERS
EW lab report: volt-ohm milliammeters. J. D. Hirsch. il Electr World 85:34-8 Mr '71
Eico solid-state FET VOM. il Pop Electr 1:84-6 Ja '72
RCA WV-510A solid state VOM. il Radio-Electr 42:27+ My '71
Solid-state V.O.M.'s. J. D. Hirsch. il Electr World 85:39-42+ Ap '71
Use a VOM as a dwell meter. H. Zave. il Radio-Electr 42:75 Ag '71

VOLTOVSKI, Boris
Ukraine's nation-wide movement to protect its natural resources; interview. il UNESCO Courier 24:26-9 Jl '71

VOLUME expander. See Sound—Apparatus

VOLUNTARY overseas aid week. See Special days, weeks, and months

VOLUNTEER army. See Military service, Voluntary

VOLUNTEER lawyers for the arts (organization)
Volunteer lawyers for the arts. M. Siple. Art in Am 59:31 S '71

VOLUNTEER service
ADVISE: help for London's immigrants. T. Beeson. Chr Cent 88:561-2 My 5 '71
AoA funds first 11 RSVP projects under new program; Retired senior volunteer program. Aging 201:13 Jl '71
Appalachia gets a program it trusts; ALCOR, inc. il Bsns W p54-5 O 16 '71
Are volunteers here to stay? E. Schindler-Rainman. Ment Hy 55:511-15 O '71
Big sister on Sesame street. il Seventeen 29:112+ Jl '70
Caring for others creates the spirit of a nation; interview. P. Nixon. il pors U S News 71:54-7 Ag 2 '71; Same abr with title First lady, first volunteer. Read Digest 99:125-8 N '71
Good projects for teen-agers without summer jobs. il Good H 172:190 My '71
HY volunteers reap awards. il Har Yrs 11:42-5 Ap '71
Helping out in Appalachia; work vacation of 35 New Jersey students. il Good H 172:60-1 Je '71
Maybe this is the summer to volunteer. S. Newmark and E. Fairclough. Seventeen 30:72+ Ap '71
New American samaritans. il Time 98:12-14+ D 27 '71
One woman's war against poverty; Interfaith task force for community services. C. Remsberg and B. Remsberg. il por Good H 173:91+ O '71
Plan for giving; Community care self-help program. il pors Ebony 27:96-8+ D '71
Power of a woman (cont) il Ladies Home J 88:68 Mr '71
Propose new status for volunteers; interview. E. S. Straus. McCalls 98:39 Mr '71
Rescue squad; Sun City Center, Fla. R. G. King. il Har Yrs 11:28-9 N '71
Time for participation. P. A. Dickinson. Har Yrs 11:41-8 Mr '71

VOLUNTEER service—*Continued*
Volunteering: the happening of the 1970s.
H. Roth il Parks & Rec 6:70-3+ Ag '71
See also
Camps—Volunteer workers
Community service
Health workers, Volunteer
Libraries—Volunteer workers
Recreation workers, Volunteer
School and the community
United States—Action corps
Volunteer workers in education
VOLUNTEER service, International
IVS unit expelled from South Vietnam. Chr
Cent 88:1127 S 29 '71
See also
United Nations volunteer corps
United States—Peace corps
VOLUNTEER system, Military. See Military
service, Voluntary
VOLUNTEER tutors. See Tutors and tutoring
VOLUNTEER workers. See Volunteer service
VOLUNTEER workers in education
Linking up through LINKS: Laymen in
North Kingstown schools. R.I. J. Leedom.
il Am Ed 7:31-2 Ag '71
Mothers help out at school. E. Berman. il
Parents Mag 46:58+ Ap '71
Museum for fun and learning; St Paul public
schools volunteer services program and the
Minnesota museum of art. M. A. Gross-
mann. il Am Ed 7:24-5 My '71
Tapping the community; agencies serving
Teaneck, N.J. and Minneapolis, Minn. G.
W. Weinstein. Sat R 54:53 Jl 17 '71
VOLUNTEERS in service to America
Super Peace corps at home and abroad? il
U S News 70:63-5 F 1 '71
West Virgina women find cash in quilts with
aid of VISTA man. Aging 198:14 Ap '71
Whatever happened to VISTA? il Sat R 54:
49 Ag 21 '71
VOLVO (automobile) See Automobiles, For-
eign
VOLVO company. See Automobile industry—
Sweden
VOLZ, Joseph
Congress: a family business. Nation 212:819-
20 Je 28 '71
VON BÉKÉSY, Georg
Auditory backward inhibition in concert halls.
bibliog il Science 171:529-36 F 12 '71
VON BRAUN, Wernher
[Articles on space technology and space
flight] See issues of Popular science month-
ly
Science and technology: a positive outlook;
excerpts from address, May 27, 1971. Space
World H-11-95:24-5 N '71
Space travel in the seventies; interview. il
por Holiday 49:8-10 Mr '71
VON BUCHAU, Stephanie
(ed) See Von Stade, F. Our friend Flicka
VONCANNON, Wanda
Freelance job idea: school public relations.
il Writers Digest 52:20-1 Ja '72
VON CLEMM, Michael
Rise of consortium banking. il Harvard Bsns
R 49:125-36+ My '71
VON DELDEN, E. K.
Auto shop series. il Hot Rod 24:62-5 S '71
VON DREELE, W. H.
Byrd wins, Teddy loses; Waldorf mixes it up;
Wailers, where are you now? poems. Nat
R 23:120. 127, 128 F 9 '71
Consternation; Two if by sea; Garbage pro-
posal; poems. Nat R 23:1216. 1217, 1218 N 5
'71
Entombed in the Times; Ghosts; poems Nat
R 23:346. 360 Ap 6 '71
Forest Hills says no; Phase II; poems. Nat R
23:1388. 1391 D 17 '71
George Meany says it's OK; Sorry about that;
poems. Nat R 23:917. 918 Ag 24 '71
Get out while we're ahead; Supremes; poems.
Nat R 23:1166, 1168 O 22 '71
Hands off Spiro Agnew; Thinking beautiful
thoughts; Lost causes; poems. Nat R 23:
178, 182 187 F 23 '71
I surrender, dear; Scenario; poems. Nat R
23:1447, 1456 D 31 '71
Let the busing commence; To your good
health; Glenda Farrell is dead; poems. Nat
R 23:512. 517, 518 My 18 '71
Mr Rehnquist's coming ordeal; Bus goes
north; poems. Nat R 23:1338. 1340 D 3 '71
Mr Wicker, please pipe down; A gathering
of eagles; poems. Nat R 23:245, 250 Mr 9 '71
Mother's little helper; poem. Nat R 23:64
Ja 26 '71
Nearer my God to thee; What am I? poems.
Nat R 23:623. 628 Je 15 '71
None dare call it hypocrisy; Muskie takes a
stand; poems. Nat R 23:296, 303 Mr 23 '71

Off to grandmother's; Reordering our prior-
ities; Rx for unhappiness; poems. Nat R
23:843, 844, 854 Ag 10 '71
Problem perspiration; Crazy journalism;
Shadows and substance; poems. Nat R 23:
1094, 1098, 1104 O 8 '71
Profiles in courage; Innocents abroad; poems.
Nat R 23:458, 467 My 4 '71
Reaganizing of Rockefeller; Intimations;
poems. Nat R 23:412, 416 Ap 20 '71
Real John Lindsay; Mr Nixon, call your con-
stituency; Depressed thoughts after read-
ing Alvin Toffler's Future shock; poems.
Nat R 23:687, 691, 709 Je 29 '71
Supercop wins; Last review; poems. Nat R
23:1272, 1282 N 19 '71
They want it, that's who; What fun to
watch Mr Nixon; poems. Nat R 23:972,
976 S 10 '71
This is ping-pong? John Tower's agony;
Shall we keep it in perspective? poems. Nat
R 23:738, 742, 746 Jl 13 '71
Tit willow; For your consideration; Bella
Abzug as Johnny Reb; Peking buddies;
poems. Nat R 23:1041, 1043, 1044, 1049 S
24 '71
To Bella Abzug; Perfectly logical conclusion;
Buying a new Sony? poems. Nat R 23:572,
576, 578 Je 1 '71
Unreliable me; Getting it all together; Rugby
Down Under; poems. Nat R 23:788,790, 796
Jl 27 '71
VON ECKARDT, Wolf
Anti-city beautiful movement. New Repub
164:32-3 Ap 3 '71
Fresh scene in the clean dream. il Sat R 54:
21-3 My 15 '71
Life-style education. il Sat R 54:64 Ap 3 '71
New towns 73 years later. il Sat R 54:61 F
6 '71
Rebuilding cities we have. Cur 125:32-5 Ja
'71
You can't see the foyer for the trees. il pors
Horizon 13:40-7 Sum '71
about
Facts vs. conclusions. N. Cousins. Sat R
54:28 S 11 '71 •
VON ENDT, D. W. and Wheeler, J. W.
1-Pentadecene production in tribolium con-
fusum. bibliog Science 172:60 Ap 2 '71
VO-nguyen-Giap
If Giap were a U.S. general. W. C. Moore. por
U S News 70:35 My 3 '71 •
Military art of people's war; selected writings
of General Vo Nguyen Giap, ed. by R.
Stetler. Review
Nation 212:764-5 Je 14 '71. L. P. Liggio •
VON HOFFMAN, Nicholas
Looking for presidents. il Harper 243:33-5+
S '71
VON KANTOR, George
Art in everyday life uncoils springs of ten-
sion. il Sch Arts 70:22-3 Ap '71
VON MATTHIESSEN, Maria
Eloquent ecologist. por Harp Baz 104:96 Jl
'71
VONNEGUT, B. and Chessin, Henry
Ice nucleation by coprecipitated silver iodide
and silver bromide. bibliog il Science 174:
945-6 N 26 '71
VONNEGUT, Kurt, 1922-
Age of Vonnegut. C. T. Samuels. New Re-
pub 164:30-2 Je 12 '71 •
Banning of Billy Pilgrim. Chr Cent 88:681
Je 2 '71 •
Masks of Kurt Vonnegut, jr. R. Todd. il pors
N Y Times Mag p 16-17+ Ja 24 '71 •
Vonnegut's otherworldly laughter. B. De-
Mott. Sat R 54:29-32+ My 1 '71 •
What are people for? E. W. Ranly. il por
Commonweal 94:267-11 My 7 '71 •
VONONES. See Harvestmen
VON PUTTKAMER, W. Jesco
Brazil protects her Cinta Largas. il Nat Geog
140:420-44 S '71
VON STADE, Frederica
Our friend Flicka; interview, ed. by S. Von
Buchau. por Opera N 35:26 Ap 10 '71
VON STRASSER, Rudolf G.
Excellence in continental glass. il Antiques
101:153-60 Ja '72
VON VOIGTLANDER, Philip F. and Moore,
K. E.
Dopamine: release from the brain in vivo by
amantadine. bibliog il Science 174:408-10 O
22 '71
VON WILLEBRAND'S disease
Factor VIII detection by hemagglutination in-
hibition: hemophilia A and von Willebrand's
disease. D. P. Stites and others. bibliog
il Science 171:196-7 Ja 15 '71
VOORHIS, Horace Jerry. See Voorhis, J.

VOORHIS, Jerry
Three saints in politics. P. H. Douglas. Am Scholar 40:223-32 Spr '71 *

VORSTER, Balthazar Johannes
South Africa's black mood. P. R. Webb. il por Newsweek 77:47-8+ My 10 '71 *

VOSBURGH, Kirby G.
Prediction of the spatial distribution of cell survival in heavy ion beams. bibliog il Science 174:1125-7 D 10 '71

VOSS, Gilbert L.
Shy monster, the octopus. il Nat Geog 140:776-99 D '71

VOSS, John. See Todd, W. M. jt. auth.

VOSTOK (space vehicle) See Space vehicles, Russian

VOTAVA, Jiri. See Weight, F. F. jt. auth.

VOTERS, Registration of
College-town worry: will 18-to-21 voters take over? il U S News 71:38-41 S 6 '71
Getting out the young vote. L. Foster. McCalls 99:48 D '71
Gown vs. town; implication of the 26th amendment for college students. Newsweek 78:27+ Ag 30 '71
Home is where the vote is; student franchise. R. G. Singer. Nation 213:202-5 S 13 '71
Pleasures and pitfalls of getting out the vote. T. Bernstein and P. Bernstein. il Seventeen 31:122+ Ja '72
Problem of student registration. Harper 243:38 S '71
Quiet revolution? first-time voters. il Newsweek 77:34+ Je 14 '71
Voting at college. W. F. Buckley, jr. Nat R 23:1259 N 5 '71
Young voters. New Repub 165:7-9 S 11 '71
Young voters surge to enroll in the system; with account by D. Wittner. il Life 71:26-33 O 15 '71

VOTING
Let a million voters bloom. M. Novak. Commonweal 94:79-81 Ap 2 '71; Discussion. 94:205+ My 7 '71
See also
Referendum
Suffrage
United Nations—Voting
United States—Congress—House—Voting
Voters, Registration of

VOTING age. See Suffrage—United States

VOUCHER plan in education
After all. S. M. Lambert. Todays Ed 60:64 My '71
Constitutional way to avoid discrimination in aiding schools; tuition grants to parents. D. Lawrence. U S News 71:88 Jl 19 '71
Education vouchers. P. A. Janssen. Ed Digest 36:5-8 Mr '71
Market economy for the schools. il Bsns W p76+ F 6 '71
Slates and hamsters. J. R. Coyne, jr. il Nat R 23:309-11 Mr 23 '71
Student-aid plan runs into a fight. il U S News 71:20-1 Ag 9 '71
Trouble with vouchers. M. R. Berube. Commonweal 93:414-17 Ja 29 '71; Discussion. 94:27+ Mr 19 '71
Voucher system? W. D. Boutwell. PTA Mag 66:12 F '71
Vouchers; schools in the marketplace. K. Branan. Schol Teach Jr/Sr High p6-8 Ja 11 '71

VOUGHT aeronautics company. See Ling-Temco-Vought, inc.

VOUGHT helicopter, inc. See Ling-Temco-Vought, inc.

VOYAGES
Alone to Hawaii. W. Amberg. il pors Yachting 130:50-1+ S '71
Cape Horn; voyage of the sailing ship, British Isles. E. Bunster. il Américas 23:2-11 Mr '71
Man who mapped the Pacific. A. Villiers. il por Nat Geog 140:297-349 S '71
North Pacific circumnavigation:
Are the Aleutians cold? H. Roth. il Yachting 130:54-5+ S '71
Northward to Hokkaido. H. Roth. il Yachting 130:52-3+ Ag '71
On to Atka. H. Roth. il Yachting 130:58-9+ O '71
Volcanos and torii. H. Roth. il Yachting 130:52-4+ Jl '71
Pacific crossing. C. Milinaire. il pors Vogue 158:194+ O 1 '71
Passaging a 12-meter; transatlantic roundtrip. G Godfray. il Yachting 130:60-1+ D '71
Passaging south; experiences in the infamous Bermuda Triangle. B. Cameron. il Yachting 130:56-7+ Ag '71
Sailor's sailor; F. Casper. S. Chasalow and H. Chasalow. il por Yachting 129:82+ Mr '71

Tahiti to Rarotonga. H. LaBorde. il Yachting 129:56+ F '71
To Alaska in 3½ days; from Seattle to Ketchikan. D. Cooper. il Yachting 129:56-7+ My '71
See also
Cruising
Ocean travel
Ra expeditions
Seafaring life
Shipwrecks

VOYAGES around the world
After 50,000 miles; appraisal of ketch, Bluebird of Thorne. Lord Riverdale. il Yachting 129:68-9+ Je '71

VRATUSA, Anton
Jugoslavia, 1971. For Affairs 50:148-62 O '71

VREELAND, Diana
Vogue for the new. pors Newsweek 77:54-5 My 31 '71

VROOM, Barbara
Oxford visit. New Yorker 47:112-15 My 8 '71

VUILLARD, Édouard
Insider. il Time 98:90-1 N 22 '71 *
Vuillard: melancholy mastered. J. Russell. il por Art N 70:48-50 S '71 *
Vuillard's housebroken muse. M. Amaya. il Art in Am 59:102-5 S '71 *

VUILLEUMIER, Beryl Simpson
Pleistocene changes in the fauna and flora of South America. bibliog il Science 173:771-80 Ag 27 '71
about
Tropics weren't so stable after all. L. Purrett. il Sci N 100:177 S 11 '71 *

VUITCH, Milan
Ambivalence on abortion. por Time 97:40 My 3 '71 *

VUKOVICH, Charles
Fine arts; The soldier in Veterans' memorial park, River Edge, N.J. C. J. McNaspy. America 124:263 Mr 13 '71

VULTURES
See also
Condors

W

W particle. See Particles (nuclear physics)

WARC conference. See World administrative radio conference

WCC. See World council of churches

WCT. See World championship tennis, inc.

WCTU. See Woman's Christian temperance union

WFLN (radio station) See Radio stations

WHDH-TV. See Television stations

WIPO. See World intellectual property organization

WJXT-TV. See Television stations

WMO. See World meteorological organization

WPA. See United States—Work projects administration

WPEN (radio station) See Radio stations

WQXR (radio station) See Radio stations

W. R. Grace and company. See Grace, W. R. and Company

WWNSS (world-wide network of standard seismograph stations) See Seismological stations

WAART, Edo de
Swinging Dutchman. il por Newsweek 77:96 Mr 15 '71 *

WACHOVIA historical museum, Old Salem. See Winston-Salem, N.C.—Galleries and museums

WACKER, Robert, Jr
(ed) What I learned from my first child. il Good H 173:114-17 N '71

WACO, Tex.
Economy-minded Waco chooses high-strength steel. J. Lykes. il Am City 86:58-9 My '71

WADDELL, Helen Jane
Peter Abelard; dramatization. See Millar, R. Abelard and Heloise

WADDINGTON, Miriam
Comment. F. D. Reeve. Poetry 118:236-7 Jl '71 *

WADE, C. M. See Hjellming, R. M. jt. auth.

WADE, Edwin C.
Fluorescent droplight. il Mech Illus 67:100+ Ja '71

WADE, J. L.
Great purple martin controversy! J. Star. il por Look 35:24-6 Ag 10 '71 *

WADLEIGH, Michael
Woodstock discovers Washington. Who? George Washington. L. Gross. il Look 35: 30+ Ag 24 '71 *

WADSWORTH, James J. and Pomerance, Jo
How the Pentagon blocks arms pacts. Cur 133:45-7 O '71

WADSWORTH, Raymond H.
Guidelines for good seeing. Arch Rec 149: 138+ Je '71

WADSWORTH, William H.
Camp environment checklist. Camp Mag 43: 11-12 Je '71

WAFFLES
Cheerful breakfasts: pineapple pancakes, kumquat waffles. il Sunset 146:241 Ap '71
Dad...treat the family to waffles. il Bet Hom & Gard 49:16 Mr '71

WAGAR, J. Alan
Challenge of environmental education. Ed Digest 36:9-12 F '71

WAGE bargaining. See Collective bargaining

WAGE differentials
Blue-collar/white-collar pay trends: analysis of occupational wage differences. A. Sackley and T. W. Gavett. bibliog il Mo Labor R 94:5-12 Je '71
Comparing union and nonunion wages in manufacturing. S. L. Mason. bibliog il Mo Labor R 94:20-6 My '71
Differences in hourly earnings between men and women. V. R. Fuchs. il Mo Labor R 94:9-15 My '71
Differentials and overlaps in annual earnings of blacks and whites; with tables. A. Strasser. bibliog Mo Labor R 94:16-26 D '71
Pay differences between men and women in the same job; with tables. J. E. Buckley. bibliog Mo Labor R 94:36-9 N '71
Regional pay differentials in white-collar occupations; with tables. H. F. Zeman. Mo Labor R 94:53-6 Ja '71
Wage differences among manufacturing establishments. W. R. Bailey and A. E. Schwenk. bibliog il Mo Labor R 94:16-19 My '71

WAGE payment plans
Blue-collar/white-collar pay trends: earnings and family income; with tables. R. L. Stein and J. N. Hedges. bibliog il Mo Labor R 94:13-24 Je '71
Time and incentive pay practices in urban areas; with table. J. H. Cox. Mo Labor R 94:53-5 D '71

WAGE-price policy
Administration blockbuster: 90-day freeze. with editorial comment. Bsns W p21-30+, 96 Ag 21 '71
After 90 days, what? D. Lawrence. U S News 71:76 Ag 30 '71
After the freeze: what comes next. il U S News 71:15-16 S 27 '71
Airlines, CAB examine effects of Phase 2. J. P. Woolsey. Aviation W 95:23 N 22 '71
Al Ullman smiles an I told you so. por Bsns W p 15-16 S 4 '71
Angry unions aim for a deal with Nixon. il por Bsns W p52-5+ Ag 28 '71
Answers to your questions. U S News 71: 19-21 Ag 30 '71
As Connally explains policy on wage-price controls; excerpts from testimony before House banking and currency committee, February 23, 1971. J. B. Connally. por U S News 70:76-7 Mr 8 '71
Bat in Mr Nixon's hand. il por Newsweek 77:75 Mr 1 '71
Battle of the bulges. Time 98:22+ D 6 '71
Bunch of violators? Newsweek 79:36 Ja 3 '72
Business agrees to grin and bear it. il Bsns W p23-4 O 16 '71
Business criticizes the new economic policy; comments by members of Dun's presidents' panel. il Duns 98:45-6 N '71
Businessmen still feel uncertain. il Bsns W p39-40 N 13 '71
Case against wage and price control. A. Reynolds. il Nat R 23:1051-5 S 24 '71; Reply. J. Davenport. 23:1116 O 8 '71
Case for an incomes policy, now; address, April 23, 1971. E. S. Adams. Vital Speeches 37:546-9 Jl 1 '71
Chance for controls as union leaders see it. il U S News 71:64-5 Ag 23 '71
Checking inflation: Nixon's new strategy. il U S News 71:17-19 Ag 16 '71
Controls: answers to your questions. U S News 71:19-22+ N 29 '71
Controls. chapter two. R. Lekachman. Duns 93:13 Je '69
Controls that labor would buy. Bsns W p48+ S 11 '71
Controls: the real test begins. il U S News 71:15-16+ S 6 '71

Double edge of price controls. Farm J 95:54 N '71
Drive to beat inflation, and Democrats; Blurry banner for Phase II; program presented by President Nixon, October 7, 1971. il por Time 98:10-12+ O 18 '71
Effect on profits. C. Morgello. il Newsweek 78:98 N 22 '71
Enforcing the freeze: an inside look; interview. A. Weber. por U S News 71:63-6 S 27 '71
Everybody is edgy about Phase two. il Newsweek 78:60-1 O 4 '71
Everything you want to know about Phase II. il Time 98:17-18 D 20 '71
Executive order on wages, prices. R. M. Nixon. U S News 71:64-5 Ag 30 '71
Expert views the freeze and the future; interview, ed. by W. A. McWhirter. O. Eckstein. por Life 71:22-6 Ag 27 '71
First outlines of Phase II. Time 98:35-6 S 27 '71
Freeze: a hot topic for teenagers? Senior youthview. il Sr Schol 99:17-18 S 27 '71
Freeze: it looks like a slow thaw. il Newsweek 78:15-16 S 6 '71
Freeze: planning for thin ice. il Newsweek 78:83-4 S 13 '71
Freeze sets in solidly. il Bsns W p24-5 O 2 '71
Freeze starts with a fever. il Bsns W p22-3 Ag 21 '71
From freeze to controlled thaw. Time 98: 28-9 N 22 '71
Full scale wage-price controls? interview. M. V. DiSalle. pors Nations Bsns 59:32-9 O '71
George Meany: fight over the freeze; with interview with G. Meany. il pors Newsweek 78:46+ S 6 '71
Getting set to start new controls. il U S News 71:26-7+ N 8 '71
Goodbye Milton Friedman. W. F. Buckley, jr. Nat R 23:1010 S 10 '71
Have controls ever worked? il Newsweek 78: 84+ S 13 '71
Headaches piling up for the Pay board. il U S News 71:104-6 D 13 '71
Here comes the thaw. il Newsweek 78:96-7 N 22 '71
Hints at wage controls: unions prepare to fight back. il U S News 70:60-2 Mr 1 '71
House divided: self discipline & economic freedom; address, October 14, 1971. R. H. Larry. Vital Speeches 38:58-61 N 1 '71
How controls will be enforced: interview. D. Rumsfeld. il por U S News 71:42-6 D 13 '71
How is the economy doing? interview, ed. by G. Farmer. O. Eckstein. por Life 71:38-9 O 8 '71
How shoppers and merchants size up the price freeze. il U S News 71:30-3 N 15 '71
How the wage-price freeze is working. il U S News 71:22-5 S 20 '71
How to control inflation: a three-stage formula; excerpt from address, January 20, 1971. R. H. Larry. por U S News 70:72-4 F 8 '71
How to stop inflation: stop raising wages. E. L. Dale, jr. il Look 35:64+ F 23 '71
If you freeze wages, freeze everything. Bsns W p29 Ag 14 '71
Impact of the Nixon program: views of top executives. il Nations Bsns 59:24-6+ O '71
Income policy and the price system. G. W. Taylor. bibliog Mo Labor R 94:45-8 Ag '71
Inflation, incomes policy and all that. B. L. Masse. America 124:398 Ap 17 '71
Investors fazed, too. C. Morgello. il Newsweek 78:104 O 18 '71
Is it constitutional? Time 98:30 N 29 '71
Is there hope for collective bargaining? the inflation threat; address, May 7, 1971. R. H. Larry. Vital Speeches 37:537-40 Je 15 '71
Is this trip necessary? Nat R 23:1280+ N 19 '71
Labor agreements breach the guidelines. il Bsns W p20-1 N 20 '71
Labor builds a stumbling block. il Time 98: 32 O 11 '71
Labor is cooling its feud with Nixon. il Bsns W p 16 S 4 '71
Labor trio in a vital role. il U S News 71:67 S 6 '71
Latest rulings on wage-price problems (title varies) il U S News 71:17 S 6; 17 S 13; 25 S 20; 24 O 11; 26 O 25; 18-19 D 6; 17 D 20; 49 D 27 '71; 72:23 Ja 10 '72
Letter from Washington; ninety-day freeze. R. H. Rovere. New Yorker 47:116-17 S 18 '71
Lid on wage gains? R. Lekachman. Duns 97: 13 My '71
Little brothers are watching. Time 98:27 O 4 '71

WAGE price policy—*Continued*
Little grumbling as controls take hold. il U S News 71:61-2 S 27 '71
Looking beyond wage-price freeze; interview. G. P. Shultz. il pors U S News 71:32-6 S 6 '71
Many are chilled, few are frozen. il Newsweek 78:87-8 N 8 '71
Meany's idea for wage controls after the freeze; excerpts from interview. G. Meany. por U S News 71:58-61 S 13 '71
Mr Nixon's puzzling wage ploy. il Newsweek 77:79 Mr 8 '71
Mr Nixon's reactionary revolution. M. Harrington. Commonweal 95:199-202 N 26 '71
Needed: a new form of wage and price control. D. Lawrence. U S News 70:92 Ja 25 '71
New controls get their opening test; with editorial comment. Bsns W p35, 128 Ap 10 '71
New pay-price rules; how Phase 2 will work. il U S News 71:21-3 N 22 '71
Next moves in the battle to hold down pay and prices; suspension of the Davis-Bacon act. il U S News 70:23-4 Mr 8 '71
Nixon-Burns battle? R. Lekachman. Duns 97:9 F '71
Nixon speaks out: China, prices, controls; news conference. August 4, 1971. R. M. Nixon. por U S News 71:76-80 Ag 16 '71
Nixon: we have an obligation to the next generation; address, November 19, 1971. R. M. Nixon. por U S News 71:87-90 D 6 '71; Excerpts. 71:87 N 29 '71
Nixon's freeze and the mood of labor. il por Time 98:9-15 S 6 '71
Nixon's frozen, floating dollar. il Newsweek 78:10-21 Ag 30 '71
Nixon's grand design for recovery. il por Time 98:4-14+ Ag 30 '71
Nixon's 90-day economic gamble. il Sr Schol 99:13-15 S 27 '71
Nixon's pay guidelines; the record to date. il U S News 70:53-4 My 3 '71
Nixon's plan for more controls. il U S News 71:18-19 N 1 '71
One town's hot & cold views of the freeze; Pittsfield, Mass. G. Nikolaieff. il Sr Schol 99:11-13 O 11 '71
Out of phase. J. Osborne. New Repub 165:11-13 O 23 '71
Phase 2 a creaky beginning. Life 71:42 D 3 '71
Phase 2 controls; with text of Nixon's address, October 7, 1971. il U S News 71:21-6+ O 18 '71
Phase II gets off to a confused start. il Bsns W p44-5 O 23 '71
Phase two has a lot going for it. Fortune 84:119-20 N '71
Phase II: holding down those prices. Time 99:60 Ja 3 '72
Phase II: how it will work. il Bsns W p21-3 O 16 '71
Phase two: living with controls. il pors Newsweek 78:26-32 O 18 '71
Phase II planners: close to consensus. il Bsns W p 17-19 S 18 '71
Phase two price controls. G. Ackley. por Duns 98:11 D '71
Phase II: whose pill? Nat R 23:1391-2 D 17 '71
Phase two: will it work? For whom? D. Deitch. Nation 213:678-82 D 27 '71
Phase three. H. C. Wallich. Newsweek 78:109 N 22 '71
Price controls get tougher. U S News 71:40 D 13 '71
Profits and Phase two. M. L. Weidenbaum. Duns 98:11 N '71
Report for shoppers; interview. V. H. Knauer. por U S News 71:53-4 Ag 30 '71
Rhetoric of Phase II. F. S. Meyer. Nat R 23:1240 N 5 '71
Search for equity. il Time 98:73-4 S 13 '71
Seasonal prices and wages: the official policy; statement, August 28, 1971. A. Weber. por U S News 71:19 S 13 '71
Specter of Phase 1/2. Time 98:23 N 15 '71
Squeeze-freeze dilemma; address, January 20, 1971. R. H. Larry. Vital Speeches 37:253-6 F 1 '71; Excerpts. por U S News 70:72-4 F 8 '71
Squeeze of the freeze. Time 98:24 S 20 '71
Stop it now. Nat R 23:1218-19 N 5 '71
Storm signals flying for wage-price controls. U S News 71:17-19 D 6 '71
TRB from Washington: bending the wind. New Repub 165:6 S 11 '71
TRB from Washington: taking stock. New Repub 165:4 N 27 '71
Talking wage and price controls. il Newsweek 77:49-50 F 1 '71
Teeth for the jawbone. H. C. Wallich. Newsweek 77:60 F 15 '71
Teeth in Phase two. il por Newsweek 78:84+ S 27 '71

There's also the risk of frostbite, Mr President. Nat R 23:969 S 10 '71
Tide turns toward an incomes policy. il Bsns W p76+ Ag 14 '71
Trials of office. W. F. Buckley, jr. Nat R 23:1074 S 24 '71
UAW plan for wages and prices. B. L. Masse. America 124:221 Mr 6 '71
Union threats that haunt the Pay board; with editorial comment. il Bsns W p78+, 128 O 23 '71
Unions begin a fight. il U S News 71:73-5 Ag 30 '71
Unions' worry: White House crackdown on wage demands. il U S News 70:63-4 F 22 '71
Vote for Nixonomics; how Americans feel now about the freeze. il Newsweek 78:75 O 11 '71
Wage & price controls. Bsns W p43 N 6; 51 N 13; 30+ N 20; 31 N 27; 34+ D 4; 41 D 11; 31 D 18; 22 D 25 '71; 24 Ja 1 '72
Wage and price controls; pro and con discussion. Sr Schol 98:16-17 Ap 5 '71
Wage-price controls: a real possibility? excerpts from interview. J. B. Connally. U S News 71:78-9 Ag 9 '71
Wage-price freeze and the book industry. R. H. Smith. Pub W 200:241 Ag 30 '71
Wage-price freeze: Phase two. R. H. Smith. Pub W 200:21 O 25 '71
Wage-price Phase two. il Sr Schol 99:12-14 N 8 '71
Wage-price plan. il Newsweek 77:65+ Ap 5 '71
Wages. H. C. Wallich. Newsweek 77:78 Je 28 '71
Wages, prices, profits. New Repub 165:7 O 23 '71
Way station? Nat R 23:1165 O 22 '71
We don't want to be heavy-handed. il Newsweek 78:73-4 S 20 '71
What Nixon told AFL-CIO; excerpts from address, November 19, 1971. R. M. Nixon. il por U S News 71:87 N 29 '71
What prices? New Repub 165:9-10 O 30 '71
What the economists are saying. W. F. Buckley, jr. Nat R 23:1486-7 D 31 '71
What to do in Phase II. il Time 98:31-2+ O 11 '71
What to expect in controls. il U S News 72:22-3 Ja 10 '72
What to watch for in prices, pay, profits, rents; interview. H. Stein. il pors U S News 71:28-32 N 8 '71
What's happening to pay and prices; views of businessmen. il U S News 71:15-17 N 29 '71
Where the shoe pinches; actions of the Pay board and the Price commission. New Repub 165:9 N 20 '71
Where's Phase II? R. W. Dietsch. New Repub 165:11-12 D 18 '71
Who's at the controls? il Newsweek 78:87-8 O 25 '71
Will controls work? R. J. Saulnier. por Nations Bsns 59:64-6 D '71
Will the kettle explode? M. Friedman. Newsweek 78:30 O 18 '71
Will the new economic policy work? R. Lekachman. Duns 98:99 O '71
Wrong ways to think about business. Fortune 84:67 O '71

See also
United States—Emergency preparedness. Office of
also subhead Wages and hours under various subjects, e.g. Construction industry—Wages and hours

Anecdotes, facetiae, satire, etc.
Everything you didn't want to know about Phase 2. W. Zinsser. il Life 71:56A+ N 19 '71

Legal aspects
And is it legal? Newsweek 78:88 O 25 '71
Legal snags that threaten controls. il Bsns W p45-6 O 23 '71

Belgium
Belgium's formula for economic stability. il U S News 71:25 Ag 30 '71

Canada
Canada may import controls from the U.S. Bsns W p24 O 30 '71

Europe, Western
Controls: lessons for U.S. from experience in Europe. il U S News 71:29-30 O 25 '71
Incomes policies: what Europe learned. il Bsns W p 142+ N 13 '71

WAGE price policy—*Continued*

Great Britain

How Britain's government views Ford pact.
U S News 70:110 Ap 19 '71

When a government cracks down on pay raises. il U S News 70:78 F 15 '71

When the British imposed controls. U S News 71:25 Ag 30 '71

Russia

Purchasing power of workers in the Soviet Union. E. Nash. bibliog il Mo Labor R 94:39-45 My '71

WAGE stabilization. See Wages—Regulation

WAGENER, James W.
New role for foundations courses in teacher education. Ed Digest 36:29-31 Mr '71

WAGENVOORD, Anita (Laidman)
Power of a woman. il pors Ladies Home J 88:68 Mr '71 *

WAGES
Foreign labor briefs. See issues of Monthly labor review
See also
Bonus system
Income
Labor cost
Non-wage payments
Profit sharing
Salaries
Tipping
Trade unions

Economic aspects

Union power and the new inflation. G. Burck. il Fortune 83:65-9+ F '71; Same abr. with title High cost of wage inflation. Read Digest 98:139-43 Ap '71
See also
Wage-price policy

Regulation

Any cure for big strikes? interview. J. D. Hodgson. il pors U S News 71:68-72 N 29 '71

Flexible guide on wages. il Time 98:29 N 22 '71

Labor can make or break the stabilization program. A. M. Louis. il Fortune 84:140-3+ N '71

Pay raises that have been put on ice. il U S News 71:94-6 S 20 '71

Phase II gets the Dunlop touch. por Bsns W p23 O 2 '71
See also
United States—Pay board
Wage-price policy

Statistics

Blue-collar/white-collar pay trends: compensation per man-hour and take-home pay. J. Alterman. bibliog il Mo Labor R 94:25-34 Je '71
See also
Wage differentials

Women

See Equal pay for equal work; Wage differentials

Russia

Purchasing power of workers in the Soviet Union. E. Nash. bibliog il Mo Labor R 94:39-45 My '71

United States

Blue-collar/white-collar pay trends; symposium. bibliog il Mo Labor R 94:3-36 Je '71

Calendar of wage increases and negotiations for 1971; with tables. L. Bornstein and L. W. Bolton. Mo Labor R 94:31-44 Ja '71

Coal miners, others to get bigger pay. U S News 71:62 N 29 '71

Confusion at Pay board as Congress moves in. U S News 71:47 D 27 '71

Developing a general wage index. N. J. Samuels. il Mo Labor R 94:3-8 Mr '71

Fight over retroactive pay. U S News 71:89 N 15 '71

Hours and earnings, private nonagricultural payrolls; tables. See issues of Monthly labor review

How workers are doing in race with prices. il U S News 70:70-1 Mr 15 '71

Labor closes in on retroactive pay. Bsns W p 19 N 27 '71

No letup in wage pressure despite Nixon's warnings. U S News 70:80-1 Mr 29 '71

Nobody wins at leapfrog; unions and real wages. H. Hazlitt. Nat R 23:83-5+ Ja 26 '71

Nonagricultural employment payroll data: tables. See issues of Monthly labor review

Raises running too high? A debate that is heating up. il U S News 71:88-9 D 20 '71

Research summaries. See issues of Monthly labor review

Swallowing hard. il Newsweek 78:69-70 D 20 '71

Three unions give up part of pay. U S News 70:58 Ja 18 '71

Uncertainty leads to higher wages. Bsns W p 17-18 My 8 '71

Unions set a minimum raise. Bsns W p 101 Mr 27 '71

Wage spiral: too late to slow it down in '71? U S News 70:86-7 Je 21 '71

Why those jeans jingle. il Nations Bsns 59:91 S '71

Young workers and their earnings; with tables. V. C. Perrella. il Mo Labor R 94:3-11 Jl '71
See also
Equal pay for equal work
Government employees—Salaries, allowances, etc.
Minimum wage—United States
Municipal employees—Salaries, allowances, etc.
Office workers—Salaries, allowances, etc.
United States—Pay board
Wages—Regulation
also subhead Wages and hours under names of industries. e.g. Construction industry—Wages and hours

WAGGONER, Paul E.
Environmental dilemma. il Horticulture 49:30-3+ My '71

WAGGONER, William
Turning a sander into a sander-grinder. il Mech Illus 67:114-15+ N '71

WAGGONER, William T.
Mostest hoss: Man o' War. P. Chew. il Am Heritage 22:24-9+ Ap '71 *

WAGNER, Barbra
Can a nose job change your life? pors Seventeen 30:136+ N '71

In my opinion. por Seventeen 30:166 Jl '71

WAGNER, C. Peter
Street seminaries of Chile. il Chr Today 15:5-8 Ag 6 '71

WAGNER, Evelyn D.
Fear of failure and other handicaps. il PTA Mag 66:24-6+ N '71

WAGNER, Frank E.
Recruitment: forum or bazaar? Sch & Soc 99:86-7 F '71

WAGNER, J. Mike
Growing tomatoes in Louisiana. il por Org Gard & Farm 18:72-3 Mr '71

WAGNER, John E.
Church's mission: let the laity do it. Chr Today 15:21 S 10 '71

WAGNER, Richard, 1813-1883
Boulez Parsifal. R. Lawrence. Sat R 54:83 O 30 '71 *

Bumper crop of Wagner operas. P. G. Davis; C. L. Osborne; D. Hamilton. il por Hi Fi 21:75-81 D '71 *

Dream of love. S. Jenkins. il Opera N 36:24-5 D 18 '71 *

Falla on Wagner; tr. by F. Grunfeld and J. Grunfeld. M. de Falla. por Opera N 35:24-6 Ap 3 '71 *

Flying Dutchman (Der fliegende Holländer)
  Criticism
New Yorker 47:85 S 4 '71 *

On watching Parsifal with Molly. O. Friedrich. il Esquire 75:144-8+ My '71; Reply. P. J. Smith. 76.24 Ag '71 *

Parsifal. Criticism
Hi Fi il 21:MA14-15+ F '71 *
Opera N il 35:17-20 Ap 3 '71 *
Vogue 157:86 F 15 '71 *

Parsifal at Bayreuth. D. Hamilton. il Hi Fi 21:85-6 N '71 *

Records. D. Hamilton. Nation 214:62 Ja 10 '72 *

Report:
  Concert performance of Rheingold, Georg Solti conducting. S. Jenkins. Opera N 35:22 Je 12 '71 *

Tristan und Isolde. Criticism
Nation 213:220 S 13 '71 *
Nation 213:670 D 20 '71 *
New Yorker 47:132-3 D 4 '71 *
Newsweek il 78:98 N 29 '71 *
Opera N il 36:17-20 D 18 '71 *
Sat R 54:37-8 D 4 '71 *
Sat R 54:25 D 18 '71 *
Time il 98:63 N 29 '71 *

Wagner lives. B. Evans. Nat R 23:1427-8 D 17 '71
See also
Bayreuth festival

WAGNER, Walter F. Jr
Editorial. See issues of Architectural record

WAGNER, William
Honey makes money. il Har Yrs 11:11-13 Ap '71

WAGON caravans. See Caravans
WAGONER, David
Break of day; poem. Mlle 72:116 Mr '71
For a man who died in his sleep; poem. New
   Yorker 47:42 Ap 3 '71
Gathering of the loons; poem. New Yorker
   47:40 My 29 '71
Lost; Riverbed; Old man, old man; Fog;
   poems. Poetry 118:219-22 Jl '71
Makers of rain; poem. New Yorker 47:40
   Jl 24 '71
Northwest. Mlle 72:246+ Ap '71
Other side of the mountain; poem. Am Schol-
   ar 40:233-4 Spr '71
Survivor; poem. Sat R 54:24 Ag 7 '71
Trail horse; poem. New Yorker 47:36 Je 12 '71
Trying to pray; poem. New Yorker 47:117 S
   25 '71
about
Comment. S. Dobyns. Poetry 117:397-8 Mr
   '71 •
WAGONER, David E.
Where school desegregation isn't happening.
   il Ed Digest 37:21-4 D '71
WAHL, Paul
Action for shooters: five new-product reports.
   il Pop Sci 199:48-9 Jl '71
Cruise aboard this space-age sailing ship. il
   Pop Sci 198:48-9 Je '71
Empty cans give scientists double-edged
   dome. il Pop Sci 199:82 O '71
Man-powered flight. il Pop Sci 198:43-5+ Ja
   '71
Personal rapid transit. il Pop Sci 199:73-7+
   N '71
STOL flying boat makes a splash. il Pop Sci
   198:54 My '71
Shooter's guide to .22 ammo; with tables. il
   Pop Sci 199:62-3+ O '71
Suit yourself, with mirrors. il Pop Sci 198:
   57 F '71
Sun machine previews shadows. il Pop Sci
   199:121 Ag '71
WAHLBERG, Rachel Conrad
Movies (title varies) Chr Cent 88:1143-4, 1364-5
   S 29, N 17 '71
Woman and the fetus: one flesh? Chr Cent
   88:1045-8 S 8 '71
WAHLER, H. J.
Winning and losing in life: a survey of
   opinions about causes. bibliog Ment Hy 55:
   91-5 Ja '71
WAHLFELDT, Bette
Hanging baskets. Org Gard & Farm 18:114-
   15 O '71
Propagating your favorites by sand-rooting.
   il Org Gard & Farm 18:54-5 F '71
WAHLÖÖ, Per
Copology; interview. New Yorker 47:28 My
   22 '71
about
Authors & editors. B. A. Bannon. il por Pub
   W 200:13-15 S 6 '71 •
WAHTERA, John
Holy Child is everywhere; story. il Redbook
   138:161-83 D '71
WAINWRIGHT, Loudon
Another sort of love story. Life 70:2B Ja 22
   '71; Same abr. Read Digest 98:86-8 My '71
Guardian of a great legacy. il pors Life 70:
   44-55 Je 11 '71
Home is where it used to be. Life 70:77-8
   F 19 '71
My new best friend is a bile-green wheel. il
   Life 71:36-7 Jl 30 '71
Old pro gets his shot at the moon. por Read
   Digest 98:88-92 Ja '71
People lost in hate. il Life 71:20-5 Ag 20
   '71
Roads to summers past. il Life 71:50-1 S
   3 '71
View from here. il por Life 72:10 Ja 14 '72
WAITE, Virginia
With Scott in the land of Brigadoon. il Sat
   R 54:37-9+ Mr 13 '71
WAITERS and waitresses
Wages and tips in restaurants and hotels;
   with tables and a chart. C. M. O'Connor.
   Mo Labor R 94:47-51 Jl '71
WAITING for daddy; story. See Wolitzer, H.
WAITING for Godot; drama. See Beckett, S.
WAITRESSES. See Waiters and waitresses
WAKABAYASHI, Masami
Life inside a Chinese commune; interview.
   ed. by K. M. Chrysler. il por U S News
   70:70-1 F 15 '71
WAKAIZUMI, Kei
Japan and southeast Asia in the 1970's. il
   Cur Hist 60:200-6+ Ap '71
WAKE turbulence. See Atmospheric turbulence
WAKEFIELD, Dan
Taking it big: a memoir of C. Wright Mills.
   il Atlan 228:65-71 S '71

WAKEFIELD scholarship fund. See Loucye
   Gordy Wakefield scholarship
WAKEFULNESS. See insomnia
WAKELIN, James Henry, 1911-
Two views of US technology and world
   trade. S. M. Hein. pors Phys Today 24:69-70
   D '71 •
WAKITA, Hiroshi, and Schmitt, R. A.
Lunar anorthosites: rare-earth and other
   elemental abundances. bibliog il Science
   170:969-74 N 27 '70; Correction. 172:184 Ap
   9 '71
WAKOSKI, Diane
Smudging; poem. Poetry 117:351-5 Mr '71
Songs & notes. Poetry 118:355-8 S '71
WALCOTT, Derek
Man of the theatre; interview. New Yorker
   47:30-1 Je 26 '71
about
Dream on Monkey Mountain. Criticism
   New Yorker 47:83-5 Mr 27 '71 •
WALCOTT, Joe
In Camden County, Jersey Joe is the arm of
   the law. pors Life 71:97 D 10 '71 •
WALD, George
Man and meaning; excerpts from address,
   November 1970. por Sr Schol Teach ed 97:
   4 Ja 11 '71
Unfinished business of America. Look 35:62
   Jl 13 '71
about
Union and campus: talking together. J.
   Higgins. Nation 213:171-4 S 6 '71 •
WALDEN, Amelia Elizabeth
I live my novel. Writer 84:26-8 O '71
WALDEN, John C.
Proposal for professional control of educator
   performance. bibliog Sch & Soc 99:39-41
   Ja '71
WALDHEIM, Kurt
New S-G. por Newsweek 79:24 Ja 3 '72 •
U.N: madness or heroism? Chr Cent 89:3
   Ja 5 '72 •
Viennese compromise. il por Time 99:39-40
   Ja 3 '72 •
WALDMAN, Anne
Queen Anne. S. Braudy. por Newsweek 78:
   128-9 N 22 '71 •
WALDMAN, Diane
Holes without history. bibliog f il Art N 70:
   44-8+ My '71
Kelly, collage and color. bibliog il Art N 70:
   44-7+ D '71
WALDMAN, Max
Generations; photographs. Life 71:104-10+ D
   17 '71
Lovely new swan alights: Natalya Maka-
   rova; photographs. Life 70:38-43 Ja 22 '71
Swinging Shakespeare; photographs. Life 70:
   64-7+ Ap 9 '71
WALDRON, Eli
Land of the fifth season. il Holiday 49:72-4+
   Ap '71
Oscar's. il Holiday 48:91-2 S '70
WALDRON, Marilyn
Redbook reader Marilyn Waldron: a well-
   dressed life. il Redbook 137:92-5 Ag '71 •
WALDROP, Keith
To Rosemarie in Bad Kissingen; poem. New
   Yorker 47:142 O 30 '71
WALEN, Harry L.
English teaching: past, present, and future.
   Engl J 60:1072-9 N '71
WALES
See also
National parks and reserves—Wales
Towy River
National library
Llyfrgell Genedlaethol Cymru: the National
   library of Wales. W. Ready. bibliog il Wil-
   son Lib Bul 45:962-5 Je '71
WALEY, Arthur
Books. G. Steiner. New Yorker 47:110-14 Je
   12 '71 •
WALKER, Alice
Growing strength of Coretta King. por Red-
   book 137:96-7 S '71
Third life of Grange Copeland; story. Red-
   book 137:173-95 My '71
about
Comment. L. Mueller. Poetry 117:328 F
   '71 •
WALKER, Barbara K.
Folks who tell folk tales: field collecting in
   Turkey. il Horn Bk 47:636-42 D '71
WALKER, Biron
End of the affair; poem. Commonweal 95:352
   Ja 14 '72
No easy reach; poem. Commonweal 94:40 Mr
   19 '71

WALKER, Daniel
Defying the bosses in Illinois & Texas. P Wieck. New Repub 164:12-13 F 27 '71 *
Journey of 1,000 miles. por Newsweek 78:45 N 8 '71 *

WALKER, David
Baptist church in Maine; poem. New Yorker 47:34 Ag 28 '71

WALKER, Eric Arthur
Higher education faces real disaster; address, January 28, 1971. Vital Speeches 37:270-3 F 15 '71

WALKER, Evan Harris
Consciousness as a hidden variable. por Phys Today 24:39 Ap '71

WALKER, Frank
Art from dry plant stems. il Sch Arts 70:18-21 F '71

WALKER, Geoffrey F.
SCR power supplies. il Electr World 86:36-8+ O '71

WALKER, Harry
Big man on campus. il pors Ebony 26:106-8+ Ag '71 *

WALKER, Harry D.
Conductor design with thin-film insulated aluminum. il Electr World 83:39+ D '71

WALKER, James R.
Pinpoint propane torch. il Mech Illus 67:92 Ja '71

WALKER, James W.
Unique type of angiosperm pollen from the family annonaceae. bibliog il Science 172:565-7 My 7 '71

WALKER, Leroy
Africa, U.S. begin track series. il por Ebony 26:143-6+ O '71 *

WALKER, Lester, and others
You gain more than space when you add greenhouse bays. il Pop Sci 198:90-3 Ap '71

WALKER, Mark
All aboard BART, the commuter's dream. il Read Digest 99:97-100 Jl '71
BART: the way to go for the '70s. il Pop Sci 198:50-3+ My '71
Big bubble atop the South Pole. il Pop Sci 199:56-9 Ag '71
One million kilowatts from a mountain cave. il Pop Mech 136:104-5 N '71

WALKER, Peter Edward
Conversation with Britain's environmental chief; interview, ed. by S. Lindsay. il por Sat R 55:64+ Ja 1 '72

WALKER, R. M. See Crozaz, G. jt. auth.

WALKER, Ted
After drought; poem. New Yorker 47:38 Ap 3 '71
Interpreter; story. McCalls 99:56 D '71
Night out; story. New Yorker 46:26-30 Ja 30 '71
Night rain on roses; poem. New Yorker 47:86 Ag 21 '71
One of ours; story. New Yorker 47:36-9 O 16 '71
Skein; story. New Yorker 47:38-41 Mr 6 '71
Snow in southern England; poem. New Yorker 46:32 Ja 23 '71
Stephen, Steve, Stevie; story. New Yorker 47:30-5 Jl 24 '71

WALKER, Theodore J.
California gray whale comes back. il Nat Geog 139:394-415 Mr '71

WALKER art center, Minneapolis
Museum in action. il Newsweek 77:69 Je 7 '71
New art action in Minneapolis. B. Rose. il por Vogue 158:70 Ag '71

WALKER cup. See Golf

WALKERS, Infants
Walkers, jumpers and bouncers for children can be dangerous. Good H 173:188 O '71

WALKERSVILLE, Md.
Recycling of the greens. B. Gilford. il Org Gard & Farm 18:74-5 D '71

WALKING
Back-country Switzerland. B. Ellison. il Travel 135:50-3 My '71
Backpacker's notebook. C. B. Colby. il Outdoor Life 148:10+ D '71
Backpacking with young children? Sunset 146:42 F '71
Equipment basics for the backpacker. J. R. Stebbins. il Field & S 76:72-3+ Je '71
Hike to visit marmots; Mount Rainier National Park. il Sunset 147:34+ Jl '71
Join the backpack boom? C. B. Colby. il Outdoor Life 148:12+ O '71
Legs are coming back. B. Hackett. il Am For 77:5+ S '71
Now everybody's backpacking! il Changing T 25:46-7 Jl '71
Thirty-year hike; Liberty Lake, Nev. C. R. Madsen. il Har Yrs 11:24-6 Je '71
Travel notes; walking in Paris and Rome. R. Joseph. Esquire 76:50+ S '71
Trouble afoot. R. Starnes. Field & S 75:8+ Mr '71

What this Sierra hike offers is variety; California's Toiyabe national forest. il Sunset 147:40+ S '71
Whistle walking. H. Gilberts. Har Yrs 11:34 My '71
Women in the wilderness. A. Tussing. il Liv Wildn 34:44-9 Aut '70
See also
Hitchhiking
Trails

WALKS (paths) See Garden walks

WALKS for development. See American freedom from hunger foundation

WALL, Dana
State of grammar in the state of Iowa. Engl J 60:1127-30 N '71

WALL, Mary B.
Analogies in chemistry. il Chem 44:31 N '71

WALL, Virginia. See Dobbs, R. C. jt. auth.

WALL clocks. See Clocks

WALL coverings
Using the new do-it-yourself fabric wall coverings. E. Taylor. il Good H 172:170 My '71

WALL decoration. See Mural painting and decoration

WALL hangings
Sheila Hicks at Rabat. B. Werther. il por Craft Horiz 31:30-3 Je '71
See also
Maps, Decorative

WALL painting. See Mural painting and decoration

WALL Street
Patient is feeling better but he isn't really cured; interview. R. Cantor. por Forbes 108:42-3 Jl 1 '71
Wall Street view. See occasional issues of Forbes

WALL Street Journal
One story the Wall Street journal won't print. C. J. Loomis. il Fortune 84:140-3+ Ag '71

WALLACE, Cornelia
Drum majorette, saxophonist and wife to George Wallace. M. Byers. il por Life 71:93 O 8 '71 *

WALLACE, George Corley
Third man in? interview. por Nations Bsns 59:74-5 N '71
Unfinished business of America. Look 35:57+ Jl 13 '71
about
As Wallace looks ahead to 1972. por U S News 71:77 N 29 '71 *
Br'er George. Newsweek 78:21 Ag 23 '71 *
Down, George! New Repub 164:7 Je 5 '71 *
Electing a president. New Repub 164:12-13 F 13 '71 *
George Wallace's shadow cabinet. il por Newsweek 78:24 D 6 '71 *
Outflanking the President. Time 98:10-11 Ag 23 '71 *
Outsider. il por Newsweek 78:18+ Jl 19 '71 *
Wallace factor. il por Time 99:17-18 Ja 17 '72 *
Who knows what frustrations lurk in the hearts of X million Americans. S. Lesher. il N Y Times Mag p9+ Ja 2 '72 *

WALLACE, Irving
Authors & editors; interview, ed. by P. Bosworth. por Pub W 201:21-3 Ja 3 '72
Lovers; excerpt from The nympho and other maniacs. pors Ladies Home J 88:127-33 F '71

WALLACE, James N.
In wake of India's victory, storm signals still flying. il U S News 71:20-3 D 27 '71

WALLACE, John J.
International 110. il Yachting 129:73+ F '71

WALLACE, Marcia
Barefoot in the kitchen; excerpts. il Am Home 74:64-72+ Je '71
Numbers game. il Am Home 74:56+ N '71
Today parties: just for fun. il Am Home 74:48+ N '71

WALLACE, Robert
Compasses of storm; poem. Sat R 54:42 F 6 '71

WALLACE, Robert K.
Build a tenoning attachment for your table saw. il Pop Mech 136:146-7 Jl '71
Make this supersafe pusher jig. il Pop Mech 136:188-9 N '71

WALLACE, Weldon
Backlash and the bishops. Commonweal 94:253-4 My 21 '71

WALLACH, Laurence
(tr) See Becker-Carsten, W. Current chronicle

WALLACK, Stanley S.
Inflation versus unemployment: another view of the trade-off. bibliog Mo Labor R 94:49-54 N '71

WALLED cities. See Cities and towns—Protection

WALLENBERG, Marc
Legacy left by Marc Wallenberg. Bsns W p28 N 27 '71 •
WALLENBERG family
Legacy left by Marc Wallenberg. Bsns W p28 N 27 '71
WALLENSTEIN, Barry
Are children poets? Commonweal 93:448-50 F 5 '71
WALLEYE fishing. See Perch fishing
WALLEYED pike fishing. See Perch fishing
WALLICH, Henry C.
Brewing interest in VAT. il Fortune 83:94-5+ Ap '71
[Column on economic questions] See issues of Newsweek
WALLOON language question. See Belgium—Languages
WALLPAPER removal. See Paper-hanging
WALLPAPERING. See Paper-hanging
WALLS
Quickie rustic wall. il Mech Illus 67:116 O '71
Three strikes against the white wall. il House B 113:74-5 Ja '71
See also
Mural painting and decoration
Paneling
Partitions
Retaining walls
Storage walls
WALNUT trees
Carpathians: better walnuts for the Midwest. B. Most. il Org Gard & Farm 18:56-9 N '71
Mike Frome; question of the vanishing American black walnut. M. Frome. Am For 77:7+ My '71
WALORDY, Alex
Wee woodworking workshop. il Mech Illus 68:101-2 Ja '72
WALRUSES
Visit to a walrus island. L. L. Rue, 3d. il Audubon 73:36-7 My '71
WALSH, Chad
God at large; excerpts. Chr Cent 88:244, 276, 308,332, 364, 396, 420 F 24-Ap 7 '71
God has left the bright sky; poem; excerpt from God at large. Chr Cent 88:244 F 24 '71
Grant Wood Gothic Turks; poem. Nation 212:600 My 10 '71
Jesus climbed the drunken tree; poem. Chr Cent 88:792 Je 30 '71
Love is not dogma; poem. Chr Cent 88:1132 S 29 '71
Time-motion study; poem. Chr Cent 88:584 My 12 '71
WALSH, Denny
Gorilla cowed his keepers. il pors Life 70:42-8+ Je 25 '71
Second business at our airports: theft. il Life 70:16-23 F 12 '71
WALSH, Don, jr
How to catch big walleyes. il pors Outdoor Life 148:66-7+ N '71
WALSH, Jim
Favorite pioneer recording artists. See issues of Hobbies
WALSH, John
Curriculum vitae: a man of his times; poem. Science 172:1218 Je 18 '71
WALSH, Mary Ellen
New leader for trail riders. il por Am For 77:36 Mr '71 •
WALSH, Moira
Films. See issues of America
WALSH, W. M. jr
Magnetic resonances and waves in simple metals. bibliog il Science 171:36-42 Ja 8 '71
WALSTON and company
Another big firm seeks Perot's aid. Bsns W p74 Ap 3 '71
WALT Disney productions. See Disney, Walt, productions
WALT Disney world, Fla. See Disney world, Fla.
WALT Whitman: poet of democracy; drama. See Cote. C. K.
WALTER, Jim, corporation
Interesting profits. A. A. Butkus. Duns 97:70 Ap '71
WALTER, Nina Willis
How to win poetry contests. Writers Digest 51:25-7 S '71
WALTER, Richard
How to compost leaves. il por Am City 86:115-17 Je '71
WALTER, Roderich, and others
Leucylglycinamide released from osytocin by human uterine enzyme. bibliog il Science 173:827-9 Ag 27 '71
WALTER, William Grey. See Grey Walter W.
WALTER Kidde & company. See Kidde, Walter and company

WALTERS, Barbara
Following their footsteps. K. Maloney. il pors Seventeen 30:96-7+ Ja '71
For Today's Barbara Walters, it's all uphill before the dawn's early light. W. J. McKean. il pors Look 35:58-63 F 9 '71 •
(ed) See Nixon, R. M. Interview
WALTERS, Eugene
How to control your hi-fi from any room in the house. il Pop Mech 136:132-7 O '71
Stereo on wheels. il Radio-Electr 42:41-3 Ap '71
WALTERS, Raymond
Obituary
Sch & Soc por 99:20+ Ja '71
WALTERS, Robert
Thinking about the thinkable. Nation 212:725-6 Je 7 '71
WALTNER, Elma, and Waltner, Willard
Build the 'glass-top' wagon-wheel table. il Pop Mech 135:182D-182G F '71
WALTNER, Willard. See Waltner, E. jt. auth.
WALTON, Hanes, jr
Black politics in the South. il Ebony 26:140-3 Ag '71
WALTON, Ray
Working at a life of leisure. J. Kirshenbaum. il Sports Illus 34:52-6+ F 1 '71 •
WALTON, Roy A.
Precision square-wave audio generator. il Electr World 85:54-5 My '71
Solid-state darkroom timer. il Electr World 85:66-7 Je '71
WALTON, Terry
Pioneer: big city schooner. il Motor B & S 128:22 Ag '71
WALTON, Sir William Turner
Menuhin plays Walton, a brilliant show. S. Fleming. Hi Fi 21:80 My '71 •
WALTZ, Jon R.
Conspiracy trial. Nation 212:589-92 My 10 '71
Mayor Daley's way with justice. il Nation 213:460-8 N 8 '71
On being monitored. Nation 212:113-14 Ja 25 '71
Staked out for slaughter. Nation 213:19-20 Jl 5 '71
WAMBAUGH, Joseph
Authors & editors; interview. ed. by J. Weisman. por Pub W 200:33-5 Ag 23 '71
Trade winds; interview. ed. by C. Amory. Sat R 54:12-13 Mr 13 '71
WANAMAKER, Rick
Ho, ho, ho went the jolly white giant. W. F. Reed. il por Sports Illus 34:20-1 Je 21 '71 •
WANAQUE, N.J, free public library
How Wanaque got a library. A. Eisenberg and H. Eisenberg. il Good H 172:47-8+ F '71
WANDERERS; story. See Henderson, R.
WANG laboratories, Inc.
Wang challenges mighty IBM for a market. il Bsns W p102+ N 13 '71
WANKEL engines. See Automobile engines
WANTAGH, N.Y. public library
Wantagh, N.Y: efficiency and beauty. il Library J 96:3982 D 1 '71
WAR
How not to win a war. C. Barnett. il Horizon 13:48-53 Sum '71
Illusion of victory; excerpt from Why don't we learn from history. B. H. Liddell Hart. il Harper 243:20-1 S '71
Speaking of unnecessary wars . . . R. L. Tobin. Sat R 54:20 Jl 17; Discussion. 54:17 Ag 28; 28 O 2 '71
See also
Atomic warfare
Guerrilla warfare
Intervention (international law)
Peace
Strategy
Vietnamese war, 1957-
War and society
World war, 1939-1945
Economic aspects
See also
Industrial demobilization
Vietnamese war, 1957- —Economic aspects
Moral aspects
See War and morals
Political aspects
See Politics and war
Psychological aspects
See also
Vietnamese war, 1957- —Psychological aspects
Social aspects
See War and society

WAR, Causes of
Herman Kahn thinks about the thinkable: most of the traditional causes of war have disappeared; interview, ed. by G. R. Urban; excerpt from Can we survive our future? H. Kahn. il por N Y Times Mag p 12-13+ Je 20 '71

WAR, Ethics of. See War and morals

WAR, Laws of
Laws of war 25 years after Nuremberg. T. J. Farer. bibliog f por Int Concil 583:5-54 My '71
Ounce of prevention; army course on laws of land warfare. il Newsweek 77:30+ Ap 19 '71
What army is doing to prevent another My Lai. il U S News 70:24-5 Ap 12 '71
Whose war crimes? views of Telford Taylor. il Newsweek 77:29 F 22 '71
Why the Calley case opens up worldwide debate. D. Lawrence. U S News 70:96 Ap 12 '71
See also
Vietnamese war, 1957- —Atrocities

WAR, Prevention of
See also
International peace academy

WAR aims
See also
Vietnamese war, 1957- —War aims

WAR and animals. See Animals, War use of
WAR and children. See Children and war
WAR and Christianity. See War and religion
WAR and college students. See College students and war

WAR and education
Education for peace. C. R. Deonanan. Clear House 46:223-6 D '71

WAR and emergency powers

Canada
Strong-arm rule in Canada; effect of the War measures act. R. N. Williams. New Repub 164:15-18 Ja 30 '71; Discussion. 164: 33-4 F 27 '71

Israel
Terrorism & preventive detention: the case of Israel. A. M. Dershowitz; discussion. Commentary 51:33-4+ Je '71

United States
Congress, the president, and the war powers; statement, May 14, 1971. W. P. Rogers. bibliog f Dept State Bul 64:721-33 Je 7 '71
Permanent emergency; Roosevelt and Truman emergency proclamations still in effect. Nation 212:772 Je 21 '71
Stretch points of liberty. A. Dershowitz. Nation 212:329-34 Mr 15 '71
War powers legislation: practical and constitutional problems; statement, June 2, 1971. J. R. Stevenson. Dept State Bul 64: 833-6 Je 28 '71

WAR and high school students. See High school students and war

WAR and literature
War in literature and film: a guided independent project. H. D. Nadig. jr. Engl J 60:906-8+ O '71

WAR and morals
Notes and comments; senselessness of wars. New Yorker 47:28-9 My 15 '71
See also
Vietnamese war, 1957- —Moral and religious aspects

WAR and politics. See Politics and war

WAR and religion
Bearing the burden of the Berrigan brothers. E. Duff. New Repub 164:18-23 Mr 6 '71
Catholics and peace. Commonweal 95:315-16 Ja 7 '72
Conscientious objection: no longer un-Catholic. J. Pisani. Chr Cent 87:876-8 Jl 21 '71
Gloomy thoughts for a merry Christmas. G. W. Ball. Newsweek 78:50 D 20 '71
Great Catholic upheaval; significance of Catholic opposition to war. G. Zahn. il Sat R 54:24-7+ S 11 '71
Scandal of silence; U.S. Catholic conference memorandum. G. C. Zahn. Commonweal 95: 79-85 O 22 '71
Time to draft the clergy. P. J. Riga. America 125:456-7 N 27 '71
See also
Conscientious objectors
Vietnamese war, 1957- —Moral and religious aspects

WAR and science
Era of big science; adaptation of address, December, 1970. E. Teller. il Bul Atom Sci 27:34-6 Ap '71
See also
Operations research

WAR and society
American manifesto, by R. J. Barnet and M. G. Raskin. Review
New Repub 164:29 Ja 2 '71
Herman Kahn thinks about the thinkable: most of the traditional causes of war have disappeared; interview, ed. by G. R. Urban; excerpt from Can we survive our future? H. Kahn. il por N Y Times Mag p 12-13+ Je 20 '71
Vietnam: what is left of conscience? B. Moyers. Sat R 54:20-1 F 13 '71

WAR casualties
See also
Geneva conventions
Vietnamese war, 1957- —Casualties

WAR correspondents
Protection of journalists; preliminary draft international convention. UN Mo Chron 8:65-7 Je '71
See also
Vietnamese war, 1957- —War correspondents and photographers

WAR crime trials
See also
Nuremberg trials

WAR crimes
After Vietnam, another witchhunt? L. J. Halle. il N Y Times Mag p36:8+ Je 6 '71
Beyond atrocity; excerpt from introd. to Crimes of war. R. J. Lifton. Sat R 54:23-5+ Mr 27 '71; Same abr. with title Reflections on Hiroshima and beyond. Cur 130: 48-54 Je '71
Convention relating to war crimes enters into force. UN Mo Chron 7:99-100 D '70
When is a crime a war crime? excerpts. E. Van Den Haag. il Nat R 23:1227-32 N 5 '71
Who else is guilty? K. Auchincloss. il Newsweek 77:30-2 Ap 12 '71
See also
Philippines—History—Insurrection, 1899-1901
Vietnamese war, 1957- —Atrocities
Vietnamese war, 1957- —Atrocities—My Lai massacre

WAR drama. See War in literature

WAR finance
See also
Vietnamese war, 1957- —Cost

WAR gases. See Gases, Asphyxiating and poisonous

WAR heroes. See Heroes

WAR in art
See also
Vietnamese war, 1957- —Art

WAR in fiction. See War in literature

WAR in literature
Rabe: two plays about the Vietnam war; interview. D. Rabe. New Yorker 47:48-9 N 20 '71
War novel: from Mailer to Vonnegut. A. Kazin. Sat R 54:13-15+ F 6 '71

WAR materials
See also
Vietnamese war, 1957- —Equipment and supplies

WAR memorials
Pillow for el Caudillo? National foundation of the Holy Cross of the Valley of the fallen. J. Bryan, 3d. Nat R 23:1314-15 N 19 '71
See also
Unknown soldiers

WAR news
See also
Vietnamese war, 1957- —Censorship
Vietnamese war, 1957- —Press reports

WAR objectors. See Conscientious objectors

WAR of secession. See United States—History—Civil war

WAR on poverty. See United States—Social policy

WAR powers. See Presidents—United States—Powers and duties

WAR profits
War profiteers, by R. F. Kaufman. Review
Sat R 54:29-30 Je 5 '71. W. Shelton

WAR propaganda
See also
Moving pictures—Propaganda films
Vietnamese war, 1957- —Propaganda

WAR records. See World war, 1939-1945—Documents, sources, etc.

WARD, Barbara
On urbanization: a worldwide process; excerpts from address, November 1970. por Sr Schol Teach ed 97:3 Ja 11 '71

WARSAW pact, 1955—*Continued*
Troop balance: NATO vs. Warsaw pact. il Newsweek 77:27+ My 31 '71
U.S. to participate in conference on revision of Warsaw convention; text of letter. November 17, 1970. C. F. Butler. Dept State Bul 63:751 D 21 '70

WARSH, Lewis
Comment. P. Schjeldahl. Poetry 117:266-7 Ja '71

WARSHIPS
United States
Drive for modern navy, warships that fly: surface-effect ships. il U S News 71:53-4 D 6 '71
First look at the navy's new destroyer. M. Schultz. il Pop Mech 136:78-81 Jl '71

WARSHOFSKY, Fred
Accounting for taste. Read Digest 98:31-2+ Je '71

WARTIAINEN, Peter, Jr
One-acre garden for $10.50. il Org Gard & Farm 18:86 My '71

WARTS
It's barefoot time, so it's time for warts. il Changing T 25:44 Ag '71

WARWICK, James F.
Impressed clay jewelry. il Sch Arts 71:16-17 S '71

WASER, Peter G. See Mikeš, F. jt. auth.

WASERMAN, Barbara, and Waserman, Manfred
History of medicine. il pors Library J 97:37-41 Ja 1 '72

WASERMAN, Manfred. See Waserman, B. jt. auth.

WASHERS (plumbing) See Plumbing

WASHING machines
Automatic washing machines. il Consumer Bul 54:7-12 Ap '71
Compact washing machines. il Consumer Bul 54:7-10 F '71
For laundry that needs tender loving care. il House B 113:60 O '71
Washing machines. il Consumer Rep 36:504-13 Ag '71

Maintenance and repair
Basics of washer repair. L. Buckwalter. il Mech Illus 67:91-3+ D '71

WASHING of clothes. See Laundry

WASHINGTON, Booker Taliaferro
Dark and stormy night in the life of Booker T. Washington. L. R. Harlan and P. Daniel. por Negro Hist Bul 33:159-61 N '70
William H. Ferris criticizes Booker T. Washington (1898); reprint from a Negro newspaper of 1898. G. P. Marks, 3d. il por Negro Hist Bul 33:162-3 N '70 •

WASHINGTON, George
Drama
Washington's paper army. M. A. Nicholson. Plays 30:65-8, 96 F '71

WASHINGTON, D.C.
Ever been arrested? DC court of appeals decision on arrest records. R. Cassidy. New Repub 165:14-16 D 4 '71
Tourists flocking back to Washington; photographs. U S News 71:38-40 Jl 26 '71
See also
White House

Airports
Air cushion to Dulles. Sci N 99:144 F 27 '71
Transpo seeks traffic solution; highway access to Dulles international airport. D. A. Brown. Aviation W 95:22 N 29 '71

Architecture
See also
Washington, D.C.—Public buildings

Bridges
New steel median barrier introduced; Washington, D.C. il Am City 86:112 Mr '71

Churches
Case of the flowing roof; lead roof of Washington national cathedral. C. P. Saylor. il Chem 44:19-20 D '71
Eight sides to this conversation piece; Christian Science Third church. il Chr Today 15:31 Ja 29 '71

City planning
Face-lifting of Washington: a more monumental city. il U S News 71:68-70 N 8 '71

Clubs
Boys' night out! group protests stag party at Gridiron club. Newsweek 77:69-70 Mr 22 '71

License plates of Burning Tree. New Yorker 46:20-2 Ja 30 '71
See also
National press club

Crime
Capital crime drop. Newsweek 77:59-60 F 8 '71
Crime drops in D.C. Am City 86:30 D '71
Is curfew the cure? il Newsweek 78:36+ S 6 '71

Education
Teaching survival in the sales jungle; high school course taught by law students. R. R. Morris. il Am Ed 7:28-31 Ap '71
Wright and Clark, dynamic duo, order to equalize per pupil expenditure. Sat R 54:52 Jl 17 '71
You've got to get them involved; Alice Deal junior high. S. McBee. il por McCalls 98:28+ My '71

Galleries and museums
Black American heritage; Museum of African art. W. Wood. il Am Ed 7:16-22 Ag '71
Totem and taboo; Museum of African art. il Newsweek 77:85-6 Je 21 '71
See also
Corcoran gallery of art, Washington, D.C.
National gallery of art
Smithsonian institution

Hotels, restaurants, etc.
Troubles of a famed capital hotel; the Mayflower in financial trouble. il U S News 71:55 N 1 '71

Housing
Legacy of David Scull; Emergency homes, inc. J. E. Roper. por Read Digest 99:33-6 Ag '71
Where the tenants have a say in the plans; Sursum corda development. il Bsns W p 132+ S 11 '71
Libraries
See also
Washington, D.C. public library

Monuments, statues, etc.
Where are they now? proposed F. D. Roosevelt memorial. il Newsweek 78:13 S 20 '71

Music
Grand night in a superbunker; opening performances at Kennedy center. il Time 98:40-40C S 20 '71
Music; first performances at Kennedy center. D. Hamilton. Nation 213:284-5 S 27 '71
New chamber music; fourteenth Chamber music festival. M. Steinberg. Hi Fi 21:MA28+ Mr '71
See also
Inter-American music festival
John F. Kennedy center for the performing arts
National cherry blossom festival
Poems against the sky. il Holiday 49:58-9 Ap '71

Negroes
Confronting the President; black caucus on home rule for the District. il por Time 97:13-14 Ap 5 '71

Newspapers
See also
I. F. Stone's bi-weekly

Parades
It rained on McIntire's victory parade. E. E. Plowman. il por Chr Today 15:30-2 Je 4 '71
Washington: the monks at Eighth and I; weekly parade at the marine barracks. il Time 98:23 Ag 9 '71

Parks and playgrounds
Capital gets some culture. A. Cross. il Am For 77:14-19 N '71

Police
Capital crime drop. Newsweek 77:59-60 F 8 '71
Washington's capital crime-stopper; police chief J. Wilson. R. MacLeish. Read Digest 98:53-4+ My '71

Politics and government
At last: Congress seat for nation's capital, but . . . il U S News 70:82-3 Ap 5 '71
Confronting the President; black caucus on home rule for the District. il por Time 97:13-14 Ap 5 '71
Little Lord; District of Columbia's Democratic primary. New Repub 166:12 Ja 1 '72

WASHINGTON, D.C.—*Continued*

Poor

Legacy of David Scull; Emergency homes. inc. J. E. Roper. por Read Digest 99:33-6 Ag '71

Prisons and reformatories

Inside the woodstockade; makeshift jail for those arrested during Mayday demonstrations. R. Anson. Time 97:15 My 17 '71

Protests, demonstrations, etc.

Another plea for peace and a reservation. America 124:474 My 8 '71

Beleaguered Washington: only recourse was mass arrests; interview. J. V. Wilson. il pors U S News 70:53-5 My 24 '71

Biggest bust. il Newsweek 77:24-8+ My 17 '71

Close down Washington! How the conspiracy was blocked; with photo report. U S News 70:9-10+ My 17 '71

Day Washington did not shut down; with report on police chief. J. Wilson, by J. Neary. il Life 70:30-9 My 14 '71

Different kind of protest for peace; Mennonites clean up. il U S News 70:29 Je 7 '71

Dissent and disorder. New Repub 164:7-8 My 15 '71

Hearts with one purpose alone. M. McGrory. America 124:476 My 8 '71

Jailed with the Mayday tribe. J. Mathews. Nation 212:646-8 My 24 '71

May day: anatomy of the movement. M. P. Lerner. il Ramp Mag 10:18-25+ Jl '71; Discussion. 10:71-2 O '71

May day at the APA. Sci N 99:315-16 My 8 '71

Mayday! Mayday! R. M. Nixon's news conference on Washington's Mayday arrests. il Newsweek 77:27-8 Je 14 '71

Nixon talks about drugs, mass arrests, Vietnam POW's; text of news conference, June 1, 1971. R. M. Nixon. il por U S News 70: 79-82 Je 14 '71

Notes and comment. New Yorker 47:27 Je 12 '71

Notes and comment; crowd's size. New Yorker 47:29-30 My 8 '71

Once more a time for protest. il Newsweek 77: 24-5 My 3 '71

Peace demonstrations, 1971. Nation 212:578-9 My 10 '71

Protracted legal conflict. Nat R 23:573+ Je 1 '71

Self-defeat for the army of peace. il Time 97: 13-15 My 17 '71

Setting an example; strategy used against Mayday antiwar demonstrators in Washington. il Newsweek 77:23 My 24 '71

Something different this spring. H. Sidey. Life 70:2B Ap 23 '71

TRB from Washington; April march on Washington. New Repub 164:4 My 8 '71

Those mass arrests. Nation 212:610 My 17 '71

Time for unity; comment on attempt to close down the government. D. Lawrence. U S News 70:104 My 17 '71

Totting up the protest costs. il U S News 70: 29 My 24 '71

Vietnam vets: the anti-war army. A. Goldberg. il Ramp Mag 10:10-15 Jl '71

Warriors oppose the war. T. M. Gannon. il America 124:516-18 My 15 '71

What price protest? Washington spring offensive against the war. il Newsweek 77:25-6 My 10 '71

Public buildings

Washington, D.C; James Forrestal building. D. R. Dibner. il Arch Forum 134:46-9 Ja '71

See also
United States—Capitol

Recreation

Maintenance team is born. E. B. Willard. il Parks & Rec 6:53-4+ My '71

Religious institutions and affairs

Advance in due process; dispute between Cardinal Patrick O'Boyle and suspended priests. America 124:165 F 20 '71

Vatican findings on Washington 19. America 124:500 My 15 '71

Social conditions

See also
Washington, D.C.—Poor

Social life and customs

Capital dance with Potomac setting. J. B. Lewis. il Dance Mag 45:24-5 S '71

See also
White House

Subway

It's full speed ahead for Washington's Metro. Sci N 100:389 D 11 '71

Theater

Arena stage: full speed ahead. H. Hewes. il Sat R 54:63-5 Mr 27 '71

Lincolniana in 1970; related Civil war activities. B. E. Wheeler. il Hobbies 75:116-21 F '71

Theater; current productions. H. Hewes. Sat R 54:12+ D 11 '71

See also
John F. Kennedy center for the performing arts

Transit systems

See also
Washington, D.C.—Subway

WASHINGTON, D.C. Federal city college

Libraries

FCC librarians association to launch investigation. Library J 97:16+ Ja 1 '72

WASHINGTON, D.C. public library

DCLA new careers program reports good progress. il Library J 96:2034-6 Je 15 '71

DCPL outlines proposals for library-based cable TV. Library J 96:3554-5 N 1 '71

WASHINGTON (state)

See also
Architecture, Domestic—Washington (state)
Camps—Washington (state)
Cascade Range
Columbia River
Fishing—Washington (state)
Forests and forestry—Washington (state)
Geology—Washington (state)
North Cascades National Park
Olympic National Park
Prisons—Washington (state)
Rainier, Mount
San Juan Islands
Stevens Pass
Water pollution—Washington (state)
Wilderness areas—Washington (state)

Description and travel

Washington: a state for all seasons. J. Reddy. il Read Digest 99:142-8 D '71

Historic houses, etc.

Not quite, but almost, a ghost; Molson. il Sunset 147:70 O '71

WASHINGTON (state). University, Seattle

ASTRA project monitors atmospheric pollution. G. B. Lubkin. il Phys Today 24:20 Ja '71

Oceanographic odyssey. R. W. Sternberg and others. il Travel 137:50-3 Ja '72

Reverse discrimination. Time 98:78 O 11 '71

College of forest resources

Outdoor classroom. D. R. Potter. il Am For 77:44-6 O '71

U.W: an old established firm. J. Murphy. il Am For 77:28-31+ O '71

WASHINGTON COUNTY, Pa.

New type water plant makes water contaminated by mine waste potable. il Am City 86:56-7 My '71

WASHINGTON monthly

Low-keyed muckrakers. il Time 97:51 Mr 29 '71

WASHINGTON national cathedral. See Washington. D.C.—Churches

WASHINGTON post

Busted backgrounder. il Time 98:52-3 D 27 '71

Government vs. the press; Pentagon study of the war in Vietnam. il por Newsweek 78:17-19 Jl 5 '71

In the courts: the government vs. the press; Pentagon papers. il por Newsweek 77:27+ Je 28 '71

Legal battle over censorship. il Time 97:17-19 Je 28 '71

1984: closer than we'd thought? publication of Vietnam papers. Pub W 199:45 Je 28 '71

Press wins and presses roll. il Time 98:10-12 Jl 12 '71

Right to publish; Supreme court's Pentagon papers decision. N. Lewin. New Repub 165: 11-13 Jl 10 '71

Truth or consequences; controversy over anonymity of government sources. il Newsweek 78:53-4 D 27 '71

Victory for the press; Supreme court ruling on publication of the secret Pentagon history of the Vietnam war; with excerpts from opinions of 5 justices. il Newsweek 78:16-19 Jl 12 '71

WASHINGTON post company

Opening the books. Time 97:45 My 24 '71

WASHINGTON Redskins (football club) See
    Football clubs
WASHINGTON Senators (baseball) See Base-
    ball clubs
WASHINGTON state penitentiary. See Prisons
    —Washington (state)
WASHINGTON university, St Louis, Mo.
        Libraries
Approach to special collections. W. Mathe-
    son. il Am Lib 2:1151-6 D '71
WASHINGTON'S paper army; drama. See
    Nicholson, M. A.
WASHOE COUNTY, Nev.
        Education
Washoe County teachers association. P.
    Dorazio. Todays Ed 60:53 Ja '71
WASKOW, Arthur I.
    . . . I am not free. Sat R 55:20-1 Ja 8 '72
Twenty-one theses; a radical perspective on
    the '70s. Commonweal 93:463-5 F 12 '71
WASSERMAN, Burton
Art appreciation in the elementary school. il
    Sch Arts 70:12-13 Mr '71
Making the gallery scene. il Sch Arts 71:30-3
    O; 28-31 N '71
WASSERMAN, Dale
One flew over the cockoos' nest; dramatiza-
    tion of novel by K. Kesey. Criticism
    Nation 212:442-3 Ap 5 '71 *
WASSERMAN, Ernest N.
Navigating by the stars. il Yachting 129:62-3+
    Ap '71
WASSERMAN, Lauren M.
Minibikes and motorbikes only. il Am City
    86:100 Ag '71
WASSERMAN, R. H. See Corradino, R. A. jt.
    auth.
WASSERMAN, Richard M.
Over the wall at Levitt. por Bsns W p36 My 8
    '71 *
WASSERMAN, Rona B.
Can good P.R. sell your camp? It sure can
    help! Camp Mag 43:12-13 N '71
WASSERSUG, Joseph D.
Diseases you can get from medicines. il Sci
    Digest 69:80-4 Je '71
WASSON, Donald
(comp) Source material. See issues of Foreign
    affairs
WASTE, Utilization of
    See also
Refuse, Utilization of
Sewage as fertilizer
WASTE disposal in the ocean
Flying Dutchman of garbage. il Time 98:
    35-6 Ag 16 '71
Geophysical garbage dump. il Time 97:70 Ap
    5 '71
Marine pollution, potential for catastrophe.
    O. Schachter and D. Serwer. UN Mo Chron
    8:28-49 Mr '71
Minisub probes ocean dumping. S. Lindsay.
    il Sat R 54:87 N 6 '71
No dumping place at sea; Stella Maris epi-
    sode. S. Lindsay. Sat R 54:57 S 4 '71
Public views sought on convention on ocean
    dumping. Dept State Bul 65:251 Ag 30 '71
Stop killing our oceans. G. Nelson. Read
    Digest 98:132-6 F '71
Threatened coastlines. il Time 98:32-3 Ag
    30 '71
    See also
Hazardous substances—Disposal in the ocean
WASTE disposal plants. See Sewage disposal
    plants
WASTE disposers. See Refuse grinders
WASTE heat
Flow of energy in an industrial society. E.
    Cook. il Sci Am 225:134-42+ bibliog (p244)
    S '71
WASTE in government spending. See United
    States—Appropriations and expenditures
WASTE injection. See Trade waste disposal
WASTE paper
    See also
Feeding and feeding stuffs— Paper
WASTE paper, Recycled. See Refuse, Utiliza-
    tion of
WASTE products
Buy wastes whenever you can. J. Olds. Org
    Gard & Farm 18:53-5 Je '71
    See also
Corncobs
Feeding and feeding stuffs—Waste products
WASTE recycling. See Refuse, Utilization of
WASTE water, Reclamation of. See Water re-
    use
WASTE water purification. See Sewage puri-
    fication
WASTE water reclamation. See Water reuse

WASYLUKA, Ray G.
New blood for tired hospitals. bibliog f il
    Harvard Bsns R 48:65-74 S '70; 49:34+ Ja
    '71
WATCH Industry
    See also
Elgin national watch company
Hamilton watch company
        Japan
Making love to one wife; K. Hattori and
    Seiko watches. Forbes 108:90 N 15 '71
        Switzerland
Self-winding industry of Switzerland. J. K.
    Galbraith. il Holiday 49:8+ F '71
WATCHDOGS
Pet news. il Ladies Home J 88:74 Mr '71
        Anecdotes, facetiae, satire, etc.
Field editor's memo to farm dogs. D. Seim.
    Farm J 95:33 Je '71
WATCHES
Counterfeit watch racket. O. Schisgall and
    D. Garr. il Pop Sci 199:54-6 D '71
On time. O. R. Hagans. See issues of Hob-
    bies
        Caricatures and cartoons
Timepieces in cartoons. Hobbies 76:126 Ja
    '72
        Purchasing
Consumer's guide to wristwatches. il Mech
    Illus 67:108 F '71
WATER
By the sweat of their brow; polywater pooh-
    poohed. il Sci N 99:62-3 Ja 23 '71
Echoes in a conch shell. H. Borland. il Audu-
    bon 73:12-13 Mr '71
Goodby, polywater? Sci Digest 69:17 Je '71
Hydrogen-bond stereochemistry and anom-
    alous water. B. Kamb. bibliog il Science
    172:231-42 Ap 16 '71; Discussion. 173:1252
    S 24 '71
Polywater and sweat: similarities between
    the infrared spectra. D. L. Rousseau. bib-
    liog il Science 171:170-2 Ja 15 '71
Polywater: evidence from electron spectro-
    scopy for chemical analysis (ESCA) of a
    complex salt mixture. R. E. Davis and
    others. bibliog il Science 171:167-70 Ja 15 '71
Polywater or sodium acetate? W. M. Madigo-
    sky. bibliog il Science 172:264-5 Ap 16 '71
Preparing polywater and other anomalous
    liquids. P. A. Christian and L. H. Berka.
    bibliog il pors Chem 44:25-8 Ja '71
Some tips on studying water as a resource.
    J. A. Weeks. bibliog il Cons 25:48-9+ F '71
Structure of water in microemulsions: elec-
    trical, birefringence, and nuclear magnetic
    resonance studies. D. O. Shah and R. M.
    Hamlin, jr. bibliog il Science 171:483-5 F
    5 '71
Water. C. Hall. bibliog il por Chem 44:6-10
    S '71
    See also
Drops
Floods
Ice
Lakes
Ocean
Rain and rainfall
Runoff
Sea water
Springs
        Aeration
Aeration saves a lake; Lake Francis in
    Florida. D. H. Fletcher. il Parks & Rec 6:
    23-4+ N '71
        Analysis
Arsenic in potable desert groundwater: an
    analysis problem. G. C. Whitnack and H.
    H. Martens. bibliog il Science 171:383-5
    Ja 29 '71
        Composition
Mechanisms controlling world water chemis-
    try. R. J. Gibbs; reply with rejoinder. J. H.
    Feth. bibliog il Science 172:870-2 My 21 '71
        Pollution
See Water pollution
        Purification
See Water purification
        Supercooling
See Supercooling
        Superheating
See Superheating
        Therapeutic use
See Hydrotherapy

WATER, Bottled
Bird-dogging the bottlers. il Time 98:78 S 13 '71
Connoisseur's guide to H_2O. W. Zinsser. Life 71:15 N 26 '71
Hitting the bottle. il Newsweek 78:52+ Ag 2 '71
Water, the new beauty drink. il Vogue 157:170-2 F 1 '71

WATER, Distilled
Modified superheating of purified water. K. Hickman and I. White. bibliog il Science 172:718-22 My 14 '71

WATER, Freezing of. See Freezing

WATER, Saline. See Saline water

WATER, Underground
Arsenic in potable desert groundwater: an analysis problem. G. C. Whitnack and H. H. Martens. bibliog il Science 171:383-5 Ja 29 '71
See also
Springs
Wells

WATER ballet. See Swimming, Synchronized

WATER birds
Birding by boat. B. Shemella. il Motor B & S 128:52-3 bibliog(p 58) Jl '71
See also names of water birds, e.g. Pelicans

Accidents and hazards
See Birds—Accidents and hazards

WATER bloom
Nitrogen, phosphorus, and eutrophication in the coastal marine environment. J. H. Ryther and W. M. Dunstan. bibliog il Science 171:1008-13 Mr 12 '71

WATER closets. See Toilets

WATER coagulation. See Water purification

WATER color painting
Chen Chi: the way of the heart. D. Marron. il por Am Artist 36:40-5 Ja '72
Tom Hill: the American artist in Mexico. T. Hill. il por Am Artist 35:56-61 F '71
Watercolor page:
  Bogomir Bogdanovic. il Am Artist 35:56-9 D '71
  Edmond J. Fitzgerald. il por Am Artist 35:60-3+ Je '71
  Grace Huntley Pugh. il por Am Artist 35:62-5+ My '71
  Hardie Gramatky. il Am Artist 35:38-41+ S '71
  Margery Soroka. il por Am Artist 35:48-9+ F '71
  Nicholas Reale. il por Am Artist 35:56-7+ Mr '71; Reply. G. C. Moore. 35:5 O '71
  Paul Strisik. il por Am Artist 35:50-1+ Ap '71
  Phil Austin. il Am Artist 35:48-51 O '71
  Richard Treaster. il Am Artist 36:36-9+ Ja '72
  Ronald Thomason. il Am Artist 35:30-3+ N '71
  Salvator Indiviglia. il Am Artist 35:34-7 Ag '71

WATER conservation
Six ways to cut your water bill. Changing T 25:28 N '71
Ways to hold the water your field crops need. P. Jones. il Suc Farm 69:38-9 My '71
See also
Terraces (agriculture)
Water reuse

WATER cress
Watercress, storehouse of vitamins and minerals. M. Findley. il Org Gard & Farm 18:45 Ap '71

WATER cycle. See Hydrologic cycle

WATER distribution
Computer bills, pays, operates; Monroe County water authority. il Am City 86:22 O '71
Little Guatemalan pipeline. Am City 86:8 Ag '71
See also
Water pipes
Water tanks
Water towers

WATER drops. See Drops

WATER erosion. See Erosion

WATER films. See Films

WATER filters. See Filters and filtration

WATER fountains. See Fountains

WATER gardens
Give your garden that final touch. W. C. Lammey. il Nat Wildlife 9·17 Ag '71
Water garden in a barrel. il Sunset 147:148-9 Jl '71

WATER heaters
Extend your swimming season with sun power. E. McGough. il Mech Illus 67:98-9 S '71

Water heaters. il Consumer Bul 54:18-22 Ag '71
Ways to baby your water heater. il Sunset 146:68 Ja '71

WATER hens. See Gallinules

WATER hoops. See Hoops

WATER in the body
State of water in red cells. A. K. Solomon. il Sci Am 224:88-96 F '71
See also
Dehydration (physiology)

WATER jet engines. See Motor boat engines

WATER lilies
American waterlilies. C. O. Masters. il Horticulture 49:26-9 Jl '71
See also
Lotus

WATER mains. See Water pipes

WATER meter reading. See Meter reading

WATER meters

Maintenance and repair
Readable meters make happy customers; Fort Worth, Tex. G. O. Muller. il Am City 86:65-6 Ja '71

WATER milfoil
Striking the balance; TVA use of 2,4-D to control Eurasian watermilfoil. E. Hirst and H. Bank. bibliog il Environ 13:34-41 N '71

WATER picks, Electric. See Toothpicks, Electric

WATER pipes
Cellular glass floats support twin intake lines; Lake Liberty, Carroll County, Md. il Am City 86:32 Ag '71
Primer on water pipery. il Mech Illus 67:95-7+ Mr '71
See also
Pipe laying
Water distribution

Maintenance and repair
Pipeline rehabilitation proved better, cheaper; methods employed in Vernon, Calif. R. H. King. il por Am City 86:80+ O '71

WATER pipes, Plastic
Plastic water main for hot soil; Denver. C. Carlson. il Am City 86:70 Je '71

WATER plants. See Aquatic plants

WATER pollution
Echoes in a conch shell. H. Borland. il Audubon 73:12-13 Mr '71
Ecology crisis, what you can do; with editorial comment. B. Emory. il Yachting 130:33, 56-7+ Jl '71
Effect of chemical fertilizers in water pollution. J. I. Rodale. Org Gard & Farm 18:26-8+ Ap '71
How to beautify a dirty river. il Audubon 73:38-9 Ja '71
Impacts of nuclear power plants on the environment; question of thermal pollution. A. W. Eipper and others. bibliog f il Liv Wildn 34:5-12 Aut '70
Nader's waders. Newsweek 77:72+ Ap 26 '71
Nation's rivers. M. G. Wolman. bibliog il Science 174:905-18 N 26 '71
Nature worst water polluter. Am City 86:62 Ap '71
New target in the antipollution drive; sewage treatment, with editorial comment. il Bsns W p 104-5+ 112 Ja 16 '71
Nuclear plant controversy. R. E. Lapp. New Repub 164:20-3 F 6 '71
One man's fight; the Ouachita River. E. E. Guess. il pors Outdoor Life 147:4+ F '71
Paddle your own canoe. S. K. Summers and A. P. Teton. il por Parks & Rec 6:35-6 Jl '71
Le panorama ecologique fantastique: where you won't swim this summer. J. Shepherd. il Look 35:24-5 My 4 '71
Proliferating at home; thermal pollution. J. Deedy. Commonweal 94:226 My 14 '71
To swim or not to swim. Time 98:41 Jl 26 '71
Verses from The brook by A. Tennyson; sketches. A. Getz. Audubon 73:10-11 Mr '71
See also
Atomic power plants—Pollution
Cruisers (pleasure boats)—Pollution
Detergent pollution of rivers, lakes, etc.
Eutrophication
Hydroelectric plants—Pollution
Marine pollution
Mercury pollution of rivers, lakes, etc
Oil pollution of rivers, harbors, etc.
Paper mills—Pollution
Sewage disposal
Steel works—Pollution
Trade waste
Water bloom

WATER pollution—*Continued*

Control
Answer the ecologists; Richmond's pollution abatement program. P. D. Eimon. il Am City 86:118+ O '71
Case of the offending effluent. R. Charan and N. Wormald. il Harvard Bsns R 49:148-50+ Jl '71
Fishermen of the world, unite! M. Frome. Field & S 76:26+ D '71
Pollution and policing; Lake George patrol. M. Crook. il Yachting 129:70+ Je '71
Sewage pollution: what can be done and when? il Bet Hom & Gard 49:20+ My '71
These farmers got cash, everybody gets a cleaner lake; Lake Mendota, Wis. B. Coffman. il Farm J 95:22E-22F Jl '71
Wanted clean water, but how clean? il Consumer Bul 55:2+ Ja '72
See also
United States—Environmental protection agency—Water quality office

History
? pollution of the water supply of—; 1887 lawsuit against industries polluting the Passaic River. il Chem 44:19-20 Ap '71

Laws and legislation
Big cleanup; Edmund Muskie's bill. Newsweek 78:76 N 1 '71
Bounty hunter wore sneakers. M. Michaelson. il Todays Health 49:41-3+ Ap '71
Burns case. il por Time 97:43 Ja 25 '71
Challenge for the President; proposed bill of Senator Muskie's subcommittee. J. Lear. Sat R 54:47 S 4 '71
Clean water: how high the cost? Sci N 100:419 D 25 '71
Court challenges licenses to pollute. Bsns W p21 Ja 1 '72
Hold your nose; Administration fighting to defeat bills. New Repub 165:9-10 D 25 '71
Industries miss deadlines; water-discharge permits. Sci N 100:23 Jl 10 '71
Law that could clean up our rivers; Federal refuse act of 1899. J. N. Miller. Read Digest 98:31-2+ My '71
Muddied waters. il Newsweek 78:70+ O 4 '71
Muskie package to Congress. Sci N 100:108 Ag 14 '71
Nader on water. Time 97:59 Ap 26 '71
Pressure against a pollution bill. Bsns W p70 N 20 '71
Sewer shortage halts the builders. il Bsns W p54+ O 2 '71
Tapping an old law to catch polluters; permit system. il Bsns W p 158 My 15 '71
Torrent of trouble. il Nations Bsns 59:20-3 Ag '71
Water polluters tangle with the law, and lose; Armco and U.S. steel cases. il Bsns W p64-5 O 9 '71
Water pollution: conservationists criticize new permit program. R. J. Bazell. Science 171:266-8 Ja 22 '71
Water pollution; permit program. New Repub 164:8-9 Mr 27 '71
What have we really done about water pollution? il Mech Illus 67:80-1+ Mr '71
Who's Mr Clean? concerning Nader's task force report. New Repub 164:7-8 My 1 '71

Statistics
Water; EQ index. il Nat Wildlife 9:28-9 O '71

California
Imminent death of San Francisco Bay. L. Green. il Field & S 75:10+ Ap '71
It's about too late for Tahoe. W. Bronson. il Audubon 73:46-62+ My '71
Sorry story of California's salmon and steelhead. Sunset 147:39 N '71

Europe, Western
Last year at Deauville. S. Novick. il Environ 13:36-7 Jl '71

Florida
Don't broadcast this, but pollution can get you fired! reporting of pollution in the Jacksonville area; reprint. C. Gillespie. il Audubon 73:103-5 Ja '71

Great Lakes Region
IJC completes report on pollution of the lower Great Lakes; statement, with Department announcement. W. P. Rogers. Dept State Bul 64:203-5 F 15 '71
U.S. and Canada hold meeting on Great Lakes pollution; joint communique, June 10, 1971. Dept State Bul 64:828-31 Je 28 '71

Italy
Dead sea II. R. Starnes. il Field & S 76:8+ Jl '71
Is the Mediterranean dying? J. Cornwell. il N Y Times Mag p24-5+ F 21 '71

Nevada
It's about too late for Tahoe. W. Bronson. il Audubon 73:46-62+ My '71

New York (state)
Hudson River lives. R. H. Boyle. il Audubon 73:14-17+ Mr '71
State's thermal profile; temperature of New York's waters. D. H. Shafer. il Cons 25:31-2 F '71

Russia
Our far-flung correspondents; Lake Baikal. M. I. Goldman. New Yorker 47:58-66 Je 19 '71
Pollution kills fish in Caspian Sea. I. Agnew. Sci Digest 71:54 Ja '72
Saving Lake Baikal. Newsweek 78:52+ N 22 '71

Switzerland
Rescuing Swiss lakes. il Time 98:56 S 13 '71

Washington (state)
How Seattle cleaned up. E. W. Kenworthy. il Audubon 73:105-6 Ja '71

WATER power electric plants. See Hydroelectric plants

WATER purification
Liquid coagulant eases operating problems; Princeton, Ill. E. Finn. il Am City 86:24 D '71
See also
Filters and filtration
Water—Aeration
Water reuse
Water softening
Water treatment plants

WATER quality office. See United States—Environmental protection agency—Water quality office

WATER rates
Modern water rates. il Am City 86:66-7+ N; 61+ D '71 (to be cont)

WATER reclamation. See Water reuse

WATER repellents
Powder that keeps things drier; Silanox hydrophobic powder. il Bsns W p68 S 11 '71

WATER reservoirs. See Reservoirs

WATER reuse
Drinkable sewage? C. F. Newstrand. il Mech Illus 67:148-9 N '71
Fall and rise of sewage salvage; use of reclaimed water for Santee Lakes. W. Marx. il Bul Atom Sci 27:10-15 My '71
Power plant to run on reclaimed water; Amarillo, Tex. il Am City 86:24 F '71
Pure water from sewage; industrial water for boilers and cooling towers; San Diego, Calif. R. E. Dodson. il por Am City 86:43-4 F '71
Recycled water: pure enough to drink because of cobalt-60. E. Hartley. il Sci Digest 70:82-6 N '71
Renovated wastewater for industry? Contra Costa County, Calif. il Am City 86:118+ Je '71
This is no ordinary lake; Indian Creek reservoir, California. il Am City 86:34 O '71

WATER skis and skiing
How to win your ski legs. F. M. Paulson. il Field & S 76:136-8+ Ag '71
Waterskiing champions and tyros. P. Keese. il Motor B & S 127:86-7+ Mr '71

WATER snails. See Snails

WATER softening
Better water for your home; an institute report. il Good H 172:6 My '71
Portable water softening. il Consumer Bul 54:22-3 D '71
Water was too hard; Cocoa, Fla. G. C. Folkes and J. Sellers. il Am City 86:49+ Jl '71

WATER sports. See Aquatic sports

WATER sprinklers. See Sprinklers

WATER storage
See also
Reservoirs
Water tanks
Water towers

WATER supply
Water supply and treatment. See issues of American city
Waterwise. A. Rango. il Weatherwise 24:69-73 Ap '71
See also
Arid regions
Boats—Water supply
Dams

WATER supply—See also—*Continued*
Droughts
Irrigation
Reservoirs
Water purification
Water rates
Water reuse
Waterworks
Wells

Arsenic content

Arsenic in potable desert groundwater: an analysis problem. G. C. Whitnack and H. H. Martens. bibliog il Science 171:383-5 Ja 29 '71

Fluoridation

Fluoridation: New York city. New Yorker 46:21-2 Ja 9 '71

Manganese content

Don't color the water black; Boonton, N.J. F. J. Costabile and C. H. Perron. il Am City 86:46-7 Ja '71

Nitrogen content

Fertilizer nitrogen: contribution to nitrate in surface water in a Corn Belt watershed. D. H. Kohl and others. bibliog il Science 174:1331-4 D 24 '71

California

Arsenic in potable desert groundwater: an analysis problem. G. C. Whitnack and H. H. Martens. bibliog il Science 171:383-5 Ja 29 '71
Fall and rise of sewage salvage; use of reclaimed water for Santee Lakes. W. Marx. il Bul Atom Sci 27:10-15 My '71

Canada

Recent resource development. G. S. Tomkins. il Focus 21:10-12 Je '71

Guatemala

Little Guatemalan pipeline. Am City 86:8 Ag '71

Illinois

Fertilizer nitrogen: contribution to nitrate in surface water in a Corn Belt watershed. D. H. Kohl and others. bibliog il Science 174:1331-4 D 24 '71

New York (state)

Airplanes and hydrologists: a beneficial alliance. J. M. Whipple. il Cons 26:17-21 O '71
Water, water everywhere; surveillance program. R. E. Maylath. il Cons 25:14-17+ Ap '71

Southwestern states

Southwest bakes in a ruinous drought. il Life 70:26-31 Je 4 '71

Texas

See also
Irrigation—Texas

United States

Nader on water. Time 97:59 Ap 26 '71
Seven out of ten drink it; urban water problem. Sci N 100:123 Ag 21 '71
    See also subhead Water supply under names of cities, e.g. San Diego, Calif.—Water supply

WATER supply, Industrial
Renovated wastewater for industry? Contra Costa County, Calif. il Am City 86:118+ Je '71

WATER supply, Rural
How does your water supply score? P. B. Jones and R. Lutz. Suc Farm 69:J14+ N '71

WATER supply engineering
    See also
Dams
Pipe laying
Water distribution
Water purification
Water supply, Industrial
Water treatment plants
Waterworks

WATER tanks
Decorative panels solve tank-location problem; Ilion, N.Y. il Am City 86:14 My '71
No outside help wanted; Toledo, Ore. C. R. Meek. il Am City 86:79 Mr '71
Water reservoir shows its colors; Bowling Green, Ky. il Am City 86:16 Jl '71
    See also
Water towers
Waterworks

WATER tanks, Boat. See Boats—Water supply
WATER towers
Observation deck added to water tower; Peoria, Ill. il Am City 86:34 Je '71

WATER toys. See Toys
WATER treatment plants
More water from the same plant; techniques used in Corvallis, Ore. F. Collins and C. Y. Shieh. il pors Am City 86:96-7 O '71
New type water plant makes water contaminated by mine waste potable; Smith Township in Washington County, Pa. il Am City 86:56-7 My '71
Wage-price freeze on water, wastewater construction. G. R. Boyce. Am City 86:29 N '71
Water supply and treatment. See issues of American city

WATER vapor
Clustering of sulfur dioxide and water vapor about oxonium and nitric oxide ions. A. W. Castleman, jr. and others. bibliog il Science 173:1025-6 S 10 '71
Particle formation during water-vapor photolysis. I. D. Clark and J. F. Noxon. bibliog Science 174:941-4 N 26 '71
Possible observation of water vapor on the moon. Sci N 100:277 O 23 '71
Water vapor could speed base on moon. Aviation W 95:15 O 25 '71
Water vapor: stratospheric injection by thunderstorms. P. M. Kuhn and others. bibliog il Science 174:1319-21 D 24 '71

WATER wagon. See Boats and boating
WATER wells. See Wells
WATER works. See Waterworks
WATERBEDS. See Beds
WATERCOLOR painting. See Water color painting
WATERCOLOR paper. See Paper
WATERCRESS. See Water cress
WATERFALLS
    See also
Niagara Falls

WATERFRONT thieves. See Stealing
WATERING of gardens, lawns, etc.
How to take the work out of watering. W. Meachem. il Home Gard 58:34-7 Ag '71
    See also
Garden hose
Sprinklers

WATERING of plants
Editors' tests: automatic pot waterer. il Home Gard 58:12 F '71

WATERLILIES. See Water lilies
WATERLOO, Belgium
Waterloo: old name for a new Scarsdale. Bsns W p31 Jl 3 '71

WATERLOO, Iowa

Education

New horizons for WEA. L. L. Kelley. Todays Ed 60:76 S '71

WATERMAN, Thomas Talbot
Last stone age American; excerpt from The first American. C. W. Ceram. il pors Am Heritage 22:14-19+ Ag '71 *

WATERMILFOIL. See Water milfoil
WATERPROOF clothing. See Clothing, Waterproof
WATERPROOF gloves. See Gloves, Rubber
WATERPROOFING
    See also
Water repellents

WATERS, Earl Jacob
All about inductors. il Radio-Electr 42:51-4 N '71
All about resistors. il Radio-Electr 42:58-61 S '71

WATERS, Muddy
Down home and Dirty. por Time 98:46 Ag 9 '71 *
Records. D. Lupoff. il Ramp Mag 10:67-8 N '71 *

WATERSHEDS
Fertilizer nitrogen: contribution to nitrate in surface water in a Corn Belt watershed. D. H. Kohl and others. bibliog il Science 174:1331-4 D 24 '71

Research

Western phenomenon, the origin and development of watershed research: Manti, Utah, 1889. A. Antrei. il Am West 8:42-7+ Mr '71

WATERWAYS
    See also
Canals
Rivers

Canada

Any season: hop aboard the Hope. P. Blaze. il Travel 135:63-5 My '71
    See also
St Lawrence Seaway

France

    See also
Canals—France

WATERWAYS—*Continued*

Great Britain

See also
Canals—Great Britain

United States

Any season: hop aboard the Hope. P. Blaze. il Travel 135:63-5 My '71

Benefits or baloney? Tennessee-Tombigbee waterway project. Newsweek 78:65 S 13 '71

Montreal to Tampico; ed. by G. F. Hammond. J. Desjardins. il por Motor B & S 127:56-9+ My; 61-3+ Je '71

Now: traffic jams on U.S. rivers. il U S News 71:66-8 S 20 '71

Riverine revolution; address, October 6, 1971. W. R. Anderson. Vital Speeches 38:90-2 N 15 '71

Sails across Florida; from Atlantic to Gulf on Florida's Okeechobee Waterway. M. Rumsey. il Motor B & S 127:66-7+ F '71

Transport of delight on rivers and canals. J. Gooding. il Fortune 84:68-73 Jl '71

See also
Arkansas River Waterway
Cross Florida Barge Canal
Great Lakes
Intracoastal Waterway
St Lawrence Seaway

WATERWORKS

Unmanned satellite water plants; Orlando, Fla. W. L. Birdyshaw. il Am City 86:97-9 Ag '71

Water supply and treatment. See issues of American city

West View's water plant is different. E. R. Powell. il Am City 86:103-4+ Je '71

See also
Dams
Water tanks

WATKINS, Arthur Martin

Can we build enough homes for everybody? Redbook 136:75+ Ap '71

Homes for young couples who can't afford castles. il Redbook 138:86-7+ N '71

How to get your money's worth from central air conditioning; excerpt from The home owner's survival kit. House & Gard 139:56+ My '71

WATKINS, Gordon R.

Same old tunnel. R. L. Shayon. Sat R 54:46 S 4 '71 *

WATKINS, John V.

Yaupon. il Horticulture 49:20 F '71

WATKINS, Lucy Scott

Conservation, for whom? Liv Wildn 34:51-2 Aut '70

WATKINS, N. D. and Kennett, J. P.

Antarctic bottom water: major change in velocity during the late Cenozoic between Australia and Antarctica. bibliog il Science 173:813-18 Ag 27 '71

WATKINS, T. H.

Gardener in Eden. Am West 8:42-7 N '71

Golden dreams and silver realities; excerpts from Gold and silver in the West. il Am West 8:34-43 My '71

Homestake gold; 1971; excerpts from Gold and silver in the West. il Am West 8:24-31 S '71

Lion at bay. il Am West 8:30-5+ Ja '71

WATKINS Glen Grand prix circuit. See Speedways

WATMAN, Thomas J.

Labor-management: a potent teaching unit. Clear House 45:493-5 Ap '71

Process for improvement (title varies) Clear House 46:190-2, 254-6 N-D '71

WATNEY Mann, ltd.

Red-stamping a new beer brand. il Bsns W p77 Jl 10 '71

WATSON, Barbara M.

International travel; address, February 16, 1971. Vital Speeches 37:463-5 My 15 '71

about

Top woman in history at the State department. il por Vogue 157:92-3 Je '71 *

WATSON, James Dewey

Moving toward the clonal man. il Atlan 227:50-3 My '71

WATSON, Lucille McWane

Virginia planter-painter Henry James Brown. il Antiques 100:591-5 O '71

WATSON, Neale, academic publications

New firm to publish in history of science. Pub W 200:24 D 6 '71

WATSON, Robert

Christmas in Las Vegas; Divorcée; Glass door; poems. Poetry 118:83-5 My '71

Fat cat; poem. Nation 212:286 Mr 1 '71

J. Goldsborough Bruff; poem. Am Scholar 40:466-8 Sum '71

WATSON, Ruth J.

Record (title varies) Chr Cent 88:1423-4 D 1 '71

WATSON, Samuel H.

Excerpt from statement, November 1971. Cong Digest 50:307+ D '71

WATSON, Thomas John, 1914-

Health service; address, November 19, 1970. Vital Speeches 37:249-51 F 1 '71

about

Watson dynasty ends at IBM. Bsns W p20 Jl 3 '71 *

WATT, Bill

Staying serene in Indiana. Travel 135:9 My '71

WATT, Kenneth E. F.

Long arm of biological law; or, How Charles Darwin and his lot will inherit the earth; with biographical sketch. Natur Hist 80:6, 14-16+ bibliog(p84) Ap '71

WATTMETERS

Build a liquid-crystal wattmeter. J. P. Shields. il Radio-Electr 42:43-4 D '71

Using the wattmeter. J. Darr. il Radio-Electr 42:26+ Mr '71

WATTS, André

André Watts on André Watts: I'm doing all right, I'm never good enough, but I'm not standing still. J. Conaway. il pors N Y Times Mag p 14-15+ S 19 '71 *

WATTS, C. Robert, and Stokes, A. W.

Social order of turkeys; with biographical sketches. il Sci Am 224:17, 112-18 Je '71

WATTS, Chester Burleigh

Obituary
Sky & Tel por 42:131 S '71

WATTS, Frances B.

Finnegan at the fair; drama. Plays 30:39-44, 78 Mr '71

King's valentine tarts; drama. Plays 30:39-46 F '71

WATTS, John

Composers theater presents a provocative May festival. A. Derhen. Hi Fi 21:MA14 Ag '71 *

WATTS, Raymond N. Jr

[Articles on astronomy, space flight, etc] See issues of Sky and telescope

WATTS, Risher, Jr

Caring for the community. il por Time 97: 45 F 15 '71 *

WATTS-DUNTON, Theodore

At the pines, by M. Panter-Downes. Review Sat R il 54:23 Ag 21 '71. L. Untermeyer *

Profiles. M. Panter-Downes. il New Yorker 46:40-4+ Ja 23; 31-43 Ja 30; 40-6+ F 6 '71 *

WATTS, Calif. See Los Angeles

WATTS manufacturing company

West Pointer for Watts mfg. por Bsns W p29 O 2 '71

WATTS towers, Los Angeles. See Architecture, Fantastic

WAUGH, Alec

Delectations. Nat R 23:87, 200+ Ja 26, F 23 '71

WAUGH, Auberon

Letter from Europe. Esquire 75:8+ Ap; 10+ Je; 76:230 N '71

WAUGH, Jack

Smog over the Great Plains. Nation 212:753-5 Je 14 '71

Who will win the shuttle port? Nation 212: 679-80 My 31 '71

Wild, wild WEST. New Repub 164:10 Mr 27 '71

WAUGH, John. See Waugh, L. jt. auth.

WAUGH, Lynne, and Waugh, John

Albuquerque's free-wheeling library. il Am Ed 7:33-5 Ag '71

WAUSAU, LAKE

Vacuum unit helps clean up local oil spill. il Am City 86:12 Jl '71

WAVE mechanics

See also
Energy band theory of solids

WAVES

Real sea; wave forecasting; excerpt from The seas in motion. F. G. W. Smith. il Sea Front 17:298-311 S '71

Sea and the sky. P. Rockwell. il Motor B & S 128:44-5 bibliog(p 58) Jl '71

See also
Gravity waves
Ocean waves
Shock waves
Sound waves
Tidal waves

WAVES, Brain. See Brain waves

WAX cylinder records. See Phonograph records

WAX engraving

Wax engraving technique of Roy P. Madsen. F. Whitaker. il Am Artist 35:50-5+ My '71

WAX painting. See Encaustic painting
WAXES
Floor waxes, floor finishes, and wax removers. il Consumer Bul 54:21-4 Mr '71
WAXWINGS; story. See Norris, L.
WAY, Florine
DOVACK's machines help children read. M. Wills. il por Am Ed 7:3-8 Je '71 *
WAY, Right of. See Right of way
WAY it is with girls; story. See Lenord, S.
WAY of a loving girl; story. See Laut, N.
WAYMAN, Stan
Gallery; photograph. Life 70:8-9 My 14 '71
WAYNE, John
Do you ever think of Duke as big daddy? interview, ed. by E. Miller. il pors Seventeen 30:122-3+ O '71
Two screen cowboys talk about the reel West & the real West; interview, ed. by M. Ronan. il pors Sr Schol 99:10-11 D 6 '71

about

John Wayne: his wife explains the man behind the legend; ed. by V. Scott. P. Palette. il pors Ladies Home J 88:72+ N '71 *
WAYS, Max
Don't we know enough to make better public policies? il Fortune 83:64-7+ Ap '71
More power to everybody. Read Digest 98:199+ Je '71
New nation gropes for better government. il Fortune 84:136-9+ Ag '71
WAYS and means committee. See United States—Congress—House—Ways and means, Committee on
WAYSON, William W.
New kind of principal. Ed Digest 36:1-4 My '71
WE are the fine musicians; story. See Boles, P. D.
WE love you, pass it on . . . we love you, pass it on. . ; story. See Naughton, P. J.
WEAKFISH fishing
Weaks are back. G. Heinold. il Outdoor Life 148:90+ Ag '71
WEALES, Gerald
Bits and pieces. Sat R 54:67+ Mr 27 '71
Stage. See issues of Commonweal to January 22, 1971
WEALTH
See also
Gross national product
Income

Pakistan

Pakistan: all in the family. Newsweek 79:26 Ja 10 '72
WEALTH, Distribution of
Rich, poor and in between. B. L. Masse. America 124:120-2 F 6 '71
WEAND, Barron L.
Lithium: the lightest metal. il por Chem 44:10-12 Jl '71
WEAPONS
Honor system; Army research and development achievement awards. J. Rowen. Ramp Mag 10:12-13 D '71
See also
Atomic weapons
Firearms
Lasers—Military use
Pistols
WEAPONS control. See Disarmament
WEAPONS systems
Status of major U.S. European defense, aerospace programs (cont) Aviation W 94:14-18 Mr 8 '71
Weapons in the deep sea. S. Hirdman. bibliog il Environ 13:28-42 Ap '71
See also
Chemical and biological weapons

Cost

Major weapon cost trends; table. Aviation W 95:55 D 6 '71
WEAR, John W.
Computerized total-cost bidding. il Am City 86:60-1 F '71
WEARLY, William Levi
Won't you come back, John Lewis? il Forbes 108:59-60 O 1 '71 *
WEASELS
See also
Fishers (animals)
WEATHER
Circulation and weather of 1970. J. F. Andrews. il Weatherwise 24:4-11+ F '71
Weather: how to beat it? Q. Crewe. Vogue 158:128+ O 15 '71

Weatherwatch. See issues of Weatherwise
See also
Atmospheric pressure
Climate
Droughts
Evaporation
Meteorological instruments
Rain and rainfall
Snow
Storms
Winds

Bibliography

Views on science books. H. C. Stubbs. Horn Bk 47:186-8 Ap '71

History

Century of American weather: the outstanding events, decade 1911-1920. Weatherwise 23:295-9 D '70
Eighteen-hundred-and-froze-to-death; snowfilled summer of 1816. G. S. Fichter. il Sci Digest 69:62-6 F '71

Mental and physiological effects

Hippocrates, thermal stress, and stroke mortality, 1966. L. A. Helfand and C. Bridger. il Weatherwise 24:100-4 Je '71
WEATHER, Prehistoric. See Paleoclimatology
WEATHER and health. See Weather—Mental and physiological effects
WEATHER bureau (United States) See United States—National weather service
WEATHER control
Meteorology; summaries of papers presented at the International conference on weather modification. Sci N 100:192 S 18 '71
Physical view of cloud seeding; address, April 1970. M. Tribus; reply. W. C. Mayes and F. W. Decker. Science bibliog 171:215 Ja 15 '71
Search for a way to suppress hail. K. Frazier. il Sci N 99:200-2 Mr 20 '71
Spreading out Buffalo's burden of snow. il Sci N 100:341 N 20 '71
Weather modification: a technology coming of age. A. L. Hammond. Science 172:548-9 My 7 '71
See also
Rain making
WEATHER forecasting
After a freakish winter, trends the weathermen see. il U S News 70:29-30 Mr 1 '71
Odds for good harvest weather. C. E. Sommers. il Suc Farm 69:A8 O '71
Translating what the weatherman says. il Good H 173:223 N '71
Weather business. J. N. Myer and J. J. Cahir. bibliog il Weatherwise 24:64-7+ Ap '71
Winter weather, what to expect. il U S News 71:28-9 D 13 '71
See also
Radio broadcasting—Weather forecasts
United States—National weather service
Weather lore
World meteorological organization
WEATHER instruments. See Meteorological instruments
WEATHER lore
Nature's weathermen. D. Austin. il Field & S 76:126+ N '71
WEATHER maps
[Daily weather maps] See issues of Weatherwise
WEATHER models. See Meteorological models
WEATHER modification. See Weather control
WEATHER predictions. See Weather forecasting
WEATHER records
Century of American weather (cont) D. M. Ludlum. Weatherwise 24:74-8, 125-9, 179-83, 238-42 Ap-O '71
Extremes of snowfall: United States and Canada; with editorial comment. Weatherwise 23:259, 286-94 D '70
WEATHER research
Annual report on World weather program transmitted to Congress; letter of transmittal, April 15, 1971. R. M. Nixon. Dept State Bul 64:625 My 10 '71
Global meteorology:
Experiments in the tropics: BOMEX, GARP and GATE. A. L. Hammond. il Science 174:278-9 O 15 '71
Numerical models of the atmosphere. A. L. Hammond. Science 174:393-5 O 22 '71
WEATHER satellites. See Artificial satellites—Meteorological use
WEATHER stations. See Meteorological stations

WEATHERING
Duricrusts and deep-weathering profiles in southwestern Wisconsin. G. H. Dury and J. C. Knox. bibliog Science 174:291 O 15 '71
See also
Erosion
Rocks—Weathering

WEATHERMEN (organization)
Diana, by T. Powers, and Weatherman, ed. by H. Jacobs. Reviews
Commonweal 95:91-3 O 22 '71. G. A. White
Revolutionary karma vs. revolutionary politics. D. Horowitz. il Ramp Mag 9:27-33 Mr '71; Reply. P. Greenberg and B. Brogans. 9: 60-1 Je '71
Weatherman, ed. by H. Jacobs. Review
Nation 212:635-6 My 17 '71. R. Neufeld

WEAVER, DeWitt
Heads roll at head to head. D. Jenkins. il por Sports Illus 35:12-16 S 6 '71 *

WEAVER, Earl
Tightening up in Baltimore. M. Mulvoy. Sports Illus 35:42 Jl 12 '71 *

WEAVER, John D.
Copenhagen. il Holiday 49:56-9+ F '71
Miracle of the vine. il Holiday 49:64-5+ Ap '71

WEAVER, Kenneth F.
Maui, where old Hawaii still lives. il Nat Geog 139:514-43 Ap '71

WEAVER, Robert L.
Current chronicle. il Mus Q 57:317-22 Ap '71

WEAVER, William
Maggio musicale & Spoleto. il Hi Fi 21: MA30-1 O '71
Merits of Mercadante. Hi Fi 21:MA29-30 My '71
Music. il Sat R 54:45-7 D 25 '71
New man at the Met. il por Sat R 54:33-5+ Je 26 '71

WEAVING
Dorothy Liebes: her approach to design and weaving. il Am Artist 35:44-9+ Ap '71
Weaving by computer. il Design 73:22-3 Fall '71
Your loom is a deck of weaving cards. il Sunset 147:126+ O '71
See also
Spinning

Study and teaching
Colonial weaving. J. F. Presta. il Sch Arts 70: 22-3 Mr '71
Wire tapestry. G. Culverhouse. il Sch Arts 71:14-15 Ja '72

WEBB, Aileen O.
America House 1940-1971. Craft Horiz 31:11 Ap '71

WEBB, Catherine M.
And now there are nine. Time 97:27 My 10 '71 *
And now there are ten. por Time 97:33 My 3 '71 *
Kate Webb's story. il por Newsweek 77:59-60 My 24 '71 *

WEBB, Dwight
What will your counselors communicate to campers? Camp Mag 43:14+ Ap '71

WEBB, Gordon
Sunk by a whale! il por Motor B & S 128: 38-40+ Ag '71
—and Webb, Jenifer
Staying alive in a raft. il Motor B & S 128: 41+ Ag '71

WEBB, Jenifer. See Webb, G. jt. auth.

WEBB, Jimmy Layne
Jimmy L. Webb; interview. New Yorker 46: 24-5 Ja 9 '71
about
Jimmy Webb. B. Korall. Sat R 54:76 S 25 '71 *

WEBB, Lee
Computerized police systems in the U.S? Cur 132:14-20 S '71
Who owns Vermont? excerpt from Colonialism and underdevelopment in Vermont. Ramp Mag 10:13 D '71

WEBB, Peter R.
South Africa's black mood. il por Newsweek 77:47-8+ My 10 '71

WEBB, S. J. and Booth, A. D.
Microwave absorption by normal and tumor cells. bibliog il Science 174:72-4 O 1 '71

WEBB, Susan Howard
What camping means to kids. il Parents Mag 46:42-3+ Ap '71

WEBB, Wilse B. and Agnew, H. W. Jr
Stage 4 sleep: influence of time course variables bibliog Science 174:1354-6 D 24 '71
—and Friel, Janette
Sleep stage and personality characteristics of natural long and short sleepers. bibliog il Science 171:587-8 F 12 '71

WEBBER, Andrew Lloyd
Rock gets religion; interview, ed. by E. Miller. pors Seventeen 30:156-7+ Mr '71
about
Jesus Christ superstar. Criticism
America 125:352-3 O 30 '71 *
Bsns W p46-7 S 11 '71 *
Cath World 213:217-21 Ag '71 *
Chr Cent 88:1333-4 N 10 '71 *
Chr Today 16:42-3 D 3 '71 *
Life il 70:20B-26 My 28 '71 *
Mlle il por 74:102-5 D '71 *
Nation 213:444 N 1 '71 *
New Repub 165:24 N 6 '71 *
New Yorker 47:109 O 23 '71
Newsweek il pors 78:84-5 O 25 '71 *
Sat R 54:38 O 30 '71 *
Sat R il 54:65-7+ O 30 '71 *
Sr School 99:10-11 D 13 '71 *
Time il 98:64-8+ O 25 '71 *
Vogue il 158:102-3 D '71 *

WEBER, Arnold R.
Enforcing the freeze: an inside look; interview. por US News 71:63-6 S 27 '71
Seasonal prices and wages: the official policy; statement, August 28, 1971. por US News 71:19 S 13 '71
about
He has to make the freeze work. por Bsns W p64 Ag 21 '71 *
Shrewd diplomat. G. R. Rosen. por Duns 98: 59 Jl '71 *

WEBER, Bruce E.
Is Dominica's forest doomed? il Am For 77: 12-15 Jl '71

WEBER, Edward J.
Strangers in the hallways. Clear House 46: 141-2 N '71

WEBER, Eugen
Gymnastics and sports in fin-de-siècle France: opium of the classes? bibliog f il Am Hist R 76:70-98 F '71

WEBER, Joseph
Detection of gravitational waves; with biographical sketch. il Sci Am 224:12, 22-9 bibliog(p 132) My '71

WEBER, Karl Maria von
Der freischütz. Criticism
Nation 213:443 N 1 '71 *
New Yorker 47:131-3 O 9 '71 *
Opera N il 36:22-3 N '71 *
Sat R 54:94 O 16 '71 *
Kubelik-Nilsson Oberon. I. Kolodin. Sat R 54:74 N 27 '71 *
Weber's English opera in German. D. Hamilton. Hi Fi 21:108 O '71 *

WEBER, Larry J.
Inequities in athletics. Ed Digest 36:46-8 F '71

WEBER, Lillian
Joy of learning in the open corridor. W. Schneir and M. Schneir. il por N Y Times Mag p30-1+ Ap 4 '71; Discussion. p95-6+ My 2 '71 *
Open school: an experiment in learning through joy. S. G. Lanes. il Parents Mag 46:56-9 S '71 *
Sober chaos. il por Time 99:44 Ja 3 '72 *

WEBER, Paul J.
School aid: will Illinois find a way? America 124:534-8 My 22 '71

WEBER, Tom, Jr
Doc psychs big bass. il por Outdoor Life 147: 86-8+ Je '71

WEBERMAN, Alan J.
Art of garbage analysis. il Esquire 76:113-17 N '71
about
Dylanologist. il por Newsweek 77:123 Ap 12 '71 *

WEBERN, Anton von
Webern's twelve-tone sketches. G. Perle. bibliog f il Mus Q 57:1-25 Ja '71 *

WEBORG, Jan
Gallery; photographs. Life 70:4-5 F 12 '71

WEBSTER, Brenda
Yeats' The shadowy waters: oral motifs and identity in the drafts. bibliog f Am Imago 28:3-16 Spr '71

WEBSTER, John White
Disappearance of Dr Parkman, by R. Sullivan. Review
Newsweek 78:77-8+ Ag 23 '71. A. Cooper *

WEBSTER, Noah
Drama
On camera, Noah Webster! C. Boiko. Plays 31:57-62 N '71

WEBSTER, Paul
High country in season; excerpt from The mighty Sierra; portrait of a mountain world. il Am West 8:20-9 N '71

WECHSBERG, Joseph
Logistics of glut. il Esquire 76:188-93+ D '71
Vienna: it's still an operetta. il Holiday 49:
74-7+ D '70
WECHSLER, Jill
Personal imagery of Zevi Blum. il por Am
Artist 36:46-51+ Ja '72
WEDDING anniversaries
Ode to the romance and the reality of marriage; silver-anniversary salute to the brides
of 1946. S. Lindsay and S. Nirenberg. House
B 113:18+ My '71
WEDDING clothes
Instant wedding dress. il Life 71:57-8 D 3 '71
Shipboard wedding. il Holiday 49:82-4 F '71
WEDDING gifts
On and off the avenue. J. Malcolm. New
Yorker 47:46-52 Jl 3 '71
WEDDING invitations. See Invitations
WEDDING is on Tuesday; story. See O'Malley,
J.
WEDDING meals
Wedding feast, 1971 style. il McCalls 98:90-1+
My '71
WEDDING of Iphigenia plus Iphigenia in concert; musical comedy. See Musical comedies, revues, etc.—Criticisms, plots, etc.
WEDDING photography. See Photography of
weddings
WEDDINGS
Behind the main event; backstage at a White
House wedding. il pors Life 70:40-9 Je 18 '71
Day all the daughters left home; the Hunds
of San Bernardino, Calif; with report by
R. B. Stolley. il Life 71:28-36 O 22 '71
Here come the brides! B. Diamonstein. il
Good H 172:90-3+ Je '71
High price of weddings; excerpt from For
richer, for poorer. K. Hanson. Read Digest
98:99-102 F '71
Marriage is easy, if you can survive the wedding. A. Chamberlin. il McCalls 98:86-9 My
'71
Marriage the new natural way. J. A. Segal
and E. Alston. il Look 35:44-7 Je 29 '71
Mr Cox takes a June bride. il pors Time 97:16
Je 21 '71
New brides ring out the old traditions. il
Bsns W p 114-15 Je 19 '71
Simple spectacular at the White House. il pors
Time 97:13-17 Je 14 '71
Tricia got her rose garden. M. Seligson. il
pors Life 70:32-5 Je 25 '71
Wedding and new wine. R. Haughton. Cath
World 213:62-3 My '71
Wedding in the garden; T. Nixon and E. F.
Cox. il pors Newsweek 77:20-1 Je 21 '71
When Tricia Nixon marries—. il por U S News
70:54 Je 14 '71
White House wedding. il pors Newsweek 77:
30-4 Je 14 '71
See also
Marriage customs and rites
Photography of weddings
Wedding gifts
Wedding meals

Anecdotes, facetiae, satire, etc.
Where have all the orange blossoms gone?
trend to far-out weddings. T. Meehan. Mlle
72:113+ Ja '71
WEDDLE, Ferris
Intruder in a cageless zoo. il Org Gard &
Farm 18:66-71 F '71
WEDEL, Cynthia C.
Hope and joy of Christmas. Chr Cent 88:
1460 D 15 '71
WEDGE, Bryant
International propaganda and statecraft. il
Ann Am Acad 398:36-43 N '71
WEED control
Keep weeds out of sorghum. Suc Farm 69:
no5 D3 Mr '71
Put a goose run in your garden. L. Hall. il
Org Gard & Farm 18:56-7 Je '71
Short tips on pest control. C. E. Sommers.
Suc Farm 69:no4 C34 Mr '71
Ultrahigh-frequency electromagnetic fields
for weed control phytotoxicity and selectivity. F. S. Davis and others. bibliog il
Science 173:535-7 Ag 6 '71
Weed and insect control guide; symposium,
ed. by C. E. Sommers. il Suc Farm 69:no3
39-42+ F '71
See also
Aquatic weed control

Biological control
Old weapons are best. K. P. Shea. bibliog il
Environ 13:40-9 Je '71

Chemical control
How to get the most out of chemical weed
killers. Home Gard 58:70-2 F '71
Keep weeds out of small grains. Suc Farm
69:F8 Ap '71
Piggyback sprays: new way to clean out
weeds in soybeans. D. Seim. il Farm J 95:
29 Ap '71
Romance of roadside ragweed. F. E. Egler.
Cons 26:27 Ag '71
Use herbicides piggyback style for soybeans? il Suc Farm 69:B10 My '71
See also
Herbicides
WEED killers. See Herbicides
WEEDEN, Robert B.
Letter from Alaska: plan or plunder for the
American Arctic? il Liv Wildn 35:35-40
Sum '71
WEEDMAN, Daniel W. See Khachikian, E. E.
jt. auth.
WEEDS
See also
Cockleburs
Fireweed
Greens, Edible
Ragweed

Chemical control
See Weed control—Chemical control
Control
See Weed control
WEEKEND excursions. See Vacations
WEEKEND guests. See Guests
WEEKEND houses. See Vacation houses
WEEKS, Edward Augustus
Peripatetic reviewer. See issues of Atlantic
WEEKS, John. See Best, G. jt. auth.
WEEKS, John A.
Homemade weather station. il Cons 26:48+ D
'71
Some tips on studying water as a resource.
bibliog il Cons 25:48-9+ F '71
WEEKS, Louis
Father takes care of the baby. il Parents
Mag 46:60-1+ F '71
WEEMS, David B.
Case for the single woofer. il Pop Electr 34:
33-5+ My '71
Colossal woofer. il Pop Electr 34:47-53 Je '71
Continental speaker system. il Pop Electr
35:41-7 Ag '71
Labyrinth speakers for hi-fi. il Pop Electr
1:40-5 Ja '72
WEEPING. See Crying
WEESNER, Theodore
Hearing; story. New Yorker 47:35-41 Ap 10
'71
WEETE, John D. See Laseter, J. L. jt. auth.
WEEVILS
See also
Alfalfa weevils
WEEWIS; ballet. See Ballets—Criticisms
WEGENER woods, Mo. See Forests, State
WEHINGER, Peter A. and Mohler, O. C.
New Michigan 52-inch reflector. il Sky &
Tel 41:72-5 F '71
WEHMILLER, John, and Hare, P. E.
Racemization of amino acids in marine sediments. bibliog il Science 173:907-11 S 3 '71
WEHRLE, Leroy S.
Affluence and the world tomorrow. For Affairs 49:419-28 Ap '71
WEIDENAAR, Ilse Eerdmans
Children in pastel. il Design 72:32-3 midWint '71
WEIDENBAUM, Murray L.
Economy. See issues of Dun's November 1971-
about
Dun's newest faces. Duns 98:3 N '71 •
WEIDENFELD, Sir George
Authors & editors; B. A. Bannon. por Pub
W 199:17-19 Je 21 '71 •
WEIDER, Matt
Hike for Hope. il por Seventeen 30:20+ Ag
'71
WEIDLEIN, Edward R.
What's wrong with college admissions? Ed
Digest 37:35-8 D '71
WEIDNER, Edward W.
Communiversity. Nat Parks & Con Mag 45:
20 My '71
WEIGEL, Richard G. and others
Differences in course grades and student ratings of teacher performance. bibliog Sch &
Soc 99:60-2 Ja '71

WEIGHING machines
Swan song of mechanical weighing? J. Frye. Electr World 86:58-9 N '71
  See also
Scales (weighing instruments)

WEIGHT, Forrest F. and Votava, Jiri
Slow synaptic excitation in sympathetic ganglion cells: evidence for synaptic inactivation of potassium conductance. bibliog il Science 170:755-8; 172; 504 N 13 '70, Ap 30 '71

WEIGHT (physiology)
Height and weight at menarche and a hypothesis of critical body weights and adolescent events. R. E. Frisch and R. Revelle; discussion. bibliog Science 174:1148-9 D 10 '71
  See also
Corpulence
Diet
Exercise

WEIGHT reducing preparations
Are diet pills still a health menace? il Good H 172:197-9 Ap '71

WEIGHT throwing. See Shot putting

WEIGHT watchers, inc.
Weight watchers, beware! il Newsweek 77: 91 Ja 25 '71

WEIGHTLESSNESS
New experiments in space test physical effects of zero gravity. il Aviation W 94: 24 F 15 '71

WEIGHTS and measures
  See also
Cookery—Measurements
Gravity
Metric system
Scales (weighing instruments)
United States—Standards, National bureau of

WEIGL, Henry
Getting to the bakery on time. il pors Nations Bsns 59:90+ Ja '71

WEIKEL, Charles P.
Afloat with freight. il Har Yrs 11:19-23 O; 20-3 D '71

WEIL, Rolf A.
College youth attitudes today. Sch & Soc 99:246-7 Ap '71

WEIL, Simone
On the meaning of work. R. Coles. Atlan 228:103-4 O '71 •

WEIMAR republic. See Germany—History—1918-1933

WEIN, Bibi
Couple who live in the clouds. il Redbook 138:51+ D '71

WEINBERG, Abraham
Self-hypnosis diet. E. Frances. il Ladies Home J 88:52+ Je '71 •

WEINBERG, Alvin M.
Nuclear energy: a prelude to H. G. Wells' dream. For Affairs 49:407-18 Ap '71

WEINBERG, Carl
Schools and social change. Sch & Soc 99: 487-9+ D '71

WEINBERGER, Paul E. See Elder, M. E. jt. auth.

WEINER, Bernard
Orderly perversion of justice. Nation 212: 145-8 F 1 '71
(ed) See De Antonio, E. Radical scavenging

WEINER, Richard
Artists in prison. Am Artist 36:8 Ja '72

WEINER, Richard J. and others
Electrical activity of the hypothalamus: effects of intraventricular catecholamines. bibliog il Science 171:411-12 Ja 29 '71

WEINRAUB, Bernard
If you don't show violence the way it is . . . il pors N Y Times Mag p36-7+ D 12 '71

WEINSHEIMER, Doris Wilson
Put sugar peas on your list. il Horticulture 49:45 Je '71

WEINSHILBOUM, Richard M. and Axelrod, Julius
Serum dopamine-β-hydroxylase: decrease after chemical sympathectomy. bibliog il Science 173:931-4 S 3 '71
—and others
Proportional release of norepinephrine and dopamine-β-hydroxylase from sympathetic nerves. bibliog il Science 174:1349-51 D 24 '71

WEINSTEIN, Allen
Alger Hiss case revisited. Am Scholar 41: 121-32 Wint '71

WEINSTEIN, Arnold
Metamorphoses; dramatization of fables by Ovid. Criticism
  America 124:637 Je 19 '71 •
  Nation 212:606 My 10 '71 •
  New Yorker 47:89 My 8 '71 •
  Sat R 54:17 My 15 '71 •
  Time il 97:62 My 3 '71 •

WEINSTEIN, David
Do you call that a union? Nation 213:242-5 S 20 '71

WEINSTEIN, George W. and others
Extracellular recordings from human retinal ganglion cells. bibliog il Science 171:1021-2 Mr 12 '71

WEINSTEIN, Grace W.
Moving made easy. il Parents Mag 46:70-1+ F '71
Psychiatry comes of age. il Parents Mag 46: 66-7+ N '71
Schools where education comes alive. il Parents Mag 46:33-5+ Je '71
Tapping community talent. il Schol Teach Jr/Sr High p 14-15 N '71
Tapping the community. Sat R 54:53 Jl 17 '71

WEINSTEIN, Martin E.
Japan and the continental giants. bibliog f Cur Hist 60:193-9+ Ap '71

WEINSTEIN, Raymond M. and Brill, N. Q.
Conceptions of mental illness by patients and normals. bibliog il Ment Hy 55:101-8 Ja '71

WEINSTOCK, Herbert
Recordings. Sat R 54:79 Mr 27; 55 Ap 24; 52 Ag 28 '71
Obituary
  Sat R 54:79 N 27 '71. I. Kolodin

WEINTRAUB, Arthur E. and Knorr, D. J.
Mid-Hudson. il Cons 25:6-9 F '71

WEINTRAUB, Herbert
Getting passive students to speak up. il Todays Ed 60:21 Mr '71

WEINTRAUB, Sidney
U.S. policy toward a changing Latin America; adaptation of address, January 29, 1971. Dept State Bul 64:550-4 Ap 26 '71

WEIS, Norman D.
Triple take at Double Lake. il Outdoor Life 148:66-9+ O '71

WEISBERG, Barry
Letter from Singapore. Nation 214:51-2 Ja 10 '72
Offshore oil boom. il Nation 212:294-5 Mr 8 '71; Same with title Will an oil boom change U.S. policies? Cur 129:47-51 My '71

WEISBERGER, Bernard A.
Liberty and disunion. il Am Heritage 22:22-5+ O '71
Paper trust. il Am Heritage 22:38-41+ Ap '71

WEISINGER, Mort
Play the calorie game. il Todays Health 49: 58-60 Jl '71
Trade winds; Miss America; interview. ed. by C. Amory. Sat R 54:8+ O 2 '71

WEISKOPF, Herman
Archery. il Sports Illus 34:52+ F 15 '71
Baseball's week. Sports Illus 35:107 S 27; 84 O 4 '71
Bowling. il Sports Illus 35:44-5 Ag 2 '71
Give me a brr, bmm, bmm, brr, bmm, bmm. il por Sports Illus 34:33-5 Mr 29 '71

WEISMAN, John
(ed) See Wambaugh, J. Authors and editors

WEISMILLER, Edward
Common enough story; poem. Am Scholar 41:63 Wint '71

WEISS, Bette F. and others
L-Dopa disaggregation of brain polysomes and elevation of brain tryptophan. bibliog il Science 173:833-5 Ag 27 '71

WEISS, Herbert V. and others
Mercury in a Greenland ice sheet: evidence of recent input by man. bibliog il Science 174:692-4 N 12 '71
Selenium and sulfur in a Greenland ice sheet: relation to fossil fuel combustion. bibliog il Science 172:261-3 Ap 16 '71

WEISS, Jay M.
Rat race. il por Newsweek 78:74-5 S 27 '71 •

WEISS, Jeffrey H.
How auxiliaries increase productivity of dentists. Mo Labor R 94:63-4 Ap '71

WEISS, Margaret R.
Cartier-Bresson's France. il Sat R 54:46-8 F 13 '71
Photography (cont) il Sat R 54:84-5 Mr 13; 44-5 Ap 3; 52-3 My 15; 44-5 Je 12; 30-1 Jl 3; 36-7 Ag 7; 58-9 O 2; 20-1 D 18 '71

WEISS, Peter, 1916-
Hölderlin. Criticism
  Newsweek 78:92 O 11 '71 •

WEISS, Robert Frank, and others
Altruism is rewarding. bibliog il Science 171: 1262-3 Mr 26 '71

WEISS, W. H.
Breaking the fear barrier. il Nations Bsns 59:64-5 Jl '71

WEISS-ROSMARIN, Trude
Is God she? And so what? Commonweal 94:374 Jl 23 '71

WEISSLER, Paul
Facts on glass tire. il Mech Illus 67:65-7 Ja
'71
WEIZMANN, Chaim
Young Weizmann. Commentary 51:83-7 Je
'71 *
WELCH, Claude
Boom in religion studies. por Time 98:83-4
O 18 '71 *
WELCH, James
Inner world where poets wander. J. Kessler.
Sat R 54:50 O 2 '71 *
WELCH, Louie
City-county drainage plans come first. il Am
City 86:70+ Ag '71
WELCH, Mary Scott
Hypoglycemia. Ladies Home J 88:98+ N '71
Secondhouse dilemma: where do you really
live? House B 113:71+ Je '71
WELCH, Susan
Vietnam: how the press went along; ex-
cerpt from Communication in international
politics, ed. by R. L. Merritt. Nation 213:
327-30 O 11 '71
WELCOME to Charnel Castle; story. See Don-
leavy, J. P.
WELD, Tuesday
If it's Monday, it must be Tuesday; inter-
view, ed. by M. Ronan. por Sr Schol 99:
24 D 13 '71
WELDERS
Welders that can weld you dead. il Con-
sumer Rep 36:584-5 O '71
Welding equipment for the home shop. B.
Berger. il Mech Illus 67:106-7+ D '71
WELDING
See also
Steel—Welding

Safety measures
Tips for safe farm welding. Suc Farm 69:C22
N '71
WELDING machines. See Welders
WELDON, Dawn
Nocturne; poem. Seventeen 31:90 Ja '72
WELDY, Gilbert R.
Should we enter that contest? Ed Digest 37:
39-41 D '71
WELDY, Keith
How to install a holding tank on your boat.
il Mech Illus 67:100+ Ap '71
WELFARE. See Public welfare
WELFARE workers. See Social workers
WELISH, Marjorie
Calder tapestries. il Craft Horiz 31:40-1 D
'71
WELKE, Elton
Hawaii. il Bet Hom & Gard 49:163-8+ N '71
WELKE, Harold C.
Mr Barr; story. Todays Ed 60:22-3 My '71
WELL-loved wife; story. See Gordon, E. E.
WELLEN, Edward
Adaptation, year 2000; poem. Sat R 54:4 Je
19 '71
WELLER, Dorothy
Our finest achievement. Chr Cent 88:1263-4
O 27 '71
WELLER, Michael
Moonchildren. Criticism
Newsweek il 78:114-15 D 13 '71 *
Sat R 54:12+ D 11 '71 *
WELLER, Ralph Albert
World's fair stunt that lifted skylines. il
pors Nations Bsns 59:82-3 Ja '71
WELLER method of tornado detection. See
Television in meteorology
WELLES, Benjamin
H-L-S of the C.I.A. il pors N Y Times Mag
p34-5+ Ap 18 '71
WELLES, Orson
All's Welles. C. L. Westerbeck, jr. Common-
weal 94:286-7 My 28 '71 *
Night the martians didn't land. il Life
70:56B F 19 '71 *
Onward and upward with the arts. P. Kael.
por New Yorker 47:43-52+ F 20; 44-50+
F 27 '71 *
WELLFLEET. See Cape Cod
WELLINGTON estate. See Virginia—Historic
houses, etc.
WELLMAN, Harry
Driver falls into drink as Home Brew spills.
il Motor B & S 127:33 My '71 *
WELLMAN, Harvey R.
Department discusses international aspects
of President Nixon's drug control program;
statement, July 8, 1971. Dept State Bul 65:
157-60 Ag 9 '71
Drug abuse: a challenge to U.S.-Turkish cooperation in the seventies; address, December 14, 1970. Dept State Bul 64:140-6 F 1 '71

International aspects of drug abuse control;
address, April 16, 1971. il Dept State Bul
64:639-47 My 17 '71
WELLMAN industries
Listening to America. B. Moyers; discussion.
Harper 242:6+ F '71
WELLS, Chris
Sociology of dumb; one evening too many
with Carson, Griffin, and Cavett. il Esquire
75:102-8+ My '71
WELLS, H. G.
H. G. Wells: the man who discovered tomor-
row. J. Williamson. il pors Sat R 55:12-15
Ja 1 '72 *
WELLS, Jerry
Many moods of modular. B. Plumb. il pors
Am Home 74:76+ O '71 *
WELLS, R. A.
First Newtonian. bibliog il por Sky & Tel
42:342-4 D '71
WELLS, William
Contact. il Flying 90:54-5+ Ja '72
WELLS
Old records and new technology find a water
supply; Marion, Ind. P. J. Satterthwaite. il
Am City 86:68+ S '71
See also
Springs
WELLS, Waste disposal. See Trade waste dis-
posal
WELLS Fargo bank, San Francisco. See San
Francisco—Banks
WELLS Fargo express company
Wells, Fargo's Jekyll and Hyde. R. H. Dil-
lon. il por Am West 8:28-33+ Mr '71
WELSH, Pat M. and Liepman, P.
This is earth calling Berkeley. il pors Pub
W 200:38-40 Jl 5; 62-3 Jl 12 '71
WELSH pottery. See Pottery, Welsh
WELTON, C. G.
Freelance job aid: promotion packet. il Writ-
ers Digest 51:27 Ag '71
WELTY, Eudora
Eudora Welty's world in the '30s; excerpts
from One time, one place. il Mlle 73:162-
5+ S '71
about
Inconstant past. B. Gill. New Yorker 47:66-8
D 25 '71 *
Symbol and theme in Eudora Welty's Petri-
fied man. L. J. Richmond. Engl J 60:1201-
3 D '71 *
WEMYSS, William Hatch
Living with antiques. T. K. Connor. il An-
tiques 100:606-10 O '71 *
WENATCHEE national forest, Wash. See Na-
tional forests
WENDELBURG, Tom
Can we save Rock Creek? il Outdoor Life
147:64-7+ F '71
WENDELL, Barbara. See Wood, P. jt. auth.
WENESE S.A. See Atomic power industry—
Europe, Western
WENNERSTROM, Bruce
How we captured the world land speed record
for electric cars. il Mech Illus 67:72-5+
D '71
We ride the moon car! il Mech Illus 67:37-
8+ Ag '71
WENSEL, Floyd
Iowa eye-opener. il Outdoor Life 147:96-7+ Ap
'71
WENTZ, Richard E.
I'd rather dance with the Jews. Chr Cent 88:
830-2 Jl 7 '71
WERNER, Alfred
Albrecht Dürer: master draftsman. il por
Am Artist 35:24-9+ S '71
Gerhard Marcks, the form of nature. il por
Am Artist 35:32-7+ D '71
WERNER, Jesse
GAF's anchor man. por Bsns W p76 Mr 20
'71 *
Inside the GAF battle. N. A. Martin. il pors
Duns 97:45-7 Ap '71 *
WERNER, M. R.
Horse racing. Sports Illus 34:69-70 Je 14 '71
WERNER, Walt
Man who busts avalanches. il Mech Illus 68:
97+ Ja '72 *
WERNER, Walter
Thebouidienne; interview. New Yorker 47:44-
5 N 6 '71
—See Cary, W. L. jt. auth.
WERTHER, Betty
Sheila Hicks at Rabat. il por Craft Horiz 31:
30-3 Je '71
WERTHER; opera. See Massenet, J.
WERTHER (literary character) See Characters
in literature
WESLEY, Charles Harris
Negro history week, 1971. por Negro Hist
Bul 34:59 Mr '71 *

WESLEY, Donald A.
Classroom control should be a vital part of teacher education. bibliog Clear House 45: 346-9 F '71

WESLEY, Richard
Black terror. Criticism
  America 125:534 D 18 '71 *
  Nation 213:572-3 N 29 '71 *
  New Yorker 47:119-20 N 20 '71 *
  Newsweek 78:110 N 29 '71 *
  Sat R 55:38 Ja 8 '72

WESLEYAN church. See Methodist church in the United States

WESLEYAN university press
Reprieve for Wesleyan; advisory group formed. Pub W 199:44 Je 21 '71

WESSEL, Morris A.
Toilet training the easy way. il Parents Mag 46:36-7+ Je '71

WESSELLS, Norman K.
How living cells change shape; with biographical sketch. il Sci Am 225:12, 76-82 O '71
—and others
Microfilaments in cellular and developmental processes. bibliog il Science 171:135-43; 173: 358-9 Ja 15, Jl 23 '71

WESSELLS, R. G.
Tips on purchasing from the British. il Am City 86:90+ Mr '71

WESSON, Robert G.
German policy toward east Europe. Cur Hist 60:295-301+ My '71

WEST, Anne Grant
Women's liberation: or, Exploding the fairy princess myth. bibliog f Schol Teach Jr/Sr High p6-11 N '71

WEST, Anthony
Can love medicines make you sexier? il Vogue 158:160-1+ O 1 '71
Great romantic travellers. il Vogue 157:90-3+ Ap 15 '71
Love flowers. Vogue 158:150-5+ D '71
Movies. Vogue 157:71 Mr 15 '71
Nakedness v. nudity. il Vogue 157:116-19 My '71

WEST, Carolyn
Lure of Baja. il Yachting 129:48-9+ Ap '71

WEST, Charles C.
Mission eastern Europe: toward a new agenda. Chr Cent 89:13-15 Ja 5 '72

WEST, Jack
Anatomy of a powerboat (cont) il Yachting 129:70-1+ F; 70-1+ Mr '71
How's the weather? il Yachting 130:68-9+ D '71
Speed curves. il Yachting 130:58-9+ Ag '71
Why? When? What? about DSB, SSB and VHF radiotelephones? il Yachting 130:63+ Jl '71

WEST, Jessamyn
Be gentle, be happy and give your child the stars for Christmas. il Redbook 138:66-7+ D '71
Real Pat Nixon. il pors Good H 172:66-71+ F '71; Same abr. with title Pat Nixon: as she is. Read Digest 98:129-33 Ap '71

WEST, John Carl
John West of South Carolina. por Time 97:18 My 31 '71 *

WEST, Morris Langlo
Exclusive interview with Morris West; ed. by S. Steiner. por Writers Digest 51:30-3+ F '71

WEST, Dame Rebecca
Q: do the claims of conscience outweigh the duties of citizenship? por Esquire 76: 157+ D '71

WEST, Thomas
Master-planned for progress. il Parks & Rec 6:36+ Mr '71

WEST, William W.
English literature for the disadvantaged; here's how, but why? Engl J 60:902-5 O '71

WEST
Two screen cowboys talk about the reel West & the real West; interviews, ed. by M. Ronan. J. Wayne; B. Johnson. il pors Sr Schol 99:10-11 D 6 '71
  See also
Camping—Western states
Fishing—Western states
Frontier and pioneer life—United States
Gardens—Western states
Geology—Western states
Hunting—Western states
Irrigation—Western states
Land—Western states
Northwest
Paleontology
Skis and skiing—Western states
Wildlife conservation—Western states

Bibliography
Books in brief. J. M. Offers. See issues of American West

Description and travel
[Month] travel in and beyond the West. See issues of Sunset
West coast wanderings. C. Pepper. See issues of Travel
  See also
Pacific Crest trail
Southwest—Description and travel

History
Exploitation of the American frontier; excerpts. W. R. Jacobs. Am West 8:48 My '71
  See also
California—History
California trail
Lewis and Clark expedition
Wells Fargo express company

Social history
Mercer girls. S. C. Shulsinger. il por Am West 8:28-9 Jl '71

WEST AFRICAN literature. See African literature

WEST ALLIS, Wis.
Trash-box demise improves environment. il Am City 86:8 Ja '71

WEST BERLIN. See Berlin (West Berlin)

WEST CHESTER, Pa.
Keep that stored water fresh. J. R. McCullough. il por Am City 86:63-5 Ap '71

WEST COAST commodity exchange. See Commodity exchanges

WEST COVINA, Calif.
Instant communication. W. Vanettes. il Am City 86:130+ My '71

WEST in art
Gold rush in Western art. il U S News 70:81-2 My 17 '71
Paul Kane's frontier. ed. by J. R. Harper Review
  Am West 8:49 S '71. D. G. Pike
Wide open approach to the wide open spaces; publication of The art of the Old West, by David C. Hunt and Paul A. Rossi. A. DeMirjian, jr. il Pub W 200:30-3 N 1 '71

WEST in literature
It don't hurt much, ma'am; gunfight myths of western fiction and film. J. S. Packer. il Am Heritage 22:66-9 F '71
  See also
Southwest in literature

WEST INDIAN cookery. See Cookery, West Indian

WEST INDIAN prints. See Prints

WEST INDIES
  See also
Anguilla (island)
Antigua (island)
Dominican Republic
Fishing—West Indies
Grenada
Jamaica
Leeward Islands
St Martin (island)
Virgin Islands

Description and travel
West Indies vacation. il Ebony 26:148-50+ Je '71
  See also
Barbados—Description and travel

Economic conditions
Black nationalism: a growing worry in the Caribbean. C. Migdail. il U S News 70:52-4 Mr 29 '71

WEST INDIES, BRITISH
  See also
Anguilla (island)
Bahama Islands
Bequia (island)
British Virgin Islands
Cayman Islands
Church and state in Jamaica
Dominica (island)
Grenadines (islands)
Tortola (island)

WEST INDIES, FRENCH
Guide to the beauty of the French West Indies. H. Sutton. il McCalls 99:90-1+ N '71
  See also
Martinique

WEST INDIES in art
Colonial life in the West Indies as depicted in prints. N. Connell. il Antiques 99:732-7 My '71
Some early printed views of the West Indies. N. Connell. il Antiques 99:127-31 Ja '71

WEST NEW YORK, N.J.
Garbage compactors end air-pollution problem. il Am City 86:28 Je '71
WEST PAKISTAN. See Pakistan
WEST POINT military academy. See United States military academy, West Point
WEST side, New York. See New York (city)
WEST VIEW, Pa.
West View's water plant is different. E. R. Powell. il Am City 86:103-4+ Je '71
WEST VIRIGINIA
See also
Libraries—West Virginia
New River
Public health—West Virginia
Reclamation of land—West Virginia
Wilderness areas—West Virginia

Description and travel
Going west to West Virginia. L. W. Swift and R. W. Swift. il pors Am For 77:16-19 Mr '71
West Virginia: the paradox of a forgotten state. M. Brooks. il Nat Wildlife 10:56-63 D '71

Politics and government
Break for West Virginia. W. E. Chilton, 3d. Nation 213:390-2 O 25 '71

Social conditions
Mending lives at a PCC. the West Virginia parent and child center. M. P. Berson. il Am Ed 7:22-7 D '71
WESTBERG, Karl, and others
Carbon monoxide: its role in photochemical smog formation. bibliog il Science 171:10-13 15 Mr 12 '71
WESTCHESTER classic golf tournament. See Golf—Tournaments
WESTCHESTER golf classic. See Golf—Tournaments
WESTER, R. E. and Parker, W. R.
Mini hotbed and propagating frame. il Horticulture 49:42-3 Mr '71
WESTERBECK, Colin L. jr
Importance of being Oscar. il Commonweal 94:139-44 Ap 16 '71
Screen. See occasional issues of Commonweal
WESTERFIELD, Nancy G.
Air horns: poem. Horn Bk 47:461 O '71
Martha, who has chosen the lesser part; poem. Chr Cent 88:1105 S 22 '71
Tomb effigies in a village church, Sussex; poem. Nation 213:158 Ag 30 '71
WESTERMARK, Tory. See Gooch, B. N. S. jt. auth.
WESTERN air lines
American-Western merger opposed. L. Doty. Aviation W 96:20 Ja 3 '72
Triple play; Anchorage, Honolulu and Los Angeles. M. Miller. il Travel 136:74-5 Ag '71
Western holders favor merger. Aviation W 94:27 Mr 29 '71
WESTERN amateur astronomers (organization)
Western amateurs meet in Hawaii. M. J. Morrow. il Sky & Tel 42:285-6 N '71
WESTERN antique auto supply (firm)
Vintage tin Canadian style. J. Chalmers. il Hot Rod 24:120-2 O '71
WESTERN civilization. See Civilization
WESTERN cookery. See Cookery, American
WESTERN energy supply and transmission associates
Smog over the Great Plains; WEST companies in the Four Corners region. J. Waugh. Nation 212:753-5 Je 14 '71
Wild, wild WEST. J. Waugh. New Repub 164:10 Mr 27 '71
WESTERN films. See Moving pictures—Western films
WESTERN forestry center, Portland, Ore.
Land of the trees. J. B. Craig. il Am For 77:10-11 S '71
WESTERN hemisphere
See also
Airlines—International services—Western hemisphere
America
WESTERN hemlock. See Hemlock
WESTERN home awards
Announcing the 1971-72 Western home awards. il Sunset 146:98-9 F '71
Eighth biennial round of the American institute of architects-Sunset magazine Western home awards. il Sunset 147:76-89 O '71
1971-72 Western home awards. il Sunset 146: 125 Je '71

WESTERN Michigan university, Kalamazoo
Black Americana studies. C. L. Lee. Negro Hist Bul 34:114-15 My '71
WESTERN music. See Folk music, American
WESTERN opera theater. See San Francisco opera association
WESTERN Pacific railroad company
Railroad doctor. T. J. Murray. por Duns 98: 68 S '71
WESTERN red cedar. See Arborvitæ
WESTERN states. See West
WESTERN Teton wilderness area (proposed) See Wilderness areas—Wyoming
WESTERN union corporation
Getting the message at Western union. A. A. Butkus. il por Duns 98:39-42 O '71
WESTERN union telegraph company
What hath profit wrought! Nation 212:677 My 31 '71
WESTERNERS
Two screen cowboys talk about the reel West & the real West; interviews, ed. by M. Ronan. J. Wayne; B. Johnson. il pors Sr Schol 99:10-11 D 6 '71
WESTING, Arthur H.
Big bomb. il por Environ 13:13-15 N '71
Ecocide in Indochina; with biographical sketch. il Natur Hist 80:8. 56-61 Mr '71
Leveling the jungle. il Environ 13:8-12 N '71
—See Haseltine, W. jt. auth.
WESTINGHOUSE, George
Mighty transformation in electricity. G. L. Wilcox. il pors Nations Bsns 59:92-3 Ja '71 •
WESTINGHOUSE electric corporation
Mighty transformation in electricity. G. L. Wilcox. il pors Nations Bsns 59:92-3 Ja '71
Westinghouse gets torpedoed. Bsns W p 19 Jl 10 '71
Westinghouse's third big step is overseas. il Bsns W p64-7 O 2 '71
WESTINGHOUSE electric nuclear systems Europe. See Atomic power industry—Europe. Western
WESTLAKE, Donald Edwin
In Anguilla it's the spirit of '71. il N Y Times Mag p24-5+ My 23 '71
WESTMINSTER, Colo.
City maps that work. H. B. Browning. il Am City 86:74-5 Je '71
3 cities, innovative reporting. il Am City 86:132+ Je '71
WESTMORELAND, William Childs
General and the Christian college: where was the dissent? D. M. Lynch. Chr Cent 88: 724-6 Je 9 '71 •
WESTMORELAND coal company
Coal king from Philly. por Forbes 108:29-30 S 1 '71
WESTON, Edward
Gallery; photographs. Life 71:6-7 S 24 '71
WESTON, Melissa
One girl five looks. pors Mlle 74:142-5 N '71 •
WESTOVER air force base. See Air bases
WESTPHALEN, Leonard
What Westphalen is doing. H. Keppler. il Mod Phot 35:76-7+ O '71 •
WETBACKS. See Mexicans in the United States
WETHERILL, George W.
Of time and the moon. bibliog il Science 173: 383-92 Jl 30 '71
WETLANDS
Prairie potholes. K. W. Harmon. il Nat Parks & Con Mag 45:25-8 Mr '71
See also
Marshes
WEXFORD festival. See Music festivals—Ireland
WEXLER, Jacqueline (Grennan)
We encourage our youth to rebel. por McCalls 98:63+ Ap '71
WEXLER, Jodi
That magnificent girl in The love machine. M. English. il pors Look 35:30-3 Ag 10 '71 •
WEYDEN, Roger van der
Out of a cottage; rediscovered masterpiece: Saint Ivo of Chartres. il Time 97:66-7 Ap 5 '71 •
WEYERHAEUSER, John Philip, 1899-1956
Tree farm and how it grew. J. E. Nolan. il por Nations Bsns 59:94-5 Ja '71 •
WEYERHAEUSER company
Brash challenger and the angry giant. il Forbes 108:30 D 15 '71
Ecologist in the paper industry. il Bsns W p54 Mr 6 '71
Tree farm and how it grew. J. E. Nolan. il por Nations Bsns 59:94-5 Ja '71
WEYR, Thomas
Letter from Vienna. Pub W 200:pt2 178-80 S 27 '71
WHALE sounds. See Animal sounds

WHIRLWINDS
Amateur scientist; experiments with wind; a pendulum anemometer and miniature torture tornadoes. V. G. Blanchette. il Sci Am 225:110-12 O '71

WHISKEY
Billion-dollar gamble in whisky; promoting light whiskey. il Time 97:84-5 Ap 12 '71
Blithe spirits: American light whiskey. il Esquire 76:136-7 O '71
Delectations; a visit to the Beam bourbon plant in Kentucky. N. Hazelton. Nat R 23: 533+, 770 My 18, Jl 13 '71
Distillers serve up new brands. il Bsns W p80-2 Mr 6 '71
Light whiskey: will it be your cup of tea. R. J. Misch. House B 113:114 S '71
Scotch makers play it straight; boom in malt whiskey, with editorial comment. il Bsns W p33, 68 Ag 28 '71
Those new light whiskeys. H. Shuldiner. il Pop Sci 199:69-71+ O '71
    See also
Distilleries

Prices
Import thaw is no help to Scotch; Japan. il Bsns W p51 Jl 17 '71

WHISTLER, James Abbott McNeill
Butterfly and the old ox. T. Reff. il pors Art N 70:26-31+ Mr '71 •

WHISTLERS (radio waves) See Radio waves

WHISTLES
    See also
Locomotives—Whistles

WHITAKER, Frederic
Colorful Southwest of R. Brownell McGrew. il Am Artist 35:72-9+ Mr '71
Wax engraving technique of Roy P. Madsen. il Am Artist 35:50-5 My '71

WHITAKER, Harry A. See McAdam, D. W. jt. auth.

WHITCOMB, Carl E.
Maximizing tree growth. Horticulture 49:44-5+ Ap '71

WHITCOMB, Roberta J.
Trail cookery simplified. il Outdoor Life 147: 74-7+ Je '71

WHITCOMB, Roger S.
United States and east Europe. bibliog f Cur Hist 60:263-8+ My '71

WHITE, B. Frank, and Barnes, L. B.
Power networks in the appraisal process. bibliog f il Harvard Bsns R 49:101-9 My '71

WHITE, Carrie
Hair talk; interview with California haircutter; ed. by N. Bertin. pors Mlle 73:208-9 My '71

WHITE, Clarence H.
Gallery; photographs. Life 71:8-9 S 10 '71

WHITE, Donald F.
Excerpt from testimony, March 4, 1971. Cong Digest 50:284+ N '71

WHITE, Dori
Flight from fear; story. Good H 172:88-9 F '71

WHITE, Dorothy Ann
Die honkie die; poem. Negro Hist Bul 34: 87 Ap '71

WHITE, Eartha M. M.
Eartha M. M. White, 94, daughter of slave, gets Lane Bryant award. il por Aging 198:11 Ap '71 •

WHITE, Edgar
Life and times of J. Walter Smintheus. Criticism
New Yorker 47:96 My 1 '71 •

WHITE, Ellington
Not a place that appeals to everyone. il Sports Illus 34:40-2+ My 31 '71

WHITE, Elwyn Brooks
Faith of a writer; remarks, December 2, 1971. Pub W 200:29 D 6 '71
Letter from the East. New Yorker 47:35-7 Mr 27; 27-9 Jl 24 '71

    about
Book committee elects Stevens, honors E. B. White. il Pub W 200:34 D 20 '71 •
E. B. White receives National literature medal. por Pub W 200:17 N 29 '71 •

WHITE, Eula T. and Friedman, Roberta
Sex is not a four-lettered word. bibliog il pors Wilson Lib Bul 46:153-62 O '71

WHITE, Fred R.
And don't forget the old products. il Hi Fi 21:62-4 O '71

WHITE, Henry C.
What one state is doing about the burden of relief; interview. il por U S News 71: 65-8 O 25 '71

WHITE, Ian. See Hickman, K. jt. auth.

WHITE, Irvin L.
Energy policy-making: limitations of a conceptual model. il por Bul Atom Sci 27: 20-6 O '71

WHITE, Jack E. Jr
Unchanged South. il Ebony 26:126-8+ Ag '71

WHITE, Jean
Programed tutor. il Am Ed 7:18-21 D '71

WHITE, Jim
Transmitter for the neglected band. il Pop Electr 1:58-61 Ja '72

WHITE, John B.
American heritage dictionary. il Wilson Lib Bul 45:674-8 Mr '71

WHITE, Joshua
Videomagnifier; interview. New Yorker 47: 19-20 Ag 28 '71

WHITE, Joyce L.
Church libraries: unrecognized resources. il Am Lib 2:397-9 Ap '71

WHITE, Ken
American designer looks at European bookstores. il Pu bW 199:117-19 My 31 '71

WHITE, M. G. and others
Acceleration of nitrogen ions to 7.4 Gev in the Princeton particle accelerator. bibliog il Science 174:1121-3 D 10 '71

WHITE, Margaret Bourke-. See Bourke-White, M.

WHITE, Nancy
Grande dame departs. il por Time 98:47 D 13 '71 •

WHITE, Oswald
Why minority publishing? ed. by B. Chambers. il pors Pub W 199:50 Mr 15 '71

WHITE, Peter T.
Barehanded battle to cleanse the Bay. il Nat Geog 139:866-81 Je '71
It's here, the computer revolution. Read Digest 98:133-7 My '71
Mosaic of cultures. il Nat Geog 139:296-329 Mr '71

WHITE, Philip L.
(ed) Let's talk about food; questions and answers. See issues of Today's health
Which diets work, which don't; interview. ed. by R. Petty. il Todays Health 49:58-62 S '71

WHITE, Ralph K.
Propaganda: morally questionable and morally unquestionable techniques. bibliog f Ann Am Acad 398:26-35 N '71

WHITE, Robert J.
Antivivisection: the reluctant Hydra. Am Scholar 40:503-512 Sum '71

WHITE, Robert Mayer
Congratulations, Dr White. il por(p53) Weatherwise 24:55 Ap '71 •

WHITE, Robin
Mixed relations; story. Seventeen 29:122-3 N '70

WHITE, Stanley
Classical walk. New Yorker 47:47-8 N 20 '71 •

WHITE, Theodore H.
Lindsay choice now: to preach or to run. il por Life 71:66-7 Ag 20 '71

WHITE, William D. and Robbins, Anthony
Role of on-the-job training in a clinical laboratory. bibliog f il Mo Labor R 94:65-9 Mr '71

WHITE, William Mathews, 1939-
Bitter lessons. por Forbes 108:52 N 15 '71 •

WHITE Bull (Sioux chief)
Echoes of the Little Bighorn. D. H. Miller. il pors Am Heritage 22:35-6 Je '71

WHITE Cloud wilderness area. See Wilderness areas—Idaho

WHITE collar workers. See Office workers

WHITE consolidated industries, inc.
White frees Allis in record stock sale. Bsns W p25-6 F 13 '71

WHITE Cow Bull (Sioux Indian)
Echoes of the Little Bighorn. D. H. Miller. il pors Am Heritage 22:32-4 Je '71 •

WHITE deer. See Deer

WHITE dwarf stars. See Stars, Dwarf

WHITE footed mice. See Mice, White footed

WHITE gospel music. See Church music

WHITE holes (astronomy) See Astrophysics

WHITE House
Christmas at the White House. P. R. Nixon. il House & Gard 140:62-9 D '71
Grand acquisitor; curator. C. E. Conger. il por Newsweek 77:26+ Mr 1 '71
Kennedy portraits; portraits by Aaron Shikler. pors U S News 70:88 F 15 '71
Praying with the President in the White House. E. B. Friske. il N Y Times Mag p 14-15+ Ag 8 '71
Something different this spring. H. Sidey. Life 70:2B Ap 23 '71

WHITE House—*Continued*
White House Christmas, 1971; photo report.
U S News 71:40-1 D 27 '71
See also
Presidents—United States
WHITE House conference of mayors
Cities are finished. S. Alsop. Newsweek 77:
100 Ap 5 '71
WHITE House conference on aging, 1971
Aging conference staff draws early criticism.
Har Yrs 11:5+ Ap '71
Aging groups trained in policy formulation
as preparation for White House conference.
il Aging 196:3 F '71
Arkansas artist wins portrait contest plus
trip to White House conference. Aging 205:9
N '71
Arthur Flemming named chairman White
House conference on aging. T. Schuchat.
Har Yrs 11:4 Je '71
Congress responds to proposals raised for
conference on aging. T. Schuchat. Har
Yrs 11:4-5 O '71
Delegates to White House conference being
named by states, organizations. Aging 201:
6+ Jl '71
Flemming named conference chairman; planning board rules on delegates. il Aging
199:3-4+ My '71
Invitation to a design world: second reader.
O. W. Coulter and D. J. Lewis. il Aging
199:13-28 My '71
More than 4,000 to attend White House con-
ference on aging. il Aging 205:4-5 N '71
1971 White House conference on aging, first
reader. il Aging 195:15-22 Ja '71
1971 White House conference work seen vi-
tal to aging now and in 21st century. Ag-
ing 199:6 My '71
Open forum night at conference on aging.
Har Yrs 11:5 Ag '71
Panel debate possible outcome of White
House conference on aging; symposium. il
Aging 205:13+ N '71
Portrait contest opens for cover of White
House conference program. il Aging 198:5
Ap '71
Quotations from state executives on aging.
Aging 205:11 N '71
Second White House conference hopes to
avoid mistakes of past. T. Schuchat. Har
Yrs 11:4 N '71
Senator Church views the conference: inter-
view. F. Church. pors Har Yrs 11:9-12 N '71
Senior voters. il Time 98:12-13 D 13 '71
Toward a national policy on aging: every
person counts; address, May 15, 1971. B. A.
Gunn. Vital Speeches 37:597-9 Jl 15 '71
WHCOA stamped envelopes, 40 million, is-
sued to honor conference. il Aging 205:8 N
'71
White House conference. il Har Yrs 11:6-8
N '71
White House conference program planned for
open discussion. il Aging 204:3-4 O '71
Year of the White House conference: toward
a national policy on aging. J. B. Martin.
Aging 195:3 Ja '71
WHITE House conference on children, 1970
1970 White House conference; recommenda-
tions. il PTA Mag 65:27-8 Ja '71
White House conference on children. T. J.
Cottle. il Sat R 54:56-7+ F 20 '71
White House conference on children. D. R.
Dunn. il Parks & Rec 6:25-8+ Mr '71
WHITE House conference on the industrial
world ahead (proposed)
Will the businessman become master of
change? Nations Bsns 59:72 D '71
WHITE House conference on youth, 1971
Discontent of the straights; gathering at
Y.M.C.A. camping center in the Colorado
Rockies. il Time 97:39 My 3 '71
Game plan for a youth conference. J.
Mathews. Nation 212:627-8 My 17 '71
Heavy snow and cheerless rhetoric in the
mountains of Colorado. D. Mitchell. Harper
243:24-6 Ag '71
Snow country; meeting at Estes Park, Colo.
J. Morgenstern. il Newsweek 77:28 My 3
'71
White House conference on youth. B. B.
Stretch. il Sat R 54:66-7+ My 22 '71
White House youth conference hits religious
hypocrisy, other evils. Chr Cent 88:615 My
19 '71
Youth conference in Colorado. V. Sims. il
Sr Schol 98:14-15 My 17 '71
WHITE House council on environmental qual-
ity. See United States—Council on environ-
mental quality
WHITE House dogs. See Dogs
WHITE House entertaining. See Government
entertaining
WHITE House fellows. See Scholarships and
fellowships

WHITE House helicopters. See Helicopters,
Government
WHITE House office. See United States—Ex-
ecutive office of the president
WHITE House receptions. See Government en-
tertaining
WHITE House staff. See Public officers
WHITE House weddings. See Weddings
WHITE motor corporation
Bunkie Knudsen redesigns White motor. il
por Bsns W p44+ O 30 '71
Knudsen returns in a White truck. Bsns W
p22-3 My 1 '71
WHITE MOUNTAIN national forest. See Na-
tional forests
WHITE-Negro relations. See Race relations
WHITE owls. See Owls
WHITE PLAINS, N.Y, public library
Parking under a library. il Am City 86:124-5
S '71
WHITE racism. See Racism
WHITE SANDS NATIONAL MONUMENT
White sands are for sliding. il Sunset 147:
28 S '71
WHITE Sox (baseball) See Baseball clubs
WHITE tailed deer hunting. See Deer hunting
WHITE whales. See Whales
WHITE wines. See Wine
WHITEFISH
See also
Cookery—Fish
WHITEFISH fishing
New ice-fishing action. J. O. Cartier. il por
Outdoor Life 147:58-9+ Mr '71
WHITEHEAD, Edwin C.
Man in a fish bowl. il por Forbes 107:19-20
Je 15 '71 *
WHITEHEAD, James
Poetry quarterly. Sat R 54:37-41+ D 18 '71
WHITEHILL, Walter Muir
Peruvian problem in historic preservation. il
Antiques 99:720-4 My '71
WHITEHORN, Ethel
Motion picture previews. See issues of PTA
magazine
WHITELEATHER, Melvin K.
(ed) Seven polarizing issues in America to-
day. bibliog f il Ann Am Acad 397:1-139
S '71
WHITESEL, Lita
Designing cardboard play equipment. il Sch
Arts 70:24-5 Mr '71
WHITESIDE, Thomas
Reporter at large (cont) New Yorker 47:54+
Ag 14 '71
Selling death: cigarette ads in the maga-
zines. New Repub 164:15-17 Mr 27 '71
WHITEWATER; story. See Horgan, P.
WHITING, Allen S.
China: the struggle for power. New Repub
165:19-21 D 4 '71
Negotiating with China. New Repub 165:17-
19 Jl 10 '71
That Chinese threat; adaptation of address.
New Repub 164:18-20 Ap 3 '71
WHITING, C. R.
Let's mass produce an electric car now. il Sci
Digest 70:67-71 Ag '71
WHITLEY, Penny
Long, long trail awinding. il por Am For
77:16-18+ F '71
WHITMAN, Alden
Allan Nevins, 1890-1971. Sat R 54:24 Mr 20 '71
Return of Charles Lindbergh. il pors N Y
Times Mag p28-9+ My 23 '71; Same abr.
Read Digest 99:190-2+ S '71
So you want to be an obit writer. Sat R
54:70-1 D 11 '71
Trade winds; interview, ed. by C. Amory.
Sat R 54:10 F 27 '71
WHITMAN, Ardis
Prejudice. Seventeen 29:118-19+ D '70
—See Jourard, S. M. jt. auth.
WHITMAN, Howard
Who would want to be a cop? Read Digest
99:168-9 S '71
WHITMAN, Walt
Specimen days, by W. Whitman. Review
Sat R il pors 54:50 N 27 '71. M. R. Weiss *
Drama
Walt Whitman: poet of democracy. C. K.
Cote. Plays 30:77-84+ F '71
WHITMER, Martin Linwood
Meetings; poem. Chr Cent 88:487 Ap 21 '71
WHITNACK, G. C. and Martens, H. H.
Arsenic in potable desert groundwater: an
analysis problem. bibliog il Science 171:
383-5 Ja 29 '71
WHITNEY, Alan R. and others
Quasars revisited: rapid time variations ob-
served via very-long-baseline interferome-
try. bibliog il Science 173:225-30 Jl 16 '71

WHITNEY, Phyllis A.
Listen for the whisperer; story. Redbook
137:147-69 Ag '71
Where it happens. Writer 85:14-15+ Ja '72
WHITNEY museum of American art, New York
Art. B. Rose. il Vogue 158:284-5 S 1 '71
Hopper bequest at the Whitney. B. O'Doher-
ty. il Art in Am 59:68-72 S '71
Three at the Whitney museum; exhibitions. il
Craft Horiz 31:30-45+ D '71
WHITNEY stakes. See Horse racing
WHITON, Louis C.
Under the power of the Gran Gadu; with
biographical sketch. il Natur Hist 80:4, 14-
16+ Ag '71
WHITTAKER, James K.
Mental hygiene influences in children's insti-
tutions: organization and technology for
treatment. bibliog Ment Hy 55:444-50 O
'71
WHITTAKER, John Barnard
John Barnard Whittaker, Brooklyn artist. C.
S. Marlor. il Antiques 100:775-7 N '71 •
WHITTAKER, Johnson Chesnut
Black cadet at West Point. J. F. Marszalek,
jr. il pors Am Heritage 22:30-7+ Ag '71;
Reply. T. J. Fleming. 22:111 O '71
WHITTAKER, R. H. and Feeny, P. P.
Allelochemics: chemical interactions between
species. bibliog il Science 171:757-70 F 26 '71
WHITTAKER corporation
Ailing Whittaker tries to slim down. il
Bsns W p30 Mr 20 '71
Whittaker reverses its empire-building. Bsns
W p24 Ag 28 '71
WHITTEMORE, Reed
Eat-mit-fingah shaggy; poem. New Repub
165:24 Ag 21 '71
Mother's breast and the father's house; poem.
New Repub 165:23-5 D 4 '71
WHITTEMORE, Thomas
Sailing; poem. Seventeen 29:180 O '70
WHITTEN, M. J.
Insect control by genetic manipulation of
natural populations. bibliog il Science 171:
682-4 F 19 '71
WHITTEN, W. K.
Parthenogenesis: does it occur spontaneously
in mice? bibliog Science 171:406-7 Ja 29
'71
WHITTIER, Susan
Susan, our beginning cook. See issues of
Good housekeeping
WHITTINGTON, Dick
Radio stunt man. il por Newsweek 77:64 My
17 '71 •
WHITTINGTON, H. G.
Police: ally or enemy of the comprehensive
community mental health center? bibliog
Ment Hy 55:55-9 Ja '71
WHITTLE, Tomás Sepúlveda. See Sepúlveda
Whittle, T.
WHITTON, John B.
Hostile international propaganda and interna-
tional law. bibliog f Ann Am Acad 398:14-25
N '71
WHITTOW, G. Causey
Tropical seals; with biographical sketch. il
Sea Front 17:285-7, 319 S '71
WHITWORTH, Kathrynne Ann
Whoopee for the proettes. il por Time 97:63
Je 28 '71 •
WHITWORTH, William
Our far-flung correspondents. il New Yorker
46:64+ Ja 30 '71
Profiles; J. Franklin. por New Yorker 47:
44-6+ My 22 '71
Profiles; D. Lefkowitz. New Yorker 47:38-
42+ D 18 '71
WHOLE earth catalog. See Catalogs, Mail
order
WHOLESALE trade
Finance
Ratios of the wholesalers; with table (cont)
Duns 98:64-5 O '71
WHOLESALERS, Book. See Book wholesalers
WHO'S compatible? drama. See Nolan, P. T.
WHO'S who in library service
See also
Biographical directory of librarians in the
United States and Canada
WHY are the trees moving? story. See
Goldreich, G.
WHY haven't you written? story. See Gordi-
mer, N.
WHY the peacock is proud; drama. See
Swortzell, L.
WHYTE, Jenny Bell
Museum fashions. il Time 97:62 My 24 '71 •
WHYTE, Lancelot Law
Science and our understanding of ourselves.
Bul Atom Sci 27:32-3 Mr '71

WICHARD, Gary
At C.W. on L.I. the QB is O.K. says
Y.A. W. F. Reed. il por Sports Illus 35:71-
2 N 15 '71 •
Gary who from C. W. where? por Time 98:76
D 6 '71 •
WICHITA, Kan.
Lighting
More light, less vandalism and fewer acci-
dents. il Am City 86:82 F '71
WICHITA MOUNTAINS wilderness. See Wild-
erness areas—Oklahoma
WICKELGREN, Barbara G.
Superior colliculus: some receptive field pro-
perties of bimodally responsive cells. bib-
liog il Science 173:69-72 Jl 2 '71
WICKER, Brian
Has Britain got a chance? Commonweal 95:
220-1 D 3 '71
WICKER, Tom
Heartbreaking. por Newsweek 78:34 S 27 '71
Nobody dares to pick his successor. Life 70:
44-5 Ap 9 '71
Notes and comment; excerpts from address,
February 22, 1971. New Yorker 47:27-9 Mr 6
'71
about
Getting to the core. pors Time 98:63 S 20
'71 •
WICKERD, Fran. See Wickerd, R. jt. auth.
WICKERD, Ron, and Wickerd, Fran
In quest of King Arthur. il Travel 136:54-61
S '71
WICKS, Harry. See Warren, D. jt. auth.
WICKS, Sid
In this corner. H. L. Masin. il por Sr Schol
98:19 Mr 8 '71 •
WIDE-angle photography. See Photography,
Wide-angle
WIDEMAN, John
Fear in the streets. Am Scholar 40:611-22
Aut '71
WIDENER, Warren
Guard changes in Berkeley. J. Slater. il
pors Ebony 26:74-6+ O '71 •
New blood and brains. J. Morgenstern. News-
week 77:17 My 10 '71 •
Welcome to the system. il por Time 97:16
Ap 19 '71 •
WIDICK, B. J.
Labor's new style. Nation 212:358-60 Mr 22
'71
1971: labor's rough year. il Nation 213:166-71
S 6 '71
WIDOWS
When your wife is a widow, what then? il
Changing T 25:6-9 Je '71
Adjustment
For women alone; Widows consultation
center. McCalls 98:45 F '71
I barely feel whole. il Todays Health 49:50-7
Ag '71
WIDOWS consultation center. See Widows—
Adjustment
WIECEK, William M.
Imaginary geography. il Am West 8:10-
12 S '71
WIECK, Paul R.
Another President Jackson? New Repub 165:
17-21 S 18 '71
For God and country: the presidential can-
didacy of Harold Hughes. New Repub 164:
19-24 My 15 '71
McCarthy in '72. New Repub 165:13-16 Ag
7 '71
McGovern's campaign. New Repub 165:15-20
O 30 '71
Muskie campaign. New Repub 165:15-20 N 27
'71
On the Chisholm campaign trail. New Repub
165:16-18 D 4 '71
President dumping. New Repub 164:11-14 Ap
24 '71
Wilbur Mills' noncandidacy. New Repub 165:
17-19 Jl 24 '71
Young man from Indiana. New Repub 164:23-
7 Je 26 '71
WIEDEMANN, R. E.
Exchange water keeps Denver's taps flow-
ing. il por Am City 86:79-80+ Je '71
WIENER, Joan. See Rosenberg, S. jt. auth.
WIESBADEN, Germany
Music
Byways of Europe: Wiesbaden; Hessian state
theater. E. Gerken. il Opera N 35:20-1 My 15
'71
WIESNER, Jerome B.
After the Pentagon papers: talk with Kistia-
kowsky, Wiesner; interview, ed. by E.
Langer. pors Science 174:923-8 N 26 '71

WIESNER, Jerome B.—*Continued*
Reaction against universities, views of a noted educator. il por U S News 71:36-7 D 20 '71

about
New team at MIT. il por Newsweek 77:93 Mr 15 '71 *
Transition at M.I.T. por Time 97:51-2 Mr 15 '71 *

WIFE and mother; story. See Ross, M.

WIGGIN, Blanton C.
Excerpt from statements prepared in 1970 and 1971. Cong Digest 50:311+ D '71

WIGGINS, Sam P.
Matter of principals. il PTA Mag 65:2-5 bibliog(p32) Je '71

WIGLETS. See Wigs

WIGREN, Klinton M.
Shadows on the wall. il Cons 26:30-1 Ag '71

WIGS
Beauty & the bath; today's synthetic wig. S. Lindsay. House B 113:34+ Ap '71
Easy pretty head: wigs, coiffures; the shortest, kindest cut. il Vogue 157:110-15 Ap 1 '71
Great hair put-ons. il Harp Baz 104:33 Jl '71
Hairpieces: pretty new additions. il Ladies Home J 88:68 S '71
Heady stuff. S. Lord. il Harp Baz 105:84-5 N '71
No-set designer wig. C. Bartel. il Am Home 74:12+ Jl '71
One-minute hair change. il Mlle 72:208-11 Ap Ap '71
6 easy pieces. il Ladies Home J 88:92-5 Jl '71
Ten years younger in ten minutes. J. K. Lester. il Har Yrs 11:34 F '71
Travel light, travel pretty: put-ons. il Seventeen 30:125-6 Ap '71
Wig and you? answers to all your questions. il Vogue 158:110-17 O 15 '71
Wigs are for everyone! T. Pavlik. il Good H 173:104-7 S '71
Wigs for women on the go. il Ladies Home J 88:128-9+ N '71
Wigs today: going to everybody's head. il Vogue 158:108-9 O 15 '71
Wigs: what to look for, how to look after them. il Harp Baz 104:8 Je '71
Wigs work wonders. il McCalls 98:88-9+ Je '71
Words of wisdom. il Vogue 157:27 F 15 '71

WILBERFORCE university, Wilberforce, Ohio
Wilberforce university: the reality of Bishop Payne's dream. C. Killian. bibliog il por Negro Hist Bul 34:83-7 Ap '71

WILBRICHT, Sue
Overdue. por Wilson Lib Bul 46:186-7 O '71

WILBUR, Richard
Wood; poem. il Am For 77:32 Ap '71
Writer; poem. New Repub 165:33 Jl 17 '71
(tr) See Molière, J. B. P. School for wives

WILBUR, Robert Hunter
China and the UN. New Repub 165:10-12 S 18 '71

WILCOX, George Latimer
Mighty transformation in electricity. il pors Nations Bsns 59:92-3 Ja '71

WILCOX, John M. and Gonzalez, Walter
Rotating solar magnetic dipole observed from 1926 to 1968. bibliog il Science 174:820-1 N 19 '71

WILCOX, Thomas Robert
From bank to board. por Bsns W p82 Ag 14 '71 *

WILCOXON, Hardy C. and others
Illness-induced aversions in rat and quail: relative salience of visual and gustatory cues. bibliog il Science 171:826-8 F 26 '71

WILD, Jonathan
Rufflers and ripping coves. J. Skow. por Time 97:92+ My 24 '71 *

WILD animal pets. See Pets

WILD animal racing
Backer of a bearback ride. P. Putnam. il por Sports Illus 34:36-8+ Je 28 '71

WILD animals in art. See Animals in art

WILD cat family. See Felidae

WILD dogs
Life and times of Shag, a feral dog in Baltimore. A. M. Beck. il Natur Hist 80:58-65 O '71

WILD flower conservation. See Plant conservation

WILD flower gardens. See Gardens, Wild

WILD flowers
How much do you know about wildflowers? quiz. J. Daugherty and M. Daugherty. il Sci Digest 69:70-1+ Mr '71
Our wildflowers. A. Holweg. il Cons 26:14-16 Ag '71
Preserving the wild in your garden. C. Sauerland. il Org Gard & Farm 18:44-6 Je '71

Try growing wild flowers at your doorstep. il Changing T 25:13-14 Mr '71
Wild flowers in the mountains. G. W. Kelly. il Horticulture 49:26-9 Ag '71
Wild flowers on a balcony. T. H. Cain. il Horticulture 49:24-5+ S '71
See also
Buds

WILD food. See Food, Wild

WILD gardens. See Gardens, Wild

WILD geese. See Geese, Wild

WILD horses. See Horses

WILD oats. See Bellworts

WILD pigeon shooting. See Pigeon shooting

WILD rivers. See Rivers

WILD turkeys. See Turkeys, Wild

WILDCAT hunting. See Bobcat hunting

WILDCATS. See Bobcats

WILDE, Patricia
Patricia Wilde a full life. T. Tobias. il pors Dance Mag 45:68-75 S '71 *

WILDEBOER, Henry
Rebuilding martial fidelity. Chr Today 15:19 Je 18 '71

WILDER, Alec
Alec Wilder; interview. New Yorker 47:22-4 S 4 '71

WILDER, Amos N.
Electric chimes or rams' horns; reprint. Chr Cent 88:103 Ja 27 '71

WILDER, Ira
Public relations for today's school. Clear House 45:537 My '71

WILDER, Laura (Ingalls)
Fine way back to our prairie past. G. McGovern. il Life 71:12 Jl 2 '71 *

WILDER garden; story. See Eden, D.

WILDERNESS areas
Gleason: presenting a rare collection of early wilderness photography; excerpts from The call of the mountains. L. Jeffers. il Am West 8:16-27 Jl '71
Loci of conflict and compromise; preservation and consumption; address, December 5, 1970. R. A. Brown. Vital Speeches 37:247-9 F 1 '71
Of wilderness. P. L. Errington. Liv Wildn 34:49-51 Wint '70
Our research natural areas. E. P. Cliff. il Am For 77:36-8+ O '71
Profiles: D. Brower. J. McPhee. por New Yorker 47:42-8+ Mr 20; 42-8+ Mr 27; 41-4+ Ap 3 '71
Pursuit of wilderness. by P. Brooks. Review Liv Wildn 35:42-3 Sum '71. W. O. Douglas
Six wild havens to explore. il Life 71:52-9 S 3 '71
Universe of the wilderness is vanishing; reprint from April, 1937 issue of Nature magazine. R. Marshall. il por Liv Wildn 35:8-14 Sum '71
Wilderness act as Congress intended. J. T. Keane. il Am For 77:40-3+ F '71
Wilderness legislation in Congress: status as of July 15, 1971. Liv Wildn 35:7 Sum '71
Wilderness: the last refuge. il Sr Schol 98:8-9 Mr 15 '71

Roads
White Clouds road ordered closed. Liv Wildn 34:60 Aut '70

Alaska
Alaska wilderness, by R. Marshall. Review Liv Wildn 34:55-7 Aut '70. M. J. Mattes
Bob Marshall and the Alaska Arctic wilderness. G. Marshall. bibliog f por Liv Wildn 34:29-32 Aut '70
Nameless valley, shining mountains; excerpts. J. P. Milton. il Liv Wildn 34:10-17 Wint '70
To jump three thousand years; Brooks Range wilderness. S. Wright. il por Am West 8:24-7 Mr '71

Canada
British Columbia wilderness; excerpt from address. W. C. Yeomans. il Liv Wildn 34:40-3 Wint '70

Europe, Western
Is there wilderness in western Europe? R. M. Pyle. il Liv Wildn 34:44-8 Wint '70

Florida
Suwannee River wilderness. il Travel 135:11 My '71

Idaho
Idaho's rugged land, still untouched; with photographs by J. Dominis. Life 70:38-49 Ap 23 '71
Lost men of Muldoon Canyon. J. Neary. il pors Life 70:50D-50F+ Mr 19 '71

WILDERNESS areas—Idaho—*Continued*
Storm signals over the Sawtooth. V. Fischer.
il por Am For 77:32-5+ Ja '71
White Clouds road ordered closed. Liv Wildn
34:60 Aut '70

Minnesota
President's Quetico-Superior committee. Liv
Wildn 34:54-8 Wint '70

Montana
Return to wilderness; Bob Marshall wilder-
ness. L. C. Merriam, jr. il Nat Parks &
Con Mag 45:28-31 Je '71

Northwestern state
See also
Wilderness areas—Washington (state)

Oklahoma
Oklahoma's new wilderness; Charons Garden
and North Mountain in Wichita Mountains
wilderness. A. Halloran. il Liv Wildn 35:
9-12 Spr '71

Russia
Soviet system of protected natural areas. V.
A. Borissoff. il Nat Parks & Con Mag 45:
8-14 Je '71

Texas
See also
Big Thicket

Washington (state)
Cascades wilderness additions urged. il Liv
Wildn 34:60-1 Aut '70
Profiles: C. Park and D. Brower. J. McPhee.
por New Yorker 47:42-8+ Mr 20 '71

West Virginia
West Virginia wilderness bills introduced;
Otter Creek basin, Dolly Sods area, and
Cranberry back country in the Mononga-
hela national forest. H. McGinnis. Liv
Wildn 34:62 Aut '70

Wyoming
Behind the Sleeping Indian: the Gros Ventre
wilderness. V. Huser. il Liv Wildn 35:4-8
Spr '71
Forgotten side of the Tetons; proposed
Western Teton wilderness area. B. Nor-
ton. il Liv Wildn 35:31-4 Sum '71
WILDERNESS camping. See Camping
WILDERNESS society
Home for the spirit. R. Nash. bibliog il Am
West 8:40-7 Ja '71
1971 Murie-Broome awards. Liv Wildn 35:3
Spr '71
Wilderness outings, some 1971 choices. Sun-
set 146:69 Mr '71
Women in the wilderness. A. Tussing. il Liv
Wildn 34:44-9 Aut '70
WILDERNESS survival
How to survive in the desert. K. Anderson.
il Pop Mech 136:108-11 Ag '71
Lost in an icy hell. W. Garde. il Outdoor
Life 147:54-5+ F '71
Lost men of Muldoon Canyon. J. Neary. il
pors Life 70:50D-50F+ Mr 19 '71
Ordeal on Mount Hood; ed by D. Holm. D.
Moon. il pors Nat Wildlife 9:36-9 Je '71
Survival training: bonus for life; sixth-
graders at Orange Grove school, Sacra-
mento, Calif. K. Hoff. bibliog il School
Teach Jr/Sr High p 18-19+ O '71
What's your survival quotient? true or false
quiz. A. W. Pond. Field & S 75:72-3+ Mr '71
Wild survival challenge in Arizona. E. Gib-
bons. Org Gard & Farm 18:121-2+ Mr '71
Winter survival. F. Katz. il Todays Health
49:44-7+ D '71
WILDERNESS walk. See Walking
WILDFLOWER exhibits. See Flower exhibits
WILDFLOWERS. See Wild flowers
WILDFOWL decoys. See Decoys (hunting)
WILDFOWLING. See Fowling
WILDI, Ernst
Wildi's wild pinwheels. il Pop Phot 68:96-7+
Je '71
WILDLIFE
Can you match them up? quiz. D. Mech. il
Outdoor Life 147:176-7+ Ap '71
Intruder in a cageless zoo. F. Weddle. il
Org Gard & Farm 18:66-71 F '71
WILDLIFE and pesticides. See Pesticides and
wildlife
WILDLIFE conservation
Fight to save wild horses. il Time 98:48-51
Jl 12 '71
New zoo view. R. T. Reuther. il Parks & Rec
6:17-19+ S '71
War on wildlife. F. McNulty. il Nat Parks &
Con Mag 45:11-17 Mr '71

Where the wolves are and how they stand.
L. D. Mech. Natur Hist 80:26-9 Ap '71
Wildlife; EQ index. il Nat Wildlife 9:34 O '71
Wildlife: the path of the dodo? il Sr Schol 98:
10 Mr 15 '71
See also
Animals—Protection
Birds of prey—Protection
Marine parks and reserves
National wildlife federation
Patuxent wildlife research center
Pesticides and wildlife
Rare animals
Wetlands
Wilderness areas
Wildlife management
World wildlife fund

Laws and legislation
Adventures in the skin trade. F. W. King. il
Natur Hist 80:8-10+ bibliog(P104) My '71

Africa
African round-up: adventure in ecology. W.
Nussey and H. Reuter. il Sci Digest 69:42-8
Je '71

Alaska
Alaska's agony; illegal hunting. B. East. il
Outdoor Life 147:33-5+ Ja '71

Arizona
Wildlife versus irrigation; phreatophyte removal. R. H. Gilluly. il Sci N 99:184-5 Mr
13 '71

California
Fur seals are coming back to California.
R. S. Peterson and B. J. Le Boeuf. il Sci
Digest 69:74-9 Ap '71

Florida
Her home is a sanctuary for injured wild-
life; R. Collett of Florida. W. Hartley and
E. Hartley. il pors Good H 173:78+ O '71

India
Tiger. A. Singh. il Nat Parks & Con Mag
45:18-21 Ag '71
Tragedy of India's wildlife. E. A. Bauer.
il Outdoor Life 147:49-53+ F '71

South Carolina
Death hovers over Santeeland; South Carolina public service authority vs the forces
of conservation. J. Rutherfoord. Field &
S 76:124+ Je '71

Western states
Mustang controversy. R. H. Gilluly. il Sci N
99:219-20 Mr 27 '71
WILDLIFE control. See Animal populations—
Control
WILDLIFE management
Wildlife ranching. D. Lipton. Sci Digest 70:
76-9 Ag '71

Texas
Boom in exotic big game. B. W. Dalrymple.
il Field & S 75:70-1+ Ap '71
WILDLIFE photographs. See Animals—Photo-
graphs
WILDLIFE photography. See Photography of
animals
WILDLIFE research
See also
Patuxent wildlife research center
WILDLIFE sanctuaries
Forest management on National wildlife
refuges. V. E. Carter. il Am For 77:22-5+
Ag '71
U.S. wildlife refuges. J. Craw. il Travel 136:
46-51 D '71

Alaska
Nameless valleys, shining mountains; excerpts, Arctic wildlife range. J. P. Milton.
il Liv Wildn 34:10-17 Wint '70

See also
Macquarie Island

Australia

Hawaii
Then came man and a mustard seed; Ha-
waiian Islands national wildlife refuge. B.
Gilbert. il Sports Illus 35:96-9+ S 13 '71

Montana
See also
National bison range

New York (state)
Black mayonnaise at the bottom of Jamaica
Bay; Jamaica Bay wildlife refuge. M.
Harwood. il N Y Times Mag p9-11+
F 7 '71

WILDLIFE sanctuaries—*Continued*
South Dakota
Carnage at Sand Lake. G. Sherwood; discussion. Audubon 72:140-1 N '70; 73:102-6 Mr '71
Virginia
Wildlife refuge overrun by dune buggies; Back Bay national wildlife refuge. Nat Parks & Con Mag 45:31-2 Jl '71

WILDLIFE telemetry. See Biotelemetry

WILE, Georgia
Early concepts of morality. il PTA Mag 66: 25-7+ bibliog(p34) D '71

WILES, Peter
Crisis prediction. Ann Am Acad 393:32-9 Ja '71

WILEY, Dorothy
Women, wives, film-makers; interview. ed. by B. Richardson. il Film Q 25:34-40 Fall '71

WILEY, John, and sons, inc.
Wiley forms new division and acquires new firm. Pub W 200:30 Ag 9 '71

WILEY, John P. Jr
Immortality and the freezing of human bodies. il Natur Hist 80:12-15 D '71
Sky reporter. See issues of Natural history

WILEY, Marcia
Cabin talk. See issues of Yachting
It's a different kind of cruising. il Yachting 129:58-9+ F '71

WILEY, William Thomas
Funky Wiley; retrospective at the Institute of contemporary art, Philadelphia. D. Davis. Newsweek 78:113 D 13 '71 *
Quirky angler. R. Hughes. il por Time 99:38-9 Ja 17 '72 *

WILFRED, Thomas
Light fantastic; retrospective at New York's Museum of modern art. D. Davis. il por Newsweek 78:83 Ag 23 '71 *

WILHELM Foerster observatory. See Astronomical observatories—Germany (Federal Republic)

WILHELM Tell festival. See Festivals—Wisconsin

WILK, Peter
America's vagabond ambassadors; interview. ed. by D. Butwin. il por Sat R 54:59-62+ F 20 '71

WILKE, L. A.
Let your gun rack work year round. il Pop Mech 135:114 F '71

WILKES, Paul
As the blacks move in, the ethnics move out. il por N Y Times Mag p9-11+ Ja 24 '71
Leonard Boudin: the left's lawyer's lawyer. il por N Y Times Mag p38-40+ N 14 '71
Mother superior to Women's lib. il por N Y Times Mag p27-9+ N 29 '70; 47 Ja 24 '71
When do we have the right to die. il Life 72:48+ Ja 14 '72
With Oscar and Lew, Milwaukee is basketball's best, but . . . pors Look 35:68-70 Ap 6 '71
Yale is no. 1 with the promoter & the idol. il pors Look 35:60-2 Ap 6 '71

WILKES-BARRE, Pa.
Oh! Fashion! One man's look at the preening of America. S. Blum. il Redbook 136: 79+ Ap '71

WILKIE, Frances, and Eisdorfer, Carl
Intelligence and blood pressure in the aged. bibliog il Science 172:959-62 My 28 '71

WILKIE, Jane
Dick Van Dyke: having it his way. il pors Good H 173:92-3+ S '71
Goldie Hawn. il pors Good H 172:54-6+ My '71

WILKING, S. Vincent
Tale of two men, two businesses and two profit performances. Pub W 199:26-8 Ap 19 '71

WILKINS, Gordon
Ford's new mid-engine sports car. il Mech Illus 67:48-9 Jl '71
Hot air engine runs quietly and cleanly. il Mech Illus 67:68+ O '71
We test a $1,000 car. il por Mech Illus 67:58-9 Je '71

WILKINSON, Billy R.
Screaming success as study halls; address, July 1970. bibliog il por Library J 96:1567-71 My 1 '71

WILKINSON, Fred T.
We're reaping a harvest of permissiveness; interview. il por U S News 71:22 S 27 '71

WILKINSON, Rachel D.
Community relations for special programs in higher education. Sch & Soc 99:170-2 Mr '71

WILKINSON, Stephan
Back to basics. Flying 89:55+ N '71
Reporting points. See issues of Flying

WILKINSON, Sylvia
To be king of the mountain. il Sports Illus 34:84-6+ Ap 19 '71

WILL, George F.
Letter from Washington. Nat R 23:196-7 F 23 '71

WILLARD, Edward B.
Maintenance team is born. il Parks & Rec 6:53-4+ My '71

WILLBERN, David P.
Thomas Kyd's The Spanish tragedy: inverted vengeance. bibliog f Am Imago 28:247-67 Fall '71

WILLERMAN, Lee, and others
Intellectual development of children from interracial matings. bibliog il Science 170: 1329-31; 172:12 D 18 '70, Ap 2 '71
Intelligence and race. Sci Am 224:46 F '71 *

WILLEY, Carolyn
Belonging; poem. Seventeen 30:132 Jl '71

WILLEY, Patsy
Frontier of faith, geography of joy: a librarian's testament. il pors Wilson Lib Bul 45: 856-63 My '71

WILLI, Doris
Oakland's theme playgrounds. il Parks & Rec 6:27 F '71

WILLIAM Jeanes memorial library, Whitemarsh Township, Lafayette Hill, Pa.
Lafayette Hill, Pa: friendly in Pennsylvania. il Library J 96:3984 D 1 '71

WILLIAMS, A. Cecil
Glide to glory. L. Robinson. il por Ebony 26:44-6+ Jl '71 *

WILLIAMS, Andrew
Whistle-blowing on Wall Street. D. McClintick. New Repub 165:20-5 S 4 '71 *

WILLIAMS, Andy
Ethel & Andy. M. Cheshire. il pors Ladies Home J 88:86+ O '71 *

WILLIAMS, Barbara Fischer-. See Fischer-Williams, B.

WILLIAMS, C. K.
Innings; Undead; Clay out of silence; Rampage; poems. Poetry 118:78-80 My '71
Keep it; poem. New Yorker 47:32 Jl 31 '71
about
Comment. M. L. Rosenthal. Poetry 119:101-2 N '71 *

WILLIAMS, C. M.
Little Johnny slept here. il Read Digest 98:82-5 F '71

WILLIAMS, Daniel Hale
Provident hospital. il por Ebony 26:64-6+ Je '71 *

WILLIAMS, David R. See Gamzu, E. jt. auth.

WILLIAMS, Dick
Riot act changes the scene. W. Leggett. il Sports Illus 34:20-1 My 3 '71 *

WILLIAMS, Donald M.
Close-up of the Jesus people. Chr Today 15: 5-7 Ag 27 '71

WILLIAMS, Donn L.
Doing business in Japan; address, October 19, 1971. Vital Speeches 38:76-80 N 15 '71
New challenge; excerpts from address. Aviation W 94:9 F 22 '71

WILLIAMS, Emmett L.
Transactional curriculum for the transescent learner; address, November 1970. il Engl J 60:599-602 My '71

WILLIAMS, George L.
Middle school reform in Italy. bibliog f Clear House 46:245-9 D '71

WILLIAMS, Gunther Gebel-. See Gebel-Williams, G.

WILLIAMS, Gurney, 3d
Radioactive accidents. il Sci Digest 70:10-14 Ag '71

WILLIAMS, Hank
Hank Williams remembered. D. Halberstam. Look 35:42 Jl 13 '71 *

WILLIAMS, Harrison A. Jr
Williams has what labor likes. por Bsns W p82+ F 13 '71 *

WILLIAMS, Heathcote
AC/DC. Criticism
America 124:408-9 Ap 17 '71 *
Nation 212:347 Mr 15 '71
Newsweek 77:84 Mr 8 '71 *

WILLIAMS, Herb
Year of the giant steelhead. il Field & S 76:58-9+ O '71

WILLIAMS, Hermann Warner, Jr
Young America. il Am Heritage 22:16-32 F '71

WILLIAMS, Hibbard E. and Smith, L. H. Jr
Hyperoxaluria in L-glyceric aciduria: possible pathogenic mechanism. bibliog il Science 171:390-1 Ja 29 '71

WILLIAMS, Jack. See Williams, J. R.

WILLIAMS, John H.
Living dangerously. il Forbes 108:48 O 15 '71 *

WILLIAMS, John Richard
Taking over the OEO. J. R. Hood. Nation 213:646-9 D 20 '71 *
WILLIAMS, Jonathan
Comment. R. J. Mills, jr. Poetry 117:331-2 F '71 *
Sound of our speaking. R. Morgan. Nation 213:188-9 S 6 '71 *
WILLIAMS, Kim
Requiem for a river; poem. Liv Wildn 35:8 Spr '71
WILLIAMS, Lawrence
Decision; story. Good H 173:92-3 Jl '71
When hearts are young; story. Good H 174: 64-5 Ja '72
WILLIAMS, Lois
Governance is integral to accountability. Todays Ed 60:59-60 Ap '71
WILLIAMS, Lydia, pseud.
Loneliness of being black. il Seventeen 30: 118+ Jl '71
WILLIAMS, Lynne
Taxes: the crucial sixty days. il Duns 98:71-2 N '71
WILLIAMS, Martin
Video. Nat R 23:823-4, 1005, 1192, 1315 Jl 27, S 10, O 22, N 19 '71
WILLIAMS, Mary Lou
Spirit of Mary Lou. H. Saal. il por Newsweek 78:67 D 20 '71 *
Whatever happened to Mary Lou Williams? il pors Ebony 26:202 O '71 *
WILLIAMS, Maurice Jacoutat
U.S. support for relief efforts in south Asia; statement, October 4, 1971. Dept State Bul 65:500-2 N 1 '71

about

Mr Williams named coordinator of U.S. relief to East Pakistan. Dept State Bul 65: 259 S 6 '71 *
WILLIAMS, Norman, jr
(ed) Zoning and planning decisions. See issues of American city
WILLIAMS, Paul
Home: today's most provocative four-letter word. Mlle 74:124-5+ D '71
WILLIAMS, Peggy Lenore
Subject was laughter. L. Foster. McCalls 98: 40 Ag '71 *
WILLIAMS, R. B. and Eichelman, B.
Social setting: influence on the physiological response to electric shock in the rat. bibliog il Science 174:613-14 N 5 '71
WILLIAMS, Raymond
Downhill to Dutschke. Nation 212:210-12 F 15 '71
WILLIAMS, Robert Francis
Odyssey of Robert Williams. G. A. Geyer. New Repub 164:15-17 Mr 20 '71 *
WILLIAMS, Rod
Cooperation in the Caribbean. Yachting 129: 61-2+ Je '71
WILLIAMS, Roger J.
Biology of behavior. Sat R 54:17-19+ Ja 30 '71
WILLIAMS, Roger M.
Emancipation of black scholars; excerpt from The Bonds: an American family. il Sat R 54:54-6+ D 18 '71
WILLIAMS, Roger Neville
Strong-arm rule in Canada. New Repub 164: 15-18 Ja 30 '71
WILLIAMS, Sam
Time for turbines. Time 98:101 N 8 '71 *
WILLIAMS, Stuart
(ed) Shooting. See issues of Field & stream November 1971-

about

Two new shooting editors for a growing sport. M. J. O'Neill and C. Conley. pors Field & S 76:8-9 O '71 *
WILLIAMS, Ted
Baseball's odd couple meets the wild bunch. J. Mann. il pors Look 35:71-2+ My 4 '71 *
Ted's (sob) hitless ballgame. R. Blount, jr. Sports Illus 34:64+ My 17 '71 *
They're ho-hummers no more. J. Underwood. il por Sports Illus 34:26-8+ Mr 15 '71 *
WILLIAMS, Tennessee
Demolition downtown; text. il Esquire 75: 124-7+ Je '71
Tennessee Williams turns sixty; interview, ed. by R. Reed. por Esquire 76:105-8+ S '71

about

Lee Hoiby. Tennessee Williams. S. Fleming. pors Hi Fi 21:MA16+ Jl '71 *
WILLIAMS, William
William Williams, novelist and painter of colonial America 1727-1791, by D. H. Dickason. Review
Antiques il 100:920+ D '71 *

WILLIAMS, William T.
652 Broadway. D. Shapiro. il por Art N 70: 50-2+ Ap '71 *
WILLIAMS brothers company. See Williams companies
WILLIAMS companies
Living dangerously. il Forbes 108:48 O 15 '71
WILLIAMS FORK reservoir, Colo. See Reservoirs
WILLIAMSBURG, Va.
Welcome to Williamsburg for Christmas. il Horticulture 49:30-3 D '71
See also
Colonial Williamsburg garden symposium
WILLIAMSBURG garden symposium. See Colonial Williamsburg garden symposium
WILLIAMSBURG student burgesses. See Forums (discussion and debate)
WILLIAMSON, Alan
Five poets. Poetry 118:169-74 Je '71
Hotel with a view of the Jungfrau; poem. Yale R 61:80-1 O '71
WILLIAMSON, Dereck
Cement mixing made easy. Sat R 54:12 Ap 17 '71
Driving you to drink. Sat R 54:4 D 25 '71
Moving plastic writes. Sat R 54:19 Mr 13 '71
Mudbacks. Sat R 54:6 Ja 30 '71
Once again, the purple finger. il Sat R 54: 6+ S 4 '71
So you want the right tool for the job? excerpt from The complete book of pitfalls. il Read Digest 98:148-50 Mr '71
Spring hangup; excerpt from The complete book of pitfalls. Sat R 54:6+ My 15 '71
You can't miss it! Sat R 54.18 Ag 7 '71
WILLIAMSON, Jack
H. G. Wells: the man who discovered tomorrow. il pors Sat R 55:12-15 Ja 1 '72
Science fiction: emerging from its exile in limbo. il Pub W 200:16-20 Jl 5 '71
WILLIAMSON, Ruth Lundgren
Companionway. See issues of Motor boating & sailing
Why don't they call them homeboats? il Motor B & S 127:66-9+ Mr '71
WILLIAMSTOWN, Mass.

Theater

Theater; production of Cyrano de Bergerac at the Williamstown theatre. H. Hewes. Sat R 54:18 Ag 21 '71
WILLIS, E. Sidney
Retirement age dilemma; address, November 9, 1970. Vital Speeches 37:204-6 Ja 15 '71
WILLIS, Ellen
Rock, etc (cont) New Yorker 47:58 Jl 10; 81-2 Ag 14; 78+ Ag 28; 120+ S 25; 168-70+ O 23 '71
WILLIS, Robert J.
Church's changing face. Commonweal 95:204-5 N 26 '71
Election time comes to Saigon. il America 125:400-2 N 13 '71
WILLIS, Thayer
Teleguide. il Schol Teach Jr/Sr High p35 My 3 '71
WILLMENT, Frank
Swifty; drama. Plays 31:1-15 O '71
WILLOUGHBY, William
World Methodists: revival in '75? Chr Today 15:45 S 10 '71
WILLOWS, A. O. D.
Giant brain cells in mollusks; with biographical sketch. il Sci Am 224:12, 68-75 F '71
WILLS, Garry
Memories of a Catholic boyhood. il Esquire 75:102-5+ F '71
Thinking of positive power. il Esquire 75:98-101+ Mr '71

about

Critics of Richard Nixon. W. F. Buckley, jr. Nat R 23:496-7 My 4 '71 *
Hoover-Berrigan-Wills. Nat R 23:578 Je 1 '71 *
WILLS, Marie
Our rotating compost. Org Gard & Farm 18: 81 My '71
WILLS, Martee
DOVACK's machines help children read. il por Am Ed 7:3-8 Je '71
WILLS
Are you in your husband's will? I. Barmash. Harp Baz 104:96 Je '71
Soul searching; controversy over the will of J. Kidd. Newsweek 77:65 F 8 '71 *
Willing to please; lawyer charged with adjusting wills. por Time 98:71+ D 6 '71
Willing your child. F. Sabin. Ladies Home J 88:194 My '71
See also
Executors and administrators
WILLSTATTER, Richard
Chemists' involvement in society. R. Ferreira. bibliog pors Chem 44:20 F '71 *

WILMERDING, John
Robert Salmon: painter of ship and shore.
il Antiques 99:257-61 F '71

WILMINGTON, Del.

Education

Alfred I. DuPont education association. B.
Sarra. Todays Ed 60:56 Ap '71

WILSON, Arnold
Sharples family of painters. il Antiques 100:
740-3 N '71

WILSON, Carroll L.
Environment: preparing for the crunch. il
Sat R 54:42-3+ Ja 23 '71

WILSON, Charles B.
Every gardener his own seedsman? Horticulture 49:46-8 D '71

WILSON, Charles Morrow
Plant roots and productive growth. Org Gard
& Farm 18:114-16 Ja '71

WILSON, Craig
Your garage can be a screened summer room.
il Pop Mech 135:160-1 Ag '71

WILSON, E. O. See Regnier, F. E. jt. auth.

WILSON, Edmund
Upstate diary. New Yorker 47:46-8+ Je 5;
43-4+ Je 12 '71
Edmund Wilson as provincial Plutarch. W.
Berthoff. il por Sat R 54:19-21 Ag 28 '71 •
Edmund Wilson: still a standard of sanity in
this culture. L. Kriegel. Commonweal 95:
135-6 N 5 '71 •
Man of property. R. Berman. Nat R 23:
1124-5 O 8 '71 •
Midtown and the Village. A. Kazin. il Harper
242:82-9 Ja '71 •
Upstate. by E. Wilson. Review
Newsweek il por 78:79 Ag 30 '71. P. S.
Prescott •

WILSON, Eugene S. See Lass, A. H. jt. auth.

WILSON, F. Perry
New boss puts ecology on top. por Bsns W
p55 F 6 '71 •

WILSON, Flip
Flip Wilson, etc. J. Leonard. il pors Life
70:12 Ja 22 '71 •
Many faces of Flip Wilson. B. Davidson. il
pors Good H 172:15+ Ap '71 •

WILSON, Frederick A. and others
Unstirred water layers in intestine: rate determinant of fatty acid absorption from
micellar solutions. bibliog il Science 174:
1031-3 D 3 '71

WILSON, Geoffrey
Ideological balance in the Free library of
Philadelphia book collections; ed. by J. F.
Krug and J. A. Harvey. Am Lib 2:156-7 F
'71

WILSON, H. H.
FBI today. Nation 212:169-72 F 8 '71; Same.
Cur 128:53-8 Ap '71

WILSON, Harold
When the war might have ended: excerpt
from The labour government, 1964-70. il
pors Life 70:54B-56+ My 21 '71

about

Britain in Europe: undecided Harold Wilson.
A. Howard. New Repub 165:8-9 Jl 10 '71 •
Britain: Labor's dark hour. pors Newsweek
78:30+ Ag 2 '71 •
Flip flop Wilson. il Time 98:30 Ag 2 '71 •
He wuz robbed. A. Howard. New Repub 165:
23-6 D 4 '71 •
Politics of power. T. Beeson. Chr Cent 88:
993 Ag 25 '71 •
Saying no to Europe. A. Howard. New
Repub 165:10-11 O 23 '71 •
Wilson agonistes. C. Brogan. Nat R 23:930+
Ag 24 '71 •

WILSON, Hazel
Books for boys and girls. See occasional
issues of Parents' magazine & better family living

WILSON, Henry H.
Bitter fruit from the EEC. por Nations Bsns
59:42 N '71

WILSON, Ian H.
Toward a new reformation. Cur 131:18-23 Jl
'71

WILSON, James Q.
Crime & the liberal audience. Commentary
51:71-8 Ja; 28+ My '71

WILSON, James W.
Shock treatment. il por Newsweek 77:68 Je
14 '71 •

WILSON, Jerry Vernon
Beleaguered Washington: only recourse was
mass arrests: interview. il pors U S News
70:53-5 My 24 '71

How to solve the police crisis; interview, ed.
by G. M. Chamberlain. pors Am City 86:
94-5+ S; 88+ O; 106-8 N '71

about

President wants firm law enforcement; with
editorial comment. J. Neary. il pors Life
70:3, 32-9 My 14 '71 •
Washington's capital crime-stopper. R. Mac-
Leisch. Read Digest 98:53-4+ My '71 •

WILSON, John A. See Mecklenburger, J. A.
jt. auth.

WILSON, John Anthony Burgess. See Burgess,
A. pseud.

WILSON, John S.
Jazz. See issues of High fidelity and Musical
America

WILSON, John W. See Changnon, S. A. jr, jt.
auth.

WILSON, José
Top of the morning party drinks. House &
Gard 139:54+ Mr '71

WILSON, Joseph Chamberlain
Original copier. por Time 98:97-8 D 6 '71 •
Why of Xerox. L. L. L. Golden. Sat R 54:53-
4 Ag 14 '71 •

WILSON, Karen
Student makes music in Siena. il Hi Fi 21:
MA10-11 Ap '71

WILSON, Mary (Baldwin)
Love poems; excerpt from Selected poems.
por Ladies Home J 88:54 F '71

WILSON, Nancy
Interview of the week; ed. by R. Hemming.
por Sr Schol 98:22 F 1 '71

WILSON, Norman W.
Marketing change that meant everyone won.
R. D. DeVitt. il pors Nations Bsns 59:
64-5 Ja '71 •

WILSON, Paul E.
Squares's night behind bars. por Nation 212:
200-6 F 15 '71

WILSON, Ralph C. jr
Mud flies all over the track. R. H. Boyle. il
por Sports Illus 35:30-1 N 1 '71 •

WILSON, Ramsay
Game gets more dangerous; interview. pors
Forbes 108:39-42 Ag 1 '71

WILSON, Robert M.
Non-verbal; Deafman glance. New Yorker 47:
29-30 Mr 27 '71 •
Staged dream time; Prologue. M. Gottfried.
Vogue 158:286 S 1 '71 •
Theatre in dreamtime; Deafman glance. M.
Gottfried. Vogue 157:195 My '71 •

WILSON, Robley, Jr
Animals; poem. Atlan 228:94 D '71
Armatures; poem. Esquire 75:36 My '71
October; poem. Esquire 75:32 Je '71

WILSON, Thornton Arnold
Wilson of Boeing. il por Forbes 107:53 My
15 '71 •

WILSON, W. Cody
Facts versus fears: why should we worry
about pornography? bibliog f Ann Am
Acad 397:105-17 S '71
No evidence pornography causes crime; in-
terview. por U S News 70:74 Ja 25 '71

WILSON, W. E. and others
DDT: participation in ultraviolet-detectable,
charge-transfer complexation. bibliog il
Science 171:180-2 Ja 15 '71

WILSON, W. Frederic
Auto flash is here! il Pop Phot 68:82-5 My '71

WILSON, Will R. 1912-
Enforcer steps down. Time 98:16+ O 25 '71 •
Promoter and the crime buster. D. Jackson.
il pors Life 71:59-60+ S 24 '71 •
Taint in the Justice department. por Time
98:12-13 S 13 '71 •
Will Wilson's loans. il pors Newsweek 78:16-17
S 13 '71 •

WILSON, William Griffith
Anonymous ally. il por Time 97:52 F 8 '71 •

WILSON, Woodrow
Wilsonian principle after half a century. R.
M. Nixon; remarks, February 18, 1971. Dept
State Bul 64:312-14 Mr 15 '71 •
Woodrow Wilson's fight for peace. T. Flem-
ing. il por Read Digest 99:87-91 S '71 •

WILSON Hicks International conference on
communications arts. See Photographic
conferences

WILSON Junior high, Cherokee, Ia. See
Cherokee, Ia.—Education

WILSON'S disease. See Hepatolenticular degeneration

WILT, Richard
Low-distortion hi-fi volume expander. il
Electr World 85:54-5 Je '71

WILTWYCK school for boys, Yorktown
Heights, N.Y.
Wiltwyck school: a new campus but a con-
tinuing, vital community service. il Arch
Rec 149:136-8 My '71

WILUSZ, Arthur F.
Super-roundhouse for public works. il **Am City** 86:84+ Ag '71
WIMBLEDON tennis tournament. See Tennis
WIMBUSH, Roger
Behind the scenes. il por **Hi Fi** 21:17-18 Ag '71
WINCELBERG, Jacob
(tr) See Marateck, J. Blow struck for the revolution
WINCHELL, Walter
Winchell, by B. Thomas. Review
Bsns W por p8 S 4 '71. D. Dunn •
Sat R 54:52 Ag 14 '71. S. W. Little •
WINCHES
Stuck? Mount a winch on your wheel. P. Mc-Cafferty. il **Pop Sci** 199:69 N '71
WINCHESTER, Alice
Perspective. il **Antiques** 101:144-52 Ja '72
WINCHESTER, James H.
Airplanes that fly from downtown. il **Read Digest** 98:186-9+ F '71
Beware charter-flight cheats. **Read Digest** 98:97-100 Ja '71
I'm not superstitious, but... il **Read Digest** 98:21-4 F '71
Nightmare in Laurel. il **Read Digest** 99:82-6 Jl '71
Top of the world. il **Travel** 136:55-9 Ag '71
WINCHESTER, Mass.

Education
Helping spend school dollars wisely; teachers councils on curriculum development. D. J. Stangel. **Todays Ed** 60:38-9 Ja '71
WIND, Herbert Warren
Profiles; P. G. Wodehouse. por **New Yorker** 47:43-6+ My 15 '71
Sporting scene (cont) **New Yorker** 47:107-14 Mr 27; 112-18+ Ap 3; 100+ Ap 10; 95-101 My 8; 56-8+ Jl 17; 98-108+ O 2 '71
WIND
See also
Winds
WIND, Solar. See Solar wind
WIND CAVE NATIONAL PARK
Wind Cave National Park. R. B. Rodgers and R. C. Ernst. il **Nat Parks & Con Mag** 45:15-17 Je '71
WIND instruments
See also
Ocarina
WIND mills. See Windmills
WIND pressure
Dampers blunt the wind's force on tall buildings; World trade center, New York city. il **Arch Rec** 150:155-8 S '71
See also
Anemometers
WINDCHY, Eugene G.
On reading the Pentagon papers. **New Repub** 165:21-5 Ag 7 '71
WINDERMERE, Fla.
Can you trim trees with a tractor? il **Am City** 86:12 My '71
WINDHAUSER, Eileen. See Miller, W. H. jt. auth.
WINDISCH-GRAETZ, Stephanie
Beauty in a classic way. pors **Vogue** 158:64-5 Ag 1 '71 •
WINDLE, Jerry
Rock painting for fun and profit. il pors **Design** 72:20-1 mid-Wint '71
WINDMILLER, Marshall
Agents of the new empire. **Nation** 212:592-6 My 10 '71
WINDMILLS
Homage to windmills. S. L. Udall. il **Read Digest** 98:95-6 My '71
See also
Heller-Aller company
WINDMILLS, Remodeled. See Houses, Remodeled
WINDOLPH, George
Building and using the 2XY calibrator. il **Pop Electr** 34:34-5+ Mr '71
WINDOW air conditioners. See Air conditioning equipment
WINDOW boxes. See Flower boxes, planters, etc.
WINDOW curtains and draperies. See Curtains and draperies
WINDOW gardening
See also
Flower boxes, planters, etc.
WINDOW gaskets. See Gaskets
WINDOW glass, Sealed double. See Glass
WINDOW screens. See Screens (doors, windows, etc)
WINDOWS
All about windows; glossary. il **Redbook** 136:91-4 F '71
Do this if you don't like the view. M. B. Smith. il **Bet Hom & Gard** 49:60-3 My '71

Historical view of the window. M. K. Albers. il **Design** 72:12-15 Sum '71
This tinted glass cuts the glare and beats the heat; storm windows. E. F. Lindsley. il **Pop Sci** 199:65 O '71
Work wonders with your windows. il **House B** 113:99-108 Ap '71
See also
Skylights

Maintenance and repair
Care & repair of aluminum doors & windows. il **Mech Illus** 67:115-16+ My '71
WINDOWS, Stained glass. See Glass painting and staining
WINDS
Circulation and weather of 1970. J. F. Andrews. il **Weatherwise** 24:4-11+ F '71
Curing an ill wind; khamsin. il **Time** 97:73 Je 14 '71
Sea and the sky P. Rockwell. il **Motor B & S** 128:44-5 bibliog(p58) Jl '71
Ways of the wind. R. E. Falconer. il **Cons** 26:22-7+ D '71
Winds that blow the earth. J. A. Maxtone-Graham. il **Am For** 77:12-15+ Mr '71
See also
Hurricanes
Storms
Whirlwinds
Wind-pressure

Measurement
Beaufort wind scale; photographs. J. C. Maddox. **Art in Am** 59:90-1 Ja '71
WINDSHIELD washers. See Automobiles—Windshield washers
WINDSHIELD wipers. See Automobiles—Windshield wipers
WINDSHIELDS. See Boats—Windshields
WINDSOR, Charles R. See Fox, S. W. jt. auth.
WINDSOR chairs. See Chairs
WINDSOR fund. See Investment trusts
WINE
And now, pop wines. **Time** 97:62 My 24 '71
Bulletin from the vineyards. R. J. Misch. il **McCalls** 98:46 Mr '71
California's wine boom. J. Wilson. **House & Gard** 140:115+ N '71
California's wines: their time is now. G. Henle. il **House B** 113:96-8+ Mr '71
Do people snigger when you order the wine? R. A. De Groot. **Esquire** 75:142-3+ My '71
Europe warily sips those U.S. vintages. il **Bsns W** p41 Ag 14 '71
Grape's the thing; American wine; with report by E. Alston. il **Look** 35:30-3 Je 15 '71
Kir. J. O'Reilly. il **Holiday** 48:68-9 S '70
Parting shots; $5,000 bet on a bottle of wine. il **Life** 70:74-5 Je 18 '71
Practical wine rack, and what to put in it. il **Mech Illus** 68:110+ Ja '72
Red table wines; Bordeaux, Burgundy, Italian and Italian-type. New York, and proprietary vinifera wines. il **Consumer Rep** 36:600-5 O '71
Rosé wines. il **Consumer Rep** 37:52-4 Ja '72
Spanish wines, overlooked and undervalued. J. Donovan. **House B** 113:100 F '71
Synergy of ethanol and a natural soporific—gamma hydroxybutyrate. E. R. McCabe and others. bibliog il **Science** 171:404-6 Ja 29 '71
What goes with what? R. A. De Groot. **House B** 113:140-1+ N '71
White table wines; bordeaux, burgundy, German and miscellaneous wines. il **Consumer Rep** 36:673-8 N '71
Wines. A. Fraser. **Mlle** 72:136+ Ap; 73:30-1 S '71
See also
Champagne
Viticulture

Bibliography
Bottle in the book. G. Henle. **House B** 113:124 Ap '71

Storage
Wine in waiting. il **Sunset** 147:64-7 S '71
WINE as gifts
Wine and spirit gifts and drinks for holiday parties; with recipes. J. Ellis. **House & Gard** 140:34+ D '71
WINE in religion, folklore, etc.
Use of the word wine in Scripture, by K. Jolly. Review
Chr Cent 88:1543 D 29 '71
WINE industry
Europe warily sips those U.S. vintages. il **Bsns W** p41 Ag 14 '71
Happy days for California wines. C. G. Burck. il **Fortune** 84:78-82+ S '71
See also
Wineries

WINE labels
How to read a wine label. W. Clifford. il House B 113:88-9+ Je; 74-6 Jl; 68+ Ag '71

WINE making
New wines, new bottles il Life 71:91-4 D 10 '71

WINE punch. See Punch (beverage)

WINE racks
Practical wine rack, and what to put in it. il Mech Illus 68:108-10 Ja '72

WINE trade. See Wine industry

WINERIES
California wine rush. il Time 97:76 Mr 1 '71
Miracle of the vine. J. D. Weaver. il Holiday 49:64-5+ Ap '71

WINFIELD, Dick
Tell it like it was, exactly; excerpt from One way to write your novel. il Writers Digest 51:34-6 F '71

WINFREY, Carey
Tip on a lost race. il pors Harper 242:64-70 Je '71

WING, Lucy
Special on meat: the new pork and how to cook it. il Good H 174:129 Ja '72

WING, R. Cliff, and Mack, P. H.
Wide open for learning. Ed Digest 36:19-21 F '71

WING chairs. See Chairs

WINGO, Hal
Busby Berkeley's girls glitter again. il por Life 70:42-3 F 19 '71
Consumer champion lays down the law. il pors Life 71:22-9 Jl 16 '71

WINGS, Airplane. See Airplane wings

WINGSHOOTING. See Shooting

WINGSPREAD project. See Chicago—Education

WINICK, Charles
Story behind the book. L. P. Freilicher. Pub W 199:53 My 24 '71 •

WINICKOFF, Susan A. and Resnik, H. L. P.
Student suicide. bibliog Todays Ed 60:30-2+ Ap '71

WINN, Ira Jay
Change and resistance to the new social studies. bibliog Sch & Soc 99:182-4+ Mr '71
Greetings from Los Angeles; with biographical sketch. il Natur Hist 80:2, 12-14+ bibliog(p 108) O '71
Toward a new definition of national security. Bul Atom Sci 27:35-7 Mr '71

WINNBERG, Anders
Computer-run radio telescope spectrograph. il Sky & Tel 42:274-6 N '71

WINNER family
Winner coat-of-arms. H. K. Eilers. il Hobbies 76.150-1 Ag '71

WINNING. See Success

WINSLOW, Miriam
Miriam Winslow: dancer-sculptress. W. Terry. il pors Dance Mag 45:25-7 D '71 •

WINSLOW, Pete
Fallout from the peaceful atom. Nation 212:557-61, 738 My 3, Je 14 '71

WINSTON, Sheldon
Vice principal: more than a disciplinarian. Clear House 46:78-81 O '71

WINSTON-SALEM, N.C.
Old Salem: a Moravian memoir. V. D. Hahn. il Am Home 74:28+ D '71
Peaceful people. M. Evans. il Am Home 74:44-9+ D '71

Galleries and museums
Dolls of Old Salem; Wachovia historical museum, Old Salem. M. L. Morris. il Hobbies 76:42+ Jl '71

Sanitary affairs
It's not sludge, it's fertilizer. F. Styers. il Am City 86:48-50 F '71

WINTER, Bill. See Winter, N. A. Jr

WINTER, Colin, bp
South African bishop attacks apartheid. Chr Cent 88:1287 N 3 '71 •

WINTER, Lon
Where's Tricia? por Ladies Home J 88:76+ N '71

WINTER, N. A. Jr
There's thunder in the Canyon. il Nat Wildlife 10:17-20 D '71

WINTER, Ruth
Biological superiority: female or male? il Sci Digest 70:44-7+ Ag '71
Dream city. il Sci Digest 69:52-5 Ap '71

WINTER
Early winter. il Cons 26:41 D '71
Letter from the East. E. B. White. New Yorker 47:35-7 Mr 27 '71
See also
Snow
Snowstorms

WINTER camping. See Camping

WINTER conditioning of automobiles. See Automobiles—Maintenance and repair

WINTER cruises. See Cruising

WINTER driving. See Automobile driving

WINTER fishing. See Fishing, Winter

WINTER flowers. See Flowers

WINTER flying. See Aviation—Winter flying

WINTER gardening
See also
Artificial light gardening

WINTER Olympic games, 1972. See Olympic games (winter)

WINTER Olympic games, 1976. See Olympic games (winter)

WINTER Olympics. See Olympic games (winter)

WINTER protection of plants. See Plants, Protection of

WINTER resorts
Action is hot when the weather is cold; Bear Valley, Calif. D. Messinesi. il Vogue 158:173 N 1 '71
From tennis courts to skating rinks, fast; Vail, Colo. il Am City 86:28 My '71
Ski bums' plight; unemployed college dropouts at Aspen and Vail, Colo. M. Kasindorf. il Newsweek 78:88+ D 20 '71
See also
Squaw Valley

WINTER sports
Frapped fun: putting your hobbies on ice. N. Levy. il Har Yrs 11:30-3 Ja '71
Sporting winter. il Seventeen 29:106-7+ D '70
See also
Hockey
Skis and skiing
Sleighs and sleighing
Snowshoeing

WINTER surfing. See Surf riding

WINTER survival. See Wilderness survival

WINTERS, Anne
Paolo Uccello; poem. Poetry 118:8-9 Ap '71

WINTERS, Daniel
Who are the youthful rebels? il PTA Mag 65:10-12+ bibliog(p33) Je '71

WINTERS, Helen M.
Is this any way to plan a retirement? Motor B & S 128:90 S '71

WINTER'S girl; story. See Warner, L.

WINTER'S tale; drama. See Shakespeare, W. —Plays

WINTERTHUR gardens. See Gardens—Delaware

WINTERTHUR museum. See Henry Francis du Pont Winterthur museum

WINTERTON, Cordys, and Winterton, James
Happy classroom home. Todays Ed 60:69 S '71

WINTERTON, James. See Winterton, C. jt. auth.

WINTHER, Barbara
Greatest treasure; dramatization of a Dutch folk tale. Plays 31:59-66 D '71
Shine on, Pecos Bill; drama. Plays 30:43-50 My '71
Sleeping mountains; dramatization of a Mexican folk tale. Plays 30:43-50 Ap '71

WIRE
See also
Electric wire and wiring
National standard company

WIRE, Tire. See Tire fabrics

WIRE sculpture
Art of wire sculpture. il Design 72:4-5 mid-Wint '71

WIRE tapping
Facts about wiretapping; views of L. Powell. N. Lewin. New Repub 165:16-17 N 20 '71
Thirty years of wire tapping. A. G. Theoharis. Nation 212:744-50 Je 14 '71
Wiretaps & national security; question of constitutionality of warrantless taps. A. M. Dershowitz. Commentary 53:56-61 Ja '72
See also
Electronics in criminal investigation, espionage, etc.

WIRE weaving. See Weaving

WIRETAPPING. See Wire tapping

WIRING, Electric. See Electric wire and wiring

WIRSIG, Woodrow
Six steps to smarter shopping. Read Digest 99:29-30+ D '71

WIRT, Eileen E.
Flying vigilantes help stop rustlers. il Farm J 95:19 F '71

WISCASSET, Me.
Fly to Wiscasset. S. Wilkinson. il Flying 89:56-9 Jl '71

WISCONSIN
See also
Architecture, Domestic—**Wisconsin**
Camps—Wisconsin
Delavan Lake
Festivals—Wisconsin
Fishing—Wisconsin
Geology—**Wisconsin**
Mendota, Lake
Wausau, Lake

WISCONSIN. University
Far Eastern students in a big university, subcultures within a subculture. M. H. Klein and others. Bul Atom Sci 27:10+ Ja '71

EDSAT center
Educational satellite telecommunication: the challenge of a new technology. D. D. Smith. il Bul Atom Sci 27:14-18 Ap '71

Green Bay campus
Communiversity. E. W. Weidner. Nat Parks & Con Mag 45:20 My '71
Ecology U. Newsweek 77:77 Je 14 '71
Survival U is alive and burgeoning in Green Bay, Wisconsin. J. Fischer. Harper 242: 20+ F '71; Same abr. with title New university for survival. Cur 128:12-18 Ap '71

Madison campus
Care and feeding of an arts administrator. F. Taylor. Hi Fi 21:MA10-11 S '71
Mood in Madison. il Newsweek 78:65 O 11 '71
New math: the day they bombed Wisconsin; Army mathematics research center. J. S. Rock. Ramp Mag 9:32-4 F '71
Wisconsin physicists pick up the pieces and get back to work. G. B. Lubkin. il Phys Today 24:69+ Mr '71

WISDOM
Wisdom, cry out! T. E. Clarke. il America 125:151-2 S 11 '71

WISE, Arthur E.
California doctrine. il Sat R 54:78-9+ N 20 '71

WISE, C. David. See Stein, L. jt. auth.

WISE, Charles N.
Forgotten AD note. Flying 88:73 My '71

WISE, Charles W. and Simpson, R. H.
Tropical analysis program of the National hurricane center. bibliog il Weatherwise 24: 164-73 Ag '71

WISE, John E.
Science and human values. bibliog Sch & Soc 99:90-2 F '71

WISE, Paul S.
Case against no-fault auto insurance. por Pop Sci 198:57+ Ja '71

WISE, Rick
Enter an all-round Wise guy. W. Leggett. il por Sports Illus 35:40 Jl 5 '71 *

WISE, Robert
Robert Wise: mythmaker. N. Gittelson. Harp Baz 104:8+ My '71 *

WISE, Wes
Up the establishment. Newsweek 77:32 My 3 '71 *

WISE men. See Magi

WISEMAN, Denis V.
Runner; poem. Chr Cent 88:518 Ap 28 '71

WISEMAN, Frederick
Public documents. il por Newsweek 78:99 O 4 '71 *

WISTER, Gertrude
Graceful Japanese peonies. il **Horticulture** 49:20-2 O '71

WIT and humor. See Humor

WITCH doctors. See Medicine men

WITCHCRAFT
Charming power of witchcraft; black magic practices in England. J. D. Douglas. Chr Today 15:41-2 Mr 26 '71
Evil. anyone? il Newsweek 78:56-7 Ag 16 '71
Further conversations with Don Juan; excerpt from A separate reality. C. Castaneda. il Esquire 75:75-89+ Mr '71; Discussion. 75:14 My '71
Separate reality, by C. Castaneda. Review Life 70:20 My 14 '71. B. Darrach
Sins of Salem. K. Bryn. Sci Digest 69:29-31 My '71
Why we fear witches. M. Mead. Redbook 138: 49+ N '71
Witches are rising. B. Vachon. il pors Look 35:40-4 Ag 24 '71
Witches in our midst. D. Cohen. il Sci Digest 69:22-6 Je '71
See also
Medicine men

WITCHCRAFT in literature. See Childrens literature—Themes

WITH all flags flying; story. See Tyler. A.
WITH all my heart; story. See Coffer, H. L.

WITHERUP, William
Fable; poem. Nation 212:796 Je 21 '71

WITHINGTON, William A.
Cambodia. bibliog il Focus 21:1-9 F '71
Indonesia. bibliog il Focus 21:1-12 My '71

WITKOWSKY, Jack
Education of a school board member. il por Sat R 54:90-2 N 20 '71

WITNESS; story. See Petry, A.

WITNESS bearing (Christianity)
Demonstrating for Jesus; recent antiwar demonstrations. E. E. Plowman. Chr Today 15:41-2 My 21 '71
Jesus movement is upon us; California. B. Vachon. il Look 35:15-21 F 9 '71
Laws of men and the law of God. G. W. Glick. Chr Cent 88:1225-9 O 20 '71
New evangelism. K. Hamilton. Chr Today 15:4-7 Ja 29 '71
Wave of witness. E. E. Plowman. il Chr Today 15:34-5 My 7 '71
Witness. L. N. Bell. Chr Today 16:21 D 17 '71

WITNESSES
Anachronisms of another day; two librarians as witnesses in connection with Kissinger kidnap plot. W. R. Eshelman. Wilson Lib Bul 45:719 Ap '71

WITT, Harold
Givers. Poetry 118:41-5 Ap '71

WITT, Linda
Stew: heterogenius mix. il Todays Health 49: 48-51 Mr '71

WITT, Ronald G.
Landlord and the economic revival of the middle ages in northern Europe, 1000-1250. bibliog f Am Hist R 76:965-88 O '71

WITTER, William D.
Rolling with the punches. por Forbes 107: 59-60 Ap 15 '71 *

WITTER, William D, Inc.
House of Witter. il Bsns W p82-3 N 6 '71

WITTLIN, Byron J. See Resnik. H. L. P. jt. auth.

WITTMER, Joe
Amish schools today. Sch & Soc 99:227-30 Ap '71

WITTNER, Dale
On the streets and the beaches, mobilizers sign up new recruits. il Life 71:28-32 O 15 '71
Quiet falls across the plains. il Life 70:22-31 Je 25 '71

WIVES
I like having a husband, but I don't want to be a wife; interview. ed. by S. Nirenberg. A. Jackson. il por House B 113:35+ O '71
Runaway wives. il Time 98:64 D 20 '71
Swapping family roles; role-swapping experiment by couples in Norway. il Time 98:72+ N 22 '71
Wives; excerpt from Wives: an investigation. R. Thorp and R. Blake. il Ladies Home J 88:186-91 S '71
See also
Desertion and non-support
Executives wives
Housewives
Husbands
Marriage
Marriage counseling
Married women
Policemens wives
Separation (law)
Service mens wives
Widows

Anecdotes, facetiae. satire, etc.
Four faces of Erma. E. Bombeck. il Todays Health 49:30-3 Ag '71

Employment
See Married women—Employment

WIXOM, Hartt
How to fish low water. il Field & S 76:64-5+ Je '71
How to fool big brown trout. il Field & S 76: 56-7+ My '71
See more shootable deer. il Field & S 76:46-7+ O '71

WODEHOUSE, Pelham Grenville
Exclusive interview: P. G. Wodehouse: ed. by D. Bensen. por Writers Digest 51:22-4+ O '71
about
Flea forever. J. Finn. New Repub 164:30-2 Ap 24 '71 *
Profiles. H. W. Wind. por New Yorker 47: 53-6+ My 15 '71 *
Talk of the town: ninetieth birthday party. New Yorker 47:40-1 O 30 '71 *
Wodehouse Aeternus. G. Clarke. il por Time 98:91-2 O 25 '71

WOESSNER, Warren
Eagles; poem. Nation 213:350 O 11 '71
Return from absolute zero; Operation; Black crow; Laos in the air; Getting the laundry; poems. Poetry 118:10-12 Ap '71

WOFFORD, Harris
College presidents and students; interview. Mlle 73:246+ Ag '71

WOHL, Paul
Merit of Ulbricht. Nation 212:613 My 17 '71
Opening to the East. il Nation 212:142-5 F 1 '71
Slow and serene; interview. New Yorker 47:30-2 My 1 '71

WOHLNER, Grace L.
How children learn to handle money. il Parents Mag 46:46-7+ Je '71

WOHLSTATTAR, Tessie
Salami; story. Todays Ed 60:20-1 My '71

WOIWODE, Larry
Fragment; poem. Mlle 72:114 F '71
Marie; story. New Yorker 47:32-8 D 25 '71
Old Halvorson place; story. New Yorker 47:35-43 My 8 '71
Pneumonia, 1945; story. New Yorker 46:38-44 F 13 '71

WOJCIECHOWSKA, Maia Teresa
Who should write for young readers? Writer 84:19-20 Ap '71

about

Maia Wojciechowska: controversial and committed. D. Chubb. Writer 84:21 Ap '71 *

WOJCIK, Fred
For your mini-compact: build the PS minicamper. il Pop Sci 198:100-2 My '71

WOJTOWICZ, Raymond J.
Don't laugh at Hamtramck. por Newsweek 77:95-6 My 17 '71 *

WOK (utensil) See Kitchen utensils

WOK, Electric (utensil) See Household appliances, Electric

WOLBACH, William Wellington
Navigation guide for pension funds. Nations Bsns 59:78A-78D Ap '71

WOLBRECHT, Walter F.
Cold and cruel. Chr Cent 88:1102 S 22 '71 *

WOLD, Finn. See Brown, W. E. jt. auth.

WOLDT, Arthur
Lunkers at large. il Cons 25:2-3 Je '71
1971 legislative session and the environment. Cons 26:17+ Ag '71

WOLF, Anne M.
Why I became a nun. pors Ladies Home J 88:94+ My '71

WOLF, Barbara
Those *longuers* in Japanese films. Nation 213:152-4 Ag 30 '71

WOLF, Charles, Jr
Military-industrial complexities. Bul Atom Sci 27:19-22 F '71

WOLF, John B.
Lebanon: the politics of survival. bibliog f Cur Hist 62:20-4+ Ja '72

WOLF, Rodney A.
Osmotic pump, an unusual timer and how to enhance contrast in astronomical photographs. il Sci Am 225:100-3 D '71

WOLF TRAP FARM PARK for the performing arts
Capital gets some culture. A. Cross. il Am For 77:14-19 N '71
Wolf Trap, a gala opening; Filene center and the national park. B. Belt. por Hi Fi 21:MA20+ O '71
Wolf trap: something new: Wolf trap farm park for the performing arts. S. Fleming. il Hi Fi 21:MA10+ Mr '71

WOLFE, Bertram David
Government of Doctor Caligari: address, December 3, 1971. Nat R 23:1461-2 D 31 '71

WOLFE, Don M.
Autobiography: the gold of writing power. Engl J 60:937-46 O '71

WOLFE, Gerald E.
Tidewater cats. il Outdoor Life 148:62-3+ S '71

WOLFE, Thomas K.
Sissy bars will be lower this year. il Esquire 75:60-3+ F '71

about

Dazzle-dust: a Wolfe in chic clothing. L. Kuehl. pors Commonweal 94:212-16 My 7 '71 *
Sketchbook of snobs. J. R. Coyne, jr. Nat R 23:90-1 Ja 26 '71 *
Tom Wolfe: reactionary chic. J. Gordon. por Ramp Mag 10:58-62 Ja '72 *

WOLFE, Tom. See Wolfe, T. K.

WOLFE, Walter M.
Question of sterilization: ed. by E. Edelson. Redbook 136:22+ Mr '71

WOLFF, Anthony
Big schemes for little ants. il Audubon 73:120-4 Mr '71

WOLFF, Christoph
New research on Bach's Musical offering. bibliog f il Mus Q 57:379-408 Jl '71

WOLFF, Klaus, and Konrad, Klaus
Melanin pigmentation: an in vivo model for studies of melanosome kinetics within keratinocytes. bibliog il Science 174:1034-5 D 3 '71

WOLFFE, Andrew J. See Wolffe, L. L. jt. auth.

WOLFFE, Lenard L. and Wolffe, A. J.
Zoning changes are coming: are you ready? House B 113:46 O '71

WOLFGANG, Myra K.
Excerpt from testimony before the Subcommittee on constitutional amendments, May 6, 1970. Cong Digest 50:19+ Ja '71

WOLFLE, Dael
Supernatural department. Science 173:109 Jl 9 '71
—and Kidd, C. V.
Future market for Ph.D.'s. bibliog il Science 173:784-93 Ag 27 '71

WOLFMAN, Augustus
Wolfman on printing. See issues of Modern photography

WOLFSON, Bernice J. See MacDonald, J. B. jt. auth.

WOLITZER, Hilma
Waiting for daddy; story. Esquire 76:98-9 Jl '71

WOLK, Donald J.
Drug abusers. il Todays Ed 60:49-50+ N '71

WOLKOWITZ, Carol
America's vagabond ambassadors; interview, ed. by D. Butwin. il por Sat R 54:59-62+ F 20 '71

WOLKSTEIN, Diane
Old and new sexual messages in fairy tales. il Wilson Lib Bul 46:163-6 O '71

WOLLETT, Bill. See Wollett, M. jt. auth.

WOLLETT, Mary, and Wollett, Bill
American historical glass. il Hobbies 76:72 N; 98Z D '71; 99 Ja '72

WOLMAN, M. Gordon
Nation's rivers. bibliog il Science 174:905-18 N 26 '71

WOLSTENHOLME, Carol
Our winter greenhouse. il Org Gard & Farm 18:103-4 N '71

WOLVERTON, Mike. See Wolverton, R. jt. auth.

WOLVERTON, Ruth, and Wolverton, Mike
Frank Kriwanek. il por Ceram Mo 19:13-15 Ja '71
To market, to market! il Ceram Mo 19:21+ My; 27+ Je '71

WOLVES
Beast of Gévaudan. C. H. D. Clarke. bibliog Natur Hist 80:44-51+ Ap '71
Harold and the wolf. il Time 97:56 Ap 26 '71
Way of life of the timber wolf. D. H. Pimlott. il Liv Wildn 34:20-8 Aut '70
Where the wolves are and how they stand. L. D. Mech. Natur Hist 80:26-9 Ap '71
Wolf music. J. B. Theberge. il Natur Hist 80:36-43 bibliog(p 84) Ap '71

WOLVES in literature. See Animals in literature

WOMAN
Female eunuch; excerpt. G. Greer. il McCalls 98:92-3+ Mr '71
Of two minds. D. Rodgers and M. Rodgers. pors McCalls 98:18+ F '71
On being a woman. J. Brothers. See issues of Good housekeeping
Right now: a monthly newsletter for women. See issues of McCall's
Tough cookies; categorizing females. D. Newman and R. Benton. il Mlle 74:20 Ja '72
What is a beautiful woman? G. Guinness. il Harp Baz 104:124-5 Ap '71
Woman problem. il Life 71:40-7 Ag 13; 40-52A Ag 20; 46-51 Ag 27 '71
You: the woman of today. il Vogue 159:36-43 Ja 1 '72
See also
Beauty, Personal
Education of women
Housewives
Marriage
Sex differences
Single women
Widows
Wives
Women and the church
Women in art

Aging
See Aging

Crime
See also
Shoplifting

WOMAN—*Continued*

Diseases
See also
Gynecology

Dress
See Clothing and dress

Education
See Education of women

Employment
Career is all in your head. N. A. Comer.
Mlle 72:119+ Ja '71
Economics of sex bias. B. M. Gray. il Nation 212:742-4 Je 14 '71
Healthy anger; discrimination against women librarians. H. Lowenthal. bibliog il Library J 96:2597-9 S 1 '71
Jobs down for women, survey finds. il McCalls 98:39 Ap '71
Motherhood vs. the job. L. Kanowitz. McCalls 98:43 My '71
Some second thoughts on Women's lib. T. Thomson. Read Digest 98:95-7 Je '71
What bfog means to you. L. Kanowitz. McCalls 98:45 S '71
Why women work, what a study finds. U S News 71:66 Ag 23 '71
Women filing classified complaints. L. Foster. McCalls 98:46 Mr '71
Women in academic libraries; discrimination. H. W. Tuttle. Library J 96:2594-6 S 1 '71; Discussion. 96:3255 O 15 '71
Women in labor. M. Sueizle. il Trans-Action 8:50-8 N '70
Working woman. L. C. Pogrebin. See issues of Ladies' home journal
You still have a long way to go, baby. il Bsns W p74-6+ S 25 '71
See also
Discrimination in employment
Equal pay for equal work
Hours of labor
Household employees
Married women—Employment
Woman—Equal rights
Woman—Occupations

Equal rights
Achieving equal rights other ways. P. A. Freund. Cur 134:32-9 N '71
Are myths about misses amiss? Report says yes; NEA findings. il Sr Schol 99:12-13 O 25 '71
Are TV commercials insulting to women? GH poll. il Good H 172:68+ My '71
Double standard; sex discrimination in civil service employment. New Repub 164:12+ My 29 '71
Facing equality for women; proposed constitutional amendment. il Time 98:58-9 O 4 '71
Fighting hard. B. Abzug. por Vogue 157:94-5 Je '71
First no to sex bias; victory for Mrs Sally Reed of Boise, Idaho. Time 98:71 D 6 '71
Inside HEW: women protest sex discrimination. J. Chase. Science 174:270-4 O 15 '71
Ladies day; victory for Mrs Sally Reid in sex bias case. Newsweek 78:23-4 D 6 '71
Liberating academe. il Sat R 54:48 Mr 20 '71
Macmillan executive victim of discrimination. Pub W 199:35-6 Je 7 '71
Men, women and the Constitution. America 125:501 D 11 '71
Ms America; ending Miss and Mrs as form of address. Newsweek 77:61-2 Ap 26 '71
Newest campus crusade: equal rights for women; with address by A. Pifer. il U S News 71:79-82 D 13 '71
Power of the purse; drive for faculty equality. Newsweek 78:81-2 D 6 '71
Race & sex bias are issues as Ringer takes LC to court. pors Library J 96:3262-3 O 15 '71
Set stage for new equal rights battle. S. B. Conroy. por McCalls 98:37 My '71
Sex discrimination; campuses face contract loss over HEW demands. R. J. Bazell; reply. F. Moog. Science 171:236 Ja 22 '71
Supporting an equal rights amendment. T. L. Emerson. Cur 134:25-32 N '71
Tally's triumph; T. Palmer wins sex discrimination case. por Time 98:20 S 6 '71
This month's feature: Congress & the Equal rights amendment. Cong Digest 50:1-32 Ja '71
Time is here for Women's liberation. K. T. Romer and C. Secor. Ann Am Acad 397:129-39 S '71
Up from slavery. J. H. Plumb. il Horizon 13:80-1 Sum '71

What can I do about sex discrimination? K. Branan. Schol Teach Jr/Sr High p20 N '71
Why women are tougher. E. Ramey. Read Digest 98:73-5 Ap '71
Womanpower problem: sex discrimination on campus. D. Zwerdling. New Repub 164:11-13 Mr 20 '71
Women profs fight back; discrimination against women. il Newsweek 77:99-100+ My 17 '71
Women: the new image; address, June 3, 1971. A. S. Fraser. Vital Speeches 37:599-605 Jl 15 '71
Women's lib in Congress; Equal rights amendment. J. K. Javits. Esquire 76:76+ O '71
Women's rights: action in court and Congress. U S News 71:86 D 6 '71
Women's rights: how GH readers feel about liberation and equality. il Good H 172:34+ Mr '71
Working women and the equal rights amendment. J. Jordan. Trans-Action 8:16+ N '70
See also
Woman—Employment
Womens liberation movement

Anecdotes, facetiae, satire, etc.
Good Lord, grandpa, it all came true. C. Davidson. il Am Heritage 22:70-1 F '71

Health and hygiene
Feminine hygiene mystique: the whats, whens, whys. Mlle 73:146-7+ Je '71
How to use your head when your hair starts falling out. J. Snyder. il Todays Health 49:32-4+ Jl '71
Latest medical facts about douching. Good H 172:179 Je '71
Over-medicated woman. H. R. Berg. il McCalls 98:67+ S '71
Why health hazards are rising for women smokers. Good H 173:195 O '71
Your health. See occasional issues of Redbook
See also
Abortion—Psychological aspects
Beauty, Personal
Menopause
Menstruation
Pregnancy
Sanitary napkins, tampons, etc.

History
Adam's rib: or, The woman within. U. Stannard. il Trans-Action 8:24-32+ N '70

Intelligence
See Intelligence levels—Women

Legal status, laws, etc.
Dimensions of the oppression of women; address, December 5, 1970. P. J. Springen. Vital Speeches 37:265-7 F 15 '71
Legal status of women. K. A. Cassell. bibliog il Library J 96:2600-3 S 1 '71; Discussion. 96:3700 N 15 '71
Women in Congress; legislative proposals and government policies. F. Lang. il Ramp Mag 9:10+ My '71
Women's legal rights in 50 states. il McCalls 98:90-5 F '71
See also
Divorce
Woman—Employment
Woman—Equal rights

Occupations
Face to face with a female Senate page; ed. by M. E. Kinsley. E. McConnell. por Seventeen 30:52 N '71
Good job opportunities for women in the health-care field. Good H 174:144 Ja '72
If you want to resume a full-time job. il Good H 172:187 My '71
Living off the fat of the land; food jobs you've heard of and some you haven't. A. M. Cunningham. il Mlle 72:178-9+ F '71
Ms Plumber. il Newsweek 79:53 Ja 10 '72
On the road; highway flag girl. T. Mocabee. il Seventeen 30:70 Jl '71
They laughed when I quit my job; a career in knitting. T. Blitz. por Redbook 136:10+ Ja '71
Women go marching on. America 124:60-1 Ja 23 '71
See also
Business and professional women
Cottage industries
Models (persons)
Negro women—Occupations
Secretaries
Telephone operators
also headings beginning Women as, e.g. Women as public relations directors

WOMAN—*Continued*

Psychology

Abortion and suicidal behaviors: observations on the concept of endangering the mental health of the mother. H. L. P. Resnik and B. J. Wittlin. bibliog Ment Hy 55:10-20 Ja '71

Anais Nin on women; interview. ed. by J. Oringer. il Ramp Mag 9:43-5 My '71

Facing up to disappointments. J. Brothers. il Good H 174:52+ Ja '72

Farewell to Heloise. M. Lukas. il Cath World 213:174-7 Jl '71

Growing up girlish; excerpt from Roles women play: readings towards women's liberation. ed. by M. H. Garskof. J. Freeman. il Trans-Action 8:36-43 N '70

How ideology shapes woman's lives. J. Lipman-Blumen. il Sci Am 226:34-42 Ja '72

Myths that keep women down. C. Bird. Ladies Home J 88:68+ N '71

On being a woman. J. Brothers. See issues of Good housekeeping

Report on a consciousness-raising group. il Mlle 73:80-1+ Jl '71

Ties women cannot shake, and have. E. Hardwick. por Vogue 157:86-7 Je '71

What do you want for Christmas? M. Reznikoff and G. Domino. Ladies Home J 88:62+ D '71

Woman and the fetus: one flesh? R. C. Wahlberg. Chr Cent 88:1045-8 S 8 '71; Discussion. il 88:1450-1 D 8 '71

Woman's intuition; symposium. Vogue 158:60-1+ S 15 '71
See also
Abortion—Psychological aspects
Intelligence levels—Women

Religious life
See also
Women and the church

Rights of women
See Woman—Equal rights

Social and moral questions

American woman; symposium. bibliog il Trans-Action 8:12-14+ N '70

Annals of justice; G. Russier case in Marseille. M. Gallant. New Yorker 47:47-52+ Je 26 '71

Liberated woman. M. Decter; discussion. Commentary 51:12+ F '71
See also
Divorce
Prostitution
Womens liberation movement

Wages
See Equal pay for equal work; Wage differentials

WOMAN as president. See Women as public officers

WOMAN in literature. See Women in literature

WOMAN suffrage

Liechtenstein

Close call. Newsweek 77:53 Mr 15 '71

Keeping up with Kuwait; vote against woman suffrage. il Time 97:39 Mr 15 '71

United States

Women's fight for the vote. E. Kern. il Life 71:40-50A Ag 20 '71

WOMAN who couldn't lie; story. See Smith, E. G.

WOMAN without a shadow; opera. See Strauss, R.

WOMAN'S Christian temperance union
Jesus, women, and temperance. Chr Today 15:37 Ag 27 '71

WOMAN'S day magazine
How to sell a magazine one issue at a time. G. Rhoads. il por Sat R 54:61-3 S 11 '71

WOMAN'S luck; story: See Chekhov, A.

WOMB, Artificial. See Uterus, Artificial

WOMEN
GH poll, the ten most admired women. il Good H 174:14+ Ja '72
See also
Christmas gifts for women
Jewish women
Negro women
Stunt women

Arab states

Shedding the veil. il Newsweek 78:59-60 O 25 '71

Canada

Canadian report on status of women: packed with dynamite. G. Lane. Chr Cent 88:345 Mr 17 '71

China (People's Republic)

China; women's liberation movement. H. Yu. Chr Cent 88:270 F 24 '71

How Chinese women live and work. L. W. Snow. Vogue 158:157+ D '71

Liberated women. il Newsweek 78:32 Ag 16 '71

Women inside China; with introduction. S. Attwood; J. Garavente. il pors McCalls 99:77-9+ N '71

Greece, Modern

Only on Sundays. M. Schein. il Natur Hist 80:52-61 Ap '71

Japan

Japanese women join the lib movement. il Bsns W p70+ Ap 10 '71

Sob sisters. B. Krisher. il Newsweek 77:50+ Je 7 '71

Morocco

Veiled Morocco; with photographs by I. Penn. A. Sefrioui. Vogue 158:116-23+ D '71

Northern Ireland

Fierce women of Ulster; with report by J. Bonfante. il Life 71:24B-30 D 3 '71

Keepers of the flame; women of the IRA. il Newsweek 78:33-4 N 29 '71

Women of Belfast; Women together movement. E. McCallion. il America 125:453-6 N 27 '71

Southern states

Belles of the South. il Ebony 26:158-62 Ag '71

Sweden

Sweden's liberated men and women. S. Kelman. New Repub 164:21-3 Mr 13 '71; Discussion. 164:30 Ap 10 '71

Turkey
See also
Harem

United States

American woman; symposium. bibliog il Trans-Action 8:12-14+ N '70

America's seventy-five most important women. D. Robinson. pors Ladies Home J 88:71-3 Ja '71

Flock of first ladies, and maybe Ms. President. il Life 71:54-5 D 31 '71

Mlle award winners: 7 women who know the answers. il Mlle 74:66-8 Ja '72

Where the women are. S. Alexander. il McCalls 98:85-7 F '71

You, the American woman; symposium. il Vogue 157:70-111+ Je '71
See also
Divorce—United States
Married women
Negro women
Woman—Equal rights
Woman suffrage—United States

History

Women's rights and American feminism. G. Lerner. Am Scholar 40:235-48 Spr '71

Zambia

Zambian women recommend reform in marriage laws. O. Eby. Chr Cent 88:112-14 S 22 '71

WOMEN, Famous
America's seventy-five most important women. D. Robinson. pors Ladies Home J 88:71-3 Ja '71

Heavenly mirrors; six faces. il Vogue 158:91-2+ D '71

History's love stories: down heartthrob lane with Kleenex and camera. D. Kaye. il Sat R 54:38-9+ Mr 13 '71

WOMEN, Jewish. See Jewish women

WOMEN, Negro. See Negro women

WOMEN alcoholics. See Alcoholics

WOMEN and advertising. See Advertising and women

WOMEN and men
Adam's rib; or, The woman within. U. Stannard. il Trans-Action 8:24-32+ N '70

Album of older women. S. Kauffmann. Harper 242:67-8+ My '71

Bad dudes; opinions about notable men by four members of the Women's liberation movement. il Esquire 76:132-5 N '71

Born free but not liberated. G. Culligan. Sat R 54:25-8 Je 5 '71

Christian breakthrough in Women's lib. P. F. Palmer. America 124:634-7 Je 19 '71

Equality seesaw: how men fail their wives and daughters. R. F. Capon. il Redbook 137:73+ Je '71

Essays on sex equality. by J. S. Mill and H. T. Mill. Review
Nation 213:405-6 O 25 '71. V. Held

WOMEN and men—*Continued*
Female sexuality: what it is and isn't; symposium. il Mlle 73:108-17 Jl '71
How men will benefit from the women's power revolution. M. Mannes. il PTA Mag 65:6-8 Ja '71
In my opinion; liberated girls need tender loving care! M. Millenson. por Seventeen 30:160 D '71
Jesus and the liberated woman. B. Graham; discussion. Ladies Home J 88:80-1 Mr '71
Male role in home economics. L. G. Baker, jr. Ed Digest 37:48-9 D '71
Man talk; brides of Frankenstein. D. Newman and R. Benton. Mlle 73:124 Ag '71
Man talk: power play. D. Newman and R. Benton. Mlle 72:96 Mr '71
Marya Mannes. B. L. Freund. Harp Baz 105:109 D '71
Opinion: on man and woman. J. M. Ganguli. por Mlle 73:38+ My '71
Opinion thoughts after an evening with Norman Mailer, Germaine Greer, Diana Trilling, Jill Johnston, Jacqueline Ceballos and a cast of thousands. M. Cantwell. Mlle 73:36+ Jl '71
Poetry, sex and women's rights. J. D. Floerke. Chr Cent 88:737 Je 16 '71
Sexual politics. by K. Millett. Review
Harper 241:110+ D '70. I. Howe; Discussion. 242:6+ Mr '71
Some second thoughts on Women's lib. T. Thomson. Read Digest 98:95-7 Je '71
Theology confronts women's liberation. E. Woo America 124:257-9 Mr 13 '71
Tyranny of the male therapist; interview. ed. by C. Bigwood. P. Chesler. Harp Baz 104:52-3 Jl '71
Why women are tougher. E. Ramey. Read Digest 98:73-5 Ap '71
With Norman Mailer at the sex circus. V. S. Pritchett; J. C. Oates. Atlan 228:40-5 Jl '71
Woman and man, man and woman. il Mlle 73:73-7 Jl '71
Women and the church: poor psychology, worse theology. S. D. Collins; discussion. Chr Cent 88:227-8 F 17 '71
See also
Sex differences
Sex role

Bibliography
Up for discussion; the skirts in fiction about boys: a maxi mess. D. G. Stavn. Library J 96:282-6 Ja 15 '71

WOMEN and peace
See also
Another mother for peace (organization)

WOMEN and politics
Men, women, and politics. L. Romney. Look 35:11 Ap 6 '71
Power of a woman. See issues of Ladies's home Journal
See also
National women's political caucus
Women in politics

WOMEN and religion
After the death of God the father. M. Daly. Commonweal 94:7-11 Mr 12 '71; Discussion. 94:275+ My 28 '71
From Adam's rib to Women's lib. K. L. Woodward. il McCalls 98:77+ Je '71
Pronoun envy; protest by female students at the Harvard divinity school. il Newsweek 78:58 D 6 '71

WOMEN and the church
Beyond sexual politics; conference of religious feminists at Graymoor, N.Y. D. Grumbach. Commonweal 95:292-3 D 24 '71
Feminist scholars criticize male-dominated theology. Chr Cent 88:648 My 26 '71
Onward Christian sisters. S. Cunneen. Chr Cent 88:245-6 F 24 '71
St Paul and the liberated woman. C. Miller. Chr Today 15:13-14 Ag 6 '71
Spirit and the human person, by J. M. Ford. Review
Cath World 213:248 Ag '71. H. Gow
Unequal in the sight of God; interviews. ed. by G. MacEoin. il McCalls 98:78-9+ Je '71
Women and the church: poor psychology, worse theology. S. D. Collins; discussion. Chr Cent 88:227-8 F 17 '71
Women of the reformation in Germany and Italy, by R. H. Bainton. Review
Chr Cent 88:1008 Ag 25 '71. M. Fousek
Women seeking bigger role in churches. il U S News 70:24-5 Ja 18 '71
Women's liberation and the church, ed. by S. B. Doely. Review
Cath World 213:99-100 My '71. D. Kolmer
Commonweal 94:114-16 Ap 9 '71. S. Cunneen
Women's liberation: tending toward idolatry. J. Hitchcock. il Chr Cent 88:1104-7 S 22 '71

Year of the woman for Baptists, Presbyterians. E. E. Plowman. por Chr Today 15:27 Je 4 '71

WOMEN as artists
Invisible woman is visible. D. Davis. il Newsweek 78:130-1 N 15 '71
Sexual politics, art style. L. R. Lippard. Art in Am 59:19-20 S '71
Women artists? M. Batterberry and A. Batterberry. Harp Baz 104:73 Jl '71
Womens liberation, woman artists and art history; symposium; discussion. Art N 69:49 Ja '71; Newsweek 77:77 Ja 18 '71

WOMEN as astronauts
No space for women? I. Asimov. il Ladies Home J 88:115+ Mr '71

WOMEN as athletes
And now for the resurrection: Mrs Swan and her Cygnets. R. Blount. il por Sports Illus 34:96-100+ Ap 12 '71
Can a man lose to a woman in a love game? Yes, but. . . S. de Gramont. Vogue 157:130+ My '71
Don't tell the girls how pretty they are; U.S. gymnasts; photographs by P. Leonian; with account by H. Weiskopf. Sports Illus 34:28-35 Mr 29 '71
Girl has to suffer. J. Lebow. il Look 35:60-2+ Je 29 '71
See also
Gibson, A.
Sports for women

WOMEN as bankers
All bankers don't have to be stodgy old men. il pors Ebony 26:58+ S '71

WOMEN as chemists
Some salaries are more equal than others. J. Zimmerman. Chem 44:4 F '71

WOMEN as city commissioners. See Women as municipal officers

WOMEN as clowns. See Clowns

WOMEN as college professors and instructors
Liberating academe. il Sat R 54:48 Mr 20 '71
Newest campus crusade: equal rights for women; with address by A. Pifer. il U S News 71:79-82 D 13 '71
Power of the purse; drive for faculty equality. Newsweek 78:81-2 D 6 '71
Womanpower problem: sex discrimination on campus. D. Zwerdling. New Repub 164:11-13 Mr 20 '71
Women in academia; study of the hiring decision in departments of physical science. A. Y. Lewin and L. Duchan. bibliog Science 173:892-5 S 3 '71

WOMEN as composers. See Women as musicians

WOMEN as detectives. See Detectives

WOMEN as doctors. See Women as physicians

WOMEN as executives
Executive mother: J. Glynn. L. Botto. il por Look 35:73+ Ja 26 '71
Rarest breed of women: black businesswomen in the executive suites. il Time 98:102 N 8 '71
Women in management: pattern for change. C. D. Orth, 3d. and F. Jacobs. bibliog f Harvard Bsns R 49:139-47 Jl '71; Discussion. 49:15-16 N '71

WOMEN as farmers
Wanted: woman to run 200-sow hog farm. R. Wilmore. il Farm J 95:H6-8 My '71

WOMEN as foreign correspondents
Hey, lady, what are you doing here? G. Emerson. il por McCalls 98:61+ Ag '71

WOMEN as foreign service employees
Department strengthens policy on equal opportunities for women. Dept State Bul 65:315 S 20 '71

WOMEN as foresters
Women as forest workers. R. M. Shaw. il Liv Wildn 35:30-1 Spr '71

WOMEN as investors
Money club: B&C investment club, for Buy and cry. M. Gunther. McCalls 98:44 Jl '71

WOMEN as jockeys
Jockey was a lady. il Sports Illus 35:24-9 Jl 5 '71

WOMEN as journalists
Open sesame! women journalists in National press club. S. McBee. McCalls 98:45 Jl '71
See also
Women as reporters

WOMEN as judges
Should a woman be on the Supreme court? Certainly. D. Lawrence. U S News 71:104 O 25 '71
Time for a madame justice. Life 71:36 O 1 '71

WOMEN as lawyers
See also
Women as judges

WOMEN as members of Congress. See Congresswomen

WOMEN as ministers
Anglicans relent; permission to ordain women. Time 97:42 Mr 22 '71
Uncorinthian Philadelphians: Suzanne Radley Hiatt ordained in the Episcopal church. T. W. Moore. por Chr Cent 88:930-1 Ag 4 '71
When the minister is a woman, by E. Gibson. Review
  Chr Cent 88:132 Ja 27 '71. H. W. Stroup. jr

WOMEN as moving picture directors
Women, wives, film-makers; interview, ed. by B. Richardson. G. Nelson; D. Wiley. il Film Q 25:34-40 Fall '71

WOMEN as municipal officers
I hope I'm not a token: New York's Commissioner of human rights. C. Dreifus. por McCalls 99:51 O '71

WOMEN as musicians
Against the odds; interviews with Carol Rosenberger, Dory Previn. rock group Fanny. C. Irving. il McCalls 99:17+ N '71
Brava, maestra! C. Contos. il Hi Fi 21:MA7-10 My '71
Male oppression of women composers. R. L. Greene. il Sat R 55:6 Ja 8 '72
Spirit of Mary Lou; composer M. L. Williams. H. Saal. il por Newsweek 78:67 D 20 '71

WOMEN as orchestral conductors. See Women as musicians

WOMEN as painters. See Women as artists

WOMEN as photographers
Children's photographer. J. Kuh. Ladies Home J 88:64 Ja '71

WOMEN as physicians
Why can't more women be doctors? F. M. Eckman. Redbook 137:77+ My '71
Women doctors preferred? H. Alpert. il Har Yrs 11:36-40 Ag '71

WOMEN as pianists. See Women as musicians

WOMEN as prisoners. See Prisoners, Women

WOMEN as public officers
Let's put women in their place like, for instance, city hall. J. Mayer. McCalls 98:74+ F '71
Shaker-upper wants to be Madame President Chisholm. J. Howard. por Life 71:81 N 5 '71
What it will be like when we elect a woman president; interview, ed. by D. Sendler. H. G. Brown. il por Todays Health 49:26-31 Jl '71
Woman could be president; address, February 25, 1971. J. B. Spain. Vital Speeches 37:357-9 Ap 1 '71

WOMEN as public relations directors
Opening door. L. L. L. Golden. Sat R 54:47-8 Jl 10 '71

WOMEN as reporters
Women wave makers. il Time 97:45 My 24 '71
  See also
Women as foreign correspondents

WOMEN as scientists
Women in physics. G. B. Lubkin. il por Phys Today 24:23-7 Ap '71
Women physicists speak up. Chem 44:4 Je '71
  See also
Women as chemists

WOMEN as skiers
Aspen's new kind of ski bum. il Life 70:62-7 Mr 5 '71

WOMEN as stewards
  See also
Airlines—Hostesses

WOMEN as stockholders. See Stockholders

WOMEN as Supreme court judges. See Women as judges

WOMEN as teachers
Discriminating against the pregnant teacher. il Todays Ed 60:33-5 D '71
What can I do about sex discrimination? R. Branan. Schol Teach Jr/Sr High p20 N '71
Working woman. L. C. Pogrebin. Ladies Home J 88:54+ O '71

WOMEN as theologians
Feminine 'theologique'; first national conference of women theologians. America 124:626 Je 19 '71; Discussion. 125:49 Ag 7 '71

WOMEN as travelers
Women's where: for women on the go; symposium. il Ladies Home J 88:56+ My '71

WOMEN golf players. See Golfers

WOMEN in agriculture
More women in ag careers. B. S. Snyder. il Farm J 95:22-3+ O '71

WOMEN in airplane racing. See Airplane racing

WOMEN in archery. See Archery

WOMEN in art
Myth, muse and mom; Pride and prejudice: A woman's exhibition at the Brooklyn museum. S. K. Oberbeck. il Newsweek 77:85 Je 21 '71

WOMEN in boating
Cabin talk. M. Wiley. See issues of Yachting
Companionway. R. L. Williamson. See issues of Motor boating & sailing
Streak of adventure. M. J. Hayes. il por Yachting 129:54-5+ Mr '71
When a lady cruises solo. J. M. Lang. il por Yachting 130:56-7+ S '71
Why can't a woman take to cruising like a man? M. Taliaferro. il Yachting 129:65+ My '71
Wives are for cruising with. M. L. Lesser. il Motor B & S 128:108-11 S '71

WOMEN in business. See Business and professional women

WOMEN in literature
Feminist look at children's books. il Library J 96:235-40 Ja 15 '71; Discussion. 96:1401+ Ap 15 '71
Harmful lessons little girls learn in school. B. Miles. il Redbook 136:86-7+ Mr '71
Make no mystique about it. Z. Sutherland. Sat R 54:30 Mr 20 '71
Sex stereotypes in readers. Library J 96:680 F 15 '71
Sugar and spice; childrens books. P. Schuman. Library J 96:221 Ja 15 '71
  See also
Shakespeare, W.—Characters

WOMEN in moving pictures
Current cinema; Billy Jack. P. Kael New Yorker 47:148+ N 27 '71

WOMEN in politics
Bellacose Abzug. pors Time 98:14+ Ag 16 '71
Goodwill toward women. New Repub 165:5-6 D 25 '71
It's nonsense that there are no qualified women to run for office. B. Friedan. McCalls 98:52+ S '71
Up with women in politics. J. Egan. il McCalls 98:47 S '71
Women's Political caucus: what it is, what it wants. il US News 71:67-8 Ag 16 '71
  See also
Women as public officers

WOMEN in sports. See Sports for women

WOMEN in television
Ecumenical group reflects on woman's image in the media. F. S. Smith. Chr Cent 88:1002+ Ag 25 '71
New breed; female reporters. il Newsweek 78:62 Ag 30 '71
Upsurge in TV news girls. il Ebony 26:168-70+ Je '71

WOMEN in the Bible
Christian breakthrough in Women's lib. P. F. Palmer. America 124:634-7 Je 19 '71
Jesus and the liberated woman. B. Graham; discussion. Ladies Home J 88:80-1 Mr '71

WOMEN in trade unions. See Trade unions—Membership

WOMEN prisoners. See Prisoners, Women

WOMEN shoppers. See Shopping and shoppers

WOMEN tennis players. See Tennis players

WOMENS clothes. See Clothing and dress

WOMENS clubs and societies
Backlash against Women's lib! Pussycat league, Fascinating womanhood, etc. B. Rollin. il Look 35:15-19 Mr 9 '71

WOMENS colleges. See Colleges for women

WOMEN'S history research center
Bell & Howell to microfilm Women's lib materials. Library J 96:3933 D 1 '71

WOMEN'S international league for peace and freedom
For peace and freedom. Nation 213:68-9 Ag 2 '71

WOMENS lib magazine. See Periodicals for women

WOMEN'S lib, the tooth fairy and other myths; story. See Ellingson, M.

WOMEN'S liberation movement
Airline's ad encounters some turbulence. il Life 71:75-6 O 29 '71
Authors & editors; interview, ed. by L. P. Freilicher. G. Greer. por Pub W 199:13-14 My 10 '71
Backlash against Women's lib! B. Rollin. il Look 35:15-19 Mr 9 '71
Black liberation and Women's lib. L. J. M. La Rue. il Trans-Action 8:59-64 N '70
Black woman and Women's lib. H. H. King. il Ebony 26:68-70+ Mr '71
Conversion to Women's lib. A. L. Micossi. il Trans-Action 8:82-90 N '70
Dialectic of sex, by S. Firestone. Review
  Cath World 213:288-9 S '71. M. C. Segers

WOMENS liberation movement—*Continued*
Farm wife stands up for Women's lib. P. Leimbach. il Farm J 95:28+ N '71
Feminine mistake. il Esquire 75:82-5+ Ja '71
Discussion. 75:22 Mr; 18+ Ap '71
Feminine utopia. W. Karp. il Horizon 13:4-13 Spr '71
For the liberated female; Ms. magazine. il Time 98:52 D 20 '71
Germaine Greer. J. Bonfante. il pors Life 70:30-3 My 7 '71
Gloria Steinem, writer and social critic, talks about sex, politics and marriage; interview, ed. by L. Smith. G. Steinem. il Redbook 138:68-76 Ja '72
How is women's liberation doing in the high schools? S. Edmiston. Seventeen 30:48+ Ap '71
How men will benefit from the women's power revolution. M. Mannes. il PTA Mag 65:6-8 Ja '71
I can't call you my sister yet; interview, ed. by M. Cantwell. D. Pitman. por Mlle 73:182-3+ My '71
Ibsen's Nora and ours; meeting of the Theatre for ideas. J. Richardson. Commentary 52:77-80 Jl '71
Is Women's lib a dirty word in Milwaukee? J. Howard. il Life 71:46-51 Ag 27 '71
Liberated woman. M. Decter; discussion. Commentary 51:12+ F '71
Liberating magazines. il Newsweek 77:101 F 8 '71
Liberation of Betty Friedan. L. Tornabene. il McCalls 98:84-5+ My '71
Loveable woman. J. Poppy. Look 35:45-6 Ja 12 '71
Mental health movement meets women's lib; interview. E. Tobach; N. Shainess; D. Headley. Ment Hy 55:1-9 Ja '71
Mother superior to Women's lib; B. Friedan. P. Wilkes; reply with rejoinder. L. Komisar. N Y Times Mag p44+ Ja 24 '71
Prisoner of sex. N. Mailer. bibliog f il por (p4) Harper 242:41-6+ Mr '71; Discussion. 242:6+ Je; 243:16+ Jl '71
Sex and the super-groupie. por Time 97:75 Ap 12 '71
Sexism in the head. A. Croce. bibliog f Commentary 51:63-8 Mr '71
Time is here for Women's liberation. K. T. Romer and C. Secor. Ann Am Acad 397:129-39 S '71
What McCall's readers think about women's liberation. il McCalls 98:68+ Mr '71
What the black woman thinks about Women's lib. T. Morrison. il N Y Times Mag p 14-15+ Ag 22 '71; Discussion. p26 S 5 '71
What the feminists are reading. McCalls 98:44 Ap '71
What to tell your daughter about Women's lib; questions and answers, ed. by T. Langleben. A. Landers. il pors Todays Health 49:52-5+ O '71
What's women's lib doing to the family? Plenty! B. Rollin. Look 35:40 Ja 26 '71
Women's lib. D. Reuben. il por McCalls 98:60 S '71
Women's lib: beyond sexual politics; Time essay. R. Brine. il Time 98:36-7 Jl 26 '71
Women's lib: Mailer v. Millett. il pors Time 97:71 F 22 '71
Women's liberation and the church. ed. by S. B. Doely. Review
Cath World 213:99-100 My '71. D. Kolmer
Commonweal 94:114-16 Ap 9 '71. S. Cunneen
Women's liberation: humanizing rather than polarizing. J. D. Mandle. bibliog f Ann Am Acad 397:118-28 S '71
Women's liberation: or, Exploding the fairy princess myth. A. G. West. bibliog f Schol Teach Jr/Sr High p6-11 N '71
Women's liberation: tending toward idolatry. J. Hitchcock. il Chr Cent 88:1104-7 S 22 '71
Women's lit; the feminist press. il Newsweek 77:65 Ap 26 '71
See also
National women's political caucus

Bibliography

Five-foot shelf for women's lib. K. Mulherin. Commonweal 94:90-2 Ap 2 '71
Resources for women's studies. Schol Teach Jr/Sr High p 12-13 N '71
Sisterhood is serious: an annotated bibliography. P. Schuman and G. Detlefsen. il pors Library J 96:2587-94 S 1 '71; Correction. 96:3086 O 1 '71

Caricatures and cartoons

Liberty belles. Read Digest 98:106-7 Ja '71

WOMENS pages in newspapers. See Newspapers—Womens pages
WOMENS periodicals. See Periodicals for women
WOMENS prisons. See Prisons for women
WOMENS studies. See Colleges and universities—Curriculum
WOMEN'S wear daily
Fresh Eye. il Newsweek 78:48 S 13 '71
Women's wear daily takes wider aim. il Bsns W p26 Jl 10 '71
WONDER
Gift forever. Cons 26:2 D '71
WONG, May
Waiting for God; Landscape; poems. Poetry 118:14-15 Ap '71
WOO, Esther
Theology confronts women's liberation. America 124:257-9 Mr 13 '71
WOOD, Abigail
Young living; questions and answers. See issues of Seventeen
WOOD, Alexander
Origins of hypodermic medication. N. Howard-Jones. il por Sci Am 224:96-102 bibliog(p 122) Ja '71 *
WOOD, Ann Douglas
Reconsiderations. New Repub 166:27-9 Ja 1 '72
WOOD, Charles C. and others
Auditory evoked potentials during speech perception. bibliog il Science 173:1248-51 S 24 '71
WOOD, F. G.
In which Bahamian fishermen recount their adventures with the beast; with biographical sketch. Natur Hist 80:6, 84+ Mr '71
Stupefying colossus of the deep; with biographical sketch. il Natur Hist 80:6, 14-16+ Mr '71
WOOD, Frank Bradshaw
AAAS council resolutions. Science 173:769 Ag 27 '71
WOOD, Irving W.
Guidelines for good sound. il Arch Rec 150:123-5 Jl '71
WOOD, John E. Jr. See Simon, W. B. jt. auth.
WOOD, Marilyn
Self in city space and in clothed space. B. Schwartz. il por Craft Horiz 31:30-5 Ag '71 *
WOOD, Merle W.
New skills for tomorrow's office worker. Ed Digest 36:50-2 My '71
WOOD, Nancy
Clearcut; excerpts. il Am West 8:10-15+ N '71
WOOD, Pam, and Wendell, Barbara
Politics and punch lines. Library J 96:2454-5 Ag '71
WOOD, Peggy
I remember Emma. por Opera N 35:26-9 F 6 '71
WOOD, Peggy Baber
Sensitivity training starts early. il PTA Mag 65:20-2+ bibliog (p32) Je '71
WOOD, Robert Coldwell
Mandate for change. il por Newsweek 79:34 Ja 3 '72 *
WOOD, Thornley B. Jr
Paternalism dies at Samsonite. il por Bsns W p58 D 25 '71 *
WOOD, Tim
Ice man, nice man. H. L. Masin. por Sr Schol 98:18-19 Mr 15 '71 *
WOOD, Walter
Black American heritage. il Am Ed 7:16-22 Ag '71
Cargo of career education. il Am Ed 7:16-20 O '71
This mini seems here to stay. il Am Ed 7:14-17 D '71
Where it's always 1850. il Am Ed 7:17-23 Je '71
WOQD-PRINCE, Alain. See Prince, A. W.
WOOD
See also
Lumber
Plywood
Timber

Identification

What is it? J. A. Starkey. il Am For 77:44-5 Je '71

Moisture content

Is that wood dry enough? wood-moisture-content meter. R. M. Benrey. il Pop Sci 199:88-9+ Jl '71
WOOD bending
Basics of wood bending; kerf bending and other methods. R. Capotosto. il Mech Illus 67:78-80 Jl '71
WOOD brothers
Pit crew. il Life 70:65-8 Mr 26 '71
WOOD burning work. See Pyrography

WOODWORKING machinery
Wee woodworking workshop; System zenses.
A. Walordy. il Mech Illus 68:101-2 Ja '72
See also
Jointers (woodworking machinery)
Sanding machines
Shapers
Tenoning machines
Vises

WOODY plants
See also
Shrubs

WOOFER speakers. See Loud speaking apparatus

WOOL, Robert
Harboring of Daniel Berrigan. il Esquire
76:156-61+ N '71
Metamorphosis of a hawk: why an ex-navy
hero from Tennessee attacked J. Edgar
Hoover. il pors N Y Times Mag p22-3+
Ap 25 '71
Stalking of the president. il Esquire 76:85-
7+ Jl '71

WOOL industry
Bid for power in Yorkshire wool. por Bsns
W p55 Je 19 '71

WOOLF, Gregory
Current chronicle. R. L. Weaver. il Mus Q
57:317-22 Ap '71 *

WOOLF, Leonard
Literature in a technological age: maintaining the wonder. Engl J 60:1217-20+ D '71

WOOLF, Robert
Woolf at the door. il por Time 98:69 N 29
'71 *

WOOLLEY, A. E.
How to get wedding pictures you'll love,
honor, & cherish. il Todays Health 49:
38-43 Je '71

WOOLLEY, Ken
Australia's terrace houses. il Arch Forum
134:46-51 My '71

WOOLMAN, John
Man for all souls. B. Burwell. il Am Heritage
23:13-16 D '71 *

WOOLNER, Frank
Woodcock! Flights and fancies. il Field & S
76:62-3+ N '71

WOOTEN, James T.
Colonel Herbert tried to go by the book
in Vietnam: how a supersoldier was fired
from his command. il pors N Y Times Mag
p 10-11+ S 5 '71
Life and death of Atlanta's hip strip. il N Y
Times Mag p34-5+ Mr 14 '71

WOOTTERS, John
Cat comes calling. il Outdoor Life 148:70-1+
O '71
Secret of the Rock. il Outdoor Life 147:60-
1+ F '71

WORCESTER, Mass.

Galleries and museums
Addition to Worcester; education wing. il
Arch Forum 135:34-9 S '71

Housing
Discouraging a do-gooder. il Time 98:80 N
15 '71

WORDEN, Alfred M.
Apollo 15: three views of the moon. Read
Digest 99:76-7 N '71

about
High-flying crew for Apollo. por Time 98:
39 Ag 2 '71 *
Mission into the moon's past. E. Driscoll.
il pors Sci N 100:28-30 Jl 10 '71 *
See also
Space flight to the moon—Manned flights—
Apollo 15 flight

WORDS
Words: how to use them effectively; excerpt
from The golden book on writing. D. Lambuth and others. Writers Digest 51:35-7 Ag
'71
See also
English language—Etymology
Semantics
Vocabulary

WORDS in art
Can epistemology be entertaining? Arakawa's
word paintings. J. G. Bowles. il por Art N
70:34-5+ My '71

WORK
Christian work ethic. C. F. H. Henry. Chr
Today 16:22-3 Ja 7 '72
Communes and the work crisis. L. M. Andrews. Cur 126:34-9 F '71
Is hard work going out of style? interview.
E. Ginzberg. il por U S News 71:52-6 Ag 23
'71

Nixon in the pulpit: economic evangelism;
summary of address, September 6, 1971. R.
M. Nixon. il por Time 98:11-12 S 20 '71; Excerpts with title Hard work out of style?
President answers. U S News 71:34 S 20 '71
On avoiding work. B. C. Lambert. Chr Today 15:7-8 Ag 27 '71
Protestant ethic, Chinese style. Nation 213:67-
8 Ag 2 '71
Time, work and leisure today. G. J. Dahl. Chr
Cent 88:185-9 F 10 '71
See also
Job satisfaction
Labor and laboring classes

Psychological aspects
Hooked on work; workaholism. Time 98:
42 Jl 5 '71
Working stiffs. C. McCarthy. New Repub 165:
13-15 S 4 '71

WORK benches
Basic 2x4 workbench. J. Capotosto. il Mech
Illus 67:99-102 My '71
Cabinet workbench for the man with a small
shop. W. C. Leckey. il Pop Mech 136:132-5
D '71
Space-age workbench has color-coded storage. A. Stimson. il Pop Sci 199:88-90+ S
'71
2 dream workbenches (title varies) il Radio-
Electr 42:36-45+ Ag; 84-5+ S '71

WORK clothes. See Clothing and dress—Work
clothes

WORK communities. See Collective settlements

WORK experience. See Education. Cooperative

WORK gloves. See Gloves

WORK measurement
Measurement of the man-day. E. S. Ferguson. il Sci Am 225:96-103 O '71

WORK projects administration. See United
States—Work projects administration

WORK rules
Work rules: the main barrier to productivity.
il Bsns W p54-5 Ag 28 '71
See also
Railroads—Work rules

WORK satisfaction. See Job satisfaction

WORK simplification. See Home economics

WORK stoppages. See Strikes

WORK-study program. See Education. Cooperative

WORKBENCHES. See Work benches

WORKERS education. See Labor and laboring
classes—Education

WORKING classes. See Labor and laboring
classes

WORKING day. See Hours of labor

WORKING life, Length of
Table of expected working life for men, 1968.
H. N. Fullerton. bibliog il Mo Labor R
94:49-55 Je '71

WORKING mothers. See Married women—
Employment

WORKING week. See Hours of labor

WORKMENS compensation. See Insurance,
Workmens compensation

WORKS progress administration. See United
States—Work projects administration

WORKSHOPS
Build a home repair center that stores in
a corner. A. Lees and L. Walker. il Pop
Sci 198:98-9 Ap '71
Workshop crammed with ideas you can use.
H. Wicks. il Pop Mech 135:138-43 Je '71

Equipment
Welding equipment for the home shop. B.
Berger. il Mech Illus 67:106-7+ D '71
See also
Tools

Heating and ventilation
Happiness is a warm shop. R. Capotosto. il
Mech Illus 67:97-9+ D '71

WORKSHOPS, Authors. See Authors conferences

WORKSHOPS, Library. See Library institutes
and workshops

WORLD, End of the. See End of the world

WORLD administrative radio conference
Report on the World administrative radio
conference. R. G. Gould. Pop Electr 35:69-
70+ D '71
Satellite radio spectrum expanded. P. J. Klass.
Aviation W 95:14-15 Ag 2 '71

WORLD airways, inc.
World buys DC-8-63 in fleet realignment.
Aviation W 94:185 Mr 8 '71

WORLD bank. See International bank for reconstruction and development

WORLD championship tennis, inc.
Rhubarb divides the tennis world; ILTF vs. WCT on open tennis. Bsns W p34 Ag 14 '71
WORLD chess tournament, Vancouver. See Chess
WORLD conference of religion for peace
World religions search for peace: the Kyoto conference and beyond. H. A. Jack. Chr Cent 88:161 F 3 '71
WORLD conference on Soviet Jewry
Brussels declaration. Chr Cent 88:334 Mr 17 '71
Cries from the heart. Newsweek 77:70+ Mr 8 '71
Mazel tov, comrade! il Time 97:27 Mr 8 '71
Show of support. H. J. Morgenthau. New Repub 164:10-11 Mr 13 '71
WORLD council of churches
Addis assertions. J. D. Douglas. Chr Today 15:46-7 F 12 '71
Burying an epoch of ecumenical politics; analysis of the Commission of the churches on international affairs. J. Hilke. Chr Cent 88:493-5 Ap 21 '71; Reply. A. R. Booth. 88:729-30 Je 9 '71
East German churches support controversial WCC program. F. Lüpsen. Chr Cent 88:258 F 24 '71
Forward with brakes on! P. Verghese. Chr Cent 88:848 Jl 14 '71
From proclamation to dialogue: a new profile for Christians. J. C. Haughey. America 124:483-5 My 8 '71
How I learned to stop worrying and to enjoy life on the far right. M. E. Marty. Chr Cent 88:1279 O 27 '71
Must our churches finance revolution? C. W. Hall. Read Digest 99:95-100 O '71; Discussion. Chr Cent 88:1219, 1504-5 O 20, D 22 '71
No myopia in Ethiopia. J. R. Nelson. Chr Cent 88:180-2 F 10 '71
No utopia in Ethiopia. J. R. Nelson. Chr Cent 88:214-16 F 17 '71
RGAE rejects WCC grant. Chr Cent 88:1159 O 6 '71
Reader's digest views of regrettable views of WCC actions. R. C. Campion. America 125:inside cover N 6 '71
Rebutting Dr Ramsey; WCC grants. T. Beeson. Chr Cent 88:364-5 Mr 24 '71
Rome-Geneva: a long and difficult way. W. Triggs. Chr Cent 88:582-3 My 12 '71
Theology en masse. T. Beeson. Chr Cent 88:1016-17 S 1 '71; Reply. G. G. Beazley, jr. 88:1305 N 3 '71
Through different spectacles; WCC grants. J. D. Douglas. Chr Today 15:45-6 Mr 26 '71
Tight money at WCC's U.S. office: preview of things to come? Friends of the WCC. M Hyer Chr Cent 88:197-8 F 10 '71
WCC consultation in South Africa postponed due to restrictions. Chr Cent 88:794 Je 30 '71
WCC: Indonesia in '75. Chr Cent 88:1157 O 6 '71
WCC racism grants: repeat performance. Chr Today 16:56 O 8 '71
Warfare on the ecumenical frontier. Chr Cent 88:713 Je 9 '71
Which way the World council of churches? C. W. Hall. Read Digest 99:177-8+ N '71; Reply. Chr Cent 88:1342 N 17 '71
See also
Joint committee for society, development and peace
WORLD court. See International court of justice. The Hague
WORLD crafts council
Last year in Ireland: pre-history recalled to life. A. Kasuba. Craft Horiz 31:5+ Ag '71
WORLD cup championship. See Golf—Tournaments
WORLD economics. See Economic conditions
WORLD field research, inc.
What we know about World field research. Consumer Rep 36:66 F '71
WORLD food supply. See Food supply
WORLD government. See International organization
WORLD history

Historiography

Europe's "discovery" of China and the writing of world history. E. J. Van Kley. bibliog f Am Hist R 76:358-85 Ap '71

Textbooks

History as taught through East German textbooks. T. Huebener. Sch & Soc 99:56-9 Ja '71
WORLD intellectual property organization
New directions in international production and intellectual property; address, May 6, 1971. E. M. Braderman. Dept State Bul 64:772-7 Je 14 '71

WORLD law. See International law
WORLD law day. See Special days, weeks, and months
WORLD meteorological organization
Tropical analysis program of the National hurricane center. C. W. Wise and R. H. Simpson. bibliog il Weatherwise 24:164-73 Ag '71
WORLD Methodist conference. See Methodist world conference
WORLD military expenditures. See Armed forces—Appropriations and expenditures
WORLD ocean racing championship. See Yacht racing
WORLD politics
See also
International relations
Propaganda, International
WORLD politics, 1945-
Current documents. See issues of Current history
In deference to Pope Gregory. G. W. Ball. Newsweek 79:32 Ja 10 '72
International dissent, by W. O. Douglas; and The common sense of politics, by M. J. Adler. Reviews
Sat R 54:30 My 8 '71. A. M. Bingham
Letter to a Soviet friend. C. Yost. por Life 71:4 S 24 '71
U.S. & world affairs annual. il Sr Schol 99:2-22+ O 4 '71
Why Nixon is going to Moscow. il por U S News 71:19-21 O 25 '71
See also
Balance of power
Communist strategy
Current events
International relations
WORLD population. See Population
WORLD pro-am surfing championship. See Surf riding
WORLD publishing company
World gets rights to German spymaster's memoirs. Pub W 200:44 S 27 '71
WORLD records
Parting shots: OK, who ordered the burger with 500 pickles? Guinness book of world records. il Life 71:68 Ag 27 '71
See also
Automobile speed records
Aviation records
WORLD revolution. See Social revolution
WORLD security. See International security
WORLD series (baseball)
Back-to-the-wall effect? W. Simon. il Science 174:774-5 N 19 '71
Birdbath for the Pirates. R. Fimrite. il Sports Illus 35:20-3 O 18 '71
Bucs and Birds battle it out. il Time 98:74 O 25 '71
Champagne and aspirin; Pittsburgh Pirates and Baltimore Orioles. pors Newsweek 78:75 O 25 '71
Some kind of a comeback: Pirates the World champions. W. Leggett. il Sports Illus 35:18-23 O 25 '71
Sporting scene (cont) R. Angell. New Yorker 47:138+ N 6 '71
WORLD series of golf. See Golf—Tournaments
WORLD shooting championships. See Shooting—Competitions
WORLD ski championship. See Skis and skiing
WORLD table tennis championship. See Table tennis
WORLD team championship. See Bridge tournaments
WORLD temperature changes. See Global temperature changes
WORLD to share; story. See Hickman, M. W.
WORLD trade. See Commerce
WORLD trade center. See New York (city)—World trade center
WORLD trade corporation. See International business machines corporation
WORLD trade institute
Foreign exporters learn the ropes. Bsns W p38-9 O 2 '71
WORLD trade week
World trade week, 1971, proclamation. R. M. Nixon. Dept State Bul 64:647 My 17 '71
WORLD travel photo contest. See Photography—Competitions
WORLD war, 1939-1945

Aerial operations

See also
London—Air raids

Atrocities

See also
World war, 1939-1945—Jews

WORLD war, 1939-1945—*Continued*

Campaigns and battles
See also
World war, 1939-1945—Japan

Burma
Retreat from Burma; excerpts from Stilwell and the American experience in China, 1911-45. B. W. Tuchman. il pors Am Heritage 22:38-43+ F '71

Germany
Why Ike didn't capture Berlin: an untold story. il por U S News 70:70-3 Ap 26 '71

Pacific
See also
Pearl Harbor, Attack on, 1941

Russia
Forgotten soldier, by G. Sajer. Review
Bsns W il p6 Ja 23 '71. S. Brown

Western
See also
Arnhem, Battle of, 1944

Caricatures and cartoons
My confrontation with General Patton; excerpt from The brass ring. B. Mauldin. il pors Life 71:50-2+ Ag 6 '71

Diplomatic history
Now told: secret history of World war II, records of the combined chiefs of staff. il U S News 70:37-41 Ja 25 '71

Documents, sources, etc.
Funds asked for declassification of World war II documents; text of letter, August 3, 1971. R. M. Nixon. Dept State Bul 65:249 Ag 30 '71
Now told: secret history of World war II, records of the combined chiefs of staff. il U S News 70:37-41 Ja 25 '71

Evacuation of civilians
Co-opting the oppressors: the case of the Japanese-Americans. R. O. Haak. il Trans-Action 7:23-31 O '70

Fiction
Multitudes, multitudes! T. Foote. il por Time 98:111+ N 22 '71

Jews
My life was like a game of Russian roulette; interview, ed. by R. Hemming. S. Comissiona. por Sr Schol 99:22-3 O 25 '71
Story behind the book: The book of Alfred Kantor; interview, ed. by D. G. Maryles. A. Kantor. il Pub W 200:28-9 O 25 '71
See also
Jews in Poland

Medical and sanitary affairs
Disaster at Bari; excerpts. G. Infield. il por Am Heritage 22:60-4 +O '71

Personal narratives
Forgotten soldier, by G. Sajer. Review
Bsns W il p6 Ja 23 '71. S. Brown
Siege and survival, by E. Skrjabina. Review
Sat R 54:98 O 23 '71. S. Jacoby
Story behind the book: The book of Alfred Kantor; interview, ed. by D. G. Maryles. A. Kantor. il Pub W 200:28-9 O 25 '71

Prisoners and prisons
See also
Concentration camps

Science
Strange, unfinished saga of Peking man. H. L. Shapiro. il Natur Hist 80:8-10+ N '71

Secret service
Double-cross system; British intelligence. por Newsweek 78:58+ N 22 '71

Strategy
History of the second World war, by B. H. Liddell-Hart. Review
Nation 212:725-6 Je 7 '71. R. Walters

Underground movement
Germany
See also
Anti-Nazi movement

Asia
Who really won World war II in Asia; 30 years after Pearl Harbor; interview. R. P. Martin. il U S News 71:67-70+ D 13 '71

China
Strange, unfinished saga of Peking man. H. L. Shapiro. il Natur Hist 80:8-10+ N '71

France
Sorrow and the pity; documentary film. il Newsweek 78:60+ O 25 '71

Germany
See also
Germany—Army
World war, 1939-1945—Campaigns and battles—Russia

Great Britain
See also
London—Air raids

Japan
Emperor who meets the President today. T. Oka. N Y Times Mag p59-60+ S 26 '71
Hirohito of Japan, was he a war criminal? por U S News 71:76-7 D 13 '71
Is Hirohito the war's real villain? views of D. Bergamini. il por Time 98:43-4 O 4 '71
Japan's imperial conspiracy, D. Bergamini. Review
Bsns W por p 15 D 4 '71. G. Ringwald
Life por 71:11 O 15 '71. C. Elliott
Japan's imperial conspiracy: the story behind David Bergamini's controversial book; interview. ed. by A. H. Johnston. D. Bergamini. il por Pub W 200:26-7 O 4 '71
See also
Pearl Harbor, Attack on, 1941

Poland
See also
Jews in Poland

Russia
Notes from the Russian front. R. E. Walters. Nation 213:248-50 S 20 '71
See also
World war, 1939-1945—Campaigns and battles—Russia

United States
My confrontation with General Patton; excerpt from The brass ring. B. Mauldin. il pors Life 71:50-2+ Ag 6 '71

WORLD weather program. See Weather research

WORLD-wide network of standard seismograph stations. See Seismological stations

WORLD wildlife fund
U.N. of conservation. Time 98:79 N 1 '71

WORLD woman's Christian temperance union. See Woman's Christian temperance union

WORLD'S Christian endeavor union
Christian endeavor at ninety. Chr Today 15: 22 Ja 29 '71

WORLDVIEW (periodical)
Speaking truth to power. Newsweek 79:47 Ja 10 '72

WORLDWIDE church of God
Examining his Worldwide church of God. J. M. Hopkins. Chr Today 16:6-9 D 17 '71

WORLEY, James
After the suicide; poem. Chr Cent 88:584 My 12 '71
Six seconds in Dallas; poem. Chr Cent 88: 1346 N 17 '71

WORLOCK, Derek John Harford, bp
Church and youth; Bishop Worlock at Isle of Wight rock festival. Commonweal 94:442 S 3 '71 *

WORMALD, Nicola. See Charan, R. jt. auth.

WORMAN, Charles G.
Firearms. See issues of Hobbies

WORMS
See also
Earthworms

WORMS, intestinal and parasitic
Worming pigs is not old-fashioned. il Suc Farm 69:no4 H10-11 Mr '71
See also
Lungworms
Schistosomes

WORN-out farms. See Farms, Worn-out

WORRY
God and man in the aspirin age. Chr Today 16:33 O 8 '71
How I found therapy in thistles. E. D. Hunt. Farm J 95:44 My '71

Anecdotes, facetiae, satire, etc.
It pays to increase your worry power. J. Lubold. Read Digest 98:116-18 F '71

WORSHIP
Forbidden worship? house churches of Britain. T. Beeson. Chr Cent 88:1042 S 8 '71
See also
Church attendance
Prayer

WORSLEY, Gump
Minnies who are no moochers. M. Mulvoy. il pors Sports Illus 35:28-9 N 22 '71 *
WORSTHORNE, Peregrine
Snobberies of the left. Nat R 23:76+ Ja 26 '71
WORTH, C. Brooke
Immortality; excerpt from Mosquito safari. il Audubon 73:28-31 Jl '71
WORTH, Don
Gallery; photographs. Life 70:6-7 My 7 '71
WORTH, Frank
Mechanic turns artist. il por Design 72:11 mid-Sum '71
WORTH
Little boy taught me... T. Guyant. il Nat Wildlife 10:13-15 D '71
See also
Social values
WORTHAM, Robert
Spanish-style chest with a marproof top. il Pop Mech 136:148-50 S '71
WORTHINGTON, Minn.

Lighting

New city lights honor United Nations. il Am City 86:86 Jl '71
WORTMAN, Sterling
Social impact of the green revolution; comment. bibliog f il pors Int Concil 581:51-4 Ja '71
WOTTON, Michael
Making trees work harder. il Am For 77:20-1+ O '71
WOUK, Herman
Herman Wouk surfaces again. J. Howard. il pors Life 71:53-4+ N 26 '71 *
Multitudes, multitudes! il por Time 98:111+ N 22 '71 *
WOUK, Victor
Electric cars: the battery problem; adaptation of address, December, 1970. il Bul Atom Sci 27:19-22 Ap '71
WOUND healing
See also
Granulation tissue
WOUNDED, Vietnamese war. See Vietnamese war. 1957- —Casualties
WOUNDS
See also subhead Wounds and injuries under names of organs and regions of the body, e.g. Eye—Wounds and injuries
WOY, James B.
(comp) Business books of 1970. il por Library J 96:793-6 Mr 1 '71
WRAPPING of packages
Bags as wraps, useful later. il Sunset 147:92 D '71
Beautiful Christmas you make yourself. il House & Gard 140:42-9 D '71
Good things in pretty packages; box social fund-raising event. il Ladies Home J 88:104-5+ O '71
Ways to reuse Christmas cards and decorations. Good H 173:169 D '71
WREATHS, Christmas. See Christmas wreaths
WRECKING
See also
Automobiles—Wrecking
WRECKS. See Shipwrecks
WREN, Christopher S.
Country music. il Look 35:11-13 Jl 13 '71
If it's 3-to-1 against Anderson: can a congressman afford a conscience? il pors Look 35:44+ Ap 20 '71
Nixon's Haldeman: power is proximity. il pors Look 35:15-19 Ag 24 '71
Scoop Jackson: an alternative for cautious Democrats. il pors Look 35:19-21 S 21 '71
Trade winds; interview, ed. by C. Amory. Sat R 54:8+ Mr 27 '71
Was the Wichita state crash avoidable? il Look 35:73-6 Mr 9 '71
West Pointer's wild preview of the volunteer army. il pors Look 35:24-7 F 23 '71
Winners got scars too; condensation. por McCalls 98:99-106 Ag '71
WRENCHES
See also
Torque wrenches
WRENN, Roger
Don't throw away that can. il Design 72:28-9 Spr '71
Painting with beads. il por Design 72:8-11 Sum '71
WRESTLING
Artists in the peanut gallery; wrist-wrestling contest. Petaluma, Calif. R. Drexler. il Sports Illus 34:78-80+ My 10 '71
Little agony, a little ecstasy; B. Sammartino. L. A. Gutkind. il por Sports Illus 35:36-8+ S 27 '71
WRICE, Herman
Businessmen go to the ghetto to learn. il pors Bsns W p 102+ Je 19 '71 *

WRIGHT, Alfred
New breed, new ideas, new taxes. il pors Sports Illus 34:48-53 Je 7 '71
Tennis (cont) Sports Illus 34:56-7 Mr 29 '71
Thanks for the memory. il pors Sports Illus 34:12-15 F 22 '71
WRIGHT, Betty Ren
Godmothers & all that; story. Ladies Home J 88:134-5 My '71
WRIGHT, Charles David
Comment. L. Mueller. Poetry 117:325-6 F '71 *
WRIGHT, David
Five songs; Stream; Moon; Valley; River; Mountain; poems. Poetry 119:130-3 D '71
WRIGHT, Don
Bush power wins Alaskan land claims. por Bsns W p23 D 18 '71 *
WRIGHT, Doris G.
Twelve days of Christmas; drama. Plays 31:77-80, 95 D '71
WRIGHT, Elliott. See Wright, H. E.
WRIGHT, Frank
Land of milk and money. Nation 213:657-9 D 20 '71
WRIGHT, Frank Lloyd
Frank Lloyd Wright's Hall of justice. R. Montgomery. il Arch Forum 133:54-9 D '70 *
Natural house. R. W. Kennedy. New Repub 165:30-2 O 30 '71 *
WRIGHT, Frederick W. Jr
Novel approaches to azalea culture. il Horticulture 49:30-3 Ap '71
WRIGHT, H. Elliott
Church and Gay liberation. il Chr Cent 88:281-5 Mr 3 '71
WRIGHT, Henry N.
Radburn revisited. bibliog il Arch Forum 135:52-7 Jl '71
WRIGHT, James
October ghosts; poem. New Yorker 47:40 O 2 '71
Old dog in the ruins of the graves at Arles; poem. Esquire 75:18B F '71
Red jacket's grave; poem. New Yorker 47:40 Mr 13 '71
Secret gratitude; poem. New Yorker 47:38 Mr 27 '71
So she said; poem. Harper 242:60 Ja '71

about

Fashionable poet? B. Deutsch. New Repub 165:27 Jl 17 '71 *
WRIGHT, James, 1927?-
Willing to please. por Time 98:71+ D 6 '71 *
WRIGHT, James C. 1922-
It's enough to drive you D-O-T; poem. Nations Bsns 59:42 O '71
WRIGHT, James E. and others
Ovarian maturation in stable flies: inhibition by 20-hydroxyecdysone. bibliog il Science 172:1247-8 Je 18 '71
WRIGHT, James R.
Performance criteria in building; with biographical sketch. il Sci Am 224:14, 16-25 Mr '71
WRIGHT, James R. (librarian)
Overdue. por Wilson Lib Bul 45:987 Je '71
WRIGHT, Jay
Albuquerque graveyard; poem. Nation 212:636 My 17 '71
Night ride; poem. New Repub 165:20-1 O 16 '71
Preparing to leave home; poem. Harper 243:84 Ag '71
WRIGHT, John D. and Hassall, D. R.
Trends in water financing. il Am City 86:61+ D '71
WRIGHT, Olgivanna Lloyd
Guardian of a great legacy; with editorial comment. L. Wainwright. il pors Life 70:3, 44-55 Je 11 '71 *
WRIGHT, Rebecca
Brief biography. S. Goodman. pors Dance Mag 45:66-7 Ag '71 *
3 nice times. J. Leichtling. por Sr Schol 98:32 My 17 '71 *
WRIGHT, Richard
Furnace and the tower: a new look at the symbols in Native son. D. R. Merkle. Engl J 60:735-9 S '71 *
WRIGHT, Russell
Garden of woodland paths. il House & Gard 140:80-5 D '71
WRIGHT, Samuel
Eskimo village. il Liv Wildn 34:3-9 Wint '70
Last frontier (cont) il pors Am West 8:24-7 Mr: 36-9 Jl: 16-19 N '71
WRIGHT, Shirley
My husband, the locomotive tycoon. il Read Digest 99:159-60+ N '71
WRIGHT brothers
Those early airplanes. J. Gilbert. il Flying 89:34-40+ D '71

WRIGHTSMAN, Charles Bierer
Wrightsman collection. R. Davidson. il Antiques 99:702-11 My '71*
WRIGHTSMAN, Jayne (Larkin)
Wrightsman collection. R. Davidson. il Antiques 99:702-11 My '71 *
WRINKLE prints. See Prints
WRINKLE resistant textile fabrics. See Textile fabrics, Wrinkle resistant
WRIST watches. See Watches
WRIST wrestling. See Wrestling
WRISTON, Walter Bigelow
How it feels to be Naderized. J. Tompkins. il por Time 98:63-4 Jl 5 '71 *
WRISTWATCHES. See Watches
WRITERS. See Authors
WRITERS colonies. See Authors colonies
WRITERS conferences. See Authors conferences
WRITERS digest (periodical)
1971 Writer's digest writing contest winners. Writers Digest 51:31-3+ O '71
Winners: Writer's digest & Great books of the western world essay contest. N. Kephart. Writers Digest 51:33-4 D '71
WRITERS notebooks. See Notebooks
WRITING
See also
Penmanship
WRITING (authorship) See Authorship; Creative writing
WRITING (composition) See English language —Composition
WRITING, Chinese. See Chinese language—Writing
WRITING for the press. See Journalism—Authorship
WRONG, Dennis H.
Case of the New York review. Commentary 50:49-63 N '70; 51:22+ Mr '71
WROTH, Lawrence Counselman
Obituary
Pub W 199:48 Ja 11 '71
WROUGHT iron work. See Ironwork
WU, Annie
Cry; poem. Ment Hy 55:263 Ap '71
Lilac in my winter yard; poem. Ment Hy 55:279 Ap '71
WU, Cheng-wen. See Hammes, G. G. jt. auth.
WU, Jin
Evaporation retardation by monolayers: another mechanism. bibliog il Science 174:283-5 O 15 '71
WU, Yuan-li
Food and agriculture in mainland China. bibliog f Cur Hist 61:160-4 S '71
WUJCIK, Edward R.
Highland Park's yes. Am City 86:92+ Jl '71
WUJEK, Joseph H. Jr
CMOS logic: low powered and versatile. il Electr World 85:42-3+ Je '71
Low-power crystal-controlled oscillator. il Electr World 86:69 D '71
WULFF, Lee
Lee Wulff: the complete angler; excerpt from introd. to Fishing with Lee Wulff, by E. C. Janes. A. Gingrich. por Field & S 76:50-1+ N '71 *
WUNDERLE, Terry M.
Easy fox hunting. il Field & S 76:60-1+ N '71
WUORINEN, Charles
Music to my ears; performance of The politics of harmony. I. Kolodin. Sat R 54:38+ O 16 '71 *
WUPATKI NATIONAL MONUMENT
Arizona prehistory, a loop north of Flagstaff. il Sunset 147:56-7 O '71
WURLITZER, Rudolph, and Corry, Will
Two lane blacktop; screenplay; text. Esquire 75:104-14+ Ap '71
WURMAN, Richard Saul
Flexible planning creates a world of uses for city living. il Am Home 74:56-8+ F '71
WURSTER, Charles F.
Aldrin and dieldrin. bibliog il Environ 13:33-41 O '71
WURTMAN, Richard J. See Fernstrom, J. D; Shoemaker, W. J. jt. auths.
WURTZ, Robert H. and Goldberg, M. E.
Superior colliculus cell responses related to eye movements in awake monkeys. bibliog il Science 171:82-4 Ja 8 '71
WYANDOTTE, Mich.

Recreation
Sure you can ice skate in warm weather. B. F. Yack. il Am City 86:54 Ap '71

WYANT, Rowena
Business failures. See issues of Dun's
Businessmen's expectations. il Duns 98:75 D '71
about
Pursuit of failure. Duns 98:3 Ag '71 *
WYANT, William K. Jr
Coming home with a habit. Nation 213:7-10 Jl 5 '71
Hell in a very small place. Nation 213:132 Ag 30 '71
WYATT, G. R. See Pan, M. L. jt. auth.
WYATT, Joan
Battle of the Boyne II. Commonweal 94:162-5 Ap 23 '71
WYATT, Lowry
Economy & environment; address, April 28, 1971. Vital Speeches 37:509-12 Je 1 '71
WYDEN, Barbara W.
Growth: 45 crucial months. il Life 71:93+ D 17 '71
Parent and child (cont) il N Y Times Mag p67+ Mr 21 '71
WYETH, Andrew
Brandywine school. D. Davis. il Newsweek 77:93 Je 28 '71 *
WYETH, Newell Convers
The Wyeths, ed. by B. J. Wyeth. Review Sat R 54:58 D 11 '71. F. Schulze *
Wyeths' kind of Christmas magic; excerpts from letters, ed. by R. Meryman. il por Life 71:122-9 D 17 '71 *
WYKERT, John. See Calabro, J. J. jt. auth.
WYLER, Armand
Mathematician's version of the fine-structure constant. G. B. Lubkin. bibliog il por Phys Today 24:17-19 Ag '71 *
WYLIE, Evan McLeod
Birth control for men. Read Digest 98:53-6 Ja '71
Day-care centers. Good H 173:102-3+ S '71
Last-ditch fight for life. il Good H 172:98-9+ My '71
New birth-control freedom for women. Read Digest 99:153-6 Ag '71
Ups and downs of young marriage. il Seventeen 30:236-7+ Ag '71
WYLIE, I. A. R.
Are you a bore? reprint. Read Digest 98:128-30 Mr '71
WYLIE, Max
Maybe your whole family needs a psychiatrist and you don't know it. il Ladies Home J 88:110+ Mr '71
WYLIE, Philip
Our old people: part of their lonely exile is their own fault. il Todays Health 49:10-11 Ag '71
Obituary
Pub W 200:21 N 1 '71
WYLY, Sam
Wyly's Texas-style dream. A. A. Butkus. por Duns 98:54 Ag '71 *
WYMAN, Donald
Woody vines. il Horticulture 49:32-3+ Ag '71
WYMAN, Karen
Star is born, and starts to grow up. il pors Life 71:64-7 Jl 9 '71 *
WYNDER, Ernest Ludwig
Heart-disease epidemic, ways to cut the toll. U S News 71:94-5 N 29 '71 *
WYNDHAM, Robert J.
Iris: beautiful, but hard to discourage. il Org Gard & Farm 18:60-2 N '71
WYNETTE, Tammy
Songs of non-liberation. por Newsweek 78:81+ Ag 2 '71 *
WYNNE, Jim
New approach to an ancient route. il Yachting 130:54-5+ D '71
WYNOT, Edward D. Jr
Necessary cruelty: the emergence of official anti-Semitism in Poland, 1936-39. bibliog f Am Hist R 76:1035-58 O '71
WYOMING
See also
Fishing—Wyoming
Grand Teton National Park
Green River
Hunting—Wyoming
Public health—Wyoming
Recreation areas—Wyoming
Roads—Wyoming
Wilderness areas—Wyoming
Yellowstone National Park

Antiquities
Big Horn medicine wheel, an American Stonehenge? J. E. Ransom. il Am West 8:16-17+ Mr '71; Reply with rejoinder. L. A. Brown. 8:48+ S '71

WYOMING library association
Of note; annual conference. M. R. Rogers.
il Am Lib 2:680-1 Jl '71
WYSE, Lois
More love poems for the very married. Ladies
Home J 88:63 Je '71
Trade winds; interview. ed. by C. Amory.
Sat R 54:6 Ag 21 '71
WYSOR, Bettie
Encounter games: a dangerous new trend.
Harp Baz 104:60-1 Je '71
Husbands who are married to their jobs. il
Ladies Home J 88:65+ F '71
Sex: up with the stock market. Vogue 157:87-
8+ F 15 '71

X

X RAY astronomy
Lunokhod 1 on the expansion of the uni-
verse. S. Mandelshtam. Space World H-4-
88:46 Ap '71
Soft X-rays from the Cygnus loop; inter-
pretation. W. H. Tucker. bibliog il Science
172:372-4 Ap 23 '71
X-ray structure of the Cygnus loop. P.
Gorenstein and others. bibliog il Science
172:369-72 Ap 23 '71
X-ray survey of Centaurus A. E. T. Byram
and others; reply with rejoinder. R. Ramaty.
bibliog il Science 171:500-1 F 5 '71
**X RAY crystallography. See Crystallography—
X ray studies**
X RAY fluorescence analysis. See Fluorimetry
X RAY photography. See Radiography
X RAY stars. See Stars—Radiation
X RAYS
X-ray parametric conversion: two photons
for one; use of beryllium crystal. M. S.
Rothenberg. Phys Today 24:17+ Ap '71
See also
Diagnosis. Radioscopic
Radiography
Archeological use
Examining fossils by X-ray. il Chem 44:21 Je
'71
Probing the New Kingdom pharaohs with
X-rays. il Sci N 100:245 O 9 '71
Diffraction
X-ray diffraction patterns of transfer RNA
consistent with the presence of short par-
allel helices in the molecule. T. Sakurai
and others. bibliog il Science 172:1234-7 Je
18 '71
Measurement
Measuring color-TV generated X-rays. J. G.
Ello. il Electr World 86:37-9+ Jl '71
Physiological effects
Never do harm. K. Z. Morgan. bibliog il
Environ 13:28-38 Ja '71
**X-RAYS in airplane hijacking prevention. See
Airplane hijacking—Prevention**
XANTEN, William A.
Let's speak up on solid wastes, truthfully. il
Am City 86:100-1 Je '71
XANTHIUM. See Cockleburs
XENON
Antiprismatic coordination about xenon:
the structure of nitrosonium octafluorox-
enate(VI) S. W. Peterson and others. bib-
liog il Science 173:1238-9 S 24 '71
Iodine-129 in terrestrial ores. B. Srinivasan
and others. bibliog il Science 173:327-8 Jl
23 '71
Xenon as a nucleophile in gas-phase dis-
placement reactions: formation of the
methyl xenonium ion. D. Holtz and J. L.
Beauchamp. bibliog il Science 173:1237-8
S 24 '71
Isotopes
Xenon record of extinct radioactivities in the
earth. M. S. Boulos and O. K. Manuel.
bibliog il Science 174:1334-6 D 24 '71
XENON compounds
Xenon hexafluoride: structural crystallography of tetrameric phases. R. D. Burbank and G. R. Jones. bibliog il Science 171:
485-7 F 5 '71
**XERODERMA pigmentosum. See Skin—Dis-
eases**
XEROGRAPHY. See Copying processes
XERORADIOGRAPHY. See Radiography

XEROX corporation
Apple for Xerox? Forbes 108:32-4 Jl 1 '71
At Xerox: giving but not forcing. V.
Louviere. Nations Bsns 59:18 D '71
Growth, it's wonderful. il Fortune 83:252 My
'71
My years at Xerox, by J. H. Dessauer. Re-
view
Bsns W il p 18+ N 13 '71. R. King
New fringe: T-shirt and trunks. il Duns 98:
79 S '71
No. 2 at Xerox. por Bsns W p76 Mr 20 '71
Original copier; beginnings of the Xerox
machine. por Time 98:97-8 D 6 '71
Where the mouth is; social service leave
plan. Newsweek 78:82+ S 20 '71
Why of Xerox. L. L. L. Golden. Sat R 54:53-4
Ag 14 '71
Xerox machine that prints X-rays. il Bsns W
p60 My 29 '71
Xerox sabbaticals. Time 98:69 S 20 '71
Xeroxing of social service. Bsns W p41 S
11 '71
Xerox's social concern; new Social service
leave program. America 125:219 O 2 '71
See also
Rank-Xerox, ltd.
XYLAN. See Metal coating

Y

**YAF. See Young Americans for freedom (or-
ganization)**
**YASD. See American library association—
Young adult services division**
**YCC. See United States—Youth conservation
corps**
**YES (Youth employment service) See Student
employment**
YABLONSKI, Joseph A.
Bombshell from the Yablonski trial. Bsns W
p30 Je 26 '71 *
Man named Tony. il por Newsweek 78:56 Jl
5 '71 *
YACHT building
See also
Morgan yacht corporaton
YACHT clubs
Toms River challenge cup is the sport's old-
est continuous competition. B. Robinson.
il Yachting 130:60-1+ Jl '71
YACHT racing
America's cup news. See occasional issues
of Yachting to July 1971
Charley Morgan speaks up; interview. ed.
by G. F. Hammond. C. Morgan. il por
Motor B & S 127:58-60+ Je '71
Chicago-Mackinac: what really happened. B.
D. Barker, 3d. Yachting 129:52+ F '71
College racing. G. Hall. Yachting 130:168 N;
134-5 D '71
Congressional cup: best test in the West. L.
J. Kennedy. il Motor B & S 127:37+ Mr '71
Deep water racing. B. D. Barker, 3d. See
issues of Yachting
Dropout problem. Yachting 129:39 Mr '71
Fair wind for Montego Bay; Miami-Jamaica
race. C. Mitchell. il Sports Illus 34:46-8+
My 24 '71
Ficker wins California cup. L. J. Kennedy.
Motor B & S 127:39 Mr '71
Get out of the boat and go; with photographs
by J. Zimmerman; account by H. D. Whall.
Sports Illus 34:38-43 Je 21 '71
How to win the Admiral's cup. S. Colgate. il
Yachting 130:52+ O '71
In the wake of the capsize kid; Ted Turner.
C. Phinizy. il por Sports Illus 35:28-30+
Jl 12 '71
Mackinacs. G. Hall; G. E. Van. il Yachting
130:43+ S '71
Midnight sailors of Buzzards Bay. H. D.
Whall. il Sports Illus 35:22-3 S 13 '71
Month in yachting. See issues of Yachting
Oh, how she scoons! G. F. Hammond. il
Motor B & S 128:48-9+ Ag '71
One ton trend; boat-for boat racing. G. F.
Hammond. il Motor B & S 128:56-9+ O '71
Organizing for offshore; how Ondine's 21-
man crew works together. D. Bertram. il
Motor B & S 128:26+ O '71
"Passage" evens the score; Transpac race.
B. Crabtree. il Yachting 130:60-2+ S '71
Queasiness in rough cup waters; moment of
decision for the New York yacht club.
H. D. Whall. Sports Illus 34:46 Ja 25 '71
Racing clinic. D. Rose; G. Hall. See issues
of Yachting

YALE, W. W.
Climate's all wrong. Nat R 23:651-2+ Je 15 '71

YALE college. See Yale university

YALE university
Alternative: publication of the party of the Right at Yale. W. F. Buckley, jr. Nat R 23:331 Mr 23 '71
Cafe, Yale freshman commons. il Arch Rec 149:100-1 Ja '71
Going to Yale on a 35-year loan. Bsns W p32 F 13 '71
How reformers bombed in New Haven. D. Hale. Commonweal 94:473-7 S 17 '71; Reply with rejoinder. R. H. Bainton. 95:123+ N 5 '71
Informal notes, taken on reading John Hersey on Yale. R. Moses. Nat R 23:142-4+ F 9 '71
Learn now, pay later. New Repub 164:12-13 F 20 '71
Pay as you earn. Newsweek 77:69 F 15 '71
Study now, pay later: Pay as you earn plan. Time 98:66 N 1 '71
Tale of two universities. E. Holsendolph. il Fortune 83:104-8+ F '71
Yale faculty makes the scene. T. Meehan. il N Y Times Mag p 12-13+ F 7 '71; Discussion. p4 F 28; 12+ Mr 7 '71
Yale plan: study now, pay for 35 years. U S News 70:28 F 22 '71
Yale's tuition postponement plan. Sch & Soc 99:273-5 Sum '71

Libraries
China records project at Yale. R. P. Morris. Chr Cent 88:832-3 Jl 7 '71

Summer school of music
See Music schools

YAMANO, Mike
Greening of America. Newsweek 78:109+ N 22 '71 *

YAMAUCHI, Edwin M.
Historical notes on the (in) comparable Christ. il Chr Today 16:7-11 O 22 '71
Historical notes on the trial and crucifixion of Jesus Christ. Chr Today 15:6-11 Ap 9 '71

YANG, Chen Ning
C. N. Yang discusses physics in People's Republic of China. G. B. Lubkin. il pors Phys Today 24:61-3 N '71 *

YANGTAOS
New fruit from China via New Zealand: Chinese gooseberry or kiwi berry. D. Elliot. il Horticulture 49:42-3+ F '71

YANKEE atomic nuclear power station. See Atomic power plants

YANKEE stadium. See Stadiums

YANKELOVICH, Daniel, inc.
Guarded optimism at the top; new Fortune 500-Yankelovich survey. R. Loving, jr. il Fortune 83:168-9+ My '71

YANNACONE, Victor John, Jr
Courtroom shootouts. J. B. Craig. Am For 77:11 Jl '71 *

YAQUI Indians
Further conversations with Don Juan; excerpt from A separate reality. C. Castaneda. il Esquire 75:75-89+ Mr '71; Discussion. 75:14 My '71

YARBOROUGH, Ralph Webster
Defying the bosses in Illinois & Texas. P. R. Wieck. New Repub 164:12-13 F 27 '71 *

YARD lighting. See Lighting, Outdoor

YARMOUTH, Me.
Education
Environmental encounters. V. A. Schlich. il Am Ed 7:23-6 Ag '71

YASHIN, Lev Ivanovich. See Iashin, L. I.

YASMINEH, Walid G. See Yunis, J. J. jt. auth.

YASSIN, my son; drama. See Halawa, F.

YASTRZEMSKI, Carl
Who's in charge here? il por Newsweek 78: 61 Jl 12 '71 *

YATES, Brock
Captain Marvel presents Captain Nice. il por Sports Illus 35:18-19 Jl 12 '71

YATES CENTER, Kan.
Greatest athlete in Yates Center, Kansas. W. Johnson. il pors Sports Illus 35:26-31 Ag 9 '71

YATVIN, Joanne
Things ain't the way they used to be in the English classroom. Engl J 60:1080-5 N '71

YAUPON. See Cassena

YAZEJIAN, Ann
(ed) Books to come. Library J 96:1145-71, 3497-527 Mr 15, O 15 '71
(comp) Children's paperbacks. Library J 96:1837-9, 2863-5 My 15, S 15 '71

YAZOO CITY, Miss.
Education
Yazoo, by W. Morris. Review Sat R 54:31-3 Je 6 '71. W. F. Holmes

YEAGER, Robert O.
Slurry seal for maintenance, remix for reconstruction. il Am City 86:54-5 Jl '71

YEAR round schools. See School year

YEARBOOKS, College. See College annuals

YEARWOOD, Randall Nile
Keys to growth: quality, cost control and service. il Arch Rec 149:67-70 Ap '71 *

YEARWOOD and Johnson, inc.
Keys to growth: quality, cost control and service. il Arch Rec 149:67-70 Ap '71

YEAST mitochondria. See Mitochondria

YEASTS
Preparation of highly labeled [³²P]nucleic acids from yeast; isolation of denaturable leucine acceptor transfer RNA. S. Kowalski and J. R. Fresco. bibliog il Science 172: 384-5 Ap 23 '71
Selection of ribosomal mutants by antibiotic suppression in yeast. F. T. Bayliss and R. T. Vinopal. bibliog il Science 174:1339-41 D 24 '71

YEATS, William Butler
Yeats' The shadowy waters: oral motifs and identity in the drafts. B. Webster. bibliog f Am Imago 28:3-16 Spr '71 *

YEE, Linda
College presidents and students; interview. Mlle 73:350-1 Ag '71

YEFIMOV, Victor, and others
What Soviet spacemen eat. Space World H-3-87:40 Mr '71

YELLOW transit freight lines, inc.
Golden profits of Yellow freight. il Fortune 84:63+ Jl '71

YELLOWSTONE NATIONAL PARK
Last chance for Yellowstone? P. Friggens. il Read Digest 98:190-2+ Mr '71
Nature's chaperones. M. D. McLean. il Am For 77:32-4 N '71
1,000 wonders: Yellowstone at 100. J. V. Young. il Travel 137:34-9+ Ja '72
Postscript to tragedy: a father's crusade. M. Cohen. il Redbook 137:76-7+ Je '71
Snowmobiling in Yellowstone. B. Behme. il Field & S 76:38-9 D '71
Yellowstone canoe trip. B. Thomas. il Travel 136:37-9+ Jl '71
Yellowstone nobody knows. C. Nansen. il Field & S 76:44-5+ Jl '71

YEMEN
Politics and government
Crossed wires. por Newsweek 78:53 S 20 '71
Crossed wires; Hassan Amri. il por Time 98: 35 S 20 '71

YENAY, Ehud
Fuel that truly is pollution-free. il Mech Illus 67:63-5+ Mr '71

YENSER, Stephen
Moving again; Racket; Calypso on Tinos; poems. Poetry 118:255-9 Ag '71

YEOMANS, W. C.
British Columbia wilderness; excerpt from address. il Liv Wildn 34:40-3 Wint '70

YERGANIAN, George. See Lavappa, K. S. jt. auth.

YERGIN, Dan
Peckinpah's progress. il pors N Y Times Mag p 16-17+ O 31 '71

YERKES, Robert Mearns
Reporter at large. E. Hahn. New Yorker 47:46-8+ Ap 17; 46-50+ Ap 24 '71 *

YERKES laboratories of primate biology
See also
Emory university, Atlanta—Yerkes primate research center

YERMA; opera. See Villa-Lobos, H.

YESHIVA university, New York
Stern college for women
American thing: grooving on your heritage? or assimilation? Jews at Stern college. J. Marks. Mlle 72:205-6+ Ap '71

YESSNE, Peter
Cracks in Daley. Nation 212:360-5 Mr 22 '71

YEUNG, Yue-man
Singapore. bibliog il Focus 21:1-12 Ap '71

YEVTUSHENKO, Yevgeny Aleksandrovich. See Evtushenko, E. A.

YGLESIAS, José
Conservative; story. New Yorker 47:32-9 Je 12 '71
Guns in the closet; story. New Yorker 47: 50-8 N 20 '71

YGLESIAS, José—*Continued*
   Romeo & Julieta. New Yorker 47:107-8+ O
      16 '71
   Walking my dog on the West side. il Esquire
      75:120-3 Je '71
YIDDISH language
   In praise of Yiddish, by M. Samuel. Review
      Sat R 54:30 Jl 17 '71
YIDDISH literature

Translations in English

   Blow struck for the revolution; tr. by J.
      Wincelberg. M. Marateck. Commentary 53:
      62-6 Ja '72
YIDDISH poetry
   Journey of a poet. I. Howe. Commentary 53:
      75-7 Ja '72
   Treasury of Yiddish poetry, ed. by I. Howe
      and E. Greenberg. Review
         Poetry 118:354-5 S '71. R. Whitman
YIN, Lo I. and others
   Core binding energy difference between bridg-
      ing and nonbridging oxygen atoms in a sil-
      icate chain. bibliog il Science 173:633-5 Ag
      13 '71
YIU, Myung-kun
   Prospect of Japanese rearmament. bibliog f il
      Cur Hist 60:231-6 Ap '71
YLVISAKER, William Townend
   Merger, factory style. por Forbes 108:54
      O 1 '71 *
YOCK, P. C. M.
   Twelve subnucleons. Sci N 99:144 F 27 '71 *
YODER, R. A.
   Clay is fun. il Sch Arts 71:20-1 O '71
   I can't draw people. il Sch Arts 71:16-17
      N '71
YOELI, Meir, and Most, Harry
   Sporozoite-induced infections of plasmodium
      berghei administered by the oral route.
      bibliog il Science 173:1031-2 S 10 '71
YOGA
   And now, the Yoga retreat. G. A. Maloney.
      America 124:591-3 Je 5 '71
   Rush for instant salvation. S. Davidson. il
      Harper 243:40-2+ Jl '71
   Yoga proves valuable camp program addition.
      L. T. Singer. il Camp Mag 43:13 N '71
YOGTIBA, Gilbert
   Summer diplomat, U.S.A. A. Adams. por
      Seventeen 29:270-1+ Ag '70 *
YOGURT
   Last word on yogurt-making. G. A. Gara-
      bedian. Science 171:847-8 Mr 5 '71
YOLEN, Jane
   Peter Rabbit, say good-bye to Snow White.
      il por Pub W 199:79-80 F 22 '71
YOLK protein. See Proteins
YOLLES, Melanie Ann
   Psychiatrist and his daughter talk frankly
      about marijuana; interview, ed. by A.
      Bramson. pors Seventeen 29:134-5+ O '70
YOLLES, Stanley Faust
   Psychiatrist and his daughter talk frankly
      about marijuana; interview, ed. by A.
      Bramson. pors Seventeen 29:134-5+ O '70
   Student use of drugs: facts and fables. Ed
      Digest 37:13-16 N '71
YONEZAWA, Takeshi. See Robbins, N. jt.
      auth.
YORK (Negro servant)
   This nation never saw a black man before.
      D. Zochert. il por Am Heritage 22:8-9 F
      '71 *
YORK, Carl M.
   Steps toward a national policy for academic
      science. bibliog il Science 172:643-8 My 14
      '71
YORK, Herbert F.
   Danger of partial disarmament steps. Cur
      133:41-5 O '71
YORK university, Toronto. See Colleges and
      universities—Canada
YORKTOWN, Va.

Siege, 1781

   Surrender at Yorktown: the world turn'd up-
      side down. T. Fleming. il Read Digest 98:
      162-4+ Ja '71
YORTY, Samuel William
   Another candidate heard from. il por News-
      week 78:18-19 N 29 '71 *
   California's mad mix. M. E. Leary. Nation
      212:685-7 My 31 '71 *
   Mayor Sam Yorty's one-man bandwagon. B.
      Boyarsky. New Repub 165:14+ D 18 '71 *
YOSEMITE NATIONAL PARK
   Hassles in the park. J. Hope. il Natur Hist
      80:20-3+ bibliog(p 104) My '71
   Park that caught urban blight. E. Abbey. il
      Life 71:40+ S 3 '71
   Yosemite's generation gap. J. H. Harring-
      ton. Am For 77:3 Ja '71

Yosemite's pioneer museum. il Sunset 146:64
      Ap '71
      See also
   Hetch Hetchy Valley
YOSEMITE VALLEY
   Yosemite Valley's new traffic pattern. il Sun-
      set 146:56 Je '71
YOSHIMURA, Fumio
   Fumio Yoshimura. S. Edmiston. il por Craft
      Horiz 31:22-5+ Ag '71 *
YOST, Charles W.
   Instruments of American foreign policy. For
      Affairs 50:59-68 O '71
   Last chance for peace in the Mideast. por
      Life 70:4 Ap 9 '71
   Letter to a Soviet friend. por Life 71:4 S
      24 '71
   U.N. General assembly urges humane treat-
      ment of prisoners of war; statement,
      December 1, 1970. Dept State Bul 64:11-12
      Ja 4 '71
   U.S. abstains on Security council resolution
      on Guinea; statement, December 8, 1970.
      Dept State Bul 64:98-101 Ja 18 '71
   U.S. informs U.N. of withdrawal from de-
      colonization committee; text of letter,
      January 11, 1971. Dept State Bul 64:186 F
      8 '71
   United States calls for concrete actions to
      strengthen U.N. peacekeeping; statement,
      November 13, 1970. Dept State Bul 64:89-92
      Ja 18 '71
   United States reviews major disarmament
      issues facing the U.N. General assembly;
      statement, November 2, 1970. Dept State
      Bul 63:803-6 D 28 '70
YOST, Nicholas
   Lifestyle. il por Am Home 74:8 Je '71 *
YOU want to go to Pittsburgh; story. See
      Shyer, M. F.
YOUMANS, Hubert L.
   Career opportunities in chemistry. bibliog il
      por Chem 44:18-20 Mr '71
YOUNG, A. S.
   Black athlete in the golden age of sports
      (title varies) (cont) il Ebony 26:44-6+ Ja;
      96-8+ Mr; 139-42+ Ap '71
YOUNG, Allan, and Marshall, Wayne
   Controlling shareholder servicing costs. bib-
      liog f il Harvard Bsns R 49:71-8 Ja '71
YOUNG, Allen
   Out of the closet: a gay manifesto. il Ramp
      Mag 10:52-9 N '71
YOUNG, Allen (writer)
   Englishman comes to Denver. por Hi Fi 21:
      MA30 Je '71
YOUNG, Andrew J. 1932-
   Whitney Young: working from the middle.
      por Life 70:4 Mr 26 '71
YOUNG, Andrew T.
   Seeing and scintillation. bibliog il Sky & Tel
      42:139-41+ S '71
YOUNG, Anne B. and others
   Nuclear localization of histamine in neonatal
      rat brain. bibliog il Science 173:247-9 Jl 16
      '71
YOUNG, Charlotte M.
   Fat child. Todays Ed 60:58-9 Mr '71
YOUNG, Chester W.
   Zener diode voltage-regulator nomograms.
      il Electr World 86:32-3+ Jl '71
YOUNG, Clarence, 3d
   Perry's mission. Criticism
      New Yorker 46:56 Ja 30 '71 *
YOUNG, Clemewell
   Same train; poem. Horn Bk 47:185 Ap '71
YOUNG, David P.
   Accident; poem. New Repub 165:39 O 16 '71
YOUNG, David Paris
   Science alone is not enough. il por Chem 44:
      14-16 N '71
YOUNG, Elizabeth
   To guard the sea. For Affairs 50:136-47 O '71
YOUNG, Francis A.
   Profile for posterity: saving the skylines of
      Vermont. il Nat Parks & Con Mag 45:20-4
      F '71
YOUNG, Gordon
   That dammed Missouri River. il Nat Geog
      140:374-413 S '71
YOUNG, Graham
   Killer shark may save your life. il Pop Mech
      135:70-4+ Je '71
—and Dempewolff, R. F.
   Mamba! il Sci Digest 70:58-64 Jl '71
YOUNG, James. See Hope, M. jt. auth.
YOUNG, John V.
   1,000 wonders: Yellowstone at 100. il Travel
      137:34-9+ Ja '72
YOUNG, Katherine
   (tr) See Pico, J. V. Exploring Spanish caves
      for cave-man art
YOUNG, Kenneth, case. See Kidnapping

YOUNG, Kenneth Todd
Thailand and multipolarity. bibliog f Cur
Hist 61:327-31+ D '71
YOUNG, Neil
After the gold rush; song. il Sr Schol 98:22
F 15 '71
YOUNG, Norman
New city in a hurry. R. Levy. por Duns 97:
63 Je '71 *
YOUNG, Peter
Allende: a special kind of Marxist. il pors
Life 71:38-40 Jl 16 '71
George Bush ran all the way. Life 71:32-4 N
5 '71
YOUNG, Ray
What to do 'til the compost comes. Org
Gard & Farm 18:51-3 D '71
YOUNG, Robert
Robert Young: TV's Dr Welby; his frank and
personal replies to fans; ed. by C. Schroeder.
il pors Good H 172:42-4+ Je '71

about

Robert Young's toughest role. B. Ellison. il
pors Todays Health 49:25-7+ My '71 *
TV's Dr Marcus Welby. G. Astor. il pors
Look 35:56-9 Mr 23 '71 *
YOUNG, Robert W.
College admissions policies. Ed Digest 36:
19-21 Ja '71
YOUNG, Russell D.
Surface microtopography; adaptation of ad-
dress. March 1971. bibliog il Phys Today
24:42-9 N '71
YOUNG, Stanley P.
Bobcat facts; excerpt from The bobcat of
North America. il Field & S 76:28 Je '71
YOUNG, Vernon R. and Scrimshaw, N. S.
Physiology of starvation; with biographical
sketches. il Sci Am 225:12, 14-21 bibliog (p
120) O '71
YOUNG, Warren R.
Magic of good posture. Read Digest 99:151-2+
N '71
YOUNG, Whitney Moore, 1921-1971
America mourns Whitney M. Young jr; with
editorial comment. S. Booker. il pors
Ebony 26:31-4+, 144 My '71 *
Kind of bridge. por Time 97:20 Mr 22 '71 *
Lost black leader. E. Dunbar. Look 35:76 Ap
20 '71 *
Obituary
America 124:307 Mr 27 '71
Chr Cent 88:367 Mr 24 '71
Chr Cent 88:395 Mr 31 '71
Negro Hist Bul por(p73) 34:94-5 Ap '71
Sr Schol 98:10 Mr 29 '71
Whitney Young: he was a doer. il por News-
week 77:29 Mr 22 '71 *
Whitney Young: working from the middle.
A. J. Young. por Life 70:4 Mr 26 '71 *
Whitney Young's open society; address, April
1971, with questions and answers. H. R.
Sims. Ann Am Acad 396:70-8 Jl '71 *
YOUNG adults literature
Innocence is a cop-out. J. B. Mercer. il Wil-
son Lib Bul 46:144-6 O '71
Popular, but not just a part of the crowd: im-
plications of formula fiction for teenagers.
B. Martinec. Engl J 60:339-44 Mr '71
Thought, not necessarily the deed: sex in
some of today's juvenile novels. J. Neu-
feld. il Wilson Lib Bul 46:147-52 O '71

Bibliography
Adult books for young adults; ed. by R.
Minudri. See second issue of each month
of Library journal
Best books for spring 1971; ed. by L. N.
Gerhardt and others. Library J 96:1783 My
15 '71
Best books for young adults. 1970. Todays
Ed 60:10-11 Ap '71; Same. PTA Mag 65:36
My; 30-1 Je '71
Book marks. J. W. Conner. See issues of
English journal
Books by young writers. M. A. Hardy. por
Seventeen 30:14 Ja '71
Books for young people. Z. Sutherland. See
issues of Saturday review
Digging the scene; books on contemporary
life. il Schol Teach Jr/Sr High p 18-19 Ap 5
'71
Mini reference library: 21 paperbacks. J.
Higgins and A. Stellwag. il pors Library
J 96:245-7 Ja 15 '71
Outlook tower; books of interest to high
school students. M. S. Cosgrave. See issues
of Horn book magazine

34 choice teen books announced by ALA. Li-
brary J 96:1764 My 15 '71
Up for discussion; the skirts in fiction about
boys: a maxi mess. D. G. Stavn. Library J
96:282-6 Ja 15 '71
YOUNG adults reading
Siddhartha; craze for works of H. Hesse.
F. Trippett. il Look 35:46-54+ F 23 '71
YOUNG Americans for freedom (organization)
Scenes from Houston; YAF at eleven. J. C.
Lobdell. Nat R 23:1111+ O 8 '71
YOUNG automobile drivers. See Automobile
drivers
YOUNG girl's heart; story. See Dowty, L.
YOUNG great society. See Negroes—Clubs,
societies, etc.
YOUNG men
See also
Youth
YOUNG militants
Diana: the making of a terrorist, by T.
Powers. Review
Sat R 54:35 My 1 '71. F. J. Cook
Don't blame me! answers to accusations of
permissiveness. B. Spock. Look 35:37-8 Ja
26 '71; Same abr. with title Doctor Spock
speaks out. Cur 127:19-23 Mr '71
Don't shoot: we are your children, by J. A.
Lukas. Review
New Repub 164:36-7 My 29 '71. J. Yardley
Radical chic is dead. S. Alsop. Read Digest
98:103-4 F '71
Radical family. J. Poppy. il Look 35:81-2+
Ja 26 '71
Radicals in America: who, what, where,
and why? Sr Schol 98:4-14 Ap 19 '71
Whatever happened to, Chicago 7 after the
trial? il U S News 70:76-7 Mr 15 '71
Who are the youthful rebels? with study-
discussion program, by C. Smallenburg and
H. Smallenburg. D. Winters. bibliog il PTA
Mag 65:10-12+, 33 Je '71
See also
Student militants
YOUNG peoples concerts. See Concerts
YOUNG women
Must marriage cheat today's young women?
P. E. Slater. il Redbook 136:66-7+ F '71
Young women of the year. il Mlle 72:61-3+
Ja '71
See also
Girls
Youth
YOUNGBLOOD, Rufus
Hero Rufus Youngblood gets the secret ser-
vice brush-off. S. Wright. il por Life 71:81
N 5 '71 *
YOUNGERMAN, Jack
Jack Youngerman. B. Rose. por Vogue 157:
143 F 1 '71 *
YOUNGMAN, Wilbur H.
Systemics. il Horticulture 49:18-19+ Jl '71
YOUNT, David E. See Murphy, F. V. jt. auth.
YOURGRAU, Wolfgang
Nominator. Nation 213:453 N 8 '71 *
YOUTH
Adolescent grievances: at home; with study-
discussion program, by C. Smallenburg
and H. Smallenburg. M. J. Bienvenu bib-
liog il PTA Mag 66:18-20, 35 S '71
Mind bright and strong; Unesco's activities.
W. McEwing. il UNESCO Courier 24:26-9
Ag '71
Natural history of the young. R. W. Murphy.
Atlan 229:36-8 Ja '72
Youth of the world. youth of Unesco. R. Ma-
heu. UNESCO Courier 24:4-5 Ag '71
See also
Adolescence
Boys
Church work with youth
Dating
Dropouts
Girls
High school students
Hippies
Indians of North America—Youth
Libraries—Services to young people
Negro youth
Smoking and youth
Students

Adjustment
See Adjustment, Social

Attitudes
Communes and the work crisis. L. M. An-
drews. Cur 126:34-9 F '71
Contemporary youth inherit a strange and
awesome world. R. E. Forbes. il Cath
World 213:21-6 Ag '71
New generation; address, June 15, 1971. J. W.
McKinney, jr. Vital Speeches 37:665-9 Ag
15 '71

YOUTH—Attitudes—*Continued*
Taking a one-world approach to the young.
  V. Louvière. il Nations Bsns 59:18 O '71
Toward a culture of unreason? D. Bazelon.
  Cur 131:51-6 Jl '71
What young America wants: change, not
  revolution. il Read Digest 98:85-7 Je '71
Youth in America: cultural and educational
  problems; symposium. bibliog Sch & Soc
  99:245-54 Ap '71
Youth's heroes have no haloes. C. Quigley.
  Todays Ed 60:28-9 F '71; Same abr. Ed
  Digest 38:46-8 Ap '71
    See also
Youth—Political attitudes

Conduct of life
Staying hip; the relevant teenager. 1966 and
  1971. S. B. Chickering. il Harper 243:62-5 S
  '71
    See also
Counter culture

Employment
Cool capitalists; teen-run enterprises. il Sev-
  enteen 29:130-1 O '70
Employment of high school graduates and
  dropouts. A. M. Young. il Mo Labor R 94:
  33-8 My '71
Employment of school-age youth; with tables
  and chart. H. Hayghe. bibliog Mo Labor
  R 94:13-18 Ag '71
Is hard work going out of style? interview. E.
  Ginzberg. il por U S News 71:52-6 Ag 23
  '71
Making more jobs for young Americans. il
  Nations Bsns 59:88-90 S '71
Preparing youth for reality; address, October
  29, 1971. J. D. Hodgson. Vital Speeches 38:
  166-8 Ja 1 '72
Young workers and their earnings; with
  tables. V. C. Perrella. il Mo Labor R 94:
  3-11 Jl '71
    See also
Junior achievement companies
Student employment

Health and hygiene
Can hypnosis help you? L. David. il Seventeen 30:94-5+ Jl '71

Law
Face to face with a boy who took his own
  case to court. G. W. Pratt, 3d. por Seven-
  teen 30:139 Jl '71
Growing up in America. M. J. Green. New
  Repub 165:14-17 S 18 '71
How fair a fair trial can you get today? il
  Sr Schol 99:2-5+ N 8 '71
Law and you. il Sr Schol 98:6-9 Ap 26 '71

Management and training
    See also
Camp discipline
Parent-child relationship

Nutrition
Those mushrooming food fads. J. N. Bell. il
  Seventeen 30:110-11+ Jl '71

Political activities
Candidates answer Senior's queries: most effective participation by persons under 18
  in 1972 campaign? il Sr Schol 99:4-13 N 1
  '71
First-time voters: what they want in a candidate; Senior youthview. il Sr Schol 99:
  14-15 N 1 '71
How will youth vote? il Newsweek 78:28-
  30+ O 25 '71
Inventing the young. J. Adelson. Commen-
  tary 51:43-8 My '71
Pleasures and pitfalls of getting out the vote.
  T. Bernstein and P. Bernstein. il Seventeen
  31:122+ Ja '72
Story behind the author; interview, ed. by
  E. Lottman. T. Moffett. por Pub W 200:
  28-9 N 22 '71
Young good guys. S. Schlesinger. il Vogue
  158:112-15 Ag 1 '71
Young voters surge to enroll in the system;
  with account by D. Wittner. il Life 71:26-33
  O 15 '71
Youth, change, and foreign policy; address,
  November 12, 1970. R. F. Pedersen. Dept
  State Bul 63:718-22 D 14 '70

Political attitudes
How will youth vote? il Newsweek 78:28-30+
  O 25 '71

Reading
    See Young adults reading

Recreation
Baseball where the players are; Cincinnati
  junior baseball program. J. Twyman. il
  Parks & Rec 6:27+ S '71
Establishing a harmonious relationship be-
  tween recreation departments and orga-
  nized youth leagues. W. D. Martin. il
  Parks & Rec 6:42-3+ Jl '71
    See also
Recreation centers

Religion
Close-up of the Jesus people. D. M. Williams.
  Chr Today 15:5-7 Ag 27 '71
Fellow traveling with Jesus; The Way, and
  The Process. il Time 98:54-5 S 6 '71
Going east: neomysticism and Christian
  faith. G. Fackre. il Chr Cent 88:457-61 Ap
  14 '71
Greening of revival: the Jesus revolution
  and other signs. E. Jorstad. il Cath World
  213:265-8 S '71
Groovy Christians of Rye, N.Y. J. Howard.
  il Life 70:78-82+ My 14 '71
Is it so odd to seek God? questions and
  answers. A. Wood. Seventeen 29:130+ D '70
Jesus craze. il Life 71:38-9 D 31 '71
Jesus movement is upon us; California. B.
  Vachon. il Look 35:15-21 F 9 '71
New religion. J. B. Sheerin. Cath World
  212:283-4 Mr '71
No circus act; letter to editor. S. Perrin.
  Chr Cent 88:1026 S 1 '71
Now that Jesus is in again. Chr Cent 88:767
  Je 23 '71
Open the shutters and let the godforce
  through; Brotherhood of the spirit com-
  mune in Massachusetts. M. Cantwell. il Mlle
  74:142-3+ D '71
Predicament of youth. L. N. Bell. Chr Today
  15:34 S 24 '71
Rapping with the Jesus people; Senior youth-
  view, ed. by A. Rubin. il Sr Schol 99:12-14
  D 13 '71
Rock and the Jesus movement. il Sr Schol 99:
  6-12 D 13 '71
Rush for instant salvation. S. Davidson. il
  Harper 243:40-2+ Jl '71
Searching for a new faith. D. A. Sugarman
  and R. Hochstein. il Seventeen 29:134-5+ S
  '70
Shape of the coming renewal. R. Lovelace.
  il Chr Cent 88:1164-7 O 6 '71
Siddhartha; craze for works of H. Hesse.
  F. Trippett. il Look 35:46-54+ F 23 '71
Summer abroad. E. E. Plowman. Chr Today
  15:42 S 10 '71
Wave of witness. E. E. Plowman. il Chr
  Today 15:34-5 My 7 '71
Winds from the East; youth and counter-
  cults. J. Needleman. il Commonweal 94:188-
  90 Ap 30 '71
Youth lead more revivals. Chr Today 15:
  50 Mr 12 '71
    See also
Children of God (movement)
Hippies—Religion
Revivals

    Anecdotes, facetiae, satire, etc.
Scenario for the movement: the Jesus revolution. Chr Cent 88:843 Jl 7 '71

Suicide
    See Suicide

Unemployment
    See Unemployment—United States

Asia
Premature aging of the Asian youth; address,
  October 29, 1971. J. K. C. Oh. Vital Speeches
  38:186-8 Ja 1 '72

Canada
Summerpower! Canada gives youth its head,
  and bread; Opportunities for youth program. I. Mothner. il Look 35:48-53 Ag 24
  '71

China (People's Republic)
China; youth and the economic development
  goals. H. Yu. Chr Cent 88:810 Je 30 '71

Czechoslovakia
How long will the winter last? A. Levy. il
  Seventeen 30:250-1+ Ag '71

Germany (Democratic Republic)
American teens in Berlin; symposium, ed.
  by R. Hemming. il Sr Schol 98:9-10 Mr 8
  '71

YOUTH—*Continued*

Germany (Federal Republic)
American teens in Berlin; symposium, ed. by R. Hemming. il Sr Schol 98:9-10 Mr 8 '71
See also
German students

Israel
Israeli youth: the coming explosion. J. R. Moskin. il Look 35:20-4+ Je 15 '71

Malaysia
Possibilities for violence in Malaysia. P. Pedersen. bibliog f Cur Hist 61:339-44+ D '71

United States
Analysis of 1970-71 campus peace. Sch & Soc 99:462 D '71
Auto accidents; top killer of U.S. youths. il U S News 71:57 S 13 '71
Blueing of America. P. L. Berger and B. Berger. New Repub 164:20-3 Ap 3 '71; Same. Cur 131:56-62 Jl '71
Contemporary youth inherit a strange and awesome world. R. E. Forbes. il Cath World 213:21-6 Ap '71
Death of the American ethic. O. S. Kramer. Yale R 61:69-75 O '71
Decline of flower power. P. C. Rule. America 124:141-5 F 13 '71
Don't shoot—We are your children, by J. A. Lukas. Review
　Commonweal 94:410-12 Ag 6 '71. W. Gaylin
Earth from far away, and close up; interview, ed. by P. Goldberger. M. Collins. por Sr Schol 98:16 Mr 15 '71
End of the youth revolt? il U S News 71:26-31 Ag 9 '71
For now (cont) C. H. Simonds. por Nat R 23:145, 1305 F 9, N 19 '71
Greening of America, by C. A. Reich. Review
Bul Atom Sci 27:33-7 N '71. E. Rabinowitch
　Cur 125:9-11 Ja '71. H. Marcuse
　Cur 125:11-14 Ja '71. P. Marin
Have we forsaken our teen-agers? L. Strauth. il Parents Mag 46:54-6+ My '71
If they're old enough to vote... Nations Bsns 59:26 S '71
In my opinion; everyone should be a full citizen at eighteen, not twenty-one! R. Alexander. por Seventeen 30:212 O '71
In my opinion; pep rallies really aren't such clean, wholesome, all-American fun. E. Silberman. por Seventeen 30:186 N '71
Inventing the young. J. Adelson. Commentary 51:43-8 My '71
Is there a new now? interview, ed. by M. Ronan. A. MacGraw. por Sr Schol 98:3+ F 15 '71
Now generation in U.S. il U S News 70:64 Mr 22 '71
On the up and up. New Repub 164:5-6 Je 19 '71
Profile of the new voter. il Newsweek 78:38+ O 25 '71
Reconciling youth and the Establishment; excerpt from address, December, 1970. J. D. Rockefeller, 3d. Sat R 54:27-9+ Ja 23 '71
Senile society: a theory. S. Goldberg. Yale R 61:1-25 O '71
Showdown at generation gap. W. L. Thomas. il Farm J 95:32-3+ Mr '71
Six cheers for our children. J. Zeliff. Good H 172:63+ F '71
Sweet bird of youth. I. J. Hutchison, Jr. il Parks & Rec 6:46-7+ O '71
This was the year the kids cooled it. il Life 71:26-7 D 31 '71
Time's children, by T. J. Cottle. Review
Sat R 54:90 O 16 '71. L. Y. Jones, jr
Two! Four! Six! Eight! Who do we appreciate? Senior youthview. il Sr Schol 99:10-11 N 8 '71
Young good guys. S. Schlesinger. il Vogue 158:112-15 Ag '71
Your whole life catalog; looking back on past years. il Seventeen 31:50-3 Ja '72
Youth, rebellion & the environment. G. Stucker. il Nat Parks & Con Mag 45:6-9 Ap '71
See also
College students
Counter culture
Dating
Volunteer service
White House conference on youth, 1971

YOUTH-adult relationship
Accent on youth. A. H. Leitch. Chr Today 16:48+ D 3 '71
Adolescent-adult bond. Sch & Soc 99:468 D '71

Adolescent grievances: at home; with study-discussion program, by C. Smallenburg and H. Smallenburg. M. J. Bienvenu. bibliog il PTA Mag 66:18-20, 35 S '71
Great white son turns left. E. G. Dalbey, jr. il Chr Cent 88:716-20 Je 9 '71
Joys and terrors of sending the kids to college. H. Swados. il N Y Times Mag p 12-13+ F 14 '71
NCTE presidential address: imagination and the health of everyman; November 1970. J. E. Miller, jr. Engl J 60:189-98 F '71
Reconciling youth and the Establishment; excerpt from address, December, 1970. J. D. Rockefeller, 3d. Sat R 54:27-9+ Ja 23 '71
U.S. journal: Florida; student spring vacations in Fort Lauderdale and Daytona Beach. C. Trillin. New Yorker 47:104+ My 1 '71
Will youth take over? J. Brothers. Good H 172:58+ Mr '71
See also
Generation gap
Parent-child relationship

YOUTH and environmental problems. See Environmental movement

YOUTH and moving pictures. See Moving pictures and youth

YOUTH and narcotics. See Narcotics and youth

YOUTH and race relations. See Interracial cooperation

YOUTH and society. See Individual and society

YOUTH art month. See Childrens art—Exhibitions

YOUTH as guides. See Guides

YOUTH associations
See also
Young Americans for freedom (organization)

YOUTH centers. See Recreation centers

YOUTH conferences
See also
International youth conference on problems of the human environment

YOUTH conservation corps. See United States—Youth conservation corps

YOUTH employment service. See Student employment

YOUTH fares. See Airlines—Fares

YOUTH forums. See Forums (discussion and debate)

YOUTH group achievement awards
Parents' magazine seventeenth annual youth achievement awards. Parents Mag 46:68 O '71

YOUTH in moving pictures
Movies from behind the barricades; student protest movies. S. Farber. il Film Q 24:24-33 Wint '70

YOUTH leagues (baseball) See Little leagues

YOUTH market
Consuming youth. H. C. Wallich. Newsweek 77:75 Ap 5 '71
What youth wants. il Newsweek 77:65 Ja 18 '71
See also
College marketing and research corporation
National student marketing corporation

YOUTH movement
See also
Counter culture
Student movement

China (People's Republic)
Red guard, by G. A. Bennett and R. N. Montaperto. Review
Time 97:80 Mr 1 '71. C. Elliott

Germany
Arrogant cult of youth. M. Geltman. Nat R 23:140-1 F 9 '71
Psychohistorical origins of the Nazi youth cohort. P. Loewenberg. bibliog f il Am Hist R 76:1457-502 D '71

YOUTH volunteer service. See Volunteer service

YOUTH vote. See Suffrage—United States

YO-YO. See Toys

YU, Hwa
China. See issues of Christian century continuing New Christian

YUBA CITY murders. See Murder

YUCATAN

Description and travel
Yucatan: Mexico's world of the Mayas. I. Stanger. il Harp Baz 104:84+ S '71

YUCCA
Three visitors from Mexico: red yucca, Mexican abelia and red cestrum. il Sunset 147:184 S '71
Tree that is not a tree: Joshua tree. C. G. Maxwell. il Am For 77:4-5 Mr '71

YUDKEN, Joel
Lockheed's life and hard times. il Ramp Mag 10:47-9 S '71

YUGOSLAV students
See also
Student demonstrations—Yugoslavia

YUGOSLAVIA
See also
Agriculture—Yugoslavia
Bosnia and Herzegovina
Electric power—Yugoslavia
Labor and laboring classes—Yugoslavia
Russia—Foreign relations—Yugoslavia

Armed forces
Every man a fighting man. il Time 98:44-5 O 18 '71

Description and travel
Red star over Cynthia R. R. S. Carter. il Motor B & S 127:60-1+ My '71

Economic conditions
Experiments with liberty. C. Bourdet. Nation 213:234-8 S 20 '71

Economic policy
Yugoslavia's future. S. S. Anderson. bibliog f Cur Hist 60:277-81 My '71

Foreign relations
Closing the triangle. il por Time 98:42 N 1 '71
Jugoslavia, 1971. A. Vratusa. For Affairs 50:148-62 O '71

Russia
See Russia—Foreign relations—Yugoslavia

Industries
See also
Airplane industry—Yugoslavia

Labor policy
Labor problems in Yugoslavia. Mo Labor R 94:62-3 O '71

Nationalism
Balkanization in Titoland. M. M. Mestrovic. Commonweal 94:252-3 My 21 '71
Yugoslavia at the crossroads. G. J. Prpic. il America 125:147-50 S 11 '71

Politics and government
Balkanization in Titoland. M. M. Mestrovic. Commonweal 94:252-3 My 21 '71
Experiments with liberty. C. Bourdet. Nation 213:234-8 S 20 '71
Jugoslavia, 1971. A. Vratusa. For Affairs 50:148-62 O '71
Tito's way. por Newsweek 77:42 My 17 '71
Working against time. por Time 97:37 My 17 '71
Yugoslavia at the crossroads. G. J. Prpic. il America 125:147-50 S 11 '71
Yugoslavia: Tito's daring experiment. il Time 98:24+ Ag 9 '71
Yugoslavia's future. S. S. Anderson. bibliog f Cur Hist 60:277-81 My '71
Yugoslavia's future: Tito as Diocletian; rioting in the Croatian capital of Zagreb. M. M. Mestrovic. Commonweal 95:317-18 Ja 7 '72

YULETIDE. See Christmas

YUNCKER, Barbara
Keep up with medicine. See issues of Good housekeeping

YUNGE, Gloria
White cane. il por Good H 172:71+ Je '71

YUNICK, Henry. See Yunick, S.

YUNICK, Smokey
Say, Smokey; questions and answers. See issues of Popular science monthly

about
Say, Smokey: a steam engine? E. F. Lindsley. il Pop Sci 199:48-9 D '71 *

YUNIS, Jorge J. and Yasmineh, W. G.
Heterochromatin, satellite DNA, and cell function. bibliog il Science 174:1200-9 D 17 '71

YURCHENKOV, V. D.
Behind the scenes. Hi Fi 21:12+ Je '7

YURIKO
Yuriko and company, 92nd street Y, NYC. D. Hering. il por Dance Mag 45:91 My '71*

YURKA, Blanche
Flowermaiden; interview. ed. by R. Zachary. il por Opera N 35:12-13 Ap 3 '71

YUTANG, Lin
Mellowness; poem. Read Digest 99:112 O '71

Z

De **ZAANSE SCHANS, Netherlands.** See Villages, Restored

ZABALETA, Nicanor
Music to my ears; performance with the Chamber music of society of Lincoln Center. I. Kolodin. Sat R 54:44 F 20 '71 *

ZACHARY, Ralph
Dames at sea goes dancing. il Dance Mag 45:28-31 O '71
Eastman. il Opera N 35:26-30 F 20 '71
Films. il Opera N 35:33 F 27 '71
Grand night for drinking. il Opera N 35:26-8 F 13 '71
(ed) See Yurka, B. Flowermaiden

ZADAN, Craig
Two for the show. il Dance Mag 45:67-73+ O '71

ZADIG, Ernest A.
Apollo 15: drilling into the moon's surface. il Pop Sci 199:58-9 D '71
Barnacles and grasses are a pain on the bottom. Motor B & S 127:90-1+ Je '71
Digging the world's first freeze-dried tunnel. il Pop Sci 198:56-7 Mr '71
I'll bet you don't know this one. il Motor B & S 127:62-5 F '71
New navigator that never sleeps. il Motor B & S 127:128+ Mr '71

ZAFFIRO, Vince
It's time to stop the gypsy moth, sanely. il Org Gard & Farm 18:59-63 O '71

ZAGORIN, Bernard
United States discusses report of economic and social council; statement, October 11, 1971. Dept State Bul 65:605-7 N 22 '71

ZAHL, Paul A.
Nature's night lights. il Nat Geog 140:45-69 Jl '71
What's so special about spiders? il Nat Geog 140:190-219 Ag '71

ZAHN, Gordon C.
Berrigans: radical activism personified (cont) Cath World 212:285 Mr '71
Great Catholic upheaval. il Sat R 54:24-7+ S 11 '71
Religious pacifist looks at abortion. Commonweal 94:279-82 My 28 '71
Scandal of silence. Commonweal 95:79-85 O 22 '71

ZAHNISER, Don V. See Miller, J. M. jt. auth.

ZAHNISER, Edward DeFrance. See DeFrance, E. pseud.

ZAÏRE (Democratic Republic)
Business African style. A. Jaffe. il Newsweek 78:104+ N 22 '71
How now, Diogo Cao? Time 98:51 N 8 '71

ZAKARIASEN, William
Montserrat. il Opera N 35:14-16 Ap 3 '71
Musician as activist. il Hi Fi 21:50-5 Jl '71
We choristers. il Opera N 35:27-9 Ja 30 '71
(ed) See Allen, B. Gypsy

ZALBA, Serapio R.
Battered child; reprint. il Sci Digest 70:8-13+ D '71

ZAMBEZI sharks. See Sharks

ZAMBIA
At play in African villages. E. Leacock. il Natur Hist 80:60-5 D '71
See also
Marriage law—Zambia
Railroads—Zambia
United Nations—Zambia
Visitors, Foreign—Zambia
Women—Zambia

Nationalism
Black Africa: the white man's future. C. W. Casewit. il America 125:15-17 Jl 10 '71

ZAMENHOF, Stephen, and others
DNA (cell number) in neonatal brain: second generation (F_2) alteration by maternal (F_0) dietary protein restriction. bibliog il Science 172:850-1 My 21 '71
Prenatal cerebral development: effect of restricted diet, reversal by growth hormone. bibliog il Science 174:954-5 N 26 '71

ZAMIR, Batya
Batya Zamir Emmanuel midtown Y, NYC. T. Borek. Dance Mag 45:24 Je '71 *

ZAMPINO. See Cookery—Meat

ZANESVILLE, Ohio

Politics and government
Zanesville: the mood of the president makers. R. Stout. il Newsweek 77:31 Mr 15 '71

ZANG, Elden G.
Non-objective sculpture. il Sch Arts 71:26-7 S '71

ZANUCK, Darryl Francis
Don't say yes until I finish talking, by M. Gussow. Review
  Newsweek il por 77:92 F 22 '71. P. D. Zimmerman *
Last tycoon. por Newsweek 77:66+ **My 31** '71 *

ZANUCK, Richard Darryl
Son of Zanuck returns. por Bsns W p32 Mr 6 '71 *

ZANUSSI (firm) See Electric industries

ZAPPA, Frank
Rock family affair. il por Life 71:46-7 S 24 '71 *

ZARIN, Neil A.
Controlling the thrust of rocket engines. il por Space World H-5-89:30-4 My '71
Die ZAUBERFLÖTE; opera. See Mozart, J. C. W. A.

ZAUNER, Phyllis
Finding the real Reno. il Travel 136:56-9+ D '71

ZAX, Manuel
Outstanding teachers: who are they? bibliog Clear House 45:285-9 Ja '71

ZAYAS, Rodrigo de
Musical events; second recital in series: A renaissance of lute song in Alice Tully Hall. W. Sargeant. New Yorker 47:98-9 N 27 '71 *

ZBAR, Berton, and Tanaka, Tomiko
Immunotherapy of cancer: regression of tumors after intralesional injection of living mycobacterium bovis. bibliog il Science 172: 271-3 Ap 16 '71

ZEA mays. See Corn

ZECKENDORF, William, 1905-
Master pitchman for a jetport. il por Bsns W p60 Mr 27 '71 *

ZEFFIRELLI, Franco
Sorcerer's apprenticeship, ed. by F. Rizzo. il pors Opera N 35:6-10 F 13 '71

ZEIGLER, G. S. and others
Mt Rainier: now you see it, now you don't. bibliog il Weatherwise 24:114-19 Je '71

ZEIGLER, John A.
Adman battles society's ills. il por Bsns W p 108+ S 11 '71 *

ZEILLER, Warren
Naked gills and recycled stings; with biographical sketch. il Natur Hist 80:2, 36-41 D '71
—and Compton, G. W.
Purple wind; with biographical sketches. il Sea Front 17:372-7, 382-3 N '71

ZEISEL, Hans
Crime and law-and-order. Am Scholar 40: 624-33 Aut '71

ZEISS (firm) See Photographic apparatus and supplies industry—Germany (Federal Republic)

ZEITLIN, Lawrence R.
One touch of larceny. Newsweek 77:84+ Je 14 '71 *

ZEITLIN, Maurice
Chilean revolution: the bullet or the ballot. il Ramp Mag 9:20-8 Ap '71

ZEITZ, Harold, and Domsky, Marvin
Why isn't my child a deep-water swimmer? il Camp Mag 43:17 Je '71

ZELAZNY, Roger
Science fiction and how it got that way. Writer 84:15-17 My '71

ZELDIN, Marvin
Oil pollution. il Audubon 73:99-119 My '71

ZELIFF, Jane Seely
Six cheers for our children. Good H 172:63+ F '71

ZELIGS, Dorothy F.
Moses encounters the daemonic aspect of God. bibliog Am Imago 27:379-91 Wint '70

ZELMANOFF, Marci
Jewelry of Marci Zelmanoff. R. Lusker. il Craft Horiz 31:16-19 F '71 *

ZEMBORAIN DE TORRES DUGGAN, Esther.
See Duggan, E. Z. de T.

ZEN Buddhism
Zen in the art of archery: a bridge to the East. C. Edwards. America 125:31 Jl 24 '71

ZEN diet. See Diet

ZÉNDEGUI, Guillermo de
Architecture, style and environment. **Américas** 23:S2-13 Ap '71
(ed) Colonial art. il Américas 23:S1-24 **Ap** '71 (to be cont)
(ed) Dream that became a reality. il Américas 23:S1-16 Ja '71
Our America. il Américas 22:S1-48 N '70
That August third. il Américas 23:S3-6 O '71

ZENER diodes. See Diodes

ZENGER, John Peter
Case of John Peter Zenger. L. Barnett. il pors Am Heritage 23:33-41+ D '71 *

ZENITH radio corporation
Zenith tunes in on a new president. por Bsns W p24 My 22 '71

ZENKER, Hans
Without snow or sand still they ski. il Travel 135:66-9 My '71

ZERN, Ed
Exit, laughing. See issues of Field & stream
Good guys, bad guys and the bighorn. il por Sports Illus 34:20-2+ Je 28 '71

ZERO gravity. See Weightlessness

ZESCHIN, Robert
Savoyard ring; or, A tetralogy in patter song. Opera N 35:6-7 Ap 3 '71

ZHUKOV, Gennadii Petrovich
Moon and international law: problems and prospects. Space World H-12-96:45-6 D '71

ZHUKOV, Georgii Konstantinovich
Memoirs of Marshal Zhukov, by G. K. Zhukov. Review
  Nation 213:248-50 S 20 '71. R. E. Walters
  Sat R il por 54:40-1 O 9 '71. H. Schwartz *
Soldier as propagandist. S. L. A. Marshall. Nat R 23:764-5 Jl 13 '71 *
Zhukov, by O. P. Chaney, jr. Review
  Sat R il por54:40-1 O 9 '71. H. Schwartz *

ZIDE, Larry
Tape up to date. il Hi Fi 21:42-7 Ag '71
Turntables and changers up to date. il Hi Fi 21:44-9 My '71

ZIEGEL, Vic
106 ways to make money on the worst team in baseball. il Look 35:67-8+ Ap 20 '71

ZIEGENFUSS, W. Beatrice
Recipe for reading. il Todays Ed 60:44-5 O '71

ZIEGFELD follies
Once and future Follies. il Time 97:70-4 My 3 '71

ZIEGLER, Henri
Aerospatiale head hits back at critics of Concorde in France. Aviation W 94:18 Mr 22 '71 *

ZIEGLER, Ronald Lewis
How the 2d best-informed man in the White House briefs the 2d worst-informed group in Washington. J. M. Naughton. il pors N Y Times Mag p9+ My 30 '71 *

ZIGMAN, Seymour
Eye lens color: formation and function. bibliog il Science 171:807-9; 173:655 F 26, **Ag** 13 '71

ZIGZAG sewing machines. See Sewing machines

ZIMA, Joseph P. and Smith, G. A.
High school students, drugs, and teachers. Sch & Soc 99:250-3 Ap '71

ZIMAN, John
Winter college format. Science 171:352-4 Ja 29 '71

ZIMBABWE
Ancient Zimbabwe empire. J. G. Spady. il Negro Hist Bul 34:33-4 F '71

ZIMBALIST, Efrem, 1923-
Save-Hoover drive. Nation 213:5-6 Jl 5 '71 *

ZIMBEL, George S.
It's what's inside that counts. il Sat R 54: 50-1 Jl 17 '71

ZIMMER, Fred A.
Green is for coolness, yellow for good auspices; with biographical sketch. il Natur Hist 80:4, 54-9 Ja '71

ZIMMER, Paul
Comment. D. Aldan. Poetry 118:39-40 Ap '71 *

ZIMMERMAN, D. W.
Uranium distributions in archeologic ceramics: dating of radioactive inclusions. bibliog il Science 174:818-19 N 19 '71

ZIMMERMAN, David R.
Last hope for the ospreys of Long Island Sound. il por N Y Times Mag p38-40+ D 12 '71
Medicine learned how to save Katie Peck. il por Todays Health 49:20-3+ D '71
Medicine today. See issues of Ladies' home journal

ZIMMERMAN, Joan
Finding records of ancient man in the soil. il Chem 44:12-14 My '71
In the footsteps of ancient man. il Chem 44:16-17 F '71

ZIMMERMAN, William F. and Goldsmith, T. H.
Photosensitivity of the circadian rhythm and of visual receptors in carotenoid-depleted drosophila. bibliog il Science 171:1167-9 Mr 19 '71

ZIMMERMANN, Karl R.
I got those disappearing railroad blues. il Sr Schol 99:30-1 D 13 '71
Miracle of rare device. Nat R 23:655+ Je 15 '71
Saints preserved. Nat R 23:882 Ag 10 '71

ZINBERG, Norman E.
G.I.'s and O.J.'s in Vietnam. il N Y Times Mag p37+ D 5 '71

ZINC in the body
Mineral element correlation with adeno-hypophyseal-adrenal cortex function and stress. A. Flynn and others. bibliog il Science 173:1035-6 S 10 '71
Teratogenic effects of a chelating agent and their prevention by zinc. H. Swenerton and L. S. Hurley. bibliog il Science 173:62-4 Jl 2 '71; Reply with rejoinder. R. D. Hamilton. 174:102-3 O 8 '71

ZINDEL, Paul
And Miss Reardon drinks a little. Criticism
  Nation 212:347-8 Mr 15 '71 *
  New Yorker 47:67 Mr 6 '71 *
  Sat R 54:10 Mr 20 '71 *
  Time 97:47 Mr 8 '71 *
Effect of gamma rays on man-in-the-mari-golds. Criticism
  Time il 97:66 My 17 '71 *
Prizewinning Marigolds. il por Time 97:66 My 17 '71 *

ZINKANN, Fred R.
Primavera; poem. Liv Wildn 34:43 Aut '70

ZINN, Howard
Two days in May. D. Brudnoy. Nat R 23:573 Je 1 '71 *

ZINNER, Ernst
Explorer of the past. por Sky & Tel 41:199 Ap '71 *

ZINSSER, William Knowlton
Annual meeting of the corporation. il N Y Times Mag p9+ My 16 '71
Boycott to Zeppelin with nary a quibble. il Life 70:10 F 5 '71
Check and supercheck il Life 71:14 O 22 '71
Connoisseur's guide to H$_2$O. Life 71:15 N 26 '71
Everything you didn't want to know about Phase 2. il Life 71:56A+ N 19 '71
It's fine, too, for Monopoly. il Life 70:54 Mr 12 '71
Letter from the golf committee. il Life 70:13 Je 11 '71
Memories of an old soldier. Sat R 54:6-7 Jl 3 '71
On winding down. il Life 70:4 My 21 '71
Parting shots: My 19,000 per cent overrun. il Life 70:59-60 F 12 '71
Quizzing the collegians. Life 70:14 My 7 '71

ZIOLKOWSKI, Korczak
Mountain versus Korczak Ziolkowski. R. Bongartz. il Esquire 75:112-13+ Mr '71 *

ZIONISM
Israel quagmire: thoughts for the U.S. citizen; address, December 3, 1970. A. M. Lilienthal. Vital Speeches 37:206-9 Ja 15 '71
My Jewish problem, and ours. S. Stern. il Ramp Mag 10:30-40 Ag '71
Normalizing the Jews; theories of M. Selzer. H. Halkin; reply with rejoinder. M. Selzer. Commentary 51:22+ My '71
  See also
Israel
Jewish-Arab relations
Jews

ZIPERMAN, H. Haskell
Panama Canal: a medical history. il Américas 23:8-18 Je '71

ZISK, S. H. and others
Lunar Apennine-Hadley Region: geological implications of earth-based radar and infrared measurements. bibliog il Science 173:808-12 Ag 27 '71

ZITHER
  See also
Autoharp

ZITO, Tom
Sound of music, music, music, music. il Esquire 76:162-4+ N '71

ŽIVKOVIĆ, B. See Bulat, M. jt. auth.

ZIVNUSKA, John A.
Conservation; address, January 22, 1971. Vital Speeches 37:304-7 Mr 1 '71; Same. Am For 77:8-9+ Jl '71

ZMUDA, Joseph P.
New electrics make performance break-throughs. il Pop Sci 198:55-6 F '71
New pollution solution: dual-fuel Cal-gas car. il Pop Sci 198:12 Ap '71

ZOANTHUS
Palytoxin: a new marine toxin from a co-elenterate. R. E. Moore and P. J. Scheuer. bibliog il Science 172:495-8 Ap 30 '71

ZOBEL, Bruce J.
Genetic improvement of southern pines; with biographical sketch. il Sci Am 225:12, 94-103 bibliog(p 138) N '71

ZOCHERT, Donald
Elusive seringo, with biographical sketch. il Natur Hist 80:2, 8-10 D '71
This nation never saw a black man before. il por Am Heritage 22:8-9 F '71

el-ZOGHBY, Gamal
Space as live-in sculpture. il House B 113:44-9 Jl '71 *

ZOISITE
Ordering of V^{2+}, Mn^{3+}, and Fe^{3+} ions in zoisite, Ca$_2$Al$_3$Si$_3$O$_{12}$(OH) S. Ghose and T. Tsang. bibliog il Science 171:374-6 Ja 29 '71; Reply. D. R. Hutton and others. 174:1259 D 17 '71

ZOLL, Donald Atwell
My Lai and the state of the army. Nat R 23:1112-14 O 8 '71
Wistful goodbye to capital punishment. Nat R 23:1351-4 D 3 '71

ZOLOTH, Stephen R. See Adler, N. T. jt. auth.

ZONING
Battle of the suburbs. il Newsweek 78:61-4+ N 15 '71
City and suburb: instead of shouting, how about talking? W. F. Wagner, jr. Arch Rec 150:9-10 O '71
Fixing the odds in Black Jack; zoning controversy. il Time 97:19-20 Ap 26 '71
For farmers mainly; rural zoning. R. Steffen. Org Gard & Farm 18:132-3 Ap '71
Higher wall around suburbia; Supreme court decision on discriminatory local zoning ordinances. Bsns W p24 My 1 '71
New set of rules to reshape New York. il Bsns W p70-2 F 13 '71
Wall of zoning; suburban racial and economic front. J. Patterson. Commonweal 94:283-5 My 28 '71
What can you do about ethnic change? plan of Decatur, Ga. P. Stevens, jr. il Am City 86:99-100 N '71
Zoning and planning decisions; ed. by N. Williams, jr. See issues of American city
Zoning by referendum; Polk County, Fla. il Am City 86:98+ D '71
Zoning changes are coming: are you ready? L. L. Wolffe and A. J. Wolffe. House B 113:46 O '71

ZONING law
Fellow Americans, keep out! regional isolationism. il Forbes 107:22-4+ Je 15 '71; Same abr. Read Digest 99:129-32 S '71
New assault on suburban zoning; Black Jack, Mo. il Bsns W p30 Ja 16 '71
Wear and tear in the communes. A. Solnit. il Nation 212:524-7 Ap 26 '71; Same abr. Cur 130:22-6 Je '71
When can a home be used for business? L. M. Brown. Bet Hom & Gard 49:100 My '71
  See also
Building laws and regulations

ZONING maps. See Municipal maps

ZOO, Central park. See New York (city)—Parks and playgrounds

ZOO animals, Tattooing of. See Tattooing

ZOOLOGICAL gardens
American zoos; with state summaries. il Parks & Rec 6:48-9+ Ag '71
Lead poisoning: zoo animals may be the first victims; study of Bronx and Staten Island zoo. J. Bazell. Science 173:130-1 Jl 7 '71
New zoo view. R. T. Reuther. il Parks & Rec 6:17-19+ S '71
Zoo story. il Time 98:54 O 18 '71
  See also
Menageries
New York zoological park

ZOOLOGY
Natural sciences. Sci N 100:174, 407 S 11, D 18 '71
Zoology. Sci N 100:265 O 16 '71
  See also
Cave fauna and flora
Primates

Ecology
  See also
Wildlife management

Nomenclature
Stability in zoological nomenclature; International code of zoological nomenclature. E. Mayr and others. Science 174:1041-2 D 3 '71

Africa
Death of an elephant. il Life 70:60-5 F 26 '71

Arctic Regions
  See also
Walruses

Australia
  See also
Tasmanian devils

Ceylon
Jungle adventure in Ceylon. E. A. Bauer. il Outdoor Life 148:46-9+ D '71

ZOOLOGY—*Continued*

Galápagos Islands

Evolution islands. D. C. Fales. il Sci Digest 69:16-21 F '71

Seychelles (Islands)

Tourists find the forgotten islands; with photographs by T. Spencer. Life 71:44-51 O 29 '71

ZOOLOGY, Economic
See also
Predation (zoology)

ZOOLOGY, Marine. See Marine fauna

ZORZA, Victor
Computerizing Soviet society. Cur 132:23-30 S '71

ZOSCHKE, David C. and Bach, F. H.
Specificity of allogeneic cell recognition by human lymphocytes in vitro. bibliog il Science 172:1350-2 Je 25 '71

ZOSIMUS (historian)
Zosimus, the first historian of Rome's fall. W. Goffart. bibliog f Am Hist R 76:412-41 Ap '71 *

ZOTTELE, Pedro
Chile's municipal elections show added support for Allende. Chr Cent 88:702-4+ Je 2 '71

ZOYSIA lawn. See Lawns

ZSCHOCK, Dieter K. See Schuyler, G. W. jt. auth.

ZUBRYD, Frances
Ideas on trial. America 124:486 My 8 '71

ZUCKER, Robert S. and others
Neuronal circuit mediating escape responses in crayfish. bibliog il Science 173:645-50 Ag 13 '71

ZUCKERMAN, Harriet, and Merton, R. K.
Sociology of refereeing. bibliog il Phys Today 24:28-33 Jl '71

ZUDÁÑEZ, Jaime
Jaime Zudáñez, illustrious unknown. T. Sepúlveda Whittle. il Américas 23:9-13 O '71 *

ZUFFA, Ann Sekuris
I won't look back. Har Yrs 11:42-3 S '71

ZULU, Alphaeus Hamilton, bp
Arresting a bishop. J. Deedy Commonweal 94:154 Ap 23 '71 *

ZULULAND, Alphaeus Hamilton Zulu, bp of.
See Zulu, A. H.

ZULUS
Last Zulu war. il Time 98:34 D 13 '71
Zulus: black nation in a land of apartheid. J. Judge. il Nat Geog 140:738-51 D '71

Religion

Zulu Zionism. J. W. Fernandez. il Natur Hist 80:44-51 Je '71

ZUMETA, Bertram W.
Road to 1976. por Nations Bsns 59:32 Ag '71

ZUMWALT, Elmo Russell, Jr
Personal accountability; address, June 9, 1971. Vital Speeches 37:605-8 Jl 15 '71
Where Russian threat keeps growing; interview. il por U S News 71:72-7 S 13 '71

about

Military goes mod. Read Digest 98:100-4 Mr '71 *

ZURICH

Music

Report:
Alberto Ginastera's Bomarzo. E. V. Epstein. Opera N 35:31-2 Ja 23 '71
Donizetti's Roberto Devereux. E. V. Epstein. il Opera N 35:31 Ap 10 '71
Parsifal. E. V. Epstein. il Opera N 35: 24-5 Je 12 '71

ZUSMAN, Jack
Evaluating the quality of mental health services: criteria for rapid informal judgement. Mental Hy 55:478-86 O '71

ZWEIG, M. B.
Wilhelm Reich's theory: ethical implications. Am Imago 28:268-86 Fall '71

ZWEIG, Paul
About angels; poem. Nation 212:220 F 15 '71
Encounter; poem. Nation 212:250 F 22 '71

ZWERDLING, Daniel
Block those buses. New Repub 165:14-17 O 23 '71
Food pollution. il Ramp Mag 9:30-7+ Je '71
Womanpower problem. New Repub 164:11-13 Mr 20 '71

ZYGOTES
See also
Sporozoites

ZYLBER, Ester A. and Penman, Sheldon
Synthesis of 5S and 4S RNA in metaphase-arrested HeLa cells. bibliog il Science 172: 947-9 My 28 '71